THE AUTHORITY SINCE 1868

THE WORLD ALMANAC®
AND BOOK OF FACTS
2012

P9-DMO-371

WORLD ALMANAC BOOKS

THE AUTHORITY SINCE 1868

THE WORLD ALMANAC
AND BOOK OF FACTS
2012

Senior Editor: Sarah Janssen
Editor: M. L. Liu **Associate Editor:** Shmuel Ross
Index Editor: Nan Badgett
Contributors: Rachel Bozek, Jason Brainard, Jeremy Eagle, Brian Fitzgerald, Marshall Gerometta, Jacqueline Laks Gorman, Richard Hantula, Geoffrey M. Horn, Michael J. Kaufman, John Mastroberardino, William A. McGeveran Jr., Carmen Morais, Lisa Renaud, John Rosenthal, George W. Smith, Andrew Steinitz, Steven Stern, Edward A. Thomas, Lori P. Wiesenfeld

Production: Newgen North America
Design and Production, Year in Pictures: Bill Smith Group
Design, Cover: Takeshi Takahashi
Photo Research: Edward A. Thomas

For Infobase Learning:
Editorial Director: Laurie E. Likoff
Project Editor: Edward A. Thomas

World Almanac® Books
An imprint of Infobase Learning
132 West 31st Street
New York, NY 10001

Hardcover
ISBN-13: 978-1-60057-147-3
ISBN-10: 1-60057-147-6

Paperback
ISBN-13: 978-1-60057-148-0
ISBN-10: 1-60057-148-4

The World Almanac® and Book of Facts is available at special discounts when purchased in bulk quantities for businesses, associations, institutions, or sales promotions. Please call our sales department at (212) 967-8800 or (800) 322-8755.

You can find The World Almanac® and Book of Facts on the Internet at www.worldalmanac.com.
Email: almanac@infobaselearning.com

The World Almanac® and Book of Facts 2012
Book printed and bound by RR Donnelly, Crawfordsville, IN
Date printed: November 2011
Printed in the United States of America
RRD 10 9 8 7 6 5 4 3 2 1

CONTENTS

2011: SPECIAL FEATURES AND YEAR IN REVIEW

2011: YEAR IN PICTURES

THE WORLD ALMANAC AND BOOK OF FACTS 2012

Top Ten News Topics of 2011

1. "Arab Spring" Uprisings Sweep North Africa and Middle East. Soaring food prices, high youth unemployment, economic inequality, religious tensions, and government corruption and repression fueled a wave of discontent that challenged entrenched Arab regimes from the northwest corner of Africa to the Persian Gulf. Mass protests forced the ouster of Tunisian Pres. Zine al-Abidine Ben Ali, Jan. 14, and Egyptian Pres. Hosni Mubarak, Feb. 11. With NATO military backing, insurgents overthrew Libyan dictator Muammar al-Qaddafi Aug. 23; he was killed Oct. 20. Yemeni Pres. Ali Abdullah Saleh was seriously wounded in a June 3 rocket attack but continued to cling to power, while Syrian Pres. Bashar al-Assad launched a ferocious offensive against antigovernment protesters.

2. Japan Earthquake, Tsunami Cause Nuclear Disaster. A magnitude 9.0 earthquake, the most powerful in modern Japanese history, struck Mar. 11 about 20 mi below the surface of the Pacific Ocean and 80 mi from the city of Sendai, on Honshu Island. The quake generated a powerful tsunami, which rolled over low-lying coastal towns. The confirmed death toll approached 16,000; property damage was estimated at $325 bil. A 46-ft-high wall of water overwhelmed a seawall designed to protect the Fukushima Daiichi nuclear power plant, leading to meltdowns at 3 of the plant's 6 nuclear reactors. Criticized for his handling of the disaster, Prime Min. Naoto Kan submitted his resignation Aug. 26 and was succeeded by Finance Min. Yoshihiko Noda, the seventh person in five years to head Japan's government.

3. Commando Raid in Pakistan Kills Osama bin Laden. Shortly after midnight May 2, in Abbottabad, Pakistan, a CIA-led squadron of U.S. Navy SEALs killed al-Qaeda leader Osama bin Laden, whose trail of terror included the Sept. 11, 2001, attacks against the U.S. Bin Laden's hideout was located less than a mile from the Pakistan Military Academy. No warning of the raid was given to Pakistani authorities, straining tensions between Pakistan and the U.S. Another U.S. target in the war against terror, Yemeni-American cleric Anwar al-Awlaki, was killed Sept. 30 by a missile launched from a U.S. drone aircraft over Yemen. Awlaki had been linked to several jihadist attacks, including a failed Dec. 2009 plot to blow up a Detroit-bound jetliner by "underwear bomber" Umar Farouk Abdulmutallab, who pled guilty in federal court Oct. 12.

4. U.S. Sets Troop Pullouts From Afghanistan and Iraq. Even as war continued to rage in Afghanistan, Pres. Barack Obama outlined plans June 22 to withdraw 10,000 U.S. troops by the end of 2011, another 23,000 by Sept. 2012, and the remaining 68,000 U.S. forces by the end of 2014. The U.S. Aug. 6 suffered its single deadliest day in the 10-year Afghan war, as insurgents used a rocket-propelled grenade to shoot down a Chinook transport helicopter, killing 30 U.S. service members and 8 others. Obama announced Oct. 21 that the nearly 40,000 U.S. troops still serving in Iraq would be pulled out by the end of the year.

5. Debt Crises Raise Fears of Default. Awash in red ink, Greece received a bailout pledge July 21 of 109 bil euros ($157 bil) from eurozone leaders. The deal soon ran into resistance from some European Union members and from the Greek public, which opposed the austerity measures imposed on their country by international lenders. In late Oct., Europe faced a new debt crisis, inflamed by fears that other eurozone members might be at risk. The U.S. narrowly averted default when, after weeks of wrangling between Pres. Obama and Republican leaders, Congress Aug. 2 enacted a measure to raise the statutory debt ceiling above the $14.3 tril limit set in 2010. The legislation included mechanisms to match debt increases with spending cuts, some of which would be proposed by a 12-member supercommittee. On Aug. 5, Standard & Poor's credit rating agency downgraded the nation's credit rating for the first time, from the top-grade AAA to AA+.

6. Ailing Economy Sparks Budget Clashes, Street Protests. As the U.S. unemployment rate hovered above 9%, more than 40 states were dealing with a cumulative projected shortfall of more than $100 bil for the 2012 fiscal year. Clashes over budget deficits and the power of public employee unions led to a long, bitter partisan battle in Wisconsin. In July, a conflict between Minnesota Democrats and Republicans over how to close a $5 bil budget gap caused a 20-day government shutdown. Denouncing a growing concentration of economic and political power in the hands of America's wealthiest 1%, a left-wing protest movement launched Sept. 17 as "Occupy Wall Street" in New York City. It had spread to dozens of U.S. cities and overseas by Oct. 15.

7. Weather Extremes Batter U.S. At least 753 tornadoes struck the U.S. during Apr., and more than 320 twisters hit the U.S. in May, with 549 tornado-related fatalities in 2011. A tornado outbreak Apr. 27 killed at least 248 people in Alabama. Another powerful twister May 22 claimed 162 lives in Joplin, MO. Torrential rains and melting snows in May swelled the Mississippi River and its tributaries from Illinois to Louisiana, inundating millions of acres. Heavy rains and snowmelt caused flooding in the Northern Plains in June. Hurricane Irene slammed into the Eastern seaboard Aug. 27-28, swamping parts of Vermont and New York state. Meanwhile, unusually hot, dry, and windy conditions in the Southwest and Southern Plains contributed to record-setting wildfires in Arizona, New Mexico, and Texas.

8. Parties Gear Up for 2012 Election. Facing a clear path to the Democratic nomination, Pres. Obama officially opened his reelection campaign Apr. 4. Republicans hoping to unseat him met in eight debates and at other forums between May 5 and Oct. 18. The GOP race remained fluid. Though former Massachusetts Gov. Mitt Romney was consistently at or near the top of polls of Republican voters' preferences, he rarely scored higher than 25%. Romney's main challengers included Texas Gov. Rick Perry, radio talk-show host and former Godfather's Pizza chief executive Herman Cain, Rep. Ron Paul (TX), and Rep. Michele Bachmann (MN).

9. Britain Buoyed by Royal Wedding, Then Rocked by Scandal and Riots. Televised worldwide Apr. 29 from London, the wedding of Prince William, second in line to the British throne, to his longtime girlfriend, Catherine (Kate) Middleton, provided Britons with a rare day of romance and pageantry before a troubled summer. On July 10, the top-selling tabloid *News of the World*, part of Rupert Murdoch's global media empire, shut itself down following reports of widespread phone hacking. The weekly paper had a reputation for breaking into the voicemail and e-mail accounts of royals, athletes, and celebrities, but revelations that its operatives had also tapped into the voicemail of Milly Dowler, a teenage murder victim, and soldiers killed in Iraq and Afghanistan triggered public outrage. The scandal was an embarrassment to Prime Min. David Cameron, who had employed a former editor of the paper as his communications director. Cameron confronted a more immediate crisis Aug. 6-10, when more than 1,700 people were arrested in 5 days of rioting that began in London and quickly spread to other major British cities.

10. Same-Sex Marriage Advances, "Don't Ask, Don't Tell" Ends. U.S. Attorney Gen. Eric Holder notified Congress Feb. 23 that the Obama administration now regarded as unconstitutional a key provision of the 1996 Defense of Marriage Act that defined marriage as "a legal union between one man and one woman as husband and wife." The New York state legislature passed a marriage equality measure June 24, and the state began issuing marriage licenses to same-sex couples 30 days later. The "Don't Ask, Don't Tell" policy that had prevented gay men and lesbians from serving openly in the U.S. armed forces expired Sept. 20.

THE WORLD
AT A GLANCE

Surprising Facts

Only 14.0 million **smartphones** were sold in the U.S. in 2006; an estimated 78.6 million were sold in 2011. *(p. 363)*

Sales of **LP and EP records** have steadily increased in the past half-decade, from $14.2 million in sales in 2005 to $87.0 million in sales in 2010. However, that is a small share of all music sales when compared to the $2.2 billion in digital music sales in 2010. *(p. 254)*

In 2009, 23.3%, of Americans smoked **cigarettes**, down significantly from 38.7% of Americans in 1985. Yet Americans spent $94.4 billion on tobacco products in 2010—more than twice the $41.0 billion they spent in 1990. *(pp. 54, 147)*

Americans paid an average of 22.9% of their total income in **income tax and Social Security** payments in 2010 (down from 24.7% in 2008); Belgians paid 42.1%. *(p. 736)*

In 1990, the average U.S. **movie ticket** cost $4.23; the average ticket in 2010 cost $7.89. *(p. 246)*

U.S. **public debt** has more than doubled since 2000, from $20,106 per capita to $44,174 per capita in 2010. However, as a percentage of federal outlays, public debt was 20.2% in 2000, and an estimated 11.5% in 2010. *(p. 63)*

Since 1975, the **fuel efficiency** of U.S. cars has increased from 13.5 miles per gallon to 25.8 miles per gallon. *(p. 86)*

In almost half (45.6%) of **motor vehicle accidents** in 2009, state traffic authorities reported that no improper driving had occurred. *(p. 171)*

The number of **triplets** born in the U.S. has more than doubled since 1990, from 2,830 to 5,877 in 2008. The number of **twins** born leapt from 93,865 to 138,660 in the same period. *(p. 167)*

More than half of U.S. **undergraduate students** took out loans, for an average of $8,200, in the 2007-08 academic year. *(p. 391)*

Number Ones

Most-visited **social networking website** . . . . Facebook, 160.9 million unique visitors in June 2011 *(p. 366)*

Most-used **search engine** . . . . Google, 12.1 billion searches by 180.5 million unique visitors in June 2011 *(p. 366)*

Airline that carried the most passengers . . . . .Delta, 110.9 million in 2010 *(p. 91)*

Busiest **U.S. airport** by passenger traffic . . . . . . Hartsfield-Jackson Airport (Atlanta, GA), 89.3 million passengers in 2010 *(p. 91)*

Top U.S. state by domestic **traveler spending**. . . . . California, $89.2 billion in 2009 *(p. 90)*

Top-selling **light truck** in the U.S. . . . . Ford F-Series, 502,125 sold in 2010 (110,013 more than in 2009) *(p. 85)*

Most popular light **truck color** in the U.S. . . . . White/white pearl, 35% of 2010 model year light trucks *(p. 85)*

Top-selling **passenger car** in the U.S. . . . . Toyota Camry, 327,804 sold in 2010 (29,020 fewer than in 2009) *(p. 85)*

Most popular **compact/sports car color** in the U.S. . . Black/black effect, 19% of 2010 model year compact/sports cars *(p. 85)*

Most popular **full-size/intermediate car color** in the U.S. . . . Silver, 19% of 2010 model year full-size/intermediate cars *(p. 85)*

Fastest **roller coaster** in the world .Formula Rossa, 149.1 mph (Ferrari World Abu Dhabi, U.A.E.) *(p. 92)*

Nation with the most **paid days off of work** per year . . . . Brazil, 41 paid days off *(p. 92)*

Nation with largest crude **oil reserves**. . . Saudi Arabia, 262.6 billion barrels in 2011 (U.S. reserves, 20.7 billion barrels) *(p. 116)*

Nation most dependent on **nuclear energy** . . . . France, 74.1% of electricity was nuclear-generated in 2010 *(p. 118)*

America: By the Numbers

47.6 million: number of students enrolled in U.S. public schools in 2008-09 school year *(p. 389)*

1.4 million: number of students enrolled in U.S. charter schools in 2008-09 school year *(p. 389)*

89.6%: public high school graduation rate in Wisconsin, the highest in the U.S. *(p. 386)*

51.3%: public high school graduation rate in Nevada, the lowest in the U.S. *(p. 386)*

28.2: median age at first marriage for U.S. men in 2010 (the highest it has ever been) *(p. 165)*

26.1: median age at first marriage for U.S. women in 2010 (the highest it has ever been) *(p. 165)*

48: average total hours of TV viewed per week by U.S. women over age 55 *(p. 256)*

43: average total hours of TV viewed per week by U.S. men over age 55 *(p. 256)*

24: average total hours of TV viewed per week by young adults ages 12-17 *(p. 256)*

18.3: average total hours U.S. Internet users spent online per week in 2010 *(p. 367)*

80%: percentage of U.S. Internet users who checked their e-mail at least once daily in 2010 *(p. 367)*

91%: percentage of U.S. households with at least one cell phone in 2010 *(p. 368)*

24.6%: percentage of the population of Texas without health insurance in 2010, higher than any other U.S. state *(p. 143)*

24.6%: percentage of U.S. deaths in 2010 caused by heart disease, the leading cause of death *(p. 172)*

67.4%: percentage of U.S. population that was overweight or obese between 2005 and 2008 *(p. 163)*

1,046.1%: change in U.S. annual per capita consumption of fresh broccoli since 1970 *(p. 97)*

-19.9%: change in U.S. annual per capita consumption of red meat since 1970 *(p. 98)*

104.4%: change in U.S. annual per capita consumption of chicken since 1970 *(p. 98)*

Money in America (pp. 47-76)

Median income for U.S. men in constant dollars . . . . .in 2005: $34,929. . . . . .in 2010: $32,137

Median income for U.S. women in constant dollars. . . . . .in 2005: $20,747. . . . . .in 2010: $20,831

Amount of money that Americans put in savings. .in 2005: $143.2 bil . . . . .in 2010: $592.8 bil

Percent of disposable income that Americans put in savings. . . . . .in 2005: 1.5% . . . . .in 2010: 5.3%

If all circulating U.S. dollars and coins were equally distributed among the nation's population, in 2010 every American would receive $3,302.

Personal expenditures, 2000-10 (p. 54)

	2000	2010
Health care	$918.4 bil	$1,667.4 bil
Housing	$1,010.5 bil	$1,583.8 bil
Food and beverages	$537.5 bil	$766.4 bil
Clothing and shoes	$280.8 bil	$334.3 bil
Gasoline and oil	$188.8 bil	$354.1 bil
New automobiles	$210.7 bil	$178.5 bil
Higher education	$76.8 bil	$154.9 bil
Casino gambling	$67.6 bil	$99.6 bil
Tobacco products	$68.5 bil	$94.4 bil
Books	$24.4 bil	$30.4 bil

Spending on selected food products, 2010-11 (p. 73)

	Sales	% change
Beer	$9.7 bil	1.9%
Soft drinks	$8.4 bil	2.2%
Cereal	$6.4 bil	−0.4%
Cookies	$4.2 bil	2.5%
Ice cream	$4.0 bil	1.9%
Bottled water	$3.9 bil	2.6%
Ground coffee	$2.7 bil	12.3%
Chocolate candy	$2.2 bil	5.4%
Dog food (dry)	$2.1 bil	0.2%
Cat food (dry)	$1.1 bil	−2.3%

Wealthiest American, 2010 (p. 52)
Bill Gates, $59.0 billion net worth

Corporation with largest revenues, 2011 (p. 57)
Wal-Mart, $421.8 billion

Top of the World, 2010

Top tourist destinations
(millions of visitors, p. 89)

France	76.8
U.S.	59.7
China	55.7
Spain	52.7
Italy	43.6

Top world airports
(millions of passengers, p. 91)

Beijing Capital	73.9
London Heathrow	65.9
Tokyo Haneda	64.2
Paris Charles de Gaulle	58.2
Frankfurt, Germany	53.0

Top cell phone usage
(subscriptions per 100 pop., p. 368)

Saudi Arabia	187.86
Vietnam	175.30
Russia	166.26
Portugal	142.33
Argentina	141.79

Top computer usage
(millions in use, p. 362)

U.S.	287.92
China	135.33
Japan	94.07
Germany	68.19
UK	51.88

Top gross domestic product
(per capita, p. 735)

Qatar	$179,000
Liechtenstein	$141,000
Luxembourg	$82,600
Singapore	$62,100
Norway	$54,600

Top U.S. trade partners
(millions, p. 77)

Canada	$526,752.5
China	$456,824.5
Mexico	$393,380.9
Japan	$181,030.8
Germany	$130,589.8

Top motor vehicle producers
(thousands of vehicles, p. 83)

China	16,144
Japan	9,197
U.S.	7,632
Germany	5,700
South Korea	4,184

Top health care spenders
(per capita of 50 most populous countries, p. 143)

U.S.	$7,164
France	$4,966
Germany	$4,720
Canada	$4,445
UK	$3,771

Top countries for U.S. foreign adoptions (p. 167)

China	3,401
Ethiopia	2,513
Russia	1,082
South Korea	863
Ukraine	445

Entertainment Award Winners, Then and Now (pp. 258-78)

	1961	2011
Highest-rated TV show	Gunsmoke (1960-61); 37.3% of TVs tuned in	American Idol (2010-11); 14.5% of TVs tuned in
Best Picture Oscar[1]	The Apartment, directed by Billy Wilder	The King's Speech, directed by Tom Hooper
Emmy Awards		
Comedy	Jack Benny Show	Modern Family
Drama	Hallmark Hall of Fame: Macbeth	Mad Men
Album of the Year Grammy[1]	Button Down Mind, Bob Newhart	The Suburbs, Arcade Fire
Record of the Year Grammy[1]	"Theme From a Summer Place," Percy Faith	"Need You Now," Lady Antebellum
Tony Awards		
Play	Becket	War Horse
Musical	Bye, Bye Birdie	The Book of Mormon
Pulitzer Prizes		
Fiction	To Kill a Mockingbird, Harper Lee	A Visit From the Goon Squad, Jennifer Egan
Drama	All the Way Home, Tad Mosel	Clybourne Park, Bruce Norris

(1) Awarded for works released in 1960 (Then) or 2010 (Now).

Thespians of the Year, 2011 (pp. 272-76)

	Best Actor	Best Actress
Academy Awards[1]	Colin Firth, *The King's Speech*	Natalie Portman, *Black Swan*
Golden Globes[1]		
Dramatic Film	Colin Firth, *The King's Speech*	Natalie Portman, *Black Swan*
Comedy/Musical Film	Paul Giamatti, *Barney's Version*	Annette Bening, *The Kids Are All Right*
TV Drama	Steve Buscemi, *Boardwalk Empire*	Katey Sagal, *Sons of Anarchy*
TV Comedy	Jim Parsons, *The Big Bang Theory*	Laura Linney, *The Big C*
Emmy Awards		
Drama	Kyle Chandler, *Friday Night Lights*	Julianna Margulies, *The Good Wife*
Comedy	Jim Parsons, *The Big Bang Theory*	Melissa McCarthy, *Mike & Molly*
Tony Awards		
Play	Mark Rylance, *Jerusalem*	Frances McDormand, *Good People*
Musical	Norbert Leo Butz, *Catch Me if You Can*	Sutton Foster, *Anything Goes*

Best Sellers, 2010 (pp. 246-50, 363)

DVD	*Couples Retreat*
Video game	*Call of Duty: Black Ops*
Computer game[2]	*Starcraft II: Wings of Liberty*
Newspaper	*Wall Street Journal*
Magazine	*AARP The Magazine*
Fiction book	*The Girl Who Kicked the Hornet's Nest*, Stieg Larsson
Nonfiction book	*Decision Points*, George W. Bush

Moviegoing in the U.S. (p. 246)

	1975	2010	% change
Total box office	$2.1 bil	$10.7 bil	407.9%
Admissions	1.03 bil	1.34 bil	29.8%
Theater screens	15,030	39,547	163.1%
Avg. ticket price	$2.05	$7.89	284.9%
Films produced	258	754	192.2%
Films released	233	560	140.3%

More Entertainment Number Ones (pp. 244-57)

#1 top-grossing U.S. movie, 2010	*Avatar*, $476.9 mil[3]
#1 top-grossing U.S. movie, all-time	*Avatar*, $760.5 mil[3]
#1 syndicated TV program, 2010-11	*Wheel of Fortune*, 6.8% of TV households
#1 basic-cable TV program, 2010-11	*Jersey Shore Season 4*, 6.4% of TV households
#1 premium-cable TV program, 2010-11	*True Blood*, 0.8% of TV households
#1 most-watched TV program, all-time	Super Bowl XLV, Feb. 6, 2011, 53.4 mil households
#1 commercial radio format, 2011	Country, 1,988 U.S. stations
#1 top-grossing North American concert tour, all-time	Rolling Stones (2005), $162.0 mil
#1 top-selling U.S. albums, all-time	*Thriller*, Michael Jackson, 29 mil copies / *Eagles/Their Greatest Hits 1971-75*, Eagles, 29 mil copies
#1 longest-running Broadway show	*The Phantom of the Opera* (1988-), 9,803 performances[4]

Milestone Birthdays in 2012 (pp. 174-236)

90	70	50	40
Betty White, Jan. 17	Paul McCartney, June 18	Axl Rose, Feb. 6	Eminem, Oct. 17
Norman Lear, July 27	Brian Wilson, June 20	Garth Brooks, Feb. 7	Brad Paisley, Oct. 28
Sid Caesar, Sept. 8	Harrison Ford, July 13	Sheryl Crow, Feb. 11	Tony Collette, Nov. 1
	Martin Scorsese, Nov. 17	John Stockton, Mar. 26	Jude Law, Dec. 29
80	Joe Biden, Nov. 20	Tom Cruise, July 3	
Milos Forman, Feb. 18		Steve Carell, Aug. 16	**30**
Debbie Reynolds, Apr. 1	**60**	Jerry Rice, Oct. 13	Dwyane Wade, Jan. 17
Donald Rumsfeld, July 9	David Byrne, May 14	Demi Moore, Nov. 11	Seth Rogen, Apr. 15
Peter O'Toole, Aug. 2	George Strait, May 18	Jodie Foster, Nov. 19	Kelly Clarkson, Apr. 24
	Liam Neeson, June 7	Jon Stewart, Nov. 28	Kirsten Dunst, Apr. 30
70	Pat Summit, June 14		Prince William, June 21
Stephen Hawking, Jan. 8	Isabella Rossellini, June 18	**40**	LeAnn Rimes, Aug. 28
Muhammad Ali, Jan. 17	John Goodman, June 20	Shaquille O'Neal, Mar. 6	Anne Hathaway, Nov. 12
Michael R. Bloomberg, Feb. 14	Dan Aykroyd, July 1	Jennifer Garner, Apr. 17	
Lou Reed, Mar. 2	David Hasselhoff, July 17	Ben Affleck, Aug. 15	**18**
Aretha Franklin, Mar. 25	Pee-Wee Herman, Aug. 27	Cameron Diaz, Aug. 30	Justin Bieber
Barbra Streisand, Apr. 24	David Petraeus, Nov. 7	Gwyneth Paltrow, Sept. 28	

(1) Awarded in 2011 for works released in 2010. (2) July 2010-June 2011. (3) *Avatar* was released Dec. 18, 2009, and grossed $283.6 mil by the end of the calendar year, making it the fifth highest grossing film of 2009, the top-grossing film of 2010, and the top-grossing film of all-time. (4) Through Sept. 1, 2011; show was still playing.

ELECTION PREVIEW, 2012:
RACE TO THE WHITE HOUSE

On Nov. 6, 2012, American voters will elect a president, at least 33 U.S. senators, and 435 members of the U.S. House of Representatives, as well as governors in at least 11 states and other state and local officials.

This will be the first national election held after congressional representative reapportionment based on the results of the 2010 census. Southern and Western states gained some influence at the expense of the Northeast and Midwest, as Texas claimed 4 new House seats and electoral votes, Florida gained 2, and 6 other states (AZ, GA, NV, SC, UT, WA) gained 1 each. Ohio and New York each lost 2 seats, while 8 other states (IL, IA, LA, MA, MI, MO, NJ, PA) lost 1 each.

As of mid-Oct. 2011, Democrats held 51 of 100 Senate seats, with 2 more held by independents who vote with the Democratic caucus. Republicans controlled the House of Representatives; as of mid-Oct. 2011, they held 242 of 435 seats. For information on all members of Congress and the results of the 2010 midterm election, see pp. 555-62.

In the presidential contest, incumbent Pres. Barack Obama was expected to win nomination by the Democratic Party without significant opposition.

Former Minnesota Gov. Tim Pawlenty entered the race May 23, 2011, but withdrew Aug. 14 after placing third in the Ames, IA, straw poll. Former Alaska governor and 2008 vice-presidential nominee Sarah Palin announced she was not running for the GOP nomination in Oct. 2011. Former Arkansas Gov. Mike Huckabee and former New York City Mayor Rudy Giuliani, both 2008 Republican presidential contenders, also decided not to run. Indiana Gov. Mitch Daniels, Mississippi Gov. Haley Barbour, and New Jersey Gov. Chris Christie, as well as real estate developer Donald Trump, all decided against running.

As of mid-Oct. 2011, there were nine declared GOP candidates who had participated in at least some debates. They are briefly profiled below, along with Pres. Obama. Many additional minor figures had declared their candidacy but did not qualify for participation in the debates, including former Louisiana Gov. Buddy Roemer and political consultant and gay rights activist Fred Karger.

For detailed past presidential results, see pp. 511-43.

Presidential Candidates, 2012

Sources: Federal Election Commission (FEC); World Almanac research. **Net worth,** Center for Responsive Politics and 24/7 Wall St., based on FEC data. **Opinion polls** are averages for specified period, RealClearPolitics (straw polls not included).

Democratic Candidate

Pres. Barack Obama

Full name: Barack Hussein Obama. **Born:** Aug. 4, 1961, Honolulu, HI. **Home state:** IL. **Education:** Occidental College, Los Angeles, CA, 1979-81. Columbia Univ., B.A., 1983; Harvard Univ., J.D., 1991. **Religion:** Protestant. **Military service:** none. **Family:** married Michelle Robinson, 1992; 2 children: Malia, Sasha. **Net worth:** $2.25-$7.67 mil.

Career highlights: Community organizer, Chicago, 1985-88; lecturer, then senior lecturer, Univ. of Chicago Law School, 1992-2004; state senator (IL), 1996-2004; keynote speaker, Dem. Natl. Convention, 2004; U.S. senator, 2005-08; 44th president, 2009-present. Awarded Nobel Peace Prize, 2009.

Announced candidacy: Apr. 4, 2011. **Campaign finances** (Apr. 1-Sept. 30, 2011, as reported to FEC): $88.4 mil received; $28.9 mil spent; $61.4 mil on hand, Sept. 30; $1.7 mil in debt.

Opinion polls. Job approval, Oct. 13-31, 2011: 44.0%; highest 2011 rating: 60% (AP, May 5-9).

Record/issues. Barack Obama's presidency has been dominated by the economy. Despite a $787 bil stimulus bill, enacted with his support in Feb. 2009, unemployment continued to rise. Democrats blamed failed policies under former president George W. Bush and claimed government spending had created jobs and averted worse problems. Republicans called for tax cuts and deregulation to spur growth. Obama's top policy priority, a health care reform bill, passed in Mar. 2010 despite strong GOP opposition, as did the Dodd-Frank Wall Street reform bill, July 2010.

With Republicans poised to take control of the House following the Nov. 2010 midterm elections, the stage was set for political gridlock. In Congress's lame-duck session before power changed hands in Jan. 2011, Obama negotiated a controversial compromise that continued George W. Bush-era tax cuts in exchange for Democratic priorities such as extended unemployment insurance. In 2011, Tea Party Republicans, devoted to shrinking government, resisted raising the federal debt ceiling. A U.S. default was averted by a late compromise Aug. 2011, with many compensating cuts to be worked out by a supercommittee. In Sept. 2011, Obama traveled to promote a new jobs bill, painting GOP opposition as politically motivated obstruction. The jobs bill was to be funded largely with tax increases on the wealthy, eliciting Republican accusations of "class warfare."

In foreign policy, Obama set a tone emphasizing diplomacy and multilateralism, the latter illustrated by the limited U.S. intervention in Libya. While moving toward a total U.S. withdrawal from Iraq, he stepped up involvement in Afghanistan, authorized drone attacks in Pakistan and elsewhere, and ordered the May 2011 operation that tracked down and killed al-Qaeda leader Osama bin Laden, the architect of the Sept. 11, 2001, terrorist attacks.

Website: www.barackobama.com

Republican Candidates

Rep. Michele Bachmann

Full name: Michele Marie Bachmann (née Amble). **Born:** Apr. 6, 1956, Waterloo, IA. **Home state:** MN. **Education:** Winona State Univ., MN, B.A., 1978; Oral Roberts Univ., J.D., 1986; Coll. of William & Mary, LL.M., 1988. **Religion:** Lutheran. **Military service:** none. **Family:** married Marcus Bachmann, 1978; 5 children: Lucas, Harrison, Elisa, Caroline, Sophia; 23 foster children. **Net worth:** $1.3-$2.8 mil.

Career highlights: IRS tax attorney, 1988-93; state senator (MN), 2001-07; U.S. representative (MN), 2007-present. Founded House Tea Party caucus, July 2010.

Announced candidacy: June 13, 2011. **Campaign finances** (June 13-Sept. 30, 2011): $7.5 mil received; $6.2 mil spent; $1.3 mil on hand, Sept. 30; $550,000 in debt.

Opinion polls. Republican support, Oct. 13-25, 2011: 34.8%; highest 2011 rating: 19% (Rasmussen, June 14).

Record/issues. An evangelical Christian, Bachmann ran unsuccessfully in 1999 for the local school board on a platform opposing government influence in education. As a Minnesota state legislator, Bachmann focused on education and led calls for a state constitutional amendment barring same-sex marriage in 2003. An ardent Tea Party supporter, she opposed the Troubled Asset Relief Program (TARP) legislation and urged repeal of "Obamacare" and the Dodd-Frank Wall Street reform act. She voted against 2009 cap and trade legislation and against raising the debt ceiling, Aug. 2011. Her American Jobs, Right Now plan advocates tax and spending cuts, repeal of "job-killing" government regulations, favorable tax treatment of repatriated corporate profits, elimination of Fannie Mae and Freddie Mac, and tough enforcement of immigration laws. She called for strong defense, promising on her campaign website to "stand up for our friends ... stand up to our foes."

Notes/sidelights. Bachmann won the closely watched Iowa straw poll, Aug. 13, but lost momentum as Perry, then Cain, gained popularity. She has become known for gaffes on the campaign trail, such as her assertion that the Founding Fathers battled slavery or that there was a link between a vaccine for human papillomavirus and mental retardation.

Website: www.michelebachmann.com

Herman Cain

Full name: Herman Cain. **Born:** Dec. 13, 1945, Memphis, TN. **Home state:** GA. **Education:** Morehouse College, B.A., 1967; Purdue Univ., M.S., 1971. **Religion:** Baptist. **Military service:** none. **Family:** married Gloria Etchison, 1968; 2 children: Melanie, Vincent. **Net worth:** $2.9-$6.6 mil.

Career highlights: Systems analyst, Coca-Cola Co., 1970s; executive, Pillsbury Co.,

1977-86; pres. and CEO, Godfather's Pizza, 1986-96; chairman (1994-95) and pres. (1996-99), Natl. Restaurant Assn.; deputy chair, then chairman, Kansas City Federal Reserve Bank, 1992-96; senior adviser, Dole-Kemp presidential campaign, 1996; radio talk show host; columnist/author.

Announced candidacy: May 21, 2011. **Campaign finances** (Dec. 17, 2010-Sept. 30, 2011): $5.4 mil received; $4.0 mil spent; $1.3 mil on hand, Sept. 30; $675,000 in debt.

Opinion polls. Republican support, Oct. 13-25, 2011: 25.0%; highest 2011 rating: 30% (Public Policy Polling, Oct. 7-10).

Record/issues. An African American who grew up in the segregated South and became highly successful in business, Cain has never held elective office. He presents himself as a conservative nonpolitician with business experience and bold solutions. His 9-9-9 tax plan, a centerpiece of his campaign, proposed replacing current federal taxes (including FICA) with a 9% flat tax on individual income, a 9% flat corporate tax, and a 9% national sales tax, then transitioning to a single "fair tax," eliminating the IRS. Cain called his plan "simple, transparent, efficient, fair, and neutral," and contended it would boost job creation and transform the economy. Rivals held that it could not pass, and that the sales tax would open up a new revenue stream for the federal government. Many outside the party attacked the plan as regressive. Generally conservative on social issues, Cain criticized Pres. Obama's Feb. 2011 decision not to enforce the federal Defense of Marriage Act as "bordering on treason." He called strong national defense the "principal duty of a limited federal government" and opposed any timetable for U.S. withdrawal from Iraq. Cain was criticized for a joke about not knowing the name of Uzbekistan's president; critics said he was wrong in calling that country "insignificant" to U.S. security interests. Past sexual harassment allegations became an issue in Nov. 2011.

Notes/sidelights. Regarded as a long shot, Cain nevertheless proved his appeal to conservatives by winning the Florida straw poll Sept. 24, 2011. As Perry began to decline in the polls, Cain rose and by mid-Oct. was neck-and-neck with presumed frontrunner Romney. Cain's lagging fundraising and lack of campaign infrastructure remained a problem.

Website: www.hermancain.com

Newt Gingrich

Full name: Newton Leroy Gingrich. **Born:** June 17, 1943, Harrisburg, PA. **Home state:** GA. **Education:** Emory Univ., B.A., 1965; Tulane Univ., Ph.D., 1971. **Religion:** Roman Catholic. **Military service:** none. **Family:** married Jackie Battley, 1962, divorced, 1981; 2 children: Kathleen, Jacqueline; married Marianne Ginther, 1981, divorced, 2000; married Callista Bisek, 2000. **Net worth:** $6.7+ mil.

Career highlights: Asst. professor, West Georgia Coll. (now Univ. of West Georgia), 1970-78; U.S. representative (GA), 1979-99; minority whip, 1989-95; Speaker of the House, 1995-99. Named *Time* magazine Man of the Year, 1995.

Announced candidacy: May 11, 2011. **Campaign finances** (Apr. 1-Sept. 30, 2011): $2.9 mil received; $2.6 mil spent; $350,000 on hand, Sept. 30; $1.2 mil in debt.

Opinion polls. Republican support, Oct. 13-25, 2011: 9.3%; highest 2011 rating: 20% (Public Policy Polling, May 5-8).

Record/issues. Credited with masterminding the Republican sweep in 1994 congressional elections, Gingrich as House speaker won passage in 1995 of the party's conservative Contract With America legislation, which included welfare reform, tax cuts, and other economic incentives. But he was blamed for a budget stalemate that led to two partial government shutdowns the same year and was fined and reprimanded by Congress, 1997, for improper use of a tax-exempt organization. He pressed for the 1998 impeachment of Pres. Bill Clinton and resigned after a lackluster GOP performance in 1998 midterm elections. Gingrich received Republican criticism in May 2011 when he called a proposal to change Medicare to a voucher system "right-wing social engineering." In his campaign, he promoted strong border security but also backed a guest worker program, and criticized the health care reform law as putting medical decisions in the hands of government bureaucrats. He blamed the government for the 2008 economic crisis and called for the firing of Federal Reserve chairman Ben Bernanke and Treasury Sec. Timothy Geithner.

Notes/sidelights. Gingrich was popular in pre-2011 polls, but his acknowledged infidelities and multiple marriages were potential problems for his campaign. He is the author of some 2 dozen books. An often confrontational and skilled debater, Gingrich was not always active on the campaign trail. Senior advisers left his campaign en masse in June after he went on a 2-week cruise.

Website: www.newt.org

Jon Huntsman

Full name: Jon Meade Huntsman Jr. **Born:** Mar. 26, 1960, Palo Alto, CA. **Home state:** UT. **Education:** Univ. of Pennsylvania, B.A., 1987. **Religion:** Mormon. **Military service:** none. **Family:** married Mary Kaye Cooper, 1983; 7 children: Mary Anne, Abigail, Elizabeth, Jon, William, Gracie Mei, Asha Bharati. **Net worth:** $16-$71 mil.

Career highlights: Deputy asst. sec. of commerce, 1989-91; U.S. ambassador to Singapore, 1992-93; executive in family-owned Huntsman Corp., 1993-2001; deputy U.S. trade ambassador, 2001-03; UT governor, 2004-09; U.S. ambassador to China, 2009-11.

Announced candidacy: June 21, 2011. **Campaign finances** (May 17-Sept. 30, 2011): $4.5 mil received; $4.2 mil spent; $300,000 on hand, Sept. 30; $3.1 mil in debt.

Opinion polls. Republican support, Oct. 13-25, 2011: 1.0%; highest 2011 rating: 4% (Fox, Sept. 25-27).

Record/issues. As Utah governor, Huntsman replaced the state income tax with a flat tax and cut taxes overall. Utah had one of the highest job growth rates in the nation, and he enjoyed popularity ratings above 80%. Huntsman signed pro-life legislation as governor and supported civil unions for same-sex couples but not marriage. He resigned to become Pres. Obama's ambassador to China. On the campaign trail, he promoted his experience in business, stressed the importance of fostering economic growth and innovation, aggressively promoted free trade, and called for negotiation to resolve trade issues with China. He advocated prompt withdrawal of U.S. troops from Afghanistan, replaced by a narrower counterinsurgency strategy. Huntsman drew some criticism for supporting the Aug. 2011 measure raising the debt ceiling and for refusing to sign pledges, including a no-tax pledge circulated by Grover Norquist and Americans for Tax Reform that was signed by the other Republican candidates.

Notes/sidelights. Huntsman dropped out of high school to join a rock band. He later served two years as a missionary in Taiwan. His father founded a family business, which developed the Big Mac "clamshell" sandwich container among other packaging products. Huntsman failed to make a strong showing in early debates and was expected to have to rely on infusions of personal funds to stay afloat.

Website: www.jon2012.com

Gary Johnson

Full name: Gary Earl Johnson. **Born:** Jan. 1, 1953, Minot, SD. **Home state:** NM. **Education:** Univ. of New Mexico, B.A., 1975. **Religion:** Lutheran. **Military service:** none. **Family:** married Denise Simms, 1977, divorced, 2005; 2 children: Seah, Erik. **Net worth:** $3-$10.5 mil.

Career highlights: Founded Big J Enterprises construction company, 1976; NM governor, 1995-2003.

Announced candidacy: Apr. 21, 2011. **Campaign finances** (Apr. 1-Sept. 30, 2011): $415,000 received; $405,000 spent; $10,000 on hand, Sept. 30; $240,000 in debt.

Opinion polls. Not included in most polls.

Record/issues. A fiscal conservative, Johnson vetoed more than 750 bills as New Mexico governor, cut 1,200 government jobs without layoffs, and left the state with a budget surplus. He opposed federal bailouts and raising the debt ceiling, and called for simplifying the tax code, eliminating corporate income taxes, and dissolving Fannie Mae and Freddie Mac. Johnson supported using block grants to transfer Medicare and Medicaid to states, promised to submit a balanced federal budget by 2013, and advocated reducing or eliminating federal involvement in education. On the campaign trail, Johnson called himself a libertarian and "not a social conservative" who believed government should be "neutral on personal beliefs." Pro-choice on abortion up to the point of viability, he also supported same-sex civil unions and the legalization of marijuana. He called for allowing the Patriot Act to expire and opposed U.S. intervention in Iraq.

Notes/sidelights. Johnson is notable for his physical prowess. He climbed Mt. Everest in 2003 and has competed in several Iron Man triathlons. As a candidate, he had low name recognition and was excluded from most debates.

Website: www.garyjohnson2012.com

CAMPAIGN TRAIL QUOTES, 2011

"Time has come around to the point where the people are agreeing with much of what I've been saying for 30 years."
—Rep. Ron Paul (R, TX), who is known for libertarian views, announcing his third presidential run May 13.

"Ultimately . . . business is my greatest passion, and I am not ready to leave the private sector."
—Real estate mogul and reality TV star Donald Trump, announcing May 16 that he would not run for president, despite a "strong conviction" that he would win if he did.

"I want to announce tonight President Obama is a one-term President."
—Rep. Michele Bachmann (R, MN), announcing she had filed paperwork to be a GOP candidate, during a candidates' debate, June 13 in Manchester, NH.

"It is a Ponzi scheme for these young people. The idea that they're working and paying into Social Security today, that the current program is going to be there for them, is a lie."
—Texas Gov. Rick Perry speaking in Iowa on Aug. 27.

"[A]ll I'm saying is that, in order for the Republican Party to win, we can't run from science. We can't run from mainstream conservative philosophy. We've got to win voters."
—Former Utah Gov. John Huntsman, in a Sept. 7 GOP debate in Simi Valley, CA.

"If you're dealt four aces, that doesn't make you a great poker player."
—Former Massachusetts Gov. Mitt Romney, assessing the job creation record of Texas Gov. Rick Perry, in a Republican debate Sept. 12 in Tampa, FL.

"My next-door neighbor's two dogs have created more shovel-ready projects than this current administration."
—Former New Mexico Gov. Gary Johnson, in GOP debate, Sept. 22 in Orlando, FL, using a one-liner borrowed from radio commentator Rush Limbaugh.

"So, New Jersey, whether you like it or not, you're stuck with me."
—New Jersey Gov. Chris Christie, in Trenton Oct. 4, ending speculation that he would enter the 2012 Republican presidential race, as some Republicans had urged.

"I believe that at this time I can be more effective in a decisive role to help elect other true public servants to office—from the nation's governors to congressional seats and the presidency."
—Former Alaska Gov. and 2008 Republican vice-presidential nominee Sarah Palin, saying she would not be running for the nomination in 2012, in a statement released Oct. 5.

"I am running because I want to win, not because I'm trying to raise my profile or get a TV show."
—Herman Cain, former Godfather's Pizza CEO, Oct. 13, after appearing at a Faith and Freedom Coalition rally at Ohio Christian Univ.

"I'm going to wait until everybody is voted off the island before . . . Once they narrow it down to one or two, I'll start paying attention."
—Pres. Barack Obama, joking Oct. 26 on *The Tonight Show With Jay Leno* about ignoring the current field of candidates for the Republican presidential nomination.

Rep. Ron Paul

Full name: Ronald Ernest Paul. **Born:** Aug. 20, 1935, Pittsburgh, PA. **Home state:** TX. **Education:** Gettysburg College, PA, B.A., 1957; Duke Univ., M.D., 1961. **Religion:** Protestant. **Military service:** Flight surgeon, Air Force, 1963-65; flight surgeon, Air National Guard, 1965-68. **Family:** married Carol Wells, 1957; 5 children: Ronald, Lori, Rand, Robert, Joy. **Net worth:** $2.25-$5 mil.
Career highlights: Obstetrician/gynecologist in private practice, beginning 1968; U.S. representative (TX), 1976-77, 1979-85, 1997-present; Libertarian Party presidential candidate, 1998; ran for GOP presidential nomination, 2008.
Announced candidacy: May 13, 2011. **Campaign finances** (Jan. 14-Sept. 30, 2011): $12.8 mil received; $9.1 mil spent; $3.7 mil on hand, Sept. 30; no debt.
Opinion polls. Republican support, Oct. 13-25, 2011: 8.5%; highest 2011 rating: 14% (USA Today/Gallup, Aug. 4-7).
Record/issues. A libertarian, Paul advocated "limited, constitutional government" and argued that an unfettered free market was crucial to future peace and prosperity. A fervent opponent of Keynesianism, he called for "sound money" and abolition of the Federal Reserve, and opposed TARP as well as U.S. involvement in Iraq and Afghanistan. Paul's Plan to Restore America went further than the other Republican candidates' economic plans, calling for $1 tril in budget cuts in just one year, with a balanced budget by 2015. His plan would freeze most spending at 2006 levels, eliminate five cabinet-level departments, and cut 10% of the federal workforce, block-grant Medicaid and other welfare programs to states, and allow young people to opt out of Medicare and Social Security. Paul also promised to "end all foreign wars" and eliminate foreign aid. Many economists say his plan, if it could be enacted, would lead to severe short-term recession; Paul contended it would restore long-term economic health.
Notes/sidelights. A pro-life campaign ad promoted Paul's experience as an obstetrician who has delivered 4,000 babies. His economic plan would lower his salary as president to $39,336, around the median U.S income. True to his principles, Paul had no campaign debt at the end of Sept. 2011, unlike most other candidates.
Website: ronpaul2012.com

Gov. Rick Perry

Full name: James Richard Perry. **Born:** Mar. 4, 1950, Paint Creek, TX. **Home state:** TX. **Education:** Texas A&M Univ., B.S., 1972. **Religion:** Methodist. **Military service:** Captain, Air Force, 1972-77. **Family:** married Anita Thigpen, 1982; 2 children: Griffin, Sydney. **Net worth:** $1.1+ mil.
Career highlights: Farmer and rancher; state representative (TX), 1984-90; TX agricultural commissioner, 1991-99; TX lieutenant governor, 1999-2000; TX governor, 2000-present; chairman, Republican Governors Assn., 2008, 2011.
Announced candidacy: Aug. 13, 2011. **Campaign finances** (July 1-Sept. 30, 2011): $17.2 mil received; $2.1 mil spent; $15.1 on hand, Sept. 30; $340,000 in debt.
Opinion polls. Republican support, Oct. 13-25, 2011: 10.5%; highest 2011 rating: 38% (NBC News/*Wall Street Journal*, Aug. 27-31).
Record/issues. An evangelical Christian, Perry addressed a prayer rally attended by some 30,000 in a Houston stadium, Aug. 6, 2011, then entered the race a week later. Perry called himself "an authentic conservative, not a conservative of convenience," in an apparent jab at Romney, though Perry was once a registered Democrat. He cited his executive experience and job creation record as a popular Texas governor since 2000 and emphasized energy deregulation and exploitation of domestic energy resources to create jobs and achieve energy independence. His Cut, Balance, and Grow plan would reduce corporate taxes and give individual taxpayers the option of paying a 20% flat rate; it also proposed fixes for Medicare and Social Security. As governor, Perry prioritized Operation Border Star, a military-style border operation launched in 2007 against Mexican drug cartels and gangs. He came under fire from rivals for signing legislation in 2001 that granted in-state tuition to children of illegal immigrants. He was criticized by Bachmann and other

candidates for a 2007 executive order mandating vaccinations for girls against a virus known to cause cervical cancer. He defended it on humanitarian grounds, but some critics tied the legislation to lobbying by his former chief of staff.

Notes/sidelights. Perry's initial popularity slid sharply in the wake of several weak debate performances. But he appeared to have the time, conservative credentials, and money, mostly from wealthy donors, to stage a possible rally. As of Sept. 30, Perry's campaign had more cash on hand than that of any GOP rival.

Website: www.rickperry.org

Mitt Romney

Full name: Willard Mitt Romney. **Born:** Mar. 12, 1947, Detroit, MI. **Home state:** MA. **Education:** Brigham Young Univ., B.A., 1971; Harvard, M.B.A., 1975, J.D., 1975. **Religion:** Mormon. **Military service:** none. **Family:** married Ann Lois Davies, 1969; 5 children: Tagg, Matt, Josh, Ben, Craig. **Net worth:** $190-$250 mil.

Career highlights: Investment banker, founder, CEO, Bain Capital, 1984-99; vice-pres., Bain & Co. consulting firm, 1977-84, 1991-92; CEO, organizing committee for 2002 Salt Lake City Olympics; MA governor, 2003-07; chairman, Republican Governors Assn., 2006; ran for GOP presidential nomination, 2008.

Announced candidacy: June 2, 2011. **Campaign finances** (Apr. 1-Sept. 30, 2011): $32.6 mil received; $17.9 mil spent; $14.7 mil on hand, Sept. 30; no debt.

Opinion polls. Republican support, Oct. 13-25, 2011: 24.3%; highest 2011 rating: 33% (Rasmussen, June 14).

Record/issues. Romney touted his business and government experience and stressed his ability as a leader to bring about consensus and solutions. His 59-point plan for jobs and economic growth called for extending the George W. Bush tax cuts, cutting corporate tax rates, abolishing the estate tax, and eliminating the capital gains tax for those making under $200,000 a year. Critics accused Romney of "flip-flopping" and especially focused on "Romneycare," a Massachusetts health care program, which he passed as governor. Romney has sought to distinguish it from the controversial 2010 health care reform law signed by Pres. Obama, in part by arguing that the state program was not meant as a workable model for the nation. While he campaigned for governor in 2002 as a pro-choice candidate, he took pro-life positions in the presidential race, though he declined to sign a broad pro-life pledge because of concerns of "unintended consequences." Romney advocated "peace through strength," indicating he would put carrier forces in the eastern Mediterranean and Persian Gulf and reverse cuts to missile defense. When Texas evangelical pastor and Perry supporter Robert Jeffress denounced Mormonism as a "cult" at a

Values Voter Summit in Oct. 2011, Romney condemned religious bigotry in response.

Notes/sidelights. Having campaigned unsuccessfully for nomination in 2008, Romney was a more experienced campaigner and debater by 2011. He had raised and spent more money than any other Republican as of Sept. 30 and was considered to be more electable nationally than his rivals by many political analysts. He had modest leads in GOP polls for most of 2011 but was not a favorite of conservatives.

Website: www.mittromney.com

Rick Santorum

Full name: Richard John Santorum. **Born:** May 10, 1958, Winchester, VA. **Home state:** PA. **Education:** Pennsylvania State Univ., B.A., 1980; Univ. of Pittsburgh, M.B.A., 1981; Dickinson Law School at Penn State, J.D., 1986. **Religion:** Roman Catholic. **Military service:** none. **Family:** married Karen Garver, 1990; 7 children: Elizabeth, Richard, Daniel, Sarah Maria, Peter, Patrick, Isabella. **Net worth:** $880,000-$1.9 mil.

Career highlights: Administrative assistant, PA state senate, 1981-86; attorney in private practice, 1986-91; U.S. representative (PA), 1991-95; U.S senator (PA), 1995-2007; Republican conference chairman, 2001-07.

Announced candidacy: June 6, 2011. **Campaign finances** (Apr. 1-Sept. 30, 2011): $1.3 mil received; $1.1 mil spent; $190,000 on hand, Sept. 30; $70,000 in debt.

Opinion polls. Republican support, Oct. 13-25, 2011: 2.0%; highest 2011 rating: 6% (Rasmussen, June 14).

Record/issues. As U.S. representative from Pennsylvania, Santorum was one of the "Gang of Seven" freshman Republicans who pressed for a probe of the 1992 House Bank scandal. A strong social conservative, he sponsored legislation—vetoed by Pres. Bill Clinton, but signed by Pres. G. W. Bush in 2003—to ban so-called partial birth abortions and signed a broad anti-abortion pledge. Santorum called for a constitutional ban on same-sex marriage and opposed repeal of the "don't ask, don't tell" policy on gays in the military. On the economy, he stressed the importance of bringing back manufacturing jobs and criticized flat tax proposals as not pro-family. Santorum supported a balanced budget amendment and denounced "Islamic fascism."

Notes/sidelights. Defeated 59% to 41% in his 2006 Senate reelection bid, Santorum remained active as a conservative advocate. In a 2003 interview, he argued that the U.S. constitution does not protect privacy rights and expressed support for anti-sodomy laws. In response, sex advice columnist Dan Savage spearheaded a protest that made a lewd definition of "santorum" the first search result for his name in Google results.

Website: www.ricksantorum.com

Election Calendar, 2012

Source: National Association of Secretaries of State, World Almanac research

Primaries and Caucuses

List indicates dates of primaries for both parties except where indicated. D = Democratic, R = Republican, * = caucus, # = pending court challenge. Dates are as of Nov. 2, 2011, and subject to change. Dates for caucuses denote first day of process.

January 2012
Jan. 3: IA*
Jan. 10: NH
Jan. 21: NV (D*), SC (R#)
Jan. 28: SC (D)
Jan. 31: FL

February 2012
Feb. 4: ME, NV (both R*)
Feb. 7: CO, MN (both R*);
   MO (nonbinding)
Feb. 28: AZ, MI

March 2012
Mar. 3: WA (R*)
Mar. 6, Super Tuesday: GA, MA, OK, TN,
   TX, VT, VA; AK, ID, ND, WY (all R*); CO,
   MN (both D*)
Mar. 7: HI (D*)
Mar. 10: KS (R*)
Mar. 11: ME (D*)
Mar. 13: AL, MS; HI (R*); UT (D*)
Mar. 17: MO (R*)
Mar. 20: IL
Mar. 24: LA

April 2012
Apr. 3: DC, MD, WI
Apr. 14: ID, KS, NE, WY (all D*)
Apr. 15: AK, FL, WA (all D*)
Apr. 24: CT, DE, NY, PA, RI

May 2012
May 5: MI (D*)
May 8: IN, NC, WV
May 15: NE, OR
May 22: AK, KY

June 2012
June 5: CA, MT, NJ, NM, SD; ND (D*)
June 12: OH
June 26: UT

Other Key Election Dates

Aug. 27-30, 2012: Republican National Convention, Tampa, FL
Sept. 3-6, 2012: Democratic National Convention, Charlotte, NC
Nov. 6, 2012: Election Day
Dec. 17, 2012: Electoral College members meet in each state to cast votes.

Jan. 6, 2013: Electoral votes officially tallied before both houses of Congress.
Jan. 20, 2013: Presidential inauguration day.
   (Because the date falls on a Sunday, the oath may be publicly administered the following day.)

THE CHANGING UNITED STATES:
A STATISTICAL PORTRAIT

Source (unless otherwise noted): Decennial Censuses, American Community Survey 2010, U.S. Census Bureau, U.S. Dept. of Commerce

Change in Population and Congressional House Seats by State, 2000-10

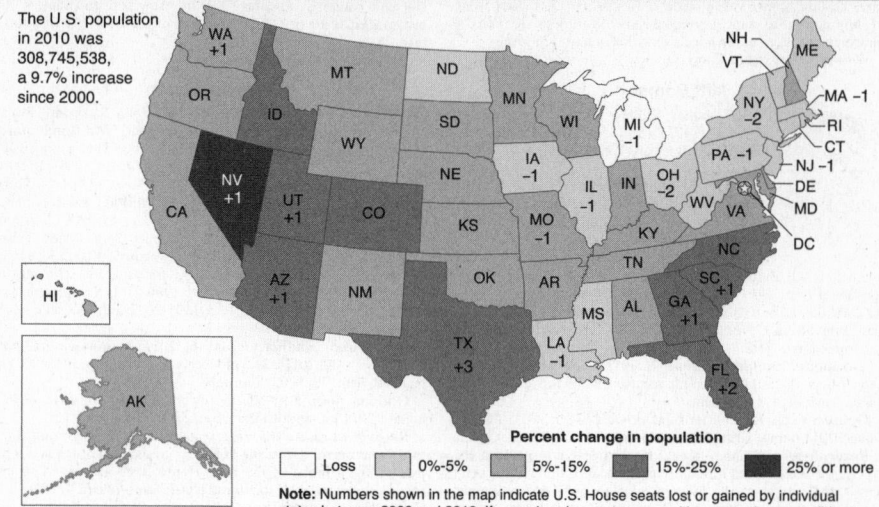

The U.S. population in 2010 was 308,745,538, a 9.7% increase since 2000.

Percent change in population

Loss · 0%-5% · 5%-15% · 15%-25% · 25% or more

Note: Numbers shown in the map indicate U.S. House seats lost or gained by individual states between 2000 and 2010. If a number does not appear with a state, that state did not experience a change in representation.

Fastest-Growing States

Rank	State	% change, 2000-10	Rank	State	% change, 2000-10
1.	Nevada	35.1	6.	North Carolina	18.5
2.	Arizona	24.6	7.	Georgia	18.3
3.	Utah	23.8	8.	Florida	17.6
4.	Idaho	21.1	9.	Colorado	16.9
5.	Texas	20.6	10.	South Carolina	15.3

Slowest-Growing States

Rank	State	% change, 2000-10	Rank	State	% change, 2000-10
1.	Michigan	-0.6	6.	West Virginia	2.5
2.	Rhode Island	0.4	7.	Vermont	2.8
3.	Louisiana	1.4	8.	Massachusetts	3.1
4.	Ohio	1.6	9.	Illinois	3.3
5.	New York	2.1	10.	Pennsylvania	3.4

Median Age by State, 2010

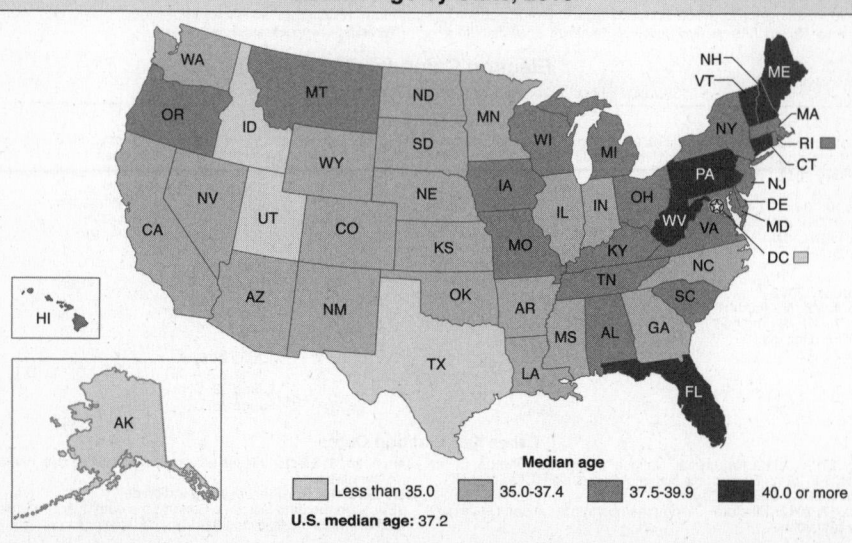

Median age

Less than 35.0 · 35.0-37.4 · 37.5-39.9 · 40.0 or more

U.S. median age: 37.2

Fastest-Growing Metropolitan Areas, 2000-10

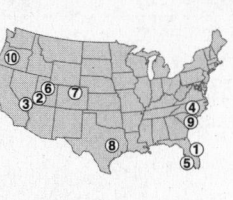

Rank	Metropolitan statistical area (MSA)	Population 2000	Population 2010	% change, 2000-10
1.	Palm Coast, FL	49,832	96,696	92.0
2.	St. George, UT	90,354	138,115	52.9
3.	Las Vegas-Paradise, NV	1,375,765	1,951,269	41.8
4.	Raleigh-Cary, NC	797,071	1,130,490	41.8
5.	Cape Coral-Fort Myers, FL	440,888	618,754	40.3
6.	Provo-Orem, UT	376,774	526,810	39.8
7.	Greeley, CO	180,926	252,825	39.7
8.	Austin-Round Rock-San Marcos, TX	1,249,763	1,716,289	37.3
9.	Myrtle Beach-N. Myrtle Beach-Conway, SC	196,629	269,291	37.0
10.	Bend, OR	115,367	157,733	36.7

Note: MSAs are defined as at least one core urbanized area of 50,000 or more, plus adjacent area closely integrated with the core, as measured by commuting ties.

Population Change in Largest U.S. Cities, 2000-10

Most Growth

Rank	City	Population 2000	Population 2010	% change, 2000-10
1.	Louisville-Jefferson Co., KY [1]	256,231	597,337	133.1
2.	North Las Vegas, NV	115,488	216,961	87.9
3.	Irvine, CA	143,072	212,375	48.4
4.	Henderson, NV	175,381	257,729	47.0
5.	Raleigh, NC	276,093	403,892	46.3
6.	Bakersfield, CA	247,057	347,483	40.6
7.	Chula Vista, CA	173,556	243,916	40.5
8.	Fort Worth, TX	534,694	741,206	38.6
9.	Charlotte, NC	540,828	731,424	35.2
10.	Chandler, AZ	176,581	236,123	33.7

(1) 2000 population is for Louisville prior to consolidation with Jefferson Co.; 2010 pop. doesn't include semi-independent incorporated places within area.

Rank	City	Population 2000	Population 2010	% change, 2000-10
1.	New Orleans, LA	484,674	343,829	−29.1
2.	Detroit, MI	951,270	713,777	−25.0
3.	Cleveland, OH	478,403	396,815	−17.1
4.	Birmingham, AL	242,820	212,237	−12.6
5.	Buffalo, NY	292,648	261,310	−10.7
6.	Cincinnati, OH	331,285	296,943	−10.4
7.	Honolulu, HI	371,657	337,256	−9.3
8.	Pittsburgh, PA	334,563	305,704	−8.6
9.	Toledo, OH	313,619	287,208	−8.4
10.	St. Louis, MO	348,189	319,294	−8.3

Greatest Decline

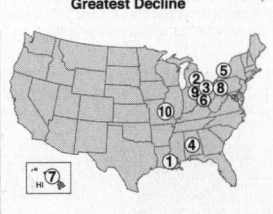

Population Change in Select Cities, 1900-2010

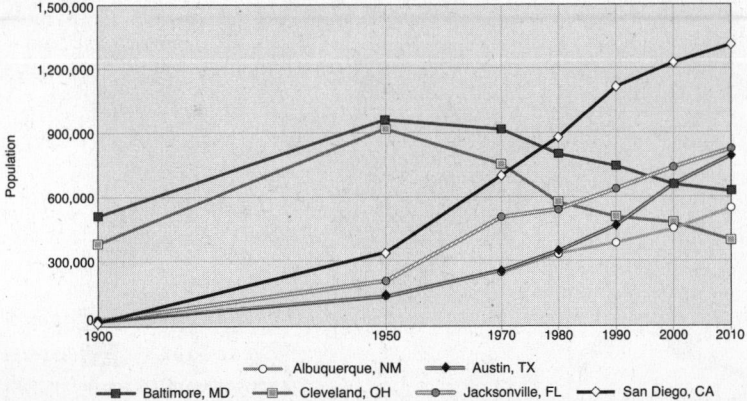

Hispanic or Latino by Type, 2010

In the U.S. Census, Hispanic or Latino refers to a person "of Cuban, Mexican, Puerto Rican, South or Central American, or other Spanish culture or origin regardless of race."

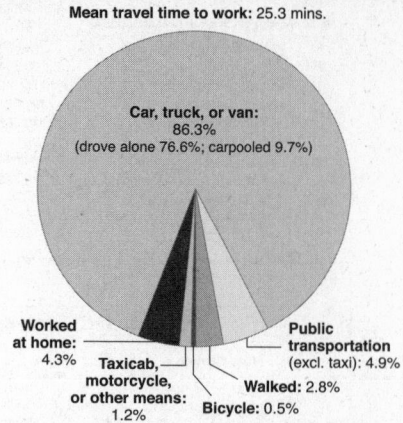

UNITED STATES

Mexican, 62.99%

Caribbean: 15.5%
Cuban, 3.54%
Dominican, 2.80% (Dominican Rep.)
Puerto Rican, 9.16%

Central American: 7.92%
Guatemalan, 2.07%
Salvadoran, 3.27%
Honduran, 1.25%
Nicaraguan, 0.69%
Costa Rican, 0.25%
Panamanian, 0.33%

South American: 5.49%
Venezuelan, 0.43%
Colombian, 1.80%
Ecuadoran, 1.12%
Peruvian, 1.05%
Bolivian, 0.20%
Chilean, 0.25%
Paraquayan, 0.04%
Uruguayan, 0.11%
Argentinean, 0.45%

Other Hispanic or Latino (incl. Spaniard, Spanish, and Spanish American): **8.10%**

Note: The percentage that appears with each country indicates the Hispanic or Latino population's self-reported country of origin, whether born in that country, the U.S., or elsewhere. Data identifies ethnicity, not country of birth.

Means of Transportation to Work, 2010

Mean travel time to work: 25.3 mins.

Car, truck, or van: 86.3%
(drove alone 76.6%; carpooled 9.7%)

Worked at home: 4.3%

Taxicab, motorcycle, or other means: 1.2%

Bicycle: 0.5%

Walked: 2.8%

Public transportation (excl. taxi): 4.9%

Note: As percentage of workers 16 years of age and over. Incl. members of the military and civilians who were at work in week prior to survey response. Data based on sample of 136,941,010 respondents from 12 states (CT, ME, MA, MI, MN, NH, NJ, NY, PA, RI, VT, WI). Figures may not add up to 100% due to rounding.

Hispanic or Latino Concentration by State, 2010

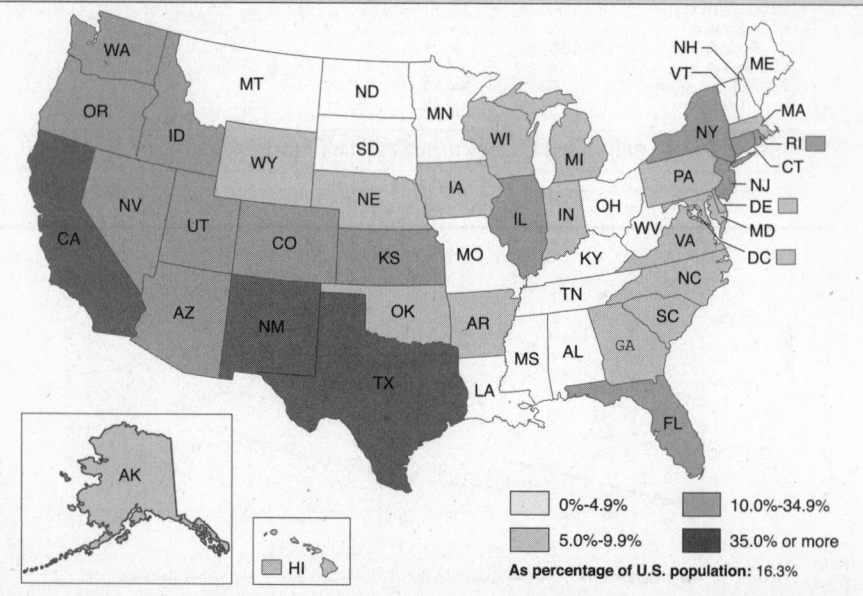

0%-4.9%
5.0%-9.9%
10.0%-34.9%
35.0% or more

As percentage of U.S. population: 16.3%

Median Earnings by Industry and Sex, 2010

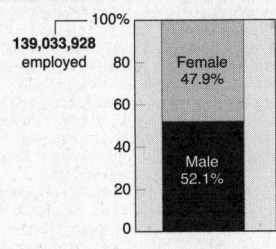

139,033,928 employed

Female 47.9%

Male 52.1%

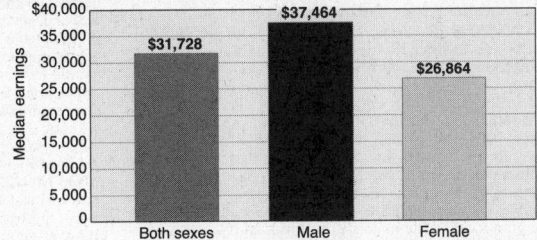

Both sexes $31,728 · Male $37,464 · Female $26,864

Industry	Total employed	Male (%)	Female (%)	Median earnings	Median earnings (male)	Median earnings (female)
Agriculture; forestry; fishing, hunting; mining	2,646,975	82.2	17.8	$27,790	$30,545	$18,906
Arts, entertainment, recreation; accommodation, food services	12,859,572	48.7	51.3	15,009	17,518	12,402
Construction	8,686,813	90.8	9.2	32,068	32,127	31,454
Educational services; health care, social assistance	32,311,107	25.3	74.7	32,509	42,252	30,845
Finance, insurance; real estate, rental, leasing	9,275,465	44.6	55.4	41,446	52,360	36,135
Information	3,015,521	56.6	43.4	43,874	51,360	36,208
Manufacturing	14,439,691	70.7	29.3	40,237	43,339	31,001
Other services, except public administration	6,913,449	47.0	53.0	21,586	29,451	16,570
Professional, scientific, management; administrative, waste management services	14,710,089	57.9	42.1	39,197	45,915	31,940
Public administration	7,187,193	55.1	44.9	48,331	55,225	41,077
Retail trade	16,203,408	50.2	49.8	21,098	26,143	17,151
Transportation, warehousing; utilities	6,843,579	75.8	24.2	41,313	43,600	34,196
Wholesale trade	3,941,066	70.2	29.8	39,367	41,821	31,690

Note: For the civilian employed population 16 years of age and over including workers not employed full-time.

How Americans Spent Their Time, 2010

Source: American Time Use Survey, Bureau of Labor Statistics, U.S. Dept. of Labor

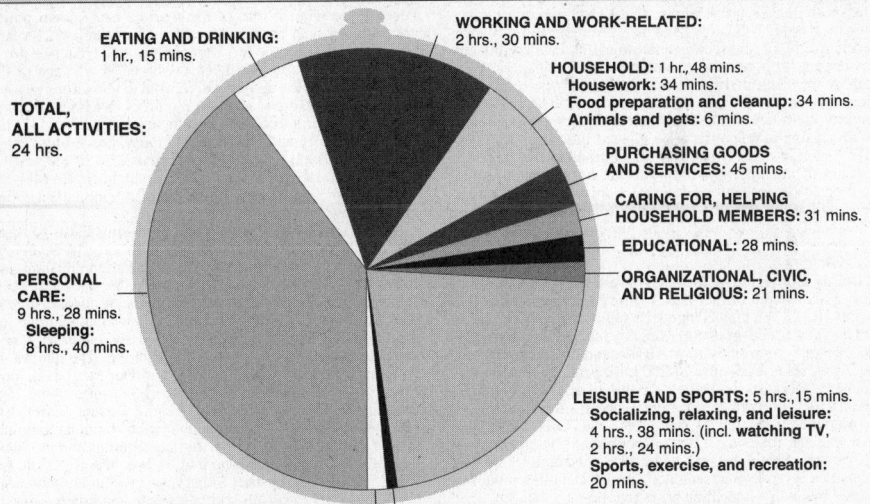

EATING AND DRINKING: 1 hr., 15 mins.

WORKING AND WORK-RELATED: 2 hrs., 30 mins.

TOTAL, ALL ACTIVITIES: 24 hrs.

HOUSEHOLD: 1 hr., 48 mins.
Housework: 34 mins.
Food preparation and cleanup: 34 mins.
Animals and pets: 6 mins.

PURCHASING GOODS AND SERVICES: 45 mins.

CARING FOR, HELPING HOUSEHOLD MEMBERS: 31 mins.

EDUCATIONAL: 28 mins.

ORGANIZATIONAL, CIVIC, AND RELIGIOUS: 21 mins.

PERSONAL CARE: 9 hrs., 28 mins.
Sleeping: 8 hrs., 40 mins.

LEISURE AND SPORTS: 5 hrs.,15 mins.
Socializing, relaxing, and leisure: 4 hrs., 38 mins. (incl. watching TV, 2 hrs., 24 mins.)
Sports, exercise, and recreation: 20 mins.

OTHER ACTIVITIES: 21 mins.[1]   TELEPHONE CALLS, MAIL, AND E-MAIL: 11 mins.

Note: For the civilian, noninstitutionalized population 15 years of age and over, both employed and not employed. Time spent is on primary, or main, activity (indicated by all caps) and selected secondary activities and includes related travel time. Data based on sample of 13,200 respondents. (1) Includes "missing activities," i.e., periods of time for which respondents could not remember what they did.

November 2010

National

In Midterm Elections, Republicans Capture House— U.S. voters frustrated with Pres. Barack Obama, congressional Democratic leaders, and the slow pace of economic recovery turned over control of the House of Representatives to the Republican Party in midterm elections Nov. 2. Final tallies showed the GOP picking up 63 seats in the House—the most for any party since 1948, when Democrats gained 75 seats—enough to ensure that a Republican would replace Rep. Nancy Pelosi (D, CA) as speaker of the House when the 112th Congress convened in Jan. 2011. Republicans also gained 6 seats in the Senate. Democrats held onto their Senate majority, however, and Senate Majority Leader Harry Reid (D, NV) beat back a challenge from Sharron Angle (R), a favorite of conservative Tea Party activists. Two other Republicans with Tea Party support, Marco Rubio (FL) and Rand Paul (KY), won Senate seats from their respective states. In a major upset in Alaska, incumbent Sen. Lisa Murkowski, who had lost the Republican party primary to a challenger backed by the Tea Party and former Alaska Gov. Sarah Palin, retained her seat by running as a write-in candidate.

In state races, Republicans made a net gain of 6 governorships and picked up more than 675 legislative seats, giving the party a significant advantage in states where results of the 2010 census will require state legislatures to redraw congressional district boundaries. Andrew Cuomo (D), son of former Gov. Mario Cuomo (D), won the New York state governorship, while former California Gov. Jerry Brown (D) won a 3rd term 28 years after finishing his 2nd term. Rick Perry (R), the longest-serving governor in Texas history, easily won reelection to a 3rd full term. Republicans also captured governorships in Florida, Pennsylvania, Ohio, Michigan, Wisconsin, and Iowa—states that are likely to be major battlegrounds in the 2012 presidential election.

According to calculations by the U.S. Elections Project, based at George Mason Univ., nearly 90.7 mil people, representing 41.6% of eligible voters, cast ballots in the 2010 general election.

Airports Implement Enhanced Screening Procedures— Under revamped airport procedures effective Nov. 1, the Transportation Security Admin. (TSA) began requiring passengers at many U.S. airports to pass through full-body scanners capable of producing anatomically detailed images. Passengers who refused to submit to an enhanced body scan or were selected for further screening would receive a thorough pat-down from a TSA employee. The aggressive security measures, which drew criticism from civil liberties groups, came in response to an alleged plot Dec. 25, 2009, by a Nigerian man, Umar Farouk Abdulmutallab, who was accused of attempting to blow up a Detroit-bound jetliner by detonating an explosive device concealed in his underwear. Different security guidelines for airline pilots were announced Nov. 19 after their unions complained that repeated use of the scanners would subject pilots to excessive radiation.

DeLay Convicted of Money Laundering— A Texas jury Nov. 24 convicted former U.S. House Majority Leader Tom DeLay (R, TX) on money laundering and conspiracy charges. DeLay was found guilty of illegally channeling $190,000 in corporate contributions to GOP candidates running for the Texas state legislature in 2002. The money, donated by company lobbyists to DeLay's political action committee, Texans for a Republican Majority, had been transferred to the Republican National Committee (RNC). The RNC had then sent the funds to 7 Texas Republican candidates, 6 of whom won seats in the state house of representatives. DeLay received a 3-year prison sentence Jan. 10, 2011, but remained free on bail while appealing his conviction.

Persistent Unemployment, Soaring Deficits Raise Concerns about U.S. Economy— Labeling the pace of recovery "disappointingly slow," the Federal Reserve announced Nov. 3 that it would pump another $600 bil into the U.S. economy by expanding its holdings of Treasury securities, a technique known as quantitative easing. Data released by the Labor Dept. a month later showed that the U.S. had added 172,000 jobs in Oct. but only 39,000 jobs in Nov., causing the unemployment rate to rise from 9.6% to 9.8%. Other economic indicators for Nov. were more positive, including an expansion of factory output, a surge in retail sales, and the largest initial public offering in history for shares of General Motors. The successful GM IPO, valued at more than $23 bil, raised hopes that taxpayers would fully recoup their $50 bil investment in the automaker in the 2009 bailout.

On Nov. 29, Pres. Obama proposed a freeze on the salaries of most federal employees. The freeze, which did not affect uniformed military personnel, was expected to save $5 bil over the first 2 years and $28 bil over a 5-year period—a relatively small sum when compared with the estimated 2010 and 2011 federal deficits of more than $1 tril. John Gage, president of the American Federation of Government Employees, AFL-CIO, called the move a "symbolic, political, public-relations stunt." The freeze was announced as the bipartisan National Commission on Fiscal Responsibility and Reform, appointed by Obama and co-chaired by former Sen. Alan Simpson (R, WY) and former White House Chief of Staff Erskine Bowles (D, NC), was preparing to issue its recommendations on deficit reduction. The commission report, released Dec. 1, proposed trimming the federal workforce by 10%, raising the Social Security retirement age to 68 by 2050, tightening cost controls on Medicare and Medicaid, and revising the federal tax code so that dividends and capital gains would be taxed at the same rate as ordinary income.

The Dow Jones Industrial Average closed Nov. 30 at 11,006.02, down 1% for the month. The Nasdaq Composite Index closed at 2.498.23, and the S&P 500 finished at 1,180.55; each declined by less than 1% for the month. Gold prices during the month spiked above $1,400 an ounce, a new record.

International

Myanmar Holds Election, Frees Aung San Suu Kyi— Six days after conducting Myanmar's first national election since 1990, the military-dominated State Peace and Development Council on Nov. 13 released pro-democracy activist Aung San Suu Kyi from house arrest. The 1991 Nobel Peace Prize winner, one of the world's best-known political prisoners, had been detained for 15 of the last 21 years. Her National League for Democracy, the country's leading opposition party, had been dissolved in advance of the Nov. 7 vote, and the regime had refused to allow foreign journalists or international election monitors to witness the balloting. According to official results announced Nov. 17, the Union Solidarity and Development Party, headed by former Prime Min. Thein Sein, won more than 75% of the seats at stake in national, regional, and state assemblies. On Mar. 30, 2011, Thein Sein became president of a nominally civilian government.

Jury Reaches Split Verdict in Bombing Case— Facing 285 criminal charges in connection with terrorist bombings in 2 African capitals in 1998, Ahmed Khalfan Ghailani was convicted Nov. 17 on a single count of conspiracy to destroy U.S. government buildings and property. A federal jury in New York City acquitted Ghailani, a Tanzanian national, on the other 284 charges, including conspiracy to murder Americans and use weapons of mass destruction. The attacks on U.S. embassies in Nairobi, Kenya, and Dar es Salaam, Tanzania, killed 224 people and wounded thousands more. The trial was an important test case for the Obama administration, which chose to prosecute Ghailani through the criminal justice system rather than by military commission at Guantánamo Bay, Cuba, where he had been held since 2006. On Jan. 25, 2011, U.S. District Judge Lewis A. Kaplan sentenced Ghailani to life in prison without parole and ordered him to pay $33 mil in restitution.

29 Die in New Zealand Mine Blast— An explosion Nov. 19 at the Pike River coal mine near Greymouth, on New Zealand's South Island, claimed the lives of 29 men. Rescue efforts, slowed by the presence of dangerous levels of carbon monoxide and explosive methane gas, were abandoned Nov. 24 after a second blast erased any hope that the men might have survived.

Cambodia Bridge Stampede Kills Hundreds—Water Festival celebrations in Cambodia's capital of Phnom Penh ended in tragedy Nov. 22 when thousands of people attempted to cross a narrow bridge between Diamond Island and the mainland. Fearful that the bridge might collapse, the crowd panicked, causing a stampede in which more than 350 people were killed. Most of the fatalities occurred because of suffocation or internal injuries, while some victims drowned after leaping off the bridge into the Bassac River.

EU Approves Ireland Bailout—At a Nov. 28 meeting in Brussels, Belgium, finance ministers from European Union member countries approved an 85 bil euro ($115 bil) program to rescue Ireland from financial crisis. The emergency loan package, requested by the Irish government a week earlier, included 50 bil euros to enable Ireland to meet its debt obligations and 35 bil euros for the nation's ailing banks. To fund the program, the EU agreed to provide 45 bil euros and the International Monetary Fund committed 22.5 bil euros; the Irish government pledged the remaining 17.5 bil euros from its cash reserves and the national pension fund to help Ireland's banks cover their losses. In exchange for international assistance, Irish Prime Min. Brian Cowen promised to restructure the nation's banking sector and to implement austerity measures—including tax increases and cuts in welfare spending, public employment, and the minimum wage—which met with widespread domestic opposition.

WikiLeaks Publishes Secret U.S. Diplomatic Cables—WikiLeaks, an international media group that makes confidential documents public online, began publishing Nov. 28 what it claimed was a collection of 251,287 previously undisclosed U.S. embassy cables. The cables, spanning the period from Dec. 1966 to Feb. 2010, represented confidential communications between the U.S. State Dept. and its diplomats worldwide. The overwhelming majority of the cables were from the last decade. Before posting an initial group of several hundred cables on its website, WikiLeaks reportedly provided the entire collection of "Cablegate" documents to mainstream media organizations in Germany, Spain, France, and the UK. (Britain's *Guardian* newspaper then passed the documents on to the *New York Times*.) Asked Nov. 30 to assess the impact of the disclosures, U.S. Defense Sec. Robert Gates qualified the release was "embarrassing" and "awkward" but described consequences for U.S. foreign policy as being "fairly modest."

On Nov. 29, U.S. Atty. Gen. Eric Holder indicated that the Justice Dept. had launched a criminal investigation against WikiLeaks. Although the organization refused to name the source of the cables, U.S. investigators continued to focus on Pfc. Bradley Manning, an Army intelligence analyst who had been arrested in May 2010 in connection with earlier WikiLeaks disclosures. On Dec. 15, Glenn Greenwald of Salon.com reported that Manning was being held 23 hrs. a day in solitary confinement at the U.S. Marine brig in Quantico, VA. Meanwhile, prosecutors in Sweden continued to pursue charges of rape and sexual molestation against WikiLeaks founder Julian Assange, who surrendered to British police in London Dec. 7. A British court ruled Feb. 24, 2011, that Assange must be extradited to Sweden to face questioning on the sexual-assault allegations, but he was allowed to remain free on bail while appealing the decision.

General

Giants Win World Series—The San Francisco Giants captured their first World Series title since 1954 and their first since the franchise moved from New York to California in 1958, defeating the Texas Rangers, 4 games to 1. In Game 5, played Nov. 1 at Rangers Ballpark in Arlington, TX, the Giants won 3-1 behind a dominant pitching performance by two-time Cy Young Award winner Tim Lincecum and a three-run homer by shortstop Edgar Rentería, who was named World Series MVP. The Rangers were making their first World Series appearance in the franchise's 50-year history.

Blame Upsets Zenyatta in Breeders' Cup—Ridden by jockey Garrett Gomez, Blame held off a thrilling stretch run

by the overwhelming favorite, Zenyatta, to win the $5 mil Breeders' Cup Classic Nov. 6 at Churchill Downs in Louisville, KY. Undefeated in her previous 19 starts, the 6-year-old Zenyatta, ridden by Mike Smith, was the oldest horse in the race and the only female. Lane's End Farm near Versailles, KY, announced Nov. 17 that Zenyatta would be moved there to serve as a broodmare. Two months later, she was named 2010 Horse of the Year in joint balloting by the National Thoroughbred Racing Association, the National Turf Writers and Broadcasters, and the *Daily Racing Form*.

Pacquiao Captures Boxing Crown in 8th Weight Division—Filipino fighter Manny Pacquiao pounded Mexican-born boxer Antonio Margarito Nov. 13 at Cowboys Stadium in Arlington, TX, in a 12-round bout billed as a super welterweight title match by the World Boxing Council. Pacquiao's victory by unanimous decision over an opponent who outweighed him by 17 pounds made him the first boxer in history to win titles in 8 different weight classifications. Pacquiao, who weighed in before the Margarito fight at 144.6 lbs, won his first world title in 1998 as a flyweight at 112 lbs.

Jimmie Johnson Takes 5th Straight Cup Series Title—With a second-place finish Nov. 21 in NASCAR's season-ending Ford 400 at Homestead-Miami Speedway, Jimmie Johnson clinched an unprecedented fifth consecutive Cup Series championship. Johnson, who trailed in the Cup Series point standings when the race began, ended the day 39 points ahead of runner-up Denny Hamlin, who finished 14th in the NASCAR season finale. Johnson's winnings for the season exceeded $7.2 mil.

December 2010
National

Congress Extends Tax Cuts, Repeals "Don't Ask, Don't Tell"; Other Legislative Developments—The 111th Congress adjourned Dec. 22 after a post-election session in which Democratic leaders passed and Pres. Barack Obama signed a flurry of major measures. An $858-bil compromise package negotiated by the White House with congressional Republicans included a cut in the Social Security payroll tax rate for 2011, an extension through 2011 of long-term unemployment benefits, and a 2-year extension of lower income tax rates for taxpayers in all brackets. The final provision represented a reversal for Obama and congressional Democrats, who had called for an end to the Bush tax cuts originally enacted in 2001 for individuals earning more than $200,000 a year. The Senate passed the measure Dec. 15 by a vote of 81-19, the House followed suit Dec. 16 by 277-148, and Pres. Obama signed it into law the following day.

By a 250-175 vote Dec. 15 in the House and a 65-31 vote Dec. 18 in the Senate, Congress acted to repeal the "Don't Ask, Don't Tell" policy that had prevented gay and bisexual men and women from serving openly in the U.S. armed forces. On Dec. 22, Pres. Obama signed the measure, which supporters regarded as a step forward for civil rights. After the Obama administration formally certified July 22, 2011, that the military was prepared to allow homosexuals to serve openly, "Don't Ask, Don't Tell" expired Sept. 20. In another bipartisan victory for the White House, the Senate voted 71-26 on Dec. 22 to ratify New START, a nuclear arms control treaty with Russia. Other legislation enacted by Congress and signed by Obama during the month included the Healthy, Hunger-Free Kids Act, which revamped nutritional standards for school meals; a food-safety law that expanded the powers of the federal Food and Drug Admin.; a measure providing health care benefits and monetary compensation to first responders who became sick as a result of the Sept. 11, 2001, terrorist attacks; and a stopgap funding bill providing $250 bil for U.S. government operations through Mar. 4, 2011.

One of the few high-profile bills Democrats failed to pass was the Development, Relief, and Education of Alien Minors Act, popularly known as the DREAM Act. It provided a path for certain illegal immigrants brought to the U.S. as children to eventually obtain U.S. citizenship by attending college and enlisting in the military, and by meeting other requirements. In a test Dec. 18, senators voted 55-41 in favor of the measure, but the DREAM Act remained 5 short of the number needed to overcome a Republican filibuster. Speaking on Dec. 22, Obama called the failure of the DREAM Act his "biggest disappointment."

House Votes to Censure Rangel—On Dec. 2, a month after he was reelected by an 80% majority to his 21st congressional term, Rep. Charles Rangel (D, NY) was censured by the House of Representatives in a bipartisan vote of 333-79. The vote followed the recommendation of the House Committee on Standards of Official Conduct (commonly known as the Ethics Committee), which on Nov. 16 had convicted the Harlem congressman on 11 ethics charges, including failure to pay taxes on rental income. Rangel had led the House Ways and Means Committee, which writes federal tax laws, since Jan. 2007, until forced by the ethics probe to give up the chairmanship in Mar. 2010.

Senate Trial Ends in Judge's Ouster—For the first time since 1989 and only the 8th time in history, the Senate voted Dec. 8 to convict a federal judge who had been impeached by the House on charges of official corruption. At his Senate trial, House prosecutors argued that Judge Thomas Porteous of New Orleans had accepted cash and other favors from lawyers and bail bondsmen with business before his court, made false claims during his personal bankruptcy case, and misled the Senate during his confirmation hearings in 1994. The Senate approved all 4 articles of impeachment against Porteous, thereby removing him from the federal bench and disqualifying him from a $174,000 annual pension. In a separate vote, the Senate passed, 94-2, a resolution barring him from holding future federal office.

Settlement Reclaims $7.2 Billion for Victims in Madoff Fraud Case—Two years after Wall Street investment adviser Bernard Madoff admitted running a multibillion-dollar Ponzi scheme, the trustee gathering assets to compensate Madoff's victims reached agreement Dec. 17 on the recovery of $7.2 bil from the estate of Jeffry Picower, an investor and philanthropist who died in Oct. 2009. The settlement, approved by Picower's widow, boosted to nearly $10 bil the victim-compensation fund controlled by Irving H. Picard, the court-appointed trustee in the Madoff case. During a 3-week period ending Dec. 12, Picard filed nearly 5 dozen lawsuits seeking more than $40 bil from individuals, banks, and hedge funds that had profited from their investments with Madoff. After pleading guilty to 11 counts of fraud, money laundering, perjury, and theft, Madoff had received a 150-year prison sentence in June 2009.

On Dec. 11, the 2nd anniversary of Madoff's arrest, his older son Mark was found dead in his Manhattan apartment; medical examiners ruled his death a suicide. The 46-year-old Madoff, who had worked in his father's investment firm, was named in at least 9 lawsuits seeking to recover damages from his father's fraudulent activities.

U.S. Population Reaches 308.7 Million; Texas Gains 4 House Seats—Results from the 2010 census released Dec. 21 showed a U.S. resident population of 308,745,538, including the 50 states and DC. California remained the nation's most populous state, with 37,253,956 residents; other population leaders were Texas (25,145,561), New York (19,378,102), and Florida (18,801,310). Despite a population gain of 14.1% over 10 years, Wyoming (563,626) remained the nation's least populous state.

The South was the nation's fastest-growing region, gaining 14.3% since the 2000 census, followed by the West with 13.8%. Two Western states, Nevada (35.1%) and Arizona (24.6%), had the highest growth rates during the decade. Texas, which grew by nearly 4.3 mil, will gain 4 House seats (and 4 electoral votes) in the 2012 election. With a population increase of more than 2.8 mil, Florida will pick up 2 seats in the House. New York and Ohio, which will each lose 2 House seats, were part of a broader demographic trend that saw the Midwest and Northeast grow at slower rates (3.9% and 3.2%). With a 0.6% drop, Michigan was the only state to lose population in 2000-10. The overall U.S. growth rate of 9.7% for the decade was the slowest since the 1940 census.

Year-End Data Show Economic Rebound—The Labor Dept. announced Dec. 30 that initial claims for unemployment benefits had fallen to a seasonally adjusted 388,000

the previous week, the lowest total since July 2008. Monthly unemployment figures, released Jan. 11, 2011, put the jobless rate for Dec. at 9.4%, down from 9.9% a year earlier. Nonfarm payrolls rose slowly but steadily, adding 1.1 mil jobs during the 12-month period. Holiday retail sales jumped more than 5% over the comparable 50-day span in 2009, according to MasterCard Advisors Spending Pulse.

Annual trading volume on Wall Street declined 16% from 2009, but those investors who remained in stocks enjoyed another banner year. The Dow Jones Industrial Average closed Dec. 31 at 11,577.51, for an annual gain of 11.0%. The S&P 500 rose to 1,257.64, up 12.8% for the year, and the Nasdaq Composite Index finished at 2,652.87, an increase of 16.9%.

International

Violence Follows Disputed Presidential Vote in Côte d'Ivoire—Nearly 200 people lost their lives in 4 weeks of chaos and confusion that followed the release of conflicting results in Côte d'Ivoire's long-delayed presidential election. Incumbent Pres. Laurent Gbagbo had led his main challenger, former Prime Min. Alassane Ouattara, by 38% to 32% in the first round of presidential balloting Oct. 31. After a runoff election Nov. 28, the country's Independent Election Commission announced Dec. 2 that Ouattara had won by 54% to 46%. On Dec. 3, however, the Constitutional Council disallowed some 500,000 ballots from Ouattara strongholds and declared Gbagbo the winner by a 51%-49% margin. The following day, the council swore in Gbagbo for a new 5-year presidential term. Meanwhile, Ouattara—who had the backing of the UN, the U.S., France, and the Economic Community of West African States (a 15-nation bloc)—established his own government, which included Prime Min. Guillaume Soro, a former rebel leader who had held the same position under Gbagbo since 2007. Gbagbo retained the support of security forces, and as international pressure intensified, his followers launched a campaign of violence and intimidation against Ouattara loyalists. By the end of the year, as the crisis deepened, more than 20,000 Ivorians had fled to neighboring Liberia.

Iran Reports Self-Sufficiency in Uranium Production as Nuclear Talks Resume—Ali Akbar Salehi, the head of Iran's Atomic Energy Organization, announced Dec. 5 that the country had succeeded in making yellowcake (a concentrated form of uranium) from uranium ore mined at Gachin, in southern Iran, and had delivered the yellowcake for enrichment at the Natanz nuclear installation in Isfahan. Western observers viewed the announcement as an attempt by Iran to bolster its bargaining position as international talks on the nation's nuclear program were about to resume Dec. 6-7 in Geneva, Switzerland. Although Iran claims its nuclear program is for civilian purposes, the U.S. and its allies have accused the country of seeking to develop nuclear weapons.

Iran's nuclear effort had suffered a series of recent setbacks, the first reportedly stemming from an infection by the Stuxnet computer worm, the second involving separate bomb attacks in Tehran Nov. 29 that killed one Iranian nuclear scientist, Majid Shahriari, and wounded another, Fereidoun Abbasi. On Dec. 21, the U.S. Treasury Dept. announced new sanctions targeting companies linked to Iran's nuclear program.

Cancún Conferees Reach Limited Accord on Climate Change—Concluding a 12-day, UN-backed conference in Cancún, Mexico, delegates from more than 190 countries endorsed Dec. 11 the establishment of a Green Climate Fund, potentially worth up to $100 bil, that would enable poorer countries to adapt to global climate change. Other modest steps in the Cancún agreement included incentives to preserve tropical rain forests, new mechanisms for sharing clean-energy technologies, and a strengthening of pledges to cut greenhouse gas emissions. The accord was approved over the opposition of Bolivia's chief climate negotiator, Pablo Solón, who objected that the emissions cuts envisioned at Cancún "won't stop temperatures from rising by 4°C, and we know that 4°C is unsustainable."

Maliki Heads Unity Government in Baghdad; Other Iraq, Afghanistan Developments—More than 9 months of political deadlock ended when Iraqi Prime Min. Nouri al-Maliki was sworn in for a 2nd term Dec. 21, heading a unity government that included representatives from all major Shiite, Sunni, and Kurdish factions. Only 31 of 42 cabinet posts were filled, and Maliki assigned himself the sensitive defense, interior, and national security portfolios until the factions could agree on permanent appointees. At the end of the month, U.S. troop strength stood at about 48,000, down from 110,000 a year earlier. U.S. military fatalities dropped to 60 in 2010, less than half of the 2009 total. According to the nongovernmental organization Iraq Body Count, 4,038 Iraqi civilians were killed in 2010, a 14% decline from 2009 and the lowest annual total since the war began.

The U.S. had about 100,000 troops in Afghanistan, up from 68,000 in Dec. 2009; forces supplied by coalition partners numbered more than 41,000 by the end of 2010. U.S. military fatalities during the year reached 499, the highest annual figure since Operation Enduring Freedom began in Oct. 2001; losses by other coalition members totaled 212. During a surprise visit to Afghanistan Dec. 3, Pres. Obama told U.S. troops at Bagram Air Base, "Today we can be proud that there are fewer areas under Taliban control and more Afghans have a chance to build a more hopeful future." U.S. policymaking in the region received a setback when veteran diplomat Richard C. Holbrooke, the Obama administration's special envoy for Afghanistan and Pakistan, died Dec. 13 during surgery to repair a torn aorta.

Cyclone Tasha Triggers Massive Floods in Australia—One of the worst natural disasters in Australian history began Dec. 25, when Cyclone Tasha made landfall south of Cairns, Queensland, in northeastern Australia. Tasha's torrential downpours, along with other rains associated with an exceptionally strong La Niña current in the Pacific, drenched Queensland with its wettest Dec. on record. In Brisbane, the state's capital and largest city, nearly 19 in. of rain fell during the month. Floods inundated Queensland in late Dec. and early Jan., with three-fourths of the state declared a disaster zone. By late Jan. the flood death toll had reached 35 and property damage was estimated at up to $5 bil.

Former Israeli President Convicted of Rape—In the most serious conviction of a senior government official in Israel's history, Moshe Katsav, the country's former president (2000-07) and tourism minister (1996-99), was found guilty by a Tel Aviv court Dec. 30 of rape, sexual assault, sexual harassment, and obstruction of justice. Before he left the largely ceremonial office of president in mid-2007, his lawyers had negotiated a plea bargain under which the most serious charges would have been dropped and Katsav would have received a suspended sentence. But Katsav rejected the plea deal, seeking to prove his innocence. After a year-long trial, conducted mostly behind closed doors, a 3-judge panel concluded that his testimony was "riddled with lies." On Mar. 22, 2011, he received a 7-year prison sentence and was ordered to pay compensation to 2 of his victims.

General

Commercial Firm Launches, Recovers Space Capsule—In a first for a privately owned company, Space Exploration Technologies Corp., or SpaceX, on Dec. 8 successfully blasted their Dragon space capsule into low Earth orbit and then recovered it after splashdown in the Pacific Ocean. The test flight was conducted as part of NASA's Commercial Orbital Transportation Services program, under which Dragon would be used to ferry cargo to the International Space Station after the U.S. space shuttle fleet was retired.

Newton Captures Heisman Trophy—Auburn Univ. quarterback Cam Newton, who led the top-ranked Tigers to a 13-0 regular-season record and a Southeastern Conference championship, won the Heisman Trophy Dec. 11 as the nation's most outstanding collegiate football player. Newton, a junior, set Auburn single-season records by passing for 28 touchdowns and rushing for 20 more, while throwing only 6 interceptions. In the Heisman balloting, Newton easily outpolled Stanford Univ. QB Andrew Luck despite ethical questions surrounding both Newton's departure from the Univ. of Florida in 2008 and his recruitment a year later. Newton's

father, Cecil, reportedly received payments of more than $100,000 from Mississippi State in exchange for persuading his son to transfer to that school, but the National Collegiate Athletic Association (NCAA) ruled Dec. 1 that Newton was unaware of the transaction.

UConn Women Set Consecutive Basketball Win Mark—Propelled by Maya Moore's career-high 41 points, the Univ. of Connecticut women's basketball team won their 89th consecutive game Dec. 21, crushing Florida State, 93-62, at the XL Center in Hartford, CT. The UConn Huskies, led by head coach Geno Auriemma, eclipsed the previous NCAA Div. I mark of 88 straight wins set 1971-74 by a UCLA men's team under coach John Wooden. The Huskies extended their win streak to 90 before losing, 71-59, to Stanford Univ. Dec. 30 in Palo Alto, CA. UConn's record fell short of the all-time college mark of 131 consecutive victories set 1953-58 by a women's basketball squad at Wayland Baptist Univ. of Plainview, TX, long before the NCAA began sponsoring women's athletics.

January 2011
National

112th Congress Convenes—The 112th Congress convened Jan. 5, with Republicans taking command of the House of Representatives and Democrats retaining control of the Senate. Eleven-term Rep. John Boehner (R, OH), was elected speaker of the House with 241 votes, all of them from GOP members; of 192 Democrats casting ballots, 173 voted for the outgoing speaker, Nancy Pelosi (D, CA), and 11 of the remaining 19 supported Pelosi rival Heath Shuler (D, NC), a member of the conservative Blue Dog Coalition. With Boehner elevated to the speaker's chair, the former House minority whip, Eric Cantor (R, VA), became majority leader, and Pelosi became minority leader. Other House leaders included Majority Whip Kevin McCarthy (R, CA) and Minority Whip Steny Hoyer (D, MD). In the Senate, where the Democrats held a 53-47 majority, including two Democratic-leaning independents, Harry Reid (D, NV) remained majority leader and Mitch McConnell (R, KY) held onto his minority leadership; Richard Durbin (D, IL) and Jon Kyl (R, AZ) stayed on as their party's whips.

Dozens of 1st-term House Republican conservatives who swept into office with Tea Party support lost little time in making their influence felt. Revisions to House rules imposed "cut as you go" language requiring that all new spending be offset by cuts, barring the imposition of tax hikes to offset spending increases, but permitting tax cuts without corresponding reductions in spending. On Jan. 19, by a 245-189 margin, the House voted to repeal the landmark health care legislation enacted by Congress and signed by Pres. Barack Obama in Mar. 2010. The repeal effort, opposed by Obama and congressional Democrats, was given little chance of success in the Democratic-controlled Senate.

6 Killed, Congresswoman Wounded at Arizona Shopping Center—A gunman armed with a semiautomatic pistol opened fire on the morning of Jan. 8 at a Tucson, AZ, shopping mall, killing 6 people and injuring 13 others, including U.S. Rep. Gabrielle Giffords (D, AZ). The dead included John Roll, 63, a federal judge for 20 years; Gabe Zimmerman, 30, a Giffords staff member; and a 9-year-old girl, Christina Taylor Green.

Bystanders subdued the assailant, later identified as Jared Lee Loughner, as he attempted to reload after emptying a 33-round magazine. Arrested by police at the crime scene, the 22-year-old Loughner was initially charged Jan. 9 with killing a federal employee and attempting to assassinate a member of Congress. Prosecutors disclosed that Loughner had legally purchased his pistol in Tucson Nov. 30, 2010, and that an FBI investigator had found an envelope on which Loughner had allegedly written Giffords's name and the words "My assassination" and "I planned ahead."

The shooting took place outside a Safeway supermarket, where the 40-year-old Giffords, a Tucson native who had represented the city in Congress since 2007, was meeting constituents in a publicly scheduled event called "Congress on Your Corner." Critically injured with a gunshot wound to the head, Giffords was airlifted to Tucson's University Medical Center, where she underwent emergency surgery. Pres. Obama eulogized the victims Jan. 12 in Tucson and pleaded for greater civility in public discourse: "Rather than pointing fingers or assigning blame, let us use this occasion to expand our moral imaginations, to listen to each other more carefully, to sharpen our instincts for empathy, and remind ourselves of all the ways that our hopes and dreams are bound together."

Giffords's condition improved enough to allow her transfer Jan. 21 to Memorial Hermann-Texas Medical Center in Houston, TX, where she began a prolonged period of rehabilitation. While still undergoing treatment there, she traveled to the Kennedy Space Center in Florida, where she saw her husband, NASA astronaut Mark Kelly, launch into space May 16 as commander of the space shuttle *Endeavour*. Meanwhile, federal prosecutors Mar. 4 unsealed a 49-count superseding indictment against Loughner, including more than a dozen capital charges. On May 25, following a series of psychiatric evaluations, he was ruled mentally incompetent to stand trial by U.S. District Court Judge Larry Burns, who ordered Loughner to undergo treatment at the U.S. Medical Center for Federal Prisoners in Springfield, MO.

Senators Announce Retirements as Election Cycle Begins—Several prominent U.S. senators, most of them Democrats, announced that they would not be candidates for reelection when their current terms expired in 2012. On Jan. 19, Sen. Joe Lieberman, the Democratic vice-presidential nominee in 2000, announced that he would not seek a 5th term from Connecticut voters. Lieberman, who was elected as an independent after losing a Democratic primary in 2006, had been expected to face a tough reelection fight in 2012. Similar announcements of impending retirements came from 3-term Sen. Kay Bailey Hutchison (R, TX) Jan. 13; 4-term Sen. Kent Conrad (D, ND) Jan. 18; Sen. Jim Webb (D, VA), a 1st-termer, Feb. 9; 3-term Sen. Jon Kyl (R, AZ), the Senate minority whip, Feb. 10; and 5-term Sen. Jeff Bingaman (D, NM), Feb. 18. Political observers noted that the retirements dimmed Democrats' prospects for retaining control of the Senate in the Nov. 2012 election, when Democrats must defend 23 seats and the Republicans only 10.

On the 7th round of balloting Jan. 14, the Republican National Committee chose Reince Priebus, a Wisconsin state GOP chairman, to lead the national party. The incumbent RNC leader, Michael Steele, criticized as gaffe-prone and a poor financial manager, withdrew his bid for a 2nd term after the 4th round of voting. The leader of the Democratic National Committee, former Gov. Tim Kaine (VA), announced Apr. 5 that he would run for Webb's Senate seat; Rep. Debbie Wasserman Schultz (D, FL), was named to replace him as DNC chair the following month.

Staff Changes Mark Midpoint of Obama Presidential Term—Two years after taking office, Pres. Obama shuffled his White House staff and accelerated preparations for his 2012 presidential campaign. On Jan. 5, Press Sec. Robert Gibbs announced he would leave the White House and serve as a paid consultant to the president's reelection effort. Named Jan. 27 to replace him as the president's official spokesman was Jay Carney, a former Washington bureau chief for *Time* magazine and communications director for Vice Pres. Joe Biden.

On Jan. 6, Obama chose lawyer and corporate executive William Daley as his chief of staff to replace Rahm Emanuel, who had resigned Oct. 2010 to run for mayor of Chicago. Daley, the son and brother of Chicago mayors, had served as Pres. Bill Clinton's commerce secretary (1997-2000). Emanuel was temporarily knocked off the mayoral ballot Jan. 24 when an appellate panel ruled that his prolonged service in Washington, DC, made him ineligible to claim Chicago residency. Reinstated on the ballot 3 days later, Emanuel went on to win the Chicago mayoralty by a landslide Feb. 22.

Corporate Earnings, Consumer Spending Boost Stocks; Employment Picture Mixed—Favorable retail sales and corporate earnings reports helped the Dow Jones Industrial Average cross the 12,000-mark Jan. 26 for the 1st time since June 2008. The Dow closed Jan. 31 at 11,891.93, up 2.72% for the month. The S&P 500 jumped 2.26%, closing at 1,286.12, while the Nasdaq Composite Index rose 1.78% to 2,700.08. Data released Feb. 4 by the Labor Dept. showed that nonfarm payrolls expanded by only 36,000 during the month, but the seasonally adjusted unemployment rate dropped to 9.0% from 9.4% in Dec. 2010.

International

Protests Topple Tunisian Government, Spread to Other Arab Countries—A protest movement known as the "Arab Spring" began to spread across North Africa and the Middle East, overturning the long-entrenched government of Tunisia and challenging autocratic regimes throughout the region. Rising food prices, high youth unemployment, economic inequality, religious tensions, and government corruption and repression fueled a wave of popular discontent that by the end of the month had sparked self-immolations and mass demonstrations in Algeria, Jordan, Egypt, Yemen, and other countries.

In Tunisia, protesters forced the ouster of Pres. Zine al-Abidine Ben Ali, whose 23-year rule ended Jan. 14 when he fled with his family to Saudi Arabia. The unrest had begun Dec. 17, 2010, in the town of Sidi Bouzid, where a 26-year-old fruit vendor, Mohamed Bouazizi, set fire to himself after a run-in with local authorities. By the time Bouazizi died Jan. 4, his alleged humiliation by a female police officer, her aides, and other provincial officials had become a rallying cry for antigovernment protests in Sidi Bouzid, Sfax, Monastir, and the capital city of Tunis. The movement spread swiftly, propelled by cell phones, Internet social networking sites, and satellite television coverage, and dozens of dissidents were killed in clashes with police. On Jan. 14, as thousands of protesters gathered in central Tunis, Ben Ali dismissed his government, declared a state of emergency, promised legislative elections within 6 months, and left the country. The following day, Tunisia's Constitutional Court declared Ben Ali's office vacant, and Parliament Speaker Fouad Mebazaa became interim president. Holdover Prime Min. Mohamed Ghannouchi Jan. 17 named a transitional government in which members of Ben Ali's ruling party retained key positions. Subsequent protests led to Ghannouchi's forming a new government Jan. 27 with fewer ties to the old regime and, a month later, to Ghannouchi's own resignation as prime minister.

South Sudanese Vote for Independence—Nearly 4 mil southern Sudanese voted overwhelmingly in favor of secession from Sudan in balloting held Jan. 9-15. The final tally announced Feb. 7 by the Southern Sudan Referendum Commission indicated that nearly 99% of voters favored becoming an independent African nation. The referendum fulfilled a 2005 peace deal that ended more than 2 decades of war between southern rebels and the Sudanese central government, based in the northern city of Khartoum. An estimated 2 mil people died during the conflict, in which troops from the predominantly Muslim north battled secessionists, who were mostly Christians or followers of traditional African religions.

The referendum opened the way for improved relations between Sudan and the U.S., which since 1993 had designated the Khartoum regime as a state sponsor of terrorism. It also eased pressure on Bashir, whom the International Criminal Court in The Hague, Netherlands, had accused of committing crimes against humanity in Sudan's Darfur region. Although voting in most of southern Sudan proceeded peacefully, clashes Jan. 7-10 claimed the lives of at least 3 dozen people in oil-rich Abyei, a disputed region on the north-south border. South Sudan was expected to declare independence by July 9, 2011.

Floods, Mudslides Kill More than 900 in Brazil—Heavy downpours Jan. 11-12 dropped 10 in. of rain in a 24-hour period, triggering floods and mudslides in mountain towns of Rio de Janeiro state in southeastern Brazil. The Brazilian newspaper *O Globo* reported Feb. 16 that the confirmed death toll had reached 904, including 426 in the municipality of Nova Friburgo and 381 in Teresópolis. The flooding left an estimated 25,000 people homeless.

General

Auburn Captures Collegiate Football Championship— Wes Byrum's 19-yd field goal as the clock ran out boosted the Auburn Tigers to a 22-19 victory over Oregon in the Bowl Championship Series title game Jan. 10 in Glendale, AZ. The win earned the Tigers their 1st national championship since 1957. Freshman tailback Michael Dyer carried the ball 22 times for 143 yds, including a memorable 4th-quarter ramble in which he rolled over an Oregon tackler, turning an 8-yd run into a 37-yd gain that brought the Tigers within field-goal range.

Clijsters, Djokovic Win Australian Tennis Titles—Kim Clijsters of Belgium won her 1st Australian Open singles championship Jan. 29, outplaying China's Li Na, 3-6, 6-3, 6-3, at Rod Laver Arena in Melbourne. The following night, Serbian Novak Djokovic captured his 2nd Australian men's singles crown, dominating Andy Murray of Scotland, 6-4, 6-2, 6-3. The 3rd-seeded Djokovic had defeated the 2010 champion, Switzerland's Roger Federer, in straight sets to reach the finals.

February 2011
National

Wisconsin Governor Leads Effort to Limit Collective Bargaining—Swept into office Nov. 2010 on a Republican electoral tide that also gave the GOP control of both houses of Wisconsin's state legislature, Gov. Scott Walker (R) on Feb. 11 proposed measures that would restrict collective bargaining by some 170,000 public-sector employees. Walker cited Wisconsin's state budget deficit to justify his proposal to deny public-employee unions the ability to negotiate health-insurance and pension-fund contributions, instead requiring the employees to set aside 5.8% of their salaries toward pensions and pay 12.6% of their health insurance costs. In 1959, Wisconsin had been the first state to extend full collective bargaining rights to public employees.

Thousands of demonstrators converged on the state capitol to oppose the plan, and all 14 of the state's Democratic senators temporarily fled to Illinois in hopes of denying Republican legislators the quorum needed to pass the bill. Those efforts failed, however, and Mar. 9-11, the state legislature passed and the governor signed a measure prohibiting strikes by public-sector employees, restricting most public-sector unions' collective bargaining powers, banning the automatic deduction of union dues from most government employees' paychecks, and requiring the unions to hold annual elections by secret ballot in order to retain the right to represent their members. Meanwhile, Republican-controlled governments in Ohio and other states launched similar efforts to curb public-employee union powers.

Wisconsin's law was struck down on procedural grounds by a circuit court judge May 26, but reinstated June 14 by a 4-3 decision of the state supreme court. Republicans beat back efforts by Democrats to regain control of the state senate in recall elections Aug. 9.

Congressman Quits Over Shirtless Photo—U.S. Rep. Christopher Lee (R, NY) resigned his seat Feb. 9, 3 hours after the gossip website Gawker published a flirtatious email exchange between the married congressman and a 34-year-old woman. The exchange began Jan. 14 when the woman posted a personal ad on Craigslist, asking for contacts from "financially & emotionally secure" men who didn't "look like toads." Lee responded, saying he was a divorced lobbyist, describing himself as a "very fit fun classy guy," and attaching a shirtless photo of himself. After discovering that Lee had lied about his identity, the woman sent the emails to Gawker. Lee, a 2nd-term congressman from a conservative district, initially claimed his email account had been hacked before publicly acknowledging his indiscretion.

Obama Administration Withdraws Support for Defense of Marriage Act—In a letter to Congress Feb. 23, U.S. Attorney Gen. Eric Holder disclosed that the Obama administration now regarded as unconstitutional a key provision of the federal Defense of Marriage Act (DOMA) defining marriage as "a legal union between one man and one woman as husband and wife." Holder said the Justice Dept. would no longer defend DOMA against legal challenges, although it would continue to enforce the law until the provision was repealed by Congress or definitively overturned by the courts. DOMA was found unconstitutional by a federal judge in Massachusetts in July 2010 and by a federal bankruptcy court in Los Angeles, CA, June 13, 2011, but a definitive decision on DOMA would likely require a ruling from the U.S. Supreme Court.

Enacted in 1996, DOMA prohibited the federal government from legally recognizing same-sex marriages, and allowed states to ignore same-sex marriages that had been performed in other states where the unions were permitted. The federal law faced multiple court challenges, and the Obama administration, which initially upheld DOMA's legality, came under increasing pressure from gay rights groups to reverse its position.

To defend DOMA, Republicans in the House of Representatives hired former U.S. Solicitor Gen. Paul Clement, a partner in the Atlanta, GA-based King & Spalding law firm. After pressure from gay rights activists, however, King & Spalding canceled the contract Apr. 25, leading Clement to resign from the firm, take a position with Washington, DC-based Bancroft PLLC, and sign a new contract with House Republicans. Pres. Obama specifically endorsed congressional legislation to repeal DOMA July 19.

Stocks Rise as Unemployment Rate Falls Below 9%—Boosted by mid-month reports that Home Depot planned to hire more than 60,000 seasonal workers and that Intel would take on 4,000 "permanent, highly skilled employees," stocks pushed upward for a 3rd consecutive month. The Dow Jones Industrial Average closed Feb. 28 at 12,226.34, for a monthly increase of 2.8%, while the S&P 500 (1,327.22) grew 3.2% and the Nasdaq Composite Index (2,782.27) gained 3%. The Labor Dept. reported Mar. 4 that in Feb., the unemployment rate dropped to 8.9%, and U.S. payrolls increased by 192,000, reflecting a rebound in the manufacturing, construction, and transportation sectors.

International

Mubarak Resigns in Egypt as "Arab Spring" Protests Spread—The wave of uprisings sweeping the Arab world, which had toppled the Tunisian government Jan. 14, claimed a second triumph when Egyptian Pres. Hosni Mubarak ceded power Feb. 11 to the Supreme Council of the Armed Forces, headed by Field Marshal Mohamed Hussein Tantawi. The 82-year-old Mubarak had ruled Egypt for nearly 30 years, during which his autocratic regime curbed domestic dissent, suppressed Islamist political activity, preserved a peace accord with Israel, and was both a reliable U.S. ally and a leading recipient of U.S. aid.

Mubarak's fall followed 18 days of mass demonstrations in Cairo's Tahrir Square and elsewhere. During that period, at least 846 people died in clashes between protesters and Mubarak supporters. As calls for his resignation grew louder, Mubarak offered political concessions, while his security forces and loyalists made violent efforts to intimidate the demonstrators. On the night of Feb. 10, hundreds of thousands of people gathered in Tahrir Square expecting to hear Mubarak surrender power. When he instead vowed to retain his presidential office until new elections could be held in Sept., the crowd reacted in fury, and the military (which had refused to intervene to suppress the protests) took swift action to end the crisis the following day. During the next 3 months,

Egyptian prosecutors launched investigations into allegations of corruption and human rights violations by Mubarak and his aides and family. His political party was disbanded, and a court ordered his name and likeness removed from all public places.

Throughout North Africa and the Middle East, "Arab Spring" demonstrators targeted other entrenched regimes. In Jordan, King Abdullah II reacted to 3 weeks of protests Feb. 1 by replacing his prime minister. In Syria, Pres. Bashar al-Assad deployed his security forces to stall protests planned for Feb. 4-5. In Iraq, where 47,000 U.S. troops were still deployed, at least 29 people were killed Feb. 25 when security forces opened fire on protesters participating in a "Day of Rage." In the Persian Gulf region, dissidents staged large-scale protests in Bahrain and Yemen. In Libya, located between Tunisia and Egypt, protesters seized control of Benghazi and other eastern cities, mounting the most serious and sustained challenge to Muammar al-Qaddafi since the Libyan dictator seized power in 1969.

Chevron Ordered to Pay $8.6 Billion in Ecuador Pollution Case—In the largest environmental damage ruling to date, Ecuadoran Judge Nicolas Zambrano on Feb. 14 ordered Chevron, a U.S.-based multinational energy company, to pay $8.6 bil to clean up oil pollution in a rain forest region of northeastern Ecuador. The court warned Chevron that if the company did not accept the judgment and issue a public apology within 15 days, the fine would be doubled. When Chevron instead vowed to appeal, the company's total liability (including an additional judgment of $860 mil for reparations to the Amazon Defense Coalition, a group representing the plaintiffs) rose to more than $18 bil. Chevron, which had no known assets in Ecuador, inherited the case through its takeover in 2001 of Texaco, which was responsible for the disputed oil operations, 1965-92.

German Defense Minister Charged with Plagiarism—Defense Min. Karl-Theodor zu Guttenberg, one of Germany's fastest-rising politicians, was forced to step down after a Munich-based newspaper, *Süddeutsche Zeitung*, published allegations Feb. 16 that the ally of Chancellor Angela Merkel had plagiarized large chunks of his doctoral dissertation. Guttenberg completed his doctoral thesis in 2006, when he was already a member of Germany's parliament. Guttenberg initially dismissed the plagiarism charges as "absurd," but the Univ. of Bayreuth revoked his doctoral title Feb. 23. Under pressure from senior members of Merkel's center-right coalition and from Germany's academic community, Guttenberg resigned his office Mar. 1, after which Interior Min. Thomas de Maizière, Merkel's former chief of staff, received the defense post.

Earthquake Kills 181 in Christchurch, New Zealand—For the 2nd time since Sept. 2010, an earthquake near Christchurch, on New Zealand's South Island, caused widespread damage. Although the magnitude 6.3 quake that struck Christchurch Feb. 22 was less powerful than the 7.1 temblor that rocked New Zealand's 2nd-largest city less than 6 months earlier, the human loss from the 2nd quake was much greater, with the official death toll reaching 181 by June 1. Unlike the Sept. 2010 disaster, which occurred early in the morning, the Feb. 22 event, classified as an aftershock of the earlier quake, took place at midday. The 2nd quake also struck closer to the surface, was nearer to the city center, and toppled buildings that may already have been damaged by the first. About one-third of the central business district was destroyed, with property damage estimated at NZ$15 bil.

Voters in Ireland Oust Fianna Fáil Government—Fianna Fáil, the party that had dominated Irish politics since the 1930s, suffered a crushing defeat in Feb. 25 elections, winning only 20 seats in the 166-seat Dáil Eireann, the lower house of parliament. Voters blamed Fianna Fáil and its departing leader, Prime Min. Brian Cowen, for the financial crisis of 2008-10 and for agreeing to impose unpopular austerity measures as part of an 85 bil euro ($115 bil) bailout accord with the European Union and International Monetary Fund. Cowen announced Jan. 22 that he would step down as Fianna Fáil leader. On Feb. 1, he called elections a year ahead of schedule. The vote count, completed Mar. 2, showed the center-right Fine Gael with 76 seats in the Dáil Eireann and the center-left Labour Party with 37. Agreement on a Fine Gael-Labour coalition was reached Mar. 4, and Fine Gael leader Enda Kenny became prime minister 5 days later. Kenny had said he would try to renegotiate the terms of the bailout, which he called "a bad deal for Ireland and a bad deal for Europe."

General

Packers Triumph in Super Bowl—In a matchup of 2 of the NFL's marquee teams and top-rated quarterbacks, Aaron Rodgers outpassed Ben Roethlisberger to lead the Green Bay Packers to a 31-25 victory over the Pittsburgh Steelers in Super Bowl XLV, played Feb. 6 at Cowboys Stadium in Arlington, TX. The Packers romped to a 21-3 lead in the 2nd quarter, then held off a furious Steelers rally. Rodgers, who completed 24 of 39 passes for 304 yds and 3 touchdowns, was named Super Bowl MVP.

Lady Antebellum Tops Grammy Honors—At the Grammy Awards ceremonies in Los Angeles, CA, Feb. 13, country-pop trio Lady Antebellum collected 5 awards, including Record of the Year and Song of the Year for "Need You Now." Album of the Year honors went to *The Suburbs*, by Canadian rock band Arcade Fire, while jazz bassist and vocalist Esperanza Spalding upset pop sensations Justin Bieber and Drake in balloting for Best New Artist.

Bayne Becomes Youngest Daytona 500 Champion—One day after celebrating his 20th birthday, Trevor Bayne Feb. 20 became the youngest-ever winner of the Daytona 500 in Daytona Beach, FL. The victory, coming in Bayne's 2nd Sprint Cup start, earned his racing team a $1,462,563 payday and eclipsed the previous youth mark set by Jeff Gordon, who won the Daytona 500 in 1997 at the age of 25.

King's Speech Takes Oscar Crown—*The King's Speech*, a drama about a stammering British monarch and his vocal coach, earned 4 Academy Awards Feb. 27, including Oscars for Best Picture, Directing (Tom Hooper), Actor in a Leading Role (Colin Firth as King George VI), and Original Screenplay (David Seidler). *Inception* won 4 Oscars, chiefly for its technical acumen, while *The Social Network* garnered 3 awards, including Adapted Screenplay (Aaron Sorkin). Natalie Portman (*Black Swan*) won for Actress in a Leading Role, and the Danish drama *In a Better World* was honored as Best Foreign Language Film.

March 2011

National

Supreme Court Upholds Religious Protests at Military Funerals—By an 8-1 majority, the U.S. Supreme Court Mar. 2 ruled that an antigay religious group, the Westboro Baptist Church of Topeka, KS, had a constitutional right to hold a public protest at the funeral of Marine Lance Cpl. Matthew Snyder, who died in Iraq. Members of the church, led by pastor Fred Phelps, claimed the killing of U.S. soldiers was God's punishing the U.S. for its growing tolerance of homosexuality. The father of the slain marine contended in his lawsuit that by carrying placards such as "God blew up the troops" and "Thank God for dead soldiers," the protesters had inflicted emotional distress on the mourners and violated their privacy.

In his majority decision in *Snyder v. Phelps*, Chief Justice John Roberts acknowledged that the church's message was hurtful but maintained that the religious group had a First Amendment right to address "matters of import on public property, in a peaceful manner, in full compliance with the guidance of local officials," about 1,000 ft from the church where the funeral was held.

Overcoming Volatility, Stocks Post Best 1st Quarter in 12 Years—The Dow Jones Industrial Average closed Mar. 31 at 12,319.73, up 6.4% since the year began; during the same 3-month period, the S&P 500 (1,325.83) increased 5.4%, and the Nasdaq Composite Index (2,781.07) rose 4.8%. En route to its best 1st-quarter performance since 1999, the Dow bounced back from a sharp drop during the first half of Mar., when investors, already nervous about the weak U.S. housing market, rising oil prices, and the continuing European debt crisis, were shaken by a catastrophic earthquake and tsunami in Japan.

Data released Apr. 1 by the Labor Dept. showed a slight dip in the U.S. unemployment rate to 8.8% and a rise of 216,000 jobs on nonfarm payrolls. On a more sobering note, the civilian labor force participation rate continued to languish at 64.2%, lower than at any time since the mid-1980s, and more than 8 mil U.S. workers held part-time rather than full-time jobs either because their hours had been cut or because they were unable to find full-time employment.

International

NATO Aids Rebels in Libya; Violence Grows in Syria, Yemen—The wave of "Arab Spring" rebellions that overturned the governments of Tunisia (Jan. 14) and Egypt (Feb. 11) plunged Libya into civil war and international conflict. As the month began, the regime of Muammar al-Qaddafi held power in western Libya, including the capital of Tripoli, while ill-equipped and poorly organized rebels controlled much of the eastern region, including Benghazi, Libya's 2nd-largest city. The UN and U.S. had imposed economic sanctions on the Qaddafi government in late Feb., and the U.S., UK, and France had closed their embassies in Tripoli. Casualties escalated Mar. 1-10, as Qaddafi loyalists launched a ferocious counterattack against rebel-held towns.

With the rebels pleading for foreign military support, the Arab League, which had already suspended Libya's membership, requested Mar. 12 the UN Security Council impose a no-fly zone that would limit progress of Qaddafi's forces. By a vote of 10-0, with Brazil, China, Germany, India, and Russia abstaining, the Security Council on Mar. 17 adopted Resolution 1973, calling for a cease-fire, tightening sanctions on the Qaddafi regime, and authorizing the establishment of a no-fly zone. Two days later, the U.S., France, and UK began aerial bombardment of Libyan air defenses, command and control centers, and air and ground forces that had targeted Benghazi and other rebel strongholds. On Mar. 23, NATO warships and aircraft took over enforcement of the no-fly zone and the arms embargo against Qaddafi, in Operation Unified Protector.

On Mar. 28, in a televised speech at Ft. McNair in Washington, DC, Pres. Obama stated that the U.S. and its allies had intervened to halt Qaddafi's "brutal repression and a looming humanitarian crisis" but would not seek to overthrow Qaddafi by force. Although Obama administration officials insisted that no U.S. ground troops would be deployed to Libya, press reports indicated that U.S. and British intelligence operatives had been providing rebel assistance there for weeks. The allies claimed a high-level defection Mar. 30 when Libyan Foreign Min. Moussa Koussa fled to Tunisia and then to the UK. Koussa, a former Libyan intelligence chief, had long been suspected of involvement in the 1988 bombing of Pan Am Flight 103 over Lockerbie, Scotland, in which 270 people were killed.

In Syria, meanwhile, a demonstration erupted in Damascus Mar. 15 against the Baathist regime that had held power for 4 decades under Pres. Hafez al-Assad (1971-2000) and, since 2000, under his son Bashar. The protests spread Mar. 18, as Syrian Muslims gathered for Friday prayers; one of the largest demonstrations was in the city of Daraa, where the government launched a crackdown that left more than 30 people dead. Tens of thousands of antigovernment protesters took

to the streets Mar. 25, with the most violent confrontations occurring in the western city of Latakia. Police responded with batons and tear gas, and in some cases, fired on the crowds, killing unknown numbers of people.

In Yemen, where the U.S. had long supported embattled Pres. Ali Abdullah Saleh as an ally in efforts to defeat al-Qaeda, some 100,000 people in Sana'a', the capital, participated in a demonstration Mar. 11. A week later, government forces opened fire on protesters in Sana'a', killing at least 50. On Mar. 27, as pressure mounted on Saleh to step down, he acknowledged that 6 of the nation's 18 provinces were under rebel control. An explosion Mar. 28 at a munitions plant that had been raided by militants in southern Yemen claimed some 150 lives. In Bahrain, a strong U.S. ally in the Persian Gulf, huge antigovernment demonstrations in Pearl Square in the capital city of Manama were suppressed after a Saudi-led force of about 1,600 entered the country Mar. 14 at the request of the Bahraini monarchy.

Japan Earthquake, Tsunami Trigger Nuclear Emergency—A magnitude 9.0 earthquake, the most powerful in modern Japanese history, struck Mar. 11 at 2:46 PM about 20 mi below the surface of the Pacific Ocean. The epicenter was 80 mi from the city of Sendai, on Honshu Island, and 230 mi northeast of Tokyo. Even more devastating was a tsunami generated by the quake, which rolled over low-lying coastal towns in Miyagi, Iwate, and Fukushima prefectures. Damage assessments issued by Japan's National Police Agency showed (as of Oct. 2011) a confirmed death toll of 15,800, with 3,800 still listed as missing; property damage was estimated at $325 bil. More than 106,000 buildings were completely destroyed, and another 108,000 structures showed major damage. Destruction of buildings, bridges, and rail lines was especially severe in Miyagi Prefecture, which accounted for 60% of the known fatalities. Disruptions in water and power supplies, transportation systems, and corporate infrastructure took a 15.3% bite out of Japan's monthly industrial production, slowing the world economy.

An immediate consequence of the earthquake and tsunami was the worst nuclear disaster since Ukraine's Chernobyl catastrophe in 1986. Less than an hour after the quake, a 46-ft-high wall of water overwhelmed a seawall designed to protect the Fukushima Daiichi nuclear power plant against a tsunami up to 19 ft high. Seawater flooded backup generators and electrical switching networks, crippling emergency cooling systems and leading to meltdowns at 3 of the plant's 6 nuclear reactors. Multiple explosions in reactor buildings allowed dangerous levels of radiation to escape. While a small number of emergency workers remained on site in a desperate effort to contain the damage, the Japanese government advised civilians living within 19 mi of the nuclear plant to evacuate the area, and the U.S. embassy in Japan recommended Americans stay at least 50 mi away from the facility.

As concern over the radiation leak deepened, food-safety authorities in the European Union, the U.S., and elsewhere increased surveillance on imports of milk, vegetables, fish, and other Japanese products. Japan, which already relied on nuclear energy to generate about 30% of its electricity, shelved plans to expand its nuclear dependence to 50%. In May, the Swiss government, which generated nearly 40% of its electricity from nuclear power, announced it would phase out all 5 of its nuclear power facilities when they reached the end of their lifetimes between 2019 and 2034. Germany, where nuclear power accounts for 28% of electricity, said it would close all of its 17 nuclear power plants by 2022.

Islamists Retaliate for Koran Burning in U.S.—After a religious group in Gainesville, FL, burned a copy of the Koran Mar. 20, militants in Afghanistan and Pakistan responded with deadly violence. The book-burning was held by Terry Jones, pastor of the Dove World Outreach Center, who had called off earlier plans to burn the Islamic holy book on Sept. 11, 2010, after a direct appeal from Defense Sec. Robert Gates. Afghan Pres. Hamid Karzai denounced the Koran burning Mar. 24. The following day, in Mazar-i-Sharif, an angry mob attacked a UN compound, killing 3 UN staff members and 4 Nepalese security guards. The U.S. had about 100,000 troops deployed in Afghanistan, and other NATO members were contributing more than 42,000 troops to the International Security Assistance Force (ISAF) there. Coalition fatalities during Jan.-Mar. numbered 109, including 76 from the U.S.

When reports of the Koran burning reached Pakistan, Pres. Asif Ali Zardari opened an address to a joint parliamentary session Mar. 22 by condemning the desecration. Islamists staged protests in Lahore, Karachi, and other cities, and leaders of the banned militant group Jamaat-ud-Dawah offered a $2.2 mil reward for anyone who killed Jones. Anti-U.S. sentiment in Pakistan had been inflamed by a Jan. 27 incident in which Raymond Davis, a security contractor with the Central Intelligence Agency, killed 2 Pakistani men on a crowded Lahore street; he was released by Pakistani authorities Mar. 16 after the victims' families were each promised up to $1 mil in compensation.

Frayed relations between Pakistan and the U.S. contributed to the instability of the Zardari government, which was already under intense Islamist pressure. On Jan. 4, Punjab's provincial Gov. Salman Taseer—a Zardari ally and an opponent of Pakistan's blasphemy laws, which required the death penalty for anyone who insulted Islam—was assassinated by one of his security guards in the Pakistani capital of Islamabad. Also in Islamabad, gunmen Mar. 2 killed Shahbaz Bhatti, the only Christian in Pakistan's federal cabinet and a proponent of tolerance for the nation's religious minorities.

General

TV Star Charlie Sheen Fired From Top-Rated Sitcom—Following weeks of bizarre behavior that had become gossip fodder, Charlie Sheen, star of the TV comedy *Two and a Half Men*, was dropped from the show Mar. 7. Warner Bros. Television and CBS had halted production on the series Feb. 24 after Sheen blasted the show and executives in charge of it. In a letter to Sheen's attorney explaining the dismissal, lawyers for Warner Bros. accused Sheen of "reckless and dangerous conduct," including allegations of drug- and alcohol-fueled binges and spousal abuse. CBS and Warner Bros. announced May 13 that the show would resume production with actor Ashton Kutcher in a lead role. Sheen reportedly received $25 mil in a legal settlement with Warner Bros. announced Sept. 26.

Problems Plague *Spider-Man* Musical—Producers of *Spider-Man: Turn Off the Dark* disclosed Mar. 9 that they had dismissed acclaimed writer-director Julie Taymor from the $70-mil spectacle, the most expensive show in Broadway history. Along with Bono and The Edge of the rock group U2, who composed the music, Taymor was responsible for turning the comic-book superhero story into a musical. The production, which involved daring aerial maneuvers, had been plagued by serious injuries to cast members, technical breakdowns, multiple delays, and savage reviews from theater critics. Mostly negative reviews accompanied the production's official opening June 14 after a record 183 previews.

April 2011
National

Budget Deal Averts Government Shutdown; Other Economic Developments—After relying for more than 6 months on a series of short-term, stopgap bills to keep the U.S. government running, Congress Apr. 14-15 passed and Pres. Obama signed an omnibus appropriations measure funding federal government operations through Sept. 30, 2011. Obama, House Speaker John Boehner (R, OH), and Senate Majority Leader Harry Reid (D, NV) reached agreement on the measure on the night of Apr. 8, only hours before

the government was due to shut down. A final stopgap bill, approved Apr. 9, gave Congress a week to consider the omnibus legislation. Pressed by Republicans to make drastic spending reductions, Obama and congressional Democrats agreed to roughly $38 bil in cutbacks.

The wrangling over fiscal 2011 funding reflected a deeper partisan divide over federal taxes and spending. On Feb. 14, the Obama administration had unveiled a budget calling for $3.73 tril in spending and $2.63 tril in revenues during the 2012 fiscal year; the budget forecast annual deficits of $1.6 tril in fiscal 2011 and $1.1 tril in fiscal 2012. Pres. Obama outlined a plan Apr. 13 to slash $4 tril from projected deficits over a 12-year period by cutting spending and raising taxes on the wealthy. Two days later, House Republicans pushed through an alternative deficit-reduction plan championed by House Budget Committee Chairman Paul Ryan (R, WI). Approved by a vote of 235-193, the House resolution promised to balance the budget by 2040, reduce taxes on individuals and corporations, cut spending by $4.4 tril over a 10-year period, replace Medicaid with block grants to states, and gradually transform the government-run Medicare program into a voucher system under which seniors would receive limited federal subsidies to purchase private insurance. Democrats, eager to highlight the resolution's unpopular Medicare overhaul, brought the Ryan plan up for a vote May 25 in the Senate, where it was defeated 57-40. Meanwhile, credit-rating agencies warned that the nation's top-rated credit might be downgraded.

The Commerce Dept. reported Apr. 28 that the U.S. gross domestic product, which had grown 3.1% Oct.-Dec. 2010, had grown by only 1.8% Jan.-Mar. 2011. Corporate earnings remained strong, however, and stocks enjoyed a banner month. The Dow Jones Industrial Average closed Apr. 29 at 12,810.54, for a monthly gain of 4.3%. The S&P 500 rose 3.4% to 1,363.61, and the Nasdaq Composite Index increased 4.2% to 2,873.54.

Tornadoes Hit Alabama, Other Southeastern States—A record 753 tornadoes struck the U.S. during Apr., eclipsing the previous one-month mark of 542 set in May 2003. The tornadoes, concentrated in the Southeast, were blamed for an estimated 364 deaths, with approximately 248 of the fatalities occurring during an Apr. 27 outbreak in Alabama. The devastation was especially intense in and around Tuscaloosa, AL, where a single tornado carved a path of destruction 1 mi wide. Property damage in the state was estimated at more than $3 bil.

Obama Launches Reelection Campaign, Debunks "Birther" Rumors—Pres. Barack Obama (D) officially began his reelection campaign Apr. 4, contacting supporters via e-mail, YouTube video, and Twitter, filing fundraising documents with the Federal Election Commission (FEC), and hosting a conference call with grassroots organizers and major donors. The announcement came as Obama saw his approval ratings dip to the lowest point of his presidency; a 3-day tracking poll taken Apr. 12-14 found only 41% of Americans approved of his performance as president, while 50% disapproved. According to a CBS/*New York Times* survey released Apr. 21, 25% of the U.S. population, including 45% of Republicans and 45% of Tea Party supporters, believed Obama had been born overseas—a groundless assertion spread by conspiracy theorists who contended that he was not a native-born U.S. citizen and thus not qualified to be president. The rumors, embraced by some mainstream figures such as real-estate developer and celebrity Donald Trump, flourished despite extensive evidence (including the official state short-form birth certificate) proving Obama was born in Honolulu, HI, in 1961. On Apr. 27, Obama denounced the rumors in a statement to the White House press corps, and a copy of his long-form birth certificate—signed in Honolulu in 1961 by his mother, the attending physician, and a local registrar—was posted on the White House website.

Fatigue Blamed for Air Traffic Controller Errors—Following a series of episodes in which air traffic controllers in various U.S. cities reportedly fell asleep while on duty, federal transportation officials took steps to discipline offenders and adjust schedules to lessen fatigue. On Apr. 13, Transportation Sec. Ray LaHood ordered a 2nd overnight controller into each of the 27 towers that had cut costs by employing only a single controller on midnight shifts. The order came in response to an incident in which a flight controller at Nevada's Reno-Tahoe International Airport reportedly dozed off while an air ambulance carrying a critically ill passenger tried to land. Three days later, after a controller in Miami, FL, was found napping, the Federal Aviation Admin. announced it would revamp scheduling practices that allowed controllers to pile up shifts with little turnaround time in-between. Another air traffic control error was blamed for an Apr. 18 incident in which a jet carrying First Lady Michelle Obama and Jill Biden, wife of Vice Pres. Joe Biden, flew too close to a military cargo plane.

Ensign Quits Senate in Ethics Scandal—Nearly 2 years after he first admitted having an affair with Cynthia Hampton, his former campaign treasurer, 2-term Sen. John Ensign (R, NV) announced Apr. 21 that he would resign his Senate seat effective May 3. Ensign left office as the Senate Ethics Committee was wrapping up its inquiry into whether he had violated Senate rules and federal law by pressuring Nevada business leaders to hire Cynthia's husband Doug as a lobbyist and by arranging to have his parents write checks totaling $96,000 to the Hampton family. Ensign had been under increasing pressure from national GOP leaders to give up his seat, and on Mar. 7—as Rep. Dean Heller (R, NV) was preparing to launch a primary challenge against him—the incumbent senator announced he would not run for reelection in 2012. After Ensign stepped down, Nevada Gov. Brian Sandoval (R) appointed Heller to fill the seat, and he was sworn in May 9. Three days later, the Senate Ethics Committee issued a report urging the Justice Dept. to consider bringing criminal charges against Ensign.

Panetta Moves to Defense, Petraeus to CIA—Pres. Obama announced Apr. 28 that he would nominate CIA Director Leon Panetta to replace the retiring Robert Gates as defense secretary. Gates, the lone holdover from the cabinet of Pres. George W. Bush, had been responsible for U.S. defense policy since Dec. 2006 and had overseen U.S. military operations in Iraq, Afghanistan, Pakistan, Libya, and elsewhere. At a Pentagon farewell ceremony June 30, Obama presented Gates with the Presidential Medal of Freedom. The popular Panetta, who had served in the CIA post since Feb. 2009, was unanimously confirmed by the Senate June 21 and sworn in at the Pentagon July 1. To replace Panetta at the CIA, Obama nominated Gen. David Petraeus, the commander of U.S. and allied troops in Afghanistan. The Senate confirmed him June 30 by a vote of 94-0. At ceremonies in Kabul July 18, Petraeus transferred his Afghanistan command to Gen. John Allen.

International

NATO Steps Up Attacks in Libya; Other "Arab Spring" Developments—Hostilities escalated in Libya, Syria, and Yemen, as Arab Spring uprisings continued to send shockwaves through North Africa and the Middle East. Much of the fighting in Libya centered around efforts by forces loyal to Muammar al-Qaddafi to besiege the port of Misurata, the nation's 3rd-largest city and the only large population center in Western Libya controlled by anti-Qaddafi rebels. Estimates of the death toll in Misurata had risen to more than 1,000 by the end of the month; 2 well-known photojournalists, British-born documentary filmmaker Tim Hetherington and U.S. news photographer Chris Hondros, were killed Apr. 20 while covering the fighting. Seeking to ease the siege of Misurata and to disrupt other military operations by the Qaddafi regime, NATO (acting under a UN Security Council mandate) carried out airstrikes against what were described as "command and control" buildings in Tripoli, Libya's capital and most populous city. An aerial assault on a house in Tripoli Apr. 30 reportedly killed Qaddafi's youngest son and 3 of the Libyan leader's grandchildren. NATO officials denied the airstrike was an attempt to assassinate Qaddafi, although he and his wife were believed to have been present around the time of the attack.

In Syria, demonstrations against the regime of Bashar al-Assad intensified, as did government actions to suppress them. At least 75 people died Apr. 22 when forces fired on crowds of protesters who had gathered after Friday prayers in many Syrian cities. In Yemen, where at least 130 street protesters had been killed in clashes with security forces, Pres. Ali Abdullah Saleh said Apr. 23 that he had agreed to resign in exchange for a grant of immunity from prosecution for himself and his family. Within the week, however, Saleh appeared to back away from the plan, which had been brokered by the Gulf Cooperation Council, a Saudi-led regional group.

Responding to shifting political realities in the Middle East, 2 feuding Palestinian factions, Fatah and Hamas, declared Apr. 27 that they had agreed to a reconciliation agreement mediated by Egypt's transitional government. Under the accord signed in Cairo May 4, Fatah (which held power in the West Bank) and Hamas (which ruled Gaza) would form a joint caretaker government and hold elections throughout Palestine.

Capture of Gbagbo Ends Côte d'Ivoire Standoff—With support from French armored vehicles and UN helicopter gunships, forces loyal to former Prime Min. Alassane Ouattara captured incumbent Pres. Laurent Gbagbo Apr. 11 in Abidjan, Côte d'Ivoire, ending a violent power struggle that had claimed an estimated 3,000 lives and displaced at least 1 mil people. The standoff stemmed from a disputed presidential election Nov. 2010 with both men claiming victory. While Gbagbo and allies clung to power in Abidjan, the nation's commercial capital and largest city, Ouattara gained backing from the U.S., UN, France, and the Economic Community of West African States. In early Apr., as Gbagbo, his family, and his closest aides retreated to a bunker beneath his presidential residence, Ouattara's forces entered Abidjan and consolidated control over the rest of the country. Human Rights Watch reported June 2 that since taking power, Ouattara's troops had killed at least 149 suspected Gbagbo supporters.

Violence Follows Reelection of Nigerian President—Incumbent Pres. Goodluck Jonathan, a Christian from the southern Niger Delta region, won reelection Apr. 16 with nearly 59% of the vote, defeating his closest rival, Muhammadu Buhari, a northern-based Muslim who received 32% of the vote. Although the election was generally regarded as free and fair by international monitors, the results exposed the deep ethnic, religious, and regional divisions in Nigeria. Jonathan had become head of state in May 2010 after the death of Pres. Umaru Yar'Adua, a Muslim. Many Muslim Nigerians had hoped that Jonathan would step aside to allow another Muslim to serve what would have been Yar'Adua's 2nd term. Instead, Jonathan secured the nomination of the ruling People's Democratic Party by defeating a Muslim rival in a party primary Jan. 13. News of his reelection victory over Buhari, who had ruled Nigeria as the head of a military council in the mid-1980s, triggered 3 days of rioting in 12 northern provinces, leaving more than 800 people dead.

Musician Elected President in Haiti—Michel Martelly, an entertainer who performed under the stage name Sweet Micky, was proclaimed president-elect by Haiti's electoral council Apr. 20. Martelly had finished 3rd behind law professor and former first lady Mirlande Manigat and ruling party candidate Jude Célestin in the initial round of balloting Nov. 28, 2010. But after violent protests by Martelly supporters, allegations of electoral fraud from international observers, and diplomatic pressure from the U.S. and other donor countries, Célestin was bumped from the ballot and Martelly was declared eligible for a runoff election against Manigat,

Mar. 20, 2011. He won, 68% to 32%, and was inaugurated May 14. Haiti was still suffering from the effects of the Jan. 2010 earthquake in which, according to official statistics, more than 220,000 people lost their lives. The International Organization for Migration estimated that more than 600,000 Haitians were still living in displacement camps at the time Martelly took office.

Hundreds of Bodies Found in Mass Graves in Mexico—Authorities in Mexico announced the discovery of mass graves holding nearly 300 bodies, apparently victims of the drug wars that have claimed close to 35,000 lives since 2006. Newly appointed Mexican Attorney Gen. Marisela Morales disclosed Apr. 26 that a total of 183 bodies had been discovered in 40 mass graves in the state of Tamaulipas, which shares a border with Texas. The following day, officials in Durango, a state in northwestern Mexico, reported that they had exhumed 104 bodies from mass graves during the month. Although most of the bodies had yet to be identified, Mexican national security spokesman Alejandro Poiré Romero said many of the Tamaulipas victims may have been killed after refusing to serve as drug traffickers.

General

UConn, Texas A&M Capture College Basketball Titles—Bruising defense by the Univ. of Connecticut and dismal shooting by Butler combined to give the Huskies a 53-41 victory in the NCAA Division I men's basketball championship game Apr. 4 at Reliant Stadium in Houston, TX. The title was UConn's 3rd under Jim Calhoun, who at 68 became the oldest coach to win the men's Division I crown. With 16 points and 9 rebounds in the title game, Huskies guard Kemba Walker was named most outstanding player. In a high-energy women's final Apr. 5 at Conseco Fieldhouse in Indianapolis, IN, the Aggies of Texas A&M won the school's first national basketball championship, defeating Notre Dame 76-70. Aggies forward Danielle Adams, who won most outstanding player honors, starred in the title game with 30 points and 9 rebounds.

Schwartzel Triumphs in Masters Golf Tournament—Charl Schwartzel of South Africa birdied his last 4 holes Apr. 10 at the Augusta (GA) National Golf Club to win the 75th Masters golf tournament. With a 6-under-par 66 in the final round, Schwartzel finished with a 14-under-par 274 for the tournament, 2 strokes ahead of his closest competitors, Australia's Jason Day and Adam Scott. The 3rd-round leader, Rory McIlroy of Northern Ireland, shot 8-over-par in the final round and finished 10 strokes behind the leader.

Bonds Found Guilty in Steroids Case—Former slugger Barry Bonds was convicted Apr. 13 of obstructing justice in 2003 when he gave evasive answers to a grand jury investigating the use of banned performance-enhancing drugs. The federal jury in San Francisco, where Bonds had set Major League Baseball career and single-season home-run records, deadlocked on charges that he had also committed perjury when he told the grand jury that he had never knowingly taken steroids or human growth hormone, and had never received injections from anyone other than his doctors. Prosecutors had a hard time making their perjury case after Bonds's former personal trainer, Greg Anderson, chose to be jailed on contempt of court charges rather than testify against the 7-time National League MVP.

Mutai Smashes Boston Marathon Record—Pushed by a tail wind of up to 20 mph, Geoffrey Mutai of Kenya ran the fastest-ever Boston Marathon Apr. 18, completing the 26.2-mi run in 2:03:02. Mutai's time eclipsed by nearly a minute the world record of 2:03:59 set in Sept. 2008 by Ethiopia's Haile Gebrselassie, but the International Association of Athletics Federations (IAAF) declined to certify Mutai's feat as a new world mark because the venerable Boston course does not meet IAAF specifications. Caroline Kilel of Kenya won the women's race in 2:22:36, only 2 seconds ahead of Desiree Davila, whose time was the best ever for an American in the Boston competition.

Prince William and Kate Middleton Marry in London—In ceremonies broadcast worldwide Apr. 29, Prince William, 2nd in line to the British throne, married his longtime girlfriend, Catherine (Kate) Middleton. The bride and groom met about 10 years earlier when both were students at the Univ. of St. Andrews, Scotland. Their engagement had been announced Nov. 16, 2010, by Prince William's father, Prince Charles. Kate's engagement ring was the same Charles had given in 1981 to William's mother, Diana. At the wedding, the groom wore a scarlet military uniform, and the bride wore a lace and ivory satin dress designed by Sarah Burton for Alexander McQueen, along with a diamond tiara loaned to her by Queen Elizabeth II. The royal couple received the new titles duke and duchess of Cambridge.

May 2011
National

GOP Presidential Field Takes Shape—A handful of candidates for the 2012 Republican presidential nomination met May 5 in Greenville, SC, for the 1st televised debate of the GOP primary season. Participants included former New Mexico Gov. Gary Johnson, who declared his candidacy Apr. 21; U.S. Rep. Ron Paul (TX), who formally joined the race May 13; radio talk-show host and former Godfather's Pizza chief executive Herman Cain, who officially entered May 21; former Minnesota Gov. Tim Pawlenty, who had spent months on the campaign trail before making his announcement in a YouTube video released May 22; and former Sen. Rick Santorum (PA), who made his intentions official June 6.

Joining the fray for the 2nd Republican debate on June 13 at New Hampshire's Saint Anselm College were former Speaker of the House Newt Gingrich (GA); U.S. Rep. Michele Bachmann (MN); and businessman and former Massachusetts Gov. Mitt Romney, who, like Paul, also ran in 2008. Gingrich made his formal announcement May 11 but lagged in fundraising and saw his top campaign aides resign en masse June 9. When Romney made his official declaration June 2, most polls showed him as the early front-runner to face Pres. Barack Obama (D) in 2012. Former Utah Gov. Jon Huntsman, who had served as Obama's ambassador to China, entered the race June 21.

Prominent Republicans who explicitly declined to run included Mississippi Gov. Haley Barbour, Apr. 25; former Arkansas Gov. Mike Huckabee (a 2008 runner-up), May 14; business tycoon and TV personality Donald Trump, May 16; and Indiana Gov. Mitch Daniels, May 22. Press attention also focused on 2 other well-known Republicans who had made appearances in key states: Texas Gov. Rick Perry and former Alaska Gov. Sarah Palin, the party's vice-presidential nominee in 2008.

Rajaratnam Convicted of Insider Trading—A federal jury in New York, NY, ended 12 days of deliberations May 11 by convicting Raj Rajaratnam, the billionaire co-founder of the Galleon Group hedge fund, on 14 counts of securities fraud and conspiracy. To prove Rajaratnam had made more than $63 mil in illicit profits, prosecutors presented jurors with 46 secretly recorded phone conversations in which company insiders tipped off the Sri Lankan-born financier about upcoming earnings reports and corporate takeovers. U.S. District Judge Richard Holwell sentenced him Oct. 13 to 11 years in prison and fined him $10 mil.

Tornadoes, Floods Batter Midwest—According to preliminary estimates by the National Weather Service, about 320 tornadoes struck the U.S. during the month. Among them was the single deadliest U.S. tornado in more than a half-century, a category EF-5 storm May 22 that claimed an estimated 162 lives in Joplin, MO. The tornado, ¾-mi wide and packing winds of more than 200 mph, devastated nearly everything in its path for a distance of 6 mi. Another 18 people died May 24 when at least 12 tornadoes struck Oklahoma, Kansas, and Arkansas. Meanwhile, torrential rains and melting snows swelled the Mississippi River and its tributaries from Illinois to Louisiana, flooding millions of acres of cropland, disrupting commerce, and displacing tens of thousands of people. The rising river crested at record levels at Vicksburg and Natchez, MS, and approached record heights in Memphis, TN. The U.S. Army Corps of Engineers deliberately blasted a levee in southwestern Missouri to save the city of Cairo, IL, from a devastating flood, and opened spillways in Louisiana to ease the threat to Baton Rouge and New Orleans.

Supreme Court Rules on Prisons, Immigration—By a 5-4 majority, the U.S. Supreme Court May 23 held that overcrowding in California prisons violated the Eighth Amendment ban on "cruel and unusual punishments." Associate Justice Anthony Kennedy's majority decision in *Brown v. Plata* affirmed a 2009 ruling by a 3-judge federal court requiring California to reduce its prison population to about 110,000. At the time of ruling, the state correctional system had held some 156,000 inmates, nearly double the system's designed capacity; in the interim, California had released about 9,000 inmates, but another 37,000 would need to be freed in order to meet the target upheld by the Supreme Court. Justice Kennedy's opinion pointed out that overcrowded conditions had denied prisoners access to adequate physical and mental health treatment, and that the suicide rate among California inmates was nearly 80% higher than the national prison average. In his dissenting opinion, Associate Justice Samuel Alito warned that "the majority is gambling with the safety of the people of California."

A 5-3 majority May 26 upheld the Legal Arizona Workers Act (2007), which penalizes employers who knowingly hire illegal immigrants. Businesses that violate the statute may have their licenses suspended for a 1st offense and revoked for a repeat violation. An unusual coalition of business and civil rights groups had opposed the Arizona legislation, claiming that it infringed on federal immigration enforcement responsibilities. Writing for the majority in *Chamber of Commerce v. Whiting*, Chief Justice John Roberts found that the licensing penalties fell "well within the confines of the authority Congress chose to leave to the States." Eight states had recently enacted similar laws, and 13 states had filed a brief supporting the Arizona statute.

Stocks Sag as Economy Stalls—After beating forecasts by adding 244,000 jobs in Apr., the nation's economy lagged in May, as nonfarm payrolls inched upward by only 54,000 and the unemployment rate rose to 9.1%. Reports issued May 31-June 1 indicated that manufacturing growth had faltered and that home prices during the 1st quarter of 2011 had slumped to levels not seen since 2002. Stocks posted their worst monthly performance since Aug. 2010, with the Dow Jones Industrial Average closing May 31 at 12,569.79, a decline of 1.9%. The S&P 500 dropped 1.4% to 1,345.20, and the Nasdaq Composite Index fell 1.3% to 2,835.30.

International

U.S. Commandos Kill Osama Bin Laden—Shortly after midnight May 2, in Abbottabad, Pakistan, a CIA-led squadron of elite U.S. Navy SEALs breached the hideout of Osama bin Laden and killed the al-Qaeda leader, whose trail of terror included the attacks against the U.S. that had claimed the lives of nearly 3,000 people on Sept. 11, 2001. The commando raid, carried out by helicopter from Jalalabad, Afghanistan, was launched without prior warning to Pakistani authorities, some of whom had long been suspected of harboring the Saudi-born bin Laden.

The al-Qaeda leader was shot twice, in the head and the chest; after his body was taken to Afghanistan for identification, it was transferred to the U.S. aircraft carrier *Carl Vinson*, where, after brief religious rites, he was buried at sea. One of bin Laden's sons was also killed in the raid along with Abu Ahmed al-Kuwaiti, the al-Qaeda courier whose movements, tracked for years by the CIA, had led the raiders to

their target. The decision to launch a commando strike rather than obliterate the compound by aerial bombardment paid dividends when the assault team was able to retrieve a trove of documents and computer hardware along with bin Laden's body. In a statement posted on jihadist websites, al-Qaeda acknowledged bin Laden's death May 6 and vowed revenge against the U.S. The Egyptian-born Ayman al-Zawahiri succeeded bin Laden as al-Qaeda's leader.

The 2001 attacks, which bin Laden plotted while living in Afghanistan, had prompted the U.S. and its allies to intervene in that country and to launch a global war against terrorism. The U.S. still maintained about 90,000 troops in Afghanistan, serving alongside more than 42,000 troops from coalition partners; U.S. and allied military fatalities through May totaled nearly 2,500. In other strikes at suspected terrorists, a U.S. drone attack in Yemen May 5 apparently missed radical Yemeni-American cleric Anwar al-Awlaki, but Somali transitional government troops June 7 killed Fazul Abdullah Mohammed, a top al-Qaeda leader in East Africa and the alleged mastermind of the Aug. 1998 bombings at U.S. embassies in Kenya and Tanzania.

Conservatives Gain Mandate in Canadian Election—Conservative Prime Min. Stephen Harper, who had led Canada since 2006 as the head of a minority government, won a convincing mandate in federal elections May 2. Final results for the 308-member House of Commons gave the Conservatives 166 seats, a gain of 23 since the last election in 2008. The New Democratic Party, led by Jack Layton, emerged as Canada's official opposition party, gaining 67 seats to finish with 103, while the Liberals plummeted from 77 seats to 34, their weakest showing in history. Michael Ignatieff, who lost his Ontario district in the election, announced his resignation as Liberal Party leader May 3. Former Ontario Premier Bob Rae was chosen as interim leader May 25. The 61-year-old Layton died Aug. 22, leaving Nycole Turmel as interim NDP leader.

Other parties represented in Parliament were the French separatist Bloc Québécois (which dropped from 47 seats to 4) and the Green Party (1). The elections had been called after Harper's government fell on a parliamentary vote of no confidence Mar. 25.

IMF Chief Accused of Sexual Assault—International Monetary Fund Managing Director Dominique Strauss-Kahn, a prominent figure in France's Socialist Party, was arrested in New York City May 14 and charged with sexually assaulting a housekeeper at the Sofitel New York hotel. His accuser, later identified as Nafissatou Diallo, a 32-year-old Guinean immigrant, told police the 62-year-old financial executive had attacked her and forced her to perform oral sex when she entered Strauss-Kahn's suite to clean it. Lawyers for Strauss-Kahn denied the assault charge, contending the encounter had been consensual. On May 18, he resigned his IMF post, and on June 28, French Finance Min. Christine Lagarde became the 1st woman to hold the fund's managing directorship. Meanwhile, follow-up inquiries by New York City police raised doubts about Diallo's allegations, background, and associates. Strauss-Kahn was released from house arrest July 1 after prosecutors informed his lawyers that her credibility as a witness had been compromised. All criminal charges against him were dropped Aug. 23, but he still faced a civil suit filed by Diallo Aug. 8.

Clashes Continue in North Africa and Middle East—Violent confrontations between "Arab Spring" dissidents and entrenched regimes continued in Libya, Yemen, and Syria. While Libyan troops loyal to the regime of Muammar al-Qaddafi faced opposition from rebel forces and NATO, José Luis Moreno-Ocampo, chief prosecutor for the International Criminal Court at The Hague, Netherlands, announced May 16 that he would seek a warrant to arrest Qaddafi for crimes against humanity.

Heavy fighting between Yemeni government forces and opponents of Pres. Ali Abdullah Saleh broke out May 23 after Saleh repeatedly refused to sign an agreement brokered by the Gulf Cooperation Council that would have led to his resignation in exchange for a grant of immunity from prosecution.

The Israeli government accused Syria's Bashar al-Assad of seeking to divert attention from his regime's continuing violent crackdown against dissidents by fomenting a confrontation between Palestinians and Israeli troops. Israeli forces killed at least 14 Palestinians as thousands of protesters tried to cross from Lebanon and Syria into Israeli-controlled territory on May 15, the day on which Palestinians annually commemorate *al-Nakba* (Arabic for "the catastrophe"), the displacement of hundreds of thousands of Palestinian Arabs by the creation of the State of Israel. The U.S. May 18 imposed sanctions directly on Assad and other top Syrian officials.

In a major policy speech delivered May 19 at the U.S. State Dept. in Washington, DC, Pres. Obama expressed support for the Arab Spring movement and called for a negotiated two-state solution to the Israeli-Palestinian conflict. Industrialized nations belonging to the Group of 8 endorsed May 27 a $40 bil program to support the transition to democracy in Tunisia and Egypt, where mass protests had toppled autocratic governments earlier in 2011. About $20 bil would come from multilateral financial institutions, $10 bil directly from G-8 members, and $10 bil from Saudi Arabia, Qatar, and Kuwait. The IMF agreed June 5 to lend Egypt $3 bil to shore up its struggling economy.

Mladic Arrested in Serbia—Ratko Mladic, the Bosnian Serb military commander accused of directing the 1995 massacre of 8,000 Muslims in Srebrenica, was arrested May 26 after he was discovered hiding in his cousin's house in Lazarevo, Serbia. He was extradited to The Hague, where he had been indicted by the International Criminal Tribunal for the Former Yugoslavia on charges of genocide and other crimes against humanity. The extradition of Mladic removed an obstacle to Serbia's eventual entry into the European Union, which at Dutch insistence had balked at admitting Serbia as long as that country (long suspected of sheltering Mladic) did not fully cooperate with war crimes investigations. The Srebrenica slaughter remained a sensitive issue for the Dutch government because the 400 lightly armed Dutch members of a UN peacekeeping force assigned to protect the Bosnian Muslim safe haven had been overrun by Bosnian Serb attackers.

General

Animal Kingdom Takes Kentucky Derby, Loses to Shackleford in Preakness—Running for the 1st time on a natural dirt track, the lightly raced Animal Kingdom won the Kentucky Derby May 7 at Churchill Downs in Louisville, KY. Jockey John Velazquez, a replacement rider for the injured Robby Albarado, won his 1st Derby in 13 appearances. Two weeks later at Pimlico in Baltimore, MD, Shackleford, the 4th-place Derby finisher, held off a late charge by the favored Animal Kingdom to capture the Preakness Stakes. The event yielded the 1st Triple Crown win for 38-year-old Mexican-born jockey Jesus Castanon and marked the 33rd consecutive year that no thoroughbred had swept all 3 Triple Crown races.

Oprah Ends TV Talk Show—Oprah Winfrey, the queen of daytime TV, ended her long-running syndicated program May 25. In a 25-year span that included more than 4,500 episodes and featured some 30,000 guests, *The Oprah Winfrey Show* reached millions of people daily in the U.S. and more than 140 other countries. Regularly ranked among the world's wealthiest, most influential, and most admired women, the Chicago-based entertainer and entrepreneur was expected to devote her energies to the Oprah Winfrey Network (OWN), a cable channel that debuted Jan. 1.

Wheldon Wins Indy 500—Overtaking rookie U.S. driver J. R. Hildebrand, who crashed on the final turn, British-born Dan Wheldon won his 2nd career Indianapolis 500 auto race at Indianapolis Motor Speedway May 29. Wheldon, who had won in 2005 and finished in 2nd place in 2009 and 2010, didn't lead until the final seconds of the 2011 competition, which marked the 100th anniversary of the 500-mi race. A video review showed that Wheldon passed Hildebrand's crumpled car just before the yellow caution light appeared.

Barcelona Triumphs in Champions League, as Scandal Hits FIFA—Argentina's Lionel Messi scored the go-ahead goal for Barcelona as the Spanish professional football (soccer) club defeated the UK's Manchester United, 3-1, to win the Champions League title match May 28 at Wembley Stadium in London, England. The annual club competition, the most prestigious in Europe, was sponsored by the Union of European Football Associations. The tournament took place as soccer's world governing body, International Federation of Association Football (FIFA), was wracked by a scandal involving alleged vote-buying in the election of FIFA's president and in the Dec. 2010 decision to choose Russia as the World Cup host country in 2018 and Qatar in 2022. A target of a FIFA ethics probe, Mohamed bin Hammam of Qatar, president of the Asian Football Confederation, withdrew his FIFA presidential candidacy May 28 and was suspended by FIFA the following day. The lone remaining candidate, Joseph "Sepp" Blatter of Switzerland, won reelection to a 4th term as FIFA president June 1.

June 2011
National

Wildfires Rage in Southwest, as Floods Hit Northern Plains—Unusually hot, dry, and windy conditions in the Southwest and Southern Plains contributed to outbreaks of wildfires throughout the region. According to the National Climatic Data Center of the National Oceanic and Atmospheric Admin., 6,567 wildfires burned a total of 1.3 mil acres during the month, with record-setting blazes in Arizona and New Mexico. Exceptional drought conditions prevailed in southern Arizona, most of New Mexico, and large sections of Texas, Louisiana, and Georgia. In the Northern Plains, meanwhile, heavy rains and snowmelt caused flooding along the Missouri River system and the Souris River, which flows from Saskatchewan, Canada, into North Dakota. Flood damage was especially heavy in Minot, ND, where the Souris crested June 26 at a record 1,561.72 ft, nearly 4 ft higher than the previous mark set in 1881.

Edwards Charged With Using Campaign Funds to Cover Up Affair—Former Sen. John Edwards (D, NC), the 2004 Democratic vice-presidential nominee, was indicted June 3 for violating campaign finance laws and lying to the Federal Election Commission. A federal grand jury in Greensboro, NC, charged that during his 2008 presidential campaign, he had used about $925,000 from 2 wealthy donors to pay off a mistress, Rielle Hunter, and a political aide, Andrew Young, in order to keep voters from learning that Edwards and not Young was the father of Hunter's child. Edwards pleaded not guilty, claiming that the funds had been used for personal rather than political purposes—to conceal the affair from his wife Elizabeth Edwards. The former senator, who had repeatedly denied tabloid reports concerning his infidelity, admitted to the affair in Aug. 2008, long after he had dropped out of the presidential race, and acknowledged paternity in Jan. 2010. Elizabeth Edwards died after a six-year struggle with breast cancer Dec. 7, 2010.

Weiner Quits Congress After Posting Lewd Photos—U.S. Rep. Anthony Weiner (D, NY), an influential 7-term legislator, announced June 16 that he would resign after sexually suggestive photos he had sent via Twitter, an online social-networking service, began circulating. The married Weiner, who had been preparing to run for mayor of New York City in 2013, at first claimed his Twitter account had been hacked but admitted June 6 to having had inappropriate online contact with several women. Democratic leaders including Pres. Obama called for his resignation, and he left the House June 21.

New York Approves Same-Sex Marriage—Championed by 1st-term Gov. Andrew Cuomo (D), a measure legalizing same-sex marriage in New York state gained approval June 24. The marriage equality bill, which had passed the Democratic-controlled state assembly June 15 by an 80-63 margin, was approved after an emotional debate by a 33-29 vote in the state senate—the 1st time a state legislative chamber controlled by Republicans endorsed a measure extending full marriage rights to same-sex couples. Gov. Cuomo signed the bill into law shortly before midnight June 24, and the state began issuing same-sex marriage licenses 30 days later.

Supreme Court Ends Term With Free Speech Rulings—The U.S. Supreme Court concluded its 2010-11 term June 27 with 2 major decisions in First Amendment cases. In *Brown v. Entertainment Merchants Association*, an unusual 7-2 coalition of conservative and liberal justices struck down a California law that banned the sale of violent video games to minors under 18 years old. "No doubt a State possesses legitimate power to protect children from harm," Associate Justice Antonin Scalia wrote in the majority opinion, "but that does not include a free-floating power to restrict the ideas to which children may be exposed." In a concurring opinion, Associate Justice Samuel Alito faulted the statute on technical grounds, but said the court might be justified in upholding other efforts to regulate the sale of video games that allow "troubled teens to experience in an extraordinarily personal and vivid way what it would be like to carry out unspeakable acts of violence."

The court split along more traditional lines in two consolidated cases, *Arizona Free Enterprise Club v. Bennett* and *McComish v. Bennett*, with the conservative faction of the court overturning provisions of the Arizona Citizens Clean Elections Act (1998) that offered supplemental matching funds to publicly financed candidates who faced privately financed opponents. In his 5-4 majority decision, Chief Justice John Roberts contended that the Arizona law violated the First Amendment rights of privately financed groups and candidates who might feel compelled to suppress their own constitutionally protected speech rather than risk triggering the matching fund provisions. In her dissent, Associate Justice Elena Kagan defended the statute as a legitimate attempt to prevent money from corrupting the electoral process.

In other notable decisions, the court June 16 expanded Fifth Amendment protections against self-incrimination in juvenile justice cases, and June 20 threw out a class-action lawsuit against Wal-Mart, the nation's largest retailer. The Wal-Mart suit, alleging sex discrimination against up to 1.5 mil women, was blocked unanimously on procedural grounds, although the 4 liberal justices found merit in the plaintiffs' claim that "gender bias suffused Wal-Mart's corporate culture."

Blagojevich Convicted of Corruption—A federal jury in Chicago June 27 convicted former Illinois Gov. Rod Blagojevich (D) on 17 felony corruption charges, including allegations that he had tried to sell the U.S. Senate seat vacated by Barack Obama after the Nov. 2008 presidential election. A previous trial had ended Aug. 2010 with a jury convicting Blagojevich on a single count of making false statements to the FBI but unable to reach a verdict on the remaining counts against him. Blagojevich had been impeached and removed from office in Jan. 2009. He was the 4th Illinois governor since the 1960s to be convicted of a crime.

Markets End Turbulent 2nd Quarter on Upswing; Other Economic Developments—Overcoming uncertainty about European and U.S. debt problems and lagging U.S. job growth, stocks June 27-30 recorded their best week in 2 years. The Dow Jones Industrial average closed June 30 at 12,414.34, up more than 7% since Jan. 1; the S&P 500 (1,320.64) and Nasdaq Composite Index (2,773.52) posted 6-month gains of 5% and 4.6%, respectively.

With crude petroleum trading at more than $100 a barrel, in part because of a disruption in oil supplies from Libya, members of the International Energy Agency agreed June 23 to release 60 mil barrels of oil from their strategic stockpiles over a 30-day period. The Obama administration pledged to supply 50% of that amount from the Strategic Petroleum Reserve, in an effort to push down U.S. gasoline prices that were averaging more than $3.50 per gallon.

Bank of America, one of the nation's largest banks, continued to struggle with the consequences of its 2008 acquisition of troubled mortgage lender Countrywide Financial. The company agreed June 29 to pay $8.5 bil to cover losses by major institutional investors on mortgage-backed securities issued by Countrywide that went sour when the mortgage market collapsed. It also announced that it would set aside $5.5 bil to deal with future claims on toxic assets as well as cover more than $6 bil in other Countrywide-related charges. The bank, based in Charlotte, NC, reported July 19 a net loss of $8.8 bil in the 2nd quarter of 2011, and announced Aug. 25 that it would receive a $5 bil cash infusion from Warren Buffett's Berkshire Hathaway holding company.

International

Conflicts Intensify in Yemen and Libya as U.S. Involvement Deepens—Pres. Ali Abdullah Saleh and other leading Yemeni officials were wounded June 3 in a rocket attack on the presidential compound in Sana'a'. Vice Pres. Abd al-Rab Mansur al-Hadi was named acting president the following day. Saleh was flown to Riyadh, Saudi Arabia, where doctors reportedly treated him for extensive burns, shrapnel wounds, and cranial bleeding. Saleh, in office since 1978 and a U.S. ally in the war against al-Qaeda, had been the target of escalating protests by an alliance of disaffected tribes and pro-democracy dissidents. Fearful that a power vacuum in Sana'a' would provide an opening for jihadists, the U.S. stepped up its military activities in Yemen, using drone aircraft and fighter jets to strike at suspected militants.

By the beginning of June, U.S. aircraft and missile support for NATO operations aiding "Arab Spring" insurgents against Libyan leader Muammar al-Qaddafi had cost the U.S. more than $700 mil. In a report to Congress June 15, the Obama administration declared it did not need congressional approval under the 1973 War Powers Resolution because U.S. military activities in Libya "do not involve sustained fighting or active exchanges of fire with hostile forces, nor do they involve the presence of U.S. ground troops." Members of the U.S. House expressed their discontent with the policy June 24 by defeating, 295-123, a bill that would have authorized U.S. military operations in Libya, but also rejecting, 238-180, a measure that would have sharply restricted such operations. In other Libya developments, the U.S. and its allies pledged June 9 to provide up to $1 bil to the anti-Qaddafi rebels, and the International Criminal Court in The Hague, Netherlands, issued a warrant June 27 for Qaddafi's arrest for crimes against humanity.

Socialists Ousted in Portuguese Election—Little more than a month after Portugal's Socialist government negotiated a 78 bil euro ($116 bil) bailout package from international lenders, Portuguese voters June 5 delivered a parliamentary election victory to the center-right Social Democratic Party, headed by Pedro Passos Coelho. He was sworn in as prime minister June 21, leading a coalition government with a smaller conservative group, the Democratic and Social Center-People's Party. In office for 6 years, Socialist Prime Min. José Sócrates had resigned Mar. 23 when Portugal's parliament rejected an austerity budget intended to avert a bailout. Under the terms of its rescue agreement with the European Union and International Monetary Fund, Portugal was required to reduce its annual budget deficit from more than 9% of its gross domestic product in 2010 to 5.9% in 2011 and 3% by 2013. Passos Coelho, a former businessman with a degree in economics, pledged to restore the country to fiscal health by trimming state agencies and privatizing government assets.

Leftist Wins Peruvian Presidency—In a presidential runoff election June 5, Ollanta Humala Tasso, a leftist former military officer, defeated legislator Keiko Fujimori, the daughter of jailed former Pres. Alberto Fujimori, by a margin of 51.4% to 48.6%. Humala and Fujimori had finished with 31.7% and 23.6%, respectively, in the 1st round of presidential elections Apr. 10, in which 3 candidates regarded as centrists—including former Pres. Alejandro Toledo and former Prime Min. Pedro Pablo Kuczynski—split 45% of the vote. Humala, who participated in counterinsurgency operations in the 1990s and led a military uprising in 2000 against the Fujimori regime, had campaigned unsuccessfully for the presidency in 2006 as an admirer of Venezuela's left-wing leader Hugo Chávez. In the 2011 campaign, he took a more moderate tone, pledging to preserve democracy, respect freedom of the press, and help the poor by following the example of Brazil, which has invested heavily in Peruvian industries and infrastructure. He took office July 28.

Islamic Government Retains Power in Turkey—The Justice and Development Party (AKP), an Islamic group headed by incumbent Prime Min. Recep Tayyip Erdogan, won about 50% of the popular vote in Turkish parliamentary elections June 12, nearly double the vote total for its main secularist rival, the Republican People's Party. The results marked a 3rd consecutive victory for the AKP, which won pluralities in 2002 and 2007. Final results gave the AKP 327 seats in the 550-seat legislature, short of the two-thirds majority that would have allowed the party unilaterally to change the constitution, which was drafted in the early 1980s when the armed forces dominated Turkish politics. Following the election, a power struggle intensified between Erdogan's Islamic government and military leaders who saw themselves as guardians of Turkey's secular republic. Since early 2010, at least 250 officers, including more than 40 generals, had been detained for allegedly plotting to overthrow the AKP government. Turkey's armed forces chief and the heads of the army, navy, and air force resigned en masse July 29, the same day nearly two dozen new arrest warrants were issued. Breaking with a tradition that had allowed the military to promote its own leaders, Pres. Abdullah Gül appointed a new quartet of top military commanders Aug. 4.

U.S. Sets Troop Withdrawal Timetable From Afghanistan—In a televised address by Pres. Obama and briefings by administration officials, the U.S. on June 22 outlined plans for drawing down military forces from Afghanistan. The timetable called for a pullout of 10,000 U.S. troops by the end of 2011 and another 23,000 by Sept. 2012; the combined total of 33,000 roughly matched the number of troops dispatched to Afghanistan under the surge strategy announced in Dec. 2009. The remaining 68,000 U.S. forces would be pulled out by the end of 2014. French Pres. Nicolas Sarkozy announced June 23 that his nation would initiate a gradual withdrawal of the 4,000 troops it had deployed to Afghanistan. British Prime Min. David Cameron had confirmed May 17 that the UK, which had more than 9,500 troops in Afghanistan, would pull out 400 by Feb. 2012.

Dramatizing the challenges the Kabul government and coalition forces continued to face in the fight against Taliban insurgents, at least 21 people died when 9 suicide bombers breached the fortified Inter-Continental Hotel in the Afghan capital June 28. A UN study issued July 14 reported 1,462 civilian deaths in Afghanistan during Jan.-June 2011, a 15% increase over the comparable period in 2010. Coalition fatalities in Afghanistan during the 1st half of 2011 numbered 282, of whom 204 were from the U.S.

Iraq, with a residual U.S. force of 46,000 troops, also witnessed an upsurge in violence; 15 American soldiers were killed in Iraq in June, the highest monthly total in 2 years.

General

Li, Nadal Take French Open Tennis Titles—Li Na became the first Chinese tennis player to win a Grand Slam singles title when she dethroned the 2010 champion, Italy's Francesca Schiavone, 6-4, 7-6 (0), in the women's final June 4 at the French Open (Roland Garros) in Paris. The following day, Spain's Rafael Nadal defeated Swiss rival Roger Federer, 7-5, 7-6 (3), 5-7, 6-1, to win the men's singles championship for a 6th time, tying the career mark set by Sweden's Björn Borg in 1981.

Ruler on Ice Wins Rainy Belmont Stakes—Ridden by Jose Valdivia Jr., Ruler on Ice, a 24-1 long shot, outran Kentucky Derby winner Animal Kingdom and Preakness Stakes champion Shackleford to capture the Belmont Stakes June 11 in Elmont, NY. The chestnut gelding had skipped the Derby and Preakness and been winless since Feb. 12. Shackleford, the early leader at Belmont Park, faded to 5th in the stretch, while Animal Kingdom finished 6th after stumbling badly at the start on the sloppy track.

***The Book of Mormon* and *War Horse* Top Tony Awards**—*The Book of Mormon*, an irreverent extravaganza from Trey Parker and Matt Stone (creators of TV's *South Park*) and composer Robert Lopez, won 9 Tony Awards June 12, including Best Musical. Nick Stafford's *War Horse* won 5 Tonys, including Best Play, plus a special award to South Africa's Handspring Puppet Company for the production's extraordinarily lifelike puppetry. Another major winner was *The Normal Heart*, Larry Kramer's 1985 AIDS drama that took home Tonys for Best Revival of a Play and for featured performances by John Benjamin Hickey and Ellen Barkin.

Mavericks Upset Heat in NBA Finals—In a 6th and deciding game June 12 in Miami, FL, the Dallas Mavericks outmuscled the Miami Heat, 105-95, to win their 1st NBA championship. Making his 11th playoff run in his 13th U.S. pro season, all with Dallas, forward Dirk Nowitzki of Germany was named MVP after a series in which the Mavs humbled the Heat and their hyped superstar, LeBron James.

Bruins' Stanley Cup Victory Over Canucks Ignites Riot in Vancouver—The Boston Bruins defeated the Vancouver Canucks, 4-0, at Rogers Arena, Vancouver, BC, Can., on June 15 to win their 1st Stanley Cup in 39 years. Frustrated Canucks fans who had gathered in downtown Vancouver to watch the finale on large outdoor screens rioted after the game, damaging dozens of local businesses. At least 140 people were injured, and more than 100 were arrested. Bruins goaltender Tim Thomas, winner of the Conn Smythe Trophy as series MVP, made 37 saves in the 1st shutout victory by a road team in a Game 7 final. Thomas received the Vezina Trophy June 22 as the NHL's best regular-season goalie after leading the league with a record-high .938 save percentage.

Golfer McIlroy Smashes U.S. Open Record—Rory McIlroy shrugged off his epic 4th-round collapse in the Masters Tournament 10 weeks earlier to score a sensational triumph June 19 in the U.S. Open Championship at Congressional Country Club in Bethesda, MD. The 22-year-old McIlroy became the youngest U.S. Open champion in 88 years and, following Graeme McDowell in 2010, the 2nd successive golfer from Northern Ireland to win the title. With rounds of 65, 66, 68, and 69, McIlroy finished 16 strokes under par—a tournament record—and 8 strokes ahead of his closest competitor, Australian Jason Day.

Boston Crime Boss Captured After 16-Year Manhunt—James "Whitey" Bulger, the inspiration for the mob boss in the film *The Departed* (2006), was arrested by federal agents June 22 in Santa Monica, CA, where the 81-year-old was living with his longtime girlfriend, Catherine Greig. Bulger had fled Boston in 1995 after he learned he was about to be indicted. Reputedly the former leader of Boston's Winter Hill Gang, Bulger also served as an FBI informant. Accused of murder, narcotics distribution, and other crimes, he was added to the FBI's 10 Most Wanted list in 1999.

July 2011
National

Agreement to Raise Debt Ceiling Reached; Other Economic Developments—Weeks of wrangling between Pres. Barack Obama and congressional Republican leaders over the mounting federal debt ended July 31 with an agreement to raise the statutory debt ceiling by more than $2 tril. The Treasury Dept. had warned that unless the debt ceiling was lifted by Aug. 2, the U.S. government would run out of borrowing authority and default on its obligations, which Treasury Sec. Tim Geithner said would have "catastrophic economic consequences." The congressionally mandated debt limit, which had risen from $5.5 tril to $6.4 tril between 1996 and 2002, ballooned to $14.3 tril by 2010; as a share of the nation's gross domestic product, the debt limit grew from 56.6% in 2001 to 92.1% at the end of the decade. Historically, Congress has viewed increases in the debt ceiling as a relatively routine task that allowed federal agencies to borrow funds that Congress had already approved. This time, however, conservative Republicans in the House insisted on budget cuts that would match or exceed any debt ceiling increase.

Congressional deadlock developed after May 31, when the House rejected a bill that would have raised the debt limit to $16.7 tril without corresponding deficit reductions. Talks between Obama and House Speaker John Boehner (R, OH) on a "grand bargain" that would have cut federal budget deficits by up to $4 tril over a 10-year period collapsed July 22. Vice Pres. Joe Biden and Senate Republican leader Mitch McConnell (KY) continued to negotiate behind the scenes, and their work reportedly shaped the final agreement.

The Budget Control Act of 2011 outlined more than $900 bil in spending cuts over a 10-year period and provided for a 3-stage rise in the debt ceiling. The 1st stage called for an immediate $400 bil increase to avert a government default. In the 2nd stage, the president could request an additional $500 bil hike, which Congress could not reject except by a two-thirds majority. In the 3rd stage, the debt ceiling would be raised between $1.2 tril and $1.5 tril, tied to equivalent spending cuts recommended by a 12-member "supercommittee" of legislators (6 from each party). The supercommittee would need to make its recommendations by Nov. 23, subject to an up-or-down vote in both houses of Congress by Dec. 23. If the supercommittee recommendations failed to pass, $1.2 tril in across-the-board spending reductions would be imposed. The agreement also required the scheduling of House and Senate votes on a Balanced Budget Amendment to the Constitution. The Budget Control Act passed Aug. 1-2 on bipartisan votes in the House (269-161) and the Senate (74-26), and was signed into law Aug. 2 by Pres. Obama.

Stocks slumped, as concerns about anemic economic growth, political gridlock, and the threat of default eroded investor confidence. The Labor Dept. reported July 8 that employers added only 18,000 nonfarm jobs in June, as the unemployment rate rose to 9.2%. Data released by the Commerce Dept. July 29 showed that the U.S. economy grew at an annual rate of 1.3% in the Apr.-June quarter, while consumer spending was nearly flat. U.S. stocks registered their worst weekly performance in more than a year July 25-29. The Dow Jones Industrial Average closed July 29 at 12,143.24, down 2.2% for the month. The S&P 500 (1,292.28) declined 2.1%, and the Nasdaq Composite Index (2,756.38) dropped less than 1%.

Budget Deal Ends Minnesota Government Shutdown—Minnesota Gov. Mark Dayton (D) signed a 2-year, $35 bil budget bill July 20, ending a 20-day state government shutdown that had forced the closure of state parks and highway rest stops, interruption of road construction projects, suspension of lottery sales, and furloughs of some 22,000 state employees. The longest shutdown in state history began when Democratic lawmakers (who wanted to raise taxes on the wealthy) and Republicans (who opposed any tax increases) were unable to agree on how to close a $5 bil budget gap through mid-2013. The breakthrough came when Dayton agreed to make up $1.4 bil of the deficit by deferring payments to local school districts and borrowing against future revenues from a 1998 settlement with the tobacco industry. A June report by the nonpartisan Center on Budget and Policy Priorities found that 42 states and the District of Columbia were dealing with a cumulative projected shortfall of about $103 bil for the 2012 fiscal year.

Oregon Congressman Resigns in Sex Scandal—U.S. Rep. David Wu (D, OR) announced July 26 that he was resigning his House seat, 4 days after the *Portland Oregonian* reported that in Nov. 2010, the 7-term Democrat had made unwanted sexual advances on the 18-year-old daughter of a friend and campaign donor. Earlier in 2011, several of Wu's staffers had quit because of the congressman's erratic behavior, such as e-mailing photos of himself in a tiger costume. Born in Taiwan, Wu in 1998 became the first Chinese-American elected to the House. A special election to fill the vacancy was set for Jan. 2012.

International

South Sudan Declares Independence—Dozens of African leaders and other dignitaries, including UN Sec. Gen. Ban Ki-moon and former U.S. Sec. of State Colin Powell, joined thousands of revelers in Juba July 9 to celebrate the independence of the Republic of South Sudan. Upon signing South Sudan's interim constitution, former rebel leader Salva Kiir Mayardit became president of Africa's 54th nation. Also participating in the ceremonies was the president of Sudan, Omar Hassan Ahmad Al-Bashir, who had long resisted the southerners' secessionist demands and who was indicted by the International Criminal Court in 2009 for crimes against humanity in Sudan's Darfur region.

Independence for South Sudan marked the culmination of a decades-long struggle in which an estimated 2 mil people lost their lives. A 2005 peace accord between southern rebels and the Sudanese government in Khartoum led to a Jan. 2011 referendum in which 99% of South Sudanese voters supported secession. On July 8, the UN Security Council authorized the UN Mission in the Republic of South Sudan (UNMISS) with up to 7,900 uniformed peacekeepers. South Sudan became the UN's 193rd member state July 14.

British Phone Hacking Scandal Implicates Murdoch Media Empire—*News of the World*, the UK's top-selling weekly newspaper, with an estimated circulation of 2.7 mil, abruptly closed its doors July 10 following fresh revelations of widespread "phone hacking," or illegal interception of telephone voicemails and e-mails. The tabloid had long been suspected of hacking into the accounts of athletes and other celebrities: the paper's royal correspondent, Clive Goodman, went to prison in 2007 for intercepting the royal household's voicemails. But public outrage erupted July 4 when the *Guardian*, a British daily newspaper, reported that *News of the World* had hacked into the voicemail of 13-year-old Milly Dowler. Milly had disappeared in Mar. 2002 and her body was found 6 months later. Hackers hired by the paper deleted some messages left on her voicemail account to make room for newer messages that could be used in subsequent stories. The tabloid's operatives had also hacked into the voicemails of the families of British soldiers killed in Iraq and Afghanistan, bribed British police for news tips, and used their influence at Scotland Yard to cover up their illegal activities.

News of the World was owned by News International Ltd., a British subsidiary of News Corp., the global media empire led by Rupert Murdoch. With holdings that include the *Times* and the *Sun* newspapers in the UK and the *Wall Street Journal* and Fox News Channel in the U.S., the Murdoch empire wielded enormous political influence on both sides of the Atlantic, as well as in Australia, where Murdoch was born. Questioned before a parliamentary committee July 19 in London, both Murdoch and his son James Murdoch, a News

Corp. executive, apologized but denied responsibility for any illegal activities. Facing a suddenly hostile climate, News Corp. withdrew its controversial $12 bil bid to gain control of the British satellite broadcaster known as BSkyB. The scandal was also an embarrassment for Prime Min. David Cameron, who had hired a former *News of the World* editor, Andy Coulson, as his communications director. Coulson, who had held a similar post with the Conservative Party after he left *News of the World* in 2007, resigned from Cameron's staff Jan. 31 and was arrested by British police July 8.

Powerful Karzai Family Member Assassinated in Afghanistan—Ahmed Wali Karzai, a half-brother of Afghanistan Pres. Hamid Karzai and a potent figure in Afghanistan, was shot to death July 12 at his home in Kandahar. Western and Afghan officials had long suspected Ahmed Wali Karzai of drug trafficking, money laundering, and shadowy dealings with both the Taliban and the U.S. Central Intelligence Agency. His death left a power vacuum in the pivotal Kandahar region that Pres. Karzai moved to fill July 13 by naming another half-brother, Shah Wali Karzai, to head Kandahar's provincial council. Taliban insurgents, who claimed responsibility for Karzai's killing, also targeted 2 other prominent figures in the next 3 weeks: Jan Muhammad Khan, a senior adviser to Pres. Karzai, was killed in Kabul July 17, and Kandahar Mayor Ghulam Haidar Hamidi died in a suicide bomb attack 10 days later. The assassination campaign occurred as Gen. John Allen was taking command of U.S. and allied troops in Afghanistan, replacing Gen. David Petraeus, who returned to the U.S. to head the CIA. Coalition military fatalities during the month totaled 53, of whom 37 were U.S. personnel.

Greece Gains New Bailout Pledge—Greece, which weathered a debt crisis in May 2010 with help from a 110 bil euro ($146 bil) loan package from other eurozone countries and the International Monetary Fund, received a 2nd bailout pledge July 21 of 109 bil euros ($157 bil). The accord, embraced by German Chancellor Angela Merkel, required private-sector bondholders to swap their Greek debt for new 30-year bonds, taking a loss of about 21%. European leaders regarded the swaps (which amounted to a limited default by Greece) as one of several necessary steps to prevent the debt crisis from spreading to other vulnerable eurozone economies. The agreement required approval of all EU members using the euro, a number that had grown to 17 with the addition of Estonia in 2011. The deal ran into trouble during the next 2 months, as some eurozone members, notably Finland, pushed for additional collateral from Greece, and as European financial authorities demanded that Greece implement additional austerity measures before funds payable under the 2010 bailout could be released. Such measures were extremely unpopular with the Greek public.

77 Die in Norway Terror Attacks—In the deadliest terrorist attack in Norway's history, right-wing extremist Anders Behring Breivik July 22 killed 77 people and injured more than 150 in two incidents. In the 1st attack, a car bomb exploded in central Oslo, killing 8 people and damaging the oil and finance ministries along with the headquarters of Prime Min. Jens Stoltenberg, who was unharmed. Less than 2 hours later, the 32-year-old Breivik, heavily armed and impersonating a police officer, went to the small island of Utøya, about 20 mi northwest of the capital. At Utøya, the site of a summer camp sponsored by the ruling Labor Party, he went on a shooting spree, murdering another 69 people before police arrived and took him into custody. Breivik had planned the attack for months in hopes of sparking an uprising against Muslim immigration. At a court session July 25 he claimed to have had accomplices, but Norwegian police said they had no evidence of a broader conspiracy.

High-Speed Rail Crash in China Kills at Least 40—Two bullet trains collided during a lightning storm July 23 near the eastern Chinese city of Wenzhou. Official reports placed the death toll at 40, with nearly 200 others injured.

Unofficial accounts put the number of dead much higher. The apparent failure of the rail line's signaling systems, which should have prevented the crash, focused attention on broader safety problems within China's high-speed rail network. China planned to invest up to $300 bil in the project under a 15-year program that would connect 24 major cities with nearly 10,000 mi of high-speed track. A bullet train linking Beijing with Shanghai had made its inaugural run with great fanfare June 30. Shortly after the Wenzhou collision, the government dismissed 3 high-ranking railway officials and suspended operation of 58 trains pending a system-wide safety check. On Aug. 10, Chinese authorities announced they were halting approvals for new high-speed rail lines while investigations continued.

General

Kvitova, Djokovic Take Wimbledon Tennis Titles—Petra Kvitova of the Czech Republic won her 1st Grand Slam tennis tournament July 2, defeating Russian-born Maria Sharapova, 6-3, 6-4, to capture the Wimbledon women's singles championship at the All England Lawn Tennis Club. Sharapova, a 2004 Wimbledon winner, was making her 1st appearance in a Grand Slam final since a 2008 shoulder surgery. On July 3, Serbia's Novak Djokovic won his 1st Wimbledon title, humbling Spain's Rafael Nadal, 6-4, 6-1, 1-6, 6-3.

Jury Acquits Casey Anthony on Murder Charge—On July 5, in a climax to a case that had become a cable-TV and Internet sensation, a jury in Orlando, FL, found Casey Anthony not guilty of killing her 2-year-old daughter, Caylee. Anthony had been charged in Oct. 2008 with first-degree murder, and prosecutors alleged, based on circumstantial evidence, that she had drugged her daughter with chloroform, suffocated her with duct tape, and disposed of the body in a wooded area near the home Caylee shared with her mother and grandparents. Anthony's attorneys asserted that Caylee had drowned in a swimming pool and that a panicked Casey, along with her father, had sought to cover up the accident. The jury convicted her on a misdemeanor charge of lying to investigators, and she was released from jail shortly after midnight July 17.

South Korea to Host 2018 Winter Olympics—The International Olympic Committee July 6 chose Pyeongchang, South Korea, to host the Olympic Winter Games in Feb. 2018. Pyeongchang won on the 1st ballot, easily outdistancing bids by Munich, Germany, and Annecy, France. Seoul, the South Korean capital, had hosted the 1988 Summer Olympics.

Ohio State Football Program Punished for Rules Violations—Responding to charges that some of its star players had traded football memorabilia for cash and tattoos, Ohio State Univ. agreed July 8 to vacate all of its wins in 2010, including its Big Ten Conference championship and its 31-26 Sugar Bowl victory over Arkansas, Jan. 4, 2011. Ohio State coach Jim Tressel, who had known as early as Apr. 2010 about his players' involvement with a local tattoo parlor owner, was forced to resign in May 2011.

Jeter Gets 3,000th Hit—With a 3rd-inning solo home run July 9 off Tampa Bay left-hander David Price, Derek Jeter became the 28th major leaguer—and the 1st New York Yankee—to reach the 3,000-hit milestone. The Yankee captain had a 5-for-5 day, including an 8th-inning single that drove in the go-ahead run in a 5-4 New York victory.

Mistrial Declared in Clemens Case—Admonishing prosecutors for their use of evidence he had already ruled inadmissible as hearsay, U.S. District Judge Reggie Walton declared a mistrial July 14 in the case against MLB pitcher Roger Clemens. The right-hander, who ended his major-league career in 2007 with 354 regular-season wins, was accused of lying to a congressional committee in Feb. 2008, when he denied he had used steroids or human growth hormone (HGH). On Sept. 2, the judge granted prosecutors' motion for a new trial, scheduled to begin Apr. 17, 2012.

Clarke Wins British Open—Darren Clarke of Northern Ireland won the British Open July 17 at Royal St. George's Golf Club in Sandwich, Kent, England. Clarke, 42, won his 1st major championship in more than 2 decades as a pro, finishing the 72-hole tournament with a 5-under par 275; his score was 3 strokes ahead of 2 U.S. golfers, Phil Mickelson and Dustin Johnson.

Atlantis **Flight Ends Space Shuttle Era**—After 30 years and 135 missions, NASA's space shuttle program came to an end July 21, as the shuttle *Atlantis* concluded a 13-day journey to the International Space Station with a perfect predawn landing at Florida's Kennedy Space Center. The end of the shuttle program left Russia's *Soyuz* as the only vehicle capable of ferrying astronauts to the station, at a current price of $63 mil per seat. NASA has purchased 46 seats on *Soyuz* flights through 2016, when the U.S. hopes to deploy a new, commercially developed space transport system.

August 2011
National

U.S. Credit Rating Downgraded; Other Economic Developments—Less than a week after squabbling between the White House and congressional Republicans over the federal debt had brought the U.S. to the brink of default, the Standard & Poor's rating agency Aug. 5 downgraded the nation's credit standing to AA+ from the top-grade AAA. Although a last-minute agreement on raising the statutory debt ceiling had been reached, S&P said that "the downgrade reflects our view that the effectiveness, stability, and predictability of American policymaking and political institutions have weakened at a time of ongoing fiscal and economic challenges." The S&P decision diverged from those of 2 other investor services, Moody's and Fitch, which retained their AAA ratings for U.S. obligations.

Employment data released Aug. 5 showed an increase of 117,000 jobs in July, but figures issued 4 weeks later showed virtually no monthly job growth in Aug. Continued uncertainty about the economy contributed to volatility on Wall Street and pushed gold prices to record highs of more than $1,800 an ounce. Closing stock prices Aug. 31 registered one-month declines of 4.4% in the Dow Jones Industrial Average (11,613.53), 5.7% in the S&P 500 (1,218.89), and 6.4% in the Nasdaq Composite Index (2,579.46).

Bachmann Wins Iowa Straw Poll; Perry Enters Race, Pawlenty Quits—In an early test of Republican presidential hopefuls' popularity and organizational strength, Rep. Michele Bachmann (MN), who was born in Iowa, took 1st place in the Ames (IA) Straw Poll Aug. 13, edging out Rep. Ron Paul (TX). Although the event, held on the Iowa State Univ. campus, had no official or legal status and served mainly to generate revenue and publicity for the Iowa Republican Party, the 9 candidates on the ballot spent hundreds of thousands of dollars in hopes of winning a top spot in the poll. Former Minnesota Gov. Tim Pawlenty, whose campaign strategy required a strong showing in Iowa, finished a distant 3rd and dropped out of the race the following morning.

Casting a shadow over Bachmann's victory was Texas Gov. Rick Perry, who declared his presidential candidacy Aug. 13 in Charleston, SC. Two days later, Perry drew criticism from all sides when he answered a question about the Federal Reserve by suggesting that the monetary policies of Fed Chairman Ben Bernanke might be "treasonous."

Earthquake, Hurricane Irene Hit Eastern U.S.—A magnitude 5.8 earthquake, unusually strong for the eastern U.S., rattled central Virginia and Washington, DC, on Aug. 23 and sent shockwaves as far north as Canada. The National Cathedral sustained an estimated $15 mil in damage, and the Washington Monument had to be closed indefinitely for repairs. The epicenter of the quake, near Mineral, VA, was only about 11 mi from the North Anna nuclear plant, which was shut down safely.

Later that week, Hurricane Irene slammed into the eastern seaboard, making landfall Aug. 27 at Cape Lookout, NC, and Aug. 28 along the New Jersey shore. Power outages were widespread, and downpours from the slow-moving storm caused flooding in many areas, including Philadelphia and upstate New York. Some of the worst flooding occurred in Vermont, hundreds of miles inland. At least 44 deaths in 13 states were attributed to the storm, which caused more than $7 bil in damage.

Top Officials Replaced in "Fast and Furious" Scandal—U.S. Attorney Gen. Eric Holder announced Aug. 30 the departure of 2 senior Justice Dept. officials who had overseen Operation Fast and Furious. The sting operation had attempted to snare high-level traffickers by tracking some 2,000 weapons smuggled into Mexico. But it drew harsh congressional criticism after agents lost track of hundreds of guns, some of which turned up at crime scenes in the U.S. and Mexico. Two of the weapons were found at the scene where U.S. border agent Brian Terry was murdered in Arizona in Dec. 2010; a .50 caliber gun was used by traffickers to attack a Mexican police helicopter in May 2011. Carlos Canino, acting attaché in Mexico for the U.S. Bureau of Alcohol, Tobacco, and Firearms, called the operation a "perfect storm of idiocy."

Mexican officials cited an influx of weapons from the U.S. as a cause of drug-related violence that by Sept. had claimed more than 40,000 lives in Mexico since 2006. In one horrific episode Aug. 25, gunmen stormed a Monterrey casino and set the building ablaze, killing at least 52 people, most of them women.

International

Libyan Rebels Take Power in Tripoli, Toppling Qaddafi Regime—The wave of Arab uprisings that had ousted entrenched regimes in Tunisia and Egypt early in 2011 claimed another victory Aug. 21-23, as insurgents stormed into Tripoli and took command of the Libyan capital. After a day-long firefight Aug. 23 the rebels, with military backing from NATO and diplomatic support from the UN Security Council and the Arab League, entered Bab al-Aziziya, the heavily fortified headquarters of Muammar al-Qaddafi. The Libyan dictator had gone into hiding and at the end of the month, his whereabouts remained unknown. The insurgents began governing through the Libyan Interim National Transitional Council (NTC), headed by Mustafa Abdul Jalil, as the former insurgents moved to subdue remaining Qaddafi loyalists, especially in his hometown of Sirte.

Other Arab regimes facing popular uprisings included Yemen, where mass protests entered their 7th month, and Syria, where Pres. Bashar al-Assad launched a ferocious new offensive against dissidents in the city of Hama, Aug. 4, killing at least 45 people. On Aug. 8, King Abdullah of Saudi Arabia took the unusual step of telling the Syrian government to "stop the killing machine" and U.S., Canadian, and European Union leaders called on Assad to step down. UN High Commissioner for Human Rights Navi Pillay reported Aug. 22 that more than 2,200 people had been killed in Syria's 5-month-long crackdown on antigovernment demonstrations.

Shinawatra Family Regains Power in Thailand—By a margin of 296-3, with 197 abstentions, the lower house of Thailand's parliament voted Aug. 5 to make Yingluck Shinawatra, the sister of former Prime Min. Thaksin Shinawatra, the nation's 1st female head of government. Thaksin, a wealthy former telecommunications executive, had been accused of corruption and ousted in a Sept. 2006 military coup. His brother-in-law Somchai Wongsawat became prime minister in Sept. 2008, but he was barred from politics and his People Power Party (PPP) was dissolved because of election fraud. Supporters of Thaksin's populist programs then staged mass protests in 2009-10, and reconstituted the banned PPP as the Pheu Thai ("For Thais") Party.

In July 3 elections, Pheu Thai, headed by Yingluck Shinawatra, won 265 of 500 seats in the lower house of parliament. Thaksin, who had fled Thailand in 2008 to avoid facing corruption charges, pledged that he would not interfere in an administration run by his sister. Soon after her government was sworn in, however, he began to exercise power behind the scenes, and his supporters pressed for an amnesty that would allow him to return from exile without fear of imprisonment.

Riots Erupt in London, Other English Cities—More than 1,700 people were arrested and charged with burglary, violent disorder, arson, muggings, and other crimes stemming from 5 days of rioting Aug. 6-10 that began in London and spread to Birmingham, Bristol, Liverpool, Manchester, and elsewhere. At least 5 people were killed in the disturbances, which began in London's Tottenham district in response to the fatal shooting of a local resident by police Aug. 4. A protest demonstration Aug. 6 in Tottenham began peacefully but turned violent, with stores looted and shops and cars set ablaze. During the next 2 nights, the rioting spread to other London districts and then to outlying cities. Prime Min. David Cameron deployed an additional 10,000 police on London's streets to restore order. Many of those arrested were young, unemployed, and poorly educated, and a majority had had previous run-ins with authorities. Judges who meted out maximum sentences for crimes committed during the disturbances won praise from Cameron, who also suggested that rioters and their families should be evicted from public housing.

U.S. Helicopter Shot Down in Afghanistan; Other War News—The U.S. suffered its single deadliest day in 10 years of fighting in Afghanistan, as Taliban insurgents shot down a Chinook transport helicopter Aug. 6 over the Tangi Valley of eastern Afghanistan. The dead included 30 U.S. service members, of whom 22 were elite Navy SEAL commandos, along with 7 Afghan troops and an Afghan translator. Coalition fatalities for the month totaled 81, of whom 70 were Americans.

In a report submitted to the U.S. Congress Aug. 31, the Commission on Wartime Contracting calculated that during the Afghanistan and Iraq wars, poor planning and ineffective oversight of contractors had cost the U.S. at least $31 bil in losses. Cumulative U.S. spending on civilian contractors in the 2 wars was projected to exceed $206 bil by the end of 2011. For the first time since the Iraq War began, no U.S. military fatalities were recorded during the month, but a spike in violence Aug. 15 involving more than 40 coordinated attacks by insurgents against Iraqi civilians and security forces left at least 89 people dead and 315 wounded.

Noda Succeeds Kan as Japanese Prime Minister—After a tumultuous 15-month term that included the Mar. 11 earthquake, tsunami, and nuclear disaster, Prime Min. Naoto Kan of Japan submitted his resignation Aug. 26. Three days later, legislators from the ruling Democratic Party of Japan elected Finance Min. Yoshihiko Noda to succeed Kan. The lower house of the Japanese parliament confirmed him Aug. 30, and he was sworn in Sept. 2. Noda was the 7th person in 5 years to head Japan's government.

Famine Spreads in Somalia as Fighting Continues—Surveys conducted during the month by the UN Food and Agriculture Organization (FAO) found that 4 mil people in Somalia were experiencing a food crisis. In a statement released Sept. 5, the FAO's Food Security and Nutrition Analysis Unit forecast that 750,000 Somalis were at risk of dying of starvation before the end of the year. Severe drought represented a threat throughout much of East Africa, but conditions in Somalia were exacerbated by 2 decades of civil war, which continued to disrupt famine relief efforts. Under pressure from a 9,000-member African Union peacekeeping force, the insurgent group al-Shabaab withdrew from Somalia's capital city of Mogadishu Aug. 6. But the radical Islamists, who had ties to al-Qaeda, continued to control much of southern Somalia and to launch attacks on the capital. An al-Shabaab suicide bomb attack Oct. 4 on government buildings in the capital left at least 100 people dead.

General

Bradley Wins PGA Tournament—Keegan Bradley captured his 1st major golf title Aug. 14, winning the PGA Championship at the Atlanta Athletic Club in Johns Creek, GA. In his 4th year as a pro, Bradley recovered from a triple bogey on the 15th hole and hit 2 birdies in the last 3 holes to tie Jason Dufner with an 8-under-par 272 at the end of 72 holes. Keegan then bested Dufner in a 3-hole playoff.

Thome Hits 600th Career Home Run—Minnesota Twins designated hitter Jim Thome joined one of baseball's most elite clubs Aug. 15, becoming the 8th player in major-league history to blast 600 career home runs. The home run, his 2nd of the game, came in the 7th inning at Detroit's Comerica Park and boosted the Twins to a 9-6 victory. A 21-year veteran, Thome was traded Aug. 25 to the Cleveland Indians, where he had risen to stardom from 1991-2002.

September 2011
National

Obama, Federal Reserve Propose New Measures to Spur Economy—With job growth weak and the unemployment rate hovering at 9.1%, Pres. Barack Obama Sept. 8 proposed the American Jobs Act, a $447 bil economic stimulus plan. Outlined in a speech to a joint session of Congress, Obama's plan included $240 bil in payroll tax cuts for employers and employees, $140 bil in investments for education and infrastructure, and $62 bil in aid for the unemployed. On Sept. 12 the White House proposed financing the jobs bill by limiting tax breaks for oil companies, corporate jet owners, investment fund managers, and families with taxable income of at least $250,000 a year—measures that stood little chance of passage by the Republican-controlled House of Representatives. In a separate effort to boost the economy, the Federal Reserve announced Sept. 21 that it would shift its $2.65 tril securities portfolio, buying more long-term U.S. Treasury bonds and mortgage-backed securities in order to reduce long-term borrowing costs for businesses and consumers.

Data released Sept. 13 by the U.S. Census Bureau offered a sobering picture of challenges facing poor and middle-class Americans. The bureau reported that 46.2 mil Americans in 2010 were living below the poverty line, with annual incomes at or below $22,314 per year for a family of 4 or $11,139 for an individual. The number of those living in poverty was the highest ever measured, and their 15.1% share of the total U.S. population was the highest since 1993. Adjusted for inflation, median household income ($49,445 in 2010) fell for the 3rd year in a row and was barely more than in 1996.

Another volatile month on Wall Street ended with a sharp dip, producing the worst quarter for stocks since 2009. The Dow Jones Industrial Average closed Sept. 30 at 10,913.38, down 12.1% since the end of June. The S&P 500 finished at 1,131.42, for a 3-month plunge of 14.3%, and the Nasdaq Composite Index ended the month at 2,415.40, for a quarterly drop of 12.9%.

Texas Wildfire Ravages More Than 1,600 Homes—A wildfire that ignited Sept. 4 in Bastrop Co., TX, charred at least 34,000 acres and destroyed more than 1,600 homes, the most of any fire in the state's history. The fire was contained by the end of the month but not officially declared controlled until Oct. 10. As of mid-Sept., a total of 14 large wildfires were active in Texas, which was experiencing its most severe drought since the 1950s. During the first 9 months of 2011, wildfires consumed an estimated 3.7 mil acres in Texas. The cumulative economic impact of the drought and wildfires was estimated at $5.4 bil.

Solar Energy Firm Favored by White House Goes Bankrupt—Solyndra, a California-based solar panel manufacturer, filed for bankruptcy Sept. 6. Two days later, agents from the FBI and the inspector general's office of the Dept. of Energy raided the company's headquarters in Fremont, CA, seeking to determine whether executives of the company had knowingly misled federal officials when the firm received $535 mil in federal loan guarantees. Although the loan approval process for Solyndra had begun well before Pres. Obama took office, the bankruptcy was a major embarrassment for the Obama administration, which had touted Solyndra in 2009-10 as evidence of its support for clean energy and green jobs. Obama visited the Fremont facility in May 2010, despite a warning 2 months earlier by the accounting firm PricewaterhouseCoopers LLP that Solyndra faced serious financial problems. The bankruptcy filing included the closure of the Fremont factory, which had employed 1,100 people. Solyndra executives invoked their Fifth Amendment privilege against self-incrimination at a congressional hearing Sept. 23. Jonathan Silver, the director of the Dept. of Energy loan office that had approved Solyndra's guarantees, announced his resignation Oct. 6.

GOP Wins Special Elections for Vacant House Seats— In special elections Sept. 13 for the U.S. House of Representatives, businessman Bob Turner (R) upset New York State Assemblyman David Weprin (D) to capture a district in New York City, and State Sen. Mark Amodei, former chairman of the Nevada GOP, scored a landslide victory over state treasurer Kate Marshall (D) in a Republican-leaning district that comprises most of Nevada's land area outside Las Vegas. The New York seat, formerly occupied by Rep. Anthony Weiner (D), who resigned in June because of a sex scandal, had not elected a Republican to Congress since 1920. The Nevada district had become open in May when Gov. Brian Sandoval (R) appointed 3rd-term U.S. Rep. Dean Heller (R) to fill the unexpired term of Sen. John Ensign (R); Ensign resigned in May while under investigation for ethical and legal violations stemming from an acknowledged affair with his former campaign treasurer. After Turner and Marshall were sworn in Sept. 15, the House had 242 Republicans and 192 Democrats, with 1 seat vacant.

28 Die in Listeria Outbreak—In the worst outbreak of food-borne illness to strike the U.S. in more than 25 years, more than 2 dozen people died after eating cantaloupes contaminated with the bacillus *Listeria monocytogenes*. The outbreak, which began in late July, was traced to cantaloupes shipped under the Rocky Ford brand by Jensen Farms of Holly, CO; the company issued a recall order Sept. 14 for millions of melons. More than a month later, the Food and Drug Admin. disclosed that the pathogen had been identified at multiple locations in a Jensen Farms packing shed. On Oct. 25, the Centers for Disease Control and Prevention reported that the outbreak had sickened 133 people in 26 states. In a separate case of listeria contamination, True Leaf Farms of San Juan Bautista, CA, recalled about 30,000 lb of chopped lettuce on Sept. 30.

Crash at Reno Air Show Kills 11—The National Championship Air Races and Air Show ended in tragedy Sept. 16 when a vintage P-51 Mustang flown by Jimmy Leeward plunged into a crowd of onlookers at Nevada's Reno-Stead Airport. Eleven people were killed, including the 74-year-old stunt pilot, and at least 74 others were injured. According to the *Reno Gazette-Journal*, 17 participants had died in previous Reno air championships since the competition began in 1946, but no spectators had been killed or seriously hurt.

International

Swiss Bank Blames $2.3 Billion Loss on Rogue Trader— The troubled global financial firm UBS AG, with headquarters in Zürich and Basel, Switzerland, accused a London-based rogue trader in its investment banking unit of fraudulent practices that had cost the bank $2.3 bil. Press reports identified the trader as Ghanaian-born Kweku Adoboli, hired by UBS as a trainee in 2006. Arrested by London police Sept. 15, he was charged with financial misconduct beginning as far back as Oct. 2008, which raised questions about how others could have been unaware of his activities over a 3-year period. On Sept. 24, the UBS board of directors accepted the immediate resignation of Chief Executive Officer Oswald Grübel, who had run the firm since 2009.

Former Pres. Rabbani Assassinated in Afghanistan— Burhanuddin Rabbani, a former guerrilla leader who had served as Afghan president (1992-96) until ousted by Taliban insurgents, was killed at his home in Kabul by a suicide bomber Sept. 20. Since 2010, Rabbani had led the Afghan High Peace Council, a government-sponsored effort to reach political accommodation with the Taliban. The assassin, identified as Mullah Esmatullah, had gained access to Rabbani by claiming he had an important message from the Taliban that would advance the cause of peace. According to an eyewitness, Esmatullah embraced Rabbani as he triggered the explosives he had hidden in his turban.

Other violence during the month included a truck bombing Sept. 11 in Wardak Province that killed 5 Afghan civilians and wounded 77 NATO soldiers; and attacks Sept. 13 on the U.S. embassy, NATO headquarters, and other targets in Kabul that claimed the lives of 5 Afghan police and 11 civilians. At a hearing of the Senate Armed Services Committee Sept. 22, Adm. Mike Mullen, chairman of the Joint Chiefs of Staff, accused Pakistani agents of providing direct assistance to the Haqqani network, an insurgent group based in the tribal areas of NW Pakistan which he called "a veritable arm of Pakistan's Inter-Services Intelligence Agency." Military fatalities during the month included 42 from the U.S. and 11 from NATO coalition partners.

Palestinians Seek Full UN Membership as Independent State; Other Middle East Developments—In a speech Sept. 23 to the UN General Assembly, Palestinian Authority Pres. Mahmoud Abbas officially applied for full UN membership for an independent Palestinian state. The application enjoyed widespread support but was strongly opposed by Israel and the U.S. In his own address to the UN 2 days earlier, Pres. Obama had expressed support for "an independent, sovereign state of Palestine," but only as part of a peace agreement with Israel. The Palestinian membership bid was referred to the Security Council, where the U.S. held veto power.

Arab Spring uprisings left Israel feeling increasingly isolated in its relationships with neighboring Arab states. Gaza militants had launched attacks Aug. 18 along Israel's border with Egypt, killing 8 Israelis; retaliatory fire by Israel killed at least 7 of the attackers along with at least 3 Egyptian security officers. On Sept. 9, thousands of protesters stormed the Israeli embassy in Cairo, leading Israel to evacuate its diplomats from Egypt. Meanwhile a series of demonstrations in Israel protested growing social and economic inequality and the rising cost of living; at least 400,000 protesters participated in the "March of the Million" Sept. 3 in Tel Aviv, Jerusalem, and other major cities.

Ripples from the Arab Spring movement also reached deeply conservative Saudi Arabia, where King Abdullah announced Sept. 25 that women would have the right to vote and run for local office by 2015. Saudi women, who face many restrictions, had also campaigned for the right to drive. On Sept. 28, the king reportedly revoked a sentence of 10 lashes a Jiddah court had imposed on a Saudi woman, Shaima Ghassaniya, for driving a car without government permission. Saudi Arabia is the only country where women may not receive drivers' licenses.

Putin Plans Return to Russian Presidency in 2012— Speaking at a convention of the ruling United Russia party Sept. 24, Pres. Dmitri Medvedev disclosed that he would step aside so that Prime Min. Vladimir Putin could run for president in Mar. 2012. Putin had won Russia's presidential elections by huge margins in 2000 and 2004, but because of constitutionally mandated term limits he had backed Medvedev, his protégé, in the 2008 presidential race. The same day he was sworn in, Pres. Medvedev had then named Putin to head the government. The announcement that Putin and Medvedev planned to swap titles occurred after Russia had enacted constitutional changes that would allow Putin to serve 2 additional 6-year terms, potentially holding the presidency until 2024. Putin nominated Medvedev to head the party's list in Dec. 2011 parliamentary elections.

U.S. Drone Strike in Yemen Kills Radical Muslim Cleric—A 2-year manhunt by U.S. and Yemeni agents ended Sept. 30 when a missile from a U.S. drone aircraft over Yemen killed radical Muslim cleric Anwar al-Awlaki, a U.S. citizen born to Yemeni parents in New Mexico. Awlaki had been linked to several high profile terrorist incidents in the U.S.: the Nov. 2009 shooting rampage at Fort Hood, TX, by Army psychiatrist Maj. Nidal Malik Hasan, the failed Dec. 2009 plot to blow up a Detroit-bound jetliner by "underwear bomber" Umar Farouk Abdulmutallab, and an unsuccessful attempt to explode a car bomb in New York City's Times Square in May 2010. In targeting Awlaki for assassination, U.S. authorities believed the radical preacher had also assumed an operational role with al-Qaeda in the Arabian Peninsula (AQAP). AQAP acknowledged Awlaki's death Oct. 10. Killed along with him was another U.S. citizen, Samir Khan, the editor of the AQAP online magazine *Inspire*, which in Oct. 2010 had published his article "I Am Proud to be a Traitor to America."

Even as Yemeni officials were playing up their role in tracking down Awlaki, the U.S. continued to press for the resignation of Pres. Ali Abdullah Saleh, who returned to Yemen Sept. 23 after receiving extended medical treatment in Saudi Arabia for injuries suffered in a June bomb attack. Mass Arab Spring protests in Sana'a', the national capital, had been demanding an end to Saleh's regime since early 2011.

General

Stosur, Djokovic Win U.S. Open Tennis Titles—Samantha Stosur of Australia won her first Grand Slam tennis championship Sept. 11, trouncing Serena Williams, 6-2, 6-3, to capture the U.S. Open women's singles title at Arthur Ashe Stadium in Flushing, NY. Williams was fined $2,000 for verbally abusing an official after a disputed call in the 2nd set. Serbian Novak Djokovic dethroned Spain's Rafael Nadal, 6-2, 6-4, 6-7(3), 6-1, to earn the men's singles title Sept. 12. The match marked the 6th time in 2011 that Djokovic had faced and beaten Nadal in a tournament final. In a semifinal match 2 days earlier, Djokovic had fought off 2 match points to gain a thrilling come-from-behind victory over Switzerland's Roger Federer.

Modern Family, Mad Men Take Top Emmy Honors—At the Primetime Emmy Awards Sept. 18, *Modern Family* was honored for the 2nd year in a row as Outstanding Comedy Series, winning 5 Emmys in all, including supporting actor awards for Julie Bowen and Ty Burrell. *Mad Men* won as Outstanding Drama Series for the 4th consecutive year, and *The Daily Show With Jon Stewart* earned its 9th consecutive Emmy as Outstanding Variety, Music, or Comedy Series.

Rivera Breaks Career Save Record—Mariano Rivera, the celebrated relief pitcher for the NY Yankees, preserved a 6-4 victory over Minnesota Sept. 19 to earn the 602nd save of his career, a new all-time record. The Panamanian closer, a 17-year veteran with the Yankees, surpassed the previous career save record of 601, set by Trevor Hoffman with the Milwaukee Brewers in 2010.

October 2011

National

Obama, Perry, Romney Lead in 2012 Campaign Fundraising—Pres. Barack Obama (D) and the Republican presidential contenders vying to oppose him continued to gear up for the 2012 election campaign. According to documents filed with the Federal Election Commission, Obama raised $42.1 mil during July-Sept. and had $61.4 mil cash on hand as the month began. For the same period, Texas Gov. Rick Perry (R) raised $17.2 mil and had $15.1 mil in his campaign war chest, while former Massachusetts Gov. Mitt Romney (R) collected $14.2 mil and had $14.7 mil available to spend. Meanwhile, New Jersey Gov. Chris Christie declared his

non-candidacy Oct. 4 and endorsed Romney a week later. Former Alaska Gov. Sarah Palin, the GOP vice-presidential nominee in 2008, said Oct. 6 that she too had decided not to run.

The GOP race remained fluid, with Romney the consensus front-runner. But Romney rarely scored higher than 25% in polls of Republicans' presidential preferences, with first Perry and then radio talk-show host and former Godfather's Pizza chief executive Herman Cain rising to challenge him. Cain pushed his "9-9-9" plan, calling for a uniform individual income tax rate of 9%, a 9% corporate tax rate, and a new 9% national sales tax that his opponents were quick to criticize. He was put on the defensive when the website Politico published a report Oct. 30 alleging that at least 2 female employees had accused him of making inappropriate comments or unwanted advances while Cain headed the National Restaurant Assn. in the 1990s.

Thousands Join Occupy Wall Street Protests; Other Economic Developments—A left-wing movement that began in New York City Sept. 17 as "Occupy Wall Street" expanded Oct. 15 to include demonstrations in dozens of cities in the U.S. and overseas. Thousands of demonstrators protested economic inequality, corporate greed, spending on foreign wars, the influence of money in politics, and banks that had profited from the 2008 bailouts. Most of the Oct. 15 demonstrations were peaceful except in Rome, where rioters clashed with police. Violence also erupted Oct. 25, when police in Oakland, CA, used force to keep protesters from reestablishing a tent camp in a downtown plaza from which they had earlier been evicted.

Data released by the Labor Dept. Oct. 7 showed the unemployment rate holding steady at 9.1%, with 103,000 jobs added the previous month. The Social Security Admin. announced Oct. 19 that monthly benefits for more than 60 mil Americans would increase 3.6% in 2012—the 1st cost-of-living adjustment since 2009—but retiree benefits were likely to be eroded by Medicare premium increases. A bright spot was the Commerce Dept. estimate Oct. 27 that the nation's gross domestic product had increased at an annual rate of 2.5% during July-Sept. Stocks rallied for their best single-month performance in years, with the Dow Jones Industrial Average closing Oct. 31 at 11,955.01, an increase of 9.5%. The S&P 500 (1,253.30) jumped 10.8%, and the Nasdaq Composite Index (2,684.41) was up 11.1%. The closing averages reflected a dip at the end of the month, reflecting concern over the bankruptcy of securities firm MF Global and renewed worries about a possible debt default by Greece.

"Underwear Bomber" Pleads Guilty—The trial of Umar Farouk Abdulmutallab came to an abrupt halt Oct. 12 in Detroit, MI, when the 24-year-old Nigerian changed his plea to guilty and admitted attempting to blow up a Detroit-bound jetliner Dec. 25, 2009, by igniting explosives hidden in his underwear. The so-called underwear bomber, who was tried in civilian proceedings in federal court, said he had waged jihad against the U.S. after being inspired by Anwar al-Awlaki, the Yemeni-American cleric killed Sept. 30 by a U.S. drone strike in Yemen. Sentencing of Abdulmutallab on 8 terrorism-related charges was scheduled for Jan. 2012.

Long-Term Care Insurance Plan Scrapped—Health and Human Services Sec. Kathleen Sebelius announced Oct. 14 that the Obama administration was unable to implement the Community Living Assistance Services and Supports (CLASS) Act, which was intended to provide long-term care for people with chronic illnesses or severe disabilities. Championed by the late Sen. Edward M. Kennedy (D, MA), the CLASS Act had been passed by Congress as part of the Patient Protection and Affordable Care Act in Mar. 2010. Sebelius said that experts had been unable to come up with a mechanism that would make the CLASS program financially self-sustaining. The Obama administration Sept. 28 asked the Supreme Court to accelerate its review of several lower-court rulings that addressed the constitutionality of the 2010 health-care overhaul.

International

Qaddafi Killed in Libya, as Conflict Continues in the Arab World—Muammar al-Qaddafi, the eccentric dictator who had ruled Libya for 42 years, was killed Oct. 20 in the coastal city of Sirte. Ousted from power 2 months earlier, Qaddafi had found a temporary haven in his hometown, but decided to flee Sirte as pressure from transitional government troops and NATO forces increased. A convoy transporting Qaddafi and his supporters had traveled about 2 mi when it was hit by a French warplane and a U.S. drone. Qaddafi abandoned his vehicle and hid in a large drainpipe, but was taken into custody by Libyan fighters. Libyan officials initially said he was killed in a crossfire, but a widely circulated video showed him being abused before he was apparently executed. The UN and human rights groups called for an inquiry into the circumstances surrounding his death.

Elsewhere in the Middle East, security forces continued violent crackdowns on antigovernment protesters in Syria and Yemen, and at least 24 people were killed and more than 200 injured Oct. 9 in Egypt in the worst outbreak of violence since the Feb. 11 collapse of the Mubarak regime. In Tunisia, where Arab Spring uprisings began, voters went to the polls Oct. 23 to elect a constituent assembly; a moderate Islamist party won a 90-seat plurality in the 217-seat chamber, which was empowered to appoint an interim government and draft a new constitution.

Sporadic clashes continued between Israel and Hamas, which dominates Gaza. But the 2 sides agreed to a prisoner swap in which Israel freed about 1,000 Palestinian and Israeli Arab detainees in exchange for the release Oct. 18 of Gilad Shalit, an Israeli soldier who had been held by Hamas militants for more than 5 years. Egypt, which had brokered the Shalit deal, carried out its own prisoner swap with Israel Oct. 27.

ETA Says It Has Ended Armed Struggle in Spain—In a written statement and video Oct. 20, the Basque separatist group commonly known by the initials ETA, proclaimed the cessation of its military activity. Classified as a terrorist organization by the European Union, U.S., and other countries, ETA was responsible for bombings that had killed about 830 people since 1968. The organization had been greatly weakened in recent years, and more than 700 ETA members reportedly were in prison. The ETA did not spell out a timetable for laying down its arms, and said it remained committed to seeking the establishment of a Basque homeland fully independent from Spain.

U.S. Troops to Leave Iraq by End of 2011—Pres. Obama announced Oct. 21 that the nearly 40,000 U.S. troops still serving in Iraq would be withdrawn by the end of the year, as called for under the 2008 Status of Forces Agreement between Iraq and the U.S. Some U.S. military leaders had hoped to keep a residual force of up to 20,000 in Iraq, but negotiations with the Baghdad government broke down over the question of legal immunity. A small number of U.S. military personnel were expected to remain as liaison officers and embassy guards. The U.S. still had roughly 98,000 troops in Afghanistan fighting alongside more than 40,000 troops from coalition partners.

According to the website icasualties.org, U.S. military fatalities in Iraq numbered 5 for the month, 52 for the year, and 4,482 since the war began in 2003. Coalition troop deaths in Afghanistan in Oct. totaled 40, of whom 29 were Americans. Cumulative U.S. losses in Operation Enduring Freedom totaled 1,828 during the 10-year period from Oct. 2001 through Oct. 2011.

Obama notified Congress Oct. 14 that the U.S. was sending up to 100 military trainers and advisers to combat the Lord's Resistance Army, a renegade group that has committed atrocities in at least 4 central African countries.

Earthquake in Turkey Kills More Than 500—A 7.2-magnitude earthquake shook the city of Van in southeastern Turkey Oct. 23, killing more than 500 people and injuring thousands more. The predominantly Kurdish region was already one of the nation's poorest. Relief efforts organized through online social media helped provide temporary shelter for the many thousands left homeless by the quake.

Monsoon Rains Inundate Thailand—Exceptionally heavy monsoon rains since July caused floods throughout Southeast Asia. Thailand experienced its worst flooding in a half century, with about ⅓ of the country under water. Districts just north of Bangkok were particularly affected, submerging crops, homes, and factories. The Chao Phraya River, which runs through the capital, reached record highs Oct. 28. By Nov. 2, the flood death toll stood at 427.

World Population Reaches 7 Billion—According to the UN Population Fund, the world population surpassed the 7 bil mark Oct. 31. The UN agency estimated that the global population had doubled since 1968, with about 97% of the increase occurring in less-developed countries. The UN's median projection called for the population to grow to 8 bil by 2025 and 9 bil by 2043.

General

Italian Court Exonerates Amanda Knox—Nearly 2 years after a trial court in Perugia, Italy, convicted U.S. exchange student Amanda Knox and her Italian boyfriend Raffaele Sollecito of sexually assaulting and murdering her British student housemate, Meredith Kercher, an Italian appellate tribunal Oct. 3 reversed the earlier verdicts and freed both defendants. The lurid case had drawn worldwide attention, especially in the UK, where tabloids vilified her as "Foxy Knoxy." The largely circumstantial case collapsed when independent experts found that DNA evidence used at the trial had been mishandled by police. In a separate trial in 2008, Rudy Guede, a Côte d'Ivoire national, had also been convicted of killing Kercher and was sentenced to 30 years in prison. His sentence was shortened to 16 years in 2009. Although Knox was cleared of the most serious charges, the appellate court let stand a verdict that she had slandered Diya (Patrick) Lumumba, a Congolese bar owner in Perugia, when she initially accused him of committing the murder.

Contract Dispute Delays Pro Basketball Season—National Basketball Association Commissioner David Stern Oct. 10 canceled the first 2 weeks of the pro basketball season, scheduled to begin Nov. 1, because of a dispute between team owners and NBA Players Association over how to divide some $4 bil in revenues. The owners had declared a lockout July 1 after negotiations for a new collective bargaining agreement broke down. On Oct. 28, with the labor dispute still unresolved, Stern canceled the entire Nov. schedule.

Wheldon Killed in Las Vegas Auto Race—British racecar driver Dan Wheldon died Oct. 16 after a fiery 15-car pileup at Las Vegas Motor Speedway. The 33-year-old Wheldon, a 2-time winner of the Indianapolis 500, was fatally injured in the 12th lap when his No. 77 vehicle hit another car, sailed into the air, slammed into a catch fence, and exploded. His death was the 1st in the IndyCar Series since 2006.

St. Louis Cardinals Win World Series—The St. Louis Cardinals captured their 11th World Series championship Oct. 28, defeating the Texas Rangers, 6-2, in Game 7 at Busch Stadium in St. Louis, MO. The Cardinals had surged from 10½ games behind on Aug. 25 to snag a wild-card playoff spot on the final day of the season. Twice in Game 6 they were only one strike away from elimination before rallying and ultimately beating the Rangers in an 11-inning seesaw struggle. MVP David Freese, the Cardinals' third baseman, had clutch hits in Games 6 and 7; in Game 3, first baseman Albert Pujols joined Babe Ruth and Reggie Jackson as the only players ever to hit 3 home runs in a World Series game. Manager Tony La Russa, who won his 2nd World Series with the Cardinals and his 3rd overall, announced Oct. 31 that he was stepping down. After 33 seasons with the Cardinals, Chicago White Sox, and Oakland As, the 67-year-old La Russa ranked 3rd among all managers in career regular-season victories (2,728) and 2nd in playoff game wins (70).

OBITUARIES

A

Anderson, George "Sparky," 76, Major League Baseball manager; won World Series titles in both the National and American Leagues; Thousand Oaks, CA, Nov. 4, 2010.

Arness, James (born James Aurness), 88, actor best known for playing Matt Dillon on TV's *Gunsmoke* (1955-75); Los Angeles, CA, June 3, 2011.

Ashford, Nick(olas), 70, half of husband and wife songwriting team Ashford and (Valerie) Simpson, famous for Motown hits including "Ain't No Mountain High Enough"; New York, NY, Aug. 22, 2011.

Al-Awlaki, Anwar, 40, U.S.-born Islamic cleric; operative for al-Qaeda terrorist network; killed in U.S. drone attack, Yemen, Sept. 30, 2011.

B

Ballas, George, 85, inventor of the Weed Eater, a string trimmer used for landscaping; Houston, TX, June 25, 2011.

Ballesteros, Seve(riano), 54, Spanish golfer who was the first European to win the Masters tournament (1980); Pedreña, Spain, May 7, 2011.

Banner, Bob, 89, Emmy Award-winning TV producer who created *Candid Camera* and *Star Search*; Woodland Hills, CA, June 15, 2011.

Baran, Paul, 84, Polish-American computer pioneer who invented packet switching, a breakthrough that led to the creation of the Internet; Palo Alto, CA, Mar. 26, 2011.

Barbour, Ross, 82, singer and original member of quartet the Four Freshmen; Simi Valley, CA, Aug. 20, 2011.

Barry, John, 77, British-born film composer who scored 11 James Bond films; won Academy Awards for *Born Free* (1966), *Out of Africa* (1985), and other films; New York, Jan. 30, 2011.

Bell, Daniel (born Daniel Bolotsky), 91, influential sociologist best known for *The End of Ideology* (1980), a study of post-industrialism; Cambridge, MA, Jan. 25, 2011.

Bell, Derrick, 80, civil rights lawyer; first African-American faculty member to be given tenure at Harvard Law School; New York, NY, Oct. 5, 2011.

Bender, Frank, 70, forensic sculptor whose facial reconstructions of victims and criminals helped law enforcement officials solve crimes; Philadelphia, PA, July 28, 2011.

Betz Addie, Pauline, 91, tennis player who won 5 women's Grand Slam singles titles (1942-46); banned from the sport in 1947 when she publicly considered playing professionally; Potomac, MD, May 31, 2011.

Swami Bhaktipada (born Keith Ham), 74, former leader of U.S. Hare Krishna community; fled after being convicted of racketeering and conspiracy to commit murder; near Mumbai, India, Oct. 24, 2011.

Bin Laden, Osama, 54, founder of the al-Qaeda terrorist network; the jihadist group responsible for the Sept. 11, 2001, terrorist attacks; killed by U.S. forces, Abbottabad, Pakistan, May 1, 2011.

Blumberg, Baruch, 85, Nobel Prize-winning biochemist who identified the hepatitis-B virus and developed a vaccine to fight it; Moffett Field, CA, Apr. 5, 2011.

Bock, Jerry, 81, Tony Award-winning composer best known for *Fiorello!* (1959) and *Fiddler on the Roof* (1964); Mount Kisco, NY, Nov. 3, 2010.

Bonner, Yelena, 88, Soviet human rights activist; widow of famed dissident physicist Andrei Sakharov; Boston, MA, June 18, 2011.

Boyle, Willard, 86, Nobel Prize-winning Canadian physicist who co-invented the charge coupled device (CCD), a component essential to digital cameras; Truro, NS, Canada, May 7, 2011.

Broder, David, 81, *Washington Post* political columnist; won a Pulitzer for his coverage of the Watergate scandal (1973); Arlington, VA, Mar. 9, 2011.

Brooks, Joseph, 73, songwriter and director who wrote the 1977 Academy and Grammy Award-winning ballad "You Light Up My Life"; New York, NY, May 22, 2011.

Buckles, Frank, 110, last surviving U.S. veteran of World War I; Charles Town, WV, Feb. 27, 2011.

Burns, Pat, 58, Canadian National Hockey League coach who led the NJ Devils to the 2003 Stanley Cup title; Sherbrooke, QC, Canada, Nov. 19, 2010.

C

Carey, Hugh, 92, New York governor (D, 1975-82) who kept the state from defaulting by issuing government bonds; Shelter Island, NY, Aug. 7, 2011.

Carrington, Leonora, 94, surrealist painter and sculptor whose works were inspired by animals, mythology, and occult symbolism; Mexico City, Mexico, May 25, 2011.

Chervokas, John, 74, advertising writer who created Charmin toilet paper's "Mr. Whipple" campaign; New York, NY, July 23, 2011.

Chiluba, Frederick, 68, first democratically elected president of Zambia; Lusaka, Zambia, June 18, 2011.

Christopher, Warren, 85, U.S. secretary of state (1993-97) who held key diplomatic posts under several presidents; played an essential role in negotiating the 1981 release of 52 U.S. citizens held hostage in Iran; Los Angeles, CA, Mar. 18, 2011.

Clark, Huguette, 104, copper heiress who was a well-known New York City socialite before becoming a recluse from the late 1930s until her death; New York, NY, May 24, 2011.

Clayburgh, Jill, 66, Oscar-nominated actress best known for portrayals of strong-willed women; Lakeville, CT, Nov. 5, 2010.

Clemons, Clarence, 69, tenor saxophonist for Bruce Springsteen's E Street Band, 1972-2011; Palm Beach, FL, June 18, 2011.

Cohen, Samuel, 89, nuclear physicist who invented the neutron bomb; Los Angeles, CA, Nov. 28, 2010.

Colan, Gene, 84, comic-book artist best known for his work with Marvel Comics; Bronx, NY, June 23, 2011.

Conaway, Jeff, 60, actor best known for his role on the TV series *Taxi* (1978-82); Encino, CA, May 27, 2011.

Cooper, Jackie, 88, Oscar-nominated child actor with a long career in TV, film, and theater; best known for *Skippy* (1931); Santa Monica, CA, May 3, 2011.

Coover, Harry, Jr., 94, chemist who developed the adhesive compound later sold as Super Glue and Instant Krazy Glue; Kingsport, TN, Mar. 26, 2011.

Corwin, Norman, 101, writer, director, and producer known for radio dramas of the 1930s-40s; Los Angeles, CA, Oct. 18, 2011.

Cuénod, Hughes-Adhémar, 108, Swiss tenor known for interpretations of French art songs; Vevey, Switzerland, Dec. 6, 2010.

D

Davies, John Howard, 72, British director and producer of TV comedies including *Fawlty Towers*; as a child actor, starred in *Oliver Twist* (1948); Blewbury, Eng., UK, Aug. 22, 2011.

Davis, Al, 82, principal owner and executive officer of the NFL's Oakland Raiders; Oakland, CA, Oct. 8, 2011.

Davis, Madelyn Pugh, 90, TV writer who co-wrote most *I Love Lucy* (1951-57) episodes and 4 other Lucille Ball series; Los Angeles, CA, Apr. 20, 2011.

De Laurentiis, Dino, 91, Italian film producer whose films included Federico Fellini's *La Strada* (1954), *Serpico* (1973), and David Lynch's *Blue Velvet* (1986); Beverly Hills, CA, Nov. 10, 2010.

Dogg, Nate (born Nathaniel Hale), 41, rap and hip-hop singer known for collaboration with other artists; Long Beach, CA, Mar. 15, 2011.

Doyle, Geraldine, 86, metal presser during World War II; believed to have been the inspiration for the Rosie the Riveter character; Lansing, MI, Dec. 26, 2010.

Dunn, Ryan, 34, TV personality and daredevil known for appearances in the *Jackass* TV show and movies; West Goshen Township, PA, June 20, 2011.

E

Eagleburger, Lawrence, 80, U.S. diplomat and adviser who served in 5 presidential administrations and was briefly secretary of state (42 days, 1992); Charlottesville, VA, June 4, 2011.

Edwards, Blake (born William Blake Crump), 88, director, screenwriter, and producer best known for *Victor/Victoria* (1982) and the *Pink Panther* movies; Santa Monica, CA, Dec. 15, 2010.

Edwards, David "Honeyboy," 96, Delta blues guitarist and singer; Chicago, IL, Aug. 29, 2011.

Edwards, Elizabeth, 61, attorney and health-care advocate; estranged wife of 2004 Democratic vice-presidential candidate John Edwards; Chapel Hill, NC, Dec. 7, 2010.

F

Falk, Peter, 83, Emmy Award-winning actor best known for his eponymous role on the long-running TV series *Columbo* (1971-2003); Beverly Hills, CA, June 23, 2011.

Feller, Bob, 92, Cleveland Indians pitcher who won 266 games and pitched 3 no-hitters; Cleveland, OH, Dec. 15, 2010.

Ferraro, Geraldine, 75, U.S. rep. (D, NY, 1979-85) and Democratic vice-presidential nominee (1984); first woman to be nominated for the post by a major political party; Boston, MA, Mar. 26, 2011.

Fickett, Mary, 83, actress best known for the long-running role of Ruth Martin on *All My Children* (1970-96, 1998-2000); Callao, VA, Sept. 8, 2011.

Flanigan, Bob, 84, singer and founding member of the Four Freshmen; he sang with the group from 1948 to 1992; Las Vegas, NV, May 15, 2011.

Flesh, Ed, 79, art director who designed the wheel used on the *Wheel of Fortune* TV game show; Mission Hills, CA, July 15, 2011.

Ford, Betty, 93, former U.S. first lady known for candor and support for equal rights and feminist issues; founder of the Betty Ford Center for people struggling with chemical dependencies, which she famously fought herself; Rancho Mirage, CA, July 8, 2011.

Francis, Anne (born Ann Marvak), 80, actress known for her roles in the sci-fi film *Forbidden Planet* (1956) and 1960s TV series *Honey West*; Santa Barbara, CA, Jan. 2, 2011.

Freud, Lucian, 88, British painter known for his stark nude portraits; London, Eng., UK, July 20, 2011.

G

Gallo, Bill, 88, sports cartoonist and columnist at the NY *Daily News* for more than 50 years; White Plains, NY, May 10, 2011.

Galvin, Robert, 89, Motorola CEO; Chicago, IL, Oct. 11, 2011.

Gardner, Carl, 83, lead singer of the Coasters singing group of the 1950s; best known for song "Yakety Yak"; Port St. Lucie, FL, June 12, 2011.

Garrett, Betty, 91, comic actress in supporting roles, well known for appearances on *All in the Family* (1973-75) and *Laverne & Shirley* (1976-81); Los Angeles, CA, Feb. 12, 2011.

Getty, John Paul, III, 54, heir to Getty oil fortune and victim of kidnappers (1973) who famously removed one of his ears; Wormsley, Eng., UK, Feb. 5, 2011.

Gilchrist, Carlton "Cookie," 75, All-Pro football fullback who was an early American Football League star; Pittsburgh, PA, Jan. 10, 2011.

Gough, Michael, 94, British character actor known for his role as butler Alfred Pennyworth in 4 *Batman* movies; London, Eng., UK, Mar. 17, 2011.

Granger, Farley, 85, actor best known for Alfred Hitchcock thrillers, including *Rope* (1948) and *Strangers on a Train* (1951); New York, NY, Mar. 27, 2011.

Greatbatch, Wilson, 92, biomedical engineer who invented the implantable cardiac pacemaker; Williamsville, NY, Sept. 27, 2011.

Greenspan, (Jonah) Bud, 84, filmmaker known for documenting Olympic athletes; New York, NY, Dec. 25, 2010.

Gussow, Roy, 92, abstract sculptor known for stainless steel works exhibited in outdoor locations; Queens, NY, Feb. 11, 2011.

H

Haberman, Alan, 81, supermarket executive credited with popularizing the use of UPC barcodes; Newton, MA, June 12, 2011.

Hamilton, Richard, 89, British painter and collage artist known as the UK's "Father of Pop Art"; Eng., UK, Sept. 13, 2011.

Handler, Elliot, 95, co-founder of Mattel toy company; developed Barbie dolls and Hot Wheels cars; Los Angeles, CA, July 21, 2011.

Handlin, Oscar, 95, Pulitzer Prize-winning historian who studied immigration, social, and ethnic history; Cambridge, MA, Sept. 20, 2011.

Harman, Sidney, 92, audio pioneer who marketed the first integrated hi-fi stereo receiver; purchased *Newsweek* magazine (2010); Washington, DC, Apr. 12, 2011.

Hart, Michael, 64, inventor of electronic books and founder of Project Gutenberg, a digital library of public domain works; Urbana, IL, Sept. 6, 2011.

Hatfield, Mark, 89, governor (1959-67) and U.S. senator (R, OR, 1967-97); early opponent of the Vietnam War; Portland, OR, Aug. 7, 2011.

Heimerdinger, Mike, 58, NFL coach for the Denver Broncos, NY Jets, and Tennessee Titans; Mexico, Sept. 30, 2011.

Holbrooke, Richard, 69, U.S. diplomat credited with brokering the Dayton accords (1995), which ended the Bosnian War; Washington, DC, Dec. 13, 2010.

Hope, Dolores, 102, singer and widow of comedian Bob Hope; Los Angeles, CA, Sept. 19, 2011.

Horton, Gladys, 66, lead singer of the Marvelettes; their hit "Please Mr. Postman" was Motown Records' first #1 hit; Sherman Oaks, CA, Jan. 26, 2011.

I

Irabu, Hideki, 42, Japanese pitcher signed by the NY Yankees in 1997 for $12.8 mil but failed to meet high expectations; Rancho Palos Verdes, CA, July 27, 2011.

J

Jacques, Brian, 71, British author of the *Redwall* children's fantasy series; Liverpool, Eng., UK, Feb. 5, 2011.

Jobs, Steve, 56, visionary co-founder of Apple; revolutionized personal computing with the Macintosh and changed the way people consume media with introduction of iTunes and the iPod, iPhone, and iPad; Palo Alto, CA, Oct. 5, 2011.

Johnson, Norma Holloway, 79, first African-American woman to serve as a U.S. district court chief judge; Lake Charles, LA, Sept. 18, 2011.

Jones, Diana Wynne, 76, British writer of children's fantasy and science fiction; Bristol, Eng., UK, Mar. 26, 2011.

K

Kahn, Alfred, 93, economist who oversaw the deregulation of the U.S. airline industry in the 1970s; Ithaca, NY, Dec. 27, 2010.

Kahn, Leo, 94, co-founder of office supply store Staples; Boston, MA, May 11, 2011.

Kameny, Franklin, 86, gay rights activist who filed a lawsuit challenging his firing from the Army Map Service for being homosexual; Washington, DC, Oct. 11, 2011.

Kato, David, 46, Ugandan teacher and gay rights activist who fought the nation's 2009 anti-homosexual bill; Mukono Town, Uganda, Jan. 26, 2011.

Kaufman, Elaine, 81, restaurateur whose Manhattan eatery Elaine's was a meeting place for celebrities for nearly 50 years; New York, NY, Dec. 3, 2010.

Kershner, Irvin (born Isadore Kershner), 87, film director best known for *The Empire Strikes Back* (1980); Los Angeles, CA, Nov. 27, 2010.

Kevorkian, Jack, 83, pathologist and physician-assisted suicide advocate known as "Dr. Death"; served 8 years of a 10-to-25-year sentence for 2nd-degree murder; Royal Oak, MI, June 3, 2011.

Kheel, Theodore, 96, labor lawyer who was New York City's chief labor negotiator (1956-82); New York, NY, Nov. 12, 2010.

Kihara, Nobutoshi, 84, Sony engineer who invented Japan's first transistor radio and Betamax video recorder; helped develop the Walkman portable stereo; Japan, Feb. 13, 2011.

Killebrew, Harmon, 74, baseball player for the Washington Senators/Minnesota Twins franchise who hit 573 career home runs; Scottsdale, AZ, May 17, 2011.

Kirk, Claude R., Jr., 85, first Republican elected governor of Florida in the 20th century (1967-71); West Palm Beach, FL, Sept. 28, 2011.

Kirkland, Eddie, 87, blues singer; Tampa, FL, Feb. 27, 2011.

Kirshner, Don, 76, music producer who helped launch the careers of Neil Diamond and Carole King and was an early promoter of the Monkees; Boca Raton, FL, Jan. 17, 2011.

L

LaLanne, Jack (born Francois Henri LaLanne), 96, health and fitness advocate whose exercise program was televised nationally (1959-85); Morro Bay, CA, Jan. 23, 2011.

Landau, Moshe, 99, presiding judge in the 1961 war crimes trial of Holocaust planner Adolf Eichmann in Israel; Jerusalem, Israel, May 1, 2011.

Laurents, Arthur (born Arthur Levine), 93, playwright, screenwriter, and director who wrote the books for the renowned musicals *West Side Story* (1957) and *Gypsy* (1959); New York, NY, May 5, 2011.

Leiber, Jerry, 78, lyricist who with his partner Mike Stoller wrote rock and roll classics, including "Hound Dog," "Stand By Me," and "Jailhouse Rock"; Los Angeles, CA, Aug. 22, 2011.

Lesser, Len, 88, actor best known for his role as Uncle Leo on the TV show *Seinfeld*; Burbank, CA, Feb. 16, 2011.

Levine, Milton, 97, novelty-toy entrepreneur and co-inventor of the classic ant farm; Thousand Oaks, CA, Jan. 16, 2011.

Licitra, Salvatore, 43, Italian operatic tenor; Catania, Sicily, Italy, Sept. 5, 2011.

Lomma, Ralph, 87, miniature golf course developer who helped popularize the sport by creating obstacles and moving figures; Scranton, PA, Sept. 12, 2011.

Louvin, Charlie, 83, country singer who performed with brother Ira as the Louvin Brothers; Wartrace, TN, Jan. 26, 2011.

Lumet, Sidney, 86, film director whose work dealt with corruption and morality; his best-known films include *12 Angry Men* (1957), *Dog Day Afternoon* (1975), and *Network* (1976); New York, NY, Apr. 9, 2011.

Luper, Clara, 88, civil rights activist who led sit-ins at Oklahoma City drugstore lunch counters in 1958 in struggle for integration; Oklahoma City, OK, June 8, 2011.

Lyon, Norma, 81, farmer and artist who sculpted butter into life-size cows, people, and famous paintings; Marshalltown, IA, June 26, 2011.

M

Maathai, Wangari Muta, 71, environmental and social activist; first African woman awarded the Nobel Peace Prize (2004); Nairobi, Kenya, Sept. 25, 2011.

Mackey, John, 69, 5-time Pro Bowl tight end, mostly for the Baltimore Ravens (1963-71); fought for free agency as president of the NFL Players Assn.; suffered dementia later in life; Baltimore, MD, July 6, 2011.

Martin, Hugh, 96, composer and lyricist best known for the score to *Meet Me in St. Louis* (1944); co-writer of "Have Yourself a Merry Little Christmas"; Encinitas, CA, Mar. 11, 2011.

Masini, Al, 80, TV producer who created *Entertainment Tonight* (1981-present), *Lifestyles of the Rich and Famous* (1984-95), and *Star Search* (1983-95); Honolulu, HI, Nov. 29, 2010.

Massey, Anna, 73, British actress in film, TV, and on stage; London, Eng., UK, July 3, 2011.

Matson, Ollie, 80, NFL running back (1952-66) who retired with 12,884 net yards; won 2 medals as a sprinter in the 1952 Olympics; Los Angeles, CA, Feb. 19, 2011.

McCulloch, Ernest, 84, Canadian scientist who, with biophysicist James E. Till, isolated the first stem cell; Toronto, ON, Canada, Jan. 20, 2011.

Mengers, Sue, 79, Hollywood agent who represented actors incl. Barbra Streisand and Steve McQueen; Beverly Hills, CA, Oct. 15, 2011.

Meredith, Don, 72, Dallas Cowboys quarterback (1960-68); commentator for *Monday Night Football* (1971-73, '77-'84); Santa Fe, NM, Dec. 5, 2010.

Monicelli, Mario, 95, prolific Italian film director and screenwriter; best known for *I Soliti Ignoti* [*Big Deal on Madonna Street*] (1958); Rome, Italy, Nov. 29, 2010.

Monroe, Bill, 90, TV journalist who moderated *Meet the Press* (1975-84); Potomac, MD, Feb. 17, 2011.

Moody, James, 85, jazz saxophonist and flutist; best known for "Moody's Mood for Love" (1949) as a member of Dizzy Gillespie's band; San Diego, CA, Dec. 9, 2010.

Moore, Gary, 58, Irish-born rock and blues guitarist best known as a member of Thin Lizzy; Estepona, Spain, Feb. 6, 2011.

Morello, Joe, 82, jazz drummer known for his tenure with the Dave Brubeck Quartet; Irvington, NJ, Mar. 12, 2011.

N

Nelson, David, 74, actor, director, and producer; last surviving member of *The Adventures of Ozzie and Harriet* (1952-66) TV sitcom family; Los Angeles, CA, Jan. 11, 2011.

Neuberger, Roy, 107, stockbroker and art collector; amassed one of the U.S.'s largest private collections of 20th-century art; New York, NY, Dec. 24, 2010.

Madame Nhu (born Tran Le Xuan), 86, de facto first lady during South Vietnamese Pres. Ngo Dinh Diem's 1955-63 rule; known internationally as the "Dragon Lady"; Rome, Italy, Apr. 24, 2011.

Niehaus, Dave, 75, longtime play-by-play announcer for the Seattle Mariners (1977-2010); Bellevue, WA, Nov. 10, 2010.

Nielsen, A(rthur) C(harles), Jr., 92, businessman who transformed his family's firm, A.C. Nielsen, into an international leader in TV ratings and market research; Winnetka, IL, Oct. 3, 2011.

Nielsen, Leslie, 84, Canadian-born actor known for comedic roles in *Airplane!* (1980) and *The Naked Gun* film series (1988-94); Fort Lauderdale, FL, Nov. 28, 2010.

O

Ohga, Norio, 81, president and chairman of Sony who mass-marketed the compact disc (CD); Tokyo, Japan, Apr. 23, 2011.

P

Peek, Dan, 60, rock singer and musician best known as a founding member of the band America; Farmington, MO, July 24, 2011.

Pemper, Mietek, 91, concentration camp survivor who as a prisoner collaborated with Oskar Schindler on a list of more than 1,200 Jews who were saved from the Nazis; Augsburg, Germany, June 7, 2011.

Percy, Charles, 91, U.S. senator (R, IL, 1967-85); went against party by sponsoring the resolution for a Watergate special prosecutor; Washington, DC, Sept. 17, 2011.

Perkins, Joe Willie "Pinetop," 97, Delta blues pianist and singer; oldest ever Grammy winner (2011); Austin, TX, Mar. 21, 2011.

Petit, Roland, 87, French choreographer who co-founded the Ballets des Champs-Élysées (1945); also known for work on films *Hans Christian Andersen* (1951) and *Anything Goes* (1956); Geneva, Switzerland, July 10, 2011.

Pierpont, Robert, 86, CBS News correspondent on radio and TV; Santa Barbara, CA, Oct. 22, 2011.

Postlethwaite, Pete, 64, British-born character actor known for his ruddy features and self-deprecating humor; Shrewsbury, Eng., UK, Jan. 2, 2011.

Price, (Edward) Reynolds, 77, novelist known for poetic depictions of rural Southern life; Durham, NC, Jan. 20, 2011.

Q

al-Qaddafi, Muammar, 69, Libyan dictator (1969-2011) who was indicted for crimes against humanity as his nation rebelled (2011); also known for bizarre behavior and flamboyant dress; near Sirte, Libya, Oct. 20, 2011.

R

Rafferty, Gerry, 63, Scottish singer whose songs included "Stuck in the Middle With You" (1972) and "Baker Street" (1978); Dorset, Eng., UK, Jan. 4, 2011.

Robertson, Cliff, 88, actor who won an Oscar for *Charly* (1968); blacklisted for exposing a studio forgery scandal, 1977; recently appeared in *Spider-Man* films (2002-07); Stony Brook, NY, Sept. 10, 2011.

Robinson, Sylvia, 76, singer, songwriter, and record producer who founded Sugar Hill Records and was a guiding force behind early rap music; Edison, NJ, Sept. 29, 2011.

Roszak, Theodore, 77, historian best known for *The Making of a Counter Culture* (1969); Berkeley, CA, July 5, 2011.

Rusher, William, 87, political strategist and columnist; published William Buckley's *National Review* (1957-88) and helped make it a preeminent conservative platform; San Francisco, CA, Apr. 16, 2011.

Russell, Jane, 89, voluptuous actress who rose to fame in Howard Hughes's *The Outlaw* (1943), which violated Hollywood's motion picture production code; Santa Maria, CA, Feb. 28, 2011.

S

Sai Baba, Sathya (born Sathyanarayana Raju), 84, spiritual leader who amassed a following of millions; Puttaparthi, Andhra Pradesh, India, Apr. 24, 2011.

Sandage, Allan, 84, astronomer who first determined a reasonably accurate age for the universe and the value of the Hubble constant, or rate of expansion of the universe; San Gabriel, CA, Nov. 13, 2010.

Sarrazin, Michael (born Jacques Michel Andre Sarrazin), 70, Canadian actor best known for *They Shoot Horses, Don't They?* (1969); Montréal, QC, Canada, Apr. 17, 2011.

Savage, Randy (born Randy Poffo), 58, professional wrestling superstar known as Macho Man; Seminole, FL, May 20, 2011.

Schlafly, Hubert, 91, electrical engineer who co-invented the teleprompter; Stamford, CT, Apr. 20, 2011.

Schneider, Maria (born Marie Gélin), 58, French actress known for role opposite Marlon Brando in the sexually explicit *Last Tango in Paris* (1972); Paris, France, Feb. 3, 2011.

Schwartz, Sherwood, 94, TV writer and producer who created *Gilligan's Island* (1964-67) and *The Brady Bunch* (1969-74); Los Angeles, CA, July 12, 2011.

Scott-Heron, Gil, 62, writer, poet, and spoken-word jazz musician best known for "The Revolution Will Not Be Televised" (1970); New York, NY, May 27, 2011.

Self, William, 89, TV producer and executive whose hit shows included *Batman, Peyton Place,* and *M*A*S*H*; Los Angeles, CA, Nov. 15, 2010.

Shalikashvili, John, 75, Polish-born 4-star U.S. Army general who served as chairman of the Joints Chiefs of Staff (1993-97); first foreign-born general to hold that position; Madigan Army Medical Center, WA, July 23, 2011.

Shearing, George, 91, British-born blind pianist who wrote over 300 songs including "Lullaby of Birdland"; New York, NY, Feb. 14, 2011.

Shriver, (Robert) Sargent, 95, diplomat and founding director of the Peace Corps; led Office of Economic Opportunity, which created the Head Start and Job Corps programs; Democratic vice-presidential nominee (1972); Bethesda, MD, Jan. 18, 2011.

Shuttlesworth, Fred L. (born Freddie Lee Robinson), 89, co-founder of civil rights organization Southern Christian Leadership Conference; Birmingham, AL, Oct. 5, 2011.

Sisulu, Albertina (born Nontsikelelo Thethiwe), 92, South African antiapartheid activist; Johannesburg, South Africa, June 2, 2011.

Skelton (Erde), Betty, 85, daredevil aviatrix and stock-car driver who became known as the "first lady of firsts"; The Villages, FL, Aug. 31, 2011.

Smith, (Charles) Bubba, 66, pro football player turned actor; best known for his role as Hightower in the *Police Academy* movie series (1984-89); Los Angeles, CA, Aug. 3, 2011.

Snider, (Edwin) Duke, 84, Hall of Fame center fielder who helped the Dodgers win the World Series in Brooklyn (1955) and after moving to Los Angeles (1959); only player to hit 4 home runs in a World Series twice; Escondido, CA, Feb. 27, 2011.

Snow, Phoebe (born Phoebe Laub), 60, singer, songwriter, and guitarist best known for her "Poetry Man" (1974); Edison, NJ, Apr. 26, 2011.

Stanley, Bear (Owsley), 76, countercultural icon who in the 1960s was a prolific distributor of the hallucinogenic drug LSD and sound engineer for the Grateful Dead rock band; Queensland, Australia, Mar. 13, 2011.

Steiner, Fred, 88, composer who wrote the *Perry Mason* TV theme song and the score for the film *The Color Purple* (1985); Ajijic, Jalisco, Mexico, June 23, 2011.

Stern, Leonard B., 88, Emmy Award-winning TV writer better known for co-creating the word game Mad Libs; Beverly Hills, CA, June 7, 2011.

Styrene, Poly (born Marianne Eliot-Said), 53, punk rock pioneer and feminist; leader of the band X-Ray Spex; East Sussex, Eng., UK, Apr. 25, 2011.

T

Tarplin, Marv, 70, Motown songwriter and guitarist for Smoky Robinson and the Miracles; co-wrote their hit "The Tracks of My Tears" (1965); Las Vegas, NV, Sept. 30, 2011.

Taylor, Billy, 89, jazz pianist and composer of more than 300 songs, including "I Wish I Knew How It Would Feel to Be Free" (1967); New York, NY, Dec. 28, 2010.

Taylor, Elizabeth, 79, British-born Hollywood legend whose beauty, acting, and tempestuous personal life fascinated for 4 decades; won Best Actress Oscars for *BUtterfield 8* (1960) and *Who's Afraid of Virginia Woolf?* (1966); co-founder of American Foundation for AIDS Research (1985); Los Angeles, CA, Mar. 23, 2011.

Teena Marie (born Mary Christine Brockert), 54, rhythm-and-blues singer; among her best-known songs were "Lovergirl" (1984) and "Ooo La La La" (1988); Pasadena, CA, Dec. 26, 2010.

Thompson, Sada, 83, stage and TV actress; won an Emmy for her matriarch role on *Family* (1976-80); Danbury, CT, May 4, 2011.

Tooker, George, 90, figurative painter known for work that expressed the anxiety of 20th-century life; Hartland, VT, Mar. 27, 2011.

Twombly, (Edwin) Cy, 83, artist known for his sparse and chaotic abstract paintings; Rome, Italy, July 5, 2011.

Tyson, Donald, 80, businessman who built his family's agricultural business, Tyson Foods Inc., into the world's largest poultry producer; Fayetteville, AR, Jan. 6, 2011.

V

Verrett, Shirley, 79, operatic mezzo-soprano who gravitated to soprano roles in the 1970s; Ann Arbor, MI, Nov. 5, 2010.

Villchur, Edgar M., 94, inventor of the acoustic suspension woofer, which revolutionized high-fidelity sound equipment; Woodstock, NY, Oct. 17, 2011.

W

Waitz, Grete, 57, Norwegian long-distance runner who won 9 New York City Marathons between 1978 and 1988; Oslo, Norway, Apr. 19, 2011.

Wanjiru, Sammy, 24, long-distance runner who became Kenya's first Olympic marathon champion at the Beijing Games (2008); Nyahururu, Kenya, May 15, 2011.

West, Arch, 94, Frito-Lay executive who helped develop Doritos corn chips; Dallas, TX, Sept. 20, 2011.

Wheldon, Dan, 33, British race-car driver who twice won the Indianapolis 500 (2005, '11); died from injuries after collision at Las Vegas Motor Speedway, Las Vegas, NV, Oct. 16, 2011.

Whitfield, Andy, 39, Welsh model and actor best known for leading role on the TV series *Spartacus: Blood and Sand*; Sydney, Australia, Sept. 11, 2011.

Whiting, Margaret, 86, rhythm-and-blues singer who popularized the songs "It Might As Well Be Spring" and "Moonlight in Vermont"; Englewood, NJ, Jan. 10, 2011.

Williams, Dick, 82, Hall of Fame baseball manager who took 3 different teams to the World Series; Las Vegas, NV, July 7, 2011.

Williams, Roger (born Louis Jacob Weertz), 87, pianist best known for his Billboard No. 1 instrumental hit "Autumn Leaves"; Los Angeles, CA, Oct. 8, 2011.

Williams, Vesta, 53, rhythm-and-blues singer best known for "Congratulations" (1989); El Segundo, CA, Sept. 22, 2011.

Wilson, Lanford, 73, prolific playwright whose work examined the predicaments of those on the fringes of society; *Talley's Folly* (1980) won a Pulitzer Prize; Wayne, NJ, Mar. 24, 2011.

Wilson, Tom, 80, cartoonist who created the comic-strip character Ziggy; Cincinnati, OH, Sept. 16, 2011.

Winehouse, Amy, 27, British soul singer who won 5 Grammy awards, including Record of the Year for "Rehab" (2007); struggled publicly with substance abuse; London, Eng., UK, July 23, 2011.

Winters, Richard "Dick," 92, Army commander whose World War II heroism was immortalized in the book and TV miniseries *Band of Brothers*; Campbelltown, PA, Jan. 2, 2011.

Wolff, William, 94, surgeon who co-developed the colonoscopy; New York, NY, Aug. 20, 2011.

Wright, Johnnie, 97, country music singer-songwriter as member of the duo Johnnie and Jack; husband of Kitty Wells; Madison, TN, Sept. 27, 2011.

Y

Yalow, Rosalyn Sussman, 89, Nobel Prize-winning medical physicist who co-developed radioimmunoassay; Bronx, NY, May 30, 2011.

Yates, Peter, 81, British-born film director and producer famous for action sequences, including those in the police thriller *Bullitt* (1968); London, Eng., UK, Jan. 9, 2011.

York, Susannah (born Susannah Yolande Fletcher), 72, British-born, Oscar-nominated actress best known for *They Shoot Horses, Don't They?* (1969); London, Eng., UK, Jan. 15, 2011.

Z

Ziskin, Laura, 61, pioneering film producer best known for *Pretty Woman* (1990) and the *Spider-Man* film trilogy (2002-07); Santa Monica, CA, June 12, 2011.

STATE GOVERNMENT

Governors of the 50 States

Source: National Governors Association; Council of State Governments; World Almanac research

As of Oct. 2011, of the 50 state governors, 29 are Republicans, 20 are Democrats, and 1 is Independent. Salary information is as of Mar. 2010.

State	Capital, ZIP code	Governor	Party	Term years	Term expires	Annual salary
Alabama	Montgomery, 36130	Robert Bentley	Rep.	4	Jan. 2015	$112,895
Alaska	Juneau, 99811	Sean Parnell	Rep.	4	Dec. 2014	125,000
Arizona	Phoenix, 85007	Jan Brewer	Rep.	4	Jan. 2015	95,000
Arkansas	Little Rock, 72201	Mike Beebe	Dem.	4	Jan. 2015	87,352
California	Sacramento, 95814	Jerry Brown	Dem.	4	Jan. 2015	173,987
Colorado	Denver, 80203	John Hickenlooper	Dem.	4	Jan. 2015	90,000
Connecticut	Hartford, 06106	Dan Malloy	Dem.	4	Jan. 2015	150,000
Delaware	Dover, 19902	Jack A. Markell	Dem.	4	Jan. 2013	171,000
Florida	Tallahassee, 32399	Rick Scott	Rep.	4	Jan. 2015	130,273
Georgia	Atlanta, 30334	Nathan Deal	Rep.	4	Jan. 2015	139,339
Hawaii	Honolulu, 96813	Neil Abercrombie	Dem.	4	Dec. 2014	117,312
Idaho	Boise, 83702	C. L. "Butch" Otter	Rep.	4	Jan. 2015	115,348
Illinois	Springfield, 62706	Patrick Quinn	Dem.	4	Jan. 2015	177,500
Indiana	Indianapolis, 46204	Mitch E. Daniels Jr.	Rep.	4	Jan. 2013	95,000
Iowa	Des Moines, 50319	Terry Branstad	Rep.	4	Jan. 2015	130,000
Kansas	Topeka, 66612	Sam Brownback	Rep.	4	Jan. 2015	110,707
Kentucky	Frankfort, 40601	Steven L. Beshear	Dem.	4	Dec. 2011	145,885[1]
Louisiana	Baton Rouge, 70804	Bobby Jindal	Rep.	4	Jan. 2012	130,000
Maine	Augusta, 04333	Paul LePage	Rep.	4	Jan. 2015	70,000
Maryland	Annapolis, 21401	Martin O'Malley	Dem.	4	Jan. 2015	150,000
Massachusetts	Boston, 02133	Deval Patrick	Dem.	4	Jan. 2015	140,535
Michigan	Lansing, 48909	Rick Snyder	Rep.	4	Jan. 2015	177,000
Minnesota	St. Paul, 55155	Mark Dayton	Dem.	4	Jan. 2015	120,303
Mississippi	Jackson, 39205	Haley Barbour	Rep.	4	Jan. 2012	122,160
Missouri	Jefferson City, 65102	Jay Nixon	Dem.	4	Jan. 2013	133,821
Montana	Helena, 59620	Brian Schweitzer	Dem.	4	Jan. 2013	100,121
Nebraska	Lincoln, 68509	David Heineman	Rep.	4	Jan. 2015	105,000
Nevada	Carson City, 89701	Brian Sandoval	Rep.	4	Jan. 2015	141,000
New Hampshire	Concord, 03301	John H. Lynch	Dem.	2	Jan. 2013	113,834
New Jersey	Trenton, 08625	Chris Christie	Rep.	4	Jan. 2014	175,000
New Mexico	Santa Fe, 87300	Susana Martinez	Rep.	4	Jan. 2015	110,000
New York	Albany, 12224	Andrew Cuomo	Dem.	4	Jan. 2015	179,000
North Carolina	Raleigh, 27699	Beverly Perdue	Dem.	4	Jan. 2013	139,590
North Dakota	Bismarck, 58505	Jack Dalrymple	Rep.	4	Dec. 2012	105,036
Ohio	Columbus, 43215	John Kasich	Rep.	4	Jan. 2015	144,269
Oklahoma	Oklahoma City, 73105	Mary Fallin	Rep.	4	Jan. 2015	147,000
Oregon	Salem, 97301	John Kitzhaber	Dem.	4	Jan. 2015	93,600
Pennsylvania	Harrisburg, 17120	Tom Corbett	Rep.	4	Jan. 2015	174,914
Rhode Island	Providence, 02903	Lincoln Chafee	Ind.	4	Jan. 2015	117,817
South Carolina	Columbia, 29201	Nikki R. Haley	Rep.	4	Jan. 2015	106,078
South Dakota	Pierre, 57501	Dennis Daugaard	Rep.	4	Jan. 2015	115,331
Tennessee	Nashville, 37243	Bill Haslam	Rep.	4	Jan. 2015	170,340
Texas	Austin, 78711	Rick Perry	Rep.	4	Jan. 2015	150,000
Utah	Salt Lake City, 84114	Gary R. Herbert	Rep.	4	Jan. 2013	109,900
Vermont	Montpelier, 05609	Peter Shumlin	Dem.	2	Jan. 2013	142,542
Virginia	Richmond, 23219	Bob McDonnell	Rep.	4	Jan. 2014	175,000
Washington	Olympia, 98504	Christine Gregoire	Dem.	4	Jan. 2013	166,891
West Virginia	Charleston, 25305	Earl Ray Tomblin	Dem.	4	Jan. 2013	95,000
Wisconsin	Madison, 53707	Scott Walker	Rep.	4	Jan. 2015	137,092
Wyoming	Cheyenne, 82002	Matthew Mead	Rep.	4	Jan. 2015	105,000

Note: Kentucky, Massachusetts, Pennsylvania, and Virginia are self-designated commonwealths. (1) Reflects a voluntary 10% salary reduction.

Governors of U.S. Commonwealths and Territories

Commonwealth/ Territory	Capital, ZIP code	Governor	Party	Term years	Term expires	Annual salary
American Samoa	Pago Pago, 96799	Togiola T.A. Tulafono	Dem.	4	Jan. 2013	$50,000
Guam	Agana, 96932	Eddie Calvo	Rep.	4	Jan. 2015	90,000
Northern Mariana Islands	Saipan, 96950	Benígno Fitial	Rep.	4	Jan. 2015	70,000
Puerto Rico	San Juan, 00902	Luis G. Fortuño	PNP[1]	4	Jan. 2013	70,000
Virgin Islands	St. Thomas, 00802	John deJongh Jr.	Dem.	4	Jan. 2015	80,000

(1) New Progressive Party (pro-statehood). Gov. Fortuño is also a registered Republican.

U.S. SUPREME COURT

The U.S. Supreme Court's 2010-11 term began Oct. 4, 2010, and concluded June 27, 2011, for its summer recess. The justices decided 82 cases (75 of which carried signed opinions) and issued 16 rulings (20%) by a 5-4 majority.

Membership. Chief Justice John G. Roberts Jr. presided over his sixth full term on the court. The eight associate justices, by order of seniority, were Antonin Scalia, Anthony M. Kennedy, Clarence Thomas, Ruth Bader Ginsburg, Stephen G. Breyer, Samuel A. Alito Jr., Sonia Sotomayor, and Elena Kagan, who served her first term as long-serving Associate Justice John Paul Stevens's replacement after being sworn in by Chief Justice Roberts Aug. 7, 2010. Kagan recused herself from about one-third of the Court's decisions due to her previous involvement in those cases as solicitor general.

In 2010-11, Roberts, Scalia, Thomas, and Alito tended to vote together as a conservative bloc, while Ginsburg, Breyer, Sotomayor, and Kagan comprised the court's liberal wing. Kennedy was often the swing vote on key 5-4 rulings, but in 10 decisions out of 14, he voted with conservative members on cases that were divided along ideological lines. Associate Justice Kennedy was in the majority 94% of the time; Chief Justice Roberts was in the majority 91% of the time.

Following are summaries of major decisions issued during the 2010-11 term. Detailed information on Supreme Court activities and opinions may be accessed at www.supremecourtus.gov. A more extensive archive of recent and historic rulings is available through Cornell Law School's Legal Information Institute: www.law.cornell.edu/supct/.

Notable Supreme Court Decisions, 2010-11

Note: The columns on the right provide information on how each justice voted. Gray shading indicates a justice who was part of the majority; black indicates a justice recused herself or otherwise did not participate in the decision. MO = justice authored majority opinion; CO = justice authored concurring opinion; DO = justice authored dissenting opinion; CD in part = justice authored opinion containing both concurring and dissenting opinions.

Business

The Supreme Court Apr. 27 ruled, 5-4, that state courts could not override contract clauses that prevented customers from bringing class-action lawsuits against companies. The case was *AT&T Mobility LLC v. Concepcion*.

The court June 20 blocked a massive class-action gender-discrimination lawsuit that had been brought against retail giant Wal-Mart. In a 5-4 decision, the court ruled that the 1.5 mil current and former female employees who had been potentially affected by the suit could not unite to file a common complaint because they had failed to show that Wal-Mart had instituted a company-wide discrimination policy. The case was *Wal-Mart Stores, Inc. v. Dukes*.

The court June 23 ruled, 5-4, that generic drug makers could not be sued under state law for failing to update their drug labels with warnings of dangerous side effects. The case was *Pliva Inc. v. Mensing*.

Environment

In a unanimous decision, the Supreme Court June 20 ruled, 8-0, to block a suit brought by six states and others to force utilities to reduce their greenhouse gas emissions. The court said the suit was preempted by the Clean Air Act, which gave the federal Environmental Protection Agency (EPA) the authority to regulate greenhouse gas emissions. The case was *American Electric Power Co., Inc. v. Connecticut*.

Free Speech

In *Snyder v. Phelps*, the Supreme Court Mar. 2 ruled, 8-1, that the father of a Marine killed in Iraq could not sue an antigay church whose members had held protests at his son's funeral denouncing homosexuals and the U.S. military. The court said the protests were protected by the free speech rights enshrined in the First Amendment.

The Supreme Court June 27 ruled, 7-2, to strike down a California law that banned minors from buying violent video games, saying it violated the First Amendment's guarantees of free speech. The case was *Brown v. Entertainment Merchants Association*.

The court June 27 ruled, 5-4, to strike down a provision of an Arizona campaign finance law that provided matching funds to publicly financed candidates facing wealthier opponents who raised money from private sources or were supported by independent groups. The court said the threat of matching funds inhibited privately financed candidates and independent groups from spending money on electioneering, thus violating their free speech rights. The decision consolidated the cases *Arizona Free Enterprise Club v. Bennett* and *McComish v. Bennett*.

Immigration

The Supreme Court May 26 ruled, 5-3, to uphold an Arizona law that allowed the state to revoke a business's license if it was twice found to have knowingly hired illegal immigrants. The decision, *Chamber of Commerce v. Whiting*, was seen as a victory for Arizona and other states that had moved more aggressively than the federal government to crack down on the hiring of illegal immigrants.

Inmates' Rights

The Supreme Court Mar. 29 ruled, 5-4, to dismiss a $14 mil jury award given to an exonerated death row inmate who had sued the district attorney's office in New Orleans, LA, for withholding evidence that would have proved his innocence at trial. The case was *Connick v. Thompson*.

The Supreme Court May 23 ruled, 5-4, to uphold a lower court ruling ordering California to release tens of thousands of convicts from state prisons. The majority said California's severely overcrowded prisons had led to "needless suffering and death," violating the Eighth Amendment's ban on cruel and unusual punishment. The case was *Brown v. Plata*.

Religion

The Supreme Court Apr. 4 ruled, 5-4, that Arizona taxpayers did not have legal standing to sue the state for offering a tax credit to those who made donations to private schools, including religious schools. The court in its decision consolidated two cases related to Arizona's policy, *Arizona Christian School Tuition Organization v. Winn* and *Garriott v. Winn*.

Case	Kagan	Sotomayor	Breyer	Ginsburg	Kennedy	Scalia	Thomas	Roberts	Alito
Business									
AT&T Mobility LLC v. Concepcion			DO			MO	CO		
Wal-Mart Stores, Inc. v. Dukes				CD in part		MO			
Pliva Inc. v. Mensing		DO					MO		
Environment									
American Electric Power Co. v. Connecticut		(recused)				MO			CO
Free Speech									
Snyder v. Phelps				CO				MO	DO
Brown v. Entertainment Merchants Assn.				DO		MO	DO		CO
Arizona Free Enterprise Club v. Bennett	DO							MO	
Immigration									
Chamber of Commerce v. Whiting	(recused)	DO	DO					MO	
Inmates' Rights									
Connick v. Thompson				DO		CO	MO		
Brown v. Plata					MO	DO			DO
Religion									
Arizona Christian School Tuition Org. v. Winn	DO					MO	CO		

NOTABLE QUOTES, 2011

National News

"The people voted to end business as usual, and today we begin to carry out their instructions."
—Newly installed House Speaker John Boehner (R, OH) Jan. 5, 2011, following Nov. 2010 elections that gave Republicans the House majority.

"In 30 minutes, 18 state senators undid 50 years of civil rights in Wisconsin."
—Mark Miller (D), Wisconsin state senate minority leader, after Republicans Mar. 9 passed a bill restricting collective bargaining by public employee unions.

"We can't keep kicking this can down the road. The president has punted."
—U.S. Rep. Paul Ryan (R, WI), contending Apr. 3 that Pres. Obama was not seriously addressing the nation's debt problem.

"It was like Dorothy in The Wizard of Oz. I just held my little dogs and prayed."
—Sharon Blue, on the tornadoes that devastated her Alabama community and many others in southeastern states, Apr. 25-28.

"It is in the DNA of our great country to reach for the stars and explore. We must not stop."
—Mark Kelly, mission commander of space shuttle Endeavour, which lifted off for the last time May 16. Kelly's wife, U.S. Rep. Gabrielle Giffords (D, AZ) was recuperating from a brain injury suffered in a mass shooting on Jan. 8.

"We're running out of runway. We're almost at the edge."
—U.S. Treasury Sec. Timothy Geithner, July 24, referring to the stalemate in Congress over raising the debt ceiling limit, eight days before the deadline to avoid U.S. government default.

"This seems like it's a prank to make fun of my name. You know, when you're named Weiner, that happens a lot."
—U.S. Rep. Anthony Weiner (D, NY), denying responsibility June 1 for a lewd photo; he later admitted having had inappropriate online exchanges and resigned.

"The downgrade reflects our view that the effectiveness, stability, and predictability of American policymaking and political institutions have weakened at a time of ongoing fiscal and economic challenge."
—From a Standard & Poor's statement explaining the rating agency's Aug. 5 downgrade of the U.S.'s sovereign credit rating.

"My friends and I have been coddled long enough by a billionaire-friendly Congress."
—Warren Buffett, Berkshire-Hathaway chairman and CEO and one of the world's richest people, in a New York Times op-ed, Aug. 14.

"We no longer search for the best ideas or the best policies . . . Now you are either an ally or a traitor."
—Longtime U.S. Rep. Jim Cooper (D, TN), criticizing Congress as dysfunctional in the New York Times Sept. 5.

"This is not class warfare—it's math."
—Pres. Barack Obama, Sept. 19, defending a plan to reduce the deficit and pay for his proposed jobs bill by increasing taxes on the rich.

Around the World

"Today we are proud of Egyptians. We have restored our rights, restored our freedom, and what we have begun cannot be reversed."
—Mohamed ElBaradei, Nobel laureate and diplomat, speaking to antigovernment protesters in Cairo's Tahrir Square, Jan. 30.

"If the Queen asks you to a party, you say yes. If the Italian prime minister asks you to a party, it's probably safe to say no. "
—British Prime Min. David Cameron Feb. 10, in a jibe at Italian Prime Min. Silvio Berlusconi for his involvement in several sex scandals.

"He has to leave as soon as possible. He has to stop killing the Libyan people."
—Ibrahim Dabbashi, Libya's deputy ambassador to the UN, at a news conference Feb. 21, defecting from the government of Libyan leader Muammar al-Qaddafi.

"The current situation of the earthquake, tsunami, and the nuclear plants is in a way the most severe crisis in the past 65 years since World War II."
—Japanese Prime Min. Naoto Kan, addressing the nation after a Mar. 11 earthquake, Japan's biggest quake on record. He later resigned amid controversy over his handling of the disaster.

"This assault . . . is by a bunch of fascists who will end up in the dustbin of history."
—Libyan leader Muammar al-Qaddafi, Mar. 22, condemning NATO air strikes amid a spreading revolt against his rule.

"We oppose any country using human rights issues as an excuse to interfere in China's domestic affairs."
—A Chinese foreign ministry spokesman, speaking on Apr. 26 ahead of U.S.-China talks on human rights.

"And on nights like this one, we can say to those families who have lost loved ones to al-Qaeda's terror: Justice has been done."
—Pres. Obama announcing May 1 that al-Qaeda leader Osama bin Laden was killed in a U.S. Navy SEALs operation in Pakistan.

"We are right, we have the law, and we have the strength. We will win."
—Mexican Pres. Felipe Calderon, refusing to abandon the government's war on drug cartels May 5, despite the thousands of lives lost.

"There is only one act of patriotism: consensus and cooperation. . . . Fiscal suicide is not an alternative."
—Elsa Papadimitriou, an opposition legislator, explaining June 29 why she was voting for bitterly contested austerity measures to deal with Greece's ongoing debt crisis.

"This is the most humble day of my life."
—Rupert Murdoch, chairman and CEO of News Corp., during a British parliamentary hearing July 19 over a phone-hacking scandal involving the company's News of the World tabloid.

"He was just an ordinary Norwegian, a well-behaved boy."
—Tove Oevermo, former stepmother of Anders Behring Breivik, who admitted responsibility for the July 22 terrorist attacks in Norway that killed more than 70 people.

"[I]t was a moral weakness, a moral mistake, and I'm not proud of this."
—Former IMF head Dominique Strauss-Kahn, in an interview Sept. 18, 4 months after his arrest for rape in New York City, May 14. Criminal charges were dropped.

People

"I for one welcome our new computer overlords."
—Ken Jennings, a former Jeopardy! champion, writing on his "Final Jeopardy" screen, Feb. 16; he and another former champion were soundly defeated in a match against Watson, a specially programmed computer.

"The only thing I'm addicted to is winning."
—Actor Charlie Sheen, in part of a long rant on the Alex Jones Radio Show, Feb. 24. Sheen was ultimately fired from his lead role on the CBS sitcom Two and a Half Men.

"While I deserve your attention and criticism, my family does not."
—Former California Gov. Arnold Schwarzenegger, publicly admitting, May 17, that he had fathered a child more than a decade ago with a member of his household staff.

"You and this show have been the great love of my life."
—Oprah Winfrey, to her studio audience in Chicago, May 25, ending her TV show's 25th and final season.

"I did not say she was innocent. I just said there was not enough evidence . . . we were sick to our stomach to get that verdict."
—Jennifer Ford, juror in the high-profile Casey Anthony trial, on the verdict July 5 that acquitted Anthony of murdering her 2-year-old daughter.

"We feel a little more human today."
—Ray Durand, age 68, shortly after marrying his partner of 42 years July 24, the day same-sex marriage became legal in New York state.

"I'm paying with my life for things that I didn't do."
—Former American exchange student Amanda Knox speaking before an Italian appeals court, which Oct. 3 overturned her conviction for the 2007 murder of her British apartment-mate Meredith Kercher.

"[T]here may be no greater tribute to Steve's success than the fact that much of the world learned of his passing on a device he invented."
—Pres. Obama, in tribute to Apple co-founder Steve Jobs, who died Oct. 5.

The Goose Is Cooked

Captain Chesley "Sully" Sullenberger and Flight 1549 were forced to make a memorable landing in the Hudson River in Jan. 2009, narrowly averting a disastrous crash. The engine failure that forced the landing was caused by the plane's engines colliding with Canada geese. The birds didn't survive the incident, but about 25,000 of their kind remained in the New York metropolitan area.

The U.S. Dept. of Agriculture (USDA) began taking steps to control the Canada goose population by conducting mass exterminations of the geese near New York City airports and disposing of the remains in landfills. Animal rights activists, who would have preferred a non-lethal solution, protested. Others, including hunters in the community, pointed out that the USDA was wasting perfectly good poultry (and targets).

New York state's Dept. of Environmental Protection decided that was a fair point, so in 2011, workers began catching Canada geese in the New York City area and sending them to food banks. New York's food banks won't be set up to process the meat until 2012. In the meantime, Pennsylvania food banks have been accepting the culled geese for distribution. The skies above New York are safer, and everyone wins—except, perhaps, the Canada geese.

Actually, It's *Speed 2* That Kills

What would it take to rename a town of 45 people in the Australian outback? Just a good cause … plus 10,000 "likes" on Facebook. Deaths on rural roads in the Australian state of Victoria increased significantly in 2010, and efforts to get drivers to slow down had mostly been fruitless. So the Victoria Transport Accident Commission (TAC) went to the tiny town of Speed (about 250 miles north of Melbourne) with a proposal: Would residents agree to rename the town SpeedKills for a month if 10,000 Facebook users joined a group for that purpose? The TAC would make a donation to the local Lions Club, and the Internet and television publicity might get people to slow down. The town agreed.

The campaign ended up with more than 30,000 "likes" by Feb. 18, 2011, when the town officially changed its name. Local farmer Phil Down even changed his name to Phil Slow Down for the month. The TAC hoped to spread the idea around the world, finding five small towns named Speed in the United States that it hoped would also consider name changes.

Snake, Snake, Oh, It's a Snake...

When a 20-inch Egyptian cobra went missing from New York City's Bronx Zoo Mar. 25, 2011, it would have been easy to respond with panic. Cobras are highly venomous, and one bite can kill a person in about 15 minutes. Zoo officials closed and secured the reptile house, confident that it was still inside … somewhere.

The unofficial @BronxZoosCobra Twitter account begged to differ. In the course of a few days, it picked up more than 200,000 followers with updates like "Does anyone know if the Whole Foods in Columbus Circle sells organic mice?" and "If you see a bag of peanuts inexplicably moving along the ground at Yankee Stadium today. Just ignore it. It's probably nothing."

After several days of fun and mild paranoia among nearby residents, the cobra was found Mar. 31 in a dark corner of the reptile house. On Apr. 7, a poll run by the zoo gave her a name: Mia, short for "Missing In Action." The unofficial Twitter account had the last word: "So, the vote is in. They want to name me Mia. But in my heart I'll always know that my true name is Mrs. Justin Bieber."

Want Gold? Here's the Scoop

New Taipei City, Taiwan, had a problem keeping the sidewalks clean: too many dog owners just didn't clean up after their pets, and there was no real incentive for them to change. But on Aug. 1, 2011, the city began offering an incentive in the form of free garbage bags, which could be exchanged for raffle tickets when turned in filled with dog waste. The top prize, to be awarded in Oct. 2011, would be a gold ingot worth about $2,000. Collectors didn't have to own the dogs themselves; whoever turned in waste-deposits would get a ticket.

Taichung, Taiwan, tried a similar incentive in 2009, offering small shopping vouchers for each kilogram of waste, but it was ridiculed and ultimately unsuccessful. New Taipei City hoped its large prize would be more of a draw, especially with the ever increasing value of gold.

What Is Watson?

Nearly 15 years have passed since IBM's Deep Blue computer impressed nonprogrammers around the world by beating world chess champion Garry Kasparov in a six-game match. IBM couldn't just rest on its laurels, so company researchers invented Watson—a supercomputer designed to combine complex linguistic analysis and a strong sense of wordplay with encyclopedic knowledge—to challenge *Jeopardy!* champions. The supercomputer's true test aired on TV Feb. 14-16, 2011, when Watson trounced Ken Jennings and Brad Rutter—the most successful *Jeopardy!* contestants of all time—in a tournament-style match. Apologists for humans might note that Watson had superior buzzer-clicking reflexes. Meanwhile, Jennings and Rutter were better at the wordplay sometimes specified by a category. For example, given a clue about a type of loose-fitting dress in the category On The Keyboard, Watson asked, "What is a chemise?" instead of "shift." And in the first Final Jeopardy, Watson resorted to "What is Toronto?????" in answering a clue in the category U.S. Cities. But these were exceptions, and Watson ended the tournament with $77,147, far ahead of Jennings ($24,000) and Rutter ($21,600).

The winnings went to charity, and Watson went to medical school: in cooperation with WellPoint, Inc., IBM plans to use Watson technology to assist doctors and nurses in diagnosing patients' conditions and recommending treatments.

Ve Haff Vays of Making You Talk (Like This)

If you wanted to change your accent, you could take elocution lessons, live abroad, or spend years immersing yourself in another language. Or you could just go to the dentist. Karen Butler, a 56-year-old Oregon tax consultant, went under general anesthesia to have teeth removed in late 2009. When she woke up, she "talked funny," with an accent verging on cartoonish Transylvanian.

The dentist told Butler, a lifelong American who has never traveled to Europe, that she'd talk normally again once she got used to her new dentures. But by Apr. 2011, 18 months after the surgery, she still didn't sound anything like her old self. Strangers think she sounds British, perhaps Irish or Scottish.

Butler is the first known case in Oregon of foreign accent syndrome, a rare condition with fewer than 100 documented cases worldwide. Historically, the condition results from a brain injury, suggesting that she might have had a minor stroke. Fortunately, Butler enjoys her new accent—it's a good conversation starter.

Braaaaaaaaaaaaaaaains...

The Centers for Disease Control and Prevention (CDC), a division of the U.S. Dept. of Health and Human Services, thinks of everything. As part of its mission to protect the public's health, the CDC website includes tips to prepare people for epidemics, natural disasters, biological warfare, and naturally, the inevitable zombie apocalypse. "You may laugh now," explains one of the zombie pages, originally posted May 16, 2011, on the CDC Public Health Matters blog, "but when it happens you'll be happy you read this."

After a quick overview of where zombies come from (with citations from the movie *Night of the Living Dead*), the CDC provided a list of items to have on hand in the event of a zombie visitation: water, food, medications, duct tape, a battery-powered radio—all of which happen to be good things to have around for more common emergencies. CDC experts don't specifically mention defensive weaponry or flaming torches, preferring that citizens leave any zombie-hunting to trained professionals in the police, military, and "your local zombie response team."

CDC officials had hoped to get more people to check out the useful information available on their website, and they certainly managed that: high Internet traffic crashed the site as word spread.

Catch the Wave

It is a truth universally acknowledged that parents of adolescents delight in embarrassing their children. Dale Price, of American Fork, UT, is simply better at it than most. On the first day of the 2010-11 school year, Price waved at his 10th-grade son Rain's bus as it went by their home. That probably would have been a one-time occurrence, except Price overheard Rain asking his mother to keep his father from doing it again. Price took that as a challenge. The next day, he waved at the bus again, this time while wearing a San Diego Chargers helmet and jersey. Price went on to wave at the bus every day that school year and never wore the same outfit twice, dressing as a referee, a zombie, a bride, a ninja, a doctor, Batgirl, and the Little Mermaid. A cardboard cutout took his place one day when he was sick, and his younger son stood in as "Mini Me" on another day, but those were the only exceptions. After the school year ended, Price decided one year of waving was enough. But all of the past costumes can be seen online at waveatthebus.blogspot.com. There's also a Wave at the Bus iPhone or iPad app (proceeds go to Rain's college fund).

HISTORICAL ANNIVERSARIES

1912 – 100 Years Ago

The Republic of China is established Jan. 1; the Kuomintang party is founded Aug. 25.

The U.S. admits a 47th state, New Mexico, Jan. 6, and a 48th state, Arizona, Feb. 14.

On its maiden voyage, the HMS *Titanic* strikes an iceberg in the N Atlantic Apr. 14 and sinks several hours later Apr. 15; lacking adequate lifeboats, 1,503 of 2,224 people aboard die.

After unsuccessfully pursuing the Republican nomination for president, former Pres. Theodore Roosevelt is nominated in Aug. by the newly formed Progressive "Bull Moose" Party. Roosevelt is shot but not seriously injured by a would-be assassin while campaigning in Milwaukee, WI, Oct. 14.

The First Balkan War begins as Montenegro declares war on Turkey Oct. 8; Greece, Bulgaria, and Serbia join the fight Oct. 17.

With the Republican vote split by incumbent Pres. William Howard Taft and former Pres. Roosevelt, Democratic nominee New Jersey Gov. Woodrow Wilson is elected president Nov. 5.

Art. Marc Chagall's *Golgotha*; Marcel Duchamp's *Nu descendant un escalier no. 2* [*Nude Descending a Staircase, No. 2*]; Egon Schiele's *Dirne* [*Prostitute*]; John Singer Sargent's *In the Generalife*; Frank Lloyd Wright's clerestory windows in his Avery Coonley Playhouse.

Film. *Les Amours de la reine Élisabeth* starring Sarah Bernhardt; *From the Manger to the Cross*; *The Land Beyond the Sunset*.

Literature. Edgar Rice Burroughs's *Tarzan of the Apes*; Sir Arthur Conan Doyle's *The Lost World*; Thomas Mann's *Der Tod in Venedig* [*Death in Venice*].

Music. Sergei Prokofiev completes *Piano Concerto No. 1 in D-flat Major*; Gustav Mahler's *Symphony No. 9* and Arnold Schoenberg's *Pierrot Lunaire* premiere.

Nonfiction. James Harvey Robinson's *The New History*; Bertrand Russell's *The Problems of Philosophy*.

Pop music. "My Melancholy Baby," "When Irish Eyes Are Smiling," W. C. Handy's "The Memphis Blues," and Jack Judge and Harry Williams's "It's a Long Way to Tipperary" are published.

Science and technology. Casimir Funk introduces the word "vitamine." MDMA (later known as ecstasy) is synthesized by Merck pharmaceutical company.

Sports. Olympic Games are held in Stockholm, Sweden; American Jim Thorpe wins medals in pentathlon and decathlon; races are timed electronically for the first time. Fenway Park baseball stadium opens in Boston.

Theater. *Little Women*, *Peg O' My Heart*, and *Within the Law* are hits on Broadway.

Miscellaneous. Russian newspaper *Pravda* is founded. The Girl Scouts is founded (as American Girl Guides).

1962 – 50 Years Ago

Former colonies and territories gaining independence include Western Samoa, Jan. 1; Rwanda and Burundi, both July 1; Jamaica, Aug. 6; Trinidad and Tobago, Aug. 31; and Uganda, Oct. 9.

Pres. John F. Kennedy Feb. 14 declares that U.S. military advisers in Vietnam would fire if fired upon but are not "combat troops in the generally understood sense of the word."

John H. Glenn Jr. becomes the first U.S. astronaut to orbit the Earth Feb. 20 in the Mercury capsule *Friendship 7*.

Gen. Ne Win overthrows the government of Burma in a non-violent military coup Mar. 2, beginning a 26-year rule; he nationalizes the banks and other major industries Mar. 28.

The U.S. Supreme Court rules against state-sanctioned school prayer June 25 in *Engel v. Vitale*.

Algeria gains independence July 5 after seven years of civil war and 132 years of French rule.

An earthquake in NW Iran kills more than 12,000 people and leaves 100,000 homeless.

Escorted by federal troops, James Meredith enrolls at the Univ. of Mississippi Oct. 1 as the institution's first black student.

In the wake of Europe's thalidomide tragedy, the U.S. Congress Oct. 3-4 passes a prescription drug regulation bill to safeguard against harmful and ineffective drugs.

The first meeting of the Second Vatican Council convenes Oct. 11 in Rome.

The Cuban missile crisis begins Oct. 22 as Pres. Kennedy orders a naval and air quarantine of Cuba in response to the presence of Soviet missile bases on the island. He and Soviet Premier Nikita Khrushchev agree Oct. 28 on a formula to end the standoff, narrowly avoiding war.

Art. Diane Arbus's *Child With Toy Hand Grenade in Central Park, N.Y.C.*; Eero Saarinen's TWA Terminal is completed; Andy Warhol exhibits pop-art work, including first paintings of Marilyn Monroe and Campbell's soup cans.

Film. *Dr. No*, starring Sean Connery, launches the James Bond movie franchise. *Lawrence of Arabia* starring Peter O'Toole, Alec Guinness, and Anthony Quinn; Stanley Kubrick's *Lolita*; *The Longest Day*; *The Manchurian Candidate*; John Ford's *The Man Who Shot Liberty Valance* starring James Stewart and John Wayne; *The Miracle Worker*; *The Music Man*; *Sweet Bird of Youth* starring Paul Newman; *To Kill a Mockingbird* starring Gregory Peck; *What Ever Happened to Baby Jane?* starring Bette Davis and Joan Crawford.

Literature. Jorge Luis Borges's *Labyrinths* (in English); Anthony Burgess's *A Clockwork Orange*; William Faulkner's *The Reivers*; Ian Fleming's *The Spy Who Loved Me*; Ken Kesey's *One Flew Over the Cuckoo's Nest*; Madeleine L'Engle's *A Wrinkle in Time*; Katherine Anne Porter's *Ship of Fools*; Kurt Vonnegut's *Mother Night*; Elie Wiesel's *Day*.

Music. Benjamin Britten's *War Requiem*; John Cage's *0'00"*; Dmitri Shostakovich's *Symphony No. 13* ("Babi Yar").

Nonfiction. Helen Gurley Brown's *Sex and the Single Girl*; Milton Friedman's *Capitalism and Freedom*; Barbara Tuchman's *The Guns of August*.

Pop music. The Beach Boys' "Surfin' Safari"; Tony Bennett's *I Left My Heart in San Francisco*; Ray Charles's "I Can't Stop Loving You"; Bob Dylan's eponymous debut album; The Four Seasons' "Big Girls Don't Cry" and "Sherry"; Henry Mancini's "The Days of Wine and Roses"; Elvis Presley's "Good Luck Charm" and "Return to Sender"; Neil Sedaka's "Breaking Up Is Hard to Do."

Science and technology. Rachel Carson's *Silent Spring* highlights pollution and environmental issues; Telstar satellite relays the first live transatlantic television broadcast.

Sports. Sonny Liston defeats Floyd Patterson in the first round of their heavyweight title fight. Wilt Chamberlain scores 100 points in a single game, setting an NBA record that still stands. Jack Nicklaus wins golf's U.S. Open, the first of 18 career major tournament wins.

Television. *The Bob Newhart Show* and *The Defenders* win Emmy awards; Johnny Carson takes over NBC's *Tonight Show* hosting duties; Walter Cronkite becomes anchor of the *CBS Evening News*.

Theater. Broadway hits include *A Funny Thing Happened on the Way to the Forum*, *I Can Get It for You Wholesale*, *Never Too Late*, *Stop the World—I Want to Get Off*, and *Who's Afraid of Virginia Woolf?*

Miscellaneous. The discount retail chain is born: Kmart, Target, and Walmart all open first stores.

1987 – 25 Years Ago

Pres. Ronald Reagan introduces the nation's first trillion-dollar budget Jan. 5.

The FDA gives fast-track approval Mar. 20 to AZT, the first drug shown effective in treating HIV and AIDS; Pres. Reagan makes his first extensive public remarks on the epidemic Apr. 1.

Joint congressional hearings investigate the Iran-Contra affair May 5-Aug. 3. Former National Security Council staff member Lt. Col. Oliver North states his belief that all his activities were authorized. Pres. Reagan, Aug. 12, denies knowing of diversion of funds to contras in Nicaragua.

Sen. Gary Hart (D, CO), the presumed frontrunner for the 1988 Democratic presidential nomination, announces May 8 that he would abandon his campaign after newspaper reports of infidelity.

Two Iraqi missiles, apparently fired accidentally, kill 37 American sailors on the USS *Stark* in the Persian Gulf, May 17.

Five Central American nations sign a regional peace plan Aug. 7 in Guatemala City that would end fighting in El Salvador, Nicaragua, and Guatemala.

The stock market crashes Oct. 19 with the Dow Jones Industrial Average plummeting a record 508 points to 1,738.

The U.S. Senate Oct. 23 rejects Pres. Reagan's nomination of Appellate Court Judge Robert H. Bork to the Supreme Court.

Pres. Reagan and Soviet leader Mikhail Gorbachev sign a pact to dismantle short- and mid-range missiles Dec. 8.

A Palestinian uprising begins Dec. 9 in Israeli-occupied Gaza and spreads to the West Bank; Israeli troops respond with force. Sheik Ahmed Yassin founds the Hamas movement.

South Korea holds its first direct presidential election in 16 years Dec. 16; Roh Tae Woo of the ruling Democratic Justice Party wins the presidency.

The Philippine ferry *Doña Paz* and oil tanker *Victor* collide in the Tablas Strait Dec. 20; 4,341 die.

Art. Gilbert and George's *Here*; Jenny Holzer's *I Am a Man*; Ed Ruscha's *Parts Per Trillion*.

Film. *Dirty Dancing*; *Fatal Attraction* starring Michael Douglas and Glenn Close; Stanley Kubrick's *Full Metal Jacket*; *Good Morning, Vietnam*; Bernardo Bertolucci's *The Last Emperor*; *Lethal Weapon* starring Mel Gibson and Danny Glover; *The Lost Boys*; *Moonstruck* starring Cher and Nicolas Cage; *Predator*; *The Princess Bride*; Joel and Ethan Coen's *Raising Arizona*; Mel Brooks's *Spaceballs*; Brian De Palma's

The Untouchables starring Kevin Costner, Sean Connery, and Robert De Niro; Oliver Stone's *Wall Street* starring Michael Douglas and Charlie Sheen; *The Witches of Eastwick*.

Literature. Tom Clancy's *Patriot Games*; Bret Easton Ellis's *The Rules of Attraction*; Fannie Flagg's *Fried Green Tomatoes at the Whistle Stop Cafe*; Stephen King's *Misery* and *The Tommyknockers*; Toni Morrison's *Beloved*; Rosamunde Pilcher's *The Shell Seekers*; Scott Turow's *Presumed Innocent*; Tom Wolfe's *The Bonfire of the Vanities*.

Music. John Adams's *Nixon in China*.

Nonfiction. Allan Bloom's *The Closing of the American Mind*; Randy Shilts's *And the Band Played On: Politics, People, and the AIDS Epidemic*; Peter Wright's *Spycatcher: The Candid Autobiography of a Senior Intelligence Officer*.

Pop music. Rick Astley's "Never Gonna Give You Up"; Bon Jovi's "Wanted Dead or Alive"; Guns 'n' Roses' *Appetite for Destruction*; Whitney Houston's "I Wanna Dance With Somebody (Who Loves Me)"; Michael Jackson's *Bad*; Los Lobos's "La Bamba"; George Michael's "Faith"; Pixies' *Come on Pilgrim*; Prince's *Sign o' the Times*; R.E.M.'s *Document*; Sonic Youth's *Sister*; U2's *The Joshua Tree*.

Science and technology. Astronomers Jan. 5 report witnessing a galaxy being born for the first time. The FDA approves Prozac for treatment of depression. Arcade game *Street Fighter* and Nintendo game *Legend of Zelda* are released in the U.S. for the first time.

Sports. Kansas City Royals outfielder Bo Jackson, the 1985 Heisman Trophy winner, signs a contract to play professional football for the L.A. Raiders. The NFL Players Association strikes; games scheduled for the third week are cancelled, and weeks 4-6 of the season are played by replacement players.

Television. The FOX network debuts in prime time; *The Simpsons* appears as a series of animated shorts on FOX's *The Tracey Ullman Show*. *A Different World*, *Full House*, *Married With Children*, *Star Trek: The Next Generation*, and *thirtysomething* premiere.

Theater. *Les Misérables* begins a 16-year run on Broadway; *Into the Woods* and *Fences* also make Broadway debuts.

Miscellaneous. Televangelist Jim Bakker resigns amid sex scandal. The "Baby M." custody dispute occupies newspaper headlines after surrogate Mary Beth Whitehead refuses to surrender parental rights.

WORLD ALMANAC EDITORS' PICKS
2011 Time Capsule

The editors of *The World Almanac* have selected the following items as representative of the year 2011.

- Twitter messages posted by Arab Spring protestors in Egypt, Tunisia, and other nations where activists organized against oppressive regimes throughout 2011.

- The flag of South Sudan, the world's newest nation, which became independent July 9, 2011, and Libya's new flag, which replaced dictator Muammar al-Qaddafi's all-green flag at Libya's embassies around the world beginning in Feb. 2011.

- Geiger counter readings from Japan's Fukushima Daiichi nuclear power plant, after a tsunami caused meltdown conditions at the 6-reactor facility in Mar. 2011.

- The much-discussed "toilet seat" hat worn by Princess Beatrice at the UK royal wedding of Prince William and Kate Middleton Apr. 29, 2011.

- A death certificate for Osama bin Laden and some of the items seized from the al-Qaeda terrorist organization leader's hideout in Abbottabad, Pakistan, after he was shot by U.S. Navy SEALs in a nighttime raid, May 1, 2011.

- A heat tile from space shuttle *Atlantis*, and a ticket on a Russian *Soyuz* spacecraft. *Soyuz* is the only way astronauts can travel to the International Space Station since *Atlantis* made its final flight July 8-21, 2011.

- The bat New York Yankee Derek Jeter used for his memorable 3,000th hit July 9, 2011, and the last ball Mariano Rivera threw in his record-setting 602nd save Sept. 19, 2011.

- The final edition of the UK weekly tabloid *News of the World*, which Rupert Murdoch shut down July 10, 2011, because of the "phone hacking" scandal that engulfed his News Corp. media empire.

- A solar panel from Solyndra, the green-energy company favored by the Obama administration with $535-million worth of loan guarantees before it went bankrupt Aug. 31, 2011.

- A copy of the NFL labor agreement that finally brought four months of disputes between players and owners to an end and allowed the 2011 NFL season to begin as scheduled Sept. 8, 2011.

- "We are the 99%" sign from the Occupy Wall Street demonstrations, which began in New York City Sept. 17, 2011.

- The iPhone 4S, announced by Apple the day before the company's co-founder and chairman, computer pioneer Steve Jobs, died Oct. 5, 2011.

ECONOMICS

Index of Leading Economic Indicators
Source: The Conference Board

The index of leading economic indicators is used to project the U.S. economy's performance. The index is made up of 10 measurements of economic activity that tend to change direction in advance of the overall economy. The index has predicted economic downturns from 8 to 20 months in advance and recoveries from 1 to 10 months in advance; however, it can be inconsistent, and has occasionally shown false signals of recessions. The components that make up the Leading Economic Index are listed below, along with their weighted percentages.

- Money supply: M-2, adjusted for inflation: 32.30%
- Average weekly hours of production workers in manufacturing: 27.37%
- Interest rate spread, 10-yr Treasury bonds less federal funds: 10.52%
- Manufacturers' new orders for consumer goods and materials, adjusted for inflation: 8.17%
- Vendor performance (slower deliveries diffusion index): 7.17%

- New private housing units authorized by local building permits: 3.70%
- Average weekly initial claims for unemployment insurance, state programs: 3.22%
- Consumer expectations (researched by Univ. of Michigan): 2.96%
- Manufacturers' new orders, nondefense capital goods industries, adjusted for inflation: 2.64%
- Stock prices, 500 common stocks: 1.95%

U.S. Gross Domestic Product, Gross National Product, Net National Product, National Income, and Personal Income, 1970-2010
Source: Bureau of Economic Analysis, U.S. Dept. of Commerce
(in billions of current dollars, revised)

	1970	1980	1990	2000	2005	2008	2009	2010
Gross domestic product	$1,038.3	$2,788.1	$5,800.5	$9,951.5	$12,623.0	$14,291.5	$13,939.0	$14,526.5
Gross national product	1,044.7	2,822.3	5,835.0	9,989.2	12,720.1	14,460.7	14,091.2	14,715.9
Less: Consumption of fixed capital	108.3	344.1	691.2	1,184.3	1,541.4	1,854.1	1,866.2	1,874.9
Net national product	936.4	2,478.2	5,143.7	8,804.9	11,178.7	12,606.6	12,225.0	12,841.0
Less: Statistical discrepancy	6.9	45.3	84.2	-134.0	-95.1	-2.4	77.4	0.8
Equals: National income	929.5	2,433.0	5,059.5	8,938.9	11,273.8	12,609.1	12,147.6	12,840.1
Less: Corporate profits with inventory valuation and capital consumption adjustments	82.5	201.4	434.4	819.2	1,456.1	1,248.4	1,362.0	1,800.1
Taxes on production and imports less subsidies[1]	86.6	190.5	398.0	662.7	869.3	985.7	958.2	996.7
Contributions for government social insurance	46.4	166.2	410.1	705.8	872.7	987.3	964.1	986.8
Net interest and miscellaneous payments on assets	39.1	181.8	444.2	539.3	543.0	870.1	656.7	564.3
Business current transfer payments (net)	4.5	14.7	40.1	87.0	95.9	123.0	132.0	136.7
Current surplus of government enterprises	0.0	-5.1	1.6	9.1	-3.5	-16.0	-14.9	-15.7
Wage accruals less disbursements	0.0	0.0	0.1	0.0	5.0	-5.0	5.0	0.0
Plus: Personal income receipts on assets	93.5	338.7	920.8	1,360.7	1,542.0	2,165.4	1,707.7	1,721.2
Personal current transfer receipts	74.7	279.5	594.9	1,083.0	1,508.6	1,879.2	2,138.1	2,281.2
Equals: Personal income	838.6	2,301.5	4,846.7	8,559.4	10,485.9	12,460.2	11,930.2	12,373.5

(1) Subsidies are included net of the current surplus of government enterprises.

U.S. Gross Domestic Product, 2000-11
Source: Bureau of Economic Analysis, U.S. Dept. of Commerce

	Billions of current dollars				Billions of constant (2005) dollars			
	2000	2005	2010	2011[1]	2000	2005	2010	2011[1]
Gross domestic product	$9,951.5	$12,623.0	$14,526.5	$14,996.8	$11,216.4	$12,623.0	$13,088.0	$13,260.5
Personal consumption expenditures	6,830.4	8,803.5	10,245.5	10,667.0	7,604.6	8,803.5	9,220.9	9,386.7
Goods	2,459.1	3,076.7	3,387.0	3,624.4	2,518.2	3,076.7	3,230.7	3,332.8
Durable goods	915.8	1,123.4	1,085.5	1,144.3	818.0	1,123.4	1,188.3	1,260.8
Nondurable goods	1,543.4	1,953.4	2,301.5	2,480.0	1,714.5	1,953.4	2,041.3	2,077.5
Services	4,371.2	5,726.8	6,858.5	7,042.6	5,093.6	5,726.8	5,991.8	6,059.7
Gross private domestic investment	1,772.2	2,172.3	1,795.1	1,895.7	1,963.1	2,172.3	1,714.9	1,778.1
Fixed investment	1,717.7	2,122.3	1,728.2	1,840.0	1,906.8	2,122.3	1,648.4	1,734.6
Nonresidential	1,268.7	1,347.3	1,390.1	1,504.9	1,311.3	1,347.3	1,319.2	1,411.7
Structures	318.1	351.8	374.4	400.2	440.0	351.8	309.1	317.3
Equipment and software	950.5	995.6	1,015.7	1,104.8	889.2	995.6	1,019.4	1,107.6
Residential	449.0	775.0	338.1	335.1	580.0	775.0	330.8	323.8
Change in private inventories	54.5	50.0	66.9	55.6	60.2	50.0	58.8	40.6
Net exports of goods and services	-382.1	-722.7	-516.9	-604.2	-451.3	-722.7	-421.8	-421.3
Exports	1,093.2	1,305.1	1,839.8	2,082.2	1,187.4	1,305.1	1,663.2	1,762.8
Goods	784.3	906.1	1,277.8	1,474.1	843.4	906.1	1,164.9	1,243.9
Services	308.9	399.0	562.0	608.0	343.5	399.0	498.8	519.5
Imports	1,475.3	2,027.8	2,356.7	2,686.4	1,638.7	2,027.8	2,085.0	2,184.0
Goods	1,246.5	1,708.0	1,947.3	2,260.1	1,366.7	1,708.0	1,729.3	1,827.1
Services	228.8	319.8	409.4	426.2	271.7	319.8	357.4	358.9
Government consumption expenditures and gross investment	1,731.0	2,369.9	3,002.8	3,038.3	2,097.8	2,369.9	2,556.8	2,508.4
Federal	576.1	876.3	1,222.8	1,237.1	698.1	876.3	1,075.9	1,058.5
National defense	371.0	589.0	819.2	830.6	453.5	589.0	718.3	706.0
Nondefense	205.0	287.3	403.6	406.5	244.4	287.3	357.7	352.5
State and local	1,154.9	1,493.6	1,780.0	1,801.2	1,400.1	1,493.6	1,487.0	1,456.0

(1) Second quarter.

U.S. Gross Domestic Product, 1930-2010

Source: Bureau of Economic Analysis, U.S. Dept. of Commerce

(in billions of current dollars)

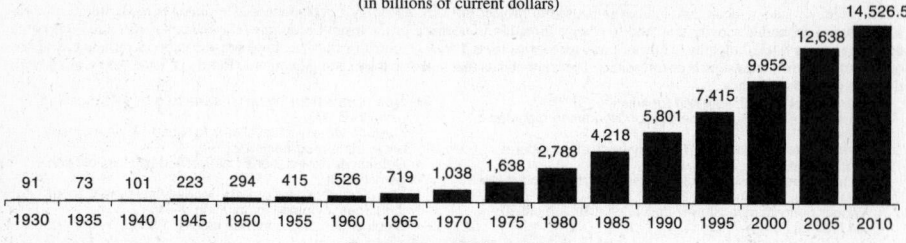

1930	1935	1940	1945	1950	1955	1960	1965	1970	1975	1980	1985	1990	1995	2000	2005	2010
91	73	101	223	294	415	526	719	1,038	1,638	2,788	4,218	5,801	7,415	9,952	12,638	14,526.5

Consumer Price Index

The Consumer Price Index (CPI) is a measure of the change in prices over time of one or more kinds of basic consumer goods and services.

From Jan. 1978, the Bureau of Labor Statistics began publishing CPIs for two population groups: (1) a CPI for all urban consumers (CPI-U), which covers about 87% of the total population; and (2) a CPI for urban wage earners and clerical workers (CPI-W), which covers about 32% of the total population. The CPI-U includes, in addition to wage earners and clerical workers, groups such as professional, managerial, and technical workers, the self-employed, short-term workers, the unemployed, retirees, and others not in the labor force.

The CPI is based on prices of food, clothing, shelter, and fuels; transportation fares; charges for doctors' and dentists' services; drug prices; and prices of other goods and services bought for day-to-day living. The index currently measures price changes from a designated reference period, 1982-84, which equals 100.0. Use of this reference period began in Jan. 1988.

U.S. Consumer Price Index, 1913-2010

Source: Bureau of Labor Statistics, U.S. Dept. of Labor

(Data are for all urban consumers. **1982-84 = 100**, unless otherwise noted.)

Year	All items	Apparel	Food and beverages	Housing	Transpor- tation	Medical care	Recreation[1]	Educ. & communi- cation[1]	Other goods & services
1913	9.9	14.9	—	—	—	—	—	—	—
1915	10.1	15.3	—	—	—	—	—	—	—
1920	20.0	43.1	—	—	—	—	—	—	—
1925	17.5	26.3	—	—	—	—	—	—	—
1930	16.7	24.2	—	—	—	—	—	—	—
1935	13.7	20.8	—	—	14.2	10.2	—	—	—
1940	14.0	21.8	—	—	14.2	10.4	—	—	—
1945	18.0	31.4	—	—	15.9	11.9	—	—	—
1950	24.1	40.3	—	—	22.7	15.1	—	—	—
1955	26.8	42.9	—	—	25.8	18.2	—	—	—
1960	29.6	45.7	—	—	29.8	22.3	—	—	—
1965	31.5	47.8	—	—	31.9	25.2	—	—	—
1970	38.8	59.2	40.1	36.4	37.5	34.0	—	—	40.9
1975	53.8	72.5	60.2	50.7	50.1	47.5	—	—	53.9
1980	82.4	90.9	86.7	81.1	83.1	74.9	—	—	75.2
1985	107.6	105.0	105.6	107.7	106.4	113.5	—	—	114.5
1990	130.7	124.1	132.1	128.5	120.5	162.8	—	—	159.0
1995	152.4	132.0	148.9	148.5	139.1	220.5	94.5	92.2	206.9
2000	172.2	129.6	168.4	169.6	153.3	260.8	103.3	102.5	271.1
2001	177.1	127.3	173.6	176.4	154.3	272.8	104.9	105.2	282.6
2002	179.9	124.0	176.8	180.3	152.9	285.6	106.2	107.9	293.2
2003	184.0	120.9	180.5	184.8	157.6	297.1	107.5	109.8	298.7
2004	188.9	120.4	186.6	189.5	163.1	310.1	108.6	111.6	304.7
2005	195.3	119.5	191.2	195.7	173.9	323.2	109.4	113.7	313.4
2006	201.6	119.5	195.7	203.2	180.9	336.2	110.9	116.8	321.7
2007	207.3	119.0	203.3	209.6	184.7	351.1	111.4	119.6	333.3
2008	215.3	118.9	214.2	216.2	195.5	364.1	113.3	123.6	345.4
2009	214.5	120.0	218.2	217.1	179.3	375.6	114.3	127.4	368.6
2010	218.1	119.5	220.0	216.3	193.4	388.4	113.3	129.9	381.3

— = Comparable data not available. (1) Dec. 1997 = 100.

Consumer Price Index, 1913-2010

Source: Bureau of Labor Statistics, U.S. Dept. of Labor

(Annual averages of monthly figures, specified for all urban consumers. **1982-84 = 100.**)

Until 2009, prices as measured by the U.S. Consumer Price Index had risen steadily since World War II. What cost $1.00 in 1982-84 cost about $0.10 in 1913, $0.18 in 1945, and $2.23 in 2010.

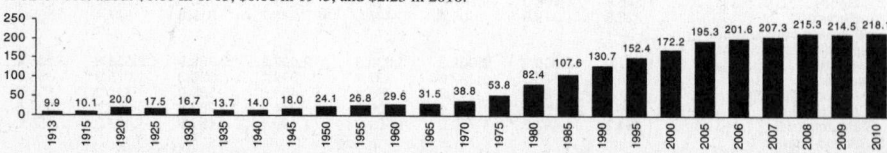

U.S. Consumer Price Indexes for Selected Items and Groups, 1970-2010

Source: Bureau of Labor Statistics, U.S. Dept. of Labor
(Annual averages of monthly figures, specified for all urban consumers. 1982-84 = 100, unless otherwise noted.)

	1970	1975	1980	1985	1990	1995	2000	2005	2006	2007	2008	2010
ALL ITEMS	38.8	53.8	82.4	107.6	130.7	152.4	172.2	195.3	201.6	207.3	215.3	218.1
Food and beverages	40.1	60.2	86.7	105.6	132.1	148.9	168.4	191.2	195.7	203.3	214.2	220.0
Food	39.2	59.8	86.8	105.6	132.4	148.4	167.8	190.7	195.2	202.9	214.1	219.6
Food at home	39.9	61.8	88.4	104.3	132.3	148.8	167.9	189.8	193.1	201.2	214.1	215.8
Cereals and bakery products	37.1	62.9	83.9	107.9	140.0	167.5	188.3	209.0	212.8	222.1	244.9	250.4
Meats, poultry, fish, and eggs	44.6	67.0	92.0	100.1	130.0	138.8	154.5	184.7	186.6	195.6	204.7	207.7
Dairy products	44.7	62.6	90.9	103.2	126.5	132.8	160.7	182.4	181.4	194.8	210.4	199.2
Fruits and vegetables	37.8	56.9	82.1	106.4	149.0	177.7	204.6	241.4	252.9	262.6	278.9	273.5
Sugar and sweets	30.5	65.3	90.5	105.8	124.7	137.5	154.0	165.2	171.5	176.8	186.6	201.2
Fats and oils	39.2	73.5	89.3	106.9	126.3	137.3	147.4	167.7	168.0	172.9	196.8	200.6
Nonalcoholic beverages	27.1	41.3	91.4	104.3	113.5	131.7	137.8	144.4	147.4	153.4	160.0	161.6
Other foods	39.6	58.9	83.6	106.4	131.2	151.1	172.2	182.5	185.0	188.2	198.1	204.6
Food away from home	37.5	54.5	83.4	108.3	133.4	149.0	169.0	193.4	199.4	206.7	215.8	226.1
Alcoholic beverages	52.1	65.9	86.4	106.4	129.3	153.9	174.7	195.9	200.7	207.0	214.5	223.3
Housing	36.4	50.7	81.1	107.7	128.5	148.5	169.6	195.7	203.2	209.6	216.3	216.3
Shelter	35.5	48.8	81.0	109.8	140.0	165.7	193.4	224.4	232.1	240.6	246.7	248.4
Rent of primary residence	46.5	58.0	80.9	111.8	138.4	157.8	183.9	217.3	225.1	234.7	243.3	249.4
Fuel and other utilities	29.1	45.4	75.4	106.5	111.6	123.7	137.9	179.0	194.7	200.6	220.0	214.2
Gas (piped) and electricity	25.4	40.1	71.4	107.1	109.3	119.2	128.0	166.5	182.1	186.3	202.2	189.7
Household furnishings and operations	46.8	63.4	86.3	103.8	113.3	123.0	128.2	126.1	127.0	126.9	127.8	125.5
Apparel	59.2	72.5	90.9	105.0	124.1	132.0	129.6	119.5	119.5	119.0	118.9	119.5
Men's and boys'	62.2	75.5	89.4	105.0	120.4	126.2	129.7	116.1	114.1	112.4	113.0	111.9
Women's and girls'	71.8	85.5	96.0	104.9	122.6	126.9	121.5	110.8	110.7	110.3	107.5	107.1
Footwear	56.8	69.6	91.8	102.3	117.4	125.4	123.8	122.6	123.5	122.4	124.2	128.0
Transportation	37.5	50.1	83.1	106.4	120.5	139.1	153.3	173.9	180.9	184.7	195.5	193.4
Private	37.5	50.6	84.2	106.2	118.8	136.3	149.1	170.2	177.0	180.8	191.0	188.7
New vehicles	53.0	62.9	88.4	106.1	121.4	139.0	142.8	137.9	137.6	136.3	134.2	138.0
Used cars and trucks	31.2	43.8	62.3	113.7	117.6	156.5	155.8	139.4	140.0	135.7	134.0	143.1
Gasoline	27.9	45.1	97.5	98.6	101.0	99.8	128.6	194.7	219.9	238.0	277.5	238.6
Public	35.2	43.5	69.0	110.5	142.6	175.9	209.6	217.3	226.6	230.0	250.5	251.4
Medical care	34.0	47.5	74.9	113.5	162.8	220.5	260.8	323.2	336.2	351.1	364.1	388.4
Entertainment/recreation[1]	47.5	62.0	83.6	107.9	132.4	153.9	103.3	109.4	110.9	111.4	113.3	113.3
Other goods and services	40.9	53.9	75.2	114.5	159.0	206.9	271.1	313.4	321.7	333.3	345.4	381.3
Tobacco products	43.1	54.7	72.0	116.7	181.5	225.7	394.9	502.8	519.9	554.2	588.7	807.3
Personal care	43.5	57.9	81.9	106.3	130.4	147.1	165.6	185.6	190.2	195.6	201.3	206.6
Personal care products	42.7	58.0	79.6	107.6	128.2	143.1	153.7	154.4	155.8	158.3	159.3	161.1
Personal care services	44.2	57.7	83.7	106.9	132.8	151.5	178.1	203.9	209.7	216.6	223.7	229.6

(1) Dec. 1997 = 100. Entertainment was reclassified as Recreation in 1997.

Consumer Price Indexes by Region and Major Cities, 1990-2010

Source: Bureau of Labor Statistics, U.S. Dept. of Labor
(For all urban consumers; % change not annualized. 1982-84 = 100, unless otherwise noted.)

Region and city	1990	1995	2000	2005	2008	2009	2010
U.S. city average	130.7	152.4	172.2	195.3	215.3	214.5	218.1
Northeast urban	136.3	159.1	179.4	207.5	229.3	229.3	233.9
Boston-Brockton-Nashua, MA-NH-ME-CT	138.9	158.6	183.6	216.4	235.4	233.8	237.4
New York-Northern New Jersey-Long Island, NY-NJ-CT-PA	138.5	162.2	182.5	212.7	235.8	236.8	240.9
Philadelphia-Wilmington-Atlantic City, PA-NJ-DE-MD	135.8	158.7	176.5	204.2	224.1	223.3	227.7
Pittsburgh, PA	126.2	149.2	168.0	189.8	211.3	212.1	215.4
Midwest urban	127.4	148.4	168.3	188.4	205.4	204.1	208.0
Chicago-Gary-Kenosha, IL-IN-WI	131.7	153.3	173.8	194.3	212.5	210.0	212.9
Cincinnati-Hamilton, OH-KY-IN	126.5	146.2	164.8	181.6	201.5	200.6	204.7
Cleveland-Akron, OH	129.0	147.9	168.0	187.9	203.0	200.5	204.6
Detroit-Ann Arbor-Flint, MI	128.6	148.6	169.8	190.8	204.7	203.5	205.1
Kansas City, MO-KS	126.0	145.3	166.6	185.3	201.2	201.0	205.4
Milwaukee-Racine, WI	126.2	151.0	168.6	185.2	203.0	203.0	209.6
Minneapolis-St. Paul, MN-WI	127.0	147.0	170.1	193.1	209.0	207.9	211.7
St. Louis, MO-IL	128.1	145.2	163.1	186.2	198.7	198.5	203.2
South urban	127.9	149.0	167.2	188.3	208.7	207.8	211.3
Atlanta, GA	131.7	150.9	170.6	188.9	206.5	201.0	203.5
Dallas-Fort Worth, TX	125.1	144.9	164.7	184.7	201.8	200.5	201.6
Houston-Galveston-Brazoria, TX	120.6	139.8	154.2	175.6	190.0	190.5	194.2
Miami-Fort Lauderdale, FL	128.0	148.9	167.8	194.3	222.1	221.4	223.1
Tampa-St. Petersburg-Clearwater, FL	111.7	129.7	145.7	168.5	190.1	189.9	193.5
Washington-Baltimore, DC-MD-VA-WV[1]	NA	NA	107.6	124.3	139.5	139.8	142.2
West urban	131.5	153.5	174.8	198.9	219.6	218.8	221.2
Anchorage, AK	118.6	138.9	150.9	171.8	189.5	191.7	195.1
Denver-Boulder-Greeley, CO	120.9	147.9	173.2	190.9	209.9	208.5	212.4
Honolulu, HI	138.1	168.1	176.3	197.8	228.9	230.0	234.9
Los Angeles-Riverside-Orange County, CA	135.9	154.6	171.6	201.8	225.0	223.2	225.9
Phoenix-Mesa, AZ	NA	NA	NA	108.3	119.3	117.6	118.2
Portland-Salem, OR-WA	127.4	153.2	178.0	196.0	215.4	215.6	218.3
San Diego, CA	138.4	156.8	182.8	220.6	242.3	242.3	245.5
San Francisco-Oakland-San Jose, CA	132.1	151.6	180.2	202.7	222.8	224.4	227.5
Seattle-Tacoma-Bremerton, WA	126.8	152.3	179.2	200.2	224.7	226.0	226.7

NA = Not available. (1) Nov. 1996 = 100.

U.S. National Income by Type, 1930-2010

Source: Bureau of Economic Analysis, U.S. Dept. of Commerce
(in billions of current dollars)

	1930	1940	1950	1960	1970	1980	1990	2000	2009	2010
NATIONAL INCOME[1,2]	$83.1	$90.9	$263.9	$473.9	$929.5	$2,433.0	$5,059.5	$8,938.9	$12,147.6	$12,840.1
Employee compensation	46.9	52.2	155.3	296.4	617.2	1,647.6	3,326.3	5,788.8	7,806.4	7,971.4
Wage and salary accruals	46.2	49.9	147.3	272.9	551.6	1,373.4	2,741.2	4,827.7	6,275.3	6,408.2
Government	5.2	8.5	22.6	49.2	117.2	261.5	519.0	779.7	1,175.3	1,190.8
Supplements to wages and salaries	0.7	2.3	8.0	23.6	65.7	274.2	585.1	961.2	1,531.1	1,563.1
Employer contributions for employee pension and insurance funds	0.6	0.9	4.7	14.3	41.8	185.2	378.6	615.9	1,073.1	1,089.9
Employer contributions for government social insurance	0.0	1.4	3.4	9.3	23.8	88.9	206.5	345.2	458.0	473.2
Proprietors' income with inventory valuation and capital consumption adjustments	11.1	12.3	37.5	50.7	78.5	173.5	365.1	817.5	941.2	1,036.4
Farm	4.0	4.1	12.9	10.6	12.9	11.7	32.2	29.6	39.2	52.2
Nonfarm	7.0	8.2	24.6	40.1	65.6	161.8	333.0	787.8	902.0	984.2
Rental income of persons with capital consumption adjustments	5.5	3.9	9.1	17.0	21.1	28.5	49.8	215.3	305.9	350.2
Corporate profits with inventory valuation and capital consumption adjustment	7.5	9.6	35.6	53.1	82.5	201.4	434.4	819.2	1,362.0	1,800.1
Taxes on corporate income	0.8	2.8	17.9	22.8	34.8	87.2	145.4	265.1	272.4	411.1
Profits after tax with inventory valuation and capital consumption adjustments	6.6	6.8	17.7	30.3	47.7	114.2	289.0	554.1	1,089.6	1,389.1
Net dividends	5.5	4.0	8.8	13.4	24.3	64.1	169.1	377.9	620.0	737.3
Undistributed profits with inventory valuation and capital consumption adjustments	1.1	2.8	8.9	16.9	23.4	50.2	120.0	176.3	469.6	651.7
Net interest and miscellaneous payments	4.8	3.3	3.2	10.6	39.1	181.8	444.2	539.3	656.7	564.3

(1) Figures may not add up to totals because of rounding and incomplete enumeration. (2) National income is the aggregate of labor and property earnings that arise in the production of goods and services. It is the sum of employee compensation, proprietors' income, rental income, adjusted corporate profits, and net interest. It measures the total factor costs of goods and services produced by the economy. Income is measured before deduction of taxes. Total national income figures include adjustments not itemized.

U.S. National Income by Industry, 2000-10

Source: Bureau of Economic Analysis, U.S. Dept. of Commerce
(in billions of current dollars)

	2000	2005	2006	2007	2008	2009	2010
National income without capital consumption adjustment	$8,817.9	$11,353.9	$12,126.9	$12,500.0	$12,532.1	$12,108.1	$12,643.7
Domestic industries	8,780.2	11,256.8	12,054.4	12,376.7	12,363.0	11,955.8	12,454.3
Private industries	7,762.4	9,921.4	10,655.9	10,908.1	10,819.7	10,358.7	10,819.8
Agriculture, forestry, fishing, and hunting	71.4	92.8	91.9	110.5	120.7	108.5	120.0
Arts, entertainment, recreation, accommodation, and food services	339.4	434.8	460.6	490.3	475.6	458.3	484.1
Construction	478.0	657.0	701.8	685.8	629.0	541.7	527.9
Educ. services, health care, social assistance	692.2	993.5	1,059.4	1,114.8	1,189.4	1,241.7	1,295.5
Finance, insurance, real estate, rental, and leasing	1,539.3	1,998.5	2,140.8	2,160.3	2,130.5	2,153.0	2,342.8
Information	296.0	408.1	424.5	452.6	439.2	421.9	412.9
Manufacturing	1,194.6	1,304.8	1,400.9	1,409.1	1,333.0	1,172.2	1,229.2
Durable goods	723.8	744.0	791.3	800.9	750.1	642.2	694.9
Nondurable goods	470.9	560.8	609.5	608.2	583.0	530.0	534.3
Mining	92.5	163.1	198.8	204.5	251.8	134.0	156.0
Professional and business services	1,120.7	1,490.3	1,623.2	1,684.9	1,752.6	1,713.6	1,778.5
Retail trade	674.1	859.6	903.8	902.1	837.0	832.9	863.7
Transportation and warehousing	272.7	332.9	360.7	361.0	362.6	340.5	349.1
Utilities	136.2	161.3	196.5	198.4	183.2	175.0	174.3
Wholesale trade	570.8	688.4	741.2	769.1	754.8	707.0	716.8
Other services, except government	284.5	336.3	351.7	364.8	360.3	358.5	369.1
Government	1,017.8	1,335.3	1,398.5	1,468.6	1,543.2	1,597.1	1,634.5
Rest of the world	37.7	97.1	72.4	123.3	169.2	152.3	189.4

Distribution of U.S. Total Personal Income, 1930-2010

Source: Bureau of Economic Analysis, U.S. Dept. of Commerce
(in billions of current dollars)

Year	Personal income	Personal taxes and nontax payments	Disposable personal income	Personal outlays	Personal savings Amount	Personal savings As % of disposable income
1930	$76.1	$1.6	$74.6	$71.6	$2.9	4.0%
1940	78.4	1.7	76.8	72.4	4.3	5.7
1950	228.0	18.9	209.9	195.0	14.9	7.1
1960	411.3	46.1	365.2	338.9	26.3	7.2
1970	838.6	103.1	735.5	666.1	69.4	9.4
1980	2,301.5	298.9	2,002.7	1,806.4	196.3	9.8
1990	4,846.7	592.7	4,254.0	3,977.3	276.7	6.5
2000	8,559.4	1,232.3	7,327.2	7,114.1	213.1	2.9
2005	10,485.9	1,208.6	9,277.3	9,149.6	143.2	1.5
2006	11,268.1	1,352.4	9,915.7	9,659.1	256.6	2.6
2007	11,912.3	1,488.7	10,423.6	10,174.9	248.7	2.4
2008	12,460.2	1,435.7	11,024.5	10,432.2	592.3	5.4
2009	11,930.2	1,141.4	10,788.8	10,236.3	552.6	5.1
2010	12,373.5	1,193.9	11,179.7	10,586.9	592.8	5.3

Note: Personal income minus taxes/nontax payments equals disposable income; disposable income minus outlays equals savings. Figures may not add up to totals because of rounding.

Median Income by Race, Hispanic Origin, and Sex, 1947-2010

Source: *Current Population Survey*, U.S. Census Bureau, U.S. Dept. of Commerce

	Year	Male No. with income (thous.)	Male Current dollars	Male 2010 dollars	Female No. with income (thous.)	Female Current dollars	Female 2010 dollars
All races	2010	105,351	$32,137	$32,137	106,142	$20,831	$20,831
	2009	105,025	32,184	32,715	106,229	20,957	21,303
	2008	105,428	33,161	33,580	106,403	20,867	21,131
	2005	102,986	31,275	34,929	104,245	18,576	20,747
	2000	98,504	28,343	35,885	101,704	16,063	20,338
	1990	88,220	20,293	32,817	92,245	10,070	16,285
	1980	78,661	12,530	31,567	80,826	4,920	12,395
	1970	65,008	6,670	33,423	51,647	2,237	11,210
	1960	55,172	4,080	26,286	36,526	1,261	8,124
	1950	47,585	2,570	20,319	24,651	953	7,535
	1947	46,813	2,230	19,041	21,479	1,017	8,684
White	2010	87,430	34,047	34,047	85,524	20,947	20,947
	2009	87,400	33,748	34,305	85,760	21,118	21,467
	2008	87,581	35,120	35,564	86,228	20,950	21,215
	2005	85,996	32,179	35,939	84,768	18,669	20,850
	2000	83,372	29,797	37,726	84,123	16,079	20,358
	1990	76,480	21,170	34,236	78,566	10,317	16,684
	1980	69,420	13,328	33,577	70,573	4,947	12,463
	1970	58,447	7,011	35,132	45,288	2,266	11,355
	1960	49,788	4,296	27,678	32,001	1,352	8,710
	1950	NA	2,709	21,418	NA	1,060	8,381
	1948	NA	2,510	19,844	NA	1,133	8,958
White, not Hispanic	2010	73,491	37,037	37,037	74,365	21,754	21,754
	2009	73,485	36,785	37,392	74,693	21,939	22,301
	2008	73,748	37,409	37,882	75,322	21,749	22,024
	2005	73,219	35,345	39,475	75,014	19,451	21,724
	2000	72,530	31,508	39,893	75,206	16,665	21,100
	1990	69,987	21,958	35,510	72,939	10,581	17,111
	1980	65,564	13,681	34,466	67,084	4,980	12,546
Black	2010	11,258	23,061	23,061	13,931	19,634	19,634
	2009	11,064	23,674	24,065	13,793	19,413	19,733
	2008	11,183	25,118	25,436	13,616	20,203	20,459
	2005	10,651	22,609	25,251	13,237	17,595	19,651
	2000	9,905	21,343	27,023	12,461	15,881	20,107
	1990	8,820	12,868	20,810	10,687	8,328	13,468
	1980	7,387	8,009	20,177	8,596	4,580	11,538
	1970	5,844	4,157	20,831	5,844	2,063	10,338
	1960	5,384	2,260	14,560	4,525	837	5,393
	1950	NA	1,471	11,630	NA	474	3,748
	1948	NA	1,363	10,776	NA	492	3,890
Asian	2010	4,922	35,622	35,622	5,047	23,664	23,664
	2009	4,828	36,886	37,495	4,923	24,170	24,569
	2008	4,788	36,204	36,662	4,787	23,015	23,306
	2005	4,518	33,036	36,896	4,520	21,623	24,150
	2000	4,303	30,833	39,038	4,192	17,356	21,975
	1999	3,934	27,878	36,480	4,003	16,797	21,980
	1990	2,235	19,394	31,363	2,333	11,086	17,928
Hispanic (any race)	2010	14,965	22,233	22,233	12,122	16,269	16,269
	2009	14,919	22,256	22,623	12,035	16,210	16,478
	2008	14,855	24,003	24,307	11,828	16,417	16,625
	2005	13,714	22,089	24,670	10,638	15,036	16,793
	2000	11,343	19,498	24,687	9,431	12,248	15,507
	1990	6,767	13,470	21,783	5,903	7,532	12,181
	1980	3,996	9,659	24,334	3,617	4,405	11,097

NA = Not available. **Note:** Income for persons 15 years of age and over beginning in Mar. 1980; 14 years of age and over as of Mar. of the following year for previous years. Beginning in 2005, Black and Asian totals include those who identify themselves as being in combination with some other race. Asian totals before 2005 include Pacific Islanders.

Consumer Credit Outstanding, 2007-10

Source: Federal Reserve System

(in billions of dollars as of Dec. of year shown, not seasonally adjusted)

	2008	2009	2010		2008	2009	2010
TOTAL	$2,594.1	$2,478.8	$2,434.7	Credit unions	$33.4	$35.4	$36.3
Major holders				Fed. govt. and Sallie Mae	NA	NA	NA
Commercial banks	878.6	855.3	1,098.7	Savings institutions	39.6	38.1	49.6
Finance companies	575.8	487.8	518.6	Nonfinancial business	8.7	8.8	8.8
Credit unions[1]	236.2	237.2	226.5	Pools of securitized assets[1]	442.4	402.8	44.9
Fed. govt. and Sallie Mae	111.0	186.0	316.4				
Savings institutions	86.3	77.5	86.8	**Nonrevolving[2]**	**1,605.0**	**1,584.9**	**1,608.0**
Nonfinancial business	59.8	57.2	56.0	Commercial banks	488.1	492.9	483.6
Pools of securitized assets[1]	646.4	577.9	131.7	Finance companies	501.3	441.3	446.7
				Credit unions	202.8	201.7	190.1
Major types of credit				Fed. govt. and Sallie Mae	111.0	186.0	316.4
Revolving	**989.1**	**894.0**	**826.7**	Savings institutions	46.8	39.5	37.2
Commercial banks	390.6	362.4	615.1	Nonfinancial business	51.1	48.4	47.2
Finance companies	74.4	46.4	71.9	Pools of securitized assets[1]	204.0	175.1	86.8

NA = Not available. (1) Outstanding balances of pools upon which securities have been issued; these balances are no longer carried on the balance sheets of the loan originators. (2) Includes estimates for holders that do not separately report consumer credit holding by type.

Stock Ownership of U.S. Families, by Income and Age, 1989-2007

Source: *Survey of Consumer Finances* (triennial), Federal Reserve System

		Families having direct or indirect stock holdings[1]				Median value of portfolios (thous. of 2007 dollars)				Stock holdings as share of financial assets[2]			
		1989	2001	2004	2007	1989	2001	2004	2007	1989	2001	2004	2007
All families		31.7%	52.2%	50.2%	51.1%	$12.5	$40.4	$35.7	$35.0	27.8%	56.1%	51.3%	53.3%
Percentile of income:	Less than 20	3.3	12.9	11.7	13.6	29.3	8.8	8.2	6.5	13.6	37.4	32.0	39.0
	20-39.9	15.2	34.1	29.6	34.0	8.8	9.1	11.0	8.8	10.0	35.6	30.9	34.3
	40-59.9	28.6	52.5	51.7	49.5	6.8	17.5	16.5	17.7	16.7	46.8	43.4	38.3
	60-79.9	44.0	75.7	69.9	70.5	8.5	33.5	28.7	34.1	21.8	52.0	41.7	52.5
	80-89.9	57.6	82.0	83.8	84.4	13.9	75.6	60.9	62.0	26.1	57.3	48.8	49.3
	90-100	76.9	89.7	92.7	91.0	57.9	289.7	225.2	219.0	34.3	60.5	57.5	57.6
By age of family head (years):	Under 35	22.4	49.0	40.8	38.6	4.4	8.2	8.8	7.0	20.2	52.5	40.3	44.3
	35-44	39.0	59.5	54.5	53.5	7.6	32.2	22.0	26.0	29.4	57.2	53.7	53.7
	45-54	41.8	59.3	56.5	60.4	19.3	58.5	54.9	45.0	33.5	59.1	53.8	53.0
	55-64	36.2	57.4	62.8	58.9	27.0	94.2	78.0	78.0	27.7	56.2	55.0	55.0
	65-74	26.7	40.0	46.9	52.1	29.8	175.8	76.9	57.0	26.0	55.4	51.5	55.3
	75+	25.9	35.7	34.8	40.1	36.7	128.7	94.3	41.0	25.0	51.8	39.3	48.1

(1) Indirect holdings are those in mutual funds, retirement accounts, and other managed assets. (2) Among stock-holding families.

Wealthiest Americans, 2011

Source: *Forbes* magazine
(as of Sept. 1, 2011)

Rank	Name	Net worth (bil)	Age	Residence	Source
1.	William Gates III	$59.0	55	Medina, WA	Microsoft
2.	Warren Buffett	39.0	81	Omaha, NE	Berkshire Hathaway
3.	Lawrence Ellison	33.0	67	Woodside, CA	Oracle
4.	Charles Koch	25.0	75	Wichita, KS	Manufacturing, energy
	David Koch	25.0	71	New York, NY	Manufacturing, energy
6.	Christy Walton	24.5	56	Jackson, WY	Wal-Mart
7.	George Soros	22.0	81	Katonah, NY	Hedge funds
8.	Sheldon Adelson	21.5	78	Las Vegas, NV	Sands casinos
9.	Jim C. Walton	21.1	63	Bentonville, AR	Wal-Mart
10.	Alice Walton	20.9	61	Fort Worth, TX	Wal-Mart
11.	S. Robson Walton	20.5	67	Bentonville, AR	Wal-Mart
12.	Michael Bloomberg	19.5	69	New York, NY	Bloomberg, LP
13.	Jeff Bezos	19.1	47	Seattle, WA	Amazon.com
14.	Mark Zuckerberg	17.5	27	Palo Alto, CA	Facebook
15.	Sergey Brin	16.7	38	Los Altos, CA	Google
	Larry Page	16.7	38	Palo Alto, CA	Google
17.	John Paulson	15.5	55	New York, NY	Hedge funds
18.	Michael Dell	15.0	46	Austin, TX	Dell
19.	Steve Ballmer	13.9	55	Hunts Point, WA	Microsoft
20.	Forrest Mars	13.8	80	Big Horn, WY	Mars candy
	Jacqueline Mars	13.8	71	The Plains, VA	Mars candy
	John Mars	13.8	75	Jackson, WY	Mars candy
23.	Paul Allen	13.2	58	Mercer Isl., WA	Microsoft
24.	Phil Knight	13.1	73	Hillsboro, OR	Nike
25.	Carl Icahn	13.0	75	New York, NY	Leveraged buyouts

Poverty Rate

Source: U.S. Census Bureau, U.S. Dept. of Commerce

The poverty rate is the proportion of the population whose income falls below the government's official poverty level and is adjusted each year for inflation. The national poverty rate was 15.1% in 2010, the highest it has been since 1983. More than 46 mil people in the U.S. were in poverty in 2010, up from 31.6 mil in 2000. In 2010, 22.0% of children under 18 and 9.0% of people aged 65 and older were defined as poor.

Persons Below Poverty Level, 1960-2010

Source: U.S. Census Bureau, U.S. Dept. of Commerce

Year	Number below poverty level (millions)					% of subgroup below poverty level					Avg. income cut-offs, family of 4 at poverty level[4]
	All races[1]	Asian[2]	White	Black	Hispanic[3]	All races[1]	Asian[2]	White	Black	Hispanic[3]	
1960	39.9	NA	28.3	NA	NA	22.2%	NA	17.8%	NA	NA	$3,022
1970	25.4	NA	17.5	7.5	NA	12.6	NA	9.9	33.5%	NA	3,968
1980	29.3	NA	19.7	8.6	3.5	13.0	NA	10.2	32.5	25.7%	8,414
1990	33.6	0.9	22.3	9.8	6.0	13.5	12.2%	10.7	31.9	28.1	13,359
1993	39.3	1.1	26.2	10.9	8.1	15.1	15.3	12.2	33.1	30.6	14,763
1994	38.1	1.0	25.4	10.2	8.4	14.5	14.6	11.7	30.6	30.7	15,141
1995	36.4	1.4	24.4	9.9	8.6	13.8	14.6	11.2	29.3	30.3	15,569
1996	36.5	1.5	24.7	9.7	8.7	13.7	14.5	11.2	28.4	29.4	16,036
1997	35.6	1.5	24.4	9.1	8.3	13.3	14.0	11.0	26.5	27.1	16,400
1998	34.5	1.4	23.5	9.1	8.1	12.7	12.5	10.5	26.1	25.6	16,660
1999	32.8	1.3	21.2	8.4	7.9	11.9	10.7	9.8	23.6	22.7	17,029
2000	31.6	1.3	21.6	8.0	7.7	11.3	9.9	9.5	22.5	21.5	17,063
2002	34.6	1.2	23.5	8.9	8.6	12.1	10.0	10.2	8.9	21.8	18,556
2003	35.9	1.5	24.3	9.1	9.1	12.5	11.8	10.5	9.1	22.5	18,979
2004	37.0	1.3	25.3	9.4	9.1	12.7	9.7	10.8	9.4	21.9	19,307
2005	37.0	1.5	24.9	9.5	9.4	12.6	10.9	10.6	9.5	21.8	19,971
2006	36.5	1.5	24.4	9.5	9.2	12.3	10.1	10.3	9.5	12.3	20,614
2007	37.2	1.5	25.1	9.7	9.9	12.5	10.2	10.5	9.7	21.5	21,203
2008	39.8	1.7	27.0	9.9	11.0	13.2	11.6	11.2	9.9	23.2	22,025
2009	43.6	1.9	29.8	10.6	12.4	14.3	12.4	12.3	10.6	25.3	21,954
2010	46.1	1.9	31.6	11.4	13.2	15.1	11.9	13.0	11.4	26.6	22,314

NA = Not available. **Note:** Because of a change in the definition of poverty, data prior to 1980 are not directly comparable to data since 1980. (1) Includes other races not shown separately. (2) Beginning in 2002, Black and Asian totals include those who identify themselves as being in combination with some other race. Asian includes Pacific Islanders 1990-2000. (3) Persons of Hispanic origin may be of any race. (4) Figures for 1960-80 represent only nonfarm families.

Poverty Thresholds by Family Size, 1980-2010

Source: U.S. Census Bureau, U.S. Dept. of Commerce
(weighted average; not used for computing poverty data)

	1980	1990	2000	2010		1980	1990	2000	2010
1 person	$4,190	$6,652	$8,794	$11,139	3 people	$6,565	$10,419	$13,738	$17,374
Under age 65	4,290	6,800	8,959	11,344	4 people	8,414	13,359	17,603	22,314
Age 65 or older	3,949	6,268	8,259	10,458	5 people	9,966	15,792	20,819	26,439
2 people	5,363	8,509	11,239	14,218	6 people	11,269	17,839	23,528	29,897
Householder under age 65	5,537	8,794	11,590	14,676	7 people	12,761	20,241	26,754	34,009
Householder age 65 or older	4,983	7,905	10,419	13,194	8 people	14,199	22,582	29,701	37,934
					9 people or more	16,896	26,848	35,060	45,220

Poverty by Family Status, Sex, and Race, 1990-2010

Source: U.S. Census Bureau, U.S. Dept. of Commerce
(numbers in thousands)

	1990 No.	%[1]	1995 No.	%[1]	2000 No.	%[1]	2008 No.	%[1]	2009 No.	%[1]	2010 No.	%[1]
TOTAL POOR	33,585	13.5%	36,425	13.8%	31,581	11.3%	39,829	13.2%	43,569	14.3%	46,180	15.1%
In families	25,232	12.0	27,501	12.3	22,347	9.6	28,564	11.5	31,197	12.5	33,007	13.2
Head of household	7,098	10.7	7,532	10.8	6,400	8.7	8,147	10.3	8,792	11.1	9,221	11.7
Related children	12,715	19.9	13,999	20.2	11,005	15.6	13,507	18.5	14,774	20.1	15,730	21.5
Families, female householder, no husband present	12,578	37.2	14,205	36.5	10,926	28.5	13,812	31.4	14,746	32.5	15,895	34.2
Head of household	3,768	33.4	4,057	32.4	3,278	25.4	4,163	28.7	4,441	29.9	4,745	31.6
Related children	7,363	53.4	8,364	50.3	6,300	40.0	7,587	43.5	7,942	44.4	NA	NA
Unrelated individuals	7,446	20.7	8,247	20.9	8,653	19.0	10,710	20.8	11,678	22.0	12,422	22.9
Unrelated female individuals	4,589	24.0	4,865	23.5	5,071	21.6	5,951	22.6	6,424	24.0	6,626	24.1
Unrelated male individuals	2,857	16.9	3,382	18.0	3,548	16.0	4,759	18.9	5,255	20.0	5,796	21.7
Total white poor[2]	22,326	10.7	24,423	11.2	21,645	9.5	26,990	11.2	29,830	12.3	31,650	13.0
In families	15,916	9.0	17,593	9.6	14,692	7.8	18,558	9.4	20,701	10.5	21,965	11.1
Head of household	4,622	8.1	4,994	8.5	4,333	7.1	5,414	8.4	5,994	9.3	NA	NA
Related children	7,696	15.1	8,474	15.5	6,834	12.4	8,441	15.3	9,440	17.0	9,982	18.1
Families, female householder, no husband present	6,210	29.8	7,047	29.7	5,609	23.2	7,340	27.2	8,283	29.4	8,934	31.2
Unrelated individuals	5,739	18.6	6,336	19.0	6,454	17.1	7,982	19.1	8,580	19.9	9,105	20.8
Total black poor[2]	9,837	31.9	9,872	29.3	7,982	22.5	9,379	24.7	9,944	25.8	10,675	27.4
In families	8,160	31.0	8,189	28.5	6,221	21.2	7,339	23.7	7,642	24.4	8,140	26.0
Head of household	2,193	29.3	2,127	26.4	1,686	19.3	2,055	22.0	2,125	22.7	NA	NA
Related children	4,412	44.2	4,644	41.5	3,495	30.9	3,781	34.4	3,919	35.3	4,282	39.2
Families, female householder, no husband present	6,005	50.6	6,553	48.2	4,774	38.6	5,533	40.5	5,427	39.7	5,830	41.0
Unrelated individuals	1,491	35.1	1,551	32.6	1,702	28.9	1,970	28.8	2,209	31.1	2,454	33.4

NA = Not available. (1) Percentage of total U.S. population in each category who fell below poverty level and are enumerated here. For example, of all persons in families in 2010, 13.2%, or 33,007, were poor. (2) Data are for one race only. The Census Bureau revised race categories in 2002, so data after 2002 is not directly comparable with previous years.

Poverty Rates by State, 1990-2010

Source: U.S. Census Bureau, U.S. Dept. of Commerce

State	1990	2000	2005	2009	2010	State	1990	2000	2005	2009	2010
Alabama	19.2%	13.3%	16.7%	16.6%	17.3%	Montana	16.3%	14.1%	13.8%	13.5%	14.0%
Alaska	11.4	7.6	10.0	11.7	12.4	Nebraska	10.3	8.6	9.5	9.9	10.2
Arizona	13.7	11.7	15.2	21.2	18.6	Nevada	9.8	8.8	10.6	13.0	16.4
Arkansas	19.6	16.5	13.8	18.9	15.5	New Hampshire	6.3	4.5	5.6	7.8	6.6
California	13.9	12.7	13.2	15.3	16.3	New Jersey	9.2	7.3	6.8	9.3	10.7
Colorado	13.7	9.8	11.4	12.3	12.2	New Mexico	20.9	17.5	17.9	19.3	18.6
Connecticut	6.0	7.7	9.3	8.4	8.3	New York	14.3	13.9	14.5	15.8	16.0
Delaware	6.9	8.4	9.2	12.3	12.1	North Carolina	13.0	12.5	13.1	16.9	17.4
Dist. of Columbia	21.1	15.2	21.3	17.9	19.9	North Dakota	13.7	10.4	11.2	10.9	12.2
Florida	14.4	11.0	11.1	14.6	16.0	Ohio	11.5	10.0	12.3	13.3	15.3
Georgia	15.8	12.1	14.4	18.4	18.7	Oklahoma	15.6	14.9	15.6	12.9	16.3
Hawaii	11.0	8.9	8.6	12.5	12.1	Oregon	9.2	10.9	12.0	13.4	14.2
Idaho	14.9	12.5	9.9	13.7	14.0	Pennsylvania	11.0	8.6	11.2	11.1	12.2
Illinois	13.7	10.7	11.5	13.2	14.1	Rhode Island	7.5	10.2	12.1	13.0	13.6
Indiana	13.0	8.5	12.6	16.1	16.3	South Carolina	16.2	11.1	15.0	13.7	17.0
Iowa	10.4	8.3	11.3	10.7	10.3	South Dakota	13.3	10.7	11.8	14.1	13.2
Kansas	10.3	8.0	12.5	13.7	14.3	Tennessee	16.9	13.5	14.9	16.5	16.7
Kentucky	17.3	12.6	14.8	17.0	17.7	Texas	15.9	15.5	16.2	17.3	18.4
Louisiana	23.6	17.2	18.3	14.3	21.6	Utah	8.2	7.6	9.2	9.7	10.0
Maine	13.1	10.1	12.6	11.4	12.5	Vermont	10.9	10.0	7.6	9.4	10.8
Maryland	9.9	7.4	9.7	9.6	10.8	Virginia	11.1	8.3	9.2	10.7	10.7
Massachusetts	10.7	9.8	10.1	10.8	10.6	Washington	8.9	10.8	10.2	11.7	11.5
Michigan	14.3	9.9	12.0	14.0	15.5	West Virginia	18.1	14.7	15.4	15.8	16.9
Minnesota	12.0	5.7	8.1	11.1	10.5	Wisconsin	9.3	9.3	10.2	10.8	9.9
Mississippi	25.7	14.9	20.1	23.1	22.7	Wyoming	11.0	10.8	10.6	9.2	9.6
Missouri	13.4	9.2	11.6	15.5	14.8	**United States**	13.5	11.3	12.6	14.3	15.1

Selected Personal Consumption Expenditures in the U.S., 1990-2010

Source: Bureau of Economic Analysis, U.S. Dept. of Commerce
(in billions of dollars)

	1990	1995	2000	2005	2008	2009	2010
Personal consumption expenditures	$3,835.5	$4,987.3	$6,830.4	$8,803.5	$10,035.5	$9,866.1	$10,245.5
Goods	1,491.3	1,815.5	2,459.1	3,076.7	3,381.7	3,197.5	3,387.0
Durable goods........................	497.1	635.7	915.8	1,123.4	1,108.9	1,029.6	1,085.5
Motor vehicles and parts	205.1	255.7	363.2	408.2	339.3	316.5	340.1
New motor vehicles	134.7	147.5	210.7	248.9	185.2	165.9	178.5
Motor vehicle parts and accessories.......	28.3	35.4	41.8	46.6	48.9	46.4	49.2
Furniture and durable household equipment	120.9	146.7	208.1	261.3	257.9	235.3	243.8
Furniture and furnishings	69.2	83.4	121.7	153.0	150.9	136.4	141.0
Household appliances	23.7	26.6	34.1	43.3	43.2	39.5	40.5
Glassware, tableware, and household utensils..	18.4	23.7	35.3	42.7	41.6	39.3	41.5
Recreational goods and vehicles..........	105.6	153.7	234.1	312.8	344.0	316.6	329.8
Video, audio, and information processing equipment	56.1	84.7	130.9	182.9	210.7	197.7	207.4
Sporting equipment, guns, and ammunition	19.9	27.2	39.1	50.7	55.7	51.6	53.3
Sports and recreational vehicles	16.6	22.5	34.9	45.7	42.7	33.5	33.7
Recreational books	10.9	16.4	24.4	28.1	29.6	29.0	30.4
Other durable goods..................	65.5	79.6	110.4	141.1	167.7	161.2	171.8
Jewelry and watches..................	30.3	37.8	49.1	58.1	63.4	58.1	61.5
Therapeutic appliances and equipment.....	18.4	21.0	32.2	41.5	49.8	50.2	54.9
Nondurable goods......................	994.2	1,179.8	1,543.4	1,953.4	2,272.8	2,167.8	2,301.5
Food and beverages purchased for off-premise consumption...............	391.2	443.7	537.5	644.5	746.4	746.0	766.4
Food and nonalcoholic beverages purchased for off-premises consumption	341.2	388.3	463.1	558.2	647.4	645.3	659.4
Alcoholic beverages purchased for off-premises consumption	49.3	55.0	74.0	86.0	98.7	100.4	106.6
Clothing and footwear	195.2	231.2	280.8	314.0	330.9	318.2	334.3
Women's and girls' clothing	94.5	108.9	132.7	152.5	160.1	153.7	161.2
Men's and boys' clothing	57.4	72.2	85.9	91.0	94.5	91.1	95.5
Footwear	35.3	41.2	50.8	57.7	62.8	60.3	63.9
Gasoline and other energy goods..........	124.2	133.4	188.8	303.8	410.5	299.4	354.1
Motor vehicle fuels, lubricants, and fluids ...	111.4	120.4	172.9	283.8	384.5	279.1	331.4
Other nondurable goods................	283.6	371.4	536.2	691.1	785.1	804.1	846.7
Pharmaceutical and medical products	59.1	85.1	159.0	254.7	302.5	316.8	330.6
Recreational items	50.9	68.9	93.7	119.1	138.7	132.8	141.4
Household supplies	54.2	70.4	86.7	102.2	112.0	110.1	114.1
Personal care products	39.3	50.2	68.5	81.5	90.8	89.9	95.2
Tobacco	41.0	49.2	68.5	71.1	75.7	87.9	94.4
Magazines, newspapers, and stationery ...	36.5	46.1	56.6	57.5	58.9	58.8	64.6
Services..............................	2,344.2	3,171.7	4,371.2	5,726.8	6,653.8	6,668.7	6,858.5
Housing...........................	570.4	756.2	1,010.5	1,328.9	1,529.9	1,574.9	1,583.8
Rental of tenant-occupied nonfarm housing	150.7	186.2	227.9	264.7	330.3	353.2	359.4
Imputed rental of owner-occupied housing ..	412.8	559.8	768.9	1,044.5	1,179.1	1,201.0	1,203.1
Household utilities....................	125.9	157.6	188.1	253.7	301.1	296.7	309.4
Water supply and sanitation	27.1	39.3	50.4	63.7	77.4	81.3	85.7
Electricity...........................	71.8	87.6	98.4	128.7	155.8	157.4	168.4
Natural gas	27.0	30.7	39.3	61.2	67.9	58.0	55.4
Health care.........................	506.2	719.9	918.4	1,308.9	1,532.6	1,604.2	1,667.4
Physician services	134.8	177.8	229.2	330.5	377.9	387.8	391.9
Dental services......................	32.4	45.4	63.6	89.1	104.4	104.4	106.0
Paramedical services	64.9	113.4	143.8	206.3	246.2	258.0	269.1
Hospital and nursing home services	274.1	383.3	481.8	683.0	804.1	854.0	900.4
Transportation services................	126.4	177.9	262.3	286.0	305.9	287.1	295.5
Motor vehicle services	87.2	129.1	189.3	209.6	221.9	209.6	211.6
Public transportation..................	39.2	48.8	73.0	76.3	84.0	77.4	83.9
Ground transportation	12.9	16.7	21.6	26.2	29.7	29.9	30.9
Air transportation	25.9	31.1	49.2	47.7	51.6	45.1	50.5
Recreation services...................	121.8	181.1	255.5	328.2	381.9	371.2	382.6
Membership clubs, sports centers, parks, theaters, and museums................	49.7	69.5	91.9	115.2	135.0	131.6	136.3
Audio-video, photographic, and information processing equipment services.........	37.9	50.0	70.1	85.4	99.9	100.7	102.7
Gambling	23.7	45.4	67.6	92.9	103.8	98.0	99.6
Food services and accommodations	262.7	316.7	410.1	533.9	618.3	610.3	638.0
Food services.......................	235.1	280.2	354.9	461.3	529.2	526.7	547.4
Accommodations	27.6	36.6	55.2	72.7	89.1	83.6	90.6
Financial services and insurance	253.2	364.7	570.0	698.4	807.0	747.8	780.2
Financial services....................	141.5	212.5	370.0	424.0	524.9	481.5	514.5
Insurance	111.7	152.2	199.9	274.4	282.1	266.3	265.8
Other services.......................	297.9	390.5	591.1	777.1	892.6	896.2	921.4
Communication......................	68.3	95.9	156.6	184.4	216.6	215.9	223.4
Telecommunication services	60.7	85.2	130.2	145.9	164.4	159.1	161.1
Internet access	0.1	1.6	16.4	29.9	42.9	48.0	53.8
Education services	60.7	85.5	125.2	170.3	209.3	221.7	236.0
Higher education.....................	34.7	51.9	76.8	108.7	134.3	144.3	154.9
Nursery, elementary, secondary schools..	14.8	19.2	24.1	31.7	38.0	39.9	41.4
Commercial and vocational schools	11.1	14.4	24.3	29.9	37.0	37.5	39.6
Professional and other services	67.7	82.8	113.0	148.6	168.5	163.0	163.3
Personal care and clothing services	44.9	56.5	80.2	102.5	113.9	111.2	112.2
Social services and religious activities	41.2	58.1	85.0	121.0	144.0	147.6	154.1
Household maintenance	25.4	34.5	47.7	55.3	63.0	57.6	55.2
Net foreign travel.....................	−10.3	−23.0	−16.5	−5.0	−22.7	−20.8	−22.8
Foreign travel by U.S. residents	42.7	54.7	84.3	99.8	119.8	106.1	115.4
Less: Expenditures in the U.S. by nonresidents	53.0	77.7	100.8	104.7	142.5	126.9	138.2
Final consumption expenditures of nonprofit institutions serving households (NPISHs)[1]	79.6	107.2	165.4	211.7	284.6	280.3	280.2

Note: Subtotals may not add up to totals due to rounding or incomplete enumeration.

Leading U.S. Businesses, 2011

Source: *Fortune* magazine

(in millions of revenue-dollars; rank among all businesses by 2010 revenue)

Company (rank)	Revenue
Advertising, Marketing	
Omnicom Group (195)	$12,542
Interpublic Group (355)	6,532
Aerospace and Defense	
Boeing (36)	$64,306
United Technologies (44)	54,326
Lockheed Martin (52)	46,890
Northrop Grumman (72)	34,757
Honeywell International (81)	33,370
General Dynamics (86)	32,466
Raytheon (104)	25,183
L-3 Communications (159)	15,680
ITT (217)	11,155
Textron (233)	10,525
Goodrich (337)	6,967
Precision Castparts (409)	5,540
Airlines	
Delta Air Lines (88)	$31,755
United Continental Holdings (114)	23,229
AMR (118)	22,170
Southwest Airlines (205)	12,104
US Airways Group (208)	11,908
Apparel	
Nike (135)	$19,014
VF (310)	7,703
Automotive Retailing, Services	
AutoNation (197)	$12,502
Penske Automotive Group (228)	10,734
CarMax (311)	7,690
Hertz Global Holdings (315)	7,562
Sonic Automotive (339)	6,936
Group 1 Automotive (413)	5,509
Avis Budget Group (432)	5,185
Beverages	
Coca-Cola (70)	$35,119
Coca-Cola Enterprises (347)	6,714
Dr Pepper Snapple Group (404)	5,636
Chemicals	
Dow Chemical (45)	$53,674
DuPont (84)	32,733
PPG Industries (181)	13,423
Monsanto (234)	10,502
Praxair (241)	10,116
Huntsman (264)	9,302
Air Products & Chemicals (271)	9,026
Ashland (272)	9,012
Sherwin-Williams (308)	7,776
Mosaic (346)	6,759
Eastman Chemical (348)	6,691
Avery Dennison (356)	6,513
Ecolab (378)	6,090
Celanese (388)	5,918
Lubrizol (423)	5,418
Momentive Specialty Chemicals (433)	5,174
Commercial Banks	
Bank of America Corp. (9)	$134,194
J.P. Morgan Chase & Co. (13)	115,475
Citigroup (14)	111,055
Wells Fargo (23)	93,249
Goldman Sachs Group (54)	45,967
Morgan Stanley (63)	39,320
American Express (91)	30,242
U.S. Bancorp (126)	20,518
Capital One Financial (134)	19,067
Ally Financial (149)	17,373
PNC Financial Services Group (151)	17,096
Bank of New York Mellon Corp. (165)	14,929
BB&T Corp. (220)	11,072
SunTrust Banks (244)	10,072
State Street Corp. (253)	9,716
Discover Financial Services (291)	8,241
Regions Financial (293)	8,220
Fifth Third Bancorp (326)	7,218
CIT Group (364)	6,362
KeyCorp (417)	5,458
Computer Peripherals	
EMC (152)	$17,015
Western Digital (251)	9,850
Computer Software	
Microsoft (38)	$62,484
Oracle (96)	26,820
Symantec (382)	5,985
Computers, Office Equipment	
Hewlett-Packard (11)	$126,033
Apple (35)	62,255

Company (rank)	Revenue
Dell (41)	61,494
Xerox (121)	21,633
Pitney Bowes (421)	5,425
Construction and Farm Machinery	
Caterpillar (58)	$42,588
Deere (98)	26,004
Cummins (186)	13,226
AGCO (340)	6,897
Diversified Financials	
Fannie Mae (5)	$153,825
General Electric (6)	151,628
Freddie Mac (20)	98,368
INTL FCStone (51)	46,940
Marsh & McLennan (225)	10,931
Ameriprise Financial (246)	10,046
Aon (286)	8,512
SLM (344)	6,776
Diversified Outsourcing	
Aramark (194)	$12,572
Automatic Data Processing (275)	8,945
Education	
Apollo Group (452)	$4,958
Washington Post (470)	4,817
Electronics, Electrical Equipment	
Emerson Electric (120)	$21,866
Whirlpool (143)	18,366
Energy	
AES (150)	$17,138
American Electric Power (169)	14,427
Constellation Energy (172)	14,340
Williams (257)	9,616
NRG Energy (276)	8,849
Energy Future Holdings (292)	8,235
Global Partners (306)	7,802
Calpine (349)	6,637
UGI (407)	5,592
Engineering, Construction	
Fluor (124)	$20,849
KBR (242)	10,099
Peter Kiewit Sons' (249)	9,938
Jacobs Engineering Group (250)	9,916
URS (267)	9,177
Shaw Group (336)	7,001
AECOM Technology (353)	6,559
CH2M Hill (422)	5,423
Emcor Group (439)	5,121
Entertainment	
Walt Disney (65)	$38,063
News Corp. (83)	32,778
Time Warner (95)	26,888
CBS (174)	14,060
Viacom (180)	13,497
CC Media Holdings (391)	5,866
Live Nation Entertainment (444)	5,064
Financial Data Services	
First Data (236)	$10,380
Visa (297)	8,065
MasterCard (410)	5,539
Fidelity National Information Svcs. (426)	5,331
Western Union (431)	5,193
SunGard Data Systems (434)	5,172
Food Consumer Products	
PepsiCo (43)	$57,838
Kraft Foods (49)	49,542
General Mills (166)	14,796
Sara Lee (191)	12,919
Kellogg (199)	12,397
ConAgra Foods (200)	12,370
Dean Foods (203)	12,149
Land O'Lakes (218)	11,146
H.J. Heinz (232)	10,558
Campbell Soup (312)	7,676
Hormel Foods (325)	7,221
Dole Food (341)	6,894
Hershey (402)	5,671
Food and Drug Stores	
CVS Caremark (21)	$96,413
Kroger (25)	82,189
Walgreen (32)	67,420
Safeway (60)	41,050
Supervalu (61)	40,597
Rite Aid (100)	25,669
Publix Super Markets (102)	25,328
Whole Foods Market (273)	9,006
Great Atlantic & Pacific Tea (278)	8,814
Winn-Dixie Stores (324)	7,248

Company (rank)	Revenue
Food Production	
Archer Daniels Midland (39)	$61,682
Tyson Foods (893)	28,430
Smithfield Foods (216)	11,203
Food Services	
McDonald's (111)	$24,075
Yum Brands (214)	11,343
Starbucks (229)	10,707
Darden Restaurants (332)	7,113
Forest and Paper Products	
International Paper (105)	$25,179
Weyerhaeuser (354)	6,552
Domtar (394)	5,850
General Merchandisers	
Wal-Mart Stores (1)	$421,849
Target (33)	67,390
Sears Holdings (57)	43,326
Macy's (107)	25,003
Kohl's (142)	18,391
J.C. Penney (146)	17,759
Dollar General (188)	13,035
Nordstrom (254)	9,700
Family Dollar Stores (302)	7,867
Dillard's (370)	6,254
Health Care: Insurance & Managed Care	
UnitedHealth Group (22)	$94,155
WellPoint (42)	58,802
Aetna (77)	34,246
Humana (79)	33,869
Cigna (122)	21,253
Health Net (179)	13,620
Coventry Health Care (212)	11,588
Amerigroup (396)	5,806
Universal American (401)	5,687
WellCare Health Plans (420)	5,440
Health Care: Medical Facilities	
HCA Holdings (90)	$30,683
Community Health Systems (190)	12,986
Tenet Healthcare (266)	9,233
DaVita (359)	6,447
Universal Health Services (408)	5,572
Health Management Associates (435)	5,169
Health Care: Pharmacy and Other Services	
Medco Health Solutions (34)	$65,986
Express Scripts (55)	44,990
Quest Diagnostics (320)	7,369
Omnicare (371)	6,200
Laboratory Corp. of America (447)	5,004
Home Equipment, Furnishings	
Stanley Black & Decker (288)	$8,410
Masco (314)	7,592
Fortune Brands (352)	6,570
Jarden (379)	6,023
Newell Rubbermaid (397)	5,759
Homebuilders	
PulteGroup (486)	$4,569
D.R. Horton (499)	4,400
Hotels, Casinos, Resorts	
Marriott International (210)	$11,691
Caesar's Entertainment (277)	8,819
Las Vegas Sands (342)	6,853
MGM Mirage (380)	6,019
Starwood Hotels & Resorts (441)	5,071
Household and Personal Products	
Procter & Gamble (26)	$79,689
Kimberly-Clark (130)	19,746
Colgate-Palmolive (160)	15,564
Avon Products (226)	10,863
Estée Lauder (307)	7,796
Clorox (411)	5,534
Industrial Machinery	
Illinois Tool Works (156)	$15,870
Eaton (178)	13,715
Parker Hannifin (248)	9,993
Dover (331)	7,142
Information Technology Services	
International Business Machines (18)	$99,870
Computer Sciences (155)	16,128
SAIC (219)	11,117
Booz Allen Hamilton Holding (438)	5,123
Insurance: Life, Health (Mutual)	
New York Life Insurance (71)	$34,941
TIAA-CREF (87)	32,225
Massachusetts Mutual Life Insurance (101)	25,647

Company (rank)	Revenue
Northwestern Mutual (112)	23,384
Guardian Life Ins. Co. of America (245)	10,050
Thrivent Financial for Lutherans (318)	7,470
Mutual of Omaha Insurance (399)	5,724
Insurance: Life, Health (Stock)	
MetLife (46)	$52,717
Prudential Financial (64)	38,414
AFLAC (125)	20,732
Lincoln National (235)	10,410
Unum Group (239)	10,193
Genworth Financial (243)	10,089
Principal Financial (268)	9,159
Reinsurance Group of America (290)	8,262
Pacific Life (405)	5,603
Insurance: Property & Casualty (Mutual)	
State Farm Insurance Cos. (37)	$63,177
Auto-Owners Insurance (425)	5,396
Insurance: Property & Casualty (Stock)	
Berkshire Hathaway (7)	$136,185
American International Group (17)	104,417
Liberty Mutual Insurance Group (82)	33,193
Allstate (89)	31,400
Travelers Cos. (106)	25,112
Hartford Financial Services (117)	22,383
Nationwide (127)	20,265
United Services Automobile Assn. (145)	17,946
Progressive (164)	14,963
Loews (168)	14,621
Chubb (185)	13,319
Assurant (285)	8,528
American Family Insurance Group (358)	6,492
Fidelity National Financial (398)	5,740
Internet Services and Retailing	
Amazon.com (78)	$34,204
Google (92)	29,321
Liberty Media (224)	10,982
eBay (269)	9,156
Yahoo (365)	6,325
Mail, Package, Freight Delivery	
United Parcel Service (48)	$49,545
FedEx (73)	34,743
Medical Products and Equipment	
Medtronic (158)	$15,817
Baxter International (192)	12,843
Boston Scientific (305)	7,806
Becton Dickinson (316)	7,540
Stryker (323)	7,320
St. Jude Medical (436)	5,165
Metals	
Alcoa (123)	$21,013
United States Steel (148)	17,374
Nucor (157)	15,845
Commercial Metals (361)	6,429
Steel Dynamics (368)	6,301
AK Steel Holding (383)	5,986
Mining, Crude Oil Production	
Occidental Petroleum (129)	$19,857
Freeport-McMoRan Copper & Gold (136)	18,982
Apache (206)	12,092
Anadarko Petroleum (223)	10,984
Devon Energy (231)	10,633
Newmont Mining (260)	9,540
Chesapeake Energy (263)	9,366
Peabody Energy (338)	6,944
EOG Resources (377)	6,100
Consol Energy (428)	5,236
Miscellaneous	
3M (97)	$26,662
Spectrum Group International (381)	6,012
Mattel (392)	5,856
Mohawk Industries (427)	5,319
CB Richard Ellis Group (440)	5,119
Motor Vehicles and Parts	
General Motors (8)	$135,592
Ford Motor (10)	128,954
Chrysler Group (59)	41,946
Johnson Controls (76)	34,305
Goodyear Tire & Rubber (139)	18,832
TRW Automotive Holdings (171)	14,383
Navistar International (204)	12,145
Lear (207)	11,955
Paccar (238)	10,293
Oshkosh (252)	9,842
Icahn Enterprises (270)	9,119
Visteon (319)	7,466

Company (rank)	Revenue
Autoliv (329)	7,171
Dana Holding (376)	6,109
Tenneco (386)	5,937
BorgWarner (403)	5,653
Network and Other Communications Equipment	
Cisco Systems (62)	$40,040
Motorola (116)	22,823
Qualcomm (222)	10,991
Corning (350)	6,632
Harris (429)	5,206
Avaya (445)	5,060
Oil and Gas Equipment Services	
Halliburton (144)	$17,973
Baker Hughes (170)	14,414
National Oilwell Varco (202)	12,156
Cameron International (375)	6,135
Packaging, Containers	
Ball (300)	$7,948
Crown Holdings (301)	7,941
Owens-Illinois (345)	6,762
Smurfit-Stone Container (369)	6,286
MeadWestvaco (373)	6,168
Petroleum Refining	
Exxon Mobil (2)	$354,674
Chevron (3)	196,337
ConocoPhillips (4)	184,966
Valero Energy (24)	86,034
Marathon Oil (29)	68,413
Sunoco (68)	35,453
Hess (74)	34,613
Murphy Oil (113)	23,345
Tesoro (128)	20,253
Holly (289)	8,323
Western Refining (298)	7,965
Frontier Oil (389)	5,885
Pharmaceuticals	
Pfizer (31)	$67,809
Johnson & Johnson (40)	61,587
Merck (53)	45,987
Abbott Laboratories (69)	35,167
Eli Lilly (115)	23,076
Bristol-Myers Squibb (131)	19,484
Amgen (163)	15,053
Gilead Sciences (299)	7,949
Mylan (418)	5,450
Pipelines	
Enterprise Products Partners (80)	$33,739
Plains All American Pipeline (99)	25,893
Oneok (189)	13,030
Kinder Morgan (294)	8,191
Enbridge Energy Partners (309)	7,736
Energy Transfer Equity (351)	6,598
Targa Resources (416)	5,469
Spectra Energy (441)	5,071
Publishing, Printing	
R.R. Donnelley & Sons (247)	$10,019
McGraw-Hill (372)	6,168
Gannett (415)	5,471
Railroads	
Union Pacific (153)	$16,965
CSX (230)	10,686
Norfolk Southern (261)	9,516
Scientific, Photo, Control Equipment	
Danaher (187)	$13,203
Thermo Fisher Scientific (237)	10,789
Eastman Kodak (327)	7,187
Agilent Technologies (419)	5,444
Securities	
KKR (256)	$9,668
BlackRock (282)	8,612
Franklin Resources (393)	5,853
Semiconductors and Other Electronic Components	
Intel (56)	$43,623
Texas Instruments (175)	13,966
Jabil Circuit (182)	13,409
Applied Materials (259)	9,549
Micron Technology (287)	8,482
Broadcom (343)	6,818
Advanced Micro Devices (357)	6,494
Sanmina-SCI (366)	6,319
Specialty Retailers: Apparel	
TJX (119)	$21,942
Gap (167)	14,664
Limited Brands (258)	9,613
Ross Stores (303)	7,866
Foot Locker (446)	5,049
Specialty Retailers: Other	
Costco Wholesale (28)	$77,946
Home Depot (30)	67,997
Best Buy (47)	49,694
Lowe's (50)	48,815

Company (rank)	Revenue
Staples (108)	24,545
Toys "R" Us (176)	13,864
Office Depot (211)	11,633
BJ's Wholesale Club (221)	11,025
GameStop (262)	9,474
Bed Bath & Beyond (304)	7,829
AutoZone (322)	7,363
OfficeMax (330)	7,150
Pantry (363)	6,368
TravelCenters of America (385)	5,962
Advance Auto Parts (387)	5,925
Dollar Tree (390)	5,882
Barnes & Noble (395)	5,811
PetSmart (400)	5,694
O'Reilly Automotive (424)	5,398
Telecommunications	
AT&T (12)	$124,629
Verizon Communications (16)	106,565
Comcast (66)	37,937
Sprint Nextel (85)	32,563
DirecTV (110)	24,102
Time Warner Cable (137)	18,868
DISH Network (193)	12,641
Qwest Communications (209)	11,730
Liberty Global (255)	9,668
Cablevision Systems (321)	7,363
Charter Communications (333)	7,059
CenturyLink (334)	7,042
Virgin Media (374)	6,138
NII Holdings (406)	5,601
Temporary Help	
Manpower (138)	$18,866
Tobacco	
Philip Morris International (94)	$27,208
Altria Group (154)	16,892
Reynolds American (284)	8,551
Transportation and Logistics	
C.H. Robinson Worldwide (301)	$9,274
Expeditors Intl. of Washington (384)	5,968
Trucking, Truck Leasing	
Ryder System (437)	$5,136
Utilities: Gas and Electric	
Exelon (141)	$18,644
Southern (147)	17,456
NextEra Energy (161)	15,317
Dominion Resources (162)	15,264
Duke Energy (173)	14,272
PG&E Corp. (177)	13,841
FirstEnergy (183)	13,339
Consolidated Edison (184)	13,325
Edison International (198)	12,409
Public Service Enterprise Group (201)	12,195
Entergy (213)	11,488
Xcel Energy (237)	10,311
Progress Energy (240)	10,190
Sempra Energy (274)	9,003
CenterPoint Energy (279)	8,785
PPL (280)	8,638
DTE Energy (283)	8,557
Ameren (313)	7,638
Pepco Holdings (335)	7,039
CMS Energy (360)	6,442
NiSource (362)	6,423
Integrys Energy Group (430)	5,203
Waste Management	
Waste Management (196)	$12,515
Republic Services (296)	8,107
Wholesalers: Diversified	
World Fuel Services (133)	$19,131
Genuine Parts (215)	11,208
W.W. Grainger (205)	7,182
Reliance Steel & Aluminum (367)	6,313
Anixter International (414)	5,472
Wesco International (443)	5,064
Wholesalers: Electronics and Office Equipment	
Ingram Micro (75)	$34,589
Tech Data (109)	24,376
Avnet (132)	19,160
Arrow Electronics (140)	18,745
Synnex (281)	8,617
Wholesalers: Food and Grocery	
Sysco (67)	$37,244
CHS (103)	25,268
Core-Mark Holding (412)	5,510
Wholesalers: Health Care	
McKesson (15)	$108,702
Cardinal Health (19)	98,602
AmerisourceBergen (27)	77,954
Owens & Minor (295)	8,124
Henry Schein (317)	7,527

100 U.S. Corporations with Largest Revenues, 2011

Source: *Fortune* magazine

(in millions of dollars; ranked by 2010 revenues)

Rank	Company (2009 rank)	Revenues	Profits	Rank	Company (2009 rank)	Revenues	Profits
1.	Wal-Mart Stores (1)	$421,849.0	$16,389.0	51.	INTL FCStone (49)	$46,940.3	$5.4
2.	Exxon Mobil (2)	354,674.0	30,460.0	52.	Lockheed Martin (44)	46,890.0	2,926.0
3.	Chevron (3)	196,337.0	19,024.0	53.	Merck (85)	45,987.0	861.0
4.	ConocoPhillips (6)	184,966.0	11,358.0	54.	Goldman Sachs Group (39)	45,967.0	8,354.0
5.	Fannie Mae (81)	153,825.0	−14,014.0	55.	Express Scripts (96)	44,989.7	1,181.2
6.	General Electric (4)	151,628.0	11,644.0	56.	Intel (62)	43,623.0	11,464.0
7.	Berkshire Hathaway (11)	136,185.0	12,967.0	57.	Sears Holdings (48)	43,326.0	133.0
8.	General Motors (15)	135,592.0	6,172.0	58.	Caterpillar (66)	42,588.0	2,700.0
9.	Bank of America Corp. (5)	134,194.0	−2,238.0	59.	Chrysler Group (NA)	41,946.0	−652.0
10.	Ford Motor (8)	128,954.0	6,561.0	60.	Safeway (52)	41,050.0	589.8
11.	Hewlett-Packard (10)	126,033.0	8,761.0	61.	Supervalu (47)	40,597.0	393.0
12.	AT&T (7)	124,629.0	19,864.0	62.	Cisco Systems (58)	40,040.0	7,767.0
13.	JP Morgan Chase & Co. (9)	115,475.0	17,370.0	63.	Morgan Stanley (70)	39,320.0	4,703.0
14.	Citigroup (12)	111,055.0	10,602.0	64.	Prudential Financial (65)	38,414.0	3,195.0
15.	McKesson (14)	108,702.0	1,263.0	65.	Walt Disney (57)	38,063.0	3,963.0
16.	Verizon Communications (13)	106,565.0	2,549.0	66.	Comcast (55)	37,937.0	3,635.0
17.	American International Group (16)	104,417.0	7,786.0	67.	Sysco (55)	37,243.5	1,180.0
18.	International Business Machines (49)	99,870.0	14,833.0	68.	Sunoco (78)	35,453.0	234.0
				69.	Abbott Laboratories (75)	35,166.7	4,626.2
19.	Cardinal Health (17)	98,601.9	642.2	70.	Coca-Cola (72)	35,119.0	11,809.0
20.	Freddie Mac (54)	98,368.0	−14,025.0	71.	New York Life Insurance (64)	34,947.2	1,091.5
21.	CVS Caremark (18)	96,413.0	3,427.0	72.	Northrop Grumman (61)	34,757.0	2,053.0
22.	UnitedHealth Group (21)	94,155.0	4,634.0	73.	FedEx (60)	34,734.0	1,184.0
23.	Wells Fargo (19)	93,249.0	12,362.0	74.	Hess (79)	34,613.0	2,125.0
24.	Valero Energy (26)	86,034.0	324.0	75.	Ingram Micro (80)	34,589.0	318.1
25.	Kroger (23)	82,189.4	1,116.3	76.	Johnson Controls (83)	34,305.0	1,491.0
26.	Procter & Gamble (22)	79,689.0	12,736.0	77.	Aetna (63)	34,246.0	1,766.8
27.	AmerisourceBergen (24)	77,954.0	636.7	78.	Amazon.com (100)	34,204.0	1,152.0
28.	Costco Wholesale (25)	77,946.0	1,303.0	79.	Humana (73)	33,868.2	1,099.4
29.	Marathon Oil (41)	68,413.0	2,568.0	80.	Enterprise Products Partners (NA)	33,739.3	320.8
30.	Home Depot (29)	67,997.0	3,338.0	81.	Honeywell International (74)	33,370.0	2,022.0
31.	Pfizer (40)	67,809.0	8,257.0	82.	Liberty Mutual Insurance Group (71)	33,193.0	1,678.0
32.	Walgreen (32)	67,420.0	2,091.0				
33.	Target (30)	67,390.0	2,920.0	83.	News Corp. (76)	32,778.0	2,539.0
34.	Medco Health Solutions (35)	65,968.3	1,427.3	84.	DuPont (86)	32,733.0	3,031.0
35.	Apple (56)	65,225.0	14,013.0	85.	Sprint Nextel (67)	32,563.0	−3,465.0
36.	Boeing (28)	64,306.0	3,307.0	86.	General Dynamics (69)	32,466.0	2,624.0
37.	State Farm Insurance Cos. (34)	63,176.7	1,762.8	87.	TIAA-CREF (90)	32,224.9	1,405.9
38.	Microsoft (36)	62,484.0	18,760.0	88.	Delta Air Lines (84)	31,755.0	593.0
39.	Archer Daniels Midland (27)	61,682.0	1,930.0	89.	Allstate (68)	31,400.0	928.0
40.	Johnson & Johnson (33)	61,587.0	13,334.0	90.	HCA Holdings (77)	30,683.0	1,207.0
41.	Dell (38)	61,494.0	2,635.0	91.	American Express (88)	30,242.0	4,057.0
42.	WellPoint (31)	58,801.8	2,887.1	92.	Google (102)	29,321.0	8,505.0
43.	PepsiCo (80)	57,838.0	6,320.0	93.	Tyson Foods (87)	28,430.0	780.0
44.	United Technologies (37)	54,326.0	4,373.0	94.	Philip Morris International (94)	27,208.0	7,259.0
45.	Dow Chemical (46)	53,674.0	2,310.0	95.	Time Warner (82)	26,888.0	2,578.0
46.	MetLife (51)	52,717.0	2,790.0	96.	Oracle (105)	26,820.0	6,135.0
47.	Best Buy (45)	49,694.0	1,317.0	97.	3M (106)	26,662.0	4,085.0
48.	United Parcel Service (43)	49,545.0	3,488.0	98.	Deere (107)	26,004.6	1,865.0
49.	Kraft Foods (53)	49,542.0	4,114.0	99.	Plains All American Pipeline (128)	25,893.0	505.0
50.	Lowe's (42)	48,815.0	2,010.0	100.	Rite Aid (89)	25,669.1	−506.7

NA = Not available.

Top U.S. Franchises, 2011

Source: *Entrepreneur* magazine

Rank	Company	Type of business	Locations	Startup costs[1]
1.	Hampton Hotels	Mid-priced hotels	1,864	$3.8 mil-$13.1mil
2.	ampm	Convenience store & gas station	3,183	$1.8 mil-$7.6 mil
3.	McDonald's	Hamburgers, chicken, salads	32,805	$1.1 mil-$1.9 mil
4.	7-Eleven Inc.	Convenience store	37,496	$30,800-$604,500
5.	Supercuts	Hair salon	2,130	$119,350-$196,550
6.	Days Inn	Hotels	1,877	$211,170-$6.8 mil
7.	Vanguard Cleaning Systems	Commercial cleaning	2,155	$8,200-$38,100
8.	Servpro	Insurance/disaster restoration & cleaning	1,572	$132,050-$180,450
9.	Subway	Submarine sandwiches & salads	34,871	$84,300-$258,300
10.	Denny's Inc.	Full-service family restaurant	1,668	$1.1 mil-$2.4 mil
11.	Jan-Pro Franchising Intl. Inc.	Commercial cleaning	12,394	$3,150-$50,410
12.	Hardee's	Burgers, chicken, biscuits	1,901	$1.2 mil-$1.6 mil
13.	Pizza Hut Inc.	Pizza, pasta, wings	13,281	$295,000-$2.2 mil
14.	Kumon Math & Reading Centers	Supplemental education	25,199	$67,760-$145,320
15.	Dunkin' Donuts	Coffee, doughnuts, baked goods	9,947	$358,200-$2.0 mil
16.	KFC Corp.	Chicken	16,224	$1.3 mil-$2.5 mil
17.	Jazzercise Inc.	Dance fitness classes	7,683	$2,980-$75,500
18.	Anytime Fitness	Fitness center	1,618	$44,070-$300,070
19.	Matco Tools	Mechanics' tools & service equipment	1,431	$82,300-$191,820
20.	Stratus Building Solutions	Commercial cleaning	5,018	$3,450-$57,750

Note: Franchises are ranked by a combination of factors, including financial strength and stability, growth rate, number of locations, startup costs, and whether the company provides financing. (1) This number does not include franchise fee, which varies.

United States Mint

Source: United States Mint, U.S. Dept. of the Treasury

The United States Mint was created on Apr. 2, 1792, by an act of Congress, which established the U.S. national coinage system. In 1799 the mint became an independent agency reporting directly to the president. It was made a statutory bureau of the Treasury Department in 1873, with a director appointed by the president. The mint manufactures and ships all U.S. coins for circulation to Federal Reserve banks and branches, which in turn issue coins to the public and business community through depository institutions. The mint also safeguards the Treasury Department's stored gold and silver, as well as other monetary assets.

The composition of dimes, quarters, and half dollars, traditionally produced from silver, was changed by the Coinage Act of 1965, which mandated that these coins from then on be minted from a cupronickel-clad alloy and reduced the silver content of the half dollar to 40%. In 1970, legislative action mandated that the half dollar and a dollar coin be minted from the same alloy.

Mint headquarters are in Washington, DC. Mint production facilities are in Philadelphia, Denver, San Francisco, and West Point, NY. In addition, the mint is responsible for the U.S. Bullion Depository at Fort Knox, KY.

The mint offers free public tours and operates sales centers at the U.S. mints in Denver and Philadelphia. Further information is available from the U.S. Mint, Customer Care Center, 801 9th St. NW, Washington, DC 20220; (800) USA-MINT. **Website:** www.usmint.gov.

New Circulating and Commemorative Coins

Source: United States Mint, U.S. Dept. of the Treasury

Dollar coins. A large, unwieldy dollar coin featuring the likeness of Pres. Dwight D. Eisenhower was minted 1971-78. The smaller Susan B. Anthony dollar, minted 1979-81, marked the first time that a woman other than a mythical figure appeared on a generally circulated U.S. coin. A golden dollar coin was first minted in 2000. It depicts Sacagawea (a Shoshone woman who helped guide explorers Lewis and Clark) on the obverse. The reverse shows an eagle and 17 stars, one for each of the states at the time of the Lewis and Clark expedition. In 2007, the Mint began issuing a series of golden dollar coins featuring U.S. presidents on the front and the Statue of Liberty on the back. Each includes the president's name, likeness, and years of service. Four are to be issued each year in the order in which the presidents served. Andrew Johnson, Ulysses S. Grant, Rutherford B. Hayes, and James Garfield were honored in 2011; Chester A. Arthur, Grover Cleveland, and Benjamin Harrison will be honored in 2012. Cleveland will appear on two coins because he served nonconsecutive terms as president. Only presidents deceased more than two years will be honored, so the program is currently slated to end in 2016 with coins commemorating Richard Nixon, Gerald Ford, and Ronald Reagan. From 2009-11, the Mint also issued golden dollar coins whose reverse sides celebrated the important contributions made by American Indian tribes to the development of the U.S. The 2009 coin featured a woman planting seeds; the 2010 issue depicted the Hiawatha belt binding five arrows; and the 2011 coin celebrated the Wampanoag Treaty of 1621.

America the Beautiful quarters. In 2010, the U.S. Mint began an initiative to honor 56 national parks and other sites of national importance. Five new reverse designs will appear on the quarter-dollar each year 2010-21; the order of issuance corresponds to the order in which the featured site was first established. The 2011 quarters commemorated Gettysburg Military National Park, PA; Glacier National Park, MT; Olympic National Park, WA; Vicksburg Military National Park, MS; and Chickasaw National Recreation Area, OK. The 2012 coins will commemorate El Yunque National Forest, PR; Chaco Culture National Historical Park, NM; Acadia National Park, ME; Hawai'i Volcanoes National Park, HI; and Denali National Park, AK.

Commemorative coins. From 1892 to 1954, and again since 1982, Congress has authorized the Mint to produce more than 50 different commemorative coins. Recent issues include the 2007 Little Rock Central High School Desegregation silver dollar coin; the 2009 Louis Braille Bicentennial-Braille Literacy silver dollar coin; the 2010 Boy Scouts of America Centennial silver dollar coin; and the 2011 Medal of Honor gold 5-dollar coin and silver dollar coin.

Bureau of Engraving and Printing

Source: Bureau of Engraving and Printing, U.S. Dept. of the Treasury

The Bureau of Engraving and Printing manufactures the financial and other securities of the United States. It designs and prints a variety of products, including Federal Reserve notes (bills in various denominations), Treasury securities, identification cards, naturalization certificates, and other special security documents. Denominations of the various types of printings produced by the bureau range from a 1/5-cent wine stamp to a $100,000,000 International Monetary Fund special note. Among its products are all hand-engraved invitations issued by the White House.

The first general circulation of paper money by the federal government dates back to 1861, prior to the establishment of the bureau, when, to finance the Civil War, Congress authorized the U.S. Treasury to issue non-interest-bearing demand notes, nicknamed "greenbacks" because of their color. A portrait of Pres. Abraham Lincoln appeared on the face of the first $10 notes. By 1862, the design of U.S. currency incorporated fine-line engraving, intricate geometric lathe work patterns, a Treasury seal, and engraved signatures to aid in counterfeit deterrence. All U.S. currency issued since 1861 remain valid and redeemable at full face value.

The Bureau of Engraving and Printing began operations by 1862, originally separating and sealing bank notes that were printed by private companies. In 1877, the bureau became the sole producer of U.S. currency. In 1894, it also began producing postage stamps. On June 10, 2005, the bureau printed its last stamps, a roll of 37-cent flag stamps; stamps are now produced by private printers.

The Federal Reserve Act of 1913 created the Federal Reserve as the nation's central bank, and provided for currency called Federal Reserve notes. The first notes, issued the following year, were $10 notes bearing a portrait of Pres. Andrew Jackson. In 1929, the look of U.S. currency was standardized. The national motto, "In God We Trust," was added to paper money in 1957.

The Bureau of Engraving and Printing currently operates two facilities, one in Washington, DC, opened in 1914, and one in Fort Worth, TX, which began operations in 1991.

Denominations of U.S. Currency

Since 1969 the largest denomination of U.S. currency that has been issued is the $100 bill. As larger-denomination bills reach the Federal Reserve Bank, they are removed from circulation. Because some discontinued currency is expected to be in the hands of holders for many years, the description of the various denominations below is continued.

Note	Portrait	Embellishment on back	Note	Portrait	Embellishment on back
$1	George Washington	Great Seal of U.S.	$500	William McKinley	Ornate denominational marking
2	Thomas Jefferson	Signers of Declaration	1,000	Grover Cleveland	Ornate denominational marking
5	Abraham Lincoln	Lincoln Memorial	5,000	James Madison	Washington resigning as Army commander
10	Alexander Hamilton	U.S. Treasury	10,000	Salmon Chase	Embarkation of the Pilgrims
20	Andrew Jackson	White House	100,000*	Woodrow Wilson	Ornate denominational marking
50	Ulysses S. Grant	U.S. Capitol			
100	Benjamin Franklin	Independence Hall			

*For use only in transactions between Federal Reserve System and Treasury Department.

Portraits on U.S. Treasury Bills, Bonds, Notes, and Savings Bonds

The U.S. Treasury discontinued issuing treasury bill, bond, and note certificates in 1986. Since then, all issues of market-able treasury securities have been available only in book-entry form, although some certificates remain in circulation.

Denomination	EE savings bonds	Treasury bills	Treasury bonds	Treasury notes
$50	George Washington		Thomas Jefferson	
75	John Adams			
100	Thomas Jefferson		Andrew Jackson	
200	James Madison			
500	Alexander Hamilton (Treasury Sec., 1789-95)		George Washington	
1,000	Benjamin Franklin	Hugh McCulloch (Treasury Sec., 1865-69; 1884-85)	Abraham Lincoln	Abraham Lincoln
5,000	Paul Revere	John G. Carlisle (Treasury Secretary, 1893-97)	James Monroe	James Monroe
10,000	James Wilson (Supreme Court Justice, 1789-98)	John Sherman (Treasury Sec., 1877-81)	Grover Cleveland	Grover Cleveland
50,000	Carter Glass (Treasury Sec., 1918-20)			
100,000		Albert Gallatin (Treasury Sec., 1801-14)	Ulysses S. Grant	Ulysses S. Grant
1,000,000		Oliver Wolcott (Treasury Sec., 1795-1800)	Theodore Roosevelt	Theodore Roosevelt
100,000,000				James Madison
500,000,000				William McKinley

U.S. Currency Designs

The U.S. Dept. of the Treasury, the Board of Governors of the Federal Reserve System, and the U.S. Secret Service unveiled a new design for the $100 note Apr. 21, 2010. A number of new security and anti-counterfeiting features were included in the redesign, including a blue 3-D security ribbon and the image of a bell in an inkwell on the front of the note. The security ribbon contains images of bells and numeral "100"s that change from one to the other as the note is tilted. The bell in the copper-colored inkwell changes color from copper to green when the note is tilted. The new notes were initially scheduled for release in Feb. 2011, but problems in the printing process has postponed the release indefinitely. Upon the issue date of the new currency, older $100 notes will remain legal tender and do not need to be exchanged for new currency.

The new $100 bill is considered the last denomination of the major currency redesign that the Treasury launched in 2003: on Oct. 9, 2003, the U.S. Treasury introduced a new $20 note, using background colors for the first time since 1905. The notes have a security thread running vertically up one side, with "USA TWENTY" and a small U.S. flag; the thread glows green under UV light. Other security features include color-shifting ink in the number "20" in the lower right corner on the note's face. A new $50 note with similar security features was released Sept. 28, 2004, followed by a $10 note on Mar. 2, 2006, and a $5 note Mar. 13, 2008.

Website: www.newmoney.gov.

The U.S. $1 Bill

Plate position: Shows where on the 32-note plate this bill was printed.

Serial number Each bill has its own.

Federal Reserve District Number: Shows which district issued the bill.

Federal Reserve District Seal: The name of the Federal Reserve Bank that issued the bill is printed in the seal. The letter tells you quickly where the bill is from. Here are the letter codes for the 12 Federal Reserve Districts:

A: Boston
B: New York
C: Philadelphia
D: Cleveland
E: Richmond
F: Atlanta
G: Chicago
H: St. Louis
I: Minneapolis
J: Kansas City
K: Dallas
L: San Francisco

Treasurer of the U.S. signature

Series indicator (year note's design was first used)

Secretary of the Treasury signature

The Treasury Department seal: The balancing scales represent justice. The pointed stripe across the middle has 13 stars for the original 13 colonies. The key represents authority.

Plate serial number Shows which printing plate was used for the face of the bill.

Plate serial number Shows which plate was used for the back.

Front of the Great Seal of the United States: The bald eagle is the national bird. The shield has 13 stripes for the 13 original colonies. The eagle holds 13 arrows (symbol of war) and an olive branch (symbol of peace). Above the eagle is the motto "E Pluribus Unum," Latin for "out of many, one," and a constellation of 13 stars.

Reverse of the Great Seal of the United States: The pyramid symbolizes something that endures for ages. The eye, known as the "Eye of Providence," probably comes from an ancient Egyptian symbol. The pyramid has 13 levels; at its base are the Roman numerals for 1776, the year of American independence. "Annuit Coeptis" is Latin for "God has favored our undertaking." "Novus Ordo Seclorum" is Latin for "a new order of the ages." Both phrases are from the works of the Roman poet Virgil.

U.S. Currency and Coin

Source: Financial Management Service, U.S. Dept. of the Treasury; as of June 30, 2011

Total Money in Circulation, 1955-2011

Date	Dollars (mil)	Per capita[1]	Date	Dollars (mil)	Per capita[1]	Date	Dollars (mil)	Per capita[1]
June 30, 1955	$30,229	$183	Sept. 30, 1985	$187,337	$782	June 30, 2009	$909,697	$2,963
June 30, 1960	32,064	177	Sept. 30, 1990	278,903	1,105	June 30, 2010	945,138	3,051
June 30, 1965	39,719	204	Sept. 30, 1995	409,272	1,553	Apr. 30, 2011	1,013,376	3,256
June 30, 1970	54,351	265	Sept. 30, 2000	568,614	2,061	May 31, 2011	1,025,087	3,292
June 30, 1975	81,196	380	Sept. 30, 2005	766,487	2,578	June 30, 2011	1,028,910	3,302
Sept. 30, 1980	129,916	581	June 30, 2008	826,314	2,676			

(1) Based on U.S. Census Bureau population estimates.

Currency in Circulation by Denominations, 2011

Denomination	Total currency in circulation	Federal Reserve notes[1]	U.S. notes	Currency no longer issued
$1	$9,813,612,968	$9,671,610,324	$143,503	$141,859,141
$2	1,834,819,666	1,702,826,476	131,980,618	12,572
$5	11,348,207,260	11,213,973,940	108,442,610	25,790,710
$10	16,444,843,570	16,424,166,020	6,300	20,671,250
$20	134,976,537,960	134,956,433,100	3,840	20,101,020
$50	67,796,754,100	67,785,258,000	500	11,495,600
$100	745,181,164,800	745,159,184,400	NA	21,980,400
$500	142,177,500	141,987,500	5,500	184,500
$1,000	165,495,000	165,286,000	5,000	204,000
$5,000	1,765,000	1,710,000	NA	55,000
$10,000	3,450,000	3,360,000	NA	90,000
Fractional notes[2]	600	NA	90	510
Total currency	$987,708,828,424	$987,225,795,760	$240,587,961	$242,444,703

NA = Not available. (1) Issued on or after July 1, 1929. (2) Represents the value of certain partial denominations not presented for redemption.

Budget Receipts and Outlays, 1789-1940

Source: U.S. Dept. of the Treasury
(in thousands of dollars; annual statements for years ending June 30, unless otherwise noted)

Yearly average	Receipts	Outlays	Yearly average	Receipts	Outlays	Yearly average	Receipts	Outlays
1789-1800[1]	$5,717	$5,776	1866-1870	$447,301	$377,642	1906-1910	$628,507	$639,178
1801-1810[2]	13,056	9,086	1871-1875	336,830	287,460	1911-1915	710,227	720,252
1811-1820[2]	21,032	23,943	1876-1880	288,124	255,598	1916-1920	3,483,652	8,065,333
1821-1830[2]	21,928	16,162	1881-1885	366,961	257,691	1921-1925	4,306,673	3,578,989
1831-1840[2]	30,461	24,495	1886-1890	375,448	279,134	1926-1930	4,069,138	3,182,807
1841-1850[2]	28,545	34,097	1891-1895	352,891	363,599	1931-1935	2,770,973	5,214,874
1851-1860	60,237	60,163	1896-1900	434,877	457,451	1936-1940	4,960,614	10,192,367
1861-1865	160,907	683,785	1901-1905	559,481	535,559			

(1) Average for period Mar. 4, 1789, to Dec. 31, 1800. (2) Years 1801-42 end Dec. 31; average for 1841-50 is for the period Jan. 1, 1841, to June 30, 1850.

U.S. Budget Receipts and Outlays, Fiscal Years 2000-10

Source: Congressional Budget Office; Budget of the U.S. Government, Office of Mgt. and Budget, Exec. Office of the President

A $236 bil budget surplus in 2000 turned into a $1.3 tril deficit as of 2010. From 2000 to 2010, the amount the federal government received in taxes declined, as outlays more than doubled for national defense, Medicare, and other health and income security programs.

(In millions of current dollars. Figures may not add up to totals because of independent rounding or omitted subcategories, including some subcategories with negative values.)

Function and subfunction	2000	2005	2007	2008	2009	2010
NET RECEIPTS	$2,025,191	$2,153,611	$2,567,985	$2,523,991	$2,104,989	$2,162,724
Individual income taxes	1,004,462	927,222	1,163,472	1,145,747	915,308	898,549
Corporation income taxes	207,289	278,282	370,243	304,346	138,229	191,437
Social insurance and retirement receipts	652,852	794,125	869,607	900,155	890,917	864,814
Employment and general retirement	620,451	747,664	824,258	856,459	848,885	815,894
Old-age and survivors insurance (off-budget)	411,677	493,646	542,901	562,519	559,067	539,996
Disability insurance (off-budget)	68,907	83,830	92,188	95,527	94,942	91,691
Hospital insurance	135,529	166,068	184,908	193,980	190,663	180,068
Railroad retirement/pension fund	2,688	2,284	2,309	2,404	2,301	2,285
Railroad social security equivalent account	1,650	1,836	1,952	2,029	1,912	1,854
Unemployment insurance	27,640	42,002	41,091	39,527	37,889	44,823
Other retirement	4,761	4,459	4,258	4,169	4,143	4,097
Excise taxes	68,865	73,094	65,069	67,334	62,483	66,909
Federal funds	22,692	22,547	11,076	15,726	13,854	18,256
Alcohol	8,140	8,111	8,648	9,283	9,903	9,329
Tobacco	7,221	7,920	7,556	7,639	12,841	17,160
Telephone	5,670	6,047	-2,125	1,048	1,115	993
Transportation fuels	819	-770	-3,291	-5,127	-10,324	-11,030
Trust funds	46,173	50,547	53,993	51,608	48,629	48,653
Transportation	34,972	37,892	39,361	36,385	34,961	34,992
Airport and airway	9,739	10,314	11,468	11,992	10,569	10,612
Black lung disability	518	610	639	653	645	615
Inland waterway	101	91	91	88	76	74
Oil spill liability	182	NA	452	333	447	476
Aquatic resources	342	429	581	595	576	580
Leaking underground storage tank	184	189	226	171	169	169
Tobacco assessments	NA	899	934	1,140	951	937
Vaccine injury compensation	133	92	241	251	235	218
Other receipts	91,723	80,888	99,594	106,409	98,052	141,015

Function and subfunction	2000	2005	2007	2008	2009	2010
OUTLAYS	$1,788,950	$2,471,957	$2,728,686	$2,982,544	$3,517,677	$3,456,213
National defense	294,363	495,308	551,271	616,073	661,049	693,586
Department of Defense—Military	281,029	474,071	528,548	594,632	636,742	666,703
Military personnel	75,950	127,463	127,544	138,940	147,348	155,690
Operation and maintenance	105,812	188,118	216,631	244,836	259,312	275,988
Procurement	51,696	82,294	99,647	117,398	129,218	133,603
Research, development, test, and evaluation	37,602	65,694	73,136	75,120	79,030	76,990
Military construction	5,109	5,331	7,899	11,563	17,614	21,169
Family housing	3,413	3,720	3,473	3,590	2,721	3,173
Atomic energy defense activities	12,138	18,042	17,050	17,126	17,552	19,315
Defense-related activities	1,196	3,195	5,673	4,315	6,755	7,568
International affairs	17,213	34,565	28,482	28,857	37,529	45,195
International development and humanitarian assistance	6,516	17,696	15,524	14,074	22,095	19,014
International security assistance	6,387	7,895	7,982	9,480	6,247	11,363
Conduct of foreign affairs	4,708	9,148	8,379	10,388	12,152	13,557
Foreign information and exchange activities	817	1,129	1,220	1,330	1,330	1,485
International financial programs	−1,215	−1,303	−4,623	−6,415	−4,295	−224
General science, space, and technology	23,597	25,525	27,731	29,449	31,047	23,597
General science and basic research	8,819	10,267	10,531	11,052	12,677	8,819
Space flight, research, and supporting activities	14,778	15,258	17,200	18,397	18,370	14,778
Energy	−761	429	−860	628	4,749	11,613
Energy supply	−1,818	−940	−1,991	−416	2,045	5,796
Energy conservation	666	883	580	409	1,432	4,997
Emergency energy preparedness	162	162	195	179	754	199
Energy information, policy, and regulation	229	324	356	456	518	621
Natural resources and environment	25,003	27,980	31,716	31,817	35,568	43,662
Water resources	5,078	5,723	5,099	6,071	8,063	11,656
Conservation and land management	6,762	6,226	9,646	8,718	9,813	10,783
Recreational resources	2,540	2,990	2,956	3,208	3,550	3,911
Pollution control and abatement	7,395	8,065	8,410	8,079	8,270	10,842
Agriculture	36,458	26,565	17,662	18,387	22,237	21,356
Farm income stabilization	33,446	22,048	13,094	13,762	17,635	16,605
Agricultural research and services	3,012	4,517	4,568	4,625	4,602	4,751
Commerce and housing credit	3,207	7,566	487	27,870	291,535	−82,298
Mortgage credit	−3,335	−862	−4,986	17	99,760	35,804
Postal Service	2,129	−1,223	−3,161	−3,074	−978	−682
Deposit insurance	−3,053	−1,371	−1,492	18,760	22,573	−32,033
Transportation	46,853	67,894	72,905	77,616	84,289	91,972
Ground transportation	31,697	42,317	46,818	49,978	54,103	60,784
Air transportation	10,571	18,807	18,096	19,399	20,799	21,431
Water transportation	4,394	6,439	7,695	8,121	9,093	9,351
Community and regional development	10,623	26,262	29,567	23,952	27,650	23,804
Community development	5,480	5,861	11,834	10,198	7,719	9,901
Area and regional development	2,538	2,745	2,514	2,584	3,221	3,249
Disaster relief and insurance	2,605	17,656	15,219	11,170	16,710	10,654
Education, training, employment, and social services	53,764	97,555	91,656	91,287	79,749	127,710
Elementary, secondary, and vocational education	20,578	38,271	38,427	38,918	53,206	73,261
Higher education	10,115	31,442	24,637	23,566	−3,258	20,023
Research and general education aids	2,543	3,124	3,153	3,194	3,456	3,631
Training and employment	6,777	6,852	7,080	7,181	7,652	9,854
Social services	12,557	16,251	16,724	16,805	17,047	19,176
Health	154,504	250,548	266,382	280,599	334,335	369,054
Health care services	136,201	219,559	233,878	247,739	300,013	330,710
Health research and training	15,979	28,050	29,279	29,883	30,570	34,200
Consumer and occupational health and safety	2,324	2,939	3,225	2,977	3,752	4,144
Medicare	197,113	298,638	375,407	390,758	430,093	451,636
Income security	253,724	345,847	365,975	431,313	533,224	622,210
Retirement and disability insurance (excl. social security)	5,189	6,976	7,829	8,899	8,218	6,564
Federal employee retirement and disability	77,152	93,351	103,916	108,998	118,119	119,867
Unemployment compensation	23,012	35,435	35,107	45,340	122,537	160,145
Housing assistance	28,949	37,899	39,715	40,556	50,913	58,651
Food and nutrition assistance	32,483	50,833	54,458	60,673	79,080	95,110
Social security	409,423	523,305	586,153	617,027	682,963	706,737
Veterans benefits and services	46,989	70,120	72,818	84,653	95,429	108,384
Income security for veterans	24,907	35,767	35,684	41,338	45,952	49,163
Veterans education, training, and rehabilitation	1,285	2,790	2,713	2,730	3,495	8,089
Hospital and medical care for veterans	19,516	28,754	32,294	36,974	41,882	45,714
Veterans housing	364	860	−868	−419	−578	540
Administration of justice	28,499	40,019	41,244	47,138	51,549	53,436
Federal law enforcement activities	12,121	19,912	19,617	24,615	27,552	27,766
Federal litigative and judicial activities	7,762	9,641	10,954	11,781	12,083	13,073
Federal correctional activities	3,707	5,862	6,328	6,888	7,298	7,748
Criminal justice assistance	4,909	4,604	4,345	3,854	4,616	4,849
General government	13,013	16,997	17,425	20,323	22,017	23,031
Legislative functions	2,223	3,451	3,541	3,658	3,815	4,089
Executive direction and management	456	569	490	525	535	528
Central fiscal operations	8,285	9,515	10,298	10,553	10,752	11,906
General property and records management	−32	472	285	570	554	1,194
Central personnel management	184	101	−20	−12	102	338
General purpose fiscal assistance	2,084	3,333	3,556	4,089	4,097	5,082
Deductions for offsetting receipts	−2,383	−2,841	−2,346	−462	−1,012	−1,704
Net interest	222,949	183,986	237,109	252,757	186,902	196,194
Undistributed offsetting receipts	−42,581	−65,224	−82,238	−86,242	−92,639	−82,116
Employer share, employee retirement (on-budget)	−30,214	−47,977	−49,476	−53,033	−56,431	−62,100
Total surplus/deficit	236,241	−318,346	−160,701	−458,553	−1,412,688	−1,293,489

Federal Receipts, Outlays, and Surpluses or Deficits, 1901-2012

Source: *Budget of the U.S. Government*, Fiscal Year 2012, Office of Management and Budget
(in millions of current dollars)

Fiscal year	Receipts	Outlays	Surplus or deficit (–)	Fiscal year	Receipts	Outlays	Surplus or deficit (–)	Fiscal year	Receipts	Outlays	Surplus or deficit (–)
1901	$588	$525	**$63**	1939	$6,295	$9,141	$–2,846	1976	$298,060	$371,792	$–73,732
1902	562	485	**77**	1940	6,548	9,468	–2,920	1977	355,559	409,218	–53,659
1903	562	517	**45**	1941	8,712	13,653	–4,941	1978	399,561	458,746	–59,185
1904	541	584	–43	1942	14,634	35,137	–20,503	1979	463,302	504,028	–40,726
1905	544	567	–23	1943	24,001	78,555	–54,554	1980	517,112	590,941	–73,830
1906	595	570	**25**	1944	43,747	91,304	–47,557	1981	599,272	678,241	–78,968
1907	666	579	**87**	1945	45,159	92,712	–47,553	1982	617,766	745,743	–127,977
1908	602	659	–57	1946	39,296	55,232	–15,936	1983	600,562	808,364	–207,802
1909	604	694	–89	1947	38,514	34,496	**4,018**	1984	666,438	851,805	–185,367
1910	676	694	–18	1948	41,560	29,764	**11,796**	1985	734,037	946,344	–212,308
1911	702	691	**11**	1949	39,415	38,835	**580**	1986	769,155	990,382	–221,227
1912	693	690	**3**	1950	39,443	42,562	–3,119	1987	854,288	1,004,017	–149,730
1913	714	715	—	1951	51,616	45,514	**6,102**	1988	909,238	1,064,416	–155,178
1914	725	726	—	1952	66,167	67,686	–1,519	1989	991,105	1,143,744	–152,639
1915	683	746	–63	1953	69,608	76,101	–6,493	1990	1,031,958	1,252,994	–221,036
1916	761	713	**48**	1954	69,701	70,855	–1,154	1991	1,054,988	1,324,226	–269,238
1917	1,101	1,954	–853	1955	65,451	68,444	–2,993	1992	1,091,208	1,381,529	–290,321
1918	3,645	12,677	–9,032	1956	74,587	70,640	**3,947**	1993	1,154,335	1,409,386	–255,051
1919	5,130	18,493	–13,363	1957	79,990	76,578	**3,412**	1994	1,258,566	1,461,753	–203,186
1920	6,649	6,358	**291**	1958	79,636	82,405	–2,769	1995	1,351,790	1,515,742	–163,952
1921	5,571	5,062	**509**	1959	79,249	92,098	–12,849	1996	1,453,053	1,560,484	–107,431
1922	4,026	3,289	**736**	1960	92,492	92,191	**301**	1997	1,579,232	1,601,116	–21,884
1923	3,853	3,140	**713**	1961	94,388	97,723	–3,335	1998	1,721,728	1,652,458	**69,270**
1924	3,871	2,908	**963**	1962	99,676	106,821	–7,146	1999	1,827,452	1,701,842	**125,610**
1925	3,641	2,924	**717**	1963	106,560	111,316	–4,756	2000	2,025,191	1,788,950	**236,241**
1926	3,795	2,930	**865**	1964	112,613	118,528	–5,915	2001	1,991,082	1,862,846	**128,236**
1927	4,013	2,857	**1,155**	1965	116,817	118,228	–1,411	2002	1,853,136	2,010,894	–157,758
1928	3,900	2,961	**939**	1966	130,835	134,532	–3,698	2003	1,782,314	2,159,899	–377,585
1929	3,862	3,127	**734**	1967	148,822	157,464	–8,643	2004	1,880,114	2,292,841	–412,727
1930	4,058	3,320	**738**	1968	152,973	178,134	–25,161	2005	2,153,611	2,471,957	–318,346
1931	3,116	3,577	–462	1969	186,882	183,640	**3,242**	2006	2,406,869	2,655,050	–248,181
1932	1,924	4,659	–2,735	1970	192,807	195,649	–2,842	2007	2,567,985	2,728,686	–160,701
1933	1,997	4,598	–2,602	1971	187,139	210,172	–23,033	2008	2,523,991	2,982,544	–458,553
1934	2,955	6,541	–3,586	1972	207,309	230,681	–23,373	2009	2,104,989	3,517,617	–1,412,688
1935	3,609	6,412	–2,803	1973	230,799	245,707	–14,908	2010	2,162,724	3,456,213	–1,293,489
1936	3,923	8,228	–4,304	1974	263,224	269,359	–6,135	2011E	2,173,700	3,818,819	–1,645,119
1937	5,387	7,580	–2,193	1975	279,090	332,332	–53,242	2012E	2,627,449	3,728,686	–1,101,237
1938	6,751	6,840	–89								

— = $500,000 or less. E = Estimate, as of Feb. 1, 2011. Figures in **bold** denote annual surpluses. **Note:** Budget figures prior to 1933 are based on the "Administrative Budget" concepts rather than the "Unified Budget" concepts. Through 1976, fiscal years end June 30; after 1976, fiscal years end Sept. 30. Surplus or deficit column may not equal difference between figures because of rounding.

Budget Deficits as Percent of GDP, Selected Countries, 1995-2012

Source: Organization for Economic Cooperation and Development (OECD)

Country	1995	2000	2005	2006	2007	2008	2009	2010	2011	2012
Australia	–3.9%	0.4%	1.2%	1.3%	1.4%	–0.2%	–4.9%	–5.9%	–2.8%	–1.4%
Austria	–5.9	–1.9	–1.8	–1.7	–1.0	–1.0	–4.2	–4.6	–3.7	–3.2
Belgium	–4.5	–0.1	–2.8	0.1	–0.4	–1.3	–6.0	–4.2	–3.6	–2.8
Canada	–5.3	2.9	1.5	1.6	1.4	0.0	–5.5	–5.5	–4.9	–3.5
Czech Republic	–13.4	–3.7	–3.6	–2.6	–0.7	–2.7	–5.8	–4.7	–3.8	–2.8
Denmark	–2.9	2.2	5.0	5.0	4.8	3.3	–2.8	–2.9	–3.8	–3.0
Estonia	1.1	–0.2	1.6	2.4	2.5	–2.9	–1.8	0.1	–0.5	–1.7
Finland	–6.2	6.8	2.5	3.9	5.2	4.2	–2.9	–2.8	–1.4	–0.6
France	–5.5	–1.5	–3.0	–2.3	–2.7	–3.3	–7.5	–7.0	–5.6	–4.6
Germany	–9.7	1.3	–3.3	–1.6	0.3	0.1	–3.0	–3.3	–2.1	–1.2
Greece	–9.1	–3.7	–5.3	–6.0	–6.7	–9.8	–15.6	–10.4	–7.5	–6.5
Hungary	–8.7	–3.0	–7.9	–9.3	–5.0	–3.6	–4.4	–4.2	2.6	–3.3
Iceland	–3.0	1.7	4.9	6.3	5.4	–13.5	–10.0	–7.8	–2.7	–1.4
Ireland	–2.1	4.8	1.6	2.9	0.1	–7.3	–14.3	–32.4	–10.1	–8.2
Israel	NA	–4.0	–4.9	–2.5	–1.5	–3.7	–6.4	–5.0	–3.7	–2.9
Italy	–7.4	–0.9	–4.4	–3.3	–1.5	–2.7	–5.3	–4.5	–3.9	–2.6
Japan	–4.7	–7.6	–6.7	–1.6	–2.4	–2.2	–8.7	–8.1	–8.9	–8.2
Korea, South	3.5	5.4	3.4	3.9	4.7	3.0	–1.1	0.0	0.5	1.3
Luxembourg	2.4	6.0	0.0	1.4	3.7	3.0	–0.9	–1.7	–0.9	0.0
Netherlands	–9.2	2.0	–0.3	0.5	0.2	0.5	–5.5	–5.3	–3.7	–2.1
New Zealand	2.5	1.8	4.7	5.3	4.5	0.4	–2.6	–4.6	–8.5	–5.8
Norway	3.2	15.4	15.1	18.4	17.5	19.1	10.5	10.5	12.5	11.9
Poland	–4.4	–3.0	–4.1	–3.6	–1.9	–3.7	–7.4	–7.9	–5.8	–3.7
Portugal	–5.0	–2.9	–5.9	–4.1	–3.2	–3.6	–10.1	–9.2	–5.9	–4.5
Slovak Republic	–3.4	–12.3	–2.8	–3.2	–1.8	–2.1	–8.0	–7.9	–5.1	–4.0
Slovenia	–8.4	–3.7	–1.5	–1.4	–0.1	–1.8	–6.0	–5.6	–5.6	–4.1
Spain	–6.5	–1.0	1.0	2.0	1.9	–4.2	–11.1	–9.2	–6.3	–4.4
Sweden	–7.3	3.6	1.9	2.2	3.6	2.2	–0.9	–0.3	0.3	1.4
Switzerland	–2.0	0.1	–0.7	0.8	1.7	2.3	1.2	0.5	0.6	0.9
Turkey	NA	NA	NA	0.8	–1.2	–2.2	–6.7	–4.6	–3.3	–3.0
United Kingdom	–5.8	3.7	–3.3	–2.7	–2.8	–4.8	–10.8	–10.3	–8.7	–7.1
United States	–3.3	1.5	–3.3	–2.2	–2.9	–6.3	–11.3	–10.6	–10.1	–9.1
Euro area	–7.5	–0.1	–2.6	–1.4	–0.7	–2.1	–6.3	–6.0	–4.2	–3.0
Total OECD	**–4.8**	**0.1**	**–2.8**	**–1.3**	**–1.3**	**–3.3**	**–8.2**	**–7.7**	**–6.7**	**–5.6**

NA = Not available. **Note:** Financial balances include revenues from the sale of mobile telephone licenses in some years.

Public Debt of the U.S., 1870-2010

Source: Bureau of Public Debt, U.S. Dept. of the Treasury; World Almanac research

Fiscal year	Debt (bil)	Debt per cap. (dollars)	Interest paid (bil)	% of federal outlays	Fiscal year	Debt (bil)	Debt per cap. (dollars)	Interest paid (bil)	% of federal outlays
1870	$2.4	$61.06	—	—	1989	$2,857.4	$11,545	$240.9	21.0%
1880	2.0	41.60	—	—	1990	3,233.3	13,000	264.8	21.1
1890	1.1	17.80	—	—	1991	3,665.3	14,436	285.5	21.6
1900	1.2	16.60	—	—	1992	4,064.6	15,846	292.3	21.2
1910	1.1	12.41	—	—	1993	4,411.5	17,105	292.5	20.8
1920	24.2	228	—	—	1994	4,692.8	18,025	296.3	20.3
1930	16.1	131	—	—	1996	5,224.8	19,805	344.0	22.0
1940	43.0	325	$1.0	10.5%	1997	5,413.1	20,026	355.8	22.2
1950	256.1	1,688	5.7	13.4	1998	5,526.2	20,443	363.8	22.0
1960	284.1	1,572	9.2	10.0	1999	5,656.3	20,746	353.5	20.7
1970	370.1	1,814	19.3	9.9	2000	5,674.2	20,106[1]	362.0	20.2
1977	698.8	3,170	41.9	10.2	2001	5,807.5	20,361[1]	359.5	19.3
1978	771.5	3,463	48.7	10.6	2002	6,228.2	21,616[1]	332.5	16.5
1979	826.5	3,669	59.8	11.9	2003	6,783.2	23,326[1]	318.1	14.7
1980	907.7	3,985	74.9	12.7	2004	7,379.1	25,130[1]	321.6	14.0
1981	997.9	4,338	95.6	14.1	2005	7,932.7	26,754[1]	352.4	14.3
1982	1,142.0	4,913	117.4	15.7	2006	8,507.0	28,414[1]	405.9	15.3
1983	1,377.2	5,870	128.8	15.9	2007	9,007.7	29,804[1]	430.0	15.8
1984	1,572.3	6,640	153.8	18.1	2008	10,025.0	33,237[1]	451.2	15.1
1986	2,125.3	8,774	190.2	19.2	2009	11.956.6	38,850[1]	383.1	9.6[1]
1987	2,350.3	9,615	195.4	19.5	2010	13,561.6	44,174[1]	414.0	11.5[1]
1988	2,602.3	10,534	214.1	20.1					

Note: As of end of fiscal year. Through 1976, the fiscal year ended June 30. From 1977 on, the fiscal year ends Sept. 30. (1) Estimated.

State Finances: Revenues, Taxes, Expenditures, and Debt, 2009

Source: U.S. Census Bureau, U.S. Dept. of Commerce

(in thousands of dollars; fiscal year)

State	Total revenue	Revenues General revenues	Intergovt. revenue	Taxes	Total expenditures	Debt at end of fiscal year
Alabama	$21,399,611	$21,998,366	$8,622,220	$8,306,446	$26,422,115	$8,155,943
Alaska	8,868,005	11,529,146	2,391,445	4,953,342	11,337,809	6,589,698
Arizona	23,962,367	26,277,519	10,402,074	11,864,046	31,516,818	12,324,879
Arkansas	12,879,574	15,210,774	4,949,582	7,467,679	16,168,717	4,135,051
California	113,389,307	186,314,745	60,516,817	101,007,459	254,334,062	134,571,934
Colorado	10,336,795	19,302,583	5,576,955	8,682,822	24,886,401	17,202,374
Connecticut	21,699,529	21,846,755	5,518,398	12,927,619	25,683,688	28,394,151
Delaware	5,787,487	6,700,350	1,575,270	2,806,031	7,360,953	5,984,645
Florida	45,494,740	64,241,428	21,083,791	31,956,841	75,688,040	38,885,422
Georgia	33,614,408	34,365,954	12,830,886	16,077,948	41,452,427	13,455,164
Hawaii	6,751,116	9,163,828	2,225,268	4,712,651	11,199,768	6,880,242
Idaho	5,537,466	6,409,721	2,153,027	3,171,863	8,217,478	3,508,973
Illinois	40,318,260	55,579,661	17,409,027	29,268,349	68,449,721	56,962,364
Indiana	27,947,393	29,944,355	9,383,442	14,900,123	32,718,561	23,711,889
Iowa	13,206,904	16,245,544	5,670,077	6,984,279	18,303,986	6,353,306
Kansas	11,654,910	13,575,933	3,815,931	6,694,630	15,832,222	5,857,295
Kentucky	19,007,789	21,486,569	7,487,283	9,755,544	26,853,131	13,364,138
Louisiana	22,912,894	27,203,538	12,521,094	10,014,637	31,098,759	17,504,772
Maine	6,462,297	8,138,033	3,101,082	3,489,105	8,780,506	5,396,983
Maryland	23,912,955	29,517,988	8,775,964	15,126,893	36,023,284	23,472,579
Massachusetts	36,942,312	41,254,783	12,178,164	19,699,494	47,910,538	74,597,901
Michigan	46,252,494	49,587,193	16,475,729	22,757,818	59,191,176	29,591,278
Minnesota	22,781,153	29,042,836	8,006,629	17,161,299	36,308,889	10,524,424
Mississippi	14,373,978	16,819,004	8,209,225	6,470,593	19,246,076	6,208,639
Missouri	17,980,899	24,452,996	9,581,085	10,345,250	28,650,820	19,217,206
Montana	4,827,179	5,710,939	2,097,188	2,407,400	6,267,753	4,763,503
Nebraska	7,380,731	8,403,141	2,770,131	4,000,939	9,034,186	2,516,775
Nevada	7,484,428	9,383,361	2,510,358	5,564,170	12,056,208	4,444,804
New Hampshire	5,639,852	5,721,403	1,952,361	2,125,722	6,956,174	8,411,660
New Jersey	43,345,635	49,062,785	12,424,668	27,074,472	62,044,123	56,897,866
New Mexico	9,665,796	13,512,204	5,072,725	4,851,689	17,111,701	8,001,721
New York	92,385,804	135,223,957	49,089,065	65,029,871	163,706,192	122,651,630
North Carolina	31,576,121	43,398,303	16,092,266	20,496,106	48,585,352	19,910,714
North Dakota	4,372,199	4,913,149	1,349,857	2,414,010	4,486,613	1,752,558
Ohio	24,963,618	54,443,346	19,265,922	23,952,422	71,600,146	27,949,184
Oklahoma	17,444,346	18,664,169	6,553,620	8,160,670	21,355,940	9,855,393
Oregon	7,811,596	18,056,866	5,867,264	7,419,494	24,381,062	12,494,686
Pennsylvania	38,795,484	60,725,555	18,314,112	30,071,179	77,564,247	41,924,042
Rhode Island	4,710,553	6,527,473	2,420,320	2,586,184	7,346,662	9,180,938
South Carolina	19,407,037	21,141,141	8,195,615	7,146,034	28,663,666	15,313,021
South Dakota	2,445,674	3,745,652	1,542,361	1,333,835	4,109,493	3,626,024
Tennessee	18,760,246	23,665,207	8,507,222	10,442,552	27,815,474	4,847,786
Texas	81,143,583	95,252,084	35,574,008	40,786,857	110,725,780	30,438,160
Utah	8,783,428	12,837,189	3,853,815	5,422,858	15,568,462	6,267,888
Vermont	4,559,326	4,977,974	1,573,825	2,505,665	5,449,237	3,426,670
Virginia	25,948,782	34,747,884	8,058,669	16,331,388	42,052,695	24,301,179
Washington	24,478,110	32,521,403	9,829,012	16,408,838	43,443,430	24,603,219
West Virginia	11,113,352	11,113,930	3,775,786	4,788,157	11,481,561	6,501,995
Wisconsin	8,473,697	29,437,323	8,796,443	14,402,506	35,646,272	20,913,355
Wyoming	4,784,765	6,037,408	2,331,836	2,760,491	5,577,990	1,320,852
United States[1]	$1,123,775,985	$1,495,253,448	$498,278,914	$715,086,270	$1,826,666,364	$1,045,166,873

(1) Figures may not add up to totals because of rounding.

State and Local Government Receipts and Current Expenditures, 1990-2010

Source: Bureau of Economic Analysis, U.S. Dept. of Commerce

(in billions of current dollars; as of Sept. 2011)

	1990	1995	2000	2005	2006	2007	2008	2009	2010
Receipts.	$738.0	$991.9	$1,322.6	$1,730.4	$1,829.7	$1,923.1	$1,944.8	$1,953.6	$2,064.7
Current tax receipts	519.1	672.1	893.2	1,163.1	1,249.0	1,313.6	1,326.4	1,252.8	1,307.9
Personal current taxes	122.6	158.1	236.7	276.7	302.5	323.1	334.4	284.8	297.5
Income taxes	109.6	141.7	217.4	251.7	276.1	295.9	307.7	256.6	266.9
Other.	13.0	16.4	19.4	25.0	26.4	27.2	26.7	28.2	30.6
Taxes on production and imports	374.1	482.4	621.3	831.4	887.4	932.7	944.6	920.6	952.6
Sales taxes.	184.3	242.7	316.8	402.2	430.4	447.1	444.0	421.8	438.3
Property taxes	161.5	202.6	254.7	346.9	370.1	396.0	408.3	419.8	430.6
Other.	28.3	37.0	49.8	82.3	86.9	89.7	92.3	79.0	83.6
Taxes on corporate income	22.5	31.7	35.2	54.9	59.2	57.8	47.4	47.4	57.9
Contributions for government social insurance	10.0	13.6	10.8	24.8	21.8	18.9	19.0	20.2	20.8
Income receipts on assets	68.5	68.5	94.3	88.3	103.5	114.5	106.8	93.3	90.9
Interest receipts	64.1	63.0	86.7	76.4	90.9	100.6	91.9	78.7	75.0
Dividends	0.2	1.0	1.4	2.1	2.3	2.4	2.9	2.5	2.6
Rents and royalties.	4.2	4.5	6.3	9.8	10.3	11.5	12.0	12.1	13.4
Current transfer receipts.	133.5	224.2	313.9	454.3	456.7	485.1	505.0	597.8	655.9
Federal grants-in-aid	111.4	184.2	247.3	361.2	359.0	380.8	395.5	482.4	531.5
From business (net)	7.1	13.5	28.6	36.5	38.4	41.3	44.3	46.1	50.3
From persons	14.9	26.5	38.0	56.5	59.2	63.1	65.2	69.4	74.1
Current surplus of government enterprises	6.9	13.5	10.4	0.1	–1.3	–9.1	–12.3	–10.5	–10.8
Expenditures.	731.8	982.7	1,281.3	1,704.5	1,778.6	1,910.8	2,017.0	2,031.7	2,090.0
Consumption expenditures.	547.0	701.3	930.6	1,212.0	1,282.3	1,368.9	1,449.2	1,425.5	1,443.5
Government social benefit payments to persons	127.7	217.6	271.4	404.8	402.9	433.7	456.7	498.1	534.6
Interest payments.	56.8	63.5	78.8	87.3	93.0	101.1	108.1	106.7	110.4
Subsidies	0.4	0.3	0.5	0.4	0.4	7.1	3.0	1.4	1.6
Less: Wage accruals less disbursements	0.0	0.0	0.0	0.0	0.0	0.0	0.0	0.0	0.0
Net state and local government saving	6.2	9.2	41.3	25.9	51.0	12.2	–72.2	–78.0	–25.3
Social insurance funds	2.0	4.0	2.0	7.4	4.7	1.9	1.2	1.7	1.9
Other.	4.2	5.1	39.3	18.5	46.4	10.4	–73.4	–79.7	–27.3
Addenda:									
Total receipts	762.9	1,024.2	1,366.4	1,786.7	1,887.1	1,982.0	2,007.6	2,020.9	2,143.0
Current receipts	738.0	991.9	1,322.6	1,730.4	1,829.7	1,923.1	1,944.8	1,953.6	2,064.7
Capital transfer receipts	25.0	32.4	43.8	56.2	57.4	58.9	62.8	67.3	78.3
Total expenditures	801.7	1,060.1	1,404.5	1,852.6	1,931.4	2,075.0	2,188.8	2,196.3	2,237.0
Current expenditures	731.8	982.7	1,281.3	1,704.5	1,778.6	1,910.8	2,017.0	2,031.7	2,090.0
Gross government investment	127.2	154.0	224.3	281.6	304.4	329.0	348.8	349.3	336.5
Net purchases of nonproduced assets	5.7	6.6	8.6	10.3	11.1	13.8	14.1	14.4	14.5
Less: Consumption of fixed capital.	63.0	83.1	109.7	150.1	162.7	178.7	191.2	199.0	204.0
Net lending or net borrowing (–)	–38.8	–35.9	–38.1	–66.0	–44.3	–93.1	–181.1	–175.4	–94.0

Federal Deposit Insurance Corporation (FDIC)

The Federal Deposit Insurance Corporation (FDIC) was created by Congress during the height of the Depression to maintain stability and public confidence in the nation's banking system. It covered depositors for up to $2,500 in case of bank failure in 1934; the limit today is 100 times that much, or $250,000. In its unique role as deposit insurer of banks and savings associations, and in cooperation with other federal and state regulatory agencies, the FDIC seeks to promote the safety and soundness of insured depository institutions in the U.S. financial system.

The quarterly premiums on deposit insurance are paid by the banks rather than by consumers. The amount of the premium is based on the institution's balance of insured deposits for the preceding quarter and the institution's risk to the insurance fund. In 2009, Congress permanently increased the limit that the Corporation may borrow from the U.S. Treasury from $30 bil to $100 bil.

U.S. Banks, 1935-2010

Source: Federal Deposit Insurance Corp.; as of June 30, 2010

	Total number of banks					Total deposits (mil dollars)				
	All banks	Commercial banks[1]			All savings	All deposits	Commercial banks[1]			All savings
Year		National charter	State charter	Non-members			National charter	State charter	Non-members	
1935	15,295	5,386	1,001	7,735	1,173	$45,102[2]	$24,802	$13,653	$5,669	$978[2]
1940	15,772	5,144	1,342	6,956	2,330	67,494	35,787	20,642	7,040	4,025
1950	16,500	4,958	1,912	6,576	3,054	171,963	84,941	41,602	19,726	25,694
1960	17,549	4,530	1,641	6,955	4,423	310,262	120,242	65,487	34,369	90,164
1970	18,205	4,621	1,147	7,743	4,694	686,901	285,436	101,512	95,566	204,367
1980	18,763	4,425	997	9,013	4,328	1,832,716	656,752	191,183	344,311	640,470
1990	15,158	3,979	1,009	7,355	2,815	3,637,292	1,558,915	397,797	693,438	987,142
2000	9,905	2,230	991	5,094	1,590	4,914,808	2,250,464	1,032,110	894,000	738,234
2003	9,182	2,001	935	4,833	1,413	5,954,288	2,786,756	1,195,914	1,046,195	925,423
2004	8,976	1,907	919	4,805	1,345	6,584,200	3,581,416	872,228	1,139,168	991,388
2005	8,832	1,818	907	4,802	1,305	7,141,178	3,850,051	936,299	1,286,983	1,067,845
2006[3]	8,767	1,780	903	4,796	1,276	6,449,864	3,190,482	818,565	1,311,720	1,118,948
2007[3]	8,605	1,676	888	4,786	1,244	6,702,212	3,273,531	831,081	1,425,607	1,165,119
2008[3]	8,441	1,585	874	4,744	1,227	7,025,790	3,596,712	857,003	1,432,609	1,132,360
2009[3]	8,185	1,505	858	4,632	1,180	7,559,616	4,141,792	962,232	1,512,703	936,101
2010[3]	7,821	1,427	836	4,413	1,130	7,675,621	4,304,392	1,002,473	1,464,022	891,159

Note: Comprises all FDIC-insured commercial and savings banks, including savings and loan institutions (S&Ls). (1) "Nonmembers" are banks that are not members of the Federal Reserve System; "National charter" and "State charter" institutions are Federal Reserve members. (2) Figures for 1935 do not include data for S&Ls (not available). (3) June 30.

U.S. Bank Failures, 1934-2011

Source: Federal Deposit Insurance Corp.

As of Sept 22, 2011. Covers all FDIC-insured commercial and savings banks, including savings and loan institutions (S&Ls) 1980 and after.

Year	Closed or assisted	Year	Closed or assisted	Year	Closed or assisted	Year	Closed or assisted	Year	Closed or assisted
1934	9	1950-59	28	1986	204	1995	8	2004	4
1935	25	1960-69	44	1987	262	1996	6	2005	0
1936	69	1970-79	79	1988	470	1997	1	2006	0
1937	75	1980	22	1989	534	1998	3	2007	3
1938	74	1981	40	1990	382	1999	8	2008	30
1939	60	1982	119	1991	271	2000	7	2009	148
1940	43	1983	99	1992	181	2001	4	2010	157
1941	15	1984	106	1993	50	2002	11	2011	71
1942	20	1985	180	1994	15	2003	3	**Total, 1934-2011**	**3,961**

50 Largest U.S. Bank Holding Companies, 2011

Source: National Information Center, Federal Financial Institutions Examinations Council
(as of June 30, 2011; ranked by total assets, in thousands)

Rank	Institution name, location	Total assets	Rank	Institution name, location	Total assets
1.	Bank of America Corporation, Charlotte, NC	$2,264,435,837	25.	RBC USA Holdco Corp., New York, NY	$84,883,726
2.	JPMorgan Chase & Co., New York, NY	2,246,764,000	26.	UnionBanCal Corp., San Francisco, CA	80,093,962
3.	Citigroup Inc., New York, NY	1,956,626,000	27.	M&T Bank Corp., Buffalo, NY	77,727,154
4.	Wells Fargo & Company, San Francisco, CA	1,259,734,000	28.	Harris Financial Corp., Wilmington, DE	75,329,920
5.	Goldman Sachs Group, Inc., New York, NY	937,192,000	29.	Bancwest Corp., Honolulu, HI	74,273,023
6.	Morgan Stanley, New York, NY	830,747,000	30.	Discover Financial Services, Riverwoods, IL	64,304,907
7.	MetLife, Inc., New York, NY	771,482,771	31.	BBVA USA Bancshares, Inc., Houston, TX	62,686,049
8.	Taunus Corporation, New York, NY	412,229,000	32.	Comerica Incorporated, Dallas, TX	54,244,445
9.	HSBC North America Holdings Inc., New York, NY	366,343,136	33.	Huntington Bancshares Inc., Columbus, OH	53,050,039
10.	U.S. Bancorp, Minneapolis, MN	320,874,000	34.	Zions Bancorporation, Salt Lake City, UT	51,363,791
11.	Bank of New York Mellon Corporation, New York, NY	304,952,000	35.	Utrecht-America Holdings, Inc., New York, NY	49,893,000
12.	PNC Financial Services Group, Inc., Pittsburgh, PA	263,259,894	36.	CIT Group Inc., Livingston, NJ	48,018,164
13.	Capital One Financial Corporation, McLean, VA	199,753,113	37.	Marshall & Ilsley Corp. , Milwaukee, WI	46,516,330
14.	TD Bank US Holding Company, Portland, ME	189,724,467	38.	New York Community Bancorp, Inc., Westbury, NY	40,612,271
15.	State Street Corporation, Boston, MA	188,984,931	39.	Popular, Inc., San Juan, PR	39,013,000
16.	Ally Financial Inc., Detroit, MI	178,889,000	40.	First Niagara Financial Group, Inc., Buffalo, NY	30,909,214
17.	Suntrust Banks, Inc., Atlanta, GA	172,236,691	41.	Synovus Financial Corp., Columbus, GA	28,313,910
18.	BB&T Corporation, Winston-Salem, NC	159,309,671	42.	First Horizon National Corp., Memphis, TN	25,054,784
19.	American Express Company, New York, NY	146,701,000	43.	BOK Financial Corp., Tulsa, OK	24,203,542
20.	Citizens Financial Group, Inc., Providence, RI	131,799,704	44.	City National Corp., Los Angeles, CA	22,532,087
			45.	Associated Banc-Corp, Green Bay, WI	22,048,475
21.	Regions Financial Corp., Birmingham, AL	130,907,840	46.	East West Bancorp, Inc., Pasadena, CA	21,872,774
22.	Fifth Third Bancorp, Cincinnati, OH	110,804,760	47.	First Citizens Bancshares, Inc., Raleigh, NC	21,021,650
23.	Northern Trust Corp., Chicago, IL	97,398,269	48.	Commerce Bancshares, Inc., Kansas City, MO	19,590,328
24.	Keycorp, Cleveland, OH	88,858,600	49.	TCF Financial Corp., Wayzata, MN	18,859,945
			50.	Webster Financial Corp., Waterbury, CT	17,811,483

Note: Includes foreign-owned banks with a strong presence in the U.S.

Status of Top Recipients of Treasury Department "Bailout" Funds, 2011

Source: ProPublica; as of Sept. 22, 2011

	Disbursed (bil)	Returned to govt. (bil)	Dividends to govt. (mil)		Disbursed (bil)	Returned to govt. (bil)	Dividends to govt. (mil)
Auto industry				**Financial services**			
General Motors	$50.7	$22.8	$231.0	GMAC (now Ally Financial)	$16.3	$2.7	$2,336.5
Chrysler	10.8	7.3	401.0	American Express	3.4	3.4	74.4
Banks (public)				Chrysler	1.5	1.5	0.0
Bank of America	45.0	45.0	2,729.3	Discover	1.2	1.2	67.7
Citigroup	45.0	45.0	2,944.1	**Govt.-sponsored enterprise**			
JPMorgan Chase	25.0	25.0	795.1	Fannie Mae	103.8	0.0	14,670.0
Wells Fargo	25.0	25.0	1,440.9	Freddie Mac	65.2	0.0	13,248.0
Goldman Sachs	10.0	10.0	318.1	**Insurance**			
Morgan Stanley	10.0	10.0	318.1	AIG	67.8	17.3	0.0
PNC Financial Services	7.6	7.6	421.1	Hartford Financial Services	3.4	3.4	108.1
U.S. Bancorp	6.6	6.6	195.2	**Investment funds**			
SunTrust	4.9	4.8	497.3	AG GECC PPIF Master Fund	3.3	0.0	75.2
Capital One Financial Corp	3.6	3.6	105.2	AllianceBernstein Legacy Securities Master Fund	2.9	0.0	102.7
Regions Financial Corp.	3.5	0.0	438.0	Wellington Management Legacy Securities PPIF Master Fund	2.6	0.0	55.1
Fifth Third Bancorp	3.4	3.4	313.3	RLJ Western Asset PPMF	1.9	0.0	63.5
BB&T	3.1	3.1	92.7	Invesco Legacy Securities Master Fund	1.7	0.8	417.6
Bank of New York Mellon	3.0	3.0	95.4	Blackrock PPIF	1.6	0.0	1.3
KeyCorp	2.5	2.5	297.2	Marathon Legacy Securities PPIP	1.3	0.0	7.7
CIT Group	2.3	0.0	43.7				
Comerica Incorporated	2.3	2.2	140.9				
State Street	2.0	2.0	63.6				
Marshall & Ilsley	1.7	1.7	214.6				
Northern Trust	1.6	1.6	46.6				
Zions Bancorp	1.4	0.0	175.2				
Huntington Bancshares	1.4	1.4	147.2				

Federal Reserve System

The Federal Reserve System is the central bank for the U.S. The system was established on Dec. 23, 1913, originally to give the country an elastic currency, provide facilities for discounting commercial paper, and improve the supervision of banking. Since then, the system's responsibilities have been broadened. Over the years, stability and growth of the economy, a high level of employment, stability in the purchasing power of the dollar, and reasonable balance in transactions with other countries have come to be recognized as primary objectives of governmental economic policy.

The Federal Reserve System consists of the Board of Governors, the 12 District Reserve Banks and their branch offices, and the Federal Open Market Committee. Several advisory councils help the board meet its varied responsibilities.

The hub of the system is the 7-member Board of Governors in Washington, DC. The members of the board are appointed by the president and confirmed by the Senate, to serve 14-year terms. The president also appoints the chairman and vice chairman of the board from among the board members for 4-year terms that may be renewed. As of Sept. 2011, the board members included: Ben S. Bernanke, chair; Janet L. Yellen, vice-chair; Elizabeth A. Duke; Daniel K. Tarullo; and Sarah Bloom Raskin. Republicans in Congress have blocked nominees to fill the two vacancies since Barack Obama became President in 2009.

The 12 **District Reserve Banks** and their branch offices serve as the decentralized portion of the system, carrying out day-to-day operations such as circulating currency and coin and providing fiscal agency functions and payments mechanism services. The 12 are in Boston, New York, Philadelphia, Cleveland, Richmond, Atlanta, Chicago, St. Louis, Minneapolis, Kansas City, Dallas, and San Francisco.

The system's principal function is monetary policy, which it controls using three tools: reserve requirements, the discount rate, and open market operations.

Uniform **reserve requirements**, set by the board, are applied to the transaction accounts and nonpersonal time deposits of all depository institutions. Responsibility for setting the **discount rate** (the interest rate at which depository institutions can borrow money from the Reserve Banks) is shared by the Board of Governors and the Reserve Banks. Changes in the discount rate are recommended by the individual boards of directors of the Reserve Banks and are subject to approval by the Board of Governors.

The most important tool of monetary policy is **open market operations** (the purchase and sale of government securities). Responsibility for influencing the cost and availability of money and credit through the purchase and sale of government securities lies with the **Federal Open Market Committee** (FOMC), which is composed of the 7 members of the Board of Governors, the president of the Federal Reserve Bank of New York, and 4 other Federal Reserve Bank presidents, who each serve 1-year terms on a rotating basis. The committee bases its decisions on economic and financial developments and outlook, setting yearly growth objectives for key measures of money supply and credit. The decisions of the committee are carried out by the Domestic Trading Desk of the Federal Reserve Bank of New York.

A Federal Advisory Council meets with the Federal Reserve Board four times a year to discuss business and financial conditions, as well as to make recommendations.
Website: www.federalreserve.gov.

Federal Reserve Board Discount Rates, 1955-2010

The interest rate that the Federal Reserve charges its member banks to borrow money overnight is often referred to as the "discount rate." On Jan. 9, 2003, the Fed divided the discount window into two categories: primary credit, for banks in sound financial condition, and secondary credit, for banks that do not qualify for primary credit. The secondary credit rate is 1/2 a percentage point higher than the primary credit rate. Banks typically raise or lower the rates they extend to their customers to track changes in the discount rate.

Effective date	Rate	Effective date	Rate	Effective date	Rate	Effective date	Rate	Effective date	Rate
1955:		**1970:**		**1979:**		**1990:**		**2003:**	
Jan. 3	1½	Nov. 13	5¾	July 20	10	Dec. 18	6½	Jan. 9	2¼[1]
Apr. 15	1¾	Dec. 4	5½	Aug. 17	10½	**1991:**		June 25	2
Aug. 5	2	**1971:**		Sept. 19	11	Apr. 30	5½	**2004:**	
Sept. 9	2¼	Jan. 8	5¼	Oct. 8	12	Sept. 13	5	June 30	2¼
Nov. 18	2½	Jan. 22	5	**1980:**		Nov. 6	4½	Aug. 10	2½
1956:		Feb. 19	4¾	Feb. 15	13	Dec. 20	3½	Sept. 21	2¾
Apr. 13	2¾	July 16	5	May 30	12	**1992:**		Nov. 10	3
Aug. 24	3	Nov. 19	4¾	June 13	11	July 2	3	Dec. 14	3¼
1957:		Dec. 17	4½	July 28	10	**1994:**		**2005:**	
Aug. 23	3½	**1973:**		Sept. 26	11	May 17	3½	Feb. 2	3½
Nov. 15	3	Jan. 15	5	Nov. 17	12	Aug. 16	4	Mar. 22	3¾
1958:		Feb. 26	5½	Dec. 5	13	Nov. 15	4¾	May 3	4
Jan. 24	2¾	May 4	5¾	**1981:**		**1995:**		June 30	4¼
Mar. 7	2¼	May 11	6	May 5	14	Feb. 1	5	Aug. 9	4½
Apr. 18	1¾	June 11	6½	Nov. 2	13	**1996:**		Sept. 20	4¾
Sept. 12	2	July 2	7	Dec. 4	12	Jan. 31	5	Nov. 1	5
Nov. 7	2½	Aug. 14	7½	**1982:**		**1998:**		Dec. 13	5¼
1959:		**1974:**		July 20	11½	Oct. 15	4¾	**2006:**	
Mar. 6	3	Apr. 25	8	Aug. 2	11	Nov. 17	4½	Jan. 31	5½
May 29	3½	Dec. 9	7¾	Aug. 16	10	**1999:**		Mar. 28	5¾
Sept. 11	4	**1975:**		Aug. 27	10	Aug. 24	4¾	May 10	6
1960:		Jan. 10	7¼	Oct. 12	9½	Nov. 16	5	June 29	6¼
June 10	3½	Feb. 5	6¾	Dec. 15	8½	**2000:**		**2007:**	
Aug. 12	3	Mar. 19	6¼	**1984:**		Feb. 2	5¼	Aug. 17	5¾
1963:		May 16	6	Apr. 9	9	Mar. 21	5½	Sept.18	5¼
July 17	3½	**1976:**		Nov. 21	8½	May 16	6	Nov. 1	5
1964:		Jan. 19	5½	Dec. 24	8	**2001:**		Dec. 12	4¾
Nov. 24	4	Nov. 22	5¼	**1985:**		Jan. 3	5¾	**2008:**	
1965:		**1977:**		May 20	7½	Jan. 3	5	Jan. 22	4
Dec. 6	4½	Aug. 31	5¾	**1986:**		Mar. 20	4½	Jan. 30	3½
1967:		Oct. 26	6	Mar. 7	7	Apr. 18	4	Mar. 17	3¼
Apr. 7	4	**1978:**		Apr. 21	6½	May 15	3½	Mar. 18	2½
Nov. 20	4½	Jan. 9	6½	July 11	6	June 27	3¼	Apr. 30	2¼
1968:		May 11	7	Aug. 21	5½	Aug. 21	3	Oct. 8	1¾
Mar. 22	5	July 3	7¼	**1987:**		Sept. 17	2½	Oct. 29	1¼
Apr. 19	5½	Aug. 21	7¾	Sept. 4	6	Oct. 2	2	Dec. 16	½
Aug. 30	5¼	Sept. 22	8	**1988:**		Dec. 11	1¼	**2010:**	
Dec. 18	5½	Oct. 16	8½	Aug. 9	6½	**2002:**		Feb. 19	¾[2]
1969:		Nov. 1	9½	**1989:**		Nov. 6	¾		
Apr. 4	6			Feb. 24	7				

(1) Adjustment credit rate replaced with primary credit rate. See note above. (2) Rate in effect as of Oct. 3, 2011.

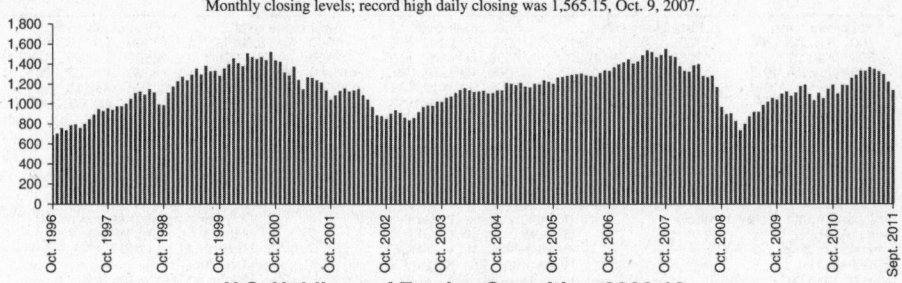

Standard & Poor's 500 Index, 1996-2011
Monthly closing levels; record high daily closing was 1,565.15, Oct. 9, 2007.

U.S. Holdings of Foreign Securities, 2006-10
Source: *U.S. Portfolio Holdings of Foreign Securities*, U.S. Dept. of the Treasury
(in billions of dollars)

	2006	2007	2008	2009	2010[1]		2006	2007	2008	2009	2010[1]
Europe.............	$3,129	$3,652	$2,172	$3,001	$3,154	Latin America and					
United Kingdom....	1,076	1,142	647	958	1,001	Caribbean.........	$946	$1,300	$733	$965	$1,064
France............	402	448	285	362	366	Cayman Islands.....	376	544	315	373	366
Switzerland........	264	288	218	305	327	Brazil.............	110	189	91	213	235
Germany..........	292	426	255	294	299	Bermuda..........	208	273	163	148	159
Netherlands........	234	235	169	233	233	Mexico............	108	110	65	88	109
Ireland...........	121	132	63	120	132	Netherlands Antilles.	58	89	38	57	83
Sweden...........	102	112	59	76	122	Asia..............	1,166	1,325	775	1,053	1,342
Luxembourg........	60	95	60	94	100	Japan.............	596	594	403	419	519
Spain............	111	146	93	113	87	South Korea.......	124	140	56	105	148
Canada.............	478	586	378	540	695	Hong Kong........	88	121	65	93	135
Africa..............	57	76	43	67	99	China, mainland....	75	97	55	102	102
South Africa.......	43	53	32	54	78	Taiwan...........	74	81	41	77	95
Australia...........	173	223	146	276	323	India.............	49	85	32	65	91
(1) Preliminary.						Total holdings.......	$5,991	$7,220	$4,291	$5,977	$6,763

Record One-Day Gains and Losses of the Dow Jones Industrial Average
Source: Dow Jones & Co., Inc.
(Ranked by largest one-day losses and gains for two terms; as of Oct. 3, 2011.)
Over a 4-day stretch in Aug. 2011, the Dow Jones Industrial Average experienced extreme volatility, falling by more than 600 points on Aug. 8, rebounding by 429 points the following day, dropping another 519 points on Aug. 10, and recovering 423 points on Aug. 11. The overall 4-day decline was 301.30 points.

Greatest % losses

Rank	Date	Close	Net chg.	% chg.
1.	10/19/1987	1738.74	−508.00	−22.61%
2.	10/28/1929	260.64	−38.33	−12.82
3.	10/29/1929	230.07	−30.57	−11.73
4.	11/6/1929	232.13	−25.55	−9.92
5.	12/18/1899	58.27	−5.57	−8.72
6.	8/12/1932	63.11	−5.79	−8.40
7.	3/14/1907	76.23	−6.89	−8.29
8.	10/26/1987	1793.93	−156.83	−8.04
9.	10/15/2008	8577.91	−733.08	−7.87
10.	7/21/1933	88.71	−7.55	−7.84

Greatest point losses

Rank	Date	Close	Net chg.	% chg.
1.	9/29/2008	10365.45	−777.68	−6.98%
2.	10/15/2008	8577.91	−733.08	−7.87
3.	9/17/2001	8920.70	−684.81	−7.13
4.	12/1/2008	8149.09	−679.95	−7.70
5.	10/9/2008	8579.19	−678.92	−7.33
6.	8/08/2011	10809.85	−634.76	−5.55
7.	4/14/2000	10305.78	−617.78	−5.66
8.	10/27/1997	7161.14	−554.26	−7.18
9.	8/10/2011	10719.94	−519.83	−4.62
10.	10/22/2008	8519.21	−514.45	−5.69

Greatest % gains

Rank	Date	Close	Net chg.	% chg.
1.	3/15/1933	62.10	8.26	15.34%
2.	10/6/1931	99.34	12.86	14.87
3.	10/30/1929	258.47	28.40	12.34
4.	9/21/1932	75.16	7.67	11.36
5.	10/13/2008	9387.61	936.42	11.08
6.	10/28/2008	9065.12	889.35	10.88
7.	10/21/1987	2027.85	186.84	10.15
8.	8/3/1932	58.22	5.06	9.52
9.	2/11/1932	78.60	6.80	9.47
10.	11/14/1929	217.28	18.59	9.36

Greatest point gains

Rank	Date	Close	Net chg.	% chg.
1.	10/13/2008	9387.61	936.42	11.08%
2.	10/28/2008	9065.12	889.35	10.88
3.	11/13/2008	8835.25	552.60	6.67
4.	3/16/2000	10630.61	499.19	4.93
5.	3/23/2009	7775.86	497.48	6.84
6.	11/21/2008	8046.42	494.14	6.54
7.	7/24/2002	8191.29	488.95	6.35
8.	9/30/2008	10850.66	485.21	4.68
9.	7/29/2002	8711.88	447.48	5.41
10.	8/09/2011	11143.31	423.37	3.95

Dow Jones Industrial Average, 1965-2011
Source: Dow Jones & Co., Inc.
(as of Oct. 3, 2011)

Year	Highest close		Lowest close		Year	Highest close		Lowest close	
1965	Dec. 31	969.26	June 28	840.59	1995	Dec. 13	5216.47	Jan. 30	3832.08
1970	Dec. 29	842.00	May 6	631.16	1996	Dec. 27	6560.91	Jan. 10	5032.94
1975	July 15	881.81	Jan. 2	632.04	1997	Aug. 6	8259.31	Apr. 11	6391.69
1980	Nov. 20	1000.17	Apr. 21	759.13	1998	Nov. 23	9374.27	Aug. 31	7539.07
1981	Apr. 27	1024.05	Sept. 25	824.01	1999	Dec. 31	11497.12	Jan. 22	9120.67
1982	Dec. 27	1070.55	Aug. 12	776.92	2000	Jan. 14	11722.98	Mar. 7	9796.03
1983	Nov. 29	1287.20	Jan. 3	1027.04	2001	May 21	11337.92	Sept. 21	8235.81
1984	Jan. 6	1286.64	July 24	1086.57	2002	Mar. 19	10635.25	Oct. 9	7286.27
1985	Dec. 16	1553.10	Jan. 4	1184.96	2003	Dec. 31	10453.90	Mar. 11	7524.06
1986	Dec. 2	1955.57	Jan. 22	1502.29	2004	Dec. 28	10854.54	Oct. 25	9749.99
1987	Aug. 25	2722.42	Oct. 19	1738.74	2005	Mar. 4	10940.50	Apr. 20	10012.36
1988	Oct. 21	2183.50	Jan. 20	1879.14	2006	Dec. 27	12510.57	Jan. 20	10667.39
1989	Oct. 9	2791.41	Jan. 3	2144.64	2007	Oct. 9	14164.53*	Mar. 5	12050.41
1990	July 16	2999.75	Oct. 11	2365.10	2008	Jan. 3	13056.72	Nov. 20	7552.29
1991	Dec. 31	3168.83	Jan. 9	2470.30	2009	Oct. 19	10092.19	Mar. 9	6547.05
1992	June 1	3413.21	Oct. 9	3136.58	2010	Apr. 26	11205.03	Dec. 29	11585.38
1993	Dec. 29	3794.33	Jan. 20	3241.95	2011	May 2	12928.45	Sept. 22	10572.20
1994	Jan. 31	3978.36	Apr. 4	3593.35					

*Record high closing.

Milestones of the Dow Jones Industrial Average
(as of Oct. 3, 2011)

First close over...	First close over...	First close over...	First close over...	First close over...
100 Jan. 12, 1906	3000 Apr. 17, 1991	6000 Oct. 14, 1996	9000 Apr. 6, 1998	12000 Oct. 19, 2006
500 Mar. 12, 1956	3500 May 19, 1993	6500 Nov. 25, 1996	9500 Jan. 6, 1999	12500 Dec. 27, 2006
1000 Nov. 14, 1972	4000 Feb. 23, 1995	7000 Feb. 13, 1997	10000 Mar. 29, 1999	13000 Apr. 25, 2007
1500 Dec. 11, 1985	4500 June 16, 1995	7500 June 10, 1997	10500 Apr. 21, 1999	13500 May 18, 2007
2000 Jan. 8, 1987	5000 Nov. 21, 1995	8000 July 16, 1997	11000 May 3, 1999	14000 July 19, 2007
2500 July 17, 1987	5500 Feb. 8, 1996	8500 Feb. 27, 1998	11500 Jan. 7, 2000	

Components of the Dow Jones Averages
(as of Oct. 3, 2011)

Dow Jones Industrial Average

Company name (ticker symbol)	Company name (ticker symbol)	Company name (ticker symbol)
Alcoa (AA)	General Electric Co. (GE)	Merck & Co. Corp. (MRK)
American Express Co. (AXP)	Hewlett-Packard Co. (HPQ)	Microsoft Corp. (MSFT)
AT&T Inc. (T)	Home Depot Inc. (HD)	Pfizer Inc. (PFE)
Bank of America Corp. (BAC)	Intel Corp. (INTC)	Procter & Gamble Co. (PG)
Boeing Co. (BA)	International Business Machines Co.	Travelers Companies, Inc. (TRV)
Caterpillar Inc. (CAT)	(IBM)	3M Co. (MMM)
Chevron Corp. (CVX)	Johnson & Johnson (JNJ)	United Technologies Corp. (UTX)
Cisco Systems, Inc. (CSCO)	JPMorgan Chase & Co. (JPM)	Verizon Communications Inc. (VZ)
Coca-Cola Co. (KO)	Kraft Foods Inc. (KFT)	Wal-Mart Stores Inc. (WMT)
E. I. DuPont de Nemours & Co. (DD)	McDonald's Corp. (MCD)	Walt Disney Co. (DIS)
Exxon Mobil Corp. (XOM)		

Dow Jones Utility Average

Company name (ticker symbol)	Company name (ticker symbol)	Company name (ticker symbol)
AES Corp. (AES)	Duke Energy Corp. (DUK)	PG&E Corp. (PCG)
American Electric Power Co.	Edison International (EIX)	Public Service Enterprise Group
Inc. (AEP)	Exelon Corp. (EXC)	Inc. (PEG)
CenterPoint Energy (CNP)	FirstEnergy Corp. (FE)	Southern Co. (SO)
Consolidated Edison Inc. (ED)	NextEra Energy Inc. (NEE)	Williams Cos. (WMB)
Dominion Resources Inc. (Virginia) (D)	NiSource Inc. (NI)	

Dow Jones Transportation Average

Company name (ticker symbol)	Company name (ticker symbol)	Company name (ticker symbol)
Alexander & Baldwin Inc. (ALEX)	FedEx Corp. (FDX)	Overseas Shipholding Group Inc.
AMR (American Airlines) Corp. (AMR)	GATX Corp. (GMT)	(OSG)
C.H. Robinson Worldwide Inc. (CHRW)	J.B. Hunt Transportation Services Inc.	Ryder System Inc. (R)
Con Way Inc. (CNW)	(JBHT)	Southwest Airlines Co. (LUV)
CSX Corp. (CSX)	JetBlue Airways Corp. (JBLU)	Union Pacific Corp. (UNP)
Delta Air Lines Inc. (DAL)	Kansas City Southern (KSU)	United Continental Holdings (UAL)
Expeditors Intl. of Washington	Landstar System Inc. (LSTR)	United Parcel Service Inc. C.I.B.
Inc. (EXPD)	Norfolk Southern Corp. (NSC)	(UPS)

Record One-Day Gains and Losses on the Nasdaq Stock Market
Source: Nasdaq Stock Market; as of Oct. 4, 2011
(ranked by largest one-day losses and gains for two terms)

	Greatest point gains			Greatest % gains			Greatest point losses			Greatest % losses	
Rank	Date	Change	Rank	Date	% change	Rank	Date	Change	Rank	Date	% change
1.	1/3/2001	324.83	1.	1/3/2001	14.17%	1.	4/14/2000	−355.49	1.	10/19/1987	−11.35%
2.	12/5/2000	274.05	2.	10/13/2008	11.81	2.	4/3/2000	−349.15	2.	4/14/2000	−9.67
3.	4/18/2000	254.41	3.	12/5/2000	10.48	3.	4/12/2000	−286.27	3.	9/29/2008	−9.14
4.	5/30/2000	254.37	4.	10/28/2008	9.53	4.	4/10/2000	−258.25	4.	10/20/1987	−9.00
5.	10/19/2000	247.04	5.	4/5/2001	8.92	5.	1/4/2000	−229.46	5.	10/26/1987	−9.00
6.	10/13/2000	242.09	6.	4/18/2001	8.12	6.	3/14/2000	−200.61	6.	12/1/2008	−8.95
7.	6/2/2000	230.88	7.	5/30/2000	7.94	7.	5/10/2000	−200.28	7.	8/31/1998	−8.56
8.	4/25/2000	228.75	8.	10/13/2000	7.87	8.	5/23/2000	−199.66	8.	10/15/2008	−8.47
9.	4/17/2000	217.87	9.	10/19/2000	7.79	9.	9/29/2008	−199.61	9.	4/3/2000	−7.64
10.	10/13/2008	194.74	10.	5/8/2002	7.78	10.	10/25/2000	−190.22	10.	1/2/2001	−7.23

Nasdaq Stock Market, 1971-2011

Year	High	Low	Year	High	Low	Year	High	Low	Year	High	Low
1971	114.12	99.68	1982	241.63	158.92	1992	676.95	545.85	2002	2059.38	1114.11
1972	135.15	113.65	1983	329.11	229.88	1993	790.56	645.02	2003	2009.88	1271.47
1973	136.84	88.67	1984	288.41	223.91	1994	803.93	691.23	2004	2178.00	1752.00
1974	96.53	54.87	1985	325.53	245.82	1995	1072.82	740.53	2005	2273.37	1904.18
1975	88.00	60.70	1986	411.21	322.14	1996	1328.45	978.17	2006	2465.98	2020.39
1976	97.88	78.06	1987	456.27	288.49	1997	1748.62	1194.39	2007	2811.61	2340.68
1977	105.05	93.66	1988	397.54	329.00	1998	2200.63	1357.09	2008	2609.63	1505.90
1978	139.25	99.09	1989	487.60	376.87	1999	4090.61	2193.13	2009	2167.70	1265.52
1979	152.29	117.84	1990	470.30	322.93	2000	5048.62*	2332.78	2010	2671.48	2091.79
1980	208.29	124.09	1991	586.35	352.85	2001	2892.36	1387.06	2011	2873.54	2335.83
1981	223.96	170.80									

*Record high closing, Mar. 10, 2000; as of Oct. 4, 2011.

Milestones of the Nasdaq Stock Market
Source: Nasdaq Stock Market; as of Oct. 21, 2011

First close over...	First close over...	First close over...	First close over...	First close over...
100 Feb. 5, 1971	400 May 30, 1986	1,500 July 11, 1997	3,000 Nov. 3, 1999	4,500 Feb. 17, 2000
200 Nov. 13, 1980	500 Apr. 12, 1991	2,000 July 16, 1998	3,500 Dec. 3, 1999	5,000 Mar. 9, 2000
300 May 6, 1983	1,000 July 17, 1995	2,500 Jan. 29, 1999	4,000 Dec. 29, 1999	

Average Yields of Long-Term Treasury, Corporate, and Municipal Bonds

Source: Office of Market Finance, U.S. Dept. of the Treasury; Federal Reserve System

Period	Treasury 30-year bonds[1]	New Aa corporate bonds[2]	New Aa municipal bonds[3]
1986			
June	7.57	9.39	7.87
Dec.	7.37	8.87	6.87
1987			
June	8.57	9.64	7.79
Dec.	9.12	10.22	7.96
1988			
June	9.00	10.08	7.78
Dec.	9.01	10.05	7.61
1989			
June	8.27	9.24	7.02
Dec.	7.90	9.23	6.98
1990			
June	8.46	9.69	7.24
Dec.	8.24	9.55	7.09
1991			
June	8.47	9.37	7.13
Dec.	7.70	8.55	6.69
1992			
June	7.84	8.45	6.49
Dec.	7.44	8.12	6.22
1993			
June	6.81	7.48	5.63
Dec.	6.25	7.22	5.35
1994			
June	7.40	8.16	6.11
Dec.	7.87	8.66	6.80

Period	Treasury 30-year bonds[1]	New Aa corporate bonds[2]	New Aa municipal bonds[3]
1995			
June	6.57	7.42	5.84
Dec.	6.06	7.02	5.45
1996			
June	7.06	8.00	6.02
Dec.	6.55	7.45	5.64
1997			
June	6.77	7.71	5.53
Dec.	5.99	6.68	5.19
1998			
June	5.70	6.43	5.12
Dec.	5.06	6.13	4.98
1999			
June	6.04	7.21	5.37
Dec.	6.35	7.55	5.95
2000			
June	5.93	7.75	5.80
Dec.	5.49	7.21	5.22
2001			
June	5.67	7.11	5.20
Dec.	5.48	6.80	5.25
2002			
June	5.65	6.57	5.09
Dec.	5.01	5.93	4.85
2003			
June	4.34	4.97	4.33
Dec.	5.11	5.62	4.65

Period	Treasury 30-year bonds[1]	New Aa corporate bonds[2]	New Aa municipal bonds[3]
2004			
June	5.45	6.01	5.05
Dec.	4.88	5.47	4.49
2005			
June	4.35	4.96	4.23
Dec.	4.73	5.37	4.46
2006			
June	5.15	5.89	4.60
Dec.	4.68	5.32	4.11
2007			
June	5.20	5.79	4.60
Dec.	4.53	5.49	4.42
2008			
June	4.69	5.68	4.69
Dec.	2.87	5.05	5.56
2009			
June	4.52	5.61	4.81
Dec.	4.49	5.26	4.21
2010			
June	4.13	4.88	4.36
Dec.	4.42	5.02	4.92
2011			
June	4.23	4.99	4.59

(1) On Feb. 18, 2002, the U.S. treasury discontinued the 30-year constant maturity yield and reintroduced it on Feb. 9, 2006; rates in the interim are for 20-year yields. (2) Treasury series based on 3-week moving average of reoffering yields of new corporate bonds rated Aa by Moody's Investors Service with an original maturity of at least 20 years. Treasury discontinued yield index after Jan. 31, 2003. Rates thereafter are for Moody's seasoned Aaa corporate bonds as listed by Federal Reserve. (3) Index of new reoffering yields on 20-year general obligations rated Aa by Moody's Investors Service; discontinued by Treasury Jan. 31, 2003; rates thereafter are from Bond Buyer Index of general obligation, 20-year-to-maturity, mixed quality state and local bonds.

Ownership of U.S. Treasury Securities, 2001-10

Source: *Treasury Bulletin, June 2011*, Financial Management Service, U.S. Dept. of the Treasury
(in billions of dollars)

In 2001, just over 17% of U.S. treasury securities were held by foreign and international investors. By 2010, the total public debt had nearly tripled, while the portion held by investors outside the U.S. had nearly doubled, to 31.6%.

	2001	2002	2003	2004	2005	2006	2007	2008	2009	2010
Total public debt	$5,943.4	$6,405.7	$6,998.0	$7,596.1	$8,170.4	$8,680.2	$9,229.2	$10,699.8	$12,311.3	$14,025.2
Federal Reserve and intra-governmental holdings	3,123.9	3,387.2	3,620.1	3,905.6	4,199.8	4,558.1	4,833.5	4,806.4	5,276.9	5,656.2
Total privately held	2,819.5	3,018.5	3,377.9	3,690.5	3,970.6	4,122.1	4,395.7	5,893.4	7,034.4	8,368.9
Depository institutions	181.5	222.6	153.1	125.0	117.1	114.8	129.8	105.0	206.4	315.7
U.S. savings bonds	190.3	194.9	203.9	204.5	205.2	202.4	196.5	194.1	191.3	187.9
Private pension funds[1]	145.8	153.8	172.2	173.7	184.9	207.5	257.6	297.2	429.8	615.9
Pension funds of state and local governments	155.1	158.9	148.6	151.0	153.8	156.2	141.6	146.4	174.5	185.8
Insurance companies	105.7	139.7	136.5	188.5	202.3	197.9	141.9	171.4	222.0	253.0
Mutual funds	261.9	281.0	280.9	254.1	251.3	250.7	362.9	768.8	666.2	636.4
State and local governments	328.4	354.7	364.2	389.1	481.4	516.9	537.6	485.5	505.6	519.8
Foreign and international	1,040.1	1,235.6	1,523.1	1,849.3	2,033.9	2,103.1	2,353.2	3,077.2	3,685.1	4,437.9
Other investors[2]	410.7	277.4	395.4	355.4	340.6	372.5	274.6	647.9	953.5	1,216.6

(1) Includes securities held by the Federal Employees Retirement System Thrift Savings Plan "G Fund." (2) Includes individuals, government-sponsored enterprises, brokers and dealers, bank personal trusts and estates, corporate and noncorporate businesses, and other investors.

2011 Federal Corporate Tax Rates

Personal service corporations (used by incorporated professionals such as attorneys and doctors) pay a flat rate of 35%.

Taxable income amount	Tax rate	Taxable income amount	Tax rate
Not more than $50,000	15%	$335,001 to $10,000,000	34%
$50,001 to $75,000	25%	$10,000,001 to $15,000,000	35%
$75,001 to $100,000	34%	$15,000,001 to $18,333,333	38%
$100,001 to $335,000	39%	More than $18,333,333	35%

Characteristics of Mutual Fund Investors, 2011

Source: Chicago Board of Trade

Median age	50	Employed	73%
Median annual household income	$80,000	Married or living with a partner	75%
Median household financial assets[1]	$200,000	Four-year college degree or more	46%
Median mutual fund assets	$100,000	Invest to save for retirement	93%
Median number of funds owned	4	Own Individual Retirement Accounts (IRAs)	68%

(1) Excluding primary residence.

Performance of Mutual Funds by Type, 2010

Source: *Kiplinger* magazine
(as of Aug. 31, 2010)

Fund type/fund objective	Average annual return 1-year	3-year	5-year	Fund type/fund objective	Average annual return 1-year	3-year	5-year
Large-Company				**Sector**			
Growth	12.41%	–8.10%	–0.17%	Financial	13.78%	–16.90%	–6.73%
Blend	13.45	–9.93	–0.81	Precious Metals	40.50	12.25	20.79
Value	13.69	–11.49	–1.48	Health	10.30	–3.39	1.84
Midsize-Company				Natural Resources	7.86	–9.94	5.32
Growth	19.62	–7.76	1.28	Realty	51.22	–9.73	–0.69
Blend	21.41	–8.80	0.35	Technology	18.18	–4.66	3.05
Value	23.65	–9.20	0.50	Utilities	7.75	–8.26	2.48
Small-Company				Hybrid	13.57	–4.31	1.58
Growth	19.07	–8.61	0.53	**International**			
Blend	21.98	–8.86	0.38	Diversified	7.41	–12.86	1.33
Value	25.83	–8.25	0.66	Small/Midsize Diversified	15.91	–12.23	3.55
Taxable Government Bond				Specialized	13.22	–8.95	5.98
Short-Term	4.26	4.86	4.00	**Corporate Bond**			
Intermediate-Term	8.12	6.92	4.91	High Yield	23.93	3.45	5.06
Long-Term	14.04	11.58	5.27	Short-Term	6.69	3.27	3.31
Tax-Free Government Bond				Intermediate-Term	13.10	6.09	4.55
Long-Term Municipal	10.69	3.44	3.04	Long-Term	19.31	6.97	4.95

Mutual Fund Ownership, 1940-2010

Source: The Investment Company Institute

Year	Mutual funds	Mutual fund accounts (thous.)	Households owning mutual funds (mil)	Total net assets (bil)	Exchange-traded funds (ETFs) Number of funds	Total net assets (bil)
1940	68	296	NA	$0.45	NA	NA
1950	98	939	NA	2.53	NA	NA
1960	161	4,898	NA	17.03	NA	NA
1970	361	10,690	NA	47.62	NA	NA
1980	564	12,088	4.6	134.76	NA	NA
1990	3,079	61,948	NA	1,065.19	NA	NA
2000	8,155	244,705	51.7	6,964.63	80	$65.58
2005	7,974	275,479	53.7	8,891.11	204	300.82
2006	8,118	288,596	54.9	10,397.94	359	422.55
2007	8,027	292,590	51.0	12,002.28	629	608.42
2008	8,022	264,599	52.5	9,603.60	728	531.29
2009	7,685	269,224	50.4	11,120.20	797	777.13
2010	7,581	292,109	51.6	11,820.68	923	991.99

NA = Not available. **Note:** Does not include data for funds that invest primarily in other mutual funds. Mutual fund accounts data include both individual and omnibus accounts.

Chicago Futures and Options, 2009-10

Source: Chicago Mercantile Exchange Group, Inc.

Futures group	2009	2010	% change, 2009-10	Futures group	2009	2010	% change, 2009-10
Futures	2,222,038,766	2,635,732,459	15.7	Interest rate	223,923,696	268,726,554	16.7
Commodities and				Metals	5,840,736	9,411,086	37.9
alternative investments	154,150,587	189,280,189	18.6	Energy	64,372,011	71,126,103	9.5
Equities	703,169,398	695,233,561	–1.1	**Combined futures**			
FX products	152,704,645	221,551,655	31.1	**and options**	2,584,920,558	3,078,148,667	16.0
Interest rate	849,626,800	1,109,855,510	23.4	Commodities and			
Metals	50,845,639	70,475,603	27.8	alternative investments	186,554,920	231,113,311	19.2
Energy	311,541,697	349,335,941	10.8	Equities	734,978,313	735,530,779	0.1
Options	362,881,792	442,416,208	18.0	FX products	157,236,746	232,573,780	32.4
Commodities and				Interest rate	1,073,550,496	1,378,582,064	22.1
alternative investments	32,404,333	41,833,122	22.5	Metals	56,686,375	79,886,689	29.0
Equities	31,808,915	40,297,218	21.1	Energy	375,913,708	420,462,044	10.6
FX products	4,532,101	11,022,125	58.9				

Gold Owned by the U.S., 2011

Source: *Status Report of U.S. Treasury-Owned Gold*, Financial Management Service, U.S. Dept. of the Treasury
(as of Sept. 30, 2011)

	Fine troy ounces	Book value		Fine troy ounces	Book value
Total Treasury-owned gold	261,498,899	$11,041,058,821	**Held by the Federal Reserve**		
Gold bullion	258,641,851	10,920,427,976	**Bank**	13,452,784	$568,006,121
Gold coins, blanks,			Gold bullion	13,378,954	564,888,890
miscellaneous	2,857,048	120,630,845	Federal Reserve Banks–NY		
Held by the U.S. Mint	248,046,116	10,473,052,700	vault	13,376,961	564,804,728
Denver, CO, deep storage	43,853,707	1,851,599,996	Federal Reserve Banks–display	1,993	84,162
Fort Knox, KY, deep storage	147,341,858	6,221,097,413	Gold coins	73,829	3,117,230
West Point, NY, deep storage	54,067,331	2,282,841,677	Federal Reserve Banks–NY		
Minting of Congressionally			vault	73,809	3,116,377
authorized coins	2,783,219	117,513,615	Federal Reserve Banks–display	20	853

World Gold Production, 1980-2010

Source: U.S. Geological Survey, U.S. Dept. of the Interior

(in thousands of troy ounces, rounded)

Year	World prod.	North and South America				Other				South Africa	Russia[1]
		Canada	Mexico	Peru	U.S.	Australia	China	Ghana	Indonesia		
1980	39,200	1,630	196	142	970	548	NA	353	55	21,700	8,430
1985	49,300	2,820	266	213	2,430	1,880	1,950	299	84	21,600	8,700
1990	70,200	5,450	311	293	9,460	7,850	3,220	541	360	19,500	9,710
1995	71,800	4,890	652	1,860	10,200	8,150	4,500	1,710	2,060	16,800	4,250
1996	73,600	5,350	787	2,080	10,500	9,310	4,660	1,580	2,690	16,000	3,960
1997	78,900	5,510	836	2,540	11,600	10,100	5,630	1,760	2,790	15,800	3,990
1998	80,300	5,320	817	3,030	11,800	10,000	5,720	2,330	3,990	15,000	3,690
1999	82,600	5,070	764	4,130	11,000	9,680	5,560	2,570	4,090	14,500	4,050
2000	81,700	5,020	848	4,260	11,300	9,530	5,790	2,320	4,010	13,900	5,000
2001	81,700	5,110	757	4,450	10,800	9,000	5,950	2,200	5,340	12,700	4,900
2002	81,300	4,880	686	5,060	9,580	8,560	6,170	2,230	4,580	12,800	5,410
2003	81,800	4,530	656	5,550	8,900	9,070	6,590	2,270	4,530	12,000	5,470
2004	77,800	4,160	701	5,570	8,290	8,330	6,910	2,030	2,950	10,800	5,250
2005	79,500	3,840	976	6,690	8,220	8,420	7,230	2,150	4,200	9,470	5,280
2006	76,200	3,330	1,250	6,520	8,100	7,940	7,880	2,240	3,000	8,750	5,120
2007	75,600	3,290	1,270	5,470	7,650	7,940	8,840	2,320	3,790	8,120	5,050
2008	73,300	3,060	1,620	5,780	7,490	6,910	9,160	2,350	2,070	6,840	5,530
2009	79,100	3,130	1,650	5,860	7,170	7,200	10,300	2,570	4,180	6,350	6,200
2010[P]	82,300	2,930	2,330	5,270	7,330	8,390	11,100	2,640	3,860	6,070	6,170

P = Preliminary. NA = Not available. (1) 1980-94 figures for USSR as constituted prior to Dec. 1991; after 1994, Russia only.

Prices of Precious Metals, 1990-2010

Source: *Minerals Yearbook* and *Minerals Commodities Summaries*, U.S. Geological Survey, U.S. Dept. of the Interior

Year	Dollars per troy ounce			Dollars per pound			
	Platinum[1]	Gold	Silver	Copper[2]	Lead	Tin[3]	Zinc[4]
1990	$ 467	$ 385	$ 4.82	$1.23	$0.46	$3.86	$0.75
1995	425	386	5.15	1.38	0.42	4.16	0.56
1996	398	389	5.19	1.09	0.49	4.12	0.51
1997	397	332	4.89	1.07	0.47	3.81	0.65
1998	375	295	5.54	0.79	0.45	3.73	0.51
1999	379	280	5.25	0.76	0.44	3.66	0.53
2000	549	280	5.00	0.88	0.44	3.70	0.56
2001	533	272	4.39	0.77	0.44	3.15	0.44
2002	543	311	4.62	0.76	0.44	2.92	0.39
2003	694	365	4.91	0.85	0.44	3.40	0.41
2004	849	411	6.69	1.34	0.55	5.47	0.52
2005	900	446	7.34	1.74	0.61	4.83	0.67
2006	1,144	606	11.61	3.15	0.77	5.65	1.59
2007	1,308	699	13.43	3.28	1.24	8.99	1.54
2008	1,578	768	15.02	3.19	1.20	11.30	0.89
2009	1,208	975	14.69	2.41	0.87	8.37	0.78
2010	1,600	1,200	17.75	3.49	1.09	10.79	1.04

(1) Average annual dealer prices. (2) U.S. producer price for cathode copper. (3) New York market price. (4) Platt's Metals Week price for North American Special High Grade zinc except for 1990, which shows average prices for High Grade Zinc.

Economic and Financial Glossary

Source: Reviewed by William M. Gentry, Graduate School of Business, Columbia University

Annuity contract: An investment vehicle sold by insurance companies. Annuity buyers can elect to receive periodic payments for the rest of their lives. Annuities provide insurance against outliving one's wealth.

Arbitrage: A form of hedged investment meant to capture slight differences in the prices of two related securities—for example, buying gold in London and selling it at a higher price in New York.

Balanced budget: A budget is balanced when receipts equal expenditures. When receipts exceed expenditures, there is a **surplus**; when they fall short of expenditures, there is a **deficit**.

Balance of payments: The difference between all payments, for some categories of transactions, made to and from foreign countries over a set period of time. A favorable balance of payments exists when more payments are coming in than going out; an unfavorable balance of payments obtains when the reverse is true. Payments may include gold, the cost of merchandise and services, interest and dividend payments, money spent by travelers, and repayment of principal on loans.

Balance of trade (trade gap): The difference between exports and imports, in both actual funds and credit. A nation's balance of trade is favorable when exports exceed imports and unfavorable when the reverse is true.

Bear market: A market in which prices are falling.

Bearer bond: A bond issued in bearer form rather than being registered in a specific owner's name. Ownership is determined by possession.

Bond: A written promise, or IOU, by the issuer to repay a fixed amount of borrowed money on a specified date and generally to pay interest at regular intervals in the interim.

Bull market: A market in which prices are on the rise.

Capital gain (loss): An increase (decrease) in the market value of an asset over some period of time. For tax purposes, capital gains are typically calculated from when an asset is bought to when it is sold.

Commercial paper: An extremely short-term corporate IOU, generally due in 270 days or less.

Consumer price index (CPI): A statistical measure of the change in the price of consumer goods.

Convertible bond: A corporate bond (see below) that may be converted into a stated number of shares of common stock. Its price tends to fluctuate along with fluctuations in the price of the stock and with changes in interest rates.

Corporate bond: A bond issued by a corporation. The bond normally has a stated life and pays a fixed rate of interest. Considered safer than the common or preferred stock of the same company.

Cost of living: The cost of maintaining a standard of living measured in terms of purchased goods and services. Inflation typically measures changes in the cost of living.

Cost-of-living adjustments: Changes in promised payments, such as retirement benefits, to account for changes in the cost of living.

Credit crunch (liquidity crisis): A situation in which cash for lending is in short supply.

Debenture: An unsecured bond backed only by the general credit of the issuing corporation.

Deficit spending: Government spending in excess of revenues, generally financed with the sale of bonds. A deficit increases the government debt.

Deflation: A decrease in the level of prices.

Depression: A long period of economic decline marked by low prices, high unemployment, and many business failures.

Derivatives: Financial contracts, such as options, whose values are based on, or derived from, the price of an underlying financial asset or indicator such as a stock or an interest rate.

Devaluation: The official lowering of a nation's currency, decreasing its value in relation to foreign currencies.

Discount rate: The rate of interest set by the Federal Reserve that member banks are charged when borrowing money through the Federal Reserve System.

Disposable income: Income after taxes that is available to persons for spending and saving.

Diversification: Investing in more than one asset in order to reduce the riskiness of the overall asset portfolio. By holding more than one asset, losses on some assets may be offset by gains realized on other assets.

Dividend: Discretionary payment by a corporation to its shareholders, usually in the form of cash or stock shares.

Dow Jones Industrial Average: An index of stock market prices, based on the prices of 30 companies, 28 of which are on the New York Stock Exchange.

Econometrics: The use of statistical methods to study economic and financial data.

Federal Deposit Insurance Corp. (FDIC): A U.S. government-sponsored corporation that insures accounts in national banks and other qualified institutions against bank failures.

Federal Reserve System: The entire banking system of the U.S., incorporating 12 Federal Reserve banks (one in each of 12 Federal Reserve districts), 25 Federal Reserve branch banks, all national banks, and state-chartered commercial banks and trust companies that have been admitted to its membership. The governors of the system greatly influence the nation's monetary and credit policies.

Full employment: The economy is said to be at full employment when everyone who wishes to work at the going wage-rate for his or her type of labor is employed, save only for the small amount of unemployment due to the time it takes to switch from one job to another.

Futures: A futures contract is an agreement to buy or sell a specific amount of a commodity or financial instrument at a particular price at a set date in the future. For example, futures based on a stock index (such as the Dow Jones Industrial Average) are bets on the future price of that group of stocks.

Golden parachute: Provisions in contracts of some high-level executives guaranteeing substantial severance benefits if they lose their position in a corporate takeover.

Government bond: A bond issued by the U.S. Treasury, considered a safe investment. These are divided into 2 categories—marketable and not marketable. Savings bonds cannot be bought and sold once the original purchase is made. Marketable bonds fall into several categories. Treasury bills are short-term U.S. obligations, maturing in 3, 6, or 12 months. Treasury notes mature in up to 10 years. Treasury bonds mature in 10 to 30 years. Indexed bonds are adjusted for inflation.

Greenmail: A company buying back its own shares for more than the going market price to avoid a threatened hostile takeover.

Gross domestic product (GDP): The market value of all goods and services that have been bought for final use during a period of time. It became the official measure of the size of the U.S. economy in 1991, replacing gross national product (GNP), in use since 1941. GDP covers workers and capital employed within the nation's borders. GNP covers production by U.S. residents regardless of where it takes place. The switch aligned U.S. terminology with that of most other industrialized countries.

Hedge fund: A flexible investment fund for a limited number of large investors (the minimum investment is typically $1 mil). Hedge funds use a variety of investment techniques, including those forbidden to mutual funds, such as short-selling and heavy leveraging.

Hedging: Taking two positions whose gains and losses will offset each other if prices change, in order to limit risk.

Individual retirement account (IRA): A self-funded tax-advantaged retirement plan that allows employed individuals to contribute up to a maximum yearly sum. With a traditional IRA, individuals contribute pre-tax earnings and defer income taxes until retirement. With a Roth IRA, individuals contribute after-tax earnings but do not pay taxes on future withdrawals (the interest is never taxed). 401(k) plans are employer-sponsored plans similar to traditional IRAs, but having higher contribution limits.

Inflation: An increase in the level of prices.

Insider information: Important facts about the condition or plans of a corporation that have not been released to the general public.

Interest: The cost of borrowing money.

Investment bank: A financial institution that arranges the initial issuance of stocks and bonds and offers companies advice about acquisitions and divestitures.

Junk bonds: Bonds issued by companies with low credit ratings. They typically pay relatively high interest rates because of the fear of default.

Leading indicators: A series of 11 indicators from different segments of the economy used by the U.S. Commerce Department to predict when changes in the level of economic activity will occur.

Leverage: The extent to which a purchase was paid for with borrowed money. Amplifies the potential gain or loss for the purchaser.

Leveraged buyout (LBO): An acquisition of a company in which much of the purchase price is borrowed, with the debt to be repaid from future profits or by subsequently selling off company assets. A leveraged buyout is typically carried out by a small group of investors, often including incumbent management.

Liquid assets: Assets consisting of cash and/or items that are easily converted into cash.

Margin account: A brokerage account that allows a person to trade securities on credit. A **margin call** is a demand for more collateral on the account.

Money supply: The currency held by the public, plus checking accounts in commercial banks and savings institutions.

Mortgage-backed securities: Created when a bank, builder, or government agency gathers together a group of mortgages and then sells bonds to other institutions and the public. The investors receive their proportionate share of the interest payments

on the loans as well as the principal payments. Usually, the mortgages in question are guaranteed by the government.

Municipal bond: Issued by governmental units such as states, cities, local taxing authorities, and other agencies. Interest is exempt from U.S.—and sometimes state and local—income tax. Municipal bond unit investment trusts offer a portfolio of many different municipal bonds chosen by professionals. The income is exempt from federal income taxes.

Mutual fund: A portfolio of professionally bought and managed financial assets in which you pool your money along with that of many other people. A share price is based on net asset value, or the value of all the investments owned by the funds, less any debt, and divided by the total number of shares. The major advantage, relative to investing individually in only a small number of stocks, is less risk—the holdings are spread out over many assets and if one or two do badly the remainder may shield you from the losses. Bond funds are mutual funds that deal in the bond market exclusively. Money market mutual funds buy in the so-called money market—institutions that need to borrow large sums of money for short terms. These funds often offer special checking account advantages.

National debt: The debt of the national government, as distinguished from the debts of political subdivisions of the nation and of private business and individuals.

National debt ceiling: Total borrowing limit set by Congress beyond which the U.S. national debt cannot rise. This limit is periodically raised by congressional vote.

Option: A type of contractual agreement between a buyer and a seller to buy or sell shares of a security. A **call** option contract gives the right to purchase shares of a specific stock at a stated price within a given period of time. A **put** option contract gives the buyer the right to sell shares of a specific stock at a stated price within a given period of time.

Per capita income: The total income of a group divided by the number of people in the group.

Prime interest rate: The rate charged by banks on short-term loans to large commercial customers with the highest credit rating.

Producer price index: A statistical measure of the change in the price of wholesale goods. It is reported for 3 different stages of the production chain: crude, intermediate, and finished goods.

Program trading: Trading techniques involving large numbers and large blocks of stocks, usually used in conjunction with computer programs. Techniques include index arbitrage, in which traders profit from price differences between stocks and futures contracts on stock indexes, and portfolio insurance, which is the use of stock-index futures to protect stock investors from potentially large losses when the market drops.

Public debt: The total of a nation's debts owed by state, local, and national government. Increases in this sum, reflected in public-sector deficits, indicate how much of the nation's spending is being financed by borrowing rather than by taxation.

Recession: A mild decrease in economic activity marked by a decline in real (inflation-adjusted) GDP, employment, and trade, usually lasting from 6 months to a year, and marked by widespread decline in many sectors of the economy.

Savings Association Insurance Fund (SAIF): Created in 1989 to insure accounts in savings and loan associations up to $100,000.

Seasonal adjustment: Statistical changes made to compensate for regular fluctuations in data that are so great they tend to distort the statistics and make comparisons meaningless. For instance, seasonal adjustments are made for a slowdown in housing construction in midwinter and for the rise in farm income in the fall after summer crops are harvested.

Short-selling: Borrowing shares of stock from a brokerage firm and selling them, hoping to buy the shares back at a lower price, return them, and realize a profit from the decline in prices.

Stagnation: Economic slowdown in which there is little growth in the GDP, capital investment, and real income.

Stock: Common stocks are shares of ownership in a corporation. For publicly held firms, the stock typically trades on an exchange, such as the New York Stock Exchange; for closely held firms, the founders and managers own most of the stock. There can be wide swings in the prices of this kind of stock. Preferred stock is a type of stock on which a fixed dividend must be paid before holders of common stock are issued their share of the issuing corporation's earnings. Preferred stock is less risky than common stock. Convertible preferred stock can be converted into the common stock of the company that issued the preferred. Over-the-counter stock is not traded on the major or regional exchanges, but rather through dealers from whom you buy directly. Blue chip stocks are so called because they have been leading stocks for a long time. Growth stocks are from companies that reinvest their earnings, rather than pay dividends, with the expectation of future stock price appreciation.

Supply-side economics: A school of thinking about economic policy holding that lowering income tax rates will inevitably lead to enhanced economic growth and general revitalization of the economy.

Takeover: Acquisition of one company by another company or group by sale or merger. A friendly takeover occurs when the acquired company's management is agreeable to the merger; when management is opposed to the merger, it is a hostile takeover.

Tender offer: A public offer to buy a company's stock; usually priced at a premium above the market.

Zero coupon bond: A corporate or government bond that is issued at a deep discount from the maturity value and pays no interest during the life of the bond. It is redeemable at face value.

Top Brands in Selected Categories, 2010-11

Source: Information Resources, Inc., a Chicago-based marketing research company

Figures for 52-week period ending Sept. 4, 2011. Sales in millions of dollars; change represents dollar sales change in 2010-11 over same period in 2009-10.

	Sales	% change	Market share		Sales	% change	Market share
Baby food				**Dog food (dry)**			
Gerber Second Foods	$246.5	−5.57%	27.84%	Private label	$208.0	−10.39%	9.76%
Gerber	91.5	−2.51	10.34	Pedigree	169.1	−5.60	7.94
Gerber Graduates	81.3	−0.77	9.18	Purina Beneful	130.9	4.11	6.14
Beechnut Stage 2	50.1	−1.08	5.66	Purina Beneful Healthy Weight	117.4	7.69	5.51
Gerber Third Foods	46.8	−13.47	5.29	Kibbles 'n' Bits	98.9	6.64	4.64
Total sales	885.1	−0.48		Total sales	2,130.5	0.15	
Batteries (alkaline)				**Ice cream**			
Duracell Coppertop	$462.5	2.23%	41.75%	Private label	$1,018.0	2.90%	25.26%
Energizer Max	331.1	3.74	29.88	Breyers	413.1	−5.05	10.25
Private label	209.7	−0.37	18.93	Blue Bell	330.5	11.43	8.20
Ray O Vac	24.2	4.59	2.18	Dreyer's Edy's Slow Churned	282.2	−4.97	7.00
Duracell Ultra	20.5	0.53	1.85	Häagen-Dazs	260.6	5.69	6.47
Total sales	1,107.8	−1.51		Total sales	4,029.8	1.85	
Beer				**Paper towels**			
Bud Light	$1,445.1	1.57%	14.96%	Bounty	$977.7	3.47%	38.79%
Coors Light	748.2	3.46	7.75	Private label	630.7	−1.37	25.02
Miller Lite	667.8	1.24	6.92	Kleenex Viva	179.6	−5.04	7.12
Budweiser	610.7	−2.07	6.32	Bounty Basic	172.0	1.91	6.82
Corona Extra	414.2	−2.69	4.29	Sparkle	132.8	25.21	5.27
Total sales	9,656.6	1.85		Total sales	2,520.4	0.90	
Bottled water				**Pizza (frozen)**			
Private label	$874.9	5.43%	22.35%	DiGiorno	$707.4	5.50%	22.58%
Aquafina	350.8	−0.65	8.96	Private label	312.4	2.22	9.97
Dasani	305.7	5.15	7.81	Red Baron	278.2	2.52	8.88
Glaceau Vitamin Water	278.9	−3.28	7.12	Tombstone	239.6	−8.37	7.65
Poland Spring	256.6	−4.14	6.55	Totino's Party Pizza	168.8	1.60	5.39
Total sales	3,914.6	2.57		Total sales	3,132.5	−1.75	
Cat food (dry)				**Potato chips**			
Private label	$96.4	−10.02%	8.53%	Lay's	$718.9	−26.64%	19.77%
Purina Cat Chow Complete Formula	88.0	6.44	7.79	Lay's Natural	418.9	4,490.81	11.52
Meow Mix	81.7	−0.23	7.24	Private label	259.1	5.68	7.13
Purina Cat Chow Indoor Formula	76.2	−1.14	6.75	Ruffles	334.5	2.02	9.20
Purina Kit 'N' Ka Boodle	57.2	1.25	5.06	Wavy Lay's	301.2	−4.74	8.28
Total sales	1,129.6	−2.30		Total sales	3,636.7	2.47	
Chocolate candies				**Salad dressing**			
M&Ms	$318.0	7.00%	14.38%	Hidden Valley Ranch	$229.5	0.43%	16.64%
Hershey's	197.9	0.79	8.95	Kraft	193.6	2.10	14.03
Reese's	122.0	21.39	5.52	Private label	190.1	−1.27	13.78
Hershey's Kisses	963	1.87	4.35	Wishbone	163.8	−2.32	11.87
Lindt Lindor	84.2	16.98	3.81	Ken's Steak House	154.7	5.75	11.22
Total sales	2,211.6	5.38		Total sales	1,379.2	−0.29	
Coffee (ground)				**Soft drinks**			
Folgers	$774.2	16.21%	28.68%	Coke Classic	$1,804.6	2.12%	21.49%
Maxwell House	433.8	7.50	16.07	Pepsi	1,275.2	−1.82	15.18
Private label	282.8	18.70	10.48	Mountain Dew	772.7	4.25	9.20
Starbucks	258.2	13.63	9.57	Dr Pepper	666.2	4.47	7.93
Dunkin' Donuts	178.2	15.47	6.60	Private label	652.4	0.95	7.77
Total sales	2,699.6	12.31		Total sales	8,398.6	2.20	
Cold cereals (ready-to-eat)				**Soft drinks (low calorie)**			
Private label	$647.4	−1.72%	10.05%	Diet Coke	$1,160.2	0.87%	24.23%
General Mills Honey Nut Cheerios	340.3	2.33	5.28	Diet Pepsi	669.2	−4.55	13.98
Post Honey Bunches of Oats	302.5	−4.28	4.70	Diet Dr Pepper	345.9	2.82	7.23
General Mills Cheerios	288.9	2.82	4.48	Coke Zero	332.8	14.95	6.95
Kelloggs Frosted Flakes	254.4	5.53	3.95	Diet Mountain Dew	328.4	7.10	6.86
Total sales	6,442.5	−0.44		Total sales	4,787.5	1.31	
Cookies				**Toothpaste**			
Private label	$637.4	−0.72%	15.12%	Crest Whitening plus Scope	$101.2	−4.80%	7.45%
Nabisco Chips Ahoy	323.8	3.10	7.68	Crest Pro Health	98.7	37.10	7.27
Nabisco Oreo	317.2	9.19	7.52	Colgate Total	94.6	4.99	6.97
Nabisco Oreo Double Stuf	$147.0	−8.44	3.49%	Crest	93.0	−5.27	6.85
Lofthouse	137.7	3.25	3.27	Sensodyne	63.3	12.79	4.67
Total sales	4,215.8	2.45		Total sales	1,357.6	5.16	

Note: For all categories, brands are ranked by dollar sales at supermarkets, drugstores, and mass merchandisers, excluding Wal-Mart. "Private label" represents the aggregated sales figures for store-branded products in that category. Total category sales include other brands not listed here.

Who Owns What: Familiar Consumer Products and Services

The following is a partial list of well-known consumer brands with their (U.S.) parent companies as of Oct. 2011. Among brands not listed are many brands whose parent companies have the same or a similar name (e.g., Colgate is a product of Colgate-Palmolive Co.).

A&W root beer: Dr Pepper Snapple Group
ABC broadcasting: Walt Disney
Advil: Pfizer
Ajax cleanser: Colgate-Palmolive
Altoids mints: Mars
Amana appliances: Whirlpool Corp.
American Girl: Mattel
Aquafina water: PepsiCo
Arm & Hammer: Church & Dwight
Arrid antiperspirant: Church & Dwight
Aunt Jemima Pancake mix: PepsiCo
Band-Aid bandages: Johnson & Johnson
Barbie dolls: Mattel
Betty Crocker prods.: General Mills
Bounty paper towels: Procter & Gamble
Brillo soap pads: Armaly Brands
Brita water systems: Clorox
Calphalon cookware: Newell Rubbermaid
Canada Dry ginger ale: Dr Pepper Snapple Group
Cap'n Crunch cereal: PepsiCo
Champion athletic apparel: Hanesbrands
Charmin toilet tissue: Procter & Gamble
Cheer detergent: Procter & Gamble
Cheerios cereal: General Mills
Cheez Whiz: Kraft
Chef Boyardee: ConAgra
Chips Ahoy!: Kraft
Clairol hair products.: Procter & Gamble
Claritin allergy products: Merck
Coppertone sunscreen: Merck
Crest toothpaste: Procter & Gamble
Crisco shortening: J.M. Smucker
Dasani water: Coca-Cola
Dial soap: Henkel
Dr. Scholl's: Merck
Doritos chips: PepsiCo
Dove soap: Unilever
Dreyer's ice cream: Nestlé
Duracell batteries: Procter & Gamble
Fantastik: S.C. Johnson
Febreze: Procter & Gamble
Fisher-Price toys: Mattel
Folger's coffee: J.M. Smucker
Formula 409 spray cleaner: Clorox
Friskies cat food: Nestlé
Frito-Lay's snacks: PepsiCo
Fruit of the Loom apparel: Berkshire Hathaway
Gatorade: PepsiCo
Gerber baby food: Nestlé
Gillette razors: Procter & Gamble
Glad products: Clorox
Glade air fresheners: S.C. Johnson
Green Giant vegetables: General Mills
Häagen-Dazs: General Mills
Halls cough drops: Kraft
Hamburger Helper: General Mills
Head & Shoulders shampoo: Procter & Gamble

Healthy Choice meals: ConAgra
Hebrew National meats: ConAgra
Hellmann's mayonnaise: Unilever
Hillshire Farm meats: Sara Lee
Hostess cupcakes: Interstate Bakeries
Hot Wheels/Matchbox cars: Mattel
Huggies diapers: Kimberly-Clark
Hunt's tomatoes: ConAgra
Iams pet food: Procter & Gamble
Irish Spring soap: Colgate-Palmolive
Ivory soap: Procter & Gamble
Jell-O: Kraft
Jennie-O turkey: Hormel
Jif peanut butter: J.M. Smucker
Jimmy Dean sausages: Sara Lee
Keebler cookies: Kellogg Co.
KFC restaurants: Yum! Brands
Kibbles 'n Bits pet food: Del Monte
Kingsford charcoal: Clorox
Kit Kat candy: Hershey
KitchenAid appliances: Whirlpool
Kleenex: Kimberly-Clark
Kmart: Sears Holdings Corp.
Knorr soups: Unilever
Kool-Aid: Kraft
Lee jeans: V.F. Corp.
L'eggs hosiery: Hanesbrands
Lipton tea: Unilever
Listerine mouthwash: Johnson & Johnson
Max Factor beauty products: Procter & Gamble
Maxwell House coffee: Kraft
Maytag appliances: Whirlpool
Metamucil: Procter & Gamble
Milton Bradley games: Hasbro
Minute Maid juices: Coca-Cola
Mr. Clean: Procter & Gamble
Mountain Dew soda: PepsiCo
Neosporin: Johnson & Johnson
Neutrogena soap: Johnson & Johnson
9 Lives cat food: Del Monte
OFF! insect repellents: S.C. Johnson
Olay: Procter & Gamble
Old Navy clothing: Gap
Oreo cookies: Kraft
Oscar Mayer meats: Kraft
Pampers: Procter & Gamble
Pantene shampoo: Procter & Gamble
Paper Mate pens: Newell Rubbermaid
Parker Bros. games: Hasbro
Pedigree pet food: Mars
Pepperidge Farm prods.: Campbell Soup
Pepto-Bismol: Procter & Gamble
Philadelphia cream cheese: Kraft
Pillsbury: General Mills
Pine-Sol cleaner: Clorox
Pizza Hut restaurants: Yum! Brands
Planters nuts: Kraft
Playskool toys: Hasbro

Playtex apparel: Hanesbrands
Post cereals: Ralcorp
Post-it notes: 3M
Prego pasta sauce: Campbell Soup
Preparation H: Pfizer
Pringles snacks: Procter & Gamble
Prozac: Eli Lilly
Purina pet foods: Nestlé
Q-Tips: Unilever
Ragu sauce: Unilever
Raid insecticide: S.C. Johnson
Reese's candy: Hershey
Rice-A-Roni: PepsiCo
Right Guard deodorant: Henkel
Ritz crackers: Kraft
Robitussin: Pfizer
Rogaine hair-growth aide: Johnson & Johnson
Ruffles chips: PepsiCo
Saran wrap: S.C. Johnson
Schick razors: Energizer
Schweppes ginger ale: Dr Pepper Snapple Group
Scope mouthwash: Procter & Gamble
Scotch tape: 3M
Scott tissue: Kimberly-Clark
7Up: Dr Pepper Snapple Group
Skippy peanut butter: Unilever
SlimFast: Unilever
S.O.S. soap pads: Clorox
Splenda sweetener: Johnson & Johnson
Sprite soda: Coca-Cola
Sudafed: Johnson & Johnson
Swanson broth: Campbell Soup
Taco Bell restaurants: Yum! Brands
Tampax tampons: Procter & Gamble
Tide detergent: Procter & Gamble
Timberland apparel: V.F. Corp.
Trident gum: Kraft
Triscuit crackers: Kraft
Trojan condoms: Church & Dwight
Tropicana juice: PepsiCo
Twizzlers candy: Hershey
Tylenol: Johnson & Johnson
Uncle Ben's rice: Mars
V8 vegetable juice: Campbell Soup
Vans apparel: V.F. Corp.
Vaseline: Unilever
Velveeta cheese products: Kraft
Viagra: Pfizer
Vicks cold medicines: Procter & Gamble
Visine eye drops: Johnson & Johnson
Wheaties cereal: General Mills
Windex: S.C. Johnson
Wonder bread: Interstate Bakeries
Wonderbra: Hanesbrands
Wrigley's candy and gum: Mars
Xanax: Pfizer
Ziploc storage bags: S.C. Johnson

U.S. Home Ownership Rates, by Selected Characteristics, 2005, 2011

Source: U.S. Census Bureau, U.S. Dept. of Commerce

Region	2005	2011	Age	2005	2011	Race/ethnicity[1]	2005	2011	Income	2005	2011
Northeast	64.7%	63.0%	Under 35	42.8%	37.5%	White, non-			Median family		
Midwest	73.4	70.0	35-44	68.7	63.8	Hispanic	75.6%	73.7%	income or more	84.0%	81.2%
South	70.4	68.2	45-54	76.3	72.3	Black	48.0	44.2	Below median		
West	63.8	60.3	55-64	81.3	77.8	Hispanic	49.2	46.6	family income	52.7	50.6
			65+	80.3	80.8	Other	58.0	56.0	Total U.S.	68.6%	65.9%

Note: Figures are for 2nd quarter of the year shown. Not seasonally adjusted. (1) Hispanic householders may be of any race. "Other" includes householders reporting Asian, Native Hawaiian/Pacific Islander, and Native American/Alaska Native, as well as combinations of two or more races/ethnicities.

U.S. Housing Affordability, 1990-2011

Source: National Association of REALTORS®

Year	Median priced existing home	Avg. mortgage rate[1]	Monthly principal & interest payment	Payment as % of median monthly income	Year	Median priced existing home	Avg. mortgage rate[1]	Monthly principal & interest payment	Payment as % of median monthly income
1990	$92,000	10.04%	$648	22.0%	2001	$147,800	7.03%	$789	18.4%
1991	97,100	9.30	642	21.4	2002	158,100	6.55	804	18.3
1992	99,700	8.11	591	19.3	2003	180,200	5.74	840	19.1
1993	103,100	7.16	558	18.1	2004	195,200	5.73	909	20.2
1994	107,200	7.47	598	18.5	2005	219,000	5.91	1,040	22.4
1995	110,500	7.85	639	18.9	2006	221,900	6.58	1,131	23.2
1996	115,800	7.71	661	18.8	2007	217,900	6.52	1,104	21.7
1997	121,800	7.68	693	18.7	2008	196,600	6.15	958	18.1
1998	128,400	7.10	690	17.4	2009	172,100	5.14	751	14.8
1999	133,300	7.33	733	18.0	2010	173,100	4.89	734	14.4
2000	139,000	8.03	818	19.3	2011[2]	168,400	4.69	698	13.6

(1) All figures assume a down payment of 20% of the home price. Based on effective rate on loans closed on existing homes for the period shown. (2) Preliminary figures, as of Aug. 2011.

Median Price of Existing Single-Family Homes, by Metropolitan Area, 2008-11

Source: National Association of REALTORS®

Median prices are in thousands of dollars and based on all transactions within time period shown. 2nd qtr. 2011 figures are preliminary.

Metropolitan area	2008	2010	2nd qtr. 2011
Akron, OH.	$100.5	$108.9	$100.2
Albany-Schenectady-Troy, NY	197.9	195.7	195.6
Albuquerque, NM	192.6	178.7	166.8
Allentown-Bethlehem-Easton, PA-NJ	243.6	224.0	191.7
Amarillo, TX	124.7	124.7	130.3
Anaheim-Santa Ana-Irvine, CA	533.2	544.7	536.7
Atlanta-Sandy Springs-Marietta, GA	149.5	114.8	102.1
Atlantic City, NJ	253.3	226.4	237.0
Austin-Round Rock, TX	188.6	193.6	199.3
Baltimore-Towson, MD	274.1	246.1	234.7
Barnstable Town, MA	341.9	326.0	309.7
Baton Rouge, LA	165.0	169.6	168.4
Beaumont-Port Arthur, TX	127.4	125.1	129.0
Birmingham-Hoover, AL	153.9	143.0	146.3
Bismarck, ND	155.2	163.4	169.0
Bloomington-Normal, IL	159.8	157.9	156.2
Boise City-Nampa, ID	188.7	136.2	136.0
Boston-Cambridge-Quincy, MA-NH	361.1	357.3	355.7
Boulder, CO	359.6	358.1	370.3
Bridgeport-Stamford-Norwalk, CT	437.9	408.6	NA
Buffalo-Niagara Falls, NY	105.4	121.2	113.0
Burlington-South Burlington, VT	248.8	261.2	276.2
Cape Coral-Fort Myers, FL	152.6	88.9	110.9
Cedar Rapids, IA	136.5	144.7	141.5
Champaign-Urbana, IL	141.9	141.9	145.0
Charleston, WV	126.9	129.1	134.7
Charleston-North Charleston, SC	206.2	200.5	198.1
Charlotte-Gastonia-Concord, NC-SC	197.8	191.0	211.1
Chattanooga, TN-GA	129.1	121.4	115.5
Chicago-Naperville-Joliet, IL	245.6	191.4	185.0
Cincinnati-Middletown, OH-KY-IN	131.8	128.0	127.3
Cleveland-Elyria-Mentor, OH	108.5	114.5	108.5
Colorado Springs, CO	205.5	195.5	183.9
Columbia, MO.	146.3	146.3	150.1
Columbia, SC	145.0	142.6	147.8
Columbus, OH	139.3	136.4	130.9
Corpus Christi, TX	139.1	135.1	132.1
Dallas-Fort Worth-Arlington, TX	145.8	143.8	151.5
Davenport-Moline-Rock Island, IA-IL	94.2	112.2	116.6
Dayton, OH.	107.0	103.6	96.8
Deltona-Daytona Beach-Ormond Beach, FL	164.1	115.6	112.2
Denver-Aurora, CO.	219.3	232.4	232.7
Des Moines, IA	153.2	150.9	155.5
Dover, DE.	206.2	193.3	169.3
Durham, NC	180.6	177.9	NA
El Paso, TX.	137.5	134.3	132.5
Erie, PA	99.5	107.7	113.4
Eugene-Springfield, OR	224.7	196.3	188.4
Ft. Wayne, IN	92.6	97.4	97.8
Gainesville, FL	188.6	161.6	151.3
Gary-Hammond, IN	127.7	122.9	128.5
Glens Falls, NY	161.1	147.5	161.6
Grand Rapids, MI	100.9	91.5	103.1
Green Bay, WI	146.2	130.4	137.8
Greensboro-High Point, NC	145.3	129.8	129.8
Greenville, SC	155.7	145.3	146.5
Gulfport-Biloxi, MS.	140.2	125.0	111.0
Hagerstown-Martinsburg, MD-WV	185.8	144.4	139.0
Hartford-West Hartford-East Hartford, CT.	246.2	235.8	236.8
Honolulu, HI	624.0	607.6	609.5
Houston-Baytown-Sugar Land, TX.	151.6	155.0	156.5
Indianapolis, IN.	111.2	123.3	127.2
Jackson, MS.	128.7	133.2	136.4
Jacksonville, FL	174.6	137.7	134.2
Kansas City, MO-KS.	144.3	141.6	137.0
Knoxville, TN	149.1	140.9	142.9
Lansing-E.Lansing, MI	97.7	84.4	85.9
Las Vegas-Paradise, NV	220.5	138.0	126.2
Lexington-Fayette, KY	144.3	143.2	138.9
Lincoln, NE.	135.2	133.6	131.0
Little Rock-N. Little Rock, AR	129.8	132.5	130.9
Los Angeles-Long Beach-Santa Ana, CA	$402.1	$316.7	$292.3
Louisville, KY-IN.	132.2	134.6	129.9
Madison, WI	226.6	217.7	212.7
Manchester-Nashua, NH	242.8	232.0	225.7
Memphis, TN-MS-AR	119.3	120.2	112.6
Miami-Fort Lauderdale-Miami Beach, FL	285.1	201.9	186.3
Milwaukee-Waukesha-West Allis, WI	212.3	205.9	186.6
Minneapolis-St. Paul-Bloomington, MN-WI	202.0	170.6	145.0
Mobile, AL.	134.2	121.0	111.4
Montgomery, AL	135.2	129.0	131.9
New Haven-Milford, CT	263.8	231.0	228.1
New Orleans-Metairie-Kenner, LA	160.5	159.7	158.3
New York-Northern New Jersey-Long Island, NY-NJ-PA	437.9	393.7	384.8
New York-Wayne-White Plains, NY-NJ	494.3	450.0	448.7
NY: Edison, NJ.	365.2	345.4	328.6
NY: Nassau-Suffolk, NY.	435.8	387.0	383.5
NY: Newark-Union, NJ-PA	417.2	379.2	374.9
Norwich-New London, CT	236.6	204.7	185.9
Oklahoma City, OK.	128.1	145.7	143.2
Omaha, NE-IA	135.2	137.3	138.9
Orlando, FL.	208.9	134.7	125.6
Palm Bay-Melbourne-Titusville, FL.	144.7	103.0	108.7
Pensacola-Ferry Pass-Brent, FL	155.7	141.0	133.5
Peoria, IL	122.1	116.9	114.8
Philadelphia-Camden-Wilmington, PA-NJ-DE-MD.	231.4	214.9	215.1
Phoenix-Mesa-Scottsdale, AZ	191.3	139.2	126.0
Pittsfield, MA.	212.6	195.5	197.1
Portland-South Portland-Biddeford, ME	229.3	218.0	219.3
Portland-Vancouver-Beaverton, OR-WA.	280.1	237.3	220.6
Providence-New Bedford-Fall River, RI-MA.	250.6	228.5	224.8
Raleigh-Cary, NC.	223.4	217.6	NA
Reading, PA.	155.7	153.3	144.5
Reno-Sparks, NV.	259.1	179.5	156.6
Riverside-San Bernardino-Ontario, CA	234.2	179.3	171.5
Rochester, NY.	117.0	118.9	118.9
Sacramento-Arden-Arcade-Roseville, CA	216.7	183.6	168.0
Saint Louis, MO-IL	133.2	131.1	129.0
Salem, OR.	208.8	173.5	136.8
Salt Lake City, UT	229.6	206.5	188.5
San Antonio, TX.	152.8	151.0	152.4
San Diego-Carlsbad-San Marcos, CA	385.6	385.2	379.3
San Francisco-Oakland-Fremont, CA	622.0	525.3	515.1
San Jose-Sunnyvale-Santa Clara, CA	668.0	602.4	610.0
Sarasota-Bradenton-Venice, FL.	240.6	164.6	157.0
Seattle-Tacoma-Bellevue, WA	357.2	295.7	287.2
Shreveport-Bossier City, LA	138.5	156.6	158.9
Sioux Falls, SD.	142.3	143.3	141.2
Spartanburg, SC.	127.3	118.2	114.8
Spokane, WA	191.2	172.2	158.5
Springfield, IL	108.0	124.0	127.4
Springfield, MA.	200.6	190.0	182.4
Springfield, MO.	121.1	109.1	114.8
Syracuse, NY	120.2	125.1	125.4
Tallahassee, FL	179.9	152.8	147.8
Tampa-St. Petersburg-Clearwater, FL	173.0	134.2	129.6
Toledo, OH.	91.2	81.5	75.2
Topeka, KS.	108.0	107.2	104.4
Trenton-Ewing, NJ	303.2	250.7	255.4
Tucson, AZ.	204.3	156.6	136.5
Tulsa, OK	136.9	132.3	130.7
Virginia Beach-Norfolk-Newport News, VA-NC.	220.0	205.0	184.9
Washington-Arlington-Alexandria, DC-VA-MD-WV.	343.4	325.3	340.9
Wichita, KS.	121.8	118.7	118.7
Worcester, MA	237.1	223.3	221.2

NA = Not available.

Characteristics of American Housing Units, 2009

Source: *American Housing Survey, 2009,* U.S. Dept. of Housing and Urban Development

Characteristic	Number of homes (thous.)	% of all homes	Characteristic	Number of homes (thous.)	% of all homes
Total units	130,112	100.0%	Square footage of unit[1]		
Units in structure			Less than 500	988	1.1%
1, detached.	82,472	63.4	500-749	2,765	3.0
1, attached.	7,053	5.4	750-999	6,440	7.0
2-4.	10,160	7.8	1,000-1,499	21,224	23.3
5-9.	6,347	4.9	1,500-1,999	20,636	22.6
10-19.	5,722	4.4	2,000-2,499	14,361	15.7
20-49.	4,525	3.5	2,500-2,999	7,589	8.3
50 or more	5,063	3.9	3,000-3,999	7,252	8.0
Manufactured/mobile home or trailer	8,769	6.7	4,000 or more	4,456	4.9
Cooperatives.	844	0.6	Not reported or don't know	5,529	6.1
Condominiums	8,741	6.7	Median square footage	1,700	
Year built			**Lot size[2]**		
2005-09.	7,324	5.6	Less than 1/8 acre	13,931	14.6
2000-04.	9,158	7.0	1/8 to 1/4 acre	25,008	26.3
1995-99.	8,821	6.8	1/4 to 1/2 acre	17,825	18.7
1990-94.	7,060	5.4	1/2 to 1 acre	11,292	11.9
1985-89.	8,804	6.8	1 to 5 acres	19,172	20.1
1980-84.	7,478	5.8	5 to 10 acres	3,104	3.3
1975-79.	13,731	10.6	10 acres or more	4,885	5.1
1970-74.	11,068	8.5	Median lot size.	0.26	
1960-69.	15,261	11.7	**Equipment**		
1950-59.	13,222	10.2	Lacking full kitchen facilities	5,586	4.3
1940-49.	7,945	6.1	Kitchen sink	128,769	99.0
1930-39.	5,840	4.5	Refrigerator	126,534	97.2
1920-29.	5,164	4.0	Cooking stove or range	126,744	97.4
1919 or earlier.	9,235	7.1	Dishwasher	82,397	63.3
Median year built	1974	1.5	Washing machine	101,387	77.9
Location			Clothes dryer	98,657	75.8
Inside metropolitan statistical areas	102,679	78.9	Disposal in kitchen sink	63,776	49.0
In central cities	37,604	28.9	Trash compactor	4,511	3.5
Suburbs	65,075	50.0	Air conditioning	109,325	84.1
Outside metropolitan statistical areas	27,433	21.0	Central air	82,475	63.4
Number of bedrooms			1 room unit	13,020	10.0
None	1,265	1.0	2 room units	8,670	6.7
1.	14,690	11.3	3 room units or more	5,160	4.0
2.	34,514	53.0	**Main source of heating[3]**		
3.	53,734	123.9	Piped gas	63,361	49.0
4 or more	25,909	19.9	Fuel oil	9,065	7.0
Number of complete bathrooms			Bottled gas	7,366	5.7
None	1,678	1.3	Wood	2,215	1.7
1.	46,977	36.1	Kerosene or other liquid fuel	732	0.6
1-1/2	17,233	13.2	Coal or coke	126	0.1
2 or more	64,223	49.4	Solar energy	18	0.0
			Other	359	0.3

(1) Percentages based on 91,241 single detached homes and trailers. (2) Percentages based on 95,216 total single-unit structures. (3) Percentages based on 129,181 homes with heat.

Fair Market Rents for Select Metropolitan Areas, 2012

Source: *Fair Market Rents 2012,* U.S. Dept. of Housing and Urban Development

Metropolitan area	Number of bedrooms 0	1	2	3	4	Metropolitan area	Number of bedrooms 0	1	2	3	4
Atlanta-Sandy Springs-Marietta, GA	$699	$757	$842	$1,025	$1,118	Minneapolis-St. Paul-Bloomington, MN-WI.	$632	$745	$904	$1,183	$1,330
Austin-Round Rock-San Marcos, TX	713	812	989	1,331	1,516	Nashville-Davidson-Murfreesboro-Franklin, TN . .	572	653	751	974	1,003
Baltimore-Towson, MD.	907	1,025	1,231	1,581	1,952	New Orleans-Metairie-Kenner, LA	732	811	948	1,217	1,258
Birmingham-Hoover, AL	605	673	750	952	980	New York, NY.	1,183	1,280	1,424	1,752	1,970
Boston-Cambridge-Quincy, MA-NH	1,099	1,166	1,369	1,637	1,799	Oklahoma City, OK.	526	574	697	941	1,009
Buffalo-Niagara Falls, NY	597	599	719	889	982	Orlando-Kissimmee-Sanford, FL	753	819	936	1,172	1,380
Charlotte-Gastonia-Rock Hill, NC-SC.	657	713	791	997	1,160	Philadelphia-Camden-Wilmington, PA-NJ-DE-MD. .	788	899	1,075	1,315	1,586
Chicago-Joliet-Naperville, IL. . .	745	853	958	1,171	1,323	Phoenix-Mesa-Glendale, AZ . .	619	721	870	1,267	1,483
Cincinnati-Middleton, OH-KY-IN	471	558	723	968	1,005	Pittsburgh, PA.	528	579	693	861	930
Cleveland-Elyria-Mentor, OH . .	520	603	727	932	990	Portland-Vancouver-Hillsboro, OR-WA	665	771	891	1,297	1,558
Columbus, OH	537	625	790	994	1,080	Providence-Fall River, RI-MA. .	710	790	910	1,087	1,341
Dallas, TX.	649	719	868	1,130	1,337	Raleigh-Cary, NC	681	763	849	1,067	1,105
Denver-Aurora-Broomfield, CO	619	705	893	1,268	1,478	Richmond, VA.	725	786	878	1,171	1,399
Detroit-Warren-Livonia, MI	586	667	798	954	984	St. Louis, MO-IL	588	638	792	1,020	1,068
Houston-Baytown-Sugar Land, TX	694	772	937	1,249	1,570	Salt Lake City, UT.	591	642	774	1,089	1,268
Indianapolis, IN.	543	629	747	967	1,023	San Antonio-New Braunfels, TX	553	616	760	980	1,191
Jacksonville, FL.	630	716	834	1,047	1,199	San Diego-Carlsbad-San Marcos, CA	984	1,126	1,378	1,960	2,421
Kansas City, MO-KS.	547	657	754	1,020	1,073	San Francisco, CA	1,238	1,522	1,905	2,543	2,688
Las Vegas-Paradise, NV	739	870	1,024	1,423	1,713	San Jose-Sunnyvale-Santa Clara, CA	1,165	1,350	1,623	2,334	2,569
Los Angeles-Long Beach, CA	961	1,159	1,447	1,943	2,338	Seattle-Bellevue, WA	800	912	1,098	1,551	1,895
Louisville, KY-IN.	509	588	698	975	1,036	Washington-Arlington-Alexandria, DC-VA-MD.	1,166	1,328	1,506	1,943	2,542
Memphis, TN-MS-AR	594	645	717	955	985						
Miami-Miami Beach-Kendall, FL	819	927	1,125	1,439	1,682						
Milwaukee-Waukesha-West Allis, WI.	577	688	822	1,036	1,067						

Note: Figures are projections made in the previous year.

TRADE

U.S. Trade With Selected Countries and Major Areas, 2010

Source: U.S. Census Bureau and U.S. Bureau of Economic Analysis, U.S. Dept. of Commerce
(in millions of dollars; top 25 countries are ranked by amount of total trade with U.S.)

Rank	Country	Total trade with U.S.	U.S. exports to	Rank[1]	U.S. imports from	Rank[1]	U.S. trade balance with	Rank[2]
1.	Canada	$526,752.5	$249,105.0	1	$277,647.5	2	–$28,542.5	5
2.	China[3]	456,824.5	91,880.6	3	364,943.9	1	–273,063.2	1
3.	Mexico	393,380.9	163,473.0	2	229,907.9	3	–66,434.9	2
4.	Japan	181,030.8	60,485.6	4	120,545.2	4	–60,059.6	3
5.	Germany	130,589.8	48,160.7	6	82,429.1	5	–34,268.4	4
6.	United Kingdom	98,188.5	48,413.5	5	49,775.0	6	–1,361.5	45
7.	South Korea	87,720.3	38,845.7	7	48,874.6	7	–10,028.9	20
8.	France	65,323.0	26,968.5	11	38,354.5	8	–11,386.0	15
9.	Taiwan	61,889.4	26,043.4	13	35,846.0	9	–9,802.6	21
10.	Brazil	59,383.0	35,425.1	8	23,957.9	18	11,467.2	228
11.	Netherlands	53,994.1	34,939.2	9	19,054.9	22	15,884.3	231
12.	India	48,782.7	19,250.1	17	29,532.6	14	–10,282.5	19
13.	Singapore	46,444.6	29,017.4	10	17,427.2	23	11,590.2	229
14.	Venezuela	43,356.8	10,649.4	25	32,707.4	11	–22,058.0	8
15.	Saudi Arabia	42,969.1	11,556.3	22	31,412.8	12	–19,856.5	9
16.	Italy	42,724.2	14,219.2	18	28,505.0	15	–14,285.8	11
17.	Ireland	41,123.2	7,275.6	31	33,847.6	10	–26,572.1	6
18.	Belgium	41,007.3	25,455.7	14	15,551.6	26	9,904.1	226
19.	Malaysia	39,980.1	14,079.9	19	25,900.3	16	–11,820.5	14
20.	Switzerland	39,823.4	20,687.3	16	19,136.1	21	1,551.2	211
21.	Nigeria	34,583.6	4,067.7	44	30,515.9	13	–26,448.3	7
22.	Israel	32,276.8	11,294.4	23	20,982.4	20	–9,688.0	22
23.	Russia	31,697.4	6,006.4	37	25,691.0	17	–19,684.7	10
24.	Thailand	31,670.2	8,977.0	28	22,693.2	19	–13,716.2	12
25.	Hong Kong	30,866.5	26,570.3	12	4,296.2	45	22,274.1	232

Major area/group							
North America	$920,133.4	$412,578.0		$507,555.4		–$94,977.4	
Europe	667,408.0	285,596.2		381,811.8		–96,215.6	
Euro Area	418,802.2	176,586.8		242,215.4		–65,628.6	
EU	558,778.1	239,583.3		319,194.8		–79,611.5	
Africa	113,354.8	28,346.9		85,007.9		–56,661.0	
OECD	1,842,261.0	807,784.7		1,034,476.3		–226,691.6	
Pacific Rim Countries	980,285.3	326,396.8		653,888.5		–327,491.6	
Asia Near East	123,237.7	48,742.2		74,495.5		–25,753.2	
NICS	226,920.6	120,476.7		106,443.9		14,032.8	
Asia/South	63,320.5	24,091.4		39,229.1		–15,137.7	
ASEAN	178,125.5	70,404.9		107,720.6		–37,315.7	
APEC	2,011,722.5	775,101.6		1,236,620.9		–461,519.2	
South/Central America	269,494.4	138,602.9		130,891.5		7,711.5	
Twenty Latin American Republics	638,441.3	287,271.8		351,169.5		–63,897.7	
Central American Common Market	37,714.4	17,678.8		20,035.6		–2,356.8	
LAFTA	581,903.8	255,373.8		326,530.0		–71,156.3	
NATO Allies	1,038,341.6	485,475.1		552,866.5		–67,391.4	
OPEC	204,187.5	54,294.4		149,893.1		–95,598.7	
World total	**$3,191,423.3**	**$1,278,263.2**		**$1,913,160.1**		**–$634,896.8**	

Note: Figures may not equal totals due to rounding. Country grouping data reflect the groups as they were at reporting time. (1) Rank shown is for column to the left. Ranking includes territories as well as nations. (2) Rank by size of U.S. trade deficit. Ranking includes territories as well as nations. (3) Not including Hong Kong, Macao, and Taiwan. **Definitions of major areas/groups used in table, as provided by source: North America**—Canada, Mexico. **Europe**—Albania, Andorra, Armenia, Austria, Azerbaijan, Belarus, Belgium, Bosnia-Herzegovina, Bulgaria, Croatia, Cyprus, Czech Republic, Denmark, Estonia, Faroe Isls., Finland, France, Georgia, Germany, Gibraltar, Greece, Hungary, Iceland, Ireland, Italy, Jan Mayen Isl., Kazakhstan, Kosovo, Kyrgyzstan, Latvia, Liechtenstein, Lithuania, Luxembourg, Macedonia, Malta, Moldova, Monaco, Montenegro, Netherlands, Norway, Poland, Portugal, Romania, Russia, San Marino, Serbia, Slovakia, Slovenia, Spain, Svalbard, Sweden, Switzerland, Tajikistan, Turkey, Turkmenistan, Ukraine, United Kingdom, Uzbekistan, Vatican City. **Euro Area**—Austria, Belgium, Cyprus, Finland, France, Germany, Greece, Ireland, Italy, Luxembourg, Malta, Netherlands, Portugal, Slovenia, Spain. **EU (European Union)**—Euro Area plus Bulgaria, Cyprus, Czech Republic, Denmark, Estonia, Hungary, Latvia, Lithuania, Poland, Romania, Slovakia, Sweden, United Kingdom. **Africa**—Algeria, Angola, Benin, Botswana, British Indian Ocean Territories, Burkina, Burundi, Cameroon, Cape Verde, Central African Republic, Chad, Comoros, Congo Republic, Côte d'Ivoire, Dem. Rep. of Congo, Djibouti, Egypt, Equatorial Guinea, Eritrea, Ethiopia, French Southern and Antarctic Lands, Gabon, Gambia, Ghana, Guinea, Guinea-Bissau, Kenya, Lesotho, Liberia, Libya, Madagascar, Malawi, Mali, Mauritania, Mauritius, Mayotte, Morocco, Mozambique, Namibia, Niger, Nigeria, Réunion, Rwanda, St. Helena, São Tomé and Príncipe, Senegal, Seychelles, Sierra Leone, Somalia, South Africa, Sudan, Swaziland, Tanzania, Togo, Tunisia, Uganda, Western Sahara, Zambia, Zimbabwe. **OECD (Org. for Economic Cooperation and Development)**—Australia, Austria, Belgium, Canada, Czech Republic, Denmark, Finland, France, Germany, Greece, Hungary, Iceland, Ireland, Italy, Japan, Luxembourg, Mexico, Netherlands, New Zealand, Norway, Poland, Portugal, Slovakia, South Korea, Spain, Sweden, Switzerland, Turkey, United Kingdom. **Pacific Rim Countries**—Australia, Brunei, China, Hong Kong, Indonesia, Japan, Macao, Malaysia, New Zealand, Philippines, Singapore, South Korea, Taiwan. **Asia Near East**—Bahrain, Iran, Iraq, Israel, Jordan, Kuwait, Lebanon, Oman, Qatar, Saudi Arabia, Syria, United Arab Emirates, Yemen. **NICS (Newly Industrialized Countries)**—Hong Kong, Singapore, South Korea, Taiwan. **Asia/South**—Afghanistan, Bangladesh, India, Nepal, Pakistan, Sri Lanka. **ASEAN (Assn. of Southeast Asia Nations)**—Brunei, Cambodia, Indonesia, Laos, Malaysia, Myanmar, Philippines, Singapore, Thailand, Vietnam. **APEC (Asia-Pacific Economic Cooperation)**—Australia, Brunei, Canada, Chile, China, Hong Kong, Indonesia, Japan, Malaysia, Mexico, New Zealand, Papua New Guinea, Peru, Philippines, Russia, Singapore, South Korea, Taiwan, Thailand, Vietnam. **South/Central America**—Anguilla, Antigua and Barbuda, Argentina, Aruba, Bahamas, Barbados, Belize, Bermuda, Bolivia, Brazil, British Virgin Isls., Cayman Isls., Chile, Colombia, Costa Rica, Cuba, Dominica, Dominican Republic, Ecuador, El Salvador, Falkland Isls., French Guiana, Grenada, Guadeloupe, Guatemala, Guyana, Haiti, Honduras, Jamaica, Martinique, Montserrat, Netherlands Antilles, Nicaragua, Panama, Paraguay, Peru, St. Kitts and Nevis, St. Lucia, St. Vincent and the Grenadines, Suriname, Trinidad and Tobago, Turks and Caicos Isls., Uruguay, Venezuela. **Twenty Latin American Republics**—Argentina, Bolivia, Brazil, Chile, Colombia, Costa Rica, Cuba, Dominican Republic, Ecuador, El Salvador, Guatemala, Haiti, Honduras, Mexico, Nicaragua, Panama, Paraguay, Peru, Uruguay, Venezuela. **Central American Common Market**—Costa Rica, El Salvador, Guatemala, Honduras, Nicaragua. **LAFTA (Latin American Free Trade Assn.)**—Argentina, Bolivia, Brazil, Chile, Colombia, Ecuador, Mexico, Paraguay, Peru, Uruguay, Venezuela. **NATO (North Atlantic Treaty Org.) Allies**—Belgium, Bulgaria, Canada, Czech Republic, Denmark, Estonia, France, Germany, Greece, Hungary, Iceland, Italy, Latvia, Lithuania, Luxembourg, Netherlands, Norway, Poland, Portugal, Romania, Slovakia, Slovenia, Spain, Turkey, United Kingdom. **OPEC (Org. of the Petroleum Exporting Countries)**—Algeria, Angola, Ecuador, Iran, Iraq, Kuwait, Libya, Nigeria, Qatar, Saudi Arabia, United Arab Emirates, Venezuela.

U.S. Exports and Imports by Principal Commodity Groupings, 2010

Source: U.S. Census Bureau and U.S. Bureau of Economic Analysis, U.S. Dept. of Commerce

Item[1]	Exports (mil)	Imports (mil)	Item	Exports (mil)	Imports (mil)
TOTAL[1]	$1,278,263	$1,913,160	Liquefied propane/butane	$2,448	$2,541
Manufactured goods[2]	873,246	1,438,617	Live animals	797	2,355
Agricultural commodities[2]	115,786	82,015	Meat and preparations	13,216	5,071
Mineral fuels[2]	80,460	354,968	Metal manufactures[3]	17,491	25,913
			Metal ores; scrap	28,366	7,293
Selected commodities[2]			Metalworking machines	5,330	5,565
ADP equipment; office machinery	22,238	113,476	Mineral fuels, other	7,434	3,410
Airplanes, engines, and parts	74,741	22,417	Natural gas	4,921	17,402
Alcoholic bev., distilled	1,126	5,608	Nickel	1,130	2,976
Aluminum	5,171	10,815	Oils/fats, vegetable	2,650	3,940
Animal feeds	8,996	1,349	Optical goods	3,278	5,507
Artwork/antiques	3,034	6,268	Paper and paperboard	14,920	15,285
Basketware, etc.	8,360	13,316	Petroleum preparations	53,528	67,409
Cereal flour	3,037	4,519	Photographic equipment	3,345	2,048
Chemicals-cosmetics	12,488	9,564	Plastic articles[3]	9,710	16,042
Chemicals-dyeing	7,407	3,105	Platinum	1,370	4,146
Chemicals-fertilizers	3,731	6,647	Pottery	98	1,501
Chemicals-inorganic	11,806	13,833	Power generating machines	33,013	42,465
Chemicals-medicinal	41,960	65,170	Printed materials	5,879	4,585
Chemicals-organic	37,494	45,792	Pulp and waste paper	8,640	3,887
Chemicals-plastics	42,019	17,825	Records/magnetic media	4,424	5,296
Chemicals[3]	24,136	11,379	Rice	2,328	574
Cigarettes	371	182	Rubber articles[3]	2,049	3,310
Clothing	3,197	78,518	Rubber tires and tubes	4,159	10,673
Coal	10,100	2,018	Scientific instruments	44,276	37,795
Coffee	6	4,055	Ships, boats	2,498	1,588
Copper	3,496	7,821	Silver and bullion	1,672	4,383
Cork, wood, and lumber	4,732	4,479	Soybeans	18,589	220
Corn	10,181	300	Specialized industrial machines	46,754	30,912
Cotton, raw and linters	5,896	8	Sugar	65	1,236
Crude fertilizers	2,367	2,257	Televisions, VCRs, etc.	21,511	137,305
Crude oil	1,368	260,105	Textile yarn, fabric	11,384	22,120
Electrical machinery	77,019	119,634	Tobacco, unmanufactured	1,167	701
Fish and preparations	4,223	14,576	Toys, games, and sporting goods	4,245	30,630
Footwear	728	20,902	Travel goods	463	8,012
Furniture and bedding	4,821	31,124	Vegetables and fruits	15,712	20,915
Gem diamonds	2,862	18,599	Vehicles	88,119	178,946
General industrial machines	51,793	60,624	Watches, clocks, and parts	379	3,747
Glass	3,380	2,588	Wheat	6,769	563
Glassware	1,015	2,339	Wood manufactures	2,053	6,920
Gold, nonmonetary	17,458	12,491	**Re-exports**	**155,847**	**NA**
Hides and skins	2,039	56	Agricultural commodities	3,529	NA
Iron and steel mill products	15,720	24,440	Manufactured goods	150,277	NA
Jewelry	4,848	10,085	Mineral fuels	825	NA
Lighting, plumbing	2,509	7,397			

NA = Not applicable. **Note:** Commodity group totals include products not listed here. Figures may not add up to totals due to rounding. (1) Both domestic and foreign exports (re-exports). (2) Domestic exports. (3) Not specified elsewhere.

Trends in U.S. Foreign Trade, 1790-2010

Source: U.S. Census Bureau and U.S. Bureau of Economic Analysis, U.S. Dept. of Commerce

In 1790, U.S. exports and imports combined came to $43 mil, and there was a $3 mil trade deficit. The global recession caused total U.S. trade and the overall trade deficit to fall in 2009, but they both resumed the ever-upward path they had been following since the last recorded surplus in 1975.

(in millions of dollars)

Year	Exports	Imports	Trade balance	Year	Exports	Imports	Trade balance	Year	Exports	Imports	Trade balance
1790	$20	$23	-$3	1885	$742	$578	$165	1980	$220,626	$244,871	-$24,245
1795	48	70	-22	1890	858	789	69	1985	213,133	345,276	-132,143
1800	71	91	-20	1895	808	732	76	1990	394,030	495,042	-101,012
1805	96	121	-25	1900	1,394	850	545	1995	584,742	743,445	-158,703
1810	67	85	-19	1905	1,519	1,118	401	1996	625,075	795,289	-170,214
1815	53	113	-60	1910	1,745	1,557	188	1997	689,182	870,671	-181,489
1820	70	74	-5	1915	2,769	1,674	1,094	1998	682,138	911,896	-229,758
1825	91	90	1	1920	8,228	5,278	2,950	1999	695,797	1,024,618	-328,821
1830	72	63	9	1925	4,910	4,227	683	2000	781,918	1,218,022	-436,104
1835	115	137	-22	1930	3,843	3,061	782	2001	729,100	1,140,999	-411,899
1840	124	98	25	1935	2,283	2,047	235	2002	693,103	1,161,366	-468,263
1845	106	113	-7	1940	4,021	2,625	1,396	2003	724,771	1,257,121	-532,350
1850	144	174	-29	1945	9,806	4,159	5,646	2004	818,775	1,469,704	-650,930
1855	219	258	-39	1950	9,997	8,954	1,043	2005	905,978	1,673,455	-767,477
1860	334	354	-20	1955	14,298	11,566	2,732	2006	1,036,635	1,853,939	-817,304
1865	166	239	-73	1960	19,659	15,073	4,586	2007	1,162,479	1,956,962	-794,483
1870	393	436	-43	1965	26,742	21,520	5,222	2008	1,287,442	2,103,641	-816,199
1875	513	533	-20	1970	42,681	40,356	2,325	2009	1,056,043	1,559,625	-503,582
1880	836	668	168	1975	107,652	98,503	9,149	2010	1,278,263	1,913,160	-634,897

World Trade Organization (WTO)

The World Trade Organization is an international body that seeks to promote free trade by eliminating barriers to trade. Founded in 1995, the WTO had grown to 153 member countries as of Aug. 2011, with 31 others, including Russia and Vatican City, granted observer status. International intergovernmental organizations, such as the International Monetary Fund and the World Bank, may also be granted observer status. With the exception of Vatican City, observers must start accession negotiations within five years of becoming observers.

Foreign Exchange Rates, 1970-2010

Source: Federal Reserve Board

(national currency units per U.S. dollar except as noted; annual average rates of exchange)

Year	Australia[1] (dollar)	Austria[1] (schilling; euro)	Belgium[1] (franc; euro)	Canada (dollar)	China (yuan)	Denmark (krone)	France[1] (franc; euro)	Germany[1,2] (deutsche mark; euro)	Greece[1] (drachma; euro)
1970	1.1136	25.8800	49.6800	1.0103	NA	7.4890	5.5200	3.6480	30.0000
1975	1.3077	17.4430	36.7990	1.0175	NA	5.7480	4.2876	2.4613	32.2900
1980	1.1400	12.9450	29.2370	1.1693	NA	5.6340	4.2250	1.8175	42.6200
1985	0.7003	20.6900	59.3780	1.3655	NA	10.5960	8.9852	2.9440	138.1200
1990	0.7813	11.3700	33.4180	1.1668	NA	6.1890	5.4453	1.6157	158.5100
1995	0.7415	10.0810	29.4800	1.3724	8.3700	5.6020	4.9915	1.4331	231.6600
2000	0.5815	0.9232	0.9232	1.4855	8.2784	8.0950	0.9232	0.9232	365.9200
2005	0.7627	1.2449	1.2449	1.2115	8.1936	5.9953	1.2449	1.2449	1.2449
2006	0.7535	1.2563	1.2563	1.1340	7.9723	5.9422	1.2563	1.2563	1.2563
2007	0.8391	1.3711	1.3711	1.0734	7.6058	5.4413	1.3711	1.3711	1.3711
2008	0.8537	1.4726	1.4726	1.0660	6.9477	5.0885	1.4726	1.4726	1.4726
2009	0.7927	1.3935	1.3935	1.1412	6.8307	5.3574	1.3935	1.3935	1.3935
2010	0.9200	1.3261	1.3261	1.0298	6.7696	5.6266	1.3261	1.3261	1.3261

Year	Hong Kong (dollar)	India (rupee)	Ireland[1] (pound; euro)	Italy[1] (lira; euro)	Japan (yen)	Malaysia (ringgit)	Mexico (peso)	Netherlands[1] (guilder; euro)	Norway (krone)
1970	NA	7.576	2.3959	623.0000	357.60	3.0900	NA	3.5970	7.1400
1975	NA	8.409	2.2216	653.0000	296.78	2.4030	NA	2.5293	5.2282
1980	NA	7.887	2.0577	856.0000	226.63	2.1767	NA	1.9875	4.9381
1985	NA	12.369	1.0656	1,909.0000	238.54	2.4830	NA	3.3214	8.5972
1990	NA	17.504	1.6585	1,198.0000	144.79	2.7049	2.812	1.8209	6.2597
1995	7.7357	32.427	1.6038	1,628.9000	94.06	2.5044	6.419	1.6057	6.3352
2000	7.7925	45.000	0.9232	0.9232	107.80	3.8000	9.459	0.9232	8.8131
2005	7.7775	44.000	1.2449	1.2449	110.11	3.7869	10.894	1.2449	6.4412
2006	7.7681	45.190	1.2563	1.2563	116.31	3.6661	10.906	1.2563	6.4095
2007	7.8016	41.180	1.3711	1.3711	117.76	3.4354	10.928	1.3711	5.8557
2008	7.7862	43.390	1.4726	1.4726	103.39	3.3292	11.143	1.4726	5.6365
2009	7.7514	48.330	1.3935	1.3935	93.68	3.5231	13.498	1.3935	6.2908
2010	7.7687	45.65	1.3261	1.3261	87.78	3.2175	12.623	1.3261	6.0451

Year	Portugal[1] (escudo; euro)	Singapore (dollar)	South Korea (won)	Spain[1] (peseta; euro)	Sweden (krona)	Switzerland (franc)	Taiwan (dollar)	Thailand (baht)	UK[1] (pound)
1970	28.7500	3.0800	310.57	69.7200	5.1700	4.3160	NA	21.000	2.3959
1975	25.5100	2.3713	484.00	57.4300	4.1530	2.5839	NA	20.379	2.2216
1980	50.0800	2.1412	607.43	71.7600	4.2309	1.6772	NA	20.476	2.3243
1985	170.3900	2.2002	870.02	170.0400	8.6039	2.4571	NA	27.159	1.2963
1990	142.5500	1.8125	707.76	101.9300	5.9188	1.3892	NA	25.585	1.7847
1995	151.1100	1.4174	771.27	124.6900	7.1333	1.1825	26.495	24.915	1.5785
2000	0.9232	1.7250	1,130.90	0.9232	9.1735	1.6904	31.260	40.210	1.5156
2005	1.2449	1.6639	1,023.75	1.2449	7.4710	1.2459	32.131	40.252	1.8204
2006	1.2563	1.5882	54.32	1.2563	7.3718	1.2532	32.506	37.876	1.8434
2007	1.3711	1.5065	928.97	1.3711	6.7550	1.1999	32.852	32.203	2.0020
2008	1.4726	1.4140	1,098.71	1.4726	6.5846	1.0816	31.521	32.962	1.8545
2009	1.3935	1.4543	1,274.63	1.3935	7.6539	1.0860	33.020	34.310	1.5661
2010	1.3261	1.3629	1,155.74	1.3261	7.2053	1.0432	31.498	31.700	1.5452

NA = Not available. **Note:** The euro, the European Union's single currency, replaced the national currencies in the EU nations shown above. Exchange rates have been in euros since 1999 for the following countries: Austria, Belgium, France, Germany, Ireland, Italy, Netherlands, Portugal, Spain. For Greece, exchange rates from 2001 on are in euros. (1) U.S. dollars per unit of national currency. (2) West Germany before 1991.

North American Free Trade Agreement (NAFTA)

NAFTA, a free trade pact between the U.S., Canada, and Mexico, took effect Jan. 1, 1994. Major provisions, which were fully implemented Jan. 1, 2008, are as follows:

Agriculture: With limited exceptions, tariffs on all agricultural products to be eliminated over 15 years. Domestic price-support systems may continue provided they do not distort trade.

Automobiles: At least 62.5% of an automobile's value must have been produced in North America for it to qualify for duty-free status. Tariffs to be phased out over 10 years.

Disputes: Special judges have jurisdiction to resolve disagreements within strict timetables.

Energy: Mexico bars foreign ownership of its oil fields but, as of 2004, U.S. and Canadian companies could bid on contracts offered by Mexico's state-owned oil and electricity monopolies.

Environment: The trade agreement cannot be used to overrule national and state environmental, health, or safety laws.

Finance: Limits on ownership of banks, insurance companies, and brokerages eliminated by Jan. 1, 2000.

Immigration: Restrictions on the movement of business executives and professionals eased.

Jobs: Barriers to limit Mexican migration to U.S. remain unaffected by NAFTA.

Patent and copyright protection: Mexico strengthened its laws providing protection to intellectual property and agreed to honor pharmaceutical patents for 20 years.

Tariffs: Tariffs on 10,000 customs goods to be eliminated over 15 years. One-half of U.S. exports to Mexico were considered duty-free by 1999.

Textiles: A "rule of origin" provision requires most garments to be made from yarn and fabric that have been produced in North America. Most tariffs phased out by 1999.

Trucking: Trucks to have free access throughout the 3 countries by 1999, but the U.S. restricted Mexican trucks to a 20-mi comm. zone at the border. In 2001, an arbitration panel ruled the restrictions were in violation of NAFTA. In 2008, the U.S. House terminated a pilot program, begun in 2007, granting limited access to some Mexican trucks.

U.S. Trade With Mexico and Canada, 1996-2010

Source: U.S. Census Bureau and U.S. Bureau of Economic Analysis, U.S. Dept. of Commerce

(in millions of dollars)

Year	WITH MEXICO Exports	Imports	U.S. trade balance[1]	Year	WITH CANADA Exports	Imports	U.S. trade balance[1]
1996	$56,792	$74,297	–$17,506	1996	$134,210	$155,893	–$21,682
1998	78,773	94,629	–15,857	1998	156,603	173,256	–16,653
2000	111,349	135,926	–24,577	2000	178,941	230,838	–51,897
2001	101,297	131,338	–30,041	2001	163,424	216,268	–52,844
2002	97,470	134,616	–37,146	2002	160,923	209,088	–48,165
2003	97,412	138,060	–40,648	2003	169,924	221,595	–51,671
2004	110,835	155,902	–45,067	2004	189,880	256,360	–66,480
2005	120,365	170,109	–49,744	2005	211,899	290,384	–78,486
2006	133,979	198,253	–64,274	2006	230,656	302,438	–71,782
2007	136,092	210,714	–74,622	2007	248,888	317,057	–68,169
2008	151,220	215,942	–64,722	2008	261,150	339,491	–78,342
2009	128,892	176,654	–47,762	2009	204,658	226,248	–21,591
2010	163,473	229,908	–66,435	2010	249,105	277,648	–28,543

(1) Figures may not add up to totals due to rounding.

Central American Free Trade Agreement (CAFTA)

CAFTA (also known as CAFTA-DR) is a free trade agreement between the U.S. and Costa Rica, Dominican Republic, El Salvador, Guatemala, Honduras, and Nicaragua. The U.S. and El Salvador approved the agreement Mar. 1, 2006; Nicaragua joined a month later, and Guatemala entered into the accord July 1, 2006. The Dominican Republic approved CAFTA Mar. 1, 2007, and Costa Rica completed the treaty by signing on Jan. 1, 2009. Some highlights of the agreement:

Agriculture: Tariffs on 50% of U.S. farm goods eliminated; other goods deemed "sensitive"—including corn, milk, and potatoes—to have tariffs reduced to zero over 20 years. Sugar imports to the U.S. allowed to rise to 1.2% of annual U.S. production, up to 1.7% over 15 years.

Automobiles: Tariffs on autos and auto parts to be phased out over 5 years.

Environment and labor: Party nations agree to enforce local labor and environmental protections, although no mechanisms to monitor enforcement currently exist.

Intellectual property: Party nations agree to uphold international standards of trademark, copyright, and patent protection to which the U.S. is a signatory. This includes seizing pirated and counterfeit goods and prosecuting those who traffic in them.

Manufacturing: Tariffs eliminated on 80% of U.S. goods.

Market barriers: Barriers for services such as telecommunications, insurance, and financial services eliminated or reduced.

Pharmaceuticals: U.S. pharmaceuticals given 5-year patent protection from their date of introduction to CAFTA markets, regardless of date introduced in U.S.

Textiles and clothing: Elimination of duties on nearly all textiles and clothing instituted, retroactive to Jan. 1, 2004.

Busiest U.S. Ports, 2009

Source: U.S. Army Corps of Engineers, Dept. of the Army, U.S. Dept. of Defense

(figures in tons; ranked by total tonnage handled)

Rank	Port	Total	Domestic	Foreign	Imports	Exports
1.	South Louisiana, LA	212,580,811	109,503,355	103,077,456	36,016,778	67,060,678
2.	Houston, TX	211,340,972	63,371,521	147,969,451	84,629,722	63,339,729
3.	New York, NY-NJ	144,689,593	61,220,507	83,469,086	64,032,262	19,436,824
4.	Long Beach, CA	72,500,221	13,927,612	58,572,609	37,283,269	21,289,340
5.	Corpus Christi, TX	68,230,968	17,435,654	50,804,314	39,673,722	11,130,592
6.	New Orleans, LA	68,126,087	37,068,258	31,057,829	14,143,810	16,914,019
7.	Beaumont, TX	67,715,469	24,428,821	43,286,648	36,873,234	6,413,414
8.	Huntington, WV-KY-OH	59,171,545	59,171,545	0	0	0
9.	Los Angeles, CA	58,406,060	7,006,435	51,399,625	31,278,985	20,120,640
10.	Texas City, TX	52,632,461	16,156,660	36,475,801	31,701,199	4,774,602
11.	Lake Charles, LA	52,252,099	19,630,344	32,621,755	27,564,890	5,056,865
12.	Mobile, AL	52,219,034	24,382,600	27,836,434	15,595,340	12,241,094
13.	Baton Rouge, LA	51,917,597	34,083,670	17,833,927	11,225,382	6,608,545
14.	Plaquemines, LA	50,869,280	34,708,400	16,160,880	2,215,295	13,945,585
15.	Norfolk Harbor, VA	40,325,961	6,602,211	33,723,750	8,192,966	25,530,784
16.	Pascagoula, MS	36,617,585	8,407,935	28,209,650	21,506,634	6,703,016
17.	Tampa, FL	34,888,052	22,804,143	12,083,909	5,767,967	6,315,942
18.	Valdez, AK	34,473,090	34,465,431	7,659	7,659	0
19.	Port Arthur, TX	33,804,199	9,418,964	24,385,235	14,440,672	9,944,563
20.	Pittsburgh, PA	32,891,355	32,891,355	0	0	0
21.	Savannah, GA	32,338,995	1,950,236	30,388,759	16,694,456	13,694,303
22.	Philadelphia, PA	31,750,604	11,431,769	20,318,835	19,899,793	419,042
23.	St. Louis, MO-IL	31,336,831	31,336,831	0	0	0
24.	Paulsboro, NJ	30,258,416	11,357,129	18,901,287	16,904,554	1,996,733
25.	Duluth-Superior, MN-WI	30,226,449	22,470,989	7,755,460	509,088	7,246,372
26.	Baltimore, MD	30,136,169	9,882,907	20,253,262	10,472,328	9,780,934
27.	Freeport, TX	27,362,765	4,025,067	23,337,698	21,093,998	2,243,700
28.	Richmond, CA	25,362,626	10,992,049	14,370,577	12,384,960	1,985,617
29.	Seattle, WA	24,607,832	5,162,695	19,445,137	6,881,937	12,563,200
30.	Marcus Hook, PA	24,568,869	8,129,616	16,439,253	16,159,451	279,802
31.	Portland, OR	23,307,489	8,925,675	14,381,814	2,335,009	12,046,805
32.	Tacoma, WA	23,165,295	5,558,302	17,606,993	4,634,259	12,972,734
33.	Portland, ME	21,001,697	1,467,705	19,533,992	19,517,986	16,006
34.	Boston, MA	20,455,925	6,952,251	13,503,674	11,961,078	1,542,596
35.	Port Everglades, FL	20,058,993	10,456,994	9,601,999	6,777,336	2,824,663
36.	Chicago, IL	19,228,125	15,740,113	3,488,012	2,592,408	895,604
37.	Newport News, VA	18,043,126	4,142,003	13,901,123	227,030	13,674,093
38.	Jacksonville, FL	17,686,279	7,047,676	10,638,603	9,040,120	1,598,483
39.	Oakland, CA	17,405,784	2,400,343	15,005,441	5,434,688	9,570,753
40.	Charleston, SC	15,834,464	2,378,893	13,455,571	8,436,693	5,018,878
41.	Memphis, TN	13,980,433	13,980,433	0	0	0
42.	Cincinnati, OH	11,767,981	11,767,981	0	0	0
43.	San Juan, PR	11,295,229	6,322,003	4,973,226	4,224,628	748,598
44.	Anacortes, WA	10,430,937	8,217,953	2,212,984	916,798	1,296,186
45.	New Haven, CT	10,135,297	6,900,810	3,234,487	2,856,482	378,005
46.	Kalama, WA	9,911,832	609,812	9,302,020	283,096	9,018,924
47.	Galveston, TX	9,791,907	5,248,200	4,543,707	1,105,885	3,437,822
48.	Toledo, OH	9,682,178	3,846,704	5,835,474	3,137,788	2,697,686
49.	Barbers Point, Oahu, HI	9,669,583	1,304,611	8,364,972	8,124,112	240,860
50.	Honolulu, HI	9,161,378	8,369,248	792,130	501,943	290,187
51.	Detroit, MI	9,014,002	5,895,713	3,118,289	2,704,474	413,815
52.	Indiana Harbor, IN	8,197,993	7,903,530	294,463	212,031	82,432
53.	St. Clair, MI	8,073,962	8,073,962	0	0	0
54.	New Castle, DE	7,582,549	3,659,819	3,922,730	3,660,307	262,423
55.	Albany, NY	7,177,977	6,301,957	876,020	470,069	405,951
56.	Two Harbors, MN	7,095,686	7,095,686	0	0	0
57.	Presque Isle, MI	6,989,563	5,205,787	1,783,776	0	1,783,776
58.	Matagorda, TX	6,950,790	1,390,861	5,559,929	3,718,460	1,841,469
59.	Providence, RI	6,927,656	3,077,152	3,850,504	3,561,111	289,393
60.	Vancouver, WA	6,818,889	1,691,264	5,127,625	762,702	4,364,923
61.	Miami, FL	6,771,535	519,139	6,252,396	3,061,298	3,191,098
62.	Wilmington, NC	6,715,576	1,836,703	4,878,873	3,544,741	1,334,132
63.	Gary, IN	6,388,914	5,999,234	389,680	356,620	33,060
64.	Cleveland, OH	6,075,920	4,642,106	1,433,814	1,269,813	164,001
65.	Camden-Gloucester, NJ	5,699,995	2,131,944	3,568,051	2,502,445	1,065,606
66.	Mount Vernon, IN	5,554,763	5,554,763	0	0	0
67.	Louisville, KY	5,352,587	5,352,587	0	0	0
68.	Longview, WA	5,100,195	1,188,699	3,911,496	852,602	3,058,894
69.	Escanaba, MI	4,854,640	4,800,757	53,883	35,888	17,995
70.	Stoneport, MI	4,847,228	4,603,544	243,684	0	243,684
71.	Calcite, MI	4,796,170	4,047,323	748,847	0	748,847
72.	Brownsville, TX	4,674,329	1,530,570	3,143,759	2,928,230	215,529
73.	Bridgeport, CT	4,576,963	2,710,536	1,866,427	1,866,427	0
74.	Wilmington, DE	4,482,223	1,221,247	3,260,976	2,703,968	557,008
75.	St. Paul, MN	4,148,342	4,148,342	0	0	0

U.S. Railroad Freight and Miles, 1890-2010

Source: Assn. of American Railroads; Bureau of Transportation Statistics, Research and Innovative Technology Admin., U.S. Dept. of Transportation

(in billion ton-miles)

Year	Class I freight[1]	All freight	Miles[2]	Year	Class I freight[1]	All freight	Miles[2]	Year	Class I freight[1]	All freight	Miles[2]
1890...	NA	76	163,597	1950...	589	592	223,779	2005...	1,696	1,733	140,810
1900...	NA	142	193,346	1960...	572	575	217,552	2006...	1,772	1,856	140,490
1910...	NA	255	240,293	1970...	765	771	205,782	2007...	1,771	1,820	140,695
1920...	410	414	252,845	1980...	919	932	178,056	2008...	1,777	1,730	139,326
1930...	383	386	249,052	1990...	1,034	1,064	145,979	2009...	1,532	NA	139,118
1940...	373	375	233,670	2000...	1,466	1,546	144,473	2010...	1,691	NA	NA

NA = Not available. **Note:** A ton-mile equals one ton of freight transported one statute mile. (1) Largest class of freight railroad companies, determined by annual operating revenue. (2) Aggregate length of operating roadway in U.S., excluding yard tracks, sidings, and parallel tracks.

Merchant Fleets of the World, 2009

Source: Maritime Administration, U.S. Dept. of Transportation
(self-propelled oceangoing vessels of 10,000 gross deadweight tons or more)

Flag of registry	All vessels No.	All vessels Tons (thous.)	Tanker No.	Tanker Tons (thous.)	Dry bulk carrier No.	Dry bulk carrier Tons (thous.)	Container No.	Container Tons (thous.)	Other[1] No.	Other[1] Tons (thous.)
Panama............	4,436	273,571	894	75,391	2,173	152,791	685	33,350	684	12,039
Liberia............	2,083	136,934	746	67,126	433	34,335	754	32,600	150	2,873
Hong Kong........	1,088	71,462	210	18,779	561	40,217	213	9,496	104	2,969
Marshall Islands.....	1,069	73,707	491	43,763	341	23,396	186	5,285	51	1,263
Singapore..........	1,005	57,868	447	30,770	178	14,519	280	10,138	100	2,441
China[2].............	955	38,546	135	8,169	484	22,186	117	4,716	219	3,475
Malta.............	885	52,109	261	20,398	465	27,380	66	2,515	93	1,816
Bahamas..........	821	56,294	344	36,479	212	12,713	39	1,487	226	5,615
Greece............	605	66,307	316	42,686	246	21,029	36	2,469	7	123
Cyprus............	567	29,865	109	10,282	256	14,009	149	4,502	53	1,072
Antigua and Barbuda	429	9,067	1	10	33	1,170	290	6,479	105	1,408
Germany...........	349	17,298	22	667	6	853	302	15,437	19	340
Norway (NIS)[3]......	333	17,672	199	11,098	46	3,824	0	0	88	2,750
United Kingdom....	325	15,097	53	1,815	30	2,790	179	9,486	63	1,007
Italy..............	317	15,106	165	7,801	61	4,955	22	1,086	69	1,264
South Korea.......	257	17,046	33	1,920	169	14,075	27	640	28	411
Denmark (DIS)[4]....	197	12,587	104	5,302	4	497	79	6,649	10	139
United States......	196	9,202	58	4,060	13	574	81	3,638	44	930
India.............	194	13,418	110	9,157	71	3,939	11	293	2	28
Isle of Man........	187	14,929	134	11,202	34	3,425	5	131	14	172
Japan............	140	12,280	47	5,795	62	5,772	2	138	29	574
Malaysia..........	128	7,998	83	6,747	13	482	21	632	11	136
Bermuda..........	106	8,784	54	4,626	23	3,339	17	667	12	152
France[5]..........	77	7,762	49	5,610	2	345	25	1,793	1	14
Belgium...........	56	6,251	29	3,302	19	2,764	4	122	4	64
Top 25 (as ranked above)	16,805	1,041,158	5,094	432,954	5,935	411,379	3,590	153,749	2,186	43,076
World total.......	19,462	1,133,450	5,850	469,812	6,750	444,688	3,865	161,493	2,997	57,457
Top 25 as % of total ...	86.3%	91.9%	87.1%	92.2%	87.9%	92.5%	92.9%	95.2%	72.9%	75.0%

(1) Includes roll-on/roll-off, gas carriers, general cargo carriers, partial container ships, refrigerated cargo ships, barge carriers, and specialized cargo ships. (2) Excludes Hong Kong. (3) Norwegian Intl. Ship Register. (4) Danish Intl. Ship Register. (5) French Intl. Ship Register.

U.S. International Transactions, 1970-2010

Source: U.S. Bureau of Economic Analysis, U.S. Dept. of Commerce
(in millions of dollars; revised as of July 2011)

	1970	1980	1990	1995	2000	2005	2009	2010
CURRENT ACCT.								
Exports of goods and services, and income receipts	$68,387	$344,440	$706,975	$1,004,631	$1,425,260	$1,824,780	$2,174,533	$2,500,817
Goods, BOP basis[1]	42,469	224,250	387,401	575,204	784,781	911,686	1,069,491	1,288,699
Services	14,171	47,584	147,832	219,183	288,002	375,755	505,547	548,878
Income receipts on U.S.-owned assets abroad........................	11,748	72,606	170,570	208,065	348,083	532,542	594,319	657,963
Imports of goods and services and income payments	−59,901	−333,774	−759,290	−1,080,124	−1,782,832	−2,464,813	−2,427,804	−2,835,620
Goods, BOP basis[1]	−39,866	−249,750	−498,438	−749,374	−1,230,568	−1,692,416	−1,575,400	−1,934,555
Services	−14,520	−41,491	−117,659	−141,397	−218,964	−303,649	−380,909	−403,048
Income payments on foreign-owned assets in U.S.	−5,515	−42,532	−139,728	−183,090	−322,345	−453,800	−457,261	−483,504
Unilateral current transfers, net	−6,156	−8,349	−26,654	−38,074	−58,767	−105,741	−123,280	−136,095
CAPITAL ACCT.: Transactions, net ..	NA	NA	−7,220	−222	−1	13,116	−140	−152
FINANCIAL ACCT.								
U.S.-owned assets abroad (decrease/ financial outflow [−])[2]	−9,337	−86,967	−81,234	−352,264	−560,523	−546,631	−139,330	−1,005,182
U.S. official reserve assets	2,481	−8,155	−2,158	−9,742	−290	14,096	−52,256	−1,834
U.S. govt. assets, other than official reserve assets	−1,589	−5,162	2,317	−984	−941	5,539	541,342	7,540
U.S. private assets................	−10,229	−73,651	−81,393	−341,538	−559,292	−566,266	−628,417	−1,010,888
Foreign-owned assets in U.S. (increase/financial inflow [+])[2]	7,226	62,037	139,357	435,102	1,038,224	1,247,347	335,793	1,245,736
Stat. discrepancy (sum of above with sign reversed)...............	−219	22,613	28,066	30,951	−61,361	31,942	130,773	216,761
BALANCE ON CURRENT ACCT.	2,331	2,317	−78,968	−113,567	−416,338	−745,774	−376,551	−470,898

NA = Not available or applicable. (1) BOP = Balance of payments. Excl. exports of goods under U.S. military agency sales contracts identified in Census export documents, excl. imports of goods under direct defense expenditures identified in Census import documents, and reflects various other adjustments. (2) Excl. financial derivatives.

Foreign Direct Investment in the U.S. by Selected Countries and Territories, 1995-2010

Source: U.S. Bureau of Economic Analysis, U.S. Dept. of Commerce

(in millions of dollars)

	2010	2000	1995
All countries[1]	$2,342,829	$1,256,867	$535,553
Canada	206,139	114,309	45,618
Europe[1]	1,697,196	887,014	332,374
Austria	4,353	3,007	1,553
Belgium	43,236	14,787	4,397
Denmark	9,285	4,025	3,444
Finland	6,558	8,875	2,710
France	184,762	125,740	36,167
Germany	212,915	122,412	46,017
Ireland	30,583	25,523	4,749
Italy	15,689	6,576	3,062
Liechtenstein	NA	319	176
Luxembourg	181,203	58,930	5,756
Netherlands	217,050	138,894	65,116
Norway	10,356	2,665	2,172
Spain	40,723	5,068	3,237
Sweden	40,758	21,991	9,584
Switzerland	192,231	64,719	27,458
United Kingdom	432,488	277,613	116,272
Latin America and other Western Hemisphere[1]	60,074	53,691	27,873
South and Central America[1]	19,206	13,384	8,067
Brazil	1,093	882	750
Mexico	12,591	7,462	1,850
Panama	1,485	3,819	4,939
Venezuela	2,857	792	-152
Other Western Hemisphere[1]	$40,869	$40,307	$19,806
Bahamas	128	1,254	1,286
Bermuda	5,142	18,336	2,626
Netherlands Antilles	3,680	3,807	8,044
UK isls., Caribbean	31,150	15,191	7,207
Africa[1]	2,010	2,700	1,113
South Africa	687	704	-3
Middle East[1]	15,407	6,506	5,801
Israel	7,231	3,012	1,883
Kuwait	347	908	2,525
Lebanon	NA	1	-9
Saudi Arabia	NA	NA	1,211
United Arab Emirates	591	64	98
Asia and Pacific[1]	362,003	192,647	122,774
Australia	49,543	18,775	10,356
China	3,150	NA	NA
Hong Kong	4,272	1,493	1,511
India	3,344	NA	NA
Japan	257,273	159,690	104,997
Malaysia	362	310	400
New Zealand	556	395	149
Philippines	NA	47	75
Singapore	21,831	5,087	1,637
South Korea	15,213	3,110	692
Taiwan	5,180	3,174	2,142
European Union[1,2]	1,484,806	814,033	302,193
OPEC[1,3]	11,437	4,330	3,854

NA = Not available. **Note:** On a historical cost basis for comparison purposes. Foreign direct investment in all industries. Book value of foreign direct investors' equity in, and net outstanding loans to, their U.S. affiliates. A U.S. affiliate is a U.S. business enterprise in which a single foreign direct investor owns at least 10% of the voting securities or the equivalent. (1) May include countries or territories not shown in table. (2) European Union members in 2010: Austria, Belgium, Bulgaria, Cyprus, Czech Republic, Denmark, Estonia, Finland, France, Germany, Greece, Hungary, Ireland, Italy, Latvia, Lithuania, Luxembourg, Malta, Netherlands, Poland, Portugal, Romania, Slovakia, Slovenia, Spain, Sweden, and the United Kingdom. (3) Org. of the Petroleum Exporting Countries in 2010: Algeria, Angola, Ecuador, Iran, Iraq, Kuwait, Libya, Nigeria, Qatar, Saudi Arabia, United Arab Emirates, and Venezuela.

U.S. Direct Investment Abroad in Selected Countries and Territories, 1995-2010

Source: U.S. Bureau of Economic Analysis, U.S. Dept. of Commerce

(in millions of dollars)

	2010	2000	1995
All countries[1]	$3,908,231	$1,316,247	$699,015
Canada	296,691	132,472	83,498
Europe[1]	2,185,898	687,320	344,596
Austria	16,876	2,872	2,829
Belgium	73,526	17,973	18,706
Czech Republic	5,909	1,228	NA
Denmark	9,828	5,270	2,161
Finland	1,472	1,342	965
France	92,820	42,628	33,358
Germany	105,828	55,508	44,242
Greece	1,798	795	533
Hungary	4,863	1,920	NA
Ireland	190,478	35,903	7,996
Italy	29,015	23,484	17,096
Luxembourg	274,923	27,849	5,929
Netherlands	521,427	115,429	42,113
Norway	33,843	4,379	4,741
Poland	12,684	3,884	NA
Portugal	2,639	2,664	1,413
Russia	9,880	1,147	NA
Spain	58,053	21,236	10,856
Sweden	29,444	25,959	6,816
Switzerland	143,627	55,377	31,125
Turkey	5,693	1,826	973
United Kingdom	508,369	230,762	106,332
Latin America and other Western Hemisphere[1]	724,405	266,576	131,377
South America[1]	136,401	84,220	49,170
Argentina	12,111	17,488	7,660
Brazil	66,021	36,717	25,002
Chile	26,260	10,052	6,216
Colombia	6,574	3,693	3,506
Ecuador	1,250	832	889
Peru	7,907	3,130	1,335
Venezuela	13,693	10,531	3,634
Central America[1]	104,127	73,841	33,493
Costa Rica	1,651	1,716	921
Guatemala	NA	NA	233
Honduras	$1,027	$399	$68
Mexico	90,304	39,352	16,873
Panama	6,040	30,758	15,123
Other Western Hemisphere[1]	483,877	108,515	48,714
Bahamas	NA	NA	1,768
Barbados	5,710	2,141	698
Bermuda	264,442	60,114	28,374
Dominican Republic	1,344	1,143	330
Jamaica	NA	NA	1,287
Netherlands Antilles	NA	NA	6,835
Trinidad and Tobago	NA	NA	673
UK isls., Caribbean	149,039	33,451	8,358
Africa[1]	53,522	11,891	6,017
Egypt	11,746	1,998	1,093
Nigeria	5,224	470	629
South Africa	6,503	3,562	1,422
Middle East[1]	36,573	10,863	7,198
Israel	9,694	3,735	1,831
Saudi Arabia	8,005	3,661	2,741
United Arab Emirates	4,271	683	500
Asia and Pacific[1]	611,143	207,125	122,774
Australia	133,990	34,838	24,328
China	60,452	11,140	2,765
Hong Kong	54,035	27,447	11,768
India	27,066	2,379	1,105
Indonesia	15,502	8,904	6,777
Japan	113,263	57,091	37,309
Malaysia	15,982	7,910	4,237
New Zealand	6,872	4,271	4,601
Philippines	6,579	3,638	2,719
Singapore	106,042	24,133	12,140
South Korea	30,165	8,968	5,557
Taiwan	20,977	7,836	4,293
Thailand	12,701	5,824	4,283
European Union[1,2]	1,945,326	609,674	301,345
OPEC[1,3]	56,379	28,545	15,546

NA = Not available. **Note:** On a historical cost basis for comparison purposes. U.S. direct investment in all industries. Book value of U.S. direct investors' equity in, and net outstanding loans to, their foreign affiliates. A foreign affiliate is a foreign business enterprise in which a single U.S. investor owns at least 10% of the voting securities or the equivalent. (1) May include countries or territories not shown in table. (2) European Union members in 2010: Austria, Belgium, Bulgaria, Cyprus, Czech Republic, Denmark, Estonia, Finland, France, Germany, Hungary, Ireland, Italy, Latvia, Lithuania, Luxembourg, Malta, Netherlands, Poland, Portugal, Romania, Slovakia, Slovenia, Spain, Sweden, and the United Kingdom. (3) Org. of the Petroleum Exporting Countries in 2010: Algeria, Angola, Ecuador, Iran, Iraq, Kuwait, Libya, Nigeria, Qatar, Saudi Arabia, United Arab Emirates, and Venezuela.

TRANSPORTATION AND TRAVEL

Top Motor Vehicle Producing Nations, 2010

Source: R.L. Polk
(numbers in thousands of units; ranked by total production)

	Total motor vehicles	Cars	Trucks[1]	% change 2009-10		Total motor vehicles	Cars	Trucks[1]	% change 2009-10
China[2]	16,144	11,365	4,780	31.96%	Malaysia	550	403	146	15.79%
Japan	9,197	8,307	890	20.25	Slovakia	530	530	NA	7.29
U.S.	7,632	2,845	4,788	36.51	Belgium	524	524	NA	-0.57
Germany	5,700	5,500	200	13.34	South Africa	487	319	168	21.14
South Korea	4,184	3,866	318	22.16	Romania	431	403	28	12.24
Brazil	3,152	2,824	580	12.60	Taiwan	298	253	45	34.23
India	3,405	2,849	303	33.16	Australia	239	205	34	7.17
Spain	2,370	1,914	457	9.82	Hungary	224	224	NA	-24.07
Mexico	2,257	1,396	861	50.07	Uzbekistan	218	218	NA	6.34
France	2,181	1,918	262	8.72	Slovenia	212	206	5	0.95
Canada	2,074	977	1,097	40.51	**Asia-Pacific/**				
UK	1,382	1,270	111	27.96	**Middle East**	36,971	28,886	8,084	26.49
Thailand	1,344	503	841	31.64	**Western Europe**	13,450	12,146	1,304	12.01
Russia	1,332	1,208	124	98.51	**North America**	12,083	5,338	6,745	40.99
Iran	1,200	1,046	154	4.90	**Central & Eastern**				
Turkey	1,059	603	455	24.44	**Europe**	5,921	5,218	703	16.85
Czech Republic	1,050	1,047	3	8.25	**South America**	4,326	3,492	834	16.01
Poland	887	799	88	-1.44	**Africa**	560	388	172	13.36
Italy	806	573	233	-1.59	**World**	73,311	55,468	17,843	24.05
Argentina	717	516	201	40.59					

NA = Not available. **Note:** Regional and world totals include only countries or territories not listed. (1) Light commercial vehicles (pickup trucks and vans). (2) Not including Taiwan.

World Motor Vehicle Production, 1950-2010

Source: For 1950-97, American Automobile Manufacturers Assn.; for 1998 and on, Automotive News Data Center and R.L. Polk
(thousands of units)

Year	United States	Canada	Europe[1]	Japan	Other	World total	U.S. % of world total
1950	8,006	388	1,991	32	160	10,577	75.7%
1960	7,905	398	6,837	482	866	16,488	47.9
1970	8,284	1,160	13,049	5,289	1,637	29,419	28.2
1980	8,010	1,324	15,496	11,043	2,692	38,565	20.8
1985	11,653	1,933	16,113	12,271	2,939	44,909	25.9
1990	9,783	1,928	18,866	13,487	4,496	48,554	20.1
1995	11,985	2,408	17,045	10,196	8,349	49,983	24.0
1996	11,799	2,397	17,550	10,346	9,241	51,332	23.0
1997	12,119	2,571	17,773	10,975	10,024	53,463	22.7
1998	12,047	2,568	16,332	10,050	12,844	53,841	22.4
1999	13,107	3,042	17,603	9,985	14,050	57,787	22.7
2000	12,832	2,952	17,678	10,145	16,098	59,704	21.5
2001	11,518	2,535	17,825	9,777	16,170	57,705	19.7
2002	12,328	2,624	17,419	10,240	16,975	59,587	20.7
2003	12,145	2,547	16,943	10,286	19,641	61,562	19.7
2004	12,021	2,698	20,850	10,512	16,573	65,654	18.3
2005	12,018	2,665	20,855	10,800	20,691	67,892	17.7
2006	11,351	2,545	21,490	11,486	23,180	70,992	16.0
2007	10,611	2,602	22,858	11,596	26,019	74,647	14.2
2008	8,503	2,046	21,608	10,969	31,224	67,602	12.6
2009	5,591	1,476	17,075	7,648	32,374	59,096	9.5
2010	7,632	2,074	19,371	9,197	35,036	73,311	10.4

Note: Data for 1998 and on not fully comparable with earlier years because derived from different source. Number of units may not add up to totals due to rounding. (1) Prior to 2004, numbers exclude Eastern European production.

New and Used Passenger Cars Imported into the U.S. by Country of Origin, 1970-2010

Source: Foreign Trade Division, U.S. Census Bureau
(in number of units)

Year	Japan	Germany[1]	Italy	United Kingdom	Sweden	France	South Korea	Mexico	Canada	Total[2]
1970	381,338	674,945	42,523	76,257	57,844	37,114	NA	NA	692,783	2,013,420
1975	695,573	370,012	102,344	67,106	51,993	15,647	NA	0	733,766	2,074,653
1980	1,991,502	338,711	46,899	32,517	61,496	47,386	NA	1	594,770	3,116,448
1985	2,527,467	473,110	8,689	24,474	142,640	42,882	NA	13,647	1,144,805	4,397,679
1988	2,123,051	264,249	6,053	31,636	108,006	15,990	455,741	148,065	1,191,357	4,450,213
1989	2,051,525	216,881	9,319	29,378	101,571	4,885	270,609	133,049	1,151,122	4,042,728
1990	1,867,794	245,286	11,045	27,271	93,084	1,976	201,475	215,986	1,220,221	3,944,602
1995	1,114,360	204,932	1,031	42,450	82,593	14	131,718	462,800	1,552,691	3,624,428
1996	1,190,896	234,909	1,365	44,373	86,619	27	225,623	550,867	1,690,733	4,069,113
1997	1,387,812	300,489	1,912	43,691	79,780	67	211,650	584,795	1,837,615	4,673,418
1998	1,456,081	373,330	2,104	49,891	84,543	186	372,965	639,878	2,170,427	5,639,616
1999	1,707,277	461,061	1,697	68,394	83,399	186	568,121	934,000	2,138,811	6,324,284
2000	1,839,093	488,323	3,125	81,196	86,707	134	633,769	861,853	1,855,789	6,065,138
2001	1,790,346	494,131	2,580	82,487	92,439	92	633,769	845,181	1,882,660	6,477,659
2002	2,046,902	574,455	3,504	157,633	87,709	150	627,881	845,181	1,882,660	6,477,659
2003	1,770,355	561,482	2,943	207,158	119,773	298	692,863	680,214	1,811,892	6,127,485
2004	1,727,065	547,008	3,373	185,621	98,131	2,417	860,424	652,509	2,035,345	6,521,248
2005	1,832,534	547,191	5,377	184,716	93,736	412	730,500	693,149	1,967,985	6,564,844
2006	2,347,532	532,022	5,469	148,014	81,008	567	697,061	947,824	1,963,922	7,380,077
2007	2,300,913	466,458	5,650	108,576	92,600	1,746	676,594	889,474	1,912,744	7,220,792
2008	2,190,013	502,971	5,783	110,737	59,638	28,198	612,300	928,273	1,609,005	6,525,836
2009	1,238,773	348,093	3,067	78,999	27,017	16,900	476,912	649,740	1,164,849	4,276,163
2010	1,569,190	506,053	4,298	96,689	38,749	4,153	515,601	902,565	1,741,493	5,668,081

NA = Not available. **Note:** Excludes cars assembled in U.S. foreign trade zones. (1) Figures prior to 1991 are for West Germany. (2) Includes units imported from countries not shown in table.

Passenger Car Production in U.S. Plants, 2009-10

Source: Ward's AutoInfoBank, Ward's Automotive Group, Penton Media Inc.

(in number of units)

	2010	2009		2010	2009
AUTOALLIANCE TOTAL[1]	122,754	102,003	Cruze	66,303	—
Ford Mustang	77,586	69,921	Malibu	235,956	160,855
Mazda6	45,168	32,082	Volt	1,219	—
CHRYSLER TOTAL	169,398	84,069	Chevrolet total	411,065	247,524
200 Series	2,197	—	Pontiac G6	1	50,758
Sebring Convertible	7,829	4,489	HONDA TOTAL	426,119	391,550
Sebring Sedan	32,157	18,907	Acura TL	35,294	28,841
Chrysler total	42,183	23,396	Honda Accord	295,709	279,408
Avenger	59,170	35,315	Honda Civic	95,116	83,301
Caliber	67,586	25,020	HYUNDAI TOTAL	238,387	103,876
Viper	459	338	Hyundai Elantra	19,780	—
Dodge total	127,215	60,673	Hyundai Sonata	218,607	103,876
FORD TOTAL	298,639	236,606	MITSUBISHI TOTAL	22,969	14,798
Focus	199,502	166,453	Mitsubishi Eclipse	6,424	2,653
Taurus	83,052	50,976	Mitsubishi Galant	16,545	12,145
Ford total	282,554	217,429	NISSAN TOTAL	346,891	259,093
Lincoln MKS	16,085	15,378	Nissan Altima	275,115	205,637
GENERAL MOTORS TOTAL	600,703	413,750	Nissan Maxima	71,776	53,456
LaCrosse	73,480	25,632	NUMMI[2] TOTAL	63,319	201,437
Lucerne	29,654	22,957	Toyota Corolla	63,319	172,988
Buick total	103,134	48,589	SUBARU TOTAL	131,522	166,958
CTS	60,688	36,496	Subaru Legacy	43,791	79,032
DTS	21,023	12,807	Toyota Camry	87,731	87,926
STS	4,792	2,945	TOYOTA TOTAL	310,404	272,341
Cadillac total	86,503	52,482	Toyota Avalon	40,155	27,513
Cobalt	91,796	79,314	Toyota Camry	270,249	244,828
Corvette	15,791	7,355	TOTAL CARS	2,731,105	2,246,481

— = No production. (1) Joint venture between Ford and Mazda. (2) NUMMI (New United Motor Manufacturing, Inc.) was a joint venture between GM and Toyota (1984-2010).

Domestic and Imported Retail Car Sales in the U.S., 1980-2010

Source: Ward's AutoInfoBank, Ward's Automotive Group, Penton Media Inc.

(in number of units)

	Cars			Light trucks			All vehicles		
	Domestic[1]	Imports	Total cars	Domestic[1]	Imports	Total light trucks	Domestic[1]	Imports	Total vehicles
1980	6,579,778	2,369,457	8,949,235	1,750,735	478,887	2,229,622	8,330,513	2,848,344	11,178,857
1981	6,180,784	2,308,418	8,489,202	1,591,575	461,975	2,053,550	7,772,359	2,770,393	10,542,752
1982	5,756,658	2,199,802	7,956,460	1,968,534	430,330	2,398,864	7,725,192	2,630,132	10,355,324
1983	6,795,297	2,352,739	9,148,038	2,477,259	496,969	2,974,228	9,272,558	2,849,708	12,122,266
1984	7,951,523	2,372,172	10,323,695	3,208,371	674,153	3,882,524	11,159,894	3,046,325	14,206,219
1985	8,204,670	2,774,517	10,979,187	3,629,080	832,186	4,461,266	11,833,750	3,606,703	15,440,453
1986	8,215,017	3,189,222	11,404,239	3,675,914	977,920	4,653,834	11,890,931	4,167,142	16,058,073
1987	7,085,279	3,106,598	10,191,877	3,791,882	921,698	4,713,580	10,877,161	4,028,296	14,905,457
1988	7,543,116	3,003,692	10,546,808	4,199,643	710,661	4,910,304	11,742,759	3,714,353	15,457,112
1989	7,098,098	2,680,419	9,778,517	4,113,441	641,387	4,754,828	11,211,539	3,321,806	14,533,345
1990	6,918,869	2,384,346	9,303,215	3,956,756	611,941	4,568,697	10,875,625	2,996,287	13,871,912
1991	6,161,573	2,023,406	8,184,979	3,605,633	538,008	4,143,641	9,767,206	2,561,414	12,328,620
1992	6,285,916	1,927,197	8,213,113	4,247,097	408,003	4,655,100	10,533,013	2,335,200	12,868,213
1993	6,741,667	1,776,192	8,517,859	5,000,482	377,639	5,378,121	11,742,149	2,153,831	13,895,980
1994	7,255,303	1,735,214	8,990,517	5,658,302	409,759	6,068,061	12,913,605	2,144,973	15,058,578
1995	7,113,902	1,506,257	8,620,159	5,705,708	402,181	6,107,889	12,819,610	1,908,438	14,728,048
1996	7,206,349	1,272,196	8,478,545	6,179,881	438,757	6,618,638	13,386,230	1,710,953	15,097,183
1997	6,862,175	1,355,305	8,217,480	6,324,758	579,483	6,904,241	13,186,933	1,934,788	15,121,721
1998	6,705,208	1,379,781	8,084,989	6,802,016	656,002	7,458,018	13,507,224	2,035,783	15,543,007
1999	6,918,781	1,718,927	8,637,708	7,480,607	775,223	8,255,830	14,399,388	2,494,150	16,893,538
2000	6,761,603	2,016,120	8,777,723	7,719,707	852,325	8,572,032	14,481,310	2,868,445	17,349,755
2001	6,254,371	2,097,629	8,352,000	7,789,089	981,280	8,770,369	14,043,460	3,078,909	17,122,369
2002	5,816,671	2,225,584	8,042,255	7,707,738	1,066,375	8,774,113	13,524,409	3,291,959	16,816,368
2003	5,472,500	2,083,051	7,555,551	7,856,322	1,227,180	9,083,502	13,328,822	3,310,231	16,639,053
2004	5,333,496	2,149,059	7,482,555	8,138,107	1,246,258	9,384,365	13,471,603	3,395,317	16,866,920
2005	5,473,450	2,186,533	7,659,983	8,072,456	1,215,315	9,287,771	13,545,906	3,401,848	16,947,754
2006	5,416,828	2,344,764	7,761,592	7,396,058	1,346,750	8,742,808	12,812,886	3,691,514	16,504,400
2007	5,197,271	2,365,063	7,562,334	7,138,803	1,388,085	8,526,888	12,336,074	3,753,148	16,089,222
2008	4,490,836	2,278,271	6,769,107	5,329,165	1,096,469	6,425,634	9,820,001	3,374,740	13,194,741
2009	3,557,608	1,843,282	5,400,890	4,116,550	884,242	5,000,792	7,674,158	2,727,524	10,401,682
2010	3,791,877	1,843,556	5,635,433	5,020,441	898,644	5,919,085	8,812,318	2,742,200	11,554,518

Note: Vehicles are cars and light trucks belonging to Gross Vehicle Weight (GVW) classes 1-3 (under 14,001 lbs). (1) Includes the U.S., Canada, and Mexico.

U.S. Retail Car Sales by Vehicle Size and Type, 1985-2010

Source: Ward's Automotive Group, a division of Penton Media Inc.
(percent of total U.S. sales)

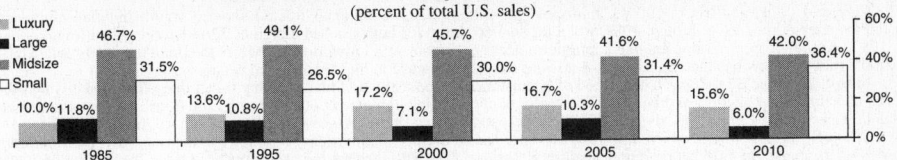

U.S. Light Truck Sales by Type, 1985-2010

Source: Ward's Automotive Group, a division of Penton Media Inc.
(percent of total U.S. sales)

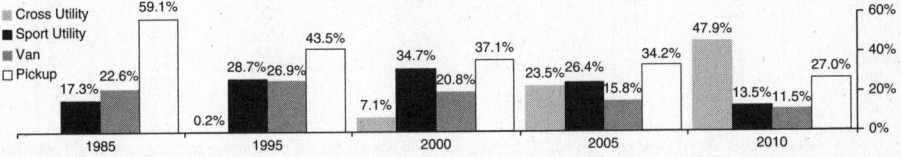

Note: Comm. chassis sales (not shown) were 1.0% for 1985, 0.7% for 1995, 0.2% for 2000, 0.1% for 2005, and 0.1% for 2010.

Top-Selling Passenger Cars in the U.S., 2007-10

Source: Ward's Automotive Group, a division of Penton Media Inc.
(ranked by number of vehicles sold)

Rank, car	2010 sales	Rank, car	2010 sales	Rank, car	2010 sales
1. Toyota Camry	327,804	8. Hyundai Sonata	196,623	15. BMW 3-Series	100,910
2. Honda Accord	282,530	9. Ford Focus	172,421	16. Nissan Versa	99,705
3. Toyota Corolla/Matrix	266,082	10. Chevrolet Impala	172,078	17. Chevrolet Cobalt	97,376
4. Honda Civic	260,218	11. Toyota Prius	140,928	18. Nissan Sentra	94,065
5. Nissan Altima	229,263	12. Hyundai Elantra	132,246	19. Chevrolet Camaro	81,299
6. Ford Fusion	219,219	13. Volkswagen Jetta	123,213	20. Dodge Charger	75,397
7. Chevrolet Malibu	198,770	14. Mazda3	106,353		

Rank, car	2009 sales	Rank, car	2008 sales	Rank, car	2007 sales
1. Toyota Camry	356,824	1. Toyota Camry	436,617	1. Toyota Camry	473,108
2. Toyota Corolla/Matrix	296,874	2. Honda Accord	372,789	2. Honda Accord	392,231
3. Honda Accord	287,492	3. Toyota Corolla/Matrix	351,007	3. Toyota Corolla/Matrix	371,390
4. Honda Civic	259,722	4. Honda Civic	339,289	4. Honda Civic	331,095
5. Nissan Altima	203,568	5. Nissan Altima	269,668	5. Chevrolet Impala	311,128
6. Ford Fusion	180,671	6. Chevrolet Impala	265,840	6. Nissan Altima	284,762
7. Chevrolet Impala	165,565	7. Ford Focus	195,823	7. Chevrolet Cobalt	200,620
8. Chevrolet Malibu	161,568	8. Chevrolet Cobalt	188,045	8. Toyota Prius	181,221
9. Ford Focus	160,433	9. Chevrolet Malibu	178,253	9. Ford Focus	173,213
10. Toyota Prius	139,682	10. Toyota Prius	158,884	10. Pontiac G6	150,001

Top-Selling Light Trucks in the U.S., 2008-10

Source: Ward's Automotive Group, a division of Penton Media Inc.
(ranked by number of vehicles sold)

Rank, truck	2010 sales	Rank, truck	2009 sales	Rank, truck	2008 sales
1. Ford F-Series	502,125	1. Ford F-Series	392,112	1. Ford F-Series	476,469
2. Chevrolet Silverado	370,135	2. Chevrolet Silverado	316,544	2. Chevrolet Silverado	465,065
3. Honda CR-V	203,714	3. Honda CR-V	191,214	3. Dodge Ram Pickup	240,454
4. Ram Pickup	194,175	4. Ram Pickup	173,066	4. Honda CR-V	197,279
5. Ford Escape	191,026	5. Ford Escape	173,044	5. GMC Sierra	168,544
6. Toyota RAV4	170,877	6. Toyota RAV4	149,088	6. Ford Escape	156,544
7. Chevrolet Equinox	149,979	7. GMC Sierra	111,842	7. Toyota Tacoma	144,655
8. GMC Sierra	129,794	8. Toyota Tacoma	111,824	8. Toyota Tundra	137,249
9. Ford Edge	118,637	9. Honda Odyssey	100,133	9. Toyota RAV4	137,020
10. Chrysler Town & Country	112,275	10. Lexus RX	93,379	10. Honda Odyssey	135,493

Most Popular Colors, by Vehicle Type, 2010

Source: Ward's Automotive Group, a division of Penton Media Inc.; Du Pont Automotive Products; for 2010 model year

Luxury cars		Full size/intermediate cars		Compact/sports cars		Light trucks	
Color	Percent	Color	Percent	Color	Percent	Color	Percent
Black/black effect	27%	Silver	19%	Black/black effect	19%	White/white pearl	35%
Gray	20	Black/black effect	18	Gray	19	Black/black effect	18
Silver	14	Gray	17	Silver	19	Silver	12
White/white pearl	13	White/white pearl	16	Blue	14	Red	12
Red	12	Red	10	White/white pearl	13	Gray	10
Beige/brown	9	Blue	9	Red	10	Blue	8
Blue	4	Beige/brown	6	Beige/brown	4	Beige/brown	2
Yellow/gold	1	Green	3	Yellow/gold	1	Green	2
Green	<1	Yellow/gold	2	Green	1	Yellow/gold	2
Other	<1	Other	<1	Other	<1	Other	<1

U.S. Light-Duty Vehicle Fuel Efficiency, 1975-2010

Source: Natl. Vehicle and Fuel Emissions Laboratory, Office of Transportation and Air Quality, U.S. Environmental Protection Agency

Cars and light-duty trucks (SUVs, minivans, passenger vans, and pickup trucks) showed significant fuel-efficiency improvements from 1975 through 1987, when the fuel economy for both reached a high of 22 miles per gallon (mpg). After 1987, the fuel economy value entered a long-term decline, reaching 19.3 mpg in 2004 before the trend reversed itself. Since 2005, fuel economy has increased. Most of this increase has been due to higher truck fuel economy.

In Dec. 2006, the EPA changed its method of calculating adjusted real-world fuel economy values due to changed driving habits, including more aggressive driving and increased air conditioning use, among other factors. Data from 1986 on were revised under this method. Comparing laboratory 55/45 fuel economy values, however, shows an all-time high was reached in 2010.

Sales of light-duty trucks, which in recent years have had an average fuel efficiency 5-7 mpg less than cars, accounted for only 19% of the market in 1975 but have been at about 50% since 2002. This increase has been a major factor in the leveling off in the fuel efficiency of the average light-duty vehicle. But technological innovations have helped to boost fuel efficiency in recent years.

Year[1]	Cars (mpg[2])	Light-duty trucks (mpg[2])	All light-duty vehicles (mpg[2])	Year[1]	Cars (mpg[2])	Light-duty trucks (mpg[2])	All light-duty vehicles (mpg[2])
1975	13.5	11.6	13.1	2001	23.0	16.7	19.6
1980	20.0	15.8	19.2	2002	23.1	16.7	19.4
1985	23.0	17.5	21.3	2003	23.3	16.9	19.6
1990	23.3	17.4	21.2	2004	23.1	16.7	19.3
1995	23.4	17.0	20.5	2005	23.5	17.2	19.9
1996	23.3	17.2	20.4	2006	23.3	17.5	20.1
1997	23.4	17.0	20.1	2007	24.1	17.7	20.6
1998	23.4	17.1	20.1	2008	24.3	18.2	21.0
1999	23.0	16.7	19.7	2009	25.4	19.0	22.4
2000	22.9	16.9	19.8	2010	25.8	19.1	22.5

(1) Because of changes in methodology, mpg figures from before 1986 are not entirely comparable with later values. (2) Adjusted composite values (city and highway fuel efficiency combined in a 55%/45% ratio) reflecting real-world use.

Registered Cars in the U.S., 1900-2009

Source: Office of Highway Policy Information, Federal Highway Administration, U.S. Dept. of Transportation

(includes automobiles for public and private use)

Year	Reg. cars	Year	Reg. cars	Year	Reg. cars	Year	Reg. cars	Year	Reg. cars
1900	8,000	1940	27,465,826	1980	121,600,843	1996	129,728,311	2003	135,669,897
1905	77,400	1945	25,796,985	1985	127,885,193	1997	129,748,704	2004	136,430,651
1910	458,377	1950	40,339,077	1990	133,700,497	1998	131,838,538	2005	136,568,083
1915	2,332,426	1955	52,144,739	1991	128,299,601	1999	132,432,044	2006	135,399,945
1920	8,131,522	1960	61,671,390	1992	126,581,148	2000	133,621,420	2007	135,932,930
1925	17,481,001	1965	75,257,588	1993	127,327,189	2001	137,633,467	2008	137,079,843
1930	23,034,753	1970	89,243,557	1994	127,883,469	2002	135,920,677	2009	134,879,600
1935	22,567,827	1975	106,705,934	1995	128,386,775	2002	135,920,677		

Note: There were no publicly owned vehicles before 1925; statistics also exclude military vehicles for all years. Alaska and Hawaii data included since 1960.

Licensed Drivers, by Age and Sex, 1980-2009

Source: Office of Highway Policy Information, Federal Highway Administration, U.S. Dept. of Transportation

(numbers in thousands)

Age	1980 Male	1980 Female	1980 Total[1]	1990 Male	1990 Female	1990 Total[1]	2009 Male	2009 Female	2009 Total[1]	% total drivers
Under 16	52	41	93	23	20	43	206	204	410	0.2%
16	1,001	822	1,823	769	674	1,443	662	654	1,315	0.6
17	1,530	1,260	2,790	1,136	996	2,132	1,074	1,038	2,112	1.0
18	1,763	1,484	3,247	1,378	1,217	2,595	1,455	1,371	2,826	1.3
19	1,900	1,643	3,542	1,608	1,429	3,037	1,682	1,587	3,269	1.6
19 and under	6,246	5,249	11,496	4,913	4,336	9,249	5,079	4,854	9,932	4.7
20	1,930	1,706	3,636	1,691	1,538	3,229	1,725	1,665	3,390	1.6
21	1,961	1,772	3,733	1,694	1,555	3,249	1,737	1,701	3,438	1.6
22	1,998	1,813	3,811	1,701	1,561	3,262	1,748	1,721	3,470	1.7
23	2,062	1,876	3,938	1,767	1,631	3,398	1,784	1,756	3,540	1.7
24	2,047	1,868	3,915	1,951	1,807	3,758	1,809	1,796	3,606	1.7
20-24	9,998	9,034	19,032	8,804	8,093	16,897	8,803	8,640	17,443	8.3
25-29	9,865	9,060	18,925	10.239	9,656	19,895	9,221	9,260	18,481	8.8
30-34	9,010	8,359	17,369	10,507	10,071	20,578	8,921	8,925	17,846	8.5
35-39	7,113	6,583	13,696	9,684	9,371	19,055	9,425	9,366	18,792	9.0
40-44	5,828	5,306	11,134	8,610	8,295	16,905	9,729	9,638	19,367	9.2
45-49	5,311	4,765	10,076	6,642	6,378	13,020	10,577	10,611	21,189	10.1
50-54	5,351	4,739	10,090	5,376	5,108	10,484	10,177	10,300	20,477	9.8
55-59	5,198	4,572	9,770	4,855	4,583	9,438	8,925	9,082	18,007	8.6
60-64	4,439	3,793	8,232	4,738	4,497	9,235	7,513	7,637	15,150	7.2
65-69	3,631	2,949	6,580	4,266	4,109	8,375	5,470	5,618	11,088	5.3
70-74	NA	NA	NA	NA	NA	NA	3,939	4,098	8,037	3.8
75-79	NA	NA	NA	NA	NA	NA	2,943	3,173	6,116	2.9
80-84	NA	NA	NA	NA	NA	NA	2,060	2,354	4,414	2.1
85 and over	NA	NA	NA	NA	NA	NA	1,480	1,799	3,280	1.6
Total	77,187	68,108	145,295	85,792	81,223	167,015	104,262	105,357	209,618	100.0

NA = Not available. (1) Figures may not add up to totals due to rounding.

Selected Motor Vehicle Statistics

Source: Federal Highway Admin., U.S. Dept. of Transportation; Insurance Inst. for Highway Safety; American Petroleum Inst.

Driver's license age requirements, state gas tax, and safety belt use laws (incl. laws passed, but not in effect) as of 2011. Other figures are for 2009.

STATE	Driver's license age requirements Learner's permit	Regular[1]	State gas tax (cents/gal.)	Safety belt use law[6]	Licensed drivers Per 1,000 total resident pop.	Per reg. motor vehicle	Reg. motor vehicles per 1,000 pop.	Fuel use per reg. motor vehicle (gallons)	Annual miles driven Per gal. used	Per reg. vehicle	Per lic. driver
Alabama	15	17	16.0	P	803	0.83	979	714	17.02	12,158	14,822
Alaska	14	16y, 6m	8.0	P	727	0.75	995	808	8.78	7,095	9,715
Arizona	15y, 6m	16y, 6m	18.0	S	668	1.02	661	773	18.30	14,143	13,996
Arkansas	14	18	21.5	P	715	1.03	705	1,010	16.15	16,305	16,086
California	15y, 6m	17	35.3	P	641	0.70	932	510	18.48	9,424	13,703
Colorado	15	17	22.0	S(a)	737	2.67	284	1,834	17.65	32,373	12,492
Connecticut	16	18[2]	25.0	P	829	0.96	873	580	17.65	10,229	10,775
Delaware	16	17[2]	23.0	P	791	0.84	953	613	17.57	10,766	12,976
Dist. of Columbia	16	18[3]	23.5	P	627	1.83	363	653	25.37	16,577	9,594
Florida	15	18	4.0	P	755	0.94	826	631	20.14	12,711	13,899
Georgia	15	18[2]	7.5	P	642	0.75	866	716	17.95	12,843	17,301
Hawaii	15y, 6m	17[2]	17.0	P	687	1.01	691	560	19.90	11,139	11,207
Idaho	14y, 6m	16[2]	25.0	S	683	0.78	889	648	17.43	11,296	14,718
Illinois	15	18[2]	19.0	P	643	0.85	766	637	16.80	10,701	12,751
Indiana	15	18[2]	18.0	P	864	0.97	910	719	18.23	13,104	13,806
Iowa	14	17[2]	21.0	P	713	0.65	1,118	672	13.75	9,237	14,480
Kansas	14	16y, 6m	24.0	S(a)	726	0.85	860	730	16.66	12,163	14,422
Kentucky	16	17[2]	21.1	P	681	0.83	831	826	16.00	13,211	16,110
Louisiana	15	17[2]	20.0	P	687	0.78	898	742	14.99	11,123	14,538
Maine	15	16y, 6m[2]	29.5	P	769	0.98	801	819	16.76	13,724	14,298
Maryland	15y, 9m	18	23.5	P	685	0.88	787	794	15.53	12,332	14,161
Massachusetts	16	18[2]	21.0	S	702	0.89	798	602	17.30	10,417	11,839
Michigan	14y, 9m	17[2]	19.0	P	710	0.91	794	676	18.10	12,229	13,662
Minnesota	15	16y, 6m[2]	27.1	P	616	0.68	911	657	18.05	11,858	17,524
Mississippi	15	16y, 6m	18.0	P	654	0.97	686	1,052	18.97	19,957	20,940
Missouri	15	17y, 11m	17.0	S(a)	704	0.87	819	847	16.61	14,070	16,360
Montana	14y, 6m	16[2]	27.0	S	757	0.82	949	793	15.01	11,904	14,921
Nebraska	15	17	26.4	S	751	0.77	998	680	15.88	10,797	14,347
Nevada	15y, 6m	18[2]	23.0	S	640	1.23	529	1,016	14.41	14,638	12,100
New Hampshire	15y, 6m	18	18.0	None	781	0.87	915	669	16.00	10,701	12,545
New Jersey	16	18	10.5	P	680	0.99	702	824	14.50	11,945	12,329
New Mexico	15	16y, 6m[2]	17.0	P	686	0.87	806	867	18.52	16,050	18,878
New York	16	18[2,4]	8.1	P	580	1.03	575	623	19.06	11,871	11,783
North Carolina	15	16y, 6m[2]	32.5	P(b)	693	1.10	645	888	19.41	17,241	16,029
North Dakota	14	16	23.0	S	737	0.67	1,116	793	14.24	11,293	17,110
Ohio	15y, 6m	18[2]	28.0	S	688	0.73	955	577	17.40	10,038	13,939
Oklahoma	15y, 6m	17[4]	16.0	P	629	0.70	921	758	18.27	13,837	20,249
Oregon	15	17[2]	30.0	P	743	0.96	796	671	16.62	11,152	11,954
Pennsylvania	16	18[4]	12.0	S	689	0.89	782	656	16.06	10,538	11,958
Rhode Island	16	17y, 6m[2]	32.0	S(a,c)	708	0.96	749	573	18.25	10,461	11,059
South Carolina	15	16y, 6m	16.0	P	717	0.92	792	931	14.60	13,593	15,031
South Dakota	14	16	22.0	S	741	0.67	1,140	700	14.81	10,372	15,954
Tennessee	15	17	20.0	P	711	0.89	816	776	17.60	13,664	15,688
Texas	15	17[4]	20.0	P	620	0.87	735	867	14.59	12,654	14,987
Utah	15	17[5]	24.5	S(a,c)	618	0.71	881	605	17.70	10,703	15,270
Vermont	15	16y, 6m[2]	19.0	S(a)	815	0.93	896	698	19.66	13,718	15,082
Virginia	15y, 6m	18[2]	17.5	S	678	0.86	799	777	16.53	12,842	15,133
Washington	15	17[2]	37.5	P	754	0.91	837	593	17.06	10,109	11,224
West Virginia	15	17	20.5	S	730	0.97	776	783	17.72	13,881	14,753
Wisconsin	15y, 6m	16y, 9m[2]	30.9	P	726	0.85	862	656	18.20	11,931	14,167
Wyoming	15	16y, 6m[2]	13.0	S	755	0.65	1,199	1,064	13.78	14,668	23,290
U.S. AVERAGE			20.6		683	0.87	802	699	17.15	11,992	14,090

Note: Most states have graduated licensing systems that phase in full driving privileges. During the learner's stage, driving generally is not permitted without adult supervision. In an intermediate stage, young licensees may be allowed to drive unsupervised only under certain conditions. (1) Min. age at which all restrictions may be lifted on private passenger car operation. (2) Applicants under a specified age (typically between 17 and 19) must complete driver education. Some states allow applicants to substitute home training, state-sponsored traffic school, or a number of hrs. of supervised driving for driver ed. (3) Learner's stage mandatory for all license applicants regardless of age. (4) Minimum age for an unrestricted driver's license may be lower if the applicant has completed driver education. Unsupervised driving in New York City prohibited for all drivers under 18. (5) Driver ed. required regardless of age. (6) P = Officer may stop vehicle for violation (primary); S = officer may issue seat belt citation only when vehicle is stopped for another moving violation (secondary). (a) Primary enforcement for children under a specified age. (b) Secondary enforcement for rear seat occupants. (c) Primary enforcement for driver.

Handheld Phone and Texting Device Laws for Drivers, 2011

Source: Insurance Institute for Highway Safety; as of July 2011

State	Handheld ban	Texting ban	Enforcement	State	Handheld ban	Texting ban	Enforcement
AL	(1)	(1)	P	MT	No	No	NA
AK	No	Yes	P	NE	No	Yes	S
AZ	No	No	NA	NV	Yes[10]	Yes[10]	P[10]
AR	(2)	Yes	(3)	NH	No	Yes	P
CA	Yes	Yes	P[4]	NJ	Yes	Yes	P
CO	No	Yes	P	NM	No	(9)	P
CT	Yes	Yes	P	NY	Yes	Yes	P
DE	Yes	Yes	P	NC	No	Yes	P
DC	Yes	Yes	P	ND	No	Yes	P
FL	No	No	NA	OH	No	No	NA
GA	No	Yes	P	OK	(9)	(11)	P
HI	No	No	NA	OR	Yes	Yes	P
ID	No	No	NA	PA	No	No	NA
IL	(5)	Yes	P	RI	No	Yes	P
IN	No	Yes	P	SC	No	No	NA
IA	No	Yes	(6)	SD	No	No	NA
KS	No	Yes	P	TN	No	Yes	P
KY	No	Yes	P	TX	(12)	(13)	P
LA	(7)	Yes	P	UT	Yes	Yes	S[8]
ME	No	Yes	P	VT	No	Yes	P
MD	Yes	Yes	S[8]	VA	No	Yes	(14)
MA	No	Yes	P	WA	Yes	Yes	P
MI	No	Yes	P	WV	No	(15)	P
MN	No	Yes	P	WI	No	Yes	P
MS	No	(9)	P	WY	No	Yes	P
MO	No	(2)	P				

Note: Laws shown for licensed passenger car drivers. Different laws and regulations apply to school bus, municipal transit, and other mass transit operators. NA = Not available/not applicable. P = Officer may stop vehicle for violation (primary); S = officer may issue citation only when vehicle is stopped for another moving violation (secondary). (1) Drivers ages 16 and 17 who have held an intermediate license for fewer than 6 months. (2) Drivers 21 and younger. (3) Primary for texting by all drivers and cell phone use by school bus drivers; secondary for cell phone use by young drivers. (4) Secondary for hands-free cell phone use by young drivers. (5) Drivers in construction and school speed zones. (6) Primary for learner's permit and intermediate license holders; secondary for texting. (7) All learner's permit holders and all intermediate license holders are prohibited from driving while using a handheld cell phone, and all drivers younger than 18 are prohibited from using any cell phone. All drivers issued a first driver's license are prohibited from using a cell phone for one year. The cell phone ban is secondary for novice drivers age 18 and older. (8) Primary for texting. (9) Learner's permit and intermediate license holders. (10) As of Jan. 1, 2012. (11) Learner's permit holders, intermediate license holders, school bus drivers, and public transit drivers. (12) Drivers in school crossing zones. (13) Bus drivers when a passenger 17 and younger is present, drivers in school crossing zones, and drivers younger than 18. (14) Secondary; primary for school bus drivers. (15) Drivers younger than 18 who hold either a learner's permit or an intermediate license.

Tourism Trends

World tourist arrivals increased 2.1% between 2007 and 2008 and decreased 3.8% between 2008 and 2009, according to the World Tourism Organization's (UNWTO) *Barometer* publication. The number of international tourist arrivals in 2010 was an estimated 940 mil, an increase of 6.6% over the previous year. Worldwide tourism receipts, as measured in constant U.S. dollars, increased 8.0% from 2009 to 2010, to a value of $919 bil. Europe as a region again commanded the largest share of international tourist arrivals (51%) and receipts (44%) in 2009. Asia and the Pacific posted the second-largest share in each category, with 22% of international tourist arrivals and 27% of receipts worldwide. With 150 mil arrivals, the Americas held a 16% share of the world total. Although all regions showed an increase in the number of international tourist arrivals in 2010 compared to 2009, the Middle East had the greatest increase (14.1%).

Preliminary data for the first four months of 2011 indicated a growth of about 4.5% in international tourist arrivals, compared with the same period in 2010. Despite recent developments in the Middle East and North Africa, as well as the tragic events in Japan (the Mar. 2011 earthquake that generated a tsunami and damaged a nuclear power plant), the UNWTO predicted a growth in global tourism in 2011.

The International Air Transport Association (IATA) reported an 8.2% increase in actual international passenger traffic (as measured in revenue passenger kilometers) in 2010. It expected a decrease in the global airline industry's net profits in 2011. The price of fuel remains a challenge, having risen from 13% of airline operating costs in 2001 to 26% in 2010, although this is lower than the high of 33% from 2 years earlier. IATA forecasted that fuel will have accounted for 30% of operating costs in 2011.

World Tourism Receipts, 1990-2010

Source: World Tourism Organization (UNWTO), © UNWTO, 9284402711
(in billions of U.S. dollars)

Year	Receipts[1]	Year	Receipts[1]	Year	Receipts[1]	Year	Receipts[1]	Year	Receipts[1]	Year	Receipts[1]
1990	$264	1994	$356	1998	$445	2002	$484	2005	$679	2008	$942
1991	278	1995	405	1999	458	2003	533	2006	744	2009	851
1992	317	1996	439	2000	478	2004	634	2007	857	2010	919*
1993	323	1997	443	2001	466						

*Preliminary. (1) Total of all transactions made by or on behalf of visitors for the duration of their visit. Does not include receipts from international passenger transport contracted from companies outside a traveler's country of residence.

Top 10 Countries in Tourism Earnings, 2010

Source: World Tourism Organization (UNWTO), © UNWTO, 9284402711
(in billions of U.S. dollars; ranked by receipts from most recent year)

		Receipts[1]		%			Receipts[1]		%
Rank	Country	2010*	2009	change	Rank	Country	2010*	2009	change
1.	United States	$103.1	$93.9	9.8%	6.	Germany	$34.7	$34.6	5.3%
2.	Spain	52.5	53.2	3.9	7.	United Kingdom	30.4	30.1	1.7
3.	France	46.3	49.4	-1.3	8.	Australia	30.1	25.4	0.8
4.	China[2]	45.8	39.7	15.5	9.	Hong Kong	23.0	16.4	39.8
5.	Italy	38.8	40.2	1.4	10.	Turkey	20.8	21.3	-2.1

*Preliminary. (1) Excluding receipts from international passenger transport contracted from companies outside a traveler's country of residence. (2) Not including Hong Kong, Macao, and Taiwan.

World's Top 10 Tourist Destinations, 2010

Source: World Tourism Organization (UNWTO), © UNWTO, 9284402711

(ranked by number of arrivals in millions; preliminary)

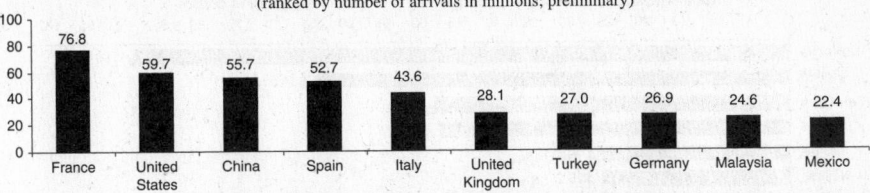

France	United States	China	Spain	Italy	United Kingdom	Turkey	Germany	Malaysia	Mexico
76.8	59.7	55.7	52.7	43.6	28.1	27.0	26.9	24.6	22.4

International Travel to the U.S., 1986-2010

Source: Office of Travel and Tourism Industries, Intl. Trade Admin., U.S. Dept. of Commerce; World Tourism Organization

(Visitors in millions; some figures are revised and may differ from other sources.)

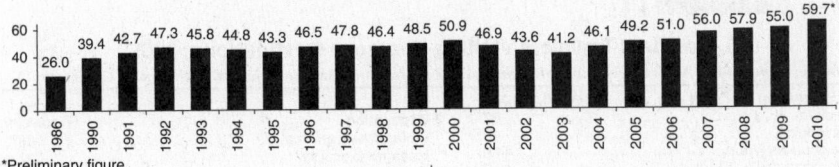

1986	1990	1991	1992	1993	1994	1995	1996	1997	1998	1999	2000	2001	2002	2003	2004	2005	2006	2007	2008	2009	2010
26.0	39.4	42.7	47.3	45.8	44.8	43.3	46.5	47.8	46.4	48.5	50.9	46.9	43.6	41.2	46.1	49.2	51.0	56.0	57.9	55.0	59.7*

*Preliminary figure.

International Visitors to the U.S. by Top Countries of Origin, 2010

Source: Office of Travel and Tourism Industries, Intl. Trade Admin., U.S. Dept. of Commerce

(ranked by number of visitors; excludes cruise travelers)

Country of origin	Visitors	Expenditures (mil)[1]	Expenditures per visitor	Country of origin	Visitors	Expenditures (mil)[1]	Expenditures per visitor
1. Canada........	19,959,000	$20,823	$104.33	12. India..........	650,935	$3,991	$6,131.18
2. Mexico	13,423,000	8,729	650.30	13. Spain	639,654	NA	NA
3. UK.............	3,850,864	11,566	3,003.48	14. Netherlands	570,179	1,860	3,262.13
4. Japan	3,386,076	14,558	4,299.37	15. Colombia	494,739	NA	NA
5. Germany.......	1,726,193	5,782	3,349.56	16. Venezuela......	491,604	2,475	5,034.54
6. France	1,342,207	4,090	3,047.21	17. Argentina......	436,192	2,110	4,837.32
7. Brazil.........	1,197,866	5,919	4,941.28	18. Switzerland.....	390,591	NA	NA
8. South Korea	1,107,518	3,430	3,097.02	19. Sweden........	371,853	NA	NA
9. Australia	904,247	3,973	4,393.71	20. Ireland........	360,492	NA	NA
10. Italy...........	838,225	3,212	3,831.91	All countries.......	59,744,616	134,436	2,250.18
11. China[2]........	801,738	5,005	6,242.69				

NA = Not available. (1) Does not include fares received by U.S. air carriers from international visitors for travel between the U.S. and foreign countries and between two foreign points. (2) Not including Hong Kong, Macao, and Taiwan.

Traveler Spending in the U.S., 1987-2010

Source: Office of Travel and Tourism Industries, Intl. Trade Admin., U.S. Dept. of Commerce; U.S. Travel Assn.

(in billions of dollars)

Year	Traveler spending Domestic	International	Year	Traveler spending Domestic	International	Year	Traveler spending Domestic	International
1987	$235	$31	1995	$360	$63	2003	$496	$65
1988	258	38	1996	385	70	2004	532	75
1989	273	47	1997	406	73	2005	572	82
1990	291	43	1998	425	71	2006	610	86
1991	296	48	1999	458	75	2007	641	97
1992	306	55	2000	503	82	2008	662	110
1993	323	58	2001	484	72	2009	610	94
1994	340	58	2002	478	67	2010	656	104

U.S. Domestic Leisure Travel Volume, 1995-2009

Source: U.S. Travel Assn.

(in millions of person-trips of 50 mi or more, one-way)

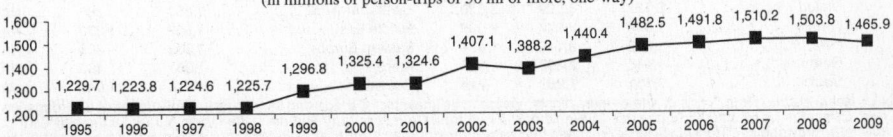

1995	1996	1997	1998	1999	2000	2001	2002	2003	2004	2005	2006	2007	2008	2009
1,229.7	1,223.8	1,224.6	1,225.7	1,296.8	1,325.4	1,324.6	1,407.1	1,388.2	1,440.4	1,482.5	1,491.8	1,510.2	1,503.8	1,465.9

Note: Method of collecting travel data has been revised; data for earlier years have been adjusted to maintain comparability.

Top 10 U.S. States by Traveler Spending, 2009

Source: U.S. Travel Assn.

(domestic and international traveler spending within state, in billions of dollars)

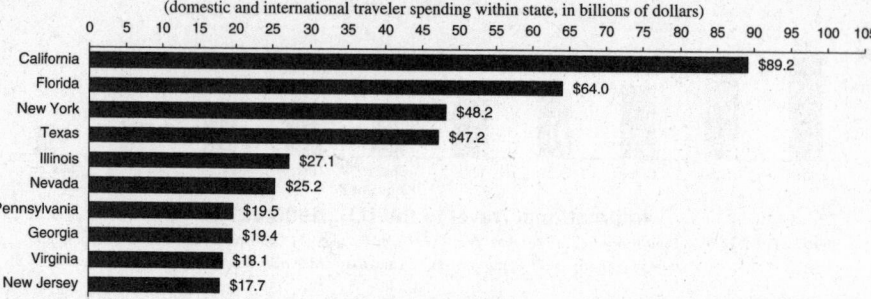

State	Spending
California	$89.2
Florida	$64.0
New York	$48.2
Texas	$47.2
Illinois	$27.1
Nevada	$25.2
Pennsylvania	$19.5
Georgia	$19.4
Virginia	$18.1
New Jersey	$17.7

U.S. Resident Travelers Visiting Overseas Destinations, 2009

Source: Survey of Intl. Air Travelers, Office of Travel and Tourism Industries, Intl. Trade Admin., U.S. Dept. of Commerce

Total U.S. resident travelers	30,300,000
Males (adults)	52%
Females (adults)	48%
Avg. age of males (yrs.)	44.8
Avg. age of females (yrs.)	42.7
Median annual household income	$99,600
Avg. total trip expend. per visitor (incl. airfare)	$2,708
Avg. expend. outside the U.S. per visitor per day	$72
Median number of nights	10.0

Region of residence	% of travelers
Middle Atlantic	39%
South Atlantic (incl. Florida, DC metro area)	19
Pacific (incl. California, Washington)	14
New England	8
East North Central (incl. Illinois, Ohio)	7
West South Central (incl. Texas)	5
Mountain	4
West North Central	2
East South Central	2

Main purpose of trip	% of travelers
Leisure/recreation/holiday	40%
Visit friends/relatives	37
Business	16
Study/teaching	4
Convention/conference	2
Religion/pilgrimage	2
Health treatment	1

Occupation	% of travelers
Professional/technical	39%
Manager/executive	22
Retired	11
Student	10
Homemaker	5
Clerical/sales	5
Craftsman/factory worker	3
Government/military	3

Leisure/recreational activities[1]	% of travelers
Dining in restaurants	82%
Shopping	72
Visit historical places	50
Visit small towns/villages	42
Sightseeing in cities	41
Cultural heritage sights	33
Touring the countryside	32
Water sports/sunbathing	25
Art gallery, museum	24
Nightclub/dancing	21
Guided tours	17
Ethnic heritage sites	13
Concert, play, musical	11
Amusement/theme parks	11
Visit national parks	11

(1) Percentages based on multiple responses.

U.S. Resident Travel Abroad, 1997-2009

Source: Office of Travel and Tourism Industries, Intl. Trade Admin., U.S. Dept. of Commerce

(numbers in thousands; regions ranked by most recent numbers)

Region/country[1]	2009	2000	1997	Region/country[1]	2009	2000	1997
Total outbound[2]	61,419	61,327	52,735	Asia	6,333	4,914	NA
				Japan	1,515	1,262	1,082
Mexico	19,452	19,285	17,909	China[4]	1,182	644	476
Canada	11,667	15,189	13,401	India	1,061	457	NA
				Caribbean	5,696	3,867	NA
Overseas subtotal[3]	30,300	26,853	21,634	Dominican Rep.	1,454	NA	NA
Europe	10,635	13,373	NA	South America	2,818	2,095	NA
Western Europe	9,848	12,916	NA	Central America	2,060	886	NA
United Kingdom	2,727	4,189	3,570	Middle East	1,909	1,370	NA
France	1,909	2,927	2,098	Eastern Europe	1,303	806	NA
Italy	1,848	2,148	1,471	Africa	1,061	483	NA
Germany	1,545	2,309	1,796	Oceania	818	1,047	NA
Spain	1,151	1,262	714				

NA = Not available. **Note:** Visits of one or more nights. Visitation estimates for Canada and Mexico include all modes of transportation used. Estimates for all other countries are available only for air travel to that country and are based upon data from the airlines that voluntarily provided it. (1) Only individual countries that received more than 1 mil visitors in 2009 are shown. Region figures include U.S. resident travelers to all countries in region. (2) To Canada, Mexico, and overseas. (3) To all countries except Canada and Mexico. (4) Not including Hong Kong, Macao, and Taiwan.

Airline Safety, U.S. Scheduled Commercial Carriers, 1985-2010

Source: National Transportation Safety Board; Federal Aviation Administration, U.S. Dept. of Transportation

Year	Departures (mil)	Fatal accidents	Fatalities[1]	Rate of fatal accidents[2]	Year	Departures (mil)	Fatal accidents	Fatalities[1]	Rate of fatal accidents[2]
1985	6.1	4	197	0.066	2001[3]	10.6	6	531	0.019
1990	7.8	6	39	0.077	2002	10.3	0	0	0.000
1992	7.5	4	33	0.053	2003	10.2	2	22	0.020
1993	7.7	1	1	0.013	2004	10.8	1	13	0.009
1994[3]	7.8	4	239	0.051	2005	10.9	3	22	0.027
1995	8.1	1	160	0.012	2006	10.6	2	50	0.019
1996	7.9	3	342	0.038	2007	10.7	0	0	—
1997	9.9	3	3	0.030	2008	10.3	0	0	—
1998	10.5	1	1	0.009	2009	10.2	1	50	0.010
1999	10.9	2	12	0.018	2010*	9.4	0	0	—
2000	11.1	2	89	0.018					

*Preliminary. (1) Includes deaths that occurred on the ground as a result of an accident, except for fatalities resulting from the Sept. 11, 2001, terrorist attacks. (2) Per 100,000 departures. (3) An illegal act, such as suicide or sabotage, was counted among fatal accidents and fatalities for this year but was not used in the calculation of accident rates.

U.S. Scheduled Airline Traffic, 2000-10

Source: Courtesy of Air Transport Association of America, Inc. Reprinted with permission. Copyright © 2010 by Air Transport Association of America, Inc. All rights reserved.

(in millions, except where otherwise noted)

	2000	2004	2005	2006	2007	2008	2009	2010
Passengers enplaned..........	666.2	702.9	738.3	744.2	769.2	741.4	703.9	720.5
Revenue passenger miles[1]........	692,757	733,680	778,563	796,795	829,033	811,440	769,485	798,008
Available seat miles[2]	956,950	971,466	1,002,735	1,005,534	1,037,116	1,020,147	957,198	972,561
Cargo revenue (ton miles)[1]........	23,888	27,978	28,036	29,339	29,524	28,383	25,002	27,884
% of seating utilized ...	72.4	75.5	77.6	79.2	79.9	79.5	80.4	82.1
Passenger operating revenue	$93,622	$85,646	$93,500	$101,419	$107,011	$111,535	$91,331	$103,978
Net profit[3]......	$2,486	-$7,643	-$5,782	$3,123	$4,998	-$9,464	-$2,528	$3,600
Total employment[4]	679,967	569,498	562,467	545,695	560,997	556,920	536,236	514,209

(1) One fare-paying passenger or one ton of revenue cargo transported one mile. (2) One seat transported one mile. (3) For all years except 2009, excludes bankruptcy-related charges (reorganization expenses and fresh-start accounting gains). (4) Not in millions. Figures are of avg. full-time equivalents (FTE), i.e., the number of full-time employees that could have been employed if the reported number of hours worked by part-time employees had been worked by full-time employees. In this table, part-time employees are treated as 0.5 FTEs.

Top 25 U.S. Passenger Airlines, 2010

Source: Courtesy of Air Transport Association of America, Inc. Reprinted with permission. Copyright © 2011 by Air Transport Association of America, Inc. All rights reserved.

(in thousands; ranked by number of passengers)

Rank	Airline	Passengers	Rank	Airline	Passengers	Rank	Airline	Passengers	Rank	Airline	Passengers
1.	Delta	110,925	8.	SkyWest	24,218	14.	Republic	11,038	20.	Spirit	6,751
2.	Southwest ..	106,228	9.	JetBlue	24,199	15.	Pinnacle	10,875	21.	Comair	6,449
3.	American	86,129	10.	Alaska	16,478	16.	Frontier......	9,241	22.	Mesaba......	6,160
4.	United	54,080	11.	ExpressJet ..	16,315	17.	Mesa........	9,042	23.	Air Wisconsin	5,891
5.	US Airways ..	51,814	12.	American Eagle	16,246	18.	Hawaiian	8,418	24.	Chautauqua ..	5,838
6.	Continental...	43,479	13.	Atlantic		19.	Horizon......	6,819	25.	Allegiant	5,610
7.	AirTran	24,558		Southeast ..	13,931						

Note: Domestic and international. Does not include passengers on flights with both origin and destination in a foreign country.

Top North American Airports by Passenger Traffic, 2010

Source: *2010 World Annual Traffic Report*, Airports Council Intl.

City/airport name (airport code)	Total passengers[1]
1. Hartsfield-Jackson Atlanta Intl. (ATL)	89,331,622
2. Chicago O'Hare Intl. (ORD)	66,774,738
3. Los Angeles Intl. (LAX)	59,070,127
4. Dallas/Fort Worth Intl. (DFW)	56,906,610
5. Denver Intl. (DEN)	52,209,377
6. New York John F. Kennedy Intl. (JFK)	46,514,154
7. Houston George Bush Intercontinental (IAH) ...	40,479,569
8. Las Vegas McCarran Intl. (LAS)	39,757,359
9. San Francisco Intl. (SFO)	39,253,999
10. Phoenix Sky Harbor Intl. (PHX)	38,554,215
11. Charlotte Douglas Intl. (CLT)	38,254,207
12. Miami Intl. (MIA)	35,698,025
13. Orlando Intl. (MCO)	34,877,899
14. Newark Liberty Intl. (EWR)	33,107,041
15. Minneapolis-St. Paul Intl. (MSP)	32,839,441
16. Detroit Metro. Wayne County (DTW)	32,377,064
17. Toronto Pearson Intl. (YYZ)	31,934,395
18. Seattle-Tacoma Intl. (SEA)	31,553,166
19. Philadelphia Intl. (PHL)................	30,775,961
20. Boston Logan Intl. (BOS)	27,428,962
21. New York LaGuardia (LGA)	23,983,082
22. Washington Dulles Intl. (IAD)	23,591,554
23. Fort Lauderdale-Hollywood Intl. (FLL).......	22,412,627
24. Baltimore/Wash. Intl. Thurgood Marshall (BWI) ...	21,949,902
25. Salt Lake City Intl. (SLC)...............	21,016,686

Top World Airports by Passenger Traffic, 2010

Source: *2010 World Annual Traffic Report*, Airports Council Intl.

City/airport name (country; airport code)	Total passengers[1]
1. Beijing Capital Intl. (China; PEK)	73,948,113
2. London Heathrow (UK; LHR)	65,884,143
3. Tokyo Haneda Intl. (Japan; HND)	64,211,074
4. Paris Charles de Gaulle (France; CDG)	58,167,062
5. Frankfurt Intl. (Germany; FRA)	53,009,221
6. Hong Kong Intl. (China; HKG).............	50,348,960
7. Madrid-Barajas (Spain, MAD).............	49,844,596
8. Dubai Intl. (United Arab Emirates; DXB).....	47,180,628
9. Amsterdam Schiphol (Netherlands; AMS)	45,211,749
10. Jakarta Soekarno-Hatta Intl. (Indonesia; CGK) ..	44,355,998
11. Bangkok Intl. Suvarnabhumi (Thailand; BKK)..	42,784,967
12. Singapore Changi (Singapore; SIN)	42,038,777
13. Guangzhou Baiyun Intl. (China; CAN)	40,975,673
14. Shanghai Pudong Intl. (China; PVG)	40,578,621
15. Rome Leonardo da Vinci-Fiumicino (Italy; FCO) ..	36,227,778
16. Sydney (Australia; SYD)................	35,991,917
17. Munich (Germany; MUC)...............	34,721,605
18. Kuala Lumpur Intl. (Malaysia; KUL)	34,087,636
19. Tokyo Narita Intl. (Japan; NRT)	33,815,906
20. Seoul Incheon Intl. (South Korea; ICN)......	33,605,579
21. Istanbul Ataturk (Turkey; IST)............	32,165,817
22. London Gatwick (UK; LGW)	31,379,968
23. Shanghai Hongqiao Intl. (China; SHA)	31,298,812
24. Barcelona El Prat (Spain; BCN)	29,197,805
25. Delhi Indira Gandhi Intl. (India; DEL)	28,531,607

Note: World list excludes North American airports and airports that do not participate in ACI's Airport Traffic Statistics collection. (1) Arriving and departing passengers and direct transit passengers counted once.

Top Travel Websites, 2011

Source: comScore Media Metrix
(ranked by number of visitors)

Rank	Website	Visitors (thous.)[1]	% of all travel websites	Rank	Website	Visitors (thous.)[1]	% of all travel websites
1.	Expedia Inc.	28,150	24.2%	10.	Kayak.com Network	6,276	5.4%
2.	TravelAdNetwork	18,117	15.6	11.	Delta Airlines	5,779	5.0
3.	Yahoo! Travel	14,972	12.9	12.	Bing Travel	5,752	5.0
4.	Priceline.com Incorporated	13,493	11.6	13.	Hilton Hotels	5,434	4.7
5.	Orbitz Worldwide	10,880	9.4	14.	Marriott	5,413	4.7
6.	Southwest Airlines Co.	9,649	8.3	15.	American Airlines	4,845	4.2
7.	Fareportal Media Group	7,514	6.5		**Total travel audience**[2]	**116,110**	**100.0**
8.	Travelocity	7,121	6.1		**Total Internet audience**[2]	**214,474**	**—**
9.	AOL Travel	6,822	5.9				

(1) Number of unique users who visited at least once in June 2011. (2) Audience comprises all persons older than 2 years of age, at U.S. home/work locations.

Number of Paid Days Off Per Year in Selected Countries

Source: *2009 Worldwide Benefit and Employment Guidelines*, Mercer

The figures below represent the amount of paid time off that workers in selected countries are entitled to each year by law. Individual employers may offer additional paid time off beyond the legal guaranteed minimum. Countries may refer to workdays, calendar days, or weeks in their legal mandates. Ranked by total paid days off.

Country	Paid vacation days	Paid holidays	Total paid days off	Country	Paid vacation days	Paid holidays	Total paid days off	Country	Paid vacation days	Paid holidays	Total paid days off
Brazil	30	11	41	Norway	25	10	35	Ireland	20	9	29
Lithuania	28	13	41	Portugal	22	13	35	Switzerland	20	9[2]	29
Finland	30	10	40	Slovakia	20	15	35	Australia	20	8	28
France	30	10	40	Denmark	25	9	34	Netherlands	20	8	28
Russia	28	12	40	South Korea	19	15	34	Taiwan	15	13	28
Austria	25	13	38	Hungary	23[1]	10	33	India	12	16[2]	28
Greece	25[1]	12	37	South Africa	21	12	33	Hong Kong	14	12	26
UK	28	8	36	Czech Republic	20	12	32	Singapore	14	11	25
Poland	26	10	36	Italy	20	11	31	China	10	11	21
Sweden	25	11	36	New Zealand	20	11	31	Canada	19[2]	9	19
Spain	22	14	36	Belgium	20	10	30	U.S.	0[3]	10	10
Japan	20	16	36	Germany	20	10[2]	30				

Note: The figures are based on statutory entitlements for an employee working five days a week with 10 years' service at the same employer. (1) Number varies according to age, ranging from 20 to 30. (2) Number varies across states, cantons, municipalities, or provinces. (3) No mandatory requirement. Typical total is 15 days.

Record-Breaking Roller Coasters

Source: UltimateRollerCoaster.com; speeds measured in mph, lengths and heights in ft

Steel-Tracked Roller Coasters

Fastest — Roller coaster — Theme park, location
- 149.1 mph — Formula Rossa — Ferrari World Abu Dhabi, United Arab Emirates
- 128 — Kingda Ka — Six Flags Great Adventure, Jackson, NJ
- 120 — Top Thrill Dragster — Cedar Point, Sandusky, OH
- 106.8 — Dodonpa — Fuji-Q High Land, Fujiyoshida-shi, Japan
- 100 — Tower of Terror — Dreamworld, Gold Coast, Australia
- 100 — Superman the Escape — Six Flags Magic Mountain, Valencia, CA

Tallest
- 456 ft — Kingda Ka — Six Flags Great Adventure, Jackson, NJ
- 420 — Top Thrill Dragster — Cedar Point, Sandusky, OH
- 415 — Superman the Escape — Six Flags Magic Mountain, Valencia, CA
- 377 — Tower of Terror — Dreamworld, Gold Coast, Australia
- 318 — Steel Dragon 2000 — Nagashima Spa Land, Mie, Japan

Largest drop
- 418 ft — Kingda Ka — Six Flags Great Adventure, Jackson, NJ
- 400 — Top Thrill Dragster — Cedar Point, Sandusky, OH
- 306 — Steel Dragon 2000 — Nagashima Spa Land, Mie, Japan
- 300 — Millennium Force — Cedar Point, Sandusky, OH
- 300 — Intimidator 305 — Kings Dominion, Doswell, VA

Longest
- 8,133 ft — Steel Dragon 2000 — Nagashima Spa Land, Mie, Japan
- 7,450 — The Ultimate — Lightwater Valley, UK
- 6,709 — Fujiyama — Fuji-Q High Land, Fujiyoshida-shi, Japan
- 6,595 — Millennium Force — Cedar Point, Sandusky, OH
- 6,562 — Formula Rossa — Ferrari World Abu Dhabi, United Arab Emirates

Most inversions
- 10 — Colossus — Thorpe Park, Surrey, UK
- 10 — 10 Inversion Roller Coaster — Chimelong Paradise, Guangzhou, China

Wood-Tracked Roller Coasters

Fastest — Roller coaster — Theme park, location
- 74.6 mph — Colossos — Heide Park, Soltau, Germany
- 70 — El Toro — Six Flags Great Adventure, Jackson, NJ
- 67.4 — The Voyage — Holiday World & Splashin' Safari, Santa Claus, IN
- 66.3 — The Boss — Six Flags St. Louis, Eureka, MO
- 66 — American Eagle — Six Flags Great America, Gurnee, IL

Tallest
- 197 ft — Colossos — Heide Park, Soltau, Germany
- 183 — T Express — Everland, Yongin, S. Korea
- 181 — El Toro — Six Flags Great Adventure, Jackson, NJ
- 179 — The Rattler — Six Flags Fiesta Texas, San Antonio, TX
- 173 — The Voyage — Holiday World & Splashin' Safari, Santa Claus, IN

Largest drop
- 176 ft — El Toro — Six Flags Great Adventure, Jackson, NJ
- 159 — Colossos — Heide Park, Soltau, Germany
- 155 — Mean Streak — Cedar Point, Sandusky, OH
- 154 — The Voyage — Holiday World & Splashin' Safari, Santa Claus, IN
- 151 — T Express — Everland, Yongin, S. Korea

Longest
- 7,400 ft — The Beast — Kings Island, Cincinnati, OH
- 6,442 — The Voyage — Holiday World & Splashin' Safari, Santa Claus, IN
- 5,578 — White Cyclone — Nagashima Spa Land, Mie, Japan
- 5,427 — Mean Streak — Cedar Point, Sandusky, OH
- 5,384 — Shivering Timbers — Michigan's Adventure, Muskegon, MI

Passports, Health Regulations, and Travel Warnings for Foreign Travel

Source: Bureau of Consular Affairs, U.S. Dept. of State; Centers for Disease Control and Prevention (CDC), U.S. Dept. of Health and Human Services; World Health Organization (WHO); Transportation Security Administration (TSA), U.S. Dept. of Homeland Security

Passports, Visas

Passports are issued by the Dept. of State to U.S. citizens and nationals to provide documentation for foreign travel. As of Oct. 2011, the fees for a new passport for persons ages 16 and over total $135; provided certain criteria are met, passports can be renewed for $110.

In July 2008, the U.S. government began issuing passport cards. Travelers arriving by land or sea from Canada, Mexico, the Caribbean (17 nations), and Bermuda may present a passport card to enter the U.S. Passport cards may not be used for air travel, however. The fees for a new passport card for persons ages 16 and over total $55.

A U.S. passport is often sufficient for U.S. citizens to gain admission for a limited stay in another country. Some countries also require a visa to enter. Each country has its own specific guidelines concerning length and purpose of visit, among other considerations. Visitors may need to provide proof of sufficient funds for their intended stay, onward/return tickets, and/or at least 6 months remaining validity on their U.S. passports.

All persons traveling by air outside of the U.S. (excluding direct travel to and from a U.S. territory) are required to present a passport or other valid document upon reentering the U.S.

For up-to-date passport and international travel information, visit the Consular Affairs website (travel.state. gov) or call the National Passport Information Center at 1-877-4USA-PPT (1-877-487-2778).

Health Regulations

Under WHO regulations, first instituted in 1969, member countries agree to abide by resolutions meant to contain the spread of disease. For example, some countries require travelers to provide proof of vaccination against yellow fever before entering.

Detailed information can be found in *Health Information for International Travel*, or the "yellow book," published every two years by the CDC. The book is written primarily for health care providers but may be of use to other travelers. The CDC also issues travel notices on outbreaks, health precautions, and health warnings. For current notices and more on travelers' health, visit www.cdc. gov/travel/.

WHO publishes a more technical guide, *International Travel and Health*, which can be found online at www. who.int/ith/.

Travel Warnings and Alerts

The State Dept. issues travel warnings as recommendations that Americans avoid travel to certain countries. Long-term conditions in such countries may be dangerous or unstable; because of an embassy closure or limited personnel, the U.S. government's ability to assist U.S. citizens is also reduced. As of Oct. 2011, travel warnings were in effect for the following countries: Afghanistan, Algeria, Burundi, Central African Republic, Chad, Colombia, Côte d'Ivoire, Dem. Rep. of the Congo, Eritrea, Guinea, Haiti, Iran, Iraq, Israel (incl. West Bank and Gaza), Kenya, Lebanon, Libya, Mali, Mauritania, Mexico, Nepal, Niger, Nigeria, North Korea, Pakistan, Philippines, Saudi Arabia, Somalia, South Sudan, Sudan, Syria, Uzbekistan, and Yemen.

The department issues travel alerts when it has concerns about short-term conditions—natural disasters, terrorist attacks, anniversaries of attacks, election-related demonstrations, and regional sporting events, among others. For the latest travel warnings and alerts, see travel. state.gov.

Summary of TSA Regulations

Airplane carry-ons. TSA promotes the "3-1-1" rule regarding carry-on items. Containers with liquids, gels, or aerosols may hold only **3.4** oz or less; these containers should be packed inside a single **1**-quart, clear plastic, zip-top bag; and this **1** bag must be X-rayed when going through security. Exceptions to the 3-1-1 rule include medication, baby formula and food, and breast milk. Travelers must declare any exceptions at security.

Security checkpoint identification. Adult travelers (18 years of age and over) must present a U.S. federal or state-issued photo ID. The ID must have name, date of birth, sex, expiration date, and a tamper-resistant feature. Acceptable documents: U.S. passport or passport card; foreign government-issued passport; state-issued drivers license; permanent resident card; or U.S. military ID, among others.

Screening process. Travelers may wear loose fitting or religious garments (incl. head coverings) through security. They may be subject to additional screening if clothing could potentially conceal prohibited items. Travelers may request a private area if selected for personal screening. In most cases, travelers will be screened by someone of the same gender.

Disability-related permitted carry-on items:

- Wheelchairs
- Crutches, canes, and walkers
- Personal supplemental oxygen
- Slate and stylus
- Medications and associated supplies
- Service animals

Permitted carry-on items:

- Safety razors (incl. disposable razors)
- Eye drops and saline solution (amounts greater than 3.4 oz must be declared)
- Nail clippers, tweezers
- Blunt-tipped plastic or metal scissors
- Mobile phones
- Umbrellas (must be inspected at security)
- Common lighters
- Beverages (any size) purchased after security screening
- Musical instruments (one per traveler going through security, though some airlines prohibit musical instruments as carry-ons)

Prohibited carry-on items:

- Knives (except for plastic or round-bladed butter knives), incl. knives that are religious objects
- Baseball bats, golf clubs
- Flares
- Realistic firearm replicas
- Hammers, screwdrivers, wrenches, pliers, and other tools more than 7 in. in length
- Brass knuckles
- Lighter fluid
- Liquid bleach
- Spray paint
- Snow globes

For complete travel information, visit www.tsa.gov/travelers/.

Road Mileage Between Selected U.S. Cities

	Atlanta	Boston	Chicago	Cincinnati	Cleveland	Dallas	Denver	Des Moines	Detroit	Houston
Atlanta, GA........	...	1,037	674	440	672	795	1,398	870	699	789
Boston, MA........	1,037	...	963	840	628	1,748	1,949	1,280	695	1,804
Chicago, IL........	674	963	...	287	335	917	996	327	266	1,067
Cincinnati, OH	440	840	287	...	244	920	1,164	571	259	1,029
Cleveland, OH	672	628	335	244	...	1,159	1,321	652	170	1,273
Dallas, TX........	795	1,748	917	920	1,159	...	781	684	1,143	243
Denver, CO	1,398	1,949	996	1,164	1,321	781	...	669	1,253	1,019
Detroit, MI........	699	695	266	259	170	1,143	1,253	584	...	1,265
Houston, TX	789	1,804	1,067	1,029	1,273	243	1,019	905	1,265	...
Indianapolis, IN....	493	906	181	106	294	865	1,058	465	278	987
Kansas City, MO ...	798	1,391	499	591	779	489	600	195	743	710
Los Angeles, CA...	2,182	2,979	2,054	2,179	2,367	1,387	1,059	1,727	2,311	1,538
Memphis, TN	371	1,296	530	468	712	452	1,040	599	713	561
Milwaukee, WI	761	1,050	87	374	422	991	1,029	361	353	1,142
Minneapolis, MN...	1,068	1,368	405	692	740	936	841	252	671	1,157
New Orleans, LA ...	479	1,507	912	786	1,030	496	1,273	978	1,045	356
New York, NY......	841	206	802	647	473	1,552	1,771	1,119	637	1,608
Omaha, NE........	986	1,412	459	693	784	644	537	132	716	865
Philadelphia, PA....	741	296	738	567	413	1,452	1,691	1,051	573	1,508
Pittsburgh, PA	687	561	452	287	129	1,204	1,411	763	287	1,313
Portland, OR.......	2,601	3,046	2,083	2,333	2,418	2,009	1,238	1,786	2,349	2,205
St. Louis, MO	541	1,141	289	340	529	630	857	333	513	779
San Francisco, CA ..	2,496	3,095	2,142	2,362	2,467	1,753	1,235	1,815	2,399	1,912
Seattle, WA	2,618	2,976	2,013	2,300	2,348	2,078	1,307	1,749	2,279	2,274
Tulsa, OK.........	772	1,537	683	736	925	257	681	443	909	478
Washington, DC....	608	429	671	481	346	1,319	1,616	984	506	1,375

	Indianapolis	Kansas City	Los Angeles	Louisville	Memphis	Milwaukee	Minneapolis	New Orleans	New York	Omaha
Atlanta, GA........	493	798	2,182	382	371	761	1,068	479	841	986
Boston, MA........	906	1,391	2,979	941	1,296	1,050	1,368	1,507	206	1,412
Chicago, IL........	181	499	2,054	292	530	87	405	912	802	459
Cincinnati, OH	106	591	2,179	101	468	374	692	786	647	693
Cleveland, OH	294	779	2,367	345	712	422	740	1,030	473	784
Dallas, TX........	865	489	1,387	819	452	991	936	496	1,552	644
Denver, CO	1,058	600	1,059	1,120	1,040	1,029	841	1,273	1,771	537
Detroit, MI........	278	743	2,311	360	713	353	671	1,045	637	716
Houston, TX	987	710	1,538	928	561	1,142	1,157	356	1,608	865
Indianapolis, IN....	...	485	2,073	111	435	268	586	796	713	587
Kansas City, MO ...	485	...	1,589	520	451	537	447	806	1,198	201
Los Angeles, CA...	2,073	1,589	...	2,108	1,817	2,087	1,889	1,883	2,786	1,595
Memphis, TN	435	451	1,817	367	...	612	826	390	1,100	652
Milwaukee, WI	268	537	2,087	379	612	...	332	994	889	493
Minneapolis, MN...	586	447	1,889	697	826	332	...	1,214	1,207	357
New Orleans, LA ...	796	806	1,883	685	390	994	1,214	...	1,311	1,007
New York, NY......	713	1,198	2,786	748	1,100	889	1,207	1,311	...	1,251
Omaha, NE........	587	201	1,595	687	652	493	357	1,007	1,251	...
Philadelphia, PA....	633	1,118	2,706	668	1,000	825	1,143	1,211	100	1,183
Pittsburgh, PA	353	838	2,426	388	752	539	857	1,070	368	895
Portland, OR.......	2,272	1,809	959	2,320	2,259	2,010	1,678	2,505	2,885	1,654
St. Louis, MO	235	257	1,845	263	285	363	552	673	948	449
San Francisco, CA ..	2,293	1,835	379	2,349	2,125	2,175	1,940	2,249	2,934	1,683
Seattle, WA	2,194	1,839	1,131	2,305	2,290	1,940	1,608	2,574	2,815	1,638
Tulsa, OK.........	631	248	1,452	659	401	757	695	647	1,344	387
Washington, DC....	558	1,043	2,631	582	867	758	1,076	1,078	233	1,116

	Philadelphia	Pittsburgh	Portland, OR	St. Louis	Salt Lake City	San Francisco	Seattle	Toledo	Tulsa	Wash., DC
Atlanta, GA........	741	687	2,601	541	1,878	2,496	2,618	640	772	608
Boston, MA........	296	561	3,046	1,141	2,343	3,095	2,976	739	1,537	429
Chicago, IL........	738	452	2,083	289	1,390	2,142	2,013	232	683	671
Cincinnati, OH	567	287	2,333	340	1,610	2,362	2,300	200	736	481
Cleveland, OH	413	129	2,418	529	1,715	2,467	2,348	111	925	346
Dallas, TX........	1,452	1,204	2,009	630	1,242	1,753	2,078	1,084	257	1,319
Denver, CO	1,691	1,411	1,238	857	504	1,235	1,307	1,218	681	1,616
Detroit, MI........	576	287	2,349	513	1,647	2,399	2,279	59	909	506
Houston, TX	1,508	1,313	2,205	779	1,438	1,912	2,274	1,206	478	1,375
Indianapolis, IN....	633	353	2,272	235	1,504	2,293	2,194	219	631	558
Kansas City, MO ...	1,118	838	1,809	257	1,086	1,835	1,839	687	248	1,043
Los Angeles, CA...	2,706	2,426	959	1,845	715	379	1,131	2,276	1,452	2,631
Memphis, TN	1,000	752	2,259	285	1,535	2,125	2,290	654	401	867
Milwaukee, WI	825	539	2,010	363	1,423	2,175	1,940	319	757	758
Minneapolis, MN...	1,143	857	1,678	552	1,186	1,940	1,608	637	695	1,076
New Orleans, LA ...	1,211	1,070	2,505	673	1,738	2,249	2,574	986	647	1,078
New York, NY......	100	368	2,885	948	2,182	2,934	2,815	578	1,344	233
Omaha, NE........	1,183	895	1,654	449	931	1,683	1,638	681	387	1,116
Philadelphia, PA....	...	288	2,821	868	2,114	2,866	2,751	514	1,264	133
Pittsburgh, PA	288	...	2,535	588	1,826	2,578	2,465	228	984	221
Portland, OR.......	2,821	2,535	...	2,060	767	636	172	2,315	1,913	2,754
St. Louis, MO	868	588	2,060	...	1,337	2,089	2,081	454	396	793
San Francisco, CA ..	2,866	2,578	636	2,089	752	...	808	2,364	1,760	2,799
Seattle, WA	2,751	2,465	172	2,081	836	808	...	2,245	1,982	2,684
Tulsa, OK.........	1,264	984	1,913	396	1,172	1,760	1,982	850	...	1,189
Washington, DC....	133	221	2,754	793	2,047	2,799	2,684	447	1,189	...

Air Distances Between Selected World Cities

Point-to-point measurements, in miles, are usually from City Hall or its equivalent.

	Bangkok	Beijing	Berlin	Cairo	Cape Town	Caracas	Chicago	Hong Kong	Honolulu	Lima
Bangkok.........	...	2,046	5,352	4,523	6,300	10,555	8,570	1,077	6,609	12,244
Beijing...........	2,046	...	4,584	4,698	8,044	8,950	6,604	1,217	5,077	10,349
Berlin...........	5,352	4,584	...	1,797	5,961	5,238	4,414	5,443	7,320	6,896
Cairo............	4,523	4,698	1,797	...	4,480	6,342	6,141	5,066	8,848	7,726
Cape Town.......	6,300	8,044	5,961	4,480	...	6,366	8,491	7,376	11,535	6,072
Caracas.........	10,555	8,950	5,238	6,342	6,366	...	2,495	10,165	6,021	1,707
Chicago.........	8,570	6,604	4,414	6,141	8,491	2,495	...	7,797	4,256	3,775
Hong Kong.......	1,077	1,217	5,443	5,066	7,376	10,165	7,797	...	5,556	11,418
Honolulu.........	6,609	5,077	7,320	8,848	11,535	6,021	4,256	5,556	...	5,947
London..........	5,944	5,074	583	2,185	5,989	4,655	3,958	5,990	7,240	6,316
Los Angeles.....	7,637	6,250	5,782	7,520	9,969	3,632	1,745	7,240	2,557	4,171
Madrid..........	6,337	5,745	1,165	2,087	5,308	4,346	4,189	6,558	7,872	5,907
Melbourne........	4,568	5,643	9,918	8,675	6,425	9,717	9,673	4,595	5,505	8,059
Mexico City......	9,793	7,753	6,056	7,700	8,519	2,234	1,690	8,788	3,789	2,639
Montreal.........	8,338	6,519	3,740	5,427	7,922	2,438	745	7,736	4,918	3,970
Moscow..........	4,389	3,607	1,006	1,803	6,279	6,177	4,987	4,437	7,047	7,862
New York, NY....	8,669	6,844	3,979	5,619	7,803	2,120	714	8,060	4,969	3,639
Paris............	5,877	5,120	548	1,998	5,786	4,732	4,143	5,990	7,449	6,370
Rio de Janeiro....	9,994	10,768	6,209	6,143	3,781	2,804	5,282	11,009	8,288	2,342
Rome............	5,494	5,063	737	1,326	5,231	5,195	4,824	5,774	8,040	6,750
San Francisco.....	7,931	5,918	5,672	7,466	10,248	3,902	1,859	6,905	2,398	4,518
Singapore........	883	2,771	6,164	5,137	6,008	11,402	9,372	1,605	6,726	11,689
Stockholm........	5,089	4,133	528	2,096	6,423	5,471	4,331	5,063	6,875	7,166
Tokyo...........	2,865	1,307	5,557	5,958	9,154	8,808	6,314	1,791	3,859	9,631
Warsaw..........	5,033	4,325	322	1,619	5,935	5,559	4,679	5,147	7,366	7,215
Washington, DC...	8,807	6,942	4,181	5,822	7,895	2,047	596	8,155	4,838	3,509

	London	Los Angeles	Madrid	Melbourne	Mexico City	Montreal	Moscow	New Delhi	New York, NY	Paris
Bangkok.........	5,944	7,637	6,337	4,568	9,793	8,338	4,389	1,813	8,669	5,877
Beijing...........	5,074	6,250	5,745	5,643	7,753	6,519	3,607	2,353	6,844	5,120
Berlin...........	583	5,782	1,165	9,918	6,056	3,740	1,006	3,598	3,979	548
Cairo............	2,185	7,520	2,087	8,675	7,700	5,427	1,803	2,758	5,619	1,998
Cape Town.......	5,989	9,969	5,308	6,425	8,519	7,922	6,279	5,769	7,803	5,786
Caracas.........	4,655	3,632	4,346	9,717	2,234	2,438	6,177	8,833	2,120	4,732
Chicago.........	3,958	1,745	4,189	9,673	1,690	745	4,987	7,486	714	4,143
Hong Kong.......	5,990	7,240	6,558	4,595	8,788	7,736	4,437	2,339	8,060	5,990
Honolulu.........	7,240	2,557	7,872	5,505	3,789	4,918	7,047	7,412	4,969	7,449
London..........	...	5,439	785	10,500	5,558	3,254	1,564	4,181	3,469	214
Los Angeles.....	5,439	...	5,848	7,931	1,542	2,427	6,068	7,011	2,451	5,601
Madrid..........	785	5,848	...	10,758	5,643	3,448	2,147	4,530	3,593	655
Melbourne........	10,500	7,931	10,758	...	8,426	10,395	8,950	6,329	10,359	10,430
Mexico City......	5,558	1,542	5,643	8,426	...	2,317	6,676	9,120	2,090	5,725
Montreal.........	3,254	2,427	3,448	10,395	2,317	...	4,401	7,012	331	3,432
Moscow..........	1,564	6,068	2,147	8,950	6,676	4,401	...	2,698	4,683	1,554
New York, NY.....	3,469	2,451	3,593	10,359	2,090	331	4,683	7,318	...	3,636
Paris............	214	5,601	655	10,430	5,725	3,432	1,554	4,102	3,636	...
Rio de Janeiro....	5,750	6,330	5,045	8,226	4,764	5,078	7,170	8,753	4,801	5,684
Rome............	895	6,326	851	9,929	6,377	4,104	1,483	3,684	4,293	690
San Francisco.....	5,367	347	5,803	7,856	1,887	2,543	5,885	7,691	2,572	5,577
Singapore........	6,747	8,767	7,080	3,759	10,327	9,203	5,228	2,571	9,534	6,673
Stockholm........	942	5,454	1,653	9,630	6,012	3,714	716	3,414	3,986	1,003
Tokyo...........	5,959	5,470	6,706	5,062	7,035	6,471	4,660	3,638	6,757	6,053
Warsaw..........	905	5,922	1,427	9,598	6,337	4,022	721	3,277	4,270	852
Washington, DC....	3,674	2,300	3,792	10,180	1,885	489	4,876	7,500	205	3,840

	Rio de Janeiro	Rome	San Francisco	Singapore	Stockholm	Tehran	Tokyo	Vienna	Warsaw	Wash., DC
Bangkok.........	9,994	5,494	7,931	883	5,089	3,391	2,865	5,252	5,033	8,807
Beijing...........	10,768	5,063	5,918	2,771	4,133	3,490	1,307	4,648	4,325	6,942
Berlin...........	6,209	737	5,672	6,164	528	2,185	5,557	326	322	4,181
Cairo............	6,143	1,326	7,466	5,137	2,096	1,234	5,958	1,481	1,619	5,822
Cape Town.......	3,781	5,231	10,248	6,008	6,423	5,241	9,154	5,656	5,935	7,895
Caracas.........	2,804	5,195	3,902	11,402	5,471	7,320	8,808	5,372	5,559	2,047
Chicago.........	5,282	4,824	1,859	9,372	4,331	6,502	6,314	4,698	4,679	596
Hong Kong.......	11,009	5,774	6,905	1,605	5,063	3,843	1,791	5,431	5,147	8,155
Honolulu.........	8,288	8,040	2,398	6,726	6,875	8,070	3,859	7,632	7,366	4,838
London..........	5,750	895	5,367	6,747	942	2,743	5,959	771	905	3,674
Los Angeles.....	6,330	6,326	347	8,767	5,454	7,682	5,470	6,108	5,922	2,300
Madrid..........	5,045	851	5,803	7,080	1,653	2,978	6,706	1,128	1,427	3,792
Melbourne........	8,226	9,929	7,856	3,759	9,630	7,826	5,062	9,790	9,598	10,180
Mexico City......	4,764	6,377	1,887	10,327	6,012	8,184	7,035	6,320	6,337	1,885
Montreal.........	5,078	4,104	2,543	9,203	3,714	5,880	6,471	4,009	4,022	489
Moscow..........	7,170	1,483	5,885	5,228	716	1,532	4,660	1,043	721	4,876
New York, NY.....	4,801	4,293	2,572	9,534	3,986	6,141	6,757	4,234	4,270	205
Paris............	5,684	690	5,577	6,673	1,003	2,625	6,053	645	852	3,840
Rio de Janeiro....	...	5,707	6,613	9,785	6,683	7,374	11,532	6,127	6,455	4,779
Rome............	5,707	...	6,259	6,229	1,245	2,127	6,142	477	820	4,497
San Francisco.....	6,613	6,259	...	8,448	5,399	7,362	5,150	5,994	5,854	2,441
Singapore........	9,785	6,229	8,448	...	5,936	5,936	4,103	6,035	5,843	9,662
Stockholm........	6,683	1,245	5,399	5,936	...	2,173	5,053	780	494	4,183
Tokyo...........	11,532	6,142	5,150	3,300	5,053	4,775	...	5,689	5,347	6,791
Warsaw..........	6,455	820	5,854	5,843	494	1,879	5,689	347	...	4,472
Washington, DC....	4,779	4,497	2,441	9,662	4,183	6,341	6,791	4,438	4,472	...

AGRICULTURE

Number and Acreage of Farms by State, 2000, 2010

Source: National Agricultural Statistics Service, U.S. Dept. of Agriculture

State	No. of farms (thous.) 2010	2000	Acreage in farms (mil) 2010	2000	Acreage per farm 2010	2000
AL.....	48.5	47.0	9.0	9.0	186	191
AK.....	0.7	0.6	0.9	0.9	1,294	1,569
AZ.....	15.5	10.7	26.1	26.9	1,684	2,518
AR.....	49.3	48.0	13.7	14.6	278	304
CA.....	81.7	83.1	25.4	28.0	311	337
CO.....	36.1	30.0	31.2	31.6	864	1,060
CT.....	4.9	4.2	0.4	0.4	82	86
DE.....	2.5	2.6	0.5	0.6	198	215
FL.....	47.5	44.0	9.3	10.4	195	238
GA.....	47.4	49.1	10.3	10.9	217	223
HI.....	7.5	5.5	1.1	1.4	148	251
ID.....	25.7	24.5	11.4	11.9	444	486
IL.....	76.0	77.0	26.7	27.5	351	357
IN.....	62.0	63.4	14.8	15.2	239	240
IA.....	92.4	94.0	30.8	32.5	333	346
KS.....	65.5	64.5	46.2	47.5	705	736
KY.....	85.7	90.0	14.0	13.7	163	152
LA.....	30.0	29.0	8.1	8.0	268	277
ME.....	8.1	7.1	1.4	1.4	167	190
MD.....	12.8	12.4	2.1	2.1	160	172
MA.....	7.7	6.1	0.5	0.5	68	89
MI.....	54.9	53.0	10.0	10.2	182	192
MN.....	81.0	81.0	26.9	27.9	332	344
MS.....	42.4	42.0	11.2	11.2	263	266
MO.....	108.0	109.0	29.1	30.2	269	277
MT.....	29.4	27.8	60.8	59.3	2,068	2,133
NE.....	47.2	46.1	45.6	46.1	966	887
NV.....	3.1	3.1	5.9	6.4	1,903	2,065
NH.....	4.2	3.3	0.5	0.4	113	133
NJ.....	10.3	9.7	0.7	0.8	71	86
NM.....	21.0	18.0	43.2	44.9	2,057	2,494
NY.....	36.3	37.5	7.0	7.7	193	205
NC.....	52.4	55.5	8.6	9.2	164	166
ND.....	31.9	30.8	39.6	39.4	1,241	1,279
OH.....	74.7	79.0	13.7	14.8	183	187
OK.....	86.5	84.5	35.2	33.8	407	401
OR.....	38.8	40.0	16.4	17.3	423	433
PA.....	63.2	59.0	7.8	7.7	123	130
PR[1].....	10.4	NA	0.5	NA	43	NA
RI.....	1.2	0.8	0.1	0.1	57	75
SC.....	27.0	24.2	4.9	4.9	181	203
SD.....	31.8	32.4	43.7	44.0	1,374	1,358
TN.....	78.3	88.0	10.9	11.8	139	134
TX.....	247.5	228.3	130.4	130.9	527	573
UT.....	16.6	15.5	11.1	11.6	669	747
VT.....	7.0	6.6	1.2	1.3	174	192
VA.....	47.3	48.5	8.1	8.7	170	180
WA.....	39.5	37.0	14.8	15.6	375	420
WV.....	23.0	20.8	3.7	3.6	159	173
WI.....	78.0	77.5	15.2	16.0	195	206
WY.....	11.0	9.2	30.2	34.5	2,745	3,750
U.S.[1]...	2,200.9	2,166.8	920.0	945.1	418	436

NA = Not available. (1) Puerto Rico not included in U.S. total.

Number and Average Size of U.S. Farms, 1940-2010

Source: National Agricultural Statistics Service, U.S. Dept. of Agriculture

The number of farms in the United States in 2010 was estimated at 2.2 million, about 720 more than in 2009. Total land in farms increased 100,000 acres from 2009 to 920.0 million acres. The average farm size in 2010 was 418 acres, unchanged from the previous year.

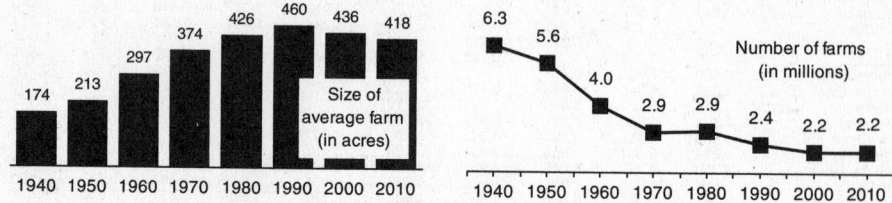

Size of average farm (in acres): 174 (1940), 213 (1950), 297 (1960), 374 (1970), 426 (1980), 460 (1990), 436 (2000), 418 (2010)

Number of farms (in millions): 6.3 (1940), 5.6 (1950), 4.0 (1960), 2.9 (1970), 2.9 (1980), 2.4 (1990), 2.2 (2000), 2.2 (2010)

U.S. Federal Food Assistance Programs, 1990-2010

Source: Food and Nutrition Service (FNS), U.S. Dept. of Agriculture

(in millions of dollars)

Program[1]	1990	1995	2000	2005	2006	2007	2008	2009	2010
Supplemental Nutrition Assistance Program (SNAP)[2]..........	$15,491	$24,620	$17,054	$31,073	$32,903	$33,191	$37,640	$53,626	$68,307
Puerto Rico nutrition asst.[3]..........	937	1,131	1,268	1,495	1,518	1,551	1,623	2,001	2,001
Natl. school lunch[4]..................	3,834	5,160	6,149	8,031	8,190	8,739	9,318	9,992	10,878
School breakfast[4,5].................	596	1,048	1,393	1,927	2,042	2,163	2,366	2,583	2,859
WIC (Women, Infants, and Children)[6]...	2,122	3,440	3,982	4,994	5,073	5,409	6,192	6,470	6,704
Summer food service[7]..............	164	237	267	267	276	290	326	348	359
Child and adult care[8]	813	1,464	1,683	2,111	2,152	2,237	2,403	2,535	2,639
Special milk[9]......................	19	17	15	16	15	14	15	14	12
Nutrition for the elderly (NSIP)[10].......	142	148	137	4	3	3	2	2	3
Food distrib. to Indian reserv.[11]........	66	65	76	76	76	81	96	100	95
Commodity supp. food prog.[11]........	85	99	98	156	131	142	161	155	165
Food dist. to charitable inst.[12]........	104	64	2	4	3	0	0	0	1
Emergency food assistance[13]........	334	135	225	373	300	255	283	617	631
Total[14]	$24,707	$37,628	$32,317	$50,673	$52,868	$54,254	$60,625	$78,995	$95,327

(1) Data are for fiscal years ending Sept. 30. All 2010 data are preliminary; all data subject to revision by the FNS. (2) Formerly known as the Food Stamp Program. Includes benefits and admin. expenses. (3) Provides benefits analogous to SNAP. (4) Data are 9-month averages (summer months excluded). (5) Costs are cash payments (federal reimbursements to states). (6) Includes food benefits, nutrition services and admin. funds, Farmers' Market Nutrition Program, infrastructure, breastfeeding promotion and peer counseling, program evaluation, and technical assistance. (7) Includes cash payments, commodity costs, and admin. expenditures. Similar services provided by Natl. School Lunch and Breakfast programs. (8) Includes cash payments, entitlement and bonus commodities, cash-in-lieu of commodities, sponsor admin. costs, start-up costs, and audits. (9) Costs are cash payments. (10) For years 2003 and on, program is administered by the Agency on Aging; FNS costs limited to value of commodities distributed. (11) Includes commodity distribution costs and admin. expenses. (12) Includes summer camps. (13) Food made available to hunger relief orgs. such as food banks and soup kitchens. (14) Figures may not add up to totals because of rounding and administrative costs not shown.

U.S. Cost of Food, 2010

Source: Center for Nutrition Policy and Promotion, U.S. Dept. of Agriculture

	Weekly cost[1]				Monthly cost[1]			
	Thrifty plan	Low-cost plan	Mod.-cost plan	Liberal plan	Thrifty plan	Low-cost plan	Mod.-cost plan	Liberal plan
Individual child, age[2]								
1 year	$20.10	$26.80	$30.60	$37.10	$86.90	$115.90	$132.60	$160.70
2-3 years	21.70	27.50	33.30	40.50	94.00	119.30	144.30	175.40
4-5 years	22.70	28.70	35.50	43.30	98.30	124.20	153.80	187.40
6-8 years	28.80	39.20	48.20	56.90	124.90	170.00	208.90	246.50
9-11 years	33.00	43.40	56.10	65.50	143.20	188.00	242.90	283.70
Individual male, age[2]								
12-13 years	35.10	49.50	61.70	72.70	152.10	214.30	267.20	315.00
14-18 years	36.20	50.80	63.80	73.40	157.00	219.90	276.40	318.00
19-50 years	39.00	50.30	62.90	77.10	169.10	217.90	272.80	334.30
51-70 years	35.60	47.60	58.60	71.10	154.40	206.30	253.70	307.90
71+ years	35.80	47.00	58.50	71.90	155.20	203.60	253.40	311.40
Individual female, age[2]								
12-13 years	35.30	42.90	51.90	63.00	152.80	186.00	224.90	273.00
14-18 years	34.80	43.10	52.00	63.90	150.70	186.70	225.20	277.00
19-50 years	34.70	43.70	53.80	69.00	150.30	189.30	233.00	299.10
51-70 years	34.30	42.50	52.90	63.50	148.70	184.40	229.20	275.10
71+ years	33.80	42.10	52.50	63.40	146.30	182.30	227.60	274.50
2-person family[3], age								
19-50 years	81.10	103.40	128.40	160.80	351.30	447.90	556.30	696.70
51-70 years	76.90	99.20	122.60	148.00	333.40	429.70	531.20	641.20
4-person family[4] **2 children, ages**								
2-3 and 4-5 years	118.10	150.20	185.50	229.90	511.60	650.60	803.90	996.20
6-8 and 9-11 years	135.60	176.60	221.00	268.50	587.40	765.20	957.60	1,163.50

Note: The Food Plans represent a nutritious diet at four different cost levels. The nutritional bases of the Food Plans are the 1997-2005 Dietary Reference Intakes, 2005 Dietary Guidelines for Americans, and 2005 MyPyramid food intake recommendations. In addition to cost, differences among plans are in specific foods and quantities of foods. Another basis of the Food Plans is that all meals and snacks are prepared at home. For specific foods and quantities in the Food Plans, see *Thrifty Food Plan, 2006* and *The Low-Cost, Moderate-Cost, and Liberal Food Plans, 2007* from the source. All four food plans are based on 2001-02 data and updated to current dollars using the consumer price index for specific food items. (1) All costs are rounded to nearest 10 cents. (2) The costs given are for individuals in 4-person families. (3) Ten percent added for family size adjustment. (4) Defined as a couple, 19-50 years old, and two children.

U.S. Annual Per Capita Consumption of Selected Foods, 1970-2009

Source: Economic Research Service, U.S. Dept. of Agriculture

(fruits and vegetables in pounds, beverages in gallons)

	1970	1990	2009	% change, 1970-2009		1970	1990	2009	% change, 1970-2009
Fresh fruit	96.2	111.0	121.0	25.8%	**Fresh vegetables**	154.3	176.4	184.8	19.8%
Apples	16.3	18.8	15.8	-3.5	Bell peppers	2.0	5.4	8.6	333.3
Avocados	0.4	1.3	3.9	820.1	Broccoli	0.5	3.1	5.6	1,046.1
Bananas	17.4	24.3	24.7	42.3	Cabbage	8.1	7.8	6.8	-15.8
Cherries	0.5	0.4	1.4	196.8	Carrots	5.8	8.0	7.2	23.8
Grapes	2.6	7.1	7.2	174.5	Cauliflower	0.7	2.0	1.4	104.6
Melons	19.6	22.3	23.9	21.7	Celery	6.8	6.7	5.6	-16.7
Grapefruit	8.0	4.3	2.7	-66.0	Cucumbers	2.6	4.3	6.1	134.1
Oranges	15.7	12.0	8.8	-43.9	Garlic	0.4	1.1	2.0	457.1
Peaches/nectarines	5.5	5.3	4.2	-24.2	Head lettuce	20.8	25.8	15.9	-23.6
Pears	1.8	3.1	3.0	67.9	Mushrooms	0.3	1.9	2.2	736.8
Pineapples	0.7	1.9	4.8	627.4	Onions	9.5	14.2	18.1	89.8
Plums/prunes	1.4	1.5	0.7	-50.0	Potatoes	59.3	44.9	35.0	-41.0
Strawberries	1.6	3.0	6.6	313.3	Snap beans	1.5	1.0	1.5	5.4
					Squash	1.2	3.2	4.0	232.1
Canned vegetables	100.6	110.3	100.4	-0.2	Sweet corn	7.2	6.2	8.3	16.2
Carrots	2.1	1.2	0.8	-62.6	Tomatoes	10.3	13.2	16.4	58.8
Green peas	3.2	1.9	1.2	-61.5					
Snap beans	4.7	3.7	3.6	-22.8	**Beverages**				
Sweet corn	14.3	10.9	7.6	-46.7	Bottled water	NA	8.8	NA	NA
Tomatoes	62.1	75.3	70.2	13.1	Carbonated soft drinks	24.3	46.2	NA	NA
					Regular	22.2	35.6	NA	NA
Frozen vegetables	43.8	66.8	71.3	62.7	Diet	2.1	10.7	NA	NA
Broccoli	1.0	2.2	2.5	151.1	Coffee	33.4	26.8	23.3	-30.0
Carrots	1.4	2.3	1.4	-5.3	Fruit juice	5.5	7.0	7.4	33.7
Green peas	1.9	2.2	1.7	-12.7	Beer	18.5	23.9	21.5	16.5
Potatoes	28.5	46.4	50.3	76.5	Wine	1.3	2.0	2.5	87.4
Sweet corn	5.8	8.6	8.8	52.8	Distilled spirits	1.8	1.5	1.4	-21.2

NA = Not available. **Note:** All figures are rounded. Percent change based on unrounded raw data.

U.S. Meat Production and Consumption, 1940-2011

Source: Economic Research Service, U.S. Dept. of Agriculture

(in millions of pounds)

Year	Beef Prod.	Beef Cons.	Veal Prod.	Veal Cons.	Lamb and mutton Prod.	Lamb and mutton Cons.	Pork Prod.	Pork Cons.	All red meats[1] Prod.	All red meats[1] Cons.	All poultry Prod.	All poultry Cons.
1940	7,175	7,257	981	981	876	873	10,044	9,701	19,076	18,812	NA	NA
1950	9,534	9,529	1,230	1,206	597	596	10,714	10,390	22,075	21,721	3,174	3,097
1960	14,728	15,465	1,109	1,118	769	857	13,905	14,057	30,511	31,497	6,310	6,168
1970	21,684	23,451	588	613	551	669	14,699	14,957	37,522	39,689	10,193	9,981
1980	21,643	23,560	400	420	318	351	16,617	16,838	38,978	41,170	14,173	13,525
1990	22,743	24,030	327	325	363	397	15,354	16,025	38,787	40,778	23,468	22,152
1995	25,222	25,534	319	319	285	346	17,849	17,768	43,675	43,967	30,393	25,944
2000	26,888	27,338	225	225	234	354	18,952	18,643	46,299	46,560	36,073	30,508
2005	26,787	27,754	165	164	191	355	20,705	19,112	45,848	47,385	40,935	34,947
2006	26,256	28,137	156	155	190	356	21,074	19,048	47,675	47,696	41,231	35,544
2007	26,523	28,144	145	144	188	384	21,962	19,763	48,817	48,435	42,117	35,667
2008	26,663	27,302	152	150	180	343	23,367	19,415	50,361	47,210	43,235	35,379
2009	25,965	26,904	147	147	177	338	22,999	19,839	49,274	47,227	41,673	34,116
2010	26,304	26,392	145	150	168	317	22,437	19,072	49,039	45,931	43,058	35,201
2011*	26,266	26,034	131	142	157	313	22,615	18,649	49,164	45,138	43,614	36,206

*Preliminary. NA = Not available. (1) Numbers may not add up to total because of rounding.

U.S. Per Capita Consumption of Meat and Dairy, 1910-2009

Source: Economic Research Service, U.S. Dept. of Agriculture

(in pounds per capita, unless otherwise noted)

	1910	1930	1950	1970	1990	2000	2009	% change, 1910-2009
Meat								
Beef.	48.5	33.7	44.6	79.6	63.9	64.5	58.1	19.7%
Chicken	11.0	11.1	14.3	27.4	42.4	54.2	56.0	410.5
Fish/shellfish	11.2	10.2	11.9	11.7	14.9	15.2	15.8	40.8
Pork.	38.2	41.1	43.0	48.1	46.4	47.8	46.6	21.7
Red meat.	96.0	83.6	95.8	131.9	112.2	113.7	105.7	10.2
Dairy								
Butter.	18.4	17.6	10.9	5.4	4.0	4.5	4.9	−73.1
American cheese.	2.5	3.2	5.5	7.0	11.1	12.7	13.4	384.0
Other cheese.	1.4	1.5	2.2	4.4	13.5	17.1	19.5	1,185.1
Skim/lower fat milk (gallons) . . .	7.1	5.0	3.0	5.8	15.2	14.4	14.6	107.5
Whole milk (gallons)	25.2	28.2	34.3	25.5	10.5	8.1	5.9	−76.4
Ice cream.	1.9	9.7	17.4	17.8	15.8	16.7	13.4	590.5

Note: All figures are rounded. Percent change based on unrounded raw data.

U.S. Organic Farmland and Animals, 1995-2008

Source: Economic Research Service, U.S. Dept. of Agriculture

Crop	1995	2000	Organic acreage[1] 2002	2003	2004	2005	2008	% change, 2000-08	Total U.S. farmland[2]
Grains									
Corn	32,650	77,912	96,270	105,574	99,111	130,672	194,637	149.8%	93,600,000
Wheat	120,820	206,474	217,611	234,221	214,244	293,824	415,902	101.4	60,433,000
Oats	13,250	29,771	53,459	46,074	42,616	46,465	57,374	92.7	3,760,000
Barley	17,150	41,904	34,031	30,265	26,629	39,271	46,954	12.1	4,020,000
Rice	8,400	26,870	22,381	20,152	22,173	26,428	49,638	84.7	2,761,000
Beans									
Soybeans	47,200	136,071	126,540	122,403	114,239	122,217	125,621	−7.7	63,631,000
Dry beans	NA	14,010	2,430	9,836	7,642	10,561	16,465	17.5	1,526,900
Dry peas & lentils	5,900	10,144	7,476	16,188	15,893	17,757	16,987	67.5	571,000
Hay and silage	84,100	231,207	267,827	327,538	356,590	411,342	793,442	243.2	61,625,000
All vegetables	NA	62,342	69,887	78,905	86,822	98,525	177,049	184.0	2,045,020
All fruits	NA	43,481	60,693	77,989	80,707	97,277	121,066	178.4	3,839,300
Other crops									
Cotton	32,850	15,027	10,551	9,875	9,213	9,537	15,377	2.3	10,830,300
Peanuts.	NA	2,085	5,134	5,698	9,514	11,940	16,776	704.6	1,230,000
Potatoes	NA	5,433	6,593	6,569	7,300	6,581	8,273	52.3	1,148,800
Trees for maple syrup	10,200	11,965	1,121	1,514	13,357	12,247	31,340	161.9	NA
Fallow land	NA	57,688	64,668	83,003	116,582	198,650	194,428	237.0	37,968,749
Total cropland . . .	638,500	1,218,905	1,299,632	1,451,601	1,452,353	1,723,271	2,655,382	117.8	370,653,755
Total pasture and rangeland	276,300	557,167	625,902	745,273	1,592,756	2,331,158	2,160,577	287.8	473,212,960
Total farmland . . .	914,800	1,776,073	1,925,534	2,196,874	3,045,109	4,054,429	4,815,959	171.2	843,866,715

Animal	1995	2000	Number of organic animals[1] 2002	2003	2004	2005	2008	% change, 2000-08	Total U.S. animals
Total livestock	NA	56,028	108,362	124,346	157,253	196,506	475,829	749.3%	167,512,858
Beef cows	NA	13,829	23,384	27,285	36,662	36,113	63,680	360.5	32,834,801
Milk cows	NA	38,196	67,207	74,435	74,840	87,082	249,766	553.9	9,266,574
Other cows[3]	NA	NA	10,103	11,501	36,598	58,822	144,817	NA	54,246,483
Hogs and pigs	NA	1,724	2,753	6,564	4,883	10,018	10,111	486.5	65,110,000
Sheep and lambs . . .	NA	2,279	4,915	4,561	4,270	4,471	7,455	227.1	6,055,000
Total poultry	NA	3,159,050	6,270,181	8,780,152	7,304,566	13,757,270	15,518,075	391.2	9,632,362,000
Layer hens	NA	1,113,746	1,052,272	1,591,181	1,787,901	2,415,056	5,538,011	397.2	377,492,000
Broilers	NA	1,924,807	3,032,189	6,301,014	4,769,104	10,405,879	9,015,984	368.4	8,882,000,000
Turkeys	NA	9,138	305,605	217,353	164,292	144,086	398,531	4,261.2	262,460,000
Other/unclassified. . . .	NA	111,359	1,880,115	670,604	583,269	792,249	565,549	407.9	110,410,000

NA = Not available. (1) Based on information from USDA-accredited state and private organic certifiers. (2) Total organic and nonorganic land used for agricultural purposes. (3) Includes breeding stock, replacement heifers, and unclassified cows.

Production of Principal U.S. Crops, 1990-2010

Source: National Agricultural Statistics Service, U.S. Dept. of Agriculture

Year	Corn for grain (1,000 bu)	Oats (1,000 bu)	Barley (1,000 bu)	Sorghum for grain (1,000 bu)	All wheat (1,000 bu)	Rye (1,000 bu)	Flaxseed (1,000 bu)	Cotton (upland) (1,000 b)	Cottonseed (1,000 t)
1990	7,934,028	357,654	422,196	573,303	2,729,778	10,176	3,812	15,505.4	5,968.5
1995	7,373,876	162,027	359,562	460,373	2,182,591	10,064	2,211	17,532.2	6,848.7
1996	9,293,435	155,273	395,751	802,974	2,285,133	9,016	1,602	18,413.5	7,143.5
1997	9,206,832	167,246	359,878	633,545	2,481,466	8,132	2,420	18,245.0	6,934.6
1998	9,758,685	165,981	352,125	519,933	2,547,321	12,161	6,708	13,475.9	5,365.4
1999	9,430,612	146,193	280,292	595,166	2,299,010	11,038	7,864	16,293.7	6,354.0
2000	9,915,051	149,545	318,728	470,526	2,232,460	8,386	10,730	16,799.2	6,435.6
2001	9,506,840	117,024	249,420	514,524	1,957,043	6,971	11,445	19,602.4	7,452.2
2002	8,966,787	116,002	226,906	360,713	1,605,878	6,488	11,863	16,530.3	6,183.9
2003	10,089,222	144,383	278,283	411,237	2,344,760	8,634	10,516	17,822.9	6,664.6
2004	11,807,086	115,695	279,743	453,654	2,158,245	8,255	10,368	22,505.1	8,242.1
2005	11,114,082	114,878	211,896	392,933	2,104,690	7,537	19,695	23,259.7	8,172.1
2006	10,534,868	93,638	180,165	277,538	1,812,036	7,193	11,019	20,822.4	7,347.9
2007	13,037,875	90,430	210,110	497,445	2,051,088	6,311	5,896	18,355.1	6,588.7
2008	12,091,648	89,135	240,193	472,342	2,499,164	7,979	5,716	12,384.5	4,300.3
2009[1]	13,091,862	93,081	227,323	382,983	2,218,061	6,993	7,423	11,787.6	4,148.8
2010	12,446,865	81,190	180,268	345,395	2,208,391	7,431	9,056	17,817.0	6,191.0

Year	Tobacco (1,000 lb)	All hay (1,000 t)	Beans, dry edible (1,000 cwt)	Peas, dry edible (1,000 cwt)	Peanuts[2] (1,000 lb)	Soybeans[3] (1,000 bu)	Potatoes (1,000 cwt)	Sweet potatoes (1,000 cwt)
1990	1,626,380	146,212	32,379	2,372	3,602,770	1,925,947	402,110	12,594
1995	1,268,538	154,166	30,812	4,765	4,247,455	2,176,814	443,606	12,906
1996	1,517,334	149,457	27,960	2,671	3,661,205	2,382,364	498,633	13,456
1997	1,787,399	152,536	29,370	5,752	3,539,380	2,688,750	467,091	13,327
1998	1,479,867	151,780	30,418	5,934	3,963,440	2,741,014	475,771	12,382
1999	1,292,692	159,707	33,085	4,773	3,829,490	2,653,758	478,216	12,234
2000	1,052,999	151,921	26,409	3,474	3,265,505	2,757,810	513,621	13,794
2001	991,223	156,764	19,583	3,763	4,276,704	2,890,682	437,888	14,637
2002	871,122	149,467	30,312	4,727	3,321,040	2,756,147	458,171	12,799
2003	802,560	157,585	22,492	5,202	4,144,150	2,453,665	457,814	15,891
2004	881,973	158,247	17,788	11,419	4,288,200	3,123,686	456,041	16,112
2005	645,015	151,017	26,772	14,003	4,869,860	3,063,237	423,926	15,730
2006	727,347	142,336	24,247	13,203	3,464,250	3,188,247	441,348	16,248
2007	787,653	146,901	25,586	16,287	3,672,250	2,667,117	444,875	18,070
2008	800,504	146,270	25,558	12,270	5,162,400	2,967,007	415,055	18,443
2009	822,581	147,700	25,427	17,137	3,691,650	3,359,011	431,318	19,469
2010	719,786	145,556	31,801	14,221	4,155,600	3,329,341	397,077	23,845

Year	Rice (1,000 cwt)	Sugarcane (1,000 t)	Sugar beets (1,000 t)	Pecans[4] (1,000 lb)	Apples (1,000 t)	Grapes (1,000 t)	Peaches (1,000 t)	Oranges[5] (1,000 bx)	Grapefruit[5] (1,000 bx)
1990	156,088	28,136	27,513	205,000	4,828	5,660	1,121	184,415	49,300
1995	173,871	30,944	27,954	268,000	5,293	5,922	1,150	263,605	71,050
1996	171,321	29,462	26,680	209,500	5,196	5,554	1,058	263,890	66,200
1997	182,992	31,709	29,886	335,000	5,162	7,291	1,312	292,620	70,200
1998	184,443	32,743	32,499	146,400	5,823	5,820	1,190	315,525	63,150
1999	206,027	35,299	33,420	406,100	5,316	6,236	1,252	224,580	61,200
2000	190,872	36,114	32,541	209,850	5,291	7,688	1,276	299,760	66,980
2001	215,270	34,587	25,764	338,500	4,712	6,569	1,204	280,935	59,750
2002	210,960	35,553	27,707	172,900	4,262	7,339	1,268	283,760	58,660
2003	199,897	33,858	30,710	282,100	4,397	6,664	1,260	267,040	50,080
2004	232,362	29,013	30,021	185,800	5,220	6,240	1,307	294,620	52,540
2005	223,235	26,606	27,433	280,250	4,853	7,814	1,185	216,500	25,640
2006	193,736	29,564	34,064	207,300	4,912	6,378	1,010	210,750	30,600
2007	198,388	29,969	31,834	387,305	4,545	7,057	1,127	177,280	39,900
2008	203,733	27,603	26,881	202,080	4,817	7,319	1,135	234,376	37,900
2009[1]	219,850	30,432	29,783	302,020	4,853	7,307	1,104	210,709	32,025
2010	243,104	29,635	29,451	293,740	4,641	7,414	1,150	191,735	30,100

b = bale; bu = bushel; bx = box; cwt = hundred weight. **Note:** Some 2010 figures are preliminary estimates. (1) Some totals revised. (2) Harvested for nuts. (3) Harvested for beans. (4) Utilized production only. (5) Crop year ending in year cited.

Livestock on Farms in the U.S., 1900-2011

Source: National Agricultural Statistics Service, U.S. Dept. of Agriculture

(in thousands)

Year (on Jan. 1)	All cattle[1]	Milk cows	Sheep and lambs	Hogs and pigs[2]	Year (on Jan. 1)	All cattle[1]	Milk cows	Sheep and lambs	Hogs and pigs[2]
1900	59,739	16,544	48,105	51,055	1995	102,755	9,487	8,886	57,150
1910	58,993	19,450	50,239	48,072	2000	98,199	9,183	7,036	59,335
1920	70,400	21,455	40,743	60,159	2001	97,298	9,172	6,908	59,110
1930	61,003	23,032	51,565	55,705	2002	96,723	9,106	6,623	59,722
1940	68,309	24,940	52,107	61,165	2003	96,100	9,142	6,321	59,554
1950	77,963	23,853	29,826	58,937	2004	94,888	8,990	6,105	60,444
1955	96,592	23,462	31,582	50,474	2005	95,838	9,005	6,135	60,975
1960	96,236	19,527	33,170	59,026	2006	96,702	9,063	6,230	61,449
1965	109,000	16,981	25,127	56,106	2007	97,003	9,132	6,165	62,490
1970	112,369	12,091	20,423	57,046	2008	96,035	9,257	5,950	66,963
1975	132,028	11,220	14,515	54,693	2009	94,521	9,333	5,747	66,768
1980	111,242	10,758	12,699	67,318	2010	93,881	9,086	5,620	65,327
1985	109,582	10,777	10,716	54,073	2011	92,582	9,150	5,530	64,625
1990	95,816	10,015	11,358	53,788					

(1) From 1970, includes milk cows and heifers that have calved. (2) As of Dec. 1 of preceding year.

Animal Products: Average Prices Received by U.S. Farmers, 1940-2010

Source: National Agricultural Statistics Service, U.S. Dept. of Agriculture

Figures below represent dollars per 100 lb for beef cattle, veal calves, hogs, lambs, milk (wholesale), and sheep; dollars per head for milk cows; cents per lb for broilers, chickens, turkeys, and wool; cents per dozen for eggs; weighted calendar year prices for livestock and livestock products other than wool. For 1943-63, wool prices were weighted on marketing year basis. The marketing year was changed in 1964 from a calendar year to a Dec.-Nov. basis for broilers, chickens, eggs, and hogs.

Year	Broilers	Calves (veal)	Cattle (beef)	Chickens (excl. broilers)	Eggs	Hogs	Lambs	Milk cows	Milk	Sheep	Turkeys	Wool
1940	17.3	8.83	7.56	13.0	18.0	5.39	8.10	61	1.82	3.95	15.2	28.4
1950	27.4	26.30	23.30	22.2	36.3	18.00	25.10	198	3.89	11.60	32.8	62.1
1960	16.9	22.90	20.40	12.2	36.1	15.30	17.90	223	4.21	5.61	25.4	42.0
1970	13.6	34.50	27.10	9.1	39.1	22.70	26.40	332	5.71	7.51	22.6	35.4
1975	26.3	27.20	32.20	9.9	54.5	46.10	42.10	412	8.75	11.30	34.8	44.8
1980	27.7	76.80	62.40	11.0	56.3	38.00	63.60	1,190	13.05	21.30	41.3	88.1
1985	30.1	62.10	53.70	14.8	57.1	44.00	67.70	860	12.76	23.90	49.1	63.3
1990	32.6	95.60	74.60	9.3	70.9	53.70	55.50	1,160	13.74	23.20	39.4	80.0
1995	34.4	73.10	61.80	6.5	62.4	40.50	78.20	1,130	12.78	28.00	41.6	104.0
2000	33.6	104.00	68.60	5.7	61.8	42.30	79.80	1,340	12.40	34.30	40.7	33.0
2001	39.3	106.00	71.30	4.5	62.2	44.30	66.90	1,500	15.04	34.60	39.0	36.0
2002	30.5	96.40	66.50	4.8	58.9	33.40	73.80	1,600	12.18	27.90	36.5	53.0
2003	34.6	102.00	79.70	4.9	73.2	37.20	94.40	1,340	12.55	34.90	36.1	73.0
2004	44.6	119.00	85.80	5.8	71.4	49.30	101.00	1,580	16.13	38.80	42.0	80.0
2005	43.6	135.00	89.70	6.5	54.0	50.20	110.00	1,770	15.19	45.10	44.9	71.0
2006	36.3	133.00	87.20	5.8	58.2	46.00	95.50	1,730	12.96	35.20	47.9	68.0
2007	43.6	119.00	89.90	5.6	88.5	46.60	98.50	1,830	19.21	31.00	52.3	87.0
2008	45.8	110.00	89.10	6.6	109.00	47.00	99.60	1,950	18.45	27.20	56.5	99.0
2009[1]	45.7	105.00	80.30	7.2	81.7	41.60	99.60	1,390	12.93	32.50	50.0	NA
2010	48.2	117.00	92.20	8.1	85.6	54.10	125.00	1,330	16.35	49.70	61.5	NA

NA = Not available. (1) Some prices revised.

Crops: Average Prices Received by U.S. Farmers, 1940-2010

Source: National Agricultural Statistics Service, U.S. Dept. of Agriculture

Figures below represent cents per lb for apples, cotton, and peanuts; dollars per bushel for barley, corn, oats, soybeans, and wheat; dollars per 100 lb for potatoes, rice, and sorghum; dollars per ton for cottonseed and baled hay; weighted crop year prices. The marketing year is described as follows: apples, June-May; barley, hay, oats, potatoes, and wheat, July-June; cotton, cottonseed, peanuts, and rice, Aug.-July; soybeans, Sept.-Aug.; and corn and sorghum grain, Oct.-Sept.

Year	Apples	Barley	Corn	Cotton-seed	Cotton (upland)*	Hay	Oats	Peanuts	Pota-toes	Rice	Sor-ghum	Soy-beans	Wheat
1940	NA	0.39	0.62	21.70	9.8	9.78	0.30	3.7	0.85	1.80	0.87	0.89	0.67
1950	NA	1.19	1.52	86.60	39.9	21.10	0.79	10.9	1.50	5.09	1.88	2.47	2.00
1960	2.7	0.84	1.00	42.50	30.1	21.70	0.60	10.0	2.00	4.55	1.49	2.13	1.74
1970	6.5	0.97	1.33	56.40	21.9	26.10	0.62	12.8	2.21	5.17	2.04	2.85	1.33
1975	8.8	2.42	2.54	97.00	51.1	52.10	1.45	12.8	4.48	8.35	4.21	4.92	3.55
1980	12.1	2.86	3.11	129.00	74.4	71.00	1.79	25.1	6.55	12.80	5.25	7.57	3.91
1985	17.3	1.98	2.23	66.00	56.8	67.60	1.23	24.4	3.92	6.53	3.45	5.05	3.08
1990	20.9	2.14	2.28	121.00	67.1	80.60	1.14	34.7	6.08	6.68	3.79	5.74	2.61
1995	24.0	2.89	3.24	106.00	75.4	82.20	1.67	29.3	6.77	9.15	5.69	6.72	4.55
2000	17.8	2.11	1.85	105.00	49.8	84.60	1.10	27.4	5.08	5.61	3.37	4.54	2.62
2001	22.9	2.22	1.97	90.50	29.8	96.50	1.59	23.4	6.99	4.25	4.25	4.38	2.78
2002	25.6	2.72	2.32	101.00	44.5	92.40	1.81	18.2	6.69	4.49	4.14	5.53	3.56
2003	29.4	2.83	2.42	117.00	61.8	85.50	1.48	19.3	5.89	8.08	4.26	7.34	3.40
2004	21.8	2.48	2.06	107.00	41.6	92.00	1.48	18.9	5.67	7.33	3.19	5.74	3.40
2005	24.4	2.53	2.00	96.00	47.7	98.20	1.63	17.3	7.06	7.65	3.33	5.66	3.42
2006	31.7	2.85	3.04	111.00	46.5	110.00	1.87	17.7	7.33	9.96	5.88	6.43	4.26
2007	28.8	4.02	4.20	162.00	59.3	128.00	2.63	20.5	7.51	12.80	7.28	10.10	6.48
2008[1]	23.2	5.37	4.06	223.00	47.8	152.00	3.15	23.0	9.09	16.80	5.72	9.97	6.78
2009[1]	23.1	4.66	3.55	158.00	62.9	108.00	2.02	21.7	8.19	14.40	5.75	9.59	4.87
2010[2]	23.4	3.90	5.40	161.00	80.0	112.00	2.40	21.5	8.79	12.40	9.80	11.70	5.70

*Beginning in 1964, 480-lb net weight bales. NA = Not available. (1) Some prices revised. (2) Preliminary.

Value of U.S. Agricultural Exports and Imports, 1978-2010

Source: Economic Research Service, U.S. Dept. of Agriculture

(in billions of dollars, unless otherwise noted)

Year[1]	Agric. trade surplus	Agric. exports	% of all exports	Agric. imports	% of all imports	Year[1]	Agric. trade surplus	Agric. exports	% of all exports	Agric. imports	% of all imports
1978	$13.4	$27.3	21%	$13.9	8%	1995	$26.0	$56.3	10%	$30.3	4%
1979	15.8	32.0	19	16.2	8	1996	26.8	60.3	10	33.5	4
1980	23.2	40.5	19	17.3	7	1997	21.0	57.2	9	36.1	4
1981	26.4	43.8	19	17.3	7	1998	14.9	51.8	8	36.9	4
1982	23.6	39.1	18	15.5	6	1999	10.7	48.4	8	37.7	4
1983	18.5	34.8	18	16.3	7	2000	12.3	51.3	7	39.0	3
1984	19.1	38.0	18	18.9	6	2001	14.3	53.7	8	39.4	3
1985	11.5	31.2	15	19.7	6	2002	11.2	53.1	8	41.9	4
1986	5.4	26.3	13	20.9	6	2003	12.0	59.4	9	47.4	4
1987	7.2	27.9	12	20.7	5	2004	7.4	61.4	8	54.0	4
1988	14.3	35.3	12	21.0	5	2005	3.9	63.2	8	59.3	4
1989	18.1	39.7	12	21.6	5	2006	5.6	70.9	8	65.3	4
1990	16.6	39.5	11	22.9	5	2007	18.1	90.0	9	71.9	4
1991	16.4	39.3	10	22.9	5	2008	34.3	114.8	10	80.5	4
1992	18.3	43.1	10	24.8	5	2009	26.8	98.5	11	71.7	5
1993	17.7	42.9	10	25.1	4	2010	34.0	115.8	10	81.9	4
1994	19.2	46.2	10	27.0	4						

(1) Fiscal year (Oct.-Sept.).

World Meat Production, 2000, 2009

Source: UN Food and Agriculture Organization; in thousands of metric tons; ranked by top producers in 2009

Rank	Top beef producers Country	2000	2009	Rank	Top pork producers Country	2000	2009	Rank	Top poultry producers Country	2000	2009
1.	U.S.	12,298	11,891	1.	China	40,752	49,879	1.	U.S.	16,416	18,953
2.	Brazil.	6,579	9,024	2.	U.S.	8,597	10,442	2.	China	12,689	16,438
3.	China	5,156	6,425	3.	Germany.	3,982	5,277	3.	Brazil.	6,125	10,385
4.	Argentina	2,718	2,830	4.	Spain	2,905	3,291	4.	Mexico	1,868	2,633
5.	India	2,237	2,313	5.	Brazil.	2,600	2,924	5.	Russia.	775	2,360
6.	Australia	1,988	2,148	6.	Vietnam	1,409	2,553	6.	France.	2,220	1,720
7.	Russia.	1,894	1,741	7.	Russia.	1,569	2,169	7.	Iran	815	1,682
8.	Mexico	1,409	1,667	8.	France	2,312	2,004	8.	UK.	1,513	1,652
9.	France	1,528	1,467	9.	Poland	1,923	1,735	9.	Indonesia	818	1,435
10.	Pakistan	886	1,441	10.	Philippines	1,213	1,710	10.	Japan	1,195	1,394
11.	Canada.	1,263	1,288	11.	Italy.	1,479	1,588	11.	Germany.	801	1,316
12.	Germany.	1,304	1,193	12.	Denmark.	1,625	1,585	12.	Turkey.	661	1,308
13.	Italy.	1,153	1,057	13.	Japan	1,256	1,310	13.	Canada.	1,065	1,212
14.	Colombia	745	936	14.	Netherlands	1,623	1,275	14.	Spain	987	1,205
15.	UK.	705	850	15.	Mexico	1,030	1,163	15.	Argentina	1,000	1,204
16.	South Africa	625	777	16.	Belgium.	1,042	1,082	16.	Poland	589	1,155
17.	New Zealand	572	637	17.	Thailand	475	756	17.	Italy.	1,092	1,154
18.	Uzbekistan	390	623	18.	UK.	899	720	18.	Thailand	1,194	1,105
19.	Egypt	544	608	19.	Indonesia	413	637	19.	Malaysia	714	1,042
20.	Spain	651	598	20.	Austria	620	540	20.	Colombia	504	1,020
21.	Uruguay	453	588	21.	Serbia	—	528	21.	South Africa	821	981
22.	Japan	530	517	22.	Ukraine	676	527	22.	Peru	542	964
23.	Ireland.	577	514	23.	Chile	261	514	23.	Ukraine	193	894
24.	Venezuela.	429	483	24.	India	466	481	24.	Australia	643	880
25.	Ukraine	754	454	25.	Romania	502	471	25.	Netherlands	766	834
	Africa	4,318	5,191		Africa	771	1,143		Africa	2,982	3,821
	Asia	13,026	15,703		Asia	47,788	59,755		Asia	22,480	31,120
	Europe	11,777	10,880		Europe	25,379	26,006		Europe	11,885	15,721
	North America	13,561	13,179		North America	10,237	12,383		North America	17,480	20,165
	Oceania	2,581	2,805		Oceania	489	461		Oceania	767	1,039
	South America	11,846	15,058		South America	3,774	4,668		South America	9,741	15,466
	World total	65,146	59,100		World total	89,787	106,069		World total	68,198	91,308

World Corn, Rice, and Wheat Production, 2000, 2009

Source: UN Food and Agriculture Organization; in millions of metric tons; ranked by top producers in 2009

Rank	Top corn producers Country	2000	2009	Rank	Top rice producers Country	2000	2009	Rank	Top wheat producers Country	2000	2009
1.	U.S.	251.9	333.0	1.	China	189.8	197.3	1.	China	99.6	115.0
2.	China	106.2	163.1	2.	India	127.5	131.3	2.	India	76.4	80.7
3.	Brazil	31.9	51.2	3.	Indonesia	51.9	64.4	3.	Russia	34.5	61.7
4.	Mexico	17.6	20.2	4.	Bangladesh	37.6	45.1	4.	U.S.	60.6	60.3
5.	Indonesia	9.7	17.6	5.	Vietnam	32.5	38.9	5.	France	37.4	38.3
6.	India	12.0	17.3	6.	Thailand	25.8	31.5	6.	Canada	26.5	26.5
7.	France	16.0	15.3	7.	Philippines	12.4	16.3	7.	Germany	21.6	25.2
8.	Argentina	16.8	13.1	8.	Brazil	11.1	12.6	8.	Pakistan.	21.1	24.0
9.	South Africa	11.4	12.1	9.	Japan	11.9	10.6	9.	Australia	22.1	21.7
10.	Ukraine	3.8	10.5	10.	Pakistan	7.2	10.3	10.	Ukraine	10.2	20.9
11.	Canada	7.0	9.6	11.	U.S.	8.7	10.0	11.	Turkey	21.0	20.6
12.	Romania	4.9	8.0	12.	Cambodia	4.0	7.6	12.	Kazakhstan	9.1	17.1
13.	Italy.	10.1	7.9	13.	Egypt	6.0	7.5	13.	UK	16.7	14.4
14.	Hungary	5.0	7.5	14.	Nepal	4.2	4.5	14.	Iran	8.1	13.5
15.	Philippines	4.5	7.0	15.	Sri Lanka	2.9	3.7	15.	Poland	8.5	9.8
16.	Egypt	6.5	6.8	16.	Laos	2.2	3.1	16.	Egypt	6.6	8.5
17.	Serbia	0.0	6.4	17.	Peru	1.9	3.0	17.	Argentina	16.1	7.6
18.	Thailand	4.5	4.6		Colombia	2.7	3.0	18.	Uzbekistan	3.5	6.6
19.	Germany.	3.3	4.5	19.	Malaysia	2.1	2.5	19.	Italy	7.5	6.3
20.	Vietnam	2.0	4.4	20.	Iran	2.0	2.3	20.	Denmark	4.7	6.0
21.	Turkey.	2.3	4.3	21.	Mali	0.7	2.0	21.	Romania	4.5	5.2
22.	Russia.	1.5	4.0	22.	Ecuador	1.2	1.6	22.	Afghanistan	1.5	5.1
23.	Ethiopia.	2.7	3.9	23.	Italy	1.2	1.5	23.	Brazil	1.7	5.0
24.	Pakistan	1.6	3.5	24.	Argentina	0.9	1.3	24.	Spain	7.3	4.8
	Spain	4.0	3.5		Uruguay	1.2	1.3	25.	Hungary	3.7	4.4
	Africa	44.3	56.7		Africa	17.5	24.4		Africa	14.3	22.1
	Asia	149.1	233.6		Asia	545.5	611.7		Asia	254.5	301.0
	Europe	63.5	84.0		Europe	3.2	4.1		Europe	183.6	228.7
	North America	258.8	342.6		North America	8.7	10.0		North America	87.2	86.8
	Oceania	0.6	0.6		Oceania	1.1	0.3		Oceania	22.4	22.1
	South America	55.4	75.6		South America	20.9	25.6		South America	20.2	17.1
	World total	592.5	817.1		World total	599.4	678.7		World total	585.7	681.9

Note: North America comprises Bermuda, Canada, Greenland, Saint Pierre and Miquelon, and the U.S.

Crop Consumption Per Capita in Selected Nations, 1980-2007

Source: UN Food and Agriculture Organization
(in kg per capita per year)

Country	Corn 1980	1990	2007	% change, 1980-2007	Rice 1980	1990	2007	% change, 1980-2007	Wheat 1980	1990	2007	% change, 1980-2007
Australia	2	4	5	150.0%	8	8	10	25.0%	81	70	70	-13.6%
Bangladesh	0	0	6	NA	132	148	160	21.2	26	20	15	-42.3
Brazil	22	22	25	13.6	39	41	33	-15.4	50	44	53	6.0
Cambodia	11	7	16	45.5	133	155	152	14.3	4	0	3	-25.0
Canada	4	3	19	375.0	3	5	9	200.0	76	78	89	17.1
Chad	5	4	12	140.0	6	10	6	0.0	2	4	10	400.0
China	5	4	7	40.0	77	84	77	0.0	60	80	67	11.7
Congo Republic	5	3	5	0.0	2	4	24	1,100.0	33	38	49	48.5
Cuba	0	0	33	NA	51	48	64	25.5	78	74	51	-34.6
Egypt	49	56	54	10.2	27	30	37	37.0	131	147	137	4.6
France	2	13	12	500.0	4	4	5	25.0	95	92	100	5.3
Germany	3	7	13	333.3	2	2	4	100.0	69	68	82	18.8
India	8	8	6	-25.0	64	79	71	10.9	45	42	60	33.3
Indonesia	23	29	28	21.7	124	132	125	0.8	10	9	22	120.0
Iran	1	1	2	100.0	29	30	29	0.0	152	163	152	0.0
Israel	11	23	22	100.0	6	8	10	66.7	137	123	114	-16.8
Italy	5	3	4	-20.0	5	5	6	20.0	173	148	146	-15.6
Japan	14	19	12	-14.3	73	65	57	-21.9	44	43	45	2.3
Kenya	114	84	80	-29.8	2	1	8	300.0	20	18	26	30.0
Korea, North	43	56	42	-2.3	72	69	77	6.9	32	22	18	-43.8
Korea, South	2	13	14	600.0	138	97	76	-44.9	49	48	51	4.1
Mexico	120	128	123	2.5	5	4	6	20.0	43	43	36	-16.3
New Zealand	1	3	2	100.0	2	4	9	350.0	78	69	75	-3.8
Nigeria	6	32	25	316.7	14	20	21	50.0	15	3	21	40.0
Pakistan	6	6	7	16.7	22	14	14	-36.4	110	123	106	-3.6
Philippines	22	19	7	-68.2	95	93	129	35.8	17	20	19	11.8
Rwanda	14	15	13	-7.1	2	1	6	200.0	2	3	7	250.0
Saudi Arabia	12	13	22	83.3	34	18	31	-8.8	90	104	94	4.4
South Africa	120	108	104	-13.3	4	8	20	400.0	56	57	60	7.1
Spain	1	1	2	100.0	6	6	7	16.7	98	93	87	-11.2
Thailand	5	5	8	60.0	141	117	103	-27.0	4	6	15	275.0
Turkey	8	20	20	150.0	3	6	9	200.0	200	215	191	-4.5
United Arab Emirates	1	1	1	0.0	34	40	42	23.5	318	494	204	-35.8
United Kingdom	3	3	3	0.0	2	2	6	200.0	82	82	97	18.3
United States	8	13	13	62.5	4	7	8	100.0	70	81	85	21.4
Uruguay	23	28	27	17.4	8	10	19	137.5	50	51	52	4.0
Venezuela	75	54	58	-22.7	21	13	20	-4.8	105	96	123	17.1
Vietnam	7	7	11	57.1	132	150	166	25.8	17	3	15	-11.8
Africa	37	40	41	10.8	14	16	20	42.9	45	45	46	2.2
Asia	8	9	9	12.5	79	84	78	-1.3	53	61	64	20.8
Central America	109	116	106	-2.8	8	7	11	37.5	38	39	35	-7.9
Europe	3	4	7	133.3	5	4	5	0.0	116	115	108	-6.9
North America	7	12	13	85.7	4	7	8	100.0	71	81	85	19.7
Oceania	2	4	4	100.0	9	10	13	44.4	79	69	71	-10.1
South America	23	23	27	17.4	29	32	29	0.0	58	53	56	-3.4
World per capita consumption	13	15	17	30.8%	50	55	53	6.0%	64	67	66	3.1%

Meat Consumption Per Capita in Selected Nations, 1980-2007

Source: UN Food and Agriculture Organization
(in kg per capita per year)

Country	Beef 1980	1990	2007	% change, 1980-2007	Pork 1980	1990	2007	% change, 1980-2007	Poultry 1980	1990	2007	% change, 1980-2007
Australia	53	47	44	-17.0%	15	18	23	53.3%	21	24	40	90.5%
Bangladesh	1	1	1	0.0	0	0	0	NA	1	1	1	0.0
Brazil	23	28	37	60.9	8	7	11	37.5	10	14	32	220.0
Cambodia	2	4	5	150.0	1	6	9	800.0	1	2	2	100.0
Canada	40	36	33	-17.5	35	28	27	-22.9	22	28	37	68.2
Chad	7	12	8	14.3	0	0	0	NA	1	1	0	-100.0
China	0	1	5	NA	12	21	33	175.0	2	3	12	500.0
Congo Republic	4	1	2	-50.0	1	1	3	200.0	2	5	10	400.0
Cuba	15	13	5	-66.7	5	10	18	260.0	9	12	14	55.6
Egypt	7	8	11	57.1	0	0	0	NA	4	5	8	100.0
France	33	33	27	-18.2	37	34	32	-13.5	16	21	21	31.3
Germany	23	22	13	-43.5	61	60	56	-8.2	10	11	16	60.0
India	2	2	2	0.0	0	0	0	NA	0	0	1	NA
Indonesia	2	2	2	0.0	1	3	3	200.0	1	3	6	500.0
Iran	6	6	6	0.0	0	0	0	NA	6	7	20	233.3
Israel	13	14	27	107.7	2	2	3	50.0	35	39	68	94.3
Italy	26	27	24	-7.7	25	32	45	80.0	18	20	16	-11.1
Japan	5	8	9	80.0	13	15	20	53.8	10	14	17	70.0
Kenya	12	9	12	0.0	0	0	0	NA	2	1	1	-50.0
Korea, North	2	2	1	-50.0	10	11	7	-30.0	2	3	2	0.0
Korea, South	3	6	11	266.7	8	13	31	287.5	2	6	13	550.0
Mexico	11	14	18	63.6	18	10	14	-22.2	6	10	29	383.3
New Zealand	57	39	32	-43.9	12	14	23	91.7	10	17	35	250.0

Country	Beef				Pork				Poultry			
	1980	1990	2007	% change, 1980-2007	1980	1990	2007	% change, 1980-2007	1980	1990	2007	% change, 1980-2007
Nigeria	5	2	2	−60.0%	1	1	1	0.0%	2	2	2	0.0%
Pakistan	5	6	8	60.0	0	0	0	NA	1	1	3	200.0
Philippines	3	2	4	33.3	9	11	19	111.1	5	4	8	60.0
Rwanda	2	2	2	0.0	0	0	1	NA	0	0	0	NA
Saudi Arabia	6	4	6	0.0	0	0	0	NA	24	29	41	70.8
South Africa	20	17	16	−20.0	3	4	4	33.3	8	15	25	212.5
Spain	11	13	15	36.4	31	48	62	100.0	21	23	28	33.3
Thailand	6	6	4	−33.3	6	6	13	116.7	7	9	11	57.1
Turkey	3	7	6	100.0	0	0	0	NA	5	7	14	180.0
United Arab Emirates	14	13	9	−35.7	0	0	0	NA	43	37	61	41.9
United Kingdom	23	21	22	−4.3	26	25	28	7.7	14	19	29	107.1
United States	47	43	41	−12.8	33	28	30	−9.1	26	39	51	96.2
Uruguay	76	47	15	−80.3	9	7	9	0.0	5	7	14	180.0
Venezuela	22	18	21	−4.5	6	5	6	0.0	17	13	29	70.6
Vietnam	2	2	4	100.0	5	11	30	500.0	2	3	7	250.0
Africa	7	6	6	−14.3	1	1	1	0.0	2	3	5	150.0
Asia	2	3	4	100.0	6	10	14	133.3	2	3	8	300.0
Central America	11	13	16	45.5	8	8	11	−21.4	6	9	27	350.0
Europe	24	25	17	−29.2	32	35	36	12.5	12	15	20	66.7
North America	47	43	40	−14.9	33	28	29	−12.1	26	38	49	88.5
Oceania	50	43	40	−20.0	14	17	22	57.1	18	22	37	105.6
South America	28	27	30	7.1	7	6	10	42.9	9	12	27	200.0
World per capita consumption	11	10	10	−0.1%	12	13	15	25.0%	6	8	13	116.7%

Trade in Wheat, Rice, Corn, and Meat, 1998, 2008

Source: UN Food and Agriculture Organization; in thousands of dollars

Wheat exports

Rank	Country	1998	Country	2008
1.	U.S.	$3,714,000	U.S.	$11,306,300
2.	Canada	2,796,400	Canada	6,727,650
3.	Australia	2,210,150	France	5,598,810
4.	France	1,960,430	Australia	3,240,620
5.	Argentina	1,298,340	Russia	2,864,430
6.	Germany	810,309	Argentina	2,547,290
7.	UK	581,744	Germany	2,534,300
8.	Kazakhstan	255,546	Ukraine	1,605,250
9.	Ukraine	193,000	Kazakhstan	1,458,780
10.	Turkey	163,366	UK	740,358

Wheat imports

Rank	Country	1998	Country	2008
1.	Italy	$1,213,910	Japan	$3,291,570
2.	Japan	1,093,660	Algeria	3,055,210
3.	Egypt	816,170	Egypt	2,461,720
4.	Brazil	813,919	Italy	2,277,540
5.	Algeria	689,309	Indonesia	1,975,480
6.	S. Korea	662,737	Brazil	1,873,590
7.	Indonesia	630,422	Iran	1,801,340
8.	Iran	530,028	Morocco	1,609,100
9.	Spain	522,016	Turkey	1,483,190
10.	Iraq	469,080	Spain	1,430,390

Rice exports

Rank	Country	1998	Country	2008
1.	U.S.	$415,866	U.S.	$744,440
2.	Uruguay	40,203	China	39,643
3.	Argentina	29,489	France	12,977
4.	Greece	17,482	Paraguay	9,705
5.	France	12,718	Italy	8,466
6.	Spain	7,852	Brazil	8,060
7.	Italy	7,072	Greece	7,491
8.	Australia	6,442	Spain	6,749
9.	China	2,487	Argentina	5,418
10.	Guyana	2,295	India	4,447

Rice imports

Rank	Country	1998	Country	2008
1.	Brazil	$151,644	Mexico	$312,900
2.	Mexico	92,743	Nicaragua	72,951
3.	Colombia	84,407	Costa Rica	47,376
4.	Ecuador	39,954	Honduras	46,914
5.	Costa Rica	34,196	Panama	38,513
6.	Bangladesh	33,424	Guatemala	36,423
7.	Panama	21,681	Saudi Arabia	36,306
8.	Portugal	18,799	Italy	35,710
9.	Botswana	14,954	El Salvador	31,132
10.	Italy	10,406	Venezuela	22,472

Corn exports

Rank	Country	1998	Country	2008
1.	U.S.	$4,619,040	U.S.	$13,884,500
2.	France	1,409,540	Argentina	3,531,051
3.	Argentina	1,335,160	France	2,298,110
4.	China	531,740	Brazil	1,405,170
5.	Hungary	204,077	Hungary	986,101
6.	South Africa	125,636	India	780,636
7.	Chile	84,327	Ukraine	670,165
8.	Germany	74,610	South Africa	531,521
9.	Indonesia	65,453	Canada	268,496
10.	Zimbabwe	52,033	Germany	255,420

Corn imports

Rank	Country	1998	Country	2008
1.	Japan	$2,113,810	Japan	$5,602,460
2.	S. Korea	910,828	S. Korea	2,819,960
3.	China	640,352	Mexico	2,391,400
4.	Mexico	624,134	Spain	1,629,760
5.	Spain	403,995	China	1,164,811
6.	Egypt	379,420	Netherlands	1,107,990
7.	Netherlands	295,030	Egypt	1,036,640
8.	Colombia	267,962	Colombia	935,065
9.	Germany	232,560	Germany	736,020
10.	UK	229,484	Italy	727,011

Meat exports

Rank	Country	1998	Country	2008
1.	U.S.	$5,832,261	Brazil	$14,089,482
2.	France	3,769,101	U.S.	11,783,486
3.	Netherlands	3,680,481	Germany	9,714,489
4.	Denmark	3,521,558	Netherlands	9,169,846
5.	Belgium-Luxembourg	2,567,233	Australia	5,701,143
6.	Australia	2,336,196	Denmark	5,604,979
7.	Germany	1,967,054	France	5,128,593
8.	Canada	1,635,708	Belgium	4,664,826
9.	Brazil	1,574,738	Spain	4,051,411
10.	Ireland	1,539,138	Canada	3,878,402

Meat imports

Rank	Country	1998	Country	2008
1.	Japan	$6,238,648	Japan	$9,997,085
2.	Germany	4,406,222	UK	8,440,575
3.	Italy	3,470,021	Germany	8,290,444
4.	UK	3,285,673	Russia	6,511,137
5.	U.S.	2,940,383	Italy	6,298,682
6.	France	2,912,651	France	5,903,647
7.	Russia	2,191,638	U.S.	5,071,107
8.	China[1]	1,310,530	Netherlands	4,759,635
9.	Netherlands	1,068,512	Mexico	2,894,406
10.	Belgium-Luxembourg	1,007,719	China	2,628,619

Note: Data for China excludes Hong Kong and Macao unless otherwise noted. (1) Includes Hong Kong.

World Capture of Fish, Crustaceans, and Mollusks, 2000-08

Source: UN Food and Agriculture Organization

(in thousands of metric tons; ranked by 2008 captures; total includes nations not shown)

Country	2000	2005	2006	2007	2008	Country	2000	2005	2006	2007	2008
China	14,649	14,589	14,631	14,659	14,791	Thailand	2,997	2,814	2,699	2,305	2,457
Peru	10,657	9,388	7,017	7,211	7,363	Norway	2,699	2,393	2,256	2,379	2,431
Indonesia	4,081	4,709	4,813	5,050	4,957	Vietnam	1,623	1,930	1,971	2,020	2,088
U.S.	4,718	4,893	4,852	4,768	4,350	South Korea	1,825	1,646	1,758	1,870	1,944
Japan	5,055	4,291	4,305	4,297	4,249	Mexico	1,316	1,320	1,357	1,484	1,589
India	3,666	3,691	3,845	3,859	4,105	Bangladesh	1,004	1,334	1,436	1,494	1,558
Chile	4,300	4,328	4,161	3,819	3,555	Malaysia	1,289	1,214	1,286	1,386	1,396
Russia	3,974	3,198	3,284	3,454	3,384	Iceland	1,983	1,665	1,327	1,399	1,284
Philippines	1,896	2,270	2,319	2,500	2,561	Taiwan	1,094	1,017	967	1,174	1,016
Myanmar						Morocco	905	1,027	877	879	996
(Burma)	1,093	1,732	2,007	2,236	2,494	**World total**	**93,505**	**92,057**	**89,712**	**89,899**	**89,741**

World Aquaculture Production, 2000-08

Source: UN Food and Agriculture Organization

Country	Metric tons (thous.)					Value (mil)				
	2000	2005	2006	2007	2008	2000	2005	2006	2007	2008
China	21,522	28,121	29,857	31,420	32,736	$21,292	$29,954	$33,299	$44,374	$50,639
India	1,943	2,967	3,181	3,112	3,479	2,511	3,760	4,178	4,980	5,044
Vietnam	499	1,437	1,658	2,085	2,462	991	2,931	3,316	4,028	4,600
Indonesia	789	1,197	1,293	1,393	1,690	2,246	1,999	2,255	2,462	2,814
Thailand	738	1,304	1,407	1,351	1,374	2,514	1,741	2,240	2,482	2,202
Bangladesh	657	882	892	946	1,006	1,039	1,246	1,359	1,523	1,766
Norway	491	662	712	842	844	1,385	2,136	2,749	2,999	3,119
Chile	392	724	794	780	843	1,250	3,229	4,350	4,866	4,503
Philippines	394	557	623	710	741	681	794	982	1,234	1,576
Japan	763	746	734	772	732	3,317	3,178	3,099	3,197	3,104
Egypt	340	540	595	636	694	815	792	951	1,193	1,251
Myanmar (Burma)	99	485	575	605	675	781	959	1,119	778	817
U.S.	456	513	519	525	500	843	882	988	943	937
South Korea	293	437	514	606	474	573	1,195	1,419	1,577	1,287
Taiwan	244	305	310	316	324	836	969	880	991	1,069
Brazil	172	258	272	289	290	264	444	469	595	608
Spain	309	219	293	281	249	329	309	356	384	518
Malaysia	152	176	168	178	243	254	339	340	370	564
France	267	245	238	238	238	425	677	663	757	814
Italy	214	181	173	179	181	446	595	599	757	810
World total[1]	**32,416**	**44,306**	**47,351**	**49,904**	**52,546**	**$47,598**	**$65,669**	**$74,451**	**$90,246**	**$98,448**

Note: Does not include aquatic plants or marine mammals. (1) Includes nations not shown.

U.S. Commercial Landings of Fish and Shellfish, 1990-2010

Source: Natl. Marine Fisheries Service, Natl. Oceanic and Atmospheric Admin., U.S. Dept. of Commerce

Year	Landings for human food		Landings for industrial purposes[1]		Total	
	Weight (mil lbs)	Value (mil)	Weight (mil lbs)	Value (mil)	Weight (mil lbs)	Value (mil)
1990	7,041	$3,366	2,363	$156	9,404	$3,522
1991	7,031	3,169	2,453	139	9,484	3,308
1992	7,618	3,531	2,019	147	9,637	3,678
1993	8,214	3,317	2,253	154	10,467	3,471
1994	7,936	3,751	2,525	95	10,461	3,846
1995	7,667	3,625	2,121	145	9,788	3,770
1996	7,474	3,355	2,091	132	9,565	3,487
1997	7,244	3,285	2,598	163	9,842	3,448
1998	7,173	3,009	2,021	119	9,194	3,128
1999	6,832	3,265	2,507	202	9,339	3,467
2000	6,912	3,398	2,157	152	9,069	3,550
2001	7,311	3,064	2,178	154	9,489	3,218
2002	7,205	2,940	2,192	152	9,397	3,092
2003	7,521	3,185	1,986	157	9,507	3,347
2004	7,794	3,611	1,889	145	9,683	3,756
2005	7,997	3,825	1,710	117	9,707	3,942
2006	7,842	3,911	1,641	113	9,483	4,024
2007	7,490	4,015	1,819	177	9,309	4,192
2008	6,633	4,231	1,692	152	8,325	4,383
2009	6,198	3,733	1,833	158	8,031	3,891
2010[2]	6,526	4,356	1,705	164	8,231	4,520

Note: Does not include products of aquaculture, except oysters and clams. Statistics on landings are shown in round (live) weight for all items except univalve and bivalve mollusks such as clams, oysters, and scallops, which are shown in weight of meats (excluding shell). (1) Processed into meal, oil, solubles, and shell products or used as bait or animal food. (2) Preliminary.

U.S. Domestic Landings by Region, 2005, 2010

Source: Natl. Marine Fisheries Service, Natl. Oceanic and Atmospheric Admin., U.S. Dept. of Commerce

Region	2005[1]		2010[1,2]	
	Weight (thous. lbs)	Value (thous.)	Weight (thous. lbs)	Value (thous.)
New England	684,090	$971,663	576,082	$953,977
Middle Atlantic	199,937	221,505	194,085	218,683
Chesapeake	508,953	218,933	592,747	294,779
South Atlantic	122,842	125,117	119,106	164,704
Gulf	1,196,355	620,987	1,282,848	635,096
Pacific Coast incl. Alaska	6,950,647	1,700,927	5,418,416	2,150,185
Great Lakes	16,732	12,434	19,234	18,042
Hawaii	28,139	70,811	28,069	84,044
Total	**9,707,275**	**$3,942,376**	**8,230,587**	**$4,519,510**

(1) Landings reported in round (live) weight for all items except univalve and bivalve mollusks (e.g., clams, oysters, scallops), which are reported in weight of meats (excluding shell). (2) Preliminary.

EMPLOYMENT

Employment and Unemployment in the U.S., 1900-2010

Source: Bureau of Labor Statistics, U.S. Dept. of Labor

(civilian labor force, persons 16 years of age and older; annual averages, in thousands)

Year[1]	Employed	Unemployed Number	Rate	Year[1]	Employed	Unemployed Number	Rate	Year[1]	Employed	Unemployed Number	Rate
1900[2] ...	26,956	1,420	5.0%	1986 ...	109,597	8,237	7.0%	1999[6] ...	133,488	5,880	4.2%
1910[2] ...	34,599	2,150	5.9	1987 ...	112,440	7,425	6.2	2000[7] ...	136,891	5,692	4.0
1920[2] ...	39,208	2,132	5.2	1988 ...	114,968	6,701	5.5	2001 ...	136,933	6,801	4.7
1930[2] ...	44,183	4,340	8.9	1989 ...	117,342	6,528	5.3	2002 ...	136,485	8,378	5.8
1940[2] ...	47,520	8,120	14.6	1990[3] ...	118,793	7,047	5.6	2003 ...	137,736	8,774	6.0
1950 ...	58,918	3,288	5.0	1991 ...	117,718	8,628	6.8	2004 ...	139,252	8,149	5.5
1955 ...	62,170	2,852	4.4	1992 ...	118,492	9,613	7.5	2005 ...	141,730	7,591	5.1
1960 ...	65,778	3,852	5.5	1993 ...	120,259	8,940	6.9	2006 ...	144,427	7,001	4.6
1965 ...	71,088	3,366	4.5	1994[4] ...	123,060	7,996	6.1	2007 ...	146,047	7,078	4.6
1970 ...	78,678	4,093	4.9	1995 ...	124,900	7,404	5.6	2008 ...	145,362	8,924	5.8
1975 ...	85,846	7,929	8.5	1996 ...	126,708	7,236	5.4	2009 ...	139,877	14,265	9.3
1980 ...	99,303	7,637	7.1	1997[5] ...	129,558	6,739	4.9	2010 ...	139,064	14,825	9.6
1985 ...	107,150	8,312	7.2	1998[5] ...	131,463	6,210	4.5				

Note: Because of revisions in population controls, data for a given year may not be strictly comparable to other years. (1) **Other unemployment rates (1905-45)**, 14 years of age and older: 1905, 4.3; 1915, 8.5; 1925, 3.2; 1935, 20.3; 1936, 16.9; 1937, 14.3; 1938, 19.0; 1939, 17.2; 1945, 1.9. (2) Persons 14 years of age and older.

Unemployment Insurance Data by State, 2010

Source: Employment and Training Admin., U.S. Dept. of Labor; state programs only

State	Unemployment rate	Monetarily eligible claimants	Number of first payments	Number of final payments	Initial claims	Benefits paid	Average weekly benefit	Employers subject to state law
AL	9.5%	191,408	140,350	70,400	346,202	$444,462,969	$206	86,627
AK	8.0	60,204	34,516	25,653	99,757	167,687,557	239	17,276
AZ	10.0	226,000	178,856	122,103	327,189	697,566,069	214	124,542
AR	7.9	147,492	103,428	55,155	244,602	407,233,901	278	68,353
CA	12.4	1,920,637	1,523,765	951,114	3,842,150	8,505,011,667	301	1,205,034
CO	8.9	182,834	153,222	103,972	223,804	917,904,411	347	149,830
CT	9.1	236,243	174,314	87,456	282,209	950,419,616	327	97,102
DE	8.5	40,459	27,466	17,735	65,396	147,135,581	247	26,028
DC	9.9	28,937	28,355	18,837	23,297	170,405,898	299	28,734
FL	11.5	749,449	521,763	388,402	1,166,560	2,107,829,042	231	460,075
GA	10.2	426,447	299,963	182,704	810,314	1,089,576,631	273	207,887
HI	6.6	50,986	41,236	21,378	115,861	304,881,367	416	30,962
ID	9.3	93,379	75,050	41,762	167,484	266,171,134	255	48,476
IL	10.3	499,005	475,822	286,600	863,328	2,906,479,572	317	299,544
IN	10.2	279,529	222,391	136,438	443,471	977,528,739	295	129,054
IA	6.1	162,241	125,564	55,538	250,531	567,257,149	321	72,895
KS	7.0	107,982	91,193	56,014	198,720	424,998,741	326	70,243
KY	10.5	185,765	134,738	63,232	340,355	654,740,629	289	84,458
LA	7.5	162,469	107,389	67,095	220,201	484,983,791	209	104,194
ME	7.9	62,166	47,540	23,175	99,591	198,632,263	274	41,463
MD	7.5	215,381	154,725	84,093	376,836	848,262,598	316	137,619
MA	8.5	313,604	270,133	141,279	441,042	1,807,015,265	392	194,045
MI	12.5	432,087	387,386	233,020	905,747	1,975,664,593	297	204,241
MN	7.3	252,291	184,752	116,206	355,862	1,123,205,577	356	131,818
MS	10.4	113,037	79,533	41,628	167,288	268,241,907	190	55,222
MO	9.6	276,115	189,210	106,239	530,832	792,933,338	244	136,810
MT	7.2	53,991	34,424	20,882	89,586	167,958,760	272	36,628
NE	4.7	72,423	54,022	29,871	105,644	187,698,573	252	48,073
NV	14.9	152,606	128,499	91,098	276,445	783,870,610	318	56,663
NH	6.1	60,293	42,319	17,375	92,495	173,819,733	272	39,956
NJ	9.5	434,321	385,201	240,431	628,012	2,706,669,701	397	236,195
NM	8.4	88,168	53,745	36,413	101,275	327,716,119	316	44,403
NY	8.6	919,597	666,369	370,371	1,407,096	3,534,563,332	307	493,007
NC	10.6	508,975	378,791	283,304	844,817	1,720,701,213	298	197,153
ND	3.9	23,300	17,569	8,432	31,845	78,164,083	310	20,882
OH	10.1	375,647	308,311	175,676	765,591	1,679,210,344	297	225,782
OK	7.1	108,905	76,334	47,806	196,409	392,684,403	276	82,895
OR	10.8	239,726	199,506	116,422	515,637	1,052,054,455	290	109,650
PA	8.7	662,335	599,353	304,843	1,418,974	3,328,541,023	338	282,957
PR	16.1	126,462	118,744	79,910	192,036	298,024,619	118	62,490
RI	11.6	58,553	48,750	27,881	97,440	311,578,462	380	32,782
SC	11.2	226,562	149,306	95,505	336,506	547,335,401	236	97,805
SD	4.8	17,154	13,014	3,713	27,096	49,759,355	251	25,480
TN	9.7	261,503	193,834	111,383	416,250	684,021,130	223	112,194
TX	8.2	744,249	544,794	343,577	985,817	2,786,512,939	316	454,341
UT	7.7	95,475	74,936	44,688	135,217	354,342,359	316	67,829
VT	6.2	33,769	29,008	10,504	52,366	133,910,298	297	21,593
VA	6.9	273,328	177,577	95,432	395,888	726,800,273	288	189,698
VI	NA	3,107	2,496	1,631	3,898	11,953,227	302	3,535
WA	9.6	335,813	263,691	140,389	620,900	1,845,013,338	384	210,963
WV	9.1	78,872	58,082	24,699	101,129	237,077,685	255	35,810
WI	8.3	372,446	324,879	142,316	808,529	1,291,327,149	275	130,400
WY	7.0	38,391	22,368	12,510	37,346	119,947,743	337	21,755
U.S.	**9.6**	**13,782,118**	**10,738,572**	**6,374,290**	**23,592,893**	**54,737,486,332**	**299**	**7,553,445**

Unemployed Persons in the U.S. by Industry and Duration of Unemployment, 2010

Source: Bureau of Labor Statistics, U.S. Dept. of Labor

Occupation	Total	Less than 5 weeks	5 to 14 weeks	15 to 26 weeks	27 weeks and over	Average (mean) duration	Median duration
		Number of unemployed persons (thous.)				**Weeks of unemployment**	
Management, professional, and related.	2,566	444	522	398	1,203	34.9	24.3
Management, business, and financial operations	1,117	152	209	176	580	38.3	29.0
Professional and related	1,449	292	313	221	623	32.3	20.8
Service	2,819	588	674	463	1,094	29.8	18.3
Sales and office	3,315	577	690	535	1,513	34.6	23.4
Sales and related	1,596	291	349	255	701	33.1	22.1
Office and administrative support.	1,719	286	341	279	813	36.1	24.8
Natural resources, construction, and maintenance	2,504	502	557	403	1,042	32.0	20.0
Farming, fishing, and forestry.	193	56	59	34	44	19.4	11.2
Construction and extraction	1,809	366	399	295	749	32.0	19.9
Installation, maintenance, and repair.	503	80	99	75	249	36.8	26.3
Production, transportation, and material moving	2,365	391	477	356	1,142	36.3	25.5
Production occupations	1,206	193	226	173	615	37.9	28.2
Transportation and material moving	1,159	198	251	183	527	34.6	22.9
Industry[1]							
Agriculture and related industries.	218	60	66	40	52	20.3	11.7
Mining, quarrying, and oil and gas extraction	73	13	15	9	37	34.6	27.1
Construction.	1,826	345	399	309	773	32.7	20.7
Manufacturing.	1,643	231	289	234	888	39.6	31.6
Durable goods	1,091	141	178	153	619	40.8	35.3
Nondurable goods	552	91	111	81	269	37.3	26.0
Wholesale and retail trade	1,986	350	421	311	904	34.6	23.3
Transportation and utilities.	538	85	110	80	263	37.5	26.1
Information.	310	48	57	45	159	37.9	29.1
Financial activities	639	83	111	114	332	37.9	29.1
Professional and business services.	1,592	272	335	263	722	33.6	23.1
Education and health services.	1,645	348	399	254	644	29.9	18.0
Leisure and hospitality.	1,650	357	395	274	624	29.5	17.6
Other services	540	106	124	87	223	31.9	19.9
Public administration	292	59	69	43	121	31.9	19.5
No previous work experience.	1,220	261	342	210	407	27.6	14.9

(1) Includes wage and salary workers only.

Persons Not in the U.S. Labor Force, 2010

Source: Bureau of Labor Statistics, U.S. Dept. of Labor

The Labor Dept.'s unemployment rate, based on its household survey, shows the number of people out of work as a percentage of U.S. adults age 16 and older in the labor force. That rate excludes, however, the millions of adults considered not to be in the labor force.

(in thousands)

	Total	16 to 24	25 to 54	55 and over	Men	Women
		Age			**Sex**	
Total not in the labor force	83,941	17,014	22,350	44,577	33,189	50,752
Do not want a job now[1]	77,882	14,990	19,659	43,233	30,309	47,573
Want a job[1]	6,059	2,024	2,691	1,344	2,880	3,179
Did not search for work in previous year	2,948	968	1,189	791	1,279	1,669
Searched for work in previous year[2].	3,111	1,056	1,502	553	1,601	1,510
Not available to work now	623	274	284	65	264	359
Available to work now	2,487	782	1,218	487	1,337	1,151
Reason not currently looking[3]						
Discouragement over job prospects[4]	1,173	291	595	287	731	442
Reasons other than discouragement	1,315	491	623	200	606	709
Family responsibilities	286	49	171	66	83	203
In school or training	350	262	81	7	191	158
Ill health or disability.	50	4	21	25	21	29
Other[5]	629	176	350	102	311	318

(1) Includes some persons who are not asked if they want a job. (2) Persons who had a job in the prior 12 months must have searched since the end of that job to be considered unemployed. (3) Of those available to work now. (4) Includes believing no work is available, not being able to find work, lacking necessary schooling or training, thought of as too young or old by employers, and other types of discrimination. (5) Includes those who did not actively look for work in the prior 4 weeks for such reasons as child care and transportation problems, as well as a small number for which reason for nonparticipation was not ascertained.

U.S. Displaced Workers, 2010

Source: Bureau of Labor Statistics, U.S. Dept. of Labor

	Total (thous.)	Plant or company closed down or moved	Insufficient work	Position or shift abolished
		Percent distribution by reason for job loss		
Total displaced workers	6,938	30.6%	42.8%	26.6%
Age: 20 to 24 years.	227	35.9	52.6	11.5
25 to 54 years.	4,923	30.4	43.8	25.8
55 to 64 years.	1,395	32.5	38.6	28.9
65 years and over.	392	23.7	39.9	36.4
Men.	4,183	29.8	47.9	22.3
Women.	2,754	31.8	35.1	33.1
White.	5,716	29.7	42.9	27.3
Black.	761	33.9	41.7	24.4
Asian.	294	34.0	44.4	21.6
Hispanic or Latino.	993	32.4	57.0	10.6

Note: As of Jan. 2010. Displaced workers are persons 20 years or older who lost or left jobs they had held for at least 3 years. Workers in this table were displaced between Jan. 2007 and Dec. 2009. Hispanic or Latino persons may be of any race.

U.S. Unemployment Rates by Selected Characteristics, 1995-2011

Source: Bureau of Labor Statistics, U.S. Dept. of Labor

	1995	2000	2005	2006	2007	2008	2009	2010 Jan.	2010 June	2010 Yr.	2011 Jan.	2011 June
Total (all civilian workers)	5.6%	4.0%	5.1%	4.6%	4.6%	5.8%	9.3%	10.6%	9.6%	9.6%	9.8%	9.3%
Men, 20 years and older	4.8	3.3	4.4	4.0	4.1	5.4	9.6	11.6	9.4	9.8	10.2	8.7
Women, 20 years and older	4.9	3.6	4.6	4.1	4.0	4.9	7.5	8.0	8.0	8.0	8.1	8.2
Both sexes, 16 to 19 years	17.3	13.1	16.6	15.4	15.7	18.7	24.3	26.9	29.0	25.9	26.3	27.6
White	4.9	3.5	4.4	4.0	4.1	5.2	8.5	9.6	8.7	8.7	8.8	8.2
Black	10.4	7.6	10.0	8.9	8.3	10.1	14.8	17.3	15.6	16.0	16.5	16.5
Asian	—	3.6	4.0	3.0	3.2	4.0	7.3	8.4	7.7	7.5	6.9	6.8
Hispanic (of any race)	9.3	5.7	6.0	5.2	5.6	7.6	12.1	13.9	12.3	12.5	13.2	11.5
Married men, spouse present	3.3	—	—	—	—	3.4	6.6	6.6	6.8	6.8	5.8	6.2
Married women, spouse present	3.9	—	—	—	—	3.6	5.5	5.8	5.9	5.9	5.6	5.6
Women who maintain families	8.0	5.9	7.8	7.1	6.5	8.0	11.5	12.3	12.1	12.3	12.7	12.8
Occupation												
Management, professional, and related	2.4	1.8	2.3	2.1	2.1	2.7	4.6	5.0	4.9	4.7	4.7	4.7
Service	7.5	5.2	6.4	5.9	5.9	6.7	9.6	11.4	9.6	10.3	10.4	9.6
Sales and office	5.0	3.8	4.8	4.4	4.3	5.3	8.5	9.5	9.0	9.0	9.1	9.2
Nat. resources, constr., and maintenance	—	5.3	6.5	6.0	6.3	8.8	15.6	19.9	15.0	16.1	17.7	12.5
Prod., trans., and material moving	—	5.1	6.5	5.8	5.8	7.6	13.3	15.2	12.0	12.8	12.9	11.4
Industry												
Nonagricultural, private wage, and salary workers	5.8	4.1	5.2	4.7	4.7	5.9	9.8	11.1	9.7	9.9	10.0	9.0
Mining	5.2	4.4	3.1	3.2	3.4	3.1	11.6	9.1	8.2	9.4	8.5	5.2
Construction	11.5	6.2	7.4	6.7	7.4	10.6	19.0	24.7	20.1	20.6	22.5	15.6
Manufacturing	4.9	3.5	4.9	4.2	4.3	5.8	12.1	13.0	9.9	10.6	9.9	9.2
Durable goods	4.4	3.2	4.6	3.9	4.2	5.6	12.9	14.1	10.4	11.2	9.9	9.7
Nondurable goods	5.7	4.0	5.3	4.8	4.5	6.0	10.6	11.1	9.1	9.6	9.9	8.3
Wholesale and retail trade	6.5	4.3	5.4	4.9	4.7	5.9	9.0	10.5	9.3	9.5	9.1	9.7
Transportation and utilities	4.5	3.4	4.1	4.0	3.9	5.1	8.9	11.3	7.2	8.4	8.8	8.2
Information	—	3.2	5.0	3.7	3.6	5.0	9.2	10.0	8.8	9.7	7.3	7.9
Financial activities	3.3	2.4	2.9	2.7	3.0	3.9	6.4	6.6	6.9	6.9	7.2	6.8
Professional and business services	—	4.8	6.2	5.6	5.3	6.5	10.8	11.1	10.3	10.8	10.2	9.1
Education and health services	—	2.5	3.4	3.0	3.0	3.5	5.3	5.5	6.2	5.8	5.8	5.8
Leisure and hospitality	—	6.6	7.8	7.3	7.4	8.6	11.7	14.2	12.3	12.2	13.8	10.9
Other services	8.4	3.9	4.8	4.7	3.9	5.3	7.5	10.0	8.5	8.5	8.8	8.7
Agriculture and related	11.1	9.0	8.3	7.2	6.3	9.2	14.3	21.3	11.7	13.9	16.0	9.0
Government	2.9	2.1	2.6	2.3	2.3	2.4	3.6	4.3	4.4	4.4	5.0	5.8
Self-employed and unpaid family workers	—	2.1	2.7	2.7	2.8	3.6	5.5	7.2	5.0	5.9	6.8	5.7

— = Not available. **Note:** All monthly rates are unadjusted, except for married men and women, which are seasonally adjusted.

Employed Persons in the U.S. by Occupation and Sex, 2009-10

Source: Bureau of Labor Statistics, U.S. Dept. of Labor
(persons 16 or older; in thousands)

	Total 2009	Total 2010	Men 2009	Men 2010	Women 2009	Women 2010
Total	139,877	139,064	73,670	73,359	66,208	65,705
Management, professional, and related occupations	52,219	51,743	25,385	25,070	26,833	26,673
Management, business, and financial operations	21,529	20,938	12,330	11,945	9,199	8,993
Management	15,447	15,001	9,674	9,266	5,773	5,735
Business and financial operations	6,082	5,937	2,655	2,679	3,426	3,258
Professional and related	30,690	30,805	13,056	13,125	17,634	17,680
Computer and mathematical	3,481	3,531	2,618	2,620	863	911
Architecture and engineering	2,740	2,619	2,363	2,282	377	337
Life, physical, and social science	1,328	1,409	707	755	621	655
Community and social services	2,341	2,337	868	836	1,474	1,500
Legal	1,710	1,716	859	878	851	838
Education, training, and library	8,627	8,628	2,221	2,261	6,407	6,367
Arts, design, entertainment, sports, and media	2,724	2,759	1,453	1,484	1,271	1,276
Healthcare practitioner and technical	7,738	7,805	1,968	2,009	5,770	5,796
Service occupations	24,598	24,634	10,521	10,652	14,077	13,982
Healthcare support	3,309	3,332	350	370	2,959	2,962
Protective service	3,164	3,289	2,457	2,587	707	703
Food preparation and serving related	7,733	7,660	3,422	3,439	4,310	4,221
Building and grounds cleaning and maintenance	5,349	5,328	3,186	3,164	2,163	2,164
Personal care and service	5,043	5,024	1,106	1,092	3,937	3,932
Sales and office occupations	33,787	33,433	12,498	12,419	21,289	21,015
Sales and related	15,641	15,386	7,880	7,703	7,761	7,683
Office and administrative support	18,146	18,047	4,618	4,716	13,527	13,331
Natural resources, construction, and maintenance occupations	13,323	13,073	12,735	12,467	587	606
Farming, fishing, and forestry	926	987	736	755	190	231
Construction and extraction	7,439	7,175	7,248	6,990	191	185
Installation, maintenance, and repair	4,957	4,911	4,751	4,721	206	190
Production, transportation, and material moving occupations	15,951	16,180	12,530	12,751	3,421	3,429
Production	7,654	7,998	5,502	5,792	2,151	2,206
Transportation and material moving	8,297	8,182	7,028	6,959	1,269	1,224

Note: Numbers may not add up to totals because of independent rounding.

Projected Openings for Selected High-Paying Occupations, 2008-18

Source: Employment Projections Program, Bureau of Labor Statistics, U.S. Dept. of Labor

Job openings shown below represent the average number expected each year for workers in the U.S. who are entering these occupations for the first time.

Occupation	Annual avg. job openings[1]	Median annual earnings[2]	Occupation	Annual avg. job openings[1]	Median annual earnings[2]
Registered nurses	103,900	$62,450	Sales representatives[4]	45,790	$51,330
Elementary school teachers[3]	59,650	49,330	First-line retail supvrs. or mgrs.	45,010	35,310
Truck drivers, heavy and tractor-trailer.	55,460	37,270	Exec. secretaries, admin. assistants.	41,920	40,030
Postsecondary teachers	55,290	58,830	Secondary school teachers[3]	41,240	51,180
Gen. and operations mgrs.	50,220	91,570	Lic. practical and voc. nurses	39,110	39,030
Accountants and auditors	49,750	59,430	Gen. maintenance and repair workers	35,750	33,710
First-line office supvrs. or mgrs.	48,900	45,790	Carpenters	32,540	38,940
Bookkeeping, accounting, auditing clerks.	46,040	32,510			

(1) As a result of growth and net replacement needs. (2) For 2008. (3) Except special and vocational education. (4) Wholesale and manufacturing, except technical and scientific products.

Top-Paying U.S. Counties by Average Weekly Wage, 2010

Source: Bureau of Labor Statistics, U.S. Dept. of Labor

County	Avg. weekly wage	% change 4th qtr., 2009-10	County	Avg. weekly wage	% change 4th qtr., 2009-10
Santa Clara, CA	$1,943	14.4%	Fairfax, VA	$1,541	3.6%
New York, NY	1,929	2.5	Somerset, NJ	1,448	2.8
Washington, DC	1,688	4.5	Alexandria City, VA	1,441	5.0
Fairfield, CT	1,668	3.9	Morris, NJ	1,420	−0.9
Arlington, VA	1,668	4.8	Middlesex, MA	1,411	5.1
Suffolk, MA	1,651	4.4	Westchester, NY	1,333	3.0
San Francisco, CA	1,573	1.7	Montgomery, MD	1,326	2.2
San Mateo, CA	1,564	5.8	United States	971	3.0

Note: Figures shown are for 4th quarter, 2010. Horry County, SC, recorded the lowest average weekly earnings among the 334 largest counties, with an average weekly wage of $585 in the 4th quarter of 2010. It was followed by Cameron County, TX ($610); Hidalgo County, TX ($611); Yakima County, WA, and Webb County, TX ($653); and Tulare County, CA ($668). The top 15 were derived from a list of the 326 largest U.S. counties, which comprise 70.9% of total covered workers. Data include all workers covered by state and federal unemployment insurance programs.

Federal Minimum Hourly Wage Rates Since 1950

Source: Bureau of Labor Statistics, U.S. Dept. of Labor

	Nonfarm workers					Nonfarm workers			
Effective date	Under laws prior to 1966[1]	Percent of avg. earnings[2]	Under 1966 and later provis.[3]	Farm workers[4]	Effective date	Under laws prior to 1966[1]	Percent of avg. earnings[2]	Under 1966 and later provis.[3]	Farm workers[4]
Jan. 25, 1950	$0.75	54%	NA	NA	Jan. 1, 1977	(5)	(5)	$2.30	$2.20
Mar. 1, 1956	1.00	52	NA	NA	Jan. 1, 1978	$2.65	44%	2.65	2.65
Sept. 3, 1961	1.15	50	NA	NA	Jan. 1, 1979	2.90	45	2.90	2.90
Sept. 3, 1963	1.25	51	NA	NA	Jan. 1, 1980	3.10	43	3.10	3.10
Feb. 1, 1967	1.40	50	$1.00	$1.00	Jan. 1, 1981	3.35	42	3.35	3.35
Feb. 1, 1968	1.60	54	1.15	1.15	Apr. 1, 1990	3.80[6]	35	3.80	3.80[6]
Feb. 1, 1969	(5)	(5)	1.30	1.30	Apr. 1, 1991	4.25[6]	38	4.25	4.25[6]
Feb. 1, 1970	(5)	(5)	1.45	(5)	Oct. 1, 1996	4.75[7]	37	4.75	4.75[7]
Feb. 1, 1971	(5)	(5)	1.60	(5)	Sept. 1, 1997	5.15[7]	39	5.15	5.15[7]
May 1, 1974	2.00	46	1.90	1.60	July 24, 2007	5.85[7]	NA	5.85	5.85[7]
Jan. 1, 1975	2.10	45	2.00	1.80	July 24, 2008	6.55[7]	NA	6.55	6.55[7]
Jan. 1, 1976	2.30	46	2.20	2.00	July 24, 2009	7.25[7]	NA	7.25	7.25[7]

NA = Not applicable. (1) Applies to workers covered prior to 1961 amendments and, after Sept. 1965, to workers covered by 1961 amendments. Rates set by 1961 amendments: Sept. 1961, $1.00; Sept. 1964, $1.15; Sept. 1965, $1.25. (2) Percent of gross average hourly earnings of production workers in manufacturing. (3) Applies to workers newly covered by amendments of 1966, 1974, and 1977, and Title IX of education amendments of 1972. (4) Included in coverage as of 1966, 1974, and 1977 amendments. (5) No change in rate. (6) Training wage for workers ages 16-19 in first 6 months of first job: Apr. 1, 1990, $3.35; Apr. 1, 1991, $3.62. The training wage expired Mar. 31, 1993. (7) Under 1996 legislation, a subminimum training wage of $4.25 an hour was established for employees under 20 years of age during their first 90 consecutive calendar days of employment with an employer. For workers receiving gratuities, the minimum wage remained $2.13 per hour.

Fatal Occupational Injuries, 2010

Source: Census of Fatal Occupational Injuries, Bureau of Labor Statistics, U.S. Dept. of Labor, in cooperation with other agencies

	Fatalities Number	%		Fatalities Number	%
Total	4,547	100%	Contact with objects and equipment	732	16%
Transportation incidents	1,766	39	Struck by object or equipment	402	9
Highway	968	21	Struck by falling object or equipment	263	6
Collision bet. vehicles, mobile equipment	501	11	Struck by flying object or equipment	36	1
Vehicle struck object on side of road	244	5	Caught in or compressed by equipment or objects	224	5
Noncollision	195	4	Caught in running equipment or machinery	90	2
Jackknifed or overturned	173	4	Caught in or crushed in collapsing materials	91	2
Nonhighway (farm, industrial premises)	272	6	**Falls**	635	14
Overturned	154	3	**Exposure to harmful substances or environments**	409	9
Worker struck by vehicle	277	6	Contact with electric current	163	4
Railway accident	44	1	Contact with overhead power lines	76	2
Water vehicle accident	52	1	Contact with temperature extremes	45	1
Aircraft accident	151	3	Exposure to caustic, noxious, or allergenic substances	139	3
Assaults and violent acts	808	18	Inhalation of substance	57	1
Homicides	506	11	Oxygen deficiency	60	1
Shooting	401	9	Drowning, submersion	45	1
Stabbing	34	1	**Fires and explosions**	187	4
Self-inflicted injuries	258	6			

Note: Totals for categories may include subcategories not shown separately. Percentages show incidence rate per total fatalities.

U.S. Occupational Injuries or Illnesses by Industry, 2009

Source: Bureau of Labor Statistics, U.S. Dept. of Labor, unless otherwise noted

(percent distribution)

	Private indus-try[1,2]	Goods producing			Service providing					
		Natural resources, mining[1,2]	Con-struc-tion	Manu-facturing	Trade, trans., utilities[3]	Info.	Financial activities	Prof., business	Educ., health	Leisure, hospitality
Total (964,990 cases)	100.0%	100.0%	100.0%	100.0%	100.0%	100.0%	100.0%	100.0%	100.0%	100.0%
Nature of injury or illness										
Sprains, strains, tears	39.3%	31.9%	33.6%	33.9%	42.9%	50.1%	33.9%	36.4%	47.4%	31.8%
Bruises, contusions	8.6	11.2	6.2	7.0	9.2	7.7	9.8	8.3	9.8	8.4
Cuts, lacerations	7.9	7.2	10.3	10.1	7.2	4.1	9.8	6.4	2.4	15.5
Punctures	1.2	1.9	3.3	1.5	0.8	0.9	1.5	1.5	0.8	0.5
Fractures	7.8	13.2	11.2	9.1	7.4	8.2	6.5	8.1	6.0	6.6
Heat burns	1.5	1.2	1.0	1.6	0.8	0.2	0.5	0.5	0.9	6.7
Carpal tunnel syndrome	0.9	0.3	0.7	2.4	0.6	1.6	2.4	0.9	0.6	0.8
Tendonitis	0.4	0.2	0.2	0.7	0.3	0.3	0.4	0.5	0.4	0.2
Chemical burns	0.5	0.8	0.6	1.0	0.4	—	0.1	0.3	0.3	0.9
Amputations	0.6	1.2	1.0	1.7	0.3	—	0.1	1.1	0.1	0.4
Multiple traumatic injuries	4.0	4.9	3.1	3.8	3.9	3.9	4.4	5.5	4.4	3.2
Part of body affected by injury or illness										
Head	6.7%	8.1%	7.8%	7.4%	6.3%	5.3%	5.9%	7.8%	5.3%	6.8%
Eye	2.5	3.8	3.7	3.9	2.0	0.9	2.8	2.8	1.2	1.7
Neck	1.2	1.1	1.1	0.8	1.1	2.7	1.7	1.1	1.8	0.9
Trunk	33.6	31.0	31.6	31.7	36.5	35.0	27.9	29.2	39.3	25.8
Shoulder	7.0	6.6	6.9	8.8	7.7	9.4	4.7	5.8	7.1	4.7
Back	20.2	16.3	18.0	16.2	21.5	20.0	16.7	17.1	27.2	16.4
Upper extremities	22.9	21.7	25.1	33.2	19.1	15.1	25.3	23.0	16.0	32.4
Arm	4.7	3.9	5.0	5.5	4.4	3.4	6.8	4.9	4.1	5.2
Wrist	4.2	3.4	4.2	5.9	3.5	3.6	6.0	3.5	3.9	5.1
Hand, except finger	4.0	4.3	5.6	5.0	3.3	2.6	4.0	3.6	2.7	6.4
Finger	8.5	9.2	8.9	14.9	6.8	4.3	6.4	9.6	4.0	14.0
Lower extremities	22.2	25.6	23.8	18.7	23.7	25.9	21.4	22.9	20.5	21.9
Knee	8.7	8.8	8.7	7.2	9.1	11.6	10.1	8.7	9.0	7.9
Ankle	5.1	5.4	5.5	3.5	5.5	5.7	5.4	6.0	4.9	5.2
Foot, except toe	3.4	4.9	4.1	3.2	4.0	4.4	2.1	2.9	2.5	2.8
Toe	0.9	1.1	1.0	1.0	1.0	0.5	0.7	1.2	0.7	1.1
Body systems	1.7	1.8	1.3	0.8	1.4	3.8	3.3	2.1	2.0	1.7
Multiple parts	10.9	10.2	8.9	6.9	10.9	11.7	12.9	13.1	14.4	9.6
Source of injury or illness										
Chemicals and chemical products	1.5%	3.5%	1.1%	2.0%	1.2%	0.8%	1.2%	0.9%	1.3%	1.9%
Containers	11.8	6.6	5.0	11.2	19.7	5.6	8.3	9.1	5.1	15.4
Furniture and fixtures	4.0	1.1	2.4	2.5	4.1	3.5	6.1	3.8	5.1	5.6
Machinery	5.9	8.2	6.3	12.3	5.0	5.6	6.9	5.2	2.2	6.7
Parts and materials	8.9	13.0	22.3	17.1	8.7	5.2	5.8	5.7	1.5	2.0
Floors, walkways, ground surfaces	20.2	18.6	19.4	13.9	18.4	28.2	24.0	22.4	24.5	23.1
Tools, instruments, and equipment	7.1	8.8	9.9	8.0	5.6	9.3	7.9	6.7	5.0	10.7
Vehicles	8.5	8.7	5.9	4.9	13.8	9.3	9.3	9.7	5.1	4.1
Person, injured or ill worker	14.4	10.3	13.2	17.9	13.9	21.2	17.6	15.0	12.9	13.8
Worker motion or position	13.6	9.9	12.3	17.2	13.2	20.1	16.0	13.6	12.2	13.0
Person, other than injured or ill worker	6.4	0.4	0.2	0.2	0.7	0.3	2.3	1.7	29.8	2.0
Health-care patient	5.3	—	—	—	0.1	—	0.4	0.8	27.5	0.1
Event or exposure leading to injury or illness										
Contact with objects and equipment	26.4%	37.3%	32.8%	35.5%	26.2%	19.0%	23.6%	26.3%	14.1%	30.2%
Struck by object	13.5	18.7	16.9	15.7	13.6	7.4	11.2	14.0	6.9	18.0
Struck against object	6.7	8.4	8.2	6.8	6.8	7.7	6.7	7.7	4.7	7.2
Caught in equipment or object	4.5	8.3	4.8	10.8	4.2	2.1	3.0	2.8	1.7	3.1
Fall to lower level	6.6	8.7	13.1	4.6	6.1	12.9	10.3	8.0	4.5	3.9
Fall on same level	14.6	10.3	8.8	10.2	12.7	16.0	14.6	16.8	20.6	20.1
Slip, trip, loss of balance—without fall	3.4	2.7	2.8	2.6	3.7	4.2	3.5	3.2	3.5	3.7
Overexertion	23.6	15.7	18.1	21.9	27.3	16.4	17.0	17.0	31.9	15.7
Overexertion in lifting	12.1	7.1	9.5	10.8	15.4	7.1	8.6	8.6	14.0	9.0
Repetitive motion	3.2	1.4	2.6	7.4	2.3	6.4	6.2	3.3	2.2	1.9
Exposure to harmful substances	4.4	4.6	4.1	4.5	2.9	3.9	5.7	3.9	4.2	9.4
Transportation accidents	4.4	4.9	3.9	2.2	6.2	7.3	6.6	6.0	2.8	2.0
Highway accident	2.7	3.0	2.4	0.8	3.8	6.4	4.0	4.5	2.1	1.1
Fires and explosions	0.2	0.3	0.2	0.3	0.1	—	—	0.2	—	0.3
Assaults and violent acts by person	1.6	0.7	0.2	0.1	0.7	0.2	0.6	0.9	5.8	1.2
Assaults by animal	0.7	2.6	0.2	0.1	0.4	1.0	1.4	3.5	0.3	0.1

— = Not available. **Note:** Because of rounding and classifications not shown, percentages may not add up to 100. All injuries and illnesses reported involved days away from work. (1) Excludes farms with fewer than 11 employees. (2) Data conforming to Occupational Safety and Health Admin. (OSHA) definitions for mining operators in coal, metal, and nonmetal mining are provided by the Mine Safety and Health Admin., U.S. Dept. of Labor. Independent mining contractors are excluded from the coal, metal, and nonmetal industries. Data for mining include establishments not governed by Mine Safety and Health Admin. rules, such as those in oil and gas extraction. (3) Data for employers in railroad transportation are provided by the Federal Railroad Administration, U.S. Dept. of Transportation.

Civilian Employment of the Federal Government, 2009

Source: Statistical Analysis and Services Division, U.S. Office of Personnel Management

(monthly payroll in thousands of dollars; as of July 2009)

	ALL AREAS		UNITED STATES		WASH., DC[1]		OVERSEAS	
	Employ-ment	Payroll	Employ-ment	Payroll	Employ-ment	Payroll	Employ-ment	Payroll
TOTAL, ALL AGENCIES[2,3]	**2,822,561**	**$14,680,389**	**2,734,014**	**$14,190,652**	**354,589**	**$2,956,479**	**88,547**	**$489,737**
Legislative Branch[2,3]	**29,933**	**182,900**	**29,927**	**182,836**	**28,812**	**173,812**	**6**	**64**
Congress[3]	17,531	97,439	17,531	97,439	17,531	97,439	—	—
U.S. Senate[3]	6,820	38,200	6,820	38,200	6,820	38,200	—	—
House of Representatives[3]	10,711	59,239	10,711	59,239	10,711	59,239	—	—
Architect of the Capitol[3]	2,212	11,404	2,212	11,404	2,212	11,404	—	—
Congressional Budget Ofc.[3]	238	3,152	238	3,152	238	3,152	—	—
Govt. Accountability Ofc.[3]	3,191	28,564	3,191	28,564	2,308	20,701	—	—
Govt. Printing Ofc.[3]	2,378	13,882	2,378	13,882	2,188	12,936	—	—
Library of Congress[3]	3,871	24,700	3,865	24,636	3,831	24,465	6	64
U.S. Tax Court[3]	223	1,631	223	1,631	223	1,631	—	—
Judicial Branch[3]	**33,754**	**187,679**	**33,385**	**185,884**	**2,815**	**18,911**	**369**	**1,795**
Supreme Court[3]	483	2,484	483	2,484	483	2,484	—	—
U.S. Courts[3]	33,271	185,195	32,902	183,400	2,332	16,427	369	1,795
Executive Branch[2,3]	**2,758,874**	**14,309,810**	**2,670,702**	**13,821,932**	**322,962**	**2,763,756**	**88,172**	**487,878**
Exec. Ofc. of the President	1,788	13,834	1,775	13,729	1,775	13,729	13	105
White House Office	427	2,495	427	2,495	427	2,495	—	—
Ofc. of Vice President	21	172	21	172	21	172	—	—
Ofc. of Mgmt. and Budget	546	4,827	546	4,827	546	4,827	—	—
Ofc. of Administration	233	1,660	233	1,660	233	1,660	—	—
Council of Econ. Advisors	26	175	26	175	26	175	—	—
Council on Environ. Quality	23	153	23	153	23	153	—	—
Ofc. of Policy Development . . .	27	207	27	207	27	207	—	—
National Security Council	57	414	57	414	57	414	—	—
Ofc. of Natl. Drug Control Policy	85	750	85	750	85	750	—	—
Ofc. of U.S. Trade Rep.	230	2,100	217	1,995	217	1,995	13	105
Executive Departments	1,880,134	10,120,361	1,797,899	9,663,801	259,298	2,295,753	82,235	456,560
State	37,482	941,053	15,338	698,356	12,552	665,837	22,144	242,697
Treasury	112,358	619,103	111,663	615,984	15,281	121,778	695	3,119
Defense, total	734,065	2,652,278	686,843	2,511,616	71,986	288,423	47,222	140,662
Defense, mil. function	709,063	2,584,706	661,894	2,444,117	71,249	286,552	47,169	140,589
Defense, civ. function[3]	25,002	67,572	24,949	67,499	737	1,871	53	73
Dept. of the Army	281,123	777,244	260,403	717,948	21,867	46,852	20,720	59,296
Army, mil. function	256,122	709,673	235,455	650,450	21,131	44,982	20,667	59,223
Army, civil function	25,001	67,571	24,948	67,498	736	1,870	53	73
Corps of Engineers	24,932	67,396	24,879	67,323	667	1,695	53	73
Dept. of the Navy	190,021	769,445	182,453	738,534	26,637	107,860	7,568	30,911
Dept. of the Air Force	163,205	660,218	156,727	634,036	5,422	21,918	6,478	26,182
Defense Logist. Agency[3]	24,269	93,931	23,669	89,381	2,163	11,452	600	4,550
Other defense activities	75,447	351,440	63,591	331,717	15,897	100,341	11,856	19,723
Justice	112,412	749,185	110,372	734,747	24,666	190,455	2,040	14,438
Interior	79,968	375,390	79,601	374,073	7,900	51,496	367	1,317
Agriculture	108,202	531,864	107,299	526,931	11,046	79,154	903	4,933
Commerce	51,130	290,547	50,736	287,682	23,787	175,744	394	2,865
Labor	16,550	110,473	16,512	110,254	5,931	44,954	38	219
Health and Human Services . . .	66,868	455,532	66,555	453,112	30,993	237,612	318	2,420
Housing and Urban Dev.	9,956	72,287	9,877	71,750	3,581	27,559	79	537
Transportation	57,017	448,439	56,691	446,382	9,492	81,232	326	2,057
Energy	16,040	128,325	16,019	128,110	5,580	48,837	21	215
Education	4,085	31,884	4,078	31,838	3,026	24,093	7	46
Veterans Affairs	294,486	1,693,125	290,485	1,674,337	8,349	65,167	4,001	18,788
Homeland Security	179,515	1,020,876	175,830	998,629	25,128	193,412	3,685	22,247
Independent agencies[2,3]	**876,952**	**4,175,615**	**871,028**	**4,144,402**	**61,889**	**454,274**	**5,924**	**31,213**
Bd. of Govt., Fed. Rsrv. Sys.[3] . . .	1,873	13,535	1,873	13,535	1,873	13,535	—	—
Environmental Protect. Agcy	18,662	138,316	18,601	137,941	5,486	36,062	61	375
Equal Employ. Opp. Comm	2,283	14,799	2,274	14,753	478	3,842	9	46
Federal Communic. Comm.	1,847	16,012	1,845	15,993	1,561	13,811	2	19
Federal Deposit Ins. Corp.	6,246	78,461	6,224	78,259	1,644	24,000	22	202
Federal Trade Comm.[3]	1,131	8,533	1,131	8,533	976	7,287	—	—
General Svcs. Admin.	12,408	83,088	12,357	82,797	4,294	32,233	51	291
Natl. Aero. and Space Admin. . . .	18,539	152,858	18,527	152,739	4,093	35,956	12	119
Natl. Fdn. Arts and Humanities[3] . .	400	3,299	400	3,299	399	3,294	—	—
Natl. Science Foundation	1,466	12,278	1,461	12,229	1,458	12,203	5	49
Nuclear Regulatory Comm.	4,180	35,218	4,178	35,195	3,012	26,239	2	23
Ofc. of Personnel Management . .	5,319	28,577	5,305	28,552	1,718	11,845	14	25
Peace Corps.	987	5,874	640	3,986	524	3,457	347	1,888
Securities and Exch. Comm.	3,813	40,166	3,813	40,166	2,250	23,543	—	—
Small Business Admin.	3,805	24,040	3,774	23,870	1,001	7,783	31	170
Smithsonian Inst.[3]	5,028	30,329	5,006	30,150	4,631	27,841	22	179
Social Security Admin.	67,929	371,605	67,494	369,667	1,720	11,178	435	1,938
Tennessee Valley Authority	12,157	92,592	12,157	92,592	5	59	—	—
U.S. Postal Service	688,582	2,881,868	685,296	2,866,083	13,305	67,184	3,286	15,785

— = Not applicable. (1) Metropolitan statistical area. (2) Totals include agencies not listed. (3) Denotes figures that are preliminary or are based in whole or part on figures for the previous month.

U.S. Median Weekly Earnings, 2011
Source: Bureau of Labor Statistics, U.S. Dept. of Labor

Age, race, or ethnicity	Total Number of workers (thous.)	Total Median weekly earnings	Men Number of workers (thous.)	Men Median weekly earnings	Women Number of workers (thous.)	Women Median weekly earnings
All workers, by age						
16 years and over	100,593	$753	56,053	$825	44,539	$689
16 to 24 years	8,670	433	5,009	446	3,661	417
16 to 19 years	968	349	602	370	366	321
20 to 24 years	7,702	451	4,407	460	3,295	432
25 years and over	91,923	794	51,045	884	40,878	720
25 to 54 years	73,568	780	41,136	863	32,433	714
25 to 34 years	24,309	704	13,863	730	10,446	675
35 to 44 years	23,838	837	13,564	926	10,274	742
45 to 54 years	25,421	859	13,709	974	11,712	734
55 years and over	18,355	854	9,909	965	8,446	744
55 to 64 years	15,563	887	8,318	1,001	7,246	753
65 years and over	2,791	709	1,591	725	1,200	592
White						
16 years and over	81,516	770	46,572	850	34,944	705
16 to 24 years	7,180	439	4,271	450	2,909	419
25 years and over	74,336	822	42,302	909	32,034	735
25 to 54 years	58,984	806	33,833	887	25,151	728
55 years and over	15,352	888	8,469	996	6,883	762
Black						
16 years and over	11,612	623	5,376	673	6,236	592
16 to 24 years	930	405	450	398	480	412
25 years and over	10,682	650	4,926	698	5,756	610
25 to 54 years	8,870	643	4,106	689	4,763	609
55 years and over	1,813	694	820	751	992	615
Asian						
16 years and over	5,181	872	2,872	972	2,308	748
16 to 24 years	306	504	146	564	160	473
25 years and over	4,874	909	2,726	992	2,148	768
25 to 54 years	4,007	933	2,257	1,018	1,750	789
55 years and over	867	807	469	903	399	713
Hispanic[1]						
16 years and over	15,472	565	9,649	586	5,823	524
16 to 24 years	1,866	412	1,231	416	635	404
25 years and over	13,606	597	8,418	615	5,188	557
25 to 54 years	11,995	598	7,464	617	4,531	551
55 years and over	1,611	585	954	578	657	590
Occupation						
Managerial, professional, and related	39,877	1,069	19,209	1,268	20,667	931
Management, business, and financial	16,122	1,149	8,775	1,371	7,347	961
Professional and related	23,754	1,019	10,434	1,199	13,320	908
Service	14,233	489	7,430	544	6,803	439
Sales and office	23,070	645	8,940	739	14,130	606
Sales and related	9,235	674	5,099	770	4,137	576
Office and administrative support	13,835	629	3,841	693	9,994	615
Natural resources, construction, and maintenance	10,015	725	9,650	729	365	636
Farming, fishing, and forestry	743	438	622	445	121	385
Construction and extraction	5,169	719	5,095	721	74	688
Installation, maintenance, and repair	4,104	796	3,933	796	171	775
Production, transportation, and material moving	13,398	610	10,824	652	2,574	484
Production	7,011	617	5,258	674	1,753	494
Transportation and material moving	6,387	601	5,566	626	820	451

Note: Not seasonally adjusted; figures are median usual weekly earnings of full-time wage and salary workers for 2nd quarter 2011.
(1) May be of any race.

Average Hours and Earnings of U.S. Production Workers, 1969-2010
Source: Bureau of Labor Statistics, U.S. Dept. of Labor
(annual averages)

	Weekly hours	Hourly earnings	Weekly earnings		Weekly hours	Hourly earnings	Weekly earnings		Weekly hours	Hourly earnings	Weekly earnings
1969	37.5	$3.22	$120.75	1983	34.9	$8.20	$286.18	1997	34.5	$12.51	$431.86
1970	37.0	3.40	125.80	1984	35.1	8.49	298.00	1998	34.5	13.01	448.56
1971	36.8	3.63	133.58	1985	34.9	8.74	305.03	1999	34.3	13.49	463.15
1972	36.9	3.90	143.91	1986	34.7	8.93	309.87	2000	34.3	14.02	481.01
1973	36.9	4.14	152.77	1987	34.7	9.14	317.16	2001	34.0	14.54	493.79
1974	36.4	4.43	161.25	1988	34.6	9.44	326.62	2002	33.9	14.97	506.75
1975	36.0	4.73	170.28	1989	34.5	9.80	338.10	2003	33.7	15.37	518.06
1976	36.1	5.06	182.67	1990	34.3	10.20	349.75	2004	33.7	15.69	529.09
1977	35.9	5.44	195.30	1991	34.1	10.52	358.51	2005	33.8	16.13	544.33
1978	35.8	5.88	210.50	1992	34.2	10.77	368.25	2006	33.9	16.76	567.87
1979	35.6	6.34	225.70	1993	34.3	11.05	378.89	2007	33.9	17.43	590.04
1980	35.2	6.85	241.12	1994	34.5	11.34	391.22	2008	33.6	18.08	607.95
1981	35.2	7.44	261.89	1995	34.3	11.65	400.07	2009	33.1	18.63	617.18
1982	34.7	7.87	273.09	1996	34.3	12.04	413.28	2010	33.4	19.07	636.91

Note: Data refer to production workers in natural resources, mining, and manufacturing; construction workers; and non-supervisory workers in the service industries.

Elderly in U.S. Labor Force, 1890-2010

Source: Bureau of the Census, U.S. Dept. of Commerce

(labor force participation rate of persons age 65 and older; 1910 figures not available)

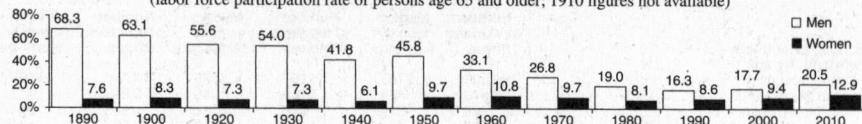

□ Men
■ Women

	1890	1900	1920	1930	1940	1950	1960	1970	1980	1990	2000	2010
Men	68.3	63.1	55.6	54.0	41.8	45.8	33.1	26.8	19.0	16.3	17.7	20.5
Women	7.6	8.3	7.3	7.3	6.1	9.7	10.8	9.7	8.1	8.6	9.4	12.9

Median Weekly Earnings of Wage and Salary Workers in the U.S. by Union Affiliation, 1996, 2010

Source: Bureau of Labor Statistics, U.S. Dept. of Labor

	1996				2010			
Sex and age	Total	Union member[1]	Represented by unions[2]	Non-union	Total	Union member[1]	Represented by unions[2]	Non-union
Total, 16 years and older . .	$490	$615	$610	$462	$747	$917	$911	$717
16 to 24 years.	298	371	362	294	432	585	580	423
25 years and older	520	625	621	498	782	931	925	755
25 to 34 years.	463	554	548	447	682	847	840	657
35 to 44 years.	559	636	632	530	824	961	954	792
45 to 54 years.	594	687	686	552	844	955	950	813
55 to 64 years.	535	620	616	505	860	975	971	828
65 years and older	384	510	510	367	684	823	821	665
Men, 16 years and older. . .	**557**	**653**	**651**	**520**	**824**	**967**	**964**	**789**
16 to 24 years.	307	375	369	303	443	610	601	430
25 years and older	599	669	668	580	874	982	979	846
25 to 34 years.	499	591	587	485	714	870	864	688
35 to 44 years.	632	683	683	617	915	1,008	1,004	893
45 to 54 years.	698	718	721	682	954	1,014	1,013	935
55 to 64 years.	643	667	664	633	979	1,010	1,012	967
65 years and older	477	589	593	424	794	903	903	770
Women, 16 years and older	**418**	**549**	**543**	**398**	**669**	**856**	**847**	**639**
16 to 24 years.	284	358	339	280	422	531	535	417
25 years and older	444	560	555	420	704	870	861	672
25 to 34 years.	415	497	495	405	648	819	811	624
35 to 44 years.	463	561	556	439	731	897	888	699
45 to 54 years.	481	620	616	445	730	874	864	702
55 to 64 years.	420	524	523	395	736	924	913	702
65 years and older	334	417	413	321	601	690	703	588

Note: Data refer to the sole or principal job of full-time workers. Excluded are self-employed workers regardless of whether or not their businesses are incorporated. (1) Including members of an employee association similar to a union. (2) Including members of a labor union or employee association similar to a union, and others whose jobs are covered by a union or an employee-association contract.

Work Stoppages (Strikes and Lockouts) in the U.S., 1950-2010

Source: Bureau of Labor Statistics, U.S. Dept. of Labor; involving 1,000 workers or more

Year	Number[1]	Workers (thous.)	Days idle (thous.)	Year	Number[1]	Workers (thous.)	Days idle (thous.)	Year	Number[1]	Workers (thous.)	Days idle (thous.)
1950	424	1,698	30,390	1984	62	376	8,499	1998	34	387	5,116
1955	363	2,055	21,180	1985	54	324	7,079	1999	17	73	1,996
1960	222	896	13,260	1986	69	533	11,861	2000	39	394	20,419
1965	268	999	15,140	1987	46	174	4,481	2001	29	99	1,151
1970	381	2,468	52,761	1988	40	118	4,381	2002	19	46	660
1975	235	965	17,563	1989	51	452	16,996	2003	14	129	4,091
1976	231	1,519	23,962	1990	44	185	5,926	2004	17	171	3,344
1977	298	1,212	21,258	1991	40	392	4,584	2005	22	100	1,736
1978	219	1,006	23,774	1992	35	364	3,989	2006	20	70	2,688
1979	235	1,021	20,409	1993	35	182	3,981	2007	21	189	1,265
1980	187	795	20,844	1994	45	322	5,020	2008	15	72	1,954
1981	145	729	16,908	1995	31	192	5,771	2009	5	13	124
1982	96	656	9,061	1996	37	273	4,889	2010	11	45	302
1983	81	909	17,461	1997	29	339	4,497				

(1) Numbers cover stoppages that began in the year indicated. Workers are counted more than once if they are involved in more than 1 stoppage during the year. For work stoppages ongoing at the end of a calendar year, days idle include only the days for the calendar year.

U.S. Union Membership, 1930-2010

Source: Bureau of Labor Statistics, U.S. Dept. of Labor

(numbers in thousands)

Year	Total employed[1]	% in unions[2]	Union members[2]	Year	Total employed[1]	% in unions[2]	Union members[2]	Year	Total employed[1]	% in unions[2]	Union members[2]
1930	29,424	11.6%	3,401	1965	60,815	28.4%	17,299	2000	120,786	13.5%	16,258
1935	27,053	13.2	3,584	1970	70,920	27.3	19,381	2005	125,889	12.5	15,685
1940	32,376	26.9	8,717	1975	76,945	25.5	19,611	2006	128,237	12.0	15,359
1945	40,394	35.5	14,322	1980	90,564	21.9	19,843	2007	129,767	12.1	15,670
1950	45,222	31.5	14,267	1985	94,521	18.0	16,996	2008	129,377	12.4	16,098
1955	50,675	33.2	16,802	1990	103,905	16.1	16,740	2009	124,490	12.3	15,327
1960	54,234	31.4	17,049	1995	110,038	14.9	16,360	2010	124,073	11.9	14,715

(1) Does not include agricultural employment; from 1985 on, does not include self-employed or unemployed persons. (2) From 1930 to 1980, includes dues-paying members of traditional trade unions, regardless of employment status; after 1980, includes employed only. From 1985 on, includes members of employee associations that engage in collective bargaining with employers.

ENERGY

U.S. Energy Overview, 1960-2010

Source: *Annual Energy Review 2010*, Energy Information Administration (EIA), U.S. Dept. of Energy; in quadrillion Btu

	1960	1965	1970	1975	1980	1985	1990	1995	2000	2005	2010[P]
Production	**42.80**	**50.68**	**63.50**	**61.36**	**67.23**	**67.80**	**70.87**	**71.32**	**71.49**	**69.59**	**75.03**
Fossil fuels	39.87	47.23	59.19	54.73	59.01	57.54	58.56	57.54	57.37	55.04	58.53
Coal[1]	10.82	13.06	14.61	14.99	18.60	19.33	22.49	22.13	22.74	23.19	22.08
Natural gas (dry)	12.66	15.78	21.67	19.64	19.91	16.98	18.33	19.08	19.66	18.56	22.10
Crude oil[2]	14.93	16.52	20.40	17.73	18.25	18.99	15.57	13.89	12.36	10.96	11.67
Natural gas plant liquids (NGPL)	1.46	1.88	2.51	2.37	2.25	2.24	2.17	2.44	2.61	2.33	2.69
Nuclear electric power	0.01	0.04	0.24	1.90	2.74	4.08	6.10	7.08	7.86	8.16	8.44
Renewable energy	2.93	3.40	4.08	4.72	5.49	6.18	6.21	6.70	6.26	6.39	8.06
Conventional hydroelectric power[3]	1.61	2.06	2.63	3.15	2.90	2.97	3.05	3.21	2.81	2.70	2.51
Biomass[4]	1.32	1.33	1.43	1.50	2.48	3.02	2.74	3.10	3.01	3.10	4.31
Geothermal	(*)	(*)	0.01	0.07	0.11	0.20	0.34	0.29	0.32	0.34	0.21
Solar	NA	NA	NA	NA	NA	(*)	0.06	0.07	0.07	0.07	0.11
Wind	NA	NA	NA	NA	NA	(*)	0.03	0.03	0.06	0.18	0.92
Imports	**4.19**	**5.89**	**8.34**	**14.03**	**15.80**	**11.78**	**18.82**	**22.26**	**28.97**	**34.71**	**29.79**
Coal	0.01	(*)	(*)	0.02	0.03	0.05	0.07	0.24	0.31	0.76	0.48
Natural gas	0.16	0.47	0.85	0.98	1.01	0.95	1.55	2.90	3.87	4.45	3.83
All crude oil and petroleum prods.[5]	4.00	5.40	7.47	12.95	14.66	10.61	17.12	18.88	24.53	29.25	25.29
Electricity[6]	0.02	0.01	0.02	0.04	0.09	0.16	0.06	0.15	0.17	0.15	0.15
Exports	**1.48**	**1.83**	**2.63**	**2.32**	**3.69**	**4.20**	**4.75**	**4.51**	**4.01**	**4.56**	**8.17**
Coal	1.02	1.24	1.94	1.76	2.42	2.44	2.77	2.32	1.53	1.27	2.10
Natural gas	0.01	0.03	0.07	0.07	0.05	0.06	0.09	0.16	0.25	0.74	1.15
All crude oil and petroleum prods.[5]	0.43	0.39	0.55	0.44	1.16	1.66	1.82	1.99	2.15	2.44	4.81
Electricity[6]	(*)	0.01	0.02	0.01	0.02	0.01	0.02	0.06	0.01	0.05	0.07
Consumption	**45.09**	**54.02**	**67.84**	**72.00**	**78.12**	**76.49**	**84.65**	**91.17**	**98.97**	**100.45**	**98.00**
Fossil fuels	42.14	50.58	63.52	65.35	69.83	66.09	72.33	77.26	84.73	85.79	81.42
Coal	9.84	11.58	12.26	12.66	15.42	17.48	19.17	20.09	22.58	22.80	20.82
Natural gas[7]	12.39	15.77	21.80	19.95	20.24	17.70	19.60	22.67	23.82	22.56	24.64
Petroleum[8]	19.92	23.25	29.52	32.73	34.20	30.92	33.55	34.44	38.26	40.39	35.97
Nuclear electric power	0.01	0.04	0.24	1.90	2.74	4.08	6.10	7.08	7.86	8.16	8.44
Renewable energy	2.93	3.40	4.08	4.72	5.49	6.18	6.21	6.71	6.26	6.41	8.05
Conventional hydroelectric power[3]	1.61	2.06	2.63	3.15	2.90	2.97	3.05	3.21	2.81	2.70	2.51
Biomass[4]	1.32	1.33	1.43	1.50	2.48	3.02	2.74	3.10	3.01	3.12	4.31
Geothermal	(*)	(*)	0.01	0.07	0.11	0.20	0.34	0.29	0.32	0.34	0.21
Solar	NA	NA	NA	NA	NA	(*)	0.06	0.07	0.07	0.07	0.11
Wind	NA	NA	NA	NA	NA	(*)	0.03	0.03	0.06	0.18	0.92

NA = Not available. P = preliminary. (*) = Less than 0.005 quadrillion Btu. **Note:** Some numbers may not add up to totals because of rounding. (1) Incl. waste coal supplied beginning in 1989 and refuse recovery beginning in 2001. (2) Incl. lease condensate. (3) Starting in 1990, pumped storage is removed and expanded coverage of industrial use of hydroelectric power is included. (4) Category known as "wood, waste, and alcohol" for years prior to 2000. Includes wood, waste, and alcohol fuels (ethanol blended into motor gasoline). Ethanol is included in both Petroleum and Biomass categories but is only counted once in totals. (5) Incl. imports of crude oil for the Strategic Petroleum Reserve, which began in 1977. (6) Small amts. transmitted across borders with Canada and Mexico. (7) Incl. supplemental gaseous fuels. (8) Petroleum products supplied, incl. natural gas plant liquids and crude oil burned as fuel.

U.S. Energy Flow, 2010

Source: *Annual Energy Review 2010*, Energy Information Administration (EIA), U.S. Dept. of Energy; in quadrillion Btu

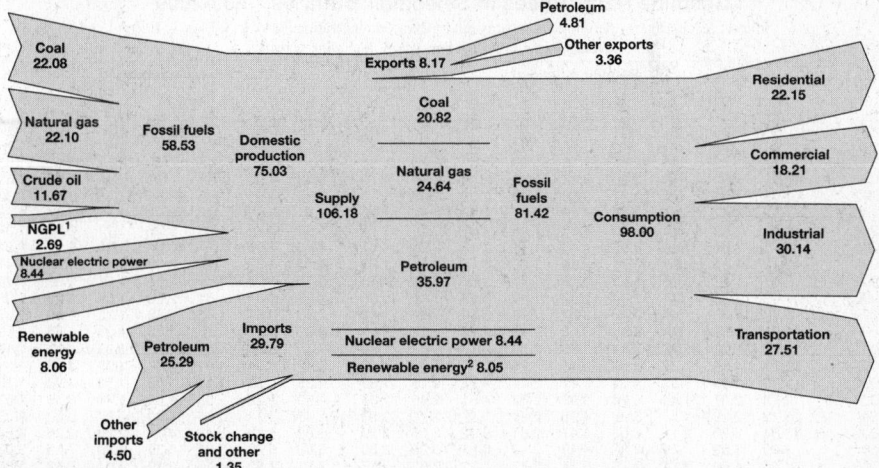

Note: Preliminary figures. Some numbers may not add up to totals because of rounding. (1) Natural gas plant liquids. (2) Conventional hydroelectric power, biomass, geothermal, solar thermal and photovoltaic, and wind.

U.S. Energy Consumption by Source, 1949-2010

Source: *Annual Energy Review 2010*, Energy Information Administration (EIA), U.S. Dept. of Energy

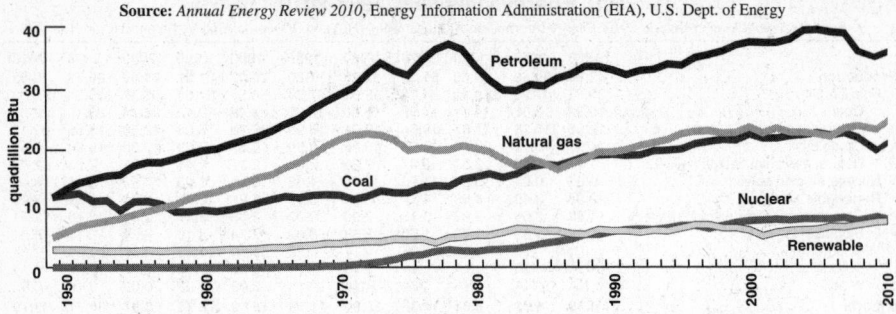

World's Largest Energy Producers and Consumers, 1980-2008

Source: *International Energy Statistics*, Energy Information Administration (EIA), U.S. Dept. of Energy
(primary energy in quadrillion Btu; ranked by top producers/consumers in 2008)

Production	1980	1985	1990	1995	2000	2005	2007	2008	% change, 1980-2008
1. China	18.122	24.303	29.385	35.045	34.200	64.447	71.552	79.108	336.5%
2. United States	67.233	67.798	70.870	71.317	71.485	69.610	71.589	73.423	9.2
3. Russia	NA	NA	NA	41.418	43.002	52.133	53.679	54.071	NA
4. Saudi Arabia	22.434	8.642	15.920	20.659	21.593	25.508	23.807	25.245	12.5
5. Canada	10.276	12.020	13.404	16.830	18.124	18.894	19.569	19.114	86.0
6. India	3.101	5.266	6.821	9.484	9.832	11.759	13.086	13.664	340.6
7. Iran	3.944	5.587	7.670	9.347	10.400	13.110	12.996	13.355	238.6
8. Australia	3.245	4.997	6.155	7.429	9.655	11.055	11.867	11.986	269.4
9. Norway	2.929	3.771	5.804	8.347	10.270	10.656	9.916	10.126	245.7
10. Indonesia	4.227	4.201	5.313	6.971	7.735	9.105	9.591	9.951	135.4
Total world production	**287.483**	**307.079**	**349.860**	**363.486**	**394.257**	**457.708**	**473.214**	**489.490**	**70.3%**

Consumption	1980	1985	1990	1995	2000	2005	2007	2008	% change, 1980-2008
1. United States	78.124	77.164	85.040	91.815	99.823	101.044	102.515	100.578	28.7%
2. China	17.287	22.006	26.999	34.756	36.352	68.246	78.001	85.060	392.0
3. Russia	NA	NA	NA	27.941	27.219	29.520	29.969	30.426	NA
4. Japan	15.210	15.706	18.779	20.965	22.436	22.675	22.590	21.874	43.8
5. India	4.041	5.914	7.879	11.443	13.462	16.363	18.848	19.954	393.8
6. Germany[1]	14.864	14.828	14.856	14.383	14.261	14.400	14.186	14.357	-3.4
7. Canada	9.695	10.152	10.979	12.211	13.062	14.164	14.072	14.029	44.7
8. France	8.389	8.350	9.125	10.052	10.850	11.353	11.194	11.290	34.6
9. Brazil	4.022	4.593	5.751	7.017	8.526	9.347	10.105	10.630	164.3
10. South Korea	1.758	2.306	3.841	6.362	7.839	9.228	9.706	9.885	462.2
Total world consumption	**283.194**	**308.968**	**347.686**	**365.393**	**397.536**	**461.601**	**482.290**	**493.014**	**74.1%**

NA = Not available. (1) Data for 1980-90 represents sum of figures for East and West Germany and may not be directly comparable to other years.

Gasoline Retail Prices in Selected Countries, 1990-2009

Source: *Annual Energy Review 2009*, Energy Information Administration (EIA), U.S. Dept. of Energy
(average price in dollars per gallon, including taxes)

	Regular unleaded									Premium unleaded						
Year	Australia	Canada	China	Germany	Japan	Mexico	S. Korea	Taiwan	U.S.	France	Italy	S. Africa	Spain	Thailand	UK	U.S.
1990	NA	$1.86	NA	$2.65	$3.16	$1.00	$2.05	$2.49	$1.16	$3.63	$4.59	NA	NA	NA	$2.82	$1.35
1991	$1.96	1.92	NA	2.90	3.46	1.30	2.49	2.39	1.14	3.45	4.50	NA	NA	NA	3.01	1.32
1992	1.89	1.73	NA	3.27	3.58	1.50	2.65	2.42	1.13	3.56	4.34	NA	$3.50	$1.35	3.06	1.32
1993	1.73	1.57	NA	3.07	4.16	1.56	2.88	2.27	1.11	3.41	3.68	NA	3.01	1.26	2.84	1.30
1994	1.84	1.45	NA	3.52	4.36	1.48	2.87	2.14	1.11	3.59	3.70	NA	2.99	1.21	2.98	1.31
1995	1.95	1.53	NA	3.96	4.43	1.11	2.93	2.23	1.15	4.26	4.00	NA	3.24	1.25	3.21	1.34
1996	2.12	1.61	NA	3.94	3.64	1.25	3.18	2.15	1.23	4.41	4.39	NA	3.32	1.49	3.34	1.41
1997	2.05	1.62	NA	3.53	3.26	1.47	3.34	2.23	1.23	4.00	4.07	$1.72	3.01	1.27	3.83	1.42
1998	1.63	1.38	NA	3.34	2.82	1.49	3.03	1.86	1.06	3.87	3.84	1.51	2.80	1.09	4.06	1.25
1999	1.72	1.52	NA	3.42	3.27	1.79	3.80	1.86	1.17	3.85	3.87	1.55	2.82	1.22	4.29	1.36
2000	1.94	1.86	NA	3.45	3.65	2.01	4.18	2.15	1.51	3.80	3.77	1.78	2.86	1.38	4.58	1.69
2001	1.71	1.72	$1.22	3.40	3.27	2.20	3.75	2.02	1.46	3.51	3.57	1.59	2.73	1.33	4.13	1.66
2002	1.76	1.69	1.21	3.67	3.15	2.24	3.84	1.93	1.36	3.62	3.74	1.41	2.90	1.35	4.16	1.56
2003	2.20	1.99	1.33	4.59	3.47	2.04	4.12	2.16	1.59	4.35	4.53	1.91	3.49	1.52	4.70	1.78
2004	2.72	2.37	1.48	5.24	3.93	2.03	4.51	2.46	1.88	4.99	5.29	2.58	4.09	1.76	5.56	2.07
2005	3.23	2.89	1.70	5.66	4.28	2.22	5.28	2.76	2.30	5.46	5.74	3.05	4.49	2.25	5.97	2.49
2006	3.54	3.26	2.11	6.03	4.47	2.31	5.92	3.05	2.59	5.88	6.10	3.42	4.84	2.76	6.36	2.81
2007	3.85	3.59	2.29	6.88	4.49	2.40	6.21	3.20	2.80	6.60	6.73	3.64	5.36	3.20	7.15	3.03
2008	4.45	4.08	3.11	7.75	5.74	2.45	5.83	3.53	3.27	7.51	7.63	4.13	6.13	4.01	7.42	3.52
2009	3.79	3.14	3.26	NA	4.85	2.12	4.69	3.01	2.35	6.36	6.47	NA	5.28	4.13	5.87	2.61

NA = Not available. **Note:** Some countries report only premium averages, and some do not sell regular unleaded gasoline.

Gasoline Retail Prices, U.S. City Average, 1973-2011

Source: *Monthly Energy Review*, Aug. 2011; *Short-Term Energy Outlook*, Sept. 2011; Energy Information Administration (EIA); U.S. Dept. of Energy
(in cents per gallon, including taxes; constant cents is price for all types using the Sept. 2011 dollar)

Year	Leaded regular	Unleaded regular	Unleaded premium	All types[1]	All types (constant cents)[1]	Year	Leaded regular	Unleaded regular	Unleaded premium	All types[1]	All types (constant cents)[1]
1973	38.8	NA	NA	NA	197.1	1993	NA	110.8	130.2	117.3	166.9
1975	56.7	NA	NA	NA	240.3	1994	NA	111.2	130.5	117.4	164.1
1976	59.0	61.4	NA	NA	236.1	1995	NA	114.7	133.6	120.5	164.7
1977	62.2	65.6	NA	NA	231.2	1996	NA	123.1	141.3	128.8	173.0
1978	62.6	67.0	NA	65.2	218.2	1997	NA	123.4	141.6	129.1	168.8
1979	85.7	90.3	NA	88.2	267.8	1998	NA	105.9	125.0	111.5	142.7
1980	119.1	124.5	NA	122.1	341.8	1999	NA	116.5	135.7	122.1	154.6
1981[2]	131.1	137.8	147.0	135.3	342.6	2000	NA	151.0	169.3	156.3	195.3
1982	122.2	129.6	141.5	128.1	294.4	2001	NA	146.1	165.7	153.1	181.9
1983	115.7	124.1	138.3	122.5	273.6	2002	NA	135.8	157.8	144.1	168.9
1984	112.9	121.2	136.6	119.8	255.7	2003	NA	159.1	177.7	163.8	191.4
1985	111.5	120.2	134.0	119.6	245.0	2004	NA	188.0	206.8	192.3	221.5
1986	85.7	92.7	108.5	93.1	182.3	2005	NA	229.5	249.1	233.8	262.8
1987	89.7	94.8	109.3	95.7	181.5	2006	NA	258.9	280.5	263.5	288.8
1988	89.9	94.6	110.7	96.3	173.7	2007	NA	280.1	303.3	284.9	305.9
1989	99.8	102.1	119.7	106.0	180.0	2008	NA	326.6	351.9	331.7	341.9
1990	114.9	116.4	134.9	121.7	194.9	2009	NA	235.0	260.7	240.1	247.5
1991	NA	114.0	132.1	119.6	182.9	2010	NA	278.8	304.7	283.6	288.3
1992	NA	112.7	131.6	119.0	175.1	2011 (July)	NA	365.4	391.5	370.3	370.3

NA = Not applicable. **Note:** Until unleaded gas became available in 1976, leaded was the only type used in automobiles. Average retail prices (in cents per gallon) for selected years preceding those in the table above were as follows: 1950: 27; 1955: 29; 1960: 31; 1965: 31; 1970: 36. Covers 56 urban areas 1974-77, 85 urban areas for 1978 and after. (1) Includes types of motor gasoline not shown separately. (2) In Sept. 1981, the Bureau of Labor Statistics changed the weights in the calculation of average motor gasoline prices. Starting in Sept. 1981, gasohol is included in average for all types, and unleaded premium is weighted more heavily.

Energy Consumption, Total and Per Capita, by State, 2009

Source: *State Energy Data Report 2009*, Energy Information Administration (EIA), U.S. Dept. of Energy

Total Consumption

Rank, state	Trillion Btu	Rank, state	Trillion Btu
1. Texas	11,297.4	27. Massachusetts	1,426.0
2. California	8,005.5	28. Iowa	1,418.5
3. Florida	4,295.2	29. Mississippi	1,138.7
4. New York	3,818.5	30. Kansas	1,084.3
5. Illinois	3,815.1	31. Oregon	1,066.5
6. Pennsylvania	3,654.1	32. Arkansas	1,054.8
7. Ohio	3,633.7	33. Connecticut	788.4
8. Louisiana	3,366.3	34. Nebraska	759.1
9. Georgia	2,949.3	35. Utah	754.5
10. Michigan	2,696.6	36. West Virginia	715.6
11. Indiana	2,622.6	37. Nevada	707.6
12. North Carolina	2,545.4	38. New Mexico	670.1
13. New Jersey	2,393.6	39. Alaska	630.4
14. Virginia	2,385.8	40. Wyoming	520.3
15. Tennessee	2,136.0	41. Idaho	509.0
16. Washington	2,032.9	42. Maine	430.5
17. Alabama	1,906.8	43. North Dakota	426.8
18. Kentucky	1,876.6	44. Montana	411.5
19. Missouri	1,817.8	45. South Dakota	359.9
20. Minnesota	1,809.5	46. New Hampshire	303.0
21. Wisconsin	1,744.6	47. Hawaii	269.8
22. South Carolina	1,581.0	48. Delaware	254.7
23. Oklahoma	1,490.6	49. Rhode Island	219.3
24. Arizona	1,454.3	50. District of Columbia	182.4
25. Colorado	1,452.2	51. Vermont	158.1
26. Maryland	1,429.3	**United States**	**94,446.9**

Note: U.S. total includes 23.8 tril Btu in coal coke imports not allocated to states.

Consumption per Capita

Rank, state	Million Btu	Rank, state	Million Btu
1. Wyoming	955.8	27. District of Columbia	304.0
2. Alaska	907.5	28. Missouri	303.9
3. Louisiana	749.8	29. Virginia	303.4
4. North Dakota	660.8	30. Georgia	300.5
5. Iowa	471.5	31. Illinois	295.9
6. Texas	456.1	32. Pennsylvania	290.0
7. South Dakota	443.8	33. Colorado	289.6
8. Kentucky	435.2	34. Delaware	288.1
9. Nebraska	422.9	35. Oregon	279.0
10. Montana	422.4	36. New Jersey	275.3
11. Indiana	408.7	37. North Carolina	272.0
12. Alabama	405.1	38. Utah	271.3
13. Oklahoma	404.4	39. Michigan	270.9
14. West Virginia	392.9	40. Nevada	268.2
15. Mississippi	386.0	41. Vermont	254.5
16. Kansas	384.9	42. Maryland	251.3
17. Arkansas	365.3	43. Florida	232.0
18. South Carolina	347.1	44. New Hampshire	229.2
19. Minnesota	343.8	45. Connecticut	224.3
20. Tennessee	339.5	46. Arizona	220.8
21. New Mexico	333.8	47. California	217.0
22. Idaho	329.5	48. Massachusetts	216.3
23. Maine	327.1	49. Hawaii	209.5
24. Ohio	315.1	50. Rhode Island	207.4
25. Wisconsin	308.7	51. New York	195.6
26. Washington	304.7	**United States**	**308.0**

U.S. Production of Crude Oil by State, 2010

Source: *Petroleum Supply Annual 2010*, Energy Information Administration (EIA), U.S. Dept. of Energy
(in thousand barrels)

Rank, state	Total	Rank, state	Total	Rank, state	Total	Rank, state	Total
1. Texas	426,700	9. Kansas	40,465	17. Arkansas	5,727	25. South Dakota	1,606
2. Alaska	218,762	10. Colorado	30,870	18. Ohio	4,785	26. Nevada	427
3. California	201,381	11. Montana	25,308	19. Pennsylvania	3,539	27. New York	384
4. North Dakota	113,033	12. Utah	24,663	20. Kentucky	2,519	28. Tennessee	257
5. Oklahoma	69,513	13. Mississippi	23,642	21. Nebraska	2,207	29. Missouri	147
6. Louisiana	67,527	14. Illinois	9,066	22. West Virginia	1,992	30. Arizona	40
7. New Mexico	65,010	15. Alabama	7,145	23. Indiana	1,835	31. Virginia	5
8. Wyoming	53,133	16. Michigan	6,438	24. Florida	1,780	**U.S.**	**1,998,137**

Note: U.S. total includes 588,232 thousand barrels of federal offshore production and offshore production by individual states (Alaska, 21,807 thousand; California, 13,027 thousand; Louisiana, 6,579 thousand; and Texas, 1,005 thousand).

U.S. Petroleum Trade, 1976-2011

Source: *Monthly Energy Review,* Aug. 2011, Energy Information Administration (EIA), U.S. Dept. of Energy
(in thousands of barrels per day; average for the year)

Year	Imports from Persian Gulf[1]	Total imports	Total exports	Net imports[2]	Petroleum products supplied[3]	Year	Imports from Persian Gulf[1]	Total imports	Total exports	Net imports[2]	Petroleum products supplied[3]
1976	1,840	7,313	223	7,090	17,461	1994	1,728	8,996	942	8,054	17,718
1977	2,448	8,807	243	8,565	18,431	1995	1,573	8,835	949	7,886	17,725
1978	2,219	8,363	362	8,002	18,847	1996	1,604	9,478	981	8,498	18,309
1979	2,069	8,456	471	7,985	18,513	1997	1,755	10,162	1,003	9,158	18,620
1980	1,519	6,909	544	6,365	17,056	1998	2,136	10,708	945	9,764	18,917
1981	1,219	5,996	595	5,401	16,058	1999	2,464	10,852	940	9,912	19,519
1982	696	5,113	815	4,298	15,296	2000	2,488	11,459	1,040	10,419	19,701
1983	442	5,051	739	4,312	15,231	2001	2,761	11,871	971	10,900	19,649
1984	506	5,437	722	4,715	15,726	2002	2,269	11,530	984	10,546	19,761
1985	311	5,067	781	4,286	15,726	2003	2,501	12,264	1,027	11,238	20,034
1986	912	6,224	785	5,439	16,281	2004	2,493	13,145	1,048	12,097	20,731
1987	1,077	6,678	764	5,914	16,665	2005	2,334	13,714	1,165	12,549	20,802
1988	1,541	7,402	815	6,587	17,283	2006	2,211	13,707	1,317	12,390	20,687
1989	1,861	8,061	859	7,202	17,325	2007	2,163	13,468	1,433	12,036	20,680
1990	1,966	8,018	857	7,161	16,988	2008	2,370	12,915	1,802	11,114	19,498
1991	1,845	7,627	1,001	6,626	16,714	2009	1,689	11,691	2,024	9,667	18,771
1992	1,778	7,888	950	6,938	17,033	2010	1,771	11,793	2,353	9,441	19,180
1993	1,782	8,620	1,003	7,618	17,237	2011[4]	NA	11,485	2,606	8,879	18,889

NA = Not available. **Note:** Beginning in Oct. 1977, imports for the Strategic Petroleum Reserves are included. U.S. exports include shipments to U.S. territories; imports include receipts from U.S. territories. Numbers may not add up to totals because of rounding. Some figures are revised. (1) Bahrain, Iran, Iraq, Kuwait, Qatar, Saudi Arabia, United Arab Emirates, and the Neutral Zone between Kuwait and Saudi Arabia. (2) Total imports minus total exports. (3) Includes domestic production and imports minus change in stocks, refinery imports, and exports. (4) Annualized 7-month average, for Jan.-July 2011. Based on estimated figures.

World Fossil Fuel Reserves

Source: International Energy Statistics Database, Energy Information Administration (EIA), U.S. Dept. of Energy

	Crude oil (bil barrels), 2011	Natural gas (tril ft[3]), 2011	Coal (mil short tons), 2008		Crude oil (bil barrels), 2011	Natural gas (tril ft[3]), 2011	Coal (mil short tons), 2008
North America[1]	209.3	343.6	269,343	Middle East	752.9	2,686.4	1,326
Canada	175.2	62.0	7,255	Bahrain	0.1	3.3	NA
Greenland	0.0	0.0	202	Iran	137.0	1,045.7	1,326
Mexico	10.4	12.0	1,335	Iraq	115.0	111.9	NA
United States[1]	20.7	272.5	260,551	Israel	0.0	7.0	NA
Central & South America	237.1	268.5	13,788	Kuwait	104.0	63.5	NA
Argentina	2.5	13.4	551	Oman	5.5	30.0	NA
Bolivia	0.5	26.5	1	Qatar	25.4	895.8	NA
Brazil	12.9	12.9	5,025	Saudi Arabia	262.6	275.7	NA
Chile	0.2	3.5	171	Syria	2.5	8.5	NA
Colombia	1.9	4.0	7,436	United Arab Emirates	97.8	227.9	NA
Cuba	0.1	2.5	NA	Yemen	3.0	16.9	NA
Ecuador	6.5	0.3	26	Africa	123.6	517.7	34,934
Peru	0.5	12.2	49	Algeria	12.2	159.0	65
Trinidad and Tobago	0.7	14.4	NA	Angola	9.5	10.9	NA
Venezuela	211.2	178.9	528	Congo	0.2	0.0	97
Europe	12.1	153.8	84,202	Egypt	4.4	77.2	18
Albania	0.2	0.0	875	Libya	46.4	54.7	NA
Bosnia and Herzegovina	0.0	0.0	3,145	Mozambique	0.0	4.5	234
Bulgaria	0.0	0.2	2,608	Namibia	0.0	2.2	NA
Czech Republic	0.0	0.1	1,213	Niger	0.0	0.0	77
Germany	0.3	6.2	44,863	Nigeria	37.2	186.9	209
Greece	0.0	0.0	3,329	South Africa	0.0	NA	33,241
Hungary	0.0	0.3	1,830	Sudan	5.0	3.0	NA
Italy	0.5	2.2	11	Swaziland	0.0	0.0	159
Macedonia	0.0	0.0	366	Tanzania	0.0	0.2	220
Montenegro	0.0	0.0	157	Zimbabwe	0.0	0.0	553
Norway	5.7	72.0	6	Asia & Oceania	40.3	537.5	293,042
Poland	0.1	5.8	6,293	Afghanistan	0.0	1.8	73
Romania	0.6	2.2	321	Australia	3.3	110.0	84,217
Serbia	0.1	1.7	15,179	Bangladesh	0.0	6.9	323
Slovakia	0.0	0.5	289	Brunei	1.1	13.8	NA
Slovenia	0.0	0.0	246	China	20.4	107.0	126,215
Spain	0.2	0.1	584	India	5.7	37.9	66,800
Turkey	0.3	0.2	2,583	Indonesia	4.0	106.0	6,095
United Kingdom	2.9	9.0	251	Japan	0.0	0.7	386
Eurasia	98.9	2,164.8	251,364	Korea, North	0.0	0.0	661
Armenia	0.0	0.0	180	Korea, South	0.0	0.0	139
Azerbaijan	7.0	30.0	NA	Laos	0.0	0.0	554
Belarus	0.2	0.1	110	Malaysia	4.0	83.0	4
Georgia	0.0	0.3	222	Mongolia	0.0	0.0	2,778
Kazakhstan	30.0	85.0	37,038	Myanmar	0.1	10.0	2
Kyrgyzstan	0.0	0.2	895	New Zealand	0.1	1.2	629
Russia	60.0	1,680.0	173,074	Pakistan	0.3	29.7	2,282
Tajikistan	0.0	0.2	413	Philippines	0.1	3.5	348
Turkmenistan	0.6	265.0	NA	Thailand	0.4	11.0	1,366
Ukraine	0.4	39.0	37,339	Vietnam	0.6	6.8	165
Uzbekistan	0.6	65.0	2,094	World[1]	1,341.6	6,289.1	948,000

NA = Not reported separately but included in regional and world totals. **Note:** Regional and world totals may include countries not shown. Proved reserves only. Some countries omitted for lack of appreciable reserves. (1) Figures for crude oil and natural gas are from 2009, the latest year available.

U.S. Crude Oil Imports by Selected Country, 1990-2010

Source: *Petroleum Supply Annual*, Energy Information Administration (EIA); U.S. Dept. of Energy

(in thousands of barrels per day; ranked by 2010 imports)

After dropping for four straight years, the United States' dependence on foreign oil increased in 2010. Imports from Organization of the Petroleum Exporting Countries (OPEC) members, non-OPEC countries, and Persian Gulf countries all rose. OPEC countries, especially those in the Persian Gulf region, have a significant production advantage because of the relatively low cost of developing their oil resources. But non-OPEC countries have also increased their oil production. Once again, Canada was the largest supplier of U.S. oil, followed by Mexico and Saudi Arabia. Despite the drawing down of U.S. troops in Iraq, imports from Baghdad declined. Sanctions do not permit the U.S. to import oil from Iran.

Country	2010	2009	2008	2007	2006	2005	2004	2000	1995	1990
Canada	1,970	1,943	1,956	1,888	1,802	1,633	1,616	1,348	1,040	643
Mexico	1,152	1,092	1,187	1,409	1,577	1,556	1,598	1,313	1,027	689
Saudi Arabia#	1,082	980	1,503	1,447	1,423	1,445	1,495	1,523	1,260	1,195
Nigeria#	983	776	922	1,084	1,037	1,077	1,078	875	621	784
Venezuela#	912	951	1,039	1,148	1,142	1,241	1,297	1,223	1,151	666
Iraq#	415	449	627	484	553	527	655	620	0	514
Angola#[1]	383	448	504	498	513	456	306	295	360	236
Colombia	338	251	178	137	141	156	142	318	207	140
Algeria#	328	281	312	443	362	228	215	1	27	63
Russia[2]	269	230	116	112	108	199	158	7	14	1
Brazil	255	295	231	165	133	94	51	5	0	0
Ecuador[3]	210	181	214	198	272	276	232	125	96	30
Kuwait#	195	180	206	175	179	227	241	263	213	79
United Kingdom	120	103	78	101	130	224	238	291	341	155
Congo Republic	70	64	67	63	27	25	8	42	20	NA
Azerbaijan	55	75	73	57	27	NA	NA	NA	NA	NA
Equatorial Guinea	50	89	74	55	57	68	66	6	NA	NA
Cameroon	50	38	10	26	2	3	18	4	2	NA
Gabon[4]	47	63	58	63	60	127	142	143	229	NA
Trinidad and Tobago	45	40	23	48	67	64	49	56	62	76
Libya#	43	61	68	84	66	44	18	0	0	0
Indonesia[5]	33	15	16	15	16	19	34	36	64	98
Argentina	29	53	29	33	29	56	59	53	44	NA
Norway	25	58	30	56	98	119	143	302	258	96
Chad	18	65	102	77	95	74	57	NA	NA	NA
Non-OPEC imports	**4,661**	**4,658**	**4,369**	**4,643**	**5,335**	**5,310**	**5,046**	**4,526**	**3,660**	**NA**
OPEC imports	**4,553**	**4,355**	**5,415**	**5,388**	**4,783**	**4,816**	**5,042**	**4,544**	**3,570**	**3,514**
Persian Gulf imports	**1,694**	**1,656**	**2,340**	**2,115**	**2,160**	**2,207**	**2,400**	**2,409**	**1,479**	**1,801**
TOTAL	**9,213**	**9,013**	**9,783**	**10,031**	**10,118**	**10,126**	**10,088**	**9,071**	**7,230**	**5,894**

= OPEC member. NA = Not available. (1) Angola became a member of OPEC as of Jan. 1, 2007, and is not included in OPEC totals from before that year. (2) May include oil from USSR states before 1992. (3) Ecuador suspended its OPEC membership Dec. 1992-Nov. 2007. Ecuador's imports between 1993 and 2007, inclusive, appear in non-OPEC totals. (4) Gabon withdrew from OPEC Dec. 31, 1994. Imports after Jan. 1, 1995, appear in non-OPEC totals. (5) Indonesia withdrew from OPEC in Jan. 2009. Imports after 2008 appear in non-OPEC totals.

U.S. Coal Production and Consumption, 1950-2010

Source: *Annual Energy Review 2010*, Energy Information Administration (EIA), U.S. Dept. of Energy

(in thousand short tons)

Year	Coal production[1]			Coal consumption				
	Surface mining	Underground mining	Total production	Residential	Commercial	Industrial	Electric power[2]	Total consumption
1950	139,388	421,000	560,388	51,562	63,021	224,637	91,871	494,102
1960	141,745	292,584	434,329	24,159	16,789	177,402	176,685	398,081
1970	272,131	340,530	612,661	9,024	7,090	186,637	320,182	523,231
1975	361,174	293,467	654,641	2,823	6,587	147,244	405,962	562,640
1980	492,192	337,508	829,700	1,355	5,097	127,004	569,274	702,730
1985	532,838	350,800	883,638	1,711	6,068	116,429	693,841	818,049
1990	604,529	424,546	1,029,076	1,345	5,379	115,207	782,567	904,498
1995	636,725	396,249	1,032,974	755	5,052	106,067	850,230	962,104
2000	699,953	373,659	1,073,612	454	3,673	94,147	985,821	1,084,095
2005	762,887	368,612	1,131,498	378	4,342	83,774	1,037,485	1,125,978
2006	803,728	359,022	1,162,750	290	2,936	82,429	1,026,636	1,112,292
2007	794,845	351,790	1,146,635	353	3,173	79,331	1,045,141	1,127,998
2008	814,729	357,079	1,171,809	351	3,155	76,463	1,040,580	1,120,548
2009	742,862	332,062	1,074,923	353	2,857	60,641	933,627	997,478
2010[3] . . .	747,876	337,405	1,085,281	339	2,741	69,628	975,588	1,048,295

(1) A small amount of refuse recovery has been included in coal production figures since 2001. (2) Electricity-only and combined-heat-and-power (CHP) plants whose primary business is to sell electricity, or electricity and heat, to the public. Through 1988, data are for electric utilities only; beginning in 1989, data are for electric utilities and independent power producers. (3) Estimated or based on preliminary figures.

World Nuclear Power Summary, 2010

Source: *Nuclear Power Reactors in the World*, International Atomic Energy Agency; as of Dec. 31, 2010

Country	Reactors in operation		Reactors under construction		Nuclear electricity supplied in 2008		Total operating experience[2]	
	No. of units	Total MW(e)	No. of units	Total MW(e)	TW(e).h[1]	% of nation's total	Years	Months
Argentina	2	935	1	692	6.7	5.9	64	7
Armenia	1	375	—	—	2.3	39.4	36	8
Belgium	7	5,926	—	—	45.7	51.2	240	7
Brazil	2	1,884	1	1,245	13.9	3.1	39	3
Bulgaria	2	1,906	2	1,906	14.2	33.1	149	3
Canada	18	12,569	—	—	85.5	15.1	600	2
China	13	10,058	28	27,230	71.0	1.8	111	2
Czech Republic	6	3,678	—	—	26.4	33.3	116	10
Finland	4	2,716	1	1,600	21.9	28.4	127	4
France	58	63,130	1	1,600	410.1	74.1	1,758	4
Germany	17	20,490	—	—	133.0	28.4	768	5
Hungary	4	1,889	—	—	14.7	42.1	102	2
India	19	4,189	6	3,766	20.5	2.8	337	3
Iran	0	0	1	915	—	—	—	—
Japan	54	46,821	2	2,650	280.2	29.2	1,494	8
Korea, South	21	18,698	5	5,560	141.9	32.2	360	1
Mexico	2	1,300	—	—	5.6	3.6	37	11
Netherlands	1	482	—	—	3.8	3.4	66	0
Pakistan	2	425	1	300	2.6	2.6	49	10
Romania	2	1,300	—	—	10.7	19.5	17	11
Russia	32	22,693	11	9,153	159.4	17.1	1,026	5
Slovakia	4	1,816	2	782	13.5	51.8	136	7
Slovenia	1	666	—	—	5.4	37.3	29	3
South Africa	2	1,800	—	—	12.9	5.2	52	3
Spain	8	7,514	—	—	59.3	20.1	277	6
Sweden	10	9,303	—	—	55.7	38.1	382	6
Switzerland	5	3,238	—	—	25.3	38.0	179	11
Taiwan	6	4,982	2	2,600	39.9	19.3	176	1
Ukraine	15	13,107	2	1,900	84.0	48.1	383	6
United Kingdom	19	10,137	—	—	56.8	15.7	1,476	8
United States	104	101,240	1	1,165	807.1	19.6	3,603	11
Total	**441**	**375,267**	**67**	**64,064**	**2,629.9**		**14,353**	**4**

MW(e) = Megawatt electricity. (1) 1 terawatt-hour [TW(e).h] = 10^6 megawatt-hour [MW(e).h]. For an average power plant, 1 TW(e).h = 0.39 megatons of coal equivalent (input) and 0.23 megatons of oil equivalent (input). (2) Through Dec. 31, 2010. Also includes shutdown plants for countries not listed here: Italy (81 years), Kazakhstan (25 years, 10 months), and Lithuania (43 years, 6 months).

Nations Most Reliant on Nuclear Energy, 2010

Source: *Nuclear Share in Electricity Generation*, International Atomic Energy Agency
(nuclear electricity generation as % of total electricity generated)

Rank	Country	Nuclear share	Rank	Country	Nuclear share	Rank	Country	Nuclear share	Rank	Country	Nuclear share
1.	France	74.1%	9.	Slovenia	37.3%	16.	Spain	20.1%	23.	South Africa	5.2%
2.	Slovakia	51.8	10.	Czech Republic	33.3	17.	United States	19.6	24.	Mexico	3.6
3.	Belgium	51.2	11.	Bulgaria	33.1	18.	Romania	19.5	25.	Netherlands	3.4
4.	Ukraine	48.1	12.	South Korea	32.2	19.	Russia	17.1	26.	Brazil	3.1
5.	Hungary	42.1	13.	Japan	29.2	20.	United Kingdom	15.7	27.	India	2.8
6.	Armenia	39.4	14.	Finland	28.4	21.	Canada	15.1	28.	Pakistan	2.6
7.	Sweden	38.1	15.	Germany	22.6	22.	Argentina	5.9	29.	China	1.8
8.	Switzerland	38.0									

U.S. Nuclear Reactors and Power Plant Operations, 1955-2010

Source: *Annual Energy Review 2010*, Energy Information Administration (EIA), U.S. Dept. of Energy

	Number of reactor units								Nuclear electricity generation (bil net KW-hrs)[6]	Nuclear share of domestic electricity generation[6]
Years	Ordered[1]	Cancelled	Construction permits[2]	Low-power licensed[3]	Full-power licensed[4]	Shutdown[5]	Operable units[6]	Capacity factor[6,7]		
1955-59	14	0	8	2	2	0	2	NA	0.2	NA
1960-64	7	0	12	13	12	1	13	NA	3.3	0.3%
1965-69	81	0	50	8	9	5	17	NA	13.9	1.0
1970-74	143	16	59	41	41	3	55	47.8%	114.0	6.1
1975-79	13	43	48	17	17	3	69	58.4	255.2	11.3
1980-84	0	54	0	24	19	1	87	56.3	327.6	13.5
1985-89	0	7	0	24	28	4	111	62.2	529.4	17.8
1990-94	0	15	0	49	58	9	109	73.8	640.4	19.7
1995-99	0	2	0	1	1	6	104	85.3	728.3	19.7
2000-04	0	0	0	0	0	0	104	90.1	788.5	19.9
2005-09	0	0	0	0	0	0	104	90.3	798.9	20.2
2010	0	0	0	0	0	0	104	91.2	807.0	19.6
Total	**259**	**124**	**177**	**132**	**132**	**28**				

NA = Not applicable. **Note:** Revised permit/license procedures eliminate the historical categories shown. According to Senate testimony, the Nuclear Regulatory Commission anticipates 16 or more new "combined license applications" over the next few years—the first of which was submitted Sept. 25, 2007—which may amount to 25 or more new reactor units. (1) Order placed by a utility or government agency for a nuclear steam supply system. (2) Permits issued in a given period, not extant permits. (3) Licenses granted to conduct testing. (4) Licenses granted for full-power operation. (5) Permanently ceased operation. (6) As of the last year of designated period. (7) The ratio of electric energy produced to the amount that could be produced at continuous full power operation.

U.S. Nuclear Reactors Generating the Most Electricity, 2009

Source: U.S. Nuclear Statistics Database, Energy Information Administration (EIA), U.S. Dept. of Energy
(in thousand net megawatt-hours)

Rank	Reactor, location	Electricity generated	Capacity[1]	Rank	Reactor, location	Electricity generated	Capacity[1]
1.	Palo Verde-1, Wintersburg, AZ	11,590	101%	14.	Peach Bottom-2, Lancaster, PA	9,942	101%
2.	South Texas-2, Bay City, TX . . .	11,304	101	15.	Nine Mile Point-2, Oswego, NY	9,922	99
3.	Grand Gulf-1, Port Gibson, MS	10,999	100	16.	San Onofre-3,		
4.	Comanche Peak-1,				San Clemente, CA	9,835	104
	Glen Rose, TX	10,641	100	17.	Braidwood-1, Braidwood, IL . . .	9,826	95
5.	Susquehanna-1, Berwick, PA	10,476	101	18.	LaSalle-1, Seneca, IL.	9,701	99
6.	Millstone-3, Waterford, CT	10,418	96	19.	Hope Creek-1, Salem, NJ	9,700	95
7.	Callaway-1, Fulton, MO . . . . :	10,247	98	20.	Byron-1, Byron, IL.	9,609	94
8.	Salem-1, Salem, NJ	10,222	99	21.	Palo Verde-3, Wintersburg, AZ	9,563	83
9.	Vogtle-2, Waynesboro, GA	10,151	101	22.	Palo Verde-2, Wintersburg, AZ	9,510	83
10.	Byron-2, Byron, IL.	10,109	102	23.	Comanche Peak-2,		
11.	South Texas-1, Bay City, TX . . .	10,052	90		Glen Rose, TX	9,501	94
12.	Limerick-1, Pottstown, PA	10,019	101	24.	Salem-2, Salem, NJ	9,428	93
13.	McGuire-1, Cowens Ford			25.	Braidwood-2, Braidwood, IL . . .	9,402	93
	Dam, NC	9,999	104				

(1) The ratio of power generated to the maximum potential generation expressed as a percentage.

Renewable Energy Sources

Source: U.S. Department of Energy

Concern over the environmental impact of burning fossil fuels has helped spur interest in alternative fuels that are less polluting. And because the supply of fossil fuels is finite and diminishing, there is interest in "renewable" sources that do not deplete existing supplies. However, renewable energy sources still make up only a small share of U.S. domestic energy production (about 8% in 2010). The main reason for this is their relatively higher cost (in some cases two to four times that of power obtained from traditional fuels). The following are the major renewable energy sources available.

Biomass is plant-derived material usable as an energy source, including wood energy crops such as hybrid poplars and willow trees, agricultural crops including soybeans and corn, and animal and other wastes. Biomass is one of the two most common renewable energy sources in the U.S. today, along with hydropower. Biomass such as wood can be burned to produce heat and generate electricity. Agricultural crops can be chemically converted into fuels such as ethanol and biodiesel; these are the only known renewable liquid energy sources and may one day replace petroleum and fossil-fuel produced diesel. But bringing ethanol and biodiesel into wide use would require more energy-efficient methods of production and transportation. Overall, biomass fuels burn much cleaner than fossil fuels, though biomass fuels still produce carbon dioxide and other pollutants.

Geothermal energy is generated from heat inside of Earth. This form of energy is both clean and renewable. The technology has caught on in countries with substantial geothermal activity such as Iceland, where it accounted for 66% of primary energy use in 2009. In the U.S., the best sources for geothermal power are in the West, where there are many underground heated lakes. Large-scale access, however, would require drilling. A major goal in this field is to find a way to harness energy directly from magma (molten rock material), which has great potential because of its high temperature.

Hydrogen is the third most abundant element on Earth. It does not naturally occur on Earth as a pure gas or liquid but is always combined with other elements (such as with oxygen, to form water, or carbon, to form methane). For energy use, it is produced from hydrocarbons using heat, from bacteria or algae through photosynthesis, or by using sunlight or electricity to split water into hydrogen and oxygen.

Hydrogen batteries, or fuel cells, were used by NASA's space shuttles. In a fuel cell, electrons are released from hydrogen atoms in a chemical reaction and flow through an external circuit as electricity. The protons combine with oxygen (and some of the electrons in the electric current) to make heat and water suitable for drinking. Fuel cells do not run down but work as long as hydrogen is supplied. Some experts think hydrogen will be the power source of the future. However, an infrastructure would need to be created for safe and cost-effective transportation and storage of hydrogen.

Hydropower, or hydroelectric power, is generated by water flowing through turbines. Along with biomass fuels, it is one of the two most common renewable energy sources in the U.S. today. A dam on a river is a common hydropower producer. No harmful greenhouse gases are produced, but the dams needed to generate the power can harm river ecosystems. Researchers are working on turbine technologies to maximize use of hydropower and reduce adverse environmental effects.

Ocean energy can be generated in two ways. Thermal ocean energy uses heat that the ocean absorbs from the sun to power generators, sometimes producing drinkable desalinated water as a by-product. Mechanical ocean energy is generated by the movement of tides and waves through a turbine. In both cases, power generation is not very efficient with current technology. Much more research is needed to make thermal ocean energy generation a reality. Mechanical ocean energy requires the building of large dams or breakwater-type structures called tidal barrages, which could harm coastal ecosystems.

Solar energy is generated using heat and light from the sun. Solar energy is an increasingly common source of electricity. Photovoltaic (PV) solar cells are made of semiconducting materials that can directly convert sunlight to electricity without producing any harmful waste. Arrays of mirrors can concentrate the sun's rays onto PV panels, making solar collectors more efficient. Sunlight can also be used to heat water directly. According to the Dept. of Energy, homes incorporating solar heating designs can save as much as 50% on heating bills. The downside to solar energy is that it depends heavily on a range of factors including location, time of year, and weather.

Wind energy uses wind turbines to produce energy. They are perched on high towers, usually 100 ft or higher, and often placed in large groups ("farms") to generate electricity for towns and cities. Farmers and homeowners sometimes use stand-alone turbines to generate supplemental electricity. In the past 20 years, tax credits to producers and government incentives for homeowners have helped lower the price of wind power by 85%, making it a more feasible option. Some people object to wind farms, however, because of their appearance or the noise the turbines make. Wind power raises few other environmental problems, but the turbines can pose a danger to birds. In addition, because weather is involved, consistent energy generation can be a challenge.

CRIME

Measuring Crime

The U.S. Dept. of Justice administers two statistical programs to measure trends in crime in the U.S. Because of differences in focus and methodology, their results are not strictly comparable.

The Federal Bureau of Investigation (FBI) conducts the **Uniform Crime Report (UCR)** program, which aims to provide statistics for law enforcement administration, operation, and management. It collects actual counts on the crimes of homicide, forcible rape, robbery, aggravated assault, burglary, larceny-theft, motor vehicle theft, and arson as they are reported to law enforcement authorities. Each year, the program releases a preliminary report in the spring, followed by a more detailed, final report in the fall.

The **National Crime Victimization Survey (NCVS)** is conducted annually by the Bureau of Justice Statistics through interviews with members of a nationally representative sample of households about their experiences with crime. The survey complements the UCR by providing alternative and previously unavailable information, including information about the victims of crime and their offenders (e.g., age, sex, ethnicity, victim-offender relationship) and information on crimes not reported to law enforcement. In contrast to the UCR, the NCVS does not cover homicide, arson, commercial crimes, or crimes against children under age 12.

Further explanation of the UCR and NCVS is available at bjs.ojp.usdoj.gov/content/pub/pdf/ntcm.pdf.

Uniform Crime Report, 2010

Source: *Crime in the United States, 2010*, Federal Bureau of Investigation, U.S. Dept. of Justice

In 2010, more than 18,000 city, county, college and university, state, tribal, and federal agencies—representing more than 308 mil people—voluntarily participated in the UCR program.

Although crime tends to rise in hard economic times, the number of reported violent crimes dropped 6.0% between 2009 and 2010, marking the fourth straight year violent crime declined. The number of property crimes reported was also down, by 2.7% from 2009, making it the eighth year in a row property crime reports declined.

The biggest decrease in violent crime was in robberies, down 10.0 percent from 2009. However, the total amount lost by victims of all property crimes, excluding arson, increased slightly from 2009 levels to $15.7 bil. Although arson is considered a property crime, it is not included in estimates of totals because of variations in the level of participation by reporting agencies.

Additional highlights from the 2010 report:

- Males accounted for 78% of all murder victims whose gender was known. Men committed 90% of the murders in which the offender's gender was known.
- Firearms were known to be used in 68% of all murders.
- Of the 7,272 murder victims whose relation to the offender was known, 24.8% were killed by a family member, and 22.2% were killed by a stranger. The other 53% were killed by an acquaintance (e.g., friend, neighbor, employee, romantic partner). Wives were more than five times as likely to kill their spouses as husbands; girlfriends were responsible for almost four times as many murders as boyfriends.
- The majority of property crimes reported were larceny-thefts (68%). Excluding motor vehicle thefts, 26% of all larceny-thefts involved items taken from motor vehicles (except for accessories), 17% were shoplifting, 11% were from buildings, and 3% were of bikes.

National Crime Victimization Survey, 2010

Source: *Criminal Victimization, 2010*, Bureau of Justice Statistics, U.S. Dept. of Justice

Victimizations of U.S. residents age 12 and over continued to decline to historic lows, according to the NCVS estimates for 2010. The violent crime rate—14.9 victimizations per 1,000 persons—was down sharply from the 2009 estimate of 17.1, and has dropped more than 40 percent since 2001. The property crime rate fell a bit more gradually to 120 victimizations per 1,000 households from 127 in 2009

and 167 in 2001. After declining 38% in 2009 from 2008, the numbers of rapes or sexual assaults increased nearly 50% in 2010. The Bureau of Justice Statistics cautions that rape and sexual assault statistics are based on a small number of incidents. The NCVS does not include figures for murders because published data are based on victim interviews.

Criminal Victimization, 2001-10

Source: *Criminal Victimization, 2010*, Bureau of Justice Statistics, U.S. Dept. of Justice

A crime committed against an individual or single household counts as one **victimization**. Because a personal crime may involve more than one victim, the number of victimizations may be greater than the number of personal crime incidents. In property crimes, the affected household is considered one victim.

Victimization rates measure the frequency with which victimizations occur. Personal crime victimization rates are based on the number of victimizations per 1,000 persons in the total population age 12 and over. Property crime victimization rates are calculated per 1,000 of total households.

| | Number of victimizations | | | Percent change | | Average annual change, |
Type of crime	2001	2009	2010	2001-10	2009-10	2001-09
All crimes	24,215,700	20,057,180	18,725,710	−22.7%	−6.6%	−2.1%
Crimes of violence[1]	5,743,820	4,343,450	3,817,380	−33.5	−12.1	−3.1
Rape/sexual assault[2]	248,250	125,920	188,380	−24.1	49.6	−7.5
Robbery	630,690	533,790	480,750	−23.8	−9.9	−1.9
Assault	4,864,890	3,683,750	3,148,250	−35.3	−14.5	−3.1
Aggravated	1,222,160	823,340	725,180	−40.7	−11.9	−4.4
Simple	3,642,720	2,860,410	2,423,060	−33.5	−15.3	−2.7
Personal theft[3]	188,370	133,210	138,340	−26.6	3.9	−3.9
Property crimes	18,283,510	15,580,520	14,769,990	−19.2	−5.2	−1.8
Household burglary	3,139,700	3,134,930	2,923,430	−6.9	−6.7	<0.5
Motor vehicle theft	1,008,730	735,770	606,990	−39.8	−17.5	−3.5
Theft	14,135,090	11,709,830	11,239,560	−20.5	−4.0	−2.1
Total population age 12 and over	229,215,290	254,105,610	255,961,940			
Total households	109,568,450	122,327,660	122,885,160			

Note: Details may not add up to totals due to rounding. (1) Excludes murder because the NCVS is based on interviews with victims. (2) Includes male as well as female victims and both heterosexual and homosexual rape. (3) Includes pocket picking, completed purse snatching, and attempted purse snatching.

Crime in the U.S., 1989-2010

Source: *Crime in the United States, 2010,* Federal Bureau of Investigation, U.S. Dept. of Justice

In the FBI's Uniform Crime Reporting (UCR) Program, offenses are classified as **violent crimes** if they involve force or the threat of force: murder and nonnegligent manslaughter, forcible rape, robbery, and aggravated assault. The following offenses are considered **property crimes**: burglary, larceny-theft, motor vehicle theft, and arson. Arson data is excluded from this table because of variations in the level of participation by reporting agencies. That data is presented separately online at www.fbi.gov/ucr/ucr.htm.

		Violent crime				Property crime			
Year(s)	Population[1]	All violent crimes	Murder & nonnegligent manslaughter	Forcible rape[2]	Robbery	Aggravated assault[3]	All property crimes	Burglary	Larceny-theft[4]	Motor vehicle theft
NUMBER OF OFFENSES										
1989	246,819,230	1,646,037	21,500	94,504	578,326	951,707	12,605,412	3,168,170	7,705,872	7,872,442
1990	249,464,396	1,820,127	23,438	102,555	639,271	1,054,863	12,655,486	3,073,909	7,945,670	1,635,907
1995	262,803,276	1,798,792	21,606	97,470	580,509	1,099,207	12,063,935	2,593,784	7,997,710	1,472,441
1997	267,783,607	1,636,096	18,208	96,153	498,534	1,023,201	11,558,475	2,460,526	7,743,760	1,354,189
1998	270,248,003	1,533,887	16,974	93,144	447,186	976,583	10,951,827	2,332,735	7,376,311	1,242,781
1999	272,690,813	1,426,044	15,522	89,411	409,371	911,740	10,208,334	2,100,739	6,955,520	1,152,075
2000	281,421,906	1,425,486	15,586	90,178	408,016	911,706	10,182,584	2,050,992	6,971,590	1,160,002
2001[5]	285,317,559	1,439,480	16,037	90,863	423,557	909,023	10,437,189	2,116,531	7,092,267	1,228,391
2002	287,973,924	1,423,677	16,229	95,235	420,806	891,407	10,455,277	2,151,252	7,057,379	1,246,646
2003	290,788,976	1,383,676	16,528	93,883	414,235	859,030	10,442,862	2,154,834	7,026,802	1,261,226
2004	293,656,842	1,360,088	16,148	95,089	401,470	847,381	10,319,386	2,144,446	6,937,089	1,237,851
2005	296,507,061	1,390,745	16,740	94,347	417,438	862,220	10,174,754	2,155,448	6,783,447	1,235,859
2006	299,398,484	1,435,123	17,309	94,472	449,246	874,096	10,019,601	2,194,993	6,626,363	1,198,245
2007	301,621,157	1,422,970	17,128	92,160	447,324	866,358	9,882,212	2,190,198	6,591,542	1,100,472
2008	304,059,724	1,394,461	16,465	90,750	443,563	843,683	9,774,152	2,228,887	6,586,206	959,059
2009	307,006,550	1,325,896	15,399	89,241	408,742	812,514	9,337,060	2,203,313	6,338,095	795,652
2010	308,745,538	1,246,248	14,748	84,767	367,832	778,901	9,082,887	2,159,878	6,185,867	737,142
PERCENT CHANGE: NUMBER OF OFFENSES										
2010/2009.........		−6.0%	−4.2%	−5.0%	−10.0%	−4.1%	−2.7%	−2.0%	−2.4%	−7.4%
2010/2006.........		−13.2	−14.8	−10.3	−18.1	−10.9	−9.3	−1.6	−6.6	−38.5
2010/2001.........		−13.4	−8.0	−6.7	−13.2	−14.3	−13.0	2.0	−12.8	−40.0
RATE PER 100,000 RESIDENTS										
1989		666.9	8.7	38.3	234.3	385.6	5,107.1	1,283.6	3,189.6	634.0
1990		729.6	9.4	41.1	256.3	422.9	5,073.1	1,232.2	3,185.1	655.8
1995		684.5	8.2	37.1	220.9	418.3	4,590.5	987.0	3,043.2	560.3
1997		611.0	6.8	35.9	186.2	382.1	4,316.3	918.8	2,891.8	505.7
1998		567.6	6.3	34.5	165.5	361.4	4,052.5	863.2	2,729.5	459.9
1999		523.0	5.7	32.8	150.1	334.3	3,743.6	770.4	2,550.7	422.5
2000		506.5	5.5	32.0	145.0	324.0	3,618.3	728.8	2,477.3	412.2
2001		504.5	5.6[5]	31.8	148.5	318.6	3,658.1	741.8	2,485.7	430.5
2002		494.4	5.6	33.1	146.1	309.5	3,630.6	747.0	2,450.7	432.9
2003		475.8	5.7	32.3	142.5	295.4	3,591.2	741.0	2,416.5	433.7
2004		463.2	5.5	32.4	136.7	288.6	3,514.1	730.3	2,362.3	421.5
2005		469.0	5.6	31.8	140.8	290.8	3,431.5	726.9	2,287.8	416.8
2006		479.3	5.8	31.6	150.0	292.0	3,346.6	733.1	2,213.2	400.2
2007		471.8	5.7	30.6	148.3	287.2	3,276.4	726.1	2,185.4	364.9
2008		458.6	5.4	29.8	145.9	277.5	3,214.6	733.0	2,166.1	315.4
2009		431.9	5.0	29.1	133.1	264.7	3,041.3	717.7	2,064.5	259.2
2010		403.6	4.8	27.5	119.1	252.3	2,941.9	699.6	2,003.5	238.8
PERCENT CHANGE: RATE PER 100,000 RESIDENTS										
2010/2009.........		−6.5%	−4.8%	−5.5%	−10.5%	−4.7%	−3.3%	−2.5%	−3.0%	−7.9%
2010/2006.........		−15.8	−17.4	−13.0	−20.6	−13.6	−12.1	−4.6	−9.5	−40.3
2010/2001.........		−20.0	−15.0	−13.8	−19.7	−20.8	−19.6	−5.7	−19.4	−44.5

Note: Figures for 2006-10 have been revised from previous reports. (1) U.S. Census Bureau estimates for July 1 of each year except for 1990 and 2000, which show Apr. 1 decennial census counts. (2) Does not include statutory rape (i.e., rape not involving force) and other offenses of a sexual nature. Also does not include sexual attacks on males, which are considered aggravated assaults or sex offenses, depending on circumstances and extent of injuries. (3) Attack upon another with the intent of doing serious bodily harm; usually accompanied by the use of a weapon or other means likely to produce death or great bodily harm. (4) The unlawful taking of another's property not involving force or fraud (e.g., theft of motor vehicle parts, shoplifting). Excludes crimes such as embezzlement and check fraud. (5) The murder and nonnegligent homicides that occurred as a result of the Sept. 11, 2001, terrorist attacks are not included.

Law Enforcement Civilian Employees and Officers, 2010

Source: *Crime in the United States, 2010; Law Enforcement Officers Killed and Assaulted, 2009;* Federal Bureau of Investigation, U.S. Dept. of Justice

As of Oct. 31, 2010, 14,744 city, county, state, college and university, and tribal agencies around the country collectively employed 1,013,608 full-time law enforcement workers. About 69.6% of employees were sworn officers. The FBI's UCR program defines a sworn **law enforcement officer** as a person who ordinarily carries a firearm and badge, has full arrest powers, and is paid from government funds specifically dedicated to law enforcement. Civilians (e.g., clerks, radio dispatchers, correctional officers) made up the remaining 30.4% of law enforcement employees.

Altogether, they provided service to an estimated 291.4 mil people around the country, meaning there were 3.5 full-time law enforcement employees (civilian and sworn officers) and 2.4 sworn officers per 1,000 residents.

The great majority of sworn officers (88.2%) are male, but females make up 60.8% of civilian employees. Not surprisingly, the most populous state, California, employed the greatest number of full-time law enforcement workers (118,884). Washington, DC, had the highest rate, with 7.4 full-time law enforcement employees (and 6.6 sworn officers) for every 1,000 residents in its population.

Nationwide, 48 law enforcement officers were killed in the line of duty in 2009, the latest year for which data is available. Of that number, 15 died in ambush situations, 8 were attacked during arrests, 8 were performing traffic stops, 5 were killed during tactical situations, and 4 died while investigating suspicious persons or circumstances. Almost all (45 of the 48 officers) were killed with firearms. The majority of these firearms (28) were handguns. Another 47 officers died accidentally while performing official duties.

U.S. Crime Rates by Region, Geographic Division, and State, 2010

Source: *Crime in the United States, 2010*, Federal Bureau of Investigation, U.S. Dept. of Justice

(per 100,000 population, as estimated by U.S. Census Bureau for July 1 of year)

	Violent crime					Property crime[1]			
	All violent crime	Murder and nonnegligent manslaughter	Forcible rape[2]	Robbery	Aggravated assault[3]	All property crime	Burglary	Larceny-theft[4]	Motor vehicle theft
Total U.S.[5,6,7]	403.6	4.8	27.5	119.1	252.3	2,941.9	699.6	2,003.5	238.8
Northeast	357.0	4.2	19.4	124.4	209.1	2,115.8	423.2	1,555.9	136.7
New England	331.9	2.9	24.6	84.1	220.3	2,320.5	520.8	1,640.8	158.9
Connecticut	281.4	3.6	16.3	99.4	162.0	2,193.2	424.5	1,581.0	187.7
Maine	122.0	1.8	29.3	31.2	59.8	2,479.3	554.0	1,850.8	74.5
Massachusetts	466.6	3.2	26.7	105.0	331.8	2,350.5	576.8	1,598.8	174.9
New Hampshire	167.0	1.0	31.3	34.3	100.4	2,186.3	413.3	1,699.5	73.5
Rhode Island	256.6	2.8	28.1	74.1	151.6	2,556.6	581.5	1,747.2	227.9
Vermont	130.2	1.1	21.1	11.8	96.2	2,282.3	537.9	1,673.9	70.5
Middle Atlantic	365.9	4.6	17.5	138.6	205.1	2,043.5	388.7	1,525.9	128.8
New Jersey	307.7	4.2	11.2	134.4	157.9	2,081.9	440.5	1,464.5	176.9
New York	392.1	4.5	14.3	146.9	226.4	1,941.2	335.3	1,500.4	105.4
Pennsylvania	366.2	5.2	26.9	128.8	205.3	2,173.0	434.3	1,607.4	131.2
Midwest[5,6]	362.5	4.4	31.1	107.7	219.3	2,833.6	668.6	1,958.5	206.5
East North Central[5,6]	377.4	4.7	30.9	126.6	215.2	2,857.4	709.7	1,935.4	212.2
Illinois[5,6]	435.2	5.5	23.6	156.3	249.7	2,681.0	587.6	1,868.9	224.4
Indiana	314.5	4.5	27.2	95.9	186.9	3,042.4	726.7	2,113.4	202.3
Michigan	490.3	5.7	47.3	116.3	321.0	2,713.6	747.4	1,689.5	276.8
Ohio	315.2	4.1	32.1	142.8	136.2	3,245.2	923.3	2,138.8	183.1
Wisconsin	248.7	2.7	20.9	79.2	145.9	2,507.7	467.1	1,897.5	143.1
West North Central[6]	328.9	3.6	31.6	65.1	228.6	2,779.6	575.4	2,010.6	193.6
Iowa	273.5	1.3	27.4	33.2	211.6	2,242.5	546.8	1,571.8	124.0
Kansas	369.1	3.5	38.8	54.1	272.7	3,119.9	680.1	2,229.2	210.6
Minnesota[6]	236.0	1.8	33.9	63.9	136.4	2,572.3	460.3	1,950.0	161.9
Missouri	455.0	7.0	23.9	102.4	321.7	3,346.4	735.4	2,343.0	268.0
Nebraska	279.5	3.0	36.8	56.1	183.6	2,673.2	455.9	2,019.4	197.9
North Dakota	225.0	1.5	35.2	13.4	174.8	1,768.5	292.3	1,348.5	127.7
South Dakota	268.5	2.8	47.9	18.9	198.9	1,852.4	390.7	1,364.1	97.6
South[7]	452.0	5.6	27.9	122.4	296.1	3,438.8	886.4	2,315.1	237.3
South Atlantic[7]	454.1	5.6	24.4	128.4	295.8	3,331.2	843.7	2,251.3	236.2
Delaware	620.9	5.3	34.7	203.7	377.1	3,448.2	836.9	2,396.5	214.8
District of Columbia[7]	1,330.2	21.9	31.1	718.8	558.4	4,778.9	703.1	3,238.9	836.9
Florida	542.4	5.2	28.6	138.7	369.8	3,558.4	899.5	2,438.4	220.5
Georgia	403.3	5.8	21.6	127.7	248.2	3,640.5	998.4	2,329.3	312.8
Maryland	547.7	7.4	21.3	191.5	327.5	2,997.4	632.9	2,051.7	312.6
North Carolina	363.4	5.0	21.1	100.8	236.5	3,447.3	1,076.9	2,178.4	192.0
South Carolina	597.7	6.1	31.7	107.7	452.3	3,900.4	997.9	2,617.2	285.3
Virginia	213.6	4.6	19.1	70.7	119.1	2,327.2	382.8	1,812.5	131.8
West Virginia	314.6	3.3	19.1	44.7	247.5	2,239.6	580.5	1,531.7	127.4
East South Central	409.6	5.6	31.4	106.6	266.0	3,252.4	906.1	2,145.6	200.8
Alabama	377.8	5.7	28.2	99.6	244.2	3,516.8	879.4	2,415.6	221.8
Kentucky	242.6	4.3	31.8	86.4	120.1	2,551.3	698.5	1,709.7	143.1
Mississippi	269.7	7.0	31.2	93.7	137.8	2,985.0	1,026.0	1,778.4	180.6
Tennessee	613.3	5.6	33.7	131.8	442.2	3,657.9	1,012.2	2,411.9	233.8
West South Central	470.0	5.8	32.0	120.4	311.9	3,710.2	946.5	2,506.0	257.7
Arkansas	505.3	4.7	45.0	81.3	374.3	3,558.9	1,114.9	2,253.8	190.1
Louisiana	549.0	11.2	27.2	114.9	395.6	3,647.5	1,002.2	2,427.1	218.2
Oklahoma	479.5	5.2	38.7	89.0	346.7	3,415.5	999.0	2,144.8	271.6
Texas	450.3	5.0	30.3	130.6	284.4	3,783.0	909.1	2,603.3	270.5
West	400.8	4.2	29.5	120.6	246.4	2,886.5	643.4	1,893.6	349.5
Mountain	386.7	4.2	37.4	84.7	260.4	3,012.7	668.4	2,083.4	260.9
Arizona	408.1	6.4	33.9	108.5	259.3	3,534.0	794.3	2,403.2	336.5
Colorado	320.8	2.4	43.7	62.3	212.4	2,684.2	520.0	1,940.5	223.6
Idaho	221.0	1.3	33.5	13.7	172.6	1,995.8	414.8	1,496.7	84.3
Montana	272.2	2.6	32.4	15.9	221.2	2,543.8	369.3	2,020.3	154.2
Nevada	660.6	5.9	35.7	196.2	422.9	2,774.7	823.0	1,574.5	377.1
New Mexico	588.9	6.9	46.5	78.4	457.1	3,435.4	1,020.5	2,160.1	254.8
Utah	212.7	1.9	34.3	45.9	130.6	3,179.6	543.3	2,421.0	215.2
Wyoming	195.9	1.4	29.1	13.5	151.9	2,461.6	381.3	1,975.4	104.9
Pacific[2]	407.0	4.2	26.1	136.5	240.2	2,830.7	632.4	1,809.6	388.7
Alaska	638.8	4.4	75.0	83.6	475.8	2,852.5	437.2	2,187.3	228.0
California	440.6	4.9	22.4	156.0	257.4	2,635.8	614.3	1,612.1	409.4
Hawaii	262.7	1.8	26.8	77.5	156.7	3,314.2	636.8	2,302.4	374.9
Oregon[2]	252.0	2.4	31.7	62.4	155.6	3,012.9	512.6	2,267.7	232.6
Washington	313.8	2.3	38.1	88.2	185.3	3,706.6	820.3	2,503.7	382.6
Puerto Rico[8]	403.6	4.8	27.5	119.1	252.3	2,941.9	699.6	2,003.5	238.8

Note: Offense totals are based on all reporting agencies and estimates for unreported areas. Figures may not add up to totals due to rounding. (1) Data for arson, considered a property crime, are not included in this table. (2) Does not include statutory rape (i.e., rape not involving force) and other offenses of a sexual nature. Also does not include sexual attacks on males, which are considered aggravated assaults or sex offenses, depending on circumstances and extent of injuries. (3) Attack upon another with the intent of doing serious bodily harm; usually accompanied by the use of a weapon or other means likely to produce death or great bodily harm. (4) The unlawful taking of another's property not involving force or fraud (e.g., theft of motor vehicle parts, shoplifting). Excludes crimes such as embezzlement and check fraud. (5) Limited data available for Illinois. (6) Illinois and Minnesota—with the exception of Rockford, IL, and Minneapolis and St. Paul, MN—collect data on forcible rape offenses using methodology not consistent with national UCR guidelines. Forcible rape offenses in the two states, with the exception of the previously mentioned cities, have been estimated for inclusion in this table. (7) Includes offenses reported by the National Zoological Park Police and Washington Metro Transit Police. (8) Data are from 2009.

State and Federal Prison Population; Death Penalty, 2000-09

Source: *Prisoners in 2009*; *Capital Punishment, 2009*; Bureau of Justice Statistics, U.S. Dept. of Justice

As of Dec. 31, 2009, 1,613,740 prisoners were under the jurisdiction, or legal authority, of state (87.1%) or federal (12.9%) correctional authorities. The prison population increased by 0.2% over 2008 figures, the slowest growth in a decade, and down considerably from the 1.8% annual average growth recorded between 2000 and 2008. Jails, which are locally operated, typically hold persons awaiting trial or sentencing as well as those sentenced to one year or less.

The imprisonment rate, or number of prisoners per 100,000 U.S. residents, also declined slightly in 2009, from 504 to 502. That's still up significantly from 478 at year-end 2000. Black males (3,119 per 100,000 U.S. residents) were incarcerated at 6.4 times the rate of white males (487 per 100,000) and 2.6 times the rate of Hispanic males (1,193 per 100,000).

There were 3,173 persons under sentence of death at year-end 2009; 52 persons were executed (nearly half of them by Texas), 27 died of other causes, and 70 were removed from death row. A total of 112 inmates were received on death row in 2009, the lowest number since 1973. Since 2000, the death row population has decreased every year, but the composition has changed little: 98% were male; 56% were white, and 42% were black. The median age of this population was 43 years.

New Mexico repealed its death penalty law for crimes committed after July 1, 2009; the repeal was not retroactive. All 36 death penalty states authorize lethal injection as a method of execution; 9 also permit electrocution, 4 permit the gas chamber, 3 allow hanging, and 2 (Oklahoma and Utah) authorize firing squads.

	Prisoners				Death penalty[1]			Executed, as of 2009[2]	
Region/jurisdiction	Year-end 2000	Year-end 2008	Year-end 2009	% change 2008-09	Death penalty statute?	Under sentence of death, year-end 2009	Executed in 2009	Since 1930	Since 1977
U.S. total	1,391,261	1,609,759	1,613,740	0.4%	—	3,173	52	5,047[3]	1,188[3]
Federal[4]	145,416	201,280	208,118	2.7	Y	55	0	36	3
State	1,245,845	1,408,479	1,405,622	0.1	36[5]	3,118	52	4,971	1,185
Northeast	174,826	178,642	177,361	0.2	—	229	0	612	4
Connecticut[6]	18,355	20,661	19,716	-2.8	Y	10	0	22	1
Maine	1,679	2,195	2,206	-1.8	N	—	—	—	—
Massachusetts . .	10,722	11,408	11,316	-0.8	N	—	—	27	—
New Hampshire . .	2,257	2,702	2,731	-4.2	Y	1	0	1	0
New Jersey	29,784	25,953	25,382	-2.3	N	—	—	74	0
New York	70,199	60,347	58,687	-3.9	Y	0	0	329	0
Pennsylvania. . . .	36,847	49,215	51,429	9.1	Y	218	0	155	3
Rhode Island[6] . . .	3,286	4,045	3,674	-5.2	N	—	—	—	—
Vermont[6]	1,697	2,116	2,220	6.2	N	—	—	4	—
Midwest	237,378	264,314	261,603	0.3	—	268	7	539	136
Illinois	45,281	45,474	45,161	0.0	Y	16	0	102	12
Indiana	20,125	28,322	28,808	7.8	Y	14	1	60	20
Iowa[7].	7,955	8,766	8,813	-3.2	N	—	—	18	—
Kansas	8,344	8,539	8,641	0.4	Y	9	0	15	0
Michigan	47,718	48,738	45,478	-6.5	N	—	—	—	—
Minnesota	6,238	9,910	9,986	1.0	N	—	—	—	—
Missouri.	27,543	30,186	30,563	-0.1	Y	51	1	129	67
Nebraska.	3,895	4,520	4,474	2.3	Y	11	0	7	3
North Dakota. . . .	1,076	1,452	1,486	-0.8	N	—	—	—	—
Ohio	45,833	51,686	51,606	1.3	Y	165	5	205	33
South Dakota . . .	2,616	3,342	3,434	2.9	Y	2	0	2	1
Wisconsin	20,754	23,379	23,153	-0.8	N	—	—	—	—
South	561,214	647,312	649,535	0.4	—	1,656	45	3,244	978
Alabama	26,332	30,508	31,874	3.9	Y	200	6	173	44
Arkansas.	11,915	14,716	15,208	5.8	Y	40	0	145	27
Delaware[6]	6,921	7,075	6,794	-3.7	Y	17	0	26	14
Florida.	71,319	102,388	103,915	2.9	Y	389	2	238	68
Georgia[7]	44,232	52,719	53,371	0.8	Y	101	3	409	46
Kentucky.	14,919	21,706	21,638	-0.8	Y	35	0	106	3
Louisiana.	35,207	38,381	39,780	2.1	Y	83	0	160	27
Maryland	23,538	23,324	22,255	-1.5	Y	5	0	73	5
Mississippi.	20,241	22,754	21,482	-3.6	Y	60	0	164	10
North Carolina. . .	31,266	39,482	39,860	3.8	Y	159	0	306	43
Oklahoma	23,181	25,864	26,397	0.1	Y	79	3	151	91
South Carolina . .	21,778	24,326	24,288	-0.9	Y	55	2	204	42
Tennessee	22,166	27,228	26,965	1.2	Y	89	2	99	6
Texas	166,719	172,506	171,249	-1.8	Y	331	24	744	447
Virginia	30,168	38,276	38,092	-1.3	Y	13	3	197	105
West Virginia. . . .	3,856	6,059	6,367	2.8	N	—	—	40	—
West.	272,427	318,211	317,123	-0.2	—	965	0	576	67
Alaska[6]	4,173	5,014	5,285	-0.4	N	—	—	—	—
Arizona[7]	26,510	39,589	40,627	3.9	Y	131	0	61	23
California.	163,001	173,670	171,275	-1.9	Y	684	0	305	13
Colorado	16,833	23,274	22,795	0.8	Y	2	0	48	1
Hawaii[6]	5,053	5,955	5,891	-0.3	N	—	—	—	—
Idaho	5,535	7,290	7,400	-0.7	Y	14	0	4	1
Montana	3,105	3,545	3,605	2.0	Y	2	0	9	3
Nevada	10,063	12,743	12,482	-2.2	Y	80	0	41	12
New Mexico	5,342	6,402	6,519	3.2	N	2	0	9	1
Oregon	10,580	14,167	14,403	2.4	Y	31	0	21	2
Utah	5,637	6,552	6,533	-0.2	Y	10	0	19	6
Washington.	14,915	17,926	18,233	3.1	Y	8	0	51	4
Wyoming	1,680	2,084	2,075	2.7	Y	1	0	8	1

— = Not available or applicable. (1) Figures do not include persons held under Armed Forces jurisdiction with a military death sentence for murder. (2) Military authorities carried out an additional 160 executions between 1930 and 1961. (3) Total executed includes 40 executions performed under the District of Columbia's jurisdiction since 1930. (4) Prisoners sentenced under DC's criminal code are housed in federal facilities. (5) The death penalty is legally authorized by 36 states. (6) Prisons and jails form one integrated system. Data includes total jail and prison population. (7) Prisoner population based on custody count.

Prison Situation Under Correctional Authorities' Jurisdiction, 2009

Source: *Prisoners in 2009*, Bureau of Justice Statistics, U.S. Dept. of Justice

Largest prison populations		Imprisonment rates of sentenced prisoners		% change in prison population, 2008-09		Avg. annual % change in prison population, 2000-08	
Jurisdiction	Number	Jurisdiction	Rate[1]	Jurisdiction	% change	Jurisdiction	% change
U.S. total . . .	1,613,740	U.S. total . . .	502	U.S. total . . .	0.2%	U.S. total[2]. . . .	1.8%
Federal[2] . . .	208,118	Federal[2]	61	Federal[2]. . .	3.4	Federal[2]	4.1
State	1,405,622	State	442	State	−0.2	State	1.5
1. California . . .	171,275	1. Louisiana . . .	881	1. Alaska[4]	5.4	1. Minnesota	6.0
2. Texas	171,249	2. Mississippi . . .	702	2. West Virginia	5.1	2. West Virginia .	5.8
3. Florida	103,915	3. Oklahoma	657	3. Vermont[4]	4.9	3. Arizona[3]	5.1
4. New York . . .	58,687	4. Alabama	650	4. Pennsylvania	4.5	4. Kentucky	4.8
5. Georgia[3]	53,371	5. Texas	648	5. Alabama	4.5	5. Florida.	4.6
6. Ohio	51,606	6. Arizona[3]	580	6. Louisiana . . .	3.6	6. Indiana	4.4
7. Pennsylvania	51,429	7. Florida.	559	7. Arkansas. . . .	3.3	7. Colorado.	4.1
8. Michigan	45,478	8. Georgia[3]	526	8. South Dakota	2.8	8. North Dakota	3.8
9. Illinois	45,161	9. Arkansas. . . .	522	9. Arizona[3]	2.6	9. Pennsylvania	3.7
10. Arizona[3]	40,627	10. South Carolina	512	10. North Dakota	2.3	10. Oregon	3.7

Note: Prisoners as of Dec. 31, 2009; excludes jail population unless otherwise noted. (1) Prisoners sentenced to more than one year. Rates are per 100,000 population, based upon census population estimates for Jan. 1, 2010. (2) Federal totals include prisoners sentenced under DC's criminal code. (3) Population based on custody count (number of prisoners held in its facilities) as opposed to jurisdiction count (number of prisoners under its legal authority). Some states are unable to provide both counts. (4) Prisons and jails form one integrated system. Data includes total jail and prison population.

Arrests by Race, 2010

Source: *Crime in the United States, 2010*, Federal Bureau of Investigation, U.S. Dept. of Justice

Each instance in which a person is arrested, cited, or summoned for an offense is counted as one arrest. The figures below therefore do not represent the number of individuals arrested but the number of times persons were arrested, as an individual may be arrested multiple times in one year. Arrest estimates are based on statistics from law enforcement agencies that reported 12 months of arrest data.

Offense charged	Total	Number of arrests where arrestee was—				% distrib. for offense charged[1]			
		White	Black	Amer. Indian/ Alaska Native	Asian/ Pacific Islander	White	Black	Amer. Indian/ Alaska Native	Asian/ Pacific Islander
PART I OFFENSES[2]									
Violent crime	429,166	254,620	163,670	5,776	5,100	59.3%	38.1%	1.3%	1.2%
Murder and nonnegligent manslaughter	8,641	4,261	4,209	91	80	49.3	48.7	1.1	0.9
Forcible rape	15,503	10,178	4,925	214	186	65.7	31.8	1.4	1.2
Robbery	87,587	37,906	48,154	617	910	43.3	55.0	0.7	1.0
Aggravated assault	317,435	202,275	106,382	4,854	3,924	63.7	33.5	1.5	1.2
Property crime	1,288,295	881,420	372,562	17,080	17,233	68.4	28.9	1.3	1.3
Burglary	225,745	152,210	69,541	1,961	2,063	67.4	30.8	0.9	0.9
Larceny-theft	998,476	687,609	282,246	14,323	14,298	68.9	28.3	1.4	1.4
Motor vehicle theft	55,278	35,009	18,797	696	776	63.3	34.0	1.3	1.4
Arson	8,766	6,592	1,978	100	96	75.2	22.6	1.1	1.1
PART II OFFENSES[3]									
Other assaults[4]	1,004,273	659,171	318,117	14,848	12,137	65.6	31.7	1.5	1.2
Forgery and counterfeiting	60,538	40,167	19,350	342	679	66.4	32.0	0.6	1.1
Fraud	144,214	95,126	46,493	1,253	1,342	66.0	32.2	0.9	0.9
Embezzlement	12,930	8,568	4,037	88	237	66.3	31.2	0.7	1.8
Stolen property: buying, receiving, possessing	74,122	48,303	24,494	598	727	65.2	33.0	0.8	1.0
Vandalism	197,015	145,284	46,306	3,279	2,146	73.7	23.5	1.7	1.1
Weapons: carrying, possessing, etc.	123,278	71,772	49,443	874	1,189	58.2	40.1	0.7	1.0
Prostitution and commercialized vice	48,154	26,156	20,405	342	1,251	54.3	42.4	0.7	2.6
Sex offenses (except forcible rape and prostitution)	56,125	41,406	13,182	744	793	73.8	23.5	1.3	1.4
Drug abuse violations	1,270,443	846,736	404,609	8,766	10,332	66.6	31.8	0.7	0.8
Gambling	7,512	2,160	5,071	32	249	28.8	67.5	0.4	3.3
Offenses against the family and children	84,812	56,233	26,470	1,533	576	66.3	31.2	1.8	0.7
Driving under the influence	1,082,301	927,516	124,467	13,980	16,338	85.7	11.5	1.3	1.5
Liquor laws	396,942	329,895	47,529	14,129	5,389	83.1	12.0	3.6	1.4
Drunkenness	440,688	362,396	66,837	8,583	2,872	82.2	15.2	1.9	0.7
Disorderly conduct	480,080	305,154	162,521	8,415	3,990	63.6	33.9	1.8	0.8
Vagrancy	24,759	14,092	9,935	567	165	56.9	40.1	2.3	0.7
All other offenses (except traffic violations)	2,877,687	1,905,436	893,018	43,634	35,599	66.2	31.0	1.5	1.2
Suspicion[5]	903	582	310	5	6	64.5	34.3	0.6	0.7
Curfew and loitering law violations	73,670	43,961	28,036	744	929	59.7	38.1	1.0	1.3
TOTAL ARRESTS	10,177,907	7,066,154	2,846,862	145,612	119,279	69.4	28.0	1.4	1.2

(1) Percentages may not add up to 100 due to rounding. (2) In the UCR program, serious crimes that occur in all areas of the country and are likely to be reported to police are classified as part I offenses. See Crime in the U.S. table footnotes, p. 128, for offense definitions. (3) Arrest data only is collected for UCR program-designated part II offenses. (4) Simple assaults, where no weapons are used and where the victim did not sustain serious injury (e.g., stalking). (5) Arrested for no specific offense and released without formal charges being placed against a person.

Imprisonment Rate by Gender, Race, Hispanic Origin, and Age, 2009

Source: *Prisoners in 2009*, Bureau of Justice Statistics, U.S. Dept. of Justice
(number of prisoners sentenced to more than one year per 100,000 of each group in the U.S. resident population)

	Male					Female			
Age	All races[1]	White	Black	Hispanic	Age	All races[1]	White	Black	Hispanic
18-19	526	242	1,512	581	18-19	23	17	42	24
20-24	1,874	886	5,339	2,365	20-24	109	86	186	124
25-29	2,211	1,001	6,927	2,682	25-29	149	115	287	164
30-34	2,348	1,204	7,721	2,481	30-34	188	155	361	178
35-39	2,226	1,220	7,490	2,305	35-39	206	164	426	187
40-44	1,949	1,121	6,447	2,054	40-44	172	131	360	171
45-49	1,219	684	4,063	1,520	45-49	94	67	205	107
50-54	712	408	2,345	1,073	50-54	45	32	101	60
55-59	424	272	1,291	732	55-59	22	18	42	29
60-64	251	180	701	490	60-64	11	9	22	22
65 or older	94	69	287	184	65 or older	3	2	6	4
Total[2]	949	487	3,119	1,193	Total[2]	67	50	142	74

Note: Rates are based on census population estimates for Jan. 1, 2009. Detailed categories exclude persons who reported two or more races. Hispanics may be of any race, but are not included in white and black population here. (1) Includes American Indians, Alaska natives, Asians, Native Hawaiians, other Pacific Islanders, and persons identifying two or more races. (2) Includes persons under age 18.

Hate Crimes by Offense Type, Bias Motivation, 2009

Source: *Hate Crime Statistics, 2009*, Federal Bureau of Investigation, U.S. Dept. of Justice

Hate crimes are defined as crimes in which victims are chosen because of one or more personal characteristics, such as race, ethnicity, or religion. Congress enacted the Hate Crime Statistics Act of 1990, which led to the collection of hate crime data as part of the FBI's Uniform Crime Report (UCR) program beginning in 1992. Not all agencies that participate in the UCR program submit hate crime data, so the data presented is not representative of the nation as a whole.

Bias motivation	Total offenses	Crimes against persons[1]					Crimes against property[2]						Total crimes against society[3]
		Aggravated assault	Simple assault	Intimidation	Other[1]	Total crimes against persons	Robbery	Burglary	Larceny-theft	Destruction/damage/vandalism	Other[2]	Total crimes against property	
Single-bias incidents	7,775	913	1,689	2,153	30	4,785	124	135	163	2,461	81	2,964	26
Race	3,816	460	804	1,194	18	2,476	57	76	79	1,079	34	1,325	15
Anti-White	652	113	191	158	10	472	31	20	47	60	16	174	6
Anti-Black	2,724	312	507	935	5	1,759	23	49	19	856	12	959	6
Anti-American Indian/ Alaskan native	84	13	31	12	3	59	3	2	9	8	2	24	1
Anti-Asian/Pacific Islander	147	15	44	40	0	99	0	0	2	45	1	48	0
Anti-multiple races, group	209	7	31	49	0	87	0	5	2	110	3	120	2
Religion	1,376	29	129	260	0	418	1	23	30	882	20	956	2
Anti-Jewish	964	9	82	172	0	263	1	13	6	671	9	700	1
Anti-Catholic	55	1	4	6	0	11	0	0	12	29	3	44	0
Anti-Protestant	40	0	0	10	0	10	0	1	1	26	2	30	0
Anti-Islamic	128	11	34	44	0	89	0	0	4	33	1	38	1
Anti-other religion	119	4	3	20	0	27	0	3	1	84	4	92	0
Anti-multiple religions, group	60	4	5	7	0	16	0	4	4	35	1	44	0
Anti-atheism/agnosticism/ etc.	10	0	1	1	0	2	0	2	2	4	0	8	0
Sexual orientation	1,436	227	493	325	7	1,052	44	16	16	295	10	381	3
Anti-male homosexual	798	137	291	170	1	599	30	7	6	152	3	198	1
Anti-female homosexual	216	36	73	47	5	161	2	4	3	43	2	54	1
Anti-homosexual	376	51	118	100	1	270	11	2	4	85	4	106	0
Anti-heterosexual	21	3	5	3	0	11	0	0	0	8	1	10	0
Anti-bisexual	25	0	6	5	0	11	1	2	3	7	0	13	1
Ethnicity/national origin	1,050	192	242	357	3	794	22	13	18	184	15	252	4
Anti-Hispanic	654	143	158	205	3	509	20	11	10	95	6	142	3
Anti-other ethnicity/ national origin	396	49	84	152	0	285	2	2	8	89	9	110	1
Disability	97	5	21	17	2	45	0	7	20	21	2	50	2
Anti-physical	25	3	4	9	0	16	0	0	4	4	0	8	1
Anti-mental	72	2	17	8	2	29	0	7	16	17	2	42	1
Multiple-bias incidents[4]	14	1	2	5	0	8	0	2	0	4	0	6	0
Total offenses	7,789	914	1,691	2,158	30	4,793	124	137	163	2,465	81	2,970	26

(1) Includes murder, non-negligent manslaughter, forcible rape, and additional offenses not shown here in details. (2) Includes arson, motor vehicle theft, and additional offenses not shown here in detail. (3) Includes drug or narcotic offenses, gambling and prostitution offenses, and weapon law violations where society as a whole is considered the victim. (4) More than one offense type must occur and at least two offense types must be motivated by different biases to count as a multiple-bias incident.

Notable Assassinations Since 1865

1865—Apr. 14: U.S. Pres. Abraham Lincoln shot by John Wilkes Booth, well-known actor with Confederate sympathies, at Ford's Theater in Washington, DC; died Apr. 15.

1881—Mar. 13: Alexander II of Russia. **July 2:** U.S. Pres. James A. Garfield shot by Charles J. Guiteau, disappointed office seeker, in Washington, DC; died Sept. 19.

1894—June 24: French Pres. Sadi Carnot, by Sante Caserio, Italian anarchist, in Lyon.

1898—Sept. 10: Empress Elizabeth of Austria stabbed by Luigi Luccheni, Italian anarchist.

1900—July 29: Umberto I, king of Italy.

1901—Sept. 6: U.S. Pres. William McKinley shot by Leon Czolgosz, anarchist, in Buffalo, NY; died Sept. 14.

1908—Feb. 1: King Carlos I of Portugal and his son Luis Felipe in Lisbon.

1913—Feb. 23: Mexican Pres. Francisco I. Madero and Vice Pres. José María Pino Suárez. **Mar. 18:** King George of Greece.

1914—June 28: Archduke Francis Ferdinand of Austria-Hungary and his wife shot by Gavrilo Princip, Serb nationalist, in Sarajevo, Bosnia.

1916—Dec. 30: Grigory Rasputin, mystic and court figure, by group of aristocrats.

1918—July 12: Grand Duke Michael of Russia, at Perm. **July 16:** Nicholas II, former (abdicated) czar of Russia; his wife, Czarina Alexandra; their son, Czarevitch Alexis; their daughters, Grand Duchesses Olga, Tatiana, Marie, Anastasia; and 4 members of household executed by Bolsheviks at Ekaterinburg.

1920—May 20: Mexican Pres. Gen. Venustiano Carranza in Tlaxcalantongo.

1922—Aug. 22: Michael Collins, Irish revolutionary, in ambush in West Cork. **Dec. 16:** Polish Pres. Gabriel Narutowicz in Warsaw.

1923—July 20: Gen. Francisco "Pancho" Villa, ex-rebel leader, in Parral, Mexico.

1928—July 17: Gen. Alvaro Obregon, president-elect of Mexico, in San Angel.

1932—May 6: French Pres. Paul Doumer shot by Russian émigré, Pavel Gorgulov, in Paris.

1934—July 25: Austrian Chancellor Engelbert Dollfuss by Nazis, in Vienna.

1935—Sept. 8: Sen. Huey P. Long, former Louisiana governor, shot by Dr. Carl Austin Weiss, son-in-law of political opponent, in Baton Rouge; died Sept. 10.

1940—Aug. 20: Leon Trotsky (Lev Bronstein), exiled Soviet commissar of war, fatally wounded with ice ax by Soviet agent near Mexico City.

1948—Jan. 30: Mohandas K. Gandhi (Mahatma) shot by Nathuram Godse, Hindu fanatic, in New Delhi. **Sept. 17:** Count Folke Bernadotte, UN mediator for Palestine, by Jewish extremists in Jerusalem.

1951—July 20: Jordanian King Abdullah ibn Hussein. **Oct. 16:** Prime Min. Liaquat Ali Khan of Pakistan shot, in Rawalpindi.

1956—Sept. 21: Pres. Anastasio Somoza of Nicaragua shot in Leon; died Sept. 29.

1957—July 26: Guatemalan Pres. Carlos Castillo Armas, in Guatemala City by one of own guards.

1958—July 14: King Faisal of Iraq, Crown Prince Abdullah, and **July 15,** Prem. Nuri as-Said, by rebels in Baghdad.

1959—Sept. 25: Prime Min. Solomon Bandaranaike of Ceylon, by Buddhist monk in Colombo.

1961—Jan. 17: Ex-Prem. Patrice Lumumba of the Congo, in Katanga Province. **May 30:** Dominican dictator Rafael Leonidas Trujillo Molina, nr. Ciudad Trujillo.

1963—June 12: Medgar Evers, NAACP's Mississippi field secretary, shot by Byron De La Beckwith in Jackson, MS. **Nov. 2:** Pres. Ngo Dinh Diem of South Vietnam and his brother, Ngo Dinh Nhu, in military coup. **Nov. 22:** U.S. Pres. John F. Kennedy shot while riding in motorcade through downtown Dallas, TX; accused gunman Lee Harvey Oswald murdered by nightclub owner Jack Ruby while awaiting trial.

1965—Jan. 21: Iranian Prem. Hassan Ali Mansour in Tehran; 4 executed. **Feb. 21:** Malcolm X, black nationalist leader, shot by three men linked to Nation of Islam at New York City rally.

1966—Sept. 6: Prime Min. Hendrik F. Verwoerd of South Africa stabbed to death in parliament at Cape Town.

1968—Apr. 4: Rev. Martin Luther King Jr. fatally shot in Memphis, TN; James Earl Ray convicted of crime. **June 5:** Sen. Robert F. Kennedy (D, NY) shot in Los Angeles; died June 6. Sirhan Sirhan convicted of crime.

1971—Nov. 28: Jordanian Prime Min. Wasfi Tal by Palestinian guerrillas, in Cairo.

1973—Mar. 2: U.S. Amb. Cleo A. Noel Jr., U.S. Charge d'Affaires George C. Moore, and Belgian Charge d'Affaires Guy Eid, by Palestinian guerrillas in Khartoum, Sudan. **Dec. 20:** Spanish Prem. Luis Carrero Blanco in car bombing by Basque separatist group ETA, in Madrid.

1974—Aug. 19: U.S. Amb. to Cyprus, Rodger P. Davies, by sniper's bullet in Nicosia.

1975—Feb. 11: Pres. Richard Ratsimandrava of Madagascar shot in Tananarive. **Mar. 25:** Saudi Arabian King Faisal shot by nephew Prince Musad Abdel Aziz, in Riyadh. **Aug. 15:** Bangladesh Pres. Sheik Mujibur Rahman killed in coup.

1976—Feb. 13: Nigerian head of state, Gen. Murtala Ramat Mohammed, by self-styled "young revolutionaries."

1977—Mar. 16: Kamal Jumblat, Lebanese Druse chieftain, shot near Beirut. **Mar. 18:** Congo Pres. Marien Ngouabi shot in Brazzaville.

1978—May 9: Former Italian Prem. Aldo Moro killed by Red Brigades terrorists who abducted him Mar. 16 in Rome, held him hostage for several weeks. **July 9:** Former Iraqi Prem. Abdul Razak Al-Naif shot in London.

1979—Feb. 14: U.S. Amb. Adolph Dubs shot by Afghan Muslim extremists in Kabul. **Aug. 27:** Lord Mountbatten, WWII hero, and 2 others killed when a bomb exploded on his fishing boat off coast of Co. Sligo, Ireland. IRA claimed responsibility. **Oct. 26:** S. Korean Pres. Park Chung Hee and 6 bodyguards fatally shot by Kim Jae Kyu, head of S. Korean CIA.

1980—Apr. 12: Liberian Pres. William R. Tolbert slain in military coup. **Sept. 17:** Former Nicaraguan Pres. Anastasio Somoza Debayle shot in Paraguay.

1981—Oct. 6: Egyptian Pres. Anwar al-Sadat shot by commandos while reviewing military parade in Cairo; 7 others killed, 28 wounded. 4 convicted as assassins and executed.

1982—Sept. 14: Lebanese Pres.-elect Bashir Gemayel killed by bomb in east Beirut.

1983—Aug. 21: Philippine opposition leader Benigno Aquino Jr. shot by gunman at Manila Intl. Airport.

1984—Oct. 31: Indian Prime Min. Indira Gandhi shot and killed by 2 Sikh bodyguards, in New Delhi.

1986—Feb. 28: Swedish Prem. Olof Palme shot by gunman on Stockholm street.

1987—June 1: Lebanese Prem. Rashid Karami killed when bomb exploded aboard helicopter.

1988—Apr. 16: PLO military chief Khalil Wazir (Abu Jihad) gunned down by Israeli commandos in Tunisia.

1989—Aug. 18: Colombian pres. candidate Luis Carlos Galan killed by Medellín cartel drug traffickers at campaign rally in Bogotá. **Nov. 22:** Lebanese Pres. Rene Moawad killed when bomb exploded next to his motorcade.

1990—Mar. 22: Colombian pres. candidate Bernardo Jaramillo Ossa shot by gunman at airport in Bogotá.

1991—May 21: Former Indian Prime Min. Rajiv Gandhi killed by bomb during election rally in Madras.

1992—June 29: Algerian Pres. Mohammed Boudiaf shot by gunman in Annaba.

1993—May 1: Sri Lankan Pres. Ranasinghe Premadasa killed by bomb in Colombo.

1994—Mar. 23: Mexican pres. candidate Luis Donaldo Colosio Murrieta shot by gunman Mario Aburto Martinez. **Apr. 6:** Burundian Pres. Cyprien Ntaryamira and Rwandan Pres. Juvenal Habyarimana killed with 8 others when their plane was apparently shot down.

1995—Nov. 4: Israeli Prime Min. Yitzhak Rabin shot by Yigal Amir, Jewish extremist, at peace rally in Tel Aviv.

1996—Oct. 2: Andrei Lukanov, former Bulgarian prime min., shot outside home by unidentified gunman.

1998—Feb. 6: Prefect of Corsica, Claude Erigmac, shot in the back by 2 unidentified gunmen while walking to concert. **Apr. 26:** Guatemalan Roman Catholic Bishop Juan Gerardi Conedera, human rights champion, found beaten to death in Guatemala City.

1999—Mar. 23: Paraguayan Vice-Pres. Luis Maria Argaña, ambushed and shot to death along with his driver, by 4 unidentified assailants, in Asunción. **Apr. 9:** Niger Pres. Ibrahim Bare Mainassara ambushed and killed by dissident soldiers. **Oct. 27:** Armenian Prime Min. Vazgen Sarkissian, along with 7 others, shot to death during session of parliament.

2000—Jan. 15: Serbian paramilitary leader Zeljko Raznjatovic (Arkan), with 2 others, shot and killed by unidentified gunman in Belgrade. **June 8:** Brig. Gen. Stephen Saunders, Britain's senior military representative in Greece, fatally shot by 2 men on motorcycle, while driving car in Athens suburb.

2001—Jan. 16: Dem. Rep. of the Congo Pres. Laurent Kabila shot to death by bodyguard at pres. palace in Kinshasa. **June 1:** Nepal's King Birendra, Queen Aiswarya, and 7 other royals fatally shot by Crown Prince Dipendra, who also fatally wounded himself. **Sept. 9:** Afghan Northern Alliance (anti-Taliban) guerrilla leader Ahmed Shah Massoud injured in suicide-attack bombing by 2 people posing as journalists, in N. Afghanistan; died Sept. 15. **Oct. 14:** Abdel Rahman Hamad, a leader of Palestinian militant group Hamas, shot by Israeli military snipers. **Oct. 17:** Israeli tourism min. Rehavam Zeevifatally shot; Popular Front for the Liberation of Palestine claimed responsibility.

2002—Mar. 16: Colombian cleric Isaias Duarte Cancino, critic of Colombian guerrillas and drug traffickers, shot by unidentified gunmen outside of church in Cali. **May 6:** Dutch right-wing politician Pim Fortuyn shot outside radio station in Hilversum. **July 6:** Afghan Vice Pres. Haji Abdul Qadir shot outside his office in Kabul. **July 23:** Salah Sherhada, a founder of armed wing of Hamas, killed with 14 others in air strike on Gaza City by Israeli fighter jet.

2003—Mar. 12: Serbian Prime Min. Zoran Djindjic shot by snipers (paramilitary) outside govt. headquarters in Belgrade. **Apr. 10:** Shiite Muslim cleric Abdul Majid al-Khoei attacked by crowd, hacked to death at Imam Ali mosque, Najaf, Iraq. **Apr. 17:** Sergei Yushenkov, former Russian legislator and Liberal Party head, shot outside apartment in Moscow. **Aug. 29:** Shiite Muslim cleric Bakir al-Hakim killed in car bombing at Imam Ali mosque in Najaf, Iraq. **Sept. 10:** Swedish Foreign Min. Anna Lindh stabbed in Stockholm dept. store; died Sept. 11.

2004—Feb. 13: Former Chechen Pres. Zelimkhan Yandarbiyev killed after car exploded in Qatar. **Mar. 22:** Sheik Ahmed Yassin, spiritual leader of Hamas, by Israeli missile attack in Gaza City. **Apr. 17:** Hamas leader Abdel Aziz Rantisi, by Israeli missile strike in Gaza City. **May 9:** Chechen Pres. Akhmad Kadyrov, by bomb explosion at WWII memorial service in Grozny. **May 17:** Iraqi Gov. Council Pres. Ezzedine Salim, by car bomb explosion at Green Zone checkpoint in Baghdad. **Nov. 2:** Filmmaker Theo van Gogh, critic of Islam and great-grandnephew of painter Vincent van Gogh, shot and stabbed by Muslim militant in Amsterdam.

2005—Jan. 4: Baghdad Gov. Ali al-Haidari gunned down by insurgents in Baghdad, Iraq. **Feb. 14:** Former Lebanese Prime Min. Rafik al-Hariri killed when motorcade bombed in Beirut. **Mar. 8:** Former Chechen pres. Aslan Maskhadov killed in raid by Russian special forces, in village outside Grozny. **July 1:** Sheik Kamaledding al-Ghuraifi, senior aide to Grand Ayatollah Ali Sistani, shot and killed on way to Friday prayers, in Baghdad.

2006—Feb. 11: Leading Kazakhstan opposition politician Altynbek Sarsenbayev (also known as Sarsenbaiuly) kidnapped, found murdered outside Almaty. **Sept. 14:** Andrei Kozlov, Russian central banker active in reforming industry, shot by unidentified gunmen in Moscow. **Oct. 7:** Anna Politkovskaya, reporter critical of Kremlin's Chechnya policies, fatally shot by unidentified gunman in apartment building in Moscow. **Nov. 21:** Pierre Gemayel, Lebanese cabinet minister opposed to Syria, shot by unknown gunmen while driving through Beirut.

2007—June 13: Walid Eido, Lebanese parliament member who was part of anti-Syria coalition, killed by car bomb in Beirut. **Aug. 2:** *Oakland Post* editor Chauncey Bailey, who was investigating financial status of black Muslim organization, shot dead in downtown Oakland, CA. **Sept. 19:** Antoine Ghanem, member of ruling anti-Syria coalition in Lebanese parliament, killed by bomb in parked car nr. Beirut. **Dec. 27:** Benazir Bhutto, former Pakistani prime min. and first female elected leader of a Muslim state, by gunfire and/or bomb as she was leaving political rally for Pakistan People's Party.

2008—Feb. 12: Imad Mughniyeh, top Hezbollah commander, by car bomb in Syria. Mughniyeh had been on FBI's Most Wanted Terrorist list and was believed to have orchestrated the 1983 bombing of U.S. embassy in Beirut. **May 8:** Edgar Eusebio Millán Gómez, Mexico's acting national police chief, by gunman outside his home in Mexico City. **Aug. 1:** Syrian Brig. Gen. and top presidential aide Mohammed Suleiman reportedly shot by sniper nr. Tartus, Syria; Suleiman had been Syria's primary contact with investigators from Intl. Atomic Energy Agency. **Oct. 23:** Ivo Pukanic, owner and editor-in-chief of Croatian political newspaper *Nacional*, killed in Zagreb when a bomb exploded near his car. The bombing was widely attributed to organized crime groups. **Oct.-Nov.:** 12 Mexico police officers, including the state police commanders in two districts, over a five-day stretch of drug-related violence.

2009—Jan.: Six candidates for elected office killed in several regions of Iraq shortly before scheduled provincial elections. **Mar. 2:** Heavily armed men launched rocket grenades into the home of Guinea-Bissau's longtime Pres. João Bernardo Vieira and Gen. Batista Tagme Na Waie, killing both men. **Mar. 31:** Sulim Yamadeyev, a former Chechen general and enemy of the Kremlin-installed president, killed by gunmen in Dubai. **May 31:** Dr. George Tiller, one of the few doctors in U.S. to perform abortions late in pregnancy, shot to death in his Wichita church by an anti-abortion activist. **June 12:** Harith al-Obaidi, a Sunni member of Iraq's Parliament, shot at point-blank range. His aide and three bodyguards also killed in the attack. **June 13:** Bashir Aushev, a former vice premier of the Ingushetia region of Russia, killed by gunmen. **Sept. 2:** Abdullah Lahgmani, deputy director of Afghanistan's National Directorate for Security, and at least 15 others killed by a suicide bomber in Mehtar Lam. **Sept. 27:** Two officials from the Russian republic of Dagestan, Alimsultan Alkhamatov and Alimsultan Atuyev, shot dead in separate incidents.

2010—Jan. 19: Mahmoud al-Mabhouh, a senior commander for Hamas, found drugged and suffocated in his Dubai, United Arab Emirates, hotel room. Suspicion immediately fell on Israel's Mossad spy agency. **Aug. 2:** Raza Haider, a member of Pakistan's parliament, and his bodyguard shot dead by four gunmen in a mosque in Karachi, Pakistan, unleashing violence that killed at least 78 others.

2011—Jan. 4: Salman Taseer, governor of Pakistan's Punjab province, killed by one of his guards in an Islamabad market. **Mar. 2:** Shahbaz Bhatti, only Christian minister in Pakistani govt. and an opponent of the nation's blasphemy laws, shot in Islamabad. **July 12:** Ahmed Wali Karzai, power-wielding half-brother of Afghan President Hamid Karzai, shot dead in his Kandahar home by a long-time confidante. Three other Karzai allies, including Kandahar mayor Ghulam Hamidi, assassinated over the next two weeks. **July 28:** Gen. Abdul Fattah Younes, Libya's top rebel commander, and two other officers killed in Benghazi. **Sept. 20:** Burhanuddin Rabbani, a former president and then-leader of Afghanistan's High Peace Council, killed in his home by an assassin with explosives hidden in turban.

Notable Assassination Attempts Since 1912

1912—Oct. 14: Former U.S. Pres. Theodore Roosevelt shot and wounded by demented man in Milwaukee, WI.

1933—Feb. 15: In Miami, FL, Joseph Zangara, anarchist, shot at Pres.-elect Franklin D. Roosevelt, but a woman seized his arm; bullet fatally wounded Chicago Mayor Anton J. Cermak, who died Mar. 6.

1944—July 20: Adolf Hitler injured when bomb, planted by a German officer, exploded in his headquarters; 1 aide killed,12 injured.

1950—Nov. 1: In attempt to assassinate Pres. Harry Truman, 2 members of a Puerto Rican nationalist movement—Griselio Torresola and Oscar Collazo—tried to shoot their way into Blair House, across the street from White House. Torresola killed. Pvt. Leslie Coffelt, White House policeman, fatally shot.

1970—Nov. 27: Pope Paul VI unharmed by knife-wielding assailant who attempted to attack him in airport in Manila, Philippines.

1972—May 15: Alabama Gov. George Wallace seriously wounded when shot in Laurel, MD, by Arthur Bremer.

1975—Sept. 5: Pres. Gerald R. Ford unharmed when Secret Service agent grabbed pistol aimed at him by Lynette (Squeaky) Fromme, a follower of cult leader Charles Manson, in Sacramento, CA. **Sept. 22:** Pres. Ford again unharmed when bystander grabbed arm of Sara Jane Moore as she fired upon Ford in San Francisco.

1980—May 29: Civil rights leader Vernon E. Jordan Jr. shot and wounded in Ft. Wayne, IN.

1981—Mar. 30: Pres. Ronald Reagan, along with Press Sec. James Brady, Secret Service agent Timothy J. McCarthy, and Washington, DC, policeman Thomas Delahanty shot and seriously wounded by John W. Hinckley Jr. in Washington, DC. **May 13:** Pope John Paul II and 2 bystanders shot and wounded by Mehmet Ali Agca, an escaped Turkish prisoner, in St. Peter's Square, Rome.

1982—May 12: Pope John Paul II wounded by ultra-conservative priest wielding bayonet, in Fatima, Portugal.

1984—Oct. 12: British Prime Min. Margaret Thatcher unharmed when a bomb, said to have been planted by the IRA, exploded at the Grand Hotel in Brighton, England, during a Party conference; 4 died, incl. a member of Parliament.

1986—Sept. 7: Chilean Pres. Gen. Augusto Pinochet Ugarte unharmed after motorcade was attacked by rebels.

1995—June 26: Egyptian Pres. Hosni Mubarak unharmed when gunmen fired on his motorcade in Addis Ababa, Ethiopia; 4 died, incl. 2 Ethiopian police officers.

1997—Feb. 12: Colombian Pres. Ernesto Samper Pizano unharmed when bomb exploded on a runway in Barranquilla as his plane was preparing to land. **Apr. 30:** Tajik Pres. Imamali Rakhmanov injured when a grenade was thrown at him.

1998—Feb. 9: Georgian Pres. Eduard A. Shevardnadze unharmed when gunmen fired on his motorcade in Tbilisi.

2000—Sept. 18: Armed men attempted to assassinate Côte d'Ivoire military leader Gen. Robert Guei in predawn raid.

2002—Apr. 14: Leading Colombian pres. candidate Alvaro Uribe Velez unharmed after bomb exploded under parked bus as his motorcade passed in Barranquilla; 3 bystanders killed. **July 14:** French Pres. Jacques Chirac unharmed after Maxime Brunerie, gunman with ties to neo-Nazi groups, fired at his open-top jeep during a Bastille Day parade in Paris. **Sept. 5:** Afghan Pres. Hamid Karzai unharmed after militant shot at car in Kandahar. **Nov. 25:** Turkmenistan Pres. Saparmurat Niyazov unharmed after gunmen opened fire on his motorcade in Ashgabat.

2003—Dec. 14: Pakistani Pres. Pervez Musharraf unharmed after bomb detonated on bridge in Rawalpindi seconds after his motorcade crossed over.

2004—Mar. 19: Taiwanese Pres. Chen Shui-bian shot while campaigning in motorcade; minor injuries. **July 13:** Separatists bombed motorcade of Sergei Abramov, Chechnya's acting pres. **Sept. 5:** Ukrainian opposition presidential candidate Viktor Yushchenko, who later won office, fell ill after meeting; diagnosed with dioxin poisoning. **Sept. 16:** Rocket fired at helicopter carrying Afghan Pres. Hamid Karzai, near Gardez.

2005—Mar. 15: Kosovo Pres. Ibrahim Rugova survived after bomb damaged the vehicle he was in as his motorcade traveled through Pristina. **July 12:** Lebanon's pro-Syrian defense min. Elias Murr wounded by car explosion in Beirut suburb.

2006—Sept. 5: Lt. Col. Samir Shehade, involved in investigation of 2005 assassination of former Lebanese Prime Min. Rafik al-Hariri, wounded by bomb as he drove in village near Sidon.

2007—June 29: Rockets hit a plane carrying former rebel chief and current Côte d'Ivoire Prime Min. Guillaume Soro, shortly after plane landed in Bouake; Soro unhurt.

2008—Feb. 11: Pres. José Ramos-Horta shot in attack led by fugitive former army official, in Dili, Timor-Leste. Ambush on Prime Min. Xanana Gusmão's motorcade a short time later unsuccessful. **Apr. 27:** Afghan President Hamid Karzai unharmed after Taliban gunmen fired on a military parade in Kabul where Karzai and other members of Parliament were in attendance.

2009—Jan. 21: Ziad al-Ani, a leader of one of Iraq's main Sunni Arab parties participating in forthcoming provincial elections, survived a car bombing that left four dead. **Apr. 30:** After a shootout, Bolivian police killed three men and captured two others whom they accused of plotting to assassinate Pres. Evo Morales. **June 22:** Yunus-Bek Yevkurov, president of the Ingushetia region of Russia, seriously wounded when a suicide bomber in a car packed with explosives crashed into his motorcade. **Sept. 2:** Hamid Saeed Kami, Pakistan's Minister of Religious Affairs, wounded by two men firing at his car from a motorcycle. **Dec. 3:** Moussa Dadis Camara, leader of Guinea's ruling military junta, shot in the head by one of his own aides.

2010—May 14: Indonesian National Police announced they broke up a plot by terrorists calling themselves al Qaeda in Aceh to assassinate Pres. Susilo Bambang Yudhoyono. **Sept. 23:** Alexander Ankvab, vice president of Georgian region of Ankhazia, survived a fourth assassination attempt in five years, a grenade fired into his Gudauta home.

2011—Jan. 8: U.S. Rep. Gabrielle Giffords (D, AZ) severely wounded by lone gunman at a public meeting near an Arizona supermarket; six others killed, including a federal judge.

Notable U.S. Kidnappings Since 1924

Bobby Franks, 14, in Chicago, **May 21, 1924**, by 2 youths from wealthy families—Richard Loeb, 18, and Nathan Leopold, 19—who killed boy. Demand for $10,000 ignored. Loeb killed in prison; Leopold paroled 1958.

Charles A. Lindbergh Jr., 20 mos. old, nr. Hopewell, NJ, **Mar. 1, 1932**; found dead **May 12**. Ransom of $50,000 paid to man identified as Bruno Richard Hauptmann, 35, paroled German convict who entered U.S. illegally. Hauptmann convicted, electrocuted in Trenton, NJ, prison, Apr. 3, 1936.

William A. Hamm Jr., 39, brewing company pres. in St. Paul, **June 15, 1933**, by Karpis-Barker gang. $100,000 paid. Alvin Karpis given life, paroled in 1969.

Charles F. Urschel, in Oklahoma City, **July 22, 1933**. Released **July 31** after $200,000 paid. George "Machine Gun" Kelly and 5 others sentenced to life.

Brooke L. Hart, 22, in San Jose, CA. Thomas Thurmond and John Holmes arrested after demanding $40,000. When Hart's body was found in San Francisco Bay, **Nov. 26, 1933**, a mob forced its way into county jail and lynched the 2 kidnappers.

June Robles, 6, abducted in Tucson, AZ, **Apr. 25, 1934**. Missing for 19 days after ransom note sent to parents. Found alive in iron cage buried in desert. No arrests ever made.

George Weyerhaeuser, 9, of Weyerhaeuser lumber company, in Tacoma, WA, **May 24, 1935**. Returned home **June 1** after $200,000 paid. Kidnappers given 20 to 60 years.

Charles Mattson, 10, in Tacoma, WA, **Dec. 27, 1936**. Kidnapper initially asked for $28,000 but subsequent communication with parents was confusing. Charles found dead **Jan. 11, 1937**.

Robert C. Greenlease, 6, son of wealthy car dealer, taken from Kansas City, MO, school **Sept. 28, 1953**, held for $600,000. Body was found **Oct. 7**. Bonnie Brown Heady and Carl A. Hall pleaded guilty, were executed.

Peter Weinberger, 32 days old, Westbury, NY, **July 4, 1956**, for $2,000 ransom, not paid. Child found dead, abandoned by kidnapper Angelo John LaMarca, 31, who was convicted, executed.

Lee Crary, 8, in Everett, WA, **Sept. 22, 1957**; $10,000 ransom, not paid. Escaped after 3 days, led police to George E. Collins, who was convicted.

Frank Sinatra Jr., 19, from hotel room in Lake Tahoe, CA, **Dec. 8, 1963**. Released **Dec. 11** after his father paid $240,000 ransom. Three men sentenced to prison.

Barbara Jane Mackle, 20, abducted **Dec. 17, 1968**, from Atlanta, GA, motel; found unharmed 3 days later, buried in a coffin-like box 18 in. underground, after her father paid $500,000 ransom. Gary Steven Krist sentenced to life, Ruth Eisenmann-Schier to 7 years.

Virginia Piper, 49, abducted **July 27, 1972**, from her home in suburban Minneapolis; found unharmed near Duluth 2 days later after husband, retired banker, paid $1 mil ransom, then largest ransom ever reported in U.S.

J. Paul Getty III, 17, grandson of the oil billionaire, disappeared **July 10, 1973**, in Italy. Reported payment of $2.8 mil ransom not made until after Getty's ear was sent to a newspaper with a warning that other parts of his body would be mutilated unless ransom was paid. Getty freed **Dec. 15**; 2 men sentenced to prison.

Patricia "Patty" Hearst, 19, taken from her Berkeley, CA, apartment **Feb. 4, 1974**; "Symbionese Liberation Army" captors demanded her father, publisher Randolph Hearst, give millions to area poor. Patricia implicated in a San Francisco bank holdup, **Apr. 15**. The FBI, **Sept. 18, 1975**, captured her and others; they were indicted on various charges. Patricia convicted of bank robbery, Mar. 20, 1976; released from prison under executive clemency, Feb. 1, 1979. In 1978, William and Emily Harris were sentenced to 10 years to life for the kidnapping; both were paroled in 1983.

J. Reginald Murphy, 40, an editor of *Atlanta Constitution* (GA), kidnapped **Feb. 20, 1974**; freed **Feb. 22** after newspaper paid $700,000 ransom. William A. H. Williams arrested; most of the money recovered.

Jack Teich, Kings Point, NY, steel executive, seized **Nov. 12, 1974**; released **Nov. 19** after payment of $750,000.

Adam Walsh, 6, abducted from a Hollywood, FL, dept. store, **July 27, 1981**. Severed head found 2 weeks later. John Walsh, Adam's father, became active in raising awareness about missing children.

Terry Anderson, 37, Middle East bureau chief for Associated Press, in Beirut, Lebanon, by members of Islamic fundamentalist group Hezbollah on **Mar. 16, 1985**. Freed **Dec. 4, 1991**. Anderson had been held hostage along with **William Buckley**, 55, CIA station chief in Beirut who was kidnapped **Mar. 16, 1984**, and died in captivity.

Jaycee Dugard, 11, kidnapped near her home in South Lake Tahoe, CA, **June 10, 1991**; held for 18 years by Nancy and Philip Garrido, who fathered two girls with Dugard during her captivity. Dugard, along with her 11- and 15-year-old daughters, was reunited with her family **Aug. 27, 2009**, after police arrested the Garridos.

Sidney J. Reso, oil company executive, seized **Apr. 29, 1992**; died **May 3**. Arthur D. Seale—former security official at oil company—and his wife, Irene, arrested June 19. Arthur pleaded guilty, sentenced to life in prison; Irene sentenced to 20-year prison term.

Polly Klaas, 12, Petaluma, CA, abducted at knife point, **Oct. 1, 1993**, during a slumber party at her home. Police arrested Richard Allen Davis on **Nov. 30**; he led them to her body, found **Dec. 4** in wooded area of Cloverdale, CA. Davis found guilty June 18, 1996, and sentenced to death Sept. 26.

Marshall I. Wais, 79, owner of 2 San Francisco steel companies, kidnapped **Nov. 19, 1996**, from his San Francisco home. Released unharmed the same day after $500,000 ransom paid; Thomas William Taylor and Michael K. Robinson arrested same day.

Tionda Z. Bradley, 10, and sister **Diamond Yvette Bradley**, 3, went missing **July 6, 2001**, in Chicago, IL. Note left by Tionda at home stated the 2 girls were going to the store and the playground. Believed kidnapped, case still unsolved.

Daniel Pearl, 38, reporter for *Wall Street Journal*, disappeared **Jan. 23, 2002**, while researching story in Karachi, Pakistan. British-born militant Ahmad Omar Saeed Sheikh **Feb. 14** admitted to organizing the kidnapping and said Pearl was dead. Sheikh and 3 others convicted July 15 of kidnapping and murder by a judge in Hyderabad.

Elizabeth Smart, 14, abducted from her home in Salt Lake City, UT, **June 5, 2002**, allegedly by Brian D. Mitchell, and forced to live with Mitchell and wife Wanda for 9 months in various U.S. cities; found walking down street with captors in Sandy, UT, 15 mi from Smart family home, **Mar. 12, 2003**.

Natalee Holloway, 18, of Birmingham, AL, vanished **May 30, 2005**, on high school graduation trip to Aruba, Netherlands dependency in West Indies. Officials believed she was kidnapped and murdered. Several suspects were detained but later released.

Jill Carroll, 28, freelance journalist, in Baghdad by group called the Revenge Brigade, **Jan. 7, 2006**. She was on assignment for the *Christian Science Monitor* when she was seized. She was released **Mar. 30**; 4 Iraqis arrested in connection with her kidnapping in Aug.

Steve Centanni, 60, a Fox News reporter released **Aug. 26, 2006** (along with a colleague), after being kidnapped and held hostage for 13 days by Palestinian militant group Holy Jihad Brigades. The group had demanded that the U.S. release all Muslims held in its prisons.

Reigh Storrow Mills, 7, abducted **July 27, 2008**, by her father Christian Gerhartsreiter (who used the alias Clark Rockefeller); reunited with her mother **Aug. 2, 2008**, by FBI agents who took Gerhartsreiter into custody.

Felix Batista, 55, who negotiated the release of numerous kidnapping victims in Latin America was abducted in Mexico in early **Dec. 2008**.

Melissa Roxas, 31, a volunteer health worker released **May 24, 2009**, five days after being kidnapped in the Philippines **May 19, 2009**.

David Rohde, 41, a *New York Times* reporter captured by the Taliban in Afghanistan **Nov. 10, 2008**, escaped **June 19, 2009**.

Notable Terrorist Incidents Worldwide Since 1971

Source: U.S. Dept. of State; *Facts On File World News Digest @ Facts.com*; World Almanac research

Selected noteworthy incidents, excluding most assassinations, kidnappings, and military targets. Does not include all incidents in Iraq or Afghanistan, 2001-present; see Chronology of the Year's Events.

1971—Mar. 1: Senate wing of U.S. Capitol Building in Wash., DC, bombed by Weather Underground; no deaths.

1972—July 21: "Bloody Friday." Provisional IRA exploded 20+ bombs across Belfast, N. Ireland; 9 killed, hundreds injured. **Sept. 5:** Members of Palestinian group Black September killed 2 Israeli athletes and seized 9 others at Olympic Village in Munich, W. Germany, during Summer Olympics. 9 hostages, 5 militants, 1 Ger. officer died in botched rescue.

1973—Dec. 17: Palestinian gunmen attacked Rome airport and bombed plane on tarmac; hijacked Lufthansa plane with 5 Italian hostages to Athens, Greece, then to Kuwait; 31 killed in all.

1974—June 17: Houses of Parliament in London, England, bombed by Provisional IRA; 11 injured.

1975—Jan. 24: Puerto Rican FALN nationalists bombed Fraunces Tavern in New York City; 4 killed, 53 injured. **Jan. 29:** U.S. State Dept. building in Wash., DC, bombed by Weather Underground; no deaths.

1976—June 27: Palestinian and Baader-Meinhof militants forced Air France jet to land at Entebbe, Uganda. Israeli army rescued 103 hostages from airport terminal in battle with terrorists and Ugandan troops, July 3-4; 32 killed in all.

1978—Mar. 11: Palestinian militants landed on beach near Haifa, Israel. Shot civilians and hijacked bus to Tel Aviv. Exploded at roadblock; 43 killed.

1979—Nov. 4: Iranian radicals seized U.S. embassy in Tehran, taking 66 Americans hostage. 52 were held until Jan. 20, 1981. **Nov. 20:** 200 Islamic terrorists seized Grand Mosque in Mecca, Saudi Arabia, and held hundreds of pilgrims hostage. Saudi forces retook mosque Dec. 4; about 250 died.

1980—Feb. 27: Members of leftist guerrilla group April 19 Movement (M-19) seized Dominican Republic embassy in Bogota, Colombia; 80 hostages taken. 18 held until Apr. 27.

1983—Apr. 18: Hezbollah suicide truck bomb at U.S. embassy in Beirut, Lebanon, killed 63. **Oct. 9:** N. Korean agents ambushed a S. Korean govt. delegation in Rangoon, Burma, killing 21. **Oct. 23:** Hezbollah suicide truck bombings of U.S. and French military bases, Beirut, Lebanon; 242 Americans, 58 French killed.

1984—Sept. 20: U.S. embassy annex nr. Beirut, Lebanon, bombed, killing approx. 20.

1985—June 14: Hezbollah members hijacked TWA Flight 847 with 153 passengers and crew to Beirut, Lebanon; 39 held for 17 days; 1 U.S. Navy sailor killed. **June 23:** Air India Flight 182 destroyed by bomb off coast of Ireland; 329 killed. Blamed on Sikh terrorists. **Apr. 12:** Bomb blast at restaurant nr. Air Force base in Torrejon, Spain; 18 killed. **Oct. 7:** Four Palestinians hijacked Italian cruise ship *Achille Lauro*; 1 passenger killed. **Nov. 23:** EgyptAir Flight 648 from Athens to Cairo hijacked to Malta by Palestinian group Abu Nidal; 60 killed in rescue. **Dec. 27:** Palestinian militants opened fire at El-Al airline counters at Rome and Vienna airports; 19 killed.

1986—Apr. 5: Nightclub in Berlin, W. Germany, bombed; 3 killed, incl. 2 U.S. servicemen, 200+ hurt. 3 Libyan embassy workers in Germany convicted in bombing.

1987—Apr. 17: Bomb in Sri Lankan capital killed 100+; blamed on Tamil rebels who, 4 days later, attacked Sinhalese travelers on highway, killing 127. **June 19:** Basque group ETA bombed supermarket garage in Barcelona, Spain; 21 killed, 45 injured. **Nov. 29:** Bomb planted by N. Korean agents exploded on Korean Air Lines Flight 858 over Indian Ocean; 115 killed.

1988—Dec. 21: Pan Am Flight 103 exploded over Lockerbie, Scotland, killing all 259 aboard and 11 on ground; Libya took responsibility for bombing in Aug. 2003.

1989—Sept. 19: French UTA Flight 722 from Congo to Paris destroyed by bomb in midair over Niger; 171 killed. Several Libyan officials convicted in absentia; no official admission.

1992—Mar. 17: Israeli embassy in Buenos Aires, Argentina, bombed; 28 killed, 200+ injured. Hezbollah suspected.

1993—Feb. 26: Truck bomb exploded in World Trade Center garage in New York City; 6 killed. Blast later linked to al-Qaeda. **Mar. 12-19:** At least 11 bombs ripped through Bombay and Calcutta, India; 300+ killed.

1994—Feb. 25: U.S.-born Israeli settler Baruch Goldstein opened fire in mosque in Hebron, West Bank; about 30 Muslim worshippers killed. **July 18:** Buenos Aires Jewish center bombed; 87 killed. Blamed on Hezbollah.

1995—Mar. 20: Twelve killed and over 5,000 injured when Japanese Aum Shinri-kyu cult members released Sarin nerve gas in several Tokyo subway cars. **Apr. 19:** Murrah Federal Building in Oklahoma City bombed, killing 168 and injuring 500+. Timothy McVeigh and Terry Nichols convicted in bombing. McVeigh executed in 2001; Nichols sentenced to life in prison, 1998 on state charges, 2004 on federal charges. **Nov. 13:** U.S. military compound in Riyadh, Saudi Arabia, bombed by Islamic Movement of Change; 7 killed.

1996—Jan. 31: Tamil Tigers drove explosives-laden truck into Central Bank in Colombo, Sri Lanka; 90 killed. **June 25:** Bomb-laden fuel truck exploded outside Khobar Towers, a U.S. military complex in Dhahran, Saudi Arabia; killed 19. **June 27:** Bomb exploded at Centennial Olympic Park in Atlanta, GA, during Summer Games; killed 2, injured 100+. Suspect Eric Robert Rudolph arrested in 2003, pleaded guilty; sentenced to life in prison, 2005. **Dec. 3:** Bomb exploded on subway train in Paris; 4 killed, 86 injured. Blamed on Algerian extremists.

1997—Nov. 17: Gamaa al-Islamiya gunmen killed 58 tourists and 4 Egyptians in Valley of the Kings near Luxor, Egypt.

1998—Aug. 7: U.S. embassies in Nairobi, Kenya, and Dar-es-Salaam, Tanzania, bombed; 257 people killed. Al-Qaeda blamed. **Aug. 15:** IRA car bomb exploded outside courthouse in Omagh, N. Ireland; killed 29, injured 300+. **Oct. 18:** National Liberation Army of Colombia blew up Ocensa oil pipeline; about 71 killed, 100+ injured.

1999—Sept. 9-16: Three apt. buildings bombed in Moscow and Volgodonsk, Russia; about 300 killed. Chechen rebels blamed.

2000—Oct. 12: Small boat assisting in docking of U.S.S. *Cole* exploded while alongside it in Aden, Yemen; 17 U.S. sailors killed, 39 injured. Blamed on al-Qaeda.

2001—Sept. 11: 19 al-Qaeda terrorists hijacked 4 U.S. domestic flights, including 2 planes that crashed into World Trade Center towers and 1 into Pentagon. Total dead minus hijackers: 2,973; deadliest attack of terrorism yet on U.S. soil. **Sept.-Nov. 7:** Letters tainted with deadly anthrax bacteria mailed through U.S. postal system killed 5.

2002—Mar. 27: Suicide bombing at hotel in Netanya, Israel, during Passover celebration; 27 killed. **Oct 12:** Resort in Bali, Indonesia, bombed; 202 dead. Jemaah Islamiah blamed. **Oct. 23:** Chechen guerrillas seized theater in Moscow, held 700+ hostages. Russian authorities gassed theater; most guerrillas and about 128 hostages killed. **Nov. 28:** Suicide bombers destroyed Israeli-owned hotel near Mombasa, Kenya; 13 killed. At same time, 2 missiles narrowly missed Israeli plane taking off from Mombasa airport; blamed on al-Qaeda. **Dec. 27:** Chechen rebels plowed truck bomb into pro-Russian gov. headquarters in Grozny, Chechnya; 80 killed, 152 injured.

2003—May 12-13: Al-Qaeda militants detonated car bombs at 3 residential complexes used by Westerners in Riyadh, Saudi Arabia; 34 killed. **May 16:** Five explosions in Casablanca, Morocco; 44 killed, 100+ wounded. Blamed on al-Qaeda. **May 17-19:** Five suicide bombings in Israel; 17 killed. Hamas and al-Aqsa Martyrs brigade blamed. **Aug. 5:** Car bomb hit Marriott hotel in Jakarta, Indonesia; 12 killed, 150 injured. Blamed on Jemaah Islamiah. **Aug. 19:** UN headquarters in Baghdad bombed by truck; 22 killed, incl. UN envoy to Iraq. **Aug. 25:** 2 bombs exploded in taxis in Mumbai (Bombay), India; 46 killed, 100+ injured. Islamic militants suspected. **Oct. 27:** Suicide bombings at Intl. Red Cross and police stations; 40 killed. **Nov. 15:** Two synagogues in Istanbul, Turkey, bombed; 25 killed. **Nov. 20:** British consulate and offices of British bank HSBC bombed in Istanbul, Turkey; 27 killed incl. Br. cons. gen. Blamed on al-Qaeda. **Dec. 5:** Suicide bombing on commuter train in Yessentuki, Russia; 44 killed, 150 injured. Blamed on Chechen rebels.

2004—Feb. 6: Bomb exploded on Moscow subway; 39 killed, 130 injured. Chechen rebels blamed. **Mar. 11:** Al-Qaeda cell bombed 4 commuter trains during morning rush hour in Madrid, Spain; 191 killed, about 1,200 injured. **Apr. 21:** Car bomb destroyed Saudi govt. security building in Riyadh; 4 killed, 148 injured. **May 29:** Al-Qaeda militants stormed foreigner compound in Khobar, Saudi Arabia, taking hostages; 22 killed. **Aug. 24:** Two Russian passenger planes crashed nearly simultaneously in diff. parts of Russia; 90 killed. Blamed on Chechen rebels. **Sept. 1:** Militants seized school in Beslan, in northern Ossetia, Russia; held 1,000+ hostage for 3 days before Russian troops stormed school. About 330 killed, incl. 27 hostage-takers. Blamed on Chechen militants.

2005—July 7: Four bombs exploded on 3 separate subways and a bus in central London, UK; 52 killed, incl. bombers, about 700 injured. **July 21:** Four bombs placed on 3 subways and a bus in London malfunction. **July 23:** Three car bombs explode nr. resorts at Sharm el Sheik, Egypt; about 90 killed. **Aug. 17:** More than 400 small bombs exploded in cities and towns across Bangladesh, killing 2 and injuring at least 125. Jamaat ul-Mujahedeen Bangladesh claimed responsibility. **Aug. 19:** Three rockets fired from Jordan hit cities of Eilat, Israel, and Aqaba, Jordan. One missile flies over a docked U.S. naval ship; 1 death. **Nov. 9:** 3 suicide bombings targeting hotels in Amman, Jordan; killed 56+, injured about 100. Al-Qaeda in Iraq took responsibility.

2006—Apr. 24: Three deadly bombs within 5 minutes struck Egyptian Red Sea resort town of Dahab; 18 killed, 85 injured. Nasser Khamis el-Mallah, supposed "mastermind and leader" of Tawhid wal Jihad (Unity and Holy War), the terrorist cell that launched the attack, reported killed during gun battle in May. **July 11:** 8 explosions struck 7 different trains and 1 station of public commuter rail system in Mumbai, India; 207 killed, 700+ wounded. Lashkar-e-Qahhar (Army of Terror) claimed responsibility.

2007—Feb. 19: Train traveling between New Delhi and border with Pakistan caught fire, 68 killed; Indian ministers blamed Muslim militants for trying to disrupt peace talks between India and Pakistan. **June 30:** In apparent attempt at suicide attack, two men crashed their SUV into the main terminal of Scotland's Glasgow Airport; both also allegedly planted bombs on two cars parked in central London before attacking airport; driver later died of burns sustained in attack. **Dec. 11:** 2 coordinated car bombs went off outside govt. building and UN office building in Algiers, Algeria; 41 killed, incl. 17 UN employees, 170 wounded.

2008—Sept. 20: Suicide bomber in truck set off explosion outside of Marriott Hotel in Islamabad, Pakistan. Hotel was popular among foreigners and wealthy residents and was located nr. prime min.'s house and parliament building; 53 killed, 271 wounded. **Nov. 26-29:** A series of attacks and bombings on luxury hotels and high profile targets in Mumbai, India; 171 killed, 300 injured. Gunmen took dozens of hostages before Mumbai police and Indian National Security Guards secured the buildings. Pakistan officials later arrested 20 suspected militant Islamic extremists in connection with the attacks.

2009—Feb. 20: Suicide bomber targeted Shiite funeral in Dera Ismail Khan, Pakistan; 30 killed, 50+ wounded. **Dec. 25:** Umar Farouk Abdulmutallab, a 23-year-old Nigerian, failed in his attempt to blow up a Northwest Airlines flight from Amsterdam to Detroit with a bomb in his underpants.

2010—Jan. 1: A Taliban suicide bomber killed more than 100 people on a playground in northwest Pakistan. **Mar. 29:** Two female Chechen separatists detonated suicide bombs at two landmark subway stations in Moscow, killing at least 40 people. **May 28:** Six men from the Pakistani Taliban attacked two mosques in Lahore, killing 86 and wounding hundreds. **July 9:** Suicide bombers attacked a group of tribal elders in Mohmand, Pakistan, killing more than 100. **July 11:** Several bombs exploded simultaneously in Kampala, Uganda, killing more than 70 people who had gathered to watch the broadcast of the World Cup final.

2011—Jan. 24: A suicide bomber killed 35 people in the international arrivals hall in Moscow's Domodedovo Airport, a location chosen to maximize deaths of foreigners. **July 22:** Anders Behring Breivik, a right-wing Norwegian extremist, set off a car bomb outside government buildings in Oslo, then donned a police uniform and traveled 25 mi to a summer camp on Tyrifjorden Lake, where he massacred dozens of young people, bringing the death toll to 77.

MILITARY AFFAIRS

Chief Commanding Officers of the U.S. Military

Chairman, Joint Chiefs of Staff: Gen. Martin E. Dempsey (U.S. Army)
Vice Chairman: Adm. James A. Winnefeld Jr. (USN)

The **Joint Chiefs of Staff** consists of the Chairman and Vice Chairman of the Joint Chiefs of Staff; the Senior Enlisted Advisor of the Chairman; the Chief of Staff, U.S. Army; the Chief of Naval Operations; the Chief of Staff, U.S. Air Force; and the Commandant of the Marine Corps. Date of rank is date when the individual achieved his or her current rank. While serving in any of these positions, or as commander of a unified or specified combatant command, basic pay is $20,263.50 per month. Officers hold positions listed as of Sept. 23, 2011.

Army

Chief of Staff	Date of rank
Odierno, Raymond T.	Aug. 2, 2011

Other Generals

Alexander, Keith B.	May 7, 2010
Austin III, Lloyd J.	July 29, 2010
Chiarelli, Peter.	June 4, 2008
Cone, Robert W.	Apr. 14, 2011
Dunwoody, Ann.	Nov. 14, 2008
Ham, Carter.	July 23, 2008
Jacoby Jr., Charles H.	Aug. 2, 2011
Rodriguez, David M.	Apr. 14, 2011
Thurman, James D.	Mar. 19, 2010

Air Force

Chief of Staff	Date of rank
Schwartz, Norton A.	Aug. 12, 2008

Other Generals

Breedlove, Philip M.	Sept. 10, 2010
Fraser, Douglas M.	June 25, 2009
Fraser III, William M.	Oct. 8, 2008
Hoffman, Donald.	Nov. 21, 2008
Hostage III, Gilmary M.	May 26, 2011
Johns Jr., Raymond E.	July 31, 2009
Kehler, C. Robert.	Oct. 12, 2007
McKinley, Craig R.	Nov. 17, 2008
North, Gary L.	Aug. 19, 2009
Rice Jr., Edward A.	May 7, 2010
Shelton, William L.	Sept. 10, 2010
Welsh III, Mark A.	Oct. 28, 2009

Navy

Chief of Naval Operations	Date of rank
Greenert, Jonathan W. (submariner).	Sept. 23, 2011

Other Admirals

Donald, Kirkland H. (submariner).	Jan. 1, 2005
Ferguson III, Mark E. (surface warfare).	Aug. 2, 2011
Harvey Jr., John C. (nuclear propulsion).	July 24, 2009
McRaven, William H. (special operations).	June 30, 2011
Stavridis, James G. (surface warfare).	Oct. 19, 2006
Walsh, Patrick M. (aviator)	Apr. 2007
Willard, Robert F. (aviator)	Mar. 18, 2005
Winnefeld Jr., James A. "Sandy" (aviator)	May 7, 2010

Marine Corps

Commandant of the Marine Corps (CMC)	Date of rank
Amos, James F.	Oct. 22, 2010

Other Generals

Allen, John R.	June 30, 2011
Dunford Jr., Joseph F.	Aug. 4, 2010
Mattis, James N.	Nov. 9, 2007

Coast Guard

Commandant, with rank of Admiral	Date of rank
Papp Jr., Robert J.	Apr. 22, 2010
Vice Commandant, with rank of Vice Admiral	
Brice-O'Hara, Sally.	May 24, 2010

Unified Combatant Commands Commanders-in-Chief

U.S. European Command, Stuttgart-Vaihingen, Germany: Adm. James Stavridis (USAF)
U.S. Pacific Command, Honolulu, Hawaii: Adm. Robert F. Willard (USN)
U.S. Special Operations Command, MacDill AFB, Florida: Adm. William H. McRaven (USN)
U.S. Transportation Command, Scott AFB, Illinois: Gen. William M. Fraser III (USAF)
U.S. Central Command, MacDill AFB, Florida: Gen. James N. Mattis (USMC)
U.S. Southern Command, Miami, Florida: Gen. Douglas Fraser (USAF)
U.S. Northern Command, Peterson AFB, Colorado: Gen. Charles H. Jacoby Jr. (U.S. Army)
U.S. Strategic Command, Offutt AFB, Nebraska: Gen. C. Robert "Bob" Kehler (USAF)
U.S. Africa Command, Kelley Barracks, Stuttgart, Germany: Gen. Carter F. Ham (U.S. Army)

North Atlantic Treaty Organization (NATO) International Commands

NATO Headquarters: Chairman, NATO Military Committee: Adm. Giampaolo Di Paola (Italian Navy)
Strategic Commands:
    Allied Command Operations (ACO): Adm. James G. Stavridis (USN), Supreme Allied Commander, Europe
    Allied Command Transformation (ACT): Gen. Stéphane Abrial (French Air Force), Supreme Allied Commander Transformation
ACO Subordinate Commands:
    Joint Force Command Brunssum (JFC Brunssum): Gen. Wolf Langheld (German Army), Commander
    Joint Force Command Naples (JFC Naples): Adm. Samuel J. Locklear III (USN), Commander
    Joint Force Command Lisbon (JHQ Lisbon): Lt. Gen. Philippe Stoltz (French Army), Commander

Chairmen of the Joint Chiefs of Staff, 1949-2011

Gen. of the Army Omar N. Bradley, USA	8/16/1949-8/15/1953	Gen. John W. Vessey Jr., USA	6/18/1982-9/30/1985
Adm. Arthur W. Radford, USN.	8/15/1953-8/15/1957	Adm. William J. Crowe Jr., USN	10/1/1985-9/30/1989
Gen. Nathan F. Twining, USAF	8/15/1957-9/30/1960	Gen. Colin L. Powell, USA.	10/1/1989-9/30/1993
Gen. Lyman L. Lemnitzer, USA.	10/1/1960-9/30/1962	Gen. John M. Shalikashvili, USA.	10/25/1993-9/30/1997
Gen. Maxwell D. Taylor, USA	10/1/1962-7/1/1964	Gen. Henry H. Shelton, USA.	9/30/1997-9/30/2001
Gen. Earle G. Wheeler, USA.	7/3/1964-7/2/1970	Gen. Richard B. Myers, USAF.	10/1/2001-9/30/2005
Adm. Thomas H. Moorer, USN	7/2/1970-7/1/1974	Gen. Peter Pace, USMC	9/30/2005-9/30/2007
Gen. George S. Brown, USAF.	7/1/1974-6/20/1978	Adm. Michael G. Mullen, USN.	10/1/2007-9/30/2011
Gen. David C. Jones, USAF	6/21/1978-6/18/1982	Gen. Martin E. Dempsey, USA	10/1/2011-

Directors of the Central Intelligence Agency

In 1942, Pres. Franklin D. Roosevelt established the Office of Strategic Services (OSS); it was disbanded in 1945. In 1946, Pres. Harry Truman established the Central Intelligence Group (CIG) to operate under the National Intelligence Authority (NIA). A 1947 law replaced the NIA with the National Security Council and the CIG with the Central Intelligence Agency.

Director	Served	Appointed by President	Director	Served	Appointed by President
Adm. Sidney W. Souers	1946	Truman	Adm. Stansfield Turner	1977-1981	Carter
Gen. Hoyt S. Vandenberg	1946-1947	Truman	William J. Casey	1981-1987	Reagan
Adm. Roscoe H. Hillenkoetter	1947-1950	Truman	William H. Webster	1987-1991	Reagan
Gen. Walter Bedell Smith	1950-1953	Truman	Robert M. Gates	1991-1993	Bush, G. H. W.
Allen W. Dulles	1953-1961	Eisenhower	R. James Woolsey.	1993-1995	Clinton
John A. McCone	1961-1965	Kennedy	John M. Deutch.	1995-1997	Clinton
Adm. William F. Raborn Jr.	1965-1966	Johnson, L. B.	George J. Tenet.	1997-2004	Clinton
Richard Helms	1966-1973	Johnson, L. B.	Porter Goss	2004-2006	Bush, G. W.
James R. Schlesinger	1973	Nixon	Gen. Michael V. Hayden	2006-2009	Bush, G. W.
William E. Colby	1973-1976	Nixon	Leon E. Panetta.	2009-2011	Obama
George H. W. Bush	1976-1977	Ford	David H. Petraeus.	2011-	Obama

U.S. Army and Air Force Units

Army Units. Squad: In infantry usually 8-16 enlisted personnel under a staff sergeant. **Platoon:** In infantry 2-4 squads under a lieutenant. **Company:** Headquarters section and 3-5 platoons under a captain. (Company-size unit in the artillery is a battery; in the cavalry, a troop.) **Battalion:** Hdqts. and 4-6 companies under a lieutenant colonel. (Battalion-size unit in the cavalry is a squadron.) **Brigade:** Hdqts. and 2-5 battalions under a colonel. (Brigade-size unit in the cavalry and rangers is a regiment; in the special forces, a group.) **Division:** Hdqts. and 3 brigades with artillery, combat support, and combat service support units under a major general. **Corps:** Two or more divisions with corps troops under a lieutenant general. **Army:** Hdqts. and 2 or more corps with operational and support responsibilities under a general.

Air Force Units. Flight: Numerically designated flights are the lowest level unit in the Air Force. They are used primarily where there is a need for small mission elements to be incorporated into an organized unit. **Squadron:** The basic unit. Designates specific operational or support capability like mission units in operational commands. **Group:** A flexible unit composed of 2 or more squadrons whose functions may be operational, support, or administrative in nature. **Wing:** A primary group with supporting groups on a distinct mission with significant scope such as combat, flying training, or airlift. **Numbered Air Forces:** Normally an operationally oriented agency, the numbered air force is designed for the control of subordinate units with the same mission and/or geographical location. **Major Command:** A major subdivision of the Air Force with full staff that manages a major segment of the USAF mission. Major Command is composed of 3 or more numbered air forces.

Active Duty U.S. Military Personnel Strength Worldwide, 2011

Source: U.S. Dept. of Defense

(as of June 30, 2011)

TOTAL WORLDWIDE[1] **1,434,312**	**EUROPE**		**EAST ASIA & PACIFIC**		
	Belgium	1,210	Australia		124
U.S. TERRITORIES &	Germany	53,951	Japan		36,712
SPEC. LOCATIONS	Greece	324	Korea, South		NA
U.S., 48 contiguous states	927,523	Greenland	135	Philippines		178
Alaska	21,502	Italy	9,467	Singapore		123
Hawaii	39,305	Netherlands	428	Thailand		158
Guam	2,981	Portugal	724	Afloat		8,388
Puerto Rico	223	Spain	1,214	**Regional total[2]**		**45,857**
Transients	55,356	Turkey	1,509	**NORTH AFRICA, NEAR EAST, &**		
Afloat	81,803	United Kingdom	9,382	**SOUTH ASIA***		
Regional total[2] **1,128,698**	Afloat	370	Afghanistan[3]		111,700
	Regional total[2]	**79,243**	Bahrain		1,403
OTHER WESTERN HEMISPHERE			Diego Garcia		226
Canada	126			Egypt		265
Colombia	62	**SUB-SAHARAN AFRICA**		Iraq[3]		91,700
Cuba (Guantánamo)	824	Djibouti	1,722	Qatar		672
Haiti	12	**Regional total[2]**	**2,132**	Saudi Arabia		437
Honduras	357			United Arab Emirates		128
Afloat	11	**FORMER SOVIET UNION**		Afloat		4,899
Regional total[2]	**1,801**	Total	155	**Regional total[2,4]**		**8,325**

NA = Not available. *Special Forces personnel involved in Operation Enduring Freedom in Afghanistan not reported by Dept. of Defense. (1) Total worldwide also includes undistributed personnel. (2) Most countries and areas with fewer than 100 assigned U.S. military members not listed; regional totals include personnel stationed in those countries and areas not shown. (3) Rounded strengths for Operation Enduring Freedom (OEF) and Operation New Dawn (OND) deployment; includes troops in surrounding areas and deployed Reserve/National Guard. (4) Excludes troops deployed for OEF/OND.

U.S. Army Personnel on Active Duty

Source: Dept. of the Army, U.S. Dept. of Defense

(as of midyear, except where noted)

Date	Total strength[1]	Commissioned officers			Warrant officers[3]		Enlisted personnel		
		Total	Male	Female[2]	Male	Female	Total	Male	Female
1940	267,767	17,563	16,624	939	763	—	249,441	249,441	—
1942	3,074,184	203,137	190,662	12,475	3,285	—	2,867,762	2,867,762	—
1943	6,993,102	557,657	521,435	36,222	21,919	—	6,413,526	6,358,200	55,325
1944	7,992,868	740,077	692,351	47,726	36,893	10	7,215,888	7,144,601	71,287
1945	8,266,373	835,403	772,511	62,892	56,216	44	7,374,710	7,283,930	90,780
1946	1,889,690	257,300	240,658	16,642	9,826	18	1,622,546	1,605,847	16,699
1950	591,487	67,784	63,375	4,409	4,760	22	518,921	512,370	6,551
1955	1,107,606	111,347	106,196	5,151	10,552	48	985,659	977,943	7,716
1960	871,348	91,056	86,832	4,224	10,141	39	770,112	761,833	8,279
1965	967,049	101,812	98,029	3,783	10,285	23	854,929	846,409	8,520
1970	1,319,735	143,704	138,469	5,235	23,005	13	1,153,013	1,141,537	11,476
1975	781,316	89,756	85,184	4,572	13,214	22	678,324	640,621	37,703
1980 (Sept. 30) . .	772,661	85,339	77,843	7,496	13,265	113	673,944	612,593	61,351
1985 (Sept. 30) . .	776,244	94,103	83,563	10,540	15,296	288	666,557	598,639	67,918
1990 (Mar. 31). . .	746,220	91,330	79,520	11,810	15,177	470	639,713	567,015	72,698
1995	521,036	72,646	62,250	10,396	12,053	599	435,807	377,832	57,975
2000	471,633	66,344	56,391	9,953	10,608	781	393,900	333,947	59,953
2002	485,536	66,446	55,715	10,731	10,900	812	404,363	341,794	62,569
2003 (Sept. 30) . .	499,301	68,198	56,980	11,218	11,273	854	414,769	351,921	62,848
2004 (Sept. 30) . .	499,543	68,640	57,245	11,395	11,414	914	414,438	354,043	60,395
2005 (Sept. 30) . .	492,728	69,174	57,675	11,499	11,506	976	406,923	346,194	57,354
2006 (Sept. 30) . .	505,402	68,742	57,318	11,424	11,931	1,035	419,353	361,528	57,825
2007 (Sept. 30) . .	522,017	70,657	58,854	11,803	13,844	1,160	433,109	374,989	58,120
2008 (Sept. 30) . .	539,170	72,650	60,357	12,293	13,428	1,246	451,846	392,163	59,683
2009 (Sept. 30) . .	553,044	75,337	63,146	12,191	13,815	1,348	457,980	398,579	59,401
2010 (Sept. 30) . .	566,045	78,588	64,952	13,636	14,106	1,434	467,248	406,871	60,377
2011	571,108	81,832	NA	NA	15,854	NA	468,753	NA	NA

NA = Not available. **Note:** Represents strength of active Army, including Philippine Scouts (1940-46), ret. Regular Army personnel on extended active duty, and National Guard and Reserve personnel on extended active duty; excl. U.S. Military Academy cadets, contract surgeons, and National Guard and Reserve personnel not on extended active duty. (1) Includes categories not listed, e.g., West Point Cadets. Data for 1940-46 include personnel in the Army Air Forces and its predecessors (Air Service and Air Corps). (2) Includes Army Nurse Corps for all years, Women's Army Corps (1942-78), Medical Specialists Corps (1949 and subsequent years). (3) Act of Congress approved Apr. 27, 1926, directed the appointment as warrant officers of field clerks still in active service. Includes flight officers as follows: 1943, 5,700; 1944, 13,615; 1945, 31,117; 1946, 2,580.

U.S. Navy Personnel on Active Duty

Source: U.S. Dept. of Defense
(as of midyear, except where noted)

Date	Officers	Nurses	Enlisted	Officer candidates	Total[1]	Date	Officers	Nurses	Enlisted	Officer candidates	Total[1]
1940	13,162	442	144,824	2,569	160,997	1998 (Sept.)	55,007	—	326,196	—	381,203
1945	320,293	11,086	2,988,207	61,231	3,380,817	1999	55,726	—	322,372	—	378,098
1950	42,687	1,964	331,860	5,037	381,538	2000 (Oct.)	53,698	—	320,212	—	373,910
1960	67,456	2,103	544,040	4,385	617,984	2005	54,039	—	305,368	—	363,858
1970	78,488	2,273	605,899	6,000	692,660	2006	53,209	—	295,773	—	353,496
1980[2]	63,100	—	464,100	—	527,200	2007 (Sept.)	51,385	—	281,772	—	337,547
1990 (Sept.)	74,429	—	530,133	—	604,562	2008	52,184	—	276,346	—	331,785
1995 (May)	61,075	—	402,626	—	463,701	2009	52,233	—	274,858	—	331,637
1996	60,013	—	376,595	—	436,608	2010	53,071	—	273,609	—	330,065
1997	57,341	—	340,616	—	397,957	2011	53,620	—	270,425	—	328,648

(1) May include categories not shown, e.g., midshipmen. (2) Starting in 1980, "Nurses" are included with "Officers," and "Officer candidates" are included with "Enlisted."

U.S. Air Force Personnel on Active Duty

Source: U.S. Dept. of Defense
(as of midyear)

Year[1]	Strength	Year[1]	Strength	Year[1]	Strength	Year[1]	Strength	Year[1]	Strength	Year[1]	Strength
1918	195,023	1943	2,197,114	1980	557,969	1993	444,351	1998	363,479	2007	340,596
1920	9,050	1944	2,372,292	1986	608,200	1994	426,327	1999	357,929	2008	328,771
1930	13,531	1945	2,282,259	1990	535,233	1995	400,051	2000	357,777	2009	334,009
1940	51,165	1950	411,277	1991	510,432	1996	389,400	2005	358,705	2010	337,505
1941	152,125	1960	814,213	1992	470,315	1997	378,681	2006	352,620	2011	333,729
1942	764,415	1970	791,078								

(1) Prior to 1947, data are for U.S. Army Air Corps and Air Service of the Signal Corps.

U.S. Marine Corps Personnel on Active Duty

Source: U.S. Dept. of Defense
(as of midyear)

Year	Officers	Enlisted	Total	Year	Officers	Enlisted	Total	Year	Officers	Enlisted	Total
1940	1,800	26,545	28,345	1994	18,430	159,949	178,379	2005	19,118	159,113	178,231
1945	37,067	437,613	474,680	1995	18,017	153,929	171,946	2006	19,218	159,705	178,923
1950	7,254	67,025	74,279	1996	18,146	154,141	172,287	2007	19,456	162,085	181,541
1960	16,203	154,418	170,621	1997	18,089	154,240	172,329	2008	20,137	172,903	193,040
1970	24,941	234,796	259,737	1998	17,984	154,648	172,632	2009	21,031	183,243	204,274
1980	18,198	170,271	188,469	1999	17,892	155,250	173,142	2010	21,680	179,446	201,126
1990	19,958	176,694	196,652	2000	17,897	154,744	172,641	2011	22,281	178,546	200,827
1993	18,878	161,205	180,083								

U.S. Coast Guard Personnel on Active Duty

Source: U.S. Dept. of Defense
(as of midyear)

Year	Total	Officers	Cadets	Enlisted	Year	Total	Officers	Cadets	Enlisted
1970	37,689	5,512	653	31,524	2006	40,639	8,032	1,004	32,001
1980	39,381	6,463	877	32,041	2007	41,265	8,231	720	32,314
1985	38,595	6,775	733	31,087	2008	42,424	8,282	1,005	33,137
1990	37,308	6,475	820	29,860	2009	43,514	8,497	993	34,024
1995	36,731	7,489	841	28,401	2010	43,135	8,678	744	33,713
2000	35,712	7,154	863	27,695	2011	43,327	8,659	1,053	33,615
2005	40,814	7,908	1,006	31,900					

Women in the U.S. Armed Forces

Source: U.S. Dept. of Defense; U.S. Census Bureau; Women In Military Service For America Memorial Foundation

Women in the Army, Navy, Air Force, Marines, and Coast Guard are fully integrated with male personnel. All enlisted jobs were open to women when the draft ended June 30, 1973. Admission to service academies began in 1976. Under rules instituted in 1993, women were allowed to fly combat aircraft and serve aboard warships. By the mid-1990s, 80% of all jobs and more than 90% of all career fields had been opened to women. The first woman achieved the rank of four-star general in 2009. In Apr. 2010, the Navy announced that women would be placed on submarine crews by Jan. 2012. Women remained restricted from service in ground combat units.

(on active duty as of Sept. 30 in year shown)

Women Active Duty Troops, 2010

Service	% women
Army	13.5
Navy	16.0
Marines	7.5
Air Force	19.2
Coast Guard	13.1

Women on Active Duty, All Services, 1973-2010

Year	% women	Year	% women
1973	2.5	1997	13.6
1975	4.6	2000	14.4
1981	8.9	2005	14.6
1987	10.2	2009	14.3
1993	11.6	2010	14.5

African American Service in U.S. Wars

Source: U.S. Dept. of Defense; U.S. Census Bureau

American Revolution. About 5,000 served in the Continental Army, mostly in integrated units, some in all-black combat units.

Civil War. Some 180,000 served in 163 units of the Union Army's U.S. Colored Troops, 200,000 worked in service units—10% of the Union Army in all; about 37,000 died, 31,000 wounded.

World War I. 350,000-400,000 served in the armed forces, 100,000 in France. Some 40,000 fought.

World War II. Some 1 mil served in the armed forces—8% of all troops—mostly in Army service units; all-black fighter and bomber AAF units and infantry divisions gave distinguished service.

Korean War. More than 600,000 served in the military; 3,075 lost their lives in combat. By 1954, armed forces were completely desegregated.

Vietnam War. 274,937 served in the armed forces (1965-74)—9.8% of all troops; 7,243 were killed in combat.

Persian Gulf War. About 104,000 served in the Kuwaiti theater—20% of all U.S. troops. 66 died in combat.

Operation Enduring Freedom. 128 military deaths and 815 wounded in Afghanistan and other locations (as of Aug. 1, 2011).

Operation Iraqi Freedom/Operation New Dawn. 433 military deaths and 2,720 wounded (as of Aug. 1, 2011).

Monthly Military Pay Scale

Source: U.S. Dept. of Defense

(effective Jan. 1, 2011; salaries rounded to nearest dollar)

	<2	2	3	4	6	8	10	12	14	16	18	20	22	24	26
Commissioned officers															
O-10[1,2]	NA	NA	NA	NA	NA	NA	NA	NA	NA	NA	NA	15,401	15,476	15,798	16,358
O-9[1]	NA	NA	NA	NA	NA	NA	NA	NA	NA	NA	NA	13,470	13,664	13,944	14,433
O-8[1]	9,531	9,843	10,050	10,108	10,367	10,798	10,899	11,309	11,426	11,780	12,291	12,762	13,077	13,077	13,077
O-7[1]	7,919	8,287	8,457	8,593	8,838	9,080	9,360	9,639	9,919	10,798	11,541	11,541	11,541	11,541	11,600
O-6	5,870	6,449	6,872	6,872	6,898	7,193	7,232	7,232	7,643	8,370	8,797	9,223	9,466	9,711	10,188
O-5	4,893	5,512	5,894	5,966	6,204	6,346	6,659	6,889	7,186	7,641	7,857	8,070	8,313	8,313	8,313
O-4	4,222	4,887	5,213	5,286	5,589	5,913	6,317	6,632	6,851	6,977	7,049	7,049	7,049	7,049	7,049
O-3	3,712	4,208	4,542	4,952	5,189	5,449	5,618	5,895	6,039	6,039	6,039	6,039	6,039	6,039	6,039
O-2	3,207	3,653	4,207	4,349	4,439	4,439	4,439	4,439	4,439	4,439	4,439	4,439	4,439	4,439	4,439
O-1	2,784	2,897	3,503	3,503	3,503	3,503	3,503	3,503	3,503	3,503	3,503	3,503	3,503	3,503	3,503
Commissioned officers with over 4 years' active duty service as enlisted member or warrant officer															
O-3[3]	NA	NA	NA	4,952	5,189	5,449	5,618	5,895	6,128	6,262	6,445	6,445	6,445	6,445	6,445
O-2[3]	NA	NA	NA	4,349	4,439	4,580	4,819	5,003	5,140	5,140	5,140	5,140	5,140	5,140	5,140
O-1[3]	NA	NA	NA	3,503	3,740	3,879	4,020	4,159	4,349	4,349	4,349	4,349	4,349	4,349	4,349
Warrant officers															
W-5	NA	NA	NA	NA	NA	NA	NA	NA	NA	NA	NA	6,821	7,167	7,425	7,710
W-4	3,836	4,127	4,245	4,361	4,562	4,761	4,961	5,264	5,530	5,782	5,988	6,190	6,485	6,728	7,006
W-3	3,503	3,649	3,799	3,848	4,005	4,314	4,635	4,786	4,961	5,142	5,466	5,685	5,816	5,956	6,145
W-2	3,100	3,393	3,483	3,545	3,746	4,059	4,214	4,366	4,553	4,698	4,830	4,988	5,092	5,174	5,174
W-1	2,721	3,014	3,092	3,259	3,456	3,746	3,881	4,070	4,257	4,403	4,538	4,702	4,702	4,702	4,702
Enlisted members															
E-9[4]	NA	NA	NA	NA	NA	NA	4,635	4,740	4,872	5,028	5,185	5,437	5,649	5,873	6,216
E-8	NA	NA	NA	NA	NA	3,794	3,962	4,066	4,190	4,325	4,568	4,692	4,902	5,018	5,305
E-7	2,637	2,879	2,989	3,135	3,249	3,445	3,555	3,751	3,914	4,025	4,143	4,189	4,343	4,426	4,740
E-6	2,281	2,510	2,621	2,729	2,841	3,094	3,192	3,383	3,441	3,484	3,533	3,533	3,533	3,533	3,533
E-5	2,090	2,230	2,338	2,448	2,620	2,801	2,948	2,966	2,966	2,966	2,966	2,966	2,966	2,966	2,966
E-4	1,916	2,014	2,123	2,231	2,326	2,326	2,326	2,326	2,326	2,326	2,326	2,326	2,326	2,326	2,326
E-3	1,730	1,839	1,950	1,950	1,950	1,950	1,950	1,950	1,950	1,950	1,950	1,950	1,950	1,950	1,950
E-2	1,645	1,645	1,645	1,645	1,645	1,645	1,645	1,645	1,645	1,645	1,645	1,645	1,645	1,645	1,645
E-1[5]	1,468	NA	NA	NA	NA	NA	NA	NA	NA	NA	NA	NA	NA	NA	NA

NA = Not applicable. **Notes:** In 2007, the military pay scale was expanded to 40 years. **Over 30 years**—O-10: 17,176; O-9: 15,155; O-8: 13,404; O-7: 11,832; O-6: 10,391; W-5: 8,096; W-4: 7,146; E-9: 6,145; E-8: 5,411. **Over 34 years**—O-10: 18,035; O-9: 15,913; O-8: 13,739; W-5: 8,501; E-9: 6,853. **Over 38 years**—O-10: 18,937; O-9: 16,709; W-5: 8,926; E-9: 7,196. (1) Basic pay for an O-7 to O-10 is limited by Level II of the Executive Schedule which is $14,975.10. Basic pay for O-6 and below is limited by Level V of the Executive Schedule which is $12,141.60. (2) While serving as Chairman, Joint Chief of Staff/Vice Chairman, Joint Chief of Staff, Chief of Navy Operations, Commandant of the Marine Corps, Army/Air Force Chief of Staff, Commander of a unified or specified combatant command, basic pay is $20,263.50. (See footnote 1.) (3) Applicable to O-1 to O-3 with at least 4 years and 1 day of active duty or more than 1,460 points as a warrant and/or enlisted member. See Department of Defense Financial Management Regulations for more detailed explanation on who is eligible for this special basic pay rate. (4) For the Master Chief Petty Officer of the Navy, Chief Master Sergeant of the Air Force, Sergeant Major of the Army or Marine Corps, or Senior Enlisted Advisor of the JCS, basic pay is $7,489.80. Combat Zone Tax Exclusion for O-1 and above is based on this basic pay rate plus Hostile Fire Pay/Imminent Danger Pay which is $225.00. (5) Applicable to E-1 with 4 months or more of active duty. Basic pay for an E-1 with less than 4 months of active duty is $1,357.20.

Outlays for Individual Payments to Veterans, 1940-2012

Source: White House Office of Management and Budget

(in millions of dollars)

Year	Total	Compensation	Pensions	Hospital/medical	Education	Insurance & burial	Year	Total	Compensation	Pensions	Hospital/medical	Education	Insurance & burial
1940	$578	$244	$185	$69	—	$80	2003	$55,792	$24,696	$3,229	$24,487	$2,049	$1,331
1950	8,827	1,533	476	764	$2,739	3,315	2004	55,021	26,297	3,334	21,590	2,408	1,392
1960	5,355	2,049	1,263	931	392	720	2005	62,206	30,877	3,663	23,073	3,224	1,369
1970	8,808	2,980	2,255	1,723	1,002	848	2006	63,658	30,991	3,547	24,445	3,325	1,350
1980	20,927	7,446	3,585	6,290	2,418	1,188	2007	69,740	31,055	3,376	30,537	3,427	1,345
1990	28,545	10,735	3,594	12,021	795	1,400	2008	76,113	36,256	3,790	31,096	3,607	1,364
1995	36,822	14,842	3,024	16,196	1,386	1,374	2009	85,501	40,399	4,161	35,264	4,308	1,369
2000	46,086	20,775	2,969	19,343	1,636	1,363	2010	95,997	43,377	4,359	38,216	8,727	1,318
2001	45,435	18,579	2,760	20,966	1,783	1,347	2011*	110,527	66,446	4,983	41,136	11,209	1,351
2002	$50,969	$22,418	$3,166	$22,384	1,681	$1,320	2012*	109,988	48,601	4,561	44,101	11,382	1,343

*Estimate. **Note:** Compensation is service-connected; pension is not.

U.S. Veteran Population, 2011

Source: U.S. Dept. of Veterans Affairs

(population projection, in thousands, as of Sept. 30)

TOTAL VETERANS IN CIVILIAN LIFE[1]	**22,234.2**
Total wartime veterans[2]	**16,502.0**
Total Gulf War[3]	5,902.0
Gulf War with no prior wartime service	5,554.4
Gulf War with service in Vietnam era	342.5
Gulf War, with service in Vietnam and Korea	4.6
Gulf War with service in Vietnam, Korea, and WWII	0.6
Total Vietnam era[3]	7,391.0
Vietnam era with no prior wartime service	6,813.1
Vietnam era with service in Korean conflict	171.0
Vietnam era with service in Korea and WWII	59.2
Total Korean conflict[3]	2,274.7
Korean conflict with no prior wartime service	1,905.5
Korean conflict with service in WWII	133.8
Total World War II[3]	1,711.0
WWII only	1,517.4
Total peacetime veterans[4]	**5,732.2**
Post Gulf War	44.2
Service between Vietnam era and Gulf War only	3,398.4
Service between Korean conflict and Vietnam era only	2,184.3
Pre-Korean conflict without service in WWII	105.3

Note: Figures are for U.S. veterans worldwide. (1) Includes those who served on active duty in Army, Navy, Air Force, Marines, Coast Guard, uniformed Public Health Service and NOAA, and reservists called to federal active duty. Excludes those dishonorably discharged, those whose only active duty was training, and those currently on active duty. (2) Veterans serving in more than one period are counted only once in total. (3) Total includes veterans who also served in previous periods. (4) Veterans with both wartime and peacetime service are counted only as "wartime veterans."

Nations With Largest Armed Forces, by Active-Duty Troop Strength

Source: *The Military Balance 2011*, International Institute for Strategic Studies, published by Routledge Journals, Taylor & Francis, UK
(As of Nov. 2010, except defense expenditure, which is for 2009.)

| | | Troop strength | | | | Navy | | Combat aircraft | |
| | | Active troops | Reserve troops | Defense expend. | Tanks (MBT) | Cruisers/ frigates/ | Sub- | FGA | FTR |
Rank	Country	(thousands)		($ bil)	(army only)	destroyers	marines	(air force only)	
1.	China	2,285	510	70,381	7,050	65F/13D	71	313+	986
2.	United States	1,564	871	661,049	5,795	22C/22F/59D*	71	978	468
3.	India	1,325	1,155	38,278	4,117+	12F/10D*	16	517	112
4.	Korea, North	1,190	600	—	3,500+	3F	70	48	458
5.	Russia	1,046	20,000	38,293	2,800+	6C/7F/18D*	67	337	707
6.	Korea, South	655	4,500	22,439	2,414	1C/12F/6D	23	234	233
7.	Pakistan	617	0	3,811	2,386+	9F	8	151	236
8.	Iran	523	350	8,636	1,613+	0	23	108	189+
9.	Turkey	511	379	10,883	4,503	17F	14	339	87
10.	Egypt	469	479	4,118	2,383	8F	4	238	156
11.	Vietnam	455	5,000	2,137	1,315	0	2	219	0
12.	Myanmar	406	0	—	150	0	0	0	69
13.	Brazil	318	1,340	25,984	267	11F/3D*	5	61	57
14.	Thailand	306	200	4,732	283	10F*	0	0	87
15.	Indonesia	302	400	4,821	0	11F	2	5	27
16.	Syria	295	314	2,229	4,950	0	0	309	158+
17.	Taiwan	290	1,657	9,500	926+	4C/22F	4	128	291
18.	Colombia	283	62	9,603	0	4F	4	31	0
19.	Mexico	280	87	4,769	0	7F	0	0	10
20.	Germany	251	40	47,466	768	13F/7D	4	175	109
21.	Japan	248	56	51,085	850	2C/16F/30D*	18	159	202
22.	Iraq	246	0	4,118	212	0	0	0	0
23.	France	239	34	54,446	254	11F/13D*	9	135	73
24.	Saudi Arabia	234	0	41,276	565	4F/3D	0	161	98
25.	Eritrea	202	120	78	270	0	0	13	14
26.	Morocco	196	150	3,061	380	2F	0	33	33
27.	Italy	185	42	30,489	320	12F/4D*	6	150	73
28.	United Kingdom	178	82	59,131	325	17F/7D*	11	177	12
29.	Israel	177	565	13,516	3,501	0	3	227	168
30.	Sri Lanka	161	6	1,485	62	0	0	16	4

— = Not available. MBT = Main battle tank. FGA = Fighter, ground attack. FTR = Fighter. *Denotes navies with aircraft carriers, as follows: United States 11, Italy 2, Brazil 1, China 1, France 1, India 1, Japan 1, Russia 1, Thailand 1, United Kingdom 1.

Budget for Global War on Terror Operations, 2001-11
Source: Congressional Research Service
(in billions of dollars)

	2001/02[1]	2003	2004	2005	2006	2007	2008	2009	2010	2011[2]	Total
Total: All missions	$33.8	$81.1	$94.1	$107.6	$121.5	$170.9	$185.6	$155.1	$165.3	$168.1	$1,283.3
Dept. of Defense.	33.0	77.4	72.4	102.6	116.8	164.9	179.2	148.3	154.3	159.1	1,208.1
Foreign aid and diplomacy[3]	0.8	3.7	21.7	4.8	4.3	5.0	5.4	5.4	9.1	6.5	66.7
Veterans Affairs medical. . . .	0.0	0.0	0.0	0.2	0.4	1.0	1.0	1.5	1.9	2.4	8.4
Op. Iraqi Freedom/New Dawn[4]	0.0	53.0	75.9	85.6	101.7	131.3	142.1	95.5	71.3	49.3	805.5
Dept. of Defense.	0.0	50.0	56.4	83.4	98.1	127.2	138.5	92.0	66.5	45.7	757.8
Foreign aid and diplomacy[3]	0.0	3.0	19.5	2.0	3.2	3.2	2.7	2.2	3.3	2.3	41.4
Veterans Affairs medical. . . .	0.0	0.0	0.0	0.2	0.4	0.9	0.9	1.2	1.5	1.3	6.3
Op. Enduring Freedom[5]	20.8	14.7	14.6	20.0	19.0	39.2	43.4	59.5	93.8	118.6	443.5
Dept. of Defense.	20.0	14.0	12.4	17.2	17.9	37.2	40.6	56.1	87.7	113.3	416.2
Foreign aid and diplomacy[3]	0.8	0.7	2.2	2.8	1.1	1.9	2.7	3.1	5.7	4.1	25.1
Veterans Affairs medical. . . .	0.0	0.0	0.0	0.0	0.0	0.1	0.1	0.2	0.5	1.1	2.1
Op. Noble Eagle[6].	13.0	8.0	3.7	2.1	0.8	0.5	0.1	0.1	0.1	0.1	28.6
Dept. of Defense unallocated	0.0	5.5	0.0	0.0	0.0	0.0	0.0	0.0	0.0	0.0	5.5

(1) Fiscal Year (FY) 2001 and FY2002 funds combined because most were obligated in FY2002 after the Sept. 11, 2001, attacks at the end of FY2001. (2) FY2011 Continuing Resolution, signed by Pres. Obama Mar. 18, 2011, extended funding for all agencies through Apr. 8, 2011. (3) Foreign aid and diplomacy figures include monies for reconstruction, development and humanitarian aid, embassy operations, counternarcotics, initial training of the Afghan and Iraqi army, foreign military sales credits, and Economic Support Funds. (4) Began in the fall of 2002 with the buildup of troops for the Mar. 2003 invasion of Iraq and continues with counterinsurgency and stability operations. (5) Covering Afghanistan and other ongoing Global War on Terror (GWOT) operations, ranging from the Philippines to Djibouti, that began immediately after the Sept. 11, 2001, attacks. (6) Dept. of Defense funds that rebuilt the Pentagon and provide higher security at U.S. military bases and other homeland security, including combat air patrol.

Leading Purchasers of U.S. Defense Articles and Services
Source: Congressional Research Service
(in current U.S. dollars)

Worldwide Deliveries[1]

	2002-05					2006-09		
1. Egypt	$6.1 billion	6. South Korea	$2.2 billion	1. Israel	$5.2 billion	6. Poland	$2.8 billion
2. Israel	4.6 billion	7. Japan	1.8 billion	2. Saudi Arabia	5.0 billion	7. South Korea	2.7 billion
3. Saudi Arabia	4.4 billion	8. UK	1.5 billion	3. Egypt	4.4 billion	8. Australia	2.7 billion
4. Taiwan	4.0 billion	9. Singapore	1.1 billion	4. Taiwan	3.5 billion	9. Greece	2.0 billion
5. Greece	3.4 billion	10. Spain	1.1 billion	5. Japan	3.0 billion	10. UK	1.8 billion

(1) Total dollar value of all U.S. defense articles and services actually delivered to top 10 purchasers worldwide. Figures include government-to-government sales through the Foreign Military Sales (FMS) system (which accounts for the overwhelming majority of U.S. conventional arms deliveries) concluded in calendar years listed, as well as commercially licensed exports concluded in pertinent fiscal years.

U.S. Foreign Military Financing, 2002-10

Source: Defense Security Cooperation Agency, U.S. Dept. of Defense, 2002-09; Office of the Director of U.S. Foreign Assistance, U.S. State Dept., 2010

(in thousands of U.S. dollars)

	2010	2002-09		2010	2002-09
Near East and South Asia....	$4,853,810	$34,991,358	Europe.....................	$137,855	$1,419,639
Afghanistan...............	0	1,051,877	Bosnia and Herzegovina	4,000	55,882
Bahrain..................	19,000	204,588	Bulgaria..................	9,000	76,403
Egypt...................	1,300,000	10,349,950	Czech Republic	6,000	62,768
Israel....................	2,775,000	18,833,604	Georgia..................	16,000	128,384
Jordan..................	300,000	2,162,317	Poland...................	47,000	261,527
Lebanon.................	100,000	99,606	Romania.................	13,000	106,645
Morocco	9,000	65,423	Turkey...................	0	170,977
Oman	8,848	189,756	Ukraine..................	11,000	50,902
Pakistan................	294,169	1,863,630	**Africa**...................	17,950	155,287
Tunisia	18,000	66,677	Djibouti..................	2,000	37,589
Yemen	12,500	72,122	Liberia...................	6,000	9,299
East Asia and Pacific	59,100	348,656	**Americas**	352,990	666,641
Indonesia	20,000	36,952	Colombia	55,000	497,400
Philippines	29,000	268,977	El Salvador	0	42,291
			Mexico	265,250	33,150
			World total................	5,476,169	37,581,582

Note: Grants extended to foreign governments in a fiscal year to pay for military equipment and services. May be from U.S. Dept. of Defense (DOD) or, for specific countries, negotiated directly with U.S. commercial suppliers with DOD approval.

Defense Contracts, 2011

Source: U.S. Dept. of Defense

(in millions of U.S. dollars)

Listed are the 50 companies or organizations receiving the largest dollar volume of prime contract awards from the U.S. Dept. of Defense during fiscal year 2011.

Rank Contractor	Contracts awarded[1]	% of total	Rank Contractor	Contracts awarded[1]	% of total
1. Lockheed Martin Corp.	$20,709.1	10.2%	27. Textron Inc.	$1,069.7	0.5%
2. The Boeing Co.	13,349.3	6.6	28. Evergreen Intl. Airlines	1,065.1	0.5
3. General Dynamics Corp.	8,327.3	4.1	29. URS Corp.	1,050.8	0.5
4. Raytheon Co.	7,574.4	3.7	30. Computershare Limited	1,036.2	0.5
5. United Technologies Corp.	5,478.3	2.7	31. FedEx Corp.	1,020.4	0.5
6. Northrop Grumman Corp.	4,927.5	2.4	32. Booz Allen Hamilton Holding Corp. ..	1,016.6	0.5
7. L-3 Communications Holdings, Inc. ...	4,006.5	2.0	33. Supreme Group Holding SARL	1,003.1	0.5
8. BAE Systems PLC	3,243.4	1.6	34. Alliant Techsystems Inc.	933.3	0.5
9. Northrop Grumman Corp.	2,770.7	1.4	35. Lockheed Martin	926.8	0.5
10. Oshkosh Corp...................	2,767.8	1.4	36. CACI International Inc	887.3	0.4
11. Health Net, Inc.	2,365.9	1.2	37. Honeywell International Inc.	796.8	0.4
12. Bell Boeing Joint Project Office	2,311.1	1.1	38. Navistar International Corp.	792.6	0.4
13. SAIC, Inc.	2,291.2	1.1	39. Amerisourcebergen Corp.	779.0	0.4
14. Triwest Healthcare Alliance.........	2,130.1	1.0	40. DDJ Capital Management, LLC	758.5	0.4
15. Humana Inc.	1,837.5	0.9	41. AM General	739.7	0.4
16. General Electric Co.	1,815.0	0.9	42. McKesson Corp.	735.7	0.4
17. Bechtel Group, Inc.	1,793.3	0.9	43. Government of the United States	719.7	0.4
18. KBR, Inc.......................	1,714.8	0.8	44. Harris Corp.	689.3	0.3
19. Cerberus Capital Management, L.P....	1,581.7	0.8	45. SOPAKCO	676.5	0.3
20. Computer Sciences Corp.	1,545.3	0.8	46. CBY Design Builders (CDM, Brasfield &		
21. Unaka Co., Inc..................	1,529.4	0.8	Gorrie, and Yates Construction) ...	675.0	0.3
22. Ameriqual Group, LLC	1,488.7	0.7	47. Government of Canada	669.4	0.3
23. ITT Corp.	1,356.7	0.7	48. Hewlett-Packard Co.	659.2	0.3
24. Fluor Corp.	1,356.3	0.7	49. Royal Dutch Shell PLC	652.9	0.3
25. Huntington Ingalls Industries, Inc.....	1,355.3	0.7	50. Rolls-Royce Group PLC	613.8	0.3
26. General Atomic Technologies Corp. ..	1,287.8	0.6	Other.........................	83,671.7	
			Total........................	203,940.0	

(1) Amounts include contracts awarded to subsidiaries of each company.

Arms Transfer Agreements With the World, by Supplier, 2003-10

Source: Congressional Research Service

(in millions of current U.S. dollars)

Supplier	2003	2004	2005	2006	2007	2008	2009	2010	2003-10
United States	$5,769	$6,810	$5,488	$8,388	$11,721	$28,452	$14,847	$14,943	$96,418
Russia	5,100	8,000	8,500	14,700	9,600	6,400	12,400	7,600	72,300
France	900	1,100	5,000	500	1,300	3,300	7,800	1,300	21,200
United Kingdom	1,900	4,100	2,800	4,000	9,500	200	1,000	1,100	24,600
China	600	1,000	2,800	1,900	2,700	2,100	2,000	900	14,000
Germany................	100	100	700	2,400	1,700	4,700	500	0	10,200
Italy...................	300	300	600	600	1,000	1,600	2,700	1,700	8,800
All other European	1,400	2,400	3,500	2,600	2,200	4,300	5,100	2,000	23,500
All others	1,400	2,600	1,000	3,000	1,800	1,700	2,700	1,200	15,400
Total..................	17,469	26,410	30,388	38,088	41,521	52,752	49,047	30,743	286,418

Note: All data are for the calendar year given except for U.S. MAP (Military Assistance Program), IMET (International Military Education, and Training), and Excess Defense Article data, which are included for the particular fiscal year. All amounts given include the values of all categories of weapons, spare parts, construction, all associated services, military assistance, excess defense articles, and training programs. Statistics for foreign countries are based upon estimated selling prices. All foreign data are rounded to the nearest $100 mil.

Personal Salutes and Honors

The U.S. **national salute**, 21 guns, is also the salute to a national flag. U.S. independence is commemorated by the salute to the Union—one gun for each state—fired at noon July 4, at all military posts provided with suitable artillery.

A 21-gun salute on arrival and departure, with 4 ruffles and flourishes, is rendered to the **president** of the United States, to a former president, and to a president-elect. The national anthem or "Hail to the Chief," as appropriate, is played for the president, and the national anthem for the others. A 21-gun salute on arrival and departure, with 4 ruffles and flourishes, also is rendered to the **sovereign or chief of state of a foreign country** or a member of a reigning royal family, and the national anthem of his or her country is played. The music is considered an inseparable part of the salute and immediately follows the ruffles and flourishes without pause. For the Honors March, generals receive the "General's March," admirals receive the "Flag Officer's March," and all others receive the 32-bar medley of "The Stars and Stripes Forever."

GRADE, TITLE, OR OFFICE	SALUTE (IN GUNS) Arriving	Leaving	Ruffles and flourishes	Music
Vice President of U.S.	19	—	4	Hail, Columbia
Speaker of the House.	19	—	4	Honors March
U.S. or foreign ambassador in country to which accredited	19	—	4	Nat. anthem of official
Premier or prime minister	19	—	4	Nat. anthem of official
Secretary of Defense, Army, Navy, or Air Force	19	19	4	Honors March
Other cabinet members, Senate president pro tempore, governor, or chief justice of U.S.	19	—	4	Honors March
Chairman, Joint Chiefs of Staff.	19	19	4	Honors March
Army chief of staff, chief of naval operations, Air Force chief of staff, Marine commandant.	19	19	4	Honors March
General of the Army, general of the Air Force, fleet admiral	19	19	4	Honors March
Generals, admirals	17	17	4	Honors March
Assistant secretaries of Defense, Army, Navy, or Air Force.	17	17	4	Honors March
Chair of a committee of Congress	17	—	4	Honors March

Other salutes (on arrival only, with Honors March) include 17 guns, with 3 ruffles and flourishes, for U.S. ambassadors returning to the U.S. on official business; 15 guns, with 3 ruffles and flourishes, for U.S. envoys or ministers, foreign envoys or ministers accredited to the U.S., and lieutenant generals or vice admirals; 13 guns, with 2 ruffles and flourishes, for a major general or rear admiral (upper half) and for U.S. ministers resident and ministers resident accredited to the U.S.; 11 guns, with 1 ruffle and flourish, for a brigadier general or rear admiral (lower half) and for U.S. chargés d'affaires and like officials accredited to the U.S.; 11 guns, no ruffles and flourishes, for consuls general accredited to the U.S.

The Medal of Honor

Source: Congressional Medal of Honor Society; Army, U.S. Dept. of Defense

(as of Oct. 1, 2011)

The Medal of Honor is the highest military award for bravery that can be given to any individual in the United States. The first Army Medals were awarded on Mar. 25, 1863; the first Navy Medals went to sailors and Marines on Apr. 3, 1863.

On Dec. 21, 1861, Pres. Abraham Lincoln signed a bill to create the Navy Medal of Honor. Lincoln, on July 14, 1862, approved a resolution providing for the presentation of Medals of Honor to enlisted men of the Army and Voluntary Forces, making it a law. The law was amended on Mar. 3, 1863, to extend its provisions to include officers as well as enlisted men.

The Medal of Honor is awarded in the name of Congress to a person who, while a member of the armed forces, distinguishes himself or herself conspicuously by gallantry and intrepidity at the risk of life above and beyond the call of duty while engaged in an action against any enemy of the United States; while engaged in military operations involving conflict with an opposing foreign force; or while serving with friendly foreign forces engaged in an armed conflict against an opposing armed force in which the United States is not a belligerent party.

The deed performed must have been one of personal bravery or self-sacrifice so conspicuous as to clearly distinguish the individual above his or her comrades and must have involved risk of life. Incontestable proof of the performance of service is required, and each recommendation for award of this decoration is considered on the standard of extraordinary merit.

Prior to World War I, the 2,625 Army Medal of Honor awards up to that time were reviewed to determine which past awards met new stringent criteria. The Army removed 911 names from the list, most of them former members of a volunteer infantry group during the Civil War who had been induced to extend their enlistments when they were promised the medal. However, in 1977 a medal was restored to Dr. Mary Walker, and in 1989 medals were restored to Buffalo Bill Cody and 7 other Indian scouts.

Medals of Honor were awarded posthumously for actions during the Battle of Mogadishu (Somalia), Oct. 3, 1993, to Army Master Sgt. Gary I. Gordon and to Sgt. First Class Randall D. Shughart. Both received the medal for voluntarily guarding a helicopter crash site and its downed crew while under heavy enemy fire until relief could arrive.

Seven African American soldiers were awarded Medals of Honor for service in World War II (6 of them posthumously) in Jan. 1997. Previously, no black soldier had received the medal for World War II service; an Army inquiry begun in 1993 con-

cluded that the prevailing political climate and Army practices of the time had prevented proper recognition of heroism on the part of black soldiers in that war. In June 2002, 22 Asian Americans received the award for World War II service.

Iraq. Four Medals of Honor have been awarded for actions in Operation Iraqi Freedom. On Apr. 4, 2003, Army Sgt. First Class Paul R. Smith was mortally wounded while holding an exposed position, near Baghdad International Airport, against enemy attack. On Apr. 14, 2004, Marine Cpl. Jason L. Dunham was mortally wounded at Karbala when he covered a live grenade with his helmet and body to protect his fellow Marines. On Sept. 29, 2006, Navy Petty Officer Second Class (SEAL) Michael A. Monsoor was mortally wounded at Ar Ramadi when he threw himself onto a grenade, saving the lives of two teammates. The most recent recipient was Army Private First Class Ross A. McGinnis, whose posthumous award was presented June 5, 2008, for covering a grenade with his body, saving his 4 Humvee crew members from serious injury.

Afghanistan. Six Medals of Honor have been awarded for actions in Afghanistan. The Medal was awarded posthumously to Navy Lt. Michael P. Murphy, whose SEAL team came under attack by Taliban fighters June 28, 2005. Heavily outnumbered and with all four team members wounded, Lt. Murphy left cover to radio for help and was shot in the back. On June 21, 2006, Army Sgt. First Class Jared C. Monti and his patrol were ambushed. Monti repeatedly tried to rescue a wounded soldier despite overwhelming gunfire and his men being outnumbered by more than 3 to 1. Monti was killed by a grenade on his third attempt and received the Medal of Honor posthumously. Special Forces Staff Sgt. Robert Miller received the Medal of Honor after dying while saving the lives of 7 U.S. and 15 Afghan Army soldiers during a battle against more than 100 insurgents on Jan. 25, 2008.

Army Staff Sgt. Salvatore Giunta on Oct. 25, 2007, advanced 3 times in the face of persistent Taliban fire to give aid to injured comrades in an ambush; he became the first surviving Medal of Honor recipient since the Vietnam War Nov. 16, 2010. A wounded Staff Sgt. Leroy Petry May 26, 2008, protected fellow injured rangers by throwing a live enemy grenade, losing his right hand as it detonated. On Sept. 8, 2009, Marine Corps Cpl. Dakota Meyer helped rescue 13 American and 23 Afghan soldiers from an ambush, manning a Humvee gun turret on 5 trips into enemy fire over 6 hours.

Other Selected Awards

Source: U.S. Army Institute of Heraldry, Navy Department Awards Web Service, Air Force Personnel Center

Distinguished Service Cross

Established in Congress July 9, 1918, on recommendation of Gen. John J. "Black Jack" Pershing, and awarded for extraordinary heroism not justifying the award of a Medal of Honor. The act or acts of heroism must have been so notable and have involved risk of life so extraordinary as to set the individual apart from his or her comrades.

Silver Star

An earlier version of this award, the Citation Star, was established by Congress on July 19, 1918, and retroactively awarded to soldiers for "gallantry in action," back to the Spanish-American War. The Silver Star medal replaced the Citation Star in 1932 and is awarded for gallantry in action which, while of a lesser degree than that required for award of the Distinguished Service Cross, must nevertheless have been performed with marked distinction.

Legion of Merit

Established by Congress on July 20, 1942, and awarded to individuals who have distinguished themselves by exceptionally meritorious conduct in the performance of outstanding services. There are different designs depending on the level of command of the award recipient.

Distinguished Flying Cross

Established by Congress July 2, 1926, and awarded for heroism or extraordinary achievement while participating in aerial flight. Awards are made only to recognize single acts of heroism or extraordinary achievement, not sustained operational activities against an armed enemy. Initial awards were given to persons who made record-breaking long-distance and endurance flights or who set altitude records. The first DFC was awarded to Cpt. Charles A. Lindbergh on May 31, 1927, and DFCs were awarded retroactively to Orville and Wilbur Wright.

Soldier's Medal

Established by Congress July 2, 1926, to recognize acts of heroism not involving actual conflict with an enemy. The same degree of heroism is required as for the award of the Distinguished Flying Cross. The performance must have involved personal hazard or danger and the voluntary risk of life under conditions not involving conflict with an armed enemy. Awards are not made solely on the basis of having saved a life.

Bronze Star

Established by Executive Order Feb. 4, 1944, largely to raise the morale of ground troops in WWII, on the recommendation of Gen. George C. Marshall. It is awarded to any person who, while serving in any capacity in or with the U.S. military, distinguishes himself or herself by heroic or meritorious achievement or service, not involving participation in aerial flight.

Purple Heart

The original Purple Heart, designated as the Badge of Military Merit, was established by Gen. George Washington on Aug. 7, 1782. Following the American Revolution, the badge fell into disuse until 1932, the 200th anniversary of Washington's birth. During WWII, the Order of the Purple Heart was awarded for both wounds received in action and for meritorious service; following the introduction of the Legion of Merit, it was awarded only for combat wounds. Today, the Purple Heart is awarded to any member of an armed force who, while serving with the U.S. Armed Services, has been wounded or killed, or who has died or may hereafter die after being wounded in action against an enemy of the U.S. or in an armed conflict in which the U.S. or friendly foreign forces are engaged; as the result of an act of any hostile foreign force; as a result of an international terrorist attack against the U.S. or a friendly foreign nation; or as a result of military operations outside the U.S. as part of a peacekeeping force. Wounds must be inflicted by weapon fire while directly engaged in armed conflict, regardless of the fire causing the wound; or while held as a prisoner of war or while being taken captive.

Air Medal

Authorized by Pres. Franklin D. Roosevelt on May 11, 1942, and awarded for heroism or meritorious achievement while participating in aerial flight. Awards may be made to recognize single acts of merit or heroism, or for meritorious service. Awards are not made to individuals who use air transportation solely for the purpose of moving from point to point in a combat zone.

Army Commendation

Established Dec. 18, 1945, and awarded for heroism, meritorious achievement, or meritorious service. It may also be awarded to a member of the Armed Forces of a friendly foreign nation who distinguishes him or herself by an act of heroism, extraordinary achievement, or meritorious service which has been of mutual benefit to a friendly nation and the United States.

U.S. Military Awards in Selected Wars and Conflicts

Source: U.S. Army Human Resources Command, U.S. Dept. of Defense

Award	Civil War	WWI	WWII	Korea	Vietnam	Gulf War	OEF[1]	Iraq[2]
Medal of Honor	1,522	119	467	136	248	0	6	4
Distinguished Service Cross	NA	6,430	4,434	724	848	0	5	15
Silver Star	NA	(3)	73,654	10,061	21,634	75	205	408
Legion of Merit	NA	NA	20,273	(3)	10,356	158	41	125
Distinguished Flying Cross	NA	NA	126,318	(3)	21,697	108	136	116
Soldier's Medal	NA	NA	12,485	581	5,402	43	33	111
Bronze Star (total)[4]	NA	NA	395,380	30,359	719,968	27,967	33,839	103,970
Purple Heart	NA	NA	(3)	(3)	220,516	504	4,483	21,406
Air Medal (total)[4]	NA	NA	1,166,471	0	1,039,124	6,399	8,310	19,897
Army Commendation (total)[4]	NA	NA	0	0	837,037	81,979	77,768	363,524

NA = Not available/not applicable. (1) Operation Enduring Freedom (primarily Afghanistan). (2) Operation Iraqi Freedom and Operation New Dawn. (3) Numbers for the individual decorations shown on these charts represent only those awards that were properly processed and reported to Headquarters, Dept. of the Army. The actual number of individual decorations awarded under combat conditions, when award approval authority is delegated to field commanders, cannot be stated with absolute certainty. These charts reflect the current statistics recorded by the Military Awards Branch, as of Feb. 24, 2011, except for MOH reported by the Congressional Medal of Honor Society as of Oct. 1, 2011. (4) Includes awards for valor/heroism and for meritorious service or achievement.

The Federal Service Academies

U.S. Military Academy, West Point, NY. Founded 1802. Awards BS degree and Army commission for a 5-year service obligation. For admissions information, write USMA Admissions, Bldg. 606, USMA, West Point, NY 10996. www.usma.edu

U.S. Naval Academy, Annapolis, MD. Founded 1845. Awards BS degree and Navy or Marine Corps commission for a 5-year service obligation. For admissions information, write Candidate Guidance Office, United States Naval Academy, 117 Decatur Rd., Annapolis, MD 21402-5018. www.usna.edu

U.S. Air Force Academy, Colorado Springs, CO. Founded 1954. Awards BS degree and Air Force commission for a 6-year service obligation. For admissions information, write HQ USAFA/RRS, 2304 Cadet Dr., Ste. 2300, USAF Academy, CO 80840-5025. www.usafa.edu

U.S. Coast Guard Academy, New London, CT. Founded 1876. Awards BS degree and Coast Guard commission for a 5-year service obligation. For admissions information, write Director of Admissions, U.S. Coast Guard Academy, 31 Mohegan Ave., New London, CT 06320-8103. www.cga.edu

U.S. Merchant Marine Academy, Kings Point, NY. Founded 1943. Awards BS degree, a license as a deck, engineer, or dual officer, and a U.S. Naval Reserve commission. Service obligations vary according to options taken by the graduate. For admissions information, write Admissions Office, U.S. Merchant Marine Academy, 300 Steamboat Rd., Kings Point, NY 11024-1699. www.usmma.edu

Casualties in Principal Wars of the U.S.

Source: U.S. Dept. of Defense, U.S. Coast Guard

Data prior to World War I are based on incomplete records in many cases. Casualty data are confined to dead and wounded personnel and, therefore, exclude personnel captured or missing in action who were subsequently returned to military control. Dash (—) indicates information is not available. off. = Officers.

	Branch of service	Number serving	CASUALTIES Battle deaths	Other deaths	Wounds not mortal[7]	Total[13]
Revolutionary War	Total	—	4,435	—	6,188	10,623
1775-83	Army	184,000	4,044	—	6,004	10,048
	Navy	to	342	—	114	456
	Marines	250,000[11]	49	—	70	119
War of 1812	Total	286,730[8]	2,260	—	4,505	6,765
1812-15	Army	—	1,950	—	4,000	5,950
	Navy	—	265	—	439	704
	Marines	—	45	—	66	111
Mexican War	Total	78,718[8]	1,733	11,550	4,152	17,435
1846-48	Army	—	1,721	11,550	4,102	17,373
	Navy	—	1	—	3	4
	Marines	—	11	—	47	58
	Coast Guard[12]	71 off.	—	—	—	—
Civil War						
Union forces	Total	2,213,363	140,414	224,097	281,881	646,392
1861-65	Army	2,128,948[8]	138,154	221,374	280,040	639,568
	Navy	84,415	2,112	2,411	1,710	6,233
	Marines	(in Navy total)	148	312	131	591
	Coast Guard[12]	219 off.	1	—	—	1
Confederate forces	Total		74,524	59,297	—	133,821
(estimate)[1]	Army	600,000	—	—	—	—
	Navy	to	—	—	—	—
	Marines	1,500,000	—	—	—	—
Spanish-American War	Total	306,760	385	2,061	1,662	4,108
1898	Army[3]	280,564	369	2,061	1,594	4,024
	Navy	22,875	10	—	47	57
	Marines	3,321	6	—	21	27
	Coast Guard[12]	660	0	—	—	—
World War I	Total	4,734,991	53,402	63,114	204,002	320,518
Apr. 6, 1917-Nov. 11, 1918	Army[4]	4,057,101	50,510	55,868	193,663	300,041
	Navy	599,051	431	6,856	819	8,106
	Marines	78,839	2,461	390	9,520	12,371
	Coast Guard	8,835	111	81	—	192
World War II	Total	16,112,566	291,557	113,842	670,846	1,076,245
Dec. 7, 1941-Dec. 31, 1946[2]	Army[5]	11,260,000	234,874	83,400	565,861	884,135
	Navy[6]	4,183,466	36,950	25,664	37,778	100,392
	Marines	669,100	19,733	4,778	67,207	91,718
	Coast Guard	241,093	574	1,343	—	1,917
Korean War[9]	Total	5,720,000	33,739	2,835	103,284	139,858
June 25, 1950-July 27, 1953	Army	2,834,000	27,731	2,125	77,596	107,452
	Navy	1,177,000	503	154	1,576	2,233
	Marines	424,000	4,267	242	23,744	28,253
	Air Force	1,285,000	1,238	314	368	1,920
	Coast Guard	44,143	—	—	—	—
Vietnam War[10]	Total	8,744,000	47,434	10,786	153,303	211,523
Aug. 4, 1964-Jan. 27, 1973	Army	4,368,000	30,963	7,261	96,802	135,026
	Navy	1,842,000	1,631	935	4,178	6,744
	Marines	794,000	13,095	1,749	51,392	66,236
	Air Force	1,740,000	1,745	841	931	3,517
	Coast Guard	8,000	7	2	60	69
Persian Gulf War	Total	2,225,000	147	235	467	850
1991	Army	782,000	98	126	354	578
	Navy	669,000	5	50	12	68
	Marines	213,000	24	44	92	160
	Air Force	561,000	20	15	9	44
	Coast Guard	400	—	—	—	—
Iraq War[14]	Total	269,363[15]	3,515	949	32,159	36,623
Mar. 19, 2003-Aug. 1, 2011	Army	99,664[15]	2,570	713	22,452	25,735
	Navy	61,018[15]	64	39	636	739
	Marines	66,166[15]	851	171	8,622	9,644
	Air Force	42,515[15]	29	26	449	504
	Coast Guard	1,250[15]	1	—	—	1

Note: As of Aug. 1, 2011, there have been 1,319 battle deaths, 356 non-hostile deaths, and 13,011 wounded in Op. Enduring Freedom, mostly in Afghanistan and the Persian Gulf area. (1) From the final report of the Provost Marshal General, 1863-66. Authoritative statistics for the Confederate forces are not available. In addition, an estimated 26,000-31,000 Confederate personnel died in Union prisons. (2) Data are for Dec. 1, 1941, through Dec. 31, 1946, when hostilities were officially terminated by presidential proclamation; few battle deaths or wounds not mortal were incurred after Japanese acceptance of Allied peace terms on Aug. 14, 1945. Numbers serving Dec. 1, 1941-Aug. 31, 1945, were: Total—14,903,213; Army—10,420,000; Navy—3,883,520; Marine Corps—599,693. (3) Number serving covers the period Apr. 21-Aug. 13, 1898, while dead and wounded data are for the period May 1-Aug. 31, 1898. Active hostilities ceased on Aug. 13, 1898, but ratifications of the treaty of peace were not exchanged between the U.S. and Spain until Apr. 11, 1899. (4) Includes Army Air Forces battle deaths and wounds not mortal, as well as casualties suffered by American forces in northern Russia to Aug. 25, 1919, and in Siberia to Apr. 1, 1920. Other deaths covered the period Apr. 1, 1917-Dec. 31, 1918. (5) Includes Army Air Forces. (6) Battle deaths and wounds not mortal include casualties incurred in Oct. 1941 due to hostile action. (7) Marine Corps data for Iraq War, World War II, the Spanish-American War, and prior wars represent the number of individuals wounded, whereas all other data in this column represent the total number (incidence) of wounds. (8) As reported by Commissioner of Pensions in his Annual Report for Fiscal Year 1903. (9) As a result of an ongoing Dept. of Defense review of Korean War casualty record information, updates to previously reported figures for battle deaths and other deaths are reflected in this table. (10) Number serving covers the period Aug. 5, 1964-Jan. 27, 1973 (date of cease-fire). Includes casualties incurred in Mayaguez incident. Wounds not mortal exclude 150,341 persons not requiring hospital care. (11) Estimated. (12) Actually the U.S. Revenue Cutter Services, predecessor to the U.S. Coast Guard. (13) Totals do not include categories for which no data are listed. (14) Military deaths during the invasion phase, which ended Apr. 30, 2003, totaled 115 combat-related and 23 other. (15) Number serving figures for the Iraq War are current as of Mar. 31, 2003, and do not include numbers of troops deployed since then.

U.S. Army, Navy, Air Force, Marine Corps, and Coast Guard Insignia

Source: Dept. of the Army, Dept. of the Navy, Dept. of the Air Force, U.S. Dept. of Defense, U.S. Coast Guard, U.S. Dept. of Homeland Security

Army

General of the Armies—Gen. John J. Pershing (1860-1948), the only person to have held this rank while living, was authorized to prescribe his own insignia but never wore in excess of four stars. The rank originally was established posthumously by Congress for George Washington in 1799, and he was promoted to the rank by joint resolution of Congress, approved by Pres. Gerald Ford, Oct. 19, 1976.

General of the Army—Five silver stars fastened together in a circle and the coat of arms of the United States in gold color metal with shield and crest enameled. Reserved for wartime use only.

Rank	Insignia
General of the Army*	Five silver stars
General	Four silver stars
Lieutenant General	Three silver stars
Major General	Two silver stars
Brigadier General	One silver star
Colonel	Silver eagle
Lieutenant Colonel	Silver oak leaf
Major	Gold oak leaf
Captain	Two silver bars
First Lieutenant	One silver bar
Second Lieutenant	One gold bar

Warrant Officers

Grade Five—Silver bar with enamel black line.
Grade Four—Silver bar with 4 enamel black squares.
Grade Three—Silver bar with 3 enamel black squares.
Grade Two—Silver bar with 2 enamel black squares.
Grade One—Silver bar with 1 enamel black square.

Noncommissioned Officers

Sergeant Major of the Army (E-9)—Three chevrons above 3 arcs, with a U.S. Coat of Arms centered on the chevrons, flanked by 2 stars—one star on each side of the eagle. Also wears distinctive red and white shield collar insignia.

Command Sergeant Major (E-9)—Three chevrons above 3 arcs with a 5-pointed star with a wreath around the star between the chevrons and arcs.

Sergeant Major (E-9)—Three chevrons above 3 arcs with a 5-pointed star between the chevrons and arcs.

First Sergeant (E-8)—Three chevrons above 3 arcs with a lozenge between the chevrons and arcs.

Master Sergeant (E-8)—Three chevrons above 3 arcs.
Sergeant First Class (E-7)—Three chevrons above 2 arcs.
Staff Sergeant (E-6)—Three chevrons above 1 arc.
Sergeant (E-5)—Three chevrons.
Corporal (E-4)—Two chevrons.

Specialists

Specialist (E-4)—Eagle device only.

Other Enlisted

Private First Class (E-3)—One chevron above 1 arc.
Private (E-2)—One chevron.
Private (E-1)—None.*

*Rank reserved for wartime use only.

Air Force

Insignia for Air Force officers are identical to those of the Army. Insignia for enlisted personnel are worn on both sleeves and consist of a star and an appropriate number of rockers. Chevrons appear above 5 rockers for the top 3 noncommissioned officer ranks, as follows (in ascending order): Master Sergeant, 1 chevron; Senior Master Sergeant, 2 chevrons; and Chief Master Sergeant, 3 chevrons. The insignia of the Chief Master Sergeant of the Air Force has 3 chevrons and a wreath around the star design. General of the Air Force is reserved for wartime use only.

Navy

The following stripes are worn on the lower sleeves of the Service Dress Blue uniform. They are of gold embroidery.

Rank	Insignia
Fleet Admiral*	1 two inch with 4 one-half inch
Admiral	1 two inch with 3 one-half inch
Vice Admiral	1 two inch with 2 one-half inch
Rear Admiral (upper half)	1 two inch with 1 one-half inch
Rear Admiral (lower half)	1 two inch
Captain	4 one-half inch
Commander	3 one-half inch
Lieutenant Commander	2 one-half inch with 1 one-quarter inch between
Lieutenant	2 one-half inch
Lieutenant (j.g.)	1 one-half inch with one-quarter inch above
Ensign	1 one-half inch
Warrant Officer W-4	½" stripe with 1 break
Warrant Officer W-3	½" stripe with 2 breaks, 2" apart
Warrant Officer W-2	½" stripe with 3 breaks, 2" apart

Enlisted personnel (noncommissioned petty officers)—A rating badge worn on the upper left sleeve, consisting of a spread eagle, appropriate number of chevrons, and centered specialty mark.

*Rank reserved for wartime use only.

Marine Corps

Marine Corps' distinctive cap and collar ornament is the Marine Corps Emblem—a combination of the American eagle, a globe, and an anchor. Marine Corps and Navy officer insignia are similar. Marine Corps enlisted insignia, although basically similar to the Army's, feature crossed rifles beneath the chevrons. Marine Corps enlisted rank insignia are as follows:

Sergeant Major of the Marine Corps (E-9)—Same as Sergeant Major (below) but with Marine Corps emblem in the center with a 5-pointed star on both sides of the emblem.

Sergeant Major (E-9)—Three chevrons above 4 rockers with a 5-pointed star in the center.

Master Gunnery Sergeant (E-9)—Three chevrons above 4 rockers with a bursting bomb insignia in the center.

First Sergeant (E-8)—Three chevrons above 3 rockers with a diamond in the middle.

Master Sergeant (E-8)—Three chevrons above 3 rockers with crossed rifles in the middle.

Gunnery Sergeant (E-7)—Three chevrons above 2 rockers with crossed rifles in the middle.

Staff Sergeant (E-6)—Three chevrons above 1 rocker with crossed rifles in the middle.

Sergeant (E-5)—Three chevrons above crossed rifles.
Corporal (E-4)—Two chevrons above crossed rifles.
Lance Corporal (E-3)—One chevron above crossed rifles.
Private First Class (E-2)—One chevron.
Private (E-1)—None.

Coast Guard

Coast Guard insignia follow Navy custom, with certain minor changes such as the officer cap insignia. The Coast Guard shield is worn on both sleeves of officers and on the right sleeve of all enlisted personnel.

For Further Information on the U.S. Armed Forces

Additional information on all the U.S. Armed Forces branches, as well as many other related organizations, can be accessed through the official Internet site of the Dept. of Defense: www.defense.gov.

Army—Office of the Chief of Public Affairs, Media Relations Division—MRD, 1500 Army Pentagon, Washington, DC 20310-1500. **Website:** www.army.mil

Navy—Chief of Information, 1200 Navy Pentagon, Washington, DC 20350-1200. **Website:** www.navy.mil

Air Force—Office of Public Affairs, 1690 Air Force Pentagon, Washington, DC 20330-1690. **Website:** www.af.mil

Marine Corps—Marine Corps Headquarters, Division of Public Affairs, 3000 Marine Corps, Pentagon, Washington, DC 20350-3000. **Website:** www.usmc.mil

Coast Guard—Commandant (CG-09222), Attn: Chief of Media Relations, U.S. Coast Guard, 2100 2nd St. SW, Stop 7362, Washington, DC 20593-7362. **Website:** www.uscg.mil

Timeline of Major Wars Since 1066

Norman Conquest
1066-71
William I, duke of Normandy, landed on the English coast near Hastings on Sept. 28, 1066, and defeated Harold II, Saxon king of England, at Battle of Hastings Oct. 14. William crowned king Dec. 25 in Westminster Abbey. Most revolts were suppressed by 1071. **Conquest linked England's interests with those of the continent and led to its rise as a powerful monarchy.**

Crusades
1095-1270/1291
Military expeditions undertaken by **Western European Christians** usually at the behest of the **papacy**, to recover **Jerusalem** and other Biblical places of pilgrimage from **Muslim** control; in the long term, stimulated trade and flow of ideas between East and West. Pope Urban II called Nov. 27, 1095, for the **First Crusade**; Crusaders took Jerusalem on July 15, 1099, massacred inhabitants, and founded four temporary states: Antioch, Edessa, Jerusalem, and Tripoli. The failed **Second Crusade** was prompted by Muslims' capture of Edessa in 1144. Jerusalem was captured by Ayyubid sultan Saladin on Oct. 2, 1187, launching the **Third Crusade**, which involved the Holy Roman emperor, Frederick I (Barbarossa); the French king, Philip II (Augustus); and the English king, Richard I (Lion-Heart), but did not lead to a Crusader victory. The **Fourth Crusade** sacked Constantinople on Apr. 13, 1204. The **Fifth Crusade** began with capture of Damietta in Egypt (1219) but failed at Cairo. A **Sixth Crusade** led to the Treaty of Jaffa in 1229, giving Jerusalem to the Crusaders until 1244, when it was taken by the Khwarizmians, launching a **Seventh Crusade**. The last crusade abruptly ended when its leader, French King Louis IX, died in 1270. The last major Crusader stronghold, Acre was lost on May 18, 1291.

Hundred Years War
1337-1453
Series of armed conflicts over rival claims to the French throne, broken by a number of truces and peace treaties. Edward III declared self king of France in 1338 and invaded, with victories at Crécy in 1346 and Poitiers in 1356. **Treaty of Brétigny** signed May 8, 1360, but French king Charles V renewed fighting in 1369. Truce from 1396 until **Henry V** of England invaded in 1415 and **defeated French army at Agincourt**, capturing land north of Loire River including Paris. **Treaty of Troyes** in 1420 made Henry VI heir of both thrones. The siege of French stronghold Orléans, lifted in 1429 with help from **Joan of Arc**, turned the tide in favor of the French. **War ended English claims to France, paved the way for French absolute monarchy.**

Wars of the Roses
1455-85
Series of dynastic civil wars in England fought by the **rival houses of Lancaster and York for the throne**. Richard, third duke of York, in conflict with the Lancastrian King **Henry VI**, won victories at St. Albans (1455) and Northampton (1460); Richard died at battle of Wakefield on Dec. 30, 1460, before coronation, leaving his son to become King Edward IV. Henry VI imprisoned in tower of London, 1465. Edward died in 1483; his brother became **Richard III** after usurping throne from Edward V. Henry Tudor defeated Richard III at the Battle of Bosworth Field (1485). As Henry VII, he married Edward's daughter Elizabeth, 1486, finally **uniting the houses**.

Thirty Years War
1618-48
A series of religious and political conflicts involving **most countries of western Europe**; most fighting in Germany, devastating it. Protestants stormed Hapsburg palace in the "Defenestration of Prague" (May 23, 1618). Major conflicts included defeat of King Christian IV of Denmark and Norway by Catholic League (1626); victories by Lutheran King Gustav II Adolph of Sweden at Breitenfeld (1631) and Lützen (1632). France, under cardinal and statesman **Richelieu**, chief minister of King Louis XIII, declared war on the Hapsburgs in May 1635; defeated Austro-Bavarian army (Aug. 3, 1645), leading to Truce of Ulm. **Peace of Westphalia** signed at Münster on Oct. 24, 1648, bringing peace by recognizing the rulers' sovereignty within their lands and their right to determine the religious beliefs of their subjects.

English Civil Wars
1638-60
Series of conflicts between followers of King Charles (Cavaliers) and Parliament (Roundheads), over divine right of king versus Parliament's right to control national finances. Presbyterian Scots, allied with Parliament, rioted and in 1640 occupied the northern counties of England. Oliver Cromwell, second in command of Parliament's New Model Army, destroyed the king's army at the Battle of Naseby (June 14, 1645); first civil war ended May 1646 when Charles surrendered to the Scots. Charles later allied with Scots, but was defeated by Cromwell at Preston Aug. 17-19, 1648, and executed Jan. 30, 1649. Parliament abolished monarchy and House of Lords. Cromwell suppressed Irish and Scottish rebellions, was briefly succeeded by son Richard after death (1658); **Charles II restored to the throne** by "The Long Parliament," May 1660.

War of the Spanish Succession
1701-14
War fought by the Grand Alliance (originally England, Netherlands, Denmark, and Austria; later also Portugal), against coalition of France, Spain, and a number of small Italian and German principalities to preserve balance of power after death of Spanish king Charles II. Opened with invasion of Italy, via Venice, by an Austrian army under Prince Eugène of Savoy in May 1701. French forced to withdraw from Netherlands and Italy in 1706 and finally defeated 1709 in bloodiest battle of the war at the French village of Malplaquet. Treaty of Rastatt and Baden signed in 1714; gave **Austria control of Spanish Netherlands and settled peace between Austria and France.**

War of the Austrian Succession
1740-48
Conflict over rival claims for the **hereditary dominions of the Habsburg family**, following death (1740) of Charles VI, Holy Roman emperor and archduke of Austria. An alliance of Bavaria, France, Spain, Sardinia, Prussia, and Saxony fought against Austria, allied with Holland and Great Britain. King Frederick the Great of Prussia captured Silesia from Austria in the First (1740-42) and Second Silesian Wars (1744-45). British king George II defeated French army at Battle of Dettingen am Main (June 27, 1743). French conquered Austrian Netherlands (1745-46). Treaty of Aix-la-Chapelle Oct. 18, 1748, **restored most original borders, and Prussia became a significant force**.

Seven Years War
1756-63
Worldwide conflicts fought for the **control of Germany** and for **supremacy in colonial N America and India**. French defeated British Gen. Edward Braddock on the Monongahela in 1754, leading to formal declaration of **French-Indian War**, May 1756. Frederick II of Prussia invaded Saxony on Aug. 29, 1756; defeated French at Rossbach (1757), Austrians at Leuthen (1757), Russians at Zorndorf (1758). By 1760, British conquered French Canada. Peter III signed armistice with Prussia, 1762. Treaty of Paris signed Feb. 10, 1763; Peace of Hubertusburg Feb. 15, 1763, between Prussia and Austria. **England emerged as leading world naval power.**

American Revolution
1775-83
Conflict between Great Britain and 13 British colonies on the eastern seaboard of North America. George Washington took command of the Continental Army, July 2, 1775, and King George III declared colonies traitors on Aug. 23. **Independence of colonies declared July 4, 1776**. France recognized the colonies' independence Feb. 6, 1778, followed by Spain on June 21, 1779; both pledged support. French fleet drove British fleet under Adm. Thomas Graves from the Chesapeake on Sept. 5, 1781. French and Americans laid siege to Yorktown Sept. 28-Oct. 19, forcing British Gen. Cornwallis to surrender. **Treaty of Paris** (Sept. 3, 1783) recognized U.S. independence.

Wars of French Revolution and Napoleonic Wars
1792-1815
Large-scale wars fought between France and two multinational coalitions. France declared war on the Austrian part of the Holy Roman Empire for aiding King Louis XVI, Apr. 20, 1792. Newly created French Republic declared war on monarchies of Britain and Holland, Feb. 1, 1793, and Spain, Mar. 7. **Napoleon Bonaparte** defeated Austria in N Italy (1796-97), captured Egypt from Britain (1798-99; Battle of the Pyramids, July 21, 1798), and became First Consul after coup d'état of Nov. 9-10, 1799. French Grande Armée later swept through Europe using innovative and aggressive tactics. French navy defeated by British under Adm. Horatio Nelson at **Trafalgar** (Oct. 21, 1805), but Napoleon defeated Austro-Russian forces at Austerlitz (Dec. 2) and controlled most of Europe except Russia and Great Britain by 1808. France suffered its first major defeat by Austria at Aspern-Essling, May 21-22, 1809. **Napoleon invaded Russia**, captured Moscow Sept. 14, 1812, but was forced to flee the bitter Russian winter and abandoned Germany after Leipzig, Oct. 16-19, 1813. Paris captured by Allied armies Mar. 30-31, 1814. Napoleon exiled to Elba May 4 but returned for "Hundred Days" reign, Mar. 20-June 28, 1815; **final defeat at Waterloo** by British and Prussian troops (June 18). The **Bourbon monarchy was restored under Louis XVIII**, and Britain, Prussia, Russia, and Austria maintained European peace.

Crimean War
1853-56

Conflict between **Russia** and a coalition of **Great Britain, France, Sardinia, and Turkey for influence over Balkans** and the straits between the Black Sea and the Mediterranean. Russia destroyed Turkish fleet at Sinope on Nov. 30, 1853. Britain and France declared war in Mar. 1854 and with Turkish troops defeated Russians at Battle of Alma River on Sept. 20. Lord Lucan of Britain prevented Russia from capturing Balaklava on Oct. 25 ("Charge of the Light Brigade"). Siege of Sevastopol ended when Russia evacuated Sept. 8, 1855. Treaty of Paris signed Mar. 30, 1856; **curbed Russian expansion and loosened European power alignments.**

American Civil War
1861-65

Conflict between the United States (the Union) and 11 secessionist Southern states, organized as the Confederate States of America. Union garrison at Fort Sumter off Charleston, SC, surrendered to Brig. Gen. Pierre Beauregard (Apr. 12-13, 1861). 22,000 Confederates under Beauregard repelled 35,000 Union troops under Gen. Irvin McDowell along Bull Run stream near Manassas, VA (July 21). The *Merrimack* (renamed the *Virginia*) battled the *Monitor* Mar. 9, 1862. In **Battle of Antietam** (Sept. 17), some 12,000 Northerners and 12,700 Southerners were killed or wounded. Pres. Abraham Lincoln announced **Emancipation Proclamation** on Sept. 22. Confederate Gen. Robert E. Lee's forces numbering 75,000 battled 88,000 Union troops under Gen. George Meade at **Gettysburg** July 1-3, 1863, forcing Lee's army back across the Potomac River. Lee surrendered to Ulysses S. Grant at **Appomattox Court House** (Apr. 9, 1865). **The Union was preserved and slavery abolished.**

Franco-Prussian War
1870-71

German states led by Prussia defeated France, seizing Alsace and part of Lorraine. French defeated in several major battles, culminating at **Sedan** Sept. 1, 1870, when Prussian forces decisively defeated the French army and captured emperor Napoleon III. Prussian king crowned William I, emperor of a unified Germany, Jan 18, 1871. **France surrendered** Jan. 28. Final treaty signed May 10; set the stage for later **German imperialistic expansion.**

Spanish-American War
1898

War waged by the U.S. to **liberate Cuba from Spanish rule.** A mysterious explosion, blamed on Spain by American newspapers, sank the U.S. battleship *Maine* in Havana's harbor (Feb. 15, 1898), killing 260. The U.S. called for Spain's withdrawal from Cuba, and Spain declared war (Apr. 24). Rufus Shafter led 17,000 U.S. troops from Daiquirí to Santiago de Cuba, taking **San Juan Hill** with help of the Rough Riders under Teddy Roosevelt. Santiago de Cuba surrendered July 17. The Treaty of Paris (Dec. 10, 1898) provided for the **independence of Cuba**; the cession by Spain to the U.S. of **Puerto Rico, Guam, and for a $20 mil payment, the Philippine Islands.**

World War I
1914-18

Local European war that grew into a global war involving 32 nations: the Allies and the Associated Powers—28 nations including Great Britain, France, Russia, Italy, and the U.S.—versus the Central Powers of Germany, Austria-Hungary, Turkey, and Bulgaria. Archduke Francis Ferdinand assassinated at Sarajevo, Bosnia (June 28, 1914). Germany invaded France through Belgium and the Netherlands; advance on Paris halted by the French under Gen. Joseph Jacques Césaire Joffre at the **First Battle of the Marne**, Sept. 5-12. Germany checked the Russian army at the Battle of Tannenberg, Aug. 26-30. The British suffered 57,470 casualties (19,240 dead) in the opening day of the **First Battle of the Somme** (July 1-Nov. 18, 1916), first of 12 battles that forced Germany back to the Hindenburg Line. **U.S. declared war on Germany Apr. 6, 1917.** Russian involvement ended when Bolshevik party seized power on Nov. 7; signed armistice Dec. 15. German offensive halted by U.S. and French troops at **Second Battle of the Marne** (July 15-Aug. 5, 1918), the turning point of the war. Allied counteroffensive broke the Hindenburg Line, and an armistice was signed Nov. 11.

World War II
1939-45

Global military conflict stemming from European unrest after World War I and Japan's aggressive expansion into Asia and the Pacific.
The War in Europe: The Nazi-Soviet nonaggression pact (Aug. 23, 1939) freed Germany and the Soviet Union to attack Poland in Sept. **Britain and France declared war on Germany** Sept. 3. German forces raced through Europe (Apr.-June 1940), capturing Paris June 14. **Italy declared war on France and Britain** June 10; German-Italian campaigns won the Balkans and N Africa by June 1941. U.S. entered war Dec. 1941. Three million Axis troops invaded Russia June 22, 1941, but Russian counterthrusts stopped the German advance (**Stalingrad,** Aug. 20, 1942-Feb. 2, 1943), and Allies took N Africa (Nov. 8, 1942-May 13, 1943), Italy (July 10, 1943-May 2, 1945). Normandy invaded on **D-Day,** June 6, 1944; Paris liberated Aug. 25. Yalta Conference (Feb. 4-11, 1945) to defeat and split Germany into quarters. Adolf Hitler committed suicide Apr. 30. **Germany surrendered unconditionally** May 7.
The War in the Pacific: Japan invaded China (July 7, 1937), joined alliance with Germany and Italy (Sept. 27, 1940) and signed nonaggression pact with Russia (Apr. 13, 1941); attacked Hawaii's Pearl Harbor, Dec. 7, 1941; U.S. declared war on Japan Dec. 8. **Battle of Midway** (June 4-7, 1942) repulsed the Japanese advance. Marines landed on Guadalcanal Aug. 7. Navy defeated Japanese fleet at **Leyte Gulf,** Oct. 23-26, 1944. B-29 bombing raids on Japan began in Nov. Marines invaded Iwo Jima (Feb. 19-Mar. 16, 1945) with heavy casualties, then Okinawa (Apr. 1-June 21). **U.S. atom bombs dropped** on Hiroshima (Aug. 6) and Nagasaki (Aug. 9) and the Soviet invasion of Manchuria (Aug. 8) **forced Japan to agree, on Aug. 14, to surrender;** formal surrender on Sept. 2.

Korean War
1950-53

Military struggle fought on the Korean Peninsula between the Democratic Peoples' Republic of Korea (N Korea) and the Republic of Korea (S Korea) that developed into an international war involving China allied with N Korea against the U.S. and other nations under the UN flag. DPRK army crossed the 38th parallel and invaded S Korea (June 25, 1950), entering Seoul (June 26). Amphibious assault launched at **Inchon** by Gen. Douglas MacArthur (Sept. 15) helped U.S. forces rout DPRK close to the Yalu River by Nov. 24. Chinese counterattack retook Seoul (Jan. 4, 1951), but forced back to the 38th parallel by Apr. 22. Armistice was signed (July 27, 1953) by the UN, DPRK, and China, but not ROK, **leaving the peninsula partitioned at about the 38th parallel.**

Vietnam War
1959-75

Struggle primarily in S Vietnam that widened into a war between S Vietnam supported mainly by the U.S. and N Vietnam supported by the USSR and China. Viet Minh, led by Communist leader Ho Chi Minh, formed the Democratic Republic of Vietnam (Sept. 2, 1945). Colonial power France withdrew after fortress at Dien Bien Phu fell (May 8, 1954). Pres. John F. Kennedy pledged U.S. commitment to S Vietnamese independence Dec. 14, 1961. USS *Maddox* destroyer damaged in **Gulf of Tonkin** (Aug. 2, 1964) prompted Congress to increase involvement. Regular bombing of N Vietnam began (Feb. 24, 1965) and the first U.S. combat ground-forces arrived (Mar. 6). North Vietnamese Army siege of **Khe Sanh** (Jan. 21-Apr. 7, 1968) and the **"Tet" offensive** (Jan. 30) aimed to cause insurrection in the south. **My Lai Massacre** by U.S. soldiers against civilians (Mar. 16, 1968) created scandal, fueled U.S. disaffection with war. U.S. forces peaked at 543,400 in Apr. 1969. NVA **"Easter Offensive"** (Mar. 30, 1972) rebuffed, and U.S. responded with aerial bombings in May and Dec. U.S. withdrew after ceasefire, Jan. 1973. **NVA offensive captured Saigon, Apr. 30, 1975, and unified Vietnam under Communist rule.**

Persian Gulf Wars
1991, 2003

Conflicts fought principally between Iraq and the U.S. concerning Iraq's influence in the Middle East and its development of weapons of mass destruction. **First Gulf War:** Iraq under dictator Saddam Hussein invaded Kuwait Aug 2, 1990, and annexed it; UN Security Council ordered Iraqi forces to withdraw by Jan. 15, 1991. Beginning Jan. 17, a multinational force (**Operation Desert Storm**) led by the U.S. bombed military targets in Iraq and Kuwait. A coordinated air-land offensive (**Operation Desert Sabre,** begun Feb. 24) retook Kuwait City Feb. 26, and permanent ceasefire was signed on Apr. 6. Iraq was ordered to pay reparations to Kuwait, reveal locations of biological and chemical weapons, and eliminate weapons of mass destruction. **Second Gulf War:** The U.S. and UK mistakenly asserted that Iraq was still producing WMD and posed an imminent threat. The UN passed Resolution 1441, Nov. 8, 2002, warning Iraq of "serious consequences" if it failed to cooperate fully and unconditionally with UN weapons inspectors. Iraq rejected a Mar. 17, 2003, U.S. ultimatum demanding Hussein and his sons leave Iraq; U.S. launched **Operation Iraqi Freedom** Mar. 19, 2003, with support from UK and other allies, but without full UN Security Council support. Baghdad fell Apr. 9, and major combat operations declared over May 1. Saddam Hussein was captured Dec. 13, but guerrilla opposition to U.S. troops and insurgent violence continued. U.S. combat operations in Iraq formally ended Aug. 31, 2010.

HEALTH

U.S. Health Expenditures, 1960-2008

Source: *Health, United States, 2010*, National Center for Health Statistics, Centers for Disease Control and Prevention

	1960	1970	1980	1990	2000	2005	2006	2007	2008
					Amount in billions				
National health expenditures	$27.5	$74.9	$253.4	$714.2	$1,352.9	$1,982.5	$2,112.5	$2,239.7	$2,338.7
					Percent distribution				
Health services and supplies	90.6%	89.6%	92.1%	93.4%	93.4%	93.4%	93.5%	93.3%	93.3%
Personal health care...............	84.8	84.1	84.8	85.1	84.2	83.5	83.4	83.3	83.5
Hospital care	33.4	36.9	39.9	35.2	30.8	30.6	30.7	30.7	30.7
Professional services	30.3	27.6	26.5	30.4	31.5	31.4	31.2	31.1	31.3
Physician and clinical services.....	19.5	18.7	18.6	22.1	21.3	21.3	21.1	21.1	21.2
Other professional services	1.4	1.0	1.4	2.5	2.9	2.8	2.8	2.8	2.8
Dental services.................	7.1	6.2	5.3	4.4	4.6	4.4	4.3	4.3	4.3
Other personal health care.......	2.2	1.7	1.3	1.3	2.7	2.9	3.0	3.0	2.9
Nursing home and home health	3.2	5.7	8.2	9.1	9.3	8.5	8.4	8.6	8.7
Home health care[1].............	0.2	0.3	0.9	1.8	2.3	2.4	2.5	2.6	2.8
Nursing home care[1]...........	3.0	5.4	7.3	7.4	7.0	6.1	5.9	5.9	5.9
Retail outlet sales of medical products	18.0	14.0	10.1	10.4	12.6	13.0	13.1	12.9	12.8
Prescription drugs	9.7	7.3	4.8	5.6	8.9	10.1	10.3	10.1	10.0
Other medical products	8.3	6.6	5.4	4.7	3.6	2.9	2.8	2.8	2.8
Government administration and net cost of private health insurance...	4.4	3.7	4.8	5.5	6.0	7.1	7.2	7.1	6.8
Government public health activities[2] ..	1.3	1.8	2.5	2.8	3.2	2.8	2.9	2.9	3.0
Investment.......................	9.4	10.4	7.9	6.6	6.6	6.6	6.5	6.7	6.7
Research[3].....................	2.5	2.6	2.1	1.8	1.9	2.1	2.0	1.9	1.9
Structures and equipment	6.9	7.8	5.7	4.9	4.7	4.5	4.5	4.8	4.9
			Average annual percent change from previous year shown						
National health expenditures	—	10.5%	13.0%	10.9%	6.6%	7.9%	6.6%	6.0%	4.4%
Health services and supplies	—	10.4	13.3	11.1	6.6	7.9	6.7	5.8	4.4
Personal health care...............	—	10.4	13.1	11.0	6.5	7.8	6.5	5.9	4.6
Hospital care	—	11.6	13.9	9.6	5.2	7.8	6.9	5.9	4.5
Professional services	—	9.5	12.5	12.4	7.0	7.8	5.9	5.9	4.8
Physician and clinical services.....	—	10.1	12.9	12.8	6.2	7.9	5.7	5.8	5.0
Other professional services	—	6.6	17.1	17.5	8.0	7.4	4.4	6.5	5.6
Dental services.................	—	9.1	11.1	9.0	7.0	6.9	5.1	6.2	5.1
Other personal health care.......	—	7.3	10.1	11.4	14.5	8.9	10.3	5.8	2.6
Nursing home and home health	—	17.2	17.2	12.1	6.8	6.1	5.6	7.6	6.0
Home health care[1].............	—	14.5	26.9	18.1	9.3	9.5	10.3	11.8	9.0
Nursing home care[1]...........	—	17.4	16.4	11.0	6.1	4.8	3.7	5.8	4.6
Retail outlet sales of medical products	—	7.8	9.4	11.2	8.7	8.7	7.6	4.6	3.4
Prescription drugs	—	7.5	8.2	12.8	11.6	10.6	8.7	4.5	3.2
Other medical products	—	8.1	10.6	9.5	3.8	3.3	4.0	4.8	4.1
Government administration and net cost of private health insurance...	—	8.6	16.0	12.4	7.6	11.4	8.3	4.3	0.7
Government public health activities[2] ..	—	13.8	16.9	12.0	8.0	5.5	7.4	7.1	7.1
Investment.......................	—	11.7	9.9	9.0	6.5	8.0	5.0	9.4	5.0
Research[3].....................	—	10.9	10.8	8.9	7.3	9.7	2.9	1.6	2.6
Structures and equipment	—	11.9	9.5	9.1	6.2	7.3	5.9	12.9	5.9

— = Not applicable. **Note:** Numbers may not add up to totals because of rounding. (1) Freestanding facilities only. Additional services of this type provided in hospital-based facilities are counted as hospital care. (2) Includes personal care services delivered by government public health agencies. (3) Excludes research and development expenditures of drug companies, other mfrs. and providers of medical equipment, and supplies. They are included in the expenditure class in which a product falls.

Health Coverage for Persons Under 65, 1984-2009

Source: *Health, United States, 2010*, National Center for Health Statistics, Centers for Disease Control and Prevention

	Private insurance				Medicaid[1]				Not covered[2]			
	1984[3]	2000	2007	2009	1984[3]	2000	2007	2009	1984[3]	2000	2007	2009
					Percent of each population group							
Total........................	76.8%	71.5%	66.8%	63.3%	6.8%	9.5%	13.9%	16.1%	14.5%	17.0%	16.6%	17.5%
Age												
Under 18 years.............	72.6	66.6	59.8	55.8	11.9	19.6	29.8	34.5	13.9	12.6	9.0	8.2
18-44 years................	76.5	70.5	65.5	61.7	5.1	5.6	8.7	10.3	17.1	22.4	23.9	25.9
45-64 years................	83.3	78.7	75.5	72.6	3.4	4.5	5.9	6.9	9.6	12.6	13.5	14.6
Race and Hispanic origin[4,5]												
White, non-Hispanic	82.4	79.5	76.2	73.3	3.7	6.1	8.5	10.4	11.9	12.5	12.6	13.2
Black, non-Hispanic	58.2	56.0	52.3	48.0	20.7	21.0	27.3	29.1	19.7	19.5	16.8	18.8
Hispanic, any race	55.7	47.8	41.7	37.3	13.3	15.5	24.7	27.6	29.5	35.6	31.8	32.9
Percent of poverty level[4]												
Below 100%	32.2	25.2	21.4	15.3	33.0	38.4	47.6	51.2	33.9	34.2	28.4	30.4
100-199%	70.3	50.1	40.0	37.4	5.3	16.2	26.1	29.0	21.8	31.0	30.0	29.8
200-399%	89.3	78.1	73.2	70.6	0.8	4.0	6.8	8.0	7.6	15.4	16.9	17.8
400% or more	95.4	91.9	91.0	90.2	0.2	0.9	1.5	1.7	3.2	5.9	5.6	5.8
Geographic region[4]												
Northeast..................	80.5	76.3	72.2	69.7	8.6	10.6	15.4	17.3	10.2	12.2	11.0	11.4
Midwest....................	80.6	78.8	72.0	67.5	7.4	8.0	13.7	16.4	11.3	12.3	13.0	14.6
South......................	74.3	66.8	62.6	59.3	5.1	9.4	12.9	14.8	17.7	20.5	20.1	21.2
West	71.9	66.5	64.0	60.6	7.0	10.4	14.5	16.8	18.2	20.7	18.9	19.4

Note: Data based on household interviews of a sample of the civilian noninstitutionalized population. Percents may not add up to 100 because other types of health insurance (e.g., Medicare, military) are not shown, and persons with both private insurance and Medicaid appear in both sections. (1) Includes Medicaid and other public assistance. (2) Includes persons not covered by private insurance, Medicaid or other public assistance, Medicare, or military plans. (3) A change in the questionnaire in 1997 prevents direct comparison with later years. (4) Age adjusted. (5) Changed reporting methods make race percentages before 1999 not strictly comparable with those from 1999 on.

Spending on Health in the 50 Most Populous Countries, 2008

Source: *World Health Statistics 2011*, World Health Organization

Country	As % of GDP	Per capita[1]	Country	As % of GDP	Per capita[1]	Country	As % of GDP	Per capita[1]	Country	As % of GDP	Per capita[1]
Afghanistan[2]	7.4%	$47	Germany	10.5%	$4,720	Myanmar	2.3%	$12	Tanzania	4.5%	$22
Algeria	5.4	272	Ghana	7.8	55	Nepal	6.0	24	Thailand	4.1	164
Argentina	7.4	610	India	4.2	45	Nigeria	5.2	73	Turkey	6.1	623
Bangladesh	3.3	17	Indonesia	2.3	51	Pakistan	2.6	22	Uganda	8.4	44
Brazil	8.4	721	Iran	5.5	254	Peru	4.5	200	Ukraine	6.8	268
Canada	9.8	4,445	Iraq[3]	3.3	109	Philippines	3.7	68	United Kingdom	8.7	3,771
China	4.3	146	Italy	8.7	3,343	Poland	7.0	971	United States	15.2	7,164
Colombia	5.9	317	Japan	8.3	3,190	Russia	4.8	568	Uzbekistan	4.9	51
Congo, Dem. Rep. of	7.3	13	Kenya	4.2	33	Saudi Arabia	3.6	676	Venezuela	5.4	597
Egypt	4.8	97	Malaysia	4.3	353	South Africa	8.2	459	Vietnam	7.2	76
Ethiopia	4.3	14	Mexico	5.9	588	South Korea	6.5	1,245	Yemen	4.8	65
France	11.2	4,966	Morocco	5.3	149	Spain	9.0	3,132	World[4]	8.5	854
			Mozambique	4.7	21	Sudan	6.9	97			

(1) At average exchange rate. (2) GDP also includes illicit GDPs (e.g., opium). Govt. expenditures include external assistance (ext. budget). (3) Not including expenditures for Northern Iraq. (4) Includes other nations not shown.

Population Not Covered by Health Insurance, by State, 1990-2010

Source: Annual Social and Economic Supplements, Current Population Survey, U.S. Census Bureau, U.S. Dept. of Commerce
(numbers in thousands)

	2010 No. not covered	2010 % pop. not covered	2000 No. not covered	2000 % pop. not covered	1990 No. not covered	1990 % pop. not covered		2010 No. not covered	2010 % pop. not covered	2000 No. not covered	2000 % pop. not covered	1990 No. not covered	1990 % pop. not covered
AL	720	15.4%	557	12.7%	710	17.4%	MT	176	18.1%	146	16.4%	115	14.0%
AK	125	18.0	114	18.3	77	15.4	NE	237	13.3	140	8.3	138	8.5
AZ	1,283	19.1	834	16.0	547	15.5	NV	563	21.3	336	16.4	201	16.5
AR	539	18.7	367	13.8	421	17.4	NH	134	10.3	99	8.0	107	9.9
CA	7,209	19.4	6,154	18.1	5,683	19.1	NJ	1,338	15.4	985	11.7	773	10.0
CO	656	13.0	598	13.8	495	14.7	NM	435	21.6	426	23.7	339	22.2
CT	384	11.0	313	9.3	226	6.9	NY	2,886	15.0	3,001	16.0	2,176	12.1
DE	99	11.3	69	8.9	96	13.9	NC	1,575	17.0	1,046	13.1	883	13.8
DC	76	12.5	75	13.6	109	19.2	ND	83	13.1	66	10.7	40	6.3
FL	3,854	20.8	2,727	17.0	2,376	18.0	OH	1,554	13.7	1,191	10.7	1,123	10.3
GA	1,905	19.4	1,145	14.1	971	15.3	OK	624	17.0	624	18.4	574	18.6
HI	97	7.7	110	9.1	81	7.3	OR	612	16.2	417	12.2	360	12.4
ID	294	19.2	194	15.0	159	15.2	PA	1,368	11.0	963	8.0	1,218	10.1
IL	1,914	14.8	1,632	13.3	1,272	10.9	RI	119	11.4	74	7.1	105	11.1
IN	855	13.4	650	10.8	587	10.7	SC	930	20.6	473	11.9	550	16.2
IA	366	12.3	239	8.4	225	8.1	SD	105	13.0	77	10.5	81	11.6
KS	350	12.7	274	10.3	272	10.8	TN	930	14.7	585	10.4	673	13.7
KY	640	14.9	521	13.0	480	13.2	TX	6,181	24.6	4,650	22.4	3,569	21.1
LA	886	20.0	755	17.3	797	19.7	UT	386	13.6	259	11.5	156	9.0
ME	121	9.4	135	10.6	139	11.2	VT	59	9.5	50	8.3	54	9.5
MD	747	13.1	511	9.7	601	12.7	VA	1,096	14.1	747	10.7	996	15.7
MA	370	5.6	527	8.4	530	9.1	WA	927	13.8	772	13.2	557	11.4
MI	1,271	13.0	838	8.5	865	9.4	WV	244	13.5	247	13.9	249	13.8
MN	509	9.8	368	7.5	389	8.9	WI	526	9.4	398	7.5	321	6.7
MS	618	21.1	361	12.9	531	19.9	WY	93	17.3	74	15.3	58	12.5
MO	835	14.0	511	9.3	665	12.7	U.S.	49,904	16.3	38,426	13.7	34,719	13.9

Persons Not Covered by Health Insurance, by Selected Characteristics, 2010

Source: Annual Social and Economic Supplements, Current Population Survey, U.S. Census Bureau, U.S. Dept. of Commerce
(numbers in thousands)

Race and Hispanic origin[1]	Number	% of pop. specified at left	Region	Number	% of pop. specified at left
White	37,385	15.4%	Northeast	6,779	12.4%
Non-Hispanic	23,093	11.7	Midwest	8,605	13.0
Black	8,132	20.8	South	21,665	19.1
Asian and Pacific Islander	2,600	18.1	West	12,855	17.9
Hispanic	15,340	30.7	**Household income**		
Nativity			Less than $25,000	16,166	26.9
Native born	36,881	13.8	$25,000 to $49,999	15,435	21.8
Foreign born	13,023	34.1	$50,000 to $74,999	8,831	15.4
Naturalized citizen	3,356	20.0	$75,000 or more	9,473	8.0
Not a citizen	9,667	45.1	**Work experience[2]**		
Age			Worked year-round	28,000	19.5
Under 65 years	49,112	18.4	Worked full-time	14,311	15.0
Under 18 years	7,307	9.8	Worked less than full-time	13,689	28.5
18 to 24 years	8,078	27.2	Did not work	13,806	28.5
25 to 34 years	11,804	28.4	**Total**	49,904	16.3
35 to 44 years	8,692	21.8			
45 to 64 years	13,231	16.3			
65 years and over	792	2.0			

(1) Persons of Hispanic origin may be of any race. (2) Of persons 18 to 64 years of age only.

Provisions of the Patient Protection and Affordable Care Act (PPACA)

Source: U.S. Dept. of Health and Human Services

On Mar. 23, 2010, Pres. Barack Obama signed a sweeping health-care reform measure into law that would extend medical insurance to an estimated 32 mil uninsured people. The legislation—the Patient Protection and Affordable Care Act (PPACA)—is projected to still leave some 23 mil people in the U.S., one-third of whom were undocumented immigrants, without insurance in 2019. The Congressional Budget Office released a Mar. 2010 report which projected that the final reform package would cost $938 bil over 10 years and reduce the budget deficit by $143 bil during the same period.

Upon signing, the PPACA activated provisions allowing health insurance tax credits to small businesses; a $15 bil fund invested in prevention and public health programs; increased payments to rural health care providers; and efforts to crack down on health care fraud, expand primary care, and hold insurance companies accountable for rate hikes. Beginning Apr. 1, 2010, more people were covered under state Medicaid programs. Beginning June 2010, coverage to early retirees was expanded, and seniors who reached the gap in Medicare prescription drug coverage known as the "donut hole" received a $250 rebate check from Medicare to pay for prescriptions. Beginning July 2010, new health insurance options were made available online, and access to insurance was extended for uninsured individuals with pre-existing conditions.

For health plan years beginning on or after Sept. 23, 2010: Insurance companies were prevented from denying coverage to children under age 19 due to a pre-existing condition and from rescinding coverage. Lifetime dollar limits on insurance coverage were eliminated, annual dollar limits on coverage were regulated, and insurance company decisions could be appealed by consumers. Insurance companies were required to cover certain preventive services for free, and young adults could stay on their parents' plan until age 26. Beginning Oct. 2010, grants were awarded to states to fund consumer assistance programs.

Note: Provisions go into effect Jan. 1 of year shown, unless otherwise noted.

2011

- Prescription drug discounts offered.
- Senior citizens: free preventive care; improved care after they leave the hospital.
- At least 85% of all premium dollars collected by insurance companies for large employer plans must be spent on health care services and health care quality improvement.
- The new Community First Choice Option allows states to offer home and community-based services to disabled individuals through Medicaid rather than institutional care in nursing homes. (Oct. 1)

2012

- Incentives for physicians to join together to form integrated health systems.
- Federal health programs required to collect and report racial, ethnic, and language data, to help reduce health disparities. (Mar.)
- Financial incentives to hospitals to improve quality of care. (Oct. 1)
- Health plans required to use electronic records. (Oct. 1)

2013

- New funding to state Medicaid programs that choose to cover preventive services for patients at little or no cost.
- Authority expanded to bundle payments to hospitals, doctors, and other providers.
- Medicaid payments increased for primary care doctors.
- Additional funding for Children's Health Insurance Program.

2014

- Strong reforms prohibiting discrimination due to pre-existing conditions or gender.
- Annual limits on insurance coverage eliminated.
- Coverage ensured for people in clinical trials.
- Tax credits to help those in the middle class not eligible for other affordable coverage.
- Affordable insurance exchanges for those whose employers do not offer insurance.
- Small-business tax credit increased.
- Access to Medicaid for those who earn less than 133% of the poverty level.

2015

- Physicians to be paid based on value, not volume.

Health Care Visits by Selected Characteristics, 1997-2009

Source: National Health Interview Survey; *Health, United States*; National Center for Health Statistics, CDC

	No visits			1-3 visits			4-9 visits			10 or more visits		
	1997	2000	2009	1997	2000	2009	1997	2000	2009	1997	2000	2009
						Percent distribution						
All persons	16.5%	16.7%	15.4%	46.2%	45.4%	46.7%	23.6%	24.6%	24.7%	13.7%	13.3%	13.2%
Age												
Under 6 years	5.0	6.3	4.4	44.9	44.5	50.5	37.0	38.1	37.3	13.0	11.1	7.8
6-17 years	15.3	15.2	11.6	58.7	58.2	60.3	19.3	20.6	22.3	6.8	6.0	5.9
18-44 years	21.7	23.5	22.7	46.7	45.2	45.7	19.0	19.1	19.3	12.6	12.2	12.3
45-64 years	16.9	15.0	15.4	42.9	43.4	43.6	24.7	25.7	24.9	15.5	15.9	16.1
65-74 years	9.8	9.0	5.6	36.9	34.5	37.6	31.6	34.5	34.6	21.6	22.1	22.2
75 years and over	7.7	5.8	3.7	31.8	29.3	31.1	33.8	39.3	38.0	26.6	25.6	27.2
Sex												
Male	21.3	21.7	20.3	47.1	45.9	47.1	20.6	22.3	22.0	11.0	10.1	10.6
Female	11.8	11.9	10.5	45.4	44.8	46.4	26.5	27.0	27.4	16.3	16.3	15.7
Race and Hispanic origin												
White, not Hispanic	14.7	14.5	12.9	46.6	45.4	47.0	24.4	25.9	25.9	14.3	14.1	14.2
Black, not Hispanic	16.9	17.1	14.4	46.1	46.8	46.6	23.1	23.5	25.2	13.8	12.6	13.8
Hispanic[1]	24.9	26.8	23.8	42.3	41.8	44.3	20.3	19.8	21.2	12.5	11.6	10.8
Health insurance status[2]												
Insured continuously	14.1	14.0	12.0	49.2	48.8	50.2	23.6	24.6	25.2	13.0	12.6	12.7
Uninsured for any period	18.9	20.6	20.8	46.0	44.5	46.4	20.8	20.8	20.7	14.4	14.1	12.0
Uninsured	39.0	43.2	43.7	41.4	39.6	40.7	13.2	12.1	10.9	6.4	5.1	4.7

Note: Covers visits to doctor's offices, emergency departments, and home visits in the 12-month period prior to interview. Estimates are age-adjusted to the year 2000 standard population. Totals include persons of races not shown separately and of unknown health insurance status. (1) Persons of Hispanic origin may be of any race. (2) In 12 months prior to interview, for under-65 population only; persons having both Medicaid and private coverage are classified as having private coverage.

Top 20 Reasons Given by Patients for Outpatient Visits, 2008

Source: National Hospital Ambulatory Medical Care Survey, National Center for Health Statistics, CDC, U.S. Dept. of Health and Human Services

Rank	Number of visits (thous.)	% distrib. Total	Rank	Number of visits (thous.)	% distrib. Total
1. Progress visit, not otherwise specified	9,029	8.2%	11. Back symptoms	1,613	1.5%
2. General medical examination	6,405	5.8	12. Stomach pain, cramps, and spasms	1,540	1.4
3. Cough	3,769	3.4	13. Fever	1,525	1.4
4. Prenatal examination, routine	2,514	2.3	14. Hypertension	1,460	1.3
5. Postoperative visit	2,257	2.1	15. Skin rash	1,315	1.2
6. Symptoms referable to throat	2,253	2.1	16. Prophylactic inoculations	1,306	1.2
7. Medication, other and unspecified kinds	2,229	2.0	17. Low back symptoms	1,305	1.2
8. Counseling, not otherwise specified	2,220	2.0	18. Knee symptoms	1,273	1.2
9. Well-baby examination	1,701	1.5	19. Earache or ear infection	1,241	1.1
10. Diabetes mellitus	1,658	1.5	20. Gynecological examination	1,090	1.0
			All other reasons	62,186	56.6
			All visits	109,889	100.0

Emergency Room Visits by Diagnosis, 2008

Source: National Hospital Ambulatory Medical Care Survey, National Center for Health Statistics, CDC, U.S. Dept. of Health and Human Services

Rank	Principal diagnosis group	Number (thous.)	% of all visits	Rank	Principal diagnosis group	Number (thous.)	% of all visits
1.	Heart disease, excluding ischemic	1,001	6.0%	12.	Chronic and unspecified bronchitis	283	1.7%
2.	Chest pain	888	5.4	13.	Fracture of the lower limb	264	1.6
3.	Pneumonia	673	4.1	14.	Abdominal pain	262	1.6
4.	Ischemic heart disease	445	2.7	15.	Syncope and collapse	250	1.5
5.	Cerebrovascular disease	443	2.7	16.	Diabetes mellitus	242	1.5
6.	Malignant neoplasms	345	2.1	17.	Anemia	217	1.3
7.	Psychoses, excluding major depressive disorder	315	1.9	18.	Dyspnea and respiratory abnormalities	194	1.2
8.	Asthma	299	1.8	19.	Noninfectious enteritis and colitis	194	1.2
9.	Cellulitis and abscess	298	1.8	20.	Fractures, excluding lower limb	190	1.1
10.	Gastrointestinal hemorrhage	291	1.8		All other diagnoses[1]	9,176	55.4
11.	Urinary tract infection, site not specified	288	1.7		All visits	16,559	100.0

(1) Includes blanks and discharges in which diagnosis was unknown.

Most Frequently Mentioned Drugs at Outpatient Department Visits, 2008

Source: National Hospital Ambulatory Medical Care Survey, National Center for Health Statistics, CDC, U.S. Dept. of Health and Human Services

Rank	Therapeutic drug category[1]	No. of mentions (thous.)	% of tot.[2]	Rank	Therapeutic drug category[1]	No. of mentions (thous.)	% of tot.[2]
1.	Analgesics	36,984	13.2%	11.	Proton pump inhibitors	7,743	2.8%
2.	Antidepressants	12,042	4.3	12.	ACE[3] inhibitors	7,487	2.7
3.	Antihyperlipidemic agents	11,864	4.2	13.	Dermatological agents	7,014	2.5
4.	Bronchodilators	11,689	4.2	14.	Viral vaccines	6,575	2.3
5.	Antidiabetic agents	11,526	4.1	15.	Antihistamines	6,548	2.3
6.	Anxiolytics, sedatives, and hypnotics	9,296	3.3	16.	Antiemetic or antivertigo agents	5,809	2.1
7.	Beta-adrenergic blocking agents	8,838	3.2	17.	Adrenal cortical steroids	5,292	1.9
8.	Diuretics	8,459	3.0	18.	Antiarrhythmic agents	4,977	1.8
9.	Antiplatelet agents	8,374	3.0	19.	Penicillins	4,667	1.7
10.	Anticonvulsants	7,990	2.9	20.	Calcium channel blocking agents	4,597	1.6

(1) Based on the Multum Lexicon second-level therapeutic drug category. (2) Based on an estimated 280,113,000 drugs provided, prescribed, or continued at outpatient department visits in 2008. (3) Angiotensin-converting enzyme.

U.S. Transplant Waiting List, June 2011

Source: Organ Procurement and Transplantation Network (OPTN), United Network for Organ Sharing (UNOS)

Type of transplant	Patients waiting	% of total
All organs[1]	121,046	100.0
Kidney	95,069	78.5
Liver	17,030	14.1
Heart	3,191	2.6
Kidney-pancreas	2,253	1.9
Lung	1,797	1.5
Pancreas	1,382	1.1
Intestine	260	0.2
Heart-lung	64	0.1

U.S. Transplants Performed, 2010

Source: Organ Procurement and Transplantation Network (OPTN), United Network for Organ Sharing (UNOS)

Type of transplant	Number	% of total
All organs	28,664	100.0
Kidney	16,900	59.0
Liver	6,291	21.9
Heart	2,333	8.1
Lung	1,770	6.2
Kidney-pancreas	828	2.9
Pancreas	350	1.2
Intestine	151	0.5
Heart-lung	41	0.1

Note: Waiting list as of June 17, 2011. (1) Figures may not add up to total because patients waiting for more than one organ are included in multiple categories.

Drug Use in the General U.S. Population, 2010

Source: Substance Abuse and Mental Health Services Administration (SAMHSA), U.S. Dept. of Health and Human Services

According to SAMHSA's 2010 annual survey, an estimated 119.5 mil Americans 12 years of age and older (or 47.1% of that population) had used an illicit drug at least once in their lifetimes. Of that number, an estimated 76.2 mil (30% of persons 12 or older) had used an illicit drug other than marijuana at least once in their lives. About 15.3% of the 12-and-older population had used an illicit drug in the previous year; 8.9% had used one in the month prior to their participation in the survey. The rate of current illicit

drug use (i.e., within the past month) in 2010 was 11.2% for men and 6.8% for women.

SAMHSA's Drug Abuse Warning Network (DAWN) reported 2.1 mil drug abuse or misuse-related visits to hospital emergency departments in 2009. Nearly half of all visits where alcohol was not also a factor (47%) involved an illicit drug. Cocaine was a factor in 20% of these. Alcohol in combination with illegal drug use was involved in 10% of emergency visits.

Illicit Drug Use Among Persons 12 or Older, 2005-10

Source: National Survey on Drug Use and Health, Substance Abuse and Mental Health Services Admin. (SAMHSA), U.S. Dept. of Health and Human Services

(numbers in thousands)

	2005 No.	%	2006 No.	%	2007 No.	%	2008 No.	%	2009 No.	%	2010 No.	%
Used in lifetime												
Illicit drugs[1]	112,085	46.1	111,774	45.4	114,275	46.1	117,325	47.0	118,705	47.1	119,508	47.1
Illicit drugs other than marijuana[1]	71,822	29.5	72,906	29.6	73,494	29.7	75,573	30.3	75,780	30.1	76,203	30.0
Used in past month												
Illicit drugs[1]	19,720	8.1	20,357	8.3	19,857	8.0	20,077	8.0	21,813	8.7	22,622	8.9
Illicit drugs other than marijuana[1]	8,963	3.7	9,615	3.9	9,270	3.7	8,565	3.4	9,157	3.6	9,017	3.6
Used in past year												
Illicit drugs[1]	35,041	14.4	35,775	14.5	35,692	14.4	35,525	14.2	37,954	15.1	38,806	15.3
Marijuana and hashish	25,375	10.4	25,378	10.3	25,085	10.1	25,768	10.3	28,521	11.3	29,206	11.5
Illicit drugs other than marijuana[1]	20,109	8.3	21,254	8.6	21,144	8.5	19,990	8.0	21,000	8.3	20,576	8.1
Cocaine	5,523	2.3	6,069	2.5	5,738	2.3	5,255	2.1	4,797	1.9	4,499	1.8
Crack	1,381	0.6	1,479	0.6	1,451	0.6	1,109	0.4	1,016	0.4	871	0.3
Heroin	379	0.2	560	0.2	366	0.1	453	0.2	605	0.2	618	0.2
Hallucinogens	3,809	1.6	3,956	1.6	3,762	1.5	3,678	1.5	4,509	1.8	4,517	1.8
LSD	563	0.2	666	0.3	620	0.3	802	0.3	779	0.3	874	0.3
PCP	164	0.1	187	0.1	137	0.1	99	0.0	122	0.0	95	0.0
Ecstasy	1,960	0.8	2,130	0.9	2,132	0.9	2,139	0.9	2,799	1.1	2,645	1.0
Inhalants	2,187	0.9	2,218	0.9	2,080	0.8	2,047	0.8	2,090	0.8	2,030	0.8
Nonmedical use of psychotherapeutics[2]	15,346	6.3	16,482	6.7	16,280	6.6	15,166	6.1	16,006	6.4	16,031	6.3
Pain relievers	11,815	4.9	12,649	5.1	12,466	5.0	11,885	4.8	12,405	4.9	12,213	4.8
OxyContin®	1,226	0.5	1,323	0.5	1,422	0.6	1,459	0.6	1,677	0.7	1,869	0.7
Tranquilizers	5,249	2.2	5,058	2.1	5,282	2.1	5,103	2.0	5,460	2.2	5,581	2.2
Stimulants	3,088	1.3	3,791	1.5	2,998	1.2	2,639	1.1	3,060	1.2	2,887	1.1
Sedatives	750	0.3	926	0.4	864	0.3	621	0.2	811	0.3	907	0.4

(1) Includes marijuana/hashish, cocaine (including crack), heroin, hallucinogens, inhalants, or prescription-type psychotherapeutics used nonmedically. (2) Includes the nonmedical use of pain relievers, tranquilizers, stimulants, or sedatives but not over-the-counter drugs.

Lifetime Prevalence of Drug Use in 12th Graders, 1975-2010

Source: Monitoring the Future study, Univ. of Michigan Inst. for Social Research; National Institute on Drug Abuse

(percent who've ever used)

Drug	1975	1980	1985	1990	1995	2000	2005	2006	2007	2008	2009	2010	2009-10 change
Any illicit drug[1,2]	55.2%	65.4%	60.6%	47.9%	48.4%	54.0%	50.4%	48.2%	46.8%	47.4%	46.7%	48.2%	1.5%
Marijuana/hashish	47.3	60.3	54.2	40.7	41.7	48.8	44.8	42.3	41.8	42.6	42.0	43.8	1.8
Inhalants[3]	—	17.3	18.1	18.5	17.8	14.6	11.9	11.5	11.0	10.1	10.2	9.0	-0.4
Amyl/butyl nitrites[4]	—	11.1	7.9	2.1	1.5	0.8	1.1	1.2	1.2	0.6	1.1	—	—
Hallucinogens[5,6]	—	15.6	12.1	9.7	13.1	13.6	9.3	8.8	8.9	9.0	8.0	8.6	1.1
LSD	11.3	9.3	7.5	8.7	11.7	11.1	3.5	3.3	3.4	4.0	3.1	4.0	0.8
PCP[4]	—	9.6	4.9	2.8	2.7	3.4	2.4	2.2	2.1	1.8	1.7	1.8	0.1
Ecstasy (MDMA)	—	—	—	—	—	11.0	5.4	6.5	6.5	6.2	6.5	7.3	0.8
Cocaine	9.0	15.7	17.3	9.4	6.0	8.6	8.0	8.5	7.8	7.2	6.0	5.5	-0.6
Crack	—	—	—	3.5	3.0	3.9	3.5	3.5	3.2	2.8	2.4	2.4	0.1
Heroin (with and without a needle)	2.2	1.1	1.2	1.3	1.6	2.4	1.5	1.4	1.5	1.3	1.2	1.6	0.3
Narcotics other than heroin[7,8]	9.0	9.8	10.2	8.3	7.2	10.6	12.8	13.4	13.1	13.2	13.2	13.0	-0.2
Amphetamines[2,7]	22.3	26.4	26.2	17.5	15.3	15.6	13.1	12.4	11.4	10.5	9.9	11.1	1.3
Methamphetamine	—	—	—	—	—	7.9	4.5	4.4	3.0	2.8	2.4	2.3	-0.1
Crystal meth. (ice)	—	—	—	2.7	3.9	4.0	4.0	3.4	3.4	2.8	2.1	1.8	-0.2
Sedatives (barbiturates)[7]	18.2	14.9	11.8	7.5	7.6	9.3	11.0	10.6	9.6	8.9	8.4	7.5	-0.7
Methaqualone[7]	8.1	9.5	6.7	2.3	1.2	0.8	1.3	1.2	1.0	0.8	0.7	0.4	-0.3
Tranquilizers[5,7]	17.0	15.2	11.9	7.2	7.1	8.9	9.9	10.3	9.5	8.9	9.3	8.5	-0.8
Alcohol[9]	90.4	93.2	92.2	89.5	80.7	80.3	75.1	72.7	72.2	71.9	72.3	71.0	-1.3
Cigarettes	73.6	71.0	68.8	64.4	64.2	62.5	50.0	47.1	46.2	44.7	43.6	42.2	-1.3
Smokeless tobacco	—	—	—	—	30.9	23.1	17.5	15.2	15.1	15.6	16.3	17.6	1.3
Steroids[7]	—	—	—	2.9	2.3	2.5	2.6	2.7	2.2	2.2	2.2	2.0	-0.2

— = Not available. (1) Includes marijuana, LSD, other hallucinogens, crack, other cocaine, or heroin; or any use of narcotics other than heroin, amphetamines, sedatives (barbiturates), methaqualone (excluded since 1990), or tranquilizers not under a doctor's orders. (2) Because of changes to question wording, data from 1982 on are not directly comparable to data from prior years. (3) Not adjusted for underreporting of amyl and butyl nitrites. (4) Because of changes to question wording, data from 1987 on are not directly comparable to data from prior years. (5) Because of changes to question wording, data from 2001 on are not directly comparable to data from prior years. (6) Not adjusted for underreporting of PCP. (7) Includes only drug use not under a doctor's orders. (8) Because of changes to question wording, data from 2002 on are not directly comparable to data from prior years. (9) Because of changes to question wording, data from 1993 on are not directly comparable to data from prior years.

Cigarette Use in the U.S., 1985-2009

Source: National Survey on Drug Use and Health, Substance Abuse and Mental Health Services Admin. (SAMHSA), U.S. Dept. of Health and Human Services

(percentage reporting use in the month prior to the survey)

	1985	2000	2005	2007	2008	2009
Total[1]	38.7	24.9	24.9	24.2	23.9	23.3
Sex						
Male	43.4	26.9	27.4	27.1	26.3	25.3
Female	34.5	23.1	22.5	21.5	21.7	21.4
Age group						
12-17 years	29.4	13.4	10.8	9.8	9.1	8.9
18-25	47.4	38.3	39.0	36.2	35.7	35.8
26 years and older	45.7[3]	24.2	24.3	24.1	23.8	23.0

	1985	2000	2005	2007	2008	2009
Race/ethnicity						
White, not Hispanic	38.9	25.9	26.0	25.6	25.2	24.5
Black, not Hispanic	38.0	23.3	24.5	23.2	24.8	22.8
Hispanic	40.0	20.7	22.1	20.5	19.4	21.2
Education[2]						
Non-high school graduate	37.3	32.4	34.8	32.9	34.4	35.4
High school graduate	37.0	31.1	31.8	31.9	30.6	30.0
Some college	32.6	27.7	28.1	26.8	26.6	25.4
College graduate	23.0	13.9	13.8	14.0	14.0	13.1

(1) Persons 12 years of age and older. (2) Persons aged 18 and older. (3) Persons aged 26 to 34 only.

Daily Use of Cigarettes by 8th, 10th, and 12th Graders, 1995-2010

Source: Monitoring the Future study, Univ. of Michigan Inst. for Social Research; National Inst. on Drug Abuse

(percent who smoked daily in last 30 days)

	8th grade						10th grade						12th grade					
	1995	2000	2005	2009	2010	2009-10 change	1995	2000	2005	2009	2010	2009-10 change	1995	2000	2005	2009	2010	2009-10 change
Total	9.3	7.4	4.0	2.7	2.9	0.2%	16.3	14.0	7.5	6.3	6.6	0.3%	21.6	20.6	13.6	11.2	10.7	−0.4%
Sex																		
Male	9.2	7.0	3.9	2.9	3.5	0.6	16.3	13.7	7.2	6.9	7.2	0.3	21.7	20.9	14.6	11.8	12.3	0.5
Female	9.2	7.5	4.0	2.3	2.3	0.0	16.1	14.1	7.7	5.6	5.9	0.3	20.8	19.7	11.9	9.9	8.7	−1.3
College plans																		
None or under 4 yrs.	22.5	21.7	14.4	10.9	12.8	1.9	32.7	28.8	19.2	17.3	19.1	1.8	33.7	31.7	24.9	20.9	21.6	0.7
Complete 4 yrs.	7.5	5.6	2.9	1.9	2.0	0.1	13.3	11.6	5.9	5.0	5.0	0.0	17.4	16.6	10.5	8.6	8.2	−0.4
Region																		
Northeast	9.2	6.9	3.2	2.1	2.4	0.3	15.8	14.1	7.6	5.3	5.7	0.4	22.5	22.8	13.3	10.8	10.3	−0.5
Midwest	11.0	9.0	4.8	3.0	3.3	0.3	17.6	16.3	8.6	5.8	7.3	1.5	25.7	23.6	16.3	15.4	12.5	−2.8
South	9.4	7.8	5.0	3.2	3.8	0.7	19.3	15.7	8.8	8.5	7.9	−0.6	21.7	19.4	15.4	11.4	12.3	0.8
West	7.0	4.9	2.4	2.0	1.4	−0.6	9.4	7.8	4.0	4.3	4.4	0.1	14.5	16.9	7.6	5.9	6.7	0.7
Race/ethnicity[1]																		
White	10.5	9.0	4.6	3.2	3.2	0.0	23.9	25.7	17.1	7.1	7.4	0.3	23.9	25.7	17.1	13.9	13.5	−0.4
Black	2.8	3.2	2.1	2.0	1.9	−0.1	6.1	8.0	5.6	3.2	3.5	0.2	6.1	8.0	5.6	5.4	5.3	−0.1
Hispanic	9.2	7.1	3.1	2.2	2.3	0.1	11.6	15.7	7.7	4.5	4.4	−0.1	11.6	15.7	7.7	6.4	5.7	−0.7

Note: Figures and percentage changes may not add up to totals because of rounding. (1) For each of these groups, data for the specified year and previous year have been combined to increase sample size and thus provide a more reliable estimate.

Alcohol Use by 8th and 12th Graders, 1980-2010

Source: Monitoring the Future study, Univ. of Michigan Inst. for Social Research; National Inst. on Drug Abuse

	1980	1990	1995	2000	2005	2006	2007	2008	2009	2010	2009-10 change
Alcohol[1]		Percent using alcohol in the month before the survey									
All 12th graders	72.0%	57.1%	51.3%	50.0%	47.0%	45.3%	44.4%	43.1%	43.5%	41.2%	−2.3%
Male	77.4	61.3	55.7	54.0	50.7	47.3	47.1	45.8	47.8	44.2	−3.6
Female	66.8	52.3	47.0	46.1	43.3	43.0	41.4	40.9	38.9	37.9	−1.0
White	75.4	63.8	54.5	55.1	52.3	50.7	49.3	48.6	47.2	45.4	−1.8
Black	47.6	35.8	35.2	30.0	29.0	29.2	28.7	28.6	30.5	31.4	0.9
Hispanic	63.6	49.1	48.7	51.2	43.3	43.4	41.4	38.9	40.1	40.1	0.0
All 8th graders	—	—	24.6	22.4	17.1	17.2	15.9	15.9	14.9	13.8	−1.2
Male	—	—	25.0	22.5	16.2	16.3	15.6	15.4	14.7	13.2	−1.5
Female	—	—	24.0	22.0	17.9	17.6	16.0	16.4	14.9	14.3	−0.6
White	—	—	25.4	24.7	17.9	16.9	15.6	15.2	15.4	13.9	−1.5
Black	—	—	18.7	16.0	14.9	13.1	12.3	12.9	12.3	11.8	−0.5
Hispanic	—	—	32.4	26.7	20.6	21.2	23.0	21.5	19.2	18.1	−1.1
Heavy alcohol[2]		Percent heavily using in the 2 weeks before the survey									
All 12th graders	41.2%	32.2%	29.8%	30.0%	27.1%	25.4%	25.9%	24.6%	25.2%	23.2%	−2.1%
Male	52.1	39.1	36.9	36.7	32.6	28.9	30.7	28.4	30.5	28.0	−2.5
Female	30.5	24.4	23.0	23.5	21.6	21.5	21.5	21.3	20.2	18.4	−1.8
White	44.3	36.6	32.3	34.6	32.5	30.4	29.7	29.9	29.0	27.6	−1.4
Black	17.7	14.4	14.9	11.5	11.3	11.4	11.5	10.9	12.0	13.1	1.1
Hispanic	33.1	25.6	26.6	31.0	23.9	23.3	22.5	21.5	22.6	22.1	−0.5
All 8th graders	—	—	12.3	11.7	8.4	8.7	8.3	8.1	7.8	7.2	−0.6
Male	—	—	12.5	11.7	8.2	8.6	8.2	8.1	7.8	6.5	−1.2
Female	—	—	12.1	11.3	8.6	8.5	8.2	8.0	7.7	7.8	0.1
White	—	—	12.1	13.0	9.0	8.4	8.0	7.8	7.7	7.1	−0.7
Black	—	—	8.3	7.3	6.1	5.7	5.6	5.7	5.2	5.3	0.1
Hispanic	—	—	18.4	16.0	12.1	11.6	12.5	12.3	11.5	10.8	−0.7

— = Data not available. **Note:** Monitoring the Future study excludes high school dropouts (about 3-6% of the class group, according to a 1996 report) and absentees (about 16-17% of 12th graders and about 9-10% of 8th graders). High school dropouts and absentees have higher alcohol usage than those included in the survey. (1) Since 1993 the alcohol question has indicated that a "drink" is defined as "more than a few sips." (2) Five or more drinks in a row at least once in the prior 2-week period.

Acquired Immune Deficiency Syndrome (AIDS)

Source: Centers for Disease Control and Prevention, www.cdc.gov

AIDS (Acquired Immune Deficiency Syndrome) is caused by the human immunodeficiency virus (**HIV**). HIV kills or disables crucial immune cells, progressively destroying the body's ability to fight disease.

HIV is commonly **spread** through unprotected sexual contact with an infected partner's semen or vaginal fluids. It is also spread through contact with infected blood. Where modern screening techniques are used, it is rare to contract HIV from transfusion or organ/tissue transplants. But it can be contracted when intravenous drug users share syringes and similar equipment with others. A woman can also transmit HIV to her child during pregnancy or delivery or through breastfeeding. With treatment, a woman can reduce her transmission rate from about 25% to less than 2%. There is no evidence HIV can spread through saliva or casual contact such as in the sharing of food utensils, towels and bedding, telephones, or toilet seats.

Some people experience flu-like symptoms a short time after infection with HIV. Even when symptoms are not present, HIV is active in the body, multiplying, infecting, and killing crucial CD4+ T cells, also known as T-lymphocytes or T-helper cells, which signal other immune cells to perform their functions.

The term **AIDS** applies to the most advanced stages of HIV infection. According to the official case definition issued by the Centers for Disease Control and Prevention (CDC), an HIV-infected person with fewer than 200 CD4+ T cells per cubic millimeter of blood can be said to have AIDS. (Healthy adults usually have 1,000 or more per cubic millimeter.) An HIV-infected person, regardless of T cell count, is diagnosed with AIDS if he or she develops 1 of 26 conditions that typically affect people with advanced HIV. Most of these conditions are opportunistic infections that occur when the immune system is so ravaged by HIV that the body cannot fight off certain bacteria, viruses, and microbes.

Months or years prior to the onset of AIDS, people may experience such **symptoms** as swollen glands, lack of energy, fevers and sweats, and skin rashes. People diagnosed with AIDS may develop infections of the intestinal tract, lungs, brain, eyes, and other organs and become severely debilitated. They also are prone to developing certain cancers, especially those caused by viruses, such as Kaposi's sarcoma, cervical cancer, and lymphoma. Children with AIDS may have delayed development or fail to thrive.

HIV is primarily **detected** by testing a person's blood for the presence of antibodies (disease-fighting proteins of the immune system) to HIV. In very rare cases, HIV antibodies may take more than six months after exposure to reach detectable levels. But in 97% of infected individuals, the antibodies are detectable in the first three months. HIV testing may also be performed on oral fluid and urine samples. New rapid HIV tests can provide preliminary results in about 20 minutes.

Patients are typically given a combination of different **drugs** to prevent the HIV virus from becoming resistant to any single one. While these drugs extend the period of time between HIV infection and the development of serious illness, they do not prevent the spread of the disease to others and can have severe side effects.

The U.S. Food and Drug Administration (FDA) has approved a number of drugs that may slow the growth of HIV in the body and treat AIDS-related infections and cancers. The first group of drugs used to treat HIV—nucleoside reverse transcriptase inhibitors (NRTIs)—include the drug zidovudine (commonly known as AZT). Non-nucleoside reverse transcriptase inhibitors (NNRTIs), as well as a third class of drugs, called protease inhibitors, have also been approved for HIV treatment. In 2003, the FDA granted accelerated approval of Fuzeon for use with other anti-HIV drugs. Fuzeon was the first among a new class of medications called fusion inhibitors; drugs in this class interfere with HIV's entry into cells by hindering the fusion of viral and cellular membranes.

The FDA in July 2006 approved Atripla, the first once-a-day, single-pill drug combination treatment for HIV. The pill combined three previously approved drugs and cost roughly $1,100 per month in the U.S. The development was regarded as a significant milestone in HIV treatment. FDA officials said complicated drug regimens dissuaded patients from taking their pills as directed.

In 2007, the FDA approved raltegravir, the first of a new class of HIV drugs called integrase inhibitors. Raltegravir is taken with other anti-HIV medications.

Since there is no vaccine or cure for AIDS, the only **protection** is to avoid activities that carry a risk. The CDC recommends abstinence (the only certain protection) if a potential partner's HIV status is unknown, mutual monogamy with an uninfected partner, or correct and consistent use of male latex condoms.

New AIDS Diagnoses in the U.S., by Transmission Category, 1985-2009

Source: *HIV Surveillance Report, 2009*; National Center for HIV/AIDS, Viral Hepatitis, STD, and TB Prevention, CDC

Transmission category	All years[1]	1985	1990	2000	2005	2006	2007	2008	2009
All males 13 years of age and older	**878,366**	**7,504**	**36,193**	**30,251**	**27,436**	**26,473**	**25,871**	**25,612**	**25,587**
Male-to-male sexual contact	529,908	5,348	23,658	13,648	16,824	16,517	16,521	16,469	17,005
Injection drug use	186,318	1,103	6,923	5,554	4,350	3,853	3,505	3,303	3,012
Male-to-male sexual contact and injection drug use	77,213	661	2,943	1,587	2,085	1,957	1,798	1,706	1,580
Heterosexual contact[2]	72,183	32	715	2,537	3,920	3,952	3,882	3,949	3,832
Other[3]	12,744	—	—	—	256	194	165	185	158
All females 13 years of age and older	**220,795**	**524**	**4,547**	**9,979**	**9,799**	**9,639**	**9,531**	**9,102**	**8,647**
Injection drug use	87,126	287	2,347	2,545	2,724	2,469	2,392	2,141	1,930
Heterosexual contact[2]	126,637	119	1,538	4,025	6,856	6,980	6,955	6,824	6,561
Other[3]	7,032	—	—	—	219	190	184	137	155
All children, under 13 years of age	**9,448**	**—**	**—**	**—**	**55**	**39**	**31**	**40**	**13**
Perinatal	8,640	—	—	—	50	36	30	35	12
Other[4]	807	—	—	—	5	3	1	5	1

Note: The definition of AIDS cases for reporting purposes was expanded in 1985, 1987, and 1993, as more was learned about the spectrum of human immunodeficiency virus-associated diseases. (1) Includes cases for years not shown, from the beginning of the epidemic (1981) through 2009. (2) Heterosexual contact with a person known to have or be at high risk for HIV infection. (3) Includes hemophilia, blood transfusion, perinatal exposure, and risk factor not reported or not identified. (4) Includes hemophilia, blood transfusion, and risk factor not reported or not identified.

AIDS Deaths and New AIDS Diagnoses in the U.S., 1981-2009

Source: HIV/AIDS Surveillance Supplemental Report; *Health, United States*; Office of Analysis and Epidemiology, National Center for Health Statistics, CDC

	% of total, all years	All years[1]	2005	2006	2007	2008
DEATHS OF PERSONS DIAGNOSED WITH AIDS, BY YEAR[2]	—	579,931	NA	15,762	14,263	12,754
CASES, BY YEAR AIDS FIRST DIAGNOSED						
All persons[3]	—	1,073,128	37,290	36,442	36,333	37,151
All males, 13 years of age and older	100.0%	851,974	27,436	26,741	26,619	27,543
Race/origin						
Not of Hispanic origin						
White	44.2	376,372	9,338	9,101	8,809	8,980
Black	37.0	315,145	11,763	11,296	11,391	11,968
Asian[4]	0.8	7,016	316	365	397	427
Native Hawaiian or other Pacific Islander	0.3	691	39	39	47	44
American Indian or Alaska Native	0.1	2,922	135	121	108	155
Hispanic[5]	17.0	144,438	5,539	5,490	5,533	5,660
Age diagnosed						
13-14 years	0.1	663	32	26	27	20
15-24 years	3.9	32,831	1,480	1,454	1,769	1,891
25-34 years	31.2	266,130	5,645	5,441	5,513	5,888
35-44 years	39.7	338,443	10,609	10,157	9,452	9,233
45-54 years	18.2	154,898	7,035	6,802	7,072	7,352
55-64 years	5.4	45,942	2,082	2,233	2,202	2,505
65 years and over	1.5	13,067	553	627	584	655
All females, 13 years of age and older	100.0%	211,804	9,799	9,661	9,683	9,567
Race/origin						
Not of Hispanic origin						
White	19.8	41,920	1,543	1,584	1,599	1,583
Black	62.3	131,988	6,458	6,267	6,303	6,336
Asian[4]	0.6	1,189	82	77	92	97
Native Hawaiian or other Pacific Islander	0.1	133	11	15	11	7
American Indian or Alaska Native	0.4	785	38	35	48	44
Hispanic[5]	16.0	33,824	1,519	1,549	1,487	1,379
Age diagnosed						
13-14 years	0.3	557	41	49	46	29
15-24 years	6.9	14,589	660	590	613	582
25-34 years	32.7	69,179	2,310	2,246	2,125	2,189
35-44 years	36.9	78,089	3,519	3,363	3,304	3,169
45-54 years	16.4	34,772	2,386	2,442	2,490	2,514
55-64 years	5.1	10,713	702	759	871	877
65 years and over	1.8	3,905	182	212	235	206
All children, under 13 years of age	100.0%	9,349	55	40	30	41
Race/origin						
Not of Hispanic origin						
White	17.2	1,612	4	3	4	7
Black	61.8	5,782	40	30	22	25
Asian[4]	0.5	49	1	1	0	1
Native Hawaiian or other Pacific Islander	0.1	7	0	0	0	0
American Indian or Alaska Native	0.4	33	0	0	0	0
Hispanic[5]	19.2	1,798	8	4	3	4

Note: Data are for the 50 states and DC and are based on reporting by state and DC health departments. (1) Based on cases reported to the CDC from the beginning of the epidemic (1981) through June 30, 2009. (2) Deaths may be due to any cause. (3) Total for all years includes 7,422 persons of unknown race or multiple races. (4) Includes persons formerly classified as "Asian or Pacific Islander," before new racial categories were implemented in 2003. (5) Persons of Hispanic origin may be of any race.

Allergies and Asthma

Source: Asthma and Allergy Foundation of America, www.aafa.org

An estimated one in five Americans suffers from **allergies**. People with allergies have immune systems that react to defend the body against normally harmless substances. Common **allergens**—the substances that may trigger such a response—include plant pollens, dust mites, or animal dander; plants such as poison ivy; certain drugs, such as penicillin; and foods such as eggs, milk, wheat, nuts, or seafood.

The **tendency to develop allergies** is usually inherited. While allergies typically manifest in childhood, they can show up at any age. Food allergies and eczema (patches of dry skin) are common allergies among infants. Older children and adults may develop allergic rhinitis, or hay fever, in reaction to an inhaled allergen. Allergic rhinitis symptoms include nasal congestion, runny nose, and sneezing.

People with allergies should avoid contact with an allergen, if feasible. **Medications**, such as antihistamines and nasal steroids, may be used to decrease an allergic reaction. Other effective allergy treatments include decongestants, eye drops, and ointments. There are also treatments aimed at gradually desensitizing a patient to an allergen.

Some allergy sufferers also have **asthma**. Asthma, which can develop at any age, is a chronic inflammation disease affecting the passageways that carry air into and out of the lungs. During what is known as an asthma attack, these inflamed, supersensitive airways tighten and fill with mucus. A person may experience wheezing, difficulty breathing, tightening of the chest, and coughing. Exposure to an allergen can set off an attack. Asthma can become life-threatening if not controlled in its early stages. The following symptoms may be indicative of an **emergency**: the patient shows no improvement minutes after initial treatment; struggles to breathe while hunched over with his or her chest and neck pulled in; has trouble walking or talking; and develops gray or blue lips or fingernails.

Besides common allergens, tobacco smoke, cold air, and pollution can trigger an asthma attack, as can viral infections or physical exercise. An accurate diagnosis by a physician is important. Although there is no cure for asthma or allergies, they can be controlled through lifestyle changes and medications.

Alzheimer's Disease

Source: Alzheimer's Association, www.alz.org

Alzheimer's disease, the most common form of dementia, is a progressive, degenerative brain disease in which nerve cells deteriorate and die. Its first symptoms usually involve impaired memory and confusion about recent events. As the disease advances, it results in greater impairment of memory, thinking, judgment, language, behavior, and physical health.

The **rate of progression** of Alzheimer's varies, ranging from 4 to 20 years. The average length of time from onset of symptoms until death is five years. As they become progressively debilitated, affected individuals grow increasingly susceptible to infections of the lungs, urinary tract, and other organs.

Alzheimer's disease affects an estimated 5.4 mil Americans, striking men and women of all races and ethnicities. Almost two-thirds of all Americans living with Alzheimer's are women. Although most people are older than age 65 when diagnosed with Alzheimer's, younger-onset, or early-onset, cases occur in people in their 40s and 50s. An estimated 13% of the U.S. population over age 65 has Alzheimer's.

Diagnosis involves a comprehensive evaluation that may include a complete health history, physical examination, neurological and mental status assessments, and other tests. Skilled health care professionals can generally diagnose Alzheimer's with about 90% accuracy. Depression, drug interactions, nutritional imbalances, and infections such as AIDS, meningitis, and syphilis can cause similar symptoms. Other forms of dementia, such as those associated with stroke, Huntington's disease, Parkinson's disease, frontotemporal dementia, and vascular disease can also appear to be Alzheimer's. Absolute confirmation of diagnosis requires a brain biopsy or autopsy.

Treatments for cognitive and behavioral symptoms are available, but no intervention has yet been developed to prevent Alzheimer's or reverse its course. The U.S. Food and Drug Administration has approved five drugs that temporarily slow worsening of symptoms for about six to twelve months. They are effective for only about half of the individuals who

take them. Some research suggests that risk factors for heart disease, such as high blood pressure, elevated cholesterol, diabetes, and excess body weight, may increase a person's risk of developing Alzheimer's. Staying physically and mentally active and socially connected may be associated with a lower risk for the disease.

Providing **care** for people with Alzheimer's is physically and psychologically demanding. About 70% of affected individuals live at home, where family or friends tend to them without pay. In the disease's advanced stages, many individuals require long-term residential care. Nearly half of all nursing home residents in the U.S. have Alzheimer's.

The costs of diagnosing, treating, and providing long-term care in this country for Alzheimer's patients are estimated to be $183 bil in 2011. People with Alzheimer's need a safe, stable environment and a regular daily schedule offering appropriate stimulation. Physical exercise and social interaction are important, as are proper nutrition and adequate pain management. Security is also a consideration, because many people with Alzheimer's tend to wander. An identification bracelet with the person's name, address, and condition may help ensure the safe return of an individual who wanders.

Warning Signs of Alzheimer's Disease

- Memory loss that disrupts daily life
- Challenges in planning or solving problems
- Difficulty completing familiar tasks at home, at work, or at leisure
- Confusion with time or place
- Trouble understanding visual images and spatial relationships
- New problems with words in speaking or writing
- Misplacing things and losing the ability to retrace steps
- Decreased or poor judgment
- Withdrawal from work or social activities
- Changes in mood and personality

Arthritis

Source: Arthritis Foundation, www.arthritis.org; Centers for Disease Control and Prevention

The term arthritis refers to more than 100 different diseases that cause pain, stiffness, swelling, and restricted movement in joints. The condition is usually chronic. The CDC estimates that nearly 50 mil adults in the United States report being told by a doctor that they had arthritis. Arthritis annually results in 44 mil ambulatory care visits and an estimated 992,100 hospitalizations. The **cause** for most types of arthritis is unknown; scientists are studying the roles played by genetics, lifestyle, and environment.

Symptoms may develop slowly or suddenly. A visit to the doctor is indicated when pain, stiffness, swelling in a joint, or difficulty in moving a joint persists for more than two weeks. To diagnose arthritis, the doctor records the patient's symptoms and examines his or her joints, looking for any swelling or limited movement. In addition, the doctor checks for other signs often seen with arthritis, such as rashes, mouth sores, or eye involvement. The doctor may test blood, urine, or joint fluid, or take X-rays of the joints.

Of the three most prevalent forms of arthritis, **osteoarthritis** is the most common, affecting approximately 27 mil Americans. It usually occurs after age 45. In patients with osteoarthritis, also called degenerative arthritis, the protective cartilage of joints is lost and changes occur in the bone, leading to pain and stiffness. It usually occurs in the fingers, knees, feet, hips, and back.

Fibromyalgia, another common arthritis condition, affects about 5 mil Americans. People suffering from fibromyalgia experience widespread pain and tenderness in muscles and their attachments to bone. Common symptoms include fatigue, disturbed sleep, stiffness, and psychological distress. More women than men are afflicted with this type of arthritis.

Rheumatoid arthritis, which affects an estimated 1.5 mil in the U.S., is one of the most serious and disabling forms of the disease. In this type—which is also more common and more degenerative in women—inflammation of the joints leads to cartilage and bone damage. The areas of the body that can be affected are the hands, wrists, feet, knees, ankles, shoulders, neck, jaw, and elbows.

Other forms of arthritis and related conditions include lupus, gout, ankylosing spondylitis, and scleroderma. Bursitis and tendinitis, which may result from injuring or overusing a joint, are also related.

Medications that relieve pain and swelling, such as analgesics, anti-inflammatory drugs, biologic response modifiers, glucocorticoids, and antirheumatic drugs, can be used to treat arthritis. They also tend to slow the disease process. Most treatment programs call for exercise, use of heat or cold, and joint-protection techniques, such as avoidance of excess stress on the joints, the use of assistive devices, and weight loss and control. In some cases, surgery may help.

Cancer Prevention

Source: American Cancer Society, Inc., www.cancer.org

PRIMARY PREVENTION: Modifiable determinants of cancer risk.

Smoking	The risk of developing lung cancer is about 23 times higher for current male smokers and 13 times higher for current female smokers than for those who have never smoked. Smoking accounts for at least 30% of all U.S. cancer deaths. Tobacco use is responsible for nearly 1 in 5 deaths in the U.S. Smoking increases the risk of the following types of cancer: nasopharynx, nasal cavity and paranasal sinuses, lip, oral cavity, pharynx, larynx, lung, esophagus, pancreas, uterine cervix, ovary (mucinous), kidney, bladder, stomach, colorectum, and acute myeloid leukemia.
Diet and physical activity	Overweight and obesity are associated with increased risk for developing many cancers, including cancers of the breast in postmenopausal women, colon, endometrium, kidney, pancreas, and adenocarcinoma of the esophagus. Evidence is suggestive that obesity also increases risk for cancers of the gallbladder, thyroid, ovary, and cervix, as well as for myeloma, Hodgkin lymphoma, and aggressive forms of prostate cancer. It's not yet known for certain how diet, nutrition intake, and the amount and distribution of body fat factor into the development of certain cancers. But eating a mostly plant-based diet, with grains and beans and five or more servings of fruits and vegetables each day, and regular physical activity can help one achieve and maintain a healthy weight. That in turn may reduce the risk for many cancers.
Sunlight	Many of the more than 2 mil skin cancers diagnosed annually in the U.S. could have been prevented by protection from the sun's rays and avoiding indoor tanning. Epidemiological evidence shows that sun exposure is a major factor in the development of melanoma and that incidence rates are increasing worldwide.
Alcohol	Heavy drinking, especially when accompanied by cigarette smoking or smokeless tobacco use, increases the risk of cancers of the mouth, larynx, pharynx, esophagus, and liver. Studies have also noted an association between regular alcohol consumption and an increased risk of breast cancer.
Smokeless tobacco	Use of chewing tobacco, snuff, and other tobacco products that are not smoked causes oral and pancreatic cancers. The excess risk of cancer of the cheek and gum may reach nearly 50-fold among long-term snuff users.
Estrogen	Menopausal hormone therapy (MHT, formerly called hormone replacement therapy) without the use of progestin can increase the risk of endometrial cancer. Combining progestin with estrogen MHT use may help minimize that risk. Studies, however, suggest that long-term use (5 years or more) of MHT increases the risk of breast cancer and may exceed the benefits. The benefits and risks of the use of estrogen by menopausal women should be discussed carefully with one's doctor.
Radiation	Excessive exposure to ionizing radiation can increase cancer risk. Medical and dental X-rays are adjusted to deliver the lowest dose possible without sacrificing image quality. Excessive radon exposure in the home may increase lung cancer risk, especially in cigarette smokers.
Environmental hazards	Exposure to various chemicals (including benzene, asbestos, vinyl chloride, arsenic, and aflatoxin) increases risk of various cancers. Risk of lung cancer from asbestos is greatly increased among smokers.
Vaccination	There are two vaccines approved for the prevention of the most common types of HPV infection that cause cervical cancer; Gardasil is recommended for use in females 9-26 years of age, and Cervarix in females 10-25 years of age.

Screening Guidelines for Early Detection of Cancer

SECONDARY PREVENTION: Steps to diagnose a cancer or precursor as early as possible after it has developed in asymptomatic people.

Cancer site	Population	Test or procedure	Frequency
Breast	Women, age 20+	Breast self-examination (BSE)	Beginning in their early 20s: women should be told about BSE. Prompt reporting of any new breast symptoms to a health professional should be emphasized. Women should receive instruction and have their technique reviewed at a periodic health exam.
		Clinical breast examination (CBE)	Women in their 20s and 30s: CBE should be part of a periodic health exam, preferably at least every 3 years. Asymptomatic women aged 40+ should continue to receive a CBE as part of a periodic health exam, preferably annually.
		Mammography	At age 40: begin annual mammography; annual clinical breast examination should be performed prior to mammography.
Colorectal[1]	Men and women, age 50+	**Tests that find polyps and cancer:** Flexible sigmoidoscopy, double-contrast barium enema (DCBE), or CT colonography (virtual colonoscopy)[2], or	Every 5 years, starting at age 50.
		Colonoscopy	Every 10 years, starting at age 50.
		Tests that mainly find cancer: Fecal occult blood test (FOBT) with at least 50% test sensitivity for cancer, or fecal immunochemical test (FIT) with at least 50% test sensitivity for cancer[2,3] or	Annual, starting at age 50.
		Stool DNA test (sDNA)[2]	Interval uncertain, starting at age 50.
Prostate	Men, age 50+	Prostate-specific antigen test (PSA) with or without digital rectal exam (DRE)	Asymptomatic men who have at least a 10-year life expectancy should have an opportunity to make an informed decision with their health care provider about screening for prostate cancer after receiving information about the uncertainties, risks, and potential benefits associated with screening. Prostate cancer screening should not occur without an informed decision-making process.[4]
Cervix	Women, age 18+	Pap test	Screening should begin about 3 years after a woman begins having vaginal intercourse, but no later than age 21. Screening should be done every year with conventional Pap tests or every 2 years using liquid-based Pap tests. At 30+ years old, women who have had 3 normal test results in a row may get screened every 2-3 years with cervical cytology alone, or every 3 years with an HPV DNA test plus cervical cytology. Women aged 70+ years who have had at least 3 normal Pap tests and no abnormal Pap tests in the past 10 years and women who have had a total hysterectomy may choose to stop cervical cancer screening.
Endometrial	Women, at menopause	At menopause, women at average risk should be informed about risks and symptoms of endometrial cancer and strongly encouraged to report any unexpected bleeding or spotting to their physicians.	
Cancer-related checkup	Men and women, age 20+	On the occasion of a periodic health exam, the cancer-related checkup should include examination for cancers of the thyroid, testicles, ovaries, lymph nodes, oral cavity, and skin, as well as health counseling about tobacco, sun exposure, diet and nutrition, risk factors, sexual practices, and environmental and occupational exposures.	

(1) Individuals with a personal or family history of colorectal cancer or adenomas, inflammatory bowel disease, or high-risk genetic syndromes should follow the most recent recommendations for individuals at increased or high risk. (2) Colonoscopy should be done if test results are positive. (3) For FOBT or FIT used as a screening test, the take-home multiple-sample method should be used. A FOBT or FIT done during a digital rectal exam in the doctor's office is not adequate for screening. (4) Information should be provided to men about the benefits and limitations of testing so that an informed decision can be made with the clinician's assistance.

Estimated New U.S. Cancer Cases and Deaths for Leading Sites, 2011

Source: *Cancer Facts & Figures 2011*, American Cancer Society, Inc.

The following estimates exclude basal and squamous cell skin cancers and in situ carcinomas (i.e., noninvasive cancers), except urinary bladder. In 2011, an estimated 57,650 new cases of carcinoma in situ of the breast and 53,360 cases of melanoma in situ are expected to be diagnosed. More than 2 mil cases of basal cell and squamous cell cancer are diagnosed yearly. They are highly curable forms of skin cancer and do not need to be reported to cancer registries.

Estimated New Cases

Both sexes		Male		Female	
Prostate	240,890	Prostate	240,890	Breast	230,480
Breast	232,620	Lung and bronchus	115,060	Lung and bronchus	106,070
Lung and bronchus	221,130	Urinary bladder	52,020	Colon	52,400
Colon	101,340	Colon	48,940	Uterine corpus	46,470
Melanoma—skin	70,230	Melanoma—skin	40,010	Thyroid	36,550
Urinary bladder	69,250	Kidney and renal pelvis	37,120	Non-Hodgkin lymphoma	30,300
Non-Hodgkin lymphoma	66,360	Non-Hodgkin lymphoma	36,060	Melanoma—skin	30,220
Kidney and renal pelvis	60,920	Rectum	22,910	Kidney and renal pelvis	23,800
Thyroid	48,020	Pancreas	22,050	Ovary	21,990
Uterine corpus	46,470	Liver and intrahepatic bile duct	19,260	Pancreas	21,980
All sites	**1,596,670**	**All sites**	**822,300**	**All sites**	**774,370**

Estimated New Deaths

Both sexes		Male		Female	
Lung and bronchus	156,940	Lung and bronchus	85,600	Lung and bronchus	71,340
Colon and rectum	49,380	Prostate	33,720	Breast	39,520
Breast	39,970	Colon and rectum	25,250	Colon and rectum	24,130
Pancreas	37,660	Pancreas	19,360	Pancreas	18,300
Prostate	33,720	Liver and intrahepatic bile duct	13,260	Ovary	15,460
Liver and intrahepatic bile duct	19,590	Esophagus	11,910	Non-Hodgkin lymphoma	9,570
Non-Hodgkin lymphoma	19,320	Urinary bladder	10,670	Uterine corpus	8,120
Ovary	15,460	Non-Hodgkin lymphoma	9,750	Liver and intrahepatic bile duct	6,330
Urinary bladder	14,990	Kidney and renal pelvis	8,270	Brain and other nervous system	5,670
Esophagus	14,710	Brain and other nervous system	7,440	Kidney and renal pelvis	4,850
All sites	**571,950**	**All sites**	**300,430**	**All sites**	**271,520**

U.S. Cancer Survival Rates by Year of Diagnosis, 1960-2007

Source: SEER (Surveillance, Epidemiology, and End Results) Cancer Statistics Review, 1975-2008, National Cancer Institute

Year	Total	Male	Female	White Total	White Male	White Female	Black Total	Black Male	Black Female
1960-63	—	—	—	39.0	—	—	27.0	—	—
1970-73	—	—	—	43.0	—	—	31.0	—	—
1975-77	49.1	41.9	56.0	50.0	42.9	56.7	39.2	32.8	46.3
1978-80	49.2	43.3	55.1	50.1	44.5	55.7	39.0	33.4	45.7
1981-83	50.4	45.4	55.3	51.5	46.8	56.1	39.0	34.3	44.6
1984-86	52.5	47.3	57.7	53.8	48.8	58.7	40.2	35.6	45.5
1987-89	55.5	51.3	59.8	56.8	53.0	60.8	43.1	39.0	47.8
1990-92	60.1	59.3	61.0	61.5	61.0	62.2	47.9	47.7	48.3
1993-95	61.4	61.0	61.9	62.5	62.1	63.0	52.7	54.4	50.6
1996-2000	64.3	64.2	64.5	65.4	65.4	65.5	56.0	58.7	52.9
2001-07	67.4	68.1	66.5	68.6	69.3	67.8	59.4	63.2	55.1

— = Statistic could not be calculated due to fewer than 25 diagnosed cases. **Note:** The geographic areas of surveillance may vary for different years. Rates are 5-year relative survival rates for all invasive cancer sites.

U.S. Cancer Survival Rate by Age at Diagnosis, 2001-07

Source: SEER (Surveillance, Epidemiology, and End Results) Cancer Statistics Review, 1975-2008, National Cancer Institute

Age	Total	Male	Female	White Total	White Male	White Female	Black Total	Black Male	Black Female
Under age 45	79.7	74.7	82.9	81.3	76.8	84.4	66.9	59.5	71.4
Ages 45-54	72.0	66.1	76.8	73.6	67.6	78.5	59.9	58.0	61.9
Ages 55-64	69.1	69.0	69.1	70.0	69.7	70.4	61.6	65.2	55.8
Under age 65	72.3	69.2	75.4	73.6	70.4	76.7	62.1	62.1	62.2
Ages 65 and older	58.4	63.1	52.9	58.9	63.2	53.9	51.8	60.0	42.0
Ages 65-74	64.5	68.0	59.4	65.0	68.2	60.5	58.7	65.6	48.3
Ages 75 and older	52.4	57.3	47.7	53.1	57.5	49.0	42.3	49.9	35.5

Note: Rates are 5-year relative survival rates for all invasive cancer sites.

Breast Cancer

Source: American Cancer Society, Inc., www.cancer.org

In 2011, an estimated 230,480 women and 2,140 men in the U.S. will be newly diagnosed with breast cancer, and about 39,520 women and 450 men will die from it. Currently, an estimated 2.6 mil women are living with a history of breast cancer, the second biggest cause of cancer death for women in the U.S. (lung cancer ranks first). But mortality rates have been declining, especially among younger women, probably because of earlier detection and improved treatment.

The **risk** for breast cancer increases with age. It is higher for women with a personal or family history of cancer, a long menstrual history (menstrual periods that started early and ended later in life), recent use of birth control pills, long-term use of postmenopausal estrogen replacement therapy, and who have no children or had no live birth until age 30 or older. Other risk factors include alcohol consumption and obesity. Inherited mutations such as in the BRCA1 and BRCA2 genes greatly increase risk, but these probably account for 5% to

10% of all breast cancers. By far the majority of women who develop breast cancer have no family history of it.

Breast cancer often **manifests** first as an abnormality on a mammogram X-ray. Physical symptoms that show up later, which may be detectable by a woman or her doctor, include a breast lump and, less commonly, breast pain or heaviness; persistent changes to the breast, such as swelling, thickening, or redness of the breast's skin; and nipple abnormalities such as spontaneous discharge, erosion, inversion, or tenderness. Breast pain is more commonly associated with benign (i.e., noncancerous) conditions.

Studies show that early **detection** increases survival and treatment options. Although most detected breast lumps are noncancerous, any suspicious lump should be biopsied.

Treatment for breast cancer may involve lumpectomy (local removal of a tumor), mastectomy (surgical removal of the breast), radiation therapy, chemotherapy, hormone therapy, and/or biologic therapy. For women with early-stage breast cancer, long-term **survival rates** following lumpectomy plus radiation therapy are similar to survival rates after a mastectomy.

Prostate Cancer

Source: Prostate Cancer Foundation, www.pcf.org; American Cancer Society, Inc., www.cancer.org

The **prostate** is a male gland located between the bladder and scrotum that secretes seminal fluid. Prostate cancer is the most common non-skin cancer in the U.S., and the second-most common cause, after lung cancer, of cancer deaths in American men. In 2011, an estimated 240,890 men will be diagnosed with prostate cancer, and about 33,720 will die from the disease. It was estimated that in 2006, 2.2 mil men with a history of prostate cancer were alive, making up nearly half of all male cancer survivors in the U.S.

The exact **cause** of prostate cancer is unknown. The most identifiable **risk factors** are age, family history, and race. About 62% of all prostate cancers are diagnosed in men over the age of 65, and the chances of developing the disease rise dramatically with age. Men with a single first-degree relative with a history of prostate cancer are twice to three times as likely to develop the disease, and those with two or more first-degree relatives are three to five times as likely to get it. African-American men are much more likely to develop prostate cancer than non-Hispanic white men and are twice as likely to die from it. The cause for this disparity remains unknown; both socioeconomic and biologic differences are likely involved.

Usually, the disease has no **symptoms** in its early stages. With more advanced disease, men may experience weak or interrupted urine flow; inability to urinate or difficulty starting or stopping the urine flow; the need to urinate frequently, especially at night; blood in the urine; or pain or burning with urination. Advanced prostate cancer commonly spreads to the bones, which can cause pain in the hips, spine, ribs, or other areas.

The American Cancer Society recommends that once they reach 50, men showing no symptoms and with no family history of prostate cancer speak with their health care provider about the benefits and risks of being **screened** through a prostate specific antigen (PSA) blood test or digital rectal exam (DRE). African-American men or those with a family history of the disease should be aware of their screening options beginning at age 40 or 45. Men under 40 seldom get prostate cancer.

Prostate cancer **treatment** may include surgery, radiation, hormonal therapy, chemotherapy, or some combination. If caught early on, while tumor cells are localized within the prostate, the five-year relative survival rate approaches 100%.

Skin Cancer

Source: American Cancer Society, Inc., www.cancer.org

Skin cancer is generally divided into two main classes, **nonmelanomas** and **melanomas**, both types affecting different types of skin cells. Melanoma develops in skin cells called melanocytes, which produce melanin, a pigment that gives skin a tan or brown color and helps to protect the deeper layers of skin from the harmful effects of the sun. Melanoma is the most dangerous type of skin cancer because it can easily spread to other parts of the body.

Although skin cancer is the most common type of cancer diagnosed in the U.S., melanoma only accounts for less than 5% of all skin cancers. The American Cancer Society estimates that in 2011, 70,230 new cases of melanoma will be diagnosed in the U.S., and about 8,790 people will die from melanoma, while 11,980 will die from any skin cancer.

The exact causes of melanoma are unclear, but there are several **risk factors** that have been associated with the disease:

- Overexposure to UV light (sunlight)
- Presence of moles; moles themselves are not harmful but are associated with an increased risk for skin cancer.
- Fair skin, freckling, and light hair
- Family history
- Use of immune suppression drugs
- Age; although melanoma is more likely to occur in older people, it is one of the most common cancers in people younger than 30.
- Gender; men get melanoma more often than women.
- Past history of melanoma
- Xeroderma pigmentosum (XP), a rare, genetic condition in which people are less able to repair damage caused by sunlight

Melanomas generally look like abnormal moles on the surface of the skin. Normal moles are most often an evenly colored brown, tan, or black spot on the skin that can be flat or raised. They normally have a distinct border that separates them from normal skin cells. Moles can be present at birth, form over time, or even disappear. Abnormal moles differ from regular skin cells and may be a sign of skin cancer. An irregular mole should be examined as soon as possible. Irregular moles generally have the following characteristics:

- Asymmetry—one half of the mole does not match the other half.
- Border—the edges are irregular, ragged, notched, or blurred.
- Color—not uniform; there may be shades of tan, brown, black, and sometimes patches of pink, red, blue, or white.
- Diameter—moles wider than ¼ inch are abnormal (however, melanomas can be smaller).

If a melanoma is suspected, the doctor will perform a biopsy using cells extracted from the suspected cancer or by removing the whole mass and examining it. If a melanoma is found, doctors will often check to see if the cancer has spread to other parts of the body. This is called **staging** and is represented by Roman numerals I through IV (1-4). The lower the number, the less the cancer has spread. This will determine what course of treatment is necessary.

If caught early, melanoma is highly curable. The five-year **survival rates** for the various stages are as follows:

- All stages   91%
- Local   98%
- Regional   62%
- Distant   16%

Treatment may include simple removal of the melanoma; amputation if the cancer is found on a finger or toe; or treatment involving chemotherapy, immunotherapy, or radiation if the melanoma has spread to other parts of the body.

Depression

Source: National Institute of Mental Health, National Institutes of Health, U.S. Dept. of Health and Human Services

Depression is a serious illness that affects thoughts, feelings, and the ability to function in everyday life. It strikes all age groups, and often goes unrecognized or is inadequately treated. The National Institute of Mental Health (NIMH) estimates that about 20.9 mil American adults age 18 and older suffer from depression or some other mood or depressive disorder in any given year; more than 16% of all Americans will have had depression at some point in life. Young people are at particular risk; in a one-year period, three times as many persons with depression were 18 to 29 years old as were 60 or older.

Nearly twice as many women as men suffer from a depressive illness in a given year. Although conventional wisdom holds that depression is most closely associated with menopause, the childbearing years, followed by the years prior to menopause, are marked by the highest rates of depression. The influence of hormones on depression in women has been an active area of NIMH research.

In a given year, 1-5% of people age 65 and older living in the community (i.e., residing outside of institutions) suffer from major depression. Depression frequently occurs with other physical illnesses including heart disease, stroke, cancer, and diabetes. It is not a normal part of aging.

Available **treatments** can alleviate symptoms, and with awareness growing, more people with depression are seeking help. But many depressed people—and those around them—still fail to realize that they have an illness or could benefit from medical help.

Symptoms and Types of Depression

- Persistent sad, anxious, or "empty" feelings
- Feelings of hopelessness and/or pessimism
- Feelings of guilt, worthlessness, and/or helplessness
- Irritability, restlessness
- Loss of interest in activities or hobbies once pleasurable, including sex
- Fatigue and decreased energy
- Difficulty concentrating, remembering details, and making decisions
- Insomnia, early-morning wakefulness, or excessive sleeping
- Overeating, or appetite loss
- Thoughts of suicide, suicide attempts
- Persistent aches or pains, headaches, cramps, or digestive problems that do not ease even with treatment

A diagnosis of **major depressive disorder** (or **unipolar major depression**) is made if an individual reports experiencing five or more of these symptoms in the same two-week period.

Bipolar disorder (or **manic-depressive illness**) is characterized by episodes of major depression alternating with periods of mania, when a person experiences a persistent, abnormally elevated mood or irritability, accompanied by feelings of inflated self-esteem, less need for sleep, increased talkativeness, racing thoughts, distractibility, agitation, and excessive involvement in pleasurable activities that have a high potential for painful consequences. While it shares some of the features of major depression, bipolar disorder is a distinct illness.

Dysthymic disorder (or **dysthymia**), a less severe yet more chronic form of depression, is diagnosed when a depressed mood persists for at least two years in adults (one year in children or adolescents) and is accompanied by at least two other depressive symptoms. Many people with dysthymic disorder also experience major depressive episodes.

In contrast to normal experiences of sadness, depression is extreme and persistent and can interfere significantly with an individual's ability to function. A study sponsored by the World Health Organization and the World Bank found unipolar major depression to be the leading cause of disability in the U.S. and worldwide.

Treatments for Depression

A variety of **medicines** are used to treat depression. These drugs influence the functioning of certain neurotransmitters in the brain, primarily serotonin and norepinephrine, known as monoamines. Older drugs—tricyclic antidepressants (TCAs) and monoamine oxidase inhibitors (MAOIs)—affect the functioning of both of these neurotransmitters. But they can have strong side effects or, in the case of MAOIs, require dietary restrictions. Newer medications, such as selective serotonin reuptake inhibitors (SSRIs), have fewer side effects. All of these medications can be effective, but some people respond to one type and not another.

NIMH research has shown that certain types of **psychotherapy**, particularly cognitive-behavioral therapy (CBT) and interpersonal therapy (IPT), can help relieve depression. CBT helps patients change the negative thinking and behaving patterns often associated with depression. IPT focuses patients on working through personal relationships that may contribute to depression. Studies of adults have shown that a combination of psychotherapy and antidepressant medication is most effective in treating moderate-to-severe depression.

Electroconvulsive therapy (ECT) has been found effective in treating some cases of severe depression, particularly those that have not responded to other forms of treatment. ECT involves producing a seizure in the brain of a patient under general anesthesia by applying electrical stimulation through electrodes placed on the scalp. Memory loss and other cognitive problems, though common side effects, are typically short-lived.

Diabetes

Source: American Diabetes Association, www.diabetes.org; Centers for Disease Control and Prevention

Diabetes is a chronic disease in which the body does not produce or properly use the hormone **insulin**. Insulin is needed to convert sugar, starches, and other foods into energy. Both genetics and environment appear to play roles in the onset of diabetes. This disease, which has no cure, is the seventh leading cause of death by disease in the U.S. According to death certificate data, 68,504 people in the U.S. died as a result of diabetes in 2009. In 2011, an estimated 25.8 mil Americans had diabetes, 7 mil of whom were undiagnosed.

The American Diabetes Association recommends the following guidelines for **diagnosing** diabetes: lowering the acceptable level of blood sugar in a fasting glucose test from 140 mg of glucose/deciliter of blood to 126 mg/deciliter; testing all adults 45 years of age and older, and then every three years if results are normal; and testing high-risk individuals starting at a younger age more frequently. The American Diabetes Association supports studies proving that detection at an earlier stage and modest lifestyle changes, such as eating better and exercising more, will help prevent or delay complications.

There are two major types of diabetes:

Type 1 (formerly known as insulin dependent, or juvenile diabetes). The body does not produce insulin; the disease most often begins in childhood or early adulthood. People with type 1 diabetes must take daily insulin injections to stay alive.

Type 2 (formerly known as non-insulin dependent, or adult-onset diabetes). The body does not produce enough or cannot properly use insulin. It is the most common form of the disease (90%-95% of diabetes cases in people over age 20) and often begins later in life.

Prediabetes

There are 79 mil people in the U.S. who have prediabetes, the state that occurs when a person's blood glucose levels are higher than normal but not high enough for a diagnosis of diabetes. One study indicated that about 11% of people with prediabetes developed type 2 diabetes each year during the average three-year study follow-up period. Other studies showed that most people with prediabetes develop type 2 diabetes within 10 years.

Complications from Diabetes

People often have diabetes many years before it is diagnosed. During that time, serious complications may develop. Potential complications include the following:

Blindness. Diabetes is the leading cause of new cases of blindness in people ages 20-74. Each year, 12,000 to 24,000 people lose their eyesight because of diabetes.

Kidney disease. 10% to 21% of all people with diabetes develop kidney disease. In 2008, a total of 48,374 people in the U.S. initiated treatment for end-stage renal disease (kidney failure) because of diabetes.

Amputations. Diabetes is the most frequent cause for nontraumatic lower limb amputations. The risk of a leg amputation is 15 to 40 times greater for a person with diabetes than for the average American. In 2006, approximately 65,700 lower-limb amputations were performed as a result of complications brought on by diabetes.

Heart disease and stroke. People with diabetes are two to four times more likely to have heart disease. They are also two to four times more likely to suffer a stroke.

Warning Signs of Diabetes

Type 1 diabetes (usually occur suddenly):
- frequent urination
- unusual thirst
- extreme hunger
- unusual weight loss
- extreme fatigue
- irritability

Type 2 diabetes (occur less suddenly):
- any type 1 symptoms
- frequent infections
- blurred vision
- cuts/bruises slow to heal
- tingling/numbness in hands or feet
- recurring skin, gum, or bladder infections

Eating Disorders

Source: National Institute of Mental Health, National Institutes of Health, U.S. Dept. of Health and Human Services

Eating disorders involve serious disturbances in eating behavior, usually in the forms of extreme and unhealthy reduction of food intake or severe overeating. They are not due to a failure of will; rather, they are real and treatable medical illnesses in which certain behavior patterns get out of control. The **main types** are anorexia nervosa, bulimia nervosa, and binge-eating disorder (technically categorized with "eating disorders not otherwise identified"). These disorders usually develop in adolescence or early adulthood and often occur with other illnesses such as depression, substance abuse, and anxiety disorders. They are much more common among females; only about 5% to 15% of anorexia or bulimia patients, and 35% of binge eaters are male.

If not treated, eating disorders can lead to serious complications, including heart conditions and kidney failure, which may result in death.

Anorexia nervosa affects an estimated 0.9% of all females. Symptoms include resistance to maintaining weight at minimally healthy levels, intense fear of gaining weight, exaggerated importance of body weight or shape in one's self image, and infrequent or absent menstrual periods. Anorexics see themselves as overweight even when they are dangerously thin. In response, they avoid food and take other extreme measures to lose weight, such as exercising compulsively or purging by means of vomiting or laxatives and enemas. While some anorexics fully recover after a single episode, others may relapse frequently or experience chronic deterioration.

Bulimia nervosa affects an estimated 0.5% of females. It is characterized by recurrent uncontrolled binge-eating episodes followed by what is believed to be compensatory behavior to prevent weight gain, such as self-induced vomiting, exercising excessively, or fasting. Persons with bulimia can weigh within the normal range for their age and height, but they still fear gaining weight and are intensely dissatisfied with their bodies. They often perform their behaviors in secret, feeling shame when they binge and relief when they purge.

Binge-eating disorder, which is not officially approved as a psychiatric diagnosis, affects an estimated 2% to 3.5% of males and females in the U.S. As with bulimia, a binge-eating disorder involves episodes of excessive eating during which the sufferer may feel a complete lack of control. But individuals with this disorder do not compensate by purging, exercising, or fasting. Many are thus overweight, and the shame they feel can lead to further bingeing.

Eating disorder sufferers may not admit they are ill. Early diagnosis and a comprehensive **treatment** program are essential to recovery. Some patients may need immediate hospitalization. For anorexia, treatment usually follows three established steps: weight restoration, usually in an inpatient hospital setting; treatment of any accompanying psychological disturbances, including the use of medications; and achieving long-term remission or recovery by reducing or eliminating negative thoughts and behaviors.

Heart and Blood Vessel Disease

Source: American Heart Association, www.heart.org; National Center for Chronic Disease Prevention and Health Promotion, Centers for Disease Control and Prevention; National Heart, Blood, and Lung Institute, National Institutes of Health, U.S. Dept. of Health and Human Services

Warning Signs of Heart Attack

- Chest discomfort. Most heart attacks involve discomfort in the center of the chest that lasts more than a few minutes or that goes away and then returns. It can feel like uncomfortable pressure, squeezing, fullness, or pain.
- Discomfort in other areas of the upper body. Symptoms can include pain or discomfort in one or both arms, the back, neck, jaw, or stomach.
- Shortness of breath. This feeling may occur with or without chest discomfort.
- Other signs may include breaking out in a cold sweat, nausea, or lightheadedness.
- The American Heart Association advises immediate action at onset of symptoms, as more than half of heart attack victims die within an hour of symptoms first manifesting. Call 9-1-1. Get to a hospital right away.

Warning Signs of Stroke

- Sudden numbness or weakness of the face, arm, or leg, especially on one side of the body.
- Sudden confusion, trouble speaking, or understanding.
- Sudden trouble seeing in one or both eyes.
- Sudden trouble walking, dizziness, loss of balance or coordination.
- Sudden severe headache with no known cause.
- Prompt treatment of a stroke can be a major factor in controlling the effects. If you have one or more stroke symptoms that last more than a few minutes, call 9-1-1 or the emergency medical service number immediately so an ambulance, ideally one with advanced life support, can be sent for you quickly.

Major Modifiable Risk Factors

High blood pressure. High blood pressure, or hypertension, increases the risk of stroke, heart attack, kidney failure, and heart failure. It affects men and women of all races, ethnic origins, and ages. Obesity, physical inactivity, and an unhealthy diet can contribute to this **often symptomless** disease. Individuals should have a blood pressure reading at least once every two years or more often if advised by a physician.

A blood pressure reading is really two measurements, with one value written above the other, such as 122/78 mmHg. The upper number (systolic pressure) represents the amount of pressure in the blood vessels when the heart contracts (beats) and pushes blood through the circulatory system. The lower number (diastolic pressure) represents the pressure in the blood vessels between beats, when the heart is resting. According to recent National Institutes of Health (NIH) guidelines, a blood pressure reading below 120/80 is considered normal, while readings from 120/80 to 139/89 are considered prehypertension.

High blood pressure is divided into two stages:
Stage 1 is 140-159 (systolic) over 90-99 (diastolic);
Stage 2 is 160+ (systolic) over 100+ (diastolic).
The diagnosis can be based on either the systolic or the diastolic reading.

High blood pressure usually cannot be cured, but it can be controlled in a variety of ways, including lifestyle modifications and medication. **Treatment** always should be at the direction and under the supervision of a physician. The treatment goal for patients with hypertension is blood pressure below 140/90. Individuals with hypertension and diabetes or chronic kidney disease should aim for blood pressure lower than 130/80.

High blood cholesterol. Cholesterol is a waxy fat-like substance found in all cells of the body. It is produced by the body and also comes in some foods. The body needs some cholesterol, but excess levels increase the risk of heart disease. High cholesterol in itself usually does not cause **symptoms**, so many people are unaware that they have a problem.

There are two major kinds of cholesterol: LDL (low-density lipoprotein), often called "bad" cholesterol, leads to narrowing of the arteries. HDL (high-density lipoprotein), known as "good" cholesterol, helps reduce that risk.

NIH guidelines classify total cholesterol levels (determined by a blood test) of less than 200 mg/dl as desirable, 200-239 as borderline high, and 240 and higher as high. About 37 mil Americans have a cholesterol level of 240 mg/dl or higher. LDL levels of less than 100 are considered optimal, 130-159 as borderline high, 160-189 as high, and 190 and higher as very high. For HDL, levels of 60 mg/dl and

higher are considered protective against heart disease, while levels under 40 mg/dl are considered a risk factor.

As with high blood pressure, high blood cholesterol can be controlled by lifestyle changes and medication and should be treated by a physician.

Triglycerides, another form of fat in the blood, can also raise the risk of heart disease. Levels that are borderline high (150-199) or high (200 or more) may need treatment.

Diabetes. Diabetes is a major risk factor for heart disease; at least 65% of people with diabetes mellitus die of some form of heart or blood vessel disease.

Smoking. Cigarette smokers are two to four times more likely to develop coronary heart disease (CHD). Smoking is also associated with the risk of sudden cardiac death.

Obesity. Using a body mass index (BMI) of 25 and higher for overweight and 30 and higher for obesity, between 60 and 70% of Americans are either overweight or obese. Of these, nearly 75 mil are obese.

Physical inactivity. A sedentary lifestyle is a risk factor for CHD. The risk increase is comparable to that observed for high blood cholesterol, high blood pressure, or cigarette smoking.

Women and Cardiovascular Disease

The American Heart Association reports that diseases of the heart and stroke, respectively, are the number one and number three killers of women over the age of 25. (Cancer is the second leading cause.) More than one in three women died of some form of cardiovascular disease in 2007. Because heart disease was long viewed as a "man's" disease, many of the major cardiovascular studies were conducted only on men. Recent attention has been directed toward understanding the influence of gender on cardiovascular disease risk and prevention, but important gaps in knowledge remain.

Women often present some of the same classic symptoms of heart attack as men, such as chest pain that spreads to the shoulders and arms. But women may more often report atypical chest pain or complain of abdominal pain, difficulty breathing (dyspnea), and nausea. Another problem in **diagnosis** is that women tend to have heart attacks later in life than men, so symptoms may be masked by other age-related diseases such as arthritis or osteoporosis. Even certain diagnostic tests and procedures such as the exercise stress test may not be as accurate in women, with the result that the disease process leading to heart attack or stroke may not be detected early on, with potentially serious consequences.

Irritable Bowel Syndrome

Source: National Institute of Diabetes and Digestive and Kidney Diseases, National Institutes of Health

Irritable Bowel Syndrome (IBS)—a functional disorder, not a disease, in the large intestine—is one of the most common disorders diagnosed by physicians. Nearly one in five Americans has IBS symptoms, and it accounts for more than 1 out of every 10 doctor visits in the U.S. IBS occurs more frequently in women than in men, and it usually begins before the age of 35 for about 50% of those affected. Though IBS causes discomfort and may even be painful, it does not damage the bowel.

Many people are uncomfortable discussing IBS because of its embarrassing **symptoms**. They may include the following:
- Abdominal pain
- Bloating
- Discomfort
- Constipation
- Mucus in the stool
- Diarrhea
- Alternating between constipation and diarrhea

For most people, IBS is a chronic condition, and there will likely be times when the symptoms may worsen or disappear altogether only to reappear in the future. Most

complications are derived from the symptoms, such as hemorrhoids, which may form as a result of diarrhea and constipation. People with chronic IBS may also go through periods of depression because of the constant discomfort and the symptoms' interference in work and personal relationships.

The specific **causes** for IBS are unknown. The walls of the intestines are lined with layers of muscle that contract and relax in a coordinated manner as they move food through the digestive system. When a person has IBS, the contractions cause food to either speed up or slow down as it moves though the bowel, subsequently causing gas, bloating, diarrhea, or constipation. Some researchers believe that people who suffer from IBS have a colon that is particularly sensitive to certain foods. Milk products, alcohol, caffeine, carbonated drinks, chocolate, and fatty foods in particular can trigger IBS symptoms. Another common factor is a low tolerance for stretching of the large intestine. Women tend to get IBS more often than men and usually have more severe symptoms during menstrual periods, leading researchers to believe that IBS may have a hormonal trigger. Recent research has shown that serotonin, a neurotransmitter hormone, may be linked with gastrointestinal functioning.

IBS can sometimes result from infection or other problems in the body. Researchers have found that people who have had gastroenteritis later develop IBS. But because IBS symptoms can match those of many serious diseases, it is important for chronic sufferers to consult their doctors. If symptoms began early in life and have remained stable, one may need to get a colonoscopy to rule out inflammatory bowel disease, such as Crohn's disease or ulcerative colitis, or even colon cancer. Those with IBS over 50 years of age should be regularly screened for colon cancer.

Despite the uncertainty over what causes IBS, there are known precautionary measures that people with sensitive digestive systems can take. Keeping a well-balanced diet is the best possible preventive. Eating foods with dietary fiber, such as whole-grain bread and cereal, as well as vegetables and beans as part of a daily diet can reduce IBS symptoms, although high–fiber diets may cause gas and bloating. Eating large meals has been shown to worsen the condition, so IBS sufferers may want to eat several smaller meals.

There is no cure for IBS. **Treatment** usually involves lessening the symptoms so that they don't interfere as much in a person's life.

Common Infectious Diseases

Source: National Institutes of Health, Centers for Disease Control and Prevention, U.S. Dept. of Health and Human Services; World Health Organization

The following is a list of major infectious diseases. It is meant to be used for reference purposes only and not as a tool for diagnosis. Statistics may appear uneven because of the different reporting methods used by the various agencies, and because not all diseases are surveyed in the same year.

Chicken pox

(*Varicella simplex*) Usually nonthreatening viral disease commonly associated with children. In adults, the disease can be serious. **Transmission:** highly contagious. Transmitted by direct contact with rash, coughing, or sneezing of infected persons. **Symptoms:** blister-like rash, discomfort, high fever. Infected people may develop shingles later in life. **Vaccine:** became available in 1995. **Treatment:** none; antibiotics in some severe cases. **Annual U.S. cases:** before 1995, about 4 mil, mostly children; 20,480 reported in 2009.

Chlamydia

(*Chlamydia trachomatis*) One of the most widely spread sexually transmitted diseases (STDs). **Transmission:** sexually transmitted. **Symptoms:** about 70% of those infected show no symptoms. In women, vaginal discharge, infection of the cervix and urinary tract, can cause pelvic inflammatory disease. In men, infection of urinary tract and epididymitis (inflammation of testicular duct); can also infect the throat, rectum, and eyes. **Treatment:** curable with antibiotics. **Annual U.S. cases:** 1,244,180 in 2009.

Common cold

(More than 200 different viruses) An upper respiratory viral infection. **Transmission:** touching one's nose, eyes, or mouth after touching something contaminated by the virus; inhalation of airborne virus. **Symptoms:** irritated nose or scratchy throat, sneezing and watery green or yellow nasal discharge, coughing, muscle aches, headache, postnasal drip, decreased appetite. **Treatment:** no cure. Over-the-counter remedies can relieve symptoms; effectiveness of antiviral drugs uncertain. **Est. annual U.S. cases:** about 1 bil.

Gonorrhea

(*Neisseria gonorrhoeae*) Common bacterial STD. **Transmission:** sexually transmitted. **Symptoms:** in men, discomfort in urethra, yellow or green discharge, burning during urination. In women, pelvic pain, bleeding associated with intercourse, burning during urination, yellow or bloody discharge. **Treatment:** highly curable with antibiotics. **Annual U.S. cases:** 301,174 in 2009.

Hepatitis

A viral disease that causes inflammation of the liver. In the U.S., five forms are endemic: A, B, C, D, and E. Forms A, B, and C are the most common. **Symptoms:** all forms have generally similar symptoms including jaundice, fatigue, abdominal pain, loss of appetite, nausea, mild flu-like symptoms. Many cases cause no symptoms. In extreme cases, liver transplants may be necessary.

Hepatitis A (*Hepatovirus picornaviridae*). **Transmission:** food or water contaminated with feces from infected persons. **Vaccine:** effective; travelers are advised to not drink tap water in countries where disease is common. **Treatment:** disease usually resolves on its own; alcohol consumption should be avoided. **Est. annual U.S. cases:** 21,000 infections in 2009; 1,987 acute lab-confirmed cases reported in 2009.

Hepatitis B (*Orthohepadnavirus hepadnaviridae*) **Transmission:** unsterilized needle sharing; contaminated blood transfusions; sexual contact. **Vaccine:** highly effective. **Treatment:** for chronic cases, drug treatment is necessary. For acute cases, disease usually resolves itself. Severe cases treated with lamivudine. **Est. annual U.S. cases:** 38,000 infections in 2009; 3,374 acute lab-confirmed cases reported in 2009.

Hepatitis C (*Hepacivirus flavinviridae*) **Transmission:** unsterilized needle sharing; contaminated blood transfusions; sexual contact. **Vaccine:** none. **Treatment:** chronic cases treated with drugs, which eliminates virus in about 50% of patients. For acute cases, treatment recommended if disease present after two to three months. **Est. annual U.S. cases:** 16,000 infections in 2009; 781 acute lab-confirmed cases reported in 2009.

HPV infection

(More than 100 strains of human papillomavirus) Common viral infection; leading cause of cervical cancer. **Transmission:** sexually transmitted. **Symptoms:** most of those infected have no symptoms but can still transmit virus. In some cases, genital warts and pre-cancerous bumps on anus, cervix or vulva, or penis. **Vaccine:** Gardasil and Cervarix. **Treatment:** while there is no cure, a healthy immune system can usually fight off HPV naturally. Women with HPV should have a pap smear and pelvic exam every six months. **Est. annual U.S. cases:** 6 mil new cases; approximately 20 mil currently infected with HPV.

Influenza

(Various influenza viruses) Highly contagious viral respiratory infection. **Transmission:** airborne; contact with face after touching infected surface. **Symptoms:** chills, fatigue, fever, headache, sore throat, sinus congestion, coughing. ("Stomach flu" is not influenza.) **Vaccine:** yearly vaccinations recommended; available as injection or nasal spray. **Treatment:** antiviral drugs; disease normally runs its course in a matter of days. **Est. annual U.S. cases:** 5%-20% of population; more than 200,000 flu-related hospitalizations, 36,000 flu-related deaths.

Lyme disease

(*Borrelia burgdorferi*) Bacterial inflammatory disease, first identified 1975 in Old Lyme, CT. Found across the U.S., usually in areas with large deer populations. **Transmission:** bite from infected deer ticks. Mice and deer are most common tick hosts. **Symptoms:** mimic those of other diseases. Flu-like symptoms: fatigue, stiff neck, joint inflammation, skin rash may appear at site of tick bite. **Treatment:** antibiotics in early stages; anti-inflammation drugs to relieve symptoms. Without treatment, long-term complications (some fatal) involving joints, heart, and nervous system. **Annual U.S. cases:** from 9,908 reported cases in 1992 to 38,468 confirmed and probable cases in 2009.

Malaria

(*Plasmodium* parasite) Infectious disease known from as early as 2700 BCE. Virtually eradicated in developed countries; still a major killer in tropical regions. **Transmission:** bite from infected mosquito. **Symptoms:** high fever, shaking chills, heavy sweating, headache, fatigue, enlarged spleen. If left untreated, organ damage and death. **Treatment:** antimalarial drugs, including chloroquine, for treatment and prevention. **Annual cases:** 1,451 in the U.S. in 2009; worldwide, an estimated 225 mil cases and 781,000 deaths, most young children in sub-Saharan Africa, in 2009.

Measles

(*Rubeola* virus) Once-common viral infection; today almost nonexistent in U.S. and Canada. **Transmission:** airborne transmission by infected persons. **Symptoms:** itchy and raised rash, sore throat, cough, pink eye, high fever; in rare cases, encephalitis, seizures, permanent deafness, death. **Vaccine:** highly effective. **Treatment:** no specific treatment; symptoms relieved with bed rest, acetaminophen, humidified air. **Annual U.S. cases:** 71 in 2009.

Mumps

(Mumps virus) Acute and contagious viral infection. **Transmission:** direct contact with mucus or saliva of infected persons. **Symptoms:** painful, visible swelling of the salivary or parotid glands in the face. Chills, headache, fever, painful swallowing. In some cases, inflammation of testes, pancreas, ovaries. In severe cases, brain swelling and symptoms ranging from nausea and drowsiness to seizures and permanent deafness. **Vaccine:** MMR vaccine is effective. **Treatment:** no specific treatment; symptoms may be relieved by applying ice or heat to swollen glands. **Annual U.S. cases:** 1,991 in 2009.

Peptic ulcer

(Most from *Helicobacter pylori* [*H. pylori*] bacteria; also overuse of aspirin or other anti-inflammatory drugs) Weakening of the stomach's protective mucous coating, allowing stomach acid and bacteria to irritate stomach lining. **Transmission:** *H. pylori* may be transmitted through food and water. **Symptoms:** indigestion; bloating; dull, transient abdominal pain or discomfort; nausea; vomiting. **Treatment:** antibiotics, acid-suppressing drugs. **Est. annual cases:** about 20% of the population under 40 years of age and half of those over 60 may be infected with *H. pylori*. An estimated 500,000 to 850,000 develop peptic ulcers each year.

Pertussis or Whooping cough

(*Bordetella pertussis* or *B. parepertussis*) Upper respiratory bacterial infection. **Transmission:** airborne transmission by infected persons; highly contagious. **Symptoms:** initially, mild cold-like symptoms, fever, diarrhea, difficulty breathing; later, violent coughing with characteristic "whooping" heard when patient tries to breathe between coughs, vomiting. In severe cases, apnea, pneumonia, seizures, encephalopathy. **Vaccine:** available as part of combination vaccine that also prevents diphtheria and tetanus. **Treatment:** antibiotics in early cases; otherwise, disease must run its course. **Annual U.S. cases:** 16,858 in 2009.

Salmonella or Salmonellosis

(*Salmonella enteritidis*) Bacterial infection. **Transmission:** eating foods contaminated by feces carrying the bacteria or undercooked meats or raw eggs contaminated by bacteria. Contact with feces of infected animal or pet. **Symptoms:** fever, diarrhea, abdominal cramps 12 to 72 hours after infection. **Treatment:** no standard treatment. Runs its course in four to seven days; antibiotics in severe cases. **Annual U.S. cases:** 49,192 in 2009.

Shigellosis

(Four species of *Shigella*: *boydii*, *dysenteriae*, *flexneri*, and *sonnei*) Bacterial infection and a form of dysentery, an intestinal disease. **Transmission:** consuming food contaminated by infected feces or vegetables grown in fields containing contaminated sewage. Swimming in contaminated water. **Symptoms:** watery or bloody diarrhea one to four days after infection, high fever, vomiting, painful bowel movements, severe diarrhea. In extreme cases, seizures in children, intestinal perforation. **Treatment:** mild infection allowed to run its course; replacement of fluids and salts lost through excessive diarrhea. Antibiotics in severe cases. Although severe diarrhea is symptomatic, antidiarrheal medicines may make illness worse. **Annual U.S. cases:** 15,931 in 2009.

Syphilis

(*Treponema pallidum*) Bacterial infection known since ancient times that spread rampantly throughout Europe in the Middle Ages. **Transmission:** sexually transmitted. **Symptoms:** primary stage: painless sore, called a chancre, where bacteria enters the body; usually heals in 3 to 12 weeks with or without treatment. Without treatment, disease enters secondary stage: skin rash as chancre is healing or weeks after it's healed. Without treatment, enters tertiary stage: mouth sores, fever, fatigue, loss of appetite, weight loss, hair loss, jaundice, syphilitic meningitis, aortal aneurysms, lesions, damage to nervous system, heart, and eyes. Most infected do not progress beyond primary or secondary stage. **Treatment:** curable with antibiotics (mostly penicillin). **Annual U.S. cases:** 44,828 total in 2009; 13,997 primary and secondary.

Tetanus or Lockjaw

(*Clostridium tetani*) Bacterial infection. **Transmission:** bacteria, found in soil, enters body through broken skin. **Symptoms:** muscle stiffness and spasms or "locking" of muscles of the jaw, neck, and limbs. **Vaccine:** four forms of immunization. **Treatment:** tetanus immune globulin to fight infection; with treatment, less than 10% of cases are fatal. **Annual U.S. cases:** 18 in 2009.

Tuberculosis

(*Mycobacterium tuberculosis*) Bacterial infection that primarily affects the lungs. **Transmission:** airborne transmission by persons with active TB infection. **Symptoms:** weight loss, fever, cough with discharge (sometimes with bloody sputum), night sweats, growing shortness of breath over time, chest pains. **Vaccine/treatment:** BCG (Bacille Calmette Guerin) vaccine only effective in protecting young children and used where TB is prevalent. Not recommended by health experts for use in the U.S. because of the low risk of infection and its variable effectiveness. **Annual U.S. cases:** 11,545 in 2009.

Yellow fever

(Yellow fever virus, in *flavivirus* group) Viral infection that has caused large epidemics in South America, the Caribbean, and Africa. **Transmission:** bite from mosquitoes carrying the virus. **Symptoms:** headaches, muscle aches, fever, jaundice (yellowing skin), nausea and vomiting, kidney failure, severe generalized pain; in severe cases, shock, coma, and death. **Vaccine:** available, safe and effective. **Treatment:** symptoms treated until disease runs its course. **Annual U.S. cases:** 0 in the U.S.; an estimated 200,000 new cases, 30,000 deaths worldwide.

Dietary Guidelines for Americans, 2010: Key Recommendations

Source: *Dietary Guidelines for Americans 2010*, U.S. Dept. of Agriculture; U.S. Dept. of Health and Human Services

Balancing Calories to Manage Weight

- Prevent and/or reduce overweight and obesity through improved eating and physical activity behaviors.
- Control total calorie intake to manage body weight.
- Increase physical activity and reduce time spent in sedentary behaviors.
- Maintain appropriate calorie balance during each stage of life.

Foods and Food Components to Reduce

- Reduce daily sodium intake to less than 2,300 mg. Further reduce intake to 1,500 mg among persons who are 51 and older and those of any age who are African American or have hypertension, diabetes, or chronic kidney disease.
- Consume less than 10% of calories from saturated fats by replacing them with monounsaturated and polyunsaturated fats.
- Consume less than 300 mg per day of dietary cholesterol.
- Keep trans fat consumption as low as possible by limiting foods that contain synthetic sources of trans fats, such as partially hydrogenated oils.
- Reduce the intake of calories from solid fats and added sugars.
- Limit the consumption of foods that contain refined grains, especially refined grain foods that contain solid fats, added sugars, and sodium.
- If alcohol is consumed, it should be consumed in moderation—up to 1 drink per day for women and 2 drinks per day for men.

For more information, visit www.dietaryguidelines.gov.

Foods and Nutrients to Increase

- Increase vegetable and fruit intake.
- Eat a variety of vegetables (especially dark-green, red, and orange vegetables), beans, and peas.
- Consume at least half of all grains as whole grains. Replace refined grains with whole grains.
- Increase intake of fat-free or low-fat milk and milk products, such as milk, yogurt, cheese, or fortified soy beverages.
- Choose a variety of protein foods, which include seafood, lean meat/poultry, eggs, beans and peas, soy products, and unsalted nuts and seeds.
- Increase seafood consumed by choosing seafood in place of some meat and poultry.
- Replace protein foods that are higher in solid fats with choices that are lower in solid fats and calories and/or are sources of oils.
- Use oils to replace solid fats where possible.
- Choose foods that provide more potassium, dietary fiber, calcium, and vitamin D, which are nutrients of concern in American diets. These foods include vegetables, fruits, whole grains, and milk and milk products.

Building Healthy Eating Patterns

- Select an eating pattern that meets nutrient needs over time at an appropriate calorie level.
- Account for all foods and beverages consumed and assess how they fit within a total healthy eating pattern.
- Follow food safety recommendations when preparing and eating foods to reduce the risk of foodborne illnesses.

Food Ingredients

Protein

Proteins, composed of amino acids, are essential to good nutrition. They build, maintain, and repair the body. Best sources: eggs, milk, fish, meat, poultry, soybeans, nuts. High-quality proteins such as eggs, meat, or fish supply all eight amino acids needed in a diet. Plant foods—whole grain breads and cereals, rice, oats, soybeans, other beans, split peas, and nuts—can be combined to meet protein needs as well.

Fats

Fats provide energy by furnishing calories to the body. They also contain vitamins A, D, E, and K. They are the most concentrated source of energy in a diet. Best sources of polyunsaturated and monounsaturated fats: margarine, vegetable/plant oils, nuts. Concentrated sources of saturated fats: meats, cheeses, butter, cream, egg yolks, lard.

Carbohydrates

Carbohydrates provide energy to the body by supplying immediate calories. The carbohydrate group includes sugars, starches, fiber, and starchy vegetables. Best sources: grains, legumes, potatoes, vegetables, fruits.

Fiber

The portion of plant foods that our bodies cannot digest is known as fiber. There are two basic types: insoluble ("roughage") and soluble. Insoluble fibers help move food materials through the digestive tract; soluble fibers tend to slow them down. Both types absorb water, thus preventing and treating constipation by softening and increasing the bulk of the undigested food components passing through the digestive tract. Soluble fibers may also be helpful in reducing blood cholesterol levels. Best sources: beans, bran, fruits, whole grains, vegetables.

Water

Water dissolves and transports other nutrients throughout the body, aiding in the processes of digestion, absorption, circulation, and excretion. It helps regulate body temperature.

Vitamins

Vitamin A—promotes good eyesight; helps keep skin and mucous membranes resistant to infection. Best sources: liver, sweet potatoes, carrots, kale, cantaloupe, turnip greens, collard greens, broccoli, fortified milk.

Vitamin B_1 (thiamine)—prevents beriberi. Essential to carbohydrate metabolism and nervous system health. Best sources: pork, enriched cereals, grains, soybeans, nuts.

Vitamin B_2 (riboflavin)—protects the skin, mouth, eyes, eyelids, and mucous membranes. Essential to protein and energy metabolism. Best sources: milk, meat, poultry, cheese, broccoli, spinach.

Vitamin B_6 (pyridoxine)—important in the regulation of the central nervous system and in protein metabolism. Best sources: whole grains, meats, fish, poultry, nuts, brewers' yeast.

Vitamin B_{12} (cobalamin)—needed to form red blood cells. Best sources: meat, fish, poultry, eggs, dairy products.

Niacin—maintains health of skin, the tongue, and the digestive system. Best sources: poultry, peanuts, fish, enriched flour, bread.

Folic acid (folacin)—required for normal blood cell formation, growth, and reproduction and for important chemical reactions in body cells. Best sources: yeast, orange juice, green leafy vegetables, wheat germ, asparagus, broccoli, nuts.

Other B vitamins—biotin, pantothenic acid.

Vitamin C (ascorbic acid)—maintains collagen, a protein necessary for the formation of skin, ligaments, and bones. Helps heal wounds and mend fractures. Aids in resisting some types of viral and bacterial infections. Best sources: citrus fruits and juices, cantaloupe, broccoli, Brussels sprouts, potatoes and sweet potatoes, tomatoes, cabbage.

Vitamin D—important for bone development. Best sources: sunlight, fortified milk and milk products, fish-liver oils, egg yolks.

Vitamin E (tocopherol)—helps protect red blood cells. Best sources: vegetable oils, wheat germ, whole grains, eggs, peanuts, margarine, green leafy vegetables.

Vitamin K—necessary for formation of prothrombin, which helps blood to clot. Also made by intestinal bacteria. Best dietary sources: green leafy vegetables, tomatoes.

Minerals

Calcium—works with phosphorus to build and maintain bones and teeth. Best sources: milk and milk products, cheese, blackstrap molasses, some types of tofu.

Phosphorus—performs more functions than any other mineral and plays a part in nearly every chemical reaction in the body. Best sources: cheese, milk, meats, poultry, fish, tofu.

Iron—necessary for the formation of myoglobin, which is a reservoir of oxygen for muscle tissue, and hemoglobin, which transports oxygen within blood. Best sources: lean meats, beans, green leafy vegetables, shellfish, enriched breads and cereals, whole grains.

Other minerals—chromium, cobalt, copper, fluorine, iodine, magnesium, manganese, molybdenum, potassium, selenium, sodium, sulfur, zinc.

Understanding Food Label Claims

Source: Center for Food Safety and Applied Nutrition, Food and Drug Admin., U.S. Dept. of Health and Human Services

The federal Nutrition Labeling and Education Act of 1990 provides that manufacturers can make certain claims on processed food labels only if they meet the definitions specified here:

Sugar

Sugar free: less than 0.5 g per serving

No added sugars; Without added sugars:
No sugars added during processing, including ingredients that contain sugars (e.g., fruit juices, applesauce, or dried fruit).
Processing does not increase sugar content above the amount naturally in the ingredients. (A functionally insignificant increase in sugars is acceptable from processes used for purposes other than increasing sugar content.)
Food for which it substitutes normally contains added sugars.

Reduced sugar: at least 25% less sugar than reference food

Fat

Fat free: less than 0.5 g of fat per serving

Saturated fat free: less than 0.5 g of saturated fat per serving, and the level of trans fatty acids does not exceed 1% of total fat

Low fat: 3 g or less per serving and, if the serving is 30 g or less or 2 tbs or less, per 50 g of the food

Low saturated fat: 1 g or less per serving and not more than 15% of calories from saturated fatty acids

Reduced fat; Less fat: at least 25% less per serving than reference food

Fiber

High fiber: 5 g or more per serving (must also meet low-fat definition or state level of total fat)

Good source of fiber: 2.5 g to 4.9 g per serving

More fiber; Added fiber: at least 2.5 g more per serving than reference food

Sodium

Sodium free: less than 5 mg per serving

Low sodium: 140 mg or less per serving and, if the serving is 30 g or less or 2 tbs or less, per 50 g of the food

Very low sodium: 35 mg or less per serving and, if the serving is 30 g or less or 2 tbs or less, per 50 g of the food

Reduced sodium; Less sodium: at least 25% less per serving than reference food

Calories

Calorie free: under 5 calories per serving

Low calorie: 40 calories or less per serving; if the serving is 30 g or less or 2 tbs or less, 40 calories or less per 50 g of food

Reduced calories; Fewer calories: at least 25% fewer calories than reference food

Cholesterol

Cholesterol free: less than 2 mg of cholesterol and 2 g or less of saturated fat per serving

Low cholesterol: 20 mg or less and 2 g or less of saturated fat per serving and, if the serving is 30 g or less or 2 tbs or less, per 50 g of the food

Reduced cholesterol; Less cholesterol: at least 25% less than reference food

Other Food Label Claims

Source: Food Safety and Inspection Service, Agricultural Marketing Service, U.S. Dept. of Agriculture

The FDA allows food producers and marketers to use language on their packaging that advertises the health benefits and production methods of their products. Products marked *certified* have been formally evaluated for class, grade, or other quality characteristics by the U.S. Dept. of Agriculture's (USDA) Food Safety and Inspection Service. Below are some common packaging terms and their meanings.

Organic: Produced by farmers who use environmentally friendly methods to raise their crops or animals. Before a product can be labeled organic, the farm where the food is grown must pass a special inspection by a USDA official. Organic foods must be produced without conventional pesticides; fertilizers made with synthetic ingredients or sewage sludge; bioengineering; or ionizing radiation.

The official *USDA organic* label may appear on vegetables, fruit, packages of meat, cartons of milk, eggs, cheese, and other single-ingredient foods. Foods with more than one ingredient can place the official seal on their packaging if at least 95% of the ingredients are organic. Products with at least 70% organic ingredients may advertise prominently on the front of the package that the item contains organic ingredients. Products with less than 70% organic ingredients may not make any organic claims on the front of the package but may list organic ingredients on the side panel. Foods that contain 100% organic ingredients may advertise that fact on the front of the packaging along with the organic seal.

Natural: A minimally processed product that does not contain any artificial ingredient or added color. The label must explain the specific use of the term *natural* with regard to the product, such as "no added colorings," "no artificial ingredients," or "minimally processed."

Free range or **free roaming:** Producers must demonstrate to the Agency that the poultry has been allowed access to the outside.

Halal and **Zabiah Halal:** Produced in federally inspected meat packing plants and handled in accordance with Islamic law and under Islamic authority.

Kosher: Meat and poultry products prepared under Rabbinical supervision.

Minimal processing: Produced using traditional physical processes that do not fundamentally alter the raw products in order to make food edible, to preserve it, or to make it safe for human consumption. Includes smoking, roasting, freezing, drying, and fermenting. Applies mostly to meat and poultry.

No hormones administered: Hormones are not allowed in raising hogs or poultry, so those products may not make this claim. If sufficient documentation is provided to the USDA proving that hormones were not used, this term may appear on packages of beef.

No antibiotics added: Claim may be made on a package (red meat and poultry) if sufficient documentation is provided to the USDA showing that the animals were raised without antibiotics.

Recommended Levels for Elements (Minerals)

Source: Food and Nutrition Board, Institute of Medicine; National Academy of Sciences, 2010

(in milligrams per day (mg/d) or micrograms per day (μg/d); asterisk denotes level defined as "adequate intake" (AI))

Life stage group		Calcium (mg/d)	Chromium (μg/d)	Copper (μg/d)	Fluoride (mg/d)	Iodine (μg/d)	Iron (mg/d)	Magnesium (mg/d)	Manganese (mg/d)	Molybdenum (μg/d)	Phosphorus (mg/d)	Selenium (μg/d)	Zinc (mg/d)
Infants	0-6 mos.	200*	0.2*	200*	0.01*	110*	0.27*	30*	0.003*	2*	100*	15*	2*
	6-12 mos.	260*	5.5*	220*	0.5*	130*	11	75*	0.6*	3*	275*	20*	3
Children	1-3 yrs.	700	11*	340	0.7*	90	7	80	1.2*	17	460	20	3
	4-8 yrs.	1,000	15*	440	1*	90	10	130	1.5*	22	500	30	5
Males	9-13 yrs.	1,300	25*	700	2*	120	8	240	1.9*	34	1,250	40	8
	14-18 yrs.	1,300	35*	890	3*	150	11	410	2.2*	43	1,250	55	11
	19-30 yrs.	1,000	35*	900	4*	150	8	400	2.3*	45	700	55	11
	31-50 yrs.	1,000	35*	900	4*	150	8	420	2.3*	45	700	55	11
	51-70 yrs.	1,000*	30*	900	4*	150	8	420	2.3*	45	700	55	11
	over 70 yrs.	1,200	30*	900	4*	150	8	420	2.3*	45	700	55	11
Females	9-13 yrs.	1,300	21*	700	2*	120	8	240	1.6*	34	1,250	40	8
	14-18 yrs.	1,300	24*	890	3*	150	15	360	1.6*	43	1,250	55	9
	19-30 yrs.	1,000	25*	900	3*	150	18	310	1.8*	45	700	55	8
	31-50 yrs.	1,000	25*	900	3*	150	18	320	1.8*	45	700	55	8
	51-70 yrs.	1,200	20*	900	3*	150	8	320	1.8*	45	700	55	8
	over 70 yrs.	1,200	20*	900	3*	150	8	320	1.8*	45	700	55	8
Pregnancy	14-18 yrs.	1,300	29*	1,000	3*	220	27	400	2.0*	50	1,250	60	12
	19-30 yrs.	1,000	30*	1,000	3*	220	27	350	2.0*	50	700	60	11
	31-50 yrs.	1,000	30*	1,000	3*	220	27	360	2.0*	50	700	60	11
Lactation	14-18 yrs.	1,300	44*	1,300	3*	290	10	360	2.6*	50	1,250	70	13
	19-30 yrs.	1,000	45*	1,300	3*	290	9	310	2.6*	50	700	70	12
	31-50 yrs.	1,000	45*	1,300	3*	290	9	320	2.6*	50	700	70	12

Recommended Levels for Vitamins

Source: Food and Nutrition Board, Institute of Medicine, National Academy of Sciences, 2010

(in milligrams per day (mg/d) or micrograms per day (μg/d); asterisk denotes level defined as "adequate intake" (AI))

Life stage group		Vitamin A (μg/d)[1]	Vitamin C (mg/d)	Vitamin D (μg/d)[2]	Vitamin E (mg/d)	Vitamin K (μg/d)	Thiamin (mg/d)	Riboflavin (mg/d)	Niacin (mg/d)[3]	Vitamin B6 (mg/d)	Folate (μg/d)[4]	Vitamin B12 (μg/d)	Pantothenic acid (mg/d)	Biotin (μg/d)	Choline (mg/d)[5]
Infants	0-6 mos.	400*	40*	10	4*	2.0*	0.2*	0.3*	2*	0.1*	65*	0.4*	1.7*	5*	125*
	6-12 mos.	500*	50*	10	5*	2.5*	0.3*	0.4*	4*	0.3*	80*	0.5*	1.8*	6*	150*
Children	1-3 yrs.	300	15	15	6	30*	0.5	0.5	6	0.5	150	0.9	2*	8*	200*
	4-8 yrs.	400	25	15	7	55*	0.6	0.6	8	0.6	200	1.2	3*	12*	250*
Males	9-13 yrs.	600	45	15	11	60*	0.9	0.9	12	1.0	300	1.8	4*	20*	375*
	14-18 yrs.	900	75	15	15	75*	1.2	1.3	16	1.3	400	2.4	5*	25*	550*
	19-30 yrs.	900	90	15	15	120*	1.2	1.3	16	1.3	400	2.4	5*	30*	550*
	31-50 yrs.	900	90	15	15	120*	1.2	1.3	16	1.3	400	2.4	5*	30*	550*
	51-70 yrs.	900	90	15	15	120*	1.2	1.3	16	1.7	400	2.4[6]	5*	30*	550*
	over 70 yrs.	900	90	20	15	120*	1.2	1.3	16	1.7	400	2.4[6]	5*	30*	550*
Females	9-13 yrs.	600	45	15	11	60*	0.9	0.9	12	1.0	300	1.8	4*	20*	375*
	14-18 yrs.	700	65	15	15	75*	1.0	1.0	14	1.2	400[7]	2.4	5*	25*	400*
	19-30 yrs.	700	75	15	15	90*	1.1	1.1	14	1.3	400[7]	2.4	5*	30*	425*
	31-50 yrs.	700	75	15	15	90*	1.1	1.1	14	1.3	400[7]	2.4	5*	30*	425*
	51-70 yrs.	700	75	15	15	90*	1.1	1.1	14	1.5	400	2.4[6]	5*	30*	425*
	over 70 yrs.	700	75	20	15	90*	1.1	1.1	14	1.5	400	2.4[6]	5*	30*	425*
Pregnancy	14-18 yrs.	750	80	15	15	75*	1.4	1.4	18	1.9	600[8]	2.6	6*	30*	450*
	19-30 yrs.	770	85	15	15	90*	1.4	1.4	18	1.9	600[8]	2.6	6*	30*	450*
	31-50 yrs.	770	85	15	15	90*	1.4	1.4	18	1.9	600[8]	2.6	6*	30*	450*
Lactation	14-18 yrs.	1,200	115	15	19	75*	1.4	1.6	17	2.0	500	2.8	7*	35*	550*
	19-30 yrs.	1,300	120	15	19	90*	1.4	1.6	17	2.0	500	2.8	7*	35*	550*
	31-50 yrs.	1,300	120	15	19	90*	1.4	1.6	17	2.0	500	2.8	7*	35*	550*

Note: For healthy breastfed infants, the AI is the mean intake. The AI for other life stage and gender groups is believed to cover needs of all individuals in the group, but lack of data or uncertainty in the data prevent being able to specify with confidence the percentage of individuals covered by this intake. (1) As retinol activity equivalents (RAEs). (2) In the absence of adequate exposure to sunlight. (3) As niacin equivalents (NEs). (4) As dietary folate equivalents (DFEs). (5) Although AIs have been set for choline, there are few data to assess whether a dietary supply of choline is needed at all stages of the life cycle. (6) Because 10%-30% of older people may malabsorb food-bound B12, it is advisable for those older than 50 years to meet their RDA mainly by consuming foods fortified with B12 or a supplement containing B12. (7) In view of evidence linking folate intake with neural tube defects in the fetus, it is recommended that all women capable of becoming pregnant consume 400 μg from supplements or fortified foods in addition to intake of food folate from a varied diet. (8) It is assumed that women will continue consuming 400 μg from supplements or fortified food until their pregnancy is confirmed and they enter prenatal care, which ordinarily occurs after the end of the periconceptional period—the critical time for formation of the neural tube.

Dietary Requirements

The Food and Nutrition Board of the National Academy of Sciences' Institute of Medicine, in reports published between 1997 and 2005, established **Dietary Reference Intakes (DRIs)**. DRIs establish daily consumption values for vitamins and elements (often called minerals) that aim to optimize health, not just guard against nutritional deficiencies, at all stages of life.

There are four DRI categories. The **Recommended Dietary Allowance (RDA)** gives intake values that meet the nutrient requirements of almost all (97%-98%) healthy individuals in a specified group. The **Estimated Average Requirement (EAR)** specifies the intake amounts meeting the estimated nutrient need of half the individuals in a specified group. **Adequate Intake (AI)** values are given when there's inadequate scientific evidence to calculate an EAR. For healthy breastfed infants, the AI is the mean intake; for other life stage groups, the AI is thought to cover the needs of all group individuals, but lack of data or uncertainty in the data prevents the percentage of individuals covered from being specified with confidence. The **Tolerable Upper Intake Level (UL)** designates the maximum intake amount that is unlikely to pose a risk of adverse health effects in almost all healthy individuals in a group. RDAs and AIs may both be used as individual intake goals.

Weight Guidelines for Adults

Source: *Dietary Guidelines for Americans, 2010,* U.S. Dept. of Agriculture; National Center for Health Statistics, CDC

Guidelines on identification, evaluation, and treatment of overweight and obesity in adults were released in June 1998 by the National Heart, Lung, and Blood Institute (NHLBI), in cooperation with the National Institute of Diabetes and Digestive and Kidney Diseases (NIDDK). The guidelines, based on research into risk factors contributing to heart disease, stroke, and other conditions, define overweight and obesity in terms of **body mass index (BMI)**. BMI is based on a person's weight and height and is strongly correlated with total body fat content. A BMI of 25-29 is said to indicate **overweight**; a BMI of 30 or higher indicates **obesity**. Weight reduction is advised for persons with a BMI of 25 or higher. Factors such as a large waist circumference, high blood pressure or cholesterol, and family medical history may increase a person's risk of developing an obesity-related disease.

The National Center for Health Statistics notes that more than ⅓ of American adults are obese. Over the past three decades, childhood obesity rates in America have tripled, and today nearly one in three children are overweight or obese. Based on directly measured weight and height, between 1988-94 and 2005-08, the proportion of adults ages 20 years and over who were obese rose by 47.8%, from 23% to 34%. During the same period, obesity increased by 54.5% in children ages 6-11, from 11% to 17%, and by 63.6% in adolescents ages 12-19, from 11% to 18%.

A high prevalence of overweight and obesity is a public health concern because excess body fat has been associated with type 2 diabetes, hypertension, dyslipidemia, cardiovascular disease, stroke, gall bladder disease, respiratory dysfunction, gout, osteoarthritis, and certain kinds of cancers.

The table below shows the BMI for certain heights and weights. For weight reduction help, contact the Weight-control Information Network, 1 WIN Way, Bethesda, MD 20892-3665; (877) 946-4627; win.niddk.nih.gov.

Body Mass Index (BMI) by Height and Weight
Weight (lbs)

Height	HEALTHY						OVERWEIGHT					OBESE									
4'10"	91	96	100	105	110	115	119	124	129	134	138	143	148	153	158	162	167	172	177	181	186
4'11"	94	99	104	109	114	119	124	128	133	138	143	148	153	158	163	168	173	178	183	188	193
5'0"	97	102	107	112	118	123	128	133	138	143	148	153	158	163	168	174	179	184	189	194	199
5'1"	100	106	111	116	122	127	132	137	143	148	153	158	164	169	174	180	185	190	195	201	206
5'2"	104	109	115	120	126	131	136	142	147	153	158	164	169	175	180	186	191	196	202	207	213
5'3"	107	113	118	124	130	135	141	146	152	158	163	169	175	180	186	191	197	203	208	214	220
5'4"	110	116	122	128	134	140	145	151	157	163	169	174	180	186	192	197	204	209	215	221	227
5'5"	114	120	126	132	138	144	150	156	162	168	174	180	186	192	198	204	210	216	222	228	234
5'6"	118	124	130	136	142	148	155	161	167	173	179	186	192	198	204	210	216	223	229	235	241
5'7"	121	127	134	140	146	153	159	166	172	178	185	191	198	204	211	217	223	230	236	242	249
5'8"	125	131	138	144	151	158	164	171	177	184	190	197	203	210	216	223	230	236	243	249	256
5'9"	128	135	142	149	155	162	169	176	182	189	196	203	209	216	223	230	236	243	250	257	263
5'10"	132	139	146	153	160	167	174	181	188	195	202	209	216	222	229	236	243	250	257	264	271
5'11"	136	143	150	157	165	172	179	186	193	200	208	215	222	229	236	243	250	257	265	272	279
6'0"	140	147	154	162	169	177	184	191	199	206	213	221	228	235	242	250	258	265	272	279	287
6'1"	144	151	159	166	174	182	189	197	204	212	219	227	235	242	250	257	265	272	280	288	295
6'2"	148	155	163	171	179	186	194	202	210	218	225	233	241	249	256	264	272	280	287	295	303
6'3"	152	160	168	176	184	192	200	208	216	224	232	240	248	256	264	272	279	287	295	303	311
6'4"	156	164	172	180	189	197	205	213	221	230	238	246	254	263	271	279	287	295	304	312	320
BMI[1]	19	20	21	22	23	24	25	26	27	28	29	30	31	32	33	34	35	36	37	38	39

(1) The BMI numbers apply to both men and women. Some very muscular people may have a high BMI without health risks.

Estimated Calorie Requirements

Source: *Dietary Guidelines for Americans, 2010*, U.S. Dept. of Agriculture, U.S. Dept. of Health and Human Services

Estimated amounts of calories, rounded to the nearest 200, needed to maintain energy balance by sex, for various age groups and levels of physical activity.

	Age (years)	Sedentary[1]	Moderately[2] active	Active[3]		Age (years)	Sedentary[1]	Moderately[2] active	Active[3]
Child	2-3	1,000-1,200	1,000-1,400	1,000-1,400					
Female[4]	4-8	1,200-1,400	1,400-1,600	1,400-1,800	Male	4-8	1,200-1,400	1,400-1,600	1,600-2,000
	9-13	1,400-1,600	1,600-2,000	1,800-2,200		9-13	1,600-2,000	1,800-2,200	2,000-2,600
	14-18	1,800	2,000	2,400		14-18	2,000-2,400	2,400-2,800	2,800-3,200
	19-30	1,800-2,000	2,000-2,200	2,400		19-30	2,400-2,600	2,600-2,800	3,000
	31-50	1,800	2,000	2,200		31-50	2,200-2,400	2,400-2,600	2,800-3,000
	51+	1,600	1,800	2,000-2,200		51+	2,000-2,200	2,200-2,400	2,400-2,800

Note: Based on Estimated Energy Requirements (EER) equations, using reference heights (average) and reference weights (healthy) for each age/gender group. For children and adolescents, reference height and weight vary. For adults, the reference man is 5 feet 10 inches tall and weighs 154 pounds. The reference woman is 5 feet 4 inches tall and weighs 126 pounds. (1) Engaging only in the light activities associated with ordinary day-to-day life. (2) Includes physical activity equivalent to walking 1.5 to 3 miles per day at 3-4 mph. (3) Includes physical activity equivalent to walking more than 3 miles per day at 3-4 mph. (4) Excludes women who are pregnant or breastfeeding.

Calories Used During Physical Activity

Source: Center for Nutrition Policy and Promotion, U.S. Dept. of Agriculture

Amounts of calories burned during physical activities are estimates for a 154-pound man. The more an individual weighs, the more calories he or she will burn up with the same degree of exercise.

Moderate physical activities	In 1 hr.	In 30 mins.	Vigorous physical activities	In 1 hr.	In 30 mins.
Hiking	370	185	Running/jogging (5 miles per hour)	590	295
Light gardening/yard work	330	165	Bicycling (more than 10 miles per hour)	590	295
Dancing	330	165	Swimming (slow freestyle laps)	510	255
Golf (walking and carrying clubs)	330	165	Aerobics	480	240
Bicycling (less than 10 miles per hour)	290	145	Walking (4½ miles per hour)	460	230
Walking (3½ miles per hour)	280	140	Heavy yard work (e.g., chopping wood)	440	220
Weight training (general light workout)	220	110	Weight lifting (vigorous effort)	440	220
Stretching	180	90	Basketball (vigorous)	440	220

Finding Your Target Heart Rate

Source: Carole Casten, EdD, *Aerobics Today*; Peg Jordan, RN, Aerobics and Fitness Assn. of America

The target heart rate is the rate of heartbeats a person should aim for during aerobic exercise (e.g., running, cycling, or cross-country skiing) to get the full benefit for cardiovascular conditioning.

First, determine the intensity level at which one would like to exercise. Someone who's led a sedentary lifestyle may want to begin an exercise regimen at the 60% level and work up to the 70% level. Athletes and highly fit individuals must work at an 85% or higher level to receive benefits. Second, calculate the target heart rate. One common way is by using the American College of Sports Medicine Method.

An individual should subtract his or her age from 220, then multiply that number by the desired intensity level of the workout. Divide the answer by 6 for a 10-second pulse count. (The 10-second pulse count is useful for checking whether the target heart rate is being achieved during the workout. One can easily check one's pulse—on the inside of the wrist or side of the neck—by counting the number of beats in 10 seconds.)

For example, a 20-year-old wishing to exercise at 70% intensity would do the following calculations to figure out his or her target heart rate:

Maximum heart rate	$220 - 20 = 200$
Target heart rate	$200 \times 0.70 = 140$
10-second pulse count	$140/6 = 23.33$

To work out at 70% intensity, this 20-year-old would strive for a target heart rate of 140 beats per minute, or a 10-second pulse count of 23.

To obtain cardiovascular fitness benefits from aerobic exercise, an individual should participate in an aerobic activity at least three to five times a week for 20-30 minutes each session. Cardiac patients and very sedentary individuals can obtain benefits with shorter periods (15-20 minutes per session). Generally, training changes occur within four to six weeks, but they can occur in as little as two weeks.

Overweight, Obesity, and Healthy Weight in the U.S., 1960-2008

Source: National Health and Nutrition Examination Survey (NHANES), National Center for Health Statistics, CDC

Weight status by sex	1960-62	1971-74	1976-80	1988-94	1999-2002	2001-04	2005-08
				Percent of population			
Overweight or obese[1]							
Both sexes[2]	44.8%	47.7%	47.4%	55.6%	65.2%	65.9%	67.4%
Male	49.5	54.7	52.9	60.1	68.8	70.3	72.5
Female[2]	40.2	41.1	42.0	51.3	61.7	61.6	62.5
Obese[3]							
Both sexes[2]	13.3	14.6	15.1	22.7	31.1	31.2	33.9
Male.	10.7	12.2	12.8	19.7	28.1	29.2	32.4
Female[2]	15.7	16.8	17.1	25.4	34.0	33.1	35.3
Healthy weight[4]							
Both sexes[2]	51.2	48.8	49.6	41.9	32.9	32.4	30.9
Male	48.3	43.0	45.4	38.7	30.2	28.6	26.5
Female[2]	54.1	54.3	53.7	45.1	35.6	36.2	35.2

Note: Data based on measured height and weight of a sample of the civilian noninstitutionalized population ages 20-74, age-adjusted to the standard population group. Percents do not add up to 100 because persons with BMIs of less than 18.5 are not included in these figures. Height was measured without shoes; two pounds were deducted from 1960-62 data to allow for weight of clothing. (1) With a body mass index (BMI) greater than or equal to 25.0. (2) Excluding pregnant women. (3) With a body mass index (BMI) greater than or equal to 30.0 (4) With a BMI greater than or equal to 18.5 and less than 25.0. See table on p. 162 to calculate BMI.

Basic First Aid

Note: This information is not intended to be a substitute for formal training. It is recommended that you contact your local American Red Cross chapter to sign up for a First Aid/CPR/AED course.

In an emergency, it is important to get medical assistance as soon as possible, but knowing what to do until a doctor or other trained person gets to the scene can save a life, especially in cases of severe bleeding, choking, poisoning, and shock.

People with special medical problems, such as diabetes, cardiovascular disease, epilepsy, or allergies, are urged to wear some sort of emblem identifying the problem as a safeguard against receiving medication that might be harmful or even fatal. Emblems may be obtained from Medic Alert Foundation, 2323 Colorado Ave., Turlock, CA 95382; (888) 633-4298; www.medicalert.org.

Animal bite: Call 9-1-1 or the local emergency number if the wound is bleeding seriously or if you suspect the animal might have rabies. Control any bleeding. Wash minor wounds with soap under running water and apply triple antibiotic ointment and a dressing. When possible, proper authorities should test the animal for rabies.

Asphyxiation: Call 9-1-1 or the local emergency number. Give care for any life-threatening conditions.

Bleeding: Use a barrier between your hand and the wound to help prevent infection. Cover wound with a sterile compress. Apply direct pressure until bleeding stops. Cover compress with a bandage. Call 9-1-1 or the local emergency number if bleeding is severe.

Burn: Check for life-threatening conditions. If the burn is mild, with skin unbroken and no blisters, flush with cold running water until pain subsides. Apply a loose, sterile dry dressing to prevent infection. If the burn is severe, call 9-1-1 or the local emergency number. Care for shock (see below). Keep the person from getting chilled or overheated until advanced medical assistance arrives. Do not try to clean a severe burn or break blisters.

Chemical in eye: Call 9-1-1 or the local emergency number. Turn the person's head to the side so that the affected eye is lower than the unaffected eye. Continuously flush the injured eye with water.

Choking: See **First Aid for Choking** below.

Convulsions (seizures): Remove nearby objects that might cause injury. Protect the person's head by placing a thin folded towel or item of clothing under it. If there is fluid in the person's mouth, roll him or her on one side so that the fluid may drain from the mouth. Do not place anything between the person's teeth. Stay with the person until he or she is fully conscious. If convulsions do not stop, get medical attention immediately.

Cut (minor): Use a clean barrier between your hand and the wound to prevent infection. Apply direct pressure for a few minutes to control any bleeding. Wash the wound thoroughly with soap and water and apply triple antibiotic ointment or cream. Cover the wound with a sterile compress and a bandage or use an adhesive bandage.

Fainting: If the person feels faint, lower him or her to the ground. Lay the person down on his or her back. If possible, elevate the person's legs 8 to 12 inches. Care for any life-threatening conditions. Loosen any restrictive clothing and check for any signs of injury. Call 9-1-1 or the local emergency number.

Foreign object in eye: If an object is embedded in someone's eye, do not remove it. If not embedded, try to remove the object by having the person blink several times. If the object doesn't come out, gently flush the eye with water. Do not rub the eye. If the object still doesn't come out, the person should receive professional medical attention.

Frostbite: Handle the frostbitten area gently. Do not rub. If there is no danger of the affected area refreezing, soak it in warm water (not warmer than 105°F). Do not allow the frostbitten area to touch the side of the water container. Keep the frostbitten part in the water until normal color returns and it feels warm. Loosely bandage the area with dry, sterile dressings. If fingers or toes are frostbitten, put sterile gauze between them. Call 9-1-1 or seek emergency help as soon as possible.

Heart attack and stroke: See p. 155.

Heat stroke and heat exhaustion: Remove the person from the heat. Loosen any tight clothing. Fan the person and apply cool, wet cloths to the skin. If the person is conscious, have him or her slowly drink some cool water. Call 9-1-1 if the person's condition does not improve or if you suspect heat stroke.

Hypothermia: Call 9-1-1 or the local emergency number. Move person to a warm place. Remove wet clothing and dry the person, if necessary. Warm the person gradually by wrapping him or her in warm blankets or clothing. Apply heat pads or other heat sources if available but do not apply directly to the body. If the person is alert, give him or her warm, non-alcoholic and decaffeinated liquids to drink.

Loss of limb: Call 9-1-1 or the local emergency number and care for any life-threatening conditions. If a limb is severed, it is important to properly protect the limb so that it can possibly be reattached. After the victim is cared for, the limb should be wrapped in sterile gauze or clean material and placed in a clean plastic bag or other suitable container. Pack ice around the limb on the outside of the bag or container to keep the limb cold. Be sure the limb is taken to the hospital with the person.

Poisoning: Care for any life-threatening conditions. Call the National Poison Control Center (800-222-1222), 9-1-1, or the local emergency number and follow their directions. Do not give the person any food or drink or induce vomiting unless specified to do so by medical professionals.

Shock (injury-related): Monitor breathing and consciousness. Have the person lie down and keep him or her as comfortable as possible. Elevate his or her legs 8 to 12 inches unless you suspect a head, neck, or back injury or broken hip or leg bones. Do not attempt to move the person if spinal injury is suspected. Maintain normal body temperature. If the weather is cold or damp, place blankets or extra clothing over and under the person; if the weather is hot, provide shade.

Snakebite: Call 9-1-1 or the local emergency number. Wash the injury. Keep the area still and at a lower level than the heart. Keep the person calm. If professional medical help cannot get to the person within 30 minutes, consider using a snakebite kit if available. Care for a bite from an elapid snake, such as a coral snake, is the same except you should apply an elastic bandage after washing the wound.

Sprains and fractures: Apply ice to reduce swelling and pain. Do not try to straighten or move broken limbs. Apply a splint to immobilize the injured area only if you have to move or transport the person to seek medical attention, and it does not cause more pain. If you suspect a serious injury, call 9-1-1 or the local emergency number.

Sting from insect: If possible, remove the stinger by scraping it away with your finger or a plastic card (like a credit card) or using tweezers. If you use tweezers, grasp the stinger, not the venom sac. Wash the area with soap and water. Cover it to keep it clean. Apply a cold pack to reduce pain and swelling. Call 9-1-1 or the local emergency number immediately if the wound does not stop swelling, the person collapses, or he or she is known to be allergic to the sting.

Unconsciousness: Call 9-1-1 or the local emergency number immediately. Care for any life-threatening conditions. If the person shows signs of life (movement and breathing), place him or her in the recovery position (i.e., lying on a side with head supported, so that the airway is open). Do not move the person if a spinal injury is suspected.

First Aid for Choking

The recommended first aid for a conscious choking victim who is unable to speak, cough, or breathe, is to deliver a series of five blows to the back and five thrusts to the abdomen. Have another person call 9-1-1 or the local emergency number. Obtain consent from the victim to treat him or her. Lean the victim forward and apply five blows to his or her back with the heel of your hand. Then stand or kneel behind the victim and wrap your arms around his or her waist. Make a fist with one hand and place the thumb side against the middle of the person's abdomen, just above the navel and well below the lower tip of the breastbone. Grasp your fist in your other hand and quickly thrust upwards into the abdomen five times. Continue back blows and abdominal thrusts until the object is dislodged, and the person can breathe or cough forcefully, or the person loses consciousness.

VITAL STATISTICS

Recent Trends in Vital Statistics

Source: National Center for Health Statistics (NCHS), U.S. Dept. of Health and Human Services

Births

An estimated 4,007,000 babies were born in the U.S. in 2010, a decrease from 4,136,000 in 2009. The birth rate decreased to 12.9 per 1,000 total population, a new record low.

The fertility rate (number of live births per 1,000 women aged 15-44 years) decreased to an estimated 64.7 for 2010, down from the 2009 rate of 66.8.

Deaths

The number of deaths during 2010 was estimated at 2,452,000 according to provisional data, up from 2,426,000 in 2009. The death rate of 7.9 deaths per 1,000 population in 2010 remained the same as in 2009. The death rate for infants under 1 year of age was 6.1 deaths per 1,000 live births in 2010, down from 6.3 in 2009.

Natural Increase

As a result of natural increase (the excess of births over deaths), an estimated 1,555,000 persons were added to the population in 2010.

Marriages

An estimated 2,080,000 marriages were performed in 2009, compared to 2,157,000 in 2008. The provisional marriage rate for 2009 (6.8 per 1,000 population) was down from the 2008 rate of 7.1.

Divorces

The 2009 divorce rate of 3.5 per 1,000 population was the same as in 2008, according to provisional data. Data are incomplete however. The NCHS does not include divorce data for California, Georgia, Hawaii, Indiana, Louisiana, and Minnesota.

Births and Deaths in the U.S., 1960-2010

Source: National Center for Health Statistics (NCHS), U.S. Dept. of Health and Human Services

Year	BIRTHS Total number	Rate	DEATHS Total number	Rate	Year	BIRTHS Total number	Rate	DEATHS Total number	Rate
1960	4,257,850	23.7	1,711,982	9.5	2000	4,058,814	14.4	2,403,351	8.5
1970	3,731,386	18.4	1,921,031	9.5	2001	4,025,933	14.1	2,416,425	8.5
1980	3,612,258	15.9	1,989,841	8.8	2002	4,021,726	13.9	2,443,387	8.5
1990	4,092,994	16.7	2,148,463	8.6	2003	4,089,950	14.1	2,448,288	8.4
1992	4,049,024	15.8	2,175,613	8.5	2004	4,112,052	14.0	2,397,615	8.2
1993	4,000,240	15.4	2,268,553	8.7	2005	4,138,349	14.0	2,448,017	8.3
1994	3,952,767	15.0	2,278,994	8.7	2006	4,265,555	14.2	2,426,264	8.1
1995	3,899,589	14.6	2,312,132	8.7	2007	4,316,233	14.3	2,423,712	8.0
1996	3,891,494	14.4	2,314,690	8.6	2008	4,247,694	14.0	2,473,018[1]	8.1[1]
1997	3,880,894	14.2	2,314,245	8.5	2009[1]	4,131,019	13.5	2,436,682	7.9
1998	3,941,553	14.3	2,337,256	8.5	2010[2]	4,007,000	12.9	2,452,000	7.9
1999	3,959,417	14.2	2,391,399	8.6					

Note: Statistics cover only events occurring within the U.S. and exclude fetal deaths. Rates per 1,000 population; enumerated as of Apr. 1 for decennial census years; estimated as of July 1 for all other years. Beginning 1970, statistics exclude births and deaths occurring among nonresidents of the U.S. (1) Preliminary. (2) Provisional.

Marriage and Divorce Rates in the U.S., 1920-2009

Source: National Center for Health Statistics (NCHS), U.S. Dept. of Health and Human Services

(Divorce rates for 2006-09 were calculated excluding data and populations from the nonreporting states California, Georgia, Hawaii, Indiana, Louisiana, and Minnesota. Some data are provisional.)

The U.S. marriage rate dipped during the Depression and peaked sharply just after World War II; the trend after that has been more gradual. The divorce rate generally rose from the 1920s through 1981, when it peaked at 5.3 per 1,000 population, before declining somewhat. The graph below shows marriage and divorce rates since 1920.

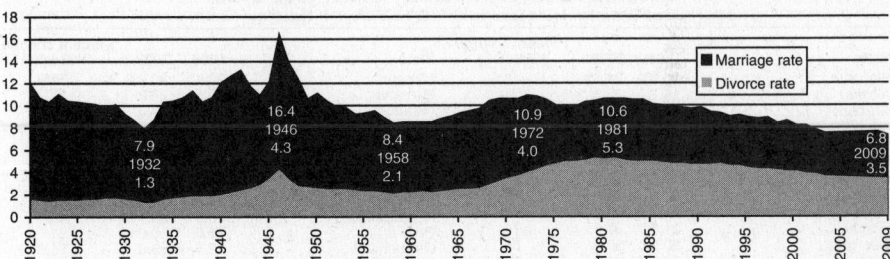

U.S. Median Age at First Marriage, 1890-2010

Source: U.S. Census Bureau, U.S. Dept. of Commerce

Year[1]	Men	Women	Year[1]	Men	Women	Year[1]	Men	Women	Year[1]	Men	Women	Year[1]	Men	Women
1890	26.1	22.0	1960	22.8	20.3	1991	26.3	24.1	1998	26.7	25.0	2005	27.1	25.3
1900	25.9	21.9	1965	22.8	20.6	1992	26.5	24.4	1999	26.9	25.1	2006	27.5	25.5
1910	25.1	21.6	1970	23.2	20.8	1993	26.5	24.5	2000	26.8	25.1	2007	27.5	25.6
1920	24.6	21.2	1975	23.5	21.1	1994	26.7	24.5	2001	26.9	25.1	2008	27.6	25.9
1930	24.3	21.3	1980	24.7	22.0	1995	26.9	24.5	2002	26.9	25.3	2009	28.1	25.9
1940	24.3	21.5	1985	25.5	23.3	1996	27.1	24.8	2003	27.1	25.3	2010	28.2	26.1
1950	22.8	20.3	1990	26.1	23.9	1997	26.8	25.0	2004	27.4	25.3			

(1) Figures after 1947 based on Current Population Survey data; earlier figures based on decennial censuses.

Divorce Rates by State, 2009

Source: National Center for Health Statistics (NCHS), U.S. Dept. of Health and Human Services

State	Divorce rate	State	Divorce rate	State	Divorce rate
Alabama	4.4	Louisiana	NA	Ohio	3.3
Alaska	4.4	Maine	4.1	Oklahoma	4.9
Arizona	3.5	Maryland	2.8	Oregon	3.9
Arkansas	5.7	Massachusetts	2.2	Pennsylvania	2.7
California	NA	Michigan	3.3	Rhode Island	3.0
Colorado	4.2	Minnesota	NA	South Carolina	3.0
Connecticut	3.1	Mississippi	4.1	South Dakota	3.3
Delaware	3.6	Missouri	3.7	Tennessee	3.9
District of Columbia	2.6	Montana	4.1	Texas	3.3
Florida	4.2	Nebraska	3.4	Utah	3.6
Georgia	NA	Nevada	6.7	Vermont	3.5
Hawaii	NA	New Hampshire	3.7	Virginia	3.7
Idaho	5.0	New Jersey	2.8	Washington	3.9
Illinois	2.5	New Mexico	4.0	West Virginia	5.2
Indiana	NA	New York	2.6	Wisconsin	3.0
Iowa	2.4	North Carolina	3.8	Wyoming	5.2
Kansas	3.7	North Dakota	2.9	**United States**	**3.5**
Kentucky	4.6				

NA = Not available. **Note:** Rate per 1,000 population. Rate includes annulments and may also include divorce petitions filed and legal separations for some counties and states.

Birth Rates and Fertility Rates by Age of Mother, 1950-2009

Source: National Center for Health Statistics (NCHS), U.S. Dept. of Health and Human Services

Live births per 1,000 women by age of mother

Year	Birth rate[1]	Fertility rate[2]	10-14 years	15-19 years Total	15-17	18-19	20-24 years	25-29 years	30-34 years	35-39 years	40-44 years	45-49 years
1950	24.1	106.2	1.0	81.6	40.7	132.7	196.6	166.1	103.7	52.9	15.1	
1960	23.7	118.0	0.8	89.1	43.9	166.7	258.1	197.4	112.7	56.2	15.5	1.2
1970	18.4	87.9	1.2	68.3	38.8	114.7	167.8	145.1	73.3	31.7	8.1	0.9
1980	15.9	68.4	1.1	53.0	32.5	82.1	115.1	112.9	61.9	19.8	3.9	0.5
1990	16.7	70.9	1.4	59.9	37.5	88.6	116.5	120.2	80.8	31.7	5.5	0.2
1992	15.8	68.4	1.4	60.3	37.6	93.6	113.7	115.7	79.6	32.3	5.9	0.3
1993	15.4	67.0	1.4	59.0	37.5	91.1	111.3	113.2	79.9	32.7	6.1	0.3
1994	15.0	65.9	1.4	58.2	37.2	90.2	109.2	111.0	80.4	33.4	6.4	0.3
1995	14.6	64.6	1.3	56.0	35.5	87.7	107.5	108.8	81.1	34.0	6.6	0.3
1996	14.4	64.1	1.2	53.5	33.3	84.7	107.8	108.6	82.1	34.9	6.8	0.3
1997	14.2	63.6	1.1	51.3	31.4	82.1	107.3	108.3	83.0	35.7	7.1	0.4
1998	14.3	64.3	1.0	50.3	29.9	80.9	108.4	110.2	85.2	36.9	7.4	0.4
1999	14.2	64.4	0.9	48.8	28.2	79.1	107.9	111.2	87.1	37.8	7.4	0.4
2000	14.4	65.9	0.9	47.7	26.9	78.1	109.7	113.5	91.2	39.7	8.0	0.5
2001	14.1	65.3	0.8	45.3	24.7	76.1	106.2	113.4	91.9	40.6	8.1	0.5
2002	13.9	64.8	0.7	43.0	23.2	72.8	103.6	113.6	91.5	41.4	8.3	0.5
2003	14.1	66.1	0.6	41.6	22.4	70.7	102.6	115.6	95.1	43.8	8.7	0.5
2004	14.0	66.3	0.7	41.1	22.1	70.0	101.7	115.5	95.3	45.4	8.9	0.5
2005	14.0	66.7	0.7	40.5	21.4	69.9	102.2	115.5	95.8	46.3	9.1	0.6
2006	14.2	68.5	0.6	41.9	22.0	73.0	105.9	116.7	97.7	47.3	9.4	0.6
2007	14.3	69.5	0.6	42.5	22.1	73.9	106.3	117.5	99.9	47.5	9.5	0.6
2008	14.0	68.6	0.6	41.5	21.7	70.6	103.0	115.1	99.3	46.9	9.8	0.7
2009[3]	13.5	66.7	0.5	39.1	20.1	66.2	96.3	110.5	97.7	46.6	10.1	0.7

(1) Live births per 1,000 population. (2) Live births per 1,000 women 15-44 years of age. (3) Preliminary.

Cesarean Delivery Rates by State, 1996-2008

Source: National Center for Health Statistics (NCHS), U.S. Dept. of Health and Human Services

State	1996	2008	Percent change 1996-2008	State	1996	2008	Percent change 1996-2008
Alabama	23.3%	34.6%	48%	Missouri	20.4%	30.8%	51%
Alaska	16.7	22.3	34	Montana	19.1	29.2	53
Arizona	16.1	27.0	68	Nebraska	19.8	31.0	57
Arkansas	25.3	34.5	36	Nevada	19.3	33.5	74
California	20.6	32.6	58	New Hampshire	20.3	31.9	57
Colorado	15.1	25.9	72	New Jersey	24.0	38.3	60
Connecticut	19.8	35.0	77	New Mexico	17.2	22.9	33
Delaware	21.0	33.2	58	New York	22.9	34.3	50
District of Columbia	21.3	31.3	47	North Carolina	21.1	30.6	45
Florida	21.6	37.6	74	North Dakota	18.9	28.1	49
Georgia	20.9	32.4	55	Ohio	19.0	30.6	61
Hawaii	17.5	26.7	53	Oklahoma	22.5	33.9	51
Idaho	16.0	24.4	53	Oregon	16.9	28.9	71
Illinois	19.3	30.6	59	Pennsylvania	19.4	30.8	59
Indiana	20.3	30.0	48	Rhode Island	17.7	33.2	88
Iowa	18.6	29.3	58	South Carolina	22.6	34.2	51
Kansas	19.2	30.1	57	South Dakota	20.8	26.6	28
Kentucky	21.3	35.0	64	Tennessee	21.7	33.8	56
Louisiana	26.4	37.9	44	Texas	23.1	34.5	49
Maine	20.8	30.3	46	Utah	15.9	21.8	37
Maryland	21.6	32.8	52	Vermont	16.5	27.2	65
Massachusetts	19.8	33.8	71	Virginia	21.1	33.8	60
Michigan	20.2	31.5	56	Washington	16.8	29.4	75
Minnesota	16.9	26.2	55	West Virginia	22.8	35.3	55
Mississippi	26.6	36.9	39	Wisconsin	15.6	25.2	62
				Wyoming	18.3	27.0	48
				United States	**20.7**	**32.2**	**56**

Note: The cesarean rate is the percentage of all live births by cesarean delivery.

Assisted Reproductive Technology (ART) Pregnancy Success Rates, 2008

Source: *2008 Assisted Reproductive Technology Success Rates: National Summary and Fertility Clinic Reports*, Centers for Disease Control (CDC), U.S. Dept. of Health and Human Services

	Age of woman[1]				
Type of cycle	Under 35	35-37	38-40	41-42	43-44
			Number		
Fresh embryos from nondonor eggs	43,296	23,326	21,793	9,783	4,907
Average number of embryos transferred	2.2	2.4	2.7	3.1	3.3
Frozen embryos from nondonor eggs	11,343	5,815	3,899	1,269	590
Average number of embryos transferred	2.2	2.2	2.3	2.3	2.4
Fresh embryos from nondonor eggs			Percent distribution		
Cycles resulting in pregnancies	47.6%	38.1%	30.3%	20.3%	10.5%
Cycles resulting in live births[2]	41.1	31.1	22.2	12.1	5.1
Retrievals resulting in live births[2]	44.3	34.9	25.9	14.7	6.3
Transfers resulting in live births[2]	47.1	37.4	28.2	16.5	7.8
Transfers resulting in singleton live births	30.4	26.2	21.1	13.9	6.9
Pregnancies with twins	33.8	27.6	21.7	14.8	9.1
Pregnancies with triplets or more	3.2	4.1	4.0	2.7	2.3
Live births having multiple infants[2]	35.4	30.0	25.2	15.9	11.3
Cancellations	7.1	10.8	14.5	17.6	19.6
Frozen embryos from nondonor eggs					
Transfers resulting in live births[2]	35.5%	29.3%	26.1%	19.5%	14.6%

	All ages combined[3]	
	Fresh embryos	Frozen embryos
Donor eggs		
Number of transfers	10,718	5,861
Average number of embryos transferred	2.1	2.2
Percentage of transfers resulting in live births[2]	55.0%	33.2%

Note: 92% (436 of 475) of ART clinics in the U.S. submitted data in 2008. A total of 148,055 cycles were reported. There were 46,326 live-birth deliveries and 61,426 infants born resulting from ART cycles in 2008. (1) Clinic-specific outcome rates are unreliable for women older than 44 undergoing ART cycles using fresh or frozen embryos with nondonor eggs. (2) A multiple-infant birth is counted as one live birth. (3) All ages (including ages over 44) are reported together because previous data show that patient age does not materially affect success with donor eggs.

Numbers of Multiple Births in the U.S., 1990-2008

Source: National Center for Health Statistics (NCHS), U.S. Dept. of Health and Human Services

The general upward trend in multiple births reflects greater numbers of births to older women and increased use of fertility drugs.

Year	Twins	Triplets	Quadruplets	Quintuplets[1]	Year	Twins	Triplets	Quadruplets	Quintuplets[1]
1990	93,865	2,830	185	13	2001	121,246	6,885	501	85
1993	96,445	3,834	277	57	2002	125,134	6,898	434	69
1994	97,064	4,233	315	46	2003	128,665	7,110	468	85
1995	96,736	4,551	365	57	2004	132,219	6,750	439	86
1996	100,750	5,298	560	81	2005	133,122	6,208	418	68
1997	104,137	6,148	510	79	2006	137,085	6,118	355	67
1998	110,670	6,919	627	79	2007	138,961	5,967	369	91
1999	114,307	6,742	512	67	2008	138,660	5,877	345	46
2000	118,916	6,742	506	77					

(1) Quintuplets and other multiple births of five or more.

Top 15 Countries for U.S. Foreign Adoptions, 2000-10

Source: Office of Immigration Statistics, U.S. Dept. of Homeland Security

Country	2010[1]	2009	2008	2007	2006	2005	2004	2003	2002	2001	2000
China	3,401	2,990	3,852	5,453	6,493	7,906	7,044	6,859	6,119	4,681	5,053
Ethiopia	2,513	2,221	1,666	1,255	732	441	289	135	105	158	95
Russia	1,082	1,580	1,859	2,310	3,706	4,639	5,865	5,209	4,939	4,279	4,269
South Korea	863	1,106	1,038	939	1,376	1,630	1,716	1,790	1,779	1,870	1,794
Ukraine	445	605	487	606	460	821	723	702	1,106	1,246	659
Taiwan	285	254	262	184	187	141	89	107	41	44	24
India	243	298	306	416	320	323	406	472	464	543	503
Colombia	235	237	308	310	344	291	287	272	334	407	246
Philippines	214	292	279	265	245	271	196	214	221	219	173
Nigeria	189	122	114	35	53	62	59	46	41	33	5
Kazakhstan	181	298	380	540	587	755	826	825	819	672	398
Haiti[2]	133	336	300	190	309	234	356	250	187	192	131
Ghana	117	104	100	33	28	16	11	6	11	17	13
Uganda	62	67	52	52	15	15	14	3	19	3	1
Jamaica	59	52	43	42	56	68	51	39	55	42	
Total[3]	11,059	12,782	17,229	19,741	20,705	22,710	22,911	21,320	20,100	19,087	18,120

(1) Ranked by 2010 totals. (2) Does not reflect approximately 1,090 Haitian children admitted as part of the Special Humanitarian Parole following the devastating 2010 earthquake in Haiti. (3) Includes countries not shown.

10 Leading Causes of Infant Death in the U.S., 2009

Source: National Center for Health Statistics (NCHS), U.S. Dept. of Health and Human Services

Cause	Number	Percent of total deaths	Mortality rate[1]
Congenital malformations, deformations, and chromosomal abnormalities	5,358	20.2%	129.7
Disorders related to short gestation and low birth weight, not elsewhere classified	4,463	16.8	108.0
Sudden infant death syndrome	2,168	8.2	52.5
Newborn affected by maternal complications of pregnancy	1,586	6.0	38.4
Accidents (unintentional injuries)	1,158	4.4	28.0
Newborn affected by complications of placenta, cord, and membranes	1,022	3.9	24.7
Bacterial sepsis[2] of newborn	682	2.6	16.5
Respiratory distress of newborn	587	2.2	14.2
Diseases of the circulatory system	565	2.1	13.7
Neonatal hemorrhage	537	2.0	13.0
All other causes	8,400	31.7	203.3
All causes	**26,526**	**100.0**	**642.1**

(1) Infant deaths per 100,000 live births. (2) Toxic condition resulting from the spread of bacteria.

Nonmarital Childbearing in the U.S., 1970-2008

Source: National Center for Health Statistics (NCHS), U.S. Dept. of Health and Human Services

	1970	1975	1980	1985	1990	1995	2000	2004	2005	2006	2007	2008
Births to unmarried mothers (thous.)	399	448	666	828	1,165	1,254	1,347	1,470	1,527	1,642	1,715	1,727
Race/Hispanic origin of mother					*Percent of live births to unmarried mothers*							
All races and origins	10.7%	14.3%	18.4%	22.0%	28.0%	32.2%	33.2%	35.8%	36.9%	38.5%	39.7%	40.6%
White	5.5	7.1	11.2	14.7	20.4	25.3	27.1	30.5	31.7	—	34.8	35.7
Black	37.5	49.5	56.1	61.2	66.5	69.9	68.5	68.8	69.3	—	71.2	71.8
American Indian or Alaska Native	22.4	32.7	39.2	46.8	53.6	57.2	58.4	62.3	63.5	64.6	65.3	65.8
Asian or Pacific Islander	—	—	7.3	9.5	13.2	16.3	14.8	15.5	16.2	16.3	16.6	16.9
Hispanic origin (selected states)[1,2]	—	—	23.6	29.5	36.7	40.8	42.7	46.4	48.0	49.9	51.3	52.6
White, non-Hispanic (selected states)[1]	—	—	9.5	12.4	16.9	21.2	22.1	24.5	25.3	26.6	27.8	28.7
Black, non-Hispanic (selected states)[1]	—	—	57.2	62.0	66.7	70.0	68.7	69.3	69.9	70.7	71.6	72.3
Maternal age					*Percent distribution of live births to unmarried mothers*							
Under 20 years	50.1%	52.1%	40.8%	33.8%	30.9%	30.9%	28.0%	23.7%	23.1%	22.7%	22.5%	22.2%
20-24 years	31.8	29.9	35.6	36.3	34.7	34.5	37.4	38.5	38.3	38.1	37.6	37.1
25 years and over	18.1	18.0	23.5	29.9	34.4	34.7	34.6	37.8	38.6	39.2	39.9	40.7
Race/Hispanic origin of mother					*Live births per 1,000 unmarried women 15-44 years of age[3]*							
All races and origins	26.4	24.5	29.4	32.8	43.8	44.3	44.0	46.1	47.5	—	52.3	52.5
White[4]	13.9	12.4	18.1	22.5	32.9	37.0	38.2	41.6	43.0	—	48.1	48.2
Black[4]	95.5	84.2	81.1	77.0	90.5	74.5	70.5	67.2	67.8	—	72.6	72.5
Hispanic origin (selected states)[1,2]	—	—	—	—	89.6	88.7	87.2	95.7	100.3	—	108.4	105.1
White, non-Hispanic	—	—	—	—	—	28.1	28.0	29.4	30.1	—	33.3	33.7

— = Not available. (1) Data for Hispanics and non-Hispanics are affected by expansion of the reporting area for a Hispanic-origin item on the birth certificate and by immigration. The states in the reporting area increased from 22 in 1980, to 23 and the District of Columbia in 1983, 48 and DC by 1990, and 50 and DC by 1993. (2) Includes mothers of all races. (3) Rates computed by relating births to unmarried mothers, regardless of mother's age, to unmarried women 15-44 years of age. (4) For 1970 and 1975, birth rates are by race of child.

Number, Ratio, and Rate of Legal Abortions in U.S., 1970-2007

Source: *Abortion Surveillance—United States, 2007*, Centers for Disease Control and Prevention, U.S. Dept. of Health and Human Services

Year	Legal abortions	Ratio[1]	Rate[2]	Year	Legal abortions	Ratio[1]	Rate[2]	Year	Legal abortions	Ratio[1]	Rate[2]
1970	193,491	52	5	1983	1,268,987	349	23	1996	1,225,937	315	21
1971	485,816	137	11	1984	1,333,521	364	24	1997	1,186,039	306	20
1972	586,760	180	13	1985	1,328,570	354	24	1998[3]	884,273	270	17
1973	615,831	196	14	1986	1,328,112	354	23	1999[3]	861,789	261	17
1974	763,476	242	17	1987	1,353,671	356	24	2000[4]	857,475	251	16
1975	854,853	272	18	1988	1,371,285	352	24	2001[4]	853,485	251	16
1976	988,267	312	21	1989	1,396,658	346	24	2002[4]	854,122	252	16
1977	1,079,430	325	22	1990	1,429,247	344	24	2003[5]	848,163	247	16
1978	1,157,776	347	23	1991	1,388,937	338	24	2004[5]	839,226	243	16
1979	1,251,921	358	24	1992	1,359,146	334	23	2005[6]	820,151	238	16
1980	1,297,606	359	25	1993	1,330,414	333	23	2006[7]	852,385	238	16
1981	1,300,760	358	24	1994	1,267,415	321	21	2007[8]	827,609	231	16
1982	1,303,980	354	24	1995	1,210,883	311	20				

(1) Number of abortions per 1,000 live births. (2) Number of abortions per 1,000 women aged 15-44 years. (3) Without estimates for AK, CA, NH, and OK. (4) Without estimates for AK, CA, and NH. (5) Without estimates for CA, NH, and WV. (6) Without estimates for CA, NH, and LA. (7) Without estimates for CA and NH. (8) Without estimates for CA, MD, and NH.

Reported Abortions by Age, Race, and Marital Status, 2007

Source: *Abortion Surveillance—United States, 2007*, Centers for Disease Control and Prevention, U.S. Dept. of Health and Human Services

Characteristic	White		Race Black		Other		Total, all races	
Age[2]	No.	%	No.	%	No.	%	No.	%
Under 15	1,232	0.4%	1,518	0.7%	129	0.3%	2,879	0.5%
15-19	51,547	16.5	34,195	16.6	4,724	12.1	90,466	16.2
20-24	105,304	33.7	66,967	32.5	10,809	27.7	183,080	32.9
25-29	73,396	23.5	52,527	25.5	9,634	24.7	135,557	24.3
30-34	41,831	13.4	29,960	14.6	6,940	17.8	78,731	14.1
35-39	28,057	9.0	15,913	7.7	4,858	12.4	48,828	8.8
40 and over	10,675	3.4	4,677	2.3	1,959	5.0	17,311	3.1
Total[1]	312,042	99.9	205,757	99.9	39,053	100.0	556,852	99.9
Marital status[3]								
Married	50,306	17.9	19,892	10.5	12,160	32.9	82,358	16.2
Unmarried	230,864	82.1	168,938	89.5	24,782	67.1	424,584	83.8
Total[2]	281,170	100.0	188,830	100.0	36,942	100.0	506,942	100.0

(1) Percentages for the individual component categories might not add up to 100 because of rounding. (2) Data from 35 reporting areas; excludes 17 areas (AZ, CA, CT, DC, FL, HI, IL, MA, NE, NH, NV, RI, UT, WA, WI, and WY) that did not report, did not report by race or age, or did not meet reporting standards for race or for age. (3) Data from 32 reporting areas; excludes 20 areas (AZ, AR, CA, CT, DC, FL, HI, IL, LA, MA, MD, NE, NV, NH, NY, RI, UT, WA, WI, and WY) that did not report, did not report by race or marital status, or did not meet reporting standards for race or for marital status.

Sexual Identity, Behavior, and Attraction in the U.S., 2011

Source: National Center for Health Statistics (NCHS), U.S. Dept. of Health and Human Services

Data released by the National Center for Health Statistics in 2011, based on surveys conducted 2006-08, show that about 96% of U.S. men and 94% of U.S. women 18-44 years of age think of themselves as heterosexual; 1.7% of men and 1.1% of women as homosexual; and 1.1% of men and 3.5% of women as bisexual. However, 5.2% of men 18-44 years of age reported ever having had sex with another male as of 2008 (up from 2.3% in 1991), and 12.5% of women reported ever having had a sexual experience with another woman (up from 4.1% in 1992).

Eleven percent of males age 15-44 had never had sex with a female, but this percentage varied greatly with age: nearly half (43%) of males age 15-19 had never had sex with a female,

but only 1.3% of males age 40-44 had not done so. Percentages were similar for women, with only 11.3% of females age 15-44 having never had sex with a male, with specific percentages ranging from 48.1% for females age 15-19 to only 0.4% for females age 40-44.

Among 18-44-year-olds, women were less likely than men to report they are attracted "only to the opposite sex"—83.3% of women compared with 93.5% of men. However, when the "only to opposite sex" and "mostly to opposite sex" categories are combined, little difference is seen between men and women. In this same age group, a greater percentage of men (1.2%) than women (0.8%) stated they were attracted "only to the same sex."

Lifetime and Median Number of Sexual Partners by Age and Race, 2008

Source: *Sexual Behavior, Sexual Attraction, and Sexual Identity in the United States*, National Center for Health Statistics (NCHS), U.S. Dept. of Health and Human Services

	Number of opposite-sex partners in lifetime, % distrib.						Median no.[2]		Number of opposite-sex partners in lifetime, % distrib.						Median no.[2]
	0	1	2	3-6	7-14	15+			0	1	2	3-6	7-14	15+	
Male, 15-44 years[1]	11.4	15.0	7.6	26.5	18.1	21.4	5.1	**Female, 15-44 years**[1]	11.3	22.2	10.7	31.6	16.0	8.3	3.2
Age								**Age**							
15-19 years	43.3	21.2	9.4	17.6	5.4	3.1	1.8	15-19 years	48.1	22.7	8.2	15.7	4.1	1.1	1.4
20-24 years	14.4	19.1	8.0	26.1	18.1	14.2	4.1	20-24 years	12.6	24.5	12.5	31.6	11.7	7.2	2.6
25-44 years	2.4	12.3	7.0	28.9	21.5	27.9	6.1	25-44 years	1.6	21.4	10.9	35.6	20.1	10.4	3.6
Race/Hispanic origin								**Race/Hispanic origin**							
White, non-Hispanic	11.6	16.1	7.3	25.7	18.4	20.9	5.1	White, non-Hispanic	11.7	19.2	9.7	31.4	18.9	8.9	3.7
Black, non-Hispanic	9.6	8.3	5.0	25.6	21.6	30.0	6.9	Black, non-Hispanic	10.5	12.3	8.3	40.9	16.7	11.3	4.4
Hispanic or Latino	7.9	12.5	10.2	32.6	17.8	19.1	4.6	Hispanic or Latina	10.7	35.0	16.7	26.6	6.6	4.4	1.6

(1) Includes people of other or multiple races and origin groups, not shown separately. (2) Excludes people who have never had sex with a partner.

Contraceptive Use in the U.S. by Age, 2006-08

Source: National Survey of Family Growth, National Center for Health Statistics (NCHS), U.S. Dept. of Health and Human Services

				Age in years			
	15-44	15-19	20-24	25-29	30-34	35-39	40-44
				Number in thousands			
All women	61,864	10,431	10,140	10,250	9,587	10,475	10,982
Contraceptive status and method				Percent distribution			
Using contraception	61.8%	28.2%	54.7%	64.2%	70.3%	75.0%	77.8%
Female sterilization	16.7	—	1.3	9.6	20.6	28.2	39.1
Male sterilization	6.1	0.0	0.4	2.1	5.8	12.4	15.3
Pill	17.3	15.2	26.2	22.6	17.4	14.4	8.6
Implant, Lunelle™, or patch	0.7	0.5	0.8	1.3	0.9	0.3	—
3-month injectable (Depo-Provera™)	2.0	2.6	2.8	3.3	1.6	0.7	0.9
Contraceptive ring	1.5	1.0	3.4	2.0	1.7	0.7	0.3
Intrauterine device (IUD)	3.4	1.0	3.2	4.0	4.7	4.4	3.2
Condom	10.0	6.4	13.4	13.1	12.0	8.4	6.8
Periodic abstinence—calendar rhythm	0.5	—	0.2	0.7	0.7	0.9	0.5
Periodic abstinence—natural family planning	0.5	0.0	0.0	0.0	0.6	—	—
Withdrawal	3.2	1.1	2.8	5.1	3.7	4.3	2.5
Other methods[1]	0.3	—	—	0.4	0.7	—	—
Not using contraception	38.2	71.8	45.3	35.8	29.7	25.0	22.2
Surgically sterile–female (noncontraceptive)	0.4	0.0	—	—	—	0.4	1.7
Nonsurgically sterile–female or male	1.7	0.0	1.5	2.6	1.6	2.2	1.8
Pregnant or postpartum	5.4	3.9	10.0	7.7	8.1	1.9	1.7
Seeking pregnancy	4.1	—	4.3	6.3	5.9	5.1	2.5
Never had intercourse or no intercourse in last 3 months	19.2	60.0	20.4	10.6	8.7	7.4	8.0
Had intercourse without contraception in last 3 months	7.3	6.5	9.1	8.6	5.3	8.0	6.4

— = Figure does not meet standard of reliability or precision. **Note:** Data was collected in interviews conducted in 2006-08 for the National Survey of Family Growth. For all methods shown, the reported standard error was less than 3.1%. (1) Includes diaphragm (with or without jelly or cream), emergency contraception, female condom or vaginal pouch, foam, cervical cap, Today™ sponge, suppository or insert, and jelly or cream (without diaphragm) among other methods.

Contraceptive Use in the U.S. by Race and Marital Status, 2006-08

Source: National Survey of Family Growth, National Center for Health Statistics (NCHS), U.S. Dept. of Health and Human Services

		Race and Hispanic origin				Marital and cohabitation status			
	Hispanic	White, single race	Black, single race	Total other or multiple races	Asian only	Currently married	Currently cohabiting	Formerly married	Never married
				Number in thousands					
All women	10,377	37,660	8,452	5,375	2,493	27,006	6,821	5,190	22,847
Contraceptive status and method				Percent distribution					
Using contraception	58.5%	64.7%	54.5%	59.2%	63.9%	78.6%	71.2%	60.6%	39.3%
Female sterilization	19.6	14.9	21.8	16.1	11.6	23.6	16.3	35.3	4.5
Male sterilization	3.4	8.3	1.1	3.9	4.5	12.7	2.2	2.3	0.3
Pill	11.4	21.2	11.4	10.9	11.1	16.3	23.2	11.4	18.1
Implant, Lunelle™, or patch	1.5	0.5	0.6	1.0	0.0	0.7	1.0	—	0.6
3-month injectable (Depo-Provera™)	2.6	1.4	4.1	1.8	—	1.4	3.1	2.6	2.2
Contraceptive ring	1.2	1.6	1.7	0.8	—	1.0	3.7	0.8	1.5
Intrauterine device (IUD)	4.8	3.3	2.8	2.2	1.9	5.3	4.7	2.1	1.1
Condom	9.4	9.5	8.8	16.2	26.1	11.7	10.2	4.1	9.1
Periodic abstinence—calendar rhythm	0.6	0.5	—	1.0	2.1	1.0	0.4	—	0.2
Periodic abstinence—natural family planning	—	—	—	—	—	0.2	—	—	—
Withdrawal	3.0	3.3	2.1	5.1	4.8	4.5	5.3	1.4	1.5
Other methods[1]	0.5	0.3	—	—	—	0.3	—	—	0.2
Not using contraception	41.5	35.3	45.5	40.8	36.1	21.4	28.8	39.4	60.7
Surgically sterile–female (noncontraceptive)	0.7	0.2	0.4	—	0.0	0.3	—	1.0	—
Nonsurgically sterile–female or male	1.8	1.6	1.8	1.9	1.2	1.0	2.2	2.7	2.1
Pregnant or postpartum	8.3	4.9	5.7	3.4	2.9	7.2	10.5	2.6	2.6
Seeking pregnancy	6.2	3.5	4.4	4.1	3.0	6.4	7.1	0.8	1.3
Never had intercourse or no intercourse in last 3 months	18.8	18.3	22.6	21.2	23.1	0.9	1.8	21.1	45.6
Had intercourse without contraception in last 3 months	5.8	6.7	10.6	9.5	5.9	5.5	6.9	11.3	8.7

— = Figure does not meet standard of reliability or precision. **Note:** Data was collected in interviews conducted in 2006-08 for the National Survey of Family Growth. For all methods shown, the reported standard error was less than 3.1%. (1) Includes diaphragm (with or without jelly or cream), emergency contraception, female condom or vaginal pouch, foam, cervical cap, Today™ sponge, suppository or insert, and jelly or cream (without diaphragm) among other methods.

Number of Opposite-Sex Partners in Past Year, 2008

Source: *Sexual Behavior, Sexual Attraction, and Sexual Identity in the United States*, National Center for Health Statistics (U.S. males and females 15-44 years of age.)

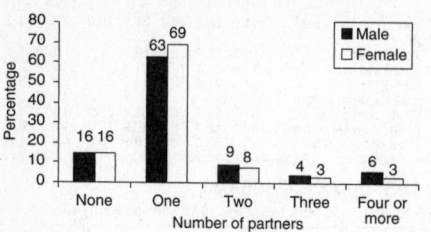

Number of Opposite-Sex Partners in Lifetime by Age, 2008

Source: *Sexual Behavior, Sexual Attraction, and Sexual Identity in the United States*, National Center for Health Statistics (U.S. males and females 15-44 years of age.)

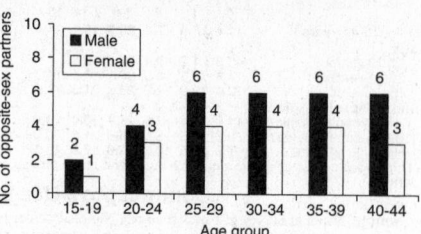

Sexual Activity of High School Students, 2009

Source: *Youth Risk Behavior Surveillance—United States, 2009*, Centers for Disease Control and Prevention

	Ever had sexual intercourse			First sexual intercourse before age 13			Currently sexually active[1]			Condom use during last sexual intercourse[2]		
	Female	Male	Total	Female	Male	Total	Female	Male	Total	Female	Male	Total
Race/ethnicity												
White[3]	44.7%	39.6%	42.0%	2.2%	4.4%	3.4%	35.4%	28.9%	32.0%	56.1%	71.0%	63.3%
Black[3]	58.3	72.1	65.2	5.6	24.9	15.2	45.0	50.3	47.7	51.8	72.5	62.4
Hispanic.	45.4	52.8	49.1	3.7	9.8	6.7	34.1	35.0	34.6	48.0	61.7	54.9
Grade												
9.	29.3	33.6	31.6	3.6	11.3	7.7	21.6	21.2	21.4	57.7	69.9	64.0
10	39.6	41.9	40.9	3.6	9.0	6.5	29.3	28.8	29.1	63.5	71.9	67.8
11	52.5	53.0	52.5	2.7	5.9	4.3	41.5	39.1	40.3	54.0	68.9	61.4
12	65.0	59.6	62.3	2.2	6.4	4.4	53.1	45.1	49.1	46.3	65.0	55.0
Total	45.7	46.1	46.0	3.1	8.4	5.9	35.6	32.6	34.2	53.9	68.6	61.1

(1) Sexual intercourse during the 3 months preceding the survey. (2) Among the 34.2% who were sexually active. (3) Non-Hispanic.

Sexual Activity of Older Adults

Source: National Social Life, Health, and Aging Project at the Univ. of Chicago

		% sexually active with a partner		% reporting sexual behavior			% reporting sexual problem[1]				
Sex	Age	In prev. 12 mos.	2-3+ times per mo.[1]	Inter-course[1]	Oral sex[1]	Mastur-bation[2]	Lack of interest	Stimulation problems	No pleasure	Anxiety	Pain
Men	57-64	83.7%	67.5%	91.1%	62.1%	63.4%	28.2%	30.7%	3.8%	25.1%	3.0%
	65-74	67.0	65.4	78.5	47.9	53.0	28.5	44.6	7.0	28.9	3.2
	75-85	38.5	54.2	83.5	28.3	27.9	24.2	43.5	5.1	29.3	1.0
Women	57-64	61.6	62.6	86.8	52.7	31.6	44.2	35.9	24.0	10.4	17.8
	65-74	39.5	65.4	85.4	46.5	21.9	38.4	43.2	22.0	12.5	18.6
	75-85	16.7	54.1	74.4	35.0	16.4	49.3	43.6	24.9	9.9	11.8

Note: Based on in-home interviews of 3,005 U.S. adults (1,550 women and 1,455 men) between July 2005 and Mar. 2006. (1) Of those who reported having sex in prev. 12 months. (2) In prev. 12 months, asked of all respondents by questionnaire.

U.S. Fires, 2010

Source: National Fire Protection Assn.

Fires

- Public fire departments responded to 1,331,500 fires in 2010, a 1.3% decrease from 2009.
- Every 24 seconds, a fire department responds to a fire somewhere in the United States.
- There were 482,000 structure fires in 2010, a very slight increase of 0.3% from 2009. Of those fires, 80% (384,000 fires) occurred in homes.
- Fires in vehicles dropped 1.6% from the previous year, totaling 215,500 in 2010.
- There were 634,000 fires in outside properties, a decrease of 2.3% from 2009.

Civilian deaths

- There were an estimated 3,120 civilian fire deaths in 2010. This was a 3.7% increase from the year before.
- The number of civilian fire deaths that occurred in home structure fires increased 2.9% to 2,640 and fires in the home caused 85% of all fire deaths.
- Fires caused an average of one civilian death every 169 minutes.

Civilian injuries

- There were an estimated 17,720 civilian fire injuries reported in 2010, a 3.9% increase from 2009. Nationwide, a civilian was injured in a fire every 30 minutes.

- Home structure fires were the site of 13,800 civilian fire injuries in 2010, and non-home structure fires accounted for 1,620 civilian injuries.

Property damage

- Direct property damage from fires amounted to an estimated $11.6 bil in 2010, a decrease of 7.5% from 2009. Structure fires accounted for $9.7 bil of property damage.
- Property loss associated with home fires came to $7.1 bil for 2010.

Intentionally set fires

- There were an estimated 27,500 intentionally set structure fires in 2010, an increase of 3.8% from 2009.
- Intentionally set structure fires are believed to have resulted in 200 civilian deaths in 2010, an increase of 17.7% from the year before. Property damage from intentionally set structure fires totaled $585 mil, a decrease of 14.5% from the 2009 figure.
- The number of intentionally set vehicle fires in 2010 was 14,000, a decrease of 6.7% from a year ago. Intentionally set vehicle fires caused an estimated $89 mil in property damage, a decrease of 17.6% from 2009.

U.S. Motor Vehicle Accidents, 2009

Source: National Safety Council (NSC); Natl. Highway Traffic Safety Admin. (NHTSA)

An estimated 35,900 people in the U.S. were killed in motor vehicle accidents in 2009, down 10% from the total for 2008. Although the number of drivers (211 mil) and the vehicle miles driven (3 tril) increased in 2009, the death rate per 100 mil vehicle miles decreased 10% to 1.21.

Motor vehicle deaths per 10,000 registered vehicles dropped from 1.55 in 2008 to 1.39 in 2009, and were down from 1.92 in 1999, a decrease of 28% over 10 years. The rate of fatalities per 100,000 population declined 25% between 1999 and 2009, and 11% between 2008 and 2009.

Male drivers were involved in about 5.4 mil accidents, whereas female drivers were in 4.2 mil. Male drivers were also involved in 73% of fatal accidents, about 32,807, compared with 11,825 accidents involving female drivers.

In 2009, 10,839 traffic fatalities, or 32%, involved an intoxicated (blood alcohol concentration of 0.08 or greater) driver or motorcycle operator, a decline of 7.9% from 2008. Driving under the influence of alcohol or drugs factored in about 15% of all traffic accidents.

Seat belt use was 85% in 2010. In 2009, safety belts and child restraints saved an estimated 13,022 lives. Another 2,381 lives were saved by frontal air bags. Women used safety belts (87%) more often than men (81%). The least likely safety belt users were urban drivers (81%) and drivers of pickup trucks (75%).

Accidents	Deaths	Injuries
All motor vehicle accidents	35,900	3,500,000
Collision between motor vehicles	13,900	2,610,000
Collision with fixed object	11,600	500,000
Pedestrian accidents	5,300	120,000
Noncollision accidents (e.g., rollovers)	4,000	160,000
Collision with pedal cycle	800	100,000
Collision with railroad train	200	1,000
Other (mostly collisions with animals)	100	9,000

Note: NSC numbers are rounded and preliminary.

Improper Driving Reported in Accidents, 2000-09

Source: National Safety Council

	Percentage of fatal accidents			Percentage of injury accidents			Percentage of all accidents		
Type	2009	2004	2000	2009	2004	2000	2009	2004	2000
Improper driving	59.5%	66.0%	61.6%	55.9%	67.1%	60.3%	54.4%	61.0%	57.8%
Speed too fast or unsafe	15.7	17.6	23.7	6.6	13.7	16.3	5.9	12.5	13.6
Right of way	10.9	13.1	18.6	15.1	19.1	19.9	13.2	15.7	20.1
Failed to yield	7.2	9.0	10.1	10.4	14.6	15.0	9.6	12.0	12.7
Disregarded signal	1.5	2.1	4.6	2.6	1.8	3.6	1.7	1.2	5.3
Passed stop sign	2.2	1.9	3.8	2.1	3.6	1.3	1.9	2.5	2.2
Drove left of center	6.9	7.3	8.2	1.5	1.7	1.1	1.2	1.3	1.0
Improper overtaking	0.9	1.3	0.9	0.8	0.9	0.6	1.1	0.9	0.9
Made improper turn	0.9	3.9	0.7	2.2	4.6	2.0	2.0	4.6	2.4
Followed too closely	1.0	0.8	0.5	6.9	7.2	4.3	9.3	8.0	5.7
Other improper driving	23.2	22.0	9.0	22.8	19.9	16.1	21.7	18.0	14.1
No improper driving stated	40.5	34.0	38.4	44.1	32.9	39.7	45.6	39.0	42.2

Note: Based on reports from state traffic authorities. When a driver was under the influence of alcohol or drugs, the accident was considered a result of the driver's physical condition—not a driving error. For this reason, accidents in which the driver was reported to be under the influence are included under "no improper driving stated."

U.S. Passenger Deaths and Death Rates, 1999-2008

Source: National Safety Council

	Passenger automobiles[1]		Vans, SUVs, pickup trucks		Buses[2]		Railroad passenger trains		Scheduled airlines[3]	
Year	Deaths	Rate[4]	Deaths	Rate[4]	Deaths	Rate[4]	Deaths	Rate[4]	Deaths	Rate[4]
1999	20,851	0.84	11,295	0.76	40	0.07	14	0.10	24	0.005
2000	20,689	0.81	11,545	0.76	3	0.01	4	0.03	94	0.02
2001	20,310	0.78	11,736	0.76	11	0.02	3	0.02	279	0.06
2002	20,564	0.78	12,278	0.78	36	0.06	7	0.05	0	0.00
2003	19,723	0.74	12,551	0.78	30	0.05	3	0.02	24	0.005
2004	19,183	0.71	12,678	0.75	27	0.05	3	0.02	13	0.002
2005	18,509	0.68	13,043	0.76	43	0.07	16	0.10	22	0.004
2006	17,792	0.66	12,723	0.72	15	0.02	2	0.01	52	0.01
2007	16,613	0.61	12,462	0.68	18	0.03	5	0.03	0	0.00
2008	14,579	0.55	10,765	0.59	50	0.08	24	0.13	0	0.00
10-year average	18,881	0.72	12,108	0.73	27	0.05	8	0.05	51	0.01

(1) Drivers of passenger automobiles are considered passengers. Includes taxi passengers. (2) Excludes school buses. (3) Excludes charter, cargo, and on-demand service and suicide/sabotage. (4) Deaths per 100 mil passenger miles.

Risk Behaviors in High School Students, 2009

Source: *Youth Risk Behavior Surveillance—United States, 2009*, Centers for Disease Control and Prevention

		Percent rarely or never wore seat belts[1]			Percent rarely or never wore bicycle helmets[2]			Percent who rode with a driver who had been drinking alcohol[3]		
		Female	Male	Total	Female	Male	Total	Female	Male	Total
Race	White, non-Hispanic	7.6%	11.2%	9.5%	80.2%	83.9%	82.3%	26.9%	25.5%	26.2%
	Black, non-Hispanic	8.3	14.8	11.7	92.7	92.9	92.8	28.7	31.2	30.0
	Hispanic	7.8	9.8	8.8	88.4	89.7	89.1	34.9	33.5	34.2
Grade	9	9.8	11.2	10.6	85.3	84.2	84.7	30.0	25.3	27.5
	10	6.8	11.7	9.4	82.8	86.9	85.2	27.6	28.3	28.0
	11	6.0	11.2	8.7	83.4	87.9	85.9	29.6	29.2	29.4
	12	8.0	12.0	10.1	79.4	84.1	82.1	27.9	28.6	28.2
Total		7.7	11.5	9.7	83.1	85.8	84.7	28.8	27.8	28.3

(1) When riding in a car driven by someone else. (2) Among the 69.5% of students who rode a bicycle during the 12 months preceding the survey. (3) In a car or other vehicle one or more times in the 30 days preceding the survey.

Death Rates for Suicide at Selected Ages, 1960-2007

Source: *Health, United States, 2010*, National Center for Health Statistics (NCHS), U.S. Dept. of Health and Human Services

	2007			2000			1980			1960		
Age	Both sexes	Male	Female	Both sexes	Male	Female	Both sexes	Male	Female	Both sexes	Male	Female
15-24	9.7	15.9	3.2	10.2	17.1	3.0	12.3	20.2	4.3	5.2	8.2	2.2
25-44	14.3	22.3	6.2	13.4	21.3	5.4	15.6	24.0	7.7	12.2	17.9	6.6
45-64	16.8	25.8	8.2	13.5	21.3	6.2	15.9	23.7	8.9	22.0	34.4	10.2
65 and older	14.3	28.6	3.9	15.2	31.1	4.0	17.6	35.0	6.1	24.5	44.0	8.4
All ages	11.3	18.4	4.7	10.4	17.7	4.0	12.2	19.9	5.7	12.5	20.0	5.6

Note: Rate is per 100,000 population.

Leading Causes of Death in the U.S., 2009

Source: National Center for Health Statistics (NCHS), U.S. Dept. of Health and Human Services

	Number	% of total deaths	Death rate[1]		Number	% of total deaths	Death rate[1]
All causes	2,436,652	100.0%	793.7	9. Kidney disease	48,714	2.0%	15.9
1. Diseases of the heart	598,607	24.6	195.0	10. Intentional self-harm (suicide)...	36,547	1.5	11.9
2. Cancer....................	568,668	23.3	185.2	11. Septicemia	35,587	1.5	11.6
3. Chronic lower respiratory diseases	137,082	5.6	44.7	12. Chronic liver disease and cirrhosis	30,444	1.2	9.9
4. Stroke	128,603	5.3	41.9	13. Hypertension and hypertensive			
5. Accidents (unintentional injuries)	117,176	4.8	38.2	renal disease	25,651	1.1	8.4
6. Alzheimer's disease...........	78,889	3.2	25.7	14. Parkinson's disease	20,552	0.8	6.7
7. Diabetes..................	68,504	2.8	22.3	15. Assault (homicide)	16,591	0.7	5.4
8. Influenza and pneumonia	53,582	2.2	17.5	All other causes (residual)........	471,455	19.3	153.6

(1) Per 100,000 population.

Principal Types of Accidental Deaths in the U.S., 1970-2009

Source: National Safety Council

Year	Total	Motor vehicle	Falls	Poisoning	Drowning	Fires, flames, smoke	Suffocation: ingestion of food, object	Firearms	Mechanical suffocation
1970	NA	54,633	16,926	5,299	7,860	6,718	2,753	2,406	NA
1980	105,718	53,172	13,294	4,331	7,257	5,822	3,249	1,955	NA
1985	93,457	45,901	12,001	5,170	5,316	4,938	3,551	1,649	NA
1990	91,983	46,814	12,313	5,803	4,685	4,175	3,303	1,416	NA
1992	86,777	40,982	12,646	7,082	3,542	3,958	3,182	1,409	NA
1993	90,437	41,893	13,141	8,537	3,807	3,900	3,160	1,521	NA
1994	91,437	42,524	13,450	8,994	3,942	3,986	3,065	1,356	NA
1995	93,320	43,363	13,986	9,072	4,350	3,761	3,185	1,225	NA
1996	94,948	43,649	14,986	9,510	3,959	3,741	3,206	1,134	NA
1997	95,644	43,458	15,447	10,163	4,051	3,490	3,275	981	NA
1998	97,835	43,501	16,274	10,801	4,406	3,255	3,515	866	NA
1999[1]	97,860	42,401	13,162	12,186	3,529	3,348	3,885	824	1,618
2000	97,900	43,354	13,322	12,757	3,482	3,377	4,313	776	1,335
2001	101,537	43,788	15,019	14,078	3,281	3,309	4,185	802	1,370
2002	106,742	45,380	16,257	17,550	3,447	3,159	4,128	762	1,389
2003	109,277	44,757	17,229	19,457	3,306	3,369	4,272	730	1,309
2004	112,012	44,933	18,807	20,950	3,308	3,229	4,470	649	1,421
2005	117,809	45,343	19,656	23,617	3,582	3,197	4,386	789	1,514
2006	121,599	45,316	20,823	27,531	3,579	3,109	4,332	642	1,580
2007[2]	123,706	43,945	22,631	29,846	3,443	3,286	4,344	613	1,653
2008[2]	125,800	39,700	24,300	34,400	3,500	3,200	4,600	610	1,700
2009[3]	128,200	35,900	26,100	39,000	3,700	3,200	4,600	600	1,800
Death rates per 100,000 population									
1970	NA	26.8	8.3	2.6	3.9	3.3	1.4	1.2	NA
1980	47.8	23.4	5.9	1.9	3.2	2.6	1.4	0.9	NA
1985	39.3	19.3	5.0	2.2	2.2	2.1	1.5	0.7	NA
1990	36.9	18.8	4.9	2.3	1.9	1.7	1.3	0.6	NA
1992	34.0	16.1	5.0	2.7	1.4	1.6	1.2	0.6	NA
1993	35.1	16.3	5.1	3.4	1.5	1.5	1.2	0.6	NA
1994	35.1	16.3	5.2	3.5	1.5	1.5	1.2	0.5	NA
1995	35.5	16.5	5.3	3.4	1.7	1.4	1.2	0.5	NA
1996	35.8	16.5	5.6	3.5	1.5	1.4	1.2	0.4	NA
1997	35.7	16.2	5.8	3.8	1.5	1.3	1.2	0.4	NA
1998	36.2	16.1	6.0	4.0	1.6	1.2	1.3	0.3	NA
1999[1]	35.9	15.5	4.8	4.5	1.3	1.2	1.4	0.3	0.6
2000	35.6	15.7	4.8	4.6	1.3	1.2	1.6	0.3	0.5
2001	35.6	15.4	5.3	4.9	1.2	1.2	1.5	0.3	0.5
2002	37.1	15.8	5.6	6.4	1.2	1.1	1.4	0.3	0.5
2003	37.6	15.4	5.9	6.7	1.1	1.2	1.5	0.3	0.4
2004	38.1	15.3	6.4	7.1	1.1	1.1	1.5	0.2	0.5
2005	39.7	15.3	6.6	8.0	1.2	1.1	1.5	0.3	0.5
2006	40.8	15.2	7.0	9.2	1.2	1.0	1.5	0.2	0.5
2007[2]	41.1	14.6	7.5	9.9	1.1	1.1	1.4	0.2	0.5
2008[2]	41.4	13.1	8.0	11.3	1.2	1.1	1.5	0.2	0.6
2009[3]	41.8	11.7	8.5	12.7	1.2	1.0	1.5	0.2	0.6

NA = Not available. **Note:** All figures include on-the-job deaths. (1) Data for 1999 and later not comparable with earlier data because of classification changes. (2) Revised data. (3) Preliminary. Totals include 13,900 other accidental deaths in 2009.

Deaths in the U.S. Involving Firearms by Age and Sex, 2007

Source: National Safety Council

	All ages	Under 5	5-14	15-19	20-24	25-44	45-64	65-74	75 & over
Total firearms deaths	31,224	85	313	2,669	4,233	11,422	8,199	1,938	2,365
Male	27,047	51	237	2,402	3,835	9,793	6,856	1,701	2,172
Female	4,177	34	76	267	398	1,629	1,343	237	193
Unintentional.............	613	19	46	73	82	185	139	31	38
Male	537	15	41	68	79	156	122	23	33
Female	76	4	5	5	3	29	17	8	5
Suicide	17,352	—	53	630	1,270	5,185	6,317	1,700	2,197
Male	15,181	—	45	572	1,155	4,426	5,374	1,539	2,070
Female	2,171	—	8	58	115	759	943	161	127
Homicide................	12,632	63	201	1,897	2,772	5,789	1,605	185	120
Male	10,767	34	141	1,696	2,503	4,969	1,243	121	60
Female	1,865	29	60	201	269	820	362	64	60
Legal intervention...........	351	0	1	24	72	183	63	5	3
Male	339	0	1	24	69	177	60	5	3
Female	12	0	0	0	3	6	3	0	0
Undetermined[1]	276	3	12	45	37	80	75	17	7
Male	223	2	9	42	29	65	57	13	6
Female	53	1	3	3	8	15	18	4	1

— = Not applicable/available. (1) The intention involved (whether accident, suicide, or homicide) could not be determined.

U.S. Infant Mortality Rates by Race and Sex, 1960-2009
Source: National Center for Health Statistics (NCHS), U.S. Dept. of Health and Human Services

Year	All races[1] Both sexes	Male	Female	White Both sexes	Male	Female	Black Both sexes	Male	Female
1960	26.0	29.3	22.6	22.9	26.0	19.6	44.3	49.1	39.4
1970	20.0	22.4	17.5	17.8	20.0	15.4	32.6	36.2	29.0
1980	12.6	13.9	11.2	11.0	12.3	9.6	21.4	23.3	19.4
1985	10.6	11.9	9.3	9.3	10.6	8.0	18.2	19.9	16.5
1989	9.8	10.8	8.8	8.1	9.0	7.1	18.6	20.0	17.2
1990	9.2	10.3	8.1	7.6	8.5	6.6	18.0	19.6	16.2
1991	8.9	10.0	7.8	7.3	8.3	6.3	17.6	19.4	15.7
1992	8.5	9.4	7.6	6.9	7.7	6.1	16.8	18.4	15.3
1993	8.4	9.3	7.4	6.8	7.6	6.0	16.5	18.3	14.7
1994	8.0	8.8	7.2	6.6	7.2	5.9	15.8	17.5	14.1
1995	7.6	8.3	6.8	6.3	7.0	5.6	15.1	16.3	13.9
1996	7.3	8.0	6.6	6.1	6.7	5.4	14.7	16.0	13.3
1997	7.2	8.0	6.5	6.0	6.7	5.4	14.2	15.5	12.8
1998	7.2	7.8	6.5	6.0	6.5	5.4	14.3	15.7	12.8
1999	7.1	7.7	6.4	5.8	6.4	5.2	14.6	15.9	13.2
2000	6.9	7.6	6.2	5.7	6.2	5.1	14.1	15.5	12.6
2001	6.8	7.5	6.1	5.7	6.2	5.1	14.0	15.5	12.5
2002	7.0	7.6	6.3	5.8	6.4	5.1	14.4	15.4	13.3
2003	6.9	7.6	6.1	5.7	6.3	5.0	14.0	15.5	12.4
2004	6.8	7.5	6.1	5.7	6.2	5.1	13.8	15.2	12.3
2005	6.9	7.6	6.2	5.7	6.3	5.1	13.7	15.2	12.3
2006	6.7	7.3	6.0	5.6	6.1	5.0	13.3	14.4	12.2
2007	6.8	7.4	6.1	5.6	6.2	5.1	13.2	14.5	11.9
2008[2]	6.6	NA	NA	5.5	NA	NA	12.7	NA	NA
2009[2]	6.4	NA	NA	5.3	NA	NA	12.7	NA	NA

NA = Not available. **Note:** Rates per 1,000 live births in specified group. (1) Includes races other than white and black. (2) Preliminary.

Years of Life Expected at Birth in U.S., 1900-2009
Source: National Center for Health Statistics (NCHS), U.S. Dept. of Health and Human Services

Year[2]	All races[1] Both sexes	Male	Female	White Both sexes	Male	Female	Black Both sexes	Male	Female
1900	47.3	46.3	48.3	47.6	46.6	48.7	NA	NA	NA
1910	50.0	48.4	51.8	50.3	48.6	52.0	NA	NA	NA
1920	54.1	53.6	54.6	54.9	54.4	55.6	NA	NA	NA
1930	59.7	58.1	61.6	61.4	59.7	63.5	NA	NA	NA
1940	62.9	60.8	65.2	64.2	62.1	66.6	NA	NA	NA
1950	68.2	65.6	71.1	69.1	66.5	72.2	NA	NA	NA
1960	69.7	66.6	73.1	70.6	67.4	74.1	NA	NA	NA
1970	70.8	67.1	74.7	71.7	68.0	75.6	64.1	60.0	68.3
1975	72.6	68.8	76.6	73.4	69.5	77.3	68.8	62.4	71.3
1980	73.7	70.0	77.5	74.4	70.7	78.1	68.1	63.8	72.5
1985	74.7	71.2	78.2	75.3	71.9	78.7	69.3	65.0	73.4
1990	75.4	71.8	78.8	76.1	72.7	79.4	69.1	64.5	73.6
1992	75.5	72.1	78.9	76.4	73.0	79.5	69.6	65.0	73.9
1993	75.5	72.1	78.9	76.3	73.0	79.5	69.2	64.6	73.7
1994	75.7	72.4	79.0	76.5	73.3	79.6	69.5	64.9	73.9
1995	75.8	72.5	78.9	76.5	73.4	79.6	69.6	65.2	73.9
1996	76.1	73.1	79.1	76.8	73.9	79.7	70.2	66.1	74.2
1997	76.5	73.6	79.4	77.1	74.3	79.9	71.1	67.2	74.7
1998	76.7	73.8	79.5	77.3	74.5	80.0	71.3	67.6	74.8
1999	76.7	73.9	79.4	77.3	74.6	79.9	71.4	67.8	74.7
2000	76.8	74.1	79.3	77.3	74.7	79.9	71.8	68.2	75.1
2001	76.9	74.2	79.4	77.4	74.8	79.9	72.0	68.4	75.2
2002	76.9	74.3	79.5	77.4	74.9	79.9	72.1	68.6	75.4
2003	77.1	74.5	79.6	77.6	75.0	80.0	72.3	68.8	75.6
2004	77.5	74.9	79.9	77.9	75.4	80.4	72.8	69.3	76.0
2005	77.4	74.9	79.9	77.9	75.4	80.4	72.8	69.3	76.1
2006	77.7	75.1	80.2	78.2	75.7	80.6	73.2	69.7	76.5
2007	77.9	75.4	80.4	78.4	75.9	80.8	73.6	70.0	76.8
2008[3]	78.0	75.5	80.5	78.4	75.9	80.8	73.9	70.9	77.4
2009[3]	78.2	75.7	80.6	78.6	76.2	80.9	74.3	70.9	77.4

NA = Not available. (1) Includes races other than white and black. (2) Data prior to 1940 does not include all states. (3) Preliminary.

U.S. Life Expectancy at Selected Ages, 2009
Source: National Center for Health Statistics (NCHS), U.S. Dept. of Health and Human Services

Exact age in years	All races[1] Both sexes	Male	Female	White Both sexes	Male	Female	Black Both sexes	Male	Female
0	78.2	75.7	80.6	78.6	76.2	80.9	74.3	70.9	77.4
1	77.7	75.3	80.0	78.0	75.6	80.3	74.2	70.9	77.2
5	73.8	71.4	76.1	74.1	71.7	76.3	70.3	67.0	73.3
10	68.8	66.4	71.2	69.1	66.8	71.4	65.4	62.1	68.4
15	63.9	61.5	66.2	64.1	61.8	66.4	60.5	57.1	63.5
20	59.0	56.7	61.3	59.3	57.0	61.5	55.7	52.4	58.6
25	54.3	52.0	56.4	54.5	52.3	56.6	51.0	47.9	53.7
30	49.5	47.3	51.6	49.8	47.6	51.8	46.3	43.3	49.0
35	44.8	42.7	46.8	45.0	43.0	47.0	41.7	38.8	44.2
40	40.1	38.0	42.0	40.3	38.3	42.2	37.1	34.3	39.6
45	35.5	33.5	37.3	35.7	33.8	37.5	32.7	30.0	35.0
50	31.1	29.1	32.8	31.2	29.4	32.9	28.5	25.8	30.7
55	26.8	25.0	28.4	26.9	25.2	28.5	24.5	22.0	26.6
60	22.7	21.1	24.1	22.8	21.2	24.1	20.9	18.6	22.7
65	18.8	17.3	20.0	18.8	17.4	20.0	17.5	15.5	18.9
70	15.1	13.8	16.1	15.1	13.9	16.1	14.3	12.6	15.4
75	11.7	10.7	12.5	11.7	10.6	12.5	11.3	9.9	12.2
80	8.8	8.0	9.4	8.8	7.9	9.3	8.8	7.7	9.4
85	6.4	5.8	6.8	6.4	5.7	6.7	6.7	5.9	7.1
90	4.6	4.1	4.8	4.5	4.1	4.7	5.0	4.4	5.2
95	3.2	2.9	3.3	3.1	2.8	3.2	3.7	3.3	3.8
100	2.2	2.0	2.2	2.2	2.0	2.2	2.7	2.5	2.7

Note: Data is preliminary. (1) Includes races other than white and black.

NOTED PERSONALITIES

Widely Known Americans of the Present

Political leaders, journalists, other prominent living persons. As of Oct. 2011. Excludes most who fall in categories listed elsewhere in Noted Personalities, such as Writers of the Present and Entertainment Personalities of the Present, or in Sports Personalities. Includes some figures active in American life but not U.S. citizens.

Roger Ailes, b 5/15/40 (Warren, OH), TV exec.

Madeleine K. Albright, b 5/15/37 (Prague, Czech.), former sec. of state.

Edwin "Buzz" Aldrin, b 1/20/30 (Montclair, NJ), former astronaut, 2nd person to walk on the Moon.

Samuel A. Alito Jr., b 4/1/50 (Trenton, NJ), Supreme Court justice.

Paul Allen, b 1/21/53 (Seattle, WA), cofounder of Microsoft.

Christiane Amanpour, b 1/12/58 (London, Eng., UK), TV journalist.

Richard K. Armey, b 7/7/40 (Cando, ND), former U.S. rep. (R, TX), House majority leader.

Neil Armstrong, b 8/5/30 (Wapakoneta, OH), former astronaut, 1st person to walk on the Moon.

John Ashcroft, b 5/9/42 (Chicago, IL), former MO gov., U.S. attorney gen.

David Axelrod, b 2/22/55 (New York, NY), sr. adviser to Pres. Obama, political strategist.

Michele Bachmann, b 4/6/56 (Waterloo, IA), U.S. rep (R, MN), 2012 pres. candidate.

F. Lee Bailey, b 6/10/33 (Waltham, MA), attorney.

Russell Baker, b 8/14/25 (Morrisonville, VA), columnist.

Dave Barry, b 7/3/47 (Armonk, NY), humorist.

Marion Barry, b 3/6/36 (Itta Bena, MS), DC city council member; former Wash., DC, mayor.

Max Baucus, b 12/11/41 (Helena, MT), senator (D, MT), Finance Committee chair.

Gary Bauer, b 5/4/46 (Covington, KY), domestic policy adviser to Pres. Reagan; founder, Campaign for Working Families.

Glenn Beck, b 2/10/64 (Mount Vernon, WA), political commentator.

William Bennett, b 7/31/43 (Brooklyn, NY), author, former education secretary.

Chris Berman, b 5/10/55 (Greenwich, CT), sportscaster.

Ben Bernanke, b 12/13/53 (Augusta, GA), Federal Reserve Chairman.

Carl Bernstein, b 2/14/44 (Washington, DC), journalist; with Woodward cracked Watergate scandal.

Jeff Bezos, b 1/12/64 (Albuquerque, NM), founder and CEO of Amazon.com.

Jill Biden, b 6/5/51 (Hammonton, NJ), English college professor, wife of vice pres. Joe Biden.

Joseph R. Biden Jr., b 11/20/42 (Scranton, PA), U.S. vice president; former senator (D, DE).

James H. Billington, b 6/1/29 (Bryn Mawr, PA), librarian of U.S. Congress.

Rod Blagojevich, b 12/10/56 (Chicago, IL), former IL governor (D).

Lloyd Blankfein, b 9/20/54 (Bronx, NY), CEO and chairman of Goldman Sachs.

Wolf Blitzer, b 3/22/48 (Augsburg, Germany), TV journalist.

Harold Bloom, b 7/11/30 (New York, NY), literary critic.

Michael R. Bloomberg, b 2/14/42 (Brighton, MA), NYC mayor; financial information/media entrepreneur.

Roy Blunt, b 1/10/50 (Niangua, MO), senator (R, MO); former U.S. rep., House minority whip.

John Boehner, b 11/17/49 (Cincinnati, OH), U.S. rep. (R, OH), speaker of the House.

Charles F. Bolden, b 8/19/46 (Columbia, SC), NASA head.

Julian Bond, b 1/14/40 (Nashville, TN), civil rights leader, former NAACP chairman.

Cory Booker, b 4/27/69 (Washington, DC), Newark, NJ, mayor.

Barbara Boxer, b 11/11/40 (Brooklyn, NY), senator (D, CA).

Bill Bradley, b 7/28/43 (Crystal City, MO), former senator (D, NJ), basketball player, pres. candidate.

James Brady, b 8/29/40 (Centralia, IL), gun control advocate; former pres. press sec.

L. Paul Bremer III, b 9/30/41 (Hartford, CT), diplomat, former top U.S. civilian administrator in Iraq.

Jimmy Breslin, b 10/17/30 (Jamaica, Queens, NY), columnist, author.

Stephen Breyer, b 8/15/38 (San Francisco, CA), Supreme Court justice.

Sergey Brin, b 8/21/73 (Moscow, Russia), cofounder of Google.

Roslyn M. Brock, b 5/30/65 (Fort Pierce, FL), NAACP chair.

Tom Brokaw, b 2/6/40 (Webster, SD), TV journalist, retired NBC anchor.

David Brooks, b 8/11/61 (Toronto, ON, Can.), columnist, political commentator.

Joyce Brothers, b 10/20/29 (New York, NY), psychologist.

Aaron Brown, b 11/10/48 (Hopkins, MN), broadcast journalist.

Jerry (Edmund G.) Brown Jr., b 4/7/38 (San Francisco, CA), CA gov (1975-83, 2011-), former atty. gen. (CA), pres. candidate.

Scott Brown, b 9/12/59 (Wakefield, MA), senator (R, MA).

Pat Buchanan, b 11/2/38 (Washington, DC), journalist, former pres. candidate.

Warren Buffett, b 8/30/30 (Omaha, NE), investor, leading philanthropist.

Roland Burris, b 8/3/37 (Centralia, IL), senator (D, IL), first African American atty. gen. of IL.

Barbara Bush, b 6/8/25 (Flushing, NY), former first lady.

Barbara Bush, b 11/25/81 (Dallas, TX), daughter of former Pres. George W. Bush.

George H. W. Bush, b 6/12/24 (Milton, MA), former U.S. president.

George W. Bush, b 7/6/46 (New Haven, CT), former U.S. president.

Laura Bush, b 11/4/46 (Midland, TX), former first lady.

Herman Cain, b 12/13/45 (Memphis, TN), former chairman and CEO of Godfather's Pizza; 2012 pres. contender.

Eric Cantor, b 6/6/63 (Richmond, VA), U.S. rep. (R, VA), House majority leader.

Tucker Carlson, b 5/16/69 (San Francisco, CA), journalist, TV commentator.

Jimmy Carter, b 10/1/24 (Plains, GA), former U.S. president; 2002 Nobel Peace Prize winner.

Rosalynn Carter, b 8/18/27 (Plains, GA), former first lady.

James Carville Jr., b 10/25/44 (Fort Benning, GA), TV political commentator.

Steve Case, b 8/21/58 (Honolulu, HI), former AOL Time Warner chairman.

Julie Chen, b 1/6/70 (New York, NY), cohost of *The Early Show* and *Big Brother*.

Dick Cheney, b 1/30/41 (Lincoln, NE), former U.S. vice president.

Lynne Cheney, b 8/14/41 (Casper, WY), political commentator, wife of Dick Cheney.

Noam Chomsky, b 12/7/28 (Philadelphia, PA), linguist; activist.

Chris Christie, b 9/6/62 (Newark, NJ), NJ governor (R).

Steven Chu, b 2/28/48 (St. Louis, MO), energy secretary, atomic physicist.

Connie Chung, b 8/20/46 (Washington, DC), TV journalist.

James R. Clapper, b 1941, director of national intelligence.

Bill Clinton, b 8/19/46 (Hope, AR), former U.S. president.

Chelsea Clinton, b 2/27/80 (Little Rock, AR), daughter of former pres. Bill Clinton and Hillary Rodham Clinton.

Hillary Rodham Clinton, b 10/26/47 (Chicago, IL), sec. of state, former senator (D, NY), former first lady, 2008 pres. contender.

James Clyburn, b 7/21/40 (Sumter, SC), U.S. rep. (D, SC), former House majority whip.

Kenneth Cole, b 3/23/54 (Brooklyn, NY), fashion designer.

Gail Collins, b 11/25/45 (Cincinnati, OH), newspaper columnist, writer.

Anderson Cooper, b 6/3/67 (New York, NY), CNN anchor.

Jon Corzine, b 1/1/47 (Willey's Station, IL), former sen. (D, NJ) and NJ governor.

Bob Costas, b 3/22/52 (Queens, NY), TV sports journalist.

Ann Coulter, b 12/8/61 (New Canaan, CT), political commentator, author.

Katie Couric, b 1/7/57 (Arlington, VA), TV journalist, former NBC morning anchor, former anchor of *CBS Evening News*.

Mark Cuban, b 7/31/58 (Pittsburgh, PA), entrepreneur, Dallas Mavericks (NBA) owner.

Andrew Cuomo, b 12/6/57 (New York, NY), NY governor (D), former state atty. gen.

Mario Cuomo, b 6/15/32 (Jamaica, Queens, NY), former NY governor.

Ann Curry, b 11/19/56 (Guam), *Today* show news anchor.

Richard M. Daley, b 4/24/42 (Chicago, IL), former Chicago mayor.

William Daley, b 8/9/48 (Chicago, IL), White House chief of staff.

Thomas Daschle, b 12/9/47 (Aberdeen, SD), former senator (D, SD) and Senate minority leader.

Howard Dean, b 11/17/48 (New York, NY), former VT gov., former Dem. Natl. Committee chair.

Oscar de la Renta, b 7/22/36 (Santo Domingo, Dominican Rep.), fashion designer.

Tom DeLay, b 4/8/47 (Laredo, TX), former U.S. rep. (R, TX), House Majority leader.

Michael Dell, b 2/23/65 (Houston, TX), founder, chairman, and CEO of Dell computers.

Alan Dershowitz, b 9/1/38 (Brooklyn, NY), attorney.

Barry Diller, b 2/2/42 (San Francisco, CA), media exec.

John Dingell, b 7/8/26 (Colorado Springs, CO), U.S. rep. (D, MI), Dean of the House.

Lou Dobbs, b 9/24/45 (Childress, TX), TV journalist.

James Dobson, b 4/21/36 (Shreveport, LA), evangelical Christian leader, chairman of Focus on the Family.

Christopher Dodd, b 5/27/44 (Willimantic, CT), Motion Picture Assn. of America chair/CEO; former senator (D, CT), 2008 pres. contender.

Elizabeth Hanford Dole, b 7/29/36 (Salisbury, NC), former senator (R, NC), Red Cross pres., cabinet member.

Robert Dole, b 7/22/23 (Russell, KS), former Senate majority leader (R, KS), 1996 pres. nominee.

Sam Donaldson, b 3/11/34 (El Paso, TX), TV journalist.

Elizabeth Drew, b 11/16/35 (Cincinnati, OH), journalist.

Matt Drudge, b 10/27/66 (Takoma Park, MD), Internet journalist.

Michael S. Dukakis, b 11/3/33 (Brookline, MA), former MA gov. (D), pres. nominee.

Arne Duncan, b 11/6/64 (Chicago, IL), education secretary.

Dick Durbin, b 11/21/44 (East St. Louis, IL), Senate majority whip (D, IL).

Bernard Ebbers, b 8/27/41 (Edmonton, AB, Can.), former WorldCom CEO; jailed for fraud.

Roger Ebert, b 6/18/42 (Urbana, IL), film critic.

Marian Wright Edelman, b 6/6/39 (Bennettsville, SC), pres. and founder of Children's Defense Fund.

John Edwards, b 6/10/53 (Seneca, SC), former senator (D, NC), 2004 vice-pres. candidate, 2008 pres. contender.

Edward Egan, b 4/2/32 (Oak Park, IL), Rom. Cath. cardinal, archbishop emeritus of New York.

Michael Eisner, b 3/7/42 (Mt. Kisco, NY), former Disney Co. CEO.

Lawrence J. Ellison, b 8/17/44 (New York, NY), Oracle Corp. founder, CEO.

Rahm Emanuel, b 11/29/59 (Chicago, IL), Chicago mayor; former White House chief of staff, U.S. rep. (D, IL).

Myrlie Evers-Williams, b 3/17/33 (Vicksburg, MS), civil rights activist.

Louis Farrakhan, b 5/11/33 (Roxbury, MA), Nation of Islam leader.

Russell Feingold, b 3/2/53 (Janesville, WI), former senator (D, WI).

Dianne Feinstein, b 6/22/33 (San Francisco, CA), senator (D, CA).

Carly (Carleton) S. Fiorina, b 9/6/54 (Austin, TX), former CEO of Hewlett-Packard, 2010 Senate candidate (R, CA).

Larry Flynt, b 11/1/42 (Lakeville, KY), publisher.

Steve (Malcolm) Forbes Jr., b 7/18/47 (Morristown, NJ), publisher, former pres. contender.

Tom Ford, b 8/27/61 (Austin, TX), fashion designer.

Barney Frank, b 3/31/40 (Bayonne, NJ), attorney, U.S. rep. (D, MA).

Al Franken, b 5/21/51 (New York, NY), senator (D, MN); humorist, political writer, radio host.

Thomas Friedman, b 7/20/53 (Minneapolis, MN), columnist, author.

Bill Gates, b 10/28/55 (Seattle, WA), software pioneer; Microsoft exec.

Henry Louis Gates Jr., b 9/16/50 (Keyser, WV), African American studies scholar.

Robert M. Gates, b 9/25/43 (Wichita, KS), former sec. of defense.

David Geffen, b 2/21/43 (Brooklyn, NY), entertainment exec.

Timothy Geithner, b 8/18/61 (New York, NY), Treasury secretary, former CEO of Federal Reserve Bank of NY.

Robert Gibbs, b 3/29/71 (Auburn, AL), White House press secretary.

Charles Gibson, b 3/4/43 (Evanston, IL), TV journalist, former host of ABC's *World News*.

Gabrielle Giffords, b 6/8/70 (Tucson, AZ), U.S. rep (D, AZ), shot in 2011 assassination attempt.

Kirsten Gillibrand, b 12/9/66 (Albany, NY), senator (D, NY), attorney.

Newt Gingrich, b 6/17/43 (Harrisburg, PA), former House speaker (R, GA), 2012 pres. contender.

Ruth Bader Ginsburg, b 3/15/33 (Brooklyn, NY), Supreme Court justice.

Rudolph Giuliani, b 5/28/44 (Brooklyn, NY), former NYC mayor.

John Glenn, b 7/18/21 (Cambridge, OH), former senator (D, OH), astronaut.

Alberto Gonzales, b 8/4/55 (San Antonio, TX), former U.S. attorney general.

Roger Goodell, b 2/19/59 (Jamestown, NY), NFL commissioner.

Ellen Goodman, b 4/11/41 (Newton, MA), columnist.

Doris Kearns Goodwin, b 1/4/43 (Brooklyn, NY), historian, TV commentator.

Berry Gordy Jr., b 11/28/29 (Detroit, MI), Motown record label founder.

Al Gore Jr., b 3/31/48 (Washington, DC), former senator (D, TN), U.S. vice president, 2000 pres. candidate; 2007 Nobel Peace Prize winner.

Tipper Gore, b 8/19/48 (Washington, DC), wife of Al Gore.

Rev. Billy Graham, b 11/7/18 (Charlotte, NC), evangelist.

(William) Franklin Graham III, b 7/14/52 (Asheville, NC), evangelist, son of Billy Graham.

Andrew Greeley, b 2/5/28 (Oak Park, IL), Rom. Cath. priest, sociologist, writer.

Jeff Greenfield, b 6/10/43 (New York, NY), TV journalist.

Alan Greenspan, b 3/6/26 (New York, NY), former Federal Reserve chairman.

Jenna Bush Hager, b 11/25/81 (Dallas, TX), daughter of former Pres. George W. Bush.

Pete Hamill, b 6/24/35 (Brooklyn, NY), journalist, author.

Lee Hamilton, b 4/20/31 (Daytona Beach, FL), 9/11 commission vice-chair, former U.S. rep. (D, IN).

Sean Hannity, b 12/30/61 (New York, NY), radio and TV host, author, political commentator.

J. Dennis Hastert, b 1/2/42 (Aurora, IL), former House speaker, U.S. rep. (R, IL).

Reed Hastings, b 10/8/60 (Boston, MA), founder, pres., CEO and board chair, Netflix, Inc.

Orrin Hatch, b 3/22/34 (Homestead Park, PA), senator (R, UT).

Hugh Hefner, b 4/9/26 (Chicago, IL), publisher.

Tommy Hilfiger, b 3/24/51 (Elmira, NY), fashion designer.

Anita Hill, b 7/30/56 (Morris, OK), legal scholar; complainant against Clarence Thomas.

Paris Hilton, b 2/17/81 (New York, NY), heiress; actress.

Perez Hilton, b 3/23/78 (Miami, FL), gossip columnist.

Christopher Hitchens, b 4/13/49 (Portsmouth, Eng., UK), journalist, author.

James P. Hoffa, b 5/19/41 (Detroit, MI), Teamsters Union head.

Eric Holder Jr., b 1/21/51 (Bronx, NY), first African American U.S. atty. gen.

David Horowitz, b 1/10/39 (New York, NY), consumer advocate, columnist, author.

Steny H. Hoyer, b 6/14/39 (New York, NY), House minority whip, former majority leader (D, MD).

Mike Huckabee, b 8/24/55 (Hope, AR), former gov. (R, AR), minister, 2008 pres. contender, TV host.

Arianna Huffington, b 7/15/50 (Athens, Greece), political commentator.

Jon Huntsman Jr., b 3/26/60 (Palo Alto, CA), former UT gov. (R), ambassador to China; 2012 pres. contender.

H. Wayne Huizenga, b 12/29/39 (Evergreen Park, IL), entrepreneur, sports exec.

Brit Hume, b 6/22/43 (Washington, DC), TV journalist on FOX.

Kay Bailey Hutchison, b 7/22/43 (Galveston, TX), senator (R, TX).

Lee Iacocca, b 10/15/24 (Allentown, PA), former auto exec.

Carl Icahn, b 2/16/36 (Queens, NY), financier.

Gwen Ifill, b 9/29/55 (Queens, NY), TV journalist, moderator on PBS.

Don Imus, b 7/23/40 (Riverside, CA), talk-show host.

Daniel Inouye, b 9/7/24 (Honolulu, HI), senator (D, HI), President pro tempore.

Patricia Ireland, b 10/19/45 (Oak Park, IL), feminist leader.

Rev. Jesse Jackson, b 10/8/41 (Greenville, SC), civil rights leader, former pres. contender.

Lisa Jackson, b 2/8/62 (Philadelphia, PA), EPA administrator.

Marc Jacobs, b 4/9/64 (New York, NY), fashion designer.

Valerie Jarrett, b 11/14/56 (Shiraz, Iran), sr. adviser to Pres. Obama.

Bobby Jindal, b 6/10/71 (Baton Rouge, LA), LA governor (R), first elected Indian American governor.

Jasper Johns, b 5/15/30 (Augusta, GA), artist.

Gary Johnson, b 1/1/53 (Minot, ND), former NM governor (R); 2012 pres. contender.

Robert L. Johnson, b 4/8/46 (Hickory, MS), Black Entertainment Television founder and CEO.

Vernon E. Jordan Jr., b 8/15/35 (Atlanta, GA), attorney, former pres. adviser, civil rights leader.

Elena Kagan, b 4/28/60 (New York, NY), Supreme Court justice.

Tim Kaine, b 2/26/58 (St. Paul, MN), former Dem Natl. Committee chair, VA governor.

Donna Karan, b 10/2/48 (Forest Hills, Queens, NY), fashion designer.

Jeffrey Katzenberg, b 12/21/50 (New York, NY), entertainment exec.

Thomas Kean, b 4/21/35 (New York, NY), 9/11 commission chair, former Drew Univ. pres., former NJ gov.

Garrison Keillor, b 8/7/42 (Anoka, MN), author, broadcaster.

Mark Kelly, b 2/21/64 (Orange, NJ), U.S. Navy capt., NASA shuttle commander.

Anthony M. Kennedy, b 7/23/36 (Sacramento, CA), Supreme Court justice.

Kirk Kerkorian, b 6/6/17 (Fresno, CA), pres. and CEO of investment firm Tracinda Corp.

Robert (Bob) Kerrey, b 8/27/43 (Lincoln, NE), former senator (D, NE); president of the New School (NYC).

John Kerry, b 12/11/43 (Aurora, CO), senator (D, MA), Foreign Relations Committee chair, 2004 pres. candidate.

Larry King, b 11/19/33 (Brooklyn, NY), TV talk show host.

Michael Kinsley, b 3/9/51 (Detroit, MI), editor, political commentator.

Calvin Klein, b 11/19/42 (Bronx, NY), fashion designer.

Philip H. Knight, b 2/24/38 (Portland, OR), founder and chairman of the board of Nike.

Edward I. Koch, b 12/12/24 (Bronx, NY), former NYC mayor.

Ted Koppel, b 2/8/40 (Lancashire, Eng., UK), former ABC network TV journalist; former anchor of *Nightline*.

Larry Kramer, b 6/25/35 (Bridgeport, CT), AIDS activist, writer.

Nicholas D. Kristof, b 4/27/59 (Chicago, IL), Pulitzer Prize winning columnist, author.

William Kristol, b 12/23/52 (New York, NY), editor, columnist.

Steve Kroft, b 8/22/45 (Kokomo, IN), TV journalist.

Paul Krugman, b 2/28/53 (Long Island, NY), economist, columnist.

Dennis Kucinich, b 10/8/46 (Cleveland, OH), U.S. rep. (D, OH), pres. contender.

Jon Kyl, b 4/25/42 (Oakland, NE), senator (R, AZ), Senate minority whip.

Brian Lamb, b 10/9/41 (Lafayette, IN), cable TV exec., journalist.

Matt Lauer, b 12/30/57 (New York, NY), TV journalist; NBC *Today* show co-host.

Ralph Lauren, b 10/14/39 (Bronx, NY), fashion designer.

Bernard F. Law, b 11/4/31 (Torreon, Mexico), cardinal archbishop emeritus of Boston.

Patrick Leahy, b 3/31/40 (Montpelier, VT), senator (D, VT), Judiciary Committee chair.

Norman Lear, b 7/27/22 (New Haven, CT), TV producer, political activist.

Jim Lehrer, b 5/19/34 (Wichita, KS), TV journalist, author.

Carl Levin, b 6/28/34 (Detroit, MI), senator (D, MI), Armed Services Committee chair.

Monica Lewinsky, b 7/23/73 (San Francisco, CA), former White House intern.

Joseph Lieberman, b 2/24/42 (Stamford, CT), senator (ind., CT), former vice pres. candidate, 2004 pres. contender.

Rush Limbaugh, b 1/12/51 (Cape Girardeau, MO), radio talk-show host.

Gary Locke, b 1/21/50 (Seattle, WA), first Chinese-Amer. U.S. ambassador to China, former commerce secretary, WA governor (D).

Trent Lott, b 10/9/41 (Grenada, MS), former senator (R, MS) and majority leader.

Shannon Lucid, b 1/14/43 (Shanghai, China), NASA scientist, astronaut.

Richard Lugar, b 4/4/32 (Indianapolis, IN), senator (R, IN).

Rachel Maddow, b 4/1/73 (Castro Valley, CA), TV/radio host, political commentator.

Bernie Madoff, b 4/29/38 (Queens, NY), financier who swindled investors; sentenced to 150 years in prison.

Roger Mahony, b 2/27/36 (Hollywood, CA), Rom. Cath. cardinal, archbishop of Los Angeles.

Mary Matalin, b 8/19/53 (Chicago, IL), political commentator.

Chris Matthews, b 12/18/45 (Philadelphia, PA), TV journalist.

John McCain, b 8/29/36 (Panama Canal Zone), senator (R, AZ), 2008 Republican presidential candidate.

Kevin McCarthy, b 1/26/65 (Bakersfield, CA), U.S. rep. (R, CA), House majority whip.

Mitch McConnell, b 2/20/42 (Tuscumbia, AL), senator (R, KY), Senate minority leader.

David McCullough, b 7/7/33 (Pittsburgh, PA), historian, biographer.

George McGovern, b 7/19/22 (Avon, SD), former senator (D, SD), 1972 pres. nominee.

Dr. Phil McGraw, b 9/1/50 (Vinita, OK), talk-show host, motivational speaker, author.

James McGreevey, b 8/6/57 (Jersey City, NJ), former NJ governor (D); resigned amid allegations of sexual harassment and admitted he was gay.

John McLaughlin, b 3/29/27 (Providence, RI), TV journalist.

Russell Means, b 11/10/39 (Pine Ridge Indian Reserv., SD), Native American activist.

Kate Michelman, b 8/4/42 (NJ), abortion-rights activist.

Kate Millett, b 9/14/34 (St. Paul, MN), author, feminist.

George Mitchell, b 8/20/33, (Waterville, ME), former spec. envoy for Middle East peace, Senate majority leader (D, ME), diplomat, Disney Co. chairman.

Walter Mondale, b 1/5/28 (Ceylon, MN), former vice pres., senator (D, MN), 1984 pres. nominee.

Michael Moore, b 4/23/54 (Davison, MI), activist, documentary filmmaker, author.

Bill Moyers, b 6/5/34 (Hugo, OK), TV journalist, author.

Robert S. Mueller III, b 8/7/44 (New York, NY), FBI director.

Michael Mullen, b 10/4/46 (Los Angeles, CA), chairman of Joint Chiefs of Staff.

Rupert Murdoch, b 3/11/31 (Melbourne, Aust.), media exec.

Ralph Nader, b 2/27/34 (Winsted, CT), consumer advocate, independent pres. cand. in 1996, 2000, 2004, and 2008.

Janet Napolitano, b 11/29/57 (New York, NY), homeland security sec., former AZ governor.

John Negroponte, b 7/21/39 (London, Eng., UK), former director of National Intelligence, former U.S. rep. to UN.

Craig Newmark, b 12/6/52 (Morristown, NY), founder of Craigslist.com.

Peggy Noonan, b 9/7/50 (Brooklyn, NY), columnist, speechwriter.

Oliver North, b 10/7/43 (San Antonio, TX), talk-show host, former Natl. Sec. Council aide, figure in Iran-contra scandal.

Eleanor Holmes Norton, b 6/13/37 (Washington, DC), U.S. House delegate for Washington, DC (D).

Sam Nunn, b 9/8/38 (Perry, GA), former senator (D, GA).

Barack Obama, b 8/4/61 (Honolulu, HI), U.S. president, former senator (D, IL).

Michelle Obama, b 1/17/64 (Chicago, IL), first lady, lawyer.

Soledad O'Brien, b 9/19/66 (Smithtown, NY), TV journalist.

Sandra Day O'Connor, b 3/26/30 (El Paso, TX), former Supreme Court justice.

Todd Oldham, b 11/22/61 (Corpus Christi, TX), fashion designer.

Keith Olbermann, b 1/27/59 (New York, NY), TV news anchor and commentator, former ESPN host.

Bill O'Reilly, b 9/10/49 (New York, NY), TV commentator, host.

Joel Osteen, b 3/5/63 (Houston, TX), televangelist, author.

Michael Ovitz, b 12/14/46 (Encino, CA), entertainment exec.

Clarence Page, b 6/2/47 (Dayton, OH), journalist, TV commentator.

Lawrence Page, b 9/26/73 (East Lansing, MI), cofounder of Google.

Camille Paglia, b 4/2/47 (Endicott, NY), scholar, author.

Sarah Palin, b 2/11/64 (Sandpoint, ID), former AK governor, 2008 Republican vice-pres. nominee.

Leon E. Panetta, b 6/28/38 (Monterey, CA), sec. of defense; former CIA director, White House chief of staff, U.S. rep. (D, CA).

Richard Parsons, b 4/4/48 (Brooklyn, NY), Citigroup chairman, former Time Warner CEO.

David Paterson, b 5/20/54 (Brooklyn, NY), attorney, former NY governor (D).

Ron Paul, b 8/20/35 (Pittsburgh, PA), physician, U.S. rep. (R, TX), pres. contender (2008, 2012).

Jane Pauley, b 10/31/50 (Indianapolis, IN), TV journalist.

Henry Paulson, b 3/28/46 (Palm Beach, FL), former sec. of treasury, former CEO/chairman of Goldman Sachs.

Tim Pawlenty, b 11/27/60 (St. Paul, MN), former MN governor (R).

Nancy Pelosi, b 3/26/40 (Baltimore, MD), U.S. rep. (D, CA); House minority leader; former House speaker.

Ross Perot, b 6/27/30 (Texarkana, TX), entrepreneur, former pres. nominee.

Rick Perry, b 3/4/50 (Paint Creek, TX), TX governor (R), 2012 pres. contender.

David Petraeus, b 11/7/52 (Cornwall-on-Hudson, NY), CIA director; former U.S. Forces Afghanistan cmdr., CENTCOM cmdr.

Colin Powell, b 4/5/37 (New York, NY), former sec. of state, natl. security adviser, Joint Chiefs of Staff chairman.

Reince Priebus, b 3/18/72 (Kenosha, WI), Rep. Natl. Committee chair.

Dan Quayle, b 2/4/47 (Indianapolis, IN), former U.S. vice pres., senator (R, IN), pres. contender.

Anna Quindlen, b 7/8/53 (Philadelphia, PA), author, columnist.

Dan Rather, b 10/31/31 (Wharton, TX), TV journalist, retired CBS anchor.

Nancy Reagan, b 7/6/21 (Flushing, Queens, NY), former first lady.

Sumner Redstone, b 5/27/23 (Boston, MA), Viacom/CBS chairman.

Ralph Reed Jr., b 6/24/61 (Portsmouth, VA), political adviser.

Robert B. Reich, b 6/24/46 (Scranton, PA), economist, author, former labor sec.

Harry Reid, b 12/2/39 (Searchlight, NV), Senate majority leader (D, NV).

Janet Reno, b 7/21/38 (Miami, FL), former U.S. attorney gen.

Condoleezza Rice, b 11/14/54 (Birmingham, AL), former sec. of state, former natl. security adviser.

Susan Rice, b 11/17/64 (Washington, DC), U.S. ambassador to UN.

Frank Rich, b 6/2/49 (Washington, DC), essayist, columnist.

Cecile Richards, b 1958, pres. of Planned Parenthood.

Bill Richardson, b 11/15/47 (Pasadena, CA), NM gov., former energy sec., UN ambassador, U.S. rep. (D, NM); 2008 pres. contender.

Sally K. Ride, b 5/26/51 (Encino, CA), former astronaut, 1st U.S. woman in space.

Tom Ridge, b 8/26/45 (Munhall, PA), former sec. of homeland security, former PA gov.

Geraldo Rivera, b 7/4/43 (New York, NY), TV journalist.

Cokie Roberts, b 12/27/43 (New Orleans, LA), TV journalist.

John G. Roberts, b 1/27/55 (Buffalo, NY), Supreme Court chief justice.

Robin Roberts, b 11/23/60 (Tuskegee, AL), *Good Morning America* co-host.

Rev. Pat Robertson, b 3/22/30 (Lexington, VA), religious broadcasting exec., former pres. contender.

V. Gene Robinson, b 5/29/47 (Lexington, KY), first openly gay Episcopal bishop.

David Rockefeller, b 6/12/15 (New York, NY), banker.

Buddy Roemer, b 10/4/43 (Shreveport, LA), former LA governor, U.S. rep (D); 2012 pres. contender.

Al Roker, b 8/20/54 (Queens, NY), TV weather person.

Mitt Romney, b 3/12/47 (Detroit, MI), Rep. pres. contender (2008, 2012); former MA governor, Olympics organizer.

Andy Rooney, b 1/14/19 (Albany, NY), TV commentator.

Charlie Rose, b 1/5/42 (Henderson, NC), TV journalist.

Karl Rove, b 12/25/50 (Denver, CO), former adviser to Pres. G. W. Bush, political commentator.

Donald Rumsfeld, b 7/9/32 (Chicago, IL), former sec. of defense.

Paul Ryan, b 1/29/70 (Janesville, WI), U.S. rep (D, WI).

Morley Safer, b 11/8/31 (Toronto, ON, Can.), TV journalist.

Ken Salazar, b 3/2/55 (Alamosa, CO), interior sec., former sen. (D, CO), rancher.

Rick Santorum, b 5/10/58 (Winchester, VA), former sen. (R, PA), U.S. rep; 2012 pres. contender.

Diane Sawyer, b 12/22/45 (Glasgow, KY), TV journalist, anchor of ABC *World News With Diane Sawyer*.

Antonin Scalia, b 3/11/36 (Trenton, NJ), Supreme Court justice.

Bob Schieffer, b 2/25/37 (Austin, TX), CBS TV news anchor.

Phyllis Schlafly, b 8/15/24 (St. Louis, MO), political activist.

Caroline Kennedy Schlossberg, b 11/27/57 (New York, NY), author, daughter of Pres. Kennedy.

Eric Schmidt, b 4/27/55 (Washington, DC), Google CEO.

Patricia Schroeder, b 7/30/40 (Portland, OR), former U.S. rep. (D, CO) Assoc. of Am. Publishers CEO.

Rev. Robert Schuller, b 9/16/26 (Alton, IA), TV evangelist.

Debbie Wasserman Schultz, b. 9/27/66 (Forest Hills, NY), U.S. rep. (D, FL), Dem. Natl. Committee chair.

Charles Schumer, b 11/23/50 (Brooklyn, NY), senator (D, NY).

Arnold Schwarzenegger, b 7/30/47 (Thal, Styria, Austria), actor, former CA governor.

H. Norman Schwarzkopf, b 8/22/34 (Trenton, NJ), former military leader.

Willard Scott, b 3/7/34 (Alexandria, VA), former TV weather person.

Kathleen Sebelius, b 5/15/58 (Cincinnati, OH), health and human services secretary, former KS governor.

Allan H. (Bud) Selig, b 7/30/34 (Milwaukee, WI), MLB commissioner.

Richard Serra, b 11/2/39 (San Francisco, CA), sculptor.

Rev. Al Sharpton, b 10/3/54 (Brooklyn, NY), activist, civil rights leader, TV personality.

Eric Shinseki, b 11/28/42 (Lihue, HI), veterans affairs sec., former Army chief of staff.

Maria Shriver, b 11/6/55 (Chicago, IL), TV journalist, former CA first lady.

George P. Shultz, b 12/13/20 (New York, NY), former sec. of state, other cabinet posts.

Russell Simmons, b 10/4/57 (Queens, NY), music producer.

Bob Simon, b 5/29/41 (Bronx, NY), TV journalist.

O. J. Simpson, b 7/9/47 (San Francisco, CA), former football star, murder defendant.

Harry Smith, b 8/21/51 (Lansing, IL), NBC TV journalist, former CBS morning anchor.

Liz Smith, b 2/2/23 (Ft. Worth, TX), gossip columnist.

Hilda Solis, b 10/20/57 (Los Angeles, CA), labor sec., former U.S. rep. (D, CA).

George Soros, b 8/12/30 (Budapest, Hungary), financier, philanthropist.

Sonia Sotomayor, b 6/25/54 (Bronx, NY), Supreme Court justice.

David H. Souter, b 9/17/39 (Melrose, MA), former Supreme Court justice.

Kate Spade, b 1962 (Kansas City, MO), fashion designer.

Arlen Specter, b 2/12/30 (Wichita, KS), former senator (R then D, PA).

Steven Spielberg, b 12/18/46 (Cincinnati, OH), movie director, producer.

Eliot Spitzer, b 6/10/59 (Bronx, NY), former NY gov. (D); resigned after involvement with prostitutes exposed.

Lesley Stahl, b 12/16/41 (Swampscott, MA), TV journalist.

Kenneth Starr, b 7/21/46 (Vernon, TX), former Whitewater indep. counsel.

Michael Steele, b 10/19/58 (Prince George's Co., MD), former Rep. Natl. Committee chair, MD lt. gov.

Shelby Steele, b 1/1/46 (Chicago, IL), scholar, critic.

Ben Stein, b 11/25/44 (Washington, DC), attorney, columnist, former speechwriter, actor, TV personality.

Gloria Steinem, b 3/25/34 (Toledo, OH), author, feminist.

Frank Stella, b 5/12/36 (Malden, MA), painter.

George Stephanopoulos, b 2/10/61 (Fall River, MA), TV journalist, former pres. adviser; *Good Morning America* co-host.

David J. Stern, b 9/22/42 (New York, NY), NBA commissioner.

Howard Stern, b 1/12/54 (Roosevelt, NY), radio talk show host.

John Paul Stevens, b 4/20/20 (Chicago, IL), former Supreme Court justice.

Martha Stewart, b 8/3/41 (Nutley, NJ), homemaking adviser, entrepreneur, TV personality.

Biz Stone, b 3/10/74 (Boston, MA), cofounder of Twitter.

Chesley (Sully) Sullenberger III, b 1/23/51 (Denison, TX), US Airways pilot who safely landed a jet in the Hudson River.

Arthur Ochs Sulzberger Jr., b 9/22/51 (Mt. Kisco, NY), newspaper publisher.

Lawrence H. Summers, b 11/30/54 (New Haven, CT), economist; former Natl. Economic Council dir., Harvard Univ. pres., sec. of treasury.

George Tenet, b 1/5/53 (Flushing, Queens, NY), former CIA director.

Clarence Thomas, b 6/23/48 (Savannah, GA), Supreme Court justice.

Helen Thomas, b 8/4/20 (Winchester, KY), former journalist.

Richard Trumka, b 7/24/49 (Waynesburg, PA), pres. of AFL-CIO.

Donald Trump, b 6/14/46 (Jamaica, Queens, NY), real estate exec., TV personality.

Ted Turner, b 11/19/38 (Cincinnati, OH), TV exec., philanthropist.

Neil deGrasse Tyson, b 10/5/58 (New York, NY), astrophysicist, director of NYC's Hayden Planetarium, author, TV host.

Abigail Van Buren, b 7/4/18 (Sioux City, IA), retired advice columnist.

Gloria Vanderbilt, b 2/20/24 (New York, NY), fashion designer, heiress.

Greta Van Susteren, b 6/11/54 (Appleton, WI), attorney, TV journalist.

Jesse Ventura, b 7/15/51 (Minneapolis, MN), former wrestler, former MN governor; radio talk show host.

Meredith Vieira, b 12/30/53 (Providence, RI), former *Today* show co-host.

Antonio Villaraigosa, b 1/23/53 (East Los Angeles, CA), 1st Hispanic mayor of L.A. since 1870s.

Paul Volcker, b 9/5/27 (Cape May, NJ), economist, former Federal Reserve chairman.

Mike Wallace, b 5/9/18 (Brookline, MA), TV journalist.

Barbara Walters, b 9/25/31 (Boston, MA), TV journalist.

Vera Wang, b 6/27/49 (New York, NY), fashion designer.

Rick Warren, b 1/28/54 (San Jose, CA), evangelical Christian pastor, founder of Saddleback Church, author.

James Watson, b 4/6/28 (Chicago, IL), biochemist, DNA pioneer, co-winner of the 1962 Nobel Prize.

Dr. Andrew Weil, b 6/8/42 (Philadelphia, PA), health adviser.

Anthony Weiner, b 9/4/64 (Brooklyn, NY), former U.S. rep. (D, NY); resigned after 2011 scandal.

Harvey Weinstein, b 3/19/52 (Flushing, Queens, NY), movie exec.

Jack Welch, b 11/19/35 (Peabody, MA), former General Electric CEO.

Jann Wenner, b 1/7/46 (New York, NY), publisher, founder of *Rolling Stone*.

Cornel West, b 6/23/53 (Tulsa, OK), African American scholar, critic.

Ruth Westheimer, b 6/4/28 (Frankfurt am Main, Germany), human sexuality expert.

Meg Whitman, b 8/4/56 (Cold Spring Harbor, NY), 2010 CA gubernatorial candidate (R), former eBay CEO; HP CEO.

Elie Wiesel, b 9/30/28 (Sighet, Romania), scholar, author, 1986 Nobel Peace Prize winner.

George Will, b 5/4/41 (Champaign, IL), journalist, author.

Brian Williams, b 5/5/59 (Elmira, NY), NBC TV news anchor.

Evan Williams, b 3/31/72 (Clarks, NE), cofounder and CEO of Twitter.

Jody Williams, b 10/9/50 (Brattleboro, VT), peace activist, 1997 Nobel Peace Prize winner.

Oprah Winfrey, b 1/29/54 (Kosciusko, MS), TV and media personality, businesswoman, actress.

Bob Woodward, b 3/26/43 (Geneva, IL), journalist; with Bernstein cracked Watergate scandal.

Steve Wynn, b 1/27/42 (New Haven, CT), casino developer.

Paula Zahn, b 2/24/56 (Omaha, NE), TV journalist.

Mark Zuckerberg, b 5/14/84 (Dobbs Ferry, NY), founder of Facebook.

Mortimer Zuckerman, b 6/4/37 (Montreal, QC, Can.), publisher, columnist.

Widely Known World Personalities of the Present

Living non-Americans only. Generally excludes current heads of state or government (see Nations chapter) and excludes most others covered elsewhere, such as in Widely Known Americans, Entertainment and Writers lists, or Sports Personalities.

Mahmoud Abbas (Abu Mazen), b 3/26/35 (Safed, Palestine [now Israel]), president of the Palestinian National Authority.

Gerry Adams, b 10/6/48 (Belfast, N. Ireland, UK), Sinn Fein leader.

Viswanathan Anand, b 12/11/69 (Chennai, Madras, India), world chess champion.

Prince Andrew, b 2/19/60 (London, Eng., UK), Duke of York (2nd son of Queen Elizabeth II).

Kofi Annan, b 4/8/38 (Kumasi, Ghana), former UN sec.-gen.; 2001 Nobel laureate.

Princess Anne, b 8/15/50 (London, Eng., UK), Princess Royal (daughter of Queen Elizabeth II).

Michael Arad, b 1969 (Jerusalem, Israel), designer of the Natl. 9/11 Memorial in NYC.

Oscar Arias Sánchez, b 9/13/41 (Heredia, Costa Rica), former Costa Rican pres., peace negotiator, 1987 Nobel laureate.

Giorgio Armani, b 7/30/34 (Piacenza, Italy), fashion designer.

Julian Assange, b 7/3/71 (Townsville, Queensland, Australia), editor-in-chief and founder of WikiLeaks media organization.

Ban Ki-Moon, b 6/13/44 (Umsong, [now] South Korea), UN sec.-gen.

Ehud Barak, b 2/12/42 (Mishmar Ha-Sharon Kibbutz, Israel), Israeli minister of defense, former Israeli prime min.

Ahmed Ben Bella, b 12/25/18 (Marnia, Algeria), 1st Algerian prime min.; revolutionary leader.

Benedict XVI (Joseph Ratzinger), b 4/16/27 (Marktl am Inn, Germany), pope of Rom. Cath. Church, elected 2005.

Boris Berezovsky, b 1/23/46 (Moscow, USSR), businessman, politician.

Tim Berners-Lee, b 6/8/55 (London, Eng., UK), World Wide Web inventor.

Tony Blair, b 5/6/53 (Edinburgh, Scot., UK), former British prime minister.

Hans Blix, b 6/28/28 (Uppsala, Swed.), former UN weapons inspector.

Bono (Paul David Hewson), b 5/20/60 (Glasnevin, Dublin, Ire., UK), musician, social activist, philanthropist.

Fernando Botero, b 4/19/32 (Medellín, Col.), Colombian artist.

Boutros Boutros-Ghali, b 11/14/22 (Cairo, Egypt), former UN sec.-gen.

Richard Branson, b 7/18/50 (S. London, Eng., UK), British Virgin Records and Airways founder.

Gordon Brown, b 2/20/51 (Glasgow, Scot., UK), former Brnstein prime minister.

Tina Brown, b 11/21/53 (Maidenhead, Eng., UK), journalist, TV talk show host, author.

Carla Bruni, b 12/23/67 (Turin, Italy), first lady of France, musician, actress, model.

Mark Burnett, b 7/17/60 (Myland, Eng., UK), reality TV producer.

Rhonda Byrne, b 3/12/51 (Australia), author, TV writer and producer.

Kim Campbell, b 3/10/47 (Port Alberni, BC, Can.), former Canadian prime min.

Pierre Cardin, b 7/7/22 (San Biaggio di Callalta, Italy), fashion designer.

Princess Caroline, b 1/23/57 (Monte Carlo, Monaco), Monaco royal (eldest daughter of Prince Rainier and Princess Grace).

Fidel Castro, b 8/13/26 (Birán, Cuba), former prime minister of Cuba.

Prince Charles, b 11/14/48 (London, Eng., UK), Prince of Wales (eldest son of Queen Elizabeth II); heir to British throne.

Jacques Chirac, b 11/29/32 (Paris, France), former president of France.

Deepak Chopra, b 1946 (New Delhi, India), new age writer.

Jean Chrétien, b 1/11/34 (Shawinigan, QC, Can.), former Canadian prime min.

Christo (Javacheff), b 6/13/35 (Gabrovo, Bulg.), artist.

Joe (Charles Joseph) Clark, b 6/5/39 (High River, AB, Can.), former Canadian prime min.

King Constantine II, b 6/2/40 (Psychiko, Greece), former king of Greece.

Simon Cowell, b 10/7/59 (Brighton, East Sussex, Eng., UK), music executive, TV producer, former *American Idol* host.

Dalai Lama (Tenzin Gyatso), b 7/6/35 (Taktser, Amdo, Tibet), Buddhist leader; 1989 Nobel Peace Prize laureate.

Richard Dawkins, b 3/26/41 (Nairobi, Kenya), ethologist, evolutionary biologist, author.

Shirin Ebadi, b 6/21/47 (Hamadan, Iran), human rights activist, 2003 Nobel Peace Prize winner.

Prince Edward, b 3/10/64 (London, Eng., UK), Earl of Essex (3rd son of Queen Elizabeth II).

Mohamed ElBaradei, b 6/17/42 (Cairo, Egypt), former director general of the International Atomic Energy Agency (IAEA); 2005 Nobel Peace Prize winner.

Prince Felipe, b 1/30/68 (Madrid, Spain), heir to Spanish throne.

Sarah Ferguson, b 10/15/58 (London, Eng., UK), Duchess of York, ex-wife of Prince Andrew.

John Galliano, b 11/28/60 (Gibraltar, UK terr.), fashion designer.

Wael Ghonim, b 12/23/80 (Cairo, Egypt), computer engineer and Internet activist who sparked Egyptian revolution (2011).

Valery Giscard d'Estaing, b 2/2/26 (Koblenz, Ger.), former French pres.

Jane Goodall, b 4/3/34 (London, Eng., UK), anthropologist, primatologist.

Mikhail Gorbachev, b 3/2/31 (Privolnoye, USSR), former Soviet pres.; 1990 Nobel Peace Prize winner.

Jürgen Habermas, b 6/18/29 (Dusseldorf, Ger.), philosopher.

Vaclav Havel, b 10/5/36 (Prague, Czech.), former Czech pres.; playwright.

Stephen Hawking, b 1/8/42 (Oxford, Eng., UK), physicist, author.

Carlos Slim Helú, 1/28/40 (Mexico City, Mexico), chairman and CEO of Telmex, Telcel and América Móvil.

Prince Henry (Harry) (of Wales), b 9/15/84 (London, Eng., UK), son of Prince Charles; 3rd in line to British throne.

Damien Hirst, b 6/7/65 (Bristol, Eng., UK), artist.

David Hockney, b 7/9/37 (Bradford, Eng., UK), artist.

Jiang Zemin, b 8/17/26 (Yangzhou, Jiangsu Prov., China), former pres. of China.

Garry Kasparov, b 4/13/63 (Baku, Azerbaijan, USSR), former world chess champion; Russian pro-democracy leader.

Ayatollah Ali Khamenei, b 7/17/39 (Mashhad, Iran), Supreme Leader and former president of Iran, cleric, author.

F. W. (Frederik Willem) de Klerk, b 3/18/36 (Johannesburg, S. Africa), former S. African pres.; 1993 Nobel Peace Prize winner.

Kim Jong-un, b 1983? (North Korea), heir apparent to North Korean leader Kim Jong-il.

Helmut Kohl, b 4/3/30 (Ludwigshafen, Ger.), former German chancellor.

Hans Kung, b 3/19/28 (Sursee, Switz.), Rom. Cath. theologian.

Karl Lagerfeld, b 9/10/38 (Hamburg, Germany), fashion designer.

Richard Leakey, b 12/19/44 (Nairobi, Kenya), anthropologist, paleontologist, conservationist.

Tzipi Livni, b 7/5/58 (Tel Aviv, Israel), attorney, head of Israeli Kadima party, foreign affairs minister of Israel.

John Major, b 3/29/43 (Wimbledon, Eng., UK), former British prime min.

Nelson Mandela, b 7/18/18 (Transkei, S. Africa), former pres. of S. Africa; 1993 Nobel Peace Prize winner.

Imelda Marcos, b 7/2/29 (Manila, Philip.), former first lady of Philippines; Philip. House of Rep. member.

Paul Martin, b 8/28/38 (Windsor, ON, Can.), former prime minister of Canada.

Peter Max, b 10/19/37 (Berlin, Ger.), artist, designer.

Stella McCartney, b 9/13/71 (London, Eng., UK), fashion designer.

Angela Merkel, b 7/17/54 (Hamburg, Ger.), 1st woman chancellor of Germany.

Jean-Marie Messier, b 12/13/56 (Grenoble, Fr.), former CEO of Vivendi Universal.

Empress Michiko, b 10/20/34 (Tokyo, Japan), empress of Japan.

Kate Middleton (Catherine, Duchess of Cambridge), b 1/9/82 (Reading, UK), wife of Prince William.

Pippa Middleton, b 9/6/83 (Reading, UK), event planner; socialite sister of Catherine, Duchess of Cambridge.

Rev. Sun Myung Moon, b 1/6/20 (Kwangju Sangsa Ri, N. Korea), Unification Church founder.

Kate Moss, b 1/16/74 (Addiscombe, Surrey, Eng., UK), model.

Mir Hussein Moussavi, b 9/29/41 (Khameneh, Iran), challenger in Iran's 2009 presidential election.

Hosni Mubarak, b 5/4/28 (Kafre al-Musailha, Egypt), deposed Egyptian president.

Brian Mulroney, b 3/20/39 (Baie-Comeau, QC, Can.), former Canadian prime min.

Prince Naruhito, b 2/23/60 (Tokyo, Japan), crown prince of Japan.

Hassan Nasrallah, b 8/31/60 (Qarantina, Lebanon), leader of the Hezbollah in Lebanon.

Queen Noor (Lisa Halaby), b 8/23/51 (Washington, DC), American-born widow of Jordan's King Hussein.

Ehud Olmert, b 9/30/45 (Binyamina, Palestine), former prime minister of Israel.

Daniel Ortega Saavedra, b 11/11/45 (La Libertad, Nicar.), Nicaraguan pres., Sandinista leader.

Camilla Parker-Bowles, Duchess of Cornwall, b 7/17/47 (London, Eng., UK), wife of Prince Charles.

Jean-Marie le Pen, b 6/20/28 (La Trinite-sur-Mer, Fr.), French right-wing politician.

Marine Le Pen, b 8/5/68 (Neuilly-sur-Seine, France), head of France's National Front Party.

Javier Perez de Cuellar, b 1/19/20 (Lima, Peru), former UN sec.-gen.

Prince Philip, b 6/10/21 (Corfu, Greece), Duke of Edinburgh (husband of Queen Elizabeth II).

Gerhard Richter, b 2/9/32 (Dresden, Ger.), artist.

Mary Robinson, b 5/21/44 (Ballina, Co. Mayo, Ireland), former Irish pres., former UN High Commissioner for Human Rights.

Ségolène Royal, b 9/22/53 (Dakar, Senegal), French socialist politician, 2007 candidate for president of France.

Muqtada al-Sadr, b 8/12/73? (Najaf, Iraq), extremist Shiite cleric.

Carlos Salinas de Gortari, b 4/3/48 (Mexico City, Mex.), former Mexican pres.

Helmut Schmidt, b 12/23/18 (Hamburg, Germany), former German chancellor.

Gerhard Schröder, b 4/7/44 (Mossenburg, Germany), former German chancellor.

Yitzhak Shamir, b 10/22/15 (Kuzinoy, Poland), former Israeli prime minister.

Ariel Sharon, b 2/26/28 (Kfar Malal, Palestine), former Israeli prime minister.

Eduard Shevardnadze, b 1/25/28 (Mamati, Georgia, USSR), former Georgian pres.

Ayatollah Ali al-Sistani, b 8/4/30 (Mashhad, Iran), major Iraqi Shiite religious leader.

Princess Stephanie, b 2/1/65 (Monte Carlo, Monaco), youngest child of Prince Rainier and Princess Grace.

Dominique Strauss-Kahn, b 4/25/49 (Neuilly-sur-Seine, France), former International Monetary Fund managing director.

Aung San Suu Kyi, b 6/19/45 (Rangoon, Myanmar), political activist, 1991 Nobel Peace Prize winner; under effective house arrest.

Valentina Tereshkova, b 3/6/37 (Maslennikovo, Russia, USSR), 1st woman in space.

Margaret Thatcher, b 10/13/25 (Grantham, Eng., UK), former British prime min.

John Napier Turner, b 6/7/29 (Richmond, Surrey, Eng., UK), former Canadian prime min.

Desmond Tutu, b 10/7/31 (Klerksdorp, Transvaal, S. Africa), former S. African archbishop; 1984 Nobel Peace Prize winner.

Lech Walesa, b 9/29/43 (Popowo, Pol.), Solidarity leader; 1983 Nobel Peace Prize winner; former president of Poland.

Prince William (of Wales), b 6/21/82 (London, Eng., UK), son of Prince Charles; 2nd in line to British throne.

Rowan Williams, b 6/14/50 (Ystradgynlais, Wales, UK), Archbishop of Canterbury.

Xi Jinping, b 6/1/53 (Shaanxi, Fuping, China), Communist party leader.

Muhammad Yunus, b 6/28/40 (Chittagong, India), 2006 Nobel Peace prize winner, economics professor.

Ayman al-Zawahiri, b 6/19/51 (Cairo, Egypt), reputed high-ranking al-Qaeda leader.

Architects

Alvar Aalto, 1898-1976, Säynätsalo, Jyväskylä, Finland; Vuoksenniska Church, Vuoksenniska, Finland.

Max Abramovitz, 1908-2004, Avery Fisher Hall, New York, NY; U.S. Steel Bldg. (now USX Towers), Pittsburgh, PA.

Tadao Ando, b 1941, Modern Art Museum, Ft. Worth, TX; Stone Hill Center, MA.

Henry Bacon, 1866-1924, Lincoln Memorial, Washington, DC.

Benjamin Banneker, 1731-1806, African American inventor, astronomer, mathematician; helped design and lay out Washington, DC.

Pietro Belluschi, 1899-1994, Juilliard School, Lincoln Center, Pan Am Bldg. (now MetLife Bldg.) with Walter Gropius, New York, NY.

Marcel Breuer, 1902-81, Whitney Museum of American Art (with Hamilton Smith), New York, NY.

Charles Bulfinch, 1763-1844, State House, Boston, MA; Capitol (part), Washington, DC.

Gordon Bunshaft, 1909-90, Lever House, Park Ave., New York, NY; Hirshhorn Museum, Washington, DC.

Daniel H. Burnham, 1846-1912, Union Station, Washington, DC; Flatiron Bldg., New York, NY.

Irwin Chanin, 1892-1988, theaters, skyscrapers, New York, NY.

David Childs, b 1941, Washington Mall Master Plan/Constitution Gardens, Washington, DC; WTC Freedom Tower, New York, NY.

Lucio Costa, 1902-98, master plan for city of Brasilia, Brazil (with Oscar Niemeyer).

Ralph Adams Cram, 1863-1942, Cath. of St. John the Divine, New York, NY; U.S. Military Acad. (part), West Point, NY.

Norman Foster, b 1935, Commerzbank Headquarters, Frankfurt-am-Main, Ger.;

London Millennium Bridge, Eng., UK; 30 St. Mary Axe, Eng., UK.

James Ingo Freed, 1930-2005, Holocaust Memorial Museum, Washington, DC; Jacob K. Javits Center, New York, NY.

R. Buckminster Fuller, 1895-1983, U.S. Pavilion (geodesic domes), Expo 67, Montreal, QC, Can.

Frank O. Gehry, b 1929, Guggenheim Museum, Bilbao, Spain; Experience Music Project, Seattle, WA; Walt Disney Concert Hall, Los Angeles, CA.

Cass Gilbert, 1859-1934, Custom House, Woolworth Bldg., New York, NY; Supreme Court Bldg., Washington, DC.

Bertram G. Goodhue, 1869-1924, Capitol, Lincoln, NE; St. Thomas's Church, St. Bartholomew's Church, New York, NY.

Michael Graves, b 1934, Portland Bldg., Portland, OR; Humana Bldg., Louisville, KY.

Walter Gropius, 1883-1969, Pan Am Bldg. (now MetLife Bldg.) (with Pietro Belluschi), New York, NY.

Zaha Hadid, b 1950, Rosenthal Center for Contemporary Art, Cincinnati, OH; London Aquatics Centre, Eng., UK.

Lawrence Halprin, 1916-2009, Ghirardelli Sq., San Francisco, CA; Nicollet Mall, Minneapolis, MN; FDR Memorial, Washington, DC.

Peter Harrison, 1716-75, Touro Synagogue, Redwood Library, Newport, RI.

Wallace K. Harrison, 1895-1981, Metropolitan Opera House, Lincoln Center, New York, NY.

Thomas Hastings, 1860-1929, NY Public Library (with John Carrère), Frick Mansion, New York, NY.

James Hoban, 1762-1831, White House, Washington, DC.

Raymond Hood, 1881-1934, Rockefeller Center (part), Daily News Bldg., New York, NY; Tribune Tower, Chicago, IL.

Richard M. Hunt, 1827-95, Metropolitan Museum (part), New York, NY; Biltmore Estate, Asheville, NC.

Helmut Jahn, b 1940, United Airlines Terminal, O'Hare Airport, Chicago, IL.

William Le Baron Jenney, 1832-1907, Home Insurance Bldg. (demolished 1931), Chicago, IL.

Philip C. Johnson, 1906-2005, AT&T headquarters (now 550 Madison Ave.), New York, NY; Transco (now Williams) Tower, Houston, TX.

Albert Kahn, 1869-1942, General Motors Bldg., Detroit, MI.

Louis Kahn, 1901-74, Salk Laboratory, La Jolla, CA; Yale Art Gallery, New Haven, CT.

Christopher Grant LaFarge, 1862-1938, Roman Catholic Chapel, West Point, NY.

Benjamin H. Latrobe, 1764-1820, Capitol (part), Washington, DC; State Capitol Bldg., Richmond, VA.

Le Corbusier (Charles-Edouard Jeanneret), 1887-1965, Salvation Army Hostel, Swiss Dormitory, Paris, France; master plan for cities of Algiers and Buenos Aires.

William Lescaze, 1896-1969, Philadelphia Savings Fund Society, PA; Borg-Warner Bldg., Chicago, IL.

Daniel Libeskind, b 1946, primary architect for the rebuilding World Trade Center site, New York, NY.

Maya Lin, b 1959, Vietnam Veterans Mem., Washington, DC.

Charles Rennie Mackintosh, 1868-1928, Glasgow School of Art; Hill House, Helensburgh, Scot., UK.

Bernard R. Maybeck, 1862-1957, Hearst Hall, Univ. of CA, Berkeley; First Church of Christ Scientist, Berkeley, CA.

Charles F. McKim, 1847-1909, Boston Public Library; Columbia Univ. (part), New York, NY.

Charles M. McKim, b 1920, KUHT-TV Transmitter Bldg., Lutheran Church of the Redeemer, Houston, TX.

Richard Meier, b 1934, Getty Center Museum, Los Angeles, CA; High Museum of Art, Atlanta, GA.

Ludwig Mies van der Rohe, 1886-1969, Seagram Bldg. (with Philip C. Johnson), New York, NY; National Gallery, Berlin, Ger.

Robert Mills, 1781-1855, Washington Monument, Washington, DC.

Charles Moore, 1925-93, Sea Ranch, nr. San Francisco, CA; Piazza d'Italia, New Orleans, LA.

Julia Morgan, 1872-1957, San Simeon, CA.

Richard J. Neutra, 1892-1970, Mathematics Park, Princeton, NJ; Orange Co. Courthouse, Santa Ana, CA.

Oscar Niemeyer, b 1907, government buildings, Brasilia Palace Hotel, all Brasilia, Braz.

Gyo Obata, b 1923, Natl. Air & Space Museum, Smithsonian Inst., Washington, DC; Dallas-Ft. Worth Airport, TX.

Frederick L. Olmsted, 1822-1903, Central Park, New York, NY; Fairmount Park, Philadelphia, PA.

I(eoh) M(ing) Pei, b 1917, East Wing, Natl. Gallery of Art, Washington, DC; Pyramid, The Louvre, Paris, Fr.; Rock & Roll Hall of Fame and Museum, Cleveland, OH.

Cesar Pelli, b 1926, World Financial Center, Carnegie Hall Tower, New York, NY; Petronas Twin Towers, Malaysia.

William Pereira, 1909-85, Cape Canaveral, FL; Transamerica Bldg., San Francisco, CA.

Renzo Piano, b 1937, Pompidou Centre, Paris, Fr.; New York Times Building, New York, NY.

John Russell Pope, 1874-1937, National Gallery, Jefferson Memorial, Washington, DC.

John Portman, b 1924, Peachtree Center, Atlanta, GA.

George Browne Post, 1837-1913, NY Stock Exchange, New York, NY; Capitol, Madison, WI.

James Renwick Jr., 1818-95, Grace Church, St. Patrick's Cathedral, New York, NY; Smithsonian Institution (Castle), Washington, DC.

Henry H. Richardson, 1838-86, Trinity Church, Boston, MA.

Kevin Roche, b 1922, Oakland Museum, Oakland, CA; Fine Arts Center, University of Massachusetts, Amherst, MA.

James Gamble Rogers, 1867-1947, Columbia-Presbyterian Medical Ctr.,

New York, NY; Northwestern Univ., Evanston, IL.

John Wellborn Root, 1887-1963, Palmolive Bldg., Chicago, IL; Hotel Statler, Washington, DC.

Paul Rudolph, 1918-97, Jewitt Art Center, Wellesley College, MA; Art & Architecture Bldg., Yale Univ., New Haven, CT.

Eero Saarinen, 1910-61, Gateway to the West Arch, St. Louis, MO; Trans World Airlines Flight Center, New York, NY.

Kazuyo Sejima, b 1956, 21st Century Museum of Contemporary Art, Kanazawa, Japan (with Ryue Nishizawa).

Norma Merrick Sklarek, b 1928, Terminal One at Los Angeles International Airport, CA.

Louis Skidmore, 1897-1962, Atomic Energy Commission town site, Oak Ridge, TN; Terrace Plaza Hotel, Cincinnati, OH.

Clarence S. Stein, 1882-1975, Temple Emanu-El, New York, NY.

Edward Durell Stone, 1902-78, interior of Radio City Music Hall, Museum of Modern Art, New York, NY.

Louis H. Sullivan, 1856-1924, Auditorium Bldg., Chicago, IL.

Kenzo Tange, 1913-2005, Hiroshima Peace Park, 1964 Tokyo Olympics twin stadiums, Japan.

Richard Upjohn, 1802-78, Trinity Church, New York, NY.

Max O. Urbahn, 1912-95, Vehicle Assembly Bldg., Cape Canaveral, FL.

Joern Utzon, 1918-2008, Sydney Opera House, Australia.

William Van Alen, 1883-1954, Chrysler Building, New York, NY.

Robert Venturi, b 1925, Gordon Wu Hall, Princeton, NJ; Mielparque Nikko Kirifuri Resort, Japan.

Ralph T. Walker, 1889-1973, NY Telephone Bldg., New York, NY; IBM Research Lab, Poughkeepsie, NY.

Roland A. Wank, 1898-1970, Cincinnati Union Terminal, OH; head architect (1933-44), Tennessee Valley Authority.

Stanford White, 1853-1906, Washington Arch in Washington Square Park, first Madison Square Garden, New York, NY.

Christopher Wren, 1632-1723, St. Paul's Cathedral, London, Eng., UK.

Frank Lloyd Wright, 1867-1959, Imperial Hotel, Tokyo, Jpn.; Guggenheim Museum, New York, NY; Kaufmann "Fallingwater" house, Bear Run, PA; Taliesin West, Scottsdale, AZ.

William Wurster, 1895-1973, Ghirardelli Sq., San Francisco, CA.

Minoru Yamasaki, 1912-86, World Trade Center (destroyed 2001), New York, NY.

Artists, Photographers, and Sculptors of the Past

Artists are painters unless otherwise indicated.

Berenice Abbott, 1898-1991, (U.S.) photographer. Documentary of New York City, *Changing New York* (1939).

Ansel Easton Adams, 1902-84, (U.S.) photographer. Landscapes of the American Southwest.

Washington Allston, 1779-1843, (U.S.) landscapist. *Belshazzar's Feast*.

Albrecht Altdorfer, 1480-1538, (Ger.) landscapist.

Andrea del Sarto, 1486-1530, (It.) frescoes. *Madonna of the Harpies*.

Fra Angelico, c. 1400-55, (It.) Renaissance muralist. *Madonna of the Linen Drapers' Guild*.

Diane Arbus, 1923-71, (U.S.) photographer. Disturbing images.

Alexsandr Archipenko, 1887-1964, (U.S.) sculptor. *Boxing Match*, *Medranos*.

Jean Arp, 1887-1966, (Fr.) sculptor and painter, founder of Dada movement.

Eugène Atget, 1856-1927, (Fr.) photographer. Paris life.

John James Audubon, 1785-1851, (U.S.) *Birds of America*.

Hans Baldung-Grien, 1484-1545, (Ger.) *Todentanz*.

Ernst Barlach, 1870-1938, (Ger.) Expressionist sculptor. *Man Drawing a Sword*.

Frédéric-Auguste Bartholdi, 1834-1904, (Fr.) *Liberty Enlightening the World* (Statue of Liberty), *Lion of Belfort*.

Fra Bartolommeo, 1472-1517, (It.) *Vision of St. Bernard*.

Romare Bearden, 1911-88, (U.S.) collage and other media. *The Visitation*.

Aubrey Beardsley, 1872-98, (Br.) illustrator. *Salome*, *Lysistrata*, *Morte d'Arthur*, *Volpone*.

Max Beckmann, 1884-1950, (Ger.) Expressionist. *The Descent From the Cross*.

Gentile Bellini, 1426-1507, (It.) Renaissance. *Procession in St. Mark's Square*.

Giovanni Bellini, 1428-1516, (It.) Renaissance. *St. Francis in Ecstasy*.

Jacopo Bellini, 1400-70, (It.) Renaissance. *Crucifixion*.

George Wesley Bellows, 1882-1925, (U.S.) sports artist, portraitist, landscapist. *Stag at Sharkey's*, *Edith Clavell*.

Thomas Hart Benton, 1889-1975, (U.S.) American regionalist. *Threshing Wheat*, *Arts of the West*.

Ruth Bernhard, 1905-2006, (Ger.-U.S.) photographer. Black-and-white studies of female nudes.

Gianlorenzo Bernini, 1598-1680, (It.) Baroque sculptor. *The Assumption*.

Albert Bierstadt, 1830-1902, (U.S.) landscapist. *The Rocky Mountains*, *Mount Corcoran*.

George Caleb Bingham, 1811-79, (U.S.) American frontier. *Fur Traders Descending the Missouri*.

William Blake, 1757-1827, (Br.) engraver. *Book of Job*, *Songs of Innocence*, *Songs of Experience*.

Rosa Bonheur, 1822-99, (Fr.) realist. *The Horse Fair*.

Pierre Bonnard, 1867-1947, (Fr.) Intimist. *The Breakfast Room*, *Girl in a Straw Hat*.

Gutzon Borglum, 1867-1941, (U.S.) sculptor. Mt. Rushmore Memorial.

Hieronymus Bosch, 1450-1516, (Flem.) religious allegories. *The Crowning With Thorns*.

Sandro Botticelli, 1444-1510, (It.) Renaissance. *Birth of Venus*, *Adoration of the Magi*, *Guiliano de'Medici*.

Louise Bourgeois, 1911-2010, (Fr.) sculptor. *Maman*.

Margaret Bourke-White, 1904-71, (U.S.) photographer, photojournalist. WWII, USSR, rural South during the Depression.

Mathew Brady, c. 1823-96, (U.S.) official photographer of the Civil War.

Constantin Brancusi, 1876-1957, (Romania-Fr.) Nonobjective sculptor. *Flying Turtle, The Kiss*.

Georges Braque, 1882-1963, (Fr.) Cubist. *Violin and Palette*.

Pieter Bruegel the Elder, c. 1525-69, (Flem.) Renaissance. *The Peasant Dance, Hunters in the Snow, Magpie on the Gallows*.

Pieter Bruegel the Younger, 1564-1638, (Flem.) Baroque. *Village Fair, The Crucifixion*.

Edward Burne-Jones, 1833-98, (Br.) Pre-Raphaelite artist-craftsman. *The Mirror of Venus*.

Alexander Calder, 1898-1976, (U.S.) sculptor. *Lobster Trap and Fish Tail*.

Julia Margaret Cameron, 1815-79, (Br.) photographer, prominent portraitist.

Robert Capa (Endre Friedmann), 1913-54, (Hung.-U.S.) photographer, war photojournalist. Invasion of Normandy.

Michelangelo Merisi da Caravaggio, 1573-1610, (It.) Baroque. *The Supper at Emmaus*.

Emily Carr, 1871-1945, (Can.) landscapist. *Blunden Harbour, Big Raven, Rushing Sea of Undergrowth*.

Carlo Carrà, 1881-1966, (It.) Metaphysical school. *Lot's Daughters, The Enchanted Room*.

Henri Cartier-Bresson, 1908-2004, (Fr.) photographer. *Imagenes à la sauvette*.

Leonora Carrington, 1917-2011, (Br.) Surrealist. *The Inn of the Dawn Horse (Self-Portrait)*.

Mary Cassatt, 1844-1926, (U.S.) Impressionist. *The Cup of Tea, Woman Bathing, The Boating Party*.

George Catlin, 1796-1872, (U.S.) American Indian life. *Gallery of Indians, Buffalo Dance*.

Benvenuto Cellini, 1500-71, (It.) Mannerist sculptor, goldsmith. *Perseus and Medusa*.

Paul Cézanne, 1839-1906, (Fr.) Post-Impressionist. *Card Players, Mont-Sainte-Victoire With Large Pine Trees*.

Marc Chagall, 1887-1985, (Russ.) Jewish life and folklore. *I and the Village, The Praying Jew*.

Jean Simeon Chardin, 1699-1779, (Fr.) still lifes. *The Kiss, The Grace*.

Giorgio de Chirico, 1888-1978, (It.) founded the Metaphysical school. *Enigma of an Autumn Night*.

Frederick Church, 1826-1900, (U.S.) Hudson River school. *Niagara, Andes of Ecuador*.

Giovanni Cimabue, 1240-1302, (It.) Byzantine mosaicist. *Madonna Enthroned With St. Francis*.

Claude (Lorrain) (Claude Gellée), 1600-82, (Fr.) Ideal-landscapist. *The Enchanted Castle*.

Thomas Cole, 1801-48, (U.S.) Hudson River school. *The Ox-Bow, In the Catskills*.

John Constable, 1776-1837, (Br.) landscapist. *Salisbury Cathedral From the Bishop's Grounds*.

John Singleton Copley, 1738-1815, (U.S.) portraitist. *Samuel Adams, Watson and the Shark*.

Lovis Corinth, 1858-1925, (Ger.) Expressionist. *Apocalypse*.

Jean-Baptiste-Camille Corot, 1796-1875, (Fr.) landscapist. *Souvenir de Mortefontaine, Pastorale*.

Correggio, 1494-1534, (It.) Renaissance muralist. *Mystic Marriages of St. Catherine*.

Gustave Courbet, 1819-77, (Fr.) Realist. *The Artist's Studio*.

Lucas Cranach the Elder, 1472-1553, (Ger.) Protestant Reformation portraitist. *Luther*.

Imogen Cunningham, 1883-1976, (U.S.) photographer, portraitist. Plant photography.

Nathaniel Currier, 1813-88, and **James M. Ives**, 1824-95, (both U.S.) lithographers. *A Midnight Race on the Mississippi, American Forest Scene—Maple Sugaring*.

John Steuart Curry, 1897-1946, (U.S.) Americana, murals. *Baptism in Kansas*.

Salvador Dalí, 1904-89, (Sp.) Surrealist. *Persistence of Memory, The Crucifixion*.

Honoré Daumier, 1808-79, (Fr.) caricaturist. *The Third-Class Carriage*.

Jacques-Louis David, 1748-1825, (Fr.) Neoclassicist. *The Oath of the Horatii*.

Arthur Davies, 1862-1928, (U.S.) Romantic landscapist. *Unicorns, Leda and the Dioscuri*.

Edgar Degas, 1834-1917, (Fr.) realist/Impressionist. *The Ballet Class*.

Willem de Kooning, 1904-97, (Neth.-U.S.) Abstract Expressionist. *Excavation, Woman I, Door to the River*.

Eugène Delacroix, 1798-1863, (Fr.) Romantic. *Massacre at Chios, Liberty Leading the People*.

Paul Delaroche, 1797-1856, (Fr.) historical themes. *Children of Edward IV*.

Luca Della Robbia, 1400-82, (It.) Renaissance terracotta. *Cantoria* (singing gallery), Florence cathedral.

Donatello, 1386-1466, (It.) Renaissance sculptor. *David, Gattamelata*.

Aaron Douglas, 1899-79, (U.S.) Harlem Renaissance illustrator and muralist.

Jean Dubuffet, 1902-85, (Fr.) painter, sculptor, printmaker. *Group of Four Trees*.

Marcel Duchamp, 1887-1968, (Fr.) Dadaist. *Nude Descending a Staircase, No. 2*.

Raoul Dufy, 1877-1953, (Fr.) Fauvist. *Chateau and Horses*.

Asher Brown Durand, 1796-1886, (U.S.) Hudson River school. *Kindred Spirits*.

Albrecht Dürer, 1471-1528, (Ger.) Renaissance painter, engraver, woodcuts. *St. Jerome in His Study, Melencolia I*.

Anthony van Dyck, 1599-1641, (Flem.) Baroque portraitist. *Portrait of Charles I Hunting*.

Thomas Eakins, 1844-1916, (U.S.) Realist. *The Gross Clinic*.

Alfred Eisenstaedt, 1898-1995, (Ger.-U.S.) photographer, photojournalist. Famous photo, V-J Day, Aug. 14, 1945.

Peter Henry Emerson, 1856-1936, (Br.) photographer. Promoted photography as an independent art form.

Jacob Epstein, 1880-1959, (Br.) religious and allegorical sculptor. *Genesis, Ecce Homo*.

Erté (Romain de Tiertoff), 1892-1990, (Fr.) painter, fashion and stage designer.

Jan van Eyck, c. 1390-1441, (Flem.) naturalistic panels. *Adoration of the Lamb*.

Roger Fenton, 1819-69, (Br.) photographer. Crimean War.

Anselm Feuerbach, 1829-80, (Ger.) Romantic Classicist. *Judgment of Paris, Iphigenia*.

John Bernard Flannagan, 1895-1942, (U.S.) animal sculptor. *Triumph of the Egg*.

Jean-Honoré Fragonard, 1732-1806, (Fr.) Rococo. *The Swing*.

Daniel Chester French, 1850-1931, (U.S.) sculptor. *The Minute Man of Concord*; seated *Lincoln*, Lincoln Memorial, Washington, DC.

Lucian Freud, 1922-2011, (Ger.-Br.) portraitist. *Girl With Roses*.

Caspar David Friedrich, 1774-1840, (Ger.) Romantic landscapist. *Man and Woman Gazing at the Moon*.

Thomas Gainsborough, 1727-88, (Br.) portraitist. *The Blue Boy, The Watering Place, Orpin the Parish Clerk*.

Alexander Gardner, 1821-82, (U.S.) photographer. Civil War, railroad construction, Great Plains Indians.

Paul Gauguin, 1848-1903, (Fr.) Post-Impressionist. *The Tahitians, Spirit of the Dead Watching*.

Lorenzo Ghiberti, 1378-1455, (It.) Renaissance sculptor. "Gates of Paradise" baptistery doors, Florence, It.

Alberto Giacometti, 1901-66, (Switz.) attenuated sculptures of solitary figures. *Man Pointing*.

Giorgione, c. 1477-1510, (It.) Renaissance. *The Tempest*.

Giotto di Bondone, 1267-1337, (It.) Renaissance. *Presentation of Christ in the Temple*.

François Girardon, 1628-1715, (Fr.) Baroque sculptor of classical themes. *Apollo Tended by the Nymphs*.

Vincent van Gogh, 1853-90, (Neth.) *The Starry Night, L'Arlesienne, Bedroom at Arles, Self-Portrait*.

Edward Gorey, 1925-2000, (U.S.) illustrator. *The Doubtful Guest*.

Arshile Gorky, 1905-48, (U.S.) Surrealist. *The Liver Is the Cock's Comb*.

Francisco de Goya y Lucientes, 1746-1828, (Sp.) painter, printmaker. *The Naked Maja, The Disasters of War* (etchings).

El Greco (Domenikos Theotokopoulos), 1541-1614, (Gr.-Sp.) painter, sculptor. *View of Toledo, Assumption of the Virgin*.

Horatio Greenough, 1805-52, (U.S.) Neo-Classical sculptor.

Matthias Grünewald, 1480-1528, (Ger.) mystical religious themes. *The Resurrection*.

Frans Hals, c. 1580-1666, (Neth.) portraitist. *Laughing Cavalier, Gypsy Girl*.

Richard Hamilton, 1922-2011, (Br.) Pop artist. *Just What Is It That Makes Today's Homes So Different, So Appealing?*

Austin Hansen, 1910-96, (U.S.) photographer. Harlem, NY, life.

Childe Hassam, 1859-1935, (U.S.) Impressionist. *Southwest Wind, July 14 Rue Daunon*.

Edward Hicks, 1780-1849, (U.S.) folk. *The Peaceable Kingdom*.

Lewis Wickes Hine, 1874-1940, (U.S.) photographer. Studies of immigrants, children in industry.

Hans Hofmann, 1880-1966, (U.S.) early Abstract Expressionist. *Spring, The Gate*.

William Hogarth, 1697-1764, (Br.) caricaturist. *The Rake's Progress*.

Katsushika Hokusai, 1760-1849, (Jpn.) printmaker. *Crabs*.

Hans Holbein the Elder, 1460-1524, (Ger.) late Gothic. *Presentation of Christ in the Temple*.

Hans Holbein the Younger, 1497-1543, (Ger.) portraitist. *Henry VIII, The French Ambassadors*.

Winslow Homer, 1836-1910, (U.S.) naturalist, marine themes. *Marine Coast, High Cliff*.

Edward Hopper, 1882-1967, (U.S.) realistic urban scenes. *Nighthawks, House by the Railroad*.

Horst P. Horst, 1906-99, (Ger.) fashion, celebrity photographer.

Jean-Auguste-Dominique Ingres, 1780-1867, (Fr.) Classicist. *Valpincon Bather*.

George Inness, 1825-94, (U.S.) luminous landscapist. *Delaware Water Gap*.

William Henry Jackson, 1843-1942, (U.S.) photographer. American West, building of Union Pacific Railroad.

Jeanne-Claude (Javacheff), 1935-2009, (Moroc.), created large-scale, temporary installations in public places with her husband, Christo.

Donald Judd, 1928-94, (U.S.) sculptor, major Minimalist.

Frida Kahlo, 1907-54, (Mex.) folkloric stylist. *Self-Portrait With Monkey*.

Wassily Kandinsky, 1866-1944, (Russ.) Abstractionist. *Capricious Forms, Improvisation 28* (second version).

Paul Klee, 1879-1940, (Switz.) Abstractionist. *Twittering Machine, Pastoral, Death and Fire*.

Gustav Klimt, 1862-1918, (Austria) cofounder of Vienna Secession Movement. *The Kiss*.

Oscar Kokoschka, 1886-1980, (Austria) Expressionist. *View of Prague, Harbor of Marseilles*.

Kathe Kollwitz, 1867-1945, (Ger.) printmaker, social justice themes. *The Peasant War*.

Gaston Lachaise, 1882-1935, (U.S.) figurative sculptor. *Standing Woman*.

John La Farge, 1835-1910, (U.S.) muralist. *Red and White Peonies, The Ascension*.

Sir Edwin (Henry) Landseer, 1802-73, (Br.) painter, sculptor. *Shoeing, Rout of Comus*.

Dorothea Lange, 1895-1965, (U.S.) photographer. Great Depression, migrant farm workers.

Fernand Léger, 1881-1955, (Fr.) Machine art. *The Cyclists*.

Leonardo da Vinci, 1452-1519, (It.) Renaissance. *Mona Lisa, Last Supper, The Annunciation*.

Emanuel Leutze, 1816-68, (U.S.) historical themes. *Washington Crossing the Delaware*.

Roy Lichtenstein, 1923-97, (U.S.) Pop Art.

Jacques Lipchitz, 1891-1973, (Fr.) Cubist sculptor. *Harpist*.

Filippino Lippi, 1457-1504, (It.) Renaissance. *Adoration of the Magi*.

Fra Filippo Lippi, 1406-69, (It.) Renaissance. *Coronation of the Virgin, Madonna and Child With Angels*.

Morris Louis, 1912-62, (U.S.) Abstract Expressionist. *Signa, Stripes, Alpha-Phi*.

René Magritte, 1898-1967, (Belg.) Surrealist. *The Descent of Man, The Betrayal of Images*.

Aristide Maillol, 1861-1944, (Fr.) sculptor. *L'Harmonie*.

Édouard Manet, 1832-83, (Fr.) forerunner of Impressionism. *Luncheon on the Grass, Olympia*.

Andrea Mantegna, 1431-1506, (It.) Renaissance frescoes. *Triumph of Caesar*.

Franz Marc, 1880-1916, (Ger.) Expressionist. *Blue Horses*.

John Marin, 1870-1953, (U.S.) Expressionist seascapes. *Maine Island*.

Reginald Marsh, 1898-1954, (U.S.) satire. *Tattoo and Haircut*.

Agnes Martin, 1912-2004, (U.S.) abstract artist. *Night Sea*.

Masaccio, 1401-28, (It.) Renaissance. *The Tribute Money*.

Henri Matisse, 1869-1954, (Fr.) Fauvist. *Woman With the Hat*.

John McCracken, 1934-2011, (U.S.) minimalist sculptor.

Michelangelo Buonarroti, 1475-1564, (It.) Renaissance. *Pietà, David, Moses, The Last Judgment*, Sistine Chapel ceiling.

Jean-Francois Millet, 1814-75, (Fr.) peasants. *The Gleaners, The Man With a Hoe*.

Joan Miró, 1893-1983, (Sp.) exuberant colors, playful images. Catalan landscape, *Dutch Interior*.

Amedeo Modigliani, 1884-1920, (It.) figurative works. *Reclining Nude*.

Piet Mondrian, 1872-1944, (Neth.) Abstractionist. *Composition With Red, Yellow and Blue*.

Claude Monet, 1840-1926, (Fr.) Impressionist. *The Bridge at Argenteuil, Haystacks, Bridge Over a Pond of Water Lillies*.

Henry Moore, 1898-1986, (Br.) sculptor of large-scale, abstract works. *Reclining Figure* (several).

Gustave Moreau, 1826-98, (Fr.) Symbolist. *The Apparition, Dance of Salome*.

James Wilson Morrice, 1865-1924, (Can.) landscapist. *The Ferry, Quebec, Venice, Looking Over the Lagoon*.

William Morris, 1834-96, (Br.) decorative artist, leader of Arts and Crafts movement.

Grandma Moses (Anna Mary Robertson Moses), 1860-1961, (U.S.) folk. *Out for the Christmas Tree, Catching the Thanksgiving Turkey*.

Edvard Munch, 1863-1944, (Nor.) Expressionist. *The Cry*.

Bartolome Murillo, 1618-82, (Sp.) Baroque religious artist. *Vision of St. Anthony, The Two Trinities*.

Elizabeth Murray, 1940-2007, (U.S.) abstract colors. *Kitchen Party*.

Eadweard Muybridge, 1830-1904, (Br.-U.S.) photographer. Studies of motion, *Animal Locomotion*.

Nadar (Gaspar-Félix Tournachon), 1820-1910, (Fr.) photographer, caricaturist, portraitist. Invented photo-essay.

Arnold Newman, 1918-2006, (U.S.) portrait photographer.

Barnett Newman, 1905-70, (U.S.) Abstract Expressionist. *Stations of the Cross*.

Isamu Noguchi, 1904-88, (U.S.) abstract sculptor, designer. *Kouros, BirdC(MU)*, sculptural gardens.

Kenneth Noland, 1924-2010 (U.S.) American color field painter, abstract.

Georgia O'Keeffe, 1887-1986, (U.S.) Southwest motifs. *Cow's Skull: Red, White, and Blue; The Shelton With Sunspots*.

José Clemente Orozco, 1883-1949, (Mex.) frescoes. *House of Tears, Pre-Columbian Golden Age*.

Timothy H. O'Sullivan, 1840-82, (U.S.) Civil War photographer.

Gordon Parks, 1912-2006, (U.S.) African American photographer, filmmaker. *Life* photographer, 1948-68.

Charles Willson Peale, 1741-1827, (U.S.) Amer. Revolutionary portraitist. *The Staircase Group*, U.S. presidents.

Rembrandt Peale, 1778-1860, (U.S.) portraitist. *Thomas Jefferson*.

Irving Penn, 1917-2009, (U.S.) portraitist, fashion photographer.

Pietro Perugino, 1446-1523, (It.) Renaissance. *Delivery of the Keys to St. Peter*.

Pablo Picasso, 1881-1973, (Sp.) painter, sculptor. *Guernica; Dove; Head of a Woman; Head of a Bull, Metamorphosis*.

Piero della Francesca, c. 1415-92, (It.) Renaissance. *Duke of Urbino, Flagellation of Christ*.

Camille Pissarro, 1830-1903, (Fr.) Impressionist. *Boulevard des Italiens, Morning, Sunlight; Bather in the Woods*.

Jackson Pollock, 1912-56, (U.S.) Abstract Expressionist. *Autumn Rhythm*.

Nicolas Poussin, 1594-1665, (Fr.) Baroque pictorial classicism. *St. John on Patmos*.

Maurice B. Prendergast, c. 1860-1924, (U.S.) Postimpressionist watercolorist. *Umbrellas in the Rain*.

Pierre-Paul Prud'hon, 1758-1823, (Fr.) Romanticist. *Crime Pursued by Vengeance and Justice*.

Pierre Cecile Puvis de Chavannes, 1824-98, (Fr.) muralist. *The Poor Fisherman*.

Raphael Sanzio, 1483-1520, (It.) Renaissance. *Disputa, School of Athens, Sistine Madonna*.

Robert Rauschenberg, 1925-2008, (U.S.) printmaker. *Combine, Bed, Revolvers, Outpost*.

Man Ray (Emmanuel Radnitsky), 1890-1976, (U.S.) Dadaist and Surrealist. *Observing Time, The Lovers, Marquis de Sade*.

Odilon Redon, 1840-1916, (Fr.) Symbolist painter, lithographer. *In the Dream, Vase of Flowers*.

Rembrandt van Rijn, 1606-69, (Neth.) painter, printmaker. *The Bridal Couple, The Night Watch*.

Frederic Remington, 1861-1909, (U.S.) painter, sculptor. Portrayer of the American West, *Bronco Buster*.

Pierre-Auguste Renoir, 1841-1919, (Fr.) Impressionist. *The Luncheon of the Boating Party, Dance in the Country*.

Joshua Reynolds, 1723-92, (Br.) portraitist. *Mrs. Siddons as the Tragic Muse*.

Herb Ritts, 1952-2002, (U.S.) photographer. Nudes, celebrities.

Diego Rivera, 1886-1957, (Mex.) frescoes. *The Fecund Earth*.

Larry Rivers, 1923-2002, (U.S.) painter, sculptor, often realistic. *Dutch Masters* series.

Henry Peach Robinson, 1830-1901, (Br.) photographer. A leader of "high art" photography.

Norman Rockwell, 1894-1978, (U.S.) painter, illustrator. *Saturday Evening Post* covers.

Auguste Rodin, 1840-1917, (Fr.) sculptor. *The Thinker*.

Milton Rogovin, 1909-2011, (U.S.) documentary photographer.

Willy Ronis, 1910-2009, (Fr.) photographer. Post-war Paris.

Joe Rosenthal, 1911-2006, (U.S.) photojournalist; photographed six marines raising the U.S. flag over Iwo Jima in WWII.

Mark Rothko, 1903-70, (U.S.) Abstract Expressionist. *Light, Earth and Blue*.

Georges Rouault, 1871-1958, (Fr.) Expressionist. *Three Judges*.

Henri Rousseau, 1844-1910, (Fr.) primitive exotic themes. *The Snake Charmer*.

Theodore Rousseau, 1812-67, (Switz.-Fr.) landscapist. *Under the Birches, Evening*.

Peter Paul Rubens, 1577-1640, (Flem.) Baroque. *Mystic Marriage of St. Catherine*.

Jacob van Ruisdael, c. 1628-82, (Neth.) landscapist. *Jewish Cemetery*.

Charles M. Russell, 1866-1926, (U.S.) Western life.

Salomon van Ruysdael, c. 1600-70, (Dutch) landscapist. *River With Ferry-Boat*.

Albert Pinkham Ryder, 1847-1917, (U.S.) seascapes, allegories. *Toilers of the Sea*.

Augustus Saint-Gaudens, 1848-1907, (U.S.) memorial statues. *Farragut, Mrs. Henry Adams (Grief)*.

Niki de Saint Phalle, 1930-2002, (Fr.) paintings, sculptures, prints, large public installations.

Andrea Sansovino, 1460-1529, (It.) Renaissance sculptor. *Baptism of Christ*.

Jacopo Sansovino, 1486-1570, (It.) Renaissance sculptor. *St. John the Baptist*.

John Singer Sargent, 1856-1925, (U.S.) Edwardian society portraitist. *The Wyndham Sisters, Madam X*.

George Segal, 1924-2000, (U.S.) sculptor. Life-sized figures realistically depicting daily life.

Georges Seurat, 1859-91, (Fr.) Pointillist. *Sunday Afternoon on the Island of La Grande Jatte*.

Gino Severini, 1883-1966, (It.) Futurist and Cubist. *Dynamic Hieroglyph of the Bal Tabarin*.

Ben Shahn, 1898-1969, (U.S.) social and political themes. Sacco and Vanzetti series, *Seurat's Lunch, Handball*.

Charles Sheeler, 1883-1965, (U.S.) abstractionist.

David Alfaro Siqueiros, 1896-1974, (Mex.) political muralist. *March of Humanity*.

David Smith, 1906-65, (U.S.) welded metal sculpture. *Hudson River Landscape, Zig, Cubi* series.

Edward Steichen, 1879-1973, (U.S.) photographer. Credited with transforming photography into an art form.

Alfred Stieglitz, 1864-1946, (U.S.) photographer, editor. Helped create acceptance of photography as art.

Paul Strand, 1890-1976, (U.S.) photographer. People, nature, landscapes.

Gilbert Stuart, 1755-1828, (U.S.) portraitist. George Washington, Thomas Jefferson, James Madison.

Thomas Sully, 1783-1872, (U.S.) portraitist. *Col. Thomas Handasyd Perkins, The Passage of the Delaware*.

William Henry Fox Talbot, 1800-77, (Br.) photographer. *Pencil of Nature*, early photographically illustrated book.

George Tames, 1919-94, (U.S.) photographer. Presidents, political leaders.

Yves Tanguy, 1900-55, (Fr.) Surrealist. *Rose of the Four Winds; Mama, Papa Is Wounded!*

Giovanni Battista Tiepolo, 1696-1770, (It.) Rococo frescoes. *The Crucifixion*.

Jacopo Tintoretto, 1518-94, (It.) Mannerist. *The Last Supper*.

Titian (Tiziano Vecellio), c. 1488-1576, (It.) Renaissance. *Venus and the Lute Player, The Bacchanal*.

Jose Rey Toledo, 1916-94, (U.S.) Native American life. Tribal dances.

George Tooker, 1920-2011, (U.S.) Magic realist. *Subway*.

Henri de Toulouse-Lautrec, 1864-1901, (Fr.) Postimpressionist. *At the Moulin Rouge*.

John Trumbull, 1756-1843, (U.S.) historical themes. *The Declaration of Independence*.

J(oseph) M(allord) W(illiam) Turner, 1775-1851, (Br.) Romantic landscapist. *Snow Storm*.

Cy Twombly, 1928-2011, (U.S.) painter and sculptor. *Leda and the Swan*.

Paolo Uccello, 1397-1475, (It.) Gothic-Renaissance. *The Rout of San Romano*.

Maurice Utrillo, 1883-1955, (Fr.) Impressionist. *Sacre-Coeur de Montmartre*.

John Vanderlyn, 1775-1852, (U.S.) Neoclassicist. *Ariadne Asleep on the Island of Naxos*.

Diego Velázquez, 1599-1660, (Sp.) Baroque. *Las Meninas, Portrait of Juan de Pareja*.

Jan Vermeer, 1632-75, (Neth.) interior genre subjects. *Young Woman With a Water Jug*.

Paolo Veronese, 1528-88, (It.) devotional themes, vastly peopled canvases. *The Temptation of St. Anthony*.

Andrea del Verrocchio, 1435-88, (It.) sculptor. *Colleoni*.

Maurice de Vlaminck, 1876-1958, (Fr.) Fauvist landscapist. *Red Trees*.

Andy Warhol, 1928-87, (U.S.) Pop Art. *Campbell's Soup Cans, Marilyn Diptych*.

Antoine Watteau, 1684-1721, (Fr.) Rococo "scenes of gallantry." *The Embarkation for Cythera*.

George Frederic Watts, 1817-1904, (Br.) painter and sculptor. Grandiose allegorical themes. *Hope*.

Benjamin West, 1738-1820, (U.S.) realistic historical themes. *Death of General Wolfe*.

Edward Weston, 1886-1958, (U.S.) photographer. Landscapes of American West.

James Abbott McNeill Whistler, 1834-1903, (U.S.) *Arrangement in Grey and Black, No. 1: The Artist's Mother*.

Archibald M. Willard, 1836-1918, (U.S.) murals. *The Spirit of '76*.

Grant Wood, 1891-1942, (U.S.) Midwestern regionalist. *American Gothic, Daughters of Revolution*.

Andrew Wyeth, 1917-2009, (U.S.), regionalist. *Christina's World*.

Ossip Zadkine, 1890-1967, (Russ.) School of Paris sculptor. *The Destroyed City, Musicians, Christ*.

Business Leaders and Philanthropists of the Past

Giovanni Agnelli, 1921-2003, (It.) industrialist; principal shareholder of Fiat.

Walter Annenberg, 1908-2002, (U.S.) publisher, founder of *TV Guide*, philanthropist.

Elizabeth Arden (F. N. Graham), 1884-1966, (U.S.) Canadian-born founder of cosmetics empire.

Philip D. Armour, 1832-1901, (U.S.) industrialist; streamlined meatpacking.

Brooke Astor, 1902-2007, (U.S.) philanthropist; president of Vincent Astor Foundation.

John Jacob Astor, 1763-1848, (U.S.) German-born fur trader, banker, real estate magnate; at death, richest in U.S.

Francis W. Ayer, 1848-1923, (U.S.) ad industry pioneer.

August Belmont, 1816-90, (U.S.) German-born financier.

James B. (Diamond Jim) Brady, 1856-1917, (U.S.) financier, philanthropist, legendary bon vivant.

Adolphus Busch, 1839-1913, (U.S.) German-born businessman; established brewery empire.

Asa Candler, 1851-1929, (U.S.) founded Coca-Cola Co.

Andrew Carnegie, 1835-1919, (U.S.) Scottish-born industrialist, philanthropist; founded Carnegie Steel Co.

Tom Carvel, 1908-89, (Gr.-U.S.) founded ice cream chain.

William Colgate, 1783-1857, (Br.-U.S.) businessman, philanthropist; founded soap-making empire.

Jay Cooke, 1821-1905, (U.S.) financier; sold $1 billion in Union bonds during Civil War.

Peter Cooper, 1791-1883, (U.S.) industrialist, inventor, philanthropist; founded Cooper Union (1859).

Ezra Cornell, 1807-74, (U.S.) businessman, philanthropist; headed Western Union, established university.

Erastus Corning, 1794-1872, (U.S.) financier; headed New York Central Railroad.

Charles Crocker, 1822-88, (U.S.) railroad builder, financier.

Samuel Cunard, 1787-1865, (Can.) pioneered transatlantic steam navigation.

Marcus Daly, 1841-1900, (U.S.) Irish-born copper magnate.

W. Edwards Deming, 1900-93, (U.S.) quality-control expert who revolutionized Japanese manufacturing.

Walt Disney, 1901-66, (U.S.) pioneer in cinema animation; built entertainment empire.

Herbert H. Dow, 1866-1930, (U.S.) founder of chemical co.

Anthony Drexel, 1826-93, (U.S.) banker, philanthropist, university founder.

James Duke, 1856-1925, (U.S.) founded American Tobacco, Duke Univ.

Eleuthère I. du Pont, 1771-1834, (Fr.-U.S.) gunpowder manufacturer; founded one of the largest business empires.

Thomas C. Durant, 1820-85, (U.S.) railroad official, financier.

William C. Durant, 1861-1947, (U.S.) industrialist; formed General Motors.

George Eastman, 1854-1932, (U.S.) inventor; manufacturer of photographic equipment.

Marshall Field, 1834-1906, (U.S.) merchant; founded Chicago's largest department store.

Harvey Firestone, 1868-1938, (U.S.) founded tire company.

Avery Fisher, 1906-94, (U.S.) industrialist, philanthropist; founded Fisher electronics.

Henry M. Flagler, 1830-1913, (U.S.) financier; helped form Standard Oil, developed Florida as resort state.

Malcolm Forbes, 1919-90, (U.S.) magazine publisher.

Henry Ford, 1863-1947, (U.S.) automaker; developed first popular low-priced car.

Henry Ford II, 1917-87, (U.S.) headed auto company founded by grandfather.

Henry C. Frick, 1849-1919, (U.S.) steel and coke magnate; had prominent role in development of U.S. Steel.

Jakob Fugger (Jakob the Rich), 1459-1525, (Ger.) headed leading banking, trading house, in 16th-cent. Europe.

Alfred C. Fuller, 1885-1973, (U.S.) Canadian-born businessman; founded brush company.

Elbert H. Gary, 1846-1927, (U.S.) one of the organizers of U.S. Steel; chaired board of directors, 1903-27.

Jean Paul Getty, 1892-1976, (U.S.) founded oil empire.

Amadeo Giannini, 1870-1949, (U.S.) founded Bank of America.

Stephen Girard, 1750-1831, (U.S.) French-born financier, philanthropist; richest man in U.S. at time of death.

Leonard H. Goldenson, 1905-99, (U.S.) turned ABC into major TV network.

Jay Gould, 1836-92, (U.S.) railroad magnate, financier.

Hetty Green, 1834-1916, (U.S.) financier, the "witch of Wall St."; richest woman in U.S. in her day.

William Gregg, 1800-67, (U.S.) launched textile industry in the South.

Meyer Guggenheim, 1828-1905, (U.S.) Swiss-born merchant, philanthropist; built merchandising, mining empires.

Armand Hammer, 1898-1990, (U.S.) headed Occidental Petroleum, promoted U.S.-Soviet ties.

Elliot Handler, 1916-2011, (U.S.) cofounder of Mattel; introduced the Barbie doll.

Edward H. Harriman, 1848-1909, (U.S.) railroad financier, administrator; headed Union Pacific.

Henry J. Heinz, 1844-1919, (U.S.) founded food empire.

Leona Helmsley, 1920-2007, (U.S.) real estate magnate, philanthropist.

Milton Snavely Hershey, 1857-1945, (U.S.) chocolate co. founder, philanthropist.

James J. Hill, 1838-1916, (U.S.) Canadian-born railroad magnate, financier; founded Great Northern Railway.

Conrad N. Hilton, 1888-1979, (U.S.) hotel chain founder.

Howard Hughes, 1905-76, (U.S.) industrialist, aviator, filmmaker.

H. L. Hunt, 1889-1974, (U.S.) oil magnate.

Collis P. Huntington, 1821-1900, (U.S.) railroad magnate.

Henry E. Huntington, 1850-1927, (U.S.) railroad builder, philanthropist.

Walter L. Jacobs, 1898-1985, (U.S.) founder of the first rental car agency, which later became Hertz.

Steve Jobs, (1955-2011), (U.S.) Apple cofounder and exec; Pixar exec.

Howard Johnson, 1896-1972, (U.S.) founded restaurants.

John H. Johnson, 1918-2005, (U.S.) built publishing empire based on *Ebony* and *Jet*.

Samuel Curtis Johnson, 1928-2004, (U.S.) headed S.C. Johnson & Sons.

Henry J. Kaiser, 1882-1967, (U.S.) industrialist; built empire in steel, aluminum.

Minor C. Keith, 1848-1929, (U.S.) railroad magnate; founded United Fruit Co.

Will K. Kellogg, 1860-1951, (U.S.) businessman, philanthropist; founded breakfast food co.

Richard King, 1825-85, (U.S.) cattleman; founded half-million-acre King Ranch in Texas.

John W. Kluge, 1914-2010, (Ger.-U.S.) Metromedia chairman; philanthropist.

William S. Knudsen, 1879-1948, (U.S.) Danish-born auto industry executive.

Samuel H. Kress, 1863-1955, (U.S.) businessman, art collector, philanthropist; founded "dime store" chain.

Ray A. Kroc, 1902-84, (U.S.) original CEO of McDonald's Corp.; oversaw company's vast expansion.

Alfred Krupp, 1812-87, (Ger.) armaments magnate.

Kenneth L. Lay, 1942-2006, (U.S.), former CEO of Enron; indicted on fraud charges.

William Levitt, 1907-94, (U.S.) industrialist; "suburb maker."

Thomas Lipton, 1850-1931, (Scot.) merchant; tea empire.

James McGill, 1744-1813, (Scot.-Can.) founded university.

Andrew W. Mellon, 1855-1937, (U.S.) financier, industrialist; benefactor of National Gallery of Art.

Charles E. Merrill, 1885-1956, (U.S.) financier; developed firm of Merrill Lynch.

John Pierpont Morgan, 1837-1913, (U.S.) most powerful figure in finance and industry at turn of the century.

Akio Morita, 1921-99, (Jpn.) cofounded Sony Corp.

Malcolm Muir, 1885-1979, (U.S.) created *Business Week* magazine; headed *Newsweek*, 1937-61.

Roy Neuberger, 1903-2010, (U.S.) financier and art patron.

Samuel Newhouse, 1895-1979, (U.S.) publishing and broadcasting magnate; built communications empire.

Aristotle Onassis, 1906-75, (Gr.) shipping magnate.

William S. Paley, 1901-90, (U.S.) built CBS communications empire.

Frederick D. Patterson, 1901-88, (U.S.) founder of United Negro College Fund, 1944.

George Peabody, 1795-1869, (U.S.) merchant, financier, philanthropist.

James C. Penney, 1875-1971, (U.S.) businessman; developed department store chain.

Frank Perdue, 1920-2005, (U.S.) founder of Perdue Farms, chicken-processing company.

William C. Procter, 1862-1934, (U.S.) headed soap co.

John D. Rockefeller, 1839-1937, (U.S.) industrialist; established Standard Oil.

John D. Rockefeller Jr., 1874-1960, (U.S.) philanthropist; established foundation, provided land for UN.

Laurance S. Rockefeller, 1910-2004, (U.S.) philanthropist, conservationist.

Meyer A. Rothschild, 1743-1812, (Ger.) founded international banking house.

Thomas Fortune Ryan, 1851-1928, (U.S.) financier; a founder of American Tobacco.

Edmond J. Safra, 1932-99, (U.S.) banker.

David Sarnoff, 1891-1971, (U.S.) broadcasting pioneer; established first radio network, NBC.

Richard Sears, 1863-1914, (U.S.) founded mail-order co.

Werner von Siemens, 1816-92, (Ger.) industrialist, inventor.

Alfred P. Sloan, 1875-1966, (U.S.) industrialist, philanthropist; headed General Motors.

A. Leland Stanford, 1824-93, (U.S.) railroad official, philanthropist; founded university.

Frank Stanton, 1908-2006, (U.S.) president of CBS network, 1946-71.

Larry Stewart, 1948-2007, (U.S.) "Kansas City's Secret Santa."

Nathan Straus, 1848-1931, (U.S.) German-born merchant, philanthropist; headed Macy's.

Levi Strauss, c. 1829-1902, (U.S.) pants manufacturer.

Clement Studebaker, 1831-1901, (U.S.) wagon, carriage maker.

Gustavus Swift, 1839-1903, (U.S.) pioneer meatpacker.

Gerard Swope, 1872-1957, (U.S.) industrialist, economist; headed General Electric.

Dave Thomas, 1932-2002, (U.S.) Wendy's founder.

James Walter Thompson, 1847-1928, (U.S.) ad executive.

Alice Tully, 1902-93, (U.S.) philanthropist, arts patron.

Theodore N. Vail, 1845-1920, (U.S.) organized Bell Telephone system, headed AT&T.

Cornelius Vanderbilt, 1794-1877, (U.S.) financier; established steamship, railroad empires.

Henry Villard, 1835-1900, (U.S.) German-born railroad executive, financier.

Charles R. Walgreen, 1873-1939, (U.S.) founded drugstore chain.

Madame C. J. Walker, 1867-1919, (U.S.) African-American hair care entrepreneur and philanthropist.

DeWitt Wallace, 1889-1981, (U.S.) and **Lila Wallace**, 1889-1984, (U.S.) cofounders of *Reader's Digest* magazine.

Sam Walton, 1918-92, (U.S.) founder of Wal-Mart stores.

John Wanamaker, 1838-1922, (U.S.) department-store merchandising pioneer.

Aaron Montgomery Ward, 1843-1913, (U.S.) established first mail-order firm.

Thomas J. Watson, 1874-1956, (U.S.) IBM head, 1914-56.

George Westinghouse, 1846-1914, (U.S) inventor, manufacturer; organized Westinghouse Electric Co., 1886.

John Hay Whitney, 1905-82, (U.S.) publisher, sportsman, philanthropist.

Charles E. Wilson, 1890-1961, (U.S.) auto exec., public official.

Frank W. Woolworth, 1852-1919, (U.S.) created five and dime chain.

William Wrigley Jr., 1861-1932, (U.S.) founded Wrigley chewing gum company.

American Cartoonists

Reviewed by Lucy Shelton Caswell, Professor and Curator, Cartoon Research Library, Ohio State University.

Scott Adams, b 1957, Dilbert.

Charles Addams, 1912-88, macabre cartoons.

Brad Anderson, b 1924, Marmaduke.

Sergio Aragones, b 1937, *MAD* magazine.

Peter Arno, 1904-68, *The New Yorker*.

Tex Avery, 1908-80, animator; Bugs Bunny, Porky Pig.

George Baker, 1915-75, The Sad Sack.

Carl Barks, 1901-2000, Donald Duck comic books.

C. C. Beck, 1910-89, Captain Marvel.

Dave Berg, 1920-2002, *Mad* magazine.

Jim Berry, b 1932, Berry's World.

Herb Block (Herblock), 1909-2001, political cartoonist.

George Booth, b 1926, *The New Yorker*.

Berkeley Breathed, b 1957, Bloom County.

Dik Browne, 1917-89, Hi & Lois, Hagar the Horrible.

Marjorie Buell, 1904-93, Little Lulu.

Ernie Bushmiller, 1905-82, Nancy.

Milton Caniff, 1907-88, Terry & the Pirates, Steve Canyon.

Al Capp, 1909-79, Li'l Abner.

Roz Chast, b 1954, *The New Yorker*.

Gene Colan, 1926-2011, *Daredevil*.

Paul Conrad, 1924-2010, political cartoonist.

Roy Crane, 1901-77, Captain Easy, Buz Sawyer.

R(obert) Crumb, b 1943, underground cartoonist.

Shamus Culhane, 1908-96, animator.

Jay N. "Ding" Darling, 1876-1962, political cartoonist.

Jack Davis, b 1926, *MAD* magazine.

Jim Davis, b 1945, Garfield.

Billy DeBeck, 1890-1942, Barney Google.

Rudolph Dirks, 1877-1968, The Katzenjammer Kids.

Walt Disney, 1901-66, produced animated cartoons; created Mickey Mouse, Donald Duck.

Steve Ditko, b 1927, Spider-Man.

Mort Drucker, b 1929, *MAD* magazine.

Will Eisner, 1917-2005, the Spirit.

Jules Feiffer, b 1929, political cartoonist.

Bud Fisher, 1884-1954, Mutt & Jeff.

Ham Fisher, 1900-55, Joe Palooka.

Max Fleischer, 1883-1972, Betty Boop.

Hal Foster, 1892-1982, Tarzan, Prince Valiant.

Fontaine Fox, 1884-1964, Toonerville Folks.

Isadore "Friz" Freleng, 1905-95, animator; Yosemite Sam, Porky Pig, Sylvester and Tweety Bird.

Rube Goldberg, 1883-1970, Boob McNutt.

Chester Gould, 1900-85, Dick Tracy.

Harold Gray, 1894-1968, Little Orphan Annie.

Matt Groening, b 1954, Life in Hell, The Simpsons.

Cathy Guisewite, b 1950, Cathy.

Bill Hanna, 1910-2001, and **Joe Barbera**, 1911-2006, animators; Tom & Jerry, Yogi Bear, Flintstones.

Oliver Harrington, 1912-95, Bootsie.

Johnny Hart, 1931-2007, BC, Wizard of Id.

Alfred Harvey, 1913-94, created Casper the Friendly Ghost.

Jimmy Hatlo, 1898-1963, Little Iodine.

John Held Jr., 1889-1958, Jazz Age.

George Herriman, 1881-1944, Krazy Kat.

Harry Hershfield, 1885-1974, Abie the Agent.

Stephen Hillenburg, b 1961, SpongeBob SquarePants.

Al Hirschfeld, 1903-2003, *NY Times* theater caricaturist.

Burne Hogarth, 1911-96, Tarzan.

Helen Hokinson, 1900-49, *The New Yorker*.

Nicole Hollander, b 1939, Sylvia.

Lynn Johnston, b 1947 (Can.), For Better or For Worse.

Oliver Johnston, 1912-2008, Disney animator.

Chuck Jones, 1912-2002, animator; Bugs Bunny, Porky Pig.

Mike Judge, b 1962, Beavis and Butthead, King of the Hill.

Bob Kane, b 1916-98, Batman.

Bil Keane, b 1922, The Family Circus.

Walt Kelly, 1913-73, Pogo.

Hank Ketcham, 1920-2001, Dennis the Menace.

Ted Key, 1912-2008, Hazel.

Frank King, 1883-1969, Gasoline Alley.

Jack Kirby, 1917-94, Fantastic Four, The Incredible Hulk.

Rollin Kirby, 1875-1952, political cartoonist.

B(ernard) Kliban, 1935-90, cat books.

Edward Koren, b 1935, *The New Yorker*.

John Kricfalusi, b 1955, Ren & Stimpy.

Harvey Kurtzman, 1921-93, *MAD* magazine.

Walter Lantz, 1900-94, Woody Woodpecker.

Gary Larson, b 1950, The Far Side.

Mell Lazarus, b 1927, Momma, Miss Peach.

Stan Lee, b 1922, Marvel Comics.

David Levine, 1926-2009, *NY Review of Books* caricatures.

Jeff MacNelly, 1947-2000, political cartoonist; Shoe.

Doug Marlette, 1949-2007, political cartoonist; Kudzu.

Don Martin, 1931-2000, *MAD* magazine.

Bill Mauldin, 1921-2003, political cartoonist.

Winsor McCay, 1872-1934, Little Nemo.

John T. McCutcheon, 1870-1949, political cartoonist.

Aaron McGruder, b 1974, The Boondocks.

George McManus, 1884-1954, Bringing Up Father.

Dale Messick, 1906-2005, Brenda Starr.

Norman Mingo, 1896-1980, Alfred E. Neuman.

Bob Montana, 1920-75, Archie.

Dick Moores, 1909-86, Gasoline Alley.

Willard Mullin, 1902-78, sports cartoonist; Dodgers "Bum," Mets "Kid."

Russell Myers, b 1938, Broom Hilda.

Thomas Nast, 1840-1902, political cartoonist; Republican elephant, Democratic donkey.

Pat Oliphant, b 1935, political cartoonist.

Frederick Burr Opper, 1857-1937, Happy Hooligan.

Richard Outcault, 1863-1928, Yellow Kid, Buster Brown.

Brant Parker, 1920-2007, Wizard of Id.

Trey Parker, b 1969, animator, co-creator of South Park.

Mike Peters, b 1943, cartoonist; Mother Goose & Grimm.

George Price, 1901-95, *The New Yorker*.

Antonio Prohias, 1921-98, Spy vs. Spy.

Alex Raymond, 1909-56, Flash Gordon, Jungle Jim.

Forrest (Bud) Sagendorf, 1915-94, Popeye.

Art Sansom, 1920-91, The Born Loser.

Charles Schulz, 1922-2000, Peanuts.

Elzie C. Segar, 1894-1938, Popeye.

Joe Shuster, 1914-92, and **Jerry Siegel**, 1914-96, Superman.

Sidney Smith, 1887-1935, The Gumps.

Otto Soglow, 1900-75, Little King.

Art Spiegelman, b 1948, Raw, Maus.

William Steig, 1907-2003, *The New Yorker*.

Matt Stone, b 1971, animator, co-creator of South Park.

James Swinnerton, 1875-1974, Little Jimmy, Canyon Kiddies.

Paul Szep, b 1941, political cartoonist.

Paul Terry, 1887-1971, animator of Mighty Mouse.

Bob Thaves, 1924-2006, Frank and Ernest.

James Thurber, 1894-61, *The New Yorker*.

Garry Trudeau, b 1948, Doonesbury.

Mort Walker, b 1923, Beetle Bailey.

Bill Watterson, b 1958, Calvin and Hobbes.

Russ Westover, 1887-1966, Tillie the Toiler.

Signe Wilkinson, b 1950, political cartoonist.

Frank Willard, 1893-1958, Moon Mullins.

J. R. Williams, 1888-1957, The Willets Family, Out Our Way.

Gahan Wilson, b 1930, *The New Yorker*.

Tom Wilson, 1931-2011, Ziggy.

Art Young, 1866-1943, political cartoonist.

Chic Young, 1901-73, Blondie.

Economists, Educators, Historians, and Social Scientists of the Past

For Psychologists, see Scientists of the Past.

Brooks Adams, 1848-1927, (U.S.) historian, political theoretician; *The Law of Civilization and Decay*.

Henry Adams, 1838-1918, (U.S.) historian, autobiographer; *The Education of Henry Adams*.

Francis Bacon, 1561-1626, (Eng.) philosopher, essayist, statesman; championed observation and induction.

George Bancroft, 1800-91, (U.S.) historian; 10-volume *History of the United States*.

Jack Barbash, 1910-94, (U.S.) labor economist; helped create the AFL-CIO.

Henry Barnard, 1811-1900, (U.S.) public school reformer.

Charles A. Beard, 1874-1948, (U.S.) historian; *The Economic Basis of Politics*.

(St.) Bede (the Venerable), c. 673-735, (Br.) scholar, historian; *Ecclesiastical History of the English People*.

Daniel Bell, 1919-2011, (U.S.) sociologist; *The End of Ideology*.

Ruth Benedict, 1887-1948, (U.S.) anthropologist; studied Indian tribes of the Southwest.

Sir Isaiah Berlin, 1909-97, (Br.) philosopher, historian; *The Age of Enlightenment*.

Leonard Bloomfield, 1887-1949, (U.S.) linguist; *Language*.

Franz Boas, 1858-1942, (U.S.) German-born anthropologist; studied American Indians.

Van Wyck Brooks, 1886-1963, (U.S.) historian; critic of New England culture, especially literature.

Edmund Burke, 1729-97, (Ire.) British parliamentarian and political philosopher; *Reflections on the Revolution in France*.

Nicholas Murray Butler, 1862-1947, (U.S.) educator; headed Columbia Univ., 1902-45; Nobel Peace Prize, 1931.

Joseph Campbell, 1904-87, (U.S.) author, editor, teacher; wrote books on mythology, folklore.

Thomas Carlyle, 1795-1881, (Scot.) historian, critic; *Sartor Resartus, Past and Present, The French Revolution*.

(Charles) Bruce Catton, 1899-1978, (U.S.) historian; *A Stillness at Appomattox*.

Edward Channing, 1856-1931, (U.S.) historian; 6-volume *History of the United States*.

Henry Steele Commager, 1902-98, (U.S.) historian, educator; *The Growth of the American Republic*.

John R. Commons, 1862-1945, (U.S.) economist, labor historian; *Legal Foundations of Capitalism*.

James B. Conant, 1893-1978, (U.S.) educator, diplomat; *The American High School Today*.

Benedetto Croce, 1866-1952, (It.) philosopher, statesman, historian; *Philosophy of the Spirit*.

Bernard A. De Voto, 1897-1955, (U.S.) historian; wrote trilogy on American West, edited Mark Twain manuscripts.

Melvil Dewey, 1851-1931, (U.S.) devised decimal system of library-book classification.

Donald Herbert Donald, 1920-2009, (U.S.) Pulitzer Prize-winning Civil War and Lincoln historian.

St. Clair Drake, 1911-90, (U.S.) sociologist, black studies pioneer; *Black Metropolis* (1945), with Horace R. Cayton.

W(illiam) E(dward) B(urghardt) Du Bois, 1868-1963, (U.S.) historian, sociologist; NAACP founder, 1909.

Will(iam), 1885-1981 (U.S.) and **Ariel Durant**, 1898-1981 (Ukraine), historians; *The Story of Civilization*.

Emile Durkheim, 1858-1917, (Fr.) a founder of modern sociology; *The Rules of Sociological Method*.

Jean Baptiste Point du Sable, c. 1750-1818, (U.S.) pioneer trader and first settler of Chicago, 1779.

Charles Eliot, 1834-1926, (U.S.) educator, Harvard president.

Friedrich Engels, 1820-95, (Ger.) political writer; with Marx wrote the *Communist Manifesto*.

Irving Fisher, 1867-1947, (U.S.) economist; contributed to the development of modern monetary theory.

John Fiske, 1842-1901, (U.S.) historian and lecturer; popularized Darwinian theory of evolution.

Charles Fourier, 1772-1837, (Fr.) utopian socialist.

John Hope Franklin, 1915-2009, (U.S.) historian; *From Slavery to Freedom: A History of African Americans*.

Sir James George Frazer, 1854-1941, (Br.) anthropologist; studied myth in religion; *The Golden Bough*.

Milton Friedman, 1912-2006, (U.S.) economist.

John Kenneth Galbraith, 1908-2006, (Can.-U.S.) economist, author, professor, former amb. to India.

Giovanni Gentile, 1875-1944, (It.) philosopher, educator; reformed Italian educational system.

Henry George, 1839-97, (U.S.) economist, reformer; led single-tax movement.

Edward Gibbon, 1737-94, (Br.) historian; *The History of the Decline and Fall of the Roman Empire*.

Francesco Guicciardini, 1483-1540, (It.) historian; *Storia d'Italia*, principal historical work of the 16th cent.

Thomas Hobbes, 1588-1679, (Eng.) philosopher, political theorist; *Leviathan*.

Richard Hofstadter, 1916-70, (U.S.) historian; *The Age of Reform*.

Charles Hamilton Houston, 1895-1950, (U.S.) African American lawyer, Howard University instructor; champion of minority rights.

Samuel Huntington, 1927-2008, (U.S.), political scientist, Harvard University professor; *The Clash of Civilizations*.

Alfred Kahn, 1917-2010, (U.S.) economist; deregulated the U.S. airline industry.

George F. Kennan, 1904-2005, (U.S.) diplomat, historian; main architect of U.S. Cold War "containment" strategy.

John Maynard Keynes, 1883-1946, (Br.) economist; principal advocate of deficit spending.

Alfred Kinsey, 1894-1956, (U.S.) zoologist; pioneering human sex researcher.

Russell Kirk, 1918-94, (U.S.), social philosopher; *The Conservative Mind*.

Alfred L. Kroeber, 1876-1960, (U.S.) cultural anthropologist; studied Indians of North and South America.

Elisabeth Kubler-Ross, 1926-2004, (Switz.) psychiatrist, author; *On Death and Dying*.

Christopher Lasch, 1932-94, (U.S.) social critic, historian; *The Culture of Narcissism*.

James L. Laughlin, 1850-1933, (U.S.) economist; helped establish Federal Reserve System.

Margaret Leech, 1893-1974 (U.S.) historian; *Reveille in Washington, 1860-1865*.

Lucien Lévy-Bruhl, 1857-1939, (Fr.) philosopher; studied the psychology of primitive societies; *Primitive Mentality*.

John Locke, 1632-1704, (Eng.) philosopher, political theorist; *Two Treatises of Government*.

Thomas B. Macaulay, 1800-59, (Br.) historian, statesman.

Niccolò Machiavelli, 1469-1527, (It.) writer, statesman; *The Prince*.

Bronislaw Malinowski, 1884-1942, (Pol.) considered the father of social anthropology.

Thomas R. Malthus, 1766-1834, (Br.) economist; *Essay on the Principle of Population*.

Horace Mann, 1796-1859, (U.S.) pioneered modern public school system.

Karl Mannheim, 1893-1947, (Hung.) sociologist, historian; *Ideology and Utopia*.

Harriet Martineau, 1802-76, (Eng.) writer, feminist; *Society in America*.

Karl Marx, 1818-83, (Ger.) political theorist, proponent of Communism; *Communist Manifesto, Das Kapital*.

Benjamin Mays, 1895-1984, (U.S.) minister, educator, civil rights leader; headed Morehouse College, 1940-67.

Giuseppe Mazzini, 1805-72, (It.) political philosopher.

William H. McGuffey, 1800-73, (U.S.) his *Reader* was a mainstay of 19th-cent. U.S. public education.

George H. Mead, 1863-1931, (U.S.) philosopher, social psychologist.

Margaret Mead, 1901-78, (U.S.) cultural anthropologist; popularized field; *Coming of Age in Samoa*.

Alexander Meiklejohn, 1872-1964, (U.S.) Br.-born educator; championed academic freedom and experimental curricula.

James Mill, 1773-1836, (Scot.) philosopher, historian, economist; a proponent of utilitarianism.

John Stuart Mill, 1806-73, (Eng.) philosopher, economist; *Utilitarianism*; eldest son of James Mill.

Perry G. Miller, 1905-63, (U.S.) historian; interpreted 17th-cent. New England.

Theodor Mommsen, 1817-1903, (Ger.) historian; *The History of Rome*.

Ashley Montagu, 1905-99, (Eng.) anthropologist; *The Natural Superiority of Women*.

Charles-Louis Montesquieu, 1689-1755, (Fr.) social philosopher; *The Spirit of Laws*.

Maria Montessori, 1870-1952, (It.) educator, physician; started Montessori method of student self-motivation.

Samuel Eliot Morison, 1887-1976, (U.S.) historian; chronicled voyages of early explorers.

Lewis Mumford, 1895-1990, (U.S.) sociologist, critic; *The Culture of Cities*.

Gunnar Myrdal, 1898-1987, (Swed.) economist, social scientist; *Asian Drama: An Inquiry Into the Poverty of Nations*.

Allan Nevins, 1890-1971, (U.S.) historian, biographer; *The Ordeal of the Union*.

José Ortega y Gasset, 1883-1955, (Sp.) philosopher; advocated control by elite; *The Revolt of the Masses*.

Robert Owen, 1771-1858, (Br.) political philosopher, reformer; pioneer in cooperative movement.

Thomas Paine, 1737-1809, (Br.-U.S.) political theorist, writer; *Common Sense*.

Vilfredo Pareto, 1848-1923, (It.) economist, sociologist.

Francis Parkman, 1823-93, (U.S.) historian; *France and England in North America*.

Elizabeth P. Peabody, 1804-94, (U.S.) education pioneer; founded 1st kindergarten in U.S., 1860.

William Prescott, 1796-1859, (U.S.) early American historian; *The Conquest of Peru*.

Pierre Joseph Proudhon, 1809-65, (Fr.) social theorist; father of anarchism; *The Philosophy of Property*.

François Quesnay, 1694-1774, (Fr.) economic theorist.

David Ricardo, 1772-1823, (Br.) economic theorist; advocated free international trade.

David Riesman, 1909-2002, (U.S.) sociologist; coauthor, *The Lonely Crowd*.

Jacqueline de Romilly, 1913-2010, (Fr.) scholar of Greek civilization and language.

Theodore Roszak, 1933-2011, (U.S.) historian; *The Making of a Counter Culture*.

Jean-Jacques Rousseau, 1712-78, (Fr.) social philosopher; the father of romantic sensibility; *Confessions*.

Paul Samuelson, 1915-2009, (U.S.) economist, famed for modern mathematical approach to economics.

Edward Sapir, 1884-1939, (Ger.-U.S.) anthropologist; studied ethnology and linguistics of U.S. Indian groups.

Ferdinand de Saussure, 1857-1913, (Switz.) a founder of modern linguistics.

Arthur Schlesinger Jr., 1917-2007, (U.S.) historian, author; *The Imperial Presidency*.

Joseph Schumpeter, 1883-1950, (Czech.-U.S.) economist, sociologist.

Elizabeth Seton, 1774-1821, (U.S.) nun; est. parochial school education in U.S., first native-born American saint.

Georg Simmel, 1858-1918, (Ger.) sociologist, philosopher; helped establish German sociology.

Robert Sklar, 1936-2011, (U.S.) film scholar.

Adam Smith, 1723-90, (Br.) economist; advocated laissez-faire economy, free trade; *The Wealth of Nations*.

Jared Sparks, 1789-1866, (U.S.) historian, educator, editor; *The Library of American Biography*.

Oswald Spengler, 1880-1936, (Ger.) philosopher, historian; *The Decline of the West*.

Leo Steinberg, 1920-2011, (Rus.-Am.) art historian.

William G. Sumner, 1840-1910, (U.S.) social scientist, economist; laissez-faire economy, Social Darwinism.

Hippolyte Taine, 1828-93, (Fr.) historian; basis of naturalistic school; *The Origins of Contemporary France*.

A(lan) J(ohn) P(ercivale) Taylor, 1906-90, (Br.) historian; *The Origins of the Second World War*.

Nikolaas Tinbergen, 1907-88, (Neth.-Br.) ethologist; pioneer in study of animal behavior.

Alexis de Tocqueville, 1805-59, (Fr.) political scientist, historian; *Democracy in America*.

Francis E. Townsend, 1867-1960, (U.S.) led old-age pension movement, 1933.

Arnold Toynbee, 1889-1975, (Br.) historian; *A Study of History*, sweeping analysis of hist. of civilizations.

George Trevelyan, 1876-1962, (Br.) historian, statesman; favored "literary" over "scientific" history; *History of England*.

Henri Troyat, 1911-2007 (Russ.-Fr.), biographies of major figures in Russian history.

Frederick J. Turner, 1861-1932, (U.S.) historian, educator; *The Frontier in American History*.

Thorstein B. Veblen, 1857-1929, (U.S.) economist, social philosopher; *The Theory of the Leisure Class*.

Giovanni Vico, 1668-1744, (It.) historian, biographer; regarded by many as first modern historian; *New Science*.

Izaak Walton, 1593-1683, (Eng.) biographer; political-philosophical study of fishing, *The Compleat Angler*.

Booker T. Washington, 1856-1915, (U.S.) founder, 1881, and first pres. of Tuskegee Institute; *Up From Slavery*.

Sidney J., 1859-1947, and **Beatrice Webb**, 1858-1943, (Br.) leading figures in Fabian Society and Labor Party.

Max Weber, 1864-1920, (Ger.) sociologist; *The Protestant Ethic and the Spirit of Capitalism*.

Walter White, 1893-1955, (U.S.) exec. sec., NAACP, 1931-55.

Roy Wilkins, 1901-81, (U.S.) exec. director, NAACP, 1955-77.

Emma Hart Willard, 1787-1870, (U.S.) pioneered higher education for women.

Carter G. Woodson, 1875-1950, (U.S.) historian; founded Assn. for the Study of Negro Life and History.

C. Vann Woodward, 1908-99, (U.S.) historian; *The Strange Career of Jim Crow*.

American Journalists of the Past

Reviewed by Dean Mills, Dean, Missouri School of Journalism.

See also Business Leaders and Philanthropists, American Cartoonists, Writers of the Past.

Franklin P. Adams (F.P.A.), 1881-1960, humorist; wrote column "The Conning Tower."

Joseph W. Alsop, 1910-89, and **Stewart Alsop**, 1914-74, Washington-based political analysts, columnists.

Jack Anderson, 1922-2006, muckraking Washington, DC, syndicated columnist.

Brooks Atkinson, 1894-1984, theater critic.

Robert L. Bartley, 1937-2003, editorial-page editor for *Wall Street Journal*.

James Gordon Bennett, 1795-1872, editor and publisher; founded *NY Herald*.

James Gordon Bennett, 1841-1918, succeeded father, financed expeditions, founded afternoon paper.

Nellie Bly (Elizabeth Cochrane), 1867-1922, pioneer woman journalist, investig. reporter; noted for series on trip around the world.

Elias Boudinot, c. 1803-39, founding editor of first Native American newspaper in U.S., *Cherokee Phoenix* (1828-34).

Ed Bradley, 1941-2006, TV journalist (*60 Minutes*); one of the first African American journalists to report on the Vietnam War.

David Brinkley, 1920-2003, co-anchor of NBC's *Huntley-Brinkley Report*, host of ABC's *This Week With David Brinkley*.

Arthur Brisbane, 1864-1936, editor; helped introduce "yellow journalism" with sensational, simply written articles.

David Broder, 1929-2011, political journalist for *The Washington Post*.

Heywood Broun, 1888-1939, author, columnist; founded American Newspaper Guild.

Art Buchwald, 1925-2007, journalist, humorist, syndicated columnist.

William F. Buckley Jr., 1925-2008, columnist and commentator; founder of *National Review*.

Herb Caen, 1916-97, longtime columnist for *San Francisco Chronicle* and *Examiner*.

John Campbell, 1653-1728, published *Boston News-Letter*, first continuing newspaper in the American colonies.

Jimmy Cannon, 1909-73, syndicated sports columnist.

John Chancellor, 1927-96, NBC reporter, anchor.

Harry Chandler, 1864-1944, *Los Angeles Times* publisher (1917-41); made it a dominant force.

Otis Chandler, 1928-2006, *Los Angeles Times* publisher (1960-80).

Marquis Childs, 1903-90, reporter and columnist for *St. Louis Post-Dispatch* and United Feature syndicate.

Craig Claiborne, 1920-2000, *NY Times* food editor and critic; key in internationalizing American tastes.

Charles Collingwood, 1917-85, CBS news correspondent.

Alistair Cooke, 1908-2004, journalist, TV narrator; naturalized American citizen, "Letter From America" series.

Howard Cosell, 1920-95, TV and radio sportscaster.

Gardner Cowles, 1861-1946, founded newspaper chain.

Walter Cronkite, 1916-2009, CBS evening news anchor, TV journalist.

Evelyn Cunningham, 1916-2010, African American civil rights reporter.

Cyrus Curtis, 1850-1933, publisher of *Saturday Evening Post*, *Ladies' Home Journal*, *Country Gentleman*.

John Charles Daly, 1914-91, war correspondent, TV journalist; Voice of America head.

Charles Anderson Dana, 1819-97, editor, publisher; made *NY Sun* famous for its news reporting.

Elmer (Holmes) Davis, 1890-1958, *NY Times* editorial writer, radio commentator.

Richard Harding Davis, 1864-1916, war correspondent, travel writer, fiction writer.

Benjamin Day, 1810-89, published *NY Sun* beginning in 1833, introducing penny press to the U.S.

Dorothy Dix (Elizabeth Meriwether Gilmer), 1861-1951, reporter; pioneer of the advice column genre.

Finley Peter Dunne, 1867-1936, humorist, social critic; wrote "Mr. Dooley" columns.

Mary Baker Eddy, 1821-1910, founded Christian Science movement and *Christian Science Monitor*.

Rowland Evans Jr., 1921-2001, Washington columnist.

Fanny Fern (Sara Willis Parton), 1811-72, newspaper columnist, author.

Marshall Field III, 1893-1956, retail magnate, *Chicago Sun* founder.

Doris Fleeson, 1901-70, war correspondent, columnist.

Benjamin Franklin, 1706-90, publisher of *Poor Richards Almanack*.

James Franklin, 1697-1735, printer, pioneer journalist; publisher of *New England Courant* and *Rhode Island Gazette*.

Fred W. Friendly, 1915-98, radio, TV reporter, producer, executive; collaborator with Edward R. Murrow.

Margaret Fuller, 1810-50, social reformer, transcendentalist, critic and foreign correspondent for *NY Tribune*.

Frank E. Gannett, 1876-1957, founded newspaper chain.

Mary Ellen Garber, 1916-2008, sports journalist.

William Lloyd Garrison, 1805-79, abolitionist; publisher of *The Liberator*.

Edwin Lawrence Godkin, 1831-1902, founder of *The Nation*, editor of *NY Evening Post*.

Katharine Graham, 1917-2001, *Washington Post* publisher.

Sheilah Graham, 1904-89, Hollywood gossip columnist.

Horace Greeley, 1811-72, editor, politician; founded *NY Tribune*.

Meg Greenfield, 1930-99, *Newsweek* columnist, *Washington Post* editorial page editor.

Gilbert Hovey Grosvenor, 1875-1966, longtime editor of *National Geographic* magazine.

John Gunther, 1901-70, *Chicago Daily News* foreign correspondent, author.

David Halberstam, 1934-2007, journalist, sports reporter, author; *The Best and the Brightest*, *Summer of '49*.

Sarah Josepha Buell Hale, 1788-1879, first female magazine editor; *Ladies' Magazine*, later *Godey's Lady's Book*.

Paul Harvey, 1918-2009, radio broadcaster and commentator.

William Randolph Hearst, 1863-1951, founder of Hearst newspaper chain, one of the pioneers of yellow journalism.

Gabriel Heatter, 1890-1972, radio commentator.

John Hersey, 1914-98, foreign correspondent for *Time*, *Life*, and *The New Yorker*; author.

Marguerite Higgins, 1920-66, reporter, war correspondent.

Hedda Hopper, 1885-1966, Hollywood gossip columnist.

Roy Howard, 1883-1964, editor, executive; Scripps-Howard papers and United Press (later United Press International).

Chet (Chester Robert) Huntley, 1911-74, co-anchor of NBC's *Huntley-Brinkley Report*.

Ralph Ingersoll, 1900-85, editor; *Fortune*, *Time*, *Life* exec.

Molly Ivins, 1944-2007, author, syndicated political columnist.

Peter Jennings, 1938-2005, ABC correspondent, anchor.

Pauline Kael, 1919-2001, film critic.

H. V. (Hans von) Kaltenborn, 1878-1965, radio commentator, reporter.

Murray Kempton, 1917-97, reporter, columnist for magazines and newspapers, including *NY Post*.

Dorothy Kilgallen, 1913-65, crime reporter, columnist.

James J. Kilpatrick, 1920-2010, political columnist, author and television personality.

John S. Knight, 1894-1981, editor, publisher; founded Knight newspaper group, which merged into Knight-Ridder.

Joseph Kraft, 1942-86, foreign policy columnist.

Irving Kristol, 1920-2009, columnist, commentator.

Arthur Krock, 1886-1974, *NY Times* political writer, Washington bureau chief.

Charles Kuralt, 1934-97, TV anchor; host of CBS "On the Road" featuring stories about life in the U.S.

Ann Landers (Eppie Lederer), 1918-2002, advice columnist.

David Lawrence, 1888-1973, reporter, columnist, publisher; founded *U.S. News & World Report*.

Frank Leslie, 1821-80, engraver, publisher of newspapers and magazines, notably *Leslie's Illustrated Newspaper*.

Alexander Liberman, 1912-99, editorial director for Condé Nast magazines.

A(bbott) J(oseph) Liebling, 1904-63, foreign correspondent, critic; principally with *The New Yorker*.

Walter Lippmann, 1889-1974, political analyst, social critic, columnist, author.

Peter Lisagor, 1915-76, Washington bureau chief, *Chicago Daily News*; broadcast commentator.

David Ross Locke, 1833-88, humorist, satirist under pseudonym P.V. Nasby; owned *Toledo (Ohio) Blade*.

Elijah Parish Lovejoy, 1802-37, abolitionist editor in St. Louis and in Alton, IL; killed by proslavery mob.

Clare Booth Luce, 1903-87, war correspondent for *Life*, diplomat, playwright.

Henry R. Luce, 1898-1967, founded *Time*, *Fortune*, *Life*, *Sports Illustrated*.

Dwight Macdonald, 1906-82, reporter, social critic.

Don Marquis, 1878-1937, humor columnist for *NY Sun* and *NY Tribune*; wrote "Archy and Mehitabel" stories.

Nancy Hicks Maynard, 1946-2008, African American publisher, journalist.

Robert Maynard, 1937-97, first African American editor and then owner of major U.S. paper, the *Oakland Tribune*.

C(harles) K(enny) McClatchy, 1858-1936, founder of McClatchy newspaper chain.

Sarah McClendon, 1910-2003, veteran White House correspondent.

Samuel McClure, 1857-1949, founder (1893) of *McClure's Magazine*, famous for its investigative reporting.

Anne O'Hare McCormick, 1889-1954, foreign correspondent; first woman on *NY Times* editorial board.

Robert R. McCormick, 1880-1955, editor, publisher, executive of *Chicago Tribune* and *NY Daily News*.

Ralph McGill, 1893-1969, crusading editor, publisher of *Atlanta Constitution*.

Mary McGrory, 1918-2004, Washington columnist.

O(scar) O(dd) McIntyre, 1884-1938, feature writer, syndicated columnist on everyday life in New York City.

Joseph Medill, 1823-99, longtime editor of the *Chicago Tribune*.

H(enry) L(ouis) Mencken, 1880-1956, reporter, editor, columnist with *Baltimore Sun* papers; anti-establishment viewpoint.

Edwin Meredith, 1876-1928, founder of magazine company.

Frank A. Munsey, 1854-1925, owner, editor, and publisher of newspapers and magazines, including *Munsey's Magazine*.

Edward R. Murrow, 1908-65, broadcast reporter, executive; reported from Britain in WWII; hosted *See It Now*, *Person to Person*.

Edwin Newman, 1919-2010, NBC news correspondent.

Louella Parsons, 1881-1972, Hollywood gossip columnist.

Ethel L. Payne, 1911-91, African American civil rights reporter.

Daniel Pearl, 1963-2002, American journalist; kidnapped and murdered in Pakistan.

Drew (Andrew Russell) Pearson, 1897-1969, investigative reporter, columnist.

(James) Westbrook Pegler, 1894-1969, reporter, columnist.

Shirley Povich, 1905-98, sports columnist.

Joseph Pulitzer, 1847-1911, *NY World* publisher; founded Columbia Journalism School, Pulitzer Prizes.

Joseph Pulitzer II, 1885-1955, longtime *St. Louis Post-Dispatch* editor, publisher; built it into major paper.

Ernie Pyle, 1900-45, reporter, war correspondent; killed in WWII.

Henry Raymond, 1820-69, cofounder, editor, *NY Times*.

Harry Reasoner, 1923-91, ABC and CBS news reporter, anchor.

John Reed, 1887-1920, reporter; foreign correspondent famous for coverage of Bolshevik Revolution; buried at the Kremlin.

Whitelaw Reid, 1837-1912, longtime editor, *NY Tribune*.

James Reston, 1909-95, *NY Times* political reporter, columnist.

Frank Reynolds, 1923-83, ABC reporter, anchor.

(Henry) Grantland Rice, 1880-1954, sportswriter.

Jacob Riis, 1849-1914, reporter, photographer; exposed slum conditions in *How the Other Half Lives*.

Max Robinson, 1939-88, first African American to anchor network news (ABC), 1978.

A. M. Rosenthal, 1922-2006, reporter, editor for *NY Times* (1943-99).

Harold Ross, 1892-1951, founder, editor, *The New Yorker*.

Carl T. Rowan, 1925-2000, reporter, columnist, author.

Mike Royko, 1932-97, Chicago newspaper columnist; wrote *Boss*, biography of Mayor Richard J. Daley (1902-76).

Louis Rukeyser, 1933-2006, TV journalist, financial analyst; hosted *Wall Street Week* on public television.

(Alfred) Damon Runyon, 1884-1946, sportswriter, columnist; stories collected in *Guys and Dolls*.

Tim Russert, 1950-2008, TV journalist; moderator of *Meet the Press* (NBC).

John B. Russwurm, 1799-1851, cofounded (1827) nation's first black newspaper, *Freedom's Journal*, in New York, NY.

William Safire, 1929-2009, Pulitzer Prizewinning columnist, *NY Times*.

Adela Rogers St. Johns, 1894-1988, reporter, sportswriter for Hearst newspapers.

Pierre Salinger, 1925-2004, press secretary under Pres. Kennedy and Johnson, foreign correspondent.

Harrison Salisbury, 1908-93, reporter, foreign correspondent; a Soviet specialist.

Daniel Schorr, 1916-2010, broadcast and print journalist.

E(dward) W(illis) Scripps, 1854-1926, founded first large U.S. newspaper chain, pioneered syndication.

Eric Sevareid, 1912-92, war correspondent, radio newscaster, CBS commentator.

Randy Shilts, 1951-94, journalist; author of *And the Band Played On*.

William L. Shirer, 1904-93, broadcaster, foreign correspondent; wrote *The Rise and Fall of the Third Reich*.

Howard K. Smith, 1914-2002, ABC news reporter, anchor.

Red (Walter) Smith, 1905-82, sportswriter.

Edgar P. Snow, 1905-71, correspondent; expert on Chinese Communist movement.

Tony Snow, 1955-2008, columnist, radio/TV journalist, White House press sec.

Tom Snyder, 1936-2007, television journalist.

Lawrence Spivak, 1900-94, co-creator, moderator, producer of *Meet the Press*.

(Joseph) Lincoln Steffens, 1866-1936, muckraking journalist.

I(sidor) F(einstein) Stone, 1907-89, one-man editor of *I. F. Stone's Weekly*.

Arthur Hays Sulzberger, 1891-1968, longtime publisher of *NY Times*.

C(yrus) L(eo) Sulzberger, 1912-93, *NY Times* foreign correspondent, columnist.

David Susskind, 1920-87, TV producer, public affairs talk-show host (*Open End*).

John Cameron Swayze, 1906-95, early TV newscaster (NBC).

Herbert Bayard Swope, 1882-1958, war correspondent, editor of *NY World*.

Ida Tarbell, 1857-1944, muckraking journalist.

Isaiah Thomas, 1750-1831, printer, publisher; cofounder of revolutionary journal, *Massachusetts Spy*.

Lowell Thomas, 1892-1981, radio newscaster, world traveler.

Dorothy Thompson, 1894-1961, foreign correspondent, columnist, radio commentator.

Hunter S. Thompson, 1937-2005, political journalist, author; *Fear and Loathing on the Campaign Trail* (1972).

Kenneth Thompson, 1923-2006, Canadian media magnate; owned Toronto *Globe and Mail* newspaper.

Ida Bell Wells-Barnett, 1862-1931, African American reporter, editor, anti-lynching crusader.

William Allen White, 1868-1944, newspaper editor, publisher.

Walter Winchell, 1897-1972, reporter, columnist, broadcaster of celebrity news.

John Peter Zenger, 1697-1746, printer, journalist; acquitted in precedent-setting libel suit (1735).

Military and Naval Leaders of the Past

Reviewed by Alan C. Aimone, USMA Library.

Alexander the Great, 356-323 BCE, (Maced.) conquered Persia and much of the world known to Europeans.

Harold Alexander, 1891-1969, (Br.) led Allied invasion of Italy, 1943, WWII.

Ethan Allen, 1738-89, (U.S.) headed Green Mountain Boys; captured Ft. Ticonderoga, 1775, Amer. Rev.

Edmund Allenby, 1861-1936, (Br.) in Boer War, WWI; led Egyptian expeditionary force, 1917-18.

Benedict Arnold, 1741-1801, (U.S.) victorious at Saratoga; tried to betray West Point to British, Amer. Rev.

Henry "Hap" Arnold, 1886-1950, (U.S.) commanded Army Air Force in WWII.

Ashurnasirpal II, 884-859 BCE, (Assyria) king; began Assyrian conquest of Middle East.

John Barry, 1745-1803, (U.S.) won numerous sea battles during Amer. Rev.

Pierre Beauregard, 1818-93, (U.S.) Confed. general; ordered bombardment of Ft. Sumter that began Civil War.

Belisarius, c. 505-565, (Byzant.) won remarkable victories for Byzantine emperor Justinian I.

Gebhard von Blücher, 1742-1819, (Ger.) helped defeat Napoleon at Waterloo.

Simón Bolívar, 1783-1830, (Venez.) S. Amer. revolutionary who liberated much of the continent from Spanish rule.

Napoleon Bonaparte, 1769-1821, (Fr.) defeated Russia and Austria at Austerlitz, 1805; invaded Russia, 1812; defeated at Waterloo, 1815.

Edward Braddock, 1695-1755, (Br.) commanded forces in French and Indian War.

Omar N. Bradley, 1893-1981, (U.S.) headed U.S. ground troops in Normandy invasion, 1944, WWII.

John Burgoyne, 1722-92, (Br.) general; defeated at Saratoga, Amer. Rev.

Julius Caesar, 100-44 BCE, (Rom.) general and politician; conquered northern Gaul, overthrew Roman Republic.

Charlemagne, 742-814, (Fr.) king of the Franks, Holy Roman Emperor; conquered most of Western Europe.

Claire Lee Chennault, 1893-1958, (U.S.) headed Flying Tigers in WWII.

El Cid (Rodrigo Diaz de Vivar), 1040-99, (Sp.) renowned knight; captured Valencia (1094), hero of "Song of Cid" epic.

Mark W. Clark, 1896-1984, (U.S.) helped plan N. African invasion in WWII; commander of UN forces, Korean War.

Karl von Clausewitz, 1780-1831, (Prus.) military theorist.

Lucius D. Clay, 1897-1978, (U.S.) led Berlin airlift, 1948-49.

Henry Clinton, 1738-95, (Br.) commander of forces in Amer. Rev., 1778-81.

Cochise, c. 1815-74, (Nat. Am.) chief of Chiricahua band of Apache Indians in Southwest.

Charles Cornwallis, 1738-1805, (Br.) victorious at Brandywine, 1777; surrendered at Yorktown, Amer. Rev.

Hernán Cortés, 1485-1547, (Sp.) led Spanish conquistadors in the defeat of the Aztec empire, 1519-28.

Crazy Horse, 1849-77, (Nat. Am.) Sioux war chief victorious at Battle of Little Bighorn.

George Armstrong Custer, 1839-76, (U.S.) army officer defeated and killed at Battle of Little Bighorn.

Benjamin O. Davis Jr., 1912-2002, (U.S.) leader of WWII black aviators; first African American general in U.S. Air Force.

Benjamin O. Davis Sr., 1877-1970, (U.S.) first African American general in U.S. Army (1940).

Moshe Dayan, 1915-81, (Isr.) directed campaigns in the 1967, 1973 Arab-Israeli wars.

Stephen Decatur, 1779-1820, (U.S.) naval hero of Barbary wars, War of 1812.

Anton Denikin, 1872-1947, (Russ.) led White forces in Russian civil war.

George Dewey, 1837-1917, (U.S.) destroyed Spanish fleet at Manila, 1898, Span.-Amer. War.

Karl Doenitz, 1891-1980, (Ger.) submarine comm. in chief and naval commander, WWII; last pres. of Third Reich.

Jimmy Doolittle, 1896-1993, (U.S.) led 1942 air raid on Tokyo and other Japanese cities in WWII.

Hugh Dowding, 1882-1970, (Br.) headed RAF Fighter Command, 1936-40, WWII.

Jubal Early, 1816-94, (U.S.) Confed. general; led raid on Washington, 1864, Civil War.

Dwight D. Eisenhower, 1890-1969, (U.S.) commanded Allied forces in Europe, WWII.

Erich von Falkenhayn, 1861-1922, (Ger.) minister of war, general, commander at Verdun in WWI.

David Farragut, 1801-70, (U.S.) Union admiral; captured New Orleans, Mobile Bay, Civil War.

John Arbuthnot Fisher, 1841-1920, (Br.) WWI admiral; naval reformer.

Ferdinand Foch, 1851-1929, (Fr.) headed victorious Allied armies, 1918, WWI.

Nathan Bedford Forrest, 1821-77, (U.S.) Confed. general; led raids against Union

supply lines, Civil War.

Frederick the Great, 1712-86, (Prus.) led Prussia in Seven Years War.

Horatio Gates, 1728-1806, (U.S.) commanded army at Saratoga, Amer. Rev.

Genghis Khan, 1162-1227, (Mongol) unified Mongol tribes, subjugated much of Asia, 1206-21.

Geronimo, 1829-1909, (Nat. Am.) leader of Chiricahua band of Apache Indians.

Charles G. Gordon, 1833-85, (Br.) led forces in China, Crimean War; killed at Khartoum.

Ulysses S. Grant, 1822-85, (U.S.) headed Union army, Civil War, 1864-65; forced Robert E. Lee's surrender, 1865.

Nathanael Greene, 1742-86, (U.S.) defeated British in Southern campaign, 1780-81, Amer. Rev.

Heinz Guderian, 1888-1954, (Ger.) tank theorist; led panzer forces in Poland, France, Russia, WWII.

Gustavus Adolphus, 1594-1632, (Swed.) king, military tactician, reformer; led forces in Thirty Years' War.

Douglas Haig, 1861-1928, (Br.) led British armies in France, 1915-18, WWI.

William F. Halsey, 1882-1959, (U.S.) defeated Japanese fleet at Leyte Gulf, 1944, WWII.

Hannibal, 247-183 BCE, (Carthage) invaded Rome, crossing Alps, in Second Punic War, 218-201 BCE.

Sir Arthur Travers Harris, 1895-1984, (Br.) led Britain's WWII bomber command.

Paul von Hindenburg, 1847-1934, (Ger.) chief of general staff, WWI; 2nd pres. of Weimar Republic.

Richard Howe, 1726-99, (Br.) commanded navy in Amer. Rev., 1776-78; June 1 victory against French, 1794.

William Howe, 1729-1814, (Br.) commanded forces in Amer. Rev., 1776-78.

Isaac Hull, 1773-1843, (U.S.) sunk British frigate *Guerriere*, War of 1812.

Thomas "Stonewall" Jackson, 1824-63, (U.S.) Confed. general; led Shenandoah Valley campaign, Civil War.

Daniel James Jr., 1920-78, (U.S.) first black 4-star general (1975); commander, N. American Air Defense Command.

Joseph Joffre, 1852-1931, (Fr.) headed Allied armies; won Battle of the Marne, 1914, WWI.

John Paul Jones, 1747-92, (U.S.) commanded *Bonhomme Richard* in victory over *Serapis*, Amer. Rev., 1779.

Chief Joseph, c. 1840-1904, (Nat. Am.) chief of the Nez Percé; forced by army to retreat and surrender.

Stephen Kearny, 1794-1848, (U.S.) headed Army of the West in Mexican War.

Albert Kesselring, 1885-1960, (Ger.) field marshal who led the defense of Italy in WWII.

Ernest J. King, 1878-1956, (U.S.) key WWII naval strategist.

Horatio H. Kitchener, 1850-1916, (Br.) led forces in Boer War, victorious at Khartoum, organized army in WWI.

Henry Knox, 1750-1806, (U.S.) general in Amer. Rev.; first sec. of war under U.S. Constitution.

Lavrenti Kornilov, 1870-1918, (Russ.) commander-in-chief, 1917; led counterrevolutionary march on Petrograd.

Thaddeus Kosciusko, 1746-1817, (Pol.) aided Amer. Rev.

Walter Krueger, 1881-1967, (U.S.) led Sixth Army in WWII in Southwest Pacific.

Mikhail Kutuzov, 1745-1813, (Russ.) fought at Borodino, Napol. Wars, 1812; abandoned Moscow, forced French retreat.

Marquis de Lafayette, 1757-1834, (Fr.) fought in, secured French aid for Amer. Rev.

T(homas) E. Lawrence (of Arabia), 1888-1935, (Br.) organized revolt of Arabs against Turks in WWI.

William Daniel Leahy, 1875-1959, (U.S.) chief of staff to Pres. Roosevelt in WWII, Fleet Admiral.

Henry (Light-Horse Harry) Lee, 1756-1818, (U.S.) cavalry officer in Amer. Rev.

Robert E. Lee, 1807-70, (U.S.) Confed. general; defeated at Gettysburg, Civil War; surrendered to Grant, 1865.

Curtis LeMay, 1906-90, (U.S.) Air Force commander in WWII, Korean War, Vietnam War.

Lyman Lemnitzer, 1899-1988, (U.S.) WWII hero; later general, chairman of Joint Chiefs of Staff.

James Longstreet, 1821-1904, (U.S.) aided Lee at Gettysburg, Civil War.

Erich Ludendorff, 1865-1937, (Ger.) general; victor at Tannenberg, WWI.

Douglas MacArthur, 1880-1964, (U.S.) commanded forces in SW Pacific in WWII; headed occupation forces in Japan, 1945-51; UN commander in Korean War.

Carl Gustaf Mannerheim, 1867-1951, (Fin.) army officer and pres. of Finland, 1944-46.

Erich von Manstein, 1887-1973, (Ger.) served WWI, WWII; planned inv. of France (1940); convicted of war crimes.

Francis Marion, 1733-95, (U.S.) led guerrilla actions in South Carolina during Amer. Rev.

Duke of Marlborough, 1650-1722, (Br.) led forces against Louis XIV in War of the Spanish Succession.

George C. Marshall, 1880-1959, (U.S.) chief of staff in WWII; authored Marshall Plan.

Maurice, Count of Nassau, 1567-1625, (Neth.) military innovator; led forces in Thirty Years' War.

George B. McClellan, 1826-85, (U.S.) Union general; commanded Army of the Potomac, 1861-62, Civil War.

George Meade, 1815-72, (U.S.) commanded Union forces at Gettysburg, Civil War.

Doris "Dorie" Miller, 1919-43, (U.S.) Navy hero of Pearl Harbor attack; first African American awarded Navy Cross.

Billy Mitchell, 1879-1936, (U.S.) WWI air-power advocate; court-martialed for insubordination, later vindicated.

Helmuth von Moltke, 1800-91, (Ger.) victorious in Austro-Prussian, Franco-Prussian wars.

Louis de Montcalm, 1712-59, (Fr.) headed troops in Canada, French and Indian War; defeated at Quebec, 1759.

Bernard Law Montgomery, 1887-1976, (Br.) stopped German offensive at Alamein, 1942, WWII; helped plan Normandy invasion.

Daniel Morgan, 1736-1802, (U.S.) victorious at Cowpens, 1781, Amer. Rev.

Louis Mountbatten, 1900-79, (Br.) Supreme Allied Commander of SE Asia, 1943-46, WWII.

Joachim Murat, 1767-1815, (Fr.) led cavalry at Marengo, Austerlitz, and Jena, Napoleonic Wars.

Horatio Nelson, 1758-1805, (Br.) naval commander; destroyed French fleet at Trafalgar.

Michel Ney, 1769-1815, (Fr.) commanded forces in Switz., Austria, Russ., Napoleonic Wars; defeated at Waterloo.

Chester Nimitz, 1885-1966, (U.S.) commander of naval forces in Pacific in WWII.

George S. Patton, 1885-1945, (U.S.) led assault on Sicily, 1943, Third Army invasion of Europe, WWII.

Oliver Perry, 1785-1819, (U.S.) won Battle of Lake Erie in War of 1812.

John Pershing, 1860-1948, (U.S.) commanded Mexican border campaign, 1916; Amer. Expeditionary Force, WWI.

Henri Philippe Pétain, 1856-1951, (Fr.) defended Verdun, 1916; headed Vichy government in WWII.

George E. Pickett, 1825-75, (U.S.) Confed. general famed for "charge" at Gettysburg, Civil War.

Charles Portal, 1893-1971, (Br.) chief of staff, Royal Air Force, 1940-45; led in Battle of Britain.

Manfred Frieherr von Richthofen (Red Baron), 1892-1918, (Ger.) WWI flying ace, led elite fighter squadron.

Hyman Rickover, 1900-86, (U.S.) father of nuclear navy.

Matthew Bunker Ridgway, 1895-1993, (U.S.) commanded Allied ground forces in Korean War.

Erwin Rommel, 1891-1944, (Ger.) headed Afrika Korps, WWII.

Gerd von Rundstedt, 1875-1953, (Ger.) supreme commander in West, 1942-45, WWII.

Saladin, 1138-93, (Kurdish Muslim) recaptured Jerusalem from Crusaders.

Aleksandr Samsonov, 1859-1914, (Russ.) led invasion of E Prussia, WWI; defeated at Tannenberg, 1914.

Antonio Lopez de Santa Anna, 1794-1876, (Mex.) defeated Texans at the Alamo; defeated in Mexican War.

Maurice, Count of Saxe, 1696-1750, (Fr.) general, noted tactician; War of Austrian Succession, War of Pol. Succession.

Scipio Africanus the Elder, 234?-183 BCE, (Rom.) hero of 2nd Punic War; defeated Hannibal, invaded N. Africa.

Winfield Scott, 1786-1866, (U.S.) hero of War of 1812; headed forces in Mexican War, took Mexico City.

Philip Sheridan, 1831-88, (U.S.) Union cavalry officer; headed Army of the Shenandoah, 1864-65, Civil War.

William T. Sherman, 1820-91, (U.S.) Union general; sacked Atlanta during "march to the sea," 1864, Civil War.

Carl Spaatz, 1891-1974, (U.S.) directed strategic bombing against Germany, later Japan, in WWII.

Raymond Spruance, 1886-1969, (U.S.) victorious at Midway Island, 1942, WWII.

Joseph W. Stilwell, 1883-1946, (U.S.) headed forces in the China, Burma, India theater in WWII.

J.E.B. Stuart, 1833-64, (U.S.) Confed. cavalry commander, Civil War.

Sun Tzu, 6th? cent. BCE, (China) general; author of *The Art of War*.

Aleksandr Suvorov, 1729-1800, (Russ.) commanded Allied Russian and Austrian armies, Russo-Turkish War.

Tamerlane, 1336-1405, (Turkoman Mongol) conqueror; established empire from India to Mediterranean Sea.

George H. Thomas, 1816-70, (U.S.) saved Union army at Chattanooga, 1863; won at Nashville, 1864, Civil War.

Semyon Timoshenko, 1895-1970, (USSR) defended Moscow, Stalingrad, WWII; led winter offensive, 1942-43.

Alfred von Tirpitz, 1849-1930, (Ger.) responsible for submarine blockade in WWI.

Henri de la Tour d'Auvergne, Viscount of Turenne, 1611-75, (Fr.) marshal; Thirty Years' War, Fronde, War of Devolution.

Sebastien Le Prestre de Vauban, 1633-1707, (Fr.) innovative military engineer, theorist.

Jonathan M. Wainwright, 1883-1953, (U.S.) forced to surrender on Corregidor, Philippines, 1942, WWII.

George Washington, 1732-99, (U.S.) led Continental army, 1775-83, Amer. Rev.

Archibald Wavell, 1883-1950, (Br.) commanded forces in N and E Africa, SE Asia in WWII.

Anthony Wayne, 1745-96, (U.S.) captured Stony Point, NY, 1779, Amer. Rev.

Duke of Wellington, 1769-1852, (Br.) defeated Napoleon at Waterloo, 1815.

William Westmoreland, 1914-2005, (U.S.) commanded forces in Vietnam, 1964-68.

William I (The Conqueror), 1027-87, (Br.) victor, Battle of Hastings, 1066; became first Norman king of England.

James Wolfe, 1727-59, (Br.) captured Quebec from French, 1759, French and Indian War.

Isoroku Yamamoto, 1884-1943, (Jpn.) cmdr. in chief of Japanese fleet, naval planner before and during WWII.

Georgi Zhukov, 1895-1974, (Russ.) defended Moscow, 1941; led assault on Berlin, 1945, WWII.

Philosophers and Religious Figures of the Past

Excludes most biblical figures and popes (see Religion). For Greeks and Romans, see also Historical Figures chapter.

Lyman Abbott, 1835-1922, (U.S.) clergyman, reformer; advocate of Christian Socialism.

Pierre Abelard, 1079-1142, (Fr.) philosopher, theologian, teacher; used dialectic method to support Christian beliefs.

Felix Adler, 1851-1933, (U.S.) German-born founder of the Ethical Culture Soc.

Mortimer Adler, 1902-2001, (U.S.) philosopher; helped create "Great Books" program.

(St.) Anselm, c. 1033-1109, (It.) philosopher-theologian, church leader; "ontological argument" for God's existence.

(St.) Thomas Aquinas, 1225-74, (It.) preeminent medieval philosopher-theologian; *Summa Theologica*.

Aristotle, 384-322 BCE, (Gr.) pioneering wide-ranging philosopher, logician, ethician, naturalist.

(St.) Augustine, 354-430, (N. Africa) philosopher, theologian, bishop; *Confessions, City of God, On the Trinity*.

J. L. Austin, 1911-60, (Br.) ordinary-language philosopher.

Averroes (Ibn Rushd), 1126-98, (Sp.) Islamic philosopher, physician.

Avicenna (Ibn Sina), 980-1037, (Iran) Islamic philosopher, scientist.

A(lfred) J(ules) Ayer, 1910-89, (Br.) philosopher, logical positivist; *Language, Truth, and Logic*.

Roger Bacon, c. 1214-94, (Eng.) philosopher, scientist.

Bahá'u'lláh (Mirza Husayn Ali), 1817-92, (Pers.) founder of Bahá'í faith.

Karl Barth, 1886-1968, (Switz.) theologian; a leading force in 20th-cent. Protestantism.

Thomas à Becket, 1118-70, (Eng.) archbishop of Canterbury; opposed Henry II, murdered by King's men.

(St.) Benedict, c. 480-547, (It.) founded the Benedictines.

Jeremy Bentham, 1748-1832, (Br.) philosopher, reformer; enunciated utilitarianism.

Henri Bergson, 1859-1941, (Fr.) philosopher of evolution.

George Berkeley, 1685-1753, (Ire.) idealist philosopher, bishop.

John Biddle, 1615-62, (Eng.) founder of English Unitarianism.

Jakob Boehme, 1575-1624, (Ger.) theosophist, mystic.

Dietrich Bonhoeffer, 1906-45, (Ger.) Lutheran theologian, pastor; executed as opponent of Nazis.

William Brewster, 1567-1644, (Eng.) led Pilgrims.

Emil Brunner, 1889-1966, (Switz.) Protestant theologian.

Giordano Bruno, 1548-1600, (It.) philosopher, pantheist.

Martin Buber, 1878-1965, (Ger.) Jewish philosopher, theologian; *I and Thou*.

Buddha (Siddhartha Gautama), c. 563-c. 483 BCE, (India) philosopher; founded Buddhism.

John Calvin, 1509-64, (Fr.) theologian; a key figure in the Protestant Reformation.

Rudolph Carnap, 1891-1970, (U.S.) German-born analytic philosopher, a founder of logical positivism.

William Ellery Channing, 1780-1842, (U.S.) clergyman; early spokesman for Unitarianism.

Auguste Comte, 1798-1857, (Fr.) philosopher; originated positivism.

Confucius, 551-479 BCE, (China) founder of Confucianism.

John Cotton, 1584-1652, (Eng.) Puritan theologian.

Thomas Cranmer, 1489-1556, (Eng.) Anglican churchman; wrote much of *Book of Common Prayer*.

Jacques Derrida, 1930-2004, (Fr.) deconstructionist philosopher.

René Descartes, 1596-1650, (Fr.) philosopher, mathematician; "father of modern philosophy"; *Discourse on Method, Meditations on First Philosophy*.

John Dewey, 1859-1952, (U.S.) philosopher, educator; instrumentalist theory of knowledge, progressive education.

Denis Diderot, 1713-84, (Fr.) philosopher, encyclopedist.

John Duns Scotus, c. 1266-1308, (Sc.) Franciscan philosopher, theologian.

Mary Baker Eddy, 1821-1910, (U.S.) founder of Christian Science; *Science and Health*.

Jonathan Edwards, 1703-58, (U.S.) preacher, theologian; "Sinners in the Hands of an Angry God."

(Desiderius) Erasmus, c. 1466-1536, (Neth.) Renaissance humanist; *On the Freedom of the Will*.

Jerry Falwell, 1933-2007, (U.S.) TV evangelist, religious commentator.

Johann Fichte, 1762-1814, (Ger.) idealist philosopher.

Michel Foucault, 1926-84, (Fr.) structuralist philosopher, historian.

George Fox, 1624-91, (Br.) founder of Society of Friends (Quakers).

(St.) Francis of Assisi, 1182-1226, (It.) espoused voluntary poverty, founded Franciscans.

al-Ghazali, 1058-1111, ([now] Iran) Islamic philosopher.

Billy James Hargis, 1925-2004, (U.S.) anti-Communist televangelist; founder of the Church of the Christian Crusade.

Georg W. F. Hegel, 1770-1831, (Ger.) idealist philosopher; *Phenomenology of Mind*.

Martin Heidegger, 1889-1976, (Ger.) existentialist philosopher; affected many fields; *Being and Time*.

Johann G. Herder, 1744-1803, (Ger.) philosopher, cultural historian; a founder of German Romanticism.

Thomas Hobbes, 1588-1679, (Eng.) philosopher, political theorist; *Leviathan*.

David Hume, 1711-76, (Scot.) empiricist philosopher; *Enquiry Concerning Human Understanding*.

Jan Hus, 1369-1415, (Czech.) religious reformer.

Edmund Husserl, 1859-1938, (Ger.) philosopher; founded the phenomenological movement.

Thomas Huxley, 1825-95, (Br.) philosopher, educator.

William Ralph Inge, 1860-1954, (Br.) theologian; explored mystic aspects of Christianity.

William James, 1842-1910, (U.S.) philosopher, psychologist, pragmatist; studied religious experience.

Karl Jaspers, 1883-1969, (Ger.) existentialist philosopher.

Joan of Arc, 1412-31, (Fr.) national heroine, a patron saint of France; key figure in the Hundred Years' War.

Immanuel Kant, 1724-1804, (Ger.) philosopher; founder of modern critical philosophy; *Critique of Pure Reason*.

Thomas à Kempis, c. 1380-1471, (Ger.) monk, devotional writer; *Imitation of Christ* attributed to him.

Soren Kierkegaard, 1813-55, (Den.) religious philosopher, pre-existentialist; *Either/Or, The Sickness Unto Death*.

John Knox, 1505-72, (Scot.) leader of Protestant Reformation in Scotland.

Lao-Tzu, 604-531 BCE, (China) philosopher; considered the founder of the Taoist religion.

Gottfried von Leibniz, 1646-1716, (Ger.) rationalist philosopher, logician, mathematician.

John Locke, 1632-1704, (Eng.) political theorist, empiricist philosopher; *Essay Concerning Human Understanding*.

(St.) Ignatius Loyola, 1491-1556, (Sp.) founder of the Jesuits; *Spiritual Exercises*.

Martin Luther, 1483-1546, (Ger.) leader of the Protestant Reformation; founded Lutheran church.

Jean-Francois Lyotard, 1924-98, (Fr.) postmodern philosopher, lecturer; *The Post-Modern Condition*.

Maimonides, 1135-1204, (Sp.) major Jewish philosopher.

Gabriel Marcel, 1889-1973, (Fr.) Rom. Cath. existentialist philosopher, dramatist.

Jacques Maritain, 1882-1973, (Fr.) neo-Thomist philosopher.

Cotton Mather, 1663-1728, (U.S.) defender of orthodox Puritanism; founded Yale, 1701.

Aimee Semple McPherson, 1890-1944, (Can.) Pentecostal evangelist.

Philipp Melanchthon, 1497-1560, (Ger.) theologian, humanist; an important voice in the Reformation.

Maurice Merleau-Ponty, 1908-61, (Fr.) existentialist philosopher; *Phenomenology of Perception*.

Thomas Merton, 1915-68, (U.S.) Trappist monk, spiritual writer; *The Seven Storey Mountain*.

Dwight Moody, 1837-99, (U.S.) evangelist.

G(eorge) E(dward) Moore, 1873-1958, (Br.) philosopher; *Principia Ethica*, "A Defense of Common Sense."

Muhammad, c. 570-632, (Arab.) prophet of Islam.

Elijah Muhammad, 1897-1975, (U.S.) founder of Black Muslim group, Nation of Islam.

Heinrich Muhlenberg, 1711-87, (Ger.) organized the Lutheran Church in America.

John H. Newman, 1801-90, (Br.) Rom. Cath. convert, cardinal; led Oxford Movement; *Apologia pro Vita Sua*.

Reinhold Niebuhr, 1892-1971, (U.S.) Protestant theologian.

Richard Niebuhr, 1894-1962, (U.S.) Protestant theologian.

Friedrich Nietzsche, 1844-1900, (Ger.) philosopher; *The Birth of Tragedy, Beyond Good and Evil, Thus Spake Zarathustra*.

Robert Nozick, 1938-2002, (U.S.) political philosopher; *Anarchy, State, and Utopia*.

Blaise Pascal, 1623-62, (Fr.) philosopher, mathematician; *Pensées*.

(St.) Patrick, c. 389-c. 461, (Br.) brought Christianity to Ireland.

Norman Vincent Peale, 1898-1993, (U.S.) minister, author; *The Power of Positive Thinking*.

C(harles) S. Peirce, 1839-1914, (U.S.) philosopher, logician; originated concept of pragmatism, 1878.

Plato, c. 428-347 BCE, (Gr.) philosopher; wrote Socratic dialogues; argued for immortality of soul, indep. reality of ideas or forms; *Republic, Meno, Phaedo, Apology*.

Plotinus, 205-70, (Rom.) a founder of neo-Platonism; *Enneads*.

W(illard) V(an) O(rman) Quine, 1908-2001, (U.S.) philosopher, logician; "On What There Is."

John Rawls, 1922-2002, (U.S.) political philosopher; *A Theory of Justice*.

Oral Roberts, 1918-2009, (U.S.) televangelist, university founder.

Moishe Rosen, 1932-2010, (U.S.) Jews for Jesus founder.

Josiah Royce, 1855-1916, (U.S.) idealist philosopher.

Bertrand Russell, 1872-1970, (Br.) philosopher, logician; one of the founders of modern logic; a prolific popular writer.

Charles T. Russell, 1852-1916, (U.S.) founder of Jehovah's Witnesses.

Gilbert Ryle, 1900-76, (Br.) analytic philosopher; *The Concept of Mind*.

George Santayana, 1863-1952, (U.S.) philosopher, writer, critic; *The Sense of Beauty, The Realms of Being*.

Jean-Paul Sartre, 1905-80, (Fr.) philosopher, novelist, playwright; *Nausea, No Exit, Being and Nothingness*.

Friedrich von Schelling, 1775-1854, (Ger.) philosopher of romantic movement.

Friedrich Schleiermacher, 1768-1834, (Ger.) theologian; a founder of modern Protestant theology.

Arthur Schopenhauer, 1788-1860, (Ger.) philosopher; *The World as Will and Idea*.

Albert Schweitzer, 1875-1965, (Ger.) theologian, social philosopher, medical missionary.

Joseph Smith, 1805-44, (U.S.) founded Latter-Day Saints (Mormon) movement, 1830.

Socrates, 469-399 BCE, (Gr.) philosopher immortalized by Plato.

Herbert Spencer, 1820-1903, (Br.) philosopher of evolution.

Herbert Spiegel, 1914-2009, (U.S.) psychiatrist who popularized hypnosis.

Baruch de Spinoza, 1632-77, (Neth.) rationalist philosopher; *Ethics*.

John Stott, 1921-2011, (Br.) evangelical Anglican cleric.

Billy Sunday, 1862-1935, (U.S.) evangelist.

Emanuel Swedenborg, 1688-1772, (Swed.) philosopher, mystic; *Principia*.

Pierre Teilhard de Chardin, 1881-1955, (Fr.) Jesuit priest, paleontologist, philosopher-theologian; *The Divine Milieu*.

Daisetz Teitaro Suzuki, 1870-1966, (Jpn.) Buddhist scholar.

(St.) Therese of Lisieux, 1873-97, (Fr.) Carmelite nun ("Little Flower"), revered for everyday sanctity; *The Story of a Soul*.

Paul Tillich, 1886-1965, (U.S.) German-born philosopher, theologian; brought depth psychology to Protestantism.

John Wesley, 1703-91, (Br.) theologian, evangelist; founded Methodism.

Alfred North Whitehead, 1861-1947, (Br.) philosopher, mathematician; *Process and Reality*.

William of Occam, c. 1285-c. 1349, (Eng.) medieval scholastic philosopher, nominalist.

Roger Williams, c. 1603-83, (U.S.) clergyman; championed religious freedom and separation of church and state.

Ludwig Wittgenstein, 1889-1951, (Austria) philosopher; major influence on contemporary language philosophy; *Tractatus Logico-Philosophicus, Philosophical Investigations*.

John Woolman, 1720-72, (U.S.) Quaker social reformer, abolitionist, writer; *The Journal*.

John Wycliffe, 1320-84, (Eng.) theologian, reformer.

(St.) Francis Xavier, 1506-52, (Sp.) Jesuit missionary; "Apostle of the Indies."

Brigham Young, 1801-77, (U.S.) Mormon leader after Joseph Smith's assassination; colonized Utah.

Huldrych Zwingli, 1484-1531, (Switz.) theologian; led Swiss Protestant Reformation.

Political Leaders of the Past

U.S. presidents, vice presidents, Supreme Court justices, signers of the Declaration of Independence listed elsewhere.

Abu Bakr, 573-634, (Arab.) Muslim leader, first caliph, chosen successor to Muhammad.

Dean Acheson, 1893-1971, (U.S.) sec. of state; architect of Cold War foreign policy.

Samuel Adams, 1722-1803, (U.S.) patriot; Boston Tea Party firebrand.

Konrad Adenauer, 1876-1967, (Ger.) first West German chancellor.

Emilio Aguinaldo, 1869-1964, (Philip.) revolutionary; fought against Spain and the U.S.

Corazon Aquino, 1933-2009, (Philip.) president of the Philippines, 1986-92.

Akbar, 1542-1605, greatest Mogul emperor of India.

Carl Albert, 1908-2000, (U.S.) House rep. (D, OK), Speaker, 1971-76.

Salvador Allende Gossens, 1908-73, (Chile) Marxist pres., 1970-73; ousted and died in coup.

Idi Amin, 1925-2003, (Uganda) Ugandan ruler, 1971-79; blamed for hundreds of thousands of deaths.

Yasir Arafat, 1929-2004, (Egypt) leader of the Palestine Liberation Organization (PLO).

Herbert H. Asquith, 1852-1928, (Br.) Liberal prime min.; instituted major social reforms.

Hafez al Assad, 1930-2000, (Syr.) Syrian ruler from 1970.

Atahualpa, 1500?-1533, (Inca) ruling chief of Peru.

Kemal Ataturk, 1881-1938, (Turk.) founded modern Turkey.

Clement Attlee, 1883-1967, (Br.) Labour party leader, prime min.; enacted natl.

health care system, nationalized many industries.

Stephen F. Austin, 1793-1836, (U.S.) led Texas colonization.

Mikhail Bakunin, 1814-76, (Russ.) revolutionary; leading exponent of anarchism.

Arthur J. Balfour, 1848-1930, (Br.) foreign sec. under Lloyd George; issued Balfour Declaration backing Zionism.

Bernard M. Baruch, 1870-1965, (U.S.) financier, govt. adviser.

Fulgencio Batista y Zaldívar, 1901-73, (Cub.) Cuban pres., 1940-44, 1952-59; overthrown by Castro.

Lord Beaverbrook, 1879-1964, (Br.) financier, statesman, newspaper owner.

Menachem Begin, 1913-92, (Isr.) Israeli prime min.; shared 1978 Nobel Peace Prize.

Eduard Benes, 1884-1948, (Czech.) pres. during interwar and post-WWII eras.

David Ben-Gurion, 1886-1973, (Isr.) first prime min. of Israel, 1948-53, 1955-63.

Thomas Hart Benton, 1782-1858, (U.S.) MO senator; championed agrarian interests and westward expansion.

Aneurin Bevan, 1897-1960, (Br.) Labour party leader.

Ernest Bevin, 1881-1951, (Br.) Labour party leader, foreign minister; helped lay foundation for NATO.

Benazir Bhutto, 1953-2007, (Pak.) former prime minister of Pakistan.

Otto von Bismarck, 1815-98, (Ger.) statesman known as the Iron Chancellor; uniter of Germany, 1870.

James G. Blaine, 1830-93, (U.S.) Republican politician, diplomat; influential in Pan-American movement.

Léon Blum, 1872-1950, (Fr.) socialist leader, writer; headed first Popular Front government.

William E. Borah, 1865-1940, (U.S.) isolationist senator; helped block U.S. membership in League of Nations.

Cesare Borgia, 1476-1507, (It.) soldier, politician; an outstanding figure of the Italian Renaissance.

P. W. Botha, 1916-2006, (S. Africa) S. African president, prime minister.

Tom Bradley, 1917-98, (U.S.) first African American mayor of L.A.

Willy Brandt, 1913-92, (Ger.) statesman, chancellor of West Germany, 1969-74; promoted East/West peace, *Ostpolitik*.

Leonid Brezhnev, 1906-82, (USSR) Soviet leader, 1964-82.

Aristide Briand, 1862-1932, (Fr.) foreign min.; chief architect of Locarno Pact and anti-war Kellogg-Briand Pact.

William Jennings Bryan, 1860-1925, (U.S.) Democratic, populist leader, orator; 3 times lost race for presidency.

Ralph Bunche, 1904-71, (U.S.) first black person to win the Nobel Peace Prize, 1950; undersecretary of the UN, 1950.

Byrd, Robert, 1917-2010, (U.S.) longest serving senator (D, WV).

John C. Calhoun, 1782-1850, (U.S.) political leader; champion of states' rights and a symbol of the Old South.

James Callaghan (Baron Callaghan), 1912-2005, (Br.) Labour party politician, prime min., 1976-79.

Robert Castlereagh, 1769-1822, (Br.) foreign sec.; guided Grand Alliance against Napoleon.

Camillo Benso Cavour, 1810-61, (It.) statesman; largely responsible for uniting Italy under the House of Savoy.

Nicolae Ceausescu, 1918-89, (Roman.) Communist leader, head of state, 1967-89; executed.

Austen Chamberlain, 1863-1937, (Br.) statesman; helped finalize Locarno Treaties, both 1925.

Neville Chamberlain, 1869-1940, (Br.) Conservative prime min. whose appeasement of Hitler led to Munich Pact.

Chiang Kai-shek, 1887-1975, (China) Nationalist Chinese pres. whose government was driven from mainland to Taiwan.

Madame Chiang Kai-shek (Mayling Soong), 1898-2003, (China) highly influential wife of Nationalist Chinese leader Chiang Kai-shek.

Shirley Chisholm, 1924-2005, (U.S.) first black woman elected to U.S. House (1968, D, NY); pres. contender, 1972.

Warren Christopher, 1925-2011, (U.S.) secretary of state, diplomat.

Winston Churchill, 1874-1965, (Br.) prime min., soldier, author; guided Britain through WWII.

Galeazzo Ciano, 1903-44, (It.) Fascist foreign minister; helped create Rome-Berlin Axis; executed by Benito Mussolini.

Henry Clay, 1777-1852, (U.S.) "The Great Compromiser"; one of the most influential pre-Civil War political leaders.

Georges Clemenceau, 1841-1929, (Fr.) twice prem.; Woodrow Wilson's antagonist at Paris Peace Conference after WWI.

DeWitt Clinton, 1769-1828, (U.S.) political leader; responsible for promoting the Erie Canal.

Robert Clive, 1725-74, (Br.) first administrator of Bengal; laid foundation for British Empire in India.

Jean Baptiste Colbert, 1619-83, (Fr.) statesman; influential under Louis XIV; created the French navy.

Bettino Craxi, 1934-2000, (It.) Italy's first post-WWII Socialist premier.

David Crockett, 1786-1836, (U.S.) frontiersman, congressman; died defending the Alamo.

Oliver Cromwell, 1599-1658, (Br.) Lord Protector of England; led parliamentary forces during Civil War.

Curzon of Kedleston, 1859-1925, (Br.) viceroy of India, foreign sec.; major force in post-WWI world.

Édouard Daladier, 1884-1970, (Fr.) Radical Socialist politician, arrested by Vichy, interned by Germans until 1945.

Richard J. Daley, 1902-76, (U.S.) Chicago mayor.

Georges Danton, 1759-94, (Fr.) leading French Rev. figure.

Jefferson Davis, 1808-89, (U.S.) pres. of the Confederacy.

Charles G. Dawes, 1865-1951, (U.S.) statesman, banker; advanced plan to stabilize post-WWI German finances.

William L. Dawson, 1886-1970, (U.S.) IL congressman; first black chairman of a major U.S. House committee.

Alcide De Gasperi, 1881-1954, (It.) prime min.; founder of Christian Democratic party.

Charles De Gaulle, 1890-1970, (Fr.) general, statesman; first pres. of the Fifth Republic.

Deng Xiaoping, 1904-97, (China) "paramount leader" of China; backed economic modernization.

Eamon De Valera, 1882-1975, (Ire.-U.S.) statesman; led fight for Irish independence.

Thomas E. Dewey, 1902-71, (U.S.) NY governor (R); twice lost in try for presidency.

Ngo Dinh Diem, 1901-63, (Viet.) South Vietnamese pres.; assassinated in government takeover.

Everett M. Dirksen, 1896-1969, (U.S.) Senate Republican minority leader, orator.

Benjamin Disraeli, 1804-81, (Br.) prime min.; considered founder of modern Conservative party.

Anatoly Dobrynin, 1919-2010, (Russ.) diplomat and Soviet amb. to U.S. (1962-86).

Engelbert Dollfuss, 1892-1934, (Austria) chancellor; assassinated by Austrian Nazis.

Andrea Doria, 1466-1560, (It.) Genoese admiral, statesman; called "Father of Peace" and "Liberator of Genoa."

Stephen A. Douglas, 1813-61, (U.S.) Democratic leader, orator; ran against Lincoln for IL sen. seat, presidency.

Alexander Dubcek, 1921-92, (Czech.) statesman whose attempted liberalization was crushed, 1968.

John Foster Dulles, 1888-1959, (U.S.) sec. of state under Eisenhower; Cold War policy maker.

Lawrence Eagleburger, 1930-2011, (U.S.) diplomat and foreign policy advisor.

Abba Eban, 1915-2002, (Isr.) diplomat; foreign min., 1966-74.

Friedrich Ebert, 1871-1925, (Ger.) Social Democratic movement leader; 1st pres., Weimar Republic, 1919-25.

Sir Anthony Eden, 1897-1977, (Br.) foreign sec., prime min. during Suez invasion of 1956.

Ludwig Erhard, 1897-1977, (Ger.) economist, West German chancellor; led nation's economic rise after WWII.

King Fahd, 1923-2005, (Saudi Arabia) monarch from 1982 but inactive after 1995 stroke; encouraged U.S. relations.

Geraldine Ferraro, 1935-2011 (U.S.) former U.S. rep. (D, NY), vice-pres. nominee.

Joao Baptista de Figueiredo, 1918-99, (Braz.) president of Brazil; restored the nation's democracy.

Hamilton Fish, 1808-93, (U.S.) sec. of state; successfully mediated disputes with Great Britain, Latin America.

James V. Forrestal, 1892-1949, (U.S.) sec. of navy, first sec. of defense.

Francisco Franco, 1892-1975, (Sp.) leader of rebel forces during Spanish Civil War, longtime ruler of Spain.

Benjamin Franklin, 1706-90, (U.S.) printer, publisher, author, inventor, scientist, diplomat.

Louis de Frontenac, 1620-98, (Fr.) governor of New France (Canada); encouraged explorations, fought Iroquois.

J. William Fulbright, 1905-95, (U.S.) senator (D, AR); leading figure in U.S. foreign policy during Cold War years.

Hugh Gaitskell, 1906-63, (Br.) Labour party leader; major force in reversing its stand for unilateral disarmament.

Albert Gallatin, 1761-1849, (U.S.) sec. of treasury; instrumental in negotiating end of War of 1812.

Léon Gambetta, 1838-82, (Fr.) statesman, politician; one of the founders of the Third Republic.

Indira Gandhi, 1917-84, (In.) daughter of Jawaharlal Nehru; prime min. of India, 1966-77, 1980-84; assassinated.

Mohandas K. Gandhi, 1869-1948, (In.) political leader, ascetic; led movement against British rule; assassinated.

Giuseppe Garibaldi, 1807-82, (It.) patriot, soldier; a leader in the Risorgimento, Italian unification movement.

William E. Gladstone, 1809-98, (Br.) prime min. 4 times; dominant force of Liberal party 1868-94.

Paul Joseph Goebbels, 1897-1945, (Ger.) Nazi propagandist; master of mass psychology.

Barry Goldwater, 1909-98, (U.S.) conservative U.S. senator (AZ), 1964 Republican pres. nominee.

Klement Gottwald, 1896-1953, (Czech.) Communist leader; ushered Communism into his country.

Alexander Hamilton, 1755-1804, (U.S.) first treasury sec.; champion of strong central government.

Dag Hammarskjold, 1905-61, (Swed.) statesman; UN sec.-general.

King Hassan II, 1929-99, (Moroc.) ruler of Morocco,1962-99.

John Hay, 1838-1905, (U.S.) sec. of state; primarily associated with Open Door Policy toward China.

Sir Edward Heath, 1916-2005, (Br.) Conservative prime min., 1970-74; promoted European unity.

Jesse Helms, 1921-2008, (U.S.) conservative senator (R, NC).

Patrick Henry, 1736-99, (U.S.) major Revolutionary War figure, orator.

Édouard Herriot, 1872-1957, (Fr.) Radical Socialist leader; twice prem., pres. of National Assembly.

Theodor Herzl, 1860-1904, (Hung.) founded modern Zionism.

Heinrich Himmler, 1900-45, (Ger.) head of Nazi SS and Gestapo.

Paul von Hindenburg, 1847-1934, (Ger.) field marshal, WWI; 2nd pres. of Weimar Republic, 1925-34.

Adolf Hitler, 1889-1945, (Ger.) dictator; built Nazism, launched WWII, presided over the Holocaust.

Ho Chi Minh, 1890-1969, (Viet.) N. Vietnamese pres., Vietnamese Communist leader.

Harry L. Hopkins, 1890-1946, (U.S.) New Deal administrator; closest adviser to Franklin D. Roosevelt during WWII.

Edward M. House, 1858-1938, (U.S.) diplomat; confidential adviser to Woodrow Wilson.

Samuel Houston, 1793-1863, (U.S.) leader of struggle for Texas independence.

Cordell Hull, 1871-1955, (U.S.) sec. of state, 1933-44; initiated reciprocal trade to lower tariffs, helped organize UN.

Hubert H. Humphrey, 1911-78, (U.S.) senator (D, MN), vice pres., pres. candidate.

King Hussein, 1935-99, (Jordan) peacemaker; ruler of Jordan, 1952-99.

Saddam Hussein, 1937-2006, (Iraq) Iraqi ruler; put to death for crimes against humanity.

Muhammad Ali Jinnah, 1876-1948, (Pak.) founder, first governor-general of Pakistan.

Barbara Jordan, 1936-96, (U.S.) congresswoman, orator, educator; first black woman to win a seat in the TX senate, 1966.

Benito Juarez, 1806-72, (Mex.) rallied his country against foreign threats; sought to create democratic, federal republic.

Constantine Karamanlis, 1907-98, (Gr.) Greek prime min.; restored democracy, later president.

Frank B. Kellogg, 1856-1937, (U.S.) sec. of state; negotiated Kellogg-Briand Pact to outlaw war.

Jack Kemp, 1935-2009, (U.S.) sec. of HUD, U.S. rep. (R, NY), football player.

Edward M. Kennedy, 1932-2009, (U.S.) senator (D, MA); championed progressive causes.

Robert F. Kennedy, 1925-68, (U.S.) attorney general, sen. (D, NY); assassinated while seeking presidency.

Aleksandr Kerensky, 1881-1970, (Russ.) headed provisional government after Feb. 1917 revolution.

Ayatollah Ruhollah Khomeini, 1900-89, (Iran), religious-political leader; spearheaded overthrow of Shah, 1979.

Nikita Khrushchev, 1894-1971, (USSR) prem., first sec. of Communist party; initiated de-Stalinization.

Kim Dae Jung, 1925-2009, (Korea) former S. Korean dissident, opposition leader, pres.; 2000 Nobel Peace Prize winner.

Kim Il Sung, 1912-94, (Korea) N. Korean dictator, 1948-94.

Lajos Kossuth, 1802-94, (Hung.) principal figure in 1848 Hungarian revolution.

Pyotr Kropotkin, 1842-1921, (Russ.) anarchist; championed the peasants but opposed Bolshevism.

Kublai Khan, c. 1215-94, (Mongol) emperor; founder of Yüan dynasty in China.

Béla Kun, 1886-c. 1939, (Hung.) member of 3rd Communist International; tried to foment worldwide revolution.

Robert M. LaFollette, 1855-1925, (U.S.) WI public official; leader of progressive movement.

Fiorello La Guardia, 1882-1947, (U.S.) New York City reform mayor.

Pierre Laval, 1883-1945, (Fr.) politician, Vichy foreign min.; executed for treason.

Andrew Bonar Law, 1858-1923, (Br.) Conservative party politician; led opposition to Irish home rule.

Vladimir Ilyich Lenin (Ulyanov), 1870-1924, (Russ.) revolutionary; founded Bolshevism; Soviet leader, 1917-24.

Ferdinand de Lesseps, 1805-94, (Fr.) diplomat, engineer; conceived idea of Suez Canal.

Rene Levesque, 1922-87, (Can.) prem. of Quebec, 1976-85; led unsuccessful separatist campaign.

Trygve Lie, 1896-1968, (Nor.) first UN sec.-gen.

Maxim Litvinov, 1876-1951, (Pol.-Russ.) revolutionary, commissar of foreign affairs; favored cooperation with West.

Liu Shaoqi, c. 1898-1969, (China) Communist leader; fell from grace during Cultural Revolution.

David Lloyd George, 1863-1945, (Br.) Liberal party prime min.; laid foundations for modern welfare state.

Henry Cabot Lodge, 1850-1924, (U.S.) Republican senator; led opposition to participation in League of Nations.

Huey P. Long, 1893-1935, (U.S.) Louisiana political demagogue, governor, U.S. senator; assassinated.

Rosa Luxemburg, 1871-1919, (Ger.) revolutionary; leader of the German Social Democratic party and Spartacus party.

J. Ramsay MacDonald, 1866-1937, (Br.) first Labour party prime min. of Great Britain.

Harold Macmillan, 1895-1986, (Br.) prime min. of Great Britain, 1957-63.

Makarios III, 1913-77, (Cyprus) Greek Orthodox archbishop; first pres. of Cyprus.

Wilma Mankiller, 1945-2010, (U.S.) first female Chief of the Cherokee Nation.

Mao Zedong, 1893-1976, (China) chief Chinese Marxist theorist, revolutionary, political leader; led revolution establishing his nation as Communist state.

Jean Paul Marat, 1743-93, (Fr.) revolutionary, politician; identified with radical Jacobins; assassinated.

Thurgood Marshall, 1908-93, (U.S.) first black U.S. solicitor general, 1965; first black justice of U.S. Supreme Court, 1967-91.

José Martí, 1853-95, (Cub.) patriot, poet; leader of Cuban struggle for independence.

Jan Masaryk, 1886-1948, (Czech.) foreign min.; died under mysterious circumstances, allegedly committed suicide following Communist coup.

Thomas G. Masaryk, 1850-1937, (Czech.) statesman, philosopher; first pres. of Czechoslovakia.

Jules Mazarin, 1602-61, (Fr.) cardinal, statesman; prime min. under Louis XIII and queen regent Anne of Austria.

Giuseppe Mazzini, 1805-72, (It.) reformer dedicated to Risorgimento movement for renewal of Italy.

Tom Mboya, 1930-69, (Kenya) political leader; instrumental in securing independence for Kenya.

Eugene McCarthy, 1916-2005, (U.S.) political leader, author; 1968 Dem. presidential contender.

Joseph R. McCarthy, 1908-57, (U.S.) senator (R, WI); extremist in searching out alleged Communists and pro-Communists.

Cosimo I de' Medici, 1519-74, (It.) Duke of Florence, grand duke of Tuscany.

Lorenzo de' Medici, the Magnificent, 1449-92, (It.) merchant prince; a towering figure in Italian Renaissance.

Catherine de Médicis, 1519-89, (Fr.) queen consort of Henry II, regent of France; influential in Catholic-Huguenot wars.

Golda Meir, 1898-1978, (Isr.) a founder of the state of Israel; prime min., 1969-74.

Klemens W. N. L. Metternich, 1773-1859, (Austria) statesman; arbiter of post-Napoleonic Europe.

Slobodan Milosevic, 1941-2006, (Serbia/Yugoslavia) former Yugoslav pres.; tried for war crimes.

François Mitterrand, 1916-96, (Fr.) pres. of France, 1981-95.

Mobutu Sese Seko, 1930-97, (Zaire) longtime ruler of Zaire (now Dem. Rep. of Congo), 1965-97; exiled after rebellion.

Guy Mollet, 1905-75, (Fr.) socialist politician, resistance leader.

Henry Morgenthau Jr., 1891-1967, (U.S.) sec. of treasury; fundraiser for New Deal and U.S. WWII activities.

Gouverneur Morris, 1752-1816, (U.S.) statesman, diplomat, financial expert; helped plan decimal coinage.

Daniel Patrick Moynihan, 1927-2003, (U.S.) senator (D, NY), diplomat, social scientist, author.

Benito Mussolini, 1883-1945, (It.) leader of the Italian fascist state; assassinated.

Imre Nagy, c. 1896-1958, (Hung.) Communist prem.; assassinated after Soviets crushed 1956 uprising.

Gamal Abdel Nasser, 1918-70, (Egypt) leader of Arab unification, 2nd Egyptian pres.

Jawaharlal Nehru, 1889-1964, (In.) prime min.; guided India through its early years of independence.

Kwame Nkrumah, 1909-72, (Ghana) 1st prime min., 1957-60; pres., 1960-66, of Ghana.

Frederick North, 1732-92, (Br.) prime min.; his inept policies led to loss of American colonies.

Julius K. Nyerere, 1922-99, (Tanz.) founding father; 1st pres., 1962-85, of Tanzania.

Daniel O'Connell, 1775-1847, (Ire.) nationalist political leader; known as The Liberator.

Omar, c. 581-644, Muslim leader; 2nd caliph, led Islam to become an imperial power.

Thomas P. (Tip) O'Neill Jr., 1912-94, (U.S.) U.S. rep. (D, MA), Speaker of the House, 1977-86.

Ignace Paderewski, 1860-1941, (Pol.) statesman, pianist, composer, briefly prime min.; ardent patriot.

Viscount Palmerston, 1784-1865, (Br.) Whig-Liberal prime min., foreign min.; embodied British nationalism.

Andreas George Papandreou, 1919-96, (Gr.) leftist politician; served twice as prem., 1981-89, 1993-96.

Georgios Papandreou, 1888-1968, (Gr.) Republican politician; served 3 times as prime min.

Franz von Papen, 1879-1969, (Ger.) politician; major role in overthrow of Weimar Republic and rise of Hitler.

Charles Stewart Parnell, 1846-1891, (Ire.) nationalist leader; "uncrowned king of Ireland."

Lester Pearson, 1897-1972, (Can.) diplomat, Liberal party leader, prime min.

Robert Peel, 1788-1850, (Br.) reformist prime min.; founder of Conservative party.

Frances Perkins, 1882-1965, (U.S.) first female cabinet member (sec. of labor).

Eva (Evita) Perón, 1919-52, (Arg.) highly influential 2nd wife of Juan Perón.

Juan Perón, 1895-1974, (Arg.) dynamic pres. of Argentina, 1946-55, 1973-74.

Joseph Pilsudski, 1867-1935, (Pol.) statesman; instrumental in reestablishing Polish state in the 20th cent.

Charles Pinckney, 1757-1824, (U.S.) founding father; his Pinckney plan largely incorporated into Constitution.

Christian Pineau, 1905-95, (Fr.) leader of French Resistance during WWII; French foreign min., 1956-58.

Augusto Pinochet (Ugarte), 1915-2006, (Chile) former Chilean ruler; indicted for human rights abuses while in office.

William Pitt the Elder, 1708-78, (Br.) statesman; the "Great Commoner," transformed Britain into imperial power.

William Pitt the Younger, 1759-1806, (Br.) prime min. during French Revolutionary wars.

Georgi Plekhanov, 1857-1918, (Russ.) revolutionary, social philosopher; called "father of Russian Marxism."

Raymond Poincaré, 1860-1934, (Fr.) 9th pres. of the Republic; advocated harsh punishment of Germany after WWI.

Pol Pot, 1925-98, (Camb.) leader of Khmer Rouge; ruled Cambodia, 1975-79; responsible for mass deaths.

Georges Pompidou, 1911-74, (Fr.) Gaullist political leader; pres., 1969-74.

Grigori Potemkin, 1739-91, (Russ.) field marshal; favorite of empress Catherine II.

Adam Clayton Powell Jr., 1908-72, (U.S.) civil rights leader; U.S. rep. (D, NY), 1945-69.

Yitzhak Rabin, 1922-95, (Isr.) military, political leader; prime min. of Israel, 1974-77, 1992-95; assassinated.

Joseph H. Rainey, 1832-87, (U.S.) first black person elected to U.S. House (1869), from SC.

Edmund Randolph, 1753-1813, (U.S.) attorney; prominent in drafting, ratification of Constitution.

John Randolph, 1773-1833, (U.S.) southern planter; strong advocate of states' rights.

Jeannette Rankin, 1880-1973, (U.S.) pacifist; first woman member of U.S. Congress (R, MT).

Walter Rathenau, 1867-1922, (Ger.) industrialist, statesman.

Sam Rayburn, 1882-1961, (U.S.) Democratic leader; representative for 47 years, House Speaker for 17.

Hiram R. Revels, 1822-1901, (U.S.) first African American U.S. senator; elected in MS, served 1870-71.

Paul Reynaud, 1878-1966, (Fr.) statesman; prem. in 1940 at time of France's defeat by Germany.

Syngman Rhee, 1875-1965, (Korea) first pres. of S. Korea.

Cecil Rhodes, 1853-1902, (Br.) imperialist, industrial magnate; established Rhodes scholarships in his will.

Ann Richards, 1933-2006, (U.S.) former TX gov.

Cardinal de Richelieu, 1585-1642, (Fr.) statesman, known as "red eminence"; chief minister to Louis XIII.

Maximilien Robespierre, 1758-94, (Fr.) leading figure in French Revolution and Reign of Terror.

Nelson Rockefeller, 1908-79, (U.S.) Republican governor of NY, 1959-73; U.S. vice pres., 1974-77.

Eleanor Roosevelt, 1884-1962, (U.S.) influential first lady, humanitarian, UN diplomat.

Elihu Root, 1845-1937, (U.S.) lawyer, statesman, diplomat; leading Republican supporter of the League of Nations.

Dean Rusk, 1909-95, (U.S.) statesman; sec. of state, 1961-69.

John Russell, 1792-1878, (Br.) Liberal prime min. during the Irish potato famine.

Anwar al-Sadat, 1918-81, (Egypt) pres., 1970-81; promoted peace with Israel; Nobel laureate; assassinated.

António de Oliveira Salazar, 1889-1970, (Port.) longtime dictator.

José de San Martin, 1778-1850, S. Amer. revolutionary; protector of Peru.

Eisaku Sato, 1901-75, (Jpn.) prime min.; presided over Japan's post-WWII emergence as major world power.

Abdul Aziz Ibn Saud, c.1880-1953, (Saudi Arabia) king of Saudi Arabia, 1932-53.

Robert Schuman, 1886-1963, (Fr.) statesman; founded European Coal and Steel Community.

Carl Schurz, 1829-1906, (U.S.) German-American political leader, journalist, orator, dedicated reformer.

Kurt Schuschnigg, 1897-1977, (Austria) chancellor; unsuccessful in stopping Austria's annexation by Germany.

William H. Seward, 1801-72, (U.S.) anti-slavery activist; as U.S. sec. of state purchased Alaska.

Carlo Sforza, 1872-1952, (It.) foreign min., anti-Fascist.

Sitting Bull, c.1831-90, (Nat. Am.) Sioux leader in Battle of Little Bighorn against George A. Custer, 1876.

Alfred E. Smith, 1873-1944, (U.S.) NY Democratic governor; first Roman Catholic to run for president.

Margaret Chase Smith, 1897-1995, (U.S.) congresswoman, senator (R, ME); 1st woman elected to both houses of Congress.

Jan C. Smuts, 1870-1950, (S. Africa) statesman, philosopher, soldier, prime min.

Paul Henri Spaak, 1899-1972, (Belg.) statesman, socialist leader.

Joseph Stalin, 1879-1953, (USSR) Soviet dictator, 1924-53; instituted forced collectivization, massive purges, and labor camps, causing millions of deaths.

Edwin M. Stanton, 1814-69, (U.S.) sec. of war, 1862-68.

Alexander Stephens, 1812-1883, (U.S.) vice pres. of the Confederacy.

Edward R. Stettinius Jr., 1900-49, (U.S.) industrialist; sec. of state who coordinated aid to WWII allies.

Adlai E. Stevenson, 1900-65, (U.S.) Democratic leader, diplomat, governor (IL), presidential candidate.

Henry L. Stimson, 1867-1950, (U.S.) statesman; served in 5 administrations, foreign policy adviser in 1930s and 1940s.

Carl Stokes, 1927-96, (U.S.) first black mayor of a major American city (Cleveland, 1967-72).

Suharto, 1921-2008, (Indon.) former longtime Indonesian ruler.

Sukarno, 1901-70, (Indon.) dictatorial first pres. of the Indonesian republic.

Sun Yat-sen, 1866-1925, (China) revolutionary; leader of Kuomintang pol. party, regarded as father of modern China.

Robert A. Taft, 1889-1953, (U.S.) conservative Senate leader (OH); called "Mr. Republican."

Charles de Talleyrand, 1754-1838, (Fr.) statesman, diplomat; the major force of the Congress of Vienna of 1814-15.

U Thant, 1909-74, (Burma) statesman, UN sec.-general.

Norman M. Thomas, 1884-1968, (U.S.) social reformer; 6 times Socialist party presidential candidate.

Josip Broz Tito, 1892-1980, (Yug.) pres. of Yugoslavia from 1953; WWII guerrilla chief, postwar rival of Stalin.

Palmiro Togliatti, 1893-1964, (It.) major Italian Communist leader.

Hideki Tojo, 1885-1948, (Jpn.) states-man, soldier; prime min. during most of WWII.

François Toussaint L'Ouverture, c.1744-1803, (Haiti) patriot, martyr; thwarted French colonial aims.

Leon Trotsky, 1879-1940, (Russ.) revolutionary; founded Red Army, expelled from party in conflict with Stalin; assassinated.

Pierre Elliott Trudeau, 1919-2000, (Can.) longtime liberal prime minister of Canada, 1968-79, 1980-84; achieved native Canadian constitution.

Rafael L. Trujillo Molina, 1891-1961, (Dominican) dictator of Dominican Republic, 1930-61; assassinated.

Moise K. Tshombe, 1919-69, (Congo) pres. of secessionist Katanga prov., prem. of Congo.

William M. Tweed, 1823-78, (U.S.) political boss of Tammany Hall, New York City's Democratic political machine.

Walter Ulbricht, 1893-1973, (Ger.) Communist leader of German Democratic Republic.

Arthur H. Vandenberg, 1884-1951, (U.S.) senator (R, MI); proponent of bipartisan anti-Communist foreign policy.

Eleutherios Venizelos, 1864-1936, (Gr.) most prominent Greek statesman of early 20th cent.

Hendrik F. Verwoerd, 1901-66, (S. Africa) prime min.; rigorously applied apartheid policy despite protest.

Kurt Waldheim, 1918-2007, (Austria) UN sec.-gen., Austrian pres.

George Wallace, 1919-98, (U.S.) former segregationist governor of Alabama, pres. candidate.

Robert Walpole, 1676-1745, (Br.) statesman; generally considered Britain's first prime min.

Harold Washington, 1922-87, (U.S.) first black mayor of Chicago.

Robert C. Weaver, 1907-97, (U.S.) first African American appointed to cabinet; sec. of Housing and Urban Development.

Daniel Webster, 1782-1852, (U.S.) orator, politician; advocate of business interests during Jacksonian agrarianism.

Caspar Weinberger, 1917-2006, (U.S.) business exec., former defense sec., other cabinet posts.

Chaim Weizmann, 1874-1952, (Russ.-Isr.) Zionist leader, scientist; first Israeli pres.

Wendell L. Willkie, 1892-1944, (U.S.) Republican who tried to unseat Franklin D. Roosevelt when he ran for his 3rd term.

Harold Wilson, 1916-95, (Br.) Labour party leader; prime min., 1964-70, 1974-76.

Boris Yeltsin, 1931-2007, (USSR-Russia) first freely elected president of post-Soviet Russia.

Coleman A. Young, 1918-97, (U.S.) first African-American mayor of Detroit, 1974-93.

Emiliano Zapata, c.1879-1919, (Mex.) revolutionary; major influence on modern Mexico.

Todor Zhivkov, 1911-98, (Bulg.) Communist ruler of Bulgaria from 1954 until ousted in a 1989 coup.

Zhou Enlai, 1898-1976, (China) diplomat, prime min.; a leading figure of the Chinese Communist party.

YEAR IN PICTURES

Tragedy in Tucson Six victims died in a shooting at a political event with Rep. Gabrielle Giffords (D, AZ) at a supermarket Jan. 8, 2011. Giffords was shot in the head and rehabilitation was ongoing throughout 2011. She appeared on the floor of the House for the first time since the tragedy Aug. 1, 2011.

Wisconsin Protests The Wisconsin state capitol came to a standstill in Feb. 2011 as thousands protested a law—ultimately passed by the Republican state legislature and signed into law by Gov. Scott Walker (R)—that would drastically alter collective bargaining and other union rights for state workers.

New Leadership Rep. Nancy Pelosi (D, CA) passed the gavel to Rep. John Boehner (R, OH) Jan. 5, 2011; Boehner became the House Speaker following 2010 midterm elections that gave the Republican Party a House majority.

The Race Begins The field of candidates for the Republican presidential nomination in 2012 began to take shape as (left to right) former House Speaker Newt Gingrich (GA), Rep. Michele Bachmann (MN), former Gov. Mitt Romney (MA), Gov. Rick Perry (TX), and Rep. Ron Paul (TX) met for a debate at the Reagan Library Sept. 7, 2011. Other contenders (not pictured) included former Sen. Rick Santorum (PA), businessman Herman Cain, former Gov. John Huntsman (UT), and former Gov. Gary Johnson (NM).

Tornado Tragedy The deadliest U.S. tornado in more than 50 years tore through Joplin, MO, May 22, 2011, claiming 162 lives.

Texas Wildfires As the state went through its worst drought in decades, dozens of wildfires in Texas consumed some 7,500 structures and 3.8 mil acres of land Dec. 2010-Sept. 2011.

Storm Surge First making landfall in North Carolina, Hurricane Irene, later downgraded to a tropical storm, swept up the East Coast of the U.S., with high winds and flooding causing more than $10 bil in damages from the Carolinas to Vermont, Aug. 27-28, 2011.

Mississippi Flooding Heavy rains and saturated ground caused flooding on the Mississippi River in May 2011; the Army Corps of Engineers responded by opening spillways into farmland to prevent downriver flooding in cities like Baton Rouge and New Orleans, LA.

Bin Laden Caught, Killed As administration officials watched May 1, 2011, from the White House Situation Room, U.S. forces killed Osama bin Laden, the leader of al Qaeda and mastermind of the Sept. 11, 2001, terrorist attacks, in a risky night raid in Abbottabad, Pakistan.

Leadership in Transition Former Central Intelligence Agency Dir. Leon Panetta (left) took over for retiring Defense Sec. Robert Gates (right) July 1, 2011. Gen. David Petraeus (center), the architect of the U.S. "surge" in Iraq, became the CIA director Sept. 6, 2011.

Dignified Return Pres. Barack Obama observed the return of the remains of 30 U.S. military personnel who died, along with 8 Afghan troops, in a Chinook helicopter crash Aug. 6, 2011; the incident was the single largest loss of life for U.S. troops in Afghanistan since the war began.

Never Forgotten Ten years after the terrorist attacks of Sept. 11, 2001, thousands gathered in New York City for memorial ceremonies and the opening of the National September 11 Memorial; similar ceremonies took place at the other attack sites.

Married in Manhattan New York became the sixth and largest state to marry same-sex couples July 24, 2011.

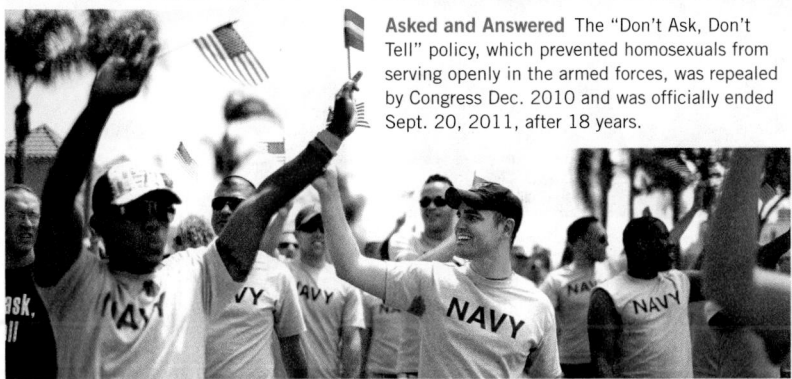

Asked and Answered The "Don't Ask, Don't Tell" policy, which prevented homosexuals from serving openly in the armed forces, was repealed by Congress Dec. 2010 and was officially ended Sept. 20, 2011, after 18 years.

Stocks Plummet U.S. stock markets saw their worst losses since the 2008 financial crisis on Aug. 8, 2011, the first trading day since Standard & Poor's announced Aug. 5 that the U.S. was being downgraded from its AAA rating for the first time.

Royal Newlyweds Prince William, second in line to the British throne, married Kate Middleton Apr. 29, 2011, in a ceremony watched worldwide.

Oprah Ovation The *Oprah Winfrey Show* concluded its 25-year run with weeks of star-studded shows, but the final broadcast May 25, 2011, featured just Oprah Winfrey herself.

Living Heroes Pres. Barack Obama presented the Medal of Honor, the highest military award for bravery, to Staff Sgt. Salvatore Giunta (above), the first living recipient of the medal since the Vietnam War, Nov. 16, 2010, and to Sgt. 1st Class Leroy Petry (below) July 12, 2011. Both were honored for actions in Afghanistan.

Farewell Steve Apple co-founder Steve Jobs resigned as CEO Aug. 24, 2011, and died Oct. 5, 2011. Under Jobs's stewardship, Apple had developed iTunes and the iPod, iPhone, and iPad and become one of the world's most profitable companies.

Wall of Shame U.S. Reps. Chris Lee (R, NY), Anthony Weiner (D, NY), and David Wu (D, OR), all resigned their offices amid controversy over personal indiscretions in 2011.

Baffling Behavior *Two and a Half Men* sitcom star Charlie Sheen, who was fired from the show Mar. 7, 2011, after making a series of odd statements (including derogatory remarks about the show's creator), toured with a live show called "My Violent Torpedo of Truth."

The Verdict A jury in Florida acquitted Casey Anthony, 25, of murder, child abuse, and manslaughter July 5, 2011, in connection with the death of her 2-year-old daughter in 2008; the investigation and trial had attacted widespread media attention.

Charges Dismissed Intl. Monetary Fund chief Dominique Strauss-Kahn, a leading French politician, was charged in May with sexual assault in New York City and resigned his post; the charges were dropped Aug. 23, 2011.

Trump Card Real estate tycoon Donald Trump toyed publicly with a presidential run in Apr. 2011, while questioning Pres. Obama's citizenship. The White House released Obama's long-form certificate for the first time Apr. 27, 2011.

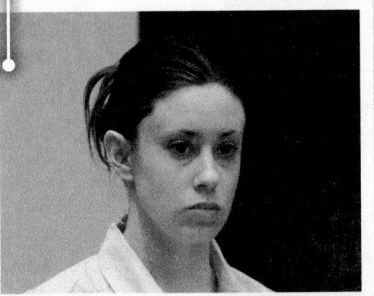

Man vs. the Machine Ken Jennings and Brad Rutter were no match for IBM's Watson, a supercomputer that handily defeated the two *Jeopardy!* champions over the course of three episodes airing in Feb. 2011.

End of an Era After 41 years, soap opera *All My Children* aired its last episode on ABC Sept. 23, 2011; another long-running soap opera, *One Life to Live*, was set to air its last ABC episode in Jan. 2012.

Rolling With It British singer Adele set records with single "Rolling in the Deep," which sold its 5 millionth digital copy in Sept. 2011.

The Good Book *The Book of Mormon*, an irreverent new musical by Roberto Lopez and *South Park* creators Trey Parker and Matt Stone, picked up nine Tony Awards June 12, 2011.

The X Factor Fox's new singing competition show reunited former *American Idol* adversaries Simon Cowell and Paula Abdul and brought in new judges L. A. Reid and Nicole Scherzinger when it debuted Sept. 21, 2011, tasking the panel with finding the U.S.'s next superstar.

Scientists of the Past

Revised by Peter Barker, Prof. and Chair, Dept. of the History of Science, Univ. of Oklahoma.

For pre-modern scientists, see also Philosophers and Religious Figures of the Past and Historical Figures chapters.

Albertus Magnus, c.1200-80, (Ger.) theologian, philosopher; helped found medieval study of natural science.

Alhazen (Ibn al-Haytham), c. 965-c. 1040, mathematician, astronomer, optical theorist.

Andre-Marie Ampère, 1775-1836, (Fr.) mathematician, chemist; founder of electrodynamics.

John V. Atanasoff, 1903-95, (U.S.) physicist; co-invented Atanasoff-Berry Computer (1939-41).

Amedeo Avogadro, 1776-1856, (It.) chemist, physicist; proposed that equal volumes of gas contain equal numbers of molecules, permitting determination of molecular weights.

John Bardeen, 1908-91, (U.S.) double Nobel laureate in physics (transistor, 1956; superconductivity, 1972).

A. H. Becquerel, 1852-1908, (Fr.) physicist; discovered radioactivity in uranium (1896).

Alexander Graham Bell, 1847-1922, (U.S.) inventor; first to patent and commercially exploit the telephone (1876).

Daniel Bernoulli, 1700-82, (Switz.) mathematician; developed fluid dynamics and kinetic theory of gases.

Clifford Berry, 1918-63, (U.S.) collaborated with John V. Atanasoff on the ABC computer (1939-41).

Jöns Jakob Berzelius, 1779-1848, (Swed.) chemist; developed modern chemical symbols and formulas.

Henry Bessemer, 1813-98, (Br.) engineer; invented Bessemer steel-making process.

Hans Bethe, 1906-2005, (Ger.-U.S.) physicist; won Nobel Prize in 1967 for describing how stars generate energy.

Bruno Bettelheim, 1903-90, (Austria-U.S.) psychoanalyst; studied disturbed children; *Uses of Enchantment* (1976).

Louis Blériot, 1872-1936, (Fr.) engineer; monoplane pioneer, first Channel flight (1909).

Franz Boas, 1858-1942, (Ger.-U.S.) founded modern anthropology; studied Pacific Coast tribes.

Niels Bohr, 1885-1962, (Den.) atomic and nuclear physicist; founded quantum mechanics.

Norman Borlaug, 1914-2009, (U.S.) plant pathologist and geneticist; father of "green" (agricultural) revolution.

Max Born, 1882-1970, (Ger.) atomic and nuclear physicist; helped develop quantum mechanics.

Satyendranath Bose, 1894-1974, (India) physicist; forerunner of modern quantum theory for integral-spin particles.

Louis de Broglie, 1892-1987, (Fr.) physicist; proposed quantum wave-particle duality.

Robert Bunsen, 1811-99, (Ger.) chemist; pioneered spectroscopic analysis; discovered rubidium, caesium.

Luther Burbank, 1849-1926, (U.S.) naturalist; developed plant breeding into a modern science.

Vannevar Bush, 1890-1974, (U.S.) electrical engineer; developed differential analyzer, an early analogue computer; headed WWII Office of Scientific Res. and Dev.

Marvin Camras, 1916-95, (U.S.) inventor, electrical engineer; invented magnetic tape recording.

Alexis Carrel, 1873-1944, (Fr.) surgeon, biologist; developed methods of suturing blood vessels, transplanting organs.

Rachel Carson, 1907-64, (U.S.) marine biologist, environmentalist; *Silent Spring* (1962).

James Chadwick, 1891-1974, (Br.) physicist; discovered the neutron (1932); led Brit. Manhattan Project group in U.S.

Albert Claude, 1898-1983, (Belg.-U.S.) a founder of modern cell biology; determined role of mitochondria.

Samuel Cohen, 1921-2010, (U.S.) physicist who invented the neutron bomb.

Nicolaus Copernicus, 1473-1543, (Pol.) first modern astronomer to propose Sun as center of the planets' motions.

Jacques Yves Cousteau, 1910-97, (Fr.) oceanographer; co-inventor, with Emile Gagnan, of the Aqualung (1943).

Seymour Cray, 1925-96, (U.S.) computer industry pioneer; developed supercomputers.

Francis Crick, 1916-2004, (Br.) biophysicist; co-discoverer of genetic code; shared 1962 Nobel Prize.

Marie, 1867-1934, (Pol.-Fr.) and **Pierre Curie**, 1859-1906, (Fr.) physical chemists; pioneer investigators of radioactivity; discovered radium and polonium (1898).

Gottlieb Daimler, 1834-1900, (Ger.) engineer, inventor; pioneer automobile manufacturer.

John Dalton, 1766-1844, (Br.) chemist, physicist; formulated atomic theory, made first table of atomic weights.

Charles Darwin, 1809-82, (Br.) naturalist; established theory of organic evolution; *Origin of Species* (1859).

Lee De Forest, 1873-1961, (U.S.) inventor of triode; pioneer in wireless telegraphy, sound pictures, television.

Pierre-Gilles de Gennes, 1932-2007, (Fr.) physicist whose research aided development of liquid-crystal-display (LCD); awarded Nobel Prize for Physics, 1991.

Max Delbruck, 1906-81, (Ger.-U.S.) founded molecular biology.

Rudolf Diesel, 1858-1913, (Ger.) mechanical engineer; patented Diesel engine (1892).

Theodosius Dobzhansky, 1900-75, (Russ.-U.S.) biologist; reconciled genetics and natural selection.

Christian Doppler, 1803-53, (Austria) physicist; showed change in wave frequency caused by motion of source, now known as Doppler effect.

J. Presper Eckert Jr., 1919-95, (U.S.) co-inventor, with John W. Mauchly, of the ENIAC computer (1943-45).

Thomas A. Edison, 1847-1931, (U.S.) inventor; held more than 1,000 patents, including incandescent electric lamp.

Paul Ehrlich, 1854-1915, (Ger.) medical researcher in immunology and bacteriology; pioneered antitoxin production.

Albert Einstein, 1879-1955, (Ger.-U.S.) theoretical physicist; founded relativity theory.

John F. Enders, 1897-1985, (U.S.) virologist; helped discover vaccines against polio, measles, mumps and chicken pox.

Erik Erikson, 1902-94, (U.S.) psychoanalyst, author; theory of developmental stages of life; *Childhood and Society* (1950).

Leonhard Euler, 1707-83, (Switz.) mathematician, physicist; pioneer of calculus; revived ideas of Fermat.

Gabriel Fahrenheit, 1686-1736, (Ger.) physicist; improved thermometers and introduced Fahrenheit temperature scale.

Michael Faraday, 1791-1867, (Br.) chemist, physicist; discovered electrical induction and invented dynamo (1831).

Philo T. Farnsworth, 1906-71, (U.S.) inventor; built first television system (San Francisco, 1928).

Pierre de Fermat, 1601-65, (Fr.) mathematician; founded modern theory of numbers.

Enrico Fermi, 1901-54, (It.-U.S.) nuclear physicist; demonstrated first controlled chain reaction (Chicago, 1942).

Richard Feynman, 1918-88, (U.S.) theoretical physicist, author; founder of Quantum Electrodynamics (QED).

Alexander Fleming, 1881-1955, (Br.) bacteriologist; discovered penicillin (1928).

Jean B. J. Fourier, 1768-1830, (Fr.) introduced Fourier Series, method of analysis in math and physics.

Sigmund Freud, 1856-1939, (Austria) psychiatrist; founder of psychoanalysis; *Interpretation of Dreams* (1901).

Erich Fromm, 1900-80, (U.S.) psychoanalyst; *Man for Himself* (1947).

Galileo Galilei, 1564-1642, (It.) physicist; used telescope to vindicate Copernicus, founded modern science of motion.

Carl Friedrich Gauss, 1777-1855, (Ger.) math. physicist; completed work of Fermat and Euler in number theory.

Josiah W. Gibbs, 1839-1903, (U.S.) theoretical physicist, chemist; founded chemical thermodynamics.

Robert H. Goddard, 1882-1945, (U.S.) physicist; invented liquid fuel rocket (1926).

George W. Goethals, 1858-1928, (U.S.) chief engineer who completed Panama Canal (1907-14).

William C. Gorgas, 1854-1920, (U.S.) physician; pioneer in prevention of yellow fever and malaria.

Stephen Jay Gould, 1941-2002, (U.S.) paleontologist, evolutionary biologist, writer.

Ernest Haeckel, 1834-1919, (Ger.) zoologist, evolutionist; early Darwinist, introduced concept of "ecology."

Otto Hahn, 1879-1968, (Ger.) chemist; with Lise Meitner discovered nuclear fission (1938).

Edmund Halley, 1656-1742, (Br.) astronomer; predicted return of 1682 comet (Halley's Comet) in 1759.

William Harvey, 1578-1657, (Br.) physician, anatomist; discovered circulation of the blood (1628).

Werner Heisenberg, 1901-76, (Ger.) physicist; developed matrix mechanics and uncertainty principle (1927).

Hermann von Helmholtz, 1821-94, (Ger.) physicist, physiologist; formulated principle of conservation of energy.

William Herschel, 1738-1822, (Ger.-Br.) astronomer; discovered Uranus (1781).

Heinrich Hertz, 1857-94, (Ger.) physicist; discovered radio waves and photo-electric effect (1886-87).

David Hilbert, 1862-1943, (Ger.) mathematician; contributed to algebra, calculus, and foundational studies (formalism).

Albert Hofmann, 1906-2008, (U.S.) father of LSD.

Edwin P. Hubble, 1889-1953, (U.S.) astronomer; discovered observational evidence of expanding universe.

Alexander von Humboldt, 1769-1859, (Ger.) naturalist, author; explored S. America, created ecology.

Edward Jenner, 1749-1823, (Br.) physician; pioneered vaccination, introduced term "virus."

James Joule, 1818-89, (Br.) physicist; found relation between heat and mechanical energy (conservation of energy).

Carl Jung, 1875-1961, (Switz.) psychiatrist; founder of analytical psychology.

Ernest Everett Just, 1883-1941, (U.S.) marine biologist; studied egg development; *Biology of Cell Surfaces* (1941).

Johannes Kepler, 1571-1630, (Ger.) astronomer; discovered laws of planetary motion.

Al-Khawarizmi, early 9th cent., (Arab.) mathematician; regarded as founder of algebra.

Robert Koch, 1843-1910, (Ger.) bacteriologist; isolated bacterial causes of tuberculosis and other diseases.

Georges Köhler, 1946-95, (Ger.) immunologist; with Cesar Milstein, developed monoclonal antibody technique.

Willem Kolff, 1911-2009, (Neth.-U.S.) physician, biomedical engineer; developed first practical kidney dialysis machine; considered the "father of artificial organs."

Jacques Lacan, 1901-81, (Fr.) influential psychoanalyst.

Joseph Lagrange, 1736-1813, (Fr.) geometer, astronomer; showed that gravity of Earth and Moon cancel, creating stable points in space around them.

Jean B. Lamarck, 1744-1829, (Fr.) naturalist; forerunner of Darwin in evolutionary theory.

Pierre Simon de Laplace, 1749-1827, (Fr.) astronomer, physicist; proposed nebular origin for solar system.

Lewis H. Latimer, 1848-1928, (U.S.) African American scientist; associate of Edison; supervised installation of first electric street lighting in New York City.

Antoine Lavoisier, 1743-94, (Fr.) a founder of modern chemistry.

Ernest O. Lawrence, 1901-58, (U.S.) physicist; invented the cyclotron.

Louis, 1903-72, and **Mary Leakey**, 1913-96, (Br.) early hominid paleoanthropologists; discovered remains in Africa.

Anton van Leeuwenhoek, 1632-1723, (Neth.) founder of microscopy.

Jerome Lejeune, 1927-94, (Fr.) geneticist; discovered chromosomal cause of Down syndrome (1959).

Claude Levi-Strauss, 1908-2009, (Belg.-Fr.) cultural anthropologist, sociologist, philosopher.

Kurt Lewin, 1890-1947, (Ger.-U.S.) social psychologist; studied human motivation and group dynamics.

Justus von Liebig, 1803-73, (Ger.) founded quantitative organic chemistry.

Joseph Lister, 1827-1912, (Br.) physician; pioneered antiseptic surgery.

Hendrik Lorentz, 1853-1928, (Neth.) physicist; developed electron theory of matter, contrib. to relativity theory.

Konrad Lorenz, 1903-89, (Austria) ethologist; pioneer in study of animal behavior.

Percival Lowell, 1855-1916, (U.S.) astronomer; predicted the existence of Pluto.

Louis, 1864-1948, and **Auguste Lumière**, 1862-1954, (Fr.) invented cinematograph, made first motion picture (1895).

Theodore H. Maiman, 1927-2007, (U.S.) physicist; invented the first workable laser, which he displayed in 1960.

Guglielmo Marconi, 1874-1937, (It.) physicist; developed wireless telegraphy.

John W. Mauchly, 1907-80, (U.S.) co-inventor, with J. Presper Eckert Jr., of computer ENIAC (1943-45).

James Clerk Maxwell, 1831-79, (Br.) physicist; unified electricity and magnetism, electromagnetic theory of light.

Maria Goeppert Mayer, 1906-72, (Ger.-U.S.) physicist; developed shell model of atomic nuclei.

Barbara McClintock, 1902-92, (U.S.) geneticist; showed that some genetic elements are mobile.

Lise Meitner, 1878-1968, (Austria) co-discoverer, with Otto Hahn, of nuclear fission (1938).

Gregor J. Mendel, 1822-84, (Austria) botanist, monk; his experiments became the foundation of modern genetics.

Dmitri Mendeleyev, 1834-1907, (Russ.) chemist; established Periodic Table of the Elements.

Bruce R. Merrifield, 1921-2006, (U.S.) chemist; discovered how to synthesize proteins quickly and efficiently.

Franz Mesmer, 1734-1815, (Ger.) physician; introduced hypnotherapy.

Albert A. Michelson, 1852-1931, (U.S.) physicist; invented interferometer.

Robert A. Millikan, 1868-1953, (U.S.) physicist; measured electronic charge.

Thomas Hunt Morgan, 1866-1945, (U.S.) geneticist, embryologist; established role of chromosomes in heredity.

Isaac Newton, 1642-1727, (Br.) natural philosopher; discovered laws of gravitation, motion; with Gottfried Wilhelm Leibniz, founded calculus.

Robert N. Noyce, 1927-90, (U.S.) invented microchip.

J. Robert Oppenheimer, 1904-67, (U.S.) physicist; scientific director of Manhattan Project.

Wilhelm Ostwald, 1853-1932, (Ger.) chemist, philosopher; main founder of modern physical chemistry.

Louis Pasteur, 1822-95, (Fr.) chemist; showed that germs cause disease and fermentation; originated pasteurization.

Linus C. Pauling, 1901-94, (U.S.) chemist; studied chemical bonds; campaigned for nuclear disarmament.

Jean Piaget, 1896-1980, (Switz.) psychologist; four-stage theory of intellectual development in children.

Max Planck, 1858-1947, (Ger.) physicist; introduced quantum hypothesis (1900).

Jules Henri Poincaré, 1854-1912, (Fr.) mathematician; founded algebraic topology, many other discoveries.

Walter S. Reed, 1851-1902, (U.S.) Army physician; proved mosquitoes transmit yellow fever.

Theodor Reik, 1888-1969, (Austria-U.S.) psychoanalyst; major Freudian disciple.

Bernhard Riemann, 1826-66, (Ger.) mathematician; developed non-Euclidean geometry used by Einstein.

Norbert Rillieux, 1806-94, (U.S.) African American inventor of a vacuum pan evaporator (1846); revolutionized sugar-refining industry.

Wilhelm Roentgen, 1845-1923, (Ger.) physicist; discovered X-rays (1895).

Carl Rogers, 1902-87, (U.S.) psychotherapist, author; originated nondirective therapy.

Ernest Rutherford, 1871-1937, (Br.) physicist; pioneer investigator of radioactivity; identified the atomic nucleus.

Albert B. Sabin, 1906-93, (Russ.-U.S.) developed oral polio live-virus vaccine.

Carl Sagan, 1934-96, (U.S.) astronomer, author.

Jonas Salk, 1914-95, (U.S.) developed first successful polio vaccine, widely used in U.S. after 1955.

Allan Sandage, 1926-2010, (U.S.) astronomer; refined the Hubble Constant, a measure of the universe's expansion.

Giovanni Schiaparelli, 1835-1910, (It.) astronomer; reported canals on Mars.

Erwin Schrödinger, 1887-1961, (Austria) physicist; developed wave equation for quantum systems.

Glenn T. Seaborg, 1912-99, (U.S.) chemist; Nobel Prize winner (1951); codiscoverer of plutonium.

Harlow Shapley, 1885-1972, (U.S.) astronomer; mapped galactic clusters and position of Sun in our own galaxy.

Norman E. Shumway, 1923-2006, (U.S.) surgeon; performed world's first successful heart-lung transplant.

B. F. Skinner, 1904-90, (U.S.) psychologist; leading advocate of behaviorism.

Richard E. Smalley, 1943-2005, (U.S.) chemist; with three other scientists, discovered buckminsterfullerenes, a previously unknown class of carbon molecules.

Roger W. Sperry, 1913-94, (U.S.) neurobiologist; established different functions of right and left sides of brain.

Benjamin Spock, 1903-98, (U.S.) pediatrician, child care expert; *Common Sense Book of Baby and Child Care.*

Charles P. Steinmetz, 1865-1923, (Ger.-U.S.) electrical engineer; developed basic ideas on alternating current.

Ernst Stuhlinger, 1913-2008, (Ger.) rocket scientist; electric propulsion for NASA in early space age.

Leo Szilard, 1898-1964, (Hung.-U.S.) physicist; helped on Manhattan Project, later opposed nuclear weapons.

Edward Teller, 1908-2003, (Hung.-U.S.) physicist; aided on Manhattan Project, had key role in development of H-bomb.

Nikola Tesla, 1856-1943, (Serb.-U.S.) invented electrical devices including AC dynamos, transformers, and motors.

William Thomson (Lord Kelvin), 1824-1907, (Br.) physicist; aided in success of transatlantic telegraph cable (1865); proposed Kelvin absolute temperature scale.

Alan Turing, 1912-54, (Br.) mathematician; helped develop basis for computers.

James Van Allen, 1914-2006, (U.S.) physicist; discovered the presence of radiation belts around Earth (Van Allen belts).

Rudolf Virchow, 1821-1902, (Ger.) pathologist; pioneered the modern theory that diseases affect the body through cells.

Alessandro Volta, 1745-1827, (It.) physicist; electricity pioneer.

Werner von Braun, 1912-77, (Ger.-U.S.) developed rockets for warfare and space exploration.

John Von Neumann, 1903-57, (Hung.-U.S.) mathematician; originated game theory; basic design for modern computers.

Alfred Russell Wallace, 1823-1913, (Br.) naturalist; proposed concept of evolution independently of Darwin.

John B. Watson, 1878-1958, (U.S.) psychologist; a founder of behaviorism.

James E. Watt, 1736-1819, (U.S.) mechanical engineer, inventor; invented modern steam engine (1765).

Alfred L. Wegener, 1880-1930, (Ger.) meteorologist, geophysicist; postulated continental drift.

Norbert Wiener, 1894-1964, (U.S.) mathematician; founder of cybernetics.

Daniel Hale Williams, 1858-1931, (U.S.) African American surgeon; performed one of first two open-heart operations (1893).

Sewall Wright, 1889-1988, (U.S.) evolutionary theorist; helped found population genetics.

Wilhelm Wundt, 1832-1920, (Ger.) founder of experimental psychology.

Qian Xuesen (Tsien Hsue-shen), 1911-2009, (China) rocket scientist; father of China's space program.

Rosalyn Yalow, 1921-2011, (U.S.), physicist; co-developer of radioimmunoassay.

Ferdinand von Zeppelin, 1838-1917, (Ger.) soldier, aeronaut, airship designer.

Social Reformers, Activists, and Humanitarians of the Past

Ralph David Abernathy, 1926-90, (U.S.) black civil rights activist; pres., 1968, Southern Christian Leadership Conf.

Jane Addams, 1860-1935, (U.S.) cofounder of Hull House; won Nobel Peace Prize, 1931.

Susan B. Anthony, 1820-1906, (U.S.) a leader in temperance, antislavery, and woman suffrage movements.

Thomas Barnardo, 1845-1905, (Br.) social reformer; pioneer in care of destitute children.

Clara Barton, 1821-1912, (U.S.) organized American Red Cross.

Daisy Bates, 1914-99, (U.S.) black civil rights leader who fought for integration; advocate for the "Little Rock 9" during Arkansas desegregation crisis in 1957.

Henry Ward Beecher, 1813-87, (U.S.) clergyman, abolitionist.

Peter Benenson, 1921-2005, (Br.) activist; founded Amnesty International, 1961.

Mary McLeod Bethune, 1875-1955, (U.S.) black educator, civil rights activist; adviser to FDR and Truman; founder, pres., Bethune-Cookman College.

Amelia Bloomer, 1818-94, (U.S.) suffragette, social reformer.

Yelena Bonner, 1923-2011, (Russ.) human rights activist in former Soviet Union.

William Booth, 1829-1912, (Br.) founded Salvation Army.

John Brown, 1800-59, (U.S.) abolitionist who led murder of 5 pro-slavery men; hanged.

Frances Xavier (Mother) Cabrini, 1850-1917, (It.-U.S.) Italian-born nun; founded charitable institutions; first American canonized as a saint, 1946.

Stokely Carmichael (Kwame Toure), 1941-98, (U.S.) black power activist; major proponent of Pan-Africanism; prime min. Black Panthers.

Carrie Chapman Catt, 1859-1947, (U.S.) suffragette.

Cesar Chavez, 1927-93, (U.S.) labor leader; helped establish United Farm Workers of America.

Eldridge Cleaver, 1935-98, (U.S.) revolutionary social critic; former minister of information for Black Panthers; *Soul on Ice*.

Clarence Darrow, 1857-1938, (U.S.) lawyer; defender of underdog, opponent of capital punishment.

Ossie Davis, 1917-2005, (U.S.) black civil rights activist, actor, director.

Dorothy Day, 1897-1980, (U.S.) founder of Catholic Worker movement.

Eugene V. Debs, 1855-1926, (U.S.) labor leader; led Pullman strike, 1894; 4-time Socialist presidential candidate.

Vine Deloria Jr., 1933-2005, (U.S.) Native American activist, author; *Custer Died for Your Sins*.

Dorothea Dix, 1802-87, (U.S.) crusader for mentally ill.

Thomas Dooley, 1927-61, (U.S.) "jungle doctor"; noted for efforts to supply medical aid to developing countries.

Marjory Stoneman Douglas, 1890-1998, (U.S.) writer, environmentalist; campaigned to save Florida Everglades.

Frederick Douglass, 1817-95, (U.S.) slave, author, editor, orator, diplomat; edited abolitionist weekly *The North Star*.

Andrea Dworkin, 1946-2005, (U.S.) radical feminist, antipornography crusader.

Medgar Evers, 1925-63, (U.S.) black civil rights leader; campaigned to register black voters; assassinated.

James Farmer, 1920-99, (U.S.) black civil rights leader; founded Congress of Racial Equality (CORE).

Betty Friedan, 1921-2006, (U.S.) author, feminist; *The Feminine Mystique*.

Millard Fuller, 1935-2009, (U.S.) founder of Habitat for Humanity.

William Lloyd Garrison, 1805-79, (U.S.) abolitionist.

Miep Gies, 1909-2010, (Neth.) protector of Anne Frank and her family during WWII.

Emma Goldman, 1869-1940, (Russ.-U.S.) published anarchist *Mother Earth*; birth-control advocate.

Samuel Gompers, 1850-1924, (U.S.) labor leader; first president of the American Federation of Labor (AFL).

Prince Hall, 1735-1807, (U.S.) activist; founded black Freemasonry; served in American Revolutionary war.

Michael Harrington, 1928-89, (U.S.) exposed poverty in affluent U.S. in *The Other America*, 1963.

Dorothy Height, 1912-2010, (U.S.) civil rights activist; pres. of the National Council of Negro Women, 1957-97.

Sidney Hillman, 1887-1946, (U.S.) labor leader; helped organize CIO.

Benjamin Hooks, 1925-2010, (U.S.) civil rights activist; exec. dir. NAACP, 1977-92.

Samuel G. Howe, 1801-76, (U.S.) social reformer; changed public attitudes toward the handicapped.

Franklin Kameny, 1925-2011, (U.S.) gay rights activist.

Helen Keller, 1880-1968, (U.S.) crusader for better treatment for the handicapped; deaf and blind herself.

Jack Kevorkian 1928-2011, (U.S.) pathologist; assisted-suicide activist.

Coretta Scott King, 1927-2006, (U.S.) black civil rights leader; wife of Rev. Martin Luther King Jr.

Rev. Martin Luther King Jr., 1929-68, (U.S.) civil rights leader; led 1955-56 Montgomery, AL, boycott; founder, pres., Southern Christian Leadership Conference, 1957; Nobel laureate, 1964; assassinated.

Maggie Kuhn, 1905-95, (U.S.) founded Gray Panthers, 1970.

William Kunstler, 1919-95, (U.S.) civil liberties attorney.

John L. Lewis, 1880-1969, (U.S.) labor leader; headed United Mine Workers, 1920-60.

Almena Lomax, 1915-2011, (U.S.) civil rights activist; journalist who founded *The Los Angeles Tribune*.

Clara Luper, 1923-2011, (U.S.) civil rights activist.

Wangari Maathai, 1940-2011, (Kenya), environmental activist; 2004 Nobel Peace Prize winner.

Robert Macauley, 1923-2010, (U.S.) founder of AmeriCares.

Malcolm X (Little), 1925-65, (U.S.) Black Muslim, black nationalist leader; promoted black pride; assassinated.

Karl Menninger, 1893-1990, (U.S.) with brother William, founded Menninger Clinic and Menninger Foundation.

Lucretia Mott, 1793-1880, (U.S.) reformer, pioneer feminist.

Philip Murray, 1886-1952, (U.S.) Scottish-born labor leader.

Huey P. Newton, 1942-89, (U.S.) cofounded Black Panther Party, 1966.

Florence Nightingale, 1820-1910, (Br.) founder of modern nursing.

Emmeline Pankhurst, 1858-1928, (Br.) woman suffragist.

Rosa Parks,1913-2005, (U.S.) black civil rights activist; her actions sparked 1955-56 Montgomery, AL, bus boycott.

A. Philip Randolph, 1889-1979, (U.S.) organized Brotherhood of Sleeping Car Porters, 1925; an organizer of 1941 and 1963 March on Washington movements.

Walter Reuther, 1907-70, (U.S.) labor leader; headed UAW.

Jacob Riis, 1849-1914, (U.S.) crusader for urban reforms.

Paul Robeson, 1898-1976, (U.S.) actor, singer, black civil rights activist.

Bayard Rustin, 1910-87, (U.S.) an organizer of the 1963 March on Washington; exec. director, A. Philip Randolph Institute.

Margaret Sanger, 1883-1966, (U.S.) social reformer; pioneered the birth-control movement.

Earl of Shaftesbury (A. A. Cooper), 1801-85, (Br.) social reformer.

Eunice Kennedy Shriver, 1921-2009, (U.S.) cofounder of Special Olympics for mentally challenged athletes.

Sargent Shriver, 1915-2011, (U.S.) founding director of Peace Corps; founder of Job Corps, Head Start.

Fred Shuttlesworth, 1922-2011, (U.S.) civil rights activist.

Albertina Sisulu, 1918-2011, (S. Africa), anti-apartheid activist.

Elizabeth Cady Stanton, 1815-1902, (U.S.) woman suffrage pioneer.

Lucy Stone, 1818-93, (U.S.) feminist, abolitionist.

Mother Teresa of Calcutta, 1910-97, (Alban.) nun; founded order to care for sick, dying poor; 1979 Nobel Peace Prize.

Willard Townsend, 1895-1957, (U.S.) organized the United Transport Service Employees (Red Caps), 1935.

Sojourner Truth (Isabella Baumfree), 1797-1883, (U.S.) preacher, abolitionist; worked for black educ. opportunity.

Harriet Tubman, 1823-1913, (U.S.) prominent figure in the Underground Railroad, which helped runaway slaves in the South reach safety in the North; nurse, spy for Union Army in the Civil War.

Nat Turner, 1800-31, (U.S.) slave who led the most significant of more than 200 slave revolts in U.S., in Southampton, VA; hanged.

Philip Vera Cruz, 1905-94, (Philip.-U.S.) helped found the United Farm Workers Union.

Edgar Wayburn, 1906-2010, (U.S.) conservationist; Sierra Club pres.

William Wilberforce, 1759-1833, (Br.) social reformer; prominent in struggle to abolish slave trade.

Frances E. Willard, 1839-98, (U.S.) temperance, women's rights leader.

Mary Wollstonecraft, 1759-97, (Br.) *Vindication of the Rights of Women*.

Sports Personalities of the Past and Present

Henry (Hank) Aaron, b 1934, Milwaukee-Atlanta outfielder; hit record 755 home runs, led NL 4 times; record 2,297 RBI.

Kareem Abdul-Jabbar, b 1947, Milwaukee, L.A. Lakers center; MVP 6 times; all-time leading NBA scorer, 38,387 points.

Andre Agassi, b 1970, won Wimbledon (1992); U.S. Open ('94, '99), Austral. Open ('95, 2000-01, '03), French Open ('99).

Troy Aikman, b 1966, quarterback; led Dallas Cowboys to Super Bowl wins in 1993-94, '96; Super Bowl MVP, 1993.

Amy Alcott, b 1956, golfer; 33 career wins (5 majors); inducted into World Golf Hall of Fame, 1999.

Grover Cleveland "Pete" Alexander, 1887-1950, pitcher; won 373 NL games; pitched 16 shutouts, 1916.

Muhammad Ali, b 1942, 3-time heavyweight champion.

Fernando Alonso, b 1981, Spanish Formula 1 racer; youngest ever to win a World Grand Prix championship, 2005; defended title, 2006.

Morten Andersen, b 1960, (Den.) kicker; NFL's career points leader, with 2,544 (1982-2007).

Gary Anderson, b 1959, (S. Afr.) kicker; NFL's 2nd in career points, with 2,434.

Sparky Anderson, 1934-2010, first manager to win World Series in the NL (Cincinnati, 1975-76) and AL (Detroit, 1984).

Mario Andretti, b 1940, race-car driver; won Daytona 500 (1967), Indy 500 (1969); Formula 1 world title (1978).

Earl Anthony, 1938-2001, bowler; won record 6 PBA Championships (1973-75, 1981-83), 43 career PBA tournaments.

Eddie Arcaro, 1916-97, only jockey to win racing's Triple Crown twice, 1941, '48; rode to 4,779 wins in his career.

Lance Armstrong, b 1971, cyclist; record 7-time winner of the Tour de France (1999-2005).

Arthur Ashe, 1943-93, tennis player; won U.S. Open (1968); Wimbledon (1975).

Evelyn Ashford, b 1957, sprinter; won 100m gold (1984) and silver (1988); member of 5 U.S. Olympic teams.

Red Auerbach, 1917-2006, coached Boston to 9 NBA titles.

Tracy Austin, b 1962, youngest player to win U.S. Open tennis title (age 16 in 1979), 2-time AP Female Athlete of the Year.

Ernie Banks, b 1931, Chicago Cubs slugger; hit 512 NL homers; twice MVP; never played in World Series.

Roger Bannister, b 1929, British physician; ran 1st sub-4-minute mile, May 6, 1954 (3 min. 59.4 sec.).

Charles Barkley, b 1963, NBA MVP, 1993; 4th player ever to surpass 20,000 points, 10,000 rebounds, 4,000 assists.

Rick Barry, b 1944, NBA scoring leader, 1967; ABA scoring leader, 1969.

Sammy Baugh, 1914-2008, Washington Redskins quarterback; held numerous records upon retirement after 16 seasons.

Elgin Baylor, b 1934, L.A. Lakers forward; 11-time all-star.

Bob Beamon, b 1946, Olympic long jump gold medalist, 1968; world record jump of 29 ft 2½ in. stood until 1991.

Boris Becker, b 1967, German tennis star; won U.S. Open 1989; Wimbledon champ 1985, '86, '89.

David Beckham, b 1975, English soccer star; captain of 2002 World Cup team; joined Los Angeles Galaxy, 2007, with record-breaking $250 mil contract.

Bill Belichick, b 1952, NFL coach; led New England Patriots to 3 Super Bowl wins (2001, '03, '04); best all-time postseason coaching record; fined $500,000 in 2007 for violating rules about videotaping opposing sideline.

Jean Beliveau, b 1931, Montreal Canadiens center; scored 507 goals; twice MVP.

Johnny Bench, b 1947, Cincinnati Reds catcher; twice MVP; led league in home runs twice, RBIs 3 times.

Patty Berg, 1918-2006, 80+ golf tournament wins; AP Woman Athlete of the Year 3 times.

Chris Berman, b 1955, sportscaster, anchor for ESPN and ABC Sports.

Yogi Berra, b 1925, Yankee catcher (1946-63); 3-time MVP.

Abebe Bikila, 1932-73, Ethiopian runner; won consecutive Olympic marathon gold medals in 1960 (barefoot), 1964.

Matt Biondi, b 1965, swimmer; won 5 golds, 1988 Olympics.

Larry Bird, b 1956, Boston Celtics forward (1979-92); NBA MVP, 1984-86; 1998 coach of the year with Indiana Pacers.

Bonnie Blair, b 1964, speed skater; won 5 individual gold medals in 3 Olympics (1988, '92, '94).

George Blanda, 1927-2010, quarterback, kicker; 26 years as active player, scored 2,002 career points.

Fanny Blankers-Koen, 1918-2004, track star; won 4 golds in 1948 Olympics.

Wade Boggs, b 1958, AL batting champ, 1983, 1985-88; reached 3,000 career hits, 1999 (3,010).

Usain Bolt, b 1986, Jamaican sprinter; won 3 golds in 2008 Olympics, world record for men's 100m, 200m runs.

Barry Bonds, b 1964, outfielder; hit record 73 homers, 2001; NL MVP, 1990, 1992-93, 2001-04; 1st all-time in HRs (762); indicted in baseball steroid scandal, 2007; convicted of obstruction of justice, 2011.

Björn Borg, b 1956, led Sweden to first Davis Cup, 1975; 6-time French Open, 5-time Wimbledon champion.

Ray Bourque, b 1960, Boston defenseman,1979-2000; 5-time Norris Trophy winner; won Stanley Cup with Colorado, 2001.

Bill Bradley, b 1943, All-American at Princeton; led NY Knicks to 2 NBA titles (1970, '73); U.S. senator, 1979-97.

Donald Bradman, 1908-2001, Australian widely regarded as greatest cricketer ever; set several batting records.

Terry Bradshaw, b 1948, quarterback; led Pittsburgh to 4 Super Bowl wins, 1975-76, 1979-80; NFL MVP, 1978.

Tom Brady, b 1977, quarterback; led New England Patriots to 3 Super Bowl titles, 2002, '04, '05; Super Bowl MVP, 2002, '04; NFL MVP, 2007, '11; most single-season TD passes (50), 2007.

Drew Brees, b 1979, New Orleans Saints quarterback; Super Bowl MVP, 2010.

Christine Brennan, b 1958, sports journalist for USA Today, radio and television commentator specializing in figure skating.

George Brett, b 1953, Kansas City Royals infielder; led AL in batting, 1976, '80, '90; MVP, 1980.

Lou Brock, b 1939, St. Louis Cardinals outfielder; stole NL single-season record 118 bases, 1974; led NL 8 times.

Jim Brown, b 1936, Cleveland fullback; 12,312 career yds.; NFL MVP 1957, '58, '65.

Paul Brown, 1908-91, football team-owner, coach; led eponymous Cleveland Browns to 3 NFL championships.

Kobe Bryant, b 1978, guard; won 3 straight titles with Lakers (2000-02); leading NBA scorer, 2005-06 and 2006-07; 2007-08 NBA MVP; NBA Finals MVP 2009, '10.

Paul "Bear" Bryant, 1913-83, college football coach with 323 wins; led Alabama to 6 national titles (1961, '64, '65, '73, '78, '79).

Sergei Bubka, b 1963, (Ukr.) pole vaulter; first to clear 20 ft.; gold medal, 1988 Olympics.

Don Budge, 1915-2000, won numerous amateur and pro tennis titles; Grand Slam, 1938.

Reggie Bush, b 1985, NFL running back drafted 2nd overall in 2006; helped USC to 2 national titles (2003-04).

Dick Butkus, b 1942, Chicago Bears linebacker; NFL defensive player of the year (1969, '70).

Dick Button, b 1929, figure skater; won 1948, 1952 Olympic gold medals; world titleholder, 1948-52.

Walter Camp, 1859-1925, Yale football player, coach, athletic director; established many rules for modern football.

Roy Campanella, 1921-93, Hall of Fame catcher for the Brooklyn Dodgers (1948-57); 3-time NL MVP.

Earl Campbell, b 1955, NFL running back; MVP 1978-79.

Jose Canseco, b 1964, outfielder; led Oakland A's to the World Series, 1988; wrote book about steroids in baseball, 2005.

Eric Cantona, b 1966, French soccer star; Manchester United (1992-97); named Manchester United Man of the Century, 2001.

Rod Carew, b 1945, AL infielder; 7 batting titles, 1977 MVP.

Steve Carlton, b 1944, NL pitcher; won 20 games 6 times; Cy Young award 4 times; 4,136 career strikeouts.

Pete Carroll, b 1951, college and pro football coach; coached the USC Trojans to 2 championships (2003-04).

Billy Casper, b 1931, PGA Player of the Year 2 times; U.S. Open champ twice.

Wilt Chamberlain, 1936-99, center; NBA leading scorer 7 times, MVP 4 times; scored 100 pts. in a game, 1962.

Bobby Clarke, b 1949, Philadelphia Flyers center; led team to 2 Stanley Cup championships; MVP 3 times.

Roger Clemens, b 1962, pitcher; 1986 AL MVP; only 7-time Cy Young winner (1986-87, '91, '97-'98, 2001, '04); twice recorded record 20 Ks in a game; 354 wins, 4,672 Ks (3rd all-time); indicted, accused of lying to Congress about using steroids, 2010.

Roberto Clemente, 1934-72, Pittsburgh Pirates outfielder; won 4 batting titles; MVP, 1966; 3,000 career hits; killed in plane crash.

Kim Clijsters, b 1983, Belgian tennis player; U.S. Open winner (2005, '09-'10), Austral. Open (2011).

Ty Cobb, 1886-1961, Detroit Tigers outfielder; record .367 lifetime batting average, 12 batting titles.

Sebastian Coe, b 1956, British runner; won Olympic 1,500m gold medal and 800m silver medal in 1980 and 1984.

Nadia Comaneci, b 1961, Romanian gymnast; won 3 gold medals, achieved 7 perfect scores, 1976 Olympics; 9 Olympic medals overall.

Maureen Connolly, 1934-69, won tennis Grand Slam, 1953; AP Woman Athlete of the Year 3 times.

Jimmy Connors, b 1952, tennis player; 5 U.S. Open, 2 Wimbledon titles.

Alberto Contador, b 1982, (Sp.) cyclist; won Tour de France 2007, '09 '10.

Cynthia Cooper, b 1963, basketball; 4-time MVP of WNBA finals; 2-time league MVP for the Houston Comets.

James J. Corbett, 1866-1933, heavyweight champion, 1892-97; credited with being the first "scientific" boxer.

Angel Cordero Jr., b 1942, jockey; leading money winner, 1976, 1982-83; rode 3 Kentucky Derby winners.

Margaret Smith Court, b 1942, Australian tennis great; won 24 Grand Slam events.

Bob Cousy, b 1928, Boston guard; 6 NBA titles, 1957 MVP.

Mark Cuban, b 1958, Dallas Mavericks owner; known for criticism of NBA.

Bjoern Daehlie, b 1967, (Nor.) cross-country skier; won record 8 Winter Olympic gold medals.

Lindsay Davenport, b 1976, tennis player; won Olympic gold, 1996; U.S. Open, 1998; Wimbledon, 1999; Austral. Open, 2000.

Al Davis, 1929-2011, Oakland Raiders owner, former coach.

Dizzy Dean, 1910-74, pitcher; St. Louis Cardinals' "Gashouse Gang" in the '30s.

Mary Decker Slaney, b 1958, runner; has held 6 separate American records from the 800m to 10,000m.

Frank Deford, b 1938, senior contributing writer for Sports Illustrated; author, commentator.

Oscar De La Hoya, b 1973, won IBF lightweight (1995); WBC super lightweight (1996); welterweight (1997-99, 2000) titles.

Juan Martin del Potro, b 1988, (Arg.) tennis player; won U.S. Open, 2009.

Jack Dempsey, 1895-1983, heavyweight champ, 1919-26.

Donna de Varona, b 1947, 2 Olympic swimming golds, 1964; 1st female sportscaster at a major network (ABC), 1965.

Gail Devers, b 1966, Olympic 100m gold medalist (1992, '96).

Joe DiMaggio, 1914-99, NY Yankees outfielder; hit safely in record 56 consecutive games, 1941; AL MVP 3 times.

Novak Djokovic, b 1987, (Serb.) tennis player; won Austral. Open (2008, '11), Wimbledon (2011), U.S. Open (2011).

Landon Donovan, b 1982, forward for L.A. Galaxy; all-time leading U.S. international goal scorer with 45; MLS MVP, 2009.

Tony Dorsett, b 1954, Heisman winner who led the Dallas Cowboys to an NFL title in his rookie year, 1977.

Tim Duncan, b 1976, San Antonio center; 3-time NBA Finals MVP, 1999, 2003, 2005; NBA MVP, 2002-03.

Roberto Duran, b 1951, (Pan.) boxer; held titles at 3 weights; lost 1980 "no mas" fight to Sugar Ray Leonard.

Leo Durocher, 1905-91, manager; won 3 NL pennants (Brooklyn, 1941; NY Giants, 1951, '54), 1954 World Series.

Dale Earnhardt Jr., b 1974, 2004 Daytona 500 winner.

Dale Earnhardt Sr., 1951-2001, 7-time NASCAR Winston Cup champ; died in a last-lap crash at 2001 Daytona 500.

Stefan Edberg, b 1966, (Swed.) tennis player; U.S. Open (1991, '92), Wimbledon (1988, '90), Austral. Open (1985, '87).

Gertrude Ederle, 1905-2003, first woman to swim English Channel; broke existing men's record, 1926.

Teresa Edwards, b 1964, 5-time basketball Olympian; gold medalist, 1984, '88, '96, 2000; bronze medalist, 1992.

Hicham El Guerrouj, b 1974, Moroccan runner; holds world records in mile (3:43.13) and 1,500m (3:26); won gold medals in 1,500m and 5,000m, 2004 Olympics.

John Elway, b 1960, quarterback; led Denver Broncos to 2 Super Bowl wins, 1998, '99; NFL MVP, 1987; Super Bowl MVP, 1999.

Julius "Dr. J" Erving, b 1950, 3-time ABA MVP, 1981 NBA MVP.

Phil Esposito, b 1942, NHL scoring leader 5 times.

Janet Evans, b 1971, 4 Olympic swimming golds, 1988, '92.

Lee Evans, b 1947, Olympic 400m gold medalist in 1968 with 43.86-sec. world record not broken until 1988.

Chris Evert, b 1954, 6-time U.S. Open tennis champ, 3-time Wimbledon champ.

Ray Ewry, 1873-1937, track-and-field star; won 8 Olympics gold medals (1900, '04, '08).

Nick Faldo, b 1957, British golfer; won Masters, British Open 3 times each.

Juan Manuel Fangio, 1911-95 (Arg.), 5-time World Grand Prix driving champ (1951, 1954-57).

Marshall Faulk, b 1973, 2000 NFL MVP; scored then-record 26 TDs, 2001; 3-time Off. Player of the Year (1999-2001).

Brett Favre, b 1969, quarterback; led Green Bay to Super Bowl win, 1997; NFL MVP, 1995, '96; co-MVP, 1997; left retirement to play for NY Jets, 2008; Minnesota Vikings, 2009-10.

Roger Federer, b 1981, (Switz.) tennis star; won Austral. Open (2004, '06-'07, '10), Wimbledon (2003-07, '09), U.S. Open (2004-08), French Open (2009).

Bob Feller, 1918-2010, Cleveland Indians pitcher; won 266 games; pitched 3 no-hitters, 12 one-hitters.

Rollie Fingers, b 1946, pitcher; 341 career saves; AL MVP, Cy Young Award, 1981; World Series MVP, 1974.

Peggy Fleming, b 1948, world figure skating champion, 1966-68; gold medalist, 1968 Olympics.

Whitey Ford, b 1928, NY Yankees pitcher; won record 10 World Series games.

George Foreman, b 1949, heavyweight champion, 1973-74, 1994-95; at 45, oldest to win a heavyweight title; gold medalist, 1968 Olympics.

Dick Fosbury, b 1947, high jumper; won 1968 Olympic gold medal; developed the "Fosbury Flop."

Jimmie Foxx, 1907-67, Red Sox, Athletics slugger; MVP 3 times; triple crown, 1933.

A. J. Foyt, b 1935, won Indy 500 4 times; U.S. Auto Club champ 7 times.

Joe Frazier, b 1944, heavyweight champion, 1970-73; gold medalist, 1964 Olympics.

Walt Frazier, b 1945, Hall of Fame guard for NY Knicks' NBA championship teams (1970, '73).

Peter Gammons, b 1945, sportswriter, broadcaster; named to Baseball Hall of Fame.

Lou Gehrig, 1903-41, NY Yankees 1st baseman; MVP, 1927, '36; triple crown, 1934; AL record 184 RBIs, 1931; played in 2,130 straight games (1925-39), a record that stood until 1995.

Althea Gibson, 1927-2003, 2-time U.S. and Wimbledon champ.

Bob Gibson, b 1935, St. Louis Cardinals pitcher; won Cy Young award twice; struck out 3,117 batters.

Josh Gibson, 1911-47, Hall of Fame catcher; known as "Babe Ruth of the Negro Leagues"; credited with as many as 84 homers in 1 season, about 800 in his career.

Marc Girardelli, b 1963, (Lux.) skier; won 5 World Cup titles.

Raul Gonzalez, b 1977, (Sp.) soccer player; led Real Madrid to 3 Champions League titles (1998, 2000, '02); all-time top UEFA goal scorer (71).

Jeff Gordon, b 1971, race-car driver; youngest to win NASCAR title 4 times (1995, '97 '98, 2001).

Steffi Graf, b 1969, (Ger.) won tennis Grand Slam 1988; U.S. Open champ 5 times; Wimbledon, 7 times; Austral. 4 times; French 6 times.

Otto Graham, 1921-2003, Cleveland quarterback; 4-time all-pro.

Red Grange, 1903-91, All-American at Univ. of Illinois, 1923-25; played for Chicago Bears, 1925-35.

"Mean" Joe Greene, b 1946, Pittsburgh Steelers lineman; twice NFL outstanding defensive player.

Wayne Gretzky, b 1961, top scorer in NHL history with record 894 goals, 1,963 assists, 2,857 points; MVP, 1980-87, '89.

Bob Griese, b 1945, All-Pro quarterback; led Miami Dolphins to 17-0 season, 1972, 2 Super Bowl titles, 1973-74.

Ken Griffey Jr., b 1969, outfielder; led AL in homers 1994, '97-'99; 1997 AL MVP; 10 gold gloves.

Archie Griffin, b 1954, Ohio State running back; only 2-time winner of the Heisman Trophy (1974-75).

Florence Griffith Joyner, 1959-98, sprinter; won 3 gold medals at 1988 Olympics; world and Olympic record for 100m.

Lefty Grove, 1900-75, pitcher; won 300 AL games.

Vladimir Guerrero, b 1975, (Dom. Rep.) right fielder; 2004 American League MVP award.

Janet Guthrie, b 1938, 1st woman driver in Indy 500 (1977).

Tony Gwynn, b 1960, 8-time NL batting champ (1984, '87-'89, '94-'97); 3,141 career hits.

Walter Hagen, 1892-1969, golfer; 5 PGA, 4 British Open titles.

Mika Hakkinen, b 1968, (Fin.) Formula One racing driver; Formula One champion, 1998, '99.

George Halas, 1895-1983, founder/player/coach of Chicago Bears; won 6 NFL championships as coach.

Roy Halladay, b 1977, pitcher; Cy Young Award, 2003, '10; pitched perfect game, 2010.

Dorothy Hamill, b 1956, figure skater; gold medalist at the Olympics and World championships, 1976.

Josh Hamilton, b 1981, Texas Rangers outfielder; AL MVP, 2010.

Scott Hamilton, b 1958, U.S. and world figure skating champion, 1981-84; Olympic gold medalist, 1984.

Mia Hamm, b 1972, soccer player; led U.S. to World Cup (1991, '99) and Olympic (1996, 2004) titles; most career intl. goals (158).

Franco Harris, b 1950, running back; 4 Super Bowls with Steelers (1975-76, 1979-80); 1,000+ yds. in a season 8 times.

Marvin Harrison, b 1972, Indianapolis Colts wide receiver; NFL record for single-season receptions (143), 2002.

Bill Hartack, 1932-2007, jockey; rode 5 Kentucky Derby winners.

Dominik Hasek, b 1965, (Czech.) NHL goaltender; won Vezina Trophy, 1994-95, '97-'99, 2001; NHL MVP, 1997-98.

John Havlicek, b 1940, Boston Celtics forward; scored 26,395 career pts.

Eric Heiden, b 1958, speed skater; won 5 Olympic golds, 1980.

Rickey Henderson, b 1958, outfielder; 1990 AL MVP; record 130 stolen bases, 1982; all-time leader in steals, runs.

Sonja Henie, 1912-69, (Nor.) world champion figure skater, 1927-36; Olympic gold medalist, 1928, '32, '36.

Martina Hingis, b 1980, (Switz.) won Austral. and U.S. Opens, Wimbledon; youngest number one player (16 yrs., 6 mos.), 1997.

Trevor Hoffman, b 1967, relief pitcher (601 career saves).

Ben Hogan, 1912-97, golfer; won 4 U.S. Open titles, 2 PGA Championships, 2 Masters.

Santonio Holmes, b 1984, wide receiver; Super Bowl MVP, 2009.

Evander Holyfield, b 1962, 4-time heavyweight champion.

Rogers Hornsby, 1896-1963, NL 2nd baseman; batted record .424, 1924; twice won triple crown.

Paul Hornung, b 1935, Green Bay Packers running back, placekicker; scored record 176 points, 1960.

Ryan Howard, b 1979, first baseman for Philadelphia Phillies; known for his hitting; 2006 NL MVP.

Gordie Howe, b 1928, hockey forward; NHL MVP 6 times; scored 801 goals in 26 NHL seasons.

Carl Hubbell, 1903-88, NY Giants pitcher; 20-game winner 5 consecutive years, 1933-37.

Bobby Hull, b 1939, NHL all-star 10 times; MVP, 1965-66.

Brett Hull, b 1964, St. Louis Blues forward; led NHL in goals, 1990-92; MVP, 1991.

Catfish Hunter, 1946-99, pitched perfect game, 1968; 20-game winner 5 times.

Don Hutson, 1913-97, Packers receiver; caught 99 TD passes; 2-time NFL MVP.

Juli Inkster, b 1960, Hall of Fame golfer; 2nd to win all 4 of LPGA's modern majors; won 7 career major titles.

Bo Jackson, b 1962, NFL running back (1987-90) and MLB outfielder (1986-91, '93-'94); 1985 Heisman Trophy winner.

Phil Jackson, b 1945, won 11 NBA titles as coach of Bulls and Lakers; 1970, '73 title as player with NY Knicks.

Reggie Jackson, b 1946, slugger; led AL in home runs 4 times; MVP, 1973; hit 5 World Series home runs, 1977.

"Shoeless" Joe Jackson, 1889-1951, outfielder; 3rd highest career batting average (.356); one of the "Black Sox" banned for allegedly throwing 1919 World Series.

Jaromir Jagr, b 1972, Czech hockey player; NHL MVP, 1999; Art Ross Trophy (leading scorer), 1995, 1998-2001.

LeBron James, b 1984, NBA forward; Rookie of the Year, 2004; 2008 scoring leader; member of 2008 U.S. Olympic gold medal team; NBA Most Valuable Player, 2008-09, 2009-10.

Ron Jaworski, b 1951, former NFL quarterback (1974-89); NFL analyst on ESPN.

Sally Jenkins, b 1960, sports journalist and writer for *The Washington Post*.

Bruce Jenner, b 1949, Olympic decathlon gold medalist, 1976.

Lynn Jennings, b 1960, runner; 3-time World, 9-time U.S. cross country champ; bronze (10,000m), 1992 Olympics.

Derek Jeter, b 1974, shortstop; led NY Yankees to 5 World Series titles; World Series MVP, 2000; 1st Yankee to reach 3,000 hits, 2011.

Earvin "Magic" Johnson, b 1959, NBA MVP, 1987, '89, '90; playoff MVP, 1980, '82, '87; 4th in career assists.

Jack Johnson, 1878-1946, heavyweight champion, 1908-15.

Jimmie Johnson, b 1975, 5-time NASCAR Sprint Cup Series champ, 2006-10; Daytona 500 winner, 2006.

Michael Johnson, b 1967, 4-time Olympic gold medalist (1992, '96, 2000); world and Olympic record, 400m and 4 × 400m.

Randy Johnson, b 1963, 5-time Cy Young winner; strikeout leader, 1992-95, 1999-2002, 2004; 4,875 strikeouts (2nd all-time); pitched perfect game, 2004.

Walter Johnson, 1887-1946, Washington Senators pitcher; won 417 games; record 110 shutouts.

Bobby Jones, 1902-71, won golf's Grand Slam, 1930; U.S. amateur champ 5 times, U.S. Open champ 4 times.

Cobi Jones, b 1970, soccer player; most U.S. national team appearances with 164.

David "Deacon" Jones, b 1938, 5-time All-Pro with L.A. Rams (1965-69); "sack" specialist credited with inventing the term.

Marion Jones, b 1975, 2000 Olympic 100m, 200m, 1,600m relay gold medalist, bronze in long jump and 400m relay; stripped of medals in 2007 after admitting use of performance-enhancing drugs.

Roy Jones Jr., b 1969, light heavyweight champ, 1999-2004.

Michael Jordan, b 1963, guard; leading NBA scorer, 1987-93, '96-'98; MVP, 1988, 1991-'92, '96, '98; playoff MVP, 1991-93, '96-'98; ESPN Athlete of the Century.

Dorothy Kamenshek, 1925-2010, led Rockford (IL) Peaches to 4 All-American Girls Baseball League titles in the 1940s.

Jackie Joyner-Kersee, b 1962, Olympic gold medalist in heptathlon (1988, '92), long jump (1988).

Harmon Killebrew, 1936-2011, Minnesota Twins slugger; led AL in home runs 6 times; 573 lifetime.

Jean Claude Killy, b 1943, (Fr.) skier; 3 Olympic golds, 1968.

Kim Yu-Na, b 1990, (S. Kor.) figure skater; Olympic gold medal winner, 2010; world champion, 2009.

Ralph Kiner, b 1922, Pittsburgh Pirates slugger; led NL in home runs 7 consecutive years, 1946-52.

Billie Jean King, b 1943, U.S. singles champ 4 times; Wimbledon champ 6 times; beat Bobby Riggs, 1973.

Peter King, b 1957, senior writer for *Sports Illustrated*.

Bob Knight, b 1940, ESPN studio analyst, ret. basketball coach; led Indiana U. to NCAA title in 1976, '81, '87; winningest men's college basketball coach (902).

Olga Korbut, b 1955, Soviet gymnast; 3 Olympic golds, 1972.

Sandy Koufax, b 1935, 3-time Cy Young winner; lowest ERA in NL, 1962-66; pitched 4 no-hitters, 1 perfect game.

Jack Kramer, 1921-2009, world's number one tennis player, 1946-53; first at Wimbledon to compete in shorts.

Ingrid Kristiansen, b 1956, (Nor.) only runner to have held world records in 5,000m, 10,000m, and marathon.

Julie Krone, b 1963, winningest female jockey; only woman to ride a winner in a Triple Crown race (Belmont, 1993).

Michelle Kwan, b 1980, figure skater; 9 U.S., 5 World titles; silver medalist at 1998 Olympics, bronze in 2002.

Guy Lafleur, b 1951, 3-time NHL scoring leader; 1977-78 MVP.

Alexi Lalas, b 1970, soccer player; first modern-era American to play in Italian League Serie A.

Kenesaw Mountain Landis, 1866-1944, 1st commissioner of baseball (1920-44);

banned the 8 "Black Sox" involved in fixing 1919 World Series.

Tom Landry, 1924-2000, Dallas Cowboys head coach, 1960-88; won 2 Super Bowls (1972, '78); 3rd in career wins (270).

Dick "Night Train" Lane, 1928-2002, Hall of Fame defensive back; intercepted an NFL season record 14 passes (1952).

Don Larsen, b 1929, as NY Yankee, pitched only World Series perfect game, Oct. 8, 1956—2-0 win over Brooklyn.

Rod Laver, b 1938, (Austral.) won tennis Grand Slam, 1962, 1969; Wimbledon champ 4 times.

Mario Lemieux, b 1965, 6-time NHL leading scorer; MVP, 1988, '93, '96; playoff MVP, 1991-92.

Greg Lemond, b 1961, cyclist; 3-time Tour de France winner (1986, '89-'90); first American to win the event.

Ivan Lendl, b 1960, (Czech.) 8 Grand Slam tennis titles, including U.S. Open, 1985-87.

Sugar Ray Leonard, b 1956, boxer; held titles in 5 different weight classes.

Lisa Leslie, b 1972, L.A. Sparks center; 3-time WNBA MVP (2001, '04, '06).

Carl Lewis, b 1961, track-and-field star; won 9 Olympic gold medals in sprinting and long jump.

Lennox Lewis, b 1965, (Br.) heavyweight champ, 1994, 1997-2004, retired undefeated; gold medalist, 1988 Olympics.

Ray Lewis, b 1975, linebacker for the Baltimore Ravens; Super Bowl MVP, 2001.

Tim Lincecum, b 1984, S.F. Giants pitcher; NL Cy Young Award, 2008-09.

Tara Lipinski, b 1982, youngest figure skater to win U.S., world championships, 1997, and Winter Olympic gold, 1998.

Vince Lombardi, 1913-70, Green Bay Packers coach; led team to 5 NFL championships, 2 Super Bowl victories.

Nancy Lopez, b 1957, Hall of Fame golfer; 4-time LPGA Player of the Year, 3-time winner of the LPGA Championship.

Greg Louganis, b 1960, won Olympic gold medals in both springboard and platform diving, 1984, 1988.

Joe Louis, 1914-81, heavyweight champion, 1937-49.

Sid Luckman, 1916-98, Chicago Bears quarterback; led team to 4 NFL championships; MVP, 1943.

Evan Lysacek, b 1985, figure skater; world champion, 2009, Olympic gold winner, 2010.

Connie Mack, 1862-1956, Philadelphia Athletics manager, 1901-50; won 9 pennants, 3 championships.

John Madden, b 1936, won Super Bowl as coach of Oakland Raiders (1977); former NFL TV analyst.

Greg Maddux, b 1966, NL pitcher; won 4 consecutive Cy Young awards, 1992-95; 355 career wins.

Karl Malone, b 1963, Utah Jazz, L.A. Lakers forward; MVP, 1997, '99; 14-time All-Star; 36,928 career points (2nd all-time).

Moses Malone, b 1955, NBA center; MVP, 1979, '82-'83.

Eli Manning, b 1981, NY Giants quarterback; Super Bowl MVP, 2008.

Peyton Manning, b 1976, Indianapolis Colts quarterback; most NFL MVP awards, 2003-04, '08-'09; Super Bowl MVP, 2007; highest single-season passer rating (121.1), 2004.

Mickey Mantle, 1931-95, NY Yankees outfielder; triple crown, 1956; 18 World Series home runs; MVP 3 times.

Diego Maradona, b 1960, (Arg.) soccer player; led Argentina to World Cup, 1986.

"Pistol" Pete Maravich, 1947-88, guard; scored NCAA record 44.2 ppg during collegiate career; led NBA in scoring, 1977.

Rocky Marciano, 1923-69, heavyweight champion, 1952-56; retired undefeated.

Dan Marino, b 1961, Miami quarterback; NFL record single-season yards passing (5,084), 1984.

Roger Maris, 1934-85, NY Yankees outfielder; hit AL record 61 home runs, 1961, record held 37 years; MVP, 1960, '61.

Marta (Marta Vieira da Silva), b 1986, (Braz.) soccer forward; FIFA World Player of the Year, 2006-10.

Curtis Martin, b 1973, Jets running back; 5-time Pro-Bowler; 4th in all-time rushing yards with 14,101.

Eddie Mathews, 1931-2001, Milwaukee-Atlanta Braves 3rd baseman; hit 512 career home runs.

Christy Mathewson, 1880-1925, pitcher; won 373 games.

Bob Mathias, 1930-2006, decathlon gold, 1948, '52 Olympics.

Hideki Matsui, b 1974, (Jpn.) designated hitter/outfielder; 1st Japanese-born World Series MVP, 2009.

Willie Mays, b 1931, NY-S.F. Giants center fielder; hit 660 home runs, led NL 4 times; had 3,283 hits; twice MVP.

Rory McIlroy, b 1989, (Ire.) golfer; won U.S. Open 16 under par, 2011.

Willie McCovey, b 1938, S.F. Giants slugger; hit 521 home runs; led NL 3 times; MVP, 1969.

John McEnroe, b 1959, U.S. Open tennis champ (1979-81, '84); Wimbledon champ (1981, '83-'84).

John McGraw, 1873-1934, NY Giants manager; led team to 10 pennants, 3 championships.

Mark McGwire, b 1963, hit then-record 70 home runs in 1998; 583 career home runs (10th); admitted career steroid use, 2010.

Tamara McKinney, b 1962, 1st U.S. skier to win overall Alpine World Cup championship (1983).

Andrea Mead Lawrence, 1932-2009, skier; first woman to win 2 gold medals in alpine skiing at one Olympics (1952).

Lionel Messi, b 1987, (Arg.) forward for FC Barcelona; FIFA World Player of the Year, 2009-10.

Mark Messier, b 1961, center; NHL MVP, 1990, '92; Conn Smythe Trophy, 1984.

Debbie Meyer, b 1952, 1st swimmer to win 3 individual Olympic golds (1968).

Al Michaels, b 1944, *NBC Sunday Night Football* announcer; 5-time Outstanding Sports Personality Emmy winner.

George Mikan, 1924-2005, Minn. Lakers center; considered the best basketball player of first half of 20th century.

Stan Mikita, b 1940, Chicago Blackhawks center; led NHL in scoring 4 times; MVP twice.

Billy Mills, b 1938, runner; upset winner of the 1964 Olympic 10,000m; only American man ever to win the event.

Joe Montana, b 1956, S.F. 49ers quarterback; Super Bowl MVP, 1982, 1985, 1990.

Archie Moore, 1913-98, light-heavyweight champ, 1952-62.

Howie Morenz, 1902-37, Montreal Canadiens forward; considered best hockey player of first half of 20th century.

Edwin Moses, b 1955, undefeated in 122 consecutive 400m hurdles races, 1977-87; Olympic gold medalist, 1976, '84.

Shirley Muldowney, b 1940, 1st woman to race National Hot Rod Assn. Top Fuel dragsters; 3-time NHRA points champ.

Eddie Murray, b 1956, 3rd player with both 3,000+ hits and 500+ home runs.

Stan Musial, b 1920, St. Louis Cardinals star; won 7 NL batting titles; MVP 3 times.

Rafael Nadal, b 1986, (Sp.) tennis player; won French Open (2005-08, '10-'11), Wimbledon (2008, '10), Australian Open (2009), U.S. Open (2010); Olympic gold medal in men's singles (2008).

Bronko Nagurski, 1908-90, Chicago Bears fullback and tackle; gained more than 4,000 yds. rushing.

Joe Namath, b 1943, Jets quarterback; 1969 Super Bowl MVP.

Steve Nash, b 1974, (Can.) Phoenix Suns point guard; NBA MVP, 2005, '06.

Martina Navratilova, b 1956, Wimbledon champ 9 times; U.S. Open champ 1983-84, '86-'87); Austral. 3 times, French 2 times.

Byron Nelson, 1912-2006, won 11 consecutive golf tournaments in 1945; twice Masters and PGA titlist.

Ernie Nevers, 1903-76, Stanford football star; selected as best college fullback to play between 1919 and 1969.

Paula Newby-Fraser, b 1962, ([now] Zimbabwe) 8-time Ironman Triathlon world champ; holds women's course record.

John Newcombe, b 1944, Australian; twice U.S. Open tennis champ; Wimbledon champ 3 times.

Jack Nicklaus, b 1940, PGA Player of the Year, 1967, 1972; leading money winner 8 times; won 18 majors (6 Masters).

Chuck Noll, b 1932, Pittsburgh coach; won 4 Super Bowls.

Dirk Nowitzki, b 1978, (Ger.) NBA forward; led Mavericks to NBA title, 2011; NBA MVP, 2007.

Paavo Nurmi, 1897-1973, (Fin.) distance runner; won 9 Olympic gold medals, 1920, 1924, 1928.

Lorena Ochoa, b 1981, (Mex.) LPGA Player of the Year, 2006-09, money leader 2006-08.

Al Oerter, 1936-2007, discus thrower; won gold medal at 4 consecutive Olympics, 1956, '60, '64, '68.

Apolo Anton Ohno, b 1982, speed skater; most decorated American Winter Olympic athlete with 2 gold, 2 silver, 4 bronze (2002, '06, '10).

Hakeem Olajuwon, b 1963, (Nigeria) Houston center; NBA MVP, 1994, playoff MVP, 1994-95; career blocked shots leader (3,830).

Barney Oldfield, 1878-1946, pioneer auto racer; was first to drive a car 60 mph, 1903.

Shaquille O'Neal, b 1972, center; led L.A. Lakers to NBA titles, 2000-02, and Miami Heat to NBA title, 2006; Finals MVP 2000-02; NBA MVP 2000.

Bobby Orr, b 1948, Boston Bruins defenseman; 8-time Norris Trophy winner; led NHL in scoring twice, assists 5 times.

Mel Ott, 1909-58, NY Giants right fielder; hit 511 home runs; led NL 6 times.

Jesse Owens, 1913-80, track and field; 4 1936 Olympic golds.

Terrell Owens, b 1973, wide receiver; NFL record for single-game receptions with 20 in 2000.

Satchel Paige, 1906-82, pitcher; starred in Negro leagues, 1924-48; entered major leagues at age 42.

Arnold Palmer, b 1929, golf's first $1 mil winner; won 4 Masters, 2 British Opens.

Jim Palmer, b 1945, Baltimore Orioles pitcher; won Cy Young award 3 times; 20-game winner 8 times.

Candace Parker, b 1986, L.A. Sparks forward; first woman to dunk in an NCAA tournament game; 2008 WNBA MVP award, Rookie of the Year.

Joe Paterno, b 1926, football coach; most wins in NCAA Div. I-A (401); led Penn St. to titles, 1982, '86.

Danica Patrick, b 1982, race car driver; 4th woman to race at Indy 500, 1st to lead, 2005.

Floyd Patterson, 1935-2006, 2-time heavyweight champion; first to ever regain the title after losing it.

Walter Payton, 1954-99, Chicago Bears running back; 2nd most rushing yards in NFL history; top NFC rusher, 1976-80.

Pelé (Edson Arantes do Nascimento), b 1940, (Braz.) soccer player; led Brazil to 3 World Cups (1958, '62, '70); scored 1,281 goals.

Bob Pettit, b 1932, first NBA player to score 20,000 points; twice NBA scoring leader.

Richard Petty, b 1937, NASCAR national champ 7 times; 7-time Daytona 500 winner.

Michael Phelps, b 1985, swimmer; holds record for most Olympic gold medals won by single athlete (14); won 8 medals (6 gold, 2 bronze) at 2004 Olympics, 8 gold in 2008.

Laffit Pincay Jr., b 1946, jockey; leading money-winner, 1970-74, '79, '85.

Jacques Plante, 1929-86, NHL goaltender; 7 Vezina trophies; first goalie to wear mask in a game.

Gary Player, b 1935, (S. Afr.) golfer; won 3 Masters, 3 British Opens, 2 PGA Championships, and U.S. Open.

Mike Powell, b 1963, track and field athlete; holds world record for long jump (29 ft, 4.5 in.).

Steve Prefontaine, 1951-75, runner; 1st to win 4 NCAA titles in same event (5,000m, 1970-73).

Kirby Puckett, 1960-2006, Minnesota Twins center fielder (1984-95); led team to World Series titles in 1987, '91.

Albert Pujols, b 1980, St. Louis first baseman; NL MVP, 2005, '08-'09.

Paula Radcliffe, b 1973, British runner; set marathon world record of 2:15:25 in London, 2003.

Kimi Räikkönen, b 1979, (Fin.) Formula One race car driver; 2007 Formula One World Drivers' Champion.

Manny Ramirez, b 1972, (Dom. Rep.) outfielder; 2004 World Series MVP; suspended for violating MLB performance-enhancing drug policy, 2009; retired after testing positive for P.E.D.s, 2011.

Willis Reed, b 1942, NY Knicks center; MVP, 1970; playoff MVP, 1970, '73.

Mary Lou Retton, b 1968, gymnast; won all-around gold medal at 1984 Olympics; also won 2 silvers, 2 bronzes.

Claudio Reyna, b 1973, midfielder; U.S. National Team; named to the FIFA World Cup All-Star team, 2002.

Jerry Rice, b 1962, receiver; 1989 Super Bowl MVP; NFL record for career touchdowns (208), receptions (1,549).

Maurice Richard, 1921-2000, Montreal Canadiens forward; scored 544 regular season goals, 82 playoff goals.

Branch Rickey, 1881-1965, MLB executive; helped break baseball's color barrier, 1947; initiated farm system, 1919.

Cal Ripken Jr., b 1960, Baltimore shortstop; AL MVP, 1983, '91; most consecutive games played (2,632).

Mariano Rivera, b 1969, (Pan.) relief pitcher; helped NY Yankees to 5 World Series titles; World Series MVP, 1999; all-time MLB leader in post-season saves with 42.

Oscar Robertson, b 1938, NBA guard; averaged career 25.7 points per game; 5th in career assists (9,887), 1964.

Brooks Robinson, b 1937, Baltimore Orioles 3rd baseman; played in 4 World Series; MVP, 1964; 16 gold gloves.

Frank Robinson, b 1935, MVP in both NL and AL; triple crown, 1966; 586 career home runs; first black manager in majors.

Jackie Robinson, 1919-72, broke baseball's color barrier with Brooklyn Dodgers, 1947; NL MVP, 1949.

Sugar Ray Robinson, 1921-89, boxer; middleweight champion 5 times; welterweight champion, 1946-51.

Knute Rockne, 1888-1931, Notre Dame football coach, 1918-31; revolutionized game by stressing forward pass.

Aaron Rodgers, b 1983, Green Bay quarterback; led Packers to victory in Super Bowl XLV.

Bill Rodgers, b 1947, runner; won Boston and New York City marathons 4 times each between 1975 and 1980.

Alex Rodriguez, b 1975, NY Yankees third baseman; AL MVP in 2003, '05, '07; 14-time All Star; youngest player to ever hit 500 HRs; admitted steroid use 2001-03.

Juan "Chi Chi" Rodriguez, b 1935, champion golfer; 8 PGA tour wins, 22 Champions tour wins.

Ben Roethlisberger, b 1982, Pittsburgh Steelers quarterback; youngest to win Super Bowl, 2005.

Ronaldinho, b 1980, (Braz.) soccer midfielder; led Brazil to World Cup Finals in 2006; FIFA World Player of the Year, 2004, '05.

Ronaldo (Ronaldo Luiz Nazario de Lima), b 1976, (Braz.) soccer forward; led Brazil to 2002 World Cup title; 3-time FIFA world player of the year, 1996-97, 2002; most World Cup goals, 15.

Art Rooney, 1901-88, NFL owner; bought Pittsburgh Pirates in 1933, renamed Steelers, 1940.

Pete Rose, b 1941, won 3 NL batting titles; hit in 44 consecutive games, 1978; most career hits, 4,256; banned for gambling, 1989; admitted betting on his team, 2004.

Ken Rosewall, b 1934, Australian tennis player; 2-time U.S. champ; 8 Grand Slam singles titles.

Patrick Roy, b 1965, Montreal-Colorado goalie; only 3-time NHL playoffs MVP (Conn Smythe Trophy), 1986, '93, 2001.

Wilma Rudolph, 1940-94, sprinter; won 3 1960 Olympic golds.

Adolph Rupp, 1901-77, NCAA basketball coach; led Kentucky to 4 national titles, 1948-49, '51, '58.

Bill Russell, b 1934, Boston Celtics center; led team to 11 NBA titles; MVP 5 times; first black coach of major pro sports team.

Babe Ruth, 1895-1948, NY Yankees outfielder; hit 60 home runs, 1927, 714 lifetime (3rd all-time); led AL 12 times.

Johnny Rutherford, b 1938, auto racer; won 3 Indy 500s.

Nolan Ryan, b 1947, pitcher; holds season (383), career (5,714) strikeout records; won 324 games (7 no-hitters).

Pete Sampras, b 1971, tennis star; 1st man in Open era to win 7 Wimbledons; 2nd-most career Grand Slam wins (14).

Joan Benoit Samuelson, b 1957, won 1st Olympic women's marathon (1984), Boston Marathon (1979, '83).

Barry Sanders, b 1968, rushed for 2,053 yards in 1997; led NFL in rushing, 1990, '94, '96, '97.

Deion Sanders, b 1967, NFL cornerback (1989-2000, '04-'05) and MLB outfielder (1989-95, '97, 2005).

Gale Sayers, b 1943, Chicago running back; twice led NFL in rushing.

Mike Schmidt, b 1949, Phillies 3rd baseman; led NL in home runs 8 times; 548 lifetime; NL MVP, 1980, '81, '86.

Michael Schumacher, b 1969, German race-car driver; 7-time Formula 1 world champ (1994-95, 2000-04).

Tom Seaver, b 1944, pitcher; won NL Cy Young award 3 times; won 311 major league games.

Monica Seles, b 1973, tennis player; won U.S. (1991-92), Austral. (1991-93, '96), French (1990-92) Opens; stabbed on court by spectator, 1993.

Maria Sharapova, b 1987, (Russ.) tennis star; won Wimbledon (2004), U.S. Open (2006), Australian Open (2008).

Patty Sheehan, b 1956, Hall of Fame golfer; 3 LPGA Championships (1983-84, '93).

Willie Shoemaker, 1931-2003, jockey; rode 4 Kentucky Derby, 5 Belmont Stakes winners.

Frank Shorter, b 1947, runner; only American to win men's Olympic marathon (1972) since 1908; silver medalist (1976).

Don Shula, b 1930, all-time winningest NFL coach (347 games).

Bill Simmons, b 1969, online columnist known as "The Sports Guy."

O. J. Simpson, b 1947, running back; rushed for 2,003 yds., 1973; AFC leading rusher 4 times; acquitted of murder, 1995; jailed after being found guilty of robbery and kidnapping, 2008.

George Sisler, 1893-1973, St. Louis Browns 1st baseman; had then-record 257 hits, 1920; batted .340 lifetime.

Dean Smith, b 1931, retired basketball coach; 879 Division I wins; led North Carolina to 2 NCAA titles (1982, '93).

Emmitt Smith, b 1969, running back; NFL and Super Bowl MVP, 1993; rushed for career record 18,355 yds.

Conn Smythe, 1895-1980, won 7 Stanley Cups as Toronto GM (1929-61); playoff MVP award named in his honor.

Sam Snead, 1912-2002, PGA and Masters champ 3 times each; record 82 PGA tournament victories.

Annika Sorenstam, b 1970, (Swed.) golfer; set LPGA 18-hole record of 59 (-13), 72-hole record of 27-under-par, 2001; won 10 LPGA majors, including career Grand Slam.

Sammy Sosa, b 1968, right fielder; 66 homers, NL MVP, 1998; 1st to hit 60+ homers 3 times (1998, '99, 2001).

Warren Spahn, 1921-2003, pitcher; won 363 NL games; 20-game winner 13 times; Cy Young award, 1957.

Tris Speaker, 1888-1958, AL outfielder; batted .345 over 22 seasons; hit record 792 career doubles.

Mark Spitz, b 1950, swimmer; won 7 golds at 1972 Olympics.

Amos Alonzo Stagg, 1862-1965, football innovator; Univ. of Chicago football coach for 41 years, 5 undefeated seasons.

Bart Starr, b 1934, Green Bay Packers quarterback; led team to 5 NFL titles, 2 Super Bowl victories.

Roger Staubach, b 1942, Dallas Cowboys quarterback; leading NFC passer 5 times.

George Steinbrenner, 1930-2010, NY Yankees owner.

Casey Stengel, 1890-1975, managed Yankees to 10 pennants, 7 World Series wins between 1949 and 1960.

Jackie Stewart, b 1939, (Scot.) auto racer; 27 Grand Prix wins.

John Stockton, b 1962, Utah Jazz guard; NBA career leader in assists, steals; NBA assists leader, 1988-96.

Picabo Street, b 1971, skier; 2-time World Cup downhill champion (1995-96); Olympic super G gold medalist, 1998.

Louise Suggs, b 1923, golfer; U.S. Women's Open champ, 1949, '52; 11 major victories, ranks 3rd all-time.

John L. Sullivan, 1858-1918, last bare-knuckle heavyweight champion, 1882-92.

Pat Summitt, b 1952, women's basketball coach; led Tennessee Lady Vols to 8 NCAA titles (1987, '89, '91, '96-'98, 2007-08); all-time winningest NCAA coach.

Ichiro Suzuki, b 1973, Japanese center fielder for the Seattle Mariners; Pacific League MVP, 1994, '95, '96; American League MVP, 2001; single-season hits record (262), 2004.

Sheryl Swoopes, b 1971, guard/forward; 1st player named WNBA MVP 3 times (2000, '02, '05).

Fran Tarkenton, b 1940, Minnesota, NY Giants quarterback; 4th in career TD passes (342); 1975 Player of the Year.

Diana Taurasi, b 1982, WNBA shooting guard, Phoenix Mercury; gold medalist, 2008 Olympics; WNBA MVP, 2009.

Lawrence Taylor, b 1959, linebacker; led NY Giants to 2 Super Bowl titles; played in 10 Pro Bowls.

Jenny Thompson, b 1973, swimmer; most decorated U.S. female Olympian; 12 medals (8 gold) in 1992, '96, 2000, '04.

Daley Thompson, b 1958, (Br.) decathlete; Olympic gold medalist in 1980, '84.

Bobby Thomson, 1923-2010, outfielder/3B; known for pennant-clinching "Shot Heard 'Round the World" for the NY Giants, 1951.

Jim Thorpe, 1888-1953, football All-American, 1911, '12; won pentathlon and decathlon, 1912 Olympics.

Bill Tilden, 1893-1953, won 7 U.S. tennis titles, 3 Wimbledon.

Y. A. Tittle, b 1926, NY Giants quarterback; MVP, 1961, '63.

Alberto Tomba "La Bomba," b 1966, (It.) skier; 5 Olympic alpine medals (3 golds, 2 silver) in 1988, '92, '94.

LaDainian "L.T." Tomlinson, b 1979, running back; NFL records for single season touchdowns (31), rushing touchdowns (28), most points scored in a single season (186).

Joe Torre, b 1940, former MLB player; managed L.A. Dodgers, NY Yankees, St. Louis Cardinals, Atlanta Braves, and NY Mets.

Lee Trevino, b 1939, golfer; won U.S., British Open twice.

Bryan Trottier, b 1956, Islanders, Penguins center for 6 Stanley Cup champs.

Gene Tunney, 1897-1978, heavyweight champion, 1926-28.

Mike Tyson, b 1966, undisputed heavyweight champ, 1987-90; at 20, youngest to win a heavyweight title (WBC, 1986).

Wyomia Tyus, b 1945, Olympic 100m gold medalist, 1964, '68.

Johnny Unitas, 1933-2002, Baltimore Colts quarterback; passed for more than 40,000 yds.; MVP, 1957, '67.

Al Unser, b 1939, Indy 500 winner 4 times.

Bobby Unser, b 1934, Indy 500 winner 3 times.

Brian Urlacher, b 1978, Chicago Bears linebacker; Defensive Rookie of the Year, 2000; 7-time Pro Bowler.

Norm Van Brocklin, 1926-83, quarterback; passed for game record 554 yds., 1951; MVP, 1960.

Amy Van Dyken, b 1973, swimmer; first American woman to win 4 gold medals in one Olympics (1996).

Michael Vick, b 1980, quarterback; suspended and convicted (2007) of illegal dog fighting, gambling activities.

Lasse Viren, b 1949, (Fin.) runner; Olympic 5,000m and 10,000m gold medalist in 1972, 1976.

Lindsey Vonn, b 1984; 1st U.S. woman to win the world super-G championship, gold medal in downhill, 2010 Olympics; 3 World Cup titles 2008-10.

Joey Votto, b 1983, (Can.) Cincinnati Reds 1st baseman; NL MVP, 2010.

Dwyane Wade, b 1982, guard; led Miami Heat to NBA title, 2006; finals MVP, 2006; NBA scoring title, 2009.

Honus Wagner, 1874-1955, Pittsburgh Pirates shortstop; 8 NL batting titles.

Grete Waitz, 1953-2011, (Nor.) 9-time winner of the New York City Marathon (1978-80, '82-'86, '88).

"Jersey" Joe Walcott, 1914-94, boxer; became heavyweight champion at age 37, 1951-52.

Bill Walton, b 1952, center; led Portland Trail Blazers to 1977 NBA title; MVP, 1978; NBA TV commentator.

Kurt Warner, b 1971, Rams, Giants, Cardinals quarterback; NFL MVP, 1999, 2001; Super Bowl MVP, 2000.

Tom Watson, b 1949, golfer; 6-time PGA Player of the Year; won 5 British Opens, 2 Masters, U.S. Open.

Karrie Webb, b 1974, Australian golfer; youngest woman (26 yrs., 6 mos.) to win career Grand Slam, 1999-2001.

Johnny Weissmuller, 1903-84, swimmer; won 52 national championships, 5 Olympic gold medals; set 67 world records.

Jerry West, b 1938, L.A. Lakers guard; had career average 27 pts. per game; first team all-star 10 times.

Dan Wheldon, 1978-2011, British race-car driver; 2-time Indy 500 winner (2005, 2011).

Byron "Whizzer" White, 1917-2002, running back; led NCAA in scoring and rushing at Colorado, 1937; led NFL in rushing twice, 1938, '40; Supreme Court justice, 1962-93.

Shaun White, b 1986, snowboarder/skateboarder, Olympic gold medalist in half-pipe (2006, '10).

Kathy Whitworth, b 1939, 7-time LPGA Player of the Year (1966-69, '71-'73); 88 tour wins, most on LPGA or PGA tour.

Michelle Wie, b 1989, golfer; in 2002 became youngest-ever qualifier for LPGA event; turned pro at age 15.

Michael Wilbon, b 1958, commentator/analyst for ESPN and ABC.

Lenny Wilkens, b 1937, 2nd winningest coach in NBA history; Hall of Fame player and coach.

Serena Williams, b 1981, tennis champ; won at Wimbledon (2002-03, '09-'10), U.S. Open (1999, 2002, '08); Australian Open (2003, '05, '07, '09, '10); French Open (2002); two-time Olympic gold medal winner in doubles (2000, '08) with sister Venus.

Ted Williams, 1918-2002, Boston Red Sox outfielder; won 6 batting titles, 2 triple crowns; hit .406 in 1941.

Venus Williams, b 1980, tennis champ at Wimbledon (2000, '01, '05, '07, '08), U.S. Open (2000, '01); Olympic gold medals in singles (2000) and doubles with sister Serena (2000, '08).

Helen Wills Moody, 1905-98, tennis star; won U.S. Open 7 times, Wimbledon 8 times.

Katarina Witt, b 1965, (Ger.) figure skater; won Olympic gold medal, 1984, '88; world champ, 1984-85, '87-'88.

John Wooden, 1910-2010, UCLA basketball coach; 10 NCAA titles.

Tiger Woods, b 1975, golfer; youngest to win career Grand Slam, at age 24 (1997-2000); 14 career major titles.

Mickey Wright, b 1935, golfer; won LPGA and U.S. Open championship 4 times; 82 career wins, including 13 majors.

Eric Wynalda, b 1969, soccer; 2nd leading U.S. international goal scorer with 34.

Kristi Yamaguchi, b 1971, figure skater; won national, world, Olympic titles, in 1992.

Yao Ming, b 1980, (Chin.) center for Houston Rockets; 8-time NBA All-Star.

Carl Yastrzemski, b 1939, Boston Red Sox slugger; won 3 batting titles; triple crown, 1967.

Cy Young, 1867-1955, pitcher; won record 511 games.

Steve Young, b 1961, 49ers quarterback; led NFL in passing, 1991-94, '96, '97; NFL MVP, 1992, '94; Super Bowl MVP, 1995.

Babe Didrikson Zaharias, 1911-56, all-around athlete; 3 track-and-field medals (2 golds), 1932 Olympics; won 10 golf majors; also played baseball; 6-time AP Female Athlete of the Year.

Emil Zátopek, 1922-2000, (Czech.) runner; won 3 gold medals at 1952 Olympics (5,000m, 10,000m, marathon).

Zinedine Zidane, b 1972, (Fr.) soccer midfielder; led France to 1998 World Cup title; named top player in 2006; 3-time FIFA world player of the year (1998, 2000, '03).

Writers of the Present

Name (Birthplace)	Birthdate
Chinua Achebe (Ogidi, Nigeria)	11/16/30
Richard Adams (Newbury, England, UK)	5/9/20
Edward Albee (Washington, DC)	3/12/28
Mitch Albom (Passaic, NJ)	5/23/58
Elizabeth Alexander (New York, NY)	5/30/62
Isabel Allende (Lima, Peru)	8/2/42
Dorothy Allison (Greenville, SC)	4/11/49
Martin Amis (Oxford, England, UK)	8/25/49
Maya Angelou (St. Louis, MO)	4/4/28
Piers Anthony (Oxford, England, UK)	8/6/34
Jeffrey Archer (Somerset, England, UK)	4/15/40
John Ashbery (Rochester, NY)	7/28/27
Margaret Atwood (Ottawa, ON, Canada)	11/18/39
David Auburn (Chicago, IL)	1969
Jean Auel (Chicago, IL)	2/18/36
Paul Auster (Newark, NJ)	2/3/47
Alan Ayckbourn (Hampstead, England, UK)	4/12/39
Nicholson Baker (New York, NY)	1/7/57
David Baldacci (Richmond, VA)	8/5/60
Russell Banks (Newton, MA)	3/28/40
John Barth (Cambridge, MD)	5/27/30
Ann Beattie (Washington, DC)	9/8/47
Alan Bennett (Leeds, UK)	5/9/34
John Berendt (Syracuse, NY)	12/5/39
Elizabeth Berg (St. Paul, MN)	12/2/48
Thomas Berger (Cincinnati, OH)	7/20/24
Maeve Binchy (Dalkey, Ireland)	3/28/40
Judy Blume (Elizabeth, NJ)	2/12/38
T. Coraghessan Boyle (Peekskill, NY)	12/2/48
Ray Bradbury (Waukegan, IL)	8/22/20
Barbara Taylor Bradford (Leeds, England, UK)	5/10/33
Christopher Bram (Buffalo, NY)	2/22/52
Geraldine Brooks (Sydney, Australia)	1955
Dan Brown (Exeter, NH)	6/22/64
Rita Mae Brown (Hanover, PA)	11/28/44
Christopher Buckley (New York, NY)	1952
James Lee Burke (Houston, TX)	12/5/36
Augusten Burroughs (Pittsburgh, PA)	10/23/65
Robert Olen Butler (Granite City, IL)	1/20/45
A. S. Byatt (Sheffield, England, UK)	8/24/36
Ethan Canin (Ann Arbor, MI)	7/19/60
Peter Carey (Bacchus-Marsh, Victoria, Australia)	5/7/43
Caleb Carr (New York, NY)	8/2/55
Michael Chabon (Washington, DC)	5/24/63
Tracy Chevalier (Washington, DC)	10/19/62
Sandra Cisneros (Chicago, IL)	12/20/54
Tom Clancy (Baltimore, MD)	4/12/47
Mary Higgins Clark (Bronx, NY)	12/24/27
Beverly Cleary (McMinnville, OR)	4/12/16
Harlan Coben (Newark, NJ)	1/4/62
Paulo Coelho (Rio de Janeiro, Brazil)	8/24/47
J(ohn) M(axwell) Coetzee (Capetown, S. Africa)	2/9/40
Billy Collins (New York, NY)	3/22/41
Jackie Collins (London, England, UK)	10/4/41
Suzanne Collins (NJ)	1964
Evan S. Connell (Kansas City, MO)	8/17/24
Pat Conroy (Atlanta, GA)	10/26/45
Robin Cook (New York, NY)	5/4/40
Patricia Cornwell (Miami, FL)	6/9/56
Harry Crews (Alma, GA)	6/6/35
Michael Cunningham (Cincinnati, OH)	11/6/52
Don DeLillo (Bronx, NY)	11/20/36
Nelson DeMille (New York, NY)	8/23/43
Junot Díaz (Santo Domingo, Dominican Republic)	12/31/68
Joan Didion (Sacramento, CA)	12/5/34
Annie Dillard (Pittsburgh, PA)	4/30/45
E. L. Doctorow (Bronx, NY)	1/6/31
Emma Donoghue (Dublin, Ireland)	10/24/69
Rita Dove (Akron, OH)	8/28/52
Roddy Doyle (Dublin, Ireland)	1958
Carol Ann Duffy (Glasgow, UK)	12/23/55
Umberto Eco (Alessandria, Italy)	1/5/32
Jennifer Egan (Chicago, IL)	9/7/62
Dave Eggers (Boston, MA)	3/12/70
Bret Easton Ellis (Los Angeles, CA)	3/7/64
James Ellroy (Los Angeles, CA)	3/4/48
Louise Erdrich (Little Falls, MN)	6/7/54
Laura Esquivel (Mexico City, Mexico)	9/30/50
Jeffrey Eugenides (Detroit, MI)	3/8/60
Janet Evanovich (South River, NJ)	4/22/43
Lawrence Ferlinghetti (Yonkers, NY)	3/24/19
Helen Fielding (Morley, Yorkshire, England, UK)	2/19/58
Fannie Flagg (Birmingham, AL)	9/21/44
Dario Fo (San Giano, Italy)	3/26/26
Ken Follett (Cardiff, Wales, UK)	6/5/49
Richard Ford (Jackson, MS)	2/16/44
Frederick Forsyth (Ashford, England, UK)	8/25/38
Paula Fox (New York, NY)	4/22/23
Jonathan Franzen (Western Springs, IL)	8/17/59
Michael Frayn (London, England, UK)	9/8/33
Charles Frazier (Asheville, NC)	11/4/50
Brian Friel (Killyclogher, N. Ireland, UK)	1/9/29
Carlos Fuentes (Panama City, Panama)	11/11/28
Ernest J. Gaines (Oscar, LA)	1/15/33
Gabriel Garcia Marquez (Aracataca, Colombia)	3/6/27
Frank Gilroy (Bronx, NY)	10/13/25
Malcolm Gladwell (Fareham, Hampshire, Eng., UK)	9/3/63
Robert Goddard (Fareham, Hampshire, Eng., UK)	11/13/54
Gail Godwin (Birmingham, AL)	6/18/37
William Goldman (Highland Park, IL)	8/12/31
Nadine Gordimer (Springs, S. Africa)	11/20/23
Mary Gordon (Far Rockaway, NY)	12/8/49
Sue Grafton (Louisville, KY)	4/24/40
Günter Grass (Danzig [now Gdansk], Poland)	10/16/27
Shirley Ann Grau (New Orleans, LA)	7/8/29
John Grisham (Jonesboro, AR)	2/8/55
John Guare (New York, NY)	2/5/38
David Handler (Los Angeles, CA)	9/14/52
Paul Harding (Wenham, MA)	12/19/67
David Hare (St. Leonards, Sussex, England, UK)	6/5/47
Jim Harrison (Grayling, MI)	12/11/37
Robert Hass (San Francisco, CA)	3/1/41
Vaclav Havel (Prague, Czech.)	10/5/36
Seamus Heaney (Mossbaum, Co. Derry, N. Ire., UK)	4/13/39
Mark Helprin (New York, NY)	6/28/47
Carl Hiaasen (Plantation, FL)	3/12/53
Oscar Hijuelos (New York, NY)	8/24/51
Laura Hillenbrand (Fairfax, VA)	5/15/67
S. E. Hinton (Tulsa, OK)	7/22/48
Alice Hoffman (New York, NY)	3/16/52
Alan Hollinghurst (Stroud, Gloucestershire, UK)	5/26/54
Khaled Hosseini (Kabul, Afghanistan)	3/4/65
John Irving (Exeter, NH)	3/2/42
Kazuo Ishiguro (Nagasaki, Japan)	11/8/54
John Jakes (Chicago, IL)	3/31/32
P. D. James (Oxford, England, UK)	8/3/20
Elfriede Jelinek (Mürzzuschlag, Austria)	10/20/46
Ha Jin (Liaoning, China)	2/21/56
Edward P. Jones (Washington, DC)	10/5/50
Erica Jong (New York, NY)	3/26/42
Sebastian Junger (Boston, MA)	1/17/62
Jan Karon (Lenoir, NC)	3/14/37
Garrison Keillor (Anoka, MN)	8/7/42
Thomas Keneally (Sydney, Australia)	10/7/35
William Kennedy (Albany, NY)	1/16/28
Sue Monk Kidd (Sylvester, GA)	8/12/48
Jamaica Kincaid (St. John's, Antigua)	5/25/49
Stephen King (Portland, ME)	9/21/47
Barbara Kingsolver (Annapolis, MD)	4/8/55
Maxine Hong Kingston (Stockton, CA)	10/27/40
Galway Kinnell (Providence, RI)	2/1/27
Dean Koontz (Everett, PA)	7/9/45
Ted Kooser (Ames, IA)	4/25/39
Jon Krakauer (Brookline, MA)	4/12/54
Judith Krantz (New York, NY)	1/9/28
Maxine Kumin (Philadelphia, PA)	6/6/25
Milan Kundera (Brno, Czechoslovakia)	4/1/29
Tony Kushner (New York, NY)	7/16/56
Jhumpa Lahiri (London, England, UK)	1967
Erik Larson (Brooklyn, NY)	1/3/54
David Leavitt (Pittsburgh, PA)	6/23/61
John Le Carré (Poole, England, UK)	10/19/31
Jean Marie Gustave Le Clézio (Nice, France)	4/13/40
Harper Lee (Monroeville, AL)	4/28/26
Ursula K. Le Guin (Berkeley, CA)	10/21/29
Elmore Leonard (New Orleans, LA)	10/11/25
Doris Lessing (Kermanshah, Persia)	10/22/19
Jonathan Lethem (Brooklyn, NY)	2/19/64
David Lodge (South London, England, UK)	1/28/35
Alison Lurie (Chicago, IL)	9/3/26
Gregory Maguire (Albany, NY)	6/9/54
David Malouf (Brisbane, Queensland, Australia)	3/20/34
Thomas Mallon (Glen Cove, NY)	11/2/51
David Mamet (Chicago, IL)	11/30/47
Yann Martel (Salamanca, Spain)	6/25/63
George R.R. Martin (Bayonne, NJ)	9/20/48
Bobbie Ann Mason (nr. Mayfield, KY)	5/1/40
Peter Matthiessen (New York, NY)	5/22/27
Armistead Maupin (Washington, DC)	4/13/44
Cormac McCarthy (Providence, RI)	7/20/33
Colleen McCullough (Wellington, NSW, Australia)	6/1/37
David McCullough (Pittsburgh, PA)	7/7/33
Alice McDermott (Brooklyn, NY)	6/27/53
Ian McEwan (Aldershot, England, UK)	6/21/48
Thomas McGuane (Wyandotte, MI)	12/11/39
Terry McMillan (Port Huron, MI)	10/18/51

Name (Birthplace)	Birthdate	Name (Birthplace)	Birthdate
Larry McMurtry (Wichita Falls, TX)	6/3/36	J. K. Rowling (Chipping Sodbury, England, UK).	7/31/65
Terrence McNally (St. Petersburg, FL)	11/3/39	Norman Rush (Oakland, CA)	10/24/33
John McPhee (Princeton, NJ)	3/8/31	Salman Rushdie (Bombay, India)	6/19/47
W(illiam) S(tanley) Merwin (New York, NY)	9/30/27	Richard Russo (Johnstown, NY)	7/15/49
Stephenie Meyer (Hartford, CT)	12/24/73	Alice Sebold (Madison, WI)	9/6/63
Steven Millhauser (New York, NY)	8/3/43	David Sedaris (Johnson City, NY)	12/26/56
Toni Morrison (Lorain, OH)	2/18/31	Vikram Seth (Calcutta, India)	6/20/52
Walter Mosley (Los Angeles, CA)	1/12/52	John Patrick Shanley (New York, NY)	10/13/50
Andrew Motion (London, England, UK)	10/26/52	Sam Shepard (Ft. Sheridan, IL)	11/5/43
Bharati Mukherjee (Calcutta, India)	7/27/40	Anne Rivers Siddons (Atlanta, GA)	1/9/36
Herta Müller (Nitzkydorf, Banat, Romania)	8/17/53	Neil Simon (Bronx, NY)	7/4/27
Alice Munro (Wingham, ON, Canada)	7/10/31	Jane Smiley (Los Angeles, CA)	9/26/49
Haruki Murakami (Kyoto, Japan)	1/12/49	Wole Soyinka (Abeokuta, Nigeria)	7/13/34
V. S. Naipaul (Chaguanas, Trinidad)	8/17/32	Nicholas Sparks (Omaha, NE)	12/31/65
Joyce Carol Oates (Lockport, NY)	6/16/38	Danielle Steel (New York, NY)	8/14/47
Edna O'Brien (Tuamgraney, Ireland)	12/15/32	Richard Stern (New York, NY)	2/25/28
Tim O'Brien (Austin, MN)	10/1/46	Mary Stewart (Sunderland, England, UK)	9/17/16
Kenzaburo Oe (Uchiko, Japan)	1/31/35	R(obert) L(awrence) Stine (Columbus, OH)	10/8/43
Michael Ondaatje (Colombo, Sri Lanka)	9/12/43	Kathryn Stockett (Jackson, MS)	1969
Cynthia Ozick (New York, NY)	4/17/28	Tom Stoppard (Zlin, Czechoslovakia)	7/3/37
Orhan Pamuk (Istanbul, Turkey)	6/7/52	Mark Strand (Summerside, PE, Canada)	4/11/34
Suzan-Lori Parks (Fort Knox, KY)	5/10/63	Elizabeth Strout (Portland, ME)	1/6/56
Ann Patchett (Los Angeles, CA)	12/2/63	Wislawa Szymborska (Kornik, Poland)	7/2/23
James Patterson (Newburgh, NY)	3/22/47	Amy Tan (Oakland, CA)	2/19/52
Jodi Picoult (New York, NY)	5/19/66	Donna Tartt (Greenwood, MS)	12/23/63
Marge Piercy (Detroit, MI)	3/31/36	Paul Theroux (Medford, MA)	4/10/41
Robert Pinsky (Long Branch, NJ)	10/20/40	Calvin Trillin (Kansas City, MO)	12/5/35
Michael Pollan (New York, NY)	2/6/55	Scott F. Turow (Chicago, IL)	4/12/49
Richard Powers (Evanston, IL)	6/18/57	Anne Tyler (Minneapolis, MN)	10/25/41
Richard Price (Bronx, NY)	10/12/49	Mario Vargas Llosa (Arequipa, Peru)	3/28/36
E. Annie Proulx (Norwich, CT)	8/22/35	Gore Vidal (West Point, NY)	10/3/25
Philip Pullman (Norwich, England, UK)	10/19/46	Paula Vogel (Washington, DC)	11/16/51
Thomas Pynchon (Glen Cove, NY)	5/8/37	Sarah Vowell (Muskogee, OK)	12/27/69
David Rabe (Dubuque, IA)	3/10/40	Derek Walcott (Castries, Saint Lucia)	1/23/30
Ishmael Reed (Chattanooga, TN)	2/22/38	Alice Walker (Eatonton, GA)	2/9/44
Ruth Rendell (London, England, UK)	2/17/30	Joseph Wambaugh (East Pittsburgh, PA)	1/22/37
Anne Rice (New Orleans, LA)	10/4/41	Edmund White (Cincinnati, OH)	1/13/40
Adrienne Rich (Baltimore, MD)	5/16/29	Elie Wiesel (Sighet, Romania)	9/30/28
Mary Roach (Etna, NH)	3/20/59	Tom Wolfe (Richmond, VA)	3/2/31
Nora Roberts (Silver Spring, MD)	10/10/50	Tobias Wolff (Birmingham, AL)	6/19/45
Marilynne Robinson (Sandpoint, IL)	11/26/43	Herman Wouk (New York, NY)	5/27/15
Philip Roth (Newark, NJ)	3/19/33	Yevgeny Yevtushenko (Zima, Russia)	7/18/33

Writers of the Past

See also Journalists, and Greeks and Romans in Historical Figures chapter.

Alice Adams, 1926-99, (U.S.) novelist, short-story writer. *Superior Woman.*

James Agee, 1909-55, (U.S.) novelist. *A Death in the Family.*

S(hmuel) Y(osef) Agnon, 1888-1970, (Isr.) Hebrew novelist. *Only Yesterday.*

Conrad Aiken, 1889-1973, (U.S.) poet, critic. *Ushant.*

Anna Akhmatova, 1889-1966, (Russ.) poet. *Requiem.*

Louisa May Alcott, 1832-88, (U.S.) novelist. *Little Women.*

Sholom Aleichem, 1859-1916, (Russ.) Yiddish writer. *Tevye's Daughters, The Old Country.*

Vicente Aleixandre, 1898-1984, (Sp.) poet. *La destrucción o el amor, Dialogolos del conocimiento.*

Horatio Alger, 1832-99, (U.S.) "rags-to-riches" books.

Jorge Amado, 1912-2001, (Brazil) novelist. *Dona Flor and Her Two Husbands, The Violent Land.*

Eric Ambler, 1909-98, (Br.) suspense novelist. *A Coffin for Dimitrios.*

Kingsley Amis, 1922-95, (Br.) novelist, critic. *Lucky Jim.*

Hans Christian Andersen, 1805-75, (Den.) author of fairy tales. *The Ugly Duckling.*

Maxwell Anderson, 1888-1959, (U.S.) playwright. *What Price Glory?, High Tor, Winterset, Key Largo.*

Sherwood Anderson, 1876-1941, (U.S.) short-story writer. "Death in the Woods," *Winesburg, Ohio.*

Reinaldo Arenas, 1943-90, (Cuba) short-story writer, novelist. *Before Night Falls.*

Ludovico Ariosto, 1474-1533, (It.) poet. *Orlando Furioso.*

Matthew Arnold, 1822-88, (Br.) poet, critic. "Thyrsis," "Dover Beach," "Culture and Anarchy."

Isaac Asimov, 1920-92, (U.S.) versatile writer, espec. of science-fiction. *I Robot.*

Miguel Angel Asturias, 1899-1974, (Guatemala) novelist. *El Señor Presidente.*

Louis Auchincloss, 1917-2010, (U.S.) novelist, memoirist, short-story writer. *The Rector of Justin.*

W(ystan) H(ugh) Auden, 1907-73, (Br.) poet, playwright, literary critic. "The Age of Anxiety."

Jane Austen, 1775-1817, (Br.) novelist. *Pride and Prejudice, Sense and Sensibility, Emma, Mansfield Park.*

Isaac Babel, 1894-1941, (Russ.) short-story writer, playwright. *Odessa Tales, Red Cavalry.*

James Baldwin, 1924-87, (U.S.) author, playwright. *The Fire Next Time, Blues for Mister Charlie.*

Honoré de Balzac, 1799-1850, (Fr.) novelist. *Le Père Goriot, Cousine Bette, Eugénie Grandet.*

James M. Barrie, 1860-1937, (Br.) playwright, novelist. *Peter Pan, Dear Brutus, What Every Woman Knows.*

Charles Baudelaire, 1821-67, (Fr.) poet. *Les Fleurs du Mal.*

L(yman) Frank Baum, 1856-1919, (U.S.) *Wizard of Oz* series.

Simone de Beauvoir, 1908-86, (Fr.) novelist, essayist. *The Second Sex, Memoirs of a Dutiful Daughter.*

Samuel Beckett, 1906-89, (Ire.) novelist, playwright. *Waiting for Godot, Endgame* (plays); *Murphy, Watt, Molloy* (novels).

Brendan Behan, 1923-64, (Ire.) playwright. *The Quare Fellow, The Hostage, Borstal Boy.*

Saul Bellow, 1915-2005, (U.S.) novelist. *The Adventures of Augie March, Humboldt's Gift.*

Robert Benchley, 1889-1945, (U.S.) humorist.

Stephen Vincent Benét, 1898-1943, (U.S.) poet, novelist. *John Brown's Body.*

Stan Berenstain, 1923-2005, (U.S.) co-writer and illustrator of *Berenstain Bears* series of children's books.

John Berryman, 1914-72, (U.S.) poet. *Homage to Mistress Bradstreet.*

Ambrose Bierce, 1842-1914, (U.S.) short-story writer, journalist. *In the Midst of Life, The Devil's Dictionary.*

Elizabeth Bishop, 1911-79, (U.S.) poet. *North and South—A Cold Spring.*

William Blake, 1757-1827, (Br.) poet, artist. *Songs of Innocence, Songs of Experience.*

Aleksandr Blok, 1880-1921, (Russ.) poet. "The Twelve," "The Scythians."

Giovanni Boccaccio, 1313-75, (It.) poet. *Decameron.*

Heinrich Böll, 1917-85, (Ger.) novelist, short-story writer. *Group Portrait With Lady.*

Jorge Luis Borges, 1900-86, (Arg.) short-story writer, poet, essayist. *Labyrinths.*

James Boswell, 1740-95, (Sc.) biographer. *The Life of Samuel Johnson.*

Pierre Boulle, 1913-94, (Fr.) novelist. *The Bridge Over the River Kwai, Planet of the Apes.*

Paul Bowles, 1910-99, (U.S.) novelist, short-story writer. *The Sheltering Sky.*

Anne Bradstreet, c. 1612-72, (U.S.) poet. *The Tenth Muse Lately Sprung Up in America.*

Bertolt Brecht, 1898-1956, (Ger.) dramatist, poet. *The Three-penny Opera, Mother Courage and Her Children.*

Joseph Brodsky, 1940-96, (Russ.-U.S.) poet. *A Part of Speech, Less Than One, To Urania.*

Charlotte Brontë, 1816-55, (Br.) novelist. *Jane Eyre.*

Emily Brontë, 1818-48, (Br.) novelist. *Wuthering Heights.*

Sterling A. Brown, 1901-89, (U.S.) poet, literature professor. *Southern Road.*

William Wells Brown, 1815-84, (U.S.) writer, memoirist; first African American to publish a novel, *Clotel*, 1853.

Elizabeth Barrett Browning, 1806-61, (Br.) poet. *Sonnets From the Portuguese, Aurora Leigh.*

Robert Browning, 1812-89, (Br.) poet. "My Last Duchess," "Fra Lippo Lippi," *The Ring and the Book.*

Pearl S. Buck, 1892-1973, (U.S.) novelist. *The Good Earth.*

Charles Bukowski, 1920-94, (U.S.) novelist, poet. *Ham on Rye, Women.*

Mikhail Bulgakov, 1891-1940, (Russ.) novelist, playwright. *The Heart of a Dog, The Master and Margarita.*

John Bunyan, 1628-88, (Br.) writer. *Pilgrim's Progress.*

Anthony Burgess, 1917-93, (Br.) author. *A Clockwork Orange.*

Frances Hodgson Burnett, 1849-1924, (Br.-U.S.) novelist. *The Secret Garden.*

Robert Burns, 1759-96, (Sc.) poet. "Flow Gently, Sweet Afton," "My Heart's in the Highlands," "Auld Lang Syne."

Edgar Rice Burroughs, 1875-1950, (U.S.) "Tarzan" books.

William S. Burroughs, 1914-97, (U.S.) novelist. *Naked Lunch.*

George Gordon, Lord Byron, 1788-1824, (Br.) poet. *Don Juan, Childe Harold, Manfred, Cain.*

Pedro Calderon de la Barca, 1600-81, (Sp.) playwright. *Life Is a Dream.*

Hortense Calisher, 1911-2009, (U.S.) novelist, short story writer. *False Entry.*

Italo Calvino, 1923-85, (It.) novelist, short-story writer. *If on a Winter's Night a Traveler.*

Luis Vaz de Camoes, 1524?-80 (Port.) poet. *The Lusiads.*

Albert Camus, 1913-60, (Fr.) writer. *The Stranger, The Fall.*

Elias Canetti, 1905-94, (Bulg.) novelist, essayist. *Auto-Da-Fe.*

Karel Capek, 1890-1938, (Czech.) playwright, novelist, essayist. *R.U.R. (Rossum's Universal Robots).*

Truman Capote, 1924-84, (U.S.) author. *Other Voices, Other Rooms; Breakfast at Tiffany's; In Cold Blood.*

Lewis Carroll (Charles Dodgson), 1832-98, (Br.) writer, mathematician. *Alice's Adventures in Wonderland.*

Barbara Cartland 1901-2000, (Br.) romance novelist.

Giacomo Casanova, 1725-98, (It.) adventurer, memoirist.

Willa Cather, 1873-1947, (U.S.) novelist. *O Pioneers!, My Antonia, Death Comes for the Archbishop.*

Constantine Cavafy, 1863-1933, (Gr.) poet. "Ithaka," "Sensual Pleasures."

Camilo Jose Cela, 1916-2001, (Sp.) novelist. *The Family of Pascual Duarte, The Hive.*

Miguel de Cervantes Saavedra, 1547-1616, (Sp.) novelist, dramatist, poet. *Don Quixote.*

Raymond Chandler, 1888-1959, (U.S.) writer of detective fiction. Philip Marlowe series.

Geoffrey Chaucer, c. 1340-1400, (Br.) poet. *The Canterbury Tales, Troilus and Criseyde.*

John Cheever, 1912-82, (U.S.) novelist, short-story writer. *The Wapshot Scandal*, "The Country Husband."

Anton Chekhov, 1860-1904, (Russ.) short- story writer, dramatist. *Uncle Vanya, The Cherry Orchard, The Three Sisters.*

Charles Waddell Chesnutt, 1858-1932, (U.S.) author known for his short stories. *The Conjure Woman.*

G(ilbert) K(eith) Chesterton, 1874-1936, (Br.) critic, novelist, relig. apologist. Father Brown series of mysteries.

Kate Chopin, 1851-1904, (U.S.) writer. *The Awakening.*

Agatha Christie, 1890-1976, (Br.) mystery writer; created Miss Marple, Hercule Poirot. *And Then There Were None, Murder on the Orient Express, Murder of Roger Ackroyd.*

James Clavell, 1924-94, (Br.-U.S.) novelist. *Shogun, King Rat.*

Arthur C. Clarke, 1917-2008, (Br.) science fiction writer. *2001: A Space Odyssey.*

Jean Cocteau, 1889-1963, (Fr.) writer, visual artist, filmmaker. *The Beauty and the Beast, Les Enfants Terribles.*

Samuel Taylor Coleridge, 1772-1834, (Br.) poet, critic. "Kubla Khan," "The Rime of the Ancient Mariner."

(Sidonie) Colette, 1873-1954, (Fr.) novelist. *Claudine, Gigi.*

Wilkie Collins, 1824-89, (Br.) novelist. *The Moonstone.*

Joseph Conrad, 1857-1924, (Br.) novelist. *Lord Jim, Heart of Darkness, The Secret Agent.*

James Fenimore Cooper, 1789-1851, (U.S.) novelist. *Leatherstocking Tales, The Last of the Mohicans.*

Pierre Corneille, 1606-84, (Fr.) dramatist. *Medeé, Le Cid.*

Hart Crane, 1899-1932, (U.S.) poet. "The Bridge."

Stephen Crane, 1871-1900, (U.S.) novelist, short-story writer. *The Red Badge of Courage*, "The Open Boat."

Michael Crichton, 1942-2008, (U.S.) writer. *The Andromeda Strain, Jurassic Park.*

Countee Cullen, 1903-46, (U.S.) poet, prominent in the Harlem Renaissance of the 1920s. *The Black Christ.*

E. E. Cummings, 1894-1962, (U.S.) poet. *Tulips and Chimneys.*

Roald Dahl, 1916-90, (Br.-U.S.) writer. *Charlie and the Chocolate Factory, James and the Giant Peach.*

Gabriele D'Annunzio, 1863-1938, (It.) poet, essayist, dramatist. *The Child of Pleasure, The Intruder, The Victim.*

Dante Alighieri, 1265-1321, (It.) poet. *The Divine Comedy.*

Robertson Davies, 1913-95, (Can.) novelist, playwright, essayist. Salterton, Deptford, and Cornish trilogies.

Daniel Defoe, 1660-1731, (Br.) writer. *Robinson Crusoe, Moll Flanders, Journal of the Plague Year.*

Charles Dickens, 1812-70, (Br.) novelist. *David Copperfield, Oliver Twist, Great Expectations, A Tale of Two Cities.*

Philip K. Dick, 1928-82, (U.S.) science fiction writer. *Do Androids Dream of Electric Sheep?*

James Dickey, 1923-97, (U.S.) poet, novelist. *Deliverance.*

Emily Dickinson, 1830-86, (U.S.) lyric poet. "Because I could not stop for Death . . .," "Success is counted sweetest . . ."

Isak Dinesen (Karen Blixen), 1885-1962, (Den.) author. *Out of Africa, Seven Gothic Tales, Winter's Tales.*

John Donne, 1573-1631, (Br.) poet. *Songs and Sonnets.*

José Donoso, 1924-96, (Chile) surreal novelist and short-story writer. *The Obscene Bird of Night.*

John Dos Passos, 1896-1970, (U.S.) novelist. *U.S.A.*

Fyodor Dostoevsky, 1821-81, (Russ.) novelist. *Crime and Punishment, The Brothers Karamazov, The Possessed.*

Arthur Conan Doyle, 1859-1930, (Br.) novelist. Sherlock Holmes mystery stories.

Theodore Dreiser, 1871-1945, (U.S.) novelist. *An American Tragedy, Sister Carrie.*

John Dryden, 1631-1700, (Br.) poet, dramatist, critic. *All for Love, Mac Flecknoe, Absalom and Achitophel.*

Alexandre Dumas (père), 1802-70, (Fr.) novelist, dramatist. *The Three Musketeers, The Count of Monte Cristo.*

Alexandre Dumas (fils), 1824-95, (Fr.) dramatist, novelist. *La Dame aux Camélias, Le Demi-Monde.*

Paul Laurence Dunbar, 1872-1906, (U.S.) poet, novelist. *Lyrics of Lowly Life.*

Lawrence Durrell, 1912-90, (Br.) novelist, poet. *Alexandria Quartet.*

Ilya G. Ehrenburg, 1891-1967, (Russ.) writer. *The Thaw.*

George Eliot (Mary Ann or Marian Evans), 1819-80, (Br.) novelist. *Silas Marner, Middlemarch.*

T(homas) S(tearns) Eliot, 1888-1965, (Br.) poet, critic. *The Waste Land*, "The Love Song of J. Alfred Prufrock."

Stanley Elkin, 1930-95, (U.S.) novelist, short story writer. *George Mills.*

Ralph Ellison, 1914-94, (U.S.) writer. *Invisible Man.*

Ralph Waldo Emerson, 1803-82, (U.S.) poet, essayist. "Brahma," "Nature," "The Over-Soul," "Self-Reliance."

James T. Farrell, 1904-79, (U.S.) novelist. *Studs Lonigan.*

Howard Fast, 1914-2003, (U.S.) novelist. *Spartacus, The Immigrants.*

William Faulkner, 1897-1962, (U.S.) novelist. *Sanctuary; Light in August; The Sound and the Fury; Absalom, Absalom!*

Edna Ferber, 1887-1968, (U.S.) novelist, short-story writer, playwright. *So Big, Cimarron, Show Boat.*

Henry Fielding, 1707-54, (Br.) novelist. *Tom Jones.*

F(rancis) Scott Fitzgerald, 1896-1940, (U.S.) short-story writer, novelist. *The Great Gatsby, Tender Is the Night.*

Gustave Flaubert, 1821-80, (Fr.) novelist. *Madame Bovary.*

Ian Fleming, 1908-64, (Br.) novelist; James Bond spy thrillers. *Dr. No, Goldfinger.*

Horton Foote, 1916-2009, (U.S.) playwright, screenwriter. *The Trip to Bountiful.*

Ford Madox Ford, 1873-1939, (Br.) novelist, critic, poet. *The Good Soldier.*

C(ecil) S(cott) Forester, 1899-1966, (Br.) writer. Horatio Hornblower books.

E(dward) M(organ) Forster, 1879-1970, (Br.) novelist. *A Passage to India, Howards End.*

Anatole France, 1844-1924, (Fr.) writer. *Penguin Island, My Friend's Book, The Crime of Sylvestre Bonnard.*

Dick Francis, 1920-2010, (Br.) crime novelist.

Marilyn French, 1929-2009, (U.S.) novelist. *The Women's Room.*

Robert Frost, 1874-1963, (U.S.) poet. "Birches," "Fire and Ice," "Stopping by Woods on a Snowy Evening."

William Gaddis, 1922-98, (U.S.) novelist. *The Recognitions.*

John Galsworthy, 1867-1933, (Br.) novelist, dramatist. *The Forsyte Saga.*

Federico Garcia Lorca, 1898-1936, (Sp.) poet, dramatist. *Blood Wedding.*

Erle Stanley Gardner, 1889-1970, (U.S.) mystery writer; created Perry Mason.

Jean Genet, 1911-86, (Fr.) playwright, novelist. *The Maids.*

Kahlil Gibran, 1883-1931, (Leban.-U.S.) mystical novelist, essayist, poet. *The Prophet.*

André Gide, 1869-1951, (Fr.) writer. *The Immoralist, The Pastoral Symphony, Strait Is the Gate.*

Allen Ginsberg, 1926-97, (U.S.) Beat poet. "Howl."

Jean Giraudoux, 1882-1944, (Fr.) novelist, dramatist. *Electra, The Madwoman of Chaillot, Ondine, Tiger at the Gate.*

Johann Wolfgang von Goethe, 1749-1832, (Ger.) poet, dramatist, novelist. *Faust, Sorrows of Young Werther.*

Nikolai Gogol, 1809-52, (Russ.) short-story writer, dramatist, novelist. *Dead Souls, The Inspector General.*

William Golding, 1911-93, (Br.) novelist. *Lord of the Flies.*

Oliver Goldsmith, 1728-74, (Br.-Ire.) dramatist, novelist. *The Vicar of Wakefield, She Stoops to Conquer.*

Maxim Gorky, 1868-1936, (Russ.) dramatist, novelist. *The Lower Depths.*

Robert Graves, 1895-1985, (Br.) poet, classical scholar, novelist. *I, Claudius; The White Goddess.*

Thomas Gray, 1716-71, (Br.) poet. "Elegy Written in a Country Churchyard," "The Progress of Poesy."

Julien Green, 1900-98, (U.S.-Fr.) expatriate American, French novelist. *Moira, Each Man in His Darkness.*

Graham Greene, 1904-91, (Br.) novelist. *The Power and the Glory, The Heart of the Matter, The Ministry of Fear.*

Zane Grey, 1872-1939, (U.S.) writer of Western stories.

Jakob, 1785-1863, (Ger.) philologist, folklorist; with brother **Wilhelm Grimm**, 1786-1859, collected *Grimm's Fairy Tales.*

Alex Haley, 1921-92, (U.S.) author. *Roots.*

Dashiell Hammett, 1894-1961, (U.S.) detective-story writer; created Sam Spade. *The Maltese Falcon.*

Jupiter Hammon, c. 1720-1800, (U.S.) poet; first African American to have his works published, 1761.

Knut Hamsun, 1859-1952, (Nor.) novelist. *Hunger.*

Lorraine Hansberry, 1930-65, (U.S.) playwright. *A Raisin in the Sun.*

Thomas Hardy, 1840-1928, (Br.) novelist, poet. *The Return of the Native, Tess of the D'Urbervilles, Jude the Obscure.*

E. Lynn Harris, 1955-2009, (U.S.) novelist. *Invisible Life, Basketball Jones.*

Joel Chandler Harris, 1848-1908, (U.S.) writer. Uncle Remus stories.

Moss Hart, 1904-61, (U.S.) playwright. *Once in a Lifetime, You Can't Take It With You, The Man Who Came to Dinner.*

Bret Harte, 1836-1902, (U.S.) short-story writer, poet. *The Luck of Roaring Camp.*

Jaroslav Hasek, 1883-1923, (Czech.) writer, playwright. *The Good Soldier Schweik.*

John Hawkes, 1925-98, (U.S.) experimental fiction writer. *The Goose on the Grave, Blood Oranges.*

Nathaniel Hawthorne, 1804-64, (U.S.) novelist, short-story writer. *The Scarlet Letter,* "Young Goodman Brown."

Heinrich Heine, 1797-1856, (Ger.) poet. *Book of Songs.*

Robert Heinlein, 1907-88, (U.S.) science-fiction writer. *Stranger in a Strange Land.*

Joseph Heller, 1923-99, (U.S.) novelist. *Catch-22.*

Lillian Hellman, 1905-84, (U.S.) playwright, memoirist. *The Little Foxes, An Unfinished Woman, Pentimento.*

Ernest Hemingway, 1899-1961, (U.S.) novelist, short-story writer. *A Farewell to Arms, For Whom the Bell Tolls.*

O. Henry (W. S. Porter), 1862-1910, (U.S.) short-story writer. "The Gift of the Magi."

George Herbert, 1593-1633, (Br.) poet. "The Altar," "Easter Wings."

Zbigniew Herbert, 1924-98, (Pol.) poet. "Apollo and Marsyas."

Robert Herrick, 1591-1674, (Br.) poet. "To the Virgins to Make Much of Time."

John Hersey, 1914-93, (U.S.) novelist, journalist. *Hiroshima, A Bell for Adano.*

Hermann Hesse, 1877-1962, (Ger.) novelist, poet. *Death and the Lover, Steppenwolf, Siddhartha.*

Tony Hillerman, 1925-2008, (U.S.) novelist. *Dance Hall of the Dead.*

James Hilton, 1900-54, (Br.) novelist. *Lost Horizon.*

Chester Himes, 1909-84, (U.S.) novelist. *Cotton Comes to Harlem.*

Oliver Wendell Holmes, 1809-94, (U.S.) poet, novelist. *The Autocrat of the Breakfast-Table.*

Gerard Manley Hopkins, 1844-89, (Br.) poet. "Pied Beauty," "God's Grandeur."

A(lfred) E. Housman, 1859-1936, (Br.) poet. *A Shropshire Lad.*

William Dean Howells, 1837-1920, (U.S.) novelist, critic. *The Rise of Silas Lapham.*

Langston Hughes, 1902-67, (U.S.) poet, lyric writer, author; a major influence in 1920s Harlem Renaissance.

Ted Hughes, 1930-98, (Br.) British poet laureate, 1984-98. *Crow, The Hawk in the Rain.*

Victor Hugo, 1802-85, (Fr.) poet, dramatist, novelist. *Notre Dame de Paris, Les Misérables.*

Zora Neale Hurston, 1903-60, (U.S.) novelist, folklorist. *Their Eyes Were Watching God, Mules and Men.*

Aldous Huxley, 1894-1963, (Br.) writer. *Brave New World.*

Henrik Ibsen, 1828-1906, (Nor.) dramatist, poet. *A Doll's House, Ghosts, The Wild Duck, Hedda Gabler.*

William Inge, 1913-73, (U.S.) playwright. *Picnic; Come Back, Little Sheba; Bus Stop.*

Eugene Ionesco, 1910-94, (Fr.) surrealist dramatist. *The Bald Soprano, The Chairs.*

Washington Irving, 1783-1859, (U.S.) writer. "Rip Van Winkle," "The Legend of Sleepy Hollow."

Christopher Isherwood, 1904-86, (Br.) novelist, playwright. *The Berlin Stories.*

Shirley Jackson, 1919-65, (U.S.) short-story writer. "The Lottery."

Henry James, 1843-1916, (U.S.) novelist, short-story writer, critic. *The Portrait of a Lady, The Ambassadors, Daisy Miller.*

Robinson Jeffers, 1887-1962, (U.S.) poet, dramatist. *Tamar and Other Poems, Medea.*

James Weldon Johnson, 1871-1938, (U.S.) poet, novelist, diplomat; lyricist for *Lift Every Voice and Sing.*

Samuel Johnson, 1709-84, (Br.) author, scholar, critic. *Dictionary of the English Language, Vanity of Human Wishes.*

Ben Jonson, 1572-1637, (Br.) dramatist, poet. *Volpone.*

James Joyce, 1882-1941, (Ire.) writer. *Ulysses, Dubliners, A Portrait of the Artist as a Young Man, Finnegans Wake.*

Ernst Junger, 1895-1998, (Ger.) novelist, essayist. *The Peace, On the Marble Cliff.*

Franz Kafka, 1883-1924, (Austria-Hung./Czech.) novelist, short-story writer. *The Trial, The Castle,* "The Metamorphosis."

George S. Kaufman, 1889-1961, (U.S.) playwright. *The Man Who Came to Dinner, You Can't Take It With You.*

Yasunari Kawabata, 1899-1972, (Jpn.) novelist. *The Sound of the Mountains.*

Nikos Kazantzakis, 1883-1957, (Gr.) novelist. *Zorba the Greek, A Greek Passion.*

Alfred Kazin, 1915-98 (U.S.) author, critic, teacher. *On Native Grounds.*

John Keats, 1795-1821, (Br.) poet. "Ode on a Grecian Urn," "Ode to a Nightingale," "La Belle Dame Sans Merci."

Jack Kerouac, 1922-69, (U.S.) author, Beat poet. *On the Road, The Dharma Bums,* "Mexico City Blues."

Joyce Kilmer, 1886-1918, (U.S.) poet. "Trees."

Rudyard Kipling, 1865-1936, (Br.) author, poet. "The White Man's Burden," "Gunga Din," *The Jungle Book.*

Jean de la Fontaine, 1621-95, (Fr.) poet. *Fables choisies.*

Pär Lagerkvist, 1891-1974, (Swed.) poet, dramatist, novelist. *Barabbas, The Sibyl.*

Selma Lagerlöf, 1858-1940, (Swed.) novelist. *Jerusalem, The Ring of the Lowen-skolds.*

Alphonse de Lamartine, 1790-1869, (Fr.) poet, novelist, statesman. *Méditations poétiques.*

Charles Lamb, 1775-1834, (Br.) essayist. *Specimens of English Dramatic Poets, Essays of Elia.*

Louis L'Amour, 1908-88, (U.S.) Western author, screenwriter. *Hondo, The Cherokee Trail.*

Giuseppe di Lampedusa, 1896-1957, (It.) novelist. *The Leopard.*

William Langland, c. 1332-1400, (Br.) poet. *Piers Plowman.*

Ring Lardner, 1885-1933, (U.S.) short-story writer, humorist.

Steig Larsson, 1954-2004, (Swed.) novelist. *The Girl With the Dragon Tattoo.*

Arthur Laurents, 1917-2011, (U.S.) playwright and director. *West Side Story.*

D(avid) H(erbert) Lawrence, 1885-1930, (Br.) novelist. *Sons and Lovers, Women in Love, Lady Chatterley's Lover.*

Halldór Laxness, 1902-98, (Iceland) novelist. *Iceland's Bell.*

Madeleine L'Engle, 1918-2007, (U.S.) novelist of young adult fiction. *A Wrinkle in Time.*

Mikhail Lermontov, 1814-41, (Russ.) novelist, poet. "Demon," *Hero of Our Time.*

Alain-René Lesage, 1668-1747, (Fr.) novelist. *Gil Blas de Santillane.*

Gotthold Lessing, 1729-81, (Ger.) dramatist, philosopher, critic. *Miss Sara Sampson, Minna von Barnhelm.*

Ira Levin, 1929-2007, (U.S.) novelist, playwright. *Deathtrap.*

C(live) S(taples) Lewis, 1898-1963, (Br.) critic, novelist, religious writer. *Allegory of Love; The Lion, the Witch and the Wardrobe; Out of the Silent Planet.*

Sinclair Lewis, 1885-1951, (U.S.) novelist. *Babbitt, Main Street, Arrowsmith, Dodsworth.*

Vachel Lindsay, 1879-1931, (U.S.) poet. *General William Booth Enters Into Heaven, The Congo.*

Li Po, 701-762, (China) poet. "Song Before Drinking," "She Spins Silk."

Hugh Lofting, 1886-1947, (Br.) writer. Dr. Doolittle series.

Jack London, 1876-1916, (U.S.) novelist, journalist. *Call of the Wild, The Sea-Wolf, White Fang.*

Henry Wadsworth Longfellow, 1807-82, (U.S.) poet. *Evangeline, The Song of Hiawatha.*

Lope de Vega, 1562-1635, (Sp.) playwright. *Noche de San Juan, Maestro de Danzar.*

H(oward) P(hillips) Lovecraft, 1890-1937, (U.S.) novelist, short-story writer. "At the Mountains of Madness."

Amy Lowell, 1874-1925, (U.S.) poet, critic. "Lilacs."

James Russell Lowell, 1819-91, (U.S.) poet, editor. *Poems, The Biglow Papers.*

Robert Lowell, 1917-77, (U.S.) poet. "Lord Weary's Castle."

Joaquim Maria Machado de Assis, 1839-1908, (Brazil) novelist, poet. *The Posthumous Memoirs of Bras Cubas.*

Archibald MacLeish, 1892-1982, (U.S.) poet. *Conquistador.*

Naguib Mahfouz, 1911-2006, (Egypt) novelist; first Arabic-language writer to win the Nobel Prize for Literature. *Cairo Trilogy.*

Norman Mailer, 1923-2007, (U.S.) novelist, essayist, journalist. *The Naked and the Dead.*

Bernard Malamud, 1914-86, (U.S.) short-story writer, novelist. "The Magic Barrel," *The Assistant, The Fixer.*

Stéphane Mallarmé, 1842-98, (Fr.) poet. *Poésies.*

Sir Thomas Malory, c. 1410-71, (Br.) writer. *Morte d'Arthur.*

Andre Malraux, 1901-76, (Fr.) novelist. *Man's Fate.*

Osip Mandelstam, 1891-1938, (Russ.) poet. *Stone, Tristia.*

Thomas Mann, 1875-1955, (Ger.) novelist, essayist. *Buddenbrooks, The Magic Mountain,* "Death in Venice."

Katherine Mansfield, 1888-1923, (Br.) short-story writer. "Bliss."

Christopher Marlowe, 1564-93, (Br.) dramatist, poet. *Tamburlaine the Great, Dr. Faustus, The Jew of Malta.*

Andrew Marvell, 1621-78, (Br.) poet. "To His Coy Mistress."

John Masefield, 1878-1967, (Br.) poet. "Sea Fever," "Cargoes," *Salt Water Ballads.*

Edgar Lee Masters, 1869-1950, (U.S.) poet, biographer. *Spoon River Anthology.*

W(illiam) Somerset Maugham, 1874-1965, (Br.) author. *Of Human Bondage, The Moon and Sixpence.*

Guy de Maupassant, 1850-93, (Fr.) novelist, short-story writer. "A Life," "Bel-Ami," "The Necklace."

François Mauriac, 1885-1970, (Fr.) novelist, dramatist. *Viper's Tangle, The Kiss to the Leper.*

Vladimir Mayakovsky, 1893-1930, (Russ.) poet, dramatist. *The Cloud in Trousers.*

Mary McCarthy, 1912-89, (U.S.) critic, novelist, memoirist. *Memories of a Catholic Girlhood.*

Frank McCourt, 1930-2009, (U.S.) memoirist. *Angela's Ashes, 'Tis, Teacher Man.*

Carson McCullers, 1917-67, (U.S.) novelist. *The Heart Is a Lonely Hunter, Member of the Wedding.*

Herman Melville, 1819-91, (U.S.) novelist, poet. *Moby-Dick, Typee, Billy Budd, Omoo.*

George Meredith, 1828-1909, (Br.) novelist, poet. *The Ordeal of Richard Feverel, The Egoist.*

Prosper Mérimée, 1803-70, (Fr.) author. *Carmen.*

James Merrill, 1926-95, (U.S.) poet. *Divine Comedies.*

James Michener, 1907-97, (U.S.) novelist. *Tales of the South Pacific.*

Edna St. Vincent Millay, 1892-1950, (U.S.) poet. *The Harp Weaver and Other Poems.*

Arthur Miller, 1915-2005, (U.S.) playwright. *The Crucible, After the Fall, Death of a Salesman.*

Henry Miller, 1891-1980, (U.S.) erotic novelist. *Tropic of Cancer.*

A(lan) A(lexander) Milne, 1882-1956, (Br.) author. *Winnie-the-Pooh.*

Czeslaw Milosz, 1911-2004, (Pol.) essayist, poet. "Esse," "Encounter."

John Milton, 1608-74, (Br.) poet, writer. *Paradise Lost, Comus, Lycidas, Areopagitica.*

Mishima Yukio (Hiraoka Kimitake) 1925-70, (Jpn.) writer. *Confessions of a Mask.*

Gabriela Mistral, 1889-1957, (Chile) poet. *Sonnets of Death.*

Margaret Mitchell, 1900-49, (U.S.) novelist. *Gone With the Wind.*

Jean Baptiste Molière, 1622-73, (Fr.) dramatist. *Tartuffe, Le Misanthrope, Le Bourgeois Gentilhomme.*

Ferenc Molnár, 1878-1952, (Hung.) dramatist, novelist. *Liliom, The Guardsman, The Swan.*

Michel de Montaigne, 1533-92, (Fr.) essayist. *Essais.*

Eugenio Montale, 1896-1981, (It.) poet.

Brian Moore, 1921-99, (Ire.-U.S.) novelist. *The Lonely Passion of Judith Hearne.*

Clement C. Moore, 1779-1863, (U.S.) poet, educator. "A Visit From Saint Nicholas."

Marianne Moore, 1887-1972, (U.S.) poet.

Alberto Moravia, 1907-90, (It.) novelist, short-story writer. *The Time of Indifference.*

Sir Thomas More, 1478-1535, (Br.) writer, statesman, saint. *Utopia.*

Wright Morris, 1910-98, (U.S.) novelist. *My Uncle Dudley.*

Murasaki Shikibu, c. 978-1026, (Jpn.) novelist. *The Tale of Genji.*

Iris Murdoch, 1919-99, (Br.) novelist, philosopher. *The Sea, The Sea.*

Alfred de Musset, 1810-57, (Fr.) poet, dramatist. *La Confession d'un Enfant du Siècle.*

Vladimir Nabokov, 1899-1977, (Russ.-U.S.) novelist. *Lolita, Pale Fire.*

R. K. Narayan, 1906-2001, (India) novelist. *The Guide.*

Ogden Nash, 1902-71, (U.S.) poet of light verse.

Irène Némirovsky, 1903-42, (Ukraine) novelist. *David Golder, Suite Française.*

Pablo Neruda, 1904-73, (Chile) poet. *Twenty Love Poems and One Song of Despair, Toward the Splendid City.*

Patrick O'Brian, 1914-2000, (Br.) historical novelist. *Master and Commander, Blue at the Mizzen.*

Sean O'Casey, 1884-1964, (Ire.) dramatist. *Juno and the Paycock, The Plough and the Stars.*

Flannery O'Connor, 1925-64, (U.S.) novelist, short-story writer. *Wise Blood,* "A Good Man Is Hard to Find."

Frank O'Connor (Michael Donovan), 1903-66, (Ire.) short-story writer. "Guests of a Nation."

Clifford Odets, 1906-63, (U.S.) playwright. *Waiting for Lefty, Awake and Sing, Golden Boy, The Country Girl.*

John O'Hara, 1905-70, (U.S.) novelist, short-story writer. *From the Terrace, Appointment in Samarra, Pal Joey.*

Omar Khayyam, c. 1028-1122, (Per.) poet. *Rubaiyat.*

Eugene O'Neill, 1888-1953, (U.S.) playwright. *Emperor Jones, Anna Christie, Long Day's Journey Into Night.*

George Orwell (Eric Arthur Blair), 1903-50, (Br.) novelist, essayist. *Animal Farm, Nineteen Eighty-Four.*

John Osborne, 1929-95, (Br.) dramatist, novelist. *Look Back in Anger, The Entertainer.*

Wilfred Owen, 1893-1918, (Br.) poet. "Dulce et Décorum Est."

Grace Paley, 1922-2007, (U.S.) short-story writer, poet. *The Little Disturbances of Man.*

Dorothy Parker, 1893-1967, (U.S.) poet, short-story writer. *Enough Rope, Laments for the Living.*

Robert B. Parker, 1932-2010, (U.S.) crime novelist. "Spenser" novels.

Boris Pasternak, 1890-1960, (Russ.) poet, novelist. *Doctor Zhivago.*

Alan Paton, 1903-88, (S. Africa) novelist. *Cry, the Beloved Country.*

Octavio Paz, 1914-98, (Mex.) poet, essayist. *The Labyrinth of Solitude, They Shall Not Pass!, The Sun Stone.*

Samuel Pepys, 1633-1703, (Br.) public official, diarist.

S(idney) J(oseph) Perelman, 1904-79, (U.S.) humorist. *The Road to Miltown, Under the Spreading Atrophy.*

Charles Perrault, 1628-1703, (Fr.) writer. *Tales From Mother Goose (Sleeping Beauty, Cinderella).*

Petrarch (Francesco Petrarca), 1304-74, (It.) poet. *Africa, Trionfi, Canzoniere.*

Harold Pinter, 1930-2008, (Br.) playwright. *The Birthday Party, The Caretaker, The Homecoming.*

Luigi Pirandello, 1867-1936, (It.) novelist, dramatist. *Six Characters in Search of an Author.*

Sylvia Plath, 1932-63, (U.S.) author, poet. *The Bell Jar.*

Edgar Allan Poe, 1809-49, (U.S.) poet, short-story writer, critic. "Annabel Lee," "The Raven," "The Purloined Letter."

Alexander Pope, 1688-1744, (Br.) poet. *The Rape of the Lock, The Dunciad, An Essay on Man.*

Katherine Anne Porter, 1890-1980, (U.S.) novelist, short-story writer. *Ship of Fools.*

Chaim Potok, 1929-2002, (U.S.) novelist. *The Chosen.*

Ezra Pound, 1885-1972, (U.S.) poet. *Cantos.*

Anthony Powell, 1905-2000, (Br.) novelist. *A Dance to the Music of Time* series.

Reynolds Price, 1933-2011, (U.S.) novelist, short-story writer, poet. *A Long and Happy Life.*

J(ohn) B(oynton) Priestley, 1894-1984, (Br.) novelist, dramatist. *The Good Companions.*

Marcel Proust, 1871-1922, (Fr.) novelist. *Remembrance of Things Past.*

Aleksandr Pushkin, 1799-1837, (Russ.) poet, novelist. *Boris Godunov, Eugene Onegin.*

Mario Puzo, 1920-99, (U.S.) novelist. *The Godfather.*

François Rabelais, 1495-1553, (Fr.) writer. *Gargantua.*

Jean Racine, 1639-99, (Fr.) dramatist. *Andromaque, Phèdre, Bérénice, Britannicus.*

Ayn Rand, 1905-82, (Russ.-U.S.) novelist, moral theorist. *The Fountainhead, Atlas Shrugged.*

Terence Rattigan, 1911-77, (Br.) playwright. *Separate Tables, The Browning Version.*

Erich Maria Remarque, 1898-1970, (Ger.-U.S.) novelist. *All Quiet on the Western Front.*

Mary Renault, 1905-1983, (Br.) novelist. *The Last of the Wine.*

Samuel Richardson, 1689-1761, (Br.) novelist. *Pamela; or Virtue Rewarded.*

Rainer Maria Rilke, 1875-1926, (Ger.) poet. *Life and Songs, Duino Elegies, Poems From the Book of Hours.*

Arthur Rimbaud, 1854-91, (Fr.) poet. *A Season in Hell.*

Harold Robbins, 1916-97, (U.S.) novelist. *The Carpetbaggers.*

Edwin Arlington Robinson, 1869-1935, (U.S.) poet. "Richard Cory," "Miniver Cheevy," *Merlin.*

Theodore Roethke, 1908-63, (U.S.) poet. *Open House, The Waking, The Far Field.*

Romain Rolland, 1866-1944, (Fr.) novelist, biographer. *Jean-Christophe.*

Pierre de Ronsard, 1524-85, (Fr.) poet. *Sonnets pour Hélène, La Franciade.*

Christina Rossetti, 1830-94, (Br.) poet. "When I Am Dead, My Dearest."

Dante Gabriel Rossetti, 1828-82, (Br.) poet, painter. "The Blessed Damozel."

Edmond Rostand, 1868-1918, (Fr.) poet, dramatist. *Cyrano de Bergerac.*

Damon Runyon, 1880-1946, (U.S.) short-story writer, journalist. *Guys and Dolls, Blue Plate Special.*

John Ruskin, 1819-1900, (Br.) critic, social theorist. *Modern Painters, The Seven Lamps of Architecture.*

François Sagan (Françoise Quoirez), 1935-2004, (Fr.) novelist. *Bonjour Tristesse.*

Antoine de Saint-Exupéry, 1900-44, (Fr.) writer. *Wind, Sand and Stars; The Little Prince.*

Saki (or H[ector] H[ugh] Munro), 1870-1916, (Br.) writer. *The Chronicles of Clovis.*

J. D. Salinger, 1919-2010, (U.S.) novelist. *The Catcher in the Rye.*

George Sand (Amandine Lucie Aurore Dupin), 1804-76, (Fr.) novelist. *Indiana, Consuelo.*

Carl Sandburg, 1878-1967, (U.S.) poet. *The People, Yes; Chicago Poems; Smoke and Steel; Harvest Poems.*

Jose Saramago, 1922-2010, (Port.) novelist. *Blindness.*

William Saroyan, 1908-81, (U.S.) playwright, novelist. *The Time of Your Life, The Human Comedy.*

Nathalie Sarraute, 1900-99, (Fr.) Nouveau Roman novelist. *Tropismes.*

May Sarton, 1914-95, (Belg.-U.S.) poet, novelist. *Encounter in April, Anger.*

Dorothy L. Sayers, 1893-1957, (Br.) mystery writer; created Lord Peter Wimsey.

Richard Scarry, 1920-94, (U.S.) author of children's books. *Richard Scarry's Best Story Book Ever.*

Friedrich von Schiller, 1759-1805, (Ger.) dramatist, poet, historian. *Don Carlos, Maria Stuart, Wilhelm Tell.*

Sir Walter Scott, 1771-1832, (Sc.) novelist, poet. *Ivanhoe.*

Gil Scott-Heron, 1949-2011, (U.S.) poet. "The Revolution Will Not Be Televised."

Jaroslav Seifert, 1902-86, (Czech.) poet.

Dr. Seuss (Theodor Seuss Geisel), 1904-91, (U.S.) children's book author and illustrator. *The Cat in the Hat.*

William Shakespeare, 1564-1616, (Br.) dramatist, poet. *Romeo and Juliet, Hamlet, King Lear, Julius Caesar, sonnets.*

Karl Shapiro, 1913-2000, (U.S.) poet. "Elegy for a Dead Soldier."

George Bernard Shaw, 1856-1950, (Ire.- Br.) playwright, critic. *St. Joan, Pygmalion, Major Barbara, Man and Superman.*

Sidney Sheldon, 1917-2007, (U.S.) screenwriter, novelist. *Rage of Angels, Memories of Midnight.*

Mary Wollstonecraft Shelley, 1797-1851, (Br.) novelist, feminist. *Frankenstein, The Last Man.*

Percy Bysshe Shelley, 1792-1822, (Br.) poet. *Prometheus Unbound, Adonais,* "Ode to the West Wind," "To a Skylark."

Richard B. Sheridan, 1751-1816, (Br.) dramatist. *The Rivals, School for Scandal.*

Robert Sherwood, 1896-1955, (U.S.) playwright, biographer. *The Petrified Forest, Abe Lincoln in Illinois.*

Mikhail Sholokhov, 1906-84, (Russ.) writer. *The Silent Don.*

Shel Silverstein, 1932-99, (U.S.) poet, writer. *The Giving Tree, Where the Sidewalk Ends.*

Georges Simenon (Georges Sims), 1903-89, (Belg.-Fr.) mystery writer; created Inspector Maigret.

Upton Sinclair, 1878-1968, (U.S.) novelist. *The Jungle.*

Isaac Bashevis Singer, 1904-91, (Pol.-U.S.) novelist, short-story writer, in Yiddish. *The Magician of Lublin.*

C(harles) P(ercy) Snow, 1905-80, (Br.) novelist, scientist. *Strangers and Brothers, Corridors of Power.*

Aleksandr Solzhenitsyn, 1918-2008, (Russ.) novelist, dramatist. *One Day in the Life of Ivan Denisovich.*

Susan Sontag, 1933-2004, (U.S.) critic, essayist, novelist. *Notes on Camp, The Volcano Lover, In America.*

Stephen Spender, 1909-95, (Br.) poet, critic, novelist. *Twenty Poems,* "Elegy for Margaret."

Edmund Spenser, 1552-99, (Br.) poet. *The Faerie Queen.*

Mickey Spillane, 1918-2006, (U.S.) novelist; series of novels with the character detective Mike Hammer. *The Killing Man.*

Johanna Spyri, 1827-1901, (Switz.) children's author. *Heidi.*

Christina Stead, 1903-83, (Austral.) novelist, short-story writer. *The Man Who Loved Children.*

Richard Steele, 1672-1729, (Br.) essayist, playwright; began the *Tatler* and *Spectator. The Conscious Lovers.*

Gertrude Stein, 1874-1946, (U.S.) writer. *Three Lives.*

John Steinbeck, 1902-68, (U.S.) novelist. *The Grapes of Wrath, Of Mice and Men, The Winter of Our Discontent.*

Stendhal (Marie Henri Beyle), 1783-1842, (Fr.) novelist. *The Red and the Black, The Charterhouse of Parma.*

Laurence Sterne, 1713-68, (Br.) novelist. *Tristram Shandy.*

Wallace Stevens, 1879-1955, (U.S.) poet. *Harmonium, The Man With the Blue Guitar, Notes Toward a Supreme Fiction.*

Robert Louis Stevenson, 1850-94, (Br.) novelist, poet, essayist. *Treasure Island, A Child's Garden of Verses.*

Bram Stoker, 1847-1912, (Br.) writer. *Dracula.*

Rex Stout, 1886-1975, (U.S.) mystery writer; created Nero Wolfe.

Harriet Beecher Stowe, 1811-96, (U.S.) novelist. *Uncle Tom's Cabin.*

Lytton Strachey, 1880-1932, (Br.) biographer, critic. *Eminent Victorians, Queen Victoria, Elizabeth and Essex.*

August Strindberg, 1849-1912, (Swed.) dramatist, novelist. *The Father, Miss Julie, The Creditors.*

William Styron, 1925-2006, (U.S.) novelist, essayist. *The Confessions of Nat Turner, Sophie's Choice, Darkness Visible: A Memoir of Madness.*

Jonathan Swift, 1667-1745, (Br.) satirist, poet. *Gulliver's Travels,* "A Modest Proposal."

Algernon C. Swinburne, 1837-1909, (Br.) poet, dramatist. *Atalanta in Calydon.*

John M. Synge, 1871-1909, (Ire.) poet, dramatist. *Riders to the Sea, The Playboy of the Western World.*

Rabindranath Tagore, 1861-1941, (In.) author, poet. *Sadhana, The Realization of Life, Gitanjali.*

Booth Tarkington, 1869-1946, (U.S.) novelist. *Seventeen.*

Peter Taylor, 1917-94, (U.S.) novelist. *A Summons to Memphis.*

Sara Teasdale, 1884-1933, (U.S.) poet. *Helen of Troy and Other Poems, Rivers to the Sea.*

Alfred, Lord Tennyson, 1809-92, (Br.) poet. *Idylls of the King, In Memoriam,* "The Charge of the Light Brigade."

William Makepeace Thackeray, 1811-63, (Br.) novelist. *Vanity Fair, Henry Esmond, Pendennis.*

Dylan Thomas, 1914-53, (Wales) poet. *Under Milk Wood, A Child's Christmas in Wales.*

Hunter S. Thompson, 1937-2005, (U.S.) author, journalist. *Hell's Angels, Fear and Loathing in Las Vegas.*

Henry David Thoreau, 1817-62, (U.S.) writer, philosopher, naturalist. *Walden,* "Civil Disobedience."

James Thurber, 1894-1961, (U.S.) humorist. "The Secret Life of Walter Mitty," *My Life and Hard Times.*

J(ohn) R(onald) R(euel) Tolkien, 1892-1973, (Br.) writer. *The Hobbit, Lord of the Rings* trilogy.

Leo Tolstoy, 1828-1910, (Russ.) novelist, short-story writer. *War and Peace, Anna Karenina,* "The Death of Ivan Ilyich."

Lionel Trilling, 1905-75, (U.S.) critic, author, teacher. *The Liberal Imagination.*

Anthony Trollope, 1815-82, (Br.) novelist. *The Warden, Barchester Towers,* the Palliser novels.

Ivan Turgenev, 1818-83, (Russ.) novelist, short-story writer. *Fathers and Sons, First Love, A Month in the Country.*

Amos Tutuola, 1920-97, (Nigeria) novelist. *The Palm-Wine Drunkard, My Life in the Bush of Ghosts.*

Mark Twain (Samuel Clemens), 1835-1910, (U.S.) novelist, humorist. *The Adventures of Huckleberry Finn.*

Sigrid Undset, 1881-1949, (Nor.) novelist. *Kristin Lavransdatter.*

John Updike, 1932-2009, (U.S.) novelist, literary critic. *Rabbit is Rich, The Witches of Eastwick.*

Paul Valéry, 1871-1945, (Fr.) poet, critic. *La Jeune Parque, The Graveyard by the Sea.*

Paul Verlaine, 1844-96, (Fr.) Symbolist poet. *Songs Without Words.*

Jules Verne, 1828-1905, (Fr.) novelist. *Twenty Thousand Leagues Under the Sea.*

François Villon, 1431-c. 1463, (Fr.) poet. *The Lays, The Grand Testament.*

Voltaire (F. M. Arouet), 1694-1778, (Fr.) writer of "philosophical romances"; philosopher, historian. *Candide.*

Kurt Vonnegut Jr., 1922-2007, (U.S.) novelist, essayist. *Cat's Cradle, Slaughterhouse-Five, Breakfast of Champions.*

David Foster Wallace, 1962-2008, (U.S.) novelist, essayist. *Infinite Jest, A Supposedly Fun Thing I'll Never Do Again.*

Robert Penn Warren, 1905-89, (U.S.) novelist, poet, critic. *All the King's Men.*

Wendy Wasserstein, 1950-2006, (U.S.) playwright. *The Heidi Chronicles.*

Evelyn Waugh, 1903-66, (Br.) novelist. *The Loved One, Brideshead Revisited, A Handful of Dust.*

H(erbert) G(eorge) Wells, 1866-1946, (Br.) novelist. *The Time Machine, The Invisible Man, The War of the Worlds.*

Eudora Welty, 1909-2001, (U.S.) Southern short story writer, novelist. "Why I Live at the P.O.," "The Ponder Heart."

Rebecca West, 1893-1983, (Br.) novelist, critic, journalist. *Black Lamb and Grey Falcon.*

Edith Wharton, 1862-1937, (U.S.) novelist. *The Age of Innocence, The House of Mirth, Ethan Frome.*

Phillis Wheatley, c. 1753-84, (U.S.) poet; 2nd American woman and first black woman to be published, 1770.

E(lwyn) B(rooks) White, 1899-1985, (U.S.) essayist, novelist. *Charlotte's Web, Stuart Little.*

Patrick White, 1912-90, (Austral.) novelist. *The Tree of Man.*

T(erence) H(anbury) White, 1906-64, (Br.) author. *The Once and Future King, A Book of Beasts.*

Walt Whitman, 1819-92, (U.S.) poet. *Leaves of Grass.*

John Greenleaf Whittier, 1807-92, (U.S.) poet, journalist. *Snow-Bound.*

Oscar Wilde, 1854-1900, (Ire.) novelist, playwright. *The Picture of Dorian Gray, The Importance of Being Earnest.*

Laura Ingalls Wilder, 1867-1957, (U.S.) novelist. *Little House on the Prairie* series of children's books.

Thornton Wilder, 1897-1975, (U.S.) playwright. *Our Town, The Skin of Our Teeth, The Matchmaker.*

Tennessee Williams, 1911-83, (U.S.) playwright. *A Streetcar Named Desire, Cat on a Hot Tin Roof, The Glass Menagerie.*

William Carlos Williams, 1883-1963, (U.S.) poet, physician. *Tempers, Al Que Quiere! Paterson*, "This Is Just to Say."

Edmund Wilson, 1895-1972, (U.S.) critic, novelist. *Axel's Castle, To the Finland Station.*

Lanford Wilson, 1937-2011, (U.S.) playwright. *Talley's Folly, Fifth of July.*

P(elham) G(renville) Wodehouse, 1881-1975, (Br.-U.S.) humorist. "Jeeves" novels, *Anything Goes.*

Thomas Wolfe, 1900-38, (U.S.) novelist. *Look Homeward, Angel; You Can't Go Home Again.*

Virginia Woolf, 1882-1941, (Br.) novelist, essayist. *Mrs. Dalloway, To the Lighthouse, A Room of One's Own.*

William Wordsworth, 1770-1850, (Br.) poet. "Tintern Abbey," "Ode: Intimations of Immortality," *The Prelude.*

Richard Wright, 1908-60, (U.S.) novelist, short-story writer. *Native Son, Black Boy, Uncle Tom's Children.*

Elinor Wylie, 1885-1928, (U.S.) poet. *Nets to Catch the Wind.*

William Butler Yeats, 1865-1939, (Ire.) poet, playwright. "The Second Coming," *The Wild Swans at Coole.*

Frank Yerby, 1916-91, (U.S.) first bestselling African American novelist. *The Foxes of Harrow.*

Émile Zola, 1840-1902, (Fr.) novelist. *Nana, Thérèsè Raquin.*

Poets Laureate

There is no record of the origin of the office of Poet Laureate of England. Henry III (1216-72) reportedly had a Versificator Regis, or King's Poet, paid 100 shillings per year. Other poets said to have filled the role include Geoffrey Chaucer (d 1400), Edmund Spenser (d 1599), Ben Jonson (d 1637), and Sir William d'Avenant (d 1668). The first official English poet laureate was John Dryden, appointed 1668, for life (as was customary). Then came Thomas Shadwell, in 1689; Nahum Tate, 1692; Nicholas Rowe, 1715; Rev. Laurence Eusden, 1718; Colley Cibber, 1730; William Whitehead, 1757; Rev. Thomas Warton, 1785; Henry James Pye, 1790; Robert Southey, 1813; William Wordsworth, 1843; Alfred, Lord Tennyson, 1850; Alfred Austin, 1896; Robert Bridges, 1913; John Masefield, 1930; C. Day Lewis, 1968; Sir John Betjeman, 1972; Ted Hughes, 1984; Andrew Motion, 1999; Carol Ann Duffy, 2009.

In the U.S., appointment is by the Librarian of Congress and is not for life: Robert Penn Warren, appointed 1986; Richard Wilbur, 1987; Howard Nemerov, 1988; Mark Strand, 1990; Joseph Brodsky, 1991; Mona Van Duyn, 1992; Rita Dove, 1993; Robert Hass, 1995; Robert Pinsky, 1997; Stanley Kunitz, 2000; Billy Collins, 2001; Louise Gluck, 2003; Ted Kooser, 2004; Donald Hall, 2006; Charles Simic, 2007; Kay Ryan, 2008; W. S. Merwin, 2010; Philip Levine, 2011.

Composers of Classical and Avant Garde Music

John Adams, b 1947, (U.S.) *Nixon in China, The Death of Klinghoffer.*

Milton Babbitt, 1916-2011, (U.S.) serial and electronic music.

Carl Philipp Emanuel Bach, 1714-88, (Ger.) cantatas, passions, numerous keyboard and instrumental works.

Johann Christian Bach, 1735-82, (Ger.) concertos, operas, sonatas. Known as the "English" Bach.

Johann Sebastian Bach, 1685-1750, (Ger.) *St. Matthew Passion, The Well-Tempered Clavier.*

Samuel Barber, 1910-81, (U.S.) *Adagio for Strings, Vanessa.*

Béla Bartók, 1881-1945, (Hung.) *Concerto for Orchestra, The Miraculous Mandarin.*

Amy Beach (Mrs. H. H. A. Beach), 1867-1944, (U.S.) *The Year's at the Spring, Fireflies, The Chambered Nautilus.*

Ludwig van Beethoven, 1770-1827, (Ger.) concertos (*Emperor*), sonatas (*Moonlight, Pathetique*), 9 symphonies.

Vincenzo Bellini, 1801-35, (It.) *I Puritani, La Sonnambula, Norma.*

Alban Berg, 1885-1935, (Austria) *Wozzeck, Lulu.*

Hector Berlioz, 1803-69, (Fr.) *Damnation of Faust, Symphonie Fantastique, Requiem.*

Leonard Bernstein, 1918-90, (U.S.) *Chichester Psalms, Jeremiah Symphony, Mass.*

Georges Bizet, 1838-75, (Fr.) *Carmen, Pearl Fishers.*

Ernest Bloch, 1880-1959, (Switz.-U.S.) *Macbeth* (opera), *Schelomo, Voice in the Wilderness.*

Luigi Boccherini, 1743-1805, (It.) chamber music and guitar pieces.

Alexander Borodin, 1833-87, (Russ.) *Prince Igor, In the Steppes of Central Asia, Polovtzian Dances.*

Pierre Boulez, b 1925, (Fr.) *Le Visage nuptial, Edats/Multiple, Domaines.*

Johannes Brahms, 1833-97, (Ger.) Liebeslieder Waltzes, Acad. Festival Overture, chamber music, 4 symphonies.

Henry Brant, 1913-2008, (Can.) spatial music.

Benjamin Britten, 1913-76, (Br.) *Peter Grimes, Turn of the Screw, A Ceremony of Carols, War Requiem.*

Anton Bruckner, 1824-96, (Austria) 9 symphonies.

Dietrich Buxtehude, 1637-1707, (Den.) organ works, vocal music.

William Byrd, 1543-1623, (Br.) masses, motets.

John Cage, 1912-92, (U.S.) *Winter Music, Fontana Mix.*

Elliott Carter, b 1908, (U.S.) *Second String Quartet, Third String Quartet.*

Emmanuel Chabrier, 1841-94, (Fr.) *Le Roi Malgré Lui, España.*

Gustave Charpentier, 1860-1956, (Fr.) *Louise.*

Frédéric Chopin, 1810-49, (Pol.) mazurkas, waltzes, etudes, nocturnes, polonaises, sonatas.

Aaron Copland, 1900-90, (U.S.) *Appalachian Spring, Fanfare for the Common Man, Lincoln Portrait.*

John Corigliano, b 1938 (U.S.) *Symphony No. 2.*

Claude Debussy, 1862-1918, (Fr.) *Pelleas et Melisande, La Mer, Prelude to the Afternoon of a Faun.*

David Del Tredici, b 1937, (U.S.) *Child Alice, In Memory of a Summer Day.*

Gaetano Donizetti, 1797-1848, (It.) *Elixir of Love, Lucia di Lammermoor, Daughter of the Regiment.*

Paul Dukas, 1865-1935, (Fr.) *Sorcerer's Apprentice.*

Antonin Dvorak, 1841-1904, (Czech.) *Songs My Mother Taught Me, Symphony in E Minor (From the New World).*

Edward Elgar, 1857-1934, (Br.) *Enigma Variations, Pomp and Circumstance.*

Manuel de Falla, 1876-1946, (Sp.) *El Amor Brujo, La Vida Breve, The Three-Cornered Hat.*

Gabriel Faurè, 1845-1924, (Fr.) *Requiem, Elègie for Cello and Piano.*

Cesar Franck, 1822-90, (Belg.) *Symphony in D minor, Violin Sonata.*

George Gershwin, 1898-1937, (U.S.) *Rhapsody in Blue, An American in Paris, Porgy and Bess.*

Philip Glass, b 1937, (U.S.) *Einstein on the Beach, The Voyage.*

Mikhail Glinka, 1804-57, (Russ.) *A Life for the Tsar, Ruslan and Ludmilla.*

Christoph W. Gluck, 1714-87, (Ger.) *Alceste, Iphigènie en Tauride.*

Charles Gounod, 1818-93, (Fr.) *Faust, Romeo and Juliet.*

Edvard Grieg, 1843-1907, (Nor.) *Peer Gynt Suite, Concerto in A minor for piano.*

George Frideric Handel, 1685-1759, (Ger.-Br.) *Messiah, Water Music.*

Howard Hanson, 1896-1981, (U.S.) Symphonies No. 1 (Nordic) and No. 2 (Romantic).

Roy Harris, 1898-1979, (U.S.) symphonies.

(Franz) Joseph Haydn, 1732-1809, (Austria) symphonies (*Clock, London, Toy*), chamber music, oratorios.

Paul Hindemith, 1895-1963, (U.S.) *Mathis der Maler.*

Gustav Holst, 1874-1934, (Br.) *The Planets.*

Arthur Honegger, 1892-1955, (Fr.) *Judith, Le Roi David, Pacific 231.*

Alan Hovhaness, 1911-2000, (U.S.) symphonies, *Magnificat.*

Engelbert Humperdinck, 1854-1921, (Ger.) *Hansel and Gretel.*

Charles Ives, 1874-1954, (U.S.) *Concord Sonata*, symphonies.

Aram Khachaturian, 1903-78, (Russ.) ballets, piano pieces, *Sabre Dance.*

Zoltán Kodaly, 1882-1967, (Hung.) *Háry János, Psalmus Hungaricus.*

Fritz Kreisler, 1875-1962, (Austria) *Caprice Viennois, Tambourin Chinois.*

Edouard Lalo, 1823-92, (Fr.) *Symphonie Espagnole.*

David Lang, b 1957, (U.S.) *The Little Match Girl Passion.*

Morten Lauridsen, 1943 (U.S.) *Lux Aeterna.*

Ruggero Leoncavallo, 1857-1919, (It.) *Pagliacci.*

Franz Liszt, 1811-86, (Hung.) 20 Hungarian rhapsodies, symphonic poems.

Edward MacDowell, 1861-1908, (U.S.) *To a Wild Rose.*

Gustav Mahler, 1860-1911, (Austria) *Das Lied von der Erde*; 9 complete symphonies.

Pietro Mascagni, 1863-1945, (It.) *Cavalleria Rusticana.*

Jules Massenet, 1842-1912, (Fr.) *Manon, Le Cid, Thaïs.*

Felix Mendelssohn, 1809-47, (Ger.) *A Midsummer Night's Dream, Songs Without Words*, violin concerto.

Gian Carlo Menotti, 1911-2007, (It.-U.S.) *The Medium, The Consul, Amahl and the Night Visitors.*

Claudio Monteverdi, 1567-1643, (It.) opera, masses, madrigals.

Wolfgang Amadeus Mozart, 1756-91, (Austria) chamber music, concertos, operas (*Magic Flute, Marriage of Figaro*), 41 symphonies.

Modest Mussorgsky, 1839-81, (Russ.) *Boris Godunov, Pictures at an Exhibition.*

Jacques Offenbach, 1819-80, (Fr.) *Tales of Hoffmann.*

Carl Orff, 1895-1982, (Ger.) *Carmina Burana.*

Johann Pachelbel, 1653-1706, (Ger.) *Canon and Fugue in D major.*

Ignacy Paderewski, 1860-1941, (Pol.) *Minuet in G.*

Niccolò Paganini, 1782-1840, (It.) *Caprices* for violin solo.

Giovanni Palestrina, c. 1525-94, (It.) masses, madrigals.

Krzysztof Penderecki, b 1933, (Pol.) *Psalmus, Polymorphia, De natura sonoris.*

Francis Poulenc, 1899-1963, (Fr.) *Dialogues des Carmélites.*

Mel Powell, 1923-98, b 1928, (U.S.) *Duplicates: A Concerto for Two Pianos and Orchestra, Cantilena Concertante.*

Sergei Prokofiev, 1891-1953, (Russ.) *Classical Symphony, Love for Three Oranges, Peter and the Wolf.*

Giacomo Puccini, 1858-1924, (It.) *La Boheme, Manon Lescaut, Tosca, Madama Butterfly.*

Henry Purcell, 1659-95, (Eng.) *Dido and Aeneas.*

Sergei Rachmaninoff, 1873-1943, (Russ.) concertos, preludes (*Prelude in C sharp minor*), symphonies.

Maurice Ravel, 1875-1937, (Fr.) *Boléro, Daphnis et Chloè*, Piano Concerto in D for Left Hand Alone.

Steve Reich, b 1936, (U.S.) *Double Sextet, Three Tales.*

Nikolai Rimsky-Korsakov, 1844-1908, (Russ.) *Golden Cockerel, Scheherazade, Flight of the Bumblebee.*

Gioacchino Rossini, 1792-1868, (It.) *Barber of Seville, Otello, William Tell.*

John Rutter, b 1945, (Br.) *Magnificat, Requiem.*

Camille Saint-Saëns, 1835-1921, (Fr.) *Carnival of Animals (The Swan), Samson and Delilah, Danse Macabre.*

Alessandro Scarlatti, 1660-1725, (It.) cantatas, oratorios, operas.

Domenico Scarlatti, 1685-1757, (It.) harpsichord works.

Alfred Schnittke, 1934-98 (Sov.-Ger.) *Life With an Idiot.*

Arnold Schoenberg, 1874-1951, (Austria) *Pelleas and Melisande, Pierrot Lunaire, Verklärte Nacht.*

Franz Schubert, 1797-1828, (Austria) chamber music (*Trout Quintet*), lieder, symphonies (*Unfinished*).

Robert Schumann, 1810-56, (Ger.) *Die Frauenliebe und Leben, Träumerei.*

Dmitri Shostakovich, 1906-75, (Russ.) symphonies, *Lady Macbeth of the District Mzensk.*

Jean Sibelius, 1865-1957, (Fin.) *Finlandia.*

Bedrich Smetana, 1824-84, (Czech.) *The Bartered Bride.*

Karlheinz Stockhausen, 1928-2008, (Ger.) *Kontra-Punkte, Kontakte for Electronic Instruments.*

Richard Strauss, 1864-1949, (Ger.) *Salome, Elektra, Der Rosenkavalier, Thus Spake Zarathustra.*

Igor Stravinsky, 1882-1971, (Russ.) *Noah and the Flood, The Rake's Progress, The Rite of Spring.*

Toru Takemitsu, 1930-96, (Jpn.) *Requiem for Strings, Dorian Horizon.*

Peter I. Tchaikovsky, 1840-93, (Russ.) *Nutcracker, Swan Lake, The Sleeping Beauty.*

Georg Philipp Telemann, 1681-1767, (Ger.) church music, orchestral suites, chamber music.

Virgil Thomson, 1896-1989, (U.S.) opera, film music, *Four Saints in Three Acts.*

Dmitri Tiomkin, 1894-1979, (Russ.-U.S.) film scores, including *High Noon.*

Sir Michael Tippett, 1905-98, (Br.) *A Child of Our Time, The Midsummer Marriage, The Knot Garden.*

Eric Whitacre, b 1970 (U.S.) *Cloudburst.*

Ralph Vaughan Williams, 1872-1958, (Br.) *Fantasia on a Theme by Thomas Tallis*, symphonies, vocal music.

Giuseppe Verdi, 1813-1901, (It.) *Aida, Rigoletto, Don Carlo, Il Trovatore, La Traviata, Falstaff, Macbeth.*

Heitor Villa-Lobos, 1887-1959, (Braz.) *Bachianas Brasileiras.*

Antonio Vivaldi, 1678-1741, (It.) Concerto grossos (*The Four Seasons*).

Richard Wagner, 1813-83, (Ger.) *Rienzi, Tannhäuser, Lohengrin, Tristan und Isolde.*

Carl Maria von Weber, 1786-1826, (Ger.) *Der Freischutz.*

Composers of Operettas, Musicals, and Popular Music

Richard Adler, b 1921, (U.S.) *Pajama Game; Damn Yankees.*

Milton Ager, 1893-1979, (U.S.) "I Wonder What's Become of Sally"; "Hard-Hearted Hannah"; "Ain't She Sweet?"

Leroy Anderson, 1908-75, (U.S.) "Sleigh Ride"; "Blue Tango"; "Syncopated Clock."

Paul Anka, b 1941, (Can.) "My Way"; *Tonight Show* theme.

Harold Arlen, 1905-86, (U.S.) "Stormy Weather"; "Over the Rainbow"; "Blues in the Night"; "That Old Black Magic."

Burt Bacharach, b 1928, (U.S.) "Raindrops Keep Fallin' on My Head"; "Walk on By"; "What the World Needs Now Is Love."

Ernest Ball, 1878-1927, (U.S.) "Mother Machree"; "When Irish Eyes Are Smiling."

John Barry, 1933-2011, (U.S.) *Born Free; Lion in Winter; Out of Africa.*

Irving Berlin, 1888-1989, (U.S.) *Annie Get Your Gun; Call Me Madam;* "God Bless America"; "White Christmas."

Leonard Bernstein, 1918-90, (U.S.) *On the Town; Wonderful Town; Candide; West Side Story.*

Eubie Blake, 1883-1983, (U.S.) *Shuffle Along;* "I'm Just Wild About Harry."

Jerry Bock, 1928-2010, (U.S.) *Mr. Wonderful; Fiorello; Fiddler on the Roof; The Rothschilds.*

Carrie Jacobs Bond, 1862-1946, (U.S.) "I Love You Truly."

Nacio Herb Brown, 1896-1964, (U.S.) "Singing in the Rain"; "You Were Meant for Me"; "All I Do Is Dream of You."

Hoagy Carmichael, 1899-1981, (U.S.) "Stardust"; "Georgia on My Mind"; "Old Buttermilk Sky."

James Cleveland, 1931-91, (U.S.) composer, musician, singer; first black gospel artist to appear at Carnegie Hall.

George M. Cohan, 1878-1942, (U.S.) "Give My Regards to Broadway"; "You're a Grand Old Flag"; "Over There."

Cy Coleman, 1929-2004, (U.S.) *Sweet Charity;* "Witchcraft."

John Frederick Coots, 1895-1985, (U.S.) "Santa Claus Is Coming to Town"; "You Go to My Head"; "For All We Know."

Noel Coward, 1899-1973, (Br.) *Bitter Sweet;* "Mad Dogs and Englishmen"; "Mad About the Boy."

Neil Diamond, b 1941, (U.S.) "I'm a Believer"; "Sweet Caroline."

Walter Donaldson, 1893-1947, (U.S.) "My Buddy"; "Carolina in the Morning"; "Makin' Whoopee."

Vernon Duke, 1903-69, (U.S.) "April in Paris."

Bob Dylan, b 1941, (U.S.) "Blowin' in the Wind"; "Like a Rolling Stone."

Gus Edwards, 1879-1945, (U.S.) "School Days"; "By the Light of the Silvery Moon"; "In My Merry Oldsmobile."

Sherman Edwards, 1919-81, (U.S.) "See You in September"; "Wonderful! Wonderful!"

Duke Ellington, 1899-1974, (U.S.) "Sophisticated Lady"; "Satin Doll"; "It Don't Mean a Thing"; "Solitude."

Sammy Fain, 1902-89, (U.S.) "I'll Be Seeing You"; "Love Is a Many-Splendored Thing."

Fred Fisher, 1875-1942, (U.S.) "Peg O' My Heart"; "Chicago."

Stephen Collins Foster, 1826-64, (U.S.) "My Old Kentucky Home"; "Old Folks at Home"; "Beautiful Dreamer."

Rudolf Friml, 1879-1972, (Czech.-U.S.) *The Firefly; Rose Marie; Vagabond King; Bird of Paradise.*

John Gay, 1685-1732, (Br.) *The Beggar's Opera.*

George Gershwin, 1898-1937, (U.S.) "Someone to Watch Over You"; "I've Got a Crush on You"; "Embraceable You."

Morton Gould, 1913-96, (U.S.) "Fall River Suite"; "Holocaust Suite"; "Spirituals for Orchestra"; "Stringmusic."

Ferde Grofe, 1892-1972, (U.S.) "Grand Canyon Suite."

Marvin Hamlisch, b 1944, (U.S.) "The Way We Were"; "Nobody Does It Better"; *A Chorus Line.*

Ray Henderson, 1896-1970, (U.S.) *George White's Scandals;* "That Old Gang of Mine"; "Five Foot Two, Eyes of Blue."

Victor Herbert, 1859-1924, (Ire.-U.S.) *Mlle. Modiste; Babes in Toyland; The Red Mill; Naughty Marietta; Sweethearts.*

Jerry Herman, b 1931, (U.S.) *Hello Dolly; Mame.*

Brian Holland, b 1941, **Lamont Dozier**, b 1941, **Eddie Holland**, b 1939, (all U.S.) "Heat Wave"; "Stop! In the Name of Love"; "Baby, I Need Your Loving."

Rupert Holmes, b 1947, (Eng.-U.S.) *The Mystery of Edwin Drood; Curtains.*

Antonio Carlos Jobim, 1927-94, (Brazil) "The Girl From Ipanema"; "Desafinado"; "One Note Samba."

Billy Joel (William Martin), b 1949, (U.S.) "Just the Way You Are"; "Honesty"; "Piano Man."

Elton John, b 1947, (Br.) *The Lion King;* "Candle in the Wind"; "Your Song."

Scott Joplin, 1868-1917, (U.S.) *Maple Leaf Rag; Treemonisha.*

John Kander, b 1927, (U.S.) *Cabaret; Chicago; Funny Lady.*

Jerome Kern, 1885-1945, (U.S.) *Sally; Sunny; Show Boat.*

Carole King, b 1942, (U.S.) "Will You Love Me Tomorrow?"; "Natural Woman"; "One Fine Day"; "Up on the Roof."

Burton Lane, 1912-97, (U.S.) *Finian's Rainbow.*

Jonathan Larson, 1960-96, (U.S.) *tick, tick... Boom!; Rent.*

Franz Lehar, 1870-1948, (Hung.) *Merry Widow.*

Jerry Leiber (1933-2011) and **Mike Stoller**, b 1933, (both U.S.) "Hound Dog"; "Searchin'"; "Yakety Yak"; "Love Me Tender."

Mitch Leigh, b 1928, (U.S.) *Man of La Mancha*.

John Lennon, 1940-80, and **Paul McCartney**, b 1942, (both Br.) "I Want to Hold Your Hand"; "She Loves You."

Jay Livingston, 1915-2001, (U.S.) "Mona Lisa"; "Que Sera, Sera."

Andrew Lloyd Webber, b 1948, (Br.) *Jesus Christ Superstar*; *Evita*; *Cats*; *The Phantom of the Opera*.

Frank Loesser, 1910-69, (U.S.) *Guys and Dolls*; *Where's Charley?*; *The Most Happy Fella*; *How to Succeed in Business....*

Frederick Loewe, 1901-88, (Austria-U.S.) *Brigadoon*; *Paint Your Wagon*; *My Fair Lady*; *Camelot*.

Henry Mancini, 1924-94, (U.S.) "Moon River"; "Days of Wine and Roses"; "Pink Panther Theme."

Barry Mann, b 1939, and **Cynthia Weil**, b 1937, (both U.S.) "You've Lost That Loving Feeling."

Hugh Martin, 1914-2011, (U.S.) "Have Yourself a Merry Little Christmas"; "The Trolley Song."

Jimmy McHugh, 1894-1969, (U.S.) "Don't Blame Me"; "I'm in the Mood for Love"; "I Feel a Song Coming On."

Alan Menken, b 1949, (U.S.) *Little Shop of Horrors*; *Beauty and the Beast*.

Joseph Meyer, 1894-1987, (U.S.) "If You Knew Susie"; "California, Here I Come"; "Crazy Rhythm."

Chauncey Olcott, 1858-1932, (U.S.) "Mother Machree."

Jerome "Doc" Pomus, 1925-91, (U.S.) "Save the Last Dance for Me"; "A Teenager in Love."

Cole Porter, 1893-1964, (U.S.) *Anything Goes*; *Kiss Me Kate*; *Can Can*; *Silk Stockings*.

Smokey Robinson, b 1940, (U.S.) "Shop Around"; "My Guy"; "My Girl"; "Get Ready."

Richard Rodgers, 1902-79, (U.S.) *Oklahoma!*; *Carousel*; *South Pacific*; *The King and I*; *The Sound of Music*.

Sigmund Romberg, 1887-1951, (Hung.) *Maytime*; *The Student Prince*; *Desert Song*; *Blossom Time*.

Harold Rome, 1908-93, (U.S.) *Pins and Needles*; *Call Me Mister*; *Wish You Were Here*; *Fanny*; *Destry Rides Again*.

Vincent Rose, 1880-1944, (U.S.) "Avalon"; "Whispering"; "Blueberry Hill."

Harry Ruby, 1895-1974, (U.S.) "Three Little Words"; "Who's Sorry Now?"

Arthur Schwartz, 1900-84, (U.S.) *The Band Wagon*; "Dancing in the Dark"; "By Myself"; "That's Entertainment."

Steven Schwartz, b 1948, (U.S.) *Godspell*; *Pippin*; *Wicked*.

Neil Sedaka, b 1939, (U.S.) "Breaking Up Is Hard to Do."

Marc Shaiman, b 1959, (U.S.) *Hairspray*.

Paul Simon, b 1942, (U.S.) "Sounds of Silence"; "I Am a Rock"; "Mrs. Robinson"; "Bridge Over Troubled Waters."

Stephen Sondheim, b 1930, (U.S.) *A Little Night Music*; *Company*; *Sweeney Todd*; *Sunday in the Park With George*.

John Philip Sousa, 1854-1932, (U.S.) *El Capitan*; "Stars and Stripes Forever."

Oskar Straus, 1870-1954, (Austrian) *Chocolate Soldier*.

Johann Strauss, 1825-99, (Austrian) *Gypsy Baron*; *Die Fledermaus*; waltzes: Blue Danube; Artist's Life.

Charles Strouse, b 1928, (U.S.) *Bye Bye, Birdie*; *Annie*.

Jule Styne, 1905-94, (Br.-U.S.) *Gentlemen Prefer Blondes*; *Bells Are Ringing*; *Gypsy*; *Funny Girl*.

Arthur S. Sullivan, 1842-1900, (Br.) *H.M.S. Pinafore*; *Pirates of Penzance*; *The Mikado*.

Deems Taylor, 1885-1966, (U.S.) *Peter Ibbetson*.

Harry Tobias, 1895-94, (U.S.) *I'll Keep the Lovelight Burning*.

Egbert van Alstyne, 1882-1951, (U.S.) "In the Shade of the Old Apple Tree"; "Memories"; "Pretty Baby."

Jimmy Van Heusen, 1913-90, (U.S.) "Moonlight Becomes You"; "Swinging on a Star"; "All the Way"; "Love and Marriage."

Albert von Tilzer, 1878-1956, (U.S.) "I'll Be With You in Apple Blossom Time"; "Take Me Out to the Ball Game."

Harry von Tilzer, 1872-1946, (U.S.) "Only a Bird in a Gilded Cage"; "On a Sunday Afternoon."

Fats Waller, 1904-43, (U.S.) "Honeysuckle Rose"; "Ain't Misbehavin."

Harry Warren, 1893-1981, (U.S.) "You're My Everything"; "We're in the Money"; "I Only Have Eyes for You."

Jimmy Webb, b 1946, (U.S.) "Up, Up and Away"; "By the Time I Get to Phoenix"; "Didn't We?"; "Wichita Lineman."

Kurt Weill, 1900-50, (Ger.-U.S.) *Threepenny Opera*; *Lady in the Dark*; *Knickerbocker Holiday*; *One Touch of Venus*.

Percy Wenrich, 1887-1952, (U.S.) "When You Wore a Tulip"; "Moonlight Bay"; "Put On Your Old Gray Bonnet."

Richard A. Whiting, 1891-1938, (U.S.) "Till We Meet Again"; "Sleepytime Gal"; "Beyond the Blue Horizon"; "My Ideal."

Fred Wildhorn, b 1959, (U.S.) *Jekyll and Hyde*; *Victor/Victoria*; *The Civil War*.

John Williams, b 1932, (U.S.) *Jaws*; *E.T.*; *Star Wars* series; *Raiders of the Lost Ark* series.

Meredith Willson, 1902-84, (U.S.) *The Music Man*.

Stevie Wonder, b 1950, (U.S.) "You Are the Sunshine of My Life"; "Signed, Sealed, Delivered, I'm Yours."

Vincent Youmans, 1898-1946, (U.S.) *Two Little Girls in Blue*; *Wildflower*; *No, No, Nanette*; *Hit the Deck*; *Rainbow*; *Smiles*.

Lyricists

Howard Ashman, 1950-91, (U.S.) *Little Shop of Horrors*; *The Little Mermaid*.

Johnny Burke, 1908-84, (U.S.) "Misty"; "Imagination."

Irving Caesar, 1895-1996, (U.S.) "Swanee"; "Tea for Two"; "Just a Gigolo."

Sammy Cahn, 1913-93, (U.S.) "High Hopes"; "Love and Marriage"; "The Second Time Around"; "It's Magic."

Leonard Cohen, b 1934, (Can.) "Suzanne"; "Stranger Song."

Betty Comden, 1917-2006, (U.S.) and **Adolph Green**, 1915-2002, (U.S.) "The Party's Over"; "New York, New York."

Hal David, b 1921, (U.S.) "What the World Needs Now Is Love."

Buddy De Sylva, 1895-1950, (U.S.) "When Day Is Done"; "Look for the Silver Lining"; "April Showers."

Howard Dietz, 1896-1983, (U.S.) "Dancing in the Dark"; "That's Entertainment."

Al Dubin, 1891-1945, (U.S.) "Tiptoe Through the Tulips"; "Lullaby of Broadway."

Fred Ebb, 1936-2004, (U.S.) *Cabaret*; *Zorba*; *Woman of the Year*; *Chicago*.

Ray Evans, 1915-2007, (U.S.) "Mona Lisa"; "Que Sera, Sera."

Dorothy Fields, 1905-74, (U.S.) "On the Sunny Side of the Street"; "Don't Blame Me"; "The Way You Look Tonight."

Ira Gershwin, 1896-1983, (U.S.) "The Man I Love"; "S'Wonderful"; "Embraceable You."

William S. Gilbert, 1836-1911, (Br.) *H.M.S. Pinafore*; *Pirates of Penzance*.

Gerry Goffin, b 1939, (U.S.) "Will You Love Me Tomorrow"; "Take Good Care of My Baby"; "Up on the Roof."

Mack Gordon, 1905-59, (Pol.-U.S.) "You'll Never Know"; "The More I See You"; "Chattanooga Choo-Choo."

Oscar Hammerstein II, 1895-1960, (U.S.) *Ol' Man River*; *Oklahoma!*; *Carousel*.

E.Y. (Yip) Harburg, 1898-1981, (U.S.) "Brother, Can You Spare a Dime"; "April in Paris"; "Over the Rainbow."

Sheldon Harnick, b 1924, (U.S.) *Fiddler on the Roof*; *She Loves Me*.

Lorenz Hart, 1895-1943, (U.S.) "Isn't It Romantic"; "Blue Moon"; "Lover"; "Manhattan"; "My Funny Valentine."

DuBose Heyward, 1885-1940, (U.S.) "Summertime."

Gus Kahn, 1886-1941, (U.S.) "Memories"; "Ain't We Got Fun."

Alan J. Lerner, 1918-86, (U.S.) *Brigadoon*; *My Fair Lady*; *Camelot*; *Gigi*; *On a Clear Day You Can See Forever*.

Johnny Mercer, 1909-76, (U.S.) "Blues in the Night"; "Come Rain or Come Shine"; "Laura"; "That Old Black Magic."

Bob Merrill, 1921-98, (U.S.) "People"; "(How Much Is That) Doggie in the Window."

Jack Norworth, 1879-1959, (U.S.) "Take Me Out to the Ball Game"; "Shine On Harvest Moon."

Mitchell Parish, 1901-93, (U.S.) "Stardust"; "Stairway to the Stars."

Andy Razaf, 1895-1973, (U.S.) "Honeysuckle Rose"; "Ain't Misbehavin."

Leo Robin, 1900-84, (U.S.) "Thanks for the Memory"; "Diamonds Are a Girl's Best Friend."

Bernie Taupin, b 1947 (Br.) "Rocket Man"; "Your Song."

Paul Francis Webster, 1907-84, (U.S.) "Secret Love"; "The Shadow of Your Smile"; "Love Is a Many-Splendored Thing."

Jack Yellen, 1892-1991, (U.S.) "Ain't She Sweet"; "Happy Days Are Here Again."

Blues and Jazz Artists of the Past

Julian "Cannonball" Adderley, 1928-75, alto sax.

Nat Adderley, 1931-2000, cornet.

Henry "Red" Allen, 1908-67, trumpet.

Louis "Satchmo" Armstrong, 1901-71, trumpet, singer, bandleader.

Albert Ayler, 1936-70, tenor sax, alto sax.

Mildred Bailey, 1907-51, singer.

Chet Baker, 1929-88, trumpet, singer.

Ray Barretto, 1930-2006, conga drummer.

William "Count" Basie, 1904-84, bandleader, piano, composer.

Sidney Bechet, 1897-1959, soprano sax, clarinet.

Bix Beiderbecke, 1903-31, cornet, composer, piano.

Rowland "Bunny" Berigan, 1908-42, trumpet.

Barney Bigard, 1906-80, clarinet.

Eubie Blake, 1883-1983, composer, piano.

Art Blakey, 1919-90, drums, bandleader.

Jimmy Blanton, 1921-42, bass.

Charles "Buddy" Bolden, 1877-1931, cornet, pioneer bandleader.

Lester Bowie, 1941-99, trumpet, composer, bandleader.

Michael Brecker, 1949-2007, saxophone.

Big Bill Broonzy, 1893-1958, blues singer, guitar.

Clarence "Gatemouth" Brown, 1924-2005, guitar, singer.

Clifford Brown, 1930-56, trumpet.

Ray Brown, 1926-2002, bass.

Don Byas, 1912-72, tenor sax.

Charlie Byrd, 1925-99, guitar; popularized bossa nova.

Cab Calloway, 1907-94, bandleader, singer.
Harry Carney, 1910-74, baritone sax, clarinet.
Benny Carter, 1907-2003, alto sax.
Betty Carter, 1930-98, jazz singer.
Sidney "Big Sid" Catlett, 1910-51, drums.
Adolphus Anthony "Doc" Cheatham, 1905-97, trumpet.
Don Cherry, 1936-95, trumpet.
Charlie Christian, 1916-42, guitar.
Kenny "Klook" Clarke, 1914-85, drums.
Buck Clayton, 1911-91, trumpet.
Al Cohn, 1925-88, tenor sax.
Nat "King" Cole, 1919-65, piano, singer.
William "Cozy" Cole, 1909-81, drums.
Alice Coltrane, 1937-2007, piano, composer.
John Coltrane, 1926-67, tenor sax, soprano sax, composer.
Eddie Condon, 1905-73, guitar, bandleader.
Tadd Dameron, 1917-65, piano, composer.
Eddie "Lockjaw" Davis, 1921-86, tenor sax.
Miles Davis, 1926-91, trumpet, composer.
Wild Bill Davison, 1906-89, cornet.
Blossom Dearie, 1924-2009, singer.
Paul Desmond, 1924-77, alto sax.
Vic Dickenson, 1906-84, trombone.
Willie Dixon, 1915-92, composer, bass.
Johnny Dodds, 1892-1940, clarinet.
Warren "Baby" Dodds, 1898-1959, drums.
Eric Dolphy, 1928-64, alto sax, bass clarinet, flute.
Jimmy Dorsey, 1904-57, alto sax, bandleader.
Tommy Dorsey, 1905-56, trombone, bandleader.
Billy Eckstine, 1914-93, singer, bandleader.
Harry "Sweets" Edison, 1915-99, trumpet.
David "Honeyboy" Edwards, 1915-2011, guitar, singer.
Roy Eldridge, 1911-89, trumpet, singer.
Duke Ellington, 1899-1974, piano, bandleader, composer.
Bill Evans, 1929-80, piano.
Gil Evans, 1912-88, composer, arranger, piano.
Art Farmer, 1928-99, trumpet, flugelhorn.
Maynard Ferguson, 1926-2006, trumpet, bandleader.
Ella Fitzgerald, 1917-96, singer.
Tommy Flanagan, 1930-2001, piano.
Erroll Garner, 1921-77, piano, composer.
Stan Getz, 1927-91, tenor sax.
Dizzy Gillespie, 1917-93, trumpet, composer, singer.
Benny Goodman, 1909-86, clarinet, bandleader.
Dexter Gordon, 1923-90, tenor sax.
Stéphane Grappelli, 1908-97, violin.
Bobby Hackett, 1915-76, trumpet, cornet.
Lionel Hampton, 1908-2002, vibraphone, bandleader.
W. C. Handy, 1873-1958, composer.
Jimmy Harrison, 1900-31, trombone.
Coleman Hawkins, 1904-69, tenor sax.
Percy Heath, 1923-2005, bass.
Fletcher Henderson, 1898-1952, bandleader, arranger.
Woody Herman, 1913-87, clarinet, alto sax, bandleader.
Jay C. Higginbotham, 1906-73, trombone.
Ruiz Hilton, 1952-2006, piano, composer.
Earl "Fatha" Hines, 1903-83, piano.
Milt Hinton, 1910-2000, bass.
Al Hirt, 1922-99, trumpet.
Johnny Hodges, 1906-70, alto sax.
Billie Holiday, 1915-59, singer.
John Lee Hooker, 1917-2001, blues guitar, singer.
Sam "Lightnin'" Hopkins, 1912-82, blues singer, guitar.
Shirley Horn, 1934-2005, piano, singer.

Howlin' Wolf (Chester Burnett), 1910-1976, blues singer, harmonica, guitar.
Alberta Hunter, 1895-1984, singer.
Mahalia Jackson, 1911-72, gospel singer.
Milt Jackson, 1923-99, vibraphone.
Elmore James, 1918-63, blues singer, guitar.
"Blind" Lemon Jefferson, 1897-1929, blues singer, guitar.
William "Bunk" Johnson, 1879-1949, trumpet.
J. J. Johnson, 1924-2001, trombone.
James P. Johnson, 1891-1955, piano, composer.
Robert Johnson, 1912-38, blues singer, guitar.
Elvin Jones, 1927-2004, drums.
Jo Jones, 1911-85, drums.
Philly Joe Jones, 1923-85, drums.
Thad Jones, 1923-86, cornet, bandleader, composer.
Scott Joplin, 1868-1917, ragtime composer.
Louis Jordan, 1908-75, singer, alto sax.
Stan Kenton, 1911-79, bandleader, composer, piano.
Barney Kessel, 1923-2004, guitar.
Albert King, 1923-92, blues guitar.
John Kirby, 1908-52, bandleader, bass.
Rahsaan Roland Kirk, 1936-77, saxophone, composer.
Gene Krupa, 1909-73, drums, bandleader.
Scott LaFaro, 1936-61, bass.
Lead Belly (Huddie Ledbetter), 1888-1949, folk and blues singer, guitar.
Peggy Lee, 1920-2002, singer.
John Lewis, 1929-90, piano, Modern Jazz Quartet founder.
Mel Lewis, 1929-90, drums, bandleader.
Jimmie Lunceford, 1902-47, bandleader.
Machito (Frank Grillo), 1908-84, Latin percussion, singer, bandleader.
Shelly Manne, 1920-84, drums, bandleader.
Jackie McLean, 1931-2006, saxophone, composer.
Jimmy McPartland, 1907-91, trumpet.
Carmen McRae, 1920-94, singer.
Glenn Miller, 1904-44, trombone, bandleader.
Charles Mingus, 1922-79, bass, composer, bandleader.
Thelonious Monk, 1917-82, piano, composer.
Wes Montgomery, 1925-68, guitar.
James Moody, 1925-2010, saxophone.
Ferdinand "Jelly Roll" Morton, 1885-1941, composer, piano.
Bennie Moten, 1894-1935, piano, bandleader.
Gerry Mulligan, 1927-96, baritone sax, composer.
Theodore "Fats" Navarro, 1923-50, trumpet.
Red Nichols, 1905-65, cornet, bandleader.
Red Norvo, 1908-99, vibraphone, xylophone, bandleader.
Anita O'Day, 1919-2006, singer.
Arturo "Chico" O'Farrill, 1921-2001, Latin composer, arranger.
King Oliver, 1885-1938, cornet, band-leader.
Sy Oliver, 1910-88, arranger, composer.
Edward "Kid" Ory, 1886-1973, trombone, bandleader.
Oran "Hot Lips" Page, 1908-54, trumpet, singer.
Charlie "Bird" Parker, 1920-55, alto sax, composer.
Joe Pass, 1929-94, guitar.
Art Pepper, 1925-82, alto sax.
Pinetop Perkins, 1913-2011, piano.
Oscar Peterson, 1925-2007, piano.
Oscar Pettiford, 1922-60, bass.
Earl "Bud" Powell, 1924-66, piano.

Chano Pozo, 1915-48, Cuban percussion, singer.
Louis Prima, 1911-78, singer, bandleader.
Tito Puente, 1923-2000, Latin percussion, bandleader.
Gertrude "Ma" Rainey, 1886-1939, blues singer.
Lou Rawls, 1933-2006, singer.
Dewey Redman, 1931-2006, tenor sax.
Don Redman (Robert Rodney Chudnick), 1900-64, composer, arranger.
Django Reinhardt, 1910-53, guitar.
Buddy Rich, 1917-87, drums.
Max Roach, 1924-2007, drums, composer.
Red Rodney (Robert Chudnick), 1927-94, trumpet.
Jimmy Rowles, 1918-96, piano.
Jimmy Rushing, 1903-72, blues and jazz singer.
Charles "Pee Wee" Russell, 1906-69, clarinet.
Artie Shaw, 1910-2004, swing-era bandleader, clarinet.
George Shearing, 1919-2011, piano.
Nina Simone (Eunice Waymon), 1933-2003, singer.
John "Zoot" Sims, 1925-85, tenor sax.
Zutty Singleton, 1898-1975, drums.
Bessie Smith, 1894-1937, blues singer.
Clarence "Pinetop" Smith, 1904-29, piano, singer, boogie woogie pioneer.
Willie "The Lion" Smith, 1897-1973, piano, composer.
Francis "Muggsy" Spanier, 1906-67, cornet.
Edward "Sonny" Stitt, 1924-82, tenor sax, alto sax.
Billy Strayhorn, 1915-67, composer, piano, Duke Ellington collaborator.
Sun Ra (Herman Blount), 1915?-93, bandleader, piano, composer.
Art Tatum, 1910-56, piano.
Art Taylor, 1929-95, drums.
Billy Taylor, 1921-2010, piano.
Jack Teagarden, 1905-64, trombone.
Mel Tormé, 1925-99, singer ("The Velvet Fog").
Dave Tough, 1908-48, drums.
Lennie Tristano, 1919-78, piano, composer.
Joe Turner, 1911-85, blues singer.
Sarah Vaughan, 1924-90, singer.
Joe Venuti, 1903-78, violin.
Aaron "T-Bone" Walker, 1910-75, blues guitar.
Thomas "Fats" Waller, 1904-43, piano, singer, composer.
Dinah Washington (Ruth Jones), 1924-63, singer.
Grover Washington Jr., 1943-99, pop-jazz sax, composer.
Ethel Waters, 1896-1977, jazz and blues singer.
Muddy Waters (McKinley Morganfield), 1915-83, blues singer, songwriter.
Julius Watkins, 1921-77, French horn.
William "Chick" Webb, 1902-39, bandleader, drums.
Ben Webster, 1909-73, tenor sax.
Junior Wells (Amos Blackmore), 1934-98, blues singer, harmonica.
Paul Whiteman, 1890-1967, bandleader.
Margaret Whiting, 1924-2011, singer.
Charles "Cootie" Williams, 1910-85, trumpet, bandleader.
Joe Williams, 1918-99, singer.
Mary Lou Williams, 1910-81, piano, composer.
Tony Williams, 1945-97, drums.
John Lee "Sonny Boy" Williamson, 1914-48, blues singer, harmonica.
Sonny Boy Williamson (Aleck "Rice" Miller), 1900?-65, blues singer, harmonica.
Teddy Wilson, 1912-86, piano.
Kai Winding, 1922-83, trombone.
Jimmy Yancey, 1894-1951, piano.
Lester "Pres" Young, 1909-59, tenor sax.

Country Music Artists of the Past and Present

Roy Acuff, 1903-92, fiddler, singer, songwriter; "Wabash Cannon Ball."

Alabama (Randy Owen, b 1949; Jeff Cook, b 1949; Teddy Gentry, b 1952; Mark Herndon, b 1955); "Feels So Right."

James "Whispering Bill" Anderson, b 1937, singer, songwriter; "Make Mine Night Time."

Eddy Arnold, 1918-2008, singer, guitarist, known as the "Tennessee Plowboy."

Chet Atkins, 1924-2001, guitarist, composer, producer; helped create the "Nashville sound."

Gene Autry, 1907-98, first great singing movie cowboy; "Back in the Saddle Again."

Clint Black, b 1962, singer, songwriter; "Killin' Time."

Garth Brooks, b 1962, singer, songwriter; "Friends in Low Places."

Brooks & Dunn (Kix Brooks, b 1955; Ronnie Dunn, b 1953); "Hard Workin' Man."

Boudleaux, 1920-87, and **Felice Bryant**, 1925-2003, songwriting team; "Hey Joe."

Glen Campbell, b 1936, singer, guitarist; "Gentle on My Mind."

Mary Chapin Carpenter, b 1958, singer, songwriter; "I Feel Lucky."

Carter Family (original members "Mother" Maybelle, 1909-78; A. P., 1891-1960; Sara, 1898-1979); "Wildwood Flower."

Johnny Cash, 1932-2003, singer, songwriter; "I Walk the Line," "Ring of Fire," "Folsom Prison Blues."

Kenny Chesney, b 1968, guitarist, singer, songwriter; "You Had Me From Hello."

Roy Clark, b 1933, guitarist, banjoist, singer, co-host *Hee Haw*; "Yesterday, When I Was Young."

Patsy Cline, 1932-63, singer; "Walkin' After Midnight," "Crazy," "Sweet Dreams."

Billy Ray Cyrus, b 1961, singer, songwriter; "Achy Breaky Heart."

Charlie Daniels, b 1936, guitarist, fiddler; "The Devil Went Down to Georgia."

Jimmy Dean, 1928-2010, singer; "Big Bad John."

John Denver, 1943-97, singer, songwriter; "Rocky Mountain High."

Dixie Chicks (Natalie Maines, b 1974; Martie Seidel, b 1969; Emily Erwin Robison, b 1972); "Wide Open Spaces."

Dale Evans, 1912-2001, singer, actress, married Roy Rogers.

Flatt & Scruggs (Lester Flatt, 1914-79; Earl Scruggs, b 1924), guitar-banjo duo and soloists; "Foggy Mountain Breakdown."

Red Foley, 1910-68, singer; "Chattanoogie Shoe Shine Boy."

Tennessee Ernie Ford, 1919-91, singer, TV host; "Sixteen Tons."

William "Lefty" Frizzell, 1928-75, singer, guitarist; "Long Black Veil."

Vince Gill, b 1957, singer, songwriter; "When I Call Your Name."

Merle Haggard, b 1937, singer, songwriter; "Okie From Muskogee."

Emmylou Harris, b 1947, singer, songwriter, folk-country crossover artist; "If I Could Only Win Your Love."

Faith Hill, b 1967, singer, songwriter; "Breathe."

Alan Jackson, b 1958, singer, songwriter; "Where Were You (When the World Stopped Turning)."

Waylon Jennings, 1937-2002, singer, songwriter, "outlaw country" pioneer; "Luckenbach, Texas."

George Jones, b 1931, singer; "He Stopped Loving Her Today."

The Judds (Naomi, b 1946; Wynonna, b 1964), mother-daughter duo; Wynonna also a solo act.

Toby Keith, b 1961, singer, songwriter; guitarist; "Should've Been a Cowboy."

Alison Krauss, b 1971, bluegrass fiddler, singer, bandleader; "When You Say Nothing at All."

Kris Kristofferson, b 1936, singer, songwriter, actor; "Me and Bobby McGee."

Lady Antebellum (Hillary Scott, b 1984; Charles Kelley, b 1981; Dave Haywood, b 1982); "I Run to You."

Miranda Lambert, b. 1983, singer, guitarist; "The House That Built Me."

Louvin Brothers (Ira, 1924-1965; Charlie, 1927-2011), singers; "If I Could Only Win Your Love."

Patty Loveless, b 1957, singer, songwriter; "How Can I Help You Say Goodbye."

Lyle Lovett, b 1957, singer, songwriter, bandleader, actor; "Cowboy Man."

Loretta Lynn, b 1935?, singer; "Coal Miner's Daughter."

Barbara Mandrell, b 1948, singer; "I Was Country When Country Wasn't Cool."

Kathy Mattea, b 1959, singer, songwriter; "Eighteen Wheels and a Dozen Roses."

Martina McBride, b 1966, singer, songwriter; "Independence Day."

Reba McEntire, b 1955, singer, songwriter, actress; "Whoever's in New England."

Tim McGraw, b 1967, singer; "It's Your Love," "I Like It, I Love It."

Roger Miller, 1936-92, singer, songwriter; "King of the Road."

Ronnie Milsap, b 1944, singer, songwriter; "There's No Gettin' Over Me."

Bill Monroe, 1911-96, singer, songwriter, mandolin player, "father of bluegrass music"; "Mule Skinner Blues."

Anne Murray, b 1945, singer; "You Needed Me."

Willie Nelson, b 1933, singer, songwriter, actor; "On the Road Again."

Mark O'Connor, b 1961, fiddler, country-classical crossover composer.

Buck Owens, 1929-2006, singer, guitarist; "Act Naturally."

Brad Paisley, b 1972, singer, songwriter; "Whiskey Lullaby," "When I Get Where I'm Going."

Dolly Parton, b 1946, singer, songwriter, actress; "Here You Come Again," "9 to 5."

Johnny Paycheck, (Don Lytle), 1938-2003, singer, guitarist; "Take This Job and Shove It."

Minnie Pearl, 1912-96, comedienne, Grand Ole Opry star.

Ray Price, b 1926, country singer, guitarist, and songwriter; "Crazy Arms."

Charley Pride, b 1938, singer, 1st African American country star; "Kiss an Angel Good Mornin'."

Eddie Rabbit, 1941-98, singer, songwriter; "I Love A Rainy Night."

Rascal Flatts (Jay DeMarcus, b 1971; Gary LeVox, b 1970; Joe Don Rooney, b 1975); "Life Is A Highway."

Jim Reeves, 1923-64, singer, songwriter; "Four Walls."

Charlie Rich, 1932-95, singer, songwriter called the "Silver Fox"; "The Most Beautiful Girl."

LeAnn Rimes, b 1982, singer; "Blue."

Tex Ritter, 1905-74, singer, songwriter; "Jingle, Jangle, Jingle."

Marty Robbins, 1925-82, singer, songwriter; "A White Sport Coat and a Pink Carnation."

Jimmie Rodgers, 1897-1933, singer, songwriter; "T for Texas."

Kenny Rogers, b 1938, singer, songwriter; "The Gambler."

Roy Rogers (Leonard Slye), 1911-98, singer, actor, "King of the Cowboys," sang with Sons of the Pioneers.

Fred Rose, 1898-1954, songwriter, singer, producer; "Blue Eyes Cryin' in the Rain."

Ricky Skaggs, b 1954, singer, songwriter, bandleader; "Don't Cheat in Our Hometown."

Ralph Stanley, b 1927, singer, banjo player; "Man of Constant Sorrow."

George Strait, b 1952, singer, bandleader; "Ace in the Hole."

Sugarland (Kristian Bush, b 1970; Jennifer Nettles, b 1974); "Stay."

Taylor Swift, b 1989, singer, songwriter; "You Belong With Me."

Lonnie "Mel" Tillis, b 1932, singer, songwriter, bandleader; "I Ain't Never."

Merle Travis, 1917-83, singer, guitarist, songwriter; "Divorce Me C.O.D."

Randy Travis, b 1959, singer, songwriter; "Forever and Ever, Amen."

Ernest Tubb, 1914-84, singer, songwriter, guitarist; "Walking the Floor Over You."

Shania Twain, b 1965, singer, songwriter; "You're Still the One."

Conway Twitty, 1933-93, singer, songwriter; "Hello Darlin'."

Carrie Underwood, b 1983, singer, *American Idol* winner.

Keith Urban, b 1967, guitarist, singer, songwriter; "It's a Love Thing."

Porter Wagoner, 1927-2007, singer, songwriter, guitarist; "I Will Always Love You."

Kitty Wells (Ellen Deason), b 1919, singer, songwriter; "It Wasn't God Who Made Honky-Tonk Angels."

Dottie West, 1932-91, singer, songwriter; "Here Comes My Baby."

Hank Williams Jr., b 1949, singer, songwriter; "Bocephus"; "All My Rowdy Friends (Have Settled Down)."

Hank Williams Sr., 1923-53, singer, songwriter; "Your Cheatin' Heart."

Bob Wills, 1905-75, Western Swing fiddler, singer, bandleader, songwriter; "New San Antonio Rose."

Lee Ann Womack, b 1966, singer, songwriter; "I Hope You Dance."

Tammy Wynette, 1942-98, singer; "Stand By Your Man."

Trisha Yearwood, b 1964, singer, songwriter; "How Do I Live."

Dwight Yoakam, b 1957, singer, songwriter, actor; "Ain't That Lonely Yet."

Zac Brown Band (Coy Bowles, b 1979, Zac Brown, b 1978, Clay Cook, Jimmy De Martini, Chris Fryar, b 1970, and John Driskell Hopkins); "Chicken Fried."

Dance Figures of the Past

Alvin Ailey, 1931-89, (U.S.) modern dancer, choreographer; melded modern dance and Afro-Caribbean techniques.

Frederick Ashton, 1904-88, (Br.) ballet choreographer; director of Great Britain's Royal Ballet, 1963-70.

Fred Astaire, 1899-1987, (U.S.) dancer, actor; teamed with dancer/actress **Ginger Rogers**, 1911-95, (U.S.) in movie musicals.

George Balanchine, 1904-83, (Russ.-U.S.) ballet choreographer, teacher; most influential exponent of neoclassical style; founded, with Lincoln Kirstein, School of American Ballet and New York City Ballet.

Pina Bausch, 1940-2009, (Ger.) modern dance choreographer influencing the Tanztheater style of dance.

Carlo Blasis, 1795-1878, (It.) ballet dancer, choreographer, writer; his teaching methods are standards of classical dance.

August Bournonville, 1805-79, (Den.) ballet dancer, choreographer, teacher; exuberant, light style.

Fernando Bujones, 1955-2005, (Cuba-U.S.) ballet dancer.

Gisella Caccianzza, 1914-98, (U.S.) ballerina; charter member of Balanchine's American Ballet.

Irene, 1893-1969, (U.S.) and **Vernon Castle**, 1887-1918, (Br.) husband-and-wife ballroom dancers.

Enrico Cecchetti, 1850-1928, (It.) ballet dancer, leading dancer of Russia's Imperial Ballet; his technique was basis for Britain's Imperial Soc. of Teachers of Dancing.

Gower Champion, 1921-80, (U.S.) dancer, choreographer, director; with wife **Marge**, b 1923, (U.S.) choreographed, danced in Broadway musicals and films.

John Cranko, 1927-73, (S. Africa) choreographer; created narrative ballets based on literary works.

Merce Cunningham, 1919-2009, (U.S.) dancer, choreographer of avant-garde dance.

Agnes de Mille, 1905-93, (U.S.) ballerina, choreographer; known for using American themes, she choreographed the ballet *Rodeo* and the musical *Oklahoma!*

Alexandra Danilova, 1903-97, (Russ.) ballerina; noted teacher at the School of American Ballet.

Dame Ninette De Valois, 1898-2001, (Br.) choreographer, founding director of London's Royal Ballet; *The Rake's Progress*.

Sergei Diaghilev, 1872-1929, (Russ.) impresario; founded Les Ballets Russes; saw ballet as art unifying dance, drama, music, and decor.

Isadora Duncan, 1877-1927, (U.S.) expressive dancer who united free movement with serious music; one of the founders of modern dance.

Katherine Dunham, 1910-2006, (U.S.) dancer, choreographer; internationally known for African, Caribbean, and African American dance forms.

Fanny Elssler, 1810-84, (Austria) ballerina of the Romantic era; known for dramatic skill, sensual style.

Michel Fokine, 1880-1942, (Russ.) ballet dancer, choreographer, teacher; rejected strict classicism in favor of dramatically expressive style.

Margot Fonteyn, 1919-91, (Br.) prima ballerina, Royal Ballet of Great Britain; famed performance partner of Rudolf Nureyev.

Bob Fosse, 1927-87, (U.S.) jazz dancer, choreographer, director; Broadway musicals and film.

Serge Golovine, 1924-98, (Fr.) ballet dancer with Grand Ballet du Marquis de Cuevas, choreographer.

Martha Graham, 1894-1991, (U.S.) modern dancer, choreographer; created and codified her own dramatic technique.

Melissa Hayden, 1923-2006, (Can.) ballet dancer.

Martha Hill, 1900-95, (U.S.) educator; leading figure in modern dance; founded American Dance Festival.

Gregory Hines, 1946-2003, (U.S.) tap-dance innovator; master of improvisation.

Doris Humphrey, 1895-1958, (U.S.) modern dancer, choreographer, writer, teacher.

Michael Jackson, 1958-2009, (U.S.) singer and dancer who perfected the "moonwalk."

Robert Joffrey, 1930-88, (U.S.) ballet dancer, choreographer; cofounded with **Gerald Arpino**, 1928-2008, (U.S.) the Joffrey Ballet.

Kurt Jooss, 1901-79, (Ger.) choreographer, teacher; created expressionist works using modern and classical techniques.

Tamara Karsavina, 1885-1978, (Russ.) prima ballerina of Russia's Imperial Ballet and Diaghilev's Ballets Russes; partner of Nijinsky.

Nora Kaye, 1920-87, (U.S.) ballerina with Metropolitan Opera Ballet and Ballet Theater (now American Ballet Theatre).

Gene Kelly, 1912-96, (U.S.) dancer, actor in movie musicals.

Michael Kidd, 1915-2003, (U.S.) dancer, film and theater choreographer.

Lincoln Kirstein, 1907-96 (U.S.) brought ballet as an art form to U.S.; founded, with George Balanchine, School of American Ballet and New York City Ballet.

Serge Lifar, 1905-86, (Russ.-Fr.) prem. danseur, choreographer; director of dance at Paris Opera, 1930-45, 1947-58.

José Limón, 1908-72, (Mex.-U.S.) modern dancer, choreographer, teacher; developed technique based on Humphrey.

Catherine Littlefield, 1908-51, (U.S.) ballerina, choreographer, teacher; pioneer of American ballet.

Kenneth MacMillan, 1929-92, (Br.) dancer, choreographer; directed Royal Ballet of Great Britain, 1970-77.

Dame Alicia Markova, 1910-2004, (Br.) ballerina; helped popularize ballet in U.S. and Britain; known for title role in *Giselle*.

Léonide Massine, 1896-1979, (Russ.-U.S.) ballet dancer, choreographer; known for his "symphonic ballet."

Fayard Nicholas, 1914-2006, (U.S.) tap dancer, choreographer, actor; together with brother **Harold Nicholas**, 1921-2000, (U.S.) formed the "Nicholas Brothers."

Vaslav Nijinsky, 1890-50, (Russ.) prem. danseur, choreographer; leading member of Diaghilev's Ballets Russes; his ballets were revolutionary for their time.

Alwin Nikolais, 1910-93, (U.S.) modern choreographer; created dance theater utilizing mixed media effects.

Jean-George Noverre, 1727-1810, (Fr.) ballet choreographer, teacher, writer; "Shakespeare of the Dance."

Rudolf Nureyev, 1938-93, (Russ.) prem. danseur, choreographer; leading male dancer of his generation; director of dance at Paris Opera, 1983-89.

Ruth Page, 1899-1991, (U.S.) ballerina, choreographer; danced, directed ballet at Chicago Lyric Opera.

Anna Pavlova, 1881-1931, (Russ.) prima ballerina; toured with her own company to world acclaim.

Marius Petipa, 1818-1910, (Fr.) ballet dancer, choreographer; ballet master of the Imperial Ballet; established Russian classicism as leading style of late 19th cent.

Roland Petit, 1924-2011, (Fr.) dancer, choreographer; founder Les Ballets de Paris.

Pearl Primus, 1919-95, (Trinidad-U.S.) modern dancer, choreographer, scholar; combined African, Caribbean, and African American styles.

Jerome Robbins, 1918-98, (U.S.) choreographer, director, dancer; *The King and I*, *West Side Story*, *Fiddler on the Roof*.

Bill "Bojangles" Robinson, 1878-1949, (U.S.) famed tap dancer; called "King of Tapology" on stage and screen.

Ruth St. Denis, 1877-1968, (U.S.) influential interpretive dancer, choreographer, teacher.

Ted Shawn, 1891-1972, (U.S.) modern dancer, choreographer; formed dance company and school with Ruth St. Denis; established Jacob's Pillow Dance Festival.

Marie Taglioni, 1804-84, (It.) ballerina, teacher; in title role of *La Sylphide* established image of the ethereal ballerina.

Glen Tetley, 1926-2007, (U.S.) dancer, choreographer, ballet director; fused elements of modern dance with ballet.

Antony Tudor, 1908-87, (Br.) choreographer, teacher; exponent of the "psychological ballet."

Galina Ulanova, 1910-98, (Russ.) revered ballerina with Bolshoi Ballet.

Agrippina Vaganova, 1879-1951, (Russ.) ballet teacher, director; codified Soviet ballet technique; called "queen of variations."

Mary Wigman, 1886-1973, (Ger.) modern dancer, choreographer, teacher; influenced European expressionist dance.

Opera Singers of the Past

Frances Alda, 1883?-1952, (N.Z.) soprano.

Pasquale Amato, 1878-1942, (It.) baritone.

Marian Anderson, 1897-1993, (U.S.) contralto.

Jussi Björling, 1911-60, (Swed.) tenor.

Lucrezia Bori, 1887-1960, (It.) soprano.

Maria Callas, 1923-77, (U.S.) soprano.

Emma Calvé, 1858-1942, (Fr.) soprano.

Enrico Caruso, 1873-1921, (It.) tenor.

Feodor Chaliapin, 1873-1938, (Russ.) bass.

Boris Christoff, 1914-93, (Bulg.) bass.

Franco Corelli, 1921-2003, (It.) tenor.

Hughes Cuenod, 1902-2010, (Switz.) tenor.

Victoria De Los Angeles, 1923-2005, (Sp.) soprano.

Giuseppe De Luca, 1876-1950, (It.) baritone.

Fernando De Lucia, 1860-1925, (It.) tenor.

Edouard De Reszke, 1853-1917, (Pol.) bass.

Jean De Reszke, 1850-1925, (Pol.) tenor.

Emmy Destinn, 1878-1930, (Czech.) soprano.

Emma Eames, 1865-1952, (U.S.) soprano.

(Carlo Broschi) Farinelli, 1705-82, (It.) castrato.

Geraldine Farrar, 1882-1967, (U.S.) soprano.

Eileen Farrell, 1920-2002, (U.S.) soprano.

Kathleen Ferrier, 1912-53, (Eng.) contralto.

Kirsten Flagstad, 1895-1962, (Nor.) soprano.

Olive Fremstad, 1871-1951, (Swed.-U.S.) soprano.
Amelita Galli-Curci, 1882-1963, (It.) soprano.
Mary Garden, 1874-1967, (Br.) soprano.
Nicolai Ghiaurov, 1929-2004, (Bulg.) bass.
Beniamino Gigli, 1890-1957, (It.) tenor.
Tito Gobbi, 1913-84, (It.) baritone.
Giulia Grisi, 1811-69, (It.) soprano.
Frieda Hempel, 1885-1955, (Ger.) soprano.
Jerome Hines, 1921-2003, (U.S.) bass.
Hans Hotter, 1909-2003, (Ger.) bass-baritone.
Maria Jeritza, 1887-1982, (Czech.) soprano.
Alexander Kipnis, 1891-1978, (Russ.-U.S.) bass.
Dorothy Kirsten, 1910-92, (U.S.) soprano.
Alfredo Kraus, 1927-99, (Sp.) tenor.
Luigi Lablache, 1794-1858, (It.) bass.
Lilli Lehmann, 1848-1929, (Ger.) soprano.
Lotte Lehmann, 1888-1976, (Ger.-U.S.) soprano.
Jenny Lind, 1820-87, (Swed.) soprano.
Cornell MacNeil, 1922-2011, (U.S.) baritone.
Maria Malibran, 1808-36, (Sp.) mezzo-soprano.
Giovanni Martinelli, 1885-1969, (It.) tenor.
John McCormack, 1884-1945, (Ire.) tenor.

Nellie Melba, 1861-1931, (Austral.) soprano.
Lauritz Melchior, 1890-1973, (Den.) tenor.
Robert Merrill, 1919-2004, (U.S.) baritone.
Zinka Milanov, 1906-89, (Yugo.) soprano.
Birgit Nilsson, 1918-2005, (Swed.) soprano.
Lillian Nordica, 1857-1914, (U.S.) soprano.
Giuditta Pasta, 1797-1865, (It.) soprano.
Adelina Patti, 1843-1919, (It.) soprano.
Luciano Pavarotti, 1935-2007, (It.) tenor.
Peter Pears, 1910-86, (Eng.) tenor.
Jan Peerce, 1904-84, (U.S.) tenor.
Ezio Pinza, 1892-1957, (It.) bass.
Lily Pons, 1898-1976, (Fr.) soprano.
Rosa Ponselle, 1897-1981, (U.S.) soprano.
Hermann Prey, 1929-98, (Ger.) baritone.
Margaret Price, 1941-2011, (U.K.) soprano.
Elisabeth Rethberg, 1894-1976, (Ger.) soprano.
Giovanni Battista Rubini, 1794-1854, (It.) tenor.
Leonie Rysanek, 1926-98, (Austria) soprano.
Dorothy Sarnoff, 1914-2008, (U.S.) soprano.
Bidú Sayão, 1902-99, (Braz.) soprano.
Friedrich Schorr, 1888-1953, (Hung.) bass-baritone.

Elisabeth Schwarzkopf, 1915-2006, (Ger.) soprano.
Marcella Sembrich, 1858-1935, (Pol.) soprano.
Cesare Siepi, 1923-2010, (It.) bass.
Beverly Sills, 1929-2007, (U.S.) soprano.
Elisabeth Söderström, 1927-2009, (Swed.) soprano.
Eleanor Steber, 1914-90, (U.S.) soprano.
Joan Sutherland, 1926-2010, (Austral.) soprano.
Ferrucio Tagliavini, 1913-95, (It.) tenor.
Renata Tebaldi, 1922-2004 (It.) soprano.
Luisa Tetrazzini, 1871-1940, (It.) soprano.
Lawrence Tibbett, 1896-1960, (U.S.) baritone.
Giorgio Tozzi, 1923-2011, (U.S.) bass-baritone.
Tatiana Troyanos, 1938-93, (U.S.) mezzo-soprano.
Richard Tucker, 1913-75, (U.S.) tenor.
Pauline Viardot, 1821-1910, (Fr.) mezzo-soprano.
Shirley Verrett, 1931-2010, (U.S.) mezzo-soprano.
William Warfield, 1920-2002, (U.S.) bass-baritone.
Leonard Warren, 1911-60, (U.S.) baritone.
Ljuba Welitsch, 1913-96, (Bulg.) soprano.
Wolfgang Windgassen, 1914-74, (Ger.) tenor.

Rock and Roll, Rhythm and Blues, and Rap Artists

Titles in quotation marks are singles; others are albums. *Inducted into Rock and Roll Hall of Fame as performer between 1986 and 2011; year is in parentheses.

Aaliyah: "More than a Woman"
*ABBA (2010): "Dancing Queen"
Paula Abdul: "Straight Up"
*AC/DC (2003): "Back in Black"
Bryan Adams: "Cuts Like a Knife"
Adele: "Rolling in the Deep"
*Aerosmith (2001): "Sweet Emotion"
Christina Aguilera: "What a Girl Wants"
Alice In Chains: "Heaven Beside You"
*The Allman Brothers Band (1995): "Ramblin' Man"
*The Animals (1994): "House of the Rising Sun"
Paul Anka: "Lonely Boy"
Fiona Apple: "Criminal"
Ashanti: "Foolish"
Frankie Avalon: "Venus"
The B-52s: "Love Shack"
Bachman Turner Overdrive: "Takin' Care of Business"
Backstreet Boys: "I Want It That Way"
Bad Company: "Can't Get Enough"
Erykah Badu: "On and On"
*La Vern Baker (1991): "I Cried a Tear"
*Hank Ballard[1] and the Midnighters (1990): "Work With Me, Annie"
*The Band (1994): "The Weight"
Barenaked Ladies: "One Week"
*The Beach Boys (1988): "Good Vibrations"
Beastie Boys: "(You Gotta) Fight for Your Right (to Party)"
*The Beatles (1988): Sgt. Pepper's Lonely Hearts Club Band
Beck: "Loser"
*Jeff Beck (2009): "Escape"
*The Bee Gees (1997): "Stayin' Alive"
Pat Benatar: "Hit Me With Your Best Shot"
Ben Folds Five: "Brick"
*Chuck Berry (1986): "Johnny B. Goode"
Beyoncé: "Crazy in Love"
The Big Bopper: "Chantilly Lace"
Björk: "Human Behavior"
The Black Crowes: "Hard to Handle"
Black Eyed Peas: Elephunk
*Black Sabbath (2006): "Paranoid"
*Bobby "Blue" Bland (1992): "Turn On Your Love Light"
Mary J. Blige: My Life
Blind Faith: "Can't Find My Way Home"
Blink-182: "All the Small Things"
*Blondie (2006): "Heart of Glass"
Blood, Sweat, and Tears: "Spinning Wheel"
Blues Traveler: "Run-Around"

Gary "U.S." Bonds: "Quarter to Three"
Bon Jovi: "Livin' on a Prayer"
*Booker T. and the M.G.'s (1992): "Green Onions"
Earl Bostic: "Flamingo"
Boston: "More Than A Feeling"
*David Bowie (1996): "Space Oddity"
Boyz II Men: "I'll Make Love to You"
Toni Braxton: "Un-Break My Heart"
Chris Brown: "Kiss Kiss"
*James Brown (1986): "Papa's Got a Brand New Bag"
*Ruth Brown (1993): "Lucky Lips"
*Jackson Browne (2004): "Doctor My Eyes"
*Buffalo Springfield (1997): "For What It's Worth"
Jimmy Buffett: "Margaritaville"
*Solomon Burke (2001): "Over and Over (Huggin' and Lovin')"
Bush: "Glycerine"
*The Byrds (1991): "Turn! Turn! Turn!"
Mariah Carey: "Vision of Love"
The Carpenters: "(They Long to Be) Close to You"
The Cars: "Shake It Up"
*Johnny Cash (1992): "I Walk the Line"
*Ray Charles (1986): "Georgia on My Mind"
Cheap Trick: "Surrender"
Chubby Checker: "The Twist"
Chicago: "Saturday in the Park"
*Eric Clapton (2000): "Layla"
Kelly Clarkson: "Since U Been Gone"
*The Clash (2003): "Rock the Casbah"
*Jimmy Cliff (2010): "I Can See Clearly Now"
*The Coasters (1987): "Yakety Yak"
*Eddie Cochran (1987): "Summertime Blues"
Joe Cocker: "With a Little Help From My Friends"
*Leonard Cohen (2008): "Suzanne"
Coldplay: "Clocks"
Collective Soul: "The World I Know"
Phil Collins: "Against All Odds"
*Sam Cooke (1986): "You Send Me"
Coolio: "Gangsta's Paradise"
*Alice Cooper (2011): "School's Out"
*Elvis Costello and the Attractions (2003): "Alison"
Counting Crows: "Mr. Jones"
*Cream (1993): "Sunshine of Your Love"
Creed: "Arms Wide Open"

*Creedence Clearwater Revival (1993): "Proud Mary"
*Crosby, Stills, and Nash (1997): "Suite: Judy Blue Eyes"
Sheryl Crow: "All I Want to Do"
The Crystals: "Da Doo Ron Ron"
The Cult: "She Sells Sanctuary"
The Cure: "Boys Don't Cry"
Cypress Hill: "Insane in the Brain"
Danny and the Juniors: "At the Hop"
*Bobby Darin (1990): "Splish Splash"
Daughtry: "It's Not Over"
*The Dave Clark Five (2008): "Glad All Over"
Dave Matthews Band: "Don't Drink the Water"
*Miles Davis (2006): Bitches Brew
Spencer Davis Group: "Gimme Some Lovin'"
Deep Purple: "Smoke on the Water"
Def Leppard: "Photograph"
*The Dells (2004): "Oh, What a Night"
Depeche Mode: "Strange Love"
Destiny's Child: "Survivor"
*Neil Diamond (2011): "Cracklin' Rosie"
*Bo Diddley (1987): "Who Do You Love?"
*Dion[1] and the Belmonts (1989): "A Teenager in Love"
Celine Dion: "Because You Loved Me"
Dire Straits: "Money for Nothing"
DMX: "What's My Name"
*Fats Domino (1986): "Blueberry Hill"
Donovan: "Mellow Yellow"
The Doobie Brothers: "What a Fool Believes"
*The Doors (1993): "Light My Fire"
Drake: "Over"
Dr. Dre: "Nothin' But a 'G' Thang"
*The Drifters (1988): "Save the Last Dance for Me"
*Dr. John (2011): "Right Place, Wrong Time"
Duran Duran: "Hungry Like the Wolf"
*Bob Dylan (1988): "Like a Rolling Stone"
*The Eagles (1998): "Hotel California"
*Earth, Wind, and Fire (2000): "Shining Star"
*Duane Eddy (1994): "Rebel-Rouser"
Missy Elliott: "Sock It 2 Me"
Eminem: "The Real Slim Shady"
En Vogue: "Hold On"
The Eurythmics: "Sweet Dreams (Are Made of This)"
Everclear: "Father Of Mine"

*The Everly Brothers (1986): "Wake Up, Little Susie"
50 Cent (Curtis Jackson): *Get Rich Or Die Tryin'*
The Five Satins: "In the Still of the Night"
Roberta Flack: "The First Time Ever I Saw Your Face"
*The Flamingos (2001): "I Only Have Eyes for You"
*Fleetwood Mac (1998): *Rumours*
The Foo Fighters: "I'll Stick Around"
Foreigner: "Double Vision"
*The Four Seasons (1990): "Sherry"
*The Four Tops (1990): "I Can't Help Myself (Sugar Pie, Honey Bunch)"
*Aretha Franklin (1987): "Respect"
Nelly Furtado: "I'm Like a Bird"
Peter Gabriel: "Shock the Monkey"
*Gamble (Kenny) and Huff (Leon) (2008): "If You Don't Know Me By Now"
*Marvin Gaye (1987): "I Heard It Through the Grapevine"
*Genesis (2010): "No Reply at All"
Goo Goo Dolls: "Iris"
Grand Funk Railroad: "We're an American Band"
*Grandmaster Flash and the Furious Five (2007): "The Message"
*The Grateful Dead (1994): "Uncle John's Band"
*Al Green (1995): "Let's Stay Together"
Green Day: "Boulevard of Broken Dreams"
The Guess Who: "American Woman"
Guns N' Roses: "Sweet Child o' Mine"
*Buddy Guy (2005): *A Man and His Blues*
*Bill Haley[1] and His Comets (1987): "Rock Around the Clock"
Hall and Oates: "Kiss on My List"
Hanson: "MMMBop"
*George Harrison (2004): "My Sweet Lord"
*Isaac Hayes (2002): "Theme From 'Shaft'"
Heart: "Barracuda"
*Jimi Hendrix (1992): "Purple Haze"
Lauryn Hill: "Doo-Wop (That Thing)"
Hole: "Doll Parts"
*The Hollies (2010): "Long Cool Woman (In a Black Dress)"
*Buddy Holly (1986): "Peggy Sue"
*John Lee Hooker (1991): "Boogie Chillen"
Hootie and the Blowfish: *Cracked Rear View*
Whitney Houston: "I Will Always Love You"
*The Impressions (1991): "For Your Precious Love"
Indigo Girls: "Closer to Fine"
INXS: "Need You Tonight"
*The Isley Brothers (1992): "It's Your Thing"
*The Jackson Five (1997): "ABC"
Janet Jackson: *Rhythm Nation*
*Michael Jackson (2001): *Thriller*
*Etta James (1993): "At Last"
Tommy James and the Shondells: "Crimson and Clover"
Jane's Addiction: "Jane Says"
Ja Rule: *Venni, Vetti, Vecci*
Jay and the Americans: "This Magic Moment"
Jay-Z: "Can I Live"
*Jefferson Airplane (1996): "White Rabbit"
Jethro Tull: *Aqualung*
Joan Jett: "I Love Rock 'n' Roll"
Jewel: "You Were Meant For Me"
*Billy Joel (1999): "Piano Man"
*Elton John (1994): "Candle in the Wind"
*Little Willie John (1996): "Sleep"
Norah Jones: *Come Away With Me*
*Janis Joplin (1995): "Me and Bobby McGee"
Journey: "Don't Stop Believin'"
K.C. and the Sunshine Band: "Get Down Tonight"
R. Kelly: "I Can't Sleep Baby (If I)"
Alicia Keys: "Fallin"
Kid Rock: "Cowboy"
*B.B. King (1987): "The Thrill Is Gone"
Carole King: *Tapestry*
*The Kinks (1990): "You Really Got Me"

Kiss: "Rock 'n' Roll All Night"
*Gladys Knight and the Pips (1996): "Midnight Train to Georgia"
Korn: "Blind"
Lenny Kravitz: "Are You Gonna Go My Way?"
Lady Gaga: "Poker Face"
*Led Zeppelin (1995): "Stairway to Heaven"
*Brenda Lee (2002): "I'm Sorry"
John Legend: "Ordinary People"
*John Lennon (1994): "Imagine"
*Jerry Lee Lewis (1986): "Whole Lotta Shakin' Going On"
Lil' Kim: "No Matter What They Say"
Limp Bizkit: "Break Stuff"
Linkin Park: "One Step Closer"
*Little Anthony and the Imperials (2009): "Tears on My Pillow"
*Little Richard (1986): "Tutti Frutti"
*Little Walter (2008): "Juke"
Live: "Lightning Crashes"
L. L. Cool J: "Mama Said Knock You Out"
Jennifer Lopez: "Love Don't Cost a Thing"
*Darlene Love (2011): "He's a Rebel"
*The Lovin' Spoonful (2000): "Summer in the City"
Ludacris: "Money Maker"
*Frankie Lymon and the Teenagers (1993): "Why Do Fools Fall in Love?"
*Lynyrd Skynyrd (2006): "Free Bird"
Madonna (2008): "Material Girl"
*The Mamas and the Papas (1998): "Monday, Monday"
Aimee Mann: "Save Me"
Marilyn Manson: "Beautiful People"
*Bob Marley (1994): *Exodus*
Maroon 5: *Songs About Jane*
Bruno Mars: "Just the Way You Are"
*Martha and the Vandellas (1995): "Dancin' in the Streets"
The Marvelettes: "Please, Mr. Postman"
Matchbox 20: "Push"
John Mayer: "Daughters"
*Curtis Mayfield (1999): "Superfly"
*Paul McCartney (1999): "Band on the Run"
Don McLean: "American Pie"
*Clyde McPhatter (1987): "A Lover's Question"
Meat Loaf: "Paradise by the Dashboard Light"
*John (Cougar) Mellencamp (2008): "Jack and Diane"
Men at Work: "Who Can It Be Now?"
*Metallica (2009): "Enter Sandman"
George Michael: "Faith"
*Joni Mitchell (1997): "Both Sides Now"
Moby: "Bodyrock"
The Monkees: "I'm a Believer"
Moody Blues: "Nights in White Satin"
*The Moonglows (2000): "Blue Velvet"
Alanis Morissette: "Ironic"
*Van Morrison (1993): "Brown-Eyed Girl"
Mötley Crüe: "Live Wire"
Motörhead: "Ace of Spades"
Jason Mraz: "I'm Yours"
Nelly: *Country Grammar*
*Ricky Nelson (1987): "Hello, Mary Lou"
Nickelback: "Photograph"
Nine Inch Nails: "Closer"
Nirvana: *Nevermind*
No Doubt: *Rock Steady*
The Notorious B.I.G.: "Mo Money Mo Problems"
'N Sync: "Bye, Bye, Bye"
Ted Nugent: "Strangehold"
N.W.A.: "Straight Outta Compton"
Oasis: "Wonderwall"
The Offspring: "Pretty Fly (For a White Guy)"
*The O'Jays (2005): "Back Stabbers"
*Roy Orbison (1987): "Oh, Pretty Woman"
Ozzy Osbourne: "Crazy Train"
OutKast: *Speakerboxxx/The Love Below*
*Parliament/Funkadelic (1997): "One Nation Under a Groove"
Pearl Jam: "Jeremy"
*Carl Perkins (1987): "Blue Suede Shoes"
Katy Perry: "I Kissed a Girl"
Peter, Paul, and Mary: "Leaving on a Jet Plane"

*Tom Petty and the Heartbreakers (2002): "Refugee"
Liz Phair: *Exile in Guyville*
Phish: "Sample in a Jar"
*Wilson Pickett (1991): "Land of 1,000 Dances"
Pink: *Missundazstood!*
*Pink Floyd (1996): *The Wall*
*Gene Pitney (2002): "Only Love Can Break a Heart"
*The Platters (1990): "The Great Pretender"
The Pointer Sisters: "I'm So Excited"
*The Police (2003): "Every Breath You Take"
Iggy Pop: "Lust for Life"
*Elvis Presley (1986): "Love Me Tender"
*The Pretenders (2005): "Back on the Chain Gang"
*Lloyd Price (1998): "Stagger Lee"
*Prince (The Artist) (2004): "Purple Rain"
Public Enemy: "Fight the Power"
Puff Daddy and the Family: *No Way Out*
*Queen (2001): "Bohemian Rhapsody"
Radiohead: *OK Computer*
Rage Against the Machine: "Bulls on Parade"
*Bonnie Raitt (2000): "Something to Talk About"
*The Ramones (2002): "I Wanna Be Sedated"
*Otis Redding (1989): "(Sittin' on) The Dock of the Bay"
Red Hot Chili Peppers: "Under the Bridge"
*Jimmy Reed (1991): "Ain't That Loving You, Baby?"
Lou Reed: "Walk on the Wild Side"
*R.E.M. (2007): "Losing My Religion"
REO Speedwagon: "Can't Fight This Feeling"
Busta Rhymes: "What's It Gonna Be?"
*The Righteous Brothers (2003): "You've Lost That Lovin' Feelin'"
Johnny Rivers: "Poor Side of Town"
*Smokey Robinson[1] and the Miracles (1987): "Shop Around"
*The Rolling Stones (1989): "Satisfaction"
*The Ronettes (2007): "Be My Baby"
Linda Ronstadt: "You're No Good"
Diana Ross: "I'm Coming Out"
*Run-D.M.C. (2009): "Raisin' Hell"
Rush: "Tom Sawyer"
Sade: "Smooth Operator"
Salt-N-Pepa: "Shoop"
*Sam and Dave (1992): "Soul Man"
*Santana (1998): "Black Magic Woman"
Seal: "Kiss From a Rose"
Neil Sedaka: "Breaking Up Is Hard to Do"
*Bob Seger (2004): "Old Time Rock & Roll"
*Sex Pistols (2006): "Anarchy in the UK"
Shaggy: "It Wasn't Me"
Shakira: "Whenever, Wherever"
Tupac Shakur: "How Do U Want It"
*Del Shannon (1999): "Runaway"
*The Shirelles (1996): "Soldier Boy"
Carly Simon: "You're So Vain"
*Paul Simon (2001): "50 Ways to Leave Your Lover"
*Simon and Garfunkel (1990): "Bridge Over Troubled Water"
*Percy Sledge (2005): "When a Man Loves a Woman"
*Sly and the Family Stone (1993): "Everyday People"
Smashing Pumpkins: "Today"
*Patti Smith (2007): "Because the Night"
Will Smith: "Gettin' Jiggy With It"
The Smiths: "This Charming Man"
Snoop Dogg: "Gin and Juice"
Sonic Youth: "Bull in the Heather"
Soundgarden: "Black Hole Sun"
Britney Spears: "Hit Me Baby One More Time"
Spice Girls: "Wannabe"
*Dusty Springfield (1999): "I Only Want to Be With You"
*Bruce Springsteen (1999): "Born to Run"
Squeeze: "Tempted"
*Staple Singers (1999): "I'll Take You There"

*Steely Dan (2001): "Rikki Don't Lose That Number"
Gwen Stefani: "Hollaback Girl"
Steppenwolf: "Born to Be Wild"
*Rod Stewart (1994): "Maggie Mae"
Sting: "If You Love Somebody, Set Them Free"
Stone Temple Pilots: "Plush"
*The Stooges (2010): "I Wanna Be Your Dog"
Styx: "Come Sail Away"
Sublime: "What I Got"
The Sugar Hill Gang: "Rapper's Delight"
Donna Summer: "Bad Girls"
*The Supremes (1988): "Stop! In the Name of Love"
Taj Mahal: "Going Up to the Country, Paint My Mailbox Blue"
*Talking Heads (2002): "Once in a Lifetime"
*James Taylor (2001): "You've Got a Friend"
*The Temptations (1989): "My Girl"
Three Dog Night: "Joy to the World"

Justin Timberlake: "SexyBack"
TLC: "Waterfalls"
T. Rex: "Bang a Gong (Get It On)"
*Traffic (2004): Traffic
*Big Joe Turner (1987): "Shake, Rattle & Roll"
*Ike and Tina Turner (1991): "Proud Mary"
*Tina Turner (1991): "What's Love Got to Do With It?"
The Turtles: "Happy Together"
*U2 (2005): "With or Without You"
Usher: "You Make Me Wanna"
*Ritchie Valens (2001): "La Bamba"
*Van Halen (2007): "Running With the Devil"
Stevie Ray Vaughan: "Crossfire"
*The Velvet Underground (1996): "Sweet Jane"
*The Ventures (2008): "Walk, Don't Run"
*Gene Vincent (1998): "Be-Bop-A-Lula"
*Tom Waits (2011): "Downtown Train"
The Wallflowers: "One Headlight"
Dionne Warwick: "I Say a Little Prayer"
*Muddy Waters (1987): "I Can't Be Satisfied"

Mary Wells: "My Guy"
Kanye West: "Gold Digger"
Whitesnake: "Here I Go Again"
The White Stripes: "Seven Nation Army"
*The Who (2001): Tommy
Lucinda Williams: Car Wheels on a Gravel Road
*Jackie Wilson (1987): "That's Why"
*Bobby Womack (2009): "Lookin' for a Love"
*Stevie Wonder (1989): "You Are the Sunshine of My Life"
Wu-Tang Clan: "Protect Ya Neck"
Weird Al Yankovic: Dare to Be Stupid
*The Yardbirds (1992): "For Your Love"
Yes: "Roundabout"
*Neil Young (1995): "Down by the River"
*The Young Rascals/The Rascals (1997): "Good Lovin' "
*Frank Zappa[1]/Mothers of Invention (1995): Hot Rats
John Zorn: News for Lulu
*ZZ Top (2004): "Legs"

(1) Only individual performer is in Rock and Roll Hall of Fame.

Entertainment Personalities of the Present

Living actors, musicians, dancers, singers, producers, directors, and radio-TV performers.

Name	Birthplace	Birthdate	Name	Birthplace	Birthdate
Abbado, Claudio	Milan, Italy	6/26/33	Apple, Fiona	New York, NY	9/13/77
Abdul, Paula	San Fernando, CA	6/19/62	Applegate, Christina	Los Angeles, CA	11/25/71
Abraham, F. Murray	Pittsburgh, PA	10/24/39	Archer, Anne	Los Angeles, CA	8/25/47
Abrams, J(effrey) J(acob)	New York, NY	6/27/66	Archuleta, David	Miami, FL	12/28/90
Adams, Amy	Aviano, Italy	8/20/74	Arkin, Adam	Brooklyn, NY	8/19/56
Adams, Bryan	Kingston, ON, Canada	11/5/59	Arkin, Alan	New York, NY	3/26/34
Adele	London, England, UK	5/5/88	Armisen, Fred	Hattiesburg, MS	12/4/66
Adjani, Isabelle	Paris, France	6/27/55	Arnaz, Desi, Jr.	Hollywood, CA	1/19/53
Ad-Rock	South Orange, NJ	10/31/66	Arnaz, Lucie	Hollywood, CA	7/17/51
Affleck, Ben	Berkeley, CA	8/15/72	Arnett, Will	Toronto, ON, Canada	5/4/70
Affleck, Casey	Falmouth, MA	8/12/75	Arnold, Tom	Ottumwa, IA	3/6/59
Aghdashloo, Shohreh	Tehran, Iran	5/11/52	Arquette, David	Winchester, VA	9/8/71
Agron, Dianna	Savannah, GA	4/30/86	Arquette, Patricia	Chicago, IL	4/8/68
Aguilera, Christina	Staten Island, NY	12/18/80	Arquette, Rosanna	New York, NY	8/10/59
Aiello, Danny	New York, NY	6/20/33	Arroyo, Martina	New York, NY	2/2/37
Aiken, Clay	Raleigh, NC	11/30/78	Ashanti (Douglas)	Glen Cove, NY	10/13/80
Aimee, Anouk	Paris, France	4/27/32	Ashley, Elizabeth	Ocala, FL	8/30/39
Alba, Jessica	Pomona, CA	4/28/81	Asner, Ed	Kansas City, KS	11/15/29
Albanese, Licia	Bari, Italy	7/22/13	Assante, Armand	New York, NY	10/4/49
Alberghetti, Anna Maria	Pesaro, Italy	5/15/36	Astin, John	Baltimore, MD	3/30/30
Albert, Marv	Brooklyn, NY	6/12/41	Astin, Sean	Santa Monica, CA	2/25/71
Alda, Alan	New York, NY	1/28/36	Atkins, Eileen	London, England, UK	6/16/34
Alexander, Jane	Boston, MA	10/28/39	Atkins, Sharif	Pittsburgh, PA	1/29/75
Alexander, Jason	Newark, NJ	9/23/59	Atkinson, Rowan	Newcastle-Upon-Tyne,	
Allen, Debbie	Houston, TX	1/16/50		England, UK	1/6/55
Allen, Joan	Rochelle, IL	8/20/56	Attenborough, Richard	Cambridge, England, UK	8/29/23
Allen, Karen	Carrollton, IL	10/5/51	Auberjonois, Rene	New York, NY	6/1/40
Allen, Kris	Jacksonville, AR	6/21/85	Austin, Patti	New York, NY	8/10/48
Allen, Ted	Columbus, OH	5/20/65	Autry, Alan	Shreveport, LA	7/31/52
Allen, Tim	Denver, CO	6/13/53	Avalon, Frankie	Philadelphia, PA	9/18/40
Allen, Woody	Brooklyn, NY	12/1/35	Aykroyd, Dan	Ottawa, ON, Canada	7/1/52
Alley, Kirstie	Wichita, KS	1/12/51	Azaria, Hank	Forest Hills, Queens, NY	4/25/64
Allman, Gregg	Nashville, TN	12/8/47	Aznavour, Charles	Paris, France	5/22/24
Alonso, Maria Conchita	Cienfuegos, Cuba	6/29/57	Babyface	Indianapolis, IN	4/10/59
Alpert, Herb	Los Angeles, CA	3/31/35	Bacall, Lauren	Bronx, NY	9/16/24
Almodóvar, Pedro	Calzada de Calatrava,		Bacon, Kevin	Philadelphia, PA	7/8/58
	Spain	9/24/49	Badalucco, Michael	Brooklyn, NY	12/20/54
Ambrose, Lauren	New Haven, CT	2/20/78	Bader, Diedrich	Alexandria, VA	12/24/66
Ames, Ed	Malden, MA	7/9/27	Badu, Erykah	Dallas, TX	2/26/71
Amos, John	Newark, NJ	12/27/41	Baez, Joan	Staten Island, NY	1/9/41
Amos, Tori	Newton, NC	8/22/63	Bain, Conrad	Lethbridge, AB, Canada	2/4/23
André 3000	Atlanta, GA	5/27/75	Baio, Scott	Brooklyn, NY	9/22/61
Anderson, Gillian	Chicago, IL	8/9/68	Baker, Anita	Toledo, OH	1/26/58
Anderson, Harry	Newport, RI	10/14/52	Baker, Carroll	Johnstown, PA	5/28/31
Anderson, Ian	Dunfermline, Scotland, UK	8/10/47	Baker, Diane	Hollywood, CA	2/25/38
Anderson, Kevin	Gurnee, IL	1/13/60	Baker, Joe Don	Groesbeck, TX	2/12/36
Anderson, Loni	St. Paul, MN	8/5/46	Baker, Kathy	Midland, TX	6/8/50
Anderson, Lynn	Grand Forks, ND	9/26/47	Baker, Simon	Launceston, Tasmania,	
Anderson, Melissa Sue	Berkeley, CA	9/26/62		Australia	7/30/69
Anderson, Pamela	Ladysmith, BC, Canada	7/1/67	Bakula, Scott	St. Louis, MO	10/9/54
Anderson, Richard	Long Branch, NJ	8/8/26	Baldwin, Alec	Massapequa, NY	4/3/58
Anderson, Richard Dean	Minneapolis, MN	1/23/50	Baldwin, Daniel	Massapequa, NY	10/5/60
Anderson, Wes	Houston, TX	5/1/69	Baldwin, Stephen	Massapequa, NY	5/12/66
Andersson, Bibi	Stockholm, Sweden	11/11/35	Baldwin, William	Massapequa, NY	2/21/63
Andress, Ursula	Bern, Switzerland	3/19/36	Bale, Christian	Pembrokeshire, Wales, UK	1/30/74
Andrews, Julie	Walton-on-Thames,		Ballard, Kaye	Cleveland, OH	11/20/26
	Surrey, England, UK	10/1/35	Bana, Eric	Melbourne, Australia	8/9/68
Andrews, Naveen	London, England, UK	1/17/69	Banderas, Antonio	Málaga, Spain	8/10/60
Andrews, Patty	Mound, MN	2/16/18	Banks, Elizabeth	Pittsfield, MA	2/10/74
Angel, Criss	East Meadow, NY	12/19/67	Banks, Tyra	Los Angeles, CA	12/4/73
Aniston, Jennifer	Sherman Oaks, CA	2/11/69	Baranski, Christine	Buffalo, NY	5/2/52
Anka, Paul	Ottawa, ON, Canada	7/30/41	Barbeau, Adrienne	Sacramento, CA	6/11/45
Ann-Margret	Stockholm, Sweden	4/28/41	Bardem, Javier	Las Palmas, Canary Islands,	
Anthony, Marc	New York, NY	9/16/68		Spain	3/1/69
Apatow, Judd	Syosset, NY	12/6/67	Bardot, Brigitte	Paris, France	9/28/34

Name	Birthplace	Birthdate	Name	Birthplace	Birthdate
Barker, Bob	Darrington, WA	12/12/23	Bogosian, Eric	Woburn, MA	4/24/53
Barkin, Ellen	Bronx, NY	4/16/55	Bologna, Joseph	Brooklyn, NY	12/30/38
Barrie, Barbara	Chicago, IL	5/23/31	Bolton, Michael	New Haven, CT	2/26/53
Barrino, Fantasia	High Point, NC	6/30/84	Bonet, Lisa	San Francisco, CA	11/16/67
Barrymore, Drew	Los Angeles, CA	2/22/75	Bonham Carter, Helena	London, England, UK	5/26/66
Bartoli, Cecilia	Rome, Italy	6/4/66	Bon Jovi, Jon	Sayreville, NJ	3/2/62
Barton, Misha	London, England, UK	1/24/86	Bono	Dublin, Ireland	5/10/60
Baryshnikov, Mikhail	Riga, Latvia	1/28/48	Boone, Debby	Hackensack, NJ	9/22/56
Basinger, Kim	Athens, GA	12/8/53	Boone, Pat	Jacksonville, FL	6/1/34
Bass, Lance	Laurel, MS	5/4/79	Boreanaz, David	Buffalo, NY	5/16/69
Bassett, Angela	New York, NY	8/16/58	Borgnine, Ernest	Hamden, CT	1/24/17
Bassey, Shirley	Cardiff, Wales, UK	1/8/37	Bosco, Philip	Jersey City, NJ	9/26/30
Bateman, Jason	Rye, NY	1/14/69	Bostwick, Barry	San Mateo, CA	2/24/45
Bateman, Justine	Rye, NY	2/19/66	Bosworth, Kate	Los Angeles, CA	1/2/83
Bates, Kathy	Memphis, TN	6/28/48	Bottoms, Timothy	Santa Barbara, CA	8/30/51
Batt, Bryan	New Orleans, LA	3/1/63	Bowen, Julie	Baltimore, MD	3/3/70
Battle, Kathleen	Portsmouth, OH	8/13/48	Bowie, David	London, England, UK	1/8/47
Baxter, Meredith	South Pasadena, CA	6/21/47	Bowles, Peter	London, England, UK	10/16/36
Bean, Orson	Burlington, VT	7/22/28	Bow Wow	Columbus, OH	3/9/87
Bean, Sean	Sheffield, England, UK	4/17/59	Boxleitner, Bruce	Elgin, IL	5/12/50
Beatty, Ned	Louisville, KY	7/6/37	Boy George	Bexleyheath, England, UK	6/14/61
Beatty, Warren	Richmond, VA	3/30/37	Boyle, Lara Flynn	Davenport, IA	3/24/70
Beauvais, Garcelle	St. Marc, Haiti	11/26/66	Bracco, Lorraine	Brooklyn, NY	10/2/55
Beck	Los Angeles, CA	7/8/70	Brady, Wayne	Orlando, FL	6/2/72
Beck, Jeff	Wallington, Surrey, Eng., UK	6/24/44	Braff, Zach	S. Orange, NJ	4/6/75
Beckham, Victoria	Hertfordshire, England, UK	4/17/74	Branagh, Kenneth	Belfast, N. Ireland, UK	12/10/60
Beckinsale, Kate	London, England, UK	7/26/73	Brand, Russell	Grays, Essex, UK	6/4/75
Bedelia, Bonnie	New York, NY	3/25/48	Brandauer, Klaus Maria	Steiermark, Austria	6/22/44
Begley, Ed, Jr.	Los Angeles, CA	9/16/49	Brandy (Norwood)	McComb, MS	2/11/79
Behar, Joy	Brooklyn, NY	10/7/43	Braschi, Nicoletta	Cesena, Italy	4/19/60
Belafonte, Harry	New York, NY	3/1/27	Bratt, Benjamin	San Francisco, CA	12/16/63
Bell, Art	Camp Lejeune, NC	6/17/45	Braugher, Andre	Chicago, IL	7/1/62
Bell, Catherine	London, England, UK	8/14/68	Braxton, Toni	Severn, MD	10/7/66
Bell, Kristen	Huntington Woods, MI	7/18/80	Bremner, Ewen	Edinburgh, Scotland, UK	1/23/72
Bello, Maria	Norristown, PA	4/18/67	Brendon, Nicholas	Los Angeles, CA	4/12/71
Belmondo, Jean-Paul	Neuilly-sur-Seine, France	4/9/33	Brennan, Eileen	Los Angeles, CA	9/3/35
Belushi, Jim	Chicago, IL	6/15/54	Brenneman, Amy	Glastonbury, CT	6/22/64
Belzer, Richard	Bridgeport, CT	8/4/44	Brenner, David	Philadelphia, PA	2/4/45
Benanti, Laura	Kinnelon, NJ	7/15/79	Bridges, Beau	Los Angeles, CA	12/9/41
Benatar, Pat	Brooklyn, NY	1/10/53	Bridges, Jeff	Los Angeles, CA	12/4/49
Benedict, Dirk	Helena, MT	3/1/45	Brightman, Sarah	Berkhamsted, England, UK	8/14/60
Benigni, Roberto	Misericordia, Italy	10/27/52	Brimley, Wilford	Salt Lake City, UT	9/27/34
Bening, Annette	Topeka, KS	5/29/58	Brinkley, Christie	Malibu, CA	2/2/54
Benjamin, Richard	New York, NY	5/22/38	Britton, Connie	Boston, MA	3/6/67
Bennett, Alan	Leeds, England, UK	5/9/34	Broadbent, Jim	Lincolnshire, England, UK	5/24/49
Bennett, Tony	Astoria, Queens, NY	8/3/26	Broderick, Matthew	New York, NY	3/21/62
Benson, George	Pittsburgh, PA	3/22/43	Brody, Adam	San Diego, CA	12/15/79
Benson, Robby	Dallas, TX	1/21/56	Brody, Adrien	New York, NY	4/14/73
Berenger, Tom	Chicago, IL	5/31/50	Brolin, James	Los Angeles, CA	7/18/40
Bergen, Candice	Beverly Hills, CA	5/9/46	Brolin, Josh	Los Angeles, CA	2/12/68
Bergen, Polly	Knoxville, TN	7/14/30	Brooks, Albert	Beverly Hills, CA	7/22/47
Bergeron, Tom	Haverhill, MA	5/6/55	Brooks, Garth	Tulsa, OK	2/7/62
Berlinger, Warren	Brooklyn, NY	8/31/37	Brooks, James L.	North Bergen, NJ	5/9/40
Berman, Shelley	Chicago, IL	2/3/26	Brooks, Mel	Brooklyn, NY	6/28/26
Bernard, Crystal	Garland, TX	9/30/61	Brosnan, Pierce	Navan, Co. Meath, Ireland	5/16/53
Bernhard, Sandra	Flint, MI	6/6/55	Brown, Blair	Washington, DC	4/23/46
Bernsen, Corbin	N. Hollywood, CA	9/7/54	Brown, Bobby	Roxbury, MA	2/5/69
Berry, Chuck	St. Louis, MO	10/18/26	Brown, Bryan	Panania, Australia	6/23/47
Berry, Halle	Cleveland, OH	8/14/66	Brown, Chris	Tappahannock, VA	5/5/89
Berry, Ken	Moline, IL	11/3/33	Brown, Foxy	Brooklyn, NY	9/6/79
Bertinelli, Valerie	Wilmington, DE	4/23/60	Browne, Jackson	Heidelberg, Germany	10/9/48
Bertolucci, Bernardo	Parma, Italy	3/16/40	Brubeck, Dave	Concord, CA	12/6/20
Bettany, Paul	London, England, UK	5/27/71	Bryson, Peabo	Greenville, SC	4/13/51
Biafra, Jello	Boulder, CO	6/17/58	Bublé, Michael	Burnaby, BC, Canada	9/9/75
Bialik, Mayim	San Diego, CA	12/12/75	Buckley, Betty	Big Spring, TX	7/3/47
Bieber, Justin	Stratford, ON, Canada	3/1/94	Buffett, Jimmy	Pascagoula, MS	12/25/46
Biel, Jessica	Ely, MN	3/3/82	Bujold, Geneviève	Montreal, QC, Canada	7/1/42
Big Boi	Savannah, GA	2/1/75	Bullock, Sandra	Arlington, VA	7/26/64
Bigelow, Kathryn	San Carlos, CA	11/27/51	Bumbry, Grace	St. Louis, MO	1/4/37
Biggs, Jason	Pompton Plains, NJ	5/12/78	Bündchen, Gisele	Horizontina, Brazil	7/20/80
Bikel, Theodore	Vienna, Austria	5/2/24	Burghoff, Gary	Bristol, CT	5/24/43
Bilson, Rachel	Los Angeles, CA	8/25/81	Burke, Delta	Orlando, FL	7/30/56
Binoche, Juliette	Paris, France	3/9/64	Burnett, Carol	San Antonio, TX	4/26/33
Birch, Thora	Beverly Hills, CA	3/11/82	Burns, Edward	Woodside, Queens, NY	1/29/68
Birney, David	Washington, DC	4/23/39	Burrell, Ty	Grants Pass, OR	8/22/67
Bisset, Jacqueline	Weybridge, England, UK	9/13/44	Burstyn, Ellen	Detroit, MI	12/7/32
Bissett, Josie	Seattle, WA	10/5/70	Burton, LeVar	Landstuhl, Germany	2/16/57
Björk	Reykjavik, Iceland	11/21/65	Burton, Tim	Burbank, CA	8/25/58
Black, Clint	Long Branch, NJ	2/4/62	Buscemi, Steve	Brooklyn, NY	12/13/57
Black, Jack	Santa Monica, CA	4/7/69	Busey, Gary	Goose Creek, TX	6/29/44
Black, Karen	Park Ridge, IL	7/1/42	Busfield, Timothy	Lansing, MI	6/12/57
Blades, Ruben	Panama City, Panama	7/16/48	Butler, Brett	Montgomery, AL	1/30/58
Blair, Linda	St. Louis, MO	1/22/59	Butler, Dan	Fort Wayne, IN	12/2/54
Blair, Selma	Southfield, MI	6/23/72	Butler, Gerard	Glasgow, Scot., UK	11/13/69
Blake, Robert	Nutley, NJ	9/18/33	Butz, Norbert Leo	St. Louis, MO	1/30/67
Blanchett, Cate	Melbourne, Australia	5/14/69	Buzzi, Ruth	Westerly, RI	7/24/36
Bledsoe, Tempestt	Chicago, IL	8/1/73	Bynes, Amanda	Thousand Oaks, CA	4/3/86
Bleeth, Yasmine	New York, NY	6/14/68	Byrne, David	Dumbarton, Scotland, UK	5/14/52
Blethyn, Brenda	Ramsgate, Kent, Eng., UK	2/20/46	Byrne, Gabriel	Dublin, Ireland	5/12/50
Blige, Mary J.	Bronx, NY	1/11/71	Byrne, Rose	Sydney, NSW, Australia	7/24/79
Bloom, Claire	London, England, UK	2/15/31	Caan, James	Bronx, NY	3/26/40
Bloom, Orlando	Canterbury, England, UK	1/13/77	Caballe, Montserrat	Barcelona, Spain	4/12/33
Blyth, Ann	Mt. Kisco, NY	8/16/28	Caesar, Sid	Yonkers, NY	9/8/22
Bochco, Steven	New York, NY	12/16/43	Cage, Nicolas	Long Beach, CA	1/7/64
Bocelli, Andrea	Lajatico, Italy	9/22/58	Cain, Dean	Mt. Clemens, MI	7/31/66
Bogdanovich, Peter	Kingston, NY	7/30/39	Caine, Michael	London, England, UK	3/14/33

Name	Birthplace	Birthdate
Caldwell, Zoe	Hawthorn, Australia	9/14/33
Callow, Simon	London, England, UK	6/15/49
Cameron, James	Kapuskasing, ON, Canada	8/16/54
Cameron, Kirk	Panorama City, CA	10/12/70
Campanella, Joseph	New York, NY	11/21/27
Campbell, Bruce	Royal Oak, MI	6/22/58
Campbell, Glen	Delight, AR	4/22/36
Campbell, Naomi	South London, Eng., UK	5/22/70
Campbell, Neve	Guelph, ON, Canada	10/3/73
Campion, Jane	Waikanae, New Zealand	4/30/54
Cannavale, Bobby	Union City, NJ	5/3/71
Cannell, Stephen J.	Pasadena, CA	2/5/41
Cannon, Dyan	Tacoma, WA	1/4/37
Cannon, Nick	San Diego, CA	10/8/80
Capshaw, Kate	Ft. Worth, TX	11/3/53
Cara, Irene	New York, NY	3/18/59
Cardellini, Linda	Redwood City, CA	6/25/75
Cardinale, Claudia	Tunis, Tunisia	4/15/38
Carell, Steve	Concord, MA	8/16/62
Carey, Drew	Cleveland, OH	5/23/58
Carey, Harry, Jr.	Saugus, CA	5/16/21
Carey, Mariah	Huntington, NY	3/27/70
Cariou, Len	St. Boniface, MB, Canada	9/30/39
Carlton, Vanessa	Milford, PA	8/16/80
Carlyle, Robert	Glasgow, Scotland, UK	4/14/61
Carmen, Eric	Cleveland, OH	8/11/49
Caron, Leslie	Boulogne, France	7/1/31
Carpenter, John	Carthage, NY	1/16/48
Carpenter, Mary Chapin	Princeton, NJ	2/21/58
Carr, Vikki	El Paso, TX	7/19/41
Carreras, Jose	Barcelona, Spain	12/5/46
Carrere, Tia	Honolulu, HI	1/2/67
Carrey, Jim	Newmarket, ON, Canada	1/17/62
Carroll, Diahann	Bronx, NY	7/17/35
Carroll, Pat	Shreveport, LA	5/5/27
Carter, Jack	Brooklyn, NY	6/24/23
Carter, Lynda	Phoenix, AZ	7/24/51
Carter, Nick	Jamestown, NY	1/28/80
Carter, Ron	Ferndale, MI	5/4/37
Cartwright, Nancy	Kettering, OH	10/25/59
Caruso, David	Forest Hills, Queens, NY	1/17/56
Carvey, Dana	Missoula, MT	6/2/55
Case, Sharon	Detroit, MI	2/9/71
Cash, Rosanne	Memphis, TN	5/24/55
Cassidy, David	New York, NY	4/12/50
Castellaneta, Dan	Chicago, IL	10/29/57
Castle-Hughes, Keisha	Donnybrook, Australia	3/24/90
Cates, Phoebe	New York, NY	7/16/63
Cattrall, Kim	Liverpool, England, UK	8/21/56
Cavanagh, Tom	Ottawa, ON, Canada	10/26/63
Cavett, Dick	Gibbon, NE	11/19/36
Cavill, Henry	Jersey, Channel Islands	5/5/83
Cedric the Entertainer	Jefferson City, MO	4/24/64
Cera, Michael	Brampton, ON, Canada	6/7/88
Chabert, Lacey	Purvis, MS	9/30/82
Chalke, Sarah	Ottawa, ON, Canada	8/27/76
Chamberlain, Richard	Beverly Hills, CA	3/31/34
Chambers, Justin	Springfield, OH	7/11/70
Chan, Jackie	Hong Kong	4/7/54
Chance, Greyson	Wichita Falls, TX	8/16/97
Chandler, Kyle	Buffalo, NY	9/17/65
Channing, Carol	Seattle, WA	1/31/21
Channing, Stockard	New York, NY	2/13/44
Chaplin, Geraldine	Santa Monica, CA	7/31/44
Chapman, Tracy	Cleveland, OH	3/30/64
Chappelle, Dave	Washington, DC	8/24/73
Charles, Josh	Baltimore, MD	9/15/71
Charo	Murcia, Spain	1/15/51?
Chase, Chevy	New York, NY	10/8/43
Chasez, J.C. (Joshua)	Washington, DC	8/8/76
Cheadle, Don	Kansas City, MO	11/29/64
Checker, Chubby	Spring Gulley, SC	10/3/41
Chenoweth, Kristin	Broken Arrow, OK	7/24/68
Cher	El Centro, CA	5/20/46
Chesney, Kenny	Lutrelle, TN	3/26/68
Chianese, Dominic	Bronx, NY	2/24/31
Chiba, Sonny	Fukuoka, Kyushu, Japan	1/23/39
Chiklis, Michael	Lowell, MA	8/30/63
Cho, Margaret	San Francisco, CA	12/5/68
Chong, Rae Dawn	Edmonton, AB, Canada	2/28/61
Chong, Thomas	Edmonton, AB, Canada	5/24/38
Chow Yun-Fat	Lamma Island, Hong Kong	5/18/55
Christensen, Hayden	Vancouver, BC, Canada	4/19/81
Christie, Julie	Chukua, Assam, India	4/14/41
Christopher, William	Evanston, IL	10/20/32
Chuck D	Roosevelt, NY	8/1/60
Church, Charlotte	Llandaff, Cardiff, Wales, UK	2/21/86
Church, Thomas Haden	El Paso, TX	6/17/61
Clapp, Gordon	North Conway, NH	9/24/48
Clapton, Eric	Ripley, Surrey, England, UK	3/30/45
Clark, Anthony	Lynchburg, VA	4/4/64
Clark, Dick	Mt. Vernon, NY	11/30/29
Clark, Petula	Epson, Surrey, England, UK	11/15/32
Clark, Roy	Meherrin, VA	4/15/33
Clarkson, Kelly	Burleson, TX	4/24/82
Clarkson, Patricia	New Orleans, LA	12/29/59

Name	Birthplace	Birthdate
Clay, Andrew Dice	Brooklyn, NY	9/29/57
Cleese, John	Weston-super-Mare, Eng., UK	10/27/39
Cliburn, Van	Shreveport, LA	7/12/34
Clooney, George	Lexington, KY	5/6/61
Close, Glenn	Greenwich, CT	3/19/47
Cocker, Joe	Sheffield, England, UK	5/20/44
Coen, Ethan	St. Louis Park, MN	9/21/57
Coen, Joel	St. Louis Park, MN	11/29/54
Cohen, Leonard	Montreal, QC, Canada	9/21/34
Cohen, Sacha Baron	London, England, UK	10/13/71
Colbert, Stephen	Charleston, SC	5/13/64
Cole, Gary	Park Ridge, IL	9/20/56
Cole, Natalie	Los Angeles, CA	2/6/50
Cole, Olivia	Memphis, TN	11/26/42
Cole, Paula	Rockport, MA	4/5/68
Coleman, Dabney	Austin, TX	1/3/32
Coleman, Ornette	Fort Worth, TX	3/19/30
Colfer, Chris	Fresno, CA	5/27/90
Collette, Toni	Blacktown, Australia	11/1/72
Collins, Joan	London, England, UK	5/23/33
Collins, Judy	Seattle, WA	5/1/39
Collins, Pauline	Exmouth, England, UK	9/3/40
Collins, Phil	London, England, UK	1/30/51
Collins, Stephen	Des Moines, IA	10/1/47
Colvin, Shawn	Vermillion, SD	1/10/56
Combs, Sean	New York, NY	11/4/69
Connelly, Jennifer	Round Top, NY	12/12/70
Connery, Sean	Edinburgh, Scotland, UK	8/25/30
Connick, Harry, Jr.	New Orleans, LA	9/11/67
Connolly, Kevin	Patchogue, NY	3/5/74
Connors, Mike	Fresno, CA	8/15/25
Conrad, Robert	Chicago, IL	3/1/35
Conroy, Frances	Monroe, GA	11/13/53
Constantine, Michael	Reading, PA	5/22/27
Conti, Tom	Paisley, Scotland, UK	11/22/41
Conway, Tim	Willoughby, OH	12/15/33
Cook, Barbara	Atlanta, GA	10/25/27
Cook, David	Houston, TX	12/20/82
Coolidge, Rita	Nashville, TN	5/1/45
Coolio	Compton, CA	8/1/63
Cooper, Alice	Detroit, MI	2/4/48
Cooper, Bradley	Philadelphia, PA	1/5/75
Cooper, Chris	Kansas City, MO	7/9/51
Copperfield, David	Metuchen, NJ	9/16/56
Coppola, Francis Ford	Detroit, MI	4/7/39
Coppola, Sofia	New York, NY	5/14/71
Corbett, John	Wheeling, WV	5/9/61
Corbin, Barry	Lamesa, TX	10/16/40
Corea, Chick	Chelsea, MA	6/12/41
Corgan, Billy	Elk Grove, IL	3/17/67
Cornell, Chris	Seattle, WA	7/20/64
Corwin, Jeff	Norwell, MA	7/11/67
Cosby, Bill	Philadelphia, PA	7/12/37
Cosgrove, Miranda	Los Angeles, CA	5/14/93
Costas, Bob	Astoria, Queens, NY	3/22/52
Costello, Elvis	London, England, UK	8/25/54
Costner, Kevin	Compton, CA	1/18/55
Cotillard, Marion	Paris, France	9/30/75
Courtenay, Tom	Hull, England, UK	2/25/37
Cowell, Simon	London, England, UK	10/7/59
Cox, Brian	Dundee, Scotland, UK	6/1/46
Cox, Ronny	Cloudcroft, NM	7/23/38
Cox Arquette, Courteney	Birmingham, AL	6/15/64
Coyote, Peter	New York, NY	10/10/42
Craig, Daniel	Chester, England, UK	3/2/68
Cranston, Bryan	San Fernando Valley, CA	3/7/56
Crawford, Cindy	DeKalb, IL	2/20/66
Crawford, Michael	Salisbury, England, UK	1/19/42
Criss, Darren	San Francisco, CA	2/5/87
Cromwell, James	Los Angeles, CA	1/27/40
Crosby, David	Los Angeles, CA	8/14/41
Cross, Ben	London, England, UK	12/16/47
Cross, Marcia	Marlborough, MA	3/25/62
Crouse, Lindsay	New York, NY	5/12/48
Crow, Sheryl	Kennett, MO	2/11/62
Crowe, Cameron	Palm Springs, CA	7/13/57
Crowe, Russell	Wellington, New Zealand	4/7/64
Crowell, Rodney	Houston, TX	8/17/50
Crudup, Billy	Manhasset, NY	7/8/68
Cruise, Tom	Syracuse, NY	7/3/62
Cruz, Penelope	Madrid, Spain	4/28/74
Cryer, Jon	New York, NY	4/16/65
Crystal, Billy	Long Beach, NY	3/14/47
Culkin, Kieran	New York, NY	9/30/82
Culkin, Macaulay	New York, NY	8/26/80
Culkin, Rory	New York, NY	7/21/89
Cullum, John	Knoxville, TN	3/2/30
Cumming, Alan	Aberfeldy, Perthshire, Scotland, UK	1/27/65
Cuoco, Kaley	Camarillo, CA	11/30/85
Curry, Tim	Grappenhall, Cheshire, England, UK	4/19/46
Curtin, Jane	Cambridge, MA	9/6/47
Curtis, Jamie Lee	Los Angeles, CA	11/22/58
Cusack, Joan	New York, NY	10/11/62
Cusack, John	Evanston, IL	6/28/66
Cyrus, Billy Ray	Flatwoods, KY	8/25/61

Name	Birthplace	Birthdate
Cyrus, Miley	Nashville, TN.	11/23/92
Dafoe, Willem	Appleton, WI	7/22/55
Dahl, Arlene	Minneapolis, MN	8/11/28
Dale, Jim	Rothwell, England, UK.	8/15/35
Dalton, Timothy	Colwyn Bay, Wales, UK	3/21/46
Daltrey, Roger	London, England, UK	3/1/44
Daly, Carson	Santa Monica, CA	6/22/73
Daly, Timothy	New York, NY	3/1/56
Daly, Tyne	Madison, WI	2/21/46
Damon, Matt	Cambridge, MA	10/8/70
Damone, Vic	Brooklyn, NY	6/12/28
Dane, Eric	San Francisco, CA.	11/9/72
Danes, Claire	New York, NY	4/12/79
D'Angelo	Richmond, VA	2/11/74
D'Angelo, Beverly	Columbus, OH.	11/15/54
Daniels, Anthony	Salisbury, England, UK	2/21/46
Daniels, Charlie	Wilmington, NC	10/28/36
Daniels, Jeff	Athens, GA	2/19/55
Daniels, William	Brooklyn, NY	3/31/27
Danner, Blythe	Rosemont, PA	2/3/43
Danson, Ted	San Diego, CA.	12/29/47
Danza, Tony	Brooklyn, NY	4/21/51
Darby, Kim	Hollywood, CA.	7/8/48
Daughtry, Chris	Roanoke Rapids, NC	12/26/79
David, Larry	Brooklyn, NY	7/2/47
Davidson, John	Pittsburgh, PA	12/13/41
Davis, Ann B.	Schenectady, NY	5/5/26
Davis, Clifton	Chicago, IL	10/4/45
Davis, Geena	Wareham, MA	1/21/56
Davis, Hope	Englewood, NJ	3/23/64
Davis, Judy	Perth, Australia	4/23/55
Davis, Kristin	Boulder, CO.	2/24/65
Davis, Mac	Lubbock, TX	1/21/42
Davis, Viola	Saint Matthews, SC	8/11/65
Dawber, Pam	Farmington Hills, MI.	10/18/51
Dawson, Richard	Gosport, Hampshire, Eng., UK	11/20/32
Dawson, Rosario	New York, NY	5/9/79
Day, Doris	Cincinnati, OH.	4/3/24
Day-Lewis, Daniel	London, England, UK	4/29/57
Dee, Ruby	Cleveland, OH	10/27/24
DeFranco, Buddy	Camden, NJ	2/17/23
DeGeneres, Ellen	Metairie, LA.	1/26/58
DeHaven, Gloria	Los Angeles, CA	7/23/25
De Havilland, Olivia	Tokyo, Japan.	7/1/16
Delaney, Kim.	Philadelphia, PA	11/29/61
Delany, Dana	New York, NY	3/13/56
De la Rocha, Zack	Long Beach, CA	1/12/70
Delon, Alain	Sceaux, France	11/8/35
Del Toro, Benicio	Santurce, Puerto Rico	2/19/67
Demme, Jonathan	Baldwin, NY.	2/22/44
De Mornay, Rebecca	Santa Rosa, CA	8/29/62
Dempsey, Patrick	Lewiston, ME.	1/13/66
Dench, Judi	York, England, UK.	12/9/34
Deneuve, Catherine	Paris, France	10/22/43
De Niro, Robert.	New York, NY	8/17/43
Dennehy, Brian	Bridgeport, CT.	7/9/38
DePalma, Brian	Newark, NJ	9/11/40
Depardieu, Gerard	Chateauroux, France	12/27/48
Depp, Johnny	Owensboro, KY	6/9/63
Derek, Bo	Long Beach, CA	11/20/56
Dern, Bruce	Winnetka, IL	6/4/36
Dern, Laura	Santa Monica, CA	2/10/67
De Rossi, Portia	Melbourne, Victoria, Austral.	1/31/73
DeVito, Danny	Neptune, NJ	11/17/44
DeWitt, Joyce	Wheeling, WV	4/23/49
DeWyze, Lee	Mount Prospect, IL	4/2/86
Dey, Susan	Pekin, IL	12/10/52
Diamond, Neil	Brooklyn, NY	1/24/41
Diaz, Cameron	San Diego, CA.	8/30/72
DiCaprio, Leonardo.	Hollywood, CA.	11/11/74
Dick, Andy	Charleston, SC	12/21/65
Dickinson, Angie	Kulm, ND.	9/30/31
Diesel, Vin.	New York, NY	7/18/67
Diggs, Taye	Essex Co., NJ	1/2/72
Diller, Phyllis	Lima, OH.	7/17/17
Dillman, Bradford	San Francisco, CA	4/14/30
Dillon, Kevin	Mamaroneck, NY.	8/19/65
Dillon, Matt	New Rochelle, NY	2/18/64
Dinklage, Peter	Mendham, NJ	6/11/69
Dion, Celine	Charlemagne, QC, Canada	3/30/68
DioGuardi, Kara	Scarsdale, NY	12/9/70
Djalili, Omid	London, England, UK	9/30/65
Dobson, Kevin	Jackson Heights, Queens, NY	3/18/43
Doherty, Shannen	Memphis, TN.	4/12/71
Dolenz, Mickey	Los Angeles, CA	3/8/45
Domingo, Placido	Madrid, Spain	1/21/41
Domino, Fats	New Orleans, LA.	2/26/28
Donahue, Phil	Cleveland, OH.	12/21/35
D'Onofrio, Vincent	Brooklyn, NY.	6/30/59
Donovan (Leitch)	Glasgow, Scotland, UK	5/10/46
Donovan, Tate.	Tenafly, NJ.	9/25/63
Dorn, Michael	Luling, TX	12/9/52
Dorough, Howie	Orlando, FL	8/22/73
Dotrice, Roy	Guernsey, England, UK	5/26/23
Douglas, Kirk	Amsterdam, NY	12/9/16
Douglas, Michael	New Brunswick, NJ	9/25/44

Name	Birthplace	Birthdate
Dourdan, Gary	Philadelphia, PA	12/11/66
Dow, Tony	Hollywood, CA.	4/13/45
Down, Lesley-Anne.	London, England, UK	3/17/54
Downey, Robert, Jr.	New York, NY	4/4/65
Downey, Roma	Derry, N. Ireland, UK	5/6/60
Downs, Hugh	Akron, OH	2/14/21
Drescher, Fran	Flushing, Queens, NY	9/30/57
Dreyfuss, Richard	Brooklyn, NY	10/29/47
Driver, Minnie	London, England, UK	1/31/70
Dryer, Fred	Hawthorne, CA	7/6/46
Duchovny, David	New York, NY	8/7/60
Duff, Haylie	Houston, TX	2/19/85
Duff, Hilary	Houston, TX	9/28/87
Duffy (Aimee Anne).	Bangor, Gwynedd, Wales, UK	6/23/84
Duffy, Julia	Minneapolis, MN	6/27/51
Duffy, Patrick	Townsend, MT	3/17/49
Duhamel, Josh	Minot, ND	11/14/72
Dukakis, Olympia	Lowell, MA.	6/20/31
Duke, Patty	Elmhurst, Queens, NY.	12/14/46
Dullea, Keir	Cleveland, OH.	5/30/36
Dunaway, Faye	Bascom, FL.	1/14/41
Duncan, Lindsay	Edinburgh, Scotland, UK	11/7/50
Duncan, Sandy	Henderson, TX	2/20/46
Dunne, Griffin	New York, NY	6/8/55
Dunst, Kirsten	Point Pleasant, NJ.	4/30/82
Durbin, Deanna	Winnipeg, MB, Canada	12/4/21
Durning, Charles.	Highland Falls, NY.	2/28/23
Dussault, Nancy	Pensacola, FL	6/30/36
Dutton, Charles S.	Baltimore, MD	1/30/51
Duvall, Robert.	San Diego, CA.	1/5/31
Duvall, Shelley	Houston, TX	7/7/49
Dylan, Bob	Duluth, MN	5/24/41
Dylan, Jakob	New York, NY	12/9/69
Dysart, Richard	Brighton, MA	3/30/29
Dzundza, George	Rosenheim, Germany	7/19/45
Eads, George	Fort Worth, TX.	3/1/67
Easton, Sheena	Bellshill, Scotland, UK	4/27/59
Eastwood, Clint	San Francisco, CA.	5/31/30
Ebersole, Christine	Chicago, IL	2/21/53
Ebert, Roger	Urbana, IL	6/18/42
Eckhart, Aaron	Cupertino, CA	3/12/68
Eden, Barbara	Tucson, AZ	8/23/34
Edwards, Anthony	Santa Barbara, CA	7/19/62
Efron, Zac	San Luis Obispo, CA	10/18/87
Ehle, Jennifer	Winston-Salem, NC	12/29/69
Eichhorn, Lisa.	Reading, PA.	2/4/52
Eikenberry, Jill	New Haven, CT	1/21/47
Eisenberg, Jesse	Bayside, NY.	10/5/83
Ekberg, Anita	Malmo, Sweden.	9/29/31
Ekland, Britt	Stockholm, Sweden.	10/6/42
Electra, Carmen	Cincinnati, OH.	4/20/72
Elfman, Jenna	Los Angeles, CA	9/30/71
Elizondo, Hector	New York, NY	12/22/36
Elliott, Bob	Boston, MA	3/26/23
Elliott, Chris	New York, NY	5/31/60
Elliott, Missy	Portsmouth, VA	7/1/71
Elliott, Sam	Sacramento, CA	8/9/44
Elvira	Manhattan, KS.	9/17/51
Emerson, Michael	Cedar Rapids, IA	9/7/54
Eminem	St. Joseph, MO	10/17/72
Enberg, Dick	Mt. Clemens, MI	1/9/35
Englund, Robert	Glendale, CA.	6/6/49
Enya	Gweedore, Ireland.	5/17/61
Ephron, Nora	New York, NY	5/19/41
Ermey, R. Lee.	Emporia, KS	3/24/44
Estefan, Gloria	Havana, Cuba	9/1/57
Estevez, Emilio	New York, NY	5/12/62
Estrada, Erik	New York, NY	3/16/49
Etheridge, Melissa	Leavenworth, KS.	5/29/61
Evans, Linda.	Hartford, CT	11/18/42
Evans, Robert.	New York, NY	6/29/30
Everett, Chad	South Bend, IN	6/11/36
Everett, Rupert	Norfolk, England, UK.	5/29/59
Everly, Don	Brownie, KY.	2/1/37
Everly, Phil	Chicago, IL	1/19/39
Evigan, Greg	South Amboy, NJ	10/14/53
Fabares, Shelley	Santa Monica, CA	1/19/44
Fabian	Philadelphia, PA	2/6/43
Fabio	Milan, Italy	3/15/61
Fabolous	Brooklyn, NY	11/18/77
Fairchild, Morgan	Dallas, TX	2/3/50
Faison, Donald	New York, NY	6/22/74
Falana, Lola	Philadelphia, PA	9/11/42
Falco, Edie	Brooklyn, NY	7/5/63
Fallon, Jimmy	Brooklyn, NY	9/19/74
Fanning, Dakota	Conyers, GA	2/23/94
Farentino, James	Brooklyn, NY	2/24/38
Fargo, Donna	Mt. Airy, NC	11/10/49
Farina, Dennis	Chicago, IL	2/29/44
Farr, Jamie	Toledo, OH	7/1/34
Farrell, Colin	Dublin, Ireland.	5/31/76
Farrell, Mike	St. Paul, Mn	2/6/39
Farrell, Perry	Bayside, Queens, NY	3/29/59
Farrelly, Bobby	Cumberland, RI.	6/17/58
Farrelly, Peter	Phoenixville, PA.	12/17/56
Farrow, Mia.	Los Angeles, CA.	2/9/45

Name	Birthplace	Birthdate
Fassbender, Michael	Heidelberg, Germany	4/2/77
Fatone, Joey	Brooklyn, NY	1/28/77
Feinstein, Michael	Columbus, OH	9/7/56
Feldon, Barbara	Bethel Park, PA	3/12/32
Feldshuh, Tovah	New York, NY	12/27/52
Feliciano, Jose	Lares, Puerto Rico	9/10/45
Fenn, Sherilyn	Detroit, MI	2/1/65
Fergie	Hacienda Heights, CA	3/27/75
Ferguson, Jesse Tyler	Missoula, MT	10/22/75
Ferrara, Jerry	Brooklyn, NY	11/29/79
Ferrell, Conchata	Charleston, WV	3/28/43
Ferrell, Will	Irvine, CA	7/16/67
Ferrera, America	Los Angeles, CA	4/18/84
Feuerstein, Mark	New York, NY	6/8/71
Fey, Tina	Upper Darby, PA	5/18/70
Field, Sally	Pasadena, CA	11/6/46
Fiennes, Joseph	Salisbury, England, UK	5/27/70
Fiennes, Ralph	Suffolk, England, UK	12/22/62
Fierstein, Harvey	Brooklyn, NY	6/6/54
50 Cent	Jamaica, Queens, NY	7/6/76
Filicia, Thom	Syracuse, NY	5/17/69
Fincher, David	Denver, CO	5/10/62
Finney, Albert	Salford, England, UK	5/9/36
Fiorentino, Linda	Philadelphia, PA	3/9/60
Firth, Colin	Grayshott, England, UK	9/10/60
Firth, Peter	Bradford, Yorkshire, Eng., UK	10/27/53
Fischer, Jenna	Ft. Wayne, IN	3/7/74
Fischer-Dieskau, Dietrich	Berlin, Germany	5/28/25
Fishburne, Laurence	Augusta, GA	7/30/61
Fisher, Carrie	Beverly Hills, CA	10/21/56
Flack, Roberta	Black Mountain, NC	2/10/39
Flanagan, Fionnula	Dublin, Ireland	12/10/41
Flavor Flav	Roosevelt, NY	3/16/59
Fleetwood, Mick	Redruth, Cornwall, Eng., UK	6/24/42
Fleming, Rhonda	Hollywood, CA	8/10/23
Fletcher, Louise	Birmingham, AL	7/22/34
Flockhart, Calista	Freeport, IL	11/11/64
Florek, Dann	Flat Rock, MI	5/1/50
Fogerty, John	Berkeley, CA	5/28/45
Foley, Dave	Etobicoke, ON, Canada	1/4/63
Fonda, Bridget	Los Angeles, CA	1/27/64
Fonda, Jane	New York, NY	12/21/37
Fonda, Peter	New York, NY	2/23/40
Fontaine, Joan	Tokyo, Japan	10/22/17
Ford, Faith	Alexandria, LA	9/14/64
Ford, Harrison	Chicago, IL	7/13/42
Forman, Milos	Caslav, Czechoslovakia	2/18/32
Forte, Will	Alameda Co., CA	6/17/70
Foster, Jodie	Los Angeles, CA	11/19/62
Foster, Sutton	Statesboro, GA	3/18/75
Fox, James	London, England, UK	5/19/39
Fox, Jorja	New York, NY	7/7/68
Fox, Matthew	Crowheart, WY	7/14/66
Fox, Megan	Rockwood, TN	5/16/86
Fox, Michael J.	Edmonton, AB, Canada	6/9/61
Fox, Vivica A.	South Bend, IN	7/30/64
Foxworth, Robert	Houston, TX	11/1/41
Foxworthy, Jeff	Atlanta, GA	9/6/58
Foxx, Jamie	Terrell, TX	12/13/67
Frampton, Peter	Kent, England, UK	4/22/50
Francis, Connie	Newark, NJ	12/12/38
Franco, James	Palo Alto, CA	4/19/78
Franken, Al	New York, NY	5/21/51
Franklin, Aretha	Memphis, TN	3/25/42
Franklin, Bonnie	Santa Monica, CA	1/6/44
Franz, Dennis	Maywood, IL	10/28/44
Fraser, Brendan	Indianapolis, IN	12/3/68
Freeman, Al, Jr.	San Antonio, TX	3/21/34
Freeman, Mona	Baltimore, MD	6/9/26
Freeman, Morgan	Memphis, TN	6/1/37
French, Dawn	Holyhead, Wales, UK	10/11/57
Fricker, Brenda	Dublin, Ireland	2/17/45
Friedkin, William	Chicago, IL	8/29/39
Frost, David	Tenterden, England, UK	4/7/39
Fry, Stephen	London, England, UK	8/24/57
Fuentes, Daisy	Havana, Cuba	11/17/66
Fuller, Robert	Troy, NY	7/29/34
Funicello, Annette	Utica, NY	10/22/42
Furlong, Edward	Pasadena, CA	8/2/77
Furtado, Nelly	Victoria, BC, Canada	12/2/78
Gabor, Zsa Zsa	Budapest, Hungary	2/6/17
Gabriel, Peter	Surrey, England, UK	2/13/50
Gaines, Boyd	Atlanta, GA	5/11/53
Galecki, Johnny	Bree, Belgium	4/30/75
Galifianakis, Zach	Wilkesboro, NC	10/1/69
Gallagher, Peter	Armonk, NY	8/19/55
Gallo, Vincent	Buffalo, NY	4/11/62
Galway, James	Belfast, N. Ireland, UK	12/8/39
Gandolfini, James	Westwood, NJ	9/18/61
Garagiola, Joe	St. Louis, MO	2/12/26
Garber, Victor	London, ON, Canada	3/16/49
Garcia, Andy	Havana, Cuba	4/12/56
Garfunkel, Art	Forest Hills, Queens, NY	11/5/41
Garlin, Jeff	Chicago, IL	6/5/62
Garner, James	Norman, OK	4/7/28
Garner, Jennifer	Houston, TX	4/17/72

Name	Birthplace	Birthdate
Garofalo, Janeane	Newton, NJ	9/28/64
Garr, Teri	Lakewood, OH	12/11/49
Garrett, Brad	Woodland Hills, CA	4/14/60
Garth, Jennie	Urbana, IL	4/3/72
Gatlin, Larry	Seminole, TX	5/2/48
Gavin, John	Los Angeles, CA	4/8/31
Gayle, Crystal	Paintsville, KY	1/9/51
Gaynor, Mitzi	Chicago, IL	9/4/31
Gazzara, Ben	New York, NY	8/28/30
Geary, Anthony	Coalville, UT	5/29/47
Gedda, Nicolai	Stockholm, Sweden	7/11/25
Gellar, Sarah Michelle	New York, NY	4/14/77
Gere, Richard	Philadelphia, PA	8/31/49
Gervais, Ricky	Reading, England, UK	6/25/61
Giannini, Giancarlo	La Spezia, Italy	8/1/42
Gibb, Barry	Isle of Man, England, UK	9/1/46
Gibb, Robin	Isle of Man, England, UK	12/22/49
Gibbons, Leeza	Hartsville, SC	3/26/57
Gibbs, Marla	Chicago, IL	6/14/31
Gibson, Deborah	Brooklyn, NY	8/31/70
Gibson, Mel	Peekskill, NY	1/3/56
Gibson, Thomas	Charleston, SC	7/3/62
Gifford, Frank	Santa Monica, CA	8/16/30
Gifford, Kathie Lee	Neuilly-sur-Seine, France	8/16/53
Gilbert, Melissa	Los Angeles, CA	5/8/64
Gilbert, Sara	Santa Monica, CA	1/29/75
Gilberto, Astrud	Salvador, Brazil	3/30/40
Gill, Vince	Norman, OK	4/12/57
Gillette, Anita	Baltimore, MD	8/16/36
Gilley, Mickey	Natchez, MS	3/9/36
Gilliam, Terry	Minneapolis, MN	11/22/40
Gilmour, David	Cambridge, England, UK	3/6/46
Gilpin, Peri	Waco, TX	5/27/61
Gilsig, Jessalyn	Montreal, QC, Canada	1971
Ginty, Robert	Brooklyn, NY	11/14/48
Givens, Robin	New York, NY	11/27/64
Glaser, Paul Michael	Cambridge, MA	3/25/43
Gleeson, Brendan	Belfast, N. Ireland, UK	11/9/55
Glenn, Scott	Pittsburgh, PA	1/26/42
Gless, Sharon	Los Angeles, CA	5/31/43
Glover, Crispin	New York, NY	4/20/64
Glover, Danny	San Francisco, CA	7/22/47
Glover, John	Kingston, NY	8/7/44
Glover, Julian	London, England, UK	3/27/35
Glover, Savion	Newark, NJ	11/19/73
Godard, Jean Luc	Paris, France	12/3/30
Goldberg, Whoopi	New York, NY	11/13/55
Goldblum, Jeff	Pittsburgh, PA	10/22/52
Goldthwait, Bobcat	Syracuse, NY	5/26/62
Goldwyn, Tony	Los Angeles, CA	5/20/60
Gooding, Cuba, Jr.	Bronx, NY	1/2/68
Goodman, John	Affton, MO	6/20/52
Gordon-Levitt, Joseph	Los Angeles, CA	2/17/81
Gorme, Eydie	Bronx, NY	8/16/32
Gosling, Ryan	London, ON, Canada	11/12/80
Gosselaar, Mark-Paul	Panorama City, CA	3/1/74
Gossett, Louis, Jr.	Brooklyn, NY	5/27/36
Gould, Elliott	Brooklyn, NY	8/29/38
Grace, Topher	New York, NY	7/12/78
Graham, Heather	Milwaukee, WI	1/29/70
Grammer, Kelsey	St. Thomas, U.S. Virgin Isls.	2/21/55
Grant, Amy	Augusta, GA	11/25/60
Grant, Hugh	London, England, UK	9/9/60
Grant, Lee	New York, NY	10/31/27
Gray, Linda	Santa Monica, CA	9/12/40
Gray, Macy	Canton, OH	9/9/70
Green, Al	Forrest City, AR	4/13/46
Green, Seth	Philadelphia, PA	2/8/74
Green, Tom	Pembroke, ON, Canada	7/30/71
Greene, Shecky	Chicago, IL	4/8/26
Greenwood, Bruce	Noranda, QC, Canada	8/12/56
Gregory, Cynthia	Los Angeles, CA	7/8/46
Gregory, Dick	St. Louis, MO	10/12/32
Grenier, Adrian	Brooklyn, NY	7/10/76
Grey, Jennifer	New York, NY	3/26/60
Grey, Joel	Cleveland, OH	4/11/32
Grier, David Alan	Detroit, MI	6/30/55
Grier, Pam	Winston-Salem, NC	5/26/49
Gries, Jon	Glendale, CA	6/17/57
Griffith, Andy	Mount Airy, NC	6/1/26
Griffith, Melanie	New York, NY	8/9/57
Griffiths, Rachel	Melbourne, Australia	12/18/68
Griffiths, Richard	Stockton-on-Tees, Eng., UK	7/31/47
Grimes, Tammy	Lynn, MA	1/30/34
Grint, Rupert	Walton-at-Stone, Hertfordshire, Eng., UK	8/24/88
Groban, Josh	Los Angeles, CA	2/27/81
Grodin, Charles	Pittsburgh, PA	4/21/35
Groff, Jonathan	Lancaster, PA	3/26/85
Grohl, David	Warren, OH	1/14/69
Grosbard, Ulu	Antwerp, Belgium	1/9/29
Gross, Michael	Chicago, IL	6/21/47
Guest, Christopher	New York, NY	2/5/48
Guillaume, Robert	St. Louis, MO	11/30/37
Gumbel, Greg	New Orleans, LA	5/3/46
Gunn, Tim	Washington, DC	7/29/53

Name	Birthplace	Birthdate
Guthrie, Arlo	Brooklyn, NY	7/10/47
Guttenberg, Steve	Brooklyn, NY	8/24/58
Guy, Buddy	Lettsworth, LA	7/30/36
Guy, Jasmine	Boston, MA	3/10/64
Gyllenhaal, Jake	Los Angeles, CA	12/19/80
Gyllenhaal, Maggie	New York, NY	11/16/77
Hackman, Gene	San Bernardino, CA	1/30/30
Hader, Bill	Tulsa, OK	6/7/78
Hagerty, Julie	Cincinnati, OH	6/15/55
Haggard, Merle	Bakersfield, CA	4/6/37
Hagman, Larry	Fort Worth, TX	9/21/31
Haid, Charles	San Francisco, CA	6/2/43
Hale, Barbara	DeKalb, IL	4/18/22
Hale, Tony	West Point, NY	9/30/70
Hall, Anthony Michael	West Roxbury, MA	4/14/68
Hall, Arsenio	Cleveland, OH	2/12/55
Hall, Daryl	Pottstown, PA	10/11/49
Hall, Deidre	Milwaukee, WI	10/31/47
Hall, Michael C.	Raleigh, NC	2/1/71
Hall, Monty	Winnipeg, MB, Canada	8/25/21
Hall, Tom T.	Olive Hill, KY	5/25/36
Halliwell, Geri	Watford, England, UK	8/6/72
Hamill, Mark	Oakland, CA	9/25/51
Hamilton, George	Memphis, TN	8/12/39
Hamilton, Linda	Salisbury, MD	9/26/56
Hamlin, Harry	Pasadena, CA	10/30/51
Hamm, Jon	St. Louis, MO	3/10/71
Hammer (M.C.)	Oakland, CA	3/30/63
Hammond, Darrell	Melbourne, FL	10/8/55
Hancock, Herbie	Chicago, IL	4/12/40
Hanks, Tom	Concord, CA	7/9/56
Hannah, Daryl	Chicago, IL	12/3/60
Hannigan, Alyson	Washington, DC	3/24/74
Hanson, Curtis	Reno, NV	3/24/45
Hanson, Isaac	Tulsa, OK	11/17/80
Hanson, Taylor	Tulsa, OK	3/14/83
Hanson, Zac	Tulsa, OK	10/22/85
Harden, Marcia Gay	La Jolla, CA	8/14/59
Harewood, Dorian	Dayton, OH	8/6/50
Hargitay, Mariska	Los Angeles, CA	1/23/64
Harmon, Angie	Highland Park, TX	8/10/72
Harmon, Mark	Burbank, CA	9/2/51
Harper, Ben	Claremont, CA	10/28/69
Harper, Tess	Mammoth Spring, AR	8/15/50
Harper, Valerie	Suffern, NY	8/22/40
Harrelson, Woody	Midland, TX	7/23/61
Harrington, Pat	New York, NY	8/13/29
Harris, Barbara	Evanston, IL	7/25/35
Harris, Ed	Tenafly, NJ	11/28/50
Harris, Emmylou	Birmingham, AL	4/2/47
Harris, Julie	Grosse Pointe Park, MI	12/2/25
Harris, Neil Patrick	Albuquerque, NM	6/15/73
Harris, Rosemary	Ashby, England, UK	9/19/27?
Harris, Steve	Chicago, IL	12/3/65
Harrison, Gregory	Avalon, CA	5/31/50
Harry, Deborah	Miami, FL	7/1/45
Hart, Mary	Madison, SD	11/8/50
Hart, Melissa Joan	Smithtown, NY	4/18/76
Hartley, Hal	Lindenhurst, NY	11/3/59
Hartley, Mariette	New York, NY	6/21/40
Hartman, David	Pawtucket, RI	5/19/35
Hartman Black, Lisa	Houston, TX	6/1/56
Hartnett, Josh	San Francisco, CA	7/21/78
Harvey, P.J.	Yeovil, Somerset, Eng., UK	10/9/69
Harvey, Steve	Welch, WV	11/23/56
Hasselbeck, Elisabeth	Cranston, RI	5/28/77
Hasselhoff, David	Baltimore, MD	7/17/52
Hatcher, Teri	Sunnyvale, CA	12/8/64
Hatfield, Juliana	Wiscasset, ME	7/27/67
Hathaway, Anne	Brooklyn, NY	11/12/82
Hauer, Rutger	Breukelen, Netherlands	1/23/44
Hawke, Ethan	Austin, TX	11/6/70
Hawn, Goldie	Washington, DC	11/21/45
Hayek, Salma	Coatzacoalcos, Mexico	9/2/66
Hayes, Sean	Glen Ellyn, IL	6/26/70
Haynes, Roy	Roxbury, MA	3/13/26
Hays, Robert	Bethesda, MD	7/24/47
Head, Anthony	Camden Town, Eng., UK	2/20/54
Heard, John	Washington, DC	3/7/45
Hearn, George	St. Louis, MO	6/18/34
Heaton, Patricia	Bay Village, OH	3/4/58
Heche, Anne	Aurora, OH	5/25/69
Heder, Jon	Fort Collins, CO	10/26/77
Hedren, Tippi	New Ulm, MN	1/19/30?
Heigl, Katherine	Washington, DC	11/24/78
Helfgott, David	Melbourne, Australia	5/19/47
Helgenberger, Marg	Fremont, NE	11/16/58
Helmond, Katherine	Galveston, TX	7/5/34
Helms, Ed	Atlanta, GA	1/24/74
Hemingway, Mariel	Mill Valley, CA	11/22/61
Hemsley, Sherman	Philadelphia, PA	2/1/38
Hemsworth, Chris	Melbourne, Victoria, Australia	8/11/83
Henderson, Florence	Dale, IN	2/14/34
Hendricks, Christina	Knoxville, TN	5/3/75
Henley, Don	Gilmer, TX	7/22/47
Henner, Marilu	Chicago, IL	4/6/52
Hennessy, Jill	Edmonton, AB, Canada	11/25/68
Henry, Buck	New York, NY	12/9/30
Herman, Pee-Wee	Peekskill, NY	8/27/52
Herrmann, Edward	Washington, DC	7/21/43
Hershey, Barbara	Hollywood, CA	2/5/48
Hesseman, Howard	Lebanon, OR	2/27/40
Hetfield, James	Downey, CA	8/3/63
Hewitt, Jennifer Love	Waco, TX	2/21/79
Hicks, Catherine	Scottsdale, AZ	8/6/51
Higgins, John Michael	Boston, MA	2/12/63
Hill, Dulé	Orange, NJ	5/3/75
Hill, Faith	Jackson, MS	9/21/67
Hill, Lauryn	South Orange, NJ	5/25/75
Hill, Steven	Seattle, WA	2/24/22
Hillerman, John	Denison, TX	12/20/32
Hilton, Paris	New York, NY	2/17/81
Hines, Cheryl	Miami Beach, FL	9/21/65
Hirsch, Emile	Palms, CA	3/13/85
Hirsch, Judd	New York, NY	3/15/35
Hodgman, John	Cambridge, MA	6/3/71
Hoffman, Dustin	Los Angeles, CA	8/8/37
Hoffman, Philip Seymour	Fairport, NY	7/23/67
Hogan, Hulk	Augusta, GA	8/11/53
Hogan, Paul	Lightning Ridge, NSW, Australia	10/8/39
Holbrook, Hal	Cleveland, OH	2/17/25
Holder, Geoffrey	Port of Spain, Trinidad	8/1/30
Holliday, Polly	Jasper, AL	7/2/37
Holliman, Earl	Delhi, LA	9/11/28
Holloway, Josh	San Jose, CA	7/20/69
Holly, Lauren	Bristol, PA	10/28/63
Holm, Celeste	New York, NY	4/29/19
Holm, Ian	Ilford, England, UK	9/12/31
Holmes, Katie	Toledo, OH	12/18/78
Hooks, Jan	Decatur, GA	4/23/57
Hopkins, Anthony	Port Talbot, South Wales, UK	12/31/37
Hopkins, Bo	Greenville, SC	2/2/42
Hopkins, Telma	Louisville, KY	10/28/48
Horne, Marilyn	Bradford, PA	1/16/34
Hornsby, Bruce	Williamsburg, VA	11/23/54
Horsley, Lee	Muleshoe, TX	5/15/55
Hoskins, Bob	Suffolk, England, UK	10/26/42
Hounsou, Djimon	Cotonou, Benin	4/24/64
Houston, Whitney	Newark, NJ	8/9/63
Howard, Ken	El Centro, CA	3/28/44
Howard, Ron	Duncan, OK	3/1/54
Howard, Terrence	Chicago, IL	3/11/69
Howell, C. Thomas	Van Nuys, CA	12/7/66
Howes, Sally Ann	St. John's Wood, London, England, UK	7/20/30
Hudgens, Vanessa	Salinas, CA	12/14/88
Hudson, Jennifer	Chicago, IL	9/12/81
Hudson, Kate	Los Angeles, CA	4/19/79
Huffman, Felicity	Bedford, NY	12/9/62
Hughley, D.L.	Los Angeles, CA	3/6/63
Hulce, Tom	Whitewater, WI	12/6/53
Humperdinck, Engelbert	Madras, India	5/2/36
Humphries, Barry	Melbourne, Australia	2/17/34
Hunt, Bonnie	Chicago, IL	9/22/64
Hunt, Helen	Culver City, CA	6/15/63
Hunt, Linda	Morristown, NJ	4/2/45
Hunter, Holly	Conyers, GA	3/20/58
Hunter, Tab	New York, NY	7/11/31
Hurley, Elizabeth	Hampshire, England, UK	6/10/65
Hurt, John	Chesterfield, England, UK	1/22/40
Hurt, Mary Beth	Marshalltown, IA	9/26/48
Hurt, William	Washington, DC	3/20/50
Huston, Anjelica	Santa Monica, CA	7/8/51
Hutton, Lauren	Charleston, SC	11/17/43
Hutton, Timothy	Malibu, CA	8/16/60
Hyman, Earle	Rocky Mount, NC	10/11/26
Ian, Janis	New York, NY	4/7/51
Ice Cube	Los Angeles, CA	6/15/69
Ice-T	Newark, NJ	2/16/58
Idle, Eric	S. Shields, England, UK	3/29/43
Idol, Billy	Middlesex, England, UK	11/30/55
Iglesias, Enrique	Madrid, Spain	5/8/75
Iglesias, Julio	Madrid, Spain	9/23/43
Iler, Robert	New York, NY	3/2/85
Iman	Mogadishu, Somalia	7/25/55
Imbruglia, Natalie	Sydney, Australia	2/4/75
Imperioli, Michael	Mount Vernon, NY	1/1/66
Imus, Don	Riverside, CA	7/23/40
Ingram, James	Akron, OH	2/16/56
Innes, Laura	Pontiac, MI	8/16/59
Ireland, Kathy	Glendale, CA	3/20/63
Irons, Jeremy	Cowes, Isle of Wight, England, UK	9/19/48
Irving, Amy	Palo Alto, CA	9/10/53
Irving, George S.	Springfield, MA	11/1/22
Irwin, Bill	Santa Monica, CA	4/11/50
Ivanek, Željko	Ljubljana, Yugoslavia	8/15/57
Ivey, Judith	El Paso, TX	9/4/51
Ivory, James	Berkeley, CA	6/7/28
Izzard, Eddie	Aden, Yemen	2/7/62

Name	Birthplace	Birthdate
Jackée (Harry)	Winston-Salem, NC	8/14/56
Jackman, Hugh	Sydney, Australia	10/12/68
Jackson, Anne	Allegheny, PA	9/3/26
Jackson, Cheyenne	Newport, WA	7/12/75
Jackson, Glenda	Birkenhead, England, UK	5/9/36
Jackson, Janet	Gary, IN	5/16/66
Jackson, Jermaine	Gary, IN	12/11/54
Jackson, Jonathan	Orlando, FL	5/11/82
Jackson, Joshua	Vancouver, BC, Canada	6/11/78
Jackson, Kate	Birmingham, AL	10/29/48
Jackson, La Toya	Gary, IN	5/29/56
Jackson, Peter	Wellington, New Zealand	10/31/61
Jackson, Samuel L.	Chattanooga, TN	12/21/48
Jacobi, Derek	London, England, UK	10/22/38
Jagger, Mick	Dartford, England, UK	7/26/43
James, Etta	Los Angeles, CA	1/25/38
James, Kevin	Mineola, NY	4/26/65
Janis, Conrad	New York, NY	2/11/28
Janney, Allison	Dayton, OH	11/19/60
Janssen, Famke	Amsterdam, Netherlands	11/5/65
Jardine, Al	Lima, OH	9/3/42
Jarmusch, Jim	Akron, OH	1/22/53
Jarreau, Al	Milwaukee, WI	3/12/40
Jarrett, Keith	Allentown, PA	5/8/45
Ja Rule	Hollis, Queens, NY	2/29/76
Jay Z	Brooklyn, NY	12/4/69
Jeffreys, Anne	Goldsboro, NC	1/26/23
Jett, Joan	Philadelphia, PA	9/22/60
Jewel	Payson, UT	5/23/74
Jewison, Norman	Toronto, ON, Canada	7/21/26
Jillette, Penn	Greenfield, MA	3/5/55
Jillian, Ann	Cambridge, MA	1/29/50
Joel, Billy	Bronx, NY	5/9/49
Johansson, Scarlett	New York, NY	11/22/84
John, Elton	Pinner, Middlesex, Eng., UK	3/25/47
Johns, Glynis	Durban, S. Africa	10/5/23
Johnson, Arte	Benton Harbor, MI	1/20/34
Johnson, Beverly	Buffalo, NY	10/13/52
Johnson, Don	Flatt Creek, MO	12/15/49
Johnson, Dwayne "The Rock"	Hayward, CA	5/2/72
Johnston, Bruce	Los Angeles, CA	6/24/42
Johnston, Kristen	Washington, DC	9/20/67
Jolie, Angelina	Los Angeles, CA	6/4/75
Jonas, Joe	Casa Grande, AZ	8/15/89
Jonas, Kevin	Teaneck, NJ	11/5/87
Jonas, Nick	Dallas, TX	9/16/92
Jones, Cherry	Paris, TN	11/21/56
Jones, Davy	Manchester, England, UK	12/30/45
Jones, Dean	Decatur, AL	1/25/31
Jones, Gemma	London, England, UK	12/4/42
Jones, George	Saratoga, TX	9/12/31
Jones, Grace	Spanish Town, Jamaica	5/19/48
Jones, Jack	Hollywood, CA	1/14/38
Jones, James Earl	Arkabutla, MS	1/17/31
Jones, January	Sioux Falls, SD	1/5/78
Jones, Mick	London, England, UK	6/26/55
Jones, Norah	New York, NY	3/30/79
Jones, Quincy	Chicago, IL	3/14/33
Jones, Shirley	Charleroi, PA	3/31/34
Jones, Star	Badin, NC	3/24/62
Jones, Tom	Pontypridd, Wales, UK	6/7/40
Jones, Tommy Lee	San Saba, TX	9/15/46
Jonze, Spike	Rockville, MD	10/22/69
Jourdan, Louis	Marseilles, France	6/19/19
Jovovich, Milla	Kiev, Ukraine	12/17/75
Judd, Ashley	Granada Hills, CA	4/19/68
Judd, Naomi	Ashland, KY	1/11/46
Judd, Wynonna	Ashland, KY	5/30/64
Kaczmarek, Jane	Milwaukee, WI	12/21/55
Kanaly, Steve	Burbank, CA	3/14/46
Kane, Carol	Cleveland, OH	6/18/52
Kaplan, Gabe	Brooklyn, NY	3/31/45
Kardashian, Kim	Los Angeles, CA	10/21/80
Karlen, John	New York, NY	5/28/33
Karn, Richard	Seattle, WA	2/17/56
Karras, Alex	Gary, IN	7/15/35
Kasem, Casey	Detroit, MI	4/27/32
Kattan, Chris	Sherman Oaks, CA	10/19/70
Kavner, Julie	Burbank, CA	9/7/51
Kazan, Lainie	New York, NY	5/15/42
Ke$ha	Los Angeles, CA	3/1/87
Keach, Stacy	Savannah, GA	6/2/41
Keaton, Diane	Santa Ana, CA	1/5/46
Keaton, Michael	Coraopolis, PA	9/9/51
Keener, Catherine	Miami, FL	3/23/59
Keillor, Garrison	Anoka, MN	8/7/42
Keitel, Harvey	Brooklyn, NY	5/13/39
Keith, David	Knoxville, TN	5/8/54
Keith, Penelope	Sutton, Surrey, Eng., UK	4/2/40
Kellerman, Sally	Long Beach, CA	6/2/37
Kelly, Minka	Los Angeles, CA	6/24/80
Kelly, R(obert)	Chicago, IL	1/8/67
Kennedy, George	New York, NY	2/18/25
Kennedy, Jamie	Upper Darby, PA	5/25/70
Kennedy, Jayne	Washington, DC	10/27/51
Kenny G	Seattle, WA	6/5/56
Kent, Allegra	Santa Monica, CA	8/11/37
Keoghan, Phil	Christchurch, New Zealand	5/31/67
Kercheval, Ken	Wolcottville, IN	7/15/35
Kerns, Joanna	San Francisco, CA	2/12/53
Keys, Alicia	New York, NY	1/25/81
Khan, Chaka	Great Lakes, IL	3/23/53
Kidder, Margot	Yellowknife, NT, Canada	10/17/48
Kidman, Nicole	Honolulu, HI	6/20/67
Kiel, Richard	Detroit, MI	9/13/39
Kilborn, Craig	Kansas City, KS	8/24/62
Kilmer, Val	Los Angeles, CA	12/31/59
Kim, Daniel Dae	Pusan, S. Korea	8/4/68
Kimmel, Jimmy	Brooklyn, NY	11/13/67
King, B.B.	Itta Bena, MS	9/16/25
King, Carole	Brooklyn, NY	2/9/42
King, Larry	Brooklyn, NY	11/19/33
King, Perry	Alliance, OH	4/30/48
Kingsley, Ben	Scarborough, England, UK	12/31/43
Kingston, Alex	London, England, UK	3/11/63
Kinnear, Greg	Logansport, IN	6/17/63
Kinney, Kathy	Stevens Point, WI	11/3/53
Kinski, Nastassja	Berlin, W. Germany	1/24/60
Kirkland, Gelsey	Bethlehem, PA	12/29/52
Kirkpatrick, Chris	Clarion, PA	10/17/71
Kirshner, Mia	Toronto, ON, Canada	1/25/75
Klein, Robert	Bronx, NY	2/8/42
Kline, Kevin	St. Louis, MO	10/24/47
Klugman, Jack	Philadelphia, PA	4/27/22
Klum, Heidi	Bergish-Gladbach, Germany	6/1/73
Knight, Gladys	Atlanta, GA	5/28/44
Knight, Shirley	Goessel, KS	7/5/36
Knight, T. R.	Minneapolis, MN	3/26/73
Knight, Wayne	New York, NY	8/7/55
Knightley, Keira	Teddington, England, UK	3/26/85
Knopfler, Mark	Glasgow, Scotland, UK	8/12/49
Knowles, Beyoncé	Houston, TX	9/4/81
Knoxville, Johnny	Knoxville, TN	3/11/71
Konitz, Lee	Chicago, IL	10/13/27
Kopell, Bernie	Brooklyn, NY	6/21/33
Kotto, Yaphet	New York, NY	11/15/37
Krakowski, Jane	Parsippany, NJ	10/11/68
Krasinski, John	Newton, MA	10/20/79
Krause, Peter	Alexandria, MN	8/12/65
Kressley, Carson	Allentown, PA	11/11/69
Kretschmann, Thomas	Dessau, E. Germany	9/8/62
Kristofferson, Kris	Brownsville, TX	6/22/36
Kudrow, Lisa	Encino, CA	7/30/63
Kunis, Mila	Kiev, Ukraine	8/14/83
Kuriyama, Chiaki	Tsuchiura, Ibaraki, Japan	10/10/84
Kurtz, Swoosie	Omaha, NE	9/6/44
Kutcher, Ashton	Cedar Rapids, IA	2/7/78
Kwan, Nancy	Hong Kong	5/19/39
LaBelle, Patti	Philadelphia, PA	5/24/44
LaBeouf, Shia	Los Angeles, CA	6/11/86
Lachey, Nick	Harlan, KY	11/9/73
Ladd, Cheryl	Huron, SD	7/12/51
Ladd, Diane	Meridian, MS	11/29/32
Lady Gaga	New York, NY	3/28/86
Lagasse, Emeril	Fall River, MA	10/15/59
Lahti, Christine	Birmingham, MI	4/4/50
Laine, Cleo	Southall, England, UK	10/28/27
Lake, Ricki	Hastings-on-Hudson, NY	9/21/68
Lamas, Lorenzo	Santa Monica, CA	1/20/58
Lambert, Adam	Indianapolis, IN	1/29/82
Lambert, Christopher	Great Neck, NY	3/29/57
Landau, Martin	Brooklyn, NY	6/20/28
Landis, John	Chicago, IL	8/3/50
Lane, Diane	New York, NY	1/22/65
Lane, Nathan	Jersey City, NJ	2/3/56
lang, k.d.	Consort, AB, Canada	11/2/61
Lang, Stephen	Jamaica Estates, Queens, NY	7/11/52
Lange, Jessica	Cloquet, MN	4/20/49
Langella, Frank	Bayonne, NJ	1/1/40
Lansbury, Angela	London, England, UK	10/16/25
LaPaglia, Anthony	Adelaide, Australia	1/31/59
Larroquette, John	New Orleans, LA	11/25/47
LaSalle, Eriq	Hartford, CT	6/23/62
Lauper, Cyndi	Ozone Park, Queens, NY	6/22/53
Laurie, Hugh	Oxford, England, UK	6/11/59
Laurie, Piper	Detroit, MI	1/22/32
Lautner, Taylor	Grand Rapids, MI	2/11/92
Lavigne, Avril	Belleville, ON, Canada	9/27/84
Lavin, Linda	Portland, ME	10/15/37
Law, Jude	London, England, UK	12/29/72
Lawless, Lucy	Mount Albert, New Zealand	3/29/68
Lawrence, Carol	Melrose Park, IL	9/5/34
Lawrence, Jennifer	Louisville, KY	8/15/90
Lawrence, Joey	Montgomery, PA	4/20/76
Lawrence, Martin	Frankfurt, Germany	4/16/65
Lawrence, Steve	Brooklyn, NY	7/8/35
Lawrence, Vicki	Inglewood, CA	3/26/49
Leach, Robin	London, England, UK	8/29/41
Leachman, Cloris	Des Moines, IA	4/30/26
Lear, Norman	New Haven, CT	7/27/22

Name	Birthplace	Birthdate
Learned, Michael	Washington, DC	4/9/39
Leary, Denis	Worcester, MA	8/18/57
LeBlanc, Matt	Newton, MA	7/25/67
LeBon, Simon	Bushey, England, UK	10/27/58
Lee, Ang	Pingtung, Taiwan	10/23/54
Lee, Brenda	Lithonia, GA	12/11/44
Lee, Christopher	London, England, UK	5/27/22
Lee, Jason	Huntington Beach, CA	4/25/70
Lee, Michele	Los Angeles, CA	6/24/42
Lee, Spike	Atlanta, GA	3/20/57
Leeves, Jane	Ilford, England, UK	4/18/61
Legrand, Michel	Paris, France	2/24/32
Leguizamo, John	Bogotá, Colombia	7/22/64
Lehmkuhl, Reichen	Cincinnati, OH	12/26/73
Leibman, Ron	New York, NY	10/11/37
Leigh, Jennifer Jason	Hollywood, CA	2/5/62
Leighton, Laura	Iowa City, IA	7/24/68
Lennox, Annie	Aberdeen, Scotland, UK	12/25/54
Leno, Jay	New Rochelle, NY	4/28/50
Leo, Melissa	New York, NY	9/14/60
Leonard, Robert Sean	Westwood, NJ	2/28/69
Leoni, Tea	New York, NY	2/25/66
Leslie, Joan	Detroit, MI	1/26/25
Leto, Jared	Bossier City, LA	12/26/71
Letterman, David	Indianapolis, IN	4/12/47
Levine, Adam	Los Angeles, CA	3/18/79
Levine, James	Cincinnati, OH	6/23/43
Levine, Ted	Bellaire, OH	5/29/57
Levinson, Barry	Baltimore, MD	4/6/42
Levy, Eugene	Hamilton, ON, Canada	12/17/46
Lewis, Huey	New York, NY	7/5/50
Lewis, Jason	Newport Beach, CA	6/25/71
Lewis, Jerry	Newark, NJ	3/16/26
Lewis, Jerry Lee	Ferriday, LA	9/29/35
Lewis, Juliette	San Fernando Valley, CA	6/21/73
Lewis, Leona	London, England, UK	4/3/85
Lewis, Richard	Brooklyn, NY	6/29/47
Li, Jet	Beijing, China	4/26/63
Light, Judith	Trenton, NJ	2/9/49
Lightfoot, Gordon	Orillia, ON, Canada	11/17/38
Lil' Kim	Brooklyn, NY	7/11/75
Lil' Romeo	New Orleans, LA	8/19/89
Lilly, Evangeline	Fort Saskatchewan, AB, Can.	8/3/79
Linden, Hal	Bronx, NY	3/20/31
Ling, Lisa	Sacramento, CA	8/30/73
Linn-Baker, Mark	St. Louis, MO.	6/17/54
Linney, Laura	New York, NY	2/5/64
Liotta, Ray	Newark, NJ	12/18/54
Lithgow, John	Rochester, NY	10/19/45
Little, Rich	Ottawa, ON, Canada	11/26/38
Little Richard	Macon, GA	12/5/32
Littrell, Brian	Lexington, KY	2/20/75
Liu, Lucy	Jackson Heights, Queens, NY	12/2/68
Lively, Blake	Tarzana, CA.	1/14/68
L. L. Cool J	St. Albans, Queens, NY	1/14/68
Lloyd, Christopher	Stamford, CT.	10/22/38
Lloyd, Emily	North London, Eng., UK	9/29/70
Lloyd Webber, Andrew	London, England, UK	3/22/48
Locke, Sondra	Shelbyville, TN.	5/28/47
Lockhart, June	New York, NY	6/25/25
Locklear, Heather	Westwood, CA.	9/25/61
Loggia, Robert	Staten Island, NY.	1/3/30
Loggins, Kenny	Everett, WA	1/7/48
Lohan, Lindsay	New York, NY	7/2/86
Lollobrigida, Gina	Subiaco, Italy	7/4/27
Lom, Herbert	Prague, Czechoslovakia	1/9/17
Lonergan, Kenneth	New York, NY	10/16/62
Long, Nia	Brooklyn, NY	10/30/70
Long, Shelley	Ft. Wayne, IN.	8/23/49
Longoria, Eva	Corpus Christi, TX	3/15/75
Lopez, George	Mission Hills, CA	4/23/61
Lopez, Jennifer	Bronx, NY	7/24/70
Lopez, Mario	San Diego, CA	10/10/73
Loren, Sophia	Rome, Italy	9/20/34
Loring, Gloria	New York, NY	12/10/46
Louis-Dreyfus, Julia	New York, NY	1/13/61
Lovato, Demi	Dallas, TX	8/20/92
Love, Courtney	San Francisco, CA	7/9/64
Love, Mike	Baldwin Hills, CA.	3/15/41
Loveless, Patty	Pikeville, KY	1/4/57
Lovett, Lyle	Klein, TX	11/1/57
Lovitz, Jon	Tarzana, CA.	7/21/57
Lowe, Rob	Charlottesville, VA	3/17/64
Lowell, Carey	Huntington, NY	2/11/61
Lucas, George	Modesto, CA	5/14/44
Lucci, Susan	Scarsdale, NY	12/23/46
Luckinbill, Laurence	Ft. Smith, AR	11/21/34
Ludacris	Champaign, IL	9/11/77
Ludwig, Christa	Berlin, Germany	3/16/24
Luhrmann, Baz	Sydney, Australia	9/17/62
LuPone, Patti	Northport, NY	4/21/49
Lynch, David	Missoula, MT.	1/20/46
Lynch, Jane	Dolton, IL.	7/14/60
Lynch, Susan	Corrinshego, N. Ireland, UK.	6/5/71
Lynley, Carol	New York, NY	2/13/42
Lynn, Loretta	Butcher Hollow, KY	1935?
Lynn, Vera	London, England, UK	3/20/17
Lynne, Shelby	Quantico, VA	10/22/68
Ma, Yo-Yo	Paris, France	10/7/55
Maazel, Lorin	Neuilly-sur-Seine, France	3/6/30
Macchio, Ralph	Huntington, NY	11/4/62
MacDonald, Kelly	Glasgow, Scotland, UK	2/23/76
MacDowell, Andie	Gaffney, SC	4/21/58
MacFarlane, Seth	Kent, CT	11/26/73
MacGowan, Shane	Tunbridge, Kent, Eng., UK	12/25/57
MacGraw, Ali	Pound Ridge, NY	4/1/38
MacLachlan, Kyle	Yakima, WA.	2/22/59
MacLaine, Shirley	Richmond, VA	4/24/34
MacLeod, Gavin	Mt. Kisco, NY	2/28/31
MacNee, Patrick	London, England, UK	2/6/22
MacNicol, Peter	Dallas, TX	4/10/54
MacPherson, Elle	Sydney, Australia	3/29/64
Macy, Bill	Revere, MA	5/18/22
Macy, William H.	Miami, FL	3/13/50
Madden, John	Austin, MN.	4/10/36
Madigan, Amy	Chicago, IL	9/11/50
Madonna (Ciccone)	Bay City, MI	8/16/58
Madsen, Michael	Chicago, IL	9/25/58
Maguire, Tobey	Santa Monica, CA	6/27/75
Maher, Bill	New York, NY	1/20/56
Mahoney, John	Blackpool, Lancashire, England, UK	6/20/40
Majors, Lee	Wyandotte, MI	4/23/39
Malick, Terrence	Ottawa, IL	11/30/43
Malick, Wendie	Buffalo, NY	12/13/50
Malina, Joshua	New York, NY	1/17/66
Malkovich, John	Christopher, IL.	12/9/53
Malone, Dorothy	Chicago, IL	1/30/25
Mamet, David	Chicago, IL	11/30/47
Manchester, Melissa	Bronx, NY	2/15/51
Mandel, Howie	Toronto, ON, Canada.	11/29/55
Mandrell, Barbara	Houston, TX	12/25/48
Mangione, Chuck	Rochester, NY	11/29/40
Manheim, Camryn	Caldwell, NJ	3/8/61
Manilow, Barry	Brooklyn, NY	6/17/46
Mann, Aimee	Richmond, VA	8/9/60
Manoff, Dinah	New York, NY	1/25/58
Manson, Marilyn	Canton, OH	1/5/69
Mantegna, Joe	Chicago, IL	11/13/47
Mantello, Joe	Rockford, IL	12/27/62
Marcil, Vanessa	Indio, CA	10/15/69
Margulies, Julianna	Spring Valley, NY	6/8/66
Marie, Constance	Hollywood, CA.	9/9/69
Marin, Cheech	Los Angeles, CA	7/13/46
Marinaro, Ed	New York, NY	3/31/50
Marriner, Neville	Lincoln, England, UK.	4/15/24
Mars, Bruno	Honolulu, HI	10/8/85
Marsalis, Branford	New Orleans, LA	8/26/60
Marsalis, Wynton	New Orleans, LA	10/18/61
Marsh, Jean	London, England, UK	7/1/34
Marshall, Garry	Bronx, NY	11/13/34
Marshall, Penny	Bronx, NY	10/15/42
Marshall, Peter	Huntington, WV	3/30/27
Martin, Chris	Devon, England, UK	3/22/77
Martin, Jesse L.	Rocky Mount, VA	1/18/69
Martin, Kellie	Riverside, CA.	10/16/75
Martin, Ricky	San Juan, Puerto Rico	12/24/71
Martin, Steve	Waco, TX.	8/14/45
Martin, Tony	Oakland, CA	12/25/13
Martindale, Margo	Jacksonville, TX.	7/18/51
Martins, Peter	Copenhagen, Denmark	10/27/46
Mason, Jackie	Sheboygan, WI	6/9/34
Mason, Marsha	St. Louis, MO.	4/3/42
Masterson, Christopher	Long Island, NY.	1/22/80
Masterson, Mary Stuart	New York, NY	6/28/66
Mastrantonio, Mary Elizabeth	Lombard, IL.	11/17/58
Masur, Kurt	Brieg, Germany	7/18/27
Masur, Richard	New York, NY	11/20/48
Mathers, Jerry	Sioux City, IA.	6/2/48
Matheson, Tim	Glendale, CA.	12/31/47
Mathis, Johnny	Gilmer, TX.	9/30/35
Matlin, Marlee	Morton Grove, IL	8/24/65
Matthews, Dave	Johannesburg, S. Africa.	1/9/67
May, Elaine	Philadelphia, PA	4/21/32
Mayer, John	Bridgeport, CT.	10/16/77
Mays, Jayma	Bristol, TN	7/16/79
Mazar, Debi	Jamaica, Queens, NY	8/13/64
Mazursky, Paul	Brooklyn, NY	4/25/30
MCA (Adam Yauch)	Brooklyn, NY	8/5/64
McAdams, Rachel	London, ON, Canada.	10/7/86
McArdle, Andrea	Abington, PA	11/5/63
McAvoy, James	Glasgow, Scotland, UK	1/1/79
McBride, Patricia	Teaneck, NJ	8/23/42
McCallum, David	Glasgow, Scotland, UK	9/19/33
McCarthy, Andrew	Westfield, NJ	11/29/62
McCarthy, Jenny	Chicago, IL	11/1/72
McCarthy, Melissa	Plainfield, IL.	8/26/70
McCartney, Paul	Liverpool, England, UK	6/18/42
McCarver, Tim	Memphis, TN.	10/16/41
McConaughey, Matthew	Uvalde, TX.	11/4/69
McCoo, Marilyn	Jersey City, NJ.	9/30/43
McCormack, Eric	Toronto, ON, Canada.	4/18/63

Name	Birthplace	Birthdate
McCormack, Mary	Plainsfield, NJ	2/8/69
McCrane, Paul	Philadelphia, PA	1/19/61
McCreery, Scotty	Garner, NC	10/9/93
McDaniel, James	Washington, DC	3/25/58
McDermott, Dylan	Waterbury, CT	10/26/61
McDiarmid, Ian	Carnoustie, Tayside, Scot., UK	4/17/47
McDonald, Audra	Berlin, Germany	7/3/70
McDonnell, Mary	Wilkes-Barre, PA	4/28/52
McDormand, Frances	Chicago, IL	6/23/57
McDowell, Malcolm	Leeds, England, UK	6/13/43
McEntire, Reba	McAlester, OK	3/28/55
McFerrin, Bobby	New York, NY	3/11/50
McGillis, Kelly	Newport Beach, CA	7/9/57
McGovern, Elizabeth	Evanston, IL	7/18/61
McGovern, Maureen	Youngstown, OH	7/27/49
McGraw, Tim	Delhi, LA	5/1/67
McGregor, Ewan	Crieff, Scotland, UK	3/31/71
McHale, Joel	Rome, Italy	11/20/71
McHale, Kevin	Plano, TX	6/14/88
McKean, Michael	New York, NY	10/17/47
McKechnie, Donna	Pontiac, MI	11/16/42
McKellen, Ian	Burnley, England, UK	5/25/39
McKenzie, Benjamin	Austin, TX	9/12/78
McKidd, Kevin	Elgin, UK	8/9/73
McLachlan, Sarah	Halifax, NS, Canada	1/28/68
McLean, A. J.	West Palm Beach, FL	1/9/78
McNichol, Kristy	Los Angeles, CA	9/11/62
McPartland, Marian	Stough, England, UK	3/20/18
McRaney, Gerald	Collins, MS	8/19/47
McShane, Ian	Blackburn, England, UK	9/29/42
Meadows, Jayne	Wu Chang, China	9/27/20
Meara, Anne	Brooklyn, NY	9/20/29
Meat Loaf	Dallas, TX	9/27/47
Meester, Leighton	Marco Island, FL	4/9/86
Mehta, Zubin	Bombay, India	4/29/36
Mellencamp, John	Seymour, IN	10/7/51
Meloni, Christopher	Washington, DC	4/2/61
Mendes, Sam	Redding, England, UK	8/1/65
Mendes, Sergio	Niteroi, Brazil	2/11/41
Menzel, Idina	Syosset, NY	5/30/71
Merchant, Natalie	Jamestown, NY	10/26/63
Merkerson, S. Epatha	Saginaw, MI	11/28/52
Merrill, Dina	New York, NY	12/9/25
Messing, Debra	Brooklyn, NY	8/15/68
Metcalf, Laurie	Carbondale, IL	6/16/55
Meyers, Seth	Bedford, NH	12/28/73
Michael, George	London, England, UK	6/25/63
Michaels, Al	Brooklyn, NY	11/12/44
Michaels, Bret	Pittsburgh, PA	3/15/63
Michaels, Lorne	Toronto, ON, Canada	11/17/44
Michele, Lea	Bronx, NY	8/29/86
Midler, Bette	Honolulu, HI	12/1/45
Midori (Goto)	Osaka, Japan	10/25/71
Mike D	Brooklyn, NY	11/20/65
Milano, Alyssa	Brooklyn, NY	12/19/72
Miles, Sarah	Ingatestone, England, UK	12/31/41
Miles, Vera	nr. Boise City, OK.	8/23/29
Miller, Dennis	Pittsburgh, PA	11/3/53
Miller, Penelope Ann	Santa Monica, CA	1/13/64
Mills, Donna	Chicago, IL	12/11/43
Mills, Hayley	London, England, UK	4/18/46
Milner, Martin	Detroit, MI	12/28/27
Milnes, Sherrill	Downers Grove, IL	1/10/35
Milsap, Ronnie	Robinsville, NC	1/16/44
Mimieux, Yvette	Hollywood, CA	1/8/42
Ming-Na (Wen)	Macao	11/20/63
Minnelli, Liza	Los Angeles, CA	3/12/46
Minogue, Kylie	Melbourne, Australia	5/28/68
Mirren, Helen	London, England, UK	7/26/45
Mitchell, Brian Stokes	Seattle, WA	10/31/57
Mitchell, Elizabeth	Los Angeles, CA	3/27/70
Mitchell, Jerry	Paw Paw, MI	1/15/60
Mitchell, Joni	Fort McLeod, AB, Canada	11/7/43
Moby	New York, NY	9/11/65
Modine, Matthew	Loma Linda, CA	3/22/59
Moffat, Donald	Plymouth, England, UK	12/26/30
Molina, Alfred	London, England, UK	5/24/53
Molinaro, Al	Kenosha, WI	6/24/19
Moll, Richard	Pasadena, CA	1/13/43
Moloney, Janel	Woodland Hills, CA	10/3/69
Monaghan, Dominic	Berlin, Germany	12/8/76
Monica (Arnold)	College Park, GA.	10/24/80
Mo'Nique	Woodlawn, MD	12/11/67
Monteith, Cory	Calgary, AB, Canada	5/11/82
Moody, Ron	London, England, UK	1/8/24
Moore, Demi	Roswell, NM	11/11/62
Moore, Julianne	Fort Bragg, NC	12/3/60
Moore, Mandy	Nashua, NH.	4/10/84
Moore, Mary Tyler	Brooklyn, NY	12/29/36
Moore, Melba	New York, NY	10/29/45
Moore, Michael	Flint, MI	4/23/54
Moore, Roger	London, England, UK	10/14/27
Moore, Terry	Los Angeles, CA	1/7/29
Morales, Esai	Brooklyn, NY	10/1/62
Moranis, Rick	Toronto, ON, Canada.	4/18/54
Moreau, Jeanne	Paris, France	1/23/28
Moreno, Rita	Humacao, Puerto Rico	12/11/31
Morgan, Harry	Detroit, MI	4/10/15
Morgan, Piers	Guildford, Surrey, UK	3/30/65
Morgan, Tracy	Bronx, NY	11/10/68
Moriarty, Michael	Detroit, MI	4/5/41
Morissette, Alanis	Ottawa, ON, Canada	6/1/74
Morris, Garrett	New Orleans, LA	2/1/37
Morrison, Matthew	Fort Ord, CA	10/30/78
Morrison, Van	Belfast, N. Ireland, UK	8/31/45
Morrissey (Steven Patrick)	Manchester, England, UK	5/22/59
Morrow, Rob	New Rochelle, NY	9/21/62
Morse, David	Beverly, MA.	10/11/53
Morse, Robert	Newton, MA.	5/18/31
Mortensen, Viggo	New York, NY	10/20/58
Mortimer, Emily	London, England, UK	12/1/71
Morton, Joe	New York, NY	10/18/47
Morton, Samantha	Nottingham, England, UK	5/13/77
Moses, William	Los Angeles, CA	11/17/59
Moss, Carrie-Anne	Vancouver, BC, Canada.	8/21/67
Moss, Elisabeth	Los Angeles, CA	7/24/82
Moss, Kate	Croydon, Surrey, Eng., UK	1/16/74
Moyer, Stephen	Brentwood, UK	10/11/69
Mueller-Stahl, Armin	Tilsit, E. Prussia	12/17/30
Muldaur, Diana	Brooklyn, NY	8/19/38
Mulgrew, Kate	Dubuque, IL	4/29/55
Mull, Martin	Chicago, IL	8/18/43
Mullally, Megan	Los Angeles, CA	11/12/58
Mullan, Peter	Peterhead, Scotland, UK	11/2/59
Mulroney, Dermot	Alexandria, VA	10/31/63
Muniz, Frankie	Ridgewood, NJ	12/5/85
Munsel, Patrice	Spokane, WA.	5/14/25
Murphy, Ben	Jonesboro, AR.	3/6/42
Murphy, Donna	Corona, Queens, NY	3/7/58
Murphy, Eddie	Brooklyn, NY	4/3/61
Murphy, Michael	Los Angeles, CA	5/5/38
Murray, Anne	Springhill, NS, Canada	6/20/45
Murray, Bill	Wilmette, IL	9/21/50
Murray, Don	Hollywood, CA.	7/31/29
Musburger, Brent	Portland, OR.	5/26/39
Muti, Riccardo	Naples, Italy.	7/28/41
Myers, Mike	Scarborough, ON, Canada	5/25/63
Nabors, Jim	Sylacauga, AL	6/12/30
Nagra, Parminder	Leicester, England, UK	10/5/75
Nash, Graham	Blackpool, England, UK.	2/2/42
Naughton, James	Middletown, CT	12/6/45
Navarro, Dave	Santa Monica, CA	6/7/67
Nealon, Kevin	St. Louis, MO.	11/18/53
Neeson, Liam	Ballymena, N. Ireland, UK	6/7/52
Neill, Sam	Ulster, N. Ireland, UK	9/14/47
Nelligan, Kate	London, ON, Canada.	3/16/51
Nelly	Austin, TX	11/2/74
Nelson, Craig T.	Spokane, WA.	4/4/44
Nelson, Ed	New Orleans, LA	12/21/28
Nelson, Judd	Portland, ME.	11/28/59
Nelson, Tracy	Santa Monica, CA	10/25/63
Nelson, Willie	Abbott, TX	4/30/33
Nero, Peter	Brooklyn, NY	5/22/34
Nesmith, Mike	Houston, TX	12/30/42
Neuwirth, Bebe	Newark, NJ	12/31/58
Neville, Aaron	New Orleans, LA	1/24/41
Newhart, Bob	Oak Park, IL	9/5/29
Newman, Randy	New Orleans, LA	11/28/43
Newton, Wayne	Norfolk, VA	4/3/42
Newton-John, Olivia	Cambridge, England, UK.	9/26/48
Nicholas, Denise	Detroit, MI	7/12/44
Nichols, Mike	Berlin, Germany	11/6/31
Nicholson, Jack	Neptune, NJ	4/22/37
Nicks, Stevie	Phoenix, AZ.	5/26/48
Nielsen, Connie	Frederikshavn, Denmark	7/3/65
Nighy, Bill	Caterham, Surrey, Eng., UK.	12/12/49
Nimoy, Leonard.	Boston, MA	3/26/31
Nixon, Cynthia	New York, NY	4/9/66
Nolte, Nick	Omaha, NE.	2/8/41
Noone, Peter	Manchester, England, UK	11/5/47
Norman, Jessye	Augusta, GA	9/15/45
Norris, Chuck	Ryan, OK.	3/10/40
Northam, Jeremy	Cambridge, England, UK.	12/1/61
Norton, Edward	Boston, MA.	8/18/69
Noth, Christopher	Madison, WI	11/13/54
Novak, Kim	Chicago, IL	2/13/33
Nuyen, France	Marseilles, France	7/31/39
Oates, John	New York, NY	4/7/49
O'Brian, Hugh	Rochester, NY	4/19/25
O'Brien, Conan	Brookline, MA	4/18/63
O'Brien, Margaret	San Diego, CA.	1/15/37
Ocean, Billy	Fyzabad, Trinidad	1/21/50
O'Connor, Sinead	Glenageary, Ireland.	12/8/66
O'Donnell, Chris	Winnetka, IL	6/26/70
O'Donnell, Rosie	Commack, NY	3/21/62
O'Grady, Gail	Detroit, MI	1/23/63
Oh, Sandra	Nepean, ON, Canada	7/20/71
O'Hara, Catherine	Toronto, ON, Canada.	3/4/54
O'Hara, Maureen	Dublin, Ireland.	8/17/20
Oka, Masi	Tokyo, Japan.	12/27/74
Oldman, Gary	South London, Eng., UK	3/21/58

Name	Birthplace	Birthdate
Olin, Ken	Chicago, IL	7/30/54
Olin, Lena	Stockholm, Sweden	3/22/55
Olmos, Edward James	E. Los Angeles, CA	2/24/47
Olsen, Ashley	Sherman Oaks, CA	6/13/86
Olsen, Mary-Kate	Sherman Oaks, CA	6/13/86
Olson, Nancy	Milwaukee, WI	7/14/28
Olyphant, Timothy	Honolulu, HI	5/20/68
O'Malley, Mike	Boston, MA	10/31/69
O'Neal, Ryan	Los Angeles, CA	4/20/41
O'Neal, Tatum	Los Angeles, CA	11/5/63
O'Neill, Ed	Youngstown, OH	4/12/46
Ontkean, Michael	Vancouver, BC, Canada	1/24/46
O'Quinn, Terry	Newbury, MI	7/15/52
Orlando, Tony	New York, NY	4/3/44
Ormond, Julia	Epsom, England, UK	1/4/65
Osbourne, Jack	London, England, UK	11/8/85
Osbourne, Kelly	London, England, UK	10/27/84
Osbourne, Ozzy	Birmingham, England, UK	12/3/48
Osbourne, Sharon	London, England, UK	10/9/52
O'Shea, Milo	Dublin, Ireland	6/2/26
Oslin, K.T.	Crossett, AR	5/15/42
Osment, Haley Joel	Los Angeles, CA	4/10/88
Osmond, Donny	Ogden, UT	12/9/57
Osmond, Marie	Ogden, UT	10/13/59
O'Toole, Annette	Houston, TX	4/1/51
O'Toole, Peter	Connemara, Ireland	8/2/32
Owen, Clive	Keresley, England, UK	10/3/64
Oz, Frank	Herford, England, UK	5/25/44
Ozawa, Seiji	Shenyang, China	9/1/35
Pacino, Al	New York, NY	4/25/40
Packer, Billy	Wellsville, NY	2/25/40
Page, Ellen	Halifax, NS, Canada	2/21/87
Page, Jimmy	Heston, England, UK	1/9/44
Page, Patti	Claremore, OK	11/8/27
Paget, Debra	Denver, CO	8/19/33
Paige, Janis	Tacoma, WA	9/16/22
Paisley, Brad	Glen Dale, WV.	10/28/72
Palin, Michael	Sheffield, England, UK.	5/5/43
Palmer, Betsy	East Chicago, IN	11/1/26
Palmer, Geoffrey	London, England, UK	6/4/27
Palminteri, Chazz	Bronx, NY	5/15/51
Paltrow, Gwyneth	Los Angeles, CA	9/28/72
Panettiere, Hayden	Palisades, NY	8/21/89
Panjabi, Archie	Edgware, England, UK	5/31/73
Pantoliano, Joe	Hoboken, NJ	9/12/51
Papas, Irene	Chiliomodi, Greece	9/3/26
Paquin, Anna	Winnipeg, MB, Canada	7/24/82
Parker, Alan	Islington, England, UK	2/14/44
Parker, Eleanor	Cedarville, OH	6/26/22
Parker, Jameson	Baltimore, MD	11/18/47
Parker, Mary-Louise	Fort Jackson, SC	8/2/64
Parker, Sarah Jessica	Nelsonville, OH	3/25/65
Parsons, Estelle	Marblehead, MA	11/20/27
Parsons, Jim	Houston, TX	3/24/73
Parton, Dolly	Sevierville, TN	1/19/46
Pasdar, Adrian	Pittsfield, MA	4/30/65
Patinkin, Mandy	Chicago, IL	11/30/52
Patric, Jason	Queens, NY.	6/17/66
Pattinson, Robert	London, England, UK	5/13/86
Patton, Will	Charleston, SC	6/14/54
Paul, Aaron	Emmett, ID	8/27/79
Paul, Adrian	London, England, UK	5/29/59
Paulson, Sarah	Tampa, FL	12/17/73
Paxton, Bill	Fort Worth, TX.	5/17/55
Pearce, Guy	Ely, England, UK	10/5/67
Peet, Amanda	New York, NY	1/11/72
Penn, Kal	Montclair, NJ	4/23/77
Penn, Sean	Burbank, CA	8/17/60
Pepper, Barry	Campbell River, BC, Can.	4/4/1970
Perez, Rosie	Brooklyn, NY	9/6/64
Perkins, Elizabeth	Queens, NY.	11/18/60
Perlman, Itzhak	Tel Aviv, Israel	8/31/45
Perlman, Rhea	Brooklyn, NY	3/31/48
Perlman, Ron	New York, NY	4/13/50
Perrine, Valerie	Galveston, TX	9/3/43
Perry, Katy	Santa Barbara, CA.	10/25/84
Perry, Luke	Mansfield, OH	10/11/65
Perry, Matthew	Williamstown, MA	8/19/69
Persoff, Nehemiah	Jerusalem, Israel	8/2/20
Pesci, Joe	Newark, NJ	2/9/43
Peters, Bernadette	Ozone Park, Queens, NY	2/28/48
Peters, Roberta	Bronx, NY	5/4/30
Petersen, Wolfgang	Emden, Germany	3/14/41
Petty, Lori	Chattanooga, TN	3/23/63
Petty, Tom	Gainesville, FL.	10/20/50
Pfeiffer, Michelle	Santa Ana, CA.	4/29/58
Phair, Liz	New Haven, CT	4/17/67
Philbin, Regis	New York, NY	8/25/31
Phillippe, Ryan	New Castle, DE.	9/10/74
Phillips, Lou Diamond	Subic Bay, Philippines	2/17/62
Phillips, Mackenzie	Alexandria, VA.	11/10/59
Phillips, Michelle	Long Beach, CA	6/4/44
Phillips, Sian	Bettws, Wales, UK.	5/14/34
Phoenix, Joaquin	San Juan, Puerto Rico.	10/28/74
Pierce, David Hyde	Albany, NY.	4/3/59
Pinchot, Bronson	New York, NY	5/20/59

Name	Birthplace	Birthdate
Pink	Doylestown, PA	9/8/79
Pinkett Smith, Jada	Baltimore, MD	9/18/71
Pirner, David	Green Bay, WI	4/16/64
Piscopo, Joe	Passaic, NJ	6/17/51
Pitt, Brad	Shawnee, OK	12/18/63
Piven, Jeremy	New York, NY	7/26/65
Plant, Robert	W. Bromwich, England, UK	8/20/48
Plimpton, Martha	New York ,NY	11/16/70
Plowright, Joan	Brigg, England, UK	10/28/29
Plummer, Amanda	New York, NY	3/23/57
Plummer, Christopher	Toronto, ON, Canada	12/13/27
Poehler, Amy	Burlington, MA.	9/16/71
Poitier, Sidney	Miami, FL	2/20/27
Polanski, Roman	Paris, France	8/18/33
Pompeo, Ellen	Everett, MA	11/10/69
Pop, Iggy	Ann Arbor, MI	4/21/47
Portman, Natalie	Jerusalem, Israel	6/9/81
Posey, Parker	Baltimore, MD	11/8/68
Post, Markie	Palo Alto, CA	11/4/50
Potente, Franka	Dulmen bei Munster, Germany	7/22/74
Potts, Annie	Nashville, TN	10/28/52
Povich, Maury	Washington, DC	1/17/39
Powell, Jane	Portland, OR	4/1/28
Powers, Stefanie	Hollywood, CA.	11/2/42
Prentiss, Paula	San Antonio, TX	3/4/39
Prepon, Laura	Watchung, NJ	3/7/80
Presley, Priscilla	Brooklyn, NY	5/24/45
Pressly, Jaime	Kinston, NC.	7/30/77
Previn, Andre	Berlin, Germany	4/6/29
Price, Leontyne	Laurel, MS.	2/10/27
Price, Molly	North Plainfield, NJ	12/15/66
Price, Ray	Perryville, TX	1/12/26
Pride, Charley	Sledge, MS	3/18/38
Priestley, Jason	Vancouver, BC, Canada	8/28/69
Prince (The Artist)	Minneapolis, MN	6/7/58
Prince, Faith	Augusta, GA	8/5/57
Principal, Victoria	Fukuoka, Japan	1/3/50
Prinze, Freddie, Jr.	Albuquerque, NM.	3/8/76
Probst, Jeff	Wichita, KS	11/4/62
Proctor, Emily	Raleigh, NC.	10/8/68
Pryce, Jonathan	Holywell, N. Wales, UK	6/1/47
Puck, Wolfgang	St. Veit, Austria	1/8/49
Pulliam, Keshia Knight	Newark, NJ	4/9/79
Pullman, Bill	Hornell, NY	12/17/53
Purcell, Sarah	Richmond, IN	10/8/48
Quaid, Dennis	Houston, TX	4/9/54
Quaid, Randy	Houston, TX	10/1/50
Queen Latifah	Newark, NJ	3/18/70
Quinn, Aidan	Chicago, IL	3/8/59
Quinn, Colin	Brooklyn, NY	8/15/59
Quinn, Martha	Albany, NY.	5/11/59
Quinto, Zachary	Pittsburgh, PA	6/2/77
Rachins, Alan	Cambridge, MA	10/3/42
Radcliffe, Daniel	London, England, UK	7/23/89
Rae, Charlotte.	Milwaukee, WI	4/22/26
Raffi	Cairo, Egypt.	7/8/48
Rainer, Luise	Vienna, Austria	1/12/10
Raitt, Bonnie	Burbank, CA	11/8/49
Ramey, Samuel.	Colby, KS.	3/28/42
Ramirez, Efren	Los Angeles, CA	10/2/73
Ramirez, Sara	Mazatlan, Mexico.	8/31/75
Ramone, Tommy	Budapest, Hungary	1/29/52
Randolph, Joyce	Detroit, MI	10/21/24
Raphael, Sally Jessy	Easton, PA.	2/25/35
Rashad, Phylicia	Houston, TX	6/19/48
Ratzenberger, John	Bridgeport, CT.	4/6/47
Raver, Kim	New York, NY	3/15/69
Ray, Rachael	Glen Falls, NY	8/25/68
Reddy, Helen	Melbourne, Australia	10/25/41
Redford, Robert	Santa Monica, CA	8/18/36
Redgrave, Vanessa	London, England, UK	1/30/37
Reed, Lou	Brooklyn, NY	3/2/42
Reed, Rex	Ft. Worth, TX	10/2/38
Reese, Della	Detroit, MI	7/6/31
Reeves, Keanu	Beirut, Lebanon.	9/2/64
Reeves, Martha	Eufaula, AL	7/18/41
Regalbuto, Joe	New York, NY	8/24/49
Reid, Tara	Wyckoff, NJ	11/8/75
Reid, Tim	Norfolk, VA	12/19/44
Reid, Vernon	London, England, UK	8/22/58
Reilly, John C.	Chicago, IL	5/24/65
Reiner, Carl	Bronx, NY	3/20/22
Reiner, Rob	Bronx, NY	3/6/47
Reinhold, Judge	Wilmington, DE	5/21/57
Reinking, Ann	Seattle, WA	11/10/49
Reiser, Paul	New York, NY	3/30/57
Reitman, Ivan	Komarno, Czechoslovakia	10/26/46
Remini, Leah	Brooklyn, NY	6/15/70
Renner, Jeremy	Modesto, CA	1/7/71
Resnik, Regina	New York, NY	8/30/22
Reynolds, Burt	Waycross, GA	2/11/36
Reynolds, Debbie	El Paso, TX	4/1/32
Reynolds, Ryan	Vancouver, BC, Canada.	10/23/76
Reznor, Trent	Mercer, PA.	5/17/65
Rhames, Ving	New York, NY	5/12/59

Name	Birthplace	Birthdate
Rhymes, Busta	Brooklyn, NY	5/20/72
Rhys Meyers, Jonathan	Dublin, Ireland	7/27/77
Ribisi, Giovanni	Los Angeles, CA	12/17/74
Ricci, Christina	Santa Monica, CA	2/12/80
Richards, Denise	Downers Grove, IL	2/17/71
Richards, Keith	Dartford, Kent, Eng., UK	12/18/43
Richards, Michael	Culver City, CA	7/24/49
Richardson, Kevin	Lexington, KY	10/3/71
Richardson, Miranda	Lancashire, England, UK	3/3/58
Richardson, Patricia	Bethesda, MD	2/23/51
Richie, Lionel	Tuskegee, AL	6/20/49
Richie, Nicole	Berkeley, CA	9/21/81
Richter, Andy	Grand Rapids, MI	10/28/66
Rickles, Don	Jackson Heights, Queens, NY	5/8/26
Rickman, Alan	Hammersmith, Eng., UK	2/21/46
Riegert, Peter	New York, NY	4/11/47
Rigg, Diana	Doncaster, England, UK	7/20/38
Rihanna	St. Michael, Barbados	2/20/88
Riley, Amber	Long Beach, CA	2/15/86
Rimes, LeAnn	Flowood, MS	8/28/82
Ringwald, Molly	Roseville, CA	2/18/68
Ripa, Kelly	Stratford, NJ	10/2/70
Rivera, Chita	Washington, DC	1/23/33
Rivera, Geraldo	New York, NY	7/4/43
Rivers, Joan	Brooklyn, NY	6/8/33
Robbins, Tim	W. Covina, CA	10/16/58
Roberts, Doris	St. Louis, MO	11/4/30
Roberts, Eric	Biloxi, MS	4/18/56
Roberts, Julia	Smyrna, GA	10/28/67
Roberts, Tony	New York, NY	10/22/39
Robertson, Dale	Harrah, OK	7/14/23
Robinson, Smokey	Detroit, MI	2/19/40
Rochon, Lela	Torrance, CA	4/17/64
Rock, Chris	Andrews, SC	2/7/65
Rodgers, Jimmy	Camas, WA	9/18/33
Rodriguez, Jai	Brentwood, NY	6/22/79
Rodriguez, Johnny	Sabinal, TX	12/10/51
Rodriguez, Michelle	Bexar County, TX	7/12/78
Rogan, Joe	Newark, NJ	8/11/67
Rogen, Seth	Vancouver, BC, Canada	4/15/82
Rogers, Kenny	Houston, TX	8/21/38
Rogers, Mimi	Coral Gables, FL	1/27/56
Rogers, Wayne	Birmingham, AL	4/7/33
Rohm, Elizabeth	Dusseldorf, Germany	4/28/73
Rollins, Henry	Washington, DC	2/13/61
Rollins, Sonny	New York, NY	9/7/30
Romano, Ray	Forest Hills, Queens, NY	12/21/57
Romijn, Rebecca	Berkeley, CA	11/6/72
Ronstadt, Linda	Tucson, AZ	7/15/46
Rooney, Mickey	Brooklyn, NY	9/23/20
Root, Stephen	Sarasota, FL	11/17/51
Rose, Axl	Lafayette, IN	2/6/62
Roseanne	Salt Lake City, UT	11/3/52
Rose Marie	New York, NY	8/15/23
Ross, Charlotte	Winnetka, IL	1/21/68
Ross, Diana	Detroit, MI	3/26/44
Ross, Katharine	Hollywood, CA	1/29/40
Ross, Marion	Albert Lea, MN	10/25/28
Rossdale, Gavin	London, England, UK	10/30/65
Rossellini, Isabella	Rome, Italy	6/18/52
Rossum, Emmy	New York, NY	9/12/86
Roth, David Lee	Bloomington, IN	10/10/55
Roth, Tim	London, England, UK	5/14/61
Rotten, Johnny	London, England, UK	1/31/56
Rourke, Mickey	Schenectady, NY	9/16/56
Routh, Brandon	Des Moines, IA	10/9/79
Routledge, Patricia	Birkenhead, England, UK	2/17/29
Rowan, Kelly	Ottawa, ON, Canada	10/26/65
Rowlands, Gena	Cambria, WI	6/19/30
Rubinstein, John	Beverly Hills, CA	12/8/46
Rudd, Paul	Passaic, NJ	4/6/1969
Rudner, Rita	Miami, FL	9/17/56
Rudolph, Maya	Gainesville, FL	7/27/72
Ruehl, Mercedes	Jackson Heights, Queens, NY	2/28/48
Ruffalo, Mark	Kenosha, WI	11/22/67
Rupp, Debra Jo	Glendale, CA	2/24/51
Rush, Barbara	Denver, CO	1/4/27
Rush, Geoffrey	Toowoomba, Australia	7/6/51
Russell, Ken	Southampton, Eng., UK	7/3/27
Russell, Keri	Fountain Valley, CA	3/23/76
Russell, Kurt	Springfield, MA	3/17/51
Russell, Leon	Lawton, OK	4/2/41
Russell, Mark	Buffalo, NY	8/23/32
Russell, Theresa	San Diego, CA	3/20/57
Russo, Rene	Burbank, CA	2/17/54
Rutherford, Ann	Vancouver, BC, Canada	11/2/20
Ruttan, Susan	Oregon City, OR	9/16/50
Ryan, Meg	Fairfield, CT	11/19/61
Ryan, Roz	Detroit, MI	7/7/51
Rydell, Bobby	Philadelphia, PA	4/26/42
Ryder, Winona	Winona, MN	10/29/71
Sabato, Antonio, Jr.	Rome, Italy	2/29/72
Sade (Adu)	Ibadan, Nigeria	1/16/59
Sagal, Katey	Hollywood, CA	1/19/54
Saget, Bob	Philadelphia, PA	5/17/56
Sagnier, Ludivine	La Celle-St.-Cloud, France	7/3/79
Sahl, Mort	Montreal, QC, Canada	5/11/27
Saint, Eva Marie	Newark, NJ	7/4/24
St. James, Susan	Hollywood, CA	8/14/46
St. John, Jill	Los Angeles, CA	8/19/40
St. Patrick, Mathew	Philadelphia, PA	3/17/68
Sajak, Pat	Chicago, IL	10/26/46
Saks, Gene	New York, NY	11/8/21
Saldana, Zoë	Passaic, NJ	6/19/78
Salling, Mark	Dallas, TX	8/17/82
Salonga, Lea	Manila, Philippines	2/22/71
Samberg, Andy	Berkeley, CA	8/18/78
Samms, Emma	London, England, UK	8/28/60
Sandler, Adam	Brooklyn, NY	9/9/66
Sands, Julian	West Yorkshire, Eng., UK	1/15/58
San Giacomo, Laura	Hoboken, NJ	11/14/62
Santana, Carlos	Autlan, Mexico	7/20/47
Sara, Mia	Brooklyn, NY	6/19/67
Sarandon, Susan	New York, NY	10/4/46
Sartain, Gailard	Tulsa, OK	9/18/46
Savage, Ben	Highland Park, IL	9/13/80
Savage, Fred	Highland Park, IL	7/9/76
Sawa, Devon	Vancouver, BC, Canada	9/7/78
Saxon, John	Brooklyn, NY	8/5/36
Sayles, John	Schenectady, NY	9/28/50
Scacchi, Greta	Milan, Italy	2/18/60
Scaggs, Boz	Canton, OH	6/8/44
Scales, Prunella	Sutton Abinger, Eng., UK	6/22/32
Scalia, Jack	Brooklyn, NY	11/10/51
Schallert, William	Los Angeles, CA	7/6/22
Schell, Maximilian	Vienna, Austria	12/8/30
Schiff, Richard	Bethesda, MD	5/27/55
Schiffer, Claudia	Rheinbach, Germany	8/25/70
Schneider, John	Mt. Kisco, NY	4/8/54
Schneider, Rob	San Francisco, CA	10/31/63
Schram, Bitty	New York, NY	7/17/68
Schreiber, Liev	San Francisco, CA	10/4/67
Schroder, Rick	Staten Island, NY	4/13/70
Schwarzenegger, Arnold	Thal, Austria	7/30/47
Schwimmer, David	Astoria, Queens, NY	11/2/66
Sciorra, Annabella	Wethersfield, CT	3/24/64
Scolari, Peter	New Rochelle, NY	9/12/54
Scorsese, Martin	Flushing, Queens, NY	11/17/42
Scott, Lizabeth	Scranton, PA	9/29/22
Scott, Ridley	South Shields, England, UK	11/30/37
Scott, Seann William	Cottage Grove, MN	10/3/76
Scott-Heron, Gil	Chicago, IL	4/1/49
Scott Thomas, Kristin	Redruth, England, UK	5/24/60
Scotto, Renata	Savona, Italy	2/24/34
Scully, Vin	Bronx, NY	11/29/27
Seacrest, Ryan	Atlanta, GA	12/24/74
Seagal, Steven	Lansing, MI	4/10/51
Secor, Kyle	Tacoma, WA	5/31/57
Sedaka, Neil	Brooklyn, NY	3/13/39
Sedgwick, Kyra	New York, NY	8/19/65
Seeger, Pete	New York, NY	5/3/19
Segal, George	Great Neck, NY	2/13/34
Seidelman, Susan	Abington, PA	12/11/52
Seinfeld, Jerry	Brooklyn, NY	4/29/54
Seldes, Marian	New York, NY	8/23/28
Sellecca, Connie	Bronx, NY	5/25/55
Selleck, Tom	Detroit, MI	1/29/45
Severinsen, Doc	Arlington, OR	7/7/27
Sevigny, Chloë	Springfield, MA	11/18/74
Sewell, Rufus	Twickenham, Middlesex, England, UK	10/29/67
Seymour, Jane	Hillingdon, England, UK	2/15/51
Shackelford, Ted	Oklahoma City, OK	6/23/46
Shaffer, Paul	Thunder Bay, ON, Canada	11/28/49
Shakira (Mebarak Ripoll)	Barranquilla, Colombia	2/2/77
Shalhoub, Tony	Green Bay, WI	10/9/53
Shandling, Garry	Chicago, IL	11/29/49
Shankar, Ravi	Benares, India	4/7/20
Shannon, Molly	Shaker Heights, OH	9/16/64
Sharif, Omar	Alexandria, Egypt	4/10/32
Shatner, William	Montreal, QC, Canada	3/22/31
Shaughnessy, Charles	London, England, UK	2/9/55
Shaver, Helen	St. Thomas, ON, Canada	2/24/51
Shawkat, Alia	Riverside, CA	4/18/89
Shea, John	N. Conway, NH	4/14/49
Shearer, Harry	Los Angeles, CA	12/23/43
Sheedy, Ally	New York, NY	6/13/62
Sheen, Charlie	Los Angeles, CA	9/3/65
Sheen, Martin	Dayton, OH	8/3/40
Sheen, Michael	Newport, Wales, UK	2/5/69
Sheindlin, Judy	Brooklyn, NY	10/21/42
Shelley, Carole	London, England, UK	8/16/39
Shepard, Sam	Ft. Sheridan, IL	11/5/43
Shepherd, Cybill	Memphis, TN	2/18/50
Shepherd, Sherri	Chicago, IL	4/22/67
Sheridan, Nicollette	Worthing, England, UK	11/21/63
Shields, Brooke	New York, NY	5/31/65
Shire, Talia	Lake Success, NY	4/25/46
Short, Martin	Hamilton, ON, Canada	3/26/50

Name	Birthplace	Birthdate
Shortz, Will	Crawfordsville, IN.	8/26/52
Show, Grant	Detroit, MI	2/27/62
Shue, Andrew	S. Orange, NJ	2/20/67
Shue, Elisabeth	Wilmington, DE	10/6/63
Shyamalan, M. Night.	Pondicherry, India	8/6/70
Sidibe, Gabourey	Brooklyn, NY	5/6/83
Sigler, Jamie-Lynn	Jericho, NY	5/15/81
Sikking, James B.	Los Angeles, CA	3/5/34
Silverman, Jonathan.	Beverly Hills, CA	8/5/66
Silverman, Sarah	Bedford, NH.	12/1/70
Silverstone, Alicia	San Francisco, CA.	10/4/76
Simmons, Gene	Haifa, Israel.	8/25/49
Simmons, Henry	Stamford, CT.	7/1/70
Simmons, Richard	New Orleans, LA.	7/12/48
Simon, Carly	New York, NY	6/25/45
Simon, Paul	Newark, NJ	10/13/41
Simpson, Ashlee.	Waco, TX.	10/3/84
Simpson, Jessica	Abilene, TX	7/10/80
Sinatra, Nancy	Jersey City, NJ.	6/8/40
Sinbad	Benton Harbor, MI	11/10/56
Singleton, John.	Los Angeles, CA	1/6/68
Sinise, Gary	Blue Island, IL	3/17/55
Sirico, Tony	Brooklyn, NY	7/29/42
Sisto, Jeremy	Grass Valley, CA	10/6/74
Sizemore, Tom	Detroit, MI	9/29/64
Skerritt, Tom	Detroit, MI	8/25/33
Slater, Christian	New York, NY	8/18/69
Slater, Helen	Massapequa, NY.	12/15/63
Slattery, John	Boston, MA	8/13/63
Sledge, Percy	Leighton, AL	11/25/40
Slezak, Erika.	Hollywood, CA.	8/5/46
Slick, Grace	Evanston, IL	10/30/39
Smirnoff, Yakov.	Odessa, Ukraine	1/24/51
Smith, Allison	New York, NY	12/9/69
Smith, Jaclyn	Houston, TX	10/26/47
Smith, Jaden	Malibu, CA.	7/8/98
Smith, Keely	Norfolk, VA	3/9/32
Smith, Kevin	Red Bank, NJ	8/2/70
Smith, Maggie	Ilford, England, UK	12/28/34
Smith, Patti	Chicago, IL	12/30/46
Smith, Robert	Blackpool, England, UK.	4/21/59
Smith, Will	Philadelphia, PA	9/25/68
Smits, Jimmy	Brooklyn, NY	7/9/55
Smothers, Dick	Governor's Island, NY	11/20/38
Smothers, Tom	Governor's Island, NY	2/2/37
Snipes, Wesley	Orlando, FL.	7/31/62
Snooki (Nicole Polizzi)	Santiago, Chile	11/23/87
Snoop Dogg	Long Beach, CA	10/20/72
Soderbergh, Steven	Atlanta, GA	1/14/63
Somers, Suzanne	San Bruno, CA	10/16/46
Sommer, Elke	Berlin, Germany	11/5/40
Sorbo, Kevin	Mound, MN	9/24/58
Sorvino, Mira	Tenafly, NJ.	9/28/67
Sorvino, Paul	Brooklyn, NY	4/13/39
Soul, David	Chicago, IL	8/28/43
Spacek, Sissy	Quitman, TX	12/25/49
Spacey, Kevin	S. Orange, NJ	7/26/59
Spade, David	Birmingham, MI	7/22/64
Spader, James	Boston, MA	2/7/60
Spalding, Esperanza.	Portland, OR	1984
Spano, Joe	San Francisco, CA.	7/7/46
Sparks, Jordin	Phoenix, AZ.	12/22/89
Spears, Britney	Kentwood, LA	12/2/81
Spears, Jamie-Lynn	McComb, MS.	4/4/91
Spector, Phil	Bronx, NY	12/26/40
Spelling, Tori	Los Angeles, CA	5/16/73
Spielberg, Steven	Cincinnati, OH	12/18/46
Spiner, Brent.	Houston, TX	2/2/49
Springer, Jerry	London, England, UK	2/13/44
Springfield, Rick	Sydney, Australia	8/23/49
Springsteen, Bruce	Freehold, NJ	9/23/49
Spurlock, Morgan	Parksburg, WV.	11/7/70
Stahl, Nick	Harlingen, TX	12/5/79
Stallone, Sylvester	New York, NY	7/6/46
Stamos, John	Cypress, CA	8/19/63
Stamp, Terence	Stepney, England, UK	7/22/39
Stanton, Harry Dean.	West Irvine, KY	7/14/26
Stapleton, Jean.	New York, NY	1/19/23
Starr, Ringo	Liverpool, England, UK	7/7/40
Steenburgen, Mary.	Newport, AR	2/8/53
Stefani, Gwen	Fullterton, CA.	10/3/69
Stein, Ben.	Washington, DC	11/25/44
Stephens, James	Mt. Kisco, NY.	5/18/51
Stern, Daniel.	Bethesda, MD	8/28/57
Stern, Howard.	Roosevelt, NY	1/12/54
Sternhagen, Frances	Washington, DC	1/13/30
Stevens, Andrew	Memphis, TN.	6/10/55
Stevens, Cat (Yusef Islam).	London, England, UK	7/21/48
Stevens, Connie	Brooklyn, NY.	8/8/38
Stevens, Rise	Bronx, NY	6/11/13
Stevens, Stella	Hot Coffee, MS	10/1/36
Stevenson, Parker	Philadelphia, PA	6/4/52
Stewart, French	Albuquerque, NM.	2/20/64
Stewart, Jon	New York, NY	11/28/62
Stewart, Kristen	Los Angeles, CA	4/9/90

Name	Birthplace	Birthdate
Stewart, Patrick.	Mirfield, England, UK	7/13/40
Stewart, Rod	London, England, UK	1/10/45
Stiers, David Ogden	Peoria, IL.	10/31/42
Stiles, Julia	New York, NY	3/28/81
Stiller, Ben	New York, NY	11/30/65
Stiller, Jerry	Brooklyn, NY	6/8/27
Stills, Stephen	Dallas, TX.	1/3/45
Sting	Newcastle upon Tyne, England, UK	10/2/51
Stipe, Michael	Decatur, GA.	1/4/60
Stockwell, Dean	North Hollywood, CA	3/5/36
Stoltz, Eric	Whittier, CA	9/30/61
Stone, Dee Wallace	Kansas City, KS.	12/14/48
Stone, Emma	Scottsdale, AZ	11/6/88
Stone, Oliver	New York, NY	9/15/46
Stone, Sharon	Meadville, PA.	3/10/58
Stonestreet, Eric	Kansas City, KS.	9/9/71
Stookey, Paul	Baltimore, MD	12/30/37
Storch, Larry	New York, NY	1/8/23
Stowe, Madeleine	Eagle Rock, CA.	8/18/58
Strait, George	Pearsall, TX.	5/18/52
Strasser, Robin	New York, NY	5/7/45
Stratas, Teresa	Toronto, ON, Canada.	5/26/38
Strathairn, David.	San Francisco, CA	1/26/49
Strauss, Peter.	Croton-on-Hudson, NY	2/20/47
Streep, Meryl	Summit, NJ	6/22/49
Streisand, Barbra	Brooklyn, NY	4/24/42
Stringfield, Sherry	Colorado Springs, CO	6/24/67
Stritch, Elaine	Detroit, MI	2/2/26
Stroman, Susan	Wilmington, DE	10/17/54
Struthers, Sally	Portland, OR	7/28/48
Studdard, Ruben	Frankfurt, Germany	9/12/78
Suchet, David	London, England, UK	5/2/46
Sullivan, Erik Per	Worcester, MA.	7/12/91
Sullivan, Susan.	New York, NY	11/18/42
Summer, Donna	Dorchester, MA	12/31/48
Sutherland, Donald.	St. John, NB, Canada	7/17/34
Sutherland, Kiefer.	London, England, UK	12/21/66
Suvari, Mena	Newport, RI	2/9/79
Swank, Hilary	Bellingham, WA.	7/30/74
Swift, Taylor.	Wyomissing, PA.	12/13/89
Swinton, Tilda	London, England, UK	11/5/60
Swit, Loretta	Passaic, NJ	11/4/37
Sykes, Wanda	Portsmouth, VA	3/7/64
Szmanda, Eric	Milwaukee, WI	7/24/75
T, Mr.	Chicago, IL	5/21/52
Takei, George	Los Angeles, CA	4/20/37
Tallchief, Maria	Fairfax, OK	1/24/25
Tamblyn, Amber	Santa Monica, CA	5/14/83
Tamblyn, Russ	Los Angeles, CA	12/30/34
Tambor, Jeffrey	San Francisco, CA.	7/8/44
Tarantino, Quentin	Knoxville, TN	3/27/63
Tautou, Audrey	Beaumont, France	8/9/78
Taylor, Buck	Hollywood, CA.	5/13/38
Taylor, James	Boston, MA	3/12/48
Taylor, Rip	Washington, DC	1/13/34
Taylor, Rod	Sydney, Australia	1/11/30
Taymor, Julie	Newton, MA.	12/15/52
Te Kanawa, Kiri	Gisborne, New Zealand	3/6/44
Teller	Philadelphia, PA	2/14/48
Temple Black, Shirley	Santa Monica, CA	4/23/28
Tennant, Victoria	London, England, UK	9/30/50
Tennille, Toni	Montgomery, AL	5/8/43
Tesh, John	Garden City, NY.	7/9/52
Tharp, Twyla	Portland, IN.	7/1/41
Thaxter, Phyllis	Portland, ME	11/20/21
Theron, Charlize	Benoni, South Africa	8/7/75
Thicke, Alan	Kirkland Lake, ON, Canada.	3/1/47
Thiessen, Tiffani	Long Beach, CA	1/23/74
Thomas, Jay	Kermit, TX.	7/12/48
Thomas, Jonathan Taylor	Bethlehem, PA.	9/8/81
Thomas, Marlo	Deerfield, MI	11/21/37
Thomas, Michael Tilson	Hollywood, CA.	12/21/44
Thomas, Philip Michael	Columbus, OH.	5/26/49
Thomas, Richard	New York, NY	6/13/51
Thomas, Sean Patrick	Wilmington, DE	12/17/70
Thompson, Emma	London, England, UK	4/15/59
Thompson, Jack	Sydney, Australia	8/31/40
Thompson, Lea	Rochester, MN.	5/31/61
Thorne-Smith, Courtney	San Francisco, CA.	11/8/67
Thornton, Billy Bob	Hot Springs, AR.	8/4/55
Thurman, Uma	Boston, MA.	4/29/70
Tiegs, Cheryl	Breckenridge, MN	9/25/47
Tierney, Maura	Boston, MA	2/3/65
Tillis, Mel	Tampa, FL.	8/8/32
Tilly, Jennifer	Harbor City, CA	9/16/58
Tilly, Meg.	Long Beach, CA	2/14/60
Timberlake, Justin.	Memphis, TN.	1/31/81
Tisdale, Ashley	West Deal, NJ	7/2/85
Tomei, Marisa	Brooklyn, NY	12/4/64
Tomlin, Lily	Detroit, MI	9/1/39
Tork, Peter	Washington, DC	2/13/42
Torn, Rip.	Temple, TX	2/6/31
Townsend, Robert	Chicago, IL	2/6/57
Townshend, Peter.	Chiswick, England, UK	5/19/45
Travanti, Daniel J.	Kenosha, WI	3/7/40

Name	Birthplace	Birthdate
Travis, Nancy	Astoria, Queens, NY	9/21/61
Travis, Randy	Marshville, NC	5/4/59
Travolta, John	Englewood, NJ	2/18/54
Trebek, Alex	Sudbury, ON, Canada	7/22/40
Tripplehorn, Jean	Tulsa, OK	6/10/63
Tritt, Travis	Marietta, GA	2/9/63
Tucci, Stanley	Katonah, NY	1/11/60
Tucker, Chris	Decatur, GA	8/31/72
Tucker, Michael	Baltimore, MD	2/6/44
Tucker, Tanya	Seminole, TX	10/10/58
Tune, Tommy	Wichita Falls, TX	2/28/39
Turlington, Christy	Walnut Creek, CA	1/2/69
Turner, Janine	Lincoln, NE	12/6/62
Turner, Kathleen	Springfield, MO	6/19/54
Turner, Tina	Brownsville, TN	11/26/39
Turturro, John	Brooklyn, NY	2/28/57
Twain, Shania	Windsor, ON, Canada	8/28/65
Twiggy (Lawson)	London, England, UK	9/19/49
Tyler, Liv	New York, NY	7/1/77
Tyler, Steven	Yonkers, NY	3/26/48
Tyson, Cicely	New York, NY	12/19/33
Uecker, Bob	Milwaukee, WI	1/26/35
Uggams, Leslie	New York, NY	5/25/43
Ullman, Tracey	Slough, England, UK	12/30/59
Ullmann, Liv	Tokyo, Japan	12/16/38
Ulrich, Skeet	Lynchburg, VA	1/20/70
Underwood, Blair	Tacoma, WA	8/25/64
Underwood, Carrie	Checotah, OK	3/10/83
Urban, Keith	Whangarei, North Island, New Zealand	10/26/67
Urie, Michael	Dallas, TX	8/8/80
Usher (Raymond IV)	Chattanooga, TN	10/14/78
Vaccaro, Brenda	Brooklyn, NY	11/18/39
Vale, Jerry	Bronx, NY	7/8/32
Valente, Caterina	Paris, France	1/14/31
Valley, Mark	Ogdensburg, NY	12/24/64
Valli, Frankie	Newark, NJ	5/3/37
Van Ark, Joan	New York, NY	6/16/43
VanCamp, Emily	Port Perry, ON, Canada	5/12/86
Vance, Courtney B.	Detroit, MI	3/12/60
Van Damme, Jean-Claude	Brussels, Belgium	10/18/60
Van Der Beek, James	Cheshire, CT	3/8/77
Van Doren, Mamie	Rowena, SD	2/6/31
Van Dyke, Dick	West Plains, MO	12/13/25
Van Dyke, Jerry	Danville, IL	7/27/31
Van Halen, Eddie	Nijmegen, Netherlands	1/26/55
Van Patten, Dick	Kew Gardens, Queens, NY	12/9/28
Van Peebles, Mario	Mexico City, Mexico	1/15/57
Van Sant, Gus	Louisville, KY	7/24/52
Van Zandt, Steven	Winthrop, MA	11/22/50
Vardalos, Nia	Winnipeg, MB, Canada	9/24/62
Vaughn, Robert	New York, NY	11/22/32
Vaughn, Vince	Minneapolis, MN	3/28/70
Vedder, Eddie	Evanston, IL	12/23/64
Vega, Alexa	Miami, FL	8/27/88
Ventimiglia, Milo	Anaheim, CA	7/8/77
Vereen, Ben	Miami, FL	10/10/46
Vergara, Sofia	Barranquilla, Colombia	7/10/72
Vickers, Jon	Prince Albert, SK, Canada	10/29/26
Vieira, Meredith	Providence, RI	12/30/53
Vigoda, Abe	New York, NY	2/24/21
Vincent, Jan-Michael	Denver, CO	7/15/44
Vinton, Bobby	Canonsburg, PA	4/16/35
Visnjic, Goran	Sibenik, Yugo. (Croatia)	9/9/72
Vitale, Dick	East Rutherford, NJ	6/9/39
Voight, Jon	Yonkers, NY	12/29/38
Von Stade, Frederica	Somerville, NJ	6/1/45
Von Sydow, Max	Lund, Sweden	4/10/29
Von Trier, Lars	Copenhagen, Denmark	4/30/56
Wagner, Jack	Washington, MO	10/3/59
Wagner, Lindsay	Los Angeles, CA	6/22/49
Wagner, Robert	Detroit, MI	2/10/30
Wahl, Ken	Chicago, IL	10/31/54
Wahlberg, Mark	Dorchester, MA	6/5/71
Wain, Bea	Bronx, NY	4/30/17
Waite, Ralph	White Plains, NY	6/22/28
Waits, Tom	Pomona, CA	12/7/49
Walden, Robert	New York, NY	9/25/43
Walken, Christopher	Astoria, Queens, NY	3/31/43
Walker, Clint	Hartford, IL	5/30/27
Wallace, Marcia	Creston, IA	11/1/42
Wallach, Eli	Brooklyn, NY	12/7/15
Walsh, Kate	San Jose, CA	10/13/67
Walter, Jessica	Brooklyn, NY	1/31/41
Ward, Fred	San Diego, CA	12/30/42
Ward, Sela	Meridian, MS	7/11/56
Ward, Simon	Kent, London, Eng., UK	10/19/41
Warfield, Marsha	Chicago, IL	3/5/54
Warner, Malcolm-Jamal	Jersey City, NJ	8/18/70
Warren, Lesley Ann	New York, NY	8/16/46
Warwick, Dionne	East Orange, NJ	12/12/40
Washington, Denzel	Mt. Vernon, NY	12/28/54
Washington, Isaiah	Houston, TX	8/3/63
Wasikowska, Mia	Canberra, Australia	10/14/89
Watanabe, Ken	Koide, Niigata, Japan	10/21/59

Name	Birthplace	Birthdate
Waters, John	Baltimore, MD	4/22/46
Waters, Roger	Great Bookham, Eng., UK	9/6/43
Waterston, Sam	Cambridge, MA	11/15/40
Watson, Emily	London, England, UK	1/14/67
Watson, Emma	Paris, France	4/15/90
Watts, Andre	Nuremberg, Germany	6/20/46
Watts, Naomi	Shoreham, England, UK	9/28/68
Wayans, Damon	New York, NY	9/4/60
Wayans, Keenen Ivory	Brooklyn, NY	6/8/58
Wayans, Marlon	New York, NY	7/23/72
Wayans, Shawn	New York, NY	1/19/71
Weathers, Carl	New Orleans, LA	1/14/48
Weaver, Fritz	Pittsburgh, PA	1/19/26
Weaver, Sigourney	New York, NY	10/8/49
Weiland, Scott	Santa Cruz, CA	10/27/67
Weir, Peter	Sydney, Australia	8/21/44
Weisz, Rachel	London, England, UK	3/7/71
Weitz, Bruce	Norwalk, CT	5/27/43
Welch, Raquel	Chicago, IL	9/5/40
Weld, Tuesday	New York, NY	8/27/43
Weller, Peter	Stevens Point, WI	6/24/47
Welling, Tom	Putnam Valley, NY	4/26/77
Wells, Kitty	Nashville, TN	8/30/19
Wendt, George	Chicago, IL	10/17/48
Wentz, Pete	Wilmette, IL	6/5/79
West, Adam	Walla Walla, WA	9/19/28
West, Kayne	Atlanta, GA	6/8/77
West, Shane	Baton Rouge, LA	6/10/78
Wettig, Patricia	Cincinnati, OH	12/4/51
Whalley, Joanne	Manchester, England, UK	8/25/64
Wheaton, Wil	Burbank, CA	7/29/72
Whitaker, Forest	Longview, TX	7/15/61
White, Betty	Oak Park, IL	1/17/22
White, Jack	Detroit, MI	7/9/75
White, Jaleel	Pasadena, CA	11/27/76
White, Vanna	N. Myrtle Beach, SC	2/18/57
Whitford, Bradley	Madison, WI	10/10/59
Whitman, Stuart	San Francisco, CA	2/1/28
Wiest, Dianne	Kansas City, MO	3/28/48
Wiig, Kristen	Canandaigua, NY	8/22/73
Wilder, Gene	Milwaukee, WI	6/11/33
Wilkinson, Tom	Leeds, England, UK	12/12/48
Williams, Andy	Wall Lake, IA	12/3/27
Williams, Armstrong	Marion, SC	2/5/59
Williams, Barry	Santa Monica, CA	9/30/54
Williams, Billy Dee	New York, NY	4/6/37
Williams, Cindy	Van Nuys, CA	8/22/47
Williams, Esther	Los Angeles, CA	8/8/21
Williams, Hal	Columbus, OH	12/14/38
Williams, Hank, Jr.	Shreveport, LA	5/26/49
Williams, JoBeth	Houston, TX	12/6/48
Williams, Kimberly	Rye, NY	9/14/71
Williams, Lucinda	Lake Charles, LA	1/26/53
Williams, Michelle	Kalispell, MT	9/9/80
Williams, Montel	Baltimore, MD	7/3/56
Williams, Paul	Omaha, NE	9/19/40
Williams, Robin	Chicago, IL	7/21/51
Williams, Treat	Rowayton, CT	12/1/51
Williams, Vanessa	Millwood, NY	3/18/63
Williamson, Kevin	New Bern, NC	3/14/65
Williamson, Nicol	Hamilton, Scotland, UK	9/14/38
Willis, Bruce	Idar-Oberstein, W. Germ.	3/19/55
Wilson, Brian	Inglewood, CA	6/20/42
Wilson, Cassandra	Jackson, MS	12/4/55
Wilson, Chandra	Houston, TX	8/27/69
Wilson, Demond	Valdosta, GA	10/13/46
Wilson, Elizabeth	Grand Rapids, MI	4/4/21
Wilson, Luke	Dallas, TX	9/21/71
Wilson, Nancy	Chillicothe, OH	2/20/37
Wilson, Owen	Dallas, TX	11/18/68
Wilson, Rainn	Seattle, WA	1/20/66
Windom, William	New York, NY	9/28/23
Winfrey, Oprah	Kosciusko, MS	1/29/54
Winger, Debra	Cleveland, OH	5/16/55
Winkler, Henry	New York, NY	10/30/45
Winningham, Mare	Phoenix, AZ	5/16/59
Winokur, Marissa Jaret	New York, NY	2/2/73
Winslet, Kate	Reading, England, UK	10/5/75
Winter, Johnny	Beaumont, TX	2/23/44
Winters, Jonathan	Dayton, OH	11/11/25
Winwood, Steve	Birmingham, England, UK	5/12/48
Withers, Jane	Atlanta, GA	4/12/26
Witherspoon, Reese	New Orleans, LA	3/22/76
Witt, Alicia	Worcester, MA	8/21/75
Wolf, Scott	Boston, MA	6/4/68
Wonder, Stevie	Saginaw, MI	5/13/50
Wong, Faye	Beijing, China	8/8/69
Woo, John	Guangzhou, China	5/1/46
Wood, Elijah	Cedar Rapids, IA	1/28/81
Woodard, Alfre	Tulsa, OK	11/8/53
Woods, James	Vernal, UT	4/18/47
Woodward, Joanne	Thomasville, GA	2/27/30
Wopat, Tom	Lodi, WI	9/9/51
Worthington Sam	Godalming, Surrey, England, UK	8/2/76
Wright, Jeffrey	Washington, DC	12/7/65

Name	Birthplace	Birthdate	Name	Birthplace	Birthdate
Wright, Max	Detroit, MI	8/2/43	Young, Sean	Louisville, KY	11/20/59
Wright, Robin	Dallas, TX	4/8/66	Zane, Billy	Chicago, IL	2/24/66
Wright, Steven	New York, NY	12/6/55	Zeffirelli, Franco	Florence, Italy	2/12/23
Wyle, Noah	Hollywood, CA	6/4/71	Zellweger, Renée	Katy, TX	4/25/69
Wyman, Bill	London, England, UK	10/24/36	Zemeckis, Robert	Chicago, IL	5/14/52
Yankovic, Weird Al	Lynwood, CA	10/23/59	Zerbe, Anthony	Long Beach, CA	5/20/36
Yanni (Chrysomallis)	Kalamata, Greece	11/14/54	Zeta-Jones, Catherine	Swansea, Wales, UK	9/25/69
Yarrow, Peter	New York, NY	5/31/38	Zimbalist, Efrem, Jr.	New York, NY	11/30/18
Yearwood, Trisha	Monticello, GA	9/19/64	Zimbalist, Stephanie	New York, NY	10/8/56
Yoakam, Dwight	Pikesville, KY	10/23/56	Zimmer, Kim	Grand Rapids, MI	2/2/55
York, Michael	Fulmer, England, UK	3/27/42	Zhang, Ziyi	Beijing, China	2/9/79
Young, Alan	North Shields, England, UK	11/19/19	Zukerman, Pinchas	Tel Aviv, Israel	7/16/48
Young, Burt	New York, NY	4/30/40	Zuniga, Daphne	Berkeley, CA	10/28/62
Young, Neil	Toronto, ON, Canada	11/12/45			

Entertainment Personalities of the Past

See also other lists for some deceased entertainers not included here.

Name	Born	Died	Name	Born	Died	Name	Born	Died
Aaliyah	1979	2001	Barrymore, Ethel	1879	1959	Bowes, Maj. Edward	1874	1946
Abbott, Bud	1895	1974	Barrymore, John	1882	1942	Bowman, Lee	1914	1979
Abbott, George	1887	1995	Barrymore, Lionel	1878	1954	Boxcar Willie	1931	1999
Acuff, Roy	1903	1992	Barrymore, Maurice	1848	1905	Boyd, Stephen	1928	1977
Adams, Don	1923	2005	Barthelmess, Richard	1895	1963	Boyd, William	1898	1972
Adams, Edie	1927	2008	Bartholomew, Freddie	1924	1992	Boyer, Charles	1899	1978
Adams, Joey	1911	1999	Barty, Billy	1924	2000	Boyle, Peter	1935	2006
Adams, Maude	1872	1953	Basehart, Richard	1914	1984	Bracken, Eddie	1915	2002
Adler, Jacob P.	1855	1926	Basie, Count	1904	1984	Brady, Alice	1892	1939
Adoree, Renee	1898	1933	Bates, Alan	1934	2003	Brando, Marlon	1924	2004
Agar, John	1921	2002	Bavier, Francis	1902	1989	Branigan, Laura	1957	2004
Aherne, Brian	1902	1986	Baxter, Anne	1923	1985	Brazzi, Rossano	1916	1994
Ailey, Alvin	1931	1989	Baxter, Warner	1889	1951	Brennan, Walter	1894	1974
Akins, Claude	1918	1994	Beaumont, Hugh	1909	1982	Brent, George	1904	1979
Albert, Eddie	1906	2005	Beavers, Louise	1902	1962	Brett, Jeremy	1935	1995
Albertson, Frank	1909	1964	Beery, Noah, Sr.	1884	1946	Brewer, Teresa	1931	2007
Albertson, Jack	1907	1981	Beery, Noah, Jr.	1913	1994	Brice, Fanny	1891	1951
Alda, Robert	1914	1986	Beery, Wallace	1885	1949	Bridges, Lloyd	1913	1998
Allen, Fred	1894	1956	Begley, Ed	1901	1970	Broderick, Helen	1891	1959
Allen, Gracie	1906	1964	Bel Geddes, Barbara	1922	2005	Bronson, Charles	1921	2003
Allen, Mel	1913	1996	Bellamy, Ralph	1904	1991	Brooks, Foster	1912	2001
Allen, Peter	1944	1992	Belushi, John	1949	1982	Brooks, Louise	1906	1985
Allen, Steve	1921	2000	Benaderet, Bea	1906	1968	Brown, Clarence	1890	1987
Allgood, Sara	1883	1950	Bendix, William	1906	1964	Brown, James	1933	2006
Allyson, June	1917	2006	Bennett, Constance	1904	1965	Brown, Joe E.	1892	1973
Altman, Robert	1925	2006	Bennett, Joan	1910	1990	Brown, Les	1912	2001
Ameche, Don	1908	1993	Bennett, Michael	1943	1987	Browne, Roscoe Lee	1925	2007
Ames, Leon	1903	1993	Benny, Jack	1894	1974	Bruce, Lenny	1925	1966
Amsterdam, Morey	1908	1996	Berg, Gertrude	1899	1966	Bruce, Nigel	1895	1953
Anderson, G. M. "Bronco Billy"	1882	1971	Bergen, Edgar	1903	1978	Bruce, Virginia	1910	1982
Anderson, Judith	1897	1992	Bergman, Ingmar	1918	2007	Brynner, Yul	1915	1985
Anderson, Marian	1897	1993	Bergman, Ingrid	1915	1982	Buchanan, Edgar	1903	1979
Andre the Giant	1946	1993	Berkeley, Busby	1895	1976	Buchholz, Horst	1933	2003
Andrews, Dana	1909	1992	Berle, Milton	1908	2002	Buñuel, Luis	1900	1983
Andrews, Laverne	1913	1967	Berlin, Irving	1888	1989	Buono, Victor	1938	1982
Andrews, Maxene	1916	1995	Bernardi, Herschel	1923	1986	Burke, Billie	1885	1970
Angeli, Pier	1932	1971	Bernhardt, Sarah	1844	1923	Burnette, Smiley	1911	1967
Antonioni, Michelangelo	1912	2007	Bernstein, Leonard	1918	1990	Burns, George	1896	1996
Arbuckle, Fatty (Roscoe)	1887	1933	Berry, Jan	1941	2004	Burr, Raymond	1917	1993
Archerd, Army	1922	2009	Bessell, Ted	1939	1996	Burton, Richard	1925	1984
Arden, Eve	1908	1990	Bickford, Charles	1889	1967	Busch, Mae	1897	1946
Arlen, Richard	1900	1976	Big Bopper, The	1930	1959	Bushman, Francis X.	1883	1966
Arliss, George	1868	1946	Billingsley, Barbara	1915	2010	Buttons, Red	1919	2006
Armstrong, Louis	1901	1971	Bing, Rudolf	1902	1997	Byington, Spring	1893	1971
Arnaz, Desi	1917	1986	Bishop, Joey	1918	2007	Cabot, Bruce	1904	1972
Arness, James	1923	2011	Bitzer, Billy	1872	1944	Cabot, Sebastian	1918	1977
Arnold, Eddy	1918	2008	Bixby, Bill	1934	1993	Cagney, James	1899	1986
Arnold, Edward	1890	1956	Blackstone, Harry, Jr.	1934	1997	Caldwell, Sarah	1924	2006
Arquette, Cliff	1905	1974	Blackstone, Harry, Sr.	1885	1965	Calhern, Louis	1895	1956
Arthur, Beatrice	1922	2009	Blaine, Vivian	1921	1995	Calhoun, Rory	1922	1999
Arthur, Jean	1900	1991	Blake, Amanda	1931	1989	Callas, Charlie	1927	2011
Ashcroft, Peggy	1907	1991	Blake, Eubie	1883	1983	Callas, Maria	1923	1977
Astaire, Fred	1899	1987	Blanc, Mel	1908	1989	Calloway, Cab	1907	1994
Astor, Mary	1906	1987	Blocker, Dan	1928	1972	Cambridge, Godfrey	1933	1976
Atkins, Chet	1924	2001	Blondell, Joan	1909	1979	Campbell, Mrs. Patrick	1865	1940
Atwill, Lionel	1885	1946	Blondin, Charles	1824	1897	Candy, John	1950	1994
Auer, Mischa	1905	1967	Blore, Eric	1887	1959	Cantinflas	1911	1993
Aumont, Jean-Pierre	1911	2001	Blue, Ben	1901	1975	Cantor, Eddie	1892	1964
Austin, Gene	1900	1972	Blyden, Larry	1925	1975	Capra, Frank	1897	1991
Autry, Gene	1907	1998	Bogarde, Dirk	1921	1999	Carey, Harry	1878	1947
Axton, Hoyt	1938	1999	Bogart, Humphrey	1899	1957	Carey, Macdonald	1913	1994
Ayres, Lew	1908	1996	Boland, Mary	1880	1965	Carle, Frankie	1903	2001
Backus, Jim	1913	1989	Boles, John	1895	1969	Carlin, George	1937	2008
Bailey, Pearl	1918	1990	Bolger, Ray	1904	1987	Carlisle Hart, Kitty	1910	2007
Bainter, Fay	1892	1968	Bond, Ward	1903	1960	Carney, Art	1918	2003
Baker, Josephine	1906	1975	Bondi, Beulah	1888	1981	Carpenter, Karen	1950	1983
Balanchine, George	1904	1983	Bono, Sonny	1935	1998	Carradine, David	1936	2009
Ball, Lucille	1911	1989	Boone, Richard	1917	1981	Carradine, John	1906	1988
Balsam, Martin	1919	1996	Booth, Edwin	1833	1893	Carrillo, Leo	1880	1961
Bancroft, Anne	1931	2005	Booth, John Wilkes	1838	1865	Carroll, Leo G.	1892	1972
Bankhead, Tallulah	1902	1968	Booth, Junius Brutus	1796	1852	Carroll, Madeleine	1906	1987
Bara, Theda	1885?	1955	Booth, Shirley	1898	1992	Carson, Jack	1910	1963
Barnett, Etta Moten	1902	2004	Borge, Victor	1909	2000	Carson, Johnny	1925	2005
Barnum, Phineas T.	1810	1891	Borzage, Frank	1893	1962	Carter, Benny	1907	2003
Barrett, Syd	1946	2006	Bosley, Tom	1927	2010	Carter, Dixie	1939	2010
Barry, Gene	1919	2009	Bow, Clara	1905	1965	Carter, Nell	1948	2003
						Caruso, Enrico	1873	1921

Name	Born	Died
Casals, Pablo	1876	1973
Cash, Johnny	1932	2003
Cash, June Carter	1929	2003
Cass, Peggy	1924	1999
Cassavetes, John	1929	1989
Cassidy, Jack	1927	1976
Castle, Irene	1893	1969
Castle, Vernon	1887	1918
Chaliapin, Feodor	1873	1938
Champion, Gower	1919	1980
Chandler, Jeff	1918	1961
Chaney, Lon	1883	1930
Chaney, Lon, Jr.	1905	1973
Chapin, Harry	1942	1981
Chaplin, Charles	1889	1977
Chapman, Graham	1941	1989
Charisse, Cyd	1921	2008
Charles, Ray	1930	2004
Chase, Ilka	1905	1978
Chatterton, Ruth	1893	1961
Cherrill, Virginia	1908	1996
Chevalier, Maurice	1888	1972
Child, Julia	1912	2004
Clair, René	1898	1981
Clayburgh, Jill	1944	2010
Clayton, Jan	1917	1983
Clemons, Clarence	1942	2011
Clift, Montgomery	1920	1966
Cline, Patsy	1932	1963
Clooney, Rosemary	1928	2002
Clyde, Andy	1892	1967
Cobain, Kurt	1967	1994
Cobb, Lee J.	1911	1976
Coburn, Charles	1877	1961
Coburn, James	1928	2002
Coca, Imogene	1908	2001
Coco, James	1930	1987
Cody, Buffalo Bill	1846	1917
Cody, Iron Eyes	1907	1999
Cohan, George M.	1878	1942
Cohen, Myron	1902	1986
Colbert, Claudette	1903	1996
Cole, Nat "King"	1919	1965
Coleman, Gary	1968	2010
Collins, Ray	1890	1965
Colman, Ronald	1891	1958
Columbo, Russ	1908	1934
Comden, Betty	1917	2006
Como, Perry	1912	2001
Conniff, Ray	1916	2002
Connors, Chuck	1921	1992
Conrad, William	1920	1994
Conried, Hans	1917	1982
Conte, Richard	1911	1975
Convy, Bert	1933	1991
Conway, Tom	1904	1967
Coogan, Jackie	1914	1984
Cook, Elisha, Jr.	1904	1995
Cooke, Alistair	1908	2004
Cooke, Sam	1931	1964
Cooper, Gary	1901	1961
Cooper, Gladys	1888	1971
Cooper, Jackie	1922	2011
Cooper, Melville	1896	1973
Copland, Aaron	1900	1990
Corby, Ellen	1913	1999
Corelli, Franco	1921	2003
Corey, Jeff	1914	2002
Corio, Ann	1914	1999
Corley, Pat	1930	2006
Cornell, Katharine	1893	1974
Correll, Charles ("Andy")	1890	1972
Costello, Dolores	1905	1979
Costello, Lou	1906	1959
Cotten, Joseph	1905	1994
Coward, Noel	1899	1973
Cox, Wally	1924	1973
Crabbe, Buster	1908	1983
Crain, Jeanne	1925	2003
Crane, Bob	1928	1978
Crawford, Broderick	1911	1986
Crawford, Joan	1904	1977
Crenna, Richard	1926	2003
Crews, Laura Hope	1880	1942
Crisp, Donald	1880	1974
Crisp, Quentin	1908	1999
Croce, Jim	1942	1973
Cronyn, Hume	1911	2003
Crosby, Bing	1903	1977
Crothers, Scatman	1910	1986
Cruz, Celia	1925	2003
Cugat, Xavier	1900	1990
Cukor, George	1899	1983
Culp, Bill	1920	1990
Culp, Robert	1930	2010
Cummings, Constance	1910	2005
Cummings, Robert	1908	1990
Curtis, Ken	1916	1991
Curtis, Tony	1925	2010
Curtiz, Michael	1888	1962
Cushing, Peter	1913	1994
Dailey, Dan	1915	1978
Dandridge, Dorothy	1923	1965
Dangerfield, Rodney	1921	2004
Daniell, Henry	1894	1963
Daniels, Bebe	1901	1971
Darin, Bobby	1936	1973
Darnell, Linda	1923	1965
Darwell, Jane	1879	1967
Da Silva, Howard	1909	1986
Davenport, Harry	1866	1949
Davies, Marion	1897	1961
Davis, Bette	1908	1989
Davis, Joan	1907	1961
Davis, Ossie	1917	2005
Davis, Sammy, Jr.	1925	1990
Day, Dennis	1917	1988
Day, Laraine	1920	2007
Dean, James	1931	1955
Dean, Jimmy	1928	2010
Dearie, Blossom	1924	2009
De Carlo, Yvonne	1922	2007
Dee, Frances	1907	2004
Dee, Sandra	1942	2005
Defore, Don	1917	1993
Dekker, Albert	1905	1968
De Laurentiis, Dino	1919	2010
Del Rio, Dolores	1905	1983
DeLuise, Dom	1933	2009
Demarest, William	1892	1983
de Mille, Agnes	1905	1993
De Mille, Cecil B.	1881	1959
Dennis, Sandy	1937	1992
Denny, Reginald	1891	1967
Denver, Bob	1935	2005
Denver, John	1943	1997
Derek, John	1926	1998
DeSica, Vittorio	1901	1974
Devine, Andy	1905	1977
Dewhurst, Colleen	1924	1991
De Wilde, Brandon	1942	1972
De Wolfe, Billy	1907	1974
Diamond, Selma	1920	1985
Diddley, Bo	1928	2008
Dietrich, Marlene	1901	1992
Disney, Walt	1901	1966
Dix, Richard	1894	1949
Dmytryk, Edward	1908	1999
Donahue, Troy	1936	2001
Donat, Robert	1905	1958
Donlevy, Brian	1901	1972
Dors, Diana	1931	1984
Dorsey, Jimmy	1904	1957
Dorsey, Tommy	1905	1956
Douglas, Melvyn	1901	1981
Douglas, Paul	1907	1959
Dove, Billie	1900	1998
Downey, Morton, Jr.	1933	2001
Doyle, David	1929	1997
Drake, Alfred	1914	1992
Draper, Ruth	1884	1956
Dressler, Marie	1869	1934
Drew, Ellen	1915	2003
Drew, Mrs. John	1820	1897
Dru, Joanne	1923	1996
Duchin, Eddy	1909	1951
Duff, Howard	1917	1990
Duggan, Andrew	1923	1988
Dumbrille, Douglass	1890	1974
Dumont, Margaret	1889	1965
Duncan, Isadora	1878	1927
Dunham, Katherine	1910	2006
Dunn, James	1905	1967
Dunne, Irene	1898	1990
Dunnock, Mildred	1901	1991
Durante, Jimmy	1893	1980
Duryea, Dan	1907	1968
Duse, Eleanora	1858	1924
Dvorak, Ann	1912	1979
Eagels, Jeanne	1894	1929
Ebsen, Buddy	1908	2003
Eckstine, Billy	1914	1993
Eddington, Paul	1927	1995
Eddy, Nelson	1901	1967
Edelman, Herb	1933	1996
Edwards, Blake	1922	2010
Edwards, Cliff	1895	1971
Edwards, Ralph	1913	2005
Edwards, Vince	1928	1996
Egan, Richard	1923	1987
Eisenstein, Sergei	1898	1948
Elam, Jack	1916	2003
Ellington, Duke	1899	1974
Elliot, Cass	1941	1974
Elliott, Denholm	1922	1992
Ellis, Mary	1897	2003
Elman, Mischa	1891	1967
Errol, Leon	1881	1951
Evans, Dale	1912	2001
Evans, Edith	1888	1976
Evans, Maurice	1901	1989
Ewell, Tom	1909	1994
Fadiman, Clifton	1904	1999
Fairbanks, Douglas	1883	1939
Fairbanks, Douglas, Jr.	1909	2000
Falk, Peter	1927	2011
Farley, Chris	1964	1997
Farmer, Frances	1913	1970
Farnsworth, Richard	1920	2000
Farnum, Dustin	1874	1929
Farnum, William	1876	1953
Farrar, Geraldine	1882	1967
Farrell, Charles	1901	1990
Farrell, Eileen	1920	2002
Fassbinder, Rainer Werner	1946	1982
Fawcett, Farrah	1947	2009
Faye, Alice	1915	1998
Fazenda, Louise	1895	1962
Feld, Fritz	1900	1993
Feldman, Marty	1933	1982
Fell, Norman	1924	1998
Fellini, Federico	1920	1993
Fenneman, George	1919	1997
Ferrer, Jose	1912	1992
Ferrer, Mel	1917	2008
Fetchit, Stepin	1898	1985
Fiedler, Arthur	1894	1979
Fiedler, John	1925	2005
Fields, Gracie	1898	1979
Fields, Totie	1930	1978
Fields, W. C.	1879	1946
Finch, Peter	1916	1977
Fine, Larry	1902	1975
Firkusny, Rudolf	1912	1994
Fisher, Eddie	1928	2010
Fiske, Minnie Maddern	1865	1932
Fitzgerald, Barry	1888	1961
Fitzgerald, Ella	1917	1996
Fitzgerald, Geraldine	1913	2005
Flagstad, Kirsten	1895	1962
Fleischer, Richard	1916	2006
Fleming, Art	1924	1995
Fleming, Victor	1889	1949
Flynn, Errol	1909	1959
Flynn, Joe	1925	1974
Foch, Nina	1924	2008
Fogelberg, Dan	1951	2007
Foley, Red	1910	1968
Fonda, Henry	1905	1982
Fontaine, Frank	1920	1978
Fontanne, Lynn	1887	1983
Fonteyn, Margot	1919	1991
Ford, Glenn	1916	2006
Ford, John	1895	1973
Ford, Paul	1901	1976
Ford, Tennessee Ernie	1919	1991
Forrest, Helen	1917	1999
Forsythe, John	1918	2010
Fosse, Bob	1927	1987
Foster, Phil	1914	1985
Foster, Preston	1901	1970
Foxx, Redd	1922	1991
Foy, Eddie	1856	1928
Franchi, Sergio	1926	1990
Franciosa, Anthony	1928	2006
Francis, Anne	1930	2011
Francis, Arlene	1907	2001
Francis, Kay	1905	1968
Franciscus, James	1934	1991
Frankenheimer, John	1930	2002
Frann, Mary	1943	1998
Frawley, William	1887	1966
Frederick, Pauline	1885	1938
Freed, Alan	1921	1965
French, Victor	1934	1989
Friganza, Trixie	1870	1955
Froman, Jane	1907	1980
Funt, Allen	1914	1999
Furness, Betty	1916	1994
Gabin, Jean	1904	1976
Gable, Clark	1901	1960
Gabor, Eva	1920	1995
Garbo, Greta	1905	1990
Garcia, Jerry	1942	1995
Gardenia, Vincent	1922	1992
Gardner, Ava	1922	1990
Garfield, John	1913	1952
Garland, Beverly	1926	2008

Name	Born	Died
Garland, Judy	1922	1969
Garrett, Betty	1919	2011
Garson, Greer	1904	1996
Gassman, Vittorio	1922	2000
Gaye, Marvin	1939	1984
Gaynor, Janet	1906	1984
Gebel-Williams, Gunther	1934	2001
Geer, Will	1902	1978
George, Gladys	1904	1954
Gershwin, George	1898	1937
Getty, Estelle	1923	2008
Ghostley, Alice	1926	2007
Gibb, Andy	1958	1988
Gibb, Maurice	1949	2003
Gibson, Henry	1935	2009
Gibson, Hoot	1892	1962
Gielgud, John	1904	2000
Gilbert, Billy	1894	1971
Gilbert, John	1895	1936
Gilford, Jack	1907	1990
Gillespie, Dizzy	1917	1993
Gillette, William	1853	1937
Gingold, Hermione	1897	1987
Gish, Dorothy	1898	1968
Gish, Lillian	1893	1993
Giulini, Carlo Maria	1914	2005
Gleason, Jackie	1916	1987
Gleason, James	1886	1959
Gluck, Alma	1884	1938
Gobel, George	1919	1991
Goddard, Paulette	1905?	1990
Godfrey, Arthur	1903	1983
Godunov, Alexander	1949	1995
Goldwyn, Samuel	1882	1974
Goodman, Benny	1909	1986
Gorcey, Leo	1917	1969
Gordon, Gale	1906	1995
Gordon, Ruth	1896	1985
Gorshin, Frank	1934	2005
Gosden, Freeman ("Amos")	1899	1982
Gottschalk, Louis	1829	1869
Gould, Glenn	1932	1982
Gould, Harold	1923	2010
Gould, Morton	1913	1996
Goulet, Robert	1933	2007
Grable, Betty	1916	1973
Graham, Martha	1894	1991
Graham, Virginia	1912	1998
Grahame, Gloria	1925	1981
Granger, Farley	1925	2011
Granger, Stewart	1913	1993
Grant, Cary	1904	1986
Granville, Bonita	1923	1988
Grapewin, Charley	1869	1956
Graves, Peter	1926	2010
Gray, Dolores	1924	2002
Gray, Spalding	1941	2004
Grayson, Kathryn	1922	2010
Greco, Jose	1918	2000
Green, Adolph	1915	2002
Greene, Lorne	1915	1987
Greenstreet, Sydney	1879	1954
Greenwood, Charlotte	1890	1978
Gregory, James	1911	2002
Griffin, Merv	1925	2007
Griffith, David Wark	1874	1948
Griffith, Hugh	1912	1980
Grizzard, George	1928	2007
Guardino, Harry	1925	1995
Guinness, Sir Alec	1914	2000
Guthrie, Woody	1912	1967
Gwenn, Edmund	1875	1959
Gwynne, Fred	1926	1993
Hackett, Buddy	1924	2003
Hackett, Joan	1934	1983
Hagen, Uta	1919	2004
Haines, William	1900	1973
Hale, Alan, Jr.	1918	1990
Hale, Alan, Sr.	1892	1950
Haley, Bill	1925	1981
Haley, Jack	1899	1979
Hall, Huntz	1919	1999
Hall, Jon	1915	1979
Hamilton, Margaret	1902	1985
Hammerstein, Oscar	1847	1919
Hammerstein II, Oscar	1895	1960
Hampton, Lionel	1908	2002
Hardwicke, Cedric	1893	1964
Hardy, Oliver	1892	1957
Harlow, Jean	1911	1937
Harris, Phil	1904	1995
Harris, Richard	1930	2002
Harrison, George	1943	2001
Harrison, Rex	1908	1990
Hart, William S.	1864	1946
Hartman, Phil	1948	1998
Harvey, Laurence	1928	1973
Harvey, Paul	1918	2009
Harwell, Ernie	1918	2010
Hatfield, Bobby	1940	2003
Haver, June	1926	2005
Havoc, June	1912	2010
Hawkins, Jack	1910	1973
Hawkins, Screamin' Jay	1929	2000
Hawks, Howard	1896	1977
Hawthorne, Nigel	1929	2001
Hayakawa, Sessue	1890	1973
Hayden, Sterling	1916	1986
Hayes, Gabby	1885	1969
Hayes, Helen	1900	1993
Hayes, Isaac	1942	2008
Hayward, Leland	1902	1971
Hayward, Louis	1909	1985
Hayward, Susan	1917	1975
Hayworth, Rita	1918	1987
Head, Edith	1897	1981
Healy, Ted	1896	1937
Heckart, Eileen	1919	2001
Heflin, Van	1910	1971
Heifetz, Jascha	1901	1987
Held, Anna	1873	1918
Hemingway, Margaux	1955	1996
Hemmings, David	1941	2003
Henderson, Skitch	1918	2005
Hendrix, Jimi	1942	1970
Henie, Sonja	1912	1969
Henreid, Paul	1908	1992
Henson, Jim	1936	1990
Hepburn, Audrey	1929	1993
Hepburn, Katharine	1907	2003
Hersholt, Jean	1886	1956
Heston, Charlton	1923	2008
Hewitt, Christopher	1922	2001
Hickey, William	1928	1997
Hickson, Joan	1906	1998
Hildegarde	1906	2005
Hill, Arthur	1922	2006
Hill, Benny	1925	1992
Hill, George Roy	1921	2002
Hiller, Wendy	1912	2003
Hines, Gregory	1946	2003
Hines, Jerome	1921	2003
Hingle, Pat	1924	2009
Hirt, Al	1922	1999
Hitchcock, Alfred	1899	1980
Ho, Don	1930	2007
Hobson, Valerie	1917	1998
Hodiak, John	1914	1955
Holden, William	1918	1981
Holiday, Billie	1915	1959
Holliday, Judy	1921	1965
Holloway, Sterling	1905	1992
Holly, Buddy	1936	1959
Holt, Jack	1888	1951
Holt, Tim	1918	1973
Homolka, Oscar	1898	1978
Hooker, John Lee	1917	2001
Hoon, Shannon	1967	1995
Hope, Bob	1903	2003
Hopkins, Miriam	1902	1972
Hopper, Dennis	1936	2010
Hopper, DeWolf	1858	1935
Hopper, Hedda	1885	1966
Hopper, William	1915	1970
Horowitz, Vladimir	1904	1989
Horne, Lena	1917	2010
Horton, Edward Everett	1886	1970
Houdini, Harry	1874	1926
Houseman, John	1902	1988
Howard (Horwitz), Curly	1903	1952
Howard, Leslie	1890	1943
Howard (Horwitz), Moe	1897	1975
Howard (Horwitz), Shemp	1895	1955
Howard, Trevor	1916	1988
Hudson, Rock	1925	1985
Hughes, Bernard	1915	2006
Hughes, John	1950	2009
Hull, Henry	1890	1977
Hull, Josephine	1886	1957
Humphrey, Doris	1895	1958
Hunter, Jeffrey	1926	1969
Hunter, Kim	1922	2002
Hunter, Ross	1920	1996
Hussey, Ruth	1911	2005
Huston, John	1906	1987
Huston, Walter	1884	1950
Hutchence, Michael	1960	1997
Hutton, Betty	1921	2007
Hutton, Jim	1934	1979
Hyde-White, Wilfrid	1903	1991
Ingram, Rex	1895	1969
Ireland, Jill	1936	1990
Ireland, John	1915	1992
Irving, Henry	1838	1905
Ives, Burl	1909	1995
Irwin, Steve	1962	2006
Iturbi, Jose	1895	1980
Jack, Wolfman	1938	1995
Jackson, Joe	1875	1942
Jackson, Mahalia	1911	1972
Jackson, Michael	1958	2009
Jackson, Milt	1923	1999
Jaeckel, Richard	1926	1997
Jaffe, Sam	1891	1984
Jagger, Dean	1903	1991
James, Dennis	1917	1997
James, Harry	1916	1983
James, Rick	1948	2004
Jam Master Jay	1965	2002
Janis, Elsie	1889	1956
Jannings, Emil	1886	1950
Janssen, David	1930	1980
Jenkins, Allen	1900	1974
Jennings, Waylon	1937	2002
Jessel, George	1898	1981
Jeter, Michael	1952	2003
Johnson, Ben	1918	1996
Johnson, Celia	1908	1982
Johnson, Chic	1892	1962
Johnson, J.J.	1924	2001
Johnson, Robert	1911	1938
Johnson, Van	1916	2008
Jolson, Al	1886	1950
Jones, Brian	1942	1969
Jones, Buck	1889	1942
Jones, Carolyn	1933	1983
Jones, Charlie	1930	2008
Jones, Elvin	1927	2004
Jones, Henry	1912	1999
Jones, Jennifer	1919	2009
Jones, Spike	1911	1965
Joplin, Janis	1943	1970
Joplin, Scott	1868	1917
Jordan, Richard	1937	1993
Jory, Victor	1902	1982
Joslyn, Allyn	1905	1981
Julia, Raul	1940	1994
Jump, Gordon	1932	2003
Jurado, Katy	1924	2002
Jurgens, Curt	1915	1982
Kahn, Madeline	1942	1999
Kane, Helen	1904	1966
Kanin, Garson	1912	1999
Karloff, Boris	1887	1969
Karns, Roscoe	1893	1970
Kaufman, Andy	1949	1984
Kaye, Danny	1913	1987
Kaye, Stubby	1918	1997
Kazan, Elia	1909	2003
Kean, Charles	1811	1868
Kean, Mrs. Charles	1806	1880
Kean, Edmund	1787	1833
Keaton, Buster	1895	1966
Keel, Howard	1919	2004
Keeler, Ruby	1910	1993
Keeshan, Bob (Captain Kangaroo)	1927	2004
Keith, Brian	1921	1997
Kellaway, Cecil	1893	1973
Kelley, DeForest	1920	1999
Kelly, Emmett	1898	1979
Kelly, Gene	1912	1996
Kelly, Grace	1929	1982
Kelly, Jack	1927	1992
Kelly, Patsy	1910	1981
Kennedy, Arthur	1914	1990
Kennedy, Edgar	1890	1948
Kerr, Deborah	1921	2007
Kibbee, Guy	1886	1956
Kilbride, Percy	1888	1964
Kiley, Richard	1922	1999
King, Alan	1927	2004
King, Henry	1896	1982
Kinski, Klaus	1926	1991
Kirby, Bruno	1949	2006
Kirby, George	1923	1995
Kirby, Durward	1912	2000
Kirsten, Dorothy	1910	1992
Kitt, Eartha	1927	2008
Klemperer, Werner	1920	2000
Knight, Ted	1923	1986
Knotts, Don	1924	2006
Korman, Harvey	1927	2008
Kostelanetz, Andre	1901	1980
Kovacs, Ernie	1919	1962
Kramer, Stanley	1913	2001
Kruger, Otto	1885	1974
Kubrick, Stanley	1928	1999

Name	Born	Died	Name	Born	Died	Name	Born	Died
Kulp, Nancy	1921	1991	MacDonald, Jeanette	1903	1965	Mills, Herbert	1912	1989
Kurosawa, Akira	1910	1998	Mack, Ted	1904	1976	Mills, John	1889	1967
Kyser, Kay	1906	1985	MacKenzie, Gisele	1927	2003	Mills, Sir John	1908	2005
Ladd, Alan	1913	1964	MacLane, Barton	1902	1969	Mineo, Sal	1939	1976
Lahr, Bert	1895	1967	MacMurray, Fred	1908	1991	Miner, Jan	1917	2004
Laine, Frankie	1913	2007	MacRae, Gordon	1921	1986	Minghella, Anthony	1954	2008
Lake, Arthur	1905	1987	Macready, George	1909	1973	Mingus, Charles	1922	1979
Lake, Veronica	1919	1973	Madison, Guy	1922	1996	Minnelli, Vincente	1903	1986
LaLanne, Jack	1914	2011	Magnani, Anna	1908	1973	Miranda, Carmen	1909	1955
Lamarr, Hedy	1913	2000	Mancini, Henry	1924	1994	Mitchell, Cameron	1918	1994
Lamas, Fernando	1915	1982	Main, Marjorie	1890	1975	Mitchell, Thomas	1892	1962
Lamour, Dorothy	1914	1996	Malden, Karl	1912	2009	Mitchum, Robert	1917	1997
Lancaster, Burt	1913	1994	Malle, Louis	1932	1995	Mix, Tom	1880	1940
Lanchester, Elsa	1902	1986	Mamoulian, Rouben	1897	1987	Monica, Corbett	1930	1998
Landis, Carole	1919	1948	Mankiewicz, Joseph	1909	1993	Moffo, Anna	1932	2006
Landis, Jessie Royce	1904	1972	Mann, Herbie	1930	2003	Monroe, Marilyn	1926	1962
Landon, Michael	1936	1991	Mansfield, Jayne	1932	1967	Monroe, Vaughn	1911	1973
Lane, Priscilla	1917	1995	Mantovani, Annunzio	1905	1980	Montalban, Ricardo	1920	2009
Lang, Fritz	1890	1976	Marais, Jean	1913	1998	Montand, Yves	1921	1991
Langdon, Harry	1884	1944	March, Fredric	1897	1975	Montez, Maria	1917	1951
Lange, Hope	1931	2003	March, Hal	1920	1970	Montgomery, Elizabeth	1933	1995
Langford, Frances	1914	2005	Marchand, Nancy	1928	2000	Montgomery, George	1916	2000
Langtry, Lillie	1853	1929	Markova, Alicia	1910	2004	Montgomery, Robert	1904	1981
Lanza, Mario	1921	1959	Marley, Bob	1945	1981	Moore, Clayton	1914	1999
LaRue, Lash (Alfred)	1917	1996	Marshall, E.G.	1910	1998	Moore, Colleen	1900	1988
Lauder, Harry	1870	1950	Marshall, Herbert	1890	1966	Moore, Dudley	1935	2002
Laughton, Charles	1899	1962	Martin, Barney	1923	2005	Moore, Garry	1915	1993
Laurel, Stan	1890	1965	Martin, Dean	1917	1995	Moore, Grace	1898	1947
Lawford, Peter	1923	1984	Martin, Dick	1922	2008	Moorehead, Agnes	1906	1974
Lawrence, Florence	1886	1938	Martin, Mary	1913	1990	Moreland, Mantan	1902	1973
Lawrence, Gertrude	1898	1952	Martin, Ross	1920	1981	Morgan, Dennis	1910	1994
Lean, David	1908	1991	Marvin, Lee	1924	1987	Morgan, Frank	1890	1949
Ledger, Heath	1979	2008	Marx, Harpo (Arthur)	1888	1964	Morgan, Helen	1900	1941
Lee, Anna	1913	2004	Marx, Zeppo (Herbert)	1901	1979	Morgan, Henry	1915	1994
Lee, Bernard	1908	1981	Marx, Groucho (Julius)	1890	1977	Morita, Pat	1932	2005
Lee, Bruce	1940	1973	Marx, Chico (Leonard)	1887	1961	Morley, Robert	1908	1992
Lee, Canada	1907	1952	Marx, Gummo (Milton)	1893	1977	Morris, Chester	1901	1970
Lee, Gypsy Rose	1914	1970	Mason, James	1909	1984	Morris, Greg	1934	1996
Lee, Peggy	1920	2002	Massey, Raymond	1896	1983	Morris, Howard	1919	2005
LeGallienne, Eva	1899	1991	Mastroianni, Marcello	1924	1996	Morris, Wayne	1914	1959
Lehmann, Lotte	1888	1976	Matthau, Walter	1920	2000	Morrison, Jim	1943	1971
Leigh, Janet	1927	2004	Mature, Victor	1913	1999	Morrow, Vic	1929	1982
Leigh, Vivien	1913	1967	Maxwell, Marilyn	1921	1972	Morton, Jelly Roll	1885	1941
Leighton, Margaret	1922	1976	Mayer, Louis B.	1885	1957	Mostel, Zero	1915	1977
Lemmon, Jack	1925	2001	Mayfield, Curtis	1942	1999	Mowbray, Alan	1897	1969
Lennon, John	1940	1980	Mayo, Virginia	1920	2005	Mulhare, Edward	1923	1997
Lenya, Lotte	1898	1981	Mazurki, Mike	1909	1990	Mulligan, Gerry	1927	1996
Leonard, Eddie	1870	1941	McCambridge, Mercedes	1916	2004	Mulligan, Richard	1932	2000
Leonard, Sheldon	1907	1997	McCarey, Leo	1898	1969	Muni, Paul	1895	1967
Leone, Sergio	1929	1989	McCarthy, Kevin	1914	2010	Munshin, Jules	1915	1970
LeRoy, Mervyn	1900	1987	McCartney, Linda	1941	1998	Murnau, F.W.	1888	1931
Levant, Oscar	1906	1972	McClanahan, Rue	1934	2010	Murphy, Audie	1924	1971
Levene, Sam	1905	1980	McClure, Doug	1935	1995	Murphy, Brittany	1977	2009
Levenson, Sam	1911	1980	McCormack, John	1884	1945	Murphy, George	1902	1992
Lewis, Al	1923	2006	McCrary, Tex	1910	2003	Murray, Arthur	1895	1991
Lewis, Joe E.	1902	1971	McCrea, Joel	1905	1990	Murray, Kathryn	1906	1999
Lewis, Shari	1934	1998	McDaniel, Hattie	1895	1952	Murray, Mae	1889	1965
Lewis, Ted	1892	1971	McDowall, Roddy	1928	1998	Nagel, Conrad	1897	1970
Liberace	1919	1987	McFarland, Spanky (George)	1928	1993	Naish, J. Carroll	1900	1973
Lillie, Beatrice	1894	1989	McGoohan, Patrick	1928	2009	Naldi, Nita	1898	1961
Lincoln, Elmo	1889	1952	McGuire, Al	1931	2001	Nance, Jack	1943	1996
Lind, Jenny	1820	1887	McGuire, Dorothy	1916	2001	Natwick, Mildred	1908	1994
Lindfors, Viveca	1920	1995	McHugh, Frank	1898	1981	Nazimova, Alla	1879	1945
Lindley, Audra	1918	1997	McIntire, John	1907	1991	Neal, Patricia	1926	2010
Linkletter, Art	1912	2010	McKern, Leo	1920	2002	Negri, Pola	1897	1987
Linville, Larry	1939	2000	McLaglen, Victor	1886	1959	Nelson, David	1936	2011
Little, Cleavon	1939	1992	McMahon, Ed	1923	2009	Nelson, Harriet (Hilliard)	1909	1994
Llewelyn, Desmond	1914	1999	McNeill, Don	1907	1996	Nelson, Ozzie	1906	1975
Lloyd, Harold	1893	1971	McQueen, Butterfly	1911	1995	Nelson, Rick	1940	1985
Lloyd, Marie	1870	1922	McQueen, Steve	1930	1980	Nesbit, Evelyn	1884	1967
Lockhart, Gene	1891	1957	Meader, Vaughn	1936	2004	Nettleton, Lois	1927	2008
Logan, Ella	1913	1969	Meadows, Audrey	1924	1996	Newley, Anthony	1931	1999
Lombard, Carole	1908	1942	Meek, Donald	1880	1946	Newman, Edwin	1919	2010
Lombardo, Guy	1902	1977	Meeker, Ralph	1920	1988	Newman, Paul	1925	2008
Long, Richard	1927	1974	Melba, Nellie	1861	1931	Newton, Robert	1905	1956
Lopes, Lisa	1971	2002	Melchior, Lauritz	1890	1973	Nicholas, Fayard	1914	2006
Lopez, Vincent	1895	1975	Menjou, Adolphe	1890	1963	Nicholas, Harold	1924	2000
Lord, Jack	1920	1998	Menken, Helen	1902	1966	Nielsen, Leslie	1926	2010
Lorne, Marion	1888	1968	Menuhin, Yehudi	1916	1999	Nijinsky, Vaslav	1890	1950
Lorre, Peter	1904	1964	Mercer, Marian	1935	2011	Nilsson, Anna Q.	1888	1974
Loudon, Dorothy	1933	2003	Mercouri, Melina	1925	1994	Niven, David	1910	1983
Lowe, Edmund	1890	1971	Mercury, Freddie	1946	1991	Nolan, Lloyd	1902	1985
Loy, Myrna	1905	1993	Meredith, Burgess	1909	1997	Normand, Mabel	1894	1930
Lubitsch, Ernst	1892	1947	Merman, Ethel	1908	1984	North, Sheree	1933	2005
Ludden, Allen	1918	1981	Merrick, David	1911	2000	Notorious B.I.G.	1972	1997
Lugosi, Bela	1882	1956	Merrill, Gary	1915	1990	Novarro, Ramon	1899	1968
Lukas, Paul	1894	1971	Milestone, Lewis	1895	1980	Nureyev, Rudolf	1938	1993
Lumet, Sidney	1924	2011	Mifune, Toshiro	1920	1997	Oakie, Jack	1903	1978
Lunt, Alfred	1892	1977	Milland, Ray	1905	1986	Oakley, Annie	1860	1926
Lupino, Ida	1918	1995	Miller, Ann	1923	2004	Oates, Warren	1928	1982
Lymon, Frankie	1942	1968	Miller, Glenn	1904	1944	Oberon, Merle	1911	1979
Lynde, Paul	1926	1982	Miller, Marilyn	1898	1936	O'Brien, Edmond	1915	1985
Lynn, Diana	1926	1971	Miller, Mitch	1911	2010	O'Brien, Pat	1899	1983
Mac, Bernie	1957	2008	Miller, Roger	1936	1992	O'Connell, Arthur	1908	1981
MacArthur, James	1937	2010	Mills, Donald	1915	1999	O'Connell, Helen	1921	1993
MacCorkindale, Simon	1952	2010	Mills, Harry	1913	1982	O'Connor, Carroll	1924	2001

Name	Born	Died
O'Connor, Donald	1925	2003
O'Connor, Una	1880	1959
Odetta	1930	2008
O'Herlihy, Daniel	1919	2005
O'Keefe, Dennis	1908	1968
Oland, Warner	1880	1938
Olcott, Chauncey	1860	1932
Oliver, Edna May	1883	1942
Olivier, Laurence	1907	1989
Olsen, Merlin	1940	2010
Olsen, Ole	1892	1963
O'Neal, Ron	1937	2004
O'Neill, James	1849	1920
Ophuls, Max	1902	1957
Orbach, Jerry	1935	2004
Orbison, Roy	1936	1988
Ormandy, Eugene	1899	1985
O'Sullivan, Maureen	1911	1998
Ouspenskaya, Maria	1876	1949
Owen, Reginald	1887	1972
Owens, Buck	1929	2006
Paar, Jack	1918	2004
Paderewski, Ignace	1860	1941
Page, Bettie	1923	2008
Page, Geraldine	1924	1987
Pakula, Alan	1928	1998
Palance, Jack	1919	2006
Pallette, Eugene	1889	1954
Palmer, Lilli	1914	1986
Palmer, Robert	1949	2003
Pangborn, Franklin	1894	1958
Parker, Fess	1925	2010
Parker, Jean	1915	2005
Parks, Bert	1914	1992
Parks, Larry	1914	1975
Pasternack, Josef A.	1881	1940
Pastor, Tony (vaudevillian)	1837	1908
Pastor, Tony (bandleader)	1907	1969
Patrick, Gail	1911	1980
Patti, Adelina	1843	1919
Patti, Carlotta	1840	1889
Paul, Les	1915	2009
Pavarotti, Luciano	1935	2007
Pavlova, Anna	1885	1931
Paycheck, Johnny	1938	2003
Payne, John	1912	1989
Pearl, Minnie	1912	1996
Peck, Gregory	1916	2003
Peckinpah, Sam	1925	1984
Peerce, Jan	1904	1984
Pendergrass, Teddy	1950	2010
Penn, Arthur	1922	2010
Penn, Chris	1965	2006
Penner, Joe	1905	1941
Peppard, George	1928	1994
Perkins, Anthony	1932	1992
Perkins, Carl	1932	1998
Perkins, Marlin	1905	1986
Peters, Brock	1927	2005
Peters, Jean	1926	2000
Peters, Susan	1921	1952
Peterson, Oscar	1925	2007
Phillips, John	1935	2001
Phoenix, River	1970	1993
Piaf, Edith	1915	1963
Pickens, Slim	1919	1983
Pickett, Wilson	1941	2006
Pickford, Mary	1893	1979
Picon, Molly	1898	1992
Pidgeon, Walter	1897	1984
Pinza, Ezio	1892	1957
Pitney, Gene	1941	2006
Pitts, Zasu	1898	1963
Plato, Dana	1964	1999
Pleasence, Donald	1919	1995
Pleshette, Suzanne	1937	2008
Pollack, Sydney	1934	2008
Pons, Lily	1904	1976
Ponselle, Rosa	1897	1981
Ponti, Carlo	1912	2007
Porter, Edwin S.	1870	1941
Porter, Eric	1928	1995
Porter, Nyree Dawn	1940	2001
Postlethwaite, Pete	1946	2011
Poston, Tom	1921	2007
Powell, Dick	1904	1963
Powell, Eleanor	1912	1982
Powell, William	1892	1984
Power, Tyrone	1914	1958
Preminger, Otto	1905	1986
Presley, Elvis	1935	1977
Preston, Billy	1946	2006
Preston, Robert	1918	1987
Price, Vincent	1911	1993
Prima, Louis	1911	1978
Prinze, Freddie	1954	1977
Prosky, Robert	1930	2008
Provine, Dorothy	1937	2010
Prowse, Juliet	1936	1996
Pryor, Richard	1940	2005
Puente, Tito	1923	2000
Pyle, Denver	1920	1997
Quayle, Anthony	1913	1989
Questel, Mae	1908	1998
Quinn, Anthony	1915	2001
Quintero, José	1924	1999
Rabb, Ellis	1930	1998
Rabbit, Eddie	1941	1998
Radner, Gilda	1946	1989
Rafferty, Gerry	1947	2011
Raft, George	1895	1980
Rains, Claude	1889	1967
Raitt, John	1917	2005
Ralston, Esther	1902	1994
Ramone, Dee Dee	1952	2002
Ramone, Joey	1951	2001
Ramone, Johnny	1948	2004
Rampal, Jean-Pierre	1922	2000
Randall, Tony	1920	2004
Randolph, John	1915	2004
Rathbone, Basil	1892	1967
Ratoff, Gregory	1897	1960
Rawls, Lou	1933	2006
Ray, Aldo	1926	1991
Ray, Johnnie	1927	1990
Ray, Nicholas	1911	1979
Rayburn, Gene	1917	1999
Raye, Martha	1916	1994
Raymond, Gene	1908	1998
Reagan, Ronald	1911	2004
Redding, Otis	1941	1967
Redgrave, Corin	1939	2010
Redgrave, Lynn	1943	2010
Redgrave, Michael	1908	1985
Reed, Donna	1921	1986
Reed, Jerry	1937	2008
Reed, Oliver	1938	1999
Reed, Robert	1932	1992
Reeve, Christopher	1952	2004
Reeves, George	1914	1959
Reeves, Steve	1926	2000
Reid, Wallace	1891	1923
Reilly, Charles Nelson	1931	2007
Reinhardt, Max	1873	1943
Remick, Lee	1935	1991
Renaldo, Duncan	1904	1980
Rennie, Michael	1909	1971
Renoir, Jean	1894	1979
Rettig, Tommy	1941	1996
Reynolds, Marjorie	1921	1997
Rich, Charlie	1932	1995
Richardson, Ian	1934	2007
Richardson, Natasha	1963	2009
Richardson, Ralph	1902	1983
Riddle, Nelson	1921	1985
Riefenstahl, Leni	1902	2003
Ripperton, Minnie	1947	1979
Ritchard, Cyril	1898	1977
Ritter, John	1948	2003
Ritter, Tex	1905	1974
Ritter, Thelma	1905	1969
Ritz, Al	1901	1965
Ritz, Harry	1906	1986
Ritz, Jimmy	1903	1985
Roach, Hall	1892	1992
Roach, Max	1924	2007
Robards, Jason	1922	2000
Robbins, Jerome	1918	1998
Robbins, Marty	1925	1982
Roberts, Pernell	1928	2010
Roberts, Rachel	1927	1980
Robertson, Cliff	1925	2011
Robeson, Paul	1898	1976
Robinson, Bill	1878	1949
Robinson, Edward G.	1893	1973
Robson, Flora	1902	1984
Roche, Eugene	1928	2004
Rochester (Eddie Anderson)	1905	1977
Roddenberry, Gene	1921	1991
Rodgers, Jimmie	1897	1933
Rogers, Buddy	1904	1999
Rogers, Fred	1928	2003
Rogers, Ginger	1911	1995
Rogers, Roy	1911	1998
Rogers, Will	1879	1935
Roland, Gilbert	1905	1994
Rolle, Esther	1920?	1998
Rollins, Howard	1950	1996
Roman, Ruth	1924	1999
Romero, Cesar	1907	1994
Rose, Billy	1899	1966
Rossellini, Roberto	1906	1977
Rostropovich, Mstislav	1927	2007
Rowan, Dan	1922	1987
Rubinstein, Artur	1887	1982
Rubenstein, Zelda	1933	2010
Ruggles, Charles	1886	1970
Russell, Harold	1914	2002
Russell, Jane	1921	2011
Russell, Lillian	1861	1922
Russell, Nipsey	1923	2005
Russell, Rosalind	1911	1976
Rutherford, Margaret	1892	1972
Ryan, Irene	1903	1973
Ryan, Robert	1909	1973
Sabu (Dastagir)	1924	1963
St. Cyr, Lili	1917	1999
St. Denis, Ruth	1877	1968
Sakall, S. Z.	1883	1955
Sale (Chic), Charles	1885	1936
Sales, Soupy	1926	2009
Sanders, George	1906	1972
Sanford, Isabel	1917	2004
Sargent, Dick	1933	1994
Sarrazin, Michael	1940	2011
Savalas, Telly	1924	1994
Scheider, Roy	1935	2008
Schell, Maria	1926	2005
Schenkel, Chris	1923	2005
Schiavelli, Vincent	1948	2005
Schildkraut, Joseph	1896	1964
Schipa, Tito	1888	1965
Schlesinger, John	1926	2003
Schnabel, Artur	1882	1951
Schneider, Maria	1952	2011
Schneider, Romy	1938	1982
Schwartzkopf, Elizabeth	1915	2006
Scofield, Paul	1922	2008
Scott, George C.	1927	1999
Scott, Gordon	1926	2007
Scott, Hazel	1920	1981
Scott, Martha	1914	2003
Scott, Randolph	1898	1987
Scott, Zachary	1914	1965
Scott-Siddons, Mrs.	1843	1896
Seberg, Jean	1938	1979
Seeley, Blossom	1892	1974
Segovia, Andres	1893	1987
Selena	1971	1995
Sellers, Peter	1925	1980
Selznick, David O.	1902	1965
Sennett, Mack	1880	1960
Señor Wences	1896	1999
Serling, Rod	1924	1975
Shakur, Tupac	1971	1996
Shaw, Artie	1910	2004
Shaw, Robert (actor)	1927	1978
Shaw, Robert (conductor)	1916	1999
Shawn, Ted	1891	1972
Shean, Al	1868	1949
Shearer, Moira	1926	2006
Shearer, Norma	1902	1983
Shearing, George	1919	2011
Sheppard, Bob	1910	2010
Sheridan, Ann	1915	1967
Shore, Dinah	1917	1994
Short, Bobby	1924	2005
Shubert, Lee	1875	1953
Shull, Richard B.	1929	1999
Siddons, Sarah	1755	1831
Sidney, Sylvia	1910	1999
Siegel, Don	1912	1991
Signoret, Simone	1921	1985
Sills, Beverly	1929	2007
Silver, Ron	1946	2009
Silverheels, Jay	1912	1980
Silvers, Phil	1912	1985
Sim, Alastair	1900	1976
Simmons, Jean	1929	2010
Simone, Nina	1933	2003
Sinatra, Frank	1915	1998
Sinclair, Madge	1938	1995
Singleton, Penny	1908	2003
Sirk, Douglas	1900	1987
Siskel, Gene	1946	1999
Sitka, Emil	1914	1998
Sjostrom, Victor	1879	1960
Skelton, Red	1913	1997
Skinner, Otis	1858	1942
Smith, Alexis	1921	1993
Smith, Bessie	1894?	1937
Smith, Buffalo Bob	1917	1998
Smith, C. Aubrey	1863	1948
Smith, Elliott	1969	2003
Smith, Jeff	1939	2004
Smith, Kate	1907	1986
Smith, Kent	1907	1985
Snodgress, Carrie	1946	2004
Snow, Hank	1914	1999

Name	Born	Died	Name	Born	Died	Name	Born	Died
Snyder, Tom	1936	2007	Thulin, Ingrid	1926	2004	Weaver, Dennis	1924	2006
Solti, George	1912	1997	Tibbett, Lawrence	1896	1960	Webb, Clifton	1891	1966
Sondergaard, Gale	1899	1985	Tierney, Gene	1920	1991	Webb, Jack	1920	1982
Sothern, Ann	1909	2001	Tiny Tim	1932	1996	Weems, Ted	1901	1963
Sousa, John Philip	1854	1932	Tippett, Sir Michael	1905	1998	Weissmuller, Johnny	1904	1984
Sparks, Ned	1884	1957	Todd, Michael	1909	1958	Welk, Lawrence	1903	1992
Spelling, Aaron	1923	2006	Todd, Richard	1919	2009	Welles, Orson	1915	1985
Spencer, John	1946	2005	Tomlinson, David	1917	2000	Wellman, William	1896	1975
Sperber, Wendy Jo	1958	2005	Tone, Franchot	1905	1968	Werner, Oskar	1922	1984
Springfield, Dusty	1939	1999	Torme, Mel	1925	1999	West, Mae	1893	1980
Stack, Robert	1919	2003	Toscanini, Arturo	1867	1957	Weston, Jack	1924	1996
Stafford, Jo	1917	2008	Tracy, Lee	1898	1968	Whale, James	1889	1957
Stander, Lionel	1908	1994	Tracy, Spencer	1900	1967	Wheeler, Bert	1895	1968
Stang, Arnold	1918	2009	Traubel, Helen	1899	1972	White, Barry	1944	2003
Stanley, Kim	1925	2001	Travers, Henry	1874	1965	White, Jesse	1919	1997
Stanwyck, Barbara	1907	1990	Travers, Mary	1936	2009	White, Pearl	1889	1938
Stapleton, Maureen	1925	2006	Treacher, Arthur	1894	1975	Whiteman, Paul	1891	1967
Steiger, Rod	1925	2002	Tree, Herbert Beerbohm	1853	1917	Whiting, Margaret	1924	2011
Sterling, Jan	1921	2004	Trevor, Claire	1909	2000	Whitmore, James	1921	2009
Stern, Isaac	1920	2001	Truex, Ernest	1890	1973	Whitty, May	1865	1948
Stevens, Craig	1918	2000	Truffaut, Francois	1932	1984	Wickes, Mary	1910	1995
Stevens, George	1904	1975	Tucker, Forrest	1919	1986	Widmark, Richard	1914	2008
Stevens, Inger	1934	1970	Tucker, Richard	1913	1975	Wilde, Cornel	1915	1989
Stevens, Mark	1916	1994	Tucker, Sophie	1884	1966	Wilder, Billy	1906	2002
Stevenson, McLean	1929	1996	Turner, Big Joe	1911	1985	Wilding, Michael	1912	1979
Stewart, James	1908	1997	Turner, Ike	1931	2008	Williams, Bert	1874	1922
Stickney, Dorothy	1896	1998	Turner, Lana	1920	1995	Williams, Guy	1924	1989
Stokowski, Leopold	1882	1977	Turpin, Ben	1869	1940	Williams, Hank, Sr.	1923	1953
Stone, Fred	1873	1959	Twelvetrees, Helen	1908	1958	Wills, Bob	1905	1975
Stone, Lewis	1879	1953	Twitty, Conway	1933	1993	Wills, Chill	1902	1978
Stone, Milburn	1904	1980	Urich, Robert	1946	2002	Wilson, Carl	1946	1998
Storm, Gale	1922	2009	Ustinov, Peter	1921	2004	Wilson, Dennis	1944	1983
Straight, Beatrice	1918	2001	Valens, Ritchie	1941	1959	Wilson, Dooley	1894	1953
Strasberg, Lee	1901	1982	Valentino, Rudolph	1895	1926	Wilson, Flip	1933	1998
Strasberg, Susan	1938	1999	Vallee, Rudy	1901	1986	Wilson, Jackie	1934	1984
Strode, Woody	1914	1994	Van, Bobby	1928	1980	Wilson, Marie	1917	1972
Strummer, Joe	1952	2002	Vance, Vivian	1912	1979	Windsor, Marie	1919	2000
Stuart, Gloria	1910	2010	Van Cleef, Lee	1925	1989	Winehouse, Amy	1983	2011
Stuarti, Enzo	1919	2005	Vandross, Luther	1951	2005	Winfield, Paul	1941	2004
Sturges, Preston	1898	1959	Van Fleet, Jo	1922	1996	Winninger, Charles	1884	1969
Sullavan, Margaret	1911	1960	Varney, Jim	1949	2000	Winters, Shelley	1920	2006
Sullivan, Barry	1912	1994	Vaughan, Sarah	1924	1990	Wise, Robert	1914	2005
Sullivan, Ed	1902	1974	Veidt, Conrad	1893	1943	Wiseman, Joseph	1918	2009
Sullivan, Francis L.	1903	1956	Velez, Lupe	1908	1944	Wong, Anna May	1907	1961
Sumac, Yma	1922	2008	Vera-Ellen (Rohe)	1926	1981	Wood, Natalie	1938	1981
Summerville, Slim	1892	1946	Verdon, Gwen	1925	2000	Wood, Peggy	1892	1978
Sutherland, Joan	1926	2010	Vernon, Jackie	1925	1987	Wood, Sam	1884	1949
Swanson, Gloria	1899	1983	Vernon, John	1932	2005	Woodard, Edward	1930	2009
Swarthout, Gladys	1904	1969	Verrett, Shirley	1931	2010	Wooley, Sheb	1921	2003
Swayze, Patrick	1952	2009	Vicious, Sid	1957	1979	Woolley, Monty	1888	1963
Sweet, Blanche	1896	1986	Vidor, King	1894	1982	Worth, Irene	1916	2002
Switzer, Carl "Alfalfa"	1927	1959	Villechaize, Herve	1943	1993	Wray, Fay	1907	2004
Talbot, Lyle	1902	1996	Vincent, Gene	1935	1971	Wright, Teresa	1918	2005
Talmadge, Constance	1900	1973	Vinson, Helen	1907	1999	Wyatt, Jane	1910	2006
Talmadge, Norma	1893	1957	Von Stroheim, Erich	1885	1957	Wyler, William	1902	1981
Tamiroff, Akim	1899	1972	Von Zell, Harry	1906	1981	Wyman, Jane	1914?	2007
Tandy, Jessica	1909	1994	Walker, Junior	1942	1995	Wynette, Tammy	1942	1998
Tanguay, Eva	1878	1947	Walker, Nancy	1922	1992	Wynn, Ed	1886	1966
Tati, Jacques	1908	1982	Walker, Robert	1918	1951	Wynn, Keenan	1916	1986
Taylor, Billy	1921	2010	Wallenda, Karl	1905	1978	Yankovic, Frank	1915	1998
Taylor, Deems	1885	1966	Walsh, J. T.	1943	1998	York, Dick	1928	1992
Taylor, Dub	1907	1994	Walsh, Raoul	1887	1980	York, Susannah	1939	2011
Taylor, Elizabeth	1932	2011	Walston, Ray	1914	2001	Young, Clara Kimball	1890	1960
Taylor, Estelle	1899	1958	Walter, Bruno	1876	1962	Young, Gig	1913	1978
Taylor, Laurette	1887	1946	Ward, Helen	1916	1998	Young, Loretta	1913	2000
Taylor, Robert	1911	1969	Warden, Jack	1920	2006	Young, Robert	1907	1998
Tebaldi, Renata	1922	2004	Waring, Fred	1900	1984	Young, Roland	1887	1953
Terry, Ellen	1847	1928	Warner, H. B.	1876	1958	Youngman, Henny	1906	1998
Thalberg, Irving	1899	1936	Warrick, Ruth	1915	2005	Zanuck, Darryl F.	1902	1979
Thaw, John	1942	2002	Washington, Dinah	1924	1963	Zappa, Frank	1940	1993
Thigpen, Lynne	1948	2003	Waters, Ethel	1896	1977	Zevon, Warren	1947	2003
Thomas, Danny	1912	1991	Waters, Muddy	1915	1983	Ziegfeld, Florenz	1869	1932
Thomas, John Charles	1891	1960	Waxman, Al	1935	2001	Zinneman, Fred	1907	1997
Thompson, Sada	1927	2011	Wayne, David	1914	1995	Zukor, Adolph	1873	1976
Thorndike, Sybil	1882	1976	Wayne, John	1907	1979			

Original Names of Selected Entertainers

Aaliyah: Aaliyah Haughton
Adele: Adele Laurie Blue Adkins
Ad-Rock: Adam Horovitz
Clay Aiken: Clayton Grissom
Eddie Albert: Edward Albert Heimberger
Alan Alda: Alphonso D'Abruzzo
Jason Alexander: Jay Greenspan
Ali G: Sacha Baron Cohen
Fred Allen: John Sullivan
Woody Allen: Allen Konigsberg
June Allyson: Ella Geisman
André 3000: Andre Benjamin
Julie Andrews: Julia Wells
Criss Angel: Christopher Sarantakos
Eve Arden: Eunice Quedens
Beatrice Arthur: Bernice Frankel
Jean Arthur: Gladys Greene
Ashanti: Ashanti Douglas
Fred Astaire: Frederick Austerlitz

Babyface: Kenneth Edmonds
Lauren Bacall: Betty Joan Perske
Erykah Badu: Erica Wright
Eric Bana: Eric Banadinovich
Anne Bancroft: Anna Maria Italiano
Theda Bara: Theodosia Goodman
Beck: Beck Hensen
Pat Benatar: Patricia Andrejewski
Tony Bennett: Anthony Benedetto
Jack Benny: Benjamin Kubelsky
Milton Berle: Mendel Berlinger
Irving Berlin: Israel Baline
Sarah Bernhardt: Henriette-Rosine Bernard
Jello Biafra: Eric Reed Boucher
Big Boi: Antwan Patton
The Big Bopper: Jiles Perry "J.P." Richardson
Joey Bishop: Joseph Gottlieb
Robert Blake: Michael James Vijencio Gubitosi

Jon Bon Jovi: John Francis Bongiovi
Björk: Björk Gudmundsdottir
Bono: Paul Hewson
Bow Wow: Shad Gregory Moss
David Bowie: David Robert Jones
Boy George: George Alan O'Dowd
Fanny Brice: Fanny Borach
Charles Bronson: Charles Buchinski
Albert Brooks: Albert Einstein
Mel Brooks: Melvin Kaminsky
Foxy Brown: Inga Marchand
George Burns: Nathan Birnbaum
Ellen Burstyn: Edna Gilhooley
Richard Burton: Richard Jenkins
Red Buttons: Aaron Chwatt
Nicolas Cage: Nicholas Coppola
Michael Caine: Maurice Micklewhite
Maria Callas: Maria Kalogeropoulos
Cedric The Entertainer: Cedric Kyles

Jackie Chan: Chan Kwong-Sung
Cyd Charisse: Tula Finklea
Ray Charles: Ray Charles Robinson
Charo: Maria Rosario Pilar Martinez Molina Baeza
Chubby Checker: Ernest Evans
Cher: Cherilyn Sarkisian
Chuck D: Carlton Ridenhour
Patsy Cline: Virginia Patterson Hensley
Claudette Colbert: Lily Chauchoin
Coolio: Artis Leon Ivey Jr.
Alice Cooper: Vincent Furnier
David Copperfield: David Kotkin
Howard Cosell: Howard Cohen
Elvis Costello: Declan McManus
Lou Costello: Louis Cristillo
Peter Coyote: Peter Cohon
Quentin Crisp: Denis Pratt
Tom Cruise: Thomas Cruise Mapother IV
Tony Curtis: Bernard Schwartz
Miley Cyrus: Destiny Hope Cyrus
Vic Damone: Vito Farinola
D'Angelo: Michael D'Angelo Archer
Rodney Dangerfield: Jacob Cohen
Bobby Darin: Walden Robert Cassotto
Doris Day: Doris von Kappelhoff
Yvonne De Carlo: Peggy Middleton
Sandra Dee: Alexandra Zuck
John Denver: Henry John Deutschendorf Jr.
Bo Derek: Mary Cathleen Collins
Portia de Rossi: Amanda Lee Rogers
Danny Devito: Daniel Michaeli
Angie Dickinson: Angeline Brown
Bo Diddley: Elias Bates
Phyllis Diller: Phyllis Driver
Divine: Harris Glenn Milstead
Dmx: Earl Simmons
Troy Donahue: Merle Johnson Jr.
Kirk Douglas: Issur Danielovitch
Melvyn Douglas: Melvyn Hesselberg
Duffy: Aimee Anne Duffy
Bob Dylan: Robert Zimmerman
Barbara Eden: Barbara Huffman
Carmen Electra: Tara Leigh Patrick
Elvira: Cassandra Peterson
Eminem: Marshall Mathers
Enya: Eithne Ni Bhraonian
Dale Evans: Frances Smith
Chad Everett: Raymon Cramton
Fabian: Fabian Anthony Forte
Fabio: Fabio Lanzoni
Fabolous: John Jackson
Douglas Fairbanks: Douglas Ullman
Morgan Fairchild: Patsy McClenny
Jamie Farr: Jameel Farah
Alice Faye: Alice Jeanne Leppert
Fergie: Stacy Ferguson
Stepin Fetchit: Lincoln Perry
W. C. Fields: William Claude Dukenfield
50 Cent: Curtis Jackson
Barry Fitzgerald: William Shields
Flavor Flav: William Drayton
Joan Fontaine: Joan de Havilland
Jodie Foster: Alicia Christian Foster
Redd Foxx: John Sanford
Arlene Francis: Arlene Kazanjian
Connie Francis: Concetta Franconero
Kenny G: Kenneth Gorelick
Greta Garbo: Greta Gustafsson
Vincent Gardenia: Vincent Scognamiglio
John Garfield: Julius Garfinkle
Judy Garland: Frances Gumm
James Garner: James Bumgarner
Crystal Gayle: Brenda Gail Webb
George Gershwin: Jacob Gershowitz
Kathie Lee Gifford: Kathie Epstein
Whoopi Goldberg: Caryn Johnson
Eydie Gorme: Edith Gormezano
Stewart Granger: James Stewart
Cary Grant: Archibald Leach
Lee Grant: Lyova Rosenthal
Robert Guillaume: Robert Williams
Buddy Hackett: Leonard Hacker
Hammer: Stanley Kirk Burrell
Jean Harlow: Harlean Carpenter
Rex Harrison: Reginald Carey Harrison
Laurence Harvey: Larushka Skikne
Helen Hayes: Helen Brown
Susan Hayward: Edythe Marrener
Rita Hayworth: Margarita Cansino
Pee-Wee Herman: Paul Reubenfeld
Charlton Heston: John Charles Carter
Perez Hilton: Mario Armando Lavandeira Jr.
Hulk Hogan: Terry Gene Bollea
William Holden: William Beedle
Billie Holiday: Eleanora Fagan
Buddy Holly: Charles Hardin Holley

Judy Holliday: Judith Tuvim
Bob Hope: Leslie Townes Hope
Harry Houdini: Erik Weisz
Leslie Howard: Leslie Stainer
Howlin' Wolf: Chester Burnett
Rock Hudson: Roy Scherer Jr. (later Fitzgerald)
Engelbert Humperdinck: Arnold Dorsey
Kim Hunter: Janet Cole
Ice Cube: O'Shea Jackson
Ice-T: Tracy Morrow
Billy Idol: William Broad
Etta James: Jamesetta Hawkins
Ja Rule: Jeffrey Atkins
Jay-Z: Shawn Carter
Jewel: Jewel Kilcher
Elton John: Reginald Dwight
Angelina Jolie: Angelina Jolie Voight
Al Jolson: Asa Yoelson
Jennifer Jones: Phylis Isley
Tom Jones: Thomas Woodward
Spike Jonze: Adam Spiegel
Louis Jourdan: Louis Gendre
Wynonna Judd: Christina Ciminella
Boris Karloff: William Henry Pratt
Danny Kaye: David Kaminsky
Ke$ha: Kesha Rose Sebert
Diane Keaton: Diane Hall
Michael Keaton: Michael Douglas
Alicia Keys: Alicia Augello Cook
Chaka Khan: Yvette Stevens
Carole King: Carole Klein
Larry King: Larry Zeiger
Ben Kingsley: Krishna Banji
Ted Knight: Tadewurz Wladziu Konopka
Cheryl Ladd: Cheryl Stoppelmoor
Lady Gaga: Stefani Germanotta
Veronica Lake: Constance Ockleman
Hedy Lamarr: Hedwig Kiesler
Dorothy Lamour: Mary Leta Dorothy Slaton
Michael Landon: Eugene Orowitz
k.d. lang: Kathryn Dawn Lang
Mario Lanza: Alfredo Cocozza
Queen Latifah: Dana Owens
Stan Laurel: Arthur Jefferson
Steve Lawrence: Sidney Leibowitz
Brenda Lee: Brenda Mae Tarpley
Gypsy Rose Lee: Rose Louise Hovick
Michelle Lee: Michelle Dusiak
Peggy Lee: Norma Egstrom
Janet Leigh: Jeanette Morrison
Vivien Leigh: Vivian Hartley
Huey Lewis: Hugh Cregg
Jerry Lewis: Joseph Levitch
Lil' Kim: Kimberly Denise Jones
Lil' Romeo: Percy Romeo Miller Jr.
Little Richard: Richard Penniman
L.L. Cool J: James Todd Smith
Carole Lombard: Jane Peters
Sophia Loren: Sophia Scicolone
Peter Lorre: Laszlo Lowenstein
Myrna Loy: Myrna Williams
Bela Lugosi: Bela Ferenc Blasko
Moms Mabley: Loretta Mary Aiken
Shirley Maclaine: Shirley Beaty
Elle Macpherson: Eleanor Gow
Madonna: Madonna Louise Veronica Ciccone
Lee Majors: Harvey Lee Yeary
Karl Malden: Mladen Sekulovich
Barry Manilow: Barry Alan Pincus
Jayne Mansfield: Vera Jane Palmer
Marilyn Manson: Brian Warner
Fredric March: Frederick Bickel
Bruno Mars: Peter Gene Hernandez
Dean Martin: Dino Crocetti
Ricky Martin: Enrique Jose Martin Morales
Groucho Marx: Julius Henry Marx
MCA: Adam Yauch
Meat Loaf: Marvin Lee Aday
Freddie Mercury: Frederick Bulsara
Ethel Merman: Ethel Zimmermann
George Michael: Georgios Panayiotou
Midori: Midori Goto
Mike D: Michael Diamond
Ray Milland: Reginald Truscott-Jones
Ann Miller: Lucille Collier
Helen Mirren: Ilynea Lydia Mironoff
Joni Mitchell: Roberta Joan Anderson
Moby: Richard Melville Hall
Mo'Nique: Monique Imes
Marilyn Monroe: Norma Jean Mortenson (later Baker)
Yves Montand: Ivo Livi
Demi Moore: Demetria Guynes
Rita Moreno: Rosita Alverio
Harry Morgan: Harry Bratsburg
Morrissey: Steven Patrick Morrissey

Mr. T: Lawrence Tureaud
Paul Muni: Mehilem Weisenfreund
Nelly: Cornell Haynes Jr.
Mike Nichols: Michael Igor Peschowsky
Chuck Norris: Carlos Ray Norris
Notorious B.I.G.: Christopher Wallace
Hugh O'Brian: Hugh Krampke
Odetta: Odetta Holmes
Maureen O'Hara: Maureen FitzSimons
Ozzy Osbourne: John Michael Osbourne
Jack Palance: Vladimir Palanuik
Minnie Pearl: Sarah Ophelia Cannon
Katy Perry: Kathryn Hudson
Bernadette Peters: Bernadette Lazzara
Edith Piaf: Edith Gassion
Slim Pickens: Louis Lindley
Mary Pickford: Gladys Smith
Pink: Alecia Moore
Iggy Pop: James Newell Osterberg
Natalie Portman: Natalie Hershlag
Robert Preston: Robert Preston Meservey
Prince: Prince Rogers Nelson
Raffi: Raffi Cavoukian
Dee Dee Ramone: Douglas Colvin
Joey Ramone: Jeffrey Hyman
Johnny Ramone: John Cummings
Tommy Ramone: Tom Erdelyi
Tony Randall: Leonard Rosenberg
Martha Raye: Margaret O'Reed
Della Reese: Delloreese Patricia Early
Busta Rhymes: Trevor Smith Jr.
Joan Rivers: Joan Sandra Molinsky
Edward G. Robinson: Emmanuel Goldenberg
The Rock: Dwayne Johnson
Ginger Rogers: Virginia McMath
Roy Rogers: Leonard Franklin Slye
Mickey Rooney: Joe Yule Jr.
Johnny Rotten: John Lydon
Lillian Russell: Helen Leonard
Meg Ryan: Margaret Hyra
Winona Ryder: Winona Horowitz
Sabu: Sabu Dastagir
Sade: Helen Folsade Abu
Soupy Sales: Milton Supman
Susan Sarandon: Susan Tomaling
Randolph Scott: George Randolph Crane
Seal: Seal Henry Olusegun Olumide Adeola Samuel
Selena: Selena Quintanilla
Jane Seymour: Joyce Frankenberg
Shakira: Shakira Isabel Mebarak Ripoll
Omar Sharif: Michael Shalhoub
Charlie Sheen: Carlos Irwin Estevez
Martin Sheen: Ramon Estevez
Talia Shire: Talia Coppola
Beverly Sills: Belle Silverman
Phil Silvers: Philip Silversmith
Gene Simmons: Chaim Witz
Sinbad: David Adkins
Anna Nicole Smith: Vickie Lynn Hogan
Snoop Dogg: Calvin Broadus
Ann Sothern: Harriette Lake
Barbara Stanwyck: Ruby Stevens
Jean Stapleton: Jeanne Murray
Ringo Starr: Richard Starkey
Cat Stevens: Stephen Demetre Georgiou
Connie Stevens: Concetta Ingolia
Jon Stewart: Jonathan Stuart Leibowitz
Sting: Gordon Sumner
Joe Strummer: John Graham Mellor
Donna Summer: La Donna Gaines
Rip Taylor: Charles Elmer Taylor Jr.
Robert Taylor: Spangler Brugh
Danny Thomas: Muzyad Yakhoob, later Amos Jacobs
Tiny Tim: Herbert Khaury
Rip Torn: Elmore Rual Torn Jr.
Randy Travis: Randy Traywick
Sophie Tucker: Sophia Kalish
Tina Turner: Annie Mae Bullock
Shania Twain: Eilleen Regina Edwards
Twiggy: Lesley Hornby
Conway Twitty: Harold Lloyd Jenkins
Usher: Usher Raymond IV
Rudolph Valentino: Rudolpho D'Antonguolla
Frankie Valli: Frank Castelluccio
Eddie Vedder: Edward Louis Seversen III
Sid Vicious: John Simon Ritchie
John Wayne: Marion Morrison
Raquel Welch: Raquel Tejada
Gene Wilder: Jerome Silberman
Shelley Winters: Shirley Schrift
Stevie Wonder: Stevland Morris
Jane Wyman: Sarah Jane Mayfield
Yanni: Yanni Chrysomallis
Loretta Young: Gretchen Michaels Young
Buckwheat Zydeco: Stanley Dural Jr.

ARTS AND MEDIA

Some Notable Movies, Sept. 2010-Aug. 2011

Film (rating)	Stars	Director
127 Hours (R)	James Franco, Amber Tamblyn, Kate Mara	Danny Boyle
The Adjustment Bureau (PG-13)	Matt Damon, Emily Blunt, Anthony Mackie, John Slattery	George Nolfi
Bad Teacher (R)	Cameron Diaz, Jason Segel, Justin Timberlake	Jake Kasdan
Battle: Los Angeles (PG-13)	Aaron Eckhart, Michelle Rodriguez, Bridget Moynahan	Jonathan Liebesman
Beginners (R)	Ewan McGregor, Christopher Plummer, Mélanie Laurent	Mike Mills
Black Swan (R)	Natalie Portman, Mila Kunis, Vincent Cassel	Darren Aronofsky
Blue Valentine (R)	Ryan Gosling, Michelle Williams	Derek Cianfrance
Bridesmaids (R)	Kristen Wiig, Rose Byrne, Maya Rudolph, Melissa McCarthy	Paul Feig
Captain America: The First Avenger (PG-13)	Chris Evans, Hugo Weaving, Stanley Tucci, Hayley Atwell	Joe Johnston
The Chronicles of Narnia: The Voyage of the Dawn Treader (PG)	Ben Barnes, Georgie Henley, Skandar Keynes	Michael Apted
The Company Men (R)	Ben Affleck, Chris Cooper, Tommy Lee Jones, Kevin Costner	John Wells
Cowboys & Aliens (PG-13)	Daniel Craig, Harrison Ford, Olivia Wilde	Jon Favreau
Crazy, Stupid, Love (PG-13)	Steve Carell, Ryan Gosling, Julianne Moore, Emma Stone	Glenn Ficarra, John Requa
The Debt (R)	Helen Mirren, Sam Worthington, Jessica Chastain, Tom Wilkinson	John Madden
The Dilemma (PG-13)	Vince Vaughn, Kevin James, Winona Ryder, Jennifer Connelly	Ron Howard
Due Date (R)	Robert Downey Jr., Zach Galifianakis	Todd Phillips
Easy A (PG-13)	Emma Stone, Amanda Bynes, Penn Badgley	Will Gluck
The Fighter (R)	Mark Wahlberg, Christian Bale, Melissa Leo, Amy Adams	David O. Russell
Friends With Benefits (R)	Mila Kunis, Justin Timberlake, Patricia Clarkson	Will Gluck
Gnomeo & Juliet (G)	James McAvoy, Emily Blunt, Maggie Smith	Kelly Asbury
The Green Hornet (PG-13)	Seth Rogen, Jay Chou, Cameron Diaz, Christoph Waltz	Michel Gondry
Green Lantern (PG-13)	Ryan Reynolds, Blake Lively, Peter Sarsgaard	Martin Campbell
The Hangover Part II (R)	Bradley Cooper, Zach Galifianakis, Ed Helms	Todd Phillips
Hanna (PG-13)	Saoirse Ronan, Eric Bana, Cate Blanchett	Joe Wright
Harry Potter and the Deathly Hallows: Part 1 (PG-13)	Daniel Radcliffe, Emma Watson, Rupert Grint, Ralph Fiennes	David Yates
Harry Potter and the Deathly Hallows: Part 2 (PG-13)	Daniel Radcliffe, Emma Watson, Rupert Grint, Ralph Fiennes	David Yates
The Help (PG-13)	Emma Stone, Viola Davis, Octavia Spencer, Bryce Dallas Howard	Tate Taylor
Hereafter (PG-13)	Matt Damon, Cécile de France, Bryce Dallas Howard	Clint Eastwood
Horrible Bosses (R)	Jason Bateman, Charlie Day, Jason Sudeikis, Jennifer Aniston	Seth Gordon
I Am Number Four (PG-13)	Alex Pettyfer, Timothy Olyphant, Dianna Agron	D.J. Caruso
Inside Job (PG-13)	documentary narrated by Matt Damon	Charles Ferguson
Jackass 3D (R)	Johnny Knoxville, Bam Margera, Steve-O	Jeff Tremaine
Just Go With It (PG-13)	Adam Sandler, Jennifer Aniston	Dennis Dugan
Justin Bieber: Never Say Never (G)	Justin Bieber	Jon M. Chu
The King's Speech (R)	Colin Firth, Geoffrey Rush, Helena Bonham Carter	Tom Hooper
Limitless (PG-13)	Bradley Cooper, Robert De Niro, Abbie Cornish	Neil Burger
Little Fockers (PG-13)	Ben Stiller, Robert De Niro, Teri Polo, Blythe Danner	Paul Weitz
Love and Other Drugs (R)	Jake Gyllenhaal, Anne Hathaway	Edward Zwick
MegaMind (PG)	Will Ferrell, Brad Pitt, Tina Fey, Jonah Hill, David Cross	Tom McGrath
Midnight in Paris (PG-13)	Owen Wilson, Rachel McAdams, Kathy Bates	Woody Allen
Mr. Popper's Penguins (PG)	Jim Carrey, Carla Gugino, Angela Lansbury	Mark Waters
No Strings Attached (R)	Natalie Portman, Ashton Kutcher, Kevin Kline	Ivan Reitman
Of Gods and Men (PG-13)	Lambert Wilson, Michael Lonsdale, Olivier Rabourdin	Xavier Beauvois
Project Nim (PG-13)	documentary	James Marsh
Rango (PG)	Johnny Depp, Abigail Breslin, Isla Fisher, Timothy Olyphant	Gore Verbinski
Red (PG-13)	Bruce Willis, Helen Mirren, John Malkovich, Morgan Freeman	Robert Schwentke
Rio (PG)	Jesse Eisenberg, Anne Hathaway, George Lopez	Carlos Saldanha
Rise of the Planet of the Apes (PG-13)	James Franco, Andy Serkis, John Lithgow, Freida Pinto	Rupert Wyatt
Scream 4 (R)	Neve Campbell, David Arquette, Courteney Cox	Wes Craven
The Social Network (PG-13)	Jesse Eisenberg, Andrew Garfield, Justin Timberlake	David Fincher
Soul Surfer (PG)	AnnaSophia Robb, Dennis Quaid, Helen Hunt	Sean McNamara
Source Code (PG-13)	Jake Gyllenhaal, Michelle Monaghan, Vera Farmiga, Jeffrey Wright	Duncan Jones
Super 8 (PG-13)	Kyle Chandler, Elle Fanning, Joel Courtney	J. J. Abrams
Tangled (PG)	Mandy Moore, Zachary Levi, Donna Murphy	Nathan Greno, Byron Howard
Terri (R)	John C. Reilly, Jacob Wysocki, Bridger Zadina	Azazel Jacobs
Thor (PG-13)	Chris Hemsworth, Natalie Portman, Anthony Hopkins	Kenneth Branagh
The Tourist (PG-13)	Angelina Jolie, Johnny Depp	Florian Henckel von Donnersmarck
The Town (R)	Ben Affleck, Jeremy Renner, Jon Hamm, Rebecca Hall	Ben Affleck
Transformers: Dark of the Moon (PG-13)	Shia LaBeouf, Rosie Huntington-Whiteley, Josh Duhamel, Tyrese Gibson	Michael Bay
The Tree of Life (PG-13)	Brad Pitt, Sean Penn, Jessica Chastain	Terrence Malick
TRON: Legacy (PG)	Garrett Hedlund, Jeff Bridges, Olivia Wilde	Joseph Kosinski
True Grit (PG-13)	Jeff Bridges, Hailee Steinfeld, Matt Damon, Josh Brolin	Joel Coen, Ethan Coen
Waiting for Superman (PG)	documentary	Davis Guggenheim
Wall Street: Money Never Sleeps (PG-13)	Michael Douglas, Shia LaBeouf, Carey Mulligan	Oliver Stone
Water for Elephants (PG-13)	Reese Witherspoon, Robert Pattinson, Christoph Waltz	Francis Lawrence
Win Win (R)	Paul Giamatti, Amy Ryan, Alex Shaffer	Thomas McCarthy
X-Men: First Class (PG-13)	James McAvoy, Michael Fassbender, Jennifer Lawrence, Kevin Bacon	Matthew Vaughn
Zookeeper (PG)	Kevin James, Rosario Dawson, Leslie Bibb	Frank Coraci

50 Top-Grossing Movies, 2010
Source: Rentrak Corporation

Rank	Title	Gross (mil)	Rank	Title	Gross (mil)
1.	Avatar	$476.9	27.	Due Date	$99.4
2.	Toy Story 3	415.0	28.	Alvin and the Chipmunks: The Squeaquel	98.9
3.	Alice in Wonderland	334.2	29.	Date Night	98.7
4.	Iron Man 2	312.1	30.	True Grit	95.4
5.	The Twilight Saga: Eclipse	300.5	31.	Sex and the City 2	95.3
6.	Inception	292.6	32.	The Book of Eli	94.8
7.	Harry Potter and the Deathly Hallows: Part 1	285.3	33.	The Social Network	93.4
8.	Despicable Me	251.3	34.	The Town	92.2
9.	Shrek Forever After	238.4	35.	Prince of Persia: The Sands of Time	90.8
10.	How to Train Your Dragon	217.6	36.	The Chronicles of Narnia: The Voyage of the Dawn Treader	89.9
11.	The Karate Kid	176.6	37.	Red	89.6
12.	Tangled	170.7	38.	Percy Jackson & the Olympians: The Lightning Thief	88.8
13.	Clash of the Titans	163.2	39.	Paranormal Activity 2	84.7
14.	Grown Ups	162.0	40.	Eat Pray Love	80.6
15.	MegaMind	144.4	41.	Dear John	80.0
16.	TRON: Legacy	138.1	42.	Unstoppable	79.7
17.	The Last Airbender	131.6	43.	The A-Team	77.2
18.	Shutter Island	128.0	44.	Knight and Day	76.4
19.	The Other Guys	119.2	45.	Dinner for Schmucks	73.0
20.	Salt	118.3	46.	It's Complicated	72.4
21.	Jackass 3D	117.2	47.	Yogi Bear	68.8
22.	Valentine's Day	110.5	48.	The Bounty Hunter	67.1
23.	Little Fockers	110.2	49.	Diary of a Wimpy Kid	64.0
24.	Sherlock Holmes	106.9	50.	The Sorcerer's Apprentice	63.2
25.	Robin Hood	105.3			
26.	The Expendables	103.1			

Note: Box-office grosses in the U.S. and Canada Jan. 1, 2010-Jan. 6, 2011; some films may have had 2009 release dates.

All-Time Top-Grossing American Movies
Source: Rentrak Corporation

Rank	Title (original release)	Gross (mil)	Rank	Title (original release)	Gross (mil)
1.	Avatar (2009)	$760.5	28.	Indiana Jones and the Kingdom of the Crystal Skull (2008)	$317.1
2.	Titanic (1997)	600.8	29.	The Lord of the Rings: The Fellowship of the Ring (2001)	314.2
3.	The Dark Knight (2008)	533.3	30.	The Lion King (1994)	312.9
4.	Star Wars (1977)	461.0	31.	Iron Man 2 (2010)	312.4
5.	Shrek 2 (2004)	436.7	32.	Star Wars: Episode II—Attack of the Clones (2002)	310.7
6.	E.T. The Extra-Terrestrial (1982)	435.0	33.	Star Wars: Episode I—The Phantom Menace (1999)	431.1
7.	Star Wars: Episode I—The Phantom Menace (1999)	431.1	34.	Star Wars: Episode VI—Return of the Jedi (1983)	309.2
8.	Pirates of the Caribbean: Dead Man's Chest (2006)	423.3	35.	Independence Day (1996)	306.2
9.	Toy Story 3 (2010)	415.0	36.	Pirates of the Caribbean: The Curse of the Black Pearl (2003)	305.4
10.	Spider-Man (2002)	403.7	37.	Harry Potter and the Half-Blood Prince (2009)	302.0
11.	Transformers: Revenge of the Fallen (2009)	402.1	38.	The Twilight Saga: Eclipse (2010)	300.5
12.	Star Wars: Episode III—Revenge of the Sith (2005)	380.3	39.	The Twilight Saga: New Moon (2009)	296.6
13.	The Lord of the Rings: The Return of the King (2003)	377.0	40.	Harry Potter and the Deathly Hallows: Part 1 (2010)	295.0
14.	Spider-Man 2 (2004)	373.4	41.	The Sixth Sense (1999)	293.5
15.	The Passion of the Christ (2004)	370.3	42.	Up (2009)	293.0
16.	Harry Potter and the Deathly Hallows: Part 2 (2011)	366.0	43.	Inception (2010)	292.6
17.	Jurassic Park (1993)	357.1	44.	Harry Potter and the Order of the Phoenix (2007)	292.0
18.	Transformers: Dark of the Moon (2011)	348.5	45.	The Chronicles of Narnia: The Lion, the Witch, and the Wardrobe (2005)	291.7
19.	The Lord of the Rings: The Two Towers (2002)	341.7	46.	Star Wars: Episode V—The Empire Strikes Back (1980)	290.3
20.	Finding Nemo (2003)	339.7	47.	Harry Potter and the Goblet of Fire (2005)	290.0
21.	Spider-Man 3 (2007)	336.5	48.	Home Alone (1990)	285.8
22.	Alice in Wonderland (2010)	334.2	49.	The Matrix Reloaded (2003)	281.5
23.	Forrest Gump (1994)	329.7	50.	Meet the Fockers (2004)	279.2
24.	Shrek the Third (2007)	322.7			
25.	Transformers (2007)	319.2			
26.	Iron Man (2008)	318.6			
27.	Harry Potter and the Sorcerer's Stone (2001)	317.6			

Note: Box-office grosses in the U.S. and Canada through Aug. 22, 2010, in absolute dollars. Rising ticket prices favor newer films. Revenues from re-releases are included.

100 Best American Movies of All Time
Source: American Film Institute

First unveiled in 1998 based on ballots sent to 1,500 individuals, mostly from the film world, in 1997. Updated in 2007 (the version shown here) to include newly eligible films and reflect shifting cultural perspectives. Criteria for judging included historical significance, cultural impact, critical recognition and awards, and popularity. The year each film was first released is in parentheses.

1. Citizen Kane (1941)
2. The Godfather (1972)
3. Casablanca (1942)
4. Raging Bull (1980)
5. Singin' in the Rain (1952)
6. Gone With the Wind (1939)
7. Lawrence of Arabia (1962)
8. Schindler's List (1993)
9. Vertigo (1958)
10. The Wizard of Oz (1939)
11. City Lights (1931)
12. The Searchers (1956)
13. Star Wars (1977)
14. Psycho (1960)
15. 2001: A Space Odyssey (1968)
16. Sunset Boulevard (1950)
17. The Graduate (1967)
18. The General (1927)
19. On the Waterfront (1954)
20. It's a Wonderful Life (1946)
21. Chinatown (1974)
22. Some Like It Hot (1959)
23. The Grapes of Wrath (1940)
24. E.T. The Extra-Terrestrial (1982)
25. To Kill a Mockingbird (1962)
26. Mr. Smith Goes to Washington (1939)
27. High Noon (1952)
28. All About Eve (1950)
29. Double Indemnity (1944)
30. Apocalypse Now (1979)
31. The Maltese Falcon (1941)
32. The Godfather Part II (1974)
33. One Flew Over the Cuckoo's Nest (1975)
34. Snow White and the Seven Dwarfs (1937)
35. Annie Hall (1977)
36. The Bridge on the River Kwai (1957)
37. The Best Years of Our Lives (1946)

38. The Treasure of the Sierra Madre (1948)
39. Dr. Strangelove (1964)
40. The Sound of Music (1965)
41. King Kong (1933)
42. Bonnie and Clyde (1967)
43. Midnight Cowboy (1969)
44. The Philadelphia Story (1940)
45. Shane (1953)
46. It Happened One Night (1934)
47. A Streetcar Named Desire (1951)
48. Rear Window (1954)
49. Intolerance (1916)
50. The Lord of the Rings: The Fellowship of the Ring (2001)
51. West Side Story (1961)
52. Taxi Driver (1976)
53. The Deer Hunter (1978)
54. M*A*S*H (1970)
55. North By Northwest (1959)
56. Jaws (1975)
57. Rocky (1976)

58. The Gold Rush (1925)
59. Nashville (1975)
60. Duck Soup (1933)
61. Sullivan's Travels (1941)
62. American Graffiti (1973)
63. Cabaret (1972)
64. Network (1976)
65. The African Queen (1951)
66. Raiders of the Lost Ark (1981)
67. Who's Afraid of Virginia Woolf? (1966)
68. Unforgiven (1992)
69. Tootsie (1982)
70. A Clockwork Orange (1971)
71. Saving Private Ryan (1998)
72. The Shawshank Redemption (1994)
73. Butch Cassidy and the Sundance Kid (1969)
74. The Silence of the Lambs (1991)
75. In the Heat of the Night (1967)
76. Forrest Gump (1994)
77. All the President's Men (1976)
78. Modern Times (1936)

79. The Wild Bunch (1969)
80. The Apartment (1960)
81. Spartacus (1960)
82. Sunrise (1927)
83. Titanic (1997)
84. Easy Rider (1969)
85. A Night at the Opera (1935)
86. Platoon (1986)
87. 12 Angry Men (1957)
88. Bringing Up Baby (1938)
89. The Sixth Sense (1999)
90. Swing Time (1936)
91. Sophie's Choice (1982)
92. Goodfellas (1990)
93. The French Connection (1971)
94. Pulp Fiction (1994)
95. The Last Picture Show (1971)
96. Do the Right Thing (1989)
97. Blade Runner (1982)
98. Yankee Doodle Dandy (1942)
99. Toy Story (1995)
100. Ben-Hur (1959)

National Film Registry, 2010
Source: National Film Registry, Library of Congress

The National Film Registry adds 25 "culturally, historically, or aesthetically significant" American films annually.

Airplane! (1980)
All the President's Men (1976)
The Bargain (1914)
Cry of Jazz (1959)
Electronic Labyrinth: THX 1138 4EB (1967)
The Empire Strikes Back (1980)

The Exorcist (1973)
The Front Page (1931)
Grey Gardens (1976)
I Am Joaquin (1969)
It's a Gift (1934)
Let There Be Light (1946)
Lonesome (1928)
Make Way for Tomorrow (1937)

Malcolm X (1992)
McCabe and Mrs. Miller (1971)
Newark Athlete (1891)
Our Lady of the Sphere (1969)
The Pink Panther (1964)
Preservation of the Sign Language (1913)
Saturday Night Fever (1977)

Study of a River (1996)
Tarantella (1940)
A Tree Grows in Brooklyn (1945)
A Trip Down Market Street (1906)

Film and Television Production by State, 2009-10
Source: Motion Picture Association of America

State	Productions, recent examples
Alabama*	11, October Baby, Due Date
Alaska*	17, Sarah Palin's Alaska (TV), Deadliest Catch (TV), Ice Road Truckers (TV)
Arizona	24, Everything Must Go, Fast Five, On the Road
Arkansas*	6, Best Laid Schemes, The Last Ride, 19 Kids & Counting (TV)
California*	1,087, American Idol (TV), The Big Bang Theory (TV), Bridesmaids, NCIS (TV)
Colorado*	20, Cool Tools (TV), Food Network Challenge (TV)
Connecticut*	26, The Jerry Springer Show (TV), Rio, Ice Age: Continental Drift, The Big C (TV)
Delaware	5, The Dish & the Spoon, Mayor Cupcake
Florida*	65, Burn Notice (TV), I Am Number Four, The Losers
Georgia*	111, The Blind Side, X-Men: First Class, The Vampire Diaries (TV), Water for Elephants
Hawaii*	23, Pirates of the Caribbean: On Stranger Tides, Rise of the Planet of the Apes, Hawaii Five-O (TV)
Idaho*	8, Finding Sky, Magic Valley, Soda Springs
Illinois*	74, Contagion, Little Fockers, Source Code, Cold Case Files (TV)
Indiana*	12, Camel Spiders, A Nightmare on Elm Street, Spooky Tales
Iowa	26, Cedar Rapids, The Crazies, Janie Jones
Kansas*	5, Earthworks, Nailbiter
Kentucky*	7, Sam Steele and the Crystal Chalice, Secretariat
Louisiana*	149, Green Lantern, Colombiana, Red, Treme (TV)
Maine*	9, 40 West, American Loggers (TV), How and Howe Tech (TV)
Maryland*	10, The Social Network, The Possession, Ace of Cakes (TV)
Massachusetts*	44, Moneyball, The Company Men, The Fighter, Ask This Old House (TV)
Michigan*	112, The Karate Kid, Red Dawn, Scream 4, Hung (TV)
Minnesota*	39, Souvenirs, Young Adult, Sweat Equity (TV)
Mississippi*	13, The Help, Rites of Spring, Where I Begin
Missouri*	15, A Horrible Way to Die, Winter's Bone, Turbine
Montana*	7, Forgotten Flag Raisers, Koani and Her Unusual Pack
Nebraska	5, Trunk'd, Up in the Air
Nevada	53, Hostel Part III, Bachelor Pad (TV), Pawn Stars (TV)
New Hampshire	15, The Resurrection of Victor Jara, The A Plate, Beneath Contempt
New Jersey*	131, Wall Street 2: Money Never Sleeps; Eat, Pray, Love; Jersey Shore (TV)
New Mexico*	51, Cowboys & Aliens, True Grit, Thor, Breaking Bad (TV)
New York*	624, The Other Guys, Black Swan, The Adjustment Bureau, 30 Rock (TV), The Good Wife (TV)
North Carolina*	30, Journey 2: The Mysterious Island, One Tree Hill (TV), Bloodworth
North Dakota*	4, The Legend of Hell's Gate: An American Conspiracy, Pinching Penny
Ohio*	18, Unstoppable, Touchback, 25 Hill
Oklahoma*	23, The Killer Inside Me, A Christmas Snow, Yellow
Oregon*	40, Shiver, Leverage (TV), Portlandia (TV)
Pennsylvania*	59, Law Abiding Citizen, Love and Other Drugs, It's Always Sunny in Philadelphia (TV)
Rhode Island*	10, Hall Pass, Body of Proof (TV), The Girl From the Naked Eye
South Carolina*	13, The Bay, Army Wives (TV), Little Red Wagon
South Dakota*	4, Full Throttle Saloon (TV), The Great Mystery
Tennessee*	26, Country Strong, Water for Elephants, Footloose
Texas*	148, True Grit, Spy Kids 4, Machete
Utah*	35, 127 Hours, John Carter of Mars, Dogtown (TV)
Vermont	4, Dug Up, Tin Can, The Sparrow and the Tigress
Virginia*	29, Almost Human, Alone Yet Not Alone, Coal (TV)
Washington*	18, The Hit List, Judas Kiss, Camilla Dickinson
Wash., DC*	32, Transformers: Dark of the Moon, Salt, Meet the Press (TV), Top Chef (TV)
West Virginia*	8, Romeo Must Hang, Super 8, Jamie Oliver's Food Revolution (TV)
Wisconsin*	13, Transformers: Dark of the Moon; No God, No Master; Feed the Fish
Wyoming*	10, Tree Fight, Wolves of Yellowstone

* = State has enacted incentives to increase production.

U.S. Movie Theaters, 1946-2010
Source: Motion Picture Association of America; Rentrak Corporation

Year	Box office (mil)	Admissions (mil)	Admissions per week (mil)	Screens	Avg. ticket price	Films produced	Films released
1946	$1,692.0	4,067.3	78.2	NA	$0.42	NA	400
1950	1,379.0	3,017.5	58.0	NA	0.46	NA	483
1955	1,204.0	2,072.3	39.9	NA	0.58	NA	319
1960	984.4	1,304.5	25.1	NA	0.76	NA	248
1965	1,041.8	1,031.5	19.8	NA	1.01	NA	279
1970	1,429.2	920.6	17.7	NA	1.55	279	306
1975	2,114.8	1,032.8	19.9	15,030	2.05	258	233
1980	2,748.5	1,021.5	19.6	17,590	2.69	214	233
1985	3,749.4	1,056.1	20.3	21,147	3.55	264	470
1990	5,021.8	1,188.6	22.9	23,689	4.23	346	410
1995	5,269.0	1,211.0	23.3	27,805	4.35	631	411
2000	7,468.0	1,383.0	26.6	37,396	5.39	683	475
2001	8,125.0	1,438.0	27.7	36,764	5.66	611	454
2002	9,272.0	1,599.0	30.8	35,280	5.81	546	475
2003	9,165.0	1,521.0	29.3	35,786	6.03	593	455
2004	9,215.0	1,484.0	28.5	36,594	6.21	611	489
2005	8,832.0	1,376.0	26.5	38,852	6.41	920	507
2006	9,138.0	1,395.0	26.8	38,415	6.55	928	594
2007	9,629.0	1,400.0	26.9	38,974	6.88	909	609
2008	9,791.0	1,364.0	26.2	38,834	7.18	759	634
2009	10,543.6	1,415.0	27.2	39,233	7.50	734	555
2010	10,741.0[1]	1,341.0	25.8	39,547	7.89	754	560

NA = Not available. (1) Box-office grosses in the U.S. and Canada, Jan. 1, 2010-Jan. 6, 2011.

Top Film Websites, June 2011
Source: comScore Media Metrix, Inc.

Rank	Website	Visitors[1]	% change[2]	Rank	Website	Visitors[1]	% change[2]
1.	IMDb.com	39,991	59.4%	11.	WarnerBros.com	2,263	51.7%
2.	Yahoo! Movies	26,774	0.6	12.	AMC Entertainment Inc.	1,995	-5.7
3.	Fandango Movies	16,935	7.8	13.	MovieFreaker.com	1,875	NA
4.	MSN Movies	14,211	30.0	14.	JudyMoodyMovie.com	1,758	NA
5.	Moviefone	12,622	-12.2	15.	Disney Movies	1,648	9.1
6.	Flixster.com	7,395	10.9	16.	Bing Movies	1,389	NA
7.	Hollywood.com sites	6,952	-23.6	17.	Cinemark.com	1,225	NA
8.	The Movie Network	6,718	30.1	18.	Comingsoon.net	1,174	NA
9.	Film.com	3,351	-25.4	19.	DreamWorks SKG	1,162	NA
10.	UGO Film-TV	3,126	26.1	20.	Regal Entertainment	1,055	-23.4

NA = Not applicable. (1) Number of unique visitors, in thousands, who visited website at least once in June 2011. (2) Percent change over June 2010.

Most Popular DVDs, 2011
Source: Rentrak Corporation

Top Rentals, 2010

Rank	Title
1.	Toy Story 3
2.	Avatar
3.	The Twilight Saga: New Moon
4.	The Twilight Saga: Eclipse
5.	The Blind Side
6.	Alice in Wonderland (2010)
7.	Alvin and the Chipmunks: The Squeakquel
8.	Iron Man 2
9.	How to Train Your Dragon
10.	Despicable Me
11.	The Princess and the Frog
12.	The Search for Santa Paws
13.	Sherlock Holmes
14.	Inception
15.	Tinker Bell and the Great Fairy Rescue
16.	The Hangover
17.	Disney's A Christmas Carol
18.	The Book of Eli
19.	The Expendables
20.	The Karate Kid

Top-Selling DVDs, 2010

Rank	Title
1.	Couples Retreat
2.	Law Abiding Citizen
3.	2012
4.	The Blind Side
5.	The Hangover
6.	The Time Traveler's Wife
7.	Sherlock Holmes
8.	Zombieland
9.	The Hurt Locker
10.	Up in the Air
11.	Surrogates
12.	The Twilight Saga: New Moon
13.	The Invention of Lying
14.	Inglourious Basterds
15.	The Men Who Stare at Goats
16.	Gamer
17.	The Book of Eli
18.	District 9
19.	Brothers (2009)
20.	Old Dogs

Note: Top-selling DVDs exclude units sold into the rental channel, online, and in Canada. Top rental DVDs exclude kiosk and online/by-mail channels.

Top-Selling Video Games, 2010
Source: The NPD Group/Retail Tracking Service; ranked by retail units sold

The video game industry (which includes hardware, software, and accessories) generated U.S. retail sales in 2010 of $25.1 bil, a 27.7% increase over $19.7 bil in 2009.

Rank	Title (console)	Rank	Title (console)
1.	Call of Duty: Black Ops* (360, NDS, PC, PS3, Wii)	6.	Wii Fit Plus* (Wii)
2.	Madden NFL 11 (360, PS3, PS2, PSP, Wii)	7.	Just Dance 2 (Wii)
3.	Halo: Reach* (360)	8.	Call of Duty: Modern Warfare 2* (360, PC, PS3)
4.	New Super Mario Bros. Wii (Wii)	9.	Assassin's Creed: Brotherhood* (360, PS3)
5.	Red Dead Redemption (360, PS3)	10.	NBA 2K11 (360, PC, PS3, PS2, PSP, Wii)

* = Includes collector's, limited, legendary, and bundled editions. 360 = Microsoft Xbox 360; NDS = Nintendo DS; PC = personal computer; PS3 = PlayStation 3; PS2 = PlayStation 2; PSP = PlayStation Portable; Wii = Nintendo Wii.

Film and TV Content Ratings

The Motion Picture Association of America (MPAA) began rating movies in 1968. The system was heavily revised in 1984 and again in 1990. The MPAA, National Cable Television Association, and National Association of Broadcasters developed and revised the TV ratings system in 1997, in accordance with the Telecommunications Act of 1996; it was implemented in Oct. 1997.

Film Ratings

G: General Audience. All ages admitted. Does not contain themes, language, nudity, sex, or violence that the MPAA ratings board believes would offend parents whose younger children see the film. Does not necessarily denote a certificate of approval nor children's movie. No nudity, sex scenes, or drug use depicted.

PG: Parental Guidance Suggested. Some material may not be suited for children. The MPAA ratings board recommends that parents determine whether the content of the film is appropriate for their children. The film may contain more mature themes, some profanity, violence, or brief nudity. No drug use depicted.

PG-13: Parents Strongly Cautioned. Some material may be inappropriate for children under 13. The MPAA urges more strongly that parents vet the movie to see if its content is appropriate for their children. Any movie depicting drug use or more than brief nudity is automatically rated at least PG-13. Violence is permitted, though it is generally not both realistic or extreme and persistent violence. The single use of one sexually-derived expletive rates a PG-13; more than one use requires at least an R rating.

R: Restricted. Under 17 requires accompanying parent or adult guardian. Movies given R ratings contain some adult material, defined as adult themes or activity, hard language, intense or persistent violence, sexually-oriented nudity, or drug abuse.

NC-17: No One 17 and Under Admitted. The ratings board considers NC-17 films those that most parents would consider too adult for children under 17. An NC-17 rating does not mean the film is obscene or pornographic. The rating can be based on violence, sex, aberrational behavior, drug abuse, or any other element that most parents would consider too adult for children.

TV Ratings

TV-Y: All Children. Program designed to be acceptable for children of all ages. Its themes and elements are designed for a very young audience.

TV-Y7: Directed to Older Children. Program designed for children ages 7 and older, and more appropriate for those who have the skills to distinguish between make-believe and reality. May include mild fantasy/comedic violence. Programs with more than mild fantasy violence are denoted with FV.

TV-G: General Audience. Program not necessarily designed for children, but most parents would find it suitable for all ages. Little or no violence, no strong language, and little or no sexual dialogue or situations.

TV-PG: Parental Guidance Suggested. Program might contain material that parents would consider inappropriate for children, such as an adult theme or one or more of the following: suggestive dialogue (D), infrequent coarse language (L), some sexual situations (S), or moderate violence (V).

TV-14: Parents Strongly Cautioned. Program contains material that many parents would consider inappropriate for children under 14, such as one or more of the following: intensely suggestive dialogue (D), strong coarse language (L), intense sexual situations (S), or intense violence (V).

TV-MA: Mature Audience Only. Program specifically designed for adults and may be unsuitable for children under 17. Contains one or more of the following: crude indecent language (L), explicit sexual activity (S), or graphic violence (V).

Longest-Running Broadway Plays

Source: The Broadway League, New York, NY

Rank	Title (run)[1]	Performances[2]	Rank	Title (run)[1]	Performances[2]	Rank	Title (run)[1]	Performances[2]
1.	*The Phantom of the Opera (1988-)	9,803	17.	Tobacco Road (1933-1941)	3,182	35.	Gemini (1977-1981)	1,819
2.	Cats (1982-2000)	7,485	18.	Hello, Dolly! (1964-1970)	2,844	36.	Deathtrap (1978-1982)	1,793
3.	Let Misérables (1987-2003)	6,680	19.	My Fair Lady (1956-1962)	2,717	37.	Harvey (1944-1949)	1,775
4.	A Chorus Line (1975-1990)	6,137	20.	Hairspray (2002-2009)	2,642	38.	Dancin' (1978-1982)	1,774
5.	*Chicago (revival, 1996-)	6,131	21.	Avenue Q (2003-2009)	2,534	39.	La Cage aux Folles (1983-1987)	1,761
6.	Oh! Calcutta! (revival, 1976-1989)	5,959	22.	The Producers (2001-2007)	2,502	40.	Hair (1968-1972)	1,750
7.	*The Lion King (1997-)	5,717	23.	*Jersey Boys (2005-)	2,393	41.	The Wiz (1975-1979)	1,672
8.	Beauty and the Beast (1994-2007)	5,461	24.	Cabaret (revival, 1998-2004)	2,377	42.	Born Yesterday (1946-1949)	1,642
9.	Rent (1996-2008)	5,123		Annie (1977-1983)	2,377	43.	Crazy For You (1992-1996)	1,622
10.	Miss Saigon (1991-2001)	4,092	26.	Man of La Mancha (1965-1971)	2,328	44.	Ain't Misbehavin' (1978-1982)	1,604
11.	*Mamma Mia! (2001-)	4,080	27.	Abie's Irish Rose (1922-1927)	2,327	45.	The Best Little Whorehouse in Texas (1978-1982)	1,584
12.	42nd Street (1980-1989)	3,486	28.	Oklahoma! (1943-1948)	2,212	46.	Spamalot (2005-2009)	1,575
13.	Grease (1972-1980)	3,388	29.	Smokey Joe's Café (1995-2000)	2,036	47.	Mary, Mary (1961-1964)	1,572
14.	Fiddler on the Roof (1964-1972)	3,242	30.	*Mary Poppins (2006-)	1,987	48.	Evita (1979-1983)	1,567
15.	*Wicked (2003-)	3,238	31.	Pippin (1972-1977)	1,944	49.	The Voice of the Turtle (1943-1948)	1,557
16.	Life With Father (1939-1947)	3,224	32.	South Pacific (1949-1954)	1,925	50.	Jekyll & Hyde (1997-2001)	1,543
			33.	The Magic Show (1974-1978)	1,920			
			34.	Aida (2000-2004)	1,852			

* = Still running Sept. 1, 2011. (1) Unless noted, listings reflect a play's first run on Broadway. (2) Number of performances through Aug. 21, 2011.

Broadway Season Statistics, 1959-2011

Source: The Broadway League, New York, NY

Season	Gross (mil $)	Attendance (mil)	Playing weeks	New productions	Season	Gross (mil $)	Attendance (mil)	Playing weeks	New productions
1959-1960	$46	7.9	1,156	58	1999-2000	$603	11.4	1,464	37
1964-1965	50	8.2	1,250	67	2004-2005	769	11.5	1,494	39
1969-1970	53	7.1	1,047	62	2005-2006	862	12.0	1,501	39
1974-1975	57	6.6	1,101	54	2006-2007	939	12.3	1,509	35
1979-1980	146	9.6	1,540	61	2007-2008	938	12.3	1,560	36
1984-1985	209	7.3	1,078	33	2008-2009	943	12.2	1,548	43
1989-1990	282	8.0	1,070	40	2009-2010	1,020	11.9	1,464	39
1994-1995	406	9.0	1,120	33	2010-2011	1,080	12.5	1,588	42

Notable U.S. Museums

This unofficial list of some of the largest (by budget) museums in the U.S. was compiled with the assistance of the American Association of Museums, a national association representing the concerns of the museum community. Association members also include zoos, aquariums, arboretums, botanical gardens, and planetariums, but these are not included in *The World Almanac* listing.

Museum	City	State
American Museum of Natural History	New York	NY
Amon Carter Museum of Western Art	Ft. Worth	TX
The Art Institute of Chicago	Chicago	IL
Boston Children's Museum	Boston	MA
Brooklyn Museum of Art	Brooklyn	NY
Busch-Reisinger Museum	Cambridge	MA
California Academy of Sciences	San Francisco	CA
California Science Center	Los Angeles	CA
Carnegie Museums of Pittsburgh	Pittsburgh	PA
Children's Museum of Indianapolis	Indianapolis	IN
Cincinnati Art Museum	Cincinnati	OH
Cincinnati Museum Center	Cincinnati	OH
Cleveland Museum of Art	Cleveland	OH
Colonial Williamsburg	Williamsburg	VA
Corning Museum of Glass	Corning	NY
Crystal Bridges Museum of American Art	Bentonville	AR
Dallas Museum of Art	Dallas	TX
Denver Art Museum	Denver	CO
Denver Museum of Nature and Science	Denver	CO
Detroit Institute of Arts	Detroit	MI
Exploratorium	San Francisco	CA
The Field Museum	Chicago	IL
Fine Arts Museums of San Francisco	San Francisco	CA
Franklin Institute	Philadelphia	PA
The Frick Collection	New York	NY
J. Paul Getty Museum	Los Angeles	CA
Harvard University Art Museums	Cambridge	MA
Henry F. Dupont Winterthur Museum	Winterthur	DE
Henry Ford Museum/Greenfield Village	Dearborn	MI
High Museum of Art	Atlanta	GA
Houston Museum of Natural Science	Houston	TX
Jamestown-Yorktown Foundation	Williamsburg	VA
Jewish Museum	New York	NY
L.A. County Museum of Art	Los Angeles	CA
Liberty Science Center, Liberty State Park	Jersey City	NJ
Maryland Science Center	Baltimore	MD
Mashantucket Pequot Museum and Research Center	Mashantucket	CT
Metropolitan Museum of Art	New York	NY
Milwaukee Public Museum	Milwaukee	WI
Minneapolis Institute of Arts	Minneapolis	MN
Museum of African American History	Detroit	MI
Museum of the American West	Los Angeles	CA
Museum of Contemporary Art	Los Angeles	CA
Museum of Fine Arts	Boston	MA
Museum of Fine Arts	Houston	TX
Museum of Modern Art	New York	NY
Museum of New Mexico	Santa Fe	NM
Museum of Science	Boston	MA
Museum of Science and Industry	Chicago	IL
Musical Instrument Museum	Phoenix	AZ
Mystic Seaport Museum	Mystic	CT
National Air and Space Museum	Washington	DC
National Baseball Hall of Fame and Museum, Inc.	Cooperstown	NY
National Constitution Center	Philadelphia	PA
National Gallery of Art	Washington	DC
National Museum of American History	Washington	DC
National Museum of the American Indian	Washington	DC
National Museum of Natural History	Washington	DC
Nelson-Atkins Museum of Art	Kansas City	MO
New York Historical Society	New York	NY
New York State Museum	Albany	NY
Peabody Essex Museum	Salem	MA
Philadelphia Museum of Art	Philadelphia	PA
Rock and Roll Hall of Fame and Museum, Inc.	Cleveland	OH
St. Louis Science Center	St. Louis	MO
San Diego Museum of Art	San Diego	CA
San Francisco Museum of Modern Art	San Francisco	CA
Science Museum of Minnesota	Saint Paul	MN
Solomon R. Guggenheim Museum of Art	New York	NY
Toledo Museum of Art	Toledo	OH
U.S. Holocaust Memorial Museum	Washington	DC
Univ. of Pennsylvania Museum of Archaeology and Anthropology	Philadelphia	PA
Virginia Museum of Fine Arts	Richmond	VA
Wadsworth Atheneum	Hartford	CT
Walker Art Center	Minneapolis	MN
Whitney Museum of American Art	New York	NY

Symphony Orchestras: Most Performed Composers, 2008-09

Source: League of American Orchestras

Composer	Performances	Composer	Performances	Composer	Performances
Ludwig Van Beethoven	872	Igor Stravinsky	265	Johann Sebastian Bach	205
Wolfgang Amadeus Mozart	705	Sergei Rachmaninoff	253	Leonard Bernstein	183
Johannes Brahms	481	Franz Joseph Haydn	237	Gustav Mahler	182
Piotr Ilyich Tchaikovsky	449	Richard Strauss	230	Samuel Barber	173
Antonín Dvořák	380	Aaron Copland	216	Dmitri Shostakovich	173
Felix Mendelssohn	330	Jean Sibelius	216	Richard Wagner	161
Maurice Ravel	323	Sergei Prokofiev	212		

Note: Scheduled performances of a given composer's work(s) during the 2008-09 season (generally Oct.-Sept.) by members of the League of American Orchestras.

Opera: Most Produced Works, 2010-11

Source: OPERA America

Work, composer	Productions	Work, composer	Productions	Work, composer	Productions
La bohème, Giacomo Puccini	12	Die Zauberflöte [The Magic Flute], Wolfgang Amadeus Mozart	7	Turandot, Giacomo Puccini	7
Le nozze di Figaro [The Marriage of Figaro], Wolfgang Amadeus Mozart	9	Lucia di Lammermoor, Gaetano Donizetti	7	Tosca, Giacomo Puccini	6
				Rigoletto, Giuseppe Verdi	6
Madama Butterfly, Giacomo Puccini	8	La traviata, Giuseppe Verdi	7	Carmen, Georges Bizet	6

Note: Scheduled productions of a given work (not individual performances) during the 2010-11 season (generally Oct.-Sept.) by members of OPERA America and Opera.ca.

Best-Selling U.S. Magazines, 2011

Source: Audit Bureau of Circulations (ABC)

General magazines, exclusive of comics; also excluding magazines that failed to file reports to ABC by press time. Based on total average paid and verified circulation during the six months ending June 30, 2011, ranked by paid circulation size.

	Publication	Paid circ.		Publication	Paid circ.		Publication	Paid circ.
1.	AARP The Magazine	22,395,670	7.	Good Housekeeping	4,336,711	15.	Cosmopolitan	3,032,211
2.	AARP Bulletin	22,236,761	8.	Woman's Day	3,863,710	16.	Prevention	2,903,417
3.	Better Homes and Gardens	7,648,900	9.	Family Circle	3,816,958	17.	Southern Living	2,830,179
			10.	People	3,556,753	18.	Maxim	2,530,440
4.	Game Informer Magazine	5,954,884	11.	Time	3,376,226	19.	AAA Living	2,477,127
			12.	Ladies' Home Journal	3,267,239	20.	O, The Oprah Magazine	2,461,464
5.	Reader's Digest	5,653,440	13.	Taste of Home	3,235,718	21.	American Legion Magazine	2,323,308
6.	National Geographic	4,445,603	14.	Sports Illustrated	3,207,861			

Publication	Paid circ.	Publication	Paid circ.	Publication	Paid circ.
22. Glamour	2,304,146	49. Bon Appetit	1,522,078	76. Country	1,103,198
23. Parenting	2,227,351	50. Playboy	1,509,982	77. Food & Family	1,077,820
24. Redbook	2,211,659	51. Fitness	1,501,244	78. Everyday Food	1,058,521
25. FamilyFun	2,128,351	52. Food Network Magazine	1,472,607	79. Essence	1,050,013
26. Smithsonian	2,075,114	53. Rolling Stone	1,467,739	80. New Yorker	1,035,579
27. Parents	2,070,645	54. Golf Magazine	1,430,563	81. Teen Vogue	1,029,336
28. Martha Stewart Living	2,060,304	55. Health	1,370,770	82. American Hunter	1,020,872
29. ESPN The Magazine	2,046,065	56. Weight Watchers	1,338,692	83. Midwest Living	979,488
30. Guideposts	2,031,000	57. All You	1,328,454	84. Travel + Leisure	970,733
31. TV Guide Magazine	2,024,092	58. First	1,310,696	85. Scouting	969,291
32. Seventeen	2,016,049	59. Woman's World	1,308,599	86. This Old House	966,525
33. Real Simple	2,011,092	60. Popular Science	1,302,472	87. Marie Claire	963,305
34. US Weekly	1,980,862	61. More	1,301,106	88. Food & Wine	954,592
35. Money	1,918,430	62. Sunset	1,262,722	89. GQ	939,067
36. Men's Health	1,892,760	63. Field & Stream	1,258,410	90. Forbes	928,900
37. American Rifleman	1,812,431	64. Vogue	1,248,121	91. Bloomberg	
38. Entertainment Weekly	1,797,384	65. Car and Driver	1,238,416	Businessweek	921,839
39. Cooking Light	1,783,808	66. Ebony	1,235,865	92. Star Magazine	880,256
40. Every Day With Rachel		67. Vanity Fair	1,227,707	93. Traditional Home	872,390
Ray	1,749,877	68. Popular Mechanics	1,214,383	94. National Geographic	
41. In Style	1,713,802	69. Boys' Life	1,154,603	International	858,301
42. Golf Digest	1,671,328	70. Reminisce	1,135,842	95. Fortune	845,043
43. Shape	1,656,678	71. Elle	1,132,860	96. Economist	844,387
44. Country Living	1,625,196	72. Motor Trend	1,129,326	97. Working Mother	833,601
45. Women's Health	1,589,342	73. Lucky	1,122,736	98. People Stylewatch	828,555
46. Self	1,545,247	74. Family Handyman	1,116,213	99. Architectural Digest	823,280
47. Birds & Blooms	1,530,672	75. Allure	1,108,834	100. House Beautiful	821,707
48. Newsweek	1,530,486				

Most Challenged Books, 2010

Source: Office for Intellectual Freedom, American Library Association (ALA)

A challenge is a formal, written complaint filed with a library or school requesting that materials be removed because of content or appropriateness. From 2001-10, 4,659 challenges were reported: 1,536 challenges due to sexually explicit material; 1,231 for offensive language; 977 for material deemed unsuited to age group; 553 for violence; 370 for homosexuality; 304 for religious viewpoints; and 121 for being anti-family. Approximately 37% of challenges were to material in classrooms; 30% in school libraries; and 24% in public libraries. ALA estimates that for every challenge received, 4 to 5 were not reported.

Rank	Title, author	Common reasons given for challenge
1.	*And Tango Makes Three*, Peter Parnell and Justin Richardson	Homosexuality, religious viewpoint, unsuited to age group
2.	*The Absolutely True Diary of a Part-Time Indian*, Sherman Alexie	Offensive language, racism, sex education, sexually explicit, unsuited to age group, violence
3.	*Brave New World*, Aldous Huxley	Insensitivity, offensive language, racism, sexually explicit
4.	*Crank*, Ellen Hopkins	Drugs, offensive language, sexually explicit
5.	*The Hunger Games*, Suzanne Collins	Sexually explicit, unsuited to age group, violence
6.	*Lush*, Natasha Friend	Drugs, offensive language, sexually explicit, unsuited to age group
7.	*What My Mother Doesn't Know*, Sonya Sones	Sexism, sexually explicit, and unsuited to age group
8.	*Nickel and Dimed*, Barbara Ehrenreich	Drugs; inaccurate, offensive language; political viewpoint; religious viewpoint
9.	*Revolutionary Voices*, edited by Amy Sonnie	Homosexuality, sexually explicit
10.	*Twilight*, Stephenie Meyer	Religious viewpoint, violence

Some Notable New Books, 2011

Source: Reference and User Services Association, American Library Association (ALA)

Fiction

Nashville Chrome, Rick Bass
Room: A Novel, Emma Donoghue
A Visit From the Goon Squad, Jennifer Egan
Crooked Letter, Crooked Letter, Tom Franklin
Freedom, Jonathan Franzen
Next, James Hynes
The Surrendered, Chang Rae Lee
Matterhorn: A Novel of the Vietnam War, Karl Marlantes
The Thousand Autumns of Jacob de Zoet: A Novel, David Mitchell
Skippy Dies, Paul Murray
The Lotus Eaters, Tatjana Soli
The Lonely Polygamist: A Novel, Brady Udall

Poetry

Unincorporated Persons in the Late Honda Dynasty: Poems, Tony Hoagland
Wait: Poems, C. K. Williams

Nonfiction

Washington: A Life, Ron Chernow
The Hare With Amber Eyes: A Family's Century of Art and Loss, Edmund de Waal
Nothing to Envy: Ordinary Lives in North Korea, Barbara Demick
Travels in Siberia, Ian Frazier
The Price of Altruism: George Price and the Search for the Origins of Kindness, Oren Harman
Last Call: The Rise and Fall of Prohibition, Daniel Okrent
Citizens of London: The Americans Who Stood With Britain in Its Darkest, Finest Hour, Lynne Olson
The Last Stand: Custer, Sitting Bull, and the Battle of the Little Bighorn, Nathaniel Philbrick
The Immortal Life of Henrietta Lacks, Rebecca Skloot
Just Kids, Patti Smith
The Tiger: A True Story of Vengeance and Survival, John Vaillant
The Warmth of Other Suns: The Epic Story of America's Great Migration, Isabel Wilkerson

Some Notable New Books for Children, 2011

Source: Association for Library Service to Children, American Library Association (ALA)

Younger Readers

April and Esme, Tooth Fairies, Bob Graham
Back of the Bus, Aaron Reynolds, Floyd Cooper (illus.)
Big Red Lollipop, Rukhsana Khan, Sophie Blackall (illus.)
Bink and Gollie, Kate DiCamillo and Alison McGhee, Tony Fucile (illus.)
Chalk, Bill Thomson
City Dog, Country Frog, Mo Willems, Jon J. Muth (illus.)
Dear Primo: A Letter to My Cousin, Duncan Tonatiuh
Fiesta Babies, Carmen Tafolla, Amy Córdova (illus.)

Grandma's Gift, Eric Velasquez
Hip-Pocket Papa, Sandra Markle, Alan Marks (illus.)
Interrupting Chicken, David Ezra Stein
In the Wild, David Elliott, Holly Meade (illus.)
Ling & Ting: Not Exactly the Same!, Grace Lin
LMNO Peas, Keith Baker
Pecan Pie Baby, Jacqueline Woodson, Sophie Blackall (illus.)
Pocketful of Posies: A Treasury of Nursery Rhymes, Salley Mavor
The Quiet Book, Deborah Underwood, Renata Liwska (illus.)

Rubia and the Three Osos, Susan Middleton Elya, Melissa Sweet (illus.)
A Sick Day for Amos McGee, Philip C. Stead, Erin E. Stead (illus.)
Tuck Me In!, Dean Hacohen, Sherry Scharschmidt (illus.)
We Are in a Book!, Mo Willems
Yucky Worms, Vivian French, Jessica Ahlberg (illus.)

Middle Readers

Ballet for Martha: Making Appalachian Spring, Jan Greenberg and Sandra Jordan, Brian Floca (illus.)
The Bat Scientists, Mary Kay Carson, Tom Uhlman (illus.)
Dave the Potter: Artist, Poet, Slave, Laban Carrick Hill, Bryan Collier (illus.)
The Fantastic Secret of Owen Jester, Barbara O'Connor
Growing Patterns: Fibonacci Numbers in Nature, Sarah C. Campbell, Sarah and Richard P. Campbell (illus.)
Guyku: A Year of Haiku for Boys, Bob Raczka, Peter H. Reynolds (illus.)
The Hive Detectives: Chronicle of a Honey Bee Catastrophe, Loree Griffin Burns, Ellen Harasimowicz (illus.)
How to Clean a Hippopotamus: A Look at Unusual Animal Partnerships, Steve Jenkins and Robin Page, Steve Jenkins (illus.)
Kakapo Rescue: Saving the World's Strangest Parrot, Sy Montgomery, Nic Bishop (illus.)
Me, Frida, Amy Novesky, David Diaz (illus.)
Nic Bishop Lizards, Nic Bishop
The Night Fairy, Laura Amy Schlitz, Angela Barrett (illus.)
Ninth Ward, Jewell Parker Rhodes
¡Ole! Flamenco, George Ancona
One Crazy Summer, Rita Williams-Garcia
Ruth and the Green Book, Calvin Alexander Ramsey and Gwen Strauss, Floyd Cooper (illus.)
Saltypie: A Choctaw Journey From Darkness Into Light, Tim Tingle, Karen Clarkson (illus.)
Shake, Rattle, & Turn That Noise Down! How Elvis Shook Up Music, Me, and Mom, Mark Alan Stamaty
Smile, Raina Telgemeier, Raina Telgemeier and Stephanie Yue (illus.)
The Strange Case of Origami Yoda, Tom Angleberger

A Tale Dark and Grimm, Adam Gidwitz
Trickster: Native American Tales: A Graphic Collection, edited by Matt Dembicki
Turtle in Paradise, Jennifer L. Holm

Older Readers

90 Miles to Havana, Enrique Flores-Galbis
Black Elk's Vision: A Lakota Story, S. D. Nelson
Countdown, Deborah Wiles
Departure Time, Truus Matti, Nancy Forest-Flier (trans.)
The Dreamer, Pam Muñoz Ryan, Peter Sís (illus.)
Fever Crumb, Philip Reeve
The Firefly Letters: A Suffragette's Journey to Cuba, Margarita Engle
Heart of a Samurai, Margi Preus
Lafayette and the American Revolution, Russell Freedman
Mockingbird, Kathryn Erskine
Moon Over Manifest, Clare Vanderpool
Nothing, Janne Teller, Martin Aitken (trans.)
Ship Breaker, Paolo Bacigalupi
They Called Themselves the K.K.K.: The Birth of an American Terrorist Group, Susan Campbell Bartoletti
A Time of Miracles, Anne-Laure Bondoux, Y. Maudet (trans.)
Ubiquitous: Celebrating Nature's Survivors, Joyce Sidman, Beckie Prange (illus.)
We Shall Overcome: A Song That Changed the World, Stuart Stotts, Terrance Cummings (illus.)
Yummy: The Last Days of a Southside Shorty, G. Neri, Randy DuBurke (illus.)

All Ages

Bones: Skeletons and How They Work, Steve Jenkins
Dark Emperor and Other Poems of the Night, Joyce Sidman, Rick Allen (illus.)
Farm, Elisha Cooper
Meanwhile, Jason Shiga
Mirror, Mirror: A Book of Reversible Verse, Marilyn Singer, Josée Masse (illus.)
Shadow, Suzy Lee

Best-Selling Books, 2010
Source: Publishers Weekly

Hardcover Fiction

1. The Girl Who Kicked the Hornet's Nest, Stieg Larsson
2. The Confession, John Grisham
3. The Help, Kathryn Stockett
4. Safe Haven, Nicholas Sparks
5. Dead or Alive, Tom Clancy
6. Sizzling Sixteen, Janet Evanovich
7. Cross Fire, James Patterson
8. Freedom, Jonathan Franzen
9. Port Mortuary, Patricia Cornwell
10. Full Dark, No Stars, Stephen King

Hardcover Nonfiction

1. Decision Points, George W. Bush
2. Broke: The Plan to Restore Our Trust, Truth, and Treasure, Glenn Beck
3. Women Food and God: An Unexpected Path to Almost Everything, Geneen Roth
4. Life, Keith Richards with James Fox
5. America by Heart: Reflections on Family, Faith, and Flag, Sarah Palin
6. The Daily Show With Jon Stewart Presents Earth (The Book): A Visitor's Guide to the Human Race, Jon Stewart
7. Sh*t My Dad Says, Justin Halpern
8. Barefoot Contessa: How Easy Is That? Ina Garten
9. Pinheads and Patriots: Where You Stand in the Age of Obama, Bill O'Reilly
10. Chelsea Chelsea Bang Bang, Chelsea Handler

Mass Market Fiction

1. The Girl With the Dragon Tattoo, Stieg Larsson
2. The Lost Symbol, Dan Brown
3. The Girl Who Played With Fire, Stieg Larsson
4. The Last Song, Nicholas Sparks
5. Ford County: Stories, John Grisham
6. Finger Lickin' Fifteen, Janet Evanovich
7. Pirate Latitudes, Michael Crichton
8. Breathless, Dean Koontz
9. I, Alex Cross, James Patterson
10. One Night, Debbie Macomber

Trade Paperback Fiction

1. The Girl With the Dragon Tattoo, Stieg Larsson
2. The Girl Who Played With Fire, Stieg Larsson
3. Eat, Pray, Love, Elizabeth Gilbert
4. The Last Song, Nicholas Sparks

5. Little Bee, Chris Cleave
6. Happy Ever After, Nora Roberts
7. Cutting for Stone, Abraham Verghese
8. Savor the Moment, Nora Roberts
9. Dear John, Nicholas Sparks
10. A Reliable Wife, Robert Goolrick

E-Books

1. The Girl Who Kicked the Hornet's Nest, Stieg Larsson
2. The Confession, John Grisham
3. Decision Points, George W. Bush
4. Sh*t My Dad Says, Justin Halpern
5. Freedom, Jonathan Franzen
6. I, Alex Cross, James Patterson
7. The Last Song, Nicholas Sparks
8. Under the Dome, Stephen King
9. Dear John, Nicholas Sparks
10. American Assassin, Vince Flynn

Children's and Young Adult Hardcover

1. The Ugly Truth (Diary of a Wimpy Kid #5), Jeff Kinney
2. The Short Second Life of Bree Tanner: An Eclipse Novella, Stephenie Meyer
3. The Wimpy Kid Movie Diary, Jeff Kinney
4. Mockingjay (Hunger Games #3), Suzanne Collins
5. The Lost Hero, Rick Riordan
6. The Red Pyramid, Rick Riordan
7. Burned (House of Night #7), PC and Kristin Cast
8. The Gift (Witch & Wizard #2), James Patterson and Ned Rust
9. Justin Bieber: First Step 2 Forever, Justin Bieber
10. Last Sacrifice (Vampire Academy #6), Richelle Mead

Children's and Young Adult Paperback

1. Eclipse (Twilight #3), Stephenie Meyer
2. Breaking Dawn (Twilight #4), Stephenie Meyer
3. The Hunger Games, Suzanne Collins
4. Max (Maximum Ride #5), James Patterson
5. Disney/Pixar Toy Story 3: Toy to Toy, Tennant Redbank, Caroline Egan (illus.)
6. The Twilight Saga: Eclipse: The Official Illustrated Movie Companion, Mark Cotta Vaz
7. Fallen, Lauren Kate
8. Disney/Pixar Toy Story 3: Toy Trouble
9. Brisingr (Inheritance Cycle #3), Christopher Paolini
10. How to Train Your Dragon, Cressida Cowell

Leading U.S. Daily Newspapers, 2009
Source: *Editor & Publisher International Yearbook*, 2010

As of Feb. 1, 2010, the number of U.S. daily newspapers had fallen to 1,397, for a net loss of 11 since Feb. 1, 2009. Average daily circulation fell by 2.3 mil, from 48.6 mil in 2008 to about 46.3 mil in 2009. The overall number of Sunday papers rose by 17, to 919. Average Sunday circulation as of Feb. 1, 2010, had fallen 2.2 mil, from 49.1 mil in 2009 to 46.9 mil in 2010.

(ranked by circulation as of Sept. 30, 2009; m = morning, d = all day)

Rank	Newspaper (edition)	Circulation	Rank	Newspaper (edition)	Circulation
1.	New York (NY) *Wall Street Journal* (m)	2,011,999	27.	Miami (FL) *Herald* (m)	225,554
2.	Arlington (VA) *USA Today* (m)	1,900,116	28.	San Jose (CA) *Mercury News* (m)	224,199
3.	New York (NY) *Times* (m)	927,851	29.	Orlando (FL) *Sentinel* (d)	216,978
4.	Los Angeles (CA) *Times* (m)	657,467	30.	Kansas City (MO) *Star* (m)	216,226
5.	Washington (DC) *Post* (m)	582,844	31.	Sacramento (CA) *Bee* (m)	215,820
6.	New York (NY) *Daily News* (m)	544,167	32.	St. Louis (MO) *Post-Dispatch* (m)	213,472
7.	New York (NY) *Post* (m)	508,042	33.	Orange County (CA) *Register* (m)	212,293
8.	Chicago (IL) *Tribune* (m)	465,892	34.	Atlanta (GA) *Journal-Constitution* (m)	211,420
9.	Houston (TX) *Chronicle* (m)	384,419	35.	Tampa (FL) *Tribune* (m)	204,106
10.	Philadelphia (PA) *Inquirer* (m)	361,480	36.	Indianapolis (IN) *Star* (m)	201,823
11.	Long Island (NY) *Newsday* (m)	357,124	37.	Ft. Lauderdale (FL) *South Florida Sun-Sentinel* (m)	200,924
12.	Denver (CO) *Post* (m)	340,949	38.	Milwaukee (WI) *Journal Sentinel* (m)	190,841
13.	Phoenix (AZ) *Republic* (m)	316,874	39.	Baltimore (MD) *Sun* (m)	186,639
14.	Minneapolis (MN) *Star Tribune* (m)	304,543	40.	San Francisco (CA) *Examiner* (m)	186,335
15.	Detroit (MI) *Free Press* (m)	298,243	41.	St. Paul (MN) *Pioneer Press* (m)	185,220
16.	St. Petersburg (FL) *Times* (m)	292,471	42.	Pittsburgh (PA) *Post-Gazette* (m)	184,234
17.	Chicago (IL) *Sun-Times* (m)	275,641	43.	Columbus (OH) *Dispatch* (m)	183,742
18.	Cleveland (OH) *Plain Dealer* (m)	271,180	44.	Detroit (MI) *News* (m)	178,280
19.	New York (NY) *am New York* (m)	266,852	45.	Louisville (KY) *Courier-Journal* (m)	176,654
20.	Boston (MA) *Globe* (m)	264,105	46.	Las Vegas (NV) *Review-Journal* (m)	175,841
21.	Dallas (TX) *Morning News* (m)	263,810	47.	Walnut Creek (CA) *Contra Costa Times* (m)	174,852
22.	Washington (DC) *Examiner* (m)	259,906	48.	Little Rock (AR) *Democrat-Gazette* (m)	169,458
23.	San Francisco (CA) *Chronicle* (d)	251,782	49.	Cincinnati (OH) *Enquirer* (m)	168,511
24.	Portland (OR) *Oregonian* (d)	249,163	50.	Greensburg (PA) *Tribune-Review* (m)	168,218
25.	Newark (NJ) *Star-Ledger* (m)	246,006			
26.	San Diego (CA) *Union-Tribune* (m)	242,705			

Paid U.S. Newspaper Circulation, 1940-2009
Source: *Editor & Publisher International Yearbook*, 2010

(circulation figures in thousands)

Year	Number of daily newspapers			Circulation of daily newspapers			Sunday newspapers	
	Morning	Evening	Total	Morning	Evening	Total	Number	Circulation
1940	380	1,498	1,878	16,114	25,018	41,132	525	32,371
1945	330	1,419	1,749	19,240	29,144	48,384	485	39,860
1950	322	1,450	1,772	21,266	32,563	53,829	549	46,582
1955	316	1,454	1,760	22,183	33,964	56,147	541	46,448
1960	312	1,459	1,763	24,029	34,853	58,882	563	47,699
1965	320	1,444	1,751	24,107	36,251	60,358	562	48,600
1970	334	1,429	1,748	25,934	36,174	62,108	586	49,217
1975	339	1,436	1,756	25,490	35,165	60,655	639	51,096
1980	387	1,388	1,745	29,414	32,787	62,202	736	54,676
1985	482	1,220	1,676	36,362	26,405	62,766	798	58,826
1990	559	1,084	1,611	41,311	21,017	62,328	863	62,635
1995	656	891	1,533	44,310	13,883	58,193	888	61,229
2000	766	727	1,480	46,772	9,000	55,773	917	59,421
2005	817	645	1,452	46,122	7,222	53,345	914	55,270
2006	833	614	1,437	45,441	6,888	52,329	907	53,179
2007	867	565	1,422	44,548	6,194	50,742	907	51,246
2008	872	546	1,408	42,758	5,840	48,598	902	49,115
2009	869	528	1,397	40,796	5,482	46,278	919	46,850

Newspaper Advertising Revenues, 1950-2010
Source: Research Dept., Newspaper Association of America

Year	National ad revenue (mil $)	Retail ad revenue (mil $)	Classified ad revenue (mil $)	Print advertising total revenue		Online advertising total revenue		Total advertising revenue	
				(mil $)	% change[1]	(mil $)	% change	(mil $)	% change
1950	$518	$1,175	$377	$2,070	—	—	—	—	—
1955	712	1,755	610	3,077	48.7%	—	—	—	—
1960	778	2,100	803	3,681	19.6	—	—	—	—
1965	783	2,429	1,214	4,426	20.2	—	—	—	—
1970	891	3,292	1,521	5,704	28.9	—	—	—	—
1975	1,109	4,966	2,159	8,234	44.4	—	—	—	—
1980	1,963	8,609	4,222	14,794	79.7	—	—	—	—
1985	3,352	13,443	8,375	25,170	70.1	—	—	—	—
1990	4,122	16,652	11,506	32,280	28.3	—	—	—	—
1995	4,251	18,099	13,742	36,092	11.8	—	—	—	—
2000	7,653	21,409	19,608	48,670	5.1	—	—	—	—
2005	7,910	22,187	17,312	47,408	1.5	$2,027	31.5%	$49,435	2.5%
2006	7,505	22,121	16,986	46,611	−1.7	2,664	31.4	49,275	−0.3
2007	7,005	21,018	14,186	42,209	−9.4	3,166	18.8	45,375	−7.9
2008	5,996	18,769	9,975	34,740	−17.7	3,109	−1.8	37,848	−16.6
2009	4,424	14,218	6,179	24,821	−28.6	2,743	−11.8	27,564	−27.2
2010	4,221	12,926	5,648	22,795	−8.2	3,042	10.9	25,838	−6.3

(1) Percent change for years 1950-2000 refers to the rate of change over the preceding 5-year period; 2005-10 figures represent the rate of change over the past year.

Leading Canadian Daily Newspapers, 2009

Source: *Editor & Publisher International Yearbook*, 2010

(ranked by circulation as of Sept. 30, 2009; all morning papers)

Newspaper	Circulation	Newspaper	Circulation
1. Toronto (ON) *Star*	430,931	6. Vancouver (BC) *Sun*	159,438
2. Toronto (ON) *Globe and Mail*	301,820	7. Vancouver (BC) *Province*	152,924
3. Montreal (QC) *Le Journal de Montreal*	265,764	8. Toronto (ON) *National Post*	150,884
4. Montreal (QC) *La Presse*	198,306	9. Montreal (QC) *Gazette*	147,668
5. Toronto (ON) *Sun*	195,211	10. Calgary (AB) *Herald*	119,131

Top Newspaper Websites, June 2011

Source: comScore Media Metrix, Inc.

Rank	Website	Visitors[1]	% change[2]	Rank	Website	Visitors[1]	% change[2]
1.	The New York Times	31,422	177.8%	12.	Guardian.co.uk	9,134	217.1%
2.	Tribune Newspapers	27,974	135.3	13.	Topix.com	9,065	48.2
3.	USA Today sites	21,803	243.8	14.	NYPost.com	6,691	124.5
4.	Advance Internet	18,026	107.0	15.	Boston.com	5,890	63.3
5.	WashingtonPost.com	16,518	108.6	16.	CSMonitor.com	5,060	NA
6.	Hearst Newspapers	15,665	131.2	17.	Sun-Times Media/Chicago		
7.	Mail Online	15,222	281.2		Region-Wide Network (CRWN)	4,665	NA
8.	McClatchy Corporation	14,256	75.0	18.	Lee Enterprises, Incorporated	4,574	–0.1
9.	Wall Street Journal Online	13,937	112.5	19.	Scripps Interactive Newspaper Group	4,382	NA
10.	MediaNews Group	11,974	100.5	20.	The Atlantic Consumer Media	3,650	NA
11.	NYDailyNews.com	10,111	56.5				

NA = Not applicable. (1) Number of unique visitors, in thousands, who visited website at least once in June 2011. (2) Percent change over June 2010.

Top News/Information Websites, June 2011

Source: comScore Media Metrix, Inc.

Rank	Website	Visitors[1]	% change[2]	Rank	Website	Visitors[1]	% change[2]
1.	Yahoo! News	83,134	75.9%	11.	Fox News Digital	23,351	167.3%
2.	CNN	72,008	115.5	12.	ABCNews Digital	19,771	98.4
3.	New York Times Digital	62,883	37.4	13.	WorldNow Sites	18,748	9.9
4.	HPMG News	57,519	NA	14.	Advance Internet	18,026	107.0
5.	MSNBC	47,650	50.1	15.	Hearst Newspapers	15,665	NA
6.	Gannett sites	40,706	92.0	16.	Mail Online	15,222	NA
7.	The Weather Channel	40,118	–3.8	17.	McClatchy Corporation	14,256	75.0
8.	Tribune Newspapers	27,974	135.3	18.	Wall Street Journal Online	13,937	NA
9.	WeatherBug Property	26,811	15.7	19.	CBS News	13,734	99.0
10.	The Washington Post Company	23,409	45.7	20.	MediaNews Group	11,974	NA

NA = Not available. (1) Number of unique visitors, in thousands, who visited website at least once in June 2011. (2) Percent change over June 2010.

Top-Selling Albums of All-Time

Source: Recording Industry Assn. of America

(As of Sept. 1, 2011; sales figures represent RIAA multi-platinum certifications, albums ranked by latest sales certification.)

Rank	Title, artist	Unit sales (mil)	Rank	Title, artist	Unit sales (mil)
1.	*Thriller*, Michael Jackson	29.0	15.	*The Beatles 1967-1970*, The Beatles	16.0
	Eagles/Their Greatest Hits 1971-1975, Eagles	29.0		*Hotel California*, Eagles	16.0
3.	*Led Zeppelin IV*, Led Zeppelin	23.0		*Greatest Hits*, Elton John	16.0
	The Wall, Pink Floyd	23.0		*Cracked Rear View*, Hootie & the Blowfish	16.0
5.	*Back in Black*, AC/DC	22.0		*Physical Graffiti*, Led Zeppelin	16.0
6.	*Double Live*, Garth Brooks	21.0		*Jagged Little Pill*, Alanis Morissette	16.0
	Greatest Hits Volume I & Volume II, Billy Joel	21.0	21.	*The Beatles 1962-1966*, The Beatles	15.0
8.	*Come on Over*, Shania Twain	20.0		*Saturday Night Fever* (soundtrack), Bee Gees	15.0
	Rumours, Fleetwood Mac	19.0		*Greatest Hits*, Journey	15.0
	The Beatles, The Beatles	19.0		*Metallica*, Metallica	15.0
11.	*Appetite for Destruction*, Guns N' Roses	18.0		*Dark Side of the Moon*, Pink Floyd	15.0
12.	*No Fences*, Garth Brooks	17.0		*Born in the U.S.A.*, Bruce Springsteen	15.0
	Boston, Boston	17.0		*Supernatural*, Santana	15.0
	The Bodyguard (soundtrack), Whitney Houston	17.0			

U.S. Commercial Radio Stations by Format, 2002-11

Source: The Radio Book by Inside Radio © 2012

Primary format	2011	2010	2009	2008	2007	2006	2005	2004	2003	2002
1. Country	1,988	1,996	1,996	2,024	2,032	2,034	2,014	2,049	2,077	2,123
2. News/Talk	1,453	1,436	1,414	1,367	1,363	1,335	1,329	1,285	1,225	1,205
3. Spanish	812	806	801	799	781	705	704	665	633	627
4. Sports	677	661	634	595	560	530	501	466	433	413
5. Classic Hits	656	624	572	519	468	425	269	234	236	249
6. Oldies	622	642	665	702	712	729	763	816	812	800
7. Adult Contemporary	609	635	627	668	664	660	683	700	680	683
8. Top 40	522	492	482	470	473	485	504	506	487	492
9. Classic Rock	478	482	479	474	456	455	461	452	427	415
10. Hot Adult Contemporary	434	421	408	372	377	375	373	420	409	400
11. Religion (Teaching, Variety)	332	324	327	298	288	313	319	335	350	340
12. Rock	302	296	295	288	281	279	271	280	275	269
13. Adult Standards	253	270	328	359	372	369	408	457	492	519
14. Black Gospel	226	233	242	244	252	266	284	273	268	251
15. Southern Gospel	188	194	212	211	208	208	208	206	207	217
Stations off the air	265	242	206	132	92	91	72	76	124	103
Total operating stations[1]	**11,351**	**11,360**	**11,310**	**11,224**	**11,161**	**11,039**	**10,916**	**10,857**	**10,906**	**10,923**

(1) As of June 2011. Totals include stations that are changing or did not report format, as well as formats not listed here.

Multi-Platinum and Platinum Awards for Recorded Music and Music Videos, 2010-11

Source: Recording Industry Assn. of America, Washington, DC

To achieve platinum status, an **album** must reach minimum total sales of 1 mil units in LPs, CDs, and digital with a manufacturer's dollar volume of at least $2 mil based on one-third of the suggested retail list price for each record, CD, or digital copy sold. To achieve multi-platinum status, an album must reach minimum total sales of at least 2 mil units in LPs, CDs, and digital with a manufacturer's dollar volume of at least $4 mil based on one-third of the list price.

Singles must sell 1 mil units to achieve a platinum award and 2 mil to achieve a multi-platinum award. **Digital singles** are certified at the same levels; the digital sales award was first created in 2004. In 1999, the Diamond Award, honoring sales of 10 mil or more copies of an album or single, was introduced. EP singles count as 2 units. Double-CD sets count as 2 units. **Music videos** (longform) must sell 100,000 units to qualify for a platinum award, more than 200,000 units for a multi-platinum award. As of July 2006, master **ringtones**—the original recording and not synthesized versions of songs—could be awarded gold (500,000 downloads), platinum (1 mil), and multi-platinum (2 mil+) status.

Awards listed here are for albums, digital singles, and music videos (released Sept. 2009-Aug. 2011) that were certified Sept. 2010-Aug. 2011. Number in parentheses = number of millions sold. Alphabetized by artist name.

Albums, Multi-Platinum

21, Adele (3)
My World 2.0, Justin Bieber (2)
The Gift, Susan Boyle (3)
Crazy Love, Michael Bublé (2)
Viva el Príncipe, Cristian Castro (2)
Recovery, Eminem (3)
Need You Now, Lady Antebellum (3)
Prince Royce, Prince Royce (2)
Speak Now, Taylor Swift (3)
Play On, Carrie Underwood (2)

Albums, Platinum

My Kinda Party, Jason Aldean
4, Beyoncé
Never Say Never: The Remixes, Justin Bieber
#1s...And Then Some, Brooks & Dunn
You Get What You Give, The Zac Brown Band
No Hay Imposibles, Chayanne
Hemingway's Whiskey, Kenny Chesney
O Holy Night, Jackie Evancho
Glee: The Music, The Christmas Album, Glee cast
Glee: The Music, Volume 1, Glee cast
A Son de Guerra, Juan Luis Guerra and 4.40
Illuminations, Josh Groban
Michael, Michael Jackson
Animal, Ke$ha
Born Free, Kid Rock
Revolution, Miranda Lambert
Drama y Luz, Maná
Doo-Wops & Hooligans, Bruno Mars
Música + Alma + Sexo, Ricky Martin
Pink Friday, Nicki Minaj
Sigh No More, Mumford & Sons
Teenage Dream, Katy Perry
Nothing Like This, Rascal Flatts
Loud, Rihanna
En Total Plenitud, Marco Antonio Solís
Telephantasm, Soundgarden
Femme Fatale, Britney Spears
The Incredible Machine, Sugarland
My Beautiful Dark Twisted Fantasy, Kanye West

Longform Videos, Multi-Platinum

I Am...World Tour, Beyoncé (2)
ISolated INcident, Dane Cook (2)
The Big 4: Live From Sofia, Bulgaria, Metallica/Slayer/ Megadeth/Anthrax (2)

Michael Jackson's Vision, Michael Jackson (5)
Beyond the Lighted Stage, Rush (2)
The 25th Anniversary Rock & Roll Hall of Fame Concert, Various (2)

Digital Singles, Platinum and Multi-Platinum

"Rolling in the Deep" (4), Adele
"Dirt Road Anthem," "Don't You Wanna Stay," "My Kinda Party," Jason Aldean
"Live Like We're Dying," Kris Allen
"If I Die Young" (2), The Band Perry
"King of Anything," Sara Bareilles
"Never Say Never," Justin Bieber
"Magic," B.o.B. feat. Rivers Cuomo
"Country Girl (Shake It For Me)," Luke Bryan
"Teach Me How to Dougie," Cali Swag District
"Somewhere With You," Kenny Chesney
"Dynamite" (5), Taio Cruz
"Break Your Heart" (3), Taio Cruz feat. Ludacris
"Ridin' Solo" (2), Jason Derülo
"Coming Home" (2), Diddy Dirty Money
"All I Do Is Win" (2), DJ Khaled feat. T-Pain, Ludacris, and Snoop Dogg
"Find Your Love," Drake
"A Little Bit Stronger," Sara Evans
"The Show Goes On," Lupe Fiasco
"Dog Days Are Over," Florence and the Machine
"Club Can't Handle Me," Flo Rida
"Pumped Up Kicks," Foster the People
"Who Says," Selena Gomez & the Scene
"F**k You/Forget You" (4), Cee Lo Green
"Pretty Girl Rock," Keri Hilson
"Tonight Tonight," Hot Chelle Rae
"I Like It" (3), Enrique Iglesias
"Tonight (I'm Lovin' You)" (2), Enrique Iglesias feat. Ludarcis and DJ Frank E
"Pray for You," Jaron and the Long Road to Love
"Down on Me" (2), Jeremih
"Price Tag," Jessie J
"Blah Blah Blah," "Take It Off," "Your Love Is My Drug" (2), Ke$ha
"Pursuit of Happiness (Nightmare)," Kid Cudi

"American Honey," "Just a Kiss," Lady Antebellum
"Bad Romance" (4), Lady Gaga
"The House That Built Me," Miranda Lambert
"6 Foot 7 Foot" (2), "How to Love," "Right Above It," Lil Wayne
"On the Floor" (3), Jennifer Lopez
"Moves Like Jagger," Maroon 5
"Grenade" (4), "Just the Way You Are" (4), Bruno Mars
"Moment 4 Life," "Super Bass," "Your Love," Nicki Minaj
"The Cave," "Little Lion Man," Mumford & Sons
"Just a Dream" (3), Nelly
"Animal," Neon Trees
"Backseat," New Boyz
"All the Right Moves," "Secrets," OneRepublic
"The Only Exception," Paramore
"Jar of Hearts" (2), Christina Perri
"E.T." (4), "Firework" (4), "Teenage Dream" (3), Katy Perry
"California Gurls" (4), Katy Perry feat. Snoop Dogg
"Rhythm of Love," Plain White T's
"Cooler Than Me" (2), "Please Don't Go," Mike Posner
"Love Like Woe," The Ready Set
"Only Girl (in the World)" (2), Rihanna
"What's My Name?" (2), Rihanna feat. Drake
"Motivation," Kelly Rowland
"I Made It (Cash Money Heroes)," Kevin Rudolf
"For the First Time," The Script
"Honey Bee," Blake Shelton
"Whip My Hair," Willow Smith
"Bottoms Up" (2), Trey Songz
"Stuck Like Glue" (2), Sugarland
"Back to December," "Mine," Taylor Swift
"Written in the Stars," Tinie Tempah
"Are You Gonna Kiss Me or Not," Thompson Square
"Marry Me," Train
"Undo It," Carrie Underwood
"Black & Yellow" (3), "Roll Up," Wiz Khalifa
"Bedrock" (3), Young Money

Top-Grossing North American Concert Tours, 1985-2010
Source: Pollstar; ranked by total gross

Rank Artist (year)	Total gross[1]	Cities/ shows	Rank Artist (year)	Total gross[1]	Cities/ shows
1. The Rolling Stones (2005)	$162.0	38/42	14. Bruce Springsteen & The E Street Band (2009)	$94.5	44/58
2. U2 (2005)	138.9	43/78	15. Céline Dion (2008)	94.0	31/47
3. The Rolling Stones (2006)	138.5	35/39	16. Barbra Streisand (2006)	92.5	16/20
4. The Police (2007)	133.2	41/54	17. Roger Waters (2010)	89.5	36/56
5. U2 (2009)	123.0	16/20	18. The Rolling Stones (1997)	89.3	26/33
6. The Rolling Stones (1994)	121.2	43/60	19. Tim McGraw/Faith Hill (2006)	88.8	55/73
7. Bruce Springsteen & The E Street Band (2003)	115.9	30/47	20. Elton John and Billy Joel (2009)	88.0	27/31
8. U2 (2001)	109.7	56/80	21. The Rolling Stones (2002)	87.9	33/34
9. Bon Jovi (2010)	108.2	38/51	22. Prince (2004)	87.4	69/96
10. Madonna (2008)	105.3	19/30	23. 'N Sync (2001)	86.8	36/43
11. Pink Floyd (1994)	103.5	39/59	24. Madonna (2006)	85.9	14/34
12. Paul McCartney (2002)	103.3	43/53	25. Britney Spears (2009)	82.5	51/61
13. The Rolling Stones (1989)	98.0	33/60			

(1) In millions. Not adjusted for inflation.

Sales of Recorded Music and Music Videos, by Units Shipped and Value, 2000-10
Source: Recording Industry Assn. of America
(in millions, net after returns)

	2000	2004	2005	2006	2007	2008	2009	2010	% change 2009-10
Physical units shipped...	1,079.2	814.1	748.7	648.2	543.9	385.5	309.2	240.5	−22.2%
Dollar value	$14,323.7	12,154.7	11,195.0	9,868.6	7,985.8	5,758.5	4,555.9	3,635.1	−20.2
Compact discs (CD)	942.5	767.0	705.4	619.7	511.1	368.4	292.9	225.8	−22.9
Dollar value.	$13,214.5	11,446.5	10,520.2	9,372.6	7,452.3	5,471.3	4,274.1	3,361.3	−21.4
Cassettes	76.0	5.2	2.5	0.7	0.4	0.1	—	—	—
Dollar value.	$626.0	23.7	13.1	3.7	3.0	0.9	—	—	—
LP/EP	2.2	1.4	1.0	0.9	1.3	2.9	3.2	4.0	25.9
Dollar value.	$27.7	19.3	14.2	15.7	22.9	56.7	60.2	87.0	44.4
CD singles	34.2	3.1	2.8	1.7	2.6	0.7	0.9	1.2	31.2
Dollar value.	$142.7	15.0	10.9	7.7	12.2	3.5	3.1	3.3	7.2
Vinyl singles	4.8	3.5	2.3	1.5	0.6	0.4	0.3	0.3	−3.9
Dollar value.	$26.3	19.9	13.2	9.9	4.0	2.9	2.5	2.2	−9.4
Music videos[1]	18.2	32.8	33.8	23.2	27.5	12.8	11.8	9.1	−22.6
Dollar value	$281.9	607.2	602.2	451.1	484.9	218.9	212.0	178.8	−15.7
Digital formats[2]	—	143.9	383.1	625.3	868.4	1,128.6	1,236.8	1,265.4	2.3
Dollar value	—	$183.4	503.6	878.0	1,257.5	1,711.5	2,030.7	2,238.1	10.2
Download albums	—	4.6	13.6	27.6	42.5	63.6	76.4	83.1	8.8
Dollar value	—	$45.5	135.7	275.9	424.9	635.3	763.4	828.8	8.6
Download singles	—	139.4	366.9	586.4	809.9	1,042.7	1,138.3	1,162.4	2.1
Dollar value	—	$138.0	363.3	580.6	801.6	1,032.2	1,220.3	1,366.8	12.0
Music videos.	—	—	1.9	2.8	14.2	20.8	20.4	18.1	−11.1
Dollar value.	—	—	$3.7	19.7	28.2	41.3	40.6	36.1	−11.1
Mobile formats[3]	—	—	170.0	315.0	362.0	405.1	305.8	220.5	−27.9
Dollar value.	—	—	$421.6	773.8	880.8	977.1	728.8	526.7	−27.7
Subscription formats[4]	—	—	1.3	1.3	1.8	1.6	1.2	1.5	29.9
Dollar value.	—	—	$149.2	206.2	201.3	221.4	213.1	200.9	−5.7
Digital performances[5]	—	6.9	27.4	31.5	47.0	100.0	155.5	249.2	60.3
Total units[6]	1,079.2	958.0	1,301.8	1,588.5	1,774.3	1,919.2	1,851.8	1,726.3	−6.8
Total value	$14,323.7	12,345.0	12,296.9	11,758.2	10,372.1	8,768.4	7,683.9	6,850.1	−10.9

— = Not available or not applicable. (1) Includes DVD videos. (2) Includes kiosk singles and albums. (3) Includes master ringtones, ringbacks, music videos, full-length downloads, and other mobile music. (4) Weighted annual average. (5) Estimated royalty payments in dollars to artists and copyright holders distributed by SoundExchange. (6) Includes albums and singles, excludes subscriptions and royalties.

Top Cable TV Networks, 2010
Source: SNL Kagan

Network (year began)	Subscribers (mil)	Network (year began)	Subscribers (mil)
1. TBS (1976)	101.0	14. TLC (1980)	99.5
2. The Weather Channel (1982)	100.6	Spike TV (2003)	99.5
3. Discovery Channel (1985)	100.5	16. HGTV (1994)	99.4
4. TNT (1988)	100.4	17. Cartoon Network (1992)	99.3
5. Nickelodeon/Nick at Nite (1979)	100.3	18. MTV (1981)	99.2
6. Food Network (1993)	100.2	19. History (1995)	99.1
7. CNN/HLN (1980)	100.1	20. Comedy Central (1991)	99.0
8. USA Network (1980)	100.0	21. FOX News (1996)	98.9
9. ESPN/ESPN HD (1979)	99.8	22. Disney Channel (1983)	98.7
A&E (1984)	99.8	VH1 (1985)	98.7
11. C-SPAN (1979)	99.7	24. ABC Family Channel (2001)	98.5
ESPN2 (1993)	99.7	25. CNBC (1989)	98.2
Lifetime Television (1984)	99.7		

U.S. Television Set Owners, 2011
Source: Nielsen Media Research, Sept. 2011

Of the 115.9 mil U.S. households that owned at least one TV set in 2011:

83.7% had 2 or more TV sets	61.9% had a VCR	90.4% received basic cable
55.3% had 3 or more TV sets	86.8% had a DVD player	53.3% received premium cable

U.S. Households With Cable Television, 1979-2011
Source: Nielsen Media Research

Year[1]	Subscribers[2] (mil)	As % of households with TVs	Year[1]	Subscribers[2] (mil)	As % of households with TVs	Year[1]	Subscribers[2] (mil)	As % of households with TVs
1979	14.9	19.4%	1990	53.9	58.6%	2001	81.5	79.8%
1980	17.7	22.6	1991	56.1	60.3	2002	87.8	83.8
1981	23.2	28.3	1992	56.2	61.1	2003	88.4	82.9
1982	27.4	33.4	1993	57.6	61.9	2004	92.4	85.3
1983	31.8	37.9	1994	59.7	63.4	2005	94.0	85.7
1984	35.8	42.5	1995	62.1	65.1	2006	95.0	86.2
1985	38.7	45.3	1996	63.6	66.3	2007	94.5	83.8
1986	40.9	47.4	1997	65.1	67.2	2008	99.7	88.2
1987	43.3	49.2	1998	65.9	67.2	2009	103.0	89.7
1988	46.3	52.0	1999	76.4	76.9	2010	104.1	90.6
1989	50.2	55.6	2000	78.6	77.9	2011	104.8	90.4

(1) After 1998, figures include wired-cable households as well as households that receive TV programming via alternate delivery systems (including satellite receivers, SMATV, MMDS). (2) Households that subscribe to basic cable service.

TV Viewing Shares by Broadcast Year, 1990-2010
Source: *Cable TV Facts*, Cable Advertising Bureau

	All television households							All cable households							Pay+cable households						
	'90	'95	'00	'05	'08	'09	'10	'90	'95	'00	'05	'08	'09	'10	'90	'95	'00	'05	'08	'09	'10
Network affiliates[1]	55	48	44	30	26	24	24	46	41	40	27	23	22	23	43	38	37	24	21	21	22
Ind. TV stations[2]	20	22	12	9	4	5	5	16	17	9	7	3	4	4	16	17	9	6	3	3	4
Public TV stations	3	3	3	2	1	1	2	3	3	2	1	1	1	1	2	2	1	1	1	1	1
Basic cable[3]	21	30	46	48	50	57	57	32	42	55	54	54	61	60	30	41	55	52	52	59	60
Pay cable	6	6	6	5	4	3	3	10	8	7	5	5	5	4	18	15	11	10	8	8	6

Note: Broadcast years represent the 12-month period of the preceding Oct. through Sept. of the year listed. Share figures refer to percentage of the viewing audience for all TV viewing, 24 hours/day. (1) Includes CBS, NBC, ABC, and FOX. (2) Stations qualifying as independent vary from year to year. (3) Includes ad-supported cable and all other cable (non-pay and non-ad-supported channels).

Selected Reality TV Show Winners, 2000-11
Numbers in parentheses represent the season, edition, or cycle of the show. As of Oct. 2011.

The Amazing Race. Debuted Aug. 2001 on CBS. Rob Frisbee & Brennan Swain (1); Chris Luca & Alex Boylan (2); Flo Pesenti & Zach Behr (3); Reichen Lehmkuhl & Chip Arndt (4); Chip & Kim McAllister (5); Freddy Holliday & Kendra Bentley (6); Uchenna & Joyce Agu (7); The Linz Family (8); B. J. Averell & Tyler Mac-Niven (9); Tyler Denk & James Branaman (10); All-Stars: Eric Sanchez & Danielle Turner (11); TK Erwin & Rachel Morales (12); Nick & Starr Spangler (13); Tammy & Victor Jih (14); Meghan Rickey & Cheyne Whitney (15); Dan & Jordan Pious (16); Natalie Strand & Katherine Chang (17); LaKisha & Jennifer Hoffman (18).

American Idol. Debuted July 2002 on Fox. Kelly Clarkson (1); Ruben Studdard (2); Fantasia Barrino (3); Carrie Underwood (4); Taylor Hicks (5); Jordin Sparks (6); David Cook (7); Kris Allen (8); Lee DeWyze (9); Scotty McCreery (10).

America's Got Talent. Debuted June 2006 on NBC. Bianca Ryan (1); Terry Fator (2); Neil E. Boyd (3); Kevin Skinner (4); Michael Grimm (5); Landau Eugene Murphy Jr. (6).

America's Next Top Model. Debuted May 2003. Adrianne Curry (1); Yoanna House (2); Eva Pigford (3); Naima Mora (4); Nicole Linkletter (5); Danielle Evans (6); CariDee English (7); Jaslene Gonzalez (8); Saleisha Stowers (9); Whitney Thompson (10); McKey Sullivan (11); Teyona Anderson (12); Nicole Fox (13); Krista White (14); Ann Ward (15); Brittani Kline (16).

The Apprentice. Debuted Jan. 2004 on NBC. Bill Rancic (1); Kelly Perdew (2); Kendra Todd (3); Randal Pinkett (4); Sean Yazbeck (5); Stefani Schaeffer (6); Brandy Kuentzel (7). *Celebrity Apprentice:* Piers Morgan (1); Joan Rivers (2); Bret Michaels (3); John Rich (4).

The Bachelor. Debuted Mar. 2002 on ABC. Alex Michel chose Amanda Marsh (1); Aaron Buerge chose Helene Eksterowicz (2); Andrew Firestone chose Jen Schefft (3); Bob Guiney chose Estella Gardinier (4); Jesse Palmer chose Jessica Bowlin (5); Byron Velvick chose Mary Delgado (6); Charlie O'Connell chose Sarah Brice (7); Travis Stork chose Sarah Stone (8); Lorenzo Borghese chose Jennifer Wilson (9); Andy Baldwin chose Tessa Horst (10); Brad Womack chose no one (11); Matt Grant chose Shayne Lamas (12); Jason Mesnick chose Melissa Rycroft (13); Jake Pavelka chose Vienna Girardi (14); Brad Womack chose Emily Maynard (15).

The Bachelorette. Debuted Jan. 2003 on ABC. Trista Rehn chose Ryan Sutter (1); Meredith Phillips chose Ian McKee (2); Jen Schefft chose Jerry Ferris (3); DeAnna Pappas chose Jesse Csincsak (4); Jillian Harris chose Ed Swiderski (5); Ali Fedotowsky chose Roberto Martinez (6); Ashley Hebert chose J. P. Rosenbaum (7).

The Biggest Loser. Debuted Oct. 2004 on NBC. Ryan Benson (1); Matt Hoover (2); Erik Chopin (3); Bill Germanakos (4); Ali Vincent (5); Michelle Aguilar (6); Helen Phillips (7); Danny Cahill (8); Michael Ventrella (9); Patrick House (10); Olivia Ward (11).

Big Brother. Debuted July 2000 on CBS. Eddie McGee (1); Will Kirby (2); Lisa Donahue (3); Jun Song (4); Drew Daniel (5); Maggie Ausburn (6); Mike Malinto (7); Dick Donato (8); Adam Jasinski (9); Dan Gheesling (10); Jordan Lloyd (11); Hayden Moss (12); Rachel Reilly (13).

Dancing With the Stars. Debuted June 2005 on ABC. Kelly Monaco & Alex Mazo (1); Drew Lachey & Cheryl Burke (2); Emmitt Smith & Cheryl Burke (3); Apolo Anton Ohno & Julianne Hough (4); Helio Castroneves & Julianne Hough (5); Kristi Yamaguchi & Mark Ballas (6); Brooke Burke & Derek Hough (7); Shawn Johnson & Mark Ballas (8); Donny Osmond & Kym Johnson (9); Nicole Scherzinger & Derek Hough (10); Jennifer Grey & Derek Hough (11); Hines Ward & Kym Johnson.

Food Network Star. Debuted June 2005 on Food Network. Steve McDonagh & Dan Smith (1); Guy Fieri (2); Amy Finley (3); Aaron McCargo Jr. (4); Melissa d'Arabian (5); Aarti Sequeria (6); Jeff Mauro (7).

Hell's Kitchen. Debuted Mar. 2005 on FOX. Michael Wray (1); Heather West (2); Rock Harper (3); Christina Machamer (4); Danny Veltri (5); Dave Levey (6); Holli Ugalde (7); Nona Sivley (8); Paul Niedermann (9).

Project Runway. Debuted Dec. 2004 on Bravo. Jay McCarroll (1); Chloe Dao (2); Jeffrey Sebelia (3); Christian Siriano (4); Leanne Marshall (5); Irina Shabayeva (6); Seth Aaron Henderson (7); Gretchen Jones (8).

So You Think You Can Dance. Debuted July 2005 on FOX. Nick Lazzarini (1); Benji Schwimmer (2); Sabra Johnson (3); Joshua Allen (4); Jeanine Mason (5); Russell Ferguson (6); Lauren Froderman (7); Melanie Moore (8).

Survivor. Debuted May 2000 on CBS. Borneo: Richard Hatch (1); Outback: Tina Wesson (2); Africa: Ethan Zohn (3); Marquesas: Vecepia Towery (4); Thailand: Brian Heidik (5); The Amazon: Jenna Morasca (6); Pearl Islands: Sandra Diaz-Twine (7); All-Stars, Panama: Amber Brkich (8); Vanuatu: Chris Daugherty (9); Palau: Tom Westman (10); Guatemala: Danni Boatwright (11); Panama: Aras Baskauskas (12); Cook Islands: Yul Kwon (13); Fiji: Earl Cole (14); China: Todd Herzog (15); Micronesia: Parvati Shallow (16); Gabon: Robert Crowley (17); Tocantins: James "JT" Thomas (18); Samoa: Natalie White (19); Heroes vs. Villains: Sandra Diaz-Twine (20); Redemption Island, Nicaragua: Rob Mariano (21).

Top Chef. Debuted Mar. 2006 on Bravo. Harold Dieterle (1); Ilan Hall (2); Hung Huynh (3); Stephanie Izard (4); Hosea Rosenberg (5); Michael Voltaggio (6); Kevin Sbraga (7); Richard Blais (8). *Top Chef Masters:* Rick Bayless (1); Marcus Samuelsson (2); Floyd Cardoz (3).

The Voice. Debuted Apr. 2011 on NBC. Javier Colon (1).

Average U.S. Television Viewing Time, 2010-11

Source: Nielsen Media Research (hours: minutes per week)

Group	Age	Total per week	M-F 7-10 AM	M-F 10 AM-4 PM	M-Sun. 8-11 PM	M-F 11:30 PM-1 AM	Sat. 7 AM-1 PM	Sunday 1-7 PM
Men	18+	34:46	1:57	4:31	8:29	1:48	1:00	1:55
	18-24	24:41	1:04	3:33	5:15	1:32	0:37	1:15
	25-54	32:31	1:46	3:47	7:59	1:51	0:59	1:48
	55+	43:05	2:41	6:15	10:43	1:49	1:13	2:23
Women	18+	38:50	2:31	5:50	9:13	1:56	1:06	1:47
	18-24	26:49	1:18	4:22	5:44	1:35	0:41	1:11
	25-54	35:25	2:17	4:54	8:30	1:55	1:02	1:38
	55+	48:15	3:18	7:48	11:32	2:04	1:21	2:12
Children	2-11	26:07	1:51	4:19	5:21	0:53	1:13	1:21
Teens	12-17	23:57	1:01	2:47	5:34	1:16	0:47	1:13
All viewers		**34:16**	**2:05**	**4:53**	**8:05**	**1:41**	**1:03**	**1:43**

Note: For viewing period Jan. 31, 2011-Aug. 24, 2011. Includes DVR playback.

Favorite Prime-Time Television Programs, 2010-11

Source: Nielsen Media Research

Data are for regularly scheduled network programs Sept. 20, 2010-Aug. 24, 2011; ranked by average audience percentage. Ratings, or average audience percentages, are estimates of the percentage of all TV-owning households that are watching a particular program live, or on DVR within 7 days of broadcast. Audience share percentages are estimates of the percentage of those watching TV that are tuned into a particular program.

Rank	Program, network	Avg. audience	Audience share	Rank	Program, network	Avg. audience	Audience share
1.	American Idol-Wednesday, FOX....	14.5%	23%	26.	Bones, FOX	7.0%	11%
2.	Dancing With the Stars-Monday, ABC	13.8	21	27.	Two and a Half Men, CBS	6.9	10
3.	American Idol-Thursday, FOX......	13.4	22	28.	Criminal Minds: Suspect Behavior,	6.9	11
4.	NBC Sunday Night Football	12.6	20		CBS		
5.	CBS NFL National Post-Gun	12.6	22	29.	The Voice: Results, NBC..........	6.8	12
6.	Dancing With the Stars: Results, ABC	11.8	18	30.	The Amazing Race 17, CBS.......	6.8	10
7.	NCIS, CBS	10.4	17	31.	Blue Bloods, CBS..............	6.8	12
8.	Sunday Night NFL Pre-Kickoff, NBC	9.2	15	32.	Hawaii Five-O, CBS	6.7	11
9.	NCIS: Los Angeles, CBS	8.9	14	33.	Castle, ABC	6.7	11
10.	America's Got Talent-Tuesday, NBC	8.4	14	34.	Secret Millionaire, ABC...........	6.6	11
11.	The Mentalist, CBS..............	8.4	14	35.	Football Night in America Part 3, NBC	6.5	11
12.	The Voice, NBC	7.9	13	36.	The Defenders, CBS.............	6.5	11
13.	The Good Wife, CBS	7.8	13	37.	$#*! My Dad Says, CBS	6.4	10
14.	Survivor: Nicaragua, CBS........	7.6	13	38.	Undercover Boss, CBS...........	6.2	10
15.	60 Minutes, CBS..............	7.6	13	39.	House, FOX	6.2	10
16.	America's Got Talent-Wednesday,	7.6	13	40.	Mike & Molly, CBS	6.2	9
	NBC			41.	CSI: Miami, CBS...............	6.2	10
17.	Criminal Minds, CBS	7.6	12	42.	Modern Family, ABC..............	6.2	10
18.	Dancing With the Stars-Tuesday, ABC	7.5	12	43.	Body of Proof, ABC..............	6.1	10
19.	Desperate Housewives, ABC	7.5	11	44.	Harry's Law, NBC..............	6.1	10
20.	Grey's Anatomy, ABC	7.5	12	45.	The Bachelorette, ABC...........	6.1	10
21.	CSI, CBS	7.4	12	46.	CSI: NY, CBS.................	6.0	11
22.	The OT, FOX.	7.3	13	47.	Glee, FOX...................	6.0	9
23.	Survivor: Redemption Island, CBS..	7.2	12	48.	The Amazing Race 18, CBS.......	5.8	9
24.	The Big Bang Theory, CBS.	7.1	12	49.	Law and Order: SVU, NBC........	5.8	9
25.	The Bachelor, ABC..............	7.0	11	50.	Brothers & Sisters, ABC	5.6	9

Favorite Syndicated Programs, 2010-11

Source: Nielsen Media Research

Average audience percentages or ratings are estimates of the percentage of TV-owning households watching a program live or on DVR within 7 days of broadcast, Sept. 20, 2010-Aug. 24, 2011.

Rank	Program	Avg. audience	Rank	Program	Avg. audience
1.	Wheel of Fortune	6.8%	14.	Dr. Phil	2.8%
2.	Two and a Half Men	6.1	15.	Everybody Loves Raymond	2.8
3.	Jeopardy.	5.8	16.	Two and a Half Men (weekend A)	2.7
4.	Judge Judy........................	5.5	17.	How I Met Your Mother..............	2.6
5.	The Oprah Winfrey Show	4.4	18.	Seinfeld..........................	2.6
6.	Family Guy	4.1	19.	Live With Regis and Kelly............	2.6
7.	Entertainment Tonight................	3.9	20.	The Office	2.5
8.	Law & Order: Criminal Intent	3.1	21.	George Lopez......................	2.5
9.	Two and a Half Men (weekend B).......	3.1	22.	Family Guy (weekend)	2.4
10.	Criminal Minds	3.1	23.	Seinfeld (weekend).................	2.4
11.	Inside Edition	2.9	24.	Monk.	2.3
12.	My Wife and Kids	2.9	25.	The Dr. Oz Show	2.3
13.	Wheel of Fortune (weekend)	2.9			

Favorite Basic Cable Programs, 2010-11

Source: Nielsen Media Research

Data are for regularly scheduled basic cable programs Sept. 27, 2010-Aug. 28, 2011. Average audience percentages, or ratings, are estimates of the percentage of TV-owning households watching a program live or on DVR within 7 days of broadcast.

Rank	Program, network	Avg. audience	Rank	Program, network	Avg. audience
1.	Jersey Shore Season 4, MTV	6.4%	17.	Law & Order: Criminal Intent (original episodes), USA	3.0%
2.	Jersey Shore Season 3, MTV	5.6			
3.	Jersey Shore Season 2, MTV	4.4	18.	Jersey Shore After Show, MTV	3.0
4.	Covert Affairs, USA	4.4	19.	Fairly Legal, USA	3.0
5.	Burn Notice, USA	4.2	20.	The Game Season 4, BET	2.9
6.	Suits, USA	4.1	21.	Army Wives, Lifetime	2.9
7.	Royal Pains, USA	4.1	22.	Teen Mom 3, MTV	2.9
8.	Walking Dead, AMC	3.9	23.	Real Housewives of New Jersey, Bravo	2.5
9.	Necessary Roughness, USA	3.8	24.	Psych, USA	2.5
10.	Teen Mom 2, MTV	3.5	25.	Victorious, Nickelodeon	2.4
11.	White Collar, USA	3.5	26.	Real Housewives of Atlanta, Bravo	2.3
12.	Jersey Shore After Show, MTV	3.4	27.	America's Election HQ, Fox News Channel	2.3
13.	In Plain Sight, USA	3.3	28.	SpongeBob SquarePants, Nickelodeon	2.2
14.	Teen Mom II, MTV	3.1	29.	Warehouse 13, Syfy Channel	2.2
15.	iCarly, Nickelodeon	3.0	30.	Real Housewives of New York City, Bravo	2.2
16.	Project Runway, Lifetime	3.0			

Favorite Premium Cable Programs, 2010-11

Source: Nielsen Media Research

Average audience percentages, or ratings, are estimates of the percentage of TV-owning households watching a program live or on DVR within 7 days of broadcast, Sept. 27, 2010-Aug. 28, 2011.

Top-Rated Series

Rank	Program, network	Avg. audience	Rank	Program, network	Avg. audience
				Top-Rated Movies	
1.	True Blood, HBO	0.8%	1.	Tangled (2010), STARZ	0.8%
2.	Entourage, HBO	0.6	2.	Toy Story 2, STARZ	0.8
3.	Game of Thrones, HBO	0.6	3.	Unstoppable, HBO	0.6
4.	Curb Your Enthusiasm, HBO	0.6	4.	Conviction, HBO	0.5
5.	Boardwalk Empire, HBO	0.6	5.	Avatar, HBO	0.5
6.	Spartacus: Gods of the Arena, STARZ	0.3	6.	Toy Story, STARZ	0.5
7.	Real Time With Bill Maher, HBO	0.3	7.	The Blind Side, HBO	0.5
8.	Big Love, HBO	0.3	8.	The Book of Eli, HBO	0.5
9.	Camelot, STARZ	0.3	9.	Knight and Day, HBO	0.5
10.	Spartacus: Blood and Sand, STARZ	0.3			
11.	Eastbound & Down, HBO	0.3			

All-Time Most Watched Television Programs

Source: Nielsen Media Research, Jan. 1961-Aug. 2011

Estimates exclude unsponsored or joint network telecasts (e.g., presidential addresses) or programs under 30 minutes long. Ranked by number of TV-owning households tuned in to the program.

Rank	Program	Telecast date	Network	Rating	Avg. audience (thous.)
1.	Super Bowl XLV	2/6/2011	FOX	46.1%	53,435
2.	Super Bowl XLIV	2/7/2010	CBS	45.2	51,873
3.	M*A*S*H (last episode)	2/28/1983	CBS	60.2	50,150
4.	Super Bowl XLII	2/3/2008	FOX	43.2	48,721
5.	Super Bowl XLIII	2/1/2009	NBC	42.1	48,239
6.	Super Bowl XLI	2/4/2007	CBS	42.7	47,535
7.	Super Bowl XL	2/5/2006	ABC	41.6	45,869
8.	XVII Winter Olympics (Women's figure skating)	2/23/1994	CBS	48.5	45,690
9.	Super Bowl XXXIX	2/6/2005	FOX	41.1	45,080
10.	Super Bowl XXXVIII	2/1/2004	CBS	41.4	44,910
11.	Super Bowl XXX	1/28/1996	NBC	46.0	44,150
12.	Super Bowl XXXII	1/25/1998	NBC	44.5	43,630
13.	Super Bowl XXXIV	1/30/2000	ABC	43.3	43,620
14.	Super Bowl XXXVII	1/26/2003	ABC	40.7	43,430
15.	Super Bowl XXVIII	1/30/1994	NBC	45.5	42,860
16.	Super Bowl XXXVI	2/3/2002	FOX	40.4	42,660
17.	Cheers	5/20/1993	NBC	45.5	42,360
18.	Super Bowl XXXI	1/26/1997	FOX	43.3	42,000
19.	Super Bowl XXVII	1/31/1993	NBC	45.1	41,990
20.	XVII Winter Olympics (Women's figure skating)	2/25/1994	CBS	44.1	41,540
21.	Super Bowl XX	1/26/1986	NBC	48.3	41,490

Highest-Rated TV Programs by Season, 1950-2011

Source: Nielsen Media Research; regular series programs, Sept.-May season

Rating is percentage of TV-owning households tuned in to the program. Data prior to 1988-89 exclude Alaska and Hawaii.

Season	Program	Rating	TV-owning households (thous.)	Season	Program	Rating	TV-owning households (thous.)
1950-51	Texaco Star Theatre	61.6%	10,320	1981-82	Dallas	28.4%	81,500
1951-52	Godfrey's Talent Scouts	53.8	15,300	1982-83	60 Minutes	25.5	83,300
1952-53	I Love Lucy	67.3	20,400	1983-84	Dallas	25.7	83,800
1953-54	I Love Lucy	58.8	26,000	1984-85	Dynasty	25.0	84,900
1954-55	I Love Lucy	49.3	30,700	1985-86	Cosby Show	33.8	85,900
1955-56	$64,000 Question	47.5	34,900	1986-87	Cosby Show	34.9	87,400
1956-57	I Love Lucy	43.7	38,900	1987-88	Cosby Show	27.8	88,600
1957-58	Gunsmoke	43.1	41,920	1988-89	Roseanne	25.5	90,400
1958-59	Gunsmoke	39.6	43,950	1989-90	Roseanne	23.4	92,100
1959-60	Gunsmoke	40.3	45,750	1990-91	Cheers	21.6	93,100
1960-61	Gunsmoke	37.3	47,200	1991-92	60 Minutes	21.7	92,100
1961-62	Wagon Train	32.1	48,555	1992-93	60 Minutes	21.6	93,100
1962-63	Beverly Hillbillies	36.0	50,300	1993-94	Home Improvement	21.9	94,200
1963-64	Beverly Hillbillies	39.1	51,600	1994-95	Seinfeld	20.5	95,400
1964-65	Bonanza	36.3	52,700	1995-96	E.R.	22.0	95,900
1965-66	Bonanza	31.8	53,850	1996-97	E.R.	21.2	97,000
1966-67	Bonanza	29.1	55,130	1997-98	Seinfeld	22.0	98,000
1967-68	Andy Griffith	27.6	56,670	1998-99	E.R.	17.8	99,400
1968-69	Rowan & Martin's Laugh-In	31.8	58,250	1999-2000	Who Wants to Be a Millionaire	18.6	100,800
1969-70	Rowan & Martin's Laugh-In	26.3	58,500	2000-01	Survivor II	17.4	102,200
1970-71	Marcus Welby, M.D.	29.6	60,100	2001-02	Friends	15.3	105,500
1971-72	All in the Family	34.0	62,100	2002-03	CSI	16.1	106,700
1972-73	All in the Family	33.3	64,800	2003-04	CSI	15.9	108,400
1973-74	All in the Family	31.2	66,200	2004-05	CSI	16.3	106,900
1974-75	All in the Family	30.2	68,500	2005-06	American Idol-Tuesday	17.6	110,200
1975-76	All in the Family	30.1	69,600	2006-07	American Idol-Wednesday	17.3	112,800
1976-77	Happy Days	31.5	71,200	2007-08	American Idol-Wednesday	16.1	113,050
1977-78	Laverne & Shirley	31.6	72,900	2008-09	American Idol-Wednesday	15.1	114,900
1978-79	Laverne & Shirley	30.5	74,500	2009-10	American Idol-Tuesday	13.7	114,900
1979-80	60 Minutes	28.2	76,300	2010-11	American Idol-Wednesday	14.5	115,900
1980-81	Dallas	31.2	79,900				

All-Time Highest-Rated Television Programs

Source: Nielsen Media Research, Jan. 1961-Aug. 2011

Estimates exclude unsponsored or joint network telecasts (e.g., presidential addresses) and programs under 30 minutes long. Ranked by rating (percentage of TV-owning households tuned in to the program). Average audience is number of TV-owning households tuned in.

Rank	Program	Telecast date	Network	Rating	Avg. audience (thous.)
1.	M*A*S*H (last episode)	2/28/1983	CBS	60.2%	50,150
2.	Dallas (Who Shot J.R.?)	11/21/1980	CBS	53.3	41,470
3.	Roots-Pt. 8	1/30/1977	ABC	51.1	36,380
4.	Super Bowl XVI	1/24/1982	CBS	49.1	40,020
5.	Super Bowl XVII	1/30/1983	NBC	48.6	40,480
6.	XVII Winter Olympics (Women's figure skating)	2/23/1994	CBS	48.5	45,690
7.	Super Bowl XX	1/26/1986	NBC	48.3	41,490
8.	Gone With the Wind-Pt. 1	11/7/1976	NBC	47.7	33,960
9.	Gone With the Wind-Pt. 2	11/8/1976	NBC	47.4	33,750
10.	Super Bowl XII	1/15/1978	CBS	47.2	34,410
11.	Super Bowl XIII	1/21/1979	NBC	47.1	35,090
12.	Bob Hope Christmas Show	1/15/1970	NBC	46.6	27,260
13.	Super Bowl XIX	1/20/1985	ABC	46.4	39,390
14.	Super Bowl XVIII	1/22/1984	CBS	46.4	38,800
15.	Super Bowl XIV	1/20/1980	CBS	46.3	35,330
16.	Super Bowl XLV	2/6/2011	FOX	46.1	53,435
17.	Super Bowl XXX	1/28/1996	NBC	46.0	44,150
18.	ABC Theater (The Day After)	11/20/1983	ABC	46.0	38,550
19.	Roots-Pt. 6	1/28/1977	ABC	45.9	32,680
20.	The Fugitive	8/29/1967	ABC	45.9	25,700
21.	Super Bowl XXI	1/25/1987	CBS	45.8	40,030
22.	Roots-Pt. 5	1/27/1977	ABC	45.7	32,540
23.	Super Bowl XXVIII	1/30/1994	NBC	45.5	42,860
24.	Cheers (last episode)	5/20/1993	NBC	45.5	42,360
25.	Ed Sullivan	2/9/1964	CBS	45.3	23,240
26.	Super Bowl XLIV	2/7/2010	CBS	45.2	51,873

AWARDS — MEDALS — PRIZES

Alfred B. Nobel Prizes, 1901-2011

Alfred B. Nobel (1833-96) bequeathed $9 mil, the interest on which was to be distributed yearly to those judged to have most benefited humankind in chemistry, literature, promotion of peace, physics, and physiology or medicine. Prizes were first awarded in 1901. The first prize in economics was awarded in 1969, funded by Sweden's central bank. Each prize is now worth 10 mil Swedish krona (about $1.5 mil). If year is omitted, no award was given. The Royal Swedish Academy selects prize winners for chemistry, economics, and physics; the Nobel Assembly at Karolinska Institutet, physiology or medicine; the Swedish Academy, literature; and the Norwegian Nobel Committee, the peace prize. The 2011 Nobel Prizes were announced Oct. 3-10.

Nobel Prizes, 2011

Chemistry: Dan Shechtman, Israel, was awarded the prize for his discovery of quasicrystals, a material with regular but non-repeating atomic patterns.

Economics: Americans Thomas J. Sargent and Christopher A. Sims shared the prize for research on the cause and effect of policy changes on the macroeconomy.

Literature: Swedish poet Tomas Tranströmer was awarded the prize "because, through his condensed, translucent images, he gives us fresh access to reality."

Peace: Liberian Pres. Ellen Johnson Sirleaf, Liberian peace activist Leymah Gbowee, and Yemeni pro-democracy activist Tawakkul Karman shared the prize "for their non-violent struggle for the safety of women and for women's rights to full participation in peace-building work."

Physics: Saul Perlmutter, U.S.; Adam G. Riess, U.S.; and Brian P. Schmidt, Australia-U.S.; were awarded the prize for their studies of a force now known as dark energy and its role in the expansion of the universe.

Physiology or Medicine: Ralph M. Steinman and Bruce A. Beutler of the U.S. and Jules A. Hoffmann of France were given the prize for their advances in immunology studies. (The status of Steinman's prize was briefly in question, as he had died after the Nobel committee's decision but before the announcement; prizes are not given posthumously. Nobel Foundation directors ultimately decided that the award was valid.)

Physics

1901 Wilhelm C. Röntgen, Ger.
1902 Hendrik A. Lorentz,
     Pieter Zeeman, Neth.
1903 Antoine Henri Becquerel, Pierre
     Curie, Fr.; Marie Curie, Pol.-Fr.
1904 Lord Rayleigh (John W. Strutt), UK
1905 Philipp E. A. von Lenard, Ger.
1906 Sir Joseph J. Thomson, UK
1907 Albert A. Michelson, U.S.
1908 Gabriel Lippmann, Fr.
1909 Carl F. Braun, Ger.;
     Guglielmo Marconi, It.
1910 Johannes D. van der Waals, Neth.
1911 Wilhelm Wien, Ger.
1912 Nils G. Dalén, Swed.
1913 Heike Kamerlingh Onnes, Neth.
1914 Max von Laue, Ger.
1915 Sir William H. Bragg,
     William L. Bragg, UK
1917 Charles G. Barkla, UK
1918 Max K. E. L. Planck, Ger.
1919 Johannes Stark, Ger.
1920 Charles E. Guillaume, Fr.-Switz.
1921 Albert Einstein, Ger.-U.S.
1922 Niels Bohr, Den.
1923 Robert A. Millikan, U.S.
1924 Karl M. G. Siegbahn, Swed.
1925 James Franck, Gustav Hertz, Ger.
1926 Jean B. Perrin, Fr.
1927 Arthur H. Compton, U.S.;
     Charles T. R. Wilson, UK
1928 Owen W. Richardson, UK
1929 Prince Louis-Victor de Broglie, Fr.
1930 Sir Chandrasekhara V. Raman,
     India
1932 Werner Heisenberg, Ger.
1933 Paul A. M. Dirac, UK;
     Erwin Schrödinger, Austria
1935 Sir James Chadwick, UK
1936 Carl D. Anderson, U.S.;
     Victor F. Hess, Austria
1937 Clinton J. Davisson, U.S.;
     Sir George P. Thomson, UK
1938 Enrico Fermi, It.-U.S.
1939 Ernest O. Lawrence, U.S.
1943 Otto Stern, U.S.
1944 Isidor Isaac Rabi, U.S.
1945 Wolfgang Pauli, U.S.-Austria
1946 Percy W. Bridgman, U.S.
1947 Sir Edward V. Appleton, UK
1948 Patrick M. S. Blackett, UK
1949 Hideki Yukawa, Jpn.
1950 Cecil F. Powell, UK

1951 Sir John D. Cockcroft, UK;
     Ernest T. S. Walton, Ire.
1952 Felix Bloch, Edward M. Purcell, U.S.
1953 Frits Zernike, Neth.
1954 Max Born, UK; Walter Bothe, Ger.
1955 Polykarp Kusch, Willis E. Lamb, U.S.
1956 John Bardeen, Walter H. Brattain,
     William Shockley, U.S.
1957 Tsung-Dao Lee, Chen Ning Yang,
     U.S.-China
1958 Pavel Cherenkov, Il'ja Frank,
     Igor Y. Tamm, USSR
1959 Owen Chamberlain,
     Emilio G. Segre, U.S.
1960 Donald A. Glaser, U.S.
1961 Robert Hofstadter, U.S.;
     Rudolf L. Mossbauer, Ger.
1962 Lev D. Landau, USSR
1963 Maria Goeppert-Mayer, Eugene P.
     Wigner, U.S.; J. Hans D. Jensen, Ger.
1964 Nicolay G. Basov,
     Aleksandr M. Prokhorov, USSR;
     Charles H. Townes, U.S.
1965 Richard P. Feynman,
     Julian S. Schwinger, U.S.;
     Sin-Itiro Tomonaga, Jpn.
1966 Alfred Kastler, Fr.
1967 Hans A. Bethe, U.S.
1968 Luis W. Alvarez, U.S.
1969 Murray Gell-Mann, U.S.
1970 Louis Néel, Fr.;
     Hannes Alfvén, Swed.
1971 Dennis Gabor, UK
1972 John Bardeen, Leon N. Cooper,
     John R. Schrieffer, U.S.
1973 Ivar Giaever, U.S.; Leo Esaki, Jpn.;
     Brian D. Josephson, UK
1974 Sir Martin Ryle, Antony Hewish, UK
1975 Leo James Rainwater, U.S.;
     Ben Mottelson, U.S.-Den.;
     Aage Bohr, Den.
1976 Burton Richter,
     Samuel C. C. Ting, U.S.
1977 John H. van Vleck,
     Philip W. Anderson, U.S.;
     Sir Nevill F. Mott, UK
1978 Pyotr Kapitsa, USSR;
     Arno Penzias, Robert Wilson, U.S.
1979 Steven Weinberg,
     Sheldon L. Glashow, U.S.;
     Abdus Salam, Pakistan
1980 James W. Cronin, Val L. Fitch, U.S.
1981 Nicolaas Bloembergen,
     Arthur Schawlow, U.S.;
     Kai M. Siegbahn, Swed.
1982 Kenneth G. Wilson, U.S.
1983 Subramanyan Chandrasekhar,
     William A. Fowler, U.S.
1984 Carlo Rubbia, It.;
     Simon van der Meer, Neth.

1985 Klaus von Klitzing, Ger.
1986 Ernest Ruska, Gerd Binnig, Ger.;
     Heinrich Rohrer, Switz.
1987 K. Alex Müller, Switz.;
     J. Georg Bednorz, Ger.
1988 Leon M. Lederman, Melvin
     Schwartz, Jack Steinberger, U.S.
1989 Norman F. Ramsey, U.S.;
     Hans G. Dehmelt, Ger.-U.S.;
     Wolfgang Paul, Ger.
1990 Richard E. Taylor, Can.; Jerome I.
     Friedman, Henry W. Kendall, U.S.
1991 Pierre-Gilles de Gennes, Fr.
1992 Georges Charpak, Pol.-Fr.
1993 Joseph H. Taylor,
     Russell A. Hulse, U.S.
1994 Bertram N. Brockhouse, Can.;
     Clifford G. Shull, U.S.
1995 Martin Perl, Frederick Reines, U.S.
1996 David M. Lee, Douglas D. Osheroff,
     Robert C. Richardson, U.S.
1997 Steven Chu, William D. Phillips,
     U.S.; Claude Cohen-Tannoudji, Fr.
1998 Robert B. Laughlin, U.S.;
     Horst L. Störmer, Ger.-U.S;
     Daniel C. Tsui, China-U.S.
1999 Gerardus 't Hooft,
     Martinus J. G. Veltman, Neth.
2000 Jack S. Kilby, U.S.;
     Herbert Kroemer, Ger.-U.S.;
     Zhores I. Alferov, Russ.
2001 Eric A. Cornell, Carl E. Wieman,
     U.S.; Wolfgang Ketterle, Ger.
2002 Raymond Davis Jr.,
     Riccardo Giacconi, U.S.;
     Masatoshi Koshiba, Jpn.
2003 Vitaly L. Ginzburg,
     Alexei A. Abrikosov, Russ.;
     Anthony J. Leggett, UK
2004 David J. Gross, H. David Politzer,
     Frank Wilczek, U.S.
2005 Roy J. Glauber, John L. Hall, U.S.;
     Theodor W. Hänsch, Ger.
2006 John C. Mather,
     George F. Smoot, U.S.
2007 Albert Fert, Fr.;
     Peter Grünberg, Ger.
2008 Yoichiro Nambu, U.S.;
     Makoto Kobayashi,
     Toshihide Maskawa, Jpn.
2009 Charles K. Kao, U.S.-UK;
     Willard S. Boyle, U.S.-Can.;
     George E. Smith, U.S.
2010 Andre Geim, Russ.-Neth.;
     Konstantin Novoselov,
     Russ.-UK

Chemistry

1901	Jacobus H. van 't Hoff, Neth.	
1902	Emil Fischer, Ger.	
1903	Svante A. Arrhenius, Swed.	
1904	Sir William Ramsay, UK	
1905	Adolf von Baeyer, Ger.	
1906	Henri Moissan, Fr.	
1907	Eduard Buchner, Ger.	
1908	Ernest Rutherford, UK	
1909	Wilhelm Ostwald, Ger.	
1910	Otto Wallach, Ger.	
1911	Marie Curie, Pol.-Fr.	
1912	Victor Grignard, Paul Sabatier, Fr.	
1913	Alfred Werner, Switz.	
1914	Theodore W. Richards, U.S.	
1915	Richard M. Willstätter, Ger.	
1918	Fritz Haber, Ger.	
1920	Walther H. Nernst, Ger.	
1921	Frederick Soddy, UK	
1922	Francis W. Aston, UK	
1923	Fritz Pregl, Austria	
1925	Richard A. Zsigmondy, Ger.	
1926	Theodor Svedberg, Swed.	
1927	Heinrich O. Wieland, Ger.	
1928	Adolf O. R. Windaus, Ger.	
1929	Sir Arthur Harden, UK; Hans von Euler-Chelpin, Swed.	
1930	Hans Fischer, Ger.	
1931	Friedrich Bergius, Carl Bosch, Ger.	
1932	Irving Langmuir, U.S.	
1934	Harold C. Urey, U.S.	
1935	Frédéric Joliot, Irene Joliot-Curie, Fr.	
1936	Peter J. W. Debye, Neth.	
1937	Walter N. Haworth, UK; Paul Karrer, Switz.	
1938	Richard Kuhn, Ger.	
1939	Adolf F. J. Butenandt, Ger.; Leopold Ruzicka, Switz.	
1943	George de Hevesy, Hung.	
1944	Otto Hahn, Ger.	
1945	Artturi I. Virtanen, Fin.	
1946	James B. Sumner, John H. Northrop, Wendell M. Stanley, U.S.	
1947	Sir Robert Robinson, UK	
1948	Arne W. K. Tiselius, Swed.	
1949	William F. Giauque, U.S.	
1950	Kurt Alder, Otto P. H. Diels, Ger.	

1951	Edwin M. McMillan, Glenn T. Seaborg, U.S.
1952	Archer J. P. Martin, Richard L. M. Synge, UK
1953	Hermann Staudinger, Ger.
1954	Linus C. Pauling, U.S.
1955	Vincent du Vigneaud, U.S.
1956	Sir Cyril N. Hinshelwood, UK; Nikolay N. Semenov, USSR
1957	Lord (Alexander R.) Todd, UK
1958	Frederick Sanger, UK
1959	Jaroslav Heyrovsky, Czech.
1960	Willard F. Libby, U.S.
1961	Melvin Calvin, U.S.
1962	John C. Kendrew, Max F. Perutz, UK
1963	Giulio Natta, It.; Karl Ziegler, Ger.
1964	Dorothy C. Hodgkin, UK
1965	Robert B. Woodward, U.S.
1966	Robert S. Mulliken, U.S.
1967	Manfred Eigen, Ger.; Ronald G. W. Norrish, George Porter, UK
1968	Lars Onsager, U.S.
1969	Derek H. R. Barton, UK; Odd Hassel, Nor.
1970	Luis F. Leloir, Arg.
1971	Gerhard Herzberg, Can.
1972	Christian B. Anfinsen, Stanford Moore, William H. Stein, U.S.
1973	Ernst Otto Fischer, Ger.; Geoffrey Wilkinson, UK
1974	Paul J. Flory, U.S.
1975	John Cornforth, Austral.-UK; Vladimir Prelog, Bosnia-Switz.
1976	William N. Lipscomb, U.S.
1977	Ilya Prigogine, Belg.
1978	Peter Mitchell, UK
1979	Herbert C. Brown, U.S.; Georg Wittig, Ger.
1980	Paul Berg, Walter Gilbert, U.S.; Frederick Sanger, UK
1981	Kenichi Fukui, Jpn.; Roald Hoffmann, U.S.
1982	Aaron Klug, UK-Lith.
1983	Henry Taube, Can.
1984	Robert Bruce Merrifield, U.S.
1985	Herbert A. Hauptman, Jerome Karle, U.S.

1986	Dudley Herschbach, Yuan T. Lee, U.S.; John C. Polanyi, Can.
1987	Donald J. Cram, Charles J. Pedersen, U.S.; Jean-Marie Lehn, Fr.
1988	Johann Deisenhofer, Robert Huber, Hartmut Michel, Ger.
1989	Thomas R. Cech, Sidney Altman, U.S.
1990	Elias James Corey, U.S.
1991	Richard R. Ernst, Switz.
1992	Rudolph A. Marcus, Can.-U.S.
1993	Kary B. Mullis, U.S.; Michael Smith, UK-Can.
1994	George A. Olah, U.S.
1995	Paul Crutzen, Neth.; Mario Molina, Mex.-U.S.; Sherwood Rowland, U.S.
1996	Sir Harold W. Kroto, UK; Robert F. Curl Jr., Richard E. Smalley, U.S.
1997	Paul D. Boyer, U.S.; John E. Walker, UK; Jens C. Skou, Den.
1998	Walter Kohn, U.S.; John A. Pople, UK
1999	Ahmed H. Zewail, U.S.
2000	Alan J. Heeger, U.S.; Alan G. MacDiarmid, N. Zea.-U.S.; Hideki Shirakawa, Jpn.
2001	K. Barry Sharpless, William S. Knowles, U.S.; Ryoji Noyori, Jpn.
2002	John B. Fenn, U.S.; Koichi Tanaka, Jpn.; Kurt Wüthrich, Switz.
2003	Peter Agre, Roderick MacKinnon, U.S.
2004	Aaron Ciechanover, Avram Hershko, Isr.; Irwin Rose, U.S.
2005	Yves Chauvin, Fr.; Robert H. Grubbs, Richard R. Schrock, U.S.
2006	Roger D. Kornberg, U.S.
2007	Gerhard Ertl, Ger.
2008	Martin Chalfie, Roger Y. Tsien, Osamu Shimomura, U.S.
2009	Venkatraman Ramakrishnan, UK; Thomas A. Steitz, U.S.; Ada E. Yonath, Isr.
2010	Richard F. Heck, U.S.; Ei-ichi Negishi, Jpn.-U.S.; Akira Suzuki, Jpn.

Physiology or Medicine

1901	Emil A. von Behring, Ger.
1902	Sir Ronald Ross, UK
1903	Niels R. Finsen, Den.
1904	Ivan P. Pavlov, Russ.
1905	Robert Koch, Ger.
1906	Camillo Golgi, It.; Santiago Ramon y Cajal, Spain
1907	Charles L. A. Laveran, Fr.
1908	Paul Ehrlich, Ger.; Ilya Mechnikov, Fr.
1909	Emil T. Kocher, Switz.
1910	Albrecht Kossel, Ger.
1911	Allvar Gullstrand, Swed.
1912	Alexis Carrel, Fr.
1913	Charles R. Richet, Fr.
1914	Robert Bárány, Austria
1919	Jules Bordet, Belg.
1920	Schack A. S. Krogh, Den.
1922	Archibald V. Hill, UK; Otto F. Meyerhof, Ger.
1923	Frederick G. Banting, Can.; John J. R. Macleod, UK
1924	Willem Einthoven, Neth.
1926	Johannes A. G. Fibiger, Den.
1927	Julius Wagner-Jauregg, Austria
1928	Charles J. H. Nicolle, Fr.
1929	Christiaan Eijkman, Neth.; Sir Frederick G. Hopkins, UK
1930	Karl Landsteiner, U.S.

1931	Otto H. Warburg, Ger.
1932	Edgar D. Adrian, Sir Charles S. Sherrington, UK
1933	Thomas H. Morgan, U.S.
1934	George R. Minot, William P. Murphy, G. H. Whipple, U.S.
1935	Hans Spemann, Ger.
1936	Sir Henry H. Dale, UK; Otto Loewi, U.S.
1937	Albert Szent-Gyorgyi, Hung.-U.S.
1938	Corneille J. F. Heymans, Belg.
1939	Gerhard Domagk, Ger.
1943	Henrik C. P. Dam, Den.; Edward A. Doisy, U.S.
1944	Joseph Erlanger, Herbert S. Gasser, U.S.
1945	Ernst B. Chain, Sir Alexander Fleming, Sir Howard W. Florey, UK
1946	Hermann J. Muller, U.S.
1947	Carl F. Cori, Gerty T. Cori, U.S.; Bernardo A. Houssay, Arg.
1948	Paul H. Müller, Switz.
1949	Walter R. Hess, Switz.; Antonio Moniz, Port.
1950	Philip S. Hench, Edward C. Kendall, U.S.; Tadeus Reichstein, Switz.
1951	Max Theiler, U.S.
1952	Selman A. Waksman, U.S.
1953	Hans A. Krebs, UK; Fritz A. Lipmann, U.S.

1954	John F. Enders, Frederick C. Robbins, Thomas H. Weller, U.S.
1955	Alex H. T. Theorell, Swed.
1956	André F. Cournand, Dickinson W. Richards, U.S.; Werner Forssmann, Ger.
1957	Daniel Bovet, It.
1958	George W. Beadle, Edward L. Tatum, Joshua Lederberg, U.S.
1959	Arthur Kornberg, Severo Ochoa, U.S.
1960	Sir Frank Macfarlane Burnet, Austral.; Peter B. Medawar, UK
1961	Georg von Békésy, U.S.
1962	Francis H. C. Crick, Maurice H. F. Wilkins, UK; James D. Watson, U.S.
1963	Sir John C. Eccles, Austral.; Alan L. Hodgkin, Andrew F. Huxley, UK
1964	Konrad E. Bloch, U.S.; Feodor Lynen, Ger.
1965	François Jacob, André Lwoff, Jacques Monod, Fr.
1966	Charles B. Huggins, Peyton Rous, U.S.
1967	Ragnar Granit, Swed.; Haldan Keffer Hartline, George Wald, U.S.

1968 Robert W. Holley,
H. Gobind Khorana,
Marshall W. Nirenberg, U.S.
1969 Max Delbrück, Alfred D. Hershey,
Salvador Luria, U.S.
1970 Julius Axelrod, U.S.;
Sir Bernard Katz, UK;
Ulf von Euler, Swed.
1971 Earl W. Sutherland Jr., U.S.
1972 Gerald M. Edelman, U.S.;
Rodney R. Porter, UK
1973 Karl von Frisch, Ger.;
Konrad Lorenz, Austria;
Nikolaas Tinbergen, UK
1974 Albert Claude, Lux.-U.S.;
George Emil Palade, Rom.-U.S.;
Christian de Duve, Belg.
1975 David Baltimore,
Howard Temin, U.S.;
Renato Dulbecco, It.-U.S.
1976 Baruch S. Blumberg,
Daniel Carleton Gajdusek, U.S.
1977 Rosalyn S. Yalow,
Roger C.L. Guillemin,
Andrew V. Schally, U.S.
1978 Daniel Nathans,
Hamilton O. Smith, U.S.;
Werner Arber, Switz.
1979 Allan M. Cormack, U.S.;
Godfrey N. Hounsfield, UK
1980 Baruj Benacerraf, George Snell,
U.S.; Jean Dausset, Fr.

1981 Roger W. Sperry, David H. Hubel,
Torsten N. Wiesel, U.S.
1982 Sune K. Bergström,
Bengt I. Samuelsson, Swed.;
John R. Vane, UK
1983 Barbara McClintock, U.S.
1984 César Milstein, UK-Arg.;
Georges J. F. Köhler, Ger.;
Niels K. Jerne, UK-Den.
1985 Michael S. Brown,
Joseph L. Goldstein, U.S.
1986 Rita Levi-Montalcini, It.-U.S.;
Stanley Cohen, U.S.
1987 Susumu Tonegawa, Jpn.
1988 Gertrude B. Elion,
George H. Hitchings, U.S;
Sir James Black, UK
1989 J. Michael Bishop,
Harold E. Varmus, U.S.
1990 Joseph E. Murray,
E. Donnall Thomas, U.S.
1991 Edwin Neher, Bert Sakmann, Ger.
1992 Edmond H. Fisher,
Edwin G. Krebs, U.S.
1993 Phillip A. Sharp, U.S.;
Richard J. Roberts, UK
1994 Alfred G. Gilman,
Martin Rodbell, U.S.
1995 Edward B. Lewis,
Eric F. Wieschaus, U.S.;
Christiane Nüsslein-Volhard, Ger.

1996 Peter C. Doherty, Austral.;
Rolf M. Zinkernagel, Switz.
1997 Stanley B. Prusiner, U.S.
1998 Robert F. Furchgott,
Louis J. Ignarro, Ferid Murad, U.S.
1999 Günter Blobel, U.S.
2000 Arvid Carlsson, Swed.;
Paul Greengard, U.S.;
Eric R. Kandel, Austria-U.S.
2001 Leland H. Hartwell, U.S.;
R. Timothy (Tim) Hunt,
Sir Paul M. Nurse, UK
2002 Sydney Brenner, John E. Sulston,
UK; H. Robert Horvitz, U.S.
2003 Paul C. Lauterbur, U.S.;
Sir Peter Mansfield, UK
2004 Richard Axel, Linda B. Buck, U.S.
2005 Barry J. Marshall,
J. Robin Warren, Austral.
2006 Andrew Z. Fire, Craig C. Mello, U.S.
2007 Mario R. Capecchi,
Oliver Smithies, U.S.;
Sir Martin J. Evans, UK
2008 Harald zur Hausen, Ger.;
Françoise Barré-Sinoussi,
Luc Montagnier, Fr.
2009 Elizabeth H. Blackburn,
Carol W. Greider,
Jack W. Szostak, U.S.
2010 Robert G. Edwards, UK

Literature

1901 Rene F. A. Sully Prudhomme, Fr.
1902 Theodor Mommsen, Ger.
1903 Bjørnstjerne Bjørnson, Nor.
1904 Frédéric Mistral, Fr.;
José Echegaray y Eizaguirre, Spain
1905 Henryk Sienkiewicz, Pol.
1906 Giosuè Carducci, It.
1907 Rudyard Kipling, UK
1908 Rudolf C. Eucken, Ger.
1909 Selma Lagerlöf, Swed.
1910 Paul J. L. Heyse, Ger.
1911 Maurice Maeterlinck, Belg.
1912 Gerhart Hauptmann, Ger.
1913 Rabindranath Tagore, India
1915 Romain Rolland, Fr.
1916 Verner von Heidenstam, Swed.
1917 Karl A. Gjellerup,
Henrik Pontoppidan, Den.
1919 Carl F. G. Spitteler, Switz.
1920 Knut Hamsun, Nor.
1921 Anatole France, Fr.
1922 Jacinto Benavente, Spain
1923 William Butler Yeats, Ire.
1924 Wladyslaw S. Reymont, Pol.
1925 George Bernard Shaw, Ire.-UK
1926 Grazia Deledda, It.
1927 Henri Bergson, Fr.
1928 Sigrid Undset, Nor.
1929 Thomas Mann, Ger.
1930 Sinclair Lewis, U.S.
1931 Erik A. Karlfeldt, Swed.
1932 John Galsworthy, UK
1933 Ivan A. Bunin, USSR
1934 Luigi Pirandello, It.
1936 Eugene O'Neill, U.S.
1937 Roger Martin du Gard, Fr.

1938 Pearl S. Buck, U.S.
1939 Frans E. Sillanpää, Fin.
1944 Johannes V. Jensen, Den.
1945 Gabriela Mistral, Chile
1946 Hermann Hesse, Ger.-Switz.
1947 André Gide, Fr.
1948 T. S. Eliot, UK
1949 William Faulkner, U.S.
1950 Bertrand Russell, UK
1951 Pär F. Lagerkvist, Swed.
1952 François Mauriac, Fr.
1953 Sir Winston Churchill, UK
1954 Ernest Hemingway, U.S.
1955 Halldór K. Laxness, Ice.
1956 Juan Ramón Jiménez, Spain
1957 Albert Camus, Fr.
1958 Boris L. Pasternak, USSR
(declined)
1959 Salvatore Quasimodo, It.
1960 Saint-John Perse, Fr.
1961 Ivo Andric, Yugo.
1962 John Steinbeck, U.S.
1963 Giorgos Seferis, Greece
1964 Jean-Paul Sartre, Fr. (declined)
1965 Mikhail Sholokhov, USSR
1966 Shmuel Yosef Agnon, Isr.;
Nelly Sachs, Swed.
1967 Miguel Angel Asturias, Guat.
1968 Yasunari Kawabata, Jpn.
1969 Samuel Beckett, Ire.
1970 Aleksandr I. Solzhenitsyn, USSR
1971 Pablo Neruda, Chile
1972 Heinrich Böll, Ger.
1973 Patrick White, Austral.
1974 Eyvind Johnson,
Harry Edmund Martinson, Swed.

1975 Eugenio Montale, It.
1976 Saul Bellow, U.S.
1977 Vicente Aleixandre, Spain
1978 Isaac Bashevis Singer, U.S.
1979 Odysseus Elytis, Greece
1980 Czeslaw Milosz, Pol.-U.S.
1981 Elias Canetti, Bulg.-UK
1982 Gabriel García Márquez, Colombia
1983 William Golding, UK
1984 Jaroslav Siefert, Czech.
1985 Claude Simon, Fr.
1986 Wole Soyinka, Nigeria
1987 Joseph Brodsky, USSR-U.S.
1988 Naguib Mahfouz, Egypt
1989 Camilo José Cela, Spain
1990 Octavio Paz, Mex.
1991 Nadine Gordimer, S. Afr.
1992 Derek Walcott, St. Lucia
1993 Toni Morrison, U.S.
1994 Kenzaburo Oe, Jpn.
1995 Seamus Heaney, Ire.
1996 Wislawa Szymborska, Pol.
1997 Dario Fo, It.
1998 Jose Saramago, Por.
1999 Günter Grass, Ger.
2000 Gao Xingjian, China-Fr.
2001 Sir V. S. Naipaul, UK
2002 Imre Kertész, Hung.
2003 J. M. Coetzee, S. Afr.
2004 Elfriede Jelinek, Austria
2005 Harold Pinter, UK
2006 Orhan Pamuk, Turk.
2007 Doris Lessing, UK
2008 Jean-Marie Gustave Le Clézio, Fr.
2009 Herta Müller, Ger.
2010 Mario Vargas Llosa, Peru

Peace

1901 Jean H. Dunant, Switz.;
Frédéric Passy, Fr.
1902 Élie Ducommun,
Charles A. Gobat, Switz.
1903 Sir William R. Cremer, UK
1904 Institute of International Law
1905 Baroness Bertha von Suttner,
Austria
1906 Theodore Roosevelt, U.S.
1907 Ernesto T. Moneta, It.;
Louis Renault, Fr.

1908 Klas P. Arnoldson, Swed.;
Fredrik Bajer, Den.
1909 Auguste M. F. Beernaert, Belg.;
Paul H. B. B. d'Estournelles
de Constant, Fr.
1910 Permanent Intl. Peace Bureau
1911 Tobias M. C. Asser, Neth.;
Alfred H. Fried, Austria
1912 Elihu Root, U.S.
1913 Henri La Fontaine, Belg.
1917 International Red Cross

1919 Woodrow Wilson, U.S.
1920 Léon V. A. Bourgeois, Fr.
1921 Karl H. Branting, Swed.;
Christian L. Lange, Nor.
1922 Fridtjof Nansen, Nor.
1925 Sir J. Austen Chamberlain, UK;
Charles G. Dawes, U.S.
1926 Aristide Briand, Fr.;
Gustav Stresemann, Ger.
1927 Ferdinand E. Buisson, Fr.;
Ludwig Quidde, Ger.

1929 Frank B. Kellogg, U.S.	1964 Martin Luther King Jr., U.S.	1990 Mikhail S. Gorbachev, USSR
1930 Nathan Söderblom, Swed.	1965 UN Children's Fund (UNICEF)	1991 Aung San Suu Kyi, Burma
1931 Jane Addams,	1968 René Cassin, Fr.	1992 Rigoberta Menchú Tum, Guat.
Nicholas Murray Butler, U.S.	1969 Intl. Labor Organization	1993 Frederik W. de Klerk,
1933 Sir Norman Angell, UK	1970 Norman E. Borlaug, U.S.	Nelson Mandela, S. Afr.
1934 Arthur Henderson, UK	1971 Willy Brandt, Ger.	1994 Yasser Arafat, Pal.; Shimon Peres,
1935 Carl von Ossietzky, Ger.	1973 Henry Kissinger, U.S.;	Yitzhak Rabin, Isr.
1936 Carlos Saavedra Lamas, Arg.	Le Duc Tho, N. Viet. (Tho declined)	1995 Joseph Rotblat, Pol.-UK;
1937 Viscount Cecil of Chelwood, UK	1974 Eisaku Sato, Jpn.;	Pugwash Conferences
1938 Nansen International Office for	Seán MacBride, Ire.	1996 Bishop Carlos Ximenes Belo,
Refugees	1975 Andrei Sakharov, USSR	José Ramos-Horta, Timor-Leste
1944 International Red Cross	1976 Mairead Corrigan,	1997 Jody Williams, U.S.; Intl. Campaign
1945 Cordell Hull, U.S.	Betty Williams, N. Ire.	to Ban Landmines
1946 Emily G. Balch, John R. Mott, U.S.	1977 Amnesty International	1998 John Hume, David Trimble, N. Ire.
1947 Friends Service Council, UK; Amer.	1978 Anwar al-Sadat, Egypt;	1999 Doctors Without Borders
Friends Service Committee, U.S.	Menachem Begin, Isr.	(Médecins Sans Frontières), Fr.
1949 Lord John Boyd Orr of Brechin, UK	1979 Mother Teresa of Calcutta,	2000 Kim Dae-Jung, S. Kor.
1950 Ralph J. Bunche, U.S.	Alb.-India	2001 UN; Kofi Annan, Ghana
1951 Léon Jouhaux, Fr.	1980 Adolfo Pérez Esquivel, Arg.	2002 Jimmy Carter, U.S.
1952 Albert Schweitzer, Fr.	1981 Office of UN High Commissioner for	2003 Shirin Ebadi, Iran
1953 George C. Marshall, U.S.	Refugees	2004 Wangari Maathai, Kenya
1954 Office of UN High Commissioner for	1982 Alva Myrdal, Swed.;	2005 Mohamed ElBaradei, Egypt; Intl.
Refugees	Alfonso García Robles, Mex.	Atomic Energy Agency, Austria
1957 Lester B. Pearson, Can.	1983 Lech Walesa, Pol.	2006 Muhammad Yunus,
1958 Georges Pire, Belg.	1984 Bishop Desmond Tutu, S. Afr.	Grameen Bank, Bangl.
1959 Philip J. Noel-Baker, UK	1985 Intl. Physicians for the Prevention	2007 Intergovernmental Panel on Climate
1960 Albert J. Lutuli, S. Afr.	of Nuclear War, U.S.	Change, Switz.;
1961 Dag Hammarskjöld, Swed.	1986 Elie Wiesel, Rom.-U.S.	Albert Arnold Gore Jr., U.S.
1962 Linus C. Pauling, U.S.	1987 Oscar Arias Sánchez, Costa Rica	2008 Martti Ahtisaari, Fin.
1963 International Red Cross,	1988 UN Peacekeeping Forces	2009 Barack H. Obama, U.S.
League of Red Cross Societies	1989 Dalai Lama (Tenzin Gyatso), Tibet	2010 Liu Xiaobo, China

Nobel Memorial Prize in Economic Sciences

1969 Ragnar Frisch, Nor.;	1985 Franco Modigliani, It.-U.S.	2000 James J. Heckman,
Jan Tinbergen, Neth.	1986 James M. Buchanan, U.S.	Daniel L. McFadden, U.S.
1970 Paul A. Samuelson, U.S.	1987 Robert M. Solow, U.S.	2001 George A. Akerlof, A. Michael
1971 Simon Kuznets, U.S.	1988 Maurice Allais, Fr.	Spence, Joseph E. Stiglitz, U.S.
1972 Kenneth J. Arrow, U.S.;	1989 Trygve Haavelmo, Nor.	2002 Daniel Kahneman, U.S.-Isr.;
John R. Hicks, UK	1990 Harry M. Markowitz,	Vernon L. Smith, U.S.
1973 Wassily Leontief, U.S.	William F. Sharpe,	2003 Robert F. Engle, U.S.;
1974 Gunnar Myrdal, Swed.;	Merton H. Miller, U.S.	Clive W. J. Granger, UK
Friedrich A. von Hayek, Austria	1991 Ronald H. Coase, UK-U.S.	2004 Finn E. Kydland, Nor.;
1975 Tjalling Koopmans, Neth.-U.S.;	1992 Gary S. Becker, U.S.	Edward C. Prescott, U.S.
Leonid Kantorovich, USSR	1993 Robert W. Fogel,	2005 Robert J. Aumann, Isr.-U.S.;
1976 Milton Friedman, U.S.	Douglass C. North, U.S.	Thomas C. Schelling, U.S.
1977 Bertil Ohlin, Swed.;	1994 John C. Harsanyi, John F. Nash,	2006 Edmund S. Phelps, U.S.
James E. Meade, UK	U.S.; Reinhard Selten, Ger.	2007 Leonid Hurwicz, Eric S. Maskin,
1978 Herbert A. Simon, U.S.	1995 Robert E. Lucas Jr., U.S.	Roger B. Myerson, U.S.
1979 Theodore W. Schultz, U.S.;	1996 James A. Mirrlees, UK;	2008 Paul Krugman, U.S.
Sir Arthur Lewis, UK	William Vickrey, Can.-U.S.	2009 Elinor Ostrom,
1980 Lawrence R. Klein, U.S.	1997 Robert C. Merton, U.S.;	Oliver E. Williamson, U.S.
1981 James Tobin, U.S.	Myron S. Scholes, Can.-U.S.	2010 Peter A. Diamond, Dale T.
1982 George J. Stigler, U.S.	1998 Amartya Sen, India	Mortensen, U.S.; Christopher A.
1983 Gerard Debreu, Fr.-U.S.	1999 Robert A. Mundell, Can.	Pissarides, Cyprus-UK
1984 Richard Stone, UK		

Pulitzer Prizes in Journalism, Letters, and Music, 1917-2011

Endowed by Joseph Pulitzer (1847-1911), publisher of the *New York World*, in a bequest to Columbia Univ. and awarded annually, in years shown, for work published the previous year. Prizes are currently $10,000 in each category, except Public Service (in Journalism), for which a gold medal is given. The prize board began considering submissions from online-only publications in 2009. For letters and music, prizes in past years are listed; if a year is omitted, no award was given that year.

Pulitzer Prizes in Journalism, 2011

Public Service: *L.A. Times*, for its exposure of city-government corruption in Bell, CA.

Breaking News Reporting: No award.

Investigative Reporting: Page St. John, *Sarasota Herald-Tribune* (FL), for examining the weaknesses in the property-insurance system for Florida homeowners.

Explanatory Reporting: Mark Johnson, Kathleen Gallagher, Gary Porter, Lou Saldivar, and Alison Sherwood of the *Milwaukee Journal Sentinel* (WI), for their examination of an effort to use genetic technology to save a sick 4-year-old boy.

Local Reporting: Frank Main, Mark Konkol, and John J. Kim of the *Chicago Sun-Times*, for documenting violence in Chicago neighborhoods—examining victims, criminals, and detectives—as a code of silence prevails.

National Reporting: Jesse Eisinger and Jake Bernstein, *ProPublica*, for exposing Wall Street's questionable practices that contributed to the nation's economic meltdown and using digital tools to explain the complex subject.

International Reporting: Clifford J. Levy and Ellen Barry, *NY Times*, for covering the faltering justice system in Russia.

Feature Writing: Amy Ellis Nutt, *Star-Ledger* (Newark, NJ), for her probing story on the mysterious sinking of a commercial fishing boat that drowned 6 men.

Commentary: David Leonhardt, *NY Times*, for covering America's complicated economic questions.

Criticism: Sebastian Smee, *Boston Globe*, for his vivid and exuberant writing about art.

Editorial Writing: Joseph Rago, *Wall Street Journal*, for editorials challenging the health care reform advocated by Pres. Barack Obama.

Editorial Cartooning: Mike Keefe, *Denver Post*.

Breaking News Photography: Carol Guzy, Nikki Kahn, and Ricky Carioti, *Washington Post*, for their portrait of grief and desperation after an earthquake struck Haiti.

Feature Photography: Barbara Davidson, *L.A. Times*, for her story of innocent victims trapped in the crossfire of gang violence.

Pulitzer Prizes in Letters, 1917-2011

Fiction

1918 Ernest Poole, *His Family*
1919 Booth Tarkington, *The Magnificent Ambersons*
1921 Edith Wharton, *The Age of Innocence*
1922 Booth Tarkington, *Alice Adams*
1923 Willa Cather, *One of Ours*
1924 Margaret Wilson, *The Able McLaughlins*
1925 Edna Ferber, *So Big*
1926 Sinclair Lewis, *Arrowsmith* (refused prize)
1927 Louis Bromfield, *Early Autumn*
1928 Thornton Wilder, *Bridge of San Luis Rey*
1929 Julia M. Peterkin, *Scarlet Sister Mary*
1930 Oliver LaFarge, *Laughing Boy*
1931 Margaret Ayer Barnes, *Years of Grace*
1932 Pearl S. Buck, *The Good Earth*
1933 T. S. Stribling, *The Store*
1934 Caroline Miller, *Lamb in His Bosom*
1935 Josephine W. Johnson, *Now in November*
1936 Harold L. Davis, *Honey in the Horn*
1937 Margaret Mitchell, *Gone With the Wind*
1938 John P. Marquand, *The Late George Apley*
1939 Marjorie Kinnan Rawlings, *The Yearling*
1940 John Steinbeck, *The Grapes of Wrath*
1942 Ellen Glasgow, *In This Our Life*
1943 Upton Sinclair, *Dragon's Teeth*
1944 Martin Flavin, *Journey in the Dark*
1945 John Hersey, *A Bell for Adano*
1947 Robert Penn Warren, *All the King's Men*
1948 James A. Michener, *Tales of the South Pacific*
1949 James Gould Cozzens, *Guard of Honor*
1950 A. B. Guthrie Jr., *The Way West*
1951 Conrad Richter, *The Town*
1952 Herman Wouk, *The Caine Mutiny*
1953 Ernest Hemingway, *The Old Man and the Sea*
1955 William Faulkner, *A Fable*
1956 MacKinlay Kantor, *Andersonville*
1958 James Agee, *A Death in the Family*
1959 Robert Lewis Taylor, *The Travels of Jaimie McPheeters*
1960 Allen Drury, *Advise and Consent*
1961 Harper Lee, *To Kill a Mockingbird*
1962 Edwin O'Connor, *The Edge of Sadness*
1963 William Faulkner, *The Reivers*
1965 Shirley Ann Grau, *The Keepers of the House*
1966 Katherine Anne Porter, *Collected Stories*
1967 Bernard Malamud, *The Fixer*
1968 William Styron, *The Confessions of Nat Turner*
1969 N. Scott Momaday, *House Made of Dawn*
1970 Jean Stafford, *Collected Stories*
1972 Wallace Stegner, *Angle of Repose*
1973 Eudora Welty, *The Optimist's Daughter*
1975 Michael Shaara, *The Killer Angels*
1976 Saul Bellow, *Humboldt's Gift*
1978 James Alan McPherson, *Elbow Room*
1979 John Cheever, *The Stories of John Cheever*
1980 Norman Mailer, *The Executioner's Song*
1981 John Kennedy Toole, *A Confederacy of Dunces*
1982 John Updike, *Rabbit Is Rich*
1983 Alice Walker, *The Color Purple*
1984 William Kennedy, *Ironweed*
1985 Alison Lurie, *Foreign Affairs*
1986 Larry McMurtry, *Lonesome Dove*
1987 Peter Taylor, *A Summons to Memphis*
1988 Toni Morrison, *Beloved*
1989 Anne Tyler, *Breathing Lessons*
1990 Oscar Hijuelos, *The Mambo Kings Play Songs of Love*
1991 John Updike, *Rabbit at Rest*
1992 Jane Smiley, *A Thousand Acres*
1993 Robert Olen Butler, *A Good Scent From a Strange Mountain*
1994 E. Annie Proulx, *The Shipping News*
1995 Carol Shields, *The Stone Diaries*
1996 Richard Ford, *Independence Day*
1997 Steven Millhauser, *Martin Dressler: The Tale of an American Dreamer*
1998 Philip Roth, *American Pastoral*
1999 Michael Cunningham, *The Hours*
2000 Jhumpa Lahiri, *Interpreter of Maladies*
2001 Michael Chabon, *The Amazing Adventures of Kavalier & Clay*
2002 Richard Russo, *Empire Falls*
2003 Jeffrey Eugenides, *Middlesex*
2004 Edward P. Jones, *The Known World*
2005 Marilynne Robinson, *Gilead*
2006 Geraldine Brooks, *March*
2007 Cormac McCarthy, *The Road*
2008 Junot Díaz, *The Brief Wondrous Life of Oscar Wao*
2009 Elizabeth Strout, *Olive Kitteridge*
2010 Paul Harding, *Tinkers*
2011 Jennifer Egan, *A Visit From the Goon Squad*

Drama

1918 Jesse Lynch Williams, *Why Marry?*
1920 Eugene O'Neill, *Beyond the Horizon*
1921 Zona Gale, *Miss Lulu Bett*
1922 Eugene O'Neill, *Anna Christie*
1923 Owen Davis, *Icebound*
1924 Hatcher Hughes, *Hell-Bent for Heaven*
1925 Sidney Howard, *They Knew What They Wanted*
1926 George Kelly, *Craig's Wife*
1927 Paul Green, *In Abraham's Bosom*
1928 Eugene O'Neill, *Strange Interlude*
1929 Elmer Rice, *Street Scene*
1930 Marc Connelly, *The Green Pastures*
1931 Susan Glaspell, *Alison's House*
1932 George S. Kaufman, Morrie Ryskind, and Ira Gershwin, *Of Thee I Sing*
1933 Maxwell Anderson, *Both Your Houses*
1934 Sidney Kingsley, *Men in White*
1935 Zoe Akins, *The Old Maid*
1936 Robert E. Sherwood, *Idiot's Delight*
1937 George S. Kaufman and Moss Hart, *You Can't Take It With You*
1938 Thornton Wilder, *Our Town*
1939 Robert E. Sherwood, *Abe Lincoln in Illinois*
1940 William Saroyan, *The Time of Your Life*
1941 Robert E. Sherwood, *There Shall Be No Night*
1943 Thornton Wilder, *The Skin of Our Teeth*
1945 Mary Chase, *Harvey*
1946 Russel Crouse and Howard Lindsay, *State of the Union*
1948 Tennessee Williams, *A Streetcar Named Desire*
1949 Arthur Miller, *Death of a Salesman*
1950 Richard Rodgers, Oscar Hammerstein II, and Joshua Logan, *South Pacific*
1952 Joseph Kramm, *The Shrike*
1953 William Inge, *Picnic*
1954 John Patrick, *Teahouse of the August Moon*
1955 Tennessee Williams, *Cat on a Hot Tin Roof*
1956 Frances Goodrich and Albert Hackett, *The Diary of Anne Frank*
1957 Eugene O'Neill, *Long Day's Journey Into Night*
1958 Ketti Frings, *Look Homeward, Angel*
1959 Archibald MacLeish, *J. B.*
1960 George Abbott, Jerome Weidman, Sheldon Harnick, and Jerry Bock, *Fiorello!*
1961 Tad Mosel, *All the Way Home*
1962 Frank Loesser and Abe Burrows, *How to Succeed in Business Without Really Trying*
1965 Frank D. Gilroy, *The Subject Was Roses*
1967 Edward Albee, *A Delicate Balance*
1969 Howard Sackler, *The Great White Hope*
1970 Charles Gordone, *No Place to Be Somebody*
1971 Paul Zindel, *The Effect of Gamma Rays on Man-in-the-Moon Marigolds*
1973 Jason Miller, *That Championship Season*
1975 Edward Albee, *Seascape*
1976 Michael Bennett, James Kirkwood, Nicholas Dante, Marvin Hamlisch, and Edward Kleban, *A Chorus Line*
1977 Michael Cristofer, *The Shadow Box*
1978 Donald L. Coburn, *The Gin Game*
1979 Sam Shepard, *Buried Child*
1980 Lanford Wilson, *Talley's Folly*
1981 Beth Henley, *Crimes of the Heart*
1982 Charles Fuller, *A Soldier's Play*
1983 Marsha Norman, *'night, Mother*
1984 David Mamet, *Glengarry Glen Ross*
1985 Stephen Sondheim and James Lapine, *Sunday in the Park With George*
1987 August Wilson, *Fences*
1988 Alfred Uhry, *Driving Miss Daisy*
1989 Wendy Wasserstein, *The Heidi Chronicles*
1990 August Wilson, *The Piano Lesson*
1991 Neil Simon, *Lost in Yonkers*
1992 Robert Schenkkan, *The Kentucky Cycle*
1993 Tony Kushner, *Angels in America: Millennium Approaches*
1994 Edward Albee, *Three Tall Women*
1995 Horton Foote, *The Young Man From Atlanta*
1996 Jonathan Larson, *Rent*
1998 Paula Vogel, *How I Learned to Drive*
1999 Margaret Edson, *Wit*
2000 Donald Margulies, *Dinner With Friends*
2001 David Auburn, *Proof*
2002 Suzan-Lori Parks, *Topdog/Underdog*
2003 Nilo Cruz, *Anna in the Tropics*
2004 Doug Wright, *I Am My Own Wife*
2005 John Patrick Shanley, *Doubt, a parable*
2007 David Lindsay-Abaire, *Rabbit Hole*
2008 Tracy Letts, *August: Osage County*
2009 Lynn Nottage, *Ruined*
2010 Tom Kitt and Brian Yorkey, *Next to Normal*
2011 Bruce Norris, *Clybourne Park*

History (U.S.)

1917 J. J. Jusserand, *With Americans of Past and Present Days*
1918 James Ford Rhodes, *History of the Civil War*
1920 Justin H. Smith, *The War With Mexico*
1921 William Sowden Sims, *The Victory at Sea*
1922 James Truslow Adams, *The Founding of New England*
1923 Charles Warren, *The Supreme Court in United States History*
1924 Charles Howard McIlwain, *The American Revolution: A Constitutional Interpretation*
1925 Frederick L. Paxton, *A History of the American Frontier*
1926 Edward Channing, *A History of the U.S.*
1927 Samuel Flagg Bemis, *Pinckney's Treaty*
1928 V. L. Parrington, *Main Currents in American Thought*
1929 Fred A. Shannon, *The Organization and Administration of the Union Army, 1861-65*
1930 Claude H. Van Tyne, *The War of Independence*
1931 Bernadotte E. Schmitt, *The Coming of the War, 1914*
1932 Gen. John J. Pershing, *My Experiences in the World War*
1933 Frederick J. Turner, *The Significance of Sections in American History*
1934 Herbert Agar, *The People's Choice*
1935 Charles McLean Andrews, *The Colonial Period of American History*
1936 Andrew C. McLaughlin, *The Constitutional History of the United States*
1937 Van Wyck Brooks, *The Flowering of New England*
1938 Paul Herman Buck, *The Road to Reunion, 1865-1900*
1939 Frank Luther Mott, *A History of American Magazines*
1940 Carl Sandburg, *Abraham Lincoln: The War Years*
1941 Marcus Lee Hansen, *The Atlantic Migration, 1607-1860*
1942 Margaret Leech, *Reveille in Washington*
1943 Esther Forbes, *Paul Revere and the World He Lived In*
1944 Merle Curti, *The Growth of American Thought*
1945 Stephen Bonsal, *Unfinished Business*
1946 Arthur M. Schlesinger Jr., *The Age of Jackson*
1947 James Phinney Baxter III, *Scientists Against Time*
1948 Bernard De Voto, *Across the Wide Missouri*
1949 Roy F. Nichols, *The Disruption of American Democracy*
1950 O. W. Larkin, *Art and Life in America*
1951 R. Carlyle Buley, *The Old Northwest: Pioneer Period 1815-1840*
1952 Oscar Handlin, *The Uprooted*
1953 George Dangerfield, *The Era of Good Feelings*
1954 Bruce Catton, *A Stillness at Appomattox*
1955 Paul Horgan, *Great River: The Rio Grande in North American History*
1956 Richard Hofstadter, *The Age of Reform*
1957 George F. Kennan, *Russia Leaves the War*
1958 Bray Hammond, *Banks and Politics in America—From the Revolution to the Civil War*
1959 Leonard D. White and Jean Schneider, *The Republican Era, 1869-1901*
1960 Margaret Leech, *In the Days of McKinley*
1961 Herbert Feis, *Between War and Peace: The Potsdam Conference*
1962 Lawrence H. Gibson, *The Triumphant Empire: Thunderclouds Gather in the West*
1963 Constance McLaughlin Green, *Washington: Village and Capital, 1800-1878*
1964 Sumner Chilton Powell, *Puritan Village: The Formation of a New England Town*
1965 Irwin Unger, *The Greenback Era*
1966 Perry Miller, *Life of the Mind in America*
1967 William H. Goetzmann, *Exploration and Empire: The Explorer and Scientist in the Winning of the American West*
1968 Bernard Bailyn, *The Ideological Origins of the American Revolution*
1969 Leonard W. Levy, *Origin of the Fifth Amendment*
1970 Dean Acheson, *Present at the Creation: My Years in the State Department*
1971 James McGregor Burns, *Roosevelt: The Soldier of Freedom*
1972 Carl N. Degler, *Neither Black nor White*
1973 Michael Kammen, *People of Paradox: An Inquiry Concerning the Origins of American Civilization*
1974 Daniel J. Boorstin, *The Americans: The Democratic Experience*
1975 Dumas Malone, *Jefferson and His Time*
1976 Paul Horgan, *Lamy of Santa Fe*
1977 David M. Potter, *The Impending Crisis*
1978 Alfred D. Chandler Jr., *The Visible Hand: The Managerial Revolution in American Business*
1979 Don E. Fehrenbacher, *The Dred Scott Case: Its Significance in American Law and Politics*
1980 Leon F. Litwack, *Been in the Storm So Long*

1981 Lawrence A. Cremin, *American Education: The National Experience, 1783-1876*
1982 C. Vann Woodward, ed., *Mary Chesnut's Civil War*
1983 Rhys L. Issac, *The Transformation of Virginia, 1740-1790*
1985 Thomas K. McCraw, *Prophets of Regulation*
1986 Walter A. McDougall, *The Heavens and the Earth*
1987 Bernard Bailyn, *Voyagers to the West*
1988 Robert V. Bruce, *The Launching of Modern American Science, 1846-1876*
1989 Taylor Branch, *Parting the Waters: America in the King Years, 1954-63*; James M. McPherson, *Battle Cry of Freedom: The Civil War Era*
1990 Stanley Karnow, *In Our Image: America's Empire in the Philippines*
1991 Laurel Thatcher Ulrich, *A Midwife's Tale: The Life of Martha Ballard, based on her diary, 1785-1812*
1992 Mark E. Neely Jr., *The Fate of Liberty: Abraham Lincoln and Civil Liberties*
1993 Gordon S. Wood, *The Radicalism of the American Revolution*
1995 Doris Kearns Goodwin, *No Ordinary Time: Franklin and Eleanor Roosevelt: The Home Front in World War II*
1996 Alan Taylor, *William Cooper's Town: Power and Persuasion on the Frontier of the Early American Republic*
1997 Jack N. Rakove, *Original Meanings: Politics and Ideas in the Making of the Constitution*
1998 Edward J. Larson, *Summer for the Gods: The Scopes Trial and America's Continuing Debate Over Science and Religion*
1999 Edwin G. Burrows and Mike Wallace, *Gotham: A History of New York City to 1898*
2000 David M. Kennedy, *Freedom From Fear: The American People in Depression and War, 1929-1945*
2001 Joseph J. Ellis, *Founding Brothers: The Revolutionary Generation*
2002 Louis Menand, *The Metaphysical Club: A Story of Ideas in America*
2003 Rick Atkinson, *An Army at Dawn: The War in North Africa, 1942-1943*
2004 Steven Hahn, *A Nation Under Our Feet: Black Political Struggles in the Rural South From Slavery to the Great Migration*
2005 David Hackett Fischer, *Washington's Crossing*
2006 David M. Oshinsky, *Polio: An American Story*
2007 Gene Roberts and Hank Klibanoff, *The Race Beat: The Press, the Civil Rights Struggle, and the Awakening of a Nation*
2008 Daniel Walker Howe, *What Hath God Wrought: The Transformation of America, 1815-1848*
2009 Annette Gordon-Reed, *The Hemingses of Monticello: An American Family*
2010 Liaquat Ahamed, *Lords of Finance: The Bankers Who Broke the World*
2011 Eric Foner, *The Fiery Trial: Abraham Lincoln and American Slavery*

Biography or Autobiography

1917 Laura E. Richards and Maude Howe Elliott, assisted by Florence Howe Hall, *Julia Ward Howe*
1918 William Cabell Bruce, *Benjamin Franklin, Self-Revealed*
1919 Henry Adams, *The Education of Henry Adams*
1920 Albert J. Beveridge, *The Life of John Marshall*
1921 Edward Bok, *The Americanization of Edward Bok*
1922 Hamlin Garland, *A Daughter of the Middle Border*
1923 Burton J. Hendrick, *The Life and Letters of Walter H. Page*
1924 Michael Pupin, *From Immigrant to Inventor*
1925 M. A. DeWolfe Howe, *Barrett Wendell and His Letters*
1926 Harvey Cushing, *Life of Sir William Osler*
1927 Emory Holloway, *Whitman: An Interpretation in Narrative*
1928 Charles Edward Russell, *The American Orchestra and Theodore Thomas*
1929 Burton J. Hendrick, *The Training of an American: The Earlier Life and Letters of Walter H. Page*
1930 Marquis James, *The Raven*
1931 Henry James, *Charles W. Eliot*
1932 Henry F. Pringle, *Theodore Roosevelt*
1933 Allan Nevins, *Grover Cleveland*
1934 Tyler Dennett, *John Hay*
1935 Douglas Southall Freeman, *R. E. Lee*
1936 Ralph Barton Perry, *The Thought and Character of William James*
1937 Allan Nevins, *Hamilton Fish: The Inner History of the Grant Administration*
1938 Odell Shepard, *Pedlar's Progress*; Marquis James, *Andrew Jackson, 2 vols.*
1939 Carl Van Doren, *Benjamin Franklin*
1940 Ray Stannard Baker, *Woodrow Wilson, Life and Letters*
1941 Ola Elizabeth Winslow, *Jonathan Edwards*
1942 Forrest Wilson, *Crusader in Crinoline*

1943 Samuel Eliot Morison, *Admiral of the Ocean Sea* (Christopher Columbus)
1944 Carleton Mabee, *The American Leonardo: The Life of Samuel F. B. Morse*
1945 Russell Blaine Nye, *George Bancroft: Brahmin Rebel*
1946 Linny Marsh Wolfe, *Son of the Wilderness*
1947 William Allen White, *Autobiography of William Allen White*
1948 Margaret Clapp, *Forgotten First Citizen: John Bigelow*
1949 Robert E. Sherwood, *Roosevelt and Hopkins*
1950 Samuel Flagg Bemis, *John Quincy Adams and the Foundations of American Foreign Policy*
1951 Margaret Louise Coit, *John C. Calhoun: American Portrait*
1952 Merlo J. Pusey, *Charles Evans Hughes*
1953 David J. Mays, *Edmund Pendleton, 1721-1803*
1954 Charles A. Lindbergh, *The Spirit of St. Louis*
1955 William S. White, *The Taft Story*
1956 Talbot F. Hamlin, *Benjamin Henry Latrobe*
1957 John F. Kennedy, *Profiles in Courage*
1958 Douglas Southall Freeman, *George Washington*, Vols. I-VI
1959 Arthur Walworth, *Woodrow Wilson: American Prophet*
1960 Samuel Eliot Morison, *John Paul Jones*
1961 David Donald, *Charles Sumner and the Coming of the Civil War*
1963 Leon Edel, *Henry James: Vols. 2-3*
1964 Walter Jackson Bate, *John Keats*
1965 Ernest Samuels, *Henry Adams*
1966 Arthur M. Schlesinger Jr., *A Thousand Days*
1967 Justin Kaplan, *Mr. Clemens and Mark Twain*
1968 George F. Kennan, *Memoirs (1925-1950)*
1969 B. L. Reid, *The Man From New York: John Quinn and His Friends*
1970 T. Harry Williams, *Huey Long*
1971 Lawrence Thompson, *Robert Frost: The Years of Triumph, 1915-1938*
1972 Joseph P. Lash, *Eleanor and Franklin*
1973 W. A. Swanberg, *Luce and His Empire*
1974 Louis Sheaffer, *O'Neill, Son and Artist*
1975 Robert A. Caro, *The Power Broker: Robert Moses and the Fall of New York*
1976 R. W. B. Lewis, *Edith Wharton: A Biography*
1977 John E. Mack, *A Prince of Our Disorder: The Life of T. E. Lawrence*
1978 Walter Jackson Bate, *Samuel Johnson*
1979 Leonard Baker, *Days of Sorrow and Pain: Leo Baeck and the Berlin Jews*
1980 Edmund Morris, *The Rise of Theodore Roosevelt*
1981 Robert K. Massie, *Peter the Great: His Life and World*
1982 William S. McFeely, *Grant: A Biography*
1983 Russell Baker, *Growing Up*
1984 Louis R. Harlan, *Booker T. Washington*
1985 Kenneth Silverman, *The Life and Times of Cotton Mather*
1986 Elizabeth Frank, *Louise Bogan: A Portrait*
1987 David J. Garrow, *Bearing the Cross: Martin Luther King Jr. and the Southern Christian Leadership Conference*
1988 David Herbert Donald, *Look Homeward: A Life of Thomas Wolfe*
1989 Richard Ellmann, *Oscar Wilde*
1990 Sebastian de Grazia, *Machiavelli in Hell*
1991 Steven Naifeh and Gregory White Smith, *Jackson Pollock: An American Saga*
1992 Lewis B. Puller Jr., *Fortunate Son: The Healing of a Vietnam Vet*
1993 David McCullough, *Truman*
1994 David Levering Lewis, *W.E.B. DuBois: Biography of a Race, 1868-1919*
1995 Joan D. Hedrick, *Harriet Beecher Stowe: A Life*
1996 Jack Miles, *God: A Biography*
1997 Frank McCourt, *Angela's Ashes: A Memoir*
1998 Katharine Graham, *Personal History*
1999 A. Scott Berg, *Lindbergh*
2000 Stacy Schiff, *Véra (Mrs. Vladimir Nabokov)*
2001 David Levering Lewis, *W.E.B. Du Bois: The Fight for Equality and the American Century, 1919-1963*
2002 David McCullough, *John Adams*
2003 Robert Caro, *The Years of Lyndon Johnson: Master of the Senate*
2004 William Taubman, *Khrushchev: The Man and His Era*
2005 Mark Stevens and Annalyn Swan, *de Kooning: An American Master*
2006 Kai Bird and Martin J. Sherwin, *American Prometheus: The Triumph and Tragedy of J. Robert Oppenheimer*
2007 Debby Applegate, *The Most Famous Man in America: The Biography of Henry Ward Beecher*
2008 John Matteson, *Eden's Outcasts: The Story of Louisa May Alcott and Her Father*
2009 Jon Meacham, *American Lion: Andrew Jackson in the White House*
2010 T. J. Stiles, *The First Tycoon: The Epic Life of Cornelius Vanderbilt*
2011 Ron Chernow, *Washington: A Life*

American Poetry

1922 Edwin Arlington Robinson, *Collected Poems*
1923 Edna St. Vincent Millay, *The Ballad of the Harp-Weaver*; *A Few Figs From Thistles*; other works
1924 Robert Frost, *New Hampshire: A Poem With Notes and Grace Notes*
1925 Edwin Arlington Robinson, *The Man Who Died Twice*
1926 Amy Lowell, *What's O'Clock*
1927 Leonora Speyer, *Fiddler's Farewell*
1928 Edwin Arlington Robinson, *Tristram*
1929 Stephen Vincent Benet, *John Brown's Body*
1930 Conrad Aiken, *Selected Poems*
1931 Robert Frost, *Collected Poems*
1932 George Dillon, *The Flowering Stone*
1933 Archibald MacLeish, *Conquistador*
1934 Robert Hillyer, *Collected Verse*
1935 Audrey Wurdemann, *Bright Ambush*
1936 Robert P. Tristram Coffin, *Strange Holiness*
1937 Robert Frost, *A Further Range*
1938 Marya Zaturenska, *Cold Morning Sky*
1939 John Gould Fletcher, *Selected Poems*
1940 Mark Van Doren, *Collected Poems*
1941 Leonard Bacon, *Sunderland Capture*
1942 William Rose Benet, *The Dust Which Is God*
1943 Robert Frost, *A Witness Tree*
1944 Stephen Vincent Benet, *Western Star*
1945 Karl Shapiro, *V-Letter and Other Poems*
1947 Robert Lowell, *Lord Weary's Castle*
1948 W. H. Auden, *The Age of Anxiety*
1949 Peter Viereck, *Terror and Decorum*
1950 Gwendolyn Brooks, *Annie Allen*
1951 Carl Sandburg, *Complete Poems*
1952 Marianne Moore, *Collected Poems*
1953 Archibald MacLeish, *Collected Poems*
1954 Theodore Roethke, *The Waking*
1955 Wallace Stevens, *Collected Poems*
1956 Elizabeth Bishop, *Poems, North and South*
1957 Richard Wilbur, *Things of This World*
1958 Robert Penn Warren, *Promises: Poems 1954-1956*
1959 Stanley Kunitz, *Selected Poems 1928-1958*
1960 W. D. Snodgrass, *Heart's Needle*
1961 Phyllis McGinley, *Times Three: Selected Verse From Three Decades*
1962 Alan Dugan, *Poems*
1963 William Carlos Williams, *Pictures From Breughel*
1964 Louis Simpson, *At the End of the Open Road*
1965 John Berryman, *77 Dream Songs*
1966 Richard Eberhart, *Selected Poems*
1967 Anne Sexton, *Live or Die*
1968 Anthony Hecht, *The Hard Hours*
1969 George Oppen, *Of Being Numerous*
1970 Richard Howard, *Untitled Subjects*
1971 William S. Merwin, *The Carrier of Ladders*
1972 James Wright, *Collected Poems*
1973 Maxine Winokur Kumin, *Up Country*
1974 Robert Lowell, *The Dolphin*
1975 Gary Snyder, *Turtle Island*
1976 John Ashbery, *Self-Portrait in a Convex Mirror*
1977 James Merrill, *Divine Comedies*
1978 Howard Nemerov, *Collected Poems*
1979 Robert Penn Warren, *Now and Then: Poems 1976-1978*
1980 Donald Justice, *Selected Poems*
1981 James Schuyler, *The Morning of the Poem*
1982 Sylvia Plath, *The Collected Poems*
1983 Galway Kinnell, *Selected Poems*
1984 Mary Oliver, *American Primitive*
1985 Carolyn Kizer, *Yin*
1986 Henry Taylor, *The Flying Change*
1987 Rita Dove, *Thomas and Beulah*
1988 William Meredith, *Partial Accounts*
1989 Richard Wilbur, *New and Collected Poems*
1990 Charles Simic, *The World Doesn't End*
1991 Mona Van Duyn, *Near Changes*
1992 James Tate, *Selected Poems*
1993 Louise Glück, *The Wild Iris*
1994 Yusef Komunyakaa, *Neon Vernacular*
1995 Philip Levine, *The Simple Truth*
1996 Jorie Graham, *The Dream of the Unified Field*
1997 Lisel Mueller, *Alive Together: New and Selected Poems*
1998 Charles Wright, *Black Zodiac*
1999 Mark Strand, *Blizzard of One*
2000 C. K. Williams, *Repair*
2001 Stephen Dunn, *Different Hours*
2002 Carl Dennis, *Practical Gods*
2003 Paul Muldoon, *Moy Sand and Gravel*
2004 Franz Wright, *Walking to Martha's Vineyard*
2005 Ted Kooser, *Delights & Shadows*

2006 Claudia Emerson, *Late Wife*
2007 Natasha Tretheway, *Native Guard*
2008 Robert Hass, *Time and Materials*; Philip Schultz, *Failure*
2009 W. S. Merwin, *The Shadow of Sirius*
2010 Rae Armantrout, *Versed*
2011 Kay Ryan, *The Best of It: New and Selected Poems*

General Nonfiction

1962 Theodore H. White, *The Making of the President 1960*
1963 Barbara W. Tuchman, *The Guns of August*
1964 Richard Hofstadter, *Anti-Intellectualism in American Life*
1965 Howard Mumford Jones, *O Strange New World*
1966 Edwin Way Teale, *Wandering Through Winter*
1967 David Brion Davis, *The Problem of Slavery in Western Culture*
1968 Will and Ariel Durant, *Rousseau and Revolution*
1969 Norman Mailer, *The Armies of the Night*;
     Rene Jules Dubos, *So Human an Animal: How We Are Shaped by Surroundings and Events*
1970 Eric H. Erikson, *Gandhi's Truth*
1971 John Toland, *The Rising Sun*
1972 Barbara W. Tuchman, *Stilwell and the American Experience in China, 1911-1945*
1973 Frances FitzGerald, *Fire in the Lake: The Vietnamese and the Americans in Vietnam*;
     Robert Coles, *Children of Crisis, Vols. II and III*
1974 Ernest Becker, *The Denial of Death*
1975 Annie Dillard, *Pilgrim at Tinker Creek*
1976 Robert N. Butler, *Why Survive? Being Old in America*
1977 William W. Warner, *Beautiful Swimmers*
1978 Carl Sagan, *The Dragons of Eden*
1979 Edward O. Wilson, *On Human Nature*
1980 Douglas R. Hofstadter, *Gödel, Escher, Bach: An Eternal Golden Braid*
1981 Carl E. Schorske, *Fin-de-Siecle Vienna: Politics and Culture*
1982 Tracy Kidder, *The Soul of a New Machine*
1983 Susan Sheehan, *Is There No Place on Earth for Me?*
1984 Paul Starr, *Social Transformation of American Medicine*
1985 Studs Terkel, *The Good War*
1986 Joseph Lelyveld, *Move Your Shadow*;
     J. Anthony Lukas, *Common Ground*
1987 David K. Shipler, *Arab and Jew*
1988 Richard Rhodes, *The Making of the Atomic Bomb*
1989 Neil Sheehan, *A Bright Shining Lie: John Paul Vann and America in Vietnam*
1990 Dale Maharidge and Michael Williamson, *And Their Children After Them*
1991 Bert Holldobler and Edward O. Wilson, *The Ants*
1992 Daniel Yergin, *The Prize: The Epic Quest for Oil*

1993 Garry Wills, *Lincoln at Gettysburg*
1994 David Remnick, *Lenin's Tomb: The Last Days of the Soviet Empire*
1995 Jonathan Weiner, *The Beak of the Finch: A Story of Evolution in Our Time*
1996 Tina Rosenberg, *The Haunted Land: Facing Europe's Ghosts After Communism*
1997 Richard Kluger, *Ashes to Ashes: America's Hundred-Year Cigarette War, the Public Health, and the Unabashed Triumph of Philip Morris*
1998 Jared Diamond, *Guns, Germs, and Steel: The Fates of Human Societies*
1999 John McPhee, *Annals of the Former World*
2000 John W. Dower, *Embracing Defeat: Japan in the Wake of World War II*
2001 Herbert P. Bix, *Hirohito and the Making of Modern Japan*
2002 Diane McWhorter, *Carry Me Home: Birmingham, Alabama, the Climactic Battle of the Civil Rights Revolution*
2003 Samantha Power, *A Problem From Hell: America and the Age of Genocide*
2004 Anne Applebaum, *Gulag: A History*
2005 Steve Coll, *Ghost Wars*
2006 Caroline Elkins, *Imperial Reckoning: The Untold Story of Britain's Gulag in Kenya*
2007 Lawrence Wright, *The Looming Tower: Al-Qaeda and the Road to 9/11*
2008 Saul Friedländer, *The Years of Extermination: Nazi Germany and the Jews, 1939-1945*
2009 Douglas A. Blackmon, *Slavery by Another Name: The Re-Enslavement of Black Americans From the Civil War to World War II*
2010 David E. Hoffman, *The Dead Hand: The Untold Story of the Cold War Arms Race and Its Dangerous Legacy*
2011 Siddhartha Mukherjee, *The Emperor of All Maladies: A Biography of Cancer*

Special Citation in Letters

1944 Richard Rodgers and Oscar Hammerstein II, for *Oklahoma!*
1957 Kenneth Roberts, for his historical novels
1960 *The Armada*, by Garrett Mattingly
1961 *American Heritage Picture History of the Civil War*
1973 *George Washington, Vols. I-IV*, by James Thomas Flexner
1977 Alex Haley, for *Roots*
1978 E. B. White
1984 Theodore Seuss Geisel (Dr. Seuss)
1992 Art Spiegelman, for *Maus*
2006 Edmund S. Morgan
2007 Ray Bradbury

Pulitzer Prizes in Music, 1943-2011

1943 William Schuman, *Secular Cantata No. 2, A Free Song*
1944 Howard Hanson, *Symphony No. 4, Op. 34*
1945 Aaron Copland, *Appalachian Spring*
1946 Leo Sowerby, *The Canticle of the Sun*
1947 Charles E. Ives, *Symphony No. 3*
1948 Walter Piston, *Symphony No. 3*
1949 Virgil Thomson, *Louisiana Story*
1950 Gian-Carlo Menotti, *The Consul*
1951 Douglas Moore, *Giants in the Earth*
1952 Gail Kubik, *Symphony Concertante*
1954 Quincy Porter, *Concerto for Two Pianos and Orchestra*
1955 Gian-Carlo Menotti, *The Saint of Bleecker Street*
1956 Ernest Toch, *Symphony No. 3*
1957 Norman Dello Joio, *Meditations on Ecclesiastes*
1958 Samuel Barber, *Vanessa*
1959 John La Montaine, *Concerto for Piano and Orchestra*
1960 Elliott Carter, *Second String Quartet*
1961 Walter Piston, *Symphony No. 7*
1962 Robert Ward, *The Crucible*
1963 Samuel Barber, *Piano Concerto No. 1*
1966 Leslie Bassett, *Variations for Orchestra*
1967 Leon Kirchner, *Quartet No. 3*
1968 George Crumb, *Echoes of Time and the River*
1969 Karel Husa, *String Quartet No. 3*
1970 Charles W. Wuorinen, *Time's Encomium*
1971 Mario Davidovsky, *Synchronisms No. 6*
1972 Jacob Druckman, *Windows*
1973 Elliott Carter, *String Quartet No. 3*
1974 Donald Martino, *Notturno*
1975 Dominick Argento, *From the Diary of Virginia Woolf*
1976 Ned Rorem, *Air Music*
1977 Richard Wernick, *Visions of Terror and Wonder*
1978 Michael Colgrass, *Deja Vu for Percussion and Orchestra*
1979 Joseph Schwantner, *Aftertones of Infinity*
1980 David Del Tredici, *In Memory of a Summer Day*
1982 Roger Sessions, *Concerto for Orchestra*
1983 Ellen T. Zwilich, *Three Movements for Orchestra*
1984 Bernard Rands, *Canti del Sole*
1985 Stephen Albert, *Symphony, RiverRun*
1986 George Perle, *Wind Quintet IV*

1987 John Harbison, *The Flight Into Egypt*
1988 William Bolcom, *12 New Etudes for Piano*
1989 Roger Reynolds, *Whispers Out of Time*
1990 Mel Powell, *Duplicates: A Concerto for Two Pianos and Orchestra*
1991 Shulamit Ran, *Symphony*
1992 Wayne Peterson, *The Face of the Night, The Heart of the Dark*
1993 Christopher Rouse, *Trombone Concerto*
1994 Gunther Schuller, *Of Reminiscences and Reflections*
1995 Morton Gould, *Stringmusic*
1996 George Walker, *Lilacs for Voice and Orchestra*
1997 Wynton Marsalis, *Blood on the Fields*
1998 Aaron Jay Kernis, *String Quartet No. 2 (musica instrumentalis)*
1999 Melinda Wagner, *Concerto for Flute, Strings, and Percussion*
2000 Lewis Spratlan, *Life is a Dream, Opera in Three Acts: Act II, Concert Version*
2001 John Corigliano, *Symphony No. 2 for String Orchestra*
2002 Henry Brant, *Ice Field*
2003 John Adams, *On the Transmigration of Souls*
2004 Paul Moravec, *Tempest Fantasy*
2005 Steven Stucky, *Second Concerto for Orchestra*
2006 Yehudi Wyner, *Piano Concerto: "Chiavi in Mano"*
2007 Ornette Coleman, *Sound Grammar*
2008 David Lang, *The Little Match Girl Passion*
2009 Steve Reich, *Double Sextet*
2010 Jennifer Higdon, *Violin Concerto*
2011 Zhou Long, *Madame White Snake*

Special Citation in Music

1974 Roger Sessions
1976 Scott Joplin
1982 Milton Babbitt
1985 William Schuman
1998 George Gershwin
1999 Edward Kennedy "Duke" Ellington
2006 Thelonious Monk
2007 John Coltrane
2008 Bob Dylan
2010 Hank Williams

Man Booker Prize for Fiction, 1969-2011

The Booker Prize for fiction, established in 1968, is awarded annually in October for what is judged the best full-length novel written in English by a citizen of the UK, the Commonwealth, or the Irish Republic. In 2002, sponsorship of the award was taken over by Man Group PLC, the name was changed to the Man Booker Prize, and the amount was increased from £20,000 to £50,000 (about $80,000).

Year	Author, book	Year	Author, book
1969	P. H. Newby, *Something to Answer For*	1991	Ben Okri, *The Famished Road*
1970	Bernice Rubens, *The Elected Member*	1992	Michael Ondaatje, *The English Patient*;
1971	V. S. Naipaul, *In a Free State*		Barry Unsworth, *Sacred Hunger*
1972	John Berger, *G*	1993	Roddy Doyle, *Paddy Clarke Ha Ha Ha*
1973	J. G. Farrell, *The Siege of Krishnapur*	1994	James Kelman, *How Late It Was, How Late*
1974	Nadine Gordimer, *The Conservationist*;	1995	Pat Barker, *The Ghost Road*
	Stanley Middleton, *Holiday*	1996	Graham Swift, *Last Orders*
1975	Ruth Prawer Jhabvala, *Heat and Dust*	1997	Arundhati Roy, *The God of Small Things*
1976	David Storey, *Saville*	1998	Ian McEwan, *Amsterdam*
1977	Paul Scott, *Staying On*	1999	J. M. Coetzee, *Disgrace*
1978	Iris Murdoch, *The Sea, The Sea*	2000	Margaret Atwood, *The Blind Assassin*
1979	Penelope Fitzgerald, *Offshore*	2001	Peter Carey, *True History of the Kelly Gang*
1980	William Golding, *Rites of Passage*	2002	Yann Martel, *Life of Pi*
1981	Salman Rushdie, *Midnight's Children*[1]	2003	DBC Pierre, *Vernon God Little*
1982	Thomas Keneally, *Schindler's Ark*	2004	Alan Hollinghurst, *The Line of Beauty*
1983	J. M. Coetzee, *Life and Times of Michael K*	2005	John Banville, *The Sea*
1984	Anita Brookner, *Hotel du Lac*	2006	Kiran Desai, *The Inheritance of Loss*
1985	Keri Hulme, *The Bone People*	2007	Anne Enright, *The Gathering*
1986	Kingsley Amis, *The Old Devils*	2008	Aravind Adiga, *The White Tiger*
1987	Penelope Lively, *Moon Tiger*	2009	Hilary Mantel, *Wolf Hall*
1988	Peter Carey, *Oscar and Lucinda*	2010	Howard Jacobson, *The Finkler Question*
1989	Kazuo Ishiguro, *The Remains of the Day*	2011	Julian Barnes, *The Sense of an Ending*
1990	A. S. Byatt, *Possession*		

(1) Rushdie's *Midnight's Children* also won the Booker of Booker prize in 1993 and the Best of the Booker prize in 2008.

Newbery Medal, 1922-2011

The Newbery Medal was awarded annually in the years shown, by the Association for Library Service to Children, a division of the American Library Association, to the author of the most distinguished contribution to American literature for children.

Year	Book, author	Year	Book, author
1922	*The Story of Mankind*, Hendrik Willem van Loon	1968	*From the Mixed-Up Files of Mrs. Basil E. Frankweiler*,
1923	*The Voyages of Dr. Dolittle*, Hugh Lofting		E. L. Konigsburg
1924	*The Dark Frigate*, Charles Boardman Hawes	1969	*The High King*, Lloyd Alexander
1925	*Tales From Silver Lands*, Charles Joseph Finger	1970	*Sounder*, William H. Armstrong
1926	*Shen of the Sea*, Arthur Bowie Chrisman	1971	*The Summer of the Swans*, Betsy Byars
1927	*Smoky, the Cowhorse*, Will James	1972	*Mrs. Frisby and the Rats of NIMH*, Robert C. O'Brien
1928	*Gay-Neck*, Dhan Gopal Mukerji	1973	*Julie of the Wolves*, Jean George
1929	*The Trumpeter of Krakow*, Eric P. Kelly	1974	*The Slave Dancer*, Paula Fox
1930	*Hitty, Her First Hundred Years*, Rachel Field	1975	*M. C. Higgins the Great*, Virginia Hamilton
1931	*The Cat Who Went to Heaven*, Elizabeth Coatsworth	1976	*Grey King*, Susan Cooper
1932	*Waterless Mountain*, Laura Adams Armer	1977	*Roll of Thunder, Hear My Cry*, Mildred D. Taylor
1933	*Young Fu of the Upper Yangtze*, Elizabeth Foreman Lewis	1978	*Bridge to Terabithia*, Katherine Paterson
1934	*Invincible Louisa*, Cornelia Lynde Meigs	1979	*The Westing Game*, Ellen Raskin
1935	*Dobry*, Monica Shannon	1980	*A Gathering of Days*, Joan Blos
1936	*Caddie Woodlawn*, Carol Ryrie Brink	1981	*Jacob Have I Loved*, Katherine Paterson
1937	*Roller Skates*, Ruth Sawyer	1982	*A Visit to William Blake's Inn: Poems for Innocent*
1938	*The White Stag*, Kate Seredy		*and Experienced Travelers*, Nancy Willard
1939	*Thimble Summer*, Elizabeth Enright	1983	*Dicey's Song*, Cynthia Voigt
1940	*Daniel Boone*, James Daugherty	1984	*Dear Mr. Henshaw*, Beverly Cleary
1941	*Call It Courage*, Armstrong Sperry	1985	*The Hero and the Crown*, Robin McKinley
1942	*The Matchlock Gun*, Walter D. Edmonds	1986	*Sarah, Plain and Tall*, Patricia MacLachlan
1943	*Adam of the Road*, Elizabeth Janet Gray	1987	*The Whipping Boy*, Sid Fleischman
1944	*Johnny Tremain*, Esther Forbes	1988	*Lincoln: A Photobiography*, Russell Freedman
1945	*Rabbit Hill*, Robert Lawson	1989	*Joyful Noise: Poems for Two Voices*, Paul Fleischman
1946	*Strawberry Girl*, Lois Lenski	1990	*Number the Stars*, Lois Lowry
1947	*Miss Hickory*, Carolyn S. Bailey	1991	*Maniac Magee*, Jerry Spinelli
1948	*Twenty-One Balloons*, William Pène Du Bois	1992	*Shiloh*, Phyllis Reynolds Naylor
1949	*King of the Wind*, Marguerite Henry	1993	*Missing May*, Cynthia Rylant
1950	*The Door in the Wall*, Marguerite de Angeli	1994	*The Giver*, Lois Lowry
1951	*Amos Fortune, Free Man*, Elizabeth Yates	1995	*Walk Two Moons*, Sharon Creech
1952	*Ginger Pye*, Eleanor Estes	1996	*The Midwife's Apprentice*, Karen Cushman
1953	*Secret of the Andes*, Ann Nolan Clark	1997	*The View From Saturday*, E. L. Konigsburg
1954	*...And Now Miguel*, Joseph Krumgold	1998	*Out of the Dust*, Karen Hesse
1955	*The Wheel on the School*, Meindert DeJong	1999	*Holes*, Louis Sachar
1956	*Carry On, Mr. Bowditch*, Jean Lee Latham	2000	*Bud, Not Buddy*, Christopher Paul Curtis
1957	*Miracles on Maple Hill*, Virginia Sorensen	2001	*A Year Down Yonder*, Richard Peck
1958	*Rifles for Watie*, Harold Keith	2002	*A Single Shard*, Linda Sue Park
1959	*The Witch of Blackbird Pond*, Elizabeth George Speare	2003	*Crispin: The Cross of Lead*, Avi
1960	*Onion John*, Joseph Krumgold	2004	*The Tale of Despereaux*, Kate DiCamillo
1961	*Island of the Blue Dolphins*, Scott O'Dell	2005	*Kira-Kira*, Cynthia Kadohata
1962	*The Bronze Bow*, Elizabeth George Speare	2006	*Criss Cross*, Lynne Rae Perkins
1963	*A Wrinkle in Time*, Madeleine L'Engle	2007	*The Higher Power of Lucky*, Susan Patron
1964	*It's Like This, Cat*, Emily Cheney Neville	2008	*Good Masters! Sweet Ladies! Voices From a Medieval*
1965	*Shadow of a Bull*, Maja Wojciechowska		*Village*, Laura Amy Schlitz
1966	*I, Juan de Pareja*, Elizabeth Borton de Trevino	2009	*The Graveyard Book*, Neil Gaiman
1967	*Up a Road Slowly*, Irene Hunt	2010	*When You Reach Me*, Rebecca Stead
		2011	*Moon Over Manifest*, Clare Vanderpool

Caldecott Medal, 1938-2011

The Caldecott Medal was awarded annually in the years shown, by the Association for Library Service to Children, a division of the American Library Association, to the illustrator of the most distinguished American picture book for children.

Year	Book, illustrator	Year	Book, illustrator
1938	*Animals of the Bible*, Dorothy P. Lathrop	1975	*Arrow to the Sun*, Gerald McDermott
1939	*Mei Li*, Thomas Handforth	1976	*Why Mosquitoes Buzz in People's Ears*, Leo & Diane Dillon
1940	*Abraham Lincoln*, Ingri and Edgar Parin d'Aulaire	1977	*Ashanti to Zulu: African Traditions*, Leo & Diane Dillon
1941	*They Were Strong and Good*, Robert Lawson	1978	*Noah's Ark*, Peter Spier
1942	*Make Way for Ducklings*, Robert McCloskey	1979	*The Girl Who Loved Wild Horses*, Paul Goble
1943	*The Little House*, Virginia Lee Burton	1980	*Ox-Cart Man*, Barbara Cooney
1944	*Many Moons*, Louis Slobodkin	1981	*Fables*, Arnold Lobel
1945	*Prayer for a Child*, Elizabeth Orton Jones	1982	*Jumanji*, Chris Van Allsburg
1946	*The Rooster Crows*, Maude and Miska Petersham	1983	*Shadow*, Marcia Brown
1947	*The Little Island*, Leonard Weisgard	1984	*The Glorious Flight: Across the Channel With Louis Bleriot*, Alice and Martin Provensen
1948	*White Snow, Bright Snow*, Roger Duvoisin		
1949	*The Big Snow*, Berta and Elmer Hader	1985	*Saint George and the Dragon*, Trina Schart Hyman
1950	*Song of the Swallows*, Leo Politi	1986	*The Polar Express*, Chris Van Allsburg
1951	*The Egg Tree*, Karherine Milhous	1987	*Hey, Al*, Richard Egielski
1952	*Finders Keepers*, Nicolas, pseud. (Nicholas Mordvinoff)	1988	*Owl Moon*, John Schoenherr
1953	*The Biggest Bear*, Lynd Ward	1989	*Song and Dance Man*, Stephen Gammell
1954	*Madeline's Rescue*, Ludwig Bemelmans	1990	*Lon Po Po: A Red-Riding Hood Story From China*, Ed Young
1955	*Cinderella, or the Little Glass Slipper*, Marcia Brown	1991	*Black and White*, David Macaulay
1956	*Frog Went A-Courtin'*, Feodor Rojankovsky	1992	*Tuesday*, David Wiesner
1957	*A Tree Is Nice*, Marc Simont	1993	*Mirette on the High Wire*, Emily Arnold McCully
1958	*Time of Wonder*, Robert McCloskey	1994	*Grandfather's Journey*, Allen Say
1959	*Chanticleer and the Fox*, Barbara Cooney	1995	*Smoky Night*, David Diaz
1960	*Nine Days to Christmas*, Marie Hall Ets	1996	*Officer Buckle and Gloria*, Peggy Rathmann
1961	*Baboushka and the Three Kings*, Nicolas Sidjakov	1997	*Golem*, David Wisniewski
1962	*Once a Mouse*, Marcia Brown	1998	*Rapunzel*, Paul O. Zelinsky
1963	*The Snowy Day*, Ezra Jack Keats	1999	*Snowflake Bentley*, Mary Azarian
1964	*Where the Wild Things Are*, Maurice Sendak	2000	*Joseph Had a Little Overcoat*, Simms Taback
1965	*May I Bring a Friend?*, Beni Montressor	2001	*So You Want to be President?*, David Small
1966	*Always Room for One More*, Nonny Hogrogian	2002	*The Three Pigs*, David Wiesner
1967	*Sam, Bang, and Moonshine*, Evaline Ness	2003	*My Friend Rabbit*, Eric Rohmann
1968	*Drummer Hoff*, Ed Emberley	2004	*The Man Who Walked Between the Towers*, Mordicai Gerstein
1969	*The Fool of the World and the Flying Ship*, Uri Shulevitz	2005	*Kitten's First Full Moon*, Kevin Henkes
		2006	*The Hello, Goodbye Window*, Chris Raschka
1970	*Sylvester and the Magic Pebble*, William Steig	2007	*Flotsam*, David Wiesner
1971	*A Story A Story*, Gail E. Haley	2008	*The Invention of Hugo Cabret*, Brian Selznick
1972	*One Fine Day*, Nonny Hogrogian	2009	*The House in the Night*, Beth Krommes
1973	*The Funny Little Woman*, Blair Lent	2010	*The Lion & the Mouse*, Jerry Pinkney
1974	*Duffy and the Devil*, Margot Zemach	2011	*A Sick Day for Amos McGee*, Erin E. Stead

National Book Awards, 1950-2010

The National Book Awards (known as American Book Awards 1980-86) are administered by the National Book Foundation and have been given annually in the years shown, since 1950. The prizes, each valued at $10,000, are awarded to U.S. citizens for works published in the U.S. In some years, multiple awards were given for nonfiction in various categories; in such cases, the history and biography winner is listed. Selected additional awards in nonfiction are listed in footnotes.

Other National Book Awards, 2010: Poetry: Terrance Hayes, *Lighthead*. Young People's Literature: Kathryn Erskine, *Mockingbird*. Distinguished Contribution to American Letters: Tom Wolfe. Literarian Award: Joan Ganz Cooney.

Fiction

Year	Author, book	Year	Author, book
1950	Nelson Algren, *The Man With the Golden Arm*	1980	William Styron, *Sophie's Choice*
1951	William Faulkner, *The Collected Stories*	1981	Wright Morris, *Plains Song*
1952	James Jones, *From Here to Eternity*	1982	John Updike, *Rabbit Is Rich*
1953	Ralph Ellison, *Invisible Man*	1983	Alice Walker, *The Color Purple*
1954	Saul Bellow, *The Adventures of Augie March*	1984	Ellen Gilchrist, *Victory Over Japan*
1955	William Faulkner, *A Fable*	1985	Don DeLillo, *White Noise*
1956	John O'Hara, *Ten North Frederick*	1986	E. L. Doctorow, *World's Fair*
1957	Wright Morris, *The Field of Vision*	1987	Larry Heinemann, *Paco's Story*
1958	John Cheever, *The Wapshot Chronicle*	1988	Pete Dexter, *Paris Trout*
1959	Bernard Malamud, *The Magic Barrel*	1989	John Casey, *Spartina*
1960	Philip Roth, *Goodbye, Columbus*	1990	Charles Johnson, *Middle Passage*
1961	Conrad Richter, *The Waters of Kronos*	1991	Norman Rush, *Mating*
1962	Walker Percy, *The Moviegoer*	1992	Cormac McCarthy, *All the Pretty Horses*
1963	J. F. Powers, *Morte d'Urban*	1993	E. Annie Proulx, *The Shipping News*
1964	John Updike, *The Centaur*	1994	William Gaddis, *A Frolic of His Own*
1965	Saul Bellow, *Herzog*	1995	Philip Roth, *Sabbath's Theater*
1966	Katherine Anne Porter, *The Collected Stories*	1996	Andrea Barrett, *Ship Fever and Other Stories*
1967	Bernard Malamud, *The Fixer*	1997	Charles Frazier, *Cold Mountain*
1968	Thornton Wilder, *The Eighth Day*	1998	Alice McDermott, *Charming Billy*
1969	Jerzy Kosinski, *Steps*	1999	Ha Jin, *Waiting*
1970	Joyce Carol Oates, *Them*	2000	Susan Sontag, *In America*
1971	Saul Bellow, *Mr. Sammler's Planet*	2001	Jonathan Franzen, *The Corrections*
1972	Flannery O'Connor, *The Complete Stories*	2002	Julia Glass, *Three Junes*
1973	John Barth, *Chimera*	2003	Shirley Hazzard, *The Great Fire*
1974	Thomas Pynchon, *Gravity's Rainbow*	2004	Lily Tuck, *The News From Paraguay*
1974	Isaac Bashevis Singer, *A Crown of Feathers*	2005	William T. Vollmann, *Europe Central*
1975	Robert Stone, *Dog Soldiers*	2006	Richard Powers, *The Echo Maker*
1976	William Gaddis, *JR*	2007	Denis Johnson, *Tree of Smoke*
1977	Wallace Stegner, *The Spectator Bird*	2008	Peter Matthiessen, *Shadow Country*
1978	Mary Lee Settle, *Blood Ties*	2009	Colum McCann, *Let the Great World Spin*
1979	Tim O'Brien, *Going After Cacciato*	2010	Jaimy Gordon, *Lord of Misrule*

Nonfiction

Year	Author, title
1950	Ralph L. Rusk, *Ralph Waldo Emerson*
1951	Newton Arvin, *Herman Melville*
1952	Rachel Carson, *The Sea Around Us*
1953	Bernard A. De Voto, *The Course of an Empire*
1954	Bruce Catton, *A Stillness at Appomattox*
1955	Joseph Wood Krutch, *The Measure of Man*
1956	Herbert Kubly, *An American in Italy*
1957	George F. Kennan, *Russia Leaves the War*
1958	Catherine Drinker Bowen, *The Lion and the Throne*
1959	J. Christopher Herold, *Mistress to an Age: A Life of Madame De Stael*
1960	Richard Ellman, *James Joyce*
1961	William L. Shirer, *The Rise and Fall of the Third Reich*
1962	Lewis Mumford, *The City in History: Its Origins, Its Transformations, and Its Prospects*
1963	Leon Edel, *Henry James: Vol. II: The Conquest of London; Vol. III: The Middle Years*
1964	William H. McNeill, *The Rise of the West: A History of the Human Community*
1965	Louis Fisher, *The Life of Lenin*
1966	Arthur M. Schlesinger Jr., *A Thousand Days: John F. Kennedy in the White House*
1967	Peter Gay, *The Enlightenment, An Interpretation, Vol I: The Rise of Modern Paganism*
1968	George F. Kennan, *Memoirs: 1925-1950*[1]
1969	Winthrop D. Jordan, *White Over Black: American Attitudes Toward the Negro, 1550-1812*[2]
1970	T. Harry Williams, *Huey Long*[3]
1971	James MacGregor Burns, *Roosevelt: The Soldier of Freedom*
1972	Joseph P. Lash, *Eleanor and Franklin: The Story of Their Relationship, Based on Eleanor Roosevelt's Private Papers*
1973	James Thomas Flexner, *George Washington, Vol. IV: Anguish and Farewell, 1793-1799*[4]
1974	John Clive, *Macaulay, The Shaping of the Historian*; Douglas Day, *Malcolm Lowry: A Biography*[5]
1975	Richard B. Sewall, *The Life of Emily Dickinson*[6]
1976	David Brion Davis, *The Problem of Slavery in the Age of Revolution, 1770-1823*
1977	W. A. Swanberg, *Norman Thomas: The Last Idealist*[7]
1978	W. Jackson Bate, *Samuel Johnson*
1979	Arthur M. Schlesinger Jr., *Robert Kennedy and His Times*
1980	Tom Wolfe, *The Right Stuff*
1981	Maxine Hong Kingston, *China Men*
1982	Tracy Kidder, *The Soul of a New Machine*

Year	Author, title
1983	Fox Butterfield, *China: Alive in the Bitter Sea*
1984	Robert V. Remini, *Andrew Jackson and the Course of American Democracy, 1833-1845*
1985	J. Anthony Lukas, *Common Ground: A Turbulent Decade in the Lives of Three American Families*
1986	Barry Lopez, *Arctic Dreams*
1987	Richard Rhodes, *The Making of the Atom Bomb*
1988	Neil Sheehan, *A Bright Shining Lie: John Paul Vann and America in Vietnam*
1989	Thomas L. Friedman, *From Beirut to Jerusalem*
1990	Ron Chernow, *The House of Morgan: An American Banking Dynasty and the Rise of Modern Finance*
1991	Orlando Patterson, *Freedom*
1992	Paul Monette, *Becoming a Man: Half a Life Story*
1993	Gore Vidal, *United States: Essays 1952-1992*
1994	Sherwin B. Nuland, *How We Die: Reflections on Life's Final Chapter*
1995	Tina Rosenberg, *The Haunted Land: Facing Europe's Ghosts After Communism*
1996	James Carroll, *An American Requiem: God, My Father, and the War That Came Between Us*
1997	Joseph J. Ellis, *American Sphinx: The Character of Thomas Jefferson*
1998	Edward Ball, *Slaves in the Family*
1999	John W. Dower, *Embracing Defeat: Japan in the Wake of World War II*
2000	Nathaniel Philbrick, *In the Heart of the Sea: The Tragedy of the Whaleship Essex*
2001	Andrew Solomon, *The Noonday Demon: An Atlas of Depression*
2002	Robert A. Caro, *Master of the Senate: The Years of Lyndon Johnson*
2003	Carlos Eire, *Waiting for Snow in Havana: Confessions of a Cuban Boy*
2004	Kevin Boyle, *Arc of Justice: A Saga of Race, Civil Rights, and Murder in the Jazz Age*
2005	Joan Didion, *The Year of Magical Thinking*
2006	Timothy Egan, *The Worst Hard Time: The Untold Story of Those Who Survived the Great American Dust Bowl*
2007	Tim Weiner, *Legacy of Ashes: The History of the CIA*
2008	Annette Gordon-Reed, *The Hemingses of Monticello: An American Family*
2009	T. J. Stiles, *The First Tycoon: The Epic Life of Cornelius Vanderbilt*
2010	Patti Smith, *Just Kids*

(1) Science, Philosophy, & Religion: Jonathan Kozol, *Death at an Early Age*. (2) Arts & Letters: Norman Mailer, *The Armies of the Night: History as a Novel, the Novel as History*. (3) Arts & Letters: Lillian Hellman, *An Unfinished Woman: A Memoir*. (4) Contemp. Affairs: Frances FitzGerald, *Fire in the Lake: The Vietnamese and the Americans in Vietnam*. (5) Arts & Letters: Pauline Kael, *Deeper Into the Movies*. (6) Arts & Letters: Roger Shattuck, *Marcel Proust*; Lewis Thomas, *The Lives of a Cell: Notes of a Biology Watcher*. (7) Contemp. Thought: Bruno Bettelheim, *The Uses of Enchantment: The Meaning and Importance of Fairy Tales*.

Journalism Awards, 2011

National Journalism Awards, by Scripps Howard Foundation. Investigative Reporting: Marshall Allen and Alex Richards, *Las Vegas Sun*. Breaking News: CNBC. Public Service Reporting: Jason Felch, Jason Song, Doug Smith, Sandra Poindexter, and Ken Schwencke, *L.A. Times*. Editorial Writing: Linda Valdez, *Arizona Republic* (Phoenix). Commentary: Laurie Roberts, *Arizona Republic* (Phoenix). Human Interest Writing: Wright Thompson, *ESPN.com*. Environmental Reporting: *Times-Picayune* (New Orleans). Washington Reporting: Adam Liptak, *NY Times*. Editorial Cartooning: Mike Thompson, *Detroit Free Press*. Photojournalism: Lisa Krantz, *San Antonio Express-News*. Business/Economics Reporting: Paige St. John, *Sarasota Herald-Tribune* (FL). Community Journalism: Tracy Loew, *Statesman Journal* (Salem, OR). Radio In-Depth Reporting: Laura Sullivan and Steve Drummond, National Public Radio. TV/Cable In-Depth Reporting: Brett Shipp, Mark Smith, and Billy Bryant, WFAA-TV, Dallas. Distinguished Service to the First Amendment: *Burlington Free Press* (VT). College Cartoonist: John Vestevich, *Ferris State Torch*, Ferris State Univ. (Big Rapids, MI). Journalism Teacher of the Year: Joe Saltzman, USC. Journalism Administrator of the Year: Paul Parsons, Elon Univ. (NC).

National Magazine Awards, by American Society of Magazine Editors and Columbia Univ. Graduate School of Journalism. Magazine of the Year: *National Geographic*. **Print awards:** General Excellence in News, Sports, and Entertainment: *New York*; Literary, Political, and Professional: *Poetry*; Fashion, Service, and Lifestyle: *Women's Health*; Food, Travel, and Design: *Garden & Gun*; Finance, Technology, and Lifestyle: *Scientific American*; Special-Interest: *Los Angeles*. Design: *GQ*. Photography: *W*. News and Documentary Photography: *NY Times Magazine*. Feature Photography: *ESPN The Magazine*. Single-Topic Issue: *National Geographic*. Magazine Section: *New York*. Personal

Service: *Men's Health*. Leisure Interests: *Men's Journal*. Public Interest: *New Yorker*. Reporting: *Harper's Magazine*. Feature Writing: *Los Angeles*. Profile Writing: *NY Times Magazine*. Essays and Criticism: *Paris Review*. Columns and Commentary: *Vanity Fair*. Fiction: *Virginia Quarterly Review*. **Digital awards:** General Excellence, Service and Lifestyle: *Epicurious*; News and Opinion: *Slate*. Mobile Edition: *Esquire*. Blogging: *Tablet Magazine*.

George Foster Peabody Awards, by Univ. of Georgia, awarded to best in electronic media. *The Promised Land*, American Public Media. *Zimbabwe's Forgotten Children*, BBC Four. *The Good Wife*, CBS. Gulf Oil Spill coverage, CNN. *C-SPAN Video Library*, C-SPAN. *30 for 30*, ESPN. *Justified*, FX. *Burma VJ*; *For Neda*; *If God Is Willing and da Creek Don't Rise*; *Magic & Bird: A Courtship of Rivals*; *The Pacific*; *Temple Grandin*; *12th & Delaware*; HBO. *Who Killed Doc?*, KSTP-TV. *Covering Pakistan: War, Flood, and Social Issues*, NPR. *Trafficked: A Youth Radio Investigation*, NPR/All Things Considered. *Behind the Bail Bond System*, NPR/All Things Considered/Morning Edition. *Seeking Justice for Campus Rapes*, NPR and npr.org. *American Experience: My Lai*; *Elia Kazan: A Letter to Elia*; *Frontline: The Wounded Platoon*; *Great Performances: Macbeth*; *Independent Lens: Reel Injun: On the Trail of the Hollywood Indian*; *LennoNYC*; *POV: The Most Dangerous Man in America*; *Sherlock: A Study in Pink*; *William Kentridge: Anything Is Possible*; PBS. *The Moth Radio Hour*, public radio stations. *Wonders of the Solar System*, Science Channel. *Degrassi: My Body Is a Cage*, TeenNick. *Men of a Certain Age*, TNT. *The Cost of War: Traumatic Brain Injury: Coming Home a Different Person*, washingtonpost.com; *Bitter Lessons*, WFAA-TV. *Lucia's Letter*, WGCU-FM. *The Lord Is Not On Trial Here Today*, WILL-TV. *Radiolab*, WNYC-FM. *Reality Check: Where Are the Jobs?*, WTHR-TV.

Reuben Award, by National Cartoonists Society. Outstanding Cartoonist of the Year: Richard Thompson.

Miscellaneous Book Awards, 2011
(Awarded in 2011 unless otherwise noted.)

Academy of American Poets Awards. Wallace Stevens Award, for poetry mastery, $100,000 (2010): Galway Kinnell. Academy Fellowship, $25,000 (2010): Khaled Mattawa. Lenore Marshall Poetry Prize, $25,000 (2010): John Koethe, *Ninety-fifth Street*. James Laughlin Award, $5,000 (2010): Michael Dickman, *Flies*. Walt Whitman Award, $5,000: Elana Bell, *Eyes, Stones*. Raizíss/de Palchi Translation Prizes: Fellowship, $25,000: Dominic Siracusa, *Oramai*, by Emilio Villa. Book, $10,000 (2010): Paul Vangelisti, *The Position of Things: Collected Poems 1961-1992*, by Adriano Spatola. Harold Morton Landon Translation Award, $1,000: Jeffrey Angles, *Forest of Eyes: Selected Poems of Tada Chimako*.

American Academy of Arts and Letters. Gold Medal for Belles Lettres and Criticism: Eric Bentley. Award of Merit Medal for Drama, $10,000: John Patrick Shanley. Academy Awards in Literature, $7,500 each: Mark Doty, Alice Fulton, John Koethe, Colum McCann, Suzan-Lori Parks, Alex Ross, Leslie Marmon Silko, and Joseph Stroud. Addison M. Metcalf Award, $10,000: Matthea Harvey. Arthur Rense Poetry Prize (triennial), $20,000: David Wagoner. Benjamin H. Danks Award, $20,000: Karen Russell. E. M. Forster Award, $20,000: Rachel Seiffert. Harold D. Vursell Memorial Award, $10,000: Thomas Mallon. John Updike Award (biennial), $20,000: Tom Sleigh. Rome Fellowships in Literature: Matt Donovan, Suzanne Rivecca. Rosenthal Family Foundation Award, $10,000: Monique Truong, *Bitter in the Mouth*. Sue Kaufman Prize for First Fiction, $5,000: Brando Skyhorse, *The Madonnas of Echo Park*.

Bollingen Prize in American Poetry, $100,000, biennially, by the Yale Univ. Library: Susan Howe.

Coretta Scott King Awards, by American Library Assn., for African American authors and illustrators of outstanding books for children and young adults. Author: Rita Williams-Garcia, *One Crazy Summer*. Illustrator: Bryan Collier, *Dave the Potter: Artist, Poet, Slave*. New Talent: (author) Victoria Bond, T. R. Simon, *Zora and Me*; (illustrator) Sonia Lynn Sadler, *Seeds of Change*. Lifetime Achievement: Dr. Henrietta Mays Smith.

Costa Book Awards (2010): Book of the Year (formerly Whitbread Award): Jo Shapcott, *Of Mutability*. Novel: Maggie O'Farrell, *The Hand That First Held Mine*. First Novel: Kishwar Desai, *Witness the Night*. Biography: Edmund de Waal, *The Hare With Amber Eyes*. Poetry: Jo Shapcott, *Of Mutability*. Children's Book: Jason Wallace, *Out of Shadows*.

Edgar Awards, by the Mystery Writers of America. Novel: *The Lock Artist*, Steve Hamilton. First Novel by an American Author: *Rogue Island*, Bruce DeSilva. Paperback Original: *Long Time Coming*, Robert Goddard. Fact Crime: *Scoreboard, Baby: A Story of College Football, Crime, and Complicity*, Ken Armstrong and Nick Perry. Critical/Biographical: *Charlie Chan: The*

Untold Story of the Honorable Detective and His Rendezvous With American History, Yunte Huang. Short Story: "The Scent of Lilacs," Doug Allyn. Juvenile: *The Buddy Files: The Case of the Lost Boy*, Dori Hillestad Butler. Young Adult: *Interrogation of Gabriel James*, Charlie Price. Play: *The Psychic*, Sam Bobrick. Teleplay: "Episode 1," *Luther*, Neil Cross (BBC America). Grandmaster: Sara Paretsky.

Golden Kite Awards, by Society of Children's Book Writers and Illustrators. Fiction: *Turtle in Paradise*, Jennifer Holm. Nonfiction: *The Good, the Bad, and the Barbie*, Tanya Lee Stone. Picture Book Text: *Big Red Lollipop*, Rukhsana Khan. Picture Book Illustration: *A Pocket Full of Posies*, Salley Mavor.

Hugo Awards, by the World Science Fiction Society (WSFS). Novel: *Blackout/All Clear*, Connie Willis. Novella: *The Lifecycle of Software Objects*, Ted Chiang. Novelette: "The Emperor of Mars," Allen M. Steele. Short Story: "For Want of a Nail," Mary Robinette Kowal. Related Work: *Chicks Dig Time Lords*, ed. by Lynne M. Thomas and Tara O'Shea. Graphic Story: *Girl Genius, Vol. 10: Agatha Heterodyne and the Guardian Muse*, Kaja and Phil Foglio. Dramatic, long form: *Inception*, Christopher Nolan. Dramatic, short form: "The Pandorica Opens/The Big Bang," *Doctor Who*, Steven Moffat. Best New Writer (not a Hugo but admin. by WSFS): Lev Grossman.

Lincoln Prize, by Gettysburg College and the Gilder Lehrman Inst. of American History, ($50,000): *The Fiery Trial: Abraham Lincoln and American Slavery*, Eric Foner.

National Book Critics Circle Awards. Fiction: Jennifer Egan, *A Visit From the Goon Squad*. Nonfiction: Isabel Wilkerson, *The Warmth of Other Suns: The Epic Story of America's Great Migration*. Biography: Sarah Bakewell, *How To Live: Or, A Life of Montaigne in One Question and Twenty Attempts at an Answer*. Autobiography: Darin Strauss, *Half a Life*. Criticism: Clare Cavanagh, *Lyric Poetry and Modern Politics: Russia, Poland, and the West*. Poetry: C. D. Wright, *One With Others [a little book of her days]*. Ivan Sandrof Lifetime Achievement Award: Dalkey Archive Press. Nona Balakian Citation for Excellence in Reviewing: Parul Sehgal.

Nebula Awards, by the Science Fiction and Fantasy Writers of America. Novel: *Blackout/All Clear*, Connie Willis. Novella: *The Lady Who Plucked Red Flowers Beneath the Queen's Window*, Rachel Swirsky. Novelette: "That Leviathan Whom Thou Hast Made," Eric James Stone. Short Story (tie): "Ponies," Kij Johnson; "How Interesting: A Tiny Man," Harlan Ellison. Ray Bradbury Award: *Inception*. Andre Norton Award: *I Shall Wear Midnight*, Terry Pratchett.

PEN/Faulkner Award, for fiction, $15,000: Deborah Eisenberg, *The Collected Stories of Deborah Eisenberg*.

Spingarn Medal, 1915-2011

The Spingarn Medal has been awarded annually since 1915 (except in 1938) by the National Assoc. for the Advancement of Colored People for outstanding achievement by an African American.

1915 Ernest E. Just	1941 Richard Wright	1964 Roy Wilkins	1988 Frederick D. Patterson
1916 Charles Young	1942 A. Philip Randolph	1965 Leontyne Price	1989 Jesse Jackson
1917 Harry T. Burleigh	1943 William H. Hastie	1966 John H. Johnson	1990 L. Douglas Wilder
1918 William S. Braithwaite	1944 Charles Drew	1967 Edward W. Brooke	1991 Gen. Colin L. Powell
1919 Archibald H. Grimké	1945 Paul Robeson	1968 Sammy Davis Jr.	1992 Barbara Jordan
1920 W. E. B. Du Bois	1946 Thurgood Marshall	1969 Clarence M. Mitchell Jr.	1993 Dorothy I. Height
1921 Charles S. Gilpin	1947 Dr. Percy L. Julian	1970 Jacob Lawrence	1994 Maya Angelou
1922 Mary B. Talbert	1948 Channing H. Tobias	1971 Leon H. Sullivan	1995 John Hope Franklin
1923 George W. Carver	1949 Ralph J. Bunche	1972 Gordon Parks	1996 A. Leon Higginbotham
1924 Roland Hayes	1950 Charles H. Houston	1973 Wilson C. Riles	1997 Carl T. Rowan
1925 James W. Johnson	1951 Mabel K. Staupers	1974 Damon Keith	1998 Myrlie Evers-Williams
1926 Carter G. Woodson	1952 Harry T. Moore	1975 Henry (Hank) Aaron	1999 Earl G. Graves Sr.
1927 Anthony Overton	1953 Paul R. Williams	1976 Alvin Ailey	2000 Oprah Winfrey
1928 Charles W. Chesnutt	1954 Theodore K. Lawless	1977 Alex Haley	2001 Vernon E. Jordan Jr.
1929 Mordecai W. Johnson	1955 Carl Murphy	1978 Andrew Young	2002 John Lewis
1930 Henry A. Hunt	1956 Jack R. Robinson	1979 Rosa L. Parks	2003 Constance Baker Motley
1931 Richard B. Harrison	1957 Martin Luther King Jr.	1980 Dr. Rayford W. Logan	2004 Robert L. Carter
1932 Robert R. Moton	1958 Daisy Bates and the	1981 Coleman Young	2005 Oliver W. Hill
1933 Max Yergan	Little Rock Nine	1982 Dr. Benjamin E. Mays	2006 Dr. Benjamin S. Carson
1934 William T. B. Williams	1959 Duke Ellington	1983 Lena Horne	2007 John Conyers Jr.
1935 Mary McLeod Bethune	1960 Langston Hughes	1984 Thomas Bradley	2008 Ruby Dee
1936 John Hope	1961 Kenneth B. Clark	1985 Bill Cosby	2009 Julian Bond
1937 Walter White	1962 Robert C. Weaver	1986 Dr. Benjamin L. Hooks	2010 Cicely Tyson
1939 Marian Anderson	1963 Medgar W. Evers	1987 Percy E. Sutton	2011 Frankie Muse Freeman
1940 Louis T. Wright			

Miscellaneous Awards, 2011

(Awarded in 2011, unless otherwise noted.)

American Academy of Arts and Letters Architecture Awards. Arthur W. Brunner Memorial Prize, $5,000: Mack Scogin and Merrill Elam. Academy Awards, $7,500 each: Sylvia Lavin, William E. Massie, Julie VandenBerg Snow, Anthony Vidler.

American Academy of Arts and Letters Art Awards. Gold Medal in Painting: Cy Twombly. Distinguished Service to the Arts: Zelda Fichandler. Academy Awards, $7,500 each: John Bradford, Jonathan Lasker, Ron Nagle, Michelle Segre, Arlene Shechet. Jimmy Ernst Award, $10,000: Sal Sirugo. Rosenthal Family Foundation Award in Painting, $10,000: Amy Bennett.

American Academy of Arts and Letters Music Awards. Academy Awards, $7,500 each: Karim Al-Zand, David Dzubay, Steven Mackey, and Lewis Spratlan. Goddard Lieberson Fellowships, $15,000 each: John Aylward, Lansing McLoskey. Walter Hinrichsen Award: Rand Steiger. Charles Ives Fellowships, $15,000 each: Dan Visconti, Jay Wadley. Charles Ives Scholarships, $7,500 each: Christopher Cerrone, Louis Chiappetta, Michael Ippolito, Bryan Jacobs, Hannah Lash, Alex Mincek. Richard Rodgers Awards for Musical Theater: *Dogfight*, Peter Duchan, Benj Pasek, Justin Paul; *Gloryana*, Andrew Gerle.

Congressional Gold Medal, by Congress: Dr. Muhammad Yunus (Oct. 5, 2010); 100th Infantry Battalion and 442nd Regimental Combat Team, U.S. Army (Oct. 5, 2010).

Intel Science Talent Search. First place, $100,000 scholarship: Evan O'Dorney, Danville, CA; second place, $75,000 scholarship: Michelle Hackman, Great Neck, NY; third place, $50,000 scholarship: Matthew Miller, Elon, NC.

John F. Kennedy Center Honors. 2010: Merle Haggard, Jerry Herman, Bill T. Jones, Paul McCartney, Oprah Winfrey. 2011: Barbara Cook, Neil Diamond, Yo-Yo Ma, Sonny Rollins, Meryl Streep.

Library of the Year Award, by Gale and Library Journal, $10,000: King County Library System, WA.

MacArthur Fellows, by the John D. and Catherine T. MacArthur Foundation, $500,000 each: Jad Abumrad, Marie-Therese Connolly, Roland Fryer, Jeanne Gang, Elodie Ghedin, Markus Greiner, Kevin Guskiewicz, Peter Hessler, Tiya Miles, Matthew Nock, Francisco Núñez, Sarah Otto, Shwetak Patel, Dafnis Prieto, Kay Ryan, Melanie Sanford, William Seeley, Jacob Soll, A. E. Stallings, Ubaldo Vitali, Alisa Weilerstein, Yukiko Yamashita.

National Humanities Medal, by National Endowment for the Humanities (2010): Daniel Aaron, Bernard Bailyn, Jacques Barzun, Wendell E. Berry, Roberto González Echevarría, Stanley Nider Katz, Joyce Carol Oates, Arnold Rampersad, Philip Roth, Gordon S. Wood.

National Medal of the Arts, by the National Endowment for the Arts and the White House: Robert Brustein, Van Cliburn, Mark di Suvero, Donald Hall, Quincy Jones, Harper Lee, Sonny Rollins, Meryl Streep, James Taylor.

Presidential Medal of Freedom, by the White House. Pres. Obama announced recipients Nov. 17, 2010; medals presented Feb. 15, 2011: John H. Adams, Maya Angelou, Warren Buffett, Pres. George H. W. Bush, Jasper Johns, Gerda Weissmann Klein, Rep. John Lewis (D, GA), Dr. Tom Little (posthumous), Yo-Yo Ma, Sylvia Mendez, Chancellor Angela Merkel, Stan Musial, Bill Russell, Jean Kennedy Smith, John J. Sweeney. Pres. Obama announced and presented June 30, 2011: Robert Gates.

Pritzker Architecture Prize, by the Hyatt Foundation, $100,000: Eduardo Souto de Moura, Portugal.

Teacher of the Year, by Council of Chief State School Officers: Michelle Shearer, Chemistry, Urbana High School, Frederick, MD.

Templeton Prize, by Templeton Foundation, £1 mil (about $1.6 mil): Martin J. Rees.

Miss America Winners, 1921-2011

1921	Margaret Gorman, Washington, DC
1922-23	Mary Campbell, Columbus, Ohio
1924	Ruth Malcolmson, Philadelphia, Pennsylvania
1925	Fay Lamphier, Oakland, California
1926	Norma Smallwood, Tulsa, Oklahoma
1927	Lois Delander, Joliet, Illinois
1933	Marion Bergeron, West Haven, Connecticut
1935	Henrietta Leaver, Pittsburgh, Pennsylvania
1936	Rose Coyle, Philadelphia, Pennsylvania
1937	Bette Cooper, Bertrand Island, New Jersey
1938	Marilyn Meseke, Marion, Ohio
1939	Patricia Donnelly, Detroit, Michigan
1940	Frances Marie Burke, Philadelphia, Pennsylvania
1941	Rosemary LaPlanche, Los Angeles, California
1942	Jo-Caroll Dennison, Tyler, Texas
1943	Jean Bartel, Los Angeles, California
1944	Venus Ramey, Washington, DC
1945	Bess Myerson, New York City, New York
1946	Marilyn Buferd, Los Angeles, California
1947	Barbara Walker, Memphis, Tennessee
1948	BeBe Shopp, Hopkins, Minnesota
1949	Jacque Mercer, Litchfield, Arizona
1951	Yolande Betbeze, Mobile, Alabama
1952	Coleen Kay Hutchins, Salt Lake City, Utah
1953	Neva Jane Langley, Macon, Georgia
1954	Evelyn Margaret Ay, Ephrata, Pennsylvania
1955	Lee Meriwether, San Francisco, California
1956	Sharon Ritchie, Denver, Colorado
1957	Marian McKnight, Manning, South Carolina
1958	Marilyn Van Derbur, Denver, Colorado
1959	Mary Ann Mobley, Brandon, Mississippi
1960	Lynda Lee Mead, Natchez, Mississippi
1961	Nancy Fleming, Montague, Michigan
1962	Maria Fletcher, Asheville, North Carolina
1963	Jacquelyn Mayer, Sandusky, Ohio
1964	Donna Axum, El Dorado, Arkansas
1965	Vonda Kay Van Dyke, Phoenix, Arizona
1966	Deborah Irene Bryant, Overland Park, Kansas
1967	Jane Anne Jayroe, Laverne, Oklahoma
1968	Debra Dene Barnes, Moran, Kansas
1969	Judith Anne Ford, Belvidere, Illinois
1970	Pamela Anne Eldred, Birmingham, Michigan
1971	Phyllis Ann George, Denton, Texas
1972	Laurie Lea Schaefer, Columbus, Ohio
1973	Terry Anne Meeuwsen, DePere, Wisconsin
1974	Rebecca Ann King, Denver, Colorado
1975	Shirley Cothran, Fort Worth, Texas
1976	Tawney Elaine Godin, Yonkers, New York
1977	Dorothy Kathleen Benham, Edina, Minnesota
1978	Susan Perkins, Columbus, Ohio
1979	Kylene Barker, Galax, Virginia
1980	Cheryl Prewitt, Ackerman, Mississippi
1981	Susan Powell, Elk City, Oklahoma
1982	Elizabeth Ward, Russellville, Arkansas
1983	Debra Maffett, Anaheim, California
1984[1]	Suzette Charles, Mays Landing, New Jersey
1985	Sharlene Wells, Salt Lake City, Utah
1986	Susan Akin, Meridian, Mississippi
1987	Kellye Cash, Memphis, Tennessee
1988	Kaye Lani Rae Rafko, Monroe, Michigan
1989	Gretchen Carlson, Anoka, Minnesota
1990	Debbye Turner, Columbia, Missouri
1991	Marjorie Vincent, Oak Park, Illinois
1992	Carolyn Suzanne Sapp, Honolulu, Hawaii
1993	Leanza Cornett, Jacksonville, Florida
1994	Kimberly Aiken, Columbia, South Carolina
1995	Heather Whitestone, Birmingham, Alabama
1996	Shawntel Smith, Muldrow, Oklahoma
1997	Tara Dawn Holland, Overland Park, Kansas
1998	Kate Shindle, Evanston, Illinois
1999	Nicole Johnson, Roanoke, Virginia
2000	Heather Renee French, Maysville, Kentucky
2001	Angela Perez Baraquio, Honolulu, Hawaii
2002	Katie Harman, Gresham, Oregon
2003	Erika Harold, Urbana, Illinois
2004	Ericka Dunlap, Orlando, Florida
2005[2]	Deidre Downs, Birmingham, Alabama
2006	Jennifer Berry, Tulsa, Oklahoma
2007	Lauren Nelson, Lawton, Oklahoma
2008	Kirsten Haglund, Farmington Hills, Michigan
2009	Katie Stam, Seymour, Indiana
2010	Caressa Cameron, Fredricksburg, Virginia
2011	Teresa Scanlan, Gering, Nebraska

(1) Miss New York, Vanessa Williams, resigned July 23, 1984. (2) The Sept. 2005 Miss America Pageant and award were postponed until Jan. 2006, when the pageant was broadcast from Las Vegas, NV, by Country Music Television (CMT).

Entertainment Awards

Tony (Antoinette Perry) Awards, 2011

Play: War Horse, Nick Stafford
Musical: The Book of Mormon
Book of a musical: Trey Parker, Robert Lopez, Matt Stone, The Book of Mormon
Original score: Trey Parker, Robert Lopez, Matt Stone, The Book of Mormon
Play revival: The Normal Heart
Musical revival: Anything Goes
Actor, play: Mark Rylance, Jerusalem
Actress, play: Frances McDormand, Good People
Actor, musical: Norbert Leo Butz, Catch Me if You Can
Actress, musical: Sutton Foster, Anything Goes
Featured actor, play: John Benjamin Hickey, The Normal Heart
Featured actress, play: Ellen Barkin, The Normal Heart
Featured actor, musical: John Larroquette, How to Succeed in Business Without Really Trying
Featured actress, musical: Nikki M. James, The Book of Mormon
Director, play: Marianne Elliott, Tom Morris, War Horse

Director, musical: Casey Nicholaw, Trey Parker, The Book of Mormon
Choreography: Kathleen Marshall, Anything Goes
Orchestrations: Larry Hochman, Stephen Oremus, The Book of Mormon
Scenic design, play: Rae Smith, War Horse
Scenic design, musical: Scott Pask, The Book of Mormon
Costume design, play: Desmond Heeley, The Importance of Being Earnest
Costume design, musical: Tim Chappel, Lizzy Gardiner, Priscilla, Queen of the Desert
Regional theater: Lookingglass Theater Company, Chicago
Special Tony Award, lifetime achievement: Athol Fugard, Philip J. Smith
Isabelle Stevenson Award: Eve Ensler
Tony Honors for Excellence in the Theatre: William Berloni; The Drama Book Shop; Sharon Jensen and Alliance for Inclusion in the Arts
Special Tony Award: Handspring Puppet Company, South Africa

Tony Awards, 1948-2011

Year	Play	Musical	Year	Play	Musical
1948	Mister Roberts	No Award	1980	Children of a Lesser God	Evita
1949	Death of a Salesman	Kiss Me Kate	1981	Amadeus	42nd Street
1950	The Cocktail Party	South Pacific	1982	The Life and Adventures of Nicholas Nickelby	Nine
1951	The Rose Tattoo	Guys and Dolls	1983	Torch Song Trilogy	Cats
1952	The Fourposter	The King and I	1984	The Real Thing	La Cage aux Folles
1953	The Crucible	Wonderful Town	1985	Biloxi Blues	Big River
1954	The Teahouse of the August Moon	Kismet	1986	I'm Not Rappaport	The Mystery of Edwin Drood
1955	The Desperate Hours	The Pajama Game	1987	Fences	Les Miserables
1956	The Diary of Anne Frank	Damn Yankees	1988	M. Butterfly	Phantom of the Opera
1957	Long Day's Journey Into Night	My Fair Lady	1989	The Heidi Chronicles	Jerome Robbins' Broadway
1958	Sunrise at Campobello	The Music Man	1990	The Grapes of Wrath	City of Angels
1959	J.B.	Redhead	1991	Lost in Yonkers	The Will Rogers Follies
1960	The Miracle Worker	Fiorello!, The Sound of Music	1992	Dancing at Lughnasa	Crazy for You
1961	Becket	Bye, Bye Birdie	1993	Angels in America: Millennium Approaches	Kiss of the Spider Woman
1962	A Man for All Seasons	How to Succeed in Business Without Really Trying	1994	Angels in America: Perestroika	Passion
1963	Who's Afraid of Virginia Woolf?	A Funny Thing Happened on the Way to the Forum	1995	Love! Valour! Compassion!	Sunset Boulevard
1964	Luther	Hello, Dolly!	1996	Master Class	Rent
1965	The Subject Was Roses	Fiddler on the Roof	1997	The Last Night of Ballyhoo	Titanic
1966	Marat/Sade	Man of La Mancha	1998	Art	The Lion King
1967	The Homecoming	Cabaret	1999	Side Man	Fosse
1968	Rosencrantz and Guildenstern Are Dead	Hallelujah, Baby!	2000	Copenhagen	Contact
1969	The Great White Hope	1776	2001	Proof	The Producers
1970	Borstal Boy	Applause	2002	Edward Albee's The Goat or Who Is Sylvia?	Thoroughly Modern Millie
1971	Sleuth	Company	2003	Take Me Out	Hairspray
1972	Sticks and Bones	Two Gentleman of Verona	2004	I Am My Own Wife	Avenue Q
1973	That Championship Season	A Little Night Music	2005	Doubt	Monty Python's Spamalot
1974	The River Niger	Raisin	2006	The History Boys	Jersey Boys
1975	Equus	The Wiz	2007	The Coast of Utopia	Spring Awakening
1976	Travesties	A Chorus Line	2008	August: Osage County	In the Heights
1977	The Shadow Box	Annie	2009	God of Carnage	Billy Elliot, The Musical
1978	Da	Ain't Misbehavin'	2010	Red	Memphis
1979	The Elephant Man	Sweeney Todd	2011	War Horse	The Book of Mormon

Selected Daytime Emmy Awards, 2011

Drama series: The Bold and the Beautiful, CBS
Game show: Jeopardy!, synd.; Wheel of Fortune, synd.
Talk show, entertainment: The Ellen DeGeneres Show, synd.
Talk show, informative: The Dr. Oz Show, synd.
Actress: Laura Wright, General Hospital, ABC
Actor: Michael Park, As the World Turns, CBS
Game show host: Ben Bailey, Cash Cab, Discovery Channel

Talk show host: Dr. Mehmet Oz, The Dr. Oz Show, synd.; Regis Philbin, Kelly Ripa, Live With Regis and Kelly, synd.
Animated children's show: Penguins of Madagascar, Nickelodeon
Children's show: The Electric Company, PBS
Culinary show: Avec Eric, PBS
Legal/courtroom show: Judge Pirro, synd.
Lifestyle show: The Martha Stewart Show, Hallmark

Selected Prime-Time Emmy Awards, 2011

Drama series: Mad Men, AMC
Comedy series: Modern Family, ABC
Miniseries or movie: Downton Abbey, PBS
Variety, music, or comedy series: The Daily Show With Jon Stewart, Comedy Central
Lead actor, drama: Kyle Chandler, Friday Night Lights, DIRECTV
Lead actress, drama: Julianna Margulies, The Good Wife, CBS
Lead actor, comedy: Jim Parsons, The Big Bang Theory, CBS
Lead actress, comedy: Melissa McCarthy, Mike & Molly, CBS
Lead actor, miniseries/movie: Barry Pepper, The Kennedys, ReelzChannel
Lead actress, miniseries/movie: Kate Winslet, Mildred Pierce, HBO
Sup. actor, drama: Peter Dinklage, Game of Thrones, HBO

Sup. actress, drama: Margo Martindale, Justified, FX
Sup. actor, comedy: Ty Burrell, Modern Family, ABC
Sup. actress, comedy: Julie Bowen, Modern Family, ABC
Sup. actor, miniseries/movie: Guy Pearce, Mildred Pierce, HBO
Sup. actress, miniseries/movie: Maggie Smith, Downton Abbey, PBS
Reality-competition program: The Amazing Race, CBS
Director, drama: Martin Scorsese, Boardwalk Empire, HBO
Director, comedy: Michael Alan Spiller, Modern Family, ABC
Writing, drama: Jason Katims, Friday Night Lights, DIRECTV
Writing, comedy: Steven Levitan, Jeffrey Richman, Modern Family, ABC
Writing, variety, music, or comedy: The Daily Show With Jon Stewart, Comedy Central

Prime-Time Emmy Awards, 1952-2011

The Academy of Television Arts and Sciences presented the first Emmy Awards in 1949. Through the years, award categories have changed, but since 1952, the Academy has given out an outstanding comedy and drama award each year.

Year	Comedy	Drama	Year	Comedy	Drama
1952	Red Skelton Show, NBC	Studio One, CBS	1978	All in the Family, CBS	The Rockford Files, NBC
1953	I Love Lucy, CBS	Robert Montgomery Presents, NBC	1979	Taxi, ABC	Lou Grant, CBS
			1980	Taxi, ABC	Lou Grant, CBS
1954	I Love Lucy, CBS	The U.S. Steel Hour, ABC	1981	Taxi, ABC	Hill Street Blues, NBC
1955	Make Room for Daddy, ABC	The U.S. Steel Hour, ABC	1982	Barney Miller, ABC	Hill Street Blues, NBC
1956	Phil Silvers Show, CBS	Producer's Showcase, NBC	1983	Cheers, NBC	Hill Street Blues, NBC
1957	Phil Silvers Show, CBS	Requiem for a Heavyweight, CBS[1]	1984	Cheers, NBC	Hill Street Blues, NBC
			1985	The Cosby Show, NBC	Cagney & Lacey, CBS
1958	Phil Silvers Show, CBS	Gunsmoke, CBS	1986	Golden Girls, NBC	Cagney & Lacey, CBS
1959[2]	Jack Benny Show, CBS	*	1987	Golden Girls, NBC	L.A. Law, NBC
1960	Art Carney Special, NBC	Playhouse 90, CBS	1988	The Wonder Years, ABC	thirtysomething, ABC
1961	Jack Benny Show, CBS	Hallmark Hall of Fame: Macbeth, NBC	1989	Cheers, NBC	L.A. Law, NBC
			1990	Murphy Brown, CBS	L.A. Law, NBC
1962	Bob Newhart Show, CBS	The Defenders, CBS	1991	Cheers, NBC	L.A. Law, NBC
1963	Dick Van Dyke Show, CBS	The Defenders, CBS	1992	Murphy Brown, CBS	Northern Exposure, CBS
1964	Dick Van Dyke Show, CBS	The Defenders, CBS	1993	Seinfeld, NBC	Picket Fences, CBS
1965	Dick Van Dyke Show, CBS	Hallmark Hall of Fame: The Magnificent Yankee, NBC	1994	Frasier, NBC	Picket Fences, CBS
			1995	Frasier, NBC	NYPD Blue, ABC
1966	Dick Van Dyke Show, CBS	The Fugitive, ABC	1996	Frasier, NBC	ER, NBC
1967	The Monkees, NBC	Mission: Impossible, CBS	1997	Frasier, NBC	Law & Order, NBC
1968	Get Smart, NBC	Mission: Impossible, CBS	1998	Frasier, NBC	The Practice, ABC
1969	Get Smart, NBC	NET Playhouse, NET	1999	Ally McBeal, Fox	The Practice, ABC
1970	My World and Welcome to It, NBC	Marcus Welby, M.D., ABC	2000	Will & Grace, NBC	The West Wing, NBC
			2001	Sex and the City, HBO	The West Wing, NBC
1971	All in the Family, CBS	The Bold Ones: "The Senator," NBC	2002	Friends, NBC	The West Wing, NBC
			2003	Everybody Loves Raymond, CBS	The West Wing, NBC
1972	All in the Family, CBS	Masterpiece Theatre: Elizabeth R, PBS	2004	Arrested Development, Fox	The Sopranos, HBO
1973	All in the Family, CBS	The Waltons, CBS	2005	Everybody Loves Raymond, CBS	Lost, ABC
1974	M*A*S*H, CBS	Masterpiece Theatre: Upstairs, Downstairs; PBS	2006	The Office, NBC	24, Fox
1975	Mary Tyler Moore Show, CBS	Masterpiece Theatre: Upstairs, Downstairs; PBS	2007	30 Rock, NBC	The Sopranos, HBO
			2008	30 Rock, NBC	Mad Men, AMC
1976	Mary Tyler Moore Show, CBS	Police Story, NBC	2009	30 Rock, NBC	Mad Men, AMC
1977	Mary Tyler Moore Show, CBS	Masterpiece Theatre: Upstairs, Downstairs; PBS	2010	Modern Family, ABC	Mad Men, AMC
			2011	Modern Family, ABC	Mad Men, AMC

(1) "Best Single Program of the Year," shown on *Playhouse 90*, which was named "Best New Series." (2) Beginning in 1959, Emmys awarded for work in the season encompassing the previous and current year. (*) *Playhouse 90* (CBS) was best drama of 1 hour or longer; *Alcoa-Goodyear Theatre* (NBC) was best drama of less than 1 hour.

Golden Globe Awards, 2011

The Hollywood Foreign Press Association (then the Hollywood Foreign Correspondents Association) presented its first awards for achievement in film in 1944; television was considered for the first time in 1955.

Film

Drama: *The Social Network*
Comedy/musical: *The Kids Are All Right*
Actress, drama: Natalie Portman, *Black Swan*
Actress, comedy/musical: Annette Bening, *The Kids Are All Right*
Actor, comedy/musical: Paul Giamatti, *Barney's Version*
Sup. actress: Melissa Leo, *The Fighter*
Sup. actor: Christian Bale, *The Fighter*
Director: David Fincher, *The Social Network*
Screenplay: Aaron Sorkin, *The Social Network*
Animated film: *Toy Story 3*
Foreign-language film: *In a Better World* (Denmark)
Original score: Trent Reznor and Atticus Ross, *The Social Network*
Original song: "You Haven't Seen the Last of Me," *Burlesque*, w/m by Diane Warren
Cecil B. DeMille Award: Robert De Niro

Television

Series, drama: *Boardwalk Empire*, HBO
Series, comedy/musical: *Glee*, FOX
Actress, drama: Katey Sagal, *Sons of Anarchy*, FX
Actor, drama: Steve Buscemi, *Boardwalk Empire*, HBO
Actress, comedy/musical: Laura Linney, *The Big C*, Showtime
Actor, comedy/musical: Jim Parsons, *The Big Bang Theory*, CBS
Miniseries or made-for-TV movie: *Carlos*, Sundance Channel
Actress, miniseries/movie: Claire Danes, *Temple Grandin*, HBO
Actor, miniseries/movie: Al Pacino, *You Don't Know Jack*, HBO
Sup. actress: Jane Lynch, *Glee*, FOX
Sup. actor: Chris Colfer, *Glee*, FOX

People's Choice Awards, 2011

The first People's Choice Awards were presented in 1975. Sponsored by Procter & Gamble, the nominees and awards were initially selected by a Gallup Poll. Since 2005, winners have been selected by Internet voting.

Film

Movie: *The Twilight Saga: Eclipse*
Action movie: *Iron Man 2*
Comedy movie: *Grown Ups*
Family movie: *Toy Story 3*
Horror movie: *A Nightmare on Elm Street*
Movie actor, actress: Johnny Depp, Kristen Stewart
Star under 25: Zac Efron
Action star: Jackie Chan
Comedic star: Adam Sandler
On-screen team: *The Twilight Saga: Eclipse*

Music

Artists: Eminem, Katy Perry
Band: Paramore
Breakout music artist: Selena Gomez & the Scene
Country artist: Taylor Swift
Hip-hop artist: Eminem

Pop artist: Rihanna
R&B artist: Usher
Song: "Love the Way You Lie," Eminem feat. Rihanna
Music video: "Love the Way You Lie," Eminem feat. Rihanna
Online sensation: Katy Perry

Television

Drama: *House*
Comedy: *Glee*
Drama actor, actress: Hugh Laurie, Lisa Edelstein
Comedy actor, actress: Neil Patrick Harris, Jane Lynch
Talk show host: Conan O'Brien
Competition show: *American Idol*
Crime drama: *Lie to Me*
Sci-fi or fantasy show: *Fringe*
TV obsession: *Dexter*
New comedy: *$#*! My Dad Says*
New drama: *Hawaii Five-O*

Academy Awards (Oscars), 1927-2010

Year	Picture	Actor	Actress	Sup. Actor[1]	Sup. Actress[1]	Director
1927 -28	*Wings*	Emil Jannings *The Way of All Flesh*	Janet Gaynor *Seventh Heaven*			Frank Borzage *Seventh Heaven;* Lewis Milestone *Two Arabian Knights*
1928 -29	*Broadway Melody*	Warner Baxter *In Old Arizona*	Mary Pickford *Coquette*			Frank Lloyd *The Divine Lady*
1929 -30	*All Quiet on the Western Front*	George Arliss *Disraeli*	Norma Shearer *The Divorcee*			Lewis Milestone *All Quiet on the Western Front*
1930 -31	*Cimarron*	Lionel Barrymore *Free Soul*	Marie Dressler *Min and Bill*			Norman Taurog *Skippy*
1931 -32	*Grand Hotel*	Fredric March *Dr. Jekyll and Mr. Hyde;* Wallace Beery *The Champ*	Helen Hayes *The Sin of Madelon Claudet*			Frank Borzage *Bad Girl*
1932 -33	*Cavalcade*	Charles Laughton *The Private Life of Henry VIII*	Katharine Hepburn *Morning Glory*			Frank Lloyd *Cavalcade*
1934	*It Happened One Night*	Clark Gable *It Happened One Night*	Claudette Colbert *It Happened One Night*			Frank Capra *It Happened One Night*
1935	*Mutiny on the Bounty*	Victor McLaglen *The Informer*	Bette Davis *Dangerous*			John Ford *The Informer*
1936	*The Great Ziegfeld*	Paul Muni *Story of Louis Pasteur*	Luise Rainer *The Great Ziegfeld*	Walter Brennan *Come and Get It*	Gale Sondergaard *Anthony Adverse*	Frank Capra *Mr. Deeds Goes to Town*
1937	*Life of Emile Zola*	Spencer Tracy *Captains Courageous*	Luise Rainer *The Good Earth*	Joseph Schildkraut *Life of Emile Zola*	Alice Brady *In Old Chicago*	Leo McCarey *The Awful Truth*
1938	*You Can't Take It With You*	Spencer Tracy *Boys Town*	Bette Davis *Jezebel*	Walter Brennan *Kentucky*	Fay Bainter *Jezebel*	Frank Capra *You Can't Take It With You*
1939	*Gone With the Wind*	Robert Donat *Goodbye Mr. Chips*	Vivien Leigh *Gone With the Wind*	Thomas Mitchell *Stage Coach*	Hattie McDaniel *Gone With the Wind*	Victor Fleming *Gone With the Wind*
1940	*Rebecca*	James Stewart *The Philadelphia Story*	Ginger Rogers *Kitty Foyle*	Walter Brennan *The Westerner*	Jane Darwell *The Grapes of Wrath*	John Ford *The Grapes of Wrath*
1941	*How Green Was My Valley*	Gary Cooper *Sergeant York*	Joan Fontaine *Suspicion*	Donald Crisp *How Green Was My Valley*	Mary Astor *The Great Lie*	John Ford *How Green Was My Valley*
1942	*Mrs. Miniver*	James Cagney *Yankee Doodle Dandy*	Greer Garson *Mrs. Miniver*	Van Heflin *Johnny Eager*	Teresa Wright *Mrs. Miniver*	William Wyler *Mrs. Miniver*
1943	*Casablanca*	Paul Lukas *Watch on the Rhine*	Jennifer Jones *The Song of Bernadette*	Charles Coburn *The More the Merrier*	Katina Paxinou *For Whom the Bell Tolls*	Michael Curtiz *Casablanca*
1944	*Going My Way*	Bing Crosby *Going My Way*	Ingrid Bergman *Gaslight*	Barry Fitzgerald *Going My Way*	Ethel Barrymore *None But the Lonely Heart*	Leo McCarey *Going My Way*
1945	*The Lost Weekend*	Ray Milland *The Lost Weekend*	Joan Crawford *Mildred Pierce*	James Dunn *A Tree Grows in Brooklyn*	Anne Revere *National Velvet*	Billy Wilder *The Lost Weekend*
1946	*The Best Years of Our Lives*	Fredric March *The Best Years of Our Lives*	Olivia de Havilland *To Each His Own*	Harold Russell *The Best Years of Our Lives*	Anne Baxter *The Razor's Edge*	William Wyler *The Best Years of Our Lives*
1947	*Gentleman's Agreement*	Ronald Colman *A Double Life*	Loretta Young *The Farmer's Daughter*	Edmund Gwenn *Miracle on 34th Street*	Celeste Holm *Gentleman's Agreement*	Elia Kazan *Gentleman's Agreement*
1948	*Hamlet*	Laurence Olivier *Hamlet*	Jane Wyman *Johnny Belinda*	Walter Huston *Treasure of Sierra Madre*	Claire Trevor *Key Largo*	John Huston *Treasure of Sierra Madre*
1949	*All the King's Men*	Broderick Crawford *All the King's Men*	Olivia de Havilland *The Heiress*	Dean Jagger *Twelve O'Clock High*	Mercedes McCambridge *All the King's Men*	Joseph L. Mankiewicz *Letter to Three Wives*
1950	*All About Eve*	Jose Ferrer *Cyrano de Bergerac*	Judy Holliday *Born Yesterday*	George Sanders *All About Eve*	Josephine Hull *Harvey*	Joseph L. Mankiewicz *All About Eve*
1951	*An American in Paris*	Humphrey Bogart *The African Queen*	Vivien Leigh *A Streetcar Named Desire*	Karl Malden *A Streetcar Named Desire*	Kim Hunter *A Streetcar Named Desire*	George Stevens *A Place in the Sun*
1952	*The Greatest Show on Earth*	Gary Cooper *High Noon*	Shirley Booth *Come Back Little Sheba*	Anthony Quinn *Viva Zapata!*	Gloria Grahame *The Bad and the Beautiful*	John Ford *The Quiet Man*
1953	*From Here to Eternity*	William Holden *Stalag 17*	Audrey Hepburn *Roman Holiday*	Frank Sinatra *From Here to Eternity*	Donna Reed *From Here to Eternity*	Fred Zinnemann *From Here to Eternity*

Year	Picture	Actor	Actress	Sup. Actor[1]	Sup. Actress[1]	Director
1954	On the Waterfront	Marlon Brando On the Waterfront	Grace Kelly The Country Girl	Edmond O'Brien The Barefoot Contessa	Eva Marie Saint On the Waterfront	Elia Kazan On the Waterfront
1955	Marty	Ernest Borgnine Marty	Anna Magnani The Rose Tattoo	Jack Lemmon Mister Roberts	Jo Van Fleet East of Eden	Delbert Mann Marty
1956	Around the World in 80 Days	Yul Brynner The King and I	Ingrid Bergman Anastasia	Anthony Quinn Lust for Life	Dorothy Malone Written on the Wind	George Stevens Giant
1957	The Bridge on the River Kwai	Alec Guinness The Bridge on the River Kwai	Joanne Woodward The Three Faces of Eve	Red Buttons Sayonara	Miyoshi Umeki Sayonara	David Lean The Bridge on the River Kwai
1958	Gigi	David Niven Separate Tables	Susan Hayward I Want to Live	Burl Ives The Big Country	Wendy Hiller Separate Tables	Vincente Minnelli Gigi
1959	Ben-Hur	Charlton Heston Ben-Hur	Simone Signoret Room at the Top	Hugh Griffith Ben-Hur	Shelley Winters Diary of Anne Frank	William Wyler Ben-Hur
1960	The Apartment	Burt Lancaster Elmer Gantry	Elizabeth Taylor Butterfield 8	Peter Ustinov Spartacus	Shirley Jones Elmer Gantry	Billy Wilder The Apartment
1961	West Side Story	Maximilian Schell Judgment at Nuremberg	Sophia Loren Two Women	George Chakiris West Side Story	Rita Moreno West Side Story	Jerome Robbins, Robert Wise West Side Story
1962	Lawrence of Arabia	Gregory Peck To Kill a Mockingbird	Anne Bancroft The Miracle Worker	Ed Begley Sweet Bird of Youth	Patty Duke The Miracle Worker	David Lean Lawrence of Arabia
1963	Tom Jones	Sidney Poitier Lilies of the Field	Patricia Neal Hud	Melvyn Douglas Hud	Margaret Rutherford The V.I.P.s	Tony Richardson Tom Jones
1964	My Fair Lady	Rex Harrison My Fair Lady	Julie Andrews Mary Poppins	Peter Ustinov Topkapi	Lila Kedrova Zorba the Greek	George Cukor My Fair Lady
1965	The Sound of Music	Lee Marvin Cat Ballou	Julie Christie Darling	Martin Balsam A Thousand Clowns	Shelley Winters A Patch of Blue	Robert Wise The Sound of Music
1966	A Man for All Seasons	Paul Scofield A Man for All Seasons	Elizabeth Taylor Who's Afraid of Virginia Woolf?	Walter Matthau The Fortune Cookie	Sandy Dennis Who's Afraid of Virginia Woolf?	Fred Zinnemann A Man for All Seasons
1967	In the Heat of the Night	Rod Steiger In the Heat of the Night	Katharine Hepburn Guess Who's Coming to Dinner	George Kennedy Cool Hand Luke	Estelle Parsons Bonnie and Clyde	Mike Nichols The Graduate
1968	Oliver!	Cliff Robertson Charly	Katharine Hepburn The Lion in Winter; Barbra Streisand Funny Girl	Jack Albertson The Subject Was Roses	Ruth Gordon Rosemary's Baby	Sir Carol Reed Oliver!
1969	Midnight Cowboy	John Wayne True Grit	Maggie Smith The Prime of Miss Jean Brodie	Gig Young They Shoot Horses Don't They?	Goldie Hawn Cactus Flower	John Schlesinger Midnight Cowboy
1970	Patton	George C. Scott Patton (refused)	Glenda Jackson Women in Love	John Mills Ryan's Daughter	Helen Hayes Airport	Franklin Schaffner Patton
1971	The French Connection	Gene Hackman The French Connection	Jane Fonda Klute	Ben Johnson The Last Picture Show	Cloris Leachman The Last Picture Show	William Friedkin The French Connection
1972	The Godfather	Marlon Brando The Godfather (refused)	Liza Minnelli Cabaret	Joel Grey Cabaret	Eileen Heckart Butterflies Are Free	Bob Fosse Cabaret
1973	The Sting	Jack Lemmon Save the Tiger	Glenda Jackson A Touch of Class	John Houseman The Paper Chase	Tatum O'Neal Paper Moon	George Roy Hill The Sting
1974	The Godfather Part II	Art Carney Harry and Tonto	Ellen Burstyn Alice Doesn't Live Here Anymore	Robert DeNiro The Godfather Part II	Ingrid Bergman Murder on the Orient Express	Francis Ford Coppola The Godfather Part II
1975	One Flew Over the Cuckoo's Nest	Jack Nicholson One Flew Over the Cuckoo's Nest	Louise Fletcher One Flew Over the Cuckoo's Nest	George Burns The Sunshine Boys	Lee Grant Shampoo	Milos Forman One Flew Over the Cuckoo's Nest
1976	Rocky	Peter Finch Network	Faye Dunaway Network	Jason Robards All the President's Men	Beatrice Straight Network	John G. Avildsen Rocky
1977	Annie Hall	Richard Dreyfuss The Goodbye Girl	Diane Keaton Annie Hall	Jason Robards Julia	Vanessa Redgrave Julia	Woody Allen Annie Hall
1978	The Deer Hunter	Jon Voight Coming Home	Jane Fonda Coming Home	Christopher Walken The Deer Hunter	Maggie Smith California Suite	Michael Cimino The Deer Hunter
1979	Kramer vs. Kramer	Dustin Hoffman Kramer vs. Kramer	Sally Field Norma Rae	Melvyn Douglas Being There	Meryl Streep Kramer vs. Kramer	Robert Benton Kramer vs. Kramer
1980	Ordinary People	Robert DeNiro Raging Bull	Sissy Spacek Coal Miner's Daughter	Timothy Hutton Ordinary People	Mary Steenburgen Melvin and Howard	Robert Redford Ordinary People
1981	Chariots of Fire	Henry Fonda On Golden Pond	Katharine Hepburn On Golden Pond	John Gielgud Arthur	Maureen Stapleton Reds	Warren Beatty Reds
1982	Gandhi	Ben Kingsley Gandhi	Meryl Streep Sophie's Choice	Louis Gossett Jr. An Officer and a Gentleman	Jessica Lange Tootsie	Richard Attenborough Gandhi
1983	Terms of Endearment	Robert Duvall Tender Mercies	Shirley MacLaine Terms of Endearment	Jack Nicholson Terms of Endearment	Linda Hunt The Year of Living Dangerously	James L. Brooks Terms of Endearment

Year	Picture	Actor	Actress	Sup. Actor[1]	Sup. Actress[1]	Director
1984	Amadeus	F. Murray Abraham *Amadeus*	Sally Field *Places in the Heart*	Haing S. Ngor *The Killing Fields*	Peggy Ashcroft *A Passage to India*	Milos Forman *Amadeus*
1985	Out of Africa	William Hurt *Kiss of the Spider Woman*	Geraldine Page *The Trip to Bountiful*	Don Ameche *Cocoon*	Anjelica Huston *Prizzi's Honor*	Sydney Pollack *Out of Africa*
1986	Platoon	Paul Newman *The Color of Money*	Marlee Matlin *Children of a Lesser God*	Michael Caine *Hannah and Her Sisters*	Dianne Wiest *Hannah and Her Sisters*	Oliver Stone *Platoon*
1987	The Last Emperor	Michael Douglas *Wall Street*	Cher *Moonstruck*	Sean Connery *The Untouchables*	Olympia Dukakis *Moonstruck*	Bernardo Bertolucci *The Last Emperor*
1988	Rain Man	Dustin Hoffman *Rain Man*	Jodie Foster *The Accused*	Kevin Kline *A Fish Called Wanda*	Geena Davis *The Accidental Tourist*	Barry Levinson *Rain Man*
1989	Driving Miss Daisy	Daniel Day-Lewis *My Left Foot*	Jessica Tandy *Driving Miss Daisy*	Denzel Washington *Glory*	Brenda Fricker *My Left Foot*	Oliver Stone *Born on the Fourth of July*
1990	Dances With Wolves	Jeremy Irons *Reversal of Fortune*	Kathy Bates *Misery*	Joe Pesci *Goodfellas*	Whoopi Goldberg *Ghost*	Kevin Costner *Dances With Wolves*
1991	The Silence of the Lambs	Anthony Hopkins *The Silence of the Lambs*	Jodie Foster *The Silence of the Lambs*	Jack Palance *City Slickers*	Mercedes Ruehl *The Fisher King*	Jonathan Demme *The Silence of the Lambs*
1992	Unforgiven	Al Pacino *Scent of a Woman*	Emma Thompson *Howards End*	Gene Hackman *Unforgiven*	Marisa Tomei *My Cousin Vinny*	Clint Eastwood *Unforgiven*
1993	Schindler's List	Tom Hanks *Philadelphia*	Holly Hunter *The Piano*	Tommy Lee Jones *The Fugitive*	Anna Paquin *The Piano*	Steven Spielberg *Schindler's List*
1994	Forrest Gump	Tom Hanks *Forrest Gump*	Jessica Lange *Blue Sky*	Martin Landau *Ed Wood*	Dianne Wiest *Bullets Over Broadway*	Robert Zemeckis *Forrest Gump*
1995	Braveheart	Nicolas Cage *Leaving Las Vegas*	Susan Sarandon *Dead Man Walking*	Kevin Spacey *The Usual Suspects*	Mira Sorvino *Mighty Aphrodite*	Mel Gibson *Braveheart*
1996	The English Patient	Geoffrey Rush *Shine*	Frances McDormand *Fargo*	Cuba Gooding Jr. *Jerry Maguire*	Juliette Binoche *The English Patient*	Anthony Minghella *The English Patient*
1997	Titanic	Jack Nicholson *As Good As It Gets*	Helen Hunt *As Good As It Gets*	Robin Williams *Good Will Hunting*	Kim Basinger *L.A. Confidential*	James Cameron *Titanic*
1998	Shakespeare in Love	Roberto Benigni *Life Is Beautiful*	Gwyneth Paltrow *Shakespeare in Love*	James Coburn *Affliction*	Judi Dench *Shakespeare in Love*	Steven Spielberg *Saving Private Ryan*
1999	American Beauty	Kevin Spacey *American Beauty*	Hilary Swank *Boys Don't Cry*	Michael Caine *The Cider House Rules*	Angelina Jolie *Girl Interrupted*	Sam Mendes *American Beauty*
2000	Gladiator	Russell Crowe *Gladiator*	Julia Roberts *Erin Brockovich*	Benicio Del Toro *Traffic*	Marcia Gay Harden *Pollock*	Steven Soderbergh *Traffic*
2001	A Beautiful Mind	Denzel Washington *Training Day*	Halle Berry *Monster's Ball*	Jim Broadbent *Iris*	Jennifer Connelly *A Beautiful Mind*	Ron Howard *A Beautiful Mind*
2002	Chicago	Adrien Brody *The Pianist*	Nicole Kidman *The Hours*	Chris Cooper *Adaptation*	Catherine Zeta-Jones, *Chicago*	Roman Polanski *The Pianist*
2003	The Lord of the Rings: The Return of the King	Sean Penn *Mystic River*	Charlize Theron *Monster*	Tim Robbins *Mystic River*	Renée Zellweger *Cold Mountain*	Peter Jackson *The Lord of the Rings: The Return of the King*
2004	Million Dollar Baby	Jamie Foxx *Ray*	Hilary Swank *Million Dollar Baby*	Morgan Freeman *Million Dollar Baby*	Cate Blanchett *The Aviator*	Clint Eastwood *Million Dollar Baby*
2005	Crash	Philip Seymour Hoffman *Capote*	Reese Witherspoon *Walk the Line*	George Clooney *Syriana*	Rachel Weisz *The Constant Gardener*	Ang Lee *Brokeback Mountain*
2006	The Departed	Forest Whitaker *The Last King of Scotland*	Helen Mirren *The Queen*	Alan Arkin *Little Miss Sunshine*	Jennifer Hudson *Dreamgirls*	Martin Scorsese *The Departed*
2007	No Country for Old Men	Daniel Day-Lewis *There Will Be Blood*	Marion Cotillard *La Vie en Rose*	Javier Bardem *No Country for Old Men*	Tilda Swinton *Michael Clayton*	Joel Coen and Ethan Coen, *No Country for Old Men*
2008	Slumdog Millionaire	Sean Penn *Milk*	Kate Winslet *The Reader*	Heath Ledger *The Dark Knight*	Penelope Cruz, *Vicky Cristina Barcelona*	Danny Boyle *Slumdog Millionaire*
2009	The Hurt Locker	Jeff Bridges *Crazy Heart*	Sandra Bullock *The Blind Side*	Christoph Waltz *Inglourious Basterds*	Mo'Nique *Precious*	Kathryn Bigelow *The Hurt Locker*
2010	The King's Speech	Colin Firth *The King's Speech*	Natalie Portman *Black Swan*	Christian Bale *The Fighter*	Melissa Leo *The Fighter*	Tom Hooper *The King's Speech*

(1) Award not given until 1936.

Other Oscar Winners, 2010

Animated film: *Toy Story 3*
Screenplay, adapted: *The Social Network*, Aaron Sorkin
Screenplay, original: *The King's Speech*, David Seidler
Art direction: *Alice in Wonderland*
Cinematography: *Inception*
Costume design: *Alice in Wonderland*
Documentary: *Inside Job*
Film editing: *The Social Network*
Foreign language film: *Hævnen* [*In a Better World*], Denmark

Makeup: *The Wolfman*
Original score: *The Social Network*, Trent Reznor and Atticus Ross
Original song: "We Belong Together," *Toy Story 3*, Randy Newman
Short films: *The Lost Thing* (animated), *Strangers No More* (documentary), *God of Love* (live-action)
Sound editing: *Inception*
Sound mixing: *Inception*
Visual effects: *Inception*

Other Film Awards, 2011
(Awarded in 2011, unless otherwise noted.)

Berlin International Film Festival

Best film (Golden Bear): *Jodaeiye Nader az Simin* [*Nader and Simin, a Separation*], Asghar Farhadi, Iran
Jury grand prix (Silver Bear): *A torinói ló* [*The Turin Horse*], Béla Tarr, Hungary
Director: Ulrich Köhler, *Schlafkrankheit* [*Sleeping Sickness*], Germany/France
Actress: Ensemble, *Jodaeiye Nader az Simin* [*Nader and Simin, a Separation*], Asghar Farhadi, Iran
Actor: Ensemble, *Jodaeiye Nader az Simin* [*Nader and Simin, a Separation*], Asghar Farhadi, Iran
Artistic achievement: Wojciech Staron (camera) & Barbara Enriquez (production design), *El premio* [*The Prize*], Mexico
Script: Joshua Marston & Andamion Murataj, *The Forgiveness of Blood*, U.S.
Alfred Bauer Prize: *Wer wenn nicht wir* [*If Not Us, Who*], Andres Veiel, Germany

British Academy of Film and Television Awards (BAFTAs)

Awarded in 2011 to films released in the UK in 2010.
Best film: *The King's Speech*
British film: *The King's Speech*
Director: David Fincher, *The Social Network*
Original screenplay: David Seidler, *The King's Speech*
Adapted screenplay: Aaron Sorkin, *The Social Network*
Foreign language film: *The Girl With the Dragon Tattoo*, Sweden
Animated film: *Toy Story 3*
Actor: Colin Firth, *The King's Speech*
Actress: Natalie Portman, *Black Swan*
Supporting actor: Geoffrey Rush, *The King's Speech*
Supporting actress: Helena Bonham Carter, *The King's Speech*

Cannes International Film Festival Awards

Feature Films
Palme d'Or: *The Tree of Life*, Terrence Malick, U.S.
Grand Prix Ex-aequo: *Bir Zamanlar Anadolu'da* [*Once Upon a Time in Anatolia*], Nuri Bilge Ceylan, Turkey/Bosnia-Herzegovina; *Le Gamin Au Vélo* [*The Kid With a Bike*], Jean-Pierre & Luc Dardenne, Belgium/France/Italy
Best Director: Nicolas Winding Refn, *Drive*, U.S.
Best Screenplay: Joseph Cedar, *Hearat Shulayim* [*Footnote*], Israel
Best Actress: Kirsten Dunst, *Melancholia*, Denmark/Sweden/France/Germany
Best Actor: Jean Dujardin, *The Artist*, France
Jury Prize: *Polisse* [*Poliss*], Maïwenn, France

Short Films
Palme d'Or: *Cross* [*Cross-Country*], Maryna Vroda, France/Ukraine
Jury Prize: *Badpakje 46* [*Swimsuit 46*], Wannes Destoop, Belgium

Genie Awards

Motion picture: *Incendies*
Actor: Paul Giamatti, *Barney's Version*
Actress: Lubna Azabal, *Incendies*
Supporting actor: Dustin Hoffman, *Barney's Version*
Supporting actress: Minnie Driver, *Barney's Version*
Documentary: *Last Train Home*
Director: Denis Villeneuve, *Incendies*

Director's Guild of America Awards

Feature film: Tom Hooper, *The King's Speech*
Documentary: Charles Ferguson, *Inside Job*

Sundance Film Festival Awards

Grand Jury Prize: *Like Crazy*, Drake Doremus (drama); *How to Die in Oregon*, Peter D. Richardson (doc.)
World Cinema Jury Prize: *Sykt Lykkelig* [*Happy, Happy*], Anne Sewitsky, Norway (drama); *Hell and Back Again*, Danfung Dennis, U.S./UK (doc.)
Audience Award: *Circumstance*, Maryam Keshavarz (drama); *Buck*, Cindy Meehl (doc.)
World Cinema Audience Award: *Kinyarwanda*, Alrick Brown, U.S./Rwanda (drama); *Senna*, Asif Kapadia, UK (doc.)
Directing: Sean Durkin, *Martha Marcy May Marlene* (drama); Jon Foy, *Resurrect Dead: The Mystery of the Toynbee Tiles* (doc.)
World Cinema Directing Award: Paddy Considine, *Tyrannosaur*, UK (drama); James Marsh, *Project Nim*, UK (doc.)
Waldo Salt Screenwriting Award: Sam Levinson, *Another Happy Day*
World Cinema Screenwriting Award: Erez Kav-El, *Restoration*, Israel
Documentary editing: Matthew Hamachek & Marshall Curry, *If a Tree Falls: A Story of the Earth Liberation Front*
World Cinema Doc. Editing Award: Göran Hugo Olsson & Hanna Lejonqvist, *The Black Power Mixtape 1967–1975*, Sweden/U.S.
Cinematography: Bradford Young, *Pariah* (drama); Eric Strauss, Ryan Hill, & Peter Hutchens, *The Redemption of General Butt Naked* (doc.)
World Cinema Cinematography Award: Diego F. Jimenez, *All Your Dead Ones*, Colombia (drama); Danfung Dennis, *Hell and Back Again*, U.S./UK (doc.)
Special Jury Prize: *Another Earth*, Mike Cahill (drama); Felicity Jones, *Like Crazy* (acting); *Being Elmo: A Puppeteer's Journey*, Constance Marks (doc.)
World Cinema Special Jury Prize: Olivia Colman & Peter Mullan, *Tyrannosaur*, UK (breakout performances); *Stand van de Sterren* [*Position Among the Stars*], Leonard Retel Helmrich, Netherlands (doc.)
Alfred P. Sloan Feature Film Prize: *Another Earth*, Mike Cahill
Short Filmmaking Jury Prize: *Brick Novax pt 1 and 2*, Matt Piedmont
International Short Filmmaking Jury Prize: *Deeper Than Yesterday*, Ariel Kleiman, Australia

Toronto International Film Festival

Prize of the International Critics (FIPRESCI Prize) for Discovery: *Avalon*, Axel Petersén, Sweden
FIPRESCI Prize for Special Presentations: *The First Man*, Gianni Amelio, France/Algeria/Italy
Cadillac People's Choice Award: *Where Do We Go Now?*, Nadine Labaki, France/Lebanon/Italy/Egypt
Cadillac People's Choice Award (documentary): *The Island President*, Jon Shenk, U.S.
Cadillac People's Choice Award (Midnight Madness): *The Raid*, Gareth Evans, Indonesia
Best Canadian Feature Film: *Monsieur Lazhar*, Philippe Falardeau
Best Canadian Short Film: *Doubles With Slight Pepper*, Ian Harnarine
Best Canadian First Feature Film: *Edwin Boyd*, Nathan Morlando

MTV Video Music Awards, 2011

Video of the year: "Firework," Katy Perry
New artist: "Yonkers," Tyler, The Creator
Female video: "Born This Way," Lady Gaga
Male video: "U Smile," Justin Bieber
Collaboration: "E.T.," Katy Perry feat. Kanye West
Video with a Message: "Born This Way," Lady Gaga
Hip-hop video: "Super Bass," Nicki Minaj
Pop video: "Till the World Ends," Britney Spears

Rock video: "Walk," Foo Fighters
Art direction: "Rolling in the Deep," Adele
Choreography: "Run the World (Girls)," Beyoncé
Cinematography: "Rolling in the Deep," Adele
Direction: "Make Some Noise," Beastie Boys
Editing: "Rolling in the Deep," Adele
Special effects: "E.T.," Katy Perry feat. Kanye West

Academy of Country Music Awards, 2011

Entertainer of the year: Taylor Swift
Album of the year: *Need You Now*, Lady Antebellum
Record of the year (single): "The House That Built Me," Miranda Lambert
Song of the year: "The House That Built Me," Miranda Lambert
Vocal event of the year: "As She's Walking Away," Zac Brown Band feat. Alan Jackson

Female vocalist: Miranda Lambert
Male vocalist: Brad Paisley
Vocal duo: Sugarland
Vocal group: Lady Antebellum
New artist: The Band Perry
New solo vocalist: Eric Church
New vocal duo/group: The Band Perry
Video of the year: "The House That Built Me," Miranda Lambert

Selected Grammy Awards, 2010

Source: National Academy of Recording Arts and Sciences.
For albums released Oct. 1, 2009-Sept. 30, 2010, awarded in Feb. 2011.

Record of the year (single): "Need You Now," Lady Antebellum
Album of the year: *The Suburbs*, Arcade Fire
Song of the year: "Need You Now," Lady Antebellum
New artist: Esperanza Spalding
Pop vocal perf., female: "Bad Romance," Lady Gaga
Pop vocal perf., male: "Just The Way You Are," Bruno Mars
Pop vocal perf., duo/group: "Hey, Soul Sister" (live), Train
Pop vocal perf., collaboration: "Imagine," Herbie Hancock, Pink, India.Arie, Seal, Konono No 1, Jeff Beck, and Oumou Sangare
Pop vocal album: *The Fame Monster*, Lady Gaga
Dance recording: "Only Girl (In The World)," Rihanna
Dance/electronic album: *La Roux*, La Roux
Rock vocal perf., solo: "Helter Skelter," Paul McCartney
Rock vocal perf., duo/group: "Tighten Up," The Black Keys
Hard rock perf.: "New Fang," Them Crooked Vultures
Rock song: "Angry World," Neil Young
Rock album: *The Resistance*, Muse
Alternative album: *Brothers*, The Black Keys
R&B vocal perf., female: "Bittersweet," Fantasia
R&B vocal perf., male: "There Goes My Baby," Usher
R&B vocal perf., duo/group: "Soldier of Love," Sade

R&B song: "Shine," John Legend & The Roots (w/m by John Stephens)
R&B album: *Wake Up!*, John Legend & The Roots
R&B album, contemporary: *Raymond v. Raymond*, Usher
Rap perf., solo: "Not Afraid," Eminem
Rap perf., duo/group: "On to the Next One," Jay-Z & Swizz Beatz
Rap song: "Empire State of Mind," Jay-Z & Alicia Keyes
Rap album: *Recovery*, Eminem
Country vocal perf., female: "The House That Built Me," Miranda Lambert
Country vocal perf., male: "'Til Summer Comes Around," Keith Urban
Country vocal perf., duo/group: "Need You Now," Lady Antebellum
Country song: "Need You Now," Lady Antebellum
Country album: *Need You Now*, Lady Antebellum
Comedy album: *Stark Raving Black*, Lewis Black
Soundtrack album, compilation: *Crazy Heart*, various artists
Soundtrack album, score: *Toy Story 3*, Randy Newman
Song, motion picture/TV: "The Weary Kind," Ryan Bingham and T Bone Burnett, *Crazy Heart*
Music video, short form: "Bad Romance," Lady Gaga
Music video, long form: *When You're Strange*, The Doors

Grammy Awards, 1958-2010

Record of the Year (single)	Year	Album of the Year
Domenico Modugno, "Nel Blu Dipinto Di Blu (Volare)"	1958	Henry Mancini, *The Music From Peter Gunn*
Bobby Darin, "Mack the Knife"	1959	Frank Sinatra, *Come Dance With Me*
Percy Faith, "Theme From a Summer Place"	1960	Bob Newhart, *Button Down Mind*
Henry Mancini, "Moon River"	1961	Judy Garland, *Judy at Carnegie Hall*
Tony Bennett, "I Left My Heart in San Francisco"	1962	Vaughn Meader, *The First Family*
Henry Mancini, "The Days of Wine and Roses"	1963	Barbra Streisand, *The Barbra Streisand Album*
Stan Getz and Astrud Gilberto, "The Girl From Ipanema"	1964	Stan Getz and João Gilberto, *Getz/Gilberto*
Herb Alpert, "A Taste of Honey"	1965	Frank Sinatra, *September of My Years*
Frank Sinatra, "Strangers in the Night"	1966	Frank Sinatra, *A Man and His Music*
5th Dimension, "Up, Up and Away"	1967	The Beatles, *Sgt. Pepper's Lonely Hearts Club Band*
Simon and Garfunkel, "Mrs. Robinson"	1968	Glen Campbell, *By the Time I Get to Phoenix*
5th Dimension, "Aquarius/Let the Sunshine In"	1969	Blood, Sweat & Tears, *Blood, Sweat & Tears*
Simon and Garfunkel, "Bridge Over Troubled Water"	1970	Simon and Garfunkel, *Bridge Over Troubled Water*
Carole King, "It's Too Late"	1971	Carole King, *Tapestry*
Roberta Flack, "The First Time Ever I Saw Your Face"	1972	George Harrison and Friends, *The Concert for Bangla Desh*
Roberta Flack, "Killing Me Softly With His Song"	1973	Stevie Wonder, *Innervisions*
Olivia Newton-John, "I Honestly Love You"	1974	Stevie Wonder, *Fulfillingness' First Finale*
Captain & Tennille, "Love Will Keep Us Together"	1975	Paul Simon, *Still Crazy After All These Years*
George Benson, "This Masquerade"	1976	Stevie Wonder, *Songs in the Key of Life*
Eagles, "Hotel California"	1977	Fleetwood Mac, *Rumours*
Billy Joel, "Just the Way You Are"	1978	Bee Gees, *Saturday Night Fever*
The Doobie Brothers, "What a Fool Believes"	1979	Billy Joel, *52nd Street*
Christopher Cross, "Sailing"	1980	Christopher Cross, *Christopher Cross*
Kim Carnes, "Bette Davis Eyes"	1981	John Lennon and Yoko Ono, *Double Fantasy*
Toto, "Rosanna"	1982	Toto, *Toto IV*
Michael Jackson, "Beat It"	1983	Michael Jackson, *Thriller*
Tina Turner, "What's Love Got to Do With It"	1984	Lionel Richie, *Can't Slow Down*
USA for Africa, "We Are the World"	1985	Phil Collins, *No Jacket Required*
Steve Winwood, "Higher Love"	1986	Paul Simon, *Graceland*
Paul Simon, "Graceland"	1987	U2, *The Joshua Tree*
Bobby McFerrin, "Don't Worry, Be Happy"	1988	George Michael, *Faith*
Bette Midler, "Wind Beneath My Wings"	1989	Bonnie Raitt, *Nick of Time*
Phil Collins, "Another Day in Paradise"	1990	Quincy Jones, *Back on the Block*
Natalie Cole, with Nat "King" Cole, "Unforgettable"	1991	Natalie Cole, with Nat "King" Cole, *Unforgettable*
Eric Clapton, "Tears in Heaven"	1992	Eric Clapton, *Unplugged*
Whitney Houston, "I Will Always Love You"	1993	Whitney Houston, *The Bodyguard*
Sheryl Crow, "All I Wanna Do"	1994	Tony Bennett, *MTV Unplugged*
Seal, "Kiss From a Rose"	1995	Alanis Morissette, *Jagged Little Pill*
Eric Clapton, "Change the World"	1996	Celine Dion, *Falling Into You*
Shawn Colvin, "Sunny Came Home"	1997	Bob Dylan, *Time Out of Mind*
Celine Dion, "My Heart Will Go On"	1998	Lauryn Hill, *The Miseducation of Lauryn Hill*
Santana feat. Rob Thomas, "Smooth"	1999	Santana, *Supernatural*
U2, "Beautiful Day"	2000	Steely Dan, *Two Against Nature*
U2, "Walk On"	2001	Various artists, *O Brother, Where Art Thou?*
Norah Jones, "Don't Know Why"	2002	Norah Jones, *Come Away With Me*
Coldplay, "Clocks"	2003	OutKast, *Speakerboxxx/The Love Below*
Ray Charles & Norah Jones, "Here We Go Again"	2004	Ray Charles and various artists, *Genius Loves Company*
Green Day, "Boulevard of Broken Dreams"	2005	U2, *How to Dismantle an Atomic Bomb*
Dixie Chicks, "Not Ready to Make Nice"	2006	Dixie Chicks, *Taking the Long Way*
Amy Winehouse, "Rehab"	2007	Herbie Hancock, *River: The Joni Letters*
Robert Plant & Alison Krauss, "Please Read the Letter"	2008	Robert Plant & Alison Krauss, *Raising Sand*
Kings of Leon, "Use Somebody"	2009	Taylor Swift, *Fearless*
Lady Antebellum, "Need You Now"	2010	Arcade Fire, *The Suburbs*

SCIENCE AND TECHNOLOGY

Science and Technology News 2011

The following were some of the more newsworthy developments in science and technology in the past year.

Einstein Once Again Proved Right

In May 2011, scientists announced that Albert Einstein's general theory of relativity, which revolutionized thinking about gravity, space, and time, had passed a major new test. In the years since it was put forth, in the early 20th century, several predictions based on it have found experimental confirmation.

According to the theory, a massive body should noticeably distort, or warp, the space and time (or space-time) around it. It should also pull space-time along with it as it rotates. Earth is large enough that these effects—sometimes called the geodetic and frame-dragging effects, respectively—ought to be detectable. NASA's *Gravity Probe B*, launched in 2004, was designed to measure them in a novel way. It carried four gyroscopes. The relativity effects were expected to cause slight drifts in the gyroscopes' spin axes relative to the position of a reference star (IM Pegasi). The first year and a half after launch were spent preparing the experimental systems and collecting data. Analysis of the data then took years. The final results, confirming the relativity effects to a reasonably high degree of accuracy, were published in the journal *Physical Review Letters* at the end of May.

Smell Builds Big Brains

When it comes to brains, humans and other mammals have the largest ones, in proportion to their body size. An intriguing study in the May 20, 2011, issue of *Science* magazine suggested that improvements in the sense of smell may have started mammals on the evolutionary path to big brains. Researchers trying to puzzle out the history of brains were long hampered by the fact that learning what was inside a fossil skull required breaking it open. Good skull specimens from the distant past were few and far between, and scientists were understandably reluctant to damage them. With modern CT scanning, however, it is possible to make a detailed image of a skull interior.

The *Science* researchers applied this technique to the skulls of two of the earliest known mammals—the tiny *Morganucodon oehleri* and *Hadrocodium wui*, dating from roughly 190 mil years ago. These two early mammals' brains were definitely larger (relative to body weight) than those of pre-mammals studied. The part of the brain that showed the most growth was the region that handled the olfactory system, or sense of smell. Univ. of Texas paleontologist Timothy Rowe, who led the study, summed up the implications for mammal evolution: "The olfactory system was the thing that drove the expansion of the brain in the first place, and once you've got a big brain you can do all kinds of things with it."

In Search of the First Americans

A report in the Mar. 25, 2011, issue of *Science* told of the discovery of a large group of artifacts suggesting that people were living in North America as far back as 15,500 years ago. According to genetic data, humans originally came to the Americas from Siberia. When they arrived has not been so clear. For decades the best evidence archaeologists could come up with pointed to the presence of a so-called Clovis people roughly 13,000 years ago. The Clovis culture used a distinctive stone blade (two-faced and fluted) that has been called the first great American invention.

Objects found in a dig near Buttermilk Creek in central Texas, about 40 mi northwest of Austin, appeared to provide solid evidence of human habitation several thousand years earlier than expected. The objects included dozens of stone tools, such as blades and spear points, along with flakes and debris from the cutting or sharpening of tools. The commonly used radiocarbon method was not usable because it only functions on organic material. Instead, a relatively new technique called optically stimulated luminescence was used. It essentially measures how much time has passed since now-buried minerals were exposed to sunlight. The dating of the objects is subject to confirmation by other researchers.

Quantum Quest Advances

New developments were reported in efforts to use the exotic world of quantum mechanics to overcome the limitations of traditional computers and communication systems. Hopes are that someday the processing and transmitting of information in

enormous amounts and at colossal speeds—far exceeding the capabilities of today's systems—will become a common occurrence thanks to quantum effects.

One notable breakthrough was made by scientists at Japan's Univ. of Tokyo and Australia's Univ. of New South Wales. The researchers accomplished the first high-speed, high-accuracy teleportation of a complex set of quantum information, expressed in packets of light. By taking advantage of the quantum principles known as entanglement and superposition, the information was destroyed in one place and re-created in another. The achievement marked a step toward the creation of truly powerful quantum computers and the ability to send quantum information across large networks. The researchers reported their experiment in the Apr. 15, 2011, issue of *Science*.

Meanwhile, in May 2011, D-Wave released what it dubbed the first commercially available quantum computer. The D-Wave One is a special-purpose machine, designed to do the mathematical operation known as discrete optimization. It features a superconducting processor that can handle 128 qubits, or quantum bits, and is housed in a cryogenics system in a shielded 100-sq-ft room. It comes with a price tag of $10 mil.

Thwarting Aging

A team of Harvard Medical School researchers reversed tissue damage associated with aging in mice. Aging is a complex process, and only some aspects of it are understood by scientists. Telomeres, for example, appear to play a role in aging in many types of organisms, such as mice and humans. These are special regions of DNA that serve as caps on the tips of chromosomes. They help keep chromosome DNA from losing key segments from its ends when it is copied during cell division. Generally when cells divide, however, the telomeres became shorter. At some point they lose their protective ability, and the cell dies or enters senescence and stops growing.

Some cells, such as fetal tissue and tumor cells in humans, naturally produce an enzyme called telomerase, which serves to lengthen telomeres. Working with mice whose telomerase production gene had been switched off, the Harvard researchers applied an experimental treatment that stimulated production of the enzyme. They found that the aging process was not only slowed down, but its effects were reversed, including the regeneration of olfactory nerves and the restoration of fertility.

Telomere shortening is not the only factor in organ deterioration, and there is evidence of a connection between telomerase and cancer. Still, someday the Harvard study may lead to treatments capable of regenerating human organs and thereby improving quality of life for the elderly. The study was published online on Nov. 28, 2010, by the journal *Nature*, and a print version appeared in the journal's Jan. 6, 2011, issue.

Arsenic-Based Life?

Arsenic is notoriously poisonous. In late 2010 a team of NASA-funded researchers reported finding a type of bacteria that not only is tolerant of arsenic but appeared to be able to use the substance instead of phosphorus as a component in its makeup.

The bacteria in question—strain GFAJ-1 in the Halomonadaceae family of Gammaproteobacteria—were found in mud from California's Mono Lake, which is salty and also contains relatively high levels of arsenic. Phosphorus is one of a few chemical elements that, as far as has been known, always appear in key biological molecules. Arsenic has a number of chemical similarities to it. When the researchers fed arsenic to the GFAJ-1 bacteria instead of phosphorus, the bacteria grew roughly 60% larger than those receiving phosphorus. Testing suggested that arsenic atoms had somehow substituted for some of the phosphorus in molecules such as DNA and the energy-transporting molecule ATP.

The study, which touched on the fundamental question of the nature of life, triggered a storm of controversy. If its findings are eventually confirmed by other researchers, they will entail an expansion of the definition of life as we know it. And this might increase the chances of finding such life on other planets. The study was published online by *Science* on its website Dec. 2, 2010; a print version appeared in the magazine issue of June 3, 2011.

Science Glossary

This glossary covers some concepts that come up frequently in the news, in biology, chemistry, geology, and physics.

Biology

Amino acid: one of about 20 similar small molecules that are the building blocks of proteins.

Antibiotic: a substance produced by or derived from a bacterium, fungus, or other organism that battles infections and diseases caused by microorganisms, especially bacteria; it works by killing the microorganism or halting its growth.

Archaea: a group of single-celled microorganisms; they are prokaryotes, like bacteria, but they share some similarities with eukaryotes.

Autoimmunity: a condition in which an individual's immune system reacts against his or her own tissues; leads to diseases such as lupus, some forms of diabetes, inflammatory bowel disease, and rheumatoid arthritis.

Bacterium (plural, bacteria): one of a large, varied class of microscopic and simple, single-celled organisms; bacteria live almost everywhere—some forms cause disease, while others are useful in digestion and other natural processes.

Biodiversity: richness of variety of life-forms—both plant and animal—in a given environment.

Cell: the smallest unit of life capable of living independently, or with other cells; usually bounded by a membrane. May include a nucleus and other specialized parts.

Cholesterol: a fatty substance found in animal tissues. It is produced by the liver in humans; is found in foods such as butter, eggs, and meat; and is an essential body constituent.

Chromosome: one of the rod-like structures in cell nuclei that carry genetic material (DNA).

Cloning: the process of copying a particular piece of DNA to allow it to be sequenced, studied, or used in some other way; can also refer to producing a genetic copy of an organism.

DNA (deoxyribonucleic acid): the chemical substance that carries genetic information, which determines the form and functioning of all living things.

Ecosystem: an interdependent community of living organisms and their climatic and geographical habitat.

Enzyme: a protein that promotes a particular chemical reaction in the body.

Estrogen: one of a group of hormones that promote development of female secondary sex characteristics and the growth and health of the female reproductive system; males also produce small amounts of estrogen.

Eukaryote: any of the group of single- or multi-celled organisms whose cells have distinct nuclei.

Evolution: the process of gradual change that may occur as a species adapts to its environment; natural selection is the process by which evolution occurs.

Gene: a portion of a DNA molecule that provides the blueprint for the assembly of a protein.

Gene pool: the collection and total diversity of genes in an interbreeding population.

Gene therapy: a treatment in which scientists try to implant functioning genes in a person's cells so the genes can produce proteins that the person lacks or that help the person fight disease.

Genetic sequencing: the process of finding the order of subunits in a gene or the order of all an organism's genes.

Genome: the complete set of an organism's genetic material.

Hormone: a substance secreted in one part of an organism that regulates the functioning of other tissues or organs.

Meiosis: the process of cell division that results in gametes (sperm or egg cells), all of which contain half the number of chromosomes as their precursor.

Metabolism: the sum total of the body's chemical processes providing energy for vital functions and enabling new material to be synthesized.

Mitosis: the process by which a cell divides its nucleus and other cell materials into two duplicate daughter cells with the same DNA.

Neuron or **nerve cell:** any of the cells in the nervous system that send electrical and chemical messages to other cells.

Nucleus (plural, nuclei): the center of an atom; or the portion of a eukaryotic cell that contains genetic material and regulates growth and metabolism.

Organism: a living entity, capable of growth, metabolism, and usually reproduction.

Phenotype: the observable properties and characteristics of an organism arising at least in part from its genetic makeup.

Pheromone: a chemical secreted by an animal or plant to influence the behavior of other members of its species.

Placebo effect: a phenomenon in which patients show improvements even though they have taken a medically inactive substance, called a placebo.

Prokaryote: a single-celled organism that does not have a distinct nucleus, such as bacteria and archaea.

Protein: a complex molecule made up of one or more chains of amino acids; essential to the structure and function of all cells.

RNA (ribonucleic acid): a complex molecule similar to the genetic material DNA but usually single-stranded; several forms of RNA translate the genetic code of DNA and use that code to assemble proteins for structural and biological functions in the body. RNA also serves as the genetic material of some viruses.

Species: a population of organisms that breed with each other in nature and produce fertile offspring; other definitions of species exist to accommodate the diversity of life on Earth.

Stem cell: a cell that can give rise to other types of cells; for instance, bone marrow stem cells may divide and produce different types of blood cells.

Steroid: a type of chemical substance with a certain molecular structure. Some steroids are hormones that can suppress immune response or influence stress reaction, blood pressure, or sexual development.

Testosterone: a steroid hormone that stimulates the development and maintenance of male sexual characteristics and the production of sperm; women also produce small amounts of testosterone.

Virus: a steroid microscopic, often disease-causing organism made of genetic material surrounded by a protein shell; can only reproduce inside a living cell.

Chemistry

Acid: a class of compound that contrasts with bases. Acids taste sour, turn litmus red/pink, and often produce hydrogen gas in contact with some metals. Acids donate protons (hydrogen atoms minus the electron) in chemical reactions.

Base: a substance that yields hydroxyl ions (OH-) when dissolved in water; any of a class of compounds whose aqueous solutions taste bitter, feel slippery, turn litmus blue, and react with acids to form salts; also known as **alkaline.**

Carbon fiber: an extremely strong, thin fiber made by pyrolyzing (decomposing by heat) synthetic fibers, such as rayon, until charred; used to make high-strength composites.

Chlorofluorocarbon (CFC): one of a group of industrial chemicals that contain chlorine, fluorine, and carbon and have been found to damage Earth's ozone layer.

Element: a substance that cannot be chemically decomposed into simpler substances; the atoms of an element all have the same number of protons and electrons.

Isotope: an atom of a chemical element with the same number of protons in its nucleus as other atoms of that element, but with a different number of neutrons.

Molecule: the basic unit of a chemical compound, composed of two or more atoms bound together.

Noble gases or inert gases: a group of gases including helium, neon, argon, krypton, xenon, and radon that are not reactive except in rare and limited instances.

Osmosis: the transfer of a fluid across a semipermeable membrane, usually from an area of higher concentration to one of lower concentration.

Phase: any of the possible states of matter—solid, liquid, gas, or plasma—that change according to temperature and pressure.

Polymer: a huge molecule containing hundreds or thousands of smaller molecules arranged in repeating units.

Salt: a neutral compound produced by the reaction of an acid and a base.

Geology

Fault, tectonic: a crack or break in Earth's crust, often due to the slippage of tectonic plates past or over one another; usually geologically unstable.

Igneous: a type of rock formed by solidification from a molten state, especially from molten magma.

Magma: hot liquid rock material under Earth's crust, from which igneous rock is formed by cooling.

Metamorphic: in geology, the name given to rocks or minerals that have recrystallized under the influence of heat and pressure since their original formation.

Pangaea: a single supercontinent that scientists believe began to break apart at least 200 mil years ago to form the current continents.

Plate tectonics: theory that Earth's lithosphere—the uppermost layer that includes the crust—is made up of many separate rigid plates of rock that float on top of hot semi-liquid rock.

Sedimentary: a type of rock formed by the buildup of material at the bottoms of bodies of water.

Physics

Absolute zero: the theoretical temperature at which all motion within a molecule stops, corresponding to −273.15°C (−459.67°F).

Antimatter: matter that consists of antiparticles, such as antiprotons, that have an opposite charge from normal particles; when matter meets antimatter, both are destroyed, and their combined mass is converted to energy. Antimatter is created in certain radioactive decay processes but appears to be present in only small amounts in the universe.

Atom: the basic unit of a chemical element.

Atomic mass: the total mass of an atom of a given element; atoms of the same element with different atomic masses (different numbers of neutrons, not protons) are called **isotopes**.

Atomic number: the number of protons in an atom of a given element in the periodic table; the characteristic that sets atoms of different elements apart.

Axion: a hypothetical subatomic particle with low mass and energy that is thought to exist because of the properties of the strong nuclear force.

Bose-Einstein condensate (BEC): a "super-atom" comprising thousands of atoms super-cooled to within a few hundred millionths of a degree of absolute zero and thus condensed into the lowest energy state; atoms bound in the BEC behave synchronously, giving the BEC wavelike properties.

Boson: force-carrying particles including photons, gluons, and the W and Z particles; one of the two primary categories of particles in the Standard Model, the other being fermions.

Dark energy: a mysterious, undefined energy leading to a repulsive forces pervading all of space-time; proposed by cosmologists as counteracting gravity and accelerating the expansion of the universe; predicted to make up 73% of the universe's composition.

Dark matter: hypothetical, invisible matter that some scientists believe makes up 83% of the matter in the universe (excluding dark energy); its existence was proposed to account for otherwise inexplicable gravitational forces observed in space.

Doppler effect: a change in the frequency of sound, light, or radio waves caused by the motion of the source emitting the waves or the motion of the person or instrument perceiving the waves.

Electron: negatively charged particle that is the least massive electrically charged fundamental particle; the most common charged lepton in the Standard Model.

Energy: capacity to perform work. Energy can take various forms, such as potential energy, kinetic energy, and chemical energy.

Entropy: a measure of disorder in a system.

Fermion: any one of a number of matter particles including electrons, protons, neutrons, and quarks; one of the two primary categories of particles in the Standard Model, the other being bosons.

Field: the effects of forces (gravitational, electric, etc.) are visualized and described mathematically by physicists in terms of fields, which show the strength and direction of a force at a given position.

Fission: a nuclear reaction that occurs when the nuclei of large, unstable atoms break apart, releasing large amounts of energy.

Fluorescence: luminescence that is caused by the absorption of radiation at one wavelength followed by an almost immediate re-radiation, usually at a different wavelength, that stops almost immediately when the radiation stops.

Force: in classical physics, a force is something that causes acceleration on a body; can be thought of as a push or pull.

Fusion: a nuclear reaction occurring when atomic nuclei collide at high temperatures and combine to form one heavier atomic nucleus, releasing enormous energy in the process.

Gravity: an attractive force between any two objects or particles, proportional to the mass (or energy) of the objects; strength of the force decreases with greater distance; the only fundamental force still unaccounted for by the Standard Model.

Half-life: the time it takes for half of a given amount of a radioactive element to decay.

Hertz (Hz): a measure of frequency, or how many times a given event occurs per second; applied to sound waves, electrical current, microchip clock speeds.

Laser: light consisting of a cascade of photons all having the same wavelength; stands for Light Amplification by Stimulated Emission of Radiation.

Light-emitting diode (LED): a semiconductor that emits light when an electrical current is passed through it. The color of the light depends on the material used in making the diode.

Neutrino: a tiny fundamental particle with no electrical charge and very small mass that moves very quickly through the universe; comes in three varieties, or flavors, called electron, muon, and tau.

Neutron: a neutral particle found in the nuclei of atoms.

Particle accelerator: a large machine with a circular or long, straight tunnel in which atoms smash into each other at high speeds; physicists use these machines to study subatomic particles.

Phosphorescence: luminescence that is caused by the absorption of radiation at one wavelength followed by a delayed re-radiation, usually at a different wavelength, that continues for at least a hundredth of a second after the radiation stops.

Photon: the elementary unit, or quantum, of light or electromagnetic radiation having no mass or electrical charge; one of the fundamental force-carrying particles, or bosons, described by the Standard Model.

Plasma: a high-energy state of matter different from solid, liquid, or gas in which atomic nuclei and the electrons orbiting them separate from each other.

Proton: a positively charged subatomic particle found in the nuclei of atoms.

Quantum: a natural unit of some physically measurable property, such as energy or electrical charge.

Quark: a fermion and a fundamental matter particle that makes up neutrons and protons, forming atomic nuclei; there are six different "flavors" of quarks grouped in pairs; up and down, charm and strange, top and bottom.

Radiation: energy emitted as rays or particles; radiation includes heat, light, ultraviolet rays, gamma rays, X-rays, cosmic rays, alpha particles, and beta particles.

Relativity, general theory of: a theory of space-time proposed by Albert Einstein in 1915; gravitational and other forces are transmitted through the effects of the curvature of space-time.

Relativity, special theory of: Einstein's theory of space and time: all laws of physics are valid in all uniformly moving frames of reference, and the speed of light in a vacuum is always the same, so long as the source and the observer are moving uniformly (not accelerating).

Standard Model: prevailing theory of the interaction of subatomic particles; matter particles are fermions: either leptons or quarks; force-carrying particles are bosons: either gluons, W or Z bosons, or photons; successfully explains three of the four elementary forces acting on particles (strong, weak, electromagnetic) but thus far has not incorporated gravity.

String theory: a theory that seeks to unify quantum mechanics and general relativity, positing that the basic constituents of matter can best be understood not as point objects but as tiny oscillating "strings."

Subatomic particle: one of the small particles, such as electrons, neutrons, and protons, which make up an atom.

Superconductivity: the property of certain materials, usually metals and chemically complex ceramics, to conduct electricity without resistance, generally at very cold temperatures.

Thermodynamics: the branch of physics that describes how energy, heat, and temperature flow in physical systems.

Ultraviolet radiation: a form of light, invisible to the human eye, that has a shorter wavelength and greater energy than visible light but a longer wavelength and less energy than X-rays.

Virtual particle: subatomic particles that rapidly pop into and out of existence and can exert real forces; usually occur in particle-antiparticle pairs and are rapidly annihilated.

Mohs Scale of Hardness

Hardness is the ability of a solid substance to resist abrasion or deformation on the surface. Soft minerals scratch more easily than hard ones. For example, a diamond will scratch graphite because the graphite is softer. In 1812, German mineralogist Frederich Mohs (1773-1839) created the arbitrary scale shown below to measure relative hardness using 10 minerals that were readily available at that time. The numbers in the Mohs scale are arranged in order of increasing hardness. An item's hardness is determined by determining which mineral in the Mohs scale can scratch it.

Mohs Scale		Selected items and their relative hardness	
1. Talc	6. Orthoclase feldspar	2.5 . . . . . . Fingernails	5.5 . . . . . Knife blade
2. Gypsum	7. Quartz	2.5-3 . . . . . Gold, silver	6-7 . . . . . Glass
3. Calcite	8. Topaz	3 . . . . . . Copper penny	6.5 . . . . . Iron pyrite
4. Fluorite	9. Corundum	4-4.5 . . Platinum	7+ . . . . . . Hardened steel file
5. Apatite	10. Diamond	4-5 . . . . . . Iron	

Chemical Elements, Atomic Numbers, Year Discovered

See Periodic Table of the Elements on page 283 for atomic weights.

Element	Symbol	Atomic number	Year discov.	Element	Symbol	Atomic number	Year discov.	Element	Symbol	Atomic number	Year discov.
Actinium	Ac	89	1899	Hafnium	Hf	72	1923	Radon	Rn	86	1900
Aluminum	Al	13	1825	Hassium	Hs	108	1984	Rhenium	Re	75	1925
Americium	Am	95	1944	Helium	He	2	1868	Rhodium	Rh	45	1803
Antimony	Sb	51	1450	Holmium	Ho	67	1878	Roentgenium	Rg	111	1995
Argon	Ar	18	1894	Hydrogen	H	1	1766	Rubidium	Rb	37	1861
Arsenic	As	33	13th cent.	Indium	In	49	1863	Ruthenium	Ru	44	1845
Astatine	At	85	1940	Iodine	I	53	1811	Rutherfordium	Rf	104	1969
Barium	Ba	56	1808	Iridium	Ir	77	1804	Samarium	Sm	62	1879
Berkelium	Bk	97	1949	Iron	Fe	26	BCE	Scandium	Sc	21	1879
Beryllium	Be	4	1798	Krypton	Kr	36	1898	Seaborgium	Sg	106	1974
Bismuth	Bi	83	15th cent.	Lanthanum	La	57	1839	Selenium	Se	34	1817
Bohrium	Bh	107	1981	Lawrencium	Lr	103	1961	Silicon	Si	14	1823
Boron	B	5	1808	Lead	Pb	82	BCE	Silver	Ag	47	BCE
Bromine	Br	35	1826	Lithium	Li	3	1817	Sodium	Na	11	1807
Cadmium	Cd	48	1817	Lutetium	Lu	71	1907	Strontium	Sr	38	1790
Calcium	Ca	20	1808	Magnesium	Mg	12	1829	Sulfur	S	16	BCE
Californium	Cf	98	1950	Manganese	Mn	25	1774	Tantalum	Ta	73	1802
Carbon	C	6	BCE	Meitnerium	Mt	109	1982	Technetium	Tc	43	1937
Cerium	Ce	58	1803	Mendelevium	Md	101	1955	Tellurium	Te	52	1782
Cesium	Cs	55	1860	Mercury	Hg	80	BCE	Terbium	Tb	65	1843
Chlorine	Cl	17	1774	Molybdenum	Mo	42	1782	Thallium	Tl	81	1861
Chromium	Cr	24	1797	Neodymium	Nd	60	1885	Thorium	Th	90	1828
Cobalt	Co	27	1735	Neon	Ne	10	1898	Thulium	Tm	69	1879
Copernicium	Cn	112	1996	Neptunium	Np	93	1940	Tin	Sn	50	BCE
Copper	Cu	29	BCE	Nickel	Ni	28	1751	Titanium	Ti	22	1791
Curium	Cm	96	1944	Niobium[2]	Nb	41	1801	Tungsten (Wolfram)	W	74	1783
Darmstadtium	Ds	110	1995	Nitrogen	N	7	1772	Ununhexium	Uuh	116	2000
Dubnium (Hahnium)[1]	Db (Ha)	105	1970	Nobelium	No	102	1958	*Ununoctium	Uuo	118	2006
Dysprosium	Dy	66	1886	Osmium	Os	76	1804	*Ununpentium	Uup	115	2004
Einsteinium	Es	99	1952	Oxygen	O	8	1774	Ununquadium	Uuq	114	1999
Erbium	Er	68	1843	Palladium	Pd	46	1803	*Ununseptium	Uus	117	2010
Europium	Eu	63	1901	Phosphorus	P	15	1669	*Ununtrium	Uut	113	2004
Fermium	Fm	100	1953	Platinum	Pt	78	1735	Uranium	U	92	1789
Fluorine	F	9	1771	Plutonium	Pu	94	1941	Vanadium	V	23	1830
Francium	Fr	87	1939	Polonium	Po	84	1898	Xenon	Xe	54	1898
Gadolinium	Gd	64	1886	Potassium	K	19	1807	Ytterbium	Yb	70	1878
Gallium	Ga	31	1875	Praseodymium	Pr	59	1885	Yttrium	Y	39	1794
Germanium	Ge	32	1886	Promethium	Pm	61	1945	Zinc	Zn	30	BCE
Gold	Au	79	BCE	Protactinium	Pa	91	1917	Zirconium	Zr	40	1789
				Radium	Ra	88	1898				

Note: 118 elements are listed here; only 114 have been independently confirmed. The most recent of these, elements 114 and 116, were discovered by a collaboration between teams at the Joint Institute for Nuclear Research in Dubna, Russia, and the Lawrence Livermore National Laboratory in California. The bulk of the work was carried out in 2004 and 2006. The discoveries were approved by the International Union of Pure and Applied Chemistry (IUPAC) in June 2011, with official names for the elements to be chosen later. (*) Indicates element whose existence has been reported or hypothesized, but not yet confirmed. Between 2004 and 2010, observation of isotopes of elements 113, 115, 117, and 118 were reported in refereed journals. These reports all await confirmation and are shown in italics in the periodic table. (1) The name Dubnium (Db) has been approved by IUPAC for element 105, but the name Hahnium (Ha) was used in most of the scientific literature before 1998 and is still sometimes used in the U.S. (2) Formerly Columbium.

Periodic Table of the Elements

Source: Lawrence Berkeley National Laboratory; International Union of Pure and Applied Chemistry (IUPAC)

Legend:
- atomic number
- 14 — approximate atomic weight
- 28.09
- Si — symbol
- Silicon — name

alkali metals

| 1 Hydrogen **H** 1.008 |
| 3 Lithium **Li** 6.94 |
| 11 Sodium **Na** 22.99 |
| 19 Potassium **K** 39.10 |
| 37 Rubidium **Rb** 85.47 |
| 55 Cesium **Cs** 132.9 |
| 87 Francium **Fr** [223]* |

alkaline earth metals

| 4 Beryllium **Be** 9.012 |
| 12 Magnesium **Mg** 24.31 |
| 20 Calcium **Ca** 40.08 |
| 38 Strontium **Sr** 87.62 |
| 56 Barium **Ba** 137.3 |
| 88 Radium **Ra** [226]* |

transitional metals

21 Scandium Sc 44.96	22 Titanium Ti 47.87	23 Vanadium V 50.94	24 Chromium Cr 52.00	25 Manganese Mn 54.94	26 Iron Fe 55.85	27 Cobalt Co 58.93	28 Nickel Ni 58.69	29 Copper Cu 63.55	30 Zinc Zn 65.38
39 Yttrium Y 88.91	40 Zirconium Zr 91.22	41 Niobium Nb 92.91	42 Molybdenum Mo 95.96	43 Technetium Tc [98]*	44 Ruthenium Ru 101.1	45 Rhodium Rh 102.9	46 Palladium Pd 106.4	47 Silver Ag 107.9	48 Cadmium Cd 112.4
57 Lanthanum La 138.9	72 Hafnium Hf 178.5	73 Tantalum Ta 180.9	74 Tungsten W 183.8	75 Rhenium Re 186.2	76 Osmium Os 190.2	77 Iridium Ir 192.2	78 Platinum Pt 195.1	79 Gold Au 197.0	80 Mercury Hg 200.6
89 Actinium Ac [227]*	104 Rutherfordium Rf [265]*	105 Dubnium Db [268]*	106 Seaborgium Sg [271]*	107 Bohrium Bh [270]*	108 Hassium Hs [277]*	109 Meitnerium Mt [276]*	110 Darmstadtium Ds [281]*	111 Roentgenium Rg [280]*	112 Copernicium Cn [285]*

other metals

| 13 Aluminum Al 26.98 |
| 31 Gallium Ga 69.72 |
| 49 Indium In 114.8 |
| 50 Tin Sn 118.7 |
| 81 Thallium Tl 204.4 |
| 82 Lead Pb 207.2 |
| 83 Bismuth Bi 209.0 |
| 84 Polonium Po [209]* |
| 113 [284]* |
| 114 [289]* |
| 115 [288]* |
| 116 [293]* |
| 117 [294]* |
| 118 [294]* |

nonmetals

| 5 Boron B 10.81 |
| 6 Carbon C 12.01 |
| 7 Nitrogen N 14.01 |
| 8 Oxygen O 16.00 |
| 9 Fluorine F 19.00 |
| 14 Silicon Si 28.09 |
| 15 Phosphorus P 30.97 |
| 16 Sulfur S 32.06 |
| 17 Chlorine Cl 35.45 |
| 32 Germanium Ge 72.63 |
| 33 Arsenic As 74.92 |
| 34 Selenium Se 78.96 |
| 35 Bromine Br 79.90 |
| 51 Antimony Sb 121.8 |
| 52 Tellurium Te 127.6 |
| 53 Iodine I 126.9 |
| 85 Astatine At [210]* |

noble gases

| 2 Helium He 4.003 |
| 10 Neon Ne 20.18 |
| 18 Argon Ar 39.95 |
| 36 Krypton Kr 83.80 |
| 54 Xenon Xe 131.3 |
| 86 Radon Rn [222]* |

Lanthanide series

| 58 Cerium Ce 140.1 | 59 Praseodymium Pr 140.9 | 60 Neodymium Nd 144.2 | 61 Promethium Pm [145]* | 62 Samarium Sm 150.4 | 63 Europium Eu 152.0 | 64 Gadolinium Gd 157.3 | 65 Terbium Tb 158.9 | 66 Dysprosium Dy 162.5 | 67 Holmium Ho 164.9 | 68 Erbium Er 167.3 | 69 Thulium Tm 168.9 | 70 Ytterbium Yb 173.1 | 71 Lutetium Lu 175.0 |

Actinide series

| 90 Thorium Th 232.0 | 91 Protactinium Pa 231.0 | 92 Uranium U 238.0 | 93 Neptunium Np [237]* | 94 Plutonium Pu [244]* | 95 Americium Am [243]* | 96 Curium Cm [247]* | 97 Berkelium Bk [247]* | 98 Californium Cf [251]* | 99 Einsteinium Es [252]* | 100 Fermium Fm [257]* | 101 Mendelevium Md [258]* | 102 Nobelium No [259]* | 103 Lawrencium Lr [262]* |

*Element has no stable nuclides. The value enclosed in brackets, e.g., [209], indicates the mass number of the longest-lived isotope of the element. However, three such elements (Th, Pa, and U) do have a characteristic terrestrial isotopic composition, and for these an atomic weight is tabulated.

Basic Laws of Physics

Isaac Newton's Laws of Motion

1. An object in motion moves at a constant velocity in a straight line unless acted upon by a force. Likewise, an object at rest will stay at rest. These two properties are known as inertia.

2. The acceleration of an object is proportional to the force acting on it and inversely proportional to the mass of an object.

Force (F) equals mass (m) times acceleration (a):

$$F = ma$$

3. For every action, there is an equal and opposite reaction. For example, if a force of 1 ton pushes down on an object, the object pushes up with an equal force. As per the 2nd law, the amount of movement (acceleration) produced in the object will depend on the object's mass.

Law of Gravity

In common usage, gravity refers to the gravitational force between planets and objects on or near them. But in scientific parlance, gravitation represents one of four basic forces controlling the interactions of matter. The others are the strong and weak nuclear forces and electromagnetic force. The gravitational force (F) between objects is proportional to the product of their masses (m_1 and m_2) and inversely proportional to the square of the distance (d) between them. G represents the gravitational constant in Newton's law of gravity, a fixed ratio of approximately 6.67384×10^{-11} newton m^2/kg^2.

The basic law of gravity is:

$$F = G\,\frac{m_1 m_2}{d_2}$$

Near Earth's surface, Earth's gravitational force is considered to pull objects downward at a constant acceleration of $g = 9.8$ m/s^2. This allows calculation of the vertical velocity (v) of an object with an initial vertical velocity of v_0 in free fall at a given point in time (t) and calculation of the distance (d) of an object from Earth at any given time with a given initial velocity (v_0) and a known initial height (a) via the following equations:

$$v = v_0 - g\,t$$

$$d = -\tfrac{1}{2}g(t^2) + v_0 t + a$$

Assuming that height is measured in feet and speeds in feet per second, the maximum height (H) reached by an object with a positive v_0 is expressed as:

$$H = a + \frac{v_0^2}{64}$$

For motion not near Earth's surface, more complicated equations are required. Also, if the object's upward velocity is very great, the object may escape Earth's gravity. Even near Earth's surface, there are slight complications. Gravity is lessened by the centrifugal force of the Earth's rotation. At the poles, where centrifugal force is absent, acceleration due to gravity is greater.

Gravity is weaker on a mountaintop than at sea level because the mountaintop is farther from Earth's center.

Conservation Laws

In physics, laws of conservation state that in a closed system, where neither mass nor energy is added or subtracted, certain measurable quantities remain constant.

Conservation of Mass: Mass is neither created nor destroyed within a closed system except when converted to energy.

Conservation of Momentum: All moving objects have momentum, and in a closed system, total momentum is always conserved. Linear momentum is the product of the mass of an object and its velocity. In the following equation, M and V represent the initial total mass and velocity of objects within a closed system. After a collision between those objects, the mass and velocity of individual objects may change (for example, one object breaks into smaller pieces, each traveling at a different velocity), but the product of the total mass and velocity in the system after the collision (mv) will remain the same.

$$MV = mv$$

Any object moving in a circle has another kind of momentum—angular momentum. This is because circular motion requires acceleration toward the center of the circle. The amount of acceleration depends on the speed of the object and the square of the radius of the circle. (Angular momentum is the product of this speed, the mass of the object, and the square of the radius.)

Conservation of Energy: The total amount of energy in a closed system will not change except when converted to mass.

Conservation of Mass-Energy: Although mass and energy can be converted into one another, the total amount of mass and energy together must be conserved. This is reflected in Einstein's famous equation, where m is mass, E is energy, and c is the speed of light in a vacuum (which is constant):

$$E = mc^2$$

Relativistic mass can describe how mass increases with velocity. The following equation—where m is the mass of a moving object, m_0 is the object's mass when not moving, v is its velocity in relation to a stationary observer, and c is the speed of light—shows the relationship:

$$m = \frac{m_0}{\sqrt{1 - \dfrac{v^2}{c^2}}}$$

The theory that no object can travel faster than the speed of light is based in this equation. As an object approaches c, so much energy is converted to mass that it no longer accelerates.

Laws of Thermodynamics

1. Heat is a form of energy. Within a closed system energy must be conserved except in nuclear reactions or other extreme conditions. It is neither created nor destroyed.

2. Within a self-sustaining system, heat can never go from an area of low temperature to an area of high temperature, for this would require added energy. Without added energy, disorder, or entropy, can only increase.

3. Absolute zero cannot be attained by any procedure in a finite number of steps. Although it can be approached asymptotically, it can never be reached.

Laws of Current Electricity

Electric current generally represents the flow of electrons through a conductor. The rate at which electrons flow can be measured in amperes, defined as the number of electrons (measured in a unit called the coulomb, equal to about 6.24 quintillion or 6.24×10^{18} electrons) moving past a particular point every second. One ampere is equal to 1 coulomb of charge passing each second. Like water, electrons tend to move from areas of high pressure to low pressure. The difference between these two pressures is known as potential difference and is measured in volts.

Certain substances, such as copper and carbon, allow electric currents to pass more readily than others—that is, they have greater conductivity. Resistance to conductivity is measured in ohms.

Ohm's Law: Electric current is directly proportional to the potential difference and inversely proportional to the total resistance of the circuit. I is electric current (measured in amperes), V is the potential difference (measured in volts), and R is resistance (measured in ohms):

$$I = \frac{V}{R}$$

Law of Electric Power: Electric power (P), measured in watts, represents the rate at which electricity is converted into some other form of energy (such as light, in the case of a lightbulb). For a direct-current circuit, P is the product of current and potential difference:

$$P = IV$$

Two Basic Laws of Quantum Physics

1. Heisenberg's uncertainty principle: Certain pairs of observable quantities like energy and time or position and momentum cannot be measured with complete accuracy simultaneously. Also known as the indeterminacy principle.

2. Pauli's exclusion principle: Two electrons in an atom cannot simultaneously occupy the same quantum or energy state. This has since been shown to be true for many subatomic particles.

Breaking the Sound Barrier; Speed of Sound

The prefix **Mach** is used to describe supersonic speed. It was named for Ernst Mach (1838-1916), a Czech-born Austrian physicist. Mach may be defined as the ratio of the velocity of an object to the velocity of sound in a particular medium. A plane moving at the speed of sound moves at Mach 1. At twice the speed of sound, it moves at Mach 2.

When a plane passes the sound barrier—flying faster than sound travels—listeners in the area hear thunderclaps, although the pilot of the plane does not.

Sound is produced by vibrations of an object and is transmitted by the alternating increase and decrease in pressure radiating outward through a material medium of molecules, like waves spreading out on a pond after a rock has been tossed in.

The **frequency of sound** is determined by the number of times the vibrating waves undulate per second and is measured in cycles per second. The slower the cycle of waves, the lower the frequency. As the frequency increases, the sound becomes higher in pitch. The human ear is sensitive to frequencies between 20 and 20,000 vibrations per second, although this range varies among individuals.

Intensity, or loudness, is the strength of the pressure of these radiating waves and is measured in decibels. (See Weights and Measures.)

The **speed of sound** is generally defined as 1,088 feet per second at sea level at 32°F. It varies in other temperatures and media. Sound travels faster in water than in air and even faster in iron and steel.

Light; Colors of the Spectrum

Light, a form of electromagnetic radiation similar to radiant heat, radio waves, and X-rays, is emitted from a source in straight lines and spreads out over larger areas as it travels. For emission from a point source, light per unit area diminishes in proportion to the square of the distance.

The English mathematician and physicist Isaac Newton (1642-1727) described light as an **emission of particles**; the Dutch astronomer, mathematician, and physicist Christiaan Huygens (1629-95) and others developed the theory that light travels in a **wave motion**. It is now believed that these two theories are essentially complementary, and the development of quantum theory has led to results where light acts like a series of particles in some experiments and like a wave in others.

The first relatively accurate measurement of the **speed of light** in a laboratory experiment was made by the French physicist Armand Hippolyte Louis Fizeau (1819-96). Today the speed of light is known very precisely as 299,792.458 km per sec (or 186,282.397 mi per sec) in a vacuum; in water the speed of light is about 25% less, and in glass, 33% less.

Color sensations are produced through the excitation of the retina of the eye by light vibrating at different frequencies. The different colors of the spectrum may be seen by viewing a light beam refracted by passage through a prism, which breaks the light into its wavelengths.

Customarily, the basic colors are taken to be the six monochromatic colors that occupy relatively large areas of the spectrum: red, orange, yellow, green, blue, and violet. So-called primary colors can be combined to produce the sensation of other colors. However, scientists disagree about how many and what primary colors to recognize. The color sensation of **black** is due to complete lack of stimulation of the retina, that of **white** to complete stimulation.

Infrared and **ultraviolet rays**, below the red (long) end of the visible spectrum and above the visible spectrum's violet (short) end, respectively, are invisible to the naked eye. Heat is the principal effect of infrared rays, and chemical action that of ultraviolet rays.

Discoveries and Innovations: Biology, Chemistry, Medicine, Physics

Discovery	Date	Discoverer(s)	Nationality
Acetylene gas	1862	Berthelot	French
ACTH	1927	Evans, Long	U.S.
Adrenaline	1901	Takamine	Japanese
Aluminum, electrolytic process	1886	Hall	U.S.
Aluminum, isolated	1825	Oersted	Danish
Anesthesia, ether	1842	Long	U.S.
Anesthesia, local	1885	Koller	Austrian
Anesthesia, spinal	1898	Bier	German
Aniline dye	1856	Perkin	English
Anti-rabies	1885	Pasteur	French
Antiseptic surgery	1867	Lister	English
Antitoxin, diphtheria	1891	Von Behring	German
Argyrol	1897	Bayer	German
Arsphenamine	1910	Ehrlich	German
Aspirin	1853	Gerhardt	French
Atabrine	1932	Mietzsch, et al.	German
Atomic numbers	1913	Moseley	English
Atomic theory	1803	Dalton	English
Atomic time clock	1948	Lyons	U.S.
Atomic time clock, cesium beam	1948	Essen	English
Atom-smashing theory	1919	Rutherford	English
Bacitracin	1943	Johnson, Meleneyl	U.S.
Bacteria, description	1676	Leeuwenhoek	Dutch
Bleaching powder	1798	Tennant	English
Blood, circulation	1628	Harvey	English
Blood plasma storage (blood bank)	1940	Drew	U.S.
Bordeaux mixture	1885	Millardet	French
Bromine from the sea	1826	Balard	French
Calcium carbide	1888	Wilson	U.S.
Calculus	1670	Newton	English
Camphor synthetic	1896	Haller	French
Canning (food)	1804	Appert	French
Carbon oxides	1925	Fisher	German
Chemotherapy	1909	Ehrlich	German
Chloramphenicol	1947	Burkholder	U.S.
Chlorine	1774	Scheele	Swedish
Chloroform	1831	Guthrie, S.	U.S.
Chlortetracycline	1948	Duggen	U.S.
Classification of plants and animals	1735	Linnaeus	Swedish
Cloning, DNA	1973	Boyer, Cohen	U.S.
Cloning, mammal	1996	Wilmut, et al.	Scottish
Cocaine	1860	Niermann	German
Combustion explained	1777	Lavoisier	French
Conditioned reflex	1914	Pavlov	Russian
Cortisone	1936	Kendall	U.S.
Cortisone, synthesis	1946	Sarett	U.S.
Cosmic rays	1910	Gockel	Swiss
Cyanamide	1905	Frank, Caro	German
Cyclotron	1930	Lawrence	U.S.
DDT (not applied as insecticide until 1939)	1874	Zeidler	German
Deuterium	1932	Urey, Brickwedde, Murphy	U.S.
DNA (structure)	1953	Crick	English
		Watson	U.S.
		Wilkins	English
Electric resistance, law of	1827	Ohm	German
Electric waves	1888	Hertz	German
Electrolysis	1852	Faraday	English
Electromagnetism	1819	Oersted	Danish
Electron	1897	Thomson, J.	English
Electron diffraction	1936	Thomson	English
		Davisson, G.	U.S.
Electroshock treatment	1938	Cerletti, Bini	Italian
Erythromycin	1952	McGuire	U.S.
Evolution, natural selection	1858	Darwin	English
Falling bodies, law of	1590	Galileo	Italian
Gases, law of combining volumes	1808	Gay-Lussac	French
Geometry, analytic	1619	Descartes	French
Gold, cyanide process for extraction	1887	MacArthur, Forest	British
Gravitation, law	1687	Newton	English
HIV (human immuno-deficiency virus)	1984	Montagnier	French
		Gallo	U.S.
Holograph	1948	Gabor	British
Human heart transplant	1967	Barnard	S. African
Indigo, synthesis of	1880	Baeyer	German
Induction, electric	1830	Henry	U.S.
Insulin	1922	Banting, Best	Canadian
		Macleod	Scottish
Intelligence testing	1905	Binet, Simon	French

Discovery	Date	Discoverer(s)	Nationality
In vitro fertilization	1978	Steptoe, Edwards	English
Isotopes, theory	1912	Soddy	English
Laser	1957	Gould	U.S.
Light, velocity	1675	Roemer	Danish
Light, wave theory	1690	Huygens	Dutch
Lithography	1796	Senefelder	Bohemian
Logarithms	1614	Napier	Scottish
LSD-25	1943	Hoffman	Swiss
Mendelian laws	1866	Mendel	Austrian
Mercator projection (map)	1568	Mercator (Kremer)	Flemish
Methanol	1661	Boyle	Irish
Milk condensation	1853	Borden	U.S.
Molecular hypothesis	1811	Avogadro	Italian
Motion, laws of	1687	Newton	English
Neomycin	1949	Waksman, Lechevalier	U.S.
Neutrino	1956	Reines, Cowan	U.S.
Neutron	1932	Chadwick	English
Nitric acid	1648	Glauber	German
Nitric oxide	1772	Priestley	English
Nitroglycerin	1846	Sobrero	Italian
Oil cracking process	1891	Dewar	U.S.
Oxygen	1774	Priestley	English
Oxytetracycline	1950	Finlay, et al.	U.S.
Ozone	1840	Schonbein	German
Paper, sulfite process	1867	Tilghman	U.S.
Paper, wood pulp, sulfate process	1884	Dahl	German
Penicillin	1928	Fleming	Scottish
Penicillin, practical use	1941	Florey, Chain	English
Periodic law and table of elements	1869	Mendeleyev	Russian
Physostigmine synthesis	1935	Julian	U.S.
Pill, birth-control	1954	Pincus, Rock	U.S.
Planetary motion, laws	1609	Kepler	German
Plutonium fission	1940	Kennedy, Wahl, Seaborg, Segre	U.S.
Polymyxin	1947	Ainsworth	English
Positron	1932	Anderson	U.S.
Proton	1919	Rutherford	N. Zealand
Psychoanalysis	1900	Freud	Austrian
Pulsars	1967	Bell	English
Quantum theory	1900	Planck	German
Quasars	1963	Matthews, Sandage	U.S.
Quinine synthetic	1946	Woodward, Doering	U.S.
Radioactivity	1896	Becquerel	French
Radiocarbon dating	1947	Libby	U.S.
Radium	1898	Curie, Pierre	French
		Curie, Marie	Pol.-Fr.
Relativity theory	1905	Einstein	German

Discovery	Date	Discoverer(s)	Nationality
Reserpine	1949	Jal Vaikl	Indian
Schick test	1913	Schick	U.S.
Silicon	1823	Berzelius	Swedish
Smallpox eradication	1979	World Health Org.	UN
Streptomycin	1944	Waksman, et al.	U.S.
Sulfanilamide	1935	Bovet, Trefouel	French
Sulfanilamide theory	1908	Gelmo	German
Sulfapyridine	1938	Ewins, Phelps	English
Sulfathiazole	1939	Fosbinder, Walter	U.S.
Sulfuric acid	1831	Phillips	English
Sulfuric acid, lead	1746	Roebuck	English
Superconductivity	1911	Onnes	Dutch
Superconductivity theory	1957	Bardeen, Cooper, Schreiffer	U.S.
Superconductors, high-temp.	1986	Bednorz, Muller	Ger., Swiss
Syphilis test	1906	Wassermann	German
Transplant, heart	1967	Barnard	S. Africa
Tuberculin	1890	Koch	German
Uranium fission, atomic reactor	1942	Fermi, Szilard	U.S.
Uranium fission theory	1939	Hahn, Meitner, Strassmann	German
		Bohr	Danish
		Fermi	Italian
		Einstein, Pegram, Wheeler	U.S.
Vaccine, measles	1963	Enders	U.S.
Vaccine, measles-mumps-rubella	1971	Hilleman	U.S.
Vaccine, meningitis (first conjugate)	1987	Gordon, et al., Connaught Lab.	U.S.
Vaccine, polio	1954	Salk	U.S.
Vaccine, polio, oral	1960	Sabin	U.S.
Vaccine, rabies	1885	Pasteur	French
Vaccine, smallpox	1796	Jenner	English
Vaccine, typhus	1909	Nicolle	French
Vaccine, varicella	1974	Takahashi	Japanese
Van Allen belts, radiation	1958	Van Allen	U.S.
Vitamin A	1913	McCollum, Davis	U.S.
Vitamin B	1916	McCollum	U.S.
Vitamin C	1928	Szent-Gyorgyi	Hungarian
		King	U.S.
Vitamin D	1922	McCollum	U.S.
Vitamin K	1935	Dam, Doisy	U.S.
Xerography	1938	Carlson	U.S.
X-ray	1895	Roentgen	German

Inventions

Invention	Date	Inventor(s)	Nationality
Adding machine	1642	Pascal	French
Adding machine	1885	Burroughs	U.S.
Aerosol spray	1926	Rotheim	Norwegian
Airbag	1952	Hetrick	U.S.
Air brake	1868	Westinghouse	U.S.
Air conditioning	1902	Carrier	U.S.
Air pump	1654	Guericke	German
Airplane, automatic pilot	1912	Sperry	U.S.
Airplane, experimental	1896	Langley	U.S.
Airplane, hydro	1911	Curtiss	U.S.
Airplane jet engine	1939	Ohain	German
Airplane with motor	1903	Wright Bros.	U.S.
Airship	1852	Giffard	French
Aqua-Lung	1943	Cousteau, Gagnan	French
Arc welder	1919	Thomson	U.S.
Aspartame	1965	Schlatter	U.S.
Autogyro	1920	de la Cierva	Spanish
Automobile, differential gear	1885	Benz	German
Automobile, electric	1892	Morrison	U.S.
Automobile, exp'mtl	1864	Marcus	Austrian
Automobile, gasoline	1889	Daimler	German
Automobile, gasoline	1892	Duryea	U.S.
Automobile magneto	1897	Bosch	German
Automobile muffler	1904	Pope	U.S.
Automobile self-starter	1911	Kettering	U.S.
Bakelite	1907	Baekeland	Belg., U.S.
Balloon	1783	Montgolfier	French
Barometer	1643	Torricelli	Italian
Bicycle, modern	1885	Starley	English
Bifocal lens	1780	Franklin	U.S.
Bottle machine	1895	Owens	U.S.
Braille printing	1829	Braille	French
Brassiere, modern	1913	Jacob	U.S
Bubble gum	1928	Diemer	U.S.
Burner, gas	1855	Bunsen	German
Calculating machine	1833	Babbage	English
Calculator, electronic pocket	1972	Merryman, Van Tassel	U.S.

Invention	Date	Inventor(s)	Nationality
Camera, digital	1977	Lloyd, Sasson	U.S.
Camera, Kodak	1888	Eastman, Walker	U.S.
Camera, Polaroid Land	1948	Land	U.S.
Can, pop-top	1959	Fraze	U.S.
Car coupler	1873	Janney	U.S.
Carburetor, gasoline	1893	Maybach	German
Carding machine	1797	Whittemore	U.S.
Carpet sweeper	1876	Bissell	U.S.
Cash register	1879	Ritty	U.S.
Cassette, audio	1963	Philips Co.	Dutch
Cassette, videotape	1969	Sony	Japanese
Cathode-ray tube	1897	Braun	German
CAT, or CT, scan	1973	Hounsfield	English
Cellophane	1908	Brandenberger	Swiss
Celluloid	1870	Hyatt	U.S.
Cement, Portland	1824	Aspdin	English
Chronometer	1735	Harrison	English
Circuit breaker	1925	Hilliard	U.S.
Circuit, integrated	1959	Kilby, Noyce, Texas Instr.	U.S.
Clock, pendulum	1657	Huygens	Dutch
Coaxial cable system	1929	Affel, Espensched.	U.S.
Coca-Cola	1885	Pemberton	U.S.
Coffeemaker, automatic drip	1963	Bunn Corp.	U.S.
Compressed air rock drill	1871	Ingersoll	U.S.
Comptometer	1887	Felt	U.S.
Computer, automatic sequence	1944	Aiken, et al.	U.S.
Computer, electronic	1942	Atanasoff, Berry	U.S.
Computer, laptop	1987	Sinclair	English
Computer, mini	1960	Digital Corp.	U.S.
Condenser microphone (telephone)	1916	Wente	U.S.
Contact lens, corneal	1948	Tuohy	U.S.
Contraceptive, oral	1954	Pincus, Rock	U.S.
Corn, hybrid	1917	Jones	U.S.
Cotton gin	1793	Whitney	U.S.
Cream separator	1878	DeLaval	Swedish

Invention	Date	Inventor(s)	Nationality
Cultivator, disc	1878	Mallon	U.S.
Cyclotron	1931	Lawrence	U.S.
Cystoscope	1878	Nitze	German
Diapers, disposable	1950	Donovan	U.S.
Diesel engine	1895	Diesel	German
Disc, compact	1972	RCA	U.S.
Disc player, compact	1979	Sony, Philips Co.	Japanese, Dutch
Dishwasher	1893	Cochrane	U.S.
Disk, floppy	1970	IBM	U.S.
Disk, video	1972	Philips Co.	Dutch
Dynamite	1866	Nobel	Swedish
Dynamo, contin. current	1871	Gramme	Belgian
Electric battery	1800	Volta	Italian
Electric fan	1882	Wheeler	U.S.
Electrocardiograph	1903	Einthoven	Dutch
Electroencephalograph.	1929	Berger	German
Electromagnet	1824	Sturgeon	English
Electronic paper (e-ink)	1974	Sheridon	U.S.
Electron microscope	1931	Ruska, Knoll	German
Electron spectrometer	1944	Deutsch, Elliott, Evans	U.S.
Electron tube multigrid	1913	Langmuir	U.S.
Electroplating	1805	Brugnatelli	Italian
Electrostatic generator	1929	Van de Graaff	U.S.
Elevator brake	1852	Otis	U.S.
Elevator, push button	1922	Larson	U.S.
Engine, automatic transmission	1910	Föttinger	German
Engine, coal-gas 4-cycle	1876	Otto	German
Engine, compression ignition	1883	Daimler	German
Engine, electric ignition	1883	Benz	German
Engine, gas, compound	1926	Eickemeyer	U.S.
Engine, gasoline	1872	Brayton, Geo.	U.S.
Engine, gasoline	1889	Daimler	German
Engine, jet	1930	Whittle	English
Engine, steam, piston	1705	Newcomen	English
Engine, steam, piston	1769	Watt	Scottish
Engraving, half-tone	1852	Talbot	U.S.
Ferris wheel	1893	Ferris	U.S.
Fiberglass	1938	Owens-Corning	U.S.
Fiber optics	1955	Kapany	English
Fiber optic wire	1970	Keck, Maurer Schulz	U.S.
Filament, tungsten	1913	Coolidge	U.S.
Flanged rail	1831	Stevens	U.S.
Flatiron, electric	1882	Seely	U.S.
Food, frozen	1923	Birdseye	U.S.
Freon	1930	Midgley, et al.	U.S.
Furnace (for steel)	1858	Siemens	German
Galvanometer	1820	Sweigger	German
Garbage bag, polyethylene	1950	Wasylyk	Canadian
Gas discharge tube	1922	Hull	U.S.
Gas lighting	1792	Murdoch	Scottish
Gas mantle	1885	Welsbach	Austrian
Gasoline, cracked	1913	Burton	U.S.
Gasoline, high octane	1930	Ipatieff	Russian
Gasoline (lead ethyl)	1922	Midgley	U.S.
Geiger counter	1913	Geiger	German
Geodesic dome	1948	Fuller	U.S.
Glass, laminated safety	1909	Benedictus	French
Glider	1853	Cayley	English
Google search software	1996	Brin, Page	U.S.
Gun, breechloader	1811	Thornton	U.S.
Gun, Browning	1897	Browning	U.S.
Gun, magazine	1875	Hotchkiss	U.S.
Gun, silencer	1908	Maxim, H. P.	U.S.
Guncotton	1847	Schoenbein	German
Gyrocompass	1911	Sperry	U.S.
Gyroscope	1852	Foucault	French
Hard drive, computer	1955	Johnson	U.S.
Harvester-thresher	1818	Lane	U.S.
Heart, artificial	1982	Jarvik	U.S.
Helicopter	1939	Sikorsky	U.S.
Hovercraft	1955	Cockerell	English
Hydrometer	1768	Baume	French
Ice resurfacing machine	1949	Zamboni	U.S.
Iron lung	1928	Drinker, Slaw	U.S.
Jet Ski	1973	Jacobsen	U.S.
Kaleidoscope	1817	Brewster	Scottish
Kevlar	1965	Kwolek, Blades	U.S.
Kidney dialysis machine	1941	Kolff	Dutch
Kinetoscope	1889	Edison	U.S.
Lamp, arc	1847	Staite	English
Lamp, fluorescent	1938	General Electric, Westinghouse	U.S.

Invention	Date	Inventor(s)	Nationality
Lamp, incandescent	1879	Edison	U.S.
Lamp, incand., gas	1913	Langmuir	U.S.
Lamp, klieg	1911	Kliegl, A. and J.	U.S.
Lamp, mercury vapor	1912	Hewitt	U.S.
Lamp, miner's safety	1816	Davy	English
Lamp, neon	1909	Claude	French
Lathe, turret	1845	Fitch	U.S.
Launderette	1934	Cantrell	U.S.
Lens, achromatic	1758	Dollond	English
Lens, fused bifocal	1908	Borsch	U.S.
Leyden jar (condenser)	1745	von Kleist	German
Lightning rod	1752	Franklin	U.S.
Linoleum	1860	Walton	English
Linotype	1884	Mergenthaler	U.S.
Linux	1991	Torvalds	Finnish
Liquid Paper	c.1951	Graham	U.S.
Lock, cylinder	1851	Yale	U.S.
Locomotive, electric	1851	Vail	U.S.
Locomotive, exp'mtl	1802	Trevithick	English
Locomotive, exp'mtl	1812	Fenton, et al.	English
Locomotive, exp'mtl	1814	Stephenson	English
Locomotive, practical	1829	Stephenson	English
Locomotive, 1st U.S.	1830	Cooper, P.	U.S.
Loom, power	1785	Cartwright	English
Loudspeaker, dynamic	1924	Rice, Kellogg	U.S.
Machine gun	1862	Gatling	U.S.
Machine gun, improved	1872	Hotchkiss	U.S.
Machine gun (Maxim)	1883	Maxim, H. S.	U.S.-Eng.
Magnet, electro	1828	Henry	U.S.
Magnetic Resonance Imaging (MRI)	1971	Damadian	U.S.
Maser	1953	Townes	U.S.
Mason jar	1858	Mason, J.	U.S.
Match, friction	1827	Walker, J.	English
Mercerized textiles	1843	Mercer, J.	English
Meter, induction	1888	Shallenberger	U.S.
Metronome	1816	Malezel	German
Microcomputer	1973	Truong, et al.	French
Micrometer	1636	Gascoigne	English
Microphone	1877	Berliner	U.S.
Microprocessor	1971	Intel Corp.	U.S.
Microscope, compound	1590	Janssen	Dutch
Microscope, electronic	1931	Knoll, Ruska	German
Microscope, field ion	1951	Mueller	German
Microwave oven	1947	Spencer	U.S.
Monitor, warship	1861	Ericsson	U.S.
Monotype	1887	Lanston	U.S.
Motor, AC	1892	Tesla	U.S.
Motor, DC	1837	Davenport	U.S.
Motor, induction	1887	Tesla	U.S.
Motorcycle	1885	Daimler	German
Mouse, computer	1968	Engelbart	U.S.
Movie machine	1894	Jenkins	U.S.
Movie, panoramic	1952	Waller	U.S.
Movie, talking	1927	Warner Bros.	U.S.
Mower, lawn	1831	Budding, Ferrabee	English
Mowing machine	1822	Bailey	U.S.
Neoprene	1930	Carothers	U.S.
Nylon	1937	DuPont lab	U.S.
Oil cracking furnace	1891	Gavrilov	Russian
Oil filled power cable	1921	Emanueli	Italian
Oleomargarine	1869	Mege-Mouries	French
Ophthalmoscope	1851	Helmholtz	German
Pacemaker	1952	Zoll	U.S.
Pacemaker, implantable cardiac	1958	Greatbatch	U.S.
Paper	105	Ts'ai	Chinese
Paper clip	1900	Waaler	Norwegian
Paper machine	1809	Dickinson	U.S.
Parachute	1785	Blanchard	French
Pen, ballpoint	1888	Loud	U.S.
Pen, fountain	1884	Waterman	U.S.
Pen, steel	1780	Harrison	English
Pendulum	1583	Galileo	Italian
Percussion cap	1807	Forsythe	Scottish
Phonograph	1877	Edison	U.S.
Photo, color	1892	Ives	U.S.
Photo film, celluloid	1893	Reichenbach	U.S.
Photo film, transparent	1884	Eastman, Goodwin	U.S.
Photocopier	1938	Carlson	U.S.
Photoelectric cell	1895	Elster	German
Photographic paper	1835	Talbot	English
Photography	1816	Niepce	French
Photography	1835	Talbot	English
Photography	1835	Daguerre	French

Invention	Date	Inventor(s)	Nationality
Photophone	1880	Bell	U.S.-Scot.
Phototelegraphy	1925	Bell Labs	U.S.
Piano	1709	Cristofori	Italian
Piano, player	1863	Fourneaux	French
Pin, safety	1849	Hunt	U.S.
Pistol (revolver)	1836	Colt	U.S.
Plow, cast iron	1785	Ransome	English
Plow, disc	1896	Hardy	U.S.
Pneumatic hammer	1890	King	U.S.
Post-it note	1980	Fry, Silver	U.S.
Potato chip	1853	Crum	U.S.
Powder, smokeless	1884	Vieille	French
Printing press, rotary	1845	Hoe	U.S.
Printing press, web	1865	Bullock	U.S.
Propeller, screw	1804	Stevens	U.S.
Propeller, screw	1837	Ericsson	Swedish
Punch card accounting	1889	Hollerith	U.S.
Radar	1940	Watson-Watt	Scottish
Radio, magnetic detector	1902	Marconi	Italian
Radio, signals	1895	Marconi	Italian
Radio amplifier	1906	De Forest	U.S.
Radio beacon	1928	Donovan	U.S.
Radio crystal oscillator	1918	Nicolson	U.S.
Radio receiver, cascade tuning	1913	Alexanderson	U.S.
Radio receiver, heterodyne	1913	Fessenden	Canadian
Radio transmitter triode modulation	1914	Alexanderson	U.S.
Radio tube diode	1904	Fleming	English
Radio tube oscillator	1915	De Forest	U.S.
Radio tube triode	1906	De Forest	U.S.
Radio FM, 2-path	1933	Armstrong	U.S.
Rayon (acetate)	1895	Cross	English
Rayon (cuprammonium)	1890	Despeissis	French
Rayon (nitrocellulose)	1884	Chardonnet	French
Razor, electric	1917	Schick	U.S.
Razor, safety	1895	Gillette	U.S.
Reaper	1834	McCormick	U.S.
Record, cylinder	1887	Bell, Tainter	U.S.
Record, disc	1887	Berliner	U.S.
Record, long playing	1947	Goldmark	U.S.
Record, wax cylinder	1888	Edison	U.S.
Refrigerator car	1868	David	U.S.
Remote control	1898	Tesla	U.S.
Resin, synthetic	1931	Hill	English
Richter scale	1935	Richter	U.S.
Rifle, repeating	1860	Henry	U.S.
Rocket, liquid fuel	1926	Goddard	U.S.
Rollerblades	1980	Olson	U.S.
Rubber, vulcanized	1839	Goodyear	U.S.
Saccharin	1879	Remsen, Fahlberg	U.S.
Saw, circular	1777	Miller	English
Scotch tape	1930	Drew	U.S.
Seat belt	1959	Volvo	Swedish
Segway human transporter	2001	Kamen	U.S.
Seismograph	1880	Milne, Ewing, Gray	British
Sewing machine	1846	Howe	U.S.
Shoe-lasting machine	1883	Matzeliger	U.S.
Shoe-sewing machine	1860	McKay	U.S.
Shrapnel shell	1784	Shrapnel	English
Shuttle, flying	1733	Kay	English
Skates, in-line	1759	Merlin	Belgian
Sleeping-car	1865	Pullman	U.S.
Slide rule	1620	Oughtred	English
Slinky	1943	James	U.S.
Smoke detector	1969	Smith, House	U.S.
Soap, hardwater	1928	Bertsch	German
Spectroscope	1859	Kirchoff, Bunsen	German
Spectroscope (mass)	1918	Dempster	U.S.
Spinning jenny	c.1764	Hargreaves	English
Spinning mule	1779	Crompton	English
Steam car	1770	Cugnot	French
Steam turbine	1884	Parsons	English
Steamboat, exp'mtl	1778	Jouffroy	French
Steamboat, exp'mtl	1785	Fitch	U.S.
Steamboat, exp'mtl	1787	Rumsey	U.S.
Steamboat, exp'mtl	1803	Fulton	U.S.
Steamboat, exp'mtl	1804	Stevens	U.S.
Steamboat, practical	1802	Symington	Scottish
Steamboat, practical	1807	Fulton	U.S.
Steel (converter)	1856	Bessemer	English

Invention	Date	Inventor(s)	Nationality
Steel alloy	1891	Harvey	U.S.
Steel alloy, high-speed	1901	Taylor, White	U.S.
Steel, manganese	1884	Hadfield	English
Steel, stainless	1916	Brearley	English
Stereoscope	1838	Wheatstone	English
Stethoscope	1819	Laennec	French
Stethoscope, binaural	1840	Cammann	U.S.
Stock ticker	1870	Edison	U.S.
Storage battery, rechargeable	1859	Plante	French
Stove, electric	1896	Hadaway	U.S.
Submarine	1891	Holland	U.S.
Submarine, even keel	1894	Lake	U.S.
Submarine, torpedo	1776	Bushnell	U.S.
Synthesizer	1964	Moog	U.S.
Tank, military	1914	Swinton	English
Tape recorder, magnetic	1899	Poulsen	Danish
Teflon	1938	Du Pont	U.S.
Telegraph, magnetic	1837	Morse	U.S.
Telegraph, quadruplex	1864	Edison	U.S.
Telegraph, railroad	1887	Woods	U.S.
Telegraph, wireless high frequency	1895	Marconi	Italian
Telephone[1]	1871	Meucci	U.S.-Italian
Telephone[1]	1876	Bell	U.S.-Scot.
Telephone amplifier	1912	De Forest	U.S.
Telephone answering machine (1st practical)	1954	Hashimoto	Japanese
Telephone, automatic	1891	Strowger	U.S.
Telephone, cellular[2]	1947	Bell Labs	U.S.
Telephone, cordless[2]	1950	Gross	U.S.
Telephone, radio	1900	Poulsen	Danish
		Fessenden	Canadian
Telephone, radio	1906	De Forest	U.S.
Telephone, radio, long dist.	1915	AT&T	U.S.
Telephone, recording	1898	Poulsen	Danish
Telescope	1608	Lippershey	Dutch
Telescope	1609	Galileo	Italian
Telescope, astronomical	1611	Kepler	German
Telescope, reflecting	1668	Newton	English
Teletype	1928	Morkrum, Kleinschmidt	U.S.
Television, color	1928	Baird	Scottish
Television, electronic	1927	Farnsworth	U.S.
Television, iconoscope	1923	Zworykin	U.S.
Television, mech. scanner	1923	Baird	Scottish
Tesla Coil	1891	Tesla	U.S.
Thermometer	1593	Galileo	Italian
Thermometer	1730	Reaumur	French
Thermometer, mercury	1714	Fahrenheit	German
Time recorder	1890	Bundy	U.S.
Tire, double-tube	1845	Thomson	Scottish
Tire, pneumatic	1888	Dunlop	Scottish
Toaster, automatic	1918	Strite	U.S.
Toilet, flush	1589	Harington	English
Tool, pneumatic	1865	Law	English
Torpedo, marine	1804	Fulton	U.S.
Tractor, crawler	1904	Holt	U.S.
Transformer, AC	1885	Stanley	U.S.
Transistor	1947	Shockley, Brattain, Bardeen	U.S.
Trolley car, electric	1884-87	Van DePoele, Sprague	U.S.
Tungsten, ductile	1912	Coolidge	U.S.
Tupperware®	1945	Tupper	U.S.
Turbine, gas	1849	Bourdin	French
Turbine, hydraulic	1849	Francis	U.S.
Turbine, steam	1884	Parsons	English
Type, movable	1447	Gutenberg	German
Typewriter	1867	Sholes, Soule, Glidden	U.S.
Universal Serial Bus (USB)	1994	Bhatt et al.	U.S.
Vacuum cleaner, electric	1907	Spangler	U.S.
Vacuum evaporating pan	1846	Rillieux	U.S.
Velcro	1948	de Mestral	Swiss
Video game ("Pong")	1972	Bushnell	U.S.
Video home system (VHS)	1975	Matsushita, JVC	Japanese

Invention	Date	Inventor(s)	Nationality	Invention	Date	Inventor(s)	Nationality
Vinyl	1926	Semon	U.S.	Windshield wiper	1903	Anderson	U.S.
Washer, electric	1901	Fisher	U.S.	Wind tunnel	1912	Eiffel	French
Welding, atomic				Wire, barbed	1874	Glidden	U.S.
hydrogen	1924	Langmuir, Palmer	U.S.	World Wide Web	1989	Berners-Lee	English
Welding, electric	1877	Thomson	U.S.	Wrench, double-acting	1913	Owen	U.S.
Wheelchair, multiterrain	1986	Twitchell	U.S.	X-ray tube	1913	Coolidge	U.S.
Wheelchair,				Zeppelin	1900	Zeppelin	German
stair-climbing	1962	Blanco	U.S.	Zipper, early model	1893	Judson	U.S.
Wiki software	1995	Cunningham	U.S.	Zipper, improved	1913	Sundback	Canadian

(1) While Alexander Graham Bell has traditionally been credited with invention of the telephone, which he patented, Antonio Meucci developed a working model before Bell. (2) Al Gross held a number of important early patents in the field of wireless communication; other people were also involved in the development of practical cordless telephones.

Top 20 Corporations Receiving U.S. Patents, 2010

Source: U.S. Patent and Trademark Office, U.S. Dept. of Commerce

Rank	Company	No. of patents	Rank	Company	No. of patents
1.	International Business Machines Corp.	5,866	11.	Hitachi, Ltd.	1,447
2.	Samsung Electronics Co., Ltd.	4,518	12.	Seiko Epson Corp.	1,438
3.	Microsoft Corp.	3,086	13.	Fujitsu Limited	1.276
4.	Canon Kabushiki Kaisha	2,551	14.	General Electric Co.	1,222
5.	Panasonic Corp.	2,443	15.	Ricoh Company, Ltd.	1,198
6.	Toshiba Corp.	2,212	16.	Cisco Technology, Inc.	1,114
7.	Sony Corp.	2,130	17.	Fujifilm Corp.	1,025
8.	Intel Corp.	1,652	18.	Honda Giken Kogyo Kabushiki Kaisha	
9.	LG Electronics Inc.	1,488		(Honda Motor Co., Ltd.)	987
10.	Hewlett-Packard Development Co., L.P.	1,480	19.	Hynix Semiconductor Inc.	973
			20.	Broadcom Corp.	958

Note: Reflects patent ownership at time of patent grant. Changes may occur after patent grant. Where more than one assignee exists, patents are attributed to first-named assignee.

Foreign Countries Receiving Most U.S. Patents, 2010

Source: U.S. Patent and Trademark Office, U.S. Dept. of Commerce

2010 rank	Country (2009 rank)	2010 patents	% change 2009-10	Share of total issued	2010 rank	Country (2009 rank)	2010 patents	% change 2009-10	Share of total issued
1.	Japan (1)	44,814	26.2%	20.4%	7.	United Kingdom (6)	4,302	35.5%	2.0%
2.	Germany (2)	12,363	37.4	5.6	8.	China (8)	2,657	60.5	1.2
3.	South Korea (3)	11,671	33.2	5.3	9.	Israel (9)	1,819	29.6	0.8
4.	Taiwan (4)	8,238	24.0	3.8	10.	Italy (10)	1,798	33.6	0.8
5.	Canada (5)	4,852	32.7	2.2		**United States**	107,792	30.8	49.1
6.	France (7)	4,450	41.7	2.0		**All countries**	219,614	31.2	100.0

Note: Country of origin is determined by residence of first-named inventor in patent.

Top 20 U.S. Patent Categories, 1990-2010

Source: U.S. Patent and Trademark Office, U.S. Dept. of Commerce
(ranked by number of patents issued in 2010)

Rank	Category	Pre-1990	1990	2000	2010	% change, 1990-2010
1.	Multiplex Communications	2,951	414	1,832	7,416	1,691.3%
2.	Active Solid-State Devices (e.g., Transistors, Solid-State Diodes)	4,616	960	2,716	6,908	619.6
3.	Semiconductor Device Manufacturing: Process	4,871	603	4,486	6,142	918.6
4.	Drug, Bio-Affecting, and Body Treating Compositions	21,445	2,355	3,949	4,686	99.0
5.	Electrical Computers and Digital Processing Systems: Multicomputer Data Transferring	244	49	1,161	4,648	9,385.7
6.	Data Processing: Database and File Management or Data Structures	227	52	862	4,445	8,448.1
7.	Telecommunications	2,537	248	1,876	4,309	1,637.5
8.	Data Processing: Financial, Business Practice, Management, or Cost/Price Determination	626	100	735	4,031	3,931.0
9.	Chemistry: Molecular Biology and Microbiology	6,400	932	3,451	3,720	299.1
10.	Image Analysis	1,649	311	1,245	3,373	984.6
11.	Computer Graphics Processing and Selective Visual Display Systems	2,690	385	1,635	3,322	762.9
12.	Pulse or Digital Communications	2,607	346	1,346	3,022	773.4
13.	Drug, Bio-Affecting, and Body Treating Compositions	6,734	1,022	2,788	2,852	179.1
14.	Static Information Storage and Retrieval	3,540	466	1,929	2,738	487.6
15.	Electricity: Electrical Systems and Devices	6,093	654	1,390	2,498	282.0
16.	Stock Material or Miscellaneous Articles	15,314	1,799	2,772	2,497	38.8
17.	Electrical Connectors	6,906	929	2,243	2,403	158.7
18.	Error Detection/Correction and Fault Detection/Recovery	2,406	300	986	2,390	696.7
19.	Optical: Systems and Elements	6,355	822	1,652	2,379	189.4
20.	Television	6,431	722	1,036	2,345	224.8

Geologic Time Scale

Our understanding of Earth's ancient history is largely a result of geoscientists' study of climate, rock strata, ice samples, mineral deposits, and fossils from around the world; clues to the planet's origin have also been found through the study of extraterrestrial bodies. Geologists divide Earth's history into the following units (MYA = million years ago):

PRECAMBRIAN TIME (4,600-542 MYA)

HADEAN EON (4,600-4,000 MYA) Earth has no continents, oceans, or life; surface conditions are defined by intense volcanic activity and widespread meteorite impact. Oldest known minerals and rocks, many of meteoric origin, date to this era.

ARCHEAN EON (4,000-2,500 MYA) Earth's surface cools and water vapor in atmosphere condenses to form early oceans, which define small protocontinents; the first single-celled organisms, bacteria and archaea, appear in these oceans.

PROTEROZOIC EON (2,500-542 MYA) Protocontinents merge into larger landmasses as Earth's crust continues to shift. Atmospheric oxygen levels increase, and first known multicellular life appears. Later, soft-bodied marine animals emerge.

PHANEROZOIC EON

Paleozoic Era (542-251 MYA)

Cambrian Period (542-488 MYA) The supercontinent known as Gondwana, or Gondwanaland, dominates the southern hemisphere. Seas experience an explosion of invertebrate animal life, including thousands of species of trilobites, and the first known vertebrates appear. There is no life on land.

Ordovician Period (488-444 MYA) Gondwanaland extends from South Pole to tropic regions; Northern Hemisphere is mostly open ocean. Average global temperatures are warmer than present era. First primitive land plants, early ancestors of starfish and mollusks, and first armored, jawless fishes appear. The period ends in extinction of a majority of species, possibly a result of a global drop in sea level due to glaciation.

Silurian Period (444-416 MYA) South Pole remains covered by supercontinent, but precursors of present-day N America, Europe, and Asia coalesce around the equator and middle latitudes. Appearance of first known vascular land plants, first freshwater fish, first jawed fish, first coral reefs, and first air-breathing animals (certain eurypterids, a scorpion-like creature).

Devonian Period (416-359 MYA) Collisions between Gondwanaland and ancestral landmasses of N America and Eurasia produce mountains visible today as northern Appalachians. Newly-formed ozone layer offers protection from sun's rays, allowing first air-breathing spiders and mites to appear on dry land; emergence of fish with fins and scales, and first amphibians.

Carboniferous Period (359-299 MYA) Precursors of modern N America and Northern Europe lie in tropical latitudes north of the Equator; warm and humid conditions there facilitate spread of lush forests and peat swamps that later form most of the world's coal and limestone. Later period sees emergence of first true conifers, lepidodendrales ("scale trees") as tall as 100 ft, and first true reptiles.

Permian Period (299-251 MYA) All major landmasses collide to form the supercontinent Pangaea, surrounded by the world ocean Panthalassa. Gradual warming through much of the Permian allows for initial flourishing of species— including dinosaur precursors (up to 10 ft in length) and marine species in shallow inland seas. The period ended with a mass extinction of as much as 95% of all marine species and most land species.

Mesozoic Era (251-65.5 MYA)

Triassic Period (251-200 MYA) Pangea separates into supercontinents of Laurasia and Gondwana; subtropical conditions extend as far north as present-day Wyoming and New England. Emergence of icthyosaurs and plesiosaurs (large marine reptiles), several species of dinosaurs (up to 15 ft long), first true mammals, and first insects to undergo metamorphosis from larva to pupa to adult.

Jurassic Period (200-145.5 MYA) N American continent drifts westward, opening Gulf of Mexico; rift forms between South America and Africa. Warm, moist climate contributes to flourishing of coral reefs and temperate and subtropical forests. Appearance of first angiosperms (flowering plants), pterosaurs (winged reptiles), the earliest known birds, and huge dinosaurs such as the carnivorous *Allosaurus* and herbivorous *Apatosaurus*.

Cretaceous Period (145.5-65.5 MYA) African continental plate drifts north, creating roots of European Alps; gap between S America and Africa broadens; western movement of N America drives formation of Sierra Nevada and Rocky Mountains, turning the western interior of continent into a vast swamp. Later, sea levels rise and cover about one-third of Earth's present land area; global climate is warm and mild. The period ends in a mass extinction of plant and animal species (including dinosaurs), likely caused by the impact of one or more asteroids or comet fragments.

Cenozoic Era (65.5 MYA-present)

Paleogene Period (65.5-23 MYA)

• **Paleocene Epoch** (65.5-55.8 MYA) Australia begins to separate from Antarctica; N America and Greenland begin to spread apart. Mammalian life predominates, including early marsupials, insectivores, creodonts (carnivorous relatives of cats and dogs), and primitive hoofed mammals.

• **Eocene Epoch** (55.8-33.9 MYA) Australia drifts farther from Antarctica; the Indian subcontinent becomes welded to Asia, and tectonic forces drive the upheaval of the Alpine-Himalayan system. Climate in N America and Europe is subtropical and moist, with temperate forests as far north as Greenland and Siberia. Ancestors of modern horses, elephants, rhinoceroses, camels, bats, primates, and squirrel-like rodents emerge; earliest known marine mammals appear in later Eocene.

• **Oligocene Epoch** (33.9-23 MYA) San Andreas fault develops between N American and Pacific plates. Mammalian species continue to diversify, producing modern horse and multiple rodent, camel, and rhinoceros-like species, as well as first known species of great ape. Long-term cooling trend begins that would later cause Pleistocene ice ages.

Neogene Period (23 MYA-2.6 MYA)

• **Miocene Epoch** (23-5.3 MYA) Crustal plate collisions continue to drive uplift of Alps, Himalayas, and Cordilleran Ranges in Americas; eroded sediment is deposited in shallow marine basins, forming reservoirs for oil fields of California, Romania, and Caspian Sea. Ocean currents prevent Antarctica from receiving warmer waters, fostering growth of Antarctic ice sheet; northern forests become grassy prairies. Large apes related to the orangutan live in Asia and southern Europe; oldest hominid fossils from Africa date to this epoch.

• **Pliocene Epoch** (5.3-2.6 MYA) Alps continue to rise in Europe, and subduction of the Pacific tectonic plate elevates the Sierra Nevada and volcanic Cascade Range. Climate becomes cooler and drier, driving formation of permanent Arctic ice cap. Rapid primate evolution produces *Australopithecus*, earliest direct ancestor of *Homo sapiens*.

Quaternary Period (2.6 MYA-present)

• **Pleistocene Epoch** (2.6 MYA-11,700 years ago) Glacier ice covers as much as 25% or more of Earth's land surface, carving numerous present-day features including the Great Lakes; increased rainfall in lower latitudes allows plant and animal life to flourish in northern and eastern Africa. Late Pleistocene brings worldwide extinction of many large mammals, including the mastodon, saber-toothed tiger, and ground sloth. Evidence of Neanderthals dates from the latter part of the Pleistocene.

• **Holocene Epoch** (11,700 years ago to the present) Melting ice caused sea levels to rise 100 ft or more in early Holocene, covering large areas of land and extending continental shelf of N America. Humans proliferate, and civilization begins.

Classification

Source: *Funk & Wagnalls New Encyclopedia*

In biology, classification is the identification, naming, and grouping of organisms into a formal system. The two fields that are most directly concerned with classification are taxonomy and systematics. Although they overlap, taxonomy is more concerned with nomenclature (naming) and with constructing hierarchical systems, and systematics with uncovering evolutionary relationships. Two kingdoms of living forms, Plantae and Animalia, have been recognized since Aristotle established the first taxonomy in the 4th century BCE. Plants and animals are examples of eukaryotes; their cells have nuclei bound by membranes. Two other kingdoms of eukaryotes that have been identified are Protista (one-celled organisms) and Fungi. The single-celled bacteria and archaea lack such nuclei. They are referred to as prokaryotes (or procaryotes) and are commonly placed in separate kingdoms. The seven basic categories of classification (from most general to most specific) are kingdom, phylum (or division), class, order, family, genus, and species. (In addition, many scientists group all eukaryotes together in a single "domain." The bacteria and archaea are also often treated as separate domains.) Below are two examples of classification:

ZOOLOGICAL HIERARCHY

Kingdom	Phylum	Class	Order	Family	Genus	Species name	Common name
Animalia	Chordata	Mammalia	Primates	Hominidae	*Homo*	*Homo sapiens*	Human

BOTANICAL HIERARCHY

Kingdom	Division*	Class	Order	Family	Genus	Species name	Common name
Plantae	Magnoliophyta	Magnoliopsida	Magnoliales	Magnoliaceae	*Magnolia*	*M. virginiana*	Sweet Bay

*In botany, the division is generally used in place of the phylum.

Gestation, Longevity, and Incubation of Selected Animals

Information reviewed by Ronald M. Nowak, author of *Walker's Mammals of the World* (6th ed., Johns Hopkins University Press, 1999). Average longevity figures supplied by Ronald T. Reuther. These apply to animals in captivity; the potential life span of animals is rarely attained in nature. Figures on gestation and incubation are averages based on estimates.

Animal	Gestation (days)	Average longevity (yrs.)	Maximum longevity (yrs.-mos.)	Animal	Gestation (days)	Average longevity (yrs.)	Maximum longevity (yrs.-mos.)
Ass	365	12	47	Leopard	98	12	23
Baboon	187	20	45	Lion	100	15	30
Bear (black)	219	18	36-10	Monkey (rhesus)	166	15	37
Bear (grizzly)	225	25	50	Moose	240	12	27
Bear (polar)	240	20	45	Mouse (domestic white)	19	3	6
Beaver	105	5	50	Mouse (meadow)	21	3	4
Bison	285	15	40	Opossum (American)	13	1	5
Camel	406	12	50	Pig (domestic)	112	10	27
Cat (domestic)	63	12	38	Puma	90	12	20
Chimpanzee	230	20	60	Rabbit (domestic)	31	5	18-10
Chipmunk	31	6	10	Rhinoceros (black)	450	15	45-10
Cow	284	15	30	Rhinoceros (white)	480	20	50
Deer (white-tailed)	201	8	20	Sea lion (California)	350	12	34
Dog (domestic)	61	12	21	Sheep (domestic)	154	12	23
Elephant (African)	660	35	70	Squirrel (gray)	44	10	23-6
Elephant (Asian)	645	40	77	Tiger	105	16	26-3
Elk	250	15	26-8	Wolf (maned)	63	5	15-8
Fox (red)	52	7	14	Zebra (Grant's)	365	15	50
Giraffe	457	10	36-2				
Goat (domestic)	151	8	18				**Incubation time (days)**
Gorilla	258	20	54	Chicken			21
Guinea pig	68	4	8	Duck			30
Hippopotamus	238	41	61	Goose			30
Horse	330	20	50	Pigeon			18
Kangaroo (gray)	36	7	24	Turkey			26

Major Venomous Animals

Snakes

Asian pit viper—2 ft to 5 ft long; throughout Asia; reactions and mortality vary, but most bites cause tissue damage, and mortality is generally low.

Australian brown snake—4 ft to 7 ft long; very slow onset of cardiac or respiratory distress; moderate mortality, but because death can be sudden and unexpected, it is the most dangerous of the Australian snakes; antivenom.

Barba Amarilla or fer-de-lance—up to 7 ft long; from tropical Mexico to Brazil; severe tissue damage common; moderate mortality; antivenom.

Black mamba—up to 14 ft long, fast-moving; S and central Africa; rapid onset of dizziness, difficulty breathing, erratic heartbeat; mortality high, nears 100% without antivenom.

Boomslang—less than 6 ft long; African savannahs; rapid onset of nausea and dizziness, often followed by slight recovery and then sudden death from internal hemorrhaging; bites rare, mortality high; antivenom.

Bushmaster—up to 12 ft long; wet tropical forests of Central and S America; few bites occur, but mortality rate is high.

Common, or Asian, cobra—4 ft to 8 ft long; throughout southern Asia; considerable tissue damage, sometimes paralysis; mortality probably not more than 10%; antivenom.

Copperhead—less than 4 ft long; from New England to Texas; pain and swelling; very seldom fatal; antivenom seldom needed.

Coral snake—2 ft to 5 ft long; in Americas south of Canada; bite may be painless; slow onset of paralysis, impaired breathing; mortalities rare, but high without antivenom and mechanical respiration.

Cottonmouth water moccasin—up to 5 ft long; wetlands of southern U.S. from Virginia to Texas; rapid onset of severe pain, swelling; mortality low, but tissue destruction can be extensive; antivenom.

Death adder—less than 3 ft long; Australia; rapid onset of faintness, cardiac and respiratory distress; at least 50% mortality without antivenom.

Desert horned viper—up to 2 ft long; dry areas of Africa and western Asia; swelling and tissue damage; low mortality; antivenom.

European viper—1 ft to 3 ft long; throughout Europe; bleeding and tissue damage; mortality low; antivenom.

Gaboon viper—more than 6 ft long, fat, 2-in. fangs; south of the Sahara; massive tissue damage, internal bleeding; few recorded bites.

King cobra—up to 16 ft long; throughout southern Asia; rapid swelling, dizziness, loss of consciousness, difficulty breathing, erratic heartbeat; mortality varies sharply with amount of venom involved, but most bites involve nonfatal amounts; antivenom.

Krait—up to 5 ft long; SE Asia; rapid onset of sleepiness, numbness; up to 50% mortality even with use of antivenom.

Puff adder—up to 5 ft long, fat; south of the Sahara, throughout the Middle East; rapid large swelling, great pain, dizziness; moderate mortality, often from internal bleeding; antivenom.

Rattlesnake—2 ft to 6 ft long; throughout W Hemisphere; rapid onset of severe pain, swelling; mortality low, but amputation of affected parts is sometimes necessary; antivenom. Mojave rattler may produce temporary paralysis.

Ringhals, or spitting, cobra—5 ft to 7 ft long; southern Africa; squirts venom through holes in front of fangs as a defense; venom is severely irritating, can cause blindness.

Russell's viper or tic-polonga—more than 5 ft long; throughout Asia; internal bleeding; bite reports common; moderate mortality rate; antivenom.

Saw-scaled, or carpet, viper—up to 2 ft long; dry areas from India to Africa; severe bleeding, fever; high mortality, causes more human fatalities than any other snake; antivenom.

Sea snakes—3 ft to 10 ft long; throughout Pacific, Indian oceans except NE Pacific; almost painless bite; variety of muscle pain, paralysis; mortality rate low, many bites not envenomed; some antivenoms.

Sharp-nosed pit viper or one hundred pace snake—up to 5 ft long; S Vietnam, S China; the most toxic of Asian pit vipers; very rapid onset of swelling and tissue damage, internal bleeding; moderate mortality; antivenom.

Taipan—up to 11 ft long; Australia and New Guinea; rapid paralysis with severe breathing difficulty; mortality nears 100% without antivenom.

Tiger snake—2 ft to 6 ft long; S Australia; pain, numbness, mental disturbances with rapid paralysis; may be deadliest of all land snakes, but antivenom is quite effective.

Yellow, or cape, cobra—7 ft long; southern Africa; most toxic venom of any cobra; rapid onset of swelling, breathing and cardiac difficulties; mortality is high without treatment; antivenom.

Note: Not all bites by venomous snakes are actually envenomed. Any animal bite, however, carries the danger of tetanus, and anyone suffering a venomous snake bite should seek medical attention. Antivenoms do not cure; they are only an aid in the treatment of bites. Mortality rates above are for envenomed bites; low mortality, c. 2% or less; moderate, 2%-5%; high, 5%-15%.

Lizards

Gila monster—up to 24 in. long, with heavy body and tail; in high desert in SW U.S. and N Mexico; immediate severe pain and transient low blood pressure; no recent mortality.

Mexican beaded lizard—similar to Gila monster; Mexican west coast; reaction and mortality rate similar to Gila monster.

Insects

Ants, bees, wasps, hornets—global distribution; usual reaction is piercing pain in area of sting; not directly fatal, except in cases of massive multiple stings, though many people suffer allergic reactions—swelling and rashes—and a few may die within minutes from severe sensitivity to the venom (anaphylactic shock).

Spiders, scorpions

Black widow—small, round-bodied with red hourglass marking; the widow and its relatives are found in tropical and temperate zones; severe musculoskeletal pain, weakness, breathing difficulty, convulsions; may be more serious in small children; low mortality; antivenom. The **redback** spider of Australia has the hourglass marking on its back, rather than on its front, but is otherwise identical to the black widow.

Brown recluse, or fiddleback, spider—small, oblong body; throughout U.S.; pain with later ulceration, which may last months, at place of bite; in severe cases fever, nausea, and stomach cramps; very low mortality.

Funnel web spider—several varieties, often large; Australia; slow onset of breathing, circulation difficulties; low mortality; antivenom.

Scorpion—crablike body with stinger in tail, various sizes; many varieties throughout tropical and subtropical areas; symptoms may include severe pain spreading from the wound, numbness, severe agitation, cramps; severe reaction may include respiratory failure; low mortality, usually in children; antivenoms.

Tarantula—large, hairy spider found around the world; the American tarantula, and probably all other tarantulas, are harmless to humans, though their bite may cause some pain and swelling.

Sea life

Cone-shell—mollusk in small, beautiful shell; S Pacific and Indian oceans; shoots barbs into victims; paralysis; low mortality.

Octopus—global distribution, usually in warm waters; rapid onset of paralysis with breathing difficulty; all varieties produce venom, but only a few can cause death.

Portuguese man-of-war—jellyfish-like, with tentacles up to 100 ft long; in most warm water areas; immediate severe pain; not directly fatal, though shock may cause death in rare cases.

Sea wasp—jellyfish, with tentacles up to 30 ft long; S Pacific; very rapid onset of circulatory problems; high mortality because of speed of toxic reaction; antivenom.

Stingray—several varieties of differing sizes; tropical and temperate seas and some fresh water; severe pain, rapid onset of nausea, vomiting, breathing difficulties; wound area may ulcerate, gangrene may appear; seldom fatal.

Stonefish—brownish fish that lies motionless on bottom of shallow waters; throughout S Pacific and Indian oceans; extraordinary pain, rapid paralysis; low mortality; antivenom available, amount determined by number of puncture wounds; warm water relieves pain.

Speeds of Selected Animals

Source: Natural History magazine. © American Museum of Natural History

Animal	mph	Animal	mph	Animal	mph
Cheetah	70	Mongolian wild ass	40	Human	27.89
Pronghorn antelope	61	Greyhound	39.35	Elephant	25
Wildebeest	50	Whippet	35.50	Black mamba snake	20
Lion	50	Rabbit (domestic)	35	Six-lined race runner (lizard)	18
Thomson's gazelle	50	Mule deer	35	Wild turkey	15
Quarterhorse	47.5	Jackal	35	Squirrel	12
Elk	45	Reindeer	32	Pig (domestic)	11
Cape hunting dog	45	Giraffe	32	Chicken	9
Coyote	43	White-tailed deer	30	Spider (Tegenaria atrica)	1.17
Gray fox	42	Wart hog	30	Giant tortoise	0.17
Hyena	40	Grizzly bear	30	Three-toed sloth	0.15
Zebra	40	Cat (domestic)	30	Garden snail	0.03

Note: Most of these measurements are for maximum speeds over approximate quarter-mile distances. Exceptions are the lion and elephant, whose speeds were clocked in the act of charging; the whippet, which was timed over a 200-yd course; the cheetah, timed over a 100-yd distance; a human, timed over a 15-yd segment of a 100-yd run; and the black mamba, six-lined race runner, spider, giant tortoise, three-toed sloth, and garden snail, which were measured over various small distances.

Top 50 American Kennel Club Registrations, 2000-10

Source: American Kennel Club (AKC), New York, NY

Breed	Rank 2010	Rank 2009	Rank 2005	Rank 2000	Breed	Rank 2010	Rank 2009	Rank 2005	Rank 2000
Labrador Retrievers	1	1	1	1	Australian Shepherds	26	28	34	35
German Shepherd Dogs	2	2	4	3	Pembroke Welsh Corgis	27	26	23	27
Yorkshire Terriers	3	3	3	7	Mastiffs	28	27	33	39
Beagles	4	5	5	5	English Springer Spaniels	29	29	28	26
Golden Retrievers	5	4	2	2	Brittanys	30	30	30	31
Bulldogs	6	7	13	21	Havanese	31	32	43	86
Boxers	7	6	7	9	Weimaraners	32	31	29	32
Dachshunds	8	8	6	4	Leonbergers[1]	33	NA	NA	NA
Poodles	9	9	8	6	West Highland White Terriers	34	36	32	30
Shih Tzu	10	10	9	10	Papillons	35	37	35	43
Rottweilers	11	13	16	11	Basset Hounds	36	34	27	22
Miniature Schnauzers	12	11	10	13	Bichons Frises	37	35	26	25
Chihuahuas	13	12	11	8	Collies	38	38	36	34
Doberman Pinschers	14	15	21	23	Bernese Mountain Dogs	39	39	47	58
Pomeranians	15	14	14	12	Miniature Pinschers	40	33	22	17
German Shorthaired Pointers	16	16	20	24	Vizslas	41	42	44	47
Great Danes	17	21	24	28	Bullmastiffs	42	40	42	52
Siberian Huskies	18	22	25	19	Bloodhounds	43	43	50	50
Shetland Sheepdogs	19	18	18	16	Newfoundlands	44	46	46	53
Boston Terriers	20	19	17	18	St. Bernards	45	45	37	36
French Bulldogs	21	24	38	71	Rhodesian Ridgebacks	46	48	54	57
Maltese	22	20	19	20	Border Collies	47	52	55	64
Cavalier King Charles Spaniels	23	25	31	54	Chesapeake Bay Retrievers	48	49	49	41
Pugs	24	17	12	15	Akitas	49	50	51	38
Cocker Spaniels	25	23	15	14	Chinese Shar-Pei	50	47	45	37

(1) Breed entered in AKC registry in 2010. The breed was not recognized by the AKC prior to that year.

Registrations for Pedigreed Cats, 2010

Source: The Cat Fanciers' Association, Alliance, OH

The breeds recognized by the Cat Fanciers' Association in 2010, listed in order of registration totals, were as follows:

Rank	Breed	Rank	Breed	Rank	Breed	Rank	Breed
1.	Persian	12.	British Shorthair	22.	Japanese Bobtail	32.	Korat
2.	Maine Coon	13.	Tonkinese	23.	Somali	33.	RagaMuffin
3.	Exotic	14.	Oriental	24.	Selkirk Rex	34.	Chartreux
4.	Ragdoll	15.	Devon Rex	25.	Turkish Angora	35.	Bombay
5.	Sphynx	16.	Scottish Fold	26.	Manx	36.	European Burmese
6.	Siamese	17.	Burmese	27.	American Curl	37.	LaPerm
7.	Abyssinian	18.	Siberian	28.	Colorpoint Shorthair	38.	American Bobtail
8.	American Shorthair	19.	Ocicat	29.	Singapura	39.	Turkish Van
9.	Cornish Rex	20.	Russian Blue	30.	Balinese/Javanese	40.	American Wirehair
10.	Birman	21.	Egyptian Mau	31.	Havana Brown	41.	Chinese Li Hua
11.	Norwegian Forest Cat						

Note: In Feb. 2011, the Cat Fanciers' Association accepted for registration the Burmilla, a 42nd breed.

Trees of the U.S.

Source: American Forests, Washington, DC

Approximately 861 native and naturalized species of trees are grown in the U.S. The trunk of the world's largest known living tree, the General Sherman giant sequoia in California, weighs almost 1,400 tons—about as much as 15 adult blue whales. Listed here are the 10 largest National Champion trees according to American Forests, as of July 1, 2011.

10 Largest National Champion Trees

Tree type	Girth at 4.5 ft (in.)	Height (ft)	Crown spread (ft)	Total points	Location
Giant sequoia (Gen. Sherman tree)	1,020	274	107	1,321	Sequoia National Park, CA
Coast redwood	950	321	75	1,290	Jedediah Smith Redwoods State Park, CA
Coast redwood	895	307	83	1,223	Jedediah Smith Redwoods State Park, CA
Coast redwood	844	349	89	1,216	Redwood National Park, CA
Coast redwood	867	299	101	1,191	Prairie Creek Redwoods State Park, CA
Western red cedar	761	159	45	931	Olympic National Park, WA
Sitka spruce	668	191	96	883	Olympic National Park, WA
Coast Douglas-fir	505	281	71	804	Olympic National Forest, WA
Port-Orford-cedar	522	242	35	773	Siskiyou National Forest, OR
Common baldcypress	647	96	74	762	Cat Island, LA

Note: American Forests uses a point system to determine the largest trees. The following calculation is used to determine a tree's points: trunk circumference (in inches) + height (in feet) + ¼ average crown spread (in feet) = total points.

ENVIRONMENT

U.S. Greenhouse Gas Emissions From Human Activities, 1990-2009
Source: U.S. Environmental Protection Agency

Gas and major source(s)	1990	1995	2000	2006	2007	2008	2009	% change, 2000-09
Carbon dioxide (CO_2)	5,099.7	5,422.8	5,975.0	6,021.1	6,120.0	5,921.4	5,505.2	–8%
Fossil fuel combustion	4,738.4	5,031.5	5,594.8	5,653.1	5,756.7	5,565.9	5,209.0	–7
Methane (CH_4)	674.9	678.0	659.9	672.1	664.6	676.7	686.3	4
Landfills	147.4	139.4	111.7	111.7	111.3	115.9	117.5	5
Enteric fermentation[1]	132.1	143.5	136.5	138.8	141.0	140.6	139.8	2
Natural gas systems	189.8	198.4	209.3	217.7	205.2	211.8	221.2	6
Coal mining	84.1	67.1	60.4	58.2	57.9	67.1	71.0	18
Nitrous oxide (N_2O)	315.2	342.8	341.0	326.4	325.1	310.8	295.6	–13
Agricultural soil management	197.8	207.6	206.8	208.9	209.4	210.7	204.6	–1
Hydrofluorocarbons (HFCs), perfluorocarbons (PFCs), and sulfur hexafluoride (SF_6)	92.0	107.2	136.8	147.4	153.7	152.2	146.1	7
Total U.S. emissions	**6,181.8**	**6,550.7**	**7,112.7**	**7,166.9**	**7,263.4**	**7,061.1**	**6,633.2**	**–7**
Net U.S. emissions[2]	**5,320.3**	**5,738.1**	**6,536.1**	**6,102.6**	**6,202.5**	**6,020.7**	**5,618.2**	**–14**

Note: Emissions given in terms of equivalent emissions of carbon dioxide (CO_2), using units of teragrams of carbon dioxide equivalents (Tg CO_2 Eq.). (1) Digestive process of ruminant animals, such as cattle and sheep, producing methane as a by-product. (2) Total emissions minus carbon dioxide absorbed by forests or other means.

U.S. Carbon Dioxide Emissions From Fossil Fuel Combustion, 1990-2009
Source: U.S. Environmental Protection Agency; in teragrams of carbon dioxide equivalents (Tg CO_2 Eq.)

The concept of Global Warming Potential (GWP) was developed by the Intergovernmental Panel on Climate Change (IPCC) to compare the ability of each greenhouse gas to trap heat in the atmosphere relative to another gas. Carbon dioxide (CO_2) from fossil fuel combustion is the largest source of U.S. greenhouse gas emissions, accounting for approximately 78% of GWP weighted emissions since 1990.

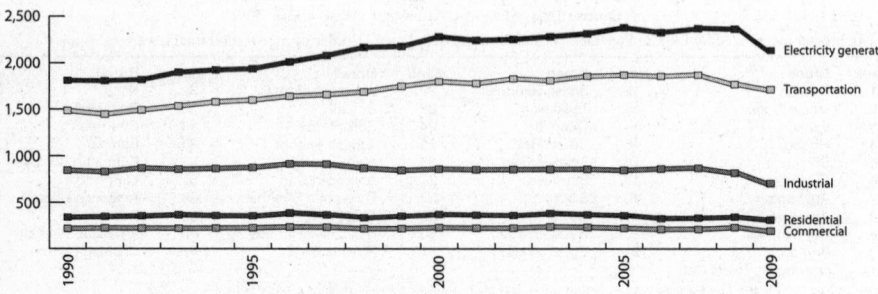

Top 15 Nations Producing Carbon Dioxide Emissions, 1980-2009
Source: U.S. Department of Energy
(in million metric tons of carbon dioxide emitted from the consumption of energy; ranked by 2009 totals)

Country	1980	1985	1990	1995	2000	2009	% change, 1980-2009	% change, 1990-2009
China	1,448.46	1,857.81	2,269.71	2,861.68	2,849.75	7,706.83	432%	240%
United States	4,776.57	4,604.84	5,041.00	5,319.89	5,861.82	5,424.53	14	8
India	291.23	447.38	578.62	870.23	1,002.95	1,591.13	446	175
Russia[1]	3,081.87	3,535.69	3,820.85	1,603.06	1,556.10	1,556.66	NA	NA
Japan	947.01	926.25	1,046.98	1,116.24	1,201.43	1,097.96	16	5
Germany[2]	759.25	688.15	698.14	890.82	854.66	765.56	NA	NA
Canada	457.45	443.67	470.59	508.74	573.27	540.97	18	15
Iran	116.83	159.94	202.11	262.20	320.62	528.60	355	162
Korea, South	131.74	172.32	242.13	381.43	438.83	528.13	301	118
United Kingdom	613.57	589.26	601.82	560.13	560.34	519.94	–15	–14
South Africa	235.03	302.05	297.98	347.47	386.01	451.22	92	51
Mexico	240.33	280.70	302.16	321.37	383.05	443.61	85	47
South Arabia	176.92	179.22	208.02	235.29	290.54	438.25	148	111
Brazil	185.66	192.66	237.33	289.09	344.36	425.17	129	79
Australia	198.83	237.70	267.60	289.07	356.31	417.68	110	56
World total[3]	18,433.92	19,542.06	21,615.99	22,150.06	23,803.63	30,313.25	64	40

NA = Not applicable. (1) Numbers for 1980-90 are for the former Soviet Union. (2) Numbers for 1980-90 are for former West Germany. (3) Includes nations not listed.

Air Pollution in Selected World Cities

Source: *World Development Indicators 2011*, The World Bank

Particulate matter in the following table refers to smoke, soot, dust, and liquid droplets from combustion that are in the air—specifically, to particulates less than 10 microns in diameter capable of reaching deep into the respiratory tract. The level of particulates, an important indicator of air quality, is significantly affected by the state of technology and pollution controls. Particulate pollution causes an estimated 500,000 premature deaths each year. **Sulfur dioxide** is a pollutant formed when fossil fuels containing sulfur are burned. **Nitrogen dioxide** is a poisonous, pungent gas formed when nitric oxide combines with hydrocarbons and sunlight, producing a photochemical reaction. Nitrogen oxides are emitted by bacteria, nitrogenous fertilizers, aerobic decomposition of organic matter, biomass combustion, and, especially, burning fuel for vehicles and industrial activities. Emissions of sulfur dioxide and nitrogen oxides lead to **acid rain**.

Data in the table are average concentrations based on reports from urban monitoring sites, measured in micrograms per cubic meter (mpcm); the figures give a general indication of air quality, but results should be interpreted with caution. World Health Organization standards for acceptable air quality are annual mean concentrations of 20 mpcm for particulate matter less than 10 microns in diameter (PM10) and 40 mpcm for nitrogen dioxide and daily mean concentrations of 20 mpcm for sulfur dioxide.

City, country	Particulate matter[1]	Sulfur dioxide[2]	Nitrogen dioxide[2]	City, country	Particulate matter[1]	Sulfur dioxide[2]	Nitrogen dioxide[2]
Accra, Ghana	24	NA	NA	Montréal, Canada	15	10	42
Amsterdam, Netherlands	31	10	58	Moscow, Russia	16	109	NA
Athens, Greece	34	34	64	Mumbai, India	51	33	39
Bangkok, Thailand	63	11	23	Nairobi, Kenya	32	NA	NA
Barcelona, Spain	29	11	43	New York, NY-Newark, NJ, U.S.	18	26	79
Beijing, China	80	90	122	Oslo, Norway	20	8	43
Berlin, Germany	18	18	26	Paris, France	10	14	57
Cairo, Egypt	124	69	NA	Prague, Czech Republic	19	14	33
Cape Town, South Africa	13	21	72	Quito, Ecuador	24	22	NA
Caracas, Venezuela	14	33	57	Rio de Janeiro, Brazil	26	129	NA
Chicago, IL, U.S.	21	14	57	Rome, Italy	25	NA	NA
Delhi, India	122	24	41	São Paulo, Brazil	30	43	83
Jakarta, Indonesia	74	NA	NA	Seoul, South Korea	33	44	60
Kolkata, India	104	49	34	Shanghai, China	65	53	73
London, United Kingdom	17	25	77	Sofia, Bulgaria	55	39	122
Los Angeles, CA, U.S.	29	9	74	Tokyo, Japan	35	18	68
Manila, Philippines	26	33	NA	Toronto, Canada	17	17	43
Mexico City, Mexico	43	74	130	Warsaw, Poland	39	16	32
Milan, Italy	26	31	248				

NA = Not available. (1) Urban-population-weighted PM10 data as of 2008. (2) As of 2001.

Air Quality of Selected U.S. Urban Areas, 2000-10

Source: Office of Air Quality Planning and Standards, U.S. Environmental Protection Agency

Data indicate the number of days metropolitan statistical areas or corresponding "core based statistical areas" failed to meet acceptable air-quality standards.

Urban area	2000	2005	2007	2008	2009	2010
Atlanta-Sandy Springs-Marietta, GA	26	5	15	4	0	2
Bakersfield, CA	62	33	29	40	23	14
Baltimore-Towson, MD	7	6	5	4	1	6
Baton Rouge, LA	19	9	5	0	0	3
Boston-Cambridge-Quincy, MA-NH	1	3	2	0	0	0
Chicago-Naperville-Joliet, IL-IN-WI	1	6	2	0	1	0
Cincinnati-Middletown, OH-KY-IN	3	5	4	0	0	0
Cleveland-Elyria-Mentor, OH	2	6	2	0	0	1
Dallas-Fort Worth-Arlington, TX	17	16	3	1	3	0
Denver-Aurora, CO	0	0	2	0	0	0
Detroit-Warren-Livonia, MI	1	7	4	1	0	0
Fresno, CA	69	19	19	17	10	11
Houston-Sugar Land-Baytown, TX	30	19	5	3	6	1
Indianapolis-Carmel, IN	6	1	0	0	0	1
Kansas City, MO-KS	6	4	2	0	0	0
Las Vegas-Paradise, NV	1	3	2	0	0	0
Los Angeles-Long Beach-Santa Ana, CA	36	29	18	31	18	4
Memphis, TN-MS-AR	6	4	2	1	0	0
Miami-Fort Lauderdale-Pompano Beach, FL	0	1	0	0	0	0
Minneapolis-St. Paul-Bloomington, MN-WI	1	2	0	0	0	0
Nashville-Davidson-Murfreesboro-Franklin, TN	5	1	2	0	0	0
New Orleans-Metairie-Kenner, LA	5	0	1	0	0	16
New York-N. New Jersey-Long Island, NY-NJ-PA	7	12	7	2	0	1
Philadelphia-Camden-Wilmington, PA-NJ-DE-MD	9	9	7	4	0	3
Phoenix-Mesa-Scottsdale, AZ	2	1	92	84	17	3
Pittsburgh, PA	7	13	8	2	3	10
Riverside-San Bernardino-Ontario, CA	65	50	52	57	47	31
Sacramento-Arden-Arcade-Roseville, CA	22	22	4	19	8	4
Salt Lake City, UT	9	2	9	1	4	5
San Francisco-Oakland-Fremont, CA	1	0	0	1	0	1
Seattle-Tacoma-Bellevue, WA	0	0	2	0	1	0
Tucson, AZ	0	0	0	0	1	0
Washington-Arlington-Alexandria, DC-VA-MD-WV	5	4	3	3	0	2
Winston-Salem, NC	4	0	2	0	1	0

U.S. Greenhouse Gas Emissions, 2009
Source: U.S. Environmental Protection Agency

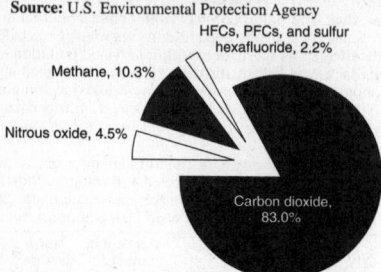

HFCs, PFCs, and sulfur hexafluoride, 2.2%
Methane, 10.3%
Nitrous oxide, 4.5%
Carbon dioxide, 83.0%

World Carbon Dioxide Emissions From the Use of Fossil Fuels, 2009
Source: U.S. Energy Information Administration

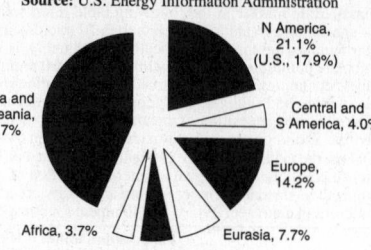

N America, 21.1% (U.S., 17.9%)
Asia and Oceania, 43.7%
Central and S America, 4.0%
Europe, 14.2%
Eurasia, 7.7%
Africa, 3.7%
Middle East, 5.6%

Note: Emissions sources are independently rounded; percentages may not add up to 100.

Atmospheric Concentration of Carbon Dioxide, 1744-2009
Sources: Carbon Dioxide Information Analysis Center, U.S. Dept. of Energy

Year[1]	CO$_2$ in ppm[2]	Year[1]	CO$_2$ in ppm[2]	Year[1]	CO$_2$ in ppm[2]	Year[1]	CO$_2$ in ppm[2]	Year[1]	CO$_2$ in ppm[2]
1744	277	1878	290	1943	308	1990	354	2006	379
1791	280	1903	295	1960	317	2000	367	2007	381
1816	284	1915	301	1970	326	2004	375	2008	383
1843	287	1927	306	1980	339	2005	377	2009	385
1869	289								

(1) Measurements for the years 1744-1943 were derived from a 200-m ice core sample drilled near Siple Station in Antarctica in 1983-84. Measurements from 1960-2004 were taken directly from the atmosphere at Mauna Loa Observatory in Hawaii. Measurements for 2005-09 were taken directly from the atmosphere at Jubany Station, Antarctica. (2) Parts per million.

Emissions of Principal Air Pollutants in the U.S., 1970-2008
Source: Office of Air Quality Planning and Standards, U.S. Environmental Protection Agency; in est. million tons

Pollutant	1970	1975	1980	1985	1990	1995	2000	2005	2008
Carbon monoxide	204.0	188.4	185.4	176.8	154.2	126.8	114.5	93.0	77.7
Nitrogen oxides[1]	26.9	26.4	27.1	25.8	25.5	25.0	22.6	19.1	16.3
Particulate matter[2]									
PM$_{10}$	13.0	7.6	7.0	41.3	27.8	25.8	23.0	18.3	11.9
PM$_{2.5}$	NA	NA	NA	NA	7.6	6.9	6.5	3.0	2.4
Sulfur dioxide	31.2	28.0	25.9	23.3	23.1	18.6	16.3	14.8	11.4
Volatile org. compounds[1]	3.5	30.8	31.1	27.4	24.1	22.06	17.5	18.4	15.9
Lead	0.221	0.160	0.074	0.022	0.005	0.004	0.003	0.001	0.001
Total[3]	278.8	281.4	276.5	294.6	254.7	91.5	193.9	163.6	133.2

NA = Not available. (1) Ozone, a major air pollutant and the primary constituent of smog, is not emitted directly to the air but is formed by sunlight acting on emissions of nitrogen oxides and volatile organic compounds. (2) PM$_{10}$, particulates 10 microns or smaller diameter. PM$_{2.5}$, particulates 2.5 microns or smaller diameter. (3) Totals are rounded, as are components of totals.

Carbon Monoxide Emission Estimates, 1970-2008
(in thousand tons)

Source	1970	1975	1980	1985	1990	1995	2000	2006	2007	2008
Fuel combustion, elec. util.	237	276	322	291	363	372	484	661	680	699
Industrial processes[1]	10,610	8,304	7,700	5,894	5,572	5,631	3,628	3,143	3,213	3,283
Transportation[2]	174,602	167,884	160,512	153,216	131,702	107,755	92,239	65,111	61,007	56,902
Total[3]	204,042	188,398	185,408	176,845	154,188	126,778	114,465	87,915	82,801	77,685

(1) Industrial fuel combustion, chemical and allied manufacturing, metals processing, and petroleum and other industrial sectors. (2) Highway and off-highway vehicles. (3) Numbers may not add up to totals because not all categories are listed.

Nitrogen Oxides Emission Estimates, 1970-2008
(in thousand tons)

Source	1970	1975	1980	1985	1990	1995	2000	2006	2007	2008
Fuel combustion, elec. util.	4,900	5,694	7,024	6,127	6,663	6,384	5,330	3,446	3,320	3,006
Industrial processes[1]	5,100	4,546	4,110	4,009	3,831	3,909	3,518	2,769	2,755	2,741
Transportation[2]	15,276	15,029	14,846	14,508	13,373	12,989	12,561	10,740	10,101	9,461
Total[3]	26,882	26,378	27,080	25,757	25,527	24,955	22,599	18,110	17,321	16,339

(1) Industrial fuel combustion, chemical and allied manufacturing, metals processing, and petroleum and other industrial sectors. (2) Highway and off-highway vehicles. (3) Numbers may not add up to totals because not all categories are listed.

Sulfur Dioxide Emission Estimates, 1970-2008
(in thousand tons)

Source	1970	1975	1980	1985	1990	1995	2000	2006	2007	2008
Fuel combustion, elec. util.	17,398	18,268	17,469	16,272	15,909	12,080	11,396	9,404	8,941	7,552
Industrial processes[1]	11,661	7,993	6,725	5,597	5,402	4,945	3,516	2,701	2,683	2,663
Transportation[2]	551	635	717	809	874	741	697	827	673	520
Total[3]	31,218	28,044	25,926	23,307	23,077	18,619	16,348	13,655	13,006	11,429

(1) Industrial fuel combustion, chemical and allied manufacturing, metals processing, and petroleum and other industrial sectors. (2) Highway and off-highway vehicles. (3) Numbers may not add up to totals because not all categories are listed.

Average Global Temperatures, 1900-2010

Source: National Oceanic and Atmospheric Administration, U.S. Dept. of Commerce; in degrees Fahrenheit

Period	Avg. °F	Period	Avg. °F	Period	Avg. °F	Period	Avg. °F	Period	Avg. °F
1900-09	56.58	1950-59	56.98	1990-99	57.64	2003	58.02	2007	58.01
1910-19	56.56	1960-69	57.04	2000	57.67	2004	57.98	2008	57.88
1920-29	56.76	1970-79	57.06	2001	57.90	2005	58.11	2009	57.99
1930-39	57.01	1980-89	57.35	2002	58.02	2006	57.99	2010	58.11
1940-49	57.13								

Note: In 2005 and 2010, the average global temperature reached 58.11°F, making them the warmest years on record. The next warmest year on record was 1998.

Toxics Release Inventory in the U.S., 2008-09

Source: U.S. Environmental Protection Agency

Releases of toxic chemicals into the environment, by manner of release and industry sector; pollutant transfers by destination of transfer. Numbers may not add up to totals because of rounding.

	2008 mil lbs	2009 mil lbs		2008 %	2009 %
Pollutant releases			**Top industries, total releases**		
Air releases	1,146	914	Metal mining	30%	34%
Surface water discharges	249	205	Electric utilities	23	24
Underground injection	188	175	Chemicals	12	12
On-site land releases	1,784	1,710	Primary metals	11	9
Off-site releases	488	371	Paper	5	5
Total on- and off-site releases	3,855	3,375	All others	18	16
Pollutant transfers	**mil lbs**	**mil lbs**	**Top carcinogens, air/water/land releases**	**mil lbs**	**mil lbs**
To recycling	1,970	1,629	Lead compounds	467	382
To energy recovery	451	365	Arsenic compounds	78	99
To treatment	257	229	Chromium compounds	45	36
To publicly owned treatment works	258	220	Nickel compounds	27	24
Other transfers	<1	<1	Styrene	34	20
Off-site to disposal	575	400	Formaldehyde	20	15
Total	3,511	2,842			

Note: This information does not indicate whether or to what degree the public has been exposed to toxic chemicals.

Total Toxics Releases by State, 2009

Source: U.S. Environmental Protection Agency

State	Total lbs	State	Total lbs	State	Total lbs	State	Total lbs
Alaska	695,927,854	Ohio	158,508,558	Indiana	132,074,361	Illinois	95,068,572
Texas	189,779,393	Utah	147,373,378	Pennsylvania	120,400,308		
Nevada	183,371,163	Kentucky	142,607,547	Louisiana	119,527,406	U.S. total*	3,374,903,304

*Includes states not shown, District of Columbia, Puerto Rico, American Samoa, Guam, Northern Marianas, and the Virgin Islands.

Hazardous Waste Sites in the U.S., 2010

Source: *National Priorities List*, U.S. Environmental Protection Agency, July 2010

State/territory	Proposed Gen.	Proposed Fed.	Final Gen.	Final Fed.	Total	State/territory	Proposed Gen.	Proposed Fed.	Final Gen.	Final Fed.	Total
Alabama	2	0	10	3	15	Nevada	0	0	1	0	1
Alaska	0	0	1	5	6	New Hampshire	1	0	19	1	21
Arizona	0	0	7	2	9	New Jersey	2	0	104	8	114
Arkansas	0	0	8	0	8	New Mexico	1	0	12	1	14
California	3	0	70	24	97	New York	2	0	83	4	89
Colorado	2	0	15	3	20	North Carolina	2	0	34	2	38
Connecticut	1	0	13	1	15	North Dakota	0	0	0	0	0
Delaware	1	0	13	1	15	Ohio	5	2	32	3	42
District of Columbia	0	0	0	1	1	Oklahoma	1	0	7	1	9
Florida	1	0	48	6	55	Oregon	2	0	11	2	15
Georgia	2	0	12	2	16	Pennsylvania	2	0	89	6	97
Hawaii	0	0	1	2	3	Rhode Island	0	0	10	2	12
Idaho	3	0	4	2	9	South Carolina	1	0	24	2	27
Illinois	5	1	40	4	50	South Dakota	0	0	1	1	2
Indiana	1	0	32	0	33	Tennessee	1	1	11	3	16
Iowa	1	0	10	1	12	Texas	2	0	45	4	51
Kansas	1	0	10	1	12	Utah	3	0	12	4	19
Kentucky	0	0	13	1	14	Vermont	0	0	11	0	11
Louisiana	3	0	7	1	11	Virginia	0	0	20	11	31
Maine	0	0	9	3	12	Washington	0	0	35	13	48
Maryland	2	0	9	10	21	West Virginia	0	0	7	2	9
Massachusetts	1	0	24	6	31	Wisconsin	1	0	38	0	39
Michigan	1	1	66	0	68	Wyoming	0	0	1	1	2
Minnesota	0	0	23	2	25	Guam	0	0	1	1	2
Mississippi	4	0	4	0	8	Puerto Rico	0	0	15	1	16
Missouri	0	0	29	3	32	Virgin Islands	0	0	1	0	1
Montana	1	0	16	0	17	**Total**	**61**	**5**	**1,130**	**158**	**1,354**
Nebraska	0	0	12	1	13						

Note: Fed. = Hazardous waste produced by federal agency; Gen. = Non-Fed. sites. Sites that have been proposed for federal Superfund financing are listed under Proposed; sites that have qualified for Superfund financing are under Final.

Renewable Water Resources, 2008

Source: Food and Agriculture Organization, United Nations

Globally, water supplies are abundant, but they are unevenly distributed among and within countries. In some areas, water withdrawals are so high, relative to supply, that surface water supplies are shrinking, and groundwater reserves are being depleted faster than they can be replenished by precipitation. The U.S. (including Alaska and Hawaii) has a total of 2,818 cubic kilometers (cubic km) of internal renewable water resources, or 9,042 cubic meters (cubic m) per capita. Totals for all countries are 43,022 cubic km of internal renewable freshwater resources and 6,383 cubic m per capita.

These numbers, and those in the tables below, were published by the Food and Agriculture Organization; the tables, which take into account countries for which data are available, draw upon studies done over a number of years and use 2008 population data. Numbers represent each given country's internal resources.

Countries With Greatest Internal Water Resources

Country	Cubic meters per capita	Total cubic km
Iceland	539,683	170.0
Guyana	315,858	241.0
Suriname	170,874	88.0
Papua New Guinea	121,788	801.0
Bhutan	113,537	78.0
Gabon	113,260	164.0
Solomon Islands	87,476	44.7
Canada	85,691	2,850.0
Norway	80,134	382.0
New Zealand	77,305	327.0

Countries With Lowest Internal Water Resources

Country	Cubic meters per capita	Total cubic km
Bahrain	5.155	0.004
Egypt	22.08	1.8
United Arab Emirates	33.44	0.15
Qatar	43.72	0.056
Bahamas	59.17	0.02
Yemen	91.64	2.1
Saudi Arabia	95.23	2.4
Libya	95.33	0.6
Maldives	98.36	0.03
Israel	106.4	0.75

Top 50 Countries by Forest Area, 1990-2010

Source: Food and Agriculture Organization, United Nations

(in square kilometers; ranked by 2010 area)

Country	Forest area, 1990	Forest area, 2010	% change, 1990-2010	% of land area covered by forest in 2010	Country	Forest area, 1990	Forest area, 2010	% change, 1990-2010	% of land area covered by forest in 2010
Russia	8,089,500	8,090,900	0.0%	49.0%	Congo	227,260	224,110	−1.4%	66.0%
Brazil	5,748,390	5,195,220	−9.6	62.0	Finland	218,890	221,570	1.2	73.0
Canada	3,101,340	3,101,340	0.0	34.0	Gabon	220,000	220,000	0.0	85.0
United States	2,963,350	3,040,220	2.6	33.0	Malaysia	223,760	204,560	−8.6	62.0
China	1,571,410	2,068,610	31.6	22.0	Cameroon	243,160	199,160	−18.1	42.0
Congo, Dem. Rep.	1,603,630	1,541,350	−3.9	68.0	Thailand	195,490	189,720	−3.0	37.0
Australia	1,545,000	1,493,000	−3.4	19.0	Spain	138,180	181,730	31.5	36.0
Indonesia	1,185,450	944,320	−20.3	52.0	Paraguay	211,570	175,820	−16.9	44.0
Sudan	763,810	699,490	−8.4	29.0	Chile	152,630	162,310	6.3	22.0
India	639,390	684,340	7.0	23.0	France	145,370	159,540	9.7	29.0
Peru	701,560	679,920	−3.1	53.0	Laos	173,140	157,510	−9.0	68.0
Mexico	702,910	648,020	−7.8	33.0	Zimbabwe	221,640	156,240	−29.5	40.0
Colombia	625,190	604,990	−3.2	55.0	Guyana	152,050	152,050	0.0	77.0
Angola	609,760	584,800	−4.1	47.0	Suriname	147,760	147,580	−0.1	95.0
Bolivia	627,950	571,960	−8.9	53.0	Vietnam	93,630	137,970	47.4	44.0
Zambia	528,000	494,680	−6.3	67.0	Madagascar	136,920	125,530	−8.3	22.0
Venezuela	520,260	462,750	−11.1	52.0	Mali	140,720	124,900	−11.2	10.0
Mozambique	433,780	390,220	−10.0	50.0	Ethiopia	151,140	122,960	−18.6	11.0
Tanzania	414,950	334,280	−19.4	38.0	Chad	131,100	115,250	−12.1	9.0
Myanmar	392,180	317,730	−19.0	48.0	Botswana	137,180	113,510	−17.3	20.0
Argentina	347,930	294,000	−15.5	11.0	Turkey	96,800	113,340	17.1	15.0
Papua New Guinea	315,230	287,260	−8.9	63.0	Germany	107,410	110,760	3.1	32.0
Sweden	272,810	282,030	3.4	69.0	Iran	110,750	110,750	0.0	7.0
Japan	249,500	249,790	0.1	69.0	Mongolia	125,360	108,980	−13.1	7.0
Central African Rep.	232,030	226,050	−2.6	36.0	Côte d'Ivoire	102,220	104,030	1.8	33.0
					World	**41,684,000**	**40,330,620**	**−3.2**	**NA**

NA = Not available.

Selected Endangered Animal Species

Source: Fish and Wildlife Service, U.S. Dept. of the Interior

Common name	Scientific name	Range
Albatross, Amsterdam	Diomedia amsterdamensis	Amsterdam Island, Indian Ocean
Antelope, giant sable	Hippotragus niger variani	Angola
Armadillo, giant	Pridontes maximus	Venezuela, Guyana to Argentina
Babirusa	Babyrousa babyrussa	Indonesia
Bandicoot, desert	Perameles eremiana	Australia
Bat, gray	Myotis grisescens	Central, southeastern U.S.
Bear, Mexican grizzly	Ursus arctos	Mexico
Bison, wood	Bison bison athabascae	Canada, northwestern U.S.
Bobcat, Mexican	Lynx rufus escuinapae	Central Mexico
Caiman, black	Melanosuchus niger	Amazon basin
Camel, Bactrian	Camelus bactrianus	Mongolia, China
Caribou, woodland	Rangifer tarandus caribou	Canada, northern U.S.

Common name	Scientific name	Range
Cheetah	Acinonyx jubatus	Africa to India
Chimpanzee, pygmy	Pan paniscus	Dem. Rep. of the Congo
Condor, California	Gymnogyps californianus	U.S. (AZ, CA, OR), Mexico (Baja California)
Crane, whooping	Grus americana	Canada, Mexico, U.S. (Rocky Mts. to Carolinas)
Crocodile, American	Crocodylus acutus	Mexico, Caribbean Sea, Central and South America
Deer, Columbian white-tailed	Odocoileus virginianus leucurus	U.S. (OR, WA)
Dolphin, Chinese river	Lipotes vexillifer	China
Dugong	Dugong dugon	East Africa to southern Japan, Palau
Elephant, Asian	Elephas maximus	South-central and southeastern Asia
Fox, northern swift	Vulpes velox hebes	U.S. (northern plains), Canada
Frog, mountain yellow-legged	Rana muscosa	Western U.S. (CA, NV)
Gorilla	Gorilla gorilla	Central and W Africa
Hartebeest, Tora	Alcelaphus buselaphus tora	Egypt, Ethiopia, Sudan
Hawk, Hawaiian	Buteo solitarius	U.S. (HI)
Hyena, brown	Parahyaena brunnea	Southern Africa
Impala, black-faced	Aepyceros melampus petersi	Angola, Namibia
Kangaroo, Tasmanian forester	Macropus giganteus tasmaniensis	Australia (Tasmania)
Leopard	Panthera pardus	Africa and Asia
Lion, Asiatic	Panthera leo persica	Turkey to India
Manatee, West Indian	Trichechus manatus	Southeastern U.S., Caribbean Sea, Mexico
Monkey, spider	Ateles geoffroyi frontatus	Costa Rica, Nicaragua, Panama
Ocelot	Leopardus pardalis	U.S. (AZ, TX) to Central and S. America
Orangutan	Pongo pygmaeus	Borneo, Sumatra
Ostrich, West African	Struthio camelus spatzi	W Sahara
Otter, marine	Lontra felina	Peru south to Straits of Magellan
Panda, giant	Ailuropoda melanoleuca	China
Panther, Florida	Puma concolor coryi	U.S. (LA and AR to SC and FL)
Parakeet, golden	Aratinga guarouba	Brazil
Parrot, imperial	Amazona imperialis	West Indies (Dominica)
Penguin, Galapagos	Spheniscus mendiculus	Ecuador (Galapagos Islands)
Puma, eastern	Puma concolor couguar	Eastern N America (presumed extinct in wild)
Python, Indian	Python molurus molurus	Sri Lanka, India
Rat-kangaroo, brush-tailed	Bettongia penicillata	Australia
Rhinoceros, black	Diceros bicornis	Sub-Saharan Africa
Rhinoceros, northern white	Ceratotherium simum cottoni	Dem. Rep. of the Congo, Sudan, Uganda, Central African Rep.
Salamander, Chinese giant	Andrias davidianus	Western China
Sea-lion, Steller	Eumetopias jubatus	Alaska, Russia
Squirrel, Carolina northern flying	Glaucomys sabrinus coloratus	U.S. (NC, TN)
Tiger	Panthera tigris	Asia
Tortoise, Galapagos	Geochelone nigra	Ecuador (Galapagos Islands)
Whale, gray	Eschrichtius robustus	Northern Pacific Ocean
Whale, humpback	Megaptera novaeangliae	All major oceans
Wolf, red	Canis rufus	Southeastern U.S.
Woodpecker, ivory-billed	Campephilus principalis	South-central and southeastern U.S., Cuba
Yak, wild	Bos mutus	China (Tibet), India
Zebra, mountain	Equus zebra zebra	South Africa

List of Endangered and Threatened Species, 2011

Source: Fish and Wildlife Service, U.S. Dept. of the Interior; as of July 2011

Group	Endangered		Threatened		Total species[1]	U.S. species with recovery plans
	U.S.	Foreign	U.S.	Foreign		
Mammals	70	256	12	16	354	60
Birds	76	198	14	14	302	85
Reptiles	13	66	23	15	117	38
Amphibians	14	8	9	1	32	17
Fishes	72	11	63	1	147	101
Clams	63	2	8	0	73	70
Snails	25	1	11	0	37	29
Insects	50	4	10	0	64	40
Arachnids	12	0	0	0	12	12
Crustaceans	19	0	3	0	22	18
Corals	0	0	2	0	2	0
Animal subtotal	**414**	**546**	**155**	**47**	**1,162**	**470**
Flowering plants	613	1	145	0	759	638
Conifers and cycads	2	0	1	2	5	3
Ferns and allies	27	0	2	0	29	26
Lichens	2	0	0	0	2	2
Plant subtotal	**644**	**1**	**148**	**2**	**795**	**669**
Grand total	**1,058**	**547**	**303**	**49**	**1,957**	**1,139**

(1) Some species are classified as both endangered and threatened. The table tallies these dual status species only once, as endangered. The dual status species, all tallied as endangered, are (U.S.) California tiger salamander, chinook salmon, chum salmon, coho salmon, gray wolf, green sea turtle, piping plover, roseate tern, sockeye salmon, steelhead, Steller sea-lion; (non-U.S.) argali, chimpanzee, dugong, leopard, saltwater crocodile.

METEOROLOGY

National Weather Service Watches and Warnings

Source: National Weather Service, National Oceanic and Atmospheric Admin. (NOAA), U.S. Dept. of Commerce; *Glossary of Meteorology*, American Meteorological Society

The National Weather Service issues watches, warnings, and advisories for specific geographic areas to alert people to the possibility or imminent arrival of severe weather or of flooding. Often the weather hazard is a convective storm (a storm involving upward and downward movement of heat and moisture). A severe thunderstorm or tornado warning is issued when a severe convective storm, covering a relatively small geographic area or moving in a narrow path, is sufficiently intense to threaten life and property. Excessive localized convective rains are not classified as severe storms but are often the product of severe local storms. Such rainfall may result in phenomena, such as flash floods, that threaten life and property. Lightning occurs with all thunderstorms and, along with flash floods, is a leading cause of storm deaths and injuries.

Cyclone: atmospheric circulation of winds rotating counterclockwise in the Northern Hemisphere and clockwise in the Southern Hemisphere. Tornadoes, hurricanes, and the lows shown on weather maps are all examples of cyclones. Cyclones are usually accompanied by precipitation or stormy weather.

Severe thunderstorm: thunderstorm (any local atmospheric disturbance) that produces a tornado, winds more than 50 knots (58 mph), and/or hail at least ¾ inch in diameter. A severe thunderstorm watch indicates conditions are favorable for the development of a severe thunderstorm within 4 to 8 hours. A severe thunderstorm warning indicates a severe thunderstorm has been sighted by radar or reported by a spotter.

Tornado: violent rotating column of air that extends from the base of a thunderstorm to the ground. On a local scale, it is the most destructive of all atmospheric phenomena. Tornado paths range from a few feet to more than 100 mi long (average 5 mi) and from a few feet to more than 1 mi in diameter (avg. 220 yds). The average forward speed is 30 mph, and wind speeds can reach to more than 200 mph. A rotating column of air over water, whether or not linked to a thunderstorm, is called a **waterspout**.

Tropical storm: cyclone that develops over tropical or subtropical waters with 1-min. sustained surface winds between 34 and 63 knots (39-73 mph). A tropical storm watch is issued when tropical storm conditions pose a threat to specified coastal areas within 48 hours. A tropical storm warning is issued when such conditions are expected in a specified coastal area within 36 hours.

Hurricane: tropical cyclone having 1-min. sustained surface winds of 64 knots (74 mph) or more. (West of the international date line, north of the equator, such storms are known as **typhoons**.) The hurricane-force winds form a circle or oval, sometimes as wide as 300 mi in diameter. In the lower latitudes, hurricanes usually move W or NW at 10-15 mph. When the center approaches 25° to 30° N lat., the direction of motion often changes to the NE, with increased forward speed. In the Atlantic, hurricane season is June 1-Nov. 30. Hurricane season is May 15-Nov. 30 in the eastern Pacific. A hurricane warning is issued when a hurricane is forecast for an area within 36 hours.

Winter storm and **blizzard:** A winter storm watch is issued when there is a potential for heavy snow or significant ice accumulations, usually at least 24-36 hours in advance. A winter storm warning is issued when a winter storm is producing or is forecast to produce heavy snow or significant ice accumulations. A blizzard warning is issued for winter storm conditions where winds are 35 mph or more, there is sufficient falling and/or blowing snow to frequently reduce visibility to less than ¼ mi, and the conditions are expected to prevail for at least 3 hours.

Floods take many forms. **River flooding:** occurs when rains, sometimes coupled with melting snow, quickly fill river basins with an excess of water. Torrential rains from decaying hurricanes or tropical systems are also a major cause. **Coastal flooding:** tropical storm and hurricane winds or intense offshore low-pressure systems can drive ocean water inland. Coastal floods can also be produced by sea waves called **tsunamis**, produced by earthquakes or underwater volcanic eruptions or landslides. **Flash flooding:** usually due to copious amounts of rain falling in a short time. Ice can also cause flash flooding. When ice accumulates at natural or artificial obstructions, it can stop the flow of water. The resulting buildup of water can lead to flooding upstream. If the jam suddenly gives way, a flash flood can occur downstream. Flash flooding typically occurs within 6 hours of the causative event.

Flash floods account for the majority of flood deaths in the U.S. and are the leading cause of deaths associated with thunderstorms. Urbanization significantly increases runoff because less rain is absorbed by the terrain, making flash flooding in urban areas extremely dangerous. Streets can become swift-moving rivers, and basements can fill with water.

A (flash) flood watch indicates flooding or flash flooding is possible within a designated area. A (flash) flood warning indicates flooding is in progress, imminent, or highly likely.

National Weather Service Marine Warnings and Advisories

Primary sources of dissemination are commercial radio, TV, U.S. Coast Guard radio stations, and NOAA VHF radio broadcasts. The NOAA Weather Radio All Hazards (NWR) network broadcasts on seven frequencies between 162.40 and 162.55 MHz. These broadcasts can usually be received within at least 25 nautical mi of the transmission site using a special radio receiver. The following are examples of the warnings and advisories that may be addressed to mariners.

Small craft advisory: alerts mariners to sustained weather and/or sea conditions, present or forecast, potentially hazardous to small boats, including winds 20-33 knots (23-38 mph) and/or dangerous wave conditions. The advisory is also issued when sea or lake ice exists that could be hazardous to small boats. Criteria vary depending on region and type of marine environment.

Special marine warning: indicates potentially hazardous weather conditions not covered by existing marine warnings. The conditions are usually of short duration (2 hours or less) and involve wind speeds of 34 knots (39 mph) or more, and/or hail at least ¾ inch in diameter or waterspouts.

Gale warning: indicates winds of 34-47 knots (39-54 mph) not directly associated with a tropical storm are forecast for the area.

Storm warning: indicates winds 48-63 knots (55-73 mph) not directly associated with a tropical storm are forecast for the area.

Monthly Normal Mean Temperatures, Precipitation in U.S. Cities

Source: National Climatic Data Center, NESDIS, NOAA, U.S. Dept. of Commerce

Normals are averages covering a 30-year period. The temperature and precipitation normals given here are based on records for 1981-2010. Temperatures listed below represent means of the normal daily maximum and normal daily minimum temperatures for each month. For stations that did not have continuous records from the same site for the entire 30 years, the means have been adjusted to the record at the present site. (*) = city station. Other figures are for airport stations. T = Temperature in Fahrenheit; P = Precipitation in inches.

	Jan.		Feb.		Mar.		Apr.		May		June		July		Aug.		Sept.		Oct.		Nov.		Dec.	
Station	T	P	T	P	T	P	T	P	T	P	T	P	T	P	T	P	T	P	T	P	T	P	T	P
Albany, NY	23	2.6	26	2.2	35	3.2	48	3.2	58	3.6	67	3.8	72	4.1	70	3.5	62	3.3	50	3.7	40	3.3	29	2.9
Albuquerque, NM	36	0.4	41	0.5	48	0.5	56	0.6	66	0.5	75	0.7	78	1.5	76	1.6	69	1.1	58	1.0	45	0.6	36	0.5
Anchorage, AK	17	0.7	20	0.7	27	0.6	37	0.5	48	0.7	55	1.0	59	1.8	57	3.3	49	3.0	35	2.0	22	1.2	19	1.1
Asheville, NC	37	3.7	40	3.8	47	3.8	55	3.3	63	3.7	71	4.7	74	4.3	73	4.4	66	3.8	56	2.9	47	3.7	39	3.6
Atlanta, GA	43	4.2	47	4.7	54	4.8	62	3.4	70	3.7	77	4.0	80	5.3	79	3.9	74	4.5	63	3.4	54	4.1	45	3.9
Atlantic City, NJ	33	3.2	35	2.9	42	4.2	52	3.6	61	3.4	71	3.1	76	3.7	74	4.1	67	3.2	56	3.4	47	3.3	37	3.7
Baltimore, MD	33	3.1	36	2.9	44	3.9	54	3.2	54	4.0	72	3.5	77	4.1	75	3.3	68	4.0	56	3.3	47	3.3	37	3.4
Barrow, AK	−13	0.1	−14	0.1	−13	0.1	2	0.2	21	0.2	36	0.3	41	1.0	39	1.1	32	0.1	17	0.4	0.1	0.2	−8	0.1
Birmingham, AL	44	4.8	48	4.5	55	5.2	63	4.4	71	5.0	78	4.4	81	4.8	81	3.9	75	3.9	64	3.4	54	4.9	46	4.5
Bismarck, ND	13	0.4	18	0.5	30	0.9	44	1.3	56	2.4	65	3.2	71	2.9	70	2.3	59	1.6	45	1.3	29	0.7	16	0.5
Boise, ID	31	1.2	37	1.0	45	1.4	51	1.2	59	1.4	68	0.7	76	0.3	75	0.2	65	0.6	53	0.8	40	1.4	31	1.6
Boston, MA	29	3.4	32	3.3	38	4.3	48	3.7	58	3.5	68	3.7	73	3.4	72	3.4	65	3.4	54	3.9	45	4.0	35	3.8
Buffalo, NY	25	3.2	26	2.5	34	2.9	46	3.0	57	3.5	66	3.7	71	3.2	70	3.3	62	3.9	51	3.5	41	4.0	30	3.9
Burlington, VT	19	2.1	22	1.8	31	2.2	45	2.8	56	3.5	66	3.7	71	4.2	69	3.9	61	3.6	48	3.6	38	3.1	26	2.4
Caribou, ME	10	2.7	14	2.2	25	2.5	39	2.7	52	3.3	61	3.5	66	4.1	64	3.8	55	3.3	43	3.5	32	3.6	18	3.3
Charleston, SC	48	3.7	52	3.0	58	3.7	65	2.9	73	3.0	79	5.7	82	6.5	81	7.2	76	6.1	67	3.8	59	2.4	51	3.1
Charleston, WV	34	3.0	38	3.2	46	3.9	56	3.2	64	4.8	72	4.3	75	4.9	74	3.7	67	3.3	57	2.7	47	3.7	37	3.3
Chicago, IL	24	1.7	28	1.8	38	2.5	49	3.4	59	3.7	69	3.5	74	3.7	72	4.9	65	3.2	53	3.2	40	3.2	28	2.3
Cleveland, OH	28	2.7	31	2.3	38	2.9	50	3.5	60	3.7	69	3.4	74	3.5	72	3.5	65	3.8	54	3.1	44	3.6	32	3.1
Columbus, OH	30	2.7	33	2.3	42	3.0	53	3.4	63	4.2	72	4.0	75	4.8	74	3.3	67	2.8	55	2.6	44	3.2	34	3.0
Dallas-Ft. Worth, TX	46	2.1	50	2.7	58	3.5	66	3.1	74	4.9	81	3.8	85	2.2	86	1.9	78	2.6	68	4.2	57	2.7	47	2.6
Denver, CO	31	0.4	33	0.3	40	0.9	47	1.7	57	2.2	67	2.0	74	3.0	73	1.6	63	1.0	51	1.0	38	0.6	30	0.3
Des Moines, IA	23	1.0	27	1.3	39	2.3	52	3.9	62	4.7	72	4.9	76	4.5	74	4.1	66	3.1	53	2.6	39	2.2	26	1.4
Detroit, MI	26	2.0	28	2.0	37	2.3	49	2.9	60	3.4	69	3.5	74	3.4	72	3.0	64	3.3	52	2.5	42	2.8	30	2.4
Dodge City, KS	32	0.6	36	0.7	44	1.6	54	1.8	64	2.9	74	3.2	80	3.1	78	2.8	69	1.7	57	1.7	43	0.8	33	0.8
Duluth, MN	10	1.0	15	0.8	26	1.5	40	2.4	51	3.2	60	4.2	66	3.9	64	3.7	56	4.1	43	2.9	29	2.1	15	1.2
Fairbanks, AK	−8	0.6	−1	0.4	11	0.3	33	0.3	49	0.6	60	1.4	63	2.2	56	1.9	45	1.1	24	0.8	3	0.7	−4	0.6
Fresno, CA	47	2.2	52	2.0	57	2.0	62	1.0	70	0.4	77	0.2	83	0.0	82	0.0	76	0.2	66	0.6	54	1.1	47	1.8
Galveston, TX*	53	3.7	55	3.0	61	2.9	68	2.2	76	3.0	82	4.8	84	3.9	84	3.4	80	5.4	73	4.2	64	3.4	56	3.4
Grand Rapids, MI	24	2.1	27	1.8	36	2.4	48	3.4	59	4.0	68	3.8	73	3.8	71	3.6	63	4.3	51	3.3	40	3.5	29	2.5
Helena, MT	23	0.4	28	0.3	36	0.6	45	1.0	54	1.9	62	2.1	70	1.2	68	1.2	58	1.1	46	0.7	33	0.5	22	0.4
Honolulu, HI	73	2.3	73	2.0	75	2.0	76	0.6	78	0.6	80	0.3	81	0.5	82	0.6	82	0.7	80	1.8	78	2.4	75	3.2
Houston, TX	53	3.4	56	3.2	63	3.4	70	3.3	77	5.1	82	5.9	84	3.8	85	3.8	80	4.1	72	5.7	62	4.3	54	3.7
Huron, SD	17	0.5	22	0.6	33	1.5	47	2.3	58	3.1	68	3.9	74	2.9	72	2.4	62	2.5	48	1.8	33	0.9	19	0.5
Indianapolis, IN	28	2.7	32	2.3	42	3.6	53	3.8	63	5.1	72	4.3	75	4.6	74	3.1	67	3.1	55	3.1	44	3.7	32	3.2
Jackson, MS	46	5.0	50	4.8	57	5.0	64	5.0	72	4.4	79	4.1	82	4.8	81	4.2	76	3.0	65	3.9	56	4.8	48	5.2
Jacksonville, FL	53	3.3	56	3.2	62	4.0	67	2.6	74	2.5	80	6.5	82	6.6	82	6.8	78	8.2	70	3.9	62	2.1	55	2.8
Juneau, AK	28	5.4	30	4.1	34	3.8	41	2.9	49	3.4	55	3.2	57	4.6	56	5.7	50	8.6	42	8.6	33	6.0	30	5.8
Kansas City, MO	29	1.1	34	1.5	44	2.4	55	3.7	65	5.2	74	5.2	78	4.5	77	3.9	68	4.6	56	3.2	44	2.2	32	1.5
Knoxville, TN	38	4.3	42	4.3	50	4.3	59	4.0	67	4.5	75	3.8	78	5.1	78	3.3	71	3.2	60	2.5	50	4.0	41	4.5
Lander, WY	22	0.4	25	0.6	36	1.2	44	1.9	53	2.2	63	1.3	71	0.8	70	0.6	59	1.1	46	1.3	31	0.9	21	0.6
Lexington, KY	33	3.2	37	3.2	46	4.1	55	3.6	64	5.3	73	4.4	76	4.7	75	3.3	68	2.9	57	3.1	46	3.5	36	3.9
Little Rock, AR	41	3.6	45	3.7	53	4.7	62	5.1	71	4.9	79	3.7	83	3.3	83	2.6	75	3.2	64	4.9	53	5.3	43	5.0
Los Angeles, CA*	58	3.1	59	3.8	61	2.4	63	0.9	66	0.3	69	0.1	73	0.0	74	0.0	73	0.2	69	0.7	62	1.0	58	2.3
Louisville, KY	35	3.2	39	3.2	48	4.2	58	4.0	67	5.3	76	3.8	79	4.2	78	3.3	71	3.1	60	3.2	49	3.6	38	3.8
Marquette, MI*	19	1.8	21	1.3	29	2.0	40	2.5	51	2.5	60	2.7	67	2.8	67	2.6	59	3.2	47	3.1	35	2.6	24	2.0
Memphis, TN	41	4.0	46	4.4	54	5.2	63	5.5	72	5.3	80	3.6	83	4.6	82	2.9	75	3.1	64	4.0	53	5.5	44	5.7
Miami, FL	68	1.6	70	2.3	73	3.0	76	3.1	80	5.3	83	9.7	84	6.5	84	8.9	83	9.9	80	6.3	75	3.3	71	2.0
Milwaukee, WI	22	1.8	26	1.7	35	2.3	46	3.6	56	3.4	66	3.9	72	3.7	71	4.0	63	3.2	51	2.7	39	2.7	27	2.0
Minneapolis, MN	16	0.9	21	0.8	33	1.9	48	2.7	59	3.4	69	4.2	74	4.0	71	4.3	62	3.1	49	2.4	34	1.8	20	1.2
Mobile, AL	50	5.7	54	5.1	60	6.1	66	4.8	74	5.1	80	6.1	82	7.2	82	7.0	78	5.1	68	3.7	60	5.1	52	5.1
Moline, IL	23	1.5	27	1.6	39	2.9	51	3.6	62	4.3	72	4.5	75	4.3	74	4.5	65	3.1	53	3.0	40	2.6	27	2.2
Nashua, NH	24	3.7	27	3.2	35	4.3	46	4.0	57	2.9	66	4.3	71	3.7	70	4.5	62	3.4	50	4.7	40	4.1	30	3.7
Nashville, TN	38	3.8	42	3.9	50	4.1	59	4.0	68	5.5	76	4.1	79	3.6	79	3.2	72	3.4	60	3.0	50	4.3	40	4.2
Newark, NJ	32	3.5	35	2.9	42	4.2	53	4.2	63	4.1	72	4.0	77	4.8	76	3.7	68	3.8	57	3.6	47	3.7	37	3.8
New Orleans, LA	53	5.2	57	5.3	63	4.6	69	4.6	77	4.6	82	8.1	83	5.9	83	6.0	80	5.1	71	3.6	63	4.5	56	5.3
New York, NY*	33	3.7	35	3.1	43	4.4	53	4.5	62	4.2	71	4.4	77	4.6	75	4.4	68	4.3	57	4.4	48	4.0	38	4.0
Norfolk, VA	40	3.4	43	3.1	49	3.7	58	3.4	67	3.4	75	4.3	80	5.1	78	5.5	72	4.8	62	3.4	53	3.2	44	3.3
Oklahoma City, OK	39	1.4	44	1.6	52	3.1	61	3.1	70	4.7	78	4.9	83	2.9	82	3.3	74	4.1	63	3.7	51	2.0	41	1.9
Omaha, NE	24	0.7	28	0.9	40	2.0	52	3.0	62	4.8	72	4.2	77	3.8	75	3.8	66	2.7	53	2.2	39	1.6	26	1.0
Philadelphia, PA	33	3.0	36	2.7	44	3.8	54	3.6	64	3.7	73	3.4	78	4.4	77	3.5	69	3.8	58	3.2	48	3.0	38	3.6
Phoenix, AZ	56	0.9	60	0.9	65	1.0	73	0.3	82	0.1	91	0.0	95	1.1	94	1.0	88	0.6	77	0.6	64	0.7	55	0.9
Pittsburgh, PA	29	2.7	32	2.7	40	3.1	52	3.2	61	4.2	69	4.0	73	3.8	72	3.5	65	3.4	53	2.5	43	3.4	33	2.9
Portland, ME	22	3.4	26	3.3	34	4.2	44	4.3	54	4.0	63	3.8	69	3.6	68	3.1	60	3.7	49	4.9	39	4.9	29	4.0
Portland, OR	41	4.9	44	3.7	48	3.7	52	2.7	58	2.5	64	1.7	69	0.7	70	0.7	65	1.5	55	3.0	47	5.6	40	5.5
Providence, RI	29	3.9	32	3.3	39	5.0	49	4.4	59	3.6	68	3.6	74	3.3	72	3.6	65	3.9	54	3.9	45	4.5	34	4.2
Raleigh, NC	41	3.5	45	3.2	52	4.1	60	2.9	68	3.3	76	3.5	80	4.7	79	4.3	72	4.4	61	3.3	52	3.1	44	3.1
Rapid City, SD	25	0.3	27	0.4	35	0.9	45	1.8	55	3.2	65	2.5	73	1.9	72	1.6	61	1.3	48	1.4	35	0.5	25	0.4
Reno, NV	36	1.0	40	1.0	46	0.8	51	0.5	60	0.5	68	0.5	75	0.2	73	0.2	65	0.4	54	0.5	43	0.8	35	1.0
Richmond, VA	38	3.0	41	2.8	49	4.0	58	3.3	66	3.8	75	3.9	79	4.5	78	4.7	71	4.1	60	3.0	50	3.2	41	3.3
St. Louis, MO	32	2.4	36	2.2	46	3.3	57	3.7	67	4.7	76	4.3	80	4.1	79	3.0	70	3.1	59	3.3	47	3.9	35	2.8
Salt Lake City, UT	30	1.3	34	1.3	44	1.8	51	2.0	60	2.0	70	1.0	79	0.6	77	0.7	66	1.2	53	1.5	40	1.5	30	1.4
San Antonio, TX	52	1.8	56	1.8	62	2.3	69	2.1	77	4.0	82	4.1	85	2.7	85	2.1	80	3.0	71	4.1	61	2.3	53	1.9
San Diego, CA	57	2.0	58	2.3	59	1.8	62	0.8	64	0.1	66	0.1	70	0.0	72	0.0	71	0.2	67	0.6	61	1.0	57	1.5
San Francisco, CA	50	4.2	53	4.1	55	3.0	57	1.3	60	0.5	62	0.1	64	0.0	65	0.0	65	0.2	62	1.0	56	2.4	51	4.0
San Juan, PR	78	3.8	78	2.4	79	2.0	80	4.7	82	5.9	83	4.4	83	5.1	84	5.5	84	5.8	83	5.6	81	6.4	79	5.0
Santa Fe, NM	32	0.6	36	0.5	43	0.8	50	0.7	60	0.9	69	1.1	73	1.8	71	2.6	64	1.6	53	1.4	40	0.7	31	0.8
Savannah, GA	50	3.7	53	2.8	59	3.7	66	3.1	73	3.0	80	6.0	83	5.6	82	6.6	77	4.6	68	3.7	59	2.4	52	3.0
Seattle, WA	42	5.6	43	3.5	47	3.7	50	2.7	56	1.9	61	1.6	66	0.7	66	0.9	61	1.5	53	3.5	45	6.6	41	5.4
Spokane, WA	30	1.8	33	1.3	40	1.6	47	1.3	55	1.6	62	1.3	70	0.6	69	0.6	60	0.7	48	1.2	36	2.3	27	2.3
Springfield, MO	33	2.5	37	2.5	46	3.6	56	4.3	65	5.1	73	4.9	78	3.7	78	3.6	69	4.6	58	3.6	46	4.2	35	3.0
Tampa, FL	61	2.2	63	2.8	67	3.0	72	2.0	78	2.1	82	6.7	83	7.1	83	7.8	82	6.3	76	2.3	69	1.6	63	2.5
Washington, DC	36	2.8	39	2.6	47	3.5	57	3.1	66	4.0	75	3.8	80	3.7	78	2.9	71	3.7	60	3.4	50	3.2	40	3.1
Wilmington, DE	32	3.0	35	2.7	43	3.9	53	3.5	63	4.0	72	3.9	77	4.6	75	3.2	68	4.3	56	3.4	47	3.1	37	3.5
Windsor Locks, CT	26	3.2	30	2.9	38	3.6	49	3.7	60	4.4	69	4.4	74	4.2	72	3.9	64	3.9	52	4.4	42	3.9	32	3.4

Normal High and Low Temperatures, Precipitation in U.S. Cities

Source: National Climatic Data Center, NESDIS, NOAA, U.S. Dept. of Commerce

The normal temperatures and precipitation data given here are based on records for the period 1981-2010. The extreme temperatures are based on records from the time of each station's installation. (*) = city station. Other figures are for airport stations.

State	Station	NORMAL TEMPERATURE (°F) January Max.	January Min.	July Max.	July Min.	EXTREME TEMPERATURE (°F) Highest	Lowest	AVG. ANNUAL PRECIPITATION (in.)
Alabama	Mobile	61	40	91	73	105	3	66.15
Alaska	Anchorage	23	11	65	52	85	−34	16.58
Alaska	Barrow	−7	−20	47	35	79	−56	4.53
Alaska	Juneau	33	24	64	50	90	−22	62.27
Arizona	Phoenix	67	46	106	78	122	17	8.03
Arkansas	North Little Rock	50	33	92	73	111	−6	50.03
California	Los Angeles	65	49	74	64	110	23	12.82
California	San Francisco	56	44	72	55	106	20	20.65
Colorado	Denver	44	17	89	59	105	−19	14.92
Connecticut	Windsor Locks	35	18	85	63	102	−26	45.85
Delaware	Wilmington	40	25	86	68	103	11	43.08
District of Columbia	Washington–Reagan	43	29	88	71	105	−5	39.74
Florida	Jacksonville	65	41	92	73	105	7	52.39
Florida	Miami	76	60	91	77	98	30	61.90
Georgia	Atlanta	52	34	89	71	105	−8	49.71
Georgia	Savannah	60	39	92	73	105	3	47.96
Hawaii	Honolulu	80	66	88	75	95	53	17.10
Idaho	Boise	38	25	91	60	111	−25	11.73
Illinois	Chicago	31	17	84	64	104	−27	36.89
Indiana	Indianapolis	36	21	85	66	104	−27	42.44
Iowa	Des Moines	31	14	86	67	108	−26	36.01
Kansas	Dodge City	44	20	93	66	110	−21	21.60
Kentucky	Lexington	41	25	86	66	103	−21	45.17
Kentucky	Louisville	43	27	89	70	106	−22	44.91
Louisiana	New Orleans	62	45	91	75	102	11	62.66
Maine	Caribou	20	1	76	55	96	−41	38.49
Maine	Portland	31	13	79	59	103	−39	47.25
Maryland	Baltimore	41	24	87	67	105	−7	41.88
Massachusetts	Boston	36	22	81	65	102	−12	43.77
Michigan	Detroit	32	19	83	64	104	−21	33.47
Michigan	Grand Rapids	31	18	83	62	100	−22	38.27
Michigan	Sault Ste. Marie	23	8	76	54	98	−36	32.95
Minnesota	Duluth	19	2	76	55	97	−39	30.96
Minnesota	Minneapolis	24	8	83	64	105	−34	30.61
Mississippi	Jackson	56	35	92	72	107	2	54.14
Missouri	Kansas City	38	20	88	68	109	−23	38.86
Missouri	St. Louis	40	24	89	71	107	−18	40.96
Montana	Helena	33	13	86	54	105	−42	11.22
Nebraska	Omaha	33	14	87	66	114	−23	30.62
Nevada	Reno	46	25	92	58	108	−16	7.40
New Hampshire	Concord	31	10	82	58	102	−37	40.61
New Jersey	Atlantic City	42	25	86	67	106	−11	41.75
New Mexico	Albuquerque	47	26	90	66	107	−17	9.45
New York	Albany	31	15	82	61	100	−28	39.35
New York	Buffalo	31	19	80	62	99	−20	40.48
New York	New York–Central Park*	38	27	84	69	106	−15	49.94
North Carolina	Raleigh	51	31	90	70	105	−9	43.34
North Dakota	Bismarck	23	2	85	57	112	−44	17.85
Ohio	Cleveland	34	22	83	64	104	−20	39.14
Ohio	Columbus	37	23	85	66	102	−22	39.31
Oklahoma	Oklahoma City	50	29	94	72	110	−8	36.52
Oregon	Portland	47	36	81	58	107	−3	36.03
Pennsylvania	Philadelphia	40	26	87	69	104	−7	41.53
Pennsylvania	Pittsburgh	36	21	83	63	103	−22	38.19
Puerto Rico	San Juan	83	72	89	78	98	60	56.35
Rhode Island	Providence	37	21	83	64	104	−13	47.18
South Carolina	Charleston	59	38	91	73	105	6	51.03
South Dakota	Huron	27	7	86	61	112	−41	22.90
South Dakota	Rapid City	37	13	87	58	111	−31	16.29
Tennessee	Memphis	50	33	92	74	108	−13	53.68
Tennessee	Nashville	47	28	89	68	107	−17	47.25
Texas	Dallas-Fort Worth	56	36	96	75	113	−1	36.14
Texas	Houston	63	43	94	75	109	7	49.77
Utah	Salt Lake City	37	22	93	65	107	−30	16.10
Vermont	Burlington	27	10	81	60	101	−30	36.82
Virginia	Norfolk	48	33	87	72	105	−3	46.53
Virginia	Richmond	47	28	90	69	105	−12	43.60
Washington	Seattle-Tacoma	47	37	76	56	103	0	37.49
Washington	Spokane	34	25	83	56	108	−25	16.56
West Virginia	Charleston	43	26	85	66	104	−16	44.03
Wisconsin	Milwaukee	29	16	80	64	103	−26	34.76
Wyoming	Lander	33	10	87	56	101	−37	12.66

Mean annual snowfall (in.): Based on climate normals 1981-2010: Boston, MA, 43.8; Sault Ste. Marie, MI, 123.4; Albany, NY, 59.1; Burlington, VT, 81.2; Lander, WY, 91.4; Anchorage, AK, 74.5.

World's wettest spot: Lloro, Colombia, may be the rainiest place in the world. It has an estimated average annual rainfall of 523.6 in.

Temperature extremes: A temperature of 136°F observed at El Azizia (Al Aziziyah), near Tripoli, Libya, on Sept. 13, 1922, is generally accepted as the world's highest temperature recorded under standard conditions. The record high in the U.S. was 134°F in Death Valley, CA, July 10, 1913. The world record low of −129°F was recorded at the Soviet station of Vostok in Antarctica on July 21, 1983. The record low in the U.S. was −80°F at Prospect Creek, AK, Jan. 23, 1971.

Annual Climatological Data for U.S. Cities, 2010

Source: National Climatic Data Center, NESDIS, NOAA, U.S. Dept. of Commerce

Station	Elev. (ft)	Highest	Date	Lowest	Date	Total (in.)	Greatest in 24 hrs. (in.)	Date	Total snowfall (in.)	Greatest in 24 hrs (in.)	Date	MPH	Date	Prec. 0.01 in. or more	Snow, sleet 1 in. or more
Albany, NY	281	96	7/6	-2	1/30	37.84	3.04	10/1	45.1	6.4	2/23	39	12/1	124	13
Albuquerque, NM	5,308	102	7/20	12	12/31	8.96	1.86	9/22-23	4.7	1.0	12/16	46	4/29	48	1
Anchorage, AK	222	76	5/27	-8	12/24	16.47	1.25	7/25-26	84.8	9.0	4/14	36	9/24	119	26
Asheville, NC	2,174	94	7/8	9	1/11	44.26	4.18	11/29-30	39.6	11.0	1/29	40	12/26	105	8
Atlanta, GA	974	97	7/23+	13	1/9	48.15	2.81	9/26	6.8	3.6	2/12	38	7/23	92	3
Atlantic City, NJ	117	102	7/6	10	2/7	42.13	2.85	3/28-29	66.4	18.4	12/26	47	3/13	102	11
Baltimore, MD	196	105	7/6	8	1/31	43.47	6.02	9/30	58.1	16.0	2/6	52	7/18	104	9
Barrow, AK	38	67	8/4	-43	3/15	5.47	0.95	7/18-19	67.9	6.4	11/17	41	11/17	98	18
Birmingham, AL	630	102	8/12	14	12/14	47.89	3.78	4/23-24	1.7	1.7	2/12	49	5/20	98	1
Bismarck, ND	1,654	104	8/22	-33	1/8	23.18	2.12	9/16	70.2	5.6	12/3	55	6/16	113	23
Boise, ID	2,861	104	8/26	7	11/25	14.98	1.41	5/22	23.0	4.1	12/1	46	8/21	108	8
Boston, MA	180	100	7/6	6	1/30	49.66	3.62	3/29-30	42.4	9.9	12/26	47	6/6	112	8
Buffalo, NY	717	92	7/8	-2	1/31	36.72	2.19	8/6	82.6	8.8	1/3	46	5/8	144	24
Burlington, VT	348	96	7/8	-6	1/10	40.73	2.18	10/15-16	107.1	18.9	1/2	36	5/4	163	22
Caribou, ME	626	93	8/31	-17	2/3	43.61	2.39	7/13-14	53.9	8.5	1/2	38	12/27	158	18
Charleston, SC	48	99	7/26	18	12/15	57.57	4.97	8/6	3.6	3.3	2/12	47	8/6	95	1
Chicago, IL	658	94	8/29	-1	1/3	37.61	6.38	7/23-24	49.6	12.6	2/9	47	4/5	116	12
Cleveland, OH	805	95	7/23	4	2/8	35.40	1.75	6/27-28	64.1	4.5	1/4	44	6/27	151	23
Columbus, OH	812	94	9/2	4	2/8	36.26	2.08	7/12	49.0	9.7	2/15	51	8/4	130	11
Dallas-Ft. Worth, TX	562	107	8/23	13	1/9	31.70	5.75	9/7-8	13.9	11.2	2/11	43	5/14	72	3
Denver, CO	5,382	102	7/17	-16	1/7	12.86	1.84	7/4	27.8	8.0	3/23	52	5/24	71	11
Des Moines, IA	971	97	7/14	-17	1/2	51.77	3.37	8/8-9	49.4	6.4	1/25	46	7/18	128	15
Detroit, MI	631	94	7/7	3	1/10	32.28	2.73	6/5-6	45.2	6.5	2/9	40	4/3	115	12
Duluth, MN	1,429	89	8/9	-26	1/3	35.59	3.93	5/23	81.3	7.8	1/24	41	9/2	113	18
Fairbanks, AK	464	91	8/15	-41	12/15	10.31	1.35	7/21	20.9	2.3	11/26	28	3/23	94	8
Fresno, CA	375	110	8/25	30	12/31	16.51	1.54	12/28-29	T	T	4/12	32	1/20	68	0
Grand Rapids, MI	788	93	8/29	4	1/30	35.87	3.27	1/15-16	47.6	8.1	2/9	51	9/21	124	12
Helena, MT	3,867	97	8/26	-20	1/7	12.97	1.15	6/16	30.2	2.6	11/28	44	5/3	100	14
Honolulu, HI	18	90	8/28	61	2/16	17.40	5.41	12/19	—	—	—	33	3/31	88	—
Houston, TX	107	102	8/23	20	1/9	42.72	5.45	7/1-2	T	T	2/23	44	7/24	85	0
Huron, SD	1,284	100	7/17	-24	1/8+	30.89	2.47	9/14-15	45.4	6.5	12/31	58	6/22	106	14
Indianapolis, IN	797	98	8/11	1	12/15	33.85	3.58	6/21-22	41.9	6.3	2/15	43	10/26	118	10
Jackson, MS	296	105	8/2	15	1/11	47.22	3.01	8/13-14	—	—	—	38	12/31	114	—
Jacksonville, FL	34	102	7/30	20	12/28+	33.40	2.93	9/26-27	—	—	—	35	6/6	85	—
Kansas City, MO	1,008	103	8/13	-5	1/7	41.91	2.59	5/12-13	30.9	7.3	3/20	47	4/2	102	10
Knoxville, TN	982	99	7/8	8	1/9	45.80	2.63	7/12-13	9.1	2.5	12/25	38	11/16	111	6
Lander, WY	5,560	97	7/26	-16	1/7	14.50	2.08	5/11-12	—	9.2	4/6	55	5/28	72	24
Lexington, KY	984	96	8/12+	2	12/15+	38.04	4.31	5/2	34.3	5.0	2/15	43	11/16	123	10
Los Angeles, CA	326	105	9/27	39	12/31	20.05	2.62	12/18-19	—	—	—	38	4/21	56	—
Louisville, KY	484	102	8/4	6	12/14	38.51	3.44	5/2	27.3	6.5	2/9	40	4/7	104	8
Marquette, MI	1,415	91	5/24	-8	12/29	34.83	2.14	9/23	200.6	9.8	4/8	—	—	173	45
Memphis, TN	286	104	8/4	9	1/8	47.90	4.58	7/11-12	7.1	5.0	2/8	40	3/11	89	2
Miami, FL	29	96	8/21+	35	1/10	65.10	5.07	9/28-29	—	—	—	35	2/12	130	—
Milwaukee, WI	680	92	8/29	2	1/10	35.98	3.61	7/22-23	34.5	8.1	2/9	44	10/26	103	9
Minneapolis, MN	874	96	8/8	-15	1/2	32.89	2.84	9/22-23	60.4	16.3	12/11	43	10/26	112	14
Mobile, AL	212	101	8/2+	14	1/11	59.87	5.94	1/20-21	0.3	0.3	2/12	38	3/1	106	0
Moline, IL	607	95	8/24	-15	1/10	45.13	2.73	7/6-7	46.2	6.9	12/24	48	6/23	127	15
Nashville, TN	574	101	8/4	8	12/14	59.08	9.09	5/1-2	11.6	3.9	1/29	37	10/26	110	4
Newark, NJ	28	103	7/6	14	1/31+	43.47	3.99	3/13	59.1	17.7	12/26	43	12/27	106	8
New Orleans, LA	7	100	8/2+	21	1/11	53.92	2.88	7/10	—	—	—	41	7/10	111	—
New York, NY	161	103	7/6	13	1/30	49.37	3.86	3/13	59.1	12.2	12/26	37	3/13	102	7
Norfolk, VA	69	105	7/25+	16	2/1	50.97	7.85	9/30	26.9	13.4	12/26	41	9/30	105	4
North Little Rock, AR	565	104	8/3	10	1/8	42.04	3.80	7/12-13	6.7	5.0	2/8	—	—	86	2
Oklahoma City, OK	1,284	104	8/23+	6	1/10	32.53	7.80	6/14-15	9.2	5.0	1/29	41	9/2	67	2
Philadelphia, PA	62	103	7/7	13	2/8	44.46	3.00	10/1	67.3	21.9	2/6	62	6/24	103	9
Phoenix, AZ	1,106	114	7/2+	32	12/31	9.14	1.33	7/31	—	—	—	43	1/21	38	—
Pittsburgh, PA	1,175	93	9/2	-1	2/7	37.85	2.95	11/30	78.8	11.4	2/5	43	10/26	139	21
Portland, ME	72	95	7/6	-1	1/10	52.51	4.24	2/24-25	36.5	7.4	1/18	49	11/7	116	10
Portland, OR	223	98	8/14	18	11/24+	46.18	1.73	12/8-9	—	—	—	39	12/18	191	—
Providence, RI	53	102	7/6	6	1/30	53.54	6.56	3/29-30	20.1	7.9	12/26	41	11/8	107	5
Raleigh-Durham, NC	430	102	7/25+	15	1/11	36.94	3.20	9/29-30	16.2	6.7	12/26	36	7/9	101	5
Rapid City, SD	3,153	102	8/27+	-18	1/8	19.24	1.81	5/10	31.6	5.8	11/22	52	10/27	103	11
Reno, NV	4,407	102	7/24	10	11/25+	9.25	1.09	10/4	28.5	10.9	2/21	48	4/27	57	6
Richmond, VA	167	105	7/25+	12	2/1	35.89	4.69	9/29-30	28.6	9.5	1/30	47	10/26	126	6
St. Louis, MO	710	102	8/3	0	1/9	39.07	3.48	11/24-25	19.3	4.4	12/12	49	8/22	109	17
Salt Lake City, UT	4,224	103	7/16	1	1/9	18.69	1.12	8/19	50.2	8.6	11/28	51	6/2	77	0
San Antonio, TX	821	103	8/24	16	1/9	37.39	6.45	9/7-8	0.2	0.2	2/23	35	1/22	60	—
San Diego, CA	81	100	11/4	42	11/30	16.26	2.90	12/21-22	—	—	—	44	5/23	80	—
San Francisco, CA	89	99	8/24	37	11/26+	24.15	1.84	1/18-19	—	—	—	33	8/30	199	0
San Juan, PR	10	94	9/2	68	12/5+	89.50	5.68	1/13-14	0.0	0.0	—	39	10/27	145	18
Sault Ste. Marie, MI	727	92	8/30	-12	1/7	30.43	3.05	9/23-24	54.4	7.5	12/2	39	6/19	82	0
Savannah, GA	143	102	7/26	20	1/11	36.35	3.26	8/22-23	0.8	0.8	2/12	52	5/24	92	12
Scottsbluff, NE	3,949	101	8/26	-15	1/8	16.13	1.48	6/9-10	47.7	7.2	5/12	52	5/2	91	9
Seattle, WA	434	96	8/15	14	11/24	46.99	4.63	12/11-12	3.0	2.5	11/22	38	12/18	190	1
Spokane, WA	2,384	95	7/26	-10	11/23	19.03	0.99	5/27-28	46.3	7.5	11/22	54	11/16	131	14
Springfield, MO	1,280	101	8/13	-7	1/10	46.16	4.62	9/1	19.3	5.2	1/29	38	8/15	107	5
Tampa, FL	40	98	6/12	25	1/11	40.34	2.12	4/25-26	0.0	0.0	—	44	1/25	100	0
Washington, DC	3	102	7/7+	16	2/7	34.78	4.70	9/29-30	41.6	9.1	2/6	44	4/8	101	9
Wilmington, DE	77	103	7/7+	11	2/7	43.96	4.32	9/30	57.0	19.4	2/6	47	6/24	104	9
Windsor Locks, CT	165	102	7/6	1	1/30	46.32	3.34	12/12	32.0	7.0	12/27	41	12/27	105	6

(+) = Indicates value for extreme also occurred on an earlier date(s). (T) = Trace amount. — = Data not available or unreported. (1) Where one date is shown, it is the starting date of the storm. (2) Comprises all forms of frozen precipitation, including hail and sleet. (3) Sustained for at least 2 mins., not peak gust.

Record Temperatures by State

Source: National Climatic Data Center, NESDIS, NOAA, U.S. Dept. of Commerce
(through 2010)

State	°F	Latest date	Station	Approx. elevation (ft)	°F	Latest date	Station	Approx. elevation (ft)
		LOWEST TEMPERATURE				HIGHEST TEMPERATURE		
Alabama	−27	Jan. 30, 1966	New Market	732	112	Sept. 6, 1925	Centerville	220
Alaska	−80	Jan. 23, 1971	Prospect Creek Camp	955	100	June 27, 1915	Fort Yukon	445
Arizona	−40	Jan. 7, 1971	Hawley Lake	8,180	128	June 29, 1994	Lake Havasu City	505
Arkansas	−29	Feb. 13, 1905	Brook Farm Pond	1,260	120	Aug. 10, 1936	Ozark	390
California	−45	Jan. 20, 1937	Boca	5,575	134	July 10, 1913	Greenland Ranch	−194
Colorado	−61	Feb. 1, 1985	Maybell	5,944	114	July 11, 1954[1]	Sedgwick	3,584
Connecticut	−32	Jan. 22, 1961[1]	Coventry	480	106	July 15, 1995[1]	Danbury	405
Delaware	−17	Jan. 17, 1893	Millsboro	20	110	July 21, 1930	Millsboro	20
Florida	−2	Feb. 13, 1899	Tallahassee	192	109	June 29, 1931	Monticello	98
Georgia	−17	Jan. 27, 1940	CCC Camp F-16	1,000	112	Aug. 20, 1983[1]	Greenville	960
Hawaii	12	May 17, 1979	Mauna Kea Obs.	13,773	100	Apr. 27, 1931	Pahala	840
Idaho	−60	Jan. 18, 1943	Island Park Dam	6,290	118	July 28, 1934	Orofino	1,320
Illinois	−36	Jan. 5, 1999	Congerville	635	117	July 14, 1954	East St. Louis	410
Indiana	−36	Jan. 19, 1994	New Whiteland	785	116	July 14, 1936	Collegeville	650
Iowa	−47	Feb. 3, 1996[1]	Elkader	788	118	July 20, 1934	Keokuk	651
Kansas	−40	Feb. 13, 1905	Lebanon	1,874	121	July 24, 1936[1]	Alton (near)	1,591
Kentucky	−37	Jan. 19, 1994	Shelbyville	730	114	July 28, 1930	Greensburg	590
Louisiana	−16	Feb. 13, 1899	Minden	200	114	Aug. 10, 1936	Plain Dealing	290
Maine	−50	Jan. 16, 2009	Big Black River	885	105	July 10, 1911[1]	North Bridgton	449
Maryland	−40	Jan. 13, 1912	Oakland	2,420	109	July 10, 1936[1]	Cumberland Frederick	899 380
Massachusetts	−35	Jan. 12, 1981[1]	Chester	640	107	Aug. 2, 1975	Chester New Bedford	640 70
Michigan	−51	Feb. 9, 1934	Vanderbilt	905	112	July 13, 1936	Mio Stanwood	960 830
Minnesota	−60	Feb. 2, 1996	Tower	1,485	115	July 29, 1917	Beardsley	1,089
Mississippi	−19	Jan. 30, 1966	Corinth	420	115	July 29, 1930	Holly Springs	502
Missouri	−40	Feb. 13, 1905	Warsaw	705	118	July 14, 1954	Warsaw Union	705 540
Montana	−70	Jan. 20, 1954	Rogers Pass	5,545	117	July 5, 1937[1]	Medicine Lake	1,942
Nebraska	−47	Dec. 22, 1989[1]	Oshkosh	3,390	118	July 24, 1936[1]	Minden	2,160
Nevada	−50	Jan. 8, 1937	San Jacinto	5,203	125	June 29, 1994	Laughlin	605
New Hampshire	−46	Jan. 8, 1968	Mt. Washington	6,267	106	July 4, 1911	Nashua	140
New Jersey	−34	Jan. 5, 1904	River Vale	70	110	July 10, 1936	Runyon	140
New Mexico	−50	Feb. 1, 1951	Gavilan	7,425	122	June 27, 1994	Waste Isolat. Pilot Plt.	3,411
New York	−52	Feb. 18, 1979	Old Forge	1,748	108	July 22, 1926	Troy	35
North Carolina	−34	Jan. 21, 1985	Mt. Mitchell	6,240	110	Aug. 21, 1983	Fayetteville	186
North Dakota	−60	Feb. 15, 1936	Parshall	1,952	121	July 6, 1936	Steele	1,885
Ohio	−39	Feb. 10, 1899	Milligan	875	113	July 21, 1934	Gallipolis (near)	669
Oklahoma	−27	Jan. 4, 1947[1]	Guthrie	1,110	120	June 27, 1994[1]	Tipton	1,269
Oregon	−54	Feb. 10, 1933[1]	Seneca	4,660	119	Aug. 10, 1898[1]	Pendleton	1,040
Pennsylvania	−42	Jan. 5, 1904	Smethport	1,469	111	July 10, 1936[1]	Phoenixville	105
Rhode Island	−28	Jan. 11, 1942	Wood River Junction	49	104	Aug. 2, 1975	Providence	60
South Carolina	−19	Jan. 21, 1985	Caesars Head	3,200	111	June 28, 1954[1]	Camden	140
South Dakota	−58	Feb. 17, 1936	McIntosh	2,175	120	July 15, 2006[1]	Fort Pierre	1,590
Tennessee	−32	Dec. 30, 1917	Mountain City	2,503	113	Aug. 9, 1930[1]	Perryville	371
Texas	−23	Feb. 8, 1933	Seminole	3,336	120	June 28, 1994[1]	Monahans	2,547
Utah	−50	Jan. 5, 1913	Strawberry Tunnel E.	7,615	117	July 5, 1985	Saint George	2,770
Vermont	−50	Dec. 30, 1933	Bloomfield	1,040	107	July 7, 1912	Vernon	226
Virginia	−30	Jan. 21, 1985	Mountain Lake Bio. Station	3,870	110	July 15, 1954[1]	Balcony Falls	732
Washington	−48	Dec. 30, 1968	Mazama Winthrop	2,106 1,749	118	Aug. 5, 1961[1]	Ice Harbor Dam	368
West Virginia	−37	Dec. 30, 1917	Lewisburg	2,251	112	July 10, 1936[1]	Martinsburg	534
Wisconsin	−55	Feb. 4, 1996[1]	Couderay	1,300	114	July 13, 1936	Wisconsin Dells	835
Wyoming	−66	Feb. 9, 1933	Riverside Ranger Sta.	6,500	115	July 15, 1988[1]	Diversion Dam	5,575

(1) Also on earlier dates at the same or other places.

Hurricane and Tornado Classifications

Source: National Weather Service, NOAA, U.S. Dept. of Commerce

The Saffir-Simpson Hurricane Wind Scale rates a hurricane's intensity from 1 to 5. The scale, updated in 2010, provides examples of the type of damage and impacts associated with winds of the indicated intensity. The Fujita (or F) Scale was created by T. Theodore Fujita in 1971 to classify tornadoes. The Enhanced Fujita Scale, an update to the original, was implemented in the U.S. in 2007. It uses 3-sec. gusts estimated at the point of damage based on a judgment of several levels of damage to 28 indicators.

Category	Winds[1]	Saffir-Simpson Wind Scale (Hurricanes) Summary of damage
1	74-95 mph	Very dangerous winds will produce some damage.
2	96-110 mph	Extremely dangerous winds will cause extensive damage.
3	111-130 mph	Devastating damage will occur.
4	131-155 mph	Catastrophic damage will occur.
5	Over 155 mph	Catastrophic damage will occur.

(1) 1-minute sustained winds.

Enhanced Fujita Scale (Tornadoes)	
Rank	3-sec. gust
EF-0	65-85 mph
EF-1	86-110 mph
EF-2	111-135 mph
EF-3	136-165 mph
EF-4	166-200 mph
EF-5	Over 200 mph

Tropical Cyclone Names in 2012

Source: National Weather Service, NOAA, U.S. Dept. of Commerce

Atlantic: Alberto, Beryl, Chris, Debby, Ernesto, Florence, Gordon, Helene, Isaac, Joyce, Kirk, Leslie, Michael, Nadine, Oscar, Patty, Rafael, Sandy, Tony, Valerie, William. If there are more than 21 named Atlantic storms in one season, remaining storms take names from the Greek alphabet, starting with Alpha.

Eastern North Pacific: Aletta, Bud, Carlotta, Daniel, Emilia, Fabio, Gilma, Hector, Ileana, John, Kristy, Lane, Miriam, Norman, Olivia, Paul, Rosa, Sergio, Tara, Vicente, Willa, Xavier, Yolanda, Zeke.

World Temperature and Precipitation

Source: World Meteorological Organization

Average daily maximum and minimum temperatures and annual precipitation based on records for the period 1961-90. Records of extreme temperatures include all available years of data for a given location and are usually for a longer period. Surface elevations are supplied by the WMO and may differ from figures in other sections of *The World Almanac.* NA = Not available.

Station	Surface elevation (ft)	Temperature (°F) AVERAGE DAILY January Max.	Min.	July Max.	Min.	EXTREME Max.	Min.	Avg. annual precipitation (in.)
Algiers, Algeria	82	61.7	42.6	87.1	65.3	NA	NA	27.0
Athens, Greece	49	56.1	44.6	88.9	73.0	NA	NA	14.6
Auckland, New Zealand	20	74.8	61.2	58.5	46.4	NA	NA	49.4
Bangkok, Thailand	66	89.6	69.8	90.9	77.0	104	51	59.0
Berlin, Germany	190	35.2	26.8	73.6	55.2	107	−4	23.3
Bogotá, Colombia	8,357	67.3	41.7	64.6	45.5	75	21	32.4
Bucharest, Romania	298	34.7	22.1	83.8	60.1	105	−18	23.4
Budapest, Hungary	456	34.2	24.8	79.7	59.7	103	−10	20.3
Buenos Aires, Argentina	82	85.8	67.3	59.7	45.7	104	22	45.2
Cairo, Egypt	243	65.8	48.2	93.9	71.1	118	34	1.0
Cape Town, South Africa	138	79.0	60.3	63.3	44.6	105	28	20.5
Caracas, Venezuela	2,739	79.9	60.8	81.3	66.0	96	45	36.1
Casablanca, Morocco	203	62.8	47.1	77.7	66.7	NA	NA	16.8
Copenhagen, Denmark	16	35.6	28.4	68.9	55.0	NA	NA	NA
Damascus, Syria	2,004	54.3	32.9	97.2	61.9	NA	NA	5.6
Dublin, Ireland	279	45.7	36.5	66.0	52.5	86	8	28.8
Geneva, Switzerland	1,364	38.3	27.9	76.3	53.2	101	−3	35.6
Havana, Cuba	164	78.4	65.5	88.3	74.8	NA	NA	46.9
Hong Kong, China	203	65.5	56.5	88.7	79.9	97	32	87.2
Istanbul, Turkey	108	47.8	37.2	82.8	65.3	105	7	27.4
Jerusalem, Israel	2,483	53.4	39.4	83.8	63.0	107	26	23.2
Lagos, Nigeria	125	90.0	72.3	82.8	72.1	NA	NA	59.3
Lima, Peru	43	79.0	66.9	66.4	59.4	NA	NA	0.2
London, England	203	44.1	32.7	71.1	52.3	99	2	29.7
Manila, Philippines	79	85.8	74.8	89.1	76.8	NA	NA	49.6
Mexico City, Mexico	7,570	70.3	43.7	73.8	53.2	100	−36	33.4
Montreal, Canada	118	21.6	5.2	79.2	59.7	100	−36	37.0
Mumbai (Bombay), India	36	85.3	66.7	86.2	77.5	110	46	85.4
Nairobi, Kenya	5,897	77.9	50.9	71.6	48.6	NA	NA	41.9
Paris, France	213	42.8	33.6	75.2	55.2	105	−1	25.6
Prague, Czech Republic	1,197	32.7	22.5	73.9	53.2	98	−16	20.7
Reykjavik, Iceland	200	35.4	26.6	55.9	46.9	76	−3	31.5
Rome, Italy	79	53.8	35.4	88.2	62.1	NA	NA	33.0
San Salvador, El Salvador	2,037	86.5	61.3	86.2	66.4	105	45	68.3
São Paulo, Brazil	2,598	81.1	65.7	71.2	53.1	NA	NA	57.4
Shanghai, China	23	45.9	32.9	88.9	76.6	104	10	43.8
Singapore	52	85.8	73.6	87.4	75.6	NA	NA	84.6
Stockholm, Sweden	171	30.7	23.0	71.4	56.1	97	−26	21.2
Sydney, Australia	10	79.5	65.5	62.4	43.9	114	32	46.4
Tehran, Iran	3,906	45.0	30.0	98.2	75.2	109	−5	9.1
Tokyo, Japan	118	49.1	34.2	83.8	72.1	NA	NA	55.4
Toronto, Canada	567	27.5	12.0	80.2	57.6	105	−26	30.8

Speed of Winds in the U.S.

Source: National Climatic Data Center, NESDIS, NOAA, U.S. Dept. of Commerce

Based on available records through 2010. Average and maximum speeds are annual. Max. speeds are highest 1-min. average.

Station	Avg. mph	Max. mph	Station	Avg. mph	Max. mph	Station	Avg. mph	Max. mph
Albuquerque, NM	8.9	53	Helena, MT[2]	7.7	73	Oklahoma City, OK	12.2	74
Anchorage, AK[1,2]	7.1	75	Honolulu, HI	11.2	46	Omaha, NE	10.5	58
Atlanta, GA	9.1	60	Houston, TX	7.6	51	Philadelphia, PA[2]	9.5	73
Baltimore, MD[2]	8.7	80	Indianapolis, IN	9.6	60	Phoenix, AZ	6.2	54
Birmingham, AL[2]	7.1	65	Jackson, MS	6.9	55	Pittsburgh, PA	8.9	58
Bismarck, ND	10.2	64	Jacksonville, FL	7.8	57	Portland, ME	8.7	57
Boise, ID[2]	8.7	61	Little Rock, AR[2]	7.7	65	Portland, OR[2]	7.9	88
Boston, MA	12.3	54	Los Angeles, CA[2]	5.0	49	Providence, RI	10.4	90
Buffalo, NY[2]	11.8	91	Louisville, KY	8.3	56	Richmond, VA	7.7	48
Burlington, VT	9.0	39	Miami, FL	9.2	86	St. Louis, MO	9.6	53
Charleston, SC	8.6	52	Milwaukee, WI	11.5	54	Salt Lake City, UT[2]	8.8	71
Chicago, IL	10.3	58	Minn.-St. Paul, MN	10.5	51	San Francisco, CA[2]	8.7	47
Cleveland, OH	10.5	58	Mobile, AL	8.8	66	San Juan, PR	8.3	79
Dallas-Ft. Worth, TX	10.7	73	Mount Washington, NH[1,2]	35.1	231	Seattle, WA[2]	8.8	66
Denver, CO	8.7	54	Nashville, TN	7.9	58	Sioux Falls, SD	11.0	70
Des Moines, IA[2]	10.7	76	Newark, NJ	10.2	82	Washington, DC	9.4	49
Detroit, MI	10.1	61	New Orleans, LA	8.2	69	Wichita, KS	12.2	70
Hartford, CT	8.4	46	New York, NY	9.1	40	Wilmington, DE	9.0	58

(1) Max. speed based on short gusts. (2) Max. speed calculated from minimum time during which 1 mi of wind passed the station.

Wind Chill Temperature

Source: National Weather Service, NOAA, U.S. Dept. of Commerce

Temperature and wind combine to cause heat loss from body surfaces. For example, a temperature of 5°F, plus a 10-mph wind, causes body heat loss equal to that which would occur in −10°F with no wind. In other words, a 10-mph wind makes 5°F feel like −10°F. Wind speeds greater than 45 mph have little additional chilling effect. Direct sunlight can increase the wind chill temperature 10° to 15°F. When the wind chill temperature falls within the shaded area, frostbite can occur in 30 mins. or less.

Wind speed (mph) \ Calm	40	35	30	25	20	15	10	5	0	−5	−10	−15	−20	−25	−30	−35	−40	−45
Air temperature (°F) ↑ / **Wind chill temperature (°F)**																		
5	36	31	25	19	13	7	1	−5	−11	−16	−22	−28	−34	−40	−46	−52	−57	−63
10	34	27	21	15	9	3	−4	−10	−16	−22	−28	−35	−41	−47	−53	−59	−66	−72
15	32	25	19	13	6	0	−7	−13	−19	−26	−32	−39	−45	−51	−58	−64	−71	−77
20	30	24	17	11	4	−2	−9	−15	−22	−29	−35	−42	−48	−55	−61	−68	−74	−81
25	29	23	16	9	3	−4	−11	−17	−24	−31	−37	−44	−51	−58	−64	−71	−78	−84
30	28	22	15	8	1	−5	−12	−19	−26	−33	−39	−46	−53	−60	−67	−73	−80	−87
35	28	21	14	7	0	−7	−14	−21	−27	−34	−41	−48	−55	−62	−69	−76	−82	−89
40	27	20	13	6	−1	−8	−15	−22	−29	−36	−43	−50	−57	−64	−71	−78	−84	−91
45	26	19	12	5	−2	−9	−16	−23	−30	−37	−44	−51	−58	−65	−72	−79	−86	−93

Heat Index

Source: National Weather Service, NOAA, U.S. Dept. of Commerce

The heat index, or apparent temperature, is a measure of how hot it feels when the relative humidity is added to the actual air temperature. For example, when air temperature is 100°F, and relative humidity is 50%, it will feel as if it's 118°F with no humidity. Full sunlight can make one feel even hotter. On the chart, the shaded area above 103°-105° apparent temperature corresponds to a level that may cause increasingly severe heat disorders with continued exposure and/or physical activity.

Relative humidity % \ Temperature (°F)	80	82	84	86	88	90	92	94	96	98	100	102	104	106	108	110
Apparent temperature (°F)																
40	80	81	83	85	88	91	94	97	101	105	109	114	119	124	130	136
45	80	82	84	87	89	93	96	100	104	109	114	119	124	130	137	
50	81	83	85	88	91	95	99	103	108	113	118	124	131	137		
55	81	84	86	89	93	97	101	106	112	117	124	130	137			
60	82	84	88	91	95	100	105	110	116	123	129	137				
65	82	85	89	93	98	103	108	114	121	126	130					
70	83	86	90	95	100	105	112	119	126	134						
75	84	88	92	97	103	109	116	124	132							
80	84	89	94	100	106	113	121	129								
85	85	90	96	102	110	117	126	135								
90	86	91	98	105	113	122	131									
95	86	93	100	108	117	127										
100	87	95	103	112	121	132										

☐ Caution   ▨ Extreme caution   ▨ Danger   ▨ Extreme danger

Ultraviolet (UV) Index Forecast

Source: National Weather Service, NOAA, U.S. Dept. of Commerce; U.S. Environmental Protection Agency; U.S. Food and Drug Administration, U.S. Dept. of Health and Human Services

The National Weather Service (NWS) and the Environmental Protection Agency (EPA) developed and began offering a UV index in 1994 in response to increasing incidences of skin cancer, cataracts, and other effects from exposure to the sun's harmful rays. In 2004, they adapted their index to the Global Solar UV Index sponsored by the World Health Organization. The UV index is now a regular element of NWS atmospheric forecasts.

The UV index, ranging from 0 to 11+, is an indication of the expected intensity of UV radiation reaching the Earth's surface during the solar noon hour (the time of day when the sun appears to have reached its highest point in the sky; it depends on location and the time of year). The lower the UV index value, the less the radiation. The UV index forecast is produced daily for 58 cities by the NWS Climate Prediction Center and uses the following scale.

UV index	Exposure	Minimum precautions
0-2	Low	Sunscreen with an SPF of at least 15
3-5	Moderate	Sunscreen, covering up
6-7	High	Sunscreen, hat, UV-blocking sunglasses, avoid sun 10 AM-4 PM
8-10	Very high	Same as above
11+	Extreme	Same as above

The index value is valid for a radius of about 30 miles around a listed city and is based on several factors:

Ozone. Ozone, a form of oxygen, the molecules of which consist of three atoms rather than two, blocks UV radiation. The more ozone, the lower the UV radiation at the surface.

Sun height. The higher the sun is in the sky, the higher the UV radiation level.

Cloudiness. UV radiation levels are highest under cloudless skies. Even with cloud cover, UV radiation levels can be high due to the scattering of UV radiation by water molecules and fine particles in the atmosphere.

Reflectivity. Reflective surfaces intensify UV exposure. White sand reflects about 15% of UV radiation reaching the surface; sea foam, 25%; snow, as much as 80%; water, up to 100% depending on reflection angle.

Elevation. At higher elevations, UV radiation travels a shorter distance to reach Earth's surface so there is less atmosphere to absorb the rays. For every 1,000 m (3,281 ft) one travels above sea level, UV levels increase by 10%-12%. Snow and lack of pollutants intensify UV exposure at higher altitudes.

Latitude. The closer a location is to the equator, the higher the UV radiation level.

SPF (sun protection factor) number. The UV index is not linked in any way to the SPF number on suntan lotions and sunscreens. The Centers for Disease Control and Prevention recommends using a sunscreen with at least SPF 15. Under a Food and Drug Administration rule taking effect in 2012, sunscreens that protect against cancer and early skin aging as well as sunburn will be labeled as "broad spectrum."

Further information. For precautions to take after learning the UV index value, call the EPA's Stratospheric Ozone Hotline (800-296-1996). For questions on scientific aspects, visit the NWS Climate Prediction Center online at www.cpc.noaa.gov.

Lightning

Source: National Weather Service, NOAA, U.S. Dept. of Commerce

Lightning is a powerful electric discharge, or spark, that can occur in the atmosphere when an imbalance of positive and negative charges develops. It may travel within a cloud, between clouds, between a cloud and clear air, or between a cloud and the ground. Lightning generally accompanies rainstorms, but it sometimes is also seen with snowstorms, volcano eruption clouds, and violent forest fires. In a common form of cloud-to-ground lightning, a negatively charged area in a thunderstorm sends charges downward, attracted to positively charged objects. Lightning can travel miles away from the area of a storm.

The transfer of charges in lightning generates a huge amount of heat, sending the temperature in the channel to 50,000°F or more and causing the air within it to expand rapidly. The sound of that expansion is thunder. Sound travels more slowly than light, so lightning is usually observed before thunder is heard.

An estimated 25 mil cloud-to-ground lightning bolts happen in the U.S. each year, killing an annual average of 55 people in 1981-2010. This is a small number compared to U.S. deaths from fire (about 3,000 a year) and motor vehicle accidents (more than 30,000 in recent years), but it is still significant. In comparison, tornadoes caused an average of 56 deaths a year and hurricanes an average of 47 over the same 30-year time period. According to preliminary figures from the National Weather Service, 29 people were struck and killed by lightning in 2010; 182 more were injured.

Most lightning deaths and injuries occur in summer when people are outdoors. If outdoors, one should run to a safe building or vehicle when the first thunder is heard, lightning is seen, or dark threatening clouds are observed developing overhead. Even while indoors, one is advised to stay away from windows and doors and avoid contact with anything conducting electricity, including corded phones, computers, and tubs, showers, and other plumbing, and stay inside until 30 mins. after the last clap of thunder is heard.

More information about lightning can be found online at www.lightningsafety.noaa.gov.

Global Measured Extremes of Temperature and Precipitation Records

Source: World Weather/Climate Extremes Archive, World Meteorological Organization Commission for Climatology
(records in each category ranked from most to least extreme)

Highest Temperature Extremes

Continent	Highest temp. (°F)	Place	Elevation (ft)	Date
Africa	136	El Azizia, Libya	367	Sept. 13, 1922
North America	134	Death Valley, CA, U.S. (Furnace Creek Ranch)	−179	July 10, 1913
Asia	129	Tirat Tsvi, Israel	−722	June 21, 1942
Australia	123	Oodnadatta, South Australia	367	Jan. 2, 1960
South America	120	Rivadavia, Argentina	2,192	Dec. 11, 1905
Europe	118.4	Athens, Greece (and Elefsina, Greece)	774	July 10, 1977
Oceania	108	Tuguegarao, Philippines	676	Apr. 29, 1912
Antarctica	59	Vanda Station (New Zealand), Wright Valley	49	May 1, 1974

Lowest Temperature Extremes

Continent	Lowest temp. (°F)	Place	Elevation (ft)	Date
Antarctica	−129	Vostok Station (Russia)	11,220	July 21, 1983
Asia	−90	Verkhoyansk, Russia	350	Feb. 5 and 7, 1892
	−90	Oimekon, Russia	2,625	Feb. 6, 1933
North America	−81.4	Snag, Yukon Territory, Canada	2,120	Feb. 3, 1947
Europe	−72.6	Ust'-Shchugor, Russia	279	Dec. 31, 1978
South America	−27	Sarmiento, Argentina	879	June 1, 1907
Africa	−11	Ifrane, Morocco	5,364	Feb. 11, 1935
Australia	−9.4	Charlotte Pass, New South Wales	5,758	June 29, 1994

Highest Measured Average Annual Precipitation Extremes

Continent	Highest avg. (in.)[1]	Place	Elevation (ft)	Years in averaging period
Asia	467.4	Mawsynram, India	4,695	38
Oceania	460	Mt. Waialeale, Kauai, HI, U.S.	5,148	30
Africa	405	Debundscha, Cameroon	30	32
South America	354	Quibdo, Colombia	230	29
Australia	316.3	Bellenden Ker, Queensland	5,102	34
North America	276	Henderson Lake, British Columbia, Canada	12	15
Europe	183	Crkvica, Bosnia-Herzegovina	4,298	22
Antarctica	>31.5[2]	Along coast of E and W and over the Antarctic Peninsula		3[3]

(1) Official greatest average annual precipitation. The average annual precipitation record of 523.6 in., set in Lloro, Colombia (14 mi SE and at a higher elevation than Quibdo), is an estimated amount. (2) Water equivalent. (3) July 1996-June 1999.

Lowest Measured Average Annual Precipitation Extremes

Continent	Lowest avg. (in.)	Place	Elevation (ft)	Years in averaging period
South America	0.03	Arica, Chile	213	59
Antarctica	0.08	Amundsen-Scott South Pole Station (U.S.)	9,301	10
Africa	<0.1	Wadi Halfa, Sudan	590	39
North America	1.2	Batagues, Mexico	69	14
Asia	1.8	Aden, Yemen	63	50
Australia	4.05	Troudaninna, South Australia	46	42
Europe	6.4	Astrakhan, Russia	66	25
Oceania	7.41	Mauna Kea Observatory, HI, U.S.	13,780	11[1]

(1) 1972-82.

OCEANOGRAPHY

Tides and Their Causes

Source: National Ocean Service, NOAA, U.S. Dept. of Commerce

The tides are natural phenomena involving the movement of waves in the Earth's large fluid bodies as a result of the gravitational attraction of the sun and moon. These two variable influences combined produce the complex recurrent cycle of the tides. Tides may occur in both oceans and seas; to a limited extent in large lakes and in the atmosphere; and, to a very minute degree, in the Earth itself. The length of time between succeeding tides can vary.

The tide-generating force represents the difference between (1) the centrifugal force produced by Earth's revolution around the common center-of-gravity of the Earth-moon system and (2) the gravitational attraction of the moon acting upon the Earth's overlying waters. The moon is about 390 times closer to Earth than is the sun. So despite its smaller mass, the moon's tide-raising force is two times greater.

The tide-generating forces of the moon and sun acting tangentially to the Earth's surface tend to cause a maximum accumulation of waters at two diametrically opposite points on the Earth's surface and to withdraw compensating amounts of water from all points 90° removed from these tidal bulges. As the Earth rotates beneath the maxima and minima of these tide-generating forces, a sequence of two high tides, separated by two low tides, is produced each lunar day (the time it takes for a specific site on the Earth to rotate from an exact point under the moon to the same point under the moon, 24 hours and 50 minutes) in what is called a **semidiurnal tide**. Each ocean basin reacts differently to tidal forces.

Twice each month, when the sun, moon, and Earth are directly aligned—the moon between the Earth and sun (at new moon) or on the opposite side of Earth from the sun (at full moon)—the sun and moon exert gravitational forces in a mutual or additive fashion. The highest high tides and lowest low tides, called **spring tides**, are produced at these times. At two positions 90° in between, the moon and sun's gravitational forces—imposed at right angles—counteract each other to the greatest extent, and the range between high and low tides is reduced, resulting in **neap tides**.

The inclination of the moon's monthly orbit and of the sun to the equator during Earth's yearly passage through its orbit produce a difference in the height of succeeding high and low tides, known as the diurnal inequality. In most cases, this produces a so-called **mixed tide**. In extreme cases, these phenomena may result in a **diurnal tide**, with only one high tide and one low tide each day. There are other monthly and yearly variations in the tides because of the elliptical shape of the orbits.

The range of tides in the open ocean is generally less than in the coastal regions, where the incoming tide can be augmented by the continental shelves, as well as by bays and estuaries. The largest tidal ranges in the world occur in the Bay of Fundy and in Ungava Bay, Canada, where the range of tide reaches 53 ft. In New Orleans, the periodic rise and fall of the diurnal tide is affected by the seasonal stages of the Mississippi River, being about 10 in. at low stage and 0 at high.

In every case, actual high or low tide can vary considerably from the average, as a result of weather conditions such as strong winds, abrupt barometric pressure changes, or prolonged periods of extreme high or low pressure.

Average Rise and Fall of Tides

(mean ranges, based on 2011 predictions)

Place	Ft	In.	Place	Ft	In.	Place	Ft	In.
Baltimore, MD	1	2	Honolulu, HI	1	3	Portland, ME	9	1
Boston, MA	9	6	Key West, FL	1	3	St. Petersburg, FL	1	7
Charleston, SC	5	3	Los Angeles, CA	3	10	San Diego, CA	4	1
Cristobal, Panama	0	8	Miami, FL	2	4	Sandy Hook, NJ	4	8
Eastport, ME	18	4	New London, CT	2	7	San Francisco, CA	4	1
Ft. Pulaski, GA	6	11	Newport, RI	3	6	San Juan, PR	1	1
Galveston, TX	1	0	New York, NY	4	6	Seattle, WA	7	8
Hampton Roads, VA	2	5	Philadelphia, PA	6	0	Washington, DC	2	9

El Niño and La Niña

Source: National Weather Service, NOAA, U.S. Dept. of Commerce

El Niño is a climatically significant disruption of the ocean-atmosphere system characterized by large-scale weakening of trade winds and warming of the surface layers in the central and eastern equatorial Pacific. The term *El Niño*, Spanish for "the little boy" or "The Christ Child," was originally used by fishermen to refer to a warm ocean current that appeared around Christmas off the west coasts of Ecuador and Peru that lasted several months. The term has come to be reserved for exceptionally strong, warm currents that bring heavy rains.

El Niño events generally occur at irregular intervals of 2 to 7 years, at an average of once every 3 to 4 years. They typically last 12 to 18 months. The intensity of El Niño events varies depending on the area encompassed by the abnormally warm ocean temperatures. Some are strong, such as in 1982-83 and 1997-98. Others are considerably weaker, such as the 2009-10 event. The eastward extent of warmer than normal water varies from episode to episode.

El Niño influences weather around the globe, and its impacts are most clearly seen in the winter. During El Niño years, winter temperatures in the continental U.S. tend to be warmer than normal in the North and West Coast states and cooler than normal in the Southeast. Conditions tend to be wetter than normal over central and southern California, the Southwest states and across much of the South, and drier than normal over the northern portions of the Rocky Mountains and in the Ohio valley. Globally, El Niño brings wetter than normal conditions to Peru and Chile and dry conditions to Australia and Indonesia. It should be noted that El Niño is only one of a number of factors influencing seasonal variations of climate.

La Niña ("the little girl") is characterized by colder than normal sea surface temperatures in the equatorial Pacific. La Niña typically brings wetter, cooler conditions to the Pacific Northwest and drier, warmer conditions to much of the southern U.S. El Niño and La Niña are opposite phases of the El Niño-Southern Oscillation (ENSO) cycle, which involves a shift in tropical sea-level pressure between the Eastern and Western hemispheres.

The National Oceanographic and Atmospheric Administration and other agencies monitor these events using satellites, weather balloons, and buoys in the Pacific Ocean. Highly sophisticated numerical computer models of the ocean and atmosphere use these data to predict the onset and evolution of El Niño and La Niña.

DISASTERS

Some Notable Aircraft Disasters Since 1937

Source: National Transportation Safety Board; World Almanac research. As of Sept. 2011.

Particularly notable disasters are in bold. Asterisk (*) indicates number of deaths includes those on ground.

Date	Aircraft	Site of accident	Deaths
1937, May 6	**German zeppelin Hindenburg**	**Burned at mooring, Lakehurst, NJ**	**36***
1944, Aug. 23	U.S. Air Force B-24 Liberator bomber	Hit school, Freckleton, England	61*
1945, July 28	U.S. Army B-25	Hit Empire State Building after getting lost in fog, New York, NY	14*
1952, Dec. 20	U.S. Air Force C-124	Crashed at Moses Lake, WA	87
1953, Mar. 3	**Canadian Pacific DH-106 Comet**	**Crashed on takeoff from Karachi, Pakistan; world's first fatal commercial passenger jet crash**	**11**
1953, June 18	U.S. Air Force C-124	Crashed, burned near Tokyo, Japan	129
1955, Oct. 6	United Airlines DC-4	Crashed in Medicine Bow Peak, WY	66
1955, Nov. 1	United Airlines DC-6	Bomb on board exploded near Longmont, CO	44[1]
1956, June 20	Venezuelan Super Constellation	Crashed into Atlantic off Asbury Park, NJ	74
1956, June 30	TWA Super Const., United DC-7	Collided over Grand Canyon, AZ	128
1960, Dec. 16	United DC-8, TWA Super Const.	Collided over New York, NY, killing all 128 on planes, 6 on ground	134*
1962, Mar. 16	Flying Tiger Super Constellation	Vanished in W Pacific en route to Philippines from Guam	107
1962, June 3	Air France Boeing 707	Crashed on takeoff from Paris, France	130
1962, June 22	Air France Boeing 707	Crashed in storm, Guadeloupe, French W Indies	113
1963, Feb. 1	Lebanese Middle East Airlines Vickers Viscount 754, Turkish Mil. Douglas C-47	Collided over Ankara, Turkey, killing all 17 on planes, 87 on ground	104*
1963, June 3	Northwest Airlines DC-7	Crashed into Pacific off British Columbia, Canada	101
1963, Nov. 29	Trans-Canada Air Lines DC-8	Crashed after takeoff from Montreal, QC, Canada	118
1965, May 20	Pakistani Boeing 720	Crashed at airport in Cairo, Egypt	121
1966, Jan. 24	Air India Boeing 707	Crashed on Mont Blanc, France-Italy	117
1966, Feb. 4	All-Nippon Boeing 727	Plunged into Tokyo Bay, Japan	133
1966, Mar. 5	BOAC Boeing 707	Crashed into Mt. Fuji, Japan, after encountering severe turbulence	124
1966, Dec. 24	U.S. military-chartered CL-44	Crashed into village in S Vietnam	129*
1967, Apr. 20	Globe Air Bristol Britannia	Crashed on approach to airport, Nicosia, Cyprus	126
1967, July 19	Piedmont Boeing 727, Cessna 310	Collided over Hendersonville, NC	82
1968, Apr. 20	S. African Airways Boeing 707	Crashed on takeoff from Windhoek, Namibia	122
1968, May 3	Braniff International Electra	Crashed in storm near Dawson, TX	85
1969, Mar. 16	Venezuelan DC-9	Crashed after takeoff from Maracaibo, Venezuela	155[2]
1969, Dec. 8	Olympic Airways DC-6B	Crashed in storm near Athens, Greece	93
1970, Feb. 15	Dominicana DC-9	Crashed into sea on takeoff from Santo Domingo, Dominican Rep.	102
1970, July 3	British-chartered DH-106 Comet	Crashed near Barcelona, Spain	112
1970, July 5	Air Canada DC-8	Crashed near Toronto Intl. Airport, ON, Canada	108
1970, Aug. 9	LANSA Lockheed L-188A Electra	Crashed on takeoff from Cuzco, Peru	101*
1970, Nov. 14	Southern Airways DC-9	Crashed into mountains near Huntington, WV	75[3]
1971, July 30	All-Nippon Boeing 727, Japan Air Force F-86 fighter	Collided over Morioka, Japan	162[4]
1971, Sept. 4	Alaska Airlines Boeing 727	Crashed into mountain near Juneau, AK	111
1972, Aug. 14	East German IL-62	Crashed on takeoff from East Berlin	156
1972, Oct. 13	Aeroflot IL-62	Crashed near Moscow, U.S.S.R.	176
1972, Dec. 3	Spanish-chartered Convair CV-990	Crashed on takeoff from Canary Islands, Spain	155
1972, Dec. 29	Eastern Airlines Lockheed Tristar	Crashed on approach to Miami Intl. Airport, FL	101
1973, Jan. 22	Nigerian-chartered Boeing 707	Burst into flames upon landing at Kano Airport, Nigeria	176
1973, Feb. 21	**Libyan Arab Boeing 727**	**Flew off course, shot down by Israeli fighter planes over Sinai Desert**	**108**
1973, Apr. 10	British Vickers Vanguard	Crashed during snowstorm on approach to Basel, Switzerland	104
1973, June 3	Soviet Supersonic Tu-144	Crashed near Goussainville, France	14[5]
1973, July 11	Brazilian Boeing 707	Crashed on approach to Orly Airport, Paris, France	122
1973, July 31	Delta Airlines DC-9	Crashed while attempting landing in fog, Logan Airport, Boston, MA	89
1974, Mar. 3	Turkish DC-10	Crashed in Ermenonville, near Paris, France	346
1974, Apr. 22	Pan American Boeing 707	Crashed in Bali, Indonesia	107
1974, Dec. 1	TWA Boeing 727	Crashed on approach in storm, Upperville, VA	92
1974, Dec. 4	Dutch-chartered DC-8	Crashed in storm near Colombo, Sri Lanka	191
1975, Apr. 4	Air Force Galaxy C-5A	Crashed on takeoff nr. Saigon, S Vietnam; carried orphans	172
1975, June 24	Eastern Airlines 727	Crashed in storm, JFK Airport, New York, NY	113
1975, Aug. 3	Alia Royal Jordanian Boeing 707	Hit mountainside in heavy fog near Agadir, Morocco	188
1976, Sept. 10	Brit. Airways Trident, Yug. DC-9	Collided near Zagreb, Yugoslavia	176
1976, Sept. 19	Turkish 727	Hit mountain in S Turkey	155
1976, Oct. 13	LAB Boeing 707	Crashed after takeoff from Santa Cruz, Bolivia	100[6]
1977, Mar. 27	**KLM 747, Pan American 747**	**Collided on runway, Tenerife, Canary Islands, Spain; world's worst airline disaster**	**583**
1977, Nov. 19	TAP Portugal Boeing 727	Crashed in Madeira, Portugal	130
1977, Dec. 4	Malaysian Airlines Boeing 737	Hijacked and forced to fly to Singapore, crashed near Johor Strait	100
1977, Dec. 13	National Jet Service DC-3	Crashed after takeoff from Evansville, IN; passengers incl. Univ. of Evansville men's basketball team	29
1978, Jan. 1	Air India 747	Crashed into sea after takeoff from Bombay, India	213
1978, Sept. 25	Boeing 727, Cessna 172	Collided over San Diego, CA	150
1978, Nov. 15	Indonesian-chartered DC-8	Crashed on approach to airport, Colombo, Sri Lanka	183
1979, May 25	**American Airlines DC-10**	**Crashed after takeoff from O'Hare Airport, Chicago, IL; highest death toll in U.S. aviation history**	**275***
1979, Aug. 11	Aeroflot/Moldova Tu-134, Aeroflot Tu-134	Collided over Ukraine	178
1979, Nov. 26	Pakistani Boeing 707	Crashed near Jidda, Saudi Arabia	156
1979, Nov. 28	Air New Zealand DC-10	Crashed into mountain after takeoff from Antarctica	257
1980, Mar. 14	PLL LOT IL-62	Crashed making emergency landing, Warsaw, Poland	87[7]
1980, Aug. 19	Saudi Arabian Tristar	Burned after emergency landing in Riyadh, Saudi Arabia	301
1981, Dec. 1	Inex Adria DC-9	Crashed into mountain on island of Corsica, France	180
1982, Jan. 13	Air Florida Boeing 737	Crashed into Potomac R. after takeoff from Washington, DC	78
1982, July 9	Pan Am Boeing 727	Crashed after takeoff from Kenner, LA, near New Orleans	153*
1983, Sept. 1	**S. Korean Boeing 747**	**Shot down after violating Soviet airspace near Sakhalin; plane apparently misidentified**	**269**
1983, Nov. 27	Avianca Boeing 747	Crashed near Barajas Airport, Madrid, Spain	183
1984, Oct. 11	Aeroflot/East Siberia Tu-154	Crashed into vehicles on runway while landing in poor weather, Omsk, Russia	178*

Date	Aircraft	Site of accident	Deaths
1985, Feb. 19	Spanish Boeing 727	Crashed into Mt. Oiz, Spain	148
1985, June 23	Air India Boeing 747	Crashed into Atlantic off Ireland after bomb detonated on board	329
1985, Aug. 2	Delta Air Lines L-1011	Crashed at Dallas-Ft. Worth Airport, TX.	137
1985, Aug. 12	**Japan Air Lines Boeing 747**	**Crashed into Mt. Ogura, Japan; world's worst single-plane disaster**	**520**
1985, Dec. 12	Arrow Air DC-8	Crashed after takeoff from Gander, NL, Canada	256[8]
1986, Mar. 31	Mexican Boeing 727	Crashed NW of Mexico City	166
1986, Aug. 31	Aeromexico DC-9, Piper PA-28	Collided over Cerritos, CA	82*
1987, May 9	Polish IL-62M	Crashed after takeoff from Warsaw, Poland.	183
1987, Aug. 16	Northwest Airlines MD-82	Crashed after takeoff from Romulus, MI.	156
1987, Nov. 28	S. African Boeing 747	Crashed into Indian Ocean near Mauritius.	159
1987, Nov. 29	S. Korean Boeing 707	Bomb planted by 2 N. Korean agents exploded while plane over Thai-Burmese border	155
1988, Mar. 17	Colombian Boeing 707	Crashed into mountainside near Venezuela border	137
1988, July 3	**Iran Air Airbus A300**	**Misidentified as hostile aircraft, shot down by U.S. Navy warship *Vincennes* over Persian Gulf.**	**290**
1988, Dec. 21	**Pan Am Boeing 747**	**Libyan agent planted bomb on board; exploded over Lockerbie, Scotland**	**270[9]**
1989, Feb. 8	U.S.-chartered Boeing 707	Crashed into mountain on Azores Isls., off Portugal	144
1989, June 7	Suriname DC-8	Crashed near Paramaribo Airport, Suriname	168
1989, July 19	United Airlines DC-10	Crashed on landing in Sioux City, IA	111
1989, Sept. 19	**UTA DC-10**	**Bomb exploded on board flight from Chad to France while over desert in Niger**	**171**
1989, Nov. 27	Avianca Boeing 727	Bomb exploded on flight from Bogotá, Colombia	107
1990, Jan. 25	Avianca Air Boeing 707	Crashed on landing at JFK Airport, New York, NY.	73
1990, Feb. 14	Indian Airlines Airbus 320.	Crashed and burned on landing in Bangalore, India	91
1990, Oct. 2	Xiamen Airlines Boeing 737	Hijacked after takeoff from Xiamen; struck empty 707, then 757 on runway, Guangzhou, China.	132
1991, May 26	Lauda-Air Boeing 767-300	Exploded over rural Thailand	223
1991, July 11	Nigerian DC-8.	Crashed on landing at Jidda, Saudi Arabia	261
1991, Oct. 5	Air Force Lockheed C-130 Hercules	Crashed after takeoff from Jakarta, Indonesia	137*
1992, July 31	Thai Airbus A300-310.	Crashed into mountain N of Kathmandu, Nepal.	113
1992, Oct. 4	**El Al Boeing 747-200F**	**Crashed into 2 apartment bldgs., Amsterdam, Netherlands**	**120***
1993, Feb. 8	Iran Air Tu-154, Iranian Air Force jet	Collided after military jet took off from Tehran, Iran	133
1993, Mar. 5	Macedonian Pal Air Fokker 100	Crashed after takeoff in snowstorm from Skopje, Macedonia	83
1994, Jan. 3	Aeroflot Tu-154.	Crashed and exploded after takeoff from Irkhutsk, Russia.	125*
1994, Apr. 26	China Airlines Airbus A300.	Crashed on approach to Nagoya Airport, Japan.	264
1994, June 6	China Northwest Airlines Tu-154	Crashed near Xian, China	160
1994, Sept. 8	USAir Boeing 737-300	Crashed near Pittsburgh Intl. Airport, Aliquippa, PA.	132
1994, Oct. 31	American Eagle ATR-72-210	Crashed in field near Roselawn, IN	68
1995, Aug. 11	Aviateca Boeing 737.	Crashed into Chichontepec volcano, El Salvador	65
1995, Dec. 20	American Airlines Boeing 757	Crashed into mountain N of Cali, Colombia	160
1996, Jan. 8	Antonov-32 cargo plane	Crashed into central market in Kinshasa, Zaire	350+*
1996, Feb. 6	Turkish Boeing 757.	Crashed into Atlantic off Dominican Republic	189
1996, Apr. 3	U.S. Air Force Boeing T-43A	Crashed into mountain near Dubrovnik, Croatia	35[10]
1996, May 11	ValuJet DC-9	Crashed into Florida Everglades after takeoff	110
1996, July 17	Trans World Airlines Boeing 747	Exploded and crashed into Atlantic off Long Island, NY.	230
1996, Aug. 29	Vnukovo Tu-154.	Crashed into mountain on Arctic island of Spitsbergen	141
1996, Oct. 2	Aeroperu Boeing 757	Crashed into Pacific after takeoff from Lima, Peru.	70
1996, Oct. 31	Brazilian TAM Fokker-100	Crashed shortly after takeoff from São Paulo, Brazil	97*
1996, Nov. 7	ADG Boeing 727.	Crashed into lagoon SE of Lagos, Nigeria	143
1996, Nov. 12	**Saudi Arabian Boeing 747, Kazakh IL-76 cargo plane**	**Collided near New Delhi, India; world's worst midair collision**	**349**
1996, Nov. 23	Ethiopian Airlines Boeing 767	Hijacked, then crashed into Indian Ocean off the Comoros	127
1997, Aug. 6	Korean Air Boeing 747-300	Crashed into jungle on Guam on approach to airport.	228
1997, Sept. 3	Vietnamese Airlines Tu-134	Crashed on approach to Phnom Penh airport, Cambodia	64
1997, Sept. 26	Indonesian Airbus A300	Crashed near airport, Medan, Indonesia	234
1997, Oct. 10	Austral Airlines DC-9-32.	Crashed and exploded near Neuvo Berlin, Uruguay	74
1997, Dec. 6	Russian AN-124 transport cargo plane	Crashed into apartment complex near Irkutsk, Siberia.	67*
1997, Dec. 15	Tajik Air Tu-154	Crashed in desert near airport, Sharja, UAE	85
1997, Dec. 17	AeroSvit Airlines Yakovlev-42	Crashed into mountains near Katerini, Greece	70
1997, Dec. 19	SilkAir Boeing 737-300.	Crashed into Musi River, Sumatra, Indonesia	104
1998, Feb. 2	Cebu Pacific Air DC-9-32.	Crashed into mountain near Cagayan de Oro, Philippines	104
1998, Feb. 16	China Airlines Airbus A300.	Crashed on approach to airport in Taipei, Taiwan.	203*
1998, Apr. 20	Air France Boeing 727-200.	Crashed into mountain after takeoff from Bogotá, Colombia	53
1998, Sept. 2	Swissair MD-11	Crashed into Atlantic off Nova Scotia, Canada	229
1998, Dec. 11	Thai Airways Airbus A310	Crashed on third landing attempt at Surat Thani Airport, Thailand	101
1999, Feb. 24	China Southwest Airlines Tu-154	Crashed on approach to airport in Wenzhou, China	61
1999, Sept. 1	LAPA Boeing 737-200	Crashed on takeoff from airport, Buenos Aires, Argentina	74*
1999, Oct. 31	EgyptAir Boeing 767	Crashed off Nantucket, MA; result of deliberate actions by copilot, motives unknown	217
2000, Jan. 30	Kenya Airways Airbus A310	Crashed into Atlantic after takeoff from Abidjan, Ivory Coast.	169
2000, Jan. 31	Alaska Airlines MD-83	Crashed into Pacific off coast of Southern CA.	88
2000, Apr. 19	Air Philippines Boeing 737-200	Crashed on approach to airport, Davao, Philippines	131
2000, July 25	**Air France Concorde**	**Crashed into hotel after takeoff from Paris; world's first Concorde crash**	**113***
2000, Aug. 23	Gulf Air Airbus A320.	Crashed into Persian Gulf on approach to airport in Bahrain.	143
2000, Oct. 31	Singapore Airlines Boeing 747.	Crashed immediately after takeoff from Taipei, Taiwan.	81
2001, July 3	Vladivostokavia Tu-154	Crashed on approach to airport, Irkutsk, Russia	145
2001, Sept. 11	**2 Boeing 767s, 2 Boeing 757s**	**September 11 terrorist attacks**	**265[11]**
2001, Oct. 4	Sibir Airlines Tu-154.	Crashed into Black Sea, off Russia, after hit by errant Ukrainian missile	78
2001, Oct. 8	Cessna 525A Citation, Scandinavian Airlines System (SAS) MD-87	Collided in heavy fog on takeoff from Milan, Italy.	118*
2001, Nov. 12	**American Airlines Airbus A300**	**Crashed after takeoff from JFK Airport, New York, NY**	**265***
2002, Jan. 28	TAME Ecuador Boeing 727	Crashed into Andes mountains, S Colombia	92
2002, Feb. 12	Iran Air Tours Tu-154	Crashed in Khorramabad, Iran.	119
2002, Apr. 15	Air China Boeing 767	Crashed into mountainside in rain and fog on approach to airport, Pusan, S. Korea	129
2002, May 4	EAS Airlines BAC 1-11.	Crashed shortly after takeoff from Kano, Nigeria	149

Date	Aircraft	Site of accident	Deaths
2002, May 7	China Northern Airlines MD-82	Plunged into sea, apparently after a passenger started fire in cabin, NE China	112
2002, May 25	China Airlines Boeing 747	Broke apart in midair, plunged into Taiwan Strait en route to Hong Kong airport	225
2002, July 1	Bashkirian Airlines Tu-154, DHL Boeing 757 cargo	Collided over S Germany	71
2002, July 27	**Ukraine Air Force Sukhoi Su-27**	**Crashed while performing, Lviv, Ukraine; world's worst air-show crash**	**77[12]**
2002, Aug. 19	Russian Mi-26 transport helicopter	Hit by Chechen missile near Grozny, Chechnya	127
2003, Jan. 8	Turkish Airlines British Aerospace RJ-100	Crashed on approach to airport in Diyarbakir, Turkey	75
2003, Feb. 19	Iranian Revolutionary Guard Il-76	Crashed into mountain near Kerman, Iran; passengers were Revolutionary Guard members	275
2003, Mar. 6	Air Algérie Boeing 737-200	Crashed on takeoff from Tamanrasset, Algeria	102
2003, May 26	Ukrain.-Medit. Airlines Yak-42	Crashed into mountain in fog approaching Trabzon, Turkey; passengers incl. Spanish peacekeepers returning from Afghan.	75
2003, July 8	Sudan Airways Boeing 737-200	Mechanical problems reported shortly after takeoff; crashed upon return to Port Sudan Airport	115
2003, Dec. 25	Union Transp. Africains Boeing 727	Overloading caused crash on takeoff from Cotonou, Benin	138
2004, Jan. 3	Flash Airlines Boeing 737-300	Crashed into Red Sea after takeoff from Sharm el-Sheik, Egypt	148
2004, Aug. 24	Volga-Aviaexpress Tu-134, Sibir Airlines Tu-154	2 planes that took off from Moscow crashed within minutes of each other; brought down by Chechen suicide bombers	90
2005, Feb. 3	Kam Air Boeing 737-200	Crashed on approach to airport in Kabul, Afghan.	104
2005, Aug. 14	Helios Airways Boeing 737-300	Crashed after air pressure failure on board, near Athens, Greece	121
2005, Aug. 16	West Caribbean Airways MD-82	Crashed after engine failure, near Machiques, Venezuela	160
2005, Sept. 5	Mandala Airlines Boeing 737-200	Crashed shortly after takeoff from Medan, Sumatra, Indonesia	145[13]
2005, Oct. 22	Bellview Airlines Boeing 737-200	Crashed during heavy electrical storm near Lagos, Nigeria	117
2005, Dec. 6	Islamic Rep. of Iran Air Force Lockheed C-130	Crashed into apartment building after reportedly attempting emergency landing back at airport, Tehran, Iran	116+[14]
2005, Dec. 10	Sosoliso Airlines DC-9-30	Crashed during storm on approach to Port Harcourt, Nigeria	107
2006, May 3	Armavia Airbus A320	Crashed into Black Sea on approach to airport, Sochi, Russia	113
2006, July 9	S7 Airlines Airbus A310	Skidded off runway, crashed into concrete barrier after landing, Irkutsk, Russia	125
2006, Aug. 22	Pulkovo Aviation Tu-154	Crashed after encountering storm, near Donetsk, Ukraine	170
2006, Aug. 27	Comair Bombardier CRJ-100	Crashed after takeoff from Lexington, KY	49
2006, Sept. 29	Gol Airlines Boeing 737	Crashed into Amazon jungle after midair collision with Embraer Legacy jet, Brazil	154
2006, Oct. 29	ADC Airlines Boeing 737-200	Crashed in stormy weather shortly after takeoff from Abuja, Nigeria	96
2007, Jan. 1	Adam Air Boeing 737-400	Crashed into sea off coast, Makassar, Indonesia	102
2007, May 5	Kenya Airways Boeing 737-800	Crashed shortly after takeoff from Douala, Cameroon	114
2007, July 17	TAM Airlines Airbus 320	Crashed into cargo depot, gas station after skidding off airport runway, São Paulo, Brazil	199*
2007, Sept. 16	One-Two-Go Airlines Boeing-MD-82	Skidded off runway, caught fire after landing, Phuket, Thailand	89
2008, Aug. 20	Spanair Boeing-MD-82	Swerved off runway, caught fire on takeoff attempt, Madrid, Spain	154
2008, Sept. 14	Aeroflot-Nord Boeing 737-500	Crashed on approach to airport, Perm, Russia	88
2009, Feb. 12	Colgan Air Bombardier Dash 8 Q400	Crashed into house near airport, Buffalo, NY	50*
2009, May 20	Indonesian military C-130 Hercules	Crashed into houses and a rice field, Java, Indonesia	98*
2009, June 1	**Air France Airbus A330**	**Plunged into Atlantic Ocean en route from Rio de Janeiro, Brazil, to Paris, France**	**228**
2009, June 29	Yemenia Airbus A310-300	Fell into Indian Ocean on approach to Moroni, Comoros	152
2009, July 15	Caspian Airlines Tupolev 154	Crashed after takeoff from Tehran, Iran	168
2010, Jan. 25	Ethiopian Airlines Boeing 737-800	Crashed into Mediterranean after takeoff from Beirut, Lebanon	90
2010, Apr. 10	Polish Air Force Tupolev 154M	Crashed on approach to Smolensk Air Base, killing President Lech Kaczynski, his wife, and several members of Poland's Parliament	96
2010, May 12	Afriqiyah Airways Airbus A330-200	Crashed short of runway in Tripoli, Libya	103
2010, May 22	Air India Express Boeing 737-800	Overran runway on landing at Mangalore, India	158
2010, July 28	Airblue Airbus 321-231	Crashed into Margalla Hills near Islamabad, Pakistan	152
2011, Jan. 9	Iran Air Boeing 727-200	Crashed during forced landing 5 mi from Orumiyeh Airport, Iran	77
2011, July 26	Royal Moroccan Air Force C-130H Hercules	Crashed on approach to Goulimime Airport, Morocco	80
2011, Sept. 15	North American Aviation P-51 Mustang	Crashed into stands at Reno, NV, air races, killing spectators	11*

(1) Bomb was planted by Jack G. Graham in insurance plot to kill his mother, Daisie E. King, a passenger. (2) 84 on plane, 71 on ground killed. (3) Incl. 43 Marshall Univ. (WV) football players and coaches. (4) Fighter pilot parachuted to safety. (5) First supersonic plane crash; killed 8 on ground. (6) Crew of 3, 97 on ground killed. (7) Incl. 22 members of U.S. amateur boxing team. (8) Incl. 248 members of U.S. 101st Airborne Division. (9) Incl. 11 on ground. (10) Incl. U.S. Sec. of Commerce Ron Brown. (11) 4 planes were hijacked and crashed, with all on board killed (265, incl. 19 hijackers). American Airlines Flight 11, a Boeing 767-200, with 81 passengers, 11 crew, crashed into Tower 1 of World Trade Center; United Airlines Flight 175, a Boeing 767-200, with 56 passengers, 9 crew, crashed into Tower 2 of World Trade Center; American Airlines Flight 77, a Boeing 757-200, with 58 passengers, 6 crew, crashed into Pentagon outside Washington, DC; United Air Lines Flight 93, a Boeing 757-200, with 37 passengers, 7 crew, crashed near Shanksville, PA. The official death toll of 2,753 (as of Aug. 9, 2011) includes all those who perished on the ground at the Pentagon and the World Trade Center, as well as those who died as many as 10 years later from pulmonary sarcoidosis, a lung disease caused by exposure to the toxic dust created by the disaster. (12) Pilots ejected to safety. All spectator deaths. (13) Incl. 44 on ground. (14) 94 on plane plus 22+ on ground.

Disaster Averted

Date: Jan. 15, 2009. **Location:** Hudson River, NY-NJ. **Fatalities:** 0.

Chesley B. "Sully" Sullenberger III, the captain of U.S. Airways Flight 1549, made a spectacular emergency landing on the surface of a chilly Hudson River after apparent bird strikes took out both of the plane's engines shortly after takeoff from New York's LaGuardia Airport. Ferry boats and other nearby watercrafts safely evacuated the five crew members and all 150 passengers to shore soon after the emergency water landing. Some passengers were treated for hypothermia, but no major injuries were reported.

Some Notable Shipwrecks Since 1854

Figures are estimated deaths. Does not include most wartime disasters.

Date—vessel(s)	Incident	Deaths
1854, Mar. 1—City of Glasgow	Brit. steamer left Liverpool for Philadelphia, never heard from again	480
1854, Sept. 27—Arctic and Vesta	U.S. Collins Line steamer sunk collided with French steamer nr. Cape Race, Canada	285-351
1856, Jan. 23—Pacific	U.S. Collins Line steamer went missing in N Atlantic	186-286
1858, Sept. 23—Austria	German steamer destroyed by fire in N Atlantic	471
1863, Apr. 27—Anglo-Saxon	Brit. steamer wrecked at Cape Race, Canada	238
1865, Apr. 27—Sultana	Mississippi R. steamer blew up nr. Memphis, TN	1,450
1869, Oct. 27—Stonewall	Steamer burned, Mississippi R. below Cairo, IL	200
1870, Jan. 25—City of Boston	Brit. Inman Line steamer vanished between New York and Liverpool	177
1870, Oct. 19—Cambria	Brit. steamer off NW Ireland	196
1872, Nov. 7—Mary Celeste	U.S. half-brig sailing from New York to Genoa, Italy, found abandoned	Unknown
1873, Jan. 22—Northfleet	Brit. steamer foundered off Dungeness, England	300
1873, Apr. 1—Atlantic	Brit. White Star steamer off Nova Scotia, Can.	585
1873, Nov. 23—Ville du Havre and Loch Earn	French steamer sank after collision with Brit. sailing ship	226
1875, May 7—Schiller	German steamer off Scilly Isles, UK	312
1875, Nov. 4—Pacific	U.S. steamer sank after collision off Cape Flattery, WA	236
1878, Sept. 3—Princess Alice	Brit. steamer sank after collision with Bywell Castle in Thames R.	700
1883, Jan. 19—Cimbria and Sultan	German steamer sank in collision with Brit. steamer in North Sea	389
1890, Feb. 17—Duburg	Brit. steamer wrecked, China Sea	400
1890, Sept. 19—Ertogrul	Turkish frigate off Japan	540
1891, Mar. 17—Utopia and Anson	Brit. steamer sank in collision with Brit. ironclad off Gibraltar	562
1895, Jan. 30—Elbe and Craithie	German steamer sank in collision with Brit. steamer in North Sea	332
1895, Mar. 11—Reina Regenta	Spanish cruiser foundered nr. Gibraltar	400
1898, Feb. 15—USS Maine	Explosion caused battleship to sink in Havana Harbor, Cuba	260
1898, July 4—La Bourgogne and Cromartyshire	French steamer in collision with Brit. sailing ship off Nova Scotia, Can.	549
1898, Nov. 26—Portland	U.S. steamer, off Cape Cod, MA	157
1904, June 15—General Slocum	Excursion steamer burned in East R., New York, NY	1,021
1904, June 28—Norge	Danish steamer wrecked on Rockall Isl., Scotland	620
1906, Aug. 4—Sirio	Italian steamer wrecked off Cape Palos, Spain	350
1908, Mar. 23—Mutsu Maru	Japanese steamer sank in collision with another steamer nr. Hakodate, Japan	300
1909, Aug. 1—Waratah	Brit. steamer vanished en route from Sydney to London	300
1910, Feb. 9—General Chanzy	French steamer wrecked off Minorca, Spain	200
1911, Sept. 25—Liberté	French battleship exploded at Toulon	285
1912, Mar. 5—Principe de Asturias	Spanish steamer wrecked off Spanish coast	500
1912, Apr. 14-15—Titanic	Brit. White Star steamer hit iceberg in N Atlantic	1,503
1912, Sept. 28—Kichemaru	Japanese steamer sank off Japan coast	1,000
1914, May 29—Empress of Ireland	Canadian Pacific steamer collided with Norwegian coal transporter Storstad in St. Lawrence R., Can.	1,014
1915, May 7—Lusitania	Brit. Cunard Line steamer torpedoed and sunk by German submarine off Ireland	1,198
1915, July 24—Eastland	Steamer capsized, Chicago R., IL	844
1916, Feb. 26—Provence	French cruiser sank in Mediterranean Sea	3,100
1916, Mar. 3—Principe de Asturias	Spanish steamer wrecked nr. Santos, Brazil	558
1917, Dec. 6—Mont Blanc and Imo	French ammunition ship and Belgian steamer collided in Halifax Harbor, Can.	1,600
1918, Apr. 25—Kiang-Kwan	Chinese steamer sank in collision off Hankow	500
1918, July 12—Kawachi	Japanese battleship blew up in Tokayama Bay	500
1918, Oct. 25—Princess Sophia	Canadian steamer sank off Alaskan coast	398
1919, Jan. 17—Chaonia	French steamer lost in Straits of Messina, Italy	460
1919, Sept. 9—Valbanera	Spanish steamer lost off FL coast	500
1921, Mar. 18—Hong Kong	Steamer wrecked, S China Sea	1,000
1922, Aug. 26—Niitaka	Japanese cruiser sank in storm off Kamchatka, USSR	300
1927, Oct. 25—Principessa Mafalda	Italian steamer blew up, sank off Porto Seguro, Brazil	314
1928, Nov. 12—Vestris	Brit. steamer sank off VA coast	113
1934, Sept. 8—Morro Castle	U.S. steamer en route from Havana to New York, burned off Asbury Park, NJ	134
1939, May 23—Squalus	U.S. submarine sank off Portsmouth, NH	26
1939, June 1—Thetis	Brit. submarine sank, Liverpool Bay	99
1942, Feb. 18—USS Truxtun and USS Pollux	Destroyer and cargo ship ran aground, sank off Newfoundland, Can.	204
1942, Oct. 2—Curacao and Queen Mary	Brit. cruiser sank after collision with liner	338
1944, Dec. 17-18	3 U.S. Third Fleet destroyers sank during typhoon, Philippine Sea	790
1945, Jan. 30—Wilhelm Gustloff	Liner with German refugees, soldiers sunk by Soviet submarine in Baltic	5,000-9,000
1945, Apr. 16—Goya	Cargo ship with German refugees, soldiers sunk by Soviet submarine in Baltic	6,000-7,000
1945, May 3—Cap Arcona and Thielbek	German liners carrying concentration camp inmates sunk by British warplanes in Lubeck Bay, Germany	7,000-8,000
1947, Jan. 19—Himera	Greek steamer hit mine off Athens, Greece	392
1947, Apr. 16—Grandcamp	French freighter exploded, Texas City, TX, harbor; started fires	576+
1948, Dec. 3—Kiangya	Chinese refugee ship wrecked in explosion S of Shanghai	1,100+
1949, Sept. 17—Noronic	Canadian Great Lakes Cruiser burned in dock, Toronto, ON, Can.	130
1952, Apr. 26—USS Hobson and USS Wasp	Destroyer and aircraft carrier collided in Atlantic	176
1954, Sept. 26—Toya Maru	Japanese ferry sank, Tsugaru Strait, Japan	1,172
1956, July 26—Andrea Doria and Stockholm	Italian liner and Swedish liner collided off Nantucket Isl., MA	51
1957, July 14—Eshghabad	Soviet ship ran aground in Caspian Sea	270
1961, Apr. 8—Dara	Brit. liner exploded in Persian Gulf	236
1961, July 8—Save	Portuguese ship ran aground off Mozambique	259
1963, Apr. 10—Thresher	U.S. Navy atomic submarine sank in N Atlantic	129
1964, Feb. 10—Voyager	Australian destroyer sank after collision with aircraft carrier Melbourne off New South Wales	82
1965, Nov. 13—Yarmouth Castle	Panamanian-registered cruise ship burned, sank off Nassau, Bahamas	89
1968, May 27—Scorpion	U.S. nuclear sub went missing, later found to have sunk in Atlantic nr. Azores	99
1969, June 2—Evans and Melbourne	U.S. destroyer cut in half by Australian carrier, S China Sea	74
1970, Dec. 15—Namyong-Ho	S. Korean ferry sank in Korea Strait	308
1974, Sept. 26	Soviet destroyer sank in Black Sea	200+
1975, Nov. 10—Edmund Fitzgerald	U.S. cargo ship sank during storm on Lake Superior	29
1976, Oct. 20—George Prince and Frosta	U.S. ferryboat and Norwegian tanker collided, Mississippi R., at Luling, LA	77
1976, Dec. 25—Patria	Egyptian liner caught fire in Red Sea	100
1979, Aug. 14	23 yachts competing in Fastnet yacht race sank or abandoned during storm in S Irish Sea	18
1980, Apr. 22—Don Juan	Sank off Mindoro Isl., Philippines, after colliding with barge	1,000+
1981, Jan. 27—Tamponas II	Indonesian passenger ship caught fire and sank in Java Sea	580
1983, Feb. 12—Marine Electric	Coal freighter sank during storm off Chincoteague, VA	33
1983, May 25—10th of Ramadan	Nile steamer caught fire and sank in Lake Nasser, Egypt	357
1986, Apr. 20—Atlas Star	Ferry sank in storm, Dhaleswari R. nr. Dhaka, Bangladesh	300+
1986, May 25—Shamia	Ferry capsized in storm, Meghna R., Bangladesh	500+

Date—vessel(s)	Incident	Deaths
1986, Sept. 1—Admiral Nakhimov and Pyotr Vasev	Soviet cruise ship collided with Soviet freighter in Black Sea	425
1987, Mar. 6—Herald of Free Enterprise	Brit. ferry capsized off Zeebrugge, Belgium	189
1987, Dec. 20—Doña Paz and Victor	Philippine ferry and oil tanker collided in Tablas Strait	4,341
1988, Aug. 6	Indian ferry capsized on Ganges R.	400+
1989, Apr. 7—Komsolets	Soviet submarine sank after fire off Norwegian coast	42
1989, Aug. 20—Bowbelle and Marchioness	Brit. barge struck Brit. pleasure cruiser on Thames R. in central London	56
1991, Apr. 10—Moby Prince and Agip Abruzzo	Auto ferry and oil tanker collided outside Livorno Harbor, Italy	140
1991, Dec. 14—Salem Express	Ferry rammed coral reef nr. Safaga, Egypt	462
1993, Feb. 17—Neptune	Ferry capsized off Port-au-Prince, Haiti	500+
1993, Oct. 10—Seohae	Capsized in Yellow Sea nr. western S. Korea during storm	285
1994, Sept. 28—Estonia	Ferry sank in Baltic Sea	852
1996, May 21—Bukoba	Overcrowded Tanzanian ferry sank in Lake Victoria	500+
1997, Feb. 20	Tamil refugee boat sank off Sri Lanka	165
1997, Mar. 28	Albanian refugee boat sank in Adriatic after being rammed by Italian navy warship Sibilla.	83
1997, Sept. 8—Pride of la Gonâve	Haitian ferry sank off Montrouis, Haiti	200+
1998, Apr. 4	Passenger boat capsized off nr. Ibaka beach, Nigeria	280
1998, Sept. 2	2 passenger boats capsized on Lake Kivu, nr. Bukavu, Congo	200+
1999, Feb. 6—Harta Rimba	Cargo ship sank off Indonesia	280+
1999, May 1—Miss Majestic	"Duck" boat on tour sank, Lake Hamilton, AR	13
1999, Nov. 24—Dashun	Passenger ferry capsized nr. Yantai, China	280
2000, June 29—Cahaya Bahari	Overloaded ferry carrying refugees from religious strife capsized in storm off Sulawesi Isl., Indonesia	500+
2000, Aug. 12—Kursk	Faulty torpedo exploded on board Russian submarine, causing it to sink in Barents Sea	118
2000, Sept. 26—Express Samina	Greek ferry sank off Paros, Greece	81+
2001, Oct. 19	Fishing boat with refugees, mainly fr. Middle East, sank off Indonesia	350+
2002, May 4—Salahuddin-2	Overloaded Bangladesh ferry sank in Meghna R.	300+
2002, Sept. 26—Joola	Overloaded Senegalese ferry capsized in ocean off The Gambia	1,863
2003, Mar. 23—Kashowgwe	Overloaded ferry capsized in Lake Tanganyika, off Burundi	111+
2003, July 8—MV-Nasrin 1	Overcrowded ferry sank nr. Chandpur in Bangladesh R.	400
2003, Oct. 15—Andrew J. Barberi	NYC ferry crashed into dock on approach to Staten Isl.	11
2003, Nov. 25—Dieu Merci.	Overloaded ferry sank on Lake Mayi Ndombe, Dem. Rep. of Congo.	130-200
2004, Jan. 26—Convoi Lengi	Ferry caught fire on Congo R., Dem. Rep. of Congo	200
2004, Mar. 11—Samson	Ferry sank off Madagascar during cyclone	113
2005, July 7—KMP Digul	Ferry capsized in rough waters nr. Merauke, Indonesia.	150+
2005, Aug. 12	Fishing boat overloaded with Ecuadorans attempting to migrate to U.S. sank off Colombia	94
2005, Oct. 2—Ethan Allen	Glass boat carrying senior citizens capsized on tour, Lake George, NY	20
2006, Feb. 3—Al-Salam Boccaccio 98	Ferry caught fire, sank in Red Sea off Egypt	1,000+
2006, Dec. 30—Senopati Nusantara	High waves capsized ferry en route to Java, Indonesia	400+
2007, May 4	Boat overloaded with illegal Haitian immigrants capsized in storm nr. Turks and Caicos Isls.	61+
2007, Nov. 23—Explorer	Canadian cruise ship sank off Antarctica, first comm. passenger ship to sink in region.	None
2008, June 23—Princess of the Stars	Philippine ferry capsized during Typhoon Fengshen nr. Manila.	800
2009, Mar. 30	Passenger boat carrying African immigrants to Italy capsized off Libyan coast	200+
2009, Aug. 5—Princess Ashika	Ferry capsized 55 mi NE of Nuku'alofa, Tonga.	74
2010, Mar. 26—Cheonan	S. Korean warship sunk by N. Korean torpedo in Yellow Sea.	46
2010, Dec. 15	Boat carrying Iraqi, Iranian, Kurdish asylum-seekers crashed into rocks off Christmas Isl., Australia	48+

Some Notable Railroad Disasters Since 1925

Date	Location	Deaths	Date	Location	Deaths
1925, June 16	Hackettstown, NJ	50	1963, Nov. 9	Yokohama, Japan.	120+
1926, Sept. 5	Waco, CO.	30	1964, July 26	Porto, Portugal	94
1937, July 16	Bhita, India	107	1967, July 6	Madgeburg, Germany.	94
1938, June 19	Saugus, MT	47	1970, Feb. 1	Buenos Aires, Argentina.	236
1939, Dec. 22	Near Magdeburg, Germany	132	1972, June 16	Vierzy, France	107
1939, Dec. 22	Near Friedrichshafen, Germany	99	1972, July 21	Seville, Spain	76
1940, Apr. 19	Little Falls, NY	31	1972, Oct. 6	Saltillo, Mexico	208
1940, July 31	Cuyahoga Falls, OH	43	1972, Oct. 30	Chicago, IL	45
1943, Sept. 6	Frankford Junction, Philad., PA	79	1974, Aug. 30	Zagreb, Yugoslavia.	153
1943, Dec. 16	Between Rennert and Buie, NC	72	1975, Feb. 28	Subway train, London, England	41
1944, Jan. 16	León Province, Spain	500	1977, Jan. 18	Granville, Australia	83
1944, Mar. 2	Salerno, Italy.	521	1981, June 6	Bihar, India.	800+
1944, July 6	High Bluff, TN.	35	1982, Jan. 27	El Asnam, Algeria.	130
1944, Aug. 4	Near Stockton, GA	47	1982, July 11	Tepic, Mexico	120
1944, Dec. 31	Bagley, UT.	50	1983, Feb. 19	Empalme, Mexico	100
1945, Aug. 9	Michigan, ND	34	1985, Feb. 23	Madhya Pradesh state, India	50
1946, Mar. 20	Aracaju, Mexico	185	1987, July 2	Kasumbalesha Shaba, Zaire	125
1946, Apr. 25	Naperville, IL.	45	1988, June 27	Gare de Lyon train station, Paris	57
1949, Oct. 22	Near Dwor, Poland.	200+	1988, Dec. 12	London, England	35
1950, Feb. 17	Rockville Centre, NY	31	1989, Jan. 15	Maizdi Khan, Bangladesh.	110+
1950, Sept. 11	Coshocton, OH.	33	1990, Jan. 4	Sindh Province, Pakistan	210+
1950, Nov. 22	Richmond Hill, NY	79	1993, Sept. 22	Big Bayou Conot, AL	47
1951, Feb. 6	Woodbridge, NJ	84	1994, Mar. 8	Near Durban, South Africa	63
1952, Mar. 4	Near Rio de Janeiro, Brazil.	119	1994, Sept. 22	Tolunda, Angola	300
1952, July 9	Rzepin, Poland.	160	1995, Aug. 20	Firozabad, India	358
1952, Oct. 8	Harrow, England.	112	1997, Mar. 3	Punjab Province, Pakistan	125
1953, Dec. 24	Tangiwai, New Zealand.	151	1997, Apr. 29	Rongjiawan, China	58
1955, Apr. 3	Guadalajara, Mexico.	300	1997, May 4	Rwandan refugees on overcrowded trains, Kisangani, Zaire.	100+
1956, Jan. 22	Los Angeles, CA.	30			
1957, Sept. 1	Kendal, Jamaica.	178	1997, Sept. 14	Madhya Pradesh state, India	77
1957, Sept. 29	Montgomery, W Pakistan	250	1998, Feb. 19	Yaounde, Cameroon	100+
1957, Dec. 4	London, England	90	1998, June 3	Eschede, Germany.	102
1958, May 8	Rio de Janeiro, Brazil	128	1998, Nov. 26	Khanna, India.	200+
1958, Sept. 15	Elizabethport, NJ	48	1998, Mar. 15	Bourbonnais, IL	11
1960, Nov. 14	Pardubice, Czechoslovakia	110	1999, Mar. 24	Nairobi, Kenya	32+
1962, Jan. 8	Woerden, Netherlands	91	1999, Aug. 2	Gauhati, India.	285+
1962, May 3	Tokyo, Japan.	163	1999, Oct. 5	London, England	31

Date	Location	Deaths	Date	Location	Deaths
2000, Jan. 4	Rena, Norway	35	2005, Oct. 29	Near Veligonda, India	114+
2000, Nov. 11	Kaprun, Austria	155	2006, Jan. 23	Podgorica, Montenegro	46
2001, June 22	Cochin, India	64	2007, Aug. 2	Nr. Benaleka, Dem. Rep. of Congo	70+
2002, Feb. 27	Train fire, Godhra, India	59	2008, July 16	Near Marsa Matruh, Egypt	37+
2002, Feb. 20	S of Cairo, Egypt	373	2008, Sept. 12	Commuter train collided head-on with freight train, Los Angeles, CA	25
2002, May 25	Muamba, Mozambique	196+			
2002, June 24	Igandu, Tanzania	281+	2009, June 22	Moving DC Metro train collided with stationary train nr. Takoma Park, MD	9
2002, Sept. 10	Bihar, India	118			
2003, Feb. 1	NW Zimbabwe	46	2010, May 28	W Bengal, India	148
2004, Feb. 18	Neyshabur, NE Iran	300+	2010, July 21	Derailment between Brazzaville and Pointe-Noire, Rep. of Congo	76
2004, Apr. 22	Ryongchon, N. Korea	161			
2004, July 22	Mekece, NW Turkey	36	2010, July 19	Express train crashed into stationary train in W Bengal, India	66
2005, Jan. 26	Glendale, CA	11			
2005, Apr. 25	Near Amagasaki, Japan	107+	2011, July 23	High speed train crashed into stationary train near Wenzhou, China	40
2005, July 13	Ghotki, Pakistan	133			

Some Notable U.S. Tornadoes Since 1925

Date	Location	Deaths	Date	Location	Deaths
1925, Mar. 18	MO, IL, IN	747	1970, May 11	Lubbock, TX	23
1927, Apr. 12	Rocksprings, TX	74	1971, Feb. 21	Mississippi Delta: MS, LA, AR, TN	110
1927, May 9	AR; Poplar Bluff, MO	92	1973, May 26-27	South, Midwest	47
1927, Sept. 29	St. Louis, MO	90	1974, Apr. 3-4	AL; GA; KY; Xenia, OH; other states	315
1930, May 6	Hill, Navarro, Ellis Cos., TX	41	1977, Apr. 4	AL, MS, GA	22
1932, Mar. 21	Alabama	268	1979, Apr. 10	TX, OK	60
1936, Apr. 5-6	Tupelo, MS; Gainesville, GA	454	1984, Mar. 28	NC, SC	57
1938, Sept. 29	Charleston, SC	32	1985, May 31	NY; PA; OH; Ontario, Can.	75
1942, Mar. 16	Central to NE Mississippi	75	1987, May 22	Saragosa, TX	30
1942, Apr. 27	Rogers and Mayes Cos., OK	52	1989, Nov. 15	Huntsville, AL	18
1944, June 23	OH, PA, WV, MD	150	1990, Aug. 28	Northern IL	25
1945, Apr. 12	OK, AR	102	1991, Apr. 26	KS, OK	23
1947, Apr. 9	TX; Woodward, OK; KS	181	1992, Nov. 21-23	South, Midwest	26
1948, Mar. 19	Bunker Hill and Gillespie, IL	33	1994, Mar. 27-28	AL, TN, GA, NC, SC	52
1949, Jan. 3	LA, AR	58	1995, May 6-7	S Oklahoma, N Texas	23
1952, Mar. 21-22	AR, MO, TN	208	1997, Mar. 1	Central AR	26
1953, May 11	Waco, TX	114	1997, May 27	Jarrell, TX	27
1953, June 8	Flint-Beecher, MI; OH	142	1998, Feb. 22-23	Central FL	42
1953, June 9	Worcester and vicinity, MA	90	1998, Apr. 8	AL, GA, MS	39
1953, Dec. 5	Vicksburg, MS	38	1999, May 3	OK, KS	54
1955, May 25	Udall, KS; MO; Blackwell, OK; TX	115	2000, Feb. 14	SW Georgia	22+
1957, May 20	KS, MO	48	2000, Dec. 16	Alabama	12
1958, June, 4	NW Wisconsin	30	2001, Nov. 23-24	AL, AR, MS	13
1959, Feb. 10	St. Louis, MO	21	2002, Nov. 10-11	AL, MS, TN, IN, OH, PA	36
1960, May 5-6	Southeastern OK, AR	30	2003, May 4-11	TN, MO, KS, IL, OK, WV, AL	48
1962, Mar. 31	Milton, FL	17	2005, Nov. 6	KY, IN	22
1965, Apr. 11	IA, IN, IL, OH, MI, WI	271	2007, Mar. 1	AL, GA, MO, Midwest	20
1966, Mar. 3	Jackson, MS	57	2008, Feb. 25	"Super Tuesday"—TN, AR, KY, AL, MO	57
1966, Mar. 3	MS, AL	61	2008, May 10	MS, OK, GA	23
1967, Jan. 24	IL, MO, IA, MI	33	2011, Apr. 14-16	Southeast, Midwest U.S., OK to VA	38
1968, May 15	Midwest	71	2011, Apr. 25-28	U.S.; 305 funnels reported from TX to NY	321
1969, Jan. 23	Mississippi	32	2011, May 22	Joplin, MO	162

Principal U.S. Mine Disasters Since 1900

Source: Bureau of Mines, U.S. Dept. of the Interior; Mine Safety and Health Admin., U.S. Dept. of Labor; World Almanac research
All are bituminous coal mines unless otherwise noted.

Date	Location	Deaths	Date	Location	Deaths	Date	Location	Deaths
1900, May 1	Scofield, UT	200	1913, Oct. 22	Dawson, NM	263	1940, Mar. 16	St. Clairesville, OH	72
1902, May 19	Coal Creek, TN	184	1914, Apr. 28	Eccles, WV	181	1942, Mar. 26	Allentown, PA[4]	31
1902, July 10	Johnstown, PA	112	1915, Mar. 2	Layland, WV	115	1943, Feb. 27	Washoe, MT	74
1903, June 30	Hanna, WY	169	1917, Apr. 27	Hastings, CO	121	1947, Mar. 25	Centralia, IL	111
1904, Jan. 25	Cheswick, PA	179	1917, June 8	Butte, MT[1]	163	1951, Dec. 21	West Frankfort, IL	119
1905, Feb. 20	Virginia City, AL	112	1919, June 5	Wilkes-Barre, PA[2]	92	1968, Mar. 6	Belle Isle, LA[5]	21
1907, Jan. 29	Stuart, WV	84	1922, Nov. 6	Spangler, PA	77	1968, Nov. 20	Farmington, WV	78
1907, Dec. 6	Monongah, WV	362	1922, Nov. 22	Dolomite, AL	90	1970, Dec. 30	Hyden, KY	38
1907, Dec. 19	Jacobs Creek, PA	239	1923, Feb. 8	Dawson, NM	120	1972, May 2	Kellogg, ID[6]	91
1908, Nov. 28	Marianna, PA	154	1923, Aug. 14	Kemmerer, WY	99	1976, Mar. 9	Oven Fork, KY	15
1909, Nov. 13	Cherry, IL	259	1924, Mar. 8	Castle Gate, UT	172	1981, Apr. 15	Redstone, CO	15
1910, Jan. 31	Primero, CO	75	1924, Apr. 28	Benwood, WV	119	1981, Dec. 8	Whitwell, TN	13
1910, May 5	Palos, AL	84	1926, Jan. 13	Wilburton, OK	91	1984, Dec. 19	Orangeville, UT	27
1910, Nov. 8	Delagua, CO	79	1926, Nov. 3	Ishpeming, MI[3]	51	1989, Sept. 13	Wheatcroft, KY	10
1911, Apr. 8	Littleton, AL	128	1927, Apr. 30	Everettville, WV	97	2001, Sept. 23	Brookwood, AL	13
1911, Dec. 9	Briceville, TN	84	1928, May 19	Mather, PA	195	2006, Jan. 2	Buckhannon, WV	12
1912, Mar. 26	Jed, WV	81	1930, Nov. 5	Millfield, OH	82	2010, Apr. 5	Montcoal, WV	29
1913, Apr. 23	Finleyville, PA	98	1940, Jan. 10	Bartley, WV	91			

Note: The world's worst mine disaster killed 1,549 workers in Manchuria, China, Apr. 25, 1942. (1) Copper mine. (2) Anthracite mine. (3) Iron mine. (4) Limestone mine. (5) Salt mine. (6) Silver mine.

A Month of Tornadoes

Date: Apr. 2011. **Location:** Midwest, southeastern U.S.
Fatalities: 364+. **Damages:** $3 bil.

Apr. 2011 proved to be one of the most active, destructive, and deadly tornado months in U.S. history, with at least 748 tornadoes on record. Wisconsin experienced its strongest tornadoes in 27 years Apr. 9-10, and the entire southeastern U.S., from Oklahoma to Virginia, was plagued by hundreds of tornadoes Apr. 14-16. The deadliest twisters tracked across the eastern half of the country Apr. 25-28, killing at least 321 people. Alabama, including cities Tuscaloosa and Birmingham, suffered some of the greatest damage: 248 deaths, more than 1,000 injured, and damages of approximately $100 mil.

Some Notable Hurricanes, Typhoons, Blizzards, Other Storms

C.—cyclone; H.—hurricane; TS.—tropical storm; T.—typhoon[1]

Date	Location	Deaths
1881, Aug. 24-29	H., GA, SC	700
1888, Mar. 11-14	Blizzard, eastern U.S.	400
1893, Aug. 15-Sept. 2	H., GA, SC	1,000+
1893, Oct. 1	H., LA	1,100+
1900, Sept. 8	H., Galveston, TX	8,000+
1906, Sept. 19-24	H., LA, MS	350
1906, Sept. 18	T., Hong Kong	10,000+
1909, Sept. 20	H., LA	350+
1915, Aug. 16	H., Galveston, TX	275
1915, Sept. 29	H., LA	275
1919, Sept. 6-14	H., Carib., FL Keys, Gulf, TX	600+[2]
1926, Sept. 11-22	H., FL, AL, MS	370+
1926, Oct. 20	H., Cuba	600
1928, Sept. 6-20	H., southern FL	2,500+
1930, Sept. 3	H., Dominican Republic	2,000
1935, Aug. 29-Sept. 10	H., Caribbean, SE U.S.	400+
1937, Sept. 2	T., "The Great Typhoon," Hong Kong	10,000+
1938, Sept. 21	H., "Long Isl. Express," NY; New England	682
1940, Nov. 11-12	Blizzard, NE, Midwest U.S.	144
1942, Oct. 15-16	H., Bengal, India	40,000
1947, Dec. 26	Blizzard, NYC, N Atl. states	55
1952, Oct. 22	T., Philippines	440
1954, Aug. 30	H. Carol, northeastern U.S.	68
1954, Oct. 5-18	H. Hazel, E Canada, U.S., Haiti	347
1955, Aug. 7-21	H. Diane, eastern U.S.	400
1955, Sept. 19	H. Hilda, Mexico	200
1956, Feb. 1-29	Blizzard, W Europe	1,000
1957, June 25-30	H. Audrey, TX to AL	390
1958, Feb. 15-16	Blizzard, northeastern U.S.	171
1959, Sept. 17-19	T. Sarah, Japan, S. Korea	2,000
1959, Sept. 26-27	T. Vera, Honshu, Japan	4,466
1960, Sept. 4-12	H. Donna, Caribbean, E U.S.	148
1961, Oct. 31	H. Hattie, Brit. Honduras.	400
1962, Sept. 1	T. Wanda, Hong Kong	130-200
1963, May 28-29	Windstorm, Bangladesh	22,000
1963, Oct. 4-8	H. Flora, Caribbean	6,000
1964, June 30	T. Winnie, N Philippines	107
1964, Sept. 5	T. Ruby, Hong Kong, China	735
1965, May 11-12	Windstorm, Bangladesh	17,000
1965, June 1-2	Windstorm, Bangladesh	30,000
1965, Sept. 7-12	H. Betsy, FL, MS, LA	74
1965, Dec. 15	Windstorm, Bangladesh	10,000
1966, June 4-10	H. Alma, Honduras, SE U.S.	51
1966, Sept. 24-30	H. Inez, Carib., FL, Mexico	293
1967, July 9	T. Billie, SW Japan	347
1967, Sept. 5-23	H. Beulah, Carib., Mex., TX	54
1967, Dec. 12-20	Blizzard, SW U.S.	51
1969, Aug. 17-18	H. Camille, MS, LA	256
1970, Sept. 15	T. Georgia, Philippines	300
1970, Oct. 14	T. Sening, Philippines	583
1970, Oct. 15	T. Titang, Philippines	526
1970, Nov. 13	C., Bay of Bengal, Bangladesh	300,000
1971, Aug. 1	T. Rose, Hong Kong	130
1972, June 19-29	T. Agnes, FL to NY	118
1972, Dec. 3	T. Theresa, Philippines	169
1973, June-Aug.	Monsoon rains, India	1,217
1974, June 11	TS. Dinah, Luzon Isl., Philippines	71
1974, July 11	H. Gilda, Japan, S. Korea	108
1974, Sept. 19-20	H. Fifi, Honduras	2,000
1975, Sept. 13-27	H. Eloise, Caribbean, NE U.S.	71
1976, May 20	T. Olga, floods, Philippines	215
1976, Sept. 25-Oct. 2	H. Liza, W Mexico	630
1978, Oct. 27	T. Rita, Philippines	400
1979, Aug. 30-Sept. 7	H. David, Caribbean, E U.S.	1,100
1980, Aug. 4-11	H. Allen, Caribbean, TX	272
1981, Nov. 25	T. Irma, Luzon Isl., Philippines	176
1983, June	Monsoon, India	900
1984, Sept. 2	T. Ike, S Philippines	1,363
1985, May 25	C., Bangladesh	10,000
1985, Oct. 26-Nov. 6	H. Juan, SE U.S.	97
1987, Nov. 25	T. Nina, Philippines	650
1988, Sept. 10-16	H. Gilbert, Carib., Gulf of Mex.	260
1989, Sept. 16-22	H. Hugo, Caribbean, SE U.S.	86
1990, May 6-11	C. (mult.), SE India	450
1991, Apr. 30	C., Bangladesh	139,000
1991, Nov. 5	TS. Thelma, flash floods, central Philippines	7,000+
1992, Aug. 24-26	H. Andrew, southern FL	65
1993, Mar. 12-14	Blizzard, eastern U.S.	270+
1993, June	Monsoon, Bangladesh	2,000
1994, Nov. 8-18	TS. Gordon, Caribbean, FL	830
1995, Oct. 2-4	H. Opal, S Mexico, FL, AL	59
1995, Nov. 2-3	T. Angela, Philippines	600+
1996, Jan. 7-8	Blizzard, northeastern U.S.	100
1996, Aug. 22	Blizzard, Himalayas, India	239
1996, Aug. 29-Sept. 6	H. Fran, Carib., NC, VA, WV	30
1996, Sept. 9	T. Sally, S China	114
1996, Nov. 6	C., Andhra Pradesh, India	1,000+
1996, Nov. 24-25	Ice storms, TX to MO	26
1996, Dec. 25	TS. Greg, E Malaysia	100+
1997, May 19	C., Bangladesh	108
1997, Aug. 18-21	T. Winnie, Taiwan, E China	140+
1997, Oct. 8-10	H. Pauline, SW Mexico	230
1998, June 9	C., Gujarat, India	1,320
1998, Aug.	Monsoon, Bangladesh	326
1998, Sept. 21-23	H. Georges, Carib., FL, U.S. Gulf	600+
1998, Oct. 27-29	H. Mitch, Honduras, Nicaragua, Guatemala, El Salvador	10,866+
1999, Sept. 4-17	H. Floyd, Baha., E seaboard U.S.	56
1999, Oct. 29	C., E India	9,392
1999, Dec. 26-29	Gales, France, Switz., Germany	120
2000, Dec. 27	Winter storm, TX, OK, AR	40+
2001, July 30	T. Toraji, Taiwan	200
2001, Nov. 6-12	T. Lingling, S Philip., Vietnam	220+
2002, July 1-11	T. Chata'an, Micron., Phil., Jpn.	70+
2002, Aug.-Sept.	T. Rusa, N. and S. Korea	115+
2003, Feb. 16-17	Blizzard, E seaboard U.S.	59
2003, Sept. 12	T. Maemi, S. Korea	130
2003, Sept. 7-19	H. Isabel, NC, VA, E seaboard.	40+
2004, Mar. 7-19	C. Gafilo, Madagascar	198
2004, May 19	C., Myanmar	220
2004, Aug. 12-15	T. Rananim, E China	164
2004, Aug. 13-14	H. Charley, FL, SC	36
2004, Sept. 5-6	H. Frances, Bahamas, FL	35
2004, Sept. 7-16	H. Ivan, Barbados, Grenada, U.S. Gulf Coast.	115
2004, Sept. 16-26	H. Jeanne, Dom. Rep., Haiti, FL.	1,500+
2005, July 7-11	H. Dennis, Jamaica, Haiti, Cuba, FL	50
2005, Aug. 25-29	H. Katrina, LA, MS, FL, AL, GA	1,833+[3]
2005, Aug. 31-Sept. 1	T. Talim, Taiwan, E China	129+
2005, Sept. 21-24	H. Rita, TX, LA	62[4]
2005, Sept. 21-28	T. Damrey, SE Asia; Philippines; Hainan, China.	145
2005, Oct. 4	H. Stan, Central Amer., Mex.	1,000+[5]
2006, Jul. 14	TS. Bilis, SE China	612
2006, Aug. 10	T. Saomai, SE China	295
2006, Nov. 30	T. Durian, Philippines	450-1,000+
2007, June 6-7	C. Gonu, Oman, Iran	54[6]
2007, Nov. 15	C. Sidr, S Bangladesh	3,363
2008, May 2-3	C. Nargis, S Myanmar	84,500-125,000
2008, June 20-25	T. Fengshen, Philippines, China	233
2008, Aug. 26-Sept. 1	H. Gustav, Haiti, Dom. Rep., U.S.	138
2008, Sept. 1-4	TS. Hanna, Haiti	529
2008, Sept. 7-13	H. Ike, Haiti; Cuba; Galveston, TX	164
2009, May 23-26	C. Alia, India, Bangladesh	260
2009, July 9	T. Morakot, mudslides, Taiwan	700+
2009, Sept. 23-30	T. Ketsana, Philippines, Vietnam, Cambodia, Laos	498+
2009, Oct. 3-10	T. Parma, Philippines	375
2009, Oct. 30-Nov. 3	T. Mirinae, Philippines, Vietnam	159+
2009, Dec. 11-22	Snowstorms, central Europe	90+
2010, Apr. 13	C., India, Bangladesh	137
2010, May 29	TS. Agatha, Guatemala, El Salvador, Honduras	184
2010, July 13-17	T. Conson, Luzon Isl., Philippines	105+

(1) What hurricanes are called W of intl. date line and N of equator. (2) Incl. about 500 lost on ships at sea. (3) Official toll as of Aug. 2006 was 1,577 in LA, 238 in MS, 14 in FL, and 2 each in AL and GA. (4) Incl. 55 indirect deaths, among them 20 people, mostly elderly evacuees from a nursing home, whose bus exploded and caught fire outside Dallas. (5) Incl. deaths from floods and landslides generated by heavy rainstorms. (6) First documented super cyclone in Arabian Sea.

Hurricane Katrina

Dates: Aug. 25-29, 2005. **Location:** FL, LA, MS, AL, other inland states.
Fatalities: 1,833+. **Damages:** $125 bil.

The costliest storm to date in U.S. history first made landfall in SE Florida, Aug. 25, as a Category 1 hurricane. Katrina brought heavy rains that led to flooding in the Florida peninsula. Katrina then weakened slightly, strengthened over the Gulf of Mexico, but was downgraded again to Category 3 status before hitting land south of Buras, LA, on Aug. 29. Despite weakening, Katrina caused massive storm surges measuring up to 25-28 ft throughout SE Louisiana, S Mississippi, and SW Alabama. These storm surges, combined with strong winds and heavy rainfall, contributed to the failure of New Orleans's levee system Aug. 30. About 80% of the city eventually flooded. Approximately 1 mil were displaced from their homes.

Some Notable Floods, Tidal Waves

Date	Location	Deaths	Date	Location	Deaths
1703	Awa, Japan	100,000+	1996, June-July	S China	950+
1889, May 31	Johnstown, PA	2,200+	1997, Mar.	Ohio R. Valley	35
1903, June 15	Heppner, OR	325	1997, July	Poland, Czech Republic	98
1911	Chang Jiang R., China	100,000	1997, Nov.	Bardera, Somalia	1,300+
1913, Mar. 25-27	OH, IN.	732	1998, Jan.	Kenya	86
1915, Aug. 17	Galveston, TX	275	1998, Mar.	SW Pakistan	300+
1927, Jan.-July	Mississippi Valley	246+	1998, July-Aug.	China	4,150
1928, Mar. 13	Dam collapse, Saugus, CA	450	1998, July-Sept.	Bangladesh	1,441
1928, Sept. 16	Lake Okeechobee, FL	1,770+	1998, July 17	Papua New Guinea	3,000
1931, Aug.	Huang He R., China	3,700,000	1999, Aug. 1-4	Philippines, SE Asia	188+
1937, Jan. 22	OH, MS valleys	250	1999, Sept.-Oct.	NE Mexico	350+
1939	N China	200,000	1999, Oct.-Dec.	Central Vietnam	700+
1946, Apr. 1	HI, AK	159	1999, Dec. 15-17	NW Venezuela	9,000+
1947, Sept. 20	Honshu Isl., Japan	1,900	2000, Feb.-Mar.	Madagascar	150+
1951, Aug.	Manchuria	1,800	2000, Feb.-Mar.	Mozambique	700
1953, Jan. 31	W Europe	2,000	2000, Aug. 2	Himachal Pradesh, India	120+
1954, Aug. 17	Farahzad, Iran	2,000	2000, Aug. 2	Bhutan	200+
1955, Oct. 7-12	India, Pakistan	1,700	2000, Sept. 19-30	India, Bangladesh	1,000+
1959, Nov. 1	W Mexico	2,000	2001, Jan.-Feb.	Mozambique	84+
1959, Dec. 2	Frejus, France	412	2001, Aug.-Nov.	S Vietnam, Cambodia	360+
1960, Oct. 10	Bangladesh	6,000	2001, Aug. 1-6	Taiwan	100+
1960, Oct. 31	Bangladesh	4,000	2001, Aug. 10-12	NE Iran	247
1962, Feb. 17	North Sea coast, Germany	343	2001, Aug.	N Thailand	170
1962, Sept. 27	Barcelona, Spain	445	2001, Nov. 9-10	N Algeria	711+
1963, Oct. 9	Dam collapse, Vaiont, Italy	1,800	2002, Jan. 30-Feb. 15	Java Isl., Indonesia	147
1966, Nov. 3-4	Florence, Venice, Italy	113	2002, Apr.-May	E Africa	150+
1967, Jan. 18-24	E Brazil	894	2002, Apr.-Aug.	China	800+
1967, Mar. 19	Rio de Janeiro, Brazil	436	2002, July-Aug.	India, Nepal, Bangladesh	1,100+
1967, Nov. 26	Lisbon, Portugal	464	2002, Aug.	Russia	110
1968, Aug. 7-14	Gujarat state, India	1,000	2002, Aug.	Germany, Hungary, Austria, Czech Rep.	100+
1968, Oct. 7	NE India	780			
1969, Jan. 18-26	Southern CA	100	2003, May 17-27	Sri Lanka	250
1969, Mar. 17	Mundau Valley, Alagoas, Brazil	218	2003, Aug.-mid-Sept.	E India	200+
1969, Aug. 20-22	Western VA	189	2003, Dec. 10- Jan. 23, 2004	Sumatra, Indonesia	148
1969, Sept. 15	South Korea	250			
1969, Oct. 1-8	Tunisia	500	2003, Dec. 19- Jan. 7, 2004	Central Philippines	200
1970, May 20	Central Romania	160	2004, Jan. 10-Mar. 8	E Brazil	161
1970, July 22	Himalayas, India	500	2004, May 23-25	Dom. Republic, Haiti	2,000
1971, Feb. 26	Rio de Janeiro, Brazil	130	2004, June-Sept.	Banglad., India, Myan., Nepal	2,000+
1972, Feb. 26	Buffalo Creek, WV	118	2004, June-Sept.	China	500
1972, June 9	Rapid City, SD	238	2004, Nov.-Dec.	Philippines	1,060+
1972, Aug. 7	Luzon Isl., Philippines	454	2004, Dec. 26	12 Indian Ocean nations	226,328[1]
1972, Aug. 19-31	Pakistan	1,500	2005, July 26-Aug. 2	W Maharashtra state, India	1,000+
1974, Mar. 29	Tubaro, Brazil	1,000	2006, Feb. 17	Leyte Isl., Philippines	1,000
1974, Aug. 12	Monty-Iago, Bangladesh	2,500	2006, July 17	S of Java, Indonesia	530+
1976, June 5	Teton Dam collapse, ID	11	2007, Aug. 19-27	MN, WI, OH	25
1976, July 31	Big Thompson Canyon, CO	140	2008, June	IL, IN, WI, MN, MO.	24
1976, Nov. 17	E Java, Indonesia	136	2008, Sept.	E Orissa, India	173
1977, July 19-20	Johnstown, PA	68	2008, Oct. 24-25	Hadramaut, Mahavra, Yemen	100
1977, Nov. 6	Toccoa, GA	39	2008, Oct.-Nov.	Central, N Vietnam	80
1978, June-Sept.	N India	1,200	2008, Nov. 22-Dec. 3	Santa Catarina, S Brazil	116
1979, Jan.-Feb.	Brazil	204	2009, Mar. 27	Jakarta, Indonesia	77+
1979, July 17	Lomblen Isl., Indonesia	539	2009, Mar.-Apr.	Zambia, Namibia	92
1979, Aug. 11	Morvi, India	15,000	2009, Sept. 29	Amer. Samoa, Samoa, Tonga	170+
1981, Apr.	N China	550	2009, Sept. 29-Oct. 14	S India	355
1981, July	Sichuan, Hubei Prov., China	1,300	2009, Nov. 4-6	El Salvador	192+
1982, Jan. 23	Near Lima, Peru	600	2009, Nov. 25	Jeddah, Saudi Arabia	106
1982, May 12	Guangdong, China	430	2010, May 1-3	KY, TN, MS, AR	29
1982, Sept. 17-21	El Salvador, Guatemala	1,300+	2010, May 1-7	Afghanistan, Tajikistan	124+
1984, Aug.-Sept.	South Korea	200+	2010, June 13-24	Cenxi, China	377+
1985, July 19	Dam collapse, N Italy	361	2010, June 28	Dazhai, China	99
1987, Aug.-Sept.	N Bangladesh	1,000+	2010, July 1-7	Qinghai, China	118
1988, Sept.	N India	1,000+	2010, July-Aug.	Pakistan	1,600+
1990, June 14	Shadyside, OH	26	2010, Aug.	Sahel region, W Africa	200+
1993, July-Aug.	Midwest, U.S.	47	2010, Oct.	W Papua, Indonesia	145+
1995, July	NE China	1,200	2011, Jan.	SE Brazil	900+
1995, Aug. 19	SW Morocco	136	2011, Mar. 11	NE Japan	15,800+
1995, Dec. 25	KwaZulu Natal, South Africa	166	2011, Apr.-May	N Colombia	425+
1996, Feb. 17	Biak Isl., Indonesia	105			
1996, Apr.	Afghanistan	100+			

(1) Based on official estimates assembled by the Intl. Fed. of Red Cross and Red Crescent Societies, including 50,773 missing; as reported Dec. 15, 2005. The nearly 176,300 listed as dead include 128,645 from Indonesia; 31,147 from Sri Lanka; 10,749 from India; and 5,395 from Thailand.

Earthquake, Tsunami, Meltdown

Dates: Beg. Mar. 11, 2011. **Location:** NE Japan.
Fatalities: 15,800+ (est.). **Damages:** $245-$600 bil (est.).

Japan experienced one of the worst disasters in its history when it was struck by a 9.0-magnitude temblor. But the earthquake was just the beginning of the tragedy. An ensuing tsunami wiped out entire towns in the northeastern provinces of Iwate, Miyagi, and Fukushima, and flooded the Fukushima Daiichi nuclear power plant. Officials released nearly 12,000 tons of radioactive water into the ocean in hopes of preventing even more toxic water from escaping the plant but could not avoid partial meltdowns in three of the plant's reactors. Some officials put the disaster on par with the 1986 Chernobyl explosion in Ukraine.

Some Major Earthquakes

Source: Global Volcanism Network, Smithsonian Institution; U.S. Geological Survey, U.S. Dept. of the Interior; World Almanac research
Magnitude of earthquakes (mag.) is a relative measurement of an earthquake's energy.

Date	Location	Deaths	Mag.
526, May 20	Antioch, Syria	250,000	NA
856	Corinth, Greece	45,000	NA
856, Dec. 22	Damghan, Iran	200,000	NA
893, Mar. 23	Ardabil, Iran	150,000	NA
1057	Chihli, China	25,000	NA
1138, Aug. 9	Aleppo, Syria	230,000	NA
1169, Feb. 11	Nr. Mt. Etna, Sicily	15,000	NA[1]
1268	Silicia, Asia Minor	60,000	NA
1290, Sept. 27	Chihli, China	100,000	NA
1293, May 20	Kamakura, Japan	30,000	NA
1531, Jan. 26	Lisbon, Portugal	30,000	NA
1556, Jan. 24	Shaanxi, China	830,000	NA
1667, Nov.	Shemakha, Caucasia	80,000	NA
1693, Jan. 11	Catania, Italy	60,000	NA
1737, Oct. 11	India, Calcutta	300,000	NA
1755, June 7	N Persia (current-day Iran)	40,000	NA
1755, Nov. 1	Lisbon, Portugal	60,000	8.75[2]
1783, Feb. 4	Calabria, Italy	30,000	NA
1797, Feb. 4	Quito, Ecuador	41,000	NA
1822, Sept. 5	Asia Minor, Aleppo	22,000	NA
1828, Dec. 28	Echigo, Japan	30,000	NA
1868, Aug. 13-15	Peru, Ecuador	40,000	NA
1875, May 16	Venezuela, Colombia	16,000	NA
1886, Aug. 31	Charleston, SC	60	6.6
1896, June 15	Sanriku, Japan (tsunami)	27,120	8.5
1902, Apr. 19	Quezaltenango and San Marcos, Guatemala	2,000	7.5
1902, Dec. 16	Uzbekistan, Russia	4,700	6.4
1903, Apr. 28	Malazgirt, Turkey	3,500	7.0
1903, May 28	Gole, Turkey	1,000	5.8
1905, Apr. 4	Kangra, India	19,000	7.5
1906, Jan. 31	Off coast of Esmeraldas, Ecuador	1,000	8.8
1906, Mar. 16	Chia-i, Taiwan	1,250	6.8
1906, Apr. 18-19	San Francisco, CA	3,000+	7.7[3]
1906, Aug. 17	Valparaiso, Chile	3,882	8.6
1907, Oct. 21	Central Asia	12,000	8.1
1908, Dec. 28	Messina, Italy	72,000	7.2
1909, Jan. 23	Silakhor, Iran	5,000-6,000	7.3
1912, Aug. 9	Murefte, Turkey	2,800	7.4
1914, Oct. 3	Burdur, Turkey	4,000	7.0
1915, Jan. 13	Avezzano, Italy	32,610	7.0
1917, July 30	Yunnan, China	1,800	7.5
1918, Feb. 13	Guangdong, China	1,000	7.4
1920, Dec. 16	Gansu, China	200,000	7.8[4]
1923, Mar. 24	Sichuan, China	3,500	7.3
1923, Mar. 25	Torbat-e Heydariyeh, Iran	2,200	5.7
1923, Sept. 1	Yokohama, Japan	142,800	7.9
1925, Mar. 16	Yunnan, China	5,800	7.0
1927, Mar. 7	Tango, Japan	3,020	7.6
1927, May 22	Gansu, China	40,900	7.6
1929, May 1	Koppeh Dagh, Iran	3,800	7.2
1930, May 6	Salmas, Iran	2,500	7.2
1930, July 23	Irpinia, Italy	1,404	6.5
1931, Mar. 31	Managua, Nicaragua	2,500	6.0
1931, Apr. 27	Armenia-Azerbaijan border	2,800	5.7
1931, Aug. 10	Xinjiang, China	10,000	8.0
1933, Mar. 2	Sanriku, Japan (tsunami)	2,990	8.4
1933, Mar. 10	Long Beach, CA	115	6.2
1933, Aug. 25	Sichuan, China	9,300	7.5
1934, Jan. 15	Bihar, India-Nepal	10,700	8.1
1935, Apr. 21	Miao-li, Taiwan	3,270	7.1
1935, May 30	Quetta, Pakistan	30,000	7.6
1939, Jan. 25	Chillan, Chile	28,000	7.8
1939, Dec. 26	Erzincan, Turkey	32,700	7.8
1940, Nov. 10	Vrancea, Romania	1,000	7.3
1942, Dec. 20	Erbaa, Turkey	1,100	7.3
1943, Sept. 10	Tottori, Japan	1,190	7.4
1943, Nov. 26	Ladik, Turkey	4,000	7.6
1944, Jan. 15	San Juan, Argentina	8,000	7.4
1944, Feb. 1	Gerede, Turkey	2,790	7.4
1945, Jan. 12	Mikawa, Japan	1,961	7.1
1945, Nov. 27	Makran Coast, Pakistan	4,000	8.0
1946, May 31	Ustukran, Turkey	1,300	5.9
1946, Nov. 10	Ancash, Peru	1,400	7.3
1946, Dec. 20	Honshu, Japan	1,362	8.1
1948, June 28	Fukui, Japan	3,769	7.3
1948, Oct. 5	Ashgabat, Turkmenistan	110,000	7.3
1949, July 10	Khait, Tajikistan	12,000	7.5
1949, Aug. 5	Pelileo, Ecuador	5,050	6.8
1950, Aug. 15	Assam, India	1,526	8.6
1951, Aug. 2	Cosiguina, Nicaragua	1,000	5.8
1953, Mar. 18	NW Turkey	1,070	7.3
1954, Sept. 9	Orleansville, Algeria	1,250	6.8
1956, June 10-17	N Afghanistan	2,000	7.7
1957, July 2	N Iran	1,200	7.1
1957, Dec. 13	W Iran	1,130	7.1
1960, Feb. 29	Agadir, Morocco	12,000	5.7
1960, May 21-30	S Chile	1,655	9.5[5]
1962, Sept. 1	NW Iran	12,255	7.1
1963, July 26	Skopje, Yugoslavia	1,100	6.0
1964, Mar. 27	Prince Wm. Sound, AK	131	9.2[6]
1966, Mar. 7	Hebei, China	1,000	7.0
1966, Mar. 22	Hebei, China	1,000	6.9
1966, Aug. 19	E Turkey	2,529	6.8
1968, Aug. 31	NE Iran	12,000	7.3
1969, July 25	Guangdong, China	3,000	5.9
1970, Jan. 5	Yunnan Prov., China	10,000	7.5
1970, Mar. 28	W Turkey	1,086	6.9
1970, May 31	Chimbote, Peru	70,000	7.9
1971, Feb. 9	San Fernando Valley, CA	65	6.6
1971, May 22	SE of Ankara, Turkey	1,000	6.9
1972, Apr. 10	S Iran	5,054	7.1
1972, Dec. 23	Managua, Nicaragua	5,000	6.2
1974, May 10	China	20,000	6.8
1974, Dec. 28	N Pakistan	5,300	6.2
1975, Feb. 4	Haicheng, China	2,000	7.0
1975, Sept. 6	E Turkey	2,300	6.7
1976, Feb. 4	Guatemala	23,000	7.5
1976, May 6	NE Italy	1,000	6.5
1976, June 25	Irian Jaya, New Guinea	422	7.1
1976, July 28	Tangshan, China	255,000	7.5
1976, Aug. 16	Mindanao, Philippines	8,000	7.9
1976, Nov. 24	NW Iran-Turkey border	5,000	7.3
1977, Mar. 4	Romania	1,500	7.2
1978, Sept. 16	NE Iran	15,000	7.8
1980, Oct. 10	NW Algeria	5,000	7.7
1980, Nov. 23	S Italy	2,735	6.5
1981, June 11	S Iran	3,000	6.9
1981, July 28	S Iran	1,500	7.3
1982, Dec. 13	W Arabian Peninsula	2,800	6.0
1983, Oct. 30	E Turkey	1,342	6.9
1985, Sept. 19	Michoacan, Mexico	9,500	8.0
1986, Oct. 10	El Salvador	1,000+	5.5
1987, Mar. 6	Colombia-Ecuador	1,000	7.0
1988, Aug. 20	India-Nepal border	1,000	6.8
1988, Dec. 7	Spitak, Armenia	25,000	6.8
1989, Oct. 17	San Francisco Bay area, CA	63	6.9
1990, June 20	W Iran	40,000+	7.4
1990, July 16	Luzon, Philippines	1,621	7.7
1991, Feb. 1	Pakistan-Afgh. border	1,200	6.8
1991, Oct. 19	N India	2,000	7.0
1992, Dec. 12	Flores Isl., Indonesia	2,500	7.5
1993, Sept. 30	Maharashtra, S India	9,748	6.2
1994, Jan. 17	Northridge, CA	61	6.8
1994, June 6	Cauca, SW Colombia	1,000	6.8
1995, Jan. 16	Kobe, Japan	5,502	6.9
1995, May 27	Sakhalin Isl., Russia	1,989	7.5
1997, Feb. 28	NW Iran	1,000+	6.1
1997, May 10	N Iran	1,567	7.3
1998, Feb. 4	Hindu Kush, Afghanistan	2,323	5.9
1998, May 30	Afghanistan-Tajikistan border	4,000+	6.6
1998, July 17	Papua New Guinea	2,183	7.0
1999, Jan. 25	Armenia, Colombia	1,185+	6.1
1999, Aug. 17	Izmit, W Turkey	17,118+	7.6
1999, Sept. 20	Taichung, Taiwan	2,400	7.6
2001, Jan. 26	Gujarat, India	20,085	7.6
2002, Mar. 25-26	Hindu Kush, Afghanistan	1,000+	6.1
2003, May 21	N Algeria	2,266	6.8
2003, Dec. 26	Bam, SE Iran	31,000	6.6
2004, Dec. 26	Sumatra-Andaman Isls., Indonesia	227,898	9.1[7]
2005, Mar. 28	N. Sumatra, Indonesia	1,313	8.6
2005, Oct. 8	Kashmir, Pakistan, India	86,000	7.6
2006, May 26	Java, Indonesia	5,749	6.3
2008, May 12	E Sichuan Prov., China	87,587	7.9
2009, Sept. 30	Sumatra, Indonesia	1,117	7.5
2010, Jan. 12	Haiti	222,570	7.0
2010, Feb. 27	Chile	800	8.8
2010, Apr. 13	S Qinghai, China	2,698	6.9
2011, Mar. 11	NE Japan	15,800+	9.0[8]

NA = Not available. (1) Once thought to have been a volcanic eruption; evidence indicates a destructive earthquake and tsunami occurred on this date. (2) This earthquake caused the most deadly tsunami to date in the Atlantic Ocean. (3) Incl. deaths from resulting fires; revised estimates of magnitude range from 7.7 to 7.9. (4) Commonly referred to as the Gansu quake; actually located within the Ningxia autonomous region. (5) The largest recorded earthquake; caused a deadly tsunami that spread across the Pacific Ocean as far as Japan. (6) The "Good Friday" earthquake sent a tsunami that hit British Columbia, Canada, and the U.S. Pacific coast. (7) This undersea earthquake triggered devastating tsunamis that hit 12 Indian Ocean nations. (8) The most powerful earthquake in Japan's history set off a tsunami that inundated much of the coast and caused a partial meltdown of the Fukushima nuclear power plant.

Some Notable Fires Since 1930

See also Some Notable Explosions Since 1920.

Date	Location	Deaths
1930, Apr. 21	Penitentiary, Columbus, OH	320
1931, July 24	Home for aged, Pittsburgh, PA	48
1934, Dec. 11	Hotel Kerns, Lansing, MI	34
1938, May 16	Terminal Hotel, Atlanta, GA	35
1940, Apr. 23	Nightclub, Natchez, MS	198
1942, Nov. 28	Cocoanut Grove Nightclub, Boston, MA	492
1942, Dec. 12	Hostel, St. John's, NL, Canada	100
1943, Sept. 7	Gulf Hotel, Houston, TX	55
1944, July 6	Ringling Circus, Hartford, CT	168
1946, June 5	LaSalle Hotel, Chicago, IL	61
1946, Dec. 7	Winecoff Hotel, Atlanta, GA	119
1946, Dec. 12	Ice plant, tenement, New York, NY	37
1949, Apr. 5	Hospital, Effingham, IL	77
1950, Jan. 7	Mercy Hospital, Davenport, IA	41
1953, Mar. 29	Nursing home, Largo, FL	35
1953, Apr. 16	Metalworking plant, Chicago, IL	35
1957, Feb. 17	Home for aged, Warrenton, MO	72
1958, Mar. 19	Loft building, New York, NY	24
1958, Dec. 1	Parochial school, Chicago, IL	95
1958, Dec. 16	Store, Bogotá, Colombia	83
1959, June 23	Resort hotel, Stalheim, Norway	34
1960, Mar. 12	Chemical plant, Pusan, Korea	68
1960, July 14	Mental hospital, Guatemala City	225
1960, Nov. 13	Movie theater, Amude, Syria	152
1960, Dec. 19	USS Constellation, Brooklyn, NY	49
1961, Jan. 6	Thomas Hotel, San Francisco, CA	20
1961, Dec. 17	Circus, Niteroi, Brazil	323
1963, May 4	Theater, Diourbel, Senegal	64
1963, Nov. 18	Surfside Hotel, Atlantic City, NJ	25
1963, Nov. 23	Rest home, Fitchville, OH	63
1963, Dec. 29	Roosevelt Hotel, Jacksonville, FL	22
1964, May 8	Apt. bldg., Manila, Philippines	30
1964, Dec. 18	Nursing home, Fountaintown, IN	20
1965, Mar. 1	Apartment, LaSalle, QC, Can.	28
1965, Aug. 11-16	Watts riot fires, Los Angeles, CA	30+
1966, Mar. 11	2 ski resorts, Numata, Japan	31
1966, Oct. 17	Bldg. (firefighters), New York, NY	12
1966, Dec. 7	Barracks, Erzurum, Turkey	68
1967, Feb. 7	Restaurant, Montgomery, AL	25
1967, May 22	Dept. store, Brussels, Belgium	322
1967, July 16	State prison, Jay, FL	37
1967, July 29	USS Forrestal, off N Vietnam	134
1968, May 11	Wedding hall, Vijayawada, India	58
1969, Dec. 2	Nursing home, Notre Dame, QC, Can.	54
1970, Jan. 9	Nursing home, Marietta, OH	27
1970, Nov. 1	Dance hall, Grenoble, France	145
1970, Dec. 20	Hotel, Tucson, AZ	28
1971, Dec., 25	Hotel, Seoul, S. Korea	162
1972, May 13	Nightclub, Osaka, Japan	116
1972, July 5	Hospital, Sherborne, England	30
1973, June 24	Bar, New Orleans, LA	32
1973, Aug. 3	Amusement park, Isle of Man, Eng.	51
1973, Sept. 1	Hotel, Copenhagen, Denmark	35
1973, Nov. 29	Dept. store, Kumamoto, Japan	107
1973, Dec. 2	Theater, Seoul, S. Korea	50
1974, Feb. 1	Bank building, São Paulo, Brazil	189
1974, June 30	Discotheque, Port Chester, NY	24
1974, Nov. 3	Hotel, disco, Seoul, S. Korea	88
1975, Dec. 12	Tent city, Mina, Saudi Arabia	138
1976, Oct. 24	Social club, Bronx, NY	25
1977, Feb. 25	Rossiya hotel, Moscow, Russia	45
1977, May 28	Nightclub, Southgate, KY	164
1977, June 9	Nightclub, Abidjan, Ivory Coast	41
1977, June 26	Jail, Columbia, TN	42
1977, Nov. 14	Hotel, Manila, Philippines	47
1978, Jan. 28	Coates House Hotel, Kansas City, MO	16
1978, Aug. 19	Movie theater, Abadan, Iran	425+
1979, July 14	Hotel, Saragossa, Spain	80
1979, Dec. 31	Social club, Chapais, QC, Can.	42
1980, May 20	Nursing home, Kingston, Jamaica	157
1980, Nov. 21	MGM Grand Hotel, Las Vegas, NV	84
1980, Dec. 4	Stouffer Inn, Harrison, NY	26
1981, Jan. 9	Boarding home, Keansburg, NJ	30
1981, Feb. 10	Las Vegas Hilton, Las Vegas, NV	8
1981, Feb. 14	Discotheque, Dublin, Ireland	44
1982, Nov. 8	County jail, Biloxi, MS	29
1983, Feb. 13	Movie theater, Turin, Italy	64
1983, Dec. 17	Discotheque, Madrid, Spain	83
1984, May 11	Great Adventure Amusement Pk., NJ	8
1985, Apr. 21	Movie theaters, Tabaco, Philippines	44
1985, Apr. 26	Hospital, Buenos Aires, Argentina	79
1985, May 11	Soccer stadium, Bradford, England	53
1985, May 13	MOVE headquarters, row houses, Philadelphia, PA	11
1986, Dec. 31	Dupont Plaza Hotel, Puerto Rico	96
1987, May 6- June 2	Forest fire, N China	193
1987, Nov. 17	Subway, London, England	30
1988, Mar. 20	About 2,000 buildings, Lashio, Burma	134
1990, Mar. 25	Social club, Bronx, NY	87
1991, Mar. 3	Munitions dump, Addis Ababa, Ethiopia	260+
1991, Sept. 3	Processing plant, Hamlet, NC	25
1991, Oct. 20-21	Wildfire, Oakland, Berkeley, CA	24
1993, Apr. 19	Cult compound, Waco, TX	72
1994, May 10	Toy factory, Bangkok, Thailand	213
1994, July 4-10	(Firefighters) Glenwood Springs, CO	14
1994, Nov. 2	Burning fuel flood, Durunka, Egypt	500
1994, Dec. 10	Theater, Karamay, China	300
1995, Oct. 28	Subway train, Baku, Azerbaijan	300
1995, Dec. 23	School, Mandi Dabwali, India	500+
1996, Mar. 19	Nightclub, Quezon City, Philippines	150+
1996, Mar. 28	Shopping mall, Bogor, Indonesia	78
1996, Nov. 20	Building, Hong Kong	39
1997, Feb. 23	Worship site, Baripada, India	164
1997, Apr. 15	Encampment, Mina, Saudi Arabia	343
1997, June 7	Temple, Thanjavur, India	60+
1997, June 13	Movie theater, New Delhi, India	60
1997, July 11	Hotel, Pattaya, Thailand	90
1997, Sept. 29	Children's home, nr. Colina, Chile	30
1998, Dec. 3	Orphanage, Manila, Philippines	28
1999, Mar. 24	Mt. Blanc Tunnel, France, Italy	40
1999, Oct. 30	Karaoke salon, Inchon, S. Korea	55+
2000, Mar. 17	Church, Kanungu, Uganda	530
2000, Oct. 20	Nightclub, Mexico City, Mexico	20
2000, Nov. 11	Cable car, Kaprun, Austria	155
2000, Dec. 25	Shopping center, Luoyang, China	309
2001, Mar. 6	School, central China	41
2001, Mar. 26	School, Machakos, Kenya	64
2001, Aug. 18	Hotel, Quezon City, Philippines	73
2001, Sept. 1	Nightclub, Tokyo, Japan	44
2001, Dec. 29	Fireworks accident, Lima, Peru	291
2002, Mar. 11	Girls' school, Mecca, Saudi Arabia	15
2002, June 16	Internet cafe, Beijing, China	24
2002, July 7	Coal mine, Donetsk region, Ukraine	34+
2002, July 20	Disco, Lima, Peru	25+
2002, July 31	Coal mine, Donetsk region, Ukraine	20
2003, Feb. 18	Subway train, Taegu, S. Korea	198
2003, Feb. 20	Pyrotechnics in nightclub, Warwick, RI	100
2003, Sept. 15	Prison, Riyadh, Saudi Arabia	94
2003, Nov. 24	Students' hostel, Moscow, Russia	36
2004, May 17	Prison, San Pedro Sula, Honduras	104
2004, July 16	Pvt. school, Kumbakonam, India	80+
2004, Aug. 1	Market, Asunción, Paraguay	400+
2004, Dec. 30	Club, Buenos Aires, Argentina	194
2005, Feb. 14	Mosque, Tehran, Iran	59
2005, Mar. 7	Prison, Higuey, Dom. Republic	159
2005, Apr. 15	Hotel, Paris, France	22
2005, Sept. 5	Theater, Beni Suef, Egypt	32
2006, Dec. 9	Drug treatment center, Moscow, Russ.	45
2007, Mar. 20	Nursing home for elderly and disabled, Kamyshevatskaya, Russia	62
2007, Aug. 24- Sept. 2	Wildfires (arson), Greece	65
2008, Apr. 26	Factory fire, Casablanca, Morocco	55
2008, Sept.	Wildfires, Mozambique, S. Africa, Swaziland	89
2009, Jan.-Feb.	Wildfires (arson), Victoria, Australia	173

Some Notable Explosions Since 1920

See also Principal U.S. Mine Disasters Since 1900. Some bombings related to political conflicts and terrorism are not included.

Date	Location	Deaths
1920, Sept. 16	Wall Street, New York, NY	30
1921, Sept. 21	Chem. storage facility, Oppau, Ger.	561
1924, Jan. 3	Food plant, Pekin, IL.	42
1927, May 18	Bath school, Lansing, MI	38
1928, Apr. 13	Dance hall, West Plains, MO	40
1937, Mar. 18	School, New London, TX	311
1940, Sept. 12	Hercules Powder factory, Kenvil, NJ	55
1942, June 5	Ordnance plant, Elwood, IL	49
1944, Apr. 14	Harbor, Bombay, India	700
1944, July 17	Munitions ships, depot, Port Chicago, CA	322
1944, Oct. 21	Liquid gas tank, Cleveland, OH	135
1947, Apr. 16	Freighter, chemical co. plant, Texas City, TX.	576
1948, July 28	Farben works, Ludwigshafen, Ger.	184
1950, May 19	Munitions barges, S. Amboy, NJ	30
1954, May 26	USS *Bennington*, off RI	103
1956, Aug. 7	Dynamite trucks, Cali, Colombia	1,100
1958, Apr. 18	Sunken munitions ship, Okinawa, Japan	40
1958, May 22	Nike missiles, Leonardo, NJ.	10
1959, Apr. 10	WWII bomb, Philippines	38
1959, June 28	Rail tank cars, Meldrim, GA	25
1959, Aug. 7	Dynamite truck, Roseburg, OR.	13
1959, Nov. 2	Explosives, Jamuri Bazar, India	46
1959, Dec. 13	2 apt. bldgs., Dortmund, Ger.	26
1960, Mar. 4	Belgian munitions ship, Havana, Cuba.	100
1962, Oct. 3	Telephone Co. office, New York, NY	23
1963, Jan. 2	Packing plant, Terre Haute, IN	17
1963, Mar. 9	Dynamite plant, S. Africa	45
1963, Aug. 13	Explosives dump, Gauhaiti, India	32
1963, Oct. 31	State Fair Coliseum, Indianapolis, IN	73
1964, July 23	Harbor munitions, Bone, Algeria.	100
1965, Aug. 9	Missile silo, Searcy, AR	53
1965, Oct. 21	Bridge, Tila Bund, Pakistan	80
1965, Nov. 24	Armory, Keokuk, IA.	20
1967, Dec. 25	Apartment bldg., Moscow, USSR.	20
1968, Apr. 6	Sports store, Richmond, IN	43
1969, Mar. 31	Coal mine, nr. Barroteran, Mexico	180
1970, Apr. 8	Subway construction, Osaka, Japan	73
1971, June 24	Tunnel, Sylmar, CA	17
1973, Feb., 10	Liquid gas tank, Staten Island, NY	40
1975, Dec. 27	Coal mine, Chasnala, India	431
1976, Apr. 13	Munitions works, Lapua, Finland	40
1977, Nov. 11	Freight train, Iri, S. Korea	57
1977, Dec. 22	Grain elevator, Westwego, LA	35
1978, Feb. 24	Derailed tank car, Waverly, TN.	12
1978, July 11	Propylene tank truck, Tarragona, Spain. .	150
1980, Oct. 23	School, Ortuella, Spain.	64
1982, Apr. 25	Antiques exhibition, Todi, Italy	33
1982, Nov. 2	Salang Tunnel, Afghanistan	1,000+
1984, Feb. 25	Oil pipeline, Cubatao, Brazil	508
1984, June 21	Naval supply depot, Severomorsk, USSR.	200+
1984, Nov. 19	Gas storage area, NE Mexico City	334
1984, Dec. 3	Chemical plant, Bhopal, India.	3,849
1984, Dec. 5	Coal mine, Taipei, Taiwan	94
1985, June 25	Fireworks factory, Hallett, OK.	21
1988, Apr. 10	Army ammunitions dump nr. Rawalpindi and Islamabad, Pakistan	100
1988, July 6	Oil rig, North Sea off NE Scotland	167
1989, June 3	Gas pipeline, between Ufa, Asha, USSR	650+
1992, Mar. 3	Coal mine, Kozlu, Turkey	270+
1992, Apr. 22	Gas leak in sewers, Guadalajara, Mexico	200+
1992, May 9	Coal mine, Plymouth, Nova Scotia.	26
1993, Feb. 26	World Trade Center, New York, NY	6
1994, July 18	Jewish com. center, Buenos Aires, Arg.	100
1995, Apr. 19	Fed. office building, Oklahoma City, OK.	168
1995, Apr. 29	Subway construction, S. Korea	110
1995, Nov. 13	Military facility, Riyadh, Saudi Arabia	7
1996, Jan. 31	Bank, Colombo, Sri Lanka	53
1996, Mar. 3-4	Jerusalem and Tel Aviv, Israel	33
1996, June 25	U.S. military housing complex, nr. Dhahran, Saudi Arabia	19
1996, July 24	Train, Colombo, Sri Lanka	86
1996, Nov. 16	Military apt., Dagestan region, Russia	68

Date	Location	Deaths
1996, Nov. 21	Propane gas leak in bldg., San Juan, Puerto Rico.	33
1996, Nov. 27	Coal mine, Shanxi Prov., China	91+
1996, Dec. 30	Train, Assam, India.	59+
1997, Dec. 2	Coal mine, Novokuznetsk, Siberia	68
1998, Feb. 14	2 oil tankers, Yaounde, Cameroon	120
1998, Feb. 14	17 bombs, Coimbatore, India	50
1998, Apr. 4	Coal mine, Donetsk, Ukraine	63
1998, Aug. 7	Bomb, U.S. emb., Nairobi, Kenya.	213
	Bomb, U.S. emb., Dar-es-Salaam, Tanz.	11
1998, Sept. 8	2 buses, São Paulo, Brazil	59
1998, Oct. 17	Oil pipeline, Jesse, Nigeria.	700+
1999, May 16	Fuel truck, Punjab Prov., Pakistan	75
1999, Sept. 9	Apartment building, Moscow, Russia	94
1999, Sept. 13	Apartment building, Moscow, Russia	118
1999, Sept. 16	Apartment building, Moscow, Russia	18
1999, Sept. 26	Fireworks factory, Celaya, Mexico	56
2000, Feb. 25	Bombs on 2 buses, Ozamis, Philippines	41
2000, Mar. 11	Coal mine, Krasnodon, Ukraine	80
2000, Apr. 16	Airport hangar, Dem. Rep. of Congo	100+
2000, July 16	Oil pipeline, Warri, Nigeria	30
2000, Sept. 9	Truck explosion, Urumqi, China	60
2000, Oct. 12	U.S. destroyer, Yemen	17
2001, Mar. 6	School, Wanzai Co., China.	41
2001, Apr. 21	Coal mine, Shaanxi, China.	51
2001, June 1	Dance club, Tel Aviv, Israel	21
2001, July 17	Coal mine, Guanxi, China.	76+
2001, Aug. 19	Coal mine, Donetsk region, Ukraine.	52
2001, Sept. 21	Chem. plant, Toulouse, France	29
2002, Jan. 21	Volcanic lava caused gas station blast, Goma, Dem. Rep. of Congo.	50+
2002, Jan. 27	Munitions dump, Lagos, Nigeria.	1,000+
2002, Apr. 11	Truck nr. synagogue, Djerba, Tunisia.	17
2002, Apr. 21	Bomb, dept. store, Mindanao, Philip.	14
2002, May 8	Bomb on bus outside hotel, Karachi, Pak.	14
2002, May 9	Land mine at parade, Kaspiisk, Russia	34+
2002, June 14	Car bomb outside U.S. consulate, Karachi, Pakistan	12
2002, June 18	Bomb on bus, Jerusalem, Israel	20
2002, July 5	Bomb in market, Larba, Algeria	35+
2002, Aug. 9	Explosion, Jalalabad, Afghanistan	25+
2002, Sept. 5	Car bomb, Kabul, Afghanistan	30
2002, Oct. 12	Nightclub bombings, Bali, Indonesia	202
2003, Aug. 25	Bombs in 2 taxis, Mumbai, India.	52
2003, Dec. 5	Bomb on train, Yessentuki, Russia.	45
2003, Dec. 23	Gas well explosion, Chongqing, China.	233
2004, Jan. 19	Natural gas facility, Skikda, Algeria	27
2004, Feb. 6	Bomb on subway car, Moscow, Russia	39
2004, Mar. 11	Bombs on commuter trains, Madrid, Spain	191
2005, Feb. 14	Coal mine, NE China	214
2005, Apr. 23	Oil refinery, Texas City, TX.	15
2005, May 2	Arms cache, Baghlan Prov., Afghan.	34+
2005, July 7	Bombs in mass transit, London, Eng.	56
2005, Oct. 1	Bombings of restaurants, Bali, Indonesia	26
2005, Nov. 27	Coal mine, NE China	161+
2006, May 12	Oil pipeline, nr. Lagos, Nigeria	200
2006, July 1	Bombings of trains, station, Mumbai, India	207
2007, Mar. 19	Coal mine, Siberia, Russia	108
2007, Mar. 22	Natl. weapons depot, Maputo, Mozambique.	117
2007, June 9	Oil pipeline, Pyongan Prov., N. Korea	110
2007, Nov. 18	Methane gas buildup in coal mine, E Ukraine	90
2008, May 15	Pipeline explosion in Lagos, Nigeria.	100+
2008, Sept. 20	Truck bomb outside hotel, Islamabad, Pakistan	40+
2009, Feb. 22	Coal mine, N China	74
2010, Apr. 5	Coal mine, WV	29
2010, Apr. 20	Oil rig, Gulf of Mexico, U.S.	11
2010, May 8-9	Coal mine, Siberia, Russia	91
2010, June 17	Coal mine, Amaga, Colombia.	73
2011, Mar. 28	Munitions factory, Abyan, Yemen.	150+

Gulf of Mexico Oil Spill

Dates: Beg. Apr. 20, 2010. **Location:** Gulf of Mexico, off the coast of LA.
Fatalities: 11. **Damages:** $20 bil.

The worst oil spill in history began with a gas explosion on the *Deepwater Horizon* platform 50 mi off Venice, LA. When the rig burned and sank, oil started gushing unabated from the ruptured pipes. After 86 days and several failed efforts, BP, the well's owner, finally capped the leak. Approximately 4.9 mil barrels of oil had spilled into the water—nearly 20 times the amount released in the 1989 Exxon *Valdez* disaster. But while a few tar balls washed up on beaches from Florida to Texas, a swirling current kept most oil swirling out to sea. By 2011, fish, shrimp, and even oysters from the Gulf were deemed safe to eat.

Notable Nuclear Accidents

Oct. 7, 1957: Fire in the Windscale plutonium production reactor N of Liverpool, England, released radioactive material; later blamed for 39 cancer deaths.

Jan. 3, 1961: Reactor explosion at a federal installation near Idaho Falls, ID, killed 3 workers. Radiation contained.

Oct. 5, 1966: Sodium cooling system malfunction caused a partial core meltdown at the Enrico Fermi demonstration breeder reactor, near Detroit, MI. Radiation contained.

Jan. 21, 1969: Coolant malfunction from an experimental underground reactor at Lucens Vad, Switzerland, released radiation into a cavern, which was then sealed.

Mar. 22, 1975: Fire at the Brown's Ferry reactor in Decatur, AL, caused dangerous lowering of cooling water levels.

Mar. 28, 1979: Worst commercial nuclear accident in the U.S. occurred as equipment failures and human mistakes led to a loss of coolant and a partial core meltdown at the Three Mile Island reactor in Middletown, PA.

Feb. 11, 1981: 8 workers were contaminated when 100,000 gallons of radioactive coolant fluid leaked into containment building of TVA's Sequoyah 1 plant near Chattanooga, TN.

Apr. 25, 1981: Some 100 workers were exposed to radiation during repairs of a nuclear plant at Tsuruga, Japan.

Jan. 6, 1986: Cylinder of nuclear material burst after being improperly heated at a Kerr-McGee plant at Gore, OK. One worker died; 100 were hospitalized.

Apr. 26, 1986: In the worst nuclear accident in the history of nuclear power, fires and explosions resulting from an unauthorized experiment at the Chernobyl nuclear power plant near Kiev, USSR (now in Ukraine), left at least 31 dead in the immediate aftermath and spread radioactive material over much of Europe. An estimated 135,000 people were evacuated from the region, some of which was uninhabitable for years. As a result of the radiation released, tens of thousands of excess cancer deaths (as well as increased birth defects) were expected.

Mar. 11, 2011: A 9.0-magnitude earthquake caused a devastating tsunami that inundated the Fukushima Daiichi nuclear power plant on Japan's NE coast. Three of the plant's reactors suffered partial meltdowns, and more than 12,000 tons of radioactive water was released into the sea.

Record Oil Spills

The exact number of barrels in a ton varies with the type of oil, but a good approximation is 7 barrels per ton. Each barrel contains 42 gallons.

Name, location	Date	Cause	Tons
BP *Deepwater Horizon* rig, Gulf of Mexico, U.S.	Apr. 20-July 15, 2010	Explosion	700,000[1]
Ixtoc I oil well, S Gulf of Mexico	June 3, 1979	Blowout	600,000
Nowruz oil field, Persian Gulf	Feb. 1983	Blowout	600,000 (est.)
Atlantic Empress and *Aegean Captain*, off Trinidad and Tobago	July 19, 1979	Collision	300,000
ABT Summer, off Angola	May 28, 1991	Explosion	260,000
Castillo de Bellver, off Cape Town, South Africa	Aug. 6, 1983	Fire	250,000
Amoco Cadiz, near Portsall, France	Mar. 16, 1978	Grounding	223,000
Torrey Canyon, off Land's End, England	Mar. 18, 1967	Grounding	119,000
Sea Star, Gulf of Oman	Dec. 19, 1972	Collision	115,000
Urquiola, La Coruna, Spain	May 12, 1976	Grounding	100,000

Other Notable Oil Spills

Name, location	Date	Cause	Gallons
Persian Gulf	Began Jan. 23, 1991	Spillage by Iraq	130,000,000[2]
Braer, off Shetland Islands, UK	Jan. 5, 1993	Grounding	26,000,000
Prestige, off N Spain	Nov. 13-19, 2002	Ship broke in half	22,600,000
Aegean Sea, off N Spain	Dec. 3, 1992	Unknown	21,500,000
Sea Empress, off SW Wales	Feb. 15, 1996	Grounding	18,000,000
World Glory, off South Africa	June 13, 1968	Hull failure	13,524,000
Newtown Creek, Greenpoint, Brooklyn, NY	Oct. 5, 1950-present	Industrial explosion, preceded by leaks in 1940s-50s	17,000,000
Exxon Valdez, Prince William Sound, AK	Mar. 24, 1989	Grounding	10,080,000
Ashland Oil facility, Floreffe, PA; Monongahela R.	Jan. 2, 1988	Storage tank collapse	3,850,000

(1) The Dept. of Energy estimated the spill at 4.9 mil barrels, or more than 200 mil gallons. (2) Est. by Saudi Arabia. Some estimates as low as 25 mil gal.

Some Notable Miscellaneous Disasters Since 1950

Date	Event	Location	Details	Est. deaths
1952, Dec.	Pollution	London, England	Heavy smog blanketed city; caused breathing difficulties	4,000
1973-74	Drought and famine	Ethiopia	Caused by 6-year drought	200,000
1974	Famine	Bangladesh	Caused by flooding	26,000+
1974-75	Famine	Sub-Saharan Africa	Drought in some regions, torrential rains in others, compounded by government mismanagement	40,000+
1980, summer	Heat wave	United States	June through Sept.	1,265
1984, Dec. 3	Industrial accident	Bhopal, India	Toxic gas leaked from a Union Carbide factory	16,000
1984	Famine	Africa, espec. Ethiopia	Several years of drought compounded by government mismanagement	800,000-1 mil
1986, Aug. 21	Gas	Nr. Lake Nyos, Cameroon	Volcanic lake released cloud of carbon dioxide gas	1,700
1990, July 2	Stampede	Mecca, Saudi Arabia	Pilgrims panicked in tunnel leading to the holy city	1,426
2003, summer	Heat wave	Europe	Abnormally high temperatures from Russia to Britain; France suffered most, with 14,800 dead	35,000
2005, Aug. 31	Stampede	Baghdad, Iraq	Fear of suicide bomber caused bridge stampede	1,000

Damn This Traffic Jam

Dates: Aug.-Sept. 2010. **Location:** Inner Mongolia to Hebei, China.

China experienced the worst traffic jam ever in 2010, when as many as 10,000 vehicles were trapped for up to 10 days along a 60-mi. stretch of the highway between Inner Mongolia and Beijing. Officials blamed roadwork, an increase in trucks carrying coal between Mongolia and the capital, and drivers who fell asleep in their cars waiting for the gridlock to unlock. Congestion isn't likely to improve as long as Beijing residents continue to buy new cars at the rate of 2,000 per day, as according to official estimates.

AEROSPACE

Memorable Moments in Human Spaceflight

Source: National Aeronautics and Space Administration (NASA); Congressional Research Service; World Almanac research.

The spaceflights listed are a selection of notable U.S. missions by NASA, unless otherwise noted, plus non-U.S. missions (shown with an asterisk). The non-U.S missions were sponsored by the USSR—later, the Commonwealth of Independent States (CIS) and, from 1997, Russia—or by China. Launch dates are Eastern standard time. EVA = extravehicular activity. ASTP = Apollo-Soyuz Test Project. STS = Space Transportation System, NASA's name for the overall shuttle program.

For shuttle flights, mission name is in parentheses following name of orbiter. Duration of flight is listed in hours:minutes for 1961-Apr. 1970; days (d.), hours (hr.), and minutes (min.) for June 1970-Nov. 1981; days only thereafter. Number of total flights taken by each crew member is given in parentheses when flight listed is not the person's first.

4/12/1961: *Vostok 1*; 1:48; Yuri A. Gagarin. **1st human orbital flight.**

5/5/1961: *Mercury-Redstone 3*; 0:15; Alan B. Shepard Jr. **1st American in space.**

7/21/1961: *Mercury-Redstone 4*; 0:15; Virgil I. Grissom. Flight successful but spacecraft sank shortly after splashdown, Grissom rescued.

8/6/1961: **Vostok 2*; 25:18; Gherman S. Titov. 1st spaceflight of more than 24 hours.

2/20/1962: *Mercury-Atlas 6*; 4:55; John H. Glenn Jr. **1st American in orbit**; 3 orbits.

5/24/1962: *Mercury-Atlas 7*; 4:56; M. Scott Carpenter. Manual retrofire error caused 250-mi landing overshoot.

8/11/1962: **Vostok 3*; 94:22; Andrian G. Nikolayev. *Vostok 3* and *4* made 1st group flight.

8/12/1962: **Vostok 4*; 70:57; Pavel R. Popovich. On 1st orbit, it came within 3 mi of *Vostok 3*.

10/3/1962: *Mercury-Atlas 8*; 9:13; Walter M. Schirra Jr. Landed 5 mi from target; 6 orbits.

5/15/1963: *Mercury-Atlas 9*; 34:19; L. Gordon Cooper. 1st U.S. evaluation of effects of one day in space on a person; 22 orbits.

6/14/1963: **Vostok 5*; 119:06; Valery F. Bykovsky. *Vostok 5* and *6* made 2nd group flight.

6/16/1963: **Vostok 6*; 70:50; Valentina V. Tereshkova. **1st woman in space**; passed within 3 mi of *Vostok 5*.

10/12/1964: **Voskhod 1*; 24:17; Vladimir M. Komarov, Konstantin P. Feoktistov, Boris B. Yegorov. 1st 3-person orbital flight; 1st without space suits.

3/18/1965: **Voskhod 2*; 26:02; Pavel I. Belyayev, Aleksei A. Leonov. Leonov made **1st "space walk"** (10 min.).

3/23/1965: *Gemini-Titan 3*; 4:53; Virgil I. Grissom (2), John W. Young. 1st piloted spacecraft to change its orbital path.

6/3/1965: *Gemini-Titan 4*; 97:56; James A. McDivitt, Edward H. White II. White was **1st American to "walk in space"** (36 min.).

8/21/1965: *Gemini-Titan 5*; 190:55; L. Gordon Cooper (2), Charles Conrad Jr. Longest-duration human flight to date.

12/4/1965: *Gemini-Titan 7*; 330:35; Frank Borman, James A. Lovell. Longest-duration *Gemini* flight.

12/15/1965: *Gemini-Titan 6A*; 25:51; Walter M. Schirra Jr. (2), Thomas P. Stafford. Completed 1st U.S. space rendezvous, with *Gemini 7*.

3/16/1966: *Gemini-Titan 8*; 10:41; Neil A. Armstrong, David R. Scott. **1st docking of one space vehicle with another**; mission aborted, control malfunction; 1st Pacific landing.

6/3/1966: *Gemini-Titan 9A*; 72:21; Thomas P. Stafford (2), Eugene A. Cernan. Performed simulation of lunar module rendezvous.

7/18/1966: *Gemini-Titan 10*; 70:47; John W. Young (2), Michael Collins. 1st use of Agena target vehicle's propulsion systems; 1st orbital docking.

9/12/1966: *Gemini-Titan 11*; 71:17; Charles Conrad Jr. (2), Richard F. Gordon Jr. 1st tethered flight; highest Earth-orbit altitude (850 mi).

11/11/1966: *Gemini-Titan 12*; 94:34; James A. Lovell (2), Edwin E. "Buzz" Aldrin Jr. Final *Gemini* mission; 5-hr. EVA.

4/23/1967: **Soyuz 1*; 26:40; Vladimir M. Komarov (2). Crashed on reentry, killing Komarov; **1st space fatality**.

10/11/1968: *Apollo-Saturn 7*; 260:09; Walter M. Schirra Jr. (3), Donn F. Eisele, R. Walter Cunningham. 1st piloted flight of *Apollo* spacecraft command-service module only; live TV footage of crew.

12/21/1968: *Apollo-Saturn 8*; 147:00; Frank Borman (2), James A. Lovell (3), William A. Anders. **1st lunar orbit** and piloted lunar return reentry (command-service module only); views of lunar surface televised to Earth.

1/14/1969: **Soyuz 4*; 71:21; Vladimir A. Shatalov. Docked with *Soyuz 5*.

1/15/1969: **Soyuz 5*; 72:54; Boris V. Volyanov, Aleksei S. Yeliseyev, Yevgeny V. Khrunov. Docked with *Soyuz 4*; Yeliseyev and Khrunov transferred to *Soyuz 4* via a spacewalk.

3/3/1969: *Apollo-Saturn 9*; 241:00; James A. McDivitt (2), David R. Scott (2), Russell L. Schweickart. 1st piloted flight of lunar module.

5/18/1969: *Apollo-Saturn 10*; 192:03; Thomas P. Stafford (3), John W. Young (3), Eugene A. Cernan (2). 1st lunar module orbit of Moon, 50,000 ft from Moon's surface.

7/16/1969: *Apollo-Saturn 11*; 195:18; Neil A. Armstrong (2), Michael Collins (2), Edwin E. "Buzz" Aldrin Jr. (2). **1st Moon landing** made by Armstrong and Aldrin (7/20); collected 48.5 lbs of soil, rock samples; lunar stay time 21:36.

10/11/1969: **Soyuz 6*; 118:43; Georgi S. Shonin, Valery N. Kubasov. 1st welding of metals in space.

10/12/1969: **Soyuz 7*; 118:40; Anatoly A. Flipchenko, Vladislav N. Volkov, Viktor V. Gorbatko. Space lab construction test made; *Soyuz 6*, *7*, and *8*: 1st time 3 spacecraft, 7 crew members orbited the Earth at once.

10/13/1969: **Soyuz 8*; 118:51; Vladimir A. Shatalov (2), Aleksei S. Yeliseyev (2). Part of space lab construction team.

11/14/1969: *Apollo-Saturn 12*; 244:36; Charles Conrad Jr. (3), Richard F. Gordon Jr. (2), Alan L. Bean. Conrad and Bean made **2nd Moon landing** (11/18); collected 74.7 lbs of samples; lunar stay time 31:31.

4/11/1970: *Apollo-Saturn 13*; 142:54; James A. Lovell (4), Fred W. Haise Jr., John L. Swigert Jr. Aborted after service module oxygen tank ruptured; crew returned in lunar module.

6/1/1970: **Soyuz 9*; 17 d., 16 hr., 59 min.; Andrian G. Nikolayev (2), Vitaliy I. Sevastyanov. Longest human spaceflight to date.

1/31/1971: *Apollo-Saturn 14*; 9 d., 2 min.; Alan B. Shepard Jr. (2), Stuart A. Roosa, Edgar D. Mitchell. Shepard and Mitchell made **3rd Moon landing** (2/3); collected 96 lbs of lunar samples; lunar stay 33:31.

4/19/1971: **Salyut 1*; launched without crew. **1st space station**.

4/22/1971: **Soyuz 10*; 1 d., 23 hr., 46 min.; Vladimir A. Shatalov (3), Aleksei S. Yeliseyev (3), Nikolay N. Rukavishnikov. **1st successful docking with a space station**; failed to enter space station.

6/6/1971: **Soyuz 11*; 23 d., 28 hr., 22 min.; Georgi T. Dobrovolskiy, Vladislav N. Volkov (2), Viktor I. Patsayev. Docked and entered *Salyut 1* space station; **crew died** during reentry from loss of pressurization.

7/26/1971: *Apollo-Saturn 15*; 12 d., 17 hr., 12 min.; David R. Scott (3), James B. Irwin, Alfred M. Worden. Scott and Irwin made **4th Moon landing** (7/30). 1st lunar rover use; 1st deep space walk; 170 lbs of samples; 66:55 stay.

4/16/1972: *Apollo-Saturn 16*; 11 d., 1 hr., 51 min.; John W. Young (4), Charles M. Duke Jr., Thomas K. Mattingly II. Young and Duke made **5th Moon landing** (4/20); collected 213 lbs of lunar samples; lunar stay 71:02.

12/7/1972: *Apollo-Saturn 17*; 12 d., 13 hr., 52 min.; Eugene A. Cernan (3), Ronald E. Evans, Harrison H. Schmitt. Cernan and Schmitt made 6th and **last lunar landing** (12/11); collected 243 lbs of samples; record lunar stay over 75 hrs.

5/14/1973: *Skylab 1*; launched without crew. **1st U.S. space station**; fell out of orbit 7/11/1979.

5/25/1973: *Skylab 2*; 28 d., 49 min.; Charles Conrad Jr. (4), Joseph P. Kerwin, Paul J. Weitz. 1st U.S.-piloted orbiting space station; crew repaired damage caused in boost.

7/28/1973: *Skylab 3*; 59 d., 11 hr., 1 min.; Alan L. Bean (2), Owen K. Garriott, Jack R. Lousma. Crew systems and operational tests; scientific activities; 3 EVAs, 13:44.

11/16/1973: *Skylab 4*; 84 d., 1 hr., 16 min.; Gerald P. Carr, Edward G. Gibson, William R. Pogue. Final *Skylab* mission.

7/15/1975: **Soyuz 19 (ASTP)*; 6 d., 11 hr., 31 min.; Aleksei A. Leonov (2), Valery N. Kubasov (2). U.S.-USSR joint flight; crews linked up in space (7/17), conducted experiments, shared meals, held a joint news conference.

7/15/1975: *Apollo (ASTP)*; 9 d., 7 hr., 28 min.; Vance D. Brand, Thomas P. Stafford (4), Donald K. Slayton. Joint flight with *Soyuz 19*.

12/10/1977: **Soyuz 26*; 96 d., 10 hr.; Yuri V. Romanenko, Georgiy M. Grechko (2). 1st multiple docking at a space station (*Soyuz 26* and *27* docked at *Salyut 6*).

1/10/1978: **Soyuz 27*; 5 d., 22 hr., 59 min.; Vladimir A. Dzhanibekov. See *Soyuz 26*.

3/2/1978: **Soyuz 28*; 7 d., 22 hr., 16 min.; Aleksei A. Gubarev (2), Vladimir Remek. 1st international crew launch; Remek was 1st Czech in space.

4/12/1981: *Columbia (STS-1)*; 2 d., 6 hr., 21 min.; John W. Young (5), Robert L. Crippen. **1st reusable space shuttle** to fly into Earth's orbit.

11/12/1981: *Columbia (STS-2)*; 3 days; Joe H. Engle, Richard H. Truly. 1st scientific payload; 1st reuse of space shuttle.

11/11/1982: *Columbia (STS-5)*; 6 days; Vance D. Brand (2), Robert F. Overmyer, William Lenoir, Joseph Allen. 1st 4-person crew.

6/18/1983: *Challenger (STS-7)*; 7 days; Robert L. Crippen (2), Frederick Hauck, Sally K. Ride, John M. Fabian, Norman E. Thagard. Ride was **1st U.S. woman in space**; 1st 5-person crew.

6/27/1983: **Soyuz T-9*; 150 days; Vladimir A. Lyakhov (2), Aleksandr Pavlovich. Docked at *Salyut 7*. 1st construction in space.

8/30/1983: *Challenger (STS-8)*; 7 days; Richard H. Truly (2), Daniel Brandenstein, William Thornton, Guion Bluford, Dale Gardner. Bluford was **1st African American in space**; **1st night launch**.

11/28/1983: *Columbia (STS-9)*; 11 days; John W. Young (6), Brewster Shaw Jr., Robert Parker, Owen K. Garriott (2), Byron Lichtenberg, Ulf Merbold. 1st 6-person crew; 1st Spacelab mission.

2/3/1984: *Challenger (41-B)*; 8 days; Vance Brand (3), Robert Gibson, Ronald McNair, Bruce McCandless, Robert Stewart. 1st untethered EVA.

2/8/1984: **Soyuz T-10B*; 63 days; Leonid Kizim, Vladimir Solovyov, Oleg Atkov. Docked with *Salyut 7*; crew set space duration record of 237 days.

4/3/1984: **Soyuz T-11*; 182 days; Yury Malyshev (2), Gennady Strekalov (2), Rakesh Sharma. Docked with *Salyut 7*; Sharma was 1st Indian in space.

4/6/1984: *Challenger (41-C)*; 7 days; Robert L. Crippen (3), Francis R. Scobee, George D. Nelson, Terry J. Hart, James D. van Hoften. 1st in-orbit satellite repair.

7/17/1984: **Soyuz T-12*; 12 days; Vladimir A. Dzhanibekov (4), Svetlana Y. Savitskaya (2), Igor P. Volk. Docked at *Salyut 7*; Savitskaya was 1st woman to perform EVA.

8/30/1984: *Discovery (41-D)*; 7 days; Henry W. Hartsfield (2), Michael L. Coats, Richard M. Mullane, Steven A. Hawley,

Judith A. Resnik, Charles D. Walker. 1st flight of U.S. non-astronaut (Walker).

10/5/1984: *Challenger (41-G)*; 9 days; Robert L. Crippen (4), Jon A. McBride, Kathryn D. Sullivan, Sally K. Ride (2), Marc Garneau, David C. Leestma, Paul D. Scully-Power. 1st 7-person crew.

11/8/1984: *Discovery (51-A)*; 8 days; Frederick Hauck (2), David M. Walker (2), Dr. Anna L. Fisher, Joseph Allen (2), Dale Gardner (2). 1st satellite retrieval/repair.

4/12/1985: *Discovery (51-D)*; 7 days; Karol J. Bobko, Donald E. Williams, Jake Garn, Charles D. Walker (2), Jeffrey A. Hoffman, S. David Griggs, M. Rhea Seddon. Garn (R, UT) was **1st U.S. senator in space**.

6/17/1985: *Discovery (51-G)*; 8 days; Daniel Brandenstein (2), John O. Creighton, Shannon W. Lucid, Steven R. Nagel, John M. Fabian (2), Prince Sultan Salman al-Saud, Patrick Baudry. Launched 3 satellites; Salman al-Saud was 1st Arab in space; Baudry was 1st French person on U.S. mission.

10/3/1985: *Atlantis (51-J)*; 5 days; Karol J. Bobko (3), Ronald J. Grabe, David C. Hilmers, Robert Stewart (2), William A. Pailes. 1st *Atlantis* flight.

10/30/1985: *Challenger (61-A)*; 8 days; Henry W. Hartsfield (3), Steven R. Nagel (2), James F. Buchli (2), Guion Bluford (2), Bonnie J. Dunbar, Wubbo J. Ockels, Richard Furrer, Ernst Messerschmid. 1st 8-person crew; 1st German Spacelab mission.

1/12/1986: *Columbia (61-C)*; 7 days; Robert Gibson (2), Charles F. Bolden Jr., Steven A. Hawley (2), George D. Nelson (2), Franklin R. Chang-Diaz, Robert J. Cenker, Bill Nelson. Nelson (D, FL) was **1st U.S. representative in space**.

1/28/1986: *Challenger (51-L)*; 73 seconds; Francis R. Scobee (2), Michael J. Smith, Judith A. Resnik, Ellison S. Onizuka (2), Ronald E. McNair, Gregory B. Jarvis, Christa McAuliffe. **Exploded 73 seconds after liftoff; all aboard were killed**, including McAuliffe, a New Hampshire schoolteacher who won a national competition to become 1st private citizen in space.

2/20/1986: **Mir[1]*; launched without crew. **Space station** with 6 docking ports launched.

3/13/1986: **Soyuz T-15*; 125 days; Leonid Kizim (3), Vladimir Solovyov (2). Ferry between stations; docked at *Mir*.

2/5/1987: **Soyuz TM-2*; 327 days; Yuri V. Romanenko (3), Aleksandr I. Laveikin. Romanenko set endurance record, since broken.

7/22/1987: **Soyuz TM-3*; 161 days; Aleksandr Viktorenko, Aleksandr Pavlovich Aleksandrov (2), Mohammed Faris. Docked with *Mir*; Faris was 1st Syrian in space.

9/29/1988: *Discovery (STS-26)*; 4 days; Frederick Hauck (3), Richard O. Covey (2), David C. Hilmers (2), George D. Nelson (3), John M. Lounge (2). **1st shuttle flight since Challenger explosion** 1/28/1986.

5/4/1989: *Atlantis (STS-30)*; 4 days; David M. Walker (2), Ronald J. Grabe (2), Norman E. Thagard (3), Mary L. Cleave (2), Mark C. Lee. Launched Venus orbiter *Magellan*.

10/18/1989: *Atlantis (STS-34)*; 5 days; Donald E. Williams (2), Michael J. McCulley, Shannon W. Lucid (2), Franklin R. Chang-Diaz (2), Ellen S. Baker. Launched Jupiter probe and orbiter *Galileo*.

4/24/1990: *Discovery (STS-31)*; 6 days; Loren J. Shriver (2), Charles F. Bolden Jr. (2), Steven A. Hawley (3), Bruce McCandless (2), Kathryn D. Sullivan (2). **Launched Hubble Space Telescope**.

10/6/1990: *Discovery (STS-41)*; 5 days; Richard N. Richards (2), Robert D. Cabana, Bruce E. Melnick, William M. Shepherd (2), Thomas D. Akers. Launched *Ulysses* spacecraft to investigate interstellar space and the Sun.

5/18/1991: **Soyuz TM-12*; 145 days; Anatoly Artsebarskiy, Sergei Krikalev (2) (to *Mir*), Helen Sharman. Docked with *Mir*; Sharman was 1st Briton in space.

3/17/1992: **Soyuz TM-14*; 146 days; Aleksandr Viktorenko (3) (to *Mir*), Alexandr Kaleri (to *Mir*), Klaus-Dietrich Flade, Aleksandr

Volkov (3) (from *Mir*), Sergei Krikalev (2) (from *Mir*). 1st human CIS space mission; docked with *Mir* 3/19; Krikalev was in space 313 days.

5/7/1992: *Endeavour (STS-49)*; 9 days; Daniel Brandenstein (4), Thomas D. Akers (2), Kevin C. Chilton, Richard J. Hieb (2), Bruce E. Melnick (2), Kathryn Thornton (2), Pierre J. Thuot (2). 1st 3-person EVA; satellite recovery and redeployment.

9/12/1992: *Endeavour (STS-47)*; 8 days; Robert Gibson (4), Jay Apt (2), Curtis L. Brown Jr. (2), N. Jan Davis (2), Mae Carol Jemison, Mark C. Lee (2), Mamoru Mohri. Jemison was **1st black woman in space**; Lee and Davis were **1st married couple to travel together in space**; 1st Japanese Spacelab.

6/21/1993: *Endeavour (STS-57)*; 10 days; Ronald J. Grabe (4), Brian J. Duffy (2), G. David Low (2), Nancy J. Sherlock, Janice E. Voss, Peter J. K. Wisoff. Carried Spacelab commercial payload module.

12/2/1993: *Endeavour (STS-61)*; 11 days; Richard O. Covey (3), Kenneth D. Bowersox (2), Claude Nicollier (2), F. Story Musgrave (5), Thomas D. Akers (3), Kathryn Thornton (3), Jeffrey A. Hoffman (4). Hubble Space Telescope repaired; Akers set new U.S. EVA duration record (29 hr., 40 min.).

2/3/1994: *Discovery (STS-60)*; 9 days; Charles F. Bolden Jr. (3), Kenneth S. Reightler Jr. (2), N. Jan Davis (2), Franklin R. Chang-Diaz (3), Ronald M. Sega, Sergei Krikalev (3). Krikalev was 1st Russian on U.S. shuttle.

7/1/1994: **Soyuz TM-19*; 126 days; Yuri I. Malenchenko, Talgat A. Musabayev, Ulf Merbold (3) (from *Mir*). Docked with *Mir*.

9/9/1994: *Discovery (STS-64)*; 11 days; Richard N. Richards (4), L. Blaine Hammond Jr. (2), Jerry M. Linenger, Susan J. Helms (2), Carl J. Meade (3), Mark C. Lee (3). Performed atmospheric research; 1st untethered EVA in more than 10 years.

2/3/1995: *Discovery (STS-63)*; 9 days; James D. Wetherbee (3), Eileen M. Collins, Bernard A. Harris (2), C. Michael Foale (3), Janice E. Voss (2), Vladimir Titov (4). *Discovery* and Russian space station rendezvous.

3/2/1995: *Endeavour (STS-67)*; 17 days; Stephen S. Oswald (3), William G. Gregory, Samuel T. Durrance (2), Ronald Parise (2), Wendy B. Lawrence, Tamara E. Jernigan (3), John M. Grunsfeld. Shuttle data made available on the Internet.

3/14/1995: **Soyuz TM-21*; 112 days; Norman E. Thagard (5), Vladimir Dezhurov, Gennady Strekalov (5). Docked with *Mir* 3/16. Thagard was 1st American onboard Russian spacecraft; Valery Polyakov returned to Earth, 3/22/1995, after record stay in space (439 days).

6/27/1995: *Atlantis (STS-71)*; 10 days; Robert Gibson (5), Charles J. Precourt (2), Ellen S. Baker (3), Gregory J. Harbaugh (3), Bonnie J. Dunbar (4), Anatoly Solovyev (4) (to *Mir*), Nikolai M. Budarin (to *Mir*), Norman E. Thagard (5) (from *Mir*), Gennady Strekalov (from *Mir*), Vladimir Dezhurov (from *Mir*). **1st shuttle-*Mir* docking**; exchanged crew members with *Mir*.

11/12/1995: *Atlantis (STS-74)*; 9 days; Kenneth D. Cameron (3), James D. Halsell Jr. (2), Chris Hadfield, Jerry L. Ross (5), William S. McArthur (2). 2nd shuttle-*Mir* docking (11/15-11/18); erected a 15-ft permanent docking tunnel to *Mir* for future use by U.S. orbiters.

2/22/1996: *Columbia (STS-75)*; 16 days; Andrew M. Allen (3), Scott J. Horowitz, Franklin R. Chang-Diaz (5), Umberto Guidoni, Jeffrey A. Hoffman (5), Maurizio Cheli, Claude Nicollier (3). Lost an Italian satellite when its tether was severed; microgravity experiments performed; singe marks found on 2 O-rings.

3/22/1996: *Atlantis (STS-76)*; 10 days; Kevin C. Chilton (3), Richard A. Searfoss (2), Ronald M. Sega (2), Michael R. Clifford (3), Linda Godwin (3), Shannon W. Lucid (5) (to *Mir*). 3rd shuttle-*Mir* docking (5 days); 2-person EVA.

9/16/1996: *Atlantis (STS-79)*; 11 days; Jay Apt (4), Terry W. Wilcutt (2), William Readdy (3), Thomas D. Akers (4), Carl E. Walz (3), Shannon W. Lucid (5) (from *Mir*), John E. Blaha (5) (to *Mir*).

Docked with *Mir* 9/18; exchanged crew members; Lucid set **U.S. and women's duration in space record** (188 days).

11/19/1996: *Columbia (STS-80)*; 18 days; Kenneth D. Cockrell (3), Kent V. Rominger (2), Tamara E. Jernigan (4), Thomas D. Jones (3), F. Story Musgrave (6). Longest-duration shuttle flight; Musgrave, 61, oldest thus far to fly in space; 2 science satellites deployed, retrieved.

1/12/1997: *Atlantis (STS-81)*; 11 days; Michael A. Baker (4), John M. Grunsfeld (2), Marsha Ivins (4), Brent W. Jett (2), Peter J. K. Wisoff (3), Jerry M. Linenger (2) (to *Mir*), John E. Blaha (5) (from *Mir*). Docked with *Mir* 1/14-1/19; Blaha spent 128 days in space.

2/11/1997: *Discovery (STS-82)*; 10 days; Kenneth D. Bowersox (4), Gregory J. Harbaugh (4), Steven A. Hawley (4), Scott J. Horowitz (2), Mark C. Lee (4), Steve Smith (2), Joe Tanner (2). Increased capabilities of Hubble Space Telescope; 5 EVAs used to service it.

5/15/1997: *Atlantis (STS-84)*; 10 days; Charles J. Precourt (3), Jean-François Clervoy (2), Eileen M. Collins (2), Elena Kondakova, Edward T. Lu, Carlos Noriega, C. Michael Foale (4) (to *Mir*), Jerry M. Linenger (2) (from *Mir*). Docked with *Mir* 5/16-5/21.

8/5/1997: **Soyuz TM-26*; 198 days; Anatoly Solovyev (5), Pavel Vinogradov. Docked with *Mir* 8/7; repaired damaged space station.

8/7/1997: *Discovery (STS-85)*; 12 days; Curtis L. Brown Jr. (4), Robert L. Curbeam Jr., N. Jan Davis (3), Stephen K. Robinson, Kent V. Rominger (3), Bjarni V. Tryggvason. Deployed and retrieved satellite designed to study Earth's middle atmosphere; demonstrated robotic arm.

9/25/1997: *Atlantis (STS-86)*; 11 days; James D. Wetherbee (4), Michael J. Bloomfield, Vladimir Titov (4), Scott Parazynski (2), Jean-Loup Chrétien (3), Wendy B. Lawrence (2), David A. Wolf (2) (to *Mir*), C. Michael Foale (4) (from *Mir*). Docked with *Mir* 9/27-10/3/1997; delivered new computer to *Mir*; stay on *Mir* marked by major collision with cargo ship 6/25/1997.

4/17/1998: *Columbia (STS-90)*; 16 days; Richard A. Searfoss (3), Scott D. Altman, Richard M. Linnehan (2), Dave R. Williams, Kathryn P. Hire, Jay C. Buckey, James A. Pawelczyk. Studied effects of microgravity on the nervous systems of the crew and more than 2,000 live animals; 1st surgery in space on animals meant to survive.

6/2/1998: *Discovery (STS-91)*; 10 days; Charles J. Precourt (4), Dominic L. Gorie, Wendy B. Lawrence (3), Franklin R. Chang-Diaz (6), Janet L. Kavandi, Valery Ryumin (2), Andrew S.W. Thomas (2) (from *Mir*). Final docking mission with *Mir*; Thomas from *Mir*, 141 days in space.

10/29/1998: *Discovery (STS-95)*; 10 days; Curtis L. Brown Jr. (5), Steven W. Lindsey (2), Scott Parazynski (3), Stephen K. Robinson (2), Pedro Duque, Chiaki Mukai (2), John H. Glenn Jr. (2). Glenn, one of the original *Mercury* astronauts, and at that point a senator (D, OH), 77, was **oldest person to fly in space**; Duque was 1st Spaniard in space; experiments to study aging performed on Glenn.

12/4/1998: *Endeavour (STS-88)*; 12 days; Robert D. Cabana (4), Frederick W. Sturckow, Nancy J. Currie (3), Jerry L. Ross (6), James H. Newman (3), Sergei Krikalev (4). **1st assembly of International Space Station (ISS)**; attached U.S.-built *Unity* connecting module to Russian-built *Zarya* control module; 1st crew to enter ISS.

7/23/1999: *Columbia (STS-93)*; 5 days; Eileen M. Collins (3), Jeffrey S. Ashby, Steven A. Hawley (5), Catherine G. Coleman (2), Michel Tognini (2). Collins was **1st woman space shuttle commander**; deployed Chandra X-ray Observatory telescope.

2/11/2000: *Endeavour (STS-99)*; 12 days; Kevin R. Kregel (4), Dominic L. Gorie (2), Janet L. Kavandi (2), Janice E. Voss (5), Mamoru Mohri (2), Gerhard P.J. Thiele (2). Used radar to make most complete topographic map of Earth's surface ever produced.

9/8/2000: *Atlantis (STS-106)*; 12 days; Terry W. Wilcutt (4), Scott D. Altman (2), Edward T. Lu (2), Richard A. Mastracchio, Daniel C. Burbank, Yuri I. Malenchenko (2), Boris V. Morukov. Prepared ISS for 1st permanent crew; 1 EVA by all 7 crew members.

10/31/2000: **Soyuz TM-31*; William M. Shepherd (4), Yuri Gidzenko (2), Sergei Krikalev (5). Established **1st permanent manning of ISS** with 3-person crew for a 4-month stay.

3/8/2001: *Discovery (STS-102)*; 13 days; James D. Wetherbee (5), James M. Kelly, Susan J. Helms (3) (to ISS), James S. Voss (5) (to ISS), Paul Richards, Andrew S.W. Thomas (2), Yuri V. Usachev (4) (to ISS), William M. Shepherd (4) (from ISS), Yuri Gidzenko (2) (from ISS), Sergei Krikalev (5) (from ISS). Transported 2nd permanent crew to ISS and returned 1st crew to Earth; 2 EVAs.

7/12/2001: *Atlantis (STS-104)*; 13 days; Steven W. Lindsey (3), Charles O. Hobaugh, Michael L. Gernhardt (4), Janet L. Kavandi (3), James F. Reilly II (2). Installed a Joint Airlock, with nitrogen and oxygen tanks to permit future spacewalks from the ISS; 3 EVAs.

3/1/2002: *Columbia (STS-109)*; 11 days; Scott D. Altman (3), Duane G. Carey, John M. Grunsfeld (4), Nancy J. Currie (4), Richard M. Linnehan (3), James H. Newman (4), Michael J. Massimino. Installed powerful new camera and upgraded other equipment in Hubble Space Telescope; 5 EVAs.

4/8/2002: *Atlantis (STS-110)*; 11 days; Michael J. Bloomfield (3), Stephen N. Frick, Rex J. Walheim, Ellen Ochoa (4), Lee M.E. Morin, Jerry L. Ross (7), Steven L. Smith (4). Installed S0 Truss, backbone for expansion of ISS; Ross set records with 7th spaceflight, 9th spacewalk.

10/30/2002: **Soyuz TMA-1*[2]; Sergei Zalyotin (2), Frank De Winne, Yuri Lonchakov (2). 1st launch of *Soyuz TMA*; (crew returned 11/10/2002 on *Soyuz TM-34* already docked at ISS).

1/16/2003: *Columbia (STS 107)*; 16 days; Rick Husband (2), William McCool, Michael Anderson (2), David Brown, Kalpana Chawla (2), Laurel Clark, Ilan Ramon. **Entire crew lost when** *Columbia* **burned** during reentry, 2/1; Ramon was 1st Israeli astronaut.

10/15/2003: **Shenzhou 5*; 21 hr.; Yang Liwei. **1st Chinese manned spacecraft.**

6/21/2004: *SpaceShipOne*; 90 min.; Mike Melvill. **1st privately funded manned spaceflight**[3].

7/26/2005: *Discovery (STS-114)*; 14 days; Charles Camarda, Eileen M. Collins (4), James M. Kelly (2), Wendy B. Lawrence (4), Soichi Noguchi, Stephen K. Robinson (3), Andrew S.W. Thomas (3). **1st space shuttle flight since** *Columbia* **disaster;** tested new safety modifications to craft.

7/4/2006: *Discovery (STS-121)*; 13 days; Steven W. Lindsey (4), Mark E. Kelly, Michael E. Fossum, Piers J. Sellers (2), Lisa M. Nowak, Thomas Reiter (to ISS), Stephanie D. Wilson. **1st shuttle to launch on Independence Day;** conducted more safety tests to craft; brought supplies to and performed maintenance on ISS.

4/7/2007: **Soyuz TMA-10*[2]; Oleg Kotov (to ISS), Sheikh Muszaphar Shukor (from ISS), Charles Simonyi (U.S.) Fyodor Yurchikhin (to ISS). Kotov and Yurchikhin joined ISS expedition 15; Simonyi became **5th space tourist** (returned on *TMA-9*); Shukor was 1st Malaysian in space (arrived on *TMA-11*).

6/8/2007: *Atlantis (STS-117)*; 14 days; Frederick Sturckow (3), Lee Archambault, Patrick Forrester (2), John "Danny" Olivas, Jim Reilly (3), Steven Swanson, Clayton Anderson (to ISS), Sunita L. Williams (from ISS). Delivered truss segments and

solar arrays to ISS; Williams set record for **longest spaceflight by a woman.**

8/8/2007: *Endeavour (STS-118)*; 13 days; Scott Kelly (2), Alvin Drew, Barbara R. Morgan, Charles O. Hobaugh (2), Tracy Caldwell, Rick Mastracchio (2), Dave R. Williams (2). Brought **Teacher in Space** project participant Morgan to ISS; attached new truss segment; repaired faulty gyroscope.

10/10/2007: **Soyuz TMA-11*[2]; Yuri I. Malenchenko (3), Sheikh Muszaphar Shukor (to ISS), Peggy A. Whitson (2) (from ISS), Yi So-Yeon (from ISS). Delivered and installed components of ISS; malfunctioned on return to Earth, landing short of its touchdown area but causing no fatalities.

10/23/2007: *Discovery (STS-120)*; 16 days; Pamela A. Melroy (3), Paolo Nespoli, Scott Parazynski (5), Douglas Wheelock, Stephanie Wilson, George Zamka, Daniel M. Tani (2) (to ISS), Clayton Anderson (from ISS). Installed living space (Harmony Node 2) on ISS.

2/7/2008: *Atlantis (STS-122)*; 13 days; Stephen N. Frick (2), Stanley G. Love, Leland D. Melvin, Alan G. Poindexter, Hans Schlegel (2), Léopold Eyharts (to ISS), Daniel M. Tani (from ISS), Rex J. Walheim (2). Installed European Space Agency's Columbus laboratory on the ISS; minor damage to a thermal plate caused concern about the shuttle's safety during reentry, but *Atlantis* landed safely.

3/11/2008: *Endeavour (STS-123)*; 16 days; Dominic L. Gorie (4), Robert L. Behnken, Takao Doi (2), Michael J. Foreman, Gregory H. Johnson, Richard M. Linnehan (4), Léopold Eyharts (from ISS), Garrett Reisman (to ISS). Delivered and installed components of the Japanese Kibo science laboratory.

4/8/2008: **Soyuz TMA-12*[2]; Oleg Kononenko, Sergei Volkov, Yi So-Yeon (to ISS); Richard Garriott (from ISS). Yi became 1st S. Korean in space.

5/31/2008: *Discovery (STS-124)*; 14 days; Mark E. Kelly (3), Michael E. Fossum (2), Ronald J. Garan Jr., Kenneth T. Ham, Akihiko Hoshide, Karen Nyberg, Gregory E. Chamitoff (to ISS), Garrett Reisman (from ISS). Delivered and installed pressurized and experimental modules of Kibo.

9/25/2008: **Shenzhou 7*; 68 hr.; Jing Haipeng, Liu Boming, Zhai Zhigang. Zhai completed 1st Chinese spacewalk.

10/12/2008: **Soyuz TMA-13*[2]; Richard Garriott (to ISS), Yuri V. Lonchakov (3), Michael Fincke. Garriott became 6th space tourist.

3/15/2009: *Discovery (STS-119)*; 13 days; Lee J. Archambault (2), Joseph M. Acaba, Dominic A. Antonelli, Richard R. Arnold, John L. Phillips, Steven Swanson (2), Koichi Wakata (to ISS), Sandra H. Magnus (from ISS). Delivered final solar panels and last U.S.-made truss segment.

5/11/2009: *Atlantis (STS-125)*; 13 days; Scott D. Altman (4), Andrew J. Feustel, Michael T. Good, John M. Grunsfeld (5), Gregory C. Johnson, Michael J. Massimino (2), K. Megan McArthur. Final Hubble Space Telescope servicing mission.

11/16/2009: *Atlantis (STS-129)*; 11 days; Charles O. Hobaugh (3), Randolph J. Bresnik, Michael J. Foreman (2), Leland D. Melvin (2), Robert L. Satcher Jr., Barry E. Wilmore, Nicole P. Stott (from ISS). Final Space Shuttle crew rotation flight.

6/15/2010: **Soyuz TMA-19*[2]; Fyodor Yurchikhin (3), Shannon Walker, Douglas H. Wheelock (2). 100th mission since launching of the International Space Station.

7/8/2011: *Atlantis (STS-135)*; 13 days; Christopher Ferguson (3), Doug Hurley (2), Sandy Magnus (3), Rex Walheim (3). Final Space Shuttle mission.

Note: Four Soviet cosmonauts have died during spaceflight: Vladimir Komarov was killed on *Soyuz 1* (1967) when parachute lines tangled during descent; the 3-person *Soyuz 11* crew (1971) was asphyxiated. Six Americans and an Israeli astronaut died aboard the *Columbia*; 7 Americans died in the *Challenger* explosion; and 3 astronauts—Virgil I. Grissom, Edward H. White, and Roger B. Chaffee—died in the Jan. 27, 1967, *Apollo 1* fire on the ground at Cape Canaveral, FL. (1) Space stations, such as the *Salyuts* and *Mir*, were used to house crews starting in 1971. (2) *Soyuz* crew often return from ISS on spacecraft that launched and were docked at the station before their arrival. (3) Date of first successful flight; later, SpaceShipOne flew at least 100 km (62 mi) into space, 9/29/2004, piloted by Mike Melvill, and 10/4/2004, piloted by Brian Binnie, winning the $10 mil Ansari Prize for first private venture to accomplish this feat twice within two weeks.

U.S. Manned Space Program

Source: National Aeronautics and Space Administration (NASA)

After 50 years of sending men and women into space, the United States ended its manned space program with the safe landing of the *Atlantis* space shuttle on July 21, 2011, at Florida's Kennedy Space Center. For the short term, U.S. astronauts will have to travel to and from the International Space Station (ISS) on Russian rockets, but NASA is hopeful that private companies will someday carry passengers to the ISS.

The era of the reusable space shuttle (1981-2011) was tempered by two tragedies: the Jan. 28, 1986, *Challenger* explosion, in which six astronauts and schoolteacher Christa McAuliffe were killed 73 seconds after liftoff; and the Feb. 1, 2003, accident in which all seven astronauts aboard died when the *Columbia* burned up on reentry.

The three remaining space shuttles have been marked for retirement in U.S. museums: *Discovery* will be displayed at the Smithsonian National Air and Space Museum's Udvar-Hazy Center in Virginia; *Endeavour* will reside at the California Science Center in Los Angeles, CA; and *Atlantis* will remain at the Kennedy Space Center in Central Florida. The *Enterprise*, a test vehicle and the first shuttle built, will be moved from the Udvar-Hazy Center to the Intrepid Sea, Air, and Space Museum in New York City.

Pres. Barack Obama announced Apr. 15, 2010, a new blueprint for NASA's efforts in the human exploration of space. NASA's plans include development of a heavy-lift rocket with the ability to efficiently send into orbit crew capsules, propulsion systems, and large quantities of supplies needed to reach deep space. By 2025, a new spacecraft designed for long journeys will carry astronauts to long-range destinations, including asteroids and Mars.

International Space Station

Source: National Aeronautics and Space Administration (NASA)

The International Space Station (ISS) is considered the largest cooperative scientific project in history. Construction began in 1998; it has been inhabited by international crew members since 2000.

16 cooperating nations: Brazil, Belgium, Canada, Denmark, France, Germany, Italy, Japan, Netherlands, Norway, Russia, Spain, Sweden, Switzerland, United Kingdom, United States.

The station when completed:
- Mass of 925,000 lbs
- 361 ft long, with almost an acre of solar panels
- Internal volume roughly equivalent to one-and-a-half 747 jumbo jets
- 6 laboratories
- Living space for up to 7 people

Examples of research conducted or planned:
- Studying the effects of long-term exposure to reduced gravity on plants, crystals, plant and animal cells, and pathogens
- Studying the effects on humans of long-term exposure to reduced gravity
- Recording large-scale long-term changes in Earth's environment by observing the planet from orbit
- Testing recycling technologies for human life support

Summary of Worldwide Successful Launches, 1957-2011

Source: National Aeronautics and Space Administration (NASA), World Almanac research

Year	Total[1]	Russia[2]	U.S.	ESA[3]	China	Japan	France	India	UK	Germany	Canada	Israel	Iran	S. Korea
1957-59	24	6	18	—	—	—	—	—	—	—	—	—	—	—
1960-69	1,035	399	614	2	—	—	4	—	1	—	—	—	—	—
1970-79	1,366	1,028	247	5	8	18	14	1	6	3	4	—	—	—
1980-89	1,431	1,132	191	14	16	26	5	9	4	7	5	—	—	—
1990-99	1,045	542	300	55	33	23	16	11	7	6	4	—	—	—
2000-09	603	246	206	63	52	18	0	13	0	0	0	3	1	1
2010-11[4]	94	38	24	9	17	3	0	2	0	0	0	1	0	0
Total[4]	5,598	3,391	1,600	148	126	88	39	36	18	16	13	4	1	1

(1) Includes launches sponsored by countries not shown. (2) Data for 1957-91 apply to the Soviet Union, for 1992-96 to the Commonwealth of Independent States, after 1996 to Russia. (3) European Space Agency. Member states are Austria, Belgium, Denmark, Finland, France, Germany, Greece, Ireland, Italy, Luxembourg, the Netherlands, Norway, Portugal, Spain, Sweden, Switzerland, and the United Kingdom. Canada, Hungary, and the Czech Republic also participate in some projects under cooperation agreements. (4) As of Aug. 1, 2011.

Notable Lunar and Planetary Science Missions

Source: National Aeronautics and Space Administration (NASA)

Spacecraft	Launch date[1]	Mission	Remarks
Mariner 2	Aug. 27, 1962	Venus	Passed within 22,000 mi of Venus 12/14/1962; confirmed high surface temperature on planet; contact lost 1/3/1963 at 54 mil mi.
Ranger 7	July 28, 1964	Moon	Yielded over 4,000 photos of lunar surface.
Mariner 4	Nov. 28, 1964	Mars	1st probe to fly by Mars; passed behind planet 7/14/1965; took 22 photos from 6,000 mi above surface.
Ranger 8	Feb. 17, 1965	Moon	Yielded over 7,000 photos of lunar surface.
Venera 3	Nov. 16, 1965	Venus	Soviet probe; 1st artificial probe to impact on the surface of another planet, 3/1/1966; probe failed to send back data.
Surveyor 3	Apr. 17, 1967	Moon	Scooped and tested lunar soil.
Mariner 5	June 14, 1967	Venus	In solar orbit; closest Venus flyby 10/19/1967; allowed scientists to obtain accurate readings on the composition of the Venusian atmosphere.
Mariner 6	Feb. 24, 1969	Mars	Came within 2,000 mi of Mars 7/31/1969; collected data, photos.
Mariner 7	Mar. 27, 1969	Mars	Came within 2,000 mi of Mars 8/5/1969.
Venera 7	Aug. 17, 1970	Venus	Soviet probe; 1st probe to land safely on the surface of another planet; because of high atmospheric temperatures, probe is thought to have melted.
Mariner 9	May 30, 1971	Mars	1st craft to orbit Mars 11/13/1971; sent back over 7,000 photos.
Pioneer 10	Mar. 2, 1972	Jupiter	Passed Jupiter 12/4/1973; took readings on Jupiter's composition, found that the planet is composed mostly of hydrogen; exited the planetary system 6/13/1983; transmission ended 3/31/1997 at 6.39 bil mi.
Pioneer 11	Apr. 5, 1973	Jupiter, Saturn	Passed Jupiter 12/3/1974, Saturn 9/1/1979; discovered an additional ring and 2 moons around Saturn; operated in outer solar system; transmission ended 9/30/1995.
Mariner 10	Nov. 3, 1973	Venus, Mercury	Passed Venus 2/5/1974, arrived at Mercury 3/29/1974. 1st time gravity of 1 planet (Venus) used to whip spacecraft toward another (Mercury); 1st probe to visit 2 planets; took cloud and wind pattern readings in Venusian atmosphere.

Spacecraft	Launch date[1]	Mission	Remarks
Viking 1	Aug. 20, 1975	Mars	Landed on Mars 7/20/1976; 1st probe to land safely on Mars; performed chemical analysis of soil; functioned 6 years.
Viking 2	Sept. 9, 1975	Mars	Sister probe of *Viking 1*; landed on Mars 9/3/1976; functioned 3 years.
Voyager 2	Aug. 20, 1977	Jupiter, Saturn, Uranus, Neptune	Encountered Jupiter 7/9/1979, Saturn 8/25/1981, Uranus 1/24/1986, Neptune 8/25/1989. Confirmed existence of rings around Neptune; observed Neptune's "great dark spot," which has since dissipated. Entered boundary of solar system 10/2007.
Voyager 1	Sept. 5, 1977	Jupiter, Saturn	Encountered Jupiter 3/5/1979; provided evidence of rings around Jupiter; passed near Saturn 11/12/1980; passed *Pioneer 10* to become most distant human-made object 2/17/1998; 8/15/2006 reached a distance of 100 AUs from Sun.
Pioneer Venus 1	May 20, 1978	Venus	Entered Venus orbit 12/4/1978; studied atmosphere, magnetic field, weather, and surface; fuel ran out and probe was destroyed in atomospheric entry, 8/1992.
Pioneer Venus 2 (multiprobe)	Aug. 8, 1978	Venus	Consisted of a "bus" carrying 1 large and 3 small atmospheric probes. All 4 probes entered the Venus atmosphere 12/9/1978, followed by the bus; took readings of Venusian atmosphere; probes impacted on surface.
Magellan	May 4, 1989	Venus	Landed on Venus 8/10/1990; monitored geological activity; mapped more than 99% of planet surface, observed more than 1,600 volcanoes and volcanic features, enabling creation of a 3-D map; showed that about 85% of the surface is covered by volcanic flows; ceased operating 10/11/1994.
Galileo	Oct. 18, 1989	Jupiter	Used Earth's gravity to propel it toward Jupiter; encountered Venus 2/1990, Jupiter 12/7/1995; encountered moons. Released probe into Jovian atmosphere; intentionally flown into Jupiter 9/21/2003 to prevent accidental contamination of Jupiter's moon Europa.
Mars Global Surveyor	Nov. 7, 1996	Mars	Began orbiting Mars 9/11/1997; began mapping survey of entire surface 3/9/1999; discovered a weak magnetic field on planet; observed Martian moon Phobos; found evidence of liquid water in past 6/22/2000.
Mars Pathfinder	Dec. 4, 1996	Mars	Landed on Mars 7/4/1997; rover *Sojourner* made measurements of climate and soil composition, sending thousands of surface images; ceased operating 9/27/1997.
Cassini-Huygens	Oct. 15, 1997	Saturn	Began orbiting Saturn 6/30/2004; 4-year mission to study planet's atmosphere, rings, and moons; spotted evidence of a subterranean ocean and 300-mi-wide hot spot region on moon Titan; detected an atmosphere on moon Enceladus. *Huygens* probe landed on Titan 1/14/2005; found a muddy surface, possible deposits of water ice, channels carved by liquid methane springs.
Lunar Prospector	Jan. 6, 1998	Moon	Began orbiting Moon 1/11/1998; mapped abundance of 11 elements on Moon's surface; discovered evidence of water ice at both lunar poles; crashed into crater near Moon's south pole 7/31/1999 to end mission.
Deep Space 1	Oct. 24, 1998	Comet Borrelly	Flew within 1,500 mi of comet; sent back photos showing a 6-mi-long nucleus.
Stardust	Feb. 7, 1999	Comet Wild-2	Reached comet 1/2/2004; gathered dust samples, returned to Earth 1/15/2006.
2001 Mars Odyssey	Apr. 7, 2001	Mars	Reached Mars 10/24/2001; detected evidence of water ice near south pole; primary mission to study climate and geologic history completed 8/2004; began extended mission, aiming to identify minerals on Mars.
Genesis	Aug. 8, 2001	Sun	Orbited Sun, collected particles from solar wind; capsule containing specimens crashed to Earth 9/8/2004; some samples survived.
Mars Express/ Beagle 2 lander	June 3, 2003	Mars	1st European Space Agency probe to another planet; arrived at Mars 12/2003; performed remote sensing including photography in search of subsurface water; *Beagle 2* lander was deployed 12/19/2003 but contact was lost soon after.
Mars Exploration Rovers	June 7 and July 10, 2003	Mars	Rovers *Spirit* and *Opportunity* landed on Mars 1/2004, found further evidence that water existed on surface; *Spirit* took 1st photo of a Martian meteor; survived severe dust storms in 2007. *Opportunity* explored massive Victoria Crater 9/2007-8/2008; sighted larger Endeavor Crater 3/2009.
MESSENGER	Mar. 2, 2004	Mercury	Flew by Mercury 10/6/2008, entered orbit 3/2011; provided images of 20% of Mercury's surface.
Deep Impact	Jan. 12, 2005	Comet Tempel 1	Reached Tempel 1; deployed an impact probe which slammed into comet 7/4/2005 with a force roughly equivalent to 5 tons of TNT. Mission extended post-impact and renamed EPOXI. Passed Comet Hartley 2, 11/4/2010.
Mars Reconnais-sance Orbiter	Aug. 12, 2005	Mars	Reached Mars 3/10/2006 and began taking detailed images of Martian surface; in 3/2008, found salt deposits suggesting ancient water supplies; 6/2008 found largest known crater in solar system.
New Horizons (Pluto)	Jan. 19, 2006	Pluto, Charon	Flew by Jupiter 7/2007. Due to reach Pluto and Charon in 7/2015; may examine other Kuiper Belt Objects.
Phoenix Mars Lander	Aug. 4, 2007	Mars	Landed on Mars 5/25/2008; examined northern polar region; monitored weather and analyzed minerals; evidence of water ice verified 7/31/2008; lost contact 11/2/2008.
Dawn	Sept. 27, 2007	Asteroid Belt (bet. Jupiter and Mars)	Will compare the evolution of Ceres, a dwarf planet, with Vesta, an asteroid, in an effort to shed light on the formation of the solar system.
Lunar CRater Observation and Sensing Satellite (LCROSS)	June 18, 2009	Moon	Launch vehicle's upper stage and LCROSS impacted Cabeus crater on 10/9/2009; impacts were intended to create plumes of lunar debris that could be analyzed for water content.
Mars Science Laboratory Curiosity Rover (Mars Rover)	Not before Nov. 25, 2011	Mars	Will assess whether Mars ever was, or is still today, able to support microbial life; will attempt to determine planet's habitability.

(1) Coordinated Universal Time.

Notable Proposed U.S. Space Missions in 2012

Source: National Aeronautics and Space Administration (NASA)

Planned Launch	Mission	Purpose
Feb. 3	Nuclear Spectroscopic Telescope Array (NuSTAR)	Launching from Kwajalein Atoll in the Marshall Islands, this Explorer program mission will allow astronomers to study the universe in high energy X-rays.
June	Tracking and Data Relay Satellite-K (TDRS-K)	This spacecraft is part of the next generation of space-based communications satellites providing tracking, telemetry, command, and high-bandwidth data services.

General Aviation and Air Taxi Active Aircraft, 2009

Source: Federal Aviation Administration; aircraft not associated with major airlines or the military

Aircraft	Total active	Personal	Busi-ness	Cor-porate	Instruc-tional	Aerial apps.	Aerial obser-vation	Other work	Sight-seeing	Air medical	Other	Air taxi	Air tours	Air med.
Fixed wing....	177,446	118,504	20,773	9,944	12,061	2,562	3,073	817	262	352	2,422	5,865	128	428
Piston........	157,123	115,749	18,007	1,655	11,912	1,407	2,707	657	261	280	1,961	2,117	71	85
Turboprop....	9,055	1,737	1,718	2,100	101	1,150	360	119	2	60	211	1,079	50	197
Turbojet	11,268	1,018	1,048	6,189	48	4	5	40	0	13	250	2,489	7	145
Rotorcraft.....	9,984	1,577	566	395	1,097	539	2,131	120	121	99	546	1,267	229	753
Piston.......	3,499	1,286	309	38	1,023	224	252	22	96	3	152	42	7	0
Turbine.......	6,485	290	256	357	74	315	1,879	98	25	95	394	1,225	222	753
Other aircraft...	5,480	4,564	14	3	308	0	10	47	454	0	68	0	11	0
Gliders	1,808	1,561	8	0	217	0	3	0	5	0	15	0	0	0
Lighter-than-air	3,672	3,003	5	3	92	0	7	47	449	0	52	0	11	0
Experimental...	24,419	21,748	1,024	155	287	58	67	188	11	35	763	40	0	19
Amateur......	20,794	19,152	840	3	196	0	11	149	2	0	440	0	0	0
Exhibition....	2,063	1,819	20	2	35	5	11	16	4	0	147	0	0	0
Other........	1,562	777	164	150	57	53	45	23	5	35	176	40	0	19
Light sport.....	6,547	5,879	68	0	377	2	7	5	2	0	207	0	0	0
Total aircraft	223,877	152,272	22,445	10,498	14,130	3,161	5,288	1,177	849	486	4,005	6,992	367	1,200

Note: Columns may not add up to totals due to rounding. **Personal**—Flying for personal reasons; **Business**—Individual or group use business transportation without a paid, professional crew; **Corporate**—Individual or group business transportation with a paid, professional crew (includes fractional ownership); **Instructional**—Flying under the supervision of a flight instructor; **Aerial applications**—Includes agriculture, forestry, public health, fire fighting, and other applications; **Aerial observation**—Includes aerial mapping/photography, patrol, search and rescue, hunting, traffic advisory, ranching, surveillance, oil and mineral exploration, etc.; **Other work**—Construction work, parachuting, aerial advertising, towing gliders, etc.; **Sight-seeing**—Commercial sight-seeing; **Air medical**—Air ambulance services, rescue, human organ transportation, emergency medical services; **Other**—Positioning flights, proficiency flights, training, ferrying, sales demos; **On demand operations**—On demand air taxi, air tours, commuter, and air medical services.

Estimated Active Airmen Certificates Held, 2010

Source: Federal Aviation Administration, U.S. Dept. of Transportation

Category	Certificates	Category	Certificates	Category	Certificates
Pilot total	**627,588**	Sport only	3,682	Parachute Rigger	8,407
Airplane[1]		Rotorcraft (helicopters) only	15,377	Ground Instructor	75,205
Private..............	202,020	Glider only	21,275	Dispatcher	20,691
Commercial...........	123,705	**Nonpilot total**	**686,717**	Flight Navigator.........	174
Airline Transport	142,198	Mechanic..............	331,989	Flight Attendant	156,946
Student	119,119	Repairmen.............	41,267	Flight Engineer	49,038
Recreational only........	212				

Note: The term airmen includes men and women certified as pilots, mechanics, or other aviation technicians. (1) Includes pilots with an airplane-only certificate as well as those with an airplane and a helicopter and/or glider certificate.

Aircraft Operating Statistics, 2011

Source: Airbus S.A.S., The Boeing Company, Embraer SA.

Manufacturer and model	Max. # of seats	Typical # of seats	Fuel capacity (gals.)	Typical cruising speed (mph)[1]	Max. range (naut. mi)	Max. thrust (thous. lbs)	Manufacturer and model	Max. # of seats	Typical # of seats	Fuel capacity (gals.)	Typical cruising speed (mph)[1]	Max. range (naut. mi)	Max. thrust (thous. lbs)
Airbus							**Boeing**						
A318	132	107	6,400	630	3,200	24.0	727-200*	189	148	9,806	605	2,500	17.4
A319	156	124	6,400	630	3,700	27.0	737-600	132	110	6,875	602	3,225	22.7
A320	180	150	6,400	630	3,300	27.0	737-700	149	126	6,875	602	3,440	26.3
A321	220	185	6,350	630	6,200	33.0	737-700C	140	126	6,875	599	3,285	27.3
A330-200	380	253	36,750	660	7,250	72.0	737-800	189	162	6,875	602	3,115	27.3
A330-300	440	295	26,765	660	5,850	72.0	737-900	215	180	7,837	599	3,265	27.3
A340-300	440	295	37,150	660	7,400	34.0	747-100	452	366	48,445	645	6,100	50.1
A340-500	375	313	56,870	660	9,000	56.0	747-200/300 ..	452	366	52,410	645	7,900	54.8
A340-600	475	380	51,750	660	7,900	60.0	747-400	524	416	57,285	653	7,260	63.3
A380	853	525	84,600	684	8,300	70.0	747-8	467	467	64,055	653	8,000	66.5
Embraer							757-200*	228	200	11,489	614	3,900	43.5
190	114	98	NA	630	2,400	20.0	757-300*	280	243	11,466	614	3,395	43.5
195	122	108	NA	630	2,200	20.0	767-200ER	255	181	23,980	614	6,385	62.1
McDonnell-Douglas							767-300ER	350	218	23,980	614	5,990	63.3
							767-400ER	375	245	23,980	614	5,625	63.5
							777-200	440	305	31,000	645	5,420	77.0
DC-10 series*..	380	250	36,650	600	6,220	24.0	777-200ER	440	301	45,220	645	7,725	93.7
MD-11*	410	285	NA	NA	7,360	NA	777-200LR	NA	301	47,890	645	9,395	115.3
MD-80 series*	172	155	5,840	584	2,504	21.0	777-300	550	368	45,220	645	6,005	98.0
MD-90 series*	172	153	7,620	584	3,205	28.0	777-300ER	NA	365	47,890	645	7,390	115.3

* = Aircraft no longer in production. NA = Not available. **Note:** Figures are for most commonly flown passenger models. When models within a series vary, maximums are shown. McDonnell-Douglas merged with Boeing in 1997. (1) Figures shown are converted from Mach speeds (speed of sound) which varies depending on altitude and temperature. For comparison purposes, this table uses 768 mph as equivalent to Mach 1.

Milestones in Aviation History

Source: National Aeronautics and Space Administration (NASA), National Air and Space Museum, Air Transport Association of America, National Museum of the U.S. Air Force, U.S. National Park Service

1903, Dec. 17: Brothers Wilbur and Orville Wright (U.S.) made the first human-carrying, powered flight near Kitty Hawk, NC. Each brother made two flights; the longest, about 852 ft, lasted 59 seconds.

1908, May 14: Charles Furnas (U.S.), worker for Wright brothers, became first American airplane passenger.

1911, Feb.: The Burgess Company and Curtis Inc. receive authorization to build Wright planes, becoming the first licensed airplane manufacturer in the U.S.

1911, Sept. 23: First transportation of mail by airplane officially approved by the U.S. Postal Service.

1914, Jan. 1: First scheduled passenger airline service began. A seaplane that landed on water, it operated between St. Petersburg and Tampa, FL.

1918, May 14: First scheduled air mail service began, between New York and Washington, DC, with intermediate stops in Philadelphia. In 1921, scheduled transcontinental airmail service began between New York City and San Francisco.

1919, June 14-15: Capt. John Alcock (UK) and Lt. Arthur W. Brown (U.S.) completed the first nonstop flight across the Atlantic Ocean. They traveled from Newfoundland, Canada, to Ireland in 16 hours and 12 minutes.

1923, Aug. 23: Rotating beacons enabled the first night flights.

1924, Apr. 6-Sept. 28: Two U.S. Army planes landed in Seattle, completing the first circumnavigation of the globe. They completed the 26,000-mi journey in 371 hours of flying time.

1926, May 12-13: Roald Amundsen (Norway), Umberto Nobile (Italy), Lincoln Ellsworth (U.S.), and Oscar Wisting (Norway) made the first flight over the North Pole, in a dirigible that flew between Spitsbergen, Norway, and Teller, AK. Two weeks earlier, Adm. Richard E. Byrd (U.S) and Floyd Bennett (U.S.) claimed to have made the first flight over the Pole (May 9, 1926) in a Fokker F-VII. But when Byrd's diary was released to the public in 1996, some historians began to question whether his plane indeed reached the Pole.

1927, May 20-21: Charles Lindbergh (U.S.) completed the first solo transatlantic flight in the *Spirit of St. Louis.* "Lucky Lindy" traveled 3,610 mi from New York to Paris in 33 hours, 29 minutes, and 30 seconds.

1929, Aug. 8-29: Hugo Eckener (Germany) piloted the *Graf Zeppelin* around the world in record time: 20,373 mi in 21 days, 5 hours, and 31 minutes.

1929, Nov. 28: Adm. Richard E. Byrd (U.S.) and Bernt Balchen (Norway) became the first to fly to the South Pole and back, in 18 hours and 41 minutes.

1930, May 15: Ellen Church (U.S.) became first flight attendant.

1931, June 23-July 1: Wiley Post (U.S.) and Harold Gatty (U.S.) broke the speed record for around-the-world flight. They traveled 15,474 mi in 8 days, 15 hours, and 51 minutes in the monoplane *Winnie Mae.*

1931, Oct. 3-5: Clyde Pangborn (U.S.) and Hugh Herndon (U.S.) completed the first nonstop transpacific flight. They traveled 4,558 mi from Misawa, Japan, to East Wenatchee, WA, in 41 hours and 34 minutes.

1932, May 20-21: Amelia Earhart (U.S.) completed first solo transoceanic flight by a woman. She completed the 2,026-mi journey from Newfoundland, Canada, to Ireland in 14 hours and 56 minutes.

1933, July 15-22: Wiley Post (U.S.) completed the first solo circumnavigation of the globe. His 15,596-mi trip took 7 days, 18 hours, and 49 minutes.

1936, June 25: American Airlines began scheduled passenger service of the first Douglas DC-3 aircraft. The DC-3 was the first aircraft with a kitchen onboard and hence offered the first in-flight hot meal service.

1937, May 6: German *Hindenburg* zeppelin exploded and burst into flames in Lakehurst, NJ, killing 35 of the 97 people aboard (and one on the ground). The airship had made 34 transatlantic flights in 1936.

1938, July 10-13: Howard Hughes (U.S.) and four assistants established a new speed record for circumnavigating the globe: 14,824 mi in 3 days, 9 hours, 17 minutes.

1939, Aug. 27: The German-made Heinkel He 178 made the first successful flight powered by a jet engine.

1947, June 17-30: Pan American Airways began the first scheduled around-the-world passenger flights, from New York or San Francisco.

1947, Oct. 14: Chuck Yeager (U.S.) broke the sound barrier, reaching Mach 1 speed in a Bell X-1 rocket-powered aircraft.

1947, Nov. 2: Howard Hughes (U.S.) piloted the *Spruce Goose* on its maiden and only flight. The largest airplane ever built, it could carry 750 troops or two Sherman tanks.

1949, Mar. 2: James Gallagher (U.S.) piloted the first round-the-world flight to be refueled in midair. The *Lucky Lady* U.S. Air Force (USAF) B-50 covered 23,452 mi in 94 hours and one minute and was refueled four times.

1950, Sept. 22: Col. David Schilling (USAF) made the first non-stop transatlantic jet flight, covering 3,300 mi in 10 hours and 1 minute.

1952, Aug. 26: The UK bomber Canberra made the first round-trip transatlantic crossing on the same day, from Northern Ireland to Newfoundland, Canada, and back in 7 hours and 59 minutes.

1953, May 18: Jacqueline Cochran (U.S.) became first woman to fly faster than the speed of sound.

1956, Mar. 10: Britain's Fairey FD-2 aircraft set a world speed record of 1,132 mph.

1956, Nov. 11: Convair B-58, first supersonic bomber, was introduced.

1957, Jan. 15-18: Three USAF B-52 Stratofortresses made the first nonstop global flight by jet planes. They were refueled in flight by KC-97 aerial tankers.

1958, Oct. 24: A Mirage III-A achieved Mach 2 (twice the speed of sound) in level flight, the first European plane to reach that speed.

1962, Nov. 29: Britain and France signed an agreement to jointly develop the Concorde, a supersonic plane that could fly twice as fast as most U.S. jets.

1969, June 5: The Soviet Tupolev Tu-144 became the first passenger airliner to reach Mach 2.

1970, May 26: The Tupolev Tu-144 reached a top speed of about 1,335 mph at 53,475 ft.

1976, Aug. 23: The Concorde began first scheduled supersonic commercial service.

1977, Aug. 23: The *Gossamer Condor*, built by Paul MacCready (U.S.), successfully demonstrated human-powered flight through pedalling, completing a figure-8 course of 1.15 mi.

1979, June 12: The human-powered *Gossamer Albatross*, also built by MacCready, crossed the English Channel in 2 hours and 49 minutes.

1981, July 7: *Solar Challenger* became the first solar-powered airplane to cross the English Channel.

1995, Aug. 15-16: The Concorde set a new around-the-world speed record of 31 hours, 27 minutes, and 49 seconds.

1999, Mar. 1-21: Bertrand Piccard (Switz.) and Brian Jones (UK) completed the first around-the-world flight in a hot-air balloon. Their 29,055-mi journey began in Chateau-d'Oex, Switzerland, and ended 19 days, 21 hours, and 55 minutes later in the Egyptian desert.

2001, Aug. 13: Solar-powered, propeller-driven plane *Helios* (NASA) reached 96,863 ft, breaking altitude record for non-rocket-powered aircraft.

2002, June 19-July 4: Steve Fossett (U.S.) completed the first nonstop solo circumnavigation of globe in a balloon.

2003, Nov. 26: The Concorde flew its final flight.

2005, Mar. 1-3: Steve Fossett (U.S.) achieved the first nonstop solo circumnavigation in an airplane without refueling.

2005, Apr. 27: The Airbus A380, the biggest-ever commercial jet, made its maiden voyage. It was 240 ft long, had a wingspan of 262 ft, and could seat a maximum of 840 passengers. Its first commercial flight was Oct. 25, 2007.

2006, Feb. 8-11: Steve Fossett (U.S.) flew the longest nonstop, non-refueled single flight (25,766 mi).

2009, Dec. 15: Boeing's 787 Dreamliner, the company's most fuel-efficient plane and the first to be constructed primarily from composite materials, made its maiden voyage, two years after it was originally scheduled.

ASTRONOMY

Edited by Michael J. Kaufman, Dept. of Physics and Astronomy, San Jose State University

Celestial Events Summary, 2012

There are 4 eclipses in 2012: one annular solar eclipse, one total solar eclipse, one partial lunar eclipse, and one penumbral lunar eclipse. The annular solar eclipse will be visible over a narrow path extending across the continental U.S. from N California to Texas. The partial lunar eclipse will be visible before sunrise over wide portions of N America from the Midwest to the West.

This year includes a rare transit of Venus, when the planet Venus crosses in front of the Sun as seen from Earth. The last transit occurred in 2004; the next will not occur until 2117, 105 years from now. Parts of the transit will be visible across the U.S., most of Europe, the eastern half of Africa, and the Middle East. The entire transit will be visible in the W Pacific, Siberia, Mongolia, E China, and E Australia, among other locations. From the U.S., the transit will begin before sunset on the evening of June 5. Observers in Asia and Africa will see the end of the transit after sunrise on June 6.

The most likely viewing successes for meteor showers will be the Perseids in Aug., the Orionids in Oct., the Leonids in Nov., and the Geminids in Dec. Meteor showers are far less affected by moonlight than they were in 2011, so viewing of these major showers should be improved.

At the start of the year Jupiter is high overhead at sunset, while Venus is further West, closer to the setting Sun. Mercury, Mars, and Saturn rise before the Sun and are visible in the East and overhead before sunrise. Venus is a bright evening object through May, becoming a morning object from late June onward. Jupiter is visible in the evening sky through Apr., then moves to the morning sky from late June through Oct.; by late fall, it is visible high in the sky throughout the night. Saturn is up much of the night through Apr., setting several hours after the Sun in summer and fall, and becoming an early morning object by the end of the year. The best opportunities for seeing Mercury occur in mid-Apr., mid-Aug., and early Dec.. in the morning sky and in early July and late Oct. in the evening sky.

The crescent Moon, with its subdued light, regularly makes pretty pairings with the 2 brightest planets, Venus and Jupiter. Waxing crescent pairings are visible in the early evening soon after sunset, while waning crescent pairings are visible in the early morning before sunrise. The waxing crescent Moon pairs with Venus in each of the months from Jan. through Apr. The waning crescent Moon pairs with Venus in all of the months from July through Dec. The waxing crescent Moon pairs with Jupiter in the evening in Mar. and Apr., and the waning crescent pairs with Jupiter twice in June, July and Aug. The waning crescent Moon joins Mercury, Venus, and Jupiter in the early morning sky Aug. 12-15 and joins Mercury, Venus, and Saturn in the early morning sky Dec. 9-11. The waxing crescent Moon joins Mars and Saturn in the evening sky Aug. 21.

Astronomical Positions and Constants

Two celestial bodies are in **conjunction** when they are due north and south of each other, either in **right ascension** (with respect to the north celestial pole) or in **celestial longitude** (with respect to the north ecliptic pole). Celestial bodies in conjunction will rise and set at nearly the same time. For the inner planets—Mercury and Venus—**inferior conjunction** occurs when either planet passes between Earth and the Sun, while **superior conjunction** occurs when either Mercury or Venus is on the far side of the Sun. Celestial bodies are in **opposition** when their right ascensions differ by exactly 12 hours, or when their celestial longitudes differ by 180°. In this case one of the 2 objects in opposition will rise while the other is setting. **Quadrature** refers to the arrangement where the coordinates of 2 bodies differ by exactly 90°. These terms may refer to the relative positions of any two bodies as seen from Earth, but one of the bodies is so frequently the Sun that mention of the Sun is omitted in that case.

When objects are in conjunction, the alignment is not perfect, and one is usually passing above or below the other.

The geocentric angular separation between the Sun and an object is termed **elongation**. Elongation is limited only for Mercury and Venus; the greatest elongation for each of these bodies is approximately the time for longest observation. **Perihelion** is the point in an orbit that is nearest to the Sun, and **aphelion** is the point farthest from the Sun. **Perigee** is the point in an orbit that is nearest Earth, **apogee** the point that is farthest from Earth. An **occultation** of a planet or a star is an eclipse of it by some other body, usually the Moon. A **transit** of the Sun occurs when Mercury or Venus passes directly between Earth and the Sun, appearing to cross the disk of the Sun.

The following were adopted as part of the International Astronomical Union System of Astronomical Constants (1976): **Speed of light**, 299,792.458 km per sec., or about 186,282 statute mi per sec.; **solar parallax**, 8".794148; **astronomical unit** (the mean distance between the Earth and the Sun), 149,597,870 km, or 92,955,807 mi; **constant of nutation**, 9".2025; and **constant of aberration**, 20".49552.

Celestial Events Highlights, 2012

(In Coordinated Universal Time, or UTC, the standard time of the prime meridian.)

January

Mercury is visible low in the SE before sunrise early in the month.
Venus is visible low in the SW after sunset all month.
Mars rises late in the evening and sets before sunrise.
Jupiter is high overhead at sunset and sets after midnight.
Saturn rises in the middle of the night and is visible high overhead at sunrise.
Uranus and **Neptune** are in the SW after sunset and set several hours later.

Jan. 1: Sun in Sagittarius, Mercury in Ophiuchus, Venus in Capricorn, Mars in Leo, Jupiter in Pisces, Saturn in Virgo, Uranus in Pisces, Neptune in Aquarius all year, Pluto in Sagittarius all year
Jan. 1: First Quarter Moon
Jan. 3: Jupiter passes 5.03° S of Moon
Jan. 5: Mercury enters Ophiuchus
Jan. 6: Aldebaran passes 5.83° S of Moon
Jan. 8: Jupiter enters Aries
Jan. 9: Full Moon, Pollux passes 10.28° N of Moon
Jan. 11: Venus enters Aquarius
Jan. 12: Regulus passes 5.91° N of Moon

Jan. 13: Neptune passes 1.16° N of Venus, Pluto passes 4.56° N of Mercury
Jan. 14: Mars passes 9.11° N of Moon
Jan. 15: Mars enters Virgo
Jan. 16: Last Quarter Moon, Spica passes 1.98° N of Moon, Saturn passes 6.37° N of Moon
Jan. 19: Antares passes 4.24° S of Moon
Jan. 20: Sun enters Capricorn
Jan. 21: Pluto passes 1.76° N of Moon
Jan. 22: Mercury passes 4.82° S of Moon
Jan. 23: New Moon
Jan. 25: Neptune passes 5.93° S of Moon
Jan. 26: Venus passes 6.78° S of Moon
Jan. 27: Mercury enters Capricorn
Jan. 28: Uranus passes 5.95° S of Moon
Jan. 30: Jupiter passes 4.54° S of Moon
Jan. 31: First Quarter Moon

February

Mercury is visible low in the SW after sunset late in the month.
Venus is visible low in the SW after sunset all month.

Mars rises late in the evening and sets before sunrise.
Jupiter is high overhead at sunset and sets several hours
after sunset.
Saturn rises late in the evening and is up much of the night.
Uranus sets several hours after the Sun.
Neptune begins the month setting just after the Sun and is
lost in the Sun's glare by the end of the month.

Feb. 2: Aldebaran passes 5.67° S of Moon
Feb. 3: Venus enters Pisces
Feb. 4: Mars enters Leo
Feb. 6: Pollux passes 10.30° N of Moon
Feb. 7: Full Moon, Mercury in superior conjunction 2.07° S
Feb. 8: Regulus passes 5.80° N of Moon
Feb. 10: Venus passes 0.34° N of Uranus, Mars passes 9.75°
N of Moon
Feb. 12: Spica passes 1.74° N of Moon, Mercury enters
Aquarius
Feb. 13: Saturn passes 6.22° N of Moon
Feb. 14: Last Quarter Moon, Mercury passes 1.30° S of
Neptune
Feb. 15: Antares passes 4.45° S of Moon
Feb. 16: Sun enters Aquarius
Feb. 17: Pluto passes 1.54° N of Moon
Feb. 19: Neptune passes 0.55° S of Sun
Feb. 21: New Moon, Neptune passes 5.89° S of Moon
Feb. 23: Mercury passes 6.05° S of Moon
Feb. 24: Uranus passes 5.70° S of Moon
Feb. 25: Venus passes 3.27° S of Moon
Feb. 26: Mercury enters Pisces
Feb. 27: Jupiter passes 3.84° S of Moon

March

Mercury is visible low in the SW after sunset the first half
of the month.
Venus is visible in the SW after sunset all month.
Mars rises around sunset and is up most of the night.
Jupiter is in the SW after sunset and sets a few hours later.
Saturn rises mid-evening and is up until the early morning.
Uranus is low in the SW at sunset at the start of the month
and lost in the Sun's glare by late in the month.
Neptune is visible low in the SE before sunrise.
Mar. 1: First Quarter Moon, Aldebaran passes 5.41° S of
Moon
Mar. 3: Mars at opposition
Mar. 4: Pollux passes 10.47° N of Moon, Venus enters Aries
Mar. 5: Mercury at greatest elongation 18.2° E
Mar. 7: Uranus passes 3.09° S of Mercury, Regulus passes
5.82° N of Moon
Mar. 8: Full Moon, Mars passes 9.84° N of Moon
Mar. 10: Spica passes 1.54° N of Moon
Mar. 11: Saturn passes 6.18° N of Moon, Sun enters Pisces
Mar. 13: Antares passes 4.72° S of Moon
Mar. 15: Last Quarter Moon, Jupiter passes 3.27° S of Venus
Mar. 16: Uranus passes 4.60° S of Mercury, Pluto passes
1.27° N of Moon
Mar. 20: Neptune passes 5.98° S of Moon, Vernal Equinox
Mar. 21: Mercury in inferior conjunction 3.28° N
Mar. 22: Mercury passes 1.56° S of Moon, Uranus passes
5.54° S of Moon
Mar. 24: Uranus passes 0.69° S of Sun
Mar. 26: Jupiter passes 3.09° S of Moon, Venus passes
1.85° N of Moon
Mar. 27: Venus at greatest elongation 46.0° E
Mar. 28: Aldebaran passes 5.16° S of Moon
Mar. 30: First Quarter Moon, Venus enters Taurus

April

Mercury is visible low in the SE before sunrise all month.
Venus is visible in the SW after sunset all month.
Mars is in the SE after sunset and up much of the night.
Jupiter is low in the SW after sunset and sets soon after the
Sun.
Saturn is up all night.

Uranus and Neptune are low in the SE at sunrise by the
end of the month.
Apr. 1: Pollux passes 10.71° N of Moon
Apr. 3: Regulus passes 5.95° N of Moon
Apr. 4: Mars passes 8.92° N of Moon
Apr. 6: Full Moon
Apr. 7: Spica passes 1.45° N of Moon, Saturn passes
6.28° N of Moon
Apr. 10: Antares passes 4.93° S of Moon
Apr. 12: Pluto passes 1.03° N of Moon
Apr. 13: Last Quarter Moon
Apr. 15: Saturn at opposition
Apr. 16: Neptune passes 6.15° S of Moon
Apr. 17: Aldebaran passes 9.97° S of Venus, Sun enters
Aries
Apr. 18: Mercury at greatest elongation 27.5° W
Apr. 19: Mercury passes 7.55° S of Moon, Uranus passes
5.51° S of Moon
Apr. 21: New Moon
Apr. 22: Uranus passes 2.13° N of Mercury, Jupiter passes
2.39° S of Moon
Apr. 23: Mercury enters Cetus
Apr. 24: Aldebaran passes 5.02° S of Moon
Apr. 25: Venus passes 5.70° N of Moon
Apr. 28: Pollux passes 10.89° N of Moon
Apr. 29: First Quarter Moon, Mercury enters Pisces

May

Mercury is visible low in the SE before sunrise the first half
of the month.
Venus is visible in the SW after sunset the first half of the
month.
Mars is high overhead at sunset and sets in the middle of
the night.
Jupiter is too close to the Sun to be visible this month.
Saturn is high in the SE at sunset and sets in the early
morning hours.
Uranus and Neptune rise a few hours before the Sun.
May 1: Regulus passes 6.10° N of Moon, Mars passes 7.86°
N of Moon
May 4: Spica passes 1.47° N of Moon, Saturn passes 6.44°
N of Moon
May 6: Full Moon
May 7: Antares passes 5.01° S of Moon
May 9: Pluto passes 0.93° N of Moon
May 11: Mercury enters Aries
May 12: Last Quarter Moon, Uranus enters Cetus
May 13: Jupiter passes 0.80° S of Moon, Neptune passes
6.29° S of Moon, Sun enters Taurus
May 14: Jupiter enters Taurus
May 16: Uranus passes 5.51° S of Moon
May 20: Annular Solar Eclipse, Mercury passes 2.06° S of
Moon, Jupiter passes 1.75° S of Moon
May 21: New Moon, Aldebaran passes 5.00° S of Moon,
Mercury enters Taurus
May 22: Mercury passes 0.41° N of Jupiter, Venus passes
4.71° N of Moon
May 25: Pollux passes 10.94° N of Moon
May 27: Mercury in superior conjunction 0.51° N
May 28: First Quarter Moon, Regulus passes 6.15° N of
Moon
May 29: Aldebaran passes 6.36° S of Mercury, Mars passes
6.90° N of Moon

June

Mercury is visible low in the SW after sunset late in the
month.
Venus and Jupiter are visible in the SE before sunrise the
second half of the month.
Mars is high overhead at sunset and sets around midnight.
Saturn is in the SE at sunset and sets in the early morning
hours.
Uranus and Neptune rise in the middle of the night and are
high overhead at sunrise.

June 1: Spica passes 1.50° N of Moon, Saturn passes 6.50° N of Moon, Venus passes 0.20° S of Mercury

June 4: Partial Lunar Eclipse, Full Moon, Antares passes 5.01° S of Moon

June 6: Transit of Venus (*N American observers will see the transit begin on the evening of June 5*); Pluto passes 0.95° N of Moon,

June 7: Mercury enters Gemini

June 10: Neptune passes 6.30° S of Moon

June 11: Last Quarter Moon

June 13: Uranus passes 5.46° S of Moon

June 15: Aldebaran passes 3.59° S of Venus

June 17: Jupiter passes 1.12° S of Moon

June 18: Venus passes 2.06° S of Moon, Aldebaran passes 5.00° S of Moon

June 19: New Moon

June 20: Summer Solstice, Sun enters Gemini

June 21: Pollux passes 5.22° N of Mercury, Pollux passes 10.89° N of Moon, Mercury passes 5.68° N of Moon, Mars enters Virgo

June 24: Regulus passes 6.07° N of Moon, Mercury enters Cancer

June 26: Mars passes 5.76° N of Moon

June 27: First Quarter Moon

June 28: Spica passes 1.42° N of Moon, Saturn passes 6.34° N of Moon

June 29: Pluto at opposition

July

Mercury is visible low in the SW after sunset early in the month.

Venus and **Jupiter** are visible in the SE before sunrise all month.

Mars and **Saturn** are high overhead at sunset and set around midnight.

Uranus and **Neptune** rise in the middle of the night and are high overhead at sunrise.

July 1: Antares passes 5.04° S of Moon, Mercury at greatest elongation 25.7° E

July 3: Full Moon, Pluto passes 0.99° N of Moon

July 7: Neptune passes 6.19° S of Moon

July 9: Aldebaran passes 0.92° S of Venus

July 10: Uranus passes 5.32° S of Moon

July 11: Last Quarter Moon

July 15: Jupiter passes 0.50° S of Moon, Aldebaran passes 4.93° S of Moon, Venus passes 3.82° S of Moon

July 19: New Moon, Pollux passes 10.85° N of Moon, Sun enters Cancer

July 20: Mercury passes 0.55° N of Moon

July 21: Regulus passes 5.94° N of Moon

July 24: Mars passes 4.23° N of Moon

July 25: Spica passes 1.22° N of Moon, Saturn passes 5.97° N of Moon

July 26: First Quarter Moon

July 28: Antares passes 5.17° S of Moon, Mercury in inferior conjunction 4.96° S

July 30: Pluto passes 0.92° N of Moon

August

Mercury is visible low in the SE before sunrise mid-month.

Venus and **Jupiter** are visible high in the SE before sunrise all month.

Mars and **Saturn** are high overhead at sunset and set around midnight.

Uranus and **Neptune** rise in the late evening and in the W at sunrise.

Aug. 2: Full Moon

Aug. 3: Aldebaran passes 4.74° S of Jupiter, Neptune passes 6.06° S of Moon

Aug. 5: Venus enters Orion

Aug. 6: Uranus passes 5.13° S of Moon

Aug. 9: Last Quarter Moon, Sun enters Leo

Aug. 11: Aldebaran passes 4.74° S of Moon, Jupiter passes 0.11° N of Moon

Aug. 12: Perseid meteor shower

Aug. 13: Spica passes 1.91° S of Mars, Venus passes 0.56° S of Moon, Venus enters Gemini

Aug. 15: Pollux passes 10.91° N of Moon, Venus at greatest elongation 45.8° W

Aug. 16: Mercury passes 3.55° N of Moon, Mercury at greatest elongation 18.7° W

Aug. 17: New Moon, Mars passes 2.90° S of Saturn

Aug. 18: Regulus passes 5.85° N of Moon

Aug. 21: Spica passes 0.99° N of Moon

Aug. 22: Saturn passes 5.47° N of Moon, Mars passes 2.31° N of Moon

Aug. 24: First Quarter Moon, Neptune at opposition

Aug. 25: Antares passes 5.40° S of Moon, Mercury enters Leo

Aug. 27: Pluto passes 0.70° N of Moon

Aug. 31: Full Moon, Neptune passes 6.02° S of Moon, Regulus passes 1.28° S of Mercury

September

Mercury is too close to the Sun to be seen this month.

Venus is high in the SE before sunrise all month.

Mars and **Saturn** are in the SW at sunset and set several hours later.

Jupiter rises near midnight and is high overhead at sunrise.

Uranus and **Neptune** rise around sunset and set near sunrise.

Sept. 1: Pollux passes 8.76° N of Venus

Sept. 3: Uranus passes 5.00° S of Moon

Sept. 4: Venus enters Cancer

Sept. 5: Mars enters Libra

Sept. 8: Last Quarter Moon, Aldebaran passes 4.49° S of Moon, Jupiter passes 0.62° N of Moon

Sept. 10: Mercury in superior conjunction 1.64° N

Sept. 11: Pollux passes 11.09° N of Moon

Sept. 12: Venus passes 3.74° N of Moon

Sept. 13: Mercury enters Virgo

Sept. 14: Regulus passes 5.89° N of Moon

Sept. 15: Sun enters Virgo

Sept. 16: New Moon, Mercury passes 5.90° N of Moon

Sept. 17: Uranus enters Pisces

Sept. 18: Spica passes 0.82° N of Moon, Saturn passes 4.99° N of Moon

Sept. 19: Mars passes 0.15° N of Moon

Sept. 21: Antares passes 5.64° S of Moon

Sept. 22: First Quarter Moon, Autumnal Equinox

Sept. 23: Pluto passes 0.38° N of Moon, Venus enters Leo

Sept. 27: Neptune passes 6.10° S of Moon

Sept. 29: Uranus at opposition

Sept. 30: Full Moon, Uranus passes 5.00° S of Moon

October

Mercury is low in the SW after sunset late in the month.

Venus is in the SE before sunrise all month.

Mars is low in the SW at sunset and sets several hours later.

Jupiter rises in the late evening and is up much of the night.

Saturn is visible low in the SW after sunset early in the month.

Uranus and **Neptune** are high in the SE at sunset and set in the early morning.

Oct. 1: Spica passes 1.79° S of Mercury

Oct. 3: Regulus passes 0.12° N of Venus

Oct. 5: Aldebaran passes 4.27° S of Moon, Jupiter passes 0.91° N of Moon

Oct. 6: Mercury passes 3.48° S of Saturn, Mars enters Scorpius

Oct. 8: Last Quarter Moon

Oct. 9: Pollux passes 11.30° N of Moon

Oct. 11: Regulus passes 6.02° N of Moon, Mercury enters Libra

Oct. 12: Venus passes 6.32° N of Moon

Oct. 15: New Moon, Spica passes 0.77° N of Moon

Oct. 16: Saturn passes 4.60° N of Moon

Oct. 17: Mercury passes 1.31° S of Moon

Oct. 18: Mars passes 2.03° S of Moon, Antares passes 5.80° S of Moon

Oct. 19: Mars enters Ophiuchus

Oct. 20: Antares passes 3.64° S of Mars, Pluto passes 0.08° N of Moon

Oct. 21: Orionid meteor shower

Oct. 22: First Quarter Moon

Oct. 23: Venus enters Virgo

Oct. 24: Neptune passes 6.23° S of Moon

Oct. 25: Saturn passes 2.23° N of Sun

Oct. 26: Mercury at greatest elongation 24.1° E

Oct. 27: Uranus passes 5.11° S of Moon

Oct. 29: Full Moon, Mercury enters Scorpius

Oct. 30: Sun enters Libra

November

Mercury is low in the SW after sunset early in the month.

Venus is in the SE before sunrise all month.

Mars is low in the SW at sunset and sets several hours later.

Jupiter rises soon after sunset and is up most of the night.

Saturn is visible low in the SE before sunrise late in the month.

Uranus and **Neptune** are high overhead at sunset and set after midnight.

Nov. 1: Aldebaran passes 4.18° S of Moon

Nov. 2: Jupiter passes 0.89° N of Moon

Nov. 5: Pollux passes 11.42° N of Moon

Nov. 7: Last Quarter Moon

Nov. 8: Regulus passes 6.12° N of Moon

Nov. 11: Venus passes 5.34° N of Moon

Nov. 12: Spica passes 0.79° N of Moon, Saturn passes 4.31° N of Moon, Mars enters Sagittarius

Nov. 13: Total Solar Eclipse, New Moon

Nov. 14: Mercury passes 1.05° S of Moon

Nov. 15: Antares passes 5.84° S of Moon, Spica passes 4.14° S of Venus, Mercury enters Libra

Nov. 16: Mars passes 4.04° S of Moon, Pluto passes 0.11° S of Moon

Nov. 17: Mercury in inferior conjunction 0.41° N, Leonid meteor shower

Nov. 20: First Quarter Moon, Neptune passes 6.29° S of Moon

Nov. 22: Sun enters Scorpius

Nov. 23: Uranus passes 5.18° S of Moon

Nov. 27: Venus passes 0.56° S of Saturn, Pluto passes 4.55° N of Mars

Nov. 28: Penumbral Lunar Eclipse, Full Moon, Aldebaran passes 4.18° S of Moon, Sun enters Ophiuchus, Venus enters Libra

Nov. 29: Jupiter passes 0.63° N of Moon

December

Mercury is low in the SE before sunrise early in the month.

Venus is low in the SE before sunrise all month.

Mars is low in the SW at sunset and sets a few hours later.

Jupiter is high in the SE at sunset and sets in the early morning hours.

Saturn is visible in the SE before sunrise all month.

Uranus and **Neptune** are overhead at sunset and in the late evening.

Dec. 2: Pollux passes 11.41° N of Moon

Dec. 3: Jupiter at opposition

Dec. 4: Mercury at greatest elongation 20.6° W

Dec. 5: Regulus passes 6.10° N of Moon

Dec. 6: Last Quarter Moon, Saturn enters Libra

Dec. 7: Aldebaran passes 4.73° S of Jupiter

Dec. 9: Spica passes 0.77° N of Moon

Dec. 10: Saturn passes 4.04° N of Moon

Dec. 11: Venus passes 1.60° N of Moon

Dec. 12: Mercury passes 1.12° N of Moon, Antares passes 5.83° S of Moon

Dec. 13: New Moon, Mercury enters Scorpius, Geminid meteor shower

Dec. 14: Pluto passes 0.21° S of Moon

Dec. 15: Mars passes 5.62° S of Moon

Dec. 16: Mercury enters Ophiuchus

Dec. 17: Antares passes 5.53° S of Mercury, Sun enters Sagittarius

Dec. 18: Neptune passes 6.20° S of Moon, Venus enters Scorpius

Dec. 20: First Quarter Moon, Uranus passes 5.08° S of Moon

Dec. 21: Winter Solstice

Dec. 22: Venus enters Ophiuchus

Dec. 23: Antares passes 5.67° S of Venus

Dec. 25: Mars enters Capricorn

Dec. 26: Jupiter passes 0.42° N of Moon, Aldebaran passes 4.17° S of Moon

Dec. 28: Full Moon

Dec. 29: Pollux passes 11.33° N of Moon, Mercury enters Sagittarius

Dec. 30: Pluto passes 3.33° N of Sun

Meteorites and Meteor Showers

When a chunk of material, ice or rock, plunges into Earth's atmosphere and burns up in a fiery display, the event is a **meteor**. While the chunk of material is still in space, it is a **meteoroid**. If a portion of the material survives passage through the atmosphere and reaches the ground, the remnant on the ground is a **meteorite**.

Meteorites found on Earth are classified into types, depending on their composition: **irons**, those composed chiefly of iron, a small percentage of nickel, and traces of other metals such as cobalt; **stones**, stony meteors consisting of silicates; and **stony irons**, containing varying proportions of both iron and stone.

Serious study of meteorites as non-earth objects began in the 20th century. Scientists use sophisticated chemical analysis, X-rays, and mass spectrography in determining their origin and composition. Although most meteorites are now believed to be fragments of asteroids or comets, geochemical studies have shown that a few Antarctic stones came from the Moon or from Mars, presumably ejected by the explosive impact of asteroids.

The **largest known meteorite**, estimated to weigh about 55 metric tons, is situated at Hoba West near Grootfontein, Namibia. The Manicouagan impact crater in Quebec, Canada, with an estimated diameter of 60 mi, is one of the largest crater structures still visible on the surface of the Earth. Although not visible to the eye, other still larger impact craters identified include the Vredefort crater in South Africa at 185 mi across and the Sudbury crater in Ontario, Canada, estimated

at 125 mi across. The Bedout impact site off the NW coast of Australia gained attention in 2004, when scientists identified further evidence in support of the idea that it may be linked to the Permian extinction event 250 mil years ago.

Meteor showers vary in strength, but usually the 3 most visible meteor showers of the year are the **Perseids**, around Aug. 13, the **Orionids**, around Oct. 21, and the **Geminids**, around Dec. 14. These showers feature meteors at the rate of about 60 per hour. Best observing conditions occur with the absence of moonlight, usually when the Moon's phase is between waning crescent Moon and waxing quarter Moon.

For most meteor showers the cometary debris is relatively uniformly scattered along the comet's orbit. However, in the case of the **Leonid** meteor shower, which occurs every year around Nov. 17-18, the cometary debris, from Comet Temple-Tuttle, seems to be bunched up in one stretch. Hence, most years when Earth crosses the orbit of this comet, the meteor shower produced is relatively weak. However, about every 33 years, Earth encounters the bunched-up debris. Sometimes the storm is a disappointment, as it was in 1899 and 1933; at other times it is a roaring success, as in 1833 and 1866. The Leonids stormed again more recently, producing rates of 1,000-3,000 meteors per hour in 2001. Viewing of the typically best showers of the year (Perseids in mid-Aug., Orionids in late Oct., Leonids in mid-Nov., and Geminids in mid-Dec.) will all be adversely affected by bright Moons during the best viewing hours.

Rising and Setting of Planets, 2012

(In Coordinated Universal Time. 0 in the *h* col. designates 12 AM.)

Venus, 2012

Date	20° N Latitude Rise	Set	30° N Latitude Rise	Set	40° N Latitude Rise	Set	50° N Latitude Rise	Set	60° N Latitude Rise	Set
	h m	h m	h m	h m	h m	h m	h m	h m	h m	h m
Jan. 1	8 53	20 03	9 09	19 47	9 29	19 27	9 56	19 00	10 41	18 15
11	8 55	20 18	9 07	20 06	9 22	19 51	9 43	19 31	10 15	18 59
21	8 54	20 32	9 02	20 24	9 12	20 14	9 25	20 01	9 46	19 41
31	8 51	20 43	8 55	20 40	9 00	20 36	9 05	20 30	9 14	20 22
Feb. 10	8 47	20 54	8 46	20 55	8 45	20 56	8 44	20 58	8 41	21 01
20	8 42	21 04	8 37	21 10	8 30	21 16	8 21	21 26	8 07	21 40
Mar. 1	8 36	21 14	8 27	21 23	8 15	21 36	7 58	21 53	7 32	22 19
11	8 31	21 22	8 17	21 36	8 00	21 54	7 36	22 19	6 57	22 58
21	8 26	21 30	8 08	21 48	7 46	22 11	7 14	22 43	6 21	23 37
31	8 21	21 37	8 00	21 58	7 33	22 25	6 54	23 04	5 45	0 11
Apr. 10	8 15	21 40	7 51	22 04	7 20	22 35	6 36	23 20	5 09	0 45
20	8 07	21 37	7 41	22 03	7 07	22 37	6 18	23 26	4 34	1 10
30	7 53	21 26	7 26	21 53	6 51	22 27	6 00	23 19	4 04	1 16
May 10	7 30	21 02	7 03	21 28	6 28	22 03	5 37	22 54	3 42	0 52
20	6 53	20 20	6 27	20 46	5 54	21 18	5 05	22 07	3 24	23 47
30	6 01	19 20	5 38	19 43	5 08	20 13	4 25	20 55	3 02	22 16
June 9	5 02	18 10	4 42	18 30	4 16	18 56	3 40	19 32	2 35	20 35
19	4 08	17 08	3 50	17 25	3 28	17 47	2 58	18 17	2 06	19 09
29	3 26	16 22	3 10	16 38	2 50	16 58	2 22	17 26	1 36	18 12
July 9	2 57	15 53	2 41	16 09	2 21	16 29	1 54	16 56	1 08	17 42
19	2 38	15 37	2 22	15 53	2 01	16 14	1 32	16 43	0 45	17 30
29	2 27	15 29	2 09	15 46	1 48	16 08	1 17	16 38	0 26	17 30
Aug. 8	2 21	15 26	2 03	15 45	1 41	16 07	1 09	16 39	0 15	17 34
18	2 21	15 28	2 03	15 46	1 40	16 09	1 07	16 42	0 12	17 37
28	2 25	15 31	2 07	15 49	1 45	16 11	1 13	16 43	0 19	17 37
Sept. 7	2 33	15 34	2 16	15 51	1 55	16 12	1 25	16 41	0 35	17 31
17	2 42	15 37	2 27	15 52	2 08	16 10	1 42	16 36	0 59	17 18
27	2 53	15 39	2 40	15 51	2 25	16 06	2 03	16 27	1 29	17 01
Oct. 7	3 04	15 39	2 55	15 48	2 43	16 00	2 27	16 15	2 02	16 39
17	3 15	15 39	3 10	15 44	3 03	15 51	2 53	16 01	2 38	16 15
27	3 27	15 38	3 25	15 40	3 23	15 42	3 19	15 45	3 14	15 50
Nov. 6	3 39	15 37	3 41	15 34	3 44	15 32	3 47	15 28	3 51	15 23
16	3 52	15 36	3 58	15 30	4 06	15 23	4 15	15 13	4 30	14 57
26	4 06	15 37	4 16	15 27	4 28	15 15	4 45	14 58	5 10	14 32
Dec. 6	4 21	15 40	4 35	15 26	4 52	15 10	5 14	14 47	5 51	14 10
16	4 38	15 46	4 54	15 29	5 15	15 08	5 44	14 39	6 31	13 51
26	4 54	15 55	5 14	15 35	5 38	15 11	6 11	14 37	7 09	13 40

Mars, 2012

Date	20° N Latitude Rise	Set	30° N Latitude Rise	Set	40° N Latitude Rise	Set	50° N Latitude Rise	Set	60° N Latitude Rise	Set
	h m	h m	h m	h m	h m	h m	h m	h m	h m	h m
Jan. 1	22 33	10 59	22 27	11 05	22 20	11 12	22 10	11 22	21 55	11 37
11	22 02	10 26	21 57	10 32	21 50	10 38	21 41	10 48	21 26	11 02
21	21 26	9 51	21 21	9 56	21 14	10 03	21 05	10 12	20 51	10 26
31	20 46	9 11	20 40	9 17	20 33	9 24	20 23	9 34	20 08	9 49
Feb. 10	19 59	8 28	19 53	8 34	19 45	8 42	19 34	8 53	19 17	9 10
20	19 08	7 40	19 00	7 47	18 51	7 57	18 38	8 10	18 18	8 30
Mar. 1	18 12	6 49	18 04	6 58	17 53	7 09	17 38	7 24	17 14	7 47
11	17 16	5 57	17 06	6 07	16 54	6 19	16 37	6 37	16 10	7 03
21	16 22	5 06	16 11	5 17	15 58	5 30	15 39	5 49	15 09	6 19
31	15 33	4 18	15 21	4 29	15 07	4 43	14 48	5 03	14 16	5 34
Apr. 10	14 49	3 34	14 37	3 45	14 23	3 59	14 03	4 19	13 32	4 50
20	14 10	2 53	13 59	3 04	13 45	3 18	13 26	3 37	12 57	4 07
30	13 36	2 17	13 26	2 27	13 13	2 40	12 56	2 58	12 28	3 25
May 10	13 07	1 44	12 57	1 53	12 46	2 04	12 30	2 20	12 06	2 45
20	12 40	1 13	12 32	1 21	12 22	1 31	12 09	1 44	11 48	2 06
30	12 17	0 44	12 10	0 51	12 02	0 59	11 51	1 10	11 34	1 27
June 9	11 55	0 17	11 50	0 22	11 44	0 28	11 36	0 37	11 23	0 50
19	11 35	23 49	11 32	23 52	11 28	23 56	11 23	0 04	11 14	0 13
29	11 17	23 24	11 16	23 25	11 14	23 27	11 12	23 29	11 08	23 33
July 9	11 00	23 01	11 01	23 00	11 01	22 59	11 02	22 58	11 03	22 57
19	10 44	22 38	10 47	22 35	10 50	22 32	10 54	22 28	11 00	22 21
29	10 29	22 16	10 34	22 11	10 40	22 06	10 48	21 58	10 59	21 46
Aug. 8	10 16	21 55	10 23	21 49	10 31	21 40	10 42	21 29	10 59	21 11
18	10 03	21 36	10 12	21 27	10 23	21 16	10 38	21 01	11 01	20 37
28	9 51	21 17	10 03	21 06	10 16	20 52	10 35	20 33	11 04	20 04
Sept. 7	9 41	20 59	9 54	20 46	10 10	20 30	10 33	20 07	11 08	19 32
17	9 31	20 43	9 47	20 28	10 05	20 09	10 31	19 43	11 13	19 01
27	9 23	20 29	9 40	20 11	10 01	19 50	10 31	19 20	11 20	18 31
Oct. 7	9 15	20 15	9 34	19 56	9 58	19 33	10 30	19 00	11 26	18 04
17	9 08	20 04	9 29	19 43	9 54	19 18	10 30	18 42	11 32	17 39
27	9 02	19 54	9 23	19 32	9 50	19 05	10 29	18 27	11 37	17 19
Nov. 6	8 56	19 45	9 18	19 23	9 46	18 55	10 26	18 15	11 38	17 03
16	8 50	19 38	9 12	19 16	9 41	18 47	10 21	18 07	11 35	16 53
26	8 43	19 33	9 06	19 10	9 34	18 42	10 14	18 02	11 27	16 49
Dec. 6	8 36	19 28	8 58	19 06	9 26	18 39	10 04	18 00	11 13	16 51
16	8 29	19 24	8 49	19 03	9 15	18 37	9 51	18 01	10 55	16 58
26	8 20	19 20	8 39	19 01	9 03	18 37	9 36	18 04	10 32	17 08

Jupiter, 2012

Date	20° N Latitude Rise h m	Set h m	30° N Latitude Rise h m	Set h m	40° N Latitude Rise h m	Set h m	50° N Latitude Rise h m	Set h m	60° N Latitude Rise h m	Set h m
Jan. 1	12 55	1 32	12 46	1 42	12 34	1 53	12 18	2 09	11 53	2 34
11	12 17	0 55	12 07	1 04	11 55	1 16	11 39	1 32	11 14	1 57
21	11 40	0 19	11 30	0 28	11 18	0 40	11 01	0 57	10 35	1 23
31	11 03	23 40	10 53	23 50	10 41	0 06	10 24	0 23	9 56	0 50
Feb. 10	10 28	23 06	10 18	23 17	10 05	23 30	9 47	23 48	9 18	0 20
20	9 54	22 34	9 43	22 45	9 29	22 59	9 10	23 17	8 40	23 47
Mar. 1	9 20	22 02	9 09	22 14	8 54	22 28	8 35	22 48	8 03	23 20
11	8 47	21 31	8 35	21 43	8 20	21 58	7 59	22 19	7 26	22 53
21	8 15	21 01	8 02	21 13	7 46	21 29	7 24	21 51	6 49	22 27
31	7 43	20 31	7 29	20 44	7 13	21 01	6 50	21 24	6 12	22 02
Apr. 10	7 11	20 01	6 57	20 15	6 40	20 33	6 15	20 57	5 36	21 37
20	6 40	19 32	6 25	19 47	6 07	20 05	5 41	20 31	5 00	21 13
30	6 09	19 03	5 54	19 19	5 34	19 38	5 08	20 05	4 24	20 49
May 10	5 38	18 35	5 22	18 51	5 02	19 10	4 34	19 38	3 48	20 25
20	5 07	18 06	4 51	18 22	4 30	18 43	4 01	19 12	3 13	20 00
30	4 37	17 37	4 20	17 54	3 58	18 16	3 28	18 46	2 38	19 36
June 9	4 06	17 08	3 48	17 26	3 26	17 48	2 55	18 19	2 03	19 11
19	3 35	16 39	3 17	16 57	2 55	17 20	2 23	17 52	1 28	18 46
29	3 04	16 09	2 46	16 28	2 23	16 51	1 50	17 24	0 54	18 20
July 9	2 33	15 39	2 14	15 58	1 51	16 22	1 17	16 56	0 19	17 54
19	2 02	15 09	1 42	15 28	1 18	15 52	0 44	16 27	23 41	17 26
29	1 29	14 38	1 10	14 57	0 45	15 22	0 11	15 57	23 06	16 58
Aug. 8	0 57	14 06	0 37	14 26	0 12	14 51	23 33	15 26	22 32	16 28
18	0 23	13 33	0 04	13 53	23 35	14 18	22 59	14 54	21 56	15 57
28	23 46	12 59	23 26	13 19	23 00	13 45	22 24	14 21	21 21	15 24
Sept. 7	23 10	12 24	22 50	12 45	22 25	13 10	21 48	13 46	20 44	14 50
17	22 34	11 48	22 14	12 08	21 48	12 34	21 12	13 10	20 07	14 15
27	21 56	11 11	21 36	11 31	21 10	11 56	20 34	12 33	19 29	13 38
Oct. 7	21 17	10 32	20 57	10 52	20 31	11 17	19 55	11 54	18 50	12 59
17	20 37	9 51	20 16	10 11	19 51	10 37	19 14	11 13	18 10	12 18
27	19 55	9 09	19 35	9 29	19 09	9 55	18 33	10 31	17 29	11 35
Nov. 6	19 12	8 26	18 52	8 46	18 26	9 11	17 50	9 47	16 47	10 51
16	18 28	7 42	18 08	8 01	17 43	8 27	17 07	9 02	16 04	10 05
26	17 43	6 56	17 24	7 16	16 59	7 41	16 23	8 17	15 21	9 19
Dec. 6	16 59	6 11	16 39	6 31	16 14	6 55	15 39	7 31	14 38	8 32
16	16 14	5 26	15 55	5 45	15 30	6 10	14 55	6 45	13 55	7 45
26	15 30	4 41	15 11	5 01	14 46	5 25	14 12	5 59	13 12	6 59

Saturn, 2012

Date	20° N Latitude Rise h m	Set h m	30° N Latitude Rise h m	Set h m	40° N Latitude Rise h m	Set h m	50° N Latitude Rise h m	Set h m	60° N Latitude Rise h m	Set h m
Jan. 1	1 18	12 56	1 26	12 49	1 34	12 40	1 46	12 28	2 04	12 10
11	0 41	12 19	0 49	12 11	0 58	12 02	1 10	11 51	1 28	11 32
21	0 04	11 41	0 11	11 33	0 20	11 24	0 32	11 12	0 51	10 54
	24 00									
31	23 22	11 02	23 29	10 55	23 38	10 46	23 50	10 34	0 13	10 15
Feb. 10	22 42	10 23	22 50	10 16	22 59	10 07	23 11	9 55	23 30	9 36
20	22 02	9 44	22 10	9 36	22 19	9 27	22 31	9 15	22 49	8 57
Mar. 1	21 22	9 03	21 29	8 56	21 38	8 47	21 49	8 36	22 08	8 17
11	20 40	8 23	20 47	8 16	20 56	8 07	21 07	7 56	21 25	7 38
21	19 59	7 42	20 05	7 35	20 14	7 26	20 25	7 15	20 42	6 58
31	19 16	7 00	19 23	6 53	19 31	6 45	19 42	6 35	19 58	6 18
Apr. 10	18 34	6 18	18 40	6 12	18 48	6 04	18 58	5 54	19 14	5 38
20	17 51	5 37	17 57	5 30	18 05	5 23	18 15	5 13	18 30	4 58
30	17 09	4 55	17 15	4 49	17 22	4 42	17 31	4 32	17 46	4 18
May 10	16 26	4 13	16 32	4 08	16 39	4 01	16 48	3 51	17 02	3 37
20	15 45	3 32	15 50	3 26	15 57	3 20	16 06	3 11	16 19	2 57
30	15 03	2 51	15 09	2 46	15 15	2 39	15 24	2 30	15 37	2 17
June 9	14 23	2 11	14 28	2 05	14 34	1 59	14 43	1 50	14 56	1 37
19	13 42	1 31	13 48	1 25	13 54	1 19	14 03	1 10	14 16	0 57
29	13 03	0 51	13 08	0 46	13 15	0 39	13 24	0 31	13 37	0 17
July 9	12 24	0 12	12 30	0 07	12 36	0 00	12 45	23 47	12 59	23 34
						23 56				
19	11 46	23 30	11 52	23 24	11 59	23 17	12 08	23 08	12 21	22 55
29	11 09	22 52	11 15	22 46	11 22	22 39	11 31	22 30	11 45	22 16
Aug. 8	10 32	22 14	10 38	22 08	10 46	22 01	10 55	21 51	11 10	21 37
18	9 56	21 37	10 02	21 31	10 10	21 23	10 20	21 13	10 36	20 58
28	9 21	21 01	9 27	20 54	9 35	20 46	9 46	20 36	10 02	20 19
Sept. 7	8 45	20 24	8 52	20 18	9 00	20 09	9 12	19 58	9 29	19 41
17	8 10	19 48	8 18	19 41	8 26	19 32	8 38	19 21	8 56	19 03
27	7 36	19 13	7 43	19 05	7 53	18 56	8 05	18 43	8 24	18 24
Oct. 7	7 02	18 37	7 09	18 29	7 19	18 19	7 32	18 06	7 52	17 46
17	6 27	18 02	6 36	17 53	6 46	17 43	6 59	17 30	7 20	17 08
27	5 53	17 26	6 02	17 18	6 12	17 07	6 27	16 53	6 49	16 31
Nov. 6	5 19	16 51	5 28	16 42	5 39	16 31	5 54	16 16	6 17	15 53
16	4 45	16 16	4 54	16 06	5 06	15 55	5 21	15 39	5 45	15 15
26	4 11	15 40	4 20	15 30	4 32	15 18	4 48	15 02	5 13	14 38
Dec. 6	3 36	15 04	3 46	14 54	3 58	14 42	4 15	14 26	4 40	14 00
16	3 01	14 28	3 11	14 18	3 24	14 06	3 41	13 49	4 07	13 22
26	2 26	13 52	2 36	13 42	2 49	13 29	3 06	13 11	3 33	12 44

Morning and Evening "Stars," 2012

(In Coordinated Universal Time)

	Morning	Evening		Morning	Evening
Jan.	Mercury Mars Saturn	Venus Jupiter Uranus Neptune	July	Mercury from July 29 Venus Jupiter Uranus Neptune	Mercury to July 28 Mars Saturn
Feb.	Mercury to Feb. 7 Mars Saturn Neptune from Feb. 20	Mercury from Feb. 8 Venus Jupiter Uranus Neptune to Feb. 19	Aug.	Mercury Venus Jupiter Uranus Neptune to Aug. 24	Mars Saturn Neptune from Aug. 25
Mar.	Mercury from Mar. 22 Mars to Mar. 3 Saturn Uranus from Mar. 25 Neptune	Mercury to Mar. 21 Venus Mars from Mar. 4 Jupiter Uranus to Mar. 24	Sept.	Mercury to Sept. 10 Venus Jupiter Uranus to Sept. 29	Mercury from Sept. 11 Mars Saturn Uranus from Sept. 30 Neptune
Apr.	Mercury Saturn to Apr. 15 Uranus Neptune	Venus Mars Jupiter Saturn from Apr. 16	Oct.	Venus Jupiter Saturn from Oct. 26	Mercury Mars Saturn to Oct. 25 Uranus Neptune
May	Mercury to May 27 Jupiter from May 14 Uranus Neptune	Mercury from May 28 Venus Mars Jupiter to May 13 Saturn	Nov.	Mercury from Nov. 18 Venus Jupiter Saturn	Mercury to Nov. 17 Mars Uranus Neptune
June	Venus from June 7 Jupiter Uranus Neptune	Mercury Venus to June 6 Mars Saturn	Dec.	Mercury Venus Jupiter to Dec. 3 Saturn	Mars Jupiter from Dec. 4 Uranus Neptune

Greenwich Sidereal Time for 0h UTC, 2012

UTC = Coordinated Universal Time. Add 12 hours to obtain right ascension of mean sun.

Date	d	h	m	Date	d	h	m	Date	d	h	m	Date	d	h	m
Jan.	1	6	40.2	Apr.	10	13	14.5	July	9	19	9.3	Oct.	7	1	4.2
	11	7	19.7		20	13	53.9		19	19	48.8		17	1	43.6
	21	7	59.1		30	14	33.4		29	20	28.2		27	2	23.0
	31	8	38.5	May	10	15	12.8	Aug.	8	21	7.6	Nov.	6	3	2.4
Feb.	10	9	17.9		20	15	52.2		18	21	47.0		16	3	41.9
	20	9	57.4		30	16	31.6		28	22	26.5		26	4	21.3
Mar.	1	10	36.8	June	9	17	11.1	Sept.	7	23	5.9	Dec.	6	5	0.7
	11	11	16.2		19	17	50.5		17	23	45.3		16	5	40.1
	21	11	55.6		29	18	29.9		27	0	24.7		26	6	19.6
	31	12	35.1												

Largest Telescopes

Astronomers indicate the size of telescopes not by length or magnification, but by the diameter of the primary light-gathering component of the system—such as the lens or mirror. This measurement is a direct indication of the telescope's light-gathering power. The bigger the diameter, the fainter the objects you are able to detect. The Earth's atmosphere limits the resolution of what you see. That is why the Hubble Space Telescope, which is outside the atmosphere, can have better resolution than larger telescopes on the Earth.

Refracting (lens) telescopes are currently not made with lens diameters of more than 40 in. Mirror telescopes can be made less expensively than lens telescopes, so all modern large optical telescopes are made with mirrors. Radio telescopes, also reflecting telescopes, view at wavelengths not visible to optical telescopes or to the human eye. Radio telescopes are made larger than optical telescopes because larger diameters are required at longer wavelengths to obtain equivalent resolution. Arrays of telescopes are used to achieve even better resolution through a technique called interferometry. Originally developed for radio telescopes, the technique is now also used with optical and infrared telescopes.

Largest refracting (lens) optical telescope: Yerkes Observatory, 1 m (40 in.), at Williams Bay, WI

Largest reflecting (mirror) optical/infrared telescope: Gran Telescopio Canarias, 10.4 m (34 ft), on La Palma, Canary Islands (segmented mirror)

Largest infrared interferometer: Four 8.2-m (27-ft) telescopes of the Very Large Telescope Interferometer (VLTI) with a 200-m (656-ft) baseline on Cerro Paranal in Chile

Largest fully steerable radio dish: Robert Byrd Green Bank Telescope (GBT), 100 m × 110 m (328 ft × 360 ft), in Green Bank, WV

Largest single radio dish: Arecibo Observatory, 305 m (1,000 ft), in Puerto Rico

Largest radio interferometer: Ten 25-m (82-ft) diameter telescopes of the Very Long Baseline Array (VLBA), dispersed from Hawaii to the Virgin Islands with a resolution equal to a radio dish of 8,600 km (5,000 mi), making it the highest resolution telescope in the solar system

Largest airborne telescope: Stratospheric Observatory for Infrared Astronomy (SOFIA), 2.5-m (8.2-ft) infrared telescope aboard a NASA 747

Constellations

Culturally, constellations are imagined patterns among the stars that, in some cases, have been recognized through millennia. Knowledge of constellations was once necessary in order to function as an astronomer. For today's astronomers, constellations are simply areas on the entire sky in which interesting objects await observation and interpretation.

Because Western culture has prevailed in establishing modern science, equally valuable and interesting constellations and celestial traditions of other cultures are not well known outside their regions of origin. Even the patterns with which we are most familiar today have undergone considerable change over the centuries.

Today, **88 constellations** are officially recognized. Although many have ancient origins, some are modern, devised out of unclaimed stars by astronomers a few centuries ago. Unclaimed stars were those too faint or inconveniently placed to be included in the more prominent constellations. Stars in a constellation are not necessarily near each other; they are just located in the same direction on the celestial sphere.

When astronomers began to travel to South Africa in the 16th and 17th centuries, they found an unfamiliar sky that showed numerous brilliant stars. Thus, we find constellations in the Southern Hemisphere that depict technological marvels of the time, as well as some arguably traditional forms, such as Musca, the fly.

Many of the commonly recognized constellations had their **origins** in ancient Asia Minor. These were adopted by the Greeks and Romans, who translated their names and stories into their own languages, modifying some details in the process. After the declines of these cultures, most such knowledge entered oral tradition or remained hidden in monastic libraries. From the 8th century, the Muslim explosion spread through the Mediterranean world. Wherever possible, everything was translated into Arabic to be taught in the universities the Muslims established all over their new-found world.

In the 13th century, Alfonso X of Castile, an avid student of astronomy, had Ptolemy's *Almagest* translated into Latin. It thus became widely available to European scholars. In the process, the constellation names were translated, but the star names were retained in their Arabic forms. Thus the names of many stars—Altair, Alnitak, and Mirfak, among others—have Arabic roots, although linguistic adaptation and the inaccuracies of transliteration have wrought changes.

Until the 1920s, astronomers used curved boundaries for the constellation areas. As these were rather arbitrary at best, the International Astronomical Union adopted new constellation boundaries that ran due north-south and east-west, filling the sky much as the contiguous states fill up the area of the lower 48 United States.

Common names of stars often referred to parts of the traditional figures they represented: Deneb, the tail of the swan; Betelgeuse, the armpit of the giant. Avoiding traditional names, astronomers may label stars by using Greek letters, generally to denote order of brightness. Thus, the "alpha star" would generally be the brightest star of that constellation. The "of" implies possession, so the genitive (possessive) form of the constellation name is used, as in Alpha Orionis, the first star of Orion (Betelgeuse). Astronomers usually use a 3-letter abbreviation for the constellation name, as indicated here.

Within these boundaries, and occasionally crossing them, popular asterisms are recognized: the so-called Big Dipper is a small part of the constellation Ursa Major, the big bear; the Sickle is the traditional head and mane of Leo, the lion; the three stars of the Summer Triangle are each in a different constellation, with Vega in Lyra the lyre, Deneb in Cygnus the swan, and Altair in Aquila the eagle; the northeast star of the Great Square of Pegasus is Alpha Andromedae.

Name	Genitive case	Abbr.	Meaning	Name	Genitive case	Abbr.	Meaning
Andromeda	Andromedae	And	Chained Maiden	Lacerta	Lacertae	Lac	Lizard
Antlia	Antliae	Ant	Air Pump	Leo	Leonis	Leo	Lion
Apus	Apodis	Aps	Bird of Paradise	Leo Minor	Leonis Minoris	LMi	Littler Lion
Aquarius	Aquarii	Aqr	Water Bearer	Lepus	Leporis	Lep	Hare
Aquila	Aquilae	Aql	Eagle	Libra	Librae	Lib	Balance
Ara	Arae	Ara	Altar	Lupus	Lupi	Lup	Wolf
Aries	Arietis	Ari	Ram	Lynx	Lyncis	Lyn	Lynx
Auriga	Aurigae	Aur	Charioteer	Lyra	Lyrae	Lyr	Lyre
Boötes	Boötis	Boo	Herdsmen	Mensa	Mensae	Men	Table Mountain
Caelum	Caeli	Cae	Chisel	Microscopium	Microscopii	Mic	Microscope
Camelopardalis	Camelopardalis	Cam	Giraffe	Monoceros	Monocerotis	Mon	Unicorn
Cancer	Cancri	Cnc	Crab	Musca	Muscae	Mus	Fly
Canes Venatici	Canum Venaticorum	CVn	Hunting Dogs	Norma	Normae	Nor	Square (rule)
Canis Major	Canis Majoris	CMa	Greater Dog	Octans	Octantis	Oct	Octant
Canis Minor	Canis Minoris	CMi	Littler Dog	Ophiuchus	Ophiuchi	Oph	Serpent Bearer
Capricornus	Capricorni	Cap	Sea-goat	Orion	Orionis	Ori	Hunter
Carina	Carinae	Car	Keel	Pavo	Pavonis	Pav	Peacock
Cassiopeia	Cassiopeiae	Cas	Queen	Pegasus	Pegasi	Peg	Flying Horse
Centaurus	Centauri	Cen	Centaur	Perseus	Persei	Per	Hero
Cepheus	Cephei	Cep	King	Phoenix	Phoenicis	Phe	Phoenix
Cetus	Ceti	Cet	Whale	Pictor	Pictoris	Pic	Painter
Chamaeleon	Chamaeleontis	Cha	Chameleon	Pisces	Piscium	Psc	Fishes
Circinus	Circini	Cir	Compasses (art)	Piscis Austrinus	Piscis Austrini	PsA	Southern Fish
Columba	Columbae	Col	Dove	Puppis	Puppis	Pup	Stern (deck)
Coma Berenices	Comae Berenices	Com	Berenice's Hair	Pyxis	Pyxidis	Pyx	Compass (sea)
Corona Australis	Coronae Australis	CrA	Southern Crown	Reticulum	Reticuli	Ret	Reticle
Corona Borealis	Coronae Borealis	CrB	Northern Crown	Sagitta	Sagittae	Sge	Arrow
Corvus	Corvi	Crv	Crow	Sagittarius	Sagittarii	Sgr	Archer
Crater	Crateris	Crt	Cup	Scorpius	Scorpii	Sco	Scorpion
Crux	Crucis	Cru	Cross (southern)	Sculptor	Sculptoris	Scl	Sculptor
Cygnus	Cygni	Cyg	Swan	Scutum	Scuti	Sct	Shield
Delphinus	Delphini	Del	Dolphin	Serpens	Serpentis	Ser	Serpent
Dorado	Doradus	Dor	Goldfish	Sextans	Sextantis	Sex	Sextant
Draco	Draconis	Dra	Dragon	Taurus	Tauri	Tau	Bull
Equuleus	Equulei	Equ	Little Horse	Telescopium	Telescopii	Tel	Telescope
Eridanus	Eridani	Eri	River	Triangulum	Trianguli	Tri	Triangle
Fornax	Fornacis	For	Furnace	Triangulum Australe	Trianguli Australis	TrA	Southern Triangle
Gemini	Geminorum	Gem	Twins	Tucana	Tucanae	Tuc	Toucan
Grus	Gruis	Gru	Crane (bird)	Ursa Major	Ursae Majoris	UMa	Greater Bear
Hercules	Herculis	Her	Hercules	Ursa Minor	Ursae Minoris	UMi	Littler Bear
Horologium	Horologii	Hor	Clock	Vela	Velorum	Vel	Sail
Hydra	Hydrae	Hya	Water Snake (female)	Virgo	Virginis	Vir	Maiden
Hydrus	Hydri	Hyi	Water Snake (male)	Volans	Volantis	Vol	Flying Fish
Indus	Indi	Ind	Indian	Vulpecula	Vulpeculae	Vul	Fox

Eclipses, 2012

(In Coordinated Universal Time, standard time of the prime meridian.)

There are four eclipses in 2012: one annular solar eclipse, one total solar eclipse, one partial lunar eclipse, and one penumbral lunar eclipse. The annular solar eclipse will be visible over a narrow path extending across the continental U.S from N California to Texas. The partial lunar eclipse will be visible before sunrise over wide portions of N America from the Midwest to the West. During an annular eclipse of the Sun, the Moon's angular diameter is not large enough to block the entire disk of the Sun, and the Sun appears as a bright ring about the dark disk of the Moon. Penumbral lunar eclipses are rather unspectacular since the Moon never enters the dark portion of the Earth's shadow. The tables below give the times, in UTC, when the Moon or Sun reaches certain phases of eclipse. In the case of the lunar eclipses, the times are relevant for any observer who can see the Moon. In the case of solar eclipses, the tabulated times refer to when the given event begins or ends from specific points along the eclipse path; as the Moon's shadow sweeps quickly across the Earth, the observed duration of totality depends precisely on the observer's location.

I. Annular Eclipse of the Sun, May 20

The annular phase of the eclipse will be visible over a narrow path which extends from SE China and Japan, across the N Pacific, and across N California through N Texas. For U.S. observers along this path, the eclipse will be visible near sunset. A partial eclipse will be visible over a much wider area extending from Indonesia to Siberia, through much of the Pacific, and from Baja California through Canada and Alaska.

Event	Date	h	m
Penumbral eclipse begins	May	20	20	56.1
Annular eclipse begins		20	22	6.3
Greatest eclipse		20	23	52.8
Annular eclipse ends		21	1	39.2
Penumbral eclipse ends		21	2	49.4

II. Partial Eclipse of the Moon, June 4

Portions of the eclipse will be visible across most of the Americas, Siberia, Central and E China, SE Asia, and W Australia, while the entire eclipse will be visble across the Pacific, New Zealand, E Australia, and New Guinea. In much of the U.S., the eclipse will be visible in the early morning of June 4 before moonset.

Event	Date	h	m
Penumbral eclipse begins	June	4	8	48.2
Partial eclipse begins		4	9	59.9
Greatest eclipse		4	11	4.3
Partial eclipse ends	June	4	12	6.5
Penumbral eclipse ends		4	13	18.2

III. Total Eclipse of the Sun, Nov. 13

The path of totality skims the Northern regions of Australia before moving over the Pacific. A partially eclipsed Sun will be visible over a much wider area extending from New Guinea and Central Australia through the Pacific, through parts of Antarctica and South America.

Event	Date	h	m
Penumbral eclipse begins	Nov.	13	19	37.9
Total eclipse begins		13	20	35.1
Greatest eclipse		13	22	11.8
Total eclipse ends		13	23	48.4
Penumbral eclipse ends		14	0	45.5

IV. Penumbral Eclipse of the Moon, Nov. 28

During a penumbral lunar eclipse, the Moon dims only slightly, and the eclipse is hardly noticeable. Portions of this eclipse will be visible over a wide area extending from Europe and N and E Africa eastward across the Pacific and most of N America.

Event	Date	h	m
Penumbral eclipse begins	Nov.	28	12	14.9
Greatest eclipse		28	14	34.1
Penumbral eclipse ends		28	16	50.9

Total Solar Eclipses, 2010-20

Total solar eclipses actually take place nearly as often as total lunar eclipses. Total lunar eclipses are visible over at least half of the Earth, while total solar eclipses can be seen only along a very narrow path up to a few hundred miles wide and a few thousand miles long. Observing a total solar eclipse is thus a rarity for most people.

Solar eclipses can be dangerous to observe. This is not because the Sun emits more potent rays, but because the Sun is always dangerous to observe directly, and people are particularly likely to stare at it during a solar eclipse.

Date	Duration[1] m	s	Width (mi)	Path of totality
2010, July 11	5	20	164	Pacific Ocean, southern S America
2012, Nov. 13	4	2	112	N Australia, Pacific Ocean
2013, Nov. 3[h]	1	40	36	Atlantic Ocean, Africa
2015, Mar. 20	2	47	304	N Atlantic Ocean, Arctic Ocean
2016, Mar. 9	4	10	96	Indonesia, Pacific Ocean
2017, Aug. 21	2	40	71	Pacific Ocean, U.S., Atlantic Ocean
2019, July 2	4	33	125	S Pacific Ocean, S America
2020, Dec. 14	2	10	56	S Pacific Ocean, S America, S Atlantic Ocean

h = Annular-total hybrid eclipse. (1) Length of time at optimal viewing area.

Total Solar Eclipses in the U.S. in the 21st Century

During the 21st century there will be 8 total solar eclipses visible somewhere in the continental U.S. The first comes after a long gap; the last total solar eclipse was on Feb. 26, 1979, in the northwestern U.S.

Date	Path of totality	Date	Path of totality
Aug. 21, 2017	Oregon to South Carolina	Mar. 30, 2052	Florida to Georgia
Apr. 8, 2024	Mexico to Texas and N through Maine	May 11, 2078	Louisiana to North Carolina
Aug. 23, 2044	Montana to North Dakota	May 1, 2079	New Jersey to the lower edge of New England
Aug. 12, 2045	N California to Florida	Sept. 14, 2099	North Dakota to Virginia

Beginnings of the Universe

One of the dominating astronomical discoveries of the 20th century was that the galaxies of the universe all seem to be moving away from us. Doppler redshifts were observed for the spiral nebulae around 1920, even though they were not yet known to be galaxies. By the early 1930s, Edwin Hubble and M. L. Humason had established that the more distant a galaxy, the faster it was receding. It turned out that they are moving away not just from us but from one another—that is, the **universe is expanding**. Scientists conclude that the universe must once, very long ago, have been extremely compact and dense, until an explosion or a similar event caused the matter to spread out. The explosion that gave birth to the universe is called the **Big Bang**.

On the subatomic level, according to this theory, there were vast changes of energy and matter and the way physical laws operated during the first few minutes. After those early minutes the percentages of the basic matter of the universe—hydrogen, helium, and lithium—were set. Everything was so compact and so hot that **radiation dominated the early universe** and there were no stable, un-ionized atoms. At first, the universe was opaque, in the sense that any energy emitted was quickly absorbed and then re-emitted by free electrons. As the universe expanded, **density and temperature continued to drop**. A few hundred thousand years after the Big Bang, the temperature dropped far enough that electrons and nuclei could combine to form stable atoms as the universe became transparent. Once that occurred, the radiation that had been trapped was free to escape.

In the 1940s, George Gamov and others predicted that astronomers should be able to see remnants of this escaped radiation. They were starting to search for this background radiation when physicists Arno Penzias and Robert Wilson, using a radio telescope, inadvertently beat them to the punch (the two were later awarded a Nobel Prize).

In 2003, NASA's Wilkinson Microwave Anisotropy Probe made measurements of the temperature of this **cosmic microwave background** radiation to within millionths of a degree. From these measurements, scientists were able to deduce that our universe is **13.7 bil years old** and that first-generation stars began to form a mere 200 mil years after the Big Bang.

A related mystery is that evidence suggests there is hidden matter and hidden energy that cannot be directly observed. This **dark matter** may be composed of gas, large numbers of cool, small objects, or even subatomic particles. The presence of dark matter is indicated by the rotation curves of galaxies and the dynamics of clusters of galaxies. Evidence for **dark energy** is derived from studies of distant Type Ia supernovae in far galaxies indicating that the expansion of the universe is accelerating, rather than slowing. The visible matter we see seems to constitute only about 4% of the total mass of the universe, while the rest of the mass of the universe is in the form of dark matter (23%) and dark energy (73%). Dark energy is a mysterious force that seems to work on the very fabric of the universe, spreading it apart.

Galaxies

The 20th century might be called the century of the galaxy. By the start of the century, more than 10,000 **nebulae**—cloud-like luminous objects in the sky—had been discovered. Some were correctly identified as star clusters and others as clouds of gas and dust. Those nebulae which were spiral or elliptical in shape were found in regions of the sky far from the glowing band that is our own Milky Way Galaxy. Immanuel Kant had written in 1775 that some of these fuzzy objects might be **"island universes"** apart from our own. But the idea remained speculative until 1923-24, when Edwin Hubble discovered the existence of variable stars in some of these nebulae. This provided conclusive evidence that these systems were outside our own island universe, the Milky Way Galaxy.

Galaxies range in size from small dwarf elliptical ones, with perhaps 1 mil stars, to spiral galaxies containing 300 bil stars, to giant elliptical galaxies that may be home to more than 10 tril stars. The diameters of galaxies range from 3,000 light-years in dwarf elliptical galaxies to over 500,000 light-years in giant elliptical galaxies. It is estimated that the Milky Way Galaxy is about 100,000 light-years in diameter with about 400 bil stars.

Galaxies also congregate into **clusters**. The smallest are poor clusters of only a few dozen galaxies, while the largest rich clusters may contain thousands of galaxies. The Milky Way is part of a poor cluster of about 3 dozen galaxies called the **Local Group**. The largest member of the Local Group is the Andromeda Galaxy, a spiral galaxy visible to the unaided eye in the constellation of Andromeda on a very dark night away from lights. The Milky Way is the second largest galaxy in this group; most other galaxies in our Local Group are small.

The Solar System

The major planets of the solar system, in order of mean distance from the Sun, are **Mercury**, **Venus**, **Earth**, **Mars**, **Jupiter**, **Saturn**, **Uranus**, and **Neptune**. The dwarf planets in order of average distance from the Sun are **Ceres** (located between Mars and Jupiter), **Pluto**, **Haumea**, **Makemake**, and **Eris**. All planets orbit counterclockwise around the Sun as viewed from above the Earth's North Pole.

Because **Mercury** and **Venus** are nearer to the Sun than is Earth, their motions about the Sun appear from Earth as wide swings first to one side of the Sun then to the other, though both planets move around the Sun in almost circular orbits. When their passage takes them between Earth and the Sun or beyond the Sun as seen from Earth, they cannot be seen.

The planets that lie farther from the Sun than does Earth may be seen for longer periods and are invisible only when so located in our sky that they rise and set at about the same time as the Sun—and thus become overwhelmed by the Sun's light.

The giant planets emit their own energy. On occasion, radio emissions from Jupiter exceed even those emitted by the Sun in intensity.

Mercury and Venus, because they are between Earth and the Sun, show phases much as the Moon does. The planets farther from the Sun are always seen as full, although Mars does occasionally present a slightly gibbous phase—like the Moon when not quite full.

The planets appear to move rapidly among the stars because they are relatively closer to Earth than the stars. The stars are also in motion, some at tremendous speeds, but they are so far away that their motion does not change their apparent positions in the heavens enough to be perceived. The nearest star is about 9,000 times farther away than Neptune. The count for identified **moons** in the solar system orbiting planets and dwarf planets stood at 176 as of Sept. 2011. Several dwarf planet candidates are also known to have moons.

Planet Superlatives			
Largest, most massive planet	Jupiter	Smallest, least massive planet	Mercury
Fastest orbiting planet	Mercury	Slowest orbiting planet	Neptune
Fastest sidereal rotation	Jupiter	Slowest sidereal rotation	Venus
Longest (synodic) day	Mercury	Shortest (synodic) day	Jupiter
Rotational pole closest to ecliptic	Uranus	Hottest planet	Venus
Most moons	Jupiter	No moons	Mercury, Venus
Planet with largest moon	Jupiter	Planet with moon with most eccentric orbit	Neptune
Greatest average density	Earth	Lowest average density	Saturn
Tallest mountain	Mars	Deepest oceans	Jupiter
Strongest magnetic fields	Jupiter	Greatest amount of liquid, surface water	Earth
Most circular orbit	Venus		

Planets and the Sun, by Selected Characteristics

Sun and planets	Radius—at unit distance[1] "	Radius—at mean least distance[2] "	in mi mean radius	Volume[3]	Mass[3]	Density[3]	Sidereal period				Gravity at surface[3]	Reflecting power (pct.)	Daytime surface temp. (°F)
							d	h	m	s			
Sun	959.50	976.0	432,500	1,304,000	333,000	0.26	25	9	7		28.00		+9,941
Mercury	3.36	6.5	1,516	0.0562	0.0553	0.98	58	15	36		0.38	0.11	845
Venus	8.34	33.0	3,760	0.857	0.815	0.95	243		30R		0.91	0.65	867
Earth	8.78	—	3,959	1.000	1.000	1.00		23	56	4.2	1.00	0.37	59
Moon	2.40	986.2	1,079	0.0203	0.0123	0.61	27	7	43	40	0.16	0.12	260
Mars	4.67	12.8	2,106	0.151	0.107	0.71		24	37	22	0.38	0.15	−24
Jupiter	96.40	24.5	43,441	1,321	317.8	0.24		9	55	30	2.53	0.52	−162
Saturn	80.29	10.05	36,184	764	95.16	0.12		10	39	20	1.06	0.47	−218
Uranus	34.97	2.05	15,759	63.1	14.54	0.23		17	14	20R	0.90	0.51	−323
Neptune	33.95	1.2	15,301	57.7	17.15	0.30		16	6	40	1.14	0.41	−330

R = Retrograde rotation. (1) Angular radius, in seconds of arc, if object were seen at a distance of 1 astronomical unit. (2) Angular radius, in seconds of arc, when object is closest to Earth. (3) Earth = 1.

Planets: Motion, Distance, and Brightness

Planet	Mean daily motion[1]	Orbital velocity mi per sec.[2]	Sidereal revolution days[3]	Synodic revolution days[4]	Distance from Sun in mil of mi Max.	Min.	Distance from Earth in mil of mi Max.	Min.	Light at[5] perihelion	aphelion
Mercury	14,732	29.75	87.97	115.9	43.4	28.6	137.9	48	10.56	4.59
Venus	5,768	21.76	224.7	583.9	67.7	66.8	162.2	23.7	1.94	1.89
Earth	3,548	18.50	365.256	—	94.5	91.4	—	—	1.03	0.97
Mars	1,887	15.00	686.98	779.9	154.9	128.4	249.4	33.9	0.52	0.36
Jupiter	299	8.12	4,332.6	398.9	507.4	460.1	602	366	0.041	0.034
Saturn	120	6.02	10,759.2	378.1	941.1	840.4	1,031	743	0.012	0.0098
Uranus	42	4.23	30,685.4	369.7	1,866.4	1,703.4	1,962	1,605	0.0030	0.0025
Neptune	22	3.37	60,189.0	367.5	2,824.5	2,761.7	2,913	2,676	0.0011	0.0011

(1) Average angular motion measured in seconds of arc per day. (2) Speed of revolution around Sun. (3) Number of Earth days to orbit Sun with respect to background stars. (4) Number of Earth days to get back to the same position in its orbit around Sun, relative to Earth. (5) Light at perihelion and aphelion is solar illumination measured in units of mean illumination at Earth.

Planets of the Solar System

Note: AU = astronomical unit (92.96 mil mi, mean distance of Earth from the Sun); **d** = 1 Earth synodic (solar) day (24 hours); **synodic day** = rotation period of a planet measured with respect to the Sun (the "true" day, i.e., the time from midday to midday, or from sunrise to sunrise); **sidereal day** = the rotation period of a planet with respect to the stars.

The International Astronomical Union (IAU) on Aug. 24, 2006, at their General Assembly in Prague, Czech Republic, agreed on a new definition for planet, and in the process effectively removed Pluto's planet status. The ruling came after years of debate as to whether Pluto, discovered in 1930, should still be considered the ninth planet in our solar system because of its size, orbit, and other characteristics. New discoveries of other Pluto-like objects in the solar system, such as the 2003 discovery of Eris, a **Kuiper Belt object** (KBO) bigger than Pluto, also contributed to the debate.

Under the IAU's new definition, Mercury, Venus, Earth, Mars, Jupiter, Saturn, Uranus, and Neptune are regarded as "classical" planets. A **planet** is now defined as a celestial body that (a) is in orbit around the Sun, (b) has sufficient mass for its self-gravity to overcome rigid body forces so that it assumes a hydrostatic equilibrium (nearly round) shape, and (c) has cleared the neighborhood around its orbit.

Pluto, Eris, Ceres, Makemake, and Haumea are now regarded as dwarf planets, with the status of Pluto's largest moon, Charon, to be determined at a later date. A **dwarf planet** is a celestial body that (a) is in orbit around the Sun, (b) has sufficient mass for its self-gravity to overcome rigid body forces so that it assumes a hydrostatic equilibrium (nearly round) shape, (c) has not cleared the neighborhood around its orbit, and (d) is not a satellite.

The IAU also created a new category, **small solar system bodies**, for all other objects orbiting the Sun, including comets, asteroids, KBOs, and other small objects, although it has not yet established a process by which other solar system objects will be classified.

Mercury

Distance from the Sun	
Perihelion	28.6 mil mi
Semi-major axis (mean distance)	36 mil mi (0.387 AU)
Aphelion	43.4 mil mi
Period of revolution around Sun	87.97 d
Orbital eccentricity	0.2056
Orbital inclination	7.00°
Synodic day (midday to midday)	175.94 d
Sidereal day	58.65 d
Rotational inclination	0.01°
Mass (Earth = 1)	0.0553
Mean radius	1,516 mi
Mean density (Earth = 1)	0.984
Natural satellites	0
Average surface temperature	333°F

Mercury, named for the Roman gods' messenger, is the closest planet to the Sun and the smallest in the solar system. Mercury is too much in line with the Sun to be observed against a dark sky; therefore it is always seen during morning or evening twilight. In 2008, the MESSENGER spacecraft made the first flybys of Mercury since the 1970s. Messenger went into orbit about Mercury in Mar. 2011, for a year-long reconnaissance mission. The goals of the mission include mapping, imaging, and measuring the surface composition of Mercury. Only preliminary results were available as of Aug. 2011, but the mission promises to revolutionize our understanding of Mercury and its environment.

Orbit and rotation. Mercury moves with great speed around the Sun, averaging about 30 mi per second to complete its orbit, which takes about 88 Earth days. Mercury takes nearly 59 days to rotate on its axis. Because its orbital period is only about 50% longer than its sidereal rotation, the time from one sunrise to the next on Mercury is about 176 days—twice as long as a Mercurial year. Oddly, Mercury has a magnetic field, albeit very weak. It has been held that both a fluid core and rapid rotation—neither of which Mercury is believed to have—are necessary for the generation of a planetary magnetic field. Mercury may demonstrate the contrary.

Atmosphere. Mercury's atmosphere is almost nonexistent. What very little it has is composed of 42% oxygen, 29% sodium, 22% hydrogen, 6% helium, 0.5% potassium, and 0.5% other particles. Because of Mercury's lack of atmosphere to regulate temperatures between day and night, the surface during the day may reach a temperature of about 845°F, while the temperature at night may fall as low as −300°F. Earth-based observation has provided evidence of water ice near the poles.

Surface and composition. Mercury's surface is rocky and cratered similar to that of the Earth's moon. The most imposing feature on Mercury, the Caloris Basin, is a huge impact crater more than 800 mi in diameter. Mercury has a huge iron core that takes up about 75% of the planet's radius; it has a higher percentage of iron than any other planet.

Venus

Distance from the Sun	
Perihelion	66.8 mil mi
Semi-major axis (mean distance)	67.2 mil mi (0.723 AU)
Aphelion	67.7 mil mi
Period of revolution around Sun	224.7 d
Orbital eccentricity	0.0067
Orbital inclination	3.39°
Synodic day (midday to midday)	116.75 d (retrograde)
Sidereal day	243.02 d (retrograde)
Rotational inclination	177.4°
Mass (Earth = 1)	0.815
Mean radius	3,760 mi
Mean density (Earth = 1)	0.951
Natural satellites	0
Average surface temperature	867°F

Mars

Distance from the Sun	
Perihelion	128.4 mil mi
Semi-major axis (mean distance)	141.6 mil mi (1.524 AU)
Aphelion	154.9 mil mi
Period of revolution around Sun	686.98 d (1.88 y)
Orbital eccentricity	0.0935
Orbital inclination	1.85°
Synodic day (midday to midday)	24h 39m 35s
Sidereal day	24h 37m 22s
Rotational inclination	25.19°
Mass (Earth = 1)	0.107
Mean radius	2,106 mi
Mean density (Earth = 1)	0.713
Natural satellites	2
Average surface temperature	−81°F

Venus, named for the Roman goddess of love, is the second planet out from the Sun. Because Venus is almost the same size as Earth, it is believed that the two planets were formed at the same time by the same general process and from the same mixture of chemical elements. Venus can easily be seen from Earth with the naked eye; it is the 3rd-brightest object in the sky, exceeded only by the Sun and the Moon.

Orbit and rotation. It takes Venus 225 Earth days to complete its orbit around the Sun. Its synodic revolution—its return to the same relationship with Earth and the Sun, which is a result of the combination of its own motion with that of Earth—is 584 days. Because of this, every 19 months Venus is closer to Earth than any other planet. The rotation period of Venus appears to be 243 days clockwise—in other words, contrary to the spin of the other planets and contrary to its own motion around the Sun. This rate and sense of rotation makes for a solar day (sunrise to sunrise) on Venus of 116.8 Earth days; night lasts 58 days and day lasts 58 days. Venus has no detectible magnetic field.

Atmosphere. The Venusian atmosphere is very thick and toxic. It is composed primarily of 96.5% carbon dioxide, 3.5% nitrogen, and trace concentrations of sulfur dioxide, argon, water, carbon monoxide, helium, and neon. In addition, it exerts an atmospheric pressure at the surface more than 90 times Earth's normal sea-level pressure. The planet is covered with a dense, white, cloudy atmosphere that conceals whatever is below it. These clouds are believed to contain sulfuric acid, meaning that when it rains on Venus, it may rain sulfuric acid. Due to the thickness of the atmosphere and resulting extreme greenhouse effect, the temperature is essentially the same day and night; the planet has an average surface temperature of about 867°F, making it the hottest planet in the solar system. Winds of about 200 mph in the clouds may account for the transfer of heat into the night side despite the low rotation speed of the planet. However, at the surface, the winds are very slow.

Surface and composition. Radar-produced maps of the planet show large craters, continent-sized highlands, and extensive dry lowlands. No tectonic activity has been found similar to Earth's moving tectonic plates, but a system of global rift zones and numerous broad, low, dome-like structures, called coronae, may have been produced by the upwelling and subsidence of magma from the mantle. Volcanic surface features, such as vast lava plains, fields of small lava domes, and large shield volcanoes, are common. About 1,600 volcanoes and volcanic features appear on the Venusian surface; more than 85% of the surface is covered by volcanic flows. Theia Mons, a huge shield volcano, has a diameter of over 600 mi and a height of over 3.5 mi. (The largest Hawaiian volcano is only about 125 mi in diameter, but rises nearly 5.5 mi from the ocean floor.) Aside from volcanoes, there are highly deformed mountain belts across Venus along with a few meteor-impact craters more than 20 mi wide. Erosion is a very slow process on Venus due to the lack of water. There are indications of some wind movement of dust and sand. The few impact craters on Venus suggest that the surface is generally geologically young—less than 800 mil years old. Despite the fact that probes have landed on Venus, there are very few pictures because the probes themselves couldn't survive the high temperature and atmospheric pressure.

Named for the Roman god of war, the "Red Planet" has some features much like Earth. Mars has climate, seasons, volcanoes, and possibly once had liquid water flowing across its surface. Mars can easily be seen with the naked eye on most clear nights, which is why it was one of the first planets to be studied by ancient astronomers. Later, when telescopes came into use, many observers claimed that canals made by Martians existed on the planet's surface, which led to speculation as to whether there was intelligent life there. Unmanned probes have since put all those theories to rest; the canals turned out to be topographic patterns and dust storms.

Orbit and rotation. Although Mars's orbital path is nearly circular, it is somewhat more eccentric than that of most other planets; Mars is more than 26 mil mi farther from the Sun at its most distant point compared to its closest approach. Its orbit and speed in relation to Earth's bring it fairly close to Earth about every 2 years. Every 15-17 years the close approaches are especially favorable for observation.

Mars rotates in 24 hours and 37 minutes, almost the same period of time as Earth. Mars's mean distance from the Sun is 142 mil mi. Because Mars's axis of rotation is inclined by about 25° from the vertical to the plane of its solar orbit about the Sun, the planet has seasons.

Unlike Earth's global magnetic field, the Martian magnetic field is small, weak, and localized and may be the remnant of a stronger field from the planet's past.

Atmosphere. The Martian atmosphere is composed primarily of 95.32% carbon dioxide, 2.7% nitrogen, 1.6% argon, 0.13% oxygen, 0.08% carbon monoxide, and in very minor quantities, water, hydrogen oxide, and neon. The atmosphere on Mars is very thin; it has an atmospheric pressure between 1% and 2% of Earth's (if Earth's atmosphere were that thin, we would not have enough oxygen to breathe). Because the Martian atmosphere is so thin and because of the planet's weak magnetic field, its surface is bombarded by cosmic radiation about 100 times as intense as on Earth.

Martian weather systems consist mainly of huge dust storms. On the poles, white caps (believed to be both water ice and carbon dioxide ice) grow in winter and shrink in summer. It is mainly the carbon dioxide that comes and goes with the seasons. The water ice is apparently in many layers with dust between them, indicating climatic cycles.

Surface and composition. Mars is an alien world with rust-red sand and pink skies. In the planet's beginning stages when it was much hotter, Mars's surface melted to a sufficient extent to separate into dense and lighter layers. At some point later, Mars cooled enough to allow liquid water to possibly flow across its surface. Today, Mars is very dry.

Natural satellites. Mars has 2 satellites called Phobos and Deimos, each discovered in 1877 by Asaph Hall. (Phobos measures about 11 by 17 mi and Deimos about 7 by 9 mi.) Deimos, the outer satellite, revolves around the planet in about 31 hours. Phobos, the inner satellite, whips around Mars in a little more than 7 hours, making 3 trips each Martian day. Since it orbits Mars faster than the planet rotates, Phobos rises in the west and sets in the east, opposite to what other bodies appear to do in the Martian sky. Both moons are irregularly shaped and pitted with numerous craters. Their origins are not known; however, some astronomers consider them to be asteroid-like objects that were captured by Mars very early in its history.

Jupiter

Distance from the Sun	
Perihelion	460.1 mil mi
Semi-major axis (mean distance)	483.8 mil mi (5.204 AU)
Aphelion	507.4 mil mi
Period of revolution around Sun	11.862 y
Orbital eccentricity	0.0489
Orbital inclination	1.304°
Synodic day (midday to midday)	9h 55m 33s
Sidereal day	9h 55m 30s
Rotational inclination	3.13°
Mass (Earth = 1)	317.8
Mean radius	43,441 mi
Mean density (Earth = 1)	0.24
Natural satellites	64
Average temperature*	−162°F

*i.e., temperature where atmosphere pressure equals 1 Earth atmosphere.

Jupiter, named for the Roman ruler of the gods, is the largest planet in the solar system (11 times the diameter of Earth). Its mass is more than twice the mass of all the other planets, moons, and asteroids put together. Visible to the naked eye and known to the ancients, it was a focus of the Italian scientist Galileo Galilei who viewed the planet and its 4 largest moons through a homemade telescope.

Orbit and rotation. Jupiter is at an average distance of 484 mil mi from the Sun and takes almost 12 Earth years to make a complete revolution. The largest of the planets, Jupiter has an equatorial diameter of 88,846 mi; however, its polar diameter is more than 5,700 mi shorter. This noticeable oblateness is a result of the liquidity of the planet and its extremely rapid rotation rate—a Jupiter day is less than 10 Earth hours long. For a planet this size, this rotational speed is amazing. A point on Jupiter's equator moves at a speed of 22,000 mph, as compared with 1,000 mph for a point on Earth's equator. Jupiter's magnetic field is by far the strongest of any planet. Electrical activity caused by this field is so strong that it discharges billions of watts into Earth's magnetic field daily.

Atmosphere. Jupiter's atmosphere is primarily composed of 90% molecular hydrogen and 10% helium. Minor constituents include methane, ammonia, hydrogen deuteride, ethane, and water. Jupiter has a turbulent atmosphere characterized by thick clouds, high winds, and huge lightning storms many times larger than those on Earth. The atmospheric temperature varies, but the temperature at the tops of clouds may be about −280°F. The Great Red Spot seen prominently on Jupiter is a huge hurricane-like storm that is three times the diameter of Earth. In 2006, the Hubble Space Telescope detected the appearance of a second, smaller red spot.

Surface and composition. Gas giant planets like Jupiter, Saturn, and Neptune do not have a surface like Earth or any of the other rocky planets. The gases become denser with depth, until they may turn into a slush or slurry. Jupiter has a liquid hydrogen ocean more than 35,000 mi deep. It likely has a rocky core about the size of Earth, but 13 times more massive. There is no sharp interface between the gaseous atmosphere and the hydrogen ocean that accounts for most of Jupiter's volume. At lower depths, under enormous pressure, the liquid hydrogen takes on the properties of a metal. It is likely that this liquid metallic hydrogen is the source for both Jupiter's persistent radio noise and for its improbably strong magnetic field.

Natural satellites. Jupiter has 64 known satellites, 24 of which were found since 2003. Four of the moons (in order of distance from Jupiter), Io, Europa, Ganymede, and Callisto—all discovered by Galileo in 1610—are large and bright and are close in diameter to Earth's moon and Mercury. Because they move so rapidly around Jupiter, their change in position from night to night can be seen from Earth using binoculars.

Io is one of the most intriguing moons because it is the most volcanically active body in the solar system. A gaseous, doughnut-shaped ring, or torus, enveloping Io's orbit around Jupiter may have been formed by material ejected from Io's active volcanoes. (This is not to be confused with Jupiter's rings.) These volcanoes, hotter than Earth's volcanoes, erupt mainly molten sulfur.

Europa may have a 30-mi-deep salty, liquid ocean beneath its icy crust, perhaps a small metallic core, and a very tenuous atmosphere. Ganymede is the biggest moon in the solar system. With a diameter of 3,120 mi, it is bigger than both the planet Mercury and dwarf planet Pluto. Ganymede also has it own magnetic field produced by a molten core perhaps of iron sulfide. Callisto has the oldest, most heavily cratered surface in the solar system, a very thin atmosphere of carbon dioxide, and possibly a subsurface liquid ocean.

The other satellites are much smaller, with 4 closer to Jupiter than Io, 5 between Ganymede and Callisto, and the rest farther out. Most of Jupiter's moons revolve around Jupiter clockwise as seen from the north, contrary to the motions of most satellites in the solar system and to the direction of revolution of planets around the Sun. These moons may be captured asteroids.

Rings. Jupiter has a set of rings that cannot be seen from Earth without powerful telescopes. They are composed of small dust grains possibly blasted off the 4 innermost moons by meteoroid impacts.

Saturn

Distance from the Sun	
Perihelion	840.44 mil mi
Semi-major axis (mean distance)	890.8 mil mi (9.582 AU)
Aphelion	941.07 mil mi
Period of revolution around Sun	29.458 y
Orbital eccentricity	0.0565
Orbital inclination	2.485°
Synodic day (midday to midday)	10h 39m 23s
Sidereal day	10h 39m 22s
Rotational inclination	26.73°
Mass (Earth = 1)	95.159
Mean radius	36,184 mi
Mean density (Earth = 1)	0.125
Natural satellites	62
Average temperature*	−218°F

*i.e., temperature where atmosphere pressure equals 1 Earth atmosphere.

Saturn, named for the Roman ruler of the Titans, is the 6th planet from the Sun and most distant of the planets visible to the unaided eye. Saturn is 2nd in size to Jupiter, but its mass is much smaller. Saturn is the only planet less dense than water, meaning that Saturn would float if there were a pool of water gigantic enough to hold it.

Orbit and rotation. Saturn's diameter is almost 74,900 mi at the equator, while its polar diameter is more than 7,300 mi shorter. Like Jupiter, its noticeable oblateness is a result of the liquidity of the planet and its extremely rapid rate of rotation; a day is little more than 10 Earth hours long.

Atmosphere. Saturn's atmosphere is composed primarily of 96.3% hydrogen, 3.3% helium, and traces of methane, ammonia, hydrogen deuteride, ethane, and water. Saturn's atmosphere is much like that of Jupiter, except that the temperature at the top of its cloud layer is at least 50°F colder.

Surface and composition. Saturn's atmosphere resembles Jupiter's; it likely has a small dense center surrounded by a deep ocean of hydrogen.

Natural satellites. Saturn has 62 known natural satellites, most of which were not discovered until space probes reached the planet. Saturn's moon Mimas has an impact crater 81 mi across (the moon itself is only 249 mi across). Enceladus has an atmosphere and shows evidence of geysers that spit water ice and vapor. Two tiny moons orbit within the rings, plowing through and making gaps in the rings along their orbits. Pan, the innermost satellite, creates the Encke Gap of Saturn's A-ring. 2005 S1 creates the Keeler Gap. The most intriguing Saturnian moon is Titan. The 2nd-biggest moon in the solar system, Titan, is bigger than Mercury. Its atmosphere is similar to Earth's atmosphere of long ago; it is made up of approximately 95% nitrogen with traces of methane. Titan's atmosphere extends about 360 mi into space whereas Earth's atmosphere extends about 37 mi. Photographs from the surface show a muddy terrain, with possible deposits of water ice, channels carved by liquid methane springs, and an interesting boundary between light and dark material on the surface. In addition, in 2006, scientists found sand dunes on Titan's surface. The "sand" is believed to be tiny water ice crystals or organic compounds. Surface phenomena such as sand dunes are signs of erosion and wind. However, unlike on Earth or Mars, Titan's winds are not the result of uneven solar heating on the moon's surface, but rather the strong gravitational pull from Saturn that creates atmospheric "tides" almost in the same way Earth's moon does to the oceans.

Rings. Saturn's ring system is the planet's most recognizable feature. It begins about 4,000 mi above the visible disk of Saturn lying above its equator and extends about 260,000 mi into space. The diameter of the ring system visible from Earth is about 170,000 mi; the rings are estimated to be about 700 ft thick. The rings are composed of rock and ice and range in size from tiny particles to large chunks of material the size of a bus. There are several divisions in the rings. The 2,920-mi Cassini division, the gap between the A and B rings, is the largest division.

Uranus

Distance from the Sun	
Perihelion	1,703.4 mil mi
Semi-major axis (mean distance)	1,784.8 mil mi (19.201 AU)
Aphelion	1,866.4 mil mi
Period of revolution around Sun	84.01 y
Orbital eccentricity	0.0457
Orbital inclination	0.772°
Synodic day (midday to midday)	17h 14m 23s (retrograde)
Sidereal day	17h 14m 24s (retrograde)
Rotational inclination	97.77°
Mass (Earth = 1)	14.536
Mean radius	15,759 mi
Mean density (Earth = 1)	0.23
Natural satellites	27
Average temperature*	−323°F

*i.e., temperature where atmosphere pressure equals 1 Earth atmosphere.

Uranus, discovered by Sir William Herschel in 1781, was the first planet discovered using a telescope. It was named for the father of the Titans in Roman mythology.

Rotation and orbit. Uranus has a diameter of over 31,000 mi and spins once in approximately 17.23 hours, according to flyby magnetic data. One of the most fascinating features of Uranus is how far over it is tipped. Its north pole lies 98° from being directly up and down to its orbit plane. Thus, its seasons are extreme. Over its 84-year orbit, when the Sun rises at the north pole, it shines there for about 42 Earth years; then it sets, and the north pole is in darkness for 42 Earth years. In addition to its rotational tilt, Uranus's magnetic field axis is tipped an incredible 58.6° from its rotational axis and is displaced about 30% of its radius away from the planet's center.

Atmosphere. The atmosphere is composed primarily of 82.5% hydrogen, 15.2% helium, 2.3% methane, with small amounts of hydrogen deuteride, ammonia ice, water ice, ammonia hydrosulfide, and methane ice.

Surface and composition. Uranus has no solid surface, and likely no rocky core but rather a mixture of rocks and assorted ices with about 15% hydrogen and some helium.

Natural satellites. Uranus has 27 known moons, which have orbits lying in the plane of the planet's equator. Five moons are relatively large, while 22 are very small and were only discovered with the *Voyager 2* mission or in later observations. Miranda has grooved markings, reminiscent of Jupiter's Ganymede, but often arranged in a chevron pattern. Rifts and channels on Ariel provide evidence of liquid flowing over its surface in the past. Umbriel is extremely dark, prompting some observers to regard its surface as among the oldest in the system. Titania has rifts and fractures, but not the evidence of flow found on Ariel. Oberon's main feature is its surface saturated with craters, unrelieved by other formations.

Rings. In the equatorial plane there is also a complex of 11 rings, 9 of which were discovered in 1978 by observers watching Uranus pass before a star.

Neptune

Distance from the Sun	
Perihelion	2,761.7 mil mi
Semi-major axis (mean distance)	2,793.1 (30.047 AU)
Aphelion	2,824.5 mil mi
Period of revolution around Sun	164.79 y
Orbital eccentricity	0.0113
Orbital inclination	1.769°
Synodic day (midday to midday)	16h 6m 37s
Sidereal day	16h 6m 36s
Rotational inclination	28.32°
Mass (Earth = 1)	17.147
Mean radius	15,301 mi
Mean density (Earth = 1)	0.297
Natural satellites	13
Average temperature*	−330°F

*i.e., temperature where atmosphere pressure equals 1 Earth atmosphere.

Named for the Roman god of the sea, Neptune was the first planet discovered through mathematical calculations and not observation. Its approximate orbit and position were first calculated independently by John Couch Adams and Urbain Le Verrier in 1845. In 1846, Johann Galle first observed Neptune through a telescope.

Orbit and rotation. Neptune orbits the Sun in 164.8 years in a nearly circular orbit. Its magnetic field is considerably asymmetric to the planet's structure, similar to, but not so extreme as, that found at Uranus. Neptune's magnetic field axis is tipped 46.9° from its rotational axis and is displaced more than 55% of its radius away from the planet's center.

Atmosphere. The Neptunian atmosphere is composed primarily of 80% hydrogen, 19% helium, 1.5% methane, and small amounts of hydrogen deuteride, ethane, ammonia ice, water ice, ammonia hydrosulfide, and methane ice. Neptune's atmosphere is quite blue, with quickly changing white clouds often suspended high above an apparent surface. A Great Dark Spot was discovered in 1989 when *Voyager 2* visited the planet, reminiscent of the Great Red Spot of Jupiter. Observations with the Hubble Space Telescope have shown that the Great Dark Spot originally seen by *Voyager* has apparently dissipated, but a new dark spot has since appeared. Lightning and auroras have been found on other giant planets, but only the aurora phenomenon has been seen on Neptune. As with the other giant planets, Neptune is emitting more energy than it receives from the Sun. The excess has been found to be 2.7 times the solar contribution.

Surface and composition. As with other giant planets, Neptune may have no solid surface, or exact diameter. However, a mean value of 30,600 mi may be assigned to a diameter between atmosphere levels where the pressure is about the same as sea level on Earth.

Natural satellites. Largest of Neptune's 13 satellites is Triton. It is the only large moon in a retrograde orbit, which suggests that it was captured rather than having been there from the beginning. Triton's large size, sufficient to raise significant tides on the planet, may one day, billions of years from now, cause Triton to come close enough to Neptune for it to be torn apart. Triton has a tenuous atmosphere of nitrogen with a trace of hydrocarbons and evidence of active geysers injecting material into it. Triton is the coldest object yet measured in the solar system with a surface temperature of −391°F. Only about half of Triton has been observed, but its terrain shows cratering and a strange regional feature described as resembling the skin of a cantaloupe. Nereid has the highest orbital eccentricity (0.75) of any moon. Its long looping orbit suggests that it was also captured. In 2003, 2 more moons, which orbit farther from their parent planet than any other moons, were discovered. The *Voyager 2* probe in 1989 confirmed the existence of 6 rings around Neptune composed of very fine particles. There may be some clumpiness in the rings' structure. It is not known whether Neptune's satellites influence the formation or maintenance of the rings.

Dwarf Planets

Note: See page 339 for the definition of a dwarf planet.

Ceres

```
Distance from the Sun
  Perihelion .................... 237 mil mi (2.55 AU)
  Semi-major axis (mean distance) ... 257 mil mi (2.77 AU)
Period of revolution around Sun.................. 4.6 y
Orbital eccentricity............................0.0789
Orbital inclination...........................10.58°
Sidereal day...........................9.075 hours
Mass (Earth = 1) ..........................0.00016
Mean radius...................................300 mi
```

Ceres was the first asteroid ever discovered, on Jan. 1, 1801, by Guiseppe Piazzi. In the 1800s, it was considered a planet, but as more asteroids were discovered, it lost that designation. In Aug. of 2006, it was designated a dwarf planet by the International Astronomical Union.

No probe has ever visited Ceres. NASA's DAWN space probe, launched in Sept. 2007, may become the first. The Dawn probe's mission is to Vesta and Ceres, the solar system's two largest asteroids. When Dawn arrives at Ceres in Feb. 2015, months before the New Horizons probe arrives at Pluto, it will be the first mission to study a dwarf planet.

Orbit and rotation. Ceres orbits the Sun in the asteroid belt region between Mars and Jupiter.

Surface and composition. Ceres is in a class of stony meteorites known as carbonaceous chondrites. These are considered to be the oldest materials in the solar system, with a composition reflecting that of the primitive solar nebula. Extremely dark in color, probably because of their hydrocarbon content, they show evidence of having absorbed water of hydration. Thus, unlike the Earth and the Moon, they have never either melted or been reheated since they first formed.

Pluto

```
Distance from the Sun
  Perihelion .......................... 2,756.9 mil mi
  Semi-major axis (mean distance).......... 3,647.2 mil mi
                                          (39.482 AU)
  Aphelion ......................... 4,583.2 mil mi
Period of revolution around Sun .............. 247.68 y
Orbital eccentricity....................... 0.2488
Orbital inclination.........................17.16°
Synodic day (midday to midday).... 6d 9h 17m (retrograde)
Sidereal day .................... 6d 9h 18m (retrograde)
Rotational inclination......................122.53°
Mass (Earth = 1)............................ 0.0021
Mean radius ...............................742.5 mi
Mean density (Earth = 1) ....................... 0.317
Natural satellites ................................ 4
Average surface temperature ................. −369°F
```

Pluto, named for the Roman god of the underworld, is the 2nd-largest-known Kuiper Belt object (KBO) in the solar system. It was first discovered in 1930 by Clyde Tombaugh and classified as a planet until 2006, when the International Astronomical Union (IAU) changed its designation to dwarf planet. The New Horizons spacecraft was launched on a voyage to Pluto and beyond in 2006; the spacecraft will make its closest approach to Pluto in July 2015. In 2008, Pluto was designated by the IAU as the prototype for a class of objects called **plutoids**, bodies (a) whose average distance from the Sun is greater than Neptune's; (b) are large enough that gravity determines their shape; and (c) have not cleared their orbit of other objects. Haumea, Makemake, and Eris are also Plutoids. At least 10 other Plutoid candidates have been identified through mid-2011.

Orbit and rotation. Pluto's orbit and rotation are highly irregular. Although on average it stays about 3.6 bil mi from the Sun, it may get as close as 2.76 bil mi, and for about 20 years of its orbit, it is closer to the Sun than Neptune. Currently, it is beyond Neptune's orbit.

Atmosphere and surface. Because no probes have visited Pluto, it is difficult for astronomers to accurately take readings of the dwarf planet's atmospheric composition. It is believed that an atmosphere of methane, nitrogen, and carbon monoxide exists when the dwarf planet is closer to the Sun. When Pluto is farther away from the Sun during its orbit, the atmosphere freezes and becomes part of the surface. Large regions on Pluto are dark, others light; Pluto has spots and perhaps polar caps. There is also evidence of temperature fluctuations on the dwarf planet that may indicate primitive weather. Its core may be rocky with a mantle of water ice surrounding it.

Natural satellites. Pluto has 4 natural satellites. Charon, the biggest, has a diameter of 737 mi—about half of Pluto's diameter of 1,485 mi. No other planet of any kind has a moon so close to its size. Discovered in 1978, Charon orbits Pluto at a distance of 12,200 mi and takes 6.39 days to move around the dwarf planet. In this same length of time, Pluto and Charon both rotate once around their axes, meaning that a person standing on Pluto would always see the same face of Charon in the same part of the sky, every day and night. The Pluto-Charon system thus appears to rotate as virtually a rigid body. Both worlds are roughly spherical and have comparable densities. Because of these similarities and their peculiar relationship, there is debate as to whether Charon should one day be designated a dwarf planet.

Two other moons, discovered in 2005 and 2006, were officially named Nix and Hydra. A 4th moon, discovered in summer 2011, had not been given an official name as of Aug. 2011; it is provisionally referred to as P4.

Haumea

```
Distance from the Sun
  Semi-major axis (mean distance)........... 43.335 AU
Period of revolution around Sun .................. 285 y
Mean radius .................................. 420 mi
Orbital eccentricity ............................ 0.189
Orbital inclination ..........................28.19°
Mass (Earth = 1)........................... 0.0007
Natural satellites.................................2
```

Haumea was discovered in 2004 and was accepted as a dwarf planet by the IAU in 2008.
Orbit and rotation. Haumea has a moderately eccentric orbit and takes about 285 years to go around the Sun.
Surface and composition. Spectra of Haumea indicate the presence of almost pure crystalline water ice. The surface reflects about 60% of sunlight shining on it. Haumea has a very oblong shape, twice as long as it is wide.
Natural satellites. Haumea has two natural satellites.

Makemake

```
Distance from the Sun
  Semi-major axis (mean distance)........... 45.791 AU
Period of revolution around Sun .................. 310 y
Mean radius .................................. 450 mi
Orbital eccentricity ............................ 0.159
Orbital inclination ..........................28.96°
Mass (Earth = 1)........................... 0.0007
```

Makemake was discovered in 2005 and was accepted as a dwarf planet by the IAU in 2008.
Orbit and rotation. Makemake has a moderately eccentric orbit and takes about 310 years to go around the Sun.
Surface and composition. Spectra of Makemake indicate the presence of frozen methane, as well as several organic compounds. The surface is highly reflective and appears similar to that of Pluto.

Eris

```
Distance from the Sun
  Semi-major axis (mean distance).......... 67.6681 AU
Period of revolution around Sun.................. 560 y
Mean radius ................................. 925 mi
Orbital eccentricity ........................... 0.44177
Orbital inclination ..........................44.177°
Natural satellites ................................ 1
Mass (Earth = 1)........................... 0.0027
```

Eris is the largest dwarf planet. Discovered in 2003 by astronomers at the California Institute of Technology, it is the most distant object ever seen in orbit around the Sun.
Orbit and rotation. Eris has a highly elliptical orbit and takes about 560 years to go around the Sun—more than twice the time it takes Pluto. Its inclination is steep, tilted at 44° to the planetary plane. It also has an extremely eccentric orbit. It will be at its closest, actually coming inside part of Pluto's orbit, in about 280 years.
Surface and composition. Eris, with a surface covered in frozen methane, may be similar to Pluto and the Neptunian moon Triton. Observations made by the Hubble Space Telescope show that Eris's surface is almost white and uniform, reflecting 86% of the light that hits it. This makes it the most reflective body in the solar system. The dwarf planet's interior is likely a mixture of rock and ice.
Natural satellites. Eris has one moon, Dysnomia.

Small Solar System Bodies: Asteroids, Comets, Kuiper Belt, and the Oort Cloud

Asteroids

Besides planets and moons, there are many smaller objects that orbit the Sun. In 2006, the IAU officially designated these objects "small solar system bodies." **Asteroids** or minor planets are found mainly in a belt between the orbits of Mars and Jupiter, but some may be found outside this region. Within this belt there may be millions of asteroids of varying sizes. Most asteroids are very small. Ceres, which can be classified both as an asteroid and a dwarf planet, is 588 mi in diameter, about one-quarter the diameter of our moon.

Some of these objects, or asteroids, are gravitationally locked with Jupiter and the Sun so that they have roughly the same orbit as Jupiter but are either 60° ahead or behind the planet. These are the **Trojan asteroids**. Many of the smaller moons of the solar system, especially those in retrograde orbits, may be captured asteroids. Asteroids whose orbits either cross or come close to the Earth's orbit are labeled **Near Earth asteroids** or NEAs. A handful of asteroids have actually been imaged by the Arecibo and Goldstone radio telescopes, and by the NEAR Shoemaker space probe, while the *Galileo* spacecraft imaged the asteroids Gaspra and Ida (including its moon Dactyl) on its way to Jupiter.

Comets

Comets are small icy bodies that orbit the Sun. When they approach the Sun, the energy from the Sun boils off material from the comet's icy nucleus, producing an enlarged head (or **coma**), and in many cases an extended tail. Because of the proximity to the Sun and the expanded head and tail, comets are brighter when near the Sun. For large comets, the head may be 100,000 mi across and the tail more than a million miles long, though both are mainly empty space.

Comets have been known since ancient times; ultimately, British astronomer Edmund Halley (1656-1742) realized that a group of historical reports were just repeated visits of the same object. Comets are the only astronomical objects named after their discoverers. In 1986, the European spacecraft *Giotto* took the first close-up images of a comet's nucleus, specifically of Comet Halley, showing it had a peanut-shaped nucleus whose longest dimension was about 10 mi.

In 1995, Alan Hale (1958-) and Thomas Bopp (1949-) independently discovered a comet that was then beyond the orbit of Jupiter. It was the farthest comet ever discovered by amateurs and one of the brightest of all time. It also holds the record for length of naked-eye visibility—19 months—and is the most photographed comet in history. In July 2009, an amateur astronomer discovered a large impact scar in the upper atmosphere of Jupiter, likely the results of another cometary impact.

Kuiper Belt

The **Kuiper Belt** is a doughnut-shaped region that extends to about 50 AU from the Sun and is thought to be the source of short-period comets such as Comet Halley or Comet Swift-Tuttle. It is filled with icy bodies that are in solar orbit. The more than 1,000 objects found in this region in recent years are called Kuiper Belt objects (KBOs). It is estimated that there are more than 70,000 objects 60 mi in diameter or larger within the Kuiper Belt. Dwarf planets Pluto and Eris are considered KBOs. There are at least 6 KBOs larger than 300 mi in diameter.

Oort Cloud

The Oort Cloud is a vast spherical shell hypothesized to exist around the Sun. Astronomer Jan Oort (1900-92) proposed its existence as the origin for long-period comets that enter the inner part of the solar system where the planets orbit. As of yet, our technology is not sufficient to detect any members of the Oort Cloud, other than those comets that have been observed that indicate the most distant parts of their orbits may reach out to 50,000 AU. Recent examples of such long-period comets are Comet Hale-Bopp and Comet Hyakutake.

The Sun

Distance from Earth, mean	92.96 mil mi (1 AU)
Sidereal day	25.38 d
Mass (Earth =1)	332,900
Mean radius	432,200 mi
Mean density (Earth =1)	0.255
Average surface temperature	9,941°F

The Sun is the Earth's primary source of light and heat, and its closest star. The biggest object in the solar system, the Sun is 332,900 times more massive than Earth and contains 99.86% of the mass of the entire solar system. On the whole, the Sun is made up of about 92.1% hydrogen and 7.8% helium, with trace amounts of other elements. It has a mass and luminosity greater than that of 90% of the stars in the Milky Way galaxy. Although most of the stars that can be easily seen on a clear night are bigger and brighter than the Sun, its proximity to Earth makes it appear tremendously large and bright. The Sun is 400,000 times as bright as the full moon, and it gives Earth 6 mil times as much light as do all other stars put together. Because of the great distance between the Sun and Earth, it takes about 499 seconds, or slightly more than 8 minutes, for light from the Sun to reach Earth.

Composition. The Sun has six regions. The first three from the inside out are the core, the radiative zone, and the convective zone. Together they form the interior. The others, which comprise the visible surface, are the photosphere, the chromosphere, and the outermost region, the corona.

The Sun's core is where its heat and energy are produced. Through a series of nuclear fusion reactions, hydrogen nuclei are converted to helium nuclei. Temperatures in the core are theorized to be 28 mil°F. From the core, photons transport the energy outward through the radiative zone. It can take photons several million years to pass through this area. In the convective zone, gases move energy outward at a faster rate. Like a boiling pot, bubbles of gas bring energy to the surface.

The photosphere is the visible surface of the Sun, that is, the light from here is what we see as sunlight. When sunlight is analyzed with a spectroscope, it is found to consist of a continuous spectrum composed of all the colors of the rainbow in order, crossed by many dark lines. The dark "absorption lines" are produced by gaseous materials in the outer layers of the Sun. More than 60 of the natural terrestrial elements have been identified in the Sun, all in gaseous form because of the Sun's intense heat.

Just above the photosphere is the chromosphere, which is visible to the naked eye only at total solar eclipses, appearing then to be a pinkish-violet layer with occasional great prominences projecting above its general level. With proper instruments, the chromosphere can be seen or photographed whenever the Sun is visible. Above the chromosphere is the corona, also visible to the naked eye only at times of total eclipse or with instruments that permit the brighter portions of the corona to be seen. The light of the corona surges millions of miles from the Sun, where atoms of which it is composed are all in a state of extreme attenuation and high ionization that indicates temperatures nearly 2 mil°F.

Sunspots. These dark, irregularly shaped regions may reach diameters of thousands of miles. There is an intimate connection between sunspots and the corona. At times of low sunspot activity, the fine streamers of the corona are longer above the Sun's equator than over the polar regions of the Sun; during periods of high sunspot activity, the corona extends fairly evenly outward from all regions of the Sun, but to a much greater distance in space. The average life of a sunspot group is 2 months, but some have lasted for more than a year.

Sunspots reach a low point, on average, every 11.3 years, with a peak of activity occurring irregularly between 2 successive periods of minimal activity. Currently, the number of sunspots is declining. Solar minimum occurred late in 2006.

Solar wind and magnetic field. Magnetic arches, called prominences, may extend tens of thousands of miles into the corona and may release enormous amounts of energy heating the corona. Coronal mass ejections are enormous releases of solar energy. Coronal holes are regions where the corona appears dark in X-rays, and are associated with open magnetic field lines, where the magnetic field lines project out into space instead of back towards the Sun. It is in these regions where the high-speed solar wind originates.

The solar wind carries the Sun's magnetic field, which extends beyond the planets. This is called the interplanetary magnetic field (IMF). Far past Pluto and the Kuiper Belt, the solar wind and the IMF lose their influence, and the boundary between them and interstellar space is called the heliopause.

Searching for Extrasolar Planets

During the last 10 years of the 20th century, astronomers began to detect the presence of planets orbiting stars other than the Sun. Except for a few possible instances, they have not seen those objects, but merely inferred their existence by their effect on their parent star. The Sun is a typical star in many respects. With over 200 bil stars in the Milky Way, it seems plausible that many other stars might have planets.

As of summer 2011, astronomers had found a total of 573 planets orbiting some 500 stars. Of those, 330 were at least as massive as Jupiter, which is about 318 times more massive than the Earth. 243 of the planets may be less massive than Jupiter. Planets with masses less than Jupiter are now regularly discovered; at the time of this writing, the minimum confirmed mass for an extrasolar planet was about 2 times the mass of the Earth.

Using the Doppler Effect to detect radial velocity changes in the motions of individual stars, astronomers are more likely to find high-mass planets in close and eccentric orbits around stars, because that situation produces larger and more noticeable changes.

In addition to the radial velocity method, astronomers are now using an optical gravitational lensing means of detecting extrasolar planets. Using this technique, Southern Hemisphere astronomers found the most distant planet yet detected, about halfway to the center of our own Milky Way galaxy.

Astronomers have also found planets by looking for the periodic dimming of starlight as orbiting planets pass in front of their host stars. About 25 planets have been discovered this way.

In 2005, astronomers obtained the first direct photograph of an extrasolar planet. The unnamed planet orbits a star called GQ Lupi, which is a star like our Sun but younger. The planet is about 100 AUs away from its star, and it is estimated to be about twice as massive as Jupiter.

In 2006, astronomers discovered what they call a "super Earth" orbiting a red dwarf star 9,000 light-years away. The planet appears to have about 13 times the mass of Earth and may be composed of rock and ice. Although the planet is similar in structure to the Earth, it is believed to orbit too far from its star for there to be any liquid on the surface. In 2007, astronomers for the first time detected water in the atmosphere of an extra-solar planet.

In Apr. 2009, NASA launched Kepler, the first telescope sensitive enough to detect Earth-sized planets around other stars. Kepler's first data release, in summer 2010, included data indicating that small planets are more common than large planets, with hints of planets with diameters as small as twice the diameter of Earth. All of the planet candidates to date orbit their stars much closer than Earth orbits the Sun. Kepler will need to observe for several more years to find evidence of Earth-sized planets at comparable distances from their stars.

Earth: Size, Computation of Time, Seasons

Distance from the Sun	
Perihelion	91.4 mil mi
Semi-major axis (mean distance)	93 mil mi (1.0000 AU)
Aphelion	94.5 mil mi
Period of revolution	365.256 d
Orbital eccentricity	0.0167
Orbital inclination	0°
Sidereal day (rotation period)	23h 56m 4.2s
Synodic day (midday to midday)	24h 0m 0s
Rotational inclination	23.45°
Mass (Earth = 1)	1
Mean radius	3,958.8 mi
Mean density (Earth = 1)	1
Natural satellites	1
Average surface temperature	59°F

Earth is the 5th-largest planet and the 3rd from the Sun. Its mass is 5.9736×10^{24} kg. Earth's equatorial diameter is 7,926 mi while its polar diameter is only 7,900 mi.

Size and dimensions. Earth is considered a solid mass, yet it has a large, liquid iron, **magnetic core** with a radius of about 2,160 mi. Surprisingly, it has a solid **inner core** that may be a large iron crystal, with a radius of 760 mi. Around the core is a thick shell, or **mantle**, of dense rock. This mantle is composed of materials rich in iron and magnesium. It is somewhat plastic-like, and under slow steady pressure, it can flow like a liquid. The mantle, in turn, is covered by a thin **crust** forming the solid granite and basalt base of the continents and ocean basins. Over broad areas of Earth's surface, the crust has a thin cover of sedimentary rock such as sandstone, shale, and limestone formed by weathering and by deposits of sands, clays, and plant and animal remains.

The temperature inside the Earth increases about 1°F with every 100 to 200 ft in depth, in the upper 100 km of Earth, and reaches nearly 8,000-9,000°F at the center. The heat is believed to come from radioactivity in rocks, pressures within Earth, and the original heat of formation.

Atmosphere of Earth. Earth's atmosphere is a blanket composed of 78% nitrogen, 21% oxygen, and 1% argon. Present in minute quantities are carbon dioxide, hydrogen, neon, helium, krypton, and xenon. Water vapor displaces other gases and varies from nearly zero to about 4% by volume. The atmosphere rests on Earth's surface with a weight equivalent to a layer of water 34 ft deep. For about 300,000 ft upward, the gases remain in the proportions stated. Gravity holds the gases to Earth. The weight of the air compresses it at the bottom so that the greatest density is at Earth's surface. Pressure and density decrease as height increases.

The lowest layer of the atmosphere extending up about 7.5 mi is the **troposphere**, which contains 90% of the air and the tallest mountains. This is also where most weather phenomena occur. The temperature drops with increasing height throughout this layer. The atmosphere for about 23 mi above the troposphere is the **stratosphere**, where the temperature generally increases with height. The stratosphere contains **ozone**, which prevents ultraviolet rays from reaching Earth's surface. Since there is very little convection in the stratosphere, jets regularly cruise in the lower parts to provide a smoother ride for passengers.

Above the stratosphere is the **mesosphere**, where the temperature again decreases with height for another 19 mi. Extending above the mesosphere to the outer fringes of the atmosphere is the **thermosphere**, a region where temperature once more increases with height to a value measured in thousands of degrees Fahrenheit. The lower portion of this region, extending from 50 to about 400 mi in altitude, is characterized by a high ion density and is thus called the **ionosphere**. Most meteors are in the lower thermosphere or the mesosphere at the time they are observed.

Longitude and latitude. Position on the globe is measured by meridians and parallels. Meridians, which are imaginary lines drawn around Earth through the poles, determine **longitude**. The meridian running through Greenwich, England, is the **prime meridian** of longitude, and all others are either E or W. Parallels, which are imaginary circles parallel with the equator, determine **latitude**. The length of a degree of longitude varies as the cosine of the latitude. At the equator a degree of longitude is 69.171 statute mi; this is gradually reduced toward the poles. Value of a longitude degree at the poles is zero.

Latitude is reckoned by the number of degrees N or S of the **equator**, an imaginary circle on Earth's surface everywhere equidistant between the two poles. According to the International Astronomical Union, the length of a degree of latitude is 68.708 statute mi at the equator and varies slightly N and S because of the oblate form of the globe; at the poles it is 69.403 statute mi.

Definitions of time. Earth rotates on its axis and follows an elliptical orbit around the Sun. The rotation makes the Sun appear to move across the sky from E to W. This rotation determines day and night, and the complete rotation, in relation to the Sun, is called the **apparent or true solar day**. A sundial thus measures **apparent solar time**. This length of time varies, but an average determines the mean solar day of 24 hours.

The mean solar day and **mean solar time** are in universal use for civil purposes. Mean solar time may be obtained from apparent solar time by correcting observations of the Sun for the **equation of time**. Mean solar time may be up to 16 minutes different from apparent solar time.

Sidereal time is the measure of time defined by the diurnal motion of the vernal equinox and is determined from observation of the meridian transits of stars. One complete rotation of Earth relative to the equinox is called the **sidereal day**. The **mean sidereal day** is 23 hours, 56 minutes, 4.2 seconds of mean solar time.

The interval required for Earth to make one absolute revolution around the Sun is a **sidereal** year; it consisted of 365 days, 6 hours, 9 minutes, and 9.5 seconds of mean solar time (approximately 24 hours per day) in 1900 and has been increasing at the rate of 0.0001 second annually.

The **tropical year**, upon which our calendar is based, is the interval between 2 consecutive returns of the Sun to the vernal equinox. The tropical year consisted of 365 days, 5 hours, 48 minutes, and 46 seconds in 1900. It has been decreasing at the rate of 0.53 second per century. The **calendar year** begins at 12 o'clock midnight precisely, local clock time, on the night of Dec. 31-Jan. 1. The day and the calendar month also begin at midnight by the clock.

On Jan. 1, 1972, the Bureau International des Poids et Mesures in Paris introduced **International Atomic Time** (TAI) as the most precisely determined time scale for astronomical usage. The fundamental unit of TAI in the international system of units is the second, defined as the duration of 9,192,631,770 periods of the radiation corresponding to the transition between 2 hyperfine levels of the ground state of the cesium-133 atom. **Coordinated Universal Time** (UTC), which serves as the basis for civil timekeeping and is the standard time of the prime meridian, is officially defined by a formula which relates UTC to mean sidereal time in Greenwich, England. (UTC has replaced GMT as the basis for standard time for the world.)

Zones and seasons. The 5 zones of Earth's surface are the Torrid, lying between the Tropics of Cancer and Capricorn; the N Temperate, between Cancer and the Arctic Circle; the S Temperate, between Capricorn and the Antarctic Circle; and the 2 Frigid Zones, between the Polar Circles and the Poles.

The inclination, or tilt, of Earth's axis, 23°45´ away from a perpendicular to Earth's orbit of the Sun, determines the seasons. These are commonly marked in the N Temperate Zone, where spring begins at the vernal equinox, summer at the summer solstice, autumn at the autumnal equinox, and winter at the winter solstice. In the S Temperate Zone, the seasons are reversed. Spring begins at the autumnal equinox, summer at the winter solstice, etc.

The points at which the Sun crosses the equator are the **equinoxes**, when day and night are most nearly equal. The points at which the Sun is at a maximum distance from the equator are the **solstices**. Days and nights are then most unequal. However, at the equator, day and night are equal throughout the year.

In June, the North Pole is tilted 23°27´ toward the Sun, and the days in the Northern Hemisphere are longer than the nights, while the days in the Southern Hemisphere are shorter than the nights. In Dec., the North Pole is tilted 23°27´ away from the Sun, and the situation is reversed.

The Seasons in 2012. In 2012, the four seasons begin in the Northern Hemisphere as shown. (Add 1 hour to Eastern Standard Time for Atlantic Time; subtract 1 hour for Central, 2 for Mountain, 3 for Pacific, 4 for Alaska, 5 for Hawaii-Aleutian. Also shown is Coordinated Universal Time.)

Seasons	Date	UTC	EST/EDT
Vernal equinox (spring)	Mar. 20	05:14	01:14 EDT
Northern solstice (summer)	June 20	23:09	19:09 EDT
Autumnal equinox (fall)	Sept. 22	14:49	10:49 EDT
Southern solstice (winter)	Dec. 21	11:12	06:12 EST

Poles of Earth. The geographic (rotation) poles, or points where Earth's axis of rotation cuts the surface, are not absolutely fixed in the body of Earth. The pole of rotation describes an irregular curve about its mean position.

Two periods have been detected in this motion: (1) an annual period due to seasonal changes in barometric pressure, to load of ice and snow on the surface, and to other seasonal phenomena; (2) a period of about 14 months due to the shape and constitution of Earth. In addition, there are small but as yet unpredictable irregularities. The whole motion is so small that the actual pole at any time remains within a circle of 30 or 40 ft in radius centered at the mean position of the pole.

The pole of rotation for the time being is of course the pole having a latitude of 90° and an indeterminate longitude.

Magnetic poles. Although Earth's magnetic field resembles that of an ordinary bar magnet, this magnetic field is probably produced by electric currents in the liquid currents of the Earth's outer core. The **north magnetic pole** of Earth is that region where the magnetic force is vertically downward, and the **south magnetic pole** is that region where the magnetic force is vertically upward. A compass placed at the magnetic poles experiences no directive force in azimuth (i.e., direction).

There are slow changes in the distribution of Earth's magnetic field. This slow temporal change is referred to as the secular change of the main magnetic field, and the magnetic poles shift due to this. The location of the N magnetic pole was first measured in 1831 at Cape Adelaide on the west coast of Boothia Peninsula in Canada's Northwest Territories (about latitude 70°N and longitude 96°W). Since then it has moved over 500 mi. It is now estimated to be at 82.7°N and 114.4°W, NW of Ellef Ringnes Island in northern Canada. Measurement for several decades by Canadian scientists indicates the motion of the pole has accelerated, now averaging about 25 mi per year.

The direction of the horizontal components of the magnetic field at any point is known as magnetic N at that point, and the angle by which it deviates E or W of true N is known as the magnetic declination.

A compass without error points in the direction of magnetic north. (In general, this is not the direction of the true rotational north pole.) If you follow the direction indicated by the N end of the compass, you will go along an irregular curve that eventually reaches the north magnetic pole (though not usually by a great-circle route). However, the action of the compass should not be thought of as due to any influence of the distant pole, but simply as an indication of the distribution of Earth's magnetism at the place of observation.

Rotation of Earth. The speed of rotation of Earth about its axis is slightly variable. The variations may be classified as:

(A) **Secular.** Tidal friction acts as a brake on the rotation and causes a slow secular increase in the length of the day, about 1 millisecond per century.

(B) **Irregular.** The speed of rotation may increase for a number of years, about 5 to 10, and then start decreasing. The maximum difference from the mean in the length of the day during a century is about 5 milliseconds. The accumulated difference in time has amounted to approximately 44 seconds since 1900. The cause is probably motion in the interior of Earth.

(C) **Periodic.** Seasonal variations exist with periods of 1 year and 6 months. The cumulative effect is such that each year, Earth is late about 30 milliseconds near June 1 and is ahead about 30 milliseconds near Oct. 1. The maximum seasonal variation in the length of the day is about 0.5 millisecond. It is believed that the principal cause of the annual variation is the seasonal change in the wind patterns of the Northern and Southern Hemispheres. The semiannual variation is due chiefly to tidal action of the Sun, which distorts the shape of Earth slightly.

The Moon

Distance from Earth	
Perigee	225,744 mi
Semi-major axis (mean distance)	238,855 mi
Apogee	251,966 mi
Period of revolution	27.322 d
Synodic orbital period (period of phases)	29.53 d
Orbital eccentricity	0.0549
Orbital inclination	5.145°
Sidereal day (rotation period)	27.322 d
Rotational inclination	6.68°
Mass (Earth = 1)	0.0123
Mean radius	1,079 mi
Mean density (Earth = 1)	0.607
Average surface temperature	–100°F

The Moon is the 2nd-brightest object in the sky (the Sun is the first). Earth's only natural satellite, the Moon is the force behind the rising and falling of tides, and it helps to regulate the Earth's orbit around the Sun. Many probes have been sent to the moon, and between 1969 and 1972, 12 U.S. astronauts walked on its surface. The Moon is the subject of renewed international interest. In 2007, Japan and China orbited satellites around the Moon, India orbited a spacecraft in fall 2008, and the U.S. sent an orbiter and impactor in 2009. It is expected that several nations, including the U.S. and China, will send humans back to the Moon in the next 15 years. In Sept. 2009, American scientists announced the discovery of a thin layer of water ice near the lunar poles. The LCROSS impactor mission impacted the lunar south polar region in Oct. 2009. The plume of material thrown up in the impact included water plus a variety of other chemical species, indicating that the lunar regolith harbors a rich and active chemistry.

Orbit and rotation. The Moon completes a circuit around Earth in a period that averages 27 days, 7 hours, 43.2 minutes. This is the Moon's sidereal period. Because of the motion of the Moon in common with Earth around the Sun, the mean duration of the lunar month—the period from one New Moon to the next New Moon—is 29 days, 12 hours, 44.05 minutes. This is the Moon's synodic period.

The mean distance of the Moon from Earth is 238,855 mi, but its orbit about Earth is elliptical, and thus the actual distance varies considerably. The maximum distance from Earth that the Moon may reach is 251,966 mi and the least distance is 225,744 mi.

The Moon rotates on its axis in a period of time that is exactly equal to its sidereal revolution about Earth—27.322 days. Thus the backside, or farside, of the Moon always faces away from Earth. But this does not mean that the backside is always dark. The farside of the Moon gets just as much direct sunlight as the nearside; at New Moon phase, the farside of the Moon is fully lit but not visible from Earth.

The Moon's revolution about Earth is irregular because of its elliptical orbit. The Moon's rotation, however, is regular, and this, together with the irregular revolution, produces what is called libration in longitude, which permits an observer on Earth to see first farther around the eastern side and then farther around the western side of the Moon. The Moon's variation north or south of the ecliptic permits one to see farther over first one pole of the Moon and then the other; this is called libration in latitude. These two libration effects permit observers on Earth to see a total of about 60% of the Moon's surface over a period of time.

Atmosphere and surface. The Moon, like the planet Mercury, has no real atmosphere to speak of. What little exists is variable and tenuous. With its long day and night, the daytime temperature can reach 260°F, while the coldest nighttime temperature may reach –280°F. This day-to-night contrast is exceeded only by that on Mercury.

The lunar surface has not changed much since humans have been observing it. The side visible from Earth has large craters and vast dark areas called *maria* that were once lava. The farside has almost no maria but is pockmarked with craters.

Recent findings show that up to 300 mil metric tons of water ice may exist in craters at the lunar poles. In its interior, the Moon may have a small core, which supports the idea that most of the mass of the Moon was ripped away from the early Earth when a Mars-size object collided with Earth. The hidden side of the Moon was first photographed in 1959 by the Soviet space probe *Lunik III*.

Harvest moon and hunter's moon. The harvest moon, the full Moon nearest the autumnal equinox, ushers in a period of several successive days when the Moon rises soon after sunset. This phenomenon gives farmers in temperate latitudes extra hours of light in which to harvest their crops before frost and winter. The 2012 harvest moon falls on Sept. 30. Harvest moon in the Southern Hemisphere temperate latitudes falls on Mar. 8.

The next full Moon after harvest moon is called the hunter's moon; it is accompanied by a similar but less marked phenomenon. In 2012, the hunter's moon occurs on Oct. 29 in the Northern Hemisphere and on Apr. 6 in the Southern Hemisphere.

Moon's Perigee and Apogee, 2012

Perigee is the point in the moon's orbit where it is closest to the Earth. Apogee is the point where it is farthest.

(In Coordinated Universal Time, standard time of the prime meridian.)

	Perigee			Perigee			Apogee			Apogee	
Month	Day	Hour	Month	Day	Hour	Month	Day	Hour	Month	Day	Hour
Jan.	17	21	July	29	9	Jan.	30	18	Aug.	10	11
Feb.	11	19	Aug.	23	20	Feb.	27	14	Sept.	7	6
Mar.	10	10	Sept.	19	3	Mar.	26	6	Oct.	5	1
Apr.	7	17	Oct.	17	1	Apr.	22	14	Nov.	1	16
May	6	4	Nov.	14	10	May	19	16	Nov.	28	20
June	3	13	Dec.	12	23	June	16	1	Dec.	25	21
July	1	18				July	13	17			

Moon Phases, 2012

(In Coordinated Universal Time, standard time of the prime meridian.)

	New Moon				Waxing Quarter				Full Moon				Waning Quarter		
Month	d	h	m	Month	d	h	m	Month	d	h	m	Month	d	h	m
Jan.	23	7	39	Jan.	1	6	15	Jan.	9	7	30	Jan.	16	9	8
Feb.	21	22	35	Jan.	31	4	10	Feb.	7	21	54	Feb.	14	17	4
Mar.	22	14	37	Mar.	1	1	21	Mar.	8	9	39	Mar.	15	1	25
Apr.	21	7	18	Mar.	30	19	41	Apr.	6	19	19	Apr.	13	10	50
May	20	23	47	Apr.	29	9	57	May	6	3	35	May	12	21	47
June	19	15	2	May	28	20	16	June	4	11	12	June	11	10	41
July	19	4	24	June	27	3	30	July	3	18	52	July	11	1	48
Aug.	17	15	54	July	26	8	56	Aug.	2	3	27	Aug.	9	18	55
Sept.	16	2	11	Aug.	24	13	54	Aug.	31	13	58	Sept.	8	13	15
Oct.	15	12	2	Sept.	22	19	41	Sept.	30	3	19	Oct.	8	7	33
Nov.	13	22	8	Oct.	22	3	32	Oct.	29	19	49	Nov.	7	0	36
Dec.	13	8	42	Nov.	20	14	31	Nov.	28	14	46	Dec.	6	15	31
				Dec.	20	5	19	Dec.	28	10	21				

CALENDAR

Julian and Gregorian Calendars; Leap Year; Century

The **Julian calendar**, under which all Western nations measured time until 1582 CE, was authorized by Julius Caesar in 46 BCE. It called for a year of 365¼ days, starting in January, with every 4th year being a **leap year** of 366 days. St. Bede, an Anglo-Saxon monk also known as the Venerable Bede, announced in 730 CE that the Julian year was 11 min., 14 sec. too long, a cumulative error of about a day every 128 years, but nothing was done about this for centuries.

By 1582 the accumulated error was estimated at 10 days. In that year Pope Gregory XIII decreed that the day following Oct. 4, 1582, should be called Oct. 15, thus dropping 10 days and initiating the **Gregorian calendar**.

The Gregorian calendar continued a system devised by the monk Dionysius Exiguus (6th century), starting from the first year following the birth of Jesus Christ, which was inaccurately taken to be the year 753 in the Roman calendar. Leap years were continued but, to prevent further displacements, centesimal years (years ending in 00) were made common years, not leap years, unless divisible by 400. Under this plan, 1600 and 2000 were leap years (as was 2004); 1700, 1800, and 1900 were not.

The Gregorian calendar was adopted at once by France, Italy, Spain, Portugal, and Luxembourg. Within 2 years most German Catholic states, Belgium, and parts of Switzerland and the Netherlands were brought under the new calendar, and Hungary followed in 1587. The rest of the Netherlands, along with Denmark and the German Protestant states, made the change in 1699-1700.

The British government adopted the Gregorian calendar and imposed it on all its possessions, including the American colonies, in 1752, decreeing that the day following Sept. 2, 1752, should be called Sept. 14, a loss of 11 days. All dates preceding were marked OS, for Old Style. In addition, New Year's Day was moved to Jan. 1 from Mar. 25 (under the old reckoning, for example, Mar. 24, 1700, had been followed by Mar. 25, 1701). Thus George Washington's birthdate, which was Feb. 11, 1731, OS, became Feb. 22, 1732, NS (New Style). In 1753 Sweden also went Gregorian.

In 1793 the French revolutionary government adopted a calendar of 12 months of 30 days each with 5 extra days in September of each common year and 6 extra days every 4th year. Napoleon reinstated the Gregorian calendar in 1806.

The Gregorian system later spread to non-European regions, replacing traditional calendars at least for official purposes. Japan in 1873, Egypt in 1875, China in 1912, and Turkey in 1925 made the change, usually in conjunction with political upheaval. In China, the republican government began reckoning years from its 1911 founding. After 1949, the People's Republic adopted the Common, or Christian Era, year count, even for the traditional lunar calendar, which it retained. In 1918 the Soviet Union decreed that the day after Jan. 31, 1918, OS, would be Feb. 14, 1918, NS. Greece changed over in 1923. For the first time in history, all major nations had one calendar. The Russian Orthodox church and some other Christian sects retained the Julian calendar.

To convert from the Julian to the Gregorian calendar, add 10 days to dates Oct. 5, 1582, through Feb. 28, 1700; after that date add 11 days through Feb. 28, 1800; 12 days through Feb. 28, 1900; and 13 days through Feb. 28, 2100.

A **century** consists of 100 consecutive years. The 1st century CE may be said to have run from the years 1 through 100. The 20th century by this reckoning consisted of the years 1901 through 2000 and ended Dec. 31, 2000, as did the 2nd millennium CE. The 21st century thus technically began Jan. 1, 2001.

For a **Perpetual Calendar**, see pages 354-55.

Gregorian Calendar

Choose the desired year from the table below or from the Perpetual Calendar (for years 1803 to 2080). The number after each year designates which calendar to use for that year, as shown in the Perpetual Calendar. (The Gregorian calendar was inaugurated Oct. 15, 1582. From that date to Dec. 31, 1582, use calendar 6.)

1583-1802

1583	7	1603	4	1623	1	1643	5	1663	2	1683	6	1703	2	1723	6	1743	3	1763	7	1783	4
1584	8	1604	12	1624	9	1644	13	1664	10	1684	14	1704	10	1724	14	1744	11	1764	8	1784	12
1585	3	1605	7	1625	4	1645	1	1665	5	1685	2	1705	5	1725	2	1745	6	1765	3	1785	7
1586	4	1606	1	1626	5	1646	2	1666	6	1686	3	1706	6	1726	3	1746	7	1766	4	1786	1
1587	5	1607	2	1627	6	1647	3	1667	7	1687	4	1707	7	1727	4	1747	1	1767	5	1787	2
1588	13	1608	10	1628	14	1648	11	1668	8	1688	12	1708	8	1728	12	1748	9	1768	13	1788	10
1589	1	1609	5	1629	2	1649	6	1669	3	1689	7	1709	3	1729	7	1749	4	1769	1	1789	5
1590	2	1610	6	1630	3	1650	7	1670	4	1690	1	1710	4	1730	1	1750	5	1770	2	1790	6
1591	3	1611	7	1631	4	1651	1	1671	5	1691	2	1711	5	1731	2	1751	6	1771	3	1791	7
1592	11	1612	8	1632	12	1652	9	1672	13	1692	10	1712	13	1732	10	1752	14	1772	11	1792	8
1593	6	1613	3	1633	7	1653	4	1673	1	1693	5	1713	1	1733	5	1753	2	1773	6	1793	3
1594	7	1614	4	1634	1	1654	5	1674	2	1694	6	1714	2	1734	6	1754	3	1774	7	1794	4
1595	1	1615	5	1635	2	1655	6	1675	3	1695	7	1715	3	1735	7	1755	4	1775	1	1795	5
1596	9	1616	13	1636	10	1656	14	1676	11	1696	8	1716	11	1736	8	1756	12	1776	9	1796	13
1597	4	1617	1	1637	5	1657	2	1677	6	1697	3	1717	6	1737	3	1757	7	1777	4	1797	1
1598	5	1618	2	1638	6	1658	3	1678	7	1698	4	1718	7	1738	4	1758	1	1778	5	1798	2
1599	6	1619	3	1639	7	1659	4	1679	1	1699	5	1719	1	1739	5	1759	2	1779	6	1799	3
1600	11	1620	11	1640	8	1660	12	1680	9	1700	6	1720	9	1740	13	1760	10	1780	14	1800	4
1601	2	1621	6	1641	3	1661	7	1681	4	1701	7	1721	4	1741	1	1761	5	1781	2	1801	5
1602	3	1622	7	1642	4	1662	1	1682	5	1702	1	1722	5	1742	2	1762	6	1782	3	1802	6

The Julian Period

How many days have you lived? To determine this, multiply your age by 365, add the number of days since your last birthday, and account for all leap years. Chances are your calculations will go wrong somewhere. Astronomers, however, find it convenient to express dates and time intervals in days rather than in years, months, and days. This is done by placing events within the Julian period.

The Julian period was devised in 1582 by the French classical scholar Joseph Scaliger (1540-1609), who named it after his father, Julius Caesar Scaliger, not after the Julian calendar as might be supposed.

Scaliger began with a zero hour, or starting time, of noon on Jan. 1, 4713 BCE (on the Julian calendar). This was the most recent time that 3 major chronological cycles began on the same day: (1) the 28-year solar cycle, after which dates in the Julian calendar (e.g., Feb. 11) return to the same days of the week (e.g., Monday); (2) the 19-year lunar cycle, after which the phases of the moon return to the same dates of the year; and (3) the 15-year indiction cycle, used in ancient Rome to regulate taxes.

It will take 7,980 years to complete the period, the product of 28, 19, and 15.

Noon (Universal Time) of Jan. 1, 2012, will be Julian Date (JD) 2,455,928; that many days will have passed since the start of the Julian period. The JD at noon of any date in 2012 may be found by adding to this figure the day of the year for that date, which can be obtained from the left half of the "How Far Apart Are Two Dates?" chart on the next page.

Julian Calendar

To find which of the 14 calendars of the Perpetual Calendar (pages 354-55) applies to any year under the Julian system, find the century for the desired year in the 3 leftmost columns below. Locate the desired year from among the 4 top rows. Then read down. The number in the intersection is the calendar designation for that year. For some years and countries the Julian new year did not start Jan. 1; to find the correct Perpetual Calendar for Britain and its possessions, you can generally add one year for dates from Jan. 1 to Mar. 24. For example, to look up Feb. 2, 1705, Old Style, use the year 1706.

Year (last 2 figures of desired year)

Century	00	01 02 03 04 05 06 07 08 09 10 11 12 13 14 15 16 17 18 19 20 21 22 23 24 25 26 27 28
		29 30 31 32 33 34 35 36 37 38 39 40 41 42 43 44 45 46 47 48 49 50 51 52 53 54 55 56
		57 58 59 60 61 62 63 64 65 66 67 68 69 70 71 72 73 74 75 76 77 78 79 80 81 82 83 84
	85 86 87 88 89 90 91 92 93 94 95 96 97 98 99	
0 700 1400	12	7 1 2 10 5 6 7 8 3 4 5 13 1 2 3 11 6 7 1 9 4 5 6 14 2 3 4 12
100 800 1500	11	6 7 1 9 4 5 6 14 2 3 4 12 7 1 2 10 5 6 7 8 3 4 5 13 1 2 3 11
200 900 1600	10	5 6 7 8 3 4 5 13 1 2 3 11 6 7 1 9 4 5 6 14 2 3 4 12 7 1 2 10
300 1000 1700	9	4 5 6 14 2 3 4 12 7 1 2 10 5 6 7 8 3 4 5 13 1 2 3 11 6 7 1 9
400 1100 1800	8	3 4 5 13 1 2 3 11 6 7 1 9 4 5 6 14 2 3 4 12 7 1 2 10 5 6 7 8
500 1200 1900	14	2 3 4 12 7 1 2 10 5 6 7 8 3 4 5 13 1 2 3 11 6 7 1 9 4 5 6 14
600 1300 2000	13	1 2 3 11 6 7 1 9 4 5 6 14 2 3 4 12 7 1 2 10 5 6 7 8 3 4 5 13

How Far Apart Are Two Dates?

This table covers a range of 2 years. To use, find the numbers listed in the tables for each date and subtract the smaller number from the larger. For example, to find the number of days between Mar. 15, 2010, and Sept. 22, 2011, subtract 74 from 630; the result is 556. For leap years, such as 2012, where Feb. 29 intervenes, one day must be added to the result; thus Feb. 4, 2012, and Mar. 13, 2013, were 403 days apart.

First year

Date	Jan.	Feb.	Mar.	Apr.	May	June	July	Aug.	Sept.	Oct.	Nov.	Dec.
1	1	32	60	91	121	152	182	213	244	274	305	335
2	2	33	61	92	122	153	183	214	245	275	306	336
3	3	34	62	93	123	154	184	215	246	276	307	337
4	4	35	63	94	124	155	185	216	247	277	308	338
5	5	36	64	95	125	156	186	217	248	278	309	339
6	6	37	65	96	126	157	187	218	249	279	310	340
7	7	38	66	97	127	158	188	219	250	280	311	341
8	8	39	67	98	128	159	189	220	251	281	312	342
9	9	40	68	99	129	160	190	221	252	282	313	343
10	10	41	69	100	130	161	191	222	253	283	314	344
11	11	42	70	101	131	162	192	223	254	284	315	345
12	12	43	71	102	132	163	193	224	255	285	316	346
13	13	44	72	103	133	164	194	225	256	286	317	347
14	14	45	73	104	134	165	195	226	257	287	318	348
15	15	46	74	105	135	166	196	227	258	288	319	349
16	16	47	75	106	136	167	197	228	259	289	320	350
17	17	48	76	107	137	168	198	229	260	290	321	351
18	18	49	77	108	138	169	199	230	261	291	322	352
19	19	50	78	109	139	170	200	231	262	292	323	353
20	20	51	79	110	140	171	201	232	263	293	324	354
21	21	52	80	111	141	172	202	233	264	294	325	355
22	22	53	81	112	142	173	203	234	265	295	326	356
23	23	54	82	113	143	174	204	235	266	296	327	357
24	24	55	83	114	144	175	205	236	267	297	328	358
25	25	56	84	115	145	176	206	237	268	298	329	359
26	26	57	85	116	146	177	207	238	269	299	330	360
27	27	58	86	117	147	178	208	239	270	300	331	361
28	28	59	87	118	148	179	209	240	271	301	332	362
29	29	—	88	119	149	180	210	241	272	302	333	363
30	30	—	89	120	150	181	211	242	273	303	334	364
31	31	—	90	—	151	—	212	243	—	304	—	365

Second year

Date	Jan.	Feb.	Mar.	Apr.	May	June	July	Aug.	Sept.	Oct.	Nov.	Dec.
1	366	397	425	456	486	517	547	578	609	639	670	700
2	367	398	426	457	487	518	548	579	610	640	671	701
3	368	399	427	458	488	519	549	580	611	641	672	702
4	369	400	428	459	489	520	550	581	612	642	673	703
5	370	401	429	460	490	521	551	582	613	643	674	704
6	371	402	430	461	491	522	552	583	614	644	675	705
7	372	403	431	462	492	523	553	584	615	645	676	706
8	373	404	432	463	493	524	554	585	616	646	677	707
9	374	405	433	464	494	525	555	586	617	647	678	708
10	375	406	434	465	495	526	556	587	618	648	679	709
11	376	407	435	466	496	527	557	588	619	649	680	710
12	377	408	436	467	497	528	558	589	620	650	681	711
13	378	409	437	468	498	529	559	590	621	651	682	712
14	379	410	438	469	499	530	560	591	622	652	683	713
15	380	411	439	470	500	531	561	592	623	653	684	714
16	381	412	440	471	501	532	562	593	624	654	685	715
17	382	413	441	472	502	533	563	594	625	655	686	716
18	383	414	442	473	503	534	564	595	626	656	687	717
19	384	415	443	474	504	535	565	596	627	657	688	718
20	385	416	444	475	505	536	566	597	628	658	689	719
21	386	417	445	476	506	537	567	598	629	659	690	720
22	387	418	446	477	507	538	568	599	630	660	691	721
23	388	419	447	478	508	539	569	600	631	661	692	722
24	389	420	448	479	509	540	570	601	632	662	693	723
25	390	421	449	480	510	541	571	602	633	663	694	724
26	391	422	450	481	511	542	572	603	634	664	695	725
27	392	423	451	482	512	543	573	604	635	665	696	726
28	393	424	452	483	513	544	574	605	636	666	697	727
29	394	—	453	484	514	545	575	606	637	667	698	728
30	395	—	454	485	515	546	576	607	638	668	699	729
31	396	—	455	—	516	—	577	608	—	669	—	730

Signs of the Zodiac

The zodiac is the apparent yearly path of the sun among the stars as viewed from Earth and was divided by the ancients into 12 equal sections or signs, each named for the constellation situated within its limits in ancient times. Astrologers claim that the temperament and destiny of each individual depend on the zodiac sign under which the person was born and the relationships between the planets at that time and throughout the person's life.

Below are the 12 traditional signs and the traditional range of dates pertaining to each:

♈ **Aries** (Ram), March 21–April 19

♉ **Taurus** (Bull), April 20–May 20

♊ **Gemini** (Twins), May 21–June 21

♋ **Cancer** (Crab), June 22–July 22

♌ **Leo** (Lion), July 23–August 22

♍ **Virgo** (Virgin), August 23–September 22

♎ **Libra** (Scales), September 23–October 23

♏ **Scorpio** (Scorpion), October 24–November 21

♐ **Sagittarius** (Archer), November 22–December 21

♑ **Capricorn** (Goat), December 22–January 19

♒ **Aquarius** (Water Bearer), January 20–February 18

♓ **Pisces** (Fishes), February 19–March 20

Calendar for the Year 2012

JANUARY	FEBRUARY	MARCH	APRIL
S M T W T F S	S M T W T F S	S M T W T F S	S M T W T F S
1 2 3 4 5 6 7	1 2 3 4	1 2 3	1 2 3 4 5 6 7
8 9 10 11 12 13 14	5 6 7 8 9 10 11	4 5 6 7 8 9 10	8 9 10 11 12 13 14
15 16 17 18 19 20 21	12 13 14 15 16 17 18	11 12 13 14 15 16 17	15 16 17 18 19 20 21
22 23 24 25 26 27 28	19 20 21 22 23 24 25	18 19 20 21 22 23 24	22 23 24 25 26 27 28
29 30 31	26 27 28 29	25 26 27 28 29 30 31	29 30

MAY	JUNE	JULY	AUGUST
S M T W T F S	S M T W T F S	S M T W T F S	S M T W T F S
1 2 3 4 5	1 2	1 2 3 4 5 6 7	1 2 3 4
6 7 8 9 10 11 12	3 4 5 6 7 8 9	8 9 10 11 12 13 14	5 6 7 8 9 10 11
13 14 15 16 17 18 19	10 11 12 13 14 15 16	15 16 17 18 19 20 21	12 13 14 15 16 17 18
20 21 22 23 24 25 26	17 18 19 20 21 22 23	22 23 24 25 26 27 28	19 20 21 22 23 24 25
27 28 29 30 31	24 25 26 27 28 29 30	29 30 31	26 27 28 29 30 31

SEPTEMBER	OCTOBER	NOVEMBER	DECEMBER
S M T W T F S	S M T W T F S	S M T W T F S	S M T W T F S
1	1 2 3 4 5 6	1 2 3	1
2 3 4 5 6 7 8	7 8 9 10 11 12 13	4 5 6 7 8 9 10	2 3 4 5 6 7 8
9 10 11 12 13 14 15	14 15 16 17 18 19 20	11 12 13 14 15 16 17	9 10 11 12 13 14 15
16 17 18 19 20 21 22	21 22 23 24 25 26 27	18 19 20 21 22 23 24	16 17 18 19 20 21 22
23 24 25 26 27 28 29	28 29 30 31	25 26 27 28 29 30	23 24 25 26 27 28 29
30			30 31

Federal Holidays and Other Notable Dates, 2012
Some dates may be subject to change.

The dates shaded on the calendar above and shown below in *italics* are U.S. federal holidays, designated by the president or Congress and applicable to federal employees and in the District of Columbia. Most U.S. states also observe these holidays, and many states observe others; practices vary from state to state. In most states the secretary of state's office can provide details.

January
1 New Year's Day
2 *New Year's Day* (federal holiday observed); Rose Bowl
3 Sugar Bowl
4 Orange Bowl
5 Fiesta Bowl
9 BCS Football Championship Game (New Orleans, LA)
16 *Martin Luther King Jr. Day*
16-29 Australian Open tennis tournament
26 Australia Day, Australia
29 NFL Pro Bowl (Honolulu, HI)

February
2 Groundhog Day
5 Super Bowl XLVI (Indianapolis, IN)
12 Lincoln's Birthday
13-14 Westminster Dog Show
14 Valentine's Day
18-21 Carnival, Brazil
20 *Washington's Birthday* (observed), Presidents' Day, or Washington-Lincoln Day (3rd Mon. in Feb.)
21 Mardi Gras
22 Ash Wednesday
26 Daytona 500; NBA All-Star Game (Orlando, FL); Academy Awards
29 Leap Day

March
3 Iditarod Trail Sled Dog Race begins
8 Purim (Feast of Lots) begins previous night
11 Daylight Saving Time begins in U.S.
17 St. Patrick's Day
20 First day of spring (Northern Hemisphere)
21 Benito Juárez's Birthday, Mexico
31-Apr. 2 NCAA men's basketball Final Four (New Orleans, LA)

April
1 April Fool's Day
1-3 NCAA women's basketball Final Four (Denver, CO)
2-8 Masters golf tournament
6 Good Friday
7 Passover, 1st full day
8 Easter
15 Easter (Orthodox)
16 Patriots' Day; Boston Marathon (3rd Mon. in Apr.)
17 Tax Day (IRS filing deadline)
22 Earth Day
26 Take Our Daughters and Sons to Work Day
27 Arbor Day, U.S.
28 Buddha's Birthday, Korea, Hong Kong

May
1 May Day
5 Kentucky Derby; Cinco de Mayo (Battle of Puebla Day), Mexico
13 Mother's Day
19 Armed Forces Day; Preakness Stakes
21 Victoria Day, Canada
27-June 10 French Open tennis tournament
28 *Memorial Day*, or Decoration Day (last Mon. in May)

June
9 Belmont Stakes
14 Flag Day
14-17 U.S. Open golf tournament (Daly City, CA)
17 Father's Day
20 First day of summer (Northern Hemisphere)
23 Dragon Boat Festival, China
25-July 8 Wimbledon tennis tournament

July
1 Canada Day, Canada
4 *Independence Day*
7-14 Running of the Bulls (Pamplona, Spain)
14 Bastille Day, France
19-22 British Open golf tournament
20 Ramadan (Islamic month of fasting), 1st full day
27-Aug. 12 Summer Olympic Games (London, England, UK)

August
9-12 PGA Championship (Kiawah Island, SC)
29-Sept. 9 Paralympic Games (London, England, UK)

September
3 *Labor Day*, U.S., Canada (1st Mon. in Sept.)
9 Grandparents' Day, U.S.
16 Independence Day, Mexico
17 Rosh Hashanah (New Year), 1st full day; Constitution Day and Citizenship Day, U.S.
22 First day of autumn (Northern Hemisphere)
26 Yom Kippur (Day of Atonement) begins previous night

October
1 U.S. Supreme Court session begins
3 German Unity Day, Germany
8 *Columbus Day* (2nd Mon. in Oct.); Thanksgiving Day, Canada
12 Día de la Raza, Spain, Mexico
31 Halloween

November
1 All Saints' Day
4 New York City Marathon; Daylight Saving Time ends in U.S.
5 Guy Fawkes Day, UK
6 Election Day (1st Tues. after 1st Mon. in Nov.)
11 Veterans Day; Remembrance Day, Canada; Remembrance Sunday, UK
12 *Veterans Day* (federal holiday observed)
15 Islamic New Year (Muharram 1) begins previous night
22 *Thanksgiving Day* (4th Thurs. in Nov.)

December
9-16 Hanukkah (Festival of Lights) begins previous night
10 Nobel Prizes awarded (winners announced in Oct.)
12 Día de la Virgen de Guadalupe, Mexico
21 First day of winter (Northern Hemisphere)
25 *Christmas Day*
26 Boxing Day, Australia, Canada, New Zealand, UK
26-Jan. 1 Kwanzaa

Chinese Calendar, Asian Festivals

The Chinese calendar, like the Jewish and Islamic calendars (see the Religion chapter), is a lunar calendar. It is divided into 12 months of 29 or 30 days (compensating for the lunar month's mean duration of 29 days, 12 hr., 44.05 min.). This calendar is synchronized with the solar year by the addition of extra months at fixed intervals.

The Chinese calendar runs on a 60-year cycle. The cycles 1876-1935 and 1936-95, with the years grouped under their 12 animal designations, are printed below, along with the first 24 years of the current cycle. This cycle began in 1996 and will last until 2055. Jan. 23, 2012, marks the beginning of the year 4710 in the Chinese calendar, and is designated the Year of the Dragon. Readers can find the animal name for the year of their birth in the chart below. (Note: The first 3-7 weeks of each Western year belong to the previous Chinese year and animal designation.)

Both the Western (Gregorian) and traditional lunar calendars are used publicly in China and in North and South Korea, and 2 New Year's celebrations are held. In Taiwan, overseas Chinese communities, and Vietnam, the lunar calendar is used only to set the dates for traditional festivals, with the Gregorian system in general use.

The 4-day Chinese New Year, the 3-day Vietnamese New Year festival, Tet, and the 3-to-4-day Korean festival, Suhl, begin at the 2nd new moon after the winter solstice. The new moon in East Asia, which is west of the International Date Line, may be a day later than the new moon in the U.S. The festivals may start, therefore, anywhere between Jan. 21 and Feb. 19 of the Gregorian calendar.

Rat	Ox	Tiger	Hare (Rabbit)	Dragon	Snake	Horse	Sheep (Goat)	Monkey	Rooster	Dog	Pig (Boar)
1876	1877	1878	1879	1880	1881	1882	1883	1884	1885	1886	1887
1888	1889	1890	1891	1892	1893	1894	1895	1896	1897	1898	1899
1900	1901	1902	1903	1904	1905	1906	1907	1908	1909	1910	1911
1912	1913	1914	1915	1916	1917	1918	1919	1920	1921	1922	1923
1924	1925	1926	1927	1928	1929	1930	1931	1932	1933	1934	1935
1936	1937	1938	1939	1940	1941	1942	1943	1944	1945	1946	1947
1948	1949	1950	1951	1952	1953	1954	1955	1956	1957	1958	1959
1960	1961	1962	1963	1964	1965	1966	1967	1968	1969	1970	1971
1972	1973	1974	1975	1976	1977	1978	1979	1980	1981	1982	1983
1984	1985	1986	1987	1988	1989	1990	1991	1992	1993	1994	1995
1996	1997	1998	1999	2000	2001	2002	2003	2004	2005	2006	2007
2008	2009	2010	2011	2012	2013	2014	2015	2016	2017	2018	2019

Other Calendars: Year and New Year's Day, 2012

Era	Year	Begins in 2012	Era	Year	Begins in 2012
Byzantine	7521	Sept. 14	Grecian (Seleucidae)	2324	Sept. 14 or Oct. 14
Jewish	5773	Sept. 17[1]	Diocletian	1729	Sept. 11
Roman (Ab Urbe Condita)	2765	Jan. 14	Indian (Saka)	1934	Mar. 22
Nabonassar (Babylonian)	2761	Apr. 23	Islamic/Muslim (Hijra)	1434	Nov. 15
Japanese (starts at 0 with new emperor)	24	Jan. 1	Chinese (Year of the Dragon)	4710	Jan. 23

(1) Year begins at sunset of the previous day.

Chronological Cycles, 2012

Dominical Letter	AG	Roman Indiction	5	Solar Cycle	5
Golden Number (Lunar Cycle)	18	Epact	6	Julian Period (year of)	6725

Special Months

There are many thousands of special months, days, and weeks because of anniversaries, official proclamations, and promotional events, both trivial and serious. Here are a few of the special months:

January: Jump Out of Bed Month, National Mentoring Month, National Poverty in America Awareness Month

February: Black History Month, American Heart Month, Library Lovers Month, Youth Leadership Month, Return Shopping Carts to the Supermarket Month

March: Irish-American Heritage Month, Women's History Month, American Red Cross Month, National Frozen Foods Month, National Talk With Your Teen About Sex Month

April: National Child Abuse Prevention Month, National Humor Month, Stress Awareness Month, Grange Month

May: Clean Air Month, Get Caught Reading Month, National Barbecue Month, Asian Pacific American Heritage Month, National Mental Health Month

June: National Candy Month, Gay and Lesbian Pride Month, Potty Training Awareness Month, National Safety Month

July: Cell Phone Courtesy Month, National Hot Dog Month, Women's Motorcycle Month

August: Black Business Month, National Inventors' Month, Happiness Happens Month, National Toddler Month

September: Library Card Sign-Up Month, National Hispanic Heritage Month (Sept. 15-Oct. 15), National Biscuit Month

October: National Domestic Violence Awareness Month, National Breast Cancer Awareness Month, Diversity Awareness Month, National Popcorn Poppin' Month

November: National AIDS Awareness Month, National American Indian Heritage Month, National Adoption Month, American Diabetes Month, Peanut Butter Lovers' Month

December: Universal Human Rights Month, National Drunk and Drugged Driving Prevention Month, National Tie Month, Colorectal Cancer Education and Awareness Month

Wedding Anniversaries

The traditional names for wedding anniversaries go back many years in social usage and have been used to suggest types of appropriate anniversary gifts. Traditional products for gifts are listed here in capital letters, with allowable revisions in parentheses, followed by common modern gifts in each category.

1st	PAPER, clocks	9th	POTTERY (CHINA), leather goods	25th	SILVER, sterling silver
2nd	COTTON, china	10th	TIN, ALUMINUM, diamond	30th	PEARL, diamond
3rd	LEATHER, crystal, glass	11th	STEEL, fashion jewelry	35th	CORAL (JADE), jade
4th	LINEN (SILK), appliances	12th	SILK, pearls, colored gems	40th	RUBY, ruby
5th	WOOD, silverware	13th	LACE, textiles, furs	45th	SAPPHIRE, sapphire
6th	IRON, wood objects	14th	IVORY, gold jewelry	50th	GOLD, gold
7th	WOOL (COPPER), desk sets	15th	CRYSTAL, watches	55th	EMERALD, emerald
8th	BRONZE, linens, lace	20th	CHINA, platinum	60th	DIAMOND, diamond

Birthstones

Source: Jewelry Industry Council

Month	Ancient	Modern	Month	Ancient	Modern
January	Garnet	Garnet	July	Onyx	Ruby
February	Amethyst	Amethyst	August	Carnelian	Sardonyx or Peridot
March	Jasper	Bloodstone or Aquamarine	September	Chrysolite	Sapphire
April	Sapphire	Diamond	October	Aquamarine	Opal or Tourmaline
May	Agate	Emerald	November	Topaz	Topaz
June	Emerald	Pearl, Moonstone, or Alexandrite	December	Ruby	Turquoise or Zircon

Standard Time and Daylight Saving Time

Source: National Institute of Standards and Technology, U.S. Dept. of Commerce
See also Time Zone map, page 460.

Standard Time

Standard Time is reckoned from the Prime Meridian of Longitude in Greenwich, England. The world is divided into 24 zones, each 15 deg of arc, or one hour in time apart. The Greenwich meridian (0 deg) extends through the center of the initial zone, and the zones to the east are numbered from 1 to 12, with the prefix "minus" indicating the number of hours to be subtracted to obtain Greenwich Time. Each zone extends 7.5 deg on either side of its central meridian.

Westward zones are similarly numbered, but prefixed "plus," showing the number of hours that must be added to get Greenwich Time. Although these zones apply generally to sea areas, the Standard Time maintained in many countries does not coincide with zone time.

The U.S. and possessions are divided into nine Standard Time zones. Each zone is approximately 15 deg of longitude in width. All places in each zone use, instead of their own local time, the time counted from the transit of the "mean sun" across the Standard Time meridian that passes near the middle of that zone. These time zones are designated as Atlantic, Eastern, Central, Mountain, Pacific, Alaska, Hawaii-Aleutian, Samoa, and Chamorro (Guam and Northern Mariana Isls.); the time in these zones is reckoned from the 60th, 75th, 90th, 105th, 120th, 135th, 150th, and 165th meridians west of Greenwich and the 150th meridian east of Greenwich. The time zone line wanders to conform to local geographical regions. The time in the various zones in the U.S. and U.S. territories west of Greenwich is earlier than Greenwich Time by 4, 5, 6, 7, 8, 9, 10, and 11 hours, respectively. However, Chamorro crosses the International Date Line and is 10 hours later than Greenwich Time.

24-Hour Time

Twenty-four-hour time is widely used in scientific work throughout the world. In the U.S. it is also used in operations of the armed forces. In Europe it is frequently used by the transportation networks in preference to the 12-hour AM and PM system. With the 24-hour system the day begins at midnight, and times are designated 00:00 through 23:59.

International Date Line

The Date Line, approximately coinciding with the 180th meridian, separates the calendar dates. The date must be advanced one day when crossing in a westerly direction and set back one day when crossing in an easterly direction. The Date Line frequently deviates from the 180th meridian because of decisions made by individual nations affected. The line is deflected eastward through the Bering Strait and westward of the Aleutians to prevent separating these areas by date. The line is deflected eastward of the Tonga and New Zealand Islands in the South Pacific for the same reason. In 1995, Kiribati announced that all of its islands east of the Date Line would observe the same date as islands to the west, though most maps and atlases do not depict this as a deviation in the Date Line. The line is established by international custom; there is no international authority prescribing its exact course.

Daylight Saving Time

Daylight Saving Time is achieved by advancing the clock one hour. Since 2007, Daylight Saving Time has begun at 2 AM on the 2nd Sunday in Mar. and ends at 2 AM on the first Sunday in Nov. **In 2012, Daylight Saving Time begins at 2 AM on Mar. 11 and ends at 2 AM on Nov. 4.** Prior to 2007, Daylight Saving Time traditionally ran from the first Sunday in Apr. to the last Sunday in Oct.

Daylight Saving Time was first observed in the U.S. during World War I, and then again during World War II. In the intervening years, some states and communities observed Daylight Saving Time, using whatever beginning and ending dates they chose. In 1966, Congress passed the Uniform Time Act, which provided that any state or territory that chooses to observe Daylight Saving Time must begin and end on the federal dates. Any state could, by law, exempt itself; a 1972 amendment to the act authorized states split by time zones to observe Daylight Saving Time in one time zone and standard time in the other time zone. Currently, most of Arizona, Hawaii, Puerto Rico, the U.S. Virgin Islands, Guam, and American Samoa do not observe Daylight Saving Time. On Apr. 2, 2006, all of Indiana observed Daylight Saving Time for the first time. The state remains divided between two time zones.

Congress and the secretary of transportation both have authority to change time zone boundaries, which they have done on a number of occasions since 1966. In addition, efforts to conserve energy have prompted various changes in the times that Daylight Saving Time is observed.

Daylight Saving Time: International Usage

Adjusting clock time so as to gain the added daylight on summer evenings is common throughout the world.

Canada, which extends over 6 time zones, generally observes Daylight Saving Time during the same period as the U.S. Most provincial governments observe the 4 week extension to Daylight Saving Time that went into effect in 2007. Most of Saskatchewan remains on standard time year-round. Communities elsewhere in Canada also may exempt themselves from Daylight Saving Time. Except for the state of Sonora, which shares a border with Arizona, most of Mexico observes Daylight Saving Time.

Member nations of the European Union (EU) observe a "summer-time period," a version of Daylight Saving Time, from the last Sunday of Mar. until the last Sunday in Oct.

Russia, which extends over 11 time zones, maintains its Standard Time 1 hour fast for its zone designation. Additionally, Russian observation of Daylight Saving Time ended in 2011. An hour of time added in Mar. 2011 was not expected to move back an hour in the fall, meaning that Standard Time in most of Russia will be 2 hours ahead of the zone designation.

China, which extends across 5 time zones, has decreed that the entire country be placed on Greenwich Time plus 8 hours. Daylight Saving Time is not observed. Japan, which lies within one time zone, also does not modify its legal time during the summer months.

Many countries in the Southern Hemisphere maintain Daylight Saving Time generally from Oct. to Mar.; however, most countries near the equator do not deviate from Standard Time.

Standard Time Differences: World Cities

The time indicated in the table is fixed by law and is called the legal time or, more generally, Standard Time. Use of Daylight Saving Time varies widely. An asterisk (*) indicates morning of the following day. At 12:00 noon, Eastern Standard Time, the Standard Time (in 24-hour time) in selected cities is as follows:

City	Time		City	Time		City	Time	
Addis Ababa	20	00	Hong Kong	1	00*	Paris	18	00
Amsterdam	18	00	Islamabad	22	00	Prague	18	00
Ankara	19	00	Istanbul	19	00	Quito	12	00
Athens	19	00	Jakarta	0	00*	Rio de Janeiro	14	00
Auckland	5	00*	Jerusalem	19	00	Riyadh	20	00
Baghdad	20	00	Johannesburg	19	00	Rome	18	00
Bangkok	0	00*	Kabul	21	50	St. Petersburg	20	00
Beijing	1	00*	Karachi	22	00	Santiago	13	00
Belfast	17	00	Kathmandu	22	45	São Paulo	14	00
Belgrade	18	00	Kiev	19	00	Sarajevo	18	00
Berlin	18	00	Kolkata (Calcutta)	22	30	Seoul	2	00*
Bogotá	12	00	Lagos	18	00	Shanghai	1	00*
Brussels	18	00	Lima	12	00	Singapore	1	00*
Bucharest	19	00	Lisbon	17	00	Stockholm	18	00
Budapest	18	00	London	17	00	Sydney	3	00*
Buenos Aires	14	00	Madrid	18	00	Taipei	1	00*
Cairo	19	00	Manila	1	00*	Tashkent	22	00
Cape Town	19	00	Mecca	20	00	Tehran	20	30
Caracas	13	00	Melbourne	3	00*	Tel Aviv	19	00
Casablanca	17	00	Montevideo	14	00	Tokyo	2	00*
Copenhagen	18	00	Moscow	20	00	Vladivostok	3	00*
Dhaka	23	00	Mumbai (Bombay)	22	30	Vienna	18	00
Dublin	17	00	Munich	18	00	Warsaw	18	00
Edinburgh	17	00	Nagasaki	2	00*	Wellington	5	00*
Geneva	18	00	Nairobi	20	00	Yangon (Rangoon)	23	30
Helsinki	19	00	New Delhi	22	30	Yokohama	2	00*
Ho Chi Minh City	0	00*	Oslo	18	00	Zurich	18	00

Standard Time Differences: North American Cities

At 12:00 noon, Eastern Standard Time, the Standard Time in selected North American cities is as follows:

City	Time			City	Time			City	Time		
Akron, OH	12	00	Noon	Fort Wayne, IN[1]	12	00	Noon	Ottawa, ON	12	00	Noon
Albuquerque, NM	10	00	AM	Frankfort, KY	12	00	Noon	*Panama City, Panama	12	00	Noon
Anchorage, AK	8	00	AM	Havana, Cuba	12	00	Noon	Peoria, IL	11	00	AM
Atlanta, GA	12	00	Noon	Helena, MT	10	00	AM	*Phoenix, AZ	10	00	AM
Austin, TX	11	00	AM	*Honolulu, HI	7	00	AM	Pierre, SD	11	00	AM
Baltimore, MD	12	00	Noon	Houston, TX	11	00	AM	Pittsburgh, PA	12	00	Noon
Birmingham, AL	11	00	AM	Indianapolis, IN[1]	12	00	Noon	*Regina, SK	11	00	AM
Bismarck, ND	11	00	AM	Jackson, MS	11	00	AM	Reno, NV	9	00	AM
Boise, ID	10	00	AM	Jacksonville, FL	12	00	Noon	Richmond, VA	12	00	Noon
Boston, MA	12	00	Noon	Juneau, AK	8	00	AM	Rochester, NY	12	00	Noon
Buffalo, NY	12	00	Noon	Kansas City, MO	11	00	AM	Sacramento, CA	9	00	AM
Butte, MT	10	00	AM	*Kingston, Jamaica	12	00	Noon	St. John's, NL	1	30	PM
Calgary, AB	10	00	AM	Knoxville, TN	12	00	Noon	St. Louis, MO	11	00	AM
Charleston, SC	12	00	Noon	Las Vegas, NV	9	00	AM	St. Paul, MN	11	00	AM
Charleston, WV	12	00	Noon	Lexington, KY	12	00	Noon	Salt Lake City, UT	10	00	AM
Charlotte, NC	12	00	Noon	Lincoln, NE	11	00	AM	San Antonio, TX	11	00	AM
Charlottetown, PE	1	00	PM	Little Rock, AR	11	00	AM	San Diego, CA	9	00	AM
Chattanooga, TN	12	00	Noon	Los Angeles, CA	9	00	AM	San Francisco, CA	9	00	AM
Cheyenne, WY	10	00	AM	Louisville, KY	12	00	Noon	San Jose, CA	9	00	AM
Chicago, IL	11	00	AM	Madison, WI	11	00	AM	*San Juan, PR	1	00	PM
Cincinnati, OH	12	00	Noon	Mexico City, Mexico	11	00	AM	Santa Fe, NM	10	00	AM
Cleveland, OH	12	00	Noon	Memphis, TN	11	00	AM	Savannah, GA	12	00	Noon
Colorado Spr., CO	10	00	AM	Miami, FL	12	00	Noon	Seattle, WA	9	00	AM
Columbus, OH	12	00	Noon	Milwaukee, WI	11	00	AM	Shreveport, LA	11	00	AM
Dallas, TX	11	00	AM	Minneapolis, MN	11	00	AM	Sioux Falls, SD	11	00	AM
*Dawson, YT	9	00	AM	Mobile, AL	11	00	AM	Spokane, WA	9	00	AM
Dayton, OH	12	00	Noon	Montréal, QC	12	00	Noon	Tampa, FL	12	00	Noon
Denver, CO	10	00	AM	Nashville, TN	11	00	AM	Toledo, OH	12	00	Noon
Des Moines, IA	11	00	AM	Nassau, Bahamas	12	00	Noon	Topeka, KS	11	00	AM
Detroit, MI	12	00	Noon	New Haven, CT	12	00	Noon	Toronto, ON	12	00	Noon
Duluth, MN	11	00	AM	New Orleans, LA	11	00	AM	*Tucson, AZ	10	00	AM
Edmonton, AB	10	00	AM	New York, NY	12	00	Noon	Tulsa, OK	11	00	AM
El Paso, TX	10	00	AM	Nome, AK	8	00	AM	Vancouver, BC	9	00	AM
Erie, PA	12	00	Noon	Norfolk, VA	12	00	Noon	Washington, DC	12	00	Noon
Evansville, IN[1]	11	00	AM	Oklahoma City, OK	11	00	AM	Wichita, KS	11	00	AM
Fairbanks, AK	8	00	AM	Omaha, NE	11	00	AM	Wilmington, DE	12	00	Noon
Flint, MI	12	00	Noon	Orlando, FL	12	00	Noon	Winnipeg, MB	11	00	AM

Note: This same table can be used for Daylight Saving Time when it is in effect, but allowance must be made for cities that do not observe it; they are marked with an asterisk (*). Daylight Saving Time is one hour later than Standard Time. (1)While most of Indiana is in the Eastern Time Zone, 18 counties in the southwestern and northwestern parts of the state observe Central Time.

Perpetual Calendar

The number shown for each year indicates which Gregorian calendar to use. For 1583–1802, see "Gregorian Calendar" on page 348. For 1803–20, use numbers for 1983–2000, respectively. For Julian Calendar, see "Julian Calendar" on page 349.

2008 — 10

SEPTEMBER, OCTOBER, NOVEMBER, DECEMBER, MAY, JUNE, JULY, AUGUST, JANUARY, FEBRUARY, MARCH, APRIL

2000 — 14

SEPTEMBER, OCTOBER, NOVEMBER, DECEMBER, MAY, JUNE, JULY, AUGUST, JANUARY, FEBRUARY, MARCH, APRIL

2016 — 9 / 13

SEPTEMBER, OCTOBER, NOVEMBER, DECEMBER, MAY, JUNE, JULY, AUGUST, JANUARY, FEBRUARY, MARCH, APRIL

2012 — 8 / 12

SEPTEMBER, OCTOBER, NOVEMBER, DECEMBER, MAY, JUNE, JULY, AUGUST, JANUARY, FEBRUARY, MARCH, APRIL

2011 — 7 / 11

SEPTEMBER, OCTOBER, NOVEMBER, DECEMBER, MAY, JUNE, JULY, AUGUST, JANUARY, FEBRUARY, MARCH, APRIL

WEIGHTS AND MEASURES

Source: National Institute of Standards and Technology, U.S. Dept. of Commerce

International System of Units (SI)

Two systems of weights and measures coexist in the U.S. today: the **U.S. Customary System** and the **International System of Units** (SI, for Système International). SI, commonly identified with the **metric system**, is actually a more complete, coherent version of it. Throughout U.S. history, the Customary System—inherited from, but now different from, the British Imperial System—has been generally used. Federal and state legislation gave it, through implication, standing as the primary weights and measures system. The metric system, however, is the only system that Congress has ever specifically sanctioned, dating back to an 1866 law that reads:

"It shall be lawful throughout the United States of America to employ the weights and measures of the metric system; and no contract or dealing, or pleading in any court, shall be deemed invalid or liable to objection because the weights or measures expressed or referred to therein are weights or measures of the metric system."

Since that time, use of the metric system in the U.S. has slowly increased, particularly in the scientific community, the pharmaceutical industry, and the manufacturing sector—the last motivated by the predominant use of the metric system in international commerce.

On Feb. 10, 1964, the National Bureau of Standards, now known as the National Institute of Standards and Technology, issued the following statement:

"Henceforth it shall be the policy of the National Bureau of Standards to use the units of the International System (SI), as adopted by the 11th General Conference on Weights and Measures (Oct. 1960), except when the use of these units would obviously impair communication or reduce the usefulness of a report."

On Dec. 23, 1975, Pres. Gerald R. Ford signed the Metric Conversion Act of 1975. It defines the metric system as being the International System of Units as interpreted in the U.S. by the secretary of commerce. The Trade Act of 1988 and other legislation declare the metric system the preferred system of weights and measures for U.S. trade and commerce, call for the federal government to adopt metric specifications, and mandate Commerce Dept. oversight of the program. However, the metric system has still not become the system of choice for most Americans' daily use.

The following are the 7 base SI units: **length**—meter; **mass**—kilogram; **time**—second; **thermodynamic temperature**—kelvin; **amount of substance**—mole; and **luminous intensity**—candela.

Frequently Used Conversions

Boldface indicates exact values. For greater accuracy, use the "multiply by" number in parentheses. For weights, avoirdupois (avdp) weight is the system applied to all goods except medicines, precious metals, and precious stones (see p. 359). For more detailed tables, see pp. 358-61.

U.S. Customary to Metric

	If you have:	Multiply by:		To get:
Length	inches	**25.4**		millimeters
	inches	**2.54**		centimeters
	inches	**0.0254**		meters
	feet	0.3	**(0.3048)**	meters
	yards	0.9	**(0.9144)**	meters
	miles[1]	1.6	**(1.609344)**	kilometers
Area	sq. inches	6.5	**(6.4516)**	sq. cm.
	sq. feet	0.09	**(0.09290304)**	sq. meters
	sq. yards	0.84	**(0.83612736)**	sq. meters
	acres	0.4	(0.4046873)	hectares
	sq. miles[1]	2.6	(2.58998811)	sq. kilometers
Weight	ounces (avdp)	28	(28.34952)	grams
	pounds (avdp)	454	**(453.59237)**	grams
	pounds (avdp)	0.45	**(0.45359237)**	kilograms
	short tons[2]	0.91	**(0.90718474)**	metric tons
	long tons[3]	1	(1.016047)	metric tons
Liquid meas.	ounces	0.03	(0.02957353)	liters
	cups	0.24	(0.23658824)	liters
	pints	0.47	(0.473176473)	liters
	quarts	0.95	(0.946352946)	liters
	gallons	3.79	(3.785412)	liters

Metric to U.S. Customary

	If you have:	Multiply by:		To get:
Length	millimeters	0.04	(0.03937)	inches
	centimeters	0.4	(0.3937)	inches
	meters	.39	(39.37)	inches
	meters	3.3	(3.280840)	feet
	meters	1.1	(1.093613)	yards
	kilometers	0.6	(0.621371)	miles[1]
Area	sq. cm.	0.16	(0.15500)	sq. inches
	sq. meters	10.8	(10.76391)	sq. feet
	sq. meters	1.2	(1.195990)	sq. yards
	hectares	2.5	(2.471044)	acres
	sq. kilometers	0.39	(0.386102)	sq. miles[1]
Weight	grams	0.035	(0.03527396)	ounces (avdp)
	grams	0.002	(0.00220462)	pounds (avdp)
	kilograms	2.2	(2.204623)	pounds (avdp)
	metric tons	1.1	(1.102311)	short tons[2]
	metric tons	0.98	(0.9842065)	long tons[3]
Liquid meas.	liters	33.8	(33.81402)	ounces
	liters	4.2	(4.226752)	cups
	liters	2.1	(2.113376)	pints
	liters	1.1	(1.056688)	quarts
	liters	0.26	(0.264172)	gallons

(1) Survey mile. (2) A short ton is 2,000 pounds. (3) A long ton is 2,240 pounds.

Temperature Conversions

The left-hand column below gives a temperature according to the **Celsius** scale, and the right-hand gives the same temperature according to the **Fahrenheit** scale. The lowest number on each scale is equivalent to absolute zero, the temperature at which all motion within a molecule must stop.

For temperatures not shown: To convert Fahrenheit to Celsius, subtract 32 degrees and divide by 1.8; to convert Celsius to Fahrenheit, multiply by 1.8 and add 32 degrees.

Celsius	Fahrenheit	Celsius	Fahrenheit	Celsius	Fahrenheit	Celsius	Fahrenheit	Celsius	Fahrenheit
−273.15	−459.67	−45.6	−50	−1.1	30	30	86	65.6	150
−250	−418	**−40**	**−40**	**0**	**32**	32.2	90	70	158
−200	−328	−34.4	−30	4.4	40	35	95	80	176
−184.4	−300	−30	−22	10	50	**37**	**98.6**	90	194
−156.7	−250	−28.9	−20	15.6	60	37.8	100	93.3	200
−150	−238	−23.3	−10	**20**	**68**	40	104	**100**	**212**
−128.9	−200	−20	−4	21.1	70	43.3	110	121.1	250
−101.1	−150	−17.8	0	23.9	75	48.9	120	148.9	300
−100	−148	−12.2	10	25	77	50	122	150	302
−73.3	−100	−10	14	26.7	80	54.4	130	200	392
−50	−58	−6.7	20	29.4	85	60	140	300	572

Note: Although the term *centigrade* is still frequently used, the International Committee on Weights and Measures and the National Institute of Standards and Technology have recommended since 1948 that this scale be called *Celsius*.

Boiling and Freezing Points

Water boils at 212°F (100°C) at sea level. For every 550 feet above sea level, boiling point of water is lower by about 1°F. Methyl alcohol boils at 148.5°F. Average human oral temperature is 98.6°F. **Water freezes** at 32°F (0°C).

Mathematical Formulas

The value of π (the Greek letter pi) is approximately 3.14159265 (equal to the ratio of the circumference of a circle to the diameter). The equivalence is typically rounded further to 3.1416 or 3.14.

Calculating Circumference
Circle: Multiply the diameter by π.

Calculating Area
Circle: Multiply the square of the radius (equal to ½ the diameter) by π.
Rectangle: Multiply the length of the base by the height.
Sphere (surface): Multiply the square of the radius by π and multiply by 4.
Square: Square the length of one side.
Trapezoid: Add the 2 parallel sides, multiply by the height, and divide by 2.
Triangle: Multiply the base by the height and divide by 2.

Calculating Volume
Cone: Multiply the square of the radius of the base by π, multiply by the height, and divide by 3.
Cube: Cube the length of one edge.
Cylinder: Multiply the square of the radius of the base by π and multiply by the height.
Pyramid: Multiply the area of the base by the height and divide by 3.
Rectangular prism: Multiply the length by the width by the height.
Sphere: Multiply the cube of the radius by π, multiply by 4, and divide by 3.

Playing Cards and Dice Chances

5-Card Poker Hands

Hand	Number possible	Odds against
Royal flush	4	649,739 to 1
Other straight flush	36	72,192 to 1
Four of a kind	624	4,164 to 1
Full house	3,744	693 to 1
Flush	5,108	508 to 1
Straight	10,200	254 to 1
Three of a kind	54,912	46 to 1
Two pairs	123,552	20 to 1
One pair	1,098,240	4 to 3 (1.37 to 1)
Nothing	1,302,540	1 to 1
Total	**2,598,960**	

Bridge

The odds—against suit distribution in a hand of 4-4-3-2 are about 4 to 1; against 5-4-2-2 about 8 to 1; against 6-4-2-1 about 20 to 1; against 7-4-1-1 about 254 to 1; against 8-4-1-0 about 2,211 to 1; and against 13-0-0-0 about 158,753,389,899 to 1.

Dice
(probabilities on 2 dice)

Total	Odds against (single toss)	Total	Odds against (single toss)
2	35 to 1	8	31 to 5
3	17 to 1	9	8 to 1
4	11 to 1	10	11 to 1
5	8 to 1	11	17 to 1
6	31 to 5	12	35 to 1
7	5 to 1		

Large Numbers

No. of zeros	U.S.	British[1], French, German	No. of zeros	U.S.	British[1], French, German
6	million	million	42	tredecillion	septillion
9	billion	milliard	45	quattuordecillion	1,000 septillion
12	trillion	billion	48	quindecillion	octillion
15	quadrillion	1,000 billion	51	sexdecillion	1,000 octillion
18	quintillion	trillion	54	septendecillion	nonillion
21	sextillion	1,000 trillion	57	octodecillion	1,000 nonillion
24	septillion	quadrillion	60	novemdecillion	decillion
27	octillion	1,000 quadrillion	63	vigintillion	1,000 decillion
30	nonillion	quintillion	100	googol	googol
33	decillion	1,000 quintillion	303	centillion	—
36	undecillion	sextillion	600	—	centillion
39	duodecillion	1,000 sextillion	googol	googolplex	googolplex

(1) In recent years, it has become more common in Britain to use U.S. terminology for large numbers.

Prime Numbers to 1,009

A prime number is any positive integer greater than 1 that is divisible only by two positive integers—1 and itself.

	2	3	5	7	11	13	17	19	23
29	31	37	41	43	47	53	59	61	67
71	73	79	83	89	97	101	103	107	109
113	127	131	137	139	149	151	157	163	167
173	179	181	191	193	197	199	211	223	227
229	233	239	241	251	257	263	269	271	277
281	283	293	307	311	313	317	331	337	347
349	353	359	367	373	379	383	389	397	401
409	419	421	431	433	439	443	449	457	461
463	467	479	487	491	499	503	509	521	523
541	547	557	563	569	571	577	587	593	599
601	607	613	617	619	631	641	643	647	653
659	661	673	677	683	691	701	709	719	727
733	739	743	751	757	761	769	773	787	797
809	811	821	823	827	829	839	853	857	859
863	877	881	883	887	907	911	919	929	937
941	947	953	967	971	977	983	991	997	1,009

Common Fractions Converted to Decimals

8ths	16ths	32nds	64ths	= decimal
			1	= 0.015625
		1	2	= 0.03125
			3	= 0.046875
	1	2	4	= 0.0625
			5	= 0.078125
		3	6	= 0.09375
			7	= 0.109375
1	2	4	8	= 0.125
			9	= 0.140625
		5	10	= 0.15625
			11	= 0.171875
	3	6	12	= 0.1875
			13	= 0.203125
		7	14	= 0.21875
			15	= 0.234375
2	4	8	16	= 0.25
			17	= 0.265625
		9	18	= 0.28125
			19	= 0.296875
	5	10	20	= 0.3125
			21	= 0.328125
		11	22	= 0.34375
			23	= 0.359375
3	6	12	24	= 0.375
			25	= 0.390625
		13	26	= 0.40625
			27	= 0.421875
	7	14	28	= 0.4375
			29	= 0.453125
		15	30	= 0.46875
			31	= 0.484375
4	8	16	32	= 0.5
			33	= 0.515625
		17	34	= 0.53125
			35	= 0.546875
	9	18	36	= 0.5625
			37	= 0.578125
		19	38	= 0.59375
			39	= 0.609375
5	10	20	40	= 0.625
			41	= 0.640625
		21	42	= 0.65625
			43	= 0.671875
	11	22	44	= 0.6875
			45	= 0.703125
		23	46	= 0.71875
			47	= 0.734375
6	12	24	48	= 0.75
			49	= 0.765625
		25	50	= 0.78125
			51	= 0.796875
	13	26	52	= 0.8125
			53	= 0.828125
		27	54	= 0.84375
			55	= 0.859375
7	14	28	56	= 0.875
			57	= 0.890625
		29	58	= 0.90625
			59	= 0.921875
	15	30	60	= 0.9375
			61	= 0.953125
		31	62	= 0.96875
			63	= 0.984375
8	16	32	64	= 1.0

Roman Numerals

I — 1	IV — 4	VII — 7	X — 10	XX — 20	L — 50	C — 100	D — 500
II — 2	V — 5	VIII — 8	XI — 11	XXX — 30	LX — 60	CC — 200	CM — 900
III — 3	VI — 6	IX — 9	XIX — 19	XL — 40	XC — 90	CD — 400	M — 1,000

Note: The numerals V, X, L, C, D, or M shown with a horizontal line on top denote 1,000 times the original value.

Ancient Measures

Biblical
Cubit	=	21.8 inches
Omer	=	0.45 peck
	=	3.964 liters
Ephah	=	10 omers
Shekel	=	0.497 ounce
	=	14.1 grams

Greek
Cubit	=	18.3 inches
Stadion	=	607.2 or 622 feet
Obolos	=	715.38 milligrams
Drachma	=	4.2923 grams
Mina	=	0.9463 pound
Talent	=	60 mina

Roman
Cubit	=	17.5 inches
Stadium	=	202 yards
As, libra, pondus	=	325.971 grams
	=	0.71864 pound

Metric System Prefixes

The following prefixes, in combination with the basic unit names, provide the multiples and submultiples in the metric system. For example, the unit name *meter*, with the prefix *kilo* added, produces *kilometer*, meaning "1,000 meters."

Prefix	Symbol	Multiples	Equivalent	Prefix	Symbol	Multiples	Equivalent
yotta	Y	10^{24}	septillionfold	deci	d	10^{-1}	tenth part
zetta	Z	10^{21}	sextillionfold	centi	c	10^{-2}	hundredth part
exa	E	10^{18}	quintillionfold	milli	m	10^{-3}	thousandth part
peta	P	10^{15}	quadrillionfold	micro	μ	10^{-6}	millionth part
tera	T	10^{12}	trillionfold	nano	n	10^{-9}	billionth part
giga	G	10^{9}	billionfold	pico	p	10^{-12}	trillionth part
mega	M	10^{6}	millionfold	femto	f	10^{-15}	quadrillionth part
kilo	k	10^{3}	thousandfold	atto	a	10^{-18}	quintillionth part
hecto	h	10^{2}	hundredfold	zepto	z	10^{-21}	sextillionth part
deka	da	10	tenfold	yocto	y	10^{-24}	septillionth part

Metric Weights and Measures

The metric system generally uses the term *mass* instead of *weight*. Mass is a measure of an object's inertial property, or the amount of matter it contains. Weight is a measure of the force exerted on an object by gravity or the force needed to support it. Also, the metric system does not make a distinction between dry volume and liquid volume.

Length

10 millimeters (mm)	= 1 centimeter (cm)
10 centimeters	= 1 decimeter (dm)
	= 100 millimeters
10 decimeters	= 1 meter (m)
	= 1,000 millimeters
10 meters	= 1 dekameter (dam)
10 dekameters	= 1 hectometer (hm)
	= 100 meters
10 hectometers	= 1 kilometer (km)
	= 1,000 meters

Area

100 square millimeters (mm²)	= 1 square centimeter (cm²)
10,000 square centimeters	= 1 square meter (m²)
	= 1,000,000 square millimeters
100 square meters	= 1 are (a)
100 ares	= 1 hectare (ha)
	= 10,000 square meters
100 hectares	= 1 square kilometer (km²)
	= 1,000,000 square meters

Volume

10 milliliters (mL)	= 1 centiliter (cL)
10 centiliters	= 1 deciliter (dL)
	= 100 milliliters
10 deciliters	= 1 liter (L)
	= 1,000 milliliters
10 liters	= 1 dekaliter (daL)
10 dekaliters	= 1 hectoliter (hL)
	= 100 liters
10 hectoliters	= 1 kiloliter (kL)
	= 1,000 liters

Volume (Cubic Measure)

1,000 cubic millimeters (mm³)	= 1 cubic centimeter (cm³)
1,000 cubic centimeters	= 1 cubic decimeter (dm³)
	= 1,000,000 cubic millimeters
1,000 cubic decimeters	= 1 cubic meter (m³)
	= 1 stere (s)
	= 1,000,000 cubic centimeters
	= 1,000,000,000 cubic millimeters

Weight (Mass)

10 milligrams (mg)	= 1 centigram (cg)
10 centigrams	= 1 decigram (dg)
	= 100 milligrams
10 decigrams	= 1 gram (g)
	= 1,000 milligrams
10 grams	= 1 dekagram (dag)
10 dekagrams	= 1 hectogram (hg)
	= 100 grams
10 hectograms	= 1 kilogram (kg)
	= 1,000 grams
1,000 kilograms	= 1 metric ton (t)

U.S. Customary Weights and Measures

Units of length, area, and chain measure are based on survey feet.

Length

12 inches (in.)	= 1 foot (ft)
3 feet	= 1 yard (yd)
5½ yards	= 1 rod (rd), pole, or perch (16½ feet)
40 rods	= 1 furlong (fur)
	= 220 yards
	= 660 feet
8 furlongs	= 1 mile (mi)
	= 1,760 yards
	= 5,280 feet
3 miles	= 1 league (on land)
	= 5,280 yards
	= 15,840 feet

Volume (Liquid Measure)

When necessary to distinguish the liquid pint or quart from the dry pint or quart, the word *liquid* (liq) is used in combination with the name or abbreviation of the liquid unit.

4 gills (gi)	= 1 pint (pt)
	= 28.875 cubic inches (in.^{3})
2 pints	= 1 quart (qt)
	= 57.75 cubic inches
4 quarts	= 1 gallon (gal)
	= 231 cubic inches
	= 8 pints
	= 32 gills

Volume (Dry Measure)

When necessary to distinguish the dry pint or quart from the liquid pint or quart, the word *dry* is used in combination with the name or abbreviation of the dry unit.

2 pints (pt.)	= 1 quart (qt)
	= 67.2006 cubic inches (in.^{3})
8 quarts	= 1 peck (pk)
	= 537.605 cubic inches
	= 16 pints
4 pecks	= 1 bushel (bu)
	= 2,150.42 cubic inches
	= 32 quarts

Area

144 square inches (in.^{2})	= 1 square foot (ft^2)
9 square feet	= 1 square yard (yd^2)
	= 1,296 square inches
30¼ square yards	= 1 square rod (rd^2)
	= 272¼ square feet
160 square rods	= 1 acre (A)
	= 4,840 square yards
	= 43,560 square feet

640 acres	= 1 square mile (mi^2)
1 mile square	= 1 section (of land)
6 miles square	= 1 township
	= 36 sections
	= 36 square miles

Cubic Measure

1 cubic foot (ft^3)	= 1,728 cubic inches (in.^{3})
27 cubic feet	= 1 cubic yard (yd^3)

Gunter's, or Surveyor's, Chain Measure

7.92 inches (in.)	= 1 link (li)
100 links	= 1 chain (ch)
	= 4 rods (rd)
	= 66 feet (ft)
80 chains	= 1 mile (mi)
	= 320 rods
	= 5,280 feet

Avoirdupois Weight

When necessary to distinguish the avoirdupois ounce or pound from the troy ounce or pound, the word *avoirdupois* (avdp) is used in combination with the name or abbreviation of the avoirdupois unit. The *grain* is the same in avoirdupois and troy weight.

27^{11}/$_{32}$ grains (gr)	= 1 dram (dr)
16 drams	= 1 ounce (oz)
	= 437½ grains
16 ounces	= 1 pound (lb)
	= 256 drams
	= 7,000 grains
100 pounds	= 1 hundredweight (cwt)*
20 hundredweights	= 1 ton (t)
	= 2,000 pounds*

In gross or long measure, the following values are recognized.

112 pounds	= 1 gross or long hundredweight*
20 gross or long hundredweights	= 1 gross or long ton
	= 2,240 pounds*

*When the terms *hundredweight* and *ton* are used unmodified, they are commonly understood to mean the 100-pound hundredweight and the 2,000-pound ton, respectively; these units may be designated *net* or *short* when necessary to distinguish them from the corresponding units in gross or long measure.

Troy Weight

24 grains (gr)	= 1 pennyweight (dwt)
20 pennyweights	= 1 ounce troy (oz t)
	= 480 grains
12 ounces troy	= 1 pound troy (lb t)
	= 240 pennyweights
	= 5,760 grains

Weight and Measurement Equivalents

In this table it is necessary to distinguish between the international and the survey foot. The international foot, defined in 1959 as exactly equal to 0.3048 meter, is shorter than the old survey foot by exactly 2 parts in 1 million. The survey foot is still used in data expressed in feet in geodetic surveys within the U.S. In this table the survey foot is indicated with capital letters, as FEET.

When the name of a unit is enclosed in brackets, e.g., [1 hand], either (1) the unit is not in general current use in the U.S. or (2) the unit is believed to be based on custom and usage rather than on formal definition.

Equivalents involving decimals are, in most instances, rounded to the 3rd decimal place; exact equivalents are so designated.

Lengths

1 angstrom (Å)	= 0.1 nanometer (exactly)
	= 0.0001 micrometer (exactly)
	= 0.0000001 millimeter (exactly)
	= 0.000000004 inch
1 cable's length	= 120 fathoms (exactly)
	= 720 FEET (exactly)
	= 219 meters
1 centimeter (cm)	= 0.3937 inch
1 chain (ch) (Gunter's or surveyor's)	= 66 FEET (exactly)
	= 20.1168 meters
1 chain (engineer's)	= 30.48 meters (exactly)
	= 100 feet
1 decimeter (dm)	= 3.937 inches
1 degree (geographical)	= 364,566.929 feet
	= 69.047 miles (avg.)
	= 111.123 kilometers (avg.)
of latitude	= 68.708 miles at equator
	= 69.403 miles at poles
of longitude	= 69.171 miles at equator

1 dekameter (dam)	= 32.808 feet
1 fathom (fath)	= 6 FEET (exactly)
	= 1.8288 meters
1 foot (ft)	= 0.3048 meters (exactly)
	= 0.015 chains (surveyor's)
1 furlong (fur)	= 660 FEET (exactly)
	= ^{1}/$_8$ survey mile (exactly)
	= 201.168 meters
[1 hand (height measure for horses, from ground to top of their shoulders)]	= 4 inches
1 inch (in.)	= 2.54 centimeters (exactly)
1 kilometer (km)	= 0.621371 mile
	= 3,280.8 feet
1 league (land)	= 3 survey miles (exactly)
	= 4.828 kilometers
1 link (Gunter's or surveyor's)	= 7.92 inches (exactly)
	= 0.201 meter
1 link (engineer's)	= 1 foot
	= 0.305 meter

1 meter (m). . . . . = 39.37 inches
= 1.09361 yards
1 micrometer (μm) . . . . = 0.001 millimeter (exactly)
= 0.00003937 inch
1 mil . . . . = 0.001 inch (exactly)
= 0.0254 millimeter (exactly)
1 mile (mi) (statute or land). . . = 5,280 FEET (exactly)
= 1.609344 kilometers (exactly)
1 international nautical mile
(nmi). . . . . = 1.852 kilometers (exactly)
= 1.151 miles
= 6,076.1 feet
1 millimeter (mm) . . . . = 0.03937 inch
1 nanometer (nm). . . . . = 0.001 micrometer (exactly)
= 0.00000003937 inch
1 pica (typography). . . . . = 12 points
1 point (pt) (typography) . . . . . . = 0.013837 inch (exactly)
= 0.351 millimeter
1 rod (rd), pole, or perch. . . . . = 16½ FEET (exactly)
= 5.029 meters
1 yard (yd) . . . . = 0.9144 meter (exactly)

Areas or Surfaces

1 acre (A) . . . . = 43,560 square FEET (exactly)
= 4,840 square yards
= 0.405 hectare
1 are (a) . . . . = 119.599 square yards
= 0.025 acre
1 bolt (cloth measure):
length . . . . = 100 yards (on modern looms)
width. . . . . = 45 or 60 inches
1 hectare (ha). . . . . = 2.471 acres
[1 square (building)] . . . . = 100 square feet
1 square centimeter (cm²) . . . . = 0.155 square inch
1 square decimeter (dm²) . . . . = 15.500 square inches
1 square foot (ft²) . . . . = 929.030 square centimeters
1 square inch (in.²) . . . . = 6.4516 square centimeters
(exactly)
1 square kilometer (km²) . . . . . = 247.104 acres
= 0.386102 square mile
1 square meter (m²) . . . . = 1.196 square yards
= 10.764 square feet
1 square mile (mi²) . . . . = 258.999 hectares
1 square millimeter (mm²) . . . . = 0.002 square inch
1 square rod (rd²), square
pole, or square perch . . . . . = 25.293 square meters
1 square yard (yd²). . . . . = 0.836127 square meter

Capacities or Volumes

1 barrel (bbl), liquid. . . . . = 31 to 42 gallons*
*There are a variety of "barrels" established by law or usage. For example, federal taxes on fermented liquors are based on a barrel of 31 gallons. Many state laws fix the "barrel for liquids" as 31½ gallons; one state fixes a 36-gallon barrel for cistern measurement. Federal law recognizes a 40-gallon barrel for "proof spirits." By custom, 42 gallons constitute a barrel of crude oil or petroleum products for statistical purposes, and this equivalent is recognized "for liquids" by some states.

1 barrel (bbl), standard for
fruits, vegetables, and other
dry commodities except dry
cranberries . . . . = 7,056 cubic inches
= 105 dry quarts
= 3.281 bushels, struck measure
1 barrel, standard, cranberry . . = 86 ⁴⁵/₆₄ dry quarts
= 2.709 bushels, struck measure
= 5,826 cubic inches
1 board foot (lumber measure) = a foot-square board 1 inch
thick
1 bushel (U.S.) (struck
measure) . . . . = 2,150.42 cu in. (exactly)
= 35.239 liters
[1 bushel, heaped (U.S.)] . . . . = 2,747.715 cubic inches
= 1.278 bushels, struck
measure**
**Frequently recognized as 1¼ bushels, struck measure.
[1 bushel (bu) (British Imperial)
(struck measure)] = 1.032 U.S. bushels, struck
measure
= 2,219.36 cubic inches
1 cord (cd) (firewood) . . . . = 128 cubic feet (exactly)

1 cubic centimeter (cm³) . . . . . = 0.061 cubic inch
1 cubic decimeter (dm³). . . . . . = 61.024 cubic inches
1 cubic inch (in³) . . . . = 0.554 fluid ounce
= 4.433 fluid drams
= 16.387 cubic centimeters
1 cubic foot (ft³) . . . . = 7.481 gallons
= 28.317 cubic decimeters
1 cubic meter (m³) . . . . = 1.308 cubic yards
1 cubic yard (yd³) . . . . = 0.765 cubic meter
1 cup, measuring . . . . = 8 fluid ounces (exactly)
= ½ liquid pint (exactly)
[1 dram, fluid (fl dr) (British)] . . = 0.961 U.S. fluid dram
= 0.217 cubic inch
= 3.552 milliliters
1 dekaliter (daL). . . . . = 2.642 gallons
= 1.135 pecks
1 gallon (gal) (U.S.) . . . . = 231 cubic inches (exactly)
= 3.785 liters
= 0.833 British gallon
= 128 U.S. fluid ounces (exactly)
[1 gallon (British Imperial)]. . . . = 277.42 cubic inches
= 1.201 U.S. gallons
= 4.546 liters
= 160 British fluid ounces
(exactly)
1 gill (gi) . . . . = 7.219 cubic inches
= 4 fluid ounces (exactly)
= 0.118 liter
1 hectoliter (hL) . . . . = 26.418 gallons
= 2.838 bushels
1 liter (L) (1 cubic decimeter
exactly). . . . . = 1.057 liquid quarts
= 0.908 dry quart
= 61.024 cubic inches
1 milliliter (mL) (1 cu cm
exactly). . . . . = 0.271 fluid dram
= 16.231 minims
= 0.061 cubic inch
1 ounce, liquid (U.S.) . . . . = 1.805 cubic inches
= 29.574 milliliters
= 1.041 British fluid ounces
[1 ounce, fluid (fl oz) (British)] = 0.961 U.S. fluid ounce
= 1.734 cubic inches
= 28.412 milliliters
1 peck (pk) . . . . = 8.810 liters
1 pint (pt), dry. . . . . = 33.600 cubic inches
= 0.551 liter
1 pint, liquid . . . . = 28.875 cubic inches (exactly)
= 0.473 liter
1 quart (qt), dry (U.S.) . . . . . . = 67.201 cubic inches
= 1.101 liters
= 0.969 British quart
1 quart, liquid (U.S.). . . . . = 57.75 cubic in ches (exactly)
= 0.946 liter
= 0.833 British quart
[1 quart (British)] . . . . = 69.354 cubic inches
= 1.032 U.S. dry quarts
= 1.201 U.S. liquid quarts
1 tablespoon (T., Tbs, tbsp.) . . = 3 teaspoons (exactly)
= 4 fluid drams
= ½ fluid ounce (exactly)
1 teaspoon (t., tsp.) . . . . = ⅓ tablespoon (exactly)
= 1⅓ fluid drams***
***The equivalent "1 teaspoon = 1⅓ fluid drams" has been found to correspond more closely with the actual capacities of teaspoons in use than the equivalent "1 teaspoon = 1 fluid dram" given by many dictionaries.

Weights or Masses

1 assay ton* (AT) . . . . = 29.167 grams
*Used in assaying. The assay ton bears the same relation to the milligram that a ton of 2,000 pounds avoirdupois bears to the ounce troy; hence, the weight in milligrams of precious metal obtained from one assay ton of ore gives directly the number of troy ounces to the net ton.

1 carat (c). . . . . = 200 milligrams (exactly)
= 3.086 grains
1 dram avoirdupois (dr avdp). . = 27¹¹/₃₂ (= 27.344) grains
= 1.772 grams
1 gamma (γ). . . . . = 1 microgram (exactly)
1 grain (gr) . . . . = 64.79891 milligrams (exactly)

1 gram (g)	= 15.432 grains
	= 0.035 ounce, avoirdupois
1 hundredweight, gross or	
long** (gross cwt)	= 112 pounds (exactly)
	= 50.802 kilograms

**The gross, or long, ton and hundredweight are used commercially in the U.S. to only a limited extent, usually in restricted industrial fields. These units are the same as the British ton and hundredweight.

1 hundredweight, gross or	
short (cwt or net cwt)	= 100 pounds (exactly)
	= 45.359 kilograms
1 kilogram (kg)	= 2.20462 pounds
1 microgram (μg)	= 0.000001 gram (exactly)
1 milligram (mg)	= 0.015 grain
1 ounce, avoirdupois (oz avdp)	= 437.5 grains (exactly)
	= 0.911 troy ounce
	= 28.3495 grams
1 ounce, troy (oz t)	= 480 grains (exactly)
	= 1.097 avoirdupois ounces
	= 31.103 grams

1 pennyweight (dwt)	= 1.555 grams
1 pound, avoirdupois (lb avdp)	= 7,000 grains (exactly)
	= 1.215 troy pounds
	= 453.59237 grams (exactly)
1 pound, troy (lb t)	= 5,760 grains (exactly)
	= 0.823 pound, avoirdupois
	= 373.242 grams
1 stone (st)	= 14 pounds avdp (exactly)
	= 6.350 kilograms
1 ton, gross or long	= 2,240 pounds (exactly)
	= 1.12 net tons (exactly)
	= 1.016 metric tons
1 ton, metric (t)	= 2,204.623 pounds
	= 0.984 gross ton
	= 1.102 net tons
1 ton, net or short (sh ton)	= 2,000 pounds (exactly)
	= 0.893 gross ton
	= 0.907 metric ton

Electrical Units

The **watt** (W) is the unit of power (electrical, mechanical, thermal). Electrical power is given by the product of the voltage and the current.

Energy is sold by the **joule** (J), but in common practice the billing of electrical energy is expressed in terms of the **kilowatt-hour** (kWh), which is 3,600,000 joules or 3.6 megajoules.

The **horsepower** (hp) is a nonmetric unit sometimes used in mechanics. It is equal to 746 watts.

The **ohm** is the unit of electrical resistance and represents the physical property of a conductor that offers a resistance to the flow of electricity, permitting just 1 ampere to flow at 1 volt of pressure.

Measures of Force and Pressure

Dyne (dyn) = force necessary to accelerate a 1-gram mass 1 centimeter per second squared = 0.000072 poundal

Poundal (pdl) = force necessary to accelerate a 1-pound mass 1 foot per second squared = 13,825.5 dynes = 0.138255 newtons

Newton (N) = force needed to accelerate a 1-kilogram mass 1 meter per second squared = 100,000 dynes (exactly)

Pascal (pressure) (Pa) = 1 newton per square meter = 0.020885 pound per square foot

Atmosphere (air pressure at sea level) (atm) = 2,116.217 pounds per square foot = 14.6959 pounds per square inch = 1.0332 kilograms per square centimeter = 101,325 newtons per square meter

Spirits Measures

Pony	= 1.0 fluid ounce
Shot	= varies, usu. 1.0-1.5 fluid ounces
Jigger	= 1.5 fluid ounces
Pint (pt)	= 16 fluid ounces
	= 0.625 fifth
Fifth	= 25.6 fluid ounces
	= 1.6 pints
	= 0.8 quart
	= 0.757 liter

Quart (qt)	= 32 fluid ounces
	= 1.25 fifths
Wine bottle (standard)	= 0.750 liter
	= 25.4 fluid ounces
Magnum	= 1.5 liters

For champagne and brandy:

Jeroboam	= 2 magnums
	= 3 liters
	= 101 fluid ounces

For champagne:

Rehoboam	= 3 magnums
Methuselah	= 4 magnums
Salmanazar	= 6 magnums
Balthazar	= 8 magnums
Nebuchadnezzar	= 10 magnums

Miscellaneous Measures

Caliber (cal)—the diameter of a gun bore. In the U.S., caliber is traditionally expressed in hundredths of inches, e.g., .22. In Britain, caliber is often expressed in thousandths of inches, e.g., .270. Now it is commonly expressed in millimeters, e.g., the 5.56 mm M16 rifle. Heavier weapons' caliber has long been expressed in millimeters, e.g., the 155 mm howitzer. Naval guns' caliber refers to the barrel length as a multiple of the bore diameter. A 5-inch, 50-caliber naval gun has a 5-inch bore and a barrel length of 250 inches.

Decibel (dB)—a measure of the relative loudness or intensity of sound. A 20-decibel sound is 10 times louder than a 10-decibel sound; 30 decibels is 100 times louder; 40 decibels is 1,000 times louder.

One decibel is the smallest difference between sounds detectable by the human ear. A 125-decibel sound is painful.

10 decibels	breathing
20	rustling leaves
30	whisper
40	refrigerator humming
50	quiet conversation
60	conversation, laughter
70	vacuum cleaner
80	city traffic
90	subway, lawn mower
100	chainsaw

Em—a printer's measure designating the square width of any given type size. For example, an em of 10-point type is 10 points. An en is half an em.

Gauge (ga)—a measure of shotgun bore diameter. Gauge numbers originally referred to the number of lead balls just fitting the gun barrel diameter required to make a pound. Thus, a 16-gauge shotgun's bore was smaller than a 12-gauge shotgun's. Today, an international agreement assigns millimeter measures to each gauge.

Gauge	Bore diameter (mm)	Gauge	Bore diameter (mm)
6	23.34	14	17.60
10	19.67	16	16.81
12	18.52	20	15.90

Horsepower (hp)—the power needed to lift 550 pounds 1 foot in 1 second or to lift 33,000 pounds 1 foot in 1 minute. Equivalent to 746 watts or 2,546 British thermal units per hour.

Karat or carat (k or c)—a measure of fineness for gold equal to 1/24 part of pure gold in an alloy. Thus 24-karat gold is pure; 18-karat gold is ¼ alloy. The carat is also used as a unit of weight for precious stones; it is equal to 200 milligrams or 3.086 grains.

Knot (kn or kt)—a measure of the speed of ships. A knot equals 1 nautical mile per hour.

Quire (qr)—25 sheets of paper of the same size and quality.

Ream (rm)—500 sheets of paper of the same size and quality.

Computer Milestones

1623: German mathematician Wilhelm Schickard developed the 1st mechanical calculator, capable of adding, subtracting, multiplying, and dividing.

1642: French mathematician Blaise Pascal built the 1st of more than 4 dozen copies of an adding and subtracting machine that he invented.

1801: French inventor Joseph Marie Jacquard demonstrated a new control system for looms. He "programmed" the loom, communicating desired weaving operations to the machine via patterns of holes in paper cards.

1833-71: British mathematician and scientist Charles Babbage used the Jacquard punch-card system in his design for a sophisticated, programmable "Analytical Engine" that foreshadowed basic features of today's computers. Babbage's conception was beyond the capabilities of the technology of his time, and the machine remained unfinished at his death in 1871.

1889: American engineer Herman Hollerith patented an electromechanical punch-card tabulating system that facilitated the handling of large amounts of statistical data and quickly found use in censuses in the U.S. and other countries.

1911: Hollerith's Tabulating Machine Company merged with 2 other enterprises to form the Computing-Tabulating-Recording Company, which was renamed the International Business Machines Corporation (IBM) in 1924.

1941: German engineer Konrad Züse completed the Z3, the 1st fully functional digital computer to be controlled by a program; the Z3 was not electronic—it was based on electrical switches called relays.

1942: Iowa State Coll. physicist John Vincent Atanasoff and his assistant Clifford Berry completed a working model of the 1st fully electronic computer using vacuum tubes, which could operate much more quickly than relays; the rudimentary machine was not programmable.

1943: IBM and Harvard professor Howard Aiken completed the 1st large-scale automatic digital computer, the Mark I, a relay-based machine 55 ft long and 8 ft high. British scientists built the Colossus, an electronic computer designed specifically for breaking German codes.

1946: ENIAC (Electronic Numerical Integrator and Computer), a 30-ton room-sized electronic computer with more than 18,000 vacuum tubes, was completed by physicist John Mauchly and engineer J. Presper Eckert at the Univ. of Pennsylvania for the U.S. Army. ENIAC could be programmed to do different tasks, but cables had to be plugged in and switches set by hand.

1951: Eckert and Mauchly's UNIVAC (Universal Automatic Computer) became the 1st computer commercially available in the U.S. The 1st customer: the Census Bureau. CBS-TV used a UNIVAC in 1952 to predict election results.

1969-71: The powerful Unix operating system was developed at Bell Laboratories; later versions became widely used on large computers and formed the basis for Linux and Macintosh OS X operating systems for personal computers.

1971: Intel released the 4004, the 1st commercial microprocessor (an entire computer processing unit on a chip).

1973: The Alto computer, developed at Xerox's Palo Alto Research Center, became operational, implementing many features used years later in commercial personal computers, including a graphical user interface (GUI) featuring windows, icons, a mouse, and pointers.

1975: The 1st widely marketed personal computer (PC), the MITS Altair 8800, was introduced in kit form, with no keyboard, video display, or printer, for under $400. Microsoft was founded by college dropouts Bill Gates and Paul Allen.

1976: The 1st word-processing program for personal computers, Electric Pencil, was written. Apple Computer Company was founded by Steven Jobs and Stephen Wozniak.

1977: Apple introduced the Apple II; capable of displaying text and graphics in color, the machine enjoyed phenomenal success.

1981: IBM unveiled its Personal Computer (IBM 5150), which used an operating system from Microsoft known as MS-DOS (disc operating system).

1984: Apple introduced the 1st Macintosh. The easy-to-use Macintosh came with a proprietary operating system and was the 1st popular computer to have a GUI and a mouse.

1990: Microsoft released Windows 3.0, the 1st workable version of its own GUI.

1991: The Linux operating system was invented for the personal computer by Helsinki Univ. student Linus Torvalds and made available for free.

1996: The Palm Pilot, the 1st widely successful handheld computer and personal information manager, arrived.

1997: The IBM computer Deep Blue beat world chess champion Garry Kasparov in a 6-game match, 2-1, with 3 draws.

2000: Microsoft was found guilty of antitrust violations by a federal district judge. Microsoft settled in 2001 by accepting certain restrictions on its competitive practices and creating an antitrust compliance committee.

2001: Apple introduced the Unix-based operating system OS X for the Macintosh.

2002: The total number of personal computers, including desktop and laptop machines of all types, shipped by manufacturers since 1975 reached 1 bil, according to computer industry research firm Gartner Dataquest.

2004: The European Union found Microsoft guilty of anticompetitive practices and fined the company $613 mil.

2006: Apple began using Intel microprocessors in its Macintosh computers instead of the IBM PowerPC.

2007: Microsoft released Windows Vista, the successor to its 6-year-old Windows XP operating system. Apple introduced the iPhone, a touchscreen-equipped smartphone. Amazon released the Kindle, a proprietary hardware/software system for displaying books electronically.

2008: Google released the Android OS for mobile devices.

2010: Apple released the iPad tablet computer and sold more than 3 mil devices in the first 80 days.

Nations With the Most Personal Computers in Use, 2010

Source: Computer Industry Almanac at www.c-i-a.com for year-end 2010

Rank	Nations	PCs in use (mil)	PCs per 1,000 pop	% of world total	Rank	Nations	PCs in use (mil)	PCs per 1,000 pop	% of world total
1.	U.S.	287.92	928.2	20.43%	10.	Brazil	41.40	205.8	2.94%
2.	China	135.33	100.5	9.60	11.	Korea	38.89	799.5	2.76
3.	Japan	94.07	741.4	6.68	12.	Canada	29.91	886.2	2.12
4.	Germany	68.19	828.7	4.84	13.	Mexico	24.28	215.9	1.72
5.	UK	51.88	846.6	3.68	14.	Spain	20.61	508.1	1.46
6.	France	50.12	802.0	3.56	15.	Australia	18.64	866.2	1.32
7.	India	47.03	39.7	3.34					
8.	Russia	47.01	337.2	3.34	**Top 15 countries**		**996.99**		**70.76**
9.	Italy	41.71	717.7	2.96	**World**		**1,409.06**		

U.S. Sales of Selected Hardware, 2004-11

Source: Consumer Electronics Association
(factory sales to dealers in millions of dollars and millions of units)

	2004		2006		2008		2010		2011	
	Sales	Units	Sales	Units	Sales	Units	Sales	Units	Sales	Units
Desktop computers..........	$7,710	10.8	$7,340	10.7	$6,744	10.2	$3,755	7.0	$3,032	5.9
Notebook computers[1]........	10,523	9.2	11,936	13.7	16,668	20.0	12,517	20.1	13,899	20.5
Netbooks[1].................	—	—	—	—	(2)	(2)	2,322	7.7	1,834	6.4
Tablets[1]..................	—	—	—	—	(2)	(2)	6,708	10.3	13,977	26.6
Smartphones	1,708	4.5	4,781	14.0	11,393	28.6	17,594	54.1	23,154	78.6
Video game consoles	3,162	—	4,425	—	7,780	—	4,532	21.5	4,154	22.1
Digital video recorders (DVRs) ..	635	3.3	975	5.0	3,237	20.2	2,618	17.0	3,477	21.0
Digital cameras.............	4,739	18.9	7,149	32.9	6,813	33.2	6,778	36.5	6,506	37.7
Digital camcorders	1,651	5.6	1,828	5.3	1,885	5.6	1,150	7.2	976	7.1
MP3 players	1,289	7.1	5,559	38.1	5,844	43.7	7,030	39.7	6,757	39.5

— = Not available. (1) U.S. consumer channels. (2) Notebooks, netbooks, and tablets were not separated.

Status of Electronics Sold in the U.S., 1980-2009

Source: U.S. Environmental Protection Agency
(in millions of units)

	Disposed or recycled		In storage		Still in use		Total
	Units	%	Units	%	Units	%	Units
Computers..............	462	53.9%	71	8.2%	325	37.9%	857
Computer displays........	422	64.6	40	6.2	191	29.2	653
Mobile devices[1].........	789	47.5	58	3.5	812	48.9	1,660
Hard copy devices[2]	262	55.6	41	8.8	167	35.5	471
Televisions[3].............	356	46.1	104	13.5	312	40.4	772
Total	2,291	51.9	314	7.1	1,807	40.9	4,413

Note: Estimates released in 2011. (1) Cell phones, personal digital assistants, smartphones, and pagers. (2) Printers, scanners, fax machines, digital copiers, and multifunction devices. (3) Monochrome, cathode ray tube, flat-panel, and projection.

Top-Selling Software, 2010-11

Source: The NPD Group/Retail Tracking Service
(based on unit U.S. sales, July 2010-June 2011; does not include software bundled with computers at point of sale)

Operating System
1. Mac OS X 10.6 Snow Leopard Upgrade (M) .... Apple
2. MS Windows 7 Home Premium Upgrade .... Microsoft
3. MS Windows 7 Home Premium .... Microsoft
4. MS Windows 7 Home Premium Family
   Pack 3-user Upgrade .... Microsoft
5. MS Windows 7 Anytime Pro Upgrade .... Microsoft

Business
1. MS Office 2010 Home & Student 3-user .... Microsoft
2. MS Office 2010 Home & Student Product Key Card.... Microsoft
3. iWork 2009 (M) .... Apple
4. MobileMe (W/M) .... Apple
5. MS Office 2011 Home & Student 3-user (M) ...... Microsoft
6. MS Office 2008 Home & Student 3-user (M) ...... Microsoft
7. MS Office 2010 Home & Business .... Microsoft
8. MS Office 2010 Home & Business Product Key Card... Microsoft
9. Quicktime 7.0 Pro .... Apple
10. Mac Box Set Snow Leopard (M)................... Apple

Education
1. Instant Immersion Spanish Levels 1, 2 & 3
   (W/M) .... Topics Entertainment
2. Oregon Trail 5.0 (W/M) .... Riverdeep Interactive
3. Jumpstart Adv Preschool 3.0 (W/M)...... Knowledge Adventure
4. Disney Learning Kindergarten 3-Pk
   (W/M) .... Disney Interactive Studios
5. Disney Learning Toddler 3-Pk (W/M) .. Disney Interactive Studios
6. Disney Learning 1st-2nd Grade (W/M) Disney Interactive Studios
7. Typing Instructor Platinum 21 (W/M)........ Individual Software
8. Disney Learning Preschool 3-Pk (W/M) Disney Interactive Studios
9. Caillou Ready for School JC (W/M) .... Brighter Minds
10. Jumpstart Adv. Kindergarten 2.0 (W/M) ... Knowledge Adventure

Finance
1. Turbotax 2010 Deluxe Federal + State + e-File (W/M) ..... Intuit
2. Turbotax 2010 Home & Business Federal + State +
   e-File (W/M) .... Intuit
3. Turbotax 2010 Premier Federal + State + e-File (W/M) ..... Intuit
4. Turbotax 2010 Deluxe Federal + e-File (W/M) ..... Intuit
5. H&R Block At Home 10 Deluxe (W/M)............. H&R Block
6. Quickbooks 2011 Pro .... Intuit
7. Quicken 2011 Deluxe .... Intuit
8. Turbotax 2010 Basic Federal + e-File (W/M) .... Intuit
9. Quicken 2011 Home & Business .... Intuit
10. Quicken 2011 Starter .... Intuit

Imaging/Graphics
1. iLife 2011 (M) .... Apple
2. Adobe Photoshop Elements 9.0 (W/M) .... Adobe
3. iLife 2011 Family Pack 5-user (M) .... Apple
4. Adobe Photoshop Elements 9.0/Premiere Elements
   9.0 (W/M) ....Adobe
5. Photo Explosion 4.0 Deluxe ....Nova Development
6. Printmaster 2011 Platinum (W/M) .... Encore
7. Anime Studio Debut 7 (W/M) .... Smith Micro
8. Corel Paint Shop Pro Photo X3 ....Corel
9. Print Shop 2.0 Deluxe .... Encore
10. Adobe Photoshop Elements 8.0....................Adobe

Games
1. Starcraft II: Wings of Liberty
   (W/M) .... Blizzard Entertainment (Activision)
2. World of Warcraft: Cataclysm Expansion
   Pack (W/M)......... Blizzard Entertainment (Activision)
3. The Sims 3 (W/M)....................... Electronic Arts
4. Civilization V............................ 2k Games (Take 2)
5. The Sims 3: Ambitions Expansion Pack (W/M) .... Electronic Arts
6. The Sims 3: Late Night Expansion Pack (W/M) ... Electronic Arts
7. Call of Duty: Black Ops.........Activision (Activision Blizzard)
8. World of Warcraft: Cataclysm Expansion
   Pack (W/M)......... Blizzard Entertainment (Activision)
9. World of Warcraft: Wrath of The Lich King Expansion
   Pack (W/M) .... Blizzard Entertainment (Activision)
10. World of Warcraft: Battle Chest
   (W/M) .... Blizzard Entertainment (Activision)

Personal Productivity
1. Easy VHS to DVD............................ Roxio
2. MS Streets & Trips 2010 .... Microsoft
3. Roxio Creator 2011 .... Roxio
4. Easy CD & DVD Burning .... Roxio
5. Cakewalk Music Creator 5.0 .... Cakewalk Music
6. Home & Landscape Design w/ Nexgen Technology ..... Encore
7. VHS to DVD 5.0 Deluxe .... Honest Technology
8. Nero 10.0 Multimedia Suite .... Nero Inc
9. 123 Copy DVD 2010 Gold .... Bling Software
10. Resumemaker Pro 16.0................Individual Software

Note: Software is Windows-only unless otherwise noted; M = Macintosh, W/M = Windows/Mac.

About the Internet

The Internet is a vast and rapidly growing computer network. In 1994, a total of 3 mil people (most of them in the U.S.) made use of it; by the end of 2010 the number of users worldwide exceeded 2 bil (Computer Industry Almanac Inc.).

The Internet is not owned or funded by any one institution, organization, or government. It has no CEO and is not a commercial service. Its development is guided by the Internet Society (ISOC), which is composed of volunteers. The ISOC appoints the Internet Architecture Board (IAB), which oversees issues of standards and network resources, among others.

Major Historical Highlights

1969: ARPANET, an experimental 4-computer network, was established by the Advanced Research Projects Agency (ARPA) of the U.S. Defense Dept. Two years later, ARPANET linked about 23 computers ("hosts") at 15 sites, including MIT and Harvard.

1978: The 1st spam, or junk e-mail, message was sent over ARPANET.

1983: The set of communications rules (protocol) known as TCP/IP became the main networking protocol of ARPANET. TCP/IP facilitates connection between networks. Its adoption was tantamount to the birth of the Internet. The military portion of ARPANET was moved onto the MILNET.

1986: The U.S. National Science Foundation (NSF) launched NSFNET, the 1st large-scale network using Internet technology.

1988: Internet Relay Chat (IRC) was developed by Finnish student Jarkko Oikarinen, enabling people to communicate via the Internet in "real time."

1988: A "worm" crafted by Cornell Univ. computer science graduate student Robert Morris Jr. infected thousands of computers, shutting many down and causing millions of dollars of damage—the 1st known case of large-scale damage caused by a computer virus spread via the Internet.

1989: The World—the 1st commercial Internet service provider supplying dial-up access—debuted.

1989-90: Tim Berners-Lee invented the World Wide Web. Created as an environment in which scientists at the European Center for Nuclear Research in Switzerland could share information, it gradually evolved into a medium with text, graphics, audio, animation, and video.

1990: ARPANET was disbanded.

1991: The NSFNET was opened to commercial traffic. Berners-Lee introduced the 1st browser, or software for accessing the web.

1993: The U.S. National Center for Supercomputing Applications released versions of Mosaic, the 1st web browser able to present both text and images in a single page.

1994: Netscape Communications released the Netscape Navigator browser.

1995: Microsoft released its Internet Explorer browser. It initially failed to make a dent in Netscape's dominance of the browser market but surpassed it by 1999.

1996: A group of universities launched Internet2, an advanced, high-performance network for the research community and a test bed for development of new capabilities that might find use in the commercial Internet.

1998: Under a contract with the U.S. Dept. of Commerce, the nonprofit Internet Corporation for Assigned Numbers and Names (ICANN) took over the management of assigning domain names and Internet (IP) addresses.

1999: Release of the free Napster file-sharing service enabled users to easily exchange files containing music or other content without regard to copyright restrictions.

2003: Niue, a self-governing Pacific island associated with New Zealand, became the 1st country to offer free nationwide wireless access to the Internet, using Wi-Fi technology.

2004: The Mozilla Foundation released the first official version of the open-source browser Mozilla Firefox.

2006: Websites with rich user interfaces that encourage collective participation and personalization through online applications and scripts, known as Web 2.0, became prevalent.

2007: Apple Inc. releases the iPhone, a touchscreen-equipped smartphone; the company sold 1 mil units within 3 days of its launch.

2010: A U.S. appellate court rules that the FCC cannot regulate an Internet provider's ability to charge tiered rates for different download speeds.

2011: ICANN allows generic top level domains to be almost any word in any alphabet.

Safety and Security on the Internet

Common sense dictates some basic security rules:

• Pick passwords that are difficult to guess, preferably consisting of both letters and numbers, and other symbols, if permitted. Using the same password at multiple websites is not recommended.

• Do not give out your phone number, address, credit card number, or other personal information unless needed for a transaction at a site you trust.

• If you feel someone is being threatening or dangerous, inform your Internet service provider.

• Use protective "firewall," antivirus, and antispyware software to guard your system against attacks by hackers.

• Be careful about opening e-mail and file attachments from unknown correspondents.

• If you have programs that can make use of macros—bits of auxiliary coding that are meant to play a helpful role but can be taken advantage of by some viruses—make sure the programs' macro virus protection is turned on. Disable macros if you do not know how to use them.

• Users of so-called **peer-to-peer** (P2P) file-sharing networks or protocols should open up only part of their computer system to sharing, not the entire hard drive.

• When manufacturers provide **patches** to solve security flaws or other problems with operating systems, software, or web browsers, it is usually advisable to install these fixes. If a fix is not available for a serious security problem, you may want to consider switching to an alternative program.

Malware. Software designed to harm a computer system—such as a virus (malicious code carried within a program) or a worm (a self-contained malicious program)—may be transmitted via the Internet, received on a disk, or communicated via e-mail.

Malicious software may install a "back door" on an infected system, giving hackers access; attempt to turn off any antivirus program on the system; or try to log the user's keystrokes.

A **Trojan horse** is computer code concealed within harmless code or data that is capable of taking control and causing damage. It can be used to mount a massive **denial-of-service** attack, which overwhelms targeted computers by inundating them with messages. The infected computers, acting under hacker control without their owners' knowledge, are called **zombies**, and the network of zombie computers that carry out an attack is called a **botnet**.

Spyware. Software that observes your computer activity without your knowledge is often regarded as a type of malware. Spyware programs, which can gain entry to your machine via a Trojan horse, may record your keystrokes and report passwords or other personal information to a hacker. Some can flood your screen with ads.

Phishing. A popular scam is **phishing**—the use of a forged e-mail message purportedly from a respectable organization, such as a bank, to elicit personal data. The e-mail typically contains a hyperlink that leads to a fabricated website resembling the site of the ostensible sender. To avoid falling victim to a phishing scam, do not click on any links in e-mails sent by companies with whom you do business. If you want to visit a company's website, open your browser and manually enter the site's address.

Spam. Junk e-mail, or **spam**, can be a time-wasting annoyance or worse—spam may offer pornography or products dangerous to health; seek to defraud the recipient; carry a destructive virus; or turn the recipient's machine into a zombie that stores illicit material, takes part in a denial-of-service attack, or distributes spam. Net administrators worry that the flood of spam could cause a breakdown in the flow of Internet traffic.

In 2003 Congress enacted a law that attempted to restrict spam, but it had little effect on the volume of spam received by e-mail accounts.

While filtering software can help reduce the deluge of spam—some e-mail programs include filters—it is not completely accurate. Experts recommend that you be wary of revealing your e-mail address as you surf the web. If possible, do not list your e-mail address on a public website.

Internet Addresses

The fundamental part of an address on the Internet is called the domain. The final part of a domain name, known as the **top-level domain (TLD)**, is its most basic part. For example, in *The World Almanac*'s web address (www.worldalmanac.com), .com is the top-level domain.

So-called generic top-level domains (gTLDs), consisting of 3 or more letters, include the following:

Domain	What it is (usually)
.aero	an organization in the air-transport industry
.asia	Pan-Asia and Asia-Pacific region legal entities
.biz	a business
.cat	a site associated with Catalan language and culture
.com	generally a commercial organization, business, or company

.coop	a nonprofit business cooperative, such as a rural electric co-op
.edu	an educational institution
.gov	a nonmilitary U.S. governmental entity, usually federal
.info	an informational site for an individual or organization
.int	an international organization
.jobs	information about employment
.mil	a U.S. military organization
.mobi	a site providing content for mobile devices
.museum	a museum
.name	an individual
.net	suggested for a network administration, but actually used by a wide variety of sites
.org	suggested for a nonprofit organization, but actually used by a wide variety of sites
.post	postal services
.pro	a professional, such as an accountant, lawyer, or physician
.tel	contact data for a group or individual
.travel	information about travel
.xxx	adult entertainment community

Domain names with 2 letters are generally for countries or regions. The **top-level domain** .us, for instance, is available to persons, organizations, and entities in the U.S. More examples: .eu (European Union), .jp (Japan), .ru (Russia), .uk (United Kingdom).

Internet Lingo

The following abbreviations are sometimes used on the Internet and in e-mail.

BTW	By the way	**GOK**	God only knows	**LOL**	Laughing out loud
CBLO	See below	**GTG**	Got to go	**PLS**	Please
F2F	Face to face; a personal meeting	**HHOK**	Ha, ha—only kidding	**ROFL**	Rolling on the floor laughing
FCOL	For crying out loud	**IMHO**	In my humble opinion	**TAFN**	That's all for now
FWIW	For what it's worth	**IMO**	In my opinion	**TTFN**	Ta-ta for now

Emoticons, or smileys, are a series of typed characters that, when turned sideways, resemble a face and express an emotion. Here are some smileys often encountered on the Internet.

:-)	Smile	:-D	Laugh	:-(	Unhappy	:-b..	Drooling
;-)	Wink	:-*	Kiss	:-o	Surprised	{*}	A hug and a kiss

Nations With the Most Internet Users, 2010

Source: Computer Industry Almanac at www.c-i-a.com for year-end 2010

Rank	Country	Internet users (mil)	Internet users per 1,000 pop	% of worldwide users	Rank	Country	Internet users (mil)	Internet users per 1,000 pop	% of worldwide users
1.	China	381.65	283.3	18.67%	10.	Indonesia ..	43.68	179.7	2.14%
2.	U.S.	254.44	820.3	12.45	11.	Italy.......	42.46	730.6	2.08
3.	India	142.46	120.3	6.97	12.	South Korea	39.37	809.4	1.93
4.	Japan	104.93	827.0	5.13	13.	Mexico	30.10	267.6	1.47
5.	Germany...	63.31	769.4	3.10	14.	Canada....	28.03	830.5	1.37
6.	Brazil.....	58.80	292.4	2.88	15.	Spain	27.33	673.8	1.34
7.	Russia.....	49.06	351.9	2.40	**Top 15 total**	....	**1,360.33**		**66.54**
8.	UK........	48.82	796.6	2.39	**World total**	....	**2,044.48**		
9.	France	45.89	734.4	2.24					

Most-Visited World Websites, June 2011

Source: comScore Media Metrix, Inc.

Some websites represent an aggregation of commonly owned domain names; popular domains within a group added in parentheses by World Almanac editors.

Rank	Website	Visitors[1]	Rank	Website	Visitors[1]
1.	Google sites (YouTube; Blogger)	1,023,643	11.	eBay (PayPal; Half.com; Stubhub)	223,520
2.	Microsoft sites (Bing; Xbox Live)...........	882,818	12.	Baidu.com Inc.	215,086
3.	Facebook.com	734,240	13.	CBS Interactive (CNET; ZDNet).	214,019
4.	Yahoo! sites (Associated Content; Flickr)	671,573	14.	Ask Network (Dictionary, Mindspark, Pronto)...	212,548
5.	Wikimedia Foundation sites (Wikipedia)......	399,362	15.	Glam Media (Glam; Brash)................	203,630
6.	Amazon sites (Zappos; Audible; IMDb; LoveFilm)	282,233	16.	Sohu.com Inc.	189,558
7.	Apple Inc. (iTunes)	246,889	17.	Viacom Digital........................	185,122
8.	Vevo	238,271	18.	BitTorrent Network	164,101
9.	AOL, Inc. (Moviefone; Patch)	231,564	19.	Alibaba.com Corporation	156,780
10.	Tencent Inc. (QQ)	229,175	20.	WordPress...........................	150,784

(1) Number of persons age 15 or older, in thousands, who visited a website from any location at least once in June 2011.

U.S. Broadband and Dial-Up Adoption, 2000-11

Source: Pew Internet and American Life Project, Aug. 2011
(% of American adults who access the Internet via dial-up or broadband)

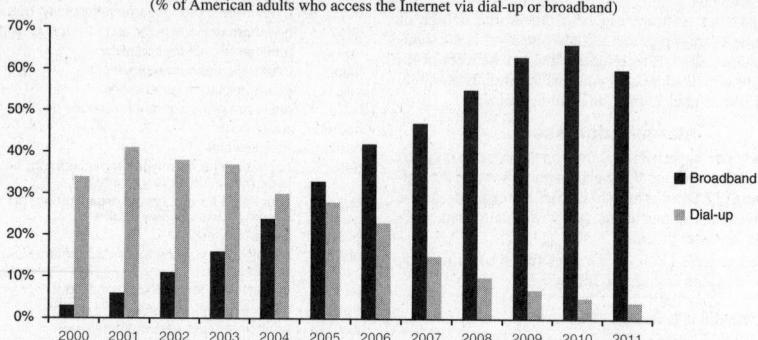

Note: Survey of adults, persons age 18 and older, on which report is based takes place annually in Mar.-June.

U.S. Broadband Internet Access by Selected Characteristics, 2010-11

Source: Pew Internet and American Life Project, Aug. 2011

	% broadband 2010	% broadband 2011		% broadband 2010	% broadband 2011		% broadband 2010	% broadband 2011
All adults	61%	62%	**Race/ethnicity**			**Annual household income**		
Gender			White	65%	66%	Less than $30,000	42%	41%
Male	63	65	Black	52	49	$30,000-$49,999	65	66
Female	60	60	Hispanic	50	51	$50,000-$74,999	80	81
Age			**Educational**			$75,000 or more	89	89
18-29	80	76	No high school diploma	23	22	**Geography**		
30-49	69	70	High school graduate	50	52	Urban	62	64
50-64	57	60	Some college	74	73	Suburban	64	65
65+	27	30	College graduate	83	85	Rural	52	55

Note: Respondents Aug. 9-Sept. 13, 2010, and July 25-Aug. 26, 2011, who had broadband Internet access at home. Adults are persons age 18 and older. Interviews were conducted in English and Spanish.

Most-Visited U.S. Websites, June 2011

Source: comScore Media Metrix

Some websites represent an aggregation of commonly owned domain names; popular domains within a group as of June 2011 added in parentheses by World Almanac editors.

All U.S. Sites

Rank	Website	Visitors[1]	Rank	Website	Visitors[1]
1.	Google sites (YouTube; Blogger)	182,537	9.	Ask Network (Dictionary, Mindspark, Pronto)	84,810
2.	Yahoo! sites (Associated Content; Flickr)	178,383	10.	Viacom Digital (BET; Comedy Central; MTV)	81,645
3.	Microsoft sites (Bing; Xbox Live)	173,562	11.	CBS Interactive (CNET; ZDNet)	73,981
4.	Facebook.com	160,879	12.	Apple Inc.	73,188
5.	AOL, Inc. (Moviefone; Patch)	110,447	13.	Wikimedia Foundation sites (Wikipedia)	71,804
6.	Amazon sites (Zappos; Audible; IMDb)	95,771	14.	Vevo	66,396
7.	Turner Digital (CNN; SI; Golf; NCAA; PGA)	93,382	15.	eBay (PayPal; Half.com; Stubhub)	65,474
8.	Glam Media (Glam; Brash)	85,987			

Video Sites

Rank	Website	Visitors[1]	Rank	Website	Visitors[1]
1.	Google sites (YouTube)	149,281	6.	Facebook.com	47,687
2.	Vevo	63,000	7.	AOL, Inc.	43,915
3.	Yahoo! sites (Associated Content; Flickr)	52,665	8.	Turner Digital (CNN; SI; Golf; NCAA; PGA)	30,063
4.	Microsoft sites (Xbox Live; Zune)	50,663	9.	Hulu	26,701
5.	Viacom Digital (BET; Comedy Central; MTV)	49,493	10.	Amazon sites (IMDb)	21,247

Blog Sites

Rank	Website	Visitors[1]
1.	Blogger	62,226
2.	Federated Media Publishing (Imgur; BoingBoing)	41,515
3.	Technorati Media	36,281
4.	WordPress	28,892
5.	Gawker Media (Gizmodo; Lifehacker)	17,696

Social Networking Sites

Rank	Website	Visitors[1]
1.	Facebook	160,879
2.	LinkedIn	33,904
3.	Myspace	33,480
4.	Twitter	30,649
5.	MyLife.com sites	13,681

Search and Navigation

Rank	Website	Searches (mil)	Searchers[1]	% of searches
1.	Google sites	12,079	180,487	64.5
2.	Yahoo! sites	3,277	117,910	17.5
3.	Microsoft sites	2,647	99,031	14.1
4.	Ask Network	478	62,345	2.6
5.	AOL, Inc.	239	16,469	1.3

E-mail

Rank	Website	Visitors[1]
1.	Yahoo! Mail	93,386
2.	Google Gmail	57,104
3.	Windows Live Hotmail	44,991
4.	AOL Email	23,720
5.	Comcast.net WebMail	9,490

(1) Number of persons age 2 and older in any U.S. location, in thousands, who visited the website at least once in June 2011.

Internet Access in the U.S., 2000-10

Source: 2011 Digital Future Report, USC Annenberg School Center for the Digital Future

Type of Internet access	% of Americans accessing Internet[1]						Avg. hours per week spent online[1]					
	2000	2002	2005	2008	2009	2010	2000	2002	2005	2008	2009	2010
All access	67%	71%	79%	80%	82%	82%	9.4	11.1	13.3	17.3	19.0	18.3
at home..................	47	59	66	72	71	76	3.3	6.8	7.8	10.1	10.6	12.3
at school[2]	55	63	67	66	66	69	NA	NA	NA	3.6	4.0	5.0
at work[3].................	42	40	55	59	59	65	NA	5.5	5.6	8.3	9.0	9.2
by cell phone/mobile devices[4]	NA	5	9	13	17	27	NA	3.6	2.0	1.7	2.5	3.9
by wireless computer[4]	NA	3	7	32	41	NA	NA	5.8	5.7	9.7	10.3	NA

NA = Not available. (1) Internet users age 12 and older who connect from all locations. (2) Percentages are from adult respondents with children in household; hours are for students using a wired PC. (3) Active use. Work outside the home. (4) Via wireless device.

Frequency of Internet Activities in the U.S., 2010

Source: 2011 Digital Future Report, USC Annenberg School Center for the Digital Future

(as % of all Internet users age 12 and older who connect from any location)

Online activity	Daily[1]	Weekly	Monthly	Less often	Never	Online activity	Daily[1]	Weekly	Monthly	Less often	Never
Use e-mail	80%	11%	4%	2%	3%	Watch/download videos	16%	23%	9%	15%	37%
Browse (surf)	57	22	6	7	9	Online banking	15	32	15	7	31
Read news	43	21	10	12	14	Read blogs	13	14	8	18	48
Social networking or video sharing	33	13	6	10	38	Make/receive phone calls	5	5	4	9	77
Find or check a fact	27	32	17	16	8	Pay bills	3	19	32	7	39
Play games...........	23	16	7	15	40	Work on a blog	3	7	3	8	79
Instant message	21	11	6	14	48	Buy things............	1	14	34	35	17
Listen/download music ..	19	19	13	19	30	Gamble..............	1	2	2	8	87

(1) One or more times daily.

Informative and Useful Websites

Name	URL	Description
Daily Data		
Federal Register	www.federalregister.gov	Online magazine approach to the government's daily journal. Browse by topic, location, agency, etc.
Flowing Data	flowingdata.com	Online data visualizations and statistics.
ResourceShelf	www.resourceshelf.com	Running list of newly published databases, reports, and other research aids.
Today's Front Pages	www.newseum.org/todaysfrontpages/	Today's front page from more than 500 newspapers worldwide.
Education and Exhibits		
American Memory	memory.loc.gov	More than 5 mil items from the Library of Congress, including audio, maps, movies, photos, prints, and sheet music.
Europeana	europeana.eu	Network of European cultural organizations linking to more than 6 mill digital items.
Internet Archive	www.archive.org	Digital library of free cultural artifacts and Internet sites.
MIT OpenCourseWare	ocw.mit.edu	Free and open educational course material from Massachusetts Institute of Technology.
New York Public Library Digital Gallery	digitalgallery.nypl.org	More than 700,000 images digitized from primary sources and printed rarities in the library's collections.
Our Documents	www.ourdocuments.gov	Digitized images and text of 100 milestone documents from America's history.
SmART History	smarthistory.org	Open educational resource on art history.
World Digital Library	www.wdl.org	Collection of significant primary documents from countries around the world.
Statistics		
DATA.gov	www.data.gov	Open access to raw government data files.
FedStats	www.fedstats.gov	Statistics by topic or program from more than 100 federal agencies.
United Nations Statistics Division	unstats.un.org	International data sets and country profiles with demographics and stats on society, industry, and the environment.
U.S. Economy at a Glance	stats.bls.gov/eag/	Quick reference tables on employment and wages from the Bureau of Labor Statistics.
Online Tools		
Kayak	www.kayak.com	One stop search of multiple travel-booking sites for the lowest fares and price trends.
LibraryThing	www.librarything.com	Track the books you've read, receive suggestions for new books, and compare lists with similar readers.
Wolfram Alpha	www.wolframalpha.com	Ready reference through computation of databases maintained by Wolfram Research.
Open Congress	www.opencongress.org	Easily follow Congress and find news about specific members, bills, committees, and issues. Receive updates by RSS feed.
Downloadable Tools		
Google Earth	earth.google.com	Free downloadable interactive world atlas and mapping software.
Stellarium	www.stellarium.org	Free downloadable planetarium that visualizes astronomical phenomena in real time from any point on Earth.

Note: Websites are subject to change. The World Almanac cannot take responsibility for contents.

Worldwide Telecommunications: Market Data, 1990-2010

Source: © International Telecommunication Union

	1990 (mil)	(per 100 pop.)	2000 (mil)	(per 100 pop.)	2005 (mil)	(per 100 pop.)	2008 (mil)	(per 100 pop.)	2009 (mil)	(per 100 pop.)	2010 (mil)	(per 100 pop.)
Fixed telephone lines	520	NA	975	15.9	1,253	19.3	1,250	18.6	1,214	17.8	1,189	17.2
Mobile cellular subscriptions	11	NA	739	12.0	2,207	33.9	4,035	59.9	4,650	68.3	5,373	78.0
Internet users	NA	NA	394	6.4	1,023	15.7	1,575	23.4	1,805	26.5	2,044	29.7
Wired broadband subscriptions	NA	NA	NA	NA	220	3.4	414	6.1	472	6.9	527	7.6
Active mobile broadband subscriptions	NA	NA	NA	NA	NA	NA	422	6.3	531	7.8	872	12.6

NA = Not available.

World Cellular Telephones Use by Nation, 2010

Source: © International Telecommunication Union, estimated; top countries ranked by subscriptions

Country	Subscriptions (thous.)	Per 100 pop.	Country	Subscriptions (thous.)	Per 100 pop.
China	859,003.0	64.04	Poland	46,000.0	120.18
India	752,190.0	61.42	Colombia	43,405.3	93.76
United States	278,900.0	89.86	Malaysia	34,456.0	121.32
Russia	237,689.2	166.26	Algeria	32,780.2	92.42
Indonesia	220,000.0	91.72	Morocco	31,982.3	100.10
Brazil	202,944.0	104.10	Peru	29,115.1	100.13
Vietnam	154,000.0	175.30	Venezuela	27,879.9	96.20
Japan	120,708.7	95.39	Taiwan	27,839.5	119.91
Germany	104,560.0	127.04	Kenya	24,968.9	61.63
Pakistan	102,777.4	59.21	Romania	24,640.0	114.68
Mexico	91,362.8	80.55	Canada	24,037.4	70.66
Nigeria	87,297.8	55.10	Iraq	24,000.0	75.78
Italy	82,000.0	135.42	Australia	22,500.0	101.04
United Kingdom	80,799.0	130.25	Tanzania	20,983.9	46.80
Philippines	79,895.6	85.67	Uzbekistan	20,952.0	76.34
Egypt	70,661.0	87.11	Chile	19,852.2	116.00
Thailand	69,683.1	100.81	Kazakhstan	19,768.5	123.35
Bangladesh	68,650.0	46.17	Netherlands	19,310.0	116.23
Iran	67,500.0	91.25	Guatemala	18,068.0	125.57
France	62,600.0	99.70	Sudan	17,654.2	40.54
Turkey	61,769.6	84.90	Ghana	17,436.9	71.49
Argentina	57,300.0	141.79	Sri Lanka	17,359.3	83.22
Ukraine	53,928.8	118.66	Portugal	15,194.9	142.33
Saudi Arabia	51,564.4	187.86	Côte d'Ivoire	14,910.0	75.54
Spain	51,492.7	111.75	Ecuador	14,780.7	102.18
Korea, South	50,767.2	105.36	Czech Republic	14,331.2	136.58
South Africa	50,372.0	100.48	World	5,373,000.0	78.00

U.S. Wireless Industry, 1985-2010

Source: The CTIA Semi-Annual Industry Survey, used with permission of CTIA. As of Dec. of year shown.

Date	Est. total subscribers	Total service revenues (thous.)	Cell phone antennas	Avg. local monthly bill	Avg. local call length (mins.)
1985	340,213	$482,428	913	NA	NA
1987	1,230,855	1,151,519	2,305	$96.83	2.33
1989	3,508,944	3,340,595	4,169	89.30	2.48
1991	7,557,148	5,708,522	7,847	72.74	2.38
1993	16,009,461	10,892,175	12,824	61.49	2.41
1995	33,785,661	19,081,239	22,663	51.00	2.15
1996	44,042,992	23,634,971	30,045	47.70	2.32
1997	55,312,293	27,485,633	51,600	42.78	2.31
1998	69,209,321	33,133,175	65,887	39.43	2.39
1999	86,047,003	40,018,489	81,698	41.24	2.38
2000	109,478,031	52,466,020	104,288	45.27	2.56
2001	128,374,512	65,316,235	127,540	47.37	2.74
2002	140,766,842	76,508,187	139,338	48.40	2.73
2003	158,721,981	87,624,093	162,986	49.91	3.07
2004	182,140,362	102,121,210	175,725	50.64	3.05
2005	207,896,198	113,538,221	183,689	49.98	3.00
2006	233,040,781	125,456,825	195,613	50.56	3.03
2007	255,395,599	138,869,304	213,299	49.79	NA
2008	270,333,881	148,084,170	242,130	50.07	2.27
2009	285,646,191	152,551,854	247,081	48.16	1.81
2010	302,859,674	159,929,648	253,086	47.21	1.79

NA = Not available.

U.S. Sales and Household Penetration of Selected Products, 1985-2010

Source: Consumer Electronics Association

Product	1985 Sales (mil)	% of all households	1990 Sales (mil)	% of all households	1995 Sales (mil)	% of all households	2000 Sales (mil)	% of all households	2005 Sales (mil)	% of all households	2010 Sales (mil)	% of all households
Cordless telephones	$280	11%	$842	28%	$1,141	55%	$1,307	80%	$943	88%	$891	91%
Pagers	NA	NA	118	1	300	11	750	23	525	11	NA	NA
Modems/fax modems	10	0	191	2.7	770	16	1,564	55	1,525	70	1,166	70
Telephone answering devices	325	7	827	35	1,077	57	984	75	1,279	76	724	69
Cellular phones	116	0.1	1,098	9	2,574	29	8,995	60	14,265	NA	7,663	91

NA = Not available.

Telephone Area Codes, by Number

As of Aug. 2011.

Code	Location or *Service*	Code	Location or *Service*	Code	Location or *Service*	Code	Location or *Service*
201	New Jersey	406	Montana	*611*	*Repair Service*	809	Dominican Republic
202	District of Columbia	407	Florida	612	Minnesota	810	Michigan
203	Connecticut	408	California	613	Ontario	*811*	*Utility location*
204	Manitoba	409	Texas	614	Ohio	812	Indiana
205	Alabama	410	Maryland	615	Tennessee	813	Florida
206	Washington	*411*	*Directory Assistance*	616	Michigan	814	Pennsylvania
207	Maine	412	Pennsylvania	617	Massachusetts	815	Illinois
208	Idaho	413	Massachusetts	618	Illinois	816	Missouri
209	California	414	Wisconsin	619	California	817	Texas
210	Texas	415	California	620	Kansas	818	California
211	*Community Info.*	416	Ontario	623	Arizona	819	Quebec
212	New York	417	Missouri	626	California	828	North Carolina
213	California	418	Quebec	630	Illinois	829	Dominican Republic
214	Texas	419	Ohio	631	New York	830	Texas
215	Pennsylvania	423	Tennessee	636	Missouri	831	California
216	Ohio	424	California	641	Iowa	832	Texas
217	Illinois	425	Washington	646	New York	843	South Carolina
218	Minnesota	430	Texas	647	Ontario	845	New York
219	Indiana	432	Texas	649	Turks and Caicos Isls.	847	Illinois
224	Illinois	434	Virginia	650	California	848	New Jersey
225	Louisiana	435	Utah	651	Minnesota	849	Dominican Republic
226	Ontario	438	Quebec	657	California	850	Florida
228	Mississippi	440	Ohio	660	Missouri	*855*	*Toll-Free Service*
229	Georgia	441	Bermuda	661	California	856	New Jersey
231	Michigan	442	California	662	Mississippi	857	Massachusetts
234	Ohio	443	Maryland	664	Montserrat	858	California
239	Florida	450	Quebec	670	N. Mariana Islands	859	Kentucky
240	Maryland	456	Inbound Intl.	671	Guam	860	Connecticut
242	Bahamas	458	Oregon	678	Georgia	862	New Jersey
246	Barbados	469	Texas	681	West Virginia	863	Florida
248	Michigan	470	Georgia	682	Texas	864	South Carolina
249	Ontario	473	Grenada	684	American Samoa	865	Tennessee
250	British Columbia	475	Connecticut	*700*	*Interexchange carriers*	*866*	*Toll-Free Service*
251	Alabama	478	Georgia	701	North Dakota	867	Yukon, NW Terr., Nunavut
252	North Carolina	479	Arkansas	702	Nevada	868	Trinidad and Tobago
253	Washington	480	Arizona	703	Virginia	869	St. Kitts and Nevis
254	Texas	484	Pennsylvania	704	North Carolina	870	Arkansas
256	Alabama	*500*	*Personal Comm. Serv.*	705	Ontario	872	Illinois
260	Indiana	501	Arkansas	706	Georgia	876	Jamaica
262	Wisconsin	502	Kentucky	707	California	*877*	*Toll-Free Service*
264	Anguilla	503	Oregon	708	Illinois	878	Pennsylvania
267	Pennsylvania	504	Louisiana	709	Newfoundland	*880*	*Paid Toll-Free Serv.*
268	Antigua/Barbuda	505	New Mexico	710	U.S. Government	*881*	*Paid Toll-Free Serv.*
269	Michigan	506	New Brunswick	*711*	*Telecommunications*	*882*	*Paid Toll-Free Serv.*
270	Kentucky	507	Minnesota		*Relay Service (TRS)*	*888*	*Toll-Free Service*
276	Virginia	508	Massachusetts	712	Iowa	*900*	*Premium Service*
281	Texas	509	Washington	713	Texas	901	Tennessee
284	British Virgin Islands	510	California	714	California	902	Nova Scotia, Prince Ed. Isl.
289	Ontario	*511*	*Traffic Info.*	715	Wisconsin	903	Texas
301	Maryland	512	Texas	716	New York	904	Florida
302	Delaware	513	Ohio	717	Pennsylvania	905	Ontario
303	Colorado	514	Quebec	718	New York	906	Michigan
304	West Virginia	515	Iowa	719	Colorado	907	Alaska
305	Florida	516	New York	720	Colorado	908	New Jersey
306	Saskatchewan	517	Michigan	721	Sint Maarten	909	California
307	Wyoming	518	New York	724	Pennsylvania	910	North Carolina
308	Nebraska	519	Ontario	727	Florida	*911*	*Emergency*
309	Illinois	520	Arizona	731	Tennessee	912	Georgia
310	California	530	California	732	New Jersey	913	Kansas
311	*Non-Emergency Access*	*533*	*Personal Comm. Serv.*	734	Michigan	914	New York
312	Illinois	534	Wisconsin	740	Ohio	915	Texas
313	Michigan	539	Oklahoma	747	California	916	California
314	Missouri	540	Virginia	754	Florida	917	New York
315	New York	541	Oregon	757	Virginia	918	Oklahoma
316	Kansas	*544*	*Personal Comm. Serv.*	758	St. Lucia	919	North Carolina
317	Indiana	551	New Jersey	760	California	920	Wisconsin
318	Louisiana	559	California	762	Georgia	925	California
319	Iowa	561	Florida	763	Minnesota	928	Arizona
320	Minnesota	562	California	765	Indiana	929	New York
321	Florida	563	Iowa	767	Dominica	931	Tennessee
323	California	567	Ohio	769	Mississippi	936	Texas
325	Texas	570	Pennsylvania	770	Georgia	937	Ohio
330	Ohio	571	Virginia	772	Florida	938	Alabama
331	Illinois	573	Missouri	773	Illinois	939	Puerto Rico
334	Alabama	574	Indiana	774	Massachusetts	940	Texas
336	North Carolina	575	New Mexico	775	Nevada	941	Florida
337	Louisiana	579	Quebec	778	British Columbia	947	Michigan
339	Massachusetts	580	Oklahoma	779	Illinois	949	California
340	U.S. Virgin Islands	581	Quebec	780	Alberta	951	California
343	Ontario	585	New York	781	Massachusetts	952	Minnesota
345	Cayman Islands	586	Michigan	784	St. Vincent and Gren.	954	Florida
347	New York	587	Alberta	785	Kansas	956	Texas
351	Massachusetts	*600*	*Canadian Services*	786	Florida	970	Colorado
352	Florida	601	Mississippi	787	Puerto Rico	971	Oregon
360	Washington	602	Arizona	*800*	*Toll-Free Service*	972	Texas
361	Texas	603	New Hampshire	801	Utah	973	New Jersey
385	Utah	604	British Columbia	802	Vermont	978	Massachusetts
386	Florida	605	South Dakota	803	South Carolina	979	Texas
401	Rhode Island	606	Kentucky	804	Virginia	980	North Carolina
402	Nebraska	607	New York	805	California	985	Louisiana
403	Alberta	608	Wisconsin	806	Texas	989	Michigan
404	Georgia	609	New Jersey	807	Ontario		
405	Oklahoma	610	Pennsylvania	808	Hawaii		

POSTAL INFORMATION

Basic U.S. Postal Service

The Postal Reorganization Act, creating a government-owned postal service under the executive branch and replacing the old Post Office Department, was signed into law by Pres. Richard Nixon, Aug. 12, 1970. The service officially came into being on July 1, 1971. The U.S. Postal Service is governed by an 11-person board of governors. Nine of the members are appointed by the president, with Senate approval. These nine choose a postmaster general. The board and the postmaster general choose the 11th member, who serves as deputy postmaster general.

Congress passed the Postal Accountability and Enhancement Act, which overhauled postal service operations for the first time since 1971, on Dec. 8, 2006. New operating provisions included the ability to adjust rates annually, negotiate for contracts, and invest profits in internal improvements. (The Postal Service last received a public service subsidy, i.e., taxpayer dollars, in 1982.)

Historical Postage Rates, 1851-2011

Postage cost for a prepaid, one-ounce letter (the first-class standard after July 1, 1885).

Effective date	Rate	2011 dollars	Effective date	Rate	2011 dollars	Effective date	Rate	2011 dollars
July 1, 1851	$0.06[1]	$1.62	Jan. 7, 1968	$0.06	$0.39	Feb. 3, 1991	$0.29	$0.48
July 1, 1863	0.06	1.09	May 16, 1971	0.08	4.45	Jan. 1, 1995	0.32	0.47
Oct. 1, 1883	0.04	0.96	Mar. 2, 1974	0.10	0.46	Jan. 10, 1999	0.33	0.45
July 1, 1885	0.02	0.50	Dec. 31, 1975	0.13	0.55	Jan. 7, 2001	0.34	0.43
Nov. 2, 1917	0.03[2]	0.53	May 29, 1978	0.15	0.52	June 30, 2002	0.37	0.46
July 1, 1919	0.02[2]	0.26	Mar. 22, 1981	0.18	0.45	Jan. 8, 2006	0.39	0.44
July 6, 1932	0.03	0.49	Nov. 1, 1981	0.20	0.50	May 14, 2007	0.41	0.45
Aug. 1, 1958	0.04	0.31	Feb. 17, 1985	0.22	0.46	May 12, 2008	0.42	0.44
Jan. 7, 1963	0.05	0.37	Apr. 3, 1988	0.25	0.48	May 11, 2009	0.44	0.46

(1) For domestic letters traveling under 3,000 miles. (2) The price increased one cent during World War I; Congress restored the prewar rate in 1919.

Status of the U.S. Postal Service, 2001-10

Source: *Postal Facts 2011*, U.S. Postal Service

	2001	2002	2003	2004	2005	2006	2007	2008	2009	2010	% change, 2001-10
Total mail items (bil)	207.5	202.8	202.1	206.1	211.7	213.1	212.2	202.7	177.0	171.0	−17.6%
First-class mail items (bil)	103.7	102.4	99.1	97.9	98.1	97.7	95.9	91.7	83.8	78.2	−24.6
Stamped mail items (bil) . .	53.6	52.0	49.2	47.7	45.9	44.4	42.2	35.3	31.8	28.6	−46.6
Standard mail items (bil) . .	89.9	87.2	90.5	95.6	100.9	102.5	103.5	99.1	82.7	82.5	−8.2
Annual revenue (bil)	$65.8	$66.4	$68.5	$68.9	$69.9	$72.7	$74.7	$74.9	$68.0	$67.1	2.0
Total retail revenue (bil) . .	$14.8	$15.0	$15.5	$15.2	$14.9	$14.5	$14.6	$14.1	$13.1	$12.5	−15.5
Total customer visits (bil)	1.4	1.3	1.3	1.2	1.3	1.3	1.2	1.2	1.1	1.1	−21.3
Delivery points (mil)	137.7	139.4	141.3	142.5	144.3	146.2	148.0	149.2	150.0	150.7	9.4
Total delivery routes	242,600	241,000	240,300	241,200	243,000	244,700	246,500	244,800	232,900	230,600	−4.9
Total retail offices	38,123	37,683	37,579	37,159	37,142	36,826	36,451	36,723	36,496	35,754	−6.2
Career employees	775,903	752,949	729,035	707,485	704,716	696,138	696,138	663,238	623,128	574,000	−26.0

U.S. Domestic Mail Rates

Source: *Price List (Notice 123)*, U.S. Postal Service. Effective June 6, 2011. Rates are for domestic retail customers unless otherwise noted. Domestic rates apply to the U.S., to its territories and possessions, and to APOs and FPOs.

First-Class Mail

First-Class Mail includes written matter such as letters, postcards, bills, account statements, and any matter sealed or closed against inspection. In most cases, **delivery is in 3 days or less.**

Written matter sealed against inspection costs 44¢ for the first ounce, 20¢ for each additional ounce or fraction thereof, up to 3.5 oz. Postcard postage is 29¢. Large envelopes measuring up to 12 in. by 15 in. (or standard envelopes over 3.5 oz.) cost 88¢ for the first ounce and 20¢ for each additional ounce or fraction thereof. Presort- and automation-compatible mail can qualify for lower rates if certain piece minimums, mailing permits, and other requirements are met.

Express Mail

Express Mail provides guaranteed expedited service for any mailable article (up to 70 lbs and not over 108 in. in combined length and girth). Offers **next day delivery** by noon to most destinations; there is a $12.50 extra charge for Sunday or holiday delivery. Second-day service is available to locations not in the Next Day Delivery Network. Prices start at $13.25 for items weighing up to 8 oz., dependent on distance. All rates include insurance up to $100, shipment receipt, record of delivery at the destination post office, and free tracking.

Express Mail Flat Rate: $18.30, regardless of weight, if matter fits into a designated Postal Service flat-rate envelope.

Pickup On Demand service is available for **$15.30** per stop, regardless of the number of pieces or service used.

Priority Mail

Due to expeditious handling and transportation, Priority Mail is **delivered in 2 days** in most cases. Priority Mail may include any mailable article up to 70 lbs and not over 108 in. in length and girth combined.

Priority Mail Flat Rate: $4.95, regardless of weight, if matter fits into a designated Postal Service flat-rate envelope. **$5.20, $10.95, or $14.95**, regardless of weight (under 70 lbs) if matter fits into special Postal Service flat-rate boxes.

Priority Mail Rates

Weight not over	Zone							
	1-2	3	4	5	6	7	8
1 lb	$5.10	$5.15	$5.25	$5.35	$5.45	$5.60	$5.95
2	5.20	5.55	6.20	7.90	8.60	9.15	10.20
3	5.95	6.80	7.80	9.35	10.35	11.15	13.20
4	6.70	7.85	8.95	12.40	13.50	14.35	15.90
5	7.95	9.10	10.25	14.05	15.45	16.50	18.35
6	8.75	10.05	11.50	15.65	17.30	18.50	20.70
7	9.30	10.95	12.40	17.45	19.15	20.85	23.30
8	10.00	11.90	13.85	18.95	21.00	22.95	26.10
9	10.65	12.85	15.00	20.55	22.90	24.90	29.05
10	11.35	13.80	16.35	22.20	24.70	27.35	31.60
11	12.15	14.75	17.60	23.95	26.55	30.20	34.70
12	13.00	15.80	18.90	25.70	28.85	32.65	37.30
13	13.80	16.80	19.95	27.20	30.95	33.95	38.60
14	14.60	17.80	21.15	28.90	32.65	35.90	40.50
15	15.25	18.80	22.35	30.60	34.10	36.65	41.65

Parcel Post

Parcel Post applies to packages not mailed as Priority Mail, Express Mail, Media Mail, or Library Mail. (Parcel Select, a separate service, is used for medium-to-large volumes of packages.) Parcel Post is a ground service for non-urgent shipping and oversized packages; delivery depends on distance and takes 2-8 days.

Any package matter may be mailed at Parcel Post rates provided it does not exceed 70 lbs or 130 in. in combined length and girth. Packages over 84 in. and up to 108 in. in combined length and girth and under 20 lbs use the 20-lb "balloon" price. Packages exceeding 108 in. use the oversized price—consult postal worker. Fractions of a pound are counted as a full pound.

Parcel Post Rates

Weight not over	Zone						
	1-2	3	4	5	6	7	8
1 lb	$5.10	$5.15	$5.25	$5.30	$5.34	$5.38	$5.41
2	5.15	5.38	5.89	7.35	7.65	7.96	8.67
3	5.65	6.39	7.14	8.23	9.00	9.48	10.69
4	6.10	7.14	7.97	9.30	10.13	10.76	11.77
5	7.23	8.28	9.02	10.12	10.82	11.39	12.29
6	7.92	9.15	9.94	10.94	11.45	12.02	13.03
7	8.37	9.86	10.49	11.80	12.36	13.01	14.15
8	8.70	10.34	10.86	12.17	12.96	13.74	15.03
9	8.95	10.69	11.24	12.55	13.56	14.47	15.90
10	9.18	11.03	11.61	12.92	14.16	15.21	16.77
11	9.49	11.38	11.99	13.29	14.76	15.94	17.65
12	9.80	11.72	12.36	13.66	15.36	16.67	18.52
13	10.11	12.06	12.74	14.03	15.96	17.40	19.39
14	10.42	12.41	13.11	14.40	16.56	18.13	20.27
15	10.73	12.75	13.49	14.77	17.16	18.86	21.14

Standard Mail

Standard Mail is limited to items less than 16 oz. such as solicitations, newsletters, advertising materials, books, cassettes, and other merchandise. It may not be used for personal correspondence. A minimum volume of 200 pieces or 50 lbs of such items is necessary, and specific bulk mail preparation and sortation requirements apply.

The minimum rate per piece for pieces 3.3 oz. or less is $0.381 for basic nonmachinable letters. Contact a post office for discounts for automation, presorted, carrier route, and destination entry, among others. Separate rates are available for some nonprofit organizations.

Any mailer who uses standard mail is required to pay an annual fee of $190, good for 365 days. Additional standards apply to mailings of nonidentical-weight pieces.

Periodicals

Periodicals include newspapers and magazines.

For the general public, the applicable retail postage is paid for periodicals.

For publishers, rates vary according to the following:

(1) whether item is sent to same county,

(2) percentage of editorial and advertising matter,

(3) whether the publisher is a nonprofit or produces educational material for use in classrooms,

(4) weight,

(5) distance,

(6) level of presort, and

(7) automation compatibility.

Library Mail

Applies to books, printed music, bound academic theses, periodicals, sound recordings, museum materials, and other library materials mailed between schools, colleges, universities, public libraries, museums, veteran and fraternal organizations, and nonprofit religious, educational, scientific, and labor organizations or associations (or to or from such organizations). Advertising restrictions apply. All packages must be marked "Library Mail" and may not exceed 108 in. in combined length and girth. Contact a post office for further information.

Rates are calculated by weight only. Single-piece rates: $2.29, up to 1 lb; 39¢ for each additional pound or fraction thereof up to 7 lbs; additional pounds thereafter, 37¢.

Media Mail

Applies to books of at least 8 printed pages; 16-mm or narrower-width films; printed music; printed test materials; sound recordings, playscripts, and manuscripts for books; printed educational charts; loose-leaf pages and binders consisting of medical information; computer-readable media. Advertising restrictions apply. Packages must be marked "Media Mail" and may not exceed 108 in. in combined length and girth. Contact a post office for further information.

Rates are calculated by weight only. Single-piece rates: $2.41, up to 1 lb; 41¢, for each additional pound or fraction thereof up to 7 lbs; additional pounds thereafter, 39¢.

Bound Printed Matter

Applies to advertising, promotional, directory, or editorial material that is bound by permanent fastening and consists of sheets of which at least 90% are imprinted by any process other than handwriting or typewriting. Does not include stationery (or pads of blank forms) or personal correspondence. Packages may not exceed 108 in. in combined length and girth and must be marked "Bound Printed Matter" or "BPM."

Bound Printed Matter Rates
(zone rate for commercial parcels)

Weight not over	Zone						
	1-2	3	4	5	6	7	8
1.0 lb	$2.34	$2.38	$2.44	$2.53	$2.64	$2.70	$2.89
1.5	2.34	2.38	2.44	2.53	2.64	2.70	2.89
2.0	2.44	2.50	2.58	2.70	2.84	2.92	3.18
2.5	2.55	2.62	2.72	2.87	3.05	3.15	3.47
3.0	2.65	2.74	2.86	3.04	3.25	3.37	3.76
3.5	2.76	2.86	3.00	3.21	3.46	3.60	4.05
4.0	2.86	2.98	3.14	3.38	3.66	3.82	4.34
4.5	2.97	3.10	3.28	3.55	3.87	4.05	4.63
5.0	3.07	3.22	3.42	3.72	4.07	4.27	4.92
6.0	3.28	3.46	3.70	4.06	4.48	4.72	5.50
7.0	3.49	3.70	3.98	4.40	4.89	5.17	6.08
8.0	3.70	3.94	4.26	4.74	5.30	5.62	6.66
9.0	3.91	4.18	4.54	5.08	5.71	6.07	7.24
10.0	4.12	4.42	4.82	5.42	6.12	6.52	7.82
11.0	4.33	4.66	5.10	5.76	6.53	6.97	8.40
12.0	4.54	4.90	5.38	6.10	6.94	7.42	8.98
13.0	4.75	5.14	5.66	6.44	7.35	7.87	9.56
14.0	4.96	5.38	5.94	6.78	7.76	8.32	10.14
15.0	5.17	5.62	6.22	7.12	8.17	8.77	10.72

Domestic Mail Special Services

Delivery Confirmation

Applies to First-Class Mail parcels, Priority Mail, and Package Services. Available for purchase at the time of mailing only. Provides mailer with the date and time an article was delivered or date and time of any unsuccessful delivery attempts. Electronic confirmation is available for bar-coded matter.

Confirmation is accessible to retail purchasers on the Internet (www.usps.com) or toll-free by phone at (800) 222-1811.

Priority Mail fees: retail, 70¢; electronic, free. First-Class Mail parcels and Package Services fees: retail, 80¢; electronic, 19¢. Standard Mail fee: electronic, 19¢.

Change of Address

The USPS will forward mail to another address provided a Change of Address (COA) card has been filed, either in person (free), on www.usps.com ($1 fee), or by phone at (800) ASK-USPS ($1). The COA card, which can be picked up at any post office or printed off the Internet, can also be dropped in any mailbox for free filing.

Special Handling

Provides preferential handling, but not preferential delivery, to the extent practicable in dispatch and transportation. Available for First-Class Mail; Priority Mail, and Package Services for the following surcharge: up to 10 lb, $7.55; over 10 lb, $10.60. Pieces must be marked "Special Handling."

> The USPS introduced the "Forever" stamp Apr. 12, 2007. The Forever stamp initially cost 41¢ and will always be valid as First-Class postage on standard envelopes weighing one ounce or less, even if rates change. The Forever stamp can be purchased at the current First-Class standard rate (44¢ as of Sept. 2011).

Registered Mail

Provides sender with mailing receipt, and a delivery record is maintained. Only matter prepaid with postage at First Class or Priority Mail rates may be registered. Stamps or meter stamps must be attached. The face of the article must be at least 5 in. long, 3.5 in. high.

Declared value	Fee
$0.00.	$10.75
$0.01 to $100.00.	11.50
$100.01 to $500.00.	13.25
$500.01 to $1,000.00.	14.65
$1,000.01 to $2,000.00.	16.05
$2,000.01 to $3,000.00.	17.45
$3,000.01 to $4,000.00.	18.85
$4,000.01 to $5,000.00.	20.25
$5,000.01 to $6,000.00.	21.65
$6,000.01 to $7,000.00.	23.05
$7,000.01 to $8,000.00.	24.45
$8,000.01 to $9,000.00.	25.85
$9,000.01 to $10,000.00.	27.25
$10,000.01 to $11,000.00	28.65
Each additional $1,000 or fraction thereof . .	1.40

Note: The mailer is required to declare the value of mail presented for registration. Fee for articles with declared value of more than $0.00 up to $25,000 includes insurance.

Collect on Delivery (C.O.D.): Fee: $5.75 for up to $50; increases incrementally. Items must be sent as bona fide orders or be in conformity with agreements between senders and addressees. Maximum amount collectible is $1,000. For details, consult a post office.

Certified mail: Available for any matter having no intrinsic value on which First Class or Priority Mail postage is paid. A receipt is furnished at the time of mailing, and evidence of delivery is obtained. Basic fee is $2.85 in addition to regular postage. Return receipt and restricted delivery available upon payment of additional fees. No indemnity.

Insured Mail

Applicable to Standard Mail, First-Class, or Priority Mail packages. Matter for sale addressed to prospective purchasers who have not ordered it or authorized its sending cannot be insured. **Note:** For Express Mail, insurance is included up to $100; additional insurance can be purchased for significantly lower fees than those shown here.

Declared value	Insured mail fee[1]
$0.01 to $50.00.	$1.80
$50.01 to $100.00.	2.30
$100.01 to $200.00.	2.85
$200.01 to $300.00.	4.75
$300.01 to $400.00.	5.80
$400.01 to $500.00.	6.85
$500.01 to $600.00.	7.90
$Each additional $100 or fraction thereof	1.05

(1) In addition to postage. (Maximum liability is $5,000.) See a post office for details on bulk discounts.

International Mail Special Services

Insurance: Available to many countries for loss of or damage to items paid at parcel post rate. Consult a post office for indemnity limits for individual countries.

Priority Mail International Insurance Rates

Limit of indemnity not over	Fee
$50	$2.30
$100	3.40
$200	4.50
$300	5.60
$400	6.70
$500	7.80
$600	8.90
$700	10.00
Each additional $100 or fraction thereof. . . .	1.10

Note: Maximum insurance $5,000 ($2,499 in Canada). Varies by country.

International postcards (single): 80¢ to Canada or Mexico; 98¢ to all other countries.

Registration: Available for letter-post items only to most countries. Fee: $11.50.

Return Receipt: Shows to whom and when item is delivered. Fee: $2.30 (must be purchased at time of mailing).

First-Class Mail International: Letter-post items weighing under 1 oz. can be sent airmail for 98¢ to most countries daily; 80¢ to Canada; 80¢ to Mexico.

International Reply Coupons (IRC): Provide foreign addressees with a prepaid means of responding to communications initiated by a U.S. sender. Each IRC is equivalent to the destination country's minimum postage rate for an unregistered airmail letter. Fee: $2.10 per coupon.

Restricted Delivery: Places restrictions on who receives an item. Available to many countries for registered mail, with some limitations. Fee: $4.50.

Post Office-Authorized Two-Letter State Abbreviations

The abbreviations below are approved by the U.S. Postal Service for use in addresses.

Alabama	AL	Hawaii	HI	Missouri	MO	Pennsylvania	PA
Alaska	AK	Idaho	ID	Montana	MT	Puerto Rico	PR
American Samoa	AS	Illinois	IL	Nebraska	NE	Rhode Island	RI
Arizona	AZ	Indiana	IN	Nevada	NV	South Carolina	SC
Arkansas	AR	Iowa	IA	New Hampshire	NH	South Dakota	SD
California	CA	Kansas	KS	New Jersey	NJ	Tennessee	TN
Colorado	CO	Kentucky	KY	New Mexico	NM	Texas	TX
Connecticut	CT	Louisiana	LA	New York	NY	Utah	UT
Delaware	DE	Maine	ME	North Carolina	NC	Vermont	VT
District of Columbia	DC	Marshall Islands[1]	MH	North Dakota	ND	Virgin Islands	VI
Federated States of		Maryland	MD	Northern Mariana Isls.	MP	Virginia	VA
Micronesia[1]	FM	Massachusetts	MA	Ohio	OH	Washington	WA
Florida	FL	Michigan	MI	Oklahoma	OK	West Virginia	WV
Georgia	GA	Minnesota	MN	Oregon	OR	Wisconsin	WI
Guam	GU	Mississippi	MS	Palau[1]	PW	Wyoming	WY

(1) Although an independent nation, this country is subject to domestic rates and fees.

Canadian Province and Territory Postal Abbreviations

Source: Canada Post

Alberta	AB	Newfoundland and		Nunavut	NU	Quebec	QC
British Columbia	BC	Labrador	NL	Ontario	ON	Saskatchewan	SK
Manitoba	MB	Northwest Territories	NT	Prince Edward Island	PE	Yukon	YT
New Brunswick	NB	Nova Scotia	NS				

Social Security Coverage

Source: Social Security Administration; World Almanac research; provisions shown are as under current law, Sept. 2011

Social Security Benefits

Social Security's **Old-Age, Survivors, and Disability Insurance (OASDI)** program benefits are based on a worker's **primary insurance amount (PIA)**, which is related by law to the average indexed monthly earnings (AIME) on which Social Security contributions have been paid. The full PIA is currently payable to a worker retiring at age 66 (varies depending on birth year), and to an entitled disabled worker at any age. Spouses and children of retired or disabled workers and survivors of deceased workers receive set proportions of the PIA subject to a family maximum amount.

The PIA is calculated by applying varying percentages to succeeding parts of the AIME. The formula is adjusted annually to reflect changes in average annual wages.

Increases in Social Security benefits are initiated for Dec. of each year, assuming the Consumer Price Index (CPI) for the 3rd calendar quarter of the year increased relative to the base quarter, which is the 3rd calendar quarter of the year in which an increase last became effective. The size of the benefit increase is determined by the percentage rise of the CPI between the quarters measured.

The **average monthly benefit** payable to all retired workers amounted to $1,175 in Dec. 2010. The average benefit for disabled workers in that month amounted to $1,068.

Maximum Monthly Retired-Worker Benefits Payable for Individuals who Retired at Age 65[1]

Year attaining age 65	Maximum benefit— Payable at retirement	Payable effective Dec. 2010
1990	$975	$1,701
1995	1,199	1,762
1996	1,248	1,789
1997	1,326	1,847
1998	1,342	1,831
1999	1,373	1,848
2000	1,435	1,885
2001	1,538	1,952
2002	1,660	2,054
2003	1,721	2,100
2004	1,784	2,133
2005	1,874	2,181
2006	1,961	2,193
2007	1,998	2,163
2008	2,030	2,148
2009	2,172	2,172
2010	2,191	2,191
2011	2,249	2,249

(1) Assumes retirement at beginning of year.

Amount of Work Required

To qualify for benefits, the worker generally must have worked a certain length of time in covered employment. Just how long depends on when the worker reaches age 62 or, if earlier, when he or she dies or becomes disabled. A person born after 1929 who dies, becomes disabled, or reaches age 62 after 1991 must generally have had at least 10 years work credit to qualify for benefits.

Contribution and Benefit Base

Calendar year	OASDI[1]	Calendar year	OASDI[1]	Calendar year	OASDI[1]
1994	$60,600	2000	$76,200	2006	$94,200
1995	61,200	2001	80,400	2007	97,500
1996	62,700	2002	84,900	2008	102,000
1997	65,400	2003	87,000	2009	106,800
1998	68,400	2004	87,900	2010	106,800
1999	72,600	2005	90,000		

(1) Old-Age, Survivors, and Disability Insurance.

A person is **fully insured** who has 1 quarter of coverage for every year after age 21 is reached (or 1950, if later) up to but not including the year the worker reaches 62, dies, or becomes disabled. In 2010, a person earns 1 quarter of coverage for each $1,120 of annual earnings in covered employment, up to 4 quarters per year.

To receive **disability benefits**, the worker, in addition to being fully insured, must generally have credit for 20 quarters of coverage out of the 40 calendar quarters before he or she became disabled. A disabled blind worker need meet only the fully insured requirement. Persons disabled before age 31 can qualify with a briefer period of coverage. Certain survivor benefits are payable if the deceased worker had 6 quarters of coverage in the 13 quarters preceding death.

Tax Rate Schedule

(percentage of covered earnings)

Year	Total	OASDI[1]	HI[2]
	(for employees and employers, each)		
1979-80	6.13%	5.08%	1.05%
1981	6.65	5.35	1.30
1982-83	6.70	5.40	1.30
1984	7.00	5.70	1.30
1985	7.05	5.70	1.35
1986-87	7.15	5.70	1.45
1988-89	7.51	6.06	1.45
1990 and after[3]	7.65	6.20	1.45
Year	**(for self-employed)**		
1979-80	8.10%	7.05%	1.05%
1981	9.30	8.00	1.30
1982-83	9.35	8.05	1.30
1984	14.00	11.40	2.60
1985	14.10	11.40	2.70
1986-87	14.30	11.40	2.90
1988-89	15.02	12.12	2.90
1990 and after[3]	15.30	12.40	2.90

(1) Old-Age, Survivors, and Disability Ins. (2) Hospital Ins. (Medicare). (3) Under Public Law 111-147, most employers were exempt from paying their share of OASDI payroll tax Mar. 19-Dec. 31, 2010, to certain qualified individuals hired after Feb. 3, 2010. Under Public Law 111-312, the OASDI payroll tax rate was reduced for 2011 by 2 percentage points for employees and for self-employed workers. Temporary reductions in revenue have been and will be made up by reimbursements from the general fund of the treasury to the OASI and DI Trust Funds.

What Aged Workers Receive

A person may receive monthly old-age benefits when he or she has enough work in covered employment and has reached retirement age—age 62 for reduced benefits, the age below for full benefits.

Full-Benefit Retirement Age (FRA) by Birth Year

Year of birth	FRA	Year of birth	FRA
1937 or earlier	65	1955	66 and 2 mos.
1938	65 and 2 mos.	1956	66 and 4 mos.
1939	65 and 4 mos.	1957	66 and 6 mos.
1940	65 and 6 mos.	1958	66 and 8 mos.
1941	65 and 8 mos.	1959	66 and 10 mos.
1942	65 and 10 mos.	1960 or	
1943-54	66	later	67

Note: If born on Jan. 1, refer to the previous birth year.

In 2000, the retirement **earnings test** was eliminated beginning with the month when the beneficiary reaches **full-benefit retirement age (FRA)**. A person at or above FRA no longer has benefits reduced because of earnings. However, in the calendar year a beneficiary reaches FRA, benefits are reduced $1 for every $3 of earnings above the limit allowed by law ($37,680 in 2011) for the months prior to FRA. For years before the beneficiary attains FRA, the reduction is $1 for every $2 of earnings over the exempt amount ($14,160 for 2011).

For workers who reached age 65 between 1982 and 1989, Social Security benefits are raised by 3% for each year for which the worker failed to receive benefits between FRA and 70 (72 before 1984), whether because of earnings from work, because the worker had not applied for benefits, or because the worker declined benefits after entitlement. The **delayed retirement credit** is 1% per year for workers who reached age 65 before 1982. The delayed retirement credit rose to 8% per year for 2008 and years after. The rate for workers who reached age 65 in 1998-99 is 5.5%; 2000-01, 6.0%; 2002-03, 6.5%; 2004-05, 7.0%. For 2006-07, it is 7.5%.

For workers retiring early, before full retirement age, benefits are permanently reduced 5/9 of 1% for each month before the FRA, up to 36 months. If the number of months exceeds 36, then the benefit is further reduced 5/12 of 1% per month.

For example, when FRA reaches 67, for workers who retire at exactly age 62, there are a total of 60 months of reduction. The reduction for the first 36 months is 5/9 of 36%, or 20%. The reduction for the remaining 24 months is 5/12 of 24%, or 10%. Thus, when the FRA reaches 67, the amount of reduction at age 62 will be 30%. The nearer to FRA the worker is when he or she begins collecting a benefit, the larger the monthly benefit will be.

Benefits for Worker's Spouse

The spouse of a worker who is getting Social Security retirement or disability payments may become entitled to an insurance benefit of **one-half of the worker's PIA** if claiming benefits at full retirement age. Reduced spouse's benefits are available at age 62 and are permanently reduced $^{25}/_{36}$ of 1% for each month before FRA, up to 36 months. If the number of months exceeds 36, then the benefit is further reduced $^{5}/_{12}$ of 1% per month. Benefits are also payable to the aged divorced spouse of an insured worker if he or she was married to the worker for at least 10 years. To qualify for divorced spouse benefits, the insured worker does not have to be receiving benefits if the divorce occurred at least 2 years earlier. Benefits received as a spouse are reduced by the amount of one's own PIA.

Benefits for Children of Workers

If a retired or disabled worker has a child under age 18, the child will usually get a benefit equal to **one-half of the worker's unreduced benefit**. So will the worker's spouse, even if under age 62, if he or she is caring for an entitled child of the worker who is under 16 or who became disabled before age 22. However, total benefits paid on a worker's earnings record are subject to a family maximum. Total monthly benefits paid to the family of a worker who retired in 2011 at age 66 and always had the maximum earnings creditable under Social Security cannot exceed $4,172.

When entitled children reach age 18, their benefits generally stop, but a child disabled before age 22 may get a benefit as long as the disability meets the definition in the law. Benefits will be paid until age 19 to a child attending elementary or secondary school full-time.

Benefits may also be paid to a grandchild or step-grandchild of a worker or of his or her spouse, in special circumstances.

OASDI Beneficiaries

Beneficiaries	May 2005	May 2006	May 2009	May 2010	May 2011
Total (in thous.)[1]	48,068	48,877	51,800	53,349	54,790
Age 65 and over, total	33,811	34,232	36,182	36,914	37,584
Retired workers.....	27,413	27,898	29,920	30,734	31,488
Disabled workers ...	112	143	336	339	344
Survivors/dependents	6,286	6,192	5,926	5,841	5,752
Under age 65, total ...	14,257	14,645	15,618	16,435	17,206
Retired workers.....	2,809	2,883	3,002	3,314	3,593
Disabled workers ...	6,239	6,465	7,227	7,628	8,027
Survivors/dependents	5,209	5,297	5,389	5,492	5,587
Total monthly benefits (in mil)	$42,074	$44,956	$54,797	$56,966	$59,042

(1) Numbers may not add up to totals due to rounding or incomplete enumeration.

What Disabled Workers Receive

A worker who becomes unable to work may be eligible for a monthly **disability benefit**. Benefits continue until it is determined that the individual is no longer disabled. When a disabled-worker beneficiary reaches FRA (66 years for workers born 1943-54), the disability benefit becomes a retired-worker benefit.

Benefits—generally like those for dependents of retired-worker beneficiaries—may be paid to dependents of disabled beneficiaries. However, the maximum family benefit in disability cases is generally lower than in retirement cases.

Survivor Benefits

If an insured worker should die, one or more types of benefits may be payable to survivors, again subject to a maximum family benefit described above.

1. If claiming benefits at FRA, the **surviving spouse** will receive a benefit equal to 100% of the deceased worker's benefit. Benefits claimed before FRA are reduced for age with a maximum reduction of 28.5% at age 60. However, if the deceased worker claimed benefits before FRA, the surviving spouse's benefits are limited to the reduced amount the worker would be getting if alive, but not less than 82.5% of the worker's PIA. Remarriage after the worker's death ends the surviving spouse's benefit rights. However, if the widow(er) marries and the marriage is ended, he or she

regains benefit rights. (A marriage after age 60, age 50 if disabled, is deemed not to have occurred for benefit purposes.) Survivor benefits may also be paid to a divorced spouse if the marriage lasted for at least 10 years.

Disabled widows and widowers may under certain circumstances qualify for benefits after attaining age 50 at the rate of 71.5% of the deceased worker's PIA. The widow or widower must have become totally disabled before or within 7 years after the spouse's death or the last month in which he or she received mother's or father's insurance benefits.

2. There is a benefit for each **child under age 18**. The monthly benefit for a child of a deceased worker is $^{3}/_{4}$ of the PIA, subject to the family maximum. A child with a disability that began before age 22 may also receive benefits. Also, a child may receive benefits until age 19 if he or she is in full-time attendance at an elementary or secondary school.

3. There is a **mother's or father's benefit** for the widow(er) if children of the worker under age 16 are in his or her care. The benefit is 75% of the PIA (subject to the family maximum), and it continues until the youngest child reaches age 16, at which time payments stop even if the child's benefit continues. However, if the widow(er) has a disabled child beneficiary age 16 or over in his or her care, benefits may continue.

4. **Dependent parents** may be eligible for benefits if they have been receiving at least half their support from the worker before his or her death, have reached age 62, and (except in certain circumstances) have not remarried since the worker's death. Each parent gets 75% of the worker's PIA; if only one parent survives, the benefit is 82%, but could be reduced for the family maximum.

5. A lump sum cash payment of **$255** is made when there is a spouse who was living with the worker or a spouse or child eligible for **immediate monthly survivor benefits**.

Self-Employed Workers

A self-employed person who has **net earnings of $400 or more** in a year must report such earnings for Social Security tax and credit purposes. The person reports net returns from the business. Income from real estate, savings, dividends, loans, pensions, or insurance policies are not included unless it is part of the business.

A self-employed person receives 1 quarter of coverage for each $1,120 (for 2011), up to a maximum of 4 quarters per year.

The nonfarm self-employed have the option of reporting their earnings as $^{2}/_{3}$ of their gross income from self-employment. This option can be used only if actual net earnings from self-employment income are less than $1,600 and less than $^{2}/_{3}$ of their gross income. The option may be used only 5 times. Also, the self-employed person must have actual net earnings of $400 or more in 2 of the 3 taxable years immediately preceding the year in which he or she uses the option.

When a person has both taxable wages and earnings from self-employment, wages are credited for Social Security purposes first; only as much self-employment income as brings total earnings up to the current taxable maximum becomes subject to the self-employment tax.

Farm Owners and Workers

Self-employed farmers whose gross annual earnings from farming are from **$600 to $2,400** may report $^{2}/_{3}$ of their gross earnings instead of net earnings for Social Security purposes. (Farmers whose gross annual earnings are under $600 cannot use the optional method.) Farmers whose gross income is over $2,400 and whose net earnings are less than $1,600 can report $1,600. Cash or crop shares received from a tenant or share farmer count if the owner participated materially in production or management. The self-employed farmer pays contributions at the same rate as other self-employed persons.

Agricultural employees. A worker's earnings from farm work count toward benefits if (1) the employer pays the worker $150 or more in cash during the year; or (2) the employer spends $2,500 or more in the year for agricultural labor. Under these rules, a person gets credit for 1 calendar quarter for each $1,120 in cash pay in 2011.

Foreign farm workers admitted to the U.S. on a temporary basis are not covered.

Household Workers

If an employer pays a household worker (e.g., maid, cook, laundry worker, nurse, babysitter, chauffeur, gardener) who is age 18 or older $1,700 or more in wages in 2011, the wages are covered under Social Security. This includes transportation costs paid for in cash. The job need not be regular or full-time.

The employee should get a Social Security card at the Social Security office and show it to the employer. The employer deducts the amount of the employee's Social Security tax from the worker's pay, adds an identical amount as the employer's Social Security tax, and sends the total amount to the federal government.

Medicare Coverage

The Medicare health insurance program provides acute-care coverage for Social Security and Railroad Retirement beneficiaries age 65 and over; workers and spouses age 65 and over with sufficient Medicare-only coverage in Federal, State, or local government employment; certain persons entitled to receive Social Security or Railroad Retirement disability benefits; certain disabled persons with Medicare-only coverage through government employment; certain persons with end-stage kidney disease; and certain persons in the vicinity of Libby, MT, with asbestos-related conditions. What follows is a basic description and may not cover all circumstances.

The **basic Medicare plan**, available nationwide, is a fee-for-service arrangement, where the beneficiary may use any provider accepting Medicare; some services are not covered, and there are some out-of-pocket costs.

Hospital insurance (Part A). The basic hospital insurance program pays covered services for hospital and post-hospital care, including the following:
- All necessary inpatient hospital care for the first 60 days of each benefit period, except for a deductible ($1,132 in 2011). For days 61-90, Medicare pays for services over and above a coinsurance amount ($283 per day in 2011). After 90 days, the beneficiary has 60 lifetime reserve days for which Medicare helps pay. The coinsurance amount for reserve days was $566 in 2011.
- Up to 100 days of care in a skilled-nursing facility in each benefit period. Hospital insurance pays for all covered services for the first 20 days; for days 21-100, the beneficiary pays coinsurance ($141.50 per day in 2011).
- Part-time home health care provided by nurses or other health workers.
- Limited coverage of hospice care for individuals certified to be terminally ill.

There is a premium for this insurance in certain—but not most—cases.

Medical insurance (Part B). Eligible elderly and disabled persons can receive benefits under this supplementary program only if they sign up for them and agree to a monthly premium. As of 2007, the monthly premium is tied to annual income. Individuals with income of $85,000 or less and couples with income of $170,000 or less pay $115.40 per person if they sign up upon becoming eligible in 2011. Part B covers certain medical services and supplies, including:

- Physicians' and surgeons' services, including some services furnished by other medical professionals.
- Services in an emergency room, outpatient clinic, or ambulatory surgical center.
- Home health care not covered under Part A.
- Laboratory tests, X-rays, and other diagnostic radiology services.
- Certain preventative care services and screening tests.
- Most physical and occupational therapy and speech pathology services.
- Comprehensive outpatient rehabilitation facility services, and mental health care in a partial hospitalization psychiatric program, if inpatient care would otherwise be required.
- Radiation therapy, renal (kidney) dialysis and transplants, heart, lung, heart-lung, liver, pancreas, bone marrow, and intestinal transplants.
- Approved durable medical equipment for home use.
- Drugs that are not usually self-administered. Certain services for diabetes.
- Ambulance services when other transportation methods are contraindicated.
- Rural health clinic and health center services, including some telemedicine.

Part B services are generally subject to a deductible ($162 in 2011), coinsurance (generally 20% of the remaining allowed charges, but with certain exceptions), a deductible for blood, and amounts above the allowed charge if the doctor or supplier is not one who accepts the Medicare-approved rate as payment in full. For outpatient mental health services, coinsurance is phasing down from 50% to 20% of allowed charges over the period 2010-14. For outpatient hospital services, coinsurance varies by service, usually falling between 20% and 50% of allowed charges. There are no deductibles or coinsurance for certain services, such as clinical lab tests, home health agency services (except some durable medical equipment, which is subject to 20% coinsurance), and some preventative care services. Payments for certain physical, speech, and occupational therapy services are subject to certain limits. Dental care, hearing aids, and routine eye care are generally not covered under the basic plan.

To get medical insurance (Part B), persons approaching age 65 may enroll during the Initial Enrollment Period that lasts from 3 months before to 3 months after the 65th birthday, and the month of their birthday. If new enrollees desire coverage to begin in the month they reach age 65, they must enroll in the 3 months before their birthday. Persons who did not enroll during their first enrollment period may enroll later, but late-enrollment premiums may apply.

The monthly premium is deducted from the cash benefit for persons receiving Social Security, Railroad Retirement, or Civil Service retirement benefits. Income from the medical premiums and the federal matching payments are put in a Supplementary Medical Insurance Trust Fund, from which benefits and administrative expenses are paid.

MedicareAdvantage (Part C) (formerly Medicare+Choice). Persons eligible for Medicare may have the option of getting services through a Medicare-certified health maintenance organization (HMO), preferred provider organization (PPO), provider-sponsored organization (PSO), or other Medicare-certified **managed care** plan. Any such plan must provide at least the same benefits as Parts A and B, except for hospice services. They may offer added benefits (such as vision or hearing coverage) or reduce cost sharing or premiums. Enrollees may be required to use the plan's network of participating providers, or may be allowed to go outside the network but pay higher out-of-pocket costs. Also available as options in some areas are Medicare-approved private fee-for-service plans and, for certain beneficiaries, special needs plans.

Prescription Drug Coverage (Part D). Effective Jan. 1, 2006, a Medicare prescription drug plan provides insurance coverage for prescription drugs. Medicare recipients pay a monthly premium (averaging $30 in 2011, depending on the provider) and a portion of drug costs. As of 2011, the monthly premium is tied to annual income. **Enrollment is scheduled to take place Nov. 15-Dec. 31 each year** and is optional. Coverage varies depending on the drug plan selected.

Part D Benefits
(Parameters determined annually by the Centers for Medicare and Medicaid Services.)

Standard benefit parameters	2010	2011
Initial coverage limit	$2,830	$2,840
Out-of-pocket threshold	4,550	4,550
Deductible	310	310
Minimum generic cost-sharing[1]	2.50	2.50
Minimum other drug cost-sharing[2]	6.30	6.30
Retiree drug subsidy		
Cost limit	$6,300	$6,300
Cost threshold	310	310

(1) For generic/preferred multi-source drugs in the catastrophic coverage phase. (2) For other (i.e., non-generic/preferred) drugs in the catastrophic coverage phase.

Further details are available on the Internet at www. medicare. gov or by calling 1-800-MEDICARE (1-800-633-4227).

Medicare card. Persons qualifying for hospital insurance under Social Security receive a health insurance card similar to cards used by other health insurers. The card indicates whether the individual has taken out medical insurance protection. It is to be shown to the hospital, skilled-nursing facility, home health agency, doctor, or whoever provides the covered services.

Payments are generally made only in the 50 states, Puerto Rico, Virgin Islands, Guam, and American Samoa.

Social Security Financing

Social Security is paid for by a tax on certain earnings (for 2011, on earnings up to $106,800) for **Old Age, Survivors, and Disability Insurance (OASDI)** and on all earnings (no upper limit) for Hospital Insurance with the **Medicare** Program; the taxable earnings base for OASDI has been adjusted annually to reflect increases in average wages. The employed worker and his or her employer share Social Security taxes equally.

Employers remit amounts withheld from employee wages for Social Security and income taxes to the Internal Revenue Service; employer Social Security taxes are also payable at the same time. (Self-employed workers pay Social Security taxes when filing their regular income tax forms.) The Social Security taxes (along with revenues arising from partial taxation of the Social Security benefits of certain high-income people) are transferred to the Social Security Trust Funds; they can be used only to pay benefits, the cost of rehabilitation services, and administrative expenses. Money not immediately needed for these purposes is by law invested in obligations of the federal government, which must pay interest on the money borrowed and must repay the principal when the obligations are redeemed or mature.

On Jan. 1, 1974, the **Supplemental Security Income (SSI)** program established by the 1972 Social Security Act amendments replaced the former federal grants to states for aid to the needy aged, blind, and disabled in the 50 states and the District of Columbia. The program provides both for federal payments, based on uniform national standards and eligibility requirements, and for state supplementary payments varying from state to state. The Social Security Administration administers the federal payments financed from general funds of the Treasury—and the state supplements as well, if the state elects to have its supplementary program federally administered. States may supplement the federal payment for all recipients and must supplement it for persons otherwise adversely affected by the transition from the former public assistance programs. In May 2011, the number of persons receiving federally administered SSI payments was 8,057,448, and the payments totaled about $4.4 bil.

The **maximum monthly federal SSI payment** for individuals without an eligible spouse and with no other countable income, living in their own household, was $674 in 2011. For couples where both members were eligible, the maximum payment was $1,011.

For further information contact the Social Security Administration toll-free at 1-800-772-1213 or visit its website at www.socialsecurity.gov.

Examples of Monthly Social Security Benefits Available, 2011

Benefit or beneficiary	For low earnings[1]	For med. earnings[1]	For max. earnings[1,2]
Primary insurance amount (worker retiring at 66 years, 0 months) ...	$908.20	$1,497.00	$2,366.10
Maximum family benefit (worker retiring at 66 years, 0 months)	1,362.30	2,733.00	4,141.80
Maximum family disability benefit (worker disabled at 55; in 2011) ...	1,320.90	2,310.00	3,666.00
Disabled worker (disabled at 55):			
Worker alone	931.70	1,540.00	2,444.00
Worker, spouse, and 1 child...................	1,319.00	2,310.00	3,666.00
Retired worker claiming benefits at age 62:			
Worker alone[3].............................	692.00	1,140.00	1,793.00
Worker with spouse claiming benefits at—			
NRA or over.............................	1,153.00	1,900.00	2,988.00
Age 62[3]................................	1,015.00	1,672.00	2,629.00
Widow or widower claiming benefits at—			
Age 66 or over[4]............................	908.00	1,497.00	2,366.00
Age 60[4].................................	652.00	1,076.00	1,701.00
Disabled widow or widower claiming benefits at age 50-59[5]	649.00	1,070.00	1,691.00
1 surviving child[4]	681.00	1,122.00	1,774.00
Widow or widower at NRA or over and 1 child[4]	1,362.00	2,619.00	4,140.00
Widowed mother or father and 1 child[4]	1,362.00	2,244.00	3,548.00
Widowed mother or father and 2 children[4]	1,362.00	2,733.00	4,141.00

NRA = Normal retirement age. **Note:** Effective Jan. 2011. (1) Career average earnings: an average of lifetime earnings indexed to the year prior to entitlement (2010 in this case). Low career average earnings = $18,829; med. = $41,843; max. = $97,706. (2) Assumes work beginning at age 22. (3) Assumes maximum reduction. (4) Assumes worker lived and worked until NRA without receiving reduced benefits. (5) Effective Jan. 1984, disabled widow(er) claiming a benefit at ages 50-59 receive a benefit equal to 71.5% of the primary insurance amount.

Social Security Recipients by Age, Sex, Race, and Hispanic Origin, 2010
Source: Social Security Administration

Social Security beneficiaries[1] (thous.)	Total[2]	White	Black	American Indian, Alaska Native	Asian	Hispanic
Total	43,624	37,767	4,570	533	1,145	3,106
Sex						
Male	19,076	16,680	1,864	226	484	1,411
Female	24,548	21,087	2,706	307	661	1,695
Age						
15-54 years............................	4,807	3,666	1,009	108	99	547
55-64 years............................	5,767	4,786	817	85	145	452
65-74 years............................	17,128	15,014	1,554	210	502	1,200
75 years or older.......................	15,922	14,301	1,189	130	399	907
Supplemental Security Income recipients[1] (thous.)						
Total	5,460	3,667	1,497	154	252	819
Sex						
Male	2,256	1,527	601	72	95	320
Female	3,204	2,140	896	83	156	499
Age						
15-54 years...........................	3,084	2,074	937	92	61	441
55-64 years...........................	1,250	895	318	34	20	155
65-74 years...........................	652	418	148	18	75	126
75 years or older.......................	474	281	93	9	95	96
Average annual benefit in 2009 (dollars)						
Social Security........................	$13,159	$13,361	$11,828	$11,843	$12,134	$11,024
Supplemental Security Income...........	7,173	7,173	6,963	6,931	6,528	6,714

Note: Race categories include people who reported being of that race, alone or in combination with another race. Persons of Hispanic origin may be of any race. (1) Persons 15 or older receiving Social Security benefits or Supplemental Security Income in Mar. 2010. (2) The sum of the individual categories may not add up to totals because of independent rounding, and because the totals include persons who reported being of more than one race.

OASDI Recipients and Monthly Payments, 1940-2010

Source: Social Security Administration

Year	Total recipients	Monthly benefits Total (thousands)	Avg.[1]	Avg. (2010 dollars)[2]	Year	Total recipients	Monthly benefits Total (thousands)	Avg.[1]	Avg. (2010 dollars)[2]
1940	222,488	$4,070	$18.29	$277.40	1990	39,832,125	$21,686,763	$544.45	$902.29
1945	1,288,107	23,801	18.48	218.45	1995	43,387,259	28,148,078	648.76	926.43
1950	3,477,243	126,857	36.48	322.49	2000	45,414,794	34,848,920	767.35	971.63
1955	7,960,616	411,613	51.71	410.33	2005	48,434,445	44,351,772	915.71	1,025.41
1960	14,844,589	936,321	63.07	453.37	2006	49,122,831	46,938,176	955.53	1,036.55
1965	20,866,767	1,516,802	72.69	490.26	2007	49,864,982	49,218,232	987.03	1,041.54
1970	26,228,629	2,628,326	100.21	549.15	2008	50,898,396	53,666,202	1,054.38	1,068.94
1975	32,085,372	5,727,903	178.52	705.24	2009	52,522,819	55,905,731	1,064.41	1,086.43
1980	35,618,840	10,694,022	300.23	774.25	2010	54,032,097	58,048,364	1,074.33	1,074.33
1985	37,058,353	15,901,643	429.10	858.29					

OASDI = Old Age, Survivors, and Disability Insurance. **Note:** Disability insurance payments began in 1957. (1) Avg. monthly benefit does not necessarily reflect individual payments to OASDI recipients. (2) Adjusted for inflation.

Social Security Trust Funds

Old-Age and Survivors Insurance Trust Fund, 1940-2010

(in millions)

Fiscal year[1]	Total	INCOME Net payroll tax contribs.	Income from taxing benefits	General fund reimburse-ments[2]	Net interest[3]	Total	DISBURSEMENTS Benefit pymts.[4]	Admin. expenses	Transfers to Railroad Retirement program	Net increase in fund[5]	Year-end balance
1940	$592	$550	—	—	$42	$28	$16	$12	—	$564	$1,745
1950	2,367	2,106	—	$4	257	784	727	57	—	1,583	12,893
1960	10,360	9,843	—	—	517	11,073	10,270	202	$600	−713	20,829
1970	31,746	29,955	—	442	1,350	27,321	26,268	474	579	4,425	32,616
1980	100,051	97,608	—	557	1,886	103,228	100,626	1,160	1,442	−3,177	24,566
1990	278,607	260,069	$2,924	1,471	14,143	223,481	218,948	1,564	2,969	55,126	203,445
1995	326,067	289,525	5,114	11	31,417	294,456	288,607	1,797	4,052	31,611	447,946
2000	484,228	418,219	12,476	1	53,532	353,396	347,868	1,990	3,538	130,832	893,003
2005	599,992	502,998	15,332	—	81,662	436,919	430,439	2,900	3,579	163,073	1,615,623
2006	632,157	530,006	15,176	−350	87,324	455,560	449,191	2,911	3,458	176,597	1,792,220
2007	663,376	553,414	16,661	—	93,300	488,553	481,828	3,151	3,575	174,822	1,967,042
2008	692,873	573,750	16,396	—	102,727	509,864	502,973	3,259	3,632	183,000	2,150,052
2009	697,326	571,228	18,967	—	107,131	551,542	544,484	3,369	3,690	145,784	2,295,835
2010	682,448	552,037	21,068	737	108,606	579,907	572,515	3,462	3,930	102,541	2,398,377

Note: Numbers may not add up to totals because of rounding. (1) Fiscal years 1980 and later consist of the 12 months ending on Sept. 30 of each year. Fiscal years prior to 1977 consisted of the 12 months ending on June 30 of each year. (2) Includes reimbursements from the General Fund of the Treasury to the OASI Trust Fund for: (a) the cost of non-contributory wage credits for military service before 1957; (b) the cost in 1971-82 of deemed wage credits for military service performed after 1956; (c) the cost of benefits to certain uninsured persons who attained age 72 before 1968; (d) the cost of payroll tax credits provided to employees in 1984 and self-employed persons in 1984-89 by Public Law 98-21; (e) the cost in 2009-17 of excluding certain self-employment earnings from SECA taxes under Public Law 110-246; and (f) payroll tax revenue foregone under the provisions of Public Law 111-147. (3) Net interest includes net profits or losses on marketable investments. Beginning in 1967, administrative expenses are charged to the trust fund on an estimated basis, with a final adjustment, including interest, made in the following fiscal year. The amounts of these interest adjustments are included in net interest. For years prior to 1967, a description of the method of accounting for administrative expenses is contained in the 1970 annual report. Beginning in Oct. 1973, the figures shown include relatively small amounts of gifts to the fund. Net interest for 1983-86 reflects payments from a borrowing trust fund to a lending trust fund for interest on amounts owed under the interfund borrowing provisions. During 1983-91, interest paid from the trust fund to the general fund on advance tax transfers is reflected. (4) Beginning in 1967, includes payments for vocational rehabilitation services furnished to disabled persons receiving benefits because of their disabilities. Beginning in 1983, amounts are reduced by amount of reimbursement for unnegotiated benefit checks. (5) Net change in assets during fiscal year, including amounts borrowed or repaid by other funds.

Disability Insurance Trust Fund, 1960-2010

(in millions)

Fiscal year[1]	Total	INCOME Net payroll tax contribs.	Income from taxing benefits	General fund reimburse-ments[2]	Net interest[3]	Total	DISBURSEMENTS Benefit pymts.[4]	Admin. expenses	Transfers to Railroad Retirement program	Net increase in fund[5]	Year-end balance
1960	$1,034	$987	—	—	$47	$533	$528	$32	−$27	$501	$2,167
1970	4,380	4,141	—	$16	223	2,954	2,795	149	10	1,426	5,104
1980	17,376	16,805	—	118	453	15,320	14,998	334	−12	2,056	7,680
1990	28,215	27,154	$158	138	766	25,124	24,327	717	80	3,091	11,455
1995	70,209	67,986	335	—	1,888	41,374	40,234	1,072	68	28,835	35,206
2000	77,023	70,001	756	—	6,266	56,008	54,244	1,608	159	21,014	113,752
2005	96,765	85,418	1,164	—	10,183	86,360	83,721	2,301	338	10,405	193,298
2006	101,571	90,001	1,174	—	10,396	92,932	90,064	2,480	388	8,640	201,938
2007	108,396	93,973	1,351	—	13,072	96,758	93,955	2,357	445	11,638	213,577
2008	109,816	97,432	1,373	8	11,003	107,153	104,222	2,513	418	2,663	216,239
2009	109,681	97,008	1,841	—	10,832	118,144	115,073	2,623	448	−8,462	207,777
2010	105,513	93,739	1,745	125	9,904	126,344	122,935	2,947	446	−20,831	186,946

Note: Numbers may not add up to totals because of rounding. (1) Fiscal years 1977 and later consist of the 12 months ending Sept. 30 of each year. Fiscal years prior to 1977 consisted of the 12 months ending June 30 of each year. (2) Includes reimbursements from the General Fund of the Treasury to the DI Trust Fund for: (a) the cost of noncontributory wage credits for military service before 1957; (b) the cost in 1971-82 of deemed wage credits for military service performed after 1956; (c) the cost of payroll tax credits provided to employees in 1984 and self-employed persons in 1984-89 by Public Law 98-21; (d) the cost in 2009-17 of excluding certain self-employment earnings from SECA taxes under Public Law 110-246; and (e) payroll tax revenue foregone under the provisions of Public Law 111-147. (3) Net interest includes net profits or losses on marketable investments. Beginning in 1967, administrative expenses are charged to the trust fund on an estimated basis, with a final adjustment, including interest, made in the following fiscal year. The amounts of these interest adjustments are included in net interest. For years prior to 1967, a description of the method of accounting for administrative expenses is contained in the 1970 annual report. Beginning in July 1974, the figures shown include relatively small amounts of gifts to the fund. Net interest for 1983-86 reflects payments from a borrowing trust fund to a lending trust fund for interest on amounts owed under the interfund borrowing provisions. During 1983-91, interest paid from the trust fund to the general fund on advance tax transfers is reflected. (4) Beginning in 1967, includes payments for vocational rehabilitation services furnished to disabled persons receiving benefits because of their disabilities. Beginning in 1983, amounts are reduced by amount of reimbursement for unnegotiated benefit checks. (5) Net change in assets during fiscal year, including amounts borrowed or repaid by other funds.

Supplementary Medical Insurance Trust Fund (Medicare SMI), 1975-2010

(in millions)

Fiscal year[1]	INCOME					DISBURSEMENTS			Net change	Year-end balance[9]
	Total	Premium from participants[2]	Govt. contribs.[3]	Transfers from states[4]	Interest and other income[5,6]	Total	Benefit pymts.[6,7,8]	Admin. expenses		
1975	$4,322	$1,887	$2,330	—	$106	$4,170	$3,765	$404	$152	$1,424
1980	10,275	2,928	6,932	—	416	10,737	10,144	593	−462	4,532
1990	46,138[10]	11,494[10]	33,210	—	1,434[10]	43,022[10]	41,498	1,524[10]	3,115[10]	14,527[10]
1995	58,169	19,244	36,988	—	1,937	65,213	63,491	1,722	−7,044	13,874
1996	82,025	18,931	61,702	—	1,392	68,946	67,176	1,771	13,079	26,953
1997	80,806	19,141	59,471	—	2,193	72,553	71,133	1,420	8,252	35,206
1998	81,955	19,427	59,919	—	2,608	76,272	74,837	1,435	5,683	40,889
1999	85,278	20,160	62,185	—	2,933	80,518	79,008	1,510	4,760	45,649
2000	89,239	20,515	65,561	—	3,164	88,992	87,212[11]	1,780	247	45,896
2001	95,336	22,307	69,838	—	3,191	99,452	97,466[11]	1,986	−4,116	41,780
2002	105,705	24,427	78,318	—	2,960	108,825	106,995[11]	1,830	−3,120	38,659
2003	110,194	26,834	80,905	—	2,455	124,055	121,699[11]	2,356	−13,861	24,799
2004	126,805	30,341	94,734	—	1,730	134,490	131,673	2,817	−7,684	17,114
2005	152,505	35,939	115,200	—	1,366	152,735	149,820[12]	2,914	−230	16,885
2006	211,951	44,241[13]	162,601	$3,630	1,478	195,557	192,083[12,13]	3,474	16,394	33,279
2007	237,864	49,640[13]	179,181	6,977	2,065	231,996	228,570[12,13]	3,426	5,867	39,146
2008	244,832	54,118[13]	180,434	7,042	3,238	224,830	221,406[13,14]	3,423	20,003	59,149
2009	262,529	57,665[13]	194,267	7,504	3,093	260,212	256,894[13]	3,318	2,317	61,466
2010	262,629	61,304[13]	213,709	4,493	3,168	272,164	268,650[13]	3,514	10,510	71,976

Note: Numbers may not add up to totals because of rounding. (1) Fiscal year 1975 consists of the 12 months ending on June 30, 1975; fiscal years 1980 and later consist of the 12 months ending Sept. 30 of each year. (2) For Part D, premiums include both amounts withheld from Social Security benefit checks (and certain other federal benefit payments) and amounts paid directly to Part D plans (estimated). (3) For Part B, includes matching payments from the general fund, plus certain interest-adjustment items. For Part D, includes all federal govt. transfers. Includes amounts for the transitional assistance benefits in 2004-06. (4) As of 2006, Medicaid is no longer the primary payer for full-benefit dual eligibles. States must pay a portion of their estimated foregone drug costs for this population. As of 2006, states pay 90% of estimated costs, with the percentage phasing down to 75% in 2015 and later. (5) "Other income" includes recoveries of amounts reimbursed from the trust fund that are not obligations of the trust fund and other small amounts of miscellaneous income. In 2008, includes an adjustment of $812 mil for interest inadvertently unearned as a result of HI hospice costs that were misallocated to, and paid from, the Part B account from May 2005 to Sept. 2007. (6) Values after 2005 include additional premiums for Medicare Advantage (MA) plans that are deducted from beneficiaries' Social Security checks, transferred to HI and SMI trust funds and then to the plans. (7) Includes costs of Peer Review Organizations in 1983-2001 and costs of Quality Review Organizations beginning in 2002. (8) For Part D, includes payments to plans, subsidies to employer-sponsored retiree drug plans, payments to states for low-income eligibility determinations, and Part D drug premiums (the amount collected from beneficiaries and transferred to plans and an estimated amount for premiums paid directly by enrollees to plans). Includes amounts for transitional assistance benefits in 2004-06. (9) The financial status of SMI depends on the assets and liabilities of the trust fund. (10) Includes the impact of the Medicare Catastrophic Coverage Act of 1988. (11) Benefit payments less monies transferred from the HI trust fund for home health agency costs. (12) Certain HI hospice costs were misallocated to, and paid from, the Part B account of the SMI trust fund. See also footnote (14). (13) Includes an estimated $1.804 bil (2006), $2.269 bil (2007), $2.930 bil (2008), $3.654 bil (2009), and $4.161 bil (2010) for premiums paid directly to Part D plans. (14) Benefit payments were $229,890 mil amount shown includes −$8,484 mil, which represents a transfer from the general fund of the Treasury to the Part B account of the SMI trust fund for HI hospice costs that were misallocated to, and paid from, the Part B account from May 2005 to Sept. 2007. (The HI trust fund, in turn, transferred $8,484 mil to the general fund.)

Hospital Insurance Trust Fund (Medicare HI), 1975-2010

(in millions)

Fiscal year[1]	INCOME								DISBURSEMENTS			Net change	Year-end balance
	Total	Payroll taxes	Taxation of benefits	Transfers from Railroad Retirement acct.	Rmbrs. for uninsured persons	Premiums from voluntary enrollees	Pymts. for military wage credits	Interest and other income[2,3]	Total	Benefit pymts.[3,4]	Admin. expenses[5]		
1975	$12,568	$11,291	—	$132	$481	$6	$48	$609	$10,612	$10,353	$259	$1,956	$9,870
1980	25,415	23,244	—	244	697	17	141	1,072	24,288	23,790	497	1,127	14,490
1990	79,563	70,655	—	367	413	113	107	7,908	66,687	65,912	774	12,876	95,631
1995	114,847	98,053	$3,913	396	462	998	61	10,963	114,883	113,583	1,300	−36	129,520
1996	121,135	106,934	4,069	401	419	1,107	−2,293[6]	10,496	125,317	124,088	1,229	−4,182	125,338
1997	128,548	112,725	3,558	419	481	1,279	70	10,017	137,836	136,175	1,661	−9,287	116,050
1998	138,203	121,913	5,067	419	34	1,320	67	9,382	137,140	135,487[7]	1,653	1,063	117,113
1999	153,015	134,385	6,552	430	652	1,401	71	9,523	131,441	129,463[7]	1,978	21,574	138,687
2000	159,681	137,738	8,787	465	470	1,392	2	10,827	130,284	127,934[7]	2,350	29,397	168,084
2005	196,921	168,954	8,765	445	286	2,303	0	16,168	184,142	181,292[8]	2,850	12,779	277,723
2006	210,309	180,392	10,319	471	408	2,632	0	16,086	184,901	181,815[8]	3,086	25,408	303,130
2007	219,207	187,992	10,593	483	468	2,761	0	16,910	202,827	200,191[8]	2,636	16,380	319,510
2008	229,729	197,195	11,733	526	506	2,913	0	16,856	230,240	227,008[9]	3,231	−511	319,000
2009	228,915	194,102	12,376	524	614	2,817	968[10]	17,514	238,001	234,659	3,343	−9,086	309,914
2010	218,004	183,603	13,760	525	−142	3,314	0	16,933	248,978	245,650	3,328	−30,975	278,939

Note: Numbers may not add up to totals because of rounding. (1) Fiscal year 1975 consists of the 12 months ending on June 30, 1975; fiscal years 1980 and later consist of the 12 months ending Sept. 30 of each year. (2) Other income includes recoveries of amounts reimbursed from the trust fund that are not obligations of the trust fund, receipts from the fraud and abuse control program, and other small amounts of miscellaneous income. In 2008, includes an adjustment of −$853 mil for interest inadvertently earned as a result of HI hospice costs that were misallocated to, and paid from, the Part B account of the SMI trust fund from May 2005 to Sept. 2007. (3) Values after 2005 include additional premiums for Medicare Advantage (MA) plans that are deducted from beneficiaries' Social Security checks, transferred to the HI and SMI trust funds, and then transferred to the plans. (These additional premiums are incurred when an MA plan is chosen with a monthly payment exceeding the benchmark amount. Enrollees may pay plans directly or have the amounts deducted from their Social Security checks.) (4) Includes costs of Peer Review Organizations from 1983 through 2001 (beginning with the implementation of the Prospective Payment System on Oct. 1, 1983), and costs of Quality Improvement Organizations beginning in 2002. (5) Includes costs of experiments and demonstration projects. Beginning in 1997, includes fraud and abuse control expenses, as provided for by PL 104-191. (6) Includes the lump-sum general revenue adjustment of −$2,366 mil, as provided for by sec. 151 of PL 98-21. (7) Includes monies transferred to the SMI trust fund for home health agency costs, as provided for by PL 105-33. (8) Certain HI hospice costs were misallocated to, and paid from, the Part B account of the SMI trust fund. (9) Benefit payments were $218,525 mil. Amount shown includes a transfer of $8,484 mil to the general fund of the Treasury for HI hospice costs that were misallocated to, and paid from, the Part B account of the SMI trust fund from May 2005 to Sept. 2007. (The general fund, in turn, transferred $8,484 mil to the Part B account.) (10) Includes the lump-sum general revenue adjustment of −$968 mil, as provided for by sec. 151 of PL 98-21.

Temporary Assistance for Needy Families, 2009

Source: Office of Family Assistance, Admin. for Children and Families, U.S. Dept. of Health and Human Services

State	Total federal and state TANF expenditures, 2009[1]	2009 average monthly expenditure per— Family	2009 average monthly expenditure per— Recipient	2009 average monthly number of— Families	2009 average monthly number of— Recipients	2009 average monthly number of— Children
Alabama	$147,259	$665.42	$283.89	18,442	43,226	33,098
Alaska	69,880	1,920.09	703.10	3,033	8,282	5,757
Arizona	387,073	851.97	392.96	37,860	82,085	61,792
Arkansas	135,918	1,338.36	589.59	8,463	19,211	14,033
California	6,525,869	1,020.48	415.82	532,907	1,307,832	1,030,805
Colorado	330,238	2,967.10	1,209.04	9,275	22,762	17,677
Connecticut	477,523	2,379.68	1,205.00	16,722	33,024	23,462
Delaware	53,235	983.39	346.69	4,511	12,796	7,899
Dist. of Columbia	172,310	1,804.92	773.85	7,956	18,555	13,949
Florida	855,916	1,294.74	731.04	55,090	97,568	78,907
Georgia	521,487	2,060.43	1,143.06	21,091	38,018	35,105
Guam	NA	NA	NA	1,376	3,250	2,423
Hawaii	336,378	3,556.40	1,300.39	7,882	21,556	15,020
Idaho	33,630	1,760.82	1,178.75	1,592	2,378	2,217
Illinois	1,090,772	4,635.06	1,734.31	19,611	52,412	47,895
Indiana	313,895	654.12	253.53	39,989	103,175	77,187
Iowa	179,630	926.62	367.68	16,155	40,712	28,155
Kansas	169,968	1,079.42	424.28	13,122	33,384	22,822
Kentucky	221,077	625.07	309.09	29,473	59,604	46,894
Louisiana	202,796	1,656.68	751.20	10,201	22,497	19,715
Maine	132,029	1,037.04	442.15	10,609	24,884	16,733
Maryland	516,131	1,918.01	807.20	22,425	53,284	39,238
Massachusetts	1,056,165	1,860.25	943.65	47,313	93,269	63,315
Michigan	1,420,537	1,902.26	751.55	62,230	157,511	118,900
Minnesota	489,660	1,874.18	865.12	21,772	47,167	36,249
Mississippi	100,719	741.33	357.31	11,322	23,490	17,754
Missouri	314,479	749.77	311.50	34,953	84,130	58,439
Montana	41,981	1,015.22	402.07	3,446	8,701	6,142
Nebraska	89,716	1,013.99	419.69	7,373	17,814	13,970
Nevada	127,533	1,275.48	500.16	8,332	21,249	15,945
New Hampshire	82,664	1,236.83	575.84	5,570	11,963	8,573
New Jersey	1,110,247	2,842.61	1,197.25	32,548	77,278	54,866
New Mexico	168,393	871.63	328.44	16,099	42,726	31,542
New York	5,092,194	3,636.42	1,633.81	116,694	259,731	195,397
North Carolina	636,721	2,066.20	1,059.07	25,680	50,101	41,294
North Dakota	36,320	1,400.65	551.50	2,161	5,488	4,032
Ohio	1,317,381	1,219.02	544.98	90,057	201,443	148,905
Oklahoma	218,385	2,081.02	949.54	8,745	19,166	15,775
Oregon	313,056	1,189.67	495.83	21,929	52,615	37,613
Pennsylvania	973,330	1,688.77	702.80	48,030	115,411	87,823
Puerto Rico	NA	NA	NA	12,178	32,817	22,225
Rhode Island	101,587	1,004.09	417.42	8,431	20,281	13,903
South Carolina	185,743	906.00	390.26	17,085	39,662	30,282
South Dakota	25,754	721.05	349.93	2,976	6,133	5,211
Tennessee	346,299	496.37	193.89	58,138	148,837	108,072
Texas	801,343	1,389.78	622.49	48,050	107,277	92,687
Utah	127,986	1,791.62	712.40	5,953	14,971	10,542
Vermont	72,577	2,109.42	956.04	2,867	6,326	4,457
Virgin Islands	NA	NA	NA	469	1,350	962
Virginia	254,814	657.10	291.95	32,315	72,734	52,308
Washington	1,451,714	2,066.71	859.95	58,536	140,678	98,395
West Virginia	147,369	1,336.10	600.31	9,192	20,457	14,917
Wisconsin	568,627	2,592.42	1,201.20	18,279	39,449	32,660
Wyoming	31,458	8,980.20	4,543.28	292	577	479
Totals by year						
2009 totals	30,577,765	1,475.65	630.53	1,726,799	4,041,292	3,084,413
2008 totals	28,129,745	1,438.71	620.06	1,629,344	3,780,543	2,911,078
2007 totals	26,921,973	1,321.70	566.92	1,697,432	3,957,330	3,047,043
2006 totals	25,593,809	1,191.88	510.33	1,789,460	4,179,295	3,207,216
2005 totals	25,580,110	1,120.87	474.21	1,901,810	4,495,175	3,428,885
2004 totals	25,821,230	1,094.51	455.63	1,965,960	4,722,588	3,581,448
2003 totals	26,339,994	1,092.22	447.88	2,009,666	4,900,889	3,693,056
2002 totals	25,414,383	1,039.00	417.89	2,038,373	5,067,963	3,791,560
2001 totals	25,667,381	1,024.57	400.86	2,087,646	5,335,891	3,968,499
2000 totals	24,780,711	926.32	353.72	2,229,315	5,838,043	4,303,943
1999 totals	23,114,572	267.99	267.99	2,673,610	7,187,658	NA
1998 totals	22,036,420	208.91	208.91	3,199,700	8,790,194	NA
1997 totals	19,010,190	144.87	144.87	3,936,610	10,935,125	NA

NA = Not available. **Note:** Under 1996 legislation, the Aid to Families with Dependent Children (AFDC) program was converted to this state block-grant program. Covers period from Oct. to Sept. in fiscal years shown. (1) In thousands.

Adults Receiving TANF Funds by Employment Status, 2009

Source: Office of Family Assistance, Admin. for Children and Families, U.S. Dept. of Health and Human Services

State	Adults	Employed	State	Adults	Employed	State	Adults	Employed	State	Adults	Employed
AL	10,128	30.1%	IL	4,517	15.2%	NE	3,844	50.5%	SC	9,381	28.6%
AK	2,526	30.3	IN	25,989	24.3	NV	5,303	40.4	SD	922	20.4
AZ	20,293	16.2	IA	12,557	37.2	NH	3,390	24.3	TN	40,765	32.1
AR	5,178	27.9	KS	10,562	28.5	NJ	22,412	12.5	TX	14,590	31.5
CA	277,027	27.6	KY	12,709	18.8	NM	11,184	20.0	UT	4,430	17.2
CO	5,085	25.5	LA	2,782	23.9	NY	64,334	26.6	VT	1,869	18.4
CT	9,561	27.3	ME	8,150	22.3	NC	8,806	14.4	Virgin Isls.	387	3.0
DE	4,897	28.5	MD	14,047	15.7	ND	1,456	39.8	VA	20,425	26.6
DC	4,606	19.9	MA	29,955	10.3	OH	52,538	16.2	WA	42,283	14.6
FL	18,662	10.9	MI	38,611	26.4	OK	3,391	9.2	WV	5,541	13.6
GA	2,913	12.3	MN	10,918	30.6	OR	15,002	7.2	WI	6,789	19.1
Guam	826	2.6	MS	5,737	21.5	PA	27,588	28.6	WY	98	9.3
HA	6,536	37.1	MO	25,692	14.9	Puerto Rico	10,592	1.0	**U.S.**	973,580	23.5
ID	160	34.2	MT	2,559	32.9	RI	6,378	17.7			

NA = Not available. **Note:** TANF = Temporary Assistance for Needy Families state block-grant program. For fiscal year 2009; covers period from Oct. 2008 to Sept. 2009.

TAXES

Federal Income Tax

Source: George W. Smith III, CPA, Managing Partner, George W. Smith & Company, P.C.

Essential Tax Return Facts

Deadline Extended. Apr. 15, the usual due date for filing an individual federal tax return falls on a Sunday in 2012; the deadline was extended to the next legal business day. Apr. 16, is Emancipation Day, a federal holiday observed in Washington, DC. As a result, the 2012 due date for filing was extended to Tue., Apr. 17, 2012.

Paperless Returns. The IRS announced June 10, 2011, that 1 bil individual tax returns had been processed since the electronic filing program began as a pilot project in 1986. More than 100 mil individual income tax returns were electronically filed in 2011. The IRS will no longer mail tax return packages to taxpayers.

Highlights of Current Legislation

Tax Relief Act of 2010

Pres. Barack H. Obama signed the Tax Relief Act into law Dec. 17, 2010. Congress temporarily extended the Tax Relief Reconciliation Act of 2001 and Jobs and Growth Tax Relief Act of 2003 for two additional years. The Tax Relief Act of 2010 will cost an estimated $850 bil and impacts hundreds of tax code provisions, including provisions that affect individual income tax rates, capital gains tax rates, and the estate tax.

Congress also extended tax credits for school teacher expenses, local sales taxes, qualified tuition, and home improvement, as well as more than 50 other tax benefits. Most provisions of the act begin with the 2011 individual tax returns filed in 2012.

Health Care and Education Reconciliation Act

On Mar. 25, 2010, Pres. Obama signed into law the 2010 Reconciliation Act. The roughly $800 bil package includes over $300 bil in revenue raisers and new taxes on employers and individuals.

Adoption. The adoption expense amount will be indexed for inflation starting in 2011. In addition, the total adoption credit is allowed even if it exceeds the filer's tax liability.

Medical Expenses. Beginning in 2013, the 7.5% adjustment for medical expense deduction on Schedule A, Form 1040 increases to 10%. For taxpayers age 65 and older, the increase begins in 2017.

Tanning Services. Effective July 1, 2010, a 10% excise tax applies to qualified indoor tanning services.

Updated 1099 Provision. In Apr. 2011, Congress passed and Pres. Obama signed legislation repealing a tax compliance mandate that would have required that businesses file paperwork (Form 1099) when paying $600 or more to corporations for goods or services.

Military Tax Relief Bill

Congress unanimously passed this legislation in May 2008. The law includes tax breaks for members of the military, tax-free combat pay, various credits, and retirement provisions.

Combat Pay. The law allows military personnel to permanently treat combat pay as tax-free. Military personnel can include tax-free combat pay to compute the earned income credit.

Extensions. The deadline for filing tax returns, paying taxes, filing claims for refunds, and taking other actions with the IRS is automatically extended for members of the military.

IRA Withdrawals. The law makes permanent the ability for military reservists to make penalty-free withdrawals from IRAs when called to active duty.

Other Recent Legislation

The **Hiring Incentives to Restore Employment (HIRE) Act** of 2010 and **American Recovery and Reinvestment Act** of 2009 provide additional tax breaks for both businesses and individuals.

American Opportunity Tax Credit. This addition to the Hope educational credit increased the credit to a maximum $2,500 per year for each eligible student. The tax credit can be claimed each year for up to four years.

Alternative Powered Vehicles. A new 10% credit up to $4,000 is available for the conversion of existing vehicles into plug-in electric drive motor vehicles converted before 2012.

Energy Credits. Beginning in 2011, the Tax Relief Act of 2010 reduced the credit for home improvements to 10% with a maximum ceiling of $500; no more than $150 for furnaces and water heaters and $200 for windows. The maximum credit was $1,500 in 2010.

IRS Rulings and Other Tax Matters

Alimony. Payments to an individual under a written separation agreement constitute alimony for federal tax purposes even if the agreement is not enforceable under state law.

Auto Damage. Damage to a person's car may be a deductible casualty loss unless it was caused by the person's willful conduct, such as drunken driving.

Bicycling. A maximum $20 per month commuting reimbursement is excludable from income for employees who bicycle between their home and work. Expenses include the purchase of a bicycle, repair, and storage.

Counseling. The parent of a child with psychological problems may deduct as a medical expense that part of a private school fee directly related to psychological aid given to the child.

Day Camp. The cost of computer camp, soccer camps, and other specialty day camps (not overnight) for children may qualify for the child care credit. The child must be under the age of 13, and the expenses must be incurred so the parent or parents can work.

Employee Parking. Reimbursement for parking expense provided to an employee who commutes caps out at $230 per month. The limit also applies to employees who commute by mass transportation.

First Job. Graduates may not deduct expenses of seeking their first job. These expenses include auto rental, plane travel, motel costs, and meals.

Garage Sales. Revenues received from a garage sale usually do not result in taxable income. In most cases, the item that was sold cost more than the revenue received. These losses are considered personal and, therefore, not deductible.

Investment Expenses. Investors may take a miscellaneous deduction on Schedule A, Form 1040, for financial newspapers, reports, and other expenses incurred in managing their investment portfolio. However, investors cannot deduct expenses for attending a convention, seminar, or similar meeting.

Madoff Response. The IRS approved a theft loss deduction and net operating loss carryback by investors who fell victim to the Ponzi scheme perpetrated by Bernard Madoff.

Mileage Use for Business. The IRS increased the standard mileage rate to 51 cents per mile for the business use of an individual's automobile from Jan. 1 to June 30, 2011, and 55.5 cents from July 1 to Dec. 31, 2011, per business mile. The business portion of parking fees and tolls may be deducted in addition to the standard mileage rate.

Mileage Use for Personal Reasons. The mileage allowance deduction for moving and medical expense was increased to 19 cents per mile from Jan. 1 to June 30, 2011, and 23.5 cents from July 1 to Dec. 31, 2011. The rate used for volunteer work for charitable activities remains at 14 cents per mile. The charitable rates are set by Congress, not the IRS.

Most Common Income Tax Errors

Periodically, the IRS issues a list of the most commonly made income tax errors.
1. Incorrect or missing Social Security numbers.
2. Incorrect tax entered from tax tables.
3. Mathematical errors or wrong ID numbers listed for tax credits.
4. Entering withholding and estimated tax payments on the wrong line.
5. General math mistakes.

Penalties. Penalties and fines paid to a governmental agency or department are not deductible. This includes parking and speeding tickets as well as penalties for late filing of a tax return.

Refunds. Not all taxpayers expecting a refund will necessarily receive one. If an individual owes taxes to the federal government, has failed to pay child support, or has unpaid education loans, the IRS can take the individual's refund to satisfy the debt.

Retirement Accounts. In a unanimous decision, the U.S. Supreme Court held that Individual Retirement Accounts (IRAs) are beyond the reach of creditors. This includes IRA assets of taxpayers who have filed for bankruptcy.

Sale of Residence. Married couples filing jointly who have lived in their principal residence for at least two years out of the last five can exclude up to $500,000 of the gain on the sale of their residence. Single taxpayers can exclude up to $250,000.

Same-Sex Marriage. The IRS ruled that it is unlawful for same-sex couples to file federal tax returns under any married status, even if the jurisdiction in which the couple lives recognizes such marriages.

Smoking. Taxpayers can deduct the cost of two types of aids for quitting cigarette smoking as a medical expense: (1) participation in a smoking-cessation program or (2) prescription drugs to alleviate the effects of nicotine withdrawal. Over-the-counter products such as nicotine patches and chewing gum remain nondeductible.

Student Full-Time. A taxpayer in 2011 may not claim a dependency exemption for an individual who qualifies as a full-time student and is over age 23 at the end of the year, unless the student's gross income is less than $3,700.

Student Loans. For taxable years beginning in 2011, the income phase-out range for the $2,500 maximum deduction for interest paid on qualified education loans is $60,000-75,000 income for single taxpayers and $120,000-150,000 for married taxpayers filing jointly.

Weekend Business Travel. If a business trip is extended over a weekend to take advantage of reduced airfares, the additional costs of meals, lodging, and other incidental expenses are deductible.

Weight Loss. The IRS allows a medical deduction for costs of certain weight-loss programs. Participation must be for treatment of a physician-diagnosed disease, including obesity. No deduction is allowed for diets that are used for purely cosmetic reasons or special diet foods.

Working Abroad. Many Americans who live and work abroad are eligible to exclude a certain amount of their pay from U.S. income taxes. The amount of earned income excludable for 2011 is $92,900, slightly more than the exclusion for 2010.

Income Tax Filing and Payment Due Dates

Due Dates for Filing. The due date for filing a 2011 U.S. Individual Income Tax Return Form 1040, 1040A, or 1040EZ is Tue., Apr. 17, 2012. Calendar year-ending 2011 U.S. partnership tax returns are also due on Apr. 17, 2011. Corporate calendar year-ending returns are due Thu., Mar. 15, 2012.

Estimated Payments. Due dates for filing individual quarterly federal estimated tax payments, Form 1040-ES: 1st quarter, Tue., Apr. 17, 2012; 2nd quarter, Fri., June 15; 3rd quarter, Mon., Sept. 17; and 4th quarter, Tue., Jan. 15, 2013. Different filing dates may apply for state/local taxes.

Filing Penalties. The IRS can levy two potential penalties after the filing due date when there is a balance owed. One penalty is for failing to file a timely tax return; the other is for failure to pay the tax when due. In addition, interest will be charged on any unpaid tax balance.

There is a $195 late filing penalty for S corporations and partnerships *per shareholder or partner* each month for up to 12 months.

Need More Time to File? Individuals who cannot file their 2011 individual income tax return by the due date, Apr. 17, 2012, may apply for an automatic six-month extension to Oct. 15, 2012. To qualify for an extension, Form 4868 must be filed no later than the tax return due date Apr. 17, 2012. Approximately 9 mil extensions were filed last year.

Refunds. Individuals can check on the status of their expected federal refund by calling the IRS toll-free number at (800) 829-4477, or by checking at www.irs.gov. For security purposes, taxpayers should request that tax refunds be deposited directly into their bank accounts.

Statute of Limitations. Taxpayers who have not yet filed their 2008 federal tax return have until Apr. 16, 2012, to file and claim their refund. After that date any refunds for income tax or withholding tax for 2008, including the refundable earned income tax credit, will be lost.

IRS Contact Information for Assistance

For Tax Questions: (800) 829-1040
Website: www.irs.gov
Fax: (703) 368-9694
For Forms/Publications: (800) TAX-FORM (829-3676)
For English and Spanish: The IRS provides videotaped instructions both in English and Spanish at participating libraries. Many IRS publications and tax forms, including instructions, are also printed in Spanish. For more information, call (800) TAX-FORM and ask for the free IRS Publication 1SP, *Derechos del Contribuyente*.
For Hearing Impaired: The IRS telephone service for hearing impaired persons is available for taxpayers with access to TDD equipment. The toll-free number is (800) 829-4059.

Meeting With a Tax Preparer

Here are some ideas to keep in mind when visiting a tax preparer:

- **Choose** wisely. New regulations in effect in 2011 require all paid tax return preparers including attorneys, CPAs, and IRS-enrolled agents to have a Preparer Tax Identification Number. Check the preparer's qualifications and history. Ask about service fees in advance.
- **Review** last year's tax return. Make notes of any changes since then such as marriage, divorce, number of dependents, retirement, job changes, additional income, new deductions, etc.
- **Organize** your records with income items first, followed by itemized deductions in sequence: medical, taxes, interest, charitable, and other miscellaneous deductions, followed by gains, losses, rentals, or other items.
- **Time** spent with your preparer may affect your bill. If you bring in jumbled records and deductions, there may

be an additional cost to have your tax preparer organize your records.
- **Prepare** a list of questions in advance. Bring with you any invoices or bills that you are not sure of.
- **Alert** your preparer if you're waiting to receive additional information. He or she can begin preparing your tax return and include the missing data later to finalize your return.
- **Don't hesitate** to call the preparer if you receive additional information at a later time. However, if you call after the return is completed, changes may cost you additional fees.
- **Review** your tax return before signing it. Ask questions about any item you don't understand. Remember, even though your preparer is required to sign the return, you are responsible for its contents.

Additional Help: For more information about choosing tax preparers, call the IRS Tele-Tax information at (800) 829-4477. Follow the prompts and select Topic 254. This information is also available online at www.irs.gov/taxtopics/tc254.html.

Individual Federal Income Tax Rates and Brackets, 2011

Tax rate	Single	Married filing jointly or qualifying widow(er)	Married filing separately	Head of household
10%	$1 to $8,500	$1 to $17,000	$1 to $8,500	$1 to $12,150
15%	$8,501 to $34,500	$17,001 to $69,000	$8,501 to $34,500	$12,151 to $46,250
25%	$34,501 to $83,600	$69,001 to $139,350	$34,501 to $69,675	$46,251 to $119,400
28%	$83,601 to $174,400	$139,351 to $212,300	$69,676 to $106,150	$119,401 to $193,350
33%	$174,401 to $379,150	$212,301 to $379,150	$106,151 to $189,575	$193,351 to $379,150
35%	Over $379,150	Over $379,150	Over $189,575	Over $379,150

Note: The 2011 income tax brackets were only slightly increased from the prior year because of mild inflation during the 12-month period from Sept. 2009 through Aug. 2010. The Tax Relief Act of 2010 extended these tax rates for two more years.

Personal Exemptions, 2011

Dollar Amounts. The personal exemption amount for each taxpayer, spouse, and dependent for 2011 is $3,700, up $50 from 2010. The exemption amount is adjusted each year for cost-of-living increases. The personal exemption of an individual who is a dependent of another taxpayer is zero.

Exemption Phase-Out. The exemption deduction phase-out rule for higher-income taxpayers was eliminated.

Standard Deduction, 2011

The standard deduction is a flat dollar amount that is subtracted from the adjusted gross income of taxpayers who do not itemize their deductions. The dollar amounts were adjusted for inflation.

Standard Deduction Amount, 2011

Single	$5,800
Married filing jointly or qualifying widow(er)	$11,600
Married filing separately	$5,800
Head of household	$8,500

Dependents Tax Returns. An individual reported as a dependent on another person's 2011 income tax return generally may claim on his or her own tax return only the greater of $950 or the sum of $300 plus earned income not to exceed the regular standard deduction.

Additional Standard Deduction, 2011

Taxpayers in 2011 who do not itemize, are 65 or older, and/or blind may claim an additional standard deduction.

Single or head of household, 65 or older OR blind	$1,450
Single or head of household, 65 or older AND blind	$2,900
Married filing jointly or qualifying widow(er), 65 or older OR blind (per person)	$1,150
Married filing jointly or qualifying widow(er), 65 or older AND blind (per person)	$2,300
Married filing separately, 65 or older OR blind	$1,150
Married filing separately, 65 or older AND blind	$2,300

Savings Plans for Traditional and Roth IRAs

Traditional IRA. For 2011 the maximum tax-deferred Individual Retirement Arrangement (IRA) deduction for a married couple filing jointly is $10,000 ($5,000 for singles). Each spouse can contribute up to $5,000 annually even if one spouse has little or no income. Individuals age 50 or older can fund an additional "catch-up" amount of $1,000. However, there are income limitations and phase-outs.

Withdrawals. There is a 10% penalty for IRA distributions before age 59½. Distributions paid to the beneficiary due to a disability or death of the owner are not subject to this penalty, nor are payments used for certain unreimbursed medical expense, higher-education expenses, or first-time homebuyer acquisition costs (up to $10,000).

Contributions to a traditional IRA or Roth IRA made after Apr. 16, 2012, will automatically be considered deposits for the year 2012.

Roth IRA. Although contributions paid into a Roth IRA are not tax deductible, distributions of funds including investment earnings held in the account for five years or longer and distributed after age 59½ are both free of income tax and the 10% early withdrawal penalty at the time of distribution. Withdrawals from the account in less than five years can be subject to income tax and the 10% withdrawal penalty regardless of age. There are income limitations on contributions.

401(k) Plan. The maximum amount that an individual under age 50 can contribute to a 401(k) plan for 2011 is $16,500. Individuals age 50 or older can put away an additional $5,500, for a total of $22,000.

Children. Kids of any age can open a Roth IRA as long as they have earned income from a job (e.g. mowing lawns, fast-food, retailing) up to a maximum $5,000. Parents and grandparents can give the children the money for the Roth, if need be.

Distributions. The owner of a traditional IRA (or a SIMPLE plan, pension, or profit-sharing plan account) must begin receiving distributions by Apr. 1 of the calendar year following the year in which he or she reaches age 70½. Any employee who works beyond 70½ and is not a 5% or more owner of the business can continue to defer profit-sharing and pension plan distributions.

IRA Publication. For more information on IRAs, call the IRS at (800) TAX-FORM (829-3676) for a free copy of Publication 590, *Individual Retirement Arrangements (IRAs)*.

Itemized Deductions, 2011

If the total amount of itemized deductions is more than the standard deduction, taxpayers generally should itemize their deductions on Schedule A, Form 1040. The following examples are just a few of the many deductions that may be itemized. Some are subject to income limitations.

Business Expenses. Deductible miscellaneous expenses include unreimbursed employee business expenses such as travel, automobile, telephone, and gifts. However, only 50% of the cost of customer meals and entertainment is deductible.

Charitable Contributions. Individuals may not deduct the value of volunteer work they personally perform for charities.

Gambling. Lottery, slots, Texas Hold-Em poker, craps, bingo, or other gambling expenses are deductible if the taxpayer itemizes on Schedule A. However, expenses are limited to gambling winnings reported on page one, Form 1040. If there are no winnings on page one, there are no deductions allowed on Schedule A.

Interest. Mortgage interest paid on a primary residence or a second home is deductible. However, there are limitations on mortgages in excess of $1 mil. Interest on home equity loans also is deductible, but only covering the first $100,000 of equity debt. Personal credit card interest is not deductible.

Lamaze Class. A mother-to-be may deduct as a medical expense the cost of classes taken for Lamaze breathing and relaxation techniques, stages of labor, and delivery procedures.

Long-Term Care Insurance. Based on various annual limits, long-term care insurance premiums are deductible as medical expenses. For 2011, taxpayers age 71 and older can claim as much as $4,240 per person; ages 61-70, up to $3,390; ages 51-60, up to $1,270; ages 41-50, up to $640; and ages 40 and younger are limited to $340.

Medical Expenses that exceed 7.5% of the taxpayer's adjusted gross income are deductible. Medicines, birth control pills, and insulin qualify if prescribed by a physician. Cosmetic surgery for congenital abnormality, for personal injury from an accident or trauma, or for a disfiguring disease is also allowed as a medical deduction.

Medical Traveling. Taxpayers may deduct part of the travel expense to seek health care. Travel can include auto and airfare expense.

Miscellaneous Deductions. Certain miscellaneous expenses are deductible, but only the amount that exceeds 2% of adjusted gross income. Expenses include investment expenses, union and professional dues, tax preparation fees, safe deposit box rental fees and most (but not all) expenses for a job search.

Moving Expenses. Taxpayers who change jobs or are transferred usually can deduct part of their moving expenses, including travel and the cost of moving household goods, but not the cost of meals.

Personal Losses. Casualty and theft losses are deductible subject to a $100 reduction and further reduced 10% for each occurrence. Separate rules apply for federally declared disasters. Unreimbursed automobile accident damage may be a deductible casualty loss.

Taxes. State and local income taxes including real estate taxes are deductible. An auto license fee based on weight, model, year, or horsepower is not deductible. A tax based on the car's value qualifies as a personal property tax deduction.

Tax Credits

A tax deduction reduces a taxpayer's taxable income, whereas tax credits reduce, dollar-for-dollar, the amount of tax owed.

Adoption Credit. The adoption credit for qualified expenses increased $190 to $13,360 in 2011. The credit limit is per person, not per year, and is adjusted annually for inflation. The exclusion phases out for taxpayers whose income is between $185,210 and $225,210 when the credit is completely phased out.

American Opportunity Tax Credit. Modifying the Hope credit, this credit provides a partially refundable $2,500 credit to cover each of four years of college. The credit begins to phase out for higher income individuals.

Earned Income Credit. Lower-income workers who maintain a household may be eligible for an Earned Income Credit (EIC). This credit is based on total earned income such as wages, commissions, and tips. Military personnel can include tax-free combat pay in income to compute the credit. There are phase-out rules. Refer to the income tax instructions for guidance.

Energy Credits. There are many energy-related credits—from the purchase of an alternative fuel vehicle, the installation of solar/fuel cell property in a residence, to the production of biodiesel or ethanol.

Alternative Minimum Tax

AMT. The Alternative Minimum Tax was established in 1969 to prevent people with very high incomes from using special tax breaks to pay little or no tax. It hasn't been indexed or adjusted for inflation. Because of changes in the tax law, this tax now affects more and more middle-income taxpayers every year.

Instructions included with tax forms 1040 and 1040A provide help for individuals to determine if they are subject to the AMT. Tax Form 6251 is used to figure how much additional tax, if any, is owed.

Estate and Gift Taxes Exclusion

Estate Tax. The Tax Relief Reconciliation Act of 2001 increased the estate tax exclusion from $675,000 in 2001 to $3.5 mil through 2009, then the estate tax was set to expire in 2010. The maximum tax rate in 2001, based on the value of an estate, was 55%. The rate was decreased over the years to a maximum 45% in 2009. The Tax Relief Act of 2010 reinstated the estate tax and increased the exemption for 2011 to $5 mil with a 35% flat rate.

Gifting. U.S. citizens, residents, and non-resident aliens have an annual gift tax exclusion of up to $13,000 per individual to as many individuals as he or she chooses. For married couples the gift is twice that amount, $26,000, even if only one spouse does all the gifting.

International Property. All property owned worldwide is subject to the U.S. estate tax rules and regulations.

Resident Aliens. Aliens residing in the U.S. are subject to the same rules as that of an American citizen.

Tax-Free. The gift tax is not applicable for most charities or for tuition that donors pay directly to schools or medical expenses paid on behalf of donees.

Taxable Social Security Benefits

Earnings Limitations. For 2011, Social Security recipients who have not reached the full retirement age of 66 will lose $1 of their benefits for every $2 of earned income over $14,160. Recipients who reached full retirement age in 2011 will not lose any benefits if they earned $37,680 or less. Recipients will have to pay back some benefits if their income exceeded that amount.

Taxable Benefits. Up to 50% of Social Security benefits may be taxable if the person's total income is more than $25,000 but less than $34,000 for a single individual, head of household, qualifying widow(er), or a married person who is filing separately if spouses lived apart all year; or more than $32,000 but less than $44,000 for married individuals filing jointly. For higher incomes, 85% of Social Security benefits may become taxable.

Tax-Free. If the only income received during the year was Social Security, these benefits are not taxable and you probably do not have to file a tax return.

Retention of Income Tax Records

How long should a taxpayer keep copies of their tax returns and supporting records? The answer is a combination of judgment and the statutes of limitations. Since federal tax returns generally can be audited for up to three years after filing, or six years if the IRS suspects underreported income, it's wise to keep copies of the income tax return and records at least seven years after a return is filed.

IRS Tax Audits

The IRS audit rate for individual returns filed last year was 1.11%, the highest number since 1997. Most taxpayers have no reason to be concerned about being audited—unless they happen to be one of the 1.11%

Decision to Audit. The IRS audit selection process is not done randomly. It is based on a set of formulas that are designed to spot questionable returns. If the IRS concludes that the taxpayer owes more tax and he or she disagrees with the findings, the taxpayer can meet with a supervisor.

If the taxpayer still does not agree, he or she can appeal to a separate Appeals Office, or take it to the U.S. Tax Court, Federal District Court, or the U.S. Court of Federal Claims.

Tax Court. The U.S. Tax Court is a federal court where taxpayers can dispute tax deficiencies as determined by the Commissioner of Internal Revenue before payment of the disputed amounts. The Tax Court is composed of presidentially appointed members. Many taxpayers will choose the Tax Court because they are not required to pay the contested tax up front.

Appeals. For more information about audits, call the IRS at (800) TAX-FORM (829-3676) for its free Publication 556, *Examination of Returns, Appeal Rights, and Claims for Refund*. Or visit www.irs.gov.

Your Rights as a Taxpayer

Congress has enacted "Taxpayer Bill of Rights" legislation and created an Office of the Taxpayer Advocate within the IRS, with authority to order IRS personnel to issue refund checks and meet deadlines for resolving disputes. Taxpayer advocates can be contacted at (877) 777-4778; (800) 829-4059 for TTY/TDD.

The IRS must pay legal fees if the taxpayer wins the case and the IRS cannot show it was "substantially justified" in pursuing the disputed amount. For more information, ask for free IRS Publication 1, *Your Rights as a Taxpayer*, by calling (800) TAX-FORM (829-3676).

Reporting Wrongdoing

To confidentially report misconduct, waste, fraud or abuse by an IRS employee, call (800) 366-4484; (800) 877-8339 for TTY/TDD.

More IRS Services

To find out what additional services are available, ask for Publication 910, *IRS Guide to Free Tax Services*. This guide contains a list of free tax publications and other information including tax education and assistance programs and a list of Tele-Tax topics.

State Government Personal Income Tax Rates, 2011

Source: Reproduced with permission from *CCH State Tax Guide*, published and copyrighted by CCH Inc., a Wolters Kluwer business

Alaska, Florida, Nevada, South Dakota, Texas, Washington, and Wyoming did not have state income taxes and are thus not listed. Tax rates apply in stages—for example, a single person in Arizona making $60,000 in taxable income would pay 2.59% on the first $10,000 of income, 2.88% on the next $15,000, and so on. For further details, see notes at end of table.

Alabama
Single, Head of household, or Married filing separately
$0 to $500.	2%
$501 to $3,000	4%
$3,001 and over	5%

Married filing jointly
$0 to $1,000	2%
$1,001 to $6,000.	4%
$6,001 and over	5%

Arizona[1]
Single or Married filing separately
$0 to $10,000	2.59%
$10,001 to $25,000.	2.88%
$25,001 to $50,000.	3.36%
$50,001 to $150,000.	4.24%
$150,001 and over	4.54%

Married filing jointly or Head of household
$0 to $20,000	2.59%
$20,001 to $50,000.	2.88%
$50,001 to $100,000.	3.36%
$100,001 to $300,000.	4.24%
$300,001 and over	4.54%

Arkansas[2,3]
Single, Head of household, Married filing jointly, or Married filing separately
$0 to $3,899.	1%
$3,900 to $7,799.	2.5%
$7,800 to $11,799.	3.5%
$11,800 to $19,599.	4.5%
$19,600 to $32,699.	6%
$32,700 and over	7%

California[1,2]
Single, Married filing separately, or Registered domestic partner filing separately
$0 to $7,316.	1%
$7,317 to $17,346.	2%
$17,347 to $27,377.	4%
$27,378 to $38,004.	6%
$38,005 to $48,029.	8%
$48,030 and over	9.3%

Head of household
$0 to $14,642	1%
$14,643 to $34,692.	2%
$34,693 to $44,721.	4%
$44,722 to $55,348.	6%
$55,349 to $65,376.	8%
$65,377 and over	9.3%

Married filing jointly, Registered domestic partner jointly, or Qualifying widow(er)
$0 to $14,632	1%
$14,633 to $34,692.	2%
$34,693 to $54,754.	4%
$54,755 to $76,008.	6%
$76,009 to $96,058.	8%
$96,059 and over	9.3%

Colorado
4.63% of federal taxable income

Connecticut
Single or Married filing separately
$0 to $10,000	3%
$10,001 to $50,000.	5%
$50,001 to $100,000.	5.5%
$100,001 to $200,000.	6%
$200,001 to $250,000.	6.5%
$250,001 and over	6.7%

Head of household
$0 to $16,000.	3%
$16,001 to $80,000.	5%
$80,001 to $160,000.	5.5%
$160,001 to $320,000.	6%
$320,001 to $400,000.	6.5%
$400,001 and over	6.7%

Delaware
Single, Head of household, Married filing jointly, or Married filing separately
$0 to $2,000	0%
$2,001 to $5,000.	2.2%
$5,001 to $10,000.	3.9%
$10,001 to $20,000.	4.8%
$20,001 to $25,000.	5.2%
$25,001 to $60,000.	5.55%
$60,001 and over	6.95%

District of Columbia
$0 to $10,000	4%
$10,001 to $40,000.	6%
$40,001 and over	8.5%

Georgia
Single
$0 to $750.	1%
$751 to $2,250	2%
$2,251 to $3,750.	3%
$3,751 to $5,250.	4%
$5,251 to $7,000.	5%
$7,001 and over	6%

Head of household, Married filing jointly, or Qualifying widow(er)
$0 to $1,000	1%
$1,001 to $3,000.	2%
$3,001 to $5,000.	3%
$5,001 to $7,000.	4%
$7,001 to $10,000.	5%
$10,001 and over	6%

Married filing separately
$0 to $500.	1%
$501 to $1,500.	2%
$1,501 to $2,500.	3%
$2,501 to $3,500.	4%
$3,501 to $5,000.	5%
$5,001 and over	6%

Hawaii
Single or Married filing separately
$0 to $2,400	1.4%
$2,401 to $4,800.	3.2%
$4,801 to $9,600.	5.5%
$9,601 to $14,400.	6.4%
$14,401 to $19,200.	6.8%
$19,201 to $24,000.	7.2%
$24,001 to $36,000.	7.6%
$36,001 to $48,000.	7.9%
$48,001 to $150,000.	8.25%
$150,001 to $175,000.	9%
$175,001 to $200,000.	10%
$200,001 and over	11%

Head of household
$0 to $3,600.	1.4%
$3,601 to $7,200.	3.2%
$7,201 to $14,400.	5.5%
$14,401 to $21,600.	6.4%
$21,601 to $28,800.	6.8%
$28,801 to $36,000.	7.2%
$36,001 to $54,000.	7.6%
$54,001 to $72,000.	7.9%
$72,001 to $225,000.	8.25%
$225,001 to $262,500	9%
$262,501 to $300,000.	10%
$300,001 and over	11%

Married filing jointly or Surviving spouse
$0 to $4,800	1.4%
$4,801 to $9,600.	3.2%
$9,601 to $19,200.	5.5%
$19,201 to $28,800.	6.4%
$28,801 to $38,400.	6.8%
$38,401 to $48,000.	7.2%
$48,001 to $72,000.	7.6%
$72,001 to $96,000.	7.9%
$96,001 to $300,000.	8.25%
$300,001 to $350,000.	9%
$350,001 to $400,000.	10%
$400,001 and over	11%

Idaho[1,2,3]
Single or Married filing separately
$0 to $1,315.	1.6%
$1,316 to $2,631.	3.6%
$2,632 to $3,947.	4.1%
$3,948 to $5,263.	5.1%
$5,264 to $6,579.	6.1%
$6,580 to $9,869.	7.1%
$9,870 to $26,319.	7.4%
$26,320 and over	7.8%

Head of household, Married filing jointly, or Surviving spouse
$0 to $2,631.	1.6%
$2,632 to $5,263.	3.6%
$5,264 to $7,895.	4.1%
$7,896 to $10,527.	5.1%
$10,528 to $13,159.	6.1%
$13,160 to $19,739.	7.1%
$19,740 to $52,639.	7.4%
$52,640 and over	7.8%

Illinois
5% of federal AGI with modifications

Indiana
3.4% of adjusted gross income

Iowa[2]
$0 to $1,439.	0.36%
$1,440 to $2,878.	0.72%
$2,879 to $5,756.	2.43%
$5,757 to $12,951.	4.5%
$12,952 to $21,585.	6.12%
$21,586 to $28,780.	6.48%
$28,781 to $43,170.	6.8%
$43,171 to $64,755.	7.92%
$64,756 and over	8.98%

Kansas
Single, Head of household, or Married filing separately
$0 to $15,000.	3.5%
$15,001 to $30,000.	6.25%
$30,001 and over	6.45%

Married filing jointly
$0 to $30,000.	3.5%
$30,001 to $60,000.	6.25%
$60,001 and over	6.45%

Kentucky
Single, Head of household, Married filing jointly, or Married filing separately
$0 to $3,000.	2%
$3,001 to $4,000.	3%
$4,001 to $5,000.	4%
$5,001 to $8,000.	5%
$8,001 to $75,000.	5.8%
$75,001 and over	6%

Louisiana[1]
Single, Head of household, or Married filing separately
$0 to $12,500	2%
$12,501 to $50,000.	4%
$50,001 and over	6%

Married filing jointly
$0 to $25,000	2%
$25,001 to $100,000.	4%
$100,001 and over	6%

Maine[2]
Single or Married filing separately
$0 to $4,999	2%
$5,000 to $9,949.	4.5%
$9,950 to $19,949.	7%
$19,950 and over	8.5%

Head of household
$0 to $7,499	2%
$7,500 to $14,899.	4.5%
$14,900 to $29,899.	7%
$29,900 and over	8.5%

Married filing jointly or Qualifying widow(er)
$0 to $9,999	2%
$10,000 to $19,949.	4.5%
$19,950 to $39,899.	7%
$39,900 and over	8.5%

Maryland
Single or Married filing separately
$0 to $1,000	2%
$1,001 to $2,000.	3%
$2,001 to $3,000.	4%
$3,001 to $150,000.	4.75%
$150,001 to $300,000.	5%
$300,001 to $500,000.	5.25%
$500,001 and over	5.5%

Head of household, Married filing jointly, or Qualifying widow(er)
$0 to $1,000	2%
$1,001 to $2,000.	3%
$2,001 to $3,000.	4%
$3,001 to $200,000.	4.75%
$200,001 to $350,000.	5%
$350,001 to $500,000.	5.25%
$500,001 and over	5.5%

Massachusetts
Short-term capital gains	12.0%
All other income	5.3%

Michigan
4.35% of taxable income

Minnesota[2]
Single
$0 to $23,100	5.35%
$23,101 to $75,890.	7.05%
$75,891 and over	7.85%

Head of household
$0 to $28,440	5.35%
$28,441 to $114,290.	7.05%
$114,291 and over	7.85%

Married filing jointly
$0 to $33,770	5.35%
$33,771 to $134,170.	7.05%
$134,171 and over	7.85%

Married filing separately
$0 to $16,890	5.35%
$16,891 to $67,090.	7.05%
$67,091 and over	7.85%

Mississippi
$0 to $5,000	3%
$5,001 to $10,000.	4%
$10,001 and over	5%

Missouri
$0 to $1,000	1.5%
$1,001 to $2,000.	2%
$2,001 to $3,000.	2.5%
$3,001 to $4,000.	3%
$4,001 to $5,000.	3.5%
$5,001 to $6,000.	4%
$6,001 to $7,000.	4.5%
$7,001 to $8,000.	5%
$8,001 to $9,000.	5.5%
$9,001 and over	6%

Montana[2]
$0 to $2,700	1%
$2,701 to $4,700.	2%
$4,701 to $7,200.	3%

$7,201 to $9,700........ 4%
$9,701 to $12,500 .... 5%
$12,501 to $16,000....... 6%
$16,001 and over 6.9%

Nebraska

Single
$0 to $2,400 .... 2.56%
$2,401 to $17,500 ..... 3.57%
$17,501 to $27,000..... 5.12%
$27,001 and over 6.84%

Head of household
$0 to $4,500 .... 2.56%
$4,501 to $28,000 ..... 3.57%
$28,001 to $40,000..... 5.12%
$40,001 and over 6.84%

Married filing jointly or Surviving spouse
$0 to $4,800 .... 2.56%
$4,801 to $35,000 ..... 3.57%
$35,001 to $54,000..... 5.12%
$54,001 and over 6.84%

Married filing separately
$0 to $2,400 .... 2.56%
$2,401 to $17,500 ..... 3.57%
$17,501 to $27,000..... 5.12%
$27,001 and over 6.84%

New Hampshire
5% on interest and dividends only

New Jersey

Single or Married/Civil union partner filing separately
$0 to $20,000 .... 1.4%
$20,001 to $35,000..... 1.75%
$35,001 to $40,000...... 3.5%
$40,001 to $75,000..... 5.525%
$75,001 to $500,000.... 6.37%
$500,001 and over 8.97%

Head of household, Married/ civil-union couple filing jointly, or Qualifying widow(er)/surviving civil-union partner
$0 to $20,000 .... 1.4%
$20,001 to $50,000..... 1.75%
$50,001 to $70,000..... 2.45%
$70,001 to $80,000...... 3.5%
$80,001 to $150,000.... 5.525%
$150,001 to $500,000... 6.37%
$500,001 and over 8.97%

New Mexico[1]

Single
$0 to $5,500 .... 1.7%
$5,501 to $11,000...... 3.2%
$11,001 to $16,000..... 4.7%
$16,001 and over 4.9%

Head of household
$0 to $8,000 .... 1.7%
$8,001 to $16,000...... 3.2%
$16,001 to $24,000..... 4.7%
$24,001 and over 4.9%

Married filing jointly or Qualifying widow(er)
$0 to $8,000 .... 1.7%
$8,001 to $16,000...... 3.2%
$16,001 to $24,000..... 4.7%
$24,001 and over 4.9%

Married filing separately
$0 to $4,000 .... 1.7%
$4,001 to $8,000....... 3.2%
$8,001 to $12,000...... 4.7%
$12,001 and over 4.9%

New York

Single or Married filing separately
$0 to $8,000 .... 4%
$8,001 to $11,000...... 4.5%
$11,001 to $13,000..... 5.25%
$13,001 to $20,000..... 5.9%
$20,001 to $200,000.... 6.85%
$200,001 to $500,000... 7.85%
$500,001 and over 8.97%

Head of household
$0 to $11,000 .... 4%
$11,001 to $15,000..... 4.5%
$15,001 to $17,000..... 5.25%
$17,001 to $30,000..... 5.9%
$30,001 to $250,000.... 6.85%
$250,001 to $500,000... 7.85%
$500,001 and over 8.97%

Married filing jointly or Qualifying widow(er)
$0 to $16,000 .... 4%
$16,001 to $22,000..... 4.5%
$22,001 to $26,000..... 5.25%
$26,001 to $40,000..... 5.9%
$40,001 to $300,000.... 6.85%
$300,001 to $500,000... 7.85%
$500,001 and over 8.97%

North Carolina

Single
$0 to $12,750 .... 6%
$12,751 to $60,000...... 7%
$60,001 and over 7.75%

Head of household
$0 to $17,000 .... 6%
$17,001 to $80,000...... 7%
$80,001 and over 7.75%

Married filing jointly or Surviving spouse
$0 to $21,250 .... 6%
$21,251 to $100,000..... 7%
$100,001 and over 7.75%

Married filing separately
$0 to $10,625 .... 6%
$10,626 to $50,000...... 7%
$50,001 and over 7.75%

North Dakota[2]

Single
$0 to $34,500 .... 1.51%
$34,501 to $83,600..... 2.82%
$83,601 to $174,400.... 3.13%
$174,401 to $379,150... 3.63%
$379,151 and over 3.99%

Head of household
$0 to $46,250 .... 1.51%
$46,251 to $119,400.... 2.82%
$119,401 to $193,350... 3.13%
$193,351 to $379,150... 3.63%
$379,151 and over 3.99%

Married filing jointly or Surviving spouse
$0 to $57,700 .... 1.51%
$57,701 to $139,350.... 2.82%
$139,351 to $212,300... 3.13%
$212,301 to $379,150... 3.63%
$379,151 and over 3.99%

Married filing separately
$0 to $28,850 .... 1.51%
$28,851 to $69,675..... 2.82%
$69,676 to $106,150.... 3.13%
$106,151 to $189,575... 3.63%
$189,576 and over 3.99%

Ohio[3]

$0 to $5,050 .... 0.587%
$5,051 to $10,100..... 1.174%
$10,101 to $15,150.... 2.348%
$15,151 to $20,200.... 2.935%
$20,201 to $40,350.... 3.521%
$40,351 to $80,700.... 4.109%
$80,701 to $100,900... 4.695%
$100,901 to $201,800.. 5.451%
$201,801 and over 5.925%

Oklahoma

Single or Married filing separately
$0 to $1,000 .... 0.5%
$1,001 to $2,500......... 1%
$2,501 to $3,750......... 2%
$3,751 to $4,900......... 3%
$4,901 to $7,200......... 4%
$7,201 to $8,700......... 5%
$8,701 and over 5.5%

Head of household, Married filing jointly, or Qualifying widow(er)
$0 to $2,000 .... 0.5%
$2,001 to $5,000......... 1%
$5,001 to $7,500......... 2%
$7,501 to $9,800......... 3%
$9,801 to $12,200....... 4%
$12,201 to $15,000...... 5%
$15,001 and over 5.5%

Oregon[2]

Single or Married filing separately
$0 to $2,000 .... 5%
$2,001 to $5,000......... 7%
$5,001 to $125,000...... 9%
$125,001 to $250,000.. 10.8%
$250,001 and over...... 11%

Married filing jointly, Head of household, or Qualifying widow(er)
$0 to $4,000 .... 5%
$4,001 to $10,000....... 7%
$10,001 to $250,000..... 9%
$250,001 to $500,000.. 10.8%
$500,001 and over 11%

Pennsylvania
3.07% of taxable compensation, net profits, net gains from the sale of property, rent, royalties, patents or copyrights, income from estates or trusts, dividends, interest, and winnings

Rhode Island[2]

Single, Head of household, Married filing jointly, Surviving spouse, or Married filing separately
$0 to $55,000 .... 3.75%
$55,001 to $125,000.... 4.75%
$125,001 and over 5.99%

South Carolina[2]

$0 to $2,760 .... 0%
$2,761 to $5,520........ 3%
$5,521 to $8,280........ 4%
$8,281 to $11,040....... 5%
$11,041 to $13,800...... 6%
$13,801 and over 7%

Tennessee
6% upon interest and dividend income

Utah
5% on state taxable income

Vermont[2,4]

Single
$0 to $34,500 .... 3.55%
$34,501 to $83,600...... 6.8%
$83,601 to $174,400..... 7.8%
$174,401 to $379,150... 8.8%
$379,151 and over 8.95%

Head of household
$0 to $46,250 .... 3.55%
$46,251 to $119,400.... 6.8%
$119,401 to $193,350... 7.8%
$193,351 to $379,150... 8.8%
$379,151 and over 8.95%

Married filing jointly, Qualifying widow(er), Civil union filing jointly
$0 to $57,650 .... 3.55%
$57,651 to $139,350.... 6.8%
$139,351 to $212,300... 7.8%
$212,301 to $379,150... 8.8%
$379,151 and over 8.95%

Married or Civil union filing separately
$0 to $28,825 .... 3.55%
$28,826 to $69,675..... 6.8%
$69,676 to $106,150.... 7.8%
$106,151 to $189,575... 8.8%
$189,576 and over 8.95%

Virginia

Single, Head of household, Married filing jointly, or Married filing separately
$0 to $3,000 .... 2%
$3,001 to $5,000........ 3%
$5,001 to $17,000....... 5%
$17,001 and over 5.75%

West Virginia

Single, Head of household, or Married filing jointly
$0 to $10,000 .... 3%
$10,001 to $25,000...... 4%
$25,001 to $40,000..... 4.5%
$40,001 to $60,000...... 6%
$60,001 and over 6.5%

Married filing separately
$0 to $5,000 .... 3%
$5,001 to $12,500....... 4%
$12,501 to $20,000..... 4.5%
$20,001 to $30,000...... 6%
$30,001 and over 6.5%

Wisconsin[1,2]

Single or Head of household
$0 to $10,180 .... 4.6%
$10,181 to $20,360.... 6.15%
$20,361 to $152,740.... 6.5%
$152,741 to $224,210.. 6.75%
$224,211 and over..... 7.75%

Married filing jointly
$0 to $13,580 .... 4.6%
$13,581 to $27,150.... 6.15%
$27,151 to $203,650... 6.5%
$203,651 to $298,940.. 6.75%
$298,941 and over 7.75%

Married filing separately
$0 to $6,790 .... 4.6%
$6,791 to $13,580..... 6.15%
$13,581 to $101,820... 6.5%
$101,821 to $149,470.. 6.75%
$149,471 and over..... 7.75%

AMT = Alternative minimum tax; AGI = Adjusted gross income; MFS = Married filing separately. (1) Community property state in which, in general, one-half of the community income is taxable to each spouse. (2) Brackets indexed for inflation annually. (3) 2011 adjusted brackets were not available. Bracketed rates listed are for 2010. (4) These are preliminary 2011 tax rates and brackets. **Arkansas:** Married filing separately combined-status couples calculate taxes separately and add the results. **California:** An additional 1% tax is imposed on taxable income in excess of $1 mil. **Colorado:** Individual taxpayers are subject to an AMT equal to the amount by which 3.47% of their Colorado alternative minimum taxable income exceeds their Colorado normal tax. **Connecticut:** Resident estates and trusts are subject to 6.7% rate on all income. **Indiana:** Counties may impose an adjusted gross income tax on residents or on nonresidents, or a county option income tax. **Iowa:** An AMT of 6.7% of alternative minimum income is imposed if the minimum tax exceeds the taxpayer's regular income tax liability. **Maine:** Additional state minimum tax is imposed equal to the amount by which the tentative minimum tax exceeds regular income tax liability. **Massachusetts:** Part A income represents either interest and dividends or short-term capital gains. Part B income represents wages, salaries, tips, pensions, state bank interest, partnership income, business income, rents, alimony, winnings, and certain other items of income. Part C income represents gains from the sale of capital assets held for more than one year. **Michigan:** Business activity attributable to Michigan is also subject to the Michigan Business Tax. **Minnesota:** A 6.4% AMT is imposed. **Montana:** Minimum tax, $1. **Nebraska:** There is an additional tax on taxpayers with federal AGI of more than a certain amount, which was $167,100 ($83,550 for MFS) in 2010. **New Mexico:** Qualified nonresident taxpayers may pay alternative tax of 0.75% of gross receipts from New Mexico sales. **New York:** A supplemental tax is imposed to recapture the tax table benefit. **Ohio:** The brackets listed for 2011 do not reflect an annual adjustment for inflation that was scheduled to take place in July 2011. **Vermont:** The tax amount in the schedules is increased or decreased by 24% of a taxpayer's federal tax liability for certain items. **West Virginia:** The West Virginia minimum tax expired for tax years on or after Jan. 1, 2010. **Wisconsin:** A permanent recycling surcharge is imposed on individuals with at least $4 mil in gross receipts at the rate of the greater of $25 or 0.2% of net business income as allocated or apportioned to Wisconsin with a maximum of $9,800.

EDUCATION

U.S. Public Schools: Students, Staff, Spending, 1899-2009
Source: National Center for Education Statistics, U.S. Dept. of Education

	1899-1900	1919-20	1939-40	1959-60	1969-70	1979-80	1989-90	1999-2000	2008-09
Population (thous.)									
Total U.S. population[1]	75,995	104,514	131,028	177,830	201,385	225,055	246,819	279,040	304,375
Population 5-17 years of age	21,573	27,571	30,151	43,881	52,386	48,043	44,947	52,811	53,277
Percentage 5-17 years of age	28.4%	26.4%	23.0%	24.7%	26.0%	21.3%	18.2%	18.9%	17.5%
Enrollment (thous.)									
Elementary and secondary[2]	15,503	21,578	25,434	36,087	45,550	41,651	40,543	46,857	49,266
Pre-kindergarten and grades 1-8	14,984	19,378	18,833	27,602	32,513	28,034	29,152	33,486	34,286
Grades 9-12	519	2,200	6,601	8,485	13,037	13,616	11,390	13,371	14,980
Percentage pop. 5-17 enrolled	71.9%	78.3%	84.4%	82.2%	87.0%	86.7%	90.2%	88.7%	92.5%
Percentage enrolled in high schools	3.3%	10.2%	26.0%	23.5%	28.6%	32.7%	28.1%	28.5%	30.4%
High school grads. (thous.)	62	231	1,143	1,627	2,589	2,748	2,320	2,554	3,005
Instructional staff (thous.)									
Total instructional staff	*	678	912	1,457	2,286	2,406	2,986	3,819	4,275
Teachers, librarians, and other nonsupervisory instructional staff	423	657	875	1,393	2,195	2,300	2,860	3,682	4,155
Revenue and expenditures (mil)									
Total revenue	$220	$970	$2,261	$14,747	$40,267	$96,881	$208,548	$372,944	$593,061
Total expenditures	215	1,036	2,344	15,613	40,683	95,962	212,770	381,838	610,110
Current expenditures[3,4]	180	861	1,942	12,329	34,218	86,984	188,229	323,889	518,997
Capital outlay	35	154	258	2,662	4,659	6,506	17,781	43,357	65,882
Interest on school debt	*	18	131	490	1,171	1,874	3,776	9,135	16,691
Others	*	3	13	133	636	598	2,983	5,457	8,539
Salaries and pupil cost									
Avg. annual salary of instruct. staff[5]	$325	$871	$1,441	$4,995	$8,626	$15,970	$31,367	$41,807	$54,319
Expenditure per capita total pop.	2.83	9.91	17.89	88	202	426	862	1,368	2,004
Current expenditure per pupil ADA[4,6]	16.67	53.32	88.09	375	816	2,272	4,980	7,394	10,591

* = Data not collected. **Note:** Because of rounding, details may not add up to totals. Prior to 1959-60, data do not include Alaska and Hawaii. (1) Data for 1899-1900 are based on total population from the decennial census. From 1919-20 to 1959-60, population data are total population, including armed forces overseas, as of July 1 preceding the school year. Data for later years are for resident population excluding armed forces overseas. (2) Data for 1899-1960 are school year enrollment; data for later years are fall enrollment. (3) In 1899-1900, includes interest on school debt. (4) Because of changes in the definition of "current expenditures," data for 1959-60 and later years are not entirely comparable with prior years. (5) Data prior to 1959-60 include supervisors, principals, teachers, and nonsupervisory instructional staff. (6) ADA = average daily attendance.

U.S. Public High School Graduation Rates, 2007-08
Source: National Center for Education Statistics, U.S. Dept. of Education

State	Rate	Rank	State	Rate	Rank	State	Rate	Rank	State	Rate	Rank
Alabama	69.0%	43	Illinois	80.4%	15	Montana	82.0%	13	Rhode Island	76.4%	25
Alaska	69.1	42	Indiana	74.1	34	Nebraska	83.8	7	South Carolina	61.9	49
Arizona	70.7	41	Iowa	86.4	3	Nevada	51.3	51	South Dakota	84.4	6
Arkansas	76.4	25	Kansas	79.0	19	New Hampshire	83.3	9	Tennessee	74.9	31
California	71.2	39	Kentucky	74.4	32	New Jersey	84.6	5	Texas	73.1	35
Colorado	75.4	30	Louisiana	63.5	48	New Mexico	66.8	45	Utah	74.3	33
Connecticut	82.2	12	Maine	79.1	18	New York	70.9	40	Vermont	89.3	2
Delaware	72.1	37	Maryland	80.4	15	North Carolina	72.8	36	Virginia	77.0	23
Dist. of Columbia	56.0	50	Massachusetts	81.5	14	North Dakota	83.8	7	Washington	71.9	38
Florida	66.9	44	Michigan	76.3	27	Ohio	79.0	19	West Virginia	77.3	22
Georgia	65.4	46	Minnesota	86.4	3	Oklahoma	78.0	21	Wisconsin	89.6	1
Hawaii	76.0	28	Mississippi	63.9	47	Oregon	76.7	24	Wyoming	76.0	28
Idaho	80.1	17	Missouri	82.4	11	Pennsylvania	82.7	10	**Total U.S.**	**74.7**	

Note: The averaged freshman graduation rate provides an estimate of the percentage of students who receive a regular diploma within 4 years of entering ninth grade. The rate uses aggregate student enrollment data to estimate the size of an incoming freshman class and aggregate counts of the number of diplomas awarded 4 years later.

High School Dropouts by Sex, Race, and Ethnicity, 1960-2009
Source: Current Population Survey, Census Bureau, U.S. Dept. of Commerce

Data for Oct. of year shown unless otherwise noted.

Year[4]	Total dropout rate				Male dropout rate				Female dropout rate			
	All races[1]	White	Black	Hispanic	All races[1]	White	Black	Hispanic	All races[1]	White	Black	Hispanic
1960[2]	27.2%	NA	NA	NA	27.8%	NA	NA	NA	26.7%	NA	NA	NA
1970[3]	15.0	13.2%	27.9%	NA	14.2	12.2%	29.4%	NA	15.7	14.1%	26.6%	NA
1975	13.9	11.4	22.9	29.2%	13.3	11.0	23.0	26.7%	14.5	11.8	22.9	31.6%
1980	14.1	11.4	19.1	35.2	15.1	12.3	20.8	37.2	13.1	10.5	17.7	33.2
1985	12.6	10.4	15.2	27.6	13.4	11.1	16.1	29.9	11.8	9.8	14.3	25.2
1990	12.1	9.0	13.2	32.4	12.3	9.3	11.9	34.3	11.8	8.7	14.4	30.3
1995	12.0	8.6	12.1	30.0	12.2	9.0	11.1	30.0	11.7	8.2	12.9	30.0
2000	10.9	6.9	13.1	27.8	12.0	7.0	15.3	31.8	9.9	6.9	11.1	23.5
2001	10.7	7.3	10.9	27.0	12.2	7.9	13.0	31.6	9.3	6.7	9.0	22.1
2002	10.5	6.5	11.3	25.7	11.8	6.7	12.8	29.6	9.2	6.3	9.9	21.2
2003[5]	9.9	6.3	10.9	23.5	11.3	7.1	12.5	26.7	8.4	5.6	9.5	20.1
2004[5]	10.3	6.8	11.8	23.8	11.6	7.1	13.5	28.5	9.0	6.4	10.2	18.5
2005[5]	9.4	6.0	10.4	22.4	10.8	6.6	12.0	26.4	8.0	5.3	9.0	18.1
2006[5]	9.3	5.8	10.7	22.1	10.3	6.4	9.7	25.7	8.3	5.3	11.7	18.1
2007[5]	8.7	5.3	8.4	21.4	9.8	6.0	8.0	24.7	7.7	4.5	8.8	18.0
2008[5]	8.0	4.8	9.9	18.3	8.5	5.4	8.7	19.9	7.5	4.2	11.1	16.7
2009[5]	8.1	5.2	9.3	17.6	9.1	6.3	10.6	19.9	7.1	4.1	8.1	16.1

NA = Not available. **Note:** Table shows "status" dropouts, defined as 16- to 24-year-old persons who are not enrolled in school and who have not completed a high school program, regardless of when they left school. People who have received GED credentials are not shown. Excludes persons in prisons or in the military, and other persons not living in households. Race categories exclude persons of Hispanic ethnicity unless otherwise noted. (1) Includes other racial/ethnic categories not separately shown. (2) Based on the Apr. 1960 decennial census. (3) White and black figures include persons of Hispanic ethnicity. (4) Because of changes in data collection procedures, data for years prior to 1992 may not be comparable to later years. (5) White and black figures exclude persons identifying themselves as being of two or more races.

Overview of U.S. Public Schools, 2009-10

Source: National Center for Education Statistics, U.S. Dept. of Education; National Education Association (NEA)

State	Local school districts	Elementary schools[1]	Secondary schools[2,3]	Classroom teachers	Total enrollment	Pupils per teacher	Teacher's avg. pay	Expend. per pupil
Alabama	132	951	395	46,285	741,115	16.0	$47,571	$9,001
Alaska	54	188	86	8,865	131,662	14.9	59,672	11,000*
Arizona	627	1,341	674	56,944*	1,077,800*	18.9*	46,952*	6,170*
Arkansas	245*	721	388	36,153*	458,237*	12.7*	46,700	11,171*
California	1,042*	6,939	2,535	291,011	6,238,244*	21.4*	68,203*	8,846*
Colorado	178	1,260	417	48,960	832,368	17.0	49,202	9,631
Connecticut	195*	827	259	43,196*	568,279*	13.2*	64,350*	14,472*
Delaware	37	149	47	8,786	126,801	14.4	57,080	13,496*
Dist. of Columbia	41*	167	37	5,791*	75,923*	13.1*	64,548*	13,519*
Florida	67*	2,634	656	166,055	2,635,115	15.9	46,708	8,963
Georgia	186	1,758	440	115,700	1,667,685	14.4	53,112	10,594*
Hawaii	1	210	52	11,682	177,800	15.2	55,063	11,521
Idaho	137	435	232	15,424*	281,003*	18.2*	46,283*	7,875*
Illinois	869*	3,179	1,019	141,596	2,105,779	14.9	62,077	11,457*
Indiana	349	1,425	434	62,515	1,046,222	16.7	49,986	10,120
Iowa	361	1,013	434	35,481	490,417	13.8	49,626	9,455
Kansas	293	965	389	34,985	480,498	13.7	46,657	9,264
Kentucky	174	986	478	41,288	651,810	15.8	49,543	9,603
Louisiana	120	984	313	49,321	690,915	14.0	48,903	10,750
Maine	229*	500	149	17,085*	189,643*	11.1*	46,106*	14,247*
Maryland	24	1,121	270	59,142	848,412	14.3	63,971	14,244*
Massachusetts	392	1,439	368	70,396	956,231	13.6	69,273	14,766
Michigan	773*	2,551	1,133	97,798*	1,673,032*	17.1*	57,958*	11,595*
Minnesota	471*	1,275	818	52,734	814,641*	15.4*	52,431	11,447*
Mississippi	152*	620	335	35,568*	495,790*	13.9*	45,644*	7,752*
Missouri	524*	1,574	658	67,882*	903,423*	13.3*	45,317*	9,076*
Montana	417	478	352	10,578	141,807	13.4	45,759	9,613*
Nebraska	253	728	310	22,054	295,402	13.4	46,227	9,760
Nevada	17*	448	105	24,314*	449,607*	18.5*	51,524*	7,813*
New Hampshire	163	384	105	15,436	196,344	12.7	51,443	12,979*
New Jersey	591	1,951	485	114,545*	1,372,731*	12.0*	65,130*	16,967*
New Mexico	89	596	224	21,907	326,558	14.9	46,258	10,812*
New York	695	3,301	1,063	226,123	2,677,369*	11.8*	71,633	16,922*
North Carolina	115	1,830	519	95,377	1,416,161	14.8	46,850	8,529
North Dakota	183	303	187	7,772	93,715	12.1	42,964	8,541
Ohio	986	2,620	1,006	110,628	1,892,137	17.1	55,958	9,528*
Oklahoma	527	1,231	562	42,355	654,542	15.5	47,691	7,968*
Oregon	196	922	307	29,969	561,698	18.7	55,224	10,476
Pennsylvania	499	2,300	826	126,828	1,780,413	14.0	59,156	12,728*
Rhode Island	49	241	80	11,132	145,118	13.0	59,686*	15,384*
South Carolina	89	895	276	48,257	712,244	14.8	47,508	9,531
South Dakota	154	433	249	9,212	123,370	13.4	38,837	9,021*
Tennessee	135*	1,312	359	65,049*	953,975*	14.7*	46,290*	8,199*
Texas	1,237	5,767	2,092	333,103	4,824,778	14.5	48,261	9,227
Utah	41	621	354	25,167	563,273	22.4	45,885	6,859*
Vermont	286*	239	72	8,905*	87,580*	9.8*	49,084*	16,308*
Virginia	132*	1,513	389	106,674*	1,245,165*	11.7*	50,015*	11,290*
Washington	295	1,450	568	53,611	1,035,887	19.3	53,003	9,900
West Virginia	55*	571	125	19,796*	282,892*	14.3*	45,959*	11,043*
Wisconsin	425	1,564	618	58,849	872,436	14.8	51,264	11,429*
Wyoming	48	238	99	7,085	87,420	12.3	55,861	15,345
Total U.S.	**15,350***	**67,148**	**24,348**	**3,215,371***	**49,141,467***	**15.3***	**55,202***	**10,586***

* = NEA estimate. (1) Includes primary and middle schools (schools with no grade higher than 8). (2) 2008-09 estimates. (3) Includes schools with no grade lower than 7.

Programs for the Disabled, 1995-2010

Source: Office of Special Education and Rehabilitative Services, U.S. Dept. of Education

Number of children and young adults 3 to 21 years old served annually in federally funded educational programs for the disabled; in thousands.

Type of disability	1995 -96	1999 -00	2000 -01	2001 -02	2002 -03	2003 -04	2004 -05	2005 -06	2006 -07	2007 -08	2008 -09	2009 -10
Learning disabilities	2,578	2,834	2,868	2,861	2,848	2,831	2,798	2,735	2,665	2,577	2,537	2,498
Speech impairments.	1,022	1,080	1,409	1,391	1,412	1,441	1,463	1,468	1,475	1,458	1,451	1,449
Mental retardation.	571	600	624	616	602	593	578	556	534	500	488	473
Emotional disturbance	437	469	481	483	485	489	489	477	464	442	421	409
Multiple disabilities	93	111	133	136	138	140	140	141	142	138	132	132
Hearing impairments	67	71	78	78	78	79	79	79	80	79	79	79
Orthopedic impairments	63	71	83	83	83	77	73	71	69	67	70	66
Other health impairments[1] . .	133	253	303	350	403	464	521	570	611	641	666	698
Visual impairments.	25	26	29	28	29	28	29	29	29	29	29	29
Autism.	28	65	94	114	137	163	191	223	258	296	338	380
Deaf-blindness	1	2	1	2	2	2	2	2	2	2	2	2
Traumatic brain injury	9	14	16	22	22	23	24	24	25	25	26	25
Developmental delay	—	19	178	242	283	305	332	339	333	358	354	368
All disabilities	**5,572**	**6,195**	**6,296**	**6,407**	**6,523**	**6,634**	**6,719**	**6,713**	**6,686**	**6,613**	**6,593**	**6,608**

— = Not available or not reliable data. **Note:** Counts based on reports from states and District of Columbia. Details may not add to totals because of rounding and/or incomplete enumeration. (1) Includes limited strength, vitality, or alertness due to chronic or acute health problems such as a heart condition, tuberculosis, rheumatic fever, nephritis, asthma, sickle cell anemia, hemophilia, epilepsy, lead poisoning, leukemia, or diabetes.

Students Reporting School Bullying and Cyberbullying, 2006-07
Source: National Center for Education Statistics, U.S. Dept. of Education

	Number of students (thous.)	Percent		Number of students (thous.)	Percent
Total students	25,721	100.0%	Excluded from activities on purpose	1,340	5.2%
Not bullied	17,556	68.3	Property destroyed on purpose	1,076	4.2
Bullied students	8,166	31.7	Not cyberbullied	24,761	96.3
Made fun of, called names, or insulted	5,390	21.0	Cyberbullied students	940	3.7
Subject of rumors	4,636	18.1	Hurtful information on Internet	408	1.6
Threatened with harm	1,487	5.8	Unwanted contact via instant messaging	538	2.1
Pushed, shoved, tripped, or spit on	2,819	11.0	Unwanted contact via text messaging	448	1.7
Tried to make do things they did not want to do	1,060	4.1			

Note: Includes school bullying among students ages 12-18, taking place in the school building, on school property, on a school bus, or going to and from school.

Trends in International Mathematics and Science Study (TIMSS), 1995-2007
Source: National Center for Education Statistics, U.S. Dept. of Education

The TIMSS is an international assessment test that was administered to 4th and 8th graders in 1995, 1999 (5th graders only), 2003, and 2007, to measure the degree to which students have learned concepts of mathematics and science. Listed below are the average scaled scores for each country. Scores are reported on a scale of 0 to 1,000, with the scale average set at 500. Student achievement is considered "high" with a score of at least 550; a score of at least 475 is considered "intermediate."

4th Grade

	Mathematics 2007	Mathematics % change, 1995-2007	Science 2007	Science % change, 1995-2007
Australia	516	22%	527	6%
Austria	505	−25	526	−12
Czech Republic	486	−54	515	−17
England	541	57	542	14
Hong Kong	607	50	554	46
Hungary	510	−12	536	28
Iran	402	15	436	55
Japan	568	1	548	−5
Latvia	537	38	542	56
Netherlands	535	−14	523	−7
New Zealand	492	23	504	−1
Norway	473	−3	477	−27
Scotland	494	1	500	−14
Singapore	599	9	587	63
Slovenia	502	40	518	54
United States	**529**	**11**	**539**	**−3**

8th Grade

	Mathematics 2007	Mathematics % change, 1995-2007	Science 2007	Science % change, 1995-2007
Australia	496	−13%	NA	NA
Bulgaria	464	−63	515	1%
Colombia	380	47	417	52
Cyprus	465	−2	452	0
Czech Republic	504	−42	539	−16
England	513	16	542	8
Hong Kong	572	4	530	20
Hungary	517	−10	539	2
Iran	403	−15	459	−4
Japan	570	−11	554	−1
Korea, South	597	17	553	7
Lithuania	506	34	519	55
Norway	469	−29	487	−28
Romania	461	−12	462	−9
Russia	512	−12	530	7
Scotland	487	−6	496	−5
Singapore	593	−16	567	−13
Slovenia	501	7	538	24
Sweden	491	−48	511	−42
United States	**508**	**16**	**520**	**7**

Mathematics, Reading, and Science Achievement of U.S. Students, 1998-2009
Source: National Assessment of Educational Progress, National Center for Education Statistics, U.S. Dept. of Education

Percent of public school students who scored at or above basic levels in national tests. Basic level denotes a partial mastery of prerequisite knowledge and skills fundamental for proficient work at each grade.

	4th Grade Math 2000	2009	Reading 1998	2009	8th Grade Math 2000	2009	Reading 1998	2009	Science 2000	2009
State										
AL	55	70	56	62	52	58	67	66	53	51
AK	NA	78	NA	59	NA	75	NA	72	NA	NA
AZ	57	71	51	56	62	67	72	68	55	54
AR	55	80	54	63	52	67	68	69	53	58
CA	50	72	48	54	52	59	63	64	38	48
CO	70	84	69	72	NA	76	77	78	NA	70
CT	76	86	76	76	72	78	81	81	64	69
DE	76	84	53	73	NA	75	64	78	NA	62
DC	24	56	27	44	23	40	44	51	NA	NA
FL	76	86	53	73	NA	70	67	76	NA	57
GA	57	78	54	63	55	67	68	72	52	58
HI	55	77	45	57	52	65	59	67	40	50
ID	68	85	NA	69	71	78	NA	77	71	72
IL	63	80	NA	65	68	73	NA	77	59	61
IN	77	87	NA	70	76	78	NA	79	66	67
IA	75	87	67	69	NA	76	NA	77	NA	72
KS	76	89	70	72	77	79	81	80	NA	NA
KY	59	81	62	72	63	70	74	79	60	71
LA	57	72	44	51	48	62	63	64	44	51
ME	73	87	72	70	76	78	83	80	72	73
MD	60	85	58	70	65	75	70	77	57	60
MA	77	92	70	80	76	85	79	83	70	74
MI	71	78	62	64	70	68	NA	72	68	66
MN	76	89	69	70	80	83	78	82	72	74
MS	45	69	47	55	41	54	62	62	41	41
MO	71	83	61	70	67	77	75	79	66	71
MT	72	88	72	73	80	82	83	84	79	79
NE	65	82	NA	70	74	75	NA	80	52	NA
NV	60	79	51	59	58	63	70	65	NA	54
NH	NA	92	75	77	NA	82	NA	81	NA	77
NJ	NA	88	NA	76	NA	80	NA	83	NA	70
NM	50	72	51	52	50	59	71	66	48	55
NY	66	83	62	71	68	73	76	75	NA	61
NC	73	87	58	65	70	74	74	70	54	56
ND	73	91	NA	76	77	86	NA	86	72	80
OH	73	85	NA	71	75	76	NA	80	72	73
OK	67	82	66	65	64	68	80	73	60	60
OR	65	80	58	65	71	75	78	76	68	68
PA	NA	84	NA	70	NA	78	NA	81	NA	66
RI	65	81	64	69	64	68	76	72	58	59
SC	59	78	53	62	55	69	66	68	48	55
SD	NA	86	NA	70	NA	83	NA	84	NA	77
TN	59	74	57	63	53	65	71	73	55	61
TX	76	85	59	65	68	78	74	73	52	64
UT	69	81	62	67	68	75	77	78	67	72
VT	73	89	NA	75	75	81	NA	84	71	NA
VA	71	85	62	74	67	76	78	78	61	70
WA	NA	84	68	68	NA	78	76	78	NA	69
WV	65	77	60	62	62	61	75	67	57	58
WI	76	85	72	67	NA	79	78	78	NA	73
WY	71	87	64	72	70	78	76	82	69	74
U.S.	**64**	**81**	**58**	**66**	**65**	**71**	**71**	**74**	**57**	**62**

NA = Not administered.

Enrollment in U.S. Public and Private Schools, 1899-2020

Source: National Center for Education Statistics, U.S. Dept. of Education

School year[1]	Public school[2]	Private school[2]	% private[3]	School year[1]	Public school[2]	Private school[2]	% private[3]
1899-1900	15,503	1,352	8.0%	1979-80	41,651	5,000[4]	10.7%
1909-10	17,814	1,558	8.0	1989-90	40,543	5,599	12.1
1919-20	21,578	1,699	7.3	1999-2000	46,857	6,018	11.4
1929-30	25,678	2,651	9.4	2007-08	49,293	5,910	10.7
1939-40	25,434	2,611	9.3	2008-09[5]	49,265	5,969	10.8
1949-50	25,111	3,380	11.9	2009-10[5]	49,312	5,970	10.8
1959-60	35,182	5,675	13.9	2019-20[5]	52,342	6,248	10.7
1969-70	45,550	5,500[3]	10.8				

Note: Private includes all nonpublic schools. (1) Fall enrollment. (2) In thousands. Data from fall 1980 onward covers an expanded universe of private schools; comparisons with earlier years should be avoided. (3) Percent of U.S. students enrolled in private schools. (4) Estimated. (5) Projected.

U.S. Religious and Nonsectarian Private Schools, 2009-10

Source: *Private School Universe Survey, 2009-10*, National Center for Education Statistics, U.S. Dept. of Education

Number and percentage distribution of private school students, by religious or nonsectarian orientation of school. Religious groups listed only if at least some data met reporting standards.

	Schools		Students		Teachers[1]	
	Number	Percent	Number	Percent	Number	Percent
Total U.S.	33,366	100.0%	4,700,119	100.0%	437,414	100.0%
Nonsectarian	10,635	31.9	938,467	20.0	122,926	28.1
Religious orientation	22,731	68.1	3,761,652	80.0	314,489	71.9
Amish	1,705	5.1	49,517	1.1	2,893	0.7
Assembly of God	345	1.0	41,933	0.9	3,614	0.8
Baptist	2,272	6.8	236,031	5.0	22,936	5.2
Brethren	86	0.3	7,420	0.2	709	0.2
Calvinist	120	0.4	26,251	0.6	1,876	0.4
Christian (unspecified)	4,702	14.1	606,555	12.9	60,070	13.7
Church of Christ	143	0.4	29,577	0.6	2,566	0.6
Church of God	130	0.4	10,989	0.2	1,103	0.3
Church of God in Christ	66	0.2	3,566	0.1	366	0.1
Church of the Nazarene	101	0.3	14,584	0.3	1,090	0.2
Episcopal	381	1.1	96,344	2.0	11,503	2.6
Friends	85	0.3	20,484	0.4	2,613	0.6
Greek Orthodox	33	0.1	3,621	0.1	484	0.1
Islamic	232	0.7	29,996	0.6	3,535	0.8
Jewish	1,015	3.0	227,506	4.8	25,403	5.8
Lutheran Church—Missouri Synod	1,068	3.2	123,987	2.6	9,813	2.2
Evangelical Lutheran Church In America	153	0.5	12,497	0.3	1,080	0.2
Wisconsin Evangelical Lutheran Synod	358	1.1	30,590	0.7	2,317	0.5
Other Lutheran	53	0.2	4,321	0.1	368	0.1
Mennonite	571	1.7	28,432	0.6	2,669	0.6
Methodist	287	0.9	18,048	0.4	2,083	0.5
Pentecostal	383	1.1	17,976	0.4	2,353	0.5
Presbyterian	254	0.8	37,992	0.8	3,829	0.9
Roman Catholic	7,115	21.3	2,009,640	42.8	142,620	32.6
Seventh-Day Adventist	849	2.5	51,393	1.1	4,205	1.0
Other	187	0.6	18,641	0.4	2,054	0.5

Note: Details may not add up to totals because of rounding and/or missing data. (1) Full-time equivalent teachers.

Characteristics of Public Charter Schools and Traditional Public Schools, 2008-09

Source: National Center for Education Statistics, U.S. Dept. of Education

Characteristic	Public charter schools Total	Elementary	Secondary	Combined	Traditional public schools Total	Elementary	Secondary	Combined
Student characteristics								
Total number	1,433,116	746,933	291,033	395,122	47,620,670	30,683,274	15,779,923	1,125,124
Sex								
Male	49.6%	50.0%	49.5%	48.9%	51.3%	51.4%	51.0%	53.4%
Female	50.4	50.0	50.5	51.1	48.7	48.6	49.0	46.6
Race/ethnicity								
White	37.9	33.6	32.4	50.0	55.4	54.0	58.0	58.6
Black	31.0	36.2	29.0	22.7	16.5	16.6	16.3	18.2
Hispanic	25.1	24.6	32.1	20.7	21.4	22.7	19.0	17.6
Asian/Pacific Islander	3.8	4.1	3.4	3.8	4.9	4.9	5.1	2.8
American Indian/ Alaska Native	1.1	0.9	1.7	1.0	1.2	1.2	1.2	2.5
School characteristics								
Total number	4,694	2,512	1,256	865	94,012	64,570	23,019	4,758
Enrollment size								
Under 300	63.7%	61.4%	76.0%	52.7%	29.8%	25.2%	35.7%	68.6%
300-499	20.4	22.7	15.9	20.3	28.0	33.5	14.4	13.3
500-999	12.6	14.3	5.6	17.7	32.8	37.4	22.9	13.9
1,000 or more	3.2	1.5	2.5	9.3	9.4	3.9	27.0	4.3
Locale								
City	55.1	57.5	56.4	46.1	24.6	26.0	20.2	25.5
Suburban	21.0	21.8	20.1	19.9	28.1	30.2	23.8	18.7
Town	7.8	6.0	9.2	11.4	14.4	13.8	16.4	12.9
Rural	16.1	14.8	14.2	22.6	32.9	30.0	39.6	42.8

Note: A public charter school is a school that provides free public education to eligible students under a specific charter granted by the state legislature or other appropriate authority. Charter schools can be administered by regular school districts, state education agencies, or chartering organizations.

Homeschooled Students

Source: National Center for Education Statistics, U.S. Dept. of Education

A total of 1,508,000 U.S. students in grades K-12 were homeschooled in 2007, 84% of them full-time, according to the latest available statistics from the U.S. Dept. of Education.

In a 2007 U.S. Dept. of Education survey of parents who homeschool their children, the reasons given as most important included concern over the school environment, including such factors as safety, drugs, or negative peer pressure (20.5%); desire to provide religious or moral instruction (35.8%); dissatisfaction with academic instruction in schools (17.1%); and a physical or mental health problem or other special need (5.7%). In all, 87.6% cited concern over school environment as one of their reasons, while 83.3% cited religious or moral instruction, and 72.7% cited dissatisfaction with academic instruction.

	1999			2007		
Characteristic	No. of students	Percentage distribution	Home-schooling rate[1]	No. of students	Percentage distribution	Home-schooling rate[1]
Total U.S.	850,000	100.0%	1.7%	1,508,000	100.0%	2.9%
Homeschooled entirely	697,000	82.0	—	1,266,000	84.0	—
Homeschooled and enrolled in school part-time	153,000	18.0	—	242,000	16.0	—
Race/ethnicity[2]						
White........	640,000	75.3	2.0	1,159,000	76.8	3.9
Black........	84,000	9.9	1.0	61,000	4.0	0.8
Hispanic	77,000	9.1	1.1	147,000	9.8	1.5
Other........	49,000	5.8	1.9	141,000	9.3	3.4
Number of children in household						
One child........	120,000	14.1	1.5	187,000	12.4	2.2
Two children	207,000	24.4	1.0	412,000	27.3	2.0
Three or more children	523,000	61.6	2.4	909,000	60.3	4.1
Household income						
$25,000 or less........	262,000	30.9	1.6	239,000	15.9	2.1
$25,001-$50,000........	278,000	32.7	1.8	364,000	24.1	3.4
$50,001-$75,000........	162,000	19.1	1.9	405,000	26.8	3.9
$75,001 or more........	148,000	17.4	1.5	501,000	33.2	2.7
Parents' education						
High school diploma or less........	160,000	18.9	0.9	206,000	13.7	1.4
Some college or vocational/technical	287,000	33.7	1.9	549,000	36.4	3.8
Bachelor's degree........	213,000	25.1	2.6	444,000	29.4	3.9
Graduate/professional degree	190,000	22.3	2.3	309,000	20.5	2.9

(1) The homeschooling rate is the percentage of the total group or subgroup within the general population that is homeschooled. For example, in 1999, 1.1% of all Hispanic students grades K-12 in the U.S. were homeschooled. (2) Hispanic or Latino persons may be of any race. Race categories include non-Hispanic population only.

Revenues for Public Elementary and Secondary Schools by State, 2008-09

Source: National Education Association (NEA); amounts in thousands

State	Total	Federal Amount	Federal % of tot. rev.	State Amount	State % of tot. rev.	Local and intermediate Amount	Local and intermediate % of tot. rev.
Alabama	$7,239,083	$777,591	10.7%	$4,166,018	57.5%	$2,295,475	31.7%
Alaska	2,262,964	314,949	13.9	1,459,658	64.5	488,356	21.6
American Samoa	79,922	68,432	85.6	11,282	14.1	209	0.3
Arizona	9,771,972	1,137,316	11.6	4,594,648	47.0	4,040,008	41.3
Arkansas	4,823,956	556,500	11.5	2,684,309	55.6	1,583,147	32.8
California	70,687,012	9,185,270	13.0	40,605,913	57.4	20,895,829	29.6
Colorado	8,353,849	578,233	6.9	3,670,240	43.9	4,105,376	49.1
Connecticut	9,871,755	440,826	4.5	3,842,177	38.9	5,588,751	56.6
Delaware	1,755,133	142,428	8.1	1,094,909	62.4	517,796	29.5
District of Columbia[1]	1,651,014	175,732	10.6	NA	NA	1,475,283	89.4
Florida	26,322,090	2,694,579	10.2	9,047,588	34.4	14,579,923	55.4
Georgia	18,017,477	1,688,274	9.4	7,780,725	43.2	8,548,478	47.4
Guam	262,823	50,170	19.1	NA	NA	212,652	80.9
Hawaii[1]	2,689,757	392,837	14.6	2,205,032	82.0	91,889	3.4
Idaho	2,243,784	229,156	10.2	1,509,815	67.3	504,812	22.5
Illinois	26,512,711	3,146,741	11.9	7,324,750	27.6	16,041,221	60.5
Indiana	12,569,782	1,432,813	11.4	4,964,928	39.5	6,172,042	49.1
Iowa	5,519,854	443,827	8.0	2,545,360	46.1	2,530,666	45.8
Kansas	5,757,927	453,608	7.9	3,323,346	57.7	1,980,973	34.4
Kentucky	6,641,128	731,351	11.0	3,802,150	57.3	2,107,627	31.7
Louisiana	8,099,981	1,264,057	15.6	3,740,262	46.2	3,095,662	38.2
Maine	2,575,516	245,719	9.5	1,127,032	43.8	1,202,765	46.7
Maryland	13,097,508	694,847	5.3	5,698,735	43.5	6,703,926	51.2
Massachusetts	15,102,480	1,276,250	8.5	6,036,202	40.0	7,790,028	51.6
Michigan	19,585,635	2,253,644	11.5	10,904,987	55.7	6,427,004	32.8
Minnesota	10,542,303	632,057	6.0	6,914,839	65.6	2,995,407	28.4
Mississippi	4,360,702	675,972	15.5	2,334,355	53.5	1,350,375	31.0
Missouri	10,042,753	833,909	8.3	3,425,716	34.1	5,783,128	57.6
Montana	1,595,197	199,017	12.5	774,091	48.5	622,089	39.0
Nebraska	3,455,794	280,666	8.1	1,213,317	35.1	1,961,810	56.8
Nevada	4,450,741	434,484	9.8	1,362,123	30.6	2,654,134	59.6
New Hampshire	2,717,115	147,318	5.4	1,003,249	36.9	1,566,547	57.7
New Jersey	25,283,290	1,040,733	4.1	10,525,550	41.6	13,717,006	54.3
New Mexico	3,820,116	569,047	14.9	2,675,916	70.0	575,152	15.1
New York	55,558,190	3,220,417	5.8	25,346,556	45.6	26,991,217	48.6
North Carolina	13,322,946	1,406,049	10.6	8,401,249	63.1	3,515,648	26.4
North Dakota	1,102,479	161,484	14.6	408,000	37.0	532,990	48.3
Northern Mariana Islands	65,538	30,711	46.9	34,602	52.8	225	0.3
Ohio	22,956,215	1,685,617	7.3	10,917,974	47.6	10,352,625	45.1
Oklahoma	5,729,610	770,745	13.5	3,042,487	53.1	1,916,378	33.4

State	Total	Federal Amount	Federal % of tot. rev.	State Amount	State % of tot. rev.	Local and intermediate Amount	Local and intermediate % of tot. rev.
Oregon	$6,145,206	$670,547	10.9%	$3,117,303	50.7%	$2,357,357	38.4%
Pennsylvania	25,632,072	1,868,034	7.3	9,920,340	38.7	13,843,699	54.0
Puerto Rico	3,542,658	1,076,147	30.4	2,462,725	69.5	3,787	0.1
Rhode Island	2,232,149	215,514	9.7	817,590	36.6	1,199,044	53.7
South Carolina	7,702,962	762,297	9.9	3,679,907	47.8	3,260,758	42.3
South Dakota	1,241,892	203,354	16.4	410,179	33.0	628,359	50.6
Tennessee	8,283,928	935,135	11.3	3,809,467	46.0	3,539,325	42.7
Texas	46,962,119	5,014,820	10.7	19,973,129	42.5	21,974,171	46.8
Utah	4,542,690	565,022	12.4	2,387,698	52.6	1,589,970	35.0
Vermont	1,571,006	102,785	6.5	1,346,300	85.7	121,922	7.8
Virgin Islands (U.S.)	243,079	40,037	16.5	NA	NA	203,042	83.5
Virginia	14,964,444	914,524	6.1	6,303,648	42.1	7,746,272	51.8
Washington	11,903,510	1,385,449	11.6	7,146,394	60.0	3,371,667	28.3
West Virginia	3,281,385	366,038	11.2	1,938,999	59.1	976,347	29.8
Wisconsin	10,832,105	1,302,449	12.0	4,809,185	44.4	4,720,471	43.6
Wyoming	1,675,896	110,634	6.6	945,167	56.4	620,095	37.0

NA = Not applicable. **Note:** Included as revenue receipts are all appropriations from general funds of federal, state, county, and local governments; receipts from taxes levied for school purposes; income from permanent school funds and endowments; and income from leases of school lands and miscellaneous sources (interest on bank deposits, tuition, gifts, school lunch charges, etc.). (1) District of Columbia and Hawaii have only one school district each; neither is comparable to other states.

Population With Upper Secondary Education in Selected Countries, 2009

Source: Organization for Economic Cooperation and Development

Percentage of the population ages 25-64 that have received at least upper secondary (senior high school) education.

Country	%	Country	%	Country	%	Country	%	Country	%
Czech Republic	91%	Switzerland	87%	Norway	81%	Ireland	72%	Greece	61%
Slovak Republic	91	Sweden	86	Hungary	81	New Zealand	72	Italy	54
Estonia	89	Germany	85	Korea, South	80	Australia	71	Spain	52
United States	89	Slovenia	83	Luxembourg	77	Belgium	71	Brazil	41
Canada	88	Austria	82	Denmark	76	France	70	Mexico	35
Poland	88	Finland	82	United Kingdom	74	Chile	69	Turkey	31
Russia	88	Israel	82	Netherlands	73	Iceland	66	Portugal	30

Loans and Grants to U.S. Undergraduate Students, 1999-2000 and 2007-08

Source: National Center for Education Statistics, U.S. Dept. of Education

	Total Loans % of students	Total Loans Average amount	Total Grants % of students	Total Grants Average amount	Federal Loans % of students	Federal Loans Average amount	Federal Grants % of students	Federal Grants Average amount
Characteristics								
			1999-2000					
Total	44.5%	$6,500	59.2%	$6,500	43.4%	$5,700	30.6%	$3,300
Dependency status and income								
Dependent undergraduates	44.4	6,000	56.9	7,100	43.2	5,100	23.4	3,100
Low-income	47.8	5,800	83.6	7,100	46.9	5,200	73.2	3,600
Middle-income	49.0	6,000	54.4	7,100	47.8	5,100	13.1	2,100
High-income	33.0	6,400	39.0	6,900	31.5	5,100	0.7	2,100
Independent undergraduates	44.8	7,900	66.2	4,900	43.9	7,300	51.7	3,500
Control and level of institution								
Public less-than-2-year	4.6	6,600	48.3	3,800	4.6	6,500	39.8	3,100
Public 2-year	12.8	4,900	49.3	3,400	11.9	4,200	32.4	3,200
Public 4-year	48.6	5,900	54.8	4,900	47.6	5,500	28.9	3,200
Private not-for-profit less-than-2-year	7.4	(1)	84.3	3,900	(1)	(1)	84.3	3,300
Private not-for-profit 2-year	26.6	6,200	72.6	6,600	26.6	5,400	35.4	3,400
Private not-for-profit 4-year	61.3	7,500	75.9	10,900	59.7	6,000	27.5	3,500
Private for-profit less-than-2-year	74.0	6,000	74.1	3,200	73.3	5,300	72.1	3,100
Private for-profit 2-year	86.7	6,800	68.9	4,700	85.7	6,000	58.1	3,300
Private for-profit 4-year	73.4	8,200	51.7	4,700	73.0	7,700	35.5	3,200
			2007-08					
Total	53.1%	$8,200	65.3%	$7,400	49.3%	$5,600	33.4%	$3,800
Dependency status and income								
Dependent undergraduates	49.5	7,900	63.1	8,100	45.6	4,900	25.4	3,800
Low-income	54.0	6,900	88.5	9,000	51.2	5,200	79.9	4,400
Middle-income	53.6	8,000	61.4	7,700	49.4	4,900	15.0	2,500
High-income	39.2	8,600	46.2	7,800	34.9	4,700	0.8	3,200
Independent undergraduates	64.2	9,200	72.4	5,400	60.8	7,100	58.6	3,700
Control and level of institution								
Public less-than-2-year	26.3	6,700	55.1	3,700	23.2	5,400	48.5	3,400
Public 2-year	22.5	5,000	55.7	3,800	19.6	4,200	36.7	3,600
Public 4-year	52.7	7,200	60.4	6,300	48.7	5,400	28.8	3,900
Private not-for-profit less-than-2-year	(1)	(1)	81.2[2]	4,100	(1)	(1)	77.2[2]	3,900
Private not-for-profit 2-year	50.7	9,300	67.0	7,200	47.6	5,600	52.4	5,100
Private not-for-profit 4-year	65.0	10,000	81.2	12,600	60.6	5,700	28.0	4,200
Private for-profit less-than-2-year	77.9	7,200	75.5	3,800	67.5	5,500	72.8	3,500
Private for-profit 2-year	95.3	10,300	79.0	4,500	94.2	6,700	73.6	3,700
Private for-profit 4-year	94.2	10,300	68.8	4,000	91.9	6,700	55.5	3,200

Note: Data for full-time, full-year undergraduates. Total loans include federal, state, institutional, and private loans. Total grants include federal, state, institutional, and private grants, including employer reimbursements. Parent Loans for Undergraduate Students (PLUS), veterans' benefits, and tax credits are not included in this table. Average aid amounts are calculated for recipients only. Income for dependent students is based on parents' annual income in the prior year. Data adjusted to 2009-10 dollars. (1) Reporting standards not met. (2) Interpret data with caution. Estimate is unstable because the standard error represents more than 30% of the estimate.

Undergraduate Students Taking Distance Education Courses, 2003-04 and 2007-08

Source: National Center for Education Statistics, U.S. Dept. of Education

	2003-04				2007-08			
	Taking any distance education courses		Taking entire program through distance education		Taking any distance education courses		Taking entire program through distance education	
Selected characteristic	Number (thous.)	Percent	Number (thous.)	Percent	Number (thous.)	Percent	Number (thous.)	Percent
Total	2,961	15.5%	973	5.1%	4,277	20.4%	769	3.7%
Sex								
Male	1,099	13.6	365	4.5	1,679	18.6	297	3.3
Female	1,862	17.0	609	5.5	2,598	21.8	472	4.0
Age								
15-23 years.	1,283	11.7	353	3.2	1,891	15.1	169	1.4
24-29 years.	592	18.4	213	6.6	938	25.9	192	5.3
30 years or older.	1,086	22.4	408	8.4	1,448	30.1	408	8.5
Attendance status								
Exclusively full-time.	1,179	12.7	360	3.9	1,648	16.5	299	3.0
Exclusively part-time.	1,251	18.7	470	7.0	1,839	24.8	373	5.0
Mixed full-time and part-time	531	17.3	143	4.7	791	22.3	97	2.7
Work status								
No job.	533	12.4	158	3.7	708	16.1	121	2.8
Regular job only	2,282	17.2	768	5.8	3,259	22.3	607	4.2
Work-study/assistantship only	60	8.8	18	2.6	112	12.9	13	1.5
Both regular job and work-study/assistantship. . . .	86	11.1	29	3.7	198	18.7	27	2.5
Housing status								
On-campus.	194	7.2	48	1.8	263	8.9	13	0.5
Off-campus.	1,851	17.7	634	6.1	2,709	24.0	606	5.4
With parents or relatives.	604	13.2	171	3.7	854	17.1	83	1.7
Attended more than one institution.	312	23.4	120	9.1	452	27.1	66	4.0
Dependency status								
Dependent	1,064	11.1	291	3.0	1,589	14.3	108	1.0
Independent, no dependents, not married	454	15.6	152	5.2	788	24.0	155	4.7
Independent, no dependents, married	269	19.6	101	7.4	356	28.7	83	6.6
Independent, with dependents, not married	522	20.5	180	7.1	712	25.5	197	7.0
Independent, with dependents, married	653	25.1	251	9.6	833	33.0	227	9.0

Note: Distance education courses include live, interactive audio- or video-conferencing; prerecorded instructional videos; webcasts; CD-ROMs or DVDs; or computer-based systems accessed over the Internet. Does not include correspondence courses. Estimates pertain to all postsecondary students who enrolled at any time during the school year at an institution participating in Title IV programs. Includes students attending more than one institution.

Charges at U.S. Institutions of Higher Education, 1969-70 to 2009-10

Source: National Center for Education Statistics, U.S. Dept. of Education

Figures for 1969-70 are average charges for full-time resident degree-credit students; figures for later years are average charges per full-time equivalent student. Room and board are based on full-time students. These figures are enrollment-weighted according to the number of full-time-equivalent undergraduates, and thus may vary from averages given elsewhere.

	Tuition and fees			Board rates			Dormitory charges		
Public (in-state)	All institutions	2-yr	4-yr	All institutions	2-yr	4-yr	All institutions	2-yr	4-yr
1969-70	$323	$178	NA	$511	$465	NA	$369	$308	NA
1979-80	583	355	$738	867	893	$865	715	574	$725
1989-90	1,356	756	1,780	1,635	1,581	1,638	1,513	962	1,557
1999-2000	2,506	1,338	3,349	2,364	1,834	2,406	2,440	1,549	2,519
2000-01	2,562	1,333	3,501	2,455	1,906	2,499	2,569	1,600	2,654
2001-02	2,700	1,380	3,735	2,598	2,036	2,645	2,723	1,722	2,816
2002-03	2,903	1,483	4,046	2,669	2,164	2,712	2,930	1,954	3,029
2003-04	3,319	1,702	4,587	2,823	2,233	2,875	3,107	2,086	3,212
2004-05	3,629	1,849	5,027	2,931	2,353	2,981	3,304	2,174	3,418
2005-06	3,874	1,935	5,351	3,035	2,306	3,093	3,545	2,251	3,664
2006-07	4,102	2,018	5,666	3,191	2,390	3,253	3,757	2,407	3,878
2007-08	4,291	2,061	5,943	3,331	2,409	3,404	3,952	2,506	4,082
2008-09	4,512	2,136	6,312	3,554	2,769	3,619	4,190	2,664	4,331
2009-10	4,751	2,285	6,695	3,653	2,574	3,754	4,399	2,845	4,565
Private									
1969-70	$1,533	$1,034	NA	$561	$546	NA	$436	$413	NA
1979-80	3,130	2,062	$3,225	955	923	$957	827	766	$831
1989-90	8,147	5,196	8,396	1,948	1,811	1,953	1,923	1,663	1,935
1999-2000	14,081	8,235	14,588	2,882	2,922	2,881	3,224	2,808	3,237
2000-01	15,000	9,067	15,470	2,993	3,000	2,993	3,374	2,722	3,392
2001-02	15,742	10,076	16,211	3,104	2,633	3,109	3,567	3,116	3,576
2002-03	16,383	10,651	16,826	3,206	3,870	3,197	3,752	3,232	3,764
2003-04	17,327	11,546	17,777	3,364	4,432	3,354	3,945	3,581	3,952
2004-05	18,154	12,122	18,604	3,485	3,728	3,483	4,171	4,243	4,170
2005-06	18,862	12,450	19,292	3,647	4,726	3,639	4,380	3,994	4,386
2006-07	20,048	12,708	20,517	3,785	3,429	3,788	4,606	4,147	4,613
2007-08	21,462	13,126	21,979	3,992	4,074	3,991	4,804	4,484	4,808
2008-09	22,299	13,562	22,852	4,209	4,627	4,206	5,025	4,537	5,032
2009-10	22,604	14,876	23,210	4,331	4,390	4,331	5,249	5,217	5,249

NA = Not available.

Top 20 Colleges and Universities in Endowment Assets, 2010

Source: *2010 NACUBO Endowment Study*, National Association of College and University Business Officers (NACUBO)

Rank	College/university	Endowment assets[1]	% change, 2009-10	Rank	College/university	Endowment assets[1]	% change, 2009-10
1.	Harvard University	$27,557,404	5.4%	11.	University of Pennsylvania	$5,668,937	9.6%
2.	Yale University	16,652,000	2.0	12.	University of Chicago	5,638,040	10.7
3.	Princeton University	14,391,450	14.1	13.	University of California	5,441,225	10.2
4.	University of Texas System	14,052,220	15.5	14.	University of Notre Dame	5,234,841	9.2
5.	Stanford University	13,851,115	9.8	15.	Duke University	4,823,572	8.6
6.	Massachusetts Institute of Technology	8,317,321	5.5	16.	Emory University	4,694,260	8.5
7.	University of Michigan	6,564,144	9.4	17.	Washington University in St. Louis	4,473,180	9.6
8.	Columbia University	6,516,512	10.6	18.	Cornell University	4,378,587	10.4
9.	Northwestern University	5,945,277	9.2	19.	University of Virginia	3,906,823	9.2
10.	Texas A&M University System and Foundations	5,738,289	12.9	20.	Rice University	3,786,548	4.8

Note: Market value of endowment assets, excluding pledges and working capital, in the fiscal year. (1) In thousands.

U.S. Higher Education Trends: Bachelor's Degrees Conferred

Source: National Center for Education Statistics, U.S. Dept. of Education

(*) figures are projected.

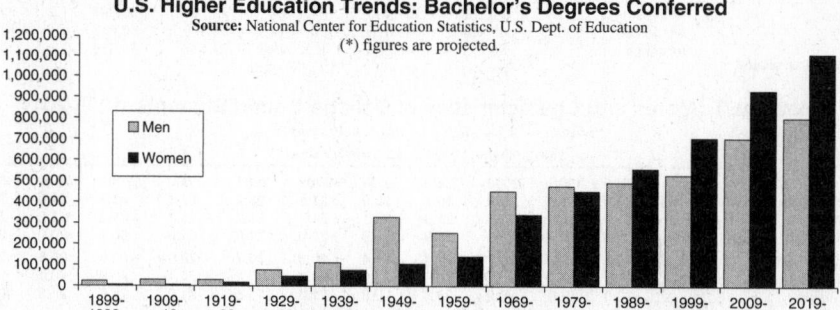

Financial Aid for College and Other Postsecondary Education

As of June 2011. Reviewed by National Assoc. of Student Financial Aid Administrators.

The cost of postsecondary education in the U.S. continues to increase, but financial aid—in the form of **grants** (no repayment needed), **loans**, and/or **work-study** programs—is widely available to help families meet these expenses. Most federal aid is limited to families that demonstrate financial need as determined by standard formulas and is designed to help students attend the college of their choice regardless of their ability to pay. Financial aid personnel at each school can provide information about all aid programs (federal, state, institutional, and private) available to students, steps to apply for them, and deadlines, all of which may vary.

All applicants for federal aid must file a Free Application for Federal Student Aid (**FAFSA**), generally as soon as possible after Jan. 1 for the academic year starting the following Sept. Figures provided should match federal income tax forms filed for the previous year. Applicants may also import certain information from their tax forms when they file their taxes online. Many other sources of aid—state governments, employers and unions, civic organizations, and the institutions themselves—also use the FAFSA to determine eligibility for aid. There are also special federal programs that pay for postsecondary education in return for service: AmeriCorps (1-800-942-2677), ROTC (1-800-USA-ROTC), and the G.I. Bill (1-888-442-4551). Additional forms and applications may be required if a student is to be considered for non-federal aid. Aid must be reapplied for annually.

A **federal formula**, based on information provided on the FAFSA, takes into account such factors as family income in the preceding calendar year, parental and student assets (excluding the parents' home, farm, or small business), length of time to parents' retirement, and unusual expenses (such as very high medical expenses). Outside scholarships (even non-need-based) are also taken into account in determining aid eligibility for federal, institutional, and state financial aid programs.

The formula determines a family's **expected family contribution** (EFC), which is divided among the number of family members—excluding parents—in college. The EFC is subtracted from the total cost of attending college for each person (including tuition and fee charges, room and board or allowance for living costs, books and supplies, transportation to and from school, and other miscellaneous costs). The difference determines financial need and the maximum federal aid for which the family may be eligible. (Some institutions use a separate formula for need-based institutional aid.) Some schools guarantee to meet the full financial need of each admitted student; most do their best to cover a student's financial need using various forms of financial aid but may not be able to because of a lack of funds.

The **aid package** offered by each school may include one or more of the following resources: Federal Pell Grants, for those who demonstrate sufficient financial need; Federal Supplemental Educational Opportunity Grants, for those who still have need after receiving Pell Grants; grants from the school; Federal Work-Study or other work programs; low-interest Perkins loans; and subsidized and unsubsidized Stafford loans. Parents of undergraduates may also apply for a Federal PLUS loan. Unsubsidized Stafford loans and all PLUS loans to parents are available to all students regardless of their financial need, but students and parents must still complete the FAFSA to get these loans.

Loans have varying interest rates and other requirements. Repayment of Perkins and Stafford loans does not begin until after graduation; deferments, income-based repayment plans, and loan forgiveness are available on federal loans for students who meet certain requirements. For PLUS loans, parents must pass a credit check and begin repayment of both principal and interest while the student is still in school.

Certain federal income **tax credits and refunds** are also available to families who meet income and other requirements; see the chapter on taxes.

Rules for financial aid are complex and changeable. *Funding Education Beyond High School: The Guide to Federal Student Aid*, a comprehensive resource on financial aid from the U.S. Dept. of Education, is available in English and Spanish on the Department's website: studentaid.ed.gov/students/publications/student_guide/index.html

Further information and FAFSA forms are available from schools or from the Federal Student Aid Information Center, P.O. Box 84, Washington, DC 20044; 1-800-4-FED-AID, Mon.-Fri., 8 AM-12 midnight EST. The Information Center also has a free booklet called *The EFC Formula Book*. FAFSA forms can be obtained online at www.fafsa.ed.gov

Average Salaries of U.S. College Professors, 2010-11

Source: American Association of University Professors

		Men			Women		
		Type of institution			Type of institution		
Teaching level		Public	Private/ independent	Church-related	Public	Private/ independent	Church-related
Doctoral level	Professor	$120,690	$159,964	$134,172	$109,032	$147,702	$122,696
	Associate	83,565	102,378	91,761	77,702	94,612	85,863
	Assistant	72,337	89,434	79,005	66,881	81,861	72,109
Master's level	Professor	90,999	103,932	93,490	87,311	95,795	86,213
	Associate	72,669	78,229	73,029	70,040	73,977	69,374
	Assistant	61,743	65,244	60,726	59,548	62,138	58,863
Baccalaureate level	Professor	85,489	101,596	76,127	82,334	96,807	72,580
	Associate	70,451	74,539	61,931	67,067	72,913	60,513
	Assistant	58,597	61,024	52,050	56,435	59,512	51,720
2-year	Professor	75,330	64,430	NA	72,784	50,897	NA
	Associate	62,433	59,418	NA	60,570	56,650	NA
	Assistant	54,471	44,733	NA	54,177	44,086	NA

NA = Not available.

Mean ACT Scores and Characteristics of College-Bound Students, 1990-2011

Source: ACT, Inc. (formerly American College Testing)

(for graduating class ending in year shown)

Scores[1]	Unit	1990	1995	2000	2004	2005	2006	2007	2008	2009	2010	2011
Composite scores	Points	20.6	20.8	21.0	20.9	20.9	21.1	21.2	21.1	21.1	21.0	21.1
Male	Points	21.0	21.0	21.2	21.0	21.1	21.2	21.2	21.2	21.3	21.2	21.2
Female	Points	20.3	20.7	20.9	20.9	20.9	21.0	21.0	21.0	20.9	20.9	21.0
English score	Points	20.5	20.2	20.5	20.4	20.4	20.6	20.7	20.6	20.6	20.5	20.6
Male	Points	20.1	19.8	20.0	19.9	20.0	20.1	20.2	20.1	20.2	20.1	20.2
Female	Points	20.9	20.6	20.9	20.8	20.8	21.0	21.0	21.0	20.9	20.8	20.9
Math score	Points	19.9	20.2	20.7	20.7	20.7	20.8	21.0	21.0	21.0	21.0	21.1
Male	Points	20.7	20.9	21.4	21.3	21.3	21.5	21.6	21.6	21.6	21.6	21.6
Female	Points	19.3	19.7	20.2	20.2	20.2	20.3	20.4	20.4	20.4	20.5	20.6
Participants												
Total number	(Thous.)	817	945	1,065	1,171	1,186	1,206	1,301	1,422	1,480	1,569	1,623
Male	Percent	46	44	43	43	44	44	42	44	45	45	46
White	Percent	79	80	72	67	66	63	60	63	64	62	60
Black	Percent	9	9	10	11	12	12	12	13	13	14	14
Hispanic[2]	Percent	4	5	5	7	7	7	7	8	9	10	12
Composite scores												
27 or above	Percent	12	13	14	14	14	14	15	9[3]	12	16	17
18 or below	Percent	35	34	32	34	34	33	32	33	34	35	34

(1) Minimum point score, 1; maximum score, 36. Test scores and characteristics of college-bound students are based on the performance of all ACT-tested students who graduated in the spring of a given school year and took the ACT assessment during junior or senior year of high school. (2) Persons of Hispanic origin may be of any race. (3) Composite scores of 28 or above.

Average ACT Composite Scores by State, 2010-11

Source: ACT, Inc. (formerly American College Testing)

State	Avg. comp. score	% grads taking ACT[1]	State	Avg. comp. score	% grads taking ACT[1]	State	Avg. comp. score	% grads taking ACT[1]
Alabama	20.3	81%	Kentucky	19.6	100%	Ohio	21.8	69%
Alaska	21.2	40	Louisiana	20.2	100	Oklahoma	20.7	76
Arizona	19.7	34	Maine	23.3	9	Oregon	21.5	35
Arkansas	19.9	91	Maryland	22.1	20	Pennsylvania	22.3	17
California	22.1	24	Massachusetts	24.2	22	Rhode Island	23.0	12
Colorado	20.7	100	Michigan	20.0	100	South Carolina	20.1	56
Connecticut	23.9	26	Minnesota	22.9	72	South Dakota	21.8	81
Delaware	22.4	16	Mississippi	18.7	100	Tennessee	19.5	100
District of Columbia	20.0	28	Missouri	21.6	71	Texas	20.8	36
Florida	19.6	66	Montana	22.1	60	Utah	21.8	73
Georgia	20.6	47	Nebraska	22.1	76	Vermont	22.7	28
Hawaii	21.3	24	Nevada	21.4	31	Virginia	22.3	24
Idaho	21.7	64	New Hampshire	23.7	18	Washington	22.8	20
Illinois	20.9	100	New Jersey	23.2	19	West Virginia	20.6	65
Indiana	22.3	29	New Mexico	19.8	72	Wisconsin	22.2	71
Iowa	22.3	61	New York	23.4	28	Wyoming	20.3	100
Kansas	22.0	79	North Carolina	21.9	18	U.S. average	21.1	49
			North Dakota	20.7	98			

(1) Totals for graduating seniors were obtained from *Knocking at the College Door—March 2008, Projections of High School Graduates by State and Race/Ethnicity 1992-2022*, Copyright © March 2008 by the Western Interstate Commission for Higher Education.

Mean SAT Scores of College-Bound Seniors, 1975-2011
Source: The College Board
(recentered scale; for school year ending in year shown)

	1975	1980	1985	1990	1995	2000	2002	2003	2004	2005	2006	2007	2008	2009	2010	2011
Critical reading scores[1]	512	502	509	500	504	505	504	507	508	508	503	502	502	501	501	497
Male	515	506	514	505	505	507	507	512	512	513	505	504	504	503	503	500
Female	509	498	503	496	502	504	502	503	504	505	502	502	500	498	498	495
**Math scores.......... **	498	492	500	501	506	514	516	519	518	520	518	515	515	515	516	514
Male	518	515	522	521	525	533	534	537	537	538	536	533	533	534	534	531
Female	479	473	480	483	490	498	500	503	501	504	502	499	500	499	500	500
**Writing scores........ **	NA	NA	NA	NA	NA	NA	NA	NA	NA	NA	497	494	494	493	492	489
Male	NA	NA	NA	NA	NA	NA	NA	NA	NA	NA	491	489	488	486	486	482
Female	NA	NA	NA	NA	NA	NA	NA	NA	NA	NA	502	500	501	499	498	496

NA = Not applicable. **Note:** In 1995, the College Board recentered the scoring scale for the SAT by reestablishing the original mean score of 500 on the 200-800 scale. Earlier scores have been adjusted to account for this recentering. The writing test was first given in Mar. 2005; however, only the scores of the first graduating class to take the revised test are given. (1) Pre-2006 scores are for the Verbal section.

Mean SAT Scores by State, 1990-2011
Source: The College Board
(recentered scale; for school year ending in year shown; V = Verbal, M = Math, CR = Critical reading, W = Writing)

	1990		2000		2005		2010[1]			2011			% grads
State	V	M	V	M	V	M	CR	M	W	CR	M	W	taking SAT[2]
Alabama	545	534	559	555	567	559	556	550	544	546	541	536	8%
Alaska	514	501	519	515	523	519	518	515	491	515	511	487	52
Arizona	521	520	521	523	526	530	519	525	500	517	523	499	28
Arkansas	545	532	563	554	563	552	566	566	552	568	570	554	5
California	494	508	497	518	504	522	501	516	500	499	515	499	53
Colorado	533	534	534	537	560	560	568	572	555	570	573	556	19
Connecticut	506	496	508	509	517	517	509	514	513	509	513	513	87
Delaware	510	496	502	496	503	502	493	495	481	489	490	476	74
District of Columbia	483	467	494	486	490	478	474	464	466	469	457	459	79
Florida	495	493	498	500	498	498	496	498	479	487	489	471	64
Georgia	478	473	488	486	497	496	488	490	475	485	487	473	80
Hawaii	480	505	488	519	490	516	483	505	470	479	500	469	64
Idaho	542	524	540	541	544	542	543	541	517	542	539	517	20
Illinois	542	547	568	586	594	606	585	600	577	599	617	591	5
Indiana	486	486	498	501	504	508	494	505	477	493	501	475	68
Iowa	584	588	589	600	596	608	603	613	582	596	606	575	3
Kansas	566	563	574	580	585	588	590	595	567	580	591	563	7
Kentucky	548	541	548	550	561	559	575	575	563	576	572	563	6
Louisiana	551	537	562	558	565	562	555	550	547	555	550	546	8
Maine	501	490	504	500	509	505	468	467	454	469	469	453	93
Maryland	506	502	507	509	511	515	501	506	495	499	502	491	74
Massachusetts	503	498	511	513	520	527	512	526	509	513	527	509	89
Michigan	529	534	557	569	568	579	585	605	576	583	604	573	5
Minnesota	552	558	581	594	592	597	594	607	580	593	608	577	7
Mississippi	552	538	562	549	564	554	566	548	552	564	543	553	4
Missouri	548	541	572	577	588	588	593	595	580	592	593	579	5
Montana	540	542	543	546	540	540	538	538	517	539	537	516	26
Nebraska	559	562	560	571	574	579	585	593	568	585	591	569	5
Nevada	511	511	510	517	508	513	496	501	473	494	496	470	47
New Hampshire	518	510	520	519	525	525	520	524	510	523	525	511	77
New Jersey	495	498	498	513	503	517	495	514	497	495	516	497	78
New Mexico	554	546	549	543	558	547	553	549	534	548	541	529	12
New York	489	496	494	506	497	511	484	499	478	485	499	476	89
North Carolina	478	470	492	496	499	511	497	511	477	493	508	474	67
North Dakota	579	578	588	609	590	605	580	594	559	586	612	561	3
Ohio	526	522	533	539	539	543	538	548	522	539	545	522	21
Oklahoma	553	542	563	560	570	563	569	568	547	571	565	547	6
Oregon	515	509	527	527	526	528	523	524	499	520	521	499	56
Pennsylvania	497	490	498	497	501	503	492	501	480	493	501	479	73
Rhode Island	498	488	505	500	503	505	494	495	488	495	493	489	68
South Carolina	475	467	484	482	494	499	484	495	468	482	490	464	70
South Dakota	580	570	587	588	589	589	592	603	571	584	591	562	4
Tennessee	558	544	563	553	572	563	576	571	565	575	568	567	10
Texas	490	489	493	500	493	502	484	505	473	479	502	465	58
Utah	566	555	570	569	566	557	568	559	547	563	559	545	6
Vermont	507	493	513	508	521	517	519	521	506	515	518	505	67
Virginia	501	496	509	500	516	514	512	512	497	512	509	495	71
Washington	513	511	526	528	532	534	524	532	508	523	529	508	57
West Virginia	520	514	526	511	523	511	515	507	500	514	501	497	17
Wisconsin	552	559	584	597	592	599	595	604	579	590	602	575	5
Wyoming	534	538	545	545	544	543	570	567	546	572	569	551	5
National average	500	501	505	514	508	520	501	516	492	497	514	489	43

Note: In 1995, the College Board recentered the scoring scale for the SAT by reestablishing the original mean score of 500 on the 200-800 scale. The College Board states that comparing states or ranking them on the basis of SAT scores alone is invalid, and the College Board discourages doing so. (1) In 2005, the SAT was changed. The verbal portion became critical reading, and a new writing test was added. The 2006 graduating class was the first to take the new test. (2) Based on number of high school graduates in 2011, as projected by the Western Interstate Commission for Higher Education, and number of students in the class of 2011 who took the SAT.

Top 100 Libraries in U.S. by Volumes Held, 2009

Source: American Library Association, *ALA Library Fact Sheet Number 22*

Rank	Institution	Volumes held	Rank	Institution	Volumes held
1.	Library of Congress	33,515,702	51.	North Carolina State Univ.	4,158,190
2.	Boston Public Library[1]	24,079,520	52.	Univ. of California–Davis	4,156,170
3.	New York Public Library[1]	16,640,294	53.	Univ. of Southern California	4,124,253
4.	Harvard Univ.	16,557,002	54.	Louisiana State Univ.	4,112,774
5.	Univ. of Illinois–Urbana-Champaign	12,780,067	55.	King County Library System (WA)	4,095,811
6.	Yale Univ.	12,564,157	56.	Texas A&M Univ.	4,088,969
7.	Univ. of California–Berkeley	11,026,554	57.	Miami-Dade Public Library System	4,086,243
8.	Columbia Univ.	10,449,223	58.	Tulane Univ.	4,004,458
9.	Univ. of Texas–Austin	9,853,414	59.	Univ. of Connecticut	3,982,991
10.	Univ. of Michigan	9,575,256	60.	San Diego Public Library	3,956,526
11.	Univ. of California–Los Angeles	9,045,818	61.	Brown Univ.	3,936,274
12.	Public Library of Cincinnati and Hamilton County (OH)	8,959,303	62.	Allen County Public Library (IN)	3,861,218
13.	Univ. of Chicago	8,830,151	63.	State Univ. of New York–Buffalo	3,852,074
14.	Indiana Univ.	8,543,025	64.	Houston Public Library	3,809,224
15.	Stanford Univ.	8,500,000	65.	Univ. of Kentucky	3,784,382
16.	Univ. of Wisconsin–Madison	8,310,732	66.	Univ. of Maryland	3,767,653
17.	Cornell Univ.	8,036,029	67.	Temple Univ.	3,761,933
18.	Univ. of Washington	7,549,765	68.	Univ. of Rochester	3,740,714
19.	Queens Borough Public Library (NY)	7,384,276	69.	Johns Hopkins Univ.	3,737,404
20.	Detroit Public Library	7,252,846	70.	Univ. of Cincinnati	3,715,957
21.	Princeton Univ.	7,075,441	71.	Univ. of South Carolina	3,675,054
22.	Univ. of Minnesota	6,975,576	72.	Wayne State Univ.	3,665,628
23.	Univ. of North Carolina–Chapel Hill	6,735,325	73.	Hawaii State Public Library System	3,657,735
24.	County of Los Angeles Public Library	6,434,367	74.	Univ. of Massachusetts–Amherst	3,654,181
25.	Univ. of Pennsylvania	6,223,214	75.	Univ. of California–San Diego	3,651,393
26.	Ohio State Univ.	6,206,443	76.	Univ. of Hawaii	3,588,005
27.	Duke Univ.	6,031,761	77.	Mid-Continent Public Library (MO)	3,565,744
28.	Univ. of Pittsburgh	5,897,931	78.	Univ. of Missouri–Columbia	3,523,795
29.	Univ. of Arizona	5,794,299	79.	Emory Univ.	3,479,536
30.	Chicago Public Library	5,743,002	80.	Univ. of Notre Dame	3,469,001
31.	Univ. of Virginia	5,605,891	81.	Vanderbilt Univ.	3,467,542
32.	Univ. of Oklahoma	5,433,036	82.	Auburn Univ.	3,459,542
33.	Pennsylvania State Univ.	5,365,489	83.	Georgetown Univ.	3,431,948
34.	Michigan State Univ.	5,292,806	84.	Buffalo & Erie County Public Library (NY)	3,431,653
35.	New York Univ.	5,191,617	85.	Univ. of Utah	3,418,976
36.	Univ. of Iowa	5,155,258	86.	Univ. of Alabama	3,396,810
37.	Free Library of Philadelphia	4,970,401	87.	St. Louis Public Library	3,396,219
38.	Northwestern Univ.	4,930,613	88.	Broward County Libraries Division (FL)	3,392,940
39.	Hennepin County Library (MN)	4,793,215	89.	Cuyahoga County Public Library (OH)	3,337,733
40.	Univ. of Georgia	4,716,401	90.	Univ. of Tennessee–Knoxville	3,322,418
41.	Rutgers Univ.	4,570,477	91.	Univ. of Miami	3,300,370
42.	Cleveland Public Library	4,565,137	92.	Univ. of Nebraska–Lincoln	3,247,311
43.	Dallas Public Library	4,511,524	93.	Syracuse Univ.	3,201,031
44.	Brooklyn Public Library (NY)	4,407,843	94.	Southern Illinois Univ.–Carbondale	3,149,701
45.	Arizona State Univ.	4,393,156	95.	Jacksonville Public Library	3,147,971
46.	Univ. of Colorado	4,348,639	96.	Univ. of California–Irvine	3,145,926
47.	Univ. of Florida	4,299,252	97.	Univ. of New Mexico	3,117,590
48.	Washington Univ.–St. Louis	4,281,213	98.	Massachusetts Institute of Technology	3,057,604
49.	Univ. of Kansas	4,271,113	99.	Florida State Univ.	3,034,491
50.	Brigham Young Univ.	4,168,102	100.	Univ. of Oregon Libraries	3,026,119

Note: For academic libraries, a volume is a single physical unit of any printed, typewritten, handwritten, mimeographed, or processed work, distinguished from other units by a separate binding, encasement, portfolio, or other clear distinction, which has been cataloged, classified, and made ready for use, and which is typically the unit used to charge circulation transactions. For public libraries, holdings are the number of cataloged items plus paperbacks and videocassettes even if uncataloged. (1) Includes both public library and research library collection numbers.

Number of Public Libraries and Operating Income by State, 2008

Source: Public Libraries Survey, Institute of Museum and Library Services

State	No.[1]	Income[2] (thous.)	State	No.[1]	Income[2] (thous.)	State	No.[1]	Income[2] (thous.)	State	No.[1]	Income[2] (thous.)
AL	210	$98,557	IL	634	$714,485	MT	80	$22,416	RI	48	$47,599
AK	86	31,847	IN	238	288,458	NE	270	48,035	SC	42	114,403
AZ	86	199,710	IA	539	99,122	NV	22	101,658	SD	114	21,664
AR	51	62,599	KS	327	108,371	NH	231	51,722	TN	187	103,860
CA	181	1,326,125	KY	116	151,674	NJ	303	495,335	TX	561	449,846
CO	115	258,686	LA	68	185,157	NM	91	47,396	UT	69	85,348
CT	195	178,261	ME	272	39,734	NY	755	1,135,733	VT	183	20,637
DE	21	25,985	MD	24	269,984	NC	77	209,891	VA	91	277,222
DC	1	45,836	MA	370	262,334	ND	81	12,832	WA	64	336,147
FL	80	661,524	MI	384	444,180	OH	251	730,592	WV	97	33,406
GA	59	208,289	MN	138	198,576	OK	115	92,084	WI	381	212,951
HI	1	35,414	MS	50	48,273	OR	126	169,587	WY	23	27,975
ID	104	42,948	MO	152	211,365	PA	457	345,622	**Total U.S.**	**9,221**	**11,391,455**

(1) Includes central libraries only. (2) Some totals may be underestimated because of nonresponse.

Four-Year Colleges and Universities
General Information for the 2010-11 Academic Year

Source: Peterson's College Database © 2011 Peterson's Nelnet, LLC. All rights reserved.

Note: These listings **include only accredited degree-granting institutions** in the U.S. and the U.S. territories with a total enrollment of 1,000 or more. Only four-year colleges and universities (which award a bachelor's degree as their highest undergraduate degree) are included. Data reported **only for institutions that provided updated information** on Peterson's Annual Survey of Undergraduate Institutions for the 2010-11 academic year.

All institutions are coeducational except those where the ZIP code is followed directly by a number in parentheses. (1) = men only, (2) = primarily men, (3) = women only, (4) = primarily women.

The **Tuition & fees** column shows the annual tuition and required fees for full-time students, or, where indicated, the tuition and standard fees per unit for part-time students. Where tuition varies according to residence, the figure is given for the most local resident and is coded as follows: (A) = area residents, (S) = state residents; all other figures apply to all students regardless of residence. Where annual expenses are expressed as a lump sum (including full-time tuition, mandatory fees, and room and board), the figure is entered under Tuition & fees and coded (C) = comprehensive fee. **Room & board** is the average cost for one academic year.

Control: 1 = independent (nonprofit), 2 = independent-religious, 3 = proprietary (profit-making), 4 = federal, 5 = state, 6 = commonwealth (Puerto Rico), 7 = territory (U.S. territories), 8 = county, 9 = district, 10 = city, 11 = state and local, 12 = state-related, 13 = private (unspecified). **Degree** means the highest degree offered: B = bachelor's, M = master's, D = doctorate.

Enrollment is the total number of matriculated undergraduate and (if applicable) graduate students.

Faculty is the total number of faculty members teaching undergraduate courses and (if available) graduate courses.

Grad. rate is the percentage of full-time, first-time bachelor's (or equivalent) degree-seeking undergraduate students who obtain their degrees within six years.

NA indicates category is inapplicable or data is not available from a consistent source.

Name, address	Year founded	Tuition & fees	Room & board	Control, degree	Enroll- ment	Faculty	Grad. rate
Abilene Christian Univ., Abilene, TX 79699-9100	1906	$22,760	$7,884	2-D	4,728	368	58.0%
Abraham Baldwin Agr. Coll., Tifton, GA 31793	1933	$3,496(S)	$7,220	5-B	3,327	162	NA
Academy of Art Univ., San Francisco, CA 94105-3410	1929	$18,050	$13,400	3-M	15,791	1,301	32.0
Adams State Coll., Alamosa, CO 81102	1921	$4,971(S)	$7,060	5-M	3,231	175	24.0
Adelphi Univ., Garden City, NY 11530-0701	1896	$26,915	$11,000	1-D	7,917	967	68.0
Adrian Coll., Adrian, MI 49221-2575	1859	$25,900	$7,900	2-B	1,469	177	50.0
Alabama A&M Univ., Huntsville, AL 35811	1875	$5,800(S)	$6,200	5-D	5,814	290	NA
Alabama State Univ., Montgomery, AL 36101-0271	1867	$7,164(S)	$4,800	5-D	5,705	407	24.0
Albany Coll. of Pharmacy & Health Sci., Albany, NY 12208	1881	$25,120	$9,400	1-D	1,597	141	68.0
Albany State Univ., Albany, GA 31705-2717	1903	$5,752(S)	$8,208	5-M	4,653	278	45.0
Albertus Magnus Coll., New Haven, CT 06511-1189	1925	$24,374	$10,460	2-M	1,961	65	54.0
Albion Coll., Albion, MI 49224-1831	1835	$30,002	$8,510	2-B	1,860	171	73.0
Albright Coll., Reading, PA 19612-5234	1856	$32,740	$8,858	2-M	2,401	168	61.0
Alcorn State Univ., Alcorn State, MS 39096-7500	1871	$4,858(S)	$7,348	5-M	3,682	210	38.0
Alfred Univ., Alfred, NY 14802-1205	1836	$25,976	$11,364	1-D	2,306	196	64.0
Allegheny Coll., Meadville, PA 16335	1815	$36,190	$9,160	1-B	2,153	197	78.0
Alliant Intl. Univ., San Diego, CA 92131-1799	1952	$16,570	$7,404	1-D	4,343	670	NA
Alma Coll., Alma, MI 48801-1599	1886	$29,230	$8,840	2-B	1,422	149	63.0
Alvernia Univ., Reading, PA 19607-1799	1958	$26,630	$9,487	2-D	2,906	308	53.0
Alverno Coll., Milwaukee, WI 53234-3922	1887	$21,063	$6,966	2-M	2,759	262	37.0
Amberton Univ., Garland, TX 75041-5595	1971	$5,600	NA	2-M	1,533	40	NA
American InterContinental Univ. Online, Hoffman Estates, IL 60192	1970	$355/credit	NA	3-M	22,424	396	NA
American Intl. Coll., Springfield, MA 01109-3189	1885	$27,535	$10,930	1-D	3,401	323	34.0
American Public Univ. System, Charles Town, WV 25414	1991	$6,000	NA	3-M	39,296	1,461	NA
American Univ., Washington, DC 20016-8001	1893	$36,697	$13,468	2-D	12,795	1,221	79.0
American Univ. of Puerto Rico, Bayamón, PR 00960-2037	1963	$4,865	NA	1-M	1,798	221	NA
Amherst Coll., Amherst, MA 01002-5000	1821	$40,862	$10,660	1-B	1,795	236	94.0
Anderson Univ., Anderson, IN 46012-3495	1917	$24,610	$8,560	2-D	2,565	279	57.0
Anderson Univ., Anderson, SC 29621-4035	1911	$22,570	$7,825	2-M	2,537	254	44.0
Andrews Univ., Berrien Springs, MI 49104	1874	$22,242	$7,140	2-D	3,487	290	52.0
Angelo State Univ., San Angelo, TX 76909	1928	$6,692(S)	$6,666	5-D	6,856	346	32.0
Anna Maria Coll., Paxton, MA 01612	1946	$418/cr. hr.	NA	2-M	1,498	221	46.0
Antioch Univ. Seattle, Seattle, WA 98121-1814	1975	$18,270	NA	1-D	1,080	NA	NA
Appalachian State Univ., Boone, NC 28608	1899	$5,175(S)	$6,600	5-D	17,222	1,216	66.0
Aquinas Coll., Grand Rapids, MI 49506-1799	1886	$23,206	$7,226	2-M	2,186	244	61.0
Arcadia Univ., Glenside, PA 19038-3295	1853	$34,150	$11,640	2-D	4,078	467	62.0
Argosy Univ., Sarasota, Sarasota, FL 34235	1974	NA	NA	3-D	NA	NA	NA
Argosy Univ., Schaumburg, Schaumburg, IL 60173-5403	1979	NA	NA	3-D	NA	NA	NA
Arizona State Univ., Tempe, AZ 85287	1885	$8,132(S)	$9,706	5-D	70,440	2,705	59.0
Arkansas State Univ., State University, AR 72467	1909	$6,640(S)	$6,544	5-D	13,415	650	33.0
Arkansas Tech. Univ., Russellville, AR 72801	1909	$5,908(S)	$5,270	5-M	9,815	463	38.0
Armstrong Atlantic State Univ., Savannah, GA 31419-1997	1935	$4,510(S)	$8,440	5-D	7,702	428	28.0
Art Ctr. Coll. of Design, Pasadena, CA 91103	1930	$32,592	NA	1-M	1,737	366	NA
Art Inst. of Boston at Lesley Univ., Boston, MA 02215-2598	1912	$27,600	$12,800	1-D	5,564	258	62.0
Asbury Univ., Wilmore, KY 40390-1198	1890	$24,229	$5,634	2-M	1,624	156	63.0
Ashford Univ., Clinton, IA 52733-2967	1918	$16,270	$6,000	3-M	10,568	748	NA
Ashland Univ., Ashland, OH 44805-3702	1878	$28,580	$9,352	2-D	6,491	591	59.0
Ashworth Coll., Norcross, GA 30092	1987	$1,846	NA	3-M	57,650	NA	NA
Assumption Coll., Worcester, MA 01609-1296	1904	$31,305	$10,260	2-M	2,562	224	72.0
Athens State Univ., Athens, AL 35611	1822	$4,860(S)	NA	5-B	3,621	210	NA
Atlanta Christian Coll., East Point, GA 30344-1999	1937	$15,902	$5,850	2-B	1,023	92	22.0
Atlantic Coll., Guaynabo, PR 00970	1983	NA	NA	1-M	1,236	NA	NA
Auburn Univ., Auburn, AL 36849	1856	$7,900(S)	$9,630	5-D	25,078	1,357	66.0
Auburn Univ. Montgomery, Montgomery, AL 36124-4023	1967	$7,280(S)	$3,820	5-D	5,800	315	23.0
Augsburg Coll., Minneapolis, MN 55454-1351	1869	$30,418	$8,072	2-D	4,073	403	62.0
Augustana Coll., Rock Island, IL 61201-2296	1860	$33,363	$8,466	2-B	2,532	273	78.0
Augustana Coll., Sioux Falls, SD 57197	1860	$25,104	$6,260	2-M	1,820	171	67.0
Augusta State Univ., Augusta, GA 30904-2200	1925	$5,184(S)	$5,250	5-M	7,061	435	21.0
Aurora Univ., Aurora, IL 60506-4892	1893	$18,700	$8,800	1-D	4,355	418	48.0
Austin Coll., Sherman, TX 75090-4400	1849	$31,270	$10,078	2-M	1,314	127	79.0
Austin Peay State Univ., Clarksville, TN 37044	1927	$6,048(S)	$6,450	5-M	10,723	592	34.0
Avila Univ., Kansas City, MO 64145-1698	1916	$21,900	$6,350	2-M	1,876	200	50.0
Azusa Pacific Univ., Azusa, CA 91702-7000	1899	$28,800	$7,082	2-D	9,258	393	67.0
Babson Coll., Babson Park, MA 02457-0310	1919	$39,040	$12,876	1-M	3,445	268	91.0
Baker Coll. of Allen Park, Allen Park, MI 48101 (4)	2003	$7,560	NA	1-B	3,926	88	NA
Baker Coll. of Auburn Hills, Auburn Hills, MI 48326-1586	1911	$7,560	NA	1-B	4,179	155	NA
Baker Coll. of Cadillac, Cadillac, MI 49601	1986	$7,560	NA	1-B	2,094	105	NA
Baker Coll. of Clinton Township, Clinton Township, MI 48035-4701	1990	$7,560	NA	1-B	6,265	208	NA

Name, address	Year founded	Tuition & fees	Room & board	Control, degree	Enrollment	Faculty	Grad. rate
Baker Coll. of Flint, Flint, MI 48507-5508	1911	$7,560	$3,000	1-B	7,166	315	NA
Baker Coll. of Jackson, Jackson, MI 49202	1994	$7,580	NA	1-B	2,917	85	NA
Baker Coll. of Muskegon, Muskegon, MI 49442-3497	1888	$7,560	$3,000	1-B	5,810	177	NA
Baker Coll. of Owosso, Owosso, MI 48867-4400	1984	$7,580	$2,700	1-B	3,532	144	NA
Baker Coll. of Port Huron, Port Huron, MI 48060-2597.	1990	$7,560	NA	1-B	1,776	126	NA
Baldwin-Wallace Coll., Berea, OH 44017-2088	1845	$25,260	$8,300	2-M	4,352	415	71.0%
Ball State Univ., Muncie, IN 47306-1099	1918	$8,214(S)	$8,208	5-D	22,083	1,207	58.0
Baptist Coll. of Health Sci, Memphis, TN 38104 (4)	1994	$10,270	$900	2-B	1,022	106	NA
Bard Coll., Annandale-on-Hudson, NY 12504	1860	$41,670	$11,810	1-D	2,264	241	76.0
Barnard Coll., New York, NY 10027-6598 (3)	1889	$40,546	$12,950	1-B	2,456	361	87.0
Barry Univ., Miami Shores, FL 33161-6695	1940	$845/credit	NA	2-D	8,995	861	37.0
Barton Coll., Wilson, NC 27893-7000.	1902	$21,784	$7,316	2-M	1,186	119	37.0
Bates Coll., Lewiston, ME 04240-6028.	1855	$53,300(C)	NA	1-B	1,725	183	88.0
Bayamón Central Univ., Bayamón, PR 00960-1725.	1970	NA	NA	2-M	2,287	NA	NA
Baylor Univ., Waco, TX 76798	1845	$29,754	$8,331	2-D	14,614	1,146	70.0
Bay Path Coll., Longmeadow, MA 01106-2292	1897	$25,515	$10,440	1-M	2,034	197	54.0
Becker Coll., Worcester, MA 01609	1784	$26,880	$10,020	1-B	1,752	184	27.0
Belhaven Univ., Jackson, MS 39202-1789	1883	$17,700	$6,500	2-M	3,099	123	54.0
Bellarmine Univ., Louisville, KY 40205-0671	1950	$30,310	$8,820	2-D	3,342	320	65.0
Bellevue Univ., Bellevue, NE 68005-3098	1965	$7,600	NA	1-M	9,448	NA	NA
Belmont Abbey Coll., Belmont, NC 28012-1802.	1876	$24,584	$10,272	2-B	1,734	154	36.0
Belmont Univ., Nashville, TN 37212-3757	1951	$23,680	$11,680	2-D	5,896	648	68.0
Beloit Coll., Beloit, WI 53511-5596.	1846	$35,038	$7,164	1-B	1,397	138	77.0
Bemidji State Univ., Bemidji, MN 56601-2699	1919	$7,513(S)	$6,480	5-M	5,365	276	52.0
Benedict Coll., Columbia, SC 29204	1870	$16,370	$7,530	2-B	2,641	NA	NA
Benedictine Coll., Atchison, KS 66002-1499	1859	$20,475	$7,375	2-M	1,959	188	52.0
Benedictine Univ., Lisle, IL 60532-0900	1887	$23,750	$7,500	2-D	6,892	337	54.0
Bentley Univ., Waltham, MA 02452-4705	1917	$38,328	$12,520	1-D	5,695	471	88.0
Berea Coll., Berea, KY 40404.	1855	$910	$5,574	1-B	1,613	158	64.0
Berkeley Coll., Woodland Park, NJ 07424-3353.	1931	$20,700	$11,100	3-B	3,709	NA	NA
Berkeley Coll.–New York City Campus, New York, NY 10017-4604	1936	$20,700	NA	3-B	4,430	NA	NA
Berklee Coll. of Music, Boston, MA 02215-3693	1945	$32,520	$15,830	1-B	4,145	530	47.0
Bernard M. Baruch Coll. of the City Univ. of New York, New York, NY 10010-5585.	1919	$5,020(S)	$9,975	11-M	16,195	1,166	60.0
Berry Coll., Mount Berry, GA 30149-0159	1902	$24,620	$8,724	2-M	2,087	218	60.0
Bethel Coll., Mishawaka, IN 46545-5591	1947	$23,030	$7,070	2-M	2,152	222	58.0
Bethel Univ., St. Paul, MN 55112-6999	1871	$29,460	$8,530	2-D	5,391	303	69.0
Bethel Univ., McKenzie, TN 38201	1842	$13,552	$7,782	2-M	3,141	291	34.0
Beth Medrash Govoha, Lakewood, NJ 08701-2797 (1)	1943	NA	NA	2-M	5,639	NA	NA
Bethune-Cookman Univ., Daytona Beach, FL 32114-3099	1904	$13,572	$7,980	2-M	3,577	230	37.0
Biola Univ., La Mirada, CA 90639-0001	1908	$28,897	$8,000	2-D	6,101	493	70.0
Birmingham-Southern Coll., Birmingham, AL 35254	1856	$27,890	$9,320	2-B	1,542	134	72.0
Black Hills State Univ., Spearfish, SD 57799	1883	$6,951(S)	$5,729	5-M	4,076	241	28.0
Bloomfield Coll., Bloomfield, NJ 07003-9981	1868	$22,400	$10,600	2-M	2,180	220	27.0
Bloomsburg Univ. of Pennsylvania, Bloomsburg, PA 17815-1301	1839	$7,456(S)	$6,890	5-D	10,091	487	63.0
Bluefield State Coll., Bluefield, WV 24701-2198.	1895	$4,596(S)	NA	5-B	2,063	147	14.0
Bluffton Univ., Bluffton, OH 45817.	1899	$26,154	$8,757	2-M	1,129	104	58.0
Bob Jones Univ., Greenville, SC 29614	1927	$12,120	$5,100	2-D	3,794	354	64.0
Boise State Univ., Boise, ID 83725-0399	1932	$5,300(S)	$5,610	5-D	19,992	1,161	28.0
Boricua Coll., New York, NY 10032-1560.	1974	$9,500	NA	1-M	1,058	133	49.0
Boston Arch Coll., Boston, MA 02115-2795	1889	$16,148	NA	1-M	1,091	229	0.0
Boston Coll., Chestnut Hill, MA 02467-3800	1863	$40,542	$12,082	2-D	14,191	1,394	91.0
Boston Univ., Boston, MA 02215	1839	$39,864	$12,260	1-D	32,727	2,630	84.0
Bowdoin Coll., Brunswick, ME 04011.	1794	$41,565	$11,315	1-B	1,762	216	93.0
Bowie State Univ., Bowie, MD 20715-9465	1865	$6,154(S)	$8,570	5-D	5,578	400	40.0
Bowling Green State Univ., Bowling Green, OH 43403	1910	$9,704(S)	$7,800	5-D	17,706	919	61.0
Bradley Univ., Peoria, IL 61625-0002	1897	$25,424	$7,950	1-D	5,800	549	78.0
Brandeis Univ., Waltham, MA 02454-9110	1948	$40,274	$11,214	1-D	5,642	506	87.0
Briarcliffe Coll., Bethpage, NY 11714	1966	NA	NA	3-B	1,779	NA	NA
Briar Cliff Univ., Sioux City, IA 51104-0100	1930	$23,418	$7,290	2-M	1,156	107	55.0
Bridgewater Coll., Bridgewater, VA 22812-1599.	1880	$25,500	$10,350	2-B	1,688	143	64.0
Bridgewater State Univ., Bridgewater, MA 02325-0001	1840	$7,053(S)	$9,670	5-M	11,220	661	53.0
Brigham Young Univ., Provo, UT 84602-1001.	1875	$4,560	$7,120	2-D	33,841	1,728	78.0
Brigham Young Univ.–Hawaii, Laie, HI 96762-1294	1955	$4,330	$4,756	2-B	2,555	228	52.0
Brigham Young Univ.–Idaho, Rexburg, ID 83460	1888	$3,660	$4,160	2-B	14,944	NA	NA
Brookline Coll., Phoenix, AZ 85021	1979	$13,000	NA	3-B	1,072	43	NA
Brooklyn Coll. of the City Univ. of New York, Brooklyn, NY 11210-2889.	1930	$5,284(S)	NA	11-D	17,094	1,401	43.0
Brooks Inst., Santa Barbara, CA 93101	1945	NA	NA	3-M	1,240	NA	NA
Brown Univ., Providence, RI 02912	1764	$42,230	$10,906	1-D	8,695	977	95.0
Bryan Coll., Dayton, TN 37321-7000	1930	$18,740	$5,454	2-M	1,304	66	55.0
Bryant & Stratton Coll., Wauwatosa, WI 53226.	1854	NA	NA	3-B	1,264	NA	NA
Bryant Univ., Smithfield, RI 02917	1863	$34,624	$12,829	1-M	3,606	288	76.0
Bryn Mawr Coll., Bryn Mawr, PA 19010-2899.	1885	$39,360	$12,420	1-D	1,755	211	87.0
Bucknell Univ., Lewisburg, PA 17837	1846	$43,866	$10,574	1-M	3,615	374	91.0
Buena Vista Univ., Storm Lake, IA 50588.	1891	$26,306	$7,582	2-M	1,073	116	58.0
Buffalo State Coll., State Univ. of New York, Buffalo, NY 14222-1095	1867	$6,053(S)	$9,748	5-M	11,714	878	48.0
Butler Univ., Indianapolis, IN 46208-3485	1855	$30,558	$10,130	1-D	4,640	479	73.0
Cabrini Coll., Radnor, PA 19087-3698	1957	$32,084	$11,400	2-M	3,440	327	53.0
Caldwell Coll., Caldwell, NJ 07006-6195	1939	$25,602	$8,990	2-M	2,284	NA	NA
California Baptist Univ., Riverside, CA 92504-3206	1950	$24,654	$8,370	2-M	4,715	334	50.0
California Coll., San Diego, CA 92108	1978	NA	NA	3-B	1,299	NA	NA
California Coll. of the Arts, San Francisco, CA 94107.	1907	$35,222	$7,000	1-M	1,881	524	55.0
California Inst. of Integral Studies, San Francisco, CA 94103.	1968	$15,060	NA	1-D	1,166	NA	NA
California Inst. of Tech., Pasadena, CA 91125-0001	1891	$37,704	$11,676	1-D	2,175	317	90.0
California Inst. of the Arts, Valencia, CA 91355-2340	1961	$38,260	$9,626	1-D	1,454	314	60.0
California Lutheran Univ., Thousand Oaks, CA 91360-2787	1959	$31,000	$10,580	2-D	3,714	324	70.0
California Polytechnic State Univ., San Luis Obispo, San Luis Obispo, CA 93407	1901	$6,480(S)	$9,992	5-M	18,360	1,220	75.0
California State Polytechnic Univ., Pomona, Pomona, CA 91768-2557	1938	$4,806(S)	$10,011	5-M	20,747	955	57.0
California State Univ.–Bakersfield, Bakersfield, CA 93311	1970	$5,314(S)	$7,041	5-M	7,598	NA	42.0
California State Univ.–Channel Islands, Camarillo, CA 93012	2002	$5,074(S)	NA	5-D	3,599	294	NA
California State Univ.–Chico, Chico, CA 95929-0722	1887	$5,620(S)	$11,138	5-M	15,989	857	58.0
California State Univ.–Dominguez Hills, Carson, CA 90747-0001	1960	$4,849(S)	$10,085	5-M	13,854	645	31.0
California State Univ.–East Bay, Hayward, CA 94542-3000	1957	$4,872(S)	$10,029	5-D	14,749	820	48.0
California State Univ.–Fresno, Fresno, CA 93740-8027	1911	$4,230(S)	$10,200	5-D	21,500	1,138	48.0
California State Univ.–Fullerton, Fullerton, CA 92834-9480	1957	$4,971(S)	$9,632	5-D	35,590	1,680	51.0
California State Univ.–Long Beach, Long Beach, CA 90840	1949	$5,464(S)	$11,294	5-D	33,416	1,886	54.0
California State Univ.–Los Angeles, Los Angeles, CA 90032-8530	1947	$4,846(S)	$9,105	5-D	20,142	1,029	38.0

Name, address	Year founded	Tuition & fees	Room & board	Control, degree	Enrollment	Faculty	Grad. rate
California State Univ.–Monterey Bay, Seaside, CA 93955-8001	1994	$4,721(S)	$8,440	5-M	4,790	NA	41.0%
California State Univ.–Northridge, Northridge, CA 91330	1958	$5,076(S)	$12,414	5-M	35,272	1,833	48.0
California State Univ.–Sacramento, Sacramento, CA 95819	1947	$5,194(S)	$9,512	5-D	29,241	1,506	44.0
California State Univ.–San Bernardino, San Bernardino, CA 92407-2397	1965	$5,189(S)	NA	5-D	16,400	795	45.0
California State Univ.–San Marcos, San Marcos, CA 92096-0001	1990	$5,044(S)	$7,500	5-M	9,389	528	46.0
California State Univ.–Stanislaus, Turlock, CA 95382	1957	$5,994(S)	$8,250	5-D	8,305	438	50.0
California Univ. of Pennsylvania, California, PA 15419-1394	1852	$8,312(S)	$9,826	5-M	9,017	NA	NA
Calumet Coll. of St. Joseph, Whiting, IN 46394-2195	1951	$14,200	NA	2-M	1,292	126	20.0
Calvin Coll., Grand Rapids, MI 49546-4388	1876	$24,870	$8,525	2-M	3,991	388	77.0
Cambridge Coll., Cambridge, MA 02138-5304	1971	$13,280	NA	1-D	4,458	530	NA
Cameron Univ., Lawton, OK 73505-6377	1908	$4,336(S)	$3,668	5-M	6,354	327	15.0
Campbellsville Univ., Campbellsville, KY 42718-2799	1906	$20,740	$6,980	2-M	3,431	310	42.0
Campbell Univ., Buies Creek, NC 27506	1887	$22,520	$7,600	2-D	4,743	305	51.7
Canisius Coll., Buffalo, NY 14208-1098	1870	$30,077	$10,980	2-M	5,111	499	70.0
Capella Univ., Minneapolis, MN 55402	1993	$10,980	NA	3-D	31,998	NA	NA
Capital Univ., Columbus, OH 43209-2394	1830	$29,310	$7,864	2-D	3,629	388	60.0
Cardinal Stritch Univ., Milwaukee, WI 53217-3985	1937	$22,750	$6,700	2-M	6,255	458	56.0
Caribbean Univ., Bayamón, PR 00960-0493	1969	$4,340	NA	1-M	1,892	NA	NA
Carleton Coll., Northfield, MN 55057-4001	1866	$42,942	$11,238	1-B	2,020	235	93.0
Carlos Albizu Univ., Miami Campus, Miami, FL 33172-2209 (4)	1980	$12,048	NA	1-D	1,169	56	24.0
Carlow Univ., Pittsburgh, PA 15213-3165 (4)	1929	$22,600	$8,960	2-D	2,803	306	54.0
Carnegie Mellon Univ., Pittsburgh, PA 15213-3891	1900	$41,940	$10,750	1-D	11,618	972	86.0
Carroll Coll., Helena, MT 59625-0002	1909	$23,594	$7,518	2-B	1,409	157	62.0
Carroll Univ., Waukesha, WI 53186-5593	1846	$25,248	$7,736	2-D	3,385	330	57.0
Carson-Newman Coll., Jefferson City, TN 37760	1851	$21,778	$6,246	2-M	2,065	204	53.0
Carthage Coll., Kenosha, WI 53140	1847	$29,750	$8,150	2-M	2,778	NA	54.0
Case Western Reserve Univ., Cleveland, OH 44106	1826	$37,648	$11,400	1-D	9,837	932	82.0
Castleton State Coll., Castleton, VT 05735	1787	$9,468(S)	$8,446	5-M	2,215	220	46.0
Catawba Coll., Salisbury, NC 28144-2488	1851	$25,160	$8,700	2-M	1,358	106	58.0
Catholic Univ. of America, Washington, DC 20064	1887	$33,780	$12,742	2-D	6,967	746	69.0
Cazenovia Coll., Cazenovia, NY 13035-1084	1824	$26,736	$11,470	1-B	1,092	129	44.0
Cedar Crest Coll., Allentown, PA 18104-6196 (4)	1867	$28,967	$9,540	2-M	1,666	177	59.0
Cedarville Univ., Cedarville, OH 45314-0601	1887	$23,500	$5,086	2-M	3,208	207	67.0
Centenary Coll., Hackettstown, NJ 07840-2100	1867	$28,890	$9,720	2-M	2,694	207	52.0
Central Coll., Pella, IA 50219	1853	$26,242	$8,702	2-B	1,648	105	64.0
Central Connecticut State Univ., New Britain, CT 06050-4010	1849	$7,861(S)	$9,576	5-D	12,477	966	48.0
Central Methodist Univ., Fayette, MO 65248-1198	1854	$19,390	$6,240	2-M	1,031	88	40.0
Central Michigan Univ., Mount Pleasant, MI 48859	1892	$10,380(S)	$8,092	5-D	28,292	1,233	54.0
Central Pennsylvania Coll., Summerdale, PA 17093-0309	1881	$14,991	$6,570	3-B	1,482	127	63.0
Central State Univ., Wilberforce, OH 45384	1887	$5,480(S)	$8,198	5-M	2,288	189	19.0
Central Washington Univ., Ellensburg, WA 98926	1891	$7,113(S)	$8,901	5-M	10,662	601	55.4
Centre Coll., Danville, KY 40422-1394	1819	$42,500(C)	NA	1-B	1,241	127	86.0
Chadron State Coll., Chadron, NE 69337	1911	$5,052(S)	NA	5-M	2,649	NA	NA
Chamberlain Coll. of Nursing, Addison, IL 60101-6106	NA	NA	NA	3	1,505	93	NA
Chamberlain Coll. of Nursing, St. Louis, MO 63139-3215	1889	$14,880	NA	3-B	7,002	219	NA
Chaminade Univ. of Honolulu, Honolulu, HI 96816-1578	1955	$17,740	$10,420	2-M	1,755	120	NA
Champlain Coll., Burlington, VT 05402-0670	1878	$28,400	$12,520	1-M	2,374	324	65.0
Chapman Univ., Orange, CA 92866	1861	$40,234	$12,957	2-D	6,881	696	70.0
Charleston Southern Univ., Charleston, SC 29423-8087	1964	$19,814	$7,616	2-M	3,286	210	39.0
Charter Oak State Coll., New Britain, CT 06053-2142	1973	$203/cr. hr.(S)	NA	5-B	2,079	107	NA
Chatham Univ., Pittsburgh, PA 15232-2826	1869	$29,188	$8,873	1-D	2,266	273	60.0
Chestnut Hill Coll., Philadelphia, PA 19118-2693	1924	$29,100	$9,340	2-D	2,414	339	43.0
Cheyney Univ. of Pennsylvania, Cheyney, PA 19319	1837	$7,718(S)	$8,486	5-M	1,488	99	29.0
Chicago State Univ., Chicago, IL 60628	1867	NA	NA	5-M	6,810	433	NA
Chowan Univ., Murfreesboro, NC 27855	1848	$19,750	$7,410	2-B	1,080	60	NA
Christian Brothers Univ., Memphis, TN 38104-5581	1871	$24,870	$6,410	2-M	1,828	167	55.5
Christopher Newport Univ., Newport News, VA 23606-2998	1960	$13,220(S)	$9,540	5-M	4,916	350	60.0
Cincinnati Christian Univ., Cincinnati, OH 45204-3200	1924	$13,780	$6,710	2-D	1,028	93	NA
Citadel, Military Coll. of South Carolina, Charleston, SC 29409 (2)	1842	$11,020(S)	$5,889	5-M	3,402	240	76.0
City Coll. of the City Univ. of New York, New York, NY 10031-9198	1847	$4,830(S)	NA	11-D	15,553	1,536	39.0
City Univ. of Seattle, Bellevue, WA 98005	1973	$15,615	NA	1-M	2,885	1,045	NA
Claflin Univ., Orangeburg, SC 29115	1869	$13,172	$7,078	2-M	1,902	158	46.0
Claremont McKenna Coll., Claremont, CA 91711	1946	$42,480	$13,120	1-M	1,278	148	93.0
Clarion Univ. of Pennsylvania, Clarion, PA 16214	1867	$8,164(S)	$7,000	5-M	7,315	366	49.0
Clark Atlanta Univ., Atlanta, GA 30314	1865	$17,954	$8,124	2-D	3,941	279	42.0
Clarke Univ., Dubuque, IA 52001-3198	1843	$24,610	$7,340	2-D	1,255	157	63.0
Clarkson Univ., Potsdam, NY 13699	1896	$36,780	$12,050	1-D	3,330	247	72.0
Clark Univ., Worcester, MA 01610-1477	1887	$37,350	$7,100	1-D	3,451	270	77.0
Clayton State Univ., Morrow, GA 30260-0285	1969	$4,566(S)	$8,352	5-M	6,603	375	22.0
Clemson Univ., Clemson, SC 29634	1889	$12,346(S)	NA	5-D	18,317	1,277	79.0
Cleveland State Univ., Cleveland, OH 44115	1964	$8,466(S)	$10,285	5-D	17,323	1,069	29.0
Coastal Carolina Univ., Conway, SC 29528-6054	1954	$9,390(S)	$7,350	5-M	8,706	613	43.0
Coe Coll., Cedar Rapids, IA 52402-5092	1851	$30,860	$7,290	2-M	1,326	NA	70.0
Colby Coll., Waterville, ME 04901-8840	1813	$51,990(C)	NA	1-B	1,825	214	89.0
Colegio Universitario de San Juan, San Juan, PR 00918	1971	NA	NA	10-B	1,785	NA	NA
Colgate Univ., Hamilton, NY 13346-1386	1819	$41,870	$10,190	1-M	2,903	332	88.0
Coll. for Creative Studies, Detroit, MI 48202-4034	1926	$32,785	NA	1-M	1,361	249	59.0
Coll. of Charleston, Charleston, SC 29424-0001	1770	$10,314(S)	$9,843	5-M	11,532	909	66.0
Coll. of Coastal Georgia, Brunswick, GA 31520	1961	$3,120(S)	NA	5-B	3,438	150	NA
Coll. of Idaho, Caldwell, ID 83605	1891	$21,050	$7,700	1-M	1,013	100	62.0
Coll. of Mount St. Joseph, Cincinnati, OH 45233-1670	1920	$23,550	$7,392	2-D	2,474	254	66.0
Coll. of Mount St. Vincent, Riverdale, NY 10471-1093	1911	$26,910	$10,380	1-M	1,896	196	55.0
Coll. of New Jersey, Ewing, NJ 08628	1855	$13,273(S)	$10,358	5-M	7,115	733	86.0
Coll. of New Rochelle, New Rochelle, NY 10805-2308 (4)	1904	$28,010	$10,176	1-M	1,820	217	57.0
Coll. of Notre Dame of Maryland, Baltimore, MD 21210-2476 (4)	1873	$28,350	$9,500	2-D	2,971	238	64.0
Coll. of St. Benedict, Saint Joseph, MN 56374 (3)	1887	$32,246	$8,652	2-B	2,082	196	80.0
Coll. of St. Elizabeth, Morristown, NJ 07960-6989 (4)	1899	$26,887	$11,340	2-D	2,112	250	66.0
Coll. of St. Mary, Omaha, NE 68106 (3)	1923	$24,350	$6,700	2-D	1,070	188	47.0
Coll. of St. Rose, Albany, NY 12203-1419	1920	$25,464	$10,534	1-M	5,130	460	58.0
Coll. of St. Scholastica, Duluth, MN 55811-4199	1912	$29,506	$7,716	2-D	3,898	361	62.0
Coll. of Staten Island of the City Univ. of New York, Staten Island, NY 10314-6600	1955	$4,978(S)	NA	11-D	13,894	1,202	48.0
Coll. of the Holy Cross, Worcester, MA 01610-2395	1843	$41,488	$11,270	2-B	2,899	315	93.0
Coll. of the Ozarks, Point Lookout, MO 65726	1906	$430	$5,600	2-B	1,371	139	58.0
Coll. of William & Mary, Williamsburg, VA 23187-8795	1693	$12,188(S)	$8,684	5-D	8,000	NA	91.0
Coll. of Wooster, Wooster, OH 44691-2363	1866	$38,290	$9,310	2-B	2,003	174	76.0
Collins Coll., Tempe, AZ 85281-5206	1978	NA	NA	3-B	1,287	NA	NA
Colorado Christian Univ., Lakewood, CO 80226	1914	$22,040	$9,120	2-M	2,511	NA	NA

Name, address	Year founded	Tuition & fees	Room & board	Control, degree	Enroll-ment	Faculty	Grad. rate
Colorado Coll., Colorado Springs, CO 80903-3294	1874	$38,948	$9,416	1-M	2,091	203	87.0%
Colorado Sch. of Mines, Golden, CO 80401-1887	1874	$13,425(S)	$8,596	5-D	5,093	331	65.0
Colorado State Univ., Fort Collins, CO 80523-0015	1870	$6,985(S)	$8,744	5-D	29,932	962	64.0
Colorado State Univ.–Pueblo, Pueblo, CO 81001-4901	1933	$5,615(S)	$8,660	5-M	7,210	418	32.0
Colorado Tech. Univ. Colorado Springs, Colorado Springs, CO 80907-3896	1965	NA	NA	3-D	2,359	343	NA
Colorado Tech. Univ. Online, Colorado Springs, CO 80907	NA	NA	NA	3-M	25,797	613	NA
Columbia Coll., Columbia, MO 65216-0002	1851	$16,532	$6,254	2-M	1,327	117	42.0
Columbia Coll., Caguas, PR 00726	1966	$9,435	NA	3-M	1,344	93	6.0
Columbia Coll., Columbia, SC 29203-5998	1854	$25,050	$6,638	2-D	1,369	147	52.0
Columbia Coll. Chicago, Chicago, IL 60605-1996	1890	$20,190	$12,680	1-M	11,922	2,108	40.0
Columbia Intl. Univ., Columbia, SC 29230-3122	1923	$17,395	$6,410	2-D	1,139	53	53.0
Columbia Southern Univ., Orange Beach, AL 36561	1993	$200/credit	NA	3-D	23,242	240	40.0
Columbia Univ., New York, NY 10027	1754	$41,160	$10,570	1-D	5,766	1,796	96.0
Columbia Univ., School of General Studies, New York, NY 10027-6939	1754	$39,900	$12,960	1-B	1,464	1,048	NA
Columbus Coll. of Art & Design, Columbus, OH 43215-1758	1879	$25,824	$9,410	1-M	1,458	201	61.0
Columbus State Univ., Columbus, GA 31907-5645	1958	$5,896(S)	$7,296	5-M	8,298	473	33.0
Concordia Coll., Moorhead, MN 56562	1891	$29,360	$6,790	2-M	2,810	261	67.0
Concordia Univ., Irvine, CA 92612-3299	1972	$27,300	$8,590	2-M	2,927	314	53.0
Concordia Univ., Ann Arbor, MI 48105-2797	1963	$20,982	$7,828	2-M	1,075	95	38.0
Concordia Univ., Portland, OR 97211-6099	1905	$24,400	$7,100	2-M	1,709	172	54.0
Concordia Univ. Chicago, River Forest, IL 60305-1499	1864	$25,631	$8,250	2-D	5,223	316	49.0
Concordia Univ., Nebraska, Seward, NE 68434-1599	1894	$23,060	$6,110	2-M	2,146	157	62.0
Concordia Univ., St. Paul, St. Paul, MN 55104-5494	1893	$28,500	$7,500	2-M	2,808	344	53.0
Concordia Univ. Texas, Austin, TX 78726	1926	$21,800	$8,160	2-M	2,185	281	37.0
Concordia Univ. Wisconsin, Mequon, WI 53097-2402	1881	$22,150	$8,310	2-D	7,485	277	60.0
Concord Univ., Athens, WV 24712-1000	1872	$4,974(S)	$6,962	5-M	2,937	207	89.0
Connecticut Coll., New London, CT 06320-4196	1911	$43,990	$9,120	1-M	1,887	241	87.0
Converse Coll., Spartanburg, SC 29302-0006	1889	$26,138	$8,032	1-M	1,720	88	64.0
Cooper Union for the Advancement of Science & Art, New York, NY 10003-7120	1859	$39,150	$13,700	1-M	1,000	226	91.0
Coppin State Univ., Baltimore, MD 21216-3698	1900	$5,545(S)	$8,108	5-M	3,800	312	15.0
Corban Univ., Salem, OR 97301-9392	1935	$25,445	$7,980	2-M	1,123	101	55.0
Cornell Coll., Mount Vernon, IA 52314-1098	1853	$32,920	$7,730	2-B	1,193	88	70.0
Cornell Univ., Ithaca, NY 14853-0001	1865	$39,666	$12,650	1-D	20,939	1,802	93.0
Cornerstone Univ., Grand Rapids, MI 49525-5897	1941	$21,178	$6,786	2-D	2,606	128	53.0
Covenant Coll., Lookout Mountain, GA 30750	1955	$26,226	$7,450	2-M	1,049	84	55.0
Creighton Univ., Omaha, NE 68178-0001	1878	$30,578	$9,164	2-D	7,662	740	77.0
Crown Coll., St. Bonifacius, MN 55375-9001	1916	$21,470	$7,380	2-M	1,176	113	52.0
The Culinary Institute of America, Hyde Park, NY 12538-1499	1946	$25,560	$8,420	1-B	2,785	189	NA
Cumberland Univ., Lebanon, TN 37087	1842	$19,200	$7,600	1-M	1,375	122	31.0
Curry Coll., Milton, MA 02186-9984	1879	$32,210	$12,285	1-M	2,983	417	47.0
Daemen Coll., Amherst, NY 14226-3592	1947	$21,460	$9,850	1-D	2,921	258	49.1
Dakota State Univ., Madison, SD 57042-1799	1881	$7,171(S)	$5,004	5-D	3,058	127	44.0
Dallas Baptist Univ., Dallas, TX 75211-9299	1965	$18,690	$5,868	2-D	5,470	532	52.0
Dalton State Coll., Dalton, GA 30720	1963	$2,536(S)	$6,750	5-B	5,988	249	32.0
Dartmouth Coll., Hanover, NH 03755	1769	$40,437	$11,838	1-D	6,141	1,004	95.0
Davenport Univ., Grand Rapids, MI 49512	1866	$11,794	$8,412	1-M	11,730	1,000	NA
Davidson Coll., Davidson, NC 28035	1837	$38,866	$10,857	2-B	1,742	174	91.0
Defiance Coll., Defiance, OH 43512-1610	1850	$25,890	$8,450	2-M	1,086	99	50.0
Delaware State Univ., Dover, DE 19901-2277	1891	$7,561(S)	NA	5-D	3,819	343	NA
Delaware Valley Coll., Doylestown, PA 18901-2697	1896	$30,646	$10,842	1-M	2,241	189	51.0
Delta State Univ., Cleveland, MS 38733-0001	1924	$4,852(S)	$6,166	5-D	4,327	254	46.0
Denison Univ., Granville, OH 43023	1831	$40,210	$9,960	1-B	2,275	223	83.0
DePaul Univ., Chicago, IL 60604-2287	1898	$28,858	$10,955	2-D	25,145	1,862	68.0
DePauw Univ., Greencastle, IN 46135	1837	$34,905	$9,180	2-B	2,390	282	85.0
DeSales Univ., Center Valley, PA 18034-9568	1964	$28,000	$10,140	2-M	3,199	293	64.0
DeVry Coll. of New York, Long Island City, NY 11101	1998	$14,826	NA	3-M	1,784	64	NA
DeVry Univ., Phoenix, AZ 85021-2995	1967	$14,826	NA	3-M	1,915	120	NA
DeVry Univ., Fremont, CA 94555	1998	$14,826	NA	3-M	1,553	231	39.0
DeVry Univ., Long Beach, CA 90806	1984	$14,826	NA	3-M	1,172	101	32.0
DeVry Univ., Pomona, CA 91768-2642	1983	$14,826	NA	3-M	3,339	111	NA
DeVry Univ., Westminster, CO 80234-2010	1945	$14,826	NA	3-M	1,129	67	NA
DeVry Univ., Miramar, FL 33027-4150	2002	$14,826	NA	3-M	1,577	67	NA
DeVry Univ., Orlando, FL 32839	2000	$14,826	NA	3-M	2,367	170	NA
DeVry Univ., Decatur, GA 30030-2556	1969	$14,826	NA	3-M	3,912	150	NA
DeVry Univ., Addison, IL 60101-6106	1982	$14,826	NA	3-B	1,508	154	36.0
DeVry Univ., Chicago, IL 60618-5994	1931	$14,826	NA	3-M	2,446	182	NA
DeVry Univ., Naperville, IL 60563-2361	NA	$14,826	NA	3-M	8,828	2,248	NA
DeVry Univ., Tinley Park, IL 60477	2000	$14,826	NA	3-M	1,471	79	39.0
DeVry Univ., Kansas City, MO 64131	1931	$14,826	NA	3-M	1,484	78	NA
DeVry Univ., North Brunswick, NJ 08902-3362	1969	$14,826	NA	3-M	1,905	158	NA
DeVry Univ., Columbus, OH 43209-2705	1952	$14,826	NA	3-M	3,807	100	NA
DeVry Univ., Fort Washington, PA 19034	2002	$14,826	NA	3-M	1,300	133	NA
DeVry Univ., Houston, TX 77041	NA	$14,826	NA	3-M	2,348	183	NA
DeVry Univ., Irving, TX 75063-2439	1969	$14,826	NA	3-D	2,292	100	NA
DeVry Univ., Arlington, VA 22202	2001	$14,826	NA	3-M	1,026	158	NA
DeVry Univ., Federal Way, WA 98001	2001	$14,826	NA	3-M	1,008	86	NA
DeVry Univ. Online, Addison, IL 60101-6106	2000	$14,826	NA	3-M	30,564	3,200	NA
Dickinson Coll., Carlisle, PA 17013-2896	1773	$41,520	$10,430	1-B	2,414	239	83.0
Dickinson State Univ., Dickinson, ND 58601-4896	1918	$6,337(S)	$4,262	5-B	2,668	233	38.0
Dillard Univ., New Orleans, LA 70122-3097	1869	$542/cr. hr.	NA	2-B	1,187	127	27.0
Dixie State Coll. of Utah, St. George, UT 84770-3876	1911	$3,490(S)	$4,100	5-B	8,553	508	31.0
Doane Coll., Crete, NE 68333-2430	1872	$22,170	$6,460	2-M	1,049	123	54.0
Dominican Coll., Orangeburg, NY 10962-1210	1952	$21,990	$10,560	1-D	2,070	232	40.0
Dominican Univ., River Forest, IL 60305-1099	1901	$25,710	$8,000	2-D	3,748	413	65.0
Dominican Univ. of California, San Rafael, CA 94901-2298	1890	$37,350	$14,460	2-M	2,267	346	54.0
Dordt Coll., Sioux Center, IA 51250-1697	1955	$23,180	$6,520	2-M	1,416	142	66.0
Dowling Coll., Oakdale, NY 11769-1999	1955	$24,630	$10,770	1-D	5,198	457	36.0
Drake Univ., Des Moines, IA 50311-4516	1881	$28,382	$8,410	1-D	5,616	435	75.0
Drew Univ., Madison, NJ 07940-1493	1867	$39,550	$10,772	2-D	2,697	256	76.0
Drexel Univ., Philadelphia, PA 19104-2875	1891	$33,005	$13,125	1-D	22,493	1,499	67.0
Drury Univ., Springfield, MO 65802	1873	$21,043	$7,466	1-M	2,076	191	66.0
Duke Univ., Durham, NC 27708-0586	1838	$40,243	$11,622	2-D	14,350	1,155	95.0
Duquesne Univ., Pittsburgh, PA 15282-0001	1878	$27,502	$9,476	2-D	10,161	992	75.0
D'Youville Coll., Buffalo, NY 14201-1084	1908	$21,060	$9,800	1-D	2,971	322	63.0
Earlham Coll., Richmond, IN 47374-4095	1847	$36,694	$7,400	2-D	1,322	101	72.0
East Carolina Univ., Greenville, NC 27858-4353	1907	$4,797(S)	$7,700	5-D	27,654	1,474	57.0
East Central Univ., Ada, OK 74820-6899	1909	$4,482(S)	$4,480	5-M	4,906	279	32.0

Name, address	Year founded	Tuition & fees	Room & board	Control, degree	Enroll-ment	Faculty	Grad. rate
Eastern Connecticut State Univ., Willimantic, CT 06226-2295	1889	$8,350(S)	$10,048	5-M	5,574	446	50.0%
Eastern Illinois Univ., Charleston, IL 61920-3099	1895	$9,987(S)	$8,584	5-M	11,630	753	62.0
Eastern Kentucky Univ., Richmond, KY 40475-3102	1906	$6,624(S)	$6,714	5-D	15,839	1,039	39.0
Eastern Mennonite Univ., Harrisonburg, VA 22802-2462	1917	$25,060	$8,040	2-D	1,525	188	62.0
Eastern Michigan Univ., Ypsilanti, MI 48197	1849	$8,378(S)	$7,785	5-D	23,504	1,364	38.0
Eastern Nazarene Coll., Quincy, MA 02170	1918	$23,772	$8,000	2-M	1,075	103	54.0
Eastern New Mexico Univ., Portales, NM 88130	1934	$3,900(S)	$5,612	5-M	5,080	336	24.0
Eastern Oregon Univ., La Grande, OR 97850-2899	1929	$6,639(S)	$8,000	5-M	4,137	144	32.0
Eastern Univ., St. Davids, PA 19087-3696	1952	$24,550	$9,090	2-D	4,331	NA	NA
Eastern Washington Univ., Cheney, WA 99004-2431	1882	$6,604(S)	$7,470	5-D	11,534	628	47.0
East Stroudsburg Univ. of Pennsylvania, East Stroudsburg, PA 18301-2999	1893	$7,778(S)	$6,658	5-M	7,387	390	59.0
East Tennessee State Univ., Johnson City, TN 37614	1911	$5,823(S)	$5,783	5-D	14,952	841	39.0
East Texas Baptist Univ., Marshall, TX 75670-1498	1912	$20,500	$5,666	2-B	1,197	98	36.0
East-West Univ., Chicago, IL 60605-2103	1978	$15,750	NA	1-B	1,170	67	22.0
Eckerd Coll., St. Petersburg, FL 33711	1958	$34,546	$9,652	2-B	1,832	163	69.0
ECPI Coll. of Tech., Virginia Beach, VA 23462	1966	NA	NA	3-B	13,717	1,371	NA
Edgewood Coll., Madison, WI 53711-1997 (4)	1927	$21,988	$7,384	2-D	2,626	332	57.0
Edinboro Univ. of Pennsylvania, Edinboro, PA 16444	1857	$7,740(S)	$7,820	5-M	8,642	407	46.0
EDP Coll. of Puerto Rico, Inc., Hato Rey, PR 00918	1968	$6,120	NA	3-M	1,016	84	40.0
Elizabeth City State Univ., Elizabeth City, NC 27909-7806	1891	$2,204(S)	$5,639	5-M	3,307	241	42.0
Elizabethtown Coll., Elizabethtown, PA 17022-2298	1899	$34,830	$8,800	2-M	2,416	282	78.0
Ellis Univ., Chicago, IL 60606-7204	2008	$452/cr. hr.	NA	3-M	1,950	NA	NA
Elmhurst Coll., Elmhurst, IL 60126-3296	1871	$30,054	$8,524	2-M	3,430	375	70.0
Elmira Coll., Elmira, NY 14901	1855	$35,900	$11,150	1-M	1,840	212	NA
Elms Coll., Chicopee, MA 01013-2839 (4)	1928	$25,780	$9,810	2-M	1,260	NA	NA
Elon Univ., Elon, NC 27244-2010	1889	$27,881	$9,090	2-D	5,709	501	81.0
Embry-Riddle Aeron Univ.–Daytona, Daytona Beach, FL 32114-3900	1926	$29,852	$9,750	1-D	5,089	341	54.0
Embry-Riddle Aeron Univ.–Prescott, Prescott, AZ 86301-3720	1978	$29,672	$8,900	1-M	1,705	111	61.0
Embry-Riddle Aeron Univ.–Worldwide, Daytona Beach, FL 32114-3900	1970	$5,580	NA	1-D	16,423	2,531	NA
Emerson Coll., Boston, MA 02116-4624	1880	$31,272	$12,881	1-D	4,546	431	78.0
Emmanuel Coll., Boston, MA 02115	1919	$30,890	$12,300	2-M	2,457	191	61.0
Emory & Henry Coll., Emory, VA 24327-0947	1836	$26,000	$8,570	2-M	1,004	127	52.0
Emory Univ., Atlanta, GA 30322-1100	1836	$39,158	$11,198	2-D	13,381	1,475	88.0
Emporia State Univ., Emporia, KS 66801-5087	1863	$4,636(S)	$6,230	5-D	6,262	273	40.0
Endicott Coll., Beverly, MA 01915-2096	1939	$26,248	$12,388	1-M	4,105	288	69.0
Eugene Lang Coll.–The New School for Liberal Arts, New York, NY 10011-8601	1978	$36,090	$15,260	1-B	1,511	157	56.0
Evangel Univ., Springfield, MO 65802	1955	$16,990	$6,000	2-M	2,072	122	49.0
Everest Univ., Pompano Beach, FL 33062	1940	$14,328	NA	3-M	1,633	NA	NA
Everest Univ., Tampa, FL 33614-5899	1890	$47,332	NA	3-M	3,430	61	NA
Everest Univ., Tampa, FL 33619	1890	$16,452	NA	3-M	12,695	61	NA
Everglades Univ., Boca Raton, FL 33431	1989	$12,920	NA	1-M	1,039	NA	NA
Evergreen State Coll., Olympia, WA 98505	1967	$6,679(S)	$8,460	5-M	4,803	247	58.0
Excelsior Coll., Albany, NY 12203-5159	1970	$335/cr. hr.	NA	1-M	31,924	404	NA
Fairfield Univ., Fairfield, CT 06824-5195	1942	$39,040	$11,740	2-D	5,181	527	84.0
Fairleigh Dickinson Univ., Coll. at Florham, Madison, NJ 07940-1099	1942	$33,410	$11,578	1-M	3,288	NA	59.0
Fairleigh Dickinson Univ., Metropolitan Campus, Teaneck, NJ 07666-1914	1942	$31,060	$11,906	1-D	9,105	NA	50.0
Fairmont State Univ., Fairmont, WV 26554	1865	$5,172(S)	$7,236	5-M	4,709	334	35.0
Farmingdale State Coll., Farmingdale, NY 11735	1912	$6,093(S)	$11,780	5-B	6,988	555	33.8
Fashion Inst. of Tech., New York, NY 10001-5992 (4)	1944	$5,668(S)	$11,700	11-M	10,386	1,016	NA
Faulkner Univ., Montgomery, AL 36109-3398	1942	$14,810	$6,570	2-D	3,076	339	21.0
Fayetteville State Univ., Fayetteville, NC 28301-4298	1867	$3,756(S)	$5,812	5-D	5,781	336	45.0
Felician Coll., Lodi, NJ 07644-2117	1942	$27,925	$10,750	2-M	2,169	233	38.0
Ferris State Univ., Big Rapids, MI 49307	1884	$9,930(S)	$9,180	5-D	14,381	918	51.0
Ferrum Coll., Ferrum, VA 24088	1913	$24,945	$8,080	2-B	1,484	123	31.0
Fisher Coll., Boston, MA 02116-1500	1903	$25,778	$13,786	1-B	1,751	155	40.0
Fitchburg State Univ., Fitchburg, MA 01420-2697	1894	$7,800(S)	$8,106	5-M	6,771	285	52.0
Five Towns Coll., Dix Hills, NY 11746-6055	1972	$18,750	$13,060	1-D	1,447	133	NA
Flagler Coll., St. Augustine, FL 32085-1027	1968	$13,860	$7,590	1-B	2,753	218	64.0
Florida A&M Univ., Tallahassee, FL 32307-3200	1887	$4,248(S)	$7,856	5-D	13,284	746	39.0
Florida Atlantic Univ., Boca Raton, FL 33431-0991	1961	$4,797(S)	$9,690	5-D	28,325	1,284	38.0
Florida Gulf Coast Univ., Fort Myers, FL 33965-6565	1991	$6,728(S)	$8,150	5-M	12,034	589	45.0
Florida Hosp Coll. of Health Sci, Orlando, FL 32803	1913	$9,580	NA	1-M	2,207	84	NA
Florida Inst. of Tech., Melbourne, FL 32901-6975	1958	$32,294	$11,210	1-D	8,985	664	57.0
Florida Intl. Univ., Miami, FL 33199	1965	$5,091(S)	$11,440	5-D	42,287	1,798	45.0
Florida Memorial Univ., Miami-Dade, FL 33054	1879	$14,024	$6,112	2-M	1,750	173	33.0
Florida Natl.Coll., Hialeah, FL 33012	1982	$13,170	NA	3-B	2,819	134	NA
Florida Southern Coll., Lakeland, FL 33801-5698	1885	$26,112	$8,808	2-M	2,149	217	52.0
Florida State Univ., Tallahassee, FL 32306	1851	$5,235(S)	$9,180	5-D	40,416	1,614	71.0
Fontbonne Univ., St. Louis, MO 63105-3098	1917	$20,380	$7,800	2-M	2,532	279	45.0
Fordham Univ., New York, NY 10458	1841	$38,277	$12,890	2-D	14,544	1,386	79.0
Fort Hays State Univ., Hays, KS 67601-4099	1902	$2,457(S)	$6,625	5-M	11,537	NA	NA
Fort Lewis Coll., Durango, CO 81301-3999	1911	$4,924(S)	$7,840	5-B	3,864	257	36.0
Fort Valley State Univ., Fort Valley, GA 31030	1895	$5,562(S)	$7,326	5-D	3,571	202	39.0
Framingham State Univ., Framingham, MA 01701-9101	1839	$7,065(S)	$7,100	5-M	5,953	251	51.0
Franciscan Univ. of Steubenville, Steubenville, OH 43952-1763	1946	$20,320	$6,900	2-M	2,725	223	73.0
Francis Marion Univ., Florence, SC 29502-0547	1970	$8,802(S)	$6,620	5-M	4,032	293	40.0
Franklin & Marshall Coll., Lancaster, PA 17604-3003	1787	$41,150	$10,920	1-B	2,179	265	85.0
Franklin Coll., Franklin, IN 46131	1834	$24,655	$7,295	2-B	1,106	105	60.0
Franklin Pierce Univ., Rindge, NH 03461-0060	1962	$28,800	$10,100	1-D	2,396	316	50.0
Franklin Univ., Columbus, OH 43215-5399	1902	$11,880	NA	1-M	8,018	713	15.0
Freed-Hardeman Univ., Henderson, TN 38340-2399	1869	$15,922	$7,216	2-D	1,992	145	56.0
Fresno Pacific Univ., Fresno, CA 93702-4709	1944	$23,904	$6,300	2-M	2,353	355	60.0
Friends Univ., Wichita, KS 67213	1898	$20,040	$5,790	2-M	2,800	339	28.0
Frostburg State Univ., Frostburg, MD 21532-1099	1898	$6,904(S)	$7,378	5-M	5,385	360	49.0
Full Sail Univ., Winter Park, FL 32792-7437 (2)	1979	NA	NA	3-M	8,921	702	NA
Furman Univ., Greenville, SC 29613	1826	$38,088	$9,572	1-M	2,996	267	84.0
Gallaudet Univ., Washington, DC 20002-3625	1864	$11,226	$9,660	1-D	1,533	NA	35.0
Gannon Univ., Erie, PA 16541-0001	1925	$24,582	$9,720	2-D	4,219	346	63.0
Gardner-Webb Univ., Boiling Springs, NC 28017	1905	$22,410	$7,220	2-D	4,310	NA	48.0
Geneva Coll., Beaver Falls, PA 15010-3599	1848	$22,236	$8,000	2-M	1,720	172	61.0
George Fox Univ., Newberg, OR 97132-2697	1891	$27,970	$8,630	2-D	3,555	382	67.0
George Mason Univ., Fairfax, VA 22030	1957	$8,684(S)	$8,220	5-D	32,067	2,200	63.0
Georgetown Coll., Georgetown, KY 40324-1696	1829	$27,640	$7,320	2-M	1,851	167	68.0
Georgetown Univ., Washington, DC 20057	1789	$40,203	$12,240	2-D	16,871	1,749	93.0
George Washington Univ., Washington, DC 20052	1821	$42,905	$10,120	1-D	25,061	2,319	81.0
Georgia Coll. & State Univ., Milledgeville, GA 31061	1889	$7,852(S)	$8,414	5-M	6,737	419	59.0
Georgia Gwinnett Coll., Lawrenceville, GA 60043	2005	$5,074(S)	$8,700	5-B	5,380	324	NA
Georgia Health Science Univ., Augusta, GA 30912	1828	$8,182(S)	NA	5-D	2,438	824	NA
Georgia Inst. of Tech., Atlanta, GA 30332-0001	1885	$8,716(S)	$8,746	5-D	20,720	1,080	80.0

Name, address	Year founded	Tuition & fees	Room & board	Control, degree	Enrollment	Faculty	Grad. rate
Georgian Court Univ., Lakewood, NJ 08701-2697 (4)	1908	$26,176	$9,856	2-M	2,885	288	58.0%
Georgia Southern Univ., Statesboro, GA 30460	1906	$6,240(S)	$8,414	5-D	19,691	838	45.0
Georgia Southwestern State Univ., Americus, GA 31709-4693	1906	$4,454(S)	$6,977	5-M	2,405	155	32.7
Georgia State Univ., Atlanta, GA 30302-3083	1913	$8,698(S)	$9,325	5-D	31,538	1,495	48.0
Gettysburg Coll., Gettysburg, PA 17325-1483	1832	$41,070	$9,810	2-B	2,493	291	85.0
Glenville State Coll., Glenville, WV 26351-1200	1872	$4,888(S)	$7,350	5-B	1,721	102	39.0
Global Univ., Springfield, MO 65804	1948	$3,520	NA	2-D	4,551	633	NA
Globe Univ., Woodbury, MN 55125	1885	$19,575	NA	3-M	1,220	NA	NA
Golden Gate Univ., San Francisco, CA 94105-2968	1901	$15,390	NA	1-D	3,528	489	NA
Goldey-Beacom Coll., Wilmington, DE 19808-1999	1886	$19,860	$5,172	1-M	1,171	52	NA
Gonzaga Univ., Spokane, WA 99258	1887	$30,925	$8,300	2-D	7,637	727	82.0
Gordon Coll., Wenham, MA 01984-1899	1889	$30,606	$8,434	2-M	1,609	171	71.0
Goshen Coll., Goshen, IN 46526-4794	1894	$24,500	$8,300	2-M	1,017	122	70.0
Goucher Coll., Baltimore, MD 21204-2794	1885	$36,553	$10,569	1-M	2,299	215	66.0
Governors State Univ., University Park, IL 60466-0975	1969	$8,746(S)	NA	5-D	5,674	390	NA
Grace Coll., Winona Lake, IN 46590-1294	1948	$21,700	$7,074	2-D	1,773	101	60.0
Graceland Univ., Lamoni, IA 50140	1895	$20,980	$7,040	2-M	2,271	122	48.0
Grambling State Univ., Grambling, LA 71245	1901	$4,428(S)	$8,236	5-D	4,992	259	29.0
Grand Canyon Univ., Phoenix, AZ 85017-1097	1949	$18,000	$12,000	2-D	NA	NA	NA
Grand Valley State Univ., Allendale, MI 49401-9403	1960	$9,088(S)	$7,624	5-D	24,541	1,618	61.0
Grand View Univ., Des Moines, IA 50316-1599	1896	$20,292	$6,732	2-M	2,108	219	44.0
Granite State Coll., Concord, NH 03301	1972	$6,435(S)	NA	11-B	1,797	185	NA
Grantham Univ., Kansas City, MO 64153	1951	$7,950	NA	3-M	6,214	183	NA
Greensboro Coll., Greensboro, NC 27401-1875	1838	$25,000	$9,100	2-M	1,264	96	43.0
Greenville Coll., Greenville, IL 62246-0159	1892	$21,658	$7,338	2-M	1,605	169	59.0
Grinnell Coll., Grinnell, IA 50112-1690	1846	$39,810	$9,334	1-B	1,655	214	87.0
Grove City Coll., Grove City, PA 16127-2104	1876	$13,088	$7,132	2-B	2,499	209	83.0
Guilford Coll., Greensboro, NC 27410-4173	1837	$28,800	$7,950	2-B	2,828	220	61.0
Gustavus Adolphus Coll., St. Peter, MN 56082-1498	1862	$33,400	$8,400	2-B	2,475	243	82.0
Gwynedd-Mercy Coll., Gwynedd Valley, PA 19437-0901	1948	$25,660	$9,760	2-M	2,636	281	69.0
Hamilton Coll., Clinton, NY 13323-1296	1812	$41,280	$10,480	1-B	1,861	221	88.0
Hamline Univ., St. Paul, MN 55104-1284	1854	$31,802	$8,504	2-D	5,003	512	72.0
Hampden-Sydney Coll., Hampden-Sydney, VA 23943 (1)	1776	$32,364	$10,126	2-B	1,058	113	68.0
Hampshire Coll., Amherst, MA 01002	1965	$42,900	$11,180	1-B	1,529	163	69.0
Hampton Univ., Hampton, VA 23668	1868	$18,074	$8,048	1-D	5,401	428	NA
Hannibal-LaGrange Univ., Hannibal, MO 63401-1999	1858	$16,890	$6,200	2-M	1,191	146	49.0
Hanover Coll., Hanover, IN 47243-0108	1827	$28,850	$8,650	2-B	1,006	99	66.0
Harding Univ., Searcy, AR 72149-0001	1924	$14,040	$5,922	2-D	6,748	463	67.0
Hardin-Simmons Univ., Abilene, TX 79698-0001	1891	$22,460	$6,804	2-D	2,312	203	49.0
Harrington Coll. of Design, Chicago, IL 60605-1496 (4)	1931	$18,600	NA	3-M	1,116	109	14.0
Harris-Stowe State Univ., St. Louis, MO 63103-2136	1857	$5,320(S)	$8,080	5-B	1,886	199	NA
Hartwick Coll., Oneonta, NY 13820-4020	1797	$34,630	$9,345	1-B	1,531	187	57.0
Harvard Univ., Cambridge, MA 02138	1636	$38(4)	$12,308	1-D	10,583	2,189	97.0
Hastings Coll., Hastings, NE 68901-7696	1882	NA	NA	2-M	1,138	123	62.3
Haverford Coll., Haverford, PA 19041-1392	1833	$40,624	$12,346	1-B	1,177	139	92.0
Hawai`i Pacific Univ., Honolulu, HI 96813	1965	$15,820	$11,648	1-M	8,339	639	39.0
Heidelberg Univ., Tiffin, OH 44883-2462	1850	$22,780	$8,636	2-M	1,656	163	54.0
Henderson State Univ., Arkadelphia, AR 71999-0001	1890	$6,444(S)	$5,084	5-M	3,712	242	33.0
Hendrix Coll., Conway, AR 72032-3080	1876	$34,230	$9,714	2-B	1,467	139	60.0
Heritage Univ., Toppenish, WA 98948-9599	1982	$13,440	NA	1-M	1,115	NA	NA
High Point Univ., High Point, NC 27262-3598	1924	$35,900(C)	NA	2-M	3,603	292	55.0
Hilbert Coll., Hamburg, NY 14075-1597	1957	$18,490	$7,990	1-B	1,046	115	50.0
Hillsdale Coll., Hillsdale, MI 49242-1298	1844	$20,500	$7,990	1-B	1,391	161	76.0
Hiram Coll., Hiram, OH 44234-0067	1850	$27,135	$9,460	1-M	1,395	139	69.0
Hobart & William Smith Coll., Geneva, NY 14456-3397	1822	$41,710	$10,548	1-M	2,173	203	75.0
Hodges Univ., Naples, FL 34119	1990	$16,940	NA	1-M	2,292	115	NA
Hofstra Univ., Hempstead, NY 11549	1935	$31,800	$11,710	1-D	11,579	1,165	60.0
Hollins Univ., Roanoke, VA 24020-1603	1842	$29,485	$10,200	1-M	1,024	99	63.0
Holy Family Univ., Philadelphia, PA 19114	1954	$24,550	$11,750	2-D	3,270	259	55.0
Holy Names Univ., Oakland, CA 94619-1699 (4)	1868	$30,390	$10,260	2-M	1,216	138	31.0
Hood Coll., Frederick, MD 21701-8575	1893	$29,860	$9,901	1-M	2,447	259	77.0
Hope Coll., Holland, MI 49422-9000	1866	$27,020	$8,260	2-B	3,202	342	79.0
Hope Intl. Univ., Fullerton, CA 92831-3138	1928	$24,235	$7,800	2-M	1,059	120	44.0
Houghton Coll., Houghton, NY 14744	1883	$25,460	$7,330	2-M	1,272	128	68.0
Houston Baptist Univ., Houston, TX 77074-3298	1960	$23,180	$6,975	2-M	2,710	246	45.0
Howard Payne Univ., Brownwood, TX 76801-2715	1889	$19,950	$5,692	2-M	1,232	144	41.0
Howard Univ., Washington, DC 20059-0002	1867	$17,905	$8,498	1-D	10,288	1,520	65.0
Humboldt State Univ., Arcata, CA 95521-8299	1913	$6,496(S)	$10,486	5-M	7,902	499	37.0
Hunter Coll. of the City Univ. of New York, New York, NY 10021-5085	1870	$5,229(S)	$5,500	11-M	22,407	1,880	46.0
Huntingdon Coll., Montgomery, AL 36106-2148	1854	$20,990	$8,000	2-B	1,107	123	47.0
Huntington Univ., Huntington, IN 46750-1299	1897	$23,210	$7,680	2-M	1,260	186	58.0
Husson Univ., Bangor, ME 04401-2999	1898	$13,960	$7,520	1-D	3,216	109	40.4
Idaho State Univ., Pocatello, ID 83209	1901	$5,416(S)	$5,274	5-D	12,595	772	NA
Illinois Inst. of Tech., Chicago, IL 60616-3793	1890	$34,880	$10,338	1-D	7,774	722	66.0
Illinois State Univ., Normal, IL 61790-2200	1857	$11,417(S)	$8,436	5-D	21,134	1,184	69.0
Illinois Wesleyan Univ., Bloomington, IL 61702-2900	1850	$35,256	$8,106	1-B	2,094	232	81.0
Immaculata Univ., Immaculata, PA 19345 (4)	1920	$27,870	$11,460	2-D	4,456	423	60.0
Indiana State Univ., Terre Haute, IN 47809	1865	$7,714(S)	$7,752	5-D	11,494	663	40.0
Indiana Tech., Fort Wayne, IN 46803-1297	1930	$23,430	$8,790	1-D	4,456	325	30.0
Indiana Univ.–Bloomington, Bloomington, IN 47405-7000	1820	$9,028(S)	$7,918	5-D	42,464	2,271	71.0
Indiana Univ.–East, Richmond, IN 47374-1289	1971	$6,069(S)	NA	5-M	3,365	228	18.0
Indiana Univ.–Kokomo, Kokomo, IN 46904-9003	1945	$6,109(S)	NA	5-M	3,109	177	23.0
Indiana Univ.–Northwest, Gary, IN 46408-1197	1959	$6,193(S)	NA	5-M	5,969	390	19.0
Indiana Univ.–Purdue Univ. Fort Wayne, Fort Wayne, IN 46805-1499	1917	$6,545(S)	$5,900	5-M	14,192	827	23.0
Indiana Univ.–Purdue Univ. Indianapolis, Indianapolis, IN 46202-2896	1969	$7,885(S)	$7,944	5-D	30,566	3,190	34.0
Indiana Univ.–South Bend, South Bend, IN 46634-7111	1922	$6,290(S)	$5,382	5-M	8,590	559	25.0
Indiana Univ.–Southeast, New Albany, IN 47150-6405	1941	$6,163(S)	$5,686	5-M	7,178	479	27.0
Indiana Univ. of Pennsylvania, Indiana, PA 15705-1087	1875	$7,571(S)	$9,300	5-D	15,126	701	54.0
Indiana Wesleyan Univ., Marion, IN 46953-4974	1920	$21,956	$7,148	2-D	3,201	284	67.0
Inter American Univ. of Puerto Rico–Aguadilla, Aguadilla, PR 00605	1957	$5,495	NA	1-M	4,502	231	20.0
Inter American Univ. of Puerto Rico–Arecibo, Arecibo, PR 00614-4050	1957	$4,596	NA	1-M	4,878	298	NA
Inter American Univ. of Puerto Rico–Barranquitas, Barranquitas, PR 00794	1957	NA	NA	1-M	2,418	135	NA
Inter American Univ. of Puerto Rico–Bayamón, Bayamón, PR 00957	1912	$5,616	NA	1-M	5,063	321	23.0
Inter American Univ. of Puerto Rico–Fajardo, Fajardo, PR 00738-7003	1965	$170/credit	NA	1-M	2,239	146	NA
Inter American Univ. of Puerto Rico–Guayama, Guayama, PR 00785	1958	$4,558	NA	1-M	2,358	203	26.0
Inter American Univ. of Puerto Rico–Metropolitan, San Juan, PR 00919-1293	1960	$5,106	NA	1-D	10,093	599	25.0
Inter American Univ. of Puerto Rico–Ponce, Mercedita, PR 00715-1602	1962	$4,596	NA	1-M	6,370	347	NA
Inter American Univ. of Puerto Rico–San Germán, San Germán, PR 00683-5008	1912	$5,616	$2,500	1-D	5,380	308	30.0

Name, address	Year founded	Tuition & fees	Room & board	Control, degree	Enroll- ment	Faculty	Grad. rate
Intl. Academy of Design & Tech., Tampa, FL 33634-7350	1984	$14,460	$6,296	3-B	1,253	115	NA
Intl. Academy of Design & Tech., Chicago, IL 60602-9736	1977	$15,030	NA	3-B	1,832	113	15.0%
Iona Coll., New Rochelle, NY 10801-1890	1940	$30,192	$12,154	2-M	4,123	385	63.0
Iowa State Univ. of Science & Tech., Ames, IA 50011	1858	$6,997(S)	$7,472	5-D	28,682	1,646	70.0
Ithaca Coll., Ithaca, NY 14850	1892	$33,630	$12,314	1-D	6,949	724	77.0
Jackson State Univ., Jackson, MS 39217	1877	$5,050(S)	$6,244	5-D	8,783	525	36.4
Jacksonville State Univ., Jacksonville, AL 36265-1602	1883	$6,780(S)	$6,162	5-M	9,504	475	33.0
Jacksonville Univ., Jacksonville, FL 32211	1934	$26,600	$9,320	1-D	3,554	271	41.0
James Madison Univ., Harrisonburg, VA 22807	1908	$8,448(S)	$8,340	5-D	19,434	1,350	82.0
Jefferson Coll. of Health Sci, Roanoke, VA 24031-3186	1982	$18,810	$4,700	1-M	1,032	128	69.0
John Brown Univ., Siloam Springs, AR 72761-2121	1919	$20,766	$7,562	2-M	2,131	131	61.0
John Carroll Univ., University Heights, OH 44118-4581	1886	$31,710	$9,150	2-M	3,692	370	75.0
John F. Kennedy Univ., Pleasant Hill, CA 94523-4817 (4)	1964	$14,760	NA	1-D	1,580	237	NA
John Jay Coll. of Criminal Justice of the City Univ. of New York, New York, NY 10019-1093	1964	$4,930(S)	NA	11-M	15,206	964	40.0
Johns Hopkins Univ., Baltimore, MD 21218-2699	1876	$40,680	$12,510	1-D	6,838	592	92.0
Johnson & Wales Univ., Denver, CO 80220	1993	$25,407	$9,261	1-B	1,532	87	53.0
Johnson & Wales Univ., North Miami, FL 33181	1992	$25,407	$9,261	1-B	2,098	90	51.0
Johnson & Wales Univ., Providence, RI 02903-3703	1914	$24,141	NA	1-B	10,974	519	56.0
Johnson & Wales Univ., Charlotte Campus, Charlotte, NC 28202	2004	$25,407	$10,314	1-B	2,587	110	62.0
Johnson C. Smith Univ., Charlotte, NC 28216-5398	1867	$16,542	$6,439	1-B	1,331	130	39.0
Johnson State Coll., Johnson, VT 05656	1828	$9,672(S)	$8,444	5-M	1,949	143	32.0
Jones Intl. Univ., Centennial, CO 80112	1995	$12,480	NA	3-D	7,987	131	29.0
Judson Univ., Elgin, IL 60123-1498	1963	$24,780	$8,500	2-M	1,231	84	48.4
Juniata Coll., Huntingdon, PA 16652-2119	1876	$34,090	$9,330	2-B	1,593	150	72.0
Kalamazoo Coll., Kalamazoo, MI 49006-3295	1833	$34,317	$7,893	2-B	1,369	112	80.0
Kansas State Univ., Manhattan, KS 66506	1863	$7,376(S)	$6,954	5-D	23,588	1,109	60.0
Kean Univ., Union, NJ 07083	1855	$9,815(S)	$12,950	5-D	15,939	1,365	47.0
Keene State Coll., Keene, NH 03435	1909	$10,140(S)	$8,670	5-M	5,340	455	53.0
Kendall Coll., Chicago, IL 60201-2899	1934	$22,920	$9,900	3-B	2,545	209	37.0
Kennesaw State Univ., Kennesaw, GA 30144-5591	1963	$5,942(S)	$7,298	5-D	23,452	1,277	41.0
Kent State Univ., Kent, OH 44242-0001	1910	$9,030(S)	$8,376	5-D	26,589	1,569	50.0
Kent State Univ. at Geauga, Burton, OH 44021-9500	1964	$5,110(S)	NA	5-B	2,199	116	24.0
Kent State Univ. at Stark, Canton, OH 44720-7599	1967	$5,110(S)	NA	5-M	4,820	243	26.7
Kentucky State Univ., Frankfort, KY 40601	1886	$6,210(S)	$6,480	12-M	2,851	180	25.0
Kenyon Coll., Gambier, OH 43022-9623	1824	$42,630	$10,020	1-B	1,632	199	86.0
Kettering Univ., Flint, MI 48504 (2)	1919	$29,116	$6,440	1-M	2,187	154	57.0
Keuka Coll., Keuka Park, NY 14478-0098	1890	$23,770	$9,500	2-M	1,867	223	52.0
Keystone Coll., La Plume, PA 18440	1868	$19,620	$9,200	1-B	1,760	265	47.0
King Coll., Bristol, TN 37620-2699	1867	$22,908	$7,790	2-M	1,949	172	56.0
King's Coll., Wilkes-Barre, PA 18711-0801	1946	$26,644	$10,068	2-M	2,725	230	67.0
Knox Coll., Galesburg, IL 61401	1837	$34,464	$7,488	1-B	1,392	120	76.0
Kutztown Univ. of Pennsylvania, Kutztown, PA 19530-0730	1866	$7,732(S)	$8,094	5-M	10,707	476	54.0
Lafayette Coll., Easton, PA 18042-1798	1826	$39,115	$11,959	2-B	2,414	259	89.0
Lake Erie Coll., Painesville, OH 44077-3389	1856	$26,550	$8,192	1-M	1,216	113	47.0
Lake Forest Coll., Lake Forest, IL 60045	1857	$35,525	$8,327	1-M	1,443	158	70.0
Lakeland Coll., Sheboygan, WI 53082-0359	1862	$19,640	$7,016	2-M	3,932	71	42.0
Lake Superior State Univ., Sault Sainte Marie, MI 49783	1946	$8,764(S)	$8,081	5-M	2,588	184	37.0
Lamar Univ., Beaumont, TX 77710	1923	$6,934(S)	$7,010	5-D	13,826	600	28.0
Lander Univ., Greenwood, SC 29649-2099	1872	$9,924(S)	$6,594	5-M	2,614	222	43.8
Lane Coll., Jackson, TN 38301-4598	1882	$8,220	$5,800	2-B	2,222	104	33.0
Langston Univ., Langston, OK 73050	1897	$3,974(S)	$4,970	5-M	2,526	NA	NA
La Roche Coll., Pittsburgh, PA 15237-5898	1963	$22,476	$8,916	2-M	1,415	171	43.0
La Salle Univ., Philadelphia, PA 19141-1199	1863	$35,140	$11,680	2-D	6,636	419	69.0
Lasell Coll., Newton, MA 02466-2709	1851	$27,500	$12,300	1-M	1,798	191	51.0
La Sierra Univ., Riverside, CA 92515	1922	$28,335	$7,350	2-D	2,096	106	35.0
Lawrence Tech. Univ., Southfield, MI 48075-1058	1932	$24,633	$9,147	1-D	4,489	429	50.0
Lawrence Univ., Appleton, WI 54911	1847	$38,481	$7,890	1-B	1,566	193	73.0
Lebanon Valley Coll., Annville, PA 17003-1400	1866	$33,200	$8,800	2-D	2,065	212	74.0
Lee Univ., Cleveland, TN 37320-3450	1918	$12,680	$6,010	2-M	4,377	344	47.0
Lehigh Univ., Bethlehem, PA 18015-3094	1865	$39,780	$10,520	1-D	7,051	666	88.0
Lehman Coll. of the City Univ. of New York, Bronx, NY 10468-1589	1931	$5,208(S)	NA	11-M	12,115	900	34.0
Le Moyne Coll., Syracuse, NY 13214	1946	$28,380	$10,890	2-M	3,502	353	74.0
Lenoir-Rhyne Univ., Hickory, NC 28601	1891	$25,290	$8,930	2-M	1,562	175	55.0
Lesley Univ., Cambridge, MA 02138-2790 (4)	1909	$29,400	$12,800	1-D	5,564	258	62.0
LeTourneau Univ., Longview, TX 75607-7001	1946	$21,980	$8,390	2-M	3,173	NA	48.0
Lewis & Clark Coll., Portland, OR 97219-7899	1867	$36,632	$9,648	1-D	3,584	360	76.0
Lewis-Clark State Coll., Lewiston, ID 83501-2698	1893	$6,230(S)	NA	5-B	4,542	252	28.0
Lewis Univ., Romeoville, IL 60446	1932	$24,770	$8,900	2-D	6,139	625	58.0
Liberty Univ., Lynchburg, VA 24502	1971	$19,154	$6,680	2-D	12,155	555	54.0
Life Univ., Marietta, GA 30060-2903	1974	$9,369	$12,480	1-D	2,437	139	19.0
LIM Coll., New York, NY 10022-5268 (4)	1939	$21,475	$19,875	3-M	1,388	170	60.0
Lincoln Memorial Univ., Harrogate, TN 37752-1901	1897	$16,200	$5,780	1-D	4,445	253	34.0
Lincoln Univ., Jefferson City, MO 65102	1866	$6,175(S)	$5,144	5-M	3,349	236	23.0
Lincoln Univ., Lincoln University, PA 19352	1854	$8,472(S)	$8,004	12-M	2,649	194	36.0
Lindenwood Univ., St. Charles, MO 63301-1695	1827	$13,600	$7,210	2-D	11,345	716	45.0
Lindsey Wilson Coll., Columbia, KY 42728	1903	$18,950	$7,645	2-M	2,554	223	23.0
Linfield Coll., McMinnville, OR 97128-6894	1849	$30,604	$8,650	2-B	1,729	201	63.0
Lipscomb Univ., Nashville, TN 37204-3951	1891	$23,494	$8,790	2-D	3,742	363	56.0
Lock Haven Univ. of Pennsylvania, Lock Haven, PA 17745-2390	1870	$7,540(S)	$6,695	5-M	5,450	253	54.0
Logan Univ.–Coll. of Chiropractic, Chesterfield, MO 63006-1065	1935	$5,790	NA	1-D	1,104	96	NA
Loma Linda Univ., Loma Linda, CA 92350	1905	NA	NA	2-D	4,270	840	NA
Long Island Univ., Brooklyn Campus, Brooklyn, NY 11201-8423	1926	$896/credit	NA	1-D	8,597	816	18.0
Long Island Univ., C.W. Post Campus, Brookville, NY 11548-1300	1954	$30,210	$10,980	1-D	11,052	822	45.0
Longwood Univ., Farmville, VA 23909	1839	$9,855(S)	$8,114	5-M	4,931	274	59.0
Loras Coll., Dubuque, IA 52004-0178	1839	$26,088	$7,306	2-M	1,576	159	61.0
Louisiana Coll., Pineville, LA 71359-0001	1906	$12,980	$4,448	2-M	1,884	109	42.0
Louisiana State Univ. & A&M Coll., Baton Rouge, LA 70803	1860	$5,764(S)	$8,210	5-D	29,451	1,414	61.0
Louisiana State Univ. at Alexandria, Alexandria, LA 71302-9121	1960	$3,817(S)	NA	5-B	2,675	NA	NA
Louisiana State Univ. Health Science Ctr., New Orleans, LA 70112-2223	1931	$4,356(S)	$6,396	5-D	2,644	893	NA
Louisiana State Univ. in Shreveport, Shreveport, LA 71115-2399	1965	$4,317(S)	NA	5-M	4,504	NA	28.0
Louisiana Tech. Univ., Ruston, LA 71272	1894	$5,643(S)	$5,160	5-D	11,264	476	46.0
Lourdes Coll., Sylvania, OH 43560-2898	1958	$15,870	$7,800	2-M	2,506	257	17.0
Loyola Marymount Univ., Los Angeles, CA 90045-2659	1911	$36,404	$13,930	2-D	9,224	1,053	80.0
Loyola Univ. Chicago, Chicago, IL 60660	1870	$33,294	$11,570	2-D	15,951	1,368	68.0
Loyola Univ. Maryland, Baltimore, MD 21210-2699	1852	$39,350	$11,730	2-D	6,061	525	82.0
Loyola Univ. New Orleans, New Orleans, LA 70118-6195	1912	$33,302	$10,990	2-D	4,772	457	59.0

Name, address	Year founded	Tuition & fees	Room & board	Control, degree	Enroll- ment	Faculty	Grad. rate
Lubbock Christian Univ., Lubbock, TX 79407-2099	1957	$16,180	$6,368	2-M	2,028	159	48.0%
Luther Coll., Decorah, IA 52101	1861	$34,885	$5,850	2-B	2,481	259	74.0
Luther Rice Univ., Lithonia, GA 30038-2454	1962	$5,376	NA	2-M	1,047	NA	NA
Lycoming Coll., Williamsport, PA 17701-5192	1812	$30,800	$8,542	2-B	1,321	124	70.0
Lynchburg Coll., Lynchburg, VA 24501-3199	1903	$30,805	$8,210	2-D	2,643	274	57.0
Lyndon State Coll., Lyndonville, VT 05851-0919	1911	$9,948(S)	$8,444	5-M	1,436	160	39.0
Lynn Univ., Boca Raton, FL 33431-5598	1962	$30,900	$11,950	1-D	2,109	157	42.0
Macalester Coll., St. Paul, MN 55105-1899	1874	$42,021	$9,396	2-B	2,033	231	88.0
Macon State Coll., Macon, GA 31206	1968	$2,936(S)	$2,250	5-B	6,244	293	NA
Madonna Univ., Livonia, MI 48150-1173	1947	$13,840	$7,120	2-D	4,571	396	45.0
Maharishi Univ. of Mgmt, Fairfield, IA 52557	1971	$24,430	$6,000	1-D	1,138	115	50.0
Malone Univ., Canton, OH 44709	1892	$23,420	$8,088	2-M	2,512	220	58.0
Manchester Coll., North Manchester, IN 46962-1225	1889	$24,920	$8,860	2-M	1,278	99	53.0
Manhattan Coll., Riverdale, NY 10471	1853	$29,800	$11,420	2-M	3,412	383	73.0
Manhattanville Coll., Purchase, NY 10577-2132	1841	$34,350	$13,920	1-D	2,695	379	63.0
Mansfield Univ. of Pennsylvania, Mansfield, PA 16933	1857	$8,058(S)	$7,070	5-M	3,411	212	45.0
Marian Univ., Indianapolis, IN 46222-1997	1851	$24,960	$7,810	2-M	2,287	202	50.0
Marian Univ., Fond du Lac, WI 54935-4699	1936	$21,490	$5,700	2-D	2,881	309	52.0
Marietta Coll., Marietta, OH 45750-4000	1835	$28,340	$8,440	1-M	1,604	147	59.0
Marist Coll., Poughkeepsie, NY 12601-1387	1929	$27,650	$12,350	1-M	6,140	586	80.0
Marquette Univ., Milwaukee, WI 53201-1881	1881	$31,822	$10,370	2-D	11,806	1,118	81.0
Marshall Univ., Huntington, WV 25755	1837	$5,285(S)	$7,858	5-D	14,192	740	46.0
Mars Hill Coll., Mars Hill, NC 28754	1856	$21,997	$7,632	2-B	1,175	147	39.0
Martin Univ., Indianapolis, IN 46218-3867	1977	$13,520	NA	1-M	1,236	43	13.0
Mary Baldwin Coll., Staunton, VA 24401-3610 (4)	1842	$25,555	$7,420	1-M	3,350	138	43.0
Marygrove Coll., Detroit, MI 48221-2599 (4).	1905	$16,800	$7,600	2-M	2,953	64	34.0
Maryland Inst. Coll. of Art, Baltimore, MD 21217	1826	$37,470	$10,770	1-M	1,975	327	77.0
Marylhurst Univ., Marylhurst, OR 97036-0261 (4)	1893	$17,730	NA	2-M	1,917	260	22.0
Marymount Manhattan Coll., New York, NY 10021-4597	1936	$23,536	$13,416	1-B	2,095	330	49.0
Marymount Univ., Arlington, VA 22207-4299	1950	$23,974	$10,580	2-D	3,572	346	57.0
Maryville Coll., Maryville, TN 37804-5907	1819	$29,924	$9,234	2-B	1,080	121	59.0
Maryville Univ. of St. Louis, St. Louis, MO 63141-7299	1872	$21,910	$8,500	1-D	3,676	410	62.0
Marywood Univ., Scranton, PA 18509-1598	1915	$27,150	$12,172	2-D	3,479	398	63.0
Massachusetts Coll. of Art & Design, Boston, MA 02115-5882	1873	$9,000(S)	$11,750	5-M	2,446	252	65.0
Massachusetts Coll. of Lib. Arts, North Adams, MA 01247-4100	1894	$7,575(S)	$8,246	5-M	1,974	176	51.0
Massachusetts Coll. of Pharm. & Health Sci., Boston, MA 02115-5896	1823	$25,480	$12,290	1-D	4,278	210	69.0
Massachusetts Inst. of Tech., Cambridge, MA 02139-4307	1861	$39,212	$11,234	1-D	10,566	1,411	93.0
Massachusetts Maritime Academy, Buzzards Bay, MA 02532-1803 (2).	1891	$11,922(A)	$9,204	5-M	1,296	100	66.0
Master's Coll. & Seminary, Santa Clarita, CA 91321-1200	1927	$26,880	$8,400	2-D	1,450	199	60.0
McDaniel Coll., Westminster, MD 21157-4390	1867	$33,280	$7,060	1-M	3,512	367	70.0
McKendree Univ., Lebanon, IL 62254-1299	1828	$25,090	$8,500	2-M	3,299	323	62.0
McMurry Univ., Abilene, TX 79697	1923	$20,680	$6,976	2-B	1,414	143	38.0
McNeese State Univ., Lake Charles, LA 70609	1939	$3,600(S)	$6,070	5-M	8,645	409	37.0
Medaille Coll., Buffalo, NY 14214-2695	1875	$20,580	$9,750	1-M	2,736	231	56.0
Medgar Evers Coll. of the City Univ. of New York, Brooklyn, NY 11225-2298.	1969	$5,132(S)	NA	11-B	6,921	518	20.0
Mercer Univ., Macon, GA 31207-0003	1833	$30,560	$10,088	2-D	6,071	660	61.0
Medical Univ. of South Carolina, Charleston, SC 29425	1824	$15,034(S)	NA	5-D	2,560	227	NA
Mercy Coll., Dobbs Ferry, NY 10522-1189	1951	$17,360	$11,480	1-D	10,851	927	30.0
Mercy Coll. of Northwest Ohio, Toledo, OH 43604 (4)	1993	$10,624	NA	2-B	1,195	144	36.0
Mercyhurst Coll., Erie, PA 16546	1926	$26,346	$9,195	2-M	3,217	207	68.0
Meredith Coll., Raleigh, NC 27607-5298	1891	$26,200	$7,500	1-M	2,262	280	57.0
Merrimack Coll., North Andover, MA 01845-5800	1947	$31,380	$10,700	2-M	2,169	227	67.0
Mesa State Coll., Grand Junction, CO 81501-3122	1925	$6,248(S)	$8,298	5-M	8,130	454	26.0
Messiah Coll., Grantham, PA 17027	1909	$28,356	$8,420	2-M	2,932	281	75.0
Methodist Univ., Fayetteville, NC 28311-1498	1956	$24,220	$8,900	2-M	2,416	213	44.0
Metropolitan Coll. of New York, New York, NY 10013 (4)	1964	$16,720	NA	1-M	1,084	183	40.0
Metropolitan State Coll. of Denver, Denver, CO 80217-3362	1963	$4,093(S)	NA	5-B	23,948	1,382	21.0
Metropolitan State Univ., St. Paul, MN 55106-5000	1971	$5,923(S)	NA	5-D	7,787	550	14.0
Miami Univ., Oxford, OH 45056	1809	$12,786(S)	$9,786	12-D	17,472	1,095	80.0
Miami Univ. Hamilton, Hamilton, OH 45011-3399	1968	$4,632(S)	NA	5-M	4,194	224	NA
Michigan State Univ., East Lansing, MI 48824	1855	$11,153(S)	$7,770	5-D	47,131	2,937	77.0
Michigan Tech. Univ., Houghton, MI 49931	1885	$12,017(S)	$8,462	5-D	7,148	445	66.0
MidAmerica Nazarene Univ., Olathe, KS 66062-1899	1966	$21,500	$7,000	2-M	1,767	247	46.0
Mid-Continent Univ., Mayfield, KY 42066-9007	1949	$13,300	$6,600	2-M	2,270	155	28.0
Middlebury Coll., Middlebury, VT 05753-6002	1800	$52,500(C)	NA	1-D	2,532	310	91.0
Middle Tennessee State Univ., Murfreesboro, TN 37132	1911	$6,298(S)	$7,132	5-D	26,430	1,346	53.0
Midland Coll., Midland, TX 79705-6399	1969	$2,290(A)	$3,900	11-B	5,739	269	NA
Midway Coll., Midway, KY 40347-1120 (4)	1847	$18,900	$7,280	2-D	1,600	118	38.0
Midwestern State Univ., Wichita Falls, TX 76308	1922	$6,720(S)	$5,940	5-M	6,426	332	28.0
Miles Coll., Fairfield, AL 35064	1905	NA	NA	2-B	1,738	147	NA
Millersville Univ. of Pennsylvania, Millersville, PA 17551-0302	1855	$7,700(S)	$8,298	5-M	8,729	431	61.0
Milligan Coll., Milligan College, TN 37682	1866	$25,260	$5,650	2-M	1,140	115	56.0
Millikin Univ., Decatur, IL 62522-2084	1901	$27,425	$8,291	2-M	2,326	289	59.0
Millsaps Coll., Jackson, MS 39210-0001	1890	$29,482	$10,312	2-M	1,060	121	68.0
Mills Coll., Oakland, CA 94613-1000	1852	$37,605	$11,644	1-D	1,589	200	61.0
Milwaukee Sch. of Engineering, Milwaukee, WI 53202-3109 (2)	1903	$30,990	$7,794	1-M	2,589	253	61.0
Minnesota State Univ. Mankato, Mankato, MN 56001	1868	$6,725(S)	$6,730	5-M	15,306	761	51.0
Minnesota State Univ. Moorhead, Moorhead, MN 56563-0002	1885	$6,923(S)	$6,468	5-D	7,497	468	43.0
Minot State Univ., Minot, ND 58707-0002	1913	$5,638(S)	$4,530	5-M	3,866	189	34.0
Misericordia Univ., Dallas, PA 18612-1098 (4)	1924	$24,990	$10,410	2-D	2,812	292	67.0
Mississippi Coll., Clinton, MS 39058.	1826	$14,038	$6,340	2-D	4,963	440	55.0
Mississippi State Univ., Mississippi State, MS 39762	1878	$5,461(S)	$7,729	5-D	19,644	912	61.0
Mississippi Univ. for Women, Columbus, MS 39701-9998 (4)	1884	$4,644(S)	$5,483	5-M	2,587	182	39.0
Mississippi Valley State Univ., Itta Bena, MS 38941-1400	1946	$5,234(S)	$5,537	5-M	2,636	158	28.0
Missouri Baptist Univ., St. Louis, MO 63141-8660	1964	$18,700	$7,440	2-D	5,062	277	37.0
Missouri Southern State Univ., Joplin, MO 64801-1595.	1937	$4,816(S)	$5,500	5-M	5,802	312	34.0
Missouri State Univ., Springfield, MO 65897	1905	$6,276(S)	$6,394	5-D	20,472	1,013	54.0
Missouri Univ. of Science & Tech., Rolla, MO 65409 (2).	1870	$8,528(S)	$8,290	5-D	7,206	445	66.0
Missouri Valley Coll., Marshall, MO 65340-3197	1889	$17,170	$6,450	2-B	1,639	90	23.0
Missouri Western State Univ., St. Joseph, MO 64507-2294	1915	$5,560(S)	$6,600	5-M	5,703	348	28.0
Molloy Coll., Rockville Centre, NY 11571-5002	1955	$22,130	NA	1-D	4,188	577	62.0
Monmouth Coll., Monmouth, IL 61462-1998	1853	$28,650	$7,300	2-B	1,347	118	59.0
Monmouth Univ., West Long Branch, NJ 07764-1898	1933	$28,000	$10,680	1-D	6,506	603	60.0
Monroe Coll., Bronx, NY 10468-5407.	1933	$11,400	$8,150	3-M	5,068	251	66.0
Monroe Coll., New Rochelle, NY 10801	1983	$11,400	$8,150	3-M	2,222	93	75.0
Montana State Univ., Bozeman, MT 59717	1893	$6,168(S)	$7,900	5-D	13,559	847	49.0
Montana State Univ. Billings, Billings, MT 59101-0298.	1927	$5,242(S)	$5,620	5-M	5,335	290	26.0

Name, address	Year founded	Tuition & fees	Room & board	Control, degree	Enroll-ment	Faculty	Grad. rate
Montana State Univ.–Northern, Havre, MT 59501-7751	1929	$4,476(S)	$6,461	5-M	1,215	NA	NA
Montana Tech. of the Univ. of Montana, Butte, MT 59701-8997	1895	$6,162(S)	$6,924	5-M	2,864	214	51.0%
Montclair State Univ., Montclair, NJ 07043-1624	1908	$7,324(S)	$10,712	5-D	18,171	1,489	62.0
Montreat Coll., Montreat, NC 28757-1267	1916	$23,164	$7,346	2-M	1,082	147	31.0
Moody Bible Inst., Chicago, IL 60610-3284	1886	$10,008	$8,240	2-D	3,031	183	NA
Moravian Coll., Bethlehem, PA 18018-6650	1742	$32,177	$9,164	2-M	2,034	202	71.0
Morehead State Univ., Morehead, KY 40351	1922	$6,492(S)	$6,582	5-M	8,842	469	40.0
Morehouse Coll., Atlanta, GA 30314 (1)	1867	$22,444	$11,494	1-B	2,579	214	57.0
Morgan State Univ., Baltimore, MD 21251	1867	$6,727(S)	$8,620	5-D	7,005	558	100.0
Morningside Coll., Sioux City, IA 51106	1894	$23,984	$7,364	2-M	1,991	172	50.0
Morris Coll., Sumter, SC 29150-3599	1908	$10,290	$4,497	2-B	1,048	65	25.0
Mountain State Univ., Beckley, WV 25802-9003	1933	$7,680	$8,865	1-D	5,550	419	14.0
Mount Aloysius Coll., Cresson, PA 16630-1999	1939	$18,000	$7,660	2-M	1,611	171	37.0
Mount Holyoke Coll., South Hadley, MA 01075 (3)	1837	$40,256	$11,780	1-M	2,345	283	82.0
Mount Ida Coll., Newton, MA 02459-3310	1899	$24,500	$12,000	1-M	1,477	193	36.0
Mount Marty Coll., Yankton, SD 57078-3724	1936	$19,932	$5,636	2-M	1,249	61	58.0
Mount Mary Coll., Milwaukee, WI 53222-4597	1913	$22,118	$7,498	2-M	1,925	208	40.0
Mount Mercy Univ., Cedar Rapids, IA 52402-4797	1928	$24,360	$7,470	2-M	1,643	148	62.0
Mount Olive Coll., Mount Olive, NC 28365	1951	$15,500	$6,200	2-B	3,855	183	44.0
Mount St. Mary Coll., Newburgh, NY 12550-3494	1960	$24,410	$12,320	1-M	2,700	265	53.0
Mount St. Mary's Coll., Los Angeles, CA 90049-1599 (4)	1925	$31,626	$10,125	2-D	2,862	375	67.0
Mount St. Mary's Univ., Emmitsburg, MD 21727-7799	1808	$31,536	$10,544	2-D	2,112	186	73.0
Mount Vernon Nazarene Univ., Mount Vernon, OH 43050-9500	1964	$22,280	$6,430	2-M	2,609	246	60.0
Muhlenberg Coll., Allentown, PA 18104-5586	1848	$38,380	$8,735	2-B	2,515	257	86.0
Murray State Univ., Murray, KY 42071	1922	$6,264(S)	$6,860	5-M	10,416	558	54.0
Musicians Inst., Hollywood, CA 90028	1976	$29,520	NA	3-B	1,528	125	NA
Muskingum Univ., New Concord, OH 43762	1837	$20,616	$8,170	2-M	2,099	NA	NA
Naropa Univ., Boulder, CO 80302-6697	1974	$26,360	$8,712	1-M	1,082	175	53.0
National-Louis Univ., Chicago, IL 60603	1886	$18,435	NA	1-D	6,475	526	20.0
National Univ., La Jolla, CA 92037-1011	1971	$11,148	NA	1-M	16,400	2,949	85.0
National Univ. Coll., Bayamón, PR 00960	NA	$6,315	NA	13-B	2,703	NA	NA
Nazareth Coll. of Rochester, Rochester, NY 14618-3790	1924	$26,184	$10,716	1-D	3,310	429	72.0
Nebraska Wesleyan Univ., Lincoln, NE 68504-2796	1887	$23,474	$6,300	2-M	2,138	175	65.0
Neumann Univ., Aston, PA 19014-1298	1965	$22,256	$10,162	2-D	3,073	315	45.0
Nevada State Coll. at Henderson, Henderson, NV 89015	2002	$3,563(S)	NA	5-B	2,988	94	17.0
Newberry Coll., Newberry, SC 29108-2197	1856	$23,993	$8,150	2-B	1,155	80	48.0
Newbury Coll., Brookline, MA 02445	1962	$25,100	$11,750	1-B	1,016	110	46.0
New England Coll., Henniker, NH 03242-3293	1946	$30,495	$10,668	1-M	2,048	150	40.0
New England Inst. of Tech., Warwick, RI 02886-2244	1940	$19,715	NA	1-M	3,298	310	NA
New Jersey City Univ., Jersey City, NJ 07305-1597	1927	$9,348(S)	$9,364	5-M	8,517	738	37.0
New Jersey Inst. of Tech., Newark, NJ 07102	1881	$13,370(S)	$10,122	5-D	8,934	654	55.0
Newman Univ., Wichita, KS 67213-2097	1933	$21,766	$6,710	2-M	2,746	183	32.0
New Mexico Highlands Univ., Las Vegas, NM 87701	1893	$2,952(S)	$6,098	5-M	3,764	274	19.0
New Mexico Inst. of Mining & Tech., Socorro, NM 87801	1889	$4,942(S)	$5,874	5-D	1,914	167	46.0
New Mexico State Univ., Las Cruces, NM 88003-8001	1888	$5,400(S)	$6,526	5-D	18,552	976	45.0
New Orleans Baptist Theological Seminary, New Orleans, LA 70126-4858 (2)	1917	NA	NA	2-D	2,036	NA	NA
The New School for General Studies, New York, NY 10011-8603	1919	$25,320	$15,260	1-M	1,958	385	NA
New York City Coll. of Tech. of the City Univ. of New York, Brooklyn, NY 11201-2983	1946	$4,939(S)	NA	11-B	15,366	1,211	25.0
New York Inst. of Tech., Old Westbury, NY 11568-8000	1955	$25,470	$11,100	1-D	11,471	1,106	47.0
New York Univ., New York, NY 10012-1019	1831	$40,082	$13,510	1-D	43,797	5,344	85.0
Niagara Univ., Niagara University, NY 14109	1856	$25,650	$10,652	2-M	4,273	351	68.0
Nicholls State Univ., Thibodaux, LA 70310	1948	$4,292(S)	$7,808	5-M	7,181	271	34.0
Nichols Coll., Dudley, MA 01571-5000	1815	$28,870	$9,330	1-M	1,547	80	38.0
Norfolk State Univ., Norfolk, VA 23504	1935	$9,162(S)	$7,719	5-D	6,993	NA	30.0
North Carolina Agr. & Tech. State Univ., Greensboro, NC 27411	1891	$4,416(S)	$6,029	5-D	10,795	570	38.0
North Carolina Central Univ., Durham, NC 27707-3129	1910	$5,280(S)	$9,509	5-D	8,587	608	44.0
North Carolina State Univ., Raleigh, NC 27695	1887	$6,529(S)	$8,154	5-D	34,376	1,918	73.0
North Carolina Wesleyan Coll., Rocky Mount, NC 27804-8677	1956	$23,500	$7,890	2-B	1,510	169	NA
North Central Coll., Naperville, IL 60566-7063	1861	$28,224	$8,463	2-M	2,902	238	68.0
Northcentral Univ., Prescott Valley, AZ 86314	1996	$8,800	NA	3-D	9,085	470	NA
North Central Univ., Minneapolis, MN 55404-1322	1930	$16,546	$5,610	2-B	1,125	102	37.0
North Dakota State Univ., Fargo, ND 58108	1890	$6,661(S)	$6,890	5-D	14,407	796	51.0
Northeastern Illinois Univ., Chicago, IL 60625-4699	1961	$9,003(S)	NA	5-M	11,746	718	20.0
Northeastern State Univ., Tahlequah, OK 74464-2399	1846	$4,385(S)	$5,020	5-D	9,588	535	28.0
Northeastern Univ., Boston, MA 02115-5096	1898	$36,792	$12,760	1-D	22,863	1,448	77.0
Northern Arizona Univ., Flagstaff, AZ 86011	1899	$7,667(S)	$8,072	5-D	25,204	1,501	49.0
Northern Illinois Univ., De Kalb, IL 60115-2854	1895	$9,854(S)	$10,366	5-D	23,850	1,173	51.0
Northern Kentucky Univ., Highland Heights, KY 41099	1968	$7,128(S)	$6,260	5-D	15,716	1,121	34.0
Northern Michigan Univ., Marquette, MI 49855-5301	1899	$8,416(S)	$8,026	5-M	9,258	462	49.0
Northern State Univ., Aberdeen, SD 57401-7198	1901	$6,351(S)	$5,068	5-M	3,200	95	44.0
North Georgia Coll. & State Univ., Dahlonega, GA 30597	1873	$6,094(S)	$6,166	5-D	5,912	380	51.0
North Greenville Univ., Tigerville, SC 29688-1892	1892	$12,820	$7,510	2-M	2,318	190	47.0
North Park Univ., Chicago, IL 60625-4895	1891	$19,900	$7,830	2-D	2,181	NA	NA
Northwestern Coll., Orange City, IA 51041-1996	1882	$23,330	$7,090	2-B	1,206	134	60.0
Northwestern Coll., St. Paul, MN 55113-1598	1902	$25,700	$8,000	2-M	1,901	196	66.0
Northwestern Oklahoma State Univ., Alva, OK 73717-2799	1897	$4,336(S)	$3,640	5-M	2,302	160	32.0
Northwestern State Univ. of Louisiana, Natchitoches, LA 71497	1884	$4,384(S)	$7,070	5-M	9,244	515	36.4
Northwestern Univ., Evanston, IL 60208	1851	$40,224	NA	1-D	18,431	1,153	93.0
Northwest Missouri State Univ., Maryville, MO 64468-6001	1905	$7,047(S)	$7,962	5-M	7,142	324	52.0
Northwest Nazarene Univ., Nampa, ID 83686-5897	1913	$24,030	$6,220	2-M	2,020	112	NA
Northwest Univ., Kirkland, WA 98033	1934	$23,400	$6,884	2-D	1,422	108	51.8
Northwood Univ., Midland, MI 48640-2398	1959	$19,272	$8,160	1-M	2,269	129	44.0
Norwich Univ., Northfield, VT 05663 (2)	1819	$28,738	$9,958	1-M	3,104	311	54.0
Notre Dame Coll., South Euclid, OH 44121-4293	1922	$23,630	$7,820	2-M	1,393	118	NA
Notre Dame de Namur Univ., Belmont, CA 94002-1908	1851	$29,980	$11,680	2-M	1,790	192	49.0
Nova Southeastern Univ., Fort Lauderdale, FL 33314-7796	1964	$22,750	$9,086	1-D	28,741	1,694	41.0
Nyack Coll., Nyack, NY 10960-3698	1882	$21,500	$8,250	2-D	3,320	290	42.0
Oakland City Univ., Oakland City, IN 47660-1099	1885	$16,000	$6,700	2-D	2,550	178	60.0
Oakland Univ., Rochester, MI 48309-4401	1957	$9,285(S)	$7,644	5-D	18,920	976	41.0
Oakwood Univ., Huntsville, AL 35896	1896	$14,250	$7,988	2-M	1,824	171	46.0
Oberlin Coll., Oberlin, OH 44074	1833	$41,577	$11,010	1-M	2,974	285	86.0
Occidental Coll., Los Angeles, CA 90041-3314	1887	$40,939	$11,360	1-M	1,989	253	87.5
Oglala Lakota Coll., Kyle, SD 57752-0490	1970	NA	NA	11-M	1,000	NA	NA
Oglethorpe Univ., Atlanta, GA 30319-2797	1835	$27,950	$9,990	1-M	1,156	111	58.0
Ohio Dominican Univ., Columbus, OH 43219-2099	1911	$25,280	$8,322	2-M	3,052	170	44.0
Ohio Northern Univ., Ada, OH 45810-1599	1871	$33,099	$9,072	2-D	3,651	314	67.0
Ohio State Univ., Columbus, OH 43210	1870	$250/ qtr. hr.(S)	$9,180	5-D	56,064	4,632	78.0

Name, address	Year founded	Tuition & fees	Room & board	Control, degree	Enroll-ment	Faculty	Grad. rate
Ohio State Univ.–Lima, Lima, OH 45804	1960	$6,102(S)	NA	5-M	1,530	86	36.0%
Ohio State Univ.–Mansfield, Mansfield, OH 44906-1599	1958	$6,102(S)	$5,205	5-M	1,405	91	31.0
Ohio State Univ.–Marion, Marion, OH 43302-5695	1958	$6,102(S)	NA	5-M	1,816	118	33.0
Ohio State Univ.–Newark, Newark, OH 43055-1797	1957	$6,102(S)	$7,185	5-M	2,562	137	37.0
Ohio Univ., Athens, OH 45701-2979	1804	$9,603(S)	$9,621	5-D	25,108	1,181	65.0
Ohio Univ.–Chillicothe, Chillicothe, OH 45601	1946	$3,060(S)	NA	5-M	2,558	NA	NA
Ohio Univ.–Lancaster, Lancaster, OH 43130-1097	1968	$3,060(S)	NA	5-M	1,728	NA	NA
Ohio Univ.–Southern Campus, Ironton, OH 45638-2214	1956	$2,930(S)	NA	5-M	1,836	NA	NA
Ohio Univ.–Zanesville, Zanesville, OH 43701-2695	1946	$4,662(S)	NA	5-B	1,983	130	NA
Ohio Wesleyan Univ., Delaware, OH 43015	1842	$36,390	$9,700	2-B	1,919	223	63.0
Oklahoma Baptist Univ., Shawnee, OK 74804	1910	$18,670	$5,630	2-M	1,764	163	54.0
Oklahoma Christian Univ., Oklahoma City, OK 73136-1100	1950	$18,456	$5,900	2-M	2,216	192	48.0
Oklahoma City Univ., Oklahoma City, OK 73106-1402	1904	$25,760	$7,500	2-D	3,770	352	52.0
Oklahoma Panhandle State Univ., Goodwell, OK 73939-0430.	1909	$5,344(S)	$3,652	5-B	1,387	91	38.0
Oklahoma State Univ., Stillwater, OK 74078.	1890	$6,779(S)	$6,680	5-D	23,522	1,285	59.0
Oklahoma Wesleyan Univ., Bartlesville, OK 74006-6299	1909	$20,160	$6,874	2-M	1,144	69	25.0
Old Dominion Univ., Norfolk, VA 23529	1930	$8,144(S)	$8,796	5-D	24,466	1,244	49.0
Olivet Coll., Olivet, MI 49076-9701	1844	$20,500	$7,000	2-M	1,049	NA	NA
Olivet Nazarene Univ., Bourbonnais, IL 60914	1907	NA	NA	2-M	4,636	NA	NA
Oral Roberts Univ., Tulsa, OK 74171	1963	$20,044	$8,304	2-D	2,923	291	53.0
Oregon Health & Science Univ., Portland, OR 97239-3098	1974	$18,996(S)	NA	12-D	2,583	NA	NA
Oregon Inst. of Tech., Klamath Falls, OR 97601-8801	1947	$7,260(S)	$8,145	5-M	3,915	247	41.0
Oregon State Univ., Corvallis, OR 97331	1868	$7,115(S)	NA	5-D	23,761	980	60.0
Otis Coll. of Art & Design, Los Angeles, CA 90045-9785	1918	$35,354	NA	1-M	1,226	326	54.0
Otterbein Univ., Westerville, OH 43081	1847	$28,413	$7,887	2-M	3,131	280	NA
Ouachita Baptist Univ., Arkadelphia, AR 71998-0001	1886	$20,630	$6,040	2-B	1,504	139	57.0
Our Lady of Holy Cross Coll., New Orleans, LA 70131-7399	1916	$8,604	NA	2-M	1,298	NA	NA
Our Lady of the Lake Coll., Baton Rouge, LA 70808 (4)	1990	$8,664	NA	2-M	1,860	240	0.0
Our Lady of the Lake Univ. of San Antonio, San Antonio, TX 78207-4689	1895	$21,900	$6,838	2-D	2,751	249	32.0
Pace Univ., New York, NY 10038	1906	$33,702	$13,800	1-D	12,752	1,208	58.0
Pacific Lutheran Univ., Tacoma, WA 98447	1890	$30,950	$9,250	2-M	3,543	310	69.0
Pacific Oaks Coll., Pasadena, CA 91103 (4)	1945	$22,064	NA	1-M	1,028	125	NA
Pacific Union Coll., Angwin, CA 94508-9707	1882	$25,965	$7,275	2-M	1,527	97	38.0
Pacific Univ., Forest Grove, OR 97116-1797	1849	$33,612	$9,208	1-D	3,363	385	65.0
Palm Beach Atlantic Univ., West Palm Beach, FL 33416-4708	1968	$23,400	$8,220	2-D	3,659	336	51.0
Palmer Coll. of Chiropractic, Davenport, IA 52803-5287	1897	$186/cr. hr.	NA	1-D	2,310	15	NA
Park Univ., Parkville, MO 64152-3795	1875	$8,898	$7,580	1-M	12,775	1,003	39.0
Parsons–The New School for Design, New York, NY 10011-8878	1896	$37,610	$15,260	1-M	4,746	1,104	71.0
Patten Univ., Oakland, CA 94601-2699	1944	$13,440	$7,380	2-M	1,050	125	37.0
Peirce Coll., Philadelphia, PA 19102-4699 (4)	1865	$15,900	NA	1-B	2,139	155	78.0
Penn State–Abington, Abington, PA 19001.	1950	$12,730(S)	NA	12-B	3,476	245	49.0
Penn State–Altoona, Altoona, PA 16601-3760	1939	$13,250(S)	$8,370	12-B	4,147	327	69.0
Penn State–Berks, Reading, PA 19610-6009	1924	$13,250(S)	$9,160	12-B	2,771	211	58.0
Penn State–Erie, The Behrend Coll., Erie, PA 16563-0001	1948	$13,250(S)	$8,370	12-M	4,359	282	70.0
Penn State–Harrisburg, Middletown, PA 17057-4898.	1966	$13,240(S)	$9,580	12-D	4,224	313	64.0
Penn State–Univ. Park, University Park, PA 16802-1503	1855	$15,250(S)	$8,370	12-D	45,233	2,888	85.0
Pennsylvania Coll. of Tech., Williamsport, PA 17701-5778	1965	$13,080(S)	$9,500	12-B	6,290	489	49.0
Pepperdine Univ., Malibu, CA 90263	1937	$39,080	$11,390	2-D	7,604	690	80.0
Peru State Coll., Peru, NE 68421	1867	$4,966(S)	$5,208	5-M	2,510	115	42.0
Pfeiffer Univ., Misenheimer, NC 28109-0960	1885	$20,687	$8,266	2-M	2,019	150	59.0
Philadelphia Biblical Univ., Langhorne, PA 19047-2990.	1913	$20,888	$8,275	2-M	1,296	121	55.0
Philadelphia Univ., Philadelphia, PA 19144	1884	$28,890	$9,502	1-D	3,619	482	61.0
Piedmont Coll., Demorest, GA 30535-0010	1897	$19,000	$7,500	2-D	2,676	218	41.0
Pikeville Coll., Pikeville, KY 41501	1889	$15,250	$6,300	2-D	1,325	82	38.0
Pittsburg State Univ., Pittsburg, KS 66762	1903	$4,848(S)	$6,016	5-M	7,130	410	52.0
Pitzer Coll., Claremont, CA 91711-6101.	1963	$41,130	$11,950	1-B	1,080	105	79.0
Plymouth State Univ., Plymouth, NH 03264-1595	1871	$9,906(S)	$8,840	5-D	6,245	416	55.2
Point Loma Nazarene Univ., San Diego, CA 92106-2899	1902	$27,100	$9,000	2-M	3,377	NA	70.0
Point Park Univ., Pittsburgh, PA 15222-1984	1960	$22,500	$9,480	1-M	4,077	451	48.0
Polytechnic Inst. of NYU, Brooklyn, NY 11201-2990	1854	$36,284	$10,080	1-D	4,432	370	55.0
Polytechnic Univ. of Puerto Rico, Hato Rey, PR 00919 (2)	1966	$7,263	$11,704	1-M	5,520	279	22.0
Pomona Coll., Claremont, CA 91711	1887	$39,883	$13,227	1-B	1,560	226	94.0
Pontifical Catholic Univ. of Puerto Rico, Ponce, PR 00717-0777	1948	$5,468	$1,300	2-D	7,682	385	39.0
Portland State Univ., Portland, OR 97207-0751.	1946	$7,130(S)	$10,065	5-D	28,035	1,564	34.0
Post Univ., Waterbury, CT 06723-2540.	1890	$25,050	$9,700	1-M	2,590	218	28.0
Prairie View A&M Univ., Prairie View, TX 77446-0519	1878	$6,855(S)	$7,064	5-D	8,781	501	32.0
Pratt Inst., Brooklyn, NY 11205-3899	1887	$39,310	$10,210	1-M	4,733	1,032	57.0
Presbyterian Coll., Clinton, SC 29325	1880	$30,180	$8,670	2-D	1,266	130	66.0
Prescott Coll., Prescott, AZ 86301	1966	$27,265	$3,810	1-D	1,156	136	40.0
Princeton Univ., Princeton, NJ 08544-1019	1746	$37,000	$12,069	1-D	7,802	1,070	96.1
Providence Coll., Providence, RI 02918	1917	$39,435	$11,690	2-M	4,592	387	88.0
Purchase Coll., State Univ. of New York, Purchase, NY 10577-1400	1967	$6,504(S)	$10,646	5-M	4,175	376	55.0
Purdue Univ., West Lafayette, IN 47907	1869	$9,069(S)	$9,120	5-D	39,726	2,464	71.0
Purdue Univ. Calumet, Hammond, IN 46323-2094.	1951	$6,654(S)	$6,924	5-M	9,807	NA	27.0
Purdue Univ. North Central, Westville, IN 46391-9542.	1967	$6,704(S)	NA	5-M	4,614	320	16.0
Queens Coll. of the City Univ. of New York, Flushing, NY 11367-1597. ...	1937	$5,047(S)	$11,125	11-M	20,906	1,536	52.0
Queens Univ. of Charlotte, Charlotte, NC 28274-0002.	1857	$23,752	$8,608	2-M	2,568	216	62.0
Quincy Univ., Quincy, IL 62301-2699	1860	$24,140	$9,420	2-M	1,907	180	44.0
Quinnipiac Univ., Hamden, CT 06518-1940	1929	$36,130	$13,430	1-D	8,166	837	75.0
Radford Univ., Radford, VA 24142	1910	$8,104(S)	$7,302	5-D	9,007	608	56.0
Ramapo Coll. of New Jersey, Mahwah, NJ 07430-1680.	1969	$11,874(S)	$10,250	5-M	6,008	452	75.0
Randolph-Macon Coll., Ashland, VA 23005-5505.	1830	$30,608	$9,326	2-B	1,222	147	62.0
Reed Coll., Portland, OR 97202-8199	1908	$41,200	$10,650	1-M	1,477	139	79.0
Regent Univ., Virginia Beach, VA 23464-9800	1977	$15,308	$5,900	2-D	5,555	588	NA
Regis Coll., Weston, MA 02493	1927	$30,300	$12,190	2-D	1,737	130	57.0
Regis Univ., Denver, CO 80221-1099.	1877	$23,882	$9,100	2-D	11,069	2,222	61.0
Reinhardt Univ., Waleska, GA 30183-2981	1883	$17,840	$6,580	2-M	1,219	174	32.0
Rensselaer Polytechnic Inst., Troy, NY 12180-3590	1824	$40,680	$11,465	1-D	7,144	484	82.0
Rhode Island Coll., Providence, RI 02908-1991.	1854	$6,986(S)	$9,326	5-D	9,155	760	46.0
Rhode Island School of Design, Providence, RI 02903-2784.	1877	$38,295	$11,310	1-D	2,259	503	90.2
Rhodes Coll., Memphis, TN 38112-1690	1848	$34,580	$8,480	1-M	1,730	196	80.0
Rice Univ., Houston, TX 77251-1892	1912	$35,551	$12,270	1-D	5,879	752	93.0
The Richard Stockton Coll. of New Jersey, Pomona, NJ 08240-0195	1969	$11,393(S)	$10,281	5-D	7,879	546	64.0
Rider Univ., Lawrenceville, NJ 08648-3001	1865	$30,470	$11,200	1-M	5,816	622	64.0
Ringling Coll. of Art & Design, Sarasota, FL 34234-5895.	1931	$30,730	$10,890	1-B	1,368	152	69.0
Ripon Coll., Ripon, WI 54971	1851	$28,689	$8,270	1-B	1,065	98	71.0
Rivier Coll., Nashua, NH 03060	1933	$25,020	$9,522	2-D	2,357	194	57.0

Name, address	Year founded	Tuition & fees	Room & board	Control, degree	Enroll- ment	Faculty	Grad. rate
Roanoke Coll., Salem, VA 24153-3794	1842	$32,900	$10,772	2-B	2,104	207	71.0%
Robert Morris Univ., Moon Township, PA 15108-1189	1921	$21,550	$10,660	1-D	4,967	411	61.0
Robert Morris Univ. Illinois, Chicago, IL 60605	1913	$21,600	$10,326	1-M	4,558	317	79.0
Roberts Wesleyan Coll., Rochester, NY 14624-1997	1866	$24,360	$8,826	2-M	1,928	248	67.0
Rochester Inst. of Tech., Rochester, NY 14623-5603	1829	$30,717	$10,044	1-D	16,773	1,426	68.0
Rockford Coll., Rockford, IL 61108-2393	1847	$24,750	$6,950	1-M	1,424	156	NA
Rockhurst Univ., Kansas City, MO 64110-2561	1910	$27,390	$7,490	2-D	2,895	228	74.0
Rogers State Univ., Claremore, OK 74017-3252	1909	$4,513(S)	$5,990	5-B	4,386	260	14.0
Roger Williams Univ., Bristol, RI 02809	1956	$29,408	$12,740	1-D	5,159	584	56.0
Rollins Coll., Winter Park, FL 32789-4499	1885	$37,640	$11,760	1-M	2,451	173	69.0
Roosevelt Univ., Chicago, IL 60605	1945	$25,000	NA	1-D	6,766	727	45.0
Rose-Hulman Inst. of Tech., Terre Haute, IN 47803-3999 (2)	1874	$36,270	$9,957	1-M	1,980	170	80.0
Rowan Univ., Glassboro, NJ 08028-1701	1923	$11,676(S)	$10,348	5-D	11,392	1,041	75.0
Rush Univ., Chicago, IL 60612-3832	1969	NA	NA	1-D	1,566	796	NA
Rutgers, State Univ. of New Jersey, Camden, NJ 08102-1401	1927	$12,364(S)	$10,362	5-D	6,158	500	64.0
Rutgers, State Univ. of New Jersey, Newark, Newark, NJ 07102	1892	$12,069(S)	$11,653	5-D	11,798	732	63.0
Rutgers, State Univ. of New Jersey, New Brunswick, Piscataway, NJ 08854-8097	1766	$12,582(S)	$11,216	5-D	38,912	2,521	77.0
Sacred Heart Univ., Fairfield, CT 06825-1000	1963	$31,440	$12,340	2-D	6,283	579	67.0
Saginaw Valley State Univ., University Center, MI 48710	1963	$7,308(S)	$7,768	5-M	10,656	597	43.0
St. Ambrose Univ., Davenport, IA 52803-2898	1882	$24,920	$8,885	2-D	3,663	415	62.0
St. Anselm Coll., Manchester, NH 03102-1310	1889	$31,555	$11,650	2-B	1,896	196	73.0
St. Augustine Coll., Chicago, IL 60640-3501	1980	$8,400	NA	1-B	1,430	154	NA
St. Augustine's Coll., Raleigh, NC 27610-2298	1867	$17,160	$7,126	2-B	1,529	134	48.0
St. Bonaventure Univ., St. Bonaventure, NY 14778-2284	1858	$26,895	$9,071	2-M	2,514	238	68.0
St. Catherine Univ., St. Paul, MN 55105	1905	$30,168	$7,658	2-D	5,328	458	67.0
St. Cloud State Univ., St. Cloud, MN 56301-4498	1869	$6,718(S)	$5,984	5-D	17,785	939	48.0
St. Edward's Univ., Austin, TX 78704	1885	$28,700	$9,784	2-M	5,454	497	68.0
St. Francis Coll., Brooklyn Heights, NY 11201-4398	1884	$17,280	NA	2-M	2,511	243	54.0
St. Francis Univ., Loretto, PA 15940-0600	1847	$26,534	$9,066	2-D	2,449	190	68.0
St. John Fisher Coll., Rochester, NY 14618-3597	1948	$25,270	$10,290	2-D	4,020	413	72.0
St. John's Univ., Collegeville, MN 56321 (1)	1857	$31,576	$8,044	2-M	2,036	181	75.0
St. John's Univ., Queens, NY 11439	1870	$31,980	$13,900	2-D	21,354	1,418	58.0
St. Joseph Coll., West Hartford, CT 06117-2700	1932	$28,530	$12,940	2-D	2,326	247	42.0
St. Joseph's Coll., Rensselaer, IN 47978	1889	$26,330	$7,980	2-M	1,033	101	55.0
St. Joseph's Coll., Long Island Campus, Patchogue, NY 11772-2399	1916	$17,565	NA	1-M	4,411	422	70.0
St. Joseph's Coll., New York, Brooklyn, NY 11205-3688	1916	$17,565	NA	1-M	1,486	176	57.0
St. Joseph's Coll. of Maine, Standish, ME 04084	1912	$27,345	$10,550	2-M	1,050	126	50.0
St. Joseph's Univ., Philadelphia, PA 19131-1395	1851	$35,230	$11,925	2-D	8,916	726	78.0
St. Lawrence Univ., Canton, NY 13617-1455	1856	$41,155	$10,615	1-M	2,423	192	83.0
St. Leo Univ., Saint Leo, FL 33574-6665	1889	$18,870	$9,120	2-M	4,665	164	44.0
St. Louis Coll. of Pharm, St. Louis, MO 63110-1088	1864	$23,770	$8,755	1-D	1,215	129	60.0
St. Louis Univ., St. Louis, MO 63103-2097	1818	$32,656	$9,170	2-D	13,785	1,104	72.0
St. Martin's Univ., Lacey, WA 98503	1895	$27,621	$8,960	2-M	1,687	204	48.0
St. Mary-of-the-Woods Coll., Saint Mary-of-the-Woods, IN 47876 (4)	1840	$24,500	$8,890	2-M	1,595	178	52.0
St. Mary's Coll., Notre Dame, IN 46556 (3)	1844	$31,020	$9,480	2-B	1,555	199	82.0
St. Mary's Coll. of California, Moraga, CA 94556	1863	$35,430	$12,350	2-D	3,917	460	64.0
St. Mary's Coll. of Maryland, St. Mary's City, MD 20686-3001	1840	$13,630(S)	$10,250	5-M	2,017	227	77.0
St. Mary's Univ., San Antonio, TX 78228-8507	1852	$22,556	$7,550	2-D	3,893	340	56.0
St. Mary's Univ. of Minnesota, Winona, MN 55987-1399	1912	$27,250	$7,150	2-D	6,058	598	59.0
St. Michael's Coll., Colchester, VT 05439	1904	$36,240	$9,030	2-M	2,456	202	77.0
St. Norbert Coll., De Pere, WI 54115-2099	1898	$28,043	$7,349	2-M	2,241	196	76.0
St. Olaf Coll., Northfield, MN 55057-1098	1874	$36,800	$8,500	2-B	3,156	336	86.0
St. Petersburg Coll., St. Petersburg, FL 33733-3489	1927	$2,822(S)	NA	11-B	31,793	1,731	28.0
St. Peter's Coll., Jersey City, NJ 07306-5997	1872	$28,332	$11,510	2-M	3,081	NA	46.0
St. Thomas Aquinas Coll., Sparkill, NY 10976	1952	$22,410	$10,300	1-M	2,080	161	49.0
St. Thomas Univ., Miami Gardens, FL 33054-6459	1961	$22,770	$6,842	2-D	2,501	242	40.0
St. Vincent Coll., Latrobe, PA 15650-2690	1846	$27,190	$9,048	2-M	1,984	187	73.0
St. Xavier Univ., Chicago, IL 60655-3105	1847	$25,520	$8,692	2-M	4,852	426	56.0
Salem Intl. Univ., Salem, WV 26426-0500	1888	$14,100	$6,400	1-M	NA	16	39.4
Salem State Univ., Salem, MA 01970-5353	1854	$7,170(S)	$7,810	5-M	9,993	779	NA
Salisbury Univ., Salisbury, MD 21801-6837	1925	$6,908(S)	$8,378	5-M	8,397	597	66.0
Salve Regina Univ., Newport, RI 02840-4192	1934	$31,450	$11,300	2-D	2,618	265	69.0
Samford Univ., Birmingham, AL 35229	1841	$23,932	$8,158	2-D	4,715	439	73.0
Sam Houston State Univ., Huntsville, TX 77341	1879	$7,000(S)	$7,022	5-D	17,291	843	50.0
Samuel Merritt Univ., Oakland, CA 94609-3108 (4)	1909	$37,648	NA	1-D	1,422	251	89.0
San Diego State Univ., San Diego, CA 92182	1897	$5,206(S)	$11,485	5-D	30,016	1,467	66.0
San Diego State Univ.–Imperial Valley Campus, Calexico, CA 92231	NA	$4,464(S)	$10,388	5-M	1,003	NA	NA
San Francisco State Univ., San Francisco, CA 94132-1722	1899	$5,668(S)	$11,408	5-D	29,718	1,580	48.0
San Jose State Univ., San Jose, CA 95192-0001	1857	$5,475(S)	$10,733	5-M	29,076	1,593	48.0
Santa Clara Univ., Santa Clara, CA 95053	1851	$37,368	$11,742	2-D	8,831	840	87.0
Santa Fe Coll., Gainesville, FL 32606	1966	$2,168(S)	NA	11-B	15,745	829	NA
Sarah Lawrence Coll., Bronxville, NY 10708-5999	1926	$45,212	$13,504	1-M	1,670	309	77.0
Savannah Coll. of Art & Design, Savannah, GA 31402-3146	1978	$31,010	$12,255	1-M	10,461	720	67.0
Savannah State Univ., Savannah, GA 31404	1890	$5,624(S)	$6,288	5-M	4,080	200	35.0
Sch. of the Art Inst. of Chicago, Chicago, IL 60603-3103	1866	$35,950	$9,800	1-M	3,170	597	63.0
Sch. of Visual Arts, New York, NY 10010-3994	1947	$28,140	$15,500	3-M	4,214	929	69.0
Schreiner Univ., Kerrville, TX 78028-5697	1923	$20,354	$9,676	2-M	1,076	114	40.0
Seattle Pacific Univ., Seattle, WA 98119-1997	1891	$30,339	$9,081	2-D	4,117	355	71.0
Seattle Univ., Seattle, WA 98122-1090	1891	$30,825	$9,315	2-D	7,751	678	73.0
Seton Hall Univ., South Orange, NJ 07079-2697	1856	$31,890	$12,050	2-D	9,616	879	63.0
Seton Hill Univ., Greensburg, PA 15601	1883	$27,548	$8,810	2-M	2,232	194	55.0
Sewanee: The Univ. of the South, Sewanee, TN 37383-1000	1857	$32,292	$9,226	2-D	1,536	172	82.0
Shawnee State Univ., Portsmouth, OH 45662-4344	1986	$6,546(S)	$8,416	5-M	4,561	327	22.0
Shaw Univ., Raleigh, NC 27601-2399	1865	$12,580	$7,560	2-D	2,538	236	34.0
Shenandoah Univ., Winchester, VA 22601-5195	1875	$25,080	$8,870	2-D	3,679	432	51.0
Shepherd Univ., Shepherdstown, WV 25443	1871	$5,234(S)	$7,720	5-M	4,234	343	43.0
Shippensburg Univ. of Pennsylvania, Shippensburg, PA 17257-2299	1871	$8,056(S)	$7,400	5-M	8,326	420	60.0
Shorter Univ., Rome, GA 30165	1873	$17,070	$8,200	2-M	1,555	174	51.0
Siena Coll., Loudonville, NY 12211-1462	1937	$28,985	$11,434	2-M	3,423	330	73.0
Siena Heights Univ., Adrian, MI 49221-1796	1919	$20,557	$7,440	2-M	2,408	216	39.0
Silicon Valley Univ., San Jose, CA 95131	NA	$295/unit	NA	3-M	1,090	31	NA
Simmons Coll., Boston, MA 02115	1899	$32,230	$12,470	1-D	4,983	590	68.0
Simpson Coll., Indianola, IA 50125-1297	1860	$28,123	$7,963	2-M	2,021	204	68.0
Simpson Univ., Redding, CA 96003-8606	1921	$21,600	$7,300	2-M	1,216	125	44.0
Skidmore Coll., Saratoga Springs, NY 12866	1903	$41,184	$10,986	1-M	2,783	343	84.0
Slippery Rock Univ. of Pennsylvania, Slippery Rock, PA 16057-1383	1889	$7,666(S)	$8,884	5-D	8,852	405	61.0

Name, address	Year founded	Tuition & fees	Room & board	Control, degree	Enroll-ment	Faculty	Grad. rate
Smith Coll., Northampton, MA 01063	1871	$38,898	$13,000	1-D	3,113	296	83.0%
Sojourner-Douglass Coll., Baltimore, MD 21205-1814 (4)	1980	$8,850	NA	1-M	1,151	NA	NA
Sonoma State Univ., Rohnert Park, CA 94928-3609	1960	$5,508(S)	$10,522	5-M	8,395	567	55.0
South Carolina State Univ., Orangeburg, SC 29117-0001	1896	$8,898(S)	$9,238	5-D	4,538	289	45.0
South Dakota Sch. of Mines & Tech., Rapid City, SD 57701-3995	1885	$7,130(S)	$5,610	5-D	2,354	152	43.0
South Dakota State Univ., Brookings, SD 57007	1881	$6,444(S)	$5,899	5-D	12,816	695	55.0
Southeastern Baptist Theological Seminary, Wake Forest, NC 27588-1889	1950	$229/cr. hr.	NA	2-M	2,283	85	NA
Southeastern Louisiana Univ., Hammond, LA 70402	1925	$4,000(S)	$6,640	5-D	15,351	613	33.0
Southeastern Oklahoma State Univ., Durant, OK 74701-0609	1909	$4,552(S)	$4,520	5-M	4,181	261	41.0
Southeastern Univ., Lakeland, FL 33801-6099	1935	$16,430	$7,900	2-M	2,779	180	46.0
Southeast Missouri State Univ., Cape Girardeau, MO 63701-4799	1873	$6,255(S)	$7,342	5-M	11,112	566	48.0
Southern Adventist Univ., Collegedale, TN 37315-0370	1892	$18,324	$5,786	2-M	3,053	269	48.0
Southern Arkansas Univ.–Magnolia, Magnolia, AR 71753	1909	$6,426(S)	$4,570	5-M	3,379	220	34.0
Southern Baptist Theological Seminary, Louisville, KY 40280-0004	1858	$8,590	NA	2-D	3,190	NA	NA
Southern Connecticut State Univ., New Haven, CT 06515-1355	1893	$8,050(S)	$9,983	5-D	11,964	1,132	42.0
Southern Illinois Univ. Carbondale, Carbondale, IL 62901-4701	1869	$11,038(S)	$8,648	5-D	20,350	1,094	44.0
Southern Illinois Univ. Edwardsville, Edwardsville, IL 62026-0001	1957	$8,401(S)	$7,821	5-D	14,133	876	51.0
Southern Methodist Univ., Dallas, TX 75275	1911	$39,430	NA	2-D	10,938	1,040	74.0
Southern Nazarene Univ., Bethany, OK 73008	1899	$19,794	$7,600	2-M	2,051	189	46.0
Southern New Hampshire Univ., Manchester, NH 03106-1045	1932	$26,442	$10,176	1-D	4,211	388	55.0
Southern Oregon Univ., Ashland, OR 97520	1926	$6,729(S)	$8,508	5-M	6,512	290	NA
Southern Polytechnic State Univ., Marietta, GA 30060-2896	1948	$6,176(S)	$6,604	5-M	5,514	287	33.0
Southern Univ. & A&M Coll., Baton Rouge, LA 70813	1880	$4,581(S)	$5,580	5-D	7,699	546	30.0
Southern Univ. at New Orleans, New Orleans, LA 70126-1009 (4)	1959	$3,410(S)	$8,236	5-M	3,141	102	5.2
Southern Utah Univ., Cedar City, UT 84720-2498	1897	$4,736(S)	$2,086	5-M	8,019	328	40.0
Southern Wesleyan Univ., Central, SC 29630-1020	1906	$20,550	$7,550	2-M	1,883	193	39.0
Southwest Baptist Univ., Bolivar, MO 65613-2597	1878	$17,280	$5,720	2-D	3,716	260	48.0
Southwestern Assemblies of God Univ., Waxahachie, TX 75165-5735	1927	$15,730	$6,426	2-M	2,064	142	39.0
Southwestern Coll., Winfield, KS 67156-2499	1885	$21,680	$6,322	2-M	1,791	107	52.0
Southwestern Oklahoma State Univ., Weatherford, OK 73096-3098	1901	$4,335(S)	$4,100	5-D	5,259	240	30.0
Southwestern Univ., Georgetown, TX 78626	1840	$31,630	$9,770	2-B	1,301	166	77.0
Southwest Florida Coll., Fort Myers, FL 33907	1940	NA	NA	1-B	1,263	NA	NA
Southwest Minnesota State Univ., Marshall, MN 56258	1963	$7,244(S)	$6,637	5-M	6,611	203	40.0
Spalding Univ., Louisville, KY 40203-2188	1814	$18,150	$5,686	2-D	2,346	168	45.0
Spelman Coll., Atlanta, GA 30314-4399 (3)	1881	$22,010	$10,464	1-B	2,177	255	73.0
Spring Arbor Univ., Spring Arbor, MI 49283-9799	1873	$20,536	$7,254	2-M	4,195	139	56.0
Springfield Coll., Springfield, MA 01109-3797	1885	$30,660	NA	1-D	5,000	342	NA
Spring Hill Coll., Mobile, AL 36608-1791	1830	$26,730	$10,250	2-M	1,601	140	64.0
Stanford Univ., Stanford, CA 94305-9991	1891	$41,006	$12,291	1-D	19,535	1,014	95.0
State Univ. of New York at Albany, Albany, NY 12222-0001	1844	$6,830(S)	$10,633	5-D	18,020	1,268	63.0
State Univ. of New York at Buffalo, Buffalo, NY 14260	1846	$7,136(S)	$10,028	5-D	29,048	1,740	67.0
State Univ. of New York at Binghamton, Binghamton, NY 13902-6000	1946	$6,881(S)	$11,244	5-D	14,895	845	78.0
State Univ. of New York at Fredonia, Fredonia, NY 14063-1136	1826	$6,333(S)	$10,110	5-M	5,769	474	64.0
State Univ. of New York at New Paltz, New Paltz, NY 12561	1828	$6,458(S)	$9,950	5-M	7,885	650	67.0
State Univ. of New York at Oswego, Oswego, NY 13126	1861	$6,186(S)	$11,610	5-M	8,297	532	63.0
State Univ. of New York at Plattsburgh, Plattsburgh, NY 12901-2681	1889	$6,143(S)	$9,000	5-M	6,441	536	59.0
State Univ. of New York Coll. at Brockport, Brockport, NY 14420-2997	1867	$6,176(S)	$9,780	5-M	8,490	597	63.0
State Univ. of New York Coll. at Cortland, Cortland, NY 13045	1868	$6,215(S)	$10,490	5-M	7,358	618	62.0
State Univ. of New York Coll. at Geneseo, Geneseo, NY 14454-1401	1871	$6,401(S)	$10,042	5-M	5,695	339	77.0
State Univ. of New York Coll. at Old Westbury, Old Westbury, NY 11568-0210	1965	$5,966(S)	$9,700	5-B	4,355	285	39.0
State Univ. of New York Coll. at Oneonta, Oneonta, NY 13820-4015	1889	$6,250(S)	$9,284	5-M	6,014	499	66.0
State Univ. of New York Coll. at Potsdam, Potsdam, NY 13676	1816	$6,183(S)	$9,630	5-M	4,413	333	58.0
State Univ. of New York Coll. of Agr. & Tech. at Cobleskill, Cobleskill, NY 12043	1916	$6,414(S)	$9,926	5-B	2,619	175	40.0
State Univ. of New York Coll. of Agr. & Tech. at Morrisville, Morrisville, NY 13408-0901	1908	$6,765(S)	$8,510	5-B	3,432	261	NA
State Univ. of New York Coll. of Environmental Science & Forestry, Syracuse, NY 13210-2779	1911	$5,941(S)	$14,032	5-D	2,343	172	65.0
State Univ. of New York Coll. of Tech. at Canton, Canton, NY 13617	1906	$6,307(S)	$9,790	5-B	3,320	200	48.0
State Univ. of New York Coll. of Tech. at Delhi, Delhi, NY 13753	1913	$6,445(S)	$9,720	5-B	3,357	214	NA
State Univ. of New York Downstate Med. Ctr., Brooklyn, NY 11203-2098	1858	$5,292(S)	$12,044	5-D	1,694	981	NA
State Univ. of New York Empire State Coll., Saratoga Springs, NY 12866-4391	1971	$5,195(S)	NA	5-M	12,009	1,318	NA
State Univ. of New York Inst. of Tech., Utica, NY 13504-3050	1966	$6,094(S)	NA	5-M	2,828	183	NA
State Univ. of New York Maritime Coll., Throggs Neck, NY 10465-4198 (2)	1874	$6,157(S)	$10,090	5-M	1,891	154	52.0
State Univ. of New York Upstate Medical Univ., Syracuse, NY 13210-2334	1950	$5,550(S)	$10,422	5-D	1,537	108	NA
Stephen F. Austin State Univ., Nacogdoches, TX 75962	1923	$6,998(S)	$7,670	5-D	12,954	NA	45.0
Stephens Coll., Columbia, MO 65215-0002 (4)	1833	$26,420	$7,170	1-M	1,122	150	51.0
Stetson Univ., DeLand, FL 32723	1883	$35,081	$10,255	1-D	3,756	357	61.0
Stevens Inst. of Tech., Hoboken, NJ 07030	1870	$39,810	$12,500	1-D	5,862	438	75.0
Stevenson Univ., Stevenson, MD 21153	1952	$22,090	$10,826	1-M	3,941	378	62.0
Stillman Coll., Tuscaloosa, AL 35403-9990	1876	$14,464	$6,524	2-B	1,048	63	9.5
Stonehill Coll., Easton, MA 02357	1948	$32,620	$12,610	2-B	2,582	261	85.0
Stony Brook Univ., State Univ. of New York, Stony Brook, NY 11794	1957	$6,580(S)	$10,142	5-D	24,594	1,482	65.0
Stratford Univ., Falls Church, VA 22043	1976	$15,330	$7,000	3-M	1,385	72	NA
Suffolk Univ., Boston, MA 02108-2770	1906	$28,526	$14,624	1-D	9,312	991	56.0
Sullivan Univ., Louisville, KY 40205	1864	$16,700	$6,345	3-M	4,538	269	NA
Sul Ross State Univ., Alpine, TX 79832	1920	$2,928(S)	$6,370	5-M	3,129	174	19.0
Susquehanna Univ., Selinsgrove, PA 17870	1858	$32,850	$9,800	2-B	2,305	244	79.0
Swarthmore Coll., Swarthmore, PA 19081-1397	1864	$39,600	$11,900	1-B	1,524	212	93.0
Syracuse Univ., NY 13244	1870	$36,302	$12,850	1-D	20,407	1,513	83.0
Tarleton State Univ., Stephenville, TX 76402	1899	$6,199(S)	$6,591	5-D	9,340	535	37.0
Taylor Univ., Upland, IN 46989-1001	1846	$27,438	$7,218	2-M	2,589	252	78.0
Temple Univ., Philadelphia, PA 19122-6096	1884	$12,424(S)	$9,550	12-D	37,367	2,936	65.0
Tennessee State Univ., Nashville, TN 37209-1561	1912	$5,744(S)	$5,760	5-D	8,254	603	NA
Tennessee Tech. Univ., Cookeville, TN 38505	1915	$5,828(S)	$7,158	5-D	11,538	640	48.0
Tennessee Wesleyan Coll., Athens, TN 37371-0040	1857	$19,100	$6,350	2-B	1,103	89	50.0
Texas A&M Intl. Univ., Laredo, TX 78041-1900	1969	$6,153(S)	$6,918	5-D	6,853	326	40.0
Texas A&M Univ., College Station, TX 77843	1876	$8,387(S)	$8,008	5-D	49,129	2,818	80.0
Texas A&M Univ.–Commerce, Commerce, TX 75429-3011	1889	$5,998(S)	$7,090	5-D	9,170	843	35.4
Texas A&M Univ.–Corpus Christi, Corpus Christi, TX 78412-5503	1947	$6,514(S)	$9,528	5-D	10,033	579	38.0
Texas A&M Univ. at Galveston, Galveston, TX 77553-1675	1962	$7,158(S)	$6,276	5-M	1,774	170	53.0
Texas A&M Univ.–Kingsville, Kingsville, TX 78363	1925	$6,346(S)	$5,130	5-D	6,586	388	34.0
Texas A&M Univ.–Texarkana, Texarkana, TX 75505-5518	1971	$4,946(S)	NA	5-M	1,653	NA	NA
Texas Christian Univ., Fort Worth, TX 76129-0002	1873	$32,490	$10,600	2-D	9,142	845	74.0
Texas Lutheran Univ., Seguin, TX 78155-5999	1891	$22,890	$6,740	2-B	1,340	140	45.0
Texas Southern Univ., Houston, TX 77004-4584	1947	$7,462(S)	$11,880	5-D	9,579	585	13.0
Texas State Univ.–San Marcos, San Marcos, TX 78666	1899	$7,838(S)	$6,810	5-D	32,572	1,546	55.0
Texas Tech. Univ., Lubbock, TX 79409	1923	$8,260(S)	$7,800	5-D	31,637	1,390	63.0

Name, address	Year founded	Tuition & fees	Room & board	Control, degree	Enrollment	Faculty	Grad. rate
Texas Wesleyan Univ., Fort Worth, TX 76105-1536	1890	$18,710	$6,910	2-D	3,378	279	34.0%
Texas Woman's Univ., Denton, TX 76201 (4)	1901	$6,960(S)	$6,210	5-D	14,180	801	45.0
Thiel Coll., Greenville, PA 16125-2181	1866	$24,856	$9,652	2-B	1,096	114	38.0
Thomas Edison State Coll., Trenton, NJ 08608-1176	1972	$4,883(S)	NA	5-M	18,736	NA	NA
Thomas Jefferson Univ., Philadelphia, PA 19107	1824	$27,139	NA	1-D	3,326	NA	NA
Thomas More Coll., Crestview Hills, KY 41017-3495	1921	$24,720	$6,790	2-M	1,886	131	45.0
Thomas Univ., Thomasville, GA 31792-7499	1950	$12,720	$3,150	1-M	1,043	49	NA
Tiffin Univ., Tiffin, OH 44883-2161	1888	$19,124	$8,750	1-M	4,940	403	38.0
Touro Coll., New York, NY 10010	1971	$14,600	$7,000	1-D	17,129	NA	NA
Towson Univ., Towson, MD 21252-0001	1866	$7,656(S)	$9,614	5-D	21,840	1,588	68.0
Transylvania Univ., Lexington, KY 40508-1797	1780	$26,740	$8,090	2-B	1,110	103	76.0
Trevecca Nazarene Univ., Nashville, TN 37210-2877	1901	$18,518	$7,734	2-D	2,345	229	46.0
Trine Univ., Angola, IN 46703-1764	1884	$26,730	$8,800	1-M	1,791	213	51.0
Trinity Christian Coll., Palos Heights, IL 60463-0929	1959	$21,508	$7,964	2-B	1,450	151	58.0
Trinity Coll., Hartford, CT 06106-3100	1823	$42,370	$10,960	1-M	2,439	239	86.0
Trinity Intl. Univ., Deerfield, IL 60015-1284	1897	$23,370	NA	2-D	2,671	82	52.0
Trinity Univ., San Antonio, TX 78212-7200	1869	$30,012	$10,312	2-M	2,619	306	78.0
Trinity Univ., Washington, DC 20017-1094	1897	$20,375	$9,060	2-M	1,630	NA	NA
Troy Univ., Troy, AL 36082	1887	$7,200(S)	$6,570	5-D	29,322	1,469	44.0
Truman State Univ., Kirksville, MO 63501-4221	1867	$6,692(S)	$7,097	5-M	6,035	382	70.0
Tufts Univ., Medford, MA 02155	1852	$42,532	$11,268	1-D	10,480	951	91.0
TUI Univ., Cypress, CA 90630	NA	$9,440	NA	1-D	7,311	268	NA
Tulane Univ., New Orleans, LA 70118-5669	1834	$41,884	$9,824	1-D	12,622	1,003	70.0
Tusculum Coll., Greeneville, TN 37743-9997	1794	$19,920	$8,000	2-M	2,203	224	40.0
Tuskegee Univ., Tuskegee, AL 36088	1881	$16,750	$7,570	1-D	2,946	294	46.0
Union Coll., Barbourville, KY 40906-1499	1879	$20,004	$6,200	2-M	1,363	109	31.0
Union Coll., Schenectady, NY 12308-2311	1795	$52,329(C)	NA	1-B	2,197	236	83.0
Union Inst. & Univ., Cincinnati, OH 45206-1925	1969	$11,132	NA	1-D	1,508	294	25.0
Union Univ., Jackson, TN 38305-3697	1823	$22,390	$7,460	2-D	3,996	237	63.0
United States Air Force Academy, USAF Academy, CO 80840-5025 (2)	1954	$0(C)	NA	4-B	4,619	569	78.0
United States Coast Guard Academy, New London, CT 06320-8100	1876	$0(C)	NA	4-B	1,017	141	79.0
United States Merchant Marine Academy, Kings Point, NY 11024-1699	1943	$0(C)	NA	4-M	1,135	NA	NA
United States Military Academy, West Point, NY 10996	1802	$0(C)	NA	4-B	4,686	615	86.0
United States Naval Academy, Annapolis, MD 21402-5000 (2)	1845	$0(C)	NA	4-B	4,603	587	89.0
United Talmudical Seminary, Brooklyn, NY 11211 (1)	1949	NA	NA	2-M	1,500	NA	NA
Universidad Adventista de las Antillas, Mayagüez, PR 00681-0118	1957	$5,670	$2,900	2-M	1,019	85	NA
Universidad del Este, Carolina, PR 00984	1949	NA	NA	1-M	13,317	NA	NA
Universidad del Turabo, Gurabo, PR 00778-3030	1972	NA	NA	1-D	16,190	NA	NA
Universidad Metropolitana, San Juan, PR 00928-1150	1980	NA	NA	1-M	12,622	903	23.0
Univ. of Advancing Tech., Tempe, AZ 85283-1042 (2)	1983	$19,500	$10,926	3-M	1,073	60	NA
Univ. of Akron, Akron, OH 44325	1870	$9,247(S)	$9,160	5-D	27,076	1,731	33.0
Univ. of Alabama, Tuscaloosa, AL 35487	1831	$8,600(S)	$8,564	5-D	30,127	1,555	67.0
Univ. of Alabama at Birmingham, Birmingham, AL 35294	1969	$6,256(S)	$8,810	5-D	17,543	931	39.0
Univ. of Alabama in Huntsville, Huntsville, AL 35899	1950	$7,492(S)	$7,540	5-D	7,614	480	44.0
Univ. of Alaska Anchorage, Anchorage, AK 99508	1954	$5,096(S)	NA	5-M	17,825	1,278	NA
Univ. of Alaska Fairbanks, Fairbanks, AK 99775-7520	1917	$6,075(S)	$6,960	5-D	9,855	1,049	32.0
Univ. of Alaska Southeast, Juneau, AK 99801	1972	$5,139(S)	$8,165	5-M	3,458	229	31.0
Univ. of Arizona, Tucson, AZ 85721	1885	$8,860(S)	$9,024	5-D	39,086	1,972	60.0
Univ. of Arkansas–Fayetteville, AR 72701-1201	1871	$6,768(S)	$8,042	5-D	21,405	1,026	58.0
Univ. of Arkansas–Fort Smith, Fort Smith, AR 72913-3649	1928	$4,918(S)	$4,000	11-B	7,751	426	21.0
Univ. of Arkansas–Little Rock, Little Rock, AR 72204-1099	1927	$6,643(S)	$3,255	5-D	13,132	749	NA
Univ. of Arkansas–Monticello, Monticello, AR 71656	1909	$4,750(S)	NA	5-M	3,479	274	19.0
Univ. of Arkansas–Pine Bluff, Pine Bluff, AR 71601-2799	1873	$4,980(S)	NA	5-M	3,428	234	24.0
Univ. of Arkansas for Medical Sciences, Little Rock, AR 72205-7199	1879	$6,856(S)	$5,900	5-D	2,836	NA	NA
Univ. of Atlanta, Atlanta, GA 30360	NA	$3,150	NA	1-D	1,410	299	NA
Univ. of Baltimore, Baltimore, MD 21201-5779	1925	$7,330(S)	NA	5-D	6,501	404	NA
Univ. of Bridgeport, Bridgeport, CT 06604	1927	$26,495	$11,400	1-D	5,155	484	30.0
Univ. of California–Berkeley, Berkeley, CA 94720-1500	1868	$12,462(S)	$15,308	5-D	35,838	2,090	91.0
Univ. of California–Davis, Davis, CA 95616	1905	$11,984(S)	$12,498	5-D	31,392	1,620	82.0
Univ. of California–Irvine, Irvine, CA 92697	1965	$11,927(S)	$11,400	5-D	26,994	1,886	83.0
Univ. of California–Los Angeles, Los Angeles, CA 90095	1919	$11,868(S)	$13,734	5-D	39,593	2,595	90.0
Univ. of California–Merced, Merced, CA 95343	NA	$10,130(S)	$12,801	5-D	4,381	242	NA
Univ. of California–Riverside, Riverside, CA 92521-0102	1954	$11,029(S)	$11,600	5-D	19,439	919	65.0
Univ. of California–San Diego, La Jolla, CA 92093	1959	$12,176(S)	$11,719	5-D	26,723	1,144	84.0
Univ. of California–Santa Barbara, Santa Barbara, CA 93106-2014	1909	$11,686(S)	$13,109	5-D	22,218	1,057	79.0
Univ. of California–Santa Cruz, Santa Cruz, CA 95064	1965	$12,447(S)	$14,610	5-D	17,175	803	73.0
Univ. of Central Arkansas, Conway, AR 72035-0001	1907	$6,777(S)	$5,030	5-D	12,974	709	41.0
Univ. of Central Florida, Orlando, FL 32816	1963	$5,020(S)	$8,765	5-D	56,235	1,799	62.9
Univ. of Central Missouri, Warrensburg, MO 64093	1871	$7,311(S)	$6,320	5-M	11,351	617	51.0
Univ. of Central Oklahoma, Edmond, OK 73034-5209	1890	$4,456(S)	$8,005	5-M	16,092	860	36.0
Univ. of Charleston, Charleston, WV 25304-1099	1888	$25,000	$8,800	1-D	1,518	130	43.0
Univ. of Chicago, Chicago, IL 60637-1513	1891	$43,780	$12,633	1-D	12,781	1,662	92.0
Univ. of Cincinnati, Cincinnati, OH 45221	1819	$10,068(S)	$9,702	5-D	32,283	1,224	56.0
Univ. of Colorado–Boulder, Boulder, CO 80309	1876	$8,511(S)	$10,792	5-D	32,378	2,050	68.0
Univ. of Colorado–Colorado Springs, Colorado Springs, CO 80933-7150	1965	$7,416(S)	$6,778	5-D	9,348	601	48.0
Univ. of Colorado–Denver, Denver, CO 80217-3364	1912	$7,214(S)	$9,956	5-D	24,108	3,158	42.0
Univ. of Connecticut, Storrs, CT 06269	1881	$10,670(S)	$11,050	5-D	25,498	NA	81.0
Univ. of Dallas, Irving, TX 75062-4736	1955	$29,325	$9,326	2-D	2,843	239	74.0
Univ. of Dayton, Dayton, OH 45469-1300	1850	$29,930	$9,400	2-D	11,214	955	78.0
Univ. of Delaware, Newark, DE 19716	1743	$10,208(S)	$9,636	12-D	20,403	1,466	77.0
Univ. of Denver, Denver, CO 80208	1864	$37,833	$10,184	1-D	11,842	1,244	76.0
Univ. of Detroit Mercy, Detroit, MI 48221	1877	$28,920	$8,590	2-D	5,725	NA	NA
Univ. of Dubuque, Dubuque, IA 52001-5099	1852	$21,590	$7,370	2-D	1,864	153	38.0
Univ. of Evansville, Evansville, IN 47722	1854	$28,076	$9,110	2-D	2,898	234	66.0
Univ. of Findlay, Findlay, OH 45840-3653	1882	$26,798	$8,810	2-D	5,542	305	57.0
Univ. of Florida, Gainesville, FL 32611	1853	$5,044(S)	$8,640	5-D	49,827	3,643	82.0
Univ. of Georgia, Athens, GA 30602	1785	$8,736(S)	$8,460	5-D	34,677	2,086	82.0
Univ. of Guam, Mangilao, GU 96923	1952	$5,818(S)	$9,559	7-M	3,639	258	24.0
Univ. of Hartford, West Hartford, CT 06117-1599	1877	$30,754	$11,920	1-D	7,180	925	58.0
Univ. of Hawaii–Hilo, Hilo, HI 96720-4091	1970	$5,416(S)	$7,134	5-D	4,079	347	33.0
Univ. of Hawaii–Manoa, Honolulu, HI 96822	1907	$8,911(S)	$9,410	5-D	20,337	1,209	48.0
Univ. of Hawaii–West Oahu, Pearl City, HI 96782-3366	1976	$5,141(S)	NA	5-B	1,471	79	NA
Univ. of Houston, Houston, TX 77204	1927	$9,000(S)	$7,300	5-D	38,752	1,757	46.0
Univ. of Houston–Clear Lake, Houston, TX 77058-1098	1971	$6,188(S)	$10,340	5-D	8,110	525	NA
Univ. of Houston–Downtown, Houston, TX 77002	1974	$5,492(S)	NA	5-M	12,900	626	12.0
Univ. of Houston–Victoria, Victoria, TX 77901-4450	1973	$5,604(S)	$6,550	5-M	4,095	195	NA

Name, address	Year founded	Tuition & fees	Room & board	Control, degree	Enroll- ment	Faculty	Grad. rate
Univ. of Idaho, Moscow, ID 83844-2282	1889	$5,402(S)	$7,194	5-D	12,302	702	55.0%
Univ. of Illinois–Chicago, Chicago, IL 60607-7128	1946	$12,056(S)	$9,994	5-D	27,850	1,540	53.0
Univ. of Illinois–Springfield, Springfield, IL 62703-5407	1969	$10,367(S)	$9,400	5-D	5,174	362	68.0
Univ. of Illinois–Urbana-Champaign, Champaign, IL 61820	1867	$14,414(S)	$10,080	5-D	43,862	1,963	84.0
Univ. of Indianapolis, Indianapolis, IN 46227-3697	1902	$22,240	$8,440	2-D	5,290	472	50.0
Univ. of Iowa, Iowa City, IA 52242-1316	1847	$7,765(S)	$8,750	5-D	29,518	1,621	70.0
Univ. of Kansas, Lawrence, KS 66045	1866	$8,733(S)	$6,982	5-D	28,696	1,700	61.0
Univ. of Kentucky, Lexington, KY 40506-0032	1865	$8,610(S)	$9,439	5-D	26,295	1,683	60.0
Univ. of La Verne, La Verne, CA 91750-4443	1891	$31,300	$11,280	1-D	4,468	435	70.0
Univ. of Louisiana–Lafayette, Lafayette, LA 70504	1898	$4,426(S)	$4,758	5-D	16,763	751	40.0
Univ. of Louisiana–Monroe, Monroe, LA 71209-0001	1931	$4,635(S)	$2,992	5-D	8,801	361	33.0
Univ. of Louisville, Louisville, KY 40292-0001	1798	$8,424(S)	$6,602	5-D	21,234	1,388	48.0
Univ. of Maine, Orono, ME 04469	1865	$10,168(S)	$8,766	5-D	11,501	749	57.0
Univ. of Maine–Augusta, Augusta, ME 04330-9410	1965	$7,125(S)	NA	5-B	5,074	274	16.7
Univ. of Maine–Farmington, Farmington, ME 04938-1990	1863	$9,022(S)	$7,854	5-M	2,392	168	58.0
Univ. of Maine–Fort Kent, Fort Kent, ME 04743-1292	1878	$7,163(S)	$7,500	5-B	1,073	69	27.0
Univ. of Maine–Presque Isle, Presque Isle, ME 04769-2888	1903	$7,235(S)	$7,046	5-B	1,434	109	35.0
Univ. of Mary, Bismarck, ND 58504-9652	1959	$13,126	$5,180	2-D	2,849	273	52.0
Univ. of Mary Hardin-Baylor, Belton, TX 76513	1845	$23,050	$6,221	2-D	2,956	233	49.0
Univ. of Maryland–Baltimore County, Baltimore, MD 21250	1963	$9,171(S)	$9,620	5-D	12,888	724	59.0
Univ. of Maryland–Coll. Park, College Park, MD 20742	1856	$8,416(S)	$9,599	5-D	37,595	2,284	81.0
Univ. of Maryland–Eastern Shore, Princess Anne, MD 21853-1299	1886	$6,305(S)	$7,458	5-D	3,762	283	37.0
Univ. of Maryland University College, Adelphi, MD 20783	1947	$6,000(S)	NA	5-D	39,577	2,193	NA
Univ. of Mary Washington, Fredericksburg, VA 22401-5358	1908	$8,800(S)	$8,900	5-M	5,203	387	75.0
Univ. of Massachusetts–Amherst, Amherst, MA 01003	1863	$11,732(S)	$9,339	5-D	27,569	1,333	69.0
Univ. of Massachusetts–Boston, Boston, MA 02125-3393	1964	$10,611(S)	NA	5-D	15,454	1,038	41.0
Univ. of Massachusetts–Dartmouth, North Dartmouth, MA 02747-2300	1895	$10,358(S)	$9,134	5-D	9,432	653	48.0
Univ. of Massachusetts–Lowell, Lowell, MA 01854-2881	1894	$10,506(S)	$9,067	5-D	14,702	1,004	51.0
Univ. of Medicine & Dentistry of New Jersey, Newark, NJ 07107-1709	1970	NA	NA	5-B	5,000	NA	NA
Univ. of Memphis, Memphis, TN 38152	1912	$6,990(S)	$6,190	5-D	22,421	1,377	37.0
Univ. of Miami, Coral Gables, FL 33124	1925	$37,836	$11,062	1-D	15,657	1,370	80.0
Univ. of Michigan, Ann Arbor, MI 48109	1817	$12,779(S)	$9,192	5-D	41,924	3,085	89.0
Univ. of Michigan–Dearborn, Dearborn, MI 48128-1491	1959	$9,456(S)	NA	5-D	8,599	535	52.0
Univ. of Michigan–Flint, Flint, MI 48502-1950	1956	$8,601(S)	$7,212	5-D	8,138	509	39.0
Univ. of Minnesota–Crookston, Crookston, MN 56716-5001	1966	$10,623(S)	$6,568	5-B	2,528	109	39.0
Univ. of Minnesota–Duluth, Duluth, MN 55812-2496	1947	$11,807(S)	$6,422	5-D	11,729	566	52.0
Univ. of Minnesota–Morris, Morris, MN 56267-2134	1959	$11,532(S)	$7,050	5-B	1,607	153	66.0
Univ. of Minnesota–Twin Cities Campus, Minneapolis, MN 55455-0213	1851	$12,203(S)	$7,774	5-D	51,721	2,706	68.0
Univ. of Mississippi, University, MS 38677	1844	$5,708(S)	NA	5-D	17,085	881	59.0
Univ. of Mississippi Medical Ctr., Jackson, MS 39216-4505	1955	NA	NA	5-D	2,092	836	NA
Univ. of Missouri, Columbia, MO 65211	1839	$8,501(S)	$8,607	5-D	32,415	1,396	48.4
Univ. of Missouri–Kansas City, Kansas City, MO 64110-2499	1929	$8,602(S)	$10,131	5-D	14,818	1,137	45.0
Univ. of Missouri–St. Louis, St. Louis, MO 63121	1963	$9,038(S)	$8,404	5-D	16,802	915	43.0
Univ. of Mobile, Mobile, AL 36613	1961	$16,120	$7,780	2-M	1,673	181	41.0
Univ. of Montana, Missoula, MT 59812-0002	1893	$5,685(S)	$6,860	5-D	14,207	800	42.0
Univ. of Montana–Western, Dillon, MT 59725-3598	1893	$3,726(S)	$5,620	5-B	1,365	82	29.0
Univ. of Montevallo, Montevallo, AL 35115	1896	$8,520(S)	$5,192	5-M	3,050	211	45.0
Univ. of Mount Union, Alliance, OH 44601-3993	1846	$24,800	$7,780	2-M	2,255	233	63.0
Univ. of Nebraska–Kearney, Kearney, NE 68849-0001	1903	$5,959(S)	$7,206	5-M	6,650	406	59.0
Univ. of Nebraska–Lincoln, Lincoln, NE 68588	1869	$7,224(S)	$7,660	5-D	24,610	1,126	64.0
Univ. of Nebraska–Omaha, Omaha, NE 68182	1908	$6,626(S)	$7,750	5-D	14,665	857	45.0
Univ. of Nebraska Medical Ctr., Omaha, NE 68198	1869	$8,030(S)	NA	5-D	3,237	1,190	NA
Univ. of Nevada–Las Vegas, Las Vegas, NV 89154	1957	$5,689(S)	$10,454	5-D	28,222	1,274	41.0
Univ. of Nevada–Reno, Reno, NV 89557	1874	$4,841(S)	$9,518	5-D	17,679	567	50.0
Univ. of New England, Biddeford, ME 04005-9526	1831	$29,330	$11,410	1-D	5,168	352	55.0
Univ. of New Hampshire–Durham, NH 03824	1866	$13,672(S)	$9,053	5-D	15,155	1,008	75.0
Univ. of New Hampshire–Manchester, Manchester, NH 03101-1113	1967	$11,226(S)	NA	5-M	1,003	98	NA
Univ. of New Haven, West Haven, CT 06516-1916	1920	$30,750	$12,778	1-M	5,949	535	53.0
Univ. of New Mexico, Albuquerque, NM 87131-2039	1889	$5,809(S)	$8,068	5-D	28,688	1,469	44.0
Univ. of New Orleans, New Orleans, LA 70148	1958	$4,811(S)	$8,127	5-D	11,724	630	22.0
Univ. of North Alabama, Florence, AL 35632-0001	1830	$6,668(S)	$5,012	5-M	7,209	468	33.0
Univ. of North Carolina–Asheville, Asheville, NC 28804-3299	1927	$4,772(S)	$7,040	5-M	3,967	309	59.0
Univ. of North Carolina–Chapel Hill, Chapel Hill, NC 27599	1789	$6,666(S)	$9,036	5-D	29,390	1,788	90.0
Univ. of North Carolina–Charlotte, Charlotte, NC 28223-0001	1946	$5,138(S)	$7,260	5-D	25,063	1,376	55.1
Univ. of North Carolina–Greensboro, Greensboro, NC 27412-5001	1891	$4,520(S)	$3,855	5-D	18,478	1,185	53.0
Univ. of North Carolina–Pembroke, Pembroke, NC 28372-1510	1887	$4,140(S)	$5,990	5-M	6,913	418	38.0
Univ. of North Carolina–Wilmington, Wilmington, NC 28403-3297	1947	$5,416(S)	$7,608	5-D	13,071	899	66.0
Univ. of North Dakota, Grand Forks, ND 58202	1883	$6,934(S)	$5,950	5-D	14,194	680	53.0
Univ. of North Florida, Jacksonville, FL 32224	1965	$5,449(S)	$8,452	5-D	16,153	821	49.0
Univ. of North Texas, Denton, TX 76203	1890	$7,960(S)	$6,716	5-D	36,067	1,456	48.0
Univ. of Northern Colorado, Greeley, CO 80639	1890	$5,997(S)	$8,920	5-D	12,358	715	48.0
Univ. of Northern Iowa, Cedar Falls, IA 50614	1876	$7,008(S)	$7,140	5-D	13,201	824	67.0
Univ. of Northwestern Ohio, Lima, OH 45805-1498	1920	NA	NA	1-B	3,848	127	NA
Univ. of Notre Dame, Notre Dame, IN 46556	1842	$41,417	$11,388	2-D	11,992	1,085	96.0
Univ. of Oklahoma, Norman, OK 73019-0390	1890	$5,477(S)	$7,826	5-D	26,478	1,376	65.0
Univ. of Oklahoma Health Science Ctr., Oklahoma City, OK 73190	1890	$5,758(S)	NA	5-D	3,854	456	NA
Univ. of Oregon, Eugene, OR 97403	1872	$8,190(S)	$9,429	5-D	23,342	1,386	68.0
Univ. of Pennsylvania, Philadelphia, PA 19104	1740	$42,098	$11,878	1-D	19,842	2,161	96.0
Univ. of Phoenix, Phoenix, AZ 85034-7209	1989	$12,550	NA	3-D	292,797	11,477	NA
Univ. of Pittsburgh, Pittsburgh, PA 15260	1787	$14,936(S)	$9,230	12-D	28,823	2,315	78.0
Univ. of Pittsburgh–Bradford, Bradford, PA 16701-2812	1963	$12,046(S)	$7,650	12-B	1,627	154	41.0
Univ. of Pittsburgh–Greensburg, Greensburg, PA 15601-5860	1963	$12,176(S)	$8,110	12-B	1,803	133	54.0
Univ. of Pittsburgh–Johnstown, Johnstown, PA 15904-2990	1927	$12,078(S)	$7,826	12-B	2,982	171	56.0
Univ. of Portland, Portland, OR 97203-5798	1901	$33,538	$9,760	2-D	3,936	321	77.0
Univ. of Puerto Rico, Aguadilla Univ. Coll., Aguadilla, PR 00604	1972	NA	NA	6-B	3,076	NA	NA
Univ. of Puerto Rico, Cayey Univ. Coll., Cayey, PR 00736	1967	$1,848(S)	$8,180	6-B	3,830	164	41.0
Univ. of Puerto Rico–Arecibo, Arecibo, PR 00613	1967	NA	NA	6-B	4,352	NA	NA
Univ. of Puerto Rico–Bayamón, Bayamón, PR 00959	1971	$2,076(S)	NA	6-B	5,184	324	38.0
Univ. of Puerto Rico–Carolina, Carolina, PR 00984-4800	1974	NA	NA	6-B	4,321	NA	NA
Univ. of Puerto Rico–Humacao, Humacao, PR 00791	1962	$2,876(S)	NA	6-B	4,314	291	41.0
Univ. of Puerto Rico–Ponce, Ponce, PR 00732-7186	1970	$3,564(S)	NA	6-D	3,438	197	51.0
Univ. of Puerto Rico–Mayagüez Campus, Mayagüez, PR 00681-9000	1911	NA	NA	6-D	13,852	NA	NA
Univ. of Puerto Rico–Medical Science Campus, San Juan, PR 00936-5067 (4)	1950	NA	NA	6-D	2,381	NA	NA
Univ. of Puerto Rico–Río Piedras, San Juan, PR 00931-3300	1903	$1,368(S)	$8,280	6-D	18,966	1,084	47.0
Univ. of Puerto Rico–Utuado, Utuado, PR 00641-2500	1979	NA	NA	6-B	1,623	107	NA
Univ. of Puget Sound, Tacoma, WA 98416	1888	$38,720	$10,020	1-D	2,867	285	80.0
Univ. of Redlands, Redlands, CA 92373-0999	1907	$35,540	$10,832	1-D	4,431	479	64.0

Name, address	Year founded	Tuition & fees	Room & board	Control, degree	Enroll-ment	Faculty	Grad. rate
Univ. of Rhode Island, Kingston, RI 02881	1892	$9,014(S)	$10,854	5-D	16,294	1,229	63.0%
Univ. of Richmond, Richmond, VA 23173	1830	$43,170	$9,250	1-D	3,618	392	87.0
Univ. of Rio Grande, Rio Grande, OH 45674	1876	$18,808	$7,828	1-M	2,261	150	37.0
Univ. of Rochester, Rochester, NY 14627	1850	$40,282	$11,640	1-D	10,111	804	80.0
Univ. of St. Francis, Joliet, IL 60435-6169	1920	$24,742	$8,176	2-D	2,171	223	59.0
Univ. of St. Francis, Fort Wayne, IN 46808-3994	1890	$22,810	$6,970	2-M	2,112	222	51.0
Univ. of St. Thomas, St. Paul, MN 55105-1096	1885	$30,493	$8,320	2-D	10,832	NA	77.0
Univ. of St. Thomas, Houston, TX 77006-4696	1947	$23,500	$7,900	2-D	3,520	299	47.0
Univ. of San Diego, San Diego, CA 92110-2492	1949	$38,578	$11,752	2-D	8,201	843	73.0
Univ. of San Francisco, San Francisco, CA 94117-1080	1855	$37,424	$12,250	2-D	9,494	962	69.0
Univ. of Science & Arts of Oklahoma, Chickasha, OK 73018	1908	$4,680(S)	$4,990	5-B	1,050	91	32.0
Univ. of Scranton, Scranton, PA 18510	1888	$36,042	$12,432	2-D	6,070	518	77.0
Univ. of Sioux Falls, Sioux Falls, SD 57105-1699	1883	$22,850	$6,570	2-M	1,564	140	49.2
Univ. of South Alabama, Mobile, AL 36688-0002	1963	$6,810(S)	$5,608	5-D	14,776	816	37.0
Univ. of South Carolina, Columbia, SC 29208	1801	$9,786(S)	$7,764	5-D	29,597	1,869	68.0
Univ. of South Carolina–Aiken, Aiken, SC 29801-6309	1961	$8,424(S)	$6,450	5-M	3,254	229	38.0
Univ. of South Carolina–Beaufort, Bluffton, SC 29909	1959	$8,020(S)	$6,380	5-B	1,754	141	NA
Univ. of South Carolina–Upstate, Spartanburg, SC 29303-4999	1967	$9,292(S)	$6,400	5-M	5,494	406	39.0
Univ. of South Dakota, Vermillion, SD 57069-2390	1862	$6,762(S)	$6,123	5-D	10,151	504	49.0
Univ. of Southern California, Los Angeles, CA 90089	1880	$41,022	$11,580	1-D	36,896	2,964	89.0
Univ. of Southern Indiana, Evansville, IN 47712-3590	1965	$5,740(S)	$6,920	5-D	10,702	656	32.0
Univ. of Southern Maine, Portland, ME 04104-9300	1878	$8,538(S)	$9,394	5-D	9,654	673	NA
Univ. of Southern Mississippi, Hattiesburg, MS 39406-0001	1910	$5,452(S)	$6,634	5-D	15,778	884	47.0
Univ. of South Florida, Tampa, FL 33620-9951	1956	$5,198(S)	$5,380	5-D	40,431	1,235	NA
Univ. of Tampa, Tampa, FL 33606-1490	1931	$23,218	$8,590	1-M	6,427	534	59.0
Univ. of Tennessee, Knoxville, TN 37996	1794	$7,382(S)	$7,800	5-D	30,312	1,911	61.0
Univ. of Tennessee–Chattanooga, Chattanooga, TN 37403-2598	1886	$6,062(S)	$8,210	5-D	10,781	740	38.0
Univ. of Tennessee–Martin, Martin, TN 38238-1000	1900	$6,190(S)	$5,104	5-M	8,469	532	45.0
Univ. of Texas–Arlington, Arlington, TX 76019	1895	$8,500(S)	$6,224	5-D	32,975	1,283	43.0
Univ. of Texas–Austin, Austin, TX 78712-1111	1883	$9,794(S)	NA	5-D	51,195	2,976	81.0
Univ. of Texas–Brownsville, Brownsville, TX 78520-4991	1973	$4,766(S)	$5,782	5-D	17,189	701	16.0
Univ. of Texas–Dallas, Richardson, TX 75080	1969	$10,744(S)	$8,210	5-D	17,128	898	63.0
Univ. of Texas–El Paso, El Paso, TX 79968-0001	1913	$6,535(S)	NA	5-D	21,011	1,158	31.0
Univ. of Texas–Pan American, Edinburg, TX 78539	1927	$4,560(S)	$5,298	5-D	18,744	800	36.0
Univ. of Texas–Permian Basin, Odessa, TX 79762-0001	1969	$5,599(S)	$6,964	5-M	4,063	197	32.0
Univ. of Texas–San Antonio, San Antonio, TX 78249-0617	1969	$8,283(S)	$8,696	5-D	30,258	1,250	26.0
Univ. of Texas–Tyler, Tyler, TX 75799-0001	1971	$6,322(S)	$8,106	5-D	6,476	383	37.0
Univ. of Texas Health Science Ctr. at Houston, Houston, TX 77225-0036	1972	$306/cr. hr.(S)	NA	5-D	3,969	44	NA
Univ. of Texas Health Science Ctr. at San Antonio, San Antonio, TX 78229-3900	1976	NA	NA	5-D	3,093	NA	NA
Univ. of Texas Medical Branch at Galveston, Galveston, TX 77555	1891	$5,740(S)	NA	5-D	2,430	NA	NA
Univ. of Texas Southwestern Medical Ctr. at Dallas, Dallas, TX 75390	1943	$5,720(S)	$11,353	5-D	2,499	2,038	NA
Univ. of the Arts, Philadelphia, PA 19102-4944	1870	$33,500	$12,300	1-M	2,355	476	64.0
Univ. of the Cumberlands, Williamsburg, KY 40769-1372	1889	$18,000	$6,826	2-D	3,300	163	38.0
Univ. of the District of Columbia, Washington, DC 20008-1175	1976	$7,000(S)	$6,600	9-M	5,518	341	8.0
Univ. of the Incarnate Word, San Antonio, TX 78209-6397	1881	$22,790	$9,658	2-D	7,214	524	38.0
Univ. of the Pacific, Stockton, CA 95211-0197	1851	$34,100	$11,142	1-D	6,717	783	69.0
Univ. of the Sacred Heart, San Juan, PR 00914-0383	1935	$5,870	$2,500	2-M	5,666	367	35.3
Univ. of the Sciences in Philadelphia, Philadelphia, PA 19104-4495	1821	$30,794	$12,034	1-D	2,868	267	65.0
Univ. of the Virgin Islands, Saint Thomas, VI 00802-9990	1962	$4,594(S)	$9,386	7-M	2,733	241	33.0
Univ. of Toledo, Toledo, OH 43606-3390	1872	$8,491(S)	$9,708	5-D	23,085	1,138	45.0
Univ. of Tulsa, Tulsa, OK 74104-3189	1894	$28,310	$9,018	1-D	4,185	395	65.0
Univ. of Utah, Salt Lake City, UT 84112-1107	1850	$6,274(S)	$6,240	5-D	30,819	1,957	57.0
Univ. of Vermont, Burlington, VT 05405	1791	$14,036(S)	$9,382	5-D	13,554	764	77.0
Univ. of Virginia, Charlottesville, VA 22903	1819	$10,628(S)	$8,652	5-D	24,391	1,309	93.0
Univ. of Virginia's Coll. at Wise, Wise, VA 24293	1954	$7,721(S)	$8,890	5-B	1,990	168	47.0
Univ. of Washington, Seattle, WA 98195	1861	$8,973(S)	$8,169	5-D	42,446	3,752	80.0
Univ. of Washington–Bothell, Bothell, WA 98011-8246	1990	$8,619(S)	$6,075	5-M	3,272	162	NA
Univ. of Washington–Tacoma, Tacoma, WA 98402-3100	1990	$8,689(S)	$8,949	5-M	3,331	197	NA
Univ. of West Alabama, Livingston, AL 35470	1835	$5,530(S)	$4,466	5-M	5,157	247	36.0
Univ. of West Florida, Pensacola, FL 32514-5750	1963	$4,794(S)	$7,856	5-D	11,599	542	47.0
Univ. of West Georgia, Carrollton, GA 30118	1933	$6,182(S)	$6,754	5-D	11,283	577	35.0
Univ. of Wisconsin–Eau Claire, Eau Claire, WI 54702-4004	1916	$7,364(S)	$5,830	5-M	11,409	529	65.0
Univ. of Wisconsin–Green Bay, Green Bay, WI 54311-7001	1968	$6,973(S)	$7,290	5-M	6,636	356	50.0
Univ. of Wisconsin–La Crosse, La Crosse, WI 54601-3742	1909	$7,911(S)	$5,630	5-D	9,948	546	71.0
Univ. of Wisconsin–Madison, Madison, WI 53706-1380	1848	$8,987(S)	$7,690	5-D	42,595	2,864	84.0
Univ. of Wisconsin–Milwaukee, Milwaukee, WI 53201-0413	1956	$9,075(S)	$4,310	5-D	30,418	1,607	NA
Univ. of Wisconsin–Oshkosh, Oshkosh, WI 54901	1871	$6,682(S)	$6,922	5-M	12,669	608	52.0
Univ. of Wisconsin–Parkside, Kenosha, WI 53141-2000	1968	$6,623(S)	$6,828	5-D	5,160	300	31.0
Univ. of Wisconsin–Platteville, Platteville, WI 53818-3099	1866	$6,456(S)	$5,628	5-M	7,874	NA	53.0
Univ. of Wisconsin–River Falls, River Falls, WI 54022	1874	$6,893(S)	$5,730	5-M	6,900	372	54.0
Univ. of Wisconsin–Stevens Point, Stevens Point, WI 54481-3897	1894	$6,849(S)	$5,760	5-D	9,489	469	60.0
Univ. of Wisconsin–Stout, Menomonie, WI 54751	1891	$8,099(S)	$5,560	5-M	9,340	453	55.0
Univ. of Wisconsin–Superior, Superior, WI 54880-4500	1893	$7,169(S)	$5,730	5-M	2,856	175	43.0
Univ. of Wisconsin–Whitewater, Whitewater, WI 53190-1790	1868	$6,836(S)	$5,402	5-M	11,557	529	56.0
Univ. of Wyoming, Laramie, WY 82070	1886	$3,927(S)	$8,360	5-D	12,911	800	55.0
Upper Iowa Univ., Fayette, IA 52142-1857	1857	$23,356	$7,070	1-M	5,741	488	38.0
Urbana Univ., Urbana, OH 43078-2091	1850	$20,838	$8,070	1-M	1,551	120	NA
Ursinus Coll., Collegeville, PA 19426-1000	1869	$40,120	$9,750	1-B	1,742	194	83.0
Ursuline Coll., Pepper Pike, OH 44124-4398 (4)	1871	$23,940	$7,970	2-D	1,485	224	43.0
Utah State Univ., Logan, UT 84322	1888	$5,150(S)	$5,070	5-D	16,472	879	56.0
Utah Valley Univ., Orem, UT 84058-5999	1941	$4,288(S)	NA	5-M	32,670	1,508	23.0
Utica Coll., Utica, NY 13502-4892	1946	$28,620	$11,590	1-D	3,273	343	49.0
Valdosta State Univ., Valdosta, GA 31698	1906	$4,972(S)	$6,520	5-D	12,898	623	40.0
Valley City State Univ., Valley City, ND 58072	1890	$6,270(S)	$5,218	5-M	1,277	102	40.0
Valley Forge Christian Coll., Phoenixville, PA 19460	1938	$16,250	$7,556	2-M	1,204	77	39.0
Valparaiso Univ., Valparaiso, IN 46383	1859	$31,040	$8,756	2-D	4,056	366	70.0
Vanderbilt Univ., Nashville, TN 37240-1001	1873	$39,930	$13,058	1-D	12,714	1,108	91.0
Vanguard Univ. of Southern California, Costa Mesa, CA 92626-9601	1920	$26,342	$8,274	2-M	1,923	150	55.0
Vassar Coll., Poughkeepsie, NY 12604	1861	$43,190	$9,900	1-M	2,446	328	93.0
Vaughn Coll. of Aeronautics & Tech., Flushing, NY 11369 (2)	1932	$18,520	$11,025	1-M	1,552	156	53.0
Vermont Tech. Coll., Randolph Center, VT 05061-0500	1866	$11,555(S)	$8,445	5-B	1,658	183	NA
Villanova Univ., Villanova, PA 19085-1699	1842	$39,665	$10,640	2-D	10,635	934	90.0
Virginia Coll. at Birmingham, Birmingham, AL 35209	1989	NA	NA	3-M	3,826	NA	NA
Virginia Commonwealth Univ., Richmond, VA 23284-9005	1838	$8,717(S)	$8,526	5-D	32,303	3,158	51.0

Name, address	Year founded	Tuition & fees	Room & board	Control, degree	Enrollment	Faculty	Grad. rate
Virginia Military Inst., Lexington, VA 24450 (2)	1839	$12,328(S)	$7,132	5-B	1,569	180	73.0%
Virginia Polytechnic Inst. & State Univ., Blacksburg, VA 24061.	1872	$9,458(S)	$6,290	5-D	31,006	1,579	80.0
Virginia State Univ., Petersburg, VA 23806-0001	1882	$6,570(S)	$8,152	5-D	5,634	456	40.0
Virginia Union Univ., Richmond, VA 23220-1170	1865	$14,630	$6,830	2-D	1,700	140	31.0
Virginia Wesleyan Coll., Norfolk, VA 23502-5599	1961	$29,680	$7,988	2-B	1,279	128	45.0
Viterbo Univ., La Crosse, WI 54601-4797.	1890	$20,850	$6,970	2-M	3,282	283	50.0
Wagner Coll., Staten Island, NY 10301-4495.	1883	$35,820	$10,680	1-M	2,271	266	66.0
Wake Forest Univ., Winston-Salem, NC 27109	1834	$41,576	$11,410	1-D	7,162	654	89.0
Walden Univ., Minneapolis, MN 55401	1970	$9,465	NA	3-D	47,456	2,362	NA
Walla Walla Univ., College Place, WA 99324-1198	1892	$23,454	$5,331	2-M	1,791	207	52.0
Walsh Coll. of Accountancy & Bus. Admin., Troy, MI 48007-7006.	1922	$11,770	NA	1-M	3,106	178	NA
Walsh Univ., North Canton, OH 44720-3396	1958	$22,280	$8,360	2-D	2,812	314	60.0
Warner Pacific Coll., Portland, OR 97215-4099	1937	$17,604	$6,980	2-M	1,333	116	53.0
Warren Wilson Coll., Asheville, NC 28815-9000.	1894	$25,944	$8,028	2-M	1,002	84	45.0
Wartburg Coll., Waverly, IA 50677-0903	1852	$30,960	$8,150	2-B	1,775	166	63.0
Washburn Univ., Topeka, KS 66621	1865	$6,296(S)	$5,982	10-D	7,230	527	41.0
Washington Adventist Univ., Takoma Park, MD 20912	1904	$20,180	$7,530	2-M	1,298	108	27.0
Washington & Jefferson Coll., Washington, PA 15301	1781	$34,610	$9,280	1-B	1,460	168	71.0
Washington & Lee Univ., Lexington, VA 24450-0303	1749	$40,387	$10,243	1-D	2,173	282	93.0
Washington Coll., Chestertown, MD 21620-1197.	1782	$36,738	$7,834	1-M	1,473	155	71.0
Washington State Univ., Pullman, WA 99164	1890	$9,489(S)	$9,644	5-D	26,308	1,640	69.0
Washington Univ. in St. Louis, St. Louis, MO 63130-4899	1853	$41,992	$13,119	1-D	13,820	1,085	94.0
Wayland Baptist Univ., Plainview, TX 79072-6998	1908	$13,340	$4,084	2-M	1,422	132	42.0
Waynesburg Univ., Waynesburg, PA 15370-1222.	1849	$18,410	$7,580	2-D	2,516	301	52.0
Wayne State Coll., Wayne, NE 68787	1910	$5,071(S)	$5,540	5-M	3,569	222	50.0
Wayne State Univ., Detroit, MI 48202	1868	$9,026(S)	$7,500	5-D	31,505	1,908	31.0
Weber State Univ., Ogden, UT 84408-1001	1889	$4,088(S)	$4,000	5-M	24,048	837	43.0
Webster Univ., St. Louis, MO 63119-3194	1915	$21,688	$9,290	1-D	8,099	783	68.0
Wellesley Coll., Wellesley, MA 02481 (3)	1870	$39,666	$12,284	1-B	2,411	323	89.0
Wentworth Inst. of Tech., Boston, MA 02115-5998.	1904	$24,000	NA	1-M	3,845	282	60.0
Wesleyan Univ., Middletown, CT 06459	1831	$42,084	$11,592	1-D	3,215	372	94.0
Wesley Coll., Dover, DE 19901-3875	1873	$20,580	NA	2-M	1,871	157	40.0
West Chester Univ. of Pennsylvania, West Chester, PA 19383.	1871	$7,680(S)	$7,188	5-M	14,490	827	65.0
West Coast Univ., North Hollywood, CA 91606	1909	NA	NA	3-B	1,792	NA	NA
Western Carolina Univ., Cullowhee, NC 28723	1889	$5,367(S)	$6,980	5-D	9,407	676	53.0
Western Connecticut State Univ., Danbury, CT 06810-6885	1903	$7,909(S)	$5,698	5-D	6,582	579	44.0
Western Governors Univ., Salt Lake City, UT 84107	1998	NA	NA	1-M	9,022	NA	NA
Western Illinois Univ., Macomb, IL 61455-1390	1899	$9,490(S)	$8,138	5-D	12,585	731	58.0
Western Intl. Univ., Phoenix, AZ 85021-2718	1978	$9,625	NA	3-M	3,079	228	NA
Western Kentucky Univ., Bowling Green, KY 42101	1906	$7,560(S)	$6,600	5-D	20,897	1,120	49.0
Western Michigan Univ., Kalamazoo, MI 49008	1903	$9,006(S)	$8,095	5-D	24,576	1,435	54.0
Western New England Univ., Springfield, MA 01119	1919	$29,812	$11,336	1-D	3,710	301	54.0
Western New Mexico Univ., Silver City, NM 88062-0680	1893	$3,589(S)	$5,200	5-M	2,697	259	NA
Western Oregon Univ., Monmouth, OR 97361-1394	1856	$8,055(S)	$8,439	5-M	6,233	452	42.0
Western State Coll. of Colorado, Gunnison, CO 81231	1901	$4,775(S)	$8,518	5-M	2,284	161	36.0
Western Washington Univ., Bellingham, WA 98225-5996	1893	$6,858(S)	$8,749	5-M	14,575	730	69.0
Westfield State Univ., Westfield, MA 01086	1838	$7,431(S)	$8,525	5-M	5,891	468	61.0
West Liberty Univ., West Liberty, WV 26074	1837	$4,880(S)	$7,310	5-M	2,737	197	47.0
Westminster Coll., Fulton, MO 65251-1299	1851	$19,740	$7,610	2-B	1,151	95	58.0
Westminster Coll., New Wilmington, PA 16172-0001	1852	$29,150	$8,840	2-M	1,593	149	76.0
Westminster Coll., Salt Lake City, UT 84105-3697.	1875	$27,182	$7,584	1-M	3,163	354	59.0
Westmont Coll., Santa Barbara, CA 93108-1099	1937	$34,460	$10,960	2-B	1,384	151	77.0
West Texas A&M Univ., Canyon, TX 79016-0001	1909	$6,236(S)	$6,000	5-M	7,535	342	42.0
West Virginia State Univ., Institute, WV 25112-1000	1891	NA	NA	5-M	4,003	196	26.0
West Virginia Univ., Morgantown, WV 26506	1867	$5,406(S)	$8,120	5-D	29,306	1,235	58.0
West Virginia Univ. Inst. of Tech., Montgomery, WV 25136.	1895	$5,164(S)	$8,130	5-M	1,244	111	24.0
West Virginia Wesleyan Coll., Buckhannon, WV 26201	1890	$23,980	$7,140	2-M	1,416	156	53.0
Westwood Coll.–Anaheim, Anaheim, CA 92806.	NA	NA	NA	3-B	1,206	82	NA
Westwood Coll.–Inland Empire, Upland, CA 91786	NA	NA	NA	3-B	1,140	94	NA
Westwood Coll.–Online Campus, Broomfield, CO 80021.	NA	NA	NA	3-M	7,584	281	NA
Wheaton Coll., Wheaton, IL 60187-5593	1860	$27,580	$8,050	2-D	3,026	291	88.0
Wheaton Coll., Norton, MA 02766	1834	$41,084	$10,180	1-B	1,635	188	75.0
Wheeling Jesuit Univ., Wheeling, WV 26003-6295.	1954	$25,010	$8,874	2-D	1,371	138	60.0
Wheelock Coll., Boston, MA 02215-4176 (4)	1888	$28,160	$11,200	1-M	1,162	87	62.0
Whitman Coll., Walla Walla, WA 99362-2083	1859	$40,496	$10,160	1-B	1,555	196	85.0
Whittier Coll., Whittier, CA 90608-0634.	1887	$35,742	$10,026	1-D	2,009	130	61.0
Whitworth Univ., Spokane, WA 99251-0001.	1890	$29,890	NA	2-M	2,607	294	74.0
Wichita State Univ., Wichita, KS 67260	1895	$5,890(S)	$6,200	5-D	14,806	487	41.0
Widener Univ., Chester, PA 19013-5792	1821	$33,270	$11,720	1-D	6,630	665	48.0
Wilkes Univ., Wilkes-Barre, PA 18766-0002	1933	$27,178	$11,470	1-D	5,926	465	64.0
Willamette Univ., Salem, OR 97301-3931	1842	$37,361	$8,900	2-D	2,851	298	78.0
William Carey Univ., Hattiesburg, MS 39401-5499	1906	$10,350	NA	2-M	3,248	NA	NA
William Jewell Coll., Liberty, MO 64068-1843	1849	$29,900	$7,560	1-B	1,060	125	65.0
William Paterson Univ. of New Jersey, Wayne, NJ 07470-8420	1855	$11,238(S)	$10,380	5-D	11,361	942	50.0
William Penn Univ., Oskaloosa, IA 52577-1799	1873	$20,234	$5,392	2-M	1,861	52	22.8
Williams Coll., Williamstown, MA 01267	1793	$41,434	$10,906	1-M	2,083	304	95.0
William Woods Univ., Fulton, MO 65251-1098	1870	$18,000	$7,200	2-M*	2,185	249	44.0
Wilmington Coll., Wilmington, OH 45177	1870	$25,714	$8,520	2-M	1,404	117	52.0
Wilmington Univ., New Castle, DE 19720-6491	1967	$7,274	NA	1-D	10,605	1,086	36.0
Wingate Univ., Wingate, NC 28174-0159	1896	$22,180	$8,770	2-D	2,373	226	53.0
Winona State Univ., Winona, MN 55987.	1858	$8,200(S)	$7,330	5-D	8,539	605	52.0
Winston-Salem State Univ., Winston-Salem, NC 27110-0003	1892	$4,088(S)	$7,106	5-M	6,427	336	37.0
Winthrop Univ., Rock Hill, SC 29733	1886	$12,176(S)	$6,922	5-M	5,998	569	57.0
Wittenberg Univ., Springfield, OH 45501-0720.	1845	$36,434	$9,294	2-M	1,909	200	66.0
Wofford Coll., Spartanburg, SC 29303-3663	1854	$31,710	$8,870	2-B	1,506	159	82.0
Woodbury Univ., Burbank, CA 91504-1099	1884	$28,855	$9,293	1-M	1,628	288	40.0
Worcester Polytechnic Inst., Worcester, MA 01609-2280.	1865	$40,030	$11,934	1-D	5,360	396	80.0
Worcester State Univ., Worcester, MA 01602-2597	1874	$7,155(S)	$9,658	5-M	5,708	412	45.0
Wright State Univ., Dayton, OH 45435	1964	$8,070(S)	$8,387	5-D	18,447	656	44.0
Xavier Univ., Cincinnati, OH 45207	1831	$29,970	$9,900	2-D	7,019	677	79.0
Xavier Univ. of Louisiana, New Orleans, LA 70125-1098.	1925	$17,100	$7,200	2-D	3,391	272	33.0
Yale Univ., New Haven, CT 06520	1701	$38,300	$11,500	1-D	11,840	1,653	98.0
Yeshiva Univ., New York, NY 10033-3201	1886	$32,094	$10,380	1-D	6,246	NA	80.0
York Coll. of Pennsylvania, York, PA 17405-7199	1787	$15,880	$8,920	2-M	5,606	540	62.0
York Coll. of the City Univ. of New York, Jamaica, NY 11451-0001	1967	$5,142(S)	NA	11-M	7,821	548	19.0
Youngstown State Univ., Youngstown, OH 44555-0001	1908	$7,199(S)	$7,600	5-D	15,180	1,032	35.0

DIRECTORY

Associations and Organizations

Source: World Almanac research

Selected list, generally by category and first distinctive key word in each title. Listed by acronym when that is the official name. Year established is in parentheses. Entries for religious organizations include addresses and leadership information for 2011.

Academic and Educational

Academies, Natl. (1863): (202) 334-2000; www.nationalacademies.org
African American Life and History, Assn. for the Study of (1915): (202) 238-5910; www.asalh.org
Alpha Delta Kappa (1947): (816) 363-5525; www.alphadeltakappa.org
AMIDEAST (America-Mideast Educational and Training Services) (1951): (202) 776-9600; www.amideast.org
Anthropological Assn., American (1902): (703) 528-1902; www.aaanet.org
Archaeological Institute of America (1879): (617) 353-9361; www.archaeological.org
Arts, Americans for the (1960): (202) 371-2830; www.artsusa.org
Arts and Sciences, American Academy of (1780): (617) 576-5000; www.amacad.org
Beta Gamma Sigma Honor Society (1913): (314) 432-5650; www.betagammasigma.org
Beta Sigma Phi Intl. (1931): (816) 444-6800; www.betasigmaphi.org
Biological Sciences, American Institute of (1947): (202) 628-1500; www.aibs.org
College Board (1900): (212) 713-8000; www.collegeboard.org
Colleges and Universities, Assn. of American (1915): (202) 387-3760; www.aacu.org
Community Colleges, American Assn. of (1920): (202) 728-0200; www.aacc.nche.edu
Consumer Interests, American Council on (1953): (812) 470-1618; www.consumerinterests.org
Delta Kappa Gamma Society Intl. (1929): (512) 478-5748; www.deltakappagamma.net
Education, American Council on (1918): (202) 939-9300; www.acenet.edu
Education, Council for Advancement and Support of (1974): (202) 328-2273; www.case.org
Education of Young Children, Natl. Assn. for the (1926): (202) 232-8777; www.naeyc.org
Educators for World Peace, Intl. Assn. of (1973): (256) 534-5501; www.iaewp.org
English-Speaking Union of the U.S. (1920): (212) 818-1200; www.esuus.org
Entomological Society of America (1889): (301) 731-4535; www.entsoc.org
Esperanto-USA (1953): (510) 653-0998; www.esperanto-usa.org
Family Relations, Natl. Council on (1938): (888) 781-9331; www.ncfr.org
Foreign Study, American Institute for (1964): (866) 906-2437; www.aifs.com
Freedom of Information Center (1958): (573) 882-5736; www.nfoic.org/foi-center
French Institute/Alliance Française (1971): (212) 355-6100; www.fiaf.org
Genealogical Society, Natl. (1903): (703) 525-0050; www.ngsgenealogy.org
Genetic Association, American (1914): (541) 867-0334; www.theaga.org
Geological Society of America (1888): (303) 357-1000; www.geosociety.org
Hemispheric Affairs, Council on (1975): (202) 223-4975; www.coha.org
Industrial and Applied Mathematics, Society for (1952): (215) 382-9800; www.siam.org
Intl. Education, Institute of (1919): (212) 883-8200; www.iie.org
Intl. Educational Exchange, Council on (1947): (207) 553-4000; www.ciee.org
Intl. Law, American Society of (1906): (202) 939-6000; www.asil.org
Irish American Cultural Inst. (1962): (973) 605-1991; www.iaci-usa.org
Law Libraries, American Assn. of (1906): (312) 939-4764; www.aallnet.org
Learned Societies, American Council of (1919): (212) 697-1505; www.acls.org
Libraries Assn., Special (1909): (703) 647-4900; www.sla.org
Linguistic Society of America (1924): (202) 835-1714; www.lsadc.org
Mathematical Society, American (1888): (401) 455-4000; www.ams.org
MENC: The Natl. Assn. for Music Education (formerly Music Educators Natl. Conference) (1907): (703) 860-4000; www.menc.org
Mensa, Ltd., American (1960): (817) 607-0060; www.us.mensa.org
Meteorological Society, American (1919): (617) 227-2425; www.ametsoc.org
Metric Assn., Inc., U.S. (1916): (818) 363-5606; www.metric.org
Microbiology, American Society for (1899): (202) 737-3600; www.asm.org
Modern Language Assn. of America (1883): (646) 576-5000; www.mla.org
Museums, American Assn. of (1906): (202) 289-1818; www.aam-us.org
Musicological Society, American (1934): (207) 798-4243; www.ams-net.org
Negro College Fund, United (1944): (800) 331-2244; www.uncf.org
Oriental Society, American (1842): (734) 647-4760; www.umich.edu/~aos/
ORT America (1922): (212) 505-7700; www.ortamerica.org
PEN American Center (1922): (212) 334-1660; www.pen.org
Phi Beta Kappa Society (1776): (202) 265-3808; www.pbk.org
Phi Theta Kappa Honor Society (1918): (601) 984-3504; www.ptk.org
Philological Association, American (1869): (215) 898-4975; www.apaclassics.org
Philosophical Assn., American (1900): (302) 831-1112; www.apaonline.org
Physics, American Inst. of (1931): (301) 209-3100; www.aip.org
Physiological Society, American (1887): (301) 634-7164; www.the-aps.org
Poetry Society of America (1910): (212) 254-9628; www.poetrysociety.org
Poets, Academy of American (1934): (212) 274-0343; www.poets.org
Political Science, Academy of (1880): (212) 870-2500; www.psqonline.org
Population Connection (1968): (202) 332-2200; www.populationconnection.org
Radio and Television Society Foundation, Intl. (1939): (212) 867-6650; www.irts.org
Reading Assn., Intl. (1956): (302) 731-1600; www.reading.org
Religion, American Academy of (1909): (404) 727-3049; www.aarweb.org
Science Fiction Society, World (1939): www.wsfs.org
Sciences, Natl. Academy of (1863): (202) 334-2000; www.nasonline.org
Sigma Beta Delta (1994): (314) 516-4723; www.sigmabetadelta.org
Sociological Assn., American (1905): (202) 383-9005; www.asanet.org
Tau Beta Pi Association (1885): (865) 546-4578; www.tbp.org
Teach For America (1990): (212) 279-2080; www.teachforamerica.org
Theological Schools in the U.S. and Canada, Assn. of (1918): (412) 788-6505; www.ats.edu
Theosophical Society in America (1875): (630) 668-1571; www.theosophical.org
Universities, Assn. of American (1900): (202) 408-7500; www.aau.edu
World Learning (1954): (802) 257-7751; www.worldlearning.org

Animal Welfare and Environment

Animals, American Society for the Prevention of Cruelty to (ASPCA) (1866): (212) 876-7700; www.aspca.org
Animals, People for the Ethical Treatment of (PETA) (1980): (757) 622-7382; www.peta.org
Animal Welfare Institute (1951): (202) 337-2332; www.awionline.org
Appalachian Trail Conservancy (1925): (304) 535-6331; www.appalachiantrail.org
Audubon Society, Natl. (1905): (212) 979-3000; www.audubon.org
Bat Conservation International (1982): (512) 327-9721; www.batcon.org
Cat Fanciers' Assn., Inc., The (1906): (732) 528-9797; www.cfa.org
Conservation International (1987): (703) 341-2400; www.conservation.org
Defenders of Wildlife (1947): (800) 385-9712; www.defenders.org
Ducks Unlimited (1937): (901) 758-3825; www.ducks.org
Foresters, Society of American (1900): (301) 897-3690; www.safnet.org
Forest History Society (1946): (919) 682-9319; www.foresthistory.org
Friends of the Earth (1969): (202) 783-7400; www.foe.org
Garden Club of America (1913): (212) 753-8287; www.gcamerica.org
Garden Clubs, Inc., National Council of State (1929): (314) 776-7574; www.gardenclub.org
Geographic Society, Natl. (1888): (813) 979-6845; www.nationalgeographic.com
Green Mountain Club (1910): (802) 244-7037; www.greenmountainclub.org
Greenpeace, Inc. (1971): (202) 462-1177; www.greenpeaceusa.org
Hiking Society, American (1976): (301) 565-6704; www.americanhiking.org
Horse Council, American (1969): (202) 296-4031; www.horsecouncil.org
Humane Society of the U.S., The (1954): (202) 452-1100; www.humanesociety.org
Natural Resources Defense Council (1970): (212) 727-2700; www.nrdc.org
Nature Conservancy, The (1951): (703) 841-5300; www.nature.org
Ocean Conservancy (1972): (202) 429-5609; www.oceanconservancy.org
Ornithologists' Union, American (1883): (505) 326-1579; www.aou.org
Recreation and Park Assn., Natl. (1965): (800) 626-6772; www.nrpa.org
Recycling Coalition, Natl. (1978): (202) 618-2107; www.nrcrecycles.org
Rose Society, American (1892): (318) 938-5402; www.ars.org
Save the Redwoods League (1918): (415) 362-2352; www.savetheredwoods.org
Sierra Club (1892): (415) 977-5500; www.sierraclub.org
Water Environment Federation (1928): (800) 666-0206; www.wef.org
Wildflower Center, Lady Bird Johnson (1982): (512) 232-0100; www.wildflower.org
Wildlife Federation, Natl. (1936): (800) 822-9919; www.nwf.org
World Wildlife Fund (1961): (202) 293-4800; www.worldwildlife.org

Children and Social Services

Big Brothers Big Sisters of America (1904): (215) 567-7000; www.bbbs.org
Boy Scouts of America (1910): (972) 580-2000; www.scouting.org
Boys & Girls Clubs of America (1906): (404) 487-5700; www.bgca.org
Camp Fire USA (formerly Camp Fire Boys & Girls) (1910): (816) 285-2010; www.campfireusa.org
Children's Aid Society (1913): (205) 251-7148; www.childrensaid.org
Children's Book Council, The (1945): (212) 966-1990; www.cbcbooks.org
Child Welfare League of America (1920): (202) 688-4200; www.cwla.org
Feeding America (formerly America's Second Harvest) (1976): (800) 771-2303; feedingamerica.org
4-H Council, Natl. (1914): (301) 961-2800; www.4-h.org
Future Business Leaders of America–Phi Beta Lambda, Inc. (1942): (800) 325-2946; www.fbla-pbl.org
Future Farmers of America Org., Natl. (1928): (317) 802-6060; www.ffa.org
Gifted Children, Natl. Assn. for (1954): (202) 785-4268; www.nagc.org
Girl Scouts of the USA (1912): (212) 852-8000; www.girlscouts.org
Honor Society, Natl. (1921): (703) 860-0200; www.nhs.us
Junior Achievement, Inc. (1919): (719) 540-8000; www.ja.org
Junior Auxiliaries, Natl. Assn. of (1941): (662) 332-3000; www.najanet.org
Junior Chamber, U.S. (1920): (800) 529-2337; www.usjaycees.org

Junior Honor Society, Natl. (1929): (703) 860-0200; www.njhs.us

Missing and Exploited Children, Natl. Center for (1984): (703) 224-2150; www.missingkids.com

Pilot Intl. Foundation (1921): (478) 477-1208; www.pilotinternational.org

Student Councils, Natl. Assn. of (1931): (703) 860-0200; www.nasc.us

Fraternal

Eagles, Fraternal Order of (1898): (614) 883-2200; www.foe.com

Eastern Star, General Grand Chapter, Order of the (1876): (202) 667-4737; www.easternstar.org

Elks of the USA, Benevolent and Protective Order of (1868): (773) 755-4700; www.elks.org

Freemasonry, Supreme Council Ancient and Accepted Scottish Rite of, Northern Masonic Jurisdiction (1813): (781) 862-4410; www.supremecouncil.org

Freemasonry, Supreme Council Ancient and Accepted Scottish Rite of, Southern Jurisdiction (1802): (202) 232-3579; www.srmason-sj.org

Free Men, Natl. Coalition of (1977): (888) 223-1280; www.ncfm.org

Kiwanis International (1915): (317) 875-8755; www.kiwanis.org

Knights of Columbus (1882): (203) 752-4000; www.kofc.org

Knights of Pythias, Order of (1864): (610) 544-3500; www.pythias.org

Lions Clubs Intl. (1917): (630) 571-5466; www.lionsclubs.org

Moose Intl., Inc. (1888): (630) 859-2000; www.mooseintl.org

Odd Fellows, Independent Order of (1819): (336) 725-5955; www.ioof.org

Rotary Intl. (1905): (847) 866-3000; www.rotary.org

Shriners International (1872): (813) 281-0300; www.shrinershq.org

Sons of Italy in America, Order (1905): (202) 547-2900; www.osia.org

Sons of Norway (1895): (612) 827-3611; www.sofn.com

Woodmen of America, Modern (1883): (309) 558-3100; www.modern-woodmen.org

Historical

Civil War Trust (1987): (202) 367-1861; www.civilwar.org

Colonial Dames XVII Century, Natl. Soc. (1915): (202) 293-1700; www.colonialdames17c.org

Daughters of the American Revolution (1890): (202) 628-1776; www.dar.org

Daughters of the Confederacy, United (1894): (804) 355-1636; www.hqudc.org

Historical Assn., American (1884): (202) 544-2422; www.historians.org

Historic Preservation, Natl. Trust for (1949): (202) 588-6000; www.preservationnation.org

Lewis and Clark Trail Heritage Foundation (1969): (888) 701-3434; www.lewisandclark.org

Mayflower Descendants, General Soc. of (1897): (508) 746-3188; www.themayflowersociety.org

Pilgrims, Natl. Soc. Sons and Daughters of the (1908): www.nssdp.com

Railway Historical Society, Natl. (1935): (215) 557-6606; www.nrhs.com

Sons of the American Revolution, Natl. Society (1889): (502) 589-1776; www.sar.org

Sons of Confederate Veterans (1896): (800) 380-1896; www.scv.org

State and Local History, American Assn. for (1940): (615) 320-3203; www.aaslh.org

Supreme Court Historical Society (1974): (202) 543-0400; www.supremecourthistory.org

Theodore Roosevelt Assn. (1920): (516) 921-6319; www.theodoreroosevelt.org

Thoreau Society (1941): (978) 369-5310; www.thoreausociety.org

Titanic Historical Society, Inc. (1963): (413) 543-4770; www.titanichistoricalsociety.org

Victorian Society in America (1966): (215) 636-9872; www.victoriansociety.org

Industrial and Trade

Aerospace Industries Assn. (1919): (703) 358-1000; www.aia-aerospace.org

Better Business Bureaus, Council of (1912): (703) 276-0100; www.bbb.org

Chamber of Commerce of the U.S.A. (1912): (202) 659-6000; www.uschamber.com

Chemistry Council, American (1872): (202) 249-7000; www.americanchemistry.com

Construction Specifications Institute (1948): (800) 689-2900; www.csinet.org

CropLife America (1933): (202) 296-1585; www.croplifeamerica.org

Cryogenic Soc. of America, Inc. (1964): (708) 383-6220; www.cryogenicsociety.org

Electrical Manufacturers Assn., Natl. (1926): (703) 841-3200; www.nema.org

Fire Protection Assn., Natl. (NFPA) (1896): (617) 770-3000; www.nfpa.org

Fisheries Soc., American (1870): (301) 897-8616; www.fisheries.org

Foreign Trade Council, Inc., Natl. (1914): (202) 887-0278; www.nftc.org

Funeral Consumers Alliance (1963): (802) 865-8300; www.funerals.org

Hotel & Lodging Assn., American (1910): (202) 289-3100; www.ahla.com

Insurance Assn., American (1866): (202) 828-7100; www.aiadc.org

Magazine Media, Assn. of (1919): (212) 872-3700; www.magazine.org

Manufacturers, Natl. Assn. of (1895): (202) 637-3000; www.nam.org

Newspaper Assn. of America (1992): (571) 366-1000; www.naa.org

Nuclear Society, American (1954): (708) 352-6611; www.ans.org

Orchestras, League of American (1942): (212) 262-5161; www.symphony.org

Petroleum Institute, American (1919): (202) 682-8000; www.api.org

Printing Industries of America, Inc. (1887): (412) 741-6860; www.printing.org

Publishers, Assn. of American (1970): (202) 347-3375; www.publishers.org

Retail Federation, Natl. (1908): (800) 673-4692; www.nrf.com

Safety Council, Natl. (1913): (630) 285-1121; www.nsc.org

Shipbuilders Council of America (1920): (202) 347-5462; www.shipbuilders.org

Small Business Assn., Natl. (1937): (202) 293-8830; www.nsba.biz

Software and Information Industry Assn. (1999): (202) 289-7442; www.siia.net

Tall Buildings and Urban Habitat, Council on (1969): (312) 567-3307; www.ctbuh.org

Toy Industry Assn., Inc. (1916): (212) 675-1141; www.toyassociation.org

Water Works Assn., American (1881): (303) 794-7711; www.awwa.org

Zoos & Aquariums, Assn. of (1924): (301) 562-0777; www.aza.org

Lifestyle and Travel

AAA (American Automobile Assn.) (1902): (407) 444-7000; www.aaa.com

AARP (formerly American Assn. of Retired Persons) (1958): (888) 687-2277; www.aarp.org

AFS Intercultural Programs USA (1947): (800) 237-4636; www.afs.org/usa

Aircraft Owners and Pilots Assn. (1939): (800) 872-2672; www.aopa.org

Appalachian Mountain Club (1876): (617) 523-0636; www.outdoors.org

Boat Owners Assn. of the U.S. (1966): (703) 461-4666; www.boatus.com

Camp Assn., American (1910): (765) 342-8456; www.acacamps.org

Consumer Federation of America (1968): (202) 387-6121; www.consumerfed.org

Consumers Union (1936): (914) 378-2000; www.consumersunion.org

Green America (formerly Co-op America) (1982): (800) 584-7336; www.greenamericatoday.org

Helicopter Society Intl., American (1943): (703) 684-6777; www.vtol.org

Hostelling Intl. USA (1934): (301) 495-1240; www.hiayh.org

Jewish Community Centers Assn. of North America (1917): (212) 532-4949; www.jcca.org

Motorcyclist Assn., American (1924): (800) 262-5646; www.americanmotorcyclist.com

Nude Recreation, American Assn. for (1931): (407) 933-2064; www.aanr.com

Parents Without Partners, Inc. (1957): (800) 637-7974; www.parentswithoutpartners.org

Planetary Society (1980): (626) 793-5100; www.planetary.org

SCRABBLE® Assn., Natl. (1978): (631) 477-0033; www.scrabble-assoc.com

Sports Car Club of America (1944): (785) 357-7222; www.scca.org

Toastmasters Intl. (1924): (949) 858-8255; www.toastmasters.org

YMCA (Young Men's Christian Assn.) of the USA (1851): (800) 872-9622; www.ymca.net

YWCA (Young Women's Christian Assn.) USA (1858): (202) 467-0801; www.ywca.org

Military and Veterans'

Air Force Assn. (1946): (703) 247-5800; www.afa.org

American Legion (1919): (317) 630-1200; www.legion.org

American Legion Auxiliary (1919): (317) 569-4500; www.legion-aux.org

AMVETS (American Veterans) (1944): (301) 459-9600; www.amvets.org

Army, Assn. of the United States (1950): (703) 841-4300; www.ausa.org

Blinded Veterans Assn. (1958): (202) 371-8880; www.bva.org

Civil Air Patrol (1941): (877) 227-9142; www.gocivilairpatrol.com

Coast Guard Combat Veterans Assn. (1985): (330) 887-5539; www.coastguardcombatvets.com

Disabled American Veterans (1920): (859) 441-7300; www.dav.org

88th Infantry Division Assn. (1948): (508) 584-4169; www.88infdiv.org

82nd Airborne Division Assn., Inc. (1944): (910) 223-1182; www.82ndassociation.org

Ex-Prisoners of War, American (1942): (817) 649-2979; www.axpow.org

Fleet Reserve Association (1924): (703) 683-1400; www.fra.org

Jewish War Veterans of the U.S.A. (1896): (202) 265-6280; www.jwv.org

Legion of Valor Museum (1991): (559) 498-0510; www.legionofvalormuseum.org

Marine Corps League (1937): (703) 207-9588; www.mcleague.org

Military Officers Assn. of America (1929): (703) 549-2311; www.moaa.org

Military Order of the World Wars (1919): (877) 320-3774; www.militaryorder.net

National Guard Assn. of the U.S. (1878): (202) 789-0031; www.ngaus.org

Naval Institute, U.S. (1873): (410) 268-6110; www.usni.org

Navy League of the United States (1902): (703) 528-1775; www.navyleague.org

Ninety-Nines, Inc. (Intl. Org. of Women Pilots) (1929): (405) 685-7969; www.ninety-nines.org

Non-Commissioned Officers Assn. (1960): (800) 662-2620; www.ncoausa.org

Paralyzed Veterans of America (1946): (800) 424-8200; www.pva.org

Purple Heart, Military Order of the (1952): (703) 354-2140; www.purpleheart.org

Reserve Officers Assn. of the U.S. (1922): (202) 479-2200; www.roa.org

Sons of the American Legion (1932): (317) 630-1200; www.sal.legion.org

Tin Can Sailors (Natl. Assn. of Destroyer Veterans) (1976): (508) 677-0515; www.destroyers.org

Uniformed Services, Natl. Assn. for (1968): (703) 750-1342; www.naus.org

USO, Inc. (United Service Org.) (1941): (888) 484-3876; www.uso.org

USS Missouri Memorial Assn., Inc. (1994): (808) 455-1600; www.ussmissouri.org

Veterans of Foreign Wars of the U.S. (1899): (816) 756-3390; www.vfw.org

Veterans of Foreign Wars of the U.S., Ladies Auxiliary to the (1914): (816) 561-8655; www.ladiesauxvfw.org

Veterans of the Vietnam War, Inc. (1978): (570) 603-9740; www.theveteranscoalition.org

War Mothers, American (1917): (202) 362-0090; www.americanwarmoms.org

Women's Army Corps Veterans' Assn. (1946): (256) 820-6824; www.armywomen.org

USS Los Angeles CA-135 Assn. (1977): c/o Jim Osborne, 1314 N. Alden Rd., Muncie, IN 47304; www.uss-la-ca135.org/2la-assoc.htm

Political

Abortion Federation, National (1977): (202) 667-5881; www.prochoice.org

Advancement and Support of Education, Council for (1974): (202) 328-2273; www.case.org

American Indians, Natl. Congress of
(1944): (202) 466-7767; www.ncai.org

American-Islamic Relations, Council on
(1994): (202) 488-8787; www.cair.com

Center for Responsive Politics (1983):
(202) 857-0044; www.opensecrets.org

Cities, Natl. League of (1924): (202) 626-3100; www.nlc.org

Civil Liberties Union, American (ACLU)
(1920): (212) 549-2500; www.aclu.org

Coffee Party USA (2010): (301) 259-1869;
www.coffeepartyusa.com

Common Cause (1970): (202) 833-1200;
www.commoncause.org

Concerned Women for America (1979):
(202) 488-7000; www.cwfa.org

Congress of Racial Equality (CORE)
(1942): (212) 598-4000; www.core-online.org

Crime and Delinquency, Natl. Council on
(1907): (510) 208-0500; www.nccd-crc.org

Democratic Natl. Committee (1848): (202) 863-8000; www.democrats.org

Feminists for Life of America (1972): (703) 836-3354; www.feministsforlife.org

Gay & Lesbian Alliance Against Defamation (GLAAD) (1985): (212) 629-3322;
www.glaad.org

Gay and Lesbian Task Force, Natl. (1973):
(202) 393-5177; www.thetaskforce.org

Governors Assn., Natl. (1908): (202) 624-5300; www.nga.org

Grange of the Order of Patrons of Husbandry, Natl. (1867): (202) 628-3507; www.nationalgrange.org

Gray Panthers (1970): (202) 737-6637; www.graypanthers.org

Greens/Green Party USA (1984): (866) 473-3672; www.greenparty.org

Homeless, Natl. Coalition for the (1984):
(202) 462-4822; www.nationalhomeless.org

Japanese American Citizens League
(1929): (415) 921-5225; www.jacl.org

Jewish Committee, American (1906): (212) 751-4000; www.ajc.org

John Birch Society (1958): (920) 749-3780;
www.jbs.org

Libertarian Party (1971): (202) 333-0008;
www.lp.org

Mayors, U.S. Conference of (1932): (202) 293-7330; www.usmayors.org

NAACP (Natl. Assn. for the Advancement of Colored People) (1909): (410) 580-5777;
www.naacp.org

National Tea Party Federation (2010): www.thenationalteapartyfederation.com

NRA (National Rifle Assn.) (1871): (800) 672-3888; www.nra.org

Parliamentarians, Natl. Assn. of (1930):
(816) 833-3892; www.parliamentarians.org

Reform Party of the U.S.A. (1995): (972) 275-9297; www.reformparty.org

Republican National Committee (1856):
(202) 863-8500; www.rnc.org

Science, American Assn. for the Advancement of (1848): (202) 326-6400; www.aaas.org

Southern Christian Leadership Conference
(1957): (404) 522-1420; sclcnational.org

Southern Poverty Law Center (1971): (334) 956-8200; www.splcenter.org

State Governments, Council of (1933):
(859) 244-8000; www.csg.org

Tax Foundation (1937): (202) 464-6200;
www.taxfoundation.org

Taxpayers Union, Natl. (1969): (703) 683-5700; www.ntu.org

Term Limits, U.S. (1992): (703) 383-0907;
www.termlimits.org

Urban League, Natl. (1910): (212) 558-5300;
www.nul.org

Women, Natl. Organization for (NOW)
(1966): (202) 628-8669; www.now.org

Women and Families, Natl. Partnership for (1971): (202) 986-2600; www.nationalpartnership.org

Women's Christian Temperance Union,
Natl. (1874): (847) 864-1397; www.wctu.org

Women Voters of the U.S., League of
(1920): (202) 429-1965; www.lwv.org

Zionist Organization of America (1897):
(212) 481-1500; www.zoa.org

Religious

African Methodist Episcopal Church
(1787): 500 8th Ave. S., Nashville, TN 37203; (615) 254-0911; www.ame-church.com; Senior Bishop, Bishop John R. Bryant

African Methodist Episcopal Zion Church
(1796): 3225 West Sugar Creek Rd., Charlotte, NC 28269; (704) 599-4630; www.amez.org; Senior Bishop, George W. C. Walker Sr.

American Baptist Churches USA (1907):
P.O. Box 851, Valley Forge, PA 19482; (610) 768-2000; www.abc-usa.org; Pres., Frank Christine

Antiochian Orthodox Christian Archdiocese of North America (1895): P.O. Box 5238, Englewood, NJ 07631; (201) 871-1355; www.antiochian.org; Primate, Archbishop, Metropolitan Philip Saliba

Armenian Apostolic Church of America:
Eastern Prelacy (1958): 138 E. 39th St., New York, NY 10016; (212) 689-7810; www.armenianprelacy.org; Prelate, Archbishop Oshagan Choloyan; *Western Prelacy* (1973): 6252 Honolulu Ave., La Crescenta, CA 91214; (818) 248-7737; www.westernprelacy.org; Prelate, Archbishop Moushegh Mardirossian

Assemblies of God USA (1914): 1445 N. Boonville Ave., Springfield, MO 65802; (417) 862-2781; www.ag.org/top; Gen. Supt., George O. Wood

Atheists, American (1963): P.O. Box 158, Cranford, NJ 07016; (908) 276-7300; www.atheists.org; Pres., David P. Silverman

Bahá'í's of the U.S., National Spiritual Assembly of the (1909): 1233 Central St., Evanston, IL 60201; (847) 733-3400; www.bahai.us; Sec., Kenneth E. Bowers

Baptist Bible Fellowship Intl. (1950): 720 E. Kearney St., Springfield, MO 65803; (417) 862-5001; www.bbfi.org; Pres., Linzy Slayden

Baptist Convention, Southern (1845): 901 Commerce St., Nashville, TN 37203; (615) 244-2355; www.sbc.net; Pres. Bryant Wright

Baptist Convention, U.S.A., Inc., National
(1895): 1700 Baptist World Center Dr., Nashville, TN 37207; (615) 228-6292; www.nationalbaptist.com; Pres., Dr. Julius R. Scruggs

Baptist Convention of America, National
(1880): 777 S.R.L. Thornton Freeway, Ste. 210, Dallas, TX 75203; (214) 942-3311; www.nbcainc.com; Pres., Rev. Stephen J. Thurston

Baptist Convention of America, National Missionary (1988): 43789 NE Langly Ct., Scissoris, RI 99870l (555) 345-9877; www.nmbca.com; Pres., Dr. C. C. Robertson

Bible Society, American (1816): 1865 Broadway, New York, NY 10023; (800) 322-4253; www.americanbible.org; Pres. and CEO, Dr. Lamar Vest

Biblical Literature, Society of (1880): 825 Houston Mill Rd., Atlanta, GA 30329; (404) 727-3100; www.sbl-site.org

B'nai B'rith Intl. (1843): 2020 K St. NW, 7th Fl., Washington, DC 20006; (202) 857-6600; www.bnaibrith.org

Brethren in Christ Church (c. 1778): 431 Grabtgan Rd., Grantham, PA 17027; (717) 697-2634; www.bic-church.org; Moderator, Dr. Warren L. Hoffman

Buddhist Churches of America (1899): 1710 Octavia St., San Francisco, CA 94109; (415) 776-5600; www.buddhistchurchesofamerica.com; Pres., Everett Watadaa

Catholic Bishops, U.S. Conference of
(2001): 3211 4th St. NE, Washington, DC 20017; (202) 541-3000; www.usccb.org; Gen. Sec., Msgr. Ronny E. Jenkins

Christian Church (Disciples of Christ)
(1832): Disciples Center, 130 E. Washington St., Indianapolis, IN 46204; (317) 635-3100; www.disciples.org; Pres., Rev. Dr. Sharon E. Watkins

Christian Methodist Episcopal Church
(1870): 4466 Elvis Presley Blvd., Memphis, TN 38116; (901) 345-0580; www.c-m-e.org; Senior Bishop, Thomas L. Hoyt, Jr.

Church of the Brethren (1708): General Offices, 1451 Dundee Ave., Elgin, IL 60120; (847) 742-5100; www.brethren.org; Moderator, Robert Alley

Church of Christ (1830): P.O. Box 472, Independence, MO 64051; (816) 833-3995; www.churchofchrist-tl.org; Council of Apostles, Sec., Apostle Smith N. Brickhouse

Church of God (Anderson, IN) (1881): Box 2420, Anderson, IN 46018; (765) 642-0256;

www.chog.org; Gen. Dir., Pres. Dr. Ronald V. Duncan

Church of God (Cleveland, TN) (1886): 2490 Keith St. NW, Cleveland, TN 37320; (423) 472-3361; www.churchofgod.org; Gen. Overseer, Dr. Raymond F. Culpepper

Church of God in Christ (1897): Mason Temple, 930 Mason St., Memphis, TN 38126; (901) 947-9300; www.cogic.org; Presiding Bishop, Bishop Charles E. Blake Sr.

Church of Jesus Christ (Bickertonites) (1862): 6th and Lincoln Sts., Monongahela, PA 15063; (412) 331-7829; www.thechurchofjesuschrist.org; Pres., Larry Watson

Church of Jesus Christ of Latter-day Saints, The (Mormons) (1830): 47 E. South Temple St., Salt Lake City, UT 84150; (801) 240-1000; www.lds.org; Pres., Thomas S. Monson

Church of the Nazarene (1908): Global Ministry Center, 17001 Prairie Star Pkwy., Lenexa, KS 66220; (913) 577-0500; www.nazarene.org; Gen. Secy., David P. Wilson

Community of Christ (reorganized Church of Jesus Christ of Latter-Day Saints) (1830): Intl. Headquarters, 1001 W. Walnut, Independence, MO 64050; (816) 833-1000; www.cofchrist.org; Pres., Stephen M. Veazey

Community Churches, International Council of (1950): 21116 Washington Pkwy., Frankfort, IL 60423; (815) 464-5690; www.icccusa.com; Exec. Dir., Michael Livingston

Conservative Judaism, United Synagogue of (1913): 820 Second Ave., New York, NY 10017; (212) 533-7800; www.uscj.org; Pres., Richard Skolnik

Converge Worldwide (formerly Baptist General Conference) (1852): 2002 S. Arlington Heights Rd., Arlington Heights, IL 60005; (800) 323-4215; www.convergeworldwide.org; Pres. and CEO, Dr. Gerald Sheveland

Cumberland Presbyterian Church (1810): 8207 Traditional Pl., Cordova, TN 38016; (901) 276-4572; www.cumberland.org; Moderator, Jonathan Clark

Episcopal Church (1789): 815 Second Ave., New York, NY 10017; (212) 716-6000; www.ecusa.anglican.org; Presiding Bishop and Primate, Most Rev. Katharine Jefferts Schori

Evangelical Lutheran Church in America
(1988): 8765 W. Higgins Rd., Chicago, IL 60631; (773) 380-2700; www.elca.org; Presiding Bishop, Rev. Mark S. Hanson

First Church of Christ, Scientist, The
(1879): 210 Massachusetts Ave., Boston, MA 02115; (617) 450-2000; www.tfccs.com; Pres., Marta Greenwood

Free Methodist Church of North America
(1860): World Ministries Center, 770 N. High School Rd., Indianapolis, IN 46214; (317) 244-3660; www.freemethodistchurch.org; The Board of Bishops

Freedom From Religion Foundation (1978): P.O. Box 750, Madison, WI 53701; (608) 256-8900; www.ffrf.org

Friends General Conference (1900): 1216 Arch St., #2B, Philadelphia, PA 19107; (215) 561-1700; www.fgcquaker.org; Gen. Sec., Bruce Birchard

Gideons Intl. (1899): P.O. Box 140800, Nashville, TN 37214; (615) 564-5000; www.gideons.org

Greek Orthodox Archdiocese of America
(1922): 8 E. 79th St., New York, NY 10075; (212) 570-3500; www.goarch.org; Primate, Archbishop Demetrios

Hadassah, the Women's Zionist Organization of America, Inc. (1912): 50 W. 58th St., New York, NY 10019; (888) 303-3640; www.hadassah.org

Interfaith Alliance, The (1994): 1212 New York Ave. NW, Ste. 1250, Washington, DC 20005; (202) 238-3300; www.interfaithalliance.org; Pres., Rev. Dr. C. Welton Gaddy

Islamic Society of North America: 6555 S. 750 East, Plainfield, IN 46168; (317) 839-8157; www.isna.net; Pres., Imam Mohamed Magid

Jehovah's Witnesses (1931): 25 Columbia Heights, Brooklyn, NY 11201; (718) 560-5000; www.watchtower.org; Pres., Don Adams

Jewish Congress, American (1918): 115 E. 57 St., New York, NY 10022; (212)

879-4500; www.ajcongress.org; Pres., Richard S. Gordon

Jewish Reconstructionist Federation (1955): Beit Devora, 101 Greenwood Ave., Ste. 430, Jenkintown, PA 19046; (215) 885-5601; www.jrf.org; Pres., Robert Barkin

Jewish Women, Natl. Council of (1893): 475 Riverside Dr., Ste. 1901, New York, NY 10115; (212) 645-4048; www.ncjw.org; Pres., Linda Slucker

Lutheran Church—Missouri Synod (1847): 1333 S. Kirkwood Rd., St. Louis, MO 63122; (800) 248-1930; www.lcms.org; Pres., Dr. Matthew C. Harrison

Mennonite Church USA (2001): 718 N. Main St., Newton, KS 67114; (316) 283-5100; www.mennoniteusa.org; Moderator, Edward D. Diller

Moravian Church in North America (1735): www.moravian.org; *Northern Prov.:* P.O. Box 1245, Bethlehem, PA 18016; (610) 867-0593; Pres., Betsy Miller; *Southern Prov.:* 459 S. Church St., Winston-Salem, NC 27101; (336) 725-5811; Pres., Rt. Rev. Wayne Burkette

North American Shia Ithna-asheri Muslim Communities, Org. of (1986) P.O. Box 29691, Minneapolis, MN 55429; (905)

763-7512; www.nasimco.info; Pres., Gulamabbas Najafi

Orthodox Union (1898): 11 Broadway, New York, NY 10004; (212) 563-4000; www.ou.org; Pres., Dr. Simcha Katz

Pentecostal Assemblies of the World, Inc. (1906): 3939 N. Meadows Dr., Indianapolis, IN 46205; (317) 547-9541; www.pawinc.org; Presiding Bishop, Charles H. Ellis, III

Presbyterian Church (U.S.A.) (1983): 100 Witherspoon St., Louisville, KY 40202; (800) 728-7228; www.pcusa.org; Exec. Dir., Linda Valentine

Progressive National Baptist Convention, Inc. (1961): 601 50th St. NE, Washington, DC 20019; (202) 396-0558; www.pnbc.org; Pres., Dr. Carroll A. Baltimore Sr.

Rabbis, Central Conference of American (1889): 355 Lexington Ave., New York, NY 10017; (212) 972-3636; www.ccarnet.org; Pres., Jonathan Stein

Reform Judaism, Union for (1873): 633 3rd Ave., New York, NY 10017; (212) 650-4000; www.urj.org; Pres., Rabbi Eric Yoffie

Secular Humanism, Council for (1980): P.O. Box 664, Amherst, NY 14226; (716) 636-7571; www.secularhumanism.org; Pres., Ronald A. Lindsay

Separation of Church and State, Americans United for (1947): 1301 K St. NW, Ste. 850, East Tower, Washington, DC 20005; (202) 466-3234; www.au.org; Exec. Dir., Rev. Barry W. Lynn

Seventh-day Adventist Church (1863): 12501 Old Columbia Pike, Silver Spring, MD 20904; (301) 680-6000; www.adventist.org; Pres., Ted N. C. Wilson

Unitarian Universalist Association of Congregations (1961): 25 Beacon St., Boston, MA 02108; (617) 742-2100; www.uua.org; Pres., Rev. Peter Morales

United Church of Christ (1957): 700 Prospect Ave., Cleveland, OH 44115; (216) 736-2100; www.ucc.org; Pres., Rev. Geoffrey A. Black

United Methodist Church (1968): 100 Maryland Ave. NE, Washington, DC 20002; (202) 488-5600; www.umc.org; Gen. Sec., James E. Winkler

United Pentecostal Church Intl. (1945): 8855 Dunn Rd., Hazelwood, MO 63042; (314) 837-7300; www.upci.org; Gen. Supt., David K. Bernard

Wesleyan Church (1843): 13300 Olio Rd., Fishers, IN 46250; (317) 774-7900; www.wesleyan.org; Gen. Sec., Dr. Ronald D. Kelly

Businesses and Corporations

Source: World Almanac research

Listed below are major corporations offering products and services to U.S. consumers, as of Aug. 2011. Alphabetization is by first key word or founder last name. Listings generally include examples of products offered.

Company name (NYSE/Nasdaq symbol, if traded on those markets): Address; Telephone number; Website; Top executive; Business, products, or services.

A&P: see Great Atlantic & Pacific Tea Co., Inc.

Abbott Laboratories (ABT): 100 Abbott Park Rd., Abbott Park, IL 60064; (847) 937-6100; www.abbott.com; Miles D. White; development, mfr. of pharmaceutical, nutritional, diagnostic prods.

Advance Publications, Inc.: 950 Fingerboard Rd., Staten Island, NY, 10305; (718) 981-1234; www.advance.net; Samuel I. Newhouse Jr.; communications, newspaper and magazine publisher (*Parade*; Condé Nast subsids.: *New Yorker*, *Vanity Fair*, *Vogue*).

Aetna, Inc. (AET): 151 Farmington Ave., Hartford, CT 06156; (860) 273-0123; www.aetna.com; Mark T. Bertolini; health care, employee benefits.

Aflac, Inc. (AFL): 1932 Wynnton Rd., Columbus, GA 31999; (706) 323-3431; www.aflac.com; Daniel P. Amos; supplemental health and life insurance.

Alaska Air Group, Inc. (ALK): 19300 International Blvd., Seattle, WA 98188; (206) 392-5040; www.alaskaair.com; William S. Ayer; airline carriers (Alaska Airlines, Horizon Air).

Alberto Culver Co.: see Unilever US.

Alcatel-Lucent (ALU): 3 av. Octave Gréard, Paris 75007, France; +33 (1) 4076-1010; www.alcatel-lucent.com; Ben Verwaayen; telecommunications equip., broadband networks.

Alcoa Inc. (AA): 201 Isabella St., Pittsburgh, PA 15212; (412) 553-4545; www.alcoa.com; Klaus Kleinfeld; prod., mgt. of aluminum, aluminum products (aerospace, automotive, industrial materials and components).

Allegheny Technologies Inc. (ATI): 1000 Six PPG Pl., Pittsburgh, PA 15222; (412) 394-2800; www.alleghenytechnologies.com; Richard J. Harshman; specialty metals mfr. (titanium, alloys).

Allstate Corp. (ALL): 2775 Sanders Rd., Northbrook, IL 60062; (847) 402-5000; www.allstate.com; Thomas J. Wilson; personal property and casualty insurance; financial services.

Altria Group, Inc. (MO): 6601 West Broad St., Richmond, VA 23230; (807) 274-2200; www.altria.com; Michael E. Szymanczyk; largest U.S. tobacco company (Philip Morris USA brands: Marlboro, Merit, Parliament, Virginia Slims). Acquired UST Inc. smokeless tobacco mfr., 1/6/2009.

Amazon.com, Inc. (AMZN): 1200 12th Ave. S., Ste. 1200, Seattle, WA 98144; (206) 266-1000; www.amazon.com; Jeffrey P. Bezos; online retailer of books, music, other consumer and household prods.

American Electric Power Co., Inc. (AEP): 1 Riverside Plz., Columbus, OH 43215; (614)

716-1000; www.aep.com; Michael G. Morris; public utilities.

American Express Co. (AXP): World Financial Ctr., 200 Vesey St., NY, NY 10285; (212) 640-2000; www.american express.com; Kenneth I. Chenault; charge and credit cards, travel-related services.

American Greetings Corp. (AM): 1 American Rd., Cleveland, OH 44144; (216) 252-7300; www.americangreetings.com; Morry Weiss; greeting cards, stationery, party goods, gift items.

American Intl. Group, Inc. (AIG): 70 Pine St., NY, NY 10270; (212) 770-7000; www.aigcorporate.com; Robert H. Benmosche; insurance, financial services. AIG received $182 bil in govt. bailouts, 2008.

American Standard Brands (AS America, Inc.): 1 Centennial Plz., Piscataway, NJ 08855; (732) 980-6000; www.american standard-us.com; Donald C. Devine; kitchen and bath prods. Formed from merger of American Standard America, Crane Plumbing, and Eljer, 2/2008.

AMR Corp. (AMR): 4333 Amon Carter Blvd., Ft. Worth, TX 76155; (817) 963-1234; www.aa.com; Gerard J. Arpey; one of the world's largest air carriers (American Airlines, American Eagle).

Anheuser-Busch InBev (BUD): Brouwerijplein 1, 3000 Leuven, Belgium; +32 (16) 247111; www.ab-inbev.com; Carlos Brito; world's largest brewer (Budweiser, Bud Light, Michelob, Busch), soft drinks. Anheuser-Busch became wholly owned subsid. of InBev, 11/18/2008; sold subsid. Busch Entertainment Corp., 2nd largest theme park operator in U.S., 12/1/2009.

Apple Inc. (AAPL): 1 Infinite Loop, Cupertino, CA 95014; (408) 996-1010; www.apple.com; Steve Jobs; mfr. of computers (Mac), digital media devices (iPod, iPhone, iPad) and distrib. (iTunes store).

ARAMARK Corp.: ARAMARK Tower, 1101 Market St., Philadelphia, PA 19107; (215) 238-3000; www.aramark.com; Joseph Neubauer; food/support services to institutions and facilities, uniforms and career apparel.

ArcelorMittal USA, Inc.: 1 South Dearborn, East Chicago, IN 46312; (312) 899-3440; www.arcelormittal.com; Michael G. Rippey; U.S. subsidiary of Arcelor Mittal, world's largest steel co., based in Luxembourg.

Archer Daniels Midland Co. (ADM): 4666 Faries Pkwy., Decatur, IL 62526; (217) 424-5200; www.adm.com; Patricia A. Woertz; agricultural commodities and prods.

Armstrong World Industries, Inc. (AWI): 2500 Columbia Ave., P.O. Box 3001,

Lancaster, PA 17604; (717) 397-0611; www.armstrong.com; Matthew J. Espe; mfr. of flooring, ceiling prods., cabinets.

ArvinMeritor, Inc. (MTOR): see Meritor, Inc.

Ashland Inc. (ASH): 50 E. RiverCenter Blvd., Covington, KY 41012; (859) 815-3333; www.ashland.com; James J. O'Brien; petroleum producer and refiner (Valvoline, plastics), chemicals, road construction. Acquired Hercules, Inc., 11/13/2008.

AT&T Inc. (T): 208 S. Akard St., Dallas, TX 75202; (210) 821-4105; www.att.com; Randall L. Stephenson; telecommunications, global information management.

AutoNation, Inc. (AN): 110 SE 6th St., Ft. Lauderdale, FL 33301; (954) 769-6000; www.autonation.com; Mike Jackson; new and used vehicles; auto parts, maintenance, and repair; auto finance and insurance.

Avon Products, Inc. (AVP): 1345 Ave. of the Americas, NY, NY 10105; (212) 282-5000; www.avon.com; Andrea Jung; cosmetics, fragrances, skin and personal care items; fashion apparel, accessories; housewares.

Bank of America Corp. (BAC): Bank of America Corporate Center, 100 N. Tryon St., 18th Fl., Charlotte, NC 28255; (704) 386-5681; www.bankofamerica.com; Brian T. Moynihan; banking and nonbanking financial services. Acquired Merrill Lynch, 1/1/2009.

Barnes & Noble, Inc. (BKS): 122 Fifth Ave., NY, NY 10011; (212) 633-3300; www.barnesandnobleinc.com; Leonard S. Riggio; leading U.S. bookseller (retail and college), publisher (Sterling Pub. Co.).

Bausch & Lomb Inc.: One Bausch & Lomb Pl., Rochester, NY 14604; (585) 338-6000; www.bausch.com; Brent L. Saunders; vision care prods., pharmaceuticals, surgical equip. Acquired by Warburg Pincus, 10/26/2007.

Baxter International Inc. (BAX): 1 Baxter Pkwy., Deerfield, IL 60015; (847) 948-2000; www.baxter.com; Robert L. Parkinson Jr.; mfr. of health care prods.

Bear Stearns Cos. Inc.: see JPMorgan Chase & Co.

Becton, Dickinson & Co. (BDX): 1 Becton Dr., Franklin Lakes, NJ 07417; (201) 847-6800; www.bd.com; Edward J. Ludwig; medical, laboratory, diagnostic prods.

BellSouth Corp.: see AT&T Inc.

Berkshire Hathaway Inc. (BRK.A): 3555 Farnam St., Ste. 1440, Omaha, NE 68131; (402) 346-1400; www.berkshirehathaway.com; Warren E. Buffett; insurance (GEICO), building materials (Benjamin Moore & Co., Shaw), apparel (Fruit of the Loom), food

(Dairy Queen). Merged Burlington Northern Santa Fe Corp. rail transportation co. into Berkshire subsidiary, 2/12/2010.

Bertelsmann AG: Carl-Bertelsmann-Str. 270, D-33311 Gütersloh, Germany; +49-5241-80-0; www.bertelsmann.de; Hartmut Ostrowski; intl. media corp., world's largest trade book publisher (Random House: Knopf, Doubleday). Sold stake in Sony BMG to Sony Corp., 10/1/2008.

Best Buy Co., Inc. (BBY): 7601 Penn Ave. S., Richfield, MN 55423; (612) 291-1000; www.bestbuy.com; Brian J. Dunn; retailer of software, appliances, consumer electronics.

Blackstone Group LP, The (BX): 345 Park Ave., NY, NY 10154; (212) 583-5000; www.blackstone.com; Stephen A. Schwarzman; asset mgmt., financial services.

Blockbuster Inc.: 3000 N. Redbud Blvd., McKinney, TX 75069; (972) 683-3854; www.blockbuster.com; Michael Kelly; in-home movie and video game rental, purchases. Filed for bankruptcy 9/23/2010; acquired by DISH Network, 4/26/2011.

Boeing Co. (BA): 100 N. Riverside, Chicago, IL 60606; (312) 544-2000; www.boeing.com; W. James McNerney Jr.; world's leading aerospace co., largest mfr. of commercial jet and military aircraft; one of the largest U.S. defense contractors.

The Brink's Co. (BCO): 1801 Bayberry Ct., Richmond, VA 23226; (804) 289-9600; www.brinkscompany.com; Michael T. Dan; security (armored transport, alarm systems, guarding services). Completed spin-off of Home Security Holdings, 10/31/2008.

Bristol-Myers Squibb Co. (BMY): 345 Park Ave., NY, NY 10154; (212) 546-4000; www.bms.com; Lamberto Andreotti; development, mfr., and sale of pharmaceuticals (Plavix, Abilify, Atripla). Acquired ZymoGenetics, Inc., 10/12/2010.

Brown-Forman Corp. (BFB): 850 Dixie Hwy., Louisville, KY 40210; (502) 585-1100; www.brown-forman.com; Paul C. Varga; distilled spirits (Jack Daniel's, Southern Comfort), wine and champagne (Fetzer, Korbel).

Brown Shoe Co., Inc. (BWS): 8300 Maryland Ave., St. Louis, MO 63105; (314) 854-4000; www.brownshoe.com; Ronald A. Fromm; shoe mfr. (Buster Brown, Naturalizer, Dr. Scholl's) and retailer (Famous Footwear, shoes.com). Acquired American Sporting Goods Corp., 2/17/2011.

Brunswick Corp. (BC): 1 N. Field Ct., Lake Forest, IL 60045; (847) 735-4700; www.brunswick.com; Dustan E. McCoy; largest U.S. maker of leisure and recreation prods., incl. marine engines and boats; billiards, bowling, and fitness equipment; bowling centers.

Burger King Holdings, Inc.: 5505 Blue Lagoon Dr., Miami, FL 33126; (305) 378-3000; www.bk.com; John W. Chidsey; fast food hamburger restaurant chain. Acquired by 3G Capital 10/19/2010.

Cablevision Systems Corp. (CVC): 1111 Stewart Ave., Bethpage, NY 11714; (516) 803-2300; www.cablevision.com; James L. Dolan; cable and Internet services provider (Optimum); local media and programming; movie theaters (Clearview). Spun off of Madison Square Garden, 2/9/2010; spun off AMC Networks, 6/30/2011.

Caesars Entertainment Corp.: One Caesars Palace Dr., Las Vegas, NV 89109; (702) 407-6000; www.harrahs.com; Gary W. Loveman; world's largest provider of branded casino entertainment (Caesars, Harrah's, Horseshoe, World Series of Poker). Changed name from Harrah's Entertainment, Inc., 11/23/2010.

Campbell Soup Co. (CPB): One Campbell Pl., Camden, NJ 08103; (856) 342-4800; www.campbellsoupcompany.com; Douglas R. Conant; world's largest soup mfr.; sauces (Pace, Prego), V8 juice, Pepperidge Farm prods.

Caterpillar Inc. (CAT): 100 NE Adams St., Peoria, IL 61629; (309) 675-1000; www.cat.com; Douglas R. Oberhelman; world's largest mfr. of construction and mining equip.

CBS Corp. (CBS): 51 W. 52nd St., NY, NY 10019; (212) 975-4321; www.cbscorporation.com; Leslie Moonves; TV networks (CBS, Showtime); TV distribution;

radio stations; book publishing (Simon & Schuster); advertising.

CenturyLink, Inc. (CTL): 100 CenturyLink Dr., Monroe, LA 71203; (318) 388-9000; www.centurylink.com; Glen F. Post III; 3rd-largest telecommunications provider in the U.S. Acquired Qwest Communications, 4/1/2011.

Chevron Corp. (CVX): 6001 Bollinger Canyon Rd., San Ramon, CA 94583; (925) 842-1000; www.chevron.com; John S. Watson; one of the world's largest integrated-energy co. Acquired Atlas Energy, 2/18/2011.

Chiquita Brands International, Inc. (CQB): 250 E. 5th St., Cincinnati, OH 45202; (513) 784-8000; www.chiquitabrands.com; Fernando Aguirre; bananas and other fruits and vegetables.

Church & Dwight Co., Inc. (CHD): 469 N. Harrison St., Princeton, NJ 08543; (609) 683-5900; www.churchdwight.com; James R. Craigie; world's largest producer of sodium bicarbonate (ARM & HAMMER baking soda); household (OxiClean) and personal care prods. (Arrid, Trojan, First Response).

CIGNA Corp. (CI): 2 Liberty Pl., 1601 Chestnut St., Philadelphia, PA 19192; (215) 761-1000; www.cigna.com; David M. Cordani; healthcare, life and accident insurance provider.

Cintas Corp. (CTAS): 6800 Cintas Blvd., Cincinnati, OH 45262; (513) 459-1200; www.cintas.com; Scott D. Farmer; largest uniform supplier in North America.

Circuit City Stores, Inc.: see Systemax Inc.

Cisco Systems, Inc. (CSCO): 170 West Tasman Dr., Bldg. 10, San Jose, CA 95134; (408) 526-4000; www.cisco.com; John T. Chambers; networking and communication products.

Citigroup, Inc. (C): 399 Park Ave., NY, NY 10043; (212) 559-1000; www.citigroup.com; Vikram Pandit; diversified financial services. Announced plans to realign into two business segments (Citicorp and Citi Holdings), 1/16/2009.

Clear Channel Communications, Inc. (CCMO): 200 E. Basse Rd., San Antonio, TX 78209; (210) 822-2828; www.clearchannel.com; Mark P. Mays; largest radio station owner in U.S. (850+ stations); outdoor advertising (billboards, mass transit ads). Acquired by CC Media Holdings, 7/30/2008.

Clorox Co. (CLX): 1221 Broadway, Oakland, CA 94612; (510) 271-7000; www.clorox.com; Donald R. Knauss; retail consumer prods. (Clorox, Formula 409, Pine-Sol, S.O.S., Tilex; Scoop Away, Fresh Step cat litters; Kingsford charcoal; Hidden Valley dressing; Glad plastic bags; Brita water systems; Burt's Bees personal care prods.).

Coca-Cola Co. (KO): 1 Coca-Cola Plz., Atlanta, GA 30313; (404) 676-2121; www.coca-cola.com; Muhtar Kent; world's largest soft drink co. (Coca-Cola, Sprite, DASANI water), world's largest dist. of juice prods. (Minute Maid).

Colgate-Palmolive Co. (CL): 300 Park Ave., NY, NY 10022; (212) 310-2000; www.colgate.com; Ian M. Cook; soap (Irish Spring), detergent (Palmolive), household cleansers (Ajax), toothpaste (Colgate, Tom's of Maine), pet food (Hill's Science Diet).

Collective Brands, Inc. (PSS): 3231 SE 6th Ave., Topeka, KS 66607; (785) 233-5171; www.collectivebrands.com; Michael J. Massey; shoe mfr./retailer. Formed by acquisition of StrideRite by Payless ShoeSource, 8/17/2007.

Comcast Corp. (CMCSA): 1 Comcast Ctr., Philadelphia, PA 19103; (215) 286-1700; www.comcast.com; Brian L. Roberts; largest U.S. cable company; broadband cable, internet, and voice services. Some programming (E!, Golf Channel).

Compaq Computer Corp.: see Hewlett-Packard Co.

CompUSA Inc.: see Systemax Inc.

Computer Sciences Corp. (CSC): 3170 Fairview Park Dr., Falls Church, VA 22042; (703) 876-1000; www.csc.com; Michael W. Laphen; technology services.

ConAgra Foods, Inc. (CAG): 1 ConAgra Dr., Omaha, NE 68102; (402) 595-4000; www.conagrafoods.com; Gary M. Rodkin; food

processor (Chef Boyardee, Healthy Choice frozen dinners, Egg Beaters, Reddi-wip); food service supplier.

ConocoPhillips Co. (COP): 600 N. Dairy Ashford, P.O. Box 2197, Houston, TX 77079; (281) 293-1000; www.conocophillips.com; James J. Mulva; 3rd-largest U.S. oil and gas company.

Consolidated Edison, Inc. (ED): 4 Irving Pl., NY, NY 10003; (212) 460-4600; www.conedison.com; Kevin Burke; electric, natural gas utilities.

Continental Airlines, Inc.: see United Continental Holdings, Inc.

Corning Inc. (GLW): 1 Riverfront Plz., Corning, NY 14831; (607) 974-9000; www.corning.com; Wendell P. Weeks; mfr. of telecommunications, specialty equipment, fiber optics.

Costco Wholesale Corp. (COST): 999 Lake Dr., Issaquah, WA 98027; (425) 313-8100; www.costco.com; James D. Sinegal; wholesale warehouse stores.

Countrywide Financial: see Bank of America Corp.

Crane Co. (CR): 100 First Stamford Pl., Stamford, CT 06902; (203) 363-7300; www.craneco.com; Eric C. Fast; mfr. of fluid control devices, vending machines, aircraft components.

A.T. Cross Co. (ATX): 1 Albion Rd., Lincoln, RI 02865; (401) 333-1200; www.cross.com; David G. Whalen; writing instruments, timepieces, personal accessories.

Crown Holdings, Inc. (CCK): 1 Crown Way, Philadelphia, PA 19154; (215) 698-5100; www.crowncork.com; John W. Conway; leading producer of packaging prods.

CSX Corp. (CSX): 500 Water St., 15th Fl., Jacksonville, FL 32202; (904) 359-3200; www.csx.com; Michael J. Ward; rail and road freight transport.

CVS Caremark Corp. (CVS): 1 CVS Dr., Woonsocket, RI 02895; (401) 765-1500; www.cvs.com; Larry J. Merlo. Acquired Eckerd Corp. in Aug. 2004, to become nation's largest drugstore chain; announced acquisition of Longs Drug Stores Corp., 8/12/2008.

Dana Holding Corp. (DAN): 4500 Dorr St., Toledo, OH 43615; (419) 535-4500; www.dana.com; Roger J. Wood; truck and auto parts, supplies; emerged from Chap. 11 reorganization, 2/1/2008.

Darden Restaurants, Inc. (DRI): 5900 Lake Ellenor Dr., Orlando, FL 32809; (407) 245-4000; www.dardenrestaurants.com; Clarence Otis Jr.; casual-dining restaurants (Red Lobster, Olive Garden).

Dean Foods Co. (DF): 2515 McKinney Ave., Ste. 1200, Dallas, TX 75201; (214) 303-3400; www.deanfoods.com; Gregg L. Engles; milk and specialty dairy products (LAND O LAKES, Horizon Organic, Silk soy milk, International Delight coffee creamers).

Deere & Co. (DE): One John Deere Pl., Moline, IL 61265; (309) 765-8000; www.deere.com; Samuel R. Allen; one of the world's largest mfrs. of farm equip.; mfr. industrial equip., lawn and garden tractors.

Dell Inc. (DELL): 1 Dell Way, Round Rock, TX 78682; (512) 338-4400; www.dell.com; Michael S. Dell; laptop and desktop computers, network accessories, peripherals, tablets, smartphones.

Delta Air Lines, Inc. (DAL): 1030 Delta Blvd., Atlanta, GA 30320; (404) 715-2600; www.delta.com; Richard H. Anderson; air transportation; emerged from Chap. 11, 4/30/2007; merged with Northwest Airlines, 10/29/2008.

Dial Corp.: 15501 N. Dial Blvd., Scottsdale, AZ 85260; (480) 754-3425; www.henkelna.com; Bradley A. Casper; consumer prods. (Dial soap, Purex detergent, Right Guard antiperspirant, Renuzit air fresheners); U.S. subsidiary of Germany's Henkel company.

Diebold, Inc. (DBD): 5995 Mayfair Rd., North Canton, OH 44720; (330) 490-4000; www.diebold.com; Thomas W. Swidarski; mfr. ATMs, security systems and prods.

Dillard's Inc. (DDS): 1600 Cantrell Rd., Little Rock, AR 72201; (501) 376-5200; www.dillards.com; William Dillard II; dept. store chain.

Walt Disney Co., The (DIS): 500 S. Buena Vista St., Burbank, CA 91521; (818) 560-1000; disney.go.com; Robert A. Iger; one of the world's largest media conglomerates;

motion pictures (Touchstone, Pixar); TV (ABC, ESPN) and radio; publishing; theme parks (Walt Disney World, Disneyland) and resorts. Acquired Marvel Entertainment, 12/31/2009. Announced sale of Miramax Films, 7/29/2010.

Doctor's Associates Inc.: 325 Bic Dr., Milford, CT 06461; (203) 877-4281; www. subway.com; Frederick A. DeLuca; restaurants (Subway).

Dole Food Co., Inc. (DOLE): One Dole Dr., Westlake Village, CA 91362; (818) 879-6600; www.dole.com; David A. DeLorenzo; food prods., fresh fruits, and vegetables. Announced plans to go public through an IPO, 8/14/2009; shares began trading 10/23/2009.

R. R. Donnelley & Sons Co. (RRD): 111 S. Wacker Dr., Chicago, IL 60606; (312) 326-8000; www.rrdonnelley.com; Thomas J. Quinlan III; commercial printing; photos/ graphics, translation; printer of *The World Almanac*.

Dow Chemical Co. (DOW): 2030 Dow Ctr., Midland, MI 48674; (989) 636-1000; www. dow.com; Andrew N. Liveris; chemicals, plastics (world's 2nd-largest chemical co.). Acquired Rohm and Haas, 4/1/2009.

Dow Jones & Co., Inc.: see News Corp.

Dr Pepper Snapple Group, Inc. (DPS): 5301 Legacy Dr., Plano, TX 75024; (972) 673-7000; www.drpeppersnapplegroup.com; Larry D. Young; bottler and distributor of non-alcoholic beverages (Dr Pepper, Hawaiian Punch, 7UP, Snapple, Mott's).

Duke Energy Corp. (DUK): 526 S. Church St., Charlotte, NC 28202; (704) 594-6200; www.duke-energy.com; James E. Rogers; utilities, fiber optics networks.

Dun & Bradstreet Corp. (DNB): 103 JFK Pkwy., Short Hills, NJ 07078; (973) 921-5500; www.dnb.com; Sara Mathew; business information, research.

E. I. du Pont de Nemours & Co. (Dupont) (DD): 1007 Market St., Wilmington, DE 19898; (302) 774-1000; www.dupont.com; Ellen J. Kullman; 3rd-largest U.S. chemical co.; petroleum, consumer prods.

Eastman Kodak Co. (EK): 343 State St., Rochester, NY 14650; (585) 724-4000; www.kodak.com; Antonio M. Perez; film; digital cameras; printers.

Eaton Corp. (ETN): Eaton Ctr., 1111 Superior Ave., Cleveland, OH 44114; (216) 523-5000; www.eaton.com; Alexander M. Cutler; mfr. vehicle components, controls.

eBay Inc. (EBAY): 2145 Hamilton Ave., San Jose, CA 95125; (408) 376-7400; www. ebay.com; John Donahoe; online auctions. Acquired StubHub.com, 2/13/2007.

Edison Intl. (EIX): 2244 Walnut Grove Ave., Rosemead, CA 91770; (626) 302-2222; www.edison.com; Theodore F. Craver Jr.; electric utilities.

Electronic Arts Inc. (ERTS): 209 Redwood Shores Pkwy., Redwood City, CA 94065; (650) 628-1500; www.ea.com; John Riccitiello; leading U.S. video game publisher (Madden NFL, Battlefield, The Sims).

Electronic Data Systems: see Hewlett-Packard Co.

Eli Lilly and Co. (LLY): Lilly Corporate Center, Indianapolis, IN 46285; (317) 276-2000; www.lilly.com; John C. Lechleiter; pharmaceutical research, development, and manufacturing (Prozac, Strattera, Cialis).

El Paso Corp. (EP): 1001 Louisiana St., Houston, TX 77002; (713) 420-2600; www. elpaso.com; Douglas L. Foshee; natural gas/oil transportation, storage, exploration, production.

EMC Corp. (EMC): 176 South St., Hopkinton, MA 01748; (508) 435-1000; www.emc.com; Joseph M. Tucci; data storage/protection.

Emerson Electric Co. (EMR): 8000 W. Florissant Ave., St. Louis, MO 63136; (314) 553-2000; www.emerson.com; David N. Farr; electrical, electronics prods. & systems.

Energizer Holdings, Inc. (ENR): 533 Maryville Univ. Dr., St. Louis, MO 63141; (314) 985-2000; www.energizer.com; Ward M. Klein; batteries, flashlights.

Estée Lauder Cos. Inc. (EL): 767 Fifth Ave., NY, NY 10153; (212) 572-4200; www. elcompanies.com; Fabrizio Freda; cosmetics (Clinique, Bobbi Brown), fragrance, skin care prods.

Exelon Corp. (EXC): 10 S. Dearborn St., 48th Fl., Chicago, IL 60680; (312) 394-7398; www.exeloncorp.com; John W. Rowe; electricity generation/distribution; natural gas.

ExxonMobil Corp. (XOM): 5959 Las Colinas Blvd., Irving, TX 75039; (972) 444-1000; www.exxonmobil.com; Rex W. Tillerson; world's largest integrated oil co.

Federal Home Loan Mortgage Corp. (Freddie Mac): 8200 Jones Branch Dr., McLean, VA 22102; (703) 903-2000; www. freddiemac.com; Charles E. Haldeman Jr.; residential mortgage provider. Taken over by U.S. government, 9/7/2008.

Federal National Mortgage Assn. (Fannie Mae): 3900 Wisconsin Ave. NW, Washington, DC 20016; (202) 752-7000; www.fanniemae.com; Michael J. Williams; largest U.S. provider of residential mortgage funds. Taken over by U.S. government, 9/7/2008.

FedEx Corp. (FDX): 942 S. Shady Grove Rd., Memphis, TN 38120; (901) 818-7500; www. fedex.com; Frederick W. Smith; world's largest express delivery service.

First Data Corp.: 5565 Glenridge Connector NE, Ste. 2000, Atlanta, GA 30342; (303) 967-8000; www.firstdata.com; Jonathan J. Judge; financial transaction processing. Acquired by Kohlberg Kravis Roberts & Co., 9/24/2007.

FirstEnergy Corp. (FE): 76 S. Main St., Akron, OH 44308; (800) 736-3402; www. firstenergycorp.com; Anthony J. Alexander; public electricity supplier.

Fluor Corp. (FLR): 6700 Las Colinas Blvd., Irving, TX 75039; (469) 398-7000; www. fluor.com; David T. Seaton; international engineering and construction co.

Foot Locker, Inc. (FL): 112 W. 34th St., NY, NY 10120; (212) 720-3700; www.footlocker-inc.com; Ken C. Hicks; retail athletic stores (Footaction, Foot Locker, Champs Sports).

Ford Motor Co. (F): 1 American Rd., Dearborn, MI 48126; (313) 322-3000; www.ford. com; William C. Ford Jr.; auto mfr.; motor vehicle sales (Ford, Lincoln); largest U.S. auto. finance co. (Ford Motor Credit).

Fortune Brands, Inc. (FO): 520 Lake Cook Rd., Deerfield, IL 60015; (847) 484-4400; www.fortunebrands.com; Bruce A. Carbonari; spirits and wine (Jim Beam, Courvoisier, Sauza); home and hardware prods. (Moen, Master Lock). Sold golf and leisure prod. div. (Titleist, FootJoy) to Fila Korea Ltd., 7/29/2011.

Gannett Co., Inc. (GCI): 7950 Jones Branch Dr., McLean, VA 22107; (703) 854-6000; www.gannett.com; Craig A. Dubow; largest U.S. newspaper publisher (*USA Today*); network and cable TV.

Gap Inc. (GPS): 2 Folsom St., San Francisco, CA 94105; (650) 952-4400; www.gapinc. com; Glenn K. Murphy; casual apparel retailer (Gap, Banana Republic, Old Navy).

Gateway, Inc.: 7565 Irvine Center Dr., Irvine, CA 92618; (949) 471-7000; www.gateway. com; personal computers, network servers, peripherals; acquired by Taiwan-based Acer Inc., 10/16/2007.

General Dynamics Corp. (GD): 2941 Fairview Park Dr., Ste. 100, Falls Church, VA 22042; (703) 876-3000; www. generaldynamics.com; Jay L. Johnson; defense contractor: aerospace, combat systems, marine systems, computing devices.

General Electric Co. (GE): 3135 Easton Tpke., Fairfield, CT 06828; (203) 373-2211; www.ge.com; Jeffrey Immelt; electrical, electronic equip., financial services, radio and TV broadcasting (NBC, Bravo, USA, Telemundo); aircraft engines, power generation, appliances.

General Mills, Inc. (GIS): One General Mills Blvd., Minneapolis, MN 55426; (763) 764-7600; www.generalmills.com; Kendall J. Powell; food mfr. (Betty Crocker, Bisquick, Cheerios, Chex, Green Giant, Häagen-Dazs, Pillsbury, Progresso, Total, Wheaties, Yoplait).

General Motors Co. (GM): 300 Renaissance Ctr., Detroit, MI 48265; (313) 556-5000; www.gm.com; Daniel F. Akerson; one of the world's largest auto mfrs. (Chevrolet, Cadillac, Buick, GMC); auto financing (GM Financial); vehicle security (OnStar). General Motors Corp. filed for

Chap. 11 reorganization, 6/1/2009; sold its profitable components to a new, smaller company called General Motors Co., 7/10/2009.

Genuine Parts Co. (GPC): 2999 Circle 75 Pkwy., Atlanta, GA 30339; (770) 953-1700; www.genpt.com; Thomas C. Gallagher; auto replacement parts distributor (NAPA).

Goldman Sachs Group, Inc. (GS): 200 West St., 29th Fl., NY, NY 10282; (212) 902-1000; www.goldmansachs.com; Lloyd C. Blankfein; investment banking, asset management, securities services.

Goodyear Tire & Rubber Co. (GT): 1144 E. Market St., Akron, OH 44316; (330) 796-2121; www.goodyear.com; Richard J. Kramer; tires and other auto prods.

Google, Inc. (GOOG): 1600 Amphitheatre Pkwy., Mountain View, CA 94043; (650) 253-0000; www.google.com; Eric E. Schmidt; leading internet search engine. Acquired YouTube, 10/9/2006, DoubleClick, 3/11/2008; announced plans to acquire Motorola Mobility Holdings, 8/15/2011.

W. R. Grace & Co. (GRA): 7500 Grace Dr., Columbia, MD 21044; (410) 531-4000; www.grace.com; Alfred E. Festa; chemicals, construction prods.

Great Atlantic & Pacific Tea Co., Inc. (GAP): 2 Paragon Dr., Montvale, NJ 07645; (201) 573-9700; www.aptea.com; Samuel Martin; supermarkets (A&P, The Food Emporium, Super Fresh, Waldbaum's, Pathmark). Acquired Pathmark, 12/3/2007. Filed for Chap. 11 reorganization, 12/12/2010.

Halliburton Co. (HAL): 5 Houston Center, 1401 McKinney St., Ste. 2400, Houston, TX 77010; (713) 759-2600; www.halliburton. com; David J. Lesar; oil field mgmt., energy services. Split off subsidiary KBR, Inc., 4/5/2007.

Hanesbrands Inc. (HBI): 1000 E. Hanes Mill Rd., Winston-Salem, NC 27105; (336) 519-8080; www.hanesbrands.com; Richard A. Noll; apparel mfr. (Hanes, L'eggs, Champion, Just My Size, Playtex, Wonderbra). Spun off from parent co. Sara Lee Corp., 9/5/2006; acquired GearCo., Inc., 11/1/2010.

Harley-Davidson, Inc. (HOG): 3700 W. Juneau Ave., Milwaukee, WI 53208; (414) 342-4680; www.harley-davidson.com; Keith E. Wandell; mfr. motorcycles, parts, and accessories.

Hartford Financial Services Group, Inc. (HIG): One Hartford Plz., Hartford, CT 06155; (860) 547-5000; www.thehartford. com; Liam E. McGee; insurance, financial services.

Hasbro, Inc. (HAS): 1027 Newport Ave., Pawtucket, RI 02862; (401) 431-8697; www. hasbro.com; Brian Goldner; toy and game mfr. (Milton Bradley, Playskool, G.I. Joe, Parker Bros., Nerf, Play-Doh).

HCA Holdings, Inc. (HCA): 1 Park Plz., Nashville, TN 37203; (615) 344-9551; www. hcahealthcare.com; Richard M. Bracken; owns and operates hospitals; other diagnostic, surgical, health treatment centers.

H. J. Heinz Co. (HNZ): 1 PPG Pl., Ste. 3100, Pittsburgh, PA 15222; (412) 456-5700; www.heinz.com; William R. Johnson; food mfr. (Ore-Ida, 57 Varieties ketchup, Weight Watchers foods).

Hershey Co., The (HSY): 100 Crystal A Dr., Hershey, PA 17033; (717) 534-4200; www.thehersheycompany.com; John P. Bilbrey; largest North American producer of chocolate prods. (Reese's, Kit Kat, Mounds, Almond Joy, Jolly Rancher, Twizzlers, Milk Duds, Good & Plenty, York).

Hertz Global Holdings, Inc. (HTZ): 225 Brae Blvd., Park Ridge, NJ 07656; (201) 307-2000; www.hertz.com; Mark P. Frissora; car rentals.

Hess Corp. (HES): 1185 Ave. of the Americas, NY, NY 10036; (212) 997-8500; www. hess.com; John B. Hess; integrated oil and gas co.

Hewlett-Packard Co. (HPQ): 3000 Hanover St., Palo Alto, CA 94304; (650) 857-1501; www.hp.com; Léo Apotheker; computers, electronic prods. and systems. Merged with Compaq, 5/3/2002. Acquired Electronic Data Systems, 8/26/2008.

Hillenbrand, Inc. (HI): One Batesville Blvd., Batesville, IN 47006; (812) 934-7000; www. hillenbrandinc.com; Kenneth A. Camp;

holder of Batesville Caskets, coffin mfr. Spun off from Hill-Rom Holdings, 4/1/2008.

Hill-Rom Holdings, Inc. (HRC): 1069 State Rte. 46 E., Batesville, IN 47006; (812) 934-7777; www.hill-rom.com; John J. Greisch; mfr. hospital beds, other hospital equip. Hill-Rom separated its funeral casket mfr., 4/1/2008.

Hilton Worldwide: 7930 Jones Branch Dr., Ste. 1100, McLean, VA 22102; (703) 883-1000; www.hiltonworldwide.com; Christopher J. Nassetta; hotels and resorts (Doubletree, Embassy, Hampton). Merged with The Blackstone Group, 10/24/2007.

Home Depot, Inc. (HD): 2455 Paces Ferry Rd. NW, Atlanta, GA 30339; (770) 433-8211; www.homedepot.com; Francis S. Blake; world's largest home improvement retailer; 4th-largest U.S. retailer; home improvement warehouse stores. Sold construction business, HD Supply, 8/30/2007.

Honeywell Intl. Inc. (HON): 101 Columbia Rd., Morristown, NJ 07962; (973) 455-2000; www.honeywell.com; David Cote; industrial and home control systems, aerospace guidance systems.

Hormel Foods Corp. (HRL): 1 Hormel Pl., Austin, MN 55912; (507) 437-5611; www.hormelfoods.com; Jeffrey M. Ettinger; meat processor; pork, turkey, and beef prods. (SPAM, Dinty Moore, Jennie-O).

Hostess Brands: 6031 Connection Dr., Ste. 600, Irving, TX 75039; (972) 532-4500; www.hostessbrands.com; Brian J. Driscoll; baked goods wholesaler, distributor (Wonder, Hostess, Dolly Madison, Drake's, Home Pride). Emerged from Chap. 11 reorganization, 2/3/2009.

Houghton Mifflin Harcourt: 222 Berkeley St., Boston, MA 02116; (617) 351-5000; www.hmhco.com; Michael Muldowney; publisher of textbooks and other educational prods. (McDougal Littell), trade and reference books.

H&R Block, Inc. (HRB): 1 H&R Block Way, Kansas City, MO 64105; (816) 854-3000; www.hrblock.com; William C. Cobb; tax return preparation; business and consulting services.

Humana Inc. (HUM): 500 W. Main St., Louisville, KY 40202; (502) 580-1000; www.humana.com; Michael B. McCallister; managed health care service provider, related specialty products.

IAC/InterActiveCorp (IACI): 555 W. 18th St., NY, NY 10011; (212) 314-7300; www.iac.com; Barry Diller; internet conglomerate (Ask.com, Match.com, Citysearch, Urbanspoon, ServiceMagic). Split off TV, leisure, and financial holdings into 5 separate cos., 8/21/2008.

Illinois Tool Works Inc. (ITW): 3600 W. Lake Ave., Glenview, IL 60026; (847) 724-7500; www.itw.com; David B. Speer; consumer, industrial tools; food equip. (Hobart), packaging (Zip-Pak).

Ingersoll-Rand plc (IR): 170/175 Lakeview Dr., Airside Business Park, Swords, Dublin, Ireland; 353-1-870-7400; company. ingersollrand.com; Michael W. Lamach; locks and security systems (Schlage, Kryptonite); refrigeration equip. (Thermo King, Hussmann); industrial equip.; air conditioning systems (Trane). Sold Bobcat, Utility Equip., & Attachments, 11/30/2007. Acquired Trane, 6/5/2008.

Intel Corp. (INTC): 2200 Mission College Blvd., Santa Clara, CA 95054; (408) 765-8080; www.intel.com; Paul S. Otellini; mfr. semiconductors, microprocessors (Core, Centrino).

International Business Machines Corp. (IBM): One New Orchard Rd., Armonk, NY 10504; (914) 499-1900; www.ibm.com; Samuel Palmisano; world's largest supplier of advanced information processing technology equip., services.

International Paper Co. (IP): 6400 Poplar Ave., Memphis, TN 38197; (901) 419-7000; www.ipaper.com; John V. Faraci Jr.; world's largest paper/forest prods. co.

International Textile Group, Inc. (ITXN): 804 Green Valley Rd., Greensboro, NC 27408; (336) 379-6220; www.itg-global.com; Joseph L. Gorga; apparel and home textiles/fabrics.

J.C. Penney Co., Inc. (JCP): 6501 Legacy Dr., Plano, TX 75024; (972) 431-1000; www. jcpenney.net; Myron E. Ullman III; dept. store retailer, general merchandise catalog sales.

J. Crew Group, Inc.: 770 Broadway, NY, NY 10003; (212) 209-2500; www.jcrew.com; Millard S. Drexler; retail and mail order apparel and accessories. Acquired by TPG Capital and Leonard Green & Partners, 3/7/2011.

JetBlue Airways Corp. (JBLU): 118-29 Queens Blvd., Forest Hills, NY 11375; (718) 286-7900; www.jetblue.com; David Barger; air transportation.

Jo-Ann Stores, Inc.: 5555 Darrow Rd., Hudson, OH 44236; (330) 656-2600; www.joann.com; Darrell D. Webb; nation's largest specialty fabric and craft stores. Announced plans to be acquired by Leonard Green & Partners, 12/23/2010.

Johnson Controls, Inc. (JCI): 5757 N. Green Bay Ave., Milwaukee, WI 53209; (414) 524-1200; www.johnsoncontrols.com; Stephen A. Roell; equipment and controls for heating, ventilating, AC, refrigeration, and building security; auto interiors, batteries.

Johnson & Johnson (JNJ): 1 Johnson & Johnson Plz., New Brunswick, NJ 08933; (732) 524-0400; www.jnj.com; William Weldon; health care prods. (Band-Aid), pharmaceuticals (Tylenol, Motrin), toiletries (Neutrogena, Aveeno); acquired Pfizer's consumer prods. division (Neosporin, Listerine, Sudafed), 12/20/2006.

S. C. Johnson & Son, Inc.: 1525 Howe St., Racine, WI 53403; (262) 260-2000; www.scjohnson.com; H. Fisk Johnson; cleaning and other household prods. (Johnson's Wax, Windex, Pledge, Fantastik, Raid, OFF!, Shout, Glade, Scrubbing Bubbles, Ziploc bags).

Jones Group, Inc. (JNY): 1411 Broadway, NY, NY 10018; (212) 642-3860; www.jny.com; Wesley R. Card; apparel (Jones New York, Gloria Vanderbilt), shoes (Nine West, Anne Klein); retail and outlet stores. Sold Barneys New York, 9/7/2007.

JPMorgan Chase & Co. (JPM): 270 Park Ave., NY, NY 10017; (212) 270-6000; www.jpmorganchase.com; James Dimon; financial service. Merged with Bank One Corp., 7/1/2004; acquired Bear Stearns, 6/2/2008; acquired Washington Mutual, 9/25/2008.

KBR, Inc. (KBR): 601 Jefferson St., Ste. 3400, Houston, TX 77002; (713) 753-3011; www.kbr.com; William P. Utt; engineering; construction mgmt. services. Separated from parent company Halliburton, 4/5/2007.

Kellogg Co. (K): One Kellogg Sq., Battle Creek, MI 49016; (269) 961-2000; www.kelloggcompany.com; John A. Bryant; world's largest mfr. of ready-to-eat cereals, other food prods. (Frosted Flakes, Rice Krispies, Froot Loops, Pop-Tarts, Nutri-Grain, Keebler, Eggo).

Kelly Services, Inc. (KELYA): 999 W. Big Beaver Rd., Troy, MI 48084; (248) 362-4444; www.kellyservices.com; Carl T. Camden; temporary staffing services.

Kimberly-Clark Corp. (KMB): P.O. Box 619100, Irving, TX 75261; (972) 281-1200; www.kimberly-clark.com; Thomas J. Falk; personal care prods. (Kleenex, Scott, Cottonelle, Huggies, Kotex).

Kmart Corp.: see Sears Holdings Corp.

Koch Industries, Inc.: P.O. Box 2256, Wichita, KS 67201; (316) 828-5500; www.kochind.com; Charles G. Koch; forest prod. mfr.; oil refineries/pipeline; chemicals; pollution-control equipment; ranching. Acquired Georgia-Pacific, 12/23/2005.

Kraft Foods Inc. (KFT): 3 Lakes Dr., Northfield, IL 60093; (847) 646-2000; www.kraftfoodscompany.com; Irene B. Rosenfeld; world's second largest food company, including Nabisco (Oreo), Jell-O, Oscar Mayer, Maxwell House, Trident. Spun off Post cereals into Ralcorp Holdings, 8/4/2008. Announced acquisition of Cadbury plc, 2/2/2010.

Kroger Co. (KR): 1014 Vine St., Cincinnati, OH 45202; (513) 762-4000; www.kroger.com; David B. Dillon; largest U.S. retail grocery chain, convenience stores, mall jewelry stores.

La-Z-Boy Inc. (LZB): 1284 N. Telegraph Rd., Monroe, MI 48162; (734) 242-1444; www.la-z-boy.com; Kurt L. Darrow; reclining chairs, other furniture.

Leggett & Platt, Inc. (LEG): No. 1 Leggett Rd., Carthage, MO 64836; (417) 358-8131; www.leggett.com; David S. Haffner; furniture and its components, industrial materials, automotive seating suspension, control and power train cable systems.

Levi Strauss & Co.: 1155 Battery St., San Francisco, CA 94111; (415) 501-6000; www.levistrauss.com; John Anderson; blue jeans, casual sportswear (Dockers).

Lexmark Intl., Inc. (LXK): 740 W. New Circle Rd., Lexington, KY 40550; (859) 232-2000; www1.lexmark.com; Paul Rooke; computer printers and peripherals.

Liberty Mutual Holding Co. Inc.: 175 Berkeley St., Boston, MA 02116; (617) 357-9500; www.libertymutual.com; David H. Long; auto, home, and life insurance.

Limited Brands, Inc. (LTD): 3 Limited Pkwy., Columbus, OH 43216; (614) 415-7000; www.limitedbrands.com; Leslie H. Wexner; apparel stores (La Senza, Victoria's Secret, PINK, Henri Bendel), home decor (White Barn Candle Co.), personal care (Bath & Body Works).

Liz Claiborne, Inc. (LIZ): 1441 Broadway, NY, NY 10018; (212) 354-4900; lizclaiborneinc.com; William L. McComb; women's apparel (kate spade, Juicy Couture, Lucky Brand Jeans).

L.L. Bean, Inc.: 3 Campus Dr., Freeport, ME 04033; (207) 552-3028; www.llbean.com; Christopher J. McCormick; catalog and retail outdoor apparel, footwear, gear.

Lockheed Martin Corp. (LMT): 6801 Rockledge Dr., Bethesda, MD 20817; (301) 897-6000; www.lockheedmartin.com; Robert J. Stevens; leading U.S. defense contractor; commercial and military aircraft, electronics, missiles, information tech., and communications.

Loews Corp. (L): 667 Madison Ave., NY, NY 10065; (212) 521-2000; www.loews.com; James S. Tisch; hotels, insurance (CNA Financial), offshore drilling (Diamond). Spun off Lorillard, Inc., tobacco prods. mfr., 12/17/2007.

Longs Drug Stores: see CVS Caremark Corp.

Lorillard, Inc. (LO): 714 Green Valley Rd., Greensboro, NC 27408; (336) 335-7000; www.lorillard.com; Murray S. Kessler; 3rd-largest U.S. cigarette mfr. (Newport, Kent). Spun off from Loews Corp., 12/17/2007.

Lowe's Cos., Inc. (LOW): 1000 Lowe's Blvd., Mooresville, NC 28117; (704) 758-1000; www.lowes.com; Robert A. Niblock; building material and home improvement superstores.

Macy's, Inc. (M): 7 W. 7th St., Cincinnati, OH 45202; (513) 579-7000; www.macysinc.com; Terry J. Lundgren; dept. stores (Macy's, Bloomingdale's).

ManpowerGroup (MAN): 100 Manpower Pl., Milwaukee, WI 53212; (414) 961-1000; www.manpowergroup.com; Jeffrey A. Joerres; employment services.

Marathon Oil Corp. (MRO): 5555 San Felipe Rd., Houston, TX 77056; (713) 629-6600; www.marathonoil.com; Clarence P. Cazalot Jr.; integrated oil co.

Marriott International, Inc. (MAR): 10400 Fernwood Rd., Bethesda, MD 20817; (301) 380-3000; www.marriott.com; J. W. Marriott Jr.; hotels (Renaissance, Courtyard, Fairfield Inn, Ritz-Carlton).

Mars, Inc.: 6885 Elm St., McLean, VA 22101; (703) 821-4900; www.mars.com; Paul S. Michaels; one of the largest food mfrs. in the world, including of chocolate (M&M's, Snickers, Dove), food (Uncle Ben's), pet food (Pedigree, Whiskas). Acquired Wm. Wrigley Jr., 10/6/2008.

Masco Corp. (MAS): 21001 Van Born Rd., Taylor, MI 48180; (313) 274-7400; www.masco.com; Timothy Wadhams; mfr. kitchen, bathroom prods. (Delta, Peerless faucets; Merillat cabinets); paints (Behr).

Massachusetts Mutual Life Insurance Co. (MassMutual Financial Group): 1295 State St., Springfield, MA 01111; (800) 767-1000; www.massmutual.com; Roger W. Crandall; financial planning and investment, life insurance.

Mattel, Inc. (MAT): 333 Continental Blvd., El Segundo, CA 90245; (310) 252-2000; www.mattel.com; Robert A. Eckert; largest U.S. toymaker (Barbie, Fisher-Price, Hot Wheels, Matchbox, American Girls).

McClatchy Co. (MNI): 2100 Q St., Sacramento, CA 95816; (916) 321-1855; www.mcclatchy.com; Gary B. Pruitt; 2nd-largest U.S. newspaper publisher. Acquired Knight Ridder papers, 6/27/2006.

McDonald's Corp. (MCD): 2111 McDonald's Dr., Oak Brook, IL 60523; (630) 623-3000; www.mcdonalds.com; James A. Skinner; world's largest fast food co.

McGraw-Hill Cos., Inc. (MHP): 1221 Ave. of the Americas, NY, NY 10020; (212) 512-2000; www.mcgraw-hill.com; Harold McGraw III; book, textbook, magazine publishing (*BusinessWeek*); information and financial services (Standard & Poor's); TV stations.

McKesson Corp. (MCK): 1 Post St., San Francisco, CA 94104; (415) 983-8300; www.mckesson.com; John H. Hammergren; distributor of drugs and toiletries; provides mgmt. software and services.

MeadWestvaco Corp. (MWV): 501 S. 5th St., Richmond, VA 23219; (804) 444-1000; www.meadwestvaco.com; John A. Luke Jr.; packaging, shipping containers, chemicals, office and school supplies.

Medco Health Solutions, Inc. (MHS): 100 Parsons Pond Dr., Franklin Lakes, NJ 07417; (201) 269-3400; www.medco.com; David B. Snow Jr.; pharmacy benefits management.

Medtronic, Inc. (MDT): 710 Medtronic Pkwy., Minneapolis, MN 55432; (763) 514-4000; www.medtronic.com; Omar Ishrak; mfr. of implantable biomedical devices.

Merck & Co., Inc. (MRK): 1 Merck Dr., Whitehouse Station, NJ 08889; (908) 423-1000; www.merck.com; Richard T. Clark; pharmaceuticals (Gardasil, Propecia, Singulair, Vytorin, Zocor); consumer health prods. (Claritin, Coppertone, Dr. Scholl's, MiraLAX). Merged with Schering-Plough Corp., 11/3/2009.

Meredith Corp. (MDP): 1716 Locust St., Des Moines, IA 50309; (515) 284-3000; www.meredith.com; Stephen M. Lacy; magazine publishing (*Better Homes and Gardens*, *Ladies' Home Journal*, *Parents*, *Family Circle*), book publishing, broadcasting.

Meritor, Inc. (MTOR): 2135 W. Maple Rd., Troy, MI 48084; (248) 435-1000; www.meritor.com; Charles G. McClure; commercial vehicles systems and components. ArvinMeritor completed divestiture of its light vehicle business, 1/2011; and changed name to Meritor, 3/30/2011.

Merrill Lynch & Co., Inc.: see Bank of America Corp.

MetLife, Inc. (MET): 200 Park Ave., NY, NY 10166; (212) 578-2211; www.metlife.com; Steven A. Kandarian; insurance, financial services. Acquired American Life Insurance Co. (Alico) from American International Group, Inc. (AIG), 11/1/2010.

MGM Resorts Intl. (MGM): 3600 Las Vegas Blvd. S., Las Vegas, NV 89109; (702) 693-7120; www.mgm-mirage.com; James J. Murren; hotel-casino operator (Mirage, New York-New York, Luxor, Bellagio, Circus Circus, Monte Carlo). Acquired Mandalay Resort Group, 4/25/2005.

Microsoft Corp. (MSFT): One Microsoft Way, Redmond, WA 98052; (425) 882-8080; www.microsoft.com; William H. Gates III; world's largest consumer software maker (Windows, Word, Excel); video game consoles (Xbox).

Miller Brewing Co.: see SABMiller plc.

Molson Coors Brewing Co. (TAP): 1225 17th St., Ste. 3200, Denver, CO 80202; (303) 279-6565; www.molsoncoors.com; Peter Swinburn; brewer (Coors, Killian's, Molson, Heineken, Miller). Announced creation of MillerCoors, joint venture with SABMiller, 7/1/2008.

Morgan Stanley (MS): 1585 Broadway, NY, NY 10036; (212) 761-4000; www.morganstanley.com; James P. Gorman; diversified financial services.

Motorola Mobility Holdings, Inc. (MMI): 600 N. U.S. Hwy. 45, Libertyville, IL 60048; (847) 523-5000; www.motorola.com; Sanjay Jha; mobile phones. Spun off from Motorola, Inc., 1/4/2011; announced plans to be acquired by Google, Inc., 8/15/2011.

Motorola Solutions, Inc. (MSI): 1303 E. Algonquin Rd., Schaumburg, IL 60196; (847) 576-5000; www.motorolasolutions.com;

Greg Brown; electronic equipment and components; communication devices. Spun off from Motorola, Inc., 1/4/2011.

National Semiconductor Corp. (NSM): 2900 Semiconductor Dr., Santa Clara, CA 95052; (408) 721-5000; www.national.com; Donald Macleod; mfr. semiconductors, integrated circuits.

Nationwide Mutual Insurance Co.: One Nationwide Plz., Columbus, OH 43215; (614) 249-7111; www.nationwide.com; Stephen S. Rasmussen; property/casualty, life insurance; financial services.

Navistar Intl. Corp. (NAV): 4201 Winfield Rd., Warrenville, IL 60555; (630) 753-5000; www.navistar.com; Daniel C. Ustian; mfr. heavy-duty trucks, parts, school buses.

NCR Corp. (NCR): 3097 Satellite Blvd., Duluth, GA 30096; (937) 445-1936; www.ncr.com; William R. Nuti; mfr. ATMs, retail technology, hardware and software; computer services and supplies.

Nestlé USA, Inc.: 800 N. Brand Blvd., Glendale, CA 91203; (818) 549-6000; www.nestleusa.com; brand/candy (Baby Ruth, Raisinets), beverages (Nestea, Juicy Juice), food (Buitoni, Coffee-Mate), frozen foods (Stouffer's, Häagen-Dazs, Lean Cuisine), pet foods (Purina, Alpo, Friskies). Subsidiary of Nestlé SA in Switzerland, world's largest food co.

Netflix, Inc. (NFLX): 100 Winchester Cir., Los Gatos, CA 95032; (408) 540-3700; www.netflix.com; Reed Hastings; online DVD rentals.

New York Life Insurance Co.: 51 Madison Ave., NY, NY 10010; (212) 576-7000; www.newyorklife.com; Theodore A. Mathas; life insurance, annuities, mutual funds.

New York Times Co. (NYT): 620 8th Ave., NY, NY 10018; (212) 556-1234; www.nytco.com; Arthur O. Sulzberger Jr.; newspapers (*New York Times*, *Boston Globe*).

Newell Rubbermaid Inc. (NWL): 3 Glenlake Pkwy., Ste. 300, Atlanta, GA 30328; (770) 418-7000; www.newellrubbermaid.com; Michael B. Polk; housewares (Rubbermaid, Levolor, Calphalon); hair accessories (Goody); writing utensils (Parker, Sharpie, Paper Mate); hardware and tools (Irwin, Amerock); juvenile prods. (Graco).

News Corp. (NWS): 1211 Ave. of the Americas, NY, NY 10036; (212) 852-7000; www.newscorp.com; K. Rupert Murdoch; newspaper, magazine, book publishing (HarperCollins); TV and CATV stations (FOX, Fox News Channel, FX); film (20th Century Fox, Fox Searchlight); websites (IGN Entertainment, hulu.com). Acquired Dow Jones (*Wall Street Journal*), 12/13/2007; sold RottenTomatoes.com to Flixter, 1/4/2010; sold MySpace.com to Specific Media Inc., 6/29/2011.

NIKE, Inc. (NKE): 1 Bowerman Dr., Beaverton, OR 97005; (503) 671-6453; www.nikebiz.com; Mark G. Parker; world's largest footwear mfr. Acquired Umbro, 1/31/2008.

Nordstrom, Inc. (JWN): 1617 6th Ave., Seattle, WA 98101; (206) 628-2111; www.nordstrom.com; Blake W. Nordstrom; upscale dept. store chain.

Norfolk Southern Corp. (NSC): Three Commercial Pl., Norfolk, VA 23510; (757) 629-2600; www.nscorp.com; Charles W. Moorman IV; railway operator; freight carrier.

Northrop Grumman Corp. (NOC): 1840 Century Park East, Los Angeles, CA 90067; (310) 553-6262; www.northropgrumman.com; Wes Bush; defense contractor: aircraft, electronics, data systems, information systems, missiles. Spun off shipbuilding sector, 3/31/2011.

Northwest Airlines Corp.: see Delta Air Lines, Inc.

Northwestern Mutual Life Insurance Co.: 720 E. Wisconsin Ave., Milwaukee, WI 53202; (414) 271-1444; www.northwesternmutual.com; John E. Schlifske; life insurance, investment products and services, annuities.

Occidental Petroleum Corp. (OXY): 10889 Wilshire Blvd., Los Angeles, CA 90024; (310) 208-8800; www.oxy.com; Stephen I. Chazen; oil, natural gas, chemicals, plastics, fertilizers.

Office Depot, Inc. (ODP): 6600 N. Military Trl., Boca Raton, FL 33496; (561) 438-4800;

www.officedepot.com; Neil R. Austrian; office supply retail stores.

Omnicom Group Inc. (OMC): 437 Madison Ave., NY, NY 10022; (212) 415-3600; www.omnicomgroup.com; John D. Wren; advertising, marketing, interactive/digital media.

Oracle Corp. (ORCL): 500 Oracle Pkwy., Redwood City, CA 94065; (650) 506-7000; www.oracle.com; Lawrence J. Ellison; database and file management software. Acquired BEA Systems, 4/29/2008; acquired Sun Microsystems, 1/27/2010.

Owens Corning (OC): 1 Owens Corning Pkwy., Toledo, OH 43659; (419) 248-8000; www.owenscorning.com; Michael H. Thaman; world leader in insulation, advanced glass, composite materials. Emerged from Chap. 11 reorganization, 10/31/2006.

Owens-Illinois, Inc. (OI): 1 Michael Owens Way, Perrysburg, OH 43551; (567) 336-5000; Albert P. L. Stroucken; www.o-i.com; mfr. glass containers. Sold plastic packaging division, 8/1/2007.

PepsiCo, Inc. (PEP): 700 Anderson Hill Rd., Purchase, NY 10577; (914) 253-2000; www.pepsico.com; Indra K. Nooyi; soft drinks and other beverages (Pepsi-Cola, Mountain Dew, Gatorade, Tropicana), snacks and cereals (Fritos, Lay's, Ruffles, Quaker). Acquired Pepsi Bottling Group and PepsiAmericas, 3/1/2010, making it largest food and beverage co. in North America.

Pfizer, Inc. (PFE): 235 E. 42nd St., NY, NY 10017; (212) 733-2323; www.pfizer.com; Ian Read; biopharmaceuticals (Celebrex, Lipitor, Viagra, Zoloft); human and animal health care prods. Acquired Wyeth, 10/15/2009.

PG&E Corp. (PCG): One Market, Spear Tower, Ste. 2400, San Francisco, CA 94105; (415) 267-7000; www.pgecorp.com; C. Lee Cox; operates Pacific Gas and Electric public utility.

Philip Morris Intl. Inc. (PM): 120 Park Ave., NY, NY 10017; (917) 663-2000; www.pmi.com; Louis C. Camilleri; mfr. and distributor of tobacco. Spun off from parent company Altria Group, 3/28/2008.

Pitney Bowes Inc. (PBI): 1 Elmcroft Rd., Stamford, CT 06926; (203) 356-5000; www.pb.com; Murray D. Martin; postage meters and mailing equip.

Plains All American Pipeline, L.P. (PAA): 333 Clay St., Ste. 1600, Houston, TX 77002; (713) 646-4100; www.plainsallamerican.com; Greg L. Armstrong; oil transportation, storage.

PPG Industries, Inc. (PPG): 1 PPG Pl., Pittsburgh, PA 15272; (412) 434-3131; www.ppg.com; Charles E. Bunch; glass prods., silicas, fiberglass, chemicals, sealants; world's leading supplier of automobile/industrial coatings. Acquired SigmaKalon, 1/2/2008.

Procter & Gamble Co. (PG): 1 Procter & Gamble Plz., Cincinnati, OH 45202; (513) 983-1100; www.pg.com; Bob McDonald; soaps and detergents (Ivory, Cheer, Tide, Mr. Clean, Zest); toiletries (Crest, Scope, Head & Shoulders, Old Spice); pharmaceuticals (Pepto-Bismol, Vicks cough medicines); food (Pringles); paper prods. (Charmin toilet tissues, Bounty towels), Tampax tampons; disposable diapers (Pampers, Luvs); CoverGirl and Max Factor cosmetics, Clairol hair care. Acquired Gillette (razors, batteries), 10/1/2005; sold Folgers to J. M. Smucker, 11/6/2008.

Prudential Financial, Inc. (PRU): 751 Broad St., Newark, NJ 07102; (973) 802-6000; www.prudential.com; John R. Strangfeld Jr.; insurance, financial services.

Publix Super Markets Inc.: 3300 Publix Corporate Pkwy., Lakeland, FL 33811; (863) 688-1188; www.publix.com; Ed Crenshaw; supermarket chain.

PVH Corp. (PVH): 200 Madison Ave., NY, NY 10016; (212) 381-3500; www.pvh.com; Emanuel Chirico; mfr. of apparel, including licensed brands (Calvin Klein, IZOD, Geoffrey Beene, Kenneth Cole, DKNY, Tommy Hilfiger, Sean John).

Quest Diagnostics Inc. (DGX): 3 Giralda Farms, Madison, NJ 07940; (800) 222-0446; www.questdiagnostics.com; Surya N. Mohapatra; leading clinical laboratory.

RadioShack Corp. (RSH): 300 RadioShack Cir., Fort Worth, TX 76102; (817) 415-3011; www.radioshack.com; James F. Gooch; consumer electronics retailer.

Ralcorp Holdings, Inc. (RAH): 800 Market St., St. Louis, MO 63101; (314) 877-7000; www.ralcorp.com; Kevin J. Hunt, David P. Skarie; private-label breakfast cereals, snack foods, pasta. Acquired Post cereals, 8/4/2008

Ralph Lauren Corp. (RL): 650 Madison Ave., NY, NY 10022; (212) 318-7000; www.ralphlauren.com; Ralph Lauren; men's and women's apparel, home furnishings, fragrances.

Raytheon Co. (RTN): 870 Winter St., Waltham, MA 02451; (781) 522-3000; www.raytheon.com; William Swanson; defense, communications systems.

Reader's Digest Assn., Inc.: 750 Third Ave., NY, NY 10017; (212) 850-5600; www.rda.com; Tom Williams; magazine publisher; marketer of books, music, video prods. Emerged from Chap. 11 reorganization, 2/22/2010.

Reebok Intl. Ltd.: 1895 J.W. Foster Blvd., Canton, MA 02021; (781) 401-5000; www.reebok.com; Uli Becker; athletic and leisure footwear, apparel. Acquired by Germany's adidas AG, 1/31/2006.

Republic Services, Inc. (RSG): 18500 N. Allied Way, Phoenix, AZ 85054; (480) 627-2700; www.republicservices.com; Donald W. Slager; waste management co. Merged with Allied Waste Industries, 12/5/2008.

Revlon, Inc. (REV): 237 Park Ave., NY, NY 10017; (212) 527-4000; www.revlon.com; Ronald O. Perelman; cosmetics, skin care.

Reynolds American Inc. (RAI): 401 N. Main St., Winston-Salem, NC 27101; (336) 741-2000; www.reynoldsamerican.com; Daniel M. Delen; 2nd-largest U.S. producer of cigarettes (Winston, Camel, Pall Mall, Kool, Doral). Acquired Conwood smokeless tobacco co., 5/31/2006.

Rite Aid Corp. (RAD): 30 Hunter Ln., Camp Hill, PA 17011; (717) 761-2633; www.riteaid.com; John T. Standley; 3rd-largest U.S. drugstore chain. Acquired Brooks and Eckerd drugstore chains, 6/4/2007.

Rockwell Automation, Inc. (ROK): 1201 S. 2nd St., Milwaukee, WI 53204; (414) 382-2000; www.rockwellautomation.com; Keith D. Nosbusch; industrial automation co.

Rohm and Haas Co.: see Dow Chemical Co.

Ryder System, Inc. (R): 11690 NW 105th St., Miami, FL 33178; (305) 500-3726; www.ryder.com; Gregory T. Swienton; truck-leasing service.

SABMiller plc: 1 Stanhope Gate, London, W1K 1AF, United Kingdom; + 44 1483 264000; www.sabmiller.com; Graham Mackay; brewing company (Miller, Peroni, Grolsch). Announced creation of MillerCoors, joint venture with Molson Coors, 7/1/2008.

Safeway Inc. (SWY): 5918 Stoneridge Mall Rd., Pleasanton, CA 94588; (925) 467-3000; www.safeway.com; Steven A. Burd; supermarkets.

Sara Lee Corp. (SLE): 3500 Lacey Rd., Downers Grove, IL 60515; (630) 598-8100; www.saralee.com; Marcel H.M. Smits; baked goods, fresh and processed meats (Ball Park, Jimmy Dean, Hillshire Farm, Kahn's). Announced plans to divide into 2 separate companies, 1/28/2011.

SBC Communications, Inc.: see AT&T Inc.

Schering-Plough Corp.: see Merck & Co., Inc.

Sears Holdings Corp. (SHLD): 3333 Beverly Rd., Hoffman Estates, IL 60179; (847) 286-2500; www.searsholdings.com; Louis J. D'Ambrosio; 4th-largest U.S. retailer; formed by merger of Kmart and Sears, 3/24/2005.

Shell Oil Co.: 910 Louisiana St., Houston, TX 77002; (713) 241-6161; www.shellus.com; Marvin Odum; integrated oil co; subsidiary of Royal Dutch Shell, world's 2nd-largest oil co.

Sherwin-Williams Co. (SHW): 101 Prospect Ave. NW, Cleveland, OH 44115; (216) 566-2000; www.sherwin-williams.com; Christopher M. Connor; largest North American paint and varnish producer (Dutch Boy, Krylon, Minwax).

Smithfield Foods, Inc. (SFD): 200 Commerce St., Smithfield, VA 23430; (757)

365-3000; www.smithfieldfoods.com; C. Larry Pope; world's largest producer of pork and processed meat products. Acquired Premium Standard Farms, 5/7/2007.

J. M. Smucker Co. (SJM): One Strawberry Ln., Orrville, OH 44667; (330) 682-3000; www.smuckers.com; Timothy P. Smucker; leading producer of fruit spreads, toppings (Magic Shell), peanut butter (Jif), oils (Crisco). Merged with Folgers Coffee Co., 11/6/2008.

Smurfit-Stone Container Corp.: 222 N. LaSalle St., Chicago, IL 60601; (312) 346-6600; www.smurfit.com; Patrick J. Moore; industry leader for corrugated containers, paper bags, and sacks. Filed for Chap. 11 reorganization, 1/26/2009. Acquired by Rock-Tenn Co., 5/27/2011.

Sony Corp. of America: 550 Madison Ave., NY, NY 10022; (212) 833-6800; www.sony.com; Howard Stringer; U.S. subsidiary of Japan-based Sony Corp.; electronics, movies, music. Acquired Bertelsmann's stake in Sony BMG and renamed it Sony Music Entertainment, 10/1/2008.

Southwest Airlines Co. (LUV): P.O. Box 36611, HDQ - 1PR, Dallas, TX 75235; (214) 792-4000; www.southwest.com; Gary C. Kelly; air transportation. Acquired AirTran Holdings, Inc., 5/2/2011.

Sprint Nextel Corp. (S): 6200 Sprint Pkwy., Overland Park, KS 66251; (703) 433-4000; www.sprint.com; Dan Hesse; wireless and long-distance telecommunications; merged with Nextel, 8/12/2005.

Stanley Black & Decker, Inc. (SWK): 1000 Stanley Dr., New Britain, CT 06053; (860) 225-5111; www.stanleyblackanddecker.com; John F. Lundgren; one of the top U.S. mfrs. of hand and power tools (DeWalt, Bostitch), household prods. (Kwikset, Baldwin). The Stanley Works and Black & Decker merged, 3/12/2010.

Staples, Inc. (SPLS): 500 Staples Dr., Framingham, MA 01702; (508) 253-5000; www.staples.com; Ronald L. Sargent; largest U.S. office-supply retailer.

Starbucks Corp. (SBUX): 2401 Utah Ave. S., Seattle, WA 98134; (206) 447-1575; www.starbucks.com; Howard D. Schultz; coffee producer; world's leading specialty coffee retailer.

Starwood Hotels & Resorts Worldwide, Inc. (HOT): 1111 Westchester Ave., White Plains, NY 10604; (914) 640-8100; www.starwoodhotels.com; Frits van Paasschen; hotel and resort co. (Westin, Sheraton, W Hotels).

State Farm Mutual Automobile Ins. Co.: 1 State Farm Plz., Bloomington, IL 61710; (309) 766-2311; www.statefarm.com; Edward B. Rust Jr.; largest U.S. provider of auto/homeowners insurance.

Sun Microsystems, Inc.: see Oracle Corp.

Sunoco, Inc. (SUN): 1735 Market St., Ste. LL, Philadelphia, PA 19103; (215) 977-3000; www.sunocoinc.com; Lynn Elsenhans; energy resources co. gasoline retailer.

SUPERVALU Inc. (SVU): 11840 Valley View Rd., Eden Prairie, MN 55344; (952) 828-4000; www.supervalu.com; Craig R. Herkert; food retailer, wholesale distrib. (Acme, Albertsons, Shoppers).

SYSCO Corp. (SYY): 1390 Enclave Pkwy., Houston, TX 77077; (281) 584-1390; www.sysco.com; William J. DeLaney; world's largest food-service distributor.

Systemax Inc. (SYX): 11 Harbor Park Dr., Port Washington, NY 11050; (516) 608-7000; www.systemax.com; Richard Leeds; computers, electronics, industrial prod. retailer. Acquired CompUSA, 1/6/2008; acquired Circuit City, 5/19/2009.

Target Corp. (TGT): 1000 Nicollet Mall, Minneapolis, MN 55403; (612) 304-6073; www.target.com; Gregg W. Steinhafel; 2nd-largest U.S. discount retailer.

Tenneco Inc. (TEN): 500 N. Field Dr., Lake Forest, IL 60045; (847) 482-5000; www.tenneco.com; Gregg M. Sherrill; automotive parts (Monroe, Walker).

Texas Instruments Inc. (TXN): 12500 TI Blvd., Dallas, TX 75266; (972) 995-2011; www.ti.com; Richard K. Templeton; processors, semiconductors, software, handheld calculators.

Textron Inc. (TXT): 40 Westminster St., Providence, RI 02903; (401) 421-2800;

www.textron.com; Scott C. Donnelly; aircraft (Cessna, Bell), industrial, automotive prods.; financial services.

3M Co. (MMM): 3M Center, St. Paul, MN 55144; (651) 733-1110; www.3m.com; George W. Buckley; abrasives, adhesives, electrical, health care, cleaning (Scotch-Brite, O-Cel-O sponges, Scotchgard), printing, consumer prods. (Scotch Tape, Post-it).

TIAA-CREF: 730 Third Ave., NY, NY 10017; (212) 490-9000; www.tiaa-cref.org; Roger W. Ferguson Jr.; financial services provider.

Timberland Co. (TBL): 200 Domain Dr., Stratham, NH 03885; (603) 772-9500; www.timberland.com; Jeffrey B. Swartz; footwear, apparel, accessories.

Time Warner Inc. (TWX): One Time Warner Ctr., NY, NY 10019; (212) 484-8000; www.timewarner.com; Jeffrey L. Bewkes; magazine publishing (*Time*, *Sports Illustrated*, *Fortune*, *Money*, *People*, DC Comics), TV and CATV (Cartoon Network, HBO, CNN, TBS, TNT), motion pictures (Warner Bros., New Line Cinema), recordings. AOL and Time Warner completed the largest corporate merger in history in 2001; Time Warner spun off AOL, 12/9/2009.

TJX Cos., Inc. (TJX): 770 Cochituate Rd., Framingham, MA 01701; (508) 390-1000; www.tjx.com; Carol Meyrowitz; world's largest off-price apparel retailer (T.J. Maxx, Marshalls); home furnishing retailer (Home Goods).

Toro Co. (TTC): 8111 Lyndale Ave. S, Bloomington, MN 55420; (952) 888-8801; www.thetorocompany.com; Michael J. Hoffman; lawn and turf maintenance prods. (Lawn-Boy), snow removal equip.; irrigation systems.

Toys "R" Us, Inc.: 1 Geoffrey Way, Wayne, NJ 07470; (973) 617-3500; www.toysrus.com; Gerald L. Storch; children's specialty retailer. Acquired FAO Schwarz, 5/28/2009.

Tribune Co.: 435 N. Michigan Ave., Chicago, IL 60611; (312) 222-9100; www.tribune.com; Sam Zell; newspapers (*Los Angeles Times*, *Chicago Tribune*), broadcasting (incl. WGN and 23 other television and radio stations), Chicago Cubs franchise. Filed for Chap. 11 reorganization, 12/8/2008.

Trinity Industries, Inc. (TRN): 2525 Stemmons Fwy., Dallas, TX 75207; (214) 631-4420; www.trin.net; Timothy R. Wallace; mfr. metal prods., rail and freight equip.

Tyco Intl. Ltd. (TYC): 9 Roszel Rd., Princeton, NJ 08540; (609) 720-4200; www.tyco.com; Edward D. Breen Jr.; security and engineered prods. Spun off health care and electronics divisions, 6/29/2007.

Tyson Foods, Inc. (TSN): 2200 Don Tyson Pkwy., Springdale, AR 72762; (479) 290-4000 www.tysonfoods.com; Donnie Smith; fresh and processed poultry; beef and pork prods.

UBS Financial Services Inc.: 1285 Ave. of the Americas, NY, NY 10019; (212) 713-2000; www.ubs.com; Philip J. Lofts; financial services; subsidiary of Switzerland's UBS AG.

Unilever USA (UN/UL): 800 Sylvan Ave., Englewood Cliffs, NJ 07632; (201) 894-4000; www.unilever.com; Paul Polman; food (Hellmann's mayonnaise, Knorr soups, Ragu pasta sauce, Wish-Bone salad dressing, Lipton, Skippy peanut butter, Slim-Fast), hygiene prods. (Dove, Q-tips, Vaseline). Subsidiary of Unilever NV (Neth.) and Unilever plc (UK). Acquired Alberto Culver, 5/10/2011.

Union Pacific Corp. (UNP): 1400 Douglas St., Omaha, NE, 68179; (402) 544-5000; www.up.com; James R. Young; one of the largest railroad freight cos. in U.S.

Unisys Corp. (UIS): 801 Lakeview Dr., Ste. 100, Blue Bell, PA 19422; (215) 986-4011; www.unisys.com; J. Edward Coleman; designs, manuf. computer information systems; IT consulting.

United Continental Holdings, Inc. (UAL): 77 W. Wacker Dr., Chicago IL 60601; (312) 997-8000; www.unitedcontinentalholdings.com; Edward A. Smisek; air transportation (United Airlines, Continental Airlines); formed by merger of United Airlines and Continental Airlines, 10/1/2010.

UnitedHealth Group Inc. (UNH): UHG Center, 9900 Bren Rd. E., Minnetonka, MN 55343; (952) 936-1300; www.unitedhealthgroup.com; Stephen J. Hemsley; health insurer.

United Parcel Service, Inc. (UPS): 55 Glenlake Pkwy. NE, Atlanta, GA 30328; (404) 828-6000; www.ups.com; D. Scott Davis; world's largest package delivery co.

United States Steel Corp. (X): 600 Grant St., Pittsburgh, PA 15219; (412) 433-1121; www.ussteel.com; John P. Surma Jr.; steel, tin prods., resource mgmt.

United Technologies Corp. (UTX): One Financial Plz., Hartford, CT 06103; (860) 728-7000; www.utc.com; Louis R. Chênevert; aerospace, industrial prods. and services (Carrier, Otis, Pratt & Whitney, Sikorsky).

US Airways Group, Inc. (LCC): 111 W. Rio Salado Pkwy., Tempe, AZ 85281; (480) 693-0800; www.usairways.com; William Douglas Parker; air transportation.

Verizon Communications Inc. (VZ): 140 West St., NY, NY 10007; (212) 395-1000; www.verizon.com; Lowell C. McAdam; broadband, wireless, wireline services provider. Acquired MCI, Inc., 1/6/2006.

V.F. Corp. (VFC): 105 Corporate Center Blvd., Greensboro, NC 27408; (336) 424-6000; www.vfc.com; Eric C. Wiseman; apparel (Lee, Wrangler, North Face).

Viacom Inc. (VIA): 1515 Broadway, NY, NY 10036; (212) 258-6000; www.viacom.com; Philippe P. Dauman; media networks (BET, Comedy Central, MTV, VH1, Nickelodeon); movies (Paramount). Spun off from company that became CBS Corp., 12/31/2005.

Visteon Corp.: One Village Center Dr., Van Buren Twp., MI 48111; (734) 710-5000; www.visteon.com; Donald J. Stebbins; automotive parts mfr. Emerged from Chap. 11 reorganization, 10/1/2010.

Walgreen Co. (Walgreens) (WAG): 200 Wilmot Rd., Deerfield, IL 60015; (847) 914-2500; www.walgreens.com; Gregory D. Wasson; retail drugstores.

Wal-Mart Stores, Inc. (WMT): 702 SW 8th St., Bentonville, AR 72716; (479) 273-4000; www.walmartstores.com; Michael T. Duke; world's largest retailer; discount stores, membership warehouse clubs (Sam's Club).

Washington Post Co. (WPO): 1150 15th St. NW, Washington, DC 20071; (202) 334-6000; www.washpostco.com; Donald E. Graham; media (newspapers, Slate.com, TV) and education (Kaplan). Sold *Newsweek*, 9/30/2010.

Waste Management, Inc. (WM): 1001 Fannin St., Ste. 4000, Houston, TX 77002; (713) 512-6200; www.wm.com; David P. Steiner; North America's largest waste co., recycler.

WellPoint, Inc. (WLP): 120 Monument Cir., Indianapolis, IN 46204; (317) 532-6000; www.wellpoint.com; Angela F. Braly; largest U.S. health benefits co.; HMOs and PPOs, an independent licensee of the Blue Cross Blue Shield Assn.

Wells Fargo & Co. (WFC): 420 Montgomery St., San Francisco, CA 94163; (866) 249-3302; www.wellsfargo.com; John G. Stumpf; financial services. Acquired Wachovia, 12/31/2008.

Wendy's Co. (WEN): 1 Dave Thomas Blvd., Dublin, OH 43017; (614) 764-3100; www.aboutwendys.com; Roland C. Smith; one of the largest fast food restaurant companies in the U.S. Sold Arby's Restaurant Group, Inc., 7/4/2011.

Western Union Co. (WU): 12500 E. Belford Ave., Englewood, CO 80112; (720) 332-1000; www.westernunion.com; Hikmet Ersek; money transfers, payment services.

Weyerhaeuser Co. (WY): 33663 Weyerhaeuser Way S., Federal Way, WA 98063; (253) 924-2345; www.weyerhaeuser.com;

Daniel S. Fulton; produces, distributes wood prods; real estate development.

Whirlpool Corp. (WHR): 2000 N. M-63, Benton Harbor, MI 49022; (269) 923-5000; www.whirlpoolcorp.com; Jeff M. Fettig; mfr. of major home appliances (KitchenAid, Amana, Maytag).

Whole Foods Market, Inc. (WFM): 550 Bowie St., Austin, TX 78703; (512) 477-4455; www.wholefoodsmarket.com; John P. Mackey; largest U.S. retailer of natural and organic foods.

Winn-Dixie Stores, Inc. (WINN): 5050 Edgewood Ct., Jacksonville, FL 32254; (904) 783-5000; www.winndixie.com; Peter Lynch; one of the largest food retailers in U.S. (Winn-Dixie, SaveRite). Emerged from Chap. 11, 11/21/2006.

Winnebago Industries, Inc. (WGO): 605 W. Crystal Lake Rd., Forest City, IA 50436; (641) 585-3535; www.winnebagoind.com; Robert J. Olson; mfr. of motor homes, or recreational vehicles (RVs).

Wm. Wrigley Jr. Co.: 410 N. Michigan Ave., Chicago, IL 60611; (312) 644-2121; www.wrigley.com; William Wrigley Jr.; mfr. of chewing gum and other confections (Juicy Fruit, Wrigley's, Altoids, Life Savers). Acquired by Mars, Inc., 10/6/2008.

Xerox Corp. (XRX): 45 Glover Ave., P.O. Box 4505, Norwalk, CT 06856; (203) 968-3000; www.xerox.com; Ursula M. Burns; printers, multifunction devices, document publishing technology and support.

Yahoo! Inc. (YHOO): 701 First Ave., Sunnyvale, CA 94089; (408) 349-3300; www.yahoo.com; Carol Bartz; Internet media company.

Yum! Brands, Inc. (YUM): 1441 Gardiner Ln., Louisville, KY 40213; (502) 874-8300; www.yum.com; David C. Novak; fast food restaurants (Pizza Hut, KFC, Taco Bell, Long John Silver's, A&W).

Labor Unions and Professional Organizations

Source: Bureau of Labor Statistics, U.S. Dept. of Labor; AFL-CIO; World Almanac research.

= Member of Change to Win coalition formed in 2005 by unions disaffiliated from AFL-CIO. * = Independent union or one not otherwise affiliated with Change to Win or AFL-CIO. All other groups listed here are affiliated with AFL-CIO as of 2011. Year established is in parenthesis.

Labor Unions

Air Line Pilots Association (ALPA) (1931): 53,000 members, 39 U.S. and Canadian airlines; (703) 689-2270; www.alpa.org

American Federation of Labor and Congress of Industrial Organizations (AFL-CIO) (1955): federation of 55 unions, 12.2 mil members; (202) 637-5000; www.aflcio.org

Automobile, Aerospace & Agricultural Implement Workers of America, International Union, United (UAW) (1935): 390,000 active (600,000 ret.) members, 750 locals; (313) 926-5000; www.uaw.org

Bakery, Confectionery, Tobacco Workers, and Grain Millers International Union (BCTGM) (1886): 100,000+ members; (301) 933-8600; www.bctgm.org

Bricklayers and Allied Craftworkers, International Union of (BAC) (1865): 100,000 members, 50 locals; (202) 783-3788; www.bacweb.org

Carpenters and Joiners of America, United Brotherhood of (UBC) (1881): 500,000+ members, 600+ locals; (732) 417-9229; www.carpenters.org

#**Change to Win Coalition** (2005): 4 unions, ex-affiliates of AFL-CIO, 5.5 mil members; (202) 721-0660; www.changetowin.org

Communications Workers of America (CWA) (1938): 700,000+ members, 1,200 locals; (202) 434-1100; www.cwa-union.org

*****Education Association, National** (NEA) (1857): 3.2 mil members, 14,000+ affiliates; (202) 833-4000; www.nea.org

Electrical Workers, International Brotherhood of (IBEW) (1891): 725,000 members, 900 locals; (202) 833-7000; www.ibew.org

Engineers, International Union of Operating (IUOE) (1896): 400,000 members, 123 locals; (202) 429-9100; www.iuoe.org

#**Farm Workers of America, United** (UFW) (1962): 27,000+ members; (661) 823-6151; www.ufw.org

*****Federal Employees, National Federation of** (NFFE; affiliated with IAMAW) (1917): 110,000 members, nearly 200 locals; (202) 216-4420; www.nffe.org

Fire Fighters, International Association of (IAFF) (1918): 298,000+ members, 3,200+ locals; (202) 737-8484; www.iaff.org

Flight Attendants, Association of (AFA-CWA) (1945): nearly 60,000+ members, 23 airlines; merged with Communications Workers of America in 2004; (202) 434-1300; www.afanet.org

#**Food and Commercial Workers International Union, United** (UFCW) (1979): 1.3 mil members, 500 locals; (202) 223-3111; www.ufcw.org

Glass, Molders, Pottery, Plastics and Allied Workers Intl. Union (GMP) (1842): 51,000 members, 250+ locals; (610) 565-5051; www.gmpiu.org

Government Employees, American Federation of (AFGE) (1932): 600,000 members; 1,100 locals; (202) 737-8700; www.afge.org

Graphic Communications Conference (GCC/IBT) (1983): 60,000+ members; merged with Teamsters in 2005; (202) 462-1400; www.gciu.org

Iron Workers, Intl. Assn. of Bridge, Structural, Ornamental, and Reinforcing (1896): 140,000 members, 213 locals; (202) 383-4800; www.ironworkers.org

Laborers' International Union of North America (LIUNA) (1903): 500,000 members, 500+ locals; (202) 737-8320; www.liuna.org

Letter Carriers, National Association of (NALC) (1889): nearly 300,000 members, 2,500 locals; (202) 393-4695; www.nalc.org

#**Locomotive Engineers and Trainmen, Brotherhood of** (BLET) (1863): 59,000+ members, 600+ divisions; (216) 241-2630; www.ble-t.org

Longshoremen's Association, Intl. (ILA) (1892): 65,000+ members, approx. 200 locals; (212) 425-1200; www.ilaunion.org

Machinists and Aerospace Workers, International Association of (IAMAW) (1888): 720,000 members (current and retired), 1,174 locals; affiliated with TCU in 2005; (301) 967-4500; www.goiam.org

Maintenance of Way Employes, Division of the Intl. Brotherhood of Teamsters; Brotherhood of (BMWED) (1887): 35,000 members, 770 locals; merged with Teamsters in 2004; (248) 948-1010; www.bmwed.org (Note: In honor of tradition, the union maintains the variant spelling of "employes" in its logo.)

Mine Workers of America, United (UMWA) (1890): 110,000 members, 600 locals; (703) 291-2400; www.umwa.org

Musicians of the United States and Canada, American Federation of (AFM) (1896): 90,000+ members, 250+ locals; (212) 869-1330; www.afm.org

Newspaper Guild—Communications Workers of America, The (TNG) (CWA) (1933): 34,000+ members, 90 locals; (202) 434-7177; www.newsguild.org

*****Nurses Association, American** (ANA) (1897): 3.1 mil members, 54 constituent state & territorial assns.; (301) 628-5000; www.nursingworld.org

Office and Professional Employees Intl. Union (OPEIU) (1945): 110,000 members, 200 locals; (800) 346-7348; www.opeiu.org

Painters and Allied Trades, International Union of (IUPAT) (1887): 160,000+

members, 425 locals; (410) 564-5900; www.iupat.org

Plumbing and Pipe Fitting Industry of the U.S. and Canada, United Assn. of Journeymen and Apprentices of the (UA) (1889): 340,000 members, 300+ locals; (410) 269-2000; www.ua.org

*Police, Fraternal Order of (1915): 325,000+ members, 2,100+ affiliates; (615) 399-0900; www.grandlodgefop.org

Police Associations, International Union of (IUPA) (1979): 80,000 members, 500 locals; (941) 487-2560; www.iupa.org

Postal Workers Union, American (APWU) (1971): 220,000+ U.S.P.S. employees, 2,000 private employees, 1,000+ locals; (202) 842-4200; www.apwu.org

Roofers, Waterproofers and Allied Workers, United Union of (1906): 22,000 members; (202) 463-7663; www.unionroofers.com

*Rural Letter Carriers' Association, National (1903): 100,000+ members; 50 state org; (703) 684-5545; www.nrlca.org

*Security, Police, and Fire Professionals of America, Intl. Union (SPFPA) (1948): 27,000+ members, 200 locals; (800) 228-7492; www.spfpa.org

#Service Employees International Union (SEIU) (1921): 2.1 mil members, 150+ locals; (202) 730-7000; www.seiu.org

Sheet Metal Workers' International Association (SMWIA) (1888): 150,000 members, 200 locals; (202) 783-5880; www.smwia.org

State, County, and Municipal Employees, American Federation of (AFSCME) (1932): 1.6 mil members (active and retired), 3,400 locals; (202) 429-1000; www.afscme.org

Steel, Paper and Forestry, Rubber, Manufacturing, Energy, Allied Industrial and Service Workers International Union, United (USW) (2005): 850,000+ members, 1,800+ locals; formed from merger of the unions United Steelworkers of America (USWA) (1936) and Paper, Allied-Industrial, Chemical and Energy Workers (PACE) (1999); (412) 562-2400; www.usw.org

Teachers, American Federation of (AFT) (1916): 1.5+ mil members, 3,000+ locals; (202) 879-4400; www.aft.org

#Teamsters, International Brotherhood of (IBT) (1903): 1.4 mil. members, 440 locals; (202) 624-6800; www.teamster.org

Theatrical Stage Employees, Moving Picture Technicians, Artists and Allied Crafts of the U.S., Its Territories, and Canada, Intl. Alliance of (IATSE) (1893): 110,000+ members, 555+ locals; (212) 730-1770; www.iatse-intl.org

Transit Union, Amalgamated (ATU) (1892): 190,000+ members, 268 locals; (202) 537-1645; www.atu.org

Transportation Communications Intl. Union (TCU) (1899): affiliated with IAMAW in 2005; see Machinists and Aerospace Workers.

Transportation Union, United (UTU) (1969): 125,000 members, 500+ locals; (216) 228-9400; www.utu.org

Transport Workers Union of America (TWU) (1934): 130,000 members, 114 locals; (212) 719-3900; www.twu.org

*Treasury Employees Union, National (NTEU) (1938): 150,000 represented, 270+ chapters; (202) 572-5500; www.nteu.org

UNITE HERE (UNITE, 1900; HERE, 1891; merged 2004): 265,000 members; (212) 265-7000; www.unitehere.org

*Workers United (affiliated with SEIU) (2009): 150,000 members; (646) 448-6402; workers-united.org

Writers Guild of America, West (1933): 12,045 members; (323) 951-4000; www.wga.org

Professional Organizations and Societies

Accountants, American Institute of Certified Public (1887): 370,000 members; (888) 777-7077; www.aicpa.org

ACMP—The Chamber Music Network (1947): 5,400 members; (212) 645-7424; www.acmp.net

Actuaries, Society of (1949): 22,000 members; (847) 706-3500; www.soa.org

Administrative Professionals, Intl. Assn. of (1942): 28,000 members; (816) 891-6600; www.iaap-hq.org

Aerospace Medical Assn. (1929): 2,600+ members; (703) 739-2240; www.asma.org

Agricultural and Biological Engineers, American Soc. of (1907): 9,000 members; (269) 429-0300; www.asabe.org

Air & Waste Management Assn. (1907): 8,000+ members; (412) 232-3444; www.awma.org

AMSUS—The Society of the Federal Health Agencies (1891): nearly 8,000 members; (301) 897-8800; www.amsus.org

APICS—The Assn. for Operations Management (1957): 43,000+ members; (773) 867-1777; www.apics.org

Architects, American Institute of (1857): 83,000+; (202) 626-7300; www.aia.org

ASIS Intl. (formerly Amer. Soc. for Industrial Security) (1955): 37,000+ members; (703) 519-6200; www.asisonline.org

Astrologers, Inc., American Federation of (1938): 4,000; (480) 838-1751; www.astrologers.com

Astronautical Society, American (1954): 1,500 members; (703) 866-0020; www.astronautical.org

Astronomical Society, American (1899): 7,000 members; (202) 328-2010 www.aas.org

Authors Guild, The (1912): 8,000+ members; (212) 563-5904; www.authorsguild.org

Bankers of America, Independent Community (1930): 5,000 members; (800) 422-8439; www.icba.org

Bar Assn., American (1878): 400,000 members; (312) 988-5000; www.abanet.org

Bar Assn., Federal (1920): 15,000+ members; (571) 481-9100; www.fedbar.org

Biochemistry and Molecular Biology, American Society for (1906): 12,000+ members; (240) 283-6600; www.asbmb.org

Broadcasters, Natl. Assn. of (1923): 8,300 members; (202) 429-5300; www.nab.org

Business Women's Assn., American (1949): 40,000 members; (800) 228-0007; www.abwa.org

Cartoonists Society, Natl. (1946): 500+ members; (407) 647-8839; www.reuben.org

Ceramic Society, American (1898): 9,500+ members; (866) 721-3322; www.ceramics.org

Chemical Society, American (1876): 163,000+ members; (202) 872-4600; www.chemistry.org

Chiefs of Police, Intl. Assn. of (1893): 20,000+ members; (703) 836-6767; www.theiacp.org

Chiropractic Assn., American (1963): 15,000 members; (703) 276-8800; www.acatoday.org

Civil Engineers, American Society of (1852): 140,000+ members; (800) 548-2723; www.asce.org

College Admission Counseling, Natl. Assn. for (1937): 11,000+ members; (703) 836-2222; www.nacacnet.org

Commercial Law League of America (1895): 3,000 members; (312) 240-1400; www.clla.org

Communication Assn., Natl. (1914): 8,000+ members; (202) 464-4622; www.natcom.org

Composers, Authors & Publishers, American Soc. of (ASCAP) (1914): 410,000+ members; (212) 621-6000; www.ascap.com

Computing Machinery, Assn. for (1947): 96,000+ members; (212) 626-0500; www.acm.org

Computing Professionals, Institute for Certification of (1973): 55,000 members; (847) 299-4227; www.iccp.org

Construction Inspectors, Assn. of (1974): 1,000; (760) 327-5284; www.aci-assoc.org

Counseling Assn., American (1952): 45,000 members; (800) 347-6647; www.counseling.org

Country Music Assn. (1958): 6,000+ members; (615) 244-2840; www.CMAworld.com

Customs Brokers and Forwarders Assn. of America, Inc., Natl. (1897): 870 cos.; (202) 466-0222; www.ncbfaa.org

Dental Assn., American (1859): 157,000+ members; (312) 440-2500; www.ada.org

Directors Guild of America (1936): 14,500 members; (310) 289-2000; www.dga.org

Electrical and Electronics Engineers, Institute of (1963): 395,000+ members; (732) 981-0060; www.ieee.org

Electronics Technicians, Intl. Soc. of Certified (1980): 50,000+ members; (800) 946-0201; www.iscet.org

Energy Engineers, Assn. of (1977): 14,000+ members; (770) 447-5083; www.aeecenter.org

Engineers, Natl. Society of Professional (1934): 45,000 members; (703) 684-2800; www.nspe.org

Environmental Assessment Association (1972): 3,500 members; (760) 327-5284; www.eaa-assoc.org

Environmental Health Assn., Natl. (1937): 4,500 members; (303) 756-9090; www.neha.org

Family Physicians, American Academy of (1947): 100,300+; (913) 906-6000; www.aafp.org

Farm Bureau Federation, American (1919): 6.2 mil members; (202) 406-3600; www.fb.org

Farmers Union, Natl. (1902): 250,000 families; (202) 554-1600; www.nfu.org

Financial Professionals, Assn. for (1979): 16,000+ members; (301) 907-2862; www.AFPonline.org

Financial Service Professionals, Soc. of (1928): 15,000 members; (610) 526-2500; www.financialpro.org

Fire Chiefs, Intl. Assn. of (1873): 12,000 members; (703) 273-0911; www.iafc.org

Fire Protection Engineers, Soc. of (1950): 4,000+ members; (301) 718-2910; www.sfpe.org

Food Technologists, Institute of (1939): 22,000 members; (312) 782-8424; www.ift.org

Forensic Sciences, American Academy of (1948): 6,260 members; (719) 636-1100; www.aafs.org

Funeral Directors Assn., Natl. (1882): 19,000 members; (262) 789-1880; www.nfda.org

General Contractors of America, Associated (1918): 33,000+ cos.; (703) 548-3118; www.agc.org

Geographers, Assn. of American (1904): 10,000 members; (202) 234-1450; www.aag.org

Graphic Arts, American Institute of (1914): 22,000 members; (212) 807-1990; www.aiga.org

Ground Water Assn., Natl. (1948): 12,000+ members; (614) 898-7791; www.ngwa.org

Heating, Refrigerating and Air-Conditioning Engineers, Inc., American Soc. of (1894): 50,000+ members; (404) 636-8400; www.ashrae.org

Home Builders, Natl. Assn. of (1942): 160,000 members; (202) 266-8200; www.nahb.org

Human Resource Management, Society for (SHRM) (1948): 250,000+ members; (703) 548-3440; www.shrm.org

Illustrators, Society of (1901): 1,000 members; (212) 838-2560; www.societyillustrators.org

Industrial Designers Society of America (1938): 3,300 members; (703) 707-6000; www.idsa.org

Intelligence Officers, Assn. of Former (1975): 24 chap., 5,000+ members; (703) 790-0320; www.afio.com

Interior Designers, American Society of (1975): 36,000+ members; (202) 546-3480; www.asid.org

Investigative Pathology, American Soc. for (1900): 1,718 members; (301) 634-7130; www.asip.org

Jail Assn., American (1981): 5,000 members; (301) 790-3930; www.aja.org

Journalists, Society of Professional (1909): 10,000 members; (317) 927-8000; www.spj.org

Journalists and Authors, American Society of (1948): 1,400+ members; (212) 997-0947; www.asja.org

Judicature Society, American (1913): 6,000 members; (515) 271-2281; www.ajs.org

Landscape Architects, American Society of (1899): 17,000 members; (202) 898-2444; www.asla.org

Legal Administrators, Assn. of (1971): 10,000+ members; (847) 267-1252; www.alanet.org

Library Assn., American (1876): 61,000+ members; (800) 545-2433; www.ala.org

Lifesaving Assn., U.S. (1964): 11,000 members; (866) 367-8752; www.usla.org

Logistics, Intl. Society of (SOLE) (1966): 3,000+ members; (301) 459-8446; www.sole.org

Magicians, Intl. Brotherhood of (1922): 13,000 members; (636) 724-2400; www.magician.org

Management Accountants, Institute of (1919): 60,000 members; (201) 573-9000; www.imanet.org

Management Assn., American (1923): 4,100 cos., 38,000 ind.; (212) 903-7976; www.amanet.org

Marketing Assn., American (1931): 100,000 members; (312) 542-9000; www.marketingpower.com

Master Brewers Association of the Americas (1887): 3,500 members; (651) 454-7250; www.mbaa.com

Material and Process Engineering, Soc. for the Advancement of (1944): 4,500 members; (626) 331-0616; www.sampe.org

Mechanical Engineers, American Soc. of (1880): 127,000 members; (973) 882-1170; www.asme.org

Medical Assn., American (1847): 250,000; (800) 621-8335; www.ama-assn.org

Medical Library Assn. (1898): 4,000 members; (312) 419-9094; www.mlanet.org

Motion Picture Arts & Sciences, Academy of (1927): 6,000+ members; (310) 247-3000; www.oscars.org

Motion Picture and Television Engineers, Soc. of (1916): 5,000+ members; (914) 761-1100; www.smpte.org

Mystery Writers of America (1945): 3,000+ members; (212) 888-8171; www.mysterywriters.org

NALS...the association for legal professionals (formerly the Natl. Assn. of Legal Secretaries), (1929): 6,000 members; (918) 582-5188; www.nals.org

Notaries, American Society of (1965): approx. 20,000 members; (850) 671-5164; www.notaries.org

Nursing, Natl. League for (1893): 33,000 members, 1,200 institutions; (212) 363-5555; www.nln.org

Operations Management, Assn. for (APICS) (1957): 43,000+ members; (773) 867-1777; www.apics.org

Optometric Assn., American (1898): 36,000 members; (800) 365-2219; www.aoa.org

Organists, American Guild of (1896): 20,000 members; (212) 870-2310; www.agohq.org

Pen Women, Natl. League of American (1897): 3,000 members; (202) 785-1997; www.americanpenwomen.org

Pharmacists Assn., American (1852): 62,000+ members; (202) 628-4410; www.pharmacist.com

Physical Therapy Assn., American (1921): 77,000+ members; (703) 684-2782; www.apta.org

Plastics Engineers, Society of (1942): 20,000 members; (203) 775-0471; www.4spe.org

Police Assn.—United States Section, Intl. (1962): 10,000 members; (248) 486-7137; www.ipa-usa.org

Population Assn. of America (1930): 3,000 members; (301) 565-6710; www.popassoc.org

Postmasters of the U.S., Natl. Assn. of (1898): 42,000 members, 95 clubs; (703) 683-9027; www.napus.org

Press Club, National (1908): 3,500+ members; (202) 662-7500; www.press.org

Professional Ball Players of America, Assn. of (1924): 11,000 members; (714) 528-2012; www.apbpa.org

Professional Beauty Assn. (1904): 12,000+ members; (800) 468-2274; www.probeauty.org

Psychiatric Assn., American (1844): 36,000+ members; (703) 907-7300; www.psych.org

Psychological Assn., American (1892): 154,000+ members; (202) 336-5500; www.apa.org

Public Administration, American Soc. for (1939): 9,000 members; (202) 393-7878; www.aspanet.org

Public Health Assn., American (1872): 50,000+ members; (202) 777-2742; www.apha.org

Public Relations Society of America (1947): 21,000+ members; (212) 460-1400; www.prsa.org

Range Management, Society for (1948): 4,000 members; (303) 986-3309; www.rangelands.org

Real Estate Appraisers, Natl. Assn. of (1966): 5,500 members; (760) 327-5284; www.narea-assoc.org

Rehabilitation Assn., Natl. (1923): 5,600 members; (703) 836-0850; www.nationalrehab.org

Road & Transportation Builders Assn., American (1902): 5,000+ members; (202) 289-4434; www.artba.org

Safety Engineers, American Soc. of (1911): 34,000+ members; (847) 699-2929; www.asse.org

School Administrators, American Assn. of (1865): 13,000+ members; (703) 528-0700; www.aasa.org

Science Teachers Assn., Natl. (1944): 60,000 members; (703) 243-7100; www.nsta.org

Science Writers, Natl. Assn. of (1955): 2,215 members; (510) 647-9500; www.nasw.org

Screen Actors Guild (1933): 120,000 members; (323) 954-1600; www.sag.com

Songwriters Guild of America (1931): 5,000+ members; (615) 742-9945; www.songwritersguild.com

Sportscasters Assn., American (1980): 500+ members; (212) 227-8080; www.americansportscastersonline.com

Surgeons, American College of (1913): 77,000 members; (312) 202-5000; www.facs.org

Tax Administrators, Federation of (1937): (202) 624-5890; www.taxadmin.org

Teachers of English, Natl. Council of (1911): 60,000+ members; (217) 328-3870; www.ncte.org

Teachers of English to Speakers of Other Languages, Inc. (1966): 12,000+ members; (703) 836-0774; www.tesol.org

Teachers of French, American Assn. of (1927): 10,000 members; (618) 453-5731; www.frenchteachers.org

Teachers of German, American Assn. of (1926): 5,500 members; (856) 795-5553; www.aatg.org

Teachers of Mathematics, Natl. Council of (1920): 90,000 members; (703) 620-9840; www.nctm.org

Teachers of Spanish and Portuguese, American Assn. of (1917): 11,000 members; (248) 960-2180; www.aatsp.org

Television Arts and Sciences, Natl. Academy of (1955): (212) 586-8424; www.emmyonline.org

Theological Library Assn., American (1946): 1,000+ members; (312) 454-5100; www.atla.com

Transportation Engineers, Inst. of (1930): 17,000 members; (202) 785-0060; www.ite.org

Travel Agents, American Soc. of (1931): 12,000 members; (703) 739-2782; www.astanet.com

Underwriters Soc., Chartered Property Casualty (1944): 25,000+ members; (800) 932-2728; www.cpcusociety.org

University Women, American Assn. of (1881): 100,000+ members; (202) 785-7700; www.aauw.org

Veterinary Medical Assn., American (1863): 81,500+ members; (800) 248-2862; www.avma.org

Women in Communications, The Assn. for (1909): 3,000+ members; (703) 370-7436; www.womcom.org

Women Engineers, Society of (1950): 17,000; (392) 596-5223; www.swe.org

Women in Media, Alliance for (1951): 10,000 members; (703) 506-3290; www.awrt.org

Sports Organizations
Source: World Almanac research

Major League Baseball
Office of the Commissioner, 245 Park Ave., 31st Fl., New York, NY 10167; www.mlb.com

American League
Baltimore Orioles (1953): 333 W. Camden St., Baltimore, MD 21201; (410) 685-9800; www.orioles.com

Boston Red Sox (1901): 4 Yawkey Way, Boston, MA 02215; (617) 226-6000; www.redsox.com

Chicago White Sox (1900, as Chicago White Stockings): 333 W. 35th St., Chicago, IL 60616; (312) 674-1000; www.whitesox.com

Cleveland Indians (1901, as Cleveland Blues): 2401 Ontario St., Cleveland, OH 44115; (216) 420-4487; www.indians.com

Detroit Tigers (1901): 2100 Woodward Ave., Detroit, MI 48201; (313) 962-4000; www.tigers.com

Kansas City Royals (1969): One Royal Way, Kansas City, MO 64129; (800) 676-9257; www.royals.com

Los Angeles Angels of Anaheim (1961): 2000 Gene Autry Way, Anaheim, CA 92806; (714) 940-2000; www.angelsbaseball.com

Minnesota Twins (1960): 1 Twins Way, Minneapolis, MN 55403; (612) 659-3400; www.twinsbaseball.com

New York Yankees (1903): One East 161st St., Bronx, NY 10451; (718) 293-4300; www.yankees.com

Oakland Athletics (1901, as Philadelphia Athletics): 7000 Coliseum Way, Oakland, CA 94621; (510) 638-4900; www.oaklandathletics.com

Seattle Mariners (1977): P.O. Box 4100, Seattle, WA 98194; (206) 346-4000; www.mariners.com

Tampa Bay Rays (1995, as Tampa Bay Devil Rays): One Tropicana Dr., St. Petersburg, FL 33705; (727) 825-3137; www.raysbaseball.com

Texas Rangers (1960, as Washington Senators): 1000 Ballpark Way, Arlington, TX 76011; (817) 273-5222; www.texasrangers.com

Toronto Blue Jays (1976): One Blue Jays Way, Ste. 3200, Toronto, ON M5V 1J1, Canada; (416) 341-1000; www.bluejays.com

National League
Arizona Diamondbacks (1998): 401 E. Jefferson St., Phoenix, AZ 85004; (602) 462-6500; www.dbacks.com

Atlanta Braves (1876, as Boston Red Stockings): 755 Hank Aaron Dr., Atlanta, GA 30315; (404) 522-7630; www.braves.com

Chicago Cubs (1876, as Chicago White Stockings): 1060 W. Addison St., Chicago, IL 60613; (773) 404-2827; www.cubs.com

Cincinnati Reds (1869, as Cincinnati Red Stockings): 100 Main St., Cincinnati, OH 45202; (513) 765-7000; www.reds.com

Colorado Rockies (1991): 2001 Blake St., Denver, CO 80205; (303) 292-0200; www.coloradorockies.com

Florida Marlins (1991): 2267 Dan Marino Blvd., Miami, FL 33056; (305) 626-7400; www.floridamarlins.com

Houston Astros (1962, as Houston Colt .45s): 501 Crawford St., Houston, TX 77002; (713) 259-8000; www.astros.com

Los Angeles Dodgers (1890): 1000 Elysian Park Ave., Los Angeles, CA 90012; (323) 224-1500; www.dodgers.com

Milwaukee Brewers (1970): One Brewers Way, Milwaukee, WI 53214; (414) 902-4400; www.brewers.com

New York Mets (1961): Citi Field, Flushing, NY 11368; (718) 507-6387; www.mets.com

Philadelphia Phillies (1883): One Citizens Bank Way, Philadelphia, PA 19148; (215) 463-6000; www.phillies.com

Pittsburgh Pirates (1887, as Pittsburgh Alleghenies): 115 Federal St., Pittsburgh, PA 15212; (412) 323-5000; www.pirates.com

St. Louis Cardinals (1892, as St. Louis Browns): 700 Clark St., St. Louis, MO 63102; (314) 345-9600; www.stlcardinals.com

San Diego Padres (1968): 100 Park Blvd., San Diego, CA 92101; (619) 795-5000; www.padres.com

San Francisco Giants (1883, as New York Gothams): 24 Willie Mays Plz., San Francisco, CA 94107; (415) 972-2000; www.sfgiants.com

Washington Nationals (1969, as Montreal Expos): 1500 South Capitol St., SE, Washington, DC 20003; (202) 349-0400; www.nationals.com

National Basketball Association

League Office, Olympic Tower, 645 Fifth Ave., New York, NY 10022; www.nba.com

Atlanta Hawks (1949, as Tri-City Blackhawks): 101 Marietta St. NW, Ste. 1900, Atlanta, GA 30303; (404) 878-3800; www.nba.com/hawks/

Boston Celtics (1946): 226 Causeway St., 4th Fl., Boston, MA 02114; (866) 423-5849; www.nba.com/celtics/

Charlotte Bobcats (2004): 333 E. Trade St., Charlotte, NC 28202; (704) 688-8600; www.nba.com/bobcats/

Chicago Bulls (1966): 1901 W. Madison St., Chicago, IL 60612; (312) 455-4000; www.nba.com/bulls/

Cleveland Cavaliers (1970): One Center Ct., Cleveland, OH 44115; (800) 820-2287; www.nba.com/cavaliers/

Dallas Mavericks (1980): 2909 Taylor St., Dallas, TX 75226; (214) 747-6287; www.nba.com/mavericks/

Denver Nuggets (1967, as Denver Rockets): 1000 Chopper Cir., Denver, CO 80204; (303) 405-1100; www.nba.com/nuggets/

Detroit Pistons (1957): Six Championship Dr., Auburn Hills, MI 48326; (248) 377-0100; www.nba.com/pistons/

Golden State Warriors (1946, as Philadelphia Warriors): 1011 Broadway, Oakland, CA 94607; (510) 986-2200; www.nba.com/warriors/

Houston Rockets (1967, as San Diego Rockets): 1510 Polk St., Houston, TX 77002; (713) 627-3865; www.nba.com/rockets/

Indiana Pacers (1967): 125 S. Pennsylvania St., Indianapolis, IN 46204; (317) 917-2500; www.nba.com/pacers/

Los Angeles Clippers (1970, as Buffalo Braves): 1111 S. Figueroa St., Ste. 1100, Los Angeles, CA 90015; (888) 895-8662; www.nba.com/clippers/

Los Angeles Lakers (1947, as Minneapolis Lakers): 555 N. Nash St., El Segundo, CA 90245; (310) 426-6000; www.nba.com/lakers/

Memphis Grizzlies (1995, as Vancouver Grizzlies): 191 Beale St., Memphis, TN 38103; (901) 888-4667; www.nba.com/grizzlies/

Miami Heat (1988): 601 Biscayne Blvd., Miami, FL 33132; (786) 777-1000; www.nba.com/heat/

Milwaukee Bucks (1968): 1001 N. 4th St., Milwaukee, WI 53203; (414) 227-0500; www.nba.com/bucks/

Minnesota Timberwolves (1989): 600 1st Ave. North, Minneapolis, MN 55403; (612) 673-1600; www.nba.com/timberwolves/

New Jersey Nets (1967, as New Jersey Americans): 390 Murray Hill Pkwy., E. Rutherford, NJ 07073; (201) 935-8888; www.nba.com/nets/

New Orleans Hornets (1988, as Charlotte Hornets): 1250 Poydras St., 19th Fl., New Orleans, LA 70113; (504) 593-4700; www.nba.com/hornets/

New York Knickerbockers (1946): Two Pennsylvania Plz., New York, NY 10121; (212) 465-6471; www.nba.com/knicks/

Oklahoma City Thunder (1967, as Seattle SuperSonics): 2 Leadership Square, 211 N. Robinson Ave., Ste. 300; Oklahoma City, OK 73102; (405) 208-4800; www.nba.com/thunder/

Orlando Magic (1989): 8701 Maitland Summit Blvd., Orlando, FL 32810; (407) 916-2400; www.nba.com/magic/

Philadelphia 76ers (1949, as Syracuse Nationals): 3601 S. Broad St., Philadelphia, PA 19148; (215) 339-7676; www.nba.com/sixers/

Phoenix Suns (1968): 201 E. Jefferson St., Phoenix, AZ 85004; (602) 379-7900; www.nba.com/suns/

Portland Trail Blazers (1970): One Center Ct., Ste. 200, Portland, OR 97227; (503) 234-9291; www.nba.com/blazers/

Sacramento Kings (1945, as Rochester Royals): One Sports Pkwy., Sacramento, CA 95834; (916) 928-0000; www.nba.com/kings/

San Antonio Spurs (1967, as Dallas Chaparrals): One AT&T Center, San Antonio, TX 78219; (210) 444-5000; www.nba.com/spurs/

Toronto Raptors (1995): 40 Bay St., Toronto, ON M5J 2X2, Canada; (416) 366-3865; www.nba.com/raptors/

Utah Jazz (1974, as New Orleans Jazz): 301 W. South Temple, Salt Lake City, UT 84101; (801) 325-2500; www.nba.com/jazz/

Washington Wizards (1963, as Baltimore Bullets): 601 F St. NW, Washington, DC 20004; (202) 661-5000; www.nba.com/wizards/

National Hockey League

NHL Headquarters, 1185 Ave. of the Americas, 15th Fl., New York, NY 10036; www.nhl.com

Anaheim Ducks (1993): 2695 E. Katella Ave., Anaheim, CA 92806; (877) 945-3946; ducks.nhl.com

Boston Bruins (1924): 100 Legends Way, Boston, MA 02114; (617) 624-1900; bruins.nhl.com

Buffalo Sabres (1970): One Seymour H. Knox III Plz., Buffalo, NY 14203; (716) 855-4100; sabres.nhl.com

Calgary Flames (1980): P.O. Box 1540, Station M, Calgary, AB T2P 3B9, Canada; (403) 777-2177; flames.nhl.com

Carolina Hurricanes (1972, as New England Whalers): 1400 Edwards Mill Rd., Raleigh, NC 27607; (919) 467-7825; hurricanes.nhl.com

Chicago Blackhawks (1926): 1901 W. Madison St., Chicago, IL 60612; (312) 455-7000; blackhawks.nhl.com

Colorado Avalanche (1972, as Quebec Nordiques): 1000 Chopper Cir., Denver, CO 80204; (303) 405-1100; avalanche.nhl.com

Columbus Blue Jackets (2000): 200 W. Nationwide Blvd., Columbus, OH 43215; (614) 246-4625; bluejackets.nhl.com

Dallas Stars (1967, as Minnesota North Stars): 2601 Ave. of the Stars, Frisco, TX 75034; (214) 387-5500; stars.nhl.com

Detroit Red Wings (1926, as Detroit Cougars): 600 Civic Center Dr., Detroit, MI 48226; (313) 983-6606; redwings.nhl.com

Edmonton Oilers (1972, as Alberta Oilers): 11230 - 110 St., Edmonton, AB T5G 3H7, Canada; (780) 414-4000; oilers.nhl.com

Florida Panthers (1993): One Panther Pkwy., Sunrise, FL 33323; (954) 835-7000; panthers.nhl.com

Los Angeles Kings (1967): 1111 S. Figueroa St., Ste. 3100, Los Angeles, CA 90015; (213) 742-7100; kings.nhl.com

Minnesota Wild (2000): 317 Washington St., St. Paul, MN 55102; (651) 602-6000; wild.nhl.com

Montreal Canadiens (1917): 1909, avenue des Canadiens-de-Montréal, Montréal, QC H3C 5L2, Canada; (514) 932-2582; canadiens.nhl.com

Nashville Predators (1998): 501 Broadway, Nashville, TN 37203; (615) 770-2355; predators.nhl.com

New Jersey Devils (1974, as Kansas City Scouts): Prudential Center, 165 Mulberry St., Newark, NJ 07102; (973) 757-6100; devils.nhl.com

New York Islanders (1972): 1255 Hempstead Tpke., Uniondale, NY 11553; (516) 501-6700; islanders.nhl.com

New York Rangers (1926): Two Pennsylvania Plz., New York, NY 10121; (212) 465-6000; rangers.nhl.com

Ottawa Senators (1901): 1000 Palladium Dr., Ottawa, ON K2V 1A5, Canada; (613) 599-0250; senators.nhl.com

Philadelphia Flyers (1967): 3601 S. Broad St., Philadelphia, PA 19148; (215) 336-3600; flyers.nhl.com

Phoenix Coyotes (1979, as Winnipeg Jets): 6751 N. Sunset Blvd. #200, Glendale, AZ 85305; (623) 772-3200; coyotes.nhl.com

Pittsburgh Penguins (1967): 1001 5th Ave., Pittsburgh, PA 15219; (412) 642-1300; penguins.nhl.com

St. Louis Blues (1967): 1401 Clark Ave. at Brett Hull Way, St. Louis, MO 63103; (314) 622-5000; blues.nhl.com

San Jose Sharks (1991): 525 W. Santa Clara St., San Jose, CA 95113; (408) 287-7070; sharks.nhl.com

Tampa Bay Lightning (1992): 401 Channelside Dr., Tampa, FL 33602; (813) 301-6500; lightning.nhl.com

Toronto Maple Leafs (1919, as Toronto St. Pats): 40 Bay St., Ste. 400, Toronto, ON M5J 2X2, Canada; (416) 815-5700; mapleleafs.nhl.com

Vancouver Canucks (1946): 800 Griffiths Way, Vancouver, BC V6B 6G1, Canada; (604) 899-7400; canucks.nhl.com

Washington Capitals (1974): 627 N. Glebe Rd., Ste. 850, Arlington, VA 22203; (202) 266-2200; capitals.nhl.com

Winnipeg Jets (1999, as Atlanta Thrashers): 260 Hargrave St., Winnipeg, MB R3C 5S5, Canada; (204) 987-7825; jets.nhl.com

National Football League

League Office, 280 Park Ave., New York, NY 10017; www.nfl.com

Arizona Cardinals (1898, as Morgan Athletic Club): P.O. Box 888, Phoenix, AZ 85001; (602) 379-0101; www.azcardinals.com

Atlanta Falcons (1965): 4400 Falcon Pkwy., Flowery Branch, GA 30542; (770) 965-3115; www.atlantafalcons.com

Baltimore Ravens (1996): 1101 Russell St., Baltimore, MD 21230; (410) 261-7283; www.baltimoreravens.com

Buffalo Bills (1960): One Bills Dr., Orchard Park, NY 14127; (716) 648-1800; www.buffalobills.com

Carolina Panthers (1993): 800 S. Mint St., Charlotte, NC 28202; (704) 358-7000; www.panthers.com

Chicago Bears (1920, as Decatur Staleys): 1920 Football Dr., Lake Forest, IL 60045; (888) 792-3277; www.chicagobears.com

Cincinnati Bengals (1968): One Paul Brown Stadium, Cincinnati, OH 45202; (513) 621-3550; www.bengals.com

Cleveland Browns (1946): 100 Alfred Lerner Way, Cleveland, OH 44114; (440) 824-6284; www.clevelandbrowns.com

Dallas Cowboys (1960): 900 E. Randol Mill Rd., Arlington, TX 76011; (817) 892-5000; www.dallascowboys.com

Denver Broncos (1960): 13655 Broncos Pkwy., Englewood, CO 80112; (303) 649-9000; www.denverbroncos.com

Detroit Lions (1934): 222 Republic Dr., Allen Park, MI 48101; (313) 262-2000; www.detroitlions.com

Green Bay Packers (1919): 1265 Lombardi Ave., Green Bay, WI 54304; (920) 569-7500; www.packers.com

Houston Texans (2002): Two Reliant Park, Houston, TX 77054; (832) 667-2002; www.houstontexans.com

Indianapolis Colts (1946, as Baltimore Colts): 7001 W. 56th St., Indianapolis, IN 46254; (317) 297-2658; www.colts.com

Jacksonville Jaguars (1995): One EverBank Field Dr., Jacksonville, FL 32202; (904) 633-6000; www.jaguars.com

Kansas City Chiefs (1960, as Dallas Texans): One Arrowhead Dr., Kansas City, MO 64129; (816) 920-9300; www.kcchiefs.com

Miami Dolphins (1966): 347 Don Shula Dr., Miami Gardens, FL 33056; (305) 943-8000; www.miamidolphins.com

Minnesota Vikings (1961): 9520 Viking Dr., Eden Prairie, MN 55344; (952) 858-6500; www.vikings.com

New England Patriots (1960): One Patriot Pl., Foxboro, MA 02035; (508) 543-8200; www.patriots.com

New Orleans Saints (1967): 5800 Airline Dr., Metairie, LA 70003; (504) 733-0255; www.neworleanssaints.com

New York Giants (1925): MetLife Stadium, E. Rutherford, NJ 07073; (201) 935-8111; www.giants.com

New York Jets (1960, as New York Titans): One Jets Dr., Florham Park, NJ 07932; (800) 469-5387; www.newyorkjets.com

Oakland Raiders (1960): 1220 Harbor Bay Pkwy., Alameda, CA 94502; (510) 864-5000; www.raiders.com

Philadelphia Eagles (1933): One NovaCare Way, Philadelphia, PA 19145; (215) 463-2500; www.philadelphiaeagles.com

Pittsburgh Steelers (1933): 100 Art Rooney Ave., Pittsburgh, PA 15212; (412) 432-7800; www.steelers.com

St. Louis Rams (1937, as Cleveland Rams): One Rams Way, St. Louis, MO 63045; (314) 982-7267; www.stlouisrams.com

San Diego Chargers (1960, as Los Angeles Chargers): 4020 Murphy Canyon Rd., San Diego, CA 92123; (858) 874-4500; www.chargers.com

San Francisco 49ers (1950): 4949 Centennial Blvd., Santa Clara, CA 95054; (408) 562-4949; www.sf49ers.com

Seattle Seahawks (1976): 12 Seahawks Way, Renton, WA 98056; (888) 635-4295; www.seahawks.com

Tampa Bay Buccaneers (1976): One Buccaneer Pl., Tampa, FL 33607; (813) 870-2700; www.buccaneers.com

Tennessee Titans (1960, as Houston Oilers): 460 Great Circle Rd., Nashville, TN 37228; (615) 565-4000; www.titansonline.com

Washington Redskins (1937): 21300 Redskin Park Dr., Ashburn, VA 20147; (703) 726-7000; www.redskins.com

Other North American Sports Organizations

American Kennel Club (1884): 260 Madison Ave., New York, NY 10016; (212) 696-8200; www.akc.org

Archery, USA (1879): 711 N. Tejon St., Colorado Springs, CO 80903; (719) 866-4576; www.usarchery.org

Athletic Union, Amateur (1888): P.O. Box 22409, Lake Buena Vista, FL 32830; (407) 934-7200; www.aausports.org

Auto Club, U.S. (1955): 4910 W. 16th St., Speedway, IN 46224; (317) 247-5151; www.usacracing.com

Badminton Assn., USA (1938): One Olympic Plz., Colorado Springs, CO 80909; (719) 866-4808; www.usabadminton.org

Baseball, Little League (1939): 539 US Rte. 15 Hwy., P.O. Box 3485, Williamsport, PA 17701; (570) 326-1921; www.littleleague.org

Baseball Congress, American Amateur (1935): 100 W. Broadway, Farmington, NM 87401; (505) 327-3120; www.aabc.us

Baseball Congress, Natl. (1935): 300 S. Sycamore, Wichita, KS 67213; (316) 264-6887; www.nbcbaseball.com

Baseball Research, Inc., Society for American (1971): 4455 E. Camelback Rd., Ste. D-140, Phoenix, AZ 85018; (800) 969-7227; www.sabr.org

Basketball Association, Women's National (WNBA) (1996): 645 Fifth Ave., New York, NY 10022; (212) 688-9622; www.wnba.com

Bowlers Assn., Professional (1958): 719 2nd Ave., Ste. 701, Seattle, WA 98104; (206) 332-9688; www.pba.com

Bowling Congress, U.S. (2005): 621 Six Flags Dr., Arlington, TX 76011; (800) 514-2695; www.bowl.com

Canadian Football League (1958): 50 Wellington St. E., 3rd Fl., Toronto, ON M5E 1C8, Canada; (416) 322-9650; www.cfl.ca

Cheer and Dance Teams, U.S. All Star Federation for (2003): 6745 Lenox Center Ct., Ste. 300, Memphis, TN 38115; (800) 929-6237; www.usasf.net

Chess Federation, U.S. (1939): P.O. Box 3967, Crossville, TN 38557; (931) 787-1234; www.uschess.org

Contract Bridge League, American (1937): 6575 Windchase Blvd., Horn Lake, MS 38637; (662) 253-3100; www.acbl.org

Curling Association, United States (1948): 5525 Clem's Way, Stevens Point, WI 54482; (715) 344-1199; www.curlingrocks.net

Cycling, USA (1920): 210 USA Cycling Pt., Ste. 100, Colorado Springs, CO 80919; (719) 434-4200; www.usacycling.org

Dance, USA (1965): P.O. Box 152988, Cape Coral, FL 33915; (800) 447-9047; www.usadance.org

Disabled Sports USA (1967): 451 Hungerford Dr., Ste. 100, Rockville, MD 20850; (301) 217-0960; www.dsusa.org

Equestrian Federation, U.S. (1917): 4047 Iron Works Pkwy., Lexington, KY 40511; (859) 258-2472; www.usef.org

Figure Skating Assn., U.S. (1921): 20 First St., Colorado Springs, CO 80906; (719) 635-5200; www.usfigureskating.org

Game Fish Assn., Intl. (1939): 300 Gulf Stream Way, Dania Beach, FL 33004; (954) 927-2628; www.igfa.org

Golf Assn., Ladies Professional (LPGA) (1950): 100 International Golf Dr., Daytona Beach, FL 32124; (386) 274-6200; www.lpga.com

Golf Assn., U.S. (1894): P.O. Box 708, Far Hills, NJ 07931; (908) 234-2300; www.usga.org

Golfers' Association of America, Professional (PGA) (1916): 100 Ave. of the Champions, Palm Beach Gardens, FL 33418; (561) 624-8400; www.pga.com

Gymnastics, USA (1963): 132 E. Washington St., Ste. 700, Indianapolis, IN 46204; (317) 237-5050; www.usa-gymnastics.org

Handball Assn., U.S. (1951): 2333 N. Tucson Blvd., Tucson, AZ 85716; (520) 795-0434; www.ushandball.org

Highpointers Club (1986): P.O. Box 6364, Sevierville, TN 37864; (303) 278-1915; www.highpointers.com

Hockey, USA (1937): 1775 Bob Johnson Dr., Colorado Springs, CO 80906; (719) 576-8724; www.usahockey.com

Hot Rod Assn., Natl. (1951): 2035 Financial Way, Glendora, CA 91741; (626) 914-4761; www.nhra.com

INDYCAR (1994): 4565 W. 16th St., Indianapolis, IN 46222; (317) 492-6526; www.indycar.com

Intercollegiate Athletics, Natl. Assn. of (1937): 1200 Grand Blvd., Kansas City, MO 64106; (816) 595-8000; www.naia.org

Lacrosse, US (1998): 113 W. University Pkwy., Baltimore, MD 21210; (410) 235-6882; www.uslacrosse.org

Muzzle Loading Rifle Assn., Natl. (1933): P.O. Box 67, Friendship, IN 47021; (812) 667-5131; www.nmlra.org

NASCAR (National Association for Stock Car Auto Racing) (1948): P.O. Box 2875, Daytona Beach, FL 32120; (386) 253-0611; www.nascar.com

NCAA (National Collegiate Athletic Association) (1906, as Intercollegiate Athletic Association of the United States): 700 W. Washington St., P.O. Box 6222, Indianapolis, IN 46206; (317) 917-6222; www.ncaa.org

Olympic Committee, U.S. (1896, as American Olympic Association): 27 S. Tejon, Colorado Springs, CO 80903; (719) 632-5551; www.usoc.org

Paralympics, U.S. (2001): One Olympic Plz., Colorado Springs, CO 80909; (719) 866-2030; www.usparalympics.org

Polo Assn., U.S. (1890): 4037 Iron Works Pkwy., Ste. 110, Lexington, KY 40511; (800) 232-8772; www.us-polo.org

Power Boat Assn., American (1903): 17640 E. Nine Mile Rd., P.O. Box 377, Eastpointe, MI 48021; (586) 773-9700; www.apba-racing.com

Rifle Assn., National (1871): 11250 Waples Mill Rd., Fairfax, VA 22030; (800) 672-3888; www.nra.org

Rodeo Cowboys Assn., Professional (1936): 101 ProRodeo Dr., Colorado Springs, CO 80919; (719) 593-8840; www.prorodeo.com

Roller Sports, USA (1937): 4730 South St., Lincoln, NE 68506; (402) 483-7551; www.usarollersports.org

Rugby, USA (1975): 2500 Arapahoe Ave., Ste. 200, Boulder, CO 80302; (303) 539-0300; www.usarugby.org

Running Assn., American (1968): 4405 East-West Hwy., Ste. 405, Bethesda, MD 20814; (800) 776-2732; www.americanrunning.org

Skeet Shooting Assn., Natl. (1926): 5931 Roft Rd., San Antonio, TX 78253; (210) 688-3371; www.mynssa.com

Ski and Snowboard Assn., U.S. (1905): 1 Victory Ln., Box 100, Park City, UT 84060; (435) 649-9090; www.ussa.org

Soccer Federation, U.S. (1913): 1801 S. Prairie Ave., Chicago, IL 60616; (312) 808-1300; www.ussoccer.com

Soccer, Major League (MLS) (1993): 420 Fifth Ave., 7th Fl., New York, NY 10018; (212) 450-1200; www.mlssoccer.com

Softball Assn. of America, Amateur (1933): 2801 NE 50th St., Oklahoma City, OK 73111; (405) 424-5266; www.softball.org

Special Olympics (1968): 1133 19th St. NW, Washington, DC 20036; (202) 628-3630; www.specialolympics.org

Speedskating, U.S. (1966): PO Box 18370, Kearns, UT 84118; (801) 417-5360; www.usspeedskating.org

Speleological Society, Natl. (1941): 2813 Cave Ave., Huntsville, AL 35810; (256) 852-1300; www.caves.org

Swimming, USA (1979): One Olympic Plz., Colorado Springs, CO 80909; (719) 866-4578; www.usaswimming.org

Table Tennis, USA (1933): One Olympic Plz., Colorado Springs, CO 80909; (719) 866-4583; www.usatt.org

Tennis Assn., U.S. (1881): 70 W. Red Oak Ln., White Plains, NY 10604; (914) 696-7000; www.usta.com

Thoroughbred Racing Associations (1942): 420 Fair Hill Dr., Ste. 1, Elkton, MD 21921; (410) 392-9200; www.tra-online.com

Track & Field, USA (1878, as Amateur Athletic Union): 132 E. Washington St., Ste. 800, Indianapolis, IN 46204; (317) 261-0500; www.usatf.org

Trapshooting Assn., Amateur (1900): 601 W. National Rd., Vandalia, OH 45377; (937) 898-4638; www.shootata.com

Trotting Assn., U.S. (1939): 750 Michigan Ave., Columbus, OH 43215; (614) 224-2291; www.ustrotting.com

Ultimate, USA (1979): 4730 Table Mesa Dr., Ste. I-200C, Boulder, CO 80305; (303) 447-3472; www.usaultimate.org

Volleyball, USA (1928): 715 S. Circle Dr., Colorado Springs, CO 80910; (719) 228-6800; www.usavolleyball.org

Wheelchair & Ambulatory Sports, USA (1956): PO Box 5266, Kendall Park, NJ 08824; (732) 266-2634; www.wsusa.org

Wrestling, USA (1968): 6155 Lehman Dr., Colorado Springs, CO 80918; (719) 598-8181; www.themat.com

Health Organizations

Source: World Almanac research

Entries are roughly alphabetized by the basic condition addressed or organization name. Year established is in parentheses. In addition to these selected sites, there is a vast array of medical information on the Internet. It is important, however, to be certain that the source of information is reliable and accurate. Always check with a physician before embarking on any new health-related undertaking.

Al-Anon Family Groups (1951): (757) 563-1600; www.al-anon.alateen.org

Alcohol and Drug Information, SAMHSA National Clearinghouse (877) SAMHSA-7 (726-4727); ncadi.samhsa.gov

Alcoholics Anonymous (1935): (212) 870-3400; www.alcoholics-anonymous.org

Alcoholism and Drug Dependence, Inc., National Council on (1944): (212) 269-7797; www.ncadd.org

Aging, National Institute on (1974): (301) 496-1752; www.nia.nih.gov

Aging's Eldercare Locator, Administration on (1991): (800) 677-1116; www.eldercare.gov

AIDSinfo: (800) HIV-0440 (448-0440); www.aidsinfo.nih.gov

AIDS Society, Canadian (1988): (613) 230-3580; www.cdnaids.ca

Allergy, Asthma, and Immunology, American Academy of (1943): (414) 272-6071; www.aaaai.org

ALS Association [Lou Gehrig's disease] (1985): (202) 407-8580; www.alsa.org

Alzheimer's Association (1979): (312) 335-8700; www.alz.org

Alzheimer Society of Canada (1978): (416) 488-8772; www.alzheimer.ca

Anorexia Nervosa and Associated Disorders, National Association of (1976): (630) 577-1333; www.anad.org

Arc of the United States, The [intellectual and developmental disabilities] (1950): (800) 433-5255; www.thearc.org

Arthritis Foundation (1948): (800) 283-7800; www.arthritis.org

Arthritis and Musculoskeletal and Skin Diseases, National Institute of (1986): (877) 226-4267; www.niams.nih.gov

Asthma and Allergy Foundation of America (1953): (800) 727-8462; www.aafa.org

Autism Society (1965): (800) 328-8476; www.autism-society.org

Blind, American Council of the (1961): (202) 467-5081; www.acb.org

Blind, Inc., Guide Dog Foundation for the (1946): (800) 548-4337; www.guidedog.org

Blind, National Federation of the (1940): (410) 659-9314; www.nfb.org

Blind and Physically Handicapped, National Library Service for the (1931): (202) 707-5100; TDD (202) 707-0744; www.loc.gov/nls/

Blindness America, Prevent (1908): (800) 331-2020; www.preventblindness.org

Blindness, Foundation Fighting (1971): (800) 683-5555; www.blindness.org

Brain Tumor Society, National (2008): (800) 770-8287; www.braintumor.org

Breast Cancer Organization, Y-ME National (1978): (800) 221-2141; www.y-me.org

Cancer Institute's Cancer Information Service, National (1975): (800) 422-6237; www.cancer.gov/aboutnci/cis/

Cancer Society, American (1913): (800) 227-2345; www.cancer.org

Cancer Society, Canadian (1938): (416) 961-7223; www.cancer.ca

Centers for Disease Control and Prevention (CDC) (1946): (800) 232-4636; www.cdc.gov

Cerebral Palsy, United (1949): (202) 776-0406; www.ucp.org

CFIDS Association of America [chronic fatigue syndrome] (1987): (704) 365-2343; www.cfids.org

Child Abuse and Family Violence, National Council on (1984): (202) 429-6695; www.nccafv.org

Childhelp National Child Abuse Hotline (1959): (800) 4-A-CHILD (422-4453); www.childhelp.org

Children, National Center for Missing and Exploited (1984): (703) 224-2150; www.missingkids.com

Children's Tumor Foundation (1978): (212) 344-6633; www.ctf.org

Chronic Pain Association, American (1980): (800) 533-3231; www.theacpa.org

Continence, National Association for (1982): (843) 377-0900; www.nafc.org

Continence, Simon Foundation for (1983): (800) 237-4666; www.simonfoundation.org

Cooley's Anemia Foundation [thalassemia major] (1954): (800) 522-7222; www.thalassemia.org

Crohn's and Colitis Foundation of America (1967): (800) 932-2423; www.ccfa.org

Crohn's and Colitis Foundation of Canada (1974): (416) 920-5035; www.ccfc.ca

Cystic Fibrosis Foundation (1955): (800) 344-4823 or (301) 951-4422; www.cff.org

Deaf, Natl. Assn. of the (1880): (301) 587-1788, TTY (301) 587-1789; www.nad.org

Depression and Bipolar Support Alliance (1985): (800) 826-3632; www.dbsalliance.org

Diabetes Association, American (1940): (800) 342-2383; www.diabetes.org

Diabetes Association, Canadian (1953): (416) 363-3373; www.diabetes.ca

Diabetes Research Foundation International, Juvenile (1970): (800) 533-2873; www.jdrf.org

Dial-A-Hearing Screening Test: (800) 222-EARS (322-3277)

Domestic Violence Hotline, National (1996): (800) 799-7233; TTY (800) 787-3224; www.thehotline.org

Down Syndrome Congress, Natl. (1973): (800) 232-6372; www.ndsccenter.org

Down Syndrome Society, National (1979): (800) 221-4602; www.ndss.org

Dyslexia Association, International (1949): (410) 296-0232; www.interdys.org

Easter Seals [disabilities, special needs] (1919): (800) 221-6827; www.easterseals.com

Endometriosis Association (1980): (414) 355-2200; www.endometriosisassn.org

Epilepsy Foundation's Answer Place (1967): (800) 332-1000; www.epilepsyfoundation.org

Fat Acceptance, Natl. Assn. to Advance (1969): (916) 558-6880; www.naafa.org

First Candle [sudden infant death syndrome] (1987): (800) 221-7437; www.sidsalliance.org

FoodSafety.gov—Gateway to Federal Food Safety Information: Food (except for meat, poultry, eggs): (888) 723-3366 (FDA Center for Food Safety and Applied Nutrition); Meat, poultry, eggs: (888) 674-6854 (USDA Meat and Poultry Hotline); Illness or food poisoning: (800) 232-4636 (CDC)

Gamblers Anonymous (1957): (213) 386-8789; www.gamblersanonymous.org

Geriatrics Society, American (1942): (212) 308-1414; www.americangeriatrics.org

Hard of Hearing Association, Canadian (1982): (613) 526-1584, TTY (613) 526-2692; www.chha.ca

Headache Foundation, National (1970): (888) 643-5552; www.headaches.org

Hearing Society, Intl. (1951): (734) 522-7200; www.ihsinfo.org

Heart Association, American (1924): (800) 242-8721; www.americanheart.org

Hearts, Inc., Mended (1950): (214) 296-9252; www.mendedhearts.org

Hospice Education Institute Hospicelink (1985): (800) 331-1620; www.hospiceworld.org

Hospice International, Children's (1983): (800) 242-4453; www.chionline.org

Hospital Association, American (1898): (312) 422-3000; www.aha.org

Huntington's Disease Society of America (1967): (800) 345-4372; www.hdsa.org

Kidney Foundation, National (1950): (212) 889-2210; www.kidney.org

Kidney Foundation of Canada (1964): (514) 369-4806; www.kidney.ca

Kidney Fund, American (1971): (800) 638-8299; www.kidneyfund.org

Kidney and Urologic Diseases Information Clearinghouse, National: (800) 891-5390; www.kidney.niddk.nih.gov

La Leche League Intl. [breastfeeding] (1957): (800) 525-3243; www.llli.org

Leukemia and Lymphoma Society (1949): (800) 955-4572; www.lls.org

Liver Foundation, American (1976): (212) 668-1000; www.liverfoundation.org

Living Bank [organ donation] (1968): (800) 528-2971; www.livingbank.org

Lung Association, American (1904): (800) 548-8252; www.lungusa.org

Lung Line (1983): (877) 225-5654; www.nationaljewish.org/about/contact/lung-line/

Lupus Foundation of America, Inc. (1977): (202) 349-1155; www.lupus.org

Lyme Disease Foundation (1988): (860) 870-0070; www.lyme.org

March of Dimes [babies' health] (1938): (914) 997-4488; www.marchofdimes.com

Marfan Foundation, Natl. (1981): (800) 8-MARFAN (862-7326); www.marfan.org

Mayo Clinic (1889): (507) 284-2511; www.mayoclinic.com

Mental Health America (1909): (800) 969-6642; www.nmha.org

Mental Health, National Institute of (1946): (301) 443-4513, TTY (301) 443-8431; www.nimh.nih.gov

Mental Illness, Natl. Alliance on (1979): (703) 524-7600; www.nami.org

Multiple Sclerosis Society, National (1946): (800) 344-4867; www.nationalmssociety.org

Multiple Sclerosis Society of Canada (1948): (416) 922-6065; www.mssociety.ca

Muscular Dystrophy Association (1950): (800) 572-1717; www.mdausa.org

Myeloma Foundation, Intl. (1990): (800) 452-2873; www.myeloma.org

Narcotics Anonymous (1953): (818) 773-9999; www.na.org

National Health Council (1920): (202) 785-3910; www.nationalhealthcouncil.org

National Health Information Center (1979): (800) 336-4797; www.health.gov/NHIC/

National Institutes of Health (NIH) (1887): (301) 496-4000; www.nih.gov

Neurological Disorders and Stroke, Natl. Institute of (1950): (800) 352-9424, TTY (301) 468-5981; www.ninds.nih.gov

Organ Sharing, United Network for (1984): (804) 782-4800; www.unos.org

Osteoporosis Foundation, National (1984): (800) 231-4222; www.nof.org

Overeaters Anonymous (1960): (505) 891-2664; www.oa.org

Parkinson Foundation, National (1957): (800) 327-4545; www.parkinson.org

Parkinson's Disease Foundation, Inc. (1957): (212) 923-4700; www.pdf.org

Parkinson Society Canada (1965): (416) 227-9700; www.parkinson.ca

Pediatrics, American Academy of (1930): (847) 434-4000; www.aap.org

Phoenix House [substance abuse] (1967): (800) DRUG-HELP (378-4435); www.phoenixhouse.org

Physically Handicapped, Inc., Natl. Assn. of the (1958): (330) 724-1994; www.naph.net

Planned Parenthood Federation of America, Inc. (1916): (212) 541-7800; www.plannedparenthood.org

Plastic Surgeons, American Society of (1931): (847) 228-9900; www.plasticsurgery.org

Post-Polio Health International (1960): (314) 534-0475; www.post-polio.org

Psoriasis Foundation, Natl. (1968): (503) 244-7404; www.psoriasis.org

Rare Disorders, Natl. Organization for (1983): (203) 744-0100; www.rarediseases.org

Rehabilitation Information Center, National (1977): (800) 346-2742; TTY (301) 459-5984; www.naric.com

Reye's Syndrome Foundation, Natl. (1974): (419) 924-9000; www.reyessyndrome.org

Runaway Switchboard, National (1971): (773) 880-9860; www.1800runaway.org

Scleroderma Foundation (1989): (800) 722-HOPE (722-4673); www.scleroderma.org

Social Health Association, American (sexual health information) (1914): (919) 361-8400; www.ashastd.org

Sickle Cell Disease Association of America (1971): (800) 421-8453; www.sicklecelldisease.org

Sjögren's Syndrome Foundation (1983): (800) 475-6473; www.sjogrens.org

Speech-Language-Hearing Association, American (1925): (800) 638-8255, TTY (301) 296-5650; www.asha.org

Spinal Cord Injury Association, National (1948): (800) 962-9629; www.spinalcord.org

Stroke Association, National (1984): (800) 787-6537; www.stroke.org

Stuttering Association, Natl. (1977): (212) 944-4050; www.nsastutter.org

Stuttering Foundation of America (1947): (800) 992-9392; www.stutteringhelp.org

Stuttering, National Center for (1974): (800) 221-2483; www.stuttering.com

Sudden Infant Death Syndrome Institute, American (1983): (239) 431-5425; www.sids.org

Suicide Prevention Lifeline, National (2004): (800) 273-TALK (273-8255); www.suicidepreventionlifeline.org

Therapy Dogs Intl. (1976): (973) 252-9800; www.tdi-dog.org

Tourette Syndrome Association (1972): (718) 224-2999; tsa-usa.org

Tuberous Sclerosis Alliance (1974): (301) 562-9890; www.tsalliance.org

Urological Association, American (1902): (866) 746-4282; www.auanet.org

Visual Impairments, Natl. Assn. for Parents of Children with (1980): (800) 562-6265; www.napvi.org

Women's Health Network, National (1975): (202) 682-2640; www.nwhn.org

HealthyWomen (1988): (877) 986-9472; www.healthywomen.com

UNITED STATES FACTS

Superlative U.S. Statistics

Source: U.S. Geological Survey, Dept. of the Interior; U.S. Census Bureau, Dept. of Commerce; World Almanac research

The 50 States

Total area for 50 states and Washington, DC		3,796,742 sq mi
Land area for 50 states and Washington, DC		3,531,905 sq mi
Water area for 50 states and Washington, DC		264,837 sq mi
Largest state	Alaska	665,384 sq mi
Smallest state	Rhode Island	1,545 sq mi
Largest county (excluding Alaska)	San Bernardino County, CA	20,105 sq mi
Smallest county	Arlington County, VA[1]	.26 sq mi
Largest incorporated city (by area, pop. 1,000+)	Sitka, AK	4,811 sq mi
Northernmost city	Barrow, AK	71°17′ N
Northernmost point	Point Barrow, AK	71°23′ N
Southernmost city	Hilo, HI	19°44′ N
Southernmost settlement	Naalehu, HI	19°03′ N
Southernmost point	Ka Lae (South Cape), island of Hawaii	18°55′ N (155°41′ W)
Easternmost city	Eastport, ME	66°59′05′′ W
Easternmost settlement[2]	Attu Station, AK	173°11′ E
Easternmost point[2]	Pochnoi Point, Semisopochnoi Island, AK	179°46′ E
Westernmost city	Adak Station, AK	173°11′ E
Westernmost settlement	Adak Station, AK	173°11′ E
Westernmost point	Amatignak Island, AK	179°06′ W
Highest settlement	Tordal Estates, CO	10,653 ft
Lowest settlement	Bombay Beach, CA	−223 ft
Highest point on Atlantic coast	Cadillac Mountain, Mount Desert Island, ME	1,530 ft
Oldest national park	Yellowstone National Park (1872), WY-MT-ID	2,219,791 acres
Largest national park	Wrangell-St. Elias, AK	8,323,147 acres
Highest waterfall	Yosemite Falls—total in 3 sections	2,425 ft
	(Upper Yosemite Fall, 1,430 ft; Cascades, 675 ft; Lower Yosemite Fall, 320 ft)	
Longest river system	Mississippi-Missouri-Red Rock	3,710 mi
Highest mountain	Mount McKinley (Denali), AK	20,320 ft
Lowest point	Death Valley, CA	−282 ft
Deepest lake	Crater Lake, OR	1,958 ft
Rainiest spot	Mount Waialeale, HI	annual avg. rainfall 424 in.
Largest gorge	Grand Canyon, Colorado River, AZ	277 mi long, 600 ft to 18 mi wide, 1 mi deep
Deepest gorge	Hells Canyon, Snake River, OR-ID	7,900 ft
Largest dam	New Cornelia Tailings, Ten Mile Wash, AZ[3]	274,026,000 cu yds material used
Tallest building	Willis Tower, Chicago, IL[4]	1,451 ft
Largest building	Boeing Manufacturing Plant, Everett, WA	472,000,000 cu ft; covers 98 acres
Largest office building	Pentagon, Arlington, VA	77,025,000 cu ft; covers 29 acres
Tallest structure	KVLY-TV Tower, Blanchard, ND	2,063 ft
Longest bridge span	Verrazano-Narrows Bridge, New York, NY	4,260 ft
Highest bridge	Royal Gorge Bridge, Cañon City, CO	1,053 ft above water
Deepest well	Bertha Rogers gas well (inactive), Washita County, OK	31,441 ft

The 48 Contiguous States

Total area for 48 states and Washington, DC		3,120,426 sq mi[5]
Land area for 48 states and Washington, DC		2,954,842 sq mi
Water area for 48 states and Washington, DC		165,585 sq mi
Largest state	Texas	268,596 sq mi
Northernmost city	Bellingham, WA	48°46′ N
Northernmost settlement	Angle Inlet, MN	49°21′ N
Northernmost point	Northwest Angle, MN	49°23′ N
Southernmost city	Key West, FL	24°33′ N
Southernmost mainland city	Florida City, FL	25°27′ N
Southernmost point	Ballast Key, FL	24°31′ N
Easternmost settlement	Lubec, ME	66°58′49′′ W
Easternmost point	West Quoddy Head, ME	66°57′ W
Westernmost town	La Push, WA	124°38′ W
Westernmost point	Bodelteh Islands, WA	124°46′ W
Highest mountain	Mount Whitney, CA	14,500 ft

(1) Smallest county by land area is New York County (Manhattan) at 23 sq mi; its total area including water is 34 sq mi. Superlative shown is for smallest total area. (2) Alaska's Aleutian Islands extend into the Eastern Hemisphere (across 180° longitude) and thus technically contain the easternmost point and settlement in the U.S. (3) The New Cornelia Tailings Dam is a privately owned industrial dam composed of tailings, remnants of a mining process. (4) Formerly called the Sears Tower. (5) Components do not add up to total due to rounding.

Additional Statistical Information About the U.S.

The annual *Statistical Abstract of the United States*, published by the Bureau of the Census, U.S. Commerce Dept., contains additional data. For information, write Supt. of Documents, P.O. Box 979050, St. Louis, MO 63197-9000; visit bookstore.gpo. gov/help/ordering.jsp, call 1-866-512-1800, or e-mail ContactCenter@gpo.gov. The *Statistical Abstract* can be viewed online at www.census.gov/compendia/statab.

Highest and Lowest Altitudes in U.S. States and Territories

Source: U.S. Geological Survey, Dept. of the Interior
(negative sign indicates below sea level)

State/territory	Highest point Name	County	Elev. (ft)	Lowest point Name	County	Elev. (ft)
Alabama	Cheaha Mountain	Cleburne	2,407	Gulf of Mexico		Sea level
Alaska	Mount McKinley/Denali	Denali	20,320	Pacific Ocean		Sea level
American Samoa	Lata Mountain	Tau Island	3,160	Pacific Ocean		Sea level
Arizona	Humphreys Peak	Coconino	12,637	Colorado R.	Yuma	70
Arkansas	Magazine Mountain	Logan	2,753	Ouachita R.	Ashley-Union	55
California	Mount Whitney	Inyo-Tulare	14,500	Death Valley	Inyo	−282
Colorado	Mount Elbert	Lake	14,440	Arikaree R.	Yuma	3,315
Connecticut	S. slope of Mt. Frissell	Litchfield	2,380	Long Island Sound		Sea level
Delaware	Ebright Azimuth	New Castle	448	Atlantic Ocean		Sea level
Dist. of Columbia	Tenleytown	NW quadrant	410	Potomac R.		1
Florida	Britton Hill	Walton	345	Atlantic Ocean		Sea level
Georgia	Brasstown Bald	Towns-Union	4,784	Atlantic Ocean		Sea level
Guam	Mount Lamlam	Agat District	1,332	Pacific Ocean		Sea level
Hawaii	Mauna Kea	Hawaii	13,796	Pacific Ocean		Sea level
Idaho	Borah Peak	Custer	12,661	Snake R.	Nez Perce	710
Illinois	Charles Mound	Jo Daviess	1,235	Mississippi R.	Alexander	279
Indiana	Hoosier Hill	Wayne	1,257	Ohio R.	Posey	320
Iowa	Hawkeye Point	Osceola	1,670	Mississippi R.	Lee	480
Kansas	Mount Sunflower	Wallace	4,039	Verdigris R.	Montgomery	679
Kentucky	Black Mountain	Harlan	4,145	Mississippi R.	Fulton	257
Louisiana	Driskill Mountain	Bienville	535	New Orleans	Orleans	−8
Maine	Mount Katahdin	Piscataquis	5,268	Atlantic Ocean		Sea level
Maryland	Hoye Crest	Garrett	3,360	Atlantic Ocean		Sea level
Massachusetts	Mount Greylock	Berkshire	3,491	Atlantic Ocean		Sea level
Michigan	Mount Arvon	Baraga	1,979	Lake Erie		571
Minnesota	Eagle Mountain	Cook	2,301	Lake Superior		601
Mississippi	Woodall Mountain	Tishomingo	806	Gulf of Mexico		Sea level
Missouri	Taum Sauk Mountain	Iron	1,772	St. Francis R.	Dunklin	230
Montana	Granite Peak	Park	12,804	Kootenai R.	Lincoln	1,800
Nebraska	Panorama Point	Kimball	5,424	Missouri R.	Richardson	840
Nevada	Boundary Peak	Esmeralda	13,146	Colorado R.	Clark	479
New Hampshire	Mount Washington	Coos	6,288	Atlantic Ocean		Sea level
New Jersey	High Point	Sussex	1,803	Atlantic Ocean		Sea level
New Mexico	Wheeler Peak	Taos	13,166	Red Bluff Reservoir	Eddy	2,842
New York	Mount Marcy	Essex	5,344	Atlantic Ocean		Sea level
North Carolina	Mount Mitchell	Yancey	6,684	Atlantic Ocean		Sea level
North Dakota	White Butte	Slope	3,506	Red R. of the North	Pembina	750
Ohio	Campbell Hill	Logan	1,550	Ohio R.	Hamilton	455
Oklahoma	Black Mesa	Cimarron	4,973	Little R.	McCurtain	289
Oregon	Mount Hood	Clackamas-Hood R.	11,240	Pacific Ocean		Sea level
Pennsylvania	Mount Davis	Somerset	3,213	Delaware R.	Delaware	Sea level
Puerto Rico	Cerro de Punta	Ponce District	4,390	Atlantic Ocean		Sea level
Rhode Island	Jerimoth Hill	Providence	812	Atlantic Ocean		Sea level
South Carolina	Sassafras Mountain	Pickens	3,560	Atlantic Ocean		Sea level
South Dakota	Harney Peak	Pennington	7,242	Big Stone Lake	Roberts	966
Tennessee	Clingmans Dome	Sevier	6,643	Mississippi R.	Shelby	178
Texas	Guadalupe Peak	Culberson	8,749	Gulf of Mexico		Sea level
Utah	Kings Peak	Duchesne	13,534	Beaver Dam Wash	Washington	2,000
Vermont	Mount Mansfield	Chittenden	4,393	Lake Champlain		95
Virginia	Mount Rogers	Grayson-Smyth	5,729	Atlantic Ocean		Sea level
Virgin Islands	Crown Mountain	St. Thomas Island	1,556	Atlantic Ocean		Sea level
Washington	Mount Rainier	Pierce	14,416	Pacific Ocean		Sea level
West Virginia	Spruce Knob	Pendleton	4,863	Potomac R.	Jefferson	240
Wisconsin	Timms Hill	Price	1,951	Lake Michigan		579
Wyoming	Gannett Peak	Fremont	13,810	Belle Fourche R.	Crook	3,099

U.S. Coastline by States

Source: National Oceanic and Atmospheric Administration, U.S. Dept. of Commerce
(in statute miles)

	Coastline[1]	Shoreline[2]		Coastline[1]	Shoreline[2]
Atlantic Coast	2,069	28,673	**Gulf Coast**	1,631	17,141
Connecticut	0	618	Alabama	53	607
Delaware	28	381	Florida	770	5,095
Florida	580	3,331	Louisiana	397	7,721
Georgia	100	2,344	Mississippi	44	359
Maine	228	3,478	Texas	367	3,359
Maryland	31	3,190			
Massachusetts	192	1,519	**Pacific Coast**	7,623	40,298
New Hampshire	13	131	Alaska	5,580	31,383
New Jersey	130	1,792	California	840	3,427
New York	127	1,850	Hawaii	750	1,052
North Carolina	301	3,375	Oregon	296	1,410
Pennsylvania	0	89	Washington	157	3,026
Rhode Island	40	384			
South Carolina	187	2,876	**Arctic Coast**	1,060	2,521
Virginia	112	3,315	**United States**	12,383	88,633

(1) Figures are lengths of general outline of seacoast. Measurements were made with a unit measure of 30 minutes of latitude on charts as near the scale of 1:1,200,000 as possible. Coastline of sounds and bays is included to a point where they narrow to width of unit measure, and includes the distance across at such point. (2) Figures obtained in 1939-40 with a recording instrument on the largest-scale charts and maps then available. Shoreline of outer coast, offshore islands, sounds, bays, rivers, and creeks is included to the head of tidewater or to a point where tidal waters narrow to a width of 100 ft.

States: Capitals, Key Dates, Geographic Data

Source: Statistical Abstract of the United States, U.S. Census Bureau, Dept. of Commerce

The 13 colonies that declared independence from Great Britain and fought the War of Independence (American Revolution) became the 13 original states. They were, in the order in which they ratified the Constitution: Delaware, Pennsylvania, New Jersey, Georgia, Connecticut, Massachusetts, Maryland, South Carolina, New Hampshire, Virginia, New York, North Carolina, and Rhode Island.

State	Settled[1]	Capital	Entered Union Date	Order	Extent (mi) Long (approx. mean)	Wide	Area (sq mi) Land	Water	Total	Rank in area[2]
AL	1702	Montgomery	Dec. 14, 1819	22	330	190	50,645	1,775	52,420	30
AK	1784	Juneau	Jan. 3, 1959	49	1,480[3]	810	570,641	94,743	665,384	1
AZ	1776	Phoenix	Feb. 14, 1912	48	400	310	113,594	396	113,990	6
AR	1686	Little Rock	June 15, 1836	25	260	240	52,035	1,143	53,179	29
CA	1769	Sacramento	Sept. 9, 1850	31	770	250	155,779	7,916	163,094	3
CO	1858	Denver	Aug. 1, 1876	38	380	280	103,642	452	104,094	8
CT	1634	Hartford	Jan. 9, 1788	5	110	70	4,842	701	5,543	48
DE	1638	Dover	Dec. 7, 1787	1	100	30	1,949	540	2,489	49
DC	NA	NA	NA	NA	NA	NA	61	7	68	51
FL	1565	Tallahassee	Mar. 3, 1845	27	500	160	53,625	12,133	65,758	22
GA	1733	Atlanta	Jan. 2, 1788	4	300	230	57,513	1,912	59,425	24
HI	1820	Honolulu	Aug. 21, 1959	50	NA	NA	6,423	4,509	10,932	43
ID	1842	Boise	July 3, 1890	43	570	300	82,643	926	83,569	14
IL	1720	Springfield	Dec. 3, 1818	21	390	210	55,519	2,395	57,914	25
IN	1733	Indianapolis	Dec. 11, 1816	19	270	140	35,826	593	36,420	38
IA	1788	Des Moines	Dec. 28, 1846	29	310	200	55,857	416	56,273	26
KS	1727	Topeka	Jan. 29, 1861	34	400	210	81,759	520	82,278	15
KY	1774	Frankfort	June 1, 1792	15	380	140	39,486	921	40,408	37
LA	1699	Baton Rouge	Apr. 30, 1812	18	380	130	43,204	9,174	52,378	31
ME	1624	Augusta	Mar. 15, 1820	23	320	190	30,843	4,537	35,380	39
MD	1634	Annapolis	Apr. 28, 1788	7	250	90	9,707	2,699	12,406	42
MA	1620	Boston	Feb. 6, 1788	6	190	50	7,800	2,754	10,554	44
MI	1668	Lansing	Jan. 26, 1837	26	490	240	56,539	40,175	96,714	11
MN	1805	St. Paul	May 11, 1858	32	400	250	79,627	7,309	86,936	12
MS	1699	Jackson	Dec. 10, 1817	20	340	170	46,923	1,509	48,432	32
MO	1735	Jefferson City	Aug. 10, 1821	24	300	240	68,742	965	69,707	21
MT	1809	Helena	Nov. 8, 1889	41	630	280	145,546	1,494	147,040	4
NE	1823	Lincoln	Mar. 1, 1867	37	430	210	76,824	524	77,348	16
NV	1849	Carson City	Oct. 31, 1864	36	490	320	109,781	791	110,572	7
NH	1623	Concord	June 21, 1788	9	190	70	8,953	397	9,349	46
NJ	1660	Trenton	Dec. 18, 1787	3	150	70	7,354	1,368	8,723	47
NM	1610	Santa Fe	Jan. 6, 1912	47	370	343	121,298	292	121,590	5
NY	1614	Albany	July 26, 1788	11	330	283	47,126	7,429	54,555	27
NC	1660	Raleigh	Nov. 21, 1789	12	500	150	48,618	5,201	53,819	28
ND	1812	Bismarck	Nov. 2, 1889	39	340	211	69,001	1,698	70,698	19
OH	1788	Columbus	Mar. 1, 1803	17	220	220	40,861	3,965	44,826	34
OK	1889	Oklahoma City	Nov. 16, 1907	46	400	220	68,595	1,304	69,899	20
OR	1811	Salem	Feb. 14, 1859	33	360	261	95,988	2,391	98,379	9
PA	1682	Harrisburg	Dec. 12, 1787	2	283	160	44,743	1,312	46,054	33
RI	1636	Providence	May 29, 1790	13	40	30	1,034	511	1,545	50
SC	1670	Columbia	May 23, 1788	8	260	200	30,061	1,960	32,020	40
SD	1859	Pierre	Nov. 2, 1889	40	380	210	75,811	1,305	77,116	17
TN	1769	Nashville	June 1, 1796	16	440	120	41,235	909	42,144	36
TX	1682	Austin	Dec. 29, 1845	28	790	660	261,232	7,365	268,596	2
UT	1847	Salt Lake City	Jan. 4, 1896	45	350	270	82,170	2,727	84,897	13
VT	1724	Montpelier	Mar. 4, 1791	14	160	80	9,217	400	9,616	45
VA	1607	Richmond	June 25, 1788	10	430	200	39,490	3,285	42,775	35
WA	1811	Olympia	Nov. 11, 1889	42	360	240	66,456	4,842	71,298	18
WV	1727	Charleston	June 20, 1863	35	240	130	24,038	192	24,230	41
WI	1766	Madison	May 29, 1848	30	310	260	54,158	11,339	65,496	23
WY	1834	Cheyenne	July 10, 1890	44	360	280	97,093	720	97,813	10

NA = Not applicable. **Note:** Land and water areas may not add up to totals because of rounding. (1) First permanent settlement by Europeans. (2) Rank is based on total area as shown. (3) Aleutian Islands and Alexander Archipelago not included.

The Continental Divide of the U.S.

The Continental Divide of the U.S., also known as the Great Divide, is located at the watershed created by the mountain ranges, or tablelands, of the Rocky Mountains. This watershed separates the waters that drain easterly into the Atlantic Ocean and its marginal seas, such as the Gulf of Mexico, from those waters that drain westerly into the Pacific Ocean. The majority of easterly flowing water in the U.S. drains into the Gulf of Mexico before reaching the Atlantic Ocean. The majority of westerly flowing water, before reaching the Pacific Ocean, drains either through the Columbia River or through the Colorado River, which flows into the Gulf of California before reaching the Pacific Ocean.

The location and route of the Continental Divide across the U.S. can briefly be described as follows:

Beginning at the U.S.-Mexican boundary, near long. 108°45′ W, the Divide, in a northerly direction, crosses New Mexico along the W edge of the Rio Grande drainage basin, entering Colorado near long. 106°41′ W.

From there by a very irregular route north across Colorado along the W summits of the Rio Grande and of the Arkansas, the South Platte, and the North Platte river basins, and across Rocky Mountain National Park, entering Wyoming near long. 106°52′ W.

From there in a northwesterly direction, forming the W rims of the North Platte, the Big Horn, and the Yellowstone river basins, crossing the SW portion of Yellowstone National Park.

From there in a westerly and then a northerly direction forming the common boundary of Idaho and Montana, to a point on said boundary near long. 114°00′ W.

From there northeasterly and northwesterly through Montana and Glacier National Park, entering Canada near long. 114°04′ W.

Chronological List of Territories, With State Admissions to Union

Source: National Archives and Records Administration

Territory	Date of act creating territory	When act took effect	Date of admission as state	Years as terr.
Northwest Territory[1]	July 13, 1787	No fixed date	Mar. 1, 1803[2]	16
Territory southwest of Ohio River	May 26, 1790	No fixed date	June 1, 1796[3]	6
Mississippi	Apr. 7, 1798	When president acted	Dec. 10, 1817	19
Indiana	May 7, 1800	July 4, 1800	Dec. 11, 1816	16
Orleans	Mar. 26, 1804	Oct. 1, 1804	Apr. 30, 1812[4]	7
Michigan	Jan. 11, 1805	June 30, 1805	Jan. 26, 1837	31
Louisiana-Missouri[5]	Mar. 3, 1805	July 4, 1805	Aug. 10, 1821	16
Illinois	Feb. 3, 1809	Mar. 1, 1809	Dec. 3, 1818	9
Alabama	Mar. 3, 1817	When MS became a state	Dec. 14, 1819	2
Arkansas	Mar. 2, 1819	July 4, 1819	June 15, 1836	17
Florida	Mar. 30, 1822	No fixed date	Mar. 3, 1845	23
Wisconsin	Apr. 20, 1836	July 3, 1836	May 29, 1848	12
Iowa	June 12, 1838	July 3, 1838	Dec. 28, 1846	8
Oregon	Aug. 14, 1848	Date of act	Feb. 14, 1859	10
Minnesota	Mar. 3, 1849	Date of act	May 11, 1858	9
New Mexico	Sept. 9, 1850	On president's proclamation	Jan. 6, 1912	61
Utah	Sept. 9, 1850	Date of act	Jan. 4, 1896	46
Washington	Mar. 2, 1853	Date of act	Nov. 11, 1889	36
Nebraska	May 30, 1854	Date of act	Mar. 1, 1867	12
Kansas	May 30, 1854	Date of act	Jan. 29, 1861	6
Colorado	Feb. 28, 1861	Date of act	Aug. 1, 1876	15
Nevada	Mar. 2, 1861	Date of act	Oct. 31, 1864	3
Dakota	Mar. 2, 1861	Date of act	Nov. 2, 1889	28
Arizona	Feb. 24, 1863	Date of act	Feb. 14, 1912	49
Idaho	Mar. 3, 1863	Date of act	July 3, 1890	27
Montana	May 26, 1864	Date of act	Nov. 8, 1889	25
Wyoming	July 25, 1868	When officers were qualified	July 10, 1890	22
Alaska[6]	May 17, 1884	No fixed date	Jan. 3, 1959	75
Oklahoma	May 2, 1890	Date of act	Nov. 16, 1907	17
Hawaii	Apr. 30, 1900	June 14, 1900	Aug. 21, 1959	59

(1) Included what is now Ohio, Indiana, Illinois, Michigan, Wisconsin, E Minnesota. (2) Ohio was the first state of NW territory admitted. (3) Admitted as the state of Tennessee. (4) Admitted as the state of Louisiana. (5) The act creating Missouri Territory (June 4, 1812) became effective Dec. 7, 1812. (6) Although the May 17, 1884, act actually constituted Alaska as a district, it was often referred to as a territory and administered as such. The Territory of Alaska was formally organized by an act of Aug. 24, 1912.

Geographic Centers, U.S. and State

Source: U.S. Geological Survey, Dept. of the Interior

There is no generally accepted definition of geographic center and no uniform method for determining it. Following the U.S. Geological Survey, the geographic center of an area is defined here as the center of gravity of the surface, or that point on which the surface would balance if it were a plane of uniform thickness. All locations in the following list are approximate.

No marked point has been officially established by any government agency as the geographic center of the 50 states, the conterminous U.S. (48 states), or the North American continent. A group of private citizens erected a monument in Lebanon, KS, marking its as geographic center of the conterminous U.S., and a cairn erected in Rugby, ND, asserts that location as the center of the North American continent.

Geographic centers as reported by the U.S. Geological Survey are indicated by county below unless otherwise noted:

United States, including Alaska and Hawaii: W of Castle Rock, Butte County, SD; lat. 44°58′ N, long. 103°46′ W
Conterminous U.S. (48 states): near Lebanon, Smith County Kansas; lat. 39°50′ N, long. 98°35′ W
North American continent: 6 mi W of Balta, Pierce County, North Dakota; lat. 48°10′ N, long. 100°10′ W
Alabama: Chilton, 12 mi SW of Clanton
Alaska: approx. 60 mi NW of Mt. McKinley; lat. 63°50′ N, long. 152° W;
Arizona: Yavapai, 55 mi E-SE of Prescott
Arkansas: Pulaski, 12 mi NW of Little Rock
California: Madera, 38 mi E of Madera
Colorado: Park, 30 mi NW of Pikes Peak
Connecticut: Hartford, at East Berlin
Delaware: Kent, 11 mi S of Dover
District of Columbia: near 4th and L Sts. NW
Florida: Hernando, 12 mi N-NW of Brooksville
Georgia: Twiggs, 18 mi SE of Macon
Hawaii: off Maui; lat. 20°15′ N, long. 156°20′ W
Idaho: Custer, SW of Challis
Illinois: Logan, 28 mi NE of Springfield
Indiana: Boone, 14 mi N-NW of Indianapolis
Iowa: Story, 5 mi NE of Ames
Kansas: Barton, 15 mi NE of Great Bend
Kentucky: Marion, 3 mi N-NW of Lebanon
Louisiana: Avoyelles, 3 mi SE of Marksville
Maine: Piscataquis, 18 mi N of Dover
Maryland: Prince George's, 4.5 mi NW of Davidsonville
Massachusetts: Worcester, N part of city

Michigan: Wexford, 5 mi N-NW of Cadillac
Minnesota: Crow Wing, 10 mi SW of Brainerd
Mississippi: Leake, 9 mi W-NW of Carthage
Missouri: Miller, 20 mi SW of Jefferson City
Montana: Fergus, 11 mi W of Lewistown
Nebraska: Custer, 10 mi NW of Broken Bow
Nevada: Lander, 26 mi SE of Austin
New Hampshire: Belknap, 3 mi E of Ashland
New Jersey: Mercer, 5 mi SE of Trenton
New Mexico: Torrance, 12 mi S-SW of Willard
New York: Madison, 12 mi S of Oneida and 26 mi SW of Utica
North Carolina: Chatham, 10 mi NW of Sanford
North Dakota: Sheridan, 5 mi SW of McClusky
Ohio: Delaware, 25 mi N-NE of Columbus
Oklahoma: Oklahoma, 8 mi N of Oklahoma City
Oregon: Crook, 25 mi S-SE of Prineville
Pennsylvania: Centre, 2.5 mi SW of Bellefonte
Rhode Island: Kent, 1 mi S-SW of Crompton
South Carolina: Richland, 13 mi SE of Columbia
South Dakota: Hughes, 8 mi NE of Pierre
Tennessee: Rutherford, 5 mi NE of Murfreesboro
Texas: McCulloch, 15 mi NE of Brady
Utah: Sanpete, 3 mi N of Manti
Vermont: Washington, 3 mi E of Roxbury
Virginia: Buckingham, 5 mi SW of Buckingham
Washington: Chelan, 10 mi W-SW of Wenatchee
West Virginia: Braxton, 4 mi E of Sutton
Wisconsin: Wood, 9 mi SE of Marshfield
Wyoming: Fremont, 58 mi E-NE of Lander

International Boundary Lines of the U.S.

The length of the N boundary of the conterminous U.S.—the U.S.-Canadian border excluding Alaska—is 3,987 mi according to the U.S. Geological Survey, Dept. of the Interior. The length of the Alaskan-Canadian border is 1,538 mi. The U.S.-Mexican border, from the Gulf of Mexico to the Pacific Ocean, is about 1,933 mi (1963 boundary agreement).

Origins of the Names of U.S. States

Source: State officials; Smithsonian Institution; Topographic Division, U.S. Geological Survey, Dept. of the Interior

Alabama: Choctaw word for a Chickasaw tribe. First noted in accounts of De Soto expedition.

Alaska: Russian version of Aleutian (Eskimo) word, *alakshak,* for "peninsula," "great lands," or "land that is not an island."

Arizona: Spanish version of Pima Indian word for "little spring place," or Aztec *arizuma,* meaning "silver-bearing."

Arkansas: Algonquin name for the Quapaw Indians, meaning "south wind."

California: Bestowed by the Spanish conquistadors (possibly by Cortez). It was the name of an imaginary island, an earthly paradise, in *Las Serges de Esplandian,* a Spanish romance written by Montalvo in 1510. *Baja* (Lower) *California* (in Mexico) was first visited by Spanish in 1533. The present U.S. state was called *Alta* (Upper) *California.*

Colorado: From Spanish for "red," first applied to Colorado River.

Connecticut: From Mohican and other Algonquin words meaning "long river place."

Delaware: Named for Lord De La Warr, early governor of Virginia; first applied to river, then to Indian tribe (Lenni-Lenape), and the state.

District of Columbia: For Christopher Columbus, 1791.

Florida: Named by Juan Ponce de León *Pascua Florida,* "Flowery Easter," on Easter Sunday, 1513.

Georgia: For King George II of England, by James Oglethorpe, colonial administrator, 1732.

Hawaii: Possibly derived from native word for homeland, *Hawaiki* or *Owhyhee.*

Idaho: Said to be a coined name with the invented meaning "gem of the mountains"; originally suggested for the Pikes Peak mining territory (Colorado), then applied to the new mining territory of the Pacific Northwest. Another theory suggests *Idaho* may be a Kiowa Apache term for the Comanche.

Illinois: French for *Illini* or "land of *Illini*," Algonquin word meaning "men" or "warriors."

Indiana: Means "land of the Indians."

Iowa: Indian word variously translated as "here I rest" or "beautiful land." Named for the Iowa River, which was named for the Iowa Indians.

Kansas: Sioux word for "south wind people."

Kentucky: Indian word that is variously translated as "dark and bloody ground," "meadowland," and "land of tomorrow."

Louisiana: Part of territory called Louisiana by Robert Cavelier Sieur de La Salle for French King Louis XIV.

Maine: From Maine, ancient French province. Also descriptive, referring to the mainland as distinct from the many coastal islands.

Maryland: For Queen Henrietta Maria, wife of Charles I of England.

Massachusetts: From Indian tribe whose name meant "at or about the Great Hill" in Blue Hills region south of Boston.

Michigan: From Chippewa words, *mici gama,* meaning "great water," after the lake of the same name.

Minnesota: From Dakota Sioux word meaning "cloudy water" or "sky-tinted water" of the Minnesota River.

Mississippi: Probably Chippewa *mici zibi,* meaning "great river" or "gathering-in of all the waters." Also Algonquin word *messipi.*

Missouri: An Algonquin Indian term meaning "river of the big canoes."

Montana: Latin or Spanish for "mountainous."

Nebraska: From Omaha or Otos Indian word meaning "broad water" or "flat river," describing the Platte River.

Nevada: Spanish, meaning "snow-clad."

New Hampshire: Named, 1629, by Capt. John Mason of Plymouth Council for his home county in England.

New Jersey: The Duke of York, 1664, gave a patent to John Berkeley and Sir George Carteret to be called *Nova Caesaria,* or New Jersey, after England's Isle of Jersey.

New Mexico: Spaniards in Mexico applied term to land north and west of Rio Grande in the 16th century.

New York: For Duke of York and Albany, who received patent to New Netherland from his brother Charles II and sent an expedition to capture it, 1664.

North Carolina: In 1619, Charles I gave a large patent to Sir Robert Heath to be called Province of Carolana, from *Carolus,* Latin name for Charles. A new patent was granted by Charles II to Earl of Clarendon and others. Divided into North and South Carolina, 1710.

North Dakota: Sioux word *Dakota,* meaning "friend" or "ally."

Ohio: Iroquois word for "fine or good river."

Oklahoma: Choctaw word meaning "red man," proposed by Rev. Allen Wright, Choctaw-speaking Indian.

Oregon: Origin unknown. One theory holds that the name possibly derives from *wauregan,* meaning "beautiful," term used by Indians in New England.

Pennsylvania: William Penn, the Quaker who was made full proprietor of this area by King Charles II in 1681, suggested "Sylvania," or "woodland," for his tract. The king's government owed Penn's father, Admiral William Penn, 16,000 pounds, and the land was granted as partial settlement. Charles II added the "Penn" to Sylvania, against the desires of the modest proprietor, in honor of the admiral.

Puerto Rico: Spanish for "rich port."

Rhode Island: Exact origin unknown. One theory notes that Giovanni de Verrazano recorded an island about the size of Rhodes in the Mediterranean in 1524, but others believe the state was named *Roode Eylandt* by Adriaen Block, Dutch explorer, because of its red clay.

South Carolina: See North Carolina.

South Dakota: See North Dakota.

Tennessee: *Tanasi* was the name of Cherokee villages on the Little Tennessee River. From 1784 to 1788, this was the State of Franklin, or Frankland.

Texas: Variant of word used by Caddo and other Indians meaning "friends" or "allies," and applied to them by the Spanish in eastern Texas. Also written *Texias, Tejas, Teysas.*

Utah: From a Navajo word meaning "upper," or "higher up," as applied to a Shoshone tribe called Ute. Spanish form is *Yutta;* the English is *Uta* or *Utah.* Proposed name *Deseret,* "land of honeybees," from Book of Mormon, was rejected by Congress.

Vermont: From French words *vert* (green) and *mont* (mountain). The Green Mountains were said to have been named by Samuel de Champlain. When the state was formed, 1777, Dr. Thomas Young suggested combining *vert* and *mont* into Vermont.

Virginia: Named by Sir Walter Raleigh, who fitted out the expedition of 1584, in honor of Queen Elizabeth, the Virgin Queen of England.

Washington: Named after George Washington. When the bill creating the Territory of Columbia was introduced in the 32nd Congress, its name was changed to Washington because of the existence of the District of Columbia.

West Virginia: So named when western counties of Virginia refused to secede from the U.S. in 1863.

Wisconsin: An Indian name, spelled *Ouisconsin* and *Mesconsing* by early chroniclers. Believed to mean "grassy place" in Chippewa. Congress made it *Wisconsin.*

Wyoming: From the Algonquin words for "large prairie place," "at the big plains," or "on the great plain."

Territorial Sea of the U.S.

According to a Dec. 27, 1988, proclamation by Pres. Ronald Reagan, "The territorial sea of the United States henceforth extends to 12 nautical miles from the baselines of the United States determined in accordance with international law. In accordance with international law, as reflected in the applicable provisions of the 1982 United Nations Convention on the Law of the Sea, within the territorial sea of the United States, the ships of all countries enjoy the right of innocent passage and the ships and aircraft of all countries enjoy the right of transit passage through international straits."

Major Accessions of Territory by the U.S.

Source: U.S. Dept. of the Interior; U.S. Census Bureau, U.S. Dept. of Commerce

Not including territories such as Panama Canal Zone and the Philippines which are no longer under U.S. jurisdiction; area figures are for total area and may differ from figures for current areas given elsewhere.

Accession	Date	Area (sq mi)	Accession	Date	Area (sq mi)	Accession	Date	Area (sq mi)
Territory in 1790[1]	NA	888,685	Mexican Cession	1848	529,017	Guam[3]	1899	212
Louisiana Purchase	1803	827,192	Gadsden Purchase	1853	29,640	American Samoa[4]	1900	76
Treaty of Florida	1819	72,003	Alaska	1867	586,412	U.S. Virgin Islands	1917	133
Texas	1845	390,143	Hawaii	1898	6,450	Northern Marianas[5]	1986	179
Oregon Territory	1846	285,680	Puerto Rico[2]	1899	3,435			

NA = Not applicable. (1) Includes that part of a drainage basin of Red River of the North, S of 49th parallel, sometimes considered part of Louisiana Purchase. (2) Ceded by Spain in 1898, ratified in 1899, and became the Commonwealth of Puerto Rico by Act of Congress on July 25, 1952. (3) Acquired in 1898; ratified 1899. (4) Acquired in 1899; ratified 1900. (5) Formerly a part of the U.S. administered Trust Territory of the Pacific Islands; became a U.S. commonwealth, Nov. 3, 1986.

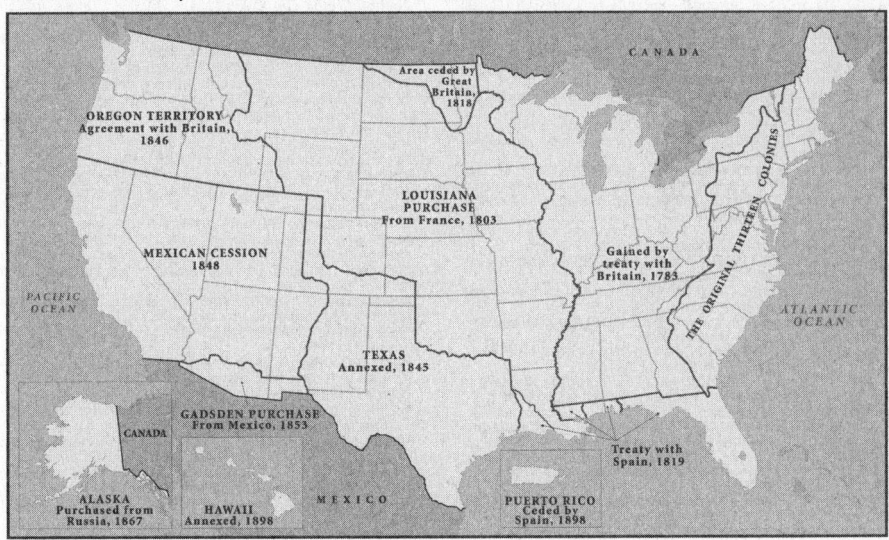

Special Areas Administered by the U.S. Forest Service, 2010

Source: U.S. Forest Service, Dept. of Agriculture

NHL = Natl. Historic Landmark; NS(A) = Natl. Scenic (Area); NM = Natl. Monument; NP = Natl. Preserve;
NRA = Natl. Recreation Area; NVM = Natl. Volcanic Monument; SRA = Scenic Recreation Area

Area	Location	Estab.	Acres[1]	Area	Location	Estab.	Acres[1]
Admiralty Island NM	AK	1980	974,278	Mount Hood NRA	OR	2009	34,474
Allegheny NRA	PA	1984	24,145	Mount Pleasant NSA	VA	1994	7,580
Arapaho NRA	CO	1978	32,521	Mount Rogers NRA	VA	1966	118,509
Bear Creek NSA	VA	2009	5,128	Mount St. Helens NVM	WA	1989	112,605
Beech Creek NSA	OK	1988	6,200	Newberry NVM	OR	1990	54,822
Cascade Head NS Research Area	OR	1974	6,637	Opal Creek SRA	OR	1996	12,645
Columbia River Gorge NSA	OR-WA	1986	72,810	Oregon Dunes NRA	OR	1972	27,232
Coosa Bald NSA	GA	1991	7,100	Pine Ridge NRA	NE	1986	6,600
Ed Jenkins NRA	GA	1991	23,166	Rattlesnake NRA	MT	1980	59,119
Flaming Gorge NRA	UT-WY	1968	189,825	Robert T. Stafford White Rocks NRA	VT	1984	36,561
Giant Sequoia NM	CA	2000	327,769	Santa Rosa and			
Grand Island NRA	MI	1990	12,974	San Jacinto Mountains NM	CA	2000	64,400
Grey Towers NHL	PA	1963	102	Sawtooth NRA	ID	1972	729,428
Hells Canyon NRA	OR-ID	1975	537,770	Seng Mountains NSA	VA	2009	5,192
Indian Nations NS & Wildlife Area	OK	1988	41,051	Smith River NRA	CA	1990	305,169
Jemez NRA	NM	1993	44,670	Spring Mountain NRA	NV	1993	314,367
Land Between the Lakes NRA	KY-TN	1998	170,310	Spruce Knob-Seneca Rocks NRA	WV	1965	57,232
Jewel Cave NM	ND	1908	1,120	Valles Caldera NP	NM	2000	89,716
Misty Fiords NM	AK	1980	2,293,760	Whiskeytown-Shasta-Trinity NRA	CA	1965	176,367
Mono Basin NSA	CA	1984	128,303	Winding Stair Mountain NRA	OK	1988	25,890
Moosalamoo NRA	VT	2006	15,912				
Mount Baker NRA	WA	1984	8,473				

(1) Area administered by the Forest Service or federally owned.

20 Most-Visited Sites in the National Park System, 2010
Source: National Park Service, Dept. of the Interior
Attendance at all areas administered by the National Park Service in 2010 totaled 281,303,769 recreation visits.

Site (location)	Recreation visits	Site (location)	Recreation visits
Blue Ridge Parkway (NC-VA)	14,517,118	Grand Canyon National Park (AZ)	4,388,386
Golden Gate Natl. Recreation Area (CA)	14,271,503	Gulf Islands National Seashore (FL-MS)	4,283,747
Great Smoky Mountains Natl. Park (NC-TN)	9,463,538	San Francisco Maritime Natl. Historical Park (CA)	4,130,970
Gateway Natl. Recreation Area (NJ-NY)	8,820,757	Castle Clinton National Monument (NY)	4,126,378
Lake Mead Natl. Recreation Area (AZ-NV)	7,080,758	Chesapeake & Ohio Canal Natl. Historical Park	
George Washington Memorial Pkwy. (VA-MD-DC)	6,925,099	(DC-MD-WV)	4,111,238
Lincoln Memorial (DC)	6,042,315	World War II Memorial (DC)	3,964,351
Natchez Trace Parkway (MS-AL-TN)	5,910,950	Yosemite National Park (CA)	3,901,408
Delaware Water Gap Natl. Recreation Area (NJ-PA)	5,285,761	Statue of Liberty National Monument (NJ-NY)	3,833,288
Cape Cod National Seashore (MA)	4,653,706	Independence National Historical Park (PA)	3,751,007
Vietnam Veterans Memorial (DC)	4,555,371		

National Parks, Other Areas Administered by National Park Service

As of Dec. 31, 2010, the National Park Service administered 84,383,361 acres of federal and non-federal land across 394 sites. Dates when sites were authorized for initial protection by Congress or by presidential proclamation are given in parentheses. If different, the date the area got its current designation, or was transferred to the National Park Service, follows. Gross area in acres, as of Dec. 31, 2010, follows date(s). Some paths, trails, and other areas are not listed.

National Parks

Acadia, ME (1916/1929): 47,455. Includes Mount Desert Isl., half of Isle au Haut, Schoodic Peninsula on mainland. Highest elevation on Eastern seaboard.

American Samoa, AS (1988): 9,000. Features a paleotropical rain forest and a coral reef.

Arches, UT (1929/1971): 76,679. Contains giant red sandstone arches and other products of erosion.

Badlands, SD (1929/1978): 242,756. Reformations and native prairie. Animal fossils 23-37 mil years old.

Big Bend, TX (1935): 801,163. Rio Grande, Chisos Mts.

Biscayne, FL (1968/1980): 172,971. Aquatic park encompassing chain of islands south of Miami.

Black Canyon of the Gunnison, CO (1933/1999): 30,750. Has a canyon 2,900 ft deep and 40 ft wide at its narrowest part.

Bryce Canyon, UT (1923/1928): 35,835. Spectacularly colorful and unusual display of erosion effects.

Canyonlands, UT (1964): 337,598. At junction of Colorado and Green Rivers; extensive evidence of prehistoric Indians.

Capitol Reef, UT (1937/1971): 241,904. A 70-mi uplift of sandstone cliffs dissected by high-walled gorges.

Carlsbad Caverns, NM (1923/1930): 46,766. Largest known caverns; not yet fully explored.

Channel Islands, CA (1938/1980): 249,561. Sea lion breeding place, nesting sea birds, unique plants.

Congaree, SC (1976/2003): 26,112. Largest intact tract of old-growth bottomland hardwood forest in the U.S.

Crater Lake, OR (1902): 183,224. Extraordinary blue lake in the crater of Mt. Mazama, a volcano that erupted about 7,700 years ago; deepest U.S. lake.

Cuyahoga Valley, OH (1974/2000): 32,856. Rural landscape along Ohio and Erie Canal system between Akron and Cleveland.

Death Valley, CA-NV (1933/1994): 3,373,042. Large desert area. Includes the lowest point in the Western Hemisphere; also includes Scotty's Castle.

Denali, AK (1917/1980): 4,740,912. Name changed from Mt. McKinley National Park. Mountains in U.S., wildlife.

Dry Tortugas, FL (1935/1992): 64,701. Ft. Jefferson and seven coral reef and sand islands near Key West.

Everglades, FL (1934): 1,509,152. Largest remaining subtropical wilderness in continental U.S.

Gates of the Arctic, AK (1978/1984): 7,523,898. Vast wilderness in north central region. Limited federal facilities.

Glacier, MT (1910): 1,013,322. Superb Rocky Mt. scenery, numerous glaciers and glacial lakes. Part of Waterton-Glacier Intl. Peace Park established by U.S. and Canada in 1932.

Glacier Bay, AK (1925/1986): 3,224,841. Great tidewater glaciers that move down mountainsides and break up into the sea; much wildlife.

Grand Canyon, AZ (1893/1919): 1,217,403. Most spectacular part of Colorado River's greatest canyon.

Grand Teton, WY (1929): 310,044. Most impressive part of the Teton Mts., winter feeding ground of largest American elk herd.

Great Basin, NV (1922/1986): 77,180. Includes Wheeler Peak, Lexington Arch, and Lehman Caves.

Great Sand Dunes, CO (1932/2000): 44,246. North America's tallest dunes.

Great Smoky Mountains, NC-TN (1926/1934): 522,051. Largest Eastern U.S. mountain range; magnificent forests.

Guadalupe Mountains, TX (1966): 86,367. Extensive Permian limestone fossil reef; tremendous earth fault.

Haleakala, HI (1916/1960): 33,223. Dormant volcano on Maui with large colorful craters.

Hawaii Volcanoes, HI (1916/1961): 323,431. Contains Kilauea and Mauna Loa, active volcanoes.

Hot Springs, AR (1832/1921): 5,550. Bathhouses are furnished with thermal waters from the park's 47 hot springs; these waters are used for bathing and drinking.

Isle Royale, MI (1931): 571,790. Largest island in Lake Superior, noted for its wilderness area and wildlife.

Joshua Tree, CA (1936/1994): 789,866. Desert region includes Joshua trees, other plant and animal life.

Katmai, AK (1918/1980): 3,674,540. "Valley of Ten Thousand Smokes," scene of 1912 volcanic eruption.

Kenai Fjords, AK (1978/1980): 669,984. Abundant marine mammals; birdlife; Harding Icefield, one of 4 major icecaps in U.S.

Kings Canyon, CA (1890/1940): 461,901. Mountain wilderness, dominated by Kings River Canyons and High Sierra; contains giant sequoias.

Kobuk Valley, AK (1978/1980): 1,750,676. Contains geological and recreational sites. Limited federal facilities.

Lake Clark, AK (1978/1980): 2,619,722. Across Cook Inlet from Anchorage. A scenic wilderness rich in fish and wildlife. Limited federal facilities.

Lassen Volcanic, CA (1907/1916): 106,452. Contains Lassen Peak, recently active volcano, and other volcanic phenomena.

Mammoth Cave, KY (1926/1941): 52,830. 365 mi of explored underground passages, beautiful natural formations, river 300 ft below surface.

Mesa Verde, CO (1906): 52,485. Most notable and best preserved prehistoric cliff dwellings in the U.S.

Mount Rainier, WA (1899): 236,381. Greatest single-peak glacial system in the U.S.

North Cascades, WA (1968): 504,781. Spectacular mountainous region with many glaciers, lakes.

Olympic, WA (1909/1938): 922,651. Mountain wilderness containing finest remnant of Pacific Northwest rain forest, active glaciers, Pacific shoreline, rare elk.

Petrified Forest, AZ (1906/1962): 221,621. Extensive petrified wood and Indian artifacts. Contains part of Painted Desert.

Redwood, CA (1968): 112,618. 40 mi of Pacific coastline, groves of ancient redwoods and world's tallest trees.

Rocky Mountain, CO (1915): 265,758. On the Continental Divide; includes peaks over 14,000 ft.

Saguaro, AZ (1933/1994): 91,440. Part of the Sonoran Desert; includes the giant saguaro cacti, unique to the region.

Sequoia, CA (1890): 404,063. Groves of giant sequoias, highest mountain in conterminous U.S.: Mt. Whitney (14,494 ft). World's largest tree.

Shenandoah, VA (1926): 199,100. Portion of the Blue Ridge Mts.; overlooks Shenandoah Valley; Skyline Drive.

Theodore Roosevelt, ND (1947/1978): 70,447. Contains part of Roosevelt's ranch and scenic badlands.

Virgin Islands, VI (1956): 14,737. Authorized to cover 75% of St. John Isl. and Hassel Isl.; lush growth, lovely beaches, Carib Indian petroglyphs, evidence of colonial Danes.

Voyageurs, MN (1971): 218,210. Abundant lakes, forests, wildlife, canoeing, boating.

Wind Cave, SD (1903): 28,291. Limestone caverns in Black Hills. Extensive wildlife includes a herd of bison.

Wrangell-St. Elias, AK (1978/1980): 8,323,147. Largest area in park system, most peaks over 16,000 ft, abundant wildlife; day's drive east of Anchorage. No federal facilities.

Yellowstone, ID-MT-WY (1872): 2,219,791. World's first national park. World's greatest geyser area has about 10,000 geysers and hot springs; spectacular falls and impressive canyons of the Yellowstone River; grizzly bear, moose, and bison.

Yosemite, CA (1890): 761,268. Yosemite Valley, the nation's highest waterfall, grove of sequoias, and mountains.

Zion, UT (1909/1919): 146,597. Unusual shapes and landscapes resulting from erosion and faulting; evidence of past volcanic activity; contains the "Great White Throne," 2,394-ft monolith.

National Historical Parks

Abraham Lincoln Birthplace, Hodgenville, KY (1916/1959): 11. Memorial building, sinking spring.

Adams, MA (1946/1998): 24. Home of Pres. John Adams, John Quincy Adams, and celebrated descendants.

Appomattox Court House, VA (1930/1954): 1,774. Where Confederate General Lee surrendered to Grant.

Boston, MA (1974): 44. Includes Faneuil Hall, Old North Church, Bunker Hill, Paul Revere House.

Cane River Creole (Gold and heritage area), LA (1994): 207. Preserves the Creole culture as it developed along the Cane River.

Cedar Creek & Belle Grove, VA (2002): 3,712. Civil War battle site and an antebellum plantation in the Shenandoah Valley.

Chaco Culture, NM (1907/1980): 33,960. Ruins of pueblos built by prehistoric Indians including the Pueblo, Hopi, and Navajo.

Chesapeake and Ohio Canal, MD-DC-WV (1938/1971): 19,616. 184-mi historic canal; DC to Cumberland, MD.

Colonial, VA (1930/1936): 8,677. Includes most of Jamestown Isl., site of first successful English colony; Yorktown, site of Cornwallis's surrender to George Washington; Colonial Parkway.

Cumberland Gap, KY-TN-VA (1940): 23,644. Mountain pass of the Wilderness Road, which carried the first great migration of pioneers into America's interior.

Dayton Aviation Heritage, OH (1992): 86. Commemorates the area's aviation heritage.

Edison, West Orange, NJ (1955/1962): 21. Inventor's home and laboratory.

George Rogers Clark, IN (1966): 26. Commemorates American defeat of British in West during Revolution.

Harpers Ferry, MD-VA-WV (1944/1963): 3,647. At the confluence of the Shenandoah and Potomac Rivers, the site of John Brown's 1859 raid on the Army arsenal.

Hopewell Culture, OH (1923/1992): 1,170. Remains of ceremonial mounds built in the Ohio River Valley, 200 BCE-500 CE.

Independence, PA (1948): 45. Contains several properties associated with the American Revolution and the founding of the U.S. Includes Independence Hall and the Liberty Bell Center.

Jean Lafitte (and preserve), LA (1907/1978): 20,001. Includes Chalmette, site of 1815 Battle of New Orleans; French Quarter.

Kalaupapa, HI (1980): 10,779. Molokai's former leper colony.

Kaloko-Honokohau, HI (1978): 1,163. Preserves the native culture of Hawaii.

Keweenaw, MI (1992): 1,870. Site of first significant copper mine in U.S.

Klondike Gold Rush, AK-WA (1976): 12,996. Preserves Chilkoot Trail used in 1898 Gold Rush. Museum in Seattle.

Lewis & Clark, OR-WA (1958/2004): 1,584. Lewis and Clark encampment, 1805-06. Incorporates former Fort Clatsop Natl. Mem. Park and OR-WA state parks.

Lowell, MA (1978): 141. Textile mills, canal, 19th-cent. structures; park shows planned city of Industrial Revolution.

Lyndon B. Johnson, TX (1969/1980): 1,570. President's birthplace, boyhood home, ranch.

Marsh-Billings-Rockefeller, VT (1992): 643. Boyhood home of conservationist George Perkins Marsh.

Minute Man, MA (1959): 1,027. Where the Minute Men battled the British, Apr. 19, 1775. Also contains Nathaniel Hawthorne's home.

Morristown, NJ (1933): 1,711. Site of important military encampments during the American Revolution; Washington's headquarters, 1779-80.

Natchez, MS (1988): 108. Mansions, townhouses, and villas related to history of Natchez.

New Bedford Whaling, MA (1996): 34. Preserves structures and relics associated with the city's 19th-cent. whaling industry.

New Orleans Jazz, LA (1994): 5. Preserves, educates, and interprets jazz as it has evolved in New Orleans.

Nez Perce, ID-MT-OR-WA (1965): 4,570. Illustrates the history and culture of the Nez Perce Indian country (38 separate sites).

Palo Alto Battlefield, TX (1978): 3,442. Scene of first battle of the Mexican War.

Pecos, NM (1965/1990): 6,703. Ruins of ancient Pueblo of Pecos, archaeological sites, and two associated Spanish colonial missions from the 17th and 18th centuries.

Pu'uhonua o Honaunau, HI (1955/1978): 420. Until 1819, a sanctuary for Hawaiians vanquished in battle and for those guilty of crimes or breaking taboos.

Rosie the Riveter/WWII Home Front, CA (2000): 145. Site of a shipyard that employed thousands of women during WWII; commemorates women who worked in wartime industries.

Salt River Bay (and ecological preserve), St. Croix, VI (1992): 982. The only known site where, in 1493, members of a Columbus party landed on what is now territory of the U.S.

San Antonio Missions, TX (1978): 826. Four of finest Spanish missions in U.S., 18th-cent. irrigation system.

San Francisco Maritime, CA (1988): 50. Artifacts, photographs, and historic vessels related to development of the Pacific Coast.

San Juan Island, WA (1966): 2,072. Commemorates peaceful relations between the U.S., Canada, and Great Britain since the 1872 boundary disputes.

Saratoga, NY (1938): 3,394. Scene of a major 1777 battle that became a turning point in the American Revolution.

Sitka, AK (1910/1972): 112. Scene of last major resistance of the Tlingit Indians to the Russians, 1804.

Tumacacori, AZ (1908/1990): 360. Historic Spanish mission building stands near site first visited by Father Kino in 1691.

Valley Forge, PA (1976): 3,466. Continental Army campsite in 1777-78 winter.

War in the Pacific, GU (1978): 2,037. Seven distinct units illustrating the Pacific theater of WWII. Limited federal facilities.

Women's Rights, NY (1980): 7. Seneca Falls site where Lucretia Mott, Elizabeth Cady Stanton organized movement in 1848.

National Battlefields/Parks/Sites

Antietam, MD (1890/1978): 3,230. Battle here ended first Confederate invasion of North, Sept. 17, 1862.

Big Hole, MT (1910/1963): 1,011. Site of major battle with Nez Perce Indians, Aug. 9-10, 1877.

Brices Cross Roads, MS (1929): 1. Site of the Confederate victory, June 10, 1864.

Cowpens, SC (1929/1972): 842. American Revolution battlefield, Jan. 17, 1781.

Fort Donelson, TN-KY (1928/1985): 1,007. Site of first major Union victory, Feb. 14-16, 1862.

Fort Necessity, PA (1931/1961): 903. Site of first battle of French and Indian War, July 3, 1754.

Kennesaw Mountain, GA (1917/1935): 2,853. Site of major battle of Atlanta campaign in Civil War.

Manassas, VA (1940): 5,073. Scene of two battles in Civil War, 1861 and 1862.

Monocacy, MD (1934/1976): 1,647. Civil War battle in defense of Washington, DC, fought here, July 9, 1864.

Moores Creek, NC (1926/1980): 88. Feb. 27, 1776, battle between Patriots and Loyalists commemorated here.

Petersburg, VA (1926/1962): 2,740. Scene of 10-month Union campaigns, 1864-65.

Richmond, VA (1936): 7,131. Site of battles defending Confederate capital.

River Raisin National Battlefield Park, MI (2010): 40. Site of major battles of War of 1812.

Stones River, TN (1927/1960): 709. Scene of battle that began federal offensive to trisect Confederacy, Dec. 31, 1862-Jan. 2, 1863.

Tupelo, MS (1929/1961): 1. Site of crucial battle over Union General Sherman's supply line, July 14-15, 1865.

Wilson's Creek, MO (1960/1970): 2,369. Scene of Civil War battle for control of Missouri, Aug. 10, 1861.

National Military Parks

Chickamauga and Chattanooga, GA-TN (1890): 9,036. Site where Gen. Sherman and Union armies gained control of TN, 1863.

Fredericksburg and Spotsylvania County, VA (1927/1933): 8,382. Sites of several major Civil War battles and campaigns.

Gettysburg, PA (1895/1933): 5,989. Site of decisive Confederate defeat in North, July 1863, and of Gettysburg Address.

Guilford Courthouse, NC (1917/1933): 243. American Revolution battle site.

Horseshoe Bend, AL (1956): 2,040. On Tallapoosa River, where Gen. Andrew Jackson's forces broke the power of the Upper Creek Indian Confederacy on Mar. 27, 1814.

Kings Mountain, SC (1931/1933): 3,945. Site of American Revolution battle, fought on Oct. 7, 1780.

Pea Ridge, AR (1956): 4,300. Scene of Civil War battle, fought Mar. 7-8, 1862.

Shiloh, TN (1894/1933): 5,964. Major Civil War battle site; includes some well-preserved Indian burial mounds.

Vicksburg, MS (1899/1933): 1,795. Union victory gave North control of the Mississippi and split the Confederate forces.

National Memorials

Arkansas Post, AR (1960): 758. First permanent French settlement in the lower Mississippi River valley.

Arlington House, The Robert E. Lee Memorial, VA (1925/1972): 28. Lee's home overlooking the Potomac River.

Chamizal, El Paso, TX (1966/1974): 55. Commemorates 1963 settlement of 99-year border dispute with Mexico.

Coronado, AZ (1941/1952): 4,750. Commemorates first European exploration of the Southwest.

De Soto, FL (1948): 30. Commemorates 16th-cent. Spanish explorations.

Federal Hall, New York, NY (1939/1955): 0.45. First seat of U.S. government under the Constitution.

Flight 93, Shanksville, PA (2002): 2,262. Commemorates the passengers and crew of Flight 93, who died thwarting an attack on Sept. 11, 2001. Permanent memorial expected for completion in 2011.

Fort Caroline, FL (1950): 138. On St. Johns River, overlooks site of a former French Huguenot colony.

Franklin Delano Roosevelt, DC (1982): 8. Statues of Pres. Roosevelt and Eleanor Roosevelt; waterfalls and gardens.

General Grant, NY (1958): 0.76. Tomb of Ulysses Grant and wife.

Hamilton Grange, NY (1962): 1. Home of Alexander Hamilton.

Jefferson National Expansion, MO (1935): 193. Commemorates westward expansion.

Johnstown Flood, PA (1964): 178. Commemorates 1889 flood.

Korean War Veterans, DC (1986): 2. Dedicated in 1995; honors those who served in the Korean War.

Lincoln Boyhood, IN (1962): 200. Site of Lincoln cabin, Lincoln's boyhood home, and grave site of Lincoln's mother.

Lincoln Memorial, DC (1911/1933): 107. Marble statue of the 16th U.S. president.

Lyndon Baines Johnson Memorial Grove on the Potomac, DC (1973): 17. Overlooks the Potomac R.; vista of the Capitol.

Mount Rushmore, SD (1925): 1,278. World-famous sculpture of 4 presidents: Washington, Jefferson, Lincoln, T. Roosevelt.

Perry's Victory and International Peace Memorial, Put-in-Bay, OH (1936/1972): 25. The world's most massive Doric column, constructed 1912-15, promotes pursuit of peace through arbitration and disarmament.

Port Chicago Naval Magazine, Danville, CA (2009): 5. 1944 munitions ship explosion killed 320 men.

Roger Williams, Providence, RI (1965): 5. Memorial to founder of Rhode Island.

Thaddeus Kosciuszko, Philadelphia, PA (1972): 0.02. Memorial to Polish hero of American Revolution.

Theodore Roosevelt Island, DC (1932/1933): 89. Statue of Roosevelt in wooded island sanctuary.

Thomas Jefferson, DC (1934): 18. Statue of Jefferson in an inscribed circular, colonnaded structure.

Vietnam Veterans, DC (1980): 2. Black granite wall inscribed with names of those missing or killed in action in Vietnam War.

Washington Monument, DC (1848/1933): 106. Obelisk honoring the first U.S. president.

World War II, DC (1994/2004): 7. Oval plaza with central pool commemorating those who fought and died.

Wright Brothers, NC (1927/1953): 428. Site of first powered flight.

National Historic Sites

Allegheny Portage Railroad, PA (1964): 1,287. Linked the Pennsylvania Canal system and the West.

Andersonville, GA (1970): 515. Noted Civil War prisoner-of-war camp.

Andrew Johnson, Greeneville, TN (1935/1963): 17. Two homes and the tailor shop of the 17th U.S. president.

Bent's Old Fort, CO (1960): 799. Replica of S. Plains outpost.

Boston African-American, MA (1980): 0.59. Pre-Civil War black-owned structures.

Brown v. Board of Education, KS (1992): 2. Commemorates the landmark 1954 U.S. Supreme Court decision, which ended legal segregation in schools.

Carl Sandburg Home, Flat Rock, NC (1968): 264.

Carter G. Woodson Home, DC (2006): 0.15.

Charles Pinckney, SC (1988): 28. Statesman's farm. Pinckney was a principal author and signer of the Constitution.

Christiansted, St. Croix, VI (1952/1961): 27. Commemorates Danish colony.

Clara Barton, Glen Echo, MD (1974): 9. Home of founder of American Red Cross.

Edgar Allan Poe, Philadelphia, PA (1978/1980): 0.52. Writer's home, where he wrote short stories.

Eisenhower, Gettysburg, PA (1967): 690. Home of 34th president.

Eleanor Roosevelt, Hyde Park, NY (1977): 181. The former first lady's personal retreat.

Eugene O'Neill, Danville, CA (1976): 13. Playwright's home where he wrote his final plays, including *The Iceman Cometh.*

First Ladies, Canton, OH (2000): 0.33. Home of first lady Ida Sexton McKinley. Library now devoted to America's first ladies.

Ford's Theatre, DC (1866/1970): 0.30. Includes theater, now restored, where Lincoln was assassinated, house where he died, and Lincoln Museum.

Fort Bowie, AZ (1964): 999. Focal point of operations against Geronimo and the Apaches.

Fort Davis, TX (1961): 474. Frontier outpost in West Texas. Established to guard the San Antonio-El Paso Road.

Fort Laramie, WY (1938/1960): 833. Military post on Oregon Trail.

Fort Larned, KS (1964/1966): 718. Military post on Santa Fe Trail.

Fort Point, San Francisco, CA (1970): 29. West Coast fortification. Protected San Francisco during and after Civil War.

Fort Raleigh, NC (1941): 513. First attempted English settlement in North America.

Fort Scott, KS (1965/1978): 17. Commemorates U.S. frontier of 1840s and '50s. Was a major focal point of black troop activity and training during Civil War.

Fort Smith, AR-OK (1961): 75. One of the earliest U.S. posts in Missouri Territory, active 1817-90.

Fort Union Trading Post, MT-ND (1966): 444. Principal fur-trading post on upper Missouri, 1829-67.

Fort Vancouver, WA-OR (1948/1961): 194. Headquarters for Hudson's Bay Company in 1825. Early political seat.

Frederick Douglass, DC (1962/1988): 9. Home of famous black abolitionist, writer, and orator.

Frederick Law Olmsted, MA (1979): 7. Home of city planner, famous for designing Central Park in NYC.

Friendship Hill, PA (1978): 675. Home of Albert Gallatin, Jefferson's and Madison's secretary of treasury.

Golden Spike, UT (1957): 2,735. Commemorates completion of first transcontinental railroad in 1869.

Grant-Kohrs Ranch, MT (1972): 1,618. Ranch house owned by John Grant, a 19th-cent. range-cattle industry pioneer.

Hampton, MD (1948): 62. 18th-cent. Georgian mansion, which in 1790 was the largest house in the U.S.

Harry S. Truman, MO (1983): 7. Home of pres. after 1919.

Herbert Hoover, West Branch, IA (1965): 187. Birthplace and boyhood home of 31st president.

Home of Franklin D. Roosevelt, Hyde Park, NY (1944): 813. FDR's birthplace, home, and "summer White House."

Hopewell Furnace, PA (1938/1985): 848. 19th-cent. iron-making village.

Hubbell Trading Post, AZ (1965): 160. Trading post that allowed interaction between the Navajo and white traders in the late 19th and 20th century. Still active today.

James A. Garfield, Mentor, OH (1980): 8. Home of 20th president. Site of his front-porch campaign.

Jimmy Carter, Plains, GA (1987): 72. Birthplace and home of 39th president.

John Fitzgerald Kennedy, Brookline, MA (1967): 0.09. Birthplace and childhood home of 35th president.

John Muir, Martinez, CA (1964): 345. Home of Sierra Club founder and "Father of the National Park Service."

Knife River Indian Villages, ND (1974): 1,758. Remnants of villages last occupied by Hidatsa and Mandan Indians.

Lincoln Home, Springfield, IL (1971): 12. Lincoln's residence at the time he was elected 16th president, 1860.

Little Rock Central High School, AR (1998): 27. Commemorates 1957 desegregation during which federal troops had to be called in to protect 9 black students.

Longfellow House–Washington's Headquarters, Cambridge, MA (1972): 2. Poet's home, 1837-82; Washington's headquarters during Boston siege, 1775-76.

Maggie L. Walker, VA (1978): 1. Richmond home of black leader and first female bank president, daughter of a former slave.

Manzanar, Lone Pine, CA (1992): 814. Commemorates Manzanar War Relocation Ctr., a Japanese-American internment camp during WWII.

Martin Luther King Jr., Atlanta, GA (1980): 39. Birthplace, grave, church of the civil rights leader.

Martin Van Buren, NY (1974): 40. Lindenwald, home of 8th president, near Kinderhook.

Mary McLeod Bethune Council House, DC (1982/1991): 0.07. Commemorates Bethune's leadership in the black women's movement.

Minidoka, ID (2008): 201. WWII Japanese internment center.

Minuteman Missile, SD (1999): 15. Missile launch facilities dating back to the Cold War era.

Nicodemus, KS (1996): 5. Only remaining Western town established by African Americans during Reconstruction.

Ninety Six, SC (1976): 1,022. Colonial trading village and the site of Gen. Nathanael Greene's siege on Loyalist-held fort in 1781.

Pennsylvania Avenue, DC (1965): 0.26. Includes area between Capitol and White House, encompassing the U.S. Navy Memorial, Freedom Plaza, Old Post Office Pavilion, and other sites.

President William Jefferson Clinton Birthplace Home, Hope, AR (2010): 1. Birthplace and early home of 42nd president.

Puukohola Heiau, HI (1972): 86. Ruins of temple built by King Kamehameha, first king of united Hawaiian islands.

Sagamore Hill, Oyster Bay, NY (1962): 83. Home of Pres. Theodore Roosevelt from 1885 until his death in 1919.

Saint-Gaudens, Cornish, NH (1964): 148. Home, studio, and gardens of American sculptor Augustus Saint-Gaudens.

Saint Paul's Church, New York, NY (1943): 6. Site associated with John Peter Zenger's "freedom of press" trial.

Salem Maritime, MA (1938): 9. Major fishing and whaling port famous for 1692 witchcraft trials.

San Juan, PR (1949): 75. 16th-cent. Spanish fortifications.

Sand Creek Massacre, CO (2000): 12,583. Site where more than 160 Cheyenne and Arapaho Indians were killed by U.S. soldiers in 1864.

Saugus Iron Works, MA (1974): 9. Reconstructed 17th-cent. colonial ironworks.

Springfield Armory, MA (1974): 55. Small-arms manufacturing center for nearly 200 years.

Steamtown, PA (1986): 62. Rail yard, roadhouse, repair shops of former Delaware, Lackawanna & Western Railroad.

Theodore Roosevelt Birthplace, New York, NY (1962): 0.11. Reconstructed brownstone where the president was born.

Theodore Roosevelt Inaugural, Buffalo, NY (1966): 1. Wilcox House, where he took oath of office, 1901.

Thomas Stone, Port Tobacco, MD (1978): 328. Home of signer of Declaration of Independence.

Tuskegee Airmen, AL (1998): 90. Airfield where pilots of all-black air corps unit of WWII received flight training.

Tuskegee Institute, AL (1974): 58. College founded by Booker T. Washington in 1881 for blacks.

Ulysses S. Grant, St. Louis Co., MO (1989): 10. Home of Grant during pre-Civil War years.

Vanderbilt Mansion, Hyde Park, NY (1940): 212. Mansion of 19th-cent. financier.

Washita Battlefield, OK (1996): 315. Scene of Nov. 27, 1868, battle between Plains tribes and the U.S. army.

Weir Farm, Wilton, CT (1990): 74. Home and studio of American impressionist painter J. Alden Weir.

Whitman Mission, WA (1936/1963): 139. Site of Protestant Missionaries to the Cayuse Indians during the mid-19th cent.

William Howard Taft, Cincinnati, OH (1969): 3.64. Birthplace and early home of the 27th president.

National Monuments

Name	State	Year[1]	Acreage
African Burial Ground	NY	2006	0.35
Agate Fossil Beds	NE	1965	3,058
Alibates Flint Quarries	TX	1965	1,371
Aniakchak[2]	AK	1978	137,176
Aztec Ruins	NM	1923	318
Bandelier	NM	1916	33,677
Booker T. Washington	VA	1956	239
Buck Island Reef	VI	1961	19,015
Cabrillo	CA	1913	160
Canyon de Chelly	AZ	1931	83,840
Cape Krusenstern[3]	AK	1978	649,085
Capulin Volcano	NM	1916	793
Casa Grande Ruins	AZ	1889	473
Castillo de San Marcos	FL	1924	19
Castle Clinton	NY	1946	1
Cedar Breaks	UT	1933	6,155
Chiricahua	AZ	1924	11,985
Colorado	CO	1911	20,534
Craters of the Moon	ID	1924	53,571
Devils Postpile	CA	1911	798
Devils Tower	WY	1906	1,347
Dinosaur	CO-UT	1915	210,278
Effigy Mounds	IA	1949	2,526
El Malpais	NM	1987	114,277
El Morro	NM	1906	1,279
Florissant Fossil Beds	CO	1969	5,998
Fort Frederica	GA	1936	284
Fort Matanzas	FL	1924	300
Fort McHenry (and Historic Shrine)	MD	1925	43
Fort Pulaski	GA	1924	5,623
Fort Stanwix	NY	1935	16
Fort Sumter	SC	1948	235
Fort Union	NM	1954	721
Fossil Butte	WY	1972	8,198
George Washington Birthplace	VA	1930	662
George Washington Carver	MO	1943	210
Gila Cliff Dwellings	NM	1907	533
Governors Island	NY	2001	23
Grand Portage	MN	1951	710
Hagerman Fossil Beds	ID	1988	4,351
Hohokam Pima[4]	AZ	1972	1,690
Homestead NM of America	NE	1936	211
Hovenweep	CO-UT	1923	785
Jewel Cave	SD	1908	1,274
John Day Fossil Beds	OR	1974	13,944
Lava Beds	CA	1925	46,560
Little Bighorn Battlefield	MT	1879	765
Montezuma Castle	AZ	1906	859
Muir Woods	CA	1908	554
Natural Bridges	UT	1908	7,636
Navajo	AZ	1909	360
Ocmulgee	GA	1934	702
Oregon Caves	OR	1909	488
Organ Pipe Cactus	AZ	1937	330,689
Papahanaumokuakea Marine	HI	2006	88,190,080
Petroglyph	NM	1990	7,533
Pinnacles	CA	1908	26,523
Pipe Spring	AZ	1923	40
Pipestone	MN	1937	282
Poverty Point[2]	LA	1988	911
Rainbow Bridge[3]	UT	1910	160
Russell Cave	AL	1961	310
Salinas Pueblo Missions	NM	1909	1,071
Scotts Bluff	NE	1919	3,005
Statue of Liberty	NJ-NY	1924	61
Sunset Crater Volcano	AZ	1930	3,040
Timpanogos Cave	UT	1922	250
Tonto	AZ	1907	1,120
Tuzigoot	AZ	1939	812
Virgin Islands Coral Reef	VI	2001	12,708
Walnut Canyon	AZ	1915	3,529
White Sands	NM	1933	143,733
World War II Valor in the Pacific	HI-CA	2008	59
Wupatki	AZ	1924	35,422
Yucca House[2]	CO	1919	34

National Preserves

Name	State	Year[1]	Acreage
Aniakchak	AK	1978	464,118
Bering Land Bridge	AK	1978	2,697,391
Big Cypress	FL	1974	720,565
Big Thicket	TX	1974	106,305
Craters of the Moon	ID	2002	410,733
Denali	AK	1917	4,740,911
Gates of the Arctic	AK	1978	7,523,897
Glacier Bay	AK	1925	58,406
Great Sand Dunes	CO	2000	41,686
Katmai	AK	1918	418,699
Lake Clark	AK	1978	1,410,293
Little River Canyon[3]	AL	1992	13,633

Name	State	Year[1]	Acreage
Mojave	CA	1994	1,536,561
Noatak	AK	1978	6,569,904
Tallgrass Prairie	KS	1996	10,894
Timucuan Ecological and Historic	FL	1988	46,301
Wrangell-St. Elias	AK	1978	4,852,652
Yukon-Charley Rivers[3]	AK	1978	2,526,512

National Seashores

Name	State	Year[1]	Acreage
Assateague Island	MD-VA	1965	39,727
Canaveral	FL	1975	57,662
Cape Cod	MA	1961	43,609
Cape Hatteras	NC	1937	30,351
Cape Lookout	NC	1966	28,243
Cumberland Island	GA	1972	36,347
Fire Island	NY	1964	19,580
Gulf Islands	FL-MS	1971	137,989
Padre Island	TX	1962	130,434
Point Reyes	CA	1962	71,070

National Parkways

Name	State	Year[1]	Acreage
Blue Ridge	NC-VA	1933	95,164
George Washington Memorial	VA-MD-DC	1930	6,997
John D. Rockefeller Jr. Mem.	WY	1972	23,777
Natchez Trace	MS-AL-TN	1938	52,316

National Lakeshores

Name	State	Year[1]	Acreage
Apostle Islands	WI	1970	69,372
Indiana Dunes	IN	1966	15,096
Pictured Rocks	MI	1966	73,236
Sleeping Bear Dunes	MI	1970	71,291

National Reserves

Name	State	Year[1]	Acreage
City of Rocks	ID	1988	14,407
Ebey's Landing Historical	WA	1978	19,333

National Rivers

Name	State	Year[1]	Acreage
Big South Fork (and Rec. Area)	KY-TN	1976	125,310
Buffalo	AR	1972	94,293
Mississippi (and Rec. Area)	MN	1988	53,775
New River Gorge	WV	1978	72,186
Ozark Riverways	MO	1964	80,785

National Wild and Scenic Rivers

Name	State	Year[1]	Acreage
Alagnak Wild	AK	1980	30,665
Bluestone Scenic[2]	WV	1978	4,310
Delaware Scenic	NY-NJ-PA	1978	1,973
Great Egg Harbor Scenic/Rec.	NJ	1992	43,311
Missouri Recreational	NE-SD	1991	34,159
Niobrara Scenic	NE	1991	23,074
Obed Wild and Scenic	TN	1976	5,073
Rio Grande Wild and Scenic[3]	TX	1978	9,600
Saint Croix Riverway	MN-WI	1968	67,469
Upper Delaware Scenic/Recreational	NY-PA	1978	75,000

National Recreation Areas

Name	State	Year[1]	Acreage
Amistad	TX	1965	58,500
Bighorn Canyon	MT-WY	1966	120,296
Boston Harbor Islands	MA	1996	1,482
Chattahoochee River	GA	1978	9,886
Chickasaw	OK	1902	9,899
Curecanti	CO	1965	41,972
Delaware Water Gap	NJ-PA	1965	66,741
Gateway	NJ-NY	1972	26,607
Gauley River[3]	WV	1988	11,560
Glen Canyon	AZ-UT	1958	1,254,117
Golden Gate	CA	1972	80,036
Lake Chelan	WA	1968	61,947
Lake Mead	AZ-NV	1936	1,495,664
Lake Meredith	TX	1965	44,978
Lake Roosevelt[5]	WA	1946	100,390
Ross Lake	WA	1968	117,575
Santa Monica Mountains[3]	CA	1978	156,670
Whiskeytown-Shasta-Trinity	CA	1965	42,503

Other Designations

Name	State	Year[1]	Acreage
Catoctin Mountain	MD	1954	5,874
Constitution Gardens	DC	1974	52
Fort Washington	MD	1930	341
Greenbelt	MD	1950	1,175
National Capital	DC	1933	6,726
National Mall	DC	1933	146
Piscataway	MD	1961	4,626
Prince William Forest	VA	1948	16,084
Rock Creek	DC	1890	1,755
White House	DC	1933	18
Wolf Trap Park for Performing Arts	VA	1966	130

International Historic Site

Name	State	Year[1]	Acreage
Saint Croix Island[3]	ME	1949	6.5

National Scenic Trails

Name	State	Year[1]	Acreage
Appalachian	ME to GA	1968	236,715
Ice Age	WI	1980	1,000
Natchez Trace	MS-TN	1983	64
North Country	NY to ND	1980	3,200
Potomac Heritage	VA to PA	1983	520

(1) Year first designated. (2) No federal facilities. (3) Limited federal facilities. (4) Not open to the public. (5) Formerly Coulee Dam National Recreation Area.

UNITED STATES HISTORY

Chronology of Events

1492 Christopher Columbus and crew sighted land Oct. 12 in present-day Bahamas.

1513 Juan Ponce de León explored Florida coast.

1524 Giovanni da Verrazano led French expedition along coast from Carolina north to Nova Scotia; entered New York Harbor.

1526 San Miguel de Guadalupe, first European settlement in what became U.S. territory, was established in the summer off South Carolina coast; abandoned in Oct.

1539 Hernando de Soto landed in Florida May 28; crossed Mississippi River, 1541.

1540 Francisco Vásquez de Coronado explored Southwest north of Rio Grande. Hernando de Alarcón reached Colorado River; García López de Cárdenas reached Grand Canyon. Others explored California coast.

1562 First French colony in what became U.S. territory founded on Parris Island off South Carolina coast; abandoned, 1564.

1565 St. Augustine, FL, oldest continuously occupied European settlement in U.S., founded Sept. 8 by Pedro Menéndez de Avilés. Spain ceded settlement to U.S. in 1821.

1579 Sir Francis Drake entered San Francisco Bay and claimed region for Britain.

1585 First English colony in America, sponsored by Sir Walter Raleigh, founded on Roanoke Island, off North Carolina coast; colony failed.

1587 Second colony attempted on Roanoke Island. Virginia Dare of colony became first English infant born in the New World. Settlers of second colony found to have vanished, 1590.

1607 Capt. John Smith and 105 cavaliers in 3 ships landed on Virginia coast, started Jamestown, first permanent English settlement in New World.

1609 Henry Hudson, English explorer of Northwest Passage, employed by Dutch, sailed into New York Harbor in Sept. and up Hudson to Albany. Samuel de Champlain explored Lake Champlain, to the north. Spaniards settled Santa Fe, NM.

1619 House of Burgesses, first representative assembly in New World, elected July 30 at Jamestown, VA. First black laborers—indentured servants—in English North American colonies, brought by Dutch to Jamestown in Aug. Chattel slavery legally recognized, 1650.

1620 Pilgrims, Puritan separatists, left Plymouth, England, Sept. 16 on *Mayflower*; reached Cape Cod Nov. 19; 103 passengers landed at Plymouth, Dec. 26. Mayflower Compact, signed Nov. 11, was agreement to form a self-government. Half of colony died during harsh winter.

1620: Pilgrims and other colonists sign the Mayflower Compact to form a "civil body politic."

1624 Dutch colonies started in Albany and in New York area, where New Netherland was established in May.

1626 Peter Minuit bought Manhattan for Dutch West India Co. from Manahatta Indians during summer for goods valued at $24; named island New Amsterdam.

1630 Settlement of Boston established by Massachusetts colonists led by John Winthrop; Winthrop began *The History of New England*. William Bradford, a governor of Plymouth Colony, began his chronicle *History of Plymouth Plantation (1620-1647)*, first published in entirety in 1856.

1634 Maryland founded as Catholic colony under charter to Lord Baltimore. Act of Toleration passed 1649 provided for religious tolerance.

1635 Boston Latin School, oldest public school in continuous existence in U.S., founded Apr. 23.

1636 Roger Williams founded Providence, RI, in June, as a democratically ruled colony with separation of church and state. Charter granted, 1644. Harvard College founded; oldest institution of higher learning in U.S.

1640 First book printed in America, the so-called *Bay Psalm Book*.

1647 Liberal constitution drafted in Rhode Island. First law in America providing for free compulsory basic education enacted in Massachusetts.

1660 British Parliament passed first Navigation Act Dec. 1, regulating colonial commerce to suit English needs.

1661 A version of the New Testament translated into Algonquian became the first Bible printed in the colonies.

1664 British troops Sept. 8 seized New Netherland from Dutch. Charles II granted New Netherland and city of New Amsterdam to brother, Duke of York; both renamed New York. Dutch recaptured colony 1673, but ceded it to Britain Nov. 10, 1674.

1670 Charles Town, SC, founded by English colonists in Apr.

1673 Regular mail service on horseback instituted Jan. 1 between New York and Boston. Jacques Marquette and Louis Jolliet reached the upper Mississippi and traveled down it.

1674 Future Salem witch trial judge Samuel Sewall began renowned diary covering events through 1729.

1676 Bloody Indian war in New England ended Aug. 12. King Philip, Wampanoag chief, and Narragansett Indians killed. Nathaniel Bacon led planters against autocratic British Gov. Sir William Berkeley, burned Jamestown, VA, Sept. 19. Rebellion collapsed when Bacon died; 23 followers executed.

1678 A book of poetry by Anne Bradstreet (first published in Britain) revised and expanded for posthumous publication in Massachusetts. Considered first female poet in American colonies.

1679 Fire destroyed 150 houses in Boston. City imported first fire engines from England.

1681 John Bunyan's *The Pilgrim's Progress* published in America; became best seller.

1682 René-Robert Cavelier, Sieur de La Salle, claimed lower Mississippi River country for France and called it Louisiana Apr. 9. Had French outposts built in Illinois and Texas, 1684. Killed during mutiny, 1687. Spanish colonists became the first Europeans to settle Texas, at site of present-day El Paso.

1683 William Penn signed treaty with Delaware Indians Apr. 23 and made payment for Pennsylvania lands. The first German colonists in America settled near Philadelphia.

1689 New York's English colonial governor, Sir Edmund Andros, resigned after armed uprising in Boston on Apr. 18.

1690 First colonial newspaper, *Publick Occurrences*, published by Benjamin Harris but promptly shut down for lack of official permission. Harris also published *New England*

Primer for use as elementary school textbook. Large-scale **whaling** operations began in Nantucket, MA.

1692 Witchcraft hysteria began in Salem Village (now Danvers), MA; 20 men and women convicted of witchcraft executed by special court.

1697 *The Essays* of **Sir Francis Bacon**, first published in England in 1597, was published in America; it became a best seller.

1699 Former privateer Capt. **William Kidd** arrested and sent to England; hanged for piracy, 1701. French settlements made in **Mississippi, Louisiana.**

1702 Legislation enacted making **Church of England** the established church in Maryland.

1704 Indians attacked Deerfield, MA, Feb. 28-29; killed 40, carried off 100. *Boston News Letter*, **first regular newspaper**, started by postmaster John Campbell.

1710 British-colonial troops captured French fort, Port Royal, Nova Scotia, in **Queen Anne's War**, 1702-13. France yielded Nova Scotia by treaty, 1713.

1712 Slaves revolted in New York Apr. 6; 21 were executed. Second uprising, 1741; 13 slaves hanged, 13 burned, 71 deported.

1716 First theater in colonies opened in Williamsburg, VA.

1726 Great Awakening, general revival of evangelical religion, began in colonies.

1731 America's **first circulating library** founded in Philadelphia by Benjamin Franklin.

1732 Benjamin Franklin published the **first *Poor Richard's Almanack***; published annually until 1757. Georgia, last of 13 colonies, chartered.

1733 Influenza epidemic swept through New York City and Philadelphia.

1735 Editor **John Peter Zenger** was acquitted of libel Aug. 5 in New York after criticizing the British governor's conduct in office.

1739 A series of **slave uprisings** put down in South Carolina.

1741 Famous sermon "Sinners in the Hands of an Angry God," delivered July 8 at Enfield, MA, by Jonathan Edwards, one of the most important preachers in the **Great Awakening** religious revival. Danish navigator **Vitus Bering**, commanding Russian expedition, reached Alaska.

1744 King George's War pitted British and colonials versus French. Colonials captured Louisbourg, Cape Breton Isl., Nova Scotia, June 17, 1745. Returned to France 1748 by Treaty of Aix-la-Chapelle.

1752 Benjamin Franklin, flying kite in thunderstorm, proved lightning is electricity, June 15; invented lightning rod. **Liberty Bell**, cast in England, was delivered to Pennsylvania.

1754 French and Indian War began with Ft. Necessity campaign in Pennsylvania. Skirmish May 28, battle at fort July 3-4. British moved Acadian French from Nova Scotia to Louisiana Oct. 8, 1755. British captured Québec Sept. 18, 1759, in battles in which French Gen. Joseph de Montcalm and British Gen. James Wolfe were killed. Peace pact signed Feb. 10, 1763. French lost Canada and Midwest. Delegates from 7 colonies to New York for **Albany Congress**, July 19, approved plan of union by Benjamin Franklin; plan rejected by the colonies.

1757 First streetlights appeared in Philadelphia.

1764 Sugar Act, Apr. 5, placed duties on lumber, foodstuffs in colonies. First law passed by Parliament to specifically raise revenue from colonies, alleviate French and Indian War debts. British enforced this act, unlike with **Molasses Act of 1733.**

1765 Stamp Act, enacted by Parliament Mar. 22, required revenue stamps to help fund royal troops. Nine colonies, at Stamp Act Congress in New York Oct. 7-25, adopted Declaration of Rights. Stamp Act repealed Mar. 17, 1766. **Quartering Act**, requiring colonists to house British troops, went into effect Mar. 24.

1767 Townshend Acts levied taxes on glass, painter's lead, paper, and tea. In 1770 all duties except on tea were repealed.

1770 British troops fired Mar. 5 into Boston mob, killed 5 including **Crispus Attucks**, a black man, reportedly leader of group; later called **Boston Massacre.**

1773 East India Co. tea ships turned back at Boston, New York, and Philadelphia in May. Cargo ship burned at Annapolis, Oct. 14; cargo thrown overboard at **Boston Tea Party,**

1765: Demonstrations erupt in Boston in response to the Stamp Act proclamations.

Dec. 16, to protest the tea tax. **First museum** in the colonies was officially established in Charleston, SC; later named the Charleston Museum.

1774 "Intolerable Acts" of Parliament curtailed Massachusetts self-rule; barred use of Boston Harbor until tea was paid for. **First Continental Congress** held in Philadelphia Sept. 5-Oct. 26; called for civil disobedience against British. Rhode Island **abolished slavery.**

1775 Patrick Henry addressed Virginia convention, Mar. 23, said, "Give me liberty or give me death!" **Paul Revere, William Dawes**, and Dr. **Samuel Prescott**, Apr. 18, rode to alert patriots that British were on their way to Concord to destroy arms. At **Lexington**, MA, Apr. 19, Minutemen lost 8. On return from **Concord**, British suffered 273 casualties. Col. Ethan Allen (joined by Col. Benedict Arnold) captured **Ft. Ticonderoga** in New York, May 10, also Crown Point. Colonials headed for **Bunker Hill**, fortified Breed's Hill, Charlestown, MA. Repulsed British under Gen. William Howe twice before retreating, June 17. Continental Congress June 15 named **George Washington** commander in chief. Established a postal system, July 26; Benjamin Franklin became the **first postmaster general.**

1776 Thomas Paine's *Common Sense*, famous pro-independence pamphlet, published Jan. 10; quickly sold some 100,000 copies. **France and Spain** agreed May 2 to provide arms to U.S. In Continental Congress June 7, Richard Henry Lee (VA) moved "that these united colonies are, and of right ought to be, free and independent states." Resolution adopted July 2. **Declaration of Independence** approved July 4, signed Aug. 2. Col. William Moultrie's batteries at **Charleston, SC**, repulsed British sea attack June 28. Washington lost **Battle of Long Island** Aug. 27; evacuated New York. **Nathan Hale** executed as spy by British Sept. 22. Brig. Gen. Arnold's **Lake Champlain** fleet was defeated at Valcour Oct. 11, but British returned to Canada. Howe failed to destroy Washington's army at White Plains, Oct. 28. Hessians captured Ft. Washington, Manhattan, and 3,000 men, Nov. 16; captured Ft. Lee, NJ, Nov. 20. Washington, in Pennsylvania, recrossed **Delaware River** Dec. 25-26, defeated Hessians at Trenton, NJ, Dec. 26.

1776: George Washington's army crosses the Delaware River to defeat Hessian forces in the Battle of Trenton.

1777 Washington defeated Lord Charles Cornwallis at **Princeton** Jan. 3. Continental Congress, June 14, authorized an **American flag**, the Stars and Stripes. Maj. Gen. John Burgoyne's force of 8,000 from Canada, captured **Ft. Ticonderoga**, July 6. Americans beat back Burgoyne at Bemis Heights, Oct. 7, cut off British escape route. Burgoyne surrendered 5,000 men at Saratoga, NY, Oct. 17. **Articles of Confederation** adopted by Continental Congress, Nov. 15; took effect Mar. 1, 1781.

1778 France signed treaty of aid with U.S. Feb. 6. Sent fleet; British evacuated Philadelphia, June 18.

1779 George Rogers Clark took Ft. Vincennes in what is now Indiana in Feb. **John Paul Jones** on the *Bonhomme Richard* defeated *Serapis* in British North Sea waters, Sept. 23.

1780 Charleston, SC, fell to the British May 12, but Loyalists were defeated in battle of **Kings Mountain**, NC, Oct. 7 in what Thomas Jefferson called "the turn of the tide of success." **Benedict Arnold** found to be a traitor Sept. 23. Arnold escaped, made brigadier general in British army.

1781 Bank of North America, **first commercial bank**, incorporated May 26. Cornwallis retired to **Yorktown, VA**. Adm. Francois Joseph de Grasse landed 3,000 French and stopped British fleet in **Hampton Roads**. Washington and Jean Baptiste de Rochambeau joined forces, arrived near Williamsburg, Sept. 26. Siege of Cornwallis began, Oct. 6; **Cornwallis surrendered** Oct. 19.

1782 New British cabinet agreed in Mar. to **recognize U.S. independence**. Preliminary agreement signed in Paris, Nov. 30. Use of **scarlet letter A**, sewn on clothing or branded on skin of adulterers, discontinued in New England.

1783 Massachusetts Supreme Court decision in final Quock Walker trial **legally ended slavery**. Newspapers typically published weekly; **first regular daily newspaper**, *Pennsylvania Evening Post*, went on sale in Philadelphia, May 30. Britain, U.S. signed **Paris peace treaty**, Sept. 3, recognizing American independence; Congress ratified it Jan. 14, 1784. **Washington ordered army disbanded** Nov. 3, bade farewell to his officers at Fraunces Tavern, New York City, Dec. 4.

1784 Thomas Jefferson's proposal to **ban slavery in new territories** after 1802 was narrowly defeated, Mar. 1.

1785 Regular stagecoach routes established between Albany, New York City, and Philadelphia.

1786 Delegates from 5 states at Annapolis, MD, Sept. 11-14 asked Congress to call a **constitutional convention**.

1787 Shays's Rebellion of debt-ridden farmers in Massachusetts failed, Jan. 25. **Constitutional convention** opened in Philadelphia, May 25, with Washington presiding. Constitution accepted by delegates, Sept. 17; Delaware became first state to ratify it, Dec. 7; Pennsylvania and New Jersey followed. **Northwest Ordinance** adopted July 13 by Continental Congress for Northwest Territory, north of Ohio River, west of New York; made rules for statehood. Guaranteed freedom of religion, support for schools, no slavery. *Federalist Papers* first appeared in *NY Independent Journal*.

1788 A large fire in New Orleans, then a Spanish territory, destroyed much of the city, Mar. 21. **Constitution adopted** June 21 after being ratified by the requisite ninth state (New Hampshire); also ratified by **Georgia, Connecticut, Massachusetts, Maryland, South Carolina, Virginia**, and **New York** throughout the year. **First U.S. senators elected** Sept. 30, from Pennsylvania.

1789 George Washington chosen president by all electors voting (73 eligible, 69 voting, 4 absent); **John Adams**, vice president, got 34 votes. **First Congress** met at Federal Hall, New York City, and declared Constitution in effect, Mar. 4; Washington inaugurated there Apr. 30; **first inaugural ball** held May 7. U.S. **State Dept.** established by Congress July 27. (Thomas Jefferson installed as first secretary of state Feb. 1790.) **War Dept.** created Aug. 7, with Henry Knox as secretary; **Treasury Dept.** created Sept. 2, with Alexander Hamilton to be secretary. **Supreme Court** created by Federal Judiciary Act, Sept. 24; **John Jay** confirmed by Congress as **first Supreme Court chief justice**, Sept. 26.

1790 First Supreme Court session held Feb. 2 in New York City. Congress, Mar. 1, authorized decennial **U.S. census**. Collection of data took 18 months. **Naturalization Act** (2-year residency) passed Mar. 26. John Carroll consecrated as **first American Catholic bishop**, Aug. 15. Congress met in **Philadelphia**, new temporary capital, Dec. 6.

1791 Bill of Rights, submitted to states, Sept. 25, 1789, went into effect Dec. 15. First Bank of the United States, **first bank to be chartered by federal government**, established in Philadelphia.

1792 Coinage Act established **U.S. Mint** in Philadelphia, Apr. 2. Gen. **"Mad" Anthony Wayne** made commander in Ohio-Indiana area, trained American Legion, established string of forts. Routed Indians at Fallen Timbers on Maumee River, Aug. 20, 1794, checked British at Fort Miami, OH, same year. **White House** cornerstone laid Oct. 13.

1793 Washington inaugurated for second term, Mar. 4, having received 132 electoral votes; **John Adams** again became vice president, having received second highest total, 77. Washington declared **U.S. neutrality**, Apr. 22, in war between Britain and France. Eli Whitney invented **cotton gin**, reviving Southern slavery.

1794 Whiskey Rebellion, western Pennsylvania farmers protesting liquor tax of 1791, suppressed by federal militia in Sept. **Jay's Treaty**, controversial treaty with Britain negotiated by John Jay, signed Nov. 19, ratified June 24, 1795. This treaty intended to settle long-standing differences between U.S. and Britain.

1795 U.S. bought peace from **Algerian pirates** by paying $1 mil ransom for 115 seamen Sept. 5, followed by annual tributes. Gen. Wayne signed **Treaty of Greenville** with Indians, opening Northwest Territory to settlers. Univ. of North Carolina became **first operating state university**.

1796 Washington's **farewell address** as president delivered Sept. 17. Warned against permanent alliances with foreign powers, big public debt, large military establishment, and devices of "small, artful, enterprising minority."

1797 John Adams inaugurated as second president Mar. 4, having received 71 electoral votes; **Thomas Jefferson** became vice president, having received 68. U.S. frigate *United States* launched at Philadelphia, July 10; *Constellation* at Baltimore, Sept. 7; *Constitution* (Old Ironsides) at Boston, Sept. 20.

1798 Alien and Sedition Acts passed by Federalists June-July; intended to silence political opposition. **War with France** threatened over French raids on U.S. shipping and rejection of U.S. diplomats. Navy (45 ships) and 365 privateers captured 84 French ships. USS *Constellation* took French warship *Insurgente*, 1799. Napoleon stopped French raids after becoming first consul.

1800 Federal government moved to **Washington, DC**.

1801 John Marshall named Supreme Court chief justice, Jan. 20. **Thomas Jefferson**, who had received same number of electoral votes as Aaron Burr in 1800 election, won out over Burr in House vote reached Feb. 17; Burr named vice president. **Tripoli declared war** June 10 against U.S., which

1793: Eli Whitney patents the cotton gin; massive growth in U.S. cotton production and expansion of Southern slavery follows.

refused added tribute to commerce-raiding Arab corsairs. Land and naval campaigns forced Tripoli to negotiate peace, June 4, 1805. **Oldest U.S. art institution,** Pennsylvania Academy of Fine Arts, founded in Philadelphia.

1802 Congress established U.S. Military Academy at **West Point,** NY.

1803 Supreme Court, in *Marbury v. Madison,* overturned U.S. law for first time, Feb. 24. Napoleon sold all of Louisiana, stretching to Canadian border, to U.S. for $11,250,000 in bonds, plus $3,750,000 indemnities to American citizens with claims against France. U.S. took title Dec. 20. **Louisiana Purchase** doubled U.S. area.

1804 **Meriwether Lewis** and **William Clark** expedition ordered by Pres. Thomas Jefferson to explore what is now Northwest U.S. Started from St. Louis May 14; ended Sept. 23, 1806, back in St. Louis. Vice Pres. **Aaron Burr** shot Alexander Hamilton in duel July 11 in Weehawken, NJ; Hamilton died next day.

1805 U.S. Marines aided by Arab mercenaries, Apr. 27, captured Tripolitan port of Derna. Major victory in war against **Barbary pirates;** inspiration for "to the shores of Tripoli" in Marines Corps song.

1807 Robert Fulton made **first practical steamboat trip;** left New York City Aug. 17, reached Albany, 150 mi away, in 32 hrs. **Embargo Act** banned all trade with foreign countries, forbidding ships to set sail for foreign ports Dec. 22.

1808 **Slave importation outlawed.** Some 250,000 slaves were illegally imported 1808-60.

1810 **Third U.S. Census** found population of 7,239,814. The slave population was put at 1,191,364, and the population of all other non-white free persons at 186,446.

1811 Indiana Territory governor William Henry Harrison defeated Indians led by Tenskwatawa, called the Prophet, in **Battle of Tippecanoe,** Nov. 7. Construction began on **Cumberland Road** in Cumberland, MD; road became important route to West. About 400 **slaves revolted** in Louisiana, killing the son of a plantation owner and marching on New Orleans. The insurrection was suppressed; some 75 slaves killed.

1812 **War of 1812** had 3 main causes: Britain seized U.S. ships trading with France; Britain had seized 4,000 naturalized U.S. sailors by 1810; Britain armed Indians, who raided Western border. U.S. stopped trade with Europe 1807 and 1809. Trade with Britain only was stopped 1810. Unaware that Britain had raised blockade against France two days before, **Congress declared war** June 18. British took **Detroit** Aug. 16.

1813 Oliver H. Perry defeated British fleet at **Battle of Lake Erie,** Sept. 10. U.S. won **Battle of the Thames,** Ontario, Oct. 5, but failed in Canadian invasion attempts. York (Toronto) and Buffalo were burned.

1814 Troops under Andrew Jackson defeated Creek Indians led by Chief Weatherford at **Battle of Horseshoe Bend** in Alabama, Mar. 29, ending **Creek Indian War,** begun a year earlier. British landed in Maryland in Aug., defeated U.S. force Aug. 24, **burned Capitol and White House.** Maryland militia stopped British advance, Sept. 12. British bombardment

of Ft. McHenry, Baltimore, for 25 hours, Sept. 13-14, failed, inspiring **Francis Scott Key** to write the words to **"The Star-Spangled Banner."** U.S. won naval **Battle of Lake Champlain** Sept. 11. Peace treaty with Great Britain signed at Ghent, Dec. 24.

1815 Some 5,300 British, unaware of peace treaty, attacked U.S. entrenchments near **New Orleans,** Jan. 8. British had more than 2,000 casualties; Americans lost 71. U.S. flotilla finally ended attacks by **pirates** from Ottoman states of Algiers, Tunis, Tripoli.

1816 **Second Bank of the U.S.** chartered Apr. 10. The **American Colonization Society,** which sought to address slavery issue by transporting freed blacks to Africa, formed in Washington, DC, Dec. 1816-Jan. 1817.

1817 Thomas Hopkins Gallaudet established the **first free public school for the deaf** in Hartford, CT.

1818 Connecticut **expanded suffrage** among white male voters. Massachusetts followed suit in 1820, and New York in 1821, reducing or eliminating property qualifications.

1819 Spain ceded **Florida** to U.S. Feb. 22. American steamship *Savannah* made **first part-steam-powered, part-sail-powered crossing of Atlantic,** traveling from Savannah, GA, to Liverpool, England, in 29 days. **Washington Irving's** *Sketch Book* became best seller.

1820 **First organized immigration of blacks to Africa** from U.S. began with 86 free blacks sailing to Sierra Leone in Feb. Henry Clay's **Missouri Compromise** bill passed by Congress, Mar. 3. Slavery was allowed in Missouri but not west of the Mississippi River, north of 36° 30′ (the southern line of Missouri). Repealed 1854.

1821 Emma Willard founded Troy Female Seminary, **first U.S. women's college.** Stephen Austin established **first American community in Texas,** San Felipe de Austin. **James Fenimore Cooper's** *The Spy,* novel set during American Revolution, published and became a best seller.

1822 Tension between sports and academics surfaced when Yale College Pres. Timothy Dwight **banned a primitive form of football,** setting fines for violators.

1823 **Monroe Doctrine,** opposing European intervention in the Americas, enunciated by Pres. James Monroe Dec. 2. The **Hudson River School,** painters who focused on the beauties of nature, began to come to public attention.

1824 Pawtucket, RI, **weavers strike,** first such action by women workers. **Slavery abolished** in state of Illinois Aug. 2.

1825 After a deadlocked election, **John Quincy Adams** was elected president by the House, Feb. 9. **Erie Canal** opened; first boat left Buffalo Oct. 26, reached New York City Nov. 4. John Stevens, of Hoboken, NJ, built and operated **first experimental steam locomotive** in U.S.

1826 Thomas Jefferson and John Adams both died July 4. **James Fenimore Cooper's** *The Last · of the Mohicans* published.

1827 Massachusetts became first state to pass a law providing for **tax-supported public high schools.**

1828 Baltimore & Ohio, the **first U.S. passenger railroad,** began operations July 4. South Carolina Dec. 19 declared right of **state nullification of federal laws,** opposing the "Tariff of Abominations." **Noah Webster** published his *American Dictionary of the English Language.*

1829 **Andrew Jackson** inaugurated as president, Mar. 4.

1830 Famous **debate** Jan. 27 between Sen. **Daniel Webster** (MA) and Robert Hayne (SC), on state right to nullify federal law. **Mormon church** organized by Joseph Smith in Fayette, NY, Apr. 6. Pres. Jackson, May 28, signed **Indian Removal Act,** granting president authority to negotiate treaties whereby Indians living east of Mississippi R. gave up lands in exchange for lands in West.

1831 William Lloyd Garrison began **abolitionist newspaper** *The Liberator* Jan. 1. **Nat Turner,** black slave in Virginia, led local slave rebellion, starting Aug. 21; 57 whites killed. Troops called in, 100 slaves killed. Turner captured, tried, hanged Nov. 11.

1832 **Black Hawk War** in Illinois and Wisconsin Apr.-Sept. pushed Sauk and Fox Indians west across Mississippi.

1833 **American Anti-Slavery Society** founded in Philadelphia, Dec. 4. **Oberlin College** became **first to adopt coeducation** in U.S.

1835 Liberty Bell cracked July 8 while tolling death of Chief Justice John Marshall. **Seminole Indians** in Florida under Osceola began attacks Nov. 1, protesting forced removal. The unpopular war ended Aug. 14, 1842; most of the Indians sent to Oklahoma. **Texas** proclaimed right to secede from Mexico; **Sam Houston** put in command of Texas army, Nov. 2-4. **Gold** discovered on Cherokee land in Georgia. Indians forced to cede lands, Dec. 20, and to cross Mississippi.

1836 Texans besieged at **Alamo** in San Antonio by Mexicans under Santa Anna, Feb. 23-Mar. 6; entire garrison killed. Texas independence declared, Mar. 2. At San Jacinto Apr. 21, Sam Houston and Texans defeated Mexicans. **Ralph Waldo Emerson** published his first work, *Nature*, espousing his philosophy of **transcendentalism**. Marcus Whitman, H. H. Spaulding, and wives reached Fort Walla Walla on Columbia River, OR, **first white women to cross the Continental Divide**, in the Rocky Mountains.

1838 Cherokee Indians forced to walk **"Trail of Tears"** from southeast U.S. to area in present-day Oklahoma. At least 4,000—nearly one-fifth of Cherokee population—are estimated to have died.

1841 First emigrant wagon train bound for California, 47 persons, left Independence, MO, May 1, reached California Nov. 4. **Edgar Allan Poe** published one of the **first American detective stories**, *The Murders in the Rue Morgue*.

1842 Webster-Ashburton Treaty signed Aug. 9, fixing U.S.-Canada border in Maine and Minnesota. **First use of anesthetic** (sulfuric ether gas).

1843 More than 1,000 settlers left Independence, MO, for Oregon May 22, arriving in Oct. via **Oregon Trail**.

1844 First message over first telegraph line sent May 24 by inventor Samuel F. B. Morse from Washington to Baltimore: "What hath God wrought?"

1845 Congress **overrode a presidential veto for the first time**, Mar. 3, after Pres. John Tyler vetoed a tariff bill. Congress of **Texas voted for annexation** by U.S., July 4. Texas admitted to Union, Dec. 29. **Edgar Allan Poe**'s poem "The Raven" published.

1846 Mexican War began after Pres. James K. Polk ordered Gen. Zachary Taylor to seize disputed Texan land settled by Mexicans. After border clash, U.S. declared war May 13; Mexico declared war May 23. About 12,000 U.S. troops took Vera Cruz Mar. 27, 1847, and Mexico City Sept. 14, 1847. Treaty signed Feb. 2, 1848, ended war, and Mexico ceded claims to Texas, California, and other territory. Bear flag of **Republic of California** raised by American settlers at Sonoma, June 14. Treaty with Britain June 15 set **Oregon territory boundary** at 49th parallel (extension of existing line). Expansionists had used slogan "54° 40′ or fight." The term **"manifest destiny,"** coined by journalist in 1845, also came into play. **Mormons**, after violent clashes with settlers over polygamy, left Nauvoo, IL, for West under Brigham Young. They settled July 1847 at Salt Lake City, UT. Elias Howe invented **sewing machine**.

1847 First adhesive U.S. postage stamps—Benjamin Franklin 5¢, Washington 10¢—sold July 1. **Henry Wadsworth Longfellow**'s *Evangeline* published.

1848 Gold discovered Jan. 24 in California; 80,000 prospectors emigrated in 1849. **Lucretia Mott and Elizabeth Cady**

1838: Cherokee Indians are marched from their homes in southeast U.S. to present-day Oklahoma on the "Trail of Tears."

Stanton led Seneca Falls, NY, **Women's Rights Convention** July 19-20.

1850 Sen. Henry Clay's **Compromise of 1850** admitted California as 31st state Sept. 9, with slavery forbidden; made Utah and New Mexico territories; made **Fugitive Slave Law** more harsh; and ended District of Columbia slave trade. **Nathaniel Hawthorne**'s *The Scarlet Letter* published.

1851 Herman Melville's *Moby-Dick* published.

1852 Harriet Beecher Stowe's *Uncle Tom's Cabin* published.

1853 Japan receives Comm. Matthew C. Perry, July 14. He negotiated **treaty to open Japan** to U.S. ships. New York City hosted **first World's Fair** in the U.S., beginning July 14. **Stephen Foster** published "My Old Kentucky Home."

1854 Republican Party formed at Ripon, WI, Feb. 28. Opposed Kansas-Nebraska Act, which left issue of slavery to vote of settlers. Act became law May 30. Treaty ratified with Mexico Apr. 25, providing for **Gadsden Purchase** of a strip of land. **Henry David Thoreau**'s *Walden* published.

1855 First railroad train crossed Mississippi River on river's first bridge, between Rock Island, IL, and Davenport, IA, Apr. 21. **Walt Whitman**'s *Leaves of Grass* published.

1856 Republican Party's **first presidential nominee**, John C. Fremont, defeated. Abraham Lincoln made 50 speeches for him. Proslavery group sacked **Lawrence, KS**, May 21; abolitionist John Brown led antislavery contingent against Missourians at Osawatomie, KS, Aug. 30. **First U.S. kindergarten** opened in Watertown, WI.

1857 In **Dred Scott** case, which involved determination of constitutionality of already-repealed Missouri Compromise, Supreme Court decided Mar. 6 that slaves did not become free in a free state, and blacks were not and could not be citizens. **Currier & Ives**, firm of American lithographers, issued their first print.

1858 First Atlantic cable completed, by Cyrus W. Field Aug. 5. **Lincoln-Douglas debates** in Illinois, Aug. 21-Oct. 15.

1859 Edwin L. Drake drilled the **first commercially productive oil well** near Titusville, PA, Aug. 27. Abolitionist **John Brown**, with 21 men, seized U.S. armory at **Harpers Ferry**, WV, Oct. 16. U.S. Marines captured raiders, killing several. Brown was hanged for treason Dec. 2.

1860 Shoeworkers in Lynn, MA, went on strike Feb. 22. Within a week, strike spread to include 20,000 shoeworkers throughout New England in country's **largest strike to date**. **First Pony Express** between Sacramento, CA, and St. Joseph, MO, started Apr. 3. Republican **Abraham Lincoln** elected president Nov. 6 in 4-way race.

1861 Seven southern states set up **Confederate States of America** Feb. 8, with **Jefferson Davis** as president. **Civil War** began as Confederates fired on **Ft. Sumter** in Charleston, SC, Apr. 12. They captured it Apr. 14. Pres. Lincoln called for 75,000 volunteers Apr. 15. By May, 11 states had **seceded**. Lincoln blockaded Southern ports Apr. 19, cutting off vital exports and aid. Confederates repelled Union forces at first **Battle of Bull Run**, July 21. **First transcontinental telegraph line** put in operation.

1862 Union forces were victorious in Western campaigns, took New Orleans May 1. Battles in East were largely inconclusive despite heavy casualties. The **Battle of Antietam**, in western Maryland Sept. 17, was bloodiest one-day battle of war; each side lost more than 2,000 men. **Homestead Act**, which granted free farms to settlers, approved May 20. **Land Grant Act**, which provided for public land sale to benefit agricultural education, approved July 7. It eventually led to establishment of state university systems.

1863 Pres. Lincoln issued **Emancipation Proclamation** Jan. 1, freeing "all slaves in areas still in rebellion." Entire Mississippi River was in Union hands by July 4. Union forces won major victory at Gettysburg, PA, July 1-3. Pres. Lincoln gave his **Gettysburg Address** Nov. 19. Confederate forces under siege surrendered **Vicksburg, MS**, to Union forces under Gen. Ulysses S. Grant, July 4. About 1,000 were killed or wounded in **draft riots** in New York City; some blacks were hanged by mobs July 13-16. Pres. Lincoln declared **Thanksgiving** a national holiday.

1864 Gen. **William Tecumseh Sherman** marched through Georgia, taking Atlanta Sept. 1 and Savannah Dec. 22. **Sand**

1863: Pres. Abraham Lincoln's Gettysburg Address eloquently commemorates the sacrifice of thousands in fewer than 300 words.

Creek massacre of Cheyenne and Arapaho Indians Nov. 29. Soldiers drove Indians out of village; about 150 killed.

1865 Gen. **Robert E. Lee surrendered** 27,800 Confederate troops to Gen. Grant at Appomattox Court House in VA, Apr. 9. J. E. Johnston surrendered 31,200 to Sherman at Durham Station, NC, Apr. 18. Last rebel troops surrendered May 26. Pres. Lincoln shot Apr. 14 by **John Wilkes Booth** in Ford's Theater, Washington, DC. Died the following morning. Vice Pres. **Andrew Johnson** was sworn in as president. Booth was hunted down and fatally wounded, perhaps by his own hand, Apr. 26. Four co-conspirators were hanged July 7. **13th Amendment**, abolishing slavery, ratified Dec. 6.

1866 Congress took control of Southern **Reconstruction**, backed freedmen's rights in legislation vetoed by Johnson; veto overridden by Congress, Apr. 9. **Ku Klux Klan** formed secretly in South to terrorize blacks who voted. Disbanded 1869-71.

1867 Alaska sold to U.S. by Russia for $7.2 mil Mar. 30, through efforts of Sec. of State William H. Seward. Fraternal society the **Grange** was organized Dec. 4 to protect farmer interests. **Horatio Alger's** *Ragged Dick* published.

1868 Pres. Johnson again dismissed Sec. of War Edwin M. Stanton after first dismissing him in 1867. **Johnson impeached** by the House Feb. 24 for violation of Tenure of Office Act but actually in response to his opposition to congressional Reconstruction. He was acquitted by the Senate Mar.-May. **14th Amendment**, providing for citizenship of all persons born or naturalized in U.S. and subject to the jurisdiction thereof, ratified July 9. Louisa May Alcott's *Little Women* published. *The World Almanac*, a publication of the *New York World*, appeared for first time.

1869 Transcontinental railroad completed; golden spike driven at Promontory Summit, UT, May 10, marking junction of Central Pacific and Union Pacific lines. Attempt to "corner" gold led to financial **"Black Friday"** in New York Sept. 24. **Woman suffrage law** passed in Wyoming Territory Dec. 10. **Knights of Labor** labor union formed in Philadelphia. By 1886, it had 700,000 members nationally.

1870 15th Amendment, making race no bar to voting rights, ratified Feb. 8. **First U.S. boardwalk** completed, in Atlantic City, NJ. **U.S. Weather Bureau** founded.

1871 Great Chicago fire destroyed city Oct. 8-11. **National Rifle Association (NRA)** founded.

1872 Amnesty Act May 22 restored civil rights to citizens of the South, except for 500 Confederate leaders. Congress established Yellowstone, **first national park**. James McNeill Whistler painted famous portrait known informally as **"Whistler's Mother."**

1873 First U.S. postal card issued May 1. **Jesse James** and his gang robbed their first passenger train July 21. Banks failed, panic began in Sept. **Depression** lasted 5 years. **"Boss" William Tweed** of New York City was convicted Nov. 19 of stealing public funds. He died in jail in 1878. New York's Bellevue Hospital started **first nursing school.**

1874 Women's Christian Temperance Union established in Cleveland. **First public zoo** in U.S. established in Philadelphia.

1875 Congress passed **Civil Rights Act** Mar. 1, giving equal rights to blacks in public accommodations and jury duty. Act invalidated in 1883 by Supreme Court. **First Kentucky Derby** held May 17. First **Jim Crow segregation law** enacted, in Tennessee.

1876 Democrat **Samuel J. Tilden** received majority of popular votes for president over Republican **Rutherford B. Hayes**, but 22 electoral votes were in dispute. Congress agreed to certify Hayes as winner in Feb. 1877 after Republicans agreed to end federal Reconstruction of South. **Alexander Graham Bell** patented the telephone Mar. 7. Col. **George A. Custer** and 264 soldiers of the 7th Cavalry were killed June 25 in "last stand," **Battle of the Little Bighorn**, MT, in Sioux Indian War.

1877 Molly Maguires—Irish terrorist society in mining areas of Scranton, PA—was broken up by hanging, June 21, of 11 leaders for murders of mine officials and police. Pres. Rutherford B. Hayes sent federal troops to control violent national railroad strike.

1878 First commercial telephone exchange opened, New Haven, CT, Jan. 28. **Thomas A. Edison** founded Edison Electric Light Co. on Oct. 15.

1879 F. W. Woolworth opened his first five-and-ten store, in Utica, NY, Feb. 22. French actress **Sarah Bernhardt** made her U.S. debut Nov. 8 at New York City's Booth Theater. Economist and social philosopher **Henry George** published *Progress & Poverty*, advocating single tax on land.

1881 Clara Barton founded **American Red Cross** May 21. Pres. **James A. Garfield** shot in Washington, DC, July 2; died Sept. 19. Famous gun battle between the Earp brothers and outlaw rustlers Oct. 26 near the **OK Corral**, Tombstone, AZ. **Booker T. Washington** founded Tuskegee Institute for blacks. **Helen Hunt Jackson's** *A Century of Dishonor*, about mistreatment of Indians, published.

1882 Chinese Exclusion Act, barring immigration of Chinese laborers for 10 years, later made permanent, passed by Congress May 6; prohibited naturalization of Chinese resident aliens.

1883 Civil Service Act, or **Pendleton Act**, passed Jan. 16, created foundations of American civil service system. The **Brooklyn Bridge** opened May 24 as world's longest suspension bridge. The **Northern Pacific Railroad** was completed Sept. 8. **Buffalo Bill Cody's** Wild West Show began its 30-year touring run.

1884 First long-distance telephone call completed, Mar. 27, between Boston and New York. Switchback Railway—**first U.S. roller coaster** built as amusement park ride—opened at Coney Island in New York City. **Mark Twain's** *The Adventures of Huckleberry Finn* published.

1885 Washington Monument dedicated Feb. 21.

1886 Haymarket riot and bombing, May 4, followed labor battles for 8-hour day in Chicago; 7 police and 4 workers died. Eight anarchists found guilty Aug. 20; 4 hanged Nov. 11. **Coca-Cola** first sold, May 8, at Jacob's Pharmacy in Atlanta. Apache Indian **Geronimo** surrendered Sept. 4, ending last major Indian war. **Statue of Liberty** dedicated Oct. 28. **American Federation of Labor** (AFL) formed Dec. 8 by 25 craft unions.

1887 Interstate Commerce Act enacted Feb. 4, created Interstate Commerce Commission.

1888 **Great blizzard** struck Eastern U.S. Mar. 11-14, causing about 400 deaths. Ernest Thayer's poem **"Casey at the Bat"** recited for first time in public at New York City theater in May.

1889 U.S. opened 2-mil acre **Oklahoma District** to settlement Apr. 22, initiating land run; "sooner" settlers illegally entered the territory before that date to stake favorable claims. More than 2,200 lives lost in **Johnstown flood** (PA) May 31. **Electric lights** installed at White House.

1890 **Sherman Antitrust Act** passed July 2, began federal effort to curb monopolies. Massacre at **Wounded Knee**, SD, Dec. 29, the last major conflict between Indians and U.S. troops; about 200 Indian men, women, and children and 29 soldiers were killed. **Jacob Riis**'s *How the Other Half Lives*, about city slums, published, instigating reform legislation in New York City. **Emily Dickinson**'s poems published, 4 years after her death.

1891 **Forest Reserve Act**, Mar. 3, let president close public forest land to settlement for establishment of national parks. **Carnegie Hall**, in New York City, opened May 5.

1892 **Ellis Island**, in New York Bay, opened Jan. 1 to receive immigrants; closed 1954. **Homestead strike** (PA) at Carnegie steel mills; 7 guards and 11 strikers and spectators shot to death July 6. James J. Corbett defeated John L. Sullivan Sept. 7 to become **first world heavyweight champion** under Marquess of Queensbury rules.

1893 **Columbian Exposition** world's fair held May-Oct. in Chicago. Financial panic led to 4-year **depression**. **Mormon Temple** dedicated in Salt Lake City, UT.

1894 Thomas A. Edison's **kinetoscope**, for motion pictures (invented 1887), given first public showing Apr. 14. **Jacob S. Coxey** led army of unemployed from the Midwest, reaching Washington, DC, Apr. 30. Coxey arrested May 1 for trespassing on Capitol grounds; his army disbanded. **Pullman strike** began May 11 at railroad car plant in Chicago. Milton Hershey started **Hershey Chocolate Company**.

1895 **"America, the Beautiful"** appeared for first time, in church publication, July 4. **Stephen Crane**'s *The Red Badge of Courage* published.

1896 Supreme Court, in *Plessy v. Ferguson*, May 18, approved racial segregation under the **"separate but equal"** doctrine. **William Jennings Bryan** delivered "Cross of Gold" speech July 9; won Democratic Party nomination. **John Philip Sousa** composed "Stars and Stripes Forever" on Dec. 25.

1897 **Olney-Pauncefote Treaty** with Britain, Jan. 11, gave wide scope to arbitration in settling disputes; never ratified by U.S. John J. McDermott won **first Boston Marathon** Apr. 19. First Klondike gold arrived in San Francisco July 14, helping set off **Klondike gold rush**. **First subway service** in country opens to public in Boston, Sept. 1.

1898 U.S. battleship *Maine* blown up Feb. 15 in Havana, Cuba; 260 killed. U.S. blockaded Cuba Apr. 22 in aid of independence forces. U.S. declared **war on Spain** Apr. 24; destroyed Spanish fleet in Philippines May 1; took Guam June 20. U.S. took **Puerto Rico** July 25-Aug. 12. Spain agreed Dec. 10 to cede Philippines, Puerto Rico, and Guam, and approved independence for Cuba. Annexation of **Hawaii** signed by Pres. William McKinley, July 7.

1899 Filipino insurgents, unable to get recognition of independence from U.S., started guerrilla war Feb. 4. Their leader, Emilio Aguinaldo, captured May 23, 1901. **Philippine insurrection** ended 1902. Killed were 20,000 Filipino troops and some 200,000 civilians, mostly from disease and starvation. Pres. McKinley signed treaty officially ending **Spanish-American War**, Feb. 10. U.S. declared **Open Door Policy** Sept. 6, to make China an open international market. Philosopher **John Dewey**'s *School and Society*, advocating progressive education ("learn by doing"), published. Pianist Scott Joplin's "Maple Leaf Rag" published, popularizing **ragtime music**.

1900 **International Ladies' Garment Workers Union** founded in New York City June 3. Fought sweatshop working conditions. **Carry Nation**, Kansas temperance leader, began raiding saloons with a hatchet. U.S. helped suppress **Boxer Rebellion** in Beijing. Eastman Kodak Co. introduced the **Brownie camera**, popularizing picture-taking.

1901 Texas had first significant oil strike at **Spindletop** well near Beaumont, Jan. 10. Pres. **McKinley** shot Sept. 6 in Buffalo, NY, by anarchist Leon Czolgosz; died Sept. 14. Vice Pres. **Theodore Roosevelt** sworn in as **youngest-ever president**, at age 42 years, 11 months. **Booker T. Washington**'s *Up from Slavery* published. U.S. withdrew troops from **Cuba** May 20, and Cuba became independent.

1902 Permanent **Bureau of the Census** established Mar. 6. **Helen Keller** autobiography appeared in serial form.

1903 Treaty between U.S. and Colombia to have U.S. dig **Panama Canal** signed Jan. 22, rejected by Colombia. Panama declared independence from Colombia with U.S. support Nov. 3; recognized by Pres. Theodore Roosevelt Nov. 6. U.S., Panama signed canal treaty Nov. 18. Wisconsin set first **direct primary voting system**, May 23. **Henry Ford** founded Ford Motor Co., June 16. Boston defeated Pittsburgh, 5 games to 3, Oct. 13 in **first modern World Series**. **First successful flight** in heavier-than-air mechanically propelled airplane by **Orville Wright** Dec. 17 near Kitty Hawk, NC, 120 ft. in 12 secs. Later flight same day by **Wilbur Wright**, 852 ft. in 59 secs. Improved plane patented, 1906. **Iroquois Theater fire** in Chicago killed about 600 out of 1,900 in audience, Dec. 30. Pioneering film *Great Train Robbery* produced.

1904 St. Louis hosted **first Olympics in U.S.**, July 1-Nov. 23. **First section of New York subway** system opened, Oct. 27. **Ida Tarbell** published muckraking *The History of the Standard Oil Company*. **Henry James**'s last great novel, *The Golden Bowl*, published.

1905 **Industrial Workers of the World**, which advocated Marxian theory of class struggle between workers and capitalists, founded in Chicago, June 27. **Rotary**, oldest service club organization in U.S., founded in Chicago.

1906 **San Francisco earthquake** and fire, Apr. 18-19, caused more than 3,000 deaths and $400 mil in damages. **Upton Sinclair**'s *The Jungle*, which exposed working conditions in meat-packing industry, published. Helped spur passage of the **Pure Food and Drug Act** and **Meat Inspection Act** June 30.

1907 Financial panic and **depression** started Mar. 13. Pres. Roosevelt sent **"Great White Fleet"** of 16 U.S. battleships around the world in show of power.

1908 Springfield, IL, torn by **anti-black rioting**, Aug. 14-15. Henry Ford introduced **Model T** car, priced at $850, Oct. 1.

1909 Adm. Robert E. Peary claimed to have reached **North Pole** Apr. 6 on sixth attempt, accompanied by black explorer Matthew Henson and 4 Inuit; may have fallen short. National Conference on the Negro convened May 30, leading to founding of **National Association for the Advancement of Colored People** (NAACP).

1910 **Boy Scouts** of America founded Feb. 8. Former Pres. Roosevelt called for **"new nationalism"** in famous speech in Kansas, Aug. 10.

1911 Building with New York City's **Triangle Shirtwaist Co.** factory caught fire Mar. 25; 146 died. Supreme Court ruled May 15 that **Standard Oil Co.** must be dissolved

1892: Ellis Island immigration station opens; it would process more than 12 million immigrants before closing in 1954.

1906: Damages caused by the San Francisco earthquake and subsequent fires leave 225,000 (more than half the area's population) homeless.

because it unreasonably restrained trade. **First transcontinental airplane flight** (with numerous stops) by C. P. Rodgers, from New York to Pasadena, CA, Sept. 17-Nov. 5; time in air 82 hrs., 4 mins.

1912 American Girl Guides founded Mar. 12; name changed in 1913 to **Girl Scouts**. U.S. Marines, Aug. 14, sent to **Nicaragua**, which was in default of loans to U.S. and Europe.

1913 **16th Amendment**, authorizing federal income tax, ratified Feb. 3. The **Armory Show** in New York City brought modern art to U.S. for first time, Feb. 17. **17th Amendment**, providing for direct popular election of U.S. senators, ratified Apr. 8. **Federal Reserve System** authorized Dec. 23, in major reform of U.S. banking and finance.

1914 Ford Motor Co. raised basic wage rates from $2.40 for 9-hr. day to $5 for 8-hr. day, Jan. 5, increasing stability in labor force. When U.S. sailors were arrested in Tampico, Mexico, Apr. 9, Atlantic fleet was sent to **Veracruz**, occupied city. Pres. Woodrow Wilson proclaimed **U.S. neutrality** in the European war, Aug. 4. The **Panama Canal** officially opened Aug. 15. The **Clayton Antitrust Act** passed Oct. 15, strengthening federal antimonopoly powers.

1915 First transcontinental telephone call, New York to San Francisco, completed Jan. 25 by Alexander Graham Bell and Thomas A. Watson. British ship *Lusitania* sunk May 7 by German submarine; 1,198 passengers died, including 128 Americans. (In notice in morning newspapers the day *Lusitania* set sail, Germany had warned Americans against taking passage on British vessels.) As result of U.S. campaign, Germany issued apology and promise of payments, Oct. 5. Pres. Wilson asked for a military fund increase, Dec. 7. U.S. troops landed in **Haiti**, July 28. Haiti became virtual U.S. protectorate under Sept. 16 treaty. D. W. Griffith's film *The Birth of a Nation* released. William J. Simmons partly inspired by film to revive **Ku Klux Klan**, which peaks in 1920s.

1916 Gen. **John J. Pershing** entered Mexico to pursue **Francisco (Pancho) Villa**, who had raided U.S. border areas. Forces withdrew Feb. 5, 1917. **Rural Credits Acts** passed July 17, followed by **Warehouse Act** Aug. 11; both provided financial aid to farmers. Bomb exploded during **San Francisco Preparedness Day parade** July 22, killed 10. Thomas J. Mooney, labor organizer, and Warren K. Billings, shoeworker, convicted 1917; both later pardoned. U.S. bought **Virgin Islands** from Denmark Aug. 4. U.S. established military government in the **Dominican Republic** Nov. 29.

Jeannette Rankin (R, MT) elected to House of Representatives, **first female member of Congress**.

1917 Germany, suffering from British blockade, declared almost unrestricted **submarine warfare** Jan. 31. U.S. cut diplomatic ties with Germany Feb. 3 and formally **declared war** Apr. 6. Jones Act, passed Mar. 2, made **Puerto Rico** a U.S. territory, its inhabitants U.S. citizens. **Conscription law** passed May 18. First U.S. troops arrived in Europe June 26.

1918 Pres. Wilson set out his **14 Points** as basis for peace, Jan. 8. More than 1 mil American troops were in Europe by July. Allied counteroffensive launched at Château-Thierry July 18. War ended with signing of **armistice** Nov. 11. **Influenza epidemic** killed an estimated 20 mil worldwide, 548,000 in U.S.

1919 18th Amendment, providing for prohibition of manufacture, sale, or transportation of alcoholic beverages, ratified Jan. 16, to take effect on Jan. 16, 1920. **First transatlantic flight**, by U.S. Navy seaplane, left Rockaway, NY, May 8, stopped at Newfoundland, Azores, Lisbon May 27. **Boston police strike** Sept. 9, earliest strike conducted by government employees. About 250 **foreign-born radicals** deported Dec. 21 to Soviet Union. **Sherwood Anderson's** *Winesburg, Ohio* published.

1920 In national **Red Scare**, some 2,700 Communists, anarchists, and other radicals were arrested Jan.-May. **League of Women Voters** founded Feb. 14. Senate refused Mar. 19 to ratify **League of Nations Covenant**. Nicola Sacco and **Bartolomeo Vanzetti** accused of killing 2 men in Massachusetts payroll holdup Apr. 15. Found guilty 1921. A 7-year campaign for their release failed; both executed Aug. 23, 1927. Verdict repudiated 1977 by proclamation of Massachusetts Gov. Michael Dukakis. **19th Amendment** ratified Aug. 18, giving women the vote. **First regular licensed radio broadcasting** began Aug. 20. **Wall St. bombing** in New York City killed 30, injured 100, did $2 mil damage, Sept. 16. **Sinclair Lewis's** *Main Street*, F. Scott Fitzgerald's *This Side of Paradise*, and Edith Wharton's *The Age of Innocence* published.

1921 Congress sharply curbed immigration, set **national quota system** May 19. Joint congressional resolution declaring **peace with Germany, Austria, and Hungary** signed July 2 by Pres. Warren G. Harding; treaties were signed in Aug. In so-called **Black Sox scandal**, 8 Chicago White Sox players were banned from baseball Aug. 4 for conspiring with gamblers to throw the 1919 **World Series**. **Limitation of Armaments Conference** met in Washington, DC, Nov. 12-Feb. 6, 1922. Major powers agreed to curtail naval construction, outlaw poison gas, restrict submarine attacks on merchant vessels, and respect China's integrity.

1922 During nationwide coal strike, union miners killed some 21 strike-breakers at Herrin, IL, June 21-22, in incident referred to as the **Herrin Massacre**. *Reader's Digest* founded. T. S. Eliot's *The Waste Land* published in London.

1923 First **sound-on-film motion picture**, *Phonofilm*, shown at Rivoli Theater, New York City, beginning in Apr. Pres. Calvin Coolidge addressed Congress, Dec. 6; **first radio broadcast of president's annual speech**.

1924 Law approved by Congress June 15 made all **Native Americans U.S. citizens**. **Nellie Tayloe Ross** elected governor of Wyoming and **Miriam (Ma) Ferguson** elected governor of Texas Nov. 9. Ross inaugurated as nation's **first female governor** Jan. 5, 1925. Ferguson installed Jan. 20, 1925. **George Gershwin** wrote "Rhapsody in Blue."

1925 John T. Scopes found guilty of having taught **evolution** in Dayton, TN, high school, fined $100 and costs, July 24. F. Scott Fitzgerald's *The Great Gatsby* published.

1926 Dr. Robert H. Goddard demonstrated practicality of rockets Mar. 16 in Auburn, MA, with **first liquid-fuel rocket**; rocket traveled 184 ft. in 2.5 secs. Congress established **Army Air Corps** July 2. **Air Commerce Act** passed Nov. 2, established government agencies for development of airports, radio navigation, and other services. **Ernest Hemingway's** *The Sun Also Rises* published.

1927 Capt. **Charles A. Lindbergh** left Roosevelt Field, NY, May 20 alone in *Spirit of St. Louis* on first New York-Paris nonstop flight. Reached Le Bourget airfield May 21, 3,610 mi. in 33½ hrs. *The Jazz Singer*, **first feature-length film** in which **spoken dialogue was part of narrative action**, released Oct. 6. Noted for line, "You ain't heard nothin' yet!" *Show Boat*, Jerome Kern and Oscar Hammerstein II's adaptation of Edna Ferber's novel, opened in New York Dec. 27. Considered musical with first serious libretto.

1929: The Great Depression devastates Americans nationwide; Dorothea Lange's iconic photo, taken in 1936, comes to represent the desperation felt.

1928 **Amelia Earhart** became first woman to fly across the Atlantic, June 17. **Herbert Hoover** elected president Nov. 6, defeating New York Gov. Alfred E. Smith, a Catholic.

1929 Gangsters killed 7 rivals in Chicago **St. Valentine's Day massacre** Feb. 14, which won Al Capone control of Chicago's underworld. Stock market crash Oct. 29 marked end of past prosperity as stock prices plummeted. Stock losses for 1929-31 estimated at $50 bil; beginning of **Great Depression**. Albert B. Fall, former secretary of the interior, was convicted of accepting $10,000 bribe in leasing of the **Elk Hills (Teapot Dome)** naval oil reserve; sentenced Nov. 1 to a year in prison and fined. **Thomas Wolfe**'s *Look Homeward, Angel* and **William Faulkner**'s *The Sound and the Fury* published.

1930 London **Naval Reduction Treaty** signed by U.S., Britain, Italy, France, and Japan Apr. 22; in effect Jan. 1, 1931; expired Dec. 31, 1936. **Hawley-Smoot Tariff** signed; rate hikes slash world trade. **Sinclair Lewis** became first American to win a **Nobel Prize in literature**. **Dashiell Hammett**'s *The Maltese Falcon*, which introduced detective Sam Spade, published.

1931 **Empire State Building** opened in New York City May 1, displacing Chrysler Building as world's tallest. **Al Capone** convicted of tax evasion Oct. 17. **Pearl Buck**'s *The Good Earth* published. **Charlie Chaplin** film *City Lights* released.

1932 **Reconstruction Finance Corp.** established Jan. 22 to stimulate banking and business. Unemployment at 12 mil. Twenty-month-old **Charles Lindbergh Jr.** kidnapped Mar. 1; found dead May 12. Bruno Hauptmann found guilty Feb. 1935; executed Apr. 3, 1936. Unemployed World War I veterans demanding Congress pay promised bonus early launched **Bonus March** on Washington, DC, May 29. **Franklin D. Roosevelt** elected president for first time in Democratic landslide, Nov. 8. Chicago Bears won **first NFL title game** Dec. 18, defeating the Portsmouth (OH) Spartans, 9-0.

1933 Pres. Roosevelt named **Frances Perkins** U.S. secretary of labor; **first woman in U.S. cabinet**. Pres. Roosevelt ordered **all U.S. banks closed** Mar. 6. In a "100 days" special session, Mar. 9-June 16, Congress passed **New Deal**, including measures to regulate banks, distribute funds to the jobless, create jobs, raise agricultural prices, and set wage and production standards for industry. **Gold standard** dropped by U.S. in favor of "modified

gold bullion standard"; announced by Pres. Roosevelt Apr. 19, ratified by Congress June 5. **Tennessee Valley Authority (TVA)** created by act of Congress, May 18. **Prohibition** ended in the U.S. as 36th state ratified **21st Amendment** Dec. 5. Pres. Roosevelt foreswore armed intervention in **Western Hemisphere** nations, Dec. 26.

1934 Pres. Roosevelt signed law creating **Securities and Exchange Commission**, June 6. U.S. troops pulled out of **Haiti**, Aug. 6.

1935 **Works Progress Administration (WPA)** instituted May 6. Rural Electrification Administration created May 11. National Industrial Recovery Act struck down by Supreme Court May 27. **Boulder Dam** (later renamed **Hoover Dam**) completed, May 29. **Social Security Act** passed by Congress Aug. 8-9. Comedian **Will Rogers** and aviator Wiley Post killed Aug. 15 in Alaska plane crash. **Huey Long**, Louisiana senator and national political leader, shot Sept. 8; died Sept. 10. George Gershwin's jazz opera *Porgy and Bess* opened Oct. 10 in New York. **Committee for Industrial Organization** (later Congress of Industrial Organizations) formed to expand industrial unionism Nov. 9.

1936 **Jesse Owens** won 4 gold medals at the **Berlin Olympics** in Aug., first American to do so in track-and-field events at single Olympics. **Baseball Hall of Fame** founded in Cooperstown, NY. **Margaret Mitchell**'s *Gone with the Wind* published.

1937 Airship *Hindenburg* caught fire, was destroyed May 6 as it was landing in Lakehurst, NJ. **Golden Gate Bridge** opened May 27, becoming suspension bridge with world's longest span. **Joe Louis** knocked out James J. Braddock to become world heavyweight champ June 22. Aviator **Amelia Earhart** and copilot Fred Noonan disappeared July 2 near Howland Island, in the Pacific. Pres. Roosevelt asked for 6 additional Supreme Court justices; **"packing" plan** defeated. **Auto, steel labor unions** won first big contracts. **Zora Neale Hurston**'s *Their Eyes Were Watching God* published.

1938 **National minimum wage** enacted June 25. Orson Welles's radio dramatization of H. G. Wells's *War of the Worlds*, Oct. 30, caused Martian invasion scare. **Seabiscuit** beat War Admiral in match race of the century, at Pimlico track, MD, Nov. 1. Artist Anna Mary Robertson, **"Grandma Moses,"** discovered. **Thornton Wilder**'s *Our Town* produced on Broadway.

1939 Opera singer **Marian Anderson** performed for integrated crowd of 75,000 at Lincoln Memorial Apr. 9. First Lady Eleanor Roosevelt had quit Daughters of the American Revolution after organization refused to let Anderson sing in DC's Constitution Hall. **New York World's Fair**—theme: "The World of Tomorrow"—opened Apr. 30, closed Oct. 31. Reopened for second season May 11, 1940, ended Oct. 27. **Lou Gehrig**, seriously ill, said farewell to fans at Yankee Stadium, July 4. Albert Einstein alerted Pres. Roosevelt to **A-bomb possibilities** in Aug. 2 letter. **U.S. declared its neutrality** in European war Sept. 5. Pres. Roosevelt proclaimed limited **national emergency** Sept. 8, unlimited emergency May 27, 1941. Both ended by Pres. Harry Truman, Apr. 28, 1952. Pocket Books, **first paperback publisher** in U.S., established. **John Steinbeck**'s *The Grapes of Wrath* published. Film versions of *Gone with the Wind*—which went on to win a record 8 Academy Awards—and *The Wizard of Oz* released.

1940 U.S. OK'd sale of **surplus war material** to Britain June 3; announced transfer of 50 overaged destroyers Sept. 3. **First peacetime military draft** in U.S. history approved, Sept. 14. **Forty-hour work week** went into effect, Oct. 24. Pres. **Roosevelt** elected Nov. 5 to third presidential term. **Carson McCullers**'s *The Heart Is a Lonely Hunter* and **Richard Wright**'s *Native Son* published.

1941 **Four Freedoms**—freedom of speech and religion, freedom from want and fear—termed essential by Pres. Roosevelt in speech to Congress Jan. 6. **Lend-Lease Act** passed Mar. 11 provided $7 bil in military credits for Britain. Lend-lease for USSR approved in Nov. Pres. Roosevelt signed executive order June 25 barring federal government and war contractors from **racial discrimination**. Order also established Fair Employment Practice Committee. The **Atlantic Charter**, 8-point declaration of principles, issued by Pres. Roosevelt and British Prime Min. Winston Churchill, Aug. 14. Japan attacked **Pearl Harbor**, Hawaii, 7:55 am Hawaiian time, Dec. 7; 19 ships sunk or damaged, 2,300 dead. Pres. Roosevelt called it "a date which will live in infamy." U.S. declared war on Japan Dec. 8. Germany and Italy declared war on U.S. Dec. 11. U.S. responded with declaration of war later on same day. Japanese invaded **Philippines**, Dec. 22; Wake Island fell, Dec. 23. *Citizen Kane*, directed by Orson Welles, released.

1942 Japanese troops took **Bataan** peninsula Apr. 8, took **Corregidor** May 6. Federal government began forcibly moving 110,000 Japanese-Americans from West Coast to **detention camps**. Exclusion lasted 3 years. **Battle of Midway** June 4-7 was Japan's first major defeat. Marines landed on **Guadalcanal** Aug. 7; last Japanese not expelled until Feb. 9, 1943. U.S., Britain invaded **North Africa** Nov. 8. **First nuclear chain reaction** (fission of uranium isotope U-235) produced at Univ. of Chicago under physicists Arthur Compton, Enrico Fermi, others, Dec. 2. The movie *Casablanca*, starring Humphrey Bogart and Ingrid Bergman, released.

1943 *Oklahoma!* opened Mar. 31 on Broadway. Pres. Roosevelt signed June 10 pay-as-you-go income tax bill. Starting July 1, wage and salary earners were subject to **paycheck withholding tax**. **Detroit race riot** June 21 left 34 dead, 700 injured. Six killed in riot in New York City's **Harlem** section Aug. 2. U.S., Britain invaded **Sicily** July 9, Italian **mainland** Sept. 3. Marines in Nov. recaptured the **Gilbert Islands**, captured by Japan in 1941 and 1942.

1944 U.S., Allied forces invaded Europe at Normandy, France, on "**D-Day**," June 6, in greatest amphibious landing in history. **Battle of the Bulge**, failed Nazi counteroffensive, waged Dec. 16 to Jan. 28, 1945. **GI Bill of Rights**, providing benefits to veterans, signed by Pres. Roosevelt June 22. Representatives of the U.S. and other major powers met at **Dumbarton Oaks**, Washington, DC, Aug. 21-Oct. 7, to work out formation of postwar world organization that would become the **United Nations**. U.S. forces landed on **Leyte**, Philippines, Oct. 20. Pres. **Roosevelt** elected to fourth term as president Nov. 7.

1945 **Yalta Conference** met in the Crimea, USSR, Feb. 4-11. Pres. Roosevelt, Prime Min. Churchill, and Soviet leader Joseph Stalin agreed that their 3 countries, plus France, would occupy Germany and that the Soviet Union would enter war against Japan. Marines landed on **Iwo Jima** Feb. 19, won control Mar. 16 after heavy casualties. U.S. forces invaded **Okinawa** Apr. 1, captured it June 21. Pres. **Roosevelt** died in Warm Springs, GA, Apr. 12; Vice Pres. **Harry S. Truman** became president. Germany surrendered May 7; May 8 proclaimed **V-E Day**. **First atomic bomb**, produced at Los Alamos, NM, exploded at Alamogordo, NM, July 16. Bomb dropped on **Hiroshima** Aug. 6, killing about 75,000; bomb dropped on **Nagasaki** Aug. 9, killing about 40,000. Japan agreed to surrender Aug. 14; formally surrendered Sept. 2. At **Potsdam Conference**, July 17-Aug. 2, leaders of U.S., USSR, and Britain agreed on disarmament of Germany, occupation zones, war crimes trials. **Empire State Building** struck accidentally by Army B-25 bomber, July 28, killing 14. U.S. forces entered **Korea** south of 38th parallel to displace Japanese Sept. 8. Gen. **Douglas MacArthur** took over supervision of Japan Sept. 9.

1944: Gen. Dwight D. Eisenhower, commander of Allied forces, prepares troops for their D-Day assault on the French coastline.

1946 **Steel strike** by 750,000 started Jan. 21, settled in 4 weeks. Strike by 400,000 **mine workers** began Apr. 1 (settled May 29); other industries (including rail, maritime) followed. Winston Churchill employed the phrase "**Iron Curtain**" in Mar. 5 speech at Westminster College in Fulton, MO. Atomic bomb tested off **Bikini Atoll** in Pacific, July 1. In all, U.S. conducted 23 nuclear tests between 1946 and 1958. **Philippines** given independence by U.S. July 4. Mother Frances Xavier Cabrini **first American to be canonized**, July 7. Dr. Benjamin Spock's *Baby and Child Care* published as **baby boom** began. **John Hersey**'s *Hiroshima* published.

1947 Pres. Truman asked Congress for financial and military aid for Greece and Turkey to help combat Communist subversion (**Truman Doctrine**), Mar. 12. Approved May 15. UN Security Council voted Apr. 2 to place under U.S. trusteeship the **Pacific islands** formerly mandated to Japan. **Jackie Robinson** joined Brooklyn Dodgers Apr. 11, breaking color barrier in major league baseball. The **Marshall Plan** for U.S. aid to European countries proposed by Sec. of State George C. Marshall June 5. Congress authorized some $12 bil in next 4 years. **Taft-Hartley Labor Act** restricting labor union power vetoed by Pres. Truman June 20; Congress overrode veto. Air Force Capt. **Chuck Yeager** broke sound barrier, Oct. 14, in X-1 rocket plane.

1948 **Organization of American States** founded Apr. 30 by 21 countries. USSR halted all surface traffic into **West Berlin** June 24; in response, U.S. and British troops launched an **airlift**. Soviet blockade halted May 12, 1949; airlift ended Sept. 30. Pres. **Truman** elected Nov. 2, defeating Gov. Thomas E. Dewey in historic upset. **Alger Hiss** indicted Dec. 15 for perjury, after denying he had passed secret documents to Whittaker Chambers to go to a Communist spy ring; convicted Jan. 21, 1950. **Kinsey Report** on sexuality in the human male published.

1949 North Atlantic Treaty Organization (**NATO**) established Aug. 24 by U.S., Canada, and 10 Western European nations, agreeing that an armed attack against one would be considered an attack against all. Eleven leaders of U.S. **Communist Party** convicted Oct. 14 of advocating violent overthrow of U.S. government; sentenced to prison. Supreme Court upheld convictions, 1951. Pres. Truman, Oct. 26, signed legislation raising **federal minimum wage** from 40¢ an hour to 75¢. **Arthur Miller**'s *Death of a Salesman* opened on Broadway.

1950 Masked bandits robbed **Brink's, Inc.**, Boston express office, Jan. 17 of $2.8 mil. Case solved 1956; 8 sentenced to life. Pres. Truman authorized production of **H-bomb** Jan. 31. Sen. **Estes Kefauver** (D, TN) chaired Special Committee to Investigate Organized Crime in Interstate Commerce, organized May 3. Also known as Kefauver Committee.

North Korean forces **invaded South Korea** June 25. UN asked for troops to restore peace. Pres. Truman ordered Air Force and Navy to Korea June 27. Truman approved ground forces, air strikes against North Korea June 30. U.S. sent 35 military advisers to **South Vietnam** June 27 and agreed to aid anti-Communist government. U.S. forces landed at **Inchon**, South Korea, Sept. 15. UN forces took Pyongyang Oct. 20, reached China border Nov. 20; China sent troops across border Nov. 26. U.S. banned shipments Dec. 8 to **Communist China** and to Asiatic ports trading with it.

Army **seized all railroads** Aug. 27 on Truman's order to prevent general strike; returned to owners in 1952. Charles Schulz's *Peanuts* comic strip first appeared in newspapers, Oct. 2. Two members of **Puerto Rican nationalist movement** tried to kill Pres. Truman Nov. 1. Variety show *Your Show of Shows* debuted on TV. David Riesman's *The Lonely Crowd* published.

1951 **22nd Amendment**, limiting presidential term of office, ratified Feb. 27. **Julius Rosenberg**; his wife, **Ethel Rosenberg**; and **Morton Sobell** found guilty Mar. 29 of conspiracy to commit wartime espionage. Rosenbergs received death penalty. Sobell sentenced to 30 years; released 1969.

Pres. Truman removed Gen. **Douglas MacArthur** from Korea command Apr. 11 for unauthorized policy statements. **Korea** cease-fire talks began in July; lasted 2 years. Fighting ended July 27, 1953.

Transcontinental TV began Sept. 4 with Pres. Truman's address at Japanese Peace Treaty Conference in San Francisco. **Japanese peace treaty** signed in San Francisco Sept. 8

by U.S., Japan, and 47 other nations. **J. D. Salinger**'s *Catcher in the Rye* published.

1952 Pres. Truman ordered **seizure of nation's steel mills** Apr. 8 to avert strike. Ruled illegal by Supreme Court June 2. **Peace contract** between West Germany, U.S., Great Britain, and France signed May 26. Last racial and ethnic barriers to naturalization removed, June 26-27, with passage of **Immigration and Naturalization Act of 1952**. **Puerto Rico** proclaimed commonwealth July 25, after referendum Mar. 3. Richard Nixon, as vice-pres. candidate, gave **"Checkers" speech**, so called because of sentimental reference to his dog Checkers, Sept. 23. **First hydrogen device explosion** Nov. 1 in Pacific. **Ralph Ellison**'s *Invisible Man* published.

1953 Federal jury in New York convicted 13 **Communist** leaders on conspiracy charges, Jan. 20. **Julius and Ethel Rosenberg** executed in Sing Sing Prison electric chair, Ossining, NY, June 19, for relaying nuclear secrets to Soviet Union. **Korean War** armistice signed July 27. California Gov. **Earl Warren** sworn in Oct. 5 as 14th chief justice of U.S. Supreme Court.

1954 *Nautilus*, **first atomic-powered submarine**, launched at Groton, CT, Jan. 21. Five members of Congress were wounded in the House Mar. 1 by 4 **Puerto Rican independence supporters** who fired at random from a spectators' gallery.

At televised Army-McCarthy hearings, Apr. 22-June 17, before a Senate subcommittee, Army officials accused Sen. **Joseph McCarthy** (R, WI) of seeking preferential treatment for a draftee, and McCarthy accused Army of hindering probe of Communist infiltration into Army. McCarthy was cleared in the hearings, but the Senate later voted to condemn him, 67-22, for his abuse of the Senate during hearings and debates.

Supreme Court ruled unanimously May 17 that racial segregation in public schools was unconstitutional, in *Brown v. Board of Education of Topeka*. **Ernest Hemingway** won Nobel Prize in literature for *The Old Man and the Sea*.

1955 U.S. agreed Feb. 12 to help train **South Vietnamese army**. Supreme Court ordered "all deliberate speed" in **integration** of public schools, May 31. A summit meeting of leaders of **Big 4**—U.S., Britain, France, and USSR—took place July 18-23 in Geneva, Switzerland.

Rosa Parks refused Dec. 1 to give her seat to white man on bus in Montgomery, AL. Her arrest, detention, and conviction sparked boycott of bus system, organized by Rev. **Martin Luther King Jr.**, by Montgomery's black community, Dec. 5. Bus segregation ordinance declared unconstitutional by federal court in 1956. Boycott ended Dec. 23 of that year.

America's 2 largest labor organizations merged Dec. 5, creating **AFL-CIO**. Russian-born U.S. citizen **Vladimir Nabokov**'s *Lolita* published.

1956 Massive resistance to **Supreme Court desegregation rulings** was called for Mar. 12 by 101 Southern congressmen. U.S. Supreme Court, Apr. 23, unanimously ruled against **racial segregation** on intrastate buses.

Federal-Aid Highway Act signed June 29, creating **interstate highway system**. **First transatlantic telephone cable** activated Sept. 25. On Oct. 8, in Game 5, Yankee right-hander Don Larsen pitched **only perfect World Series game**. **Eugene O'Neill**'s *Long Day's Journey into Night*, autobiographical play about dissolution of his family, opened in Nov. on Broadway.

1957 Congress approved **Civil Rights Act of 1957**, Apr. 29, first such bill since Reconstruction to protect voting rights. The U.S. surgeon general July 12 said studies showed "direct link" between cigarette **smoking and lung cancer**.

Arkansas Gov. Orval Faubus called National Guardsmen Sept. 4 to bar 9 black students from entering all-white high school in **Little Rock**. Faubus complied Sept. 21 with federal court order to remove Guardsmen, but local authorities ordered black students to withdraw. Pres. Eisenhower sent troops Sept. 24 to enforce court order. Pres. Eisenhower signed Civil Rights Act into law Sept. 9; provided for creation of Civil Rights Commission. **Jack Kerouac**'s *On the Road* published.

1958 Army launched **first U.S. Earth-orbiting satellite**, *Explorer I*, Jan. 31 from Cape Canaveral, FL; discovered Van Allen radiation belt. U.S. Marines sent to **Lebanon** to protect elected government from threatened overthrow July-Oct. Nuclear sub *Nautilus* made **first undersea crossing of North Pole** Aug. 5. Presidential aide **Sherman Adams** resigned Sept. 22 over scandal involving alleged improper gifts. **First**

1957: Federal troops enforce a court order to enroll the "Little Rock Nine" and integrate Central High School.

domestic jet airline passenger service in U.S. opened by National Airlines Dec. 10 between New York and Miami.

1959 Alaska admitted as 49th state, Jan. 3; **Hawaii** admitted as 50th, Aug. 21. Completion of **St. Lawrence Seaway** Apr. 25 allowed passage of oceangoing vessels between Atlantic Ocean and Great Lakes.

Vice Pres. Richard Nixon, on tour of USSR, held **"kitchen debate,"** July 24, with Soviet Prem. Nikita Khrushchev at U.S. exhibit in Moscow. Prem. **Khrushchev** paid unprecedented visit to U.S. Sept. 15-27; made transcontinental tour.

Pres. Eisenhower issued injunction Oct. 12, upheld and made effective by Supreme Court Nov. 7, ending **record 116-day steel strike**. In **quiz show scandal**, Columbia Univ. Prof. Charles Van Doren admitted to U.S. House subcommittee Nov. 2 that he had been coached before appearances on NBC-TV's *21* in 1956; he had won $129,000. William Wyler's **Ben-Hur** released; the movie won a record 11 Academy Awards the following year.

1960 Sit-ins began Feb. 1 when 4 black college students in Greensboro, NC, refused to move from a Woolworth lunch counter after being denied service. By Sept. 1961, more than 70,000 students, whites and blacks, had participated in sit-ins. Pres. Eisenhower signed **Civil Rights Act** May 6.

A U.S. **U-2 reconnaissance plane** was shot down in the Soviet Union May 1; pilot Gary Powers captured. The incident led to cancellation of a Paris summit conference. A **birth control pill** approved as safe for first time by Food and Drug Administration May 9. Vice Pres. **Richard Nixon** and Sen. **John F. Kennedy** faced each other Sept. 26 in first in series of televised debates. Kennedy defeated Nixon to win presidency, Nov. 8. U.S. announced Dec. 15 its backing of rightist group in **Laos**, which took power the next day. Alfred Hitchcock film **Psycho** released.

1961 U.S. severed diplomatic and consular relations with Cuba Jan. 3, after disputes over nationalizations of U.S. firms, U.S. military presence at Guantanamo base. U.S.-directed invasion of Cuba's **Bay of Pigs** Apr. 17 by Cuban exiles unsuccessfully attempted to overthrow the regime of Prem. Fidel Castro.

Peace Corps created by executive order, Mar. 1. **23rd Amendment**, giving DC citizens the right to vote in presidential elections, ratified Mar. 29. Comm. Alan B. Shepard Jr. rocketed from Cape Canaveral, FL, in a Mercury capsule May 5, in **first U.S.-crewed suborbital space flight**.

"Freedom Rides" from Washington, DC, across Deep South were launched May 20 to protest segregation in interstate transportation.

1962 Pres. Kennedy said Feb. 14 that U.S. military advisers in **Vietnam** would fire if fired upon. Lt. Col. John H. Glenn Jr. became **first American in orbit** Feb. 20 when he circled the Earth 3 times in the Mercury capsule *Friendship 7*.

In *Baker v. Carr*, Mar. 26, Supreme Court ruled that constitutional challenges to unequal distribution of voters among legislative districts could be resolved by federal courts. **James Meredith** became first black student at Univ. of Mississippi Oct. 1 after 3,000 troops put down riots.

A Soviet **offensive missile buildup** in Cuba was revealed Oct. 22 by Pres. Kennedy, who ordered naval and air quarantine on shipment of offensive military equipment to the island. He and Soviet Prem. Khrushchev agreed Oct. 28 on formula to end crisis. Kennedy announced Nov. 2 that missile bases in Cuba were being dismantled.

Rachel Carson's *Silent Spring* launched environmentalist movement.

1963 In *Gideon v. Wainwright*, Mar. 18, Supreme Court ruled that all criminal defendants must have counsel.

March for civil rights began May 2 in Birmingham, AL, led to desegregation accord, which in turn sparked rioting and violence. Univ. of Alabama **desegregated** after Gov. George Wallace stepped aside when confronted by federally deployed National Guard troops June 11. Civil rights leader **Medgar Evers** assassinated June 12. On Aug. 28, 200,000 joined in **March on Washington** in support of black demands for equal rights led by Rev. Martin Luther King Jr.; highlight was King's **"I Have a Dream" speech**. Four black girls killed in bombing of **16th St. Baptist Church** in Birmingham, AL, Sept. 15.

Supreme Court ruled June 17 that laws requiring **recitation of Lord's Prayer or Bible verses** in public schools were unconstitutional. Pres. Kennedy, on Europe trip, addressed huge crowd in **West Berlin**, June 23. Limited **nuclear test-ban treaty** agreed upon July 25 by the U.S., the Soviet Union, and Britain.

South Vietnam Pres. **Ngo Dinh Diem** assassinated Nov. 2; U.S. had earlier withdrawn support. Pres. **Kennedy** shot and fatally wounded Nov. 22 as he rode in motorcade through downtown Dallas, TX. Vice Pres. **Lyndon B. Johnson** sworn in as president. **Lee Harvey Oswald** arrested and charged with murder but was himself shot and fatally wounded Nov. 24. Nightclub owner **Jack Ruby** convicted of Oswald's murder; Ruby died in 1967 while awaiting retrial following reversal of his conviction. **Betty Friedan**'s feminist work *The Feminine Mystique* published.

1964 **Panama** suspended relations with U.S. Jan. 9 after riots. U.S. offered Dec. 18 to negotiate new canal treaty. **The Beatles** arrived in U.S. for first time; appeared Feb. 9 on *The Ed Sullivan Show*. Supreme Court ruled Feb. 17 in *Wesberry v. Sanders* that **congressional districts** as near as practicable be equal in population so that "one man's vote in a Congressional election is to be worth as much as another's." U.S. reported May 27 it was sending military planes to **Laos**.

1963: Martin Luther King Jr. delivers "I Have a Dream" speech before a crowd of 200,000 civil rights supporters in Washington, DC.

1963: Lyndon Johnson takes the presidential oath aboard *Air Force One*, hours after Pres. John F. Kennedy was assassinated.

Three **civil rights workers** reported missing in Mississippi June 22; bodies found Aug. 4. Eighteen white men tried. On Oct. 20, 1967, an all-white federal jury convicted 7 of conspiracy in the slayings. Omnibus **civil rights bill** signed by Pres. Johnson July 2, banning discrimination in voting, jobs, public accommodations.

Congress Aug. 7 passed **Tonkin Gulf Resolution**, authorizing presidential action in Vietnam, after North Vietnamese boats reportedly attacked 2 U.S. destroyers Aug. 2. Congress approved War on Poverty bill Aug. 11, providing for a domestic Peace Corps (**VISTA**), **Job Corps**, and antipoverty funding. The **Warren Commission** released a report Sept. 27 concluding that Lee Harvey Oswald was solely responsible for the Kennedy assassination. Pres. **Johnson** elected to full term, Nov. 3, defeating Sen. **Barry Goldwater** (R, AZ) in landslide. **Verrazano-Narrows Bridge** opened in New York City Nov. 21, with world's longest suspension span.

1965 In State of the Union address Jan. 4, Pres. Johnson outlined plans for **"Great Society,"** program of civil rights, antipoverty, and health-care legislation. Pres. Johnson in Feb. ordered continuous bombing of **North Vietnam** below 20th parallel.

Malcolm X assassinated Feb. 21 at New York City rally. **March from Selma to Montgomery**, AL, Mar. 21-25, by Rev. Martin Luther King Jr. to demand federal protection of blacks' voting rights. New **Voting Rights Act**, which banned literacy tests and other voter qualification tests, signed Aug. 6. Arrest of black motorist by white police officers precipitated **Watts riot** in predominantly-black Los Angeles neighborhood Aug. 11-16. Riots resulted in 34 deaths and $200 mil in property damage.

Some 14,000 U.S. troops sent to **Dominican Republic** during civil war Apr. 28. All troops withdrawn by next year. Bill establishing **Medicare**, government health insurance program for elderly, signed by Pres. Johnson July 30.

National **immigration quota system** abolished Oct. 3. **Electric power failure** blacked out most of northeastern U.S., parts of 2 Canadian provinces the night of Nov. 9-10.

1966 U.S. forces began firing into **Cambodia** May 1. Bombing of **Hanoi** area of North Vietnam by U.S. planes began June 29. By Dec. 31, 385,300 U.S. troops were stationed in South Vietnam, plus 60,000 offshore and 33,000 in Thailand.

Supreme Court ruled June 13, in *Miranda v. Arizona*, that suspects must be read their rights before police questioning. **Medicare** began July 1. In 96-min. shooting rampage, 25-year-old student **Charles Whitman** killed 15 and wounded 31 from atop a tower at the Univ. of Texas, Austin, Aug. 1; shot dead by police. Whitman had earlier killed his mother and wife.

Dept. of Transportation created, Oct. 15. Edward Brooke (R, MA) elected Nov. 8 as first black U.S. senator in 85 years. Robert C. Weaver named secretary of newly created Dept. of Housing and Urban Development, becoming **first black cabinet member**.

1967 Green Bay Packers beat Kansas City Chiefs, 35-10, in **first Super Bowl**, Jan. 15, in Los Angeles. Three astronauts died Jan. 27 in *Apollo 1* fire on ground at Cape Canaveral, FL. **25th Amendment**, providing for presidential succession, ratified Feb. 10. Rep. **Adam Clayton Powell** (D, NY) was denied seat Mar. 1 because of charges he misused government funds. Seated following reelection in 1968 but was fined and stripped of seniority. Pres. **Johnson** and Soviet Prem. **Aleksei Kosygin** met June 23 and 25 at Glassboro State College in New Jersey; agreed not to let any crisis push them into war.

Riots erupted among residents of predominantly black **Newark**, NJ, July 12-17; 26 killed, 1,500 injured, more than 1,000 arrested. In **Detroit**, MI, July 23-30, 43 died, 2,000 injured; 5,000 left homeless by rioting, looting, and burning in city's black neighborhoods. **Thurgood Marshall** sworn in Oct. 2 as first black Supreme Court justice. **Antiwar march** on Washington, DC, Oct. 21-22, drew 50,000 participants. Carl B. Stokes (D, Cleveland) and Richard G. Hatcher (D, Gary, IN) elected **first black mayors** of major U.S. cities Nov. 7.

1968 In **"Tet offensive,"** Communist troops attacked several provincial capitals and other major cities, including Saigon, Jan. 30, but suffered heavy casualties. Pres. Johnson **curbed bombing** of North Vietnam Mar. 31. Peace talks began in Paris May 10. All bombing of North halted Oct. 31.

Rev. **Martin Luther King Jr.** assassinated Apr. 4 in Memphis, TN. **James Earl Ray**, an escaped convict, pleaded guilty to slaying, was sentenced to 99 years. Students at **Columbia Univ.**, Apr. 23-24, seized school buildings in protest demonstrations. Sen. **Robert F. Kennedy** (D, NY) shot June 5 in Los Angeles after celebrating presidential primary victories, died June 6. **Sirhan Bishara Sirhan** convicted of murder, 1969; death sentence commuted to life in prison, 1972.

Vice Pres. Hubert Humphrey nominated for president at **Democratic National Convention** in Chicago, marred by clash between police and antiwar protestors, Aug. 26-29. Republican nominee **Richard Nixon** won presidency, defeating Humphrey in close race Nov. 5.

Apollo 8 **orbited moon** in 5-day mission, Dec. 21-27. USS *Pueblo* and 83-man crew seized in Sea of Japan Jan. 23 by North Koreans; 82 men released Dec. 22.

1969 Expanded 4-party **Vietnam peace talks** began Jan. 18. U.S. force peaked at 543,400 in Apr. Withdrawal started July 8. Pres. Nixon set Vietnamization policy Nov. 3. Earl Warren retired upon swearing in **Warren Burger**, June 23, as Supreme Court chief justice. In incident that marked birth of gay rights movement, police clashed with patrons of gay bar, the **Stonewall Inn**, in New York City June 27.

U.S. astronaut **Neil Armstrong**, commander of the *Apollo 11* mission, became the **first person to set foot on the moon**, July 20, followed by astronaut **Edwin "Buzz" Aldrin**. Astronaut **Michael Collins** remained aboard command module.

Woodstock rock music festival near Bethel, NY, drew 300,000-500,000 people, Aug. 15-18. **Anti-Vietnam War demonstrations** held in cities across the U.S., marking Vietnam Moratorium day, Oct. 15; on Nov. 15, some 250,000 marched in Washington, DC. Massacre of hundreds of civilians by U.S. troops at **My Lai**, South Vietnam, in 1968

1969: *Apollo 11* **lands on the lunar surface; Edwin "Buzz" Aldrin (pictured) and Neil Armstrong are first men to walk on the Moon.**

reported Nov. 16. **Kurt Vonnegut Jr.**'s *Slaughterhouse Five* published. *Sesame Street* launched on public TV.

1970 A federal jury Feb. 18 found the **"Chicago 7"** antiwar activists not guilty of conspiring to incite riots during 1968 Democratic National Convention. However, 5 were convicted of crossing state lines with intent to incite riots.

Three astronauts safely returned to Earth Apr. 17 after oxygen tank on *Apollo 13* ruptured. Lunar landing cancelled. Millions of Americans participated in antipollution demonstrations Apr. 22 to mark **first Earth Day**.

U.S. and South Vietnamese forces crossed **Cambodian** borders Apr. 30 to get at enemy bases. Four students killed May 4 at **Kent State Univ.** in Ohio by National Guardsmen during war protest. In protest at **Jackson State Univ.** in Mississippi, 2 killed when police fired on protesters.

Anna Mae Hayes of Army Nurse Corps and Elizabeth P. Hoisington, director of Women's Army Corps, became **first female generals** June 11. **Postal reform** measure signed Aug. 12 created an independent U.S. Postal Service. Pres. Nixon, Dec. 31, signed **clean air bill** calling for development of cleaner auto engine and national air quality standards for 10 major pollutants. Garry Trudeau's *Doonesbury* comic strip launched in 30 papers.

1971 **Charles Manson** and 3 of his cult followers found guilty Jan. 25 of first-degree murder in 1969 slaying of actress Sharon Tate and 6 others. A court-martial jury Mar. 29 convicted Lt. William L. Calley Jr. in murder of 22 South Vietnamese at **My Lai** on Mar. 16, 1968. He was sentenced to life in prison Mar. 31, later reduced to 20 years.

Pres. Nixon, Apr. 14, relaxed 20-year **trade embargo with China. 26th Amendment**, lowering the minimum voting age to 18 in all elections, ratified June 30. *New York Times* began publishing June 13 classified **Pentagon Papers**, secret Pentagon study on U.S. involvement in Vietnam. Supreme Court June 30 upheld, 6-3, right of the *Times* and *Washington Post* to publish the documents. Pres. Nixon, Aug. 15, instituted 90-day **wage and price freeze**.

U.S. bombers initiated massive 5-day strike Dec. 26 in North Vietnam in retaliation for alleged violations of agreements reached prior to 1968 bombing halt.

1972 Pres. Nixon arrived in **Beijing** Feb. 21 for 8-day visit to China, in "journey for peace." Joint communiqué released Feb. 27 called for increased Sino-U.S. contacts. Senate, Mar. 22, approved **Equal Rights Amendment** banning discrimination on basis of sex; sent measure to states for ratification.

North Vietnamese forces launched biggest attacks in 4 years across the demilitarized zone Mar. 30. The U.S. responded Apr. 15 with **resumption of bombing** of Hanoi and Haiphong after 4-year lull. Pres. Nixon announced May 8 the mining of North Vietnam ports. Last U.S. combat troops left Aug. 11.

Gov. **George C. Wallace** (D, AL), campaigning for president at Laurel, MD, shopping center May 15, shot and seriously wounded. **Arthur Bremer** convicted Aug. 4, sentenced to 63 years for shooting Wallace and 3 others. In **first visit of U.S. president to Moscow**, Pres. Nixon arrived May 22 for summit talks with Kremlin leaders that culminated in landmark strategic arms pact **(SALT I)**. Five men arrested June 17 for breaking into Democratic National Committee offices in **Watergate** office complex in Washington, DC. Supreme Court in *Furman v. Georgia* June 29 ruled **capital punishment** as currently practiced was unconstitutional.

Mark Spitz won 7 gold medals in world record times at the Munich Olympics in Aug.-Sept.

Pres. **Nixon** reelected Nov. 7 in landslide, carrying 49 states to defeat Sen. George McGovern (D, SD). Three astronauts, part of *Apollo 17*, made 6th and last lunar landing on Dec. 11. Full-scale **bombing of North Vietnam** resumed after Paris peace negotiations reached impasse Dec. 18. *The Godfather*, directed by Francis Ford Coppola and based on a Mario Puzo novel, is released.

1973 In *Roe v. Wade*, Supreme Court ruled, 7-2, Jan. 22, fetus not a person with constitutional rights and that right to privacy protected woman's decision to have abortion; states may not ban abortions during first 3 months of pregnancy and may regulate, but not ban, abortions during second trimester.

Four-party **Vietnam peace pacts** signed in Paris Jan. 27, and North Vietnam released some 590 U.S. prisoners by

Apr. 1. Last U.S. troops left Mar. 29. **End of military draft** announced Jan. 27. Pres. Nixon announced, Apr. 30, resignation of top Nixon aides H. R. Haldeman and John D. Ehrlichman and firing of White House Counsel John W. Dean III as a consequence of the widening **Watergate** scandal. John Dean told Senate hearings June 25 that Pres. Nixon, his staff and campaign aides, and Justice Dept. had conspired to cover up Watergate facts. The U.S. officially ceased bombing in **Cambodia** at midnight Aug. 14 in accord with June congressional action.

Vice Pres. **Spiro Agnew**, Oct. 10, resigned and pleaded no contest to charge of tax evasion on payments made to him by contractors when he was Maryland governor. **Gerald R. Ford**, Oct. 12, became **first appointed vice president** under 25th Amendment; sworn in Dec. 6. The **"Saturday Night Massacre"** occurred Oct. 20, when Pres. Nixon ordered Attorney Gen. Elliot Richardson to fire Watergate special prosecutor Archibald Cox, who had sought handover of Nixon's subpoenaed White House tapes. Richardson refused to comply and resigned; Dep. Attorney Gen. William Ruckelshaus refused and was fired. Solicitor Gen. Robert Bork, as acting attorney gen., then fired Cox. Nixon administration named Leon Jaworski, Nov. 1, to succeed Cox.

Skylab, **first U.S. space station**, launched May 14. **Secretariat** became first Triple Crown winner since **Citation** in 1948 by winning Belmont Stakes June 9 in record time. **Billie Jean King** defeated Bobby Riggs in 3 straight sets in tennis's nationally televised "Battle of the Sexes," Sept. 20. Total **ban on oil exports** to U.S. imposed by Arab oil-producing nations Oct. 19-21 after outbreak of an Arab-Israeli war. Ban was lifted Mar. 18, 1974. Congress overrode Nov. 7 Pres. Nixon's veto of **war powers bill**, which curbed president's power to commit forces to hostilities abroad without congressional approval.

1974 On Apr. 8, **Hank Aaron** of the Atlanta Braves hit his 715th career home run to break Babe Ruth's record.

House Judiciary Committee opened **impeachment** hearings May 9 against Pres. Nixon. John D. Ehrlichman and 3 **White House "plumbers"** found guilty July 12 of conspiring to violate the civil rights of the psychiatrist of Pentagon Papers leaker Daniel Ellsberg by breaking into psychiatrist's office. Supreme Court ruled, 8-0, July 24 that Pres. Nixon had to turn over 64 **tapes of White House conversations**. House Judiciary Committee, in televised hearings July 24-30, recommended 3 **articles of impeachment** against Pres. Nixon, involving conspiracy to obstruct justice in Watergate cover-up, abuses of power, and defiance of committee subpoenas. The House voted Aug. 20, 412-3, to accept the committee report, which included the impeachment articles.

1974: Pres. Richard Nixon resigns from office and departs the White House.

Pres. Nixon announced his **resignation**, Aug. 8, and stepped down the next day. His support in Congress had begun to collapse Aug. 5, after release of tapes appearing to implicate him in Watergate cover-up. Vice Pres. **Ford** sworn in Aug. 9 as 38th U.S. president. Pres. Ford, Aug. 20, nominated **Nelson Rockefeller** to be vice president; Rockefeller sworn in Dec. 10. Pres. Ford, Sept. 8, issued **pardon to Nixon** for any federal crimes he committed while president.

New York Times published article Dec. 22 on CIA engagement in illegal domestic surveillance. Release of article led to revelation of **"family jewels,"** compilation of CIA reports on activities it engaged in between 1950s and 1970s possibly "outside the legislative charter of this Agency."

1975 Former Atty. Gen. John Mitchell and ex-presidential advisers H. R. Haldeman and John Ehrlichman found guilty Jan. 1 of **Watergate cover-up** charges. Mitchell released 1979, last of 25 jailed over scandal to leave prison.

U.S. launched **evacuation from Saigon** of Americans and some South Vietnamese Apr. 29 as Communist forces completed takeover of South Vietnam; **South Vietnamese** government officially surrendered Apr. 30. U.S. merchant ship *Mayaguez* and its crew of 39 seized by Cambodian forces in Gulf of Siam May 12. In rescue mission, U.S. Marines attacked Tang Island, planes bombed air base; Cambodia surrendered ship and crew. Congress voted $405 mil for **South Vietnam refugees** May 16; 140,000 flown to U.S.

Publishing heiress **Patricia (Patty) Hearst**, kidnapped Feb. 5, 1974, by Symbionese Liberation Army, captured in San Francisco Sept. 18 with other militants. She was convicted Mar. 20, 1976, of bank robbery.

1976 In right-to-die case, New Jersey Supreme Court, Mar. 31, allowed comatose Karen Ann Quinlan to be removed from respirator. She survived, dying in nursing home in 1985. U.S. Supreme Court reinstated **death penalty**, July 2, subject to conditions.

U.S. celebrated **200th anniversary of independence** July 4 with festivals, parades, and New York City's Operation Sail, gathering of tall ships from around the world. **"Legionnaire's disease"** killed 29 people who attended American Legion convention July 21-24 in Philadelphia.

Viking II set down on Utopia Plains of **Mars** Sept. 3, following successful landing by *Viking I* on Chryse Plains, July 20. Two U.S. officers on routine mission near DMZ slain by **North Korean soldiers** Aug. 18; North Korea stated "regret," Aug. 21.

1977 Convicted murderer Gary Gilmore executed by Utah firing squad Jan. 17; **first use of capital punishment** in U.S. since 1967. Pres. Jimmy Carter Jan. 21 pardoned most **Vietnam War draft evaders**.

Natural gas shortage caused by severe winter weather led Congress Feb. 2 to approve emergency gas bill temporarily authorizing reallocation of interstate gas from surplus areas to shortage areas. Pres. Carter signed act Aug. 4 creating new cabinet-level **energy department**.

FBI Dec. 7 released 40,000 pages of previously secret files relating to **Kennedy assassination**. George Lucas's first *Star Wars* film produced.

1978 Senate voted, Apr. 18 to turn over **Panama Canal** to Panama on Dec. 31, 1999; Mar. 16 vote had given approval to treaty guaranteeing area's neutrality after the year 2000. Californians, June 6, approved **Proposition 13**, state constitutional amendment slashing property taxes.

Supreme Court, June 28, ruled that special admissions program—under which set number of places reserved for minorities—violated civil rights act, which forbids anyone from being excluded from federally funded program because of race, in *Regents of the Univ. of California v. Bakke*.

Egyptian Pres. **Anwar al-Sadat** and Israeli Prem. **Menachem Begin** reached accord on "framework for peace," Sept. 17, after Pres. Carter-mediated talks at Camp David. New York's Chemical Bank Dec. 20 initiated industry-wide move to raise **lending rate** to near-record 11.75%.

1979 Partial meltdown released radioactive material Mar. 28 at nuclear reactor on **Three Mile Island** near Middletown, PA. American Airlines DC-10 **jetliner crashed** May 25 after takeoff from Chicago, killing 275 people.

In speech July 15, Pres. Carter spoke of national "crisis of confidence" and outlined proposed 10-year $140 bil program to **reduce dependence on foreign oil**. Militant followers of **Ayatollah Khomeini** took hostage some 90 people, including 66 Americans, Nov. 4 at **American embassy in Tehran**, Iran. Khomeini demanded return of former Shah Muhammad Reza Pahlavi, who was undergoing medical treatment in New York City.

1980 Pres. Carter announced, Jan. 4, economic sanctions against USSR in retaliation for Soviet invasion of Afghanistan. At Carter's request, U.S. Olympic Committee voted, Apr. 12; against U.S. participation in **Moscow Summer Olympics**. **Lake Placid**, NY, hosted **Winter Olympics** for second time. The U.S. hockey team defeated heavily favored Russian team Feb. 22 en route to winning gold medal in what was called a "miracle on ice."

Eight Americans killed and 5 wounded, Apr. 24, in ill-fated attempt to rescue hostages held by Iranian militants. **Mt. St. Helens**, in Washington state, erupted May 18. The blast, with others May 25 and June 12, left 57 dead. In sweeping victory, Nov. 4, **Ronald Reagan** (R) was elected 40th president, defeating incumbent Pres. Carter. Republicans gained control of Senate. Former Beatle **John Lennon** was shot and killed by Mark David Chapman, Dec. 8, in New York City.

1981 Minutes after Reagan's inauguration Jan. 20, 52 **American hostages in Iran** were freed after being held for 444 days. Pres. **Reagan** was shot and seriously wounded, Mar. 30, in Washington, DC; also seriously wounded were a Secret Service agent, a policeman, and Press Sec. **James Brady**. **John W. Hinckley Jr.** arrested, found not guilty by reason of insanity in 1982, committed to mental institution. World's **first reusable spacecraft**, space shuttle *Columbia*, sent into space, Apr. 12. It performed its first operational mission in 1982. Members of the **Professional Air Traffic Controllers Organization**, Aug. 3, went on strike. Most defied a back-to-work order and were dismissed by Pres. Reagan Aug. 5 for violating federal law. Pres. Reagan signed into law Aug. 13 **tax-cut legislation**, expected to save taxpayers $750 bil over 5 years, largest tax cut to date. The Senate confirmed, Sept. 21, appointment of **Sandra Day O'Connor** as **first female Supreme Court justice**.

1982 The 13-year-old Justice Dept. lawsuit against **AT&T** was settled Jan. 8. AT&T agreed to give up 22 Bell System companies and was allowed to expand. **Equal Rights Amendment**, sent to states in 1972, defeated when deadline for ratification passed June 30 with only 35 of 38 necessary number of states supporting amendment. Centers for Disease Control, July 16, reported evidence of growing **AIDS epidemic**, responsible for 184 deaths in country since first reported in U.S. in June 1981. The economy showed signs of recovery from **recession** that began in mid-1981, as Dow Jones Industrial Average hit 1,016.93 Oct. 13, its highest level in 18 months.

NFL strike ended Nov. 16 after 57 days when players and team owners settled with $1.6 bil pact. Retired dentist Dr. Barney B. Clark became **first permanent artificial heart recipient**, Dec. 2; he died Mar. 23, 1983. The House, Dec. 16, cited EPA administrator Anne Gorsuch for contempt after refusing to produce certain documents concerning the **Superfund**, law that established fund for cleanup and authorized prosecution of hazardous waste dumpers. Singer **Michael Jackson**'s *Thriller* released; eventually considered best-selling album of all time.

1983 Pres. Reagan, Jan. 3, declared Times Beach, MO, a federal disaster area because of toxic **dioxin** in soil, prompting evacuation of residents and town's closure. Harold

1981: Pres. Ronald Reagan nominates Sandra Day O'Connor to be the first woman to serve on the U.S. Supreme Court.

Washington elected Apr. 12 as **first black mayor of Chicago**. On Apr. 20, Pres. Reagan signed compromise bipartisan bill designed to save **Social Security** from bankruptcy.

Sally Ride became **first American woman to travel in space**, June 18, when space shuttle *Challenger* launched from Cape Canaveral, FL. On Sept. 1, **South Korean passenger jet** infringing on Soviet air space and apparently misidentified was shot down; 269 people, including 61 Americans, killed.

On Oct. 23, 241 U.S. Marines and sailors were killed when TNT-laden **suicide truck bomb** blew up Marine barracks at Beirut International Airport in Lebanon. U.S. troops, with small force from 6 Caribbean nations, invaded **Grenada** Oct. 25. After a few days, Grenadian militia and Cuban "construction workers" were overcome, U.S. citizens were evacuated, and the Marxist regime was deposed.

1984 Seven regional companies took over **local telephone service** from AT&T, Jan. 1. On space shuttle *Challenger*'s fourth trip, launched Feb. 3, two astronauts became **first humans to fly free of a spacecraft**. On May 7, Vietnam War veterans reached out-of-court settlement with 7 chemical companies in class-action suit over the herbicide **Agent Orange**.

Former Vice Pres. **Walter Mondale** won Democratic presidential nomination, June 6. He chose Rep. **Geraldine Ferraro** (D, NY) as vice presidential candidate, first woman to be nominated for position by major political party. Pres. Reagan signed bill July 17 cutting federal transportation aid to states that keep their **drinking age** under 21. Pres. **Reagan** reelected Nov. 6 in Republican landslide, carrying 49 states for record 525 electoral votes. **Bernhard Goetz** shot and wounded 4 allegedly menacing teenage boys on NYC subway train, Dec. 22; later acquitted of major charges but was successfully sued.

1985 Visiting Germany, Pres. Reagan, May 5, laid wreath at Bergen-Belsen Nazi concentration camp site and also at military cemetery at **Bitburg**, where some Nazis were buried. Philadelphia police bombed a rowhouse occupied by **MOVE radical group**, May 13; 11 killed, and fire damaged 2 blocks of houses. On June 14, **terrorists seized TWA jet** after takeoff from Athens, Greece, with 153 passengers and crew. Thirty-nine Americans held hostage for 17 days; 1 U.S. service member killed.

Reversing an Apr. 23 decision to market "new" Coke, the **Coca-Cola Co.** said, July 10, it would resume marketing soda made under its original "Classic" formula. **Live Aid** rock concert broadcast around the world July 13, raised $70 mil for famine relief in Ethiopia.

On Oct. 7, 4 **Palestinian hijackers** seized Italian cruise ship *Achille Lauro* in the Mediterranean for 2 days. One American, Leon Klinghoffer, killed. For first time in 6 years U.S. and Soviet leaders met at **summit in Geneva**, Nov. 19-20. **General Electric** agreed Dec. 11 to buy RCA Corp. for $6.28 bil, largest merger to date outside oil industry.

1986 The U.S. officially observed **Martin Luther King Jr. Day** for first time Jan. 20. Space shuttle *Challenger* exploded 73 seconds after liftoff, Jan. 28, killing 6 astronauts and Teacher in Space Project participant Christa McAuliffe. In 4-day extravaganza in July, the U.S. celebrated 100th birthday of the **Statue of Liberty**.

The Senate confirmed, Sept. 17, Reagan's nomination of **William Rehnquist** as chief justice and **Antonin Scalia** as associate justice of Supreme Court. Congress completed action Oct. 2 overriding a veto to place economic sanctions on **South Africa**. Lebanese newspaper first broke news of **Iran-Contra scandal** Nov. 3, involving secret U.S. sale of arms to Iran and diversion of some of the proceeds to support the Contras, a right-wing, anti-Communist insurgent movement in Nicaragua.

Ivan Boesky, accused of **insider trading**, agreed Nov. 14 to pay $100 mil in fines and illicit profits and to plead guilty to an unspecified criminal count. Largest penalty to date imposed for insider trading. Robert Penn Warren named America's **first poet laureate** by the Library of Congress.

1987 Pres. Reagan produced nation's **first trillion-dollar budget**, Jan. 5. **Dow Jones** closed above 2,000 for first time, Jan. 8. The FDA approved, Mar. 20, AZT—first drug shown to be effective in **fight against AIDS**. Nearly 1.4 mil **illegal aliens** met May 4 deadline for applying for amnesty under new federal policy.

Joint public hearings by Senate and House committees investigating **Iran-Contra affair** opened May 5. Lt. Col. **Oliver North**, former National Security Council staff member, said he had believed all his activities were authorized by his

1986: The *Challenger* space shuttle explodes 73 seconds after liftoff.

superiors. Hearings end Aug. 3. Pres. Reagan, Aug. 12, denied knowing of diversion of funds to Contras.

An **Iraqi missile** killed 37 sailors on the USS *Stark* in the Persian Gulf, May 17. Iraq called it an accident. The 200th anniversary of **U.S. Constitution** signing was observed, Sept. 17, in Philadelphia and around the U.S. **Stock market crashed**, Oct. 19, with the Dow Jones plummeting a record 508 points to 1,738, ending bull market that began mid-1982. Pres. Reagan and Soviet leader Mikhail Gorbachev Dec. 8, signed **pact to dismantle** all 1,752 U.S. and 859 Soviet missiles with 300- to 3,400-mi range.

1988 In report issued May 16, Surgeon Gen. C. Everett Koop declared **cigarettes addictive**. Congress approved, in June, greatest expansion yet of **Medicare** benefits, to protect the elderly and disabled against "catastrophic" medical costs. The act was repealed in Nov. 1989. Much of U.S. suffered **worst drought** in over 50 years; by late June half the nation's agricultural counties had been declared disaster areas.

A missile, fired from U.S. Navy warship *Vincennes* in the Persian Gulf, mistakenly struck a commercial **Iranian airliner**, July 3, killing all 290 aboard. **George H. W. Bush** (R) elected 41st U.S. president, Nov. 8, decisively defeating Massachusetts Gov. **Michael Dukakis** (D). **Pan Am Flight 103** exploded and crashed, due to terrorist bomb, into town of Lockerbie, Scotland, Dec. 21, killing all 259 people aboard and 11 on the ground. **Drexel Burnham Lambert** agreed, Dec. 21, to plead guilty to insider trading and other violations, and pay penalties of $650 mil.

1989 Major oil spill occurred when *Exxon Valdez* struck Bligh Reef in Alaska's Prince William Sound, Mar. 24. Oliver North convicted, May 4, on charges related to **Iran-Contra scandal**. Conviction thrown out on appeal in 1991 because of his immunized testimony. A measure to rescue **savings and loan industry** signed into law, Aug. 9, by Pres. Bush, launching largest federal rescue to date. Army Gen. **Colin Powell** became **first black chairman of Joint Chiefs of Staff** after being nominated Aug. 10 by Pres. Bush.

Baseball legend **Pete Rose** banned from game for life Aug. 24 for involvement with gamblers. **Hurricane Hugo** swept through the Carolinas Sept. 22, causing at least 86 deaths and $7 bil damage. Just before a World Series game, Oct. 17, an **earthquake** struck the San Francisco Bay area, causing 63 deaths.

L. Douglas Wilder (D) declared governor of Virginia Nov. 27, **first elected black governor** in U.S. history. U.S. troops invaded Panama, Dec. 20, overthrowing the government of **Manuel Noriega**. Noriega, wanted by U.S. authorities on drug charges, surrendered Jan. 3, 1990.

1990 Junk bond financier **Michael Milken** pleaded guilty to fraud-related charges, Apr. 14; agreed to pay $500 mil in restitution; sentenced Nov. 21 to 10 years in prison. Justice **William Brennan** announced, July 20, resignation from U.S. Supreme Court. His replacement, Judge **David Souter**, confirmed Sept. 27. Pres. Bush signed **Americans with Disabilities Act**, barring discrimination against, and requiring accommodations for, the disabled, July 26. **Operation Desert Shield** forces left for Saudi Arabia Aug. 7, to defend that

country following invasion of **Kuwait** by Iraq, Aug. 2. Pres. Bush Nov. 15 signed into law **Clean Air Act**, strengthened version of Clean Air Act of 1970; focus on urban pollution, cancer-causing emissions from industrial sources.

1991 The U.S. and its allies defeated Iraq in **Persian Gulf War** and liberated Kuwait, which Iraq had invaded. On Jan. 17, the allies launched a devastating air attack. In rapid ground war starting Feb. 24, which lasted just 100 hours, U.S.-led forces killed or captured thousands of Iraqi soldiers and sent the rest into retreat before Pres. Bush ordered cease-fire Feb. 27.

An 8-month **recession** showed signs of having ended in Mar. The **Dow Jones** Industrial Average closed above 3,000 for first time, Apr. 17. House Speaker Tom Foley announced Oct. 3 closure of **House Bank** by end of year after revelations that House members had written numerous bad checks. Justice **Thurgood Marshall**, first black to sit on U.S. Supreme Court, announced, June 17, plans to retire. Senate approved, Oct. 15, nomination of **Clarence Thomas**, also an African American, to replace him, despite allegations that he had sexually harassed former aide Anita Hill.

1992 Retail giant **R.H. Macy & Co.** filed for bankruptcy, Jan. 27. Major U.S. carrier Trans World Airlines (**TWA**) filed for bankruptcy, Jan. 31. **Riots** swept South Central Los Angeles Apr. 29 after jury acquitted 4 white police officers on all but one count in 1991 videotaped beating of black motorist **Rodney King**. Death toll in L.A. violence was put at 53. **27th Amendment**, regarding congressional pay raises, ratified May 7.

Hurricane Andrew ravaged South Florida and Louisiana Aug. 24-26, causing 65 deaths. White supremacist and fugitive Randall Weaver surrendered Aug. 31 after 11-day **FBI siege** at his Ruby Ridge, ID, cabin, during which his wife, son, and a deputy sheriff were killed.

Bill Clinton (D) elected 42nd president, Nov. 3, defeating Pres. Bush (R) and independent Ross Perot. A UN-sanctioned military force, led by U.S. troops, arrived in **Somalia** Dec. 9. Presidents of U.S., Canada, and Mexico Dec. 17 signed **North American Free Trade Agreement** (NAFTA), which took effect Jan. 1, 1994.

1993 A postage stamp honoring the late **Elvis Presley** was introduced Jan. 8. A bomb exploded in a parking garage beneath the **World Trade Center** in New York City, Feb. 26, killing 6 people. Four men found guilty, Mar. 4, 1994. Four federal agents killed, Feb. 28, during unsuccessful raid on **Branch Davidian** compound near **Waco**, TX. A 51-day siege by agents ended Apr. 19, when the compound burned down, leaving more than 70 cult members dead. Eleven cult members acquitted Feb. 26, 1994, of deaths of federal agents.

Janet Reno became **first female attorney general** Mar. 12. Federal jury, Apr. 17, found 2 Los Angeles police officers guilty and 2 not guilty of violating civil rights of motorist **Rodney King** in 1991 videotaped beating.

Defense Sec. Les Aspin, Apr. 28, removed restrictions on aerial **combat roles for women** in the armed forces. In a May 14 plebiscite, voters in **Puerto Rico** supported continuing commonwealth status with U.S. **"Motor-voter" bill** was signed by Pres. Clinton, May 20, easing voting procedures. The **"Great Flood of 1993"** inundated at least 15 mil acres in 9 Midwestern states in summer, leaving about 50 dead and $15 bil in damages as direct result of flood.

Pres. Clinton, July 2, approved recommendations that 33 major U.S. military bases be closed. On July 19 he announced **"don't ask, don't tell, don't pursue"** policy for homosexuals in the military. Judge **Ruth Bader Ginsburg** sworn in, Aug. 10, as 107th justice and second woman on Supreme Court, replacing retiring Justice Byron White. Pres. Clinton, Aug. 10, signed measure designed to **cut federal budget deficits** by $496 bil over 5 years, through spending cuts and new taxes. **Brady Bill**, a major gun-control measure named after former Reagan press sec. James Brady, was signed into law by Pres. Clinton Nov. 30.

1994 A predawn **earthquake** in the Los Angeles area, Jan. 17, claimed 61 lives. Pres. Clinton Feb. 3 lifted 19-year ban on U.S. trade with **Vietnam**. Byron De La Beckwith convicted Feb. 5 of 1963 murder of civil rights leader **Medgar Evers**. Longtime CIA officer **Aldrich Ames** and his wife charged, Feb. 21, with spying. Under plea bargain, he received life in prison, while she drew 63 months.

U.S. troops, Mar. 25, officially ended peacekeeping and humanitarian aid mission in **Somalia**, begun in 1992.

Congressional committees, late July, began **Whitewater hearings**. Kenneth Starr named Aug. 5 as independent counsel to probe Whitewater affair. Major league **baseball players** went on **strike** following Aug. 11 games. World Series canceled; strike ended Apr. 25, 1995. Senate Majority Leader George Mitchell (D, ME), Sept. 26, dropped efforts to pass Pres. Clinton's **health-care reform** package.

Republicans gained control of both House and Senate in Nov. 8 elections after many years of Democratic control. House speaker **Tom Foley** (MA) was among the defeated Democrats.

1995 104th Congress opened, Jan. 4. **Newt Gingrich** (R, GA) elected House speaker. A bill to end Congress's exemption from federal labor laws, first in series of measures in Republicans' **"Contract with America,"** cleared Congress Jan. 17; signed into law Jan. 23. Pres. Clinton, Jan. 31, authorized $20 bil **loan to Mexico** to help it avert financial collapse. Last UN peacekeeping troops withdrew from **Somalia** Feb. 28-Mar. 3, with aid of U.S. Marines. In **Haiti**, peacekeeping responsibilities were transferred from U.S. to UN forces Mar. 31, with U.S. providing 2,400 soldiers.

Truck **bomb exploded outside Oklahoma City federal office** building Apr. 19, killing 168 people in deadliest terrorist attack up to then on U.S. soil; Timothy McVeigh arrested as key suspect, Apr. 21. U.S. space shuttle *Atlantis* made first in series of dockings with Russian space station *Mir*, June 29-July 4. The U.S. announced July 11 it was reestablishing diplomatic **relations with Vietnam**.

Ten Muslim militants convicted, Oct. 1, in failed **plot to blow up UN Headquarters** and other buildings and assassinate political leaders. Former football star **O. J. Simpson** found not guilty Oct. 3 of June 1994 murders of former wife, Nicole Brown Simpson, and a friend of hers. Hundreds of thousands of black men participated in **Million Man March** and rally in Washington, DC, Oct. 16, organized by Rev. Louis Farrakhan.

Five Americans among 7 killed, Nov. 13, in **bombing** of U.S. military post in **Riyadh, Saudi Arabia**. Budget impasse between Congress and Pres. Clinton led to partial **government shutdown** beginning Nov. 14; operations resumed Nov. 20 under continuing resolutions. After talks outside Dayton,

OH, warring parties in **Bosnia and Herzegovina** reached agreement Nov. 21 to end their conflict; treaty signed Dec. 14, after which U.S. peacekeeping troops arrived. A 1973 federal law imposing **55-mph speed limit** repealed Nov. 28.

1996 Senate, Jan. 26, approved, 87-4, **Second Strategic Arms Reduction Treaty** (START II). Congress, Mar. 27-28, approved **line item veto**; struck down by Supreme Court, June 1998.

James and Susan McDougal convicted May 28 of fraud and conspiracy in **Whitewater** case; Arkansas Gov. Jim Guy Tucker convicted on similar charges. The antitax **Freemen** surrendered to federal authorities June 13, after 81-day standoff near Jordan, MT; 4 were convicted, July 1998, of conspiring to defraud banks.

Bomb exploded at **Khobar Towers** military complex near Dhahran, Saudi Arabia, June 25, killing 19 American service personnel. Homemade pipe bomb exploded July 27 in **Atlanta**, GA, park during **Summer Olympics**; 1 person killed. Fugitive Eric Robert Rudolph, arrested in May 2003, pleaded guilty to this and other bombings, later sentenced to consecutive life terms.

Major **welfare reform bill** signed into law, Aug. 22. U.S. signed **Comprehensive Test Ban Treaty**, Sept. 24, which banned all nuclear weapons tests and explosions; Senate failed to ratify treaty. Pres. **Clinton reelected** to 2nd term, Nov. 5.

1997 **Madeleine Albright** sworn in as sec. of state Jan. 23, becoming first female State Dept. head. Former CIA official Harold Nicholson pleaded guilty, Mar. 3, to **spying for Russia**. Thirty-nine members of **Heaven's Gate** religious cult found dead in Rancho Santa Fe, CA, house Mar. 26, in apparent mass suicide.

Timothy McVeigh convicted of conspiracy and murder, June 2, in 1995 **Oklahoma City bombing**; Terry Nichols convicted Dec. 23 on related charges. Islamic militants Ramzi Ahmed Yousef and Eyad Ismoil Yousef convicted, Nov. 12, of key roles in 1993 **bombing of World Trade Center**.

1998 Media outlets reported Jan. 21 on evidence of **sexual relationship** between Pres. Clinton and former White House intern **Monica Lewinsky**; Clinton initially denied affair, but in grand jury testimony and address to the nation, Aug. 17, acknowledged his relationship with Lewinsky had been "not appropriate." On Sept. 9, independent counsel **Kenneth Starr** sent findings to House of Representatives; Judiciary Committee, Oct. 5, voted 21-16 to recommend that Clinton impeachment investigation proceed. Full House, Dec. 19, approved 2 articles of **impeachment** charging Pres. Clinton with grand jury perjury and obstruction of justice in cover-up of relationship with Lewinsky; 2 other articles failed.

"Unabomber" Theodore Kaczynski, arrested in Montana in 1993, pleaded guilty Jan. 22 to California and New Jersey bombings that killed 3 people; sentenced in May to 4 life terms plus 30 years. Texas, Feb. 3, executed its first female convict in 135 years—Karla Faye Tucker.

Bombs at U.S. embassies in Nairobi, Kenya, and Dar-es-Salaam, Tanzania, killed at least 257, Aug. 7; U.S. launched retaliatory strikes, Aug. 20, against targets in Afghanistan and Sudan. On Sept. 30, Pres. Clinton announced federal **budget surplus** of $70 bil for fiscal year 1998, the first since 1969.

Pres. Clinton, Nov. 13, settled suit by agreeing to pay $850,000 to **Paula Jones**, who alleged he had made an unwanted sexual advance in 1991. Country's 4 largest **tobacco companies**, in settlement Nov. 23, agreed to pay states and territories $206 bil over 25 years to cover public health costs related to smoking.

1999 Pres. **Clinton's impeachment trial**—2nd such trial in U.S. history—began in GOP-controlled Senate Jan. 7. He was **acquitted**, Feb. 12. Perjury article failed with 45 votes; obstruction of justice article drew 50-50 vote, with two-thirds vote needed for conviction.

Dr. **Jack Kevorkian**, who claimed to have helped 130 people kill themselves, convicted of 2nd degree murder Mar. 26 in one death; sentenced to 10-25 years. One man pleaded guilty in Apr., another convicted in Nov., in 1998 kidnapping and beating death of **Matthew Shepard**, an openly gay student at the Univ. of Wyoming.

Eric Harris, 18, and Dylan Klebold, 17, killed 12 fellow students and a teacher Apr. 20 at **Columbine High School** in Littleton, CO, then fatally shot themselves. One NYC police officer pleaded guilty to 6 charges, May 25, another convicted of assault, June 8, in 1997 police-station torture of **Abner Louima**, Haitian immigrant. **John F. Kennedy Jr.**,

1995: The Murrah Federal Building in Oklahoma City is targeted in the deadliest act of domestic terrorism in U.S. history.

son of former president, died in a plane crash, July 16, along with wife and sister-in-law.

2000 Across U.S., midnight celebrations marked changeover to year 2000 on Jan. 1; feared **Y2K** computer glitch caused only minor problems. Vermont Gov. Howard Dean (D) signed legislation Apr. 26 allowing same-sex couples in **civil unions** to gain legal rights. Scientists from U.S. and Britain announced jointly, June 26, that they had determined structure of the **human genome.**

Six-year-old **Elián González** was returned to father in Cuba June 28, 7 months after rescue from boat wreck in which his mother and other refugees drowned.

Tiger Woods became youngest player, at age 24, to win all 4 of golf's majors, with record score in British Open, July 23.

Food and Drug Administration announced, Sept. 28, approval of **RU-486**, a pill that induces abortions.

Seventeen U.S. sailors died Oct. 12 in terrorist bombing of **USS Cole**, which was refueling in Aden, Yemen.

On presidential election night, Nov. 7, the winner of **Florida's electoral votes** remained uncertain, leaving national result in doubt for weeks. Florida Supreme Court, Dec. 8, ordered manual recount of certain ballots; on Dec. 12, U.S. Supreme Court reversed that decision, and Vice Pres. **Al Gore** (D), the following day, conceded election to Texas Gov. **George W. Bush** (R).

2001 Congress, Jan. 6, certified **George W. Bush** as president by electoral vote of 271-266 (1 Gore elector abstained). He was **sworn in** as 43rd president Jan. 20.

AOL-Time Warner merger completed Jan. 11. FBI agent **Robert Hanssen** arrested Feb. 20, charged with spying for Soviet Union and Russia over 20-year period; under plea bargain, sentenced in 2002 to life in prison. **U.S. Navy spy plane** collided with Chinese fighter plane over South China Sea Apr. 1, killing fighter pilot; 24 U.S. crew members detained in Hainan until U.S. officials expressed apology, Apr. 12.

Sen. **James Jeffords** (R, VT) announced May 24 he was leaving his party, giving Democrats control of Senate. Pres. Bush signed, June 7, $1.35 tril tax-cut package. Oklahoma City bomber **Timothy McVeigh** executed June 11. Bush announced Aug. 9 he would allow federal funding of limited **stem-cell research** using human embryos.

On morning of **Sept. 11**, 2 hijacked commercial airliners struck **World Trade Center twin towers** in New York City in **worst-ever terrorist attack** on American soil. A 3rd hijacked plane destroyed a portion of the **Pentagon**; a 4th crashed in Pennsylvania field. Some 3,000 people killed, including about 2,750 at World Trade Center. Five people died and 14 became ill from exposure to **anthrax** through U.S. postal system, Oct. 4-Nov. 21; former Army microbiologist Bruce Ivins, later suspected of the crime, apparently committed suicide in July 2008.

U.S. and Britain, Oct. 7, launched air-strike campaign against Afghan-based terrorist organization **al-Qaeda** and the country's ruling **Taliban** militia. Pres. Bush created **Office of Homeland Security**, Oct. 8, and signed federal **antiterrorism bill**, Oct. 26. **Taliban** surrendered Kabul, Nov. 13, and fled from Kandahar, their stronghold, Dec. 7. Taliban member and U.S. citizen **John Walker Lindh** captured Dec. 2 in Afghanistan; under plea bargain sentenced in Oct. 2002 to 20 years. U.S. government, Dec. 11, indicted al Qaeda member **Zacarias Moussaoui** as Sept. 11 co-conspirator; he pleaded guilty, sentenced in May 2006 to life in prison. Operation in Afghanistan's **Tora Bora** cave complex, Dec. 12-17, failed to capture al-Qaeda leader **Osama bin Laden**.

Leading energy-trading company **Enron** filed for bankruptcy, Dec. 2. Pres. Bush announced, Dec. 13, U.S. withdrawal from **1972 Antiballistic Missile Treaty.**

2002 Taliban and al-Qaeda fighters captured in Afghanistan flown to U.S. naval base at **Guantánamo Bay** in Cuba, starting Jan. 11. House committee, Jan. 14, released parts of whistle-blowing letter from Enron employee Sherron Watkins to CEO **Kenneth Lay**. Lay resigned Jan. 23; Congress, Jan. 24, began hearings into **Enron bankruptcy.**

In State of the Union address, Jan. 29, Pres. Bush called **Iran, Iraq,** and **North Korea** part of **"axis of evil."** Eight U.S. troops killed Mar. 2-4 in assault against Taliban and al-Qaeda forces in Afghanistan. Mar. 6, 1,200 U.S. troops were involved in **Operation Anaconda**, which ended Mar. 12.

Independent prosecutor's report, Mar. 20, found insufficient evidence that Pres. Clinton or Hillary Clinton committed any crime in connection with **Whitewater**. Pres.

2001: The attacks of Sept. 11, 2001, kill more than 2,750 people in New York, including 343 firefighters.

Bush, Mar. 27, signed into law McCain-Feingold **campaign-finance reform bill** banning unregulated, unrestricted "soft money" donations; part of bill struck down by Supreme Court, June 2007.

Ceremonial last girder removed May 30 from **World Trade Center** site, signaling end of massive clean-up and recovery operation. Coleen Rowley testified before congressional committee June 6 that Washington FBI agents had stymied investigative efforts in Minneapolis prior to Sept. 11. WorldCom announced June 25 it had overstated its cash flow by billions; filed for bankruptcy, July 21.

Richard Reid pleaded guilty Oct. 4 to all charges stemming from incident aboard plane in Dec. 2001, when he tried to ignite explosives in his shoes; sentenced Jan. 2003 to life in prison. On Oct. 10-11 the House, 296-133, and Senate, 77-23, gave Bush backing to use **military force against Iraq**. Bush administration revealed Oct. 16 that **North Korea** had acknowledged it was developing **nuclear arms**. Pres. Bush, Nov. 25, signed legislation creating **Dept. of Homeland Security.**

U.S. Roman Catholic bishops, Nov. 13, approved revised, Vatican-vetted policies dealing with priests who **sexually abuse minors**. Cardinal **Bernard Law**, Dec. 13, resigned as archbishop of Boston; accused of covering up sexual abuse by priests. **Trent Lott** (R, MS) bowed out as new Senate majority leader Dec. 20, amid furor over comment apparently supporting segregation; Sen. **Bill Frist** (R, TN) elected as leader Dec. 23.

2003 On Jan. 10-11, Gov. George Ryan (R, IL) **pardoned or commuted death sentences** of 171 Illinois death row convicts. U.S. Senate, Jan. 22, approved Pres. Bush's nomination of **Tom Ridge** to be first sec. of homeland security.

Space shuttle **Columbia** broke apart Feb. 1 during descent toward planned landing; all 7 crew members killed. Report issued Aug. 26 blamed damage sustained during liftoff, also cited "broken safety culture" at NASA.

Senate, Mar. 6, approved the **Strategic Offensive Reductions Treaty (Moscow Treaty)** signed in 2002 by U.S. and Russian leaders. Both sides required to reduce deployed nuclear warheads to 1,700-2,200 by 2012.

U.S.-led military offensive aimed at **ousting Saddam Hussein** got underway Mar. 19, when 40 Tomahawk cruise missiles hit targets in Baghdad. U.S. forces Mar. 21 seized oil fields near Basra. On Apr. 3, U.S. Marines crossed Tigris River and moved close to **Baghdad.** By Apr. 9, U.S. forces reported control over much of Baghdad. With collapse of regime, services were disrupted and looting became widespread. Pres. Bush, speaking from aircraft carrier, declared on May 1 the **end of major combat operations in Iraq;** insurgents continued to mount attacks.

Pres. Bush signed bill May 28 providing $330 bil in **tax cuts** over several years. Under settlement in private antitrust suit brought by Netscape (unit of AOL), **Microsoft** agreed May 29 to pay **AOL Time Warner** $750 mil. A **power failure** caused blackouts affecting some 50 mil people in Ohio, Michigan, and the Northeast, as well as eastern Canada, on Aug. 14.

Roman Catholic archdiocese of Boston agreed to pay up to $85 mil in **sex abuse settlement** announced Sept. 9. Californians, Oct. 7, voted to recall Gov. Gray Davis (D) and replace him with actor-turned-politician **Arnold Schwarzenegger** (R). Rev. V. Gene Robinson consecrated Nov. 2 as Episcopal Church's **first openly gay bishop.**

Senate, Nov. 3, approved $87.5 bil for **U.S. military forces in Iraq** and help rebuilding the country. Virginia jury, Nov. 17, found **John Muhammad** guilty in 2002 Washington, DC, area **sniper attacks** that killed 10 people; sentenced to death. Another Virginia jury found **Lee Malvo** guilty of murder in the attacks, Dec. 18; sentenced to life in prison without parole. Massachusetts court decided 4-3, Nov. 18, that **gay couples had right to marry** under state constitution.

Pres. Bush signed bill Dec. 8 to overhaul **Medicare,** adding prescription drug benefit and expanding role of private insurance companies. **Saddam Hussein captured** by U.S. military forces Dec. 13, in underground hideout southeast of Tikrit.

2004 On Feb. 12, San Francisco began issuing marriage licenses to same-sex couples; process blocked Mar. 11 by state supreme court. Photos showing abuse of **Abu Ghraib prison inmates** in Iraq by American soldiers emerged Apr. 3. **National World War II Memorial** in Washington, DC, opened Apr. 29.

Ronald Reagan, 40th U.S. president, died June 5. U.S.-led coalition formally transferred power to **interim Iraqi government,** June 28. The **9/11 Commission Report,** released July 22, called for restructuring U.S. intelligence operations.

In Boston, July 28-29, Democrats nominated Sen. **John Kerry** (MA) for president and Sen. **John Edwards** (NC) for vice president. Pres. **Bush** and Vice Pres. **Cheney** renominated Sept. 1 at Republican convention in New York.

Four hurricanes hit Florida and surrounding states, Aug. 13-Sept. 25; blamed for over 50 deaths and $20 bil in damage in U.S. Number of **U.S. soldiers killed** in the Iraqi conflict reached 1,000 on Sept. 7. **Boston Red Sox** won **World Series** Oct. 27, for first time since 1918.

Pres. **Bush** reelected Nov. 2, winning 31 states; Republicans made gains in the Senate and House. U.S. forces took control of the Iraqi city of **Fallujah** from insurgents, Nov. 14. Pres. Bush signed intelligence reform bill Dec. 17, creating a **director of national intelligence.**

2005 Army Reserve Spec. Charles Graner Jr. found guilty, Jan. 14, in **Abu Ghraib prisoner abuses** in Iraq, sentenced to 10 years. Army Reserve Pfc. Lynndie England convicted Sept. 26, sentenced to 3 years.

Pres. **Bush inaugurated** for 2nd term, Jan. 20. **Condoleezza Rice** became first black woman sec. of state, Jan. 26. **Alberto Gonzales** became first Hispanic U.S. atty. gen., Feb. 3. **Terri Schiavo,** in a persistent vegetative state since 1990, died Mar. 31, 13 days after feeding tube was removed.

Vanity Fair article revealed May 31 that former FBI official **W. Mark Felt** was **"Deep Throat"**—key source for *Washington Post* reporters Bob Woodward and Carl Bernstein probing 1972 **Watergate break-in.** *Discovery* blasted off from Cape Canaveral, FL, July 26, in first shuttle launch since 2003 *Columbia* disaster.

Hurricane Katrina hit Gulf coast, Aug. 29, causing devastation in Louisiana, Mississippi, and Alabama. Breech in a levee on Lake Pontchartrain, Aug. 30, flooded **New Orleans.** Relief efforts widely criticized as insufficient.

Chief Justice **William H. Rehnquist** died Sept. 3. Bush Sept. 5 nominated as successor **John G. Roberts Jr.;** on Sept. 29 he was confirmed by Senate, 78-22, and sworn in

2005: Hurricane Katrina and subsequent failure of levees cause unprecedented destruction in New Orleans and along the Gulf coast.

as 17th chief justice. White House counsel **Harriet Miers,** nominated Oct. 3 to Supreme Court, withdrew Oct. 27. In her place, Bush, Oct. 31, nominated **Samuel A. Alito Jr.;** confirmed Jan. 31, 2006.

House Majority Leader **Tom DeLay** (R, TX) indicted in Texas Sept. 28 for allegedly conspiring to launder illegal contributions; he stepped down from his leadership post.

New York Times, Dec. 16, reported that Pres. Bush in 2002 had secretly authorized National Security Agency to **eavesdrop without court warrant** on people in U.S. suspected of terrorist activities. Senate, Dec. 21, passed $453 bil defense appropriations bill after inclusion of **anti-torture amendment.** Tropical Storm Zeta, Dec. 29, the season's 28th named storm, ended the **most active hurricane season** on record.

2006 Former top Republican lobbyist **Jack Abramoff** pleaded guilty Jan. 3 to bribery and other charges; in plea agreement, promised to cooperate with investigation into his dealings with members of Congress. Former Enron CEO **Jeffrey Skilling** convicted May 25 of fraud, conspiracy, and insider trading related to Enron's 2001 bankruptcy. **Kenneth Lay,** Enron's founder and Skilling's successor as CEO, found guilty same day of fraud and conspiracy; died July 15.

U.S. Supreme Court ruled June 29 that Pres. Bush's system for trying **terrorism detainees** at **Guantánamo** Bay was unauthorized under federal law and Geneva Conventions. Bush, July 19, issued his **first veto,** rejecting bill to end federal funding constraints on human embryonic **stem cell research.**

British authorities announced Aug. 10 they had foiled terrorist plot to use **liquid explosives** on flights between Britain and U.S.; new security restrictions prohibited passengers in U.S. from transporting most liquids in carry-on luggage. In speech Sept. 6 Bush confirmed existence of **secret overseas prisons** for terrorism suspects run by CIA.

Pres. Bush signed bill Oct. 26 authorizing construction of **700-mi fence** along U.S.-Mexico border; broader immigration bill failed in Congress.

Democrats won control of House and Senate in **midterm congressional elections** Nov. 7. Pres. Bush announced Nov. 8 that Defense Sec. **Donald Rumsfeld,** a focus of criticism over Iraq war, had resigned. **Gerald R. Ford,** 38th U.S. president, died Dec. 26 at age 93.

2007 Rep. Nancy Pelosi (D, CA) chosen Jan. 4 as **first woman Speaker of the House.** Pres. Bush announced Jan. 10 he was sending more than 20,000 additional troops to Iraq, in troop **"surge"** backed by Lt. Gen. **David Petraeus,** new top U.S. commander in Iraq.

Reports of substandard conditions at **Walter Reed Army Medical Center** in Washington, DC, resulted in dismissals of military officials, Mar. 1-2. **I. Lewis "Scooter" Libby,** former chief of staff for Vice Pres. Cheney, found guilty Mar. 6 of perjury and obstructing justice in the investigation into a leak exposing undercover CIA agent Valerie Plame Wilson; Bush commuted his prison sentence.

A senior at **Virginia Tech** killed 27 students and 5 faculty members on Apr. 16 before killing himself. On Apr. 18, Supreme Court upheld, 5-4, a 2003 federal law that banned so-called **partial birth abortions.**

U.S. Senate and House May 24 approved Iraq and Afghanistan **war-funding bill** without timetable for withdrawal of U.S. troops from Iraq; Congress also raised **minimum wage** from $5.15 to $7.25 per hour over 2 years.

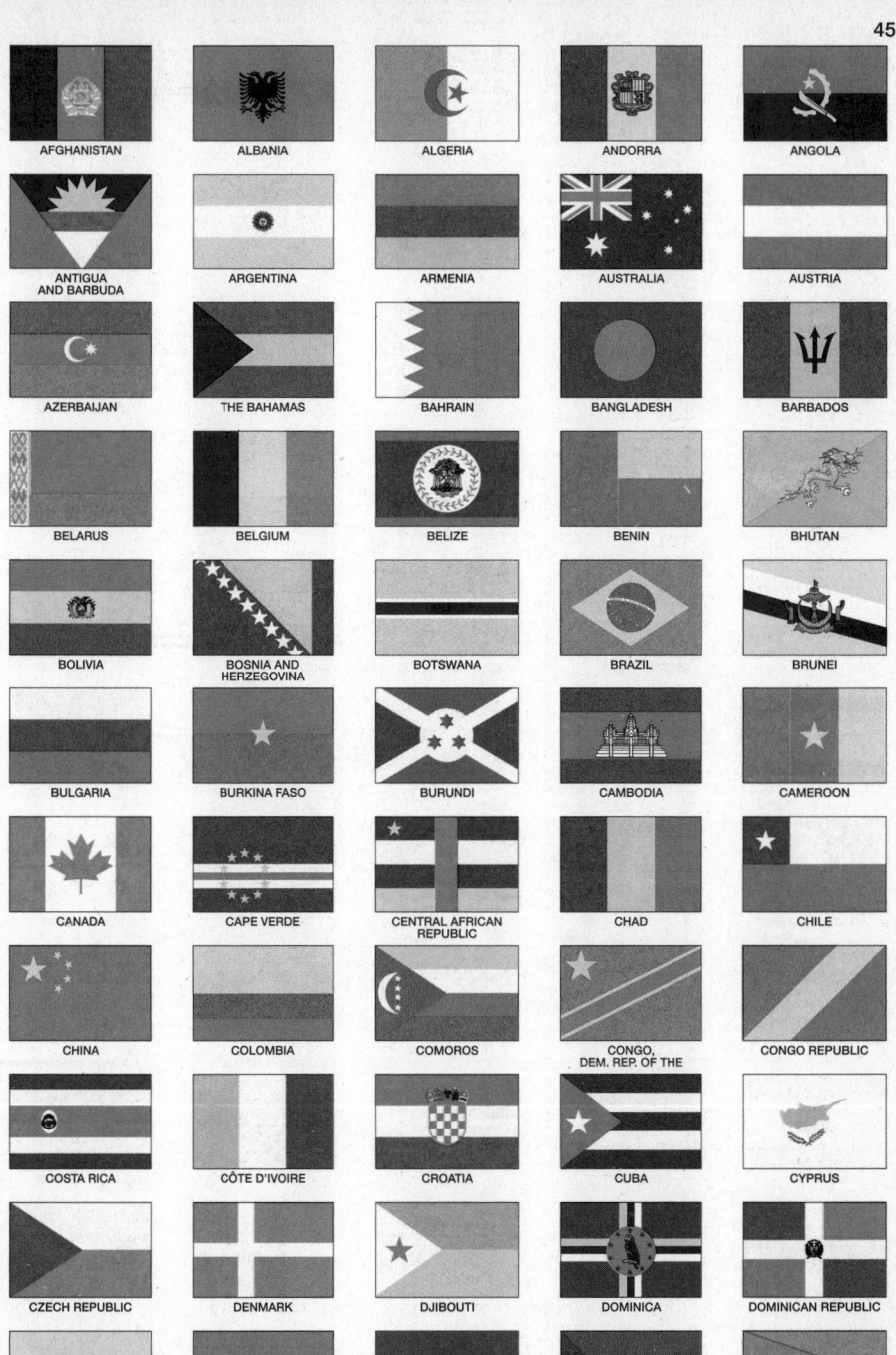

AFGHANISTAN ALBANIA ALGERIA ANDORRA ANGOLA

ANTIGUA AND BARBUDA ARGENTINA ARMENIA AUSTRALIA AUSTRIA

AZERBAIJAN THE BAHAMAS BAHRAIN BANGLADESH BARBADOS

BELARUS BELGIUM BELIZE BENIN BHUTAN

BOLIVIA BOSNIA AND HERZEGOVINA BOTSWANA BRAZIL BRUNEI

BULGARIA BURKINA FASO BURUNDI CAMBODIA CAMEROON

CANADA CAPE VERDE CENTRAL AFRICAN REPUBLIC CHAD CHILE

CHINA COLOMBIA COMOROS CONGO, DEM. REP. OF THE CONGO REPUBLIC

COSTA RICA CÔTE D'IVOIRE CROATIA CUBA CYPRUS

CZECH REPUBLIC DENMARK DJIBOUTI DOMINICA DOMINICAN REPUBLIC

ECUADOR EGYPT EL SALVADOR EQUATORIAL GUINEA ERITREA

Note: Flag proportions have been standardized to fit page.

458

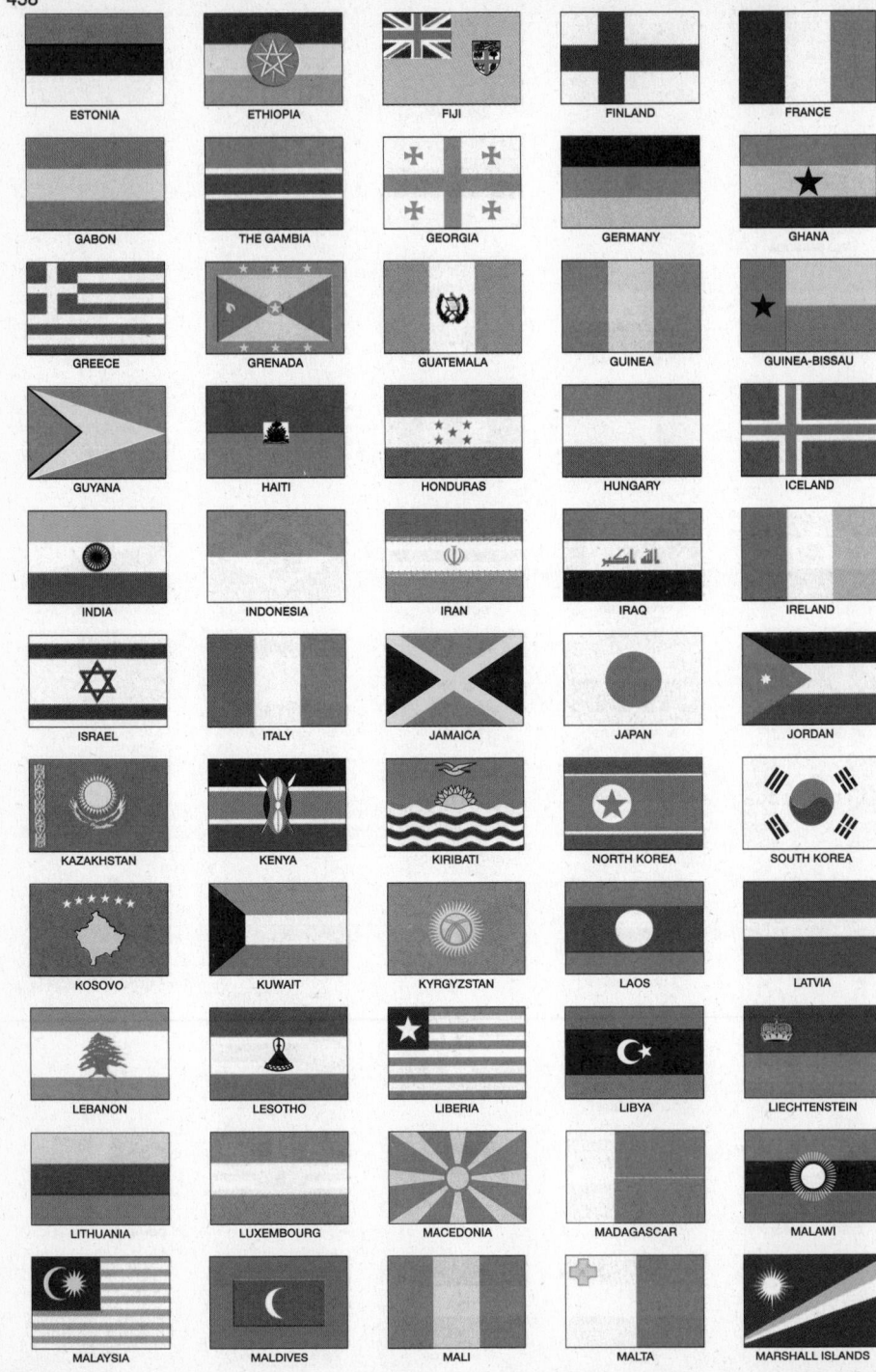

ESTONIA

ETHIOPIA

FIJI

FINLAND

FRANCE

GABON

THE GAMBIA

GEORGIA

GERMANY

GHANA

GREECE

GRENADA

GUATEMALA

GUINEA

GUINEA-BISSAU

GUYANA

HAITI

HONDURAS

HUNGARY

ICELAND

INDIA

INDONESIA

IRAN

IRAQ

IRELAND

ISRAEL

ITALY

JAMAICA

JAPAN

JORDAN

KAZAKHSTAN

KENYA

KIRIBATI

NORTH KOREA

SOUTH KOREA

KOSOVO

KUWAIT

KYRGYZSTAN

LAOS

LATVIA

LEBANON

LESOTHO

LIBERIA

LIBYA

LIECHTENSTEIN

LITHUANIA

LUXEMBOURG

MACEDONIA

MADAGASCAR

MALAWI

MALAYSIA

MALDIVES

MALI

MALTA

MARSHALL ISLANDS

Note: Flag proportions have been standardized to fit page.

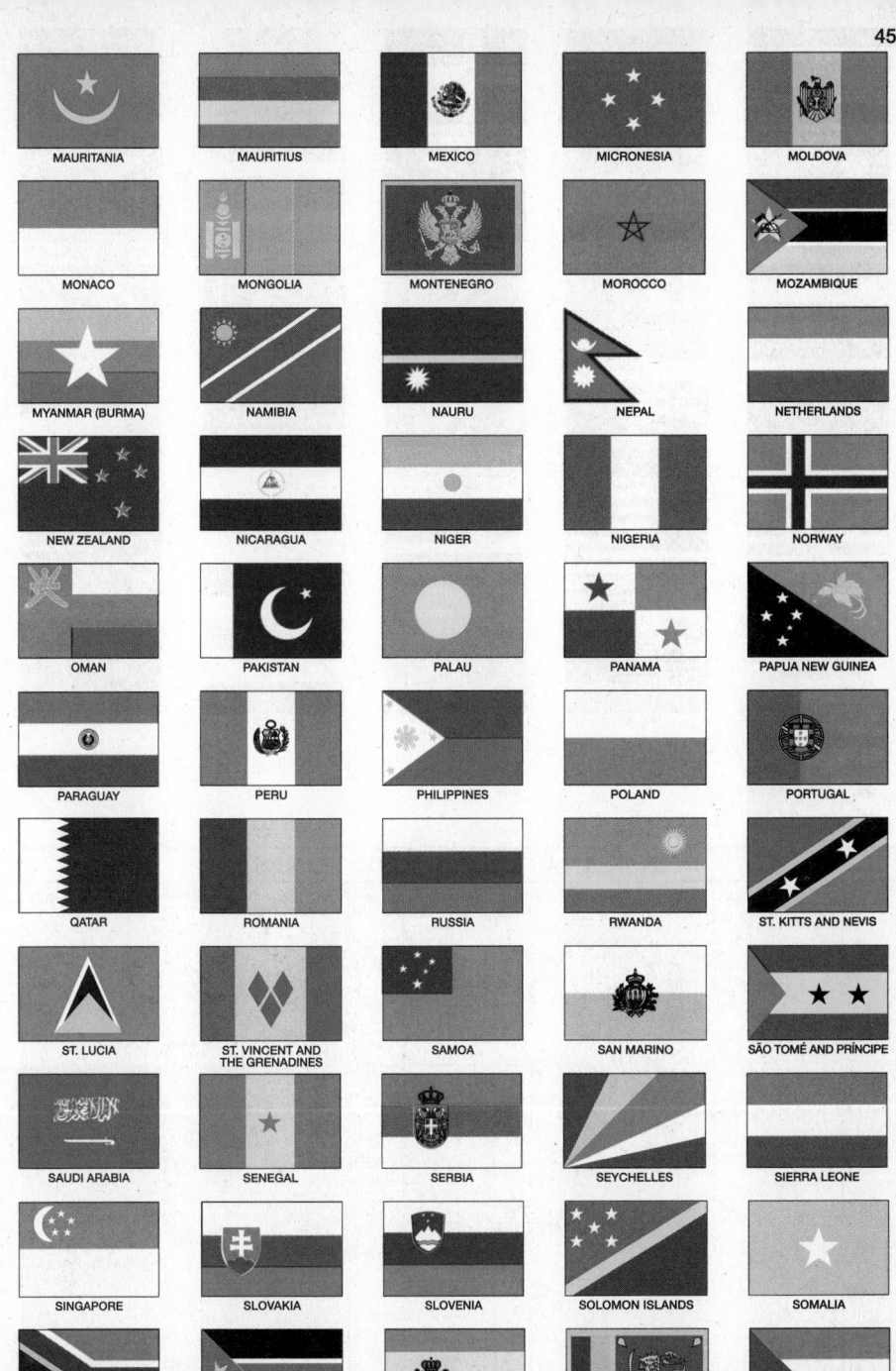

MAURITANIA	MAURITIUS	MEXICO	MICRONESIA	MOLDOVA
MONACO	MONGOLIA	MONTENEGRO	MOROCCO	MOZAMBIQUE
MYANMAR (BURMA)	NAMIBIA	NAURU	NEPAL	NETHERLANDS
NEW ZEALAND	NICARAGUA	NIGER	NIGERIA	NORWAY
OMAN	PAKISTAN	PALAU	PANAMA	PAPUA NEW GUINEA
PARAGUAY	PERU	PHILIPPINES	POLAND	PORTUGAL
QATAR	ROMANIA	RUSSIA	RWANDA	ST. KITTS AND NEVIS
ST. LUCIA	ST. VINCENT AND THE GRENADINES	SAMOA	SAN MARINO	SÃO TOMÉ AND PRÍNCIPE
SAUDI ARABIA	SENEGAL	SERBIA	SEYCHELLES	SIERRA LEONE
SINGAPORE	SLOVAKIA	SLOVENIA	SOLOMON ISLANDS	SOMALIA
SOUTH AFRICA	SOUTH SUDAN	SPAIN	SRI LANKA	SUDAN

Note: Flag proportions have been standardized to fit page.

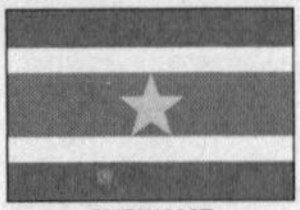
SURINAME

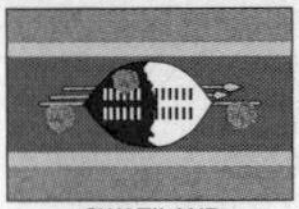
SWAZILAND

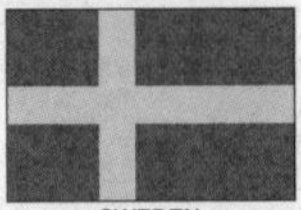
SWEDEN

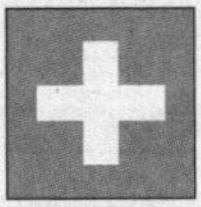
SWITZERLAND

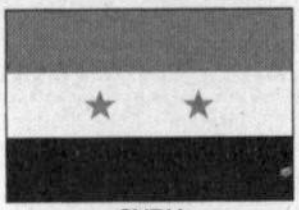
SYRIA

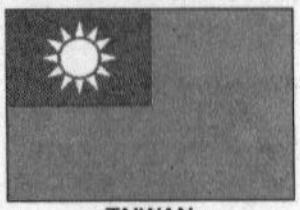
TAIWAN

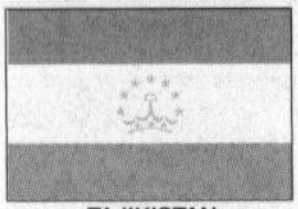
TAJIKISTAN

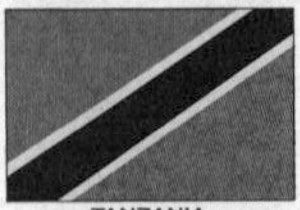
TANZANIA

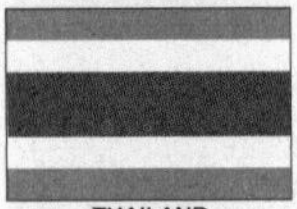
THAILAND

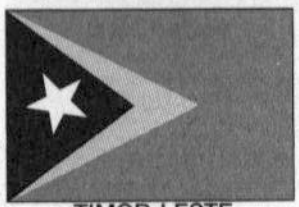
TIMOR-LESTE (EAST TIMOR)

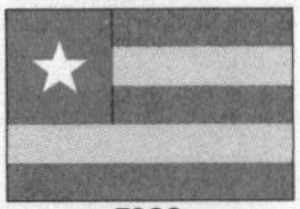
TOGO

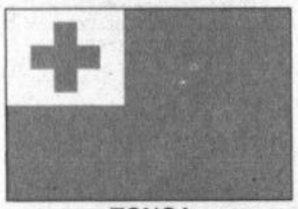
TONGA

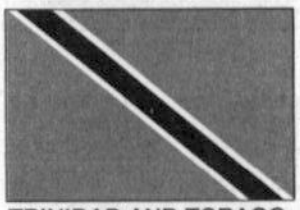
TRINIDAD AND TOBAGO

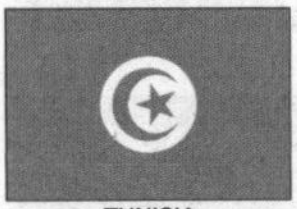
TUNISIA

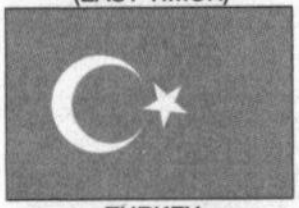
TURKEY

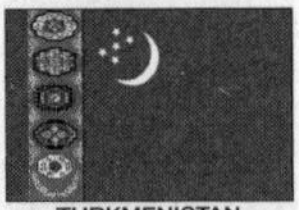
TURKMENISTAN

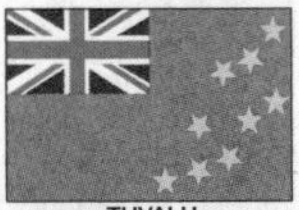
TUVALU

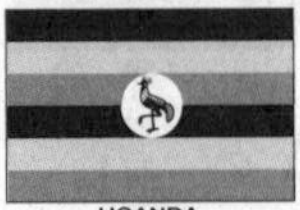
UGANDA

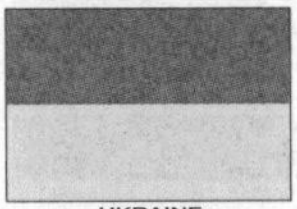
UKRAINE

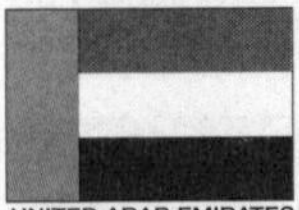
UNITED ARAB EMIRATES

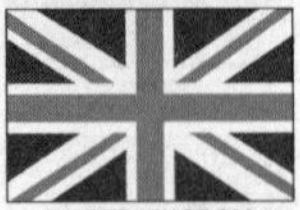
UNITED KINGDOM

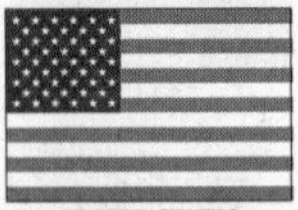
UNITED STATES

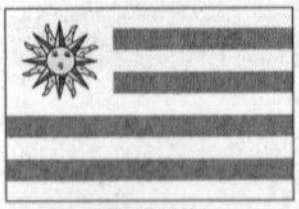
URUGUAY

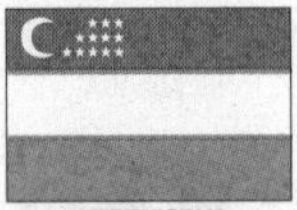
UZBEKISTAN

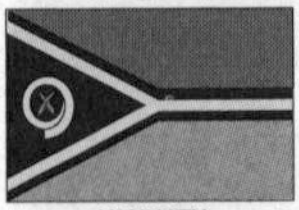
VANUATU

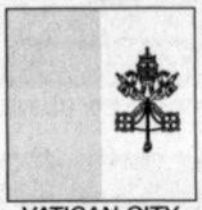
VATICAN CITY

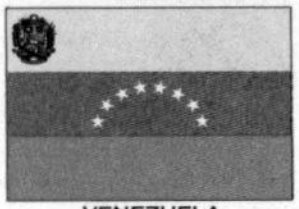
VENEZUELA

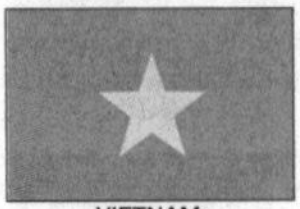
VIETNAM

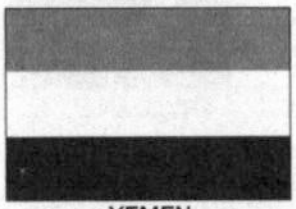
YEMEN

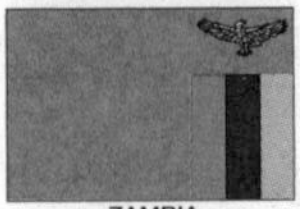
ZAMBIA

ZIMBABWE

INTERNATIONAL TIME ZONES

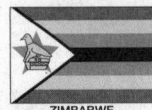

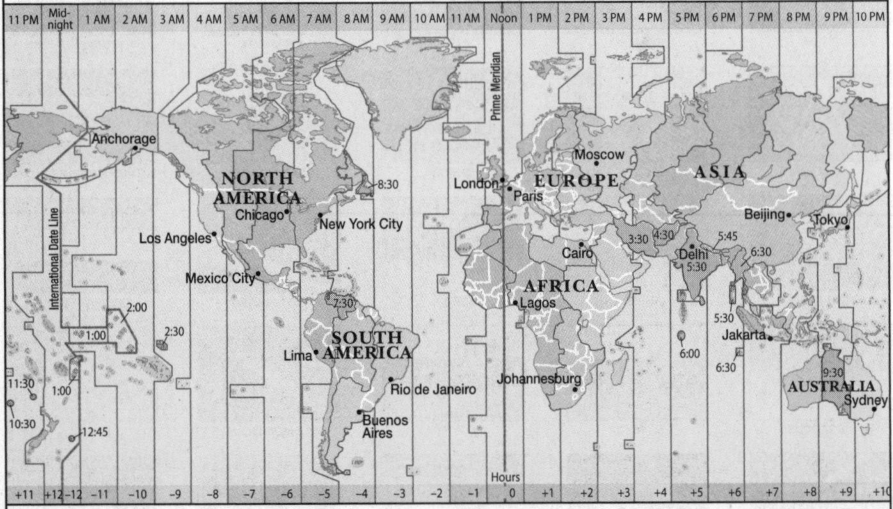
11 PM
Mid-night
1 AM
2 AM
3 AM
4 AM
5 AM
6 AM
7 AM
8 AM
9 AM
10 AM
11 AM
Noon
1 PM
2 PM
3 PM
4 PM
5 PM
6 PM
7 PM
8 PM
9 PM
10 PM
Prime Meridian
International Date Line
NORTH AMERICA
SOUTH AMERICA
EUROPE
ASIA
AFRICA
AUSTRALIA
Anchorage
Chicago
New York City
Los Angeles
Mexico City
8:30
London
Paris
Moscow
Beijing
Tokyo
Cairo
Delhi
5:30
5:45
6:30
3:30
4:30
Lagos
Lima
Rio de Janeiro
Buenos Aires
Johannesburg
Jakarta
5:30
6:00
6:30
9:30
Sydney
7:30
2:00
2:30
1:00
1:00
11:30
10:30
12:45
Hours
+11
+12
−12
−11
−10
−9
−8
−7
−6
−5
−4
−3
−2
−1
0
+1
+2
+3
+4
+5
+6
+7
+8
+9
+10

The world is divided into 24 time zones, each 15° longitude wide. The longitudinal meridian passing through Greenwich, England, is the starting point, and is called the *prime meridian.* The 12th zone is divided by the 180th meridian (International Date Line). When the line is crossed going west, the date is advanced one day; when crossed going east, the date becomes a day earlier.

UNITED STATES

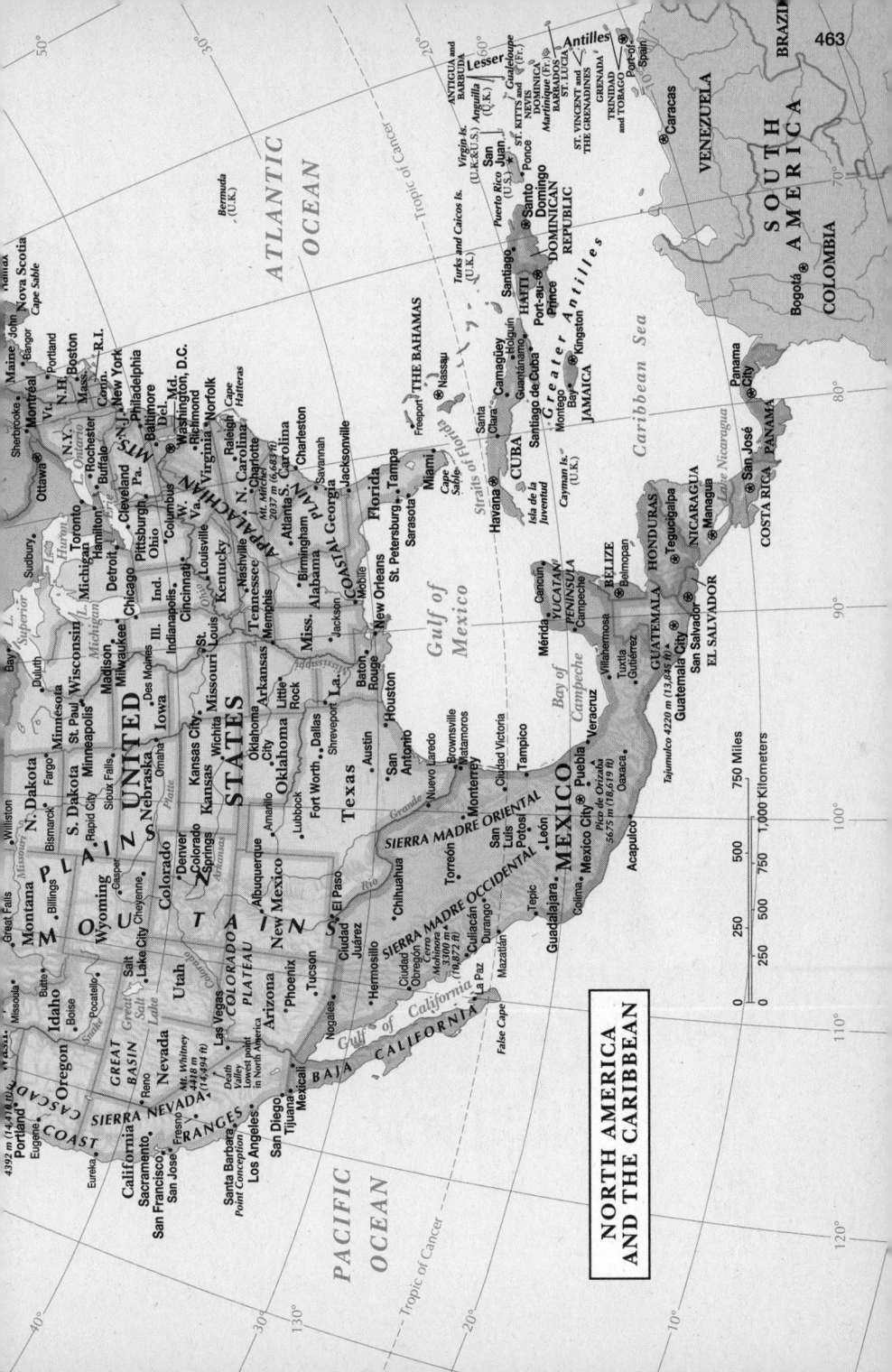

NORTH AMERICA AND THE CARIBBEAN

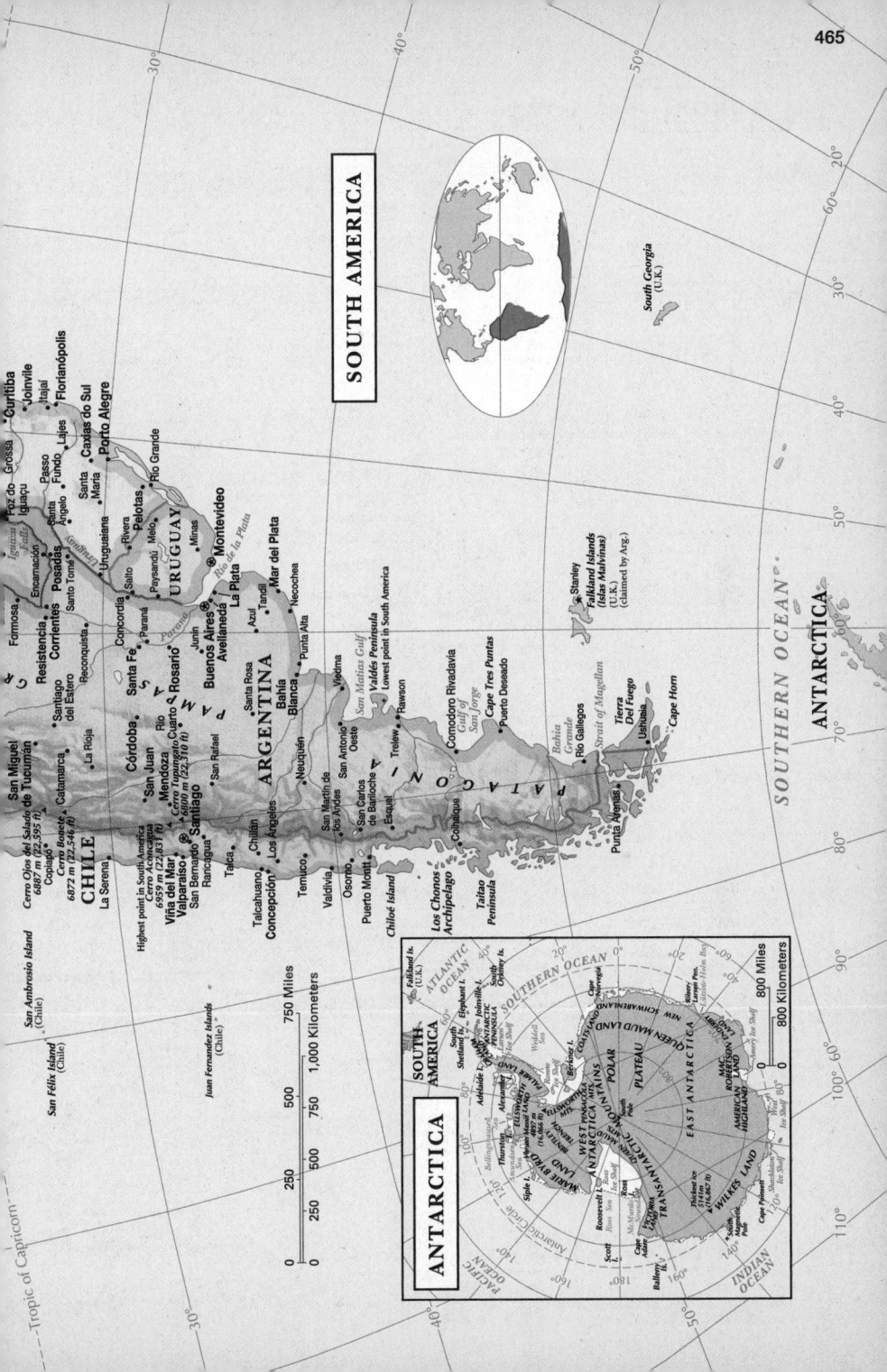

ASIA

NORTH AMERICA

Chukchi Sea · Providniya
Berin Strait
Wrangel I.
East Siberian Sea
New Siberian Islands
Bering Sea
Anadyr
Cherskiy
Laptev Sea
Nordvik
Tiksi
Verkhoyansk
Zyryanka
Susuman
Magadan
Okhotsk
Shiveluch 3283 m (10,771 ft)
Klyuchevskaya 4835 m (15,863 ft)
Karymsky 1536 m (5,039 ft)
Petropavlovsk-Kamchatskiy

TRAL RIAN TEAU
Ust'-Kut
Bratsk
Tuluh
Vilyuysk
Yakutsk
Aldan
Berkakit
Tynda
Komsomol'sk-na-Amure
Svobodny
Blagoveshchensk
Sea of Okhotsk
Okha
Sakhalin
Alaid 2339 m (7,674 ft)
Sarycheva 1496 m (4,908 ft)
Kuril Is. (Russia)

Lake Baykal
Irkutsk
Ulan-Ude
Darhan
Moron
Chita
Hailar
Khabarovsk
Yuzhno-Sakhalinsk
Tiatia 1819 m (5,968 ft)
Hokkaido
Sapporo
Hakodate

MONGOLIA
MONGOLIAN PLATEAU
Bayanhongor
Ulaanbaatar
Choybalsan
Yichun
Qiqihar
Jixi
Harbin
Jilin
Fushun
Changchun
Ussuriysk
Vladivostok
Chongjin
Sea of Japan (East Sea)
Akita
Sendai
Niigata
Honshu
Tokyo
Yokohama
Mt. Fuji 3776 m (12,388 ft)

GOBI DESERT
Hohhot
Baotou
Yumen
Yinchuan
Shenyang
Anshan
Dalian
Beijing
Tianjin
Shijiazhuang
N. KOREA
Hamhung
Pyongyang
Incheon
Seoul
Daegu
Busan
S. KOREA
Kitakyushu
Fukuoka
Kyoto
Osaka
Hiroshima
Nagoya
Kobe
Shikoku
Nagasaki
Kagoshima
Kyushu

CHINA
Xining
Lanzhou
Xi'an
Taiyuan
Handan
Jinan
Qingdao
Yellow Sea
Ryukyu Is. (Japan)

Qinghai Lake
Luoyang
Zhengzhou
Huainan
Nanjing
Shanghai
Hangzhou
Hefei
Okinawa
Naha

Chengdu
Wuhan
Nanchang
Jingdezhen
Wenzhou
East China Sea
Chongqing
Zigong
Shaoyang
Changsha
Ganzhou
Fuzhou
Gulyang
Guilin
Xiamen
Taipei
TAIWAN
Kaohsiung

Kunming
Myitkyina
Liuzhou
Guangzhou
Nanning
Macao
Hong Kong
Zhanjiang
Haikou
Hainan

Tropic of Cancer

PACIFIC OCEAN

Northern Mariana Islands (U.S.)

0   500   1,000 Miles
0   500 1,000 1,500 Kilometers

Phongsali
Haiphong
Mandalay
Taunggyi
Nay Pyi Taw
Chiang Mai
LAOS
Louangphabang
Vientiane
Hanoi
Vinh
Hue
Da Nang
Laoag
Baguio
Luzon
PHILIPPINES
Quezon City
Manila
Naga
Samar
Tacloban
Leyte
Philippine Sea
PALAU

Yangon (Rangoon)
Mawlamyine
Nakhon Sawan
Dawei
THAILAND
Nakhon Ratchasima
VIETNAM
Nha Trang
South China Sea
Mindoro
Panay
Iloilo
Cebu
Butuan
Puerto Princesa
Negros
Mindanao
Davao
Palawan
Sulu Sea
Zamboanga
Equator

Bangkok
CAMBODIA
Batdambang
Phnom Penh
Kompong Som
Ho Chi Minh City
Can Tho
Gulf of Thailand
Kota Kinabalu
Sandakan
Celebes Sea
Ternate
Halmahera
Manado
Jayapura
PAPUA NEW GUINEA
New Guinea
Port Moresby

Isthmus of Kra
Phuket
Hat Yai
Bandar Seri Begawan
BRUNEI
Tarakan
Gorontalo
Ceram
Ambon

Andaman Sea
George Town
Banda Aceh
Medan
Sibolga
Pekanbaru
Kuala Lumpur
MALAYSIA
Natuna Is.
Kuching
Samainda
Celebes
Balikpapan
Palopo
Parepare
Baubau
Banda Sea

Kelang
Singapore
SINGAPORE
Pontianak
Borneo
Sampit
Banjarmasin
Makassar
Arafura Sea

Padang
Jambi
Palembang
Bengkulu
Bandar Lampung
Jakarta
Semarang
Surabaya
Mataram
Sumba
Ende
Dili
TIMOR LESTE
Timor
Timor Sea

Bandung
Yogyakarta
Java
Malang
Bali
Kupang

Sumatra
INDONESIA

AUSTRALIA

AFRICA

ATLANTIC OCEAN

INDIAN OCEAN

SEYCHELLES

SOMALIA
Baidoa
Mogadishu
Marka
Mersabit
Kismayo

UGANDA
Kampala
Jinja

KENYA
Eldoret
Kisumu
Nairobi
Nakuru
Meru
Machakos
Lake Turkana
Mt. Kenya 5199 m (17,057 ft)

Mt. Meru 4565 m (14,977 ft)
Mombasa
Tanga
Pemba I.
Zanzibar I.
Zanzibar
Dar es Salaam

TANZANIA
Mwanza
Dodoma
Morogoro
Iringa
Arusha
SERENGETI PLAIN
HIGHLANDS
Kilimanjaro 5895 m (19,344 ft) Highest point in Africa

RWANDA
Kigali

BURUNDI
Bujumbura
Kigoma

Lake Victoria
Lake Tanganyika
Lake Albert
Lake Edward
Lake Kivu

DEMOCRATIC REPUBLIC OF THE CONGO
Kisangani
Goma
Bukavu
Kindu
Kalemie
Kabalo
Kamina
Kananga
Mbuji-Mayi
Mwene-Ditu
Kabinda
Kalemie
Likasi
Kolwezi
Lubumbashi
Kikwit
Tshikapa
Kinshasa
Ilebo
Bandundu
Mbandaka
Bumba
Buta
Isiro
Beni
Boyoma Falls
KATANGA
PLATEAU

Margherita Pk. 5119 m (16,795 ft)

MALAWI
Lilongwe
Blantyre
Chipata
Lake Nyasa

ZAMBIA
Lusaka
Ndola
Kitwe
Chingola
Kabwe
Livingstone
Mbala
Mpika
Kasama
Victoria Falls
Lake Kariba

ZIMBABWE
Harare
Bulawayo
Gweru
Mutare
Masvingo
Gwanda
Chinoyi

MOZAMBIQUE
Nampula
Nacala
Quelimane
Beira
Chimoio
Tete
Songea
Mtwara
Pemba
Inhambane
Xai-Xai
Maputo

COMOROS
Moroni
Mayotte (Fr.)

MADAGASCAR
Antananarivo
Antsiranana
Mahajanga
Toamasina
Antsirabe
Fianarantsoa
Toliara
Tolanaro

Mozambique Channel

ANGOLA
Luanda
Huambo
Lobito
Benguela
Namibe
Malanje
Menongue
Lubango
Cabinda (Angola)

NAMIBIA
Windhoek
Walvis Bay
Tsumeb
Grootfontein
Lüderitz
Keetmanshoop
NAMIB DESERT
Ruacana Falls
Augrabies Falls

BOTSWANA
Gaborone
Serowe
Palapye
Francistown
Ghanzi
Mmabatho
KALAHARI DESERT

SOUTH AFRICA
Johannesburg
Pretoria (Tshwane)
Vereeniging
Klerksdorp
Welkom
Kimberley
Bloemfontein
Upington
Springbok
Worcester
Cape Town
Cape of Good Hope
Cape Agulhas
Port Elizabeth
East London
Durban
Pietermaritzburg
Umtata
Bisho
Middelburg
Newcastle

LESOTHO
Maseru

SWAZILAND
Mbabane
Lobamba

Orange
Limpopo
Zambezi

REPUBLIC OF THE CONGO
Brazzaville
Pointe-Noire
Loubomo
Matadi
Mbanza-Ngungu
Boma

GABON
Libreville
Franceville
Lambaréné
Port-Gentil

EQUATORIAL GUINEA
Malabo
Bioko
Principe
SÃO TOMÉ AND PRÍNCIPE
São Tomé
Annobón (Eq. Guinea)

Yaoundé

Gulf of Guinea

CONGO BASIN
Congo
Ubangi
Kasai
Kwango
Kwilu
Lomami
Lualaba

RIFT VALLEY

Tropic of Capricorn

Equator

Ascension (U.K.)

750 Miles
1,000 Kilometers
500
250
750
500
250
0

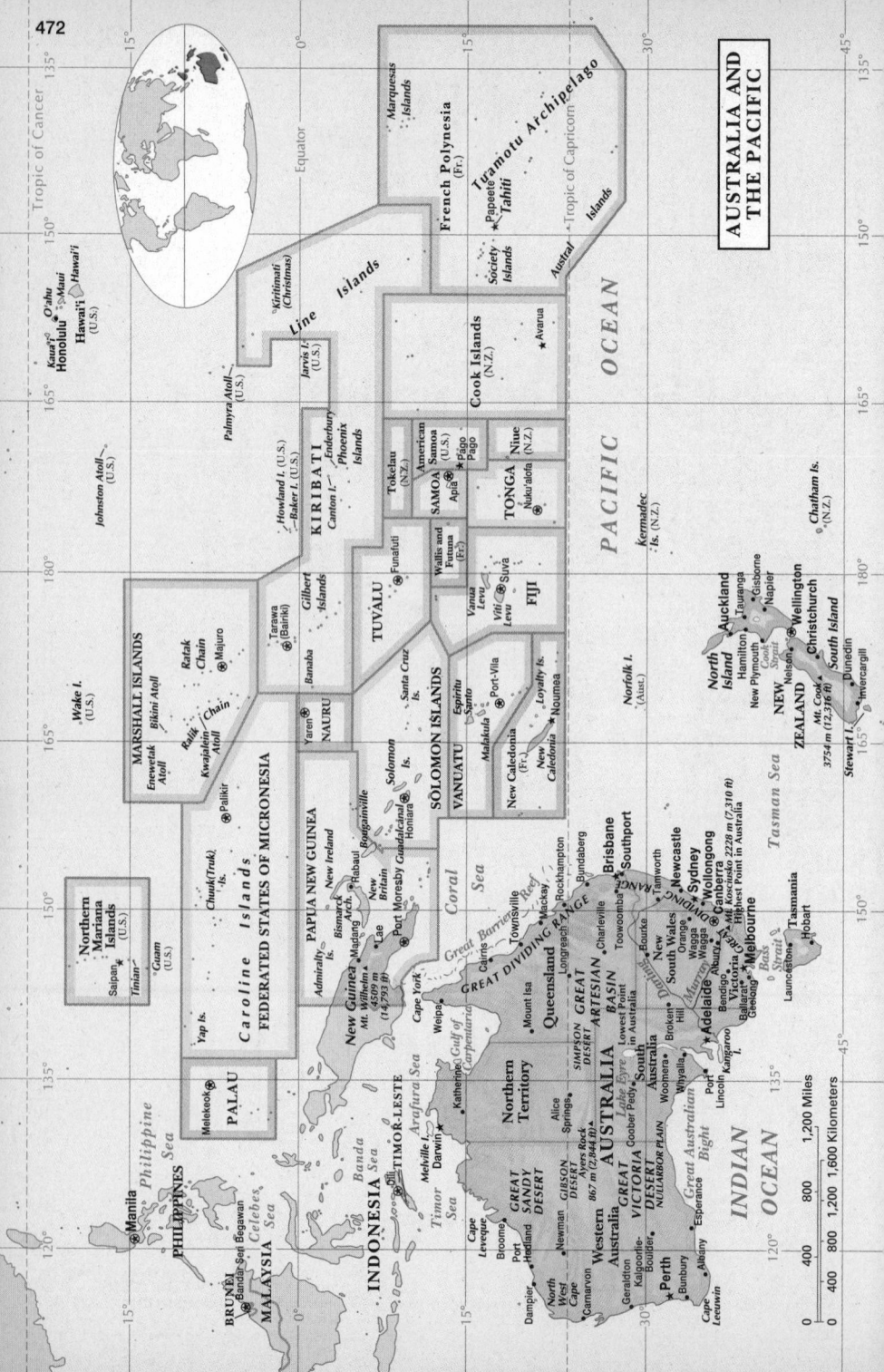

AUSTRALIA AND
THE PACIFIC

2007: Pres. George W. Bush sends a "surge" of additional U.S. troops to Iraq.

Dow Jones closed over 14,000 July 19, just 59 trading days after passing 13,000. *Harry Potter and the Deathly Hallows*, final novel in J. K. Rowling's series, released July 21, earning record U.S. sales. Pres. Bush issued an executive order July 20 requiring that **imprisoned terror suspects** receive "the basic necessities of life" and barring cruel, inhuman, or degrading treatment.

A **Minneapolis highway bridge collapsed** Aug. 1, causing the deaths of 13 people. Congress, Aug. 4, cleared measure allowing **National Security Agency** to monitor communications without court warrants if believed related to terrorism. Barry Bonds tied Major League Baseball's all-time career **home-run record** at 755—set by Hank Aaron—on Aug. 4 in San Diego; hit No. 756 on Aug. 7.

Karl Rove, Bush's chief political strategist, announced Aug. 13 that he was resigning. **José Padilla** convicted of conspiracy in terrorism case, Aug. 16; later sentenced to 17 years, 4 months in prison. Atty. Gen. **Alberto Gonzales**, blamed for alleged firing of U.S. attorneys, announced his resignation Aug. 27.

Congress voted, Nov. 6 and 8, to **overturn veto** by Pres. Bush for first time, on a $23 bil water projects bill. Report by former U.S. Sen. George J. Mitchell, released Dec. 13, presented evidence of **performance-enhancing drug use** by 86 Major League Baseball players.

On Dec. 6 Pres. Bush announced accord among mortgage lenders to impose 5-year freeze on interest rates for some mortgage holders and provide options for some homeowners to refinance. Under law signed Dec. 17, New Jersey became the first state to **repeal the death penalty** since Supreme Court reinstated it in 1976. An **energy bill** mandating an increase in automobile **fuel-economy standards** to 35 mi per gallon by 2030 signed by Pres. Bush Dec. 19.

2008 Sen. **John McCain** (AZ) won New Hampshire primary, Jan. 8; clinched 2008 Republican presidential nomination by early Mar. Among Democrats, Sen. **Barack Obama** (IL) moved ahead of closest rival Sen. **Hillary Clinton** (NY) to clinch nomination in early June.

The Federal Reserve cut key interest rates, Jan. 22 and 30, to aid U.S. economy; $168 bil **economic stimulus** package, signed Feb. 13 by Pres. Bush, provided tax rebates.

In Mar. 18 speech, Sen. Obama discussed America's racial divide and condemned inflammatory rhetoric used by Rev. **Jeremiah Wright**, his former pastor. Benedict XVI made his **first papal visit** to U.S., Apr. 15-20.

Justice Dept., Apr. 1, declassified 2003 legal brief that sanctioned use of extreme methods in questioning detainees linked to al-Qaeda. U.S. Supreme Court ruled June 12 that foreign prisoners at **Guantánamo Bay** could challenge detention by filing writs of **habeas corpus**.

Oil prices spiked above $140 per barrel in June; national average price for gallon of regular gas reached nearly $4.09 by July 1.

Sec. of State Condoleezza Rice signed agreements in Czech Republic, July 8, and Poland, Aug. 20, to place components of a U.S. **missile defense system** there (agreements rescinded by Obama administration). Measure signed July 10 by Pres. Bush expanded government power to spy on suspected terrorists. U.S. **military deaths in Iraq** dropped to 13 in July, lowest monthly total since the war began. U.S., Sept. 1, gave Iraqi forces security responsibilities in Anbar province, formerly center of a Sunni insurgency. U.S. air strike in **Afghanistan** village of Azizabad, Aug. 22, killed up to 90 civilians, according to Afghan sources. Meeting Aug. 25-28 in Denver, CO, Democrats nominated Sen.

Barack Obama (IL) for president and Sen. **Joe Biden** (DE) for vice president. Meeting Sept. 3 in St. Paul, MN, Republicans nominated Sen. **John McCain** (AZ) for president and Alaska Gov. **Sarah Palin** for vice president.

With financial system in crisis, federal government Sept. 7 took control of mortgage finance companies **Fannie Mae** and **Freddie Mac**. On Wall Street a week later, investment titan **Merrill Lynch** agreed to sell itself to Bank of America for $50 bil, and **Lehman Brothers** declared bankruptcy, after finding no buyer. The Fed Sept. 16 took control of insurance giant American International Group (**AIG**), giving it a credit line that expanded to $144 bil by Oct. 31.

On Sept. 20, a Treasury Dept. plan was introduced to purchase up to $700 bil of **"toxic" mortgage-backed securities** to restore confidence among investors and banks. Legislation to implement Troubled Assets Relief Program (**TARP**) failed in the House, Sept. 29, sending Dow Jones down 778 points. Revised **"bailout" plan** passed Senate Oct. 1, 74-25, and House Oct. 3, 263-171; gave Treasury immediate access to half of $700 bil TARP funds, with broad discretion in their use. On Oct. 21 Fed pledged $540 bil as a backup to protect money market funds.

Bush administration announced Oct. 11 it had removed **North Korea** from list of countries that sponsor terrorism, as part of June agreement for North Korea to begin dismantling nuclear weapons program.

Barack Obama elected, Nov. 4, as **first African American president** in U.S. history, earning 53% of popular vote and 365 of 538 electoral votes. Democrats also increased majorities in House and Senate. California voters approved **Proposition 8**, banning same-sex marriages in the state.

Dow Jones Industrial Average fell 427 points, or 5.1%, Nov. 19, going below 8,000 for first time since 2003. U.S. government Nov. 23 announced plan to provide $20 bil in cash and up to $306 bil more as backup to protect ailing **Citigroup** from potential mortgage losses; Dow Jones rose 397 points. Pres.-elect Obama Nov. 24 named **Timothy Geithner** as treasury sec.; he was confirmed Jan. 26, 2009. **Dow Jones** dropped 680 points Dec. 1 after reports that manufacturing had hit 26-year low and that U.S economy officially fell into **recession** in Dec. 2007.

Pres.-elect Obama named former rival **Hillary Clinton**, Dec. 1, to be sec. of state (confirmed Jan. 21, 2009). Illinois Gov. **Rod Blagojevich** (D) arrested Dec. 9, accused of seeking to sell Senate seat being vacated by Obama. Blagojevich asserted innocence and made Senate appointment, Dec. 30, choosing former state Atty. Gen. **Roland Burris. Bernard Madoff** arrested Dec. 11 on charges he had defrauded investment clients in massive **Ponzi scheme**; sentenced to 150 years in jail in guilty plea, June 2009. Fed, Dec. 16, cut benchmark interest rate to near zero. On Dec. 19, Pres. Bush announced that $17 bil in TARP funds would be used to help keep **General Motors** and **Chrysler** afloat; Treasury reported that, with this commitment, it had now allocated nearly all of its TARP funds, mostly to bolster ailing financial institutions by purchasing equity stakes in them.

2009 Illinois Gov. **Blagojevich**, impeached Jan. 9, convicted Jan. 29 by state Senate and removed from office. Treasury Dept., Jan. 15, gained access to remaining $350 bil in TARP funds and provided new funding to help prop up the troubled **Bank of America.**

Barack Obama inaugurated Jan. 20 as 44th U.S. president. On Jan. 22 issued executive orders restricting CIA interrogation practices and calling for closing of U.S. military prison at **Guantánamo** Bay, Cuba, within a year (closing blocked by Congress). Treasury Sec. Geithner, Feb. 10, outlined $2 tril program to stabilize banking and ease credit markets, with "stress tests" that led to greater capital requirements for some banks. Pres. Obama signed **economic stimulus** bill Feb. 17, providing for $212 bil in tax cuts and $575 bil in new spending; lawmakers also restricted bonuses by financial firms receiving bailout funds. Obama introduced $275 bil program Feb. 18 to help protect homeowners from **foreclosure** and ease terms for refinancing.

Pres. Obama announced, Feb. 17, that U.S. would send 17,000 more troops to **Afghanistan** and said, Feb. 27, that most U.S. troops would be out of Iraq by Aug. 2010. Strategy announced Mar. 27 called for stepped-up training of Afghan troops.

California legislators, ending 15-week deadlock, closed $42 bil budget gap, Feb. 19; revised plan passed July 24. Revised data released Feb. 27 showed U.S. **GDP fell** at 6.2% annual rate in Oct.-Dec. 2008, the steepest drop since 1982.

Bailed-out insurance giant **AIG** Mar. 2 reported **record loss** for 4th quarter 2008; new government funding granted. Treasury Sec. Geithner, Mar. 23, introduced Public-Private Investment Program (PPIP), offering incentives to encourage purchases of **"toxic assets."**

Iowa's Supreme Court Apr. 3 struck down state law barring **same-sex marriage**; measures allowing it were approved in Vermont, Apr. 7; Maine, May 6 (repealed in Nov. 3 referendum); and New Hampshire, June 3.

Justice Dept. Apr. 16 made public memos offering legal rationale for CIA detainee interrogation methods that included beatings and **waterboarding**. On Aug. 24, Atty. Gen. Eric Holder appointed a special prosecutor to investigate **possible detainee abuse**.

U.S. Navy SEALs Apr. 12 rescued American captain Richard Phillips, taken hostage by **pirates off Somali coast**. Obama administration Apr. 13 eased restrictions on family travel and remittances to **Cuba**. After outbreak of influenza A (H1N1), or **swine flu**, in Mexico and then in U.S., U.S. officials declared public health emergency Apr. 26.

Congress, with no GOP support, Apr. 29 approved $3.5 tril federal budget for fiscal 2010, with deficit of $1.2 tril. **Chrysler LLC** filed for bankruptcy protection Apr. 30; auto workers' union retirement health-care fund given 55% stake in reorganized company. Pres. Obama, May 19, tightened **fuel efficiency** standards for vehicles. **General Motors** filed for bankruptcy June 1 under plan providing $30.1 bil in new federal funds to support a leaner GM. On June 9, 10 financial firms got permission from U.S. Treasury to return some $68 bil in **TARP funds**.

George Tiller, Kansas doctor who performed **late-term abortions**, murdered May 31; anti-abortion activist was convicted Jan. 2010 and sentenced Mar. 2010 to life in prison.

Speaking June 4 in Egypt, Pres. Obama called for "new beginning" in relations with **Muslim world**. U.S. military completed **withdrawal from Iraq's cities** and towns June 30; some 130,000 U.S. troops remained at bases.

Pres. Obama, June 22, signed measure authorizing FDA to regulate content and marketing of tobacco products. Pop superstar **Michael Jackson** died June 25; death attributed to "acute propofol intoxication." Alaska Gov. **Sarah Palin** (R), July 3, announced she was resigning. Obama and Pres. Dmitri Medvedev, in Russia July 6, agreed on **reducing nuclear arsenals** and allowing U.S. flights to Afghanistan through Russian airspace.

Judge **Sonia Sotomayor**, confirmed Aug. 6 for Supreme Court vacancy left by retirement of David Souter; sworn in Aug. 8, she became first Hispanic to join the court.

Federal **"cash for clunkers"** program, for trading in old gas-guzzling vehicles, began July 24 with funding of $1 bil; renewed Aug. 7 with another $2 bil. Returning to home districts during Aug. recess, lawmakers encountered angry protesters opposed to pending **health care legislation**. Sen. Edward M. (Ted) Kennedy (D, MA) died Aug. 25.

Airport shuttle driver Najibullah Zazi arrested Sept. 19 and charged, Sept. 24, with involvement in plot to produce bombs for **terror attacks** in the New York City subway system; he

2008: Sen. Barack Obama is elected the first African American president.

later pleaded guilty. On Sept. 25, at meeting of Group of 20 (G-20) leaders in Pittsburgh, PA, Pres. Obama accused **Iran** of building secret uranium enrichment facility. In raids in 38 U.S. cities, Oct. 21-22, federal agents arrested over 300 people connected with a **Mexican drug cartel**.

Government reported Oct. 29 that real GDP grew at 3.5% annual rate in July-Sept., signaling that key sectors had **emerged from recession**. However, **unemployment** in Oct. passed 10%. Pres. Obama Nov. 6 signed measure extending unemployment benefits and $8,000 tax credit for first-time homebuyers.

Pres. Obama announced Oct. 30 end to U.S. travel and immigration restrictions on people infected with AIDS virus. On Nov. 5, 12 soldiers and a civilian were killed in **mass shooting at Ft. Hood**, TX; Army psychiatrist Maj. Nidal Malik Hasan was shot and wounded by police SWAT team, then arrested and charged in the shootings.

U.S. House Nov. 7 approved a $1.1 tril **health care reform bill**, 220-215, with only 1 Republican vote in favor; Senate Dec. 24 approved a different $871 bil version, 60-39, with no Republican votes, leaving the final fate of the legislation in limbo. Pres. Obama Dec. 1 announced a surge of 30,000 additional troops to **Afghanistan**, so as to peak at 100,000, with drawdown to begin within 18 months. Accepting **Nobel Peace Prize**, Dec. 10 in Oslo, Norway, Obama defended U.S.-led military action in Afghanistan as a "just war."

Tiger Woods Dec. 11 acknowledged infidelity in his marriage and announced he was taking a break from pro golf after a series of scandalous tabloid stories. Pres. Obama brokered 5-nation **greenhouse-gas accord**, Dec. 18 in Copenhagen, establishing nonbinding reduction goals.

On Dec. 25, people aboard an airplane approaching Detroit thwarted apparent attempt by Nigerian man to ignite **explosives hidden in his underwear**. On Dec. 30, a Jordanian CIA informant acting as a double agent set off bomb at high-level CIA meeting site near Afghan-Pakistan border, killing himself and 8 others.

U.S. stock exchanges Dec. 31 reported best gains since 2003, with Dow Jones closing 18.8% higher than a year earlier, and 59.3% from 2009 low point in early Mar.

2010 In special election Jan. 19 in Massachusetts, state Sen. **Scott Brown** (R) upset state Atty. Gen. Martha Coakley (D) to win U.S. Senate seat held by Sen. Edward Kennedy (D) for nearly 47 years; result cost Democrats their filibuster-proof majority. U.S. Supreme Court Jan. 21 held that corporations had a First Amendment right to spend unlimited funds on advertising to influence election outcomes.

The Obama administration Feb. 1 released 10-year spending plan, calling for outlays of $3.834 tril and a deficit of $1.267 tril for fiscal year 2011; White House projected declining deficits, with debt rising to $18.573 tril by 2020. Obama Feb. 18 created bipartisan National Commission on **Fiscal Responsibility and Reform**, headed by former Clinton chief of staff Erskine Bowles (D) and former Sen. Alan Simpson (R, WY).

Testifying before Congress Feb. 23-24, executives of **Toyota Motor Corp.** and its U.S. subsidiary apologized for defects that had led to recall of millions of vehicles in U.S. Toyota later agreed to pay $16.4 mil civil penalty for failing to promptly report gas pedal problems. U.S. and other coalition troops launched major offensive in **Helmand Province**, Afghanistan, Feb. 13, targeting Taliban strongholds.

Measure legalizing **same-sex marriage** in Washington, DC, came into force Mar. 3. Pres. Obama, Mar. 18, signed $18 bil **job-stimulus** measure providing tax cuts and other employer incentives.

Long effort by Democrats to enact **health care reform legislation** succeeded on Mar. 21, when the House voted, 219-212, with no Republican support, to approve bill as passed by Senate in Dec. 2009. The wide-ranging, controversial measure, signed by Pres. Obama on Mar. 23, aimed in part at extending **health insurance** to some 32 mil uninsured over 10 years; the estimated cost was $938 bil.

Community organizing group **ACORN** announced Mar. 22 that it would disband, after losses suffered as a result of videos by conservative activists showing improprieties by some ACORN workers. Explosion in **West Virginia coal mine**, Apr. 5, killed 29. Meeting Apr. 8 in Prague, Pres. Obama and Russian Pres. Dmitri Medvedev signed New Strategic Arms Reduction Treaty, or **New START** (ratified by Senate, Dec. 2010; in force, Feb. 2011). On Apr. 15, Pres. Obama outlined plans for **NASA** to send manned missions to an asteroid by 2025 and to Mars by the mid-2030s; defended decision to

2010: The *Deepwater Horizon* rig explodes, spilling oil into the Gulf of Mexico for nearly 3 months.

terminate Bush administration program to return astronauts to the moon by 2020.

A gas explosion and fire engulfed *Deepwater Horizon*, drilling platform off Louisiana coast, killing 11 people on board Apr. 20. About 4.9 mil barrels of **oil spilled into the Gulf** of Mexico over a 3-month period, damaging Gulf ecology and the regional economy. As parent company BP sought to stem the flow and clean up effects, federal government, May 27, imposed moratorium on deepwater exploratory drilling in the Gulf. After White House meeting June 16, BP executives agreed to set aside $20 bil fund to compensate persons for losses. Oil flow was stopped July 15; well declared permanently sealed Sept. 19.

Arizona state legislature passed Apr. 19, and Gov. Jan Brewer (R) signed Apr. 23, controversial **immigration measure** which, among other things, authorized police to arrest anyone reasonably suspected of being an illegal immigrant. Federal court injunction, issued July 28, blocked key provisions from taking effect.

New York City police May 1 dismantled crude **car bomb in Times Square**, traced to Faisal Shahzad, who was arrested May 3. He pleaded guilty to terrorism charges, June 21, and was sentenced to life in prison, Oct. 5.

Pres. Obama May 10 nominated **Elena Kagan** to the U.S. Supreme Court to replace retiring Justice John Paul Stevens; confirmed by Senate, Aug. 5. Long-serving Sen. Arlen Specter (D, PA), who had switched parties in 2009, was defeated for nomination in May 18 primary. Rep. **Mark Souder** (R, IN) disclosed May 18 that he would resign his seat after admitting to an affair with a married female staffer.

U.S. government officials revealed June 10 that over a 22-month period, federal law enforcement agents in 19 states had arrested more than 2,200 people suspected of having ties with **Mexican drug cartels.**

Pres. Obama June 23 named Gen. **David Petraeus** as commander of U.S. and allied troops in Afghanistan, replacing Gen. Stanley McChrystal, who was forced to resign after publication of disparaging comments made about the Obama administration by McChrystal and his staff. U.S. Supreme Court June 28 held that the **right to keep and bear arms** is a fundamental liberty that may be not be abrogated by state or local law.

Ten **Russian espionage agents** arrested June 27 were allowed to return to Russia, July 9, in exchange for 4 men imprisoned there on charges of spying for the U.S.; the Russian agents had apparently been operating under deep cover over a decade.

Investment giant **Goldman Sachs** agreed July 15 to pay $550 mil to settle case brought by the SEC, alleging the firm had duped investors into buying risky mortgage-backed securities. Pres. Obama signed **financial reform** measure July 21 that created a Consumer Financial Protection Bureau, provided for government takeovers of "too big to fail" financial firms in crisis, expanded oversight of derivatives, and limited speculative trading by banks. The bill had cleared the House, 237-192, and Senate, 60-39.

More than 75,000 Afghanistan documents, many of them classified, were published July 25 on website run by **WikiLeaks** and in *New York Times*, *Der Spiegel*, and UK's *Guardian*

newspapers. They contained evidence that Pakistan's ISI security agency aided Taliban and other Afghan insurgent groups. U.S. filed charges, July 6, against Pfc. Bradley Manning, an Army intelligence analyst who had been arrested May 26 in connection with earlier WikiLeaks disclosures.

New York City's landmark commission Aug. 3 cleared way for construction of an **Islamic cultural center** near site of former World Trade Center destroyed in Sept. 11, 2001, terrorist attack; project generated both controversy and support. Plans by a tiny Pentecostal church in Gainesville, FL, to **burn Korans** on Sept. 11 got wide attention on the Internet and sparked denunciations in the U.S. and riots abroad, before being called off.

A U.S. district court judge ruled Aug. 4 that a California measure barring **same-sex marriage**, approved by voters in Nov. 2008, violated federal constitution. Federal jury in Chicago, Aug. 17, deadlocked on 23 corruption-related counts against ousted Gov. **Rod Blagojevich** (D, IL), finding him guilty only on one felony count of making false statements to the FBI; retrial scheduled for 2011.

Last U.S. combat unit left Iraq Aug. 19 and Pres. Obama, Aug. 31, declared **U.S. combat mission in Iraq ended**; however, 50,000 troops remained in noncombat units. More than 4,400 U.S. service members had lost their lives in Iraq since beginning of U.S. engagement in Mar. 2003, and nearly 32,000 had been wounded in action.

Senate, Sept. 16, and House, Sept. 23, cleared measure establishing $30 bil loan fund and providing $12 bil in tax breaks to **aid small businesses**; signed into law Sept. 27. National Bureau of Economic Research announced Sept. 20 that the recession that began in Dec. 2007 technically ended in June 2009. During that downturn—longest recession since World War II—jobs on nonfarm payrolls shrank by more than 5%.

Pres. Obama announced Oct. 1 that **Rahm Emanuel** was resigning as White House chief of staff; a week later, national security adviser Gen. **James L. Jones** was replaced with his civilian deputy, Thomas E. Donilon.

TARP program reached 2-year mark Oct. 3, the day its authority to make new commitments expired. In report issued Oct. 5, Treasury Dept. estimated that TARP, authorized at $700 bil, would end up costing taxpayers $51 bil or less, though this figure was disputed. Taxpayers continued to pay for federal bailout of **Fannie Mae** and **Freddie Mac**; projections released Oct. 21 indicated that the two enterprises, which had already drawn $148 bil from Treasury, would need another $73 bil to $215 bil to remain solvent through Dec. 2013.

WikiLeaks released documents covering Iraq conflict Oct. 22; they provided evidence concerning civilian casualties, mistreatment of prisoners by Iraqis, and Iranian military assistance to Shiite combatants. Acting on tip from Saudi Arabia, authorities in UK and UAE Oct. 29 confiscated packages containing printer cartridges filled with a powerful explosive and rigged as bombs; shipments were from Yemen and addressed to Chicago-area destinations.

In Nov. 2 elections **Republicans gained control** of the U.S. House and picked up 6 more seats in the Senate while falling short of a majority. Among other results, Tea Party Republicans **Rand Paul** (KY) and **Mario Rubio** (FL) won Senate seats, but embattled Senate majority leader **Harry Reid** (D, NV) beat back challenge from Tea Party activist Sharron Angle. Republicans also won net total of 5 governorships, though Democrats won statehouses in both California (**Jerry Brown**) and New York (**Andrew Cuomo**).

The Fed Nov. 3 announced plan to buy $600 bil worth of Treasury securities over 8 months as means of stimulating the sluggish economy. Former House Majority Leader **Tom DeLay** (R, TX) convicted of money laundering, Nov. 24. WikiLeaks began releasing a cache of diplomatic cables in late Nov.

On Dec. 2, U.S. House voted, 333-79, to censure veteran Rep. **Charles Rangel** (D, NY) for 11 ethics violations, including failing to pay taxes on a property and failing to disclose to the House some $500,000 in assets.

Pres. Obama, Dec. 17, signed $858 bil compromise measure that extended an array of **Bush-era tax cuts** for individuals and businesses for two years, including tax cuts for the wealthy. It also extended **unemployment insurance benefits** and reduced the Social Security payroll tax rate for a year. The measure, negotiated with GOP congressional leaders, had passed in lame-duck session by votes of 81-19 in Senate and 277-148 in House. **"Don't ask, don't tell"** policy with respect to gays in the military was repealed, Dec. 22.

Patrick Henry's Speech to the Virginia Convention

The following is an excerpt from Patrick Henry's speech to the Virginia Convention, which met at St. John's Church in Richmond, on Mar. 23, 1775, to react to British oppression.

Gentlemen may cry, peace, peace—but there is no peace. The war is actually begun! The next gale that sweeps from the north will bring to our ears the clash of resounding arms! Our brethren are already in the field! Why stand we here idle? What is it that gentlemen wish? What would they have? Is life so dear, or peace so sweet, as to be purchased at the price of chains and slavery? Forbid it, Almighty God! I know not what course others may take; but as for me, give me liberty, or give me death!

Adoption of the Declaration of Independence

On June 7, 1776, Richard Henry Lee, who had issued the first call for a congress of the colonies, introduced in the Continental Congress at Philadelphia a resolution declaring "that these United Colonies are, and of right ought to be, free and independent states, that they are absolved from all allegiance to the British Crown, and that all political connection between them and the state of Great Britain is, and ought to be, totally dissolved."

The resolution, seconded by John Adams on behalf of the Massachusetts delegation, came up again on June 11 when a committee of five, headed by Thomas Jefferson, was appointed to express the purpose of the resolution in a declaration of independence. The other four were John Adams, Benjamin Franklin, Robert R. Livingston, and Roger Sherman.

Drafting the Declaration was assigned to Jefferson, who worked on a portable desk of his own construction in a room at Market and 7th St. The committee reported the result on June 28, 1776. The members of the Congress suggested a number of changes, which Jefferson called "deplorable." They did not approve Jefferson's arraignment of the British people and King George III for encouraging and fostering the slave trade, which Jefferson called "an execrable commerce." They eliminated 630 words and added 146, leaving 1,322 words in the final draft. In its final form, capitalization was erratic. Jefferson had written that men were endowed with "inalienable" rights; in the final copy it came out as "unalienable" and has been thus ever since.

The Lee-Adams resolution of independence was adopted by 12 yeas on July 2—the actual date of the act of independence. The Declaration, which explains the act, was adopted July 4.

After the Declaration was adopted, July 4, 1776, it was turned over to printer John Dunlap to be printed on broadsides. The original copy was lost and one of his broadsides was attached to a page in the journal of the Congress. It was read aloud July 8 in Philadelphia, PA; Easton, PA; and Trenton, NJ. On July 9, it was read by order of Gen. George Washington to the troops assembled on the Common in New York City (City Hall Park).

The Continental Congress of July 19, 1776, adopted the following resolution:

"Resolved, That the Declaration passed on the 4th, be fairly engrossed on parchment with the title and stile of 'The Unanimous Declaration of the thirteen United States of America' and that the same, when engrossed, be signed by every member of Congress."

Not all delegates who signed the engrossed Declaration were present on July 4. Robert Morris (PA), William Williams (CT), and Samuel Chase (MD) signed on Aug. 2; Oliver Wolcott (CT), George Wythe (VA), Richard Henry Lee (VA), and Elbridge Gerry (MA) signed in August and September; Matthew Thornton (NH) joined the Congress Nov. 4 and signed later. Thomas McKean (DE) rejoined Washington's army before signing and said later that he signed in 1781.

Charles Carroll of Carrollton was appointed a delegate by Maryland on July 4, 1776, presented his credentials July 18, and signed the engrossed Declaration on Aug. 2. Born Sept. 19, 1737, he was 95 years old and the last surviving signer when he died on Nov. 14, 1832.

Two Pennsylvania delegates who did not support the Declaration on July 4 were replaced. The four New York delegates did not have authority from their state to vote on July 4. On July 9, the New York state convention authorized its delegates to approve the Declaration, and the Congress was so notified on July 15, 1776. The four signed the Declaration on Aug. 2.

The original engrossed Declaration is preserved at the National Archives in Washington, DC.

Declaration of Independence

The Declaration of Independence was adopted by the Continental Congress in Philadelphia on July 4, 1776. John Hancock was president of the Congress, and Charles Thomson was secretary. A copy of the Declaration, engrossed on parchment, was signed by members of Congress on and after Aug. 2, 1776. On Jan. 18, 1777, Congress ordered that "an authenticated copy, with the names of the members of Congress subscribing the same, be sent to each of the United States, and that they be desired to have the same put on record." Authenticated copies were printed in broadside form in Baltimore, where the Continental Congress was then in session. The following text is that of the original printed by John Dunlap at Philadelphia for the Continental Congress. The original is on display at the National Archives.

IN CONGRESS, July 4, 1776.
A DECLARATION
By the REPRESENTATIVES of the
UNITED STATES OF AMERICA,
In GENERAL CONGRESS assembled

When in the Course of human Events, it becomes necessary for one People to dissolve the Political Bands which have connected them with another, and to assume among the Powers of the Earth, the separate and equal Station to which the Laws of Nature and of Nature's God entitle them, a decent Respect to the Opinions of Mankind requires that they should declare the causes which impel them to the Separation.

We hold these Truths to be self-evident, that all Men are created equal, that they are endowed by their Creator with certain unalienable Rights, that among these are Life, Liberty, and the Pursuit of Happiness—That to secure these Rights, Governments are instituted among Men, deriving their just Powers from the Consent of the Governed, that whenever any Form of Government becomes destructive of these Ends, it is the Right of the People to alter or to abolish it, and to institute new Government, laying its Foundation on such Principles, and organizing its Powers in such Form, as to them shall seem most likely to effect their Safety and Happiness. Prudence, indeed, will dictate that Governments long established should not be changed for light and transient Causes; and accordingly all Experience hath shewn, that Mankind are more disposed to suffer, while Evils are sufferable, than to right themselves by abolishing the Forms to which they are accustomed. But when a long Train of Abuses and Usurpations, pursuing invariably the same Object, evinces a Design to reduce them under absolute Despotism, it is their Right, it is their Duty, to throw off such Government, and to provide new Guards for their future Security. Such has been the patient Sufferance of these Colonies; and such is now the Necessity which constrains them to alter their former Systems of Government. The History of the present King of Great Britain is a History of repeated Injuries and Usurpations, all having in direct Object the Establishment of an absolute Tyranny over these States. To prove this, let Facts be submitted to a candid World.

He has refused his Assent to Laws, the most wholesome and necessary for the public Good.

He has forbidden his Governors to pass Laws of immediate and pressing Importance, unless suspended in their Operation till his Assent should be obtained; and when so suspended, he has utterly neglected to attend to them.

He has refused to pass other Laws for the Accommodation of large Districts of People, unless those People would relinquish the Right of Representation in the Legislature, a Right inestimable to them, and formidable to Tyrants only.

He has called together Legislative Bodies at Places unusual, uncomfortable, and distant from the Depository of their Public Records, for the sole Purpose of fatiguing them into Compliance with his Measures.

He has dissolved Representative Houses repeatedly, for opposing with manly Firmness his Invasions on the Rights of the People.

He has refused for a long Time, after such Dissolutions, to cause others to be elected; whereby the Legislative Powers, incapable of Annihilation, have returned to the People at large for their exercise; the State remaining in the mean time exposed to all the Dangers of Invasion from without, and Convulsions within.

He has endeavoured to prevent the Population of these States; for that Purpose obstructing the Laws for Naturalization of Foreigners; refusing to pass others to encourage their Migrations hither, and raising the Conditions of new Appropriations of Lands.

He has obstructed the Administration of Justice, by refusing his Assent to Laws for establishing Judiciary Powers.

He has made Judges dependent on his Will alone, for the Tenure of their Offices, and the Amount and payment of their Salaries.

He has erected a Multitude of new Offices, and sent hither Swarms of Officers to harrass our People, and eat out their Substance.

He has kept among us, in Times of Peace, Standing Armies, without the consent of our Legislatures.

He has affected to render the Military independent of, and superior to the Civil Power.

He has combined with others to subject us to a Jurisdiction foreign to our Constitution, and unacknowledged by our Laws; giving his Assent to their Acts of pretended Legislation:

For Quartering large bodies of armed troops among us:

For protecting them, by a mock Trial, from Punishment for any Murders which they should commit on the Inhabitants of these States:

For cutting off our Trade with all Parts of the World:

For imposing Taxes on us without our Consent:

For depriving us, in many Cases, of the Benefits of Trial by Jury:

For transporting us beyond Seas to be tried for pretended Offences:

For abolishing the free System of English Laws in a neighbouring Province, establishing therein an arbitrary Government, and enlarging its Boundaries, so as to render it at once an Example and fit Instrument for introducing the same absolute Rule into these Colonies:

For taking away our Charters, abolishing our most valuable Laws, and altering fundamentally the Forms of our Governments:

For suspending our own Legislatures, and declaring themselves invested with Power to legislate for us in all Cases whatsoever.

He has abdicated Government here, by declaring us out of his Protection and waging War against us.

He has plundered our Seas, ravaged our Coasts, burnt our towns, and destroyed the Lives of our People.

He is, at this Time, transporting large Armies of foreign Mercenaries to complete the works of Death, Desolation, and Tyranny, already begun with circumstances of Cruelty

and Perfidy, scarcely paralleled in the most barbarous Ages, and totally unworthy the Head of a civilized Nation.

He has constrained our fellow Citizens taken Captive on the high Seas to bear Arms against their Country, to become the Executioners of their Friends and Brethren, or to fall themselves by their Hands.

He has excited domestic Insurrections amongst us, and has endeavoured to bring on the Inhabitants of our Frontiers, the merciless Indian Savages, whose known Rule of Warfare, is an undistinguished Destruction, of all Ages, Sexes and Conditions.

In every stage of these Oppressions we have Petitioned for Redress in the most humble Terms: Our repeated Petitions have been answered only by repeated Injury. A Prince, whose Character is thus marked by every act which may define a Tyrant, is unfit to be the Ruler of a free People.

Nor have we been wanting in Attentions to our British Brethren. We have warned them from Time to Time of Attempts by their Legislature to extend an unwarrantable Jurisdiction over us. We have reminded them of the Circumstances of our Emigration and Settlement here. We have appealed to their native Justice and Magnanimity, and we have conjured them by the Ties of our common Kindred to disavow these Usurpations, which, would inevitably interrupt our Connections and Correspondence. They too have been deaf to the Voice of Justice and of Consanguinity. We must, therefore, acquiesce in the Necessity, which denounces our Separation, and hold them, as we hold the rest of Mankind, Enemies in War, in Peace, Friends.

We, therefore, the Representatives of the UNITED STATES OF AMERICA, in General Congress, Assembled, appealing to the Supreme Judge of the World for the Rectitude of our Intentions, do, in the Name, and by Authority of the good People of these Colonies, solemnly Publish and Declare, That these United Colonies are, and of Right ought to be, Free and Independent States; that they are absolved from all Allegiance to the British Crown, and that all political Connection between them and the State of Great Britain, is and ought to be totally dissolved; and that as Free and Independent States, they have full Power to levy War, conclude Peace, contract Alliances, establish Commerce, and to do all other Acts and Things which Independent States may of right do. And for the support of this declaration, with a firm Reliance on the Protection of Divine Providence, we mutually pledge to each other our lives, our Fortunes, and our sacred Honor.

JOHN HANCOCK, President

Attest.

CHARLES THOMSON, Secretary.

Signers of the Declaration of Independence

Delegate (state)	Occupation	Birthplace	Born	Died
Adams, John (MA)	Lawyer	Braintree (Quincy), MA	Oct. 30, 1735	July 4, 1826
Adams, Samuel (MA)	Political leader	Boston, MA	Sept. 27, 1722	Oct. 2, 1803
Bartlett, Josiah (NH)	Physician, judge	Amesbury, MA	Nov. 21, 1729	May 19, 1795
Braxton, Carter (VA)	Farmer	Newington Plantation, VA	Sept. 10, 1736	Oct. 10, 1797
Carroll, Charles of Carrollton (MD)	Merchant	Annapolis, MD	Sept. 19, 1737	Nov. 14, 1832
Chase, Samuel (MD)	Judge	Princess Anne, MD	Apr. 17, 1741	June 19, 1811
Clark, Abraham (NJ)	Surveyor	Elizabethtown, NJ	Feb. 15, 1726	Sept. 15, 1794
Clymer, George (PA)	Merchant	Philadelphia, PA	Mar. 16, 1739	Jan. 23, 1813
Ellery, William (RI)	Lawyer	Newport, RI	Dec. 22, 1727	Feb. 15, 1820
Floyd, William (NY)	Soldier	Brookhaven, NY	Dec. 17, 1734	Aug. 4, 1821
Franklin, Benjamin (PA)	Printer, publisher	Boston, MA	Jan. 17, 1706	Apr. 17, 1790
Gerry, Elbridge (MA)	Merchant	Marblehead, MA	July 17, 1744	Nov. 23, 1814
Gwinnett, Button (GA)	Merchant	Gloucester, England	c. 1735	May 19, 1777
Hall, Lyman (GA)	Physician	Wallingford, CT	Apr. 12, 1724	Oct. 19, 1790
Hancock, John (MA)	Merchant	Braintree (Quincy), MA	Jan. 12, 1737	Oct. 8, 1793
Harrison, Benjamin (VA)	Farmer	Charles City County, VA	Apr. 5, 1726	Apr. 24, 1791
Hart, John (NJ)	Farmer	Stonington, CT	c. 1711	May 11, 1779
Hewes, Joseph (NC)	Merchant	Kingston, NJ	Jan. 23, 1730	Nov. 10, 1779
Heyward, Thos. Jr. (SC)	Lawyer, farmer	St. Luke's Parish, SC	July 28, 1746	Mar. 6, 1809
Hooper, William (NC)	Lawyer	Boston, MA	June 17, 1742	Oct. 14, 1790
Hopkins, Stephen (RI)	Judge, educator	Providence, RI	Mar. 7, 1707	July 13, 1785
Hopkinson, Francis (NJ)	Judge, author	Philadelphia, PA	Oct. 2, 1737	May 9, 1791
Huntington, Samuel (CT)	Judge	Windham, CT	July 3, 1731	Jan. 5, 1796
Jefferson, Thomas (VA)	Lawyer	Shadwell, VA	Apr. 13, 1743	July 4, 1826
Lee, Francis Lightfoot (VA)	Farmer	Westmoreland County, VA	Oct. 14, 1734	Jan. 11, 1797
Lee, Richard Henry (VA)	Farmer	Westmoreland County, VA	Jan. 20, 1732	June 19, 1794
Lewis, Francis (NY)	Merchant	Llandaff, Wales	Mar. 21, 1713	Dec. 31, 1802
Livingston, Philip (NY)	Merchant	Albany, NY	Jan. 15, 1716	June 12, 1778
Lynch, Thomas Jr. (SC)	Farmer	Winyah, SC	Aug. 5, 1749	(at sea) 1779
McKean, Thomas (DE)	Lawyer	New London, PA	Mar. 19, 1734	June 24, 1817
Middleton, Arthur (SC)	Farmer	Charleston, SC	June 26, 1742	Jan. 1, 1787
Morris, Lewis (NY)	Farmer	Morrisania (Bronx County), NY	Apr. 8, 1726	Jan. 22, 1798
Morris, Robert (PA)	Merchant	Liverpool, England	Jan. 31, 1734	May 8, 1806
Morton, John (PA)	Judge	Ridley, PA	c. 1724	Apr. 1777
Nelson, Thos. Jr. (VA)	Farmer	Yorktown, VA	Dec. 26, 1738	Jan. 4, 1789
Paca, William (MD)	Judge	Abingdon, MD	Oct. 31, 1740	Oct. 23, 1799
Paine, Robert Treat (MA)	Judge	Boston, MA	Mar. 11, 1731	May 12, 1814
Penn, John (NC)	Lawyer	Caroline County, VA	May 17, 1741	Sept. 14, 1788
Read, George (DE)	Judge	Cecil County, MD	Sept. 18, 1733	Sept. 21, 1798
Rodney, Caesar (DE)	Judge	Dover, DE	Oct. 7, 1728	June 29, 1784
Ross, George (PA)	Judge	New Castle, DE	May 10, 1730	July 14, 1779
Rush, Benjamin (PA)	Physician	Byberry, PA (Philadelphia)	Jan. 4, 1746	Apr. 19, 1813
Rutledge, Edward (SC)	Lawyer	Charleston, SC	Nov. 23, 1749	Jan. 23, 1800
Sherman, Roger (CT)	Lawyer	Newton, MA	Apr. 19, 1721	July 23, 1793
Smith, James (PA)	Lawyer	Northern Ireland	c. 1719	July 11, 1806
Stockton, Richard (NJ)	Lawyer	Princeton, NJ	Oct. 1, 1730	Feb. 28, 1781
Stone, Thomas (MD)	Lawyer	Charles County, MD	c. 1743	Oct. 5, 1787
Taylor, George (PA)	Ironmaster	Ireland	c. 1716	Feb. 23, 1781
Thornton, Matthew (NH)	Physician	Ireland	c. 1714	June 24, 1803
Walton, George (GA)	Judge	Cumberland County, VA	c. 1741	Feb. 2, 1804
Whipple, William (NH)	Merchant, judge	Kittery, ME	Jan. 14, 1730	Nov. 28, 1785
Williams, William (CT)	Merchant	Lebanon, CT	Apr. 8, 1731	Aug. 2, 1811
Wilson, James (PA)	Judge	Carskerdo, Scotland	Sept. 14, 1742	Aug. 21, 1798
Witherspoon, John (NJ)	Clergyman, educator	Gifford, Scotland	Feb. 5, 1723	Nov. 15, 1794
Wolcott, Oliver (CT)	Judge	Windsor, CT	Nov. 20, 1726	Dec. 1, 1797
Wythe, George (VA)	Lawyer	Elizabeth City County, VA	c. 1726	June 8, 1806

Origin of the Constitution

The War of Independence was conducted by delegates from the original 13 states, who composed the Congress of the United States of America, known as the Continental Congress. In 1777 the Congress submitted to the legislatures of the states the Articles of Confederation and Perpetual Union, which were ratified by New Hampshire, Massachusetts, Rhode Island, Connecticut, New York, New Jersey, Pennsylvania, Delaware, Virginia, North Carolina, South Carolina, Georgia, and finally, in 1781, Maryland.

The first article read: "The stile of this confederacy shall be the United States of America." This did not signify a sovereign nation, because the states delegated only those powers they could not handle individually, such as to wage war, make treaties, and contract debts for general expenses (e.g., paying the army). Taxes for payment of such debts were levied by the individual states. The president signed himself "President of the United States in Congress assembled," but here the United States were considered in the plural, a cooperating group.

When the war was won, it became evident that a stronger federal union was needed. The Congress left the initiative to the legislatures. Virginia in Jan. 1786 appointed commissioners to meet with representatives of other states; delegates from Virginia, Delaware, New York, New Jersey, and Pennsylvania met at Annapolis. Alexander Hamilton prepared their call asking delegates from all states to meet in Philadelphia in May 1787 "to render the Constitution of the federal government adequate to the exigencies of the union." Congress endorsed the plan on Feb. 21, 1787. Delegates were appointed by all states except Rhode Island.

The convention was called for May 14, 1787, but a quorum was not present until May 25. George Washington was chosen president (presiding officer). The states certified 65 delegates, but 10 did not attend. The work was done by 55, not all of whom were present at all sessions. Of the 55 attending delegates, 16 failed to sign, and 39 actually signed Sept. 17, 1787, some with reservations. Some historians have said 74 delegates (9 more than the 65 actually certified) were named, and 19 failed to attend. These 9 additional persons refused the appointment, were never delegates, and were never counted as absentees. Washington sent the Constitution to Congress, and that body, Sept. 28, 1787, ordered it sent to the legislatures, "in order to be submitted to a convention of delegates chosen in each state by the people thereof."

The Constitution was ratified by votes of state conventions as follows: Delaware, Dec. 7, 1787, unanimous; Pennsylvania, Dec. 12, 1787, 46 to 23; New Jersey, Dec. 18, 1787, unanimous; Georgia, Jan. 2, 1788, unanimous; Connecticut, Jan. 9, 1788, 128 to 40; Massachusetts, Feb. 6, 1788, 187 to 168; Maryland, Apr. 28, 1788, 63 to 11; South Carolina, May 23, 1788, 149 to 73; New Hampshire, June 21, 1788, 57 to 46; Virginia, June 25, 1788, 89 to 79; New York, July 26, 1788, 30 to 27. Nine states were needed to establish the operation of the Constitution "between the states so ratifying the same," and New Hampshire was the 9th state. The government did not declare the Constitution in effect until the first Wednesday in Mar. 1789, which was Mar. 4. After that, North Carolina ratified it on Nov. 21, 1789, 194 to 77; and Rhode Island, May 29, 1790, 34 to 32. Vermont in convention ratified it on Jan. 10, 1791, and by act of Congress approved on Feb. 18, 1791, was admitted into the Union as the 14th state, Mar. 4, 1791.

Constitution of the United States

The Original 7 Articles

The text of the Constitution given here (except for Amendment XXVII) is from the pocket-size edition of the Constitution published by the U.S. Government Printing Office as a result of a congressional resolution to print the Constitution in its original form as amended through July 5, 1971. *Text in brackets* indicates that an item has been superseded or amended, or provides background information. **Boldface text** preceding an article, section, or amendment is a brief summary, added by *The World Almanac*.

PREAMBLE

We, the People of the United States, in Order to form a more perfect Union, establish Justice, insure domestic Tranquility, provide for the common defence, promote the general Welfare, and secure the Blessings of Liberty to ourselves and our Posterity, do ordain and establish this Constitution for the United States of America.

ARTICLE I.

Section 1—Legislative powers; in whom vested.

All legislative Powers herein granted shall be vested in a Congress of the United States, which shall consist of a Senate and House of Representatives.

Section 2—House of Representatives, how and by whom chosen. Qualifications of a Representative. Representatives and direct taxes, how apportioned. Enumeration. Vacancies to be filled. Power of choosing officers, and of impeachment.

The House of Representatives shall be composed of Members chosen every second Year by the People of the several States, and the Electors in each State shall have the Qualifications requisite for Electors of the most numerous Branch of the State Legislature.

No Person shall be a Representative who shall not have attained to the Age of twenty five Years, and been seven Years a Citizen of the United States, and who shall not, when elected, be an Inhabitant of that State in which he shall be chosen.

[Representatives and direct taxes shall be apportioned among the several States which may be included within this Union, according to their respective Numbers, which shall be determined by adding to the whole Number of free Persons, including those bound to Service for a Term of Years, and excluding Indians not taxed, three-fifths of all other persons.] [The previous sentence was superseded by Amendment XIV, section 2.] The actual Enumeration shall be made within three Years after the first Meeting of the Congress of the United States, and within every subsequent Term of ten Years, in such Manner as they shall by Law direct. The Number of Representatives shall not exceed one for every thirty Thousand, but each State shall have at Least one Representative; and until such enumeration shall be made, the State of New Hampshire shall be entitled to chuse three, Massachusetts eight, Rhode-Island and Providence Plantations one, Connecticut five, New-York six, New Jersey four, Pennsylvania eight, Delaware one, Maryland six, Virginia ten, North Carolina five, South Carolina five, and Georgia three.

When vacancies happen in the Representation from any State, the Executive Authority thereof shall issue Writs of Election to fill such Vacancies.

The House of Representatives shall chuse their Speaker and other Officers; and shall have the sole Power of Impeachment.

Section 3—Senators, how and by whom chosen. How classified. Qualifications of a Senator. President of the Senate, his right to vote. President pro tem., and other officers of the Senate, how chosen. Power to try impeachments. When President is tried, Chief Justice to preside. Sentence.

The Senate of the United States shall be composed of two Senators from each State, *[chosen by the Legislature thereof] [The preceding five words were superseded by Amendment XVII.]* for six Years; and each Senator shall have one Vote.

Immediately after they shall be assembled in Consequence of the first Election, they shall be divided as equally as may be into three Classes. The Seats of the Senators of the first Class shall be vacated at the Expiration of the second Year, of the second Class at the Expiration of the fourth Year, and of the third Class at the Expiration of the Sixth year, so that one-third may be chosen every second Year; *[and if Vacancies happen by Resignation, or otherwise, during the Recess of the Legislature of any State, the Executive thereof may make temporary Appointments until the next Meeting of the Legislature, which shall then fill such Vacancies.] [The words in brackets were superseded by Amendment XVII.]*

No Person shall be a Senator who shall not have attained to the Age of thirty Years, and been nine Years a Citizen of the United States, and who shall not, when elected, be an Inhabitant of that State for which he shall be chosen.

The Vice President of the United States shall be President of the Senate, but shall have no Vote, unless they be equally divided.

The Senate shall chuse their other Officers, and also a President pro tempore, in the absence of the Vice President, or when he shall exercise the Office of President of the United States.

The Senate shall have the sole Power to try all Impeachments. When sitting for that Purpose, they shall be on Oath or Affirmation. When the President of the United States is tried, the Chief Justice shall preside: And no Person shall be convicted without the Concurrence of two thirds of the Members present.

Judgment in Cases of Impeachment shall not extend further than to removal from Office, and disqualification to hold and enjoy any Office of honor, Trust or Profit under the United States: but the Party convicted shall nevertheless be liable and subject to Indictment, Trial, Judgment and Punishment, according to Law.

Section 4—Times, etc., of holding elections, how prescribed. One session each year.

The Times, Places and Manner of holding Elections for Senators and Representatives, shall be prescribed in each State by the Legislature thereof; but the Congress may at any time by Law make or alter such Regulations, except as to the Place of Chusing Senators.

The Congress shall assemble at least once in every Year, and such Meeting shall be *[on the first Monday in December,] [The words in brackets were superseded by Amendment XX, section 2.]* unless they shall by Law appoint a different Day.

Section 5—Membership, quorum, adjournments, rules. Power to punish or expel. Journal. Time of adjournments, how limited, etc.

Each House shall be the Judge of the Elections, Returns and Qualifications of its own Members, and a Majority of each shall constitute a Quorum to do Business; but a smaller number may adjourn from day to day, and may be authorized to compel the Attendance of absent Members, in such manner, and under such Penalties as each House may provide.

Each House may determine the Rules of its Proceedings, punish its members for disorderly Behavior, and, with the Concurrence of two thirds, expel a Member.

Each House shall keep a Journal of its Proceedings, and from time to time publish the same, excepting such Parts as may in their Judgment require Secrecy; and the Yeas and Nays of the Members of either House on any question shall, at the Desire of one fifth of those Present, be entered on the Journal.

Neither House, during the Session of Congress, shall, without the Consent of the other, adjourn for more than three days, nor to any other Place than that in which the two Houses shall be sitting.

Section 6—Compensation, privileges, disqualifications in certain cases.

The Senators and Representatives shall receive a Compensation for their Services, to be ascertained by Law, and paid out of the Treasury of the United States. They shall in all Cases, except Treason, Felony and Breach of the Peace, be privileged from Arrest during their Attendance at the Session of their respective Houses, and in going to and returning from the same; and for any Speech or Debate in either House, they shall not be questioned in any other Place.

No Senator or Representative shall, during the Time for which he was elected, be appointed to any civil Office under the Authority of the United States, which shall have been created, or the Emoluments whereof shall have been encreased during such time; and no Person holding any Office under the United States, shall be a Member of either House during his Continuance in Office.

Section 7—House to originate all revenue bills. Veto. Bill may be passed by two-thirds of each House, notwithstanding, etc. Bill, not returned in ten days, to become a law. Provisions as to orders, concurrent resolutions, etc.

All bills for raising Revenue shall originate in the House of Representatives; but the Senate may propose or concur with Amendments as on other Bills.

Every Bill which shall have passed the House of Representatives and the Senate, shall, before it become a Law, be presented to the President of the United States; If he approve he shall sign it, but if not he shall return it, with his Objections to that House in which it shall have originated, who shall enter the Objections at large on their Journal, and proceed to reconsider it. If after such Reconsideration two thirds of that House shall agree to pass the Bill, it shall be sent, together with the Objections, to the other House, by which it shall likewise be reconsidered, and if approved by two thirds of that House, it shall become a Law. But in all such Cases the Votes of both Houses shall be determined by Yeas and Nays, and the Names of the Persons voting for and against the Bill shall be entered on the Journal of each House respectively. If any Bill shall not be returned by the President within ten Days (Sundays excepted) after it shall have been presented to him, the Same shall be a Law, in like Manner as if he had signed it, unless the Congress by their Adjournment prevent its Return, in which Case it shall not be a Law.

Every order, Resolution, or Vote to which the Concurrence of the Senate and House of Representatives may be necessary (except on a question of Adjournment) shall be presented to the President of the United States; and before the Same shall take Effect, shall be approved by him, or being disapproved by him, shall be repassed by two thirds of the Senate and House of Representatives, according to the Rules and Limitations prescribed in the Case of a Bill.

Section 8—Powers of Congress.

The Congress shall have Power To lay and collect Taxes, Duties, Imposts and Excises, to pay the Debts and provide for the common Defence and general Welfare of the United States; but all Duties, Imposts and Excises shall be uniform throughout the United States;

To borrow money on the credit of the United States;

To regulate Commerce with foreign Nations, and among the several States, and with the Indian Tribes;

To establish an uniform Rule of Naturalization, and uniform Laws on the subject of Bankruptcies throughout the United States;

To coin Money, regulate the Value thereof, and of foreign Coin, and fix the Standard of Weights and Measures;

To provide for the Punishment of counterfeiting the Securities and current Coin of the United States;

To establish Post Offices and post Roads;

To promote the Progress of Science and useful Arts, by securing for limited Times to Authors and Inventors the exclusive Right to their respective Writings and Discoveries;

To constitute Tribunals inferior to the supreme Court;

To define and punish Piracies and Felonies committed on the high Seas, and Offenses against the Law of Nations;

To declare War, grant Letters of Marque and Reprisal, and make Rules concerning Captures on Land and Water;

To raise and support Armies, but no Appropriation of Money to that Use shall be for a longer Term than two Years;

To provide and maintain a Navy;

To make Rules for the Government and Regulation of the land and naval Forces;

To provide for calling forth the Militia to execute the Laws of the Union, suppress Insurrections and repel Invasions;

To provide for organizing, arming, and disciplining the Militia, and for governing such Part of them as may be employed in the Service of the United States, reserving to the States respectively, the Appointment of the Officers, and the Authority of training the Militia according to the discipline prescribed by Congress;

To exercise exclusive Legislation in all Cases whatsoever, over such District (not exceeding ten Miles square) as may, by Cession of particular States, and the acceptance of Congress, become the Seat of the Government of the United States, and to exercise like Authority over all Places purchased by the Consent of the Legislature of the State in which the Same shall be, for the Erection of Forts, Magazines, Arsenals, dock-Yards, and other needful Buildings;—And

To make all Laws which shall be necessary and proper for carrying into Execution the foregoing Powers, and all other Powers vested by this Constitution in the Government of the United States, or in any Department or Officer thereof.

Section 9—Provision as to migration or importation of certain persons. Habeas corpus, bills of attainder, etc. Taxes, how apportioned. No export duty. No commercial preference. Money, how drawn from Treasury, etc. No titular nobility. Officers not to receive presents, etc.

The Migration or Importation of such Persons as any of the States now existing shall think proper to admit, shall not be prohibited by the Congress prior to the Year one thousand eight hundred and eight, but a tax or duty may be imposed on such Importation, not exceeding ten dollars for each Person.

The privilege of the Writ of Habeas Corpus shall not be suspended, unless when in Cases of Rebellion or Invasion the public Safety may require it.

No Bill of Attainder or ex post facto Law shall be passed.

[No capitation, or other direct, Tax shall be laid, unless in Proportion to the Census or Enumeration herein before directed to be taken.] *[Words in brackets modified by Amendment XVI.]*

No Tax or Duty shall be laid on Articles exported from any State.

No Preference shall be given by any Regulation of Commerce or Revenue to the Ports of one State over those of another: nor shall Vessels bound to, or from, one State, be obliged to enter, clear, or pay Duties in another.

No Money shall be drawn from the Treasury, but in Consequence of Appropriations made by Law; and a regular Statement and Account of the Receipts and Expenditures of all publick Money shall be published from time to time.

No Title of Nobility shall be granted by the United States: and no Person holding any Office of Profit or Trust under them, shall, without the Consent of the Congress, accept of any present, Emolument, Office, or Title, of any kind whatever, from any King, Prince, or foreign State.

Section 10—States prohibited from the exercise of certain powers.

No State shall enter into any Treaty, Alliance, or Confederation; grant Letters of Marque and Reprisal; coin Money; emit Bills of Credit; make any Thing but gold and silver Coin a Tender in Payment of Debts; pass any Bill of Attainder, ex post facto Law, or Law impairing the Obligation of Contracts, or grant any Title of Nobility.

No State shall, without the Consent of the Congress, lay any Imposts or Duties on Imports or Exports, except what may be absolutely necessary for executing its inspection Laws: and the net Produce of all Duties and Imposts, laid by any State on Imports or Exports, shall be for the Use of the Treasury of the United States; and all such Laws shall be subject to the Revision and Control of the Congress.

No State shall, without the Consent of Congress, lay any duty of Tonnage, keep Troops, or Ships of War in time of Peace, enter into any Agreement or Compact with another State, or with a foreign Power, or engage in War, unless actually invaded, or in such imminent Danger as will not admit of delay.

ARTICLE II.

Section 1—President: his term of office. Electors of President; number and how appointed. Electors to vote on same day. Qualification of President. On whom his duties devolve in case of his removal, death, etc. President's compensation. His oath of office.

The executive Power shall be vested in a President of the United States of America. He shall hold his Office during the Term of four Years, and, together with the Vice President, chosen for the same Term, be elected, as follows.

Each State shall appoint, in such Manner as the Legislature thereof may direct, a Number of Electors, equal to the whole Number of Senators and Representatives to which the State may be entitled in the Congress: but no Senator or Representative, or Person holding an Office of Trust or Profit under the United States, shall be appointed an Elector.

[The Electors shall meet in their respective States, and vote by Ballot for two persons, of whom one at least shall not be an Inhabitant of the same State with themselves. And they shall make a List of all the Persons voted for, and of the Number of Votes for each; which List they shall sign and certify, and transmit sealed to the Seat of the Government of the United States, directed to the President of the Senate. The President of the Senate shall, in the Presence of the Senate and House of Representatives, open all the Certificates, and the Votes shall then be counted. The Person having the greatest Number of Votes shall be the President, if such Number be a Majority of the whole Number of Electors appointed; and if there be more than one who have such Majority, and have an equal Number of Votes, then the House of Representatives shall immediately chuse by Ballot one of them for President; and if no Person have a Majority, then from the five highest on the List the said House shall in like Manner chuse the President. But in chusing the President,

the Votes shall be taken by States, the Representation from each State having one Vote; a quorum for this Purpose shall consist of a Member or Members from two thirds of the States, and a Majority of all the States shall be necessary to a Choice. In every Case, after the Choice of the President, the Person having the greatest Number of Votes of the Electors shall be the Vice President. But if there should remain two or more who have equal Votes, the Senate shall chuse from them by Ballot the Vice-President.] [This clause was superseded by Amendment XII.]

The Congress may determine the Time of chusing the Electors, and the Day on which they shall give their Votes; which Day shall be the same throughout the United States.

No person except a natural born Citizen, or a Citizen of the United States, at the time of the Adoption of this Constitution, shall be eligible to the Office of President; neither shall any Person be eligible to that Office who shall not have attained to the Age of thirty-five Years, and been fourteen Years a Resident within the United States. *[For qualification of the Vice President, see Amendment XII.]*

[In Case of the Removal of the President from Office, or of his Death, Resignation, or Inability to discharge the Powers and Duties of the said Office, the same shall devolve on the Vice President, and the Congress may by Law, provide for the Case of Removal, Death, Resignation or Inability, both of the President and Vice President, declaring what Officer shall then act as President, and such Officer shall act accordingly, until the Disability be removed, or a President shall be elected.] [This clause was superseded by Amendments XXV.]

The President shall, at stated Times, receive for his Services, a Compensation, which shall neither be encreased nor diminished during the Period for which he shall have been elected, and he shall not receive within that Period any other Emolument from the United States, or any of them.

Before he enter on the Execution of his Office, he shall take the following Oath or Affirmation:–"I do solemnly swear (or affirm) that I will faithfully execute the Office of President of the United States, and will to the best of my Ability, preserve, protect and defend the Constitution of the United States."

Section 2—President to be Commander-in-Chief. He may require opinions of cabinet officers, etc., may pardon. Treaty-making power. Nomination of certain officers. When President may fill vacancies.

The President shall be Commander in Chief of the Army and Navy of the United States, and of the Militia of the several States, when called into the actual Service of the United States; he may require the Opinion in writing, of the principal Officer in each of the executive Departments, upon any subject relating to the Duties of their respective Offices, and he shall have Power to Grant Reprieves and Pardons for Offenses against the United States, except in Cases of Impeachment.

He shall have Power, by and with the Advice and Consent of the Senate, to make Treaties, provided two-thirds of the Senators present concur; and he shall nominate, and by and with the Advice and Consent of the Senate, shall appoint Ambassadors, other public Ministers and Consuls, Judges of the supreme Court, and all other Officers of the United States, whose Appointments are not herein otherwise provided for, and which shall be established by Law: but the Congress may by Law vest the Appointment of such inferior Officers, as they think proper, in the President alone, in the Courts of Law, or in the Heads of Departments.

The President shall have Power to fill up all Vacancies that may happen during the Recess of the Senate, by granting Commissions which shall expire at the End of their next Session.

Section 3—President shall communicate to Congress. He may convene and adjourn Congress, in case of disagreement, etc. Shall receive ambassadors, execute laws, and commission officers.

He shall from time to time give to the Congress Information of the State of the Union, and recommend to their Consideration such Measures as he shall judge necessary and expedient; he may, on extraordinary Occasions, convene both Houses, or either of them, and in Case of Disagreement between them, with Respect to the Time of Adjournment, he may adjourn them to such Time as he shall think proper; he shall receive Ambassadors and other public Ministers; he shall take Care that the Laws be faithfully executed, and shall Commission all the Officers of the United States.

Section 4—All civil offices forfeited for certain crimes.

The President, Vice President and all civil Officers of the United States, shall be removed from Office on Impeachment for, and Conviction of, Treason, Bribery, or other high Crimes and Misdemeanors.

ARTICLE III.

Section 1—Judicial powers, tenure. Compensation.

The judicial Power of the United States, shall be vested in one supreme Court, and in such inferior Courts as the Congress may from time to time ordain and establish. The Judges, both of the supreme and inferior Courts, shall hold their Offices during good Behaviour, and shall, at stated Times, receive for their Services, a Compensation, which shall not be diminished during their Continuance in Office.

Section 2—Judicial power; to what cases it extends. Original jurisdiction of Supreme Court; appellate jurisdiction. Trial by jury, etc. Trial, where.

The judicial Power shall extend to all Cases, in Law and Equity, arising under this Constitution, the Laws of the United States, and Treaties made, or which shall be made, under their Authority;–to all Cases affecting Ambassadors, other public Ministers and Consuls;–to all Cases of admiralty and maritime Jurisdiction;–to Controversies to which the United States shall be a Party;–to Controversies between two or more States; *[–between a State and Citizens of another State;–]* between Citizens of different States; – between Citizens of the same State claiming Lands under Grants of different States, *[and between a State, or the Citizens thereof, and foreign States, Citizens or Subjects.] [This section is modified by Amendment XI.]*

In all Cases affecting Ambassadors, other public Ministers and Consuls, and those in which a State shall be Party, the supreme Court shall have original Jurisdiction. In all other Cases before mentioned, the supreme Court shall have appellate Jurisdiction, both as to Law and Fact, with such Exceptions, and under such Regulations as the Congress shall make.

The trial of all Crimes, except in Cases of Impeachment, shall be by Jury; and such Trial shall be held in the State where the said Crimes shall have been committed; but when not committed within any State, the Trial shall be at such Place or Places as the Congress may by Law have directed.

Section 3—Treason Defined. Proof of. Punishment of.

Treason against the United States, shall consist only in levying War against them, or in adhering to their Enemies, giving them Aid and Comfort. No Person shall be convicted of Treason unless on the Testimony of two Witnesses to the same overt Act, or on Confession in open Court.

The Congress shall have Power to declare the Punishment of Treason, but no Attainder of Treason shall work Corruption of Blood, or Forfeiture except during the Life of the Person attainted.

ARTICLE IV.

Section 1—Each State to give credit to the public acts, etc., of every other State.

Full Faith and Credit shall be given in each State to the public Acts, Records, and judicial Proceedings of every other State. And the Congress may by general Laws prescribe the Manner in which such Acts, Records and Proceedings shall be proved, and the Effect thereof.

Section 2—Privileges of citizens of each State. Fugitives from justice to be delivered up. Persons held to service having escaped, to be delivered up.

The Citizens of each State shall be entitled to all Privileges and Immunities of Citizens in the several States.

A Person charged in any State with Treason, Felony, or other Crime, who shall flee from Justice, and be found in another State, shall on demand of the executive Authority of the State from which he fled, be delivered up, to be removed to the State having Jurisdiction of the Crime.

[No Person held to Service or Labour in one State, under the Laws thereof, escaping into another, shall, in Consequence of any Law or Regulation therein, be discharged from such Service or Labour, but shall be delivered up on Claim of the Party to whom such Service or Labour may be due.] [This clause was superseded by Amendment XIII.]

Section 3—Admission of new States. Power of Congress over territory and other property.

New States may be admitted by the Congress into this Union; but no new State shall be formed or erected within the Jurisdiction of any other State; nor any State be formed by the Junction of two or more States, or parts of States, without the Consent of the Legislatures of the States concerned as well as of the Congress.

The Congress shall have Power to dispose of and make all needful Rules and Regulations respecting the Territory or other Property belonging to the United States; and nothing in this Constitution shall be so construed as to Prejudice any Claims of the United States, or of any particular State.

Section 4—Republican form of government guaranteed. Each State to be protected.

The United States shall guarantee to every State in this Union a Republican Form of Government, and shall protect each of them against Invasion; and on Application of the Legislature, or of the Executive (when the Legislature cannot be convened) against domestic Violence.

ARTICLE V.

Constitution: how amended; proviso.

The Congress, whenever two-thirds of both Houses shall deem it necessary, shall propose Amendments to this Constitution, or, on the Application of the Legislatures of two-thirds of the several States, shall call a Convention for proposing Amendments, which, in either Case, shall be valid to all Intents and Purposes, as part of this Constitution, when ratified by the Legislatures of three-fourths of the several States, or by Conventions in three-fourths thereof, as the one or the other Mode of Ratification may be proposed by the Congress: Provided that no Amendment which may be made prior to the Year One thousand eight hundred and eight shall in any Manner affect the first and fourth Clauses in the Ninth Section of the first Article; and that no State, without its Consent, shall be deprived of its equal Suffrage in the Senate.

ARTICLE VI.

Certain debts, etc., declared valid. Supremacy of Constitution, treaties, and laws of the United States. Oath to support Constitution, by whom taken. No religious test.

All Debts contracted and Engagements entered into, before the Adoption of this Constitution, shall be as valid against the United States under this Constitution, as under the Confederation.

This Constitution, and the Laws of the United States which shall be made in Pursuance thereof; and all Treaties made, or which shall be made, under the Authority of the United States, shall be the supreme Law of the Land; and the Judges in every State shall be bound thereby, any Thing in the Constitution or Laws of any State to the Contrary notwithstanding.

The Senators and Representatives before mentioned, and the Members of the several State Legislatures, and all executive and judicial Officers, both of the United States and of the several States, shall be bound by Oath or Affirmation, to support this Constitution; but no religious Test shall ever be required as a Qualification to any Office or public Trust under the United States.

ARTICLE VII.

What ratification shall establish Constitution.

The Ratification of the Conventions of nine States shall be sufficient for the Establishment of this Constitution between the States so ratifying the Same.

Done in Convention by the Unanimous Consent of the States present the Seventeenth Day of September in the Year of our Lord one thousand seven hundred and Eighty seven and of the Independence of the United States of America the Twelfth.

In Witness whereof We have hereunto subscribed our Names.

G°. Washington, Presidt and deputy from Virginia

New Hampshire—John Langdon, Nicholas Gilman

Massachusetts—Nathaniel Gorham, Rufus King

Connecticut—Wm. Saml. Johnson, Roger Sherman

New York—Alexander Hamilton

New Jersey—Wil: Livingston, David Brearley, Wm. Paterson, Jona: Dayton

Pennsylvania—B Franklin, Thomas Mifflin, Robt. Morris, Geo. Clymer, Thos. FitzSimons, Jared Ingersoll, James Wilson, Gouv Morris

Delaware—Geo: Read, Gunning Bedford jun, John Dickinson, Richard Bassett, Jaco: Broom

Maryland—James McHenry, Dan of St Thos. Jenifer, Danl Carroll

Virginia—John Blair, James Madison Jr.

North Carolina—Wm. Blount, Rich'd Dobbs Spaight, Hu Williamson

South Carolina—J. Rutledge, Charles Cotesworth Pinckney, Charles Pinckney, Pierce Butler

Georgia—William Few, Abr Baldwin

Attest: William Jackson, Secretary.

The Bill of Rights
In force Dec. 15, 1791

[The First Congress, at its first session in the City of New York, Sept. 25, 1789, submitted to the states 12 amendments to clarify certain individual and state rights not named in the Constitution. They are generally called the Bill of Rights.

Influential in framing these amendments was the Declaration of Rights of Virginia, written by George Mason (1725-92) in 1776. Mason, a Virginia delegate to the Constitutional Convention, did not sign the Constitution and opposed its ratification on the ground that it did not sufficiently oppose slavery or safeguard individual rights.

In the preamble to the resolution offering the proposed amendments, Congress said: "The conventions of a number of the States having at the time of their adopting the Constitution, expressed a desire, in order to prevent misconstruction or abuse of its powers, that further declaratory and restrictive clauses should be added, and as extending the ground of public confidence in the government will best insure the beneficent ends of its institution, be it resolved," etc.

Ten of these amendments, now commonly known as one to 10 inclusive, but originally 3 to 12 inclusive, were ratified by the states as follows: New Jersey, Nov. 20, 1789; Maryland, Dec. 19, 1789; North Carolina, Dec. 22, 1789; South Carolina, Jan. 19, 1790; New Hampshire, Jan. 25, 1790; Delaware, Jan. 28, 1790; New York, Feb. 27, 1790; Pennsylvania, Mar. 10, 1790; Rhode Island, June 7, 1790; Vermont, Nov. 3, 1791; Virginia, Dec. 15, 1791; Massachusetts, Mar. 2, 1939; Georgia, Mar. 18, 1939; Connecticut, Apr. 19, 1939. These original 10 ratified amendments follow as Amendments I to X inclusive.

Of the two original proposed amendments that were not ratified promptly by the necessary number of states, the first related to apportionment of Representatives; the second, relating to compensation of members of Congress, was ratified in 1992 and became Amendment 27.]

AMENDMENT I.

Religious establishment prohibited. Freedom of speech, of press, right to assemble and to petition.

Congress shall make no law respecting an establishment of religion, or prohibiting the free exercise thereof; or abridging the freedom of speech, or of the press; or the right of the people peaceably to assemble, and to petition the Government for a redress of grievances.

AMENDMENT II.

Right to keep and bear arms.

A well regulated Militia, being necessary to the security of a free State, the right of the people to keep and bear Arms, shall not be infringed.

AMENDMENT III.

Conditions for quarters for soldiers.

No Soldier shall, in time of peace be quartered in any house, without the consent of the Owner, nor in time of war, but in a manner to be prescribed by law.

AMENDMENT IV.

Protection from unreasonable search and seizure.

The right of the people to be secure in their persons, houses, papers, and effects, against unreasonable searches and seizures, shall not be violated, and no Warrants shall issue, but upon probable cause, supported by Oath or affirmation, and particularly describing the place to be searched, and the persons or things to be seized.

AMENDMENT V.

Provisions concerning prosecution and due process of law. Double jeopardy restriction. Private property not to be taken without compensation.

No person shall be held to answer for a capital, or otherwise infamous crime, unless on a presentment or indictment of a Grand Jury, except in cases arising in the land or naval forces, or in the Militia, when in actual service in time of War or public danger; nor shall any person be subject for the same offence to be twice put in jeopardy of life or limb; nor shall be compelled in any criminal case to be a witness against himself, nor be deprived of life, liberty, or property, without due process of law; nor shall private property be taken for public use, without just compensation.

AMENDMENT VI.

Right to speedy trial, witnesses, etc.

In all criminal prosecutions, the accused shall enjoy the right to a speedy and public trial, by an impartial jury of the State and district wherein the crime shall have been committed, which district shall have been previously ascertained by law, and to be informed of the nature and cause of the accusation; to be confronted with the witnesses against him; to have compulsory process for obtaining witnesses in his favor, and to have the Assistance of Counsel for his defence.

AMENDMENT VII.

Right of trial by jury.

In suits at common law, where the value in controversy shall exceed twenty dollars, the right of trial by jury shall be preserved, and no fact tried by a jury, shall be otherwise reexamined in any Court of the United States, than according to the rules of the common law.

AMENDMENT VIII.

Excessive bail or fines; cruel and unusual punishment.

Excessive bail shall not be required, nor excessive fines imposed, nor cruel and unusual punishments inflicted.

AMENDMENT IX.

Rule of construction of Constitution.

The enumeration in the Constitution, of certain rights, shall not be construed to deny or disparage others retained by the people.

AMENDMENT X.

Rights of States under Constitution.

The powers not delegated to the United States by the Constitution, nor prohibited by it to the States, are reserved to the States respectively, or to the people.

Amendments Since the Bill of Rights

AMENDMENT XI.

Judicial powers construed.

The Judicial power of the United States shall not be construed to extend to any suit in law or equity, commenced or prosecuted against one of the United States by Citizens of another State, or by Citizens or Subjects of any Foreign State.

[This amendment was proposed to the Legislatures of the several States by the Third Congress on March 4, 1794, and was declared to have been ratified in a message from the President to Congress, dated Jan. 8, 1798.]

[It was on Jan. 5, 1798, that Secretary of State Pickering received from 12 of the States authenticated ratifications, and informed President John Adams of that fact.]

[As a result of later research in the Department of State, it is now established that Amendment XI became part of the Constitution on Feb. 7, 1795, for on that date it had been ratified by 12 States as follows.]

[1. New York, Mar. 27, 1794. 2. Rhode Island, Mar. 31, 1794. 3. Connecticut, May 8, 1794. 4. New Hampshire, June 16, 1794. 5. Massachusetts, June 26, 1794. 6. Vermont, between Oct. 9, 1794, and Nov. 9, 1794. 7. Virginia, Nov. 18, 1794. 8. Georgia, Nov. 29, 1794. 9. Kentucky, Dec. 7, 1794. 10. Maryland, Dec. 26, 1794. 11. Delaware, Jan. 23, 1795. 12. North Carolina, Feb. 7, 1795]

[On June 1, 1796, more than a year after Amendment XI had become a part of the Constitution—but before anyone was officially aware of this—Tennessee had been admitted as a State; but not until Oct. 16, 1797, was a certified copy of the resolution of Congress proposing the amendment sent to the Governor of Tennessee, John Sevier, by Secretary of State Pickering, whose office was then at Trenton, New Jersey, because of the epidemic of yellow fever at Philadelphia; it seems, however, that the Legislature of Tennessee took no action on Amendment XI, owing doubtless to the fact that public announcement of its adoption was made soon thereafter.]

[Besides the necessary 12 States, one other, South Carolina, ratified Amendment XI, but this action was not taken until Dec. 4, 1797; the two remaining States, New Jersey and Pennsylvania, failed to ratify.]

AMENDMENT XII.
Manner of choosing President and Vice-President.

[Proposed by Congress Dec. 9, 1803; ratified June 15, 1804.]

The Electors shall meet in their respective states and vote by ballot for President and Vice-President, one of whom, at least, shall not be an inhabitant of the same state with themselves; they shall name in their ballots the person voted for as President, and in distinct ballots the person voted for as Vice-President, and they shall make distinct lists of all persons voted for as President, and of all persons voted for as Vice-President, and of the number of votes for each, which lists they shall sign and certify, and transmit sealed to the seat of the government of the United States, directed to the President of the Senate;—the President of the Senate shall, in presence of the Senate and House of Representatives, open all the certificates and the votes shall then be counted;—The person having the greatest number of votes for President, shall be the President, if such number be a majority of the whole number of Electors appointed; and if no person have such majority, then from the persons having the highest numbers not exceeding three on the list of those voted for as President, the House of Representatives shall choose immediately, by ballot, the President. But in choosing the President, the votes shall be taken by states, the representation from each state having one vote; a quorum for this purpose shall consist of a member or members from two-thirds of the states, and a majority of all the states shall be necessary to a choice. *[And if the House of Representatives shall not choose a President whenever the right of choice shall devolve upon them, before the fourth day of March next following, then the Vice-President shall act as President, as in the case of the death or other constitutional disability of the President.] [The words in brackets were superseded by Amendment XX, section 3.]* The person having the greatest number of votes as Vice-President, shall be the Vice-President, if such number be a majority of the whole number of Electors appointed, and if no person have a majority, then from the two highest numbers on the list, the Senate shall choose the Vice-President; a quorum for the purpose shall consist of two-thirds of the whole number of Senators, and a majority of the whole number shall be necessary to a choice. But no person constitutionally ineligible to the office of President shall be eligible to that of Vice-President of the United States.

THE RECONSTRUCTION AMENDMENTS

[Amendments XIII, XIV, and XV are commonly known as the Reconstruction Amendments, inasmuch as they followed the Civil War, and were drafted by Republicans who were bent on imposing their own policy of reconstruction on the South. Postbellum legislatures there—Mississippi, South Carolina, Georgia, for example—had set up laws which, it was charged, were contrived to perpetuate Negro slavery under other names.]

AMENDMENT XIII.
Slavery abolished.

[Proposed by Congress Jan. 31, 1865; ratified Dec. 6, 1865. The amendment, when first proposed by a resolution in Congress, was passed by the Senate, 38 to 6, on Apr. 8, 1864, but was defeated in the House, 95 to 66 on June 15, 1864. On reconsideration by the House, on Jan. 31, 1865, the resolution passed, 119 to 56. It was approved by President Lincoln on Feb. 1, 1865, although the Supreme Court had decided in 1798 that the President has nothing to do with the proposing of amendments to the Constitution, or their adoption.]

1. Neither slavery nor involuntary servitude, except as a punishment for crime whereof the party shall have been duly convicted, shall exist within the United States, or any place subject to their jurisdiction.

2. Congress shall have power to enforce this article by appropriate legislation.

AMENDMENT XIV.
Citizenship rights not to be abridged.

[The following amendment was proposed to the Legislatures of the several states by the 39th Congress, June 13, 1866, ratified July 9, 1868, and declared to have been ratified in a proclamation by the Secretary of State, July 28, 1868.]

[The 14th amendment was adopted only by virtue of ratification subsequent to earlier rejections. Newly constituted legislatures in both North Carolina and South Carolina (respectively July 4 and 9, 1868), ratified the proposed amendment, although earlier legislatures had rejected the proposal. The Secretary of State issued a proclamation, which, though doubtful as to the effect of attempted withdrawals by Ohio and New Jersey, entertained no doubt as to the validity of the ratification by North and South Carolina. The following day (July 21, 1868), Congress passed a resolution which declared the 14th Amendment to be a part of the Constitution and directed the Secretary of State so to promulgate it. The Secretary waited, however, until the newly constituted Legislature of Georgia had ratified the amendment, subsequent to an earlier rejection, before the promulgation of the ratification of the new amendment.]

1. All persons born or naturalized in the United States, and subject to the jurisdiction thereof, are citizens of the United States and of the State wherein they reside. No State shall make or enforce any law which shall abridge the privileges or immunities of citizens of the United States; nor shall any State deprive any person of life, liberty, or property, without due process of law; nor deny to any person within its jurisdiction the equal protection of the laws.

2. Representatives shall be apportioned among the several States according to their respective numbers, counting the whole number of persons in each State, excluding Indians not taxed. But when the right to vote at any election for the choice of electors for President and Vice-President of the United States, Representatives in Congress, the Executive and Judicial officers of a State, or the members of the Legislature thereof, is denied to any of the male inhabitants of such State, being *[twenty-one] [The words in brackets were changed by Amendment XXVI.]* years of age, and citizens of the United States, or in any way abridged, except

for participation in rebellion, or other crime, the basis of representation therein shall be reduced in the proportion which the number of such male citizens shall bear to the whole number of male citizens twenty-one years of age in such State.

3. No person shall be a Senator or Representative in Congress, or elector of President and Vice-President, or hold any office, civil or military, under the United States, or under any State, who, having previously taken an oath, as a member of Congress, or as an officer of the United States, or as a member of any State legislature, or as an executive or judicial officer of any State, to support the Constitution of the United States, shall have engaged in insurrection or rebellion against the same, or given aid or comfort to the enemies thereof. But Congress may by a vote of two-thirds of each House, remove such disability.

4. The validity of the public debt of the United States, authorized by law, including debts incurred for payment of pensions and bounties for services in suppressing insurrection or rebellion, shall not be questioned. But neither the United States nor any State shall assume or pay any debt or obligation incurred in aid of insurrection or rebellion against the United States, or any claim for the loss or emancipation of any slave; but all such debts, obligations and claims shall be held illegal and void.

5. The Congress shall have power to enforce, by appropriate legislation, the provisions of this article.

AMENDMENT XV.

Race no bar to voting rights.

[The following amendment was proposed to the legislatures of the several States by the 40th Congress, Feb. 26, 1869, and ratified Feb. 3, 1870.]

1. The right of citizens of the United States to vote shall not be denied or abridged by the United States or by any State on account of race, color, or previous condition of servitude–

2. The Congress shall have power to enforce this article by appropriate legislation.

AMENDMENT XVI.

Income taxes authorized.

[Proposed by Congress July 12, 1909; ratified Feb. 3, 1913.]

The Congress shall have power to lay and collect taxes on incomes, from whatever source derived, without apportionment among the several States, and without regard to any census or enumeration.

AMENDMENT XVII.

United States Senators to be elected by direct popular vote.

[Proposed by Congress May 13, 1912; ratified Apr. 8, 1913.]

The Senate of the United States shall be composed of two Senators from each State, elected by the people thereof, for six years; and each Senator shall have one vote. The electors in each State shall have the qualifications requisite for electors of the most numerous branch of the State legislatures.

When vacancies happen in the representation of any State in the Senate, the executive authority of such State shall issue writs of election to fill such vacancies: *Provided,* That the legislature of any State may empower the executive thereof to make temporary appointments until the people fill the vacancies by election as the legislature may direct.

This amendment shall not be so construed as to affect the election or term of any Senator chosen before it becomes valid as part of the Constitution.

AMENDMENT XVIII.

Liquor prohibition amendment.

[Proposed by Congress Dec. 18, 1917; ratified Jan. 16, 1919. Repealed by Amendment XXI, effective Dec. 5, 1933.]

1. After one year from the ratification of this article the manufacture, sale, or transportation of intoxicating liquors within, the importation thereof into, or the exportation thereof from the United States and all territory subject to the jurisdiction thereof for beverage purposes is hereby prohibited.

2. The Congress and the several States shall have concurrent power to enforce this article by appropriate legislation.

3. This article shall be inoperative unless it shall have been ratified as an amendment to the Constitution by the legislatures of the several States as provided in the Constitution, within seven years from the date of the submission hereof to the States by the Congress.

[The total vote in the Senates of the various States was 1,310 for, 237 against—84.6% dry. In the lower houses of the States the vote was 3,782 for, 1,035 against—78.5% dry.

[The amendment ultimately was adopted by all the States except Rhode Island.]

AMENDMENT XIX.

Giving nationwide suffrage to women.

[Proposed by Congress June 4, 1919; ratified Aug. 18, 1920.]

The right of citizens of the United States to vote shall not be denied or abridged by the United States or by any State on account of sex.

Congress shall have power to enforce this Article by appropriate legislation.

AMENDMENT XX.

Terms of President and Vice President to begin on Jan. 20; those of Senators, Representatives, Jan. 3.

[Proposed by Congress Mar. 2, 1932; ratified Jan. 23, 1933.]

1. The terms of the President and Vice President shall end at noon on the 20th day of January, and the terms of Senators and Representatives at noon on the 3d day of January, of the years in which such terms would have ended if this article had not been ratified; and the terms of their successors shall then begin.

2. The Congress shall assemble at least once in every year, and such meeting shall begin at noon on the 3d day of January, unless they shall by law appoint a different day.

3. If, at the time fixed for the beginning of the term of the President, the President elect shall have died, the Vice President elect shall become President. If a President shall not have been chosen before the time fixed for the beginning of his term, or if the President elect shall have failed to qualify, then the Vice President elect shall act as President until a President shall have qualified; and the Congress may by law provide for the case wherein neither a President elect nor a Vice President elect shall have qualified, declaring who shall then act as President, or the manner in which one who is to act shall be selected, and such person shall act accordingly until a President or Vice President shall have qualified.

4. The Congress may by law provide for the case of the death of any of the persons from whom the House of Representatives may choose a President whenever the right of choice shall have devolved upon them, and for the case of the death of any of the persons from whom the Senate may choose a Vice President whenever the right of choice shall have devolved upon them.

5. Sections 1 and 2 shall take effect on the 15th day of October following the ratification of this article. *[Oct. 1933]*

6. This article shall be inoperative unless it shall have been ratified as an amendment to the Constitution by the legislatures of three-fourths of the several States within seven years from the date of its submission.

AMENDMENT XXI.

Repeal of Amendment XVIII.

[Proposed by Congress Feb. 20, 1933; ratified Dec. 5, 1933.]

1. The eighteenth article of amendment to the Constitution of the United States is hereby repealed.

2. The transportation or importation into any State, Territory, or possession of the United States for delivery or use therein of intoxicating liquors, in violation of the laws thereof, is hereby prohibited.

3. This article shall be inoperative unless it shall have been ratified as an amendment to the Constitution by conventions in the several States, as provided in the Constitution, within seven years from the date of the submission hereof to the States by the Congress.

AMENDMENT XXII.

Limiting Presidential terms of office.

[Proposed by Congress Mar. 24, 1947; ratified Feb. 27, 1951.]

1. No person shall be elected to the office of the President more than twice, and no person who has held the office of President, or acted as President, for more than two years of a term to which some other person was elected President shall be elected to the office of the President more than once. But this Article shall not apply to any person holding the office of President when this Article was proposed by the Congress, and shall not prevent any person who may be holding the office of President, or acting as President, during the term within which this Article becomes operative from holding the office of President or acting as President during the remainder of such term.

2. This article shall be inoperative unless it shall have been ratified as an amendment to the Constitution by the legislatures of three-fourths of the several States within seven years from the date of its submission to the States by the Congress.

AMENDMENT XXIII.

Presidential vote for District of Columbia.

[Proposed by Congress June 16, 1960; ratified Mar. 29, 1961.]

1. The District constituting the seat of Government of the United States shall appoint in such manner as the Congress may direct:

A number of electors of President and Vice President equal to the whole number of Senators and Representatives in Congress to which the District would be entitled if it were a State, but in no event more than the least populous State; they shall be in addition to those appointed by the States, but they shall be considered, for the purposes of the election of President and Vice President, to be electors appointed by a State; and they shall meet in the District and perform such duties as provided by the twelfth article of amendment.

2. The Congress shall have power to enforce this article by appropriate legislation.

AMENDMENT XXIV.

Barring poll tax in federal elections.

[Proposed by Congress Sept. 14, 1962; ratified Jan. 23, 1964.]

1. The right of citizens of the United States to vote in any primary or other election for President or Vice President, for electors for President or Vice President, or for Senator or Representative in Congress, shall not be denied or abridged by the United States or any State by reason of failure to pay any poll tax or other tax.

2. The Congress shall have power to enforce this article by appropriate legislation.

AMENDMENT XXV.

Presidential disability and succession.

[Proposed by Congress July 6, 1965; ratified Feb. 10, 1967.]

1. In case of the removal of the President from office or of his death or resignation, the Vice President shall become President.

2. Whenever there is a vacancy in the office of the Vice President, the President shall nominate a Vice President who shall take office upon confirmation by a majority vote of both houses of Congress.

3. Whenever the President transmits to the President pro tempore of the Senate and the Speaker of the House of Representatives his written declaration that he is unable to discharge the powers and duties of his office, and until he transmits to them a written declaration to the contrary, such powers and duties shall be discharged by the Vice President as Acting President.

4. Whenever the Vice President and a majority of either the principal officers of the executive departments or of such other body as Congress may by law provide, transmit to the President pro tempore of the Senate and the Speaker of the House of Representatives their written declaration that the President is unable to discharge the powers and duties of his office, the Vice President shall immediately assume the powers and duties of the office as Acting President.

Thereafter, when the President transmits to the President pro tempore of the Senate and the Speaker of the House of Representatives his written declaration that no inability exists, he shall resume the powers and duties of his office unless the Vice President and a majority of either the principal officers of the executive department or of such other body as Congress may by law provide, transmit within four days to the President pro tempore of the Senate and the Speaker of the House of Representatives their written declaration that the President is unable to discharge the powers and duties of his office. Thereupon Congress shall decide the issue, assembling within forty-eight hours for that purpose if not in session. If the Congress, within twenty-one days after receipt of the latter written declaration, or, if Congress is not in session, within twenty-one days after Congress is required to assemble, determines by two-thirds vote of both Houses that the President is unable to discharge the powers and duties of his office, the Vice President shall continue to discharge the same as Acting President; otherwise, the President shall resume the powers and duties of his office.

AMENDMENT XXVI.

Lowering voting age to 18 years.

[Proposed by Congress Mar. 23, 1971; ratified July 1, 1971.]

1. The right of citizens of the United States, who are eighteen years of age or older, to vote shall not be denied or abridged by the United States or by any State on account of age.

2. The Congress shall have the power to enforce this article by appropriate legislation.

AMENDMENT XXVII.

Congressional pay.

[Proposed by Congress Sept. 25, 1789; ratified May 7, 1992.]

No law, varying the compensation for the services of the Senators and Representatives, shall take effect, until an election of Representatives shall have intervened.

How a Bill Becomes a Law

A senator or representative introduces a bill in Congress by sending it to the clerk of the Senate or the House, who assigns it a number and title. This procedure is termed the first reading. The clerk then refers the bill to the appropriate committee of the Senate or House.

If the committee does not wish to consider the bill, it will table, or kill, it. Otherwise, the committee holds hearings to listen to opinions and facts offered by members and other interested parties. The committee then debates the bill and may offer amendments. A vote is taken, and if favorable, the bill is sent back to the clerk of the Senate or House.

The clerk reads the bill to the house—the second reading. Members may then debate the bill and suggest amendments.

After debate and any amendments, the bill is given a third reading, simply of the title, and put to a voice or roll-call vote.

If passed, the bill goes to the other house, where it may be defeated or passed, with or without amendments. If defeated, the bill dies. If passed with amendments, a conference committee made up of members of both houses works out the differences and arrives at a compromise.

After passage of the final version by both houses, the bill is sent to the president. If the president signs it, the bill becomes a law. The president may, however, veto the bill by refusing to sign it and sending it back to the house where it originated, with reasons for the veto.

The president's objections are then read and debated, and a roll-call vote is taken. If the bill receives less than a two-thirds majority, it is defeated. If it receives at least two-thirds, it is sent to the other house. If that house also passes it by at least a two-thirds majority, the one veto is overridden, and the bill becomes a law.

If the president neither signs nor vetoes the bill within 10 days—not including Sundays—it automatically becomes a law even without the president's signature. However, if Congress has adjourned within those 10 days, the bill is automatically killed; this indirect rejection is termed a pocket veto.

Note: Under the Line Item Veto Act, effective Jan. 1, 1997, the president was authorized, under certain circumstances, to veto a bill in part, but the legislation was found unconstitutional by the Supreme Court, June 25, 1998.

Confederate States and Secession

The American Civil War (1861-65) grew out of sectional disputes over the continued existence of slavery in the South and the contention of Southern legislators that the states retained many rights, including the right to secede.

The war was not fought by state against state but by one federal regime against another, the Confederate government in Richmond assuming control over the economic, political, and military life of the South, under protest from Georgia and South Carolina.

South Carolina voted an ordinance of secession from the Union, repealing its 1788 ratification of the U.S. Constitution on Dec. 20, 1860, to take effect on Dec. 24. Other states seceded in 1861. Their votes in conventions were: Mississippi, Jan. 9, 84-15; Florida, Jan. 10, 62-7; Alabama, Jan. 11, 61-39; Georgia, Jan. 19, 208-89; Louisiana, Jan. 26, 113-17; Texas, Feb. 1, 166-7, ratified by popular vote on Feb. 23 (for 34,794, against 11,325); Virginia, Apr. 17, 88-55, ratified by popular vote on May 23 (for 128,884;

against 32,134); Arkansas, May 6, 69-1; Tennessee, May 7, ratified by popular vote on June 8 (for 104,019, against 47,238); North Carolina, May 20.

Missouri Unionists stopped secession in conventions Feb. 28 and Mar. 9. The legislature condemned secession Mar. 7. Under the protection of Confederate troops, secessionist members of the legislature adopted a resolution of secession at Neosho, Oct. 31. The Confederate Congress seated the secessionists' representatives.

Kentucky did not secede, and its government remained Unionist. In a part of the state occupied by Confederate troops, Kentuckians approved secession, and the Confederate Congress admitted their representatives.

The Maryland legislature voted against secession Apr. 27, 53-13. Delaware did not secede. Western Virginia held conventions at Wheeling, named a pro-Union governor on June 11, 1861, and was admitted to the Union as West Virginia on June 20, and 1863. Its constitution provided for gradual abolition of slavery.

Confederate Government

Forty-two delegates from South Carolina, Georgia, Alabama, Mississippi, Louisiana, and Florida met in convention at Montgomery, AL, on Feb. 4, 1861. They adopted a provisional constitution of the Confederate States of America and elected Jefferson Davis (MS) as provisional president and Alexander H. Stephens (GA) as provisional vice president.

A permanent constitution was adopted Mar. 11. It abolished the African slave trade, but it did not bar interstate

commerce in slaves. On July 20 the Congress moved to Richmond, VA. Davis was elected president in November and was inaugurated on Feb. 22, 1862.

The Congress adopted a flag, consisting of a red field with a white stripe, and a blue jack with a circle of white stars. Later the more popular flag was the red field with blue diagonal crossbars that held 13 white stars, for the 11 states in the Confederacy plus Kentucky and Missouri.

The Gettysburg Address

Delivered by Pres. Abraham Lincoln at Gettysburg, PA, on Nov. 19, 1863.

Fourscore and seven years ago our fathers brought forth on this continent a new nation, conceived in liberty and dedicated to the proposition that all men are created equal.

Now we are engaged in a great civil war, testing whether that nation or any nation so conceived and so dedicated can long endure. We are met on a great battle field of that war. We have come to dedicate a portion of that field, as a final resting-place for those who here gave their lives that this nation might live. It is altogether fitting and proper that we should do this.

But, in a larger sense, we can not dedicate—we can not consecrate—we can not hallow—this ground. The brave men, living and dead, who struggled here, have consecrated

it, far above our poor power to add or detract. The world will little note, nor long remember, what we say here, but it can never forget what they did here. It is for us the living, rather, to be dedicated here to the unfinished work which they who fought here have thus far so nobly advanced. It is rather for us to be here dedicated to the great task remaining before us—that from these honored dead we take increased devotion to that cause for which they gave the last full measure of devotion—that we here highly resolve that these dead shall not have died in vain—that this nation, under God, shall have a new birth of freedom—and that government of the people, by the people, for the people, shall not perish from the earth.

Presidential Oath of Office

The Constitution (Article II) directs that the president-elect shall take the following oath or affirmation to be inaugurated as president: "I do solemnly swear [affirm] that I will faithfully execute the office of President of the United States, and will, to the best of my ability, preserve, protect, and defend the Constitution of the United States." (Custom decrees the addition of the words "So help me God" at the end of the oath when taken by the president-elect, with the left hand on the Bible for the duration of the oath, and the right hand slightly raised.)

Law on Succession to the Presidency

If by reason of death, resignation, removal from office, inability, or failure to qualify there is neither a president nor vice president to discharge the powers and duties of the office of president, then the speaker of the House of Representatives shall upon his resignation as speaker and as representative, act as president. The same rule shall apply in the case of the death, resignation, removal from office, or inability of an individual acting as president.

If at the time when a speaker is to begin the discharge of the powers and duties of the office of president there is no speaker, or the speaker fails to qualify as acting president, then the president pro tempore of the Senate, upon his resignation as president pro tempore and as senator, shall act as president.

An individual acting as president shall continue to act until the expiration of the then current presidential term, except that (1) if his discharge of the powers and duties of the office is founded in whole or in part in the failure of both the president-elect and the vice president-elect to qualify, then he shall act only until a president or vice president qualifies, and (2) if his discharge of the powers and duties of the office is founded in whole or in part on the inability of the president or vice president, then he shall act only until the removal of the disability of one of such individuals.

If, by reason of death, resignation, removal from office, or failure to qualify, there is no president pro tempore to act as president, then the officer of the United States who is highest on the following list, and who is not under any disability to discharge the powers and duties of president shall act as president: the secretaries of state, treasury, defense, attorney general, secretaries of interior, agriculture, commerce, labor, health and human services, housing and urban development, transportation, energy, education, veterans affairs, homeland security.

[Legislation approved July 18, 1947; amended Sept. 9, 1965, Oct. 15, 1966, Aug. 4, 1977, and Sept. 27, 1979. See also Constitutional Amendment XXV.]

Origin of the United States National Motto

In God We Trust, designated as the U.S. National Motto by Congress in 1956, originated during the Civil War as an inscription for U.S. coins, although it was used by Francis Scott Key in a slightly different form when he wrote "The Star-Spangled Banner" in 1814. On Nov. 13, 1861, when Union morale had been shaken by battlefield defeats, the Rev. M. R. Watkinson, of Ridleyville, PA, wrote to Sec. of the Treasury Salmon P. Chase. "From my heart I have felt our national shame in disowning God as not the least of our present national disasters," the minister wrote, suggesting "recognition of the Almighty God in some form on our coins." Sec. Chase ordered designs prepared with the inscription *In God We Trust* and backed coinage legislation that authorized use of this slogan. The motto first appeared on some U.S. coins in 1864, and disappeared and reappeared on various coins until 1955, when Congress ordered it placed on all paper money and all coins.

The Great Seal of the U.S.

On July 4, 1776, the Continental Congress appointed a committee consisting of Benjamin Franklin, John Adams, and Thomas Jefferson "to bring in a device for a seal of the United States of America." The designs submitted by this and a subsequent committee were considered unacceptable. After many delays, a third committee, appointed early in 1782, presented a design prepared by lawyer William Barton. Charles Thomson, the secretary of Congress, suggested certain changes, and Congress finally approved the design on June 20, 1782. The obverse side of the seal shows an American bald eagle. In its mouth is a ribbon bearing the motto E Pluribus Unum (out of many, one). In the eagle's talons are 13 arrows of war and an olive branch of peace. The reverse side shows an unfinished pyramid with an eye (Eye of Providence) above it.

The Flag of the U.S.—The Stars and Stripes

The 50-star flag of the United States was raised for the first time officially at 12:01 AM on July 4, 1960, at Fort McHenry National Monument in Baltimore, MD. The 50th star had been added for Hawaii; a year earlier the 49th, for Alaska. Before that, no star had been added since 1912, when New Mexico and Arizona were admitted to the Union.

The true history of the Stars and Stripes has become so cluttered with myth and tradition that the facts are difficult, and in some cases impossible, to establish. For example, it is not certain who designed the Stars and Stripes, who made the first such flag, or even whether it ever flew in any sea fight or land battle of the American Revolution.

All agree, however, that the Stars and Stripes originated as the result of a resolution offered by the Marine Committee of the Second Continental Congress at Philadelphia and adopted on June 14, 1777. It read:

"Resolved: that the flag of the United States be thirteen stripes, alternate red and white; that the union be thirteen stars, white in a blue field, representing a new constellation."

Congress gave no hint as to the designer of the flag, no instructions as to the arrangement of the stars, and no information on its appropriate uses. Historians have been unable to find the original flag law.

The resolution establishing the flag was not even published until Sept. 2, 1777. Despite repeated requests, Washington did not get the flags until 1783, after the American Revolution was over. And there is no certainty that they were the Stars and Stripes.

Early Flags

Many historians consider the first flag of the U.S. to have been the Grand Union (sometimes called Great Union) flag, although the Continental Congress never officially adopted it. This flag was a modification of the British Meteor flag, which had the red cross of St. George and the white cross of St. Andrew combined in the blue canton. For the Grand Union flag, 6 horizontal stripes were imposed on the red field, dividing it into 13 alternating red and white stripes. On

Jan. 1, 1776, when the Continental Army came into formal existence, this flag was unfurled on Prospect Hill, Somerville, MA. Washington wrote that "we hoisted the Union Flag in compliment to the United Colonies."

One of several flags about which controversy has raged for years is at Easton, PA. Containing the devices of the national flag in reversed order, this flag has been in the public library at Easton for more than 150 years. Some contend that this flag was actually the first Stars and Stripes, first displayed on July 8, 1776. This flag has 13 red and white stripes in the canton, 13 white stars centered in a blue field.

A flag was hastily improvised from garments by the defenders of Ft. Schuyler at Rome, NY, Aug. 3-22, 1777. Historians believe it was the Grand Union Flag.

The Sons of Liberty had a flag of 9 red and white stripes, to signify 9 colonies, when they met in New York in 1765 to oppose the Stamp Tax. By 1775, the flag had grown to 13 red and white stripes, with a rattlesnake on it.

At Concord, Apr. 19, 1775, the minutemen from Bedford, MA, are said to have carried a flag having a silver arm with sword on a red field. At Cambridge, MA, the Sons of Liberty used a plain red flag with a green pine tree on it.

In June 1775, Washington went from Philadelphia to Boston to take command of the army, escorted to New York by the Philadelphia Light Horse Troop. It carried a yellow flag that had an elaborate coat of arms—the shield charged with 13 knots, the motto "For These We Strive"—and a canton of 13 blue and silver stripes.

In Feb. 1776, Col. Christopher Gadsden, a member of the Continental Congress, gave the South Carolina Provincial Congress a flag "such as is to be used by the commander-in-chief of the American Navy." It had a yellow field, with a rattlesnake about to strike and the words "Don't Tread on Me."

At the Battle of Bennington, Aug. 16, 1777, patriots used a flag of 7 white and 6 red stripes with a blue canton extending down 9 stripes and showing an arch of 11 white stars over the figure 76 and a star in each of the upper corners. The stars are 7-pointed. This flag is preserved in the historical museum in Bennington, VT.

At the Battle of Cowpens, Jan. 17, 1781, the 3d Maryland Regiment is said to have carried a flag of 13 red and white stripes, with a blue canton containing 12 stars in a circle around one star.

Who Designed the Flag? No one knows for certain. Francis Hopkinson, designer of a naval flag, declared he also had designed the flag and in 1781 asked Congress to reimburse him for his services. Congress did not do so. Dumas Malone of Columbia University wrote: "This talented man . . . designed the American flag."

Who Called the Flag "Old Glory"? The flag is said to have been named Old Glory by William Driver, a sea captain of Salem, MA. One legend has it that when he raised the flag on his brig, the *Charles Doggett*, in 1824, he said: "I name thee Old Glory." But his daughter, who presented the flag to the Smithsonian Institution, said he named it at his 21st birthday celebration on Mar. 17, 1824, when his mother presented the homemade flag to him.

The Betsy Ross Legend. The widely publicized legend that Betsy Ross made the first Stars and Stripes in June 1776, at the request of a committee composed of George Washington, Robert Morris, and George Ross, an uncle, was first made public in 1870, by a grandson of Ross. Historians have been unable to find a historical record of such a meeting or committee.

Adding New Stars

The flag of 1777 was used until 1795. Then, on the admission of Vermont and Kentucky to the Union, Congress passed and Pres. Washington signed an act that after May 1, 1795, the flag should have 15 stripes, alternating red and white, and 15 white stars on a blue field.

When new states were admitted, it became evident that the flag would become burdened with stripes. Congress thereupon ordered that after July 4, 1818, the flag should have 13 stripes, symbolizing the 13 original states; that the union have 20 stars, and that whenever a new state was admitted a new star should be added on the July 4 following admission.

No law designates the permanent arrangement of the stars. However, since 1912, when a new state has been admitted, the new design has been announced by executive order. No star is specifically identified with any state.

Code of Etiquette for Display and Use of the U.S. Flag
Reviewed by National Flag Foundation

Although the Stars and Stripes originated in 1777, it was not until 146 years later that there was a serious attempt to establish a uniform code of etiquette for the U.S. flag. On Feb. 15, 1923, the War Department issued a circular on the rules of flag usage. These rules were adopted almost in their entirety June 14, 1923, by a conference of 68 patriotic organizations in Washington, DC. Finally, on June 22, 1942, a joint resolution of Congress, amended by Public Law 94-344, July 7, 1976, codified "existing rules and customs pertaining to the display and use of the flag."

When to Display the Flag. The flag should be displayed on all days, especially on legal holidays and other special occasions, on official buildings when in use, in or near polling places on election days, and in or near schools when in session. Citizens may fly the flag at any time. It is customary to display it only from sunrise to sunset on buildings and on stationary flagstaffs in the open. It may be displayed at night, however, on special occasions, preferably lighted. The flag now flies over the White House both day and night. It flies over the Senate wing of the Capitol when the Senate

is in session and over the House wing when that body is in session. It flies day and night over the east and west fronts of the Capitol, without floodlights at night but receiving illumination from the Capitol Dome. It flies 24 hours a day at several other places, including the Ft. McHenry National Monument in Baltimore, where it inspired Francis Scott Key to write "The Star Spangled Banner." The flag also flies 24 hours a day, properly illuminated, at U.S. Customs ports of entry.

Flying the Flag at Half-Staff. Flying the flag at half-staff, that is, halfway up the staff, is a signal of mourning. The flag should be hoisted to the top of the staff for an instant before being lowered to half-staff. It should be hoisted to the peak again before being lowered for the day or night.

As provided by presidential proclamation, the flag should fly at half-staff for 30 days from the day of death of a president or former president; for 10 days from the day of death of a vice president, chief justice or retired chief justice of the U.S., or speaker of the House of Representatives; from day of death until burial of an associate justice of the Supreme Court, cabinet member, former vice president, Senate president pro tempore, or majority or minority Senate or House leader; for a U.S. senator, representative, territorial delegate, or the resident commissioner of Puerto Rico, on day of death and the following day within the metropolitan area of the District of Columbia and from day of death until burial within the decedent's state, congressional district, territory or commonwealth; and for the death of the governor of a state, territory, or possession of the U.S., from day of death until burial.

On Memorial Day, the flag should fly at half-staff until noon and then be raised to the peak. The flag should also fly at half-staff on Korean War Veterans Armistice Day (July 27), National Pearl Harbor Remembrance Day (Dec. 7), and Peace Officers Memorial Day (May 15).

How to Fly the Flag. The flag should be hoisted briskly and lowered ceremoniously and should never be allowed to touch the ground or the floor. When the flag is hung over a sidewalk from a rope extending from a building to a pole, the union should be away from the building. When the flag is hung over the center of a street the union should be to the north in an east-west street and to the east in a north-south street. No other flag may be flown above or, if on the same level, to the right of the U.S. flag, except that at the United Nations Headquarters the UN flag may be placed above flags of all member nations and other national flags may be flown with equal prominence or honor with the flag of the U.S. At services by Navy chaplains at sea, the church pennant may be flown above the flag.

When two flags are placed against a wall with crossed staffs, the U.S. flag should be at right—its own right, and its staff should be in front of the staff of the other flag; when a number of flags are grouped and displayed from staffs, it should be at the center and highest point of the group.

Church and Platform Use. In an auditorium, the flag may be displayed flat, above and behind the speaker. When displayed from a staff in a church or in a public auditorium, the flag should hold the position of superior prominence, in advance of the audience, and in the position of honor at the speaker's right as she or he faces the audience. Any other flag so displayed should be placed on the left of the speaker or to the right of the audience.

When the flag is displayed horizontally or vertically against a wall, the stars should be uppermost and at the observer's left.

When used to cover a casket, the flag should be placed so that the union is at the head and over the left shoulder. It should not be lowered into the grave nor touch the ground.

How to Dispose of Worn Flags. When the flag is in such condition that it is no longer a fitting emblem for display,

it should be destroyed in a dignified way, preferably by burning.

When to Salute the Flag. All persons present should face the flag, stand at attention, and salute on the following occasions: (1) when the flag is passing in a parade or in a review, (2) during the ceremony of hoisting or lowering, (3) when the national anthem is played, and (4) during the Pledge of Allegiance. Those present in uniform should render the military salute. Those not in uniform should place the right hand over the heart. A man wearing a hat should remove it with his right hand and hold it to his left shoulder during the salute.

Prohibited Uses of the Flag. The flag should not be dipped to any person or thing. (An exception—customarily, ships salute by dipping their colors.) It should never be displayed with the union down save as a distress signal. It should never be carried flat or horizontally, but always aloft and free.

It should not be displayed on a float, an automobile, or a boat except from a staff. It should never be used as a covering for a ceiling, nor have placed on it any word, design, or drawing. It should never be used as a receptacle for carrying anything. It should not be used to cover a statue or a monument.

The flag should never be used for advertising purposes, nor be embroidered on such articles as cushions or handkerchiefs, printed or otherwise impressed on boxes or anything that is designed for temporary use and discard; or used as a costume or athletic uniform. Advertising signs should not be fastened to its staff or halyard.

The flag should never be used as drapery of any sort, never festooned, drawn back, nor up, in folds, but always allowed to fall free. Bunting of blue, white, and red, always arranged with the blue above and the white in the middle, should be used for covering a speaker's desk, draping the front of a platform, and for decoration in general.

An act of Congress approved on Feb. 8, 1917, provided certain penalties for the desecration, mutilation, or improper use of the flag within the District of Columbia. A 1968 federal law provided penalties of as much as a year's imprisonment or a $1,000 fine or both for publicly burning or otherwise desecrating any U.S. flag. In addition, many states have laws against flag desecration. In 1989, the Supreme Court ruled that no laws could prohibit political protesters from burning the flag. The decision had the effect of declaring unconstitutional the flag desecration laws of 48 states, as well as a similar federal statute, in cases of peaceful political expression.

The Supreme Court, in June 1990, declared that a new federal law making it a crime to burn or deface the American flag violated the free-speech guarantee of the First Amendment. The 5-4 Court decision led to renewed calls in Congress for a constitutional amendment to make it possible to prosecute flag burners.

Pledge of Allegiance to the Flag

I pledge allegiance to the flag of the United States of America and to the republic for which it stands, one nation under God, indivisible, with liberty and justice for all.

This, the current official version of the Pledge of Allegiance, has developed from the original pledge, which was first published in the Sept. 8, 1892, issue of *Youth's Companion*, a weekly magazine then published in Boston. The original pledge contained the phrase "my flag," which was changed more than 30 years later to "flag of the United States of America." A 1954 act of Congress added the words "under God." (In 2002, the 9th Circuit U.S. Court of Appeals ruled that recitation of the pledge in public schools could not include that phrase. In 2004, however, the U.S. Supreme Court voted to decline to decide the case on a technicality. The lower court's decision was thus overturned.)

The authorship of the pledge was in dispute for many years. The *Youth's Companion* stated in 1917 that the original draft was written by James B. Upham, an executive of the magazine who died in 1910. A leaflet circulated by the magazine later named Upham as the originator of the draft "afterwards condensed and perfected by him and his associates of the Companion force."

Francis Bellamy, a former member of *Youth's Companion* editorial staff, publicly claimed authorship of the pledge in 1923. In 1939, the United States Flag Association, acting on the advice of a committee named to study the controversy, upheld the claim of Bellamy, who had died 8 years earlier. In 1957 the Library of Congress issued a report attributing the authorship to Bellamy.

The History of the National Anthem

"The Star-Spangled Banner" was ordered played by the military and naval services by Pres. Woodrow Wilson in 1916. It was designated the national anthem by Act of Congress, Mar. 3, 1931. The words were written by Francis Scott Key, of Georgetown, MD, during the bombardment of Fort McHenry, Baltimore, Sept. 13-14, 1814. Key was a lawyer, a graduate of St. John's College, Annapolis, and a volunteer in a light artillery company. When a friend, Dr. Beanes, a Maryland physician, was taken aboard Admiral Cockburn's British squadron for interfering with ground troops, Key and J. S. Skinner, carrying a note from Pres. Madison, went to the fleet under a flag of truce on a cartel ship to ask Beanes's release. Cockburn consented, but as the fleet was about to sail up the Patapsco to bombard Fort McHenry, he detained them, first on HMS *Surprise* and then on a supply ship.

Key witnessed the bombardment from his own vessel. It began at 7 AM, Sept. 13, 1814, and lasted 25 hrs. The British fired more than 1,500 shells, each weighing as much as 220 lbs. They were unable to approach closely because the U.S. had sunk 22 vessels. Only 4 Americans were killed and 24 wounded. A British bomb-ship was disabled.

During the event, Key wrote a stanza on the back of an envelope. Next day at Indian Queen Inn, Baltimore, he wrote out the poem and gave it to his brother-in-law, Judge J. H. Nicholson. Nicholson suggested use of the tune, "Anacreon in Heaven" (attributed to a British composer named John Stafford Smith), and had the poem printed on broadsides, of which 2 survive. On Sept. 20 it appeared in the *Baltimore American*. Later Key made 3 copies; one is in the Library of Congress, and one in the Pennsylvania Historical Society. The copy Key wrote on Sept. 14 remained in the Nicholson family for 93 years. In 1907 it was sold to Henry Walters of Baltimore. In 1934 it was bought by Walters Art Gallery, Baltimore, for $26,400. In 1953 it was sold to the Maryland Historical Society for the same price.

The flag that Key saw during the bombardment is preserved in the Smithsonian Institution, Washington, DC. It measures 30 by 42 ft and has 15 alternating red and white stripes and 15 stars, for the original 13 states plus Kentucky and Vermont. It was made by Mary Young Pickersgill. The Baltimore Flag House, a museum, occupies her premises, which were restored in 1953.

The Star-Spangled Banner

Note: The second and third stanzas are commonly omitted as a courtesy to the British.

I

Oh, say can you see by the dawn's early light
What so proudly we hailed at the twilight's last gleaming?
Whose broad stripes and bright stars thru the perilous fight,
O'er the ramparts we watched were so gallantly streaming?
And the rocket's red glare, the bombs bursting in air,
Gave proof through the night that our flag was still there.
Oh, say does that star-spangled banner yet wave
O'er the land of the free and the home of the brave?

II

On the shore, dimly seen through the mists of the deep,
Where the foe's haughty host in dread silence reposes,
What is that which the breeze, o'er the towering steep,
As it fitfully blows, half conceals, half discloses?
Now it catches the gleam of the morning's first beam,
In full glory reflected now shines in the stream:
'Tis the star-spangled banner! Oh long may it wave
O'er the land of the free and the home of the brave!

III

And where is that band who so vauntingly swore
That the havoc of war and the battle's confusion,
A home and a country should leave us no more!
Their blood has washed out their foul footsteps' pollution.
No refuge could save the hireling and slave
From the terror of flight, or the gloom of the grave:
And the star-spangled banner in triumph doth wave
O'er the land of the free and the home of the brave!

IV

Oh! thus be it ever, when freemen shall stand
Between their loved home and the war's desolation!
Blest with victory and peace, may the heav'n rescued land
Praise the Power that hath made and preserved us a nation.
Then conquer we must, when our cause it is just,
And this be our motto: "In God is our trust."
And the star-spangled banner in triumph shall wave
O'er the land of the free and the home of the brave!

The Liberty Bell: Its History and Significance

The Liberty Bell is housed in the Liberty Bell Center, located in Philadelphia's Independence National Historical Park.

The original bell was ordered by Assembly Speaker and Chairman of the State House Superintendents Isaac Norris and was ordered from Thomas Lester, Whitechapel Foundry, London. It reached Philadelphia at the end of August 1752. It bore an inscription from Leviticus 25:10: "PROCLAIM LIBERTY THROUGHOUT ALL THE LAND UNTO ALL THE INHABITANTS THEREOF."

The bell was cracked by a stroke of its clapper in Sept. 1752 while it hung on a truss in the State House yard for testing. Pass & Stow, Philadelphia founders, recast the bell, adding 1½ ounces of copper to a pound of the original "Whitechapel" metal to reduce its high tone and brittleness. The bell then contained too much copper, injuring its tone, so Pass & Stow recast it again, this time successfully.

In June 1753 the bell was hung in the old wooden steeple of the State House. In use while the Continental Congress was in session in the State House, it rang out in defiance of British laws and trade restrictions, and it proclaimed the Boston Tea Party and, on July 8, 1776, the first public reading of the Declaration of Independence.

On Sept. 18, 1777, when the British Army was about to occupy Philadelphia, the Liberty Bell was moved in a baggage train of the American Army to Allentown, PA, where it was hidden until June 27, 1778. The bell was moved back to Philadelphia after the British left the city.

In July 1781 the wooden steeple became insecure and had to be taken down. The bell was lowered into the brick section of the tower, where it remained until 1828. Between 1828 and 1844 the old State House bell continued to ring during special occasions. According to tradition, it cracked in 1835 as it tolled the death of Chief Justice John Marshall. It rang for the last time on Feb. 23, 1846. In 1852 it was placed on exhibition in the Declaration Chamber of Independence Hall.

In 1876, when thousands of Americans visited Philadelphia for the Centennial Exposition, the bell was placed in its old wooden support in the tower hallway. In 1877 it was hung from the ceiling of the tower by a chain of 13 links. It was returned again to the Declaration Chamber and in 1896 taken back to the tower hall, where it occupied a glass case. In 1915 the case was removed so that the public might touch it. On Jan. 1, 1976, just after midnight to mark the opening of the Bicentennial Year, the bell was moved to a new glass and steel pavilion behind Independence Hall for easier viewing.

On Oct. 9, 2003, the bell was transferred to its present location, where exhibits and displays explain the history of the bell.

Measurements of the bell: circumference around the lip, 12 ft ½ in.; circumference around the crown, 6 ft 11¼ in.; lip to the crown, 3 ft; height over the crown, 2 ft 3 in.; thickness at lip, 3 in.; thickness at crown, 1¼ in.; weight, 2,080 lbs; length of clapper, 3 ft 2 in.

Statue of Liberty National Monument

Since 1886, the Statue of Liberty, formally known as "Liberty Enlightening the World," has stood as a symbol of freedom in New York harbor. It also commemorates French-American friendship, for it was given by the people of France and designed by French sculptor Frederic Auguste Bartholdi (1834-1904).

On Washington's Birthday, Feb. 22, 1877, Congress approved the use of a site on Bedloe's Island suggested by Bartholdi. This island of 12 acres had been owned in the 17th cent. by a Walloon named Isaac Bedloe. It was called Bedloe's until Aug. 3, 1956, when Pres. Dwight Eisenhower approved a measure changing the name to Liberty Island.

The statue was finished on May 21, 1884, and presented to the U.S. minister to France, Levi Parsons Morton, July 4, 1884, by Ferdinand de Lesseps, head of the Franco-American Union, promoter of the Panama Canal, and builder of the Suez Canal.

On Aug. 5, 1884, the Americans laid the cornerstone for the pedestal, to be built on the foundations of Fort Wood, erected by the government in 1811. The American committee had raised $125,000, but this was inadequate. Joseph Pulitzer, owner of the *New York World*, appealed on Mar. 16, 1885, for general donations. By Aug. 11, 1885, he had raised $100,000. The statue itself arrived dismantled, in 214 packing cases, from Rouen, France, in June 1885. The last rivet of the statue was driven on Oct. 28, 1886, when Pres. Grover Cleveland dedicated the monument.

The Statue of Liberty National Monument was designated as such in 1924. It is administered by the National Park Service. A $2.5-mil building housing the American Museum of Immigration was opened by Pres. Richard Nixon on Sept. 26, 1972, at the base of the statue. It houses a permanent exhibition tracing the history of American immigration.

Four years of restoration work funded and led by the Statue of Liberty-Ellis Island Foundation were completed before the statue's 1986 centennial. Among other repairs, the $87-mil project included replacing the 1,600 wrought

iron bands that hold the statue's copper skin to its frame, replacing its torch, and installing an elevator. A 4-day "Liberty Weekend" extravaganza of concerts, tall ships, ethnic festivals, and fireworks, July 3-6, 1986, celebrated the 100th anniversary. Chief Justice Warren E. Burger swore in 5,000 new citizens on Ellis Island, while 20,000 others across the country were sworn in through a satellite telecast. Other ceremonies followed on Oct. 28, 1986, the statue's exact 100th birthday.

Following the Sept. 11, 2001, terrorist attacks, Liberty Island was closed to visitors. On Dec. 20, 2001, the secretary of the interior reopened the island after installing airport-type screening facilities at passenger embarkation areas at Battery Park in Manhattan and Liberty State Park in New Jersey.

To open the statue, the federal government needed to increase security throughout the park. In addition to federally funded security upgrades, significant safety improvements were made to meet building codes. Access to the statue was finally restored on Aug. 3, 2004.

Following the 125th anniversary celebration Oct. 28, 2011, the statue was again scheduled to close for renovations. The work, expected to take one year and cost about $27 mil, will bring the statue up to contemporary safety standards and allow for increased visitor access. The island was to open for visitors during the renovations, and views of the statue were expected to be largely unobstructed.

Once access to the statue is restored, visitors will require reservations to visit the top of the pedestal or the statue's crown. If the past rules are retained, pedestal tickets to enter any level of the monument will be limited to 3,000 visitors per day, and access to the crown will be limited to 240 people each day. Reservations will be available by visiting www.statuecruises.com or by calling 1-877-LADY-TIX. A limited number of "walk up" reservations may also be available at ferry embarkation areas. Free, ranger-guided tours are available daily. Pedestal pass holders will be able to visit the original torch, taken down during renovation in the 1980s, and the museum. For more information, visit www.nps.gov/stli/ and www.statueofliberty.org

Statue Statistics

The statue weighs 450,000 lbs., or 225 tons. The copper sheeting weighs 200,000 lbs. There are 167 steps from the land level to the top of the pedestal, 168 steps inside the statue to the head, and 54 rungs on the ladder leading to the arm that holds the torch.

	Ft	In.		Ft	In.
Height from base to torch tip	151	1	Nose, length	4	6
Foundation of pedestal to torch tip	305	1	Right arm, length	42	0
Heel to top of head	111	1	Right arm, max. thickness	12	0
Hand, length	16	5	Thickness of waist	35	0
Index finger, length	8	0	Mouth, width	3	0
Size of fingernail		13x10	Tablet, length	23	7
Head from chin to cranium	17	3	Tablet, width	13	7
Head thickness, ear to ear	10	0			

Ellis Island

Ellis Island was the gateway to America for over 12 mil immigrants between 1892 and 1924. In the late 18th cent., Samuel Ellis, a New York City merchant, purchased the island and gave it his name. From Ellis, it passed to New York State, and the U.S. government bought it in 1808. On Jan. 1, 1892, the government opened the first federal immigration center in the U.S. there. The 27½-acre site eventually supported more than 35 buildings, including the Main Building with its Great Hall, in which as many as 5,000 people a day were processed.

Closed as an immigration station in 1954, Ellis Island was proclaimed part of the Statue of Liberty National Monument in 1965 by Pres. Lyndon B. Johnson. After a six-year, $170 mil restoration project funded by the Statue of Liberty-Ellis Island Foundation, Ellis Island was reopened as a museum in 1990. Artifacts, historic photographs and documents, oral histories, and ethnic music depicting 400 years of American immigration are housed in the museum. The museum also

includes The American Immigrant Wall of Honor (www.wallofhonor.org), which is inscribed with more than 700,000 names that have been placed in tribute. Registrations are still being accepted for inclusion in the memorial.

The American Family Immigration History Center® opened in Apr. 2001. It contains an electronic database of ship passenger arrival information through the Port of New York and Ellis Island from 1892 to 1924. Data on over 25 mil individuals are available, as well as an interactive database which features a Living Family Archive, multimedia presentations on various immigration groups and patterns, reproductions of original ships' passenger manifests, and pictures of over 800 immigrant ships (www.ellisisland.org).

In 1998, the Supreme Court ruled that nearly 90% of the island (the 24.2 acres that are landfill) lies in New Jersey, while the original 3.3 acres, on which the museum is located, are in New York.

U.S. SUPREME COURT

(as of Sept. 2011)

Justices of the U.S. Supreme Court

The Supreme Court comprises the chief justice of the U.S. and eight associate justices, all appointed for life by the president with advice and consent of the U.S. Senate. Names of chief justices are in **boldface**. Terms of service begin with the year each justice took the judicial oath. Service years are the number of complete years served by a justice. Current salaries: chief justice, $223,500; associate justice, $213,900. The U.S. Supreme Court Building is at 1 First St. NE, Washington, DC 20543. The Court website is www.supremecourt.gov.

Current membership. Chief justice: John G. Roberts Jr.; assoc. justices in seniority order: Antonin Scalia, Anthony M. Kennedy, Clarence Thomas, Ruth Bader Ginsburg, Stephen G. Breyer, Samuel A. Alito Jr., Sonia Sotomayor, Elena Kagan.

Name, appointed from	Term (Service)	Yrs.	Born	Died
John Jay, NY	1789-1795	5	1745	1829
John Rutledge, SC[1]	1790-1791	1	1739	1800
William Cushing, MA	1790-1810*	20	1732	1810
James Wilson, PA	1789-1798	8	1742	1798
John Blair, VA	1790-1795*	5	1732	1800
James Iredell, NC	1790-1799	9	1751	1799
Thomas Johnson, MD	1792-1793	<1	1732	1819
William Paterson, NJ	1793-1806	13	1745	1806
John Rutledge, SC[2,3]	1795	<1	1739	1800
Samuel Chase, MD	1796-1811	15	1741	1811
Oliver Ellsworth, CT	1796-1800	4	1745	1807
Bushrod Washington, VA	1799-1829*	30	1762	1829
Alfred Moore, NC	1800-1804	3	1755	1810
John Marshall, VA	1801-1835	34	1755	1835
William Johnson, SC	1804-1834	30	1771	1834
Henry B. Livingston, NY	1807-1823	16	1757	1823
Thomas Todd, KY	1807-1826	18	1765	1826
Gabriel Duvall, MD	1811-1835	23	1752	1844
Joseph Story, MA	1812-1845*	33	1779	1845
Smith Thompson, NY	1823-1843	20	1768	1843
Robert Trimble, KY	1826-1828	2	1777	1828
John McLean, OH	1830-1861*	31	1785	1861
Henry Baldwin, PA	1830-1844	14	1780	1844
James M. Wayne, GA	1835-1867	32	1790	1867
Roger B. Taney, MD	1836-1864	28	1777	1864
Philip P. Barbour, VA	1836-1841	4	1783	1841
John Catron, TN	1837-1865	28	1786	1865
John McKinley, AL	1838-1852*	14	1780	1852
Peter V. Daniel, VA	1842-1860*	18	1784	1860
Samuel Nelson, NY	1845-1872	27	1792	1873
Levi Woodbury, NH	1845-1851	5	1789	1851
Robert C. Grier, PA	1846-1870	23	1794	1870
Benjamin R. Curtis, MA	1851-1857	5	1809	1874
John A. Campbell, AL	1853-1861*	8	1811	1889
Nathan Clifford, ME	1858-1881	23	1803	1881
Noah H. Swayne, OH	1862-1881	18	1804	1884
Samuel F. Miller, IA	1862-1890	28	1816	1890
David Davis, IL	1862-1877	14	1815	1886
Stephen J. Field, CA	1863-1897	33	1816	1899
Salmon P. Chase, OH	1864-1873	8	1808	1873
William Strong, PA	1870-1880	10	1808	1895
Joseph P. Bradley, NJ	1870-1892	21	1813	1892
Ward Hunt, NY	1873-1882	9	1810	1886
Morrison R. Waite, OH	1874-1888	14	1816	1888
John M. Harlan, KY	1877-1911	33	1833	1911
William B. Woods, GA	1881-1887	6	1824	1887
Stanley Matthews, OH	1881-1889	7	1824	1889
Horace Gray, MA	1882-1902	20	1828	1902
Samuel Blatchford, NY	1882-1893	11	1820	1893
Lucius Q.C. Lamar, MS	1888-1893	5	1825	1893
Melville W. Fuller, IL	1888-1910	21	1833	1910
David J. Brewer, KS	1890-1910	20	1837	1910
Henry B. Brown, MI	1891-1906	15	1836	1913
George Shiras Jr., PA	1892-1903	10	1832	1924
Howell E. Jackson, TN	1893-1895	2	1832	1895
Edward D. White, LA[1]	1894-1910	16	1845	1921
Rufus W. Peckham, NY	1896-1909	13	1838	1909
Joseph McKenna, CA	1898-1925	26	1843	1926
Oliver W. Holmes, MA	1902-1932	29	1841	1935
William R. Day, OH	1903-1922	19	1849	1923
William H. Moody, MA	1906-1910	3	1853	1917
Horace H. Lurton, TN	1910-1914	4	1844	1914
Charles E. Hughes, NY[1]	1910-1916	5	1862	1948
Willis Van Devanter, WY	1911-1937	26	1859	1941
Joseph R. Lamar, GA	1911-1916	5	1857	1916
Edward D. White, LA[2]	1910-1921	10	1845	1921
Mahlon Pitney, NJ	1912-1922	10	1858	1924
James C. McReynolds, TN	1914-1941	26	1862	1946
Louis D. Brandeis, MA	1916-1939	22	1856	1941
John H. Clarke, OH	1916-1922	5	1857	1945
William H. Taft, CT	1921-1930	8	1857	1930
George Sutherland, UT	1922-1938	15	1862	1942
Pierce Butler, MN	1923-1939	16	1866	1939
Edward T. Sanford, TN	1923-1930	7	1865	1930
Harlan F. Stone, NY[1]	1925-1941	16	1872	1946
Charles E. Hughes, NY[2]	1930-1941	11	1862	1948
Owen J. Roberts, PA	1930-1945	15	1875	1955
Benjamin N. Cardozo, NY	1932-1938	6	1870	1938
Hugo L. Black, AL	1937-1971	34	1886	1971
Stanley F. Reed, KY	1938-1957	19	1884	1980
Felix Frankfurter, MA	1939-1962	23	1882	1965
William O. Douglas, CT	1939-1975	36[4]	1898	1980
Frank Murphy, MI	1940-1949	9	1890	1949
Harlan F. Stone, NY[2]	1941-1946	4	1872	1946
James F. Byrnes, SC	1941-1942	1	1879	1972
Robert H. Jackson, NY	1941-1954	13	1892	1954
Wiley B. Rutledge, IA	1943-1949	6	1894	1949
Harold H. Burton, OH	1945-1958	13	1888	1964
Fred M. Vinson, KY	1946-1953	7	1890	1953
Tom C. Clark, TX	1949-1967	17	1899	1977
Sherman Minton, IN	1949-1956	7	1890	1965
Earl Warren, CA	1953-1969	15	1891	1974
John Marshall Harlan, NY	1955-1971	16	1899	1971
William J. Brennan Jr., NJ	1956-1990	33	1906	1997
Charles E. Whittaker, MO	1957-1962	5	1901	1973
Potter Stewart, OH	1958-1981	22	1915	1985
Byron R. White, CO	1962-1993	31	1917	2002
Arthur J. Goldberg, IL	1962-1965	2	1908	1990
Abe Fortas, TN	1965-1969	3	1910	1982
Thurgood Marshall, NY	1967-1991	24	1908	1993
Warren E. Burger, VA	1969-1986	17	1907	1995
Harry A. Blackmun, MN	1970-1994	24	1908	1999
Lewis F. Powell Jr., VA	1972-1987	15	1907	1998
William H. Rehnquist, AZ[1]	1972-1986	14	1924	2005
John Paul Stevens, IL	1975-2010	34	1920	
Sandra Day O'Connor, AZ	1981-2006	24	1930	
William H. Rehnquist, VA[2]	1986-2005	18	1924	2005
Antonin Scalia, VA	1986-		1936	
Anthony M. Kennedy, CA	1988-		1936	
David H. Souter, NH	1990-2009	18	1939	
Clarence Thomas, GA	1991-		1948	
Ruth Bader Ginsburg, NY	1993-		1933	
Stephen G. Breyer, MA	1994-		1938	
John G. Roberts Jr., MD	2005-		1955	
Samuel A. Alito Jr., NJ	2006-		1950	
Sonia Sotomayor, NY	2009-		1954	
Elena Kagan, MA	2010-		1960	

*Because of inadequate government record keeping, date of oath is estimated and not absolutely certain. (1) Later, chief justice, as listed. (2) Formerly assoc. justice. (3) Named as acting chief justice; confirmation rejected by the Senate. (4) Longest term of service.

Selected Landmark Decisions of the U.S. Supreme Court, 1803-2010

1803: *Marbury v. Madison.* The Court ruled that Congress exceeded its power in the Judiciary Act of 1789. The Court thus established its power to review acts of Congress and to declare invalid those it found to be in conflict with the Constitution.

1819: *McCulloch v. Maryland.* The Court ruled that Congress had the authority to charter a national bank, under the Constitution's granting of power to enact all laws "necessary and proper" to responsibilities of government.

1819: *Trustees of Dartmouth College v. Woodward.* The Court ruled that a state could not arbitrarily alter the terms of a college's contract. The Court later used a similar principle to limit the states' ability to interfere with business contracts.

1857: *Dred Scott v. Sanford.* The Court declared unconstitutional the already-repealed Missouri Compromise of 1820 because it deprived a person of property—a slave—without due process of law. The Court also ruled that slaves were not citizens of any state nor of the U.S. The latter part of the decision was overturned by ratification of the 14th Amendment in 1868.

1896: *Plessy v. Ferguson.* The Court ruled that a state law requiring federal railroad trains to provide separate but equal facilities for black and white passengers neither infringed upon federal authority to regulate interstate commerce nor violated the 13th and 14th Amendments. The "separate but equal" doctrine remained effective until the 1954 *Brown v. Board of Education* decision.

1904: *Northern Securities Co. v. U.S.* The Court ruled that a holding company formed solely to eliminate competition between two railroad lines was a combination in restraint of trade, violating the federal antitrust act.

1908: *Muller v. Oregon.* The Court upheld a state law limiting the working hours of women. (Louis D. Brandeis, counsel for the state, cited evidence from social workers, physicians, and factory inspectors that the number of hours women worked affected their health and morals.)

1911: *Standard Oil Co. of New Jersey v. U.S.* The Court ruled that the Standard Oil Trust must be dissolved because of its unreasonable restraint of trade.

1919: *Schenck v. U.S.* The Court sustained the Espionage Act of 1917, maintaining that freedom of speech and press could be constrained if "the words used ... create a clear and present danger."

1925: *Gitlow v. New York.* The Court ruled that the 1st Amendment prohibition against government abridgment of the freedom of speech applied to the states as well as to the federal government. The decision was the first of a number of rulings holding that the 14th Amendment extended the guarantees of the Bill of Rights to state action.

1935: *Schechter Poultry Corp. v. U.S.* The Court ruled that Congress exceeded its authority to delegate legislative powers and to regulate interstate commerce when it enacted the National Industrial Recovery Act (1933), which afforded the U.S. president too much discretionary power.

1951: *Dennis v. U.S.* The Court upheld convictions under the Smith Act of 1940 for invoking Communist theory advocating the forcible overthrow of the government. In *Yates v. U.S.* (1957), the Court moderated this ruling by allowing such advocacy in the abstract, if not connected to action to achieve the goal.

1954: *Brown v. Board of Education of Topeka.* The Court ruled that separate public schools for black and white students were inherently unequal, so that state-sanctioned segregation in public schools violated the equal protection guarantee of the 14th Amendment. And in *Bolling v. Sharpe* the same year, the Court ruled that the congressionally mandated segregated public school system in the District of Columbia violated the 5th Amendment's due process guarantee of personal liberty. The Brown ruling also led to abolition of state-sponsored segregation in other public facilities.

1957: *Roth v. U.S.; Alberts v. California.* The Court ruled obscene material was not protected by 1st Amendment guarantees of freedom of speech and press, defining as obscene something "utterly without redeeming social value" in the average person's view. This definition was modified in later decisions, and the "average person" standard was replaced by the "local community" standard in *Miller v. California* (1973).

1961: *Mapp v. Ohio.* The Court ruled that evidence obtained in violation of the 4th Amendment guarantee against unreasonable search and seizure must be excluded from use in state as well as federal trials.

1962: *Engel v. Vitale.* The Court held that government bodies could not encourage the recitation of a state-composed prayer in public schools, even if nondenominational, because that would be an unconstitutional attempt to establish religion.

1962: *Baker v. Carr.* The Court held that constitutional challenges to the unequal distribution of voters among legislative districts could be resolved by federal courts.

1963: *Gideon v. Wainwright.* The Court ruled that defendants in state cases must have access to an attorney even if they could not afford one.

1964: *New York Times Co. v. Sullivan.* The Court ruled that the 1st Amendment protected the press from libel suits for defamatory reports about public officials unless an injured party could prove that a defamatory report was made out of malice or "reckless disregard" for the truth.

1965: *Griswold v. Connecticut.* The Court ruled that a state unconstitutionally interfered with personal privacy in the marriage relationship when it prohibited everyone, including married couples, from using contraceptives.

1966: *Miranda v. Arizona.* The Court ruled that, under the guarantee of due process, suspects in custody, before being questioned, must be informed that they have the right to remain silent, that anything they say may be used against them, and that they have the right to counsel.

1973: *Roe v. Wade; Doe v. Bolton.* The Court ruled that the fetus was not a "person" with constitutional rights and that a right to privacy inherent in the 14th Amendment's due process guarantee of personal liberty protected a woman's decision to have an abortion. During the first trimester of pregnancy, the Court maintained, the decision should be left entirely to a woman and her physician. Some regulation of abortion procedures was allowed in the second trimester and some restriction of abortion in the third.

1974: *U.S. v. Nixon.* The Court ruled that neither the separation of powers nor the need to preserve the confidentiality of presidential communications could alone justify an absolute executive privilege of immunity from judicial demands for evidence to be used in a criminal trial.

1976: *Gregg v. Georgia; Profitt v. Florida; Jurek v. Texas.* The Court held that death, as a punishment for persons convicted of first-degree murder, was not in and of itself cruel and unusual punishment in violation of the 8th Amendment. But the Court ruled that the sentencing judge and jury must consider the character of the offender and the circumstances of the particular crime.

1978: *Regents of the Univ. of Calif. v. Bakke.* The Court ruled that a special admissions program for a state medical school, under which a set number of places were reserved for minorities, violated the 1964 Civil Rights Act, which forbids the exclusion of anyone from a federally funded program based on race. However, the Court ruled that race could be considered as one of a complex of factors.

1986: *Bowers v. Hardwick.* The Court refused to extend any constitutional right of privacy to homosexual activity, upholding a Georgia antisodomy law that in effect made such activity a crime. However, the law was struck down by the state supreme court in 1998, and in *Lawrence v. Texas* (2003), the U.S. Supreme Court struck down all state antisodomy laws, as violations of liberty prohibited in the 14th Amendment's due process clause. In *Romer v. Evans* (1996), the Court struck down a Colorado constitutional provision that it ruled violated the 14th Amendment's Equal Protection Clause because it barred legislation whereby "homosexual orientation, conduct, practices, or relationships" granted a person "minority status, quota preferences, protected status, or claim of discrimination."

1990: *Cruzan v. Missouri.* The Court ruled that a person had the right to refuse life-sustaining medical treatment. However, the Court also ruled that, before treatment could be withheld from a comatose patient, a state could require "clear and convincing evidence" that the patient would not have wanted to live. In two 1997 rulings, *Washington v. Glucksberg* and *Vacco v. Quill,* the Court ruled that states could ban doctor-assisted suicide.

1995: *Adarand Constructors, Inc. v. Peña.* The Court held that federal programs that classify people by race, unless "narrowly tailored" to accomplish a "compelling governmental interest," may violate the right to equal protection.

1995: *U.S. Term Limits Inc. v. Thornton.* The Court ruled that neither states nor Congress could limit terms of members of Congress because the Constitution reserves to the people the right to choose federal lawmakers.

1997: *Clinton v. Jones.* Rejecting an appeal by Pres. Clinton in a sexual harassment suit, the Court ruled that a sitting president did not have temporary immunity from a lawsuit for actions outside the realm of official duties.

1997: *City of Boerne v. Flores.* The Court overturned a 1993 law banning enforcement of laws that "substantially burden" religious practice unless there is a "compelling need" to do so. The Court held that the act was an unwarranted intrusion by Congress on states' prerogatives and an infringement of the judiciary's role.

1997: *Reno v. ACLU.* Citing the right to free expression, the Court overturned a provision making it a crime to display or distribute "indecent" or "patently offensive" material on the Internet. The Court ruled, however, in *NEA v. Finley* (1998) that "general standards of decency" may be used as a criterion in federal arts funding.

1998: *Clinton v. City of New York.* The Court struck down the Line-Item Veto Act (1996), holding that it unconstitutionally gave the president "the unilateral power to change the text of duly enacted statutes."

1998: *Faragher v. City of Boca Raton; Burlington Industries, Inc. v. Ellerth.* The Court issued new guidelines for workplace sexual harassment suits, holding employers responsible for misconduct by supervisory employees. And in *Oncale v. Sundowner Offshore Services,* the Court ruled that the law against discrimination based on sex applies regardless of whether the harasser and harassed are the same sex.

1999: *Dept. of Commerce v. U.S. House.* Upholding a challenge to plans for the 2000 census, the Court prohibited statistical sampling, favored by Democrats, in apportioning seats in the U.S. House of Representatives. The Court maintained that an actual head count was required.

1999: *Alden v. Maine; Florida Prepaid v. College Savings Bank; College Savings Bank v. Florida.* In a series of rulings, the Court applied the principle of sovereign immunity to shield states in large part from being sued under federal law.

2000: *Boy Scouts of America v. Dale.* The Court ruled that the Boy Scouts could dismiss a troop leader after learning he was gay, holding that the right to freedom of association outweighed a New Jersey antidiscrimination statute.

2000: *Bush v. Gore.* The Court ruled that manual recounts of presidential ballots in the Nov. 2000 election could not proceed because inconsistent evaluation standards in different counties violated the equal protection clause. In effect, the ruling meant existing official results leaving George W. Bush as narrow winner of the election would prevail.

2001: *Good News Club v. Milford Central School.* The justices found that religious and secular organizations were entitled to equal access to public elementary school grounds for after-school meetings.

2002: *Atkins v. Virginia.* The Court ruled that the execution of mentally retarded felons violated the 8th Amendment ban on cruel and unusual punishment.

2002: *Ring v. Arizona.* The Court found that only a jury, not a judge, could decide to impose the death penalty.

2002: *Zelman v. Simmons-Harris.* The Court ruled that publicly funded tuition vouchers could be used at religious schools without violating the separation of church and state.

2002: *Federal Maritime Commission v. South Carolina State Ports Authority.* The Court ruled that the 11th Amendment gave states immunity from private lawsuits involving federal agencies.

2003: *Grotter v. Bollinger; Gratz v. Bollinger.* The Court upheld affirmative action in admission policies at the Univ. of Michigan Law School. However, in a second decision, the Court ruled against a strict point system based on racial and ethnic backgrounds, as used in the university's undergraduate admissions process.

2004: *Tennessee v. Lane.* The Court ruled that disabled individuals could sue states under the Americans with Disabilities Act (1990) for failing to provide adequate access to state courthouses, despite states' usual immunity from private lawsuits in federal court under the 11th amendment, which the Court ruled on in *Federal Maritime Commission v. South Carolina State Ports Authority* (2002).

2004: *Locke v. Davey.* The justices decided that a scholarship program provided by the state of Washington did not violate the right to free exercise of religion in denying aid to students preparing for the clergy.

2004: *Ashcroft v. ACLU.* The Court struck down the Child Online Protection Act, which Congress passed in 1998 to restrict access to online pornography by minors, on the basis that the law, as written, violated the 1st Amendment right of free speech.

2005: *Kelo v. City of New London.* The Court ruled that local governments could force property owners to sell their land in order to facilitate private development projects deemed to be economically beneficial to the community.

2005: *Roper v. Simmons.* The Court ruled that executions of convicts who committed their crimes before age 18 were prohibited under the 8th Amendment ban on cruel and unusual punishment.

2006: *Garcetti v. Ceballos.* The Court ruled that the 1st Amendment guarantee of free speech did not protect statements made by public employees in the course of their official duties.

2006: *Hamdan v. Rumsfeld.* The Court ruled that Pres. George W. Bush's system for trying terrorism detainees at the U.S. military base in Guantanamo Bay, Cuba, was unauthorized under both federal law and the international Geneva Conventions.

2007: *Gonzales v. Carhart; Gonzales v. Planned Parenthood Federation of America.* The Court upheld a 2003 federal law prohibiting the abortion procedure known as intact dilation and extraction, or "partial-birth" abortion.

2007: *Parents Involved in Community Schools v. Seattle School District No. 1; Madison v. Jefferson County Board of Education.* The Court ruled that two school districts could not, to encourage diversity, use "racial classifications in making school assignments."

2008: *Boumediene v. Bush.* The Court ruled that the guarantee of habeas corpus applied at the U.S. naval base at Guantanamo Bay, Cuba, and that detainees had a constitutional right to challenge their detention in federal court.

2008: *District of Columbia v. Heller.* The Court overturned DC's handgun ban, ruling that the 2nd Amendment protected individuals' right to own guns for personal use.

2009: *Ricci v. DeStefano.* The Court ruled that fear of litigation was not reason enough for New Haven, CT, to justify its invalidating the results of an exam to determine promotions after white firefighters outperformed minority firefighters on it.

2010: *Citizens United v. Federal Election Commission.* The Court ruled that a federal law barring corporations from using their general treasury funds to finance campaign advertisements was unconstitutional. The decision struck down provisions of two federal laws and cast doubt on the validity of state laws aimed at minimizing corporate influence in electoral politics.

See also Year in Review: Notable Supreme Court Decisions, 2010-11.

PRESIDENTS OF THE UNITED STATES

U.S. Presidents

	Name	Politics	Born	Birthplace	Inaug.	Age at inaug.	Died	Age at death
1.	George Washington	Fed.	1732, Feb. 22	VA	1789	57	1799, Dec. 14	67
2.	John Adams	Fed.	1735, Oct. 30	MA	1797	61	1826, July 4	90
3.	Thomas Jefferson	Dem.-Rep.	1743, Apr. 13	VA	1801	57	1826, July 4	83
4.	James Madison	Dem.-Rep.	1751, Mar. 16	VA	1809	57	1836, June 28	85
5.	James Monroe	Dem.-Rep.	1758, Apr. 28	VA	1817	58	1831, July 4	73
6.	John Quincy Adams	Dem.-Rep.	1767, July 11	MA	1825	57	1848, Feb. 23	80
7.	Andrew Jackson	Dem.	1767, Mar. 15	SC	1829	61	1845, June 8	78
8.	Martin Van Buren	Dem.	1782, Dec. 5	NY	1837	54	1862, July 24	79
9.	William Henry Harrison	Whig	1773, Feb. 9	VA	1841	68	1841, Apr. 4	68
10.	John Tyler	Whig	1790, Mar. 29	VA	1841	51	1862, Jan. 18	71
11.	James Knox Polk	Dem.	1795, Nov. 2	NC	1845	49	1849, June 15	53
12.	Zachary Taylor	Whig	1784, Nov. 24	VA	1849	64	1850, July 9	65
13.	Millard Fillmore	Whig	1800, Jan. 7	NY	1850	50	1874, Mar. 8	74
14.	Franklin Pierce	Dem.	1804, Nov. 23	NH	1853	48	1869, Oct. 8	64
15.	James Buchanan	Dem.	1791, Apr. 23	PA	1857	65	1868, June 1	77
16.	Abraham Lincoln	Rep.	1809, Feb. 12	KY	1861	52	1865, Apr. 15	56
17.	Andrew Johnson	(1)	1808, Dec. 29	NC	1865	56	1875, July 31	66
18.	Ulysses S. Grant	Rep.	1822, Apr. 27	OH	1869	46	1885, July 23	63
19.	Rutherford Birchard Hayes	Rep.	1822, Oct. 4	OH	1877	54	1893, Jan. 17	70
20.	James Abram Garfield	Rep.	1831, Nov. 19	OH	1881	49	1881, Sept. 19	49
21.	Chester Alan Arthur	Rep.	1829, Oct. 5	VT	1881	51	1886, Nov. 18	57
22.	Grover Cleveland	Dem.	1837, Mar. 18	NJ	1885	47	1908, June 24	71
23.	Benjamin Harrison	Rep.	1833, Aug. 20	OH	1889	55	1901, Mar. 13	67
24.	Grover Cleveland	Dem.	1837, Mar. 18	NJ	1893	55	1908, June 24	71
25.	William McKinley	Rep.	1843, Jan. 29	OH	1897	54	1901, Sept. 14	58
26.	Theodore Roosevelt	Rep.	1858, Oct. 27	NY	1901	42	1919, Jan. 6	60
27.	William Howard Taft	Rep.	1857, Sept. 15	OH	1909	51	1930, Mar. 8	72
28.	(Thomas) Woodrow Wilson	Dem.	1856, Dec. 28	VA	1913	56	1924, Feb. 3	67
29.	Warren Gamaliel Harding	Rep.	1865, Nov. 2	OH	1921	55	1923, Aug. 2	57
30.	(John) Calvin Coolidge	Rep.	1872, July 4	VT	1923	51	1933, Jan. 5	60
31.	Herbert Clark Hoover	Rep.	1874, Aug. 10	IA	1929	54	1964, Oct. 20	90
32.	Franklin Delano Roosevelt	Dem.	1882, Jan. 30	NY	1933	51	1945, Apr. 12	63
33.	Harry S. Truman	Dem.	1884, May 8	MO	1945	60	1972, Dec. 26	88
34.	Dwight David Eisenhower	Rep.	1890, Oct. 14	TX	1953	62	1969, Mar. 28	78
35.	John Fitzgerald Kennedy	Dem.	1917, May 29	MA	1961	43	1963, Nov. 22	46
36.	Lyndon Baines Johnson	Dem.	1908, Aug. 27	TX	1963	55	1973, Jan. 22	64
37.	Richard Milhous Nixon[2]	Rep.	1913, Jan. 9	CA	1969	56	1994, Apr. 22	81
38.	Gerald Rudolph Ford	Rep.	1913, July 14	NE	1974	61	2006, Dec. 26	93
39.	James Earl (Jimmy) Carter	Dem.	1924, Oct. 1	GA	1977	52		
40.	Ronald Wilson Reagan	Rep.	1911, Feb. 6	IL	1981	69	2004, June 5	93
41.	George Herbert Walker Bush	Rep.	1924, June 12	MA	1989	64		
42.	Wm. Jefferson (Bill) Clinton	Dem.	1946, Aug. 19	AR	1993	46		
43.	George Walker Bush	Rep.	1946, July 6	CT	2001	54		
44.	Barack Hussein Obama	Dem.	1961, Aug. 4	HI	2009	47		

(1) Andrew Johnson, a Democrat, was nominated vice president by Republicans and elected with Lincoln on National Union ticket.
(2) Resigned Aug. 9, 1974.

U.S. Presidents, Vice Presidents, Congresses

President	Service	Vice President	Congresses
1. George Washington	Apr. 30, 1789-Mar. 3, 1797	1. John Adams	1, 2, 3, 4
2. John Adams	Mar. 4, 1797-Mar. 3, 1801	2. Thomas Jefferson	5, 6
3. Thomas Jefferson	Mar. 4, 1801-Mar. 3, 1805	3. Aaron Burr	7, 8
	Mar. 4, 1805-Mar. 3, 1809	4. George Clinton	9, 10
4. James Madison	Mar. 4, 1809-Mar. 3, 1813	George Clinton[1]	11, 12
	Mar. 4, 1813-Mar. 3, 1817	5. Elbridge Gerry[2]	13, 14
5. James Monroe	Mar. 4, 1817-Mar. 3, 1825	6. Daniel D. Tompkins	15, 16, 17, 18
6. John Quincy Adams	Mar. 4, 1825-Mar. 3, 1829	7. John C. Calhoun	19, 20
7. Andrew Jackson	Mar. 4, 1829-Mar. 3, 1833	John C. Calhoun[3]	21, 22
	Mar. 4, 1833-Mar. 3, 1837	8. Martin Van Buren	23, 24
8. Martin Van Buren	Mar. 4, 1837-Mar. 3, 1841	9. Richard M. Johnson	25, 26
9. William Henry Harrison[4]	Mar. 4, 1841-Apr. 4, 1841	10. John Tyler	27
10. John Tyler	Apr. 6, 1841-Mar. 3, 1845	(None)	27, 28
11. James K. Polk	Mar. 4, 1845-Mar. 3, 1849	11. George M. Dallas	29, 30
12. Zachary Taylor[4]	Mar. 5, 1849-July 9, 1850	12. Millard Fillmore	31
13. Millard Fillmore	July 10, 1850-Mar. 3, 1853	(None)	31, 32
14. Franklin Pierce	Mar. 4, 1853-Mar. 3, 1857	13. William R. King[5]	33, 34
15. James Buchanan	Mar. 4, 1857-Mar. 3, 1861	14. John C. Breckinridge	35, 36
16. Abraham Lincoln	Mar. 4, 1861-Mar. 3, 1865	15. Hannibal Hamlin	37, 38
(4)	Mar. 4, 1865-Apr. 15, 1865	16. Andrew Johnson	39
17. Andrew Johnson	Apr. 15, 1865-Mar. 3, 1869	(None)	39, 40
18. Ulysses S. Grant	Mar. 4, 1869-Mar. 3, 1873	17. Schuyler Colfax	41, 42
	Mar. 4, 1873-Mar. 3, 1877	18. Henry Wilson[6]	43, 44
19. Rutherford B. Hayes	Mar. 4, 1877-Mar. 3, 1881	19. William A. Wheeler	45, 46
20. James A. Garfield[4]	Mar. 4, 1881-Sept. 19, 1881	20. Chester A. Arthur	47
21. Chester A. Arthur	Sept. 20, 1881-Mar. 3, 1885	(None)	47, 48
22. Grover Cleveland[7]	Mar. 4, 1885-Mar. 3, 1889	21. Thomas A. Hendricks[8]	49, 50
23. Benjamin Harrison	Mar. 4, 1889-Mar. 3, 1893	22. Levi P. Morton	51, 52
24. Grover Cleveland[7]	Mar. 4, 1893-Mar. 3, 1897	23. Adlai E. Stevenson	53, 54
25. William McKinley	Mar. 4, 1897-Mar. 3, 1901	24. Garret A. Hobart[9]	55, 56
(4)	Mar. 4, 1901-Sept. 14, 1901	25. Theodore Roosevelt	57
26. Theodore Roosevelt	Sept. 14, 1901-Mar. 3, 1905	(None)	57, 58
	Mar. 4, 1905-Mar. 3, 1909	26. Charles W. Fairbanks	59, 60
27. William H. Taft	Mar. 4, 1909-Mar. 3, 1913	27. James S. Sherman[10]	61, 62

President	Service	Vice President	Congresses
28. Woodrow Wilson	Mar. 4, 1913-Mar. 3, 1921	28. Thomas R. Marshall	63, 64, 65, 66
29. Warren G. Harding[4]	Mar. 4, 1921-Aug. 2, 1923	29. Calvin Coolidge	67
30. Calvin Coolidge	Aug. 3, 1923-Mar. 3, 1925	(None)	68
	Mar. 4, 1925-Mar. 3, 1929	30. Charles G. Dawes	69, 70
31. Herbert C. Hoover	Mar. 4, 1929-Mar. 3, 1933	31. Charles Curtis	71, 72
32. Franklin D. Roosevelt[11]	Mar. 4, 1933-Jan. 20, 1941	32. John N. Garner	73, 74, 75, 76, 77
	Jan. 20, 1941-Jan. 20, 1945	33. Henry A. Wallace	77, 78, 79
(4)	Jan. 20, 1945-Apr. 12, 1945	34. Harry S. Truman	79
33. Harry S. Truman	Apr. 12, 1945-Jan. 20, 1949	(None)	79, 80, 81
	Jan. 20, 1949-Jan. 20, 1953	35. Alben W. Barkley	81, 82, 83
34. Dwight D. Eisenhower	Jan. 20, 1953-Jan. 20, 1961	36. Richard M. Nixon	83, 84, 85, 86, 87
35. John F. Kennedy[4]	Jan. 20, 1961-Nov. 22, 1963	37. Lyndon B. Johnson	87, 88
36. Lyndon B. Johnson	Nov. 22, 1963-Jan. 20, 1965	(None)	88, 89
	Jan. 20, 1965-Jan. 20, 1969	38. Hubert H. Humphrey	89, 90, 91
37. Richard M. Nixon	Jan. 20, 1969-Jan. 20, 1973	39. Spiro T. Agnew[12]	91, 92, 93
(13)	Jan. 20, 1973-Aug. 9, 1974	40. Gerald R. Ford[14]	93
38. Gerald R. Ford[15]	Aug. 9, 1974-Jan. 20, 1977	41. Nelson A. Rockefeller[16]	93, 94, 95
39. Jimmy Carter	Jan. 20, 1977-Jan. 20, 1981	42. Walter F. Mondale	95, 96, 97
40. Ronald W. Reagan	Jan. 20, 1981-Jan. 20, 1989	43. George H. W. Bush	97, 98, 99, 100, 101
41. George H. W. Bush	Jan. 20, 1989-Jan. 20, 1993	44. Dan Quayle	101, 102, 103
42. Bill Clinton	Jan. 20, 1993-Jan. 20, 2001	45. Al Gore	103, 104, 105, 106, 107
43. George W. Bush	Jan. 20, 2001-Jan. 20, 2009	46. Dick Cheney	107, 108, 109, 110, 111
44. Barack H. Obama	Jan. 20, 2009-	47. Joe Biden	111, 112

(1) Died Apr. 20, 1812. (2) Died Nov. 23, 1814. (3) Resigned Dec. 28, 1832, to become U.S. senator. (4) Died in office. (5) Died Apr. 18, 1853. (6) Died Nov. 22, 1875. (7) Terms not consecutive. (8) Died Nov. 25, 1885. (9) Died Nov. 21, 1899. (10) Died Oct. 30, 1912. (11) First president to be inaugurated under 20th Amendment, Jan. 20, 1937. (12) Resigned Oct. 10, 1973. (13) Resigned Aug. 9, 1974. (14) First nonelected vice president, chosen under 25th Amendment procedure. (15) First president never elected president or vice president. (16) Second nonelected vice president, chosen under 25th Amendment. Confirmed Dec. 19, 1974.

Vice Presidents of the U.S.

The numerals given vice presidents do not coincide with those given presidents, because some presidents (Tyler, Fillmore, A. Johnson, Arthur) had none, and some had more than one.

Name	Birthplace	Year	Home	Inaug.	Politics	Place of death	Year	Age at death
1. John Adams	Quincy, MA	1735	MA	1789	Fed.	Quincy, MA	1826	90
2. Thomas Jefferson	Shadwell, VA	1743	VA	1797	Dem.-Rep.	Monticello, VA	1826	83
3. Aaron Burr	Newark, NJ	1756	NY	1801	Dem.-Rep.	Staten Island, NY	1836	80
4. George Clinton	Little Britain, NY	1739	NY	1805	Dem.-Rep.	Washington, DC	1812	73
5. Elbridge Gerry	Marblehead, MA	1744	MA	1813	Dem.-Rep.	Washington, DC	1814	70
6. Daniel D. Tompkins	Scarsdale, NY	1774	NY	1817	Dem.-Rep.	Staten Island, NY	1825	51
7. John C. Calhoun[1]	Abbeville, SC	1782	SC	1825	Dem.-Rep.	Washington, DC	1850	68
8. Martin Van Buren	Kinderhook, NY	1782	NY	1833	Dem.	Kinderhook, NY	1862	79
9. Richard M. Johnson[2]	Louisville, KY	1780	KY	1837	Dem.	Frankfort, KY	1850	70
10. John Tyler	Greenway, VA	1790	VA	1841	Whig	Richmond, VA	1862	71
11. George M. Dallas	Philadelphia, PA	1792	PA	1845	Dem.	Philadelphia, PA	1864	72
12. Millard Fillmore	Cayuga Co., NY	1800	NY	1849	Whig	Buffalo, NY	1874	74
13. William R. King	Sampson Co., NC	1786	AL	1853	Dem.	Cahaba, AL	1853	67
14. John C. Breckinridge	Lexington, KY	1821	KY	1857	Dem.	Lexington, KY	1875	54
15. Hannibal Hamlin	Paris, ME	1809	ME	1861	Rep.	Bangor, ME	1891	81
16. Andrew Johnson	Raleigh, NC	1808	TN	1865	(3)	Carter Co., TN	1875	66
17. Schuyler Colfax	New York, NY	1823	IN	1869	Rep.	Mankato, MN	1885	62
18. Henry Wilson	Farmington, NH	1812	MA	1873	Rep.	Washington, DC	1875	63
19. William A. Wheeler	Malone, NY	1819	NY	1877	Rep.	Malone, NY	1887	68
20. Chester A. Arthur	Fairfield, VT	1829	NY	1881	Rep.	New York, NY	1886	57
21. Thomas A. Hendricks	Zanesville, OH	1819	IN	1885	Dem.	Indianapolis, IN	1885	66
22. Levi P. Morton	Shoreham, VT	1824	NY	1889	Rep.	Rhinebeck, NY	1920	96
23. Adlai E. Stevenson[4]	Christian Co., KY	1835	IL	1893	Dem.	Chicago, IL	1914	78
24. Garret A. Hobart	Long Branch, NJ	1844	NJ	1897	Rep.	Paterson, NJ	1899	55
25. Theodore Roosevelt	New York, NY	1858	NY	1901	Rep.	Oyster Bay, NY	1919	60
26. Charles W. Fairbanks	Unionville Centre, OH	1852	IN	1905	Rep.	Indianapolis, IN	1918	66
27. James S. Sherman	Utica, NY	1855	NY	1909	Rep.	Utica, NY	1912	57
28. Thomas R. Marshall	N. Manchester, IN	1854	IN	1913	Dem.	Washington, DC	1925	71
29. Calvin Coolidge	Plymouth Notch, VT	1872	MA	1921	Rep.	Northampton, MA	1933	60
30. Charles G. Dawes	Marietta, OH	1865	IL	1925	Rep.	Evanston, IL	1951	85
31. Charles Curtis	Topeka, KS	1860	KS	1929	Rep.	Washington, DC	1936	76
32. John Nance Garner	Red River Co., TX	1868	TX	1933	Dem.	Uvalde, TX	1967	98
33. Henry A. Wallace	Adair County, IA	1888	IA	1941	Dem.	Danbury, CT	1965	77
34. Harry S. Truman	Lamar, MO	1884	MO	1945	Dem.	Kansas City, MO	1972	88
35. Alben W. Barkley	Graves County, KY	1877	KY	1949	Dem.	Lexington, VA	1956	78
36. Richard M. Nixon	Yorba Linda, CA	1913	CA	1953	Rep.	New York, NY	1994	81
37. Lyndon B. Johnson	Stonewall, TX	1908	TX	1961	Dem.	San Antonio, TX	1973	64
38. Hubert H. Humphrey	Wallace, SD	1911	MN	1965	Dem.	Waverly, MN	1978	66
39. Spiro T. Agnew[5]	Baltimore, MD	1918	MD	1969	Rep.	Berlin, MD	1996	77
40. Gerald R. Ford[6]	Omaha, NE	1913	MI	1973	Rep.	Rancho Mirage, CA	2006	93
41. Nelson A. Rockefeller[7]	Bar Harbor, ME	1908	NY	1974	Rep.	New York, NY	1979	70
42. Walter F. Mondale	Ceylon, MN	1928	MN	1977	Dem.			
43. George H. W. Bush	Milton, MA	1924	TX	1981	Rep.			
44. James Danforth (Dan) Quayle Jr.	Indianapolis, IN	1947	IN	1989	Rep.			
45. Albert A. Gore	Washington, DC	1948	TN	1993	Dem.			
46. Richard B. Cheney	Lincoln, NE	1941	WY	2001	Rep.			
47. Joseph R. Biden Jr.	Scranton, PA	1942	DE	2009	Dem.			

(1) Resigned Dec. 28, 1832, having been elected to the Senate to fill a vacancy. (2) Richard M. Johnson was the only vice president to be chosen by the Senate because of a tied vote in the Electoral College. (3) Andrew Johnson was a Democrat, nominated vice president by Republicans, and elected with Lincoln on the National Union Ticket. (4) Grandfather of Democratic candidate for president in 1952 and 1956. (5) Resigned Oct. 10, 1973. (6) First nonelected vice president, chosen under 25th Amendment procedure. (7) Second nonelected vice president, chosen under 25th Amendment.

Biographies of the Presidents

George Washington (1789-97), 1st president, Federalist, was born on Feb. 22, 1732, in Wakefield on Pope's Creek, Westmoreland Co., VA, the son of Augustine and Mary Ball Washington. He spent his early childhood on a farm near Fredericksburg. His father died when Washington was 11. He studied mathematics and surveying, and at 16, he went to live with his elder half brother, Lawrence, who built and named Mount Vernon in Virginia. Washington surveyed the lands of Thomas Fairfax in the Shenandoah Valley. He accompanied Lawrence to Barbados, West Indies, where he contracted smallpox and was deeply scarred. Lawrence died in 1752, and Washington inherited his property. He valued land, and when he died, he owned 70,000 acres in Virginia and 40,000 acres in what is now West Virginia.

Washington's military service began in 1753, when Lt. Gov. Robert Dinwiddie of Virginia sent him on missions deep into Ohio country. He clashed with the French and had to surrender Fort Necessity on July 3, 1754. He was an aide to the British general Edward Braddock and was at his side when the army was ambushed and defeated (July 9, 1755) on a march to Fort Duquesne. He helped take Fort Duquesne from the French in 1758.

After Washington's marriage to Martha Dandridge Custis, a widow, in 1759, he managed his family estate at Mount Vernon. Although not at first for independence, he opposed the repressive measures of the British crown and took charge of the Virginia troops before war broke out. He was made commander of the newly created Continental Army by the Continental Congress on June 15, 1775.

The American victory was due largely to Washington's leadership. He was resourceful, a disciplinarian, and the one dependable force for unity. Washington favored a federal government. He became chairman of the Constitutional Convention of 1787 and helped get the Constitution ratified. Unanimously elected president by the electoral college, he was inaugurated Apr. 30, 1789, on the balcony of New York's Federal Hall. He was reelected in 1792. Washington made an effort to avoid partisan politics as president.

Refusing to consider a third term, Washington retired to Mount Vernon in March 1797. A ride in snow and rain around his estate led to what present-day doctors believe to have been an attack of acute epiglottitis. Doctors were unsuccessful in treating the inflammation in his throat, and Washington died Dec. 14, 1799.

John Adams (1797-1801), 2nd president, Federalist, was born on Oct. 30, 1735, in Braintree (now Quincy), MA, the son of John and Susanna Boylston Adams. He was a great-grandson of Henry Adams, who came from England in 1636. He graduated from Harvard in 1755, then taught school and studied law. He married Abigail Smith in 1764. In 1765 he argued against taxation without representation before the royal governor. In 1770, he successfully defended in court the British soldiers who fired on civilians in the Boston Massacre. He was a delegate to the Continental Congress and a signer of the Declaration of Independence. In 1778, Congress sent Adams and John Jay to join Benjamin Franklin as diplomatic representatives in Europe. Because he ran second to Washington in electoral college balloting in Feb. 1789, Adams became the nation's first vice president, a post he characterized as highly insignificant; he was reelected in 1792.

In 1796 Adams was chosen president by the electors. His administration was marked by growing conflict with fellow Federalist Alexander Hamilton and with others in his own cabinet who supported Hamilton's strongly anti-French position. Adams avoided full-scale war with France but became unpopular, especially after securing passage of the Alien and Sedition Acts in 1798. His foreign policy contributed significantly to the election of Thomas Jefferson in 1800.

Adams lived for a quarter century after he left office, during which time he wrote extensively. He died July 4, 1826, on the same day as his rival Thomas Jefferson (the 50th anniversary of the Declaration of Independence).

Thomas Jefferson (1801-09), 3rd president, Democratic-Republican, was born on Apr. 13, 1743, in Shadwell in Goochland (now Albemarle) Co., VA, the son of Peter and Jane Randolph Jefferson. His father died when Jefferson was 14, leaving him 2,750 acres and his slaves. Jefferson attended (1760-62) the College of William and Mary, read Greek and Latin classics, and played the violin. In 1769 he was elected to the Virginia House of Burgesses. In 1770 he began building his home, Monticello, and in 1772 he married Martha Wayles Skelton, a wealthy widow. Jefferson helped establish the Virginia Committee of Correspondence. As a member of the 2nd Continental Congress he drafted the Declaration of Independence. He also was a member of the Virginia House of Delegates (1776-79) and was elected governor of Virginia in 1779, succeeding Patrick Henry. He was reelected in 1780 but resigned in 1781 after British troops invaded Virginia. During his term he wrote the statute on religious freedom. After his wife's death in 1782, Jefferson again became a delegate to the Congress, and in 1784 he drafted the report that was the basis for the Ordinances of 1784, 1785, and 1787. He was minister to France from 1785 to 1789, when George Washington appointed him secretary of state.

Jefferson's strong faith in the consent of the governed conflicted with the emphasis on executive control, favored by Sec. of the Treasury Alexander Hamilton, and Jefferson resigned on Dec. 31, 1793. In the 1796 election Jefferson was the Democratic-Republican candidate for president; John Adams won the election, and Jefferson became vice president. In 1800, Jefferson and Aaron Burr received equal electoral college votes; the House of Representatives elected Jefferson president. Jefferson was a strong advocate of westward expansion; major events of his first term were the Louisiana Purchase (1803) and the Lewis and Clark expedition. An important development during his second term was passage of the Embargo Act, barring U.S. ships from setting sail to foreign ports. Jefferson established the Univ. of Virginia and designed its buildings. He died July 4, 1826, on the same day as John Adams (the 50th anniversary of the Declaration of Independence).

Analysis of DNA taken from descendants of Jefferson and Sally Hemings, one of his slaves, revealed a high probability of Jefferson fathering one or more of her six children.

James Madison (1809-17), 4th president, Democratic-Republican, was born on Mar. 16, 1751, in Port Conway, King George Co., VA, the son of James and Eleanor Rose Conway Madison. Madison graduated from the College of New Jersey in 1771. He served in the Virginia Constitutional Convention (1776), and, in 1780, became a delegate to the 2nd Continental Congress. He was chief recorder at the Constitutional Convention in 1787 and supported ratification in the *Federalist Papers*, written with Alexander Hamilton and John Jay. In 1789, Madison was elected to the House of Representatives, where he helped frame the Bill of Rights and fought against passage of the Alien and Sedition Acts. In the 1790s, he helped found the Democratic-Republican Party, which ultimately became the Democratic Party. He became Jefferson's secretary of state in 1801.

Madison was elected president in 1808. His first term was marked by tensions with Great Britain, and his conduct of foreign policy was criticized by the Federalists and by his own party. Nevertheless, he was reelected in 1812, the year war was declared on Great Britain. The war that many considered a second American revolution ended with a treaty that did not settle any of the issues. Madison's most important action after the war was demilitarizing the U.S.-Canadian border.

In 1817, Madison retired to his estate, Montpelier, where he served as an elder statesman. He edited his famous papers on the Constitutional Convention and helped found the Univ. of Virginia, of which he became rector in 1826. He died June 28, 1836.

James Monroe (1817-25), 5th president, Democratic-Republican, was born on Apr. 28, 1758, in Westmoreland Co., VA, the son of Spence and Elizabeth Jones Monroe. He entered the College of William and Mary in 1774 but left to serve in the 3rd Virginia Regiment during the American Revolution. After the war, he studied law with Thomas Jefferson. In 1782 he was elected to the Virginia House of Delegates, and he served (1783-86) as a delegate to the Continental Congress. He opposed ratification of the Constitution because it lacked a bill of rights. Monroe was elected to the U.S. Senate in 1790. In 1794, Pres. Washington appointed Monroe minister to France. He served twice as governor of Virginia (1799-1802, 1811). Pres. Jefferson also sent him to France as minister (1803), and from 1803 to 1807, he served as minister to Great Britain.

In 1816 Monroe was elected president; he was reelected in 1820 with all but one electoral college vote. His administration became known as the Era of Good Feeling. He obtained Florida from Spain, settled boundary disputes with Britain over Canada, and eliminated border forts. He supported the antislavery position that led to the Missouri Compromise. His most significant contribution was the Monroe Doctrine, which opposed European intervention in the Western Hemisphere and became a cornerstone of U.S. foreign policy.

Although Monroe retired to Oak Hill, VA, financial problems forced him to sell his property and move to New York City. He died there on July 4, 1831.

John Quincy Adams (1825-29), 6th president, independent Federalist, later Democratic-Republican, was born on July 11, 1767, in Braintree (now Quincy), MA, the son of John and Abigail Adams. His father was the second president. He studied abroad and at Harvard College, from which he graduated in 1787. In 1803, he was elected to the U.S. Senate. President Monroe chose him as his secretary of state in 1817. In this capacity he negotiated the cession of Florida from Spain, supported exclusion of slavery in the Missouri Compromise, and helped formulate the Monroe Doctrine. In 1824, Adams was elected president by the House of Representatives after he failed to win an electoral college majority. His expansion of executive powers was strongly opposed, and in the 1828 election he lost to Andrew Jackson. In 1831 he entered the House of Representatives and served 17 years with distinction. He opposed slavery, the annexation of Texas, and the Mexican War. He helped establish the Smithsonian Institution.

Adams suffered a stroke in the House and died in the Speaker's Room on Feb. 23, 1848.

Andrew Jackson (1829-37), 7th president, Democratic-Republican, later a Democrat, was born on Mar. 15, 1767, in the Waxhaw district, on the border of North and South Carolina, the son of Andrew and Elizabeth Hutchinson Jackson. At the age of 13, he joined the militia to fight in the American Revolution and was captured. Orphaned at age 14, Jackson was brought up by a well-to-do uncle. By age 20, he was practicing law, and he later served as prosecuting attorney in Nashville, TN. In 1796 he helped draft the constitution of Tennessee, and for a year he occupied its one seat in the House of Representatives. The next year he served in the U.S. Senate.

In the War of 1812, Jackson crushed the Creek Indians at Horseshoe Bend, AL (1814), and, with a greatly outnumbered army consisting chiefly of backwoods militia members and volunteers, defeated Gen. Edward Pakenham's British troops at the Battle of New Orleans (1815). Nicknamed "Old Hickory" for his toughness, he emerged a national hero.

In 1818 Jackson briefly invaded Spanish Florida to quell Seminoles and outlaws who harassed frontier settlements. He ran for president against John Quincy Adams in 1824, but, although he won the most popular and electoral votes, he did not have a majority. The House of Representatives decided the election and chose Adams. In the 1828 election, however, Jackson defeated Adams, carrying the West and the South.

As president, Jackson introduced what became known as the spoils system—rewarding party members with government posts. Perhaps his most controversial act, however, was depositing federal funds in so-called pet banks, those directed by Democratic bankers, rather than in the Bank of the United States. "Let the people rule" was his slogan. In 1832, Jackson killed the congressional caucus for nominating presidential candidates and substituted the national convention. When South Carolina refused to collect imports under his protective tariff, he ordered army and naval forces to Charleston. After leaving office in 1837, he retired to the Hermitage, outside Nashville, where he died on June 8, 1845.

Martin Van Buren (1837-41), 8th president, Democrat, was born on Dec. 5, 1782, in Kinderhook, NY, the son of Abraham and Maria Hoes Van Buren. After attending local schools, he studied law and became a lawyer at the age of 20. A consummate politician, Van Buren began his career in the New York state senate and then served as state attorney general from 1816 to 1819. He was elected to the U.S. Senate in 1821. He helped swing Eastern support to Andrew Jackson in the 1828 election and then served as Jackson's secretary of state from 1829 to 1831. In 1832 he was elected vice president. Known as the "Little Magician," Van Buren was extremely influential in Jackson's administration.

In 1836, Van Buren defeated William Henry Harrison for president and took office as the financial panic of 1837 initiated a nationwide depression. Although he instituted the independent treasury system, his refusal to spend land revenues led to his defeat by William Henry Harrison in 1840. In 1844 he lost the Democratic nomination to James K. Polk. In 1848 he again ran for president on the Free Soil ticket but lost. He died in Kinderhook on July 24, 1862.

William Henry Harrison (1841), 9th president, Whig, who served only 31 days, was born on Feb. 9, 1773, in Berkeley, Charles City Co., VA, the son of Benjamin Harrison, a signer of the Declaration of Independence, and of Elizabeth Bassett Harrison. He attended Hampden-Sydney College. Harrison served as secretary of the Northwest Territory in 1798 and was its delegate to the House of Representatives in 1799. He was the first governor of Indiana Territory and served as superintendent of Indian affairs. With 900 men he put down a Shawnee uprising at Tippecanoe, IN, on Nov. 7, 1811. A generation later, in 1840, he waged a rousing presidential campaign, using the slogan "Tippecanoe and Tyler Too." The Tyler of the slogan was his running mate, John Tyler.

Although born to one of the wealthiest, most prestigious, and most influential families in Virginia, Harrison was elected president with the slogan, "Log Cabin and Hard Cider." He caught pneumonia during his inauguration and died Apr. 4, 1841, after only one month in office.

John Tyler (1841-45), 10th president, independent Whig, was born on Mar. 29, 1790, in Greenway, Charles City Co., VA, the son of John and Mary Armistead Tyler. His father was governor of Virginia (1808-11). Tyler graduated from the College of William and Mary in 1807 and in 1811 was elected to the Virginia legislature. In 1816 he was chosen for the U.S. House of Representatives. He served in the Virginia legislature again from 1823 to 1825, when he was elected governor of Virginia. After a stint in the U.S. Senate (1827-36), he was elected vice president (1840).

When William Henry Harrison died only a month after taking office, Tyler succeeded him. Because he was the first person to occupy the presidency without having been elected to that office, he was referred to as "His Accidency." He gained passage of the Preemption Act of 1841, which gave squatters on government land the right to buy 160 acres at the minimum auction price. His last act as president was to sign a resolution annexing Texas. Tyler accepted renomination in 1844 from some Democrats but withdrew in favor of the official party candidate, James K. Polk. A strong advocate of states' rights, he served briefly in the Confederate House of Representatives before he died in Richmond, VA, on Jan. 18, 1862.

James Knox Polk (1845-49), 11th president, Democrat, was born on Nov. 2, 1795, in Mecklenburg Co., NC, the son of Samuel and Jane Knox Polk. He graduated from the Univ. of North Carolina in 1818 and served in the Tennessee state legislature from 1823 to 1825. He served in the U.S. House of Representatives from 1825 to 1839, the last 4 years as Speaker. He was governor of Tennessee from 1839 to 1841. In 1844, after the Democratic National Convention became deadlocked, it nominated Polk, who became the first "dark horse" candidate for president. He was nominated primarily because he favored annexation of Texas.

As president, Polk reestablished the independent treasury system originated by Van Buren. He was so intent on acquiring California from Mexico that he sent troops to the Mexican border and, when Mexicans attacked, declared that a state of war existed. The Mexican War ended with the annexation of California and much of the Southwest as part of America's "manifest destiny." Polk compromised on the Oregon boundary ("54-40 or fight!") by accepting the 49th parallel and yielding Vancouver Island to the British. Polk died in Nashville, TN, on June 15, 1849, a few months after leaving office.

Zachary Taylor (1849-50), 12th president, Whig, who served only 16 months, was born on Nov. 24, 1784, in Orange Co., VA, the son of Richard and Sarah Strother Taylor. He grew up on his father's plantation near Louisville, KY, where he was educated by private tutors. In 1808 Taylor joined the regular army and was commissioned first lieutenant. He fought in the War of 1812, the Black Hawk War (1832), and the second Seminole War (beginning in 1837). He was called "Old Rough and Ready." In 1846 Pres. Polk sent him with an army to the Rio Grande. When the Mexicans attacked him, Polk declared war. Outnumbered four to one, Taylor defeated Antonio López de Santa Anna at Buena Vista (1847).

A national hero, Taylor received the Whig nomination in 1848 and was elected president, even though he had never bothered to vote. He resumed the spoils system and, though a slaveholder, worked to admit California as a free state. He fell ill, likely from a case of acute gastroenteritis, and died in office on July 9, 1850.

Millard Fillmore (1850-53), 13th president, Whig, was born on Jan. 7, 1800, in Cayuga Co., NY, the son of Nathaniel and Phoebe Millard Fillmore. Although he had little schooling, he became a law clerk at the age of 22 and a year later was admitted to the bar. He was elected to the New York state assembly in 1828 and served until 1831. From 1833 until 1835 and again from 1837 to 1843, he represented his district in the U.S. House of Representatives. He opposed the entrance of Texas as a slave state and voted for a protective tariff. In 1844 he was defeated for governor of New York.

In 1848 he was elected vice president, and he succeeded as president after Taylor's death. Fillmore favored the Compromise of 1850 and signed the Fugitive Slave Law. His policies pleased neither expansionists nor slaveholders, and he was not renominated in 1852. In 1856 he was nominated by the American (Know-Nothing) Party, but despite the support of the Whigs, he was defeated by James Buchanan. He died in Buffalo, NY, on Mar. 8, 1874.

Franklin Pierce (1853-57), 14th president, Democrat, was born on Nov. 23, 1804, in Hillsboro, NH, the son of Benjamin Pierce, Revolutionary War general and governor of New Hampshire, and Anna Kendrick. He graduated from Bowdoin College in 1824 and was admitted to the bar in 1827. He was elected to the New Hampshire state legislature in 1829 and was chosen Speaker in 1831. He went to the U.S. House in 1833 and was elected a U.S. senator in 1837. He enlisted in the Mexican War and became brigadier general under Gen. Winfield Scott.

In 1852 Pierce was nominated as the Democratic presidential candidate on the 49th ballot. He decisively defeated Gen. Scott, his Whig opponent, in the election. Although he was against slavery, Pierce was influenced by proslavery Southerners. He supported the controversial Kansas-Nebraska Act, which left the question of slavery in the new territories of Kansas and Nebraska to popular vote. Pierce signed a reciprocity treaty with Canada and approved the Gadsden Purchase of a border area on a proposed railroad route, from Mexico. Denied renomination, he spent most of his remaining years in Concord, NH, where he died on Oct. 8, 1869.

James Buchanan (1857-61), 15th president, Federalist, later Democrat, was born on Apr. 23, 1791, near Mercersburg, PA, the son of James and Elizabeth Speer Buchanan. He graduated from Dickinson College in 1809 and was admitted to the bar in 1812. He fought in the War of 1812 as a volunteer. He was twice elected to the Pennsylvania general assembly, and in 1821 he entered the U.S. House of Representatives. After briefly serving (1832-33) as minister to Russia, he was elected U.S. senator from Pennsylvania. As Polk's secretary of state (1845-49), he ended the Oregon dispute with Britain and supported the Mexican War and annexation of Texas. As minister to Great Britain, he signed the Ostend Manifesto (1854), declaring a U.S. right to take Cuba by force should efforts to purchase it fail.

Nominated by Democrats, Buchanan was elected president in 1856. On slavery he favored popular sovereignty and choice by state constitutions but did not consistently uphold this position. He denied the right of states to secede but opposed coercion and attempted to keep peace by not provoking secessionists. Buchanan left office having failed to deal decisively with the situation. He died at Wheatland, his estate, near Lancaster, PA, on June 1, 1868.

Abraham Lincoln (1861-65), 16th president, Whig, then Republican, was born on Feb. 12, 1809, in a log cabin on a farm in Hardin (now Larue) Co., KY, the son of Thomas and Nancy Hanks Lincoln. The Lincolns moved to Spencer Co., IN, near Gentryville, when Lincoln was 7. After Lincoln's mother died, his father married Mrs. Sarah Bush Johnston in 1819. In 1830 the family moved to Macon Co., IL.

Defeated in 1832 in a race for the state legislature, Lincoln was elected on the Whig ticket two years later and served in the lower house from 1834 to 1842. In 1837 Lincoln was admitted to the bar and became partner in a Springfield, IL, law office. He soon won recognition as an effective and resourceful attorney. In 1846, he was elected to the U.S. House of Representatives, where he attracted attention during a single term for his opposition to the Mexican War and his position on slavery. In 1856 he campaigned for the newly founded Republican Party, and in 1858 he became its senatorial candidate against Stephen A. Douglas. Although he lost the election, Lincoln gained national recognition from his debates with Douglas.

In 1860, Lincoln was nominated for president by the Republican Party on a platform of restricting slavery. He ran against Douglas, a northern Democrat; John C. Breckinridge, a Southern proslavery Democrat; and John Bell, of the Constitutional Union Party. As a result of Lincoln's winning the election, South Carolina seceded from the Union on Dec. 20, 1860, followed in 1861 by 10 other Southern states.

The Civil War erupted when Fort Sumter, which Lincoln decided to resupply, was attacked by Confederate forces on Apr. 12, 1861. Lincoln called successfully for recruits from the North. On Sept. 22, 1862, five days after the Battle of Antietam, Lincoln announced that slaves in territory then in rebellion would be free Jan. 1, 1863, the date of the Emancipation Proclamation. His speeches, including his Gettysburg and inaugural addresses, are remembered for their eloquence.

Lincoln was reelected, in 1864, over Gen. George B. McClellan, Democrat. Gen. Robert E. Lee surrendered on Apr. 9, 1865. On Apr. 14, Lincoln was shot by actor John Wilkes Booth in Ford's Theater, in Washington, DC. He died the next day.

Andrew Johnson (1865-69), 17th president, Democrat, was born on Dec. 29, 1808, in Raleigh, NC, the son of Jacob and Mary McDonough Johnson. He was apprenticed to a tailor as a youth, but ran away after two years and eventually settled in Greeneville, TN. He became popular with the townspeople and in 1829 was elected councilman and later mayor. In 1835 he was sent to the state general assembly. In 1843 he was elected to the U.S. House of Representatives, where he served for 10 years. Johnson was also governor of Tennessee from 1853 to 1857, when he was elected to the U.S. Senate. He supported John C. Breckinridge against Lincoln in the 1860 election. Although Johnson had held slaves, he opposed secession and tried to prevent Tennessee from seceding. In Mar. 1862, Lincoln appointed him military governor of occupied Tennessee.

In 1864, in order to balance Lincoln's ticket with a Southern Democrat, the Republicans nominated Johnson for vice president. He was elected vice president with Lincoln and then succeeded to the presidency upon Lincoln's death. Soon afterward, in a controversy with Congress over the president's power over the South, he proclaimed an amnesty to all Confederates, except certain leaders, if they would ratify the 13th Amendment abolishing slavery. States doing so added anti-Negro provisions that enraged Congress, which restored military control over the South. When Johnson removed Sec. of War Edwin M. Stanton, without notifying the Senate, the House impeached him in Feb. 1868. Charging him with thereby having violated the Tenure of Office Act, the House was actually responding to his opposition to harsh congressional Reconstruction, expressed in repeated vetoes. He was tried by the Senate, and in May, in two separate votes on different counts, Johnson was acquitted, both times by only one vote.

Johnson was denied renomination but remained politically active. He was reelected to the Senate in 1874. Johnson died July 31, 1875, at Carter Station, TN.

Ulysses S. Grant (1869-77), 18th president, Republican, was born on Apr. 27, 1822, in Point Pleasant, OH, the son of Jesse R. and Hannah Simpson Grant. The next year the family moved to Georgetown, OH. Grant was named Hiram Ulysses. Upon entering West Point in 1839, he found his name had been put down as Ulysses S. Grant, with his middle name first and his mother's maiden name as his middle name. He eventually adopted it as his true name but maintained the "S" did not stand for anything. Grant graduated in 1843. During the Mexican War, Grant served under both Gen. Zachary Taylor and Gen. Winfield Scott. In 1854, he resigned his commission because of loneliness and drinking problems, and in the following years he engaged in generally unsuccessful farming and business ventures. With the start of the Civil War, he was named colonel and then brigadier general of the Illinois Volunteers. He took Forts Henry and Donelson and fought at Shiloh. His brilliant campaign against Vicksburg and his victory at Chattanooga made him so prominent that Lincoln placed him in command of all Union armies. Grant accepted Lee's surrender at Appomattox Court House on Apr. 9, 1865. Pres. Johnson appointed Grant secretary of war when he suspended Stanton, but Grant was not confirmed.

Grant was nominated for president by the Republicans in 1868 and elected over Democrat Horatio Seymour. The 15th Amendment, the amnesty bill, and peaceful settlement of disputes with Great Britain were events of his administration. The Liberal Republicans and Democrats opposed him with Horace Greeley in the 1872 election, but Grant was reelected. His second administration was marked by scandals, including the Crédit Mobilier affair, the Whiskey Ring, in which high-ranked officials conspired to defraud the government of taxes, and the impeachment of his Secretary of War. An attempt by the Stalwarts (Old Guard Republicans) to nominate him in 1880 failed. In 1884 the collapse of an investment firm in which he was a partner left Grant penniless. He wrote his personal memoirs while ill with cancer and completed them shortly before his death at Mt. McGregor, NY, on July 23, 1885.

Rutherford Birchard Hayes (1877-81), 19th president, Republican, was born on Oct. 4, 1822, in Delaware, OH, the son of Rutherford and Sophia Birchard Hayes. He was reared by his uncle, Sardis Birchard. Hayes graduated from Kenyon College in 1842 and from Harvard Law School in 1845. He practiced law in Lower Sandusky (now Fremont), OH, and was city solicitor of Cincinnati from 1858 to 1861. During the Civil War, he was major of the 23rd Ohio Volunteers. He was wounded several times, and by the end of the war he had risen to the rank of brevet major general. While serving (1865-67) in the U.S. House of Representatives, Hayes supported Reconstruction and Johnson's impeachment. He was twice elected governor of Ohio (1867, 1869). After losing a race for the U.S. House in 1872, he was reelected governor of Ohio in 1875.

In 1876, Hayes was nominated for president and believed he had lost the election to Democrat Samuel J. Tilden. But a few Southern states submitted two sets of electoral votes, and the result was in dispute. An electoral commission, consisting of 8 Republicans and 7 Democrats, awarded all disputed votes to Hayes, allowing him to become president by one electoral vote. Hayes, keeping a promise to Southerners, withdrew troops from areas still occupied in the South, ending the era of Reconstruction. He proposed civil service reforms, alienating those favoring the spoils system, and advocated repeal of the Tenure of Office Act restricting presidential power to dismiss officials. He supported sound money and specie payments.

Hayes died in Fremont, OH, on Jan. 17, 1893.

James Abram Garfield (1881), 20th president, Republican, was born on Nov. 19, 1831, in Orange, Cuyahoga Co., OH, the son of Abram and Eliza Ballou Garfield. His father died in 1833, and he was reared in poverty by his mother. He worked as a canal bargeman, a farmer, and a carpenter. He attended Western Reserve Eclectic Institute and graduated from Williams College in 1856. He returned to Western Reserve to teach and in 1857, at age 25, he became the school's president. In 1859 he was elected to the Ohio legislature. Antislavery and antisecession, he volunteered for military service in the Civil War, becoming colonel of the 42nd Ohio Infantry and brigadier in 1862. He fought at Shiloh, TN, was chief of staff for Gen. William Starke Rosecrans, and was made major general for gallantry at Chickamauga, GA. He entered Congress as a radical Republican in 1863, calling for execution or exile of Confederate leaders, but he moderated his views after the Civil War. On the electoral commission in 1877 he voted for Hayes against Tilden on strict party lines.

Garfield was a senator-elect in 1880 when he became the Republican nominee for president. He was chosen as a compromise over Gen. Grant, James G. Blaine, and John Sherman, and won election despite some bitterness among Grant's supporters. For much of his brief tenure as president, Garfield was concerned with a fight with New York Sen. Roscoe Conkling, who opposed two major appointments made by Garfield. On July 2, 1881, Garfield was shot and seriously wounded by a mentally disturbed office seeker, Charles J. Guiteau, while entering a railroad station in Washington, DC. He lingered on in the White House before finally succumbing on Sept. 19, 1881, in Elberon, NJ.

Chester Alan Arthur (1881-85), 21st president, Republican, was born on Oct. 5, 1829, in Fairfield, VT, to William and Malvina Stone Arthur. He graduated from Union College in 1848, taught school in Vermont, then studied law and practiced in New York City. In 1853, he argued in a fugitive slave case that slaves transported through New York State were thereby freed. In 1871, he was appointed collector of the Port of New York. Pres. Hayes, an opponent of the spoils system, forced him to resign in 1878. This made the New York machine enemies of Hayes. Arthur and the Stalwarts (Old Guard Republicans) tried to nominate Grant for a 3rd term as president in 1880. When Garfield was nominated, Arthur was nominated for vice president in the interests of harmony.

Upon Garfield's assassination, Arthur became president. Despite his past connections, he signed major civil service reform legislation. Arthur tried to dissuade Congress from enacting the high protective tariff of 1883. He was defeated for renomination in 1884 by James G. Blaine. He died in New York City on Nov. 18, 1886.

Grover Cleveland (1885-89; 1893-97) (*According to a State Dept. ruling, Grover Cleveland should be counted as both the 22nd and the 24th president because his two terms were not consecutive*), Democrat, was born Stephen Grover Cleveland on Mar. 18, 1837, in Caldwell, NJ, the son of Richard F. and Ann Neal Cleveland. When he was a small boy, his family moved to New York. Prevented by his father's death from attending college, he studied by himself and was admitted to the bar in Buffalo, NY, in 1859. In succession he became assistant district attorney (1863), sheriff (1871), mayor (1881), and governor of New York (1882). He was an independent, honest administrator who hated corruption. Cleveland was nominated for president over Tammany Hall opposition in 1884 and defeated Republican James G. Blaine.

As president, he enlarged the civil service and vetoed many pension raids on the Treasury. In the 1888 election he was defeated by Benjamin Harrison, although his popular vote was larger. Reelected over Harrison in 1892, he faced a money crisis brought about by a lowered gold reserve, circulation of paper, and exorbitant silver purchases under the Sherman Silver Purchase Act. He obtained a repeal of the Sherman Act but was unable to secure effective tariff reform. A severe economic depression and labor troubles racked his administration, but he refused to interfere in business matters and rejected Jacob Coxey's demand for unemployment relief. In 1894, he broke the Pullman strike. Cleveland was not renominated in 1896.

He died in Princeton, NJ, on June 24, 1908.

Benjamin Harrison (1889-93), 23rd president, Republican, was born on Aug. 20, 1833, in North Bend, OH, the son of John Scott and Elizabeth Irwin Harrison. His great-grandfather, Benjamin Harrison, was a signer of the Declaration of Independence; his grandfather, William Henry Harrison, was the ninth president; his father was a member of Congress. He attended school on his father's farm and graduated from Miami University in Oxford, OH, in 1852. He was admitted to the bar in 1854 and practiced in Indianapolis, IN. During the Civil War, he rose to the rank of brevet brigadier general and fought at Kennesaw Mountain, Peachtree Creek, Nashville, and in the Atlanta campaign. He lost the 1876 gubernatorial election in Indiana but succeeded in becoming a U.S. senator in 1881.

In 1888 he defeated Cleveland for president despite receiving fewer popular votes. As president, he expanded the pension list and signed the McKinley high tariff bill, the Sherman Antitrust Act, and the Sherman Silver Purchase Act. During his administration, six states were admitted to the Union. He was defeated for reelection in 1892. He died in Indianapolis, IN, on Mar. 13, 1901.

William McKinley (1897-1901), 25th president, Republican, was born on Jan. 29, 1843, in Niles, OH, the son of William and Nancy Allison McKinley. McKinley briefly attended Allegheny College. When the Civil War broke out in 1861, he enlisted and served for the duration. He rose to captain and in 1865 was made brevet major. After studying law in Albany, NY, he opened a law office in Canton, OH (1867). He served twice in the U.S. House (1877-83; 1885-91) and led the fight there for the McKinley Tariff, passed in 1890; he was not reelected to the House as a result. He served two terms (1892-96) as governor of Ohio.

In 1896 he was elected president as a proponent of a protective tariff and sound money (gold standard) over William Jennings Bryan, the Democrat and a proponent of free silver. McKinley was reluctant to intervene in Cuba, but the loss of the battleship *Maine* at Havana crystallized opinion. He demanded

Spain's withdrawal from Cuba; Spain made some concessions, but Congress announced a state of war as of Apr. 21, 1898. He was reelected in the 1900 campaign, defeating Bryan's antiimperialist arguments with the promise of a "full dinner pail." McKinley was respected for his conciliatory nature and for his conservative stance on business issues. On Sept. 6, 1901, while welcoming citizens at the Pan-American Exposition, in Buffalo, NY, he was shot by Leon Czolgosz, an anarchist. He died Sept. 14.

Theodore Roosevelt (1901-09), 26th president, Republican, was born on Oct. 27, 1858, in New York City, the son of Theodore and Martha Bulloch Roosevelt. He was a 5th cousin of Franklin D. Roosevelt and an uncle of Eleanor Roosevelt. Roosevelt graduated from Harvard University in 1880. He attended Columbia Law School briefly but abandoned law to enter politics. He was elected to the New York State Assembly in 1881 and served until 1884. He spent the next two years ranching and hunting in the Dakota Territory. In 1886, he ran unsuccessfully for mayor of New York City. He was civil service commissioner in Washington, DC, from 1889 to 1895. From 1895 to 1897, he served as New York City's police commissioner. He was assistant secretary of the Navy under McKinley. The Spanish-American War made him nationally known. He organized the 1st U.S. Volunteer Cavalry (Rough Riders) and, as lieutenant colonel, led the charge up Kettle Hill in San Juan. Elected New York governor in 1898, he fought the spoils system and achieved taxation of corporation franchises.

Nominated for vice president in 1900, Roosevelt became the nation's youngest president when McKinley was assassinated. He was reelected in 1904. As president he fought corruption of politics by big business, dissolved the Northern Securities Co. and others for violating antitrust laws, intervened in the 1902 coal strike on behalf of the public, obtained the Elkins Law (1903) forbidding rebates to favored corporations, and helped pass the Hepburn Railway Rate Act of 1906 (extending jurisdiction of the Interstate Commerce Commission). He helped obtain passage of the Pure Food and Drug Act (1906) and of employers' liability laws. Roosevelt vigorously organized conservation efforts. He mediated the peace between Japan and Russia in 1905, for which he won the Nobel Peace Prize. He abetted the 1903 revolution in Panama that led to U.S. acquisition of territory for the Panama Canal.

In 1908 Roosevelt obtained the nomination of William H. Taft, who was elected. Feeling that Taft had abandoned his policies, he unsuccessfully sought the nomination in 1912. He then ran on the Progressive "Bull Moose" ticket against Taft and Woodrow Wilson, splitting the Republicans and ensuring Wilson's election. During the campaign he was shot by a mentally deranged man but was not seriously wounded. In 1916, after unsuccessfully seeking the presidential nomination, he supported the Republican candidate, Charles E. Hughes. A strong friend of Britain, he fought for U.S. intervention in World War I.

Roosevelt was a voracious reader and wrote some 40 books, including *The Winning of the West*. He died Jan. 6, 1919, at Sagamore Hill, his home in Oyster Bay, NY.

William Howard Taft (1909-13), 27th president, Republican, and 10th chief justice of the U.S., was born on Sept. 15, 1857, in Cincinnati, OH, the son of Alphonso and Louisa Maria Torrey Taft. His father was secretary of war and attorney general in Grant's cabinet and minister to Austria and Russia under Arthur. Taft graduated from Yale in 1878 and from Cincinnati Law School in 1880. After working as a law reporter for Cincinnati newspapers, he served as assistant prosecuting attorney (1881-82), assistant county solicitor (1885), superior court judge (1887), U.S. solicitor-general (1890), and federal circuit judge (1892). In 1900 he became head of the U.S. Philippines Commission and was the first civil governor of the Philippines (1901-04). In 1904 he served as secretary of war, and in 1906 he was sent to Cuba to help avert a threatened revolution.

Taft was groomed for the presidency by Theodore Roosevelt and elected over William Jennings Bryan in 1908.

Taft vigorously continued Roosevelt's trust-busting, instituted the Dept. of Labor, and drafted the amendments calling for direct election of senators and the income tax. However, his tariff and conservation policies angered progressives. Although renominated in 1912, he was opposed by Roosevelt, who ran on the Progressive Party ticket; the result was Democrat Woodrow Wilson's election.

Taft, with some reservations, supported the League of Nations. After leaving office, he was professor of constitutional law at Yale (1913-21) and chief justice of the U.S. (1921-30). Taft was the only person in U.S. history to have been both president and chief justice. He died in Washington, DC, on Mar. 8, 1930.

(Thomas) Woodrow Wilson (1913-21), 28th president, Democrat, was born on Dec. 28, 1856, in Staunton, VA, the son of Joseph Ruggles and Janet (Jessie) Woodrow Wilson. He grew up in Georgia and South Carolina. He attended Davidson College in North Carolina before graduating from Princeton University in 1879. He studied law at the Univ. of Virginia and political science at Johns Hopkins Univ., where he received his PhD in 1886. He taught at Bryn Mawr (1885-88) and at Wesleyan (1888-90) before joining the faculty at Princeton. He was president of Princeton from 1902 until 1910, when he was elected governor of New Jersey. In 1912 he was nominated for president with the aid of William Jennings Bryan, who sought to block James "Champ" Clark and Tammany Hall. Wilson won because the Republican vote for Taft was split by the Progressives.

As president, Wilson protected American interests in revolutionary Mexico and fought for American rights on the high seas. He oversaw the creation of the Federal Reserve system, cut the tariff, and developed a reputation as a reformer. His sharp warnings to Germany led to the resignation of his secretary of state, Bryan, a pacifist. In 1916 he was reelected by a slim margin with the slogan, "He kept us out of war," although his attempts to mediate in the war failed. After several American ships were sunk by the Germans, he secured a declaration of war against Germany on Apr. 6, 1917.

Wilson outlined his peace program on Jan. 8, 1918, in the Fourteen Points, a state paper that had worldwide influence. He enunciated a doctrine of self-determination for the settlement of territorial disputes. The Germans accepted his terms and an armistice on Nov. 11, 1918.

Wilson went to Paris to help negotiate the peace treaty, the crux of which he considered the League of Nations. The Senate demanded reservations that would not make the U.S. subordinate to the votes of other nations in case of war. Wilson refused and toured the country to get support. After Wilson suffered a severe stroke in Oct. 1919, his wife, Edith Wilson, concealed the extent of his infirmity, controlled access to him, and in effect largely acted in his place.

Wilson was awarded the 1919 Nobel Peace Prize, but the treaty embodying the League of Nations was ultimately rejected by the Senate in 1920. He left the White House in Mar. 1921. He died in Washington, DC, on Feb. 3, 1924.

Warren Gamaliel Harding (1921-23), 29th president, Republican, was born on Nov. 2, 1865, near Corsica (now Blooming Grove), OH, the son of George Tyron and Phoebe Elizabeth Dickerson Harding. He attended Ohio Central College, studied law, and became editor and publisher of a county newspaper. He entered the political arena as state senator (1901-04) and then served as lieutenant governor (1904-06). In 1910 he ran unsuccessfully for governor of Ohio; in 1914 he was elected to the U.S. Senate. In the Senate he voted for antistrike legislation, women's suffrage, and the Volstead Prohibition Enforcement Act over Pres. Wilson's veto. He opposed the League of Nations.

In 1920 he was nominated for president and defeated James M. Cox in the election. The Republicans capitalized on war weariness and fear that Wilson's League of Nations would curtail U.S. sovereignty. Harding stressed a return to "normalcy" and worked for tariff revision and the repeal of excess profits law and high income taxes. In what became known as the Teapot Dome scandal, his secretary of the interior, Albert B. Fall, resigned and was later convicted of accepting bribes in the leasing of government-owned oil reserves to private companies.

As rumors began to circulate about the corruption in his administration, Harding fell ill after a trip to Alaska, and he died suddenly in San Francisco on Aug. 2, 1923.

(John) Calvin Coolidge (1923-29), 30th president, Republican, was born on July 4, 1872, in Plymouth Notch, VT, the son of John Calvin and Victoria J. Moor Coolidge. Coolidge graduated from Amherst College in 1895. He entered Republican state politics and served as mayor of Northampton, MA, as state senator, as lieutenant governor, and, in 1919, as governor. In Sept. 1919, Coolidge attained national prominence by calling out the state guard in the Boston police strike. He declared, "There is no right to strike against the public safety by anybody, anywhere, anytime." This brought his name before the Republican convention of 1920, where he was nominated for vice president.

Coolidge succeeded to the presidency on Harding's death. As president, he opposed the League of Nations and the soldiers' bonus bill, which was passed over his veto. In 1924 he was elected to the presidency by a huge majority. He substantially reduced the national debt. He twice vetoed the McNary-Haugen farm bill, which would have provided relief to financially hardpressed farmers.

With Republicans eager to renominate him, Coolidge simply announced on Aug. 2, 1927, "I do not choose to run for president in 1928." He died in Northampton, MA, on Jan. 5, 1933.

Herbert Clark Hoover (1929-33), 31st president, Republican, was born on Aug. 10, 1874, in West Branch, IA, the son of Jesse Clark and Hulda Randall Minthorn Hoover. Hoover grew up in Indian Territory (now Oklahoma) and Oregon and graduated from Stanford University with a degree in geology in 1895. He worked briefly with the U.S. Geological Survey and then managed mines in Australia, Asia, Europe, and Africa. While chief engineer of imperial mines in China, he directed food relief for victims of the Boxer Rebellion. He gained a reputation not only as an engineer but as a humanitarian as he directed the American Relief Committee, London (1914-15) and the U.S. Commission for Relief in Belgium (1915-19). He was U.S. Food Administrator (1917-19), American Relief Administrator (1918-23), and in charge of Russian Relief (1918-23). He served as secretary of commerce under both Harding and Coolidge. Some historians believe that he was the most effective secretary of commerce ever to hold that office.

In 1928 Hoover was elected president over Alfred E. Smith. In 1929 the stock market crashed, and the economy collapsed. During the Great Depression, Hoover inaugurated some government assistance programs, but he was opposed to administration of aid through a federal bureaucracy. As the effects of the depression continued, he was defeated in the 1932 election by Franklin D. Roosevelt. Hoover remained active after leaving office. President Truman named him coordinator of the European Food Program (1946) and chairman of the Commission on Organization of the Executive Branch (1947-49); he was later appointed by President Eisenhower to serve in the same role (1953-55). Hoover died in New York City on Oct. 20, 1964.

Franklin Delano Roosevelt (1933-45), 32nd president, Democrat, was born on Jan. 30, 1882, in Hyde Park, NY, the son of James and Sara Delano Roosevelt. He graduated from Harvard University in 1903. He attended Columbia University Law School without taking a degree and was admitted to the New York State bar in 1907. His political career began when he was elected to the New York State senate in 1910. In 1913 Pres. Wilson appointed him assistant secretary of the navy, a post he held during World War I.

In 1920 Roosevelt ran for vice president with James Cox and was defeated. From 1921 to 1928 he worked in his New York law office and was also vice president of a bank. In Aug. 1921, he was stricken with poliomyelitis, which left his legs paralyzed. As a result of therapy he was able to stand, or walk a few steps, with the aid of leg braces.

Roosevelt served two terms as governor of New York (1929-33). In 1932, Democratic convention delegate W. G. McAdoo, pledged to nominee John N. Garner, threw his votes to Roosevelt, who was nominated for president. The Depression and the promise to repeal Prohibition ensured his election. He asked for emergency powers, proclaimed the New Deal, and put into effect a vast number of administrative changes. Foremost was the use of public funds for relief and public works, resulting in deficit financing. He greatly expanded the federal government's regulation of business and by an excess profits tax and progressive income taxes produced a redistribution of earnings on an unprecedented scale. He also promoted legislation establishing the Social Security system. He was the last president inaugurated on Mar. 4 (1933) and the first inaugurated on Jan. 20 (1937).

Roosevelt was the first president to use radio for "fireside chats." When the Supreme Court nullified some New Deal laws, he sought power to "pack" the Court with additional justices, but Congress refused to give him the authority. He was the first president to break the "no 3rd term" tradition (1940) and was elected to a 4th term in 1944, despite failing health.

Roosevelt was openly hostile to fascist governments before World War II and launched a lend-lease program on behalf of the Allies. With British Prime Min. Winston Churchill he wrote a declaration of principles to be followed after Nazi defeat (the Atlantic Charter of Aug. 14, 1941) and urged the Four Freedoms (freedom of speech, of worship, from want, from fear) Jan. 6, 1941. When Japan attacked Pearl Harbor on Dec. 7, 1941, the U.S. entered the war. Roosevelt guided the nation through the war and conferred with allied heads of state at Casablanca, Morocco (Jan. 1943), Quebec, Canada (Aug. 1943), Tehran, Iran (Nov.-Dec. 1943), Cairo, Egypt (Nov. and Dec. 1943), and Yalta, Ukraine (Feb. 1945).

Roosevelt did not live to see the end of the war. He died of a cerebral hemorrhage in Warm Springs, GA, on Apr. 12, 1945.

Harry S. Truman (1945-53), 33rd president, Democrat, was born on May 8, 1884, in Lamar, MO, the son of John Anderson and Martha Ellen Young Truman. A family disagreement over whether his middle name should be Shipp or Solomon, after his two grandfathers, resulted in his using only the middle initial S. After graduating from high school (1901) in Independence, MO, he worked in the mailroom of the *Kansas City Star*, as a railroad timekeeper, and as a clerk in Kansas City banks until about 1905. He ran his family's farm from 1906 to 1917, then served in France during World War I. After the war he opened a haberdashery, was a judge on the Jackson Co. Court (1922-24), and attended Kansas City School of Law (1923-25).

Truman was elected to the U.S. Senate in 1934 and reelected in 1940. In 1944, with Roosevelt's backing, he was nominated for vice president and elected. On Roosevelt's death in 1945, Truman became president. In 1948, in a famous upset victory, he defeated Republican Thomas E. Dewey to win election to a new term.

Truman authorized the first uses of the atomic bomb (Hiroshima and Nagasaki, Aug. 6 and 9, 1945), bringing World War II to a rapid end. He was responsible for what came to be called the Truman Doctrine to aid nations such as Greece and Turkey, threatened by Communist takeover, and his strong commitment to NATO and to the Marshall Plan helped bring the two about. In 1948-49, he broke a Soviet blockade of West Berlin with a massive airlift. When Communist North Korea invaded South Korea (June 1950), he won UN approval for a "police action" and, without prior congressional consent, sent in forces under Gen. Douglas MacArthur. When MacArthur opposed his policy of limited objectives, Truman removed him.

He died in Kansas City, MO, on Dec. 26, 1972.

Dwight David Eisenhower (1953-61), 34th president, Republican, was born on Oct. 14, 1890, in Denison, TX, the son of David Jacob and Ida Elizabeth Stover Eisenhower, as David Dwight Eisenhower. He grew up on a small farm in Abilene, KS, and graduated from West Point in 1915. He was on the staff of Gen. Douglas MacArthur in the Philippines from 1935 to 1939. In 1942, he was made commander of Allied forces landing in North Africa; the next year he was made full general. He became supreme Allied commander in Europe that same year and as such led the Normandy invasion (June 6, 1944). On Dec. 20, 1944, he was given the rank of general of the Army, which was made permanent in 1946.

On May 7, 1945, Eisenhower received the surrender of Germany at Rheims, France. He returned to the U.S. to serve as chief of staff (1945-48). His memoir, *Crusade in Europe* (1948), was a best-seller. In 1948 he became president of Columbia University; in 1950 he became commander of NATO forces.

Eisenhower resigned from the army and was nominated for president by the Republicans in 1952. He defeated Adlai E. Stevenson in the 1952 election and again in 1956. Eisenhower called himself a moderate, favored the "free market system" versus government price and wage controls, kept government out of labor disputes, reorganized the defense establishment, and promoted missile programs. He continued foreign aid, helped negotiate a cease fire truce in the Korean War, endorsed Taiwan and SE Asia defense treaties, backed the UN in condemning the Anglo-French raid on Egypt, and advocated the "open skies" policy of mutual inspection with the USSR. He sent U.S. troops into Little Rock, AR, in Sept. 1957, to enforce school integration.

Eisenhower died on Mar. 28, 1969, in Washington, DC.

John Fitzgerald Kennedy (1961-63), 35th president, Democrat, was born on May 29, 1917, in Brookline, MA, the son of Joseph P. and Rose Fitzgerald Kennedy. He graduated from Harvard University in 1940. While serving in the Navy (1941-45), he commanded a PT (patrol torpedo) boat in the Solomons and won the Navy and Marine Corps Medal. In 1956, while recovering from spinal surgery, he wrote *Profiles in Courage*, which won a Pulitzer Prize in 1957. He served in the House of Representatives from 1947 to 1953 and was elected to the Senate in 1952 and 1958. In 1960, he won the Democratic nomination for president and narrowly defeated Republican Vice Pres. Richard M. Nixon. Kennedy was the youngest president ever elected to the office and the first Catholic.

Despite the image of youth and vigor he conveyed to the public, Kennedy suffered from serious medical problems, including Addison's disease and severe chronic back pain that required him to wear a back brace. The public was not aware of the extent of these problems, or of his frequent sexual liaisons.

In Apr. 1961, the new Kennedy administration suffered a severe setback when an invasion force of anti-Castro Cubans, trained and directed by the CIA, failed to establish a beachhead at the Bay of Pigs in Cuba. But he weathered a major foreign crisis with his successful demand on Oct. 22, 1962, that the Soviet Union dismantle its missile bases in Cuba. Kennedy also defied Soviet attempts to force the Allies out of Berlin. He also established the Peace Corps, spurred space exploration, and won passage of other "New Frontier" legislation. But Congress balked at initiatives such as medical coverage for the aged and aid to education. After some delay he introduced major civil rights legislation, but death intervened before it could be passed.

On Nov. 22, 1963, President Kennedy was assassinated while riding in a motorcade in Dallas, TX. A commission chaired by Chief Justice Earl Warren concluded in Sept. 1964 that the sole assassin had been Lee Harvey Oswald, a former U.S. Marine and an ardent Marxist. Oswald was captured a short time after the assassination and charged with the crime. Two days later, he was shot dead by nightclub owner Jack Ruby while being moved to a county jail.

Lyndon Baines Johnson (1963-69), 36th president, Democrat, was born on Aug. 27, 1908, near Stonewall, TX, the son of Sam Ealy and Rebekah Baines Johnson. He graduated from Southwest Texas State Teachers College in 1930 and attended Georgetown University Law School. He taught public speaking in Houston (1930-31) and then served as secretary to Rep. R. M. Kleberg (1931-35). In 1937 Johnson won an election to fill the vacancy caused by the death of a U.S. representative. In 1938 he was elected to the first of five full terms. During 1941 and 1942 he also served in the Navy in the Pacific, earning a Silver Star for bravery. He was elected U.S. senator in 1948 and reelected in 1954. He became Democratic leader of the Senate in 1953. Johnson had strong support for the Democratic presidential nomination at the 1960 convention, where the nominee, John F. Kennedy, asked him to run for vice president. His campaigning helped overcome religious bias against Kennedy in the South.

Johnson became president when Kennedy was assassinated. He was elected to a full term in 1964. Johnson's domestic program was of considerable importance. He won passage of major civil rights, anti-poverty, aid to education, and health-care (Medicare, Medicaid) legislation—the "Great Society" program. However, his escalation of the war in Vietnam came to overshadow the achievements of his administration. In the face of increasing division in the nation and in his own party over his handling of the war, Johnson declined to seek another term.

Johnson died on Jan. 22, 1973, in San Antonio, TX.

Richard Milhous Nixon (1969-74), 37th president, Republican, was born on Jan. 9, 1913, in Yorba Linda, CA, the son of Francis Anthony and Hannah Milhous Nixon. He graduated from Whittier College in 1934 and from Duke University Law School in 1937. After practicing law in Whittier, CA, and serving briefly in the Office of Price Administration in 1942, he entered the Navy and served in the South Pacific. Nixon was elected to the House of Representatives in 1946 and 1948. He achieved prominence as the House Un-American Activities Committee member who forced the showdown leading to the Alger Hiss perjury conviction. In 1950 he was elected to the Senate.

Nixon was elected vice president in the Eisenhower landslides of 1952 and 1956. He won the Republican nomination for president in 1960 but was narrowly defeated by John F. Kennedy. He ran unsuccessfully for governor of California in 1962. In 1968 he again won the GOP presidential nomination, then defeated Hubert Humphrey for the presidency.

As president, Nixon appointed four Supreme Court justices, including the chief justice, moving the court to the right. As a "new federalist," he sought to shift responsibility to state and local governments. He dramatically altered relations with China, which he visited in 1972—the first U.S. president to do so. With foreign affairs adviser Henry Kissinger, he pursued détente with the Soviet Union, signing major arms limitation and other treaties and increasing trade. He began a gradual withdrawal from Vietnam, but U.S. troops remained there through his first term. He ordered an incursion into Cambodia (1970) and the bombing of Hanoi and mining of Haiphong Harbor (1972). Reelected by a large majority in Nov. 1972, he secured a Vietnam cease-fire in Jan. 1973.

Nixon's second term was cut short by scandal, after disclosures relating to a June 1972 burglary of Democratic Party headquarters in the Watergate office complex in DC. The courts and Congress sought tapes of Nixon's office conversations and called for criminal proceedings against former White House aides and for a House inquiry into possible impeachment. Nixon claimed executive privilege, but the Supreme Court ruled against him. In July 1974, the House Judiciary Committee recommended adoption of three impeachment articles charging him with obstruction of justice, abuse of power, and contempt of Congress. On Aug. 5, he released transcripts of conversations that linked him to cover-up activities. He resigned on Aug. 9, becoming the first president ever to do so.

In later years, Nixon emerged as an elder statesman. He died Apr. 22, 1994, in New York City.

Gerald Rudolph Ford (1974-77), 38th president, Republican, was born on July 14, 1913, in Omaha, NE, the son of Leslie and Dorothy Gardner King, and was named Leslie Lynch King Jr. When he was 2, his parents divorced, and he and his mother moved to Grand Rapids, MI. There she met and married Gerald R. Ford, who formally adopted him and gave him his name. Ford graduated from the Univ. of Michigan in 1935 and from Yale Law School in 1941. He began practicing law in Grand Rapids, but in 1942, he joined the Navy and served in the Pacific, leaving the service in 1946 as a lieutenant commander. He entered the House of Representatives in 1949 and spent 25 years in the House, eight of them as Republican leader.

On Oct. 12, 1973, after Vice Pres. Spiro T. Agnew resigned, Pres. Nixon nominated Ford to replace him. It was the first use of the procedures set out in the 25th Amendment. When Nixon resigned, Aug. 9, 1974, because of the Watergate scandal, Ford became president; he was the only president who was never elected either to the presidency or to the vice presidency.

Ford was widely credited with having contributed to rebuilding morale after the Nixon presidency. But he was also criticized by many when, in a controversial move, he pardoned Nixon for any federal crimes he might have committed as

president. Ford vetoed 48 bills in his first 21 months in office, mostly in the interest of fighting high inflation; he was less successful in curbing high unemployment. In foreign policy, Ford continued to pursue détente.

Ford was narrowly defeated in the 1976 election. In 1999, he received the Medal of Freedom. He died Dec. 26, 2006, at home in Rancho Mirage, CA.

James Earl (Jimmy) Carter (1977-81), 39th president, Democrat, was the first president from the Deep South since before the Civil War. He was born on Oct. 1, 1924, in Plains, GA, the son of James and Lillian Gordy Carter. Carter graduated from the U.S. Naval Academy in 1946 and in 1952 entered the Navy's nuclear submarine program as an aide to Capt. (later Adm.) Hyman Rickover. He studied nuclear physics at Union College.

Carter's father died in 1953, and he left the Navy to take over the family peanut farming businesses. He served in the Georgia state senate (1963-67) and as governor of Georgia (1971-75). In 1976, Carter won the Democratic nomination and defeated Pres. Gerald R. Ford.

On his first full day in office, Carter pardoned all Vietnam draft evaders. He played a major role in the negotiations leading to the 1979 peace treaty between Israel and Egypt, and he won passage of new treaties with Panama providing for U.S. control of the Panama Canal to end in 2000. Carter was widely criticized, however, for the poor state of the economy and was viewed by some as weak in his handling of foreign policy. In Nov. 1979, Iranian student militants attacked the U.S. embassy in Tehran and held members of the embassy staff hostage. Efforts to obtain release of the hostages were a major preoccupa-tion during the rest of his term. He reacted to the Soviet invasion of Afghanistan by imposing a grain embargo and boycotting the Moscow Olympic Games.

Carter was defeated by Ronald Reagan in the 1980 election. The 52 American hostages in Iran were finally released on inauguration day, 1981, just after Reagan officially became president. After leaving office, Carter played an active role in diplomatic and humanitarian efforts around the world, especially through the Carter Center, which he founded with his wife in 1982. He was awarded the Nobel Peace Prize in 2002.

Ronald Wilson Reagan (1981-89), 40th president, Republican, was born on Feb. 6, 1911, in Tampico, IL, the son of John Edward and Nellie Wilson Reagan. Reagan graduated from Eureka College in 1932, after which he worked as a sports announcer in Des Moines, IA. He began a successful career as an actor in 1937, starring in numerous movies, and later in television, until the 1960s. During World War II Reagan served in the Army Air Force, making training films. He was president of the Screen Actors Guild in 1947-52 and in 1959-60. Reagan was elected governor of California in 1966 and reelected in 1970.

In 1980, Reagan gained the Republican presidential nomination and won a landslide victory over Jimmy Carter. He was easily reelected in 1984. Reagan forged a bipartisan coalition in Congress, which led to enactment of his program of large-scale tax cuts, cutbacks in many government programs, and a major defense buildup. He signed a Social Security reform bill designed to provide for the long-term solvency of the system. In 1986, he signed into law a major tax-reform bill. He was shot and seriously wounded in 1981 by John Hinckley, who was tried and found not guilty by reason of insanity.

In 1982, the U.S. joined France and Italy in maintaining a peacekeeping force in Beirut, Lebanon, and the next year Reagan sent a task force to invade Grenada after two Marxist coups on the island. Reagan's opposition to international terrorism led to the U.S. bombing of Libyan military installations in 1986. He strongly supported El Salvador, the Nicaraguan contras, and other anticommunist governments and forces throughout the world. He also held four summit meetings with Soviet leader Mikhail Gorbachev. At the 1987 meeting in Washington, DC, a historic treaty eliminating short- and medium-range missiles from Europe was signed.

In 1986, it was revealed that the U.S. had sold weapons through Israeli brokers to Iran in exchange for the release of U.S.

hostages being held in Lebanon and that subsequently some of the money had been illegally diverted to the Nicaraguan contras. The scandal led to the resignation of leading White House aides, but despite several investigations no proof of Reagan's involvement was discovered. As Reagan left office in Jan. 1989, the nation was experiencing its 6th consecutive year of economic prosperity. Over the same period, however, the federal government recorded large budget deficits.

In 1994, in a letter to the American people, Reagan revealed that he was suffering from Alzheimer's disease. He died on June 5, 2004, in Los Angeles, CA, from complications of the disease.

George Herbert Walker Bush (1989-93),

41st president, Republican, was born on June 12, 1924, in Milton, MA, the son of Prescott and Dorothy Walker Bush. He served as a U.S. Navy pilot in World War II. After graduating from Yale University in 1948, he settled in Texas, where, in 1953, he helped found an oil company. After losing a bid for a U.S. Senate seat in 1964, he was elected to the House of Representatives in 1966 and 1968. He lost a second U.S. Senate race in 1970. Subsequently he served as U.S. ambassador to the United Nations (1971-73), headed the U.S. Liaison Office in Beijing (1974-75), and was director of the CIA (1976-77).

Following an unsuccessful bid for the 1980 Republican presidential nomination, Bush became Ronald Reagan's running mate, and served as vice president from 1981 to 1989.

In 1988, Bush gained the GOP presidential nomination and defeated Michael Dukakis. Bush took office faced with U.S. budget and trade deficits, and insolvent U.S. savings and loan institutions. He faced a severe budget deficit annually, struggled with military cutbacks, and vetoed abortion-rights legislation. In 1990 he agreed to a budget deficit-reduction plan that included tax hikes.

Bush supported Soviet reforms, Eastern Europe democratization, and good relations with Beijing. In Dec. 1989, he sent troops to Panama; they overthrew the government and captured military dictator Gen. Manuel Noriega.

Bush reacted to Iraq's Aug. 1990 invasion of Kuwait by sending U.S. forces to the Persian Gulf area and assembling a UN-backed coalition, including NATO and Arab League members. After a month-long air war, in Feb. 1991, Allied forces retook Kuwait in a 4-day ground assault. The quick victory, with extremely light casualties on the U.S. side, gave Bush at that time one of the highest presidential approval ratings in history. His popularity plummeted by the end of 1991, however, as the economy slipped into recession. He was defeated by Bill Clinton in the 1992 election.

Bush's oldest son, George W. Bush, was elected president in 2000 and served two terms. In 2005, Bush led campaigns with former Pres. Clinton to raise money for the victims of the Indian Ocean tsunami and Hurricane Katrina.

William Jefferson (Bill) Clinton (1993-2001),

42nd president, Democrat, was born Aug. 19, 1946, in Hope, AR, son of William Blythe and Virginia Cassidy Blythe, and was named William Jefferson Blythe IV. Blythe died in an auto accident before his son was born. His widow married Roger Clinton, whose last name Bill Clinton then took.

Clinton earned his undergraduate degree from Georgetown Univ. in 1968. He then attended Oxford University for 2 years as a Rhodes scholar. During that time he legally avoided the draft and possible service in Vietnam, according to some critics by misleading his draft board. Clinton worked on George McGovern's 1972 presidential campaign and earned a degree from Yale Law School in 1973. He taught at the Univ. of Arkansas law school until 1976, when he was elected state attorney general. In 1978 he was elected governor, becoming the nation's youngest at the time. Though defeated for reelection in 1980, he was returned to office several times thereafter. He married law school classmate Hillary Rodham in 1975; they had a daughter, Chelsea, in 1980.

Clinton won most of the 1992 presidential primaries, moving his party toward the center as he tried to broaden his appeal; as the Democratic nominee he defeated Pres. George H. W. Bush and independent candidate H. Ross Perot in the Nov. election. In 1993, Clinton won passage of a measure to reduce the federal budget deficit and won congressional approval of the North American Free Trade Agreement. However, his administration's

plan for major health care reform legislation died in Congress. After 1994 midterm elections, Clinton faced Republican majorities in both houses of Congress. He followed a centrist course at home, sent troops to Bosnia to help implement a peace settlement, and cultivated relations with Russia and China.

Though accused of improprieties in his involvement in the Whitewater Development Corp., an Arkansas land-development venture, Clinton won reelection with 49% of the vote in 1996. Independent prosecutor Kenneth Starr did not find substantial and credible evidence of impeachable wrongdoing related to Whitewater, but did report evidence of an affair between Clinton and former White House intern Monica Lewinsky. In 1998, Clinton became only the second U.S. president to be impeached by the House of Representatives. He was charged with perjury and obstruction of justice in an attempted cover-up of the affair but was acquitted by the Senate the following year.

In 1999 the United States joined other NATO nations in an aerial bombing campaign that induced Serbia to withdraw troops from Kosovo, where they had been terrorizing ethnic Albanians. In 2000 Clinton became the first president since the Vietnam War to visit Vietnam. On Clinton's last full day in office, the Whitewater investigation ended in a deal; Clinton admitted having given false testimony about his affair and agreed to give up his law license for 5 years and pay a $25,000 fine.

Both before and after leaving office, Clinton campaigned for Democratic candidates he favored, including his wife, who was elected in 2000 to the U.S. Senate from New York. Reelected in 2005, Hillary Clinton ran unsuccessfully for the 2008 Democratic presidential nomination but was subsequently named secretary of state by her chief rival, Pres. Barack Obama. In 2005 Bill Clinton founded the Clinton Global Initiative, to promote practical solutions to global problems. Later named UN special envoy to Haiti, he co-chaired a national recovery commission after that nation was devastated by an earthquake in Jan. 2010.

George Walker Bush (2001-09),

43rd president, Republican, was born on July 6, 1946, in New Haven, CT. He was the oldest of six children born to the 41st president, George Herbert Walker Bush, and the former Barbara Pierce. He became the first son of a former president to occupy the White House since John Quincy Adams took office in 1825.

Bush grew up in Midland and Houston, TX. He attended Andover Prep in Massachusetts and then Yale Univ., graduating in 1968. Eligible for the draft, he fulfilled his military service requirement with the Texas Air National Guard. After earning a master's degree from Harvard Business School, he returned to Midland in 1975 and went into the oil business. Two years later he married Laura Welch, a librarian; they had twin daughters, Barbara and Jenna, in 1981. After aiding his father's winning 1988 presidential campaign, he became managing partner of the Texas Rangers baseball team. He was elected governor of Texas in 1994 and reelected in 1998.

Campaigning as a "compassionate conservative" in 2000, Bush won the Republican presidential nomination and, with running mate Dick Cheney, defeated the Democratic ticket led by Vice Pres. Al Gore, in one of the closest-ever U.S. presidential elections. The result was not settled until a mid-Dec. ruling by the U.S. Supreme Court left Florida's crucial electoral votes in Bush's column.

In May 2001, Bush won passage of a tax cut package projected at $1.35 tril over 10 years. After the Sept. 11, 2001, terrorist attacks on the U.S., he declared a "war against terrorism." By Dec. 2001 the U.S. military, aided by forces from other nations, had deposed Afghanistan's Taliban regime, which was sheltering al-Qaeda terrorists. The new Afghan government was weak, however, and unable to maintain control over much of the countryside. In Mar. 2003, the U.S., aided mainly by UK military forces, launched an air and ground war against Iraq and deposed its autocratic leader, Saddam Hussein. However, no evidence was found that his regime had developed weapons of mass destruction, the key rationale for the war. A new Iraqi government was formed in June 2004, but insurgent violence and U.S. troop casualties continued.

Bush was reelected in Nov. 2004 with 51% of the popular vote, but his popularity declined in his 2nd term. His push for Social Security reform failed in Congress, and his administration drew criticism for its response to Hurricane Katrina in Aug.-Sept. 2005. He also failed to win passage of a broad immigration reform measure. But the Senate confirmed his nominations of John G. Roberts Jr. (2005) as chief justice and Samuel A. Alito Jr. (2006) as an associate justice of the Supreme Court. In 2006,

Bush exercised his first veto, preventing legislation to ease restrictions on federal funding for stem cell research.

After Democrats won majorities in House and Senate 2006 midterm elections, Bush accepted the resignation of Defense Sec. Donald Rumsfeld, a target of widespread criticism over the Iraq war. Two months later, he announced a "surge" in U.S. troop strength in Iraq. A sharp drop in casualties ensued, aided also by a shift in alliances, and in late 2008 the administration reached an agreement with Iraq allowing U.S. troops to remain there through but not beyond 2011. But the Taliban was gaining strength in Afghanistan and Pakistan, and the Bush administration was damaged by revelations of prisoner abuse and memos that had given legal sanction to extreme interrogation methods. North Korea emerged as an increasing threat, announcing that it would resume operations at its main nuclear reactor.

The U.S. economy fell into recession in Dec. 2007; Bush and congressional leaders responded with a $168 bil stimulus plan. Problems in home finance and credit markets triggered a deep economic crisis in Sept. The Treasury Dept. announced a bailout of mortgage finance firms Fannie Mae and Freddie Mac. Lehman Bros. filed for bankruptcy, while the Federal Reserve rescued insurance giant AIG with a line of credit reaching $144 bil. A Bush administration-backed plan to buy up to $700 bil in devalued mortgage-related assets, opposed by many Republicans and rejected by Congress in late Sept., cleared Congress Oct. 3, after a severe stock market plunge bolstered support. The economic crisis added to Bush's unpopularity and contributed to the Nov. 2008 defeat of GOP presidential candidate Sen. John McCain (AZ).

In early 2010 Bush and former Pres. Clinton established a non-profit organization to raise funds for earthquake relief in Haiti. In Nov. 2010, Bush published a memoir entitled *Decision Points*.

Barack Hussein Obama (2009-), 44th president, Democrat, was born Aug. 4, 1961, in Honolulu, HI. His father, Barack Obama Sr., was a black Kenyan, and his mother, Stanley Ann Dunham, was a white American born in Kansas. By the time Obama was 6, his parents had divorced and his mother had married an Indonesian man and moved to Indonesia. Returning to Hawaii, he lived with his grandparents while attending high school. He received a bachelor's degree (1983) from Columbia Univ., worked from the mid-1980s as a community organizer in impoverished areas of Chicago's South Side, and earned a law degree (1991) from Harvard Univ., where he was president of the law review. He then practiced civil rights law in Chicago and taught at the Univ. of Chicago Law School. In 1992, he married attorney Michelle Robinson (1964-). They have 2 daughters, Malia (1998-) and Natasha (Sasha) (2001-).

Obama won election to the Illinois state senate in 1996 and was twice reelected. He failed to capture the Democratic nomination for a U.S. House seat in 2000, but won nomination for a U.S. Senate seat in a Mar. 2004 primary. Already known to many through his 1995 memoir, *Dreams From My Father: A Story of Race and Inheritance*, he gained national attention with his keynote address at the Democratic National Convention in July 2004. He was easily elected, becoming the lone African American in the Senate, and only the 3rd since Reconstruction. His 2nd book, *The Audacity of Hope: Thoughts on Reclaiming the American Dream* (2006), was a best-seller.

In early 2007 Obama announced his candidacy for the 2008 Democratic presidential nomination. He stressed his opposition to the Iraq war and determination to bring change to Washington and transcend partisanship. With victories in the early caucuses and primaries of 2008, he pulled ahead of the expected frontrunner, Sen. Hillary Clinton (NY), and eventually clinched the nomination.

In the fall campaign, Republican nominee Sen. John McCain (AZ) and his vice-presidential pick, Alaska Gov. Sarah Palin, portrayed Obama as inexperienced and devoted to higher taxes and big government. Obama and his running mate, Sen. Joe Biden (DE), drew strength from a smooth-running campaign organization and fundraising apparatus, the unpopularity of the Iraq war and Republican Pres. George W. Bush, and an economic crisis that came to dominate the campaign. Obama won 53% of the popular vote, the biggest proportion for a Democratic national ticket in 44 years, to become the nation's first African American president.

As president-elect, Obama named a new economic team, including Timothy Geithner for treasury secretary, and chose former rival Hillary Clinton for secretary of state, while retaining Robert Gates as defense secretary. Upon becoming president, he moved to signal a change of direction. For example, he lifted restrictions on federal funding for groups that provide abortion services or counseling abroad and reversed certain Bush-era policies on interrogation of detainees suspected of terrorism. He mandated that the U.S. military detention facility at Guantánamo Bay be closed within a year, but this plan proved unworkable and fell through. He sought to strike a more cooperative and conciliatory tone in foreign relations and reach out to traditional adversaries such as Iran and North Korea. On the basis of this effort, he was awarded the 2009 Nobel Peace Prize.

Obama sought both to wind down U.S. military involvement in Iraq and step up operations in Afghanistan. In Feb. 2009, he announced that all U.S. combat units would leave Iraq by Aug. 31, 2010; this deadline was met, but some 50,000 U.S. troops remained in a technically noncombat role. In Dec. 2009, he announced the second of two surges in U.S. troop levels to counter insurgency in Afghanistan, though with withdrawals to begin in July 2011. These started as scheduled, but were gradual. Popular uprisings in Arab countries also posed challenges for the Obama administration during 2011. While voicing support for democratic change, Obama avoided military involvement. An exception was Libya, where the U.S. and other NATO countries used air strikes, with the stated aim of protecting civilians from slaughter, while also providing guidance to the ultimately successful rebels.

Obama achieved a major success when Osama bin Laden, mastermind of the terrorist attacks of Sept. 11, 2001, was tracked down in Pakistan and killed in a May 2011 operation by U.S. Navy SEALs. In general, the president's foreign policy attracted some opposition from both left and right but remained overshadowed by domestic economic concerns.

In an effort to revive the economy, the administration had won passage, in Feb. 2009, of a $787 bil stimulus package providing for tax cuts and some $575 bil in new spending. The country did technically pull out of recession in 3rd quarter 2009, but economic growth fell short of expectations and unemployment continued to be high. At least partly for this reason, Obama's approval rating, which had started out at around 70%, slid downward.

Democrats lost their filibuster-proof Senate majority after a Jan. 2010 special election in Massachusetts. Obama nevertheless secured passage, in Mar. 2010, of his top priority, a massive health care reform bill; opposed by Republicans as costly and bureaucratic, it aimed in part at extending coverage to millions of uninsured Americans. Obama in Aug. 2010 won confirmation of Elena Kagan, his second appointment to the Supreme Court; his first nominee, Sonia Sotomayor, was confirmed in 2009. In July 2010 the administration won passage of a major financial reform bill.

In Nov. 2010 elections Democrats suffered what Obama called a "shellacking," losing their majority in the House and reducing it in the Senate. The new Congress was sharply divided, and many of the new Republicans were allied with the rising "Tea Party" movement, committed to shrink the size of government and fend off tax increases. During the ensuing lame-duck session, Obama reached a controversial compromise with Republicans on an $858 bil spending plan that kept Bush tax cuts for all income levels while extending unemployment benefits and temporarily reducing the Social Security payroll tax. He also won passage of a measure to repeal the "don't ask, don't tell" policy for gays in the military.

Following the elections, the bipartisan Simpson Bowles commission, formed by the president to recommend deficit reduction measures, released a detailed $4 tril plan, calling for an ambitious, politically provocative mix of entitlement and other spending cuts along with tax reforms. Obama did not champion these proposals, but in an Apr. 2011 speech, after Republicans had issued a detailed, conservatively oriented deficit reduction plan, he outlined a general plan, with higher taxes on the wealthy and no entitlement cuts.

Conflicts over finances consumed 2011. Republicans in Congress insisted that the U.S. debt ceiling should not be raised without agreement on compensating cost savings. After tortuous negotiations between Obama and congressional leaders, a last-minute compromise to avert default was passed by Congress and signed by Obama Aug. 2, 2011. It raised the debt ceiling by up to $2.4 tril. About half of the compensating reductions were left to be determined by a special bipartisan congressional committee, to report back in Nov. 2011; if Congress failed to follow the committee recommendations, automatic cuts in both discretionary domestic programs and defense would be triggered.

The long gridlock and the terms of the final compromise itself led Standard & Poor's to downgrade the U.S. from its triple-A credit rating. These circumstances, along with indications that the economy was floundering, helped depress the stock market in Aug. 2011 and drive approval ratings for both Congress and the president down to new lows.

Wives and Children of the Presidents

Name (born-died; married)	State	Sons/ daughters	Name (born-died; married)	State	Sons/ daughters
Martha Dandridge Custis Washington (1731-1802; 1759)	VA	None	Mary Scott Lord Dimmick Harrison (1858-1948; 1896)	PA	0/1
Abigail Smith Adams (1744-1818; 1764)	MA	3/2	Ida Saxton McKinley (1847-1907; 1871)	OH	0/2
Martha Wayles Skelton Jefferson (1748-82; 1772)	VA	1/5	Alice Hathaway Lee Roosevelt (1861-84; 1880)	MA	0/1
Dolley Payne Todd Madison (1768-1849; 1794)	NC	None	Edith Kermit Carow Roosevelt (1861-1948; 1886)	CT	4/1
Elizabeth Kortright Monroe (1768-1830; 1786)	NY	1/2	Helen Herron Taft (1861-1943; 1886)	OH	2/1
Louisa Catherine Johnson Adams (1775-1852; 1797)	MD[1]	3/1	Ellen Louise Axson Wilson (1860-1914; 1885)	GA	0/3
Rachel Donelson Robards Jackson (1767-1828; 1791)	VA	1/0[2]	Edith Bolling Galt Wilson (1872-1961; 1915)	VA	None
Hannah Hoes Van Buren (1783-1819; 1807)	NY	4/0	Florence Kling De Wolfe Harding (1860-1924; 1891)	OH	None
Anna Tuthill Symmes Harrison (1775-1864; 1795)	NJ	6/4	Grace Anna Goodhue Coolidge (1879-1957; 1905)	VT	2/0
Letitia Christian Tyler (1790-1842; 1813)	VA	3/5	Lou Henry Hoover (1875-1944; 1899)	IA	2/0
Julia Gardiner Tyler (1820-89; 1844)	NY	5/2	Anna Eleanor Roosevelt (1884-1962; 1905)	NY	5/1
Sarah Childress Polk (1803-91; 1824)	TN	None	Elizabeth Virginia (Bess) Wallace Truman (1885-1982; 1919)	MO	0/1
Margaret (Peggy) Mackall Smith Taylor (1788-1852; 1810)	MD	1/5	Mamie Geneva Doud Eisenhower (1896-1979; 1916)	IA	2/0
Abigail Powers Fillmore (1798-1853; 1826)	NY	1/1	Jacqueline Lee Bouvier Kennedy (1929-94; 1953)	NY	2/1
Caroline Carmichael McIntosh Fillmore (1813-81; 1858)	NJ	None	Claudia (Lady Bird) Alta Taylor Johnson (1912-2007; 1934)	TX	0/2
Jane Means Appleton Pierce (1806-63; 1834)	NH	3/0	Thelma Catherine Patricia Ryan Nixon (1912-93; 1940)	NV	0/2
Mary Todd Lincoln (1818-82; 1842)	KY	4/0	Elizabeth (Betty) Bloomer Warren Ford (1918-2011; 1948)	IL	3/1
Eliza McCardle Johnson (1810-76; 1827)	TN	3/2	Eleanor Rosalynn Smith Carter (1927- ; 1946)	GA	3/1
Julia Boggs Dent Grant (1826-1902; 1848)	MO	3/1	Anne Frances (Nancy) Robbins Davis Reagan (1921- ; 1952)	NY	1/1[3]
Lucy Ware Webb Hayes (1831-89; 1852)	OH	7/1	Barbara Pierce Bush (1925- ; 1945)	NY	4/2
Lucretia Rudolph Garfield (1832-1918; 1858)	OH	5/2	Hillary Diane Rodham Clinton (1947- ; 1975)	IL	0/1
Ellen Lewis Herndon Arthur (1837-80; 1859)	VA	2/1	Laura Lane Welch Bush (1946- ; 1977)	TX	0/2
Frances Folsom Cleveland (1864-1947; 1886)	NY	2/3	Michelle LaVaughn Robinson Obama (1964- ; 1992)	IL	0/2
Caroline Lavinia Scott Harrison (1832-92; 1853)	OH	1/1			

Note: Pres. Buchanan was unmarried. (1) Born in London, father a MD citizen. (2) Adopted son. (3) Pres. Reagan's first wife, whom he later divorced, was Jane Wyman. They had a daughter who died in infancy, a daughter who lived past infancy, and an adopted son.

First Lady Michelle Obama

Michelle Robinson Obama was born in Chicago, IL, Jan. 17, 1964. She graduated from Princeton University, 1985, earned a law degree from Harvard University, 1988, and joined Chicago law firm Sidley & Austin. She served as assistant commissioner of planning and development for Chicago, then as founding executive director of the Chicago chapter of Public Allies, an AmeriCorps program. She began working for the Univ. of Chicago in 1996, first as associate dean of student services, then as the Univ. of Chicago Medical Center's VP of community and external affairs. Michelle and Barack Obama were married in 1992; in 1998, their daughter Malia was born, followed by Natasha (Sasha) in 2001.

As First Lady, Michelle Obama has focused on supporting military families, helping women balance career and family, encouraging national service, and promoting the arts and arts education. She has also launched a major campaign to deal with the problem of childhood obesity in the U.S.

Burial Places of the Presidents

President	Burial place	President	Burial place	President	Burial place
Washington	Mt. Vernon, VA	Pierce	Concord, NH	Wilson	Wash. Natl. Cathedral, DC
J. Adams	Quincy, MA	Buchanan	Lancaster, PA	Harding	Marion, OH
Jefferson	Charlottesville, VA	Lincoln	Springfield, IL	Coolidge	Plymouth Notch, VT
Madison	Montpelier Station, VA	A. Johnson	Greeneville, TN	Hoover	West Branch, IA
Monroe	Richmond, VA	Grant	New York, NY	F. Roosevelt	Hyde Park, NY
J. Q. Adams	Quincy, MA	Hayes	Fremont, OH	Truman	Independence, MO
Jackson	Nashville, TN	Garfield	Cleveland, OH	Eisenhower	Abilene, KS
Van Buren	Kinderhook, NY	Arthur	Albany, NY	Kennedy	Arlington Natl. Cem., VA
W. H. Harrison	North Bend, OH	Cleveland	Princeton, NJ	L. B. Johnson	Stonewall, TX
Tyler	Richmond, VA	B. Harrison	Indianapolis, IN	Nixon	Yorba Linda, CA
Polk	Nashville, TN	McKinley	Canton, OH	Ford	Grand Rapids, MI
Taylor	Louisville, KY	T. Roosevelt	Oyster Bay, NY	Reagan	Simi Valley, CA
Fillmore	Buffalo, NY	Taft	Arlington Natl. Cem., VA		

Presidential Facts

Oldest president: Ronald Reagan, who was 77 when he left office

Youngest president: Theodore Roosevelt, who was 42 when sworn in after McKinley's death

Youngest person elected president: John F. Kennedy, who was 43 when elected in 1960

Tallest president: Abraham Lincoln, who was 6 feet, 4 inches

Shortest president: James Madison, who was 5 feet, 4 inches

Heaviest president: William Howard Taft, who was 332 pounds in 1911

First president to live in the White House: John Adams, who moved there in 1800

First president inaugurated in Washington, DC: Thomas Jefferson, in 1801

First president whose parents were immigrants: Andrew Jackson; his parents immigrated from Ireland in 1765

First president born a U.S. citizen: Martin Van Buren, in Kinderhook, NY, 1782

First president born outside the original colonies: Abraham Lincoln, in Kentucky, 1809

First president born west of the Mississippi: Herbert Hoover, in West Branch, IA, 1874

Most common presidential home state: Virginia, with 8 presidents

First president born in the 20th century: John F. Kennedy, in 1917

First president born in a hospital: Jimmy Carter, in Plains, GA, 1924

First president to be photographed while in office: James K. Polk, in 1849

First president to have a telephone in the White House: Rutherford B. Hayes, in 1879

First president to address the nation on radio: Warren G. Harding, in 1922

First president to appear on TV: Franklin D. Roosevelt, at opening ceremonies for the 1939 World's Fair

First president to give a live, televised news conference: John F. Kennedy, in 1961

First president to hold an Internet chat: Bill Clinton, in 1999

Presidents who lost the popular vote while winning election: John Quincy Adams, in 1824 (elected by the House after general election failed to produce a majority); Rutherford B. Hayes, in 1876; Benjamin Harrison, in 1888; George W. Bush, in 2000. (Popular vote totals before 1824 are unknown.)

Only presidents chosen by the House of Representatives: Thomas Jefferson (1st term) and John Quincy Adams

Only president never elected either president or vice president: Gerald Ford; named vice president when Spiro Agnew reigned (1973), became president when Nixon resigned (1974)

Only left-handed presidents: James Garfield, Herbert Hoover, Harry Truman, Gerald Ford, Ronald Reagan, George H. W. Bush, Bill Clinton, and Barack Obama

Only Catholic president: John F. Kennedy; the most common religious affiliations have been Episcopalian (11) and Presbyterian (7)

Only bachelor presidents: James Buchanan, who never married, and Grover Cleveland, who married Frances Folsom in the White House in 1886

Only divorced president: Ronald Reagan; divorced from Jane Wyman in 1948, married Nancy Davis in 1952

Presidents who died on July 4: John Adams and Thomas Jefferson (both 1826) and James Monroe (1831)

Only president buried in Washington, DC: Woodrow Wilson, who was interred at Washington National Cathedral

Presidential Libraries

Presidential libraries are coordinated by the National Archives and Records Administration (www.archives.gov/presidential-libraries/). Materials for presidents before Herbert Hoover are held by private institutions. Under the Presidential Records Act, presidential records are not available to the public for the first 5 years following the end of an administration. The George W. Bush Library and Museum is scheduled to open to the public in 2013; his records will become subject to FOIA requests on Jan. 20, 2014.

Herbert Hoover Library and Museum
210 Parkside Dr.
West Branch, IA 52358
PHONE: 319-643-5301
E-MAIL: hoover.library@nara.gov
WEBSITE: hoover.archives.gov

Franklin D. Roosevelt Library and Museum
4079 Albany Post Rd.
Hyde Park, NY 12538-1990
PHONE: 800-FDR-VISIT
E-MAIL: roosevelt.library@nara.gov
WEBSITE: www.fdrlibrary.marist.edu

Harry S. Truman Library and Museum
500 West U.S. Hwy. 24
Independence, MO 64050-2481
PHONE: 800-833-1225
E-MAIL: truman.library@nara.gov
WEBSITE: www.trumanlibrary.org

Dwight D. Eisenhower Library
200 SE 4th St.
Abilene, KS 67410-2900
PHONE: 877-RING-IKE
E-MAIL: eisenhower.library@nara.gov
WEBSITE: eisenhower.archives.gov

John F. Kennedy Library and Museum
Columbia Pt.
Boston, MA 02125-3312
PHONE: 866-JFK-1960
E-MAIL: kennedy.library@nara.gov
WEBSITE: www.jfklibrary.org

Lyndon Baines Johnson Library and Museum
2313 Red River St.
Austin, TX 78705-5737
PHONE: 512-721-0200
E-MAIL: johnson.library@nara.gov
WEBSITE: www.lbjlib.utexas.edu

Richard Nixon Library and Museum
18001 Yorba Linda Blvd.
Yorba Linda, CA 92886-3903
714-983-9120
E-MAIL: nixon@nara.gov
WEBSITE: www.nixonarchives.gov
MD OFFICE: Natl. Archives at College Park
8601 Adelphi Rd.
College Park, MD 20740-6001
PHONE: 301-837-3290

Gerald R. Ford Library and Museum
LIBRARY: 1000 Beal Ave.
Ann Arbor, MI 48109-2109
PHONE: 734-205-0555
MUSEUM: 303 Pearl St. NW

Grand Rapids, MI 49504-5353
PHONE: 616-254-0400
E-MAIL: ford.library@nara.gov
WEBSITE: www.fordlibrarymuseum.gov

Jimmy Carter Library and Museum
441 Freedom Pkwy.
Atlanta, GA 30307-1498
PHONE: 404-865-7100
E-MAIL: carter.library@nara.gov
WEBSITE: www.jimmycarterlibrary.gov

Ronald Reagan Library and Museum
40 Presidential Dr.
Simi Valley, CA 93065-0600
PHONE: 800-410-8354
E-MAIL: reagan.library@nara.gov
WEBSITE: www.reagan.utexas.edu

George Bush Library and Museum
1000 George Bush Dr. West
College Station, TX 77845
PHONE: 979-691-4000
E-MAIL: library.bush@nara.gov
WEBSITE: bushlibrary.tamu.edu

William J. Clinton Library and Museum
1200 President Clinton Ave.
Little Rock, AR 72201
PHONE: 501-374-4242
E-MAIL: clinton.library@nara.gov
WEBSITE: www.clintonlibrary.gov

Presidential Impeachment in U.S. History

The U.S. Constitution provides for impeachment and removal from office of federal officials on grounds of "Treason, Bribery, or other high Crimes and Misdemeanors" (Article II, Sect. 4). Impeachment is the bringing of charges by the House of Representatives. It is followed by a Senate trial; a two-thirds majority vote of Senators present is needed for conviction and removal from office.

In 1868, **Andrew Johnson** became the first president impeached by the House, for his removal of Sec. of War Edwin M. Stanton without first notifying the Senate. He was tried but not convicted. In 1974, impeachment articles against Pres. **Richard Nixon**, in connection with the Watergate scandal, were adopted by the House Judiciary Committee. He resigned Aug. 9, and the House accepted the committee report without taking further action. In 1998, Pres. **Bill Clinton** was impeached by the House in connection with covering up a sexual relationship with former White House intern Monica Lewinsky. He was tried in the Senate in 1999 and acquitted.

PRESIDENTIAL ELECTIONS

Electoral and Popular Vote, 2004, 2008

Source: Federal Election Commission

	2008						2004					
	Electoral vote		Popular vote				Electoral vote		Popular vote			
State	Obama	McCain	Obama	McCain	Nader		Kerry	Bush	Kerry	Bush	Nader	State
AL	0	9	813,479	1,266,546	6,788		0	9	693,933	1,176,394	6,701	AL
AK	0	3	123,594	193,841	3,783		0	3	111,025	190,889	5,069	AK
AZ	0	10	1,034,707	1,230,111	11,301		0	10	893,524	1,104,294	2,773	AZ
AR	0	6	422,310	638,017	12,882		0	6	469,953	572,898	6,171	AR
CA	55	0	8,274,473	5,011,781	108,381		55	0	6,745,485	5,509,826	21,213	CA
CO	9	0	1,288,633	1,073,629	13,352		0	9	1,001,732	1,101,255	12,718	CO
CT	7	0	997,772	629,428	19,162		7	0	857,488	693,826	12,969	CT
DE	3	0	255,459	152,374	2,401		3	0	200,152	171,660	2,153	DE
DC	3	0	245,800	17,367	958		3	0	202,970	21,256	1,485	DC
FL	27	0	4,282,074	4,045,624	28,124		0	27	3,583,544	3,964,522	32,971	FL
GA	0	15	1,844,123	2,048,759	1,158		0	15	1,366,149	1,914,254	2,231	GA
HI	4	0	325,871	120,566	3,825		4	0	231,708	194,191	—	HI
ID	0	4	236,440	403,012	7,175		0	4	181,098	409,235	1,115	ID
IL	21	0	3,419,348	2,031,179	30,948		21	0	2,891,550	2,345,946	3,571	IL
IN	11	0	1,374,039	1,345,648	909		0	11	969,011	1,479,438	1,328	IN
IA	7	0	828,940	682,379	8,014		0	7	741,898	751,957	5,973	IA
KS	0	6	514,765	699,655	10,527		0	6	434,993	736,456	9,348	KS
KY	0	8	751,985	1,048,462	15,378		0	8	712,733	1,069,439	8,856	KY
LA	0	9	782,989	1,148,275	6,997		0	9	820,299	1,102,169	7,032	LA
ME	4	0	421,923	295,273	10,636		4	0	396,842	330,201	8,069	ME
MD	10	0	1,629,467	959,862	14,713		10	0	1,334,493	1,024,703	11,854	MD
MA	12	0	1,904,097	1,108,854	28,841		12	0	1,803,800	1,071,109	4,806	MA
MI	17	0	2,872,579	2,048,639	33,085		17	0	2,479,183	2,313,746	24,035	MI
MN	10	0	1,573,354	1,275,409	30,152		9[1]	0	1,445,014	1,346,695	18,683	MN
MS	0	6	554,662	724,597	4,011		0	6	458,094	684,981	3,177	MS
MO	0	11	1,441,911	1,445,814	17,813		0	11	1,259,171	1,455,713	1,294	MO
MT	0	3	231,667	242,763	3,686		0	3	173,710	266,063	6,168	MT
NE[2]	1	4	333,319	452,979	5,406		0	5	254,328	512,814	5,698	NE[2]
NV	5	0	533,736	412,827	6,150		0	5	397,190	418,690	4,838	NV
NH	4	0	384,826	316,534	3,503		4	0	340,511	331,237	4,479	NH
NJ	15	0	2,215,422	1,613,207	21,298		15	0	1,911,430	1,670,003	19,418	NJ
NM	5	0	472,422	346,832	5,327		0	5	370,942	376,930	4,053	NM
NY	31	0	4,804,945	2,752,771	41,249		31	0	4,314,280	2,962,567	99,873	NY
NC	15	0	2,142,651	2,128,474	1,448		0	15	1,525,849	1,961,166	1,805	NC
ND	0	3	141,278	168,601	4,189		0	3	111,052	196,651	3,756	ND
OH	20	0	2,940,044	2,677,820	42,337		0	20	2,741,167	2,859,768	—	OH
OK	0	7	502,496	960,165	—		0	7	503,966	959,792	—	OK
OR	7	0	1,037,291	738,475	18,614		7	0	943,163	866,831	—	OR
PA	21	0	3,276,363	2,655,885	42,977		21	0	2,938,095	2,793,847	2,656	PA
RI	4	0	296,571	165,391	4,829		4	0	259,765	169,046	4,651	RI
SC	0	8	862,449	1,034,896	5,053		0	8	661,699	937,974	5,520	SC
SD	0	3	170,924	203,054	4,267		0	3	149,244	232,584	4,320	SD
TN	0	11	1,087,437	1,479,178	11,560		0	11	1,036,477	1,384,375	8,992	TN
TX	0	34	3,528,633	4,479,328	5,751		0	34	2,832,704	4,526,917	9,159	TX
UT	0	5	327,670	596,030	8,416		0	5	241,199	663,742	11,305	UT
VT	3	0	219,262	98,974	3,339		3	0	184,067	121,180	4,494	VT
VA	13	0	1,959,532	1,725,005	11,483		0	13	1,454,742	1,716,959	2,393	VA
WA	11	0	1,750,848	1,229,216	29,489		11	0	1,510,201	1,304,894	23,283	WA
WV	0	5	303,857	397,466	7,219		0	5	326,541	423,778	4,063	WV
WI	10	0	1,677,211	1,262,393	17,605		10	0	1,489,504	1,478,120	16,390	WI
WY	0	3	82,868	164,958	2,525		0	3	70,776	167,629	2,741	WY
Total	**365**	**173**	**69,498,516**	**59,948,323**	**739,034**		**251[1]**	**286**	**59,028,444**	**62,040,610**	**465,650**	**Total**

(—) = Not listed on state's ballot. (1) Minnesota has 10 electoral votes. One elector cast a vote for John Ewards [sic] for president, presumably by mistake. All 10 electors voted for John Edwards for vice president. (2) Nebraska is one of two states (the other is Maine) that may split its electoral votes between candidates.

Presidential Popular Vote, 2008

Candidate (party)	Vote total	Percent of vote
Barack Obama (Democratic)	69,498,516	52.93%
John McCain (Republican)	59,948,323	45.65
Ralph Nader (Independent/Peace and Freedom)	739,034	0.56
Bob Barr (Libertarian)	523,715	0.40
Chuck Baldwin (Constitution/Reform/ U.S. Taxpayers)	199,750	0.15
Cynthia McKinney (Green/Independent/ Mountain)	161,797	0.12
Alan Keyes (America's Independent)	47,746	0.04
Ron Paul (Constitution/Louisiana Taxpayers)	42,426	0.03
Gloria La Riva (Socialism and Liberation)	6,818	0.01
Brian Moore (Liberty Union/Socialist)	6,538	<0.01
Róger Calero (Socialist Workers)	5,151	<0.01
Richard Duncan (Independent)	3,905	<0.01
James Harris (Socialist Workers)	2,424	<0.01
Charles Jay (Boston Tea Party/ Independent)	2,422	<0.01%
John Joseph Polachek (New)	1,149	<0.01
Frank Edward McEnulty (Unaffiliated)	829	<0.01
Jeffrey J. Wamboldt (Independent)	764	<0.01
Thomas Robert Stevens (Objectivist)	755	<0.01
Gene C. Amondson (Prohibition)	653	<0.01
Jeffrey "Jeff" Boss (Vote Here)	639	<0.01
George Phillies (Libertarian)	531	<0.01
Ted Weill (Reform)	481	<0.01
Jonathan E. Allen (HeartQuake '08)	480	<0.01
Bradford Lyttle (U.S. Pacifist)	110	<0.01
Write-In (Miscellaneous)	112,597	0.09
None of These Candidates (Nevada)	6,267	<0.01
Total votes cast	**131,313,820**	
Voting age population, Nov. 2008	225,499,000	
Percentage casting vote for president		58.23%

Note: Party designations vary from one state to another; party label listed may not necessarily represent a political party organization. Vote totals for the candidates listed above include any write-in votes they received.

The Electoral College

The president and the vice president are the only elective federal officials not chosen by direct vote of the people. They are elected by the members of the Electoral College, an institution provided for in the U.S. Constitution.

On presidential election day, the first Tuesday after the first Monday in Nov. of every fourth year, each state chooses as many electors as it has senators and representatives in Congress. In 1964, for the first time, as provided by the 23rd Amendment to the Constitution, the District of Columbia voted for three electors. Thus, with 100 senators and 435 representatives, there are 538 members of the Electoral College, with a majority of 270 electoral votes needed to elect the president and vice president.

Although political parties were not part of the original plan created by the Founding Fathers, today political parties customarily nominate their lists of electors at their respective state conventions. Some states print names of the candidates for president and vice president at the top of the Nov. ballot; others list only the electors' names. In either case, the electors of the party receiving the highest vote are elected. Two states, Maine and Nebraska, allow for proportional allocation.

The electors meet on the first Monday after the second Wednesday in Dec. in their respective state capitals or in some other place prescribed by state legislatures. By long-established custom, they vote for their party nominees, although this is not required by federal law; some states do require it.

The Constitution requires electors to cast a ballot for at least one person who is not an inhabitant of that elector's home state. This ensures that presidential and vice presidential candidates from the same party will not be from the same state. (In 2000, Republican vice presidential nominee Dick Cheney changed his voter registration to Wyoming, where he grew up and which he'd once represented in Congress, from Gov. George W. Bush's home state of Texas.) Also, an elector cannot be a member of Congress or hold federal office.

Certified and sealed lists of the votes of the electors in each state are sent to the president of the U.S. Senate, who then opens them in the presence of the members of the Senate and House of Representatives in a joint session held in early Jan., and the electoral votes of all the states are then officially counted.

If no candidate for president has a majority, the House of Representatives chooses a president from the top three candidates, with all representatives from each state combining to cast one vote for that state. The House decided the outcome of the 1800 and 1824 presidential elections. If no candidate for vice president has a majority, the Senate chooses from the top two, with the senators voting as individuals. The Senate chose the vice president following the 1836 election.

Under the electoral college system, a candidate who fails to be the top vote getter in the popular vote still may win a majority of electoral votes. This happened in the elections of 1876, 1888, and 2000.

Electoral Votes for President, 2008

Electoral votes based on the 2000 Census were in force beginning with the 2004 elections.

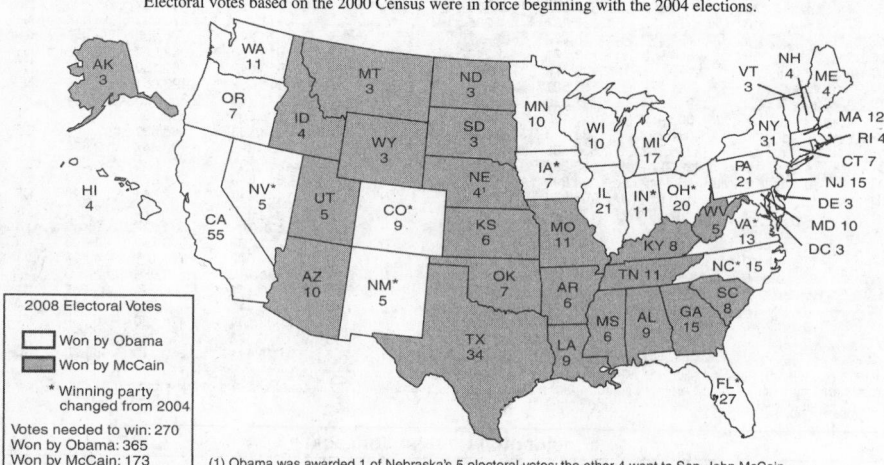

2008 Electoral Votes

☐ Won by Obama
■ Won by McCain

* Winning party changed from 2004

Votes needed to win: 270
Won by Obama: 365
Won by McCain: 173

(1) Obama was awarded 1 of Nebraska's 5 electoral votes; the other 4 went to Sen. John McCain.

Voter Turnout in Presidential Elections, 1932-2008

Source: Federal Election Commission; Center for the Study of the American Electorate, American Univ.; *Congressional Quarterly*

Year	Candidates	Voter participation (% of voting-age population)	Year	Candidates	Voter participation (% of voting-age population)
1932	Roosevelt-Hoover	52.4%	1972	Nixon-McGovern	55.2%[1]
1936	Roosevelt-Landon	56.0	1976	Carter-Ford	53.5
1940	Roosevelt-Willkie	58.9	1980	Reagan-Carter	54.0
1944	Roosevelt-Dewey	56.0	1984	Reagan-Mondale	53.1
1948	Truman-Dewey	51.1	1988	Bush-Dukakis	50.2
1952	Eisenhower-Stevenson	61.6	1992	Clinton-Bush-Perot	55.9
1956	Eisenhower-Stevenson	59.3	1996	Clinton-Dole-Perot	49.0
1960	Kennedy-Nixon	62.8	2000	Bush-Gore	51.3
1964	Johnson-Goldwater	61.9	2004	Bush-Kerry	60.7
1968	Nixon-Humphrey	60.9	2008	Obama-McCain	58.2

(1) The drop in voter participation followed the expansion of eligibility with the enfranchisement of 18- to 20-year-olds.

Major-Party Nominees for President and Vice President, 1856-2008

Asterisk (*) denotes winning ticket.

	Democratic			Republican	
Year	President	Vice President	Year	President	Vice President
1856	James Buchanan*	John Breckinridge	1856	John Frémont	William Dayton
1860	Stephen A. Douglas[1]	Herschel V. Johnson	1860	Abraham Lincoln*	Hannibal Hamlin
1864	George McClellan	G. H. Pendleton	1864	Abraham Lincoln*	Andrew Johnson
1868	Horatio Seymour	Francis Blair	1868	Ulysses S. Grant*	Schuyler Colfax
1872	Horace Greeley	B. Gratz Brown	1872	Ulysses S. Grant*	Henry Wilson
1876	Samuel J. Tilden	Thomas Hendricks	1876	Rutherford B. Hayes*	William Wheeler
1880	Winfield Hancock	William English	1880	James A. Garfield*	Chester A. Arthur
1884	Grover Cleveland*	Thomas Hendricks	1884	James G. Blaine	John Logan
1888	Grover Cleveland	A. G. Thurman	1888	Benjamin Harrison*	Levi Morton
1892	Grover Cleveland*	Adlai Stevenson	1892	Benjamin Harrison	Whitelaw Reid
1896	William J. Bryan	Arthur Sewall	1896	William McKinley*	Garret Hobart
1900	William J. Bryan	Adlai Stevenson	1900	William McKinley*	Theodore Roosevelt
1904	Alton Parker	Henry Davis	1904	Theodore Roosevelt*	Charles Fairbanks
1908	William J. Bryan	John Kern	1908	William H. Taft*	James Sherman
1912	Woodrow Wilson*	Thomas Marshall	1912	William H. Taft	James Sherman[2]
1916	Woodrow Wilson*	Thomas Marshall	1916	Charles E. Hughes	Charles Fairbanks
1920	James M. Cox	Franklin D. Roosevelt	1920	Warren G. Harding*	Calvin Coolidge
1924	John W. Davis	Charles W. Bryan	1924	Calvin Coolidge*	Charles G. Dawes
1928	Alfred E. Smith	Joseph T. Robinson	1928	Herbert Hoover*	Charles Curtis
1932	Franklin D. Roosevelt*	John N. Garner	1932	Herbert Hoover	Charles Curtis
1936	Franklin D. Roosevelt*	John N. Garner	1936	Alfred M. Landon	Frank Knox
1940	Franklin D. Roosevelt*	Henry A. Wallace	1940	Wendell L. Willkie	Charles McNary
1944	Franklin D. Roosevelt*	Harry S. Truman	1944	Thomas E. Dewey	John W. Bricker
1948	Harry S. Truman*	Alben W. Barkley	1948	Thomas E. Dewey	Earl Warren
1952	Adlai E. Stevenson	John J. Sparkman	1952	Dwight D. Eisenhower*	Richard M. Nixon
1956	Adlai E. Stevenson	Estes Kefauver	1956	Dwight D. Eisenhower*	Richard M. Nixon
1960	John F. Kennedy*	Lyndon B. Johnson	1960	Richard M. Nixon	Henry Cabot Lodge
1964	Lyndon B. Johnson*	Hubert H. Humphrey	1964	Barry M. Goldwater	William E. Miller
1968	Hubert H. Humphrey	Edmund S. Muskie	1968	Richard M. Nixon*	Spiro T. Agnew
1972	George S. McGovern	R. Sargent Shriver Jr.[3]	1972	Richard M. Nixon*	Spiro T. Agnew
1976	Jimmy Carter*	Walter F. Mondale	1976	Gerald R. Ford	Bob Dole
1980	Jimmy Carter	Walter F. Mondale	1980	Ronald Reagan*	George H. W. Bush
1984	Walter F. Mondale	Geraldine Ferraro	1984	Ronald Reagan*	George H. W. Bush
1988	Michael S. Dukakis	Lloyd Bentsen	1988	George H. W. Bush*	Dan Quayle
1992	Bill Clinton*	Al Gore	1992	George H. W. Bush	Dan Quayle
1996	Bill Clinton*	Al Gore	1996	Bob Dole	Jack Kemp
2000	Al Gore	Joseph Lieberman	2000	George W. Bush*	Richard Cheney
2004	John Kerry	John Edwards	2004	George W. Bush*	Richard Cheney
2008	Barack Obama*	Joseph Biden	2008	John McCain	Sarah Palin

(1) Douglas and Johnson were nominated at the Baltimore convention. An earlier convention in Charleston, SC, failed to reach a consensus and resulted in a split in the party. The Southern faction of the Democrats nominated John Breckinridge for president and Joseph Lane for vice president. (2) Died Oct. 30; replaced on ballot by Nicholas Butler. (3) Chosen by Democratic National Committee after Thomas Eagleton withdrew because of controversy over past treatments for depression.

Third-Party and Independent Presidential Candidates

Although many third-party candidates or independents have pursued the presidency, only 10 of these from 1832 to 2000 have polled more than a million votes. In most elections since 1860, fewer than one vote in 20 has been cast for a third-party candidate. Major vote getters among third-party and independent candidates include James B. Weaver (People's Party), 1892; former Pres. Theodore Roosevelt (Progressive Party), 1912; Robert M. La Follette (Progressive Party), 1924; George C. Wallace (American Independent Party), 1968; and H. Ross Perot, as an independent in 1992 and with the Reform Party in 1996. In these six elections, non-major-party candidates combined polled at least 10% of the vote.

Roosevelt outpolled the Republican candidate, William Howard Taft, in 1912, capturing 28% of the popular vote and 88 electoral

votes. In 1948, Strom Thurmond was able to capture 39 electoral votes (from five Southern states); however, all third parties received only 5.75% of the popular vote in the election. Twenty years later, George Wallace's popularity in the same region allowed him to get 46 electoral votes and 13.5% of the popular vote.

In 1992 Perot captured 19% of the popular vote. However, he did not win a single state. In 1996, Perot won 8% of the popular vote; all third-party candidates combined won just over 10%. In 2000, Ralph Nader won about 3% of the vote.

Despite the difficulty in winning the presidency, independent and third-party candidates often bring attention to prominent issues. They can also affect the outcome between major-party candidates.

Notable Third Party and Independent Campaigns by Year

Party	Presidential nominee	Year	Issues	Strength in
Anti-Masonic	William Wirt	1832	Against secret societies and oaths	PA, VT
Liberty	James G. Birney	1844	Anti-slavery	North
Free Soil	Martin Van Buren	1848	Anti-slavery	NY, OH
American (Know-Nothing)	Millard Fillmore	1856	Anti-immigrant	Northeast, South
Greenback	Peter Cooper	1876	For "cheap money," labor rights	National
Greenback	James B. Weaver	1880	For "cheap money," labor rights	National
Prohibition	John P. St. John	1884	Anti-liquor	National
People's (Populist)	James B. Weaver	1892	For "cheap money," end of national banks	South, West
Socialist	Eugene V. Debs	1900-12; 1920	For public ownership	National
Progressive (Bull Moose)	Theodore Roosevelt	1912	Against high tariffs	Midwest, West
Progressive	Robert M. La Follette	1924	For farmer and labor rights	Midwest, West
Socialist	Norman Thomas	1928-48	For liberal reforms	National
Union	William Lemke	1936	Anti-New Deal	National
States' Rights (Dixiecrat)	Strom Thurmond	1948	For states' rights	South
Progressive	Henry A. Wallace	1948	Anti-Cold War	NY, CA
American Independent	George C. Wallace	1968	For states' rights	South
American	John G. Schmitz	1972	For "law and order"	Far West, OH, LA
None (independent)	John B. Anderson	1980	A 3rd choice	National
None (independent)	H. Ross Perot	1992	Federal budget deficit	National
Reform	H. Ross Perot	1996	Deficit; campaign finance	National
Green, independent	Ralph Nader	2000-08	Corporate power; domestic priorities	National

Popular and Electoral Vote for President, 1789-2008

(D) Democrat; (DR) Democratic Republican; (F) Federalist; (LB) Libertarian; (LR) Liberal Republican; (NR) National Republican; (P) People's; (PR) Progressive; (R) Republican; (W) Whig; (*)–See notes at bottom.

Year	President elected	Popular	Elec.	Major losing candidate(s)	Popular	Elec.
1789	George Washington (F)	Unknown	69	No opposition	—	—
1792	George Washington (F)	Unknown	132	No opposition	—	—
1796	John Adams (F)	Unknown	71	Thomas Jefferson (DR)	Unknown	68
1800*	Thomas Jefferson (DR)	Unknown	73	Aaron Burr (DR)	Unknown	73
1804	Thomas Jefferson (DR)	Unknown	162	Charles Pinckney (F)	Unknown	14
1808	James Madison (DR)	Unknown	122	Charles Pinckney (F)	Unknown	47
1812	James Madison (DR)	Unknown	128	DeWitt Clinton (F)	Unknown	89
1816	James Monroe (DR)	Unknown	183	Rufus King (F)	Unknown	34
1820	James Monroe (DR)	Unknown	231	John Quincy Adams (DR)	Unknown	1
1824*	John Quincy Adams (DR)	113,122	84	Andrew Jackson (DR)	151,271	99
				Henry Clay (DR)	46,587	37
				William H. Crawford (DR)	44,282	41
1828	Andrew Jackson (D)	642,553	178	John Quincy Adams (NR)	500,897	83
1832	Andrew Jackson (D)	701,780	219	Henry Clay (NR)	484,205	49
1836	Martin Van Buren (D)	764,176	170	William H. Harrison (W)	550,816	73
1840	William H. Harrison (W)	1,275,390	234	Martin Van Buren (D)	1,128,854	60
1844	James K. Polk (D)	1,339,494	170	Henry Clay (W)	1,300,004	105
1848	Zachary Taylor (W)	1,361,393	163	Lewis Cass (D)	1,223,460	127
				Martin Van Buren (Free Soil)	291,501	—
1852	Franklin Pierce (D)	1,607,510	254	Winfield Scott (W)	1,386,942	42
1856	James Buchanan (D)	1,836,072	174	John C. Fremont (R)	1,342,345	114
				Millard Fillmore (W-American)	873,053	8
1860	Abraham Lincoln (R)	1,865,908	180	Stephen A. Douglas (D)	848,019	12
				John C. Breckinridge (D)	845,763	72
				John Bell (Constitutional Union)	589,581	39
1864	Abraham Lincoln (R)	2,218,388	212	George McClellan (D)	1,812,807	21
1868	Ulysses S. Grant (R)	3,013,650	214	Horatio Seymour (D)	2,708,744	80
1872*	Ulysses S. Grant (R)	3,598,235	286	Horace Greeley (D-LR)	2,834,671	—
1876*	Rutherford B. Hayes (R)	4,034,311	185	Samuel J. Tilden (D)	4,288,546	184
1880	James A. Garfield (R)	4,446,158	214	Winfield S. Hancock (D)	4,444,260	155
1884	Grover Cleveland (D)	4,874,621	219	James G. Blaine (R)	4,848,936	182
1888	Benjamin Harrison (R)	5,443,892	233	Grover Cleveland (D)	5,534,488	168
1892	Grover Cleveland (D)	5,551,883	277	Benjamin Harrison (R)	5,179,244	145
				James Weaver (P)	1,027,329	22
1896	William McKinley (R)	7,108,480	271	William J. Bryan (D-P)	6,511,495	176
1900	William McKinley (R)	7,218,039	292	William J. Bryan (D)	6,358,345	155
1904	Theodore Roosevelt (R)	7,626,593	336	Alton B. Parker (D)	5,082,898	140
1908	William H. Taft (R)	7,676,258	321	William J. Bryan (D)	6,406,801	162
1912	Woodrow Wilson (D)	6,293,152	435	Theodore Roosevelt (PR)	4,119,207	88
				William H. Taft (R)	3,483,922	8
1916	Woodrow Wilson (D)	9,126,300	277	Charles E. Hughes (R)	8,546,789	254
1920	Warren G. Harding (R)	16,153,115	404	James M. Cox (D)	9,133,092	127
1924	Calvin Coolidge (R)	15,719,921	382	John W. Davis (D)	8,386,704	136
				Robert M. La Follette (PR)	4,822,856	13
1928	Herbert Hoover (R)	21,437,277	444	Alfred E. Smith (D)	15,007,698	87
1932	Franklin D. Roosevelt (D)	22,829,501	472	Herbert Hoover (R)	15,760,684	59
1936	Franklin D. Roosevelt (D)	27,757,333	523	Alfred Landon (R)	16,684,231	8
1940	Franklin D. Roosevelt (D)	27,313,041	449	Wendell Willkie (R)	22,348,480	82
1944	Franklin D. Roosevelt (D)	25,612,610	432	Thomas E. Dewey (R)	22,117,617	99
1948	Harry S. Truman (D)	24,179,345	303	Thomas E. Dewey (R)	21,991,291	189
				Strom Thurmond (States' Rights)	1,169,021	39
				Henry A. Wallace (PR)	1,157,172	—
1952	Dwight D. Eisenhower (R)	33,936,234	442	Adlai E. Stevenson (D)	27,314,992	89
1956*	Dwight D. Eisenhower (R)	35,590,472	457	Adlai E. Stevenson (D)	26,022,752	73
1960*	John F. Kennedy (D)	34,226,731	303	Richard M. Nixon (R)	34,108,157	219
1964	Lyndon B. Johnson (D)	43,129,566	486	Barry M. Goldwater (R)	27,178,188	52
1968	Richard M. Nixon (R)	31,785,480	301	Hubert H. Humphrey (D)	31,275,166	191
				George C. Wallace (Amer. Indep.)	9,906,473	46
1972*	Richard M. Nixon (R)	47,169,911	520	George S. McGovern (D)	29,170,383	17
1976*	Jimmy Carter (D)	40,830,763	297	Gerald R. Ford (R)	39,147,793	240
1980	Ronald Reagan (R)	43,904,153	489	Jimmy Carter (D)	35,483,883	49
				John B. Anderson (independent)	5,719,437	—
1984	Ronald Reagan (R)	54,455,075	525	Walter F. Mondale (D)	37,577,185	13
1988*	George H. W. Bush (R)	48,886,097	426	Michael S. Dukakis (D)	41,809,074	111
1992	Bill Clinton (D)	44,908,254	370	George H. W. Bush (R)	39,102,343	168
				H. Ross Perot (independent)	19,741,065	—
1996	Bill Clinton (D)	45,590,703	379	Bob Dole (R)	37,816,307	159
				H. Ross Perot (Reform)	7,866,284	—
2000*	George W. Bush (R)	50,459,211	271	Al Gore (D)	51,003,894	266
				Ralph Nader (Green)	2,834,410	—
2004*	George W. Bush (R)	62,040,610	286	John Kerry (D)	59,028,444	251
2008	Barack H. Obama (D)	69,498,459	365	John McCain (R)	59,948,283	173

*1800—Elected by House of Representatives because of tied electoral vote. 1824—Elected by House of Representatives because no candidate polled a majority. By 1824, the Democratic Republicans had become a loose coalition of competing political groups. By 1828, the supporters of Jackson were known as Democrats, and the John Q. Adams and Henry Clay supporters as National Republicans. 1872—Greeley died Nov. 29, 1872. His electoral votes were split among 4 individuals. 1876—FL, LA, OR, and SC election returns were disputed. Congress in joint session (Mar. 2, 1877) declared Hayes and Wheeler elected president and vice president. 1956—Democrats elected 74 electors, but 1 from AL refused to vote for Stevenson. 1960—Sen. Harry F. Byrd (D, VA) received 15 electoral votes. 1972—John Hospers of CA received 1 vote from an elector of VA. 1976—Ronald Reagan of CA received 1 vote from an elector of WA. 1988—Sen. Lloyd Bentsen (D, TX) received 1 vote from an elector of WV. 2000—One Gore elector from Washington, DC, abstained. Nader was listed as "Independent" on the ballot in some states; he was not on the ballot in all states. 2004—One MN elector voted for VP candidate John Edwards for both president and vice president.

Presidential Election Results by State and County

Source: Alaska district results, Alaska Div. of Elections; New Hampshire and Vermont county results, respective secretary of state's office; state totals and all other state results, Federal Election Commission

All results are official. Results for Connecticut, Maine, Massachusetts, and Rhode Island are for selected cities or towns. All totals statewide.

Alabama

County	2008 Obama (D)	McCain (R)	2004 Kerry (D)	Bush (R)
Autauga	6,091	17,398	4,758	15,196
Baldwin	19,362	61,192	15,599	52,971
Barbour	5,685	5,862	4,832	5,899
Bibb	2,289	6,247	2,089	5,472
Blount	3,518	20,362	3,938	17,386
Bullock	4,001	1,389	3,210	1,494
Butler	4,174	5,472	3,413	4,979
Calhoun	16,325	32,326	15,083	29,814
Chambers	6,782	8,060	5,347	7,622
Cherokee	2,299	7,285	3,040	5,923
Chilton	3,666	13,934	3,778	12,829
Choctaw	3,633	4,220	3,303	3,897
Clarke	5,907	7,455	4,627	6,730
Clay	1,722	4,946	1,893	4,624
Cleburne	1,166	5,204	1,391	4,370
Coffee	5,068	14,909	4,480	13,019
Colbert	9,698	14,729	10,598	13,188
Conecuh	3,411	3,461	2,719	3,271
Coosa	2,269	3,245	2,055	2,905
Covington	3,238	12,431	3,423	11,119
Crenshaw	1,938	4,316	1,698	3,777
Cullman	5,855	28,837	8,045	26,818
Dale	5,257	13,873	4,484	13,621
Dallas	13,958	6,791	11,175	7,335
DeKalb	5,654	17,951	7,092	16,904
Elmore	8,268	25,695	6,471	22,056
Escambia	5,176	9,365	3,814	8,513
Etowah	13,480	30,562	15,328	26,999
Fayette	1,988	5,875	2,408	5,534
Franklin	3,469	8,048	4,514	7,690
Geneva	2,106	9,314	2,113	8,342
Greene	4,402	876	3,764	958
Hale	4,969	3,196	4,631	3,281
Henry	2,990	5,558	2,452	4,881
Houston	12,194	29,205	9,144	26,874
Jackson	6,367	14,068	8,635	11,534
Jefferson	166,015	149,843	132,286	158,680
Lamar	1,614	5,419	1,956	4,894
Lauderdale	13,318	24,050	14,628	22,161
Lawrence	5,159	9,269	6,155	7,730
Lee	21,410	32,344	16,227	27,972
Limestone	9,530	23,588	9,126	19,702
Lowndes	5,447	1,807	4,233	1,786
Macon	9,444	1,396	7,800	1,570
Madison	64,062	86,910	52,644	77,173
Marengo	5,925	5,511	5,037	5,255
Marion	2,597	9,530	3,808	8,983
Marshall	7,021	25,680	8,452	22,783
Mobile	81,741	97,670	63,732	92,014
Monroe	5,023	6,173	3,666	5,831
Montgomery	61,999	41,972	45,160	44,097
Morgan	13,882	35,986	14,131	32,477
Perry	4,423	1,676	3,767	1,738
Pickens	4,584	5,426	3,915	5,170
Pike	5,856	7,981	4,334	7,483
Randolph	3,062	7,169	2,817	6,127
Russell	10,078	8,700	8,375	8,337
St. Clair	6,088	27,630	5,456	23,500
Shelby	20,575	68,945	14,850	63,435
Sumter	5,218	1,723	4,527	1,880
Talladega	13,769	20,109	11,374	18,331
Tallapoosa	6,052	13,105	5,451	12,392
Tuscaloosa	32,738	45,351	26,447	42,877
Walker	7,418	20,719	9,016	19,167
Washington	3,032	5,592	3,145	5,060
Wilcox	4,553	1,849	3,838	1,834
Winston	1,756	8,099	2,236	8,130
Totals	**813,479**	**1,266,546**	**693,933**	**1,176,394**

Alabama Vote Since 1952

2008: McCain, R., 1,266,546; Obama, D., 813,479; Nader, Ind., 6,788; Barr, Ind., 4,991; Baldwin, Ind., 4,310.

2004: Bush, R., 1,176,394; Kerry, D., 693,933; Nader, Ind., 6,701; Badnarik, Ind., 3,529; Peroutka, Ind., 1,994.

2000: Bush, R., 941,173; Gore, D., 692,611; Nader, Ind., 18,323; Buchanan, Ind., 6,351; Browne, LB., 5,893; Phillips, Ind., 775; Hagelin, Ind., 447.

1996: Dole, R., 769,044; Clinton, D., 662,165; Perot, RF., 92,149; Browne, LB., 5,290; Phillips, Ind., 2,365; Hagelin, Natural Law, 1,697; Harris, Ind., 516.

1992: Bush, R., 804,283; Clinton, D., 690,080; Perot, Ind., 183,109; Marrou, LB., 5,737; Fulani, New Alliance, 2,161.

1988: Bush, R., 815,576; Dukakis, D., 549,506; Paul, LB., 8,460; Fulani, Ind., 3,311.

1984: Reagan, R., 872,849; Mondale, D., 551,899; Bergland, LB., 9,504.

1980: Reagan, R., 654,192; Carter, D., 636,730; Anderson, Ind., 16,481; Rarick, Amer. Ind., 15,010; Clark, LB., 13,318; Bubar, Statesman, 1,743; Hall, Comm., 1,629; DeBerry, Soc. Workers, 1,303; McReynolds, Soc., 1,006; Commoner, Citizens, 517.

1976: Carter, D., 659,170; Ford, R., 504,070; Maddox, Amer. Ind., 9,198; Bubar, Prohib., 6,669; Hall, Comm., 1,954; MacBride, LB., 1,481.

1972: Nixon, R., 728,701; McGovern, D., 219,108 plus 37,815 Natl. Dem. Party of AL; Schmitz, Conservative, 11,918; Munn, Prohib., 8,551.

1968: Wallace, 3rd party, 691,425; Humphrey, D., 196,579; Nixon, R., 146,923; Munn, Prohib., 4,022.

1964: Goldwater, R., 479,085; D. (electors unpledged), 209,848; scattered, 105.

1960: Kennedy, D., 324,050; Nixon, R., 237,981; Faubus, States' Rights, 4,367; Decker, Prohib., 2,106; King, Afro-Americans, 1,485; scattered, 236.

1956: Stevenson, D., 290,844; Eisenhower, R., 195,694; Ind. electors, 20,323.

1952: Stevenson, D., 275,075; Eisenhower, R., 149,231; Hamblen, Prohib., 1,814.

Alaska

District	2008 Obama (D)	McCain (R)	2004 Kerry (D)	Bush (R)
No. 1	2,957	4,149	1,949	4,522
No. 2	3,468	4,029	3,248	4,162
No. 3	5,657	2,828	4,808	3,031
No. 4	4,161	4,302	3,063	4,043
No. 5	3,339	3,426	2,974	3,674
No. 6	2,351	4,234	2,105	3,746
No. 7	4,283	6,297	3,259	5,272
No. 8	4,995	4,983	4,009	4,194
No. 9	2,805	4,141	2,232	3,909
No. 10	2,074	3,392	1,725	3,720
No. 11	1,924	7,736	1,523	6,416
No. 12	1,914	5,467	1,766	5,679
No. 13	2,800	8,432	2,325	6,489
No. 14	2,132	8,108	1,909	6,504
No. 15	2,510	8,227	2,331	6,030
No. 16	2,636	7,774	2,356	6,559
No. 17	2,645	6,621	2,190	6,366
No. 18	2,046	4,252	1,632	4,400
No. 19	3,095	4,106	2,521	4,087
No. 20	2,474	2,536	1,925	2,705
No. 21	3,647	4,837	2,917	4,836
No. 22	3,337	3,109	2,855	3,225
No. 23	4,075	2,808	3,449	2,789
No. 24	3,380	4,127	2,684	3,835
No. 25	3,233	3,042	2,837	3,062
No. 26	4,472	4,037	3,878	3,946
No. 27	3,130	5,159	2,670	4,713
No. 28	3,642	5,953	2,679	5,271
No. 29	2,684	4,127	2,058	3,874
No. 30	3,486	5,500	2,693	4,864
No. 31	3,596	6,419	2,853	5,803
No. 32	5,176	6,867	4,118	5,981
No. 33	2,089	6,571	1,879	5,523
No. 34	1,920	7,358	1,720	6,065
No. 35	4,959	4,254	3,780	4,442
No. 36	2,264	4,201	1,985	4,080
No. 37	1,868	2,661	1,587	2,591
No. 38	2,056	2,549	1,983	2,004
No. 39	2,323	2,695	1,963	2,407
No. 40	2,686	2,137	1,926	2,743
Totals	**123,594**	**193,841**	**111,025**	**190,889**

Alaska Vote Since 1960

2008: McCain, R., 193,841; Obama, D., 123,594; Nader, Ind., 3,783; Baldwin, AK Ind., 1,660; Barr, LB., 1,589.

2004: Bush, R., 190,889; Kerry, D., 111,025; Nader, Populist, 5,069; Peroutka, AK Ind., 2,092; Badnarik, LB., 1,675; Cobb, Green, 1,058.

2000: Bush, R., 167,398; Gore, D., 79,004; Nader, Green, 28,747; Buchanan, RF., 5,192; Browne, LB., 2,636; Hagelin, Natural Law, 919; Phillips, Const., 596.

1996: Dole, R., 122,746; Clinton, D., 80,380; Perot, RF., 26,333; Nader, Green, 7,597; Browne, LB., 2,276; Phillips, U.S. Taxpayers, 925; Hagelin, Natural Law, 729.

1992: Bush, R., 102,000; Clinton, D., 78,294; Perot, Ind., 73,481; Gritz, Populist/America First, 1,379; Marrou, LB., 1,378.

1988: Bush, R., 119,251; Dukakis, D., 72,584; Paul, LB., 5,484; Fulani, New Alliance, 1,024.

1984: Reagan, R., 138,377; Mondale, D., 62,007; Bergland, LB., 6,378.

1980: Reagan, R., 86,112; Carter, D., 41,842; Clark, LB., 18,479; Anderson, Ind., 11,155; write-in, 857.
1976: Ford, R., 71,555; Carter, D., 44,058; MacBride, LB., 6,785.
1972: Nixon, R., 55,349; McGovern, D., 32,967; Schmitz, Amer., 6,903.
1968: Nixon, R., 37,600; Humphrey, D., 35,411; Wallace, 3rd party, 10,024.
1964: Johnson, D., 44,329; Goldwater, R., 22,930.
1960: Nixon, R., 30,953; Kennedy, D., 29,809.

Arizona

County	2008		2004	
	Obama (D)	McCain (R)	Kerry (D)	Bush (R)
Apache	15,141	8,381	15,658	8,384
Cochise	18,526	28,360	17,514	26,556
Coconino	27,064	19,449	29,243	22,526
Gila	7,566	13,425	8,314	12,343
Graham	3,487	8,375	3,185	7,467
Greenlee	1,165	1,711	1,146	1,899
La Paz	1,794	3,302	1,849	3,158
Maricopa	542,206	675,027	504,849	679,455
Mohave	21,286	42,729	20,503	36,794
Navajo	14,953	19,199	14,815	17,227
Pima	191,465	168,670	193,128	171,109
Pinal	42,905	57,714	27,252	37,006
Santa Cruz	8,680	4,517	6,909	4,668
Yavapai	34,731	58,043	33,127	53,468
Yuma	17,679	23,658	16,032	22,184
Totals	**1,034,707**	**1,230,111**	**893,524**	**1,104,294**

Arizona Vote Since 1952

2008: McCain, R., 1,230,111; Obama, D., 1,034,707; Barr, LB., 12,555; Nader, New Prog., 11,301; McKinney, Green, 3,406.
2004: Bush, R., 1,104,294; Kerry, D., 893,524; Badnarik, LB., 11,856.
2000: Bush, R., 781,652; Gore, D., 685,341; Nader, Green, 45,645; Buchanan, RF., 12,373; Smith, LB., 5,775; Hagelin, Natural Law, 1,120.
1996: Clinton, D., 653,288; Dole, R., 622,073; Perot, RF., 112,072; Browne, LB., 14,358.
1992: Bush, R., 572,086; Clinton, D., 543,050; Perot, Ind., 353,741; Gritz, Populist/America First, 8,141; Marrou, LB., 6,759; Hagelin, Natural Law, 2,267.
1988: Bush, R., 702,541; Dukakis, D., 454,029; Paul, LB., 13,351; Fulani, New Alliance, 1,662.
1984: Reagan, R., 681,416; Mondale, D., 333,854; Bergland, LB., 10,585.
1980: Reagan, R., 529,688; Carter, D., 246,843; Anderson, Ind., 76,952; Clark, LB., 18,784; De Berry, Soc. Workers, 1,100; Commoner, Citizens, 551; Hall, Comm., 25; Griswold, Workers World, 2.
1976: Ford, R., 418,642; Carter, D., 295,602; McCarthy, Ind., 19,229; MacBride, LB., 7,647; Camejo, Soc. Workers, 928; Anderson, Amer., 564; Maddox, Amer. Ind., 85.
1972: Nixon, R., 402,812; McGovern, D., 198,540; Jenness, Soc. Workers, 30,945; Schmitz, Amer. Ind., 21,208.
1968: Nixon, R., 266,721; Humphrey, D., 170,514; Wallace, 3rd party, 46,573; McCarthy, New Party, 2,751; Cleaver, Peace/ Freedom, 217; Halstead, Soc. Workers, 85; Blomen, Soc. Labor, 75.
1964: Goldwater, R., 242,535; Johnson, D., 237,753; Hass, Soc. Labor, 482.
1960: Nixon, R., 221,241; Kennedy, D., 176,781; Hass, Soc. Labor, 469.
1956: Eisenhower, R., 176,990; Stevenson, D., 112,880; Andrews, Ind., 303.
1952: Eisenhower, R., 152,042; Stevenson, D., 108,528.

Arkansas

County	2008		2004	
	Obama (D)	McCain (R)	Kerry (D)	Bush (R)
Arkansas	2,616	4,184	3,110	3,789
Ashley	2,883	5,166	3,881	4,567
Baxter	6,531	12,841	7,129	11,128
Benton	23,412	50,855	20,756	46,571
Boone	4,429	10,559	4,640	9,793
Bradley	1,673	2,259	2,206	2,011
Calhoun	690	1,459	939	1,340
Carroll	4,160	6,070	4,161	6,184
Chicot	2,927	1,935	2,993	1,725
Clark	4,265	4,608	4,990	4,144
Clay	2,245	3,032	3,264	2,759
Cleburne	2,951	7,962	4,517	7,107
Cleveland	909	2,443	1,450	2,009
Columbia	3,496	5,711	4,108	5,729
Conway	3,144	4,687	3,982	4,009
Craighead	11,279	18,859	13,665	15,818
Crawford	5,265	14,746	6,764	13,391
Crittenden	9,361	7,420	8,277	6,930
Cross	2,580	4,393	3,135	3,864
Dallas	1,470	1,756	1,671	1,700
Desha	2,546	1,977	2,851	1,729
Drew	2,598	3,860	2,952	3,262
Faulkner	14,099	25,310	14,538	21,514
Franklin	1,868	4,407	3,008	4,181

County	2008		2004	
	Obama (D)	McCain (R)	Kerry (D)	Bush (R)
Fulton	1,818	2,700	2,370	2,522
Garland	14,987	25,011	18,040	21,734
Grant	1,562	5,022	2,524	4,205
Greene	4,541	8,578	6,564	7,237
Hempstead	2,861	4,252	3,817	3,580
Hot Spring	4,216	7,014	5,901	5,960
Howard	1,745	2,956	2,166	2,736
Independence	3,551	8,023	5,443	7,430
Izard	1,767	3,141	2,586	2,833
Jackson	2,220	3,146	3,515	2,624
Jefferson	18,272	10,614	19,675	10,218
Johnson	3,043	4,911	3,622	4,311
Lafayette	1,133	1,685	1,567	1,604
Lawrence	2,136	3,357	3,544	2,951
Lee	2,263	1,455	2,548	1,492
Lincoln	1,709	2,513	2,149	1,921
Little River	1,752	3,247	2,677	2,575
Logan	2,196	5,136	3,361	5,076
Lonoke	5,880	17,046	7,454	14,398
Madison	2,142	3,970	2,421	3,873
Marion	2,379	4,510	2,602	4,127
Miller	4,866	9,913	6,139	8,448
Mississippi	6,638	6,967	7,593	6,121
Monroe	1,505	1,602	2,049	1,586
Montgomery	1,090	2,359	1,524	2,367
Nevada	1,471	2,061	1,694	1,752
Newton	740	1,716	1,506	2,779
Ouachita	4,598	5,602	5,188	5,345
Perry	1,351	2,743	1,921	2,435
Phillips	5,687	3,094	5,642	3,161
Pike	1,087	2,727	1,310	2,013
Poinsett	2,740	4,900	4,069	3,555
Polk	1,955	5,470	2,473	5,192
Pope	5,986	15,535	7,100	13,614
Prairie	1,048	2,223	1,562	2,030
Pulaski	88,632	70,094	84,532	67,903
Randolph	2,460	3,601	3,412	3,158
St. Francis	5,910	3,571	5,684	3,815
Saline	12,657	30,842	14,153	24,864
Scott	1,052	2,790	1,473	2,514
Searcy	1,161	2,726	1,370	2,565
Sebastian	13,592	28,404	16,479	27,303
Sevier	1,254	3,052	2,035	2,516
Sharp	2,436	4,535	3,265	4,097
Stone	1,756	3,810	2,255	3,188
Union	6,177	10,657	7,071	10,502
Van Buren	2,145	4,269	3,310	3,988
Washington	28,965	37,915	27,597	35,726
White	6,708	19,429	9,129	17,001
Woodruff	1,350	1,135	1,972	1,021
Yell	2,001	3,805	2,913	3,678
Totals	**422,310**	**638,017**	**469,953**	**572,898**

Arkansas Vote Since 1952

2008: McCain, R., 638,017; Obama, D., 422,310; Nader, Ind., 12,882; Barr, LB., 4,776; Baldwin, Const., 4,023; McKinney, Green, 3,470; La Riva, Socialism/Liberation, 1,139.
2004: Bush, R., 572,898; Kerry, D., 469,953; Nader, Populist, 6,171; Badnarik, LB., 2,352; Peroutka, Const., 2,083; Cobb, Green, 1,488.
2000: Bush, R., 472,940; Gore, D., 422,768; Nader, Green, 13,421; Buchanan, RF., 7,358; Browne, LB., 2,781; Phillips, Const., 1,415; Hagelin, Natural Law, 1,098.
1996: Clinton, D., 475,171; Dole, R., 325,416; Perot, RF., 69,884; Nader, Ind., 3,649; Browne, Ind., 3,076; Phillips, Ind., 2,065; Forbes, Ind., 932; Collins, Ind., 823; Masters, Ind., 749; Moorehead, Ind., 747; Hagelin, Ind., 729; Hollis, Ind., 538; Dodge, Ind., 483.
1992: Clinton, D., 505,823; Bush, R., 337,324; Perot, Ind., 99,132; Phillips, U.S. Taxpayers, 1,437; Marrou, LB., 1,261; Fulani, New Alliance, 1,022.
1988: Bush, R., 466,578; Dukakis, D., 349,237; Duke, Populist, 5,146; Paul, LB., 3,297.
1984: Reagan, R., 534,774; Mondale, D., 338,646; Bergland, LB., 2,220.
1980: Reagan, R., 403,164; Carter, D., 398,041; Anderson, Ind., 22,468; Clark, LB., 8,970; Commoner, Citizens, 2,345; Bubar, Statesman, 1,350; Hall, Comm., 1,244.
1976: Carter, D., 498,604; Ford, R., 267,903; McCarthy, Ind., 639; Anderson, Amer. Ind., 389.
1972: Nixon, R., 445,751; McGovern, D., 198,899; Schmitz, Amer. Ind., 3,016.
1968: Wallace, 3rd party, 235,627; Nixon, R., 189,062; Humphrey, D., 184,901.
1964: Johnson, D., 314,197; Goldwater, R., 243,264; Kasper, Natl. States' Rights, 2,965.
1960: Kennedy, D., 215,049; Nixon, R., 184,508; Faubus, Natl. States' Rights, 28,952.
1956: Stevenson, D., 213,277; Eisenhower, R., 186,287; Andrews, Ind., 7,008.
1952: Stevenson, D., 226,300; Eisenhower, R., 177,155; Hamblen, Prohib., 886; MacArthur, Christian Nationalist, 458; Hass, Soc. Labor, 1.

California

County	2008 Obama (D)	McCain (R)	2004 Kerry (D)	Bush (R)
Alameda	489,102	119,553	422,585	130,911
Alpine	422	252	373	311
Amador	7,813	10,561	6,541	11,107
Butte	41,474	39,954	42,448	51,662
Calaveras	8,464	10,979	8,286	13,601
Colusa	2,206	3,273	1,947	4,142
Contra Costa	292,620	132,215	257,254	150,608
Del Norte	3,869	4,429	3,892	5,356
El Dorado	39,442	49,349	32,242	52,878
Fresno	127,093	124,990	103,154	141,988
Glenn	3,693	5,874	2,995	6,308
Humboldt	30,807	16,704	37,988	25,714
Imperial	17,791	10,850	17,964	15,890
Inyo	3,208	3,833	3,350	5,091
Kern	87,806	129,290	68,603	140,417
Kings	14,747	19,710	10,833	21,003
Lake	11,986	8,034	13,141	11,093
Lassen	3,586	7,483	3,158	8,126
Los Angeles	2,162,842	915,763	1,907,736	1,076,225
Madera	14,997	20,251	13,481	24,871
Marin	101,638	26,912	99,070	34,378
Mariposa	3,766	4,880	3,251	5,215
Mendocino	15,963	6,256	24,385	12,955
Merced	34,031	28,704	24,491	32,773
Modoc	1,311	2,980	1,149	3,235
Mono	2,827	2,159	2,628	2,621
Monterey	81,282	36,364	75,241	47,838
Napa	38,703	19,413	33,666	22,059
Nevada	28,037	25,211	24,220	28,790
Orange	527,334	562,211	419,239	641,832
Placer	64,460	80,209	55,573	95,969
Plumas	4,715	6,034	4,129	6,905
Riverside	210,905	197,517	228,806	322,473
Sacramento	293,516	202,433	236,657	235,539
San Benito	11,413	7,167	9,851	8,698
San Bernardino	291,717	263,044	227,789	289,306
San Diego	653,037	531,732	526,437	596,033
San Francisco	311,714	51,070	296,772	54,355
San Joaquin	105,932	87,279	87,012	100,978
San Luis Obispo	66,978	60,253	58,742	67,995
San Mateo	222,767	75,006	197,922	83,315
Santa Barbara	102,424	64,508	90,314	76,806
Santa Clara	386,279	158,630	386,100	209,094
Santa Cruz	78,495	20,063	89,102	30,354
Shasta	24,322	41,482	24,339	52,249
Sierra	743	1,157	646	1,249
Siskiyou	7,575	9,288	7,880	12,673
Solano	98,775	54,736	85,096	62,301
Sonoma	144,399	47,184	148,261	68,204
Stanislaus	75,106	74,025	58,829	85,407
Sutter	7,360	10,445	9,602	20,254
Tehama	8,801	14,618	7,504	15,572
Trinity	3,233	2,940	2,782	3,560
Tulare	33,491	46,047	32,494	65,399
Tuolumne	11,532	14,988	10,104	15,745
Ventura	164,699	130,485	148,859	160,314
Yolo	53,488	24,592	42,885	28,005
Yuba	7,107	9,608	5,687	12,076
Totals	**8,274,473**	**5,011,781**	**6,745,485**	**5,509,826**

California Vote Since 1952

2008: Obama, D., 8,274,473; McCain, R., 5,011,781; Nader, Peace/Freedom, 108,381; Barr, LB., 67,582; Alan Keyes, Amer. Ind., 40,673; McKinney, Green, 38,774.

2004: Kerry, D., 6,745,485; Bush, R., 5,509,826; Badnarik, LB., 50,165; Cobb, Green, 40,771; Peltier, Peace/Freedom, 27,607; Peroutka, Amer. Ind., 26,645.

2000: Gore, D., 5,861,203; Bush, R., 4,567,429; Nader, Green, 418,707; Browne, LB., 45,520; Buchanan, RF., 44,987; Phillips, Amer. Ind., 17,042; Hagelin, Natural Law, 10,934.

1996: Clinton, D., 5,119,835; Dole, R., 3,828,380; Perot, RF., 697,847; Nader, Green, 237,016; Browne, LB., 73,600; Feinland, Peace/Freedom, 25,332; Phillips, Amer. Ind., 21,202; Hagelin, Natural Law, 15,403.

1992: Clinton, D., 5,121,325; Bush, R., 3,630,575; Perot, Ind., 2,296,006; Marrou, LB., 48,139; Daniels, Ind., 18,597; Phillips, U.S. Taxpayers, 12,711.

1988: Bush, R., 5,054,917; Dukakis, D., 4,702,233; Paul, LB., 70,105; Fulani, Ind., 31,181.

1984: Reagan, R., 5,305,410; Mondale, D., 3,815,947; Bergland, LB., 48,400.

1980: Reagan, R., 4,524,858; Carter, D., 3,083,661; Anderson, Ind., 739,833; Clark, LB., 148,434; Commoner, Ind., 61,063; Smith, Peace/Freedom, 18,116; Rarick, Amer. Ind., 9,856.

1976: Ford, R., 3,882,244; Carter, D., 3,742,284; McCarthy, write-in, 58,412; MacBride, LB., 56,388; Maddox, Amer. Ind., 51,098; Wright, People's, 41,731; Camejo, Soc. Workers, 17,259; Hall, Comm., 12,766; write-in, 4,935.

1972: Nixon, R., 4,602,096; McGovern, D., 3,475,847; Schmitz, Amer. Ind., 232,554; Spock, Peace/Freedom, 55,167; Hospers, LB., 980; Jenness, Soc. Workers, 574; Hall, Comm., 373; Fisher, Soc. Labor, 197; Munn, Prohib., 53; Green, Universal, 21.

1968: Nixon, R., 3,467,664; Humphrey, D., 3,244,318; Wallace, 3rd party, 487,270; Peace/Freedom, 27,707; McCarthy, Alternative, 20,721; Gregory, write-in, 3,230; Blomen, Soc. Labor, 341; Mitchell, Comm., 260; Munn, Prohib., 59; Soeters, Defense, 17.

1964: Johnson, D., 4,171,877; Goldwater, R., 2,879,108; Hass, Soc. Labor, 489; DeBerry, Soc. Workers, 378; Munn, Prohib., 305; Hensley, Universal, 19.

1960: Nixon, R., 3,259,722; Kennedy, D., 3,224,099; Decker, Prohib., 21,706; Hass, Soc. Labor, 1,051.

1956: Eisenhower, R., 3,027,668; Stevenson, D., 2,420,136; Holtwick, Prohib., 11,119; Andrews, Const., 6,087; Hass, Soc. Labor, 300; Hoopes, Soc., 123; Dobbs, Soc. Workers, 96; Smith, Christian Nationalist, 8.

1952: Eisenhower, R., 2,897,310; Stevenson, D., 2,197,548; Hallinan, Prog., 24,106; Hamblen, Prohib., 15,653; MacArthur, (Tenny Ticket), 3,326; Hass, Soc. Labor, 273; Hoopes, Soc., 206; (Kellems Ticket) 178; scattered, 3,249.

Colorado

County	2008 Obama (D)	McCain (R)	2004 Kerry (D)	Bush (R)
Adams	90,113	62,321	69,122	65,912
Alamosa	3,521	2,635	3,017	3,179
Arapahoe	128,366	100,409	110,262	119,475
Archuleta	2,822	3,618	2,141	3,601
Baca	532	1,568	483	1,680
Bent	799	1,077	785	1,338
Boulder	115,339	41,644	105,564	51,586
Broomfield	16,031	12,675	10,935	12,007
Chaffee	4,827	4,832	3,766	4,875
Cheyenne	198	890	198	923
Clear Creek	3,295	2,278	2,989	2,522
Conejos	2,106	1,616	1,894	1,864
Costilla	1,236	411	1,170	566
Crowley	552	976	478	1,006
Custer	914	1,668	739	1,657
Delta	5,007	9,905	4,224	9,722
Denver	195,499	60,226	166,135	69,903
Dolores	356	803	333	785
Douglas	51,813	73,225	39,661	80,651
Eagle	13,055	8,112	9,744	8,533
Elbert	3,775	9,030	2,834	8,389
El Paso	104,670	155,914	77,648	161,361
Fremont	6,801	12,595	5,933	12,313
Garfield	10,847	10,932	9,228	11,123
Gilpin	1,944	1,249	1,807	1,329
Grand	3,961	4,088	3,243	4,260
Gunnison	5,512	3,112	4,782	3,479
Hinsdale	239	343	236	355
Huerfano	1,989	1,582	1,663	1,700
Jackson	277	624	210	710
Jefferson	155,020	129,291	126,558	140,644
Kiowa	172	630	172	712
Kit Carson	898	2,420	729	2,721
Lake	1,847	1,076	1,623	1,261
La Plata	15,422	11,170	13,409	11,704
Larimer	84,461	68,932	68,266	75,884
Las Animas	3,483	3,033	3,300	3,196
Lincoln	543	1,683	503	1,819
Logan	2,837	5,986	2,491	6,168
Mesa	23,470	43,669	19,564	41,539
Mineral	270	334	227	383
Moffat	1,566	4,101	1,355	4,247
Montezuma	4,619	6,913	3,867	6,988
Montrose	6,115	11,525	4,776	11,218
Morgan	3,762	6,222	3,039	6,787
Otero	3,454	4,324	3,164	4,947
Ouray	1,629	1,360	1,278	1,402
Park	4,196	4,835	3,445	4,781
Phillips	587	1,513	582	1,717
Pitkin	7,260	2,448	6,335	2,784
Prowers	1,464	3,026	1,308	3,392
Pueblo	38,074	28,523	35,369	31,117
Rio Blanco	654	2,425	566	2,403
Rio Grande	2,427	2,916	2,006	3,448
Routt	8,133	4,634	6,392	5,199
Saguache	1,620	913	1,594	1,163
San Juan	264	218	253	216
San Miguel	3,345	930	2,876	1,079
Sedgwick	468	857	374	971
Summit	9,700	4,845	8,144	5,370
Teller	4,370	7,939	3,556	8,094
Washington	518	1,935	455	2,050
Weld	46,644	55,913	31,868	55,551
Yuma	1,105	3,238	1,064	3,456
Totals	**1,288,633**	**1,073,629**	**1,001,732**	**1,101,255**

Colorado Vote Since 1952

2008: Obama, D., 1,288,633; McCain, R., 1,073,629; Nader, Unaff., 13,352; Barr, LB., 10,898; Baldwin, Const., 6,233; Alan Keyes, Amer. Ind., 3,051; McKinney, Green, 2,822; McEnulty, unaff., 829; Jay, Boston Tea, 598; Allen, HeartQuake '08, 348; Stevens, Objectivist, 336; Moore, Soc. USA, 226; La Riva, Socialism/Liberation, 158; Harris, Soc. Workers, 154; Lyttle, U.S. Pacifist, 110; Amondson, Prohib., 85.

2004: Bush, R., 1,101,255; Kerry, D., 1,001,732; Nader, RF., 12,718; Badnarik, LB., 7,664; Peroutka, Amer. Const., 2,562; Cobb, Green, 1,591; Andress, Ind., 804; Amondson, Concerns of People, 378; Van Auken, Soc. Equal., 329; Harris, Soc. Wkrs., 241; Brown, Soc., 216; Dodge, Prohib., 140.

2000: Bush, R., 883,748; Gore, D., 738,227; Nader, Green, 91,434; Browne, LB., 12,799; Buchanan, RF., 10,465; Hagelin, RF., 2,240; Phillips, Amer. Const., 1,319; McReynolds, Soc., 712; Harris, Soc. Workers, 216; Dodge, Prohib., 208.

1996: Dole, R., 691,848; Clinton, D., 671,152; Perot, RF., 99,629; Nader, Green, 25,070; Browne, LB., 12,392; Phillips, Amer. Const., 2,813; Collins, Ind., 2,809; Hagelin, Natural Law, 2,547; Hollis, Soc., 669; Moorehead, Workers World, 599; Templin, Amer., 557; Dodge, Prohib., 375; Harris, Soc. Workers, 244.

1992: Clinton, D., 629,681; Bush, R., 562,850; Perot, Ind., 366,010; Marrou, LB., 8,669; Fulani, New Alliance, 1,608.

1988: Bush, R., 728,177; Dukakis, D., 621,453; Paul, LB., 15,482; Dodge, Prohib., 4,604.

1984: Reagan, R., 821,817; Mondale, D., 454,975; Bergland, LB., 11,257.

1980: Reagan, R., 652,264; Carter, D., 367,973; Anderson, Ind., 130,633; Clark, LB., 25,744; Commoner, Citizens, 5,614; Bubar, Statesman, 1,180; Pulley, Soc., 520; Hall, Comm., 487.

1976: Ford, R., 584,367; Carter, D., 460,353; McCarthy, Ind., 26,107; MacBride, LB., 5,330; Bubar, Prohib., 2,882.

1972: Nixon, R., 597,189; McGovern, D., 329,980; Schmitz, Amer., 17,269; Fisher, Soc. Labor, 4,361; Spock, People's, 2,403; Hospers, LB., 1,111; Jenness, Soc. Workers, 555; Munn, Prohib., 467; Hall, Comm., 432.

1968: Nixon, R., 409,345; Humphrey, D., 335,174; Wallace, 3rd party, 60,813; Blomen, Soc. Labor, 3,016; Gregory, New Party, 1,393; Munn, Prohib., 275; Halstead, Soc. Workers, 235.

1964: Johnson, D., 476,024; Goldwater, R., 296,767; DeBerry, Soc. Workers, 2,537; Munn, Prohib., 1,356; Hass, Soc. Labor, 302.

1960: Nixon, R., 402,242; Kennedy, D., 330,629; Hass, Soc. Labor, 2,803; Dobbs, Soc. Workers, 572.

1956: Eisenhower, R., 394,479; Stevenson, D., 263,997; Hass, Soc. Labor, 3,308; Andrews, Ind., 759; Hoopes, Soc., 531.

1952: Eisenhower, R., 379,782; Stevenson, D., 245,504; MacArthur, Const., 2,181; Hallinan, Prog., 1,919; Hoopes, Soc., 365; Hass, Soc. Labor, 352.

Connecticut

City	2008		2004	
	Obama (D)	McCain (R)	Kerry (D)	Bush (R)
Bridgeport	33,941	6,501	26,280	10,326
Bristol	15,774	9,467	14,201	10,619
Danbury	15,962	10,697	13,477	12,399
Fairfield	17,236	13,071	15,068	14,706
Greenwich	16,233	13,937	14,334	15,830
Hartford	31,741	2,686	22,595	4,623
New Britain	16,742	5,442	14,122	6,560
New Haven	38,452	5,017	30,979	7,175
Norwalk	24,489	12,651	20,615	14,201
Stamford	31,733	17,510	27,588	18,866
Waterbury	22,594	12,821	16,122	15,961
West Hartford	23,576	10,021	21,612	11,641
Other	705,847	507,867	620,495	550,919
Totals	997,772	629,428	857,488	693,826

Connecticut Vote Since 1952

2008: Obama, D., 997,772; McCain, R., 629,428; Nader, Ind., 19,162.

2004: Kerry, D., 857,488; Bush, R., 693,826; Nader, petitioning cand., 12,969; Cobb, Green, 9,564; Badnarik, LB., 3,367; Peroutka, Concerned Citizens, 1,543.

2000: Gore, D., 816,015; Bush, R., 561,094; Nader, Green, 64,452; Phillips, Concerned Citizens, 9,695; Buchanan, RF., 4,731; Browne, LB., 3,484.

1996: Clinton, D., 735,740; Dole, R., 483,109; Perot, RF., 139,523; Nader, Green, 24,321; Browne, LB., 5,788; Phillips, Concerned Citizens, 2,425; Hagelin, Natural Law, 1,703.

1992: Clinton, D., 682,318; Bush, R., 578,313; Perot, Ind., 348,771; Marrou, LB., 5,391; Fulani, New Alliance, 1,363.

1988: Bush, R., 750,241; Dukakis, D., 676,584; Paul, LB., 14,071; Fulani, New Alliance, 2,491.

1984: Reagan, R., 890,877; Mondale, D., 569,597.

1980: Reagan, R., 677,210; Carter, D., 541,732; Anderson, Ind., 171,807; Clark, LB., 8,570; Commoner, Citizens, 6,130; scattered, 836.

1976: Ford, R., 719,261; Carter, D., 647,895; Maddox, George Wallace Party, 7,101; LaRouche, U.S. Labor, 1,789.

1972: Nixon, R., 810,763; McGovern, D., 555,498; Schmitz, Amer., 17,239; scattered, 777.

1968: Humphrey, D., 621,561; Nixon, R., 556,721; Wallace, 3rd party, 76,650; scattered, 1,300.

1964: Johnson, D., 826,269; Goldwater, R., 390,996; scattered, 1,313.

1960: Kennedy, D., 657,055; Nixon, R., 565,813.

1956: Eisenhower, R., 711,837; Stevenson, D., 405,079; scattered, 205.

1952: Eisenhower, R., 611,012; Stevenson, D., 481,649; Hoopes, Soc., 2,244; Hallinan, Prog., 1,466; Hass, Soc. Labor, 535; write-in, 5.

Delaware

County	2008		2004	
	Obama (D)	McCain (R)	Kerry (D)	Bush (R)
Kent	36,383	29,822	23,875	31,578
New Castle	178,712	74,595	146,179	93,079
Sussex	40,299	47,939	30,098	47,003
Totals	**255,459**	**152,374**	**200,152**	**171,660**

Delaware Vote Since 1952

2008: Obama, D., 255,459; McCain, R., 152,374; Nader, Ind. (DE), 2,401; Barr, LB., 1,109; Baldwin, Const., 626; McKinney, Green, 385; Calero, Soc. Workers, 58.

2004: Kerry, D., 200,152; Bush, R., 171,660; Nader, Ind., 2,153; Badnarik, LB., 586; Peroutka, Const., 289; Cobb, Green, 250; Brown, Natural Law, 100.

2000: Gore, D., 180,068; Bush, R., 137,288; Nader, Green, 8,307; Buchanan, RF., 777; Browne, LB., 774; Phillips, Const., 208; Hagelin, Natural Law, 107.

1996: Clinton, D., 140,355; Dole, R., 99,062; Perot, RF., 28,719; Browne, LB., 2,052; Phillips, U.S. Taxpayers, 348; Hagelin, Natural Law, 274.

1992: Clinton, D., 126,054; Bush, R., 102,313; Perot, Ind., 59,213; Fulani, New Alliance, 1,105.

1988: Bush, R., 139,639; Dukakis, D., 108,647; Paul, LB., 1,162; Fulani, New Alliance, 443.

1984: Reagan, R., 152,190; Mondale, D., 101,656; Bergland, LB., 268.

1980: Reagan, R., 111,252; Carter, D., 105,754; Anderson, Ind., 16,288; Clark, LB., 1,974; Greaves, Amer., 400.

1976: Carter, D., 122,596; Ford, R., 109,831; McCarthy, nonpartisan, 2,437; Anderson, Amer., 645; LaRouche, U.S. Labor, 136; Bubar, Prohib., 103; Levin, Soc. Labor, 86.

1972: Nixon, R., 140,357; McGovern, D., 92,283; Schmitz, Amer., 2,638; Munn, Prohib., 238.

1968: Nixon, R., 96,714; Humphrey, D., 89,194; Wallace, 3rd party, 28,459.

1964: Johnson, D., 122,704; Goldwater, R., 78,078; Munn, Prohib., 425; Hass, Soc. Labor, 113.

1960: Kennedy, D., 99,590; Nixon, R., 96,373; Faubus, States' Rights, 354; Decker, Prohib., 284; Hass, Soc. Labor, 82.

1956: Eisenhower, R., 98,057; Stevenson, D., 79,421; Oltwick, Prohib., 400; Hass, Soc. Labor, 110.

1952: Eisenhower, R., 90,059; Stevenson, D., 83,315; Hass, Soc. Lab., 242; Hamblen, Prohib., 234; Hallinan, Prog., 155; Hoopes, Soc., 20.

District of Columbia

	2008		2004	
	Obama (D)	McCain (R)	Kerry (D)	Bush (R)
Total	245,800	17,367	202,970	21,256

District of Columbia Vote Since 1964

2008: Obama, D., 245,800; McCain, R., 17,367; Nader, Ind., 958; McKinney, Green, 590.

2004: Kerry, D., 202,970; Bush, R., 21,256; Nader, Ind., 1,485; Cobb, DC Statehood Green, 737; Badnarik, LB., 502; Harris, Soc. Workers, 130.

2000: Gore, D., 171,923; Bush, R., 18,073; Nader, Green, 10,576; Browne, LB., 669; Harris, Soc. Workers, 114.

1996: Clinton, D., 158,220; Dole, R., 17,339; Nader, Green, 4,780; Perot, RF., 3,611; Browne, LB., 588; Hagelin, Natural Law, 283; Harris, Soc. Workers, 257.

1992: Clinton, D., 192,619; Bush, R., 20,698; Perot, Ind., 9,681; Fulani, New Alliance, 1,459; Daniels, Ind., 1,186.

1988: Dukakis, D., 159,407; Bush, R., 27,590; Fulani, New Alliance, 2,901; Paul, LB., 554.

1984: Mondale, D., 180,408; Reagan, R., 29,009; Bergland, LB., 279.

1980: Carter, D., 130,231; Reagan, R., 23,313; Anderson, Ind., 16,131; Commoner, Citizens, 1,826; Clark, LB., 1,104; Hall, Comm., 369; DeBerry, Soc. Workers, 173; Griswold, Workers World, 52; write-in, 692.

1976: Carter, D., 137,818; Ford, R., 27,873; Camejo, Soc. Workers, 545; MacBride, LB., 274; Hall, Comm., 219; LaRouche, U.S. Labor, 157.

1972: McGovern, D., 127,627; Nixon, R., 35,226; Reed, Soc. Workers, 316; Hall, Comm., 252.

1968: Humphrey, D., 139, 566; Nixon, R., 31,012.

1964: Johnson, D., 169,796; Goldwater, R., 28,801.

Florida

County	2008 Obama (D)	McCain (R)	2004 Kerry (D)	Bush (R)
Alachua	73,134	47,025	62,504	47,762
Baker	2,326	8,672	2,180	7,738
Bay	23,603	56,597	21,068	53,404
Bradford	3,430	8,135	3,244	7,557
Brevard	127,400	157,402	110,309	153,068
Broward	487,638	234,690	453,873	244,674
Calhoun	1,821	4,344	2,116	3,782
Charlotte	39,006	45,180	34,256	44,428
Citrus	31,428	43,666	29,277	39,500
Clay	26,635	66,847	18,971	62,078
Collier	52,710	83,238	43,892	83,631
Columbia	9,171	18,668	8,031	16,758
DeSoto	4,378	5,625	3,913	5,524
Dixie	1,921	5,188	1,960	4,434
Duval	192,173	197,171	158,610	220,190
Escambia	61,152	90,826	48,329	93,566
Flagler	24,682	23,931	18,578	19,633
Franklin	2,122	3,799	2,401	3,472
Gadsden	15,566	6,805	14,629	6,253
Gilchrist	1,993	5,654	2,017	4,936
Glades	1,674	2,533	1,718	2,443
Gulf	2,144	4,971	2,407	4,805
Hamilton	2,360	3,179	2,260	2,792
Hardee	2,561	4,758	2,149	5,049
Hendry	4,998	5,779	3,960	5,757
Hernando	18,980	25,220	37,187	42,635
Highlands	17,913	25,903	15,347	25,878
Hillsborough	219,580	209,503	214,132	245,576
Holmes	1,443	7,023	1,810	6,412
Indian River	29,565	39,972	23,956	36,938
Jackson	7,632	13,695	7,555	12,122
Jefferson	4,082	3,794	4,135	3,298
Lafayette	640	2,677	845	2,460
Lake	62,710	82,512	48,221	74,389
Lee	117,878	145,624	93,860	144,176
Leon	91,356	55,521	83,873	51,615
Levy	6,707	11,751	6,074	10,410
Liberty	892	2,337	1,070	1,927
Madison	4,270	4,544	4,050	4,191
Manatee	67,785	78,040	61,262	81,318
Marion	70,771	89,571	57,271	81,283
Martin	33,474	44,110	30,208	41,362
Miami-Dade	491,195	351,462	409,732	361,095
Monroe	20,868	18,906	19,654	19,467
Nassau	10,577	27,326	8,573	23,783
Okaloosa	25,623	68,181	19,368	69,693
Okeechobee	5,102	7,551	5,153	6,978
Orange	271,866	186,079	193,354	192,539
Osceola	59,081	39,489	38,633	43,117
Palm Beach	342,527	211,163	328,687	212,688
Pasco	102,217	109,902	84,749	103,230
Pinellas	243,994	206,909	225,460	225,686
Polk	113,552	128,658	86,009	123,559
Putnam	13,201	19,586	12,412	18,311
St. Johns	35,578	68,800	26,399	59,196
St. Lucie	66,830	52,323	51,835	47,592
Santa Rosa	19,394	55,843	14,659	52,059
Sarasota	102,413	102,650	88,442	104,692
Seminole	99,140	104,885	76,971	108,172
Sumter	17,644	30,859	11,584	19,800
Suwannee	4,572	11,672	4,522	11,153
Taylor	2,787	6,446	3,049	5,467
Union	1,299	3,933	1,251	3,396
Volusia	127,474	113,716	115,519	111,924
Wakulla	5,303	8,869	4,896	6,777
Walton	7,158	19,527	6,213	17,555
Washington	2,858	8,165	2,912	7,369
Totals	**4,282,074**	**4,045,624**	**3,583,544**	**3,964,522**

Florida Vote Since 1952

2008: Obama, D., 4,282,074; McCain, R., 4,045,624; Nader, Ecology (FL), 28,124; Barr, LB., 17,218; Baldwin, Const., 7,915; McKinney, Green, 2,887; Keyes, Amer. Ind., 2,550; La Riva, Socialism/Liberation, 1,516; Jay, Boston Tea, 795; Harris, Soc. Workers, 533; Stevens, Objectivist, 419; Moore, Soc. USA, 405; Amondson, Prohib., 293.

2004: Bush, R., 3,964,522; Kerry, D., 3,583,544; Nader, RF., 32,971; Badnarik, LB., 11,996; Peroutka, Const., 6,626; Cobb, Green, 3,917; Brown, Soc., 3,502; Harris, Soc. Workers, 2,732.

2000: Bush, R., 2,912,790; Gore, D., 2,912,253; Nader, Green, 97,488; Buchanan, RF., 17,484; Browne, LB., 16,415; Hagelin, Natural Law, 2,281; Moorehead, Workers World, 1,804; Phillips, Const., 1,371; McReynolds, Soc., 622; Harris, Soc. Workers, 562.

1996: Clinton, D., 2,545,968; Dole, R., 2,243,324; Perot, RF., 483,776; Browne, LB., 23,312.

1992: Bush, R., 2,171,781; Clinton, D., 2,071,651; Perot, Ind., 1,052,481; Marrou, LB., 15,068.

1988: Bush, R., 2,616,597; Dukakis, D., 1,655,851; Paul, LB., 19,796, Fulani, New Alliance, 6,655.

1984: Reagan, R., 2,728,775; Mondale, D., 1,448,344.

1980: Reagan, R., 2,046,951; Carter, D., 1,419,475; Anderson, Ind., 189,692; Clark, LB., 30,524; write-in, 285.

1976: Carter, D., 1,636,000; Ford, R., 1,469,531; McCarthy, Ind., 23,643; Anderson, Amer., 21,325.

1972: Nixon, R., 1,857,759; McGovern, D., 718,117; scattered, 7,407.

1968: Nixon, R., 886,804; Humphrey, D., 676,794; Wallace, 3rd party, 624,207.

1964: Johnson, D., 948,540; Goldwater, R., 905,941.

1960: Nixon, R., 795,476; Kennedy, D., 748,700.

1956: Eisenhower, R., 643,849; Stevenson, D., 480,371.

1952: Eisenhower, R., 544,036; Stevenson, D., 444,950; scattered, 351.

Georgia

County	2008 Obama (D)	McCain (R)	2004 Kerry (D)	Bush (R)
Appling	1,846	5,085	1,848	4,494
Atkinson	938	1,941	799	1,666
Bacon	817	3,089	930	2,853
Baker	846	828	936	821
Baldwin	8,587	7,823	6,775	7,709
Banks	1,027	5,120	1,149	4,410
Barrow	6,657	17,625	4,095	13,520
Bartow	9,662	25,976	7,741	22,311
Ben Hill	2,590	3,417	2,180	3,331
Berrien	1,468	4,889	1,638	3,917
Bibb	38,851	26,981	29,322	28,107
Bleckley	1,380	3,657	1,281	3,167
Brantley	1,119	5,080	1,258	4,333
Brooks	2,669	3,507	2,193	2,912
Bryan	3,630	9,105	2,590	7,363
Bulloch	9,586	14,174	6,840	12,252
Burke	5,233	4,344	4,213	4,232
Butts	3,064	5,944	2,572	5,119
Calhoun	1,342	862	1,119	890
Camden	6,482	10,502	4,637	9,488
Candler	1,209	2,286	1,096	2,048
Carroll	14,334	28,661	10,224	24,837
Catoosa	6,025	18,218	5,807	16,406
Charlton	1,193	2,458	1,064	2,311
Chatham	62,755	46,829	45,630	45,484
Chattahoochee	830	811	773	905
Chattooga	2,591	5,564	2,809	4,992
Cherokee	22,350	70,279	14,824	58,238
Clarke	29,513	15,309	21,718	15,052
Clay	879	558	798	509
Clayton	82,527	16,506	56,113	23,106
Clinch	989	1,678	750	1,501
Cobb	141,216	170,957	103,955	173,467
Coffee	4,811	8,872	3,979	8,306
Colquitt	4,139	9,185	3,378	8,296
Columbia	15,703	39,322	11,442	35,549
Cook	2,075	3,782	1,733	3,065
Coweta	15,521	37,571	10,647	31,682
Crawford	1,832	3,358	1,552	2,830
Crisp	3,078	4,423	2,357	3,865
Dade	1,608	4,698	1,823	4,368
Dawson	1,632	8,242	1,407	6,649
Decatur	4,424	5,890	3,577	5,348
DeKalb	254,594	65,581	200,787	73,570
Dodge	2,595	5,543	2,384	4,584
Dooly	2,138	1,991	1,973	1,853
Dougherty	26,135	12,547	19,805	13,711
Douglas	27,825	26,812	15,997	25,846
Early	2,602	2,709	1,701	2,495
Echols	201	981	231	757
Effingham	4,936	15,230	3,613	12,503
Elbert	3,366	4,868	2,984	4,626
Emanuel	3,068	5,110	2,774	4,666
Evans	1,374	2,462	1,213	2,291
Fannin	2,611	7,807	2,727	6,862
Fayette	20,313	38,501	14,887	37,346
Floyd	10,691	23,132	10,038	21,400
Forsyth	15,406	59,166	9,201	47,267
Franklin	1,910	6,054	2,245	5,218
Fulton	272,000	130,136	199,436	134,372
Gilmer	2,614	8,408	2,510	7,414
Glascock	210	1,202	250	1,016
Glynn	12,676	20,479	8,962	18,608
Gordon	4,268	13,113	4,028	11,671
Grady	3,539	5,775	3,092	5,068
Greene	3,339	4,532	2,774	4,069
Gwinnett	129,025	158,746	81,708	160,445
Habersham	2,900	11,766	2,750	10,434
Hall	14,457	44,962	10,514	38,883
Hancock	3,535	795	2,715	822
Haralson	2,248	8,658	2,434	7,703
Harris	4,179	10,645	3,400	8,878
Hart	3,365	6,537	3,479	5,500
Heard	1,042	3,133	1,148	2,788
Henry	40,527	47,115	21,096	42,759

County	2008 Obama (D)	McCain (R)	2004 Kerry (D)	Bush (R)
Houston	22,094	33,392	15,054	29,862
Irwin	1,197	2,605	1,051	2,347
Jackson	4,950	17,776	3,468	12,611
Jasper	1,935	3,916	1,558	3,157
Jeff Davis	1,350	3,847	1,277	3,549
Jefferson	4,149	3,061	3,447	3,066
Jenkins	1,482	1,936	1,494	1,898
Johnson	1,198	2,426	1,263	2,279
Jones	4,572	7,782	3,855	6,939
Lamar	2,745	4,871	2,432	4,027
Lanier	1,062	1,787	931	1,641
Laurens	7,769	12,052	6,281	10,883
Lee	3,100	9,923	2,182	8,201
Liberty	10,474	5,828	6,619	6,131
Lincoln	1,650	2,731	1,337	2,309
Long	1,288	2,119	1,033	1,994
Lowndes	17,405	21,085	12,516	18,981
Lumpkin	2,586	8,326	2,091	6,690
Macon	3,251	1,712	2,906	1,851
Madison	2,957	8,224	2,527	7,254
Marion	1,381	1,772	1,275	1,670
McDuffie	3,989	5,400	2,899	4,846
McIntosh	2,905	3,282	2,523	2,837
Meriwether	4,465	4,982	3,709	4,402
Miller	809	1,897	736	1,694
Mitchell	3,872	4,201	3,360	3,885
Monroe	4,106	7,933	3,216	6,522
Montgomery	1,045	2,521	1,007	2,150
Morgan	3,091	5,987	2,304	4,902
Murray	3,026	8,180	2,899	7,745
Muscogee	44,158	29,568	32,867	30,850
Newton	20,827	20,337	10,939	18,095
Oconee	4,825	12,120	3,789	10,276
Oglethorpe	2,232	4,144	1,899	3,688
Paulding	17,229	39,192	9,420	30,843
Peach	5,927	5,173	3,961	4,554
Pickens	2,595	10,004	2,444	8,115
Pierce	1,253	5,500	1,234	4,680
Pike	1,574	6,542	1,506	5,193
Polk	4,052	9,850	3,868	8,467
Pulaski	1,377	2,553	1,294	2,202
Putnam	3,102	5,966	2,880	5,188
Quitman	597	509	543	409
Rabun	2,001	5,487	1,918	4,650
Randolph	1,833	1,370	1,612	1,418
Richmond	52,100	26,842	39,262	29,764
Rockdale	20,421	16,860	12,136	18,856
Schley	479	1,252	464	1,063
Screven	3,024	3,423	2,534	3,360
Seminole	1,657	2,315	1,278	1,977
Spalding	10,141	14,885	7,460	13,461
Stephens	2,705	7,689	2,714	6,904
Stewart	1,305	783	1,220	797
Sumter	6,444	5,713	5,562	5,688
Talbot	2,367	1,300	1,830	1,103
Taliaferro	643	339	612	335
Tattnall	1,932	4,730	1,787	4,657
Taylor	1,533	2,019	1,458	1,912
Telfair	1,862	2,486	1,590	2,171
Terrell	2,501	1,890	1,951	1,859
Thomas	7,720	10,642	5,997	9,659
Tift	4,749	9,431	3,864	8,619
Toombs	2,964	6,658	2,567	6,196
Towns	1,391	4,292	1,430	3,823
Treutlen	1,112	1,826	1,052	1,691
Troup	10,438	15,374	7,630	14,183
Turner	1,427	2,096	1,135	1,815
Twiggs	2,402	2,087	2,220	2,112
Union	2,486	8,007	2,327	6,847
Upson	4,050	7,282	3,424	6,634
Walker	6,094	17,101	5,986	15,340
Walton	8,469	27,253	5,887	21,594
Ware	4,034	8,311	3,449	7,790
Warren	1,554	1,087	1,360	1,121
Washington	4,607	4,216	3,733	4,081
Wayne	2,858	7,601	2,683	6,819
Webster	515	588	515	485
Wheeler	794	1,408	847	1,192
White	2,174	8,467	2,016	7,403
Whitfield	8,167	19,230	6,933	19,297
Wilcox	978	2,159	902	1,705
Wilkes	2,315	2,705	2,028	2,490
Wilkinson	2,298	2,349	2,235	2,261
Worth	2,540	5,777	2,219	5,105
Totals	**1,844,123**	**2,048,759**	**1,366,149**	**1,914,254**

Georgia Vote Since 1952

2008: McCain, R., 2,048,759; Obama, D., 1,844,123; Barr, LB., 28,731.
2004: Bush, R., 1,914,254; Kerry, D., 1,366,149; Badnarik, LB., 18,387.
2000: Bush, R., 1,419,720; Gore, D., 1,116,230; Browne, LB., 36,332; Buchanan, Ind., 10,926.
1996: Dole, R., 1,080,843; Clinton, D., 1,053,849; Perot, RF., 146,337; Browne, LB., 17,870.
1992: Clinton, D., 1,008,966; Bush, R., 995,252; Perot, Ind., 309,657; Marrou, LB., 7,110.
1988: Bush, R., 1,081,331; Dukakis, D., 714,792; Paul, LB., 8,435; Fulani, New Alliance, 5,099.
1984: Reagan, R., 1,068,722; Mondale, D., 706,628.
1980: Carter, D., 890,955; Reagan, R., 654,168; Anderson, Ind., 36,055; Clark, LB., 15,627.
1976: Carter, D., 979,409; Ford, R., 483,743; write-in, 4,306.
1972: Nixon, R., 881,496; McGovern, D., 289,529; Schmitz, Amer., 812; scattered, 2,935.
1968: Wallace, 3rd party, 535,550; Nixon, R., 380,111; Humphrey, D., 334,440; write-in, 162.
1964: Goldwater, R., 616,600; Johnson, D., 522,557.
1960: Kennedy, D., 458,638; Nixon, R., 274,472; write-in, 239.
1956: Stevenson, D., 444,388; Eisenhower, R., 222,778; Andrews, write-in, 1,754.
1952: Stevenson, D., 456,823; Eisenhower, R., 198,979; Liberty Party, 1.

Hawaii

County	2008 Obama (D)	McCain (R)	2004 Kerry (D)	Bush (R)
Hawaii	50,808	14,865	35,116	22,032
Honolulu	213,977	88,049	152,873	144,232
Kauai	20,408	6,243	14,916	9,740
Maui	39,725	11,152	28,803	18,187
Totals	**325,871**	**120,566**	**231,708**	**194,191**

Hawaii Vote Since 1960

2008: Obama, D., 325,871; McCain, R., 120,566; Nader, Ind. (HI), 3,825; Barr, LB., 1,314; Baldwin, Const., 1,013; McKinney, Green, 979.
2004: Kerry, D., 231,708; Bush, R., 194,191; Cobb, Green, 1,737; Badnarik, LB., 1,377.
2000: Gore, D., 205,286; Bush, R., 137,845; Nader, Green, 21,623; Browne, LB., 1,477; Buchanan, RF., 1,071; Phillips, Const., 343; Hagelin, Natural Law, 306.
1996: Clinton, D., 205,012; Dole, R., 113,943; Perot, RF., 27,358; Nader, Green, 10,386; Browne, LB., 2,493; Hagelin, Natural Law, 570; Phillips, Taxpayers, 358.
1992: Clinton, D., 179,310; Bush, R., 136,822; Perot, Ind., 53,003; Gritz, Pop./America First, 1,452; Marrou, LB., 1,119.
1988: Dukakis, D., 192,364; Bush, R., 158,625; Paul, LB., 1,999; Fulani, New Alliance, 1,003.
1984: Reagan, R., 184,934; Mondale, D., 147,098; Bergland, LB., 2,167.
1980: Carter, D., 135,879; Reagan, R., 130,112; Anderson, Ind., 32,021; Clark, LB., 3,269; Commoner, Citizens, 1,548; Hall, Comm., 458.
1976: Carter, D., 147,375; Ford, R., 140,003; MacBride, LB., 3,923.
1972: Nixon, R., 168,865; McGovern, D., 101,409.
1968: Humphrey, D., 141,324; Nixon, R., 91,425; Wallace, 3rd party, 3,469.
1964: Johnson, D., 163,249; Goldwater, R., 44,022.
1960: Kennedy, D., 92,410; Nixon, R., 92,295.

Idaho

County	2008 Obama (D)	McCain (R)	2004 Kerry (D)	Bush (R)
Ada	82,023	92,879	58,523	94,641
Adams	728	1,515	555	1,468
Bannock	14,792	19,356	12,903	21,479
Bear Lake	502	2,377	494	2,506
Benewah	1,407	2,646	1,148	2,823
Bingham	4,424	12,230	3,605	12,734
Blaine	6,947	3,439	5,992	4,034
Boise	1,240	2,433	970	2,501
Bonner	7,840	11,145	6,649	10,697
Bonneville	11,415	29,324	8,356	30,048
Boundary	1,474	3,098	1,268	3,012
Butte	318	1,056	321	1,077
Camas	187	422	139	450
Canyon	20,147	42,752	13,415	41,599
Caribou	553	2,656	491	2,753
Cassia	1,305	6,240	1,153	6,562
Clark	64	305	46	302
Clearwater	1,211	2,569	1,117	2,839
Custer	620	1,704	559	1,762
Elmore	2,523	5,571	1,959	6,011
Franklin	599	4,231	456	4,527
Fremont	1,065	4,700	741	4,965
Gem	2,166	5,585	1,628	5,416
Gooding	1,485	3,764	1,278	3,973
Idaho	1,935	5,895	1,689	6,017
Jefferson	1,641	8,540	1,084	7,703
Jerome	1,794	4,897	1,344	5,177
Kootenai	22,120	38,387	17,584	36,173
Latah	9,191	7,984	8,430	8,686
Lemhi	796	2,938	915	3,079
Lewis	479	1,275	440	1,359
Lincoln	497	967	466	1,388
Madison	1,625	11,120	826	10,693
Minidoka	1,137	3,976	1,331	5,797

County	2008 Obama (D)	McCain (R)	2004 Kerry (D)	Bush (R)
Nez Perce	7,123	10,357	6,476	11,009
Oneida	381	1,724	304	1,789
Owyhee	944	3,024	685	2,859
Payette	2,415	5,988	1,848	6,256
Power	1,027	1,754	829	2,105
Shoshone	2,521	2,953	2,331	2,922
Teton	2,302	2,263	1,416	2,235
Twin Falls	8,621	19,032	6,458	19,672
Valley	2,394	2,750	1,843	2,863
Washington	1,241	3,168	1,033	3,274
Totals	236,440	403,012	181,098	409,235

Idaho Vote Since 1952

2008: McCain, R., 403,012; Obama, D., 236,440; Nader, Ind., 7,175; Baldwin, Const., 4,747; Barr, LB., 3,658.
2004: Bush, R., 409,235; Kerry, D., 181,098; Badnarik, LB., 3,844; Peroutka, Const., 3,084.
2000: Bush, R., 336,937; Gore, D., 138,637; Buchanan, RF., 7,615; Browne, LB., 3,488; Phillips, Const., 1,469; Hagelin, Natural Law, 1,177.
1996: Dole, R., 256,595; Clinton, D., 165,443; Perot, RF., 62,518; Browne, LB., 3,325; Phillips, U.S. Taxpayers, 2,230; Hagelin, Natural Law, 1,600.
1992: Bush, R., 202,645; Clinton, D., 137,013; Perot, Ind., 130,395; Gritz, Pop./America First, 10,281; Marrou, LB., 1,167.
1988: Bush, R., 253,881; Dukakis, D., 147,272; Paul, LB., 5,313; Fulani, Ind., 2,502.
1984: Reagan, R., 297,523; Mondale, D., 108,510; Bergland, LB., 2,823.
1980: Reagan, R., 290,699; Carter, D., 110,192; Anderson, Ind., 27,058; Clark, LB., 8,425; Rarick, Amer., 1,057.
1976: Ford, R., 204,151; Carter, D., 126,549; Maddox, Amer., 5,935; MacBride, LB., 3,558; LaRouche, U.S. Labor, 739.
1972: Nixon, R., 199,384; McGovern, D., 80,826; Schmitz, Amer., 28,869; Spock, People's, 903.
1968: Nixon, R., 165,369; Humphrey, D., 89,273; Wallace, 3rd party, 36,541.
1964: Johnson, D., 148,920; Goldwater, R., 143,557.
1960: Nixon, R., 161,597; Kennedy, D., 138,853.
1956: Eisenhower, R., 166,979; Stevenson, D., 105,868; Andrews, Ind., 126; write-in, 16.
1952: Eisenhower, R., 180,707; Stevenson, D., 95,081; Hallinan, Prog., 443; write-in, 23.

Illinois

County	2008 Obama (D)	McCain (R)	2004 Kerry (D)	Bush (R)
Adams	11,700	18,592	10,511	20,834
Alexander	2,189	1,692	2,016	1,831
Bond	3,832	3,938	3,228	4,068
Boone	11,324	10,396	8,286	11,132
Brown	985	1,541	895	1,679
Bureau	8,872	7,902	7,961	9,822
Calhoun	1,421	1,221	1,367	1,317
Carroll	3,956	3,589	3,537	4,534
Cass	2,690	2,617	2,492	3,163
Champaign	48,351	33,748	41,524	39,896
Christian	6,912	7,869	6,112	9,044
Clark	3,737	4,406	2,877	5,082
Clay	2,423	3,924	2,101	4,416
Clinton	7,653	9,348	6,797	10,219
Coles	11,704	10,962	9,566	13,015
Cook	1,608,870	482,395	1,439,724	597,405
Crawford	3,877	5,067	3,194	6,083
Cumberland	2,052	3,155	1,862	3,497
DeKalb	25,765	18,260	19,263	21,095
DeWitt	3,299	4,345	2,836	4,920
Douglas	3,226	5,001	2,767	5,702
DuPage	227,416	182,860	180,097	218,902
Edgar	3,737	4,393	3,093	5,258
Edwards	1,140	2,136	930	2,412
Effingham	5,256	11,313	4,388	11,774
Fayette	3,963	5,493	3,571	5,880
Ford	2,226	4,075	1,912	4,511
Franklin	8,873	9,390	8,816	10,388
Fulton	9,722	6,244	9,080	7,818
Gallatin	1,587	1,211	1,573	1,619
Greene	2,617	3,048	2,457	3,559
Grundy	9,134	9,144	8,463	11,198
Hamilton	1,794	2,353	1,814	2,653
Hancock	3,753	4,778	3,975	5,837
Hardin	892	1,330	923	1,501
Henderson	2,213	1,540	2,269	1,857
Henry	13,177	11,247	11,877	13,212
Iroquois	4,640	8,686	3,832	9,914
Jackson	15,199	9,665	14,300	11,190
Jasper	2,063	2,963	1,781	3,529
Jefferson	7,460	9,293	6,713	10,160
Jersey	5,036	5,320	4,597	5,435
Jo Daviess	6,392	5,163	5,311	6,174
Johnson	1,477	3,138	1,813	3,997
Kane	105,592	84,223	73,813	92,065
Kankakee	24,719	22,508	20,003	24,739

County	2008 Obama (D)	McCain (R)	2004 Kerry (D)	Bush (R)
Kendall	23,529	20,675	12,497	19,776
Knox	14,165	9,396	13,403	11,111
Lake	111,051	85,284	134,352	139,081
LaSalle	27,415	21,855	24,263	26,101
Lawrence	3,013	3,401	2,518	4,162
Lee	7,757	8,243	6,416	9,307
Livingston	6,184	9,180	5,632	10,316
Logan	5,245	7,424	4,273	9,112
Macon	6,780	6,047	23,341	28,118
Macoupin	12,071	9,879	11,193	11,413
Madison	68,836	57,059	63,399	59,384
Marion	8,334	8,687	7,694	9,413
Marshall	3,078	3,142	2,806	3,734
Mason	3,540	3,139	3,215	3,907
Massac	2,693	4,371	2,805	4,578
McDonough	6,780	6,047	7,119	7,656
McHenry	71,976	64,595	50,330	76,412
McLean	37,551	36,657	29,877	41,276
Menard	2,704	3,672	2,137	4,408
Mercer	4,885	3,830	4,512	4,405
Monroe	7,943	9,870	6,788	9,468
Montgomery	6,486	6,141	5,979	6,851
Morgan	7,458	7,585	5,650	9,392
Moultrie	2,663	3,466	2,388	4,028
Ogle	11,247	13,131	9,018	14,918
Peoria	44,396	33,018	41,121	41,051
Perry	4,697	5,077	4,770	5,589
Piatt	3,856	4,988	3,124	5,392
Pike	3,021	4,451	2,849	5,032
Pope	842	1,339	918	1,500
Pulaski	1,636	1,592	1,372	1,720
Putnam	1,900	1,376	1,704	1,623
Randolph	7,387	7,536	6,771	8,076
Richland	3,177	4,320	2,529	5,153
Rock Island	42,175	25,338	39,880	29,663
St. Clair	77,896	47,005	62,410	50,203
Saline	5,082	6,096	4,697	7,057
Sangamon	51,176	46,857	38,630	55,904
Schuyler	1,896	1,830	1,594	2,403
Scott	1,090	1,453	927	1,696
Shelby	4,236	6,390	3,744	6,753
Stark	1,357	1,513	1,189	1,841
Stephenson	11,010	9,686	8,913	12,212
Tazewell	29,335	33,203	25,814	36,058
Union	3,916	4,999	3,735	5,333
Vermilion	16,228	16,046	14,726	18,731
Wabash	2,462	3,252	1,752	4,212
Warren	4,286	3,637	3,938	4,474
Washington	3,338	4,468	2,986	5,072
Wayne	2,545	5,381	2,139	6,102
White	3,315	3,985	3,071	5,180
Whiteside	15,587	10,867	13,723	12,959
Will	154,691	119,049	117,172	130,728
Williamson	12,893	17,351	11,685	18,086
Winnebago	69,903	53,806	59,740	60,782
Woodford	6,969	12,137	6,005	12,698
Totals	3,419,348	2,031,179	2,891,550	2,345,946

Illinois Vote Since 1952

2008: Obama, D., 3,419,348; McCain, R., 2,031,179; Nader, Ind., 30,948; Barr, LB., 19,642; McKinney, Green, 11,838; Baldwin, Const., 8,256; Polachek, New Party, 1,149.
2004: Kerry, D., 2,891,550; Bush, R., 2,345,946; Badnarik, LB., 32,442.
2000: Gore, D., 2,589,026; Bush, R., 2,019,421; Nader, Green, 103,759; Buchanan, Ind., 16,106; Browne, LB., 11,623; Hagelin, RF., 2,127.
1996: Clinton, D., 2,341,744; Dole, R., 1,587,021; Perot, RF., 346,408; Browne, LB., 22,548; Phillips, U.S. Taxpayers, 7,606; Hagelin, Natural Law, 4,606.
1992: Clinton, D., 2,453,350; Bush, R., 1,734,096; Perot, Ind., 840,515; Marrou, LB., 9,218; Fulani, New Alliance, 5,267; Gritz, Pop./America First, 3,577; Hagelin, Natural Law, 2,751; Warren, Soc. Workers, 1,361.
1988: Bush, R., 2,310,939; Dukakis, D., 2,215,940; Paul, LB., 14,944; Fulani, Solidarity, 10,276.
1984: Reagan, R., 2,707,103; Mondale, D., 2,086,499; Bergland, LB., 10,086.
1980: Reagan, R., 2,358,049; Carter, D., 1,981,413; Anderson, Ind., 346,754; Clark, LB., 38,939; Commoner, Citizens, 10,692; Hall, Comm., 9,711; Griswold, Workers World, 2,257; DeBerry, Soc. Workers, 1,302; write-in, 604.
1976: Ford, R., 2,364,269; Carter, D., 2,271,295; McCarthy, Ind., 55,939; Hall, Comm., 9,250; MacBride, LB., 8,057; Camejo, Soc. Workers, 3,615; Levin, Soc. Labor, 2,422; LaRouche, U.S. Labor, 2,018; write-in, 1,968.
1972: Nixon, R., 2,788,179; McGovern, D., 1,913,472; Fisher, Soc. Labor, 12,344; Hall, Comm., 4,541; Schmitz, Amer., 2,471; others, 2,229.
1968: Nixon, R., 2,174,774; Humphrey, D., 2,039,814; Wallace, 3rd party, 390,958; Blomen, Soc. Labor, 13,878; write-in, 325.
1964: Johnson, D., 2,796,833; Goldwater, R., 1,905,946; write-in, 62.

1960: Kennedy, D., 2,377,846; Nixon, R., 2,368,988; Hass, Soc. Labor, 10,560; write-in, 15.
1956: Eisenhower, R., 2,623,327; Stevenson, D., 1,775,682; Hass, Soc. Labor, 8,342; write-in, 56.
1952: Eisenhower, R., 2,457,327; Stevenson, D., 2,013,920; Hass, Soc. Labor, 9,363; write-in, 448.

Indiana

County	2008 Obama (D)	McCain (R)	2004 Kerry (D)	Bush (R)
Adams	4,928	8,402	3,512	9,734
Allen	71,083	77,668	46,710	82,013
Bartholomew	13,555	17,061	9,191	19,093
Benton	1,563	2,180	1,135	2,797
Blackford	2,677	2,690	1,903	3,447
Boone	9,744	16,616	5,636	17,055
Brown	3,852	4,060	2,730	4,512
Carroll	3,733	4,845	2,689	5,868
Cass	6,995	8,339	4,315	9,480
Clark	21,918	25,299	17,648	24,495
Clay	4,954	6,264	3,333	7,361
Clinton	5,306	6,915	3,335	8,471
Crawford	2,286	2,393	1,932	2,609
Daviess	3,369	7,096	2,573	7,936
Dearborn	7,123	14,886	6,596	14,231
Decatur	3,890	6,443	2,621	7,499
DeKalb	7,169	9,771	4,810	10,468
Delaware	28,356	20,904	20,436	27,064
Dubois	8,748	9,526	5,210	11,726
Elkhart	31,289	39,344	17,966	42,967
Fayette	4,387	4,917	3,626	5,761
Floyd	16,248	19,944	13,857	19,877
Fountain	3,094	4,151	2,477	5,260
Franklin	3,404	7,017	2,925	6,977
Fulton	3,700	5,145	2,607	6,027
Gibson	6,455	8,449	5,378	9,133
Grant	11,291	14,726	8,509	18,769
Greene	5,709	7,689	4,606	8,609
Hamilton	49,691	78,391	26,388	77,887
Hancock	11,869	21,991	6,912	20,771
Harrison	7,271	10,529	6,171	11,015
Hendricks	24,394	39,578	13,548	38,430
Henry	10,058	10,894	7,176	13,137
Howard	17,803	20,207	12,998	23,714
Huntington	5,842	10,289	3,877	11,617
Jackson	7,445	9,852	5,092	11,083
Jasper	5,044	7,669	3,678	8,056
Jay	3,746	4,400	2,740	5,427
Jefferson	6,255	7,052	5,117	7,763
Jennings	5,302	6,257	3,538	6,864
Johnson	21,536	36,471	13,109	37,765
Knox	7,569	8,639	5,649	9,990
Kosciusko	9,229	20,484	5,977	22,136
LaGrange	3,659	5,697	21,114	20,916
Lake	138,603	67,417	114,743	71,903
LaPorte	28,247	17,911	21,114	20,916
Lawrence	7,208	11,018	5,346	12,207
Madison	30,152	26,403	21,882	32,526
Marion	237,275	131,459	162,249	156,072
Marshall	7,880	10,401	5,593	12,074
Martin	1,706	3,112	1,522	3,414
Miami	5,559	8,305	3,886	9,600
Monroe	41,332	21,083	26,965	22,834
Montgomery	6,005	9,055	3,536	10,901
Morgan	10,314	18,105	6,650	19,197
Newton	2,623	3,300	2,032	3,757
Noble	7,063	9,671	4,703	10,859
Ohio	1,158	1,712	1,139	1,796
Orange	3,390	4,536	2,885	5,683
Owen	3,570	4,415	2,536	5,000
Parke	2,913	3,900	2,362	4,550
Perry	5,140	3,201	4,131	4,137
Pike	2,700	3,221	2,418	3,745
Porter	39,046	33,796	29,388	34,794
Posey	5,820	6,794	4,085	7,833
Pulaski	2,466	3,368	1,750	3,797
Putnam	6,331	8,085	4,103	8,908
Randolph	4,839	5,787	3,812	7,172
Ripley	4,187	7,794	3,510	8,224
Rush	3,228	4,270	2,000	5,363
St. Joseph	68,708	48,510	52,637	55,254
Scott	4,268	4,443	3,822	4,793
Shelby	6,983	10,330	4,519	11,397
Spencer	5,037	4,998	3,920	5,934
Starke	4,778	4,473	3,987	4,846
Steuben	6,283	7,670	4,345	8,433
Sullivan	4,282	4,341	3,341	4,999
Switzerland	1,638	1,940	1,479	2,161
Tippecanoe	37,709	29,789	20,818	30,897
Tipton	3,250	4,452	2,203	5,628
Union	1,220	2,058	1,045	2,266
Vanderburgh	39,368	37,449	28,767	41,463
Vermillion	4,002	3,004	3,424	3,536
Vigo	25,023	18,111	18,426	20,988
Wabash	5,455	8,238	3,920	9,607
Warren	1,753	2,164	1,356	2,565
Warrick	12,329	16,013	8,980	16,930
Washington	4,561	6,512	3,879	6,915
Wayne	13,459	14,558	10,775	16,586
Wells	4,403	8,503	3,112	9,168
White	4,839	5,730	3,277	6,974
Whitley	5,861	9,122	3,880	9,512
Totals	**1,374,039**	**1,345,648**	**969,011**	**1,479,438**

Indiana Vote Since 1952

2008: Obama, D., 1,374,039; McCain, R., 1,345,648; Barr, LB., 29,257.
2004: Bush, R., 1,479,438; Kerry, D., 969,011; Badnarik, LB., 18,058.
2000: Bush, R., 1,245,836; Gore, D., 901,980; Buchanan, Ind., 16,959; Browne, LB., 15,530.
1996: Dole, R., 1,006,693; Clinton, D., 887,424; Perot, RF., 224,299; Browne, LB., 15,632.
1992: Bush, R., 989,375; Clinton, D., 848,420; Perot, Ind., 455,934; Marrou, LB., 7,936; Fulani, New Alliance, 2,583.
1988: Bush, R., 1,297,763; Dukakis, D., 860,643; Fulani, New Alliance, 10,215.
1984: Reagan, R., 1,377,230; Mondale, D., 841,481; Bergland, LB., 6,741.
1980: Reagan, R., 1,255,656; Carter, D., 844,197; Anderson, Ind., 111,639; Clark, LB., 19,627; Commoner, Citizens, 4,852; Greaves, Amer., 4,750; Hall, Comm., 702; DeBerry, Soc., 610.
1976: Ford, R., 1,185,958; Carter, D., 1,014,714; Anderson, Amer., 14,048; Camejo, Soc. Workers, 5,695; LaRouche, U.S. Labor, 1,947.
1972: Nixon, R., 1,405,154; McGovern, D., 708,568; Reed, Soc. Workers, 5,575; Spock, Peace/Freedom, 4,544; Fisher, Soc. Labor, 1,688.
1968: Nixon, R., 1,067,885; Humphrey, D., 806,659; Wallace, 3rd party, 243,108; Munn, Prohib., 4,616; Halstead, Soc. Workers, 1,293; Gregory, write-in, 36.
1964: Johnson, D., 1,170,848; Goldwater, R., 911,118; Munn, Prohib., 8,266; Hass, Soc. Labor, 1,374.
1960: Nixon, R., 1,175,120; Kennedy, D., 952,358; Decker, Prohib., 6,746; Hass, Soc. Labor, 1,136.
1956: Eisenhower, R., 1,182,811; Stevenson, D., 783,908; Holtwick, Prohib., 6,554; Hass, Soc. Labor, 1,334.
1952: Eisenhower, R., 1,136,259; Stevenson, D., 801,530; Hamblen, Prohib., 15,335; Hallinan, Prog., 1,222; Hass, Soc. Labor, 979.

Iowa

County	2008 Obama (D)	McCain (R)	2004 Kerry (D)	Bush (R)
Adair	1,920	2,059	1,844	2,402
Adams	1,113	1,039	977	1,317
Allamakee	3,962	2,961	3,449	3,530
Appanoose	2,964	3,081	3,063	3,340
Audubon	1,731	1,631	1,608	1,958
Benton	7,035	6,431	6,747	6,658
Black Hawk	38,564	24,467	35,392	28,046
Boone	7,333	6,265	7,027	6,870
Bremer	6,870	5,704	6,025	6,665
Buchanan	6,037	4,131	5,608	4,797
Buena Vista	4,065	4,217	3,520	4,887
Butler	3,348	3,686	3,001	4,417
Calhoun	2,335	2,747	2,243	3,255
Carroll	5,284	4,905	4,689	5,762
Cass	3,201	3,990	2,679	4,796
Cedar	5,201	4,278	4,747	4,869
Cerro Gordo	14,305	9,344	13,372	10,960
Cherokee	2,883	3,365	2,988	3,758
Chickasaw	3,897	2,536	3,708	3,040
Clarke	2,214	2,112	2,323	2,200
Clay	3,908	4,345	3,547	4,898
Clayton	5,174	3,640	4,736	4,312
Clinton	14,733	9,068	13,813	10,666
Crawford	3,697	3,338	3,220	3,955
Dallas	15,101	16,904	10,917	15,183
Davis	2,262	2,553	1,731	2,148
Decatur	1,983	2,019	1,859	2,088
Delaware	4,630	4,108	4,227	4,908
Des Moines	12,396	7,687	12,456	8,221
Dickinson	4,609	5,150	4,140	5,337
Dubuque	23,791	16,694	26,561	20,100
Emmet	2,565	2,366	2,405	2,697
Fayette	5,889	4,199	5,185	5,128
Floyd	4,797	3,044	4,349	3,745
Franklin	2,566	2,495	2,340	3,128
Fremont	2,490	2,708	1,510	2,362
Greene	2,359	2,340	2,459	2,618
Grundy	2,774	3,936	2,386	4,429
Guthrie	2,603	3,025	2,614	3,325
Hamilton	3,999	3,909	3,895	4,367
Hancock	2,790	3,008	2,484	3,368
Hardin	4,368	4,301	4,015	4,875
Harrison	3,549	3,906	2,906	4,680
Henry	5,306	5,582	4,127	5,220
Howard	2,933	1,721	2,614	2,028

County	2008		2004	
	Obama (D)	McCain (R)	Kerry (D)	Bush (R)
Humboldt	2,151	2,881	2,146	3,162
Ida	1,455	2,025	1,415	2,342
Iowa	4,173	4,173	3,841	4,544
Jackson	6,069	3,662	5,656	4,242
Jasper	10,195	8,750	10,430	9,462
Jefferson	5,028	3,321	4,490	3,648
Johnson	50,708	20,639	41,847	22,715
Jones	5,431	4,398	5,054	4,834
Keokuk	2,508	2,703	2,294	3,119
Kossuth	4,609	4,310	4,132	5,042
Lee	9,470	6,724	10,152	7,472
Linn	67,476	43,384	60,442	49,442
Louisa	2,520	2,310	2,297	2,572
Lucas	2,024	2,329	1,987	2,543
Lyon	1,673	4,461	1,303	4,751
Madison	3,702	4,525	3,380	4,538
Mahaska	4,450	6,249	3,790	6,858
Marion	7,408	9,232	6,574	9,990
Marshall	9,918	8,229	9,443	9,557
Mills	2,970	4,177	2,308	4,556
Mitchell	3,175	2,465	2,785	2,646
Monona	2,284	2,407	2,397	2,575
Monroe	1,793	1,997	1,855	2,067
Montgomery	2,318	2,878	1,899	3,601
Muscatine	10,850	7,907	9,542	9,020
O'Brien	2,333	4,883	2,330	5,328
Osceola	1,037	2,027	934	2,295
Page	2,892	4,344	2,211	5,243
Palo Alto	2,420	2,290	2,482	2,674
Plymouth	4,564	7,744	4,278	7,810
Pocahontas	1,794	2,131	1,822	2,441
Polk	119,569	88,983	105,218	95,828
Pottawattamie	20,226	21,161	16,906	24,558
Poweshiek	5,441	4,331	5,043	4,965
Ringgold	1,236	1,401	1,286	1,466
Sac	2,237	2,699	2,215	3,128
Scott	48,675	36,239	42,122	39,958
Shelby	2,847	3,472	2,355	4,256
Sioux	3,010	13,440	2,259	14,229
Story	26,268	18,812	23,296	20,819
Tama	4,859	3,813	4,487	4,456
Taylor	1,344	1,602	1,252	1,908
Union	2,990	2,774	2,747	3,165
Van Buren	1,540	1,980	1,568	2,211
Wapello	8,481	6,466	9,125	7,403
Warren	12,261	12,112	10,730	12,160
Washington	5,140	5,228	4,595	5,977
Wayne	1,356	1,563	1,379	1,733
Webster	9,847	8,299	9,561	8,959
Winnebago	3,236	2,726	2,707	3,175
Winneshiek	6,808	4,260	5,354	5,324
Woodbury	20,290	20,798	21,455	22,451
Worth	2,560	1,612	2,286	1,795
Wright	3,087	3,187	2,930	3,631
Totals	828,940	682,379	741,898	751,957

Iowa Vote Since 1952

2008: Obama, D., 828,940; McCain, R., 682,379; Nader, Peace/Freedom, 8,014; Barr, LB., 4,590; Baldwin, Const., 4,445; McKinney, Green, 1,423; Harris, Soc. Workers, 292; Moore, Soc. USA, 182; La Riva, Socialism/Liberation, 121.

2004: Bush, R., 751,957; Kerry, D., 741,898; Nader, petitioning cand., 5,973; Badnarik, LB., 2,992; Peroutka, Const., 1,304; Cobb, Green, 1,141; Harris, Soc. Workers, 373; Van Auken, petitioning cand., 176.

2000: Gore, D., 638,517; Bush, R., 634,373; Nader, Green, 29,374; Buchanan, RF., 5,731; Browne, LB., 3,209; Hagelin, Ind., 2,281; Phillips, Const., 613; Harris, Soc. Workers, 190; McReynolds, Soc., 107.

1996: Clinton, D., 620,258; Dole, R., 492,644; Perot, RF., 105,159; Nader, Green, 6,550; Hagelin, Natural Law, 3,349; Browne, LB., 2,315; Phillips, Taxpayers, 2,229; Harris, Soc. Workers, 331.

1992: Clinton, D., 586,353; Bush, R., 504,891; Perot, Ind., 253,468; Hagelin, Natural Law, 3,079; Gritz, Pop./America First, 1,177; Marrou, LB., 1,076.

1988: Dukakis, D., 670,557; Bush, R., 545,355; LaRouche, Ind., 3,526; Paul, LB., 2,494.

1984: Reagan, R., 703,088; Mondale, D., 605,620; Bergland, LB., 1,844.

1980: Reagan, R., 676,026; Carter, D., 508,672; Anderson, Ind., 115,633; Clark, LB., 13,123; Commoner, Citizens, 2,273; McReynolds, Soc., 534; Hall, Comm., 298; DeBerry, Soc. Workers, 244; Greaves, Amer., 189; Bubar, Statesman, 150; scattered, 519.

1976: Ford, R., 632,863; Carter, D., 619,931; McCarthy, Ind., 20,051; Anderson, Amer., 3,040; MacBride, LB., 1,452.

1972: Nixon, R., 706,207; McGovern, D., 496,206; Schmitz, Amer., 22,056; Jenness, Soc. Workers, 488; Hall, Comm., 272; Green, Universal, 199; Fisher, Soc. Labor, 195; scattered, 321.

1968: Nixon, R., 619,106; Humphrey, D., 476,699; Wallace, 3rd party, 66,422; Halstead, Soc. Workers, 3,377; Cleaver, Peace/Freedom, 1,332; Munn, Prohib., 362; Blomen, Soc. Labor, 241.

1964: Johnson, D., 733,030; Goldwater, R., 449,148; Munn, Prohib., 1,902; Hass, Soc. Labor, 182; DeBerry, Soc. Workers, 159.

1960: Nixon, R., 722,381; Kennedy, D., 550,565; Hass, Soc. Labor, 230; write-in, 634.

1956: Eisenhower, R., 729,187; Stevenson, D., 501,858; Andrews (A.C.P. of IA), 3,202; Hoopes, Soc., 192; Hass, Soc. Labor, 125.

1952: Eisenhower, R., 808,906; Stevenson, D., 451,513; Hallinan, Prog., 5,085; Hamblen, Prohib., 2,882; Hoopes, Soc., 219; Hass, Soc. Labor, 139; scattered, 29.

Kansas

County	2008		2004	
	Obama (D)	McCain (R)	Kerry (D)	Bush (R)
Allen	2,130	3,481	1,922	3,867
Anderson	1,161	2,329	1,295	2,500
Atchison	3,157	3,717	3,120	3,880
Barber	585	1,794	588	1,782
Barton	2,967	7,636	2,874	8,666
Bourbon	2,343	4,159	2,216	4,372
Brown	1,284	2,926	1,268	3,092
Butler	8,942	17,756	7,495	18,438
Chase	371	934	418	1,055
Chautauqua	385	1,396	404	1,529
Cherokee	3,366	5,750	3,726	6,083
Cheyenne	432	1,247	320	1,353
Clark	241	870	257	1,014
Clay	982	2,919	793	3,174
Cloud	1,213	3,070	1,210	3,221
Coffey	1,105	3,008	1,093	3,259
Comanche	194	756	200	770
Cowley	4,859	8,263	4,818	9,407
Crawford	7,646	7,453	7,617	8,626
Decatur	340	1,189	355	1,355
Dickinson	2,353	5,961	2,364	6,295
Doniphan	1,077	2,336	1,065	2,491
Douglas	33,141	17,475	28,634	20,544
Edwards	326	979	386	1,084
Elk	359	1,035	369	1,119
Ellis	3,917	8,037	4,033	7,891
Ellsworth	838	1,996	801	2,259
Finney	3,188	6,776	2,351	7,479
Ford	2,848	5,587	2,286	6,632
Franklin	4,366	6,969	3,921	7,391
Geary	3,368	4,376	2,531	4,703
Gove	257	1,120	247	1,196
Graham	323	1,043	334	1,082
Grant	616	1,941	561	2,169
Gray	416	1,585	408	1,816
Greeley	150	587	138	584
Greenwood	916	2,087	911	2,282
Hamilton	233	836	229	888
Harper	740	1,960	727	2,154
Harvey	6,185	8,865	5,331	9,534
Haskell	265	1,216	227	1,356
Hodgeman	202	836	223	953
Jackson	2,266	3,770	2,064	3,730
Jefferson	3,450	5,058	3,253	5,408
Jewell	312	1,229	385	1,495
Johnson	124,142	149,816	97,866	158,103
Kearny	302	1,138	272	1,177
Kingman	918	2,468	904	2,801
Kiowa	197	903	256	1,275
Labette	3,782	4,955	3,615	5,400
Lane	187	786	181	823
Leavenworth	12,749	16,387	11,039	15,949
Lincoln	334	1,175	391	1,368
Linn	1,401	3,029	1,631	3,048
Logan	222	1,171	248	1,255
Lyon	5,661	6,468	5,234	7,951
Marion	1,607	3,695	1,536	4,516
Marshall	1,779	3,150	1,789	3,261
McPherson	1,113	8,732	3,589	9,595
Meade	369	1,527	356	1,748
Miami	5,644	9,229	4,838	9,013
Mitchell	692	2,405	693	2,609
Montgomery	4,203	9,142	4,338	9,598
Morris	897	1,858	931	1,961
Morton	225	1,129	276	1,287
Nemaha	1,405	3,761	1,355	4,027
Neosho	2,496	4,372	2,424	4,705
Ness	283	1,197	382	1,407
Norton	488	1,836	473	2,092
Osage	2,508	4,768	2,537	4,800
Osborne	391	1,441	454	1,587
Ottawa	703	2,304	595	2,333
Pawnee	869	1,923	773	2,172
Phillips	516	2,066	557	2,256
Pottawatomie	2,552	6,816	2,176	6,326
Pratt	1,265	2,765	1,200	3,121
Rawlins	270	1,243	289	1,414
Reno	9,711	15,858	9,114	17,748
Republic	627	1,949	607	2,238
Rice	1,137	2,746	1,130	3,182
Riley	10,033	11,729	7,908	12,672
Rooks	467	2,054	534	2,121
Rush	498	1,217	517	1,226
Russell	719	2,470	810	2,671

County	2008 Obama (D)	McCain (R)	2004 Kerry (D)	Bush (R)
Saline	7,897	13,754	7,524	15,111
Scott	311	1,788	347	1,924
Sedgwick	79,175	104,119	64,839	110,381
Seward	1,376	3,620	1,122	4,272
Shawnee	40,072	40,806	36,264	44,188
Sheridan	252	1,068	239	1,144
Sherman	677	1,932	632	2,088
Smith	437	1,695	540	1,803
Stafford	535	1,483	506	1,649
Stanton	187	625	165	796
Stevens	277	1,770	310	1,936
Sumner	3,304	6,637	3,217	7,092
Thomas	761	2,762	816	3,007
Trego	415	1,215	434	1,225
Wabaunsee	1,020	2,375	1,001	2,531
Wallace	96	690	112	742
Washington	640	2,193	643	2,498
Wichita	163	835	183	869
Wilson	1,218	2,927	1,060	3,263
Woodson	507	1,045	530	1,204
Wyandotte	38,482	16,211	34,923	17,919
Totals	**514,765**	**699,655**	**434,993**	**736,456**

Kansas Vote Since 1952

2008: McCain, R., 699,655; Obama, D., 514,765; Nader, Ind., 10,527; Barr, LB., 6,706; Baldwin, RF., 4,148.
2004: Bush, R., 736,456; Kerry, D., 434,993; Nader, RF., 9,348; Badnarik, LB., 4,013; Peroutka, Ind., 2,899.
2000: Bush, R., 622,332; Gore, D., 399,276; Nader, Ind., 36,086; Buchanan, RF., 7,370; Browne, LB., 4,525; Hagelin, Ind., 1,373; Phillips, Const., 1,254.
1996: Dole, R., 583,245; Clinton, D., 387,659; Perot, RF., 92,639; Browne, LB., 4,557; Phillips, Ind., 3,519; Hagelin, Ind., 1,655.
1992: Bush, R., 449,951; Clinton, D., 390,434; Perot, Ind., 312,358; Marrou, LB., 4,314.
1988: Bush, R., 554,049; Dukakis, D., 422,636; Paul, Ind., 12,553; Fulani, Ind., 3,806.
1984: Reagan, R., 674,646; Mondale, D., 332,471; Bergland, LB., 3,585.
1980: Reagan, R., 566,812; Carter, D., 326,150; Anderson, Ind., 68,231; Clark, LB., 14,470; Shelton, Amer., 1,555; Hall, Comm., 967; Bubar, Statesman, 821; Rarick, Conservative, 789.
1976: Ford, R., 502,752; Carter, D., 430,421; McCarthy, Ind., 13,185; Anderson, Amer., 4,724; MacBride, LB., 3,242; Maddox, Conservative, 2,118; Bubar, Prohib., 1,403.
1972: Nixon, R., 619,812; McGovern, D., 270,287; Schmitz, Conservative, 21,808; Munn, Prohib., 4,188.
1968: Nixon, R., 478,674; Humphrey, D., 302,996; Wallace, 3rd party, 88,921; Munn, Prohib., 2,192.
1964: Johnson, D., 464,028; Goldwater, R., 386,579; Munn, Prohib., 5,393; Hass, Soc. Labor, 1,901.
1960: Nixon, R., 561,474; Kennedy, D., 363,213; Decker, Prohib., 4,138.
1956: Eisenhower, R., 566,878; Stevenson, D., 296,317; Holtwick, Prohib., 3,048.
1952: Eisenhower, R., 616,302; Stevenson, D., 273,296; Hamblen, Prohib., 6,038; Hoopes, Soc., 530.

Kentucky

County	2008 Obama (D)	McCain (R)	2004 Kerry (D)	Bush (R)
Adair	1,888	5,512	1,764	5,628
Allen	2,023	5,258	1,923	5,202
Anderson	3,461	6,884	3,141	6,363
Ballard	1,427	2,537	1,759	2,389
Barren	5,434	11,133	5,216	10,822
Bath	2,210	2,234	2,608	2,269
Bell	2,718	9,519	4,210	6,722
Boone	16,292	33,812	12,391	32,329
Bourbon	3,385	4,820	3,198	4,953
Boyd	8,886	11,429	10,132	11,501
Boyle	4,764	7,697	4,646	7,764
Bracken	1,241	2,066	1,213	2,363
Breathitt	2,205	2,671	3,327	2,542
Breckinridge	3,110	5,281	2,884	5,580
Bullitt	10,056	19,857	9,043	19,433
Butler	1,555	3,696	1,436	4,109
Caldwell	2,212	3,866	2,245	4,066
Calloway	6,165	8,991	5,728	9,293
Campbell	15,619	24,045	14,253	25,540
Carlisle	879	1,699	1,102	1,734
Carroll	1,716	2,032	1,688	2,175
Carter	4,314	5,252	5,577	5,422
Casey	1,219	4,679	1,174	5,109
Christian	8,822	13,515	6,970	13,935
Clark	5,749	9,664	5,661	9,540
Clay	1,552	5,710	1,901	5,726
Clinton	761	3,366	952	3,369
Crittenden	1,254	2,604	1,438	2,726
Cumberland	697	2,056	848	2,356
Daviess	19,282	23,692	15,788	25,372
Edmonson	1,652	3,562	1,856	3,595

County	2008 Obama (D)	McCain (R)	2004 Kerry (D)	Bush (R)
Elliott	1,535	902	2,064	871
Estill	1,555	3,685	1,907	3,633
Fayette	66,040	59,884	57,994	66,406
Fleming	2,279	3,432	2,406	3,749
Floyd	7,530	7,741	11,132	6,612
Franklin	11,767	11,911	11,620	12,281
Fulton	1,226	1,530	1,340	1,527
Gallatin	1,278	1,840	1,188	1,869
Garrard	2,012	5,117	1,841	4,784
Grant	3,109	5,605	2,818	5,951
Graves	5,843	10,056	6,206	9,903
Grayson	3,154	6,605	2,905	7,170
Green	1,204	3,785	1,312	3,866
Greenup	6,621	8,849	7,630	8,696
Hancock	2,128	1,924	1,709	2,286
Hardin	15,650	23,896	11,507	24,627
Harlan	2,586	7,165	4,332	6,659
Harrison	2,916	4,520	2,807	4,855
Hart	2,290	4,397	2,470	4,269
Henderson	10,049	9,523	8,101	10,467
Henry	2,724	4,081	2,366	4,094
Hickman	812	1,406	926	1,395
Hopkins	7,104	11,916	6,420	12,314
Jackson	743	4,407	769	4,369
Jefferson	196,272	153,865	170,158	164,566
Jessamine	6,236	13,710	5,476	12,972
Johnson	2,413	5,964	3,288	5,940
Kenton	26,465	40,706	22,834	43,664
Knott	2,523	2,950	4,685	2,648
Knox	3,074	8,150	3,822	8,108
LaRue	1,913	4,153	1,823	4,111
Laurel	4,593	17,563	5,297	16,819
Lawrence	2,036	3,503	2,705	3,755
Lee	752	1,978	878	2,018
Leslie	766	3,574	1,266	3,661
Letcher	2,623	5,367	4,192	4,801
Lewis	1,510	3,213	1,667	3,778
Lincoln	2,752	6,273	2,796	5,996
Livingston	1,622	2,890	2,007	2,675
Logan	3,811	6,925	3,768	6,815
Lyon	1,577	2,220	1,769	2,132
Madison	12,392	19,694	11,525	18,922
Magoffin	2,105	2,434	2,843	2,836
Marion	3,596	3,842	3,399	3,905
Marshall	5,593	9,463	6,383	9,049
Martin	808	2,824	1,504	2,996
Mason	2,891	4,102	2,644	4,381
McCracken	11,285	19,043	11,361	18,218
McCreary	1,258	4,078	1,530	4,121
McLean	1,963	2,386	1,823	2,584
Meade	4,343	6,691	3,724	7,152
Menifee	1,276	1,155	1,284	1,215
Mercer	3,159	6,781	3,224	6,745
Metcalfe	1,350	2,734	1,472	2,645
Monroe	1,067	3,537	1,158	4,657
Montgomery	4,234	5,947	4,506	5,647
Morgan	1,858	2,377	2,532	2,682
Muhlenberg	6,221	6,447	6,636	6,749
Nelson	7,654	10,139	6,524	10,161
Nicholas	1,272	1,634	1,332	1,700
Ohio	4,059	5,781	3,627	6,311
Oldham	9,996	18,992	8,080	18,801
Owen	1,694	2,969	1,615	3,084
Owsley	381	1,279	430	1,558
Pendleton	2,027	3,676	1,940	4,045
Perry	3,444	6,762	5,400	6,187
Pike	9,525	12,665	14,002	12,611
Powell	2,065	2,867	2,249	2,687
Pulaski	5,590	19,862	5,829	19,535
Robertson	451	533	413	670
Rockcastle	1,410	4,757	1,320	4,804
Rowan	4,074	3,907	4,556	4,063
Russell	1,579	5,702	1,772	6,009
Scott	7,712	11,782	6,325	10,600
Shelby	6,871	11,451	5,277	10,909
Simpson	2,775	4,437	2,730	4,273
Spencer	2,519	5,378	1,970	4,816
Taylor	3,165	7,568	2,979	7,247
Todd	1,543	3,336	1,491	3,242
Trigg	2,246	4,189	2,046	4,023
Trimble	1,484	2,239	1,428	2,332
Union	2,804	3,120	2,398	3,534
Warren	17,650	25,957	14,326	25,100
Washington	1,890	3,305	1,724	3,479
Wayne	2,201	4,868	2,616	5,027
Webster	2,390	3,037	2,304	3,207
Whitley	3,484	10,014	3,985	9,559
Wolfe	1,493	1,408	1,744	1,385
Woodford	5,027	7,130	4,480	6,937
Totals	**751,985**	**1,048,462**	**712,733**	**1,069,439**

Kentucky Vote Since 1952

2008: McCain, R., 1,048,462; Obama, D., 751,985; Nader, Ind., 15,378; Barr, LB., 5,989; Baldwin, Const., 4,694.
2004: Bush, R., 1,069,439; Kerry, D., 712,733; Nader, Ind., 8,856; Badnarik, LB., 2,619; Peroutka, Const., 2,213.
2000: Bush, R., 872,520; Gore, D., 638,923; Nader, Green, 23,118; Buchanan, RF., 4,152; Browne, LB., 2,885; Hagelin, Natural Law, 1,513; Phillips, Const., 915.
1996: Clinton, D., 636,614; Dole, R., 623,283; Perot, RF., 120,396; Browne, LB., 4,009; Phillips, U.S. Taxpayers, 2,204; Hagelin, Natural Law, 1,493.
1992: Clinton, D., 665,104; Bush, R., 617,178; Perot, Ind., 203,944; Marrou, LB., 4,513.
1988: Bush, R., 734,281; Dukakis, D., 580,368; Duke, Pop., 4,494; Paul, LB., 2,118.
1984: Reagan, R., 815,345; Mondale, D., 536,756.
1980: Reagan, R., 635,274; Carter, D., 616,417; Anderson, Ind., 31,127; Clark, LB., 5,531; McCormack, Respect For Life, 4,233; Commoner, Citizens, 1,304; Pulley, Soc., 393; Hall, Comm., 348.
1976: Carter, D., 615,717; Ford, R., 531,852; Anderson, Amer., 8,308; McCarthy, Ind., 6,837; Maddox, Amer. Ind., 2,328; MacBride, LB., 814.
1972: Nixon, R., 676,446; McGovern, D., 371,159; Schmitz, Amer., 17,627; Spock, People's, 1,118; Jenness, Soc. Workers, 685; Hall, Comm., 464.
1968: Nixon, R., 462,411; Humphrey, D., 397,547; Wallace, 3rd party, 193,098; Halstead, Soc. Workers, 2,843.
1964: Johnson, D., 669,659; Goldwater, R., 372,977; Kasper, Natl. States' Rights, 3,469.
1960: Nixon, R., 602,607; Kennedy, D., 521,855.
1956: Eisenhower, R., 572,192; Stevenson, D., 476,453; Byrd, States' Rights, 2,657; Holtwick, Prohib., 2,145; Hass, Soc. Labor, 358.
1952: Stevenson, D., 495,729; Eisenhower, R., 495,029; Hamblen, Prohib., 1,161; Hass, Soc. Labor, 893; Hallinan, Prog., 336.

Louisiana

Parish	2008		2004	
	Obama (D)	McCain (R)	Kerry (D)	Bush (R)
Acadia	7,028	19,228	8,937	16,083
Allen	2,891	6,333	3,791	5,140
Ascension	14,620	31,225	13,955	24,661
Assumption	4,756	5,981	5,585	4,966
Avoyelles	6,327	10,234	6,976	8,302
Beauregard	3,071	10,718	3,666	9,470
Bienville	3,589	3,776	3,399	3,612
Bossier	12,701	32,706	12,317	30,040
Caddo	55,220	52,105	51,739	54,292
Calcasieu	30,227	50,431	32,864	46,075
Caldwell	1,118	3,696	1,384	3,308
Cameron	613	3,089	1,367	3,190
Catahoula	1,659	3,486	1,673	3,219
Claiborne	3,025	3,750	2,854	3,704
Concordia	3,766	5,668	3,446	5,427
DeSoto	5,241	6,882	5,026	6,211
E. Baton Rouge	99,431	95,297	82,298	99,943
East Carroll	2,267	1,254	1,980	1,357
East Feliciana	4,383	5,431	4,091	5,021
Evangeline	5,852	9,792	5,757	7,949
Franklin	2,959	6,278	2,828	6,141
Grant	1,474	6,906	1,977	5,911
Iberia	12,492	20,123	12,426	19,420
Iberville	9,023	7,185	8,259	6,333
Jackson	2,456	5,190	2,525	5,038
Jefferson	64,853	113,008	72,136	117,882
Jefferson Davis	3,923	9,277	4,745	8,055
Lafayette	32,145	62,055	31,210	57,732
Lafourche	9,662	27,089	14,417	22,734
LaSalle	860	5,601	1,155	5,015
Lincoln	8,267	10,676	7,242	10,791
Livingston	6,674	43,247	9,895	33,976
Madison	3,100	2,152	2,334	2,291
Morehouse	5,789	7,258	5,336	7,471
Natchitoches	7,801	9,054	7,398	9,261
Orleans	116,042	28,041	152,610	42,847
Ouachita	24,769	41,708	22,016	41,750
Plaquemines	3,378	6,889	4,181	7,866
Pointe Coupee	5,516	6,702	5,712	5,429
Rapides	20,109	36,605	18,904	34,492
Red River	2,080	2,484	2,140	2,507
Richland	3,311	5,751	3,082	5,471
Sabine	2,245	7,226	2,743	6,711
St. Bernard	3,491	9,642	9,956	19,597
St. Charles	8,519	16,456	8,856	14,747
St. Helena	3,567	2,522	3,173	2,235
St. James	6,993	5,432	6,407	4,545
St. John the Baptist	12,420	8,908	10,305	9,039
St. Landry	20,267	21,647	18,166	18,315
St. Martin	9,419	14,443	10,321	12,095
St. Mary	9,342	13,181	9,547	12,877
St. Tammany	24,589	83,047	24,665	75,139
Tangipahoa	16,427	31,421	15,345	26,181
Tensas	1,646	1,367	1,469	1,453
Terrebonne	11,579	28,208	13,684	26,358

Parish	2008		2004	
	Obama (D)	McCain (R)	Kerry (D)	Bush (R)
Union	3,103	7,619	3,089	7,457
Vermilion	6,261	18,069	9,085	15,069
Vernon	3,534	11,946	4,035	11,032
Washington	6,122	12,215	6,554	11,006
Webster	6,610	11,417	6,833	11,070
W. Baton Rouge	5,043	6,654	4,932	5,822
West Carroll	878	4,045	1,231	3,740
W. Feliciana	2,414	3,149	2,214	2,932
Winn	2,044	4,628	2,056	4,366
Totals	782,989	1,148,275	820,299	1,102,169

Louisiana Vote Since 1952

2008: McCain, R., 1,148,275; Obama, D., 782,989; Paul, LA Taxpayers, 9,368; McKinney, Green, 9,187; Nader, Ind., 6,997; Baldwin, Const., 2,581; Harris, Soc. Workers 735; La Riva, Socialism/Liberation, 354; Amondson, Prohib., 275.
2004: Bush, R., 1,102,169; Kerry, D., 820,299; Nader, Better Life, 7,032; Peroutka, Const., 5,203; Badnarik, LB., 2,781; Brown, Protect Working Fam., 1,795; Amondson, Prohib., 1,566; Cobb, Green, 1,276; Harris, Soc. Workers, 985.
2000: Bush, R., 927,871; Gore, D., 792,344; Nader, Green, 20,473; Buchanan, RF., 14,356; Phillips, Const., 5,483; Browne, LB., 2,951; Harris, Soc. Workers, 1,103; Hagelin, Natural Law, 1,075.
1996: Clinton, D., 927,837; Dole, R., 712,586; Perot, RF., 123,293; Browne, LB., 7,499; Nader, Liberty, Ecology, Community, 4,719; Phillips, U.S. Taxpayers, 3,366; Hagelin, Natural Law, 2,981; Moorehead, Workers World, 1,678.
1992: Clinton, D., 815,971; Bush, R., 733,386; Perot, Ind., 211,478; Gritz, Pop./America First, 18,545; Marrou, LB., 3,155; Daniels, Ind., 1,663; Phillips, U.S. Taxpayers, 1,552; Fulani, New Alliance, 1,434; LaRouche, Ind., 1,136.
1988: Bush, R., 883,702; Dukakis, D., 717,460; Duke, Populist, 18,612; Paul, LB., 4,115.
1984: Reagan, R., 1,037,299; Mondale, D., 651,586; Bergland, LB., 1,876.
1980: Reagan, R., 792,853; Carter, D., 708,453; Anderson, Ind., 26,345; Rarick, Amer. Ind., 10,333; Clark, LB., 8,240; Commoner, Citizens, 1,584; DeBerry, Soc. Work., 783.
1976: Carter, D., 661,365; Ford, R., 587,446; Maddox, Amer., 10,058; Hall, Comm., 7,417; McCarthy, Ind., 6,588; MacBride, LB., 3,325.
1972: Nixon, R., 686,852; McGovern, D., 298,142; Schmitz, Amer., 52,099; Jenness, Soc. Workers, 14,398.
1968: Wallace, 3rd party, 530,300; Humphrey, D., 309,615; Nixon, R., 257,535.
1964: Goldwater, R., 509,225; Johnson, D., 387,068.
1960: Kennedy, D., 407,339; Nixon, R., 230,890; States' Rights (unpledged), 169,572.
1956: Eisenhower, R., 329,047; Stevenson, D., 243,977; Andrews, States' Rights, 44,520.
1952: Stevenson, D., 345,027; Eisenhower, R., 306,925.

Maine

City	2008		2004	
	Obama (D)	McCain (R)	Kerry (D)	Bush (R)
Auburn	6,866	4,686	6,869	5,219
Augusta	5,418	3,637	5,543	4,149
Bangor	9,405	6,257	9,162	7,135
Biddeford	6,839	2,903	6,520	3,756
Brunswick	6,502	3,371	7,288	4,248
Gorham	5,190	3,599	4,393	4,133
Lewiston	10,258	5,898	11,021	6,523
Orono	4,244	1,416	3,649	1,578
Portland	28,272	7,833	26,800	9,455
Presque Isle	2,420	2,094	2,309	2,268
Saco	6,457	3,444	5,892	3,948
Sanford	5,953	3,607	5,582	4,634
Scarborough	6,750	4,866	5,651	5,569
S. Portland	9,911	4,011	8,965	4,882
Waterville	5,070	2,109	5,056	2,413
Westbrook	5,446	3,024	5,047	3,744
Windham	5,069	3,989	4,400	4,553
Other	291,414	229,451	272,695	251,994
Totals	421,923	295,273	396,842	330,201

Maine Vote Since 1952

2008: Obama, D., 421,923; McCain, R., 295,273; Nader, Ind., 10,636; McKinney, Green, 2,900.
2004: Kerry, D., 396,842; Bush, R., 330,201; Nader, Better Life, 8,069; Cobb, Green, 2,936; Badnarik, LB., 1,965; Peroutka, Const., 735.
2000: Gore, D., 319,951; Bush, R., 286,616; Nader, Green, 37,127; Buchanan, RF., 4,443; Browne, LB., 3,074; Phillips, Const., 579.
1996: Clinton, D., 312,788; Dole, R., 186,378; Perot, RF., 85,970; Nader, Green, 15,279; Browne, LB., 2,996; Phillips, Taxpayers, 1,517; Hagelin, Natural Law, 825.
1992: Clinton, D., 263,420; Perot, Ind., 206,820; Bush, R., 206,504; Marrou, LB., 1,681.
1988: Bush, R., 307,131; Dukakis, D., 243,569; Paul, LB., 2,700; Fulani, New Alliance, 1,405.
1984: Reagan, R., 336,500; Mondale, D., 214,515.

1980: Reagan, R., 238,522; Carter, D., 220,974; Anderson, Ind., 53,327; Clark, LB., 5,119; Commoner, Citizens, 4,394; Hall, Comm., 591; write-in, 84.
1976: Ford, R., 236,320; Carter, D., 232,279; McCarthy, Ind., 10,874; Bubar, Prohib., 3,495.
1972: Nixon, R., 256,458; McGovern, D., 160,584; scattered, 229.
1968: Humphrey, D., 217,312; Nixon, R., 169,254; Wallace, 3rd party, 6,370.
1964: Johnson, D., 262,264; Goldwater, R., 118,701.
1960: Nixon, R., 240,608; Kennedy, D., 181,159.
1956: Eisenhower, R., 249,238; Stevenson, D., 102,468.
1952: Eisenhower, R., 232,353; Stevenson, D., 118,806; Hallinan, Prog., 332; Hass, Soc. Labor, 156; Hoopes, Soc., 138; scattered, 1.

Maryland

County	2008		2004	
	Obama (D)	McCain (R)	Kerry (D)	Bush (R)
Allegany	10,693	18,405	10,576	18,980
Anne Arundel	125,015	129,682	103,324	133,231
Baltimore	214,151	158,714	182,474	166,051
Calvert	20,299	23,095	15,967	23,017
Caroline	4,971	8,015	3,810	7,396
Carroll	28,060	54,503	22,974	55,275
Cecil	17,665	23,855	14,680	22,556
Charles	42,635	25,732	29,354	28,442
Dorchester	6,912	8,168	5,411	7,801
Frederick	54,013	55,170	39,503	59,934
Garrett	3,736	8,903	3,291	9,085
Harford	48,552	71,751	39,685	71,565
Howard	87,120	55,393	72,257	59,724
Kent	4,953	4,905	4,278	4,900
Montgomery	307,960	116,273	273,936	136,334
Prince George's	323,105	37,969	260,532	55,532
Queen Anne's	8,575	15,087	7,070	14,449
St. Mary's	19,023	24,705	13,776	23,725
Somerset	4,779	5,037	4,034	4,884
Talbot	9,035	10,995	7,367	11,288
Washington	26,245	34,169	20,387	36,917
Wicomico	19,436	21,849	15,137	21,998
Worcester	11,374	15,607	9,648	15,349
City				
Baltimore	214,385	28,681	175,022	36,230
Totals	**1,629,467**	**959,862**	**1,334,493**	**1,024,703**

Maryland Vote Since 1952
2008: Obama, D., 1,629,467; McCain, R., 959,862; Nader, MD Ind., 14,713; Barr, LB., 9,842; McKinney, Green, 4,747; Baldwin, RF., 3,760.
2004: Kerry, D., 1,334,493; Bush, R., 1,024,703; Nader, Populist, 11,854; Badnarik, LB., 6,094; Cobb, Green, 3,632; Peroutka, Const., 3,421.
2000: Gore, D., 1,144,008; Bush, R., 813,827; Nader, Green, 53,768; Browne, LB., 5,310; Buchanan, RF., 4,248; Phillips, Const., 918.
1996: Clinton, D., 966,207; Dole, R., 681,530; Perot, RF., 115,812; Browne, LB., 8,765; Phillips, Taxpayers, 3,402; Hagelin, Natural Law, 2,517.
1992: Clinton, D., 988,571; Bush, R., 707,094; Perot, Ind., 281,414; Marrou, LB., 4,715; Fulani, New Alliance, 2,786.
1988: Bush, R., 876,167; Dukakis, D., 826,304; Paul, LB., 6,748; Fulani, New Alliance, 5,115.
1984: Reagan, R., 879,918; Mondale, D., 787,935; Bergland, LB., 5,721.
1980: Carter, D., 726,161; Reagan, R., 680,606; Anderson, Ind., 119,537; Clark, LB., 14,192.
1976: Carter, D., 759,612; Ford, R., 672,661.
1972: Nixon, R., 829,305; McGovern, D., 505,781; Schmitz, Amer., 18,726.
1968: Humphrey, D., 538,310; Nixon, R., 517,995; Wallace, 3rd party, 178,734.
1964: Johnson, D., 730,912; Goldwater, R., 385,495; write-in, 50.
1960: Kennedy, D., 565,800; Nixon, R., 489,538.
1956: Eisenhower, R., 559,738; Stevenson, D., 372,613.
1952: Eisenhower, R., 499,424; Stevenson, D., 395,337; Hallinan, Prog., 7,313.

Massachusetts

City	2008		2004	
	Obama (D)	McCain (R)	Kerry (D)	Bush (R)
Boston	184,320	45,248	160,884	44,518
Brockton	23,206	9,611	20,091	10,058
Brookline	22,269	4,788	21,256	5,269
Cambridge	40,464	4,662	35,886	5,338
Chicopee	14,160	8,259	14,642	7,957
Fall River	22,431	7,892	23,859	7,369
Framingham	17,731	8,430	17,239	8,448
Lawrence	15,567	3,620	11,547	4,796
Lowell	20,576	10,363	18,195	10,554
Lynn	20,223	8,703	19,372	8,373
Medford	17,507	8,627	17,737	7,932
New Bedford	24,881	8,201	25,551	7,328
Newton	33,075	10,228	32,061	10,025
Quincy	22,775	15,536	24,173	13,373
Somerville	26,450	5,197	24,300	5,232
Springfield	38,228	10,976	33,583	13,028

City	2008		2004	
	Obama (D)	McCain (R)	Kerry (D)	Bush (R)
Waltham	15,233	8,372	14,517	8,228
Weymouth	14,681	12,331	15,367	10,912
Worcester	40,925	18,333	38,264	17,648
Other	1,279,365	896,551	1,227,624	858,194
Totals	**1,904,097**	**1,108,854**	**1,803,800**	**1,071,109**

Massachusetts Vote Since 1952
2008: Obama, D., 1,904,097; McCain, R., 1,108,854; Nader, Ind., 28,841; Barr, LB., 13,189; McKinney, Green, 6,550; Baldwin, RF., 4,971.
2004: Kerry, D., 1,803,800; Bush, R., 1,071,109; Badnarik, LB., 15,022; Cobb, Green, 10,623.
2000: Gore, D., 1,616,487; Bush, R., 878,502; Nader, Green, 173,564; Browne, LB., 16,366; Buchanan, RF., 11,149; Hagelin, Natural Law, 2,884.
1996: Clinton, D., 1,571,509; Dole, R., 718,058; Perot, RF., 227,206; Browne, LB., 20,424; Hagelin, Natural Law, 5,183; Moorehead, Workers World, 3,276.
1992: Clinton, D., 1,318,639; Bush, R., 805,039; Perot, Ind., 630,731; Marrou, LB., 9,021; Fulani, New Alliance, 3,172; Phillips, U.S. Taxpayers, 2,218; Hagelin, Natural Law, 1,812; LaRouche, Ind., 1,027.
1988: Dukakis, D., 1,401,415; Bush, R., 1,194,635; Paul, LB., 24,251; Fulani, New Alliance, 9,561.
1984: Reagan, R., 1,310,936; Mondale, D., 1,239,606.
1980: Reagan, R., 1,057,631; Carter, D., 1,053,802; Anderson, Ind., 382,539; Clark, LB., 22,038; DeBerry, Soc. Workers, 3,735; Commoner, Citizens, 2,056; McReynolds, Soc., 62; Bubar, Statesman, 34; Griswold, Workers World, 19; scattered, 2,382.
1976: Carter, D., 1,429,475; Ford, R., 1,030,276; McCarthy, Ind., 65,637; Camejo, Soc. Workers, 8,138; Anderson, Amer., 7,555; LaRouche, U.S. Labor, 4,922; MacBride, LB., 135.
1972: McGovern, D., 1,332,540; Nixon, R., 1,112,078; Jenness, Soc. Workers, 10,600; Schmitz, Amer., 2,877; Fisher, Soc. Labor, 129; Spock, People's, 101; Hall, Comm., 46; Hospers, LB., 43; scattered, 342.
1968: Humphrey, D., 1,469,218; Nixon, R., 766,844; Wallace, 3rd party, 87,088; Blomen, Soc. Labor, 6,180; Munn, Prohib., 2,369; scattered, 53; blank, 25,394.
1964: Johnson, D., 1,786,422; Goldwater, R., 549,727; Hass, Soc. Labor, 4,755; Munn, Prohib., 3,735; scattered, 159; blank, 48,104.
1960: Kennedy, D., 1,487,174; Nixon, R., 976,750; Hass, Soc. Labor, 3,892; Decker, Prohib., 1,633; others, 31; blank and void, 26,024.
1956: Eisenhower, R., 1,393,197; Stevenson, D., 948,190; Hass, Soc. Labor, 5,573; Holtwick, Prohib., 1,205; others, 341.
1952: Eisenhower, R., 1,292,325; Stevenson, D., 1,083,525; Hallinan, Prog., 4,636; Hass, Soc. Labor, 1,957; Hamblen, Prohib., 886; scattered, 69; blank, 41,150.

Michigan

County	2008		2004	
	Obama (D)	McCain (R)	Kerry (D)	Bush (R)
Alcona	2,896	3,404	2,871	3,592
Alger	2,472	2,188	2,395	2,318
Allegan	23,526	29,526	19,355	34,022
Alpena	7,705	7,125	7,407	7,665
Antrim	6,079	7,506	5,072	8,379
Arenac	4,155	3,807	4,076	4,071
Baraga	1,725	1,846	1,660	1,977
Barry	13,449	16,431	11,312	18,638
Bay	32,589	23,794	31,049	25,448
Benzie	5,461	4,687	4,383	5,284
Berrien	40,376	36,128	32,846	41,076
Branch	8,412	9,534	7,004	10,784
Calhoun	34,550	28,538	29,891	32,093
Cass	12,080	11,112	9,537	12,964
Charlevoix	6,817	7,306	5,729	8,214
Cheboygan	6,721	6,919	5,941	7,798
Chippewa	8,169	8,249	7,203	9,122
Clare	7,496	6,793	6,984	7,088
Clinton	20,001	19,724	15,483	21,989
Crawford	3,440	3,558	3,126	4,017
Delta	9,976	8,763	9,381	9,680
Dickinson	5,995	7,049	5,650	7,734
Eaton	30,736	25,898	25,411	29,781
Emmet	8,515	9,315	6,846	10,332
Genesee	143,919	72,445	128,334	83,870
Gladwin	6,590	6,391	6,343	6,770
Gogebic	4,757	3,330	4,421	3,935
Grand Traverse	23,255	24,713	18,256	27,446
Gratiot	9,102	8,324	7,377	9,834
Hillsdale	8,765	11,221	7,123	12,804
Houghton	7,473	8,100	6,731	8,889
Huron	8,367	8,434	7,629	9,671
Ingham	95,698	47,143	76,877	54,734
Ionia	14,808	15,850	10,647	16,621
Iosco	7,307	6,583	6,557	7,301
Iron	3,080	2,947	3,215	3,224
Isabella	16,679	11,220	12,334	11,754
Jackson	37,480	35,692	31,025	40,029
Kalamazoo	73,407	48,411	61,462	57,147
Kalkaska	3,780	4,527	3,189	5,084
Kent	149,855	148,305	116,909	171,201

County	2008 Obama (D)	McCain (R)	2004 Kerry (D)	Bush (R)
Keweenaw	610	756	630	781
Lake	2,919	2,269	2,675	2,503
Lapeer	21,457	22,831	18,086	25,556
Leelanau	7,354	6,937	6,048	7,733
Lenawee	24,638	22,223	20,787	25,675
Livingston	42,346	55,581	33,991	58,860
Luce	1,191	1,490	1,045	1,749
Mackinac	3,027	3,268	2,819	3,706
Macomb	223,754	187,645	196,160	202,166
Manistee	7,234	5,506	6,272	6,295
Marquette	19,630	12,902	17,412	14,690
Mason	7,816	7,146	6,333	8,124
Mecosta	9,099	9,235	7,730	9,710
Menominee	5,980	4,855	5,326	5,942
Midland	20,742	22,285	18,355	24,369
Missaukee	2,898	4,469	2,319	5,055
Monroe	39,180	35,852	36,089	37,470
Montcalm	13,208	13,291	11,471	14,968
Montmorency	2,403	2,841	2,196	3,300
Muskegon	53,400	28,855	44,282	35,302
Newaygo	10,788	11,862	9,057	13,608
Oakland	372,694	276,881	319,387	316,633
Oceana	6,405	5,860	5,441	6,677
Ogemaw	5,391	5,133	5,215	5,454
Ontonagon	1,966	1,823	1,863	2,262
Osceola	4,848	5,966	4,467	6,599
Oscoda	1,887	2,320	1,792	2,570
Otsego	5,634	6,752	4,674	7,470
Ottawa	51,925	84,823	35,552	92,048
Presque Isle	3,719	3,605	3,432	3,982
Roscommon	7,082	6,727	6,810	7,364
Saginaw	60,260	42,218	54,887	47,165
St. Clair	40,676	38,555	36,174	42,740
St. Joseph	12,311	12,876	9,648	15,340
Sanilac	9,047	10,678	7,883	12,632
Schoolcraft	2,184	2,058	2,137	2,058
Shiawassee	18,015	15,054	16,881	19,407
Tuscola	13,503	13,739	12,631	15,389
Van Buren	18,589	15,535	16,151	17,634
Washtenaw	130,547	53,943	109,953	61,455
Wayne	656,303	216,880	600,047	257,750
Wexford	7,357	8,044	6,034	8,986
Totals	**2,872,579**	**2,048,639**	**2,479,183**	**2,313,746**

Michigan Vote Since 1952

2008: Obama, D., 2,872,579; McCain, R., 2,048,639; Nader, Natural Law, 33,085; Barr, LB., 23,716; Baldwin, U.S. Taxpayers, 14,685; McKinney, Green, 8,892.

2004: Kerry, D., 2,479,183; Bush, R., 2,313,746; Nader, Ind., 24,035; Badnarik, LB., 10,552; Cobb, Green, 5,325; Peroutka, U.S. Taxpayers, 4,980; Brown, Natural Law, 1,431.

2000: Gore, D., 2,170,418; Bush, R., 1,953,139; Nader, Green, 84,165; Browne, LB., 16,711; Phillips, U.S. Taxpayers, 3,791; Hagelin, Natural Law, 2,426.

1996: Clinton, D., 1,989,653; Dole, R., 1,481,212; Perot, RF., 336,670; Browne, LB., 27,670; Hagelin, Natural Law, 4,254; Moorehead, Workers World, 3,153; White, Soc. Equality, 1,554.

1992: Clinton, D., 1,871,182; Bush, R., 1,554,940; Perot, Ind., 824,813; Marrou, LB., 10,175; Phillips, U.S. Taxpayers, 8,263; Hagelin, Natural Law, 2,954.

1988: Bush, R., 1,965,486; Dukakis, D., 1,675,783; Paul, LB., 18,336; Fulani, Ind., 2,513.

1984: Reagan, R., 2,251,571; Mondale, D., 1,529,638; Bergland, LB., 10,055.

1980: Reagan, R., 1,915,225; Carter, D., 1,661,532; Anderson, Ind., 275,223; Clark, LB., 41,597; Commoner, Citizens, 11,930; Hall, Comm., 3,262; Griswold, Workers World, 30; Greaves, Amer., 21; Bubar, Statesman, 9.

1976: Ford, R., 1,893,742; Carter, D., 1,696,714; McCarthy, Ind., 47,905; MacBride, LB., 5,406; Wright, People's, 3,504; Camejo, Soc. Workers, 1,804; LaRouche, U.S. Labor, 1,366; Levin, Soc. Labor, 1,148; scattered, 2,160.

1972: Nixon, R., 1,961,721; McGovern, D., 1,459,435; Schmitz, Amer., 63,321; Fisher, Soc. Labor, 2,437; Jenness, Soc. Workers, 1,603; Hall, Comm., 1,210.

1968: Humphrey, D., 1,593,082; Nixon, R., 1,370,665; Wallace, 3rd party, 331,968; Halstead, Soc. Workers, 4,099; Blomen, Soc. Labor, 1,762; Cleaver, New Politics, 4,585; Munn, Prohib., 60; scattered, 29.

1964: Johnson, D., 2,136,615; Goldwater, R., 1,060,152; DeBerry, Soc. Workers, 3,817; Hass, Soc. Labor, 1,704; Prohib. (no candidate listed), 699; scattered, 145.

1960: Kennedy, D., 1,687,269; Nixon, R., 1,620,428; Dobbs, Soc. Workers, 4,347; Decker, Prohib., 2,029; Daly, Tax Cut, 1,767; Hass, Soc. Labor, 1,718; Ind. Amer. (unpledged), 539.

1956: Eisenhower, R., 1,713,647; Stevenson, D., 1,359,898; Holtwick, Prohib., 6,923.

1952: Eisenhower, R., 1,551,529; Stevenson, D., 1,230,657; Hamblen, Prohib., 10,331; Hallinan, Prog., 3,922; Hass, Soc. Labor, 1,495; Dobbs, Soc. Workers, 655; scattered, 3.

Minnesota

County	2008 Obama (D)	McCain (R)	2004 Kerry (D)	Bush (R)
Aitkin	4,595	4,589	4,539	4,768
Anoka	86,976	91,357	80,226	91,853
Becker	7,687	8,851	6,756	9,795
Beltrami	12,019	9,762	10,592	10,237
Benton	8,454	10,338	8,059	10,043
Big Stone	1,552	1,362	1,536	1,483
Blue Earth	19,325	14,782	16,865	15,737
Brown	5,809	7,456	5,158	8,395
Carlton	11,501	6,549	11,442	6,642
Carver	20,654	28,156	16,456	28,510
Cass	7,276	8,660	6,835	8,875
Chippewa	3,280	2,907	3,424	3,089
Chisago	12,783	15,789	12,219	15,705
Clay	16,666	11,978	12,989	14,365
Clearwater	1,877	2,291	1,871	2,438
Cook	2,019	1,240	1,733	1,489
Cottonwood	2,759	3,157	2,726	3,557
Crow Wing	15,859	18,567	14,005	19,106
Dakota	116,778	104,364	104,635	108,959
Dodge	4,463	5,468	4,117	5,593
Douglas	9,256	11,241	8,219	11,793
Faribault	3,736	4,196	3,767	4,794
Fillmore	5,921	4,993	5,825	5,694
Freeborn	9,915	6,955	9,733	7,681
Goodhue	12,420	12,775	12,103	13,134
Grant	1,850	1,646	1,856	1,893
Hennepin	420,958	231,054	383,841	255,133
Houston	5,906	4,743	5,276	5,631
Hubbard	4,872	6,558	4,741	6,444
Isanti	8,248	11,324	7,883	11,190
Itasca	13,460	10,309	13,290	10,705
Jackson	2,618	2,858	2,652	3,024
Kanabec	3,743	4,479	3,592	4,527
Kandiyohi	10,125	11,319	9,337	11,704
Kittson	1,492	1,016	1,333	1,307
Koochiching	3,649	2,962	3,662	3,539
Lac Qui Parle	2,160	1,912	2,390	2,093
Lake	4,174	2,636	4,212	2,769
Lake of the Woods	971	1,278	921	1,428
Le Sueur	6,994	7,636	6,466	7,746
Lincoln	1,517	1,491	1,558	1,736
Lyon	6,110	6,315	5,292	7,203
Mahnomen	1,436	843	1,339	1,132
Marshall	2,311	2,285	2,308	3,187
Martin	4,413	6,053	4,590	6,311
McLeod	7,505	10,993	6,712	11,407
Meeker	5,380	6,737	5,292	6,854
Mille Lacs	6,072	7,049	5,677	7,194
Morrison	6,547	9,735	6,794	9,698
Mower	11,605	7,075	12,334	7,591
Murray	2,345	2,320	2,218	2,719
Nicollet	9,887	7,968	8,797	8,689
Nobles	4,244	4,368	3,898	5,159
Norman	2,129	1,204	1,954	1,794
Olmsted	38,711	36,202	33,285	37,371
Otter Tail	13,856	18,077	12,038	19,734
Pennington	3,394	3,248	3,117	3,767
Pine	7,084	6,862	7,228	7,033
Pipestone	2,023	2,652	1,900	3,066
Polk	7,850	7,148	6,729	8,724
Pope	3,317	3,069	3,301	3,303
Ramsey	182,974	88,942	171,846	97,096
Red Lake	1,120	983	963	1,164
Redwood	3,250	4,308	3,104	4,898
Renville	3,904	3,956	3,787	4,430
Rice	17,381	13,723	16,425	13,881
Rock	2,079	2,775	2,000	3,111
Roseau	3,097	4,438	2,442	5,355
St. Louis	77,351	38,742	77,958	40,112
Scott	29,208	36,724	23,958	36,055
Sherburne	17,957	26,140	15,816	25,182
Sibley	2,998	4,492	3,109	4,669
Stearns	35,690	41,194	32,659	41,726
Steele	9,016	10,068	7,994	10,389
Stevens	2,781	2,710	2,821	3,030
Swift	2,907	2,184	3,165	2,481
Todd	5,277	6,637	5,034	6,945
Traverse	1,043	933	1,026	1,076
Wabasha	5,646	5,935	5,548	6,120
Wadena	2,882	4,128	2,791	4,214
Waseca	4,401	5,211	4,179	5,457
Washington	70,277	64,334	61,395	65,751
Watonwan	2,562	2,526	2,514	2,970
Wilkin	1,550	1,786	1,169	2,303
Winona	16,308	10,975	14,231	12,686
Wright	26,343	37,779	22,618	36,176
Yellow Medicine	2,816	2,579	2,799	2,878
Totals	**1,573,354**	**1,275,409**	**1,445,014**	**1,346,695**

Minnesota Vote Since 1952

2008: Obama, D., 1,573,354; McCain, R., 1,275,409; Nader, Ind., 30,152; Barr, LB., 9,174; Baldwin, Const., 6,787; McKinney, Green, 5,174; Calero, Soc. Workers, 790.

2004: Kerry, D., 1,445,014; Bush, R., 1,346,695; Nader, Better Life, 18,683; Badnarik, LB., 4,639; Cobb, Green, 4,408; Peroutka, Const., 3,074; Harens, other, 2,387; Van Auken, Soc. Equal., 539; Calero, Soc. Workers, 416.

2000: Gore, D., 1,168,266; Bush, R., 1,109,659; Nader, Green, 126,696; Buchanan, RF. MN, 22,166; Browne, LB., 5,282; Phillips, Const., 3,272; Hagelin, RF., 2,294; Harris, Soc. Workers, 1,022.

1996: Clinton, D., 1,120,438; Dole, R., 766,476; Perot, RF., 257,704; Nader, Green, 24,908; Browne, LB., 8,271; Peron, Grass Roots, 4,898; Phillips, U.S. Taxpayers, 3,416; Hagelin, Natural Law, 1,808; Birrenbach, Ind. Grass Roots, 787; Harris, Soc. Workers, 684; White, Soc. Equality, 347.

1992: Clinton, D., 1,020,997; Bush, R., 747,841; Perot, Ind., 562,506; Marrou, LB., 3,373; Gritz, Populist/America First, 3,363; Hagelin, Natural Law, 1,406.

1988: Dukakis, D., 1,109,471; Bush, R., 962,337; McCarthy, Minn. Prog., 5,403; Paul, LB., 5,109.

1984: Mondale, D., 1,036,364; Reagan, R., 1,032,603; Bergland, LB., 2,996.

1980: Carter, D., 954,173; Reagan, R., 873,268; Anderson, Ind., 174,997; Clark, LB., 31,593; Commoner, Citizens, 8,406; Hall, Comm., 1,117; DeBerry, Soc. Workers, 711; Griswold, Workers World, 698; McReynolds, Soc., 536; write-in, 281.

1976: Carter, D., 1,070,440; Ford, R. 819,395; McCarthy, Ind., 35,490; Anderson, Amer., 13,592; Camejo, Soc. Workers, 4,149; MacBride, LB., 3,529; Hall, Comm., 1,092.

1972: Nixon, R., 898,269; McGovern, D., 802,346; Schmitz, Amer., 31,407; Fisher, Soc. Labor, 4,261; Spock, People's, 2,805; Jenness, Soc. Workers, 940; Hall, Comm., 662; scattered, 962.

1968: Humphrey, D., 857,738; Nixon, R., 658,643; Wallace, 3rd party, 68,931; Cleaver, Peace/Freedom, 935; Halstead, Soc. Workers, 808; McCarthy, write-in, 585; Mitchell, Comm., 415; Blomen, Industrial Govt., 285; scattered, 2,613.

1964: Johnson, D., 991,117; Goldwater, R., 559,624; Hass, Industrial Gov., 2,544; DeBerry, Soc. Workers, 1,177.

1960: Kennedy, D., 779,933; Nixon, R., 757,915; Dobbs, Soc. Workers, 3,077; Hass, Industrial Govt. 962.

1956: Eisenhower, R., 719,302; Stevenson, D., 617,525; Hass, Soc. Labor (Ind. Govt.), 2,080; Dobbs, Soc. Workers, 1,098.

1952: Eisenhower, R., 763,211; Stevenson, D., 608,458; Hallinan, Prog., 2,666; Hass, Soc. Labor, 2,383; Hamblen, Prohib., 2,147; Dobbs, Soc. Workers, 618.

Mississippi

County	2008		2004	
	Obama (D)	McCain (R)	Kerry (D)	Bush (R)
Adams	7,630	5,300	8,423	6,996
Alcorn	3,701	9,752	5,454	8,634
Amite	3,320	4,214	3,012	4,147
Attala	3,739	5,209	3,145	5,014
Benton	2,224	2,329	2,245	1,969
Bolivar	9,471	4,487	9,631	5,535
Calhoun	2,242	4,068	2,234	4,131
Carroll	2,027	3,886	1,900	3,664
Chickasaw	4,053	3,934	4,078	4,193
Choctaw	1,459	2,624	1,366	2,694
Claiborne	3,561	632	4,362	950
Clarke	2,727	4,679	2,402	5,068
Clay	6,424	4,412	4,753	4,342
Coahoma	6,947	2,502	6,805	3,676
Copiah	7,640	6,683	4,961	6,374
Covington	3,826	5,503	3,158	5,044
DeSoto	19,265	43,510	13,255	36,306
Forrest	11,622	15,296	10,220	16,318
Franklin	1,722	2,896	1,574	2,893
George	1,398	7,050	1,724	6,223
Greene	1,362	4,358	1,421	3,850
Grenada	4,995	6,215	4,180	5,872
Hancock	3,195	11,614	5,107	12,581
Harrison	22,175	37,927	23,076	39,703
Hinds	68,794	29,187	54,845	36,975
Holmes	6,945	1,504	6,366	1,961
Humphreys	3,180	1,243	3,168	1,679
Issaquena	523	322	516	439
Itawamba	1,938	7,240	2,802	6,833
Jackson	15,534	32,959	15,572	35,134
Jasper	4,476	3,660	4,117	3,855
Jefferson	3,295	450	2,821	630
Jefferson Davis	3,924	2,512	2,959	2,668
Jones	8,089	18,726	7,398	19,125
Kemper	2,876	1,694	2,465	2,109
Lafayette	7,997	10,278	6,218	9,004
Lamar	4,694	16,969	3,923	16,410
Lauderdale	13,048	19,368	10,292	19,736
Lawrence	2,513	4,318	2,308	3,956
Leake	3,575	4,509	3,212	4,962
Lee	11,769	22,403	10,127	20,254
Leflore	8,914	4,105	7,566	4,635
Lincoln	5,505	10,781	4,418	10,008
Lowndes	13,110	13,934	10,408	13,690

County	2008		2004	
	Obama (D)	McCain (R)	Kerry (D)	Bush (R)
Madison	18,034	24,781	13,268	24,257
Marion	3,764	7,350	3,888	7,999
Marshall	9,573	6,650	8,591	5,975
Monroe	7,137	10,165	6,237	9,308
Montgomery	2,244	2,638	2,473	3,002
Neshoba	2,584	7,205	2,600	7,780
Newton	3,063	6,338	2,280	6,165
Noxubee	4,970	1,507	4,346	1,723
Oktibbeha	9,326	9,320	7,015	9,068
Panola	8,370	7,515	6,615	6,769
Pearl River	3,727	16,156	4,472	14,896
Perry	1,521	4,040	1,261	3,747
Pike	7,958	7,441	7,881	8,660
Pontotoc	2,951	9,656	2,660	8,480
Prentiss	3,020	7,703	3,327	6,538
Quitman	2,797	1,334	2,032	1,360
Rankin	14,235	47,645	11,005	43,054
Scott	4,709	6,205	3,802	6,395
Sharkey	1,722	784	1,560	1,120
Simpson	4,393	6,660	3,272	7,138
Smith	1,821	5,715	1,496	5,577
Stone	1,746	4,661	1,528	4,146
Sunflower	7,158	2,900	6,359	3,534
Tallahatchie	3,646	2,435	3,420	2,737
Tate	4,951	7,639	4,347	6,760
Tippah	2,514	6,809	3,016	6,174
Tishomingo	1,941	6,195	2,846	5,379
Tunica	2,917	864	2,140	950
Union	2,727	8,302	2,839	7,906
Walthall	3,421	4,244	2,435	3,888
Warren	9,502	9,953	8,224	11,356
Washington	12,884	6,274	11,569	7,731
Wayne	3,860	6,056	3,193	5,562
Webster	1,321	4,032	1,341	3,708
Wilkinson	3,498	1,556	2,794	1,563
Winston	4,606	5,473	3,978	5,386
Yalobusha	3,104	3,604	2,656	3,278
Yazoo	5,725	4,219	5,013	5,672
Totals	**554,662**	**724,597**	**458,094**	**684,981**

Mississippi Vote Since 1952

2008: McCain, R., 724,597; Obama, D., 554,662; Nader, Ind., 4,011; Baldwin, Const., 2,551; Barr, LB., 2,529; McKinney, Green, 1,034; Weill, RF., 481.

2004: Bush, R., 684,981; Kerry, D., 458,094; Nader, RF., 3,177; Badnarik, LB., 1,793; Peroutka, Const., 1,759; Harris, Ind., 1,268; Cobb, Green, 1,073.

2000: Bush, R., 572,844; Gore, D., 404,614; Nader, Ind., 8,122; Phillips, Const., 2,267; Buchanan, RF., 2,265; Browne, LB., 2,009; Harris, Ind., 613; Hagelin, Natural Law, 450.

1996: Dole, R., 439,838; Clinton, D., 394,022; Perot, RF., 52,222; Browne, LB., 2,809; Phillips, U.S. Taxpayers, 2,314; Hagelin, Natural Law, 1,447; Collins, Ind., 1,205.

1992: Bush, R., 487,793; Clinton, D., 400,258; Perot, Ind., 85,626; Fulani, New Alliance, 2,625; Marrou, LB., 2,154; Phillips, U.S. Taxpayers, 1,652; Hagelin, Natural Law, 1,140.

1988: Bush, R., 557,890; Dukakis, D., 363,921; Duke, Ind., 4,232; Paul, LB., 3,329.

1984: Reagan, R., 582,377; Mondale, D., 352,192; Bergland, LB., 2,336.

1980: Reagan, R., 441,089; Carter, D., 429,281; Anderson, Ind., 12,036; Clark, LB., 5,465; Griswold, Workers World, 2,402; Pulley, Soc. Workers, 2,347.

1976: Carter, D., 381,309; Ford, R., 366,846; Anderson, Amer., 6,678; McCarthy, Ind., 4,074; Maddox, Ind., 4,049; Camejo, Soc. Workers, 2,805; MacBride, LB., 2,609.

1972: Nixon, R., 505,125; McGovern, D., 126,782; Schmitz, Amer., 11,598; Jenness, Soc. Workers, 2,458.

1968: Wallace, 3rd party, 415,349; Humphrey, D., 150,644; Nixon, R., 88,516.

1964: Goldwater, R., 356,528; Johnson, D., 52,618.

1960: D. (electors unpledged), 116,248; Kennedy, D., 108,362; Nixon, R., 73,561. Mississippi's victorious slate of 8 unpledged Democratic electors cast their votes for Sen. Harry F. Byrd (D, VA).

1956: Stevenson, D., 144,498; Eisenhower, R., 56,372 and Black and Tan Grand Old Party, 4,313 (total, 60,685); Byrd, Ind., 42,966.

1952: Stevenson, D., 172,566; Eisenhower, Ind., vote pledged to R. candidate, 112,966.

Missouri

County	2008		2004	
	Obama (D)	McCain (R)	Kerry (D)	Bush (R)
Adair	5,735	5,891	4,938	6,367
Andrew	3,345	5,279	3,069	5,135
Atchison	1,000	1,936	1,005	2,137
Audrain	4,434	6,167	4,318	6,294
Barry	4,630	9,758	4,223	9,599
Barton	1,455	4,414	1,373	4,572
Bates	3,271	4,833	3,398	5,004
Benton	3,629	5,759	3,381	5,575
Bollinger	1,690	3,972	1,754	4,102
Boone	47,062	36,849	37,643	37,801

County	2008 Obama (D)	McCain (R)	2004 Kerry (D)	Bush (R)
Buchanan	19,164	19,110	17,799	19,812
Butler	5,316	11,805	4,666	11,696
Caldwell	1,814	2,654	1,645	2,593
Callaway	7,580	11,389	6,559	11,108
Camden	7,773	14,074	6,296	13,122
Cape Girardeau	12,208	24,768	10,568	23,814
Carroll	1,535	2,955	1,568	3,155
Carter	984	1,840	964	1,797
Cass	19,844	29,695	16,681	27,253
Cedar	2,060	4,194	1,910	4,238
Chariton	1,799	2,339	1,892	2,421
Christian	11,883	25,382	9,059	22,102
Clark	1,572	1,782	1,794	1,899
Clay	53,761	54,516	44,670	51,193
Clinton	4,545	5,709	4,165	5,287
Cole	13,959	24,385	11,753	24,752
Cooper	2,996	4,902	2,400	5,058
Crawford	3,911	6,007	3,632	5,686
Dade	1,184	2,864	1,104	2,963
Dallas	2,656	4,895	2,407	4,788
Daviess	1,400	2,263	1,402	2,351
DeKalb	1,692	2,889	1,707	2,941
Dent	2,056	4,655	1,865	4,369
Douglas	2,140	4,405	1,741	4,498
Dunklin	4,540	7,044	4,901	6,720
Franklin	21,256	27,355	18,556	26,429
Gasconade	2,899	4,763	2,355	4,753
Gentry	1,235	1,964	1,201	2,085
Greene	56,181	77,683	46,657	77,885
Grundy	1,580	3,006	1,561	3,172
Harrison	1,287	2,512	1,279	2,729
Henry	4,869	6,095	4,461	6,361
Hickory	2,171	2,850	2,043	2,791
Holt	802	1,794	811	1,864
Howard	2,036	2,708	1,972	2,915
Howell	5,736	10,982	5,118	11,097
Iron	2,213	2,090	2,157	2,477
Jackson	210,824	124,687	183,654	130,500
Jasper	15,730	31,667	13,002	31,846
Jefferson	53,467	50,804	46,057	46,624
Johnson	9,480	12,183	7,790	12,257
Knox	759	1,212	761	1,207
Laclede	5,218	10,875	4,213	10,578
Lafayette	6,902	9,442	6,412	9,656
Lawrence	5,097	11,263	4,506	11,194
Lewis	1,837	2,594	1,754	2,862
Lincoln	10,234	12,924	8,368	11,316
Linn	2,638	3,140	2,440	3,422
Livingston	2,435	3,993	2,278	4,029
Macon	2,784	4,586	2,856	4,673
Madison	2,042	2,897	1,972	2,905
Maries	1,599	2,853	1,563	2,825
Marion	4,703	7,705	4,568	7,815
McDonald	2,454	5,499	2,215	5,443
Mercer	519	1,169	582	1,207
Miller	3,553	7,797	2,959	7,797
Mississippi	2,247	3,034	2,374	2,903
Moniteau	2,084	4,467	1,913	4,743
Monroe	1,703	2,533	1,647	2,632
Montgomery	2,347	3,428	2,147	3,563
Morgan	3,565	5,451	3,053	5,657
New Madrid	3,370	4,593	3,716	4,154
Newton	7,450	17,637	6,564	17,187
Nodaway	4,493	5,568	3,830	6,226
Oregon	1,811	2,652	1,823	2,769
Osage	1,907	5,062	1,673	4,975
Ozark	1,661	2,918	1,561	3,083
Pemiscot	3,029	3,954	3,381	3,398
Perry	3,005	5,527	2,621	5,583
Pettis	6,932	11,018	5,801	11,603
Phelps	7,394	11,706	6,666	11,874
Pike	3,487	4,268	3,670	4,314
Platte	21,459	24,460	18,412	23,302
Polk	4,553	8,956	3,775	8,586
Pulaski	5,249	9,552	3,551	8,618
Putnam	695	1,591	772	1,660
Ralls	2,041	2,987	2,031	2,986
Randolph	3,984	6,457	3,586	6,551
Ray	5,241	5,593	5,034	5,673
Reynolds	1,417	1,780	1,449	1,896
Ripley	1,795	3,407	1,907	3,693
St. Charles	84,183	102,550	66,855	95,826
St. Clair	1,886	2,981	1,841	3,098
St. Francois	11,540	12,660	10,748	12,087
St. Louis County	333,123	221,705	295,284	244,969
Ste. Genevieve	4,979	3,732	4,281	3,791
Saline	4,712	4,962	4,479	5,389
Schuyler	775	1,139	894	1,124
Scotland	793	1,249	828	1,352
Scott	6,258	11,563	6,057	11,330

County	2008 Obama (D)	McCain (R)	2004 Kerry (D)	Bush (R)
Shannon	1,637	2,075	1,618	2,511
Shelby	1,114	2,166	1,201	2,280
Stoddard	3,899	9,172	3,946	9,242
Stone	5,029	11,147	4,578	10,534
Sullivan	1,173	1,607	1,178	1,880
Taney	6,683	14,736	5,601	13,578
Texas	3,410	7,215	3,664	7,234
Vernon	3,381	5,334	3,206	5,732
Warren	6,705	8,675	5,461	7,883
Washington	4,711	4,706	4,459	4,641
Wayne	2,243	3,784	2,250	3,919
Webster	5,685	10,431	4,657	10,194
Worth	427	707	436	691
Wright	2,557	5,784	2,188	6,090
City				
St. Louis	132,925	24,662	116,133	27,793
Totals	1,441,911	1,445,814	1,259,171	1,455,713

Missouri Vote Since 1952

2008: McCain, R., 1,445,814; Obama, D., 1,441,911; Nader, Ind., 17,813; Barr, LB., 11,386; Baldwin, Const., 8,201.

2004: Bush, R., 1,455,713; Kerry, D., 1,259,171; Badnarik, LB., 9,831; Peroutka, Const., 5,355.

2000: Bush, R., 1,189,924; Gore, D., 1,111,138; Nader, Green, 38,515; Buchanan, RF., 9,818; Browne, LB., 7,436; Phillips, Const., 1,957; Hagelin, Natural Law, 1,104.

1996: Clinton, D., 1,025,935; Dole, R., 890,016; Perot, RF., 217,188; Phillips, U.S. Taxpayers, 11,521; Browne, LB., 10,522; Hagelin, Natural Law, 2,287.

1992: Clinton, D., 1,053,873; Bush, R., 811,159; Perot, Ind., 518,741; Marrou, LB., 7,497.

1988: Bush, R., 1,084,953; Dukakis, D., 1,001,619; Fulani, New Alliance, 6,656; Paul, write-in, 434.

1984: Reagan, R., 1,274,188; Mondale, D., 848,583.

1980: Reagan, R., 1,074,181; Carter, D., 931,182; Anderson, Ind., 77,920; Clark, LB., 14,422; DeBerry, Soc. Workers, 1,515; Commoner, Citizens, 573; write-in, 1.

1976: Carter, D., 999,163; Ford, R., 928,808; McCarthy, Ind., 24,329.

1972: Nixon, R., 1,154,058; McGovern, D., 698,531.

1968: Nixon, R., 811,932; Humphrey, D., 791,444; Wallace, 3rd party, 206,126.

1964: Johnson, D., 1,164,344; Goldwater, R., 653,535.

1960: Kennedy, D., 972,201; Nixon, R., 962,221.

1956: Stevenson, D., 918,273; Eisenhower, R., 914,299.

1952: Eisenhower, R., 959,429; Stevenson, D., 929,830; Hallinan, Prog., 987; Hamblen, Prohib., 885; MacArthur, Christian Nationalist, 302; America First, 233; Hoopes, Soc., 227; Hass, Soc. Labor, 169.

Montana

County	2008 Obama (D)	McCain (R)	2004 Kerry (D)	Bush (R)
Beaverhead	1,611	2,983	1,103	3,067
Big Horn	3,490	1,622	2,215	2,028
Blaine	1,711	1,138	1,300	1,424
Broadwater	854	1,853	533	1,778
Carbon	2,431	3,093	1,847	3,342
Carter	111	573	76	623
Cascade	17,486	16,675	13,701	19,028
Chouteau	1,118	1,625	946	1,913
Custer	2,262	3,040	1,630	3,297
Daniels	343	692	326	764
Dawson	1,587	2,626	1,494	2,884
Deer Lodge	3,341	1,481	2,700	1,725
Fallon	318	1,082	289	1,178
Fergus	1,921	4,100	1,582	4,425
Flathead	15,976	25,361	11,587	26,019
Gallatin	23,984	22,375	16,405	22,392
Garfield	109	595	52	590
Glacier	3,361	1,443	2,641	1,828
Golden Valley	122	342	119	396
Granite	601	1,013	404	1,144
Hill	3,563	2,763	2,997	3,505
Jefferson	2,574	3,525	1,881	3,844
Judith Basin	396	799	322	944
Lake	6,693	6,463	4,960	7,245
Lewis & Clark	16,939	14,794	12,717	16,494
Liberty	367	594	281	734
Lincoln	3,018	5,699	2,320	5,889
Madison	1,596	2,803	983	2,868
McCone	321	726	320	791
Meagher	298	624	247	698
Mineral	844	1,051	542	1,242
Missoula	35,701	20,266	26,983	23,989
Musselshell	615	1,552	538	1,663
Park	4,140	4,349	3,199	4,771
Petroleum	68	227	55	228
Phillips	638	1,423	456	1,677
Pondera	1,224	1,583	956	1,853
Powder River	207	797	154	856
Powell	1,021	1,679	761	1,993

County	2008 Obama (D)	McCain (R)	2004 Kerry (D)	Bush (R)
Prairie	211	503	181	546
Ravalli	8,332	12,922	6,144	13,279
Richland	1,196	3,158	1,120	3,110
Roosevelt	2,527	1,455	2,195	1,762
Rosebud	1,898	1,739	1,520	1,982
Sanders	1,964	3,556	1,502	3,461
Sheridan	953	987	846	1,159
Silver Bow	11,651	4,806	9,307	6,381
Stillwater	1,512	2,989	1,025	3,090
Sweet Grass	552	1,433	445	1,509
Teton	1,291	1,873	1,047	2,232
Toole	736	1,321	690	1,583
Treasure	154	310	121	348
Valley	1,616	2,099	1,431	2,476
Wheatland	286	632	250	706
Wibaux	146	379	144	407
Yellowstone	31,740	36,225	24,120	40,903
Totals	**231,667**	**242,763**	**173,710**	**266,063**

Montana Vote Since 1952

2008: McCain, R., 242,763; Obama, D., 231,667; Paul, Const., 10,638; Nader, Ind., 3,686; Barr, LB., 1,355.
2004: Bush, R., 266,063; Kerry, D., 173,710; Nader, Ind., 6,168; Peroutka, Const., 1,764; Badnarik, LB., 1,733; Cobb, Green, 996.
2000: Bush, R., 240,178; Gore, D., 137,126; Nader, Green, 24,437; Buchanan, RF., 5,697; Browne, LB., 1,718; Phillips, Const., 1,155; Hagelin, Natural Law, 675.
1996: Dole, R., 179,652; Clinton, D., 167,922; Perot, RF., 55,229; Browne, LB., 2,526; Hagelin, Natural Law, 1,754.
1992: Clinton, D., 154,507; Bush, R., 144,207; Perot, Ind., 107,225; Gritz, Pop./America First, 3,658.
1988: Bush, R., 190,412; Dukakis, D., 168,936; Paul, LB., 5,047; Fulani, New Alliance, 1,279.
1984: Reagan, R., 232,450; Mondale, D., 146,742; Bergland, LB., 5,185.
1980: Reagan, R., 206,814; Carter, D., 118,032; Anderson, Ind., 29,281; Clark, LB., 9,825.
1976: Ford, R., 173,703; Carter, D., 149,259; Anderson, Amer., 5,772.
1972: Nixon, R., 183,976; McGovern, D., 120,197; Schmitz, Amer., 13,430.
1968: Nixon, R., 138,835; Humphrey, D., 114,117; Wallace, 3rd party, 20,015; Munn, Prohib., 510; Caton, New RF., 470; Halstead, Soc. Workers, 457.
1964: Johnson, D., 164,246; Goldwater, R., 113,032; Kasper, Natl. States' Rights, 519; Munn, Prohib., 499; DeBerry, Soc. Workers, 332.
1960: Nixon, R., 141,841; Kennedy, D., 134,891; Decker, Prohib., 456; Dobbs, Soc. Workers, 391.
1956: Eisenhower, R., 154,933; Stevenson, D., 116,238.
1952: Eisenhower, R., 157,394; Stevenson, D., 106,213; Hallinan, Prog., 723; Hamblen, Prohib., 548; Hoopes, Soc., 159.

Nebraska

County	2008 Obama (D)	McCain (R)	2004 Kerry (D)	Bush (R)
Adams	4,624	8,163	3,791	9,233
Antelope	754	2,367	613	2,761
Arthur	39	217	24	240
Banner	61	341	56	379
Blaine	43	266	38	301
Boone	742	2,042	546	2,309
Box Butte	1,844	2,888	1,657	3,396
Boyd	250	839	228	911
Brown	311	1,208	268	1,426
Buffalo	5,768	12,920	4,100	14,222
Burt	1,406	1,895	1,272	2,349
Butler	1,175	2,534	1,068	3,016
Cass	4,709	7,076	3,619	7,763
Cedar	1,187	2,912	1,083	3,387
Chase	341	1,466	302	1,652
Cherry	599	2,360	483	2,509
Cheyenne	1,064	3,284	893	3,791
Clay	761	2,134	743	2,543
Colfax	1,125	2,014	990	2,589
Cuming	1,255	2,701	966	3,330
Custer	1,178	4,220	1,040	4,518
Dakota	2,966	3,255	3,027	3,526
Dawes	1,245	2,330	1,119	2,809
Dawson	2,352	5,368	1,728	6,149
Deuel	243	732	222	820
Dixon	946	1,785	938	2,028
Dodge	6,587	8,482	5,250	10,716
Douglas	116,893	106,419	83,330	120,813
Dundy	218	783	186	858
Fillmore	953	1,907	828	2,314
Franklin	442	1,078	412	1,277
Frontier	348	1,030	275	1,160
Furnas	556	1,725	492	1,950
Gage	4,405	5,389	3,655	6,575
Garden	283	844	201	970

County	2008 Obama (D)	McCain (R)	2004 Kerry (D)	Bush (R)
Garfield	212	800	196	806
Gosper	260	771	222	890
Grant	41	321	41	352
Greeley	457	714	361	865
Hall	7,687	12,788	6,228	14,592
Hamilton	1,322	3,362	1,012	3,785
Harlan	399	1,327	398	1,467
Hayes	85	460	66	524
Hitchcock	346	997	296	1,171
Holt	1,065	3,663	894	4,217
Hooker	75	355	64	392
Howard	1,083	1,847	900	2,020
Jefferson	1,504	2,091	1,352	2,600
Johnson	914	1,139	885	1,470
Kearney	870	2,217	707	2,621
Keith	965	2,917	743	3,356
Keya Paha	115	409	98	442
Kimball	427	1,328	366	1,491
Knox	1,248	2,724	1,086	3,062
Lancaster	63,464	57,925	52,747	69,764
Lincoln	4,937	10,609	4,905	11,056
Logan	81	327	67	357
Loup	86	302	68	314
Madison	4,076	9,542	2,934	10,981
McPherson	45	240	49	259
Merrick	978	2,356	833	2,771
Morrill	546	1,700	495	1,755
Nance	540	1,110	459	1,237
Nemaha	1,207	2,090	1,066	2,595
Nuckolls	692	1,607	541	1,884
Otoe	2,893	3,991	2,275	5,018
Pawnee	481	857	481	986
Perkins	310	1,086	262	1,285
Phelps	1,043	3,340	830	3,872
Pierce	781	2,372	546	2,824
Platte	3,734	9,279	2,657	11,130
Polk	665	1,810	549	2,146
Red Willow	1,216	3,748	1,055	4,129
Richardson	1,121	1,880	1,297	2,924
Rock	136	635	130	740
Saline	2,597	2,373	2,420	3,071
Sarpy	28,010	38,816	17,455	40,163
Saunders	3,739	6,132	2,884	6,441
Scotts Bluff	4,645	9,575	3,843	10,378
Seward	2,671	4,596	2,114	5,353
Sheridan	451	1,934	430	2,136
Sherman	583	940	541	1,072
Sioux	116	600	123	677
Stanton	657	1,772	559	2,159
Thayer	850	1,729	764	2,075
Thomas	51	331	60	378
Thurston	1,108	970	1,212	1,154
Valley	704	1,647	564	1,801
Washington	3,681	6,409	2,754	7,083
Wayne	1,249	2,503	1,059	2,971
Webster	550	1,323	557	1,403
Wheeler	96	334	81	366
York	1,594	4,807	1,304	5,393
Totals	**333,319**	**452,979**	**254,328**	**512,814**

Nebraska Vote Since 1952

2008: McCain, R., 452,979; Obama, D., 333,319; Nader, petitioning cand., 5,406; Baldwin, Nebraska, 2,972; Barr, LB., 2,740; McKinney, Green, 1,028.
2004: Bush, R., 512,814; Kerry, D., 254,328; Nader, petitioning cand., 5,698; Badnarik, LB., 2,041; Peroutka, Nebraska, 1,314; Cobb, Green, 978; Calero, petitioning cand., 82.
2000: Bush, R., 433,862; Gore, D., 231,780; Nader, Green, 24,540; Buchanan, Ind., 3,646; Browne, LB., 2,245; Hagelin, Natural Law, 478; Phillips, Ind., 468.
1996: Dole, R., 363,467; Clinton, D., 236,761; Perot, RF., 71,278; Browne, LB., 2,792; Phillips, Ind., 1,928; Hagelin, Natural Law, 1,189.
1992: Bush, R., 343,678; Clinton, D., 216,864; Perot, Ind., 174,104; Marrou, LB., 1,340.
1988: Bush, R., 397,956; Dukakis, D., 259,235; Paul, LB., 2,534; Fulani, New Alliance, 1,740.
1984: Reagan, R., 459,135; Mondale, D., 187,475; Bergland, LB., 2,075.
1980: Reagan, R., 419,214; Carter, D., 166,424; Anderson, Ind., 44,854; Clark, LB., 9,041.
1976: Ford, R., 359,219; Carter, D., 233,287; McCarthy, Ind., 9,383; Maddox, Amer. Ind., 3,378; MacBride, LB., 1,476.
1972: Nixon, R., 406,298; McGovern, D., 169,991; scattered, 817.
1968: Nixon, R., 321,163; Humphrey, D., 170,784; Wallace, 3rd party, 44,904.
1964: Johnson, D., 307,307; Goldwater, R., 276,847.
1960: Nixon, R., 380,553; Kennedy, D., 232,542.
1956: Eisenhower, R., 378,108; Stevenson, D., 199,029.
1952: Eisenhower, R., 421,603; Stevenson, D., 188,057.

Nevada

County	2008		2004	
	Obama (D)	McCain (R)	Kerry (D)	Bush (R)
Churchill	3,494	6,831	2,705	7,335
Clark	379,204	256,401	281,767	255,337
Douglas	10,671	14,645	8,275	15,192
Elko	4,537	10,958	3,050	11,938
Esmeralda	104	303	99	367
Eureka	144	564	144	571
Humboldt	1,909	3,584	1,361	3,896
Lander	574	1,462	414	1,602
Lincoln	518	1,498	418	1,579
Lyon	8,405	12,154	5,637	11,136
Mineral	1,082	1,131	931	1,336
Nye	7,223	9,535	5,616	8,487
Pershing	673	1,075	538	1,341
Storey	1,099	1,245	871	1,253
Washoe	99,395	76,743	74,841	81,545
White Pine	1,230	2,440	1,082	2,604
City				
Carson City	11,622	11,419	9,441	13,171
Totals	**533,736**	**412,827**	**397,190**	**418,690**

Nevada Vote Since 1952

2008: Obama, D., 533,736; McCain, R., 412,827; Nader, Ind., 6,150; Barr, LB., 4,263; Baldwin, Const., 3,194; McKinney, Green, 1,411; None of These Candidates, 6,267.

2004: Bush, R., 418,690; Kerry, D., 397,190; Nader, Ind., 4,838; None of These Candidates, 3,688; Badnarik, LB., 3,176; Peroutka, Ind. Amer., 1,152; Cobb, Green, 853.

2000: Bush, R., 301,575; Gore, D., 279,978; Nader, Green, 15,008; Buchanan, Citizens First, 4,747; None of These Candidates, 3,315; Browne, LB., 3,311; Phillips, Ind. Amer., 621; Hagelin, Natural Law, 415.

1996: Clinton, D., 203,974; Dole, R., 199,244; Perot, RF., 43,986; None of These Candidates, 5,608; Nader, Green, 4,730; Browne, LB., 4,460; Phillips, Ind. Amer., 1,732; Hagelin, Natural Law, 545.

1992: Clinton, D., 189,148; Bush, R., 175,828; Perot, Ind., 132,580; Gritz, Pop./America First, 2,892; Marrou, LB., 1,835.

1988: Bush, R., 206,040; Dukakis, D., 132,738; Paul, LB., 3,520; Fulani, New Alliance, 835.

1984: Reagan, R., 188,770; Mondale, D., 91,655; Bergland, LB., 2,292.

1980: Reagan, R., 155,017; Carter, D., 66,666; Anderson, Ind., 17,651; Clark, LB., 4,358.

1976: Ford, R., 101,273; Carter, D., 92,479; MacBride, LB., 1,519; Maddox, Amer., 1,497; scattered, 5,108.

1972: Nixon, R., 115,750; McGovern, D., 66,016.

1968: Nixon, R., 73,188; Humphrey, D., 60,598; Wallace, 3rd party, 20,432.

1964: Johnson, D., 79,339; Goldwater, R., 56,094.

1960: Kennedy, D., 54,880; Nixon, R., 52,387.

1956: Eisenhower, R., 56,049; Stevenson, D., 40,640.

1952: Eisenhower, R., 50,502; Stevenson, D., 31,688.

New Hampshire

County	2008		2004	
	Obama (D)	McCain (R)	Kerry (D)	Bush (R)
Belknap	16,796	16,402	14,080	17,920
Carroll	15,221	13,387	13,319	14,614
Cheshire	26,971	15,205	24,438	16,643
Coos	9,532	6,558	8,585	8,143
Grafton	31,446	17,687	26,180	20,277
Hillsborough	104,820	97,178	94,121	99,724
Merrimack	45,078	34,010	39,975	36,060
Rockingham	83,723	81,917	75,437	82,069
Strafford	37,990	25,021	32,942	25,825
Sullivan	13,249	9,169	11,434	10,142
Totals	**384,826**	**316,534**	**340,511**	**331,237**

New Hampshire Vote Since 1952

2008: Obama, D., 384,826; McCain, R., 316,534; Nader, Ind., 3,503; Barr, LB., 2,217; Phillies, LB., 531.

2004: Kerry, D., 340,511; Bush, R., 331,237; Nader, Ind., 4,479.

2000: Bush, R., 273,559; Gore, D., 266,348; Nader, Green, 22,198; Browne, LB., 2,757; Buchanan, Independence, 2,615; Phillips, Const., 328.

1996: Clinton, D., 246,166; Dole, R., 196,486; Perot, RF., 48,387; Browne, LB., 4,214; Phillips, Taxpayers, 1,344.

1992: Clinton, D., 209,040; Bush, R., 202,484; Perot, Ind., 121,337; Marrou, LB., 3,548.

1988: Bush, R., 281,537; Dukakis, D., 163,696; Paul, LB., 4,502; Fulani, New Alliance, 790.

1984: Reagan, R., 267,051; Mondale, D., 120,377; Bergland, LB., 735.

1980: Reagan, R., 221,705; Carter, D., 108,864; Anderson, Ind., 49,693; Clark, LB., 2,067; Commoner, Citizens, 1,325; Hall, Comm., 129; Griswold, Workers World, 76; DeBerry, Soc. Workers, 72; scattered, 68.

1976: Ford, R., 185,935; Carter, D., 147,645; McCarthy, Ind., 4,095; MacBride, LB., 936; Reagan, write-in, 388; LaRouche, U.S. Labor, 186; Camejo, Soc. Workers, 161; Levin, Soc. Labor, 66; scattered, 215.

1972: Nixon, R., 213,724; McGovern, D., 116,435; Schmitz, Amer., 3,386; Jenness, Soc. Workers, 368; scattered, 142.

1968: Nixon, R., 154,903; Humphrey, D., 130,589; Wallace, 3rd party, 11,173; New Party, 421; Halstead, Soc. Workers, 104.

1964: Johnson, D., 182,065; Goldwater, R., 104,029.

1960: Nixon, R., 157,989; Kennedy, D., 137,772.

1956: Eisenhower, R., 176,519; Stevenson, D., 90,364; Andrews, Const., 111.

1952: Eisenhower, R., 166,287; Stevenson, D., 106,663.

New Jersey

County	2008		2004	
	Obama (D)	McCain (R)	Kerry (D)	Bush (R)
Atlantic	62,498	46,244	55,746	49,487
Bergen	208,410	174,526	207,666	189,833
Burlington	121,222	83,078	110,411	95,936
Camden	142,433	68,072	137,765	81,427
Cape May	20,510	24,591	21,475	28,832
Cumberland	34,355	22,238	27,875	24,362
Essex	228,944	72,370	203,681	83,374
Gloucester	76,789	60,017	66,835	60,033
Hudson	141,557	51,478	127,447	60,646
Hunterdon	29,637	38,966	26,050	39,888
Mercer	99,719	47,196	91,580	56,604
Middlesex	179,924	115,969	166,628	126,492
Monmouth	147,424	159,461	133,773	163,650
Morris	101,245	122,706	98,066	135,241
Ocean	109,240	159,480	99,839	154,204
Passaic	110,331	71,850	94,962	75,200
Salem	15,909	14,763	13,749	15,721
Somerset	73,785	67,221	66,476	72,508
Sussex	28,692	43,998	23,990	44,506
Union	132,006	73,967	119,372	82,517
Warren	20,421	27,304	18,044	29,542
Totals	**2,215,422**	**1,613,207**	**1,911,430**	**1,670,003**

New Jersey Vote Since 1952

2008: Obama, D., 2,215,422; McCain, R., 1,613,207; Nader, Ind., 21,298; Barr, 8,441; Baldwin, Ind., 3,956; McKinney, Ind., 3,636; Moore, Ind., 699; Boss, Ind., 639; Calero, Ind., 523; La Riva, Ind., 416.

2004: Kerry, D., 1,911,430; Bush, R., 1,670,003; Nader, Ind., 19,418; Badnarik, Ind., 4,514; Peroutka, Ind., 2,750; Cobb, Ind., 1,807; Brown, Ind., 664; Van Auken, Ind., 575; Calero, Ind., 530.

2000: Gore, D., 1,788,850; Bush, R., 1,284,173; Nader, Ind., 94,554; Buchanan, Ind., 6,989; Browne, Ind., 6,312; Hagelin, Ind., 2,215; McReynolds, Ind., 1,880; Phillips, Ind., 1,409; Harris, Ind., 844.

1996: Clinton, D., 1,652,361; Dole, R., 1,103,099; Perot, RF., 262,134; Nader, Green, 32,465; Browne, LB., 14,763; Hagelin, Natural Law, 3,887; Phillips, U.S. Taxpayers, 3,440; Harris, Soc. Workers, 1,837; Moorehead, Workers World, 1,337; White, Soc. Equality, 537.

1992: Clinton, D., 1,436,206; Bush, R., 1,356,865; Perot, Ind., 521,829; Marrou, LB., 6,822; Fulani, New Alliance, 3,513; Phillips, U.S. Taxpayers, 2,670; LaRouche, Ind., 2,095; Warren, Soc. Workers, 2,011; Daniels, Ind., 1,996; Gritz, Pop./America First, 1,867; Hagelin, Natural Law, 1,353.

1988: Bush, R., 1,740,604; Dukakis, D., 1,317,541; Lewin, Peace/Freedom, 9,953; Paul, LB., 8,421.

1984: Reagan, R., 1,933,630; Mondale, D., 1,261,323; Bergland, LB., 6,416.

1980: Reagan, R., 1,546,557; Carter, D., 1,147,364; Anderson, Ind., 234,632; Clark, LB., 20,652; Commoner, Citizens, 8,203; McCormack, Right to Life, 3,927; Lynen, Middle Class, 3,694; Hall, Comm., 2,555; Pulley, Soc. Workers, 2,198; McReynolds, Soc., 1,973; Gahres, Down With Lawyers, 1,718; Griswold, Workers World, 1,288; Wendelken, Ind., 923.

1976: Ford, R., 1,509,688; Carter, D., 1,444,653; McCarthy, Ind., 32,717; MacBride, LB., 9,449; Maddox, Amer., 7,716; Levin, Soc. Labor, 3,686; Hall, Comm., 1,662; LaRouche, U.S. Labor, 1,650; Camejo, Soc. Workers, 1,184; Wright, People's, 1,044; Bubar, Prohib., 554; Zeidler, Soc., 469.

1972: Nixon, R., 1,845,502; McGovern, D., 1,102,211; Schmitz, Amer., 34,378; Spock, People's, 5,355; Fisher, Soc. Labor, 4,544; Jenness, Soc. Workers, 2,233; Mahalchik, Amer. First, 1,743; Hall, Comm., 1,263.

1968: Nixon, R., 1,325,467; Humphrey, D., 1,264,206; Wallace, 3rd party, 262,187; Halstead, Soc. Workers, 8,667; Gregory, Peace/Freedom, 8,084; Blomen, Soc. Labor, 6,784.

1964: Johnson, D., 1,867,671; Goldwater, R., 963,843; DeBerry, Soc. Workers, 8,181; Hass, Soc. Labor, 7,075.

1960: Kennedy, D., 1,385,415; Nixon, R., 1,363,324; Dobbs, Soc. Workers, 11,402; Lee, Conservative, 8,708; Hass, Soc. Labor, 4,262.

1956: Eisenhower, R., 1,606,942; Stevenson, D., 850,337; Holtwick, Prohib., 9,147; Hass, Soc. Labor, 6,736; Andrews, Conservative, 5,317; Dobbs, Soc. Workers, 4,004; Krajewski, Amer. Third Party, 1,829.

1952: Eisenhower, R., 1,373,613; Stevenson, D., 1,015,902; Hoopes, Soc., 8,593; Hass, Soc. Labor, 5,815; Hallinan, Prog., 5,589; Krajewski, Poor Man's, 4,203; Dobbs, Soc. Workers, 3,850; Hamblen, Prohib., 989.

New Mexico

County	2008 Obama (D)	McCain (R)	2004 Kerry (D)	Bush (R)
Bernalillo	168,406	109,212	132,252	121,454
Catron	659	1,396	551	1,427
Chaves	8,160	13,630	6,726	14,773
Cibola	3,176	1,717	3,913	3,477
Colfax	3,465	2,800	2,824	3,082
Curry	4,655	9,585	3,541	10,649
De Baca	358	676	281	706
Dona Ana	38,574	27,211	31,762	29,548
Eddy	7,289	12,468	6,880	13,268
Grant	8,092	5,381	7,095	6,135
Guadalupe	1,541	615	1,340	914
Harding	256	357	259	380
Hidalgo	990	934	861	1,081
Lea	5,084	13,301	3,646	14,430
Lincoln	3,482	5,906	2,822	6,070
Los Alamos	5,709	4,986	5,206	5,810
Luna	4,289	3,857	3,340	4,164
McKinley	15,993	6,183	13,051	7,351
Mora	2,156	565	1,876	928
Otero	8,602	12,791	6,433	14,066
Quay	1,546	2,363	1,422	2,661
Rio Arriba	11,245	3,648	9,753	5,149
Roosevelt	2,270	4,285	2,082	4,997
Sandoval	32,102	24,887	21,421	22,628
San Juan	17,645	27,418	14,843	29,525
San Miguel	10,128	2,421	8,683	3,313
Santa Fe	53,802	15,443	47,074	18,466
Sierra	2,351	3,011	1,926	3,162
Socorro	4,643	3,011	4,025	3,696
Taos	13,384	2,827	10,987	3,666
Torrance	3,068	3,721	2,386	4,026
Union	492	1,218	411	1,454
Valencia	15,142	13,033	11,270	14,474
Totals	**472,422**	**346,832**	**370,942**	**376,930**

New Mexico Vote Since 1952

2008: Obama, D., 472,422; McCain, R., 346,832; Nader, Ind., 5,327; Barr, LB., 2,428; Baldwin, Const., 1,597; McKinney, Green, 1,552.

2004: Bush, R., 376,930; Kerry, D., 370,942; Nader, Ind., 4,053; Badnarik, LB., 2,382; Cobb, Green, 1,226; Peroutka, Const., 771.

2000: Gore, D., 286,783; Bush, R., 286,417; Nader, Green, 21,251; Browne, LB., 2,058; Buchanan, RF., 1,392; Hagelin, Natural Law, 361; Phillips, Const., 343.

1996: Clinton, D., 273,495; Dole, R., 232,751; Perot, RF., 32,257; Nader, Green, 13,218; Browne, LB., 2,996; Phillips, Taxpayers, 713; Hagelin, Natural Law, 644.

1992: Clinton, D., 261,617; Bush, R., 212,824; Perot, Ind., 91,895; Marrou, LB., 1,615.

1988: Bush, R., 270,341; Dukakis, D., 244,497; Paul, LB., 3,268; Fulani, New Alliance, 2,237.

1984: Reagan, R., 307,101; Mondale, D., 201,769; Bergland, LB., 4,459.

1980: Reagan, R., 250,779; Carter, D., 167,826; Anderson, Ind., 29,459; Clark, LB., 4,365; Commoner, Citizens, 2,202; Bubar, Statesman, 1,281; Pulley, Soc. Workers, 325.

1976: Ford, R., 211,419; Carter, D., 201,148; Camejo, Soc. Workers, 2,462; MacBride, LB., 1,110; Zeidler, Soc., 240; Bubar, Prohib., 211.

1972: Nixon, R., 235,606; McGovern, D., 141,084; Schmitz, Amer., 8,767; Jenness, Soc. Workers, 474.

1968: Nixon, R., 169,692; Humphrey, D., 130,081; Wallace, 3rd party, 25,737; Chavez, 1,519; Halstead, Soc. Workers, 252.

1964: Johnson, D., 194,017; Goldwater, R., 131,838; Hass, Soc. Labor, 1,217; Munn, Prohib., 543.

1960: Kennedy, D., 156,027; Nixon, R., 153,733; Decker, Prohib., 777; Hass, Soc. Labor, 570.

1956: Eisenhower, R., 146,788; Stevenson, D., 106,098; Holtwick, Prohib., 607; Andrews, Ind., 364; Hass, Soc. Labor, 69.

1952: Eisenhower, R., 132,170; Stevenson, D., 105,661; Hamblen, Prohib., 297; Hallinan, Ind. Prog., 225; MacArthur, Christian Nationalist, 220; Hass, Soc. Labor, 35.

New York

County	2008 Obama (D)	McCain (R)	2004 Kerry (D)	Bush (R)
Albany	86,096	47,629	89,323	54,872
Allegany	6,396	10,308	6,566	12,310
Bronx[1]	300,327	38,560	283,994	56,701
Brooklyn[1]	545,785	139,594	514,973	167,149
Broome	43,510	37,773	46,281	43,568
Cattaraugus	13,858	16,975	13,514	20,051
Cayuga	16,667	14,283	17,534	17,743
Chautauqua	26,936	26,593	27,257	32,434
Chemung	17,706	18,793	17,080	21,321
Chenango	9,256	9,708	9,277	11,582
Clinton	18,232	11,535	17,124	15,330
Columbia	15,536	12,851	15,929	14,457
Cortland	10,616	8,970	10,670	11,613
Delaware	8,562	9,765	8,724	11,958
Dutchess	64,759	55,601	58,232	63,372

County	2008 Obama (D)	McCain (R)	2004 Kerry (D)	Bush (R)
Erie	218,645	154,716	251,090	184,423
Essex	9,531	7,189	8,768	9,869
Franklin	9,593	6,245	9,543	8,383
Fulton	9,147	11,537	9,202	12,570
Genesee	10,029	14,573	10,331	16,725
Greene	9,611	11,992	8,933	12,996
Hamilton	1,060	1,903	1,145	2,475
Herkimer	10,920	13,213	11,675	16,024
Jefferson	16,222	18,593	16,860	21,231
Lewis	4,813	5,700	4,546	6,624
Livingston	13,446	15,906	11,504	17,729
Madison	13,299	13,560	13,121	16,537
Manhattan[1]	490,634	79,448	526,765	107,405
Monroe	196,564	139,001	173,497	163,545
Montgomery	8,592	10,428	9,449	11,338
Nassau	316,523	272,765	323,070	288,355
Niagara	44,105	43,748	47,602	47,111
Oneida	45,531	46,555	40,792	52,392
Onondaga	118,390	80,476	116,381	94,006
Ontario	22,797	23,000	21,166	27,999
Orange	73,299	68,896	63,394	79,089
Orleans	6,142	9,166	5,959	10,317
Oswego	23,192	21,991	24,133	26,325
Otsego	12,072	11,059	12,723	13,342
Putnam	19,371	23,545	19,575	26,356
Queens[1]	436,398	144,362	433,835	165,954
Rensselaer	36,550	31,126	36,075	34,734
Rockland	65,134	58,199	64,191	65,130
St. Lawrence	21,642	15,972	22,857	18,029
Saratoga	51,932	49,734	48,730	56,158
Schenectady	35,529	28,172	35,971	32,066
Schoharie	5,760	7,520	5,630	8,591
Schuyler	3,792	4,431	3,445	4,960
Seneca	6,903	6,556	6,979	7,981
Staten Island[1]	73,192	80,853	68,448	90,325
Steuben	15,823	22,690	14,523	26,980
Suffolk	318,920	289,236	315,909	309,949
Sullivan	15,850	13,312	15,034	15,319
Tioga	9,702	12,077	9,694	13,762
Tompkins	26,401	11,004	27,229	13,994
Ulster	50,300	31,394	47,602	37,821
Warren	14,416	14,422	13,405	16,969
Washington	11,867	11,717	10,624	13,827
Wayne	16,831	21,083	15,709	24,709
Westchester	248,249	143,086	229,849	159,628
Wyoming	6,035	10,487	6,134	11,745
Yates	4,390	4,784	4,205	6,309
Totals	**4,804,945**	**2,752,771**	**4,314,280**	**2,962,567**

(1) Borough of New York City.

New York Vote Since 1952

2008: Obama, D., 4,804,945; McCain, R., 2,752,771; Nader, Populist, 41,249; Barr, LB., 19,596; McKinney, Green, 12,801; Calero, Soc. Workers, 3,615; La Riva, Socialism/Liberation, 1,639.

2004: Kerry, D., 4,314,280; Bush, R., 2,962,567; Nader, Ind., 99,873; Badnarik, LB., 11,607; Calero, Soc. Workers, 2,405.

2000: Gore, D., 4,112,965; Bush, R., 2,405,570; Nader, Green, 244,360; Buchanan, RF., 31,554; Hagelin, Independence, 24,369; Browne, LB., 7,664; Harris, Soc. Workers, 1,790; Phillips, Const., 1,503.

1996: Clinton, D., 3,756,177; Dole, R., 1,933,492; Perot, RF., 503,458; Nader, Green, 75,956; Phillips, Right to Life, 23,580; Browne, LB., 12,220; Hagelin, Natural Law, 5,011; Moorehead, Workers World, 3,473; Harris, Soc. Workers, 2,762.

1992: Clinton, D., 3,444,450; Bush, R., 2,346,649; Perot, Ind., 1,090,721; Warren, Soc. Workers, 15,472; Marrou, LB., 13,451; Fulani, New Alliance, 11,318; Hagelin, Natural Law, 4,420.

1988: Dukakis, D., 3,347,882; Bush, R., 3,081,871; Marra, Right to Life, 20,497; Fulani, New Alliance, 15,845.

1984: Reagan, R., 3,664,763; Mondale, D., 3,119,609; Bergland, LB., 11,949.

1980: Reagan, R., 2,893,831; Carter, D., 2,728,372; Anderson, Liberal, 467,801; Clark, LB., 52,648; McCormack, Right To Life, 24,159; Commoner, Citizens, 23,186; Hall, Comm., 7,414; DeBerry, Soc. Workers, 2,068; Griswold, Workers World, 1,416; scattered, 1,064.

1976: Carter, D., 3,389,558; Ford, R., 3,100,791; MacBride, LB., 12,197; Hall, Comm., 10,270; Camejo, Soc. Workers, 6,996; LaRouche, U.S. Labor, 5,413; blank, void, or scattered, 143,037.

1972: Nixon, R., 3,824,642; McGovern, D., 2,767,956 and Liberal, 183,128 (total, 2,951,084); Reed, Soc. Workers, 7,797; Fisher, Soc. Labor, 4,530; Hall, Comm., 5,641; blank, void, and scattered, 161,641.

1968: Humphrey, D., 3,378,470; Nixon, R., 3,007,932; Wallace, 3rd party, 358,864; Gregory, Peace/Freedom, 24,517; Halstead, Soc. Workers, 11,851; Blomen, Soc. Labor, 8,432; blank, void, and scattered, 171,624.

1964: Johnson, D., 4,913,156; Goldwater, R., 2,243,559; Hass, Soc. Labor, 6,085; DeBerry, Soc. Workers, 3,215; scattered, 188; blank and void, 151,383.

1960: Kennedy, D., 3,423,909 and Liberal, 406,176 (total, 3,830,085); Nixon, R., 3,446,419; Dobbs, Soc. Workers, 14,319; scattered, 256; blank and void, 88,896.

1956: Eisenhower, R., 4,340,340; Stevenson, D., 2,458,212 and Liberal, 292,557 (total, 2,750,769); Andrews, write-in, 1,027; Werdel, 492; Hass, 150; Hoopes, 82; others, 476.
1952: Eisenhower, R., 3,952,815; Stevenson, D., 2,687,890 and Liberal, 416,711 (total, 3,104,601); Hallinan, Amer. Labor, 64,211; Hoopes, Soc., 2,664; Dobbs, Soc. Workers, 2,212; Hass, Industrial Govt., 1,560; scattered, 178; blank and void, 87,813.

North Carolina

County	2008		2004	
	Obama (D)	McCain (R)	Kerry (D)	Bush (R)
Alamance	28,590	34,501	20,686	33,302
Alexander	5,153	11,747	4,618	10,928
Alleghany	2,017	3,117	1,922	2,883
Anson	6,293	4,067	5,413	3,796
Ashe	4,861	7,885	4,477	7,292
Avery	2,163	5,617	1,805	5,678
Beaufort	9,426	13,437	7,025	12,432
Bertie	6,248	3,338	4,938	3,057
Bladen	7,846	7,530	6,109	6,174
Brunswick	21,280	30,662	14,903	22,925
Buncombe	69,415	52,906	51,868	52,491
Burke	14,623	21,766	11,728	18,922
Cabarrus	31,191	45,340	19,803	40,780
Caldwell	12,007	22,397	9,999	21,186
Camden	1,587	3,118	1,339	2,480
Carteret	11,079	22,868	7,732	17,716
Caswell	5,466	5,177	4,539	4,868
Catawba	25,535	42,843	18,858	39,602
Chatham	17,783	14,591	12,897	12,892
Cherokee	3,748	8,591	3,635	7,517
Chowan	3,652	3,751	2,406	2,967
Clay	1,731	3,692	1,628	3,209
Cleveland	17,274	25,950	14,215	22,750
Columbus	11,088	12,998	10,343	10,773
Craven	17,335	23,163	14,019	23,575
Cumberland	73,926	51,596	45,788	49,139
Currituck	3,685	7,159	2,909	6,013
Dare	7,760	9,621	6,136	9,345
Davidson	22,192	45,135	17,191	42,075
Davie	6,102	13,846	4,233	12,372
Duplin	8,866	10,734	6,923	9,611
Durham	102,237	32,040	74,524	34,614
Edgecombe	17,365	8,416	12,877	8,163
Forsyth	90,712	73,304	63,340	75,294
Franklin	13,022	13,183	9,286	11,540
Gaston	31,247	52,220	20,254	43,252
Gates	2,827	2,546	2,121	1,924
Graham	1,265	2,824	1,272	2,693
Granville	13,010	11,373	9,057	9,491
Greene	3,774	4,258	2,665	3,800
Guilford	141,680	97,511	100,042	98,254
Halifax	15,726	8,867	11,528	8,088
Harnett	16,519	23,311	11,563	20,922
Haywood	12,724	14,902	11,237	14,545
Henderson	20,062	30,903	15,003	28,025
Hertford	7,479	3,083	5,141	2,942
Hoke	9,133	6,197	5,794	5,257
Hyde	1,225	1,203	1,048	1,235
Iredell	27,201	44,979	18,065	38,675
Jackson	8,671	7,793	6,737	7,351
Johnston	26,475	43,164	17,266	36,903
Jones	2,364	2,807	1,893	2,607
Lee	10,703	12,652	7,657	11,834
Lenoir	13,157	13,281	10,207	12,939
Lincoln	11,674	23,561	9,434	20,052
Macon	6,603	10,262	5,489	9,448
Madison	5,011	5,175	4,234	5,175
Martin	6,488	5,914	5,102	5,334
McDowell	6,514	11,382	5,330	10,590
Mecklenburg	252,642	152,957	166,828	155,084
Mitchell	2,220	5,472	2,080	5,686
Montgomery	4,870	6,125	4,313	5,745
Moore	17,534	27,165	13,555	24,714
Nash	23,013	23,660	15,693	21,902
New Hanover	48,588	50,004	35,572	45,351
Northampton	6,893	3,662	5,584	3,176
Onslow	19,296	29,942	11,250	25,890
Orange	53,712	20,226	42,910	20,771
Pamlico	2,820	3,809	2,335	3,679
Pasquotank	10,170	7,720	6,984	6,609
Pender	9,832	13,517	6,999	10,037
Perquimans	2,761	3,674	1,971	2,965
Person	8,410	10,007	6,198	8,973
Pitt	39,763	33,429	24,924	28,590
Polk	4,394	5,986	3,787	5,140
Randolph	16,280	40,644	12,966	37,771
Richmond	9,586	9,316	8,383	7,709
Robeson	22,315	16,883	17,868	15,909
Rockingham	16,730	22,435	14,430	22,840
Rowan	23,272	37,284	16,735	34,915
Rutherford	9,595	18,631	8,184	16,343

	2008		2004	
County	Obama (D)	McCain (R)	Kerry (D)	Bush (R)
Sampson	11,753	13,952	9,649	12,600
Scotland	8,105	5,972	6,386	5,141
Stanly	8,815	19,193	7,650	17,814
Stokes	6,816	14,335	5,767	13,583
Surry	10,399	18,574	8,304	17,587
Swain	2,803	2,896	2,419	2,593
Transylvania	7,203	9,299	6,097	9,386
Tyrrell	932	960	731	855
Union	31,038	53,882	17,974	42,820
Vance	13,095	7,584	8,762	6,884
Wake	247,914	183,291	169,909	177,324
Warren	6,663	2,992	5,171	2,840
Washington	3,734	2,667	2,969	2,484
Watauga	14,513	13,303	11,232	12,659
Wayne	22,507	26,800	15,076	24,883
Wilkes	8,889	20,152	7,862	19,197
Wilson	19,754	18,338	14,206	16,264
Yadkin	4,501	12,355	3,451	11,816
Yancey	4,470	5,021	4,434	4,940
Totals	2,142,651	2,128,474	1,525,849	1,961,166

North Carolina Vote Since 1952

2008: Obama, D., 2,142,651; McCain, R., 2,128,474; Barr, LB., 25,722.
2004: Bush, R., 1,961,166; Kerry, D., 1,525,849; Badnarik, LB., 11,731.
2000: Bush, R., 1,631,163; Gore, D., 1,257,692; Browne, LB., 13,891; Buchanan, RF., 8,874.
1996: Dole, R., 1,225,938; Clinton, D., 1,107,849; Perot, RF., 168,059; Browne, LB., 8,740; Hagelin, Natural Law, 2,771.
1992: Bush, R., 1,134,661; Clinton, D., 1,114,042; Perot, Ind., 357,864; Marrou, LB., 5,171.
1988: Bush, R., 1,237,258; Dukakis, D., 890,167; Fulani, New Alliance, 5,682; Paul, write-in, 1,263.
1984: Reagan, R., 1,346,481; Mondale, D., 824,287; Bergland, LB., 3,794.
1980: Reagan, R., 915,018; Carter, D., 875,635; Anderson, Ind., 52,800; Clark, LB., 9,677; Commoner, Citizens, 2,287; DeBerry, Soc. Workers, 416.
1976: Carter, D., 927,365; Ford, R., 741,960; Anderson, Amer., 5,607; MacBride, LB., 2,219; LaRouche, U.S. Labor, 755.
1972: Nixon, R., 1,054,889; McGovern, D., 438,705; Schmitz, Amer., 25,018.
1968: Johnson, D., 627,192; Wallace, 3rd party, 496,188; Humphrey, D., 464,113.
1964: Johnson, D., 800,139; Goldwater, R., 624,844.
1960: Kennedy, D., 713,136; Nixon, R., 655,420.
1956: Stevenson, D., 590,530; Eisenhower, R., 575,062.
1952: Stevenson, D., 652,803; Eisenhower, R., 558,107.

North Dakota

	2008		2004	
County	Obama (D)	McCain (R)	Kerry (D)	Bush (R)
Adams	434	785	353	915
Barnes	2,723	2,808	2,186	3,541
Benson	1,566	772	1,196	1,002
Billings	114	375	99	449
Bottineau	1,384	2,046	1,168	2,468
Bowman	478	1,106	397	1,280
Burke	285	639	336	808
Burleigh	15,524	25,381	11,621	26,577
Cass	37,577	32,515	26,010	39,619
Cavalier	930	1,125	887	1,522
Dickey	1,039	1,517	883	1,890
Divide	461	629	487	751
Dunn	526	1,078	571	1,178
Eddy	582	548	534	655
Emmons	545	1,226	611	1,449
Foster	687	913	518	1,219
Golden Valley	209	640	195	719
Grand Forks	16,079	14,498	12,646	17,298
Grant	402	869	264	952
Griggs	597	682	505	907
Hettinger	406	892	405	1,044
Kidder	421	751	433	902
LaMoure	868	1,307	712	1,592
Logan	299	725	265	844
McHenry	980	1,371	1,030	1,744
McIntosh	579	914	436	1,254
McKenzie	932	1,730	847	1,897
McLean	1,858	2,762	1,664	3,014
Mercer	1,472	2,788	1,245	3,285
Morton	5,073	7,853	4,073	8,325
Mountrail	1,476	1,403	1,465	1,527
Nelson	904	797	778	1,107
Oliver	332	680	310	790
Pembina	1,486	1,710	1,321	2,466
Pierce	792	1,300	686	1,475
Ramsey	2,311	2,358	1,885	2,943
Ransom	1,369	993	1,199	1,352
Renville	505	796	497	953

County	2008 Obama (D)	McCain (R)	2004 Kerry (D)	Bush (R)
Richland	3,510	3,892	2,821	5,264
Rolette	3,403	1,042	2,564	1,392
Sargent	1,112	774	1,021	1,147
Sheridan	227	550	200	727
Sioux	1,144	215	804	319
Slope	106	297	89	335
Stark	3,794	7,019	3,013	7,220
Steele	612	404	616	586
Stutsman	4,042	5,484	3,438	6,517
Towner	620	536	606	754
Traill	2,135	1,839	1,651	2,543
Walsh	2,323	2,410	1,905	3,194
Ward	10,125	15,038	8,236	17,008
Wells	840	1,468	858	1,654
Williams	2,915	6,273	2,512	6,278
Totals	**141,278**	**168,601**	**111,052**	**196,651**

North Dakota Vote Since 1952

2008: McCain, R., 168,601; Obama, D., 141,278; Nader, Ind., 4,189; Barr, LB., 1,354; Baldwin, Const., 1,199.
2004: Bush, R., 196,651; Kerry, D., 111,052; Nader, Ind., 3,756; Badnarik, LB., 851; Peroutka, Const., 514.
2000: Bush, R., 174,852; Gore, D., 95,284; Nader, Ind., 9,486; Buchanan, RF., 7,288; Browne, Ind., 660; Phillips, Const., 373; Hagelin, Ind., 313.
1996: Dole, R., 125,050; Clinton, D., 106,905; Perot, RF., 32,515; Browne, LB., 847; Phillips, Ind., 745; Hagelin, Natural Law, 349.
1992: Bush, R., 136,244; Clinton, D., 99,168; Perot, Ind., 71,084.
1988: Bush, R., 166,559; Dukakis, D., 127,739; Paul, LB., 1,315; LaRouche, Natl. Econ. Recovery, 905.
1984: Reagan, R., 200,336; Mondale, D., 104,429; Bergland, LB., 703.
1980: Reagan, R., 193,695; Carter, D., 79,189; Anderson, Ind., 23,640; Clark, LB., 3,743; Commoner, LB., 429; McLain, Natl. People's League, 296; Greaves, Amer., 235; Hall, Comm., 93; DeBerry, Soc. Workers, 89; McReynolds, Soc., 82; Bubar, Statesman, 54.
1976: Ford, R., 153,470; Carter, D., 136,078; Anderson, Amer., 3,698; McCarthy, Ind., 2,952; Maddox, Amer. Ind., 269; MacBride, LB., 256; scattered, 371.
1972: Nixon, R., 174,109; McGovern, D., 100,384; Schmitz, Amer., 5,646; Jenness, Soc. Workers, 288; Hall, Comm., 87.
1968: Nixon, R., 138,669; Humphrey, D., 94,769; Wallace, 3rd party, 14,244; Halstead, Soc. Workers, 128; Munn, Prohib., 38; Troxell, Ind., 34.
1964: Johnson, D., 149,784; Goldwater, R., 108,207; DeBerry, Soc. Workers, 224; Munn, Prohib., 174.
1960: Nixon, R., 154,310; Kennedy, D., 123,963; Dobbs, Soc. Workers, 158.
1956: Eisenhower, R., 156,766; Stevenson, D., 96,742; Andrews, Amer., 483.
1952: Eisenhower, R., 191,712; Stevenson, D., 76,694; MacArthur, Christian Nationalist, 1,075; Hallinan, Prog., 344; Hamblen, Prohib., 302.

Ohio

County	2008 Obama (D)	McCain (R)	2004 Kerry (D)	Bush (R)
Adams	4,041	6,725	4,281	7,653
Allen	16,575	26,167	16,470	32,580
Ashland	9,027	14,788	8,576	16,209
Ashtabula	24,233	18,464	24,060	21,038
Athens	19,258	9,107	18,998	10,847
Auglaize	6,492	15,938	5,903	17,016
Belmont	15,986	15,127	17,576	15,589
Brown	7,280	11,873	7,140	12,647
Butler	62,871	101,537	56,243	109,872
Carroll	6,302	6,952	6,300	7,595
Champaign	7,161	10,919	6,968	11,718
Clark	29,122	31,821	33,535	34,941
Clermont	30,124	60,287	25,887	62,949
Clinton	6,267	12,037	5,417	12,938
Columbiana	21,222	24,891	23,429	25,753
Coshocton	7,580	8,583	7,378	9,839
Crawford	8,045	12,050	7,773	13,885
Cuyahoga	441,836	196,369	448,503	221,600
Darke	7,456	17,226	7,846	18,306
Defiance	7,394	9,334	6,975	11,397
Delaware	35,848	53,670	27,048	53,143
Erie	22,277	17,080	21,421	18,597
Fairfield	28,487	40,708	24,783	42,715
Fayette	4,199	6,931	4,334	7,376
Franklin	305,144	205,338	285,801	237,253
Fulton	9,627	11,414	8,224	13,640
Gallia	4,616	8,047	5,366	8,576
Geauga	20,692	28,314	19,850	30,370
Greene	27,162	39,252	30,531	48,388
Guernsey	7,369	8,950	7,768	9,962
Hamilton	208,802	187,862	199,679	222,616
Hancock	13,357	21,898	10,352	25,105
Hardin	4,847	7,553	4,891	8,441
Harrison	3,495	3,717	3,780	4,274
Henry	6,163	8,091	5,111	9,902

County	2008 Obama (D)	McCain (R)	2004 Kerry (D)	Bush (R)
Highland	6,437	11,390	6,194	12,211
Hocking	6,083	6,201	6,175	6,936
Holmes	3,074	7,590	2,697	8,468
Huron	9,461	10,001	10,568	14,817
Jackson	5,108	7,837	5,700	8,585
Jefferson	17,266	17,216	19,024	17,185
Knox	10,702	16,207	9,820	17,068
Lake	54,786	54,441	59,049	62,193
Lawrence	10,956	15,055	12,118	15,454
Licking	19,768	30,545	30,053	49,016
Logan	7,615	13,440	6,825	14,471
Lorain	77,719	55,031	78,970	61,203
Lucas	134,729	70,865	132,715	87,160
Madison	6,193	10,178	6,203	11,117
Mahoning	76,356	44,339	83,194	48,761
Marion	12,016	14,840	11,930	17,171
Medina	24,614	31,785	36,272	48,196
Meigs	3,990	5,891	4,438	6,272
Mercer	5,636	14,730	5,118	15,650
Miami	10,739	22,217	17,606	33,992
Monroe	3,623	2,973	4,243	3,424
Montgomery	136,110	123,040	142,997	138,371
Morgan	2,921	3,387	2,875	3,758
Morrow	5,960	9,787	5,775	10,474
Muskingum	17,209	20,174	16,421	22,254
Noble	2,419	3,387	2,654	3,841
Ottawa	11,760	10,417	11,118	12,073
Paulding	4,043	5,204	3,610	6,206
Perry	7,128	7,585	7,257	7,856
Pickaway	8,229	13,087	8,579	14,161
Pike	5,833	6,005	5,989	6,520
Portage	32,160	26,959	40,675	35,583
Preble	6,846	13,340	7,274	13,734
Putnam	5,169	12,855	4,392	14,370
Richland	24,473	32,590	24,638	36,872
Ross	13,636	16,027	13,978	17,231
Sandusky	15,101	13,935	12,686	16,221
Scioto	14,470	16,472	16,827	18,259
Seneca	12,751	13,588	10,957	15,886
Shelby	6,777	15,005	6,535	16,204
Stark	66,712	63,283	95,337	92,215
Summit	151,932	107,937	156,587	118,558
Trumbull	62,254	39,319	66,673	40,977
Tuscarawas	20,957	19,940	18,853	23,829
Union	8,348	15,049	6,665	15,870
Van Wert	5,046	8,993	4,095	10,678
Vinton	2,405	2,962	2,651	3,249
Warren	32,372	69,741	26,044	68,037
Washington	12,082	16,638	12,538	17,532
Wayne	21,144	28,730	19,786	31,879
Williams	7,892	9,618	6,481	12,040
Wood	32,956	28,819	29,401	33,592
Wyandot	4,362	6,190	3,708	7,254
Totals	**2,940,044**	**2,677,820**	**2,741,167**	**2,859,768**

Ohio Vote Since 1952

2008: Obama, D., 2,940,044; McCain, R., 2,677,820; Nader, Ind., 42,337; Barr, LB., 19,917; Baldwin, Const., 12,565; McKinney, Green, 8,518; Duncan, Ind., 3,905; Moore, Soc., 2,735.
2004: Bush, R., 2,859,768; Kerry, D., 2,741,167; Badnarik, nonpartisan, 14,676; Peroutka, nonpartisan, 939.
2000: Bush, R., 2,351,209; Gore, D., 2,186,190; Nader, Ind., 117,857; Buchanan, Ind., 26,724; Browne, LB., 13,475; Hagelin, Natural Law, 6,169; Phillips, Ind., 3,823.
1996: Clinton, D., 2,148,222; Dole, R., 1,859,883; Perot, RF., 483,207; Browne, Ind., 12,851; Moorehead, Ind., 10,813; Hagelin, Natural Law, 9,120; Phillips, Ind., 7,361.
1992: Clinton, D., 1,984,942; Bush, R., 1,894,310; Perot, Ind., 1,036,426; Marrou, LB., 7,252; Fulani, New Alliance, 6,413; Gritz, Pop./America First, 4,699; Hagelin, Natural Law, 3,437; LaRouche, Ind., 2,446.
1988: Bush, R., 2,416,549; Dukakis, D., 1,939,629; Fulani, Ind., 12,017; Paul, Ind., 11,926.
1984: Reagan, R., 2,678,559; Mondale, D., 1,825,440; Bergland, LB., 5,886.
1980: Reagan, R., 2,206,545; Carter, D., 1,752,414; Anderson, Ind., 254,472; Clark, LB., 49,033; Commoner, Citizens, 8,564; Hall, Comm., 4,729; Congress, Ind., 4,029; Griswold, Workers World, 3,790; Bubar, Statesman, 27.
1976: Carter, D., 2,011,621; Ford, R., 2,000,505; McCarthy, Ind., 58,258; Maddox, Amer. Ind., 15,529; MacBride, LB., 8,961; Hall, Comm., 7,817; Camejo, Soc. Workers, 4,717; LaRouche, U.S. Labor, 4,335; scattered, 130.
1972: Nixon, R., 2,441,827; McGovern, D., 1,558,889; Schmitz, Amer., 80,067; Fisher, Soc. Labor, 7,107; Hall, Comm., 6,437; Wallace, Ind., 460.
1968: Nixon, R., 1,791,014; Humphrey, D., 1,700,586; Wallace, 3rd party, 467,495; Gregory, 372; Blomen, Soc. Labor, 120; Halstead, Soc. Workers, 69; Mitchell, Comm., 23; Munn, Prohib., 19.
1964: Johnson, D., 2,498,331; Goldwater, R., 1,470,865.
1960: Nixon, R., 2,217,611; Kennedy, D., 1,944,248.
1956: Eisenhower, R., 2,262,610; Stevenson, D., 1,439,655.
1952: Eisenhower, R., 2,100,391; Stevenson, D., 1,600,367.

Oklahoma

County	2008		2004	
	Obama (D)	McCain (R)	Kerry (D)	Bush (R)
Adair	2,049	4,636	2,562	4,971
Alfalfa	411	2,023	470	2,201
Atoka	1,370	3,509	1,946	3,142
Beaver	265	2,197	297	2,272
Beckham	1,625	5,769	1,931	5,454
Blaine	1,011	3,100	1,222	3,199
Bryan	4,423	9,295	5,745	8,615
Caddo	3,395	6,401	3,916	6,491
Canadian	11,422	36,411	9,712	33,297
Carter	5,603	13,241	6,466	12,178
Cherokee	7,193	9,182	8,623	9,569
Choctaw	1,859	3,729	2,639	3,168
Cimarron	152	1,119	184	1,242
Cleveland	39,673	64,730	34,007	65,720
Coal	570	1,609	1,203	1,396
Comanche	14,120	20,127	12,022	21,170
Cotton	690	1,793	898	1,742
Craig	2,072	3,858	2,504	3,894
Creek	8,318	20,181	9,929	18,848
Custer	2,660	7,842	2,801	7,839
Delaware	5,084	10,274	5,591	10,017
Dewey	346	1,857	408	1,843
Ellis	282	1,627	395	1,685
Garfield	5,545	17,066	5,586	17,685
Garvin	3,028	7,708	3,707	7,610
Grady	5,516	15,187	5,970	14,136
Grant	514	1,836	571	1,950
Greer	566	1,548	719	1,529
Harmon	333	757	354	838
Harper	221	1,342	268	1,397
Haskell	1,474	3,206	2,378	2,946
Hughes	1,705	3,132	2,283	3,066
Jackson	2,263	6,716	2,232	7,024
Jefferson	805	1,649	1,057	1,546
Johnston	1,246	2,707	1,713	2,635
Kay	5,462	13,229	5,957	14,121
Kingfisher	1,009	5,372	1,022	5,630
Kiowa	1,226	2,536	1,413	2,610
Latimer	1,313	2,857	1,945	2,535
Le Flore	5,136	11,603	6,741	10,683
Lincoln	3,503	10,468	4,041	10,149
Logan	5,716	12,555	4,869	11,474
Love	1,257	2,589	1,538	2,295
Major	515	2,955	537	3,122
Marshall	1,642	3,729	2,088	3,363
Mayes	5,749	10,231	6,933	9,946
McClain	3,550	11,184	3,742	10,041
McCurtain	2,792	7,744	3,684	7,472
McIntosh	3,318	4,903	4,488	4,692
Murray	1,592	3,746	2,130	3,665
Muskogee	11,286	15,276	12,585	15,124
Noble	1,174	3,881	1,335	3,993
Nowata	1,411	3,029	1,660	2,805
Okfuskee	1,478	2,642	1,743	2,542
Oklahoma	116,133	163,099	97,298	174,741
Okmulgee	6,187	8,724	7,367	8,363
Osage	7,493	12,150	8,068	11,467
Ottawa	4,266	6,904	5,086	7,443
Pawnee	2,063	4,533	2,564	4,412
Payne	10,601	18,435	10,101	19,560
Pittsburg	5,454	11,739	7,452	11,134
Pontotoc	4,511	9,749	5,165	9,647
Pottawatomie	7,906	17,728	8,638	17,215
Pushmataha	1,265	3,208	1,934	2,863
Roger Mills	286	1,502	382	1,388
Rogers	10,770	27,732	11,918	24,976
Seminole	2,977	5,599	3,648	5,624
Sequoyah	4,454	9,465	5,910	8,865
Stephens	4,538	14,392	5,515	13,646
Texas	923	5,332	1,016	5,450
Tillman	1,042	2,195	1,175	2,273
Tulsa	96,106	158,322	90,220	163,452
Wagoner	8,805	21,426	9,157	19,081
Washington	6,308	16,457	6,862	16,551
Washita	1,050	3,716	1,340	3,705
Woods	870	3,043	932	3,166
Woodward	1,348	6,402	1,458	6,193
Totals	**502,496**	**960,165**	**503,966**	**959,792**

Oklahoma Vote Since 1952
2008: McCain, R., 960,165; Obama, D., 502,496.
2004: Bush, R., 959,792; Kerry, D., 503,966.
2000: Bush, R., 744,337; Gore, D., 474,276; Buchanan, RF., 9,014; Browne, LB., 6,602.
1996: Dole, R., 582,315; Clinton, D., 488,105; Perot, RF., 130,788; Browne, LB., 5,505.
1992: Bush, R., 592,929; Clinton, D., 473,066; Perot, Ind., 319,878; Marrou, LB., 4,486.
1988: Bush, R., 678,367; Dukakis, D., 483,423; Paul, LB., 6,261; Fulani, New Alliance, 2,985.
1984: Reagan, R., 861,530; Mondale, D., 385,080; Bergland, LB., 9,066.

1980: Reagan, R., 695,570; Carter, D., 402,026; Anderson, Ind., 38,284; Clark, LB., 13,828.
1976: Ford, R., 545,708; Carter, D., 532,442; McCarthy, Ind., 14,101.
1972: Nixon, R., 759,025; McGovern, D., 247,147; Schmitz, Amer., 23,728.
1968: Nixon, R., 449,697; Humphrey, D., 301,658; Wallace, 3rd party, 191,731.
1964: Johnson, D., 519,834; Goldwater, R., 412,665.
1960: Nixon, R., 533,039; Kennedy, D., 370,111.
1956: Eisenhower, R., 473,769; Stevenson, D., 385,581.
1952: Eisenhower, R., 518,045; Stevenson, D., 430,939.

Oregon

County	2008		2004	
	Obama (D)	McCain (R)	Kerry (D)	Bush (R)
Baker	2,795	5,643	2,616	6,253
Benton	29,421	15,036	26,515	18,460
Clackamas	95,237	76,161	95,129	97,691
Clatsop	10,579	7,113	10,461	8,503
Columbia	13,253	10,351	12,563	11,868
Coos	14,270	15,236	14,393	18,291
Crook	3,623	6,348	3,024	6,830
Curry	5,216	6,626	5,220	7,332
Deschutes	38,612	38,918	31,179	41,757
Douglas	19,153	28,635	18,089	35,956
Gilliam	429	642	370	755
Grant	980	2,670	780	3,204
Harney	946	2,592	839	2,815
Hood River	6,229	3,240	5,587	4,124
Jackson	47,664	47,806	44,366	56,519
Jefferson	3,648	4,360	3,243	4,762
Josephine	17,338	22,926	15,214	26,241
Klamath	9,115	18,682	8,264	22,733
Lake	954	2,631	802	3,039
Lane	104,010	58,149	107,769	75,007
Lincoln	13,991	8,649	13,753	10,160
Linn	21,702	27,576	19,940	31,260
Malheur	2,922	7,099	2,577	8,123
Marion	55,610	53,174	57,671	69,900
Morrow	1,398	2,501	1,361	2,732
Multnomah	264,741	71,084	259,585	98,439
Polk	17,046	17,272	15,484	19,508
Sherman	382	632	390	694
Tillamook	7,018	5,732	6,750	7,003
Umatilla	9,400	15,126	8,884	17,068
Union	4,612	7,563	4,428	8,879
Wallowa	1,490	2,832	1,269	3,132
Wasco	5,649	4,900	5,691	6,119
Washington	128,402	80,203	121,140	107,223
Wheeler	276	497	245	612
Yamhill	20,494	21,068	17,572	23,839
Totals	**1,037,291**	**738,475**	**943,163**	**866,831**

Oregon Vote Since 1952
2008: Obama, D., 1,037,291; McCain, R., 738,475; Nader, Peace Party of OR, 18,614; Baldwin, Const., 7,693; Barr, LB., 7,635; McKinney, Pacific Green, 4,543.
2004: Kerry, D., 943,163; Bush, R., 866,831; Badnarik, LB., 7,260; Cobb, Pacific Green, 5,315; Peroutka, Const., 5,257.
2000: Gore, D., 720,342; Bush, R., 713,577; Nader, Green, 77,357; Browne, LB., 7,447; Buchanan, 7,063; Hagelin, RF., 2,574; Phillips, Const., 2,189.
1996: Clinton, D., 649,641; Dole, R., 538,152; Perot, RF., 121,221; Nader, Pacific, 49,415; Browne, LB., 8,903; Phillips, Taxpayers, 3,379; Hagelin, Natural Law, 2,798; Hollis, Soc., 1,922.
1992: Clinton, D., 621,314; Bush, R., 475,757; Perot, Ind., 354,091; Marrou, LB., 4,277; Fulani, New Alliance, 3,030.
1988: Dukakis, D., 616,206; Bush, R., 560,126; Paul, LB., 14,811; Fulani, Ind., 6,487.
1984: Reagan, R., 658,700; Mondale, D., 536,479.
1980: Reagan, R., 571,044; Carter, D., 456,890; Anderson, Ind., 112,389; Clark, LB., 25,838; Commoner, Citizens, 13,642; scattered, 1,713.
1976: Ford, R., 492,120; Carter, D., 490,407; McCarthy, Ind., 40,207; write-in, 7,142.
1972: Nixon, R., 486,686; McGovern, D., 392,760; Schmitz, Amer., 46,211; write-in, 2,289.
1968: Nixon, R., 408,433; Humphrey, D., 358,866; Wallace, 3rd party, 49,683; write-ins: McCarthy, 1,496; N. Rockefeller, 69; others, 1,075.
1964: Johnson, D., 501,017; Goldwater, R., 282,779; write-in, 2,509.
1960: Nixon, R., 408,060; Kennedy, D., 367,402.
1956: Eisenhower, R., 406,393; Stevenson, D., 329,204.
1952: Eisenhower, R., 420,815; Stevenson, D., 270,579; Hallinan, Ind., 3,665.

Pennsylvania

County	2008		2004	
	Obama (D)	McCain (R)	Kerry (D)	Bush (R)
Adams	17,475	26,134	13,764	28,247
Allegheny	368,453	269,819	368,912	271,925
Armstrong	10,729	17,715	12,025	18,925
Beaver	39,738	42,358	42,146	39,916
Bedford	6,001	15,928	6,016	16,606
Berks	91,803	75,868	76,309	87,122

County	2008 Obama (D)	McCain (R)	2004 Kerry (D)	Bush (R)
Blair	18,798	30,812	18,105	35,751
Bradford	10,202	14,911	8,590	16,942
Bucks	178,345	149,860	163,438	154,469
Butler	29,882	52,294	30,090	54,959
Cambria	30,697	29,981	32,591	34,048
Cameron	802	1,239	794	1,599
Carbon	13,235	12,646	12,223	12,519
Centre	41,141	32,543	30,733	33,133
Chester	135,150	112,266	109,708	120,036
Clarion	6,415	10,126	6,049	11,063
Clearfield	14,549	18,656	13,518	20,533
Clinton	6,799	7,126	5,823	8,035
Columbia	12,597	13,704	10,679	16,052
Crawford	15,684	19,265	16,013	21,965
Cumberland	45,355	59,693	37,928	67,648
Dauphin	69,352	57,964	55,299	65,296
Delaware	170,949	109,766	162,601	120,425
Elk	6,910	6,252	6,602	7,872
Erie	74,206	49,284	67,921	57,372
Fayette	25,509	25,669	29,120	25,045
Forest	1,014	1,366	989	1,571
Franklin	21,052	41,711	16,562	41,817
Fulton	1,562	4,612	1,475	4,772
Greene	7,365	7,451	7,674	7,786
Huntingdon	6,611	11,724	5,879	12,126
Indiana	16,964	19,617	15,831	20,254
Jefferson	6,132	11,248	6,073	13,371
Juniata	3,055	6,463	2,797	7,144
Lackawanna	67,112	39,198	59,573	44,766
Lancaster	97,290	124,475	74,328	145,591
Lawrence	19,371	21,496	21,387	21,938
Lebanon	22,004	32,325	18,109	37,089
Lehigh	86,226	62,668	73,940	70,160
Luzerne	71,903	60,512	69,573	64,953
Lycoming	18,335	30,215	15,681	33,961
McKean	6,186	8,835	6,294	10,941
Mercer	24,319	24,321	24,831	26,311
Mifflin	5,364	10,904	4,889	11,726
Monroe	36,655	25,892	27,967	27,971
Montgomery	249,493	163,030	222,048	175,741
Montour	3,347	4,555	2,666	4,903
Northampton	74,956	58,352	63,446	62,102
Northumberland	13,555	18,012	14,602	22,262
Perry	6,384	13,032	5,423	13,919
Philadelphia	574,930	113,260	542,205	130,099
Pike	11,448	12,456	8,656	12,444
Potter	2,277	5,073	2,268	5,640
Schuylkill	28,187	33,682	29,231	35,640
Snyder	5,375	9,895	4,348	10,566
Somerset	12,437	20,925	12,842	23,802
Sullivan	1,228	1,840	1,213	2,056
Susquehanna	8,314	10,551	7,351	11,573
Tioga	6,012	10,542	5,437	12,019
Union	7,207	9,720	5,700	10,334
Venango	8,708	12,817	9,024	14,472
Warren	8,669	9,824	8,044	10,999
Washington	44,286	48,753	48,225	47,673
Wayne	9,824	12,618	8,060	13,713
Westmoreland	69,004	96,786	77,774	100,087
Wyoming	5,631	6,494	4,982	7,782
York	81,748	107,367	63,701	114,270
Totals	**3,276,363**	**2,655,885**	**2,938,095**	**2,793,847**

Pennsylvania Vote Since 1952

2008: Obama, D., 3,276,363; McCain, R., 2,655,885; Nader, Ind., 42,977; Barr, LB., 19,912.
2004: Kerry, D., 2,938,095; Bush, R., 2,793,847; Badnarik, LB., 21,185; Cobb, Green, 6,319; Peroutka, Const., 6,318.
2000: Gore, D., 2,485,967; Bush, R., 2,281,127; Nader, Green, 103,392; Buchanan, RF., 16,023; Phillips, Const., 14,428; Browne, LB., 11,248.
1996: Clinton, D., 2,215,819; Dole, R., 1,801,169; Perot, RF., 430,984; Browne, LB., 28,000; Phillips, Const., 19,552; Hagelin, Natural Law, 5,783.
1992: Clinton, D., 2,239,164; Bush, R., 1,791,841; Perot, Ind., 902,667; Marrou, LB., 21,477; Fulani, New Alliance, 4,661.
1988: Bush, R., 2,300,087; Dukakis, D., 2,194,944; McCarthy, Consumer, 19,158; Paul, LB., 12,051.
1984: Reagan, R., 2,584,323; Mondale, D., 2,228,131; Bergland, LB., 6,982.
1980: Reagan, R., 2,261,872; Carter, D., 1,937,540; Anderson, Ind., 292,921; Clark, LB., 33,263; DeBerry, Soc. Workers, 20,291; Commoner, Consumer, 10,430; Hall, Comm., 5,184.
1976: Carter, D., 2,328,677; Ford, R., 2,205,604; McCarthy, Ind., 50,584; Maddox, Const., 25,344; Camejo, Soc. Workers, 3,009; LaRouche, U.S. Labor, 2,744; Hall, Comm., 1,891; others, 2,934.
1972: Nixon, R., 2,714,521; McGovern, D., 1,796,951; Schmitz, Amer., 70,593; Jenness, Soc. Workers, 4,639; Hall, Comm., 2,686; others, 2,715.
1968: Humphrey, D., 2,259,405; Nixon, R., 2,090,017; Wallace, 3rd party, 378,582; Gregory, Peace/Freedom, 7,821; Blomen, Soc. Labor, 4,977; Halstead, Soc. Workers, 4,862; others, 2,264.

1964: Johnson, D., 3,130,954; Goldwater, R., 1,673,657; DeBerry, Soc. Workers, 10,456; Hass, Soc. Labor, 5,092; scattered, 2,531.
1960: Kennedy, D., 2,556,282; Nixon, R., 2,439,956; Hass, Soc. Labor, 7,185; Dobbs, Soc. Workers, 2,678; scattered, 440.
1956: Eisenhower, R., 2,585,252; Stevenson, D., 1,981,769; Hass, Soc. Labor, 7,447; Dobbs, Militant Workers, 2,035.
1952: Eisenhower, R., 2,415,789; Stevenson, D., 2,146,269; Hamblen, Prohib., 8,771; Hallinan, Prog., 4,200; Hoopes, Soc., 2,684; Dobbs, Militant Workers, 1,502; Hass, Industrial Govt., 1,347; scattered, 155.

Rhode Island

City	2008 Obama (D)	McCain (R)	2004 Kerry (D)	Bush (R)
Cranston	22,520	13,981	20,331	14,471
East Providence	15,380	6,216	13,655	6,359
Pawtucket	18,486	6,098	15,567	6,394
Providence	46,252	8,545	35,917	9,787
Warwick	25,802	16,541	23,164	16,640
Other	168,107	114,008	151,126	115,395
Totals	**296,571**	**165,391**	**259,765**	**169,046**

Rhode Island Vote Since 1952

2008: Obama, D., 296,571; McCain, R., 165,391; Nader, Ind., 4,829; Barr, LB., 1,382; McKinney, Green, 797; Baldwin, Const., 675; La Riva, Socialism/Liberation, 122.
2004: Kerry, D., 259,765; Bush, R., 169,046; Nader, RF., 4,651; Cobb, Green, 1,333; Badnarik, LB., 907; Peroutka, Const., 339; Parker, Workers World, 253.
2000: Gore, D., 249,508; Bush, R., 130,555; Nader, Ind., 25,052; Buchanan, RF., 2,273; Browne, Ind., 742; Hagelin, Ind., 271; Moorehead, Ind., 199; Phillips, Ind., 97; McReynolds, Ind., 52; Harris, Ind., 34.
1996: Clinton, D., 233,050; Dole, R., 104,683; Perot, RF., 43,723; Nader, Green, 6,040; Browne, LB., 1,109; Phillips, U.S. Taxpayers, 1,021; Hagelin, Natural Law, 435; Moorehead, Workers World, 186.
1992: Clinton, D., 213,299; Bush, R., 131,601; Perot, Ind., 105,045; Fulani, New Alliance, 1,878.
1988: Dukakis, D., 225,123; Bush, R., 177,761; Paul, LB., 825; Fulani, New Alliance, 280.
1984: Reagan, R., 212,080; Mondale, D., 197,106; Bergland, LB., 277.
1980: Carter, D., 198,342; Reagan, R., 154,793; Anderson, Ind., 59,819; Clark, LB., 2,458; Hall, Comm., 218; McReynolds, Soc., 170; DeBerry, Soc. Workers, 90; Griswold, Workers World, 77.
1976: Carter, D., 227,636; Ford, R., 181,249; MacBride, LB., 715; Camejo, Soc. Workers, 462; Hall, Comm., 334; Levin, Soc. Labor, 188.
1972: Nixon, R., 220,383; McGovern, D., 194,645; Jenness, Soc. Workers, 729.
1968: Humphrey, D., 246,518; Nixon, R., 122,359; Wallace, 3rd party, 15,678; Halstead, Soc. Workers, 383.
1964: Johnson, D., 315,463; Goldwater, R., 74,615.
1960: Kennedy, D., 258,032; Nixon, R., 147,502.
1956: Eisenhower, R., 225,819; Stevenson, D., 161,790.
1952: Eisenhower, R., 210,935; Stevenson, D., 203,293; Hallinan, Prog., 187; Hass, Soc. Labor, 83.

South Carolina

County	2008 Obama (D)	McCain (R)	2004 Kerry (D)	Bush (R)
Abbeville	4,593	6,264	4,389	5,436
Aiken	26,101	42,849	19,799	39,077
Allendale	3,029	947	2,565	985
Anderson	24,132	48,690	20,697	43,355
Bamberg	4,426	2,309	3,841	2,138
Barnwell	4,931	4,769	3,982	4,606
Beaufort	30,396	37,821	21,505	33,331
Berkeley	27,755	36,205	20,142	32,104
Calhoun	3,970	3,695	3,393	3,448
Charleston	82,698	69,822	63,758	70,297
Cherokee	7,215	13,305	6,466	12,090
Chester	7,071	5,922	5,790	5,798
Chesterfield	7,842	8,325	6,729	7,252
Clarendon	8,673	6,758	7,087	6,061
Colleton	8,616	8,525	6,699	7,264
Darlington	14,505	14,544	11,829	13,416
Dillon	7,408	5,874	4,832	4,301
Dorchester	21,806	29,929	14,733	26,006
Edgefield	5,075	6,334	4,051	5,611
Fairfield	7,591	3,912	5,764	3,531
Florence	28,012	29,861	21,442	27,689
Georgetown	14,199	15,790	10,602	12,606
Greenville	70,886	116,363	55,347	111,481
Greenwood	12,348	16,995	8,954	14,264
Hampton	5,816	3,439	4,832	3,097
Horry	38,879	64,609	29,547	50,447
Jasper	5,389	3,365	3,840	2,933
Kershaw	11,226	16,466	8,515	14,160
Lancaster	12,139	16,441	7,631	12,916
Laurens	10,578	15,334	9,205	14,466
Lee	5,960	3,074	4,960	2,901
Lexington	33,303	74,960	25,393	67,132
Marion	9,608	5,416	7,767	5,589
Marlboro	6,794	3,996	4,984	3,423

County	2008 Obama (D)	McCain (R)	2004 Kerry (D)	Bush (R)
McCormick	2,755	2,437	2,648	2,396
Newberry	6,708	9,616	4,483	7,654
Oconee	9,481	21,164	8,395	18,811
Orangeburg	27,263	12,115	24,698	12,695
Pickens	11,691	32,552	10,287	29,759
Richland	105,656	57,941	76,283	56,212
Saluda	3,323	5,191	3,001	4,537
Spartanburg	41,632	65,042	33,633	62,004
Sumter	25,431	18,581	18,695	18,074
Union	5,935	7,449	5,236	6,592
Williamsburg	11,279	5,004	9,044	4,795
York	37,918	54,500	24,226	45,234
Totals	862,449	1,034,896	661,699	937,974

South Carolina Vote Since 1952

2008: McCain, R., 1,034,896; Obama, D., 862,449; Barr, LB., 7,283; Baldwin, Const., 6,827; Nader, petitioning cand., 5,053; McKinney, Green, 4,461.

2004: Bush, R., 937,974; Kerry, D., 661,699; Nader, Ind., 5,520; Peroutka, Const., 5,317; Badnarik, LB., 3,608; Brown, United Citizens, 2,124; Cobb, Green, 1,488.

2000: Bush, R., 786,892; Gore, D., 566,039; Nader, United Citizens, 20,279; Browne, LB., 4,898; Buchanan, RF., 3,309; Phillips, Const., 1,682; Hagelin, Natural Law, 943.

1996: Dole, R., 573,458; Clinton, D., 506,283; Perot, RF./Patriot, 64,386; Browne, LB., 4,271; Phillips, U.S. Taxpayers, 2,043; Hagelin, Natural Law, 1,248.

1992: Bush, R., 577,507; Clinton, D., 479,514; Perot, Ind., 138,872; Marrou, LB., 2,719; Phillips, U.S. Taxpayers, 2,680; Fulani, New Alliance, 1,235.

1988: Bush, R., 606,443; Dukakis, D., 370,554; Paul, LB., 4,935; Fulani, United Citizens, 4,077.

1984: Reagan, R., 615,539; Mondale, D., 344,459; Bergland, LB., 4,359.

1980: Reagan, R., 439,277; Carter, D., 428,220; Anderson, Ind., 13,868; Clark, LB., 4,807; Rarick, Amer. Ind., 2,086.

1976: Carter, D., 450,807; Ford, R., 346,149; Anderson, Amer., 2,996; Maddox, Amer. Ind., 1,950; write-in, 681.

1972: Nixon, R., 477,044; McGovern, D., 184,559; Schmitz, Amer., 10,075; United Citizens, 2,265; write-in, 17.

1968: Nixon, R., 254,062; Wallace, 3rd party, 215,430; Humphrey, D., 197,486.

1964: Goldwater, R., 309,048; Johnson, D., 215,700; write-ins: Wallace, 5; Nixon, 1; Powell, 1; Thurmond, 1.

1960: Kennedy, D., 198,129; Nixon, R., 188,558; write-in, 1.

1956: Stevenson, D., 136,372; Byrd, Ind., 88,509; Eisenhower, R., 75,700; Andrews, Ind., 2.

1952: Stevenson, D., 173,004. Under state law votes cast for 2 Eisenhower slates of electors could not be combined. Eisenhower, Ind., 158,289 and R., 9,793 (total, 168,082); Hamblen, Prohib., 1.

South Dakota

County	2008 Obama (D)	McCain (R)	2004 Kerry (D)	Bush (R)
Aurora	655	794	620	1,009
Beadle	3,493	4,054	3,443	4,917
Bennett	557	614	759	833
Bon Homme	1,367	1,712	1,293	2,063
Brookings	7,207	6,431	5,443	7,662
Brown	9,041	8,067	7,943	10,386
Brule	965	1,407	1,040	1,544
Buffalo	454	156	603	223
Butte	1,306	2,821	1,009	3,166
Campbell	243	591	239	708
Charles Mix	1,807	2,109	2,155	2,556
Clark	830	1,065	875	1,435
Clay	3,808	2,296	3,315	2,692
Codington	5,595	6,374	4,803	7,778
Corson	837	535	972	720
Custer	1,475	2,909	1,272	2,922
Davison	3,554	4,731	3,263	5,561
Day	1,785	1,372	1,817	1,671
Deuel	1,054	1,088	961	1,406
Dewey	1,326	658	1,606	921
Douglas	424	1,293	393	1,596
Edmunds	819	1,213	765	1,434
Fall River	1,338	2,348	1,326	2,413
Faulk	426	739	418	945
Grant	1,786	1,951	1,633	2,392
Gregory	771	1,423	813	1,685
Haakon	186	938	219	1,007
Hamlin	1,043	1,661	1,015	1,946
Hand	718	1,247	668	1,482
Hanson	961	1,426	745	1,379
Harding	135	575	94	704
Hughes	3,037	5,298	2,697	6,017
Hutchinson	1,242	2,285	1,177	2,899
Hyde	226	547	259	631
Jackson/ Washabaugh	435	668	508	726
Jerauld	535	535	482	736
Jones	147	463	134	565
Kingsbury	1,277	1,435	1,163	1,804
Lake	3,033	2,993	2,509	3,359
Lawrence	4,932	6,787	3,857	7,489
Lincoln	8,642	11,803	5,703	11,161
Lyman	710	894	872	1,029
Marshall	1,261	900	1,099	1,242
McCook	1,219	1,646	1,201	2,017
McPherson	441	915	369	1,180
Meade	3,749	7,515	2,941	8,347
Mellette	373	445	361	553
Miner	605	577	641	810
Minnehaha	39,831	39,241	32,314	44,189
Moody	1,663	1,508	1,609	1,790
Pennington	17,787	27,592	14,213	29,976
Perkins	499	1,102	418	1,329
Potter	482	937	463	1,143
Roberts	2,672	1,781	2,527	2,396
Sanborn	500	669	581	817
Shannon	2,967	330	3,566	526
Spink	1,550	1,660	1,478	2,259
Stanley	510	1,017	464	1,129
Sully	233	581	201	702
Todd	2,208	571	2,543	889
Tripp	914	1,859	972	2,230
Turner	1,681	2,538	1,646	3,084
Union	3,244	4,310	3,000	3,987
Walworth	923	1,668	878	1,967
Yankton	4,838	5,039	4,237	6,003
Ziebach	554	312	641	447
Totals	170,924	203,054	149,244	232,584

South Dakota Vote Since 1952

2008: McCain, R., 203,054; Obama, D., 170,924; Nader, Ind., 4,267; Baldwin, Const., 1,895; Barr, Ind., 1,835.

2004: Bush, R., 232,584; Kerry, D., 149,244; Nader, Ind., 4,320; Peroutka, Const., 1,103; Badnarik, Ind., 964.

2000: Bush, R., 190,700; Gore, D., 118,804; Buchanan, RF., 3,322; Phillips, Ind., 1,781; Browne, LB., 1,662.

1996: Dole, R., 150,543; Clinton, D., 139,333; Perot, RF., 31,250; Browne, LB., 1,472; Phillips, Taxpayers, 912; Hagelin, Natural Law, 316.

1992: Bush, R., 136,718; Clinton, D., 124,888; Perot, Ind., 73,295.

1988: Bush, R., 165,415; Dukakis, D., 145,560; Paul, LB., 1,060; Fulani, New Alliance, 730.

1984: Reagan, R., 200,267; Mondale, D., 116,113.

1980: Reagan, R., 198,343; Carter, D., 103,855; Anderson, Ind., 21,431; Clark, LB., 3,824; Pulley, Soc. Workers, 250.

1976: Ford, R., 151,505; Carter, D., 147,068; MacBride, LB., 1,619; Hall, Comm., 318; Camejo, Soc. Workers, 168.

1972: Nixon, R., 166,476; McGovern, D., 139,945; Jenness, Soc. Workers, 994.

1968: Nixon, R., 149,841; Humphrey, D., 118,023; Wallace, 3rd party, 13,400.

1964: Johnson, D., 163,010; Goldwater, R., 130,108.

1960: Nixon, R., 178,417; Kennedy, D., 128,070.

1956: Eisenhower, R., 171,569; Stevenson, D., 122,288.

1952: Eisenhower, R., 203,857; Stevenson, D., 90,426.

Tennessee

County	2008 Obama (D)	McCain (R)	2004 Kerry (D)	Bush (R)
Anderson	11,385	19,614	12,896	18,510
Bedford	5,026	10,215	5,268	8,351
Benton	2,644	3,695	3,869	3,161
Bledsoe	1,517	3,166	1,927	2,849
Blount	15,252	35,553	15,047	33,241
Bradley	9,353	28,324	9,431	25,951
Campbell	3,866	6,535	6,163	7,859
Cannon	2,010	3,320	2,515	2,931
Carroll	3,980	7,454	5,070	6,605
Carter	5,587	15,849	6,395	15,768
Cheatham	5,497	10,697	5,918	9,676
Chester	1,794	4,586	2,242	4,086
Claiborne	3,078	7,174	4,034	6,448
Clay	1,248	1,674	1,675	1,650
Cocke	3,340	8,945	3,935	8,297
Coffee	7,131	13,244	8,243	11,793
Crockett	1,818	3,749	2,459	3,242
Cumberland	7,889	17,436	8,327	15,144
Davidson	158,032	102,702	132,737	107,839
Decatur	1,595	3,178	2,268	2,566
DeKalb	2,832	4,085	3,445	3,685
Dickson	7,504	11,672	8,597	10,567
Dyer	4,411	9,859	5,287	8,447
Fayette	6,888	12,158	5,696	8,962
Fentress	1,831	4,789	2,371	4,293
Franklin	6,609	10,533	7,800	9,129
Gibson	7,406	13,516	8,511	10,596
Giles	4,614	6,902	5,273	6,163
Grainger	2,065	5,297	2,569	4,907
Greene	7,107	17,148	7,635	16,382
Grundy	1,969	2,561	2,789	2,107
Hamblen	6,804	15,501	7,433	14,742
Hamilton	64,205	81,666	57,302	78,547

County	2008 Obama (D)	McCain (R)	2004 Kerry (D)	Bush (R)
Hancock	604	1,587	777	1,756
Hardeman	5,919	5,225	5,685	4,704
Hardin	2,794	7,076	3,834	6,087
Hawkins	5,924	14,745	6,684	13,447
Haywood	4,891	3,165	4,359	3,140
Henderson	3,021	7,669	3,448	6,585
Henry	5,152	8,182	5,732	7,340
Hickman	3,563	4,784	4,263	4,359
Houston	1,678	1,608	2,126	1,440
Humphreys	3,600	3,818	4,485	3,261
Jackson	2,284	2,185	2,998	2,026
Jefferson	5,177	13,092	5,469	11,625
Johnson	1,837	4,620	1,812	4,634
Knox	67,923	109,847	66,013	110,803
Lake	1,024	1,175	2,634	2,078
Lauderdale	4,322	4,933	4,474	4,164
Lawrence	5,160	10,565	6,592	9,959
Lewis	1,803	2,951	2,192	2,819
Lincoln	3,694	9,226	4,546	7,829
Loudon	6,058	15,815	5,708	14,041
Macon	2,060	5,145	2,738	4,670
Madison	20,027	23,289	16,840	21,679
Marion	4,506	6,746	5,548	5,862
Marshall	4,319	6,755	4,722	5,825
Maury	13,057	20,282	12,379	17,505
McMinn	5,539	12,984	5,891	11,980
McNairy	3,131	7,134	4,101	5,787
Meigs	1,371	2,795	1,595	2,500
Monroe	5,049	11,478	5,354	10,123
Montgomery	25,634	30,103	20,070	28,627
Moore	881	2,010	1,084	1,668
Morgan	1,969	4,717	2,924	4,401
Obion	4,308	8,873	5,549	7,859
Overton	3,418	4,495	4,518	3,941
Perry	1,329	1,596	1,579	1,522
Pickett	854	1,786	1,033	1,600
Polk	2,124	4,267	2,724	3,924
Putnam	9,735	17,098	10,566	15,637
Rhea	2,905	8,033	3,665	7,301
Roane	7,222	15,643	8,706	14,467
Robertson	9,318	17,903	9,865	15,331
Rutherford	40,412	59,850	31,647	52,200
Scott	1,720	4,931	3,086	4,509
Sequatchie	1,717	3,606	1,986	2,951
Sevier	8,597	24,915	8,621	22,143
Shelby	253,633	143,422	216,945	158,137
Smith	2,990	4,561	4,044	3,739
Stewart	2,470	2,956	2,860	2,675
Sullivan	18,346	44,802	19,637	42,555
Sumner	21,486	44,947	21,458	40,181
Tipton	7,911	17,114	7,379	14,178
Trousdale	1,474	1,687	1,851	1,314
Unicoi	2,106	5,011	2,374	5,030
Union	1,828	4,461	2,524	4,145
Van Buren	849	1,293	1,209	1,120
Warren	17,650	25,957	6,808	7,503
Washington	15,894	32,216	14,944	29,735
Wayne	1,355	4,075	1,951	3,999
Weakley	4,594	8,853	5,588	7,817
White	3,369	6,100	4,147	5,269
Williamson	27,879	64,843	21,732	57,451
Wilson	15,462	33,767	15,277	28,924
Totals	**1,087,437**	**1,479,178**	**1,036,477**	**1,384,375**

Tennessee Vote Since 1952

2008: McCain, R., 1,479,178; Obama, D., 1,087,437; Nader, Ind., 11,560; Barr, Ind., 8,547; Baldwin, Ind., 8,191; McKinney, Ind., 2,499; Moore, Ind., 1,326; Jay, Ind., 1,011.

2004: Bush, R., 1,384,375; Kerry, D., 1,036,477; Nader, Ind., 8,992; Badnarik, Ind., 4,866; Peroutka, Ind., 2,570.

2000: Bush, R., 1,061,949; Gore, D., 981,720; Nader, Green, 19,781; Browne, LB., 4,284; Buchanan, RF., 4,250; Brown, Ind., 1,606; Phillips, Ind., 1,015; Hagelin, RF., 613; Venson, Ind., 535.

1996: Clinton, D., 909,146; Dole, R., 863,530; Perot, RF., 105,918; Nader, Ind., 6,427; Browne, Ind., 5,020; Phillips, Ind., 1,818; Collins, Ind., 688; Hagelin, Ind., 636; Michael, Ind., 408; Dodge, Ind., 324.

1992: Clinton, D., 933,521; Bush, R., 841,300; Perot, Ind., 199,968; Marrou, LB., 1,847.

1988: Bush, R., 947,233; Dukakis, D., 679,794; Paul, Ind., 2,041; Duke, Ind., 1,807.

1984: Reagan, R., 990,212; Mondale, D., 711,714; Bergland, LB., 3,072.

1980: Reagan, R., 787,761; Carter, D., 783,051; Anderson, Ind., 35,991; Clark, LB., 7,116; Commoner, Citizens, 1,112; Bubar, Statesman, 521; McReynolds, Soc., 519; Hall, Comm., 503; DeBerry, Soc. Workers, 490; Griswold, Workers World, 400; write-in, 152.

1976: Carter, D., 825,879; Ford, R., 633,969; Anderson, Amer., 5,769; McCarthy, Ind., 5,004; Maddox, Amer. Ind., 2,303; MacBride, LB., 1,375; Hall, Comm., 547; LaRouche, U.S. Labor, 512; Bubar, Prohib., 442; Miller, Ind., 316; write-in, 230.

1972: Nixon, R., 813,147; McGovern, D., 357,293; Schmitz, Amer., 30,373; write-in, 369.

1968: Nixon, R., 472,592; Wallace, 3rd party, 424,792; Humphrey, D., 351,233.

1964: Johnson, D., 635,047; Goldwater, R., 508,965; write-in, 34.

1960: Nixon, R., 556,577; Kennedy, D., 481,453; Faubus, States' Rights, 11,304; Decker, Prohib., 2,458.

1956: Eisenhower, R., 462,288; Stevenson, D., 456,507; Andrews, Ind., 19,820; Holtwick, Prohib., 789.

1952: Eisenhower, R., 446,147; Stevenson, D., 443,710; Hamblen, Prohib., 1,432; Hallinan, Prog., 885; MacArthur, Christian Nationalist, 379.

Texas

County	2008 Obama (D)	McCain (R)	2004 Kerry (D)	Bush (R)
Anderson	4,624	11,855	4,678	11,525
Andrews	790	3,815	677	3,837
Angelina	9,377	19,569	9,302	18,932
Aransas	3,005	6,691	2,640	6,569
Archer	739	3,591	878	3,556
Armstrong	128	856	170	830
Atascosa	4,400	5,546	4,421	7,635
Austin	2,819	8,777	2,582	8,072
Bailey	680	1,618	525	1,882
Bandera	2,248	6,934	1,738	6,933
Bastrop	11,678	13,797	9,794	13,290
Baylor	366	1,262	467	1,169
Bee	3,645	4,467	4,045	5,428
Bell	40,185	49,066	27,165	52,135
Bexar	275,023	245,932	210,976	260,698
Blanco	1,466	3,417	1,267	3,277
Borden	40	316	55	303
Bosque	1,796	5,760	1,815	5,737
Bowie	10,801	24,136	11,880	21,791
Brazoria	36,461	67,444	28,904	63,662
Brazos	20,459	37,403	16,128	37,594
Brewster	1,819	1,781	1,729	1,980
Briscoe	205	616	191	620
Brooks	1,747	556	1,823	845
Brown	2,819	12,049	2,523	11,640
Burleson	2,053	4,546	2,276	4,405
Burnet	4,596	12,034	4,147	11,456
Caldwell	5,385	6,084	5,052	6,436
Calhoun	2,727	4,106	2,561	4,348
Callahan	1,063	4,589	1,073	4,542
Cameron	48,401	26,641	33,998	34,801
Camp	1,733	2,794	1,778	2,638
Carson	406	2,547	485	2,450
Cass	3,489	8,276	4,630	7,383
Castro	719	1,561	631	1,794
Chambers	3,185	9,966	2,953	8,618
Cherokee	4,605	11,693	4,439	11,329
Childress	497	1,782	511	1,629
Clay	1,085	4,213	1,299	3,971
Cochran	284	758	249	856
Coke	297	1,252	266	1,338
Coleman	643	3,011	778	3,035
Collin	108,208	184,116	68,935	174,435
Collingsworth	292	1,052	346	1,051
Colorado	2,503	5,790	2,161	5,488
Comal	12,365	35,203	9,153	31,574
Comanche	1,339	3,807	1,431	3,813
Concho	257	807	270	911
Cooke	3,051	11,871	3,142	11,908
Coryell	6,611	11,537	5,122	12,421
Cottle	187	509	214	549
Crane	319	1,119	254	1,314
Crockett	512	1,026	473	1,248
Crosby	684	1,221	622	1,647
Culberson	510	267	375	407
Dallam	302	1,267	305	1,473
Dallas	424,468	309,477	336,641	346,246
Dawson	1,135	2,894	1,114	3,419
Deaf Smith	1,246	3,456	1,133	4,139
Delta	589	1,580	627	1,447
Denton	90,830	149,592	59,346	140,891
DeWitt	1,715	4,888	1,610	5,100
Dickens	234	730	245	815
Dimmit	2,692	874	2,365	1,188
Donley	291	1,370	349	1,429
Duval	3,298	1,076	2,916	1,160
Eastland	1,271	5,163	1,582	5,249
Ector	9,118	26,190	8,579	27,502
Edwards	346	673	217	745
El Paso	121,589	61,598	95,142	73,261
Ellis	15,315	38,046	11,640	34,602
Erath	3,126	10,757	2,710	9,506
Falls	1,958	2,975	2,427	3,454
Fannin	3,464	8,090	4,001	7,893
Fayette	3,009	7,572	2,803	7,527
Fisher	687	1,083	758	1,161

County	2008 Obama (D)	McCain (R)	2004 Kerry (D)	Bush (R)
Floyd	729	1,784	545	2,032
Foard	208	327	235	347
Fort Bend	98,136	102,846	68,722	93,625
Franklin	1,094	3,394	1,011	3,185
Freestone	2,032	5,201	2,070	5,057
Frio	2,405	1,644	1,931	1,991
Gaines	650	3,385	608	3,540
Galveston	41,543	61,844	43,919	61,290
Garza	375	1,355	326	1,480
Gillespie	2,570	9,559	2,104	9,297
Glasscock	52	502	44	488
Goliad	1,329	2,298	1,219	2,267
Gonzales	2,158	4,062	1,709	4,291
Gray	1,153	6,920	1,289	7,260
Grayson	13,892	31,122	13,452	30,777
Gregg	13,130	29,159	12,306	29,939
Grimes	2,704	5,561	2,713	5,263
Guadalupe	16,070	30,750	10,290	28,208
Hale	2,693	7,139	2,078	8,025
Hall	324	930	413	860
Hamilton	862	2,875	845	2,856
Hansford	239	1,847	240	1,903
Hardeman	373	1,199	480	1,214
Hardin	3,935	16,589	5,608	15,030
Harris	588,611	570,143	475,865	584,723
Harrison	8,874	17,085	9,642	16,473
Hartley	250	1,711	315	1,736
Haskell	699	1,388	867	1,539
Hays	28,416	29,624	20,110	27,021
Hemphill	216	1,342	257	1,380
Henderson	7,890	20,810	8,505	20,210
Hidalgo	90,122	39,614	62,369	50,931
Hill	3,802	9,220	3,751	9,225
Hockley	1,794	5,789	1,385	6,160
Hood	5,078	17,269	4,865	16,280
Hopkins	3,528	9,297	3,443	8,582
Houston	2,653	5,869	2,921	5,848
Howard	2,539	7,020	2,663	7,480
Hudspeth	430	458	302	577
Hunt	8,591	20,571	7,971	20,065
Hutchinson	1,321	7,358	1,503	7,839
Irion	164	644	141	684
Jack	470	2,527	643	2,470
Jackson	1,251	3,560	1,296	3,766
Jasper	3,636	8,960	4,471	8,347
Jeff Davis	467	746	378	764
Jefferson	44,854	42,877	47,066	44,423
Jim Hogg	1,336	472	1,344	712
Jim Wells	6,683	4,825	6,824	5,817
Johnson	12,903	36,683	12,325	34,818
Jones	1,525	4,197	1,658	4,254
Karnes	1,710	2,658	1,543	3,114
Kaufman	11,157	23,727	8,947	21,304
Kendall	3,591	12,960	2,532	11,434
Kenedy	108	93	85	82
Kent	99	342	138	382
Kerr	5,564	16,729	4,557	16,538
Kimble	341	1,487	324	1,482
King	8	151	18	137
Kinney	633	907	542	1,051
Kleberg	5,251	4,539	4,550	5,366
Knox	366	986	464	1,081
La Salle	5,240	12,940	1,229	989
La Vaca	1,156	3,344	2,152	5,974
Lamar	1,895	5,628	5,338	12,054
Lamb	1,051	713	857	3,410
Lampasas	1,867	6,286	1,593	5,422
Lee	2,000	4,312	1,899	4,160
Leon	1,415	5,563	1,754	5,023
Liberty	5,980	15,417	6,780	14,821
Limestone	2,515	5,062	2,752	5,028
Lipscomb	155	1,092	184	1,147
Live Oak	1,038	3,079	1,036	3,147
Llano	2,250	7,279	2,257	7,241
Loving	12	67	12	65
Lubbock	30,295	66,028	22,472	70,135
Lynn	623	1,469	490	1,776
Madison	1,144	2,883	1,235	2,837
Marion	1,644	2,566	1,884	2,441
Martin	314	1,389	288	1,514
Mason	546	1,543	459	1,600
Matagorda	6,682	11,929	4,355	8,119
Maverick	8,554	2,316	5,948	4,025
McCulloch	728	2,263	745	2,465
McLennan	29,959	49,005	26,760	52,090
McMullen	131	400	95	467
Medina	5,119	10,404	4,322	10,389
Menard	295	712	331	761
Midland	9,672	36,135	8,005	36,585
Milam	3,040	5,215	3,445	5,291
Mills	398	1,753	416	1,794
Mitchell	586	1,814	639	1,912
Montague	1,594	6,235	1,946	5,910
Montgomery	36,530	119,542	28,628	104,654
Moore	1,123	4,282	1,009	4,601
Morris	2,054	3,157	2,437	2,818
Motley	67	522	113	564
Nacogdoches	8,393	14,828	7,152	14,160
Navarro	5,399	10,803	5,259	10,715
Newton	1,750	3,440	2,513	3,159
Nolan	1,521	3,485	1,541	3,722
Nueces	47,811	52,264	44,439	59,359
Ochiltree	243	2,851	251	2,922
Oldham	102	813	108	733
Orange	7,646	21,509	11,476	20,292
Palo Pinto	2,499	7,264	2,816	7,137
Panola	2,586	7,582	2,958	7,021
Parker	10,429	36,646	8,966	31,795
Parmer	719	2,969	389	2,375
Pecos	1,476	2,480	1,242	3,167
Polk	6,215	13,703	6,964	13,778
Potter	8,932	20,741	7,489	21,401
Presidio	1,250	489	1,159	715
Rains	1,041	3,130	1,213	2,998
Randall	9,461	41,895	7,849	40,520
Reagan	197	795	184	956
Real	375	1,237	325	1,314
Red River	1,538	3,461	2,097	3,379
Reeves	1,605	1,444	1,600	1,777
Refugio	1,382	1,853	1,232	2,212
Roberts	41	477	46	461
Robertson	2,674	3,979	2,979	3,792
Rockwall	8,468	23,243	5,320	20,120
Runnels	720	3,118	792	3,239
Rusk	4,983	13,641	4,899	13,390
Sabine	1,077	3,749	1,476	3,138
San Augustine	1,327	2,338	1,506	2,235
San Jacinto	2,721	6,151	2,688	5,394
San Patricio	8,842	12,390	7,764	13,474
San Saba	487	1,941	529	1,894
Schleicher	322	969	312	1,012
Scurry	1,088	4,414	981	4,576
Shackelford	208	1,284	229	1,292
Shelby	2,546	6,629	2,951	6,295
Sherman	78	493	124	942
Smith	23,628	54,995	19,970	53,392
Somervell	798	2,675	831	2,701
Starr	8,233	1,488	7,199	2,552
Stephens	626	2,869	703	2,803
Sterling	97	520	71	544
Stonewall	206	524	250	499
Sutton	381	1,189	280	1,173
Swisher	812	1,676	626	1,487
Tarrant	274,101	347,843	207,286	349,462
Taylor	12,658	34,265	10,648	37,197
Terrell	186	323	159	306
Terry	1,379	2,863	794	3,166
Throckmorton	166	671	202	656
Titus	3,140	6,023	3,173	5,709
Tom Green	11,068	27,201	9,007	28,185
Travis	253,278	136,671	197,235	147,885
Trinity	1,924	4,091	2,204	3,985
Tyler	2,159	5,633	2,659	5,043
Upshur	2,106	5,871	4,225	10,232
Upton	288	898	185	1,009
Uvalde	4,120	4,585	3,298	5,148
Val Verde	6,982	5,752	4,757	6,968
Van Zandt	4,503	15,727	4,822	14,976
Victoria	9,829	19,876	8,553	20,875
Walker	7,323	11,610	5,977	11,710
Waller	7,107	8,238	6,145	7,679
Ward	899	2,667	901	2,856
Washington	4,031	10,173	3,389	9,597
Webb	33,435	13,111	23,654	17,753
Wharton	4,935	9,427	4,702	9,288
Wheeler	314	1,916	420	1,960
Wichita	13,828	31,673	12,819	32,472
Wilbarger	1,196	3,279	1,284	3,685
Willacy	3,405	1,454	2,734	2,209
Williamson	67,347	87,938	43,117	83,284
Wilson	5,360	10,903	4,409	10,400
Winkler	477	1,529	391	1,604
Wise	4,469	15,967	4,783	15,177
Wood	3,996	13,638	4,034	12,831
Yoakum	450	1,989	376	2,228
Young	1,302	5,938	1,511	5,874
Zapata	1,939	918	1,662	1,228
Zavala	3,263	596	2,332	777
Totals	3,528,633	4,479,328	2,832,704	4,526,917

Texas Vote Since 1952

2008: McCain, R., 4,479,328; Obama, D., 3,528,633 Barr, LB., 56,116.

2004: Bush, R., 4,526,917; Kerry, D., 2,832,704; Badnarik, LB., 38,787.

2000: Bush, R., 3,799,639; Gore, D., 2,433,746; Nader, Green, 137,994; Browne, LB., 23,160; Buchanan, Ind., 12,394.

1996: Dole, R., 2,736,167; Clinton, D., 2,459,683; Perot, RF., 378,537; Browne, LB., 20,256; Phillips, U.S. Taxpayers, 7,472; Hagelin, Natural Law, 4,422.

1992: Bush, R., 2,496,071; Clinton, D., 2,281,815; Perot, Ind., 1,354,781; Marrou, LB., 19,699.

1988: Bush, R., 3,036,829; Dukakis, D., 2,352,748; Paul, LB., 30,355; Fulani, New Alliance, 7,208.

1984: Reagan, R., 3,433,428; Mondale, D., 1,949,276.

1980: Reagan, R., 2,510,705; Carter, D., 1,881,147; Anderson, Ind., 111,613; Clark, LB., 37,643; write-in, 528.

1976: Carter, D., 2,082,319; Ford, R., 1,953,300; McCarthy, Ind., 20,118; Anderson, Amer., 11,442; Camejo, Soc. Workers, 1,723; write-in, 2,982.

1972: Nixon, R., 2,298,896; McGovern, D., 1,154,289; Jenness, Soc. Workers, 8,664; Schmitz, Amer., 6,039; others, 3,393.

1968: Humphrey, D., 1,266,804; Nixon, R., 1,227,844; Wallace, 3rd party, 584,269; write-in, 489.

1964: Johnson, D., 1,663,185; Goldwater, R., 958,566; Lightburn, Const., 5,060.

1960: Kennedy, D., 1,167,932; Nixon, R., 1,121,699; Sullivan, Const., 18,169; Decker, Prohib., 3,870; write-in, 15.

1956: Eisenhower, R., 1,080,619; Stevenson, D., 859,958; Andrews, Ind., 14,591.

1952: Eisenhower, R., 1,102,878; Stevenson, D., 969,228; Hamblen, Prohib., 1,983; MacArthur, Christian Nationalist, 833; MacArthur, Const., 730; Hallinan, Prog., 294.

Utah

County	2008		2004	
	Obama (D)	McCain (R)	Kerry (D)	Bush (R)
Beaver	509	1,786	493	2,023
Box Elder	3,080	14,340	2,244	15,751
Cache	9,806	27,799	6,375	32,486
Carbon	3,368	3,960	3,415	4,950
Daggett	129	294	108	380
Davis	28,831	73,317	20,893	86,187
Duchesne	897	4,592	738	4,742
Emery	965	3,338	831	3,781
Garfield	402	1,663	264	1,848
Grand	1,981	1,787	1,858	2,130
Iron	3,078	11,786	2,267	12,815
Juab	730	2,647	605	2,681
Kane	850	2,194	576	2,414
Millard	733	3,565	626	4,084
Morgan	674	3,219	472	3,301
Piute	141	635	123	646
Rich	154	829	109	922
Salt Lake	176,988	176,692	135,949	215,728
San Juan	2,322	2,586	1,906	2,971
Sanpete	1,449	6,036	1,189	7,004
Sevier	1,320	6,222	920	6,597
Summit	9,194	6,691	6,977	7,936
Tooele	5,349	10,201	4,130	12,181
Uintah	1,407	8,113	1,266	8,518
Utah	26,276	111,273	17,357	128,269
Wasatch	2,818	5,271	1,854	5,503
Washington	9,251	33,594	7,513	35,633
Wayne	333	930	279	1,062
Weber	24,028	43,250	19,862	51,199
Totals	**327,670**	**596,030**	**241,199**	**663,742**

Utah Vote Since 1952

2008: McCain, R., 596,030; Obama, D., 327,670; Baldwin, Const., 12,012; Nader, unaff., 8,416; Barr, LB., 6,966; McKinney, unaff., 982; La Riva, unaff., 262.

2004: Bush, R., 663,742; Kerry, D., 241,199; Nader, Ind., 11,305; Peroutka, Const., 6,841; Badnarik, LB., 3,375; Jay, Pers. Choice, 946; Harris, Soc. Workers, 393.

2000: Bush, R., 515,096; Gore, D., 203,053; Nader, Green, 35,850; Buchanan, RF., 9,319; Browne, LB., 3,616; Phillips, Ind. Amer., 2,709; Hagelin, Natural Law, 763; Harris, Soc. Workers, 186; Youngkeit, Ind., 161.

1996: Dole, R., 361,911; Clinton, D., 221,633; Perot, RF., 66,461; Nader, Green, 4,615; Browne, LB., 4,129; Phillips, Taxpayers, 2,601; Templin, Ind. Amer., 1,290; Crane, Ind., 1,101; Hagelin, Natural Law, 1,085; Moorehead, Workers World, 298; Harris, Soc. Workers, 235; Dodge, Prohib., 111.

1992: Bush, R., 322,632; Perot, Ind., 203,400; Clinton, D., 183,429; Gritz, Pop./America First, 28,602; Marrou, LB., 1,900; Hagelin, Natural Law, 1,319; LaRouche, Ind., 1,089.

1988: Bush, R., 428,442; Dukakis, D., 207,352; Paul, LB., 7,473; Dennis, Amer., 2,158.

1984: Reagan, R., 469,105; Mondale, D., 155,369; Bergland, LB., 2,447.

1980: Reagan, R., 439,687; Carter, D., 124,266; Anderson, Ind., 30,284; Clark, LB., 7,226; Commoner, Citizens, 1,009; Greaves, Amer., 965; Rarick, Amer. Ind., 522; Hall, Comm., 139; DeBerry, Soc. Workers, 124.

1976: Ford, R., 337,908; Carter, D., 182,110; Anderson, Amer., 13,304; McCarthy, Ind., 3,907; MacBride, LB., 2,438; Maddox, Amer. Ind., 1,162; Camejo, Soc. Workers, 268; Hall, Comm., 121.

1972: Nixon, R., 323,643; McGovern, D., 126,284; Schmitz, Amer., 28,549.

1968: Nixon, R., 238,728; Humphrey, D., 156,665; Wallace, 3rd party, 26,906; Peace/Freedom, 180; Halstead, Soc. Workers, 89.

1964: Johnson, D., 219,628; Goldwater, R., 181,785.

1960: Nixon, R., 205,361; Kennedy, D., 169,248; Dobbs, Soc. Workers, 100.

1956: Eisenhower, R., 215,631; Stevenson, D., 118,364.

1952: Eisenhower, R., 194,190; Stevenson, D., 135,364.

Vermont

County	2008		2004	
	Obama (D)	McCain (R)	Kerry (D)	Bush (R)
Addison	13,202	5,667	11,147	7,077
Bennington	12,524	6,133	11,069	7,616
Caledonia	8,900	5,472	7,106	6,765
Chittenden	59,611	22,237	49,369	26,422
Essex	1,733	1,284	1,276	1,591
Franklin	13,179	7,853	10,598	8,936
Grand Isle	2,694	1,490	2,246	1,754
Lamoille	8,914	3,515	7,636	4,260
Orange	9,799	5,047	8,159	6,421
Orleans	7,998	4,482	6,330	5,666
Rutland	19,355	11,584	15,904	14,440
Washington	22,324	9,129	19,177	11,461
Windham	17,585	5,997	15,489	7,280
Windsor	21,444	9,084	18,561	11,491
Totals	**219,262**	**98,974**	**184,067**	**121,180**

Vermont Vote Since 1952

2008: Obama, D., 219,262; McCain, R., 98,974; Nader, Ind., 3,339; Barr, LB., 1,067; Baldwin, Const., 500; Calero, Soc. Workers, 150; La Riva, Socialism/Liberation, 149; Moore, Liberty Union, 141.

2004: Kerry, D., 184,067; Bush, R., 121,180; Nader, Ind., 4,494; Badnarik, LB., 1,102; Parker, Liberty Union, 265; Calero, Soc. Workers, 244.

2000: Gore, D., 149,022; Bush, R., 119,775; Nader, Green, 20,374; Buchanan, RF., 2,192; Lane, Grass Roots, 1,044; Browne, LB., 784; Hagelin, Natural Law, 219; McReynolds, Liberty Union, 161; Phillips, Const., 153; Harris, Soc. Workers, 70.

1996: Clinton, D., 137,894; Dole, R., 80,352; Perot, RF., 31,024; Nader, Green, 5,585; Browne, LB., 1,183; Hagelin, Natural Law, 498; Peron, Grass Roots, 480; Phillips, Taxpayers, 382; Hollis, Liberty Union, 292; Harris, Soc. Workers, 199.

1992: Clinton, D., 133,590; Bush, R., 88,122; Perot, Ind., 65,985.

1988: Bush, R., 124,331; Dukakis, D., 115,775; Paul, LB., 1,000; LaRouche, Ind., 275.

1984: Reagan, R., 135,865; Mondale, D., 95,730; Bergland, LB., 1,002.

1980: Reagan, R., 94,598; Carter, D., 81,891; Anderson, Ind., 31,760; Commoner, Citizens, 2,316; Clark, LB., 1,900; McReynolds, Liberty Union, 136; Hall, Comm., 118; DeBerry, Soc. Workers, 75; scattered, 413.

1976: Ford, R., 100,387; Carter, D., 77,798 and Ind. Vermonters, 991 (total, 79,789); McCarthy, Ind., 4,001; Camejo, Soc. Workers, 430; LaRouche, U.S. Labor, 196; scattered, 99.

1972: Nixon, R., 117,149; McGovern, D., 68,174; Spock, Liberty Union, 1,010; Jenness, Soc. Workers, 296; scattered, 318.

1968: Nixon, R., 85,142; Humphrey, D., 70,255; Wallace, 3rd party, 5,104; Gregory, New Party, 579; Halstead, Soc. Workers, 295.

1964: Johnson, D., 107,674; Goldwater, R., 54,868.

1960: Nixon, R., 98,131; Kennedy, D., 69,186.

1956: Eisenhower, R., 110,390; Stevenson, D., 42,549; scattered, 39.

1952: Eisenhower, R., 109,717; Stevenson, D., 43,355; Hallinan, Prog., 282; Hoopes, Soc., 185.

Virginia

County	2008		2004	
	Obama (D)	McCain (R)	Kerry (D)	Bush (R)
Accomack	7,607	7,833	5,518	7,726
Albemarle	29,792	20,576	22,088	21,189
Alleghany	3,553	3,715	3,203	3,962
Amelia	2,488	3,970	1,862	3,499
Amherst	6,094	8,470	4,866	7,758
Appomattox	2,641	4,903	2,191	4,366
Arlington	78,994	29,876	63,987	29,635
Augusta	9,825	23,120	7,019	22,100

County	2008 Obama (D)	McCain (R)	2004 Kerry (D)	Bush (R)
Bath	1,043	1,349	828	1,432
Bedford	11,017	24,420	9,102	21,925
Bland	864	2,031	846	1,962
Botetourt	5,693	11,471	4,801	10,865
Brunswick	4,973	2,877	4,062	2,852
Buchanan	4,063	4,541	5,275	4,507
Buckingham	3,489	3,428	2,789	3,185
Campbell	8,091	17,444	6,862	15,891
Caroline	7,163	5,617	4,878	4,999
Carroll	4,108	8,186	3,888	8,173
Charles City	2,838	1,288	2,155	1,254
Charlotte	2,705	3,372	2,223	3,166
Chesterfield	74,310	86,413	49,346	83,745
Clarke	3,457	3,840	2,699	3,741
Craig	876	1,695	901	1,706
Culpeper	8,802	10,711	5,476	10,026
Cumberland	2,255	2,418	1,721	2,377
Dickenson	3,278	3,324	3,761	3,591
Dinwiddie	6,246	6,526	4,569	6,193
Essex	2,934	2,379	2,007	2,304
Fairfax	310,359	200,994	245,671	211,980
Fauquier	14,616	19,227	10,712	19,011
Floyd	2,937	4,441	2,488	4,162
Fluvanna	6,185	6,420	4,415	6,458
Franklin	9,618	15,414	8,002	14,048
Frederick	12,961	20,149	8,853	19,386
Giles	3,192	4,462	3,047	4,320
Gloucester	6,916	12,089	5,105	11,084
Goochland	4,813	7,643	3,583	6,668
Grayson	2,480	4,540	2,430	4,655
Greene	3,174	4,980	2,240	4,570
Greensville	3,122	1,729	2,514	1,732
Halifax	8,126	8,600	6,220	8,363
Hanover	18,447	37,344	13,941	35,404
Henrico	86,262	67,340	60,864	71,809
Henry	11,118	13,758	9,851	13,358
Highland	590	930	522	982
Isle of Wight	8,573	11,258	5,871	9,929
James City	17,352	20,912	11,934	18,949
King and Queen	1,918	1,763	1,506	1,737
King George	4,473	5,888	2,739	5,124
King William	3,344	4,966	2,436	4,397
Lancaster	3,235	3,647	2,477	3,724
Lee	3,219	5,825	4,005	5,664
Loudoun	74,607	63,328	47,271	60,382
Louisa	6,978	8,182	4,844	7,083
Lunenburg	2,703	2,900	2,362	2,858
Madison	2,862	3,758	2,176	3,556
Mathews	1,943	3,456	1,589	3,497
Mecklenburg	7,127	7,817	5,293	7,319
Middlesex	2,391	3,545	1,914	3,336
Montgomery	21,027	19,026	14,128	17,070
Nelson	4,391	3,647	3,543	3,539
New Kent	3,493	6,385	2,443	5,414
Northampton	3,800	2,713	2,775	2,669
Northumberland	3,312	4,041	2,548	3,832
Nottoway	3,413	3,499	2,635	3,303
Orange	7,107	8,506	5,015	7,749
Page	4,235	6,041	3,324	6,221
Patrick	2,879	5,491	2,572	5,507
Pittsylvania	11,441	18,724	9,274	17,673
Powhatan	4,237	10,088	3,112	8,955
Prince Edward	5,101	4,174	3,632	3,571
Prince George	7,130	8,752	5,066	8,131
Prince William	93,386	67,589	61,271	69,776
Pulaski	5,918	8,857	5,310	8,769
Rappahannock	2,105	2,227	1,837	2,172
Richmond	1,618	2,092	1,243	2,082
Roanoke	19,812	30,571	16,082	30,596
Rockbridge	4,347	5,732	3,627	5,412
Rockingham	10,453	22,468	7,273	21,737
Russell	4,931	6,389	5,167	6,077
Scott	2,725	6,980	3,324	6,409
Shenandoah	6,903	11,995	5,186	11,820
Smyth	4,239	7,817	4,143	7,906
Southampton	4,402	4,583	3,431	4,018
Spotsylvania	24,897	28,610	16,623	28,527
Stafford	25,716	29,221	17,208	28,500
Surry	2,626	1,663	1,954	1,543
Sussex	3,301	2,026	2,420	1,890
Tazewell	5,596	11,201	7,184	10,039

County	2008 Obama (D)	McCain (R)	2004 Kerry (D)	Bush (R)
Warren	6,997	8,879	5,241	8,600
Washington	8,063	16,077	7,339	14,749
Westmoreland	4,577	3,719	3,370	3,433
Wise	4,995	8,914	5,802	8,330
Wythe	4,107	8,207	3,581	7,911
York	13,700	19,833	10,276	19,396
City				
Alexandria	50,473	19,181	41,116	19,844
Bedford	1,208	1,497	1,042	1,472
Bristol	2,665	4,579	2,400	4,275
Buena Vista	1,108	1,282	936	1,417
Charlottesville	15,705	4,078	11,088	4,172
Chesapeake	53,993	52,624	38,744	52,283
Colonial Heights	2,562	6,161	2,061	6,129
Covington	1,304	1,020	1,179	1,104
Danville	12,352	8,361	9,436	9,399
Emporia	1,702	897	1,247	970
Fairfax	6,571	4,686	5,395	5,045
Falls Church	4,695	1,970	3,944	2,074
Franklin	2,817	1,575	1,910	1,613
Fredericksburg	6,155	3,413	4,085	3,390
Galax	1,052	1,317	987	1,336
Hampton	46,917	20,476	32,016	23,399
Harrisonburg	8,444	6,048	4,726	6,165
Hopewell	5,285	4,149	3,573	4,251
Lexington	1,540	914	1,340	982
Lynchburg	16,269	17,638	11,727	14,400
Manassas	7,518	5,975	5,562	7,257
Manassas Park	2,463	1,634	1,498	1,807
Martinsville	4,139	2,311	3,036	2,538
Newport News	51,972	28,667	35,319	32,208
Norfolk	62,819	24,814	43,518	26,401
Norton	743	744	725	768
Petersburg	13,774	1,583	9,682	2,238
Poquoson	1,748	5,229	1,424	5,004
Portsmouth	32,322	13,983	24,112	15,212
Radford	2,930	2,418	2,244	2,564
Richmond	73,180	18,472	52,167	21,637
Roanoke	24,934	15,394	18,862	16,661
Salem	5,164	7,088	4,254	7,115
Staunton	5,569	5,330	3,756	5,805
Suffolk	22,233	18,592	15,233	16,763
Virginia Beach	98,763	100,225	70,666	103,752
Waynesboro	3,906	4,815	2,792	5,092
Williamsburg	4,328	2,353	2,216	2,064
Winchester	5,268	4,725	3,967	5,283
Totals	**1,959,532**	**1,725,005**	**1,454,742**	**1,716,959**

Virginia Vote Since 1952

2008: Obama, D., 1,959,532; McCain, R., 1,725,005; Nader, Ind., 11,483; Barr, LB., 11,067; Baldwin, Ind. Green, 7,474; McKinney, Green, 2,344.

2004: Bush, R., 1,716,959; Kerry, D., 1,454,742; Badnarik, LB., 11,032; Peroutka, Const., 10,161.

2000: Bush, R., 1,437,490; Gore, D., 1,217,290; Nader, Green, 59,398; Browne, LB., 15,198; Buchanan, RF., 5,455; Phillips, Const., 1,809.

1996: Dole, R., 1,138,350; Clinton, D., 1,091,060; Perot, RF., 159,861; Phillips, Taxpayers, 13,687; Browne, LB., 9,174; Hagelin, Natural Law, 4,510.

1992: Bush, R., 1,150,517; Clinton, D., 1,038,650; Perot, Ind., 348,639; LaRouche, Ind., 11,937; Marrou, LB., 5,730; Fulani, New Alliance, 3,192.

1988: Bush, R., 1,309,162; Dukakis, D., 859,799; Fulani, Ind., 14,312; Paul, LB., 8,336.

1984: Reagan, R., 1,337,078; Mondale, D., 796,250.

1980: Reagan, R., 989,609; Carter, D., 752,174; Anderson, Ind., 95,418; Commoner, Citizens, 14,024; Clark, LB., 12,821; DeBerry, Soc. Workers, 1,986.

1976: Ford, R., 836,554; Carter, D., 813,896; Camejo, Soc. Workers, 17,802; Anderson, Amer., 16,686; LaRouche, U.S. Labor, 7,508; MacBride, LB., 4,648.

1972: Nixon, R., 988,493; McGovern, D., 438,887; Schmitz, Amer., 19,721; Fisher, Soc. Labor, 9,918.

1968: Nixon, R., 590,319; Humphrey, D., 442,387; Wallace, 3rd party, 320,272; Blomen, Soc. Labor, 4,671; Gregory, Peace/Freedom, 1,680; Munn, Prohib., 601. *10,561 votes for Wallace were omitted in the count.

1964: Johnson, D., 558,038; Goldwater, R., 481,334; Hass, Soc. Labor, 2,895.

1960: Nixon, R., 404,521; Kennedy, D., 362,327; Coiner, Conservative, 4,204; Hass, Soc. Labor, 397.

1956: Eisenhower, R., 386,459; Stevenson, D., 267,760; Andrews, States' Rights, 42,964; Hoopes, Soc. Democrat, 444; Hass, Soc. Labor, 351.

1952: Eisenhower, R., 349,037; Stevenson, D., 268,677; Hass, Soc. Labor, 1,160; Hoopes, Soc. Democrat, 504; Hallinan, Prog., 311.

Washington

County	2008		2004	
	Obama (D)	McCain (R)	Kerry (D)	Bush (R)
Adams	1,346	2,822	1,315	3,751
Asotin	4,114	5,407	3,319	5,320
Benton	23,366	40,244	21,549	44,350
Chelan	13,678	17,484	10,471	18,482
Clallam	17,512	15,978	17,049	18,871
Clark	93,541	82,631	79,538	88,646
Columbia	667	1,447	605	1,470
Cowlitz	18,944	13,969	21,589	20,217
Douglas	4,631	7,048	4,306	8,900
Ferry	1,386	1,817	1,201	2,019
Franklin	6,536	10,787	5,188	10,757
Garfield	384	966	365	935
Grant	9,364	16,756	7,779	17,799
Grays Harbor	15,759	11,614	14,583	12,871
Island	21,688	19,070	18,216	19,754
Jefferson	12,914	6,195	11,610	6,650
King	545,329	217,589	580,378	301,043
Kitsap	61,255	47,456	60,796	55,608
Kittitas	7,887	9,320	6,731	9,052
Klickitat	4,871	4,868	4,036	5,016
Lewis	11,719	17,293	10,726	21,042
Lincoln	2,024	3,794	1,706	4,015
Mason	14,934	12,512	12,894	11,987
Okanogan	6,163	6,942	6,309	9,636
Pacific	6,066	4,531	5,570	4,634
Pend Oreille	2,546	3,704	2,310	3,693
Pierce	143,491	111,851	158,231	150,783
San Juan	7,172	2,889	6,589	3,290
Skagit	28,145	23,031	25,131	26,139
Skamania	2,797	2,513	2,374	2,695
Snohomish	177,471	120,064	156,468	134,317
Spokane	102,164	105,059	87,490	111,606
Stevens	6,386	9,308	6,822	13,015
Thurston	69,999	44,565	62,650	47,992
Wahkiakum	1,112	1,100	1,021	1,171
Walla Walla	7,539	10,632	8,257	14,323
Whatcom	53,313	36,635	48,268	40,296
Whitman	7,957	7,304	8,287	9,397
Yakima	32,484	40,877	28,474	43,352
Totals	**1,750,848**	**1,229,216**	**1,510,201**	**1,304,894**

Washington Vote Since 1952

2008: Obama, D., 1,750,848; McCain, R., 1,229,216; Nader, Ind., 29,489; Barr, LB., 12,728; Baldwin, Const., 9,432; McKinney, Green, 3,819; La Riva, Socialism/Liberation, 705; Harris, Soc. Workers, 641.

2004: Kerry, D., 1,510,201; Bush, R., 1,304,894; Nader, Ind., 23,283; Badnarik, LB., 11,955; Peroutka, Const., 3,922; Cobb, Green, 2,974; Parker, Workers World, 1,077; Harris, Soc. Workers, 547; Van Auken, Soc. Equal., 231.

2000: Gore, D., 1,247,652; Bush, R., 1,108,864; Nader, Green, 103,002; Browne, LB., 13,135; Buchanan, Freedom, 7,171; Hagelin, Natural Law, 2,927; Phillips, Const., 1,989; Moorehead, Workers World, 1,729; McReynolds, Soc., 660; Harris, Soc. Workers, 304.

1996: Clinton, D., 1,123,323; Dole, R., 840,712; Perot, RF., 201,003; Nader, Ind., 60,322; Browne, LB., 12,522; Hagelin, Natural Law, 6,076; Phillips, U.S. Taxpayers, 4,578; Collins, Ind., 2,374; Moorehead, Workers World, 2,189; Harris, Soc. Workers, 738.

1992: Clinton, D., 993,037; Bush, R., 731,234; Perot, Ind., 541,780; Marrou, LB., 7,533; Gritz, Pop./America First, 4,854; Hagelin, Natural Law, 2,456; Phillips, U.S. Taxpayers, 2,354; Fulani, New Alliance, 1,776; Daniels, Ind., 1,171.

1988: Dukakis, D., 933,516; Bush, R., 903,835; Paul, LB., 17,240; LaRouche, Ind., 4,412.

1984: Reagan, R., 1,051,670; Mondale, D., 798,352; Bergland, LB., 8,844.

1980: Reagan, R., 865,244; Carter, D., 650,193; Anderson, Ind., 185,073; Clark, LB., 29,213; Commoner, Citizens, 9,403; DeBerry, Soc. Workers, 1,137; McReynolds, Soc., 956; Hall, Comm., 834; Griswold, Workers World, 341.

1976: Ford, R., 777,732; Carter, D., 717,323; McCarthy, Ind., 36,986; Maddox, Amer. Ind., 8,585; Anderson, Amer., 5,046; MacBride, LB., 5,042; Wright, People's, 1,124; Camejo, Soc. Workers, 905; LaRouche, U.S. Labor, 903; Hall, Comm., 817; Levin, Soc. Labor, 713; Zeidler, Soc., 358.

1972: Nixon, R., 837,135; McGovern, D., 568,334; Schmitz, Amer., 58,906; Spock, Ind., 2,644; Hospers, LB., 1,537; Fisher, Soc. Labor, 1,102; Jenness, Soc. Workers, 623; Hall, Comm., 566.

1968: Humphrey, D., 616,037; Nixon, R., 588,510; Wallace, 3rd party, 96,990; Cleaver, Peace/Freedom, 1,609; Blomen, Soc. Labor, 488; Mitchell, Free Ballot, 377; Halstead, Soc. Workers, 270.

1964: Johnson, D., 779,699; Goldwater, R., 470,366; Hass, Soc. Labor, 7,772; DeBerry, Freedom Soc., 537.

1960: Nixon, R., 629,273; Kennedy, D., 599,298; Hass, Soc. Labor, 10,895; Curtis, Const., 1,401; Dobbs, Soc. Workers, 705.

1956: Eisenhower, R., 620,430; Stevenson, D., 523,002; Hass, Soc. Labor, 7,457.

1952: Eisenhower, R., 599,107; Stevenson, D., 492,845; MacArthur, Christian Nationalist, 7,290; Hallinan, Prog., 2,460; Hass, Soc. Labor, 633; Hoopes, Soc., 254; Dobbs, Soc. Workers, 119.

West Virginia

County	2008		2004	
	Obama (D)	McCain (R)	Kerry (D)	Bush (R)
Barbour	2,415	3,678	2,610	4,004
Berkeley	15,945	20,779	12,244	21,293
Boone	4,490	3,603	5,933	4,207
Braxton	2,691	2,618	3,035	2,986
Brooke	4,666	4,932	5,493	5,189
Cabell	15,110	18,571	16,583	21,035
Calhoun	976	1,345	1,266	1,588
Clay	1,417	1,748	1,835	2,198
Doddridge	732	2,205	800	2,362
Fayette	7,134	7,578	8,971	7,881
Gilmer	1,117	1,578	1,159	1,665
Grant	987	3,150	963	4,063
Greenbrier	5,561	7,347	6,084	8,358
Hampshire	2,968	5,197	2,455	5,489
Hancock	5,285	7,257	6,906	7,298
Hardy	1,880	3,360	1,617	3,635
Harrison	13,488	17,715	13,238	17,111
Jackson	4,821	7,066	5,384	7,686
Jefferson	11,606	10,526	9,301	10,539
Kanawha	40,148	40,588	43,010	44,430
Lewis	2,096	4,312	2,475	4,445
Lincoln	2,972	3,556	4,048	4,102
Logan	4,862	6,297	7,877	7,047
Marion	11,507	11,389	12,771	12,150
Marshall	5,943	7,709	6,435	8,516
Mason	4,444	5,822	5,408	6,487
McDowell	3,410	2,852	4,501	2,762
Mercer	7,388	13,167	9,178	13,057
Mineral	3,717	7,546	3,518	7,854
Mingo	3,567	4,565	5,983	4,612
Monongalia	16,853	15,612	16,313	17,670
Monroe	1,969	3,344	2,311	3,590
Morgan	2,704	4,408	2,272	4,511
Nicholas	6,007	6,115	4,788	5,485
Ohio	8,481	10,590	8,543	11,694
Pendleton	1,049	1,605	1,381	2,146
Pleasants	1,127	1,753	1,349	2,061
Pocahontas	1,538	1,993	1,573	2,295
Preston	4,190	7,299	3,963	7,855
Putnam	9,424	15,295	9,301	15,716
Raleigh	10,115	17,358	11,815	18,519
Randolph	4,527	6,051	4,892	6,512
Ritchie	989	2,753	1,070	3,086
Roane	2,506	2,936	2,612	3,440
Summers	2,276	2,875	2,504	2,978
Taylor	2,420	3,518	2,617	3,893
Tucker	1,280	2,118	1,400	2,179
Tyler	1,234	2,390	1,401	2,798
Upshur	2,896	5,870	3,034	6,191
Wayne	6,101	8,890	8,411	10,070
Webster	1,543	1,374	1,965	1,724
Wetzel	2,919	3,318	3,330	3,656
Wirt	777	1,482	896	1,727
Wood	12,446	22,670	14,025	24,948
Wyoming	2,724	4,605	3,694	4,985
Totals	**303,857**	**397,466**	**326,541**	**423,778**

West Virginia Vote Since 1952

2008: McCain, R., 397,466; Obama, D., 303,857; Nader, unaff., 7,219; Baldwin, Const., 2,465; McKinney, Mountain, 2,355.

2004: Bush, R., 423,778; Kerry, D., 326,541; Nader, Ind., 4,063; Badnarik, LB., 1,405.

2000: Bush, R., 336,475; Gore, D., 295,497; Nader, Green, 10,680; Buchanan, RF., 3,169; Browne, LB., 1,912; Hagelin, Natural Law, 367.

1996: Clinton, D., 327,812; Dole, R., 233,946; Perot, RF., 71,639; Browne, LB., 3,062.

1992: Clinton, D., 331,001; Bush, R., 241,974; Perot, Ind., 108,829; Marrou, LB., 1,873.

1988: Dukakis, D., 341,016; Bush, R., 310,065; Fulani, New Alliance, 2,230.

1984: Reagan, R., 405,483; Mondale, D., 328,125.

1980: Carter, D., 367,462; Reagan, R., 334,206; Anderson, Ind., 31,691; Clark, LB., 4,356.

1976: Carter, D., 435,864; Ford, R., 314,726.

1972: Nixon, R., 484,964; McGovern, D., 277,435.

1968: Humphrey, D., 374,091; Nixon, R., 307,555; Wallace, 3rd party, 72,560.

1964: Johnson, D., 538,087; Goldwater, R., 253,953.

1960: Kennedy, D., 441,786; Nixon, R., 395,995.

1956: Eisenhower, R., 449,297; Stevenson, D., 381,534.

1952: Stevenson, D., 453,578; Eisenhower, R., 419,970.

Wisconsin

County	2008 Obama (D)	McCain (R)	2004 Kerry (D)	Bush (R)
Adams	5,808	3,976	5,447	4,890
Ashland	5,697	2,507	5,805	3,313
Barron	12,076	10,456	11,696	12,030
Bayfield	5,978	3,316	5,845	3,754
Brown	67,241	55,827	54,935	67,173
Buffalo	3,979	2,946	3,998	3,502
Burnett	4,337	4,200	4,499	4,743
Calumet	13,296	12,720	10,290	14,721
Chippewa	16,236	13,489	14,751	15,450
Clark	7,450	6,337	6,966	7,966
Columbia	16,658	12,189	14,300	14,956
Crawford	5,124	2,905	4,656	3,680
Dane	202,812	71,829	181,052	90,369
Dodge	19,178	23,013	16,690	27,201
Door	10,142	7,112	8,367	8,910
Douglas	15,827	7,833	16,537	8,448
Dunn	13,055	9,616	12,039	10,879
Eau Claire	33,143	20,944	30,068	24,653
Florence	1,134	1,512	993	1,703
Fond du Lac	23,457	28,155	19,216	33,291
Forest	2,671	1,960	2,509	2,608
Grant	14,911	9,109	12,864	12,208
Green	11,499	6,730	9,575	8,497
Green Lake	3,998	5,392	3,605	6,472
Iowa	8,076	3,915	7,122	5,348
Iron	1,915	1,470	1,956	1,884
Jackson	5,572	3,550	5,249	4,387
Jefferson	21,448	21,095	17,925	23,776
Juneau	6,209	5,187	5,734	6,473
Kenosha	45,615	31,237	40,107	35,587
Kewaunee	5,902	4,711	5,175	5,970
La Crosse	38,514	23,698	33,170	28,289
Lafayette	4,732	2,984	4,402	3,929
Langlade	5,182	5,081	4,751	6,235
Lincoln	8,419	6,510	7,484	8,024
Manitowoc	22,421	19,231	20,652	23,027
Marathon	36,363	30,339	30,899	36,394
Marinette	11,124	9,705	10,190	11,866
Marquette	4,051	3,625	3,785	4,604
Menominee	1,257	185	1,412	288
Milwaukee	316,916	147,573	297,653	180,287
Monroe	10,178	8,657	8,973	10,375
Oconto	9,926	8,754	8,534	11,043
Oneida	11,905	9,627	10,464	11,351
Outagamie	50,255	39,641	40,169	48,903
Ozaukee	20,570	32,160	17,714	34,904
Pepin	2,101	1,615	2,181	1,853
Pierce	11,695	9,715	11,176	10,437
Polk	10,876	11,282	11,173	12,095
Portage	24,815	13,807	21,861	16,546
Price	4,559	3,458	4,349	4,312
Racine	53,405	45,941	48,229	52,456
Richland	5,072	3,348	4,501	4,836
Rock	50,515	27,356	46,598	33,151
Rusk	3,855	3,253	3,820	3,985
St. Croix	20,989	22,657	18,784	22,679
Sauk	18,606	11,567	15,708	14,415
Sawyer	4,763	4,199	4,411	4,951
Shawano	10,192	9,381	8,657	12,150
Sheboygan	30,392	30,796	27,608	34,458
Taylor	4,560	4,586	3,829	5,582
Trempealeau	8,320	4,807	8,075	5,878
Vernon	8,478	5,377	7,924	6,774
Vilas	6,490	7,054	5,713	8,155
Walworth	24,176	25,482	19,177	28,754
Washburn	4,716	4,259	4,705	4,762
Washington	25,713	47,725	21,234	50,641
Waukesha	85,248	145,089	73,626	154,926
Waupaca	12,952	12,131	10,792	15,941
Waushara	5,868	5,769	5,257	6,888
Winnebago	48,156	37,943	40,943	46,542
Wood	21,705	16,576	18,950	20,592
Totals	**1,677,211**	**1,262,393**	**1,489,504**	**1,478,120**

Wisconsin Vote Since 1952

2008: Obama, D., 1,677,211; McCain, R., 1,262,393; Nader, Ind., 17,605; Barr, LB., 8,858; Baldwin, Ind., 5,072; McKinney, Green, 4,216; Wamboldt, Ind., 764; Moore, Ind., 540; La Riva, Ind., 237.
2004: Kerry, D., 1,489,504; Bush, R., 1,478,120; Nader, Ind., 16,390; Badnarik, LB., 6,464; Cobb, Green, 2,661; Brown, Ind., 471; Harris, Ind., 411.
2000: Gore, D., 1,242,987; Bush, R., 1,237,279; Nader, Green, 94,070; Buchanan, RF., 11,446; Browne, LB., 6,640; Phillips, Const., 2,042; Moorehead, Workers World, 1,063; Hagelin, RF., 878; Harris, Soc. Workers, 306.
1996: Clinton, D., 1,071,971; Dole, R., 845,029; Perot, RF., 227,339; Nader, Green, 28,723; Phillips, U.S. Taxpayers, 8,811; Browne,

LB., 7,929; Hagelin, Natural Law, 1,379; Moorehead, Workers World, 1,333; Hollis, Soc., 848; Harris, Soc. Workers, 483.
1992: Clinton, D., 1,041,066; Bush, R., 930,855; Perot, Ind., 544,479; Marrou, LB., 2,877; Gritz, Pop./America First, 2,311; Daniels, Ind., 1,883; Phillips, U.S. Taxpayers, 1,772; Hagelin, Natural Law, 1,070.
1988: Dukakis, D., 1,126,794; Bush, R., 1,047,499; Paul, LB., 5,157; Duke, Populist, 3,056.
1984: Reagan, R., 1,198,584; Mondale, D., 995,740; Bergland, LB., 4,883.
1980: Reagan, R., 1,088,845; Carter, D., 981,584; Anderson, Ind., 160,657; Clark, LB., 29,135; Commoner, Citizens, 7,767; Rarick, Const., 1,519; McReynolds, Soc., 808; Hall, Comm., 772; Griswold, Workers World, 414; DeBerry, Soc. Workers, 383; scattered, 1,337.
1976: Carter, D., 1,040,232; Ford, R., 1,004,987; McCarthy, Ind., 34,943; Maddox, Amer. Ind., 8,552; Zeidler, Soc., 4,298; MacBride, LB., 3,814; Camejo, Soc. Workers, 1,691; Wright, People's, 943; Hall, Comm., 749; LaRouche, U.S. Lab., 738; Levin, Soc. Labor, 389; scattered, 2,839.
1972: Nixon, R., 989,430; McGovern, D., 810,174; Schmitz, Amer., 47,525; Spock, Ind., 2,701; Fisher, Soc. Labor, 998; Hall, Comm., 663; Reed, Ind., 506; scattered, 893.
1968: Nixon, R., 809,997; Humphrey, D., 748,804; Wallace, 3rd party, 127,835; Blomen, Soc. Labor, 1,338; Halstead, Soc. Workers, 1,222; scattered, 2,342.
1964: Johnson, D., 1,050,424; Goldwater, R., 638,495; DeBerry, Soc. Workers, 1,692; Hass, Soc. Labor, 1,204.
1960: Nixon, R., 895,175; Kennedy, D., 830,805; Dobbs, Soc. Workers, 1,792; Hass, Soc. Labor, 1,310.
1956: Eisenhower, R., 954,844; Stevenson, D., 586,768; Andrews, Ind., 6,918; Hoopes, Soc., 754; Hass, Soc. Labor, 710; Dobbs, Soc. Workers, 564.
1952: Eisenhower, R., 979,744; Stevenson, D., 622,175; Hallinan, Ind., 2,174; Dobbs, Ind., 1,350; Hoopes, Ind., 1,157; Hass, Ind., 770.

Wyoming

County	2008 Obama (D)	McCain (R)	2004 Kerry (D)	Bush (R)
Albany	8,618	7,981	7,117	9,006
Big Horn	1,108	4,043	960	4,232
Campbell	2,986	13,001	2,464	12,415
Carbon	2,336	4,331	2,158	4,758
Converse	1,380	4,924	1,184	4,447
Crook	612	2,967	501	2,836
Fremont	6,016	11,082	5,338	11,429
Goshen	1,832	3,942	1,566	4,114
Hot Springs	618	1,834	623	1,812
Johnson	908	3,334	676	3,231
Laramie	16,070	24,549	13,171	25,951
Lincoln	1,823	6,485	1,364	6,423
Natrona	8,144	17,573	9,863	21,512
Niobrara	244	1,017	230	1,064
Park	3,757	10,838	3,007	10,917
Platte	1,407	2,993	1,328	3,149
Sheridan	4,450	10,169	4,066	9,689
Sublette	936	3,316	730	2,847
Sweetwater	5,762	10,360	5,208	10,653
Teton	7,472	4,567	5,972	5,124
Uinta	2,317	5,759	1,815	6,081
Washakie	1,042	2,956	855	3,200
Weston	658	2,618	580	2,739
Totals	**82,868**	**164,958**	**70,776**	**167,629**

Wyoming Vote Since 1952

2008: McCain, R., 164,958; Obama, D., 82,868; Nader, Ind., 2,525; Barr, LB., 1,594; Baldwin, Ind., 1,192.
2004: Bush, R., 167,629; Kerry, D., 70,776; Nader, Ind., 2,741; Badnarik, LB., 1,171; Peroutka, Ind., 631.
2000: Bush, R., 147,947; Gore, D., 60,481; Buchanan, RF., 2,724; Browne, LB., 1,443; Phillips, Ind., 720; Hagelin, Natural Law, 411.
1996: Dole, R., 105,388; Clinton, D., 77,934; Perot, RF., 25,928; Browne, LB., 1,739; Hagelin, Natural Law, 582.
1992: Bush, R., 79,347; Clinton, D., 68,160; Perot, Ind., 51,263.
1988: Bush, R., 106,867; Dukakis, D., 67,113; Paul, LB., 2,026; Fulani, New Alliance, 545.
1984: Reagan, R., 133,241; Mondale, D., 53,370; Bergland, LB., 2,357.
1980: Reagan, R., 110,700; Carter, D., 49,427; Anderson, Ind., 12,072; Clark, LB., 4,514.
1976: Ford, R., 92,717; Carter, D., 62,239; McCarthy, Ind., 624; Reagan, Ind., 307; Anderson, Amer., 290; MacBride, LB., 89; Brown, Ind., 47; Maddox, Amer. Ind., 30.
1972: Nixon, R., 100,464; McGovern, D., 44,358; Schmitz, Amer., 748.
1968: Nixon, R., 70,927; Humphrey, D., 45,173; Wallace, 3rd party, 11,105.
1964: Johnson, D., 80,718; Goldwater, R., 61,998.
1960: Nixon, R., 77,451; Kennedy, D., 63,331.
1956: Eisenhower, R., 74,573; Stevenson, D., 49,554.
1952: Eisenhower, R., 81,047; Stevenson, D., 47,934; Hamblen, Prohib., 194; Hoopes, Soc., 40; Haas, Soc. Labor, 36.

UNITED STATES GOVERNMENT

EXECUTIVE BRANCH	LEGISLATIVE BRANCH	JUDICIAL BRANCH
President	**CONGRESS**	**Supreme Court of the United States**
Vice President	**Senate/House**	Courts of Appeals
Executive Office of the President	Architect of the Capitol	District Courts
Council of Economic Advisers	U.S. Botanic Garden	Territorial Courts
Council on Environmental Quality	Government Accountability Office	Court of International Trade
Executive Residence	Government Printing Office	Bankruptcy Courts
National Security Council	Library of Congress	Court of Federal Claims
Office of Administration	Congressional Budget Office	Tax Court
Office of Management and Budget	Medicare Payment Advisory Commission	Court of Appeals for the Armed Forces
Office of National Drug Control Policy	Stennis Center for Public Service	Court of Appeals for Veterans Claims
Office of Science and Technology Policy		Administrative Office of the Courts
Office of the U.S. Trade Representative		Federal Judicial Center
Office of the Vice President		Sentencing Commission
White House Office*		Judicial Panel on Multidistrict Litigation

*Includes Domestic Policy Council, National Security Advisor, National Economic Council, Office of Cabinet Affairs, Office of the Chief of Staff, Office of Communications, Office of Digital Strategy, Office of the First Lady, Office of Legislative Affairs, Office of Management and Administration, Oval Office Operations, Office of Presidential Personnel, Office of Public Engagement and Intergovernmental Affairs, Office of Scheduling and Advance, Office of the Staff Secretary, and Office of the White House Counsel.

The Obama Administration

As of Sept. 2011; mailing addresses are for Washington, DC, except where otherwise noted.
Terms of office of the president and vice president: Jan. 20, 2009 to Jan. 20, 2013.

President: By law, Pres. Barack H. Obama received an annual salary of $400,000 (taxable) and an annual expense allowance of $50,000 (nontaxable) for costs resulting from official duties. In addition, up to $100,000 a year may be spent on travel expenses and $19,000 on official entertainment (both nontaxable). This does not include amounts available for expenditures within the Executive Office of the President, including $3,850,000 for necessary expenses for the White House and amounts for travel and entertainment.

Website: www.whitehouse.gov/administration/president-obama

Vice President: By law, Vice Pres. Joseph R. Biden received an annual salary of $230,700 (taxable) and an annual expense allowance of $20,000 for costs resulting from official duties, plus $90,000 for official entertainment expenses (nontaxable).

Website: www.whitehouse.gov/administration/vice-president-biden

Cabinet Department Heads

(Salary: $199,700 per year)

Secretary of State: Hillary Rodham Clinton
Secretary of the Treasury: Timothy F. Geithner
Secretary of Defense: Leon E. Panetta
Attorney General (Dept. of Justice): Eric H. Holder Jr.
Secretary of the Interior: Kenneth L. Salazar
Secretary of Agriculture: Thomas J. Vilsack
Secretary of Commerce: Rebecca M. Blank, acting
Secretary of Labor: Hilda L. Solis
Secretary of Health and Human Services: Kathleen Sebelius
Secretary of Housing and Urban Development: Shaun L.S. Donovan
Secretary of Transportation: Raymond L. LaHood
Secretary of Energy: Steven Chu
Secretary of Education: Arne Duncan
Secretary of Veterans Affairs: Eric K. Shinseki
Secretary of Homeland Security: Janet A. Napolitano

Executive Agencies

Council of Economic Advisers: vacant;
www.whitehouse.gov/administration/eop/cea/
Council on Environ. Quality: Nancy Sutley, chair;
www.whitehouse.gov/administration/eop/ceq/
Office of Administration: Beth Jones, dir.;
www.whitehouse.gov/administration/eop/oa/
Office of Management and Budget: Jacob J. Lew, dir.;
www.whitehouse.gov/omb/
Office of Natl. Drug Control Policy: R. Gil Kerlikowske, dir.;
www.whitehouse.gov/ondcp/
Office of Science and Technology Policy: John Holdren, dir.;
www.whitehouse.gov/administration/eop/ostp/
Office of the U.S. Trade Representative: Amb. Ronald Kirk;
www.ustr.gov

White House Staff

1600 Pennsylvania Ave. NW, 20500;
www.whitehouse.gov

Counselor to the President: Peter M. Rouse
Physician to the President: Jeffrey C. Kuhlman
Director, National Intelligence: James R. Clapper
Assistants to the President:
Chief of Staff: Bill Daley
Deputy Chief of Staff for Operations: Alyssa Mastromonaco
Deputy Chief of Staff for Policy: Nancy-Ann DeParle
Counsel to the President: Kathryn H. Ruemmler
Counselor to the Chief of Staff: David Lane
White House Press Secretary: Jay Carney
Deputy National Security Advisor: Denis R. McDonough
Director of Communications: Howard D. Pfeiffer
Domestic Policy Advisor and Director of the Domestic Policy Council: Melody C. Barnes
Economic Policy and Director of the National Economic Council: Gene B. Sperling
Homeland Security and Counterterrorism: John O. Brennan
Director of Legislative Affairs: Robert L. Nabors
Manufacturing Policy: Ron A. Bloom
National Security Advisor: Thomas E. Donilon
Director of Speechwriting: Jonathan E. Favreau
Special Advisor: Philip M. Schiliro
Senior Advisors: Valerie B. Jarrett, David Plouffe
Chief of Staff to the Vice President: Bruce Reed
White House Social Secretary: Jeremy M. Bernard
Chief of Staff to the First Lady: Christina M. Tchen
Press Secretary to the First Lady: Hannah M. August

Cabinet-Level Departments

Department of State

2201 C St. NW, 20520; www.state.gov

Conducts U.S. foreign policy. The Foreign Service protects American citizens and interests through embassies in some 180 countries. Maintains contact with foreign governments, negotiates agreements and treaties, and supports U.S. foreign trade. Promotes democracy, international security, human rights—including issues related to AIDS, human trafficking, war crimes, and migration—and arms and narcotics control. Represents the nation in international organizations. Issues passports to U.S. citizens and visas to foreigners. **Budget** (includes State Dept. and other international programs): $45.0 bil (2010); $54.8 bil (est. 2011); $62.6 bil (est. 2012).

- Intl. Boundary and Water Commission (4171 North Mesa, Ste. C-100, El Paso, TX 79902); www.ibwc.gov
- Intl. Information Programs (2201 C St. NW, SA-5, Rm. 5B17, 20520); www.state.gov/r/iip/
- Intl. Narcotics and Law Enforcement Affairs (2201 C St. NW, Rm. 7333, 20520); www.state.gov/p/inl/
- Intl. Organization Affairs (2201 C St. NW, Rm. 6323, 20520); www.state.gov/p/io/
- Population, Refugees, and Migration (2201 C St. NW, HST, Rm. 5805, 20520); www.state.gov/g/prm/
- U.S. Global AIDS Coordinator (2201 C St. NW, SA-29, Ste. 200, 20520); www.state.gov/s/gac/

Department of the Treasury

1500 Pennsylvania Ave. NW, 20220; www.treasury.gov

Responsible for the fiscal affairs of the U.S. Serves as the government's financial agent; collects, borrows, and disburses funds for the federal government. Monitors the nation's financial infrastructure and economic development; recommends domestic and international financial, monetary, economic, trade, and tax policies. Manufactures currency and coins. Carries out monetary and tax law enforcement activities, sanctions, embargoes, and fights illicit finance—counterfeiting, money laundering, narcotics trafficking, terrorist financing. **Budget:** $51.5 bil (2010); $135.2 bil (est. 2011); $129.1 bil (est. 2012).

- Alcohol and Tobacco Tax and Trade Bureau (1310 G St. NW, Ste. 300, 20220); www.ttb.gov
- Bureau of Engraving and Printing (14th and C Sts. SW, 20228); www.moneyfactory.gov
- Bureau of the Public Debt (200 3rd St., Parkersburg, WV 26106); www.publicdebt.treas.gov
- Financial Crimes Enforcement Network (P.O. Box 39., Vienna, VA 22183); www.fincen.gov
- Financial Management Service (401 14th St. SW, 20227); www.fms.treas.gov
- Internal Revenue Service (1111 Constitution Ave. NW, 20224); www.irs.gov
- U.S. Mint (801 9th St. NW, 20220); www.usmint.gov

Department of Defense

1400 Defense Pentagon, 20301; www.defense.gov

Directs and controls the armed forces and assists the president in protecting the nation's security. Military departments of the Army, Navy, and Air Force are each separately organized under its own secretary but all function under the command of the Secretary of Defense. They conduct military operations as unified commands. The chairman of the Joint Chiefs of Staff is the principal military adviser to the President. Undersecretaries supervise acquisition, technology, and logistics; intelligence; personnel and readiness; and policy. **Budget:** $666.7 bil (2010); $739.7 bil (est. 2011); $707.5 bil (est. 2012).

- Def. Advanced Research Projects Agency (3701 N. Fairfax Dr., Arlington, VA 22203); www.darpa.mil
- Def. Intelligence Agency (Bolling Air Force Base, 200 Mac-Dill Blvd., 20340-5100); www.dia.mil
- Def. Security Cooperation Agency (2800 Defense Pentagon, 20301; www.dsca.osd.mil
- Missile Def. Agency (5700 18th St., Bldg. 245, Fort Belvoir, VA 22060-5573); www.mda.mil
- Natl. Geospatial-Intelligence Agency (Springfield, VA 22150); www.nga.mil
- Natl. Security Agency/Central Security Service (Ft. Meade, MD 20755); www.nsa.gov

Department of Justice

950 Pennsylvania Ave. NW, 20530; www.justice.gov

Provides means for the enforcement of federal laws and investigating violations thereof; furnishes legal counsel in cases involving the federal government and interprets laws relating to the activities of other federal departments; supervises federal penal institutions. The Attorney General and Office of Legal Counsel render legal advice, upon request, to the president and department heads. The Solicitor General conducts all suits brought before the U.S. Supreme Court in which the federal government is concerned. The Civil Division represents the U.S. government in many civil or criminal matters. The 94 U.S. Attorneys are the principal litigators in the U.S. and its territories. Divisions for suits regarding antitrust laws, civil rights, civil and criminal statutes, natural resources and the environment, national security, and taxes. **Budget:** $29.6 bil (2010); $33.5 bil (est. 2011); $33.2 bil (est. 2012).

- Bureau of Alcohol, Tobacco, Firearms, and Explosives (99 New York Ave. NE, Rm. 5S 144, 20226); www.atf.gov
- Bureau of Prisons (320 First St. NW, 20534); www.bop.gov
- Drug Enforcement Admin. (AES, 8701 Morrissette Dr., Springfield, VA 22152); www.dea.gov
- Executive Office for Immigration Review (5107 Leesburg Pike, Falls Church, VA 22041); www.justice.gov/eoir/
- Federal Bureau of Investigation (935 Pennsylvania Ave. NW, 20535); www.fbi.gov
- U.S. Natl. Central Bureau of INTERPOL (20530); www.justice.gov/usncb/
- U.S. Marshals Service (2604 Jefferson Davis Hwy., Alexandria, VA 22301-1025); www.usmarshals.gov
- U.S. Parole Commission (90 K St. NE, 3rd Fl., 20530); www.justice.gov/uspc/

Department of the Interior

1849 C St. NW, 20240; www.doi.gov

Custodian of natural resources. Has the responsibility of protecting and conserving the country's land, water, minerals, fish and wildlife; of promoting the wise use of all these natural resources; of maintaining national parks and recreation areas; and of preserving historic places. It also provides for the welfare of American Indian reservation communities and of inhabitants of island territories under U.S. administration. **Budget:** $13.3 bil (2010); $13.1 bil (est. 2011); $13.9 bil (est. 2012).

- Bureau of Indian Affairs (1849 C Street NW, 20240); www.bia.gov
- Bureau of Land Management (1849 C St. NW, 20240); www.blm.gov
- Bureau of Ocean Energy Management, Regulation, and Enforcement (1849 C St. NW, 20240); www.boemre.gov
- Bureau of Reclamation (1849 C St. NW, 20240); www.usbr.gov
- National Park Service (1849 C St. NW, 20240); www.nps.gov
- Office of Surface Mining (1951 Constitution Ave. NW, 20240); www.osmre.gov
- U.S. Fish and Wildlife Service (1849 C St. NW, 20240); www.fws.gov
- U.S. Geological Survey (12201 Sunrise Valley Dr., Reston, VA 20192); www.usgs.gov

Department of Agriculture

1400 Independence Ave. SW, 20250; www.usda.gov

Provides leadership on food, agriculture, and natural resources; supports scientific research and education for agriculture, nutrition, and food safety. Develops nutrition assistance programs, promotes healthy eating, supplies food stamps, grades and inspects the commercial supply of food. Responsible for the health of the land through sustainable management and conservation, manages public lands in national forests and grasslands; safeguards against invasive pests and diseases; ensures the health and care of animals and plants. Oversees assistance and conservation programs for farmers and ranchers and programs to improve the rural economy and quality of life. Facilitates domestic and international marketing of U.S. agricultural products. **Budget:** $129.5 bil (2010); $152.1 bil (est. 2011); $144.0 bil (est. 2012).

- Agricultural Research Service (1400 Independence Ave. SW, 20250); www.ars.usda.gov
- Economic Research Service (1800 M St. NW, 20036); www.ers.usda.gov
- Food and Nutrition Service (3101 Park Center Dr., Alexandria, VA 22302); www.fns.usda.gov
- Food Safety and Inspection Service (1400 Independence Ave. SW, 20250); www.fsis.usda.gov
- Foreign Agricultural Service (1400 Independence Ave. SW, 20250); www.fas.usda.gov
- Forest Service (1400 Independence Ave. SW, 20250); www.fs.fed.us
- Natl. Agricultural Statistics Service (1400 Independence Ave. SW, 20250); www.nass.usda.gov
- Natural Resources Conservation Service (14th St. and Independence Ave. SW, 20250); www.nrcs.usda.gov

Department of Commerce

1401 Constitution Ave. NW, 20230; www.commerce.gov

Fosters, serves, and promotes the nation's economic development and technological advancement; supports the comprehension and use of the physical environment and its oceanic life; assists states, communities, and individuals with economic progress; promotes trade abroad and ensures an effective export control and treaty compliance system. Issues trademarks and patents, maintains measurement standards, and manages the federal telecommunications spectrum. Collects, analyzes, and distributes statistics regarding the nation and the economy through the Bureaus of the Census and Economic Analysis. The NOAA explores, monitors, and conserves oceans and coasts, tracks weather and other environmental data. **Budget:** $13.2 bil (2010); $11.9 bil (est. 2011); $13.1 bil (est. 2012).

- Bureau of the Census (4600 Silver Hill Rd., 20233); www.census.gov
- Bureau of Economic Analysis (1441 L St. NW, 20230); www.bea.gov
- Minority Business Development Agency (1401 Constitution Ave. NW, 20230); www.mbda.gov
- Natl. Institute of Standards and Technology (100 Bureau Dr., Stop 1070, Gaithersburg, MD 20899); www.nist.gov
- Natl. Oceanic and Atmospheric Admin. (1401 Constitution Ave. NW, Rm. 5128, 20230); www.noaa.gov
- Natl. Technical Information Service (5301 Shawnee Rd., Alexandria, VA 22312); www.ntis.gov
- Natl. Telecommunications and Information Admin. (1401 Constitution Ave. NW, 20230); www.ntia.doc.gov

Department of Labor

200 Constitution Ave. NW, 20210; www.dol.gov

Administers federal labor laws to foster, promote, and develop the welfare of job seekers, wage earners, and retirees of the U.S., to improve working conditions, and to advance opportunities for profitable employment. Administers standards for wages and overtime pay, safety and health conditions, workers' compensation. Tracks changes in employment, prices, and other national economic measurements. Regulates pension and welfare benefit plans, the hiring and employment of migrant and seasonal workers, and requirements pertaining to the mining, construction, and transportation industries. Monitors labor unions and their funds. **Budget:** $173.1 bil (2010); $148.0 bil (est. 2011); $109.0 bil (est. 2012).

- Bureau of Labor Statistics (2 Massachusetts Ave. NE, 20212); www.bls.gov
- Employment and Training Admin. (200 Constitution Ave. NW, 20210); www.doleta.gov
- Mine Safety and Health Admin. (1100 Wilson Blvd., 21st Fl., Arlington, VA 22209); www.msha.gov
- Occupational Safety and Health Admin. (200 Constitution Ave. NW, 20210); www.osha.gov
- Office of Federal Contract Compliance Programs (200 Constitution Ave. NW, 20210); www.dol.gov/ofccp/
- Office of Labor-Management Standards (200 Constitution Ave. NW, 20210); www.dol.gov/olms/
- Office of Workers' Compensation Programs (200 Constitution Ave. NW, 20210); www.dol.gov/owcp/
- Wage and Hour Div. (200 Constitution Ave. NW, 20210); www.dol.gov/whd/

Department of Health and Human Services

200 Independence Ave. SW, 20201; www.hhs.gov

Administers a wide range of programs in the fields of health care and social services that affect nearly all Americans. Medicare and Medicaid provide health care insurance for one in four Americans. The HRSA improves health care services for people who are uninsured, isolated, or medically vulnerable; also oversees organ, tissue, and blood cell donations. The FDA assures the safety of food, drugs, cosmetics, biological products, and medical devices. The CDC monitors and safeguards against disease outbreaks. The NIH supports research projects nationwide and 27 health institutes and centers. The Surgeon General is the nation's chief health educator and leads the U.S. Public Health Service Commissioned Corps. **Budget:** $854.2 bil (2010); $909.8 bil (est. 2011); $892.8 bil (est. 2012).

- Agency for Healthcare Research and Quality (540 Gaither Rd., Rockville, MD 20850); www.ahrq.gov
- Centers for Disease Control and Prevention (1600 Clifton Rd., Atlanta, GA 30333); www.cdc.gov
- Centers for Medicare and Medicaid Services (7500 Security Blvd., Baltimore, MD 21244); www.cms.hhs.gov
- Food and Drug Admin. (10903 New Hampshire Ave., Silver Spring, MD 20993); www.fda.gov
- Health Resources and Services Admin. (5600 Fishers Ln., Rockville, MD 20857); www.hrsa.gov
- Natl. Institutes of Health (9000 Rockville Pike, Bethesda, MD 20892); www.nih.gov
- Surgeon General (Office of the Secretary) (5600 Fishers Ln., Rm. 18-66, Rockville, MD 20857); www.surgeongeneral.gov

Department of Housing and Urban Development

451 7th St. SW, 20410; www.hud.gov

Responsible for housing needs and the improvement and development of urban areas. Supports affordable housing, provides grants for community development and redevelopment. Enforces fair and safe housing standards. Provides funds to assist homeless individuals and families with emergency and transitional shelters. The FHA provides mortgage insurance on loans made by approved lenders. **Budget:** $60.1 bil (2010); $60.8 bil (est. 2011); $49.4 bil (est. 2012).

- Fannie Mae (Federal Natl. Mortgage Association) (3900 Wisconsin Ave. NW, 20016); www.fanniemae.com
- Federal Housing Admin. (451 7th St. SW, 20410); www.fha.gov
- Freddie Mac (Federal Home Loan Mortgage Corporation) (8200 Jones Branch Dr., McLean, VA 22102); www.freddiemac.com
- Ginnie Mae (Government Natl. Mortgage Association) (451 7th St. SW, Rm. B-133, 20410); www.ginniemae.gov

Note: Fannie Mae and Freddie Mac are government-sponsored enterprises (GSEs).

Department of Transportation

1200 New Jersey Ave. SE, 20590; www.dot.gov

Promotes and develops rapid, safe, efficient, and convenient transportation in the U.S.; monitors and administers assistance to transportation industries; negotiates and implements international transportation agreements. Manages airspace, commercial space transportation, and the movement of hazardous materials. Resolves railroad rate and service disputes and reviews proposed railroad mergers. Analyzes and shares research and statistics to develop and improve transportation through RITA. Develops and enforces regulations on the nation's pipeline transportation system. The Maritime Administration maintains a fleet of cargo ships in reserve for war or national emergencies and commissions officers of the merchant marines. Operates the U.S. portion of the St. Lawrence Seaway between Montreal and Lake Erie. **Budget:** $77.8 bil (2010); $79.5 bil (est. 2011); $89.6 bil (est. 2012).

- Federal Aviation Admin. (800 Independence Ave. SW, 20591); www.faa.gov
- Federal Highway Admin. (1200 New Jersey Ave. SE, 20590); www.fhwa.dot.gov
- Federal Transit Admin. (East Bldg., 1200 New Jersey Ave. SE, 20590); www.fta.dot.gov
- Federal Railroad Admin. (1200 New Jersey Ave. SE, 20590); www.fra.dot.gov
- Maritime Admin. (1200 New Jersey Ave. SE, 20590); www.marad.dot.gov
- Natl. Highway Traffic Safety Admin. (West Bldg., 1200 New Jersey Ave. SE, 20590); www.nhtsa.gov
- Research and Innovative Technology Admin. (1200 New Jersey Ave. SE, 20590); www.rita.dot.gov

Department of Energy

1000 Independence Ave. SW, 20585; www.energy.gov

Secures the nation's energy and promotes scientific and technological innovation. Oversees the national energy supply and electric grid. Investigates and promotes clean and reliable energy. Manages and cleans up nuclear and other radioactive material, including nuclear weapons. The OSTI supports much of America's scientific research through program offices, education initiatives, national laboratories, and technology centers. Four power administrations sell hydroelectric power across the west and southeast. **Budget:** $32.1 bil (2010); $46.2 bil (est. 2011); $43.1 bil (est. 2012).

- Energy Information Admin. (1000 Independence Ave. SW, 20585); www.eia.gov
- Federal Energy Regulatory Commission (888 1st St. NE, 20426); www.ferc.gov (independent regulatory agency)
- Natl. Nuclear Security Admin. (1000 Independence Ave. SW, 20585); www.nnsa.energy.gov
- Office of Scientific and Technical Information (Oak Ridge, TN 37831); www.osti.gov

Department of Education

400 Maryland Ave. SW, 20202; www.ed.gov

Works with state agencies and local systems to ensure equal access to all levels of education and seeks to improve the quality of that education through federal support, research programs, and information sharing. Oversees a variety of financial aid distributed through competition, financial needs, or by a set formula. Sets policy goals and initiatives like No Child Left Behind. Conducts research and gathers educational information to disseminate to educators and the general public. **Budget:** $92.9 bil (2010); $79.4 bil (est. 2011); $70.9 bil (est. 2012)

Department of Veterans Affairs

810 Vermont Ave. NW, 20420; www.va.gov

Supports veterans and their families with nationwide programs for health care, financial assistance, and burial benefits. Compensates for disabilities incurred during wartime, provides pensions for veterans with low incomes, education assistance, loan guaranty, and life insurance. Manages America's largest medical education and health professions training program including hospitals, clinics, nursing homes, veterans centers, rehabilitation treatment, readjustment counseling, and home-care programs. Also funds medical research pertaining to veterans issues. Manages 131 national cemeteries, provides headstones and markers. **Budget:** $108.3 bil (2010); $141.1 bil (est. 2011); $124.3 bil (est. 2012).

Department of Homeland Security

20528 (requires no street address); www.dhs.gov

Provides a unified core for the vast national network of organizations and institutions involved in efforts to secure the U.S., its borders, infrastructure, and major events. Provides funding, intelligence, and training for law enforcement and disaster relief.

Leads and coordinates response teams to natural and man-made emergencies. Directs security for borders, customs, and transportation. Identifies threats, administers the National Terrorism Advisory System. **Budget:** $44.5 bil (2010); $48.1 bil (est. 2011); $46.9 bil (est. 2012).

- Fed. Emergency Management Agency (500 C St. SW, 20472); www.fema.gov
- Immigration and Customs Enforcement (500 12th St. SW, 20536); www.ice.gov
- Transportation Security Admin. (601 S. 12th St., Arlington, VA 20598); www.tsa.gov

- U.S. Citizenship and Immigration Services (20 Massachusetts Ave. NW, 20001); www.uscis.gov
- U.S. Coast Guard (2100 2nd St. SW, 20593); www.uscg.mil
- U.S. Customs and Border Protection (1300 Pennsylvania Ave. NW, 20229); www.cbp.gov
- U.S. Fire Admin. (16825 S. Seton Ave., Emmitsburg, MD 21727); www.usfa.dhs.gov
- U.S. Secret Service (245 Murray Dr., Bldg. 410, 20223); www.secretservice.gov

Other Notable U.S. Government Agencies

Source: The U.S. Government Manual; National Archives and Records Administration; World Almanac research
All addresses are Washington, DC, unless otherwise noted; as of Sept. 2011.

African Development Foundation: Lloyd O. Pierson, pres. and CEO (1400 I St. NW, Ste. 1000, 20005); www.adf.gov

AMTRAK (Natl. Railroad Passenger Corporation): Joseph H. Boardman, pres. and CEO (60 Mass. Ave. NE, 20002); www.amtrak.com

Broadcasting Board of Governors: Walter Isaacson, chair. (330 Independence Ave. SW, 20237); www.bbg.gov

Central Intelligence Agency: David Petraeus, dir. (20505); www.cia.gov

Commission on Civil Rights: Martin R. Castro, chair (624 9th St. NW, Ste. 500, 20425); www.usccr.gov

Commodity Futures Trading Commission: Gary Gensler, chair (3 Lafayette Ctr., 1155 21st St. NW, 20581); www.cftc.gov

Consumer Product Safety Commission: Inez Tenenbaum, chair (4330 East-West Hwy., Bethesda, MD 20814); www.cpsc.gov

Corporation for Natl. and Community Service: Robert Velasco II, act. CEO (1201 New York Ave. NW, 20525); www.nationalservice.gov

Court Services and Offender Supervision Agency for the District of Columbia: Adrienne Poteat, deputy dir. (633 Indiana Ave. NW, 20004); www.csosa.gov

Defense Nuclear Facilities Safety Board: Peter S. Winokur, chair (625 Indiana Ave. NW, Ste. 700, 20004); www.dnfsb.gov

Election Assistance Commission: Donetta Davidson, chair (1201 New York Ave. NW, Ste. 300, 20005); www.eac.gov

Environmental Protection Agency: Lisa P. Jackson, administrator (Cabinet rank) (Ariel Rios Bldg., 1200 Pennsylvania Ave. NW, 20460); www.epa.gov

Equal Employment Opportunity Commission: Jacqueline A. Berrien, chair (131 M St. NE, 20507); www.eeoc.gov

Export-Import Bank of the U.S.: Fred P. Hochberg, pres. and chair (811 Vermont Ave. NW, 20571); www.exim.gov

Farm Credit Admin.: Leland A. Strom, chair and CEO (1501 Farm Credit Dr., McLean, VA 22102); www.fca.gov

Federal Communications Commission: Julius Genachowski, chair (445 12th St. SW, 20554); www.fcc.gov

Federal Deposit Insurance Corporation: Martin J. Gruenberg, acting chair (550 17th St. NW, 20429); www.fdic.gov

Federal Election Commission: Cynthia L. Bauerly, chair (999 E St. NW, 20463); www.fec.gov

Federal Housing Finance Agency: Edward DeMarco, act. dir. (1700 G St. NW, 4th Fl., 20552); www.fhfa.gov

Federal Labor Relations Authority: Carol Waller Pope, chair (1400 K St. NW, 20424); www.flra.gov

Federal Maritime Commission: Richard A. Lidinsky Jr., chair (800 N. Capitol St. NW, 20573); www.fmc.gov

Federal Mediation and Conciliation Service: George H. Cohen, dir. (2100 K St. NW, 20427); www.fmcs.gov

Federal Mine Safety and Health Review Commission: Mary Lucille Jordan, chair (601 New Jersey Ave. NW, Ste. 9500, 20001); www.fmshrc.gov

Federal Reserve System: Ben S. Bernanke, chair (20th St. and Constitution Ave. NW, 20551); www.federalreserve.gov

Federal Retirement Thrift Investment Board: Andrew M. Saul, chair (1250 H St. NW, 20005); www.frtib.gov

Federal Trade Commission: Jon Leibowitz, chair (600 Pennsylvania Ave. NW, 20580); www.ftc.gov

General Services Admin.: Martha N. Johnson, administrator (One Constitution Sq., 1275 1st St. NE, 20417); www.gsa.gov

Institute of Museum and Library Services: Susan Hildreth, dir. (1800 M St. NW, 9th Fl., 20036); www.imls.gov

Inter-American Foundation: Robert N. Kaplan, pres. (901 N. Stuart St., 10th Fl., Arlington, VA 22203); www.iaf.gov

Merit Systems Protection Board: Susan Tsui Grundmann, chair (1615 M St. NW, 20419); www.mspb.gov

National Aeronautics and Space Admin.: Charles F. Bolden Jr., administrator (300 E St. SW, 20546); www.nasa.gov

National Archives and Records Admin.: David S. Ferriero, archivist (8601 Adelphi Rd., College Park, MD 20740); www.archives.gov

National Capital Planning Commission: L. Preston Bryant Jr., chair (401 9th St. NW, N. Lobby, Ste. 500, 20004); www.ncpc.gov

National Council on Disability: Jonathan M. Young, chair (1331 F St. NW, Ste. 850, 20004); www.ncd.gov

National Credit Union Admin.: Debbie Matz, chair (1775 Duke St., Alexandria, VA 22314); www.ncua.gov

National Endowment for the Arts: Rocco Landesman, chair (1100 Pennsylvania Ave. NW, 20506); www.arts.gov

National Endowment for the Humanities: Jim Leach, chair (1100 Pennsylvania Ave. NW, 20506); www.neh.gov

National Indian Gaming Commission: Tracie Stevens, chair (1441 L St. NW, Ste. 9100, 20005); www.nigc.gov

National Labor Relations Board: Wilma B. Liebman, chair (1099 14th St. NW, 20570); www.nlrb.gov

National Mediation Board: Linda Puchala, chair (1301 K St. NW, Ste. 250 East, 20005); www.nmb.gov

National Science Foundation: Subra Suresh, dir. (4201 Wilson Blvd., Arlington, VA 22230); www.nsf.gov

National Transportation Safety Board: Deborah A.P. Hersman, chair (490 L'Enfant Plaza SW, 20594); www.ntsb.gov

Nuclear Regulatory Commission: Gregory B. Jaczko, chair (20555); www.nrc.gov

Nuclear Waste Technical Review Board: B. John Garrick, chair (2300 Clarendon Blvd., Ste. 1300, Arlington, VA 22201); www.nwtrb.gov

Occupational Safety and Health Review Commission: Thomasina V. Rogers, chair (1120 20th St. NW, 9th Fl., 20036); www.oshrc.gov

Office of Government Ethics: Don W. Fox, act. dir. (1201 New York Ave. NW, Ste. 500, 20005); www.oge.gov

Office of Personnel Management: John Berry, dir. (1900 E St. NW, 20415); www.opm.gov

Office of Special Counsel: Carolyn Lerner, spec. counsel (1730 M St. NW, Ste. 218, 20036); www.osc.gov

Overseas Private Investment Corporation: Elizabeth L. Littlefield, pres. and CEO (1100 New York Ave. NW, 20527); www.opic.gov

Peace Corps: Aaron S. Williams, dir. (1111 20th St. NW, 20526); www.peacecorps.gov

Pension Benefit Guaranty Corporation: Joshua Gotbaum, dir. (1200 K St. NW, 20005); www.pbgc.gov

Postal Regulatory Commission: Ruth Y. Goldway, chair (901 New York Ave. NW, Ste. 200, 20268); www.prc.gov

Railroad Retirement Board: Michael S. Schwartz, chair (844 N. Rush St., Chicago, IL 60611); www.rrb.gov

Securities and Exchange Commission: Mary L. Schapiro, chair (100 F St. NE, 20549); www.sec.gov

Selective Service System: Lawrence G. Romo, dir. (Natl. Headquarters, Arlington, VA 22209); www.sss.gov

Small Business Admin.: Karen G. Mills, adm. (409 3rd St. SW, Ste. 7800, 20416); www.sba.gov

Social Security Admin.: Michael J. Astrue, comm. (6401 Security Blvd., Baltimore, MD 21235); www.ssa.gov

Tennessee Valley Authority: Tom Kilgore, CEO and pres. (400 W. Summit Hill Dr., Knoxville, TN 37902); www.tva.gov

U.S. Agency for International Development: Dr. Raj Shah, administrator (Ronald Reagan Building, 20523); www.usaid.gov

U.S. International Trade Commission: Deanna Tanner Okun, chair (500 E St. SW, 20436); www.usitc.gov

U.S. Postal Service: Patrick R. Donahoe, Postmaster General and CEO (475 L'Enfant Plaza SW, 20260); www.usps.com

U.S. Trade and Development Agency: Leocadia I. Zak, dir. (1000 Wilson Blvd., Ste. 1600, Arlington, VA 22209); www.ustda.gov

CABINETS OF THE U.S.

The U.S. Cabinet and Its Role

The heads of major executive departments of the federal government constitute the Cabinet. This institution, not provided for in the U.S. Constitution, developed as an advisory body out of the desire of presidents to consult on policy matters. Aside from its advisory role, the Cabinet as a body has no formal function and wields no executive authority. Individual members exercise authority as heads of their departments, reporting to the president. The Cabinet meets at times set by the president.

In addition to the heads of federal departments as listed below, the Cabinet commonly includes other officials designated by the president as being of Cabinet rank.

The officials so designated by Pres. Barack Obama include Vice Pres. Joseph R. Biden, Environmental Protection Agency Administrator Lisa P. Jackson, Office of Management and Budget Director Jacob J. Lew, U.S. Trade Representative Ronald Kirk, U.S. Ambassador to the United Nations Susan Rice, and White House Chief of Staff Bill Daley.

Members of Pres. Obama's Cabinet listed in this chapter are as of Oct. 1, 2011.

Secretaries of State

The Department of Foreign Affairs was created by act of Congress on July 27, 1789, and the name changed to Department of State on Sept. 15, 1789.

President	Secretary	Home	Sworn in
Washington	Thomas Jefferson	VA	1789
	Edmund Randolph	VA	1794
	Timothy Pickering	PA	1795
Adams, J.	Timothy Pickering	PA	1797
	John Marshall	VA	1800
Jefferson	James Madison	VA	1801
Madison	Robert Smith	MD	1809
	James Monroe	VA	1811
Monroe	John Quincy Adams	MA	1817
Adams, J. Q.	Henry Clay	KY	1825
Jackson	Martin Van Buren	NY	1829
	Edward Livingston	LA	1831
	Louis McLane	DE	1833
	John Forsyth	GA	1834
Van Buren	John Forsyth	GA	1837
Harrison, W. H.	Daniel Webster	MA	1841
Tyler	Daniel Webster	MA	1841
	Abel P. Upshur	VA	1843
	John C. Calhoun	SC	1844
Polk	John C. Calhoun	SC	1845
	James Buchanan	PA	1845
Taylor	James Buchanan	PA	1849
	John M. Clayton	DE	1849
Fillmore	John M. Clayton	DE	1850
	Daniel Webster	MA	1850
	Edward Everett	MA	1852
Pierce	William L. Marcy	NY	1853
Buchanan	William L. Marcy	NY	1857
	Lewis Cass	MI	1857
	Jeremiah S. Black	PA	1860
Lincoln	Jeremiah S. Black	PA	1861
	William H. Seward	NY	1861
Johnson, A.	William H. Seward	NY	1865
Grant	Elihu B. Washburne	IL	1869
	Hamilton Fish	NY	1869
Hayes	Hamilton Fish	NY	1877
	William M. Evarts	NY	1877
Garfield	William M. Evarts	NY	1881
	James G. Blaine	ME	1881
Arthur	James G. Blaine	ME	1881
	F. T. Frelinghuysen	NJ	1881
Cleveland	F. T. Frelinghuysen	NJ	1885
	Thomas F. Bayard	DE	1885
Harrison, B.	Thomas F. Bayard	DE	1889
	James G. Blaine	ME	1889
	John W. Foster	IN	1892
Cleveland	Walter Q. Gresham	IN	1893
	Richard Olney	MA	1895
McKinley	Richard Olney	MA	1897
	John Sherman	OH	1897
	William R. Day	OH	1898
	John Hay	DC	1898
Roosevelt, T.	John Hay	DC	1901
	Elihu Root	NY	1905
	Robert Bacon	NY	1909
Taft	Robert Bacon	NY	1909
	Philander C. Knox	PA	1909
Wilson	Philander C. Knox	PA	1913
	William J. Bryan	NE	1913
	Robert Lansing	NY	1915
	Bainbridge Colby	NY	1920

President	Secretary	Home	Sworn in
Harding	Charles E. Hughes	NY	1921
Coolidge	Charles E. Hughes	NY	1923
	Frank B. Kellogg	MN	1925
Hoover	Frank B. Kellogg	MN	1929
	Henry L. Stimson	NY	1929
Roosevelt, F. D.	Cordell Hull	TN	1933
	E. R. Stettinius Jr.	VA	1944
Truman	E. R. Stettinius Jr.	VA	1945
	James F. Byrnes	SC	1945
	George C. Marshall	PA	1947
	Dean G. Acheson	CT	1949
Eisenhower	John Foster Dulles	NY	1953
	Christian A. Herter	MA	1959
Kennedy	Dean Rusk	NY	1961
Johnson, L. B.	Dean Rusk	NY	1963
Nixon	William P. Rogers	NY	1969
	Henry A. Kissinger	DC	1973
Ford	Henry A. Kissinger	DC	1974
Carter	Cyrus R. Vance	NY	1977
	Edmund S. Muskie	ME	1980
Reagan	Alexander M. Haig Jr.	CT	1981
	George P. Shultz	CA	1982
Bush, G. H. W.	James A. Baker III	TX	1989
	Lawrence S. Eagleburger	MI	1992
Clinton	Warren M. Christopher	CA	1993
	Madeleine K. Albright	DC	1997
Bush, G. W.	Colin L. Powell	NY	2001
	Condoleezza Rice	AL	2005
Obama	Hillary Rodham Clinton	NY	2009

Secretaries of the Treasury

The Treasury Department was organized by act of Congress on Sept. 2, 1789.

President	Secretary	Home	Sworn in
Washington	Alexander Hamilton	NY	1789
	Oliver Wolcott	CT	1795
Adams, J.	Oliver Wolcott	CT	1797
	Samuel Dexter	MA	1801
Jefferson	Samuel Dexter	MA	1801
	Albert Gallatin	PA	1801
Madison	Albert Gallatin	PA	1809
	George W. Campbell	TN	1814
	Alexander J. Dallas	PA	1814
	William H. Crawford	GA	1816
Monroe	William H. Crawford	GA	1817
Adams, J. Q.	Richard Rush	PA	1825
Jackson	Samuel D. Ingham	PA	1829
	Louis McLane	DE	1831
	William J. Duane	PA	1833
	Roger B. Taney	MD	1833
	Levi Woodbury	NH	1834
Van Buren	Levi Woodbury	NH	1837
Harrison, W. H.	Thomas Ewing	OH	1841
Tyler	Thomas Ewing	OH	1841
	Walter Forward	PA	1841
	John C. Spencer	NY	1843
	George M. Bibb	KY	1844
Polk	Robert J. Walker	MS	1845
Taylor	William M. Meredith	PA	1849
Fillmore	Thomas Corwin	OH	1850
Pierce	James Guthrie	KY	1853
Buchanan	Howell Cobb	GA	1857
	Phillip F. Thomas	MD	1860
	John A. Dix	NY	1861

President	Secretary	Home	Sworn in
Lincoln	Salmon P. Chase	OH	1861
	William P. Fessenden	ME	1864
	Hugh McCulloch	IN	1865
Johnson, A.	Hugh McCulloch	IN	1865
Grant	George S. Boutwell	MA	1869
	William A. Richardson	MA	1873
	Benjamin H. Bristow	KY	1874
	Lot M. Morrill	ME	1876
Hayes	John Sherman	OH	1877
Garfield	William Windom	MN	1881
Arthur	Charles J. Folger	NY	1881
	Walter Q. Gresham	IN	1884
	Hugh McCulloch	IN	1884
Cleveland	Daniel Manning	NY	1885
	Charles S. Fairchild	NY	1887
Harrison, B.	William Windom	MN	1889
	Charles Foster	OH	1891
Cleveland	John G. Carlisle	KY	1893
McKinley	Lyman J. Gage	IL	1897
Roosevelt, T.	Lyman J. Gage	IL	1901
	Leslie M. Shaw	IA	1902
	George B. Cortelyou	NY	1907
Taft	Franklin MacVeagh	IL	1909
Wilson	William G. McAdoo	NY	1913
	Carter Glass	VA	1918
	David F. Houston	MO	1920
Harding	Andrew W. Mellon	PA	1921
Coolidge	Andrew W. Mellon	PA	1923
Hoover	Andrew W. Mellon	PA	1929
	Ogden L. Mills	NY	1932
Roosevelt, F. D.	William H. Woodin	NY	1933
	Henry Morgenthau Jr.	NY	1934
Truman	Fred M. Vinson	KY	1945
	John W. Snyder	MO	1946
Eisenhower	George M. Humphrey	OH	1953
	Robert B. Anderson	CT	1957
Kennedy	C. Douglas Dillon	NJ	1961
Johnson, L. B.	C. Douglas Dillon	NJ	1963
	Henry H. Fowler	VA	1965
	Joseph W. Barr	IN	1968
Nixon	David M. Kennedy	IL	1969
	John B. Connally	TX	1971
	George P. Shultz	IL	1972
	William E. Simon	NJ	1974
Ford	William E. Simon	NJ	1974
Carter	W. Michael Blumenthal	MI	1977
	G. William Miller	RI	1979
Reagan	Donald T. Regan	NY	1981
	James A. Baker III	TX	1985
	Nicholas F. Brady	NJ	1988
Bush, G. H. W.	Nicholas F. Brady	NJ	1989
Clinton	Lloyd Bentsen	TX	1993
	Robert E. Rubin	NY	1995
	Lawrence H. Summers	CT	1999
Bush, G. W.	Paul H. O'Neill	MO	2001
	John W. Snow	OH	2003
	Henry M. Paulson Jr.	FL	2006
Obama	Timothy F. Geithner	NY	2009

Secretaries of Defense

The Department of Defense, originally designated the National Military Establishment, was created on Sept. 18, 1947. It is headed by the secretary of defense, who is a member of the president's Cabinet. The departments of the Army, of the Navy, and of the Air Force function within the Defense Department. Since 1947, the secretaries of those departments have not been members of the president's Cabinet.

President	Secretary	Home	Sworn in
Truman	James V. Forrestal	NY	1947
	Louis A. Johnson	WV	1949
	George C. Marshall	PA	1950
	Robert A. Lovett	NY	1951
Eisenhower	Charles E. Wilson	MI	1953
	Neil H. McElroy	OH	1957
	Thomas S. Gates Jr.	PA	1959
Kennedy	Robert S. McNamara	MI	1961
Johnson, L. B.	Robert S. McNamara	MI	1963
	Clark M. Clifford	MD	1968
Nixon	Melvin R. Laird	WI	1969
	Elliot L. Richardson	MA	1973
	James R. Schlesinger	VA	1973

President	Secretary	Home	Sworn in
Ford	James R. Schlesinger	VA	1974
	Donald H. Rumsfeld	IL	1975
Carter	Harold Brown	CA	1977
Reagan	Caspar W. Weinberger	CA	1981
	Frank C. Carlucci	PA	1987
Bush, G. H. W.	Richard B. Cheney	WY	1989
Clinton	Les Aspin	WI	1993
	William J. Perry	CA	1994
	William S. Cohen	ME	1997
Bush, G. W.	Donald H. Rumsfeld	IL	2001
	Robert M. Gates	TX	2006
Obama	Robert M. Gates	TX	2009
	Leon E. Panetta	CA	2011

Secretaries of War

The War Department (which included jurisdiction over the Navy until 1798) was created by act of Congress on Aug. 7, 1789, and Gen. Henry Knox was commissioned secretary of war under that act on Sept. 12, 1789.

President	Secretary	Home	Sworn in
Washington	Henry Knox	MA	1789
	Timothy Pickering	PA	1795
	James McHenry	MD	1796
Adams, J.	James McHenry	MD	1797
	Samuel Dexter	MA	1800
Jefferson	Henry Dearborn	MA	1801
Madison	William Eustis	MA	1809
	John Armstrong	NY	1813
	James Monroe	VA	1814
	William H. Crawford	GA	1815
Monroe	John C. Calhoun	SC	1817
Adams, J. Q.	James Barbour	VA	1825
	Peter B. Porter	NY	1828
Jackson	John H. Eaton	TN	1829
	Lewis Cass	MI	1831
	Benjamin F. Butler	NY	1837
Van Buren	Joel R. Poinsett	SC	1837
Harrison, W. H.	John Bell	TN	1841
Tyler	John Bell	TN	1841
	John C. Spencer	NY	1841
	James M. Porter	PA	1843
	William Wilkins	PA	1844
Polk	William L. Marcy	NY	1845
Taylor	George W. Crawford	GA	1849
Fillmore	Charles M. Conrad	LA	1850
Pierce	Jefferson Davis	MS	1853
Buchanan	John B. Floyd	VA	1857
	Joseph Holt	KY	1861
Lincoln	Simon Cameron	PA	1861
	Edwin M. Stanton	PA	1862
Johnson, A.	Edwin M. Stanton	PA	1865
	John M. Schofield	IL	1868
Grant	John A. Rawlins	IL	1869
	William T. Sherman	OH	1869
	William W. Belknap	IA	1869
	Alphonso Taft	OH	1876
	James D. Cameron	PA	1876
Hayes	George W. McCrary	IA	1877
	Alexander Ramsey	MN	1879
Garfield	Robert T. Lincoln	IL	1881
Arthur	Robert T. Lincoln	IL	1881
Cleveland	William C. Endicott	MA	1885
Harrison, B.	Redfield Proctor	VT	1889
	Stephen B. Elkins	WV	1891
Cleveland	Daniel S. Lamont	NY	1893
McKinley	Russel A. Alger	MI	1897
	Elihu Root	NY	1899
Roosevelt, T.	Elihu Root	NY	1901
	William H. Taft	OH	1904
	Luke E. Wright	TN	1908
Taft	Jacob M. Dickinson	TN	1909
	Henry L. Stimson	NY	1911
Wilson	Lindley M. Garrison	NJ	1913
	Newton D. Baker	OH	1916
Harding	John W. Weeks	MA	1921
Coolidge	John W. Weeks	MA	1923
	Dwight F. Davis	MO	1925
Hoover	James W. Good	IL	1929
	Patrick J. Hurley	OK	1929
Roosevelt, F. D.	George H. Dern	UT	1933
	Harry H. Woodring	KS	1937
	Henry L. Stimson	NY	1940
Truman	Robert P. Patterson	NY	1945
	Kenneth C. Royall[1]	NC	1947

(1) Last member of the Cabinet with this title. The War Department became the Department of the Army, a branch of the Department of Defense, in 1947.

Secretaries of the Navy

The Navy Department was created by act of Congress on Apr. 30, 1798. The Marine Corps is part of this department.

President	Secretary	Home	Sworn in
Adams, J.	Benjamin Stoddert	MD	1798
Jefferson	Benjamin Stoddert	MD	1801
	Robert Smith	MD	1801
Madison	Paul Hamilton	SC	1809
	William Jones	PA	1813
	Benjamin W. Crowninshield	MA	1814
Monroe	Benjamin W. Crowninshield	MA	1817
	Smith Thompson	NY	1818
	Samuel L. Southard	NJ	1823
Adams, J. Q.	Samuel L. Southard	NJ	1825
Jackson	John Branch	NC	1829
	Levi Woodbury	NH	1831
	Mahlon Dickerson	NJ	1834
Van Buren	Mahlon Dickerson	NJ	1837
	James K. Paulding	NY	1838
Harrison, W. H.	George E. Badger	NC	1841
Tyler	George E. Badger	NC	1841
	Abel P. Upshur	VA	1841
	David Henshaw	MA	1843
	Thomas W. Gilmer	VA	1844
	John Y. Mason	VA	1844
Polk	George Bancroft	MA	1845
	John Y. Mason	VA	1846
Taylor	William B. Preston	VA	1849
Fillmore	William A. Graham	NC	1850
	John P. Kennedy	MD	1852
Pierce	James C. Dobbin	NC	1853
Buchanan	Isaac Toucey	CT	1857
Lincoln	Gideon Welles	CT	1861
Johnson, A.	Gideon Welles	CT	1865
Grant	Adolph E. Borie	PA	1869
	George M. Robeson	NJ	1869
Hayes	Richard W. Thompson	IN	1877
	Nathan Goff Jr.	WV	1881
Garfield	William H. Hunt	LA	1881
Arthur	William E. Chandler	NH	1882
Cleveland	William C. Whitney	NY	1885
Harrison, B.	Benjamin F. Tracy	NY	1889
Cleveland	Hilary A. Herbert	AL	1893
McKinley	John D. Long	MA	1897
Roosevelt, T.	John D. Long	MA	1901
	William H. Moody	MA	1902
	Paul Morton	IL	1904
	Charles J. Bonaparte	MD	1905
	Victor H. Metcalf	CA	1906
	Truman H. Newberry	MI	1908
Taft	George von L. Meyer	MA	1909
Wilson	Josephus Daniels	NC	1913
Harding	Edwin Denby	MI	1921
Coolidge	Edwin Denby	MI	1923
	Curtis D. Wilbur	CA	1924
Hoover	Charles Francis Adams	MA	1929
Roosevelt, F. D.	Claude A. Swanson	VA	1933
	Charles Edison	NJ	1940
	Frank Knox	IL	1940
	James V. Forrestal	NY	1944
Truman	James V. Forrestal[1]	NY	1945

(1) Last member of Cabinet with this title. The Navy Department became a branch of the Department of Defense when the latter was created on Sept. 18, 1947.

Attorneys General

The Office of Attorney General was established by act of Congress on Sept. 24, 1789. It officially reached Cabinet rank in Mar. 1792, when the first attorney general, Edmund Randolph, attended his initial Cabinet meeting. The Department of Justice, headed by the attorney general, was created June 22, 1870.

President	Attorney General	Home	Sworn in
Washington	Edmund Randolph	VA	1789
	William Bradford	PA	1794
	Charles Lee	VA	1795
Adams, J.	Charles Lee	VA	1797
Jefferson	Levi Lincoln	MA	1801
	John Breckenridge	KY	1805
	Caesar A. Rodney	DE	1807
Madison	Caesar A. Rodney	DE	1807
	William Pinkney	MD	1811
	Richard Rush	PA	1814
Monroe	Richard Rush	PA	1817
	William Wirt	VA	1817
Adams, J. Q.	William Wirt	VA	1825
Jackson	John M. Berrien	GA	1829
	Roger B. Taney	MD	1831
	Benjamin F. Butler	NY	1833
Van Buren	Benjamin F. Butler	NY	1837
	Felix Grundy	TN	1838
	Henry D. Gilpin	PA	1840
Harrison, W. H.	John J. Crittenden	KY	1841
Tyler	John J. Crittenden	KY	1841
	Hugh S. Legare	SC	1841
	John Nelson	MD	1843
Polk	John Y. Mason	VA	1845
	Nathan Clifford	ME	1846
	Isaac Toucey	CT	1848
Taylor	Reverdy Johnson	MD	1849
Fillmore	John J. Crittenden	KY	1850
Pierce	Caleb Cushing	MA	1853
Buchanan	Jeremiah S. Black	PA	1857
	Edwin M. Stanton	PA	1860
Lincoln	Edward Bates	MO	1861
	James Speed	KY	1864
Johnson, A.	James Speed	KY	1865
	Henry Stanbery	OH	1866
	William M. Evarts	NY	1868
Grant	Ebenezer R. Hoar	MA	1869
	Amos T. Akerman	GA	1870
	George H. Williams	OR	1871
	Edwards Pierrepont	NY	1875
	Alphonso Taft	OH	1876
Hayes	Charles Devens	MA	1877
Garfield	Wayne MacVeagh	PA	1881
Arthur	Benjamin H. Brewster	PA	1882
Cleveland	Augustus Garland	AR	1885
Harrison, B.	William H. H. Miller	IN	1889
Cleveland	Richard Olney	MA	1893
	Judson Harmon	OH	1895
McKinley	Joseph McKenna	CA	1897
	John W. Griggs	NJ	1898
	Philander C. Knox	PA	1901
Roosevelt, T.	Philander C. Knox	PA	1901
	William H. Moody	MA	1904
	Charles J. Bonaparte	MD	1906
Taft	George W. Wickersham	NY	1909
Wilson	J. C. McReynolds	TN	1913
	Thomas W. Gregory	TX	1914
	A. Mitchell Palmer	PA	1919
Harding	Harry M. Daugherty	OH	1921
Coolidge	Harry M. Daugherty	OH	1923
	Harlan F. Stone	NY	1924
	John G. Sargent	VT	1925
Hoover	William D. Mitchell	MN	1929
Roosevelt, F. D.	Homer S. Cummings	CT	1933
	Frank Murphy	MI	1939
	Robert H. Jackson	NY	1940
	Francis Biddle	PA	1941
Truman	Thomas C. Clark	TX	1945
	J. Howard McGrath	RI	1949
	J. P. McGranery	PA	1952
Eisenhower	Herbert Brownell Jr.	NY	1953
	William P. Rogers	MD	1957
Kennedy	Robert F. Kennedy	MA	1961
Johnson, L. B.	Robert F. Kennedy	MA	1963
	N. deB. Katzenbach	IL	1964
	Ramsey Clark	TX	1967
Nixon	John N. Mitchell	NY	1969
	Richard G. Kleindienst	AZ	1972
	Elliot L. Richardson	MA	1973
	William B. Saxbe	OH	1974
Ford	William B. Saxbe	OH	1974
	Edward H. Levi	IL	1975

President	Attorney General	Home	Sworn in
Carter	Griffin B. Bell	GA	1977
	Benjamin R. Civiletti	MD	1979
Reagan	William French Smith	CA	1981
	Edwin Meese III	CA	1985
	Richard Thornburgh	PA	1988
Bush, G. H. W.	Richard Thornburgh	PA	1989
	William P. Barr	NY	1991
Clinton	Janet Reno	FL	1993
Bush, G. W.	John Ashcroft	MO	2001
	Alberto Gonzales	TX	2005
	Michael Mukasey	NY	2007
Obama	Eric H. Holder Jr.	DC	2009

Secretaries of the Interior

The Department of the Interior was created by act of Congress on Mar. 3, 1849.

President	Secretary	Home	Sworn in
Taylor	Thomas Ewing	OH	1849
Fillmore	Thomas M. T. McKennan	PA	1850
	Alex H. H. Stuart	VA	1850
Pierce	Robert McClelland	MI	1853
Buchanan	Jacob Thompson	MS	1857
Lincoln	Caleb B. Smith	IN	1861
	John P. Usher	IN	1863
Johnson, A.	John P. Usher	IN	1865
	James Harlan	IA	1865
	Orville H. Browning	IL	1866
Grant	Jacob D. Cox	OH	1869
	Columbus Delano	OH	1870
	Zachariah Chandler	MI	1875
Hayes	Carl Schurz	MO	1877
Garfield	Samuel J. Kirkwood	IA	1881
Arthur	Henry M. Teller	CO	1882
Cleveland	Lucius Q. C. Lamar	MS	1885
	William F. Vilas	WI	1888
Harrison, B.	John W. Noble	MO	1889
Cleveland	Hoke Smith	GA	1893
	David R. Francis	MO	1896
McKinley	Cornelius N. Bliss	NY	1897
	Ethan A. Hitchcock	MO	1898
Roosevelt, T.	Ethan A. Hitchcock	MO	1901
	James R. Garfield	OH	1907
Taft	Richard A. Ballinger	WA	1909
	Walter L. Fisher	IL	1911
Wilson	Franklin K. Lane	CA	1913
	John B. Payne	IL	1920
Harding	Albert B. Fall	NM	1921
	Hubert Work	CO	1923
Coolidge	Hubert Work	CO	1923
	Roy O. West	IL	1929
Hoover	Ray Lyman Wilbur	CA	1929
Roosevelt, F. D.	Harold L. Ickes	IL	1933
Truman	Harold L. Ickes	IL	1945
	Julius A. Krug	WI	1946
	Oscar L. Chapman	CO	1949
Eisenhower	Douglas McKay	OR	1953
	Fred A. Seaton	NE	1956
Kennedy	Stewart L. Udall	AZ	1961
Johnson, L. B.	Stewart L. Udall	AZ	1963
Nixon	Walter J. Hickel	AK	1969
	Rogers C. B. Morton	MD	1971
Ford	Rogers C. B. Morton	MD	1971
	Stanley K. Hathaway	WY	1975
	Thomas S. Kleppe	ND	1975
Carter	Cecil D. Andrus	ID	1977
Reagan	James G. Watt	CO	1981
	William P. Clark	CA	1983
	Donald P. Hodel	OR	1985
Bush, G. H. W.	Manuel Lujan	NM	1989
Clinton	Bruce Babbitt	AZ	1993
Bush, G. W.	Gale Norton	CO	2001
	Dirk Kempthorne	ID	2006
Obama	Kenneth L. Salazar	CO	2009

Secretaries of Agriculture

The Department of Agriculture was created by act of Congress on May 15, 1862. On Feb. 8, 1889, its commissioner was renamed secretary of agriculture and became a member of the Cabinet.

President	Secretary	Home	Sworn in
Cleveland	Norman J. Colman	MO	1889
Harrison, B.	Jeremiah M. Rusk	WI	1889
Cleveland	J. Sterling Morton	NE	1893
McKinley	James Wilson	IA	1897
Roosevelt, T.	James Wilson	IA	1901
Taft	James Wilson	IA	1909
Wilson	David F. Houston	MO	1913
	Edwin T. Meredith	IA	1920
Harding	Henry C. Wallace	IA	1921
Coolidge	Henry C. Wallace	IA	1923
	Howard M. Gore	WV	1924
	William M. Jardine	KS	1925
Hoover	Arthur M. Hyde	MO	1929
Roosevelt, F. D.	Henry A. Wallace	IA	1933
	Claude R. Wickard	IN	1940
Truman	Clinton P. Anderson	NM	1945
Truman	Charles F. Brannan	CO	1948
Eisenhower	Ezra Taft Benson	UT	1953
Kennedy	Orville L. Freeman	MN	1961
Johnson, L. B.	Orville L. Freeman	MN	1963
Nixon	Clifford M. Hardin	IN	1969
	Earl L. Butz	IN	1971
Ford	Earl L. Butz	IN	1974
	John A. Knebel	VA	1976
Carter	Bob Bergland	MN	1977
Reagan	John R. Block	IL	1981
	Richard E. Lyng	CA	1986
Bush, G. H. W.	Clayton K. Yeutter	NE	1989
	Edward Madigan	IL	1991
Clinton	Mike Espy	MS	1993
	Dan Glickman	KS	1995
Bush, G. W.	Ann M. Veneman	CA	2001
	Mike Johanns	NE	2005
	Ed Schafer	ND	2008
Obama	Thomas J. Vilsack	IA	2009

Secretaries of Commerce and Labor

The Department of Commerce and Labor, created by Congress on Feb. 14, 1903, was divided by Congress Mar. 4, 1913, into two separate departments. The secretary of each was made a Cabinet member.

President	Secretary	Home	Sworn in
Roosevelt, T.	George B. Cortelyou	NY	1903
	Victor H. Metcalf	CA	1904
	Oscar S. Straus	NY	1906
Taft	Charles Nagel	MO	1909

Secretaries of Labor

President	Secretary	Home	Sworn in
Wilson	William B. Wilson	PA	1913
Harding	James J. Davis	PA	1921
Coolidge	James J. Davis	PA	1923
Hoover	James J. Davis	PA	1929
	William N. Doak	VA	1930
Roosevelt, F. D.	Frances Perkins	NY	1933
Truman	L. B. Schwellenbach	WA	1945
	Maurice J. Tobin	MA	1949
Eisenhower	Martin P. Durkin	IL	1953
	James P. Mitchell	NJ	1953
Kennedy	Arthur J. Goldberg	IL	1961
	W. Willard Wirtz	IL	1962
Johnson, L. B.	W. Willard Wirtz	IL	1963
Nixon	George P. Shultz	IL	1969
	James D. Hodgson	CA	1970
	Peter J. Brennan	NY	1973
Ford	Peter J. Brennan	NY	1974
	John T. Dunlop	CA	1975
	W. J. Usery Jr.	GA	1976
Carter	F. Ray Marshall	TX	1977
Reagan	Raymond J. Donovan	NJ	1981
	William E. Brock	TN	1985
	Ann D. McLaughlin	DC	1987
Bush, G. H. W.	Elizabeth Hanford Dole	NC	1989
	Lynn Martin	IL	1991
Clinton	Robert B. Reich	MA	1993
	Alexis M. Herman	AL	1997
Bush, G. W.	Elaine L. Chao	KY	2001
Obama	Hilda L. Solis	CA	2009

Secretaries of Commerce

President	Secretary	Home	Sworn in
Wilson	William C. Redfield	NY	1913
	Joshua W. Alexander	MO	1919
Harding	Herbert C. Hoover	CA	1921
Coolidge	Herbert C. Hoover	CA	1923
	William F. Whiting	MA	1928
Hoover	Robert P. Lamont	IL	1929
	Roy D. Chapin	MI	1932
Roosevelt, F. D.	Daniel C. Roper	SC	1933
	Harry L. Hopkins	NY	1939
	Jesse Jones	TX	1940
	Henry A. Wallace	IA	1945
Truman	Henry A. Wallace	IA	1945
	W. Averell Harriman	NY	1947
	Charles Sawyer	OH	1948
Eisenhower	Sinclair Weeks	MA	1953
	Lewis L. Strauss	NY	1958
	Frederick H. Mueller	MI	1959
Kennedy	Luther H. Hodges	NC	1961
Johnson, L. B.	Luther H. Hodges	NC	1963
	John T. Connor	NJ	1965
	Alex B. Trowbridge	NJ	1967
	Cyrus R. Smith	NY	1968
Nixon	Maurice H. Stans	MN	1969
	Peter G. Peterson	IL	1972
	Frederick B. Dent	SC	1973
Ford	Frederick B. Dent	SC	1974
	Rogers C. B. Morton	MD	1975
	Elliot L. Richardson	MA	1975
Carter	Juanita M. Kreps	NC	1977
	Philip M. Klutznick	IL	1979
Reagan	Malcolm Baldrige	CT	1981
	C. William Verity Jr.	OH	1987
Bush, G. H. W.	Robert A. Mosbacher	TX	1989
	Barbara H. Franklin	PA	1992
Clinton	Ronald H. Brown	DC	1993
	Mickey Kantor	CA	1996
	William M. Daley	IL	1997
	Norman Y. Mineta	CA	2000
Bush, G. W.	Donald L. Evans	TX	2001
	Carlos Gutierrez	MI	2005
Obama	Gary F. Locke	WA	2009

Secretaries of Housing and Urban Development

The Department of Housing and Urban Development was created by act of Congress on Sept. 9, 1965.

President	Secretary	Home	Sworn in
Johnson, L. B.	Robert C. Weaver	WA	1966
	Robert C. Wood	MA	1969
Nixon	George W. Romney	MI	1969
	James T. Lynn	OH	1973
Ford	James T. Lynn	OH	1974
	Carla Anderson Hills	CA	1975
Carter	Patricia Roberts Harris	DC	1977
	Moon Landrieu	LA	1979
Reagan	Samuel R. Pierce Jr.	NY	1981
Bush, G. H. W.	Jack F. Kemp	NY	1989
Clinton	Henry G. Cisneros	TX	1993
	Andrew M. Cuomo	NY	1997
Bush, G. W.	Mel Martinez	FL	2001
	Alphonso Jackson	TX	2004
	Steve Preston	VA	2008
Obama	Shaun L. S. Donovan	NY	2009

Secretaries of Transportation

The Department of Transportation was created by act of Congress on Oct. 15, 1966.

President	Secretary	Home	Sworn in
Johnson, L. B.	Alan S. Boyd	FL	1966
Nixon	John A. Volpe	MA	1969
	Claude S. Brinegar	CA	1973
Ford	Claude S. Brinegar	CA	1974
	William T. Coleman Jr.	PA	1975
Carter	Brock Adams	WA	1977
	Neil E. Goldschmidt	OR	1979
Reagan	Andrew L. Lewis Jr.	PA	1981
	Elizabeth Hanford Dole	NC	1983
	James H. Burnley	NC	1987
Bush, G. H. W.	Samuel K. Skinner	IL	1989
	Andrew H. Card Jr.	MA	1992
Clinton	Federico F. Peña	CO	1993
	Rodney E. Slater	AR	1997
Bush, G. W.	Norman Y. Mineta	CA	2001
	Mary E. Peters	AZ	2006
Obama	Raymond L. LaHood	IL	2009

Secretaries of Energy

The Department of Energy was created by federal law on Aug. 4, 1977.

President	Secretary	Home	Sworn in
Carter	James R. Schlesinger	VA	1977
	Charles Duncan Jr.	WY	1979
Reagan	James B. Edwards	SC	1981
	Donald P. Hodel	OR	1982
	John S. Herrington	CA	1985
Bush, G. H. W.	James D. Watkins	CA	1989
Clinton	Hazel R. O'Leary	MN	1993
	Federico F. Peña	CO	1997
	Bill Richardson	NM	1998
Bush, G. W.	Spencer Abraham	MI	2001
	Samuel W. Bodman	MA	2005
Obama	Steven Chu	CA	2009

Secretaries of Health, Education, and Welfare

The Department of Health, Education, and Welfare was created by Congress on Apr. 11, 1953. On Sept. 27, 1979, it was divided by Congress into two departments—Education, and Health and Human Services—with the secretary of each becoming a Cabinet member.

President	Secretary	Home	Sworn in
Eisenhower	Oveta Culp Hobby	TX	1953
	Marion B. Folsom	NY	1955
	Arthur S. Flemming	OH	1958
Kennedy	Abraham A. Ribicoff	CT	1961
	Anthony J. Celebrezze	OH	1962
Johnson, L. B.	Anthony J. Celebrezze	OH	1963
	John W. Gardner	NY	1965
	Wilbur J. Cohen	MI	1968
Nixon	Robert H. Finch	CA	1969
	Elliot L. Richardson	MA	1970
	Caspar W. Weinberger	CA	1973
Ford	Caspar W. Weinberger	CA	1974
	Forrest D. Mathews	AL	1975
Carter	Joseph A. Califano Jr.	DC	1977
	Patricia Roberts Harris	DC	1979

Secretaries of Health and Human Services

President	Secretary	Home	Sworn in
Carter	Patricia Roberts Harris	DC	1979
Reagan	Richard S. Schweiker	PA	1981
	Margaret M. Heckler	MA	1983
Reagan	Otis R. Bowen	IN	1985
Bush, G. H. W.	Louis W. Sullivan	GA	1989
Clinton	Donna E. Shalala	WI	1993
Bush, G. W.	Tommy Thompson	WI	2001
	Michael O. Leavitt	UT	2005
Obama	Kathleen Sebelius	KS	2009

Secretaries of Education

President	Secretary	Home	Sworn in
Carter	Shirley Hufstedler	CA	1979
Reagan	Terrel Bell	UT	1981
	William J. Bennett	NY	1985
	Lauro F. Cavazos	TX	1988
Bush, G. H. W.	Lauro F. Cavazos	TX	1989
	Lamar Alexander	TN	1991
Clinton	Richard W. Riley	SC	1993
Bush, G. W.	Roderick R. Paige	TX	2001
	Margaret Spellings	TX	2005
Obama	Arne Duncan	IL	2009

Secretaries of Veterans Affairs

The Department of Veterans Affairs was created on Oct. 25, 1988, when Pres. Ronald Reagan signed a bill that made the Veterans Administration into a Cabinet department, effective Mar. 15, 1989.

President	Secretary	Home	Sworn in
Bush, G. H. W.	Edward J. Derwinski	IL	1989
Clinton	Jesse Brown	IL	1993
	Togo D. West Jr.	NC	1998
Bush, G. W.	Anthony Principi	CA	2001
	R. James Nicholson	CO	2005
	James B. Peake	MO	2007
Obama	Eric K. Shinseki	VA	2009

Secretaries of Homeland Security

The Department of Homeland Security was created by act of Congress on Nov. 25, 2002.

President	Secretary	Home	Sworn in
Bush, G. W.	Thomas Ridge	PA	2003
	Michael Chertoff	DC	2005
Obama	Janet Napolitano	AZ	2009

CONGRESS

As of Oct. 2011.

Floor Leaders in the U.S. Senate, 1920-2011

Majority leaders				Minority leaders			
Name	Party	State	Tenure	Name	Party	State	Tenure
Charles Curtis[1]	Rep.	KS	1925-1929	Oscar W. Underwood[2]	Dem.	AL	1920-1923
James E. Watson	Rep.	IN	1929-1933	Joseph T. Robinson	Dem.	AR	1923-1933
Joseph T. Robinson	Dem.	AR	1933-1937	Charles L. McNary	Rep.	OR	1933-1944
Alben W. Barkley	Dem.	KY	1937-1947	Wallace H. White	Rep.	ME	1944-1947
Wallace H. White	Rep.	ME	1947-1949	Alben W. Barkley	Dem.	KY	1947-1949
Scott W. Lucas	Dem.	IL	1949-1951	Kenneth S. Wherry	Rep.	NE	1949-1951
Ernest W. McFarland	Dem.	AZ	1951-1953	Henry Styles Bridges	Rep.	NH	1952-1953
Robert A. Taft	Rep.	OH	1953	Lyndon B. Johnson	Dem.	TX	1953-1955
William F. Knowland	Rep.	CA	1953-1955	William F. Knowland	Rep.	CA	1955-1959
Lyndon B. Johnson	Dem.	TX	1955-1961	Everett M. Dirksen	Rep.	IL	1959-1969
Mike Mansfield	Dem.	MT	1961-1977	Hugh D. Scott	Rep.	PA	1969-1977
Robert C. Byrd	Dem.	WV	1977-1981	Howard H. Baker Jr.	Rep.	TN	1977-1981
Howard H. Baker Jr.	Rep.	TN	1981-1985	Robert C. Byrd	Dem.	WV	1981-1987
Robert J. Dole	Rep.	KS	1985-1987	Robert J. Dole	Rep.	KS	1987-1995
Robert C. Byrd	Dem.	WV	1987-1989	Thomas A. Daschle	Dem.	SD	1995-2001[3]
George J. Mitchell	Dem.	ME	1989-1995	Trent Lott	Rep.	MS	2001-2002[3,4]
Robert J. Dole	Rep.	KS	1995-1996	Thomas A. Daschle	Dem.	SD	2003-2005[5]
Trent Lott	Rep.	MS	1996-2001[3]	Harry M. Reid	Dem.	NV	2005-2007[5]
Thomas A. Daschle	Dem.	SD	2001-2003[3]	Mitch McConnell	Rep.	KY	2007-
William Frist	Rep.	TN	2003-2007[4]				
Harry M. Reid	Dem.	NV	2007-				

Note: The offices of party (majority and minority) leaders in the Senate did not evolve until the 20th century. (1) First Republican to be formally designated floor leader. Henry Cabot Lodge (MA) served as unofficial party leader prior to Curtis's election. (2) First Democrat to be designated floor leader. (3) Democrats held the majority Jan. 3, 2001, until Dick Cheney (R) was installed as vice pres., Jan. 20. Republicans subsequently lost the majority when Jim Jeffords (VT) switched from Republican to Independent, June 6, 2001. (4) Trent Lott resigned from Republican leadership Dec. 20, 2002. William Frist was elected Republican leader Dec. 23, 2002, and began service Jan. 7, 2003, as majority leader. (5) Thomas A. Daschle was defeated in the 2004 election and retired from the Senate Jan. 3, 2005; Democratic Whip Harry M. Reid was elected to the post for the 109th Congress.

Speakers of the U.S. House of Representatives, 1789-2011

Name	Party	State	Tenure	Name	Party	State	Tenure
Frederick Muhlenberg	Federalist	PA	1789-1791	Michael C. Kerr	Dem.	IN	1875-1876
Jonathan Trumbull	Federalist	CT	1791-1793	Samuel J. Randall	Dem.	PA	1876-1881
Frederick Muhlenberg	Federalist	PA	1793-1795	J. Warren Keifer	Rep.	OH	1881-1883
Jonathan Dayton	Federalist	NJ	1795-1799	John G. Carlisle	Dem.	KY	1883-1889
Theodore Sedgwick	Federalist	MA	1799-1801	Thomas B. Reed	Rep.	ME	1889-1891
Nathaniel Macon	Dem.-Rep.	NC	1801-1807	Charles F. Crisp	Dem.	GA	1891-1895
Joseph B. Varnum	Dem.-Rep.	MA	1807-1811	Thomas B. Reed	Rep.	ME	1895-1899
Henry Clay	Dem.-Rep.	KY	1811-1814	David B. Henderson	Rep.	IA	1899-1903
Langdon Cheves	Dem.-Rep.	SC	1814-1815	Joseph G. Cannon	Rep.	IL	1903-1911
Henry Clay	Dem.-Rep.	KY	1815-1820	Champ Clark	Dem.	MO	1911-1919
John W. Taylor	Dem.-Rep.	NY	1820-1821	Frederick H. Gillett	Rep.	MA	1919-1925
Philip P. Barbour	Dem.-Rep.	VA	1821-1823	Nicholas Longworth	Rep.	OH	1925-1931
Henry Clay	Dem.-Rep.	KY	1823-1825	John N. Garner	Dem.	TX	1931-1933
John W. Taylor	Dem.-Rep.	NY	1825-1827	Henry T. Rainey	Dem.	IL	1933-1934
Andrew Stevenson	Dem.	VA	1827-1834	Joseph W. Byrns	Dem.	TN	1935-1936
John Bell	Dem.	TN	1834-1835	William B. Bankhead	Dem.	AL	1936-1940
James K. Polk	Dem.	TN	1835-1839	Sam Rayburn	Dem.	TX	1940-1947
Robert M. T. Hunter	Dem.	VA	1839-1841	Joseph W. Martin Jr.	Rep.	MA	1947-1949
John White	Whig	KY	1841-1843	Sam Rayburn	Dem.	TX	1949-1953
John W. Jones	Dem.	VA	1843-1845	Joseph W. Martin Jr.	Rep.	MA	1953-1955
John W. Davis	Dem.	IN	1845-1847	Sam Rayburn	Dem.	TX	1955-1961
Robert C. Winthrop	Whig	MA	1847-1849	John W. McCormack	Dem.	MA	1962-1971
Howell Cobb	Dem.	GA	1849-1851	Carl Albert	Dem.	OK	1971-1977
Linn Boyd	Dem.	KY	1851-1855	Thomas P. O'Neill Jr.	Dem.	MA	1977-1987
Nathaniel P. Banks	American	MA	1856-1857	James Wright	Dem.	TX	1987-1989
James L. Orr	Dem.	SC	1857-1859	Thomas S. Foley	Dem.	WA	1989-1995
William Pennington	Rep.	NJ	1860-1861	Newt Gingrich	Rep.	GA	1995-1999
Galusha A. Grow	Rep.	PA	1861-1863	J. Dennis Hastert	Rep.	IL	1999-2007
Schuyler Colfax	Rep.	IN	1863-1869	Nancy Pelosi	Dem.	CA	2007-2011
Theodore M. Pomeroy	Rep.	NY	1869	John Boehner	Rep.	OH	2011-
James G. Blaine	Rep.	ME	1869-1875				

Political Divisions of the U.S. Senate and House of Representatives, 1901-2011

Source: Office of the Clerk, U.S. House of Representatives; Congressional Research Service, Library of Congress

All figures reflect immediate post-election party breakdown except where noted; **boldface** denotes party in majority immediately after election.

Congress	Years	SENATE					HOUSE OF REPRESENTATIVES				
		Total members	Dem.	Rep.	Other parties	Vacant	Total members	Dem.	Rep.	Other parties	Vacant
57th	1901-1903	90	32	**56**	2		357	151	**200**	6	
58th	1903-1905	90	33	**57**			386	176	**207**	3	
59th	1905-1907	90	32	**58**			386	135	**251**		
60th	1907-1909	92	31	**61**			391	167	**223**	1	
61st	1909-1911	92	32	**60**			391	172	**219**		
62nd	1911-1913	96	44	**52**			394	**230**	162	2	
63rd	1913-1915	96	**51**	44	1		435	**291**	134	10	
64th	1915-1917	96	**56**	40			435	**230**	196	9	
65th	1917-1919	96	**54**	42			435	214[1]	**215**	6	
66th	1919-1921	96	47	**49**			435	192	**240**	2	1
67th	1921-1923	96	37	**59**			435	131	**302**	2	
68th	1923-1925	96	42	**53**	1		435	207	**225**	3	
69th	1925-1927	96	41	**54**	1		435	183	**247**	5	
70th	1927-1929	96	46	**48**	1	1	435	194	**238**	3	
71st	1929-1931	96	39	**56**	1		435	164	**270**	1	
72nd	1931-1933	96	47	**48**	1		435	216[2]	**218**	1	

Congress	Years	SENATE Total members	Dem.	Rep.	Other parties	Vacant	HOUSE OF REPRESENTATIVES Total members	Dem.	Rep.	Other parties	Vacant
73rd	1933-1935	96	59	36	1		435	313	117	5	
74th	1935-1937	96	69	25	2		435	322	103	10	
75th	1937-1939	96	76	16	4		435	334	88	13	
76th	1939-1941	96	69	23	4		435	262	169	4	
77th	1941-1943	96	66	28	2		435	267	162	6	
78th	1943-1945	96	57	38	1		435	222	209	4	
79th	1945-1947	96	57	38	1		435	242	191	2	
80th	1947-1949	96	45	51			435	188	246	1	
81st	1949-1951	96	54	42			435	263	171	1	
82nd	1951-1953	96	49	47			435	235	199	1	
83rd	1953-1955	96	47	48	1		435	213	221	1	
84th	1955-1957	96	48	47	1		435	232	203		
85th	1957-1959	96	49	47			435	234	201		
86th	1959-1961	100	65	35			437[3,4]	283	153	1	
87th	1961-1963	100	64	36			437	263	174		
88th	1963-1965	100	66	34			435	259	176		
89th	1965-1967	100	68	32			435	295	140		
90th	1967-1969	100	64	36			435	247	187		1
91st	1969-1971	100	57	43			435	243	192		
92nd	1971-1973	100	54	44	2		435	255	180		
93rd	1973-1975	100	56	42	2		435	242	192	1	
94th	1975-1977	100	60	38	2		435	291	144		
95th	1977-1979	100	61	38	1		435	292	143		
96th	1979-1981	100	58	41	1		435	277	158		
97th	1981-1983	100	46	53	1		435	242	192	1	
98th	1983-1985	100	46	54			435	269	166		
99th	1985-1987	100	47	53			435	253	182		
100th	1987-1989	100	55	45			435	258	177		
101st	1989-1991	100	55	45			435	260	175		
102nd	1991-1993	100	56	44			435	267	167	1	
103rd	1993-1995	100	57	43			435	258	176	1	
104th	1995-1997	100	48	52			435	204	230	1	
105th	1997-1999	100	45	55			435	206	228	1	
106th	1999-2001	100	45	55			435	211	223	1	
107th	2001-2003	100	50	50[5]			435	212	221	2	
108th	2003-2005	100	48	51	1		435	204	229	1	1
109th	2005-2007	100	44	55	1		435	202	232	1	
110th	2007-2009	100	49	49	2[6]		435	233	202		
111th	2009-2011	100	57[7]	41	2[6]		435	257	178		
112th	2011-	100	51	47	2[6]		435	193	242		

(1) Democrats organized the House with help of other parties. (2) Democrats organized the House because of Republican deaths. (3) Proclamation declaring Alaska a state issued Jan. 3, 1959. (4) Proclamation declaring Hawaii a state issued Aug. 21, 1959. (5) While the Senate was split 50-50, control was held by whichever party had an incumbent vice president. Republican Sen. James M. Jeffords (VT) changed his party designation to Independent on June 6, 2001, switching control of the Senate to Democrats. (6) Both Independent senators chose to caucus with the Democrats. (7) Sen. Al Franken (D, MN) was not seated until July 7, 2009.

Congressional Bills Vetoed, 1789-2011
Source: Virtual Reference Desk, U.S. Senate

President	Regular vetoes	Pocket vetoes	Total vetoes	Vetoes overridden	President	Regular vetoes	Pocket vetoes	Total vetoes	Vetoes overridden
Washington	2	—	2	—	B. Harrison	19	25	44	1
J. Adams	—	—	—	—	Cleveland[2]	42	128	170	5
Jefferson	—	—	—	—	McKinley	6	36	42	—
Madison	5	2	7	—	T. Roosevelt	42	40	82	1
Monroe	1	—	1	—	Taft	30	9	39	1
J. Q. Adams	—	—	—	—	Wilson	33	11	44	6
Jackson	5	7	12	—	Harding	5	1	6	—
Van Buren	—	1	1	—	Coolidge	20	30	50	4
W. H. Harrison	—	—	—	—	Hoover	21	16	37	3
Tyler	6	4	10	1	F. D. Roosevelt	372	263	635	9
Polk	2	1	3	—	Truman	180	70	250	12
Taylor	—	—	—	—	Eisenhower	73	108	181	2
Fillmore	—	—	—	—	Kennedy	12	9	21	—
Pierce	9	—	9	5	L. Johnson	16	14	30	—
Buchanan	4	3	7	—	Nixon	26	17	43	7
Lincoln	2	5	7	—	Ford	48	18	66	12
A. Johnson	21	8	29	15	Carter	13	18	31	2
Grant	45	48	93	4	Reagan	39	39	78	9
Hayes	12	1	13	1	G. H. W. Bush[3]	29	15	44	1
Garfield	—	—	—	—	Clinton[4]	36	1	37	2
Arthur	4	8	12	1	G. W. Bush	12	—	12	4
Cleveland[1]	304	110	414	2	Obama	2	—	2	—
					Total[3,4]	1,498	1,066	2,564	110

— = 0. (1) First term only. (2) Second term only. (3) Excluded from the figures are two bills that Pres. Bush claimed to be vetoed but Congress considered enacted into law because the president failed to return them to Congress during a recess period. (4) Does not include line-item vetoes, which were ruled unconstitutional by the U.S. Supreme Court on June 25, 1998.

Librarians of Congress, 1802-2011
Source: Library of Congress

Librarian	Tenure	Appointed by	Librarian	Tenure	Appointed by
John J. Beckley	1802-1807	Jefferson	Herbert Putnam	1899-1939	McKinley
Patrick Magruder	1807-1815	Jefferson	Archibald MacLeish	1939-1944	F. D. Roosevelt
George Watterston	1815-1829	Madison	Luther H. Evans	1945-1953	Truman
John Silva Meehan	1829-1861	Jackson	L. Quincy Mumford	1954-1974	Eisenhower
John G. Stephenson	1861-1864	Lincoln	Daniel J. Boorstin	1975-1987	Ford
Ainsworth Rand Spofford	1864-1897	Lincoln	James H. Billington	1987-	Reagan
John Russell Young	1897-1899	McKinley			

Membership of the 112th Congress

Source: *Statistics of the Congressional Election of November 2, 2010,* Karen L. Haas, Clerk of the House of Representatives
The 112th Congress convened Jan. 5, 2011.

Members of the Senate With 2010 Election Results

51 Democrats, 47 Republicans, 1 Independent, 1 Independent Democrat. 100 total. Boldface denotes the 2010 election winner. * = Incumbent. Third-party or independent candidates receiving fewer than 10,000 votes are not listed.

Terms are for six years and end Jan. 3 of the year preceding the senator's name in the following table. Annual salary, $174,000; President Pro Tempore, Majority Leader, and Minority Leader salary, $193,400. To be eligible for the Senate, one must be at least 30 years old, a U.S. citizen for at least nine years, and a resident of the state from which chosen. Contact: U.S. Senate, Washington DC 20510; (202) 224-3121; www.senate.gov

Senate officials as of Oct. 2011: Pres. Pro Tempore, Daniel K. Inouye (HI); Majority Leader, Harry Reid (NV); Majority Whip, Richard J. Durbin (IL); Minority Leader, Mitch McConnell (KY); Minority Whip, John Kyl (AZ). The Senate had 17 women (12 D, 5 R); 2 Asian Americans (Daniel K. Inouye and Daniel K. Akaka, both D, HI); 2 Hispanics (Robert Menendez, D, NJ, and Marco Rubio, R, FL). There were no African American or Native American senators. **D** = Democrat; **R** = Republican; **Amer. Ind.** = American Independent Party; **CFL** = Connecticut for Lieberman; **CP** = Constitution Party; **DFL** = Democratic-Farmer-Labor; **DNL** = North Dakota Democratic Non-Partisan League; **I** = Independent; **Ind. Ref.** = Independent Reform; **LB** = Libertarian; **Prog.** = Progressive; **Unaff.** = Unaffiliated.

Term ends	Senator/candidate (party); service from[1]	2010 election results
Alabama		
2015	Jeff Sessions (R); 1/7/1997	
2017	**Richard Shelby* (R); 1/6/1987**	**968,181**
	William Barnes (D)	515,619
Alaska		
2015	Mark Begich (D); 1/6/2009	
2017	**Lisa Murkowski (I); 12/20/2002**	**101,091**
	Joe Miller (R)	90,860
	Scott McAdams (D)	60,045
Arizona		
2013	Jon Kyl (R); 1/4/1995	
2017	**John McCain* (R); 1/6/1987**	**1,005,615**
	Rodney Glassman (D)	592,011
	David Nolan (LB)	80,097
	Jerry Joslyn (Green)	24,603
Arkansas		
2015	Mark Pryor (D); 1/7/2003	
2017	**John Boozman (R)**	**451,618**
	Blanche L. Lincoln* (D)	288,156
	Trevor Drown (I)	25,234
	John Gray (Green)	14,430
California		
2013	Dianne Feinstein (D); 11/10/1992	
2017	**Barbara Boxer* (D); 1993**	**5,218,441**
	Carly Fiorina (R)	4,217,366
	Gail Lightfoot (LB)	175,242
	Marsha Feinland (Peace and Freedom)	135,093
	Duane Roberts (Green)	128,510
	Edward Noonan (Amer. Ind.)	125,441
Colorado		
2015	Mark Udall (D); 1/6/2009	
2017	**Michael F. Bennet* (D); 1/22/2009**	**851,590**
	Ken Buck (R)	822,731
	Bob Kinsey (Green)	38,768
	Maclyn Stringer (LB)	22,589
	Jason Napolitano (Ind. Ref.)	19,415
	Charley Miller (Unaff.)	11,330
Connecticut		
2013	Joseph Lieberman (CFL/Ind. Democrat); 1989	
2017	**Richard Blumenthal (D)**	**636,040**
	Linda McMahon (R)	498,341
	Warren Mosler (I)	11,275
Delaware		
2013	Thomas R. Carper (D); 2001	
2015	**Christopher Coons (D)[2]**	**174,012**
	Christine O'Donnell (R)	123,053
Florida		
2013	Bill Nelson (D); 2001	
2017	**Marco Rubio (R)**	**2,645,743**
	Charlie Crist (Unaff.)	1,607,549
	Kendrick Meek (D)	1,092,936
	Alexander Snitker (LB)	24,850
	Sue Askeland (Unaff.)	15,340
Georgia		
2015	Saxby Chambliss (R); 1/7/2003	
2017	**Johnny Isakson* (R); 2005**	**1,489,904**
	Michael Thurmond (D)	996,516
	Chuck Donovan (LB)	68,750
Hawaii		
2013	Daniel K. Akaka (D); 4/28/1990	
2017	**Daniel K. Inouye* (D); 1963**	**277,228**
	Cam Cavasso (R)	79,939
Idaho		
2015	Jim Risch (R); 1/6/2009	
2017	**Mike Crapo* (R); 1/6/1999**	**319,953**
	Tom Sullivan (D)	112,057
	Randy Bergquist (CP)	17,429

Term ends	Senator/candidate (party); service from[1]	2010 election results
Illinois		
2015	Richard J. Durbin (D); 1/7/1997	
2017	**Mark Kirk (R)**	**1,778,698**
	Alexi Giannoulias (D)	1,719,478
	LeAlan M. Jones (Green)	117,914
	Mike Labno (LB)	87,247
Indiana		
2013	Richard G. Lugar (R); 1977	
2017	**Dan Coats (R)**	**952,116**
	Brad Ellsworth (D)	697,775
	Rebecca Sink-Burris (LB)	94,330
Iowa		
2015	Tom Harkin (D); 1985	
2017	**Chuck Grassley* (R); 1981**	**718,215**
	Roxanne Conlin (D)	371,686
	John Heiderscheit (LB)	25,290
Kansas		
2015	Pat Roberts (R); 1/7/1997	
2017	**Jerry Moran (R)**	**587,175**
	Lisa Johnston (D)	220,971
	Michael Dann (LB)	17,922
	Joe Bellis (Reform)	11,624
Kentucky		
2015	Mitch McConnell (R); 1985	
2017	**Rand Paul (R)**	**755,706**
	Jack Conway (D)	600,052
Louisiana		
2015	Mary L. Landrieu (D); 1/7/1997	
2017	**David Vitter* (R); 2005**	**715,415**
	Charlie Melancon (D)	476,572
	Randall Hayes (LB)	13,957
Maine		
2013	Olympia J. Snowe (R); 1/4/1995	
2015	Susan M. Collins (R); 1/7/1997	
Maryland		
2013	Benjamin L. Cardin (D); 2007	
2017	**Barbara Ann Mikulski* (D); 1/6/1987**	**1,140,531**
	Eric Wargotz (R)	655,666
	Kenniss Henry (Green)	20,717
	Richard Shawver (CP)	14,746
Massachusetts		
2013	Scott P. Brown (R); 2/4/2010[3]	
2015	John F. Kerry (D); 1/2/1985	
Michigan		
2013	Debbie Stabenow (D); 2001	
2015	Carl Levin (D); 1979	
Minnesota		
2013	Amy Klobuchar (DFL); 2007	
2015	Al Franken (DFL); 7/7/2009	
Mississippi		
2013	Roger Wicker (R); 12/31/2007[4]	
2015	Thad Cochran (R); 12/27/1978	
Missouri		
2013	Claire McCaskill (D); 2007	
2017	**Roy Blunt (R)**	**1,054,160**
	Robin Carnahan (D)	789,736
	Jonathan Dine (LB)	58,663
	Jerry Beck (CP)	41,309
Montana		
2013	Jon Tester (D); 2007	
2015	Max Baucus (D); 12/15/1978	
Nebraska		
2013	Ben Nelson (D); 2001	
2015	Mike Johanns (R); 1/6/2009	

Term ends	Senator/candidate (party); service from[1]	2010 election results
Nevada		
2013	Dean Heller (R); 5/9/2011[5]	
2017	**Harry Reid* (D); 1/6/1987**	**362,785**
	Sharron Angle (R)	321,361
	None of these candidates	16,197
New Hampshire		
2015	Jeanne Shaheen (D); 1/6/2009	
2017	**Kelly Ayotte (R)**	**273,218**
	Paul Hodes (D)	167,545
New Jersey		
2013	Robert Menendez (D); 1/18/2006	
2015	Frank Lautenberg (D); 1/7/2003	
New Mexico		
2013	Jeff Bingaman (D); 1983	
2015	Tom Udall (D); 1/6/2009	
New York		
2013	**Kirsten E. Gillibrand* (D); 1/27/2009[6]**	**2,837,684**
	Joseph DioGuardi (R)	1,582,693
	Cecile Lawrence (Green)	35,489
	John Clifton (LB)	18,414
	Joseph Huff (other)	17,019
	Vivia Morgan (other)	11,787
2017	**Charles E. Schumer* (D); 1/6/1999**	**3,047,880**
	Jay Townsend (R)	1,480,423
	Colia Clark (Green)	42,341
	Randy Credico (LB)	24,871
North Carolina		
2015	Kay Hagan (D); 1/6/2009	
2017	**Richard Burr* (R); 2005**	**1,458,046**
	Elaine Marshall (D)	1,145,074
	Mike Beitler (LB)	55,687
North Dakota		
2013	Kent Conrad (DNL); 1/6/1987	
2017	**John Hoeven (R)**	**181,689**
	Tracy Potter (DNL)	52,955
Ohio		
2013	Sherrod Brown (D); 2007	
2017	**Rob Portman (R)**	**2,168,742**
	Lee Fisher (D)	1,503,297
	Eric Deaton (CP)	65,856
	Michael Pryce (I)	50,101
	Daniel LaBotz (Socialist)	26,454
Oklahoma		
2015	James M. Inhofe (R); 11/21/1994	
2017	**Tom Coburn* (R); 2005**	**718,482**
	Jim Rogers (D)	265,814
	Stephen Wallace (I)	25,048
Oregon		
2015	Jeff Merkley (D); 1/6/2009	
2017	**Ron Wyden* (D); 2/6/1996**	**825,507**
	Jim Huffman (R)	566,199
	Bruce Cronk (Working Families)	18,940
	Marc Delphine (LB)	16,028
	Rick Staggenborg (Prog.)	14,466

Term ends	Senator/candidate (party); service from[1]	2010 election results
Pennsylvania		
2013	Bob Casey Jr. (D); 2007	
2017	**Pat Toomey (R)**	**2,028,945**
	Joe Sestak (D)	1,948,716
Rhode Island		
2013	Sheldon Whitehouse (D); 2007	
2015	John F. Reed (D); 1/7/1997	
South Carolina		
2015	Lindsey Graham (R); 1/7/2003	
2017	**Jim DeMint* (R); 2005**	**810,771**
	Alvin Greene (D)	364,598
	Tom Clements (Green)	121,472
South Dakota		
2015	Tim Johnson (D); 1/7/1997	
2017	**John Thune* (R); 2005**	**Unopposed**
Tennessee		
2013	Bob Corker (R); 2007	
2015	Lamar Alexander (R); 1/7/2003	
Texas		
2013	Kay Bailey Hutchison (R); 6/5/1993	
2015	John Cornyn (R); 12/2/2002	
Utah		
2013	Orrin G. Hatch (R); 1977	
2017	**Mike Lee (R)**	**360,403**
	Sam Granato (D)	191,732
	Scott Bradley (CP)	33,095
Vermont		
2013	Bernard Sanders (I); 2007	
2017	**Patrick Leahy* (D); 1975**	**151,281**
	Len Britton (R)	72,699
Virginia		
2013	James H. "Jim" Webb Jr. (D); 2007	
2015	Mark Warner (D); 1/6/2009	
Washington		
2013	Maria Cantwell (D); 2001	
2017	**Patty Murray* (D); 1993**	**1,314,930**
	Dino Rossi (R)	1,196,164
West Virginia		
2013	**Joe Manchin (D)[7]**	**283,358**
	John Raese (R)	230,013
	Jesse Johnson (Mountain)	10,152
2015	John D. "Jay" Rockefeller IV (D); 1/15/1985	
Wisconsin		
2013	Herb Kohl (D); 1989	
2017	**Ron Johnson (R)**	**1,125,999**
	Russ Feingold* (D)	1,020,958
	Rob Taylor (CP)	23,473
Wyoming		
2013	John Barrasso (R); 6/22/2007[8]	
2015	Michael B. Enzi (R); 1/7/1997	

(1) Jan. 3, unless otherwise noted. (2) Special election to fill seat vacated by Vice Pres. Joseph Biden Jr. (D), Jan. 20, 2009. (3) Special election held Jan. 19, 2010, to fill seat vacated by death of Edward M. Kennedy (D), Aug. 25, 2009. (4) Appointed to fill seat vacated by Trent Lott (R), Dec. 31, 2007; he won a special election to keep the seat Nov. 4, 2008. (5) Appointed to fill seat vacated by John Ensign (R), May 3, 2011. (6) Special election to fill seat vacated by Hillary Rodham Clinton (D), who was appointed Sec. of State, Jan. 21, 2009. (7) Special election to fill seat vacated by death of Robert Byrd (D), June 28, 2010. (8) Appointed to fill seat vacated by death of Craig Thomas (R), June 4, 2007; he won a special election to keep the seat Nov. 4, 2008.

Members of the House of Representatives With 2010 Election Results

192 Democrats, 242 Republicans, 1 vacant. 435 total. Boldface denotes the 2010 election winner. * = Incumbent. Third-party or independent candidates receiving fewer than 10,000 votes are not listed.

Terms are for two years ending Jan. 3, 2013. Annual salary, $174,000; Majority Leader and Minority Leader salary, $196,400; Speaker of the House salary, $223,500. To be eligible for the House, a person must be at least 25 years of age, a U.S. citizen for at least seven years, and a resident of the state from which chosen. Contact: U.S. House of Representatives, Washington, DC 20515; (202) 224-3121; www.house.gov

House officials as of Oct. 2011: Speaker of the House, John Boehner (OH); Majority Leader, Eric Cantor (VA); Majority Whip, Kevin McCarthy (CA); Minority Leader, Nancy Pelosi (CA); Minority Whip, Steny Hoyer (MD). Including delegates, there were 77 women in the House (53 D, 24 R). There were 44 African Americans (42 D, 2 R), 30 Hispanics (22 D, 8 R), 9 Asian Americans (all D), and 1 Native American (Tom Cole, R, OK). **D** = Democrat; **R** = Republican; **Amer. Const.** = American Constitution; **Amer. Ind.** = American Independent Party; **CP** = Constitution Party; **DFL** = Democratic-Farmer-Labor; **I** = Independent; **IP** = Independence Party; **LB** = Libertarian; **Prog.** = Progressive; **Unaff.** = Unaffiliated.

Dist.	Representative/candidate (party)	2010 election results
Alabama		
1	**Jo Bonner* (R)**	**129,063**
	David Walter (CP)	26,357
2	**Martha Roby (R)**	**111,645**
	Bobby Bright* (D)	106,865
3	**Mike Rogers* (R)**	**117,736**
	Steve Segrest (D)	80,204
4	**Robert B. Aderholt* (R)**	**Unopposed**

Dist.	Representative/candidate (party)	2010 election results
5	**Mo Brooks (R)**	**131,109**
	Steve Raby (D)	95,192
6	**Spencer Bachus* (R)**	**Unopposed**
7	**Terri Sewell (D)**	**136,696**
	Don Chamberlain (R)	51,890
Alaska		
	Don E. Young* (R)	**175,384**
	Harry Crawford (D)	77,606

Dist.	Representative/candidate (party)	2010 election results
Arizona		
1	**Paul Gosar (R)**	**112,816**
	Ann Kirkpatrick* (D)	99,233
	Nicole Patti (LB)	14,869
2	**Trent Franks* (R)**	**173,173**
	John Thrasher (D)	82,891
	Powell Gammill (LB)	10,820
3	**Ben Quayle (R)**	**108,689**
	Jon Hulburd (D)	85,610
	Michael Shoen (LB)	10,478
4	**Ed Pastor* (D)**	**61,524**
	Janet Contreras (R)	25,300
5	**David Schweikert (R)**	**110,374**
	Harry Mitchell* (D)	91,749
	Nick Coons (LB)	10,127
6	**Jeff Flake* (R)**	**165,649**
	Rebecca Schneider (D)	72,615
7	**Raúl Grijalva* (D)**	**79,935**
	Ruth McClung (R)	70,385
8	**Gabrielle Giffords* (D)**	**138,280**
	Jesse Kelly (R)	134,124
	Steven Stoltz (LB)	11,174
Arkansas		
1	**Rick Crawford (R)**	**93,224**
	Chad Causey (D)	78,267
2	**Tim Griffin (R)**	**122,091**
	Joyce Elliott (D)	80,687
3	**Steve Womack (R)**	**148,581**
	David Whitaker (D)	56,542
4	**Mike Ross* (D)**	**102,479**
	Beth Anne Rankin (R)	71,526
California		
1	**Mike Thompson* (D)**	**147,307**
	Loren Hanks (R)	72,803
2	**Wally Herger* (R)**	**130,837**
	Jim Reed (D)	98,092
3	**Dan Lungren* (R)**	**131,169**
	Ami Bera (D)	113,128
4	**Tom McClintock* (R)**	**186,397**
	Clint Curtis (D)	95,653
	Ben Emery (Green)	22,179
5	**Doris O. Matsui* (D)**	**124,220**
	Paul Smith (R)	43,577
6	**Lynn Woolsey* (D)**	**172,216**
	Jim Judd (R)	77,361
7	**George Miller* (D)**	**122,435**
	Rick Tubbs (R)	56,764
8	**Nancy Pelosi* (D)**	**167,957**
	John Dennis (R)	31,711
9	**Barbara Lee* (D)**	**180,400**
	Gerald Hashimoto (R)	23,054
10	**John Garamendi* (D)**	**137,578**
	Gary Clift (R)	88,512
11	**Jerry McNerney* (D)**	**115,361**
	David Harmer (R)	112,703
	David Christensen (Amer. Ind.)	12,439
12	**Jackie Speier* (D)**	**152,044**
	Mike Moloney (R)	44,475
13	**Fortney Pete Stark* (D)**	**118,278**
	Forest Baker (R)	45,575
14	**Anna G. Eshoo* (D)**	**151,217**
	Dave Chapman (R)	60,917
15	**Mike Honda* (D)**	**126,147**
	Scott Kirkland (R)	60,468
16	**Zoe Lofgren* (D)**	**105,841**
	Daniel Sahagun (R)	37,913
	Edward Gonzalez (LB)	12,304
17	**Sam Farr* (D)**	**118,734**
	Jeff Taylor (R)	53,176
18	**Dennis A. Cardoza* (D)**	**72,853**
	Michael Berryhill (R)	51,716
19	**Jeff Denham (R)**	**128,394**
	Loraine Goodwin (D)	69,912
20	**Jim Costa* (D)**	**46,247**
	Andy Vidak (R)	43,197
21	**Devin G. Nunes* (R)**	**Unopposed**
22	**Kevin McCarthy* (R)**	**Unopposed**
23	**Lois Capps* (D)**	**111,768**
	Tom Watson (R)	72,744
24	**Elton Gallegly* (R)**	**144,055**
	Timothy Allison (D)	96,279

Dist.	Representative/candidate (party)	2010 election results
25	**Howard P. "Buck" McKeon* (R)**	**118,308**
	Jackie Conaway (D)	73,028
26	**David Dreier* (R)**	**112,774**
	Russ Warner (D)	76,093
	David Miller (Amer. Ind.)	12,784
27	**Brad Sherman* (D)**	**102,927**
	Mark Reed (R)	55,056
28	**Howard L. Berman* (D)**	**88,385**
	Merlin Froyd (R)	28,493
	Carlos Rodriguez (LB)	10,229
29	**Adam Schiff* (D)**	**104,374**
	John Colbert (R)	51,534
30	**Henry A. Waxman* (D)**	**153,663**
	Charles Wilkerson (R)	75,948
31	**Xavier Becerra* (D)**	**76,363**
	Stephen Smith (R)	14,740
32	**Judy Chu* (D)**	**77,759**
	Edward Schmerling (R)	31,697
33	**Karen Bass (D)**	**131,990**
	James Andion (R)	21,342
34	**Lucille Roybal-Allard* (D)**	**69,382**
	Wayne Miller (R)	20,457
35	**Maxine Waters* (D)**	**98,131**
	K. Bruce Brown (R)	25,561
36	**Janice Hahn* (D)**[1]	**47,000**
	Craig Huey (R)	38,624
37	**Laura Richardson* (D)**	**85,799**
	Star Parker (R)	29,159
	Nicholas Dibs (I)	10,560
38	**Grace F. Napolitano* (D)**	**85,459**
	Robert Vaughn (R)	30,883
39	**Linda T. Sanchez* (D)**	**81,590**
	Larry Andre (R)	42,037
40	**Ed Royce* (R)**	**119,455**
	Christina Avalos (D)	59,400
41	**Jerry Lewis* (R)**	**127,857**
	Pat Meagher (D)	74,394
42	**Gary G. Miller* (R)**	**127,161**
	Michael Williamson (D)	65,122
	Mark Lambert (LB)	12,115
43	**Joe Baca* (D)**	**70,026**
	Scott Folkens (R)	36,890
44	**Ken Calvert* (R)**	**107,482**
	Bill Hedrick (D)	85,784
45	**Mary Bono Mack* (R)**	**106,472**
	Steve Pougnet (D)	87,141
	Bill Lussenheide (Amer. Ind.)	13,188
46	**Dana Rohrabacher* (R)**	**139,822**
	Ken Arnold (D)	84,940
47	**Loretta Sanchez* (D)**	**50,832**
	Van Tran (R)	37,679
48	**John Campbell* (R)**	**145,481**
	Beth Krom (D)	88,465
49	**Darrell Issa* (R)**	**119,088**
	Howard Katz (D)	59,714
50	**Brian Bilbray* (R)**	**142,247**
	Francine Busby (D)	97,818
51	**Bob Filner* (D)**	**86,423**
	Nick Popaditch (R)	57,488
52	**Duncan D. Hunter Jr.* (R)**	**139,460**
	Ray Lutz (D)	70,870
	Michael Benoit (LB)	10,732
53	**Susan A. Davis* (D)**	**104,800**
	Michael Crimmins (R)	57,230
Colorado		
1	**Diana L. DeGette* (D)**	**140,073**
	Mike Fallon (R)	59,747
2	**Jared Polis* (D)**	**148,720**
	Stephen Bailey (R)	98,171
3	**Scott Tipton (R)**	**129,257**
	John Salazar* (D)	118,048
4	**Cory Gardner (R)**	**138,634**
	Betsy Markey* (D)	109,249
	Doug Aden (Amer. Const.)	12,312
5	**Doug Lamborn* (R)**	**152,829**
	Kevin Bradley (D)	68,039
6	**Mike Coffman* (R)**	**217,368**
	John Flerlage (D)	104,104
7	**Ed Perlmutter* (D)**	**112,667**
	Ryan Frazier (R)	88,026
	Buck Bailey (LB)	10,117

Dist.	Representative/candidate (party)	2010 election results
Connecticut		
1	**John B. Larson* (D)**	**138,440**
	Ann Brickley (R)	84,076
2	**Joe Courtney* (D)**	**147,748**
	Janet Peckinpaugh (R)	95,671
3	**Rosa L. DeLauro* (D)**	**143,565**
	Jerry Labriola (R)	74,107
4	**Jim Himes* (D)**	**115,351**
	Dan Debicella (R)	102,030
5	**Chris Murphy* (D)**	**122,879**
	Sam Caligiuri (R)	104,402
Delaware		
	John Carney (D)	**173,543**
	Glen Urquhart (R)	125,442
Florida		
1	**Jeff Miller* (R)**	**170,821**
	Joe Cantrell (Unaff.)	23,250
	John Krause (Unaff.)	18,253
2	**Steve Southerland (R)**	**136,371**
	Allen Boyd Jr.* (D)	105,211
3	**Corrine Brown* (D)**	**94,744**
	Michael Yost (R)	50,932
4	**Ander Crenshaw* (R)**	**178,238**
	Troy Stanley (Unaff.)	52,540
5	**Richard Nugent (R)**	**208,815**
	Jim Piccillo (D)	100,858
6	**Clifford "Cliff" Stearns* (R)**	**179,349**
	Steve E. Schonberg (Unaff.)	71,632
7	**John L. Mica* (R)**	**185,470**
	Heather Beaven (D)	83,206
8	**Daniel Webster (R)**	**123,586**
	Alan Grayson* (D)	84,167
9	**Gus Bilirakis* (R)**	**165,433**
	Anita de Palma (D)	66,158
10	**C.W. Bill Young* (R)**	**137,943**
	Charlie Justice (D)	71,313
11	**Kathy Castor* (D)**	**91,328**
	Mike Prendergast (R)	61,817
12	**Dennis Ross (R)**	**102,704**
	Lori Edwards (D)	87,769
	Randy Wilkinson (Tea Party)	22,857
13	**Vern Buchanan* (R)**	**183,811**
	James Golden (D)	83,123
14	**Connie Mack* (R)**	**188,341**
	James Roach (D)	74,525
	William Maverick St. Claire (Unaff.)	11,825
15	**Bill Posey* (R)**	**157,079**
	Shannon Roberts (D)	85,595
16	**Tom Rooney* (R)**	**162,285**
	Jim Horn (D)	80,327
17	**Frederica Wilson (D)**	**106,361**
	Roderick Vereen (Unaff.)	17,009
18	**Ileana Ros-Lehtinen* (R)**	**102,360**
	Rolando Banciella (D)	46,235
19	**Ted Deutch* (D)**	**132,098**
	Joe Budd (R)	78,733
20	**Debbie Wasserman Schultz* (D)**	**100,787**
	Karen Harrington (R)	63,845
21	**Mario Diaz-Balart (R)**	**Unopposed**
22	**Allen West (R)**	**118,890**
	Ron Klein* (D)	99,804
23	**Alcee Hastings* (D)**	**100,066**
	Bernard Sansaricq (R)	26,414
24	**Sandra Adams (R)**	**146,129**
	Suzanne Kosmas* (D)	98,787
25	**David Rivera (R)**	**74,859**
	Joe Garcia (D)	61,138
Georgia		
1	**Jack Kingston* (R)**	**117,270**
	Oscar L. Harris II (D)	46,449
2	**Sanford Bishop* (D)**	**86,520**
	Mike Keown (R)	81,673
3	**Lynn Westmoreland* (R)**	**168,304**
	Frank Saunders (D)	73,932
4	**Henry "Hank" Johnson* (D)**	**131,760**
	Lisbeth "Liz" Carter (R)	44,707
5	**John Lewis* (D)**	**130,782**
	Fenn Little (R)	46,622
6	**Tom Price* (R)**	**Unopposed**
7	**Rob Woodall (R)**	**160,898**
	Doug Heckman (D)	78,996

Dist.	Representative/candidate (party)	2010 election results
8	**Austin Scott (R)**	**102,770**
	Jim Marshall* (D)	92,250
9	**Tom Graves* (R)**	**Unopposed**
10	**Paul Broun* (R)**	**138,062**
	Russell Edwards (D)	66,905
11	**Phil Gingrey* (R)**	**Unopposed**
12	**John Barrow* (D)**	**92,459**
	Ray McKinney (R)	70,938
13	**David Scott* (D)**	**140,294**
	Mike Crane (R)	61,771
Hawaii		
1	**Colleen Hanabusa (D)**	**94,140**
	Charles Djou* (R)	82,723
2	**Mazie Hirono* (D)**	**132,290**
	John W. Willoughby (R)	46,404
Idaho		
1	**Raul Labrador (R)**	**126,231**
	Walt Minnick* (D)	102,135
	Dave Olson (I)	14,365
2	**Mike Simpson* (R)**	**137,468**
	Mike Crawford (D)	48,749
	Brian Schad (I)	13,500
Illinois		
1	**Bobby L. Rush* (D)**	**148,170**
	Ray Wardingley (R)	29,253
2	**Jesse Jackson Jr.* (D)**	**150,666**
	Isaac Hayes (R)	25,883
	Anthony Williams (Green)	10,564
3	**Daniel Lipinski* (D)**	**116,120**
	Michael Bendas (R)	40,479
	Laurel Lambert Schmidt (Green)	10,028
4	**Luis Gutierrez* (D)**	**63,273**
	Israel Vasquez (R)	11,711
5	**Mike Quigley* (D)**	**108,360**
	David Ratowitz (R)	38,935
6	**Peter J. Roskam* (R)**	**114,456**
	Benjamin Lowe (D)	65,379
7	**Danny Davis* (D)**	**149,846**
	Mark Weiman (R)	29,575
8	**Joe Walsh (R)**	**98,115**
	Melissa Bean* (D)	97,825
9	**Janice D. Schakowsky* (D)**	**117,553**
	Joel Pollak (R)	55,182
10	**Robert Dold (R)**	**109,941**
	Daniel Seals (D)	105,290
11	**Adam Kinzinger (R)**	**129,108**
	Debbie Halvorson* (D)	96,019
12	**Jerry Costello* (D)**	**121,272**
	Teri Newman (R)	74,046
13	**Judy Biggert* (R)**	**152,132**
	Scott Harper (D)	86,281
14	**Randy Hultgren (R)**	**112,369**
	Bill Foster* (D)	98,645
15	**Timothy V. Johnson* (R)**	**136,915**
	David Gill (D)	75,948
16	**Donald Manzullo* (R)**	**138,299**
	George Gaulrapp (D)	66,037
17	**Bobby Schilling (R)**	**104,583**
	Phil Hare* (D)	85,454
18	**Aaron Schock* (R)**	**152,868**
	Deirdre Hirner (D)	57,046
	Sheldon Schafer (Green)	11,256
19	**John M. Shimkus* (R)**	**166,166**
	Tim Bagwell (D)	67,132
Indiana		
1	**Peter J. Visclosky* (D)**	**99,387**
	Mark Leyva (R)	65,558
2	**Joe Donnelly* (D)**	**91,341**
	Jackie Walorski (R)	88,803
3	**Marlin Stutzman (R)**	**116,140**
	Thomas Hayhurst (D)	61,267
4	**Todd Rokita (R)**	**138,732**
	David Sanders (D)	53,167
	John Duncan (LB)	10,423
5	**Dan Burton* (R)**	**146,899**
	Tim Crawford (D)	60,024
	Chard Reid (LB)	18,266
	Jesse Trueblood (I)	11,218
6	**Mike Pence* (R)**	**126,027**
	Barry Welsh (D)	56,647
7	**André Carson* (D)**	**86,011**
	Marvin Scott (R)	55,213

Dist.	Representative/candidate (party)	2010 election results
8	Larry D. Bucshon (R)	117,259
	William Trent Van Haaften (D)	76,265
	John Cunningham (LB)	10,240
9	Todd Young (R)	118,040
	Baron Hill* (D)	95,353
	Gregg Knott (LB)	12,070
Iowa		
1	Bruce Braley* (D)	104,428
	Benjamin Lange (R)	100,219
2	David Loebsack* (D)	115,839
	Mariannette Miller-Meeks (R)	104,319
3	Leonard Boswell* (D)	122,147
	Brad Zaun (R)	111,925
4	Tom Latham* (R)	152,588
	Bill Maske (D)	74,300
5	Steve King* (R)	128,363
	Matthew Campbell (D)	63,160
Kansas		
1	Tim Huelskamp (R)	142,281
	Alan Jilka (D)	44,068
2	Lynn Jenkins* (R)	130,034
	Cheryl Hudspeth (D)	66,588
3	Kevin Yoder (R)	136,246
	Stephene Moore (D)	90,193
4	Mike Pompeo (R)	119,575
	Raj Goyle (D)	74,143
Kentucky		
1	Ed Whitfield* (R)	153,840
	Charles Hatchett (D)	62,090
2	Brett Guthrie* (R)	155,906
	Ed Marksberry (D)	73,749
3	John Yarmuth* (D)	139,940
	Todd Lally (R)	112,627
4	Geoff Davis* (R)	151,813
	John Waltz (D)	66,694
5	Harold "Hal" Rogers* (R)	151,019
	Jim Holbert (D)	44,034
6	Ben Chandler* (D)	119,812
	Andy Barr (R)	119,164
Louisiana		
1	Steve Scalise* (R)	157,182
	Myron Katz (D)	38,416
2	Cedric Richmond (D)	83,705
	Joseph Cao* (R)	43,378
3	Jeff Landry (R)	108,963
	Ravi Sangisetty (D)	61,914
4	John Fleming* (R)	105,223
	David Melville (D)	54,609
5	Rodney Alexander* (R)	122,033
	Tom Gibbs (Unaff.)	33,279
6	Bill Cassidy* (R)	138,607
	Merritt McDonald (D)	72,577
7	Charles Boustany* (R)	Unopposed
Maine		
1	Chellie Pingree* (D)	169,114
	Dean Scontras (R)	128,501
2	Mike Michaud* (D)	147,042
	Jason Levesque (R)	119,669
Maryland		
1	Andy Harris (R)	155,118
	Frank Kratovil* (D)	120,440
	Richard Davis (LB)	10,876
2	C. A. Dutch Ruppersberger* (D)	134,133
	Marcelo Cardarelli (R)	69,523
3	John P. Sarbanes* (D)	147,448
	Jim Wilhelm (R)	86,947
4	Donna Edwards* (D)	160,228
	Robert Broadus (R)	31,467
5	Steny Hoyer* (D)	155,110
	Charles Lollar (R)	83,575
6	Roscoe Bartlett* (R)	148,820
	Andrew Duck (D)	80,455
7	Elijah Cummings* (D)	152,669
	Frank Mirabile (R)	46,375
8	Chris Van Hollen* (D)	153,613
	Michael Philips (R)	52,421
Massachusetts		
1	John W. Olver* (D)	128,011
	Bill Gunn (R)	74,418
	Michael Engel (I)	10,880
2	Richard E. Neal* (D)	122,751
	Tom Wesley (R)	91,209

Dist.	Representative/candidate (party)	2010 election results
3	James P. McGovern* (D)	122,708
	Marty Lamb (R)	85,124
4	Barney Frank* (D)	126,194
	Sean Bielat (R)	101,517
5	Niki Tsongas* (D)	122,858
	Jon Golnik (R)	94,646
6	John Tierney* (D)	142,732
	Bill Hudak (R)	107,930
7	Edward Markey* (D)	145,696
	Gerry Dembrowski (R)	73,467
8	Michael Capuano* (D)	Unopposed
9	Stephen Lynch* (D)	157,071
	Vernon Harrison (R)	59,965
	Phil Dunkelbarger (I)	12,572
10	Bill Keating (D)	132,743
	Jeff Perry (R)	120,029
	Maryanne Lewis (I)	16,705
	Jim Sheets (I)	10,445
Michigan		
1	Dan Benishek (R)	120,523
	Gary McDowell (D)	94,824
2	Bill Huizenga (R)	148,864
	Fred Johnson (D)	72,118
3	Justin Amash (R)	133,714
	Pat Miles (D)	83,953
4	Dave Camp* (R)	148,531
	Jerry Campbell (D)	68,458
5	Dale E. Kildee* (D)	107,286
	John Kupiec (R)	89,680
6	Fred Upton* (R)	123,142
	Don Cooney (D)	66,729
7	Tim Walberg (R)	113,185
	Mark Schauer* (D)	102,402
8	Mike Rogers* (R)	156,931
	Lance Enderle (D)	84,069
9	Gary Peters* (D)	125,730
	Rocky Raczkowski (R)	119,325
10	Candice Miller* (R)	168,364
	Henry Yanez (D)	58,530
11	Thaddeus McCotter* (R)	141,224
	Natalie Mosher (D)	91,710
12	Sander Levin* (D)	124,671
	Don Volaric (R)	71,372
13	Hansen Clarke (D)	100,885
	John Hauler (R)	23,462
14	John Conyers* (D)	115,511
	Don Ukrainec (R)	29,902
15	John Dingell* (D)	118,336
	Rob Steele (R)	83,488
Minnesota		
1	Tim Walz* (DFL)	122,365
	Randy Demmer (R)	109,242
	Steven Wilson (IP)	13,242
2	John Kline* (R)	181,341
	Shelley Madore (DFL)	104,809
3	Erik Paulsen* (R)	161,177
	Jim Meffert (DFL)	100,240
	Jon Oleson (IP)	12,508
4	Betty McCollum* (DFL)	136,746
	Teresa Collett (R)	80,141
	Steve Carlson (IP)	14,207
5	Keith Ellison* (DFL)	154,833
	Joel Demos (R)	55,222
6	Michele Bachmann* (R)	159,476
	Tarryl Clark (DFL)	120,846
	Bob Anderson* (R)	17,698
7	Collin C. Peterson* (D)	133,096
	Lee Byberg (R)	90,652
8	Chip Cravaack (R)	133,490
	James L. Oberstar* (D)	129,091
	Timothy Olson (IP)	11,876
Mississippi		
1	Alan Nunnelee (R)	121,074
	Travis Childers* (D)	89,388
2	Bennie Thompson* (D)	105,327
	Bill Marcy (R)	64,499
3	Gregg Harper* (R)	132,393
	Joel Gill (D)	60,737
4	Steven Palazzo (R)	105,613
	Gene Taylor* (D)	95,243
Missouri		
1	William "Lacy" Clay* (D)	135,907
	Robyn Hamlin (R)	43,649

Dist.	Representative/candidate (party)	2010 election results
2	**Todd Akin* (R)**	**180,481**
	Arthur Lieber (D)	77,467
3	**Russ Carnahan* (D)**	**99,398**
	Ed Martin (R)	94,757
4	**Vicky Hartzler (R)**	**113,489**
	Ike Skelton* (D)	101,532
5	**Emanuel Cleaver* (D)**	**102,076**
	Jacob Turk (R)	84,578
6	**Sam Graves* (R)**	**154,103**
	Clint Hylton (D)	67,762
7	**Billy Long (R)**	**141,010**
	Scott Eckersley (D)	67,545
	Kevin Craig (LB)	13,866
8	**Jo Ann Emerson* (R)**	**128,499**
	Tommy Sowers (D)	56,377
9	**Blaine Luetkemeyer* (R)**	**162,724**
	Christopher Dwyer (LB)	46,817

Montana

	Denny Rehberg* (R)	**217,696**
	Dennis McDonald (D)	121,954
	Mike Fellows (LB)	20,691

Nebraska

Dist.		
1	**Jeff Fortenberry* (R)**	**116,871**
	Ivy Harper (D)	47,106
2	**Lee Terry* (R)**	**93,840**
	Tom White (D)	60,486
3	**Adrian Smith* (R)**	**117,275**
	Rebekah Davis (D)	29,932
	Dan Hill (other)	20,036

Nevada

Dist.		
1	**Shelley Berkley* (D)**	**103,246**
	Kenneth Wegner (R)	58,995
2	**Mark Amodei (R)[2]**	**74,976**
	Kate Marshall (D)	46,669
3	**Joe Heck (R)**	**128,916**
	Dina Titus* (D)	127,168

New Hampshire

Dist.		
1	**Frank Guinta (R)**	**121,655**
	Carol Shea-Porter* (D)	95,503
2	**Charlie Bass (R)**	**108,610**
	Ann Kuster (D)	105,060

New Jersey

Dist.		
1	**Robert Andrews* (D)**	**106,334**
	Dale Glading (R)	58,562
2	**Frank A. LoBiondo* (R)**	**109,460**
	Gary Stein (D)	51,690
3	**Jon Runyan (R)**	**110,215**
	John Adler* (D)	104,252
4	**Chris Smith* (R)**	**129,752**
	Howard Kleinhendler (D)	52,118
5	**Scott Garrett* (R)**	**124,030**
	Tod Theise (D)	62,634
6	**Frank Pallone* (D)**	**81,933**
	Anna Little (R)	65,413
7	**Leonard Lance* (R)**	**105,084**
	Ed Potosnak (D)	71,902
8	**Bill Pascrell* (D)**	**88,478**
	Roland Straten (R)	51,023
9	**Steve Rothman* (D)**	**83,564**
	Michael Agosta (R)	52,082
10	**Donald M. Payne* (D)**	**95,299**
	Michael Alonso (R)	14,357
11	**Rodney Frelinghuysen* (R)**	**122,149**
	Douglas Herbert (D)	55,472
12	**Rush Holt* (D)**	**108,214**
	Scott Sipprelle (R)	93,634
13	**Albio Sires* (D)**	**62,840**
	Henrietta Dwyer (R)	19,538

New Mexico

Dist.		
1	**Martin Heinrich* (D)**	**112,010**
	Jonathan Barela (R)	104,215
2	**Steve Pearce (R)**	**94,053**
	Harry Teague* (D)	75,708
3	**Ben R. Lujan* (D)**	**120,048**
	Tom Mullins (R)	90,617

New York

Dist.		
1	**Timothy Bishop* (D)**	**98,316**
	Randy Altschuler (R)	97,723
2	**Steve Israel* (D)**	**94,594**
	John Gomez (R)	72,029
3	**Peter King* (R)**	**131,674**
	Howard Kudler (D)	51,346
4	**Carolyn McCarthy* (D)**	**94,483**
	Francis Becker (R)	81,718
5	**Gary Ackerman* (D)**	**72,239**
	James Milano (R)	41,493

Dist.	Representative/candidate (party)	2010 election results
6	**Gregory W. Meeks* (D)**	**85,096**
	Asher Taub (R)	11,826
7	**Joseph Crowley* (D)**	**71,247**
	Ken Reynolds (R)	16,145
8	**Jerrold Nadler* (D)**	**98,839**
	Susan Kone (R)	31,996
9	**Bob Turner (R)[3]**	**33,816**
	David Weprin (D)	29,688
10	**Edolphus Towns* (D)**	**95,485**
11	**Yvette D. Clarke* (D)**	**104,297**
	Hugh Carr (R)	10,858
12	**Nydia M. Velázquez* (D)**	**68,624**
13	**Mike Grimm (R)**	**65,024**
	Michael McMahon* (D)	60,773
14	**Carolyn Maloney* (D)**	**107,327**
	Ryan Brumberg (R)	32,065
15	**Charles Rangel* (D)**	**91,225**
	Michel Faulkner (R)	11,754
16	**José E. Serrano* (D)**	**61,642**
17	**Eliot Engel* (D)**	**95,346**
	Anthony Mele (R)	29,792
18	**Nita Lowey* (D)**	**115,619**
	Jim Russell (R)	70,413
19	**Nan Hayworth (R)**	**109,956**
	John Hall* (D)	98,766
20	**Christopher Gibson (R)**	**130,178**
	Scott Murphy* (D)	107,075
21	**Paul Tonko* (D)**	**124,889**
	Theodore Danz (R)	85,752
22	**Maurice Hinchey* (D)**	**98,661**
	George Phillips (R)	88,687
23	**Bill Owens* (D)**	**82,232**
	Matthew Doheny (R)	80,237
24	**Richard Hanna (R)**	**101,599**
	Michael Arcuri* (D)	89,809
25	**Ann Marie Buerkle (R)**	**104,602**
	Daniel Maffei* (D)	103,954
26	**Kathy Hochul (D)[4]**	**52,713**
	Jane L. Corwin (R)	47,187
	Jack Davis (Tea Party)	10,029
27	**Brian Higgins* (D)**	**119,085**
	Leonard Roberto (R)	76,320
28	**Louise M. Slaughter* (D)**	**102,514**
	Jill Rowland (R)	55,392
29	**Thomas Reed (R)**	**112,314**
	Matthew Zeller (D)	86,099

North Carolina

Dist.		
1	**G. K. Butterfield* (D)**	**103,294**
	Ashley Woolard (R)	70,867
2	**Renee Ellmers (R)**	**93,876**
	Bob Etheridge* (D)	92,393
3	**Walter Jones* (R)**	**143,225**
	Johnny Rouse (D)	51,317
4	**David Price* (D)**	**155,384**
	William Lawson (R)	116,448
5	**Virginia Foxx* (R)**	**140,525**
	Billy Kennedy (D)	72,762
6	**Howard Coble* (R)**	**156,252**
	Sam Turner (D)	51,507
7	**Mike McIntyre* (D)**	**113,967**
	Ilario Pantano (R)	98,328
8	**Larry Kissell* (D)**	**88,776**
	Harold Johnson (R)	73,129
9	**Sue Myrick* (R)**	**158,790**
	Jeff Doctor (D)	71,450
10	**Patrick McHenry* (R)**	**130,813**
	Jeff Gregory (D)	52,972
11	**Heath Shuler* (D)**	**131,225**
	Jeff Miller (R)	110,246
12	**Mel Watt* (D)**	**103,495**
	Greg Dority (R)	55,315
13	**Brad Miller* (D)**	**116,103**
	William Randall (R)	93,099

North Dakota

	Rick Berg (R)	**129,802**
	Earl Pomeroy* (D)	106,542

Ohio

Dist.		
1	**Steve Chabot (R)**	**103,770**
	Steve Driehaus* (D)	92,672
2	**Jean Schmidt* (R)**	**139,027**
	Surya Yalamanchili (D)	82,431
	Marc Johnston (LB)	16,259
3	**Mike Turner* (R)**	**152,629**
	Joe Roberts (D)	71,455

Dist.	Representative/candidate (party)	2010 election results
4	**Jim Jordan* (R)**	**146,029**
	Doug Litt (D)	50,533
5	**Bob Latta* (R)**	**140,703**
	Caleb Finkenbiner (D)	54,919
	Brian Smith (LB)	11,831
6	**Bill Johnson (R)**	**103,170**
	Charlie Wilson Jr.* (D)	92,823
7	**Steve Austria* (R)**	**135,721**
	Bill Conner (D)	70,400
8	**John Boehner* (R)**	**142,731**
	Justin Coussoule (D)	65,883
9	**Marcy Kaptur* (D)**	**121,819**
	Rich Iott (R)	83,423
10	**Dennis Kucinich* (D)**	**101,343**
	Peter Corrigan (R)	83,809
11	**Marcia Fudge* (D)**	**139,693**
	Thomas Pekarek (R)	28,754
12	**Pat Tiberi* (R)**	**150,163**
	Paula Brooks (D)	110,307
13	**Betty Sutton* (D)**	**118,806**
	Tom Ganley (R)	94,367
14	**Steven LaTourette* (R)**	**149,878**
	Bill O'Neill (D)	72,604
15	**Steve Stivers (R)**	**119,471**
	Mary Jo Kilroy* (D)	91,077
16	**Jim Renacci (R)**	**114,652**
	John Boccieri* (D)	90,833
	Jeffrey Blevins (LB)	14,585
17	**Timothy Ryan* (D)**	**102,758**
	Jim Graham (R)	57,352
	James Traficant (I)	30,556
18	**Bob Gibbs (R)**	**107,426**
	Zack Space* (D)	80,756
	Lindsey Sutton (CP)	11,246
Oklahoma		
1	**John Sullivan* (R)**	**151,173**
	Angelia O'Dell (I)	45,656
2	**Dan Boren* (D)**	**108,203**
	Charles Thompson (R)	83,226
3	**Frank D. Lucas* (R)**	**161,927**
	Frankie Robbins (D)	45,689
4	**Tom Cole* (R)**	**Unopposed**
5	**James Lankford (R)**	**123,236**
	Billy Coyle (D)	68,074
Oregon		
1	**David Wu* (D)**[5]	**160,357**
	Rob Cornilles (R)	122,858
2	**Greg Walden* (R)**	**206,245**
	Joyce Segers (D)	72,173
3	**Earl Blumenauer* (D)**	**193,104**
	Delia Lopez (R)	67,714
4	**Peter DeFazio* (D)**	**162,416**
	Art Robinson (R)	129,877
5	**Kurt Schrader* (D)**	**145,319**
	Scott Bruun (R)	130,313
Pennsylvania		
1	**Robert A. Brady* (D)**	**Unopposed**
2	**Chaka Fattah* (D)**	**182,800**
	Rick Hellberg (R)	21,907
3	**Mike Kelly (R)**	**111,909**
	Kathy Dahlkemper* (D)	88,924
4	**Jason Altmire* (D)**	**120,827**
	Keith Rothfus (R)	116,958
5	**Glenn Thompson* (R)**	**127,427**
	Michael Pipe (D)	52,375
6	**Jim Gerlach* (R)**	**133,770**
	Manan Trivedi (D)	100,493
7	**Patrick Meehan (R)**	**137,825**
	Bryan Lentz (D)	110,314
8	**Michael G. Fitzpatrick (R)**	**130,759**
	Patrick Murphy* (D)	113,547
9	**Bill Shuster* (R)**	**141,904**
	Tom Conners (D)	52,322
10	**Thomas A. Marino (R)**	**110,599**
	Christopher Carney* (D)	89,846
11	**Lou Barletta (R)**	**102,179**
	Paul Kanjorski* (D)	84,618
12	**Mark Critz* (D)**	**94,056**
	Tim Burns (R)	91,170
13	**Allyson Schwartz* (D)**	**118,710**
	Dee Adcock (R)	91,987
14	**Mike Doyle* (D)**	**122,073**
	Melissa Haluszczak (R)	49,997
15	**Charles Dent* (R)**	**109,534**
	John B. Callahan (D)	79,766
	Jake Towne (other)	15,248

Dist.	Representative/candidate (party)	2010 election results
16	**Joseph Pitts* (R)**	**134,113**
	Lois Herr (D)	70,994
17	**Tim Holden* (D)**	**118,486**
	Dave Argall (R)	95,000
18	**Tim Murphy* (R)**	**161,888**
	Dan Connolly (D)	78,558
19	**Todd Platts* (R)**	**165,219**
	Ryan Sanders (D)	53,549
	Joshua Monighan (I)	10,988
Rhode Island		
1	**David Cicilline (D)**	**81,269**
	John Loughlin (R)	71,542
2	**Jim Langevin* (D)**	**104,442**
	Mark Zaccaria (R)	55,409
	John Matson (I)	14,584
South Carolina		
1	**Tim Scott (R)**	**152,755**
	Ben Frasier (D)	67,008
2	**Joe Wilson* (R)**	**138,861**
	Rob Miller (D)	113,625
3	**Jeff Duncan (R)**	**126,235**
	Jane Dyer (D)	73,095
4	**Trey Gowdy (R)**	**137,586**
	Paul Corden (D)	62,438
	Dave Edwards (CP)	11,059
5	**Mick Mulvaney (R)**	**125,834**
	John Spratt* (D)	102,296
6	**Jim Clyburn* (D)**	**125,459**
	Jim Pratt (R)	72,661
South Dakota		
	Kristi Noem (R)	**153,703**
	Stephanie Herseth Sandlin* (D)	146,589
	Thomas Marking (I)	19,134
Tennessee		
1	**Phil Roe* (R)**	**123,006**
	Michael Clark (D)	26,045
2	**John Duncan* (R)**	**141,796**
	David Hancock (D)	25,400
3	**Chuck Fleischmann (R)**	**92,032**
	John Wolfe (D)	45,387
	Savas Kyriakidis (I)	17,077
4	**Scott DesJarlais (R)**	**103,969**
	Lincoln Davis* (D)	70,254
5	**Jim Cooper* (D)**	**99,162**
	David Hall (R)	74,204
6	**Diane Black (R)**	**128,517**
	Brett Carter (D)	56,145
7	**Marsha Blackburn* (R)**	**158,916**
	Greg Rabidoux (D)	54,347
8	**Stephen Fincher (R)**	**98,759**
	Roy Herron (D)	64,960
9	**Steve Cohen* (D)**	**99,827**
	Charlotte Bergmann (R)	33,879
Texas		
1	**Louie Gohmert* (R)**	**129,398**
	Charles Parkes (LB)	14,811
2	**Ted Poe* (R)**	**130,020**
	David Smith (LB)	16,711
3	**Sam Johnson* (R)**	**101,180**
	John Lingenfelder (D)	47,848
4	**Ralph Hall* (R)**	**136,338**
	VaLinda Hathcox (D)	40,975
5	**Jeb Hensarling* (R)**	**106,742**
	Tom Berry (D)	41,649
6	**Joe Barton* (R)**	**107,140**
	David Cozad (D)	50,717
7	**John Culberson* (R)**	**143,655**
	Bob Townsend (LB)	31,704
8	**Kevin Brady* (R)**	**161,417**
	Kent Hargett (D)	34,694
9	**Al Green* (D)**	**80,107**
	Steve Mueller (R)	24,201
10	**Michael McCaul* (R)**	**144,980**
	Ted Ankrum (D)	74,086
11	**Mike Conaway* (R)**	**125,581**
	James Quillian (D)	23,989
12	**Kay Granger* (R)**	**109,882**
	Tracey Smith (D)	38,434
13	**Mac Thornberry* (R)**	**113,201**
	Keith Dyer (I)	11,192
14	**Ron Paul* (R)**	**140,623**
	Robert Pruett (D)	44,431
15	**Rubén Hinojosa* (D)**	**53,546**
	Eddie Zamora (R)	39,964
16	**Silvestre Reyes* (D)**	**49,301**
	Tim Besco (R)	31,051

Dist.	Representative/candidate (party)	2010 election results
17	Bill Flores (R)	106,696
	Chet Edwards* (D)	63,138
18	Sheila Jackson Lee* (D)	85,108
	John Faulk (R)	33,067
19	Randy Neugebauer* (R)	106,059
	Andy Wilson (D)	25,984
20	Charlie Gonzalez* (D)	58,645
	Clayton Trotter (R)	31,757
21	Lamar Smith* (R)	162,924
	Lainey Melnick (D)	65,927
22	Pete Olson* (R)	140,537
	Kesha Rogers (D)	62,082
23	Quico Canseco (R)	74,853
	Ciro Rodriguez* (D)	67,348
24	Kenny Marchant* (R)	100,078
	David Sparks (D)	22,609
25	Lloyd Doggett* (D)	99,967
	Donna Campbell (R)	84,849
26	Michael C. Burgess* (R)	120,984
	Neil Durrance (D)	55,385
27	Blake Farenthold (R)	50,976
	Solomon Ortiz* (D)	50,179
28	Henry Cuellar* (D)	62,773
	Bryan Underwood (R)	46,740
29	Gene Green* (D)	43,257
	Roy Morales (R)	22,825
30	Eddie Bernice Johnson* (D)	86,322
	Stephen Broden (R)	24,668
31	John Carter* (R)	126,384
	Bill Oliver (LB)	26,735
32	Pete Sessions* (R)	79,433
	Grier Raggio (D)	44,258
Utah		
1	Rob Bishop* (R)	135,247
	Morgan Bowen (D)	46,765
2	Jim Matheson* (D)	127,151
	Morgan Philpot (D)	116,001
3	Jason Chaffetz* (R)	139,721
	Karen Hyer (D)	44,320
Vermont		
	Peter Welch* (D)	154,006
	Paul Beaudry (R)	76,403
Virginia		
1	Robert Wittman* (R)	135,564
	Krystal Ball (D)	73,824
2	Scott Rigell (R)	88,340
	Glenn Nye* (D)	70,591
3	Bobby Scott* (D)	114,754
	Chuck Smith (R)	44,553
4	Randy Forbes* (R)	123,659
	Wynne LeGrow (D)	74,298
5	Robert Hurt (R)	119,560
	Tom Perriello* (D)	110,562
6	Bob Goodlatte* (R)	127,487
	Jeffrey Vanke (I)	21,649
	Stuart Bain (LB)	15,309

Dist.	Representative/candidate (party)	2010 election results
7	Eric Cantor* (R)	138,209
	Rick Waugh (D)	79,616
	Floyd Bayne (Independent Green)	15,164
8	Jim Moran* (D)	116,404
	Patrick Murray (R)	71,145
9	H. Morgan Griffith (R)	95,726
	Rick Boucher* (D)	86,743
10	Frank Wolf* (R)	131,116
	Jeff Barnett (D)	72,604
11	Gerry Connolly* (D)	111,720
	Keith Fimian (R)	110,739
Washington		
1	Jay Inslee* (D)	172,642
	James Watkins (R)	126,737
2	Rick Larsen* (D)	155,241
	John Koster (R)	148,722
3	Jaime Herrera (R)	152,799
	Denny Heck (D)	135,654
4	Doc Hastings* (R)	156,726
	Jay Clough (D)	74,973
5	Cathy McMorris Rodgers* (R)	177,235
	Daryl Romeyn (D)	101,146
6	Norm Dicks* (D)	151,873
	Doug Cloud (R)	109,800
7	Jim McDermott* (D)	232,649
	Bob Jeffers-Schroder (I)	47,741
8	Dave Reichert* (R)	161,296
	Suzan DelBene (D)	148,581
9	Adam Smith* (D)	123,743
	Dick Muri (R)	101,851
West Virginia		
1	David McKinley (R)	90,660
	Mike Oliverio (D)	89,220
2	Shelley Moore Capito* (R)	126,814
	Virginia Lynch Graf (D)	55,001
3	Nick Rahall* (D)	83,636
	Elliott Maynard (R)	65,611
Wisconsin		
1	Paul Ryan* (R)	179,819
	John Heckenlively (D)	79,363
2	Tammy Baldwin* (D)	191,164
	Chad Lee (R)	118,099
3	Ron Kind* (D)	126,380
	Dan Kapanke (R)	116,838
4	Gwen Moore* (D)	143,559
	Dan Sebring (R)	61,543
5	Jim Sensenbrenner* (R)	229,642
	Todd Kolosso (D)	90,634
	Robert Raymond (I)	10,813
6	Tom Petri* (R)	183,271
	Joseph Kallas (D)	75,926
7	Sean Duffy (R)	132,551
	Julie Lassa (D)	113,018
8	Reid Ribble (R)	143,998
	Steven Kagen* (D)	118,646
Wyoming		
	Cynthia Lummis* (R)	131,661
	David Wendt (D)	45,768

(1) Jane Harman (D) resigned Feb. 28, 2011. Hahn won a special election July 12, 2011, and was sworn in July 19, 2011. (2) Dean Heller (D) resigned May 9, 2011. Amodei won a special election Sept. 13, 2011, and was sworn in Sept. 15, 2011. (3) Anthony Weiner (D) resigned June 21, 2011. Turner won a special election Sept. 13, 2011, and was sworn in Sept. 15, 2011. (4) Christopher Lee (R) resigned Feb. 9, 2011. Hochul (D) won a special election May 24, 2011, and was sworn in June 1, 2011. (5) Resigned Aug. 3, 2011; a special election was scheduled for Jan. 31, 2012.

Nonvoting Members of Congress

Representative/candidate (party)	2010 election results
American Samoa	
Eni F.H. Faleomavaega* (D)	6,182
Aumua Amata (R)	4,422
District of Columbia	
Eleanor Holmes Norton* (D)	117,990
Missy Reilly Smith (R)	8,109
Guam	
Madeleine Z. Bordallo* (D)	Unopposed
Northern Mariana Islands	
Gregorio Kilili Camacho Sablan (D)	4,852
Joseph James Norita Camacho (Covenant)	2,744
Juan Nekai Babauta (D)	2,049
Jesse Camacho Borja (D)	1,707

Representative/candidate (party)	2010 election results
Puerto Rico—Resident Commissioner (2008 results)[1]	
Pedro Pierluisi (New Progressive Party)	1,010,304
Alfredo Salazar (Popular Dem. Party)	810,111
Carlos A. Velazquez Lopez (Puerto Ricans for Puerto Rico Party)	46,126
Jessica Martinez Birriel (Puerto Rican Independence Party)	37,865
Virgin Islands	
Donna M. Christensen* (D)	19,844
Jeffrey Moorhead (Unaff.)	5,063
Vincent Emile Danet (R)	2,329

(1) The resident commissioner of Puerto Rico is the only member of the U.S. House of Representatives who serves a four-year term.

────STATES AND OTHER AREAS OF THE U.S.────

Sources: Population: Decennial Census Results, U.S. Census Bureau, U.S. Dept. of Commerce. **Area:** Geography Division, U.S. Census Bureau, U.S. Dept. of Commerce. **Acres forested:** U.S. Forest Service, U.S. Dept. of Agriculture. **Chief airports:** Federal Aviation Admin., U.S. Dept. of Transportation. **Chief manuf. goods:** Manufacturing and Construction Division, U.S. Census Bureau, U.S. Dept. of Commerce. **Chief crops** and **Livestock:** Agriculture Dept., Natl. Agricultural Stat. Service, U.S. Dept. of Agriculture. Many states do not disclose broiler or hog/pig stats. **Broadband:** Industry Analysis and Tech. Division, Fed. Communications Commission. **Nonfuel minerals:** Office of Mineral Information, U.S. Dept. of Interior. **Commercial fishing:** Natl. Marine Fisheries Service, U.S. Dept. of Commerce. **Gross state product, Per capita personal income:** Bureau of Economic Analysis, U.S. Dept. of Commerce. **Sales tax:** Fed. of Tax Admin. **Employment distribution** and **Unemployment:** Bureau of Labor Statistics, U.S. Dept. of Labor. **New private housing:** Residential Construction Division, U.S. Census Bureau, U.S. Dept. of Commerce. **Finance:** Federal Deposit Insurance Corp. **Lottery figures** (not all states have a lottery): N.A. Assn. of State and Provincial Lotteries, for local fiscal year. **Federal employees:** Office of Personnel Mgmt, U.S. Dept. of Labor. **Energy:** Energy Information Admin., U.S. Dept. of Energy. Other information from sources in individual states. Some data on Outlying U.S. Areas and Other Islands provided by the CIA World Factbook.

Note: Pop. density is for land area only. Categories under racial distribution may not add up to 100% due to rounding. Hispanic population may be of any race. Source year for acres forested data may vary. Chief airports had 500,000+ boardings in 2010. Broadband internet had minimum speeds of at least 768 Kbps downstream and 200 Kbps upstream as percentage of total Internet connections. Nonfuel mineral values for some states exclude small amounts to avoid disclosing proprietary data. Employment distribution categories are nonfarm only and are not all-inclusive. Commercial bank and savings institution figures are for FDIC-insured institutions only. Notable federal facilities marked with an asterisk (*) have been recommended for realignment or closure by the U.S. Dept. of Defense, scheduled to be completed by Sept. 15, 2011. Electricity prod. excludes independent power producers; negative power generation denotes that electric power consumed for plant use exceeds gross generation. **Famous Persons lists may include nonnatives** associated with the state as well as persons born there. Websites are subject to change and are not endorsed by *The World Almanac*.

Alabama (AL)
Heart of Dixie, Camellia State

People. Population (2010): 4,779,736; rank: 23; net change (2000-10): 7.5%. **Pop. density:** 94.4 per sq mi. **Racial distribution** (2010): 68.5% white; 26.2% black; 1.1% Asian; 0.6% Native Amer./AK; 0.1% Hawaiian/Pacific Islander; 2 or more races, 1.5%. **Hispanic pop.** (any race, 2010): 3.9%.

Geography. Total area: 52,420 sq mi; rank: 30. **Land area:** 50,645 sq mi; rank: 28. **Acres forested:** 22.8 mil. **Location:** East South Central state extending N-S from Tenn. to the Gulf of Mexico; E of the Mississippi River. **Climate:** long, hot summers; mild winters; generally abundant rain. **Topography:** coastal plains, including Prairie Black Belt, give way to hills, broken terrain; highest elevation, 2,407 ft. **Capital:** Montgomery. **Chief airports:** Birmingham, Huntsville.

Economy. Chief industries: chemicals, electronics, apparel, primary metals, lumber and wood products, food processing, fabricated metals, automotive tires, oil and gas exploration. **Chief manuf. goods:** poultry processing, paper & paperboard, iron & steel, petroleum, automotive tires, aerospace, aluminum, auto body & parts. **Chief crops:** cotton, greenhouse & nursery, hay, peanuts, corn, soybeans. **Livestock** (Dec. 2010): 15.96 mil chickens (excl. broilers), 1.03 bil broilers; (Jan. 2011): 1.23 mil cattle/calves. **Broadband internet:** 72.2%. **Nonfuel minerals** (2010 prelim.): $1.0 bil; stone (crushed), cement (portland), lime, salt, sand and gravel (construction). **Commercial fishing** (2009): $40.5 mil. **Chief port:** Mobile. **Gross state product** (2010): $172.6 bil. **Sales tax** (2011): 4.0%. **Employment distrib.** (May 2011): 20.5% govt.; 19.2% trade/trans./util.; 12.6% mfg.; 11.4% ed./health; 11.3% prof./bus. serv.; 9.2% leisure/hosp.; 4.9% finance; 5.4% constr./mining/log.; 1.3% info.; 4.3% other serv. **Unemployment** (2010): 9.5%. **Per cap. pers. income** (2010 prelim.): $33,945. **New private housing** (2010): 11,261 units/$1.5 bil. **Commercial banks** (2010): 159; deposits: $79.2 bil. **Savings institutions** (2010): 14; deposits: $2.8 bil.

Federal govt. Fed. civ. employees (Mar. 2011): 43,055; **avg. salary:** $74,401. **Notable fed. facilities:** Redstone Arsenal; Ft. Rucker; Marshall Space Flight Ctr.; Anniston Army Depot; *Maxwell/Gunter AFB; U.S. Corps of Engineers, Mobile.

Energy. Electricity production (2010 kWh by source): coal: 62.6 bil; gas: 13.3 bil; nuclear: 37.9 bil; petroleum: 98 mil; hydroelectric: 9.1 bil.

State data. Motto: Audemus Jura Nostra Defendere (We dare defend our rights). **Flower:** Camellia. **Bird:** Yellowhammer. **Tree:** Southern longleaf pine. **Song:** "Alabama." **Entered union:** Dec. 14, 1819; rank: 22nd. **State fair:** no official state fair; regional and county fairs held in Sept. and Oct.

History. Alabama was inhabited by the Creek, Cherokee, Chickasaw, Alabama, and Choctaw peoples when Spanish explorers arrived in the early 1500s. The French made the first permanent settlement at Ft. Louis, 1702, and founded Mobile, 1711. France later gave up the entire region to England under the Treaty of Paris, 1763. Spanish forces took control of the Mobile Bay area, 1780, and it remained under Spanish control until seized by U.S. troops, 1813. Most of present-day Alabama was held by the Creeks until Gen. Andrew Jackson broke their power, 1814. When Alabama became a state, 1819, black slaves made up about ⅓ of the population. The Indian Removal Act of 1830 forced most remaining Creeks west. The state seceded, 1861, and the Confederate states were organized Feb. 4, at Montgomery, the first capital. The state was readmitted, 1868. Birmingham, founded 1871, became a center for iron- and steel-making. The Montgomery bus boycott, 1955, sparked by Rosa Parks, helped launch the civil rights movement. Other confrontations occurred at Birmingham, 1963, and Selma, 1965. The leading political figure from the 1960s through the '80s, 4-term gov. George Wallace, started as a segregationist but later won with black support. Growth in the auto industry boosted the state economy as the 21st cent. began. A string of tornadoes in western Alabama in Apr. 2011 killed at least 248.

Tourist attractions. First White House of the Confederacy, Civil Rights Memorial, Alabama Shakespeare Festival, in Montgomery; Ivy Green (Helen Keller's birthplace), Tuscumbia; Civil Rights Museum, statue of Vulcan, in Birmingham; Carver Museum, Tuskegee; W. C. Handy Home, Museum, & Library, Florence; Alabama Space and Rocket Center, Huntsville; Moundville State Monument; Pike Pioneer Museum, Troy; USS *Alabama* Memorial Park, Mobile; Russell Cave Natl. Monument, near Bridgeport: a detailed record of occupancy by humans from about 10,000 BCE to 1650 CE.

Famous Alabamians. Hank Aaron, Tallulah Bankhead, Hugo L. Black, Paul "Bear" Bryant, George Washington Carver, Nat King Cole, William C. Handy, Polly Holliday, Bo Jackson, Helen Keller, Coretta Scott King, Harper Lee, Joe Louis, Willie Mays, John Hunt Morgan, Jim Nabors, Jesse Owens, Condoleezza Rice, George Wallace, Booker T. Washington, Hank Williams.

Tourist information. Alabama Tourism Department, 401 Adams Ave., Ste. 126, P.O. Box 4927, Montgomery, AL 36103; 1-800-ALABAMA, (334) 242-4169; www.alabama.travel

Website. www.alabama.gov

Alaska (AK)
The Last Frontier (unofficial)

People. Population (2010): 710,231; rank: 47; net change (2000-10): 13.3%. **Pop. density:** 1.2 per sq mi. **Racial distribution** (2010): 66.7% white; 3.3% black; 5.4% Asian; 14.8% Native Amer./AK; 1% Hawaiian/Pacific Islander; 2 or more races, 7.3%. **Hispanic pop.** (any race, 2010): 5.5%.

Geography. Total area: 665,384 sq mi; rank: 1. **Land area:** 570,641 sq mi; rank: 1. **Acres forested:** 14.9 mil. **Location:** NW corner of North America, bordered on E by Canada. **Climate:** SE, SW, and central regions, moist and mild; far north extremely dry. Extended summer days, winter nights throughout. **Topography:** includes Pacific and Arctic mountain systems, central plateau, and Arctic slope. Mt. McKinley, 20,320 ft, is the highest point in North America. **Capital:** Juneau. **Chief airport:** Anchorage.

Economy. Chief industries: petroleum, tourism, fishing, mining, forestry, transportation, aerospace. **Chief manuf. goods:** petroleum, seafood. **Chief crops:** greenhouse products, barley, oats, hay, potatoes, carrots. **Livestock** (Jan. 2011): 13,500 cattle/calves. **Broadband internet:** 77.9%.

Nonfuel minerals (2010 prelim.): $3.2 bil; zinc, gold, lead, silver, sand and gravel (construction). **Commercial fishing** (2009): $1,333.5 mil. **Chief ports:** Anchorage, Dutch Harbor, Kodiak, Juneau, Sitka, Valdez. **Gross state product** (2010): $49.1 bil. **Sales tax** (2011): none. **Employment distrib.** (May 2011): 25.5% govt.; 20.1% trade/trans./util.; 2.8% mfg.; 13.2% ed./health; 8.1% prof./bus. serv.; 10.4% leisure/hosp.; 4.5% finance; 10.0% constr./mining/log.; 2.0% info.; 3.6% other serv. **Unemployment** (2010): 8.0%. **Per cap. pers. income** (2010 prelim.): $44,174. **New private housing** (2010): 904 units/$204.7 mil. **Commercial banks** (2010): 6; deposits: $8.5 bil. **Savings institutions** (2010): 2; deposits: $386 mil.

Federal govt. Fed. civ. employees (Mar. 2011): 13,358; **avg. salary:** $68,613. **Notable fed. facilities:** Joint Base Elmendorf-Richardson; Ft. Wainwright; *Eilson AFB; Ft. Greely.

Energy. Electricity production (2010 kWh by source): coal: 189 mil; gas: 3.8 bil; petroleum: 884 mil; hydroelectric: 1.3 bil.; other: 13 mil.

State data. Motto: North to the future. **Flower:** Forget-me-not. **Bird:** Willow ptarmigan. **Tree:** Sitka spruce. **Song:** "Alaska's Flag." **Entered union:** Jan. 3, 1959; rank: 49th. **State fair** at Palmer, late Aug.-early Sept.

History. Early inhabitants included the Tlingit-Haida and Athabascan peoples. Ancestors of the Aleut and Inuit (Eskimo) probably arrived from Siberia between 10,000 and 6,000 years ago. Vitus Bering, a Dane sailing for Russia, was the first European to land in Alaska, 1741. Russians, pursuing the fur trade, established a permanent settlement on Kodiak Island, 1784. Sec. of State William H. Seward bought Alaska from Russia for $7.2 mil in 1867, a deal some called "Seward's Folly." Discovery of gold in the Klondike region of Canada's Yukon Territory, 1896, triggered an Alaskan gold rush. Alaska became a territory, 1912, and a state, 1959. A huge oil find at Prudhoe Bay, 1968, led to construction of the Trans-Alaska Pipeline, 1974-77. The *Exxon Valdez* supertanker ran aground, 1989, spilling about 11 mil gallons of crude oil; the cleanup cost more than $2.2 bil. Repeated attempts by Congress members to allow oil and gas drilling in the Arctic National Wildlife Refuge have failed.

Tourist attractions. Inside Passage; Portage Glacier; Mendenhall Glacier; Ketchikan Totems; Glacier Bay Natl. Park and Preserve; Denali Natl. Park, one of N. America's great wildlife sanctuaries, surrounding Mt. McKinley, N. America's highest peak; Mt. Roberts Tramway, Juneau; Pribilof Islands for seal rookeries; restored St. Michael's Russian Orthodox Cathedral, Sitka; White Pass & Yukon Route railroad; Skagway; Katmai Natl. Park & Preserve.

Famous Alaskans. Tom Bodett, Susan Butcher, Ernest Gruening, Jewel (Kilcher), Gov. Tony Knowles, Sydney Laurence, Sarah Palin, Libby Riddles, Jefferson "Soapy" Smith.

Tourist information. Alaska Travel Industry Association, 2600 Cordova St., Ste. 201, Anchorage, AK 99503; 1-800-327-9372; www.travelalaska.com

Website. www.state.ak.us

Arizona (AZ)
Grand Canyon State

People. Population (2010): 6,392,017; rank: 14; net change (2000-10): 24.6%. **Pop. density:** 56.3 per sq mi. **Racial distribution** (2010): 73% white; 4.1% black; 2.8% Asian; 4.6% Native Amer./AK; 0.2% Hawaiian/Pacific Islander; 2 or more races, 3.4%. **Hispanic pop.** (any race, 2010): 29.6%.

Geography. Total area: 113,990 sq mi; rank: 6. **Land area:** 113,594 sq mi; rank: 6. **Acres forested:** 18.7 mil. **Location:** southwestern U.S. **Climate:** clear and dry in the southern regions and northern plateau; high central areas have heavy winter snows. **Topography:** Colorado plateau in the N, containing the Grand Canyon; Mexican Highlands running diagonally NW to SE; Sonoran Desert in the SW. **Capital:** Phoenix. **Chief airports:** Phoenix, Tucson.

Economy. Chief industries: manufacturing, construction, tourism, mining, agriculture. **Chief manuf. goods:** aerospace, semiconductors, navigational instruments, cement, plastics, structural metals, dairy, printing, furniture. **Chief crops:** cotton, grapes, apples, lettuce, hay, potatoes, sorghum, barley, corn, wheat. **Livestock** (Jan. 2011): 870,000 cattle/calves, 150,000 sheep/lambs. **Broadband internet:** 72.9%. **Nonfuel minerals** (2010 prelim.): $6.7 bil; copper, molybdenum concentrates, sand and gravel (construction), cement (portland), stone (crushed). **Gross state product**

(2010): $253.6 bil. **Sales tax** (2011): 6.6%. **Employment distrib.** (May 2011): 17.5% govt.; 19.6% trade/trans./util.; 6.2% mfg.; 14.9% ed./health; 13.9% prof./bus. serv.; 11.1% leisure/hosp.; 6.7% finance; 5.1% constr./mining/log.; 1.5% info.; 3.6% other serv. **Unemployment** (2010): 10.0%. **Per cap. pers. income** (2010 prelim.): $34,999. **New private housing** (2010): 12,370 units/$2.4 bil. **Commercial banks** (2010): 68; deposits: $79.7 bil. **Savings institutions** (2010): 13; deposits: $6.4 bil. **Lottery** (2010): total sales: $551.5 mil; profit: $141.9 mil.

Federal govt. Fed. civ. employees (Mar. 2011): 42,137; **avg. salary:** $63,750. **Notable fed. facilities:** *Luke AFB, Davis-Monthan AFB; *Ft. Huachuca; Yuma Proving Grounds.

Energy. Electricity production (2010 kWh by source): coal: 43.3 bil; gas: 9.7 bil; nuclear: 31.2 bil; petroleum: 63 mil; hydroelectric: 6.8 bil.; other: 31 mil.

State data. Motto: Ditat Deus (God enriches). **Flower:** Blossom of the saguaro cactus. **Bird:** Cactus wren. **Tree:** Paloverde. **Song:** "Arizona." **Entered union:** Feb. 14, 1912; rank: 48th. **State fair** at Phoenix, Oct.-early Nov.

History. Paleo-Indians hunted large game in the area at least 12,000 years ago. Anasazi, Mogollon, and Hohokam civilizations lived there c. 300 BCE-1300 CE; Navajo and Apache came c. 15th cent. Marcos de Niza, a Franciscan, and Estevanico, a black former slave, explored, 1539; Spanish explorer Francisco Vásquez de Coronado visited, 1540. Eusebio Francisco Kino, a Jesuit missionary, taught Indians 1692-1711, and left missions. Tubac, a Spanish fort, became the first European settlement, 1752. Spain ceded Arizona to Mexico, 1821. The U.S. took over, 1848, after the Mexican War. The area below the Gila River came from Mexico in the Gadsden Purchase, 1853. Arizona became a territory, 1863. Apache wars ended with Geronimo's surrender, 1886. Arizona became a state, 1912, and grew rapidly after 1960 with a fourfold rise in population over the next 4 decades. Barry Goldwater was a leading conservative voice in the U.S. Senate (1953-65, 1969-87). The border with Mexico is a major gateway for illegal immigration to the U.S. In 2010, the U.S. Justice Dept. challenged a controversial state immigration law, which made it a state crime to be in the U.S. illegally and gave state police the power to make arrests without a warrant if they had reasonable suspicion of an individual's illegal status, as obstructing federal policy.

Tourist attractions. Grand Canyon; Painted Desert; Petrified Forest Natl. Park; Canyon de Chelly; Meteor Crater; London Bridge, Lake Havasu City; Biosphere 2, Oracle; Navajo Natl. Monument.

Famous Arizonans. Bruce Babbitt, Cochise, Alice Cooper, Geronimo, Barry Goldwater, Zane Grey, Carl Hayden, George W. P. Hunt, Helen Jacobs, Bil Keane, Percival Lowell, John McCain, William H. Pickering, John J. Rhodes, Morris Udall, Stewart Udall, Frank Lloyd Wright.

Tourist information. Arizona Office of Tourism, 1110 W. Washington St., Ste. 155, Phoenix, AZ 85007; 1-866-275-5816; www.arizonaguide.com

Website. www.az.gov

Arkansas (AR)
Natural State, Razorback State

People. Population (2010): 2,915,918; rank: 32; net change (2000-10): 9.1%. **Pop. density:** 56 per sq mi. **Racial distribution** (2010): 77% white; 15.4% black; 1.2% Asian; 0.8% Native Amer./AK; 0.2% Hawaiian/Pacific Islander; 2 or more races, 2%. **Hispanic pop.** (any race, 2010): 6.4%.

Geography. Total area: 53,179 sq mi; rank: 29. **Land area:** 52,035 sq mi; rank: 27. **Acres forested:** 18.6 mil. **Location:** west south-central U.S. **Climate:** long, hot summers, mild winters; generally abundant rainfall. **Topography:** eastern delta and prairie, southern lowland forests, and the northwestern highlands, which include the Ozark Plateaus. **Capital:** Little Rock. **Chief airports:** Bentonville, Little Rock.

Economy. Chief industries: manufacturing, agriculture, tourism, forestry. **Chief manuf. goods:** poultry processing, motor vehicles & parts, iron & steel, paper & paperboard, plastics, preserved fruits & vegetables, aerospace, rubber. **Chief crops:** rice, soybeans, cotton, hay, wheat, corn, sorghum, tomatoes, peaches, watermelons, pecans, blueberries, grapes. **Livestock** (Dec. 2010): 20.70 mil chickens (excl. broilers), 1.04 bil broilers; (Jan. 2011): 1.72 mil cattle/calves. **Broadband internet:** 76.2%. **Nonfuel minerals** (2010 prelim.): $630 mil; bromine, stone (crushed), sand and gravel (construction), cement (portland), lime. **Chief port:** Helena. **Gross state**

product (2010): $102.6 bil. **Sales tax** (2011): 6.0%. **Employment distrib.** (May 2011): 18.7% govt.; 20.1% trade/trans./util.; 13.4% mfg.; 14.1% ed./health; 10.3% prof./bus. serv.; 9.0% leisure/hosp.; 4.3% finance; 5.1% constr./mining/log.; 1.3% info.; 3.8% other serv. **Unemployment** (2010): 7.9%. **Per cap. pers. income** (2010 prelim.): $33,150. **New private housing** (2010): 7,177 units/$880.3 mil. **Commercial banks** (2010): 139; deposits: $48.8 bil. **Savings institutions** (2010): 7; deposits: $2.1 bil. **Lottery** (2010): total sales: $383.7 mil; profit: $82.7 mil.

Federal govt. Fed. civ. employees (Mar. 2011): 14,493; **avg. salary:** $62,935. **Notable fed. facilities:** Little Rock AFB; Pine Bluff Arsenal; Natl. Ctr. for Toxicological Research, Jefferson.

Energy. Electricity production (2010 kWh by source): coal: 26.4 bil; gas: 2 bil; nuclear: 15 bil; petroleum: 38 mil; hydroelectric: 3.7 bil.

State data. Motto: Regnat Populus (The people rule). **Flower:** Apple blossom. **Bird:** Mockingbird. **Tree:** Pine. **Song:** "Arkansas." **Entered union:** June 15, 1836; rank: 25th. **State fair** at Little Rock, mid-Oct.

History. Quapaw, Caddo, Osage, Cherokee, and Choctaw peoples lived in the area at the time of European contact. The first European explorers were de Soto, 1541; Marquette and Jolliet, 1673; and La Salle, 1682. French fur trader Henri de Tonty founded the first settlement, 1686, at Arkansas Post. In 1762, the area was ceded by France to Spain, then given back, 1800, and was part of the Louisiana Purchase, 1803. It was made a territory, 1819, and entered the Union as a slave state, 1836. Arkansas seceded in 1861, after the Civil War began; it was readmitted, 1868. Pres. Eisenhower sent federal troops, 1957, to keep Gov. Orval Faubus from blocking racial integration at Central High School in Little Rock. Wal-Mart, now the world's leading retailer, opened its first store in Rogers, 1962. Elected 5 times as governor, Bill Clinton later served 2 terms in the White House (1993-2001). His presidential library opened, 2004, in Little Rock.

Tourist attractions. Hot Springs Natl. Park (water ranging 95°F-147°F); Eureka Springs; Ozark Folk Center, Blanchard Caverns, near Mountain View; Crater of Diamonds (only U.S. diamond mine) near Murfreesboro; Toltec Mounds Archeological State Park, Little Rock; Buffalo Natl. River; Mid-America Museum, Hot Springs; Pea Ridge Natl. Military Park; Tanyard Springs, Morrilton; Wiederkehr Wine Village.

Famous Arkansans. Daisy Bates, Dee Brown, Paul "Bear" Bryant, Glen Campbell, Johnny Cash, Hattie Caraway, Wesley Clark, Bill Clinton, "Dizzy" Dean, Orval Faubus, James W. Fulbright, John Grisham, John H. Johnson, Douglas MacArthur, John L. McClellan, James S. McDonnell, Scottie Pippen, Dick Powell, Brooks Robinson, Billy Bob Thornton, Winthrop Rockefeller, Mary Steenburgen, Edward Durell Stone, Sam Walton, Archibald Yell.

Tourist information. Arkansas Dept. of Parks & Tourism, 1 Capitol Mall, Little Rock, AR 72201; 1-800-NATURAL; www.arkansas.com

Website. www.state.ar.us

California (CA)
Golden State

People. Population (2010): 37,253,956; rank: 1; net change (2010-10): 10.0%. **Pop. density:** 239.1 per sq mi. **Racial distribution** (2010): 57.6% white; 6.2% black; 13% Asian; 1% Native Amer./AK; 0.4% Hawaiian/Pacific Islander; 2 or more races, 4.9%. **Hispanic pop.** (any race, 2010): 37.6%.

Geography. Total area: 163,695 sq mi; rank: 3. **Land area:** 155,779 sq mi; rank: 3. **Acres forested:** 32.9 mil. **Location:** western coast of U.S. **Climate:** moderate temperatures and rainfall along the coast; extremes in the interior. **Topography:** long mountainous coastline; central valley; Sierra Nevada on the east; desert basins of the southern interior; rugged mountains of the north. **Capital:** Sacramento. **Chief airports:** Burbank, Fresno, Long Beach, Los Angeles, Oakland, Ontario, Palm Springs, Sacramento, San Diego, San Francisco, San Jose, Santa Ana.

Economy. Chief industries: agriculture, tourism, apparel, electronics, telecommunications, entertainment. **Chief manuf. goods:** petroleum, aerospace, precision instruments, semiconductors, telecom. & broadcasting equip., pharmaceutical, wineries, plastics, medical equip., preserved fruits & vegetables, printing, dairy, cut & sew apparel, motor vehicles. **Chief crops:** grapes, nursery products, almonds, lettuce, hay, strawberries, floriculture, tomatoes, cotton, oranges, pistachios, walnuts, broccoli, carrots, rice,

peaches, lemons. **Livestock** (Dec. 2010): 24.36 mil chickens (excl. broilers); (Jan. 2011): 5.15 mil cattle/calves, 610,000 sheep/lambs. **Broadband internet:** 75.7%. **Nonfuel minerals** (2010 prelim.): $2.7 bil; sand and gravel (construction), boron minerals, cement (portland), stone (crushed), gold. **Commercial fishing** (2009): $150.0. **Chief ports:** Long Beach, Los Angeles, San Diego, Port Hueneme, Richmond, Oakland, San Francisco, Stockton. **Gross state product** (2010): $1,901.1 bil. **Sales tax** (2011): 8.25%. **Employment distrib.** (May 2011): 17.3% govt.; 18.7% trade/trans./util.; 8.9% mfg.; 13.0% ed./health; 15.0% prof./bus. serv.; 10.9% leisure/hosp.; 5.4% finance; 4.2% constr./mining/log.; 3.2% info.; 3.5% other serv. **Unemployment** (2010): 12.4%. **Per cap. pers. income** (2010 prelim.): $43,104. **New private housing** (2010): 43,716 units/$9.1 bil. **Commercial banks** (2010): 293; deposits: $814.3 bil. **Savings institutions** (2010): 30; deposits: $31.1 bil. **Lottery** (2010): total sales: $3.09 bil; profit: $1.06 bil.

Federal govt. Fed. civ. employees (Mar. 2011): 171,381; **avg. salary:** $75,153. **Notable fed. facilities:** San Diego; *USMC Camp Pendleton; Naval Base Coronado; Twentynine Palms; Miramar; Travis AFB; Naval Research Lab., Monterey; Lawrence Livermore Natl. Lab; Berkeley Natl. Lab; NASA Jet Propulsion Lab; Edwards AFB (NASA Dryden Flight Research Ctr., AF Flight Test Ctr.); San Francisco Mint.

Energy. Electricity production (2010 kWh by source): gas: 24.3 bil; nuclear: 32.2 bil; petroleum: 40 mil; hydroelectric: 32.2 bil.; other: 1.7 bil.

State data. Motto: Eureka (I have found it). **Flower:** Golden poppy. **Bird:** California valley quail. **Tree:** California redwood. **Song:** "I Love You, California." **Entered union:** Sept. 9, 1850; rank: 31st. **State fair** at Sacramento, late July-early Aug.

History. Early inhabitants included more than 100 different Native American tribes with multiple dialects. The first European explorers were Juan Rodriguez Cabrillo, 1542, and Sir Francis Drake, 1579. The first settlement was the Spanish Alta California mission at San Diego, 1769, first in a string founded by Franciscan Father Junípero Serra. California became a province of independent Mexico, 1821. U.S. traders and settlers arrived in the 19th cent. and staged the Bear Flag revolt, 1846, in protest against Mexican rule; later that year U.S. forces occupied California. At the end of the Mexican War, Mexico ceded the territory to the U.S., 1848; that same year gold was discovered, and the famed gold rush began. California became a state, 1850. An economic downturn in the 1870s spurred riots against Chinese immigrants, who had come as laborers in the boom years. An earthquake and related fires devastated San Francisco, 1906. During World War II, Japanese Americans, many of them U.S. citizens, were held in detention camps, 1942-45. Ronald Reagan, a former movie actor, became state governor (1967-75) and U.S. president (1981-89). A budget crisis, 2003, resulted in the recall of Gov. Gray Davis and the election of another actor, Arnold Schwarzenegger. Led by Hollywood in entertainment and Silicon Valley in high-tech, the state's economy dwarfs that of most nations. Still, billion-dollar budget deficits have been a perennial problem.

Tourist attractions. The *Queen Mary*, Aquarium of the Pacific, Long Beach; Palomar Mountain; Disneyland, Anaheim; Getty Center, Universal Studios, in Los Angeles; Tournament of Roses and Rose Bowl, Pasadena; Golden State Museum, Sacramento; San Diego Zoo; Yosemite Valley; Lassen and Sequoia-Kings Canyon natl. parks; Lake Tahoe; Mojave and Colorado deserts; San Francisco Bay; Napa Valley; Monterey Peninsula; oldest living things on Earth believed to be a stand of bristlecone pines in the Inyo Natl. Forest, are 4,700 years old; Redwood Natl. and State Parks.

Famous Californians. Edmund G. (Pat) Brown, Jerry Brown, Luther Burbank, Julia Child, Ted Danson, Cameron Diaz, Leonardo DiCaprio, Joe DiMaggio, Dianne Feinstein, John C. Fremont, Tom Hanks, Bret Harte, William Randolph Hearst, Helen Hunt, Jack Kemp, Monica Lewinsky, Jack London, George Lucas, Mark McGwire, Marilyn Monroe, John Muir, Richard M. Nixon, George S. Patton Jr., Gregory Peck, Nancy Pelosi, Ronald Reagan, Sally K. Ride, William Saroyan, Father Junípero Serra, O. J. Simpson, Kevin Spacey, Leland Stanford, John Steinbeck, Arnold Schwarzenegger, Shirley Temple, Earl Warren, Ted Williams, Serena Williams, Venus Williams, Tiger Woods.

Tourist information. California Tourism, P.O. Box 1499, Sacramento, CA 95812-1499; 1-877-225-4367; www.visitcalifornia.com

Website. www.ca.gov

Colorado (CO)
Centennial State

People. Population (2010): 5,029,196; rank: 22; net change (2000-10): 16.9%. **Pop. density:** 48.5 per sq mi. **Racial distribution** (2010): 81.3% white; 4.0% black; 2.8% Asian; 1.1% Native Amer./AK; 0.1% Hawaiian/Pacific Islander; 2 or more races, 3.4%. **Hispanic pop.** (any race, 2010): 20.7%.

Geography. Total area: 104,094 sq mi; rank: 8. **Land area:** 103,642 sq mi; rank: 8. **Acres forested:** 22.9 mil. **Location:** W central U.S. **Climate:** low relative humidity, abundant sunshine, wide daily, seasonal temperature ranges; alpine conditions in the high mountains. **Topography:** eastern dry high plains; hilly to mountainous central plateau; western Rocky Mts. of high ranges, with broad valleys, deep, narrow canyons. **Capital:** Denver. **Chief airports:** Colorado Springs, Denver.

Economy. Chief industries: manufacturing, construction, government, tourism, agriculture, aerospace, electronics equipment. **Chief manuf. goods:** animal slaughtering, beer, petroleum, pharmaceuticals, aerospace, medical equip., precision instruments, printing, semiconductors. **Chief crops:** hay, corn, potatoes, wheat, onions, dry edible beans, sunflowers, sugar beets, barley, proso millet, cabbage, peaches, lettuce, apples, cantaloupes. **Livestock** (Dec. 2010): 4.75 mil chickens (excl. broilers); (Jan. 2011): 2.65 mil cattle/calves, 370,000 sheep/lambs; (June 2011): 150,000 hogs/pigs. **Broadband internet:** 76.8%. **Nonfuel minerals** (2010 prelim.): $1.9 bil; molybdenum concentrates, gold, sand and gravel (construction), cement (portland), stone (crushed). **Gross state product** (2010): $257.6 bil. **Sales tax** (2011): 2.9%. **Employment distrib.** (May 2011): 18.0% govt.; 18.0% trade/trans./util.; 5.7% mfg.; 12.3% ed./health; 15% prof./bus. serv.; 11.7% leisure/hosp.; 6.2% finance; 6.4% constr./mining/log.; 3.1% info.; 4.1% other serv. **Unemployment** (2010): 8.9%. **Per cap. pers. income** (2010 prelim.): $42,802. **New private housing** (2010): 11,591 units/$2.6 bil. **Commercial banks** (2010): 173; deposits: $87.6 bil. **Savings institutions** (2010): 17; deposits: $3.6 bil. **Lottery** (2010): total sales: $501.2 mil; profit: $112.9 mil.

Federal govt. Fed. civ. employees (Mar. 2011): 40,240; **avg. salary:** $75,126. **Notable fed. facilities:** *U.S. Air Force Academy; Peterson AFB; Denver Mint; Ft. Carson; Natl. Renewable Energy Labs; U.S. Rail Transportation Test Ctr.; Cheyenne Mtn. Operations Ctr. (NORAD, U.S. Space Comm.); Denver Federal Ctr.; Natl. Ctr. for Atmospheric Research; Natl. Inst. for Standards & Technology, Boulder; Natl. Wildlife Res. Ctr.; NOAA Env. Technology Lab.

Energy. Electricity production (2010 kWh by source): coal: 34.8 bil; gas: 3.9 bil; petroleum: 12 mil; hydroelectric: 1.5 bil; other: 68 mil.

State data. Motto: Nil Sine Numine (Nothing without Providence). **Flower:** Rocky Mountain columbine. **Bird:** Lark bunting. **Tree:** Colorado blue spruce. **Songs:** "Where the Columbines Grow"; "Rocky Mountain High." **Entered union:** Aug. 1, 1876; rank 38th. **State fair** at Pueblo, mid-Aug.-early Sept.

History. Paleo-Indians hunted big game in the area at least 11,000 years ago. Anasazi cliff dwellers flourished around Mesa Verde until about 1300 CE; other Native Americans were the Ute, Pueblo, Cheyenne, and Arapaho. The region was claimed by Spain, but passed to France, 1800. The U.S. acquired eastern Colorado in the Louisiana Purchase, 1803. Lt. Zebulon M. Pike explored the area, 1806, sighting the peak that bears his name. After the Mexican War, 1846-48, U.S. immigrants settled in the east, former Mexicans in the south. Gold was discovered in 1858, causing a population boom. Congress created Colorado Territory, 1861. Conflict between newcomers and displaced Native Americans led to the Sand Creek Massacre, 1864, in which U.S. soldiers and settlers killed some 150 Cheyenne and Arapaho. Most Native Americans were later removed to Oklahoma Territory. The 1870s brought statehood, 1876, and rich silver finds that turned Leadville into a boomtown. Federal military and civilian employment in Colorado surged in the 1940s and '50s; since then, tourism and high-tech industries have fueled the economy. The state's Hispanic population grew from 5.8% in 1980 to 20.7% in 2010.

Tourist attractions. Rocky Mountain and Black Canyon of the Gunnison natl. parks; Aspen Ski Resort; Garden of the Gods, Colorado Springs; Great Sand Dunes, Dinosaur, and Colorado natl. monuments; Pikes Peak and Mt. Evans highways; Mesa Verde Natl. Park (ancient Anasazi Indian cliff dwell-ings); Grand Mesa Natl. Forest; mining towns of Central City, Silverton, Cripple Creek; Burlington's Old Town; Bent's Fort; near La Junta; Georgetown Loop Historic Mining Railroad Park, Cumbres and Toltec Scenic Railroad; limited stakes gaming in Central City, Blackhawk, Cripple Creek, Ignacio, and Towaoe.

Famous Coloradans. Tim Allen, Frederick Bonfils, Henry Brown, Molly Brown, William N. Byers, M. Scott Carpenter, Lon Chaney, Jack Dempsey, Mamie Eisenhower, Douglas Fairbanks, Barney Ford, Scott Hamilton, John Kerry, Chief Ourey, "Baby Doe" Tabor, Lowell Thomas, Byron R. White, Paul Whiteman.

Tourist information. Colorado Tourism Office, 1625 Broadway, Ste.1700, Denver, CO 80202; 1-800-COLORADO; www.colorado.com

Website. www.colorado.gov

Connecticut (CT)
Constitution State, Nutmeg State

People. Population (2010): 3,574,097; rank: 29; net change (2000-10): 4.9%. **Pop. density:** 738.1 per sq mi. **Racial distribution** (2010): 77.6% white; 10.1% black; 3.8% Asian; 0.3% Native Amer./AK; <0.05% Hawaiian/Pacific Islander; 2 or more races, 2.6%. **Hispanic pop.** (any race, 2010): 13.4%.

Geography. Total area: 5,543 sq mi; rank: 48. **Land area:** 4,842 sq mi; rank: 48. **Acres forested:** 1.6 mil. **Location:** New England state in NE corner of the U.S. **Climate:** moderate; winters avg. slightly below freezing; warm, humid summers. **Topography:** western upland, the Berkshires, in the NW, highest elevations; narrow central lowland N-S; hilly eastern upland drained by rivers. **Capital:** Hartford. **Chief airport:** Windsor Locks.

Economy. Chief industries: manufacturing, retail trade, government, services, finances, insurance, real estate. **Chief manuf. goods:** aerospace, chemicals, fabricated metals, precision instruments, toiletries, medical equip., printing, plastics. **Chief crops:** nursery stock, Christmas trees, mushrooms, sweet corn, apples, tobacco, hay. **Livestock** (Dec. 2010): 3.04 mil chickens (excl. broilers); (Jan. 2011): 49,000 cattle/calves. **Broadband internet:** 76.6%. **Nonfuel minerals** (2010 prelim.): $141 mil; stone (crushed), sand and gravel (construction), clays (common), stone (dimension), gemstones (natural). **Commercial fishing** (2009): $16.6 mil. **Chief ports:** New Haven, Bridgeport, New London. **Gross state product** (2010): $237.3 bil. **Sales tax** (2011): 6.0%. **Employment distrib.** (May 2011): 15.1% govt.; 17.8% trade/trans./util.; 10.2% mfg.; 19.3% ed./health; 12.0% prof./bus. serv.; 8.5% leisure/hosp.; 8.2% finance; 3.2% constr./mining/log.; 1.9% info.; 3.7% other serv. **Unemployment** (2010): 9.1%. **Per cap. pers. income** (2010 prelim.): $56,001. **New private housing** (2010): 3,932 units/$861.4 mil. **Commercial banks** (2010): 33; deposits: $59.6 bil. **Savings institutions** (2010): 35; deposits: $36.2 bil. **Lottery** (2010): total sales: $996.9 mil; profit: $285.5 mil.

Federal govt. Fed. civ. employees (Mar. 2011): 8,746; **avg. salary:** $77,285. **Notable fed. facilities:** U.S. Coast Guard Academy; Navy Sub Base New London.

Energy. Electricity production (2010 kWh by source): gas: 4 mil; petroleum: 3 mil; hydroelectric: 36 mil.

State data. Motto: Qui Transtulit Sustinet (He who transplanted still sustains). **Flower:** Mountain laurel. **Bird:** American robin. **Tree:** White oak. **Song:** "Yankee Doodle." **Fifth** of the 13 original states to ratify the Constitution, Jan. 9, 1788. **State fair:** no official state fair; district and local fairs, largest at Durham, late Sept.

History. At the time of European contact, inhabitants of the area were Algonquian peoples, including the Mohegan and Pequot. Dutch explorer Adriaen Block was the first European visitor, 1614. By 1634, settlers from Plymouth Bay had started colonies along the Connecticut River; in 1637 they defeated the Pequots. The Colony of Connecticut was chartered by England, 1662, adding New Haven, 1665. A Patriot stronghold in the American Revolution, the state actively supported the antislavery movement and the Union cause in the Civil War. The state economy prospered in the 20th cent. from insurance- and defense-related industries. *Nautilus*, the first nuclear-powered submarine, was launched at Groton, 1954.

Tourist attractions. Mark Twain House, Hartford; Yale University's Art Gallery, Peabody Museum, in New Haven; Mystic Seaport, Marine Life Aquarium; P. T. Barnum Museum, Bridgeport; Gillette Castle, Hadlyme; USS *Nautilus* Memorial, Groton (1st nuclear-powered submarine); Mashantucket Pequot Museum & Research Ctr., Foxwoods Resort & Casino, Ledyard; Mohegan Sun, Uncasville; Lake Compounce, Bristol.

Famous "Nutmeggers." Ethan Allen, Phineas T. Barnum, G. W. Bush, Samuel Colt, Jonathan Edwards, Nathan Hale, Katharine Hepburn, Isaac Hull, Robert Mitchum, J. Pierpont Morgan, Ralph Nader, Israel Putnam, Wallace Stevens, Harriet Beecher Stowe, Mark Twain, Noah Webster, Eli Whitney.

Tourist information. Connecticut Commission on Culture and Tourism, One Constitution Plz., 2nd Fl., Hartford, CT 06103; 1-888-CTVISIT, (860) 256-2800; www.ctvisit.com
Website. www.ct.gov

Delaware (DE)
First State, Diamond State

People. Population (2010): 897,934; rank: 45; net change (2000-10): 14.6%. **Pop. density:** 460.8 per sq mi. **Racial distribution** (2010): 68.9% white; 21.4% black; 3.2% Asian; 0.5% Native Amer./AK; <0.05% Hawaiian/Pacific Islander; 2 or more races, 2.7%. **Hispanic pop.** (any race, 2010): 8.2%.
Geography. Total area: 2,489 sq mi; rank: 49. **Land area:** 1,949 sq mi; rank: 50. **Acres forested:** 0.3 mil. **Location:** Delmarva Peninsula on the Atlantic coastal plain. **Climate:** moderate. **Topography:** Piedmont plateau to the N, sloping to a near sea-level plain. **Capital:** Dover.
Economy. Chief industries: chemicals, agriculture, finance, poultry, shellfish, tourism, auto assembly, food processing, transportation equipment. **Chief manuf. goods:** pharmaceuticals, poultry processing, soap & cleaning compounds, precision instruments, basic chemicals, plastics. **Chief crops:** soybeans, corn, greenhouse & nursery, wheat, potatoes, barley, hay, watermelons, lima beans, green peas, pumpkins, mushrooms, cabbage. **Livestock** (Dec. 2010): 235 mil broilers; (Jan. 2011): 18,000 cattle/calves. **Broadband internet:** 73.7%. **Nonfuel minerals** (2010 prelim.): $12.7 mil; magnesium compounds, sand and gravel (construction), stone (crushed), gemstones (natural). **Commercial fishing** (2009): $7.5 mil. **Chief port:** Wilmington. **Gross state product** (2010): $62.3 bil. **Sales tax** (2011): none. **Employment distrib.** (May 2011): 15.7% govt.; 17.4% trade/trans./util.; 6.3% mfg.; 15.7% ed./health; 12.7% prof./bus. serv.; 10.7% leisure/hosp.; 10.3% finance; 4.7% constr./mining/log.; 1.4% info.; 4.9% other serv. **Unemployment** (2010): 8.5%. **Per cap. pers. income** (2010 prelim.): $39,962. **New private housing** (2010): 3,072 units/$364.1 mil. **Commercial banks** (2010): 32; deposits: $199 bil. **Savings institutions** (2010): 7; deposits: $91.2 bil. **Lottery** (2010): total sales: $684.5 mil; profit: $275.5 mil.
Federal govt. Fed. civ. employees (Mar. 2011): 3,461; **avg. salary:** $65,895. **Notable fed. facilities:** Dover AFB; Federal Wildlife Refuge, Bombay Hook.
Energy. Electricity production: NA.
State data. Motto: Liberty and independence. **Flower:** Peach blossom. **Bird:** Blue hen chicken. **Tree:** American holly. **Song:** "Our Delaware." **First** of original 13 states to ratify the Constitution, Dec. 7, 1787. **State fair** at Harrington, mid-late July.
History. The Lenni Lenape (Delaware) people lived in the region at the time of European contact. Henry Hudson located the Delaware R., 1609, and in 1610, English explorer Samuel Argall entered Delaware Bay, naming the area after Virginia's governor, Lord De La Warr. Dutch, Swedish, and Finnish settlers were followed by the British, who took control in 1664. After 1682, Delaware became part of Pennsylvania, and in 1704 it was granted its own assembly. It adopted a constitution as the state of Delaware, 1776, and was first to ratify the federal Constitution, 1787. Although it remained in the Union during the Civil War, Delaware retained slavery until the 13th Amendment abolished it in 1865. The DuPont company, founded as a gunpowder mill in 1802, became an industrial giant in the 20th cent. making nylon, Teflon, and other synthetics. Pro-business laws drew many out-of-state firms to incorporate in Delaware. In 2000, Ruth Ann Minner was elected Delaware's first woman governor.
Tourist attractions. Ft. Christina Monument, site of founding of New Sweden, Holy Trinity (Old Swedes) Church, erected 1698, the oldest Protestant church in the U.S. still in use, in Wilmington; Hagley Museum, Winterthur Museum and Gardens, near Wilmington; New Castle historic district; John Dickinson "Penman of the Revolution" home, Dover; Rehoboth Beach; Dover Downs Intl. Speedway.

Famous Delawareans. Thomas F. Bayard, Joseph Biden, Henry Seidel Canby, E. I. du Pont, John P. Marquand, Howard Pyle, Caesar Rodney.
Tourist information. Delaware Tourism Office, 99 Kings Hwy., Dover, DE 19901; 1-866-2VISITDE; www.visitdelaware.com
Website. www.delaware.gov

Florida (FL)
Sunshine State

People. Population (2010): 18,801,310; rank: 4; net change (2000-10): 17.6%. **Pop. density:** 350.6 per sq mi. **Racial distribution** (2010): 75.0% white; 16.0% black; 2.4% Asian; 0.4% Native Amer./AK; 0.1% Hawaiian/Pacific Islander; 2 or more races, 2.5%. **Hispanic pop.** (any race, 2010): 22.5%.
Geography. Total area: 65,758 sq mi; rank: 22. **Land area:** 53,625 sq mi; rank: 26. **Acres forested:** 17.1 mil. **Location:** peninsula jutting southward 500 mi between the Atlantic and the Gulf of Mexico. **Climate:** subtropical N of Bradenton-Lake Okeechobee-Vero Beach line; tropical S of line. **Topography:** land is flat or rolling; highest point is 345 ft in the NW. **Capital:** Tallahassee. **Chief airports:** Ft. Lauderdale, Ft. Myers, Jacksonville, Miami, Orlando, Pensacola, Sanford, Sarasota/Bradenton, Tampa, West Palm Beach.
Economy. Chief industries: tourism, agriculture, manufacturing, construction, services, international trade. **Chief manuf. goods:** navigational instruments, medical equip., cement, broadcasting equip., beverages, phosphatic fertilizer, preserved fruits & vegetables, structural metal, printing. **Chief crops:** greenhouse & nursery, oranges, sugarcane, tomatoes, green peppers, grapefruit, strawberries, snap beans, sweet corn, potatoes, cucumbers, tangerines. **Livestock** (Dec. 2010): 11.92 mil chickens (excl. broilers), 51.70 mil broilers; (Jan. 2011): 1.63 mil cattle/calves. **Broadband internet:** 81.1%. **Nonfuel minerals** (2010 prelim.): $2.0 bil; phosphate rock, stone (crushed), cement (portland), sand and gravel (construction), zirconium concentrates. **Commercial fishing** (2009): $157.0 mil. **Chief ports:** Pensacola, Tampa, Port Manatee, Miami, Port Everglades, Jacksonville, Canaveral. **Gross state product** (2010): $747.7 bil. **Sales tax** (2011): 6.0%. **Employment distrib.** (May 2011): 15.4% govt.; 20.2% trade/trans./util.; 4.2% mfg.; 15.2% ed./health; 14.4% prof./bus. serv.; 13.4% leisure/hosp.; 6.4% finance; 4.9% constr./mining/log.; 1.8% info.; 4.3% other serv. **Unemployment** (2010): 11.5%. **Per cap. pers. income** (2010 prelim.): $39,272. **New private housing** (2010): 38,679 units/$7.8 bil. **Commercial banks** (2010): 295; deposits: $366.5 bil. **Savings institutions** (2010): 44; deposits: $43.4 bil. **Lottery** (2010): total sales: $3.9 bil; profit: $1.25 bil.
Federal govt. Fed. civ. employees (Mar. 2011): 89,931; **avg. salary:** $69,898. Notable fed. facilities:** John F. Kennedy Space Ctr.; Eglin AFB; MacDill AFB; Hurlburt Field; *Pensacola NAS; Jacksonville NAS; Mayport Naval Sta.
Energy. Electricity production (2010 kWh, by source): coal: 56.1 bil; gas: 115.7 bil; nuclear: 23.9 bil; petroleum: 5.8 bil; hydroelectric: 181 mil.; other: 3.3 bil.
State data. Motto: In God we trust. **Flower:** Orange blossom. **Bird:** Mockingbird. **Tree:** Sabal palmetto palm. **Song:** "Old Folks at Home." **Entered union:** Mar. 3, 1845; rank: 27th. **State fair** at Tampa, early-mid Feb.
History. Florida has been inhabited for at least 12,000 years. Timucua, Apalachee, and Calusa peoples were living in the region when the earliest Europeans came; later the Seminole migrated from Georgia to Florida, becoming dominant there in the early 18th cent. The first European to see Florida was Ponce de León, 1513. France established a colony, Ft. Caroline, on the St. Johns River, 1564. Spain settled St. Augustine, 1565, and Spanish troops massacred most of the French. Britain's Sir Francis Drake burned St. Augustine, 1586. In 1763, Spain ceded Florida to Great Britain, which held the area 20 years before returning it to Spain. Florida was ceded to the U.S. in the Adams-Onís Treaty, 1819. The Seminole War, 1835-42, resulted in removal of most Native Americans to Indian Territory. Florida joined the Union in 1845, seceded in 1861, and was readmitted in 1868. In the late 19th cent., hotel and railroad builder Henry M. Flagler laid the foundations of the tourism industry. The state experienced phenomenal population growth in the 20th cent., especially after 1950. The first U.S. astronaut was launched into space from Cape Canaveral, 1961. Walt Disney World opened near Orlando, 1971. Hurricane Andrew slammed S. Florida, 1992, causing at least $25 bil in property damage. A

dispute over Florida's presidential vote in 2000 led to the U.S. Supreme Court decision awarding the White House to George W. Bush; his brother Jeb was state governor 1999-2007. Four hurricanes hit the state in 2004, causing more than $40 bil in damages.

Tourist attractions. Miami Beach; Castillo de San Marcos, St. Augustine (oldest permanent European settlement in U.S.); Walt Disney World Resort, Sea World, Universal Studios, near Orlando; Kennedy Space Center and U.S. Astronaut Hall of Fame; Everglades Natl. Park; Ringling Museums of Art & the Circus, in Sarasota; Cypress Gardens, Winter Haven; Busch Gardens, Tampa; Florida Caverns State Park, near Mariana; Church St. Station, Orlando; Silver Springs, Ocala.

Famous Floridians. Edna Buchanan, Jeb Bush, Marjory Stoneman Douglas, Henry M. Flagler, Carl Hiaasen, Zora Neale Hurston, James Weldon Johnson, MacKinlay Kantor, John D. MacDonald, Chief Osceola, Claude Pepper, Henry B. Plant, A. Philip Randolph, Marjorie Kinnan Rawlings, Janet Reno, Joseph W. Stilwell, Charles P. Summerall, Ben Vereen.

Tourist information. Visit Florida, 2540 W. Executive Center Cir., Ste. 200, Tallahassee, FL 32301; 1-888-7FLA-USA; www.visitflorida.com

Website. www.myflorida.com

Georgia (GA)
Empire State of the South, Peach State

People. Population (2010): 9,687,653; rank: 9; net change (2000-10): 18.3%. **Pop. density:** 168.4 per sq mi. **Racial distribution** (2010): 59.7% white; 30.5% black; 3.2% Asian; 0.3% Native Amer./AK; 0.1% Hawaiian/Pacific Islander; 2 or more races, 2.1%. **Hispanic pop.** (any race, 2010): 8.8%.

Geography. Total area: 59,425 sq mi; rank: 24. **Land area:** 57,513 sq mi; rank: 21. **Acres forested:** 24.8 mil. **Location:** South Atlantic state. **Climate:** maritime tropical air masses dominate in summer; polar air masses in winter; E central area drier. **Topography:** most southerly of the Blue Ridge Mts. cover NE and N central; central Piedmont extends to the fall line of rivers; coastal plain levels to the coast flatlands. **Capital:** Atlanta. **Chief airports:** Atlanta, Savannah.

Economy. Chief industries: services, manufacturing, retail trade. **Chief manuf. goods:** carpet & rugs, animal slaughtering & processing, motor vehicles & parts, plastics, aircrafts, paper, chemicals, food. **Chief crops:** cotton, greenhouse & nursery, peanuts, pecans, corn, tomatoes, cucumbers, onions, watermelons, tobacco, squash, blueberries, hay, cabbage, soybeans, peaches, snap beans, wheat. **Livestock** (Dec. 2010): 24.91 mil chickens (excl. broilers), 1.31 bil broilers; (Jan. 2011): 1.02 mil cattle/calves. **Broadband internet:** 75.1%. **Nonfuel minerals** (2010 prelim.): $1.5 bil; clays (kaolin), stone (crushed), clays (fuller's earth), sand and gravel (construction), cement (portland). **Commercial fishing** (2009): $9.3 mil. **Chief ports:** Savannah, Brunswick. **Gross state product** (2010): $403.1 bil. **Sales tax** (2011): 4.0%. **Employment distrib.** (May 2011): 17.3% govt.; 21.1% trade/trans./util.; 9.1% mfg.; 12.9% ed./health; 13.9% prof./bus. serv.; 10.1% leisure/hosp.; 5.1% finance; 4.2% constr./mining/log.; 2.6% info.; 4.1% other serv. **Unemployment** (2010): 10.2%. **Per cap. pers. income** (2010 prelim.): $35,490. **New private housing** (2010): 17,265 units/$2.7 bil. **Commercial banks** (2010): 291; deposits: $175 bil. **Savings institutions** (2010): 30; deposits: $5.9 bil. **Lottery** (2010): total sales: $3.65 bil; profit: $883.9 mil.

Federal govt. fed. civ. employees (Mar. 2011): 81,600; **avg. salary:** $70,293. **Notable fed. facilities:** Ft. Benning; Ft. Stewart; Fed. Law Enforcement Training Ctr., Robins AFB; Ft. Gordon; King's Bay Naval Base; Moody AFB. Centers for Disease Control; Marine Corps Logistics.

Energy. Electricity production (2010 kWh by source): coal: 72.6 bil; gas: 11.3 bil; nuclear: 33.5 bil; petroleum: 71 mil; hydroelectric: 3.6 bil.

State data. Motto: Wisdom, justice, and moderation. **Flower:** Cherokee rose. **Bird:** Brown thrasher. **Tree:** Live oak. **Song:** "Georgia on My Mind." **Fourth** of the 13 original states to ratify the Constitution, Jan. 2, 1788. **State fair** at Macon, late Apr.-early May.

History. Creek and Cherokee peoples were living in the region when Spaniards founded Santa Catalina mission, 1566, on Saint Catherines Island. Gen. James Oglethorpe established a colony at Savannah, 1733, for the poor and religiously persecuted. Oglethorpe defeated a Spanish army from Florida at Bloody Marsh, 1742. Georgia was a battleground in the American Revolution, with the British finally evacuating Savannah in 1782. When Georgia entered the Union, 1788, its plantation economy relied on slaves for rice and cotton growing. The Cherokee were removed to Indian Territory, 1838-39, and thousands died on the long march, known as the Trail of Tears. By 1860 the number of slaves exceeded 462,000 (44% of the total population). Georgia seceded from the Union, 1861, and was invaded by Union forces, 1864, under Gen. William T. Sherman, who took Atlanta, Sept. 2, and proceeded on his famous "march to the sea," ending in Dec., in Savannah. Georgia was readmitted, 1870. Born 1929 in Atlanta, Martin Luther King Jr., made the city his base during the civil rights struggles of the 1960s. Atlanta became the leading city of the "New South," world headquarters of Coca-Cola and CNN, and host of the 1996 Summer Olympic Games. Hispanics are a rapidly growing economic and political force in the state.

Tourist attractions. State Capitol, Stone Mt. Park, Six Flags Over Georgia, Kennesaw Mt. Natl. Battlefield Park, Martin Luther King Jr. Natl. Historic Site, Underground Atlanta, Jimmy Carter Library & Museum, all Atlanta; Chickamauga and Chattanooga Natl. Military Park, near Dalton; Chattahoochee Natl. Forest; Helen alpine village; Dahlonega, site of America's first gold rush; Brasstown Bald Mt.; Lake Lanier; Franklin D. Roosevelt's Little White House, Warm Springs; Callaway Gardens, Pine Mt.; Andersonville Natl. Historic Site; Okefenokee Swamp, near Waycross; Jekyll, St. Simons, Cumberland islands; Savannah historic riverfront district.

Famous Georgians. Kim Basinger, Griffin Bell, James Bowie, James Brown, Erskine Caldwell, Jimmy Carter, Ray Charles, Lucius D. Clay, Ty Cobb, James Dickey, John C. Fremont, Newt Gingrich, Joel Chandler Harris, "Doc" Holliday, Holly Hunter, Alan Jackson, Jasper Johns, Martin Luther King Jr., Gladys Knight, Sidney Lanier, Little Richard, Juliette Gordon Low, Margaret Mitchell, Sam Nunn, Flannery O'Connor, Otis Redding, Burt Reynolds, Julia Roberts, Jackie Robinson, Clarence Thomas, Travis Tritt, Ted Turner, Carl Vinson, Alice Walker, Herschel Walker, Joseph Wheeler, Joanne Woodward, Trisha Yearwood, Andrew Young.

Tourist information. Dept. of Economic Development, 75 Fifth St., NW, Ste. 1200, Atlanta, GA 30308; 1-800-VISITGA; www.exploregeorgia.org

Website. www.georgia.gov

Hawai'i (HI)
Aloha State

People. Population (2010): 1,360,301; rank: 42; net change (2000-10): 12.3%. **Pop. density:** 211.8 per sq mi. **Racial distribution** (2010): 24.7% white; 1.6% black; 38.6% Asian; 0.3% Native Amer./AK; 10.0% Hawaiian/Pacific Islander; 2 or more races, 23.6%. **Hispanic pop.** (any race, 2010): 8.9%.

Geography. Total area: 10,932 sq mi; rank: 43. **Land area:** 6,423 sq mi; rank: 47. **Acres forested:** 1.7 mil. **Location:** Hawaiian Islands lie in the North Pacific, 2,397 mi SW from San Francisco. **Climate:** subtropical, with wide variations in rainfall; Waialeale, on Kaua'i, wettest spot in U.S. (annual rainfall 460 in.) **Topography:** islands are tops of a chain of submerged volcanic mountains; active volcanoes: Mauna Loa, Kilauea. **Capital:** Honolulu. **Chief airports:** Hilo, Honolulu, Kahului, Kailua Kona, Lihue.

Economy. Chief industries: tourism, defense, sugar, pineapples. **Chief manuf. goods:** concrete, printing, baked goods, sugar, preserved fruits & vegetables, apparel. **Chief crops:** flowers & nursery, pineapples, seed crops, sugarcane, macadamia nuts, coffee, algae, papayas, tomatoes, bananas, basil, ginger. **Livestock** (Dec. 2010): 364,000 chickens (excl. broilers); (Jan. 2011): 141,000 cattle/calves. **Broadband internet:** 85.4%. **Nonfuel minerals** (2010 prelim.): $112 mil; stone (crushed), sand and gravel (construction), gemstones (natural). **Commercial fishing** (2009): $71.2 mil. **Chief ports:** Honolulu, Hilo, Barbers Point, Kahului. **Gross state product** (2010): $66.8 bil. **Sales tax** (2011): 4.0%. **Employment distrib.** (May 2011): 21.5% govt.; 18.1% trade/trans./util.; 2.1% mfg.; 13.3% ed./health; 12.4% prof./bus. serv.; 17.0% leisure/hosp.; 4.4% finance; 4.8% constr./mining/log.; 1.9% info.; 4.5% other serv. **Unemployment** (2010): 6.6%. **Per cap. pers. income** (2010 prelim.): $41,021. **New private housing** (2010): 3,442 units/$773.0 mil. **Commercial banks** (2010): 8; deposits: $22.8 bil. **Savings institutions** (2010): 4; deposits: $5.5 bil.

Federal govt. Fed. civ. employees (Mar. 2011): 25,507; **avg. salary:** $66,050. **Notable fed. facilities:** Joint Base Pearl Harbor-Hickam; Schofield Barracks; Marine Corps Base-Kaneohe Bay; Tripler Army Med. Ctr.; Ft. Shafter; Wheeler AFB; Prince Kuhio Federal Bldg.

Energy. Electricity production (2010 kWh by source): petroleum: 6.1 bil; other: 2 mil.

State data. Motto: Ua mau ke ea o ka aina i ka pono (The life of the land is perpetuated in righteousness). **Flower:** Yellow hibiscus. **Bird:** Hawaiian goose. **Tree:** Kukui (candlenut). **Song:** "Hawai'i Pono'i" (Hawai'i's Own). **Entered union:** Aug. 21, 1959; rank: 50th. **State fair** at Honolulu, late May-June.

History. Polynesians from islands 2,000 mi to the S settled the Hawaiian Islands, probably 300-600 CE. The first European visitor was British captain James Cook, 1778. King Kamehameha I united the islands by 1810. Christian missionaries arrived, 1819, bringing Western culture. Under the reign, 1825-54, of King Kamehameha III, a constitution, legislature, and public school system were instituted. Sugar production began, 1835, and it became the dominant industry. Queen Liliuokalani was deposed, 1893, and a republic was established, 1894, headed by Sanford B. Dole. Annexation by the U.S. came in 1898. The Japanese attack on Pearl Harbor, Dec. 7, 1941, brought the U.S. into World War II. Hawai'i attained statehood, 1959. Hurricane Iniki pounded Kaua'i, 1992, causing about $1 bil in damage. In 2006, Pres. George W. Bush designated the Northwestern Hawaiian Islands National Monument, a marine area of 140,000 sq mi.

Tourist attractions. Hawaii Volcanoes, Haleakala natl. parks; Natl. Memorial Cemetery of the Pacific, Waikiki Beach, Diamond Head, in Honolulu; USS *Arizona* Memorial, Pearl Harbor; Hanauma Bay; Polynesian Cultural Ctr., Laie; Nu'uanu Pali; Waimea Canyon; Wailoa and Wailuku River state parks.

Famous Islanders. Bernice Pauahi Bishop, Tia Carrere, Father Damien de Veuster, Don Ho, Duke Kahanamoku, King Kamehameha, Brook Mahealani Lee, Daniel K. Inouye, Jason Scott Lee, Queen Liliuokalani, Bette Midler, Ellison Onizuka.

Tourist information. Hawaii Visitors and Conventions Bureau, 2270 Kalakaua Ave., Ste. 801, Honolulu, HI 96815; 1-800-GOHAWAII; www.gohawaii.com
Website. www.ehawaii.gov

Idaho (ID)
Gem State

People. Population (2010): 1,567,582; rank: 39; net change (2000-10): 21.1%. **Pop. density:** 19 per sq mi. **Racial distribution** (2010): 89.1% white; 0.6% black; 1.2% Asian; 1.4% Native Amer./AK; 0.1% Hawaiian/Pacific Islander; 2 or more races, 2.5%. **Hispanic pop.** (any race, 2010): 11.2%.

Geography. Total area: 83,569 sq mi; rank: 14. **Land area:** 82,643 sq mi; rank: 11. **Acres forested:** 21.3 mil. **Location:** northwestern Mountain state bordering on British Columbia. **Climate:** tempered by Pacific westerly winds; drier, colder, continental climate in SE; altitude an important factor. **Topography:** Snake R. plains in the S; central region of mountains, canyons, gorges (Hells Canyon, 7,900 ft, deepest in N. America); subalpine northern region. **Capital:** Boise.

Economy. Chief industries: manufacturing, agriculture, tourism, lumber, mining, electronics. **Chief manuf. goods:** computers & electronics, preserved fruits & vegetables, cheese, lumber. **Chief crops:** potatoes, wheat, hay, sugar beets, barley, greenhouse & nursery, onions, dry beans, corn, mint, apples, hops, peaches, lentils, peas, cherries, plums & prunes, oats. **Livestock** (Jan. 2011): 2.20 mil. cattle/calves, 235,000 sheep/lambs. **Broadband internet:** 70.2%. **Nonfuel minerals** (2010 prelim.): $1.2 bil; molybdenum concentrates, phosphate rock, silver, sand and gravel (construction), lead. **Chief port:** Lewiston. **Gross state product** (2010): $55.4 bil. **Sales tax** (2011): 6.0%. **Employment distrib.** (May 2011): 20.0% govt.; 20.0% trade/trans./util.; 8.7% mfg.; 14.1% ed./health; 12% prof./bus. serv.; 9.8% leisure/hosp.; 4.8% finance; 5.7% constr./mining/log.; 1.5% info.; 3.5% other serv. **Unemployment** (2010): 9.3%. **Per cap. pers. income** (2010 prelim.): $32,257. **New private housing** (2010): 4,153 units/$732.4 mil. **Commercial banks** (2010): 32; deposits: $17.2 bil. **Savings institutions** (2010): 3; deposits: $1.4 bil. **Lottery** (2010): total sales: $147 mil; profit: $36.5 mil.

Federal govt. Fed. civ. employees (Mar. 2011): 8,829; **avg. salary:** $64,192. **Notable fed. facilities:** Idaho Natl. Lab; *Mountain Home AFB.

Energy. Electricity production (2010 kWh by source): gas: 289 mil; hydroelectric: 8.4 bil.

State data. Motto: Esto Perpetua (It is perpetual). **Flower:** Syringa. **Bird:** Mountain bluebird. **Tree:** White pine. **Song:** "Here We Have Idaho." **Entered union:** July 3, 1890; rank: 43rd. **State fair** at Boise, late Aug.; at Blackfoot, early Sept.

History. Paleo-Indian hunters roamed the land over 13,000 years ago; later inhabitants included Shoshone, Northern Paiute, Bannock, and Nez Percé peoples. Meriwether Lewis and William Clark Expedition took place, 1804-06. Next came fur traders, 1809-34, and missionaries, 1830s-50s. Mormons made their first permanent settlement at Franklin, 1860. Idaho's gold rush began the same year and brought thousands of permanent settlers. A series of Indian wars followed, including a remarkable campaign by Chief Joseph and the Nez Percé that ended with his surrender in Montana, 1877. Idaho became a territory, 1863, and a state, 1890. In the 20th cent., it emerged as a leader in potato, lumber, and silver output. The Sun Valley ski resort opened in 1936, boosting tourism. Startup of Lewiston's river port, 1975, opened Idaho to oceangoing trade. Fueled by high-tech job growth, the state's population jumped 19.5% in 2000-09.

Tourist attractions. Hells Canyon, deepest gorge in N. America; World Ctr. for Birds of Prey, Boise; Craters of the Moon Natl. Monument; Sun Valley, Sawtooth Mts.; Shoshone Falls; Lava Hot Springs; Lake Pend Oreille; Lake Coeur d'Alene; Sawtooth Natl. Recreation Area, Redfish Lake; River of No Return Wilderness Area.

Famous Idahoans. William E. Borah, Frank Church, Lou Dobbs, Fred T. Dubois, Chief Joseph, Harmon Killebrew, Ezra Pound, Sacagawea, Picabo Street, Lana Turner.

Tourist information. Idaho Division of Tourism Development, 700 W. State St., P.O. Box 83720, Boise, ID 83720; 1-800-VISITID; www.visitid.org
Website. www.state.id.us

Illinois (IL)
Prairie State

People. Population (2010): 12,830,632; rank: 5; net change (2000-10): 3.3%. **Pop. density:** 231.1 per sq mi. **Racial distribution** (2010): 71.5% white; 14.5% black; 4.6% Asian; 0.3% Native Amer./AK; <0.05% Hawaiian/Pacific Islander; 2 or more races, 2.3%. **Hispanic pop.** (any race, 2010): 15.8%.

Geography. Total area: 57,914 sq mi; rank: 25. **Land area:** 55,519 sq mi; rank: 24. **Acres forested:** 4.8 mil. **Location:** East North Central state; western, southern, and eastern boundaries formed by Mississippi, Ohio, and Wabash Rivers, respectively. **Climate:** temperate; typically cold, snowy winters, hot summers. **Topography:** prairie and fertile plains throughout; open hills in the southern region. **Capital:** Springfield. **Chief airports:** Chicago (2).

Economy. Chief industries: services, manufacturing, travel, wholesale and retail trade, finance, insurance, real estate, construction, health care, agriculture. **Chief manuf. goods:** food, petroleum, plastics, chemicals, agricultural machinery, pharmaceuticals, motor vehicles, printing. **Chief crops:** corn, soybeans, hay, wheat, greenhouse & nursery, apples, peaches, sorghum. **Livestock** (Dec. 2010): 5 mil chickens (excl. broilers); (Jan. 2011): 1.10 mil cattle/calves, 56,000 sheep/lambs; (June 2011): 480,000 hogs/pigs. **Broadband internet:** 78.7%. **Nonfuel minerals** (2010 prelim.): $910 mil; stone (crushed), sand and gravel (construction), cement (portland), sand and gravel (industrial), tripoli. **Chief port:** Chicago. **Gross state product** (2010): $651.5 bil. **Sales tax** (2011): 6.25%. **Employment distrib.** (May 2011): 15.1% govt.; 20.0% trade/trans./util.; 9.9% mfg.; 15.0% ed./health; 14.4% prof./bus. serv.; 9.3% leisure/hosp.; 6.2% finance; 3.7% constr./mining/log.; 1.7% info.; 4.5% other serv. **Unemployment** (2010): 10.3%. **Per cap. pers. income** (2010 prelim.): $43,159. **New private housing** (2010): 12,318 units/$2.4 bil. **Commercial banks** (2010): 577; deposits: $337.2 bil. **Savings institutions** (2010): 87; deposits: $23.7 bil. **Lottery** (2010): total sales: $2.21 bil; profit: $657.9 mil.

Federal govt. Fed. civ. employees (Mar. 2011): 51,240; **avg. salary:** $75,642. **Notable fed. facilities:** *Great Lakes Naval Station; Fermi Natl. Accelerator Lab; Argonne Natl. Lab; Scott AFB; *Rock Island Arsenal.

Energy. Electricity production (2010 kWh by source): coal: 11.9 bil; gas: 540 mil; petroleum: 25 mil; hydroelectric: 40 mil.; other: 11 mil.

State data. Motto: State sovereignty—national union. **Flower:** Native violet. **Bird:** Cardinal. **Tree:** White oak. **Song:**

"Illinois." **Entered union:** Dec. 3, 1818; rank: 21st. **State fair** at Springfield, mid-Aug.; DuQuoin, late Aug.-Sept.

History. The region has been inhabited for at least 10,000 years; seminomadic Algonquian peoples, including the Peoria, Illinois, Kaskaskia, and Tamaroa, lived there at the time of European contact. Fur traders were the first Europeans in Illinois, followed shortly by Louis Jolliet and Jacques Marquette, 1673, and René-Robert Cavelier, sieur de La Salle, 1680, who built a fort near present-day Peoria. French priests established the first permanent settlements at Cahokia, near present-day St. Louis, 1699, and Kaskaskia, 1703. France ceded the area to Britain, 1763, and in 1778, American Gen. George Rogers Clark took Kaskaskia from the British without a shot. Illinois became a separate territory, 1809, and a state, 1818. Defeat of Native American tribes in the Black Hawk War, 1832, and canal, rail, and road construction brought rapid change. Mormon settlers at Nauvoo, 1839, met with hostility, and a Carthage mob killed Mormon leader Joseph Smith and his brother, 1844. The Great Chicago Fire, 1871, destroyed the city's downtown. Illinois became a center for the labor movement, leading to bitter conflicts such as the Haymarket riot, 1886, and Pullman strike, 1894. Social reformer Jane Addams founded Hull House, 1889, to aid immigrants and the poor. During 1900-70, as manufacturing expanded, many African Americans arrived from the southern U.S. Chicago police violently suppressed antiwar protests at the 1968 Democratic National Convention. Dennis Hastert was the longest serving Republican Speaker of the House, 1999-2007. Barack Obama, elected in 2004, was only the fifth African American to serve in the U.S. Senate; he became the 44th U.S. president in 2009. Political corruption and criminality have plagued the state for decades; since 1960, five former governors have been charged with criminal offenses.

Tourist attractions. Chicago museums and parks; Illinois State Museum, Abraham Lincoln Presidential Library and Museum, in Springfield; Cahokia Mounds, Collinsville; Starved Rock State Park; Crab Orchard Wildlife Refuge; Mormon settlement at Nauvoo; Fts. Kaskaskia, Chartres, Massac (parks); Shawnee Natl. Forest; Dickson Mounds Museum, Lewistown.

Famous Illinoisans. Jane Addams, John Ashcroft, Saul Bellow, Jack Benny, Ray Bradbury, Gwendolyn Brooks, William Jennings Bryan, St. Frances Xavier Cabrini, Hillary Rodham Clinton, Clarence Darrow, John Deere, Stephen A. Douglas, James T. Farrell, George W. Ferris, Marshall Field, Betty Friedan, Benny Goodman, Ulysses S. Grant, Dennis Hastert, Ernest Hemingway, Charlton Heston, Wild Bill Hickok, Henry J. Hyde, Abraham Lincoln, Vachel Lindsay, Edgar Lee Masters, Oscar Mayer, Cyrus McCormick, Ronald Reagan, Donald Rumsfeld, Carl Sandburg, Adlai Stevenson, James Watson, Frank Lloyd Wright, Philip Wrigley.

Tourist information. Illinois Bureau of Tourism, 100 W. Randolph St., Ste. 3-400, Chicago, IL 60601; 1-800-2CONNECT; www.enjoyillinois.com

Website. www.illinois.gov

Indiana (IN)
Hoosier State

People. Population (2010): 6,483,802; rank: 16; net change (2000-10): 6.6%. **Pop. density:** 181 per sq mi. **Racial distribution** (2010): 84.3% white; 9.1% black; 1.6% Asian; 0.3% Native Amer./AK; <0.05% Hawaiian/Pacific Islander; 2 or more races, 2.0%. **Hispanic pop.** (any race, 2010): 6.0%.

Geography. Total area: 36,420 sq mi; rank: 38. **Land area:** 35,826 sq mi; rank: 38. **Acres forested:** 4.7 mil. **Location:** East North Central state; Lake Michigan on N border. **Climate:** 4 distinct seasons with a temperate climate. **Topography:** hilly southern region; fertile rolling plains of central region; flat, heavily glaciated north; dunes along Lake Michigan shore. **Capital:** Indianapolis. **Chief airport:** Indianapolis.

Economy. Chief industries: manufacturing, services, agriculture, government, wholesale and retail trade, transportation and public utilities. **Chief manuf. goods:** motor vehicles & parts, iron & steel mills, pharmaceuticals, petroleum, plastics, medical equipment, printing. **Chief crops:** corn, soybeans, greenhouse & nursery, wheat, hay, tomatoes, watermelons, apples. **Livestock** (Dec. 2010): 30.63 mil chickens (excl. broilers); (Jan. 2011): 850,000 cattle/calves, 50,000 sheep/lambs; (June 2011): 300,000 hogs/pigs. **Broadband internet:** 73.9%. **Nonfuel minerals** (2010 prelim.): $837 mil; stone (crushed), cement (portland), sand and gravel

(construction), lime, stone (dimension). **Chief ports:** Burns Harbor-Portage, Mt. Vernon, Jeffersonville. **Gross state product** (2010): $275.7 bil. **Sales tax** (2011): 7.0%. **Employment distrib.** (May 2011): 15.4% govt.; 19.1% trade/trans./util.; 16.0% mfg.; 15.3% ed./health; 9.9% prof./bus. serv.; 10.0% leisure/hosp.; 4.7% finance; 4.4% constr./mining/log.; 1.2% info.; 3.8% other serv. **Unemployment** (2010): 10.2%. **Per cap. pers. income** (2010 prelim.): $34,943. **New private housing** (2010): 13,083 units/$2.0 bil. **Commercial banks** (2010): 140; deposits: $89.5 bil. **Savings institutions** (2010): 46; deposits: $9.0 bil. **Lottery** (2010): total sales: $739.1 mil; profit: $188.8 mil.

Federal govt. Fed. civ. employees (Mar. 2011): 24,456; **avg. salary:** $66,435. **Notable fed. facilities:** Nav. Surface Warfare Ctr., Crane Div.; Grissom Air Reserve Base.

Energy. Electricity production (2010 kWh by source): coal: 103.4 bil; gas: 3.8 bil; petroleum: 138 mil; hydroelectric: 443 mil; other: 253 mil.

State data. Motto: Crossroads of America. **Flower:** Peony. **Bird:** Cardinal. **Tree:** Tulip poplar. **Song:** "On the Banks of the Wabash, Far Away." **Entered union:** Dec. 11, 1816; rank: 19th. **State fair** at Indianapolis, mid-Aug.

History. When the Europeans arrived, Miami, Potawatomi, Kickapoo, Piankashaw, Wea, and Shawnee peoples inhabited the region. René-Robert Cavelier, sieur de La Salle visited the present South Bend area, 1679 and 1681. The first French fort was built near present-day Lafayette, 1717. A French trading post was established, 1731-32, at Vincennes. France ceded the area to Britain, 1763. During the American Revolution, American Gen. George Rogers Clark captured Vincennes, 1778, and defeated British forces, 1779. Indiana became a territory, 1800, and a state, 1816. The Miami were beaten, 1794, at Fallen Timbers, and Gen. William H. Harrison defeated Tecumseh's Indian confederation, 1811, at Tippecanoe. Manufacturing grew rapidly after the Civil War. U.S. Steel founded Gary, 1906. An automotive test track was the site of the first Indianapolis 500 race, 1911. The auto industry remains key to the state economy; in 2008, Honda opened a $550-mil plant near Greensburg. Heavy rain in June 2008 flooded southwest and central Indiana.

Tourist attractions. Lincoln Log Cabin Historic Site, near Charleston; George Rogers Clark Park, Vincennes; Wyandotte Caves; Tippecanoe Battlefield Park, near Lafayette; Benjamin Harrison home, Indianapolis 500 raceway and museum, in Indianapolis; Indiana Dunes, Chesterton; Natl. College Football Hall of Fame, South Bend; Hoosier Natl. Forest.

Famous "Hoosiers." Larry Bird, Ambrose Burnside, Hoagy Carmichael, Jim Davis, James Dean, Eugene V. Debs, Theodore Dreiser, Paul Dresser, Jeff Gordon, Benjamin Harrison, Gil Hodges, Michael Jackson, David Letterman, Carole Lombard, John Mellencamp, Jane Pauley, Cole Porter, Gene Stratton Porter, Ernie Pyle, Dan Quayle, James Whitcomb Riley, Oscar Robertson, Red Skelton, Booth Tarkington, Kurt Vonnegut, Lew Wallace, Wendell L. Willkie, Wilbur Wright.

Tourist information. Indiana Office of Tourism Development, 1 North Capital, Ste. 600, Indianapolis, IN 46204; 1-800-677-9800; www.visitindiana.com

Website. www.in.gov

Iowa (IA)
Hawkeye State

People. Population (2010): 3,046,355; rank: 30; net change (2000-10): 4.1%. **Pop. density:** 54.5 per sq mi. **Racial distribution** (2010): 91.3% white; 2.9% black; 1.7% Asian; 0.4% Native Amer./AK; 0.1% Hawaiian/Pacific Islander; 2 or more races, 1.8%. **Hispanic pop.** (any race, 2010): 5.0%.

Geography. Total area: 56,273 sq mi; rank: 26. **Land area:** 55,857 sq mi; rank: 23. **Acres forested:** 3.0 mil. **Location:** West North Central state bordered by Mississippi R. on the E and Missouri R. on the W. **Climate:** humid, continental. **Topography:** watershed from NW to SE; soil especially rich and land level in the N central counties. **Capital:** Des Moines. **Chief airport:** Des Moines.

Economy. Chief industries: agriculture, communications, construction, finance, insurance, trade, services, manufacturing. **Chief manuf. goods:** machinery, vegetable oils, animal slaughtering & processing, laundry equipment, plastics, motor vehicles & parts. **Chief crops:** corn, soybeans, hay, greenhouse & nursery, oats. **Livestock** (Dec. 2010): 66.12 mil chickens (excl. broilers); (Jan. 2011): 3.90 mil cattle/calves, 200,000 sheep/lambs; (June 2011): 1.03 mil. hogs/pigs. **Broadband internet:** 75.4%. **Nonfuel minerals** (2010 prelim.): $542 mil; stone (crushed), cement (portland), sand and gravel (construction), lime, gypsum (crude). **Gross state product** (2010): $142.7 bil. **Sales tax** (2011): 6.0%. **Employment distrib.** (May 2011): 17.3% govt.; 20.3% trade/trans./util.; 13.6% mfg.; 14.4% ed./health; 8.2% prof./bus. serv.; 9.4% leisure/hosp.; 6.6% finance; 4.5% constr./mining/log.; 1.9% info.; 3.8% other serv. **Unemployment** (2010): 6.1%. **Per cap. pers. income** (2010 prelim.): $38,281. **New private housing** (2010): 7,607 units/$1.2 bil. **Commercial banks** (2010): 364; deposits: $61.5 bil. **Savings institutions** (2010): 17; deposits: $5.0 bil. **Lottery** (2010): total sales: $256.3 mil; profit: $57.9 mil.

Federal govt. Fed. civ. employees (Mar. 2011): 9,190; **avg. salary:** $63,441. **Notable fed. facilities:** Ames Lab; Natl. Animal Disease Ctr.

Energy. Electricity production (2010 kWh by source): coal: 39.4 bil; gas: 1.5 bil; petroleum: 84 mil; hydroelectric: 825 mil; other: 4.5 bil.

State data. Motto: Our liberties we prize, and our rights we will maintain. **Flower:** Wild rose. **Bird:** Eastern goldfinch. **Tree:** Oak. **Song:** "The Song of Iowa." **Entered union:** Dec. 28, 1846; rank: 29th. **State fair** at Des Moines, mid-Aug.

History. Early inhabitants were Mound Builders who dwelt on Iowa's fertile plains. Later, Iowa and Yankton Sioux lived in the area. The first Europeans, Jacques Marquette and Louis Jolliet, gave France its claim to the area, 1673. In 1762, France ceded the region to Spain, but Napoleon took it back, 1800. It became part of the U.S. through the Louisiana Purchase, 1803. Native American Sauk and Fox tribes moved into the area but relinquished their land in defeat, after the 1832 uprising led by Sauk chieftain Black Hawk. Iowa became a territory in 1838, and entered as a free state, 1846, strongly supporting the Union. Fertile land lured farmers from eastern states, 1850-1900 and the population rose rapidly. Growth slowed in the 20th cent., as farming became mechanized. Surging demand for ethanol fuel from Iowa corn contributed more than $2.6 bil to the state economy in 2005. Severe flooding in eastern Iowa in June 2008 caused billions of dollars in damages and forced the evacuation of thousands of residents.

Tourist attractions. Herbert Hoover birthplace and library, West Branch; Effigy Mounds Natl. Monument, prehistoric Indian burial site, Marquette; Amana Colonies; Grant Wood's paintings and memorabilia, Davenport Municipal Art Gallery; Living History Farms, Des Moines; Adventureland, Prairie Meadows horse racing, in Altoona; Boone and Scenic Valley Railroad; Greyhound Parks, in Dubuque and Council Bluffs; riverboat cruises and casino gambling, Mississippi and Missouri Rivers; Iowa Great Lakes, Okoboji.

Famous Iowans. Tom Arnold, Johnny Carson, Marquis Childs, Buffalo Bill Cody, Mamie Dowd Eisenhower, Bob Feller, George Gallup, Susan Glaspell, James Norman Hall, Harry Hansen, Herbert Hoover, Ann Landers, Glenn Miller, Lillian Russell, Billy Sunday, James A. Van Allen, Abigail Van Buren, Carl Van Vechten, Henry Wallace, John Wayne, Meredith Willson, Grant Wood.

Tourist information. Iowa Tourism Office, Iowa Dept. of Economic Development, 200 E. Grand Ave., Des Moines, IA 50309; 1-888-472-6035; www.traveliowa.com

Website. www.iowa.gov

Kansas (KS)
Sunflower State

People. Population (2010): 2,853,118; rank: 33; net change (2000-10): 6.1%. **Pop. density:** 34.9 per sq mi. **Racial distribution** (2010): 83.8% white; 5.9% black; 2.4% Asian; 1.0% Native Amer./AK; 0.1% Hawaiian/Pacific Islander; 2 or more races, 3.0%. **Hispanic pop.** (any race, 2010): 10.5%.

Geography. Total area: 82,278 sq mi; rank: 15. **Land area:** 81,759 sq mi; rank: 13. **Acres forested:** 2.2 mil. **Location:** West North Central state, with Missouri R. on E. **Climate:** temperate but continental, with great extremes between summer and winter. **Topography:** hilly Osage Plains in the E; central region level prairie and hills; high plains in the W. **Capital:** Topeka. **Chief airport:** Wichita.

Economy. Chief industries: manufacturing, finance, insurance, real estate, services. **Chief manuf. goods:** animal slaughtering, aerospace, petroleum, plastics, machinery, navi-

gational instruments, printing. **Chief crops:** wheat, corn, soybeans, hay, sorghum, sunflowers, cotton, potatoes. **Livestock** (Jan. 2011): 6.3 mil cattle/calves, 70,000 sheep/lambs; (June 2011): 180,000 hogs/pigs. **Broadband internet:** 75.1%. **Nonfuel minerals** (2010 prelim.): $1.0 bil; helium (Grade-A), salt, cement (portland), stone (crushed), helium (crude). **Chief port:** Kansas City. **Gross state product** (2010): $127.2 bil. **Sales tax** (2011): 6.3%. **Employment distrib.** (May 2011): 20.2% govt.; 18.9% trade/trans./util.; 12.1% mfg.; 13.7% ed./health; 10.7% prof./bus. serv.; 8.5% leisure/hosp.; 5.1% finance; 4.7% constr./mining/log.; 2.2% info.; 3.9% other serv. **Unemployment** (2010): 7%. **Per cap. pers. income** (2010 prelim.): $39,737. **New private housing** (2010): 5,140 units/$811.6 mil. **Commercial banks** (2010): 349; deposits: $52.9 bil. **Savings institutions** (2010): 18; deposits: $7.1 bil. **Lottery** (2010): total sales: $243.7 mil; profit: $69.0 mil.

Federal govt. Fed. civ. employees (Mar. 2011): 17,884; **avg. salary:** $65,178. **Notable fed. facilities:** Fts. Riley, Leavenworth; Leavenworth Fed. Pen.; McConnell AFB; Colmery-O'Neal Veterans Hospital.

Energy. Electricity production (2010 kWh by source): coal: 32.5 bil; gas: 2.8 bil; nuclear: 9.6 bil; petroleum: 46 mil; other: 877 mil.

State data. Motto: Ad Astra per Aspera (To the stars through difficulties). **Flower:** Native sunflower. **Bird:** Western meadowlark. **Tree:** Cottonwood. **Song:** "Home on the Range." **Entered union:** Jan. 29, 1861; rank: 34th. **State fair** at Hutchinson, begins Friday after Labor Day.

History. Wichita, Pawnee, Kansa, and Osage peoples lived in the area when Francisco de Coronado explored it in 1541. These Native Americans—hunters who also farmed—were joined on the Plains by the nomadic Cheyenne, Arapaho, Comanche, and Kiowa about 1800. France claimed the region, 1682, ceded its claim to Spain, 1762, then regained control, 1800, before selling it to the U.S. in the Louisiana Purchase, 1803. After 1830, thousands of Native Americans were removed from more eastern states to Kansas. Organized as a territory, 1854, the area witnessed violent clashes between pro- and antislavery settlers and became known as "Bleeding Kansas." It entered the Union as a free state, 1861. After the Civil War, rail construction and huge cattle drives from Texas turned Abilene and Dodge City into cowboy capitals. Russian Mennonite immigrants brought a new strain of winter wheat, 1874, transforming Kansas agriculture. Carry Nation launched her anti-saloon crusade in the 1890s. Part of the "Dust Bowl," the state experienced drought and depression in the 1930s. Topeka was the focus of the famous *Brown v. Board of Education* decision, 1954, that led to desegregation of U.S. public schools. Bob Dole (R) represented Kansas in the U.S. Senate (1969-96) but failed in several efforts to win higher office.

Tourist attractions. Eisenhower Center, Abilene; Natl. Agricultural Ctr. and Hall of Fame, Bonner Springs; Dodge City-Boot Hill; Old Cowtown Museum, Wichita; Ft. Scott and Ft. Larned, restored 1800s cavalry forts; Kansas Cosmosphere and Space Center, Hutchinson; Woodlands Racetrack, Kansas City; U.S. Cavalry Museum, Ft. Riley; Heartland Park Raceway, Topeka.

Famous Kansans. Kirstie Alley, Roscoe "Fatty" Arbuckle, Ed Asner, Gwendolyn Brooks, John Brown, George Washington Carver, Wilt Chamberlain, Walter P. Chrysler, Glenn Cunningham, John Stuart Curry, Robert Dole, Amelia Earhart, Wyatt Earp, Dwight D. Eisenhower, Ron Evans, Maurice Greene, Wild Bill Hickok, Cyrus Holliday, Dennis Hopper, William Inge, Don Johnson, Walter Johnson, Nancy Landon Kassebaum, Buster Keaton, Emmett Kelly, Alf Landon, Edgar Lee Masters, Hattie McDaniel, Oscar Micheaux, Carry Nation, Georgia Neese-Gray, Charlie Parker, Gordon Parks, Jim Ryun, Barry Sanders, Vivian Vance, William Allen White, Jess Willard.

Tourist information. Kansas Dept. of Commerce, Travel and Tourism Div., 1000 SW Jackson St., Ste. 100, Topeka, KS 66612; (785) 296-2009; www.travelks.com

Website. www.kansas.gov

Kentucky (KY)
Bluegrass State

People. Population (2010): 4,339,367; rank: 26; net change (2000-10): 7.4%. **Pop. density:** 109.9 per sq mi. **Racial distribution** (2010): 87.8% white; 7.8% black; 1.1% Asian; 0.2% Native Amer./AK; 0.1% Hawaiian/Pacific Islander; 2 or more races, 1.7%. **Hispanic pop.** (any race, 2010): 3.1%.

Geography. Total area: 40,408 sq mi; rank: 37. **Land area:** 39,486 sq mi; rank: 37. **Acres forested:** 12.4 mil. **Location:** E South Central state, bordered on N by Illinois, Indiana, Ohio; on E by West Virginia and Virginia; on S by Tennessee; on W by Missouri. **Climate:** moderate, with plentiful rainfall. **Topography:** mountainous in E; rounded hills of the Knobs in the N; Bluegrass, heart of state; wooded rocky hillsides of the Pennyroyal; Western Coal Field; the fertile Purchase in the SW. **Capital:** Frankfort. **Chief airports:** Greater Cincinnati, Lexington, Louisville.

Economy. Chief industries: manufacturing, services, finance, insurance and real estate, retail trade, public utilities. **Chief manuf. goods:** motor vehicles & parts, aluminum, basic chemicals, plastics, iron & steel, rubber, printing. **Chief crops:** hay, corn, soybeans, tobacco, wheat. **Livestock** (Dec. 2010): 6.53 mil chickens (excl. broilers), 309.90 mil broilers; (Jan. 2011): 2.19 mil cattle/calves, 34,000 sheep/ lambs. **Broadband internet:** 80.1%. **Nonfuel minerals** (2010 prelim.): $742 mil; stone (crushed), lime, cement (portland), sand and gravel (construction), clays (common). **Chief ports:** Louisville, Hickman-Fulton County. **Gross state product** (2010): $163.3 bil. **Sales tax** (2011): 6.0%. **Employment distrib.** (May 2011): 18.5% govt.; 20.1% trade/trans./ util.; 11.8% mfg.; 14.1% ed./health; 10.3% prof./bus. serv.; 10.2% leisure/hosp.; 4.7% finance; 5.1% constr./mining/log.; 1.4% info.; 4.1% other serv. **Unemployment** (2010): 10.5%. **Per cap. pers. income** (2010 prelim.): $33,348. **New private housing** (2010): 7,986 units/$1.1 bil. **Commercial banks** (2010): 201; deposits: $66.4 bil. **Savings institutions** (2010): 26; deposits: $2.4 bil. **Lottery** (2010): total sales: $772.5 mil; profit: $214.3 mil.

Federal govt. Fed. civ. employees (Mar. 2011): 27,694; **avg. salary:** $59,077. **Notable fed. facilities:** U.S. Gold Bullion Depository; Ft. Knox; Ft. Campbell; Fed. Correctional Institution, Lexington; Army Corps of Engineers, Louisville.

Energy. Electricity production (2010 kWh by source): coal: 91 bil; gas: 1.5 bil; petroleum: 124 mil; hydroelectric: 2.6 bil; other: 2.3 bil.

State data. Motto: United we stand, divided we fall. **Flower:** Goldenrod. **Bird:** Cardinal. **Tree:** Tulip poplar. **Song:** "My Old Kentucky Home." **Entered union:** June 1, 1792; rank: 15th. **State fair** at Louisville, mid-Aug.

History. Paleo-Indians first arrived about 14,000 years ago. Much later, Shawnee, Wyandot, Delaware, and Cherokee peoples also used the area mostly for hunting. Explored by Thomas Walker and Christopher Gist, 1750-51, Kentucky was the first area W of the Alleghenies settled by American pioneers. The first permanent settlement was Harrodsburg, 1774. Daniel Boone blazed the Wilderness Trail through the Cumberland Gap and founded Ft. Boonesborough, 1775. Clashes with Native Americans were frequent, 1774-94. Virginia dropped its claims to the region, and Kentucky became a state, 1792. Tobacco growing, horse breeding, coal mining, and bourbon whiskey making were major industries in the 19th cent. A slave state, Kentucky tried to stay neutral in the Civil War, but then opted for the Union; many Kentuckians sided with the Confederacy. The U.S. gold depository at Ft. Knox opened, 1937. Prior to the 2008 economic downturn, auto manufacturing had grown in recent decades. An ice storm in southwestern Kentucky in Jan. 2009 killed 14 and caused severe power outages.

Tourist attractions. Churchill Downs (Kentucky Derby), Louisville; Land Between the Lakes Natl. Recreation Area, lakes Kentucky and Barkley; Mammoth Cave Natl. Park; Lake Cumberland; Lincoln's birthplace, Hodgenville; My Old Kentucky Home State Park, Bardstown; Cumberland Gap Natl. Historical Park, Middlesboro; Kentucky Horse Park, Lexington; Shaker Village, Pleasant Hill.

Famous Kentuckians. Muhammad Ali, John James Audubon, Alben W. Barkley, Daniel Boone, Louis D. Brandeis, John C. Breckinridge, Kit Carson, Albert B. "Happy" Chandler, Henry Clay, Jefferson Davis, D. W. Griffith, "Casey" Jones, Abraham Lincoln, Mary Todd Lincoln, Thomas Hunt Morgan, Carry Nation, Col. Harland Sanders, Diane Sawyer, Adlai Stevenson, Jesse Stuart, Zachary Taylor, Hunter S. Thompson, Robert Penn Warren, Whitney Young Jr.

Tourist information. Kentucky Dept. of Travel, Capital Plaza Tower, 22nd Fl., 500 Mero St., Frankfort, KY 40601; 1-800-225-8747; www.kentuckytourism.com
Website. www.kentucky.gov

Louisiana (LA)
Pelican State

People. Population (2010): 4,533,372; rank: 25; net change (2000-10): 1.4%. **Pop. density:** 104.9 per sq mi. **Racial distribution** (2010): 62.6% white; 32% black; 1.5% Asian; 0.7% Native Amer./AK; <0.05% Hawaiian/Pacific Islander; 2 or more races, 1.6%. **Hispanic pop.** (any race, 2010): 4.2%.

Geography. Total area: 52,378 sq mi; rank: 31. **Land area:** 43,204 sq mi; rank: 33. **Acres forested:** 14.2 mil. **Location:** West South Central state on the Gulf Coast. **Climate:** subtropical, affected by continental weather patterns. **Topography:** lowlands of marshes and Mississippi R. flood plain; Red R. Valley lowlands; upland hills in the Florida Parishes; avg. elevation, 100 ft. **Capital:** Baton Rouge. **Chief airport:** Metairie.

Economy. Chief industries: wholesale and retail trade, tourism, manufacturing, construction, transportation, communication, public utilities, finance, insurance, real estate, mining. **Chief manuf. goods:** petroleum, chemicals, plastics material & resin, pesticides & fertilizers, cleaning products, paper & paperboard, ships, structural metals. **Chief crops:** sugarcane, cotton, rice, soybeans, corn, sweet potatoes. **Livestock** (Dec. 2010): 2.68 mil chickens (excl. broilers); (Jan. 2011): 790,000 cattle/calves. **Broadband internet:** 80.4%. **Nonfuel minerals** (2010 prelim.): $492 mil; salt, sand and gravel (construction), stone (crushed), sand and gravel (industrial), clays (common). **Commercial fishing** (2009): $284.4 mil. **Chief ports:** New Orleans, Baton Rouge, Lake Charles, Port of S. Louisiana (La Place), Shreveport, Plaquemine, St. Bernard, Alexandria. **Gross state product** (2010): $218.9 bil. **Sales tax** (2011): 4.0%. **Employment distrib.** (May 2011): 18.9% govt.; 19.3% trade/trans./util.; 7.5% mfg.; 14.6% ed./health; 10.1% prof./bus. serv.; 10.7% leisure/hosp.; 4.8% finance; 9.1% constr./mining/log.; 1.5% info.; 3.5% other serv. **Unemployment** (2010): 7.5%. **Per cap. pers. income** (2010 prelim.): $38,446. **New private housing** (2010): 11,343 units/$1.8 bil. **Commercial banks** (2010): 137; deposits: $78.0 bil. **Savings institutions** (2010): 27; deposits: $4.8 bil. **Lottery** (2010): total sales: $372.4 mil; profit: $134.1 mil.

Federal govt. Fed. civ. employees (Mar. 2011): 21,488; **avg. salary:** $65,859. **Notable federal facilities:** Ft. Polk (Joint Readiness Training Ctr.); Barksdale AFB; Strategic Petroleum Reserve, Michoud Assembly Plant, USDA Southern Regional Research Ctr., Army Corps of Engineers, all New Orleans; New Orleans NAS.

Energy. Electricity production (2010 kWh by source): coal: 11.2 bil; gas: 18.9 bil; nuclear: 18.6 bil; petroleum: 75 mil; other: 2.8 bil.

State data. Motto: Union, justice, and confidence. **Flower:** Magnolia. **Bird:** Eastern brown pelican. **Tree:** Cypress. **Song:** "Give Me Louisiana." **Entered union:** Apr. 30, 1812; rank: 18th. **State fair** at Shreveport; late Oct.-early Nov.

History. Caddo, Tunica, Choctaw, Chitimacha, and Chawash peoples lived in the region at the time of European contact. Spanish explorers in the early 16th cent. reached the mouth of the Mississippi. René-Robert Cavelier, sieur de La Salle, 1682, claimed the region for France. Early French and Spanish settlers were the ancestors of Louisiana Creoles. Cajuns descended from the Acadians, French settlers expelled by the British from Nova Scotia, Canada, in 1755. France ceded the Louisiana region to Spain, 1762, took it back, 1800, and sold it to the U.S., 1803, in the Louisiana Purchase. Admitted as a state in 1812, Louisiana witnessed the Battle of New Orleans, 1815. Cotton and sugar plantations relied on black slaves, who made up 47% of the population in 1860, on the eve of the Civil War. Louisiana seceded, 1861, and was readmitted, 1868. Jazz was born in New Orleans in the early 20th cent. As governor (1928-32), Huey Long pushed populist programs. Many tropical storms and floods have battered Louisiana, including Hurricane Katrina and subsequent flooding, 2005, which devastated New Orleans. The offshore oil and gas industry developed after World War II. An oil rig explosion off the state's Gulf coast spilled millions of barrels of oil into the gulf, damaging coastal wetlands and many of the state's marine-dependent industries in 2010.

Tourist attractions. French Quarter and other New Orleans attractions; Jean Lafitte Natl. Hist. Park, Chalmette; Longfellow-Evangeline State Hist. Site, St. Martinville; Kent Plantation House, Alexandria; Hodges Gardens, Natchitoches; USS Kidd Memorial, Baton Rouge.

Famous Louisianans. Louis Armstrong, Pierre Beauregard, Judah P. Benjamin, Braxton Bragg, Kate Chopin, Johnnie Cochran, Harry Connick Jr., Ellen DeGeneres, Fats Domino, Lillian Hellman, Grace King, Elmore Leonard, Bob Livingston, Huey Long, Eli Manning, Peyton Manning, Wynton Marsalis, Leonidas K. Polk, Anne Rice, Henry Miller Shreve, Britney Spears, Edward D. White Jr.

Tourist information. Louisiana Office of Tourism, P.O. Box 94291, Baton Rouge, LA 70804-9291; 1-800-677-4082; www.louisianatravel.com

Website. www.louisiana.gov

Maine (ME)
Pine Tree State

People. Population (2010): 1,328,361; rank: 41; net change (2000-10): 4.2%. **Pop. density:** 43.1 per sq mi. **Racial distribution** (2010): 95.2% white; 1.2% black; 1.0% Asian; 0.6% Native Amer./AK; <0.05% Hawaiian/Pacific Islander; 2 or more races, 1.6%. **Hispanic pop.** (any race, 2010): 1.3%.

Geography. Total area: 35,380 sq mi; rank: 39. **Land area:** 30,843 sq mi; rank: 39. **Acres forested:** 17.6 mil. **Location:** New England state at northeastern tip of U.S. **Climate:** Southern interior and coastal, influenced by air masses from the S and W; northern clime harsher, avg. over 100 in. snow in winter. **Topography:** Appalachian Mts. extend through state; western borders have rugged terrain; long sand beaches on southern coast; northern coast mainly rocky promontories, peninsulas, fjords. **Capital:** Augusta. **Chief airport:** Portland.

Economy. Chief industries: manufacturing, agriculture, fishing, services, trade, government, finance, insurance, real estate, construction. **Chief manuf. goods:** paper, ships & boats, cardboard, frozen/canned fruits & vegetables, plastics, baked goods. **Chief crops:** potatoes, greenhouse & nursery, wild blueberries, apples, hay, maple syrup. **Livestock** (Dec. 2010): 3.60 mil chickens (excl. broilers); (Jan. 2011): 90,000 cattle/calves. **Broadband internet:** 77.2%. **Nonfuel minerals** (2010 prelim.): $114 mil; sand and gravel (construction), stone (crushed), cement (portland), stone (dimension), peat. **Commercial fishing** (2009): $285.9 mil. **Chief ports:** Searsport, Portland, Eastport. **Gross state product** (2010): $51.6 bil. **Sales tax** (2011): 5.0%. **Employment distrib.** (May 2011): 17.5% govt.; 19.1% trade/trans./util.; 8.6% mfg.; 20.3% ed./health; 9.4% prof./bus. serv.; 10.4% leisure/hosp.; 5.3% finance; 4.5% constr./mining/log.; 1.5% info.; 3.3% other serv. **Unemployment** (2010): 7.9%. **Per cap. pers. income** (2010 prelim.): $37,300. **New private housing** (2010): 3,034 units/$525.3 mil. **Commercial banks** (2010): 12; deposits: $18.3 bil. **Savings institutions** (2010): 21; deposits: $9.3 bil. **Lottery** (2010): total sales: $216.7 mil; profit: $52.2 mil.

Federal govt. Fed. civ. employees (Mar. 2011): 11,036; **avg. salary:** $64,615. **Notable fed. facilities:** Portsmouth Naval Shipyard; Loring AFB.

Energy. Electricity production: NA.

State data. Motto: Dirigo (I direct). **Flower:** White pine cone and tassel. **Bird:** Black-capped chickadee. **Tree:** Eastern white pine. **Song:** "State of Maine Song." **Entered union:** Mar. 15, 1820; rank: 23rd. **State fair** at Bangor, late July-early Aug.; at Skow-hegan, mid-Aug.

History. Paleo-Indians arrived about 11,500 years ago. Maine was inhabited by Algonquian peoples including the Abnaki, Penobscot, and Passamaquoddy at the time of European contact. French settled, 1604, at the St. Croix River, English, c. 1607, on the Kennebec; both settlements failed. A royal charter, 1691, made Maine part of Massachusetts. Maine broke off, 1819, and became a separate state, 1820. Drawing on vast forest resources, the pulp and paper industry developed after the Civil War. Bath Iron Works began building U.S. Navy vessels and other ships in the 1890s. Mail-order and retail giant L.L. Bean was founded, 1912. Women have fared well in state politics: Margaret Chase Smith became the first woman to serve in both houses of Congress (House, 1940-49; Senate, 1949-73), and Olympia Snowe and Susan Collins have represented Maine in the Senate since the mid-1990s.

Tourist attractions. Acadia Natl. Park, Bar Harbor, on Mt. Desert Island; Old Orchard Beach; Portland's Old Port; Kennebunkport; Common Ground Country Fair, Unity; Portland Head Light; Baxter State Park; Freeport/L.L. Bean.

Famous "Down Easters." Leon Leonwood (L.L.) Bean, James G. Blaine, Cyrus H. K. Curtis, Hannibal Hamlin, Sarah Jewett, Stephen King, Henry Wadsworth Longfellow, Sir

Hiram and Hudson Maxim, Edna St. Vincent Millay, George Mitchell, Edmund Muskie, Judd Nelson, Edwin Arlington Robinson, Joan Benoit Samuelson, Liv Tyler, Kate Douglas Wiggin, Ben Ames Williams.

Tourist information. Maine Office of Tourism, 59 State House Station, Augusta, ME 04333; 1-888-624-6345; www.visitmaine.com

Website. www.maine.gov

Maryland (MD)
Old Line State, Free State

People. Population (2010): 5,773,552; rank: 19; net change (2000-10): 9.0%. **Pop. density:** 594.8 per sq mi. **Racial distribution** (2010): 58.2% white; 29.4% black; 5.5% Asian; 0.4% Native Amer./AK; 0.1% Hawaiian/Pacific Islander; 2 or more races, 2.9%. **Hispanic pop.** (any race, 2010): 8.2%.

Geography. Total area: 12,406 sq mi; rank: 42. **Land area:** 9,707 sq mi; rank: 42. **Acres forested:** 2.4 mil. **Location:** South Atlantic state stretching from the Ocean to the Allegheny Mts. **Climate:** continental in the west; humid subtropical in the east. **Topography:** Eastern Shore of coastal plain and Maryland Main of coastal plain, Piedmont Plateau, and the Blue Ridge, separated by the Chesapeake Bay. **Capital:** Annapolis. **Chief airport:** Baltimore/Glen Burnie.

Economy. Chief industries: manufacturing, biotechnology and information technology, services, tourism. **Chief manuf. goods:** navigational instruments, pharmaceutical & medicine, broadcasting equip., plastics, printing, milk & ice cream. **Chief crops:** greenhouse & nursery, corn, soybeans, wheat, hay, tomatoes, watermelons, barley, potatoes, apples. **Livestock** (Dec. 2010): 2.86 mil chickens (excl. broilers), 300.5 mil broilers; (Jan. 2011): 195,000 cattle/calves. **Broadband internet:** 72.3%. **Nonfuel minerals** (2010 prelim.): $438 mil; stone (crushed), cement (portland), sand and gravel (construction), cement (masonry), stone (dimension). **Commercial fishing** (2009): $76.1 mil. **Chief port:** Baltimore. **Gross state product** (2010): $295.3 bil. **Sales tax** (2011): 6.0%. **Employment distrib.** (May 2011): 20.0% govt.; 17.4% trade/trans./util.; 4.5% mfg.; 15.9% ed./health; 15.6% prof./bus. serv.; 9.3% leisure/hosp.; 5.6% finance; 5.8% constr./mining/log.; 1.7% info.; 4.6% other serv. **Unemployment** (2010): 7.5%. **Per cap. pers. income** (2010 prelim.): $49,025. **New private housing** (2010): 11,931 units/$2.0 bil. **Commercial banks** (2010): 89; deposits: $104.1 bil. **Savings institutions** (2010): 45; deposits: $8.7 bil. **Lottery** (2010): total sales: $1.71 bil; profit: $510.6 mil.

Federal govt. Fed. civ. employees (Mar. 2011): 131,349; **avg. salary:** $93,483. **Notable fed. facilities:** U.S. Naval Academy; Natl. Agriculture Res. Ctr.; Ft. Meade, Aberdeen Proving Ground; Andrews AFB; Naval Air Sys. Command; Goddard Space Flight Ctr.; Natl. Inst. of Health; Natl. Inst. of Standards & Technology; Food & Drug Admin.; Bureau of the Census; Natl. Naval Med. Ctr., Bethesda; Natl. Marine Fisheries Serv.; Natl. Oceanic and Atmospheric Admin.

Energy. Electricity production (2010 kWh by source): petroleum: 4 mil.

State data. Motto: Fatti Maschii, Parole Femine (Manly deeds, womanly words). **Flower:** Black-eyed Susan. **Bird:** Baltimore oriole. **Tree:** White oak. **Song:** "Maryland, My Maryland." **Seventh** of the original 13 states to ratify the U.S. Constitution, Apr. 28, 1788. **State fair** at Timonium, late Aug.-early Sept.

History. Europeans encountered Algonquian-speaking Nanticoke and Piscataway and Iroquois-speaking Susquehannock when they first visited the area. Italian navigator Verrazano reached the Chesapeake region in the early 16th cent. English Capt. John Smith explored and mapped the area, 1608. William Claiborne set up a trading post on Kent Island in Chesapeake Bay, 1631. King Charles I granted land to Cecilius Calvert, Lord Baltimore, 1632; Calvert's brother Leonard, with about 200 settlers, founded St. Marys, 1634. During the Revolutionary War, Baltimore (1776-77) and Annapolis (1783-84) served as temporary capitals of the U.S. In the War of 1812, when a British fleet tried to take Ft. McHenry, Marylander Francis Scott Key wrote "The Star-Spangled Banner," 1814. Born into slavery at Tuckahoe in 1818, Frederick Douglass became a leading abolitionist. Although a slaveholding state, Maryland stayed in the Union during the Civil War and was the site of the battle of Antietam, 1862. Gov. Spiro Agnew elected U.S. vice pres. 1968; 1972; pleaded no contest to tax evasion and resigned 1973. Israeli and Egyptian leaders reached a historic peace accord at the Camp David presidential retreat, 1978. A major effort is under way to clean up pollution in the Chesapeake Bay watershed.

Tourist attractions. Laurel Park (Maryland Million); Ocean City; restored Ft. McHenry—near which Francis Scott Key wrote "The Star-Spangled Banner," Pimlico track (The Preakness), Edgar Allan Poe house, Camden Yards, Natl. Aquarium, Harborplace, all Baltimore; Antietam Battlefield, near Hagerstown; South Mountain Battlefield; U.S. Naval Academy, Maryland State House (oldest still in legislative use in the U.S.), Annapolis; Natl. Cryptologic Museum, Ft. Meade.

Famous Marylanders. John Astin, Benjamin Banneker, Tom Clancy, Jonathan Demme, Francis Scott Key, H. L. Mencken, Kweisi Mfume, Ogden Nash, Charles Willson Peale, William Pinkney, Edgar Allan Poe, Cal Ripken Jr., Babe Ruth, Upton Sinclair, Roger B. Taney, John Waters, Montel Williams.

Tourist information. Maryland Office of Tourism Development, 401 E. Pratt St., 14th Fl., Baltimore, MD 21202; 1-866-639-3526; www.visitmaryland.org

Website. www.maryland.gov

Massachusetts (MA)
Bay State, Old Colony

People. Population (2010): 6,547,629; rank: 15; net change (2000-10): 3.1%. **Pop. density:** 839.4 per sq mi. **Racial distribution** (2010): 80.4% white; 6.6% black; 5.3% Asian; 0.3% Native Amer./AK; <0.05% Hawaiian/Pacific Islander; 2 or more races, 2.6%. **Hispanic pop.** (any race, 2010): 9.6%.

Geography. Total area: 10,554 sq mi; rank: 44. **Land area:** 7,800 sq mi; rank: 45. **Acres forested:** 3.0 mil. **Location:** New England state along Atlantic seaboard. **Climate:** temperate, with colder and drier clime in western region. **Topography:** jagged indented coast from Rhode Island around Cape Cod; flat land yields to stony upland pastures near central region and gentle hilly country in west; except in west, land is rocky, sandy, and not fertile. **Capital:** Boston. **Chief airport:** Boston.

Economy. Chief industries: services, trade, manufacturing. **Chief manuf. goods:** electronics & instruments, pharmaceuticals, telecom. & broadcasting equip., plastics, medical equip., printing. **Chief crops:** greenhouse & nursery, cranberries, tomatoes, sweet corn, apples, hay, tobacco. **Livestock** (Dec. 2010): 138,000 chickens (excl. broilers); (Jan. 2011): 40,000 cattle/calves. **Broadband internet:** 77.0% **Nonfuel minerals** (2010 prelim.): $194 mil; stone (crushed), sand and gravel (construction), lime, stone (dimension), clays (common). **Commercial fishing** (2009): $400.2 mil. **Chief ports:** Boston, Fall River. **Gross state product** (2010): $378.7 bil. **Sales tax** (2011): 6.25%. **Employment distrib.** (May 2011): 13.6% govt.; 16.9% trade/trans./util.; 7.9% mfg.; 20.9% ed./health; 14.5% prof./bus. serv.; 9.9% leisure/hosp.; 6.4% finance; 3.4% constr./mining/log.; 2.8% info.; 3.7% other serv. **Unemployment** (2010): 8.5%. **Per cap. pers. income** (2010 prelim.): $51,552. **New private housing** (2010): 9,075 units/$1.8 bil. **Commercial banks** (2010): 49; deposits: $128.9 bil. **Savings institutions** (2010): 142; deposits: $76.3 bil. **Lottery** (2010): total sales: $4.42 bil; profit: $903.5 mil.

Federal govt. Fed. civ. employees (Mar. 2011): 29,551; **avg. salary:** $77,308. **Notable fed. facilities:** Thomas P. O'Neill Jr. Fed. Bldg.; J.W. McCormack Bldg.; JFK Fed. Bldg.; Hanscom AFB; *Natick Army Soldier Systems Ctr.

Energy. Electricity production (2010 kWh by source): gas: 511 mil; petroleum: 42 mil; hydroelectric: 237 mil; other: 13 mil.

State data. Motto: Ense Petit Placidam Sub Libertate Quietem (By the sword we seek peace, but peace only under liberty). **Flower:** Mayflower. **Bird:** Black-capped chickadee. **Tree:** American elm. **Song:** "All Hail to Massachusetts." **Sixth** of the original 13 states to ratify Constitution, Feb. 6, 1788. **State fair** at West Springfield, mid-Sept.-early Oct.

History. Early inhabitants were Algonquian peoples: Nauset, Wampanoag, Massachuset, Pennacook, Nipmuc, and Pocumtuc. Pilgrims settled in Plymouth, 1620, giving thanks for their survival with the first Thanksgiving Day, 1621. About 20,000 new settlers arrived, 1630-40. Colonist-Native American relations deteriorated, leading to King Philip's War, 1675-76, which the colonists won. Witch trials at Salem, 1692, led to the execution of 20 people. Demonstrations against British restrictions set off the Boston Massacre, 1770, and the Boston Tea Party, 1773. The first bloodshed of American

Revolution was at Lexington, 1775. After statehood, Massachusetts prospered from shipbuilding, seafaring, and the making of textiles, shoes, and metal goods, while artists, writers, and social reformers flourished. The controversial Sacco-Vanzetti case, 1920-27, ended with the execution of two Italian immigrants on murder and robbery charges. After World War II, old industries declined, knowledge-intensive enterprises thrived, and the Kennedys became a dominant political family. The state's highest court ruled, 2003, that same-sex couples could legally marry.

Tourist attractions. Provincetown arts colony; Cape Cod; Plymouth Rock, Plimoth Plantation, Mayflower II, all Plymouth; Freedom Trail, Museum of Fine Arts, New England Aquarium, and other Boston attractions; Tanglewood, Hancock Shaker Village, Berkshire Scenic Railway Museum, Norman Rockwell Museum, and other Berkshires attractions; Salem; Old Sturbridge Village; Old Deerfield Historic District; Walden Pond, Concord; Naismith Memorial Basketball Hall of Fame, Springfield.

Famous "Bay Staters." John Adams, John Quincy Adams, Samuel Adams, Louisa May Alcott, Horatio Alger, Susan B. Anthony, Crispus Attucks, Clara Barton, Alexander Graham Bell, Stephen Breyer, George H. W. Bush, John Cheever, E. E. Cummings, Emily Dickinson, Charles Eliot, Ralph Waldo Emerson, William Lloyd Garrison, Edward Everett Hale, John Hancock, Nathaniel Hawthorne, Oliver Wendell Holmes, Winslow Homer, Elias Howe, John F. Kennedy, John Kerry, Jack Kerouac, Jack Lemmon, James Russell Lowell, Cotton Mather, Samuel F. B. Morse, Edgar Allan Poe, Paul Revere, Norman Rockwell, Dr. Seuss (Theodor Seuss Geisel), Henry David Thoreau, Barbara Walters, James McNeil Whistler, John Greenleaf Whittier.

Tourist information. Massachusetts Office of Travel & Tourism, 10 Park Plz., Ste. 4510, Boston, MA 02116; 1-800-227-MASS; www.massvacation.com

Website. www.mass.gov

Michigan (MI)
Great Lakes State, Wolverine State

People. Population (2010): 9,883,640; rank: 8; net change (2000-10): –0.6%. **Pop. density:** 174.8 per sq mi. **Racial distribution** (2010): 78.9% white; 14.2% black; 2.4% Asian; 0.6% Native Amer./AK; <0.05% Hawaiian/Pacific Islander; 2 or more races, 2.3%. **Hispanic pop.** (any race, 2010): 4.4%.

Geography. Total area: 96,714 sq mi; rank: 11. **Land area:** 56,539 sq mi; rank: 22. **Acres forested:** 19.9 mil. **Location:** East North Central state bordering on 4 of the 5 Great Lakes, divided into an Upper and Lower Peninsula by the Straits of Mackinac, which link lakes Michigan and Huron. **Climate:** well-defined seasons tempered by the Great Lakes. **Topography:** low rolling hills give way to northern tableland of hilly belts in Lower Peninsula; Upper Peninsula is level in the east, with swampy areas; western region is higher and more rugged. **Capital:** Lansing. **Chief airports:** Detroit, Grand Rapids.

Economy. Chief industries: manufacturing, services, tourism, agriculture, forestry/lumber. **Chief manuf. goods:** motor vehicles & parts, plastics, metalworking machinery, non-wood office furniture, fabricated metals. **Chief crops:** greenhouse & nursery, soybeans, corn, wheat, sugar beets, apples, blueberries, potatoes, dry beans, cherries, hay, cucumbers, tomatoes, grapes. **Livestock** (Dec. 2010): 12.82 mil chickens (excl. broilers); (Jan. 2011): 1.09 mil cattle/calves, 74,000 sheep/lambs; (June 2011): 110,000 hogs/pigs. **Broadband internet:** 71.9%. **Nonfuel minerals** (2010 prelim.): $1.9 bil; iron ore (usable shipped), cement (portland), sand and gravel (construction), salt, stone (crushed). **Commercial fishing** (2009): $9.5 mil. **Chief ports:** Detroit, Escanaba, Calcite, Port Inland, Muskegon, Port Huron. **Gross state product** (2010): $384.2 bil. **Sales tax** (2011): 6.0%. **Employment distrib.** (May 2011): 15.8% govt.; 18.1% trade/trans./util.; 12.6% mfg.; 15.9% ed./health; 13.9% prof./bus. serv.; 9.6% leisure/hosp.; 4.7% finance; 3.3% constr./mining/log.; 1.4% info.; 4.3% other serv. **Unemployment** (2010): 12.5%. **Per cap. pers. income** (2010 prelim.): $35,597. **New private housing** (2010): 9,075 units/$1.6 bil. **Commercial banks** (2010): 145; deposits: $144.5 bil. **Savings institutions** (2010): 20; deposits: $11.2 bil. **Lottery** (2010): total sales: $2.35 bil; profit: $704.2 mil.

Federal govt. Fed. civ. employees (Mar. 2011): 29,829; **avg. salary:** $74,282. **Notable fed. facilities:** Detroit Arsenal

(Army TACOM Life Cycle Mgmt.); Def. Logistics Info. Serv.; Selfridge Army Garrison; Hart-Dole-Inouye Fed. Ctr.

Energy. Electricity production (2010 kWh by source): coal: 65.4 bil; gas: 1.3 bil; nuclear: 23.4 bil; petroleum: 201 mil; hydroelectric: 124 mil; other: 27 mil.

State data. Motto: Si Quaeris Peninsulam Amoenam, Circumspice (If you seek a pleasant peninsula, look about you). **Flower:** Apple blossom. **Bird:** Robin. **Tree:** White pine. **Song:** "Michigan, My Michigan." **Entered union:** Jan. 26, 1837; rank: 26th. **State fair** at Escanaba, mid-Aug.

History. Hunting and fishing peoples lived in the region as early as 11,000 years ago. Ojibwa, Ottawa, Miami, Potawatomi, and Huron inhabited the area at the time of European contact. French fur traders and missionaries arrived in the 17th cent. and established a settlement at Sault Ste. Marie, 1668. British took over, 1763, and crushed a Native American uprising led by Ottawa chieftain Pontiac. Treaty of Paris ceded the area to U.S., 1783, but British remained until 1796. Michigan was organized as a territory, 1805. The British seized Ft. Mackinac and Detroit, 1812, but the U.S. regained control, 1814. The opening of the Erie Canal, 1825, and new land laws and Native American cessions led the way for a flood of settlers. Strongly antislavery, Michigan became a state, 1837, and supplied 90,000 soldiers to the Union army in the Civil War. In the 20th cent., automobile manufacturing was the backbone of the economy. Henry Ford launched the Model T car, 1908; the United Auto Workers union was founded, 1935. Motown music flourished in Detroit in the 1960s, but riots in 1967 dealt the city a heavy blow. As the auto industry faltered, Michigan lost more than 20% of its automotive-related jobs between 2002 and 2007. In 2009, the federal government loaned billions of dollars to GM and Chrysler to keep them solvent.

Tourist attractions. Henry Ford Museum/Greenfield Village, Dearborn; Frederik Meijer Gardens and Sculpture Park, Grand Rapids; Tahquamenon (*Hiawatha*) Falls; De Zwaan windmill and Tulip Festival, Holland; "Soo Locks," St. Mary's Falls Ship Canal, Sault Ste. Marie; Air Zoo, Kalamazoo; Mackinac Island; Museum of African-American History, Motown Historical Museum, Detroit.

Famous Michiganders. Ralph Bunche, Francis Ford Coppola, Paul de Kruif, Thomas Edison, Edna Ferber, Gerald R. Ford, Henry Ford, Aretha Franklin, Edgar Guest, Lee Iacocca, Robert Ingersoll, Magic Johnson, Casey Kasem, Will Kellogg, Ring Lardner, Elmore Leonard, Charles Lindbergh, Joe Louis, Madonna, Malcolm X, Terry McMillan, Michael Moore, Pontiac, Gilda Radner, Diana Ross, Glenn Seaborg, Tom Selleck, Sinbad (David Adkins), John Smoltz, Lily Tomlin, Stewart Edward White, Serena Williams.

Tourist information. Michigan Economic Development Corp., 300 N. Washington Square, Lansing, MI 48913; 1-888-784-7328; www.michigan.org

Website. www.michigan.gov

Minnesota (MN)
North Star State, Gopher State

People. Population (2010): 5,303,925; rank: 21; net change (2000-10): 7.8%. **Pop. density:** 66.6 per sq mi. **Racial distribution** (2010): 85.3% white; 5.2% black; 4.0% Asian; 1.1% Native Amer./AK; <0.05% Hawaiian/Pacific Islander; 2 or more races, 2.4%. **Hispanic pop.** (any race, 2010): 4.7%.

Geography. Total area: 86,936 sq mi; rank: 12. **Land area:** 79,627 sq mi; rank: 14. **Acres forested:** 17.1 mil. **Location:** W North Central state bounded on the E by Wisconsin and Lake Superior, on the N by Canada, on the W by the Dakotas, and on the S by Iowa. **Climate:** northern part of state lies in the moist Great Lakes storm belt; the western border lies at the edge of the semi-arid Great Plains. **Topography:** central hill and lake region covering approx. half the state; to the NE, rocky ridges and deep lakes; to the NW, flat plain; to the S, rolling plains and deep river valleys. **Capital:** St. Paul. **Chief airport:** Minneapolis.

Economy. Chief industries: agribusiness, forest products, mining, manufacturing, tourism. **Chief manuf. goods:** petroleum & asphalt, computers & electronics, milk & cheese, printing, animal slaughtering, paper & product, medical equip. **Chief crops:** corn, soybeans, hay, sugar beets, wheat, potatoes, greenhouse & nursery, dry edible beans, green peas, sunflowers. **Livestock** (Dec. 2010): 13.58 mil chickens (excl. broilers), 42.1 mil broilers; (Jan. 2011): 2.38 mil cattle/calves, 130,000 sheep/lambs; (June 2011): 560,000 hogs/

pigs. **Broadband internet:** 75.6%. **Nonfuel minerals** (2010 prelim.): $3.8 bil; iron ore (usable shipped), sand and gravel (construction), stone (crushed), sand and gravel (industrial), lime. **Commercial fishing** (2009): $0.2 mil. **Chief ports:** Two Harbors, Silver Bay, Duluth, St. Paul. **Gross state product** (2010): $270.0 bil. **Sales tax** (2011): 6.875%. **Employment distrib.** (May 2011): 15.8% govt.; 18.4% trade/trans./util.; 11.0% mfg.; 17.5% ed./health; 12.0% prof./bus. serv.; 9.2% leisure/hosp.; 6.4% finance; 3.6% constr./mining/log.; 2.0% info.; 4.3% other serv. **Unemployment** (2010): 7.3%. **Per cap. pers. income** (2010 prelim.): $42,843. **New private housing** (2010): 9,840 units/$1.8 bil. **Commercial banks** (2010): 409; deposits: $124.7 bil. **Savings institutions** (2010): 35; deposits: $5.0 bil. **Lottery** (2010): total sales: $499.0 mil; profit: $122.3 mil.

Federal govt. Fed. civ. employees (Mar. 2011): 18,405; **avg. salary:** $70,554. **Notable fed. facilities:** Bishop Henry Whipple Fed. Bldg.; Minneapolis-St Paul Air Reserve Station.

Energy. Electricity production (2010 kWh by source): coal: 27.2 bil; gas: 3.1 bil; nuclear: 13.5 bil; petroleum: 29 mil; hydroelectric: 487 mil; other: 1 bil.

State data. Motto: L'Etoile du Nord (The star of the north). **Flower:** Pink and white lady's-slipper. **Bird:** Common loon. **Tree:** Red pine. **Song:** "Hail! Minnesota." **Entered union:** May 11, 1858; rank: 32nd. **State fair** at St. Paul, late Aug.-early Sept.

History. Inhabited for at least 10,000 years, the region was home to Dakota Sioux when Europeans arrived. French fur traders Pierre Esprit Radisson and Médard Chouart, sieur des Groseilliers, explored in the mid-17th cent. In 1679, Daniel Greysolon, sieur Duluth, claimed the entire region for France. Ojibwa arrived in the 18th cent. and warred with the Sioux for over 100 years. Britain took the area east of the Mississippi, 1763. The U.S. took over that portion after the American Revolution and gained the western area, 1803, in the Louisiana Purchase. The U.S. built Ft. St. Anthony (now Ft. Snelling), 1819, and bought Native American lands, 1837, spurring an influx of settlers from the east. Minnesota became a territory, 1849, and a state, 1858. Sioux staged a bloody uprising, the Battle of Wood Lake, 1862, and were driven from the state. Railroad construction after the Civil War spurred the growth of the grain, timber, and iron mining industries. Opening of the St. Lawrence Seaway, 1959, aided the port of Duluth. Elected as a reformer, former wrestler Jesse Ventura served as governor, 1999-2003. Two-term Sen. Paul Wellstone, one of a long line of liberal Minnesota Democrats, died when his campaign plane crashed, 2002. The I-35W Mississippi River Bridge in Minneapolis collapsed, 2007, killing 13.

Tourist attractions. Minneapolis Institute of Arts, Walker Art Center, Minneapolis Sculpture Garden, Minnehaha Falls (*Hiawatha*), Guthrie Theater, all Minneapolis; Ordway Theater, Winter Carnival, in St. Paul; Voyageurs Natl. Park; Mayo Clinic, Rochester; North Shore (of Lake Superior).

Famous Minnesotans. Warren Burger, Ethan and Joel Coen, William O. Douglas, Bob Dylan, F. Scott Fitzgerald, Al Franken, Judy Garland, Cass Gilbert, Hubert Humphrey, Garrison Keillor, Sister Elizabeth Kenny, Jessica Lange, Sinclair Lewis, Paul Manship, Roger Maris, E. G. Marshall, William and Charles Mayo, Eugene McCarthy, Walter F. Mondale, Prince (Rodgers Nelson), Charles Schulz, Harold Stassen, Thorstein Veblen, Jesse Ventura, Paul Wellstone.

Tourist information. Explore Minnesota Tourism, Metro Square, 121 7th Pl. E., Ste. 100, St. Paul, MN 55101; 1-888-TOURISM; www.exploreminnesota.com

Website. www.state.mn.us

Mississippi (MS)
Magnolia State

People. Population (2010): 2,967,297; rank: 31; net change (2000-10): 4.3%. **Pop. density:** 63.2 per sq mi. **Racial distribution** (2010): 59.1% white; 37.0% black; 0.9% Asian; 0.5% Native Amer./AK; <0.05% Hawaiian/Pacific Islander; 2 or more races, 1.1%. **Hispanic pop.** (any race, 2010): 2.7%.

Geography. Total area: 48,432 sq mi; rank: 32. **Land area:** 46,923 sq mi; rank: 31. **Acres forested:** 19.6 mil. **Location:** East South Central state bordered on the W by the Mississippi R. and on the S by the Gulf of Mexico. **Climate:** semi-tropical, with abundant rainfall, long growing season, and extreme temperatures unusual. **Topography:** low, fertile delta between the Yazoo and Mississippi Rivers; loess bluffs stretching around delta border; sandy gulf coastal terraces followed by piney woods and prairie; rugged, high sandy hills in extreme NE followed by Black Prairie Belt, Pontotoc Ridge, and flatwoods into the north central highlands. **Capital:** Jackson. **Chief airport:** Jackson.

Economy. Chief industries: warehousing & distribution, services, manufacturing, government, wholesale and retail trade. **Chief manuf. goods:** petroleum, upholstered furniture, poultry processing, motor vehicle parts, plastics, ships & boats, chemicals. **Chief crops:** cotton, soybeans, rice, hay, corn, sweet potatoes. **Livestock** (Dec. 2010): 10.22 mil chickens (excl. broilers), 807.8 mil broilers; (Jan. 2011): 900,000 cattle/calves. **Broadband internet:** 63.2%. **Nonfuel minerals** (2010 prelim.): $183 mil; sand and gravel (construction), stone (crushed), clays (fuller's earth), clays (ball), clays (bentonite). **Commercial fishing** (2009): $38.0 mil. **Chief ports:** Pascagoula, Vicksburg, Gulfport, Biloxi, Greenville. **Gross state product** (2010): $97.5 bil. **Sales tax** (2011): 7.0%. **Employment distrib.** (May 2011): 22.3% govt.; 19.5% trade/trans./util.; 12.2% mfg.; 12.2% ed./health; 8.9% prof./bus. serv.; 11.2% leisure/hosp.; 4.1% finance; 5.4% constr./mining/log.; 1.1% info.; 3.2% other serv. **Unemployment** (2010): 10.4%. **Per cap. pers. income** (2010 prelim.): $31,186. **New private housing** (2010): 5,259 units/$715.3 mil. **Commercial banks** (2010): 99; deposits: $44.6 bil. **Savings institutions** (2010): 6; deposits: $485 mil.

Federal govt. Fed. civ. employees (Mar. 2011): 19,096; **avg. salary:** $64,931. **Notable fed. facilities:** *Keesler AFB; Meridian NAS; Columbus AFB; NASA Stennis Space Ctr.; Army Corps of Eng. Waterways Experiment Sta.; Naval Constr. Battalion Ctr., Gulfport.

Energy. Electricity production (2010 kWh by source): coal: 10.3 bil; gas: 16.7 bil; nuclear: 9.6 bil; petroleum: 74 mil.

State data. Motto: Virtute et Armis (By valor and arms). **Flower:** Magnolia. **Bird:** Mockingbird. **Tree:** Magnolia. **Song:** "Go, Mississippi!" **Entered union:** Dec. 10, 1817; rank: 20th. **State fair** at Jackson, begins first Wed. in Oct.

History. Choctaw, Chickasaw, and Natchez peoples were living in the region at the time of European contact. The Spaniard Hernando de Soto explored the area, 1540-41. La Salle traced the Mississippi River from Illinois to its mouth and claimed the entire Mississippi Valley for France, 1682. The first settlement was the French Ft. Maurepas, 1699, on Biloxi Bay. The region was ceded to Britain, 1763, and claimed by Spain, 1779-98, then became a U.S. territory, 1798, and a state, 1817. Slavery spread along with cotton plantations, and slaves made up 55% of the population, 1860. Mississippi seceded, 1861. In the Civil War, Union forces captured Vicksburg, 1863, and caused extensive damage elsewhere. Mississippi reentered the Union, 1870. For the next 100 years, resistance to desegregation and violence against blacks made the state a battleground for the African American civil rights movement. Hurricanes Camille, 1969, and Katrina, 2005, caused substantial damage to the Gulf Coast. Since the early 1990s, casino gambling has boosted the economy.

Tourist attractions. Vicksburg Natl. Military Park and Cemetery, other Civil War sites; Hattiesburg; Natchez Trace; Indian mounds; Antebellum homes; pilgrimages in Natchez and some 25 other cities; Elvis Presley Birthplace and Museum, Tupelo; Smith Robertson Museum, Mynelle Gardens, in Jackson; Mardi Gras, Shrimp Festival, in Biloxi; Gulf Islands Natl. Seashore.

Famous Mississippians. Margaret Walker Alexander, Dana Andrews, Jimmy Buffett, Bo Diddley, William Faulkner, Brett Favre, Shelby Foote, Morgan Freeman, John Grisham, Fannie Lou Hamer, Jim Henson, Faith Hill, John Lee Hooker, Robert Johnson, James Earl Jones, B. B. King, L. Q. C. Lamar, Trent Lott, Gerald McRaney, Willie Morris, Walter Payton, Elvis Presley, Leontyne Price, Charley Pride, LeAnn Rimes, Muddy Waters, Eudora Welty, Tennessee Williams, Oprah Winfrey, Johnny Winter, Richard Wright, Tammy Wynette.

Tourist information. Mississippi Division of Tourism. P.O. Box 849, Jackson, MS 39205; 1-866-SEE-MISS; www. visitmississippi.org

Website. www.ms.gov

Missouri (MO)
Show Me State

People. Population (2010): 5,988,927; rank: 18; net change (2000-10): 7.0%. **Pop. density:** 87.1 per sq mi. **Racial distribution** (2010): 82.8% white; 11.6% black; 1.6% Asian; 0.5% Native Amer./AK; 0.1% Hawaiian/Pacific Islander; 2 or more races, 2.1%. **Hispanic pop.** (any race, 2010): 3.5%.

Geography. Total area: 69,707 sq mi; rank: 21. **Land area:** 68,742 sq mi; rank: 18. **Acres forested:** 15.4 mil. **Location:** West North Central state near the geographic center of the conterminous U.S.; bordered on the E by the Mississippi R., on the NW by the Missouri R. **Climate:** continental, susceptible to cold Canadian air, moist, warm gulf air, and drier SW air. **Topography:** rolling hills, open, fertile plains, and well-watered prairie N of the Missouri R.; south of the river land is rough and hilly with deep, narrow valleys; alluvial plain in the SE; low elevation in the west. **Capital:** Jefferson City. **Chief airports:** Kansas City, St. Louis.

Economy. Chief industries: agriculture, manufacturing, aerospace, tourism. **Chief manuf. goods:** motor vehicles & parts, aerospace, pharmaceuticals, plastics, soap, animal slaughtering & processing, printing. **Chief crops:** soybeans, corn, hay, cotton & cottonseed, wheat, rice, sorghum. **Livestock** (Dec. 2010): 10.08 mil chickens (excl. broilers); (Jan. 2011): 3.95 mil cattle/calves, 81,000 sheep/lambs; (June 2011): 355,000 hogs/pigs. **Broadband internet:** 77.7%. **Nonfuel minerals** (2010 prelim.): $2.1 bil; cement (portland), stone (crushed), lead, lime, sand and gravel (construction). **Gross state product** (2010): $244.0 bil. **Sales tax** (2011): 4.225%. **Employment distrib.** (May 2011): 17.1% govt.; 19.3% trade/trans./util.; 9.3% mfg.; 15.2% ed./health; 12.0% prof./bus. serv.; 10.4% leisure/hosp.; 6.1% finance; 4.1% constr./mining/log.; 2.1% info.; 4.3% other serv. **Unemployment** (2010): 9.6%. **Per cap. pers. income** (2010 prelim.): $36,979. **New private housing** (2010): 9,699 units/$1.4 bil. **Commercial banks** (2010): 354; deposits: $116.8 bil. **Savings institutions** (2010): 32; deposits: $12.1 bil. **Lottery** (2010): total sales: $971.1 mil; profit: $256.0 mil.

Federal govt. Fed. civ. employees (Mar. 2011): 40,512; avg. salary: $62,112. **Notable fed. facilities:** Federal Reserve banks; *Ft. Leonard Wood; Jefferson Barracks Natl. Cem.; Natl. Archives Civilian Personnel Records Ctr.; Whiteman AFB.

Energy. Electricity production (2010 kWh by source): coal: 75.1 bil; gas: 3.8 bil; nuclear: 9 bil; petroleum: 119 mil; hydroelectric: 2.4 bil; other: 77 mil.

State data. Motto: Salus Populi Suprema Lex Esto (The welfare of the people shall be the supreme law). **Flower:** Hawthorn. **Bird:** Bluebird. **Tree:** Dogwood. **Song:** "Missouri Waltz." **Entered union:** Aug. 10, 1821; rank: 24th. **State fair** at Sedalia, mid-Aug.; at Bethany, late Aug.-early Sept.

History. In the 17th cent., when French explorers arrived, Algonquian Sauk, Fox, and Illinois and Siouan Osage, Missouri, Iowa, and Kansa peoples were living in the region; few remained by the 1830s. French hunters and lead miners made the first settlement c. 1735, at Ste. Genevieve. The territory was ceded to Spain by the French, 1762, then returned to France, 1800, and acquired by the U.S. in the Louisiana Purchase, 1803. Powerful earthquakes rocked New Madrid, 1811-12. Missouri became a territory, 1812, and entered the Union as a slave state, 1821. St. Louis became the gateway for pioneers heading West. Though Missouri stayed with the Union, pro- and antislavery forces battled there during the Civil War. In the late 19th cent. railroad building and the cattle trade made Kansas City a boomtown. The most notable Missourian of the 20th cent., Harry S. Truman, was U.S. president, 1945-53. The state, a political bellwether, voted for the winner in every presidential election from 1960 to 2004. In May 2011, a tornado in Joplin killed about 162.

Tourist attractions. Silver Dollar City, Branson; Mark Twain Area, Hannibal; Pony Express Museum, St. Joseph; Harry S. Truman Library, Independence; Gateway Arch, St. Louis; Worlds of Fun, Kansas City; Lake of the Ozarks; Churchill Mem., Fulton; State Capitol, Jefferson City.

Famous Missourians. Maya Angelou, Robert Altman, Burt Bacharach, Josephine Baker, Scott Bakula, Thomas Hart Benton, Tom Berenger, Yogi Berra, Chuck Berry, George Caleb Bingham, Daniel Boone, Omar Bradley, William Burroughs, Kate Capshaw, Dale Carnegie, George Washington Carver, Bob Costas, Walter Cronkite, Walt Disney, T. S. Eliot, Richard Gephardt, John Goodman, Betty Grable, Edwin Hubble, Jesse James, Rush Limbaugh, Marianne Moore, Reinhold Niebuhr, J. C. Penney, John J. Pershing, Brad Pitt, Joseph Pulitzer, Ginger Rogers, Bess Truman, Harry S. Truman, Kathleen Turner, Tina Turner, Mark Twain,

Dick Van Dyke, Tennessee Williams, Lanford Wilson, Shelley Winters, Jane Wyman.

Tourist information. Missouri Division of Tourism. P.O. Box 1055, Jefferson City, MO 65102; 1-800-519-2100; www. visitmo.com

Website. www.mo.gov

Montana (MT)
Treasure State

People. Population (2010): 989,415; rank: 44; net change (2000-10): 9.7%. **Pop. density:** 6.8 per sq mi. **Racial distribution** (2010): 89.4% white; 0.4% black; 0.6% Asian; 6.3% Native Amer./AK; 0.1% Hawaiian/Pacific Islander; 2 or more races, 2.5%. **Hispanic pop.** (any race, 2010): 2.9%.

Geography. Total area: 147,040 sq mi; rank: 4. **Land area:** 145,546 sq mi; rank: 4. **Acres forested:** 25.5 mil. **Location:** Mountain state bounded on the E by the Dakotas, on the S by Wyoming, on the SSW by Idaho, and on the N by Canada. **Climate:** colder, continental climate with low humidity. **Topography:** Rocky Mts. in western third of the state; eastern two-thirds gently rolling northern Great Plains. **Capital:** Helena.

Economy. Chief industries: agriculture, timber, mining, tourism, oil and gas. **Chief manuf. goods:** sawmills, softwood veneer & plywood, petroleum. **Chief crops:** wheat, barley, hay, sugar beets, potatoes, dry beans, flaxseed, cherries, corn, oats. **Livestock** (Dec. 2010): 535,000 chickens (excl. broilers); (Jan. 2011): 2.50 mil. cattle/calves, 230,000 sheep/lambs. **Broadband internet:** 51.7%. **Nonfuel minerals** (2010 prelim.): $1.1 bil; copper, molybdenum concentrates, palladium metal, platinum metal, sand and gravel (construction). **Gross state product** (2010): $36.1 bil. **Sales tax** (2011): none. **Employment distrib.** (May 2011): 20.7% govt.; 20.5% trade/trans./util.; 3.7% mfg.; 14.8% ed./health; 8.9% prof./bus. serv.; 13.8% leisure/hosp.; 4.8% finance; 7.1% constr./mining/log.; 1.7% info.; 4.0% other serv. **Unemployment** (2010): 7.2%. **Per cap. pers. income** (2010 prelim.): $35,317. **New private housing** (2010): 2,022 units/$303.5 mil. **Commercial banks** (2010): 76; deposits: $17.3 bil. **Savings institutions** (2010): 2; deposits: $274 mil. **Lottery** (2010): total sales: $47.0 mil; profit: $10.6 mil.

Federal govt. Fed. civ. employees (Mar. 2011): 10,605; **avg. salary:** $61,937. **Notable fed. facilities:** Malmstrom AFB and missile silos; Ft. Peck, Hungry Horse, Libby, Yellowtail, and other dams.

Energy. Electricity production (2010 kWh by source): coal: 328 mil; hydroelectric: 5.8 bil; other: 69 mil.

State data. Motto: Oro y Plata (Gold and silver). **Flower:** Bitterroot. **Bird:** Western meadowlark. **Tree:** Ponderosa pine. **Song:** "Montana." **Entered union:** Nov. 8, 1889; rank: 41st. **State fair** at Great Falls, late July-early Aug.

History. Paleo-Indian hunters reached the area over 12,000 years ago. Cheyenne, Blackfoot, Crow, Assiniboin, Salish (Flatheads), Kootenai, and Kalispel peoples lived in the region before Europeans arrived. French explorers visited the region, 1742. The U.S. acquired the area partly through the Louisiana Purchase, 1803, partly through the Lewis and Clark Expedition, 1804-06. Fur traders and missionaries established posts in the early 19th cent. Gold was discovered on Grasshopper Creek, 1862, and Montana Territory was established, 1864. Indian uprisings reached their peak with the defeat of Gen. George Custer at the Battle of Little Bighorn, 1876. Chief Joseph and the Nez Percé tribe surrendered here, 1877, after a long trek across the state. Mining activity and the coming of the Northern Pacific Railway, 1883, brought population growth. Montana became a state, 1889. Copper wealth from the Butte pits resulted in the turn of the century "War of Copper Kings" as feuding factions contended for "the richest hill on earth." During the first half of the 20th cent., the Anaconda Copper firm wielded enormous political influence. Jeannette Rankin, a suffragist and pacifist, was the first woman elected to Congress, 1916. Mike Mansfield served 34 years in Congress and was Senate Democratic leader, 1961-77. An 18-year hunt for notorious "Unabomber" Theodore Kaczynski ended with his arrest, 1996, at his cabin near Lincoln.

Tourist attractions. Glacier Natl. Park; Yellowstone Natl. Park; Museum of the Rockies, Bozeman; Museum of the Plains Indian, Blackfeet Reservation, near Browning; Little Bighorn Battlefield Natl. Monument and Custer Natl. Cemetery; Flathead Lake; Helena; Lewis and Clark Caverns State Park, near Whitehall; Lewis and Clark Interpretive Ctr., Great Falls.

Famous Montanans. Dana Carvey, Gary Cooper, Marcus Daly, Chet Huntley, Will James, Myrna Loy, David Lynch, Mike Mansfield, Brent Musburger, Jeannette Rankin, Charles M. Russell, Lester Thurow.

Tourist information. Travel Montana, Dept. of Commerce, 301 S. Park Ave., P.O. Box 200533, Helena, MT 59601; 1-800-VISITMT; www.visitmt.org

Website. www.mt.gov

Nebraska (NE)
Cornhusker State

People. Population (2010): 1,826,341; rank: 38; net change (2000-10): 6.7%. **Pop. density:** 23.8 per sq mi. **Racial distribution** (2010): 86.1% white; 4.5% black; 1.8% Asian; 1% Native Amer./AK; 0.1% Hawaiian/Pacific Islander; 2 or more races, 2.2%. **Hispanic pop.** (any race, 2010): 9.2%.

Geography. Total area: 77,348 sq mi; rank: 16. **Land area:** 76,824 sq mi; rank: 15. **Acres forested:** 1.4 mil. **Location:** West North Central state with the Missouri R. for a NE and E border. **Climate:** continental semi-arid. **Topography:** till plains of the central lowland in the eastern third rising to the Great Plains and hill country of the north central and NW. **Capital:** Lincoln. **Chief airport:** Omaha.

Economy. Chief industries: agriculture, manufacturing. **Chief manuf. goods:** animal slaughtering, grain & oilseed, farm machinery, medical equip., motor vehicle parts, printing, structural metals. **Chief crops:** corn, sorghum, soybeans, hay, wheat, dry beans, oats, potatoes, sugar beets. **Livestock** (Dec. 2010): 11.59 mil chickens (excl. broilers); (Jan. 2011): 6.20 mil cattle/calves, 74,000 sheep/lambs; (June 2011): 380,000 hogs/pigs. **Broadband internet:** 65.8%. **Nonfuel minerals** (2010 prelim.): $181 mil; sand and gravel (construction), cement (portland), stone (crushed), sand and gravel (industrial), lime. **Gross state product** (2010): $89.8 bil. **Sales tax** (2011): 5.5%. **Employment distrib.** (May 2011): 17.8% govt.; 20.8% trade/trans./util.; 9.8% mfg.; 14.2% ed./health; 11.2% prof./bus. serv.; 8.8% leisure/hosp.; 7.1% finance; 4.5% constr./mining/log.; 1.8% info.; 3.9% other serv. **Unemployment** (2010): 4.7%. **Per cap. pers. income** (2010 prelim.): $39,557. **New private housing** (2010): 5,401 units/$745.0 mil. **Commercial banks** (2010): 229; deposits: $41.4 bil. **Savings institutions** (2010): 13; deposits: $1.6 bil. **Lottery** (2010): total sales: $130.6 mil; profit: $32.4 mil.

Federal govt. Fed. civ. employees (Mar. 2011): 10,755; **avg. salary:** $66,005. **Notable fed. facilities:** *Offutt AFB.

Energy. Electricity production (2010 kWh by source): coal: 23.3 bil; gas: 433 mil; nuclear: 11.1 bil; petroleum: 31 mil; hydroelectric: 449 mil; other: 263 mil.

State data. Motto: Equality before the law. **Flower:** Goldenrod. **Bird:** Western meadowlark. **Tree:** Cottonwood. **Song:** "Beautiful Nebraska." **Entered union:** Mar. 1, 1867; rank: 37th. **State fair** at Grand Island, late Aug.-early Sept.

History. When Europeans arrived, Pawnee, Ponca, Omaha, and Oto peoples lived in the region. Spanish and French explorers visited the area prior to its acquisition in the Louisiana Purchase, 1803. Meriwether Lewis and William Clark passed through, 1804-06. The first permanent settlement was Bellevue, near Omaha, 1823. The 1834 Indian Intercourse Act declared Nebraska Indian country and excluded white settlement, but conflicts with settlers eventually forced Native Americans to move to reservations. Nebraska became a territory, 1854, and a state, 1867. Many Civil War veterans settled under free land terms of the 1862 Homestead Act; as agriculture grew, struggles followed between homesteaders and ranchers. Since the mid-1930s, Nebraska has been the only state with a unicameral legislature. A leader in agribusiness, Nebraska has also become a major telemarketing center. The "Oracle of Omaha," investor Warren Buffett, one of the world's wealthiest men, announced in 2006 he would give most of his $44 bil fortune to charity.

Tourist attractions. State Museum (Elephant Hall), State Capitol, in Lincoln; Stuhr Museum of the Prairie Pioneer, Grand Island; Museum of the Fur Trade, Chadron; Boys Town, Henry Doorly Zoo, Joslyn Art Museum, Omaha; Ashfall Fossil Beds, Strategic Air and Space Museum, Ashland; Arbor Lodge State Park, Nebraska City; Buffalo Bill Ranch State Hist. Park, North Platte; Pioneer Village, Minden; Oregon Trail landmarks; Scotts Bluff Natl. Monument; Chimney Rock Natl. Historic Site; Ft. Robinson; Hastings Museum of Natural and Cultural Hist.

Famous Nebraskans. Grover Cleveland Alexander, Fred Astaire, Marlon Brando, Charles W. Bryan, William Jennings

Bryan, Warren Buffett, Johnny Carson, Willa Cather, Dick Cavett, Dick Cheney, William F. "Buffalo Bill" Cody, Loren Eiseley, Rev. Edward J. Flanagan, Henry Fonda, Gerald R. Ford, Bob Gibson, Rollin Kirby, Harold Lloyd, Malcolm X, J. Sterling Morton, John Neihardt, Nick Nolte, George Norris, Tom Osborne, John J. Pershing, Roscoe Pound, Chief Red Cloud, Mari Sandoz, Robert Taylor, Darryl F. Zanuck.

Tourist information. Nebraska Division of Travel and Tourism, 301 Centennial Mall S., Lincoln, NE 68508; 1-888-444-1867; www.visitnebraska.gov

Website. www.nebraska.gov

Nevada (NV)
Sagebrush State, Battle Born State, Silver State

People. Population (2010): 2,700,551; rank: 35; net change (2000-10): 35.1%. **Pop. density:** 24.6 per sq mi. **Racial distribution** (2010): 66.2% white; 8.1% black; 7.2% Asian; 1.2% Native Amer./AK; 0.6% Hawaiian/Pacific Islander; 2 or more races, 4.7%. **Hispanic pop.** (any race, 2010): 26.5%.

Geography. Total area: 110,572 sq mi; rank: 7. **Land area:** 109,781 sq mi; rank: 7. **Acres forested:** 11.1 mil. **Location:** Mountain state bordered on N by Oregon and Idaho, on E by Utah and Arizona, on SE by Arizona, and on SW and W by California. **Climate:** semi-arid and arid. **Topography:** rugged N-S mountain ranges; highest elevation, Boundary Peak, 13,140 ft; southern area is within the Mojave Desert; lowest elevation, Colorado River at southern tip of state, 479 ft. **Capital:** Carson City. **Chief airports:** Las Vegas, Reno.

Economy. Chief industries: gaming, tourism, mining, manufacturing, government, retailing, warehousing, trucking. **Chief manuf. goods:** gaming machines, cement & concrete, plastics, printing, architectural & structural metals, electricity instruments. **Chief crops:** hay, onions, potatoes, alfalfa, wheat, garlic, mint, barley. **Livestock** (Jan. 2011): 460,000 cattle/calves, 68,000 sheep/lambs. **Broadband internet:** 80.4%. **Nonfuel minerals** (2010 prelim.): $7.5 bil; gold, copper, sand and gravel (construction), lime, silver. **Gross state product** (2010): $125.7 bil. **Sales tax** (2011): 6.85%. **Employment distrib.** (May 2011): 13.9% govt.; 18.2% trade/trans./util.; 3.2% mfg.; 9.4% ed./health; 12.4% prof./bus. serv.; 28.5% leisure/hosp.; 4.3% finance; 6.5% constr./mining/log.; 1.1% info.; 3.1% other serv. **Unemployment** (2010): 14.9%. **Per cap. pers. income** (2010 prelim.): $36,997. **New private housing** (2010): 6,443 units/$759.7 mil. **Commercial banks** (2010): 41; deposits: $137.7 bil. **Savings institutions** (2010): 9; deposits: $45.8 bil.

Federal govt. Fed. civ. employees (Mar. 2011): 11,399; **avg. salary:** $66,040. **Notable fed. facilities:** Nevada Test Site; Hawthorne Army Depot; Creech AFB; Nellis AFB & Range Complex; Fallon NAS; Natl. Wild Horse & Burro Ctr. at Palomino Valley.

Energy. Electricity production (2010 kWh by source): coal: 5.6 bil; gas: 16 bil; petroleum: 10 mil; hydroelectric: 2.1 bil.

State data. Motto: All for our country. **Flower:** Sagebrush. **Bird:** Mountain bluebird. **Trees:** Single-leaf piñon and bristlecone pine. **Song:** "Home Means Nevada." **Entered union:** Oct. 31, 1864; rank: 36th. **State fair** at Reno, late Aug.

History. Shoshone, Paiute, Bannock, and Washoe peoples lived in the area at the time of European contact. Nevada was first explored by Spaniards, 1776. In the 1820s, fur traders Peter Skene Ogden and Jedediah Smith separately explored the area. It was acquired by the U.S., 1848, at the end of the Mexican War. A trading post at Mormon Station, now Genoa, was established, 1850. Discovery of the Comstock Lode, rich in gold and silver, 1859, spurred a population boom. Nevada became a territory, 1861, and a state, 1864. Hoover Dam was built, 1931-36. With gambling legal since 1931, a surge in resort casino construction after World War II turned Las Vegas into one of the nation's most popular tourist destinations. An influx of Hispanics and Asians, attracted by service-industry and construction jobs, helped make Nevada the fastest-growing state in the U.S. during 1990-2005, and again in 2007. The recession in recent years has had an equally powerful effect. Nevada had the highest state unemployment and home foreclosure rates in 2011.

Tourist attractions. Legalized gambling at Lake Tahoe, Reno, Las Vegas, Laughlin, Elko County, and elsewhere; Hoover Dam; Lake Mead; Great Basin Natl. Park; Valley of Fire State Park; Virginia City; Red Rock Canyon Natl. Conservation Area; Liberace Museum, The Strip, Fremont St., Atomic Testing Museum, Pinball Hall of Fame, all Las Vegas; Lamoille Canyon; Pyramid Lake; Lost City Museum, Overton; Skiing near Lake Tahoe.

Famous Nevadans. Andre Agassi, Walter Van Tilburg Clark, George Ferris, Sarah Winnemucca Hopkins, Paul Laxalt, Dat So La Lee, John William Mackay, Anne Martin, Pat McCarran, Key Pittman, William Morris Stewart.

Tourist information. Commission on Tourism, 401 N. Carson St., Carson City, NV 89701; 1-800-NEVADA8; www.travelnevada.com

Website. www.nv.gov

New Hampshire (NH)
Granite State

People. Population (2010): 1,316,470; rank: 40; net change (2000-10): 6.5%. **Pop. density:** 147 per sq mi. **Racial distribution** (2010): 93.9% white; 1.1% black; 2.2% Asian; 0.2% Native Amer./AK; <0.05% Hawaiian/Pacific Islander; 2 or more races, 1.6%. **Hispanic pop.** (any race, 2010): 2.8%.

Geography. Total area: 9,349 sq mi; rank: 46. **Land area:** 8,953 sq mi; rank: 44. **Acres forested:** 4.8 mil. **Location:** New England state bounded on S by Massachusetts, on W by Vermont, on N and NW by Canada, on E by Maine and the Atlantic Ocean. **Climate:** highly varied, due to its nearness to high mountains and ocean. **Topography:** low, rolling coast followed by countless hills and mountains rising out of a central plateau. **Capital:** Concord. **Chief airport:** Manchester.

Economy. Chief industries: tourism, manufacturing, agriculture, trade, mining. **Chief manuf. goods:** navigational instr., circuit boards, electrical equip., fabricated metal, machinery, medical equip., plastics. **Chief crops:** greenhouse & nursery, apples, sweet corn, hay, Christmas trees, berries, maple syrup. **Livestock** (Jan. 2011): 34,000 cattle/calves. **Broadband internet:** 73.1%. **Nonfuel minerals** (2010 prelim.): $100 mil; sand and gravel (construction), stone (crushed), stone (dimension), gemstones (natural). **Commercial fishing** (2009): $17.7 mil. **Chief port:** Portsmouth. **Gross state product** (2010): $60.3 bil. **Sales tax** (2011): none. **Employment distrib.** (May 2011): 15.7% govt.; 20.6% trade/trans./util.; 10.4% mfg.; 18.0% ed./health; 10.9% prof./bus. serv.; 10.4% leisure/hosp.; 5.6% finance; 3.6% constr./mining/log.; 1.8% info.; 3.1% other serv. **Unemployment** (2010): 6.1%. **Per cap. pers. income** (2010 prelim.): $44,084. **New private housing** (2010): 2,670 units/$461.8 mil. **Commercial banks** (2010): 17; deposits: $19 bil. **Savings institutions** (2010): 23; deposits: $7.3 bil. **Lottery** (2010): total sales: $233.9 mil; profit: $66.1 mil.

Federal govt. Fed. civ. employees (Mar. 2011): 4,390; **avg. salary:** $81,418. **Notable fed. facilities:** Army Cold Regions Res. & Engineering Lab.

Energy. Electricity production (2010 kWh by source): coal: 3.1 bil; gas: 175 mil; petroleum: 51 mil; hydroelectric: 329 mil; other: 342 mil.

State data. Motto: Live free or die. **Flower:** Purple lilac. **Bird:** Purple finch. **Tree:** White birch. **Song:** "Old New Hampshire." **Ninth** of the original 13 states to ratify the Constitution, June 21, 1788. **State fair:** no official state fair; many agricultural fairs statewide, July through Sept.

History. The area has been inhabited for about 10,000 years. Algonquian-speaking peoples, including the Pennacook, lived in the region when the Europeans arrived. The first explorers to visit the area were England's Martin Pring, 1603, and France's Samuel de Champlain, 1605. The first settlement was Odiorne's Point (now port of Rye), 1623. Before the American Revolution, New Hampshire residents raided a British fort at Portsmouth, 1774, and drove the royal governor out, 1775. New Hampshire became the first colony to adopt its own constitution, 1776. After statehood, 1788, New Hampshire became a textile manufacturing center. The mill towns declined in the first half of the 20th cent., but tourism and high-tech industries, lured by low taxes, have revived the economy since the 1960s. A state law requires it to hold the first primary of the presidential campaign season.

Tourist attractions. Mt. Washington, highest peak in Northeast; Lake Winnipesaukee; Crawford, Franconia, Pinkham notches, Flume Gorge, Canon Mt. aerial tramway, all White Mt. region; Strawbery Banke, Portsmouth; Canterbury Shaker Village; Saint-Gaudens, Natl. Historic Site, Cornish; Mt. Monadnock.

Famous New Hampshirites. Salmon P. Chase, Ralph Adams Cram, Mary Baker Eddy, Daniel Chester French,

Robert Frost, Horace Greeley, Sarah Buell Hale, Franklin Pierce, Augustus Saint-Gaudens, Adam Sandler, Alan Shepard, David H. Souter, Daniel Webster.

Tourist information. Division of Travel & Tourism Development, 172 Pembroke Rd., P.O. Box 1856; Concord, NH 03302; 1-800-FUNINNH; www.visitnh.gov

Website. www.nh.gov

New Jersey (NJ)
Garden State

People. Population (2010): 8,791,894; rank: 11; net change (2000-10): 4.5%. **Pop. density:** 1195.5 per sq mi. **Racial distribution** (2010): 68.6% white; 13.7% black; 8.3% Asian; 0.3% Native Amer./AK; <0.05% Hawaiian/Pacific Islander; 2 or more races, 2.7%. **Hispanic pop.** (any race, 2010): 17.7%.

Geography. Total area: 8,723 sq mi; rank: 47. **Land area:** 7,354 sq mi; rank: 46. **Acres forested:** 1.9 mil. **Location:** Middle Atlantic state bounded on N and E by New York and Atlantic Ocean, on S and W by Delaware and Pennsylvania. **Climate:** moderate, with marked difference between NW and SE extremities. **Topography:** Appalachian Valley in the NW also has highest elevation, High Pt., 1,801 ft; Appalachian Highlands, flat-topped NE-SW mountain ranges; Piedmont Plateau, low plains broken by high ridges (Palisades) rising 400-500 ft; Coastal Plain, covering three-fifths of state in SE, rises from sea level to gentle slopes. **Capital:** Trenton. **Chief airports:** Atlantic City, Newark.

Economy. Chief industries: pharmaceuticals, telecommunications, biotechnology, printing & publishing. **Chief manuf. goods:** petroleum, pharmaceuticals, toiletries, chemicals, plastics, printing, navigational instr., medical equip., paper prod. **Chief crops:** greenhouse & nursery, blueberries, peaches, corn, hay, tomatoes, bell peppers, cranberries, soybeans, apples. **Livestock** (Jan. 2011): 32,000 cattle/calves. **Broadband internet:** 73.6%. **Nonfarm minerals** (2010 prelim.): $232 mil; stone (crushed), sand and gravel (construction), sand and gravel (industrial), greensand marl, peat. **Commercial fishing** (2009): $149.0 mil. **Chief ports:** Newark-Elizabeth, Camden. **Gross state product** (2010): $487.3 bil. **Sales tax** (2011): 7.0%. **Employment distrib.** (May 2011): 16.3% govt.; 21.1% trade/trans./util.; 6.5% mfg.; 15.9% ed./health; 15.4% prof./bus. serv.; 8.8% leisure/hosp.; 6.6% finance; 3.5% constr./mining/log.; 2.0% info.; 4.1% other serv. **Unemployment** (2010): 9.5%. **Per cap. pers. income** (2010 prelim.): $50,781. **New private housing** (2010): 13,535 units/$2.0 bil. **Commercial banks** (2010): 97; deposits: $175.3 bil. **Savings institutions** (2010): 73; deposits: $71.1 bil. **Lottery** (2010): total sales: $2.61 bil; profit: $924.2 mil.

Federal govt. Fed. civ. employees (Mar. 2011): 29,176; **avg. salary:** $82,908. **Notable fed. facilities:** Joint Base McGuire-Dix-Lakehurst Picatinny Arsenal; FAA William J. Hughes Technical Ctr.

Energy. Electricity production (2010 kWh by source): hydroelectric: –194 mil.

State data. Motto: Liberty and prosperity. **Flower:** Purple violet. **Bird:** Eastern goldfinch. **Tree:** Red oak. **Third** of the original 13 states to ratify the Constitution, Dec. 18, 1787. **State fair** at Augusta, late July-early Aug.

History. The Lenni Lenape (Delaware) peoples lived in the region and had mostly peaceful relations with European colonists, who arrived after the explorers Giovanni da Verrazano, 1524, and Henry Hudson, 1609. The first permanent European settlement was Dutch, at Bergen (now Jersey City), 1660. When the British took New Netherland, 1664, the area between the Delaware and Hudson Rivers was given to Lord John Berkeley and Sir George Carteret. During the American Revolution, New Jersey was the scene of many major battles, including Trenton, 1776; Princeton, 1777; and Monmouth, 1778. New Jersey was the third state to ratify the Constitution, 1787, and the first to approve the Bill of Rights, 1789. In a duel at Weehawken, 1804, Vice Pres. Aaron Burr fatally shot Alexander Hamilton. Canal and railroad building stimulated the growth of cities and industries in the 19th cent. The 20th cent. arrival of large numbers of African Americans, Italians, Irish, European Jews, Puerto Ricans, South Asians, and other groups made New Jersey one of the most diverse states in the U.S. Construction of resort casinos in Atlantic City from the late 1970s revitalized tourism. Gov. James McGreevey resigned, 2004, after acknowledging an extramarital affair with a man identified as his former homeland security adviser.

Tourist attractions. 127 mi of beaches, boardwalks at Atlantic City (with gambling), Seaside Heights, Ocean City,

Wildwood; Grover Cleveland birthplace, Caldwell; Cape May Historic District; Edison Natl. Historic Site, W. Orange; Six Flags Great Adventure, Jackson; Liberty State Park, Liberty Science Center, Jersey City; Pine Barrens wilderness area; Princeton University; Revolutionary War sites; Adventure Aquarium, Battleship *New Jersey*, Walt Whitman house, Camden.

Famous New Jerseyans. Jason Alexander, Samuel Alito, Count Basie, Judy Blume, Jon Bon Jovi, Bill Bradley, Aaron Burr, Grover Cleveland, James Fenimore Cooper, Stephen Crane, Danny DeVito, Thomas Edison, Albert Einstein, James Gandolfini, Allen Ginsberg, Alexander Hamilton, Ed Harris, Whitney Houston, Buster Keaton, Joyce Kilmer, Norman Mailer, Jack Nicholson, Thomas Paine, Dorothy Parker, Joe Pesci, Molly Pitcher, Paul Robeson, Philip Roth, Antonin Scalia, Wally Schirra, H. Norman Schwarzkopf, Frank Sinatra, Bruce Springsteen, Martha Stewart, Meryl Streep, Dave Thomas, John Travolta, Walt Whitman, William Carlos Williams, Woodrow Wilson.

Tourist information. Dept. of State, Division of Travel and Tourism, P.O. Box 460, Trenton, NJ 08625; 1-800-VISITNJ; www.visitnj.org

Website. www.state.nj.us

New Mexico (NM)
Land of Enchantment

People. Population (2010): 2,059,179; rank: 36; net change (2000-10): 13.2%. **Pop. density:** 17 per sq mi. **Racial distribution** (2010): 68.4% white; 2.1% black; 1.4% Asian; 9.4% Native Amer./AK; 0.1% Hawaiian/Pacific Islander; 2 or more races, 3.7%. **Hispanic pop.** (any race, 2010): 46.3%.

Geography. Total area: 121,590 sq mi; rank: 5. **Land area:** 121,298 sq mi; rank: 5. **Acres forested:** 16.7 mil. **Location:** southwestern state bounded by Colorado on the N, Oklahoma, Texas, and Mexico on the E and S, and Arizona on the W. **Climate:** dry, with temperatures rising or falling 5°F with every 1,000 ft elevation. **Topography:** eastern third, Great Plains; central third, Rocky Mts. (85% of the state is over 4,000-ft elevation); western third, high plateau. **Capital:** Santa Fe. **Chief airport:** Albuquerque.

Economy. Chief industries: government, services, trade. **Chief manuf. goods:** semiconductors, medical equip., navigational/measuring/medical/control instruments, aircrafts, chemicals, jewelry. **Chief crops:** hay, pecans, corn, greenhouse & nursery, chiles, onions, cotton, wheat, peanuts. **Livestock** (Jan. 2011): 1.54 mil. cattle/calves, 110,000 sheep/lambs. **Broadband internet:** 64.6%. **Nonfarm minerals** (2010 prelim.): $1.0 bil; copper, potash, sand and gravel (construction), stone (crushed), cement (portland). **Gross state product** (2010): $79.7 bil. **Sales tax** (2011): 5.125%. **Employment distrib.** (May 2011): 25.0% govt.; 17.0% trade/trans./util.; 3.5% mfg.; 15.5% ed./health; 11.5% prof./bus. serv.; 10.6% leisure/hosp.; 4.1% finance; 7.9% constr./mining/log.; 1.7% info.; 3.6% other serv. **Unemployment** (2010): 8.4%. **Per cap. pers. income** (2010 prelim.): $33,837. **New private housing** (2010): 4,533 units/$779.5 mil. **Commercial banks** (2010): 55; deposits: $24.1 mil. **Savings institutions** (2010): 10; deposits: $1.7 bil. **Lottery** (2010): total sales: $143.6 mil; profit: $43.6 mil.

Federal govt. Fed. civ. employees (Mar. 2011): 27,232; **avg. salary:** $66,706. **Notable fed. facilities:** Kirtland, Cannon, *Holloman AF bases; Los Alamos Natl. Lab; White Sands Missile Range; Natl. Solar Observatory; Natl. Radio Astronomy Observatory; Sandia Natl. Labs.

Energy. Electricity production (2010 kWh by source): coal: 25.6 bil; gas: 4.9 bil; petroleum: 45 mil; hydroelectric: 253 mil.

State data. Motto: Crescit Eundo (It grows as it goes). **Flower:** Yucca. **Bird:** Roadrunner. **Tree:** Piñon. **Songs:** "O, Fair New Mexico"; "Asi Es Nuevo Mexico." **Entered union:** Jan. 6, 1912; rank: 47th. **State fair** at Albuquerque, mid-Sept.; at Las Cruces, late Sept.-early Oct.; at Roswell, early Oct.

History. Inhabited for more than 10,000 years, the region was home to Sandia, Clovis, Folsom, Mogollon, and Anasazi cultures, followed by the Pueblo people, Anasazi descendants; later, nomadic Navajo and Apache came. Franciscan Marcos de Niza and a former black slave, Estevanico, explored the area, 1539, seeking gold; Coronado followed, 1540. First settlements were near San Juan Pueblo, 1598, and at Santa Fe, 1610. Settlers alternately traded and fought with the Apache, Comanche, and Navajo. Trade on the Santa Fe Trail to Missouri started, 1821. After the Mexican War began, 1846, Gen.

Stephen Kearny took Santa Fe without firing a shot, and declared New Mexico part of the U.S. All Hispanic New Mexicans and Pueblo became U.S. citizens by terms of the 1848 treaty ending the war. New Mexico became a territory, 1850, but did not attain statehood until 1912. Pancho Villa raided Columbus, 1916, and U.S. troops were sent to the area. The world's first atomic bomb was exploded at a test site near Alamogordo, 1945. An underground nuclear waste depository opened near Carlsbad, 1999. Construction on a "spaceport" for space tourism, partially financed by the state, began June 2009.

Tourist attractions. Carlsbad Caverns Natl. Park, with world's largest natural underground chamber; Santa Fe, oldest capital in U.S.; White Sands Natl. Monument, world's largest gypsum deposit; Chaco Culture Natl. Hist. Park; Acoma Pueblo, "sky city" built atop a 357-ft mesa; Taos Art Colony and Ski Valley; Ute Lake State Park; Shiprock; Roswell.

Famous New Mexicans. Ben Abruzzo, Maxie Anderson, Jeff Bezos, Billy (the Kid) Bonney, Kit Carson, Bob Foster, Peter Hurd, Tony Hillerman, Archbishop Jean Baptiste Lamy, Nancy Lopez, Bill Mauldin, Georgia O'Keeffe, Bill Richardson, Kim Stanley, Al Unser, Bobby Unser, Lew Wallace.

Tourist information. New Mexico Dept. of Tourism, 491 Old Santa Fe Trl., Santa Fe, NM 87501; 1-800-733-6396; www.newmexico.org

Website. www.newmexico.gov

New York (NY)
Empire State

People. Population (2010): 19,378,102; rank: 3; net change (2000-10): 2.1%. **Pop. density:** 411.2 per sq mi. **Racial distribution** (2010): 65.7% white; 15.9% black; 7.3% Asian; 0.6% Native Amer./AK; <0.05% Hawaiian/Pacific Islander; 2 or more races, 3%. **Hispanic pop.** (any race, 2010): 17.6%.

Geography. Total area: 54,555 sq mi; rank: 27. **Land area:** 47,126 sq mi; rank: 30. **Acres forested:** 18.9 mil. **Location:** Middle Atlantic state, bordered by the New England states, Atlantic Ocean, New Jersey and Pennsylvania, Lakes Ontario and Erie, and Canada. **Climate:** variable; the SE region moderated by the ocean. **Topography:** highest and most rugged mountains in the NE Adirondack upland; St. Lawrence-Champlain lowlands extend from Lake Ontario NE along the Canadian border; Hudson-Mohawk lowland follows the flows of the rivers N and W, 10-30 mi wide; Atlantic coastal plain in the SE; Appalachian Highlands, covering half the state westward from the Hudson Valley, include the Catskill Mts., Finger Lakes; plateau of Erie-Ontario lowlands. **Capital:** Albany. **Chief airports:** Albany, Buffalo, Islip, New York (2), Rochester, Syracuse, White Plains.

Economy. Chief industries: manufacturing, finance, communications, tourism, transportation, services. **Chief manuf. goods:** pharmaceuticals, photographic chemicals, electronics, automotive parts, toiletries, printing, plastics, apparel. **Chief crops:** greenhouse & nursery, apples, corn, hay, cabbage, onions, soybeans, potatoes, snap beans, grapes, squash, pumpkins, tomatoes, wheat, cucumbers, green peas. **Livestock** (Dec. 2010): 5.53 mil chickens (excl. broilers); (Jan. 2011): 1.4 mil cattle/calves, 70,000 sheep/lambs. **Broadband internet:** 76.2%. **Nonfuel minerals** (2010 prelim.): $1.2 bil; salt, stone (crushed), sand and gravel (construction), cement (portland), clays (common). **Commercial fishing** (2009): $49.3 mil. **Chief ports:** New York, Buffalo, Albany. **Gross state product** (2010): $1,159.5 bil. **Sales tax** (2011): 4.0%. **Employment distrib.** (May 2011): 17.3% govt.; 16.9% trade/trans./util.; 5.2% mfg.; 20.1% ed./health; 13.0% prof./bus. serv.; 8.8% leisure/hosp.; 7.8% finance; 3.6% constr./mining/log.; 2.9% info.; 4.3% other serv. **Unemployment** (2010): 8.6%. **Per cap. pers. income** (2010 prelim.): $48,821. **New private housing** (2010): 19,568 units/$3.2 bil. **Commercial banks** (2010): 159; deposits: $758.5 bil. **Savings institutions** (2010): 75; deposits: $83.0 bil. **Lottery** (2010): total sales: $7.82 bil; profit: $2.67 bil.

Federal govt. Fed. civ. employees (Mar. 2011): 68,854; **avg. salary:** $73,076. **Notable fed. facilities:** Ft. Drum; West Point Military Academy; Merchant Marine Academy; NY Fed. Reserve; Griffis AFB (Research Lab), Rome; Watervliet Arsenal; Brookhaven Natl. Lab.; U.S. Mission to the United Nations.

Energy. Electricity production (2010 kWh by source): gas: 13.5 bil; petroleum: 883 mil; hydroelectric: 20.4 bil.

State data. Motto: Excelsior (Ever upward). **Flower:** Rose. **Bird:** Bluebird. **Tree:** Sugar maple. **Song:** "I Love New York."

Eleventh of the original 13 states to ratify the Constitution, July 26, 1788. **State fair** at Syracuse, late Aug.-early Sept.

History. When Europeans arrived, Algonquians including the Mahican, Wappinger, and Lenni Lenape inhabited the region, as did the Iroquoian Mohawk, Oneida, Onondaga, Cayuga, and Seneca tribes, who established the League of the Five Nations. Giovanni da Verrazano entered New York harbor, 1524. In 1609, Henry Hudson visited the river later named for him, and Samuel de Champlain explored the lake that now bears his name. The first permanent settlement was Dutch, near present-day Albany, 1624. New Amsterdam was settled, 1626, at the S tip of Manhattan island. A British fleet seized New Netherland, 1664. Key battles of the American Revolution included Saratoga, 1777. In the 19th cent., New York City emerged as one of the world's great metropolitan areas, a center for trade, finance, and arts, and a haven for millions of immigrants. Completion of Erie Canal, 1825, established the state as a gateway to the West. The first women's rights convention was held in Seneca Falls, 1848. Although the state backed the Union in the Civil War, an 1863 military draft triggered 3 days of riots in New York City. Industry declined in the 20th cent., and California and Texas passed New York in population. Attica was the scene of a bloody prison revolt, 1971. New Yorkers, 2000, elected former First Lady Hillary Rodham Clinton to the U.S. Senate. Two jet aircraft hijacked by terrorists on Sept. 11, 2001, destroyed the World Trade Center in lower Manhattan.

Tourist attractions. New York City; Adirondack and Catskill Mts.; Finger Lakes; Great Lakes; Thousand Islands; Niagara Falls; Saratoga Springs; Philipsburg Manor, Sunnyside (Washington Irving's home), Dutch Church of Sleepy Hollow, near Tarrytown; Corning Museum of Glass; Fenimore House, Natl. Baseball Hall of Fame and Museum, Cooperstown; Ft. Ticonderoga; Empire State Plaza, Albany; Lake Placid; Franklin D. Roosevelt Natl. Historic Site, Hyde Park; Long Island beaches; Theodore Roosevelt estate, Sagamore Hill, Oyster Bay; Turning Stone Casino.

Famous New Yorkers. Woody Allen, Susan B. Anthony, James Baldwin, Lucille Ball, Ann Bancroft, L. Frank Baum, Milton Berle, Humphrey Bogart, Barbara Boxer, Mel Brooks, Benjamin Cardozo, De Witt Clinton, Peter Cooper, Aaron Copland, Tom Cruise, Robert De Niro, George Eastman, Millard Fillmore, Lou Gehrig, George and Ira Gershwin, Ruth Bader Ginsburg, Rudolph Giuliani, Jackie Gleason, Stephen Jay Gould, Julia Ward Howe, Charles Evans Hughes, Washington Irving, Henry and William James, John Jay, Michael Jordan, Edward Koch, Fiorello LaGuardia, Herman Melville, Arthur Miller, J. Pierpont Morgan Jr., Eddie Murphy, Joyce Carol Oates, Carroll O'Connor, Rosie O'Donnell, Eugene O'Neill, Jerry Orbach, George Pataki, Colin Powell, Nancy Reagan, John D. Rockefeller, Nelson Rockefeller, John Roberts, Richard Rodgers, Ray Romano, Eleanor Roosevelt, Franklin D. Roosevelt, Theodore Roosevelt, Tim Russert, J. D. Salinger, Caroline Kennedy Schlossberg, Jerry Seinfeld, Al Sharpton, Paul Simon, Alfred E. Smith, Elizabeth Cady Stanton, Barbra Streisand, Donald Trump, William (Boss) Tweed, Martin Van Buren, Luther Vandross, Gore Vidal, Denzel Washington, Edith Wharton, Walt Whitman.

Tourist information. Empire State Development, Travel Information Center, 30 South Pearl St., Albany, NY 12245; 1-800-CALLNYS; www.iloveny.com

Website. www.state.ny.us

North Carolina (NC)
Tar Heel State, Old North State

People. Population (2010): 9,535,483; rank: 10; net change (2000-10): 18.5%. **Pop. density:** 196.1 per sq mi. **Racial distribution** (2010): 68.5% white; 21.5% black; 2.2% Asian; 1.3% Native Amer./AK; 0.1% Hawaiian/Pacific Islander; 2 or more races, 2.2%. **Hispanic pop.** (any race, 2010): 8.4%.

Geography. Total area: 53,819 sq mi; rank: 28. **Land area:** 48,618 sq mi; rank: 29. **Acres forested:** 18.6 mil. **Location:** South Atlantic state bounded by Virginia, South Carolina, Georgia, Tennessee, and the Atlantic Ocean. **Climate:** sub-tropical in SE, medium-continental in mountain region; tempered by the Gulf Stream and the mountains in W. **Topography:** coastal plain and tidewater, two-fifths of state, extending to the fall line of the rivers; Piedmont Plateau, another two-fifths, of gentle to rugged hills; southern Appalachian Mts. contains the Blue Ridge and Great Smoky

Mts. **Capital:** Raleigh. **Chief airports:** Charlotte, Greensboro, Raleigh.

Economy. Chief industries: manufacturing, agriculture, tourism. **Chief manuf. goods:** transportation, tobacco, pharmaceuticals, toiletries, plastics, animal slaughtering & processing, household furniture, fabric & apparel. **Chief crops:** greenhouse & nursery, tobacco, cotton, soybeans, corn, Christmas trees, sweet potatoes, wheat, peanuts, blueberries, cucumbers, tomatoes, hay, potatoes. **Livestock** (Dec. 2010): 20.95 mil chickens (excl. broilers), 766.5 mil broilers; (Jan. 2011): 780,000 cattle/calves, 27,000 sheep/lambs; (June 2011): 850,000 hogs/pigs. **Broadband internet:** 71.0%. **Nonfuel minerals** (2010 prelim.): $908 mil; stone (crushed), phosphate rock, sand and gravel (construction), sand and gravel (industrial), stone (dimension). **Commercial fishing** (2009): $77.0 mil. **Chief ports:** Morehead City, Wilmington. **Gross state product** (2010): $424.9 bil. **Sales tax** (2011): 5.75%. **Employment distrib.** (May 2011): 18.1% govt.; 18.4% trade/trans./util.; 11.1% mfg.; 13.8% ed./health; 12.7% prof./bus. serv.; 10.4% leisure/hosp.; 5.2% finance; 4.7% constr./mining/log.; 1.7% info.; 4.0% other serv. **Unemployment** (2010): 10.6%. **Per cap. pers. income** (2010 prelim.): $35,638. **New private housing** (2010): 33,889 units/$5.1 bil. **Commercial banks** (2010): 94; deposits: $200.0 bil. **Savings institutions** (2010): 35; deposits: $7.4 bil. **Lottery** (2010): total sales: $1.42 bil; profit: $430.8 mil.

Federal govt. Fed. civ. employees (Mar. 2011): 44,322; **avg. salary:** $65,658. **Notable fed. facilities:** Ft. Bragg; *Camp LeJeune Marine Base, *Cherry Point Marine Air Station; NOAA Natl. Climatic Data Ctr.; Natl. Inst. of Environmental Health Sciences, EPA Research & Dev. Labs, all in Research Triangle Park.

Energy. Electricity production (2010 kWh by source): coal: 69.3 bil; gas: 6.4 bil; nuclear: 40.7 bil; petroleum: 243 mil; hydroelectric: 4.6 bil; other: 7 mil.

State data. Motto: Esse Quam Videri (To be rather than to seem). **Flower:** Dogwood. **Bird:** Cardinal. **Tree:** Pine. **Song:** "The Old North State." **Twelfth** of the original 13 states to ratify the Constitution, Nov. 21, 1789. **State fair** at Raleigh, mid-Oct.; at Fletcher, mid-Sept.

History. Algonquian, Siouan, and Iroquoian peoples lived in the region at the time of European contact. Sir Walter Raleigh tried to found a colony, 1584-87; the "Lost Colony" on Roanoke Island, 1587, disappeared without a trace. Permanent settlers came from Virginia in the mid-17th cent. The province's congress was the first to vote for independence, 1776. In the Revolutionary War, Gen. Charles Cornwallis's forces were defeated at Kings Mountain, 1780, and forced out after Guilford Courthouse, 1781. The state ratified the Constitution, 1789, only after Congress passed the Bill of Rights. North Carolina, where one-third of the population was slaves, seceded from the Union, 1861, and provided more troops to the Confederacy than any other state; it was readmitted, 1868. The Wright brothers made the first powered airplane flight at Kitty Hawk, 1903. Sit-ins at segregated Greensboro lunch counters, 1960, drew national attention to the civil rights movement. Long reliant on tobacco, textiles, and wood products, North Carolina has prospered since the 1960s from advanced technologies in the Raleigh-Durham-Chapel Hill area and banking in Charlotte. The hurricane-prone state was hit hard by Hazel, 1954, Fran, 1996, and Floyd, 1999.

Tourist attractions. Cape Hatteras and Cape Lookout natl. seashores; Great Smoky Mts.; Guilford Courthouse and Moore's Creek parks; 66 American Revolution battle sites; Bennett Place (where last Confederate army surrendered), near Durham; Ft. Raleigh, Roanoke Island; Wright Brothers Natl. Memorial, Kitty Hawk; Battleship *North Carolina*, Wilmington; NC Zoo, Asheboro; NC Symphony, Exploris, NC museums of Art, Nat. Sciences, History, in Raleigh; Carl Sandburg Home, Hendersonville; Biltmore House and Gardens, Asheville.

Famous North Carolinians. David Brinkley, Shirley Caesar, John Coltrane, Rick Dees, Elizabeth Hanford Dole, John Edwards, Ava Gardner, Richard J. Gatling, Billy Graham, Andy Griffith, O. Henry, Andrew Jackson, Andrew Johnson, Michael Jordan, Wm. Rufus King, Charles Kuralt, Meadowlark Lemon, Dolley Madison, Thelonious Monk, Edward R. Murrow, Arnold Palmer, Richard Petty, James K. Polk, Charlie Rose, Carl Sandburg, Enos Slaughter, Dean Smith, James Taylor, Thomas Wolfe.

Tourist information. North Carolina Division of Tourism, Film and Sports Development, 4324 Mail Service Ctr., Raleigh, NC 27699; 1-800-VISIT-NC; (919) 733-8372; www.visitnc.com
Website. www.nc.gov

North Dakota (ND)
Peace Garden State

People. Population (2010): 672,591; rank: 48; net change (2000-10): 4.7%. **Pop. density:** 9.7 per sq mi. **Racial distribution** (2010): 90.0% white; 1.2% black; 1.0% Asian; 5.4% Native Amer./AK; <0.05% Hawaiian/Pacific Islander; 2 or more races, 1.8%. **Hispanic pop.** (any race, 2010): 2.0%.

Geography. Total area: 70,698 sq mi; rank: 19. **Land area:** 69,001 sq mi; rank: 17. **Acres forested:** 0.7 mil. **Location:** West North Central state, situated exactly in the middle of North America, bounded on the N by Canada, on the E by Minnesota, on the S by South Dakota, on the W by Montana. **Climate:** continental, with a wide range of temperature and moderate rainfall. **Topography:** Central Lowland in the E comprises the flat Red River Valley and the Rolling Drift Prairie; Missouri Plateau of the Great Plains on the W. **Capital:** Bismarck.

Economy. Chief industries: agriculture, mining, tourism, manufacturing, telecommunications, energy, food processing. **Chief manuf. goods:** machinery, wood product, motor vehicles & parts, furniture, processed foods. **Chief crops:** wheat, soybeans, corn, sugar beets, barley, dry beans, sunflowers, canola, potatoes, flaxseed, hay, dry peas, lentils, oats. **Livestock** (Jan. 2011): 1.70 mil cattle/calves, 78,000 sheep/lambs. **Broadband internet:** 56.9%. **Nonfuel minerals** (2010 prelim.): $88.0 mil; sand and gravel (construction), lime, stone (crushed), clays (common), sand and gravel (industrial). **Gross state product** (2010): $34.7 bil. **Sales tax** (2011): 5.0%. **Employment distrib.** (May 2011): 20.9% govt.; 21.4% trade/trans./util.; 5.9% mfg.; 14.0% ed./health; 7.3% prof./bus. serv.; 9.2% leisure/hosp.; 5.3% finance; 9.5% constr./mining/log.; 1.8% info.; 4.3% other serv. **Unemployment** (2010): 3.9%. **Per cap. pers. income** (2010 prelim.): $40,596. **New private housing** (2010): 3,833 units/$481.1 mil. **Commercial banks** (2010): 98; deposits $16.5 bil. **Savings institutions** (2010): 2; deposits: $1.1 bil. **Lottery** (2010): total sales: $24.4 mil; profit: $6.3 mil.

Federal govt. Fed. civ. employees (Mar. 2011): 6,638; **avg. salary:** $61,435. **Notable fed. facilities:** Minot AFB; *Grand Forks AFB; Northern Prairie Wildlife Res. Ctr.; Garrison Dam Nat. Fish Hatchery; Grand Forks Human Nutrition Res. Ctr.

Energy. Electricity production (2010 kWh by source): coal: 28.4 bil; petroleum: 38 mil; hydroelectric: 2 bil; other: 498 mil.

State data. Motto: Liberty and union, now and forever, one and inseparable. **Flower:** Wild prairie rose. **Bird:** Western meadowlark. **Tree:** American elm. **Song:** "North Dakota Hymn." **Entered union:** Nov. 2, 1889; rank: 39th. **State fair** at Minot, late July.

History. Paleo-Indian peoples hunted in the area at least 11,000 years ago. At the time of European contact, the Ojibwa, Yanktonai and Teton Sioux, Mandan, Arikara, and Hidatsa peoples lived in the region. Pierre de Varennes, sieur de La Vérendrye, was the first French fur trader in the area, 1738, followed by the English at the end of the 18th cent. Lewis and Clark built Ft. Mandan, near present-day Washburn, 1804-05, and wintered there. The first permanent settlement was at Pembina, 1812. Missouri River steamboats reached the area, 1832. Dakota Territory was organized, 1861. The first railroad arrived, 1872. The "bonanza farm" craze of the 1870s-80s led to statehood, 1889. The Nonpartisan League, a farmers' group favoring state ownership of industries, helped elect Lynn Frazier as governor, 1916, but he and others were ousted in a recall vote, 1921. The predominantly agricultural state had a 6.5% drop in population, 1930-2005.

Tourist attractions. North Dakota Heritage Center, Bisarck; Bonanzaville, Fargo; Ft. Union Trading Post Natl. Historic Site; Lake Sakakawea; Intl. Peace Garden; Theodore Roosevelt Natl. Park, including Elkhorn Ranch, Badlands; Ft. Abraham Lincoln State Park and Museum, near Mandan; Dakota Dinosaur Museum, Dickinson; Knife River Indian Villages-Natl. Hist. Site.

Famous North Dakotans. Maxwell Anderson, Angie Dickinson, John Bernard Flannagan, Phil Jackson, Louis L'Amour, Peggy Lee, Eric Sevareid, Ann Sothern, Vilhjalmur Stefansson, Lawrence Welk.

Tourist information. North Dakota Tourism Division, Century Center, 1600 E. Century Ave., Ste. 2, P.O. Box 2057, Bismarck, ND 58502; 1-800-435-5663; www.ndtourism.com
Website. www.nd.gov

Ohio (OH)
Buckeye State

People. Population (2010): 11,536,504; rank: 7; net change (2000-10): 1.6%. **Pop. density:** 282.3 per sq mi. **Racial distribution** (2010): 82.7% white; 12.2% black; 1.7% Asian; 0.2% Native Amer./AK; <0.05% Hawaiian/Pacific Islander; 2 or more races, 2.1%. **Hispanic pop.** (any race, 2010): 3.1%.

Geography. Total area: 44,826 sq mi; rank: 34. **Land area:** 40,861 sq mi; rank: 35. **Acres forested:** 8.0 mil. **Location:** East North Central state bounded on the N by Michigan and Lake Erie; on the E and S by Pennsylvania, West Virginia, and Kentucky; on the W by Indiana. **Climate:** temperate but variable; weather subject to much precipitation. **Topography:** generally rolling plain; Allegheny plateau in E; Lake Erie plains extend southward; central plains in the W. **Capital:** Columbus. **Chief airports:** Akron, Cleveland, Columbus, Dayton.

Economy. Chief industries: manufacturing, trade, services. **Chief manuf. goods:** motor vehicles & parts, petroleum, plastics & rubber, iron & steel, aircraft, machinery, fabricated metal, printing. **Chief crops:** corn, soybeans, hay, wheat, grapes, potatoes, tomatoes, apples, strawberries, tobacco. **Livestock** (Dec. 2010): 37.07 mil chickens (excl. broilers), 60 mil broilers; (Jan. 2011): 1.23 mil cattle/calves, 129,000 sheep/lambs; (June 2011): 165,000 hogs/pigs. **Broadband internet:** 68.2%. **Nonfuel minerals** (2010 prelim.): $1.0 bil; stone (crushed), salt, sand and gravel (construction), lime, cement (portland). **Commercial fishing** (2009): $3.4 mil. **Chief ports:** Cincinnati, Toledo, Conneaut, Cleveland, Ashtabula. **Gross state product** (2010): $477.7 bil. **Sales tax** (2011): 5.5%. **Employment distrib.** (May 2011): 15.4% govt.; 18.6% trade/trans./util.; 12.3% mfg.; 16.9% ed./health; 12.5% prof./bus. serv.; 9.8% leisure/hosp.; 5.4% finance; 3.5% constr./mining/log.; 1.5% info.; 4.2% other serv. **Unemployment** (2010): 10.1%. **Per cap. pers. income** (2010 prelim.): $36,395. **New private housing** (2010): 13,710 units/$2.3 bil. **Commercial banks** (2010): 167; deposits $194.0 bil. **Savings institutions** (2010): 101; deposits: $32.4 bil. **Lottery** (2010): total sales: $2.49 bil; profit: $728.6 mil.

Federal govt. Fed. civ. employees (Mar. 2011): 53,384; **avg. salary:** $74,380. **Notable fed. facilities:** Wright-Patterson AFB; Defense Supply Ctr., Columbus; *NASA John H. Glenn Res. Ctr.; Lima Army Tank Plant.

Energy. Electricity production (2010 kWh by source): coal: 90.3 bil; gas: 1.7 bil; petroleum: 239 mil; hydroelectric: 459 mil; other: 18 mil.

State data. Motto: With God, all things are possible. **Flower:** Scarlet carnation. **Bird:** Cardinal. **Tree:** Buckeye. **Song:** "Beautiful Ohio." **Entered union:** Mar. 1, 1803; rank: 17th. **State fair** at Columbus, late July-early Aug.

History. Paleo-Indians hunted in the area about 11,000 years ago; the Adena and Hopewell cultures followed. Wyandot, Delaware, Miami, and Shawnee peoples sparsely occupied the area when the first Europeans arrived. René-Robert Cavelier, sieur de La Salle visited the region, 1669. France claimed it, 1682, but ceded it to Britain, 1763. After the American Revolution, Ohio became part of the Northwest Territory, 1787. The first permanent settlement was at Marietta, 1788. Cincinnati was also founded, 1788; Cleveland, 1796. Indian warfare abated with the Treaty of Greenville, 1795. Ohio became a state, 1803. In the War of 1812, Oliver Hazard Perry's victory on Lake Erie and William Henry Harrison's invasion of Canada, 1813, ended British incursions. Columbus, founded 1812, became the state capital, 1816. Before the Civil War, Ohioans aided the Underground Railroad, helping runaway slaves. Agricultural for much of the 19th cent., the state became an industrial powerhouse in the 20th. Manufacturing jobs dropped by 24%, 1998-2007. No Republican has ever won the presidency without carrying Ohio, and the state's 20 electoral votes proved crucial to Pres. George W. Bush in 2004.

Tourist attractions. Mound City Group, Hopewell Culture Natl. Hist. Park; Neil Armstrong Air and Space Museum, Wapakoneta; Air Force Museum, Dayton; Pro Football Hall of Fame, Canton; King's Island amusement park, Mason; Lake Erie Islands, Cedar Point amusement park, in Sandusky; birthplaces, homes of, and memorials to U.S. Pres. W. H. Harrison, Grant, Garfield, Hayes, B. Harrison, McKinley, Harding, Taft; Amish Region, Tuscarawas/Holmes counties; German Village, Columbus; Jack Nicklaus' Golf Center, Mason; Bob Evans Farm, Rio Grande; Rock and Roll Hall of Fame and Museum, Cleveland.

Famous Ohioans. Sherwood Anderson, Neil Armstrong, George Bellows, Halle Berry, Ambrose Bierce, Erma Bombeck, Drew Carey, Hart Crane, George Custer, Clarence Darrow, Paul Laurence Dunbar, Thomas Edison, Clark Gable, John Glenn, Zane Grey, Bob Hope, William Dean Howells, Toni Morrison, Jack Nicklaus, Jesse Owens, Jack Paar, Pontiac, Eddie Rickenbacker, John D. Rockefeller Sr. and Jr., Roy Rogers, Pete Rose, Arthur Schlesinger Jr., Gen. William Sherman, Steven Spielberg, Gloria Steinem, Harriet Beecher Stowe, Charles Taft, Robert A. Taft, William H. Taft, Tecumseh, James Thurber, Ted Turner, Orville and Wilbur Wright.

Tourist information. Division of Travel and Tourism, P.O. Box 1001, Columbus, OH 43216; 1-800-BUCKEYE; www.discoverohio.com

Website. www.ohio.gov

Oklahoma (OK)
Sooner State

People. Population (2010): 3,751,351; rank: 28; net change (2000-10): 8.7%. **Pop. density:** 54.7 per sq mi. **Racial distribution** (2010): 72.2% white; 7.4% black; 1.7% Asian; 8.6% Native Amer./AK; 0.1% Hawaiian/Pacific Islander; 2 or more races, 5.9%. **Hispanic pop.** (any race, 2010): 8.9%.

Geography. Total area: 69,899 sq mi; rank: 20. **Land area:** 68,595 sq mi; rank: 19. **Acres forested:** 7.7 mil. **Location:** West South Central state bounded on the N by Colorado and Kansas; on the E by Missouri and Arkansas; on the S and W by Texas and New Mexico. **Climate:** temperate; southern humid belt merging with colder northern continental; humid eastern and dry western zones. **Topography:** high plains predominate in the W, hills and small mountains in the E; the east central region is dominated by the Arkansas R. Basin, and the Red R. Plains, in the S. **Capital:** Oklahoma City. **Chief airports:** Oklahoma City, Tulsa.

Economy. Chief industries: manufacturing, mineral and energy exploration and production, agriculture, services. **Chief manuf. goods:** animal slaughtering & processing, petroleum, plastics & rubber, fabricated metals, machinery, motor vehicles & parts. **Chief crops:** wheat, greenhouse & nursery, hay, cotton, corn, soybeans, pecans, sorghum, peanuts. **Livestock** (Dec. 2010): 4.56 mil chickens (excl. broilers), 225 mil broilers; (Jan. 2011): 5.10 mil cattle/calves, 75,000 sheep/lambs; (June 2011): 410,000 hogs/pigs. **Broadband internet:** 85.3%. **Nonfuel minerals** (2010 prelim.): $646 mil; stone (crushed), cement (portland), sand and gravel (construction), iodine, helium (Grade-A). **Chief port:** Catoosa. **Gross state product** (2010): $147.5 bil. **Sales tax** (2011): 4.5%. **Employment distrib.** (May 2011): 21.9% govt.; 17.8% trade/trans./util.; 8.5% mfg.; 13.2% ed./health; 11.3% prof./bus. serv.; 9.3% leisure/hosp.; 5.2% finance; 7.2% constr./mining/log.; 1.6% info.; 3.9% other serv. **Unemployment** (2010): 7.1%. **Per cap. pers. income** (2010 prelim.): $36,421. **New private housing** (2010): 8,140 units/$1.2 bil. **Commercial banks** (2010): 257; deposits: $61.6 bil. **Savings institutions** (2010): 7; deposits: $7.4 bil. **Lottery** (2010): total sales: $199.9 mil; profit: $70.0 mil.

Federal govt. Fed. civ. employees (Mar. 2011): 39,732; **avg. salary:** $63,554. **Notable fed. facilities:** Tinker AFB; FAA Mike Monroney Aeronautical Ctr.; *Ft. Sill; *Altus AFB; McAlester Army Ammunition Plant; Vance AFB; Natl. Severe Storms Lab.

Energy. Electricity production (2010 kWh by source): coal: 29.1 bil; gas: 25 bil; petroleum: 13 mil; hydroelectric: 2.7 bil; other: 349 mil.

State data. Motto: Labor Omnia Vincit (Labor conquers all things). **Flower:** Mistletoe. **Bird:** Scissor-tailed flycatcher. **Tree:** Redbud. **Song:** "Oklahoma!" **Entered union:** Nov. 16, 1907; rank: 46th. **State fair** at Oklahoma City, mid-Sept.; at Tulsa, 4th Thursday after Labor Day-2nd Sunday of Oct.

History. Few Native Americans inhabited the region when the Spanish explorer Coronado arrived, 1541; in the 16th and 17th cent., French traders visited. Part of the Louisiana Purchase, 1803, Oklahoma was known as Indian Country and, from 1834, Indian Territory. It became home to the "Five Civilized Tribes"—Cherokee, Choctaw, Chickasaw, Creek, and Seminole—after the forced removal of Indians from the eastern U.S., 1828-46. The land was also used by Comanche, Osage, and other Plains Indians. As white settlers pressed west, land was opened for homesteading by "runs" and lottery. The first run was in 1889; the most famous run, 1893, was to the Cherokee Outlet. Oklahoma became a state, 1907. In the early 20th cent., oil finds brought wealth to the Tulsa area; the Greenwood section of the city, then known as the "Negro Wall Street," was devastated by a white mob, 1921. Depression and drought drove many "Okies" from the Dust Bowl to California in the 1930s. A truck bomb in Oklahoma City, 1995, destroyed a federal office building, killing 168 people; Timothy McVeigh was executed for the crime, 2001.

Tourist attractions. Cherokee Heritage Center, Tahlequah; Oklahoma City Natl. Memorial; Natl. Cowboy Hall of Fame, Remington Park Race Track, White Water Bay and Frontier City theme parks, in Oklahoma City; Will Rogers Memorial, Claremore; Ft. Gibson; Ouachita Natl. Forest; Philbrook Museum of Art, Gilcrease Museum, in Tulsa; Tulsa's art deco district; Wichita Mts. Wildlife Refuge; Woolaroc Museum and Wildlife Preserve, Bartlesville; Sequoyah's Home Site, Sallisaw.

Famous Oklahomans. Troy Aikman, Carl Albert, Gene Autry, Johnny Bench, William "Hopalong Cassidy" Boyd, Garth Brooks, Lon Chaney, L. Gordon Cooper, Walter Cronkite, Jerome "Dizzy" Dean, Ralph Ellison, John Hope Franklin, James Garner, Geronimo, Woody Guthrie, Paul Harvey, Ron Howard, Gen. Patrick J. Hurley, Ben Johnson, Jeane Kirkpatrick, Louis L'Amour, Shannon Lucid, Mickey Mantle, Reba McEntire, Wiley Post, Tony Randall, Oral Roberts, Will Rogers, Sam Snead, Barry Switzer, Maria Tallchief, Jim Thorpe, J. C. Watts Jr.

Tourist information. Travel and Tourism Division, 120 N. Robinson, 6th Fl., P.O. Box 52002, Oklahoma City, OK 73152-2002; 1-800-652-6552; www.travelok.com

Website. www.ok.gov

Oregon (OR)
Beaver State

People. Population (2010): 3,831,074; rank: 27; net change (2000-10): 12.0%. **Pop. density:** 39.9 per sq mi. **Racial distribution** (2010): 83.6% white; 1.8% black; 3.7% Asian; 1.4% Native Amer./AK; 0.3% Hawaiian/Pacific Islander; 2 or more races, 3.8%. **Hispanic pop.** (any race, 2010): 11.7%.

Geography. Total area: 98,379 sq mi; rank: 9. **Land area:** 95,988 sq mi; rank: 10. **Acres forested:** 30.0 mil. **Location:** Pacific state, bounded on N by Washington; on E by Idaho; on S by Nevada and California; on W by the Pacific. **Climate:** coastal mild and humid climate; continental dryness and extreme temperatures in the interior. **Topography:** Coast Range of rugged mountains; fertile Willamette R. Valley to E and S; Cascade Mt. Range of volcanic peaks E of the valley; plateau E of Cascades, remaining two-thirds of state. **Capital:** Salem. **Chief airport:** Portland.

Economy. Chief industries: manufacturing, services, trade, finance, insurance, real estate, government, construction. **Chief manuf. goods:** wood products, frozen produce, printing, computers & electronics, transportation equipment, industrial machinery. **Chief crops:** greenhouse & nursery, grass seed, hay, wheat, potatoes, Christmas trees, onions, pears, hazelnuts, corn, grapes, cherries, blackberries, blueberries, peppermint, snap beans, apples, hops. **Livestock** (Dec. 2010): 3 mil chickens (excl. broilers); (Jan. 2011): 1.33 mil. cattle/calves, 215,000 sheep/lambs. **Broadband internet:** 80.2%. **Nonfuel minerals** (2010 prelim.): $292 mil; stone (crushed), sand and gravel (construction), cement (portland), diatomite, perlite (crude). **Commercial fishing** (2009): $102.5 mil. **Chief ports:** Portland, Coos Bay. **Gross state product** (2010): $174.2 bil. **Sales tax** (2011): none. **Employment distrib.** (May 2011): 18.8% govt.; 19.1% trade/trans./util.; 10.2% mfg.; 14.5% ed./health; 11.3% prof./bus. serv.; 10.3% leisure/hosp.; 5.7% finance; 4.5% constr./mining/log.; 2.0% info.; 3.5% other serv. **Unemployment** (2010): 10.8%. **Per cap. pers. income** (2010 prelim.): $37,095. **New private housing** (2010): 6,868 units/$1.4 bil. **Commercial banks** (2010): 49; deposits: $51.2 bil. **Savings institutions** (2010): 10; deposits: $2.5 bil. **Lottery** (2010): total sales: $1.03 bil; profit: $516.7 mil.

Federal govt. Fed. civ. employees (Mar. 2011): 20,596; **avg. salary:** $69,267. **Notable fed. facilities:** Bonneville Power Administration.

Energy. Electricity production (2010 kWh by source): coal: 4.1 bil; gas: 6.1 bil; petroleum: 3 mil; hydroelectric: 30.1 bil; other: 597 mil.

State data. Motto: She flies with her own wings. **Flower:** Oregon grape. **Bird:** Western meadowlark. **Tree:** Douglas fir. **Song:** "Oregon, My Oregon." **Entered union:** Feb. 14, 1859; rank: 33rd. **State fair** at Salem, 11 days ending with Labor Day.

History. More than 100 Native American tribes inhabited the area at the time of European contact, including the Chi-

nook, Yakima, Cayuse, Modoc, and Nez Percé. Capt. Robert Gray sighted and sailed into the Columbia River, 1792. Lewis and Clark, traveling overland, wintered at its mouth, 1805-06. Fur traders sent by John Jacob Astor established the Astoria trading post in the Columbia River region, 1811. Settlers arrived in the Willamette Valley, 1834. In 1843, the first large wave of settlers arrived via the Oregon Trail. Oregon became a territory, 1848, and a state, 1859. Early in the 20th cent., the "Oregon System"—political reforms that included initiative, referendum, recall, direct primary, and woman suffrage—was adopted. Originally dominated by forest products, the economy diversified after World War II, with high-tech firms clustering in the "Silicon Forest" area around Portland. Oregonians were the first in the U.S. to pass measures allowing physician-assisted suicide for terminally ill patients, 1994, and establishing an all-mail voting system, 1998.

Tourist attractions. John Day Fossil Beds Natl. Monument; Columbia River Gorge; Timberline Lodge, Mt. Hood Natl. Forest; Crater Lake Natl. Park; Oregon Dunes Natl. Recreation Area; Ft. Clatsop Natl. Memorial; Oregon Caves Natl. Monument; Oregon Museum of Science and Industry, Portland; Shakespeare Festival, Ashland; High Desert Museum, Bend; Multnomah Falls; Diamond Lake; "Spruce Goose," Evergreen Aviation Museum, McMinnville.

Famous Oregonians. Ernest Bloch, Bill Bowerman, Ernest Haycox, Chief Joseph, Ken Kesey, Phil Knight, Ursula K. Le Guin, Edwin Markham, Tom McCall, Dr. John McLoughlin, Joaquin Miller, Bob Packwood, Linus Pauling, Steve Prefontaine, John Reed, Alberto Salazar, Mary Decker Slaney, William Simon U'Ren.

Tourist information. Travel Oregon, 670 Hawthorne SE, Ste. 240, Salem, OR 97301; 1-800-547-7842; www.traveloregon.com

Website. www.oregon.gov

Pennsylvania (PA)
Keystone State

People. Population (2010): 12,702,379; rank: 6; net change (2000-10): 3.4%. **Pop. density:** 283.9 per sq mi. **Racial distribution** (2010): 81.9% white; 10.8% black; 2.7% Asian; 0.2% Native Amer./AK; <0.05% Hawaiian/Pacific Islander; 2 or more races, 1.9%. **Hispanic pop.** (any race, 2010): 5.7%.

Geography. Total area: 46,054 sq mi; rank: 33. **Land area:** 44,743 sq mi; rank: 32. **Acres forested:** 16.7 mil. **Location:** Middle Atlantic state, bordered on the E by the Delaware R.; on the S by the Mason-Dixon Line; on the W by West Virginia and Ohio; on the N/NE by Lake Erie and New York. **Climate:** continental with wide fluctuations in seasonal temperatures. **Topography:** Allegheny Mts. run SW-NE, with Piedmont and Coast Plain in the SE triangle; Allegheny Front a diagonal spine across the state's center; N and W rugged plateau falls to Lake Erie Lowland. **Capital:** Harrisburg. **Chief airports:** Harrisburg, Philadelphia, Pittsburgh.

Economy. Chief industries: agribusiness, advanced manufacturing, health care, travel & tourism, depository institutions, biotechnology, printing & publishing, research & consulting, trucking & warehousing, transportation by air, engineering & management, legal services. **Chief manuf. goods:** petroleum, pharmaceuticals, plastics, iron & steel, printing, paper & paperboard, confectionery & snacks, animal slaughtering & processing. **Chief crops:** greenhouse & nursery, mushrooms, corn, hay, soybeans, apples, tomatoes, wheat, grapes, peaches, potatoes, strawberries, tobacco. **Livestock** (Dec. 2010): 29.55 mil chickens (excl. broilers), 149.3 mil broilers; (Jan. 2011): 1.61 mil cattle/calves, 98,000 sheep/lambs; (June 2011): 95,000 hogs/pigs. **Broadband internet:** 75.1%. **Nonfuel minerals** (2010 prelim.): $1.5 bil; stone (crushed), cement (portland), lime, sand and gravel (construction), cement (masonry). **Commercial fishing** (2009): $100,000. **Chief ports:** Philadelphia, Pittsburgh. **Gross state product** (2010): $569.7 bil. **Sales tax** (2011): 6.0%. **Employment distrib.** (May 2011): 13.2% govt.; 19.1% trade/trans./util.; 10.0% mfg.; 20.3% ed./health; 12.2% prof./bus. serv.; 9.2% leisure/hosp.; 5.4% finance; 4.4% constr./mining/log.; 1.7% info.; 4.4% other serv. **Unemployment** (2010): 8.7%. **Per cap. pers. income** (2010 prelim.): $41,152. **New private housing** (2010): 19,740 units/$3.3 bil. **Commercial banks** (2010): 167; deposits: $222.3 bil. **Savings institutions** (2010): 91; deposits: $63.6 bil. **Lottery** (2010): total sales: $3.1 bil; profit: $915.7 mil.

Federal govt. Fed. civ. employees (Mar. 2011): 69,719; **avg. salary:** $68,152. **Notable fed. facilities:** Army War

College, Carlisle Barracks; *Naval Inventory Control Point, Mechanicsburg; Philadelphia Mint, Defense Supply Ctr., Naval Surface Warfare Ctr., in Phila.; Defense Distribution Ctr., New Cumberland; *Tobyhanna Army Depot; *Letterkenny Army Depot.

Energy. Electricity production (2010 kWh by source): hydroelectric: 1.1 bil.

State data. Motto: Virtue, liberty, and independence. **Flower:** Mountain laurel. **Bird:** Ruffed grouse. **Tree:** Hemlock. **Song:** "Pennsylvania." **Second** of the original 13 states to ratify the Constitution, Dec. 12, 1787. **State fair:** no official state fair; county and community fairs, Mar.-Oct.

History. When Europeans came, Algonquian-speaking Lenni Lenape (Delaware) and Shawnee and the Iroquoian Susquehannocks, Erie, and Seneca occupied the region. Swedish explorers made the first permanent settlement, 1643, on Tinicum Island. The Dutch seized the settlement, 1655, but lost it to the British, 1664. The region was given by Charles II to William Penn, 1681. Philadelphia ("brotherly love") was the capital of the colonies during most of the American Revolution, and of the U.S., 1790-1800; the Declaration of Independence, 1776, and Constitution, 1787, were signed here. Philadelphia was taken by the British, 1777; George Washington's troops encamped at Valley Forge in the bitter winter of 1777-78. Slavery was abolished, 1780. Union victory at the Battle of Gettysburg, July 1-3, 1863, marked a turning point in the Civil War. A dam collapse at Johnstown, 1889, killed at least 2,200 people. From the late 19th to the mid-20th cent., Pittsburgh prospered from coal and steel; later, heavy industry declined, but the city revived as a hub of finance, health care, and research. The Three Mile Island nuclear plant near Harrisburg had a near-meltdown, 1979. One of 4 hijacked planes on Sept. 11, 2001, crashed near Shanksville; a national memorial was designated on the site in 2002.

Tourist attractions. Independence Natl. Historic Park; Franklin Institute Science Museum, Philadelphia Museum of Art, in Philadelphia; Valley Forge Natl. Historic Park; Gettysburg Natl. Military Park; Pennsylvania Dutch Country; Hershey; Duquesne Incline, Carnegie Institute, Heinz Hall, in Pittsburgh; Pocono Mts.; Pennsylvania's Grand Canyon, Tioga County; Allegheny Natl. Forest; Laurel Highlands; Presque Isle State Park; Fallingwater, Mill Run; Johnstown; Steamtown, Scranton; U.S. Brig *Niagara,* Erie; Oil Heritage Region, Northwest PA.

Famous Pennsylvanians. Marian Anderson, Maxwell Anderson, George Blanda, James Buchanan, Andrew Carnegie, Rachel Carson, Perry Como, Bill Cosby, Thomas Eakins, Stephen Foster, Benjamin Franklin, Robert Fulton, Martha Graham, Milton Hershey, Gene Kelly, Grace Kelly (Princess Grace of Monaco), Dan Marino, George C. Marshall, Chris Matthews, John J. McCloy, Margaret Mead, Andrew W. Mellon, Joe Montana, Stan Musial, Joe Namath, John O'Hara, Arnold Palmer, Robert E. Peary, Mike Piazza, Tom Ridge, Mary Roberts Rinehart, Fred Rogers, Betsy Ross, Will Smith, Jimmy Stewart, Jim Thorpe, Johnny Unitas, John Updike, Honus Wagner, Andy Warhol, Benjamin West.

Tourist information. Pennsylvania Tourism Office, Department of Community and Economic Development, Commonwealth Keystone Building, 4th Fl., 400 North St., Harrisburg, PA 17120-0225; 1-800-VISITPA; www.visitpa.com

Website. www.pa.gov

Rhode Island (RI)
Little Rhody, Ocean State

People. Population (2010): 1,052,567; rank: 43; net change (2000-10): less than 0.4%. **Pop. density:** 1,018.1 per sq mi. **Racial distribution** (2010): 81.4% white; 5.7% black; 2.9% Asian; 0.6% Native Amer./AK; 0.1% Hawaiian/Pacific Islander; 2 or more races, 3.3%. **Hispanic pop.** (any race, 2010): 12.4%.

Geography. Total area: 1,545 sq mi; rank: 50. **Land area:** 1,034 sq mi; rank: 50. **Acres forested:** 0.3 mil. **Location:** New England state. **Climate:** invigorating and changeable. **Topography:** eastern lowlands of Narragansett Basin; western uplands of flat and rolling hills. **Capital:** Providence. **Chief airport:** Warwick.

Economy. Chief industries: services, manufacturing. **Chief manuf. goods:** plastics, fabricated metals, electrical equip., jewelry. **Chief crops:** greenhouse & nursery, sweet corn, berries, potatoes, apples, hay. **Livestock** (Jan. 2011):

4,900 cattle/calves. **Broadband internet:** 79.6%. **Nonfuel minerals** (2010 prelim.): $34.4 mil; stone (crushed), sand and gravel (construction), sand and gravel (industrial), gemstones (natural). **Commercial fishing** (2009): $61.7 mil. **Chief ports:** Providence, Davisville, Newport. **Gross state product** (2010): $49.2 bil. **Sales tax** (2011): 7.0%. **Employment distrib.** (May 2011): 13.2% govt.; 16.4% trade/trans./util.; 8.7% mfg.; 22.3% ed./health; 11.6% prof./bus. serv.; 11.1% leisure/hosp.; 6.4% finance; 3.6% constr./mining/log.; 2.2% info.; 4.7% other serv. **Unemployment** (2010): 11.6%. **Per cap. pers. income** (2010 prelim.): $42,579. **New private housing** (2010): 934 units/$155.1 mil. **Commercial banks** (2010): 11; deposits: $35.2 bil. **Savings institutions** (2010): 14; deposits: $4.6 bil. **Lottery** (2010): total sales: $702.4 mil; profit: $344.7 mil.

Federal govt. Fed. civ. employees (Mar. 2011): 7,176; **avg. salary:** $83,779. **Notable fed. facilities:** Naval War College; Naval Underwater Warfare Ctr.; EPA Atlantic Ecology Div. Lab.

Energy. Electricity production (2010 kWh by source): petroleum: 10 mil.

State data. Motto: Hope. **Flower:** Violet. **Bird:** Rhode Island red chicken. **Tree:** Red maple. **Song:** "Rhode Island." **Thirteenth** of original 13 states to ratify the Constitution, May 29, 1790. **State fair:** none; largest fair at Richmond, mid-Aug.

History. When Europeans arrived, Narragansett, Niantic, Nipmuc, and Wampanoag peoples lived in the region. Verrazano visited the area, 1524. The first permanent settlement was founded at Providence, 1636, by Roger Williams, who was exiled from the Massachusetts Bay Colony; Anne Hutchinson, also exiled, settled Portsmouth, 1638. Quaker and Jewish immigrants seeking freedom of worship began arriving, 1650s-60s. The colonists broke the power of the Narragansett in the Great Swamp Fight, 1675, the decisive battle in King Philip's War. The colony was the first to formally renounce all allegiance to King George III, May 4, 1776. Initially opposed to joining the Union, Rhode Island was the last of the 13 colonies to ratify the Constitution, 1790. Trade, textiles, and metal goods dominated the economy in the 19th cent., and Newport became a fashionable resort after the Civil War. The U.S. Navy was the state's largest civilian employer, 1945-73, until the destroyer force was relocated from Newport. A nightclub fire in West Warwick killed 100 people in 2003.

Tourist attractions. Newport mansions; yachting races including Newport to Bermuda; Block Island; Touro Synagogue (oldest in U.S.) Newport; First Baptist Church in America, Providence; Slater Mill Historic Site, Pawtucket; Gilbert Stuart birthplace, Saunderstown.

Famous Rhode Islanders. Ambrose Burnside, George M. Cohan, Nelson Eddy, Jabez Gorham, Nathanael Greene, Christopher and Oliver La Farge, John McLaughlin, Matthew C. and Oliver Hazard Perry, Gilbert Stuart.

Tourist information. Rhode Island Tourism Division, 315 Iron Horse Way, Ste. 101, Providence, RI 02908; 1-800-250-7384; www.visitrhodeisland.com

Website. www.ri.gov

South Carolina (SC)
Palmetto State

People. Population (2010): 4,625,364; rank: 24; net change (2000-10): 15.3%. **Pop. density:** 153.9 per sq mi. **Racial distribution** (2010): 66.2% white; 27.9% black; 1.3% Asian; 0.4% Native Amer./AK; 0.1% Hawaiian/Pacific Islander; 2 or more races, 1.7%. **Hispanic pop.** (any race, 2010): 5.1%.

Geography. Total area: 32,020 sq mi; rank: 40. **Land area:** 30,061 sq mi; rank: 40. **Acres forested:** 13.0 mil. **Location:** South Atlantic state, bordered by North Carolina on the N; Georgia on the SW and W; the Atlantic Ocean on the E, SE, and S. **Climate:** humid subtropical. **Topography:** Blue Ridge province in NW has highest peaks; piedmont lies between the mountains and the fall line; coastal plain covers two-thirds of the state. **Capital:** Columbia. **Chief airports:** Charleston, Greer, Myrtle Beach.

Economy. Chief industries: tourism, agriculture, manufacturing. **Chief manuf. goods:** chemicals & synthetics, motor vehicles & parts, plastics, paper & paper product, turbines, rubber, textiles. **Chief crops:** greenhouse & nursery, tobacco, soybeans, cotton, corn, peaches, wheat, tomatoes, peanuts. **Livestock** (Dec. 2010): 5.82 mil chickens (excl. broilers), 241 mil broilers; (Jan. 2011): 385,000 cattle/calves. **Broadband**

internet: 67.3%. **Nonfuel minerals** (2010 prelim.): $440 mil; stone (crushed), cement (portland), sand and gravel (construction), cement (masonry), sand and gravel (industrial). **Commercial fishing** (2009): $16.9 mil. **Chief ports:** Charleston, Georgetown. **Gross state product** (2010): $164.4 bil. **Sales tax** (2011): 6.0%. **Employment distrib.** (May 2011): 18.4% govt.; 19.1% trade/trans./util.; 11.6% mfg.; 11.8% ed./health; 12.2% prof./bus. serv.; 12.0% leisure/hosp.; 5.4% finance; 4.5% constr./mining/log.; 1.4% info.; 3.7% other serv. **Unemployment** (2010): 11.2%. **Per cap. pers. income** (2010 prelim.): $33,163. **New private housing** (2010): 14,021 units/$2.5 bil. **Commercial banks** (2010): 80; deposits: $64.3 bil. **Savings institutions** (2010): 27; deposits: $6.0 bil. **Lottery** (2010): total sales: $1.01 bil; profit: $272.4 mil.

Federal govt. Fed. civ. employees (Mar. 2011): 22,028; **avg. salary:** $64,948. **Notable fed. facilities:** *Ft. Jackson; Joint Base Charleston; Parris Island; Shaw AFB; USMC Air Station Beaufort; Savannah River Site.

Energy. Electricity production (2010 kWh by source): coal: 37.3 bil; gas: 9.4 bil; nuclear: 52 bil; petroleum: 146 mil; hydroelectric: 1.4 bil; other: 420 mil.

State data. Motto: Dum Spiro Spero (While I breathe, I hope). **Flower:** Yellow jessamine. **Bird:** Carolina wren. **Tree:** Palmetto. **Song:** "Carolina." **Eighth** of the original 13 states to ratify the Constitution, May 23, 1788. **State fair** at Columbia, mid-Oct.; at Aiken, late Oct.

History. When Europeans arrived, Cherokee, Catawba, and Muskogean peoples lived in the area. Spanish and French came in the 16th cent. The first English colonists settled near the Ashley River, 1670, and moved to the site of present-day Charleston, 1680. The colonists seized the government, 1775, and the royal governor fled. The British took Charleston, 1780, but were defeated at Kings Mountain that same year, and at Cowpens, 1781. In the 1830s, South Carolinians, angered by federal protective tariffs, adopted the Nullification Doctrine, holding that a state can void an act of Congress. Plantation agriculture relied on slave labor to cultivate rice and cotton; slaves made up 57% of the population in 1860, when South Carolina was the first state to secede from the Union. Confederate troops fired on and forced the surrender of U.S. troops at Ft. Sumter, in Charleston Harbor, 1861, launching the Civil War. The state was readmitted to the Union,1868. Strom Thurmond, who ran for president as a segregationist in 1948, later served 48 years in the U.S. Senate (1955-2003). Formerly dependent on textiles, the state has attracted new industries by courting foreign investment.

Tourist attractions. Historic Charleston, Charleston Museum (est. 1773, oldest in U.S.); Ft. Sumter Natl. Monument, in Charleston Harbor; Middleton Place, Magnolia Plantation, Cypress Gardens, Drayton Hall, all near Charleston; other gardens at Brookgreen, Edisto, Glencairn; Myrtle Beach; Hilton Head Island; Revolutionary War battle sites; Andrew Jackson State Park; SC State Museum, Riverbanks Zoo Columbia.

Famous South Carolinians. Charles Bolden, James F. Byrnes, John C. Calhoun, Joe Frazier, DuBose Heyward, Ernest F. Hollings, Andrew Jackson, Jesse Jackson, "Shoeless" Joe Jackson, James Longstreet, Francis Marion, Andie McDowell, Ronald McNair, Charles Pinckney, John Rutledge, Thomas Sumter, Strom Thurmond, John B. Watson.

Tourist information. SC Dept. of Parks, Recreation, & Tourism, 1205 Pendleton St., Columbia, SC 29201; 1-866-224-9339; (803) 734-1700; www.discoversouthcarolina.com.

Website. www.sc.gov

South Dakota (SD)
Coyote State, Mount Rushmore State

People. Population (2010): 814,180; rank: 46; net change (2000-10): 7.9%. **Pop. density:** 10.7 per sq mi. **Racial distribution** (2010): 85.9% white; 1.3% black; 0.9% Asian; 8.8% Native Amer./AK; <0.05% Hawaiian/Pacific Islander; 2 or more races, 2.1%. **Hispanic pop.** (any race, 2010): 2.7%.

Geography. Total area: 77,116 sq mi; rank: 17. **Land area:** 75,811 sq mi; rank: 16. **Acres forested:** 1.8 mil. **Location:** West North Central state bounded on the N by North Dakota; on the E by Minnesota and Iowa; on the S by Nebraska; on the W by Wyoming and Montana. **Climate:** characterized by extremes of temperature, persistent winds, low precipitation and humidity. **Topography:** Prairie Plains in the E; rolling hills of the Great Plains in the W; the Black Hills, rising 3,500 ft, in the SW corner. **Capital:** Pierre.

Economy. Chief industries: agriculture, services, manufacturing. **Chief manuf. goods:** animal slaughtering, machinery, semiconductors, surgical appliances. **Chief crops:** corn, soybeans, wheat, hay, sunflowers, sorghum, oats, barley. **Livestock** (Dec. 2010): 2.96 mil chickens (excl. broilers); (Jan. 2011): 3.70 mil cattle/calves, 275,000 sheep/lambs; (June 2011): 175,000 hogs/pigs. **Broadband internet:** 55.2%. **Nonfuel minerals** (2010 prelim.): $298 mil; gold, sand and gravel (construction), cement (portland), stone (crushed), stone (dimension). **Gross state product** (2010): $39.9 bil. **Sales tax** (2011): 4.0%. **Employment distrib.** (May 2011): 19.5% govt.; 19.9% trade/trans./util.; 9.4% mfg.; 16.0% ed./health; 7.0% prof./bus. serv.; 10.6% leisure/hosp.; 6.9% finance; 5.2% constr./mining/log.; 1.6% info.; 3.9% other serv. **Unemployment** (2010): 4.8%. **Per cap. pers. income** (2010 prelim.): $38,865. **New private housing** (2010): 2,946 units/$403.1 mil. **Commercial banks** (2010): 87; deposits: $105.7 bil. **Savings institutions** (2010): 6; deposits: $1.7 bil. **Lottery** (2010): total sales: $261.0 mil; profit: $116.9 mil.

Federal govt. Fed. civ. employees (Mar. 2011): 8,754; **avg. salary:** $59,505. **Notable fed. facilities:** Ellsworth AFB.

Energy. Electricity production (2010 kWh by source): coal: 3.3 bil; gas: 219 mil; petroleum: 7 mil; hydroelectric: 5.8 bil.

State data. Motto: Under God, the people rule. **Flower:** Pasqueflower. **Bird:** Chinese ring-necked pheasant. **Tree:** Black Hills spruce. **Song:** "Hail, South Dakota." **Entered union:** Nov. 2, 1889; rank: 40th. **State fair** at Huron, late Aug.-early Sept.

History. Paleo-Indians hunted in the region at least 11,500 years ago. At the time of first European contact, Mandan, Hidatsa, Arikara, and Sioux lived in the area. The French Vérendrye brothers explored the region, 1742-43. The U.S. acquired the territory in the Louisiana Purchase, 1803, and Meriwether Lewis and William Clark passed through, 1804-06. In 1817 a trading post opened at what would become Ft. Pierre. Dakota Territory was established, 1861. Gold was discovered, 1874, in the Black Hills on Sioux land; the "Great Dakota Boom" began in 1879. South Dakota became a state, 1889. The massacre of Native American families at Wounded Knee, 1890, ended Sioux resistance; 83 years later, armed supporters of the American Indian Movement, a Native American rights group, occupied the area, leading to a 70-day standoff. Major economic activities include agribusiness and, since the 1980s, credit card services. Republicans scored a key election victory, 2004, with the defeat of 3-term U.S. Sen. Tom Daschle, a national Democratic leader.

Tourist attractions. Black Hills; Mt. Rushmore; Needles Highway; Harney Peak, tallest E of Rockies; Deadwood, 1876 Gold Rush town; Custer State Park; Jewel Cave Natl. Monument; Badlands Natl. Park "moonscape"; "Great Lakes of S. Dakota;" Ft. Sisseton; Great Plains Zoo and Museum, Sioux Falls; Corn Palace, Mitchell; Wind Cave Natl. Park; Crazy Horse Memorial, mountain carving in progress.

Famous South Dakotans. Sparky Anderson, Black Elk, Bob Barker, Tom Brokaw, Crazy Horse, Thomas Daschle, Myron Floren, Mary Hart, Cheryl Ladd, Dr. Ernest O. Lawrence, George McGovern, Billy Mills, Allen Neuharth, Pat O'Brien, Sitting Bull.

Tourist information. Department of Tourism and State Development, Capitol Lake Plaza, 711 E. Wells Ave., c/o 500 E. Capitol Ave., Pierre, SD 57501; 1-800-SDAKOTA; www.travelsd.com

Website. www.sd.gov

Tennessee (TN)
Volunteer State

People. Population (2010): 6,346,105; rank: 17; net change (2000-10): 11.5%. **Pop. density:** 153.9 per sq mi. **Racial distribution** (2010): 77.6% white; 16.7% black; 1.4% Asian; 0.3% Native Amer./AK; 0.1% Hawaiian/Pacific Islander; 2 or more races, 1.7%. **Hispanic pop.** (any race, 2010): 4.6%.

Geography. Total area: 42,144 sq mi; rank: 36. **Land area:** 41,235 sq mi; rank: 34. **Acres forested:** 14.0 mil. **Location:** East South Central state bounded on the N by Kentucky and Virginia; on the E by North Carolina; on the S by Georgia, Alabama, and Mississippi; on the W by Arkansas and Missouri. **Climate:** humid continental to the N; humid subtropical to the S. **Topography:** rugged country in the E; the Great Smoky Mts. of the Unakas; low ridges of the Appalachian Valley; the flat Cumberland Plateau; slightly rolling terrain and knobs of the Interior Low Plateau, the largest region; Eastern Gulf Coastal Plain to the W, laced with streams; Mississippi Alluvial Plain, a narrow strip of swamp and flood plain in the extreme W. **Capital:** Nashville. **Chief airports:** Alcoa, Memphis, Nashville.

Economy. Chief industries: manufacturing, trade, services, tourism, finance, insurance, real estate. **Chief manuf. goods:** motor vehicles & parts, computers & electronics, food, chemicals, plastics, printing, appliances, aluminum. **Chief crops:** greenhouse & nursery, soybeans, cotton, corn, tobacco, hay, tomatoes, wheat. **Livestock** (Dec. 2010): 2.83 mil chickens (excl. broilers), 193.1 mil broilers; (Jan. 2011): 1.99 mil cattle/calves, 35,000 sheep/lambs. **Broadband internet:** 69.5%. **Nonfuel minerals** (2010 prelim.): $814 mil; stone (crushed), zinc, cement (portland), sand and gravel (industrial), sand and gravel (construction). **Chief ports:** Memphis, Nashville, Chattanooga. **Gross state product** (2010): $254.8 bil. **Sales tax** (2011): 7.0%. **Employment distrib.** (May 2011): 16.3% govt.; 21.1% trade/trans./util.; 11.4% mfg.; 14.3% ed./health; 11.6% prof./bus. serv.; 10.3% leisure/hosp.; 5.2% finance; 4.0% constr./mining/log.; 1.7% info.; 3.8% other serv. **Unemployment** (2010): 9.7%. **Per cap. pers. income** (2010 prelim.): $35,307. **New private housing** (2010): 16,475 units/$2.3 bil. **Commercial banks** (2010): 209; deposits $109.9 bil. **Savings institutions** (2010): 20; deposits: $4.8 bil. **Lottery** (2010): total sales: $1.14 bil; profit: $288.9 mil.

Federal govt. Fed. civ. employees (Mar. 2011): 28,841; **avg. salary:** $65,312. **Notable fed. facilities:** Tennessee Valley Authority; Oak Ridge Natl. Lab; Arnold Engineering Development Ctr.; Ft. Campbell; NSA Mid-South, Millington.

Energy. Electricity production (2010 kWh by source): coal: 42.3 bil; gas: 2.2 bil; nuclear: 27.7 bil; petroleum: 204 mil; hydroelectric: 8 bil.

State data. Motto: Agriculture and commerce. **Flower:** Iris. **Bird:** Mockingbird. **Tree:** Tulip poplar. **Songs:** "My Homeland, Tennessee"; "When It's Iris Time in Tennessee"; "My Tennessee"; "Tennessee Waltz"; "Rocky Top"; "Smoky Mountain Rain." **Entered union:** June 1, 1796; rank: 16th. **State fair** at Nashville, early Sept.; at Jackson, mid-Sept.

History. Inhabited for at least 20,000 years, the region was home to Creek and Yuchi peoples when the first Europeans arrived; the Cherokee moved into the region in the early 18th cent. Spanish explorers visited the area, 1540. English traders crossed the Great Smoky Mtns. from the east, while France's Marquette and Jolliet sailed down the Mississippi on the west, 1673. The first permanent settlement was of Virginians on the Watauga River, 1769. After the American Revolution, in which Tennesseans fought in eastern campaigns, the region became a territory, 1790, and a state, 1796. Slavery was widespread in western Tennessee, where cotton was the main crop, but much less common in the east. The state seceded, 1861, and saw many Civil War engagements; some 187,000 Tennesseans fought for the Confederacy and 51,000 for the Union. Tennessee was readmitted in 1866, the only former Confederate state not to have a postwar military government. The famous Scopes trial, 1925, questioned the teaching of evolution in public schools. In the 1930s, the Tennessee Valley Authority, a federal program, brought electric power to rural areas. Nashville became the capital of country music, while Memphis fostered the blues and, with Elvis Presley in the 1950s, rock 'n' roll. Martin Luther King Jr. was assassinated in Memphis, 1968. Since the 1970s, auto plants have become major employers, as has Federal Express. Al Gore Jr., U.S. vice pres. (1993-2001), lost his 2000 presidential bid partly because he failed to carry his home state of Tennessee. Record amounts of rainfall flooded parts of Tennessee, including Nashville, in May 2010.

Tourist attractions. Reelfoot Lake; Lookout Mountain, Tennessee Aquarium, Chattanooga; Fall Creek Falls; Great Smoky Mts. Natl. Park; Lost Sea, Sweetwater; Cherokee Natl. Forest; Cumberland Gap Natl. Park; Andrew Jackson's home, the Hermitage, near Nashville; homes of Pres. Polk and Andrew Johnson; American Museum of Science and Energy, Oak Ridge; Parthenon, Grand Old Opry, Opryland USA, Nashville; Dollywood theme park, Pigeon Forge; Graceland, home of Elvis Presley, Memphis; Alex Haley Home and Museum, Henning; Casey Jones Village, Jackson.

Famous Tennesseans. Roy Acuff, Davy Crockett, David Farragut, Ernie Ford, Aretha Franklin, Morgan Freeman, Bill Frist, Al Gore Jr., Alex Haley, William C. Handy, Sam Houston, Cordell Hull, Andrew Jackson, Andrew Johnson, Casey Jones, Estes Kefauver, Grace Moore, Dolly Parton, Minnie Pearl, James Polk, Elvis Presley, Dinah Shore, Bessie Smith, Fred Thompson, Hank Williams Jr., Alvin York.

Tourist information. Dept. of Tourist Development, Wm. Snodgrass/Tennessee Tower, 312 Rosa L. Parks Ave., 25th Fl., Nashville, TN 37243; 1-800-462-8366; www.tnvacation.com

Website. www.tn.gov

Texas (TX)
Lone Star State

People. Population (2010): 25,145,561; rank: 2; net change (2000-10): 20.6%. **Pop. density:** 96.3 per sq mi. **Racial distribution** (2010): 70.4% white; 11.8% black; 3.8% Asian; 0.7% Native Amer./AK; 0.1% Hawaiian/Pacific Islander; 2 or more races, 2.7%. **Hispanic pop.** (any race, 2010): 37.6%.

Geography. Total area: 268,596 sq mi; rank: 2. **Land area:** 261,232 sq mi; rank: 2. **Acres forested:** 63.3 mil. **Location:** southwestern state, bounded on the SE by the Gulf of Mexico; on the SW by Mexico, separated by the Rio Grande; surrounding states are Louisiana, Arkansas, Oklahoma, New Mexico. **Climate:** extremely varied; driest region is the Trans-Pecos; wettest is the NE. **Topography:** Gulf Coast Plain in the S and SE; North Central Plains slope upward with some hills; the Great Plains extend over the Panhandle, are broken by low mountains; the Trans-Pecos is the southern extension of the Rockies. **Capital:** Austin. **Chief airports:** Austin, Dallas, El Paso, Ft. Worth, Houston (2), Lubbock, San Antonio.

Economy. Chief industries: manufacturing, trade, oil and gas extraction, services. **Chief manuf. goods:** petroleum, chemicals & resins, computers & electronics, animal slaughtering & processing, plastics, aerospace. **Chief crops:** cotton, greenhouse & nursery, corn, wheat, sorghum, hay, peanuts, onions, rice, pecans, grapefruit. **Livestock** (Dec. 2010): 24.79 mil chickens (excl. broilers), 653.50 mil broilers; (Jan. 2011): 13.30 mil cattle/calves, 880,000 sheep/lambs; (June 2011): 70,000 hogs/pigs. **Broadband internet:** 79.3%. **Nonfuel minerals** (2010 prelim.): $2.5 bil; stone (crushed), cement (portland), sand and gravel (construction), salt, lime. **Commercial fishing** (2009): $150.2 mil. **Chief ports:** Houston, Galveston, Brownsville, Beaumont, Port Arthur, Corpus Christi, Texas City, Freeport. **Gross state product** (2010): $1,207.5 bil. **Sales tax** (2011): 6.25%. **Employment distrib.** (May 2011): 17.8% govt.; 19.6% trade/trans./util.; 7.7% mfg.; 13.5% ed./health; 12.5% prof./bus. serv.; 9.9% leisure/hosp.; 5.9% finance; 7.6% constr./mining/log.; 1.8% info.; 3.5% other serv. **Unemployment** (2010): 8.2%. **Per cap. pers. income** (2010 prelim.): $39,493. **New private housing** (2010): 88,461 units/$13.7 bil. **Commercial banks** (2010): 618; deposits: $447.5 bil. **Savings institutions** (2010): 60; deposits: $51.6 bil. **Lottery** (2010): total sales: $3.75 bil; profit: $1.1 bil.

Federal govt. Fed. civ. employees (Mar. 2011): 144,519; **avg. salary:** $68,068. **Notable fed. facilities:** *Ft. Hood; *Ft. Bliss; *Sheppard, *Dyess, Goodfellow AF Bases; Joint Base San Antonio; NASA Johnson Space Ctr.; Naval Air Training School, Corpus Christi NAS; Red River Army Depot; Ft. Worth Western Currency Facility.

Energy. Electricity production (2010 kWh by source): coal: 63.2 bil; gas: 30.1 bil; petroleum: 38 mil; hydroelectric: 994 mil; other: 66 mil.

State data. Motto: Friendship. **Flower:** Bluebonnet. **Bird:** Mockingbird. **Tree:** Pecan. **Song:** "Texas, Our Texas." **Entered union:** Dec. 29, 1845; rank: 28th. **State fair** at Dallas, late Sept.-mid-Oct.; at Beaumont, late Mar.-early Apr.; at Belton, late Aug.-early Sept.; at Denton, mid-Aug.; at Tyler, late Sept.

History. Humans have lived in the region for at least 12,000 years. Coahuiltecan, Karankawa, Caddo, Jumano, and Tonkawa peoples were in the area when the first Europeans came; later, Apache, Comanche, Cherokee, and Wichita arrived. Early Spanish explorers included Alonso de Pineda, who sailed along the Texas coast, 1519; Cabeza de Vaca, shipwrecked near Galveston along with the former slave Estevanico, 1528; and Coronado, who crossed the Panhandle, 1541. Spaniards made the first settlement at Ysleta, near El Paso, 1682. Americans moved into the land early in the 19th cent. Mexico, of which Texas was a part, won independence from Spain, 1821. Texans rebelled, 1836, losing to Santa Anna at the

Alamo, but winning decisively under Sam Houston at San Jacinto. With Houston as president, 1836-38 and 1841-44, the Republic of Texas functioned as a nation until admitted to the Union. With a slave population of 30%, Texas seceded, 1861; mostly unscathed by the Civil War, it was readmitted, 1870. In 1900 a powerful hurricane lashed Galveston, killing at least 8,000. Cotton and cattle were dominant until 1901, when the Spindletop gusher, near Beaumont, launched the petroleum and petrochemical industries. By 2000 the state population ranked 2nd in the U.S. With wealth and population came political power, notably in the presidencies of Lyndon B. Johnson (1963-69), George H. W. Bush (1989-93), and George W. Bush (2001-09).

Tourist attractions. Padre Island Natl. Seashore; Big Bend, Guadalupe Mts. natl. parks; Ft. Davis; Six Flags Over Texas, Arlington SeaWorld, Six Flags Fiesta Texas, The Alamo, San Antonio Missions Natl. Hist. Park, all San Antonio; Cowgirl Hall of Fame, Kimball Art Museum, Ft. Worth; Lyndon B. Johnson Natl. Historical Park, Johnson City; Lyndon B. Johnson Library and Museum, Austin; Texas State Aquarium, Corpus Christi; George Bush Library, College Station.

Famous Texans. Lance Armstrong, Stephen F. Austin, Lloyd Bentsen, James Bowie, Carol Burnett, George H. W. Bush, George W. Bush, Joan Crawford, J. Frank Dobie, Dwight D. Eisenhower, Morgan Fairchild, Farrah Fawcett, Sam Houston, Howard Hughes, Kay Bailey Hutchison, Molly Ivins, Lyndon B. Johnson, Tommy Lee Jones, Janis Joplin, Barbara Jordan, Mary Martin, Chester Nimitz, Sandra Day O'Connor, H. Ross Perot, Katherine Anne Porter, Dan Rather, Sam Rayburn, Ann Richards, Sissy Spacek, Kenneth Starr, George Strait.

Tourist information. Texas Tourism, P.O. Box 141009, Austin, TX 78714; (512) 486-5876; 1-800-452-9292; www.traveltex.com

Website. www.texas.gov

Utah (UT)
Beehive State

People. Population (2010): 2,763,885; rank: 34; net change (2000-10): 23.8%. **Pop. density:** 33.6 per sq mi. **Racial distribution** (2010): 86.1% white; 1.1% black; 2.0% Asian; 1.2% Native Amer./AK; 0.9% Hawaiian/Pacific Islander; 2 or more races, 2.7%. **Hispanic pop.** (any race, 2010): 13.0%.

Geography. Total area: 84,897 sq mi; rank: 13. **Land area:** 82,170 sq mi; rank: 12. **Acres forested:** 18.2 mil. **Location:** Middle Rocky Mountain state; its southeastern corner touches Colorado, New Mexico, and Arizona, and is the only spot in the U.S. where 4 states join. **Climate:** arid; ranging from warm desert in SW to alpine in NE. **Topography:** high Colorado plateau is cut by brilliantly colored canyons of the SE; broad, flat, desert-like Great Basin of the W; the Great Salt Lake and Bonneville Salt Flats to the NW; Middle Rockies in the NE run E-W; valleys and plateaus of the Wasatch Front. **Capital:** Salt Lake City. **Chief airport:** Salt Lake City.

Economy. Chief industries: services, trade, manufacturing, government, transportation, utilities. **Chief manuf. goods:** food, petroleum, nonferrous metal, motor vehicles & parts, aerospace, sporting goods, fabricated metal, computers & electronics. **Chief crops:** hay, greenhouse & nursery, wheat, cherries, onions, apples, barley, peaches, corn. **Livestock** (Dec. 2010): 4.26 mil chickens (excl. broilers); (Jan. 2011): 800,000 cattle/calves, 280,000 sheep/lambs; (June 2011): 75,000 hogs/pigs. **Broadband internet:** 78.3%. **Nonfuel minerals** (2010 prelim.): $4.4 bil; copper, molybdenum concentrates, gold, magnesium metal, potash. **Gross state product** (2010): $114.5 bil. **Sales tax** (2011): 5.95%. **Employment distrib.** (May 2011): 18.3% govt.; 19.4% trade/trans./util.; 9.5% mfg.; 12.9% ed./health; 13.4% prof./bus. serv.; 9.3% leisure/hosp.; 5.5% finance; 6.3% constr./mining/log.; 2.5% info.; 2.9% other serv. **Unemployment** (2010): 7.7%. **Per cap. pers. income** (2010 prelim.): $32,595. **New private housing** (2010): 9,171 units/$1.7 bil. **Commercial banks** (2010): 67; deposits: $244.8 bil. **Savings institutions** (2010): 7; deposits: $27.1 bil.

Federal govt. Fed. civ. employees (Mar. 2011): 30,705; avg. salary: $62,128. **Notable fed. facilities:** *Hill AFB; *Tooele Army Depot; Army Dugway Proving Ground.

Energy. Electricity production (2010 kWh by source): coal: 32.8 bil; gas: 5.6 bil; petroleum: 41 mil; hydroelectric: 784 mil; other: 274 mil.

State data. Motto: Industry. **Flower:** Sego lily. **Bird:** (California) sea gull. **Tree:** Blue spruce. **Song:** "Utah, This Is the Place." **Entered union:** Jan. 4, 1896; rank: 45th. **State fair** at Salt Lake City, early Sept.

History. Ute, Gosiute, Southern Paiute, and Navajo peoples lived in the region at the time of European contact. Spanish Franciscans visited the area, 1776; American fur traders followed. Permanent settlement began with the arrival of the Latter-day Saints, or Mormons, 1847; they made the arid land bloom and created a prosperous economy. Organized in 1849, the State of Deseret asked admission to the Union; instead, Congress established Utah Territory, 1850, and Brigham Young was appointed governor. The Union Pacific and Central Pacific railroads met near Promontory Point, May 10, 1869, creating the first transcontinental railroad. Statehood was not achieved until 1896, after a long controversy over the Mormon practices of economic isolationism and polygamy, which the church renounced in 1890. The 20th cent. brought expansion in mining, defense-related industries, and, more recently, information technologies. More than two-thirds of Utahans are Mormons; the church has its world headquarters in Salt Lake City. Utah experienced 61% population growth, 1990-2009, and has the highest birthrate and lowest median age of any state in the U.S.

Tourist attractions. Temple Square, Mormon Church headquarters, in Salt Lake City; Great Salt Lake; Zion, Canyonlands, Bryce Canyon, Arches, and Capitol Reef natl. parks; Dinosaur, Rainbow Bridge, Timpanogos Cave, and Natural Bridges natl. monuments; Lake Powell; Flaming Gorge Natl. Recreation Area.

Famous Utahans. Maude Adams, Ezra Taft Benson, John Moses Browning, Mariner Eccles, Philo Farnsworth, James Fletcher, David M. Kennedy, J. Willard Marriott, Merlin Olsen, Osmond family, Ivy Baker Priest, George Romney, Roseanne, Wallace Stegner, Brigham Young, Loretta Young.

Tourist information. Utah Office of Tourism, Council Hall/Capitol Hill, 300 N. State St., Salt Lake City, UT 84114; 1-800-200-1160; www.utah.com

Website. www.utah.gov

Vermont (VT)
Green Mountain State

People. Population (2010): 625,741; rank: 49; net change (2000-10): 2.8%. **Pop. density:** 67.9 per sq mi. **Racial distribution** (2010): 95.3% white; 1.0% black; 1.3% Asian; 0.4% Native Amer./AK; <0.05% Hawaiian/Pacific Islander; 2 or more races, 1.7%. **Hispanic pop.** (any race, 2010): 1.5%.

Geography. Total area: 9,616 sq mi; rank: 45. **Land area:** 9,217 sq mi; rank: 43. **Acres forested:** 4.6 mil. **Location:** northern New England state. **Climate:** temperate, with considerable temperature extremes; heavy snowfall in mountains. **Topography:** Green Mts. N-S slope 20-36 mi wide; avg. altitude 1,000 ft. **Capital:** Montpelier. **Chief airport:** Burlington.

Economy. Chief industries: manufacturing, tourism, agriculture, trade, finance, insurance, real estate, government. **Chief manuf. goods:** dairy, plastics, printing, wood furniture, sporting goods, metalworking machinery. **Chief crops:** greenhouse & nursery, hay, maple syrup, apples, berries, sweet corn. **Livestock** (Dec. 2010): 229,000 chickens (excl. broilers); (Jan. 2011): 270,000 cattle/calves. **Broadband internet:** 74.7%. **Nonfuel minerals** (2010 prelim.): $119 mil; stone (crushed), sand and gravel (construction), stone (dimension), talc (crude), gemstones (natural). **Gross state product** (2010): $25.6 bil. **Sales tax** (2011): 6.0%. **Employment distrib.** (May 2011): 18.9% govt.; 18.8% trade/trans./util.; 10.5% mfg.; 20.0% ed./health; 8.3% prof./bus. serv.; 9.6% leisure/hosp.; 4.2% finance; 5.0% constr./mining/log.; 1.7% info.; 3.4% other serv. **Unemployment** (2010): 6.2%. **Per cap. pers. income** (2010 prelim.): $40,283. **New private housing** (2010): 1,319 units/$227.6 mil. **Commercial banks** (2010): 13; deposits: $6.1 bil. **Savings institutions** (2010): 10; deposits: $4.5 bil. **Lottery** (2010): total sales: $97.5 mil; profit: $21.6 mil.

Federal govt. Fed. civ. employees (Mar. 2011): 4,582; avg. salary: $67,698. **Notable fed. facilities:** Law Enforcement Support Ctr.

Energy. Electricity production (2010 kWh by source): gas: 4 mil; hydroelectric: 410 mil; other: 282 mil.

State data. Motto: Freedom and unity. **Flower:** Red clover. **Bird:** Hermit thrush. **Tree:** Sugar maple. **Song:** "These

Green Mountains." **Entered union:** Mar. 4, 1791; rank: 14th. **State fair** at Rutland, early Sept.

History. Inhabited for 10,000 years or more, the region attracted Abenaki and Mahican peoples before Europeans arrived. Champlain explored the lake that now bears his name, 1609. The first European settlement was on Isle la Motte, in Lake Champlain, 1666. During the American Revolution, Ethan Allen and the Green Mountain Boys captured Ft. Ticonderoga (NY), 1775. Under a constitution that provided for public schools and abolished slavery, settlers declared a republic, 1777. Vermont joined the Union, 1791. Agriculture dominated in the 19th cent. Still mainly rural, the state expanded tourism and manufacturing after World War II, and IBM became the largest private employer. In 2000, with Howard Dean as governor (1991-2003), Vermont became the first state in the U.S. to legalize same-sex civil unions.

Tourist attractions. Shelburne Museum; Rock of Ages Quarry, Graniteville; Vermont Marble Museum, Proctor; Bennington Battle Monument; Pres. Calvin Coolidge homestead, Plymouth; Maple Grove Maple Museum, St. Johnsbury; Ben & Jerry's Factory, N. Waterbury.

Famous Vermonters. Ethan Allen, Chester A. Arthur, Calvin Coolidge, Howard Dean, John Deere, George Dewey, John Dewey, Stephen A. Douglas, Dorothy Canfield Fisher, James Fisk, James Jeffords, Rudy Vallee.

Tourist information. Vermont Dept. of Tourism and Marketing, Natl. Life Building, 6th Fl., Montpelier, VT 05620; (802) 828-3237; 1-800-VERMONT; www.vermontvacation.com
Website. www.vermont.gov

Virginia (VA)
Old Dominion

People. Population (2010): 8,001,024; rank: 12; net change (2000-10): 13.0%. **Pop. density:** 202.6 per sq mi. **Racial distribution** (2010): 68.6% white; 19.4% black; 5.5% Asian; 0.4% Native Amer./AK; 0.1% Hawaiian/Pacific Islander; 2 or more races, 2.9%. **Hispanic pop.** (any race, 2010): 7.9%.

Geography. Total area: 42,775 sq mi; rank: 35. **Land area:** 39,490 sq mi; rank: 36. **Acres forested:** 15.8 mil. **Location:** South Atlantic state bounded by the Atlantic Ocean on the E and surrounded by North Carolina, Tennessee, Kentucky, West Virginia, and Maryland. **Climate:** mild and equable. **Topography:** mountain and valley region in the W, including the Blue Ridge Mts.; rolling Piedmont Plateau; tidewater, or coastal plain, including the eastern shore. **Capital:** Richmond. **Chief airports:** Arlington, Dulles, Highland Springs, Newport News, Norfolk.

Economy. Chief industries: services, trade, government, manufacturing, tourism, agriculture. **Chief manuf. goods:** beverages & tobacco, transportation equip., animal slaughtering & processing, plastics, textiles, paper & paper product, printing, pharmaceuticals, furniture, chemicals. **Chief crops:** greenhouse & nursery, soybeans, tomatoes, corn, tobacco, hay, cotton, apples, wheat, peanuts, potatoes. **Livestock** (Dec. 2010): 4.44 mil chickens (excl. broilers), 250.40 mil broilers; (Jan. 2011): 1.54 mil. cattle/calves, 90,000 sheep/lambs. **Broadband internet:** 70.3%. **Nonfuel minerals** (2010 prelim.): $952 mil; stone (crushed); cement (portland), sand and gravel (construction), lime, zirconium concentrates. **Commercial fishing** (2009): $152.7 mil. **Chief ports:** Norfolk Harbor, Newport News, Richmond, Hopewell. **Gross state product** (2010): $423.9 bil. **Sales tax** (2011): 5.0%. **Employment distrib.** (May 2011): 19.3% govt.; 17.1% trade/trans./util.; 6.3% mfg.; 12.6% ed./health; 18.1% prof./bus. serv.; 9.3% leisure/hosp.; 4.8% finance; 5.3% constr./mining/log.; 2.0% info.; 5.1% other serv. **Unemployment** (2010): 6.9%. **Per cap. pers. income** (2010 prelim.): $44,762. **New private housing** (2010): 20,992 units/$3.2 bil. **Commercial banks** (2010): 140; deposits: $183.7 bil. **Savings institutions** (2010): 13; deposits: $30.6 bil. **Lottery** (2010): total sales: $1.44 bil; profit: $430 mil.

Federal govt. Fed. civ. employees (Mar. 2011): 147,396; **avg. salary:** $85,823. **Notable fed. facilities:** Pentagon; *Norfolk Naval Sta., Shipyard, and other Hampton Roads; *Ft. Belvoir; Joint Base Langley-Eustis; NASA Langley Res. Ctr.; CIA George Bush Ctr. for Intelligence, Langley; Quantico USMC Base, FBI Academy; *Dahlgren Nav. Surface Warfare Ctr. & Lab; USDA Food and Nutrition Serv.; U.S. Geological Survey Natl. Ctr.

Energy. Electricity production (2010 kWh by source): coal: 21.4 bil; gas: 9.6 bil; nuclear: 26.6 bil; petroleum: 1 bil; hydroelectric: –33 mil; other: 423 mil.

State data. Motto: Sic Semper Tyrannis (Thus always to tyrants). **Flower:** Dogwood. **Bird:** Cardinal. **Tree:** Dogwood. **Song emeritus:** "Carry Me Back to Old Virginia." **Tenth** of the original 13 states to ratify the Constitution, June 25, 1788. **State fair** at Doswell, late Sept.-early Oct.

History. Cherokee and Susquehanna peoples and the Algonquians of the Powhatan Confederacy were in the region when Europeans arrived. English settlers founded Jamestown, 1607. Virginians were indispensable to the founding of the American republic, and 4 of the first 5 U.S. presidents—Washington, Jefferson, Madison, and Monroe—came from there. The conclusive battle of the American Revolution took place at Yorktown, 1781. The state profited from tobacco, cotton, and the slave trade; in 1860, slaves made up nearly one-third of the population. Virginia seceded from the Union, 1861, and Richmond became the capital of the Confederacy, but Western counties, loyal to the Union, split off to become West Virginia, 1863. The war ended with Robert E. Lee's surrender to Ulysses S. Grant at Appomattox, 1865, and Virginia was readmitted to the Union, 1870. In the 20th cent., expansion of federal civilian jobs and military facilities transformed the economy. State officials pledged "massive resistance" to racial integration in the mid-1950s, but eventually accommodated. In 1989, L. Douglas Wilder became the first elected black governor in U.S. history. On Sept. 11, 2001, terrorist hijackers crashed a jet into U.S. defense headquarters at the Pentagon, in Arlington.

Tourist attractions. Colonial Williamsburg; Busch Gardens Williamsburg; Wolf Trap Farm, near Vienna; Arlington Natl. Cemetery; Mt. Vernon, home of George Washington; Jamestown Settlement; Yorktown; Jefferson's Monticello, Charlottesville; Robert E. Lee's birthplace, Stratford Hall, and grave, Lexington; Appomattox; Shenandoah Natl. Park; Blue Ridge Parkway; Virginia Beach; Kings Dominion, near Richmond.

Famous Virginians. Richard E. Byrd, James B. Cabell, Henry Clay, Katie Couric, Jubal Early, Jerry Falwell, William Henry Harrison, Patrick Henry, A. P. Hill, Thomas Jefferson, Joseph E. Johnston, Robert E. Lee, Meriwether Lewis and William Clark, James Madison, John Marshall, George Mason, James Monroe, George Pickett, Pocahontas, Edgar Allan Poe, John Randolph, Walter Reed, Rev. Pat Robertson, John Smith, J.E.B. Stuart, William Styron, Zachary Taylor, John Tyler, Maggie Walker, Booker T. Washington, George Washington, L. Douglas Wilder, Woodrow Wilson.

Tourist Information. Virginia Tourism Corp., 901 E. Byrd St., Richmond, VA 23219; 1-800-VISITVA; www.virginia.org
Website. www.virginia.gov

Washington (WA)
Evergreen State

People. Population (2010): 6,724,540; rank: 13; net change (2000-10): 14.1%. **Pop. density:** 101.2 per sq mi. **Racial distribution** (2010): 77.3% white; 3.6% black; 7.2% Asian; 1.5% Native Amer./AK; 0.6% Hawaiian/Pacific Islander; 2 or more races, 4.7%. **Hispanic pop.** (any race, 2010): 11.2%.

Geography. Total area: 71,298 sq mi; rank: 18. **Land area:** 66,456 sq mi; rank: 20. **Acres forested:** 22.3 mil. **Location:** Pacific state bordered by Canada on the N, Idaho on the E, Oregon on the S, and the Pacific Ocean on the W. **Climate:** mild, dominated by the Pacific Ocean and protected by the Cascades. **Topography:** Olympic Mts. on NW peninsula; open land along coast to Columbia R.; flat terrain of Puget Sound Lowland; Cascade Mts. region's high peaks to the E; Columbia Basin in central portion; highlands to the NE; mountains to the SE. **Capital:** Olympia. **Chief airports:** Seattle, Spokane.

Economy. Chief industries: advanced technology, aerospace, biotechnology, intl. trade, forestry, tourism, recycling, agriculture & food processing. **Chief manuf. goods:** aerospace, petroleum, food, paper, milled lumber, plastics, structural metals, computers & electronics. **Chief crops:** apples, potatoes, wheat, hay, cherries, greenhouse & nursery, forest products, pears, grapes, onions, hops, sweet corn, Christmas trees, mint, raspberries. **Livestock** (Dec. 2010): 7.66 mil chickens (excl. broilers); (Jan. 2011): 1.09 mil cattle/calves, 56,000 sheep/lambs. **Broadband internet:** 79.3%. **Nonfuel minerals** (2010 prelim.): $665 mil; gold, sand and gravel (construction), stone (crushed), cement (portland), lime. **Commercial fishing** (2009): $227.8 mil. **Chief ports:** Seattle, Tacoma, Vancouver, Kelso-Longview, Anacortes. **Gross state product** (2010): $340.5 bil. **Sales tax** (2011): 6.5%. **Employment distrib.** (May 2011): 19.6% govt.; 18.3% trade/trans./util.; 9.2% mfg.; 13.7% ed./health; 12.3% prof./bus. serv.; 9.7% leisure/hosp.; 4.9% finance; 5.2% constr./mining/log.; 3.7% info.; 3.6% other serv. **Unemployment** (2010): 9.6%. **Per cap. pers. income** (2010 prelim.): $43,564. **New private housing** (2010): 20,691 units/$3.9 bil. **Commercial banks** (2010): 92; deposits: $96.3 bil. **Savings institutions** (2010): 19; deposits: $12.9 bil. **Lottery** (2010): total sales: $491.0 mil; profit: $121.4 mil.

Federal govt. Fed. civ. employees (Mar. 2011): 57,526; avg. salary: $71,135. **Notable fed. facilities:** Bonneville Power Admin.; Lewis-McChord Joint Base; Fairchild AFB; DOE Hanford Nuclear Site; Naval Base Kitsap (Bremerton and Bangor); Whidbey Island NAS; Pacific Northwest Natl. Lab.

Energy. Electricity production (2010 kWh by source): gas: 8 bil; nuclear: 9.2 bil; hydroelectric: 66 bil; other: 2.7 bil.

State data. Motto: Alki (By and by). **Flower:** Western rhododendron. **Bird:** Willow goldfinch. **Tree:** Western hemlock. **Song:** "Washington, My Home." **Entered union:** Nov. 11, 1889; rank: 42nd. **State fairs:** no official state fair; county and area fairs, Apr.-Sept.

History. People of the Clovis culture lived in the region 11,000 years ago. At the time of European contact, Native Americans in the area included Nez Percé, Spokane, Yakima, Cayuse, Okanogan, Walla Walla, and Colville peoples in the interior, and Nooksak, Chinook, Nisqually, Clallam, Makah, Quinault, and Puyallup peoples along the coast. Spain's Bruno Hezeta sailed the coast, 1775. In 1792, British naval officer George Vancouver mapped the Puget Sound area, and American Capt. Robert Gray sailed up the Columbia River. Fur traders and missionaries arrived in the first half of the 19th cent. Final agreement on the border of Washington and Canada was made with Britain, 1846. Completion in 1883 of a transcontinental rail link between Puget Sound and the eastern U.S. aided immigration, and Washington became a state in 1889. In the 20th cent., cheap hydroelectric power spurred growth in the aluminum and aircraft industries. Founded in 1975, Microsoft became a computer software giant. Mt. St. Helens erupted, 1980. With grunge music, Starbucks coffee, and Amazon.com, Seattle became a national trendsetter in the 1990s. Violent street protests disrupted a World Trade Organization meeting there in 1999. Gary Locke, in office 1997-2005, was the first U.S. governor of Chinese ancestry.

Tourist attractions. Seattle Center, Space Needle, waterfront, Museum of Flight, Underground Tour, Seattle; Mt. Rainier, Olympic, and North Cascades natl. parks; Mt. St. Helens; Puget Sound; San Juan Islands; Grand Coulee Dam; Columbia R. Gorge Natl. Scenic Area; Spokane's Riverfront Park.

Famous Washingtonians. Raymond Carver, Kurt Cobain, Bing Crosby, William O. Douglas, Bill Gates, Jimi Hendrix, Henry M. Jackson, Gary Larson, Mary McCarthy, Robert Motherwell, Edward R. Murrow, Theodore Roethke, Ann Rule, Hilary Swank, Julia Sweeney, Adam West, Marcus Whitman, Minoru Yamasaki.

Tourist information. WA State Tourism Office, 128 10th Ave. SW, P.O. Box 42525, Olympia, WA 98504; 1-800-544-1800; www.experiencewa.com
Website. access.wa.gov

West Virginia (WV)
Mountain State

People. Population (2010): 1,852,994; rank: 37; net change (2000-10): 2.5%. **Pop. density:** 77.1 per sq mi. **Racial distribution** (2010): 93.9% white; 3.4% black; 0.7% Asian; 0.2% Native Amer./AK; <0.05% Hawaiian/Pacific Islander; 2 or more races, 1.5%. **Hispanic pop.** (any race, 2010): 1.2%.

Geography. Total area: 24,230 sq mi; rank: 41. **Land area:** 24,038 sq mi; rank: 41. **Acres forested:** 12.0 mil. **Location:** South Atlantic state bounded on the N by Ohio, Pennsylvania, Maryland; on the S and W by Virginia, Kentucky, Ohio; on the E by Maryland and Virginia. **Climate:** humid continental climate except for marine modification in the lower panhandle. **Topography:** ranging from hilly to mountainous; Allegheny Plateau in the W, covers two-thirds of the state; mountains here are the highest in the state, over 4,000 ft. **Capital:** Charleston.

Economy. Chief industries: manufacturing, services, mining, tourism. **Chief manuf. goods:** chemicals, aluminum, motor vehicle parts, lumber & plywood, primary & fabricated metals. **Chief crops:** hay, apples, corn, peaches, soybeans, tobacco, wheat. **Livestock** (Dec. 2010): 1.95 mil chickens (excl. broilers), 87.6 mil broilers; (Jan. 2011): 370,000 cattle/calves, 34,000 sheep/lambs. **Broadband internet:** 81.1%. **Nonfuel minerals** (2010 prelim.): $230 mil; stone (crushed), cement (portland), lime, sand and gravel (industrial), cement (masonry). **Chief port:** Huntington. **Gross state product** (2010): $64.6 bil. **Sales tax** (2011): 6.0%. **Employment distrib.** (May 2011): 20.3% govt.; 18.0% trade/trans./util.; 6.5% mfg.; 16.4% ed./health; 8.2% prof./bus. serv.; 9.7% leisure/hosp.; 3.7% finance; 8.5% constr./mining/log.; 1.4% info.; 7.3% other serv. **Unemployment** (2010): 9.1%. **Per cap. pers. income** (2010 prelim.): $32,641. **New private housing** (2010): 2,395 units/$345.6 mil. **Commercial banks** (2010): 79; deposits: $28.0 bil. **Savings institutions** (2010): 6; deposits: $819 mil. **Lottery** (2010): total sales: $1.36 bil; profit: $568.9 mil.

Federal govt. Fed. civ. employees (Mar. 2011): 16,224; avg. salary: $68,359. **Notable fed. facilities:** Natl. Radio Astronomy Observatory, Green Bank; Bureau of Public Debt Bldg.; Alderson Fed. Prison for Women; FBI Criminal Justice Information Services.

Energy. Electricity production (2010 kWh by source): coal: 56.2 bil; gas: 48 mil; petroleum: 149 mil; hydroelectric: 469 mil.

State data. Motto: Montani Semper Liberi (Mountaineers are always free). **Flower:** Big rhododendron. **Bird:** Cardinal. **Tree:** Sugar maple. **Songs:** "The West Virginia Hills"; "This Is My West Virginia"; "West Virginia, My Home, Sweet Home." **Entered union:** June 20, 1863; rank: 35th. **State fair** at Lewisburg, mid-Aug.

History. Sparsely inhabited at the time of European contact, the area was primarily Native American hunting grounds. British explorers Thomas Batts and Robert Fallam reached the New River, 1671. Coal, discovered in 1742, was mined extensively by the mid-19th cent. White settlement led to conflicts with Native Americans, including a major battle in which settlers defeated an Indian confederacy at Point Pleasant, 1774. The region joined the Union as part of Virginia, 1788. Longstanding tensions between the E and W parts of the state came to a head in 1861, when Virginia seceded. Delegates of the W counties, meeting at Wheeling, repudiated the act and created a new state, Kanawha, later renamed West Virginia, which was admitted to the Union in 1863. Poverty has been a problem for much of the state's subsequent history. West Virginia continued to rank low in per capita personal income, despite billions of dollars in federal contracts brought to the state by 9-term U.S. Sen. Robert Byrd, who passed away in 2010. Coal mining, though dangerous, continues to be a major industry; nearly 30 miners were killed in a mine explosion in 2010.

Tourist attractions. Harpers Ferry Natl. Historic Park; Clay Center and Avampato Discovery Museum, Charleston; White Sulphur Springs (The Greenbrier) and Berkeley Springs mineral water spas; New River Gorge Natl. River; Beckley Exhibition Coal Mine; Monongahela Natl. Forest; Fenton Glass, Williamstown; Blenko Glass, Milton; Sternwheel Regatta, Charleston; Mountain State Forest Festival, Elkins; skiing at Canaan Valley, Snowshoe, Timberline, Winterplace; Mountain State Art & Craft Festival, Ripley; Oglebay Resort, Wheeling; white-water rafting on New and Gauley Rivers.

Famous West Virginians. Newton D. Baker, Pearl Buck, Robert Byrd, John W. Davis, Thomas "Stonewall" Jackson, Don Knotts, Dwight Whitney Morrow, Michael Owens, Mary Lou Retton, Walter Reuther, Cyrus Vance, Jerry West, Charles "Chuck" Yeager.

Tourist information. West Virginia Division of Tourism, Capitol Complex, Bldg. 6, Rm. 525, Charleston, WV 25305; 1-800-CALLWVA; www.wvtourism.com

Website. www.wv.gov

Wisconsin (WI)
Badger State

People. Population (2010): 5,686,986; rank: 20; net change (2000-10): 6.0%. **Pop. density:** 105 per sq mi. **Racial distribution** (2010): 86.2% white; 6.3% black; 2.3% Asian; 1.0% Native Amer./AK; <0.05% Hawaiian/Pacific Islander; 2 or more races, 1.8%. **Hispanic pop.** (any race, 2010): 5.9%.

Geography. Total area: 65,496 sq mi; rank: 23. **Land area:** 54,158 sq mi; rank: 25. **Acres forested:** 16.7 mil. **Location:** E North Central state, bounded on the N by Lake Superior and Upper Michigan; on the E by Lake Michigan; on the S by Illinois; on the W by the St. Croix and Mississippi Rivers. **Climate:** long, cold winters and short, warm summers tempered by the Great Lakes. **Topography:** narrow Lake Superior Lowland plain met by Northern Highland, which slopes gently to the sandy crescent Central Plain; Western Upland in the SW; 3 broad parallel limestone ridges running N-S are separated by wide and shallow lowlands in the SE. **Capital:** Madison. **Chief airports:** Madison, Milwaukee.

Economy. Chief industries: services, manufacturing, trade, government, agriculture, tourism. **Chief manuf. goods:** transportation, dairy, animal slaughtering & processing, paper, printing, plastics, computers & electronics. **Chief crops:** corn, greenhouse & nursery, soybeans, potatoes, cranberries, hay, wheat, snap beans, apples, peas. **Livestock** (Dec. 2010): 6.18 mil chickens (excl. broilers), 46.9 mil broilers; (Jan. 2011): 3.45 mil cattle/calves, 90,000 sheep/lambs. **Broadband internet:** 78.5%. **Nonfuel minerals** (2010 prelim.): $651 mil; sand and gravel (construction), stone (crushed), sand and gravel (industrial), lime, stone (dimension). **Commercial fishing** (2009): $3.3 mil. **Chief ports:** Superior, Milwaukee, Green Bay. **Gross state product** (2010): $248.3 bil. **Sales tax** (2011): 5.0%. **Employment distrib.** (May 2011): 15.6% govt.; 18.4% trade/trans./util.; 15.9% mfg.; 15.4% ed./health; 9.8% prof./bus. serv.; 9.1% leisure/hosp.; 5.6% finance; 3.6% constr./mining/log.; 1.7% info.; 5.2% other serv. **Unemployment** (2010): 8.3%. **Per cap. pers. income** (2010 prelim.): $38,432. **New private housing** (2010): 10,864 units/$1.8 bil. **Commercial banks** (2010): 262; deposits: $111.6 bil. **Savings institutions** (2010): 37; deposits: $15.1 bil. **Lottery** (2010): total sales: $481.6 mil; profit: $143.1 mil.

Federal govt. Fed. civ. employees (Mar. 2011): 15,887; **avg. salary:** $65,322. **Notable fed. facilities:** *Ft. McCoy; USDA Forest Products Lab.

Energy. Electricity production (2010 kWh by source): coal: 39.6 bil; gas: 3.3 bil; petroleum: 30 mil; hydroelectric: 1.2 bil; other: 1.3 bil.

State data. Motto: Forward. **Flower:** Wood violet. **Bird:** Robin. **Tree:** Sugar maple. **Song:** "On, Wisconsin!" **Entered union:** May 29, 1848; rank: 30th. **State fair** at West Allis, early Aug.

History. At the time of European contact, Ojibwa, Menominee, Winnebago, Kickapoo, Sauk, Fox, and Potawatomi peoples inhabited the area. French explorer Jean Nicolet reached Green Bay, 1634; French missionaries and fur traders followed. The British took over, 1763. The U.S. won the land after the American Revolution but did not wield control until forts were established at Green Bay and Prairie du Chien, 1816. Native Americans rebelled against the seizure of tribal lands in the Black Hawk War, 1832, but were defeated and relocated to reservations. Wisconsin became a territory, 1836, and a state, 1848. Some 96,000 soldiers served the Union cause during the Civil War. Many immigrants arrived from Germany, Poland, and Scandinavia. Wisconsin agriculture focused on dairy; Milwaukee became a manufacturing center. As governor, 1901-06, Robert La Follette pushed Progressive reforms such as direct primary voting and consumer protection laws. An era of "McCarthyism" ended when anti-Communist crusader Sen. Joseph McCarthy (WI) was censured by the U.S. Senate, 1954. After weeks of protests in Madison, the Republican-controlled state legislature passed controversial measures in Mar. 2011 that would

restrict collective bargaining by some 170,000 public-sector employees.

Tourist attractions. Old Wade House and Carriage Museum, Greenbush; Villa Louis, Prairie du Chien; Circus World Museum, Baraboo; Wisconsin Dells; Old World Wisconsin, Eagle; Door County peninsula; Chequamegon and Nicolet natl. forests; Lake Winnebago; House on the Rock, Dodgeville; Monona Terrace, Madison.

Famous Wisconsinites. Don Ameche, Carrie Chapman Catt, Willem Dafoe, Edna Ferber, Hamlin Garland, King Camp Gillette, Harry Houdini, Robert La Follette, Alfred Lunt, Pat O'Brien, Georgia O'Keeffe, William H. Rehnquist, John Ringling, Donald K. "Deke" Slayton, Spencer Tracy, Thorstein Veblen, Orson Welles, Laura Ingalls Wilder, Thornton Wilder, Frank Lloyd Wright.

Tourist information. Wisconsin Dept. of Tourism, 201 W. Washington Ave., P.O. Box 8690, Madison, WI 53708; 1-800-432-TRIP; www.travelwisconsin.com

Website. www.wisconsin.gov

Wyoming (WY)
Equality State, Cowboy State

People. Population (2010): 563,626; rank: 51; net change (2000-10): 14.1%. **Pop. density:** 5.8 per sq mi. **Racial distribution** (2010): 90.7% white; 0.8% black; 0.8% Asian; 2.4% Native Amer./AK; 0.1% Hawaiian/Pacific Islander; 2 or more races, 2.2%. **Hispanic pop.** (any race, 2010): 8.9%.

Geography. Total area: 97,813 sq mi; rank: 10. **Land area:** 97,093 sq mi; rank: 9. **Acres forested:** 11.4 mil. **Location:** Mountain state lying in the high western plateaus of the Great Plains. **Climate:** semi-desert conditions throughout; true desert in the Big Horn and Great Divide basins. **Topography:** eastern Great Plains rise to the foothills of the Rocky Mts.; the Continental Divide crosses the state from the NW to the SE. **Capital:** Cheyenne.

Economy. Chief industries: mineral extraction, oil, natural gas, tourism and recreation, agriculture. **Chief manuf. goods:** petroleum, chemicals, fabricated metal, beet sugar, lumber. **Chief crops:** hay, sugar beets, barley, dry beans, wheat, corn, greenhouse & nursery, oats. **Livestock** (Dec. 2010): 13,000 chickens (excl. broilers); (Jan. 2011): 1.3 mil. cattle/calves, 365,000 sheep/lambs. **Broadband internet:** 54.2%. **Nonfuel minerals** (2010 prelim.): $1.8 bil; soda ash, helium (grade-A), clays (bentonite), sand and gravel (construction), stone (crushed). **Gross state product** (2010): $38.5 bil. **Sales tax** (2011): 4.0%. **Employment distrib.** (May 2011): 26.1% govt.; 17.8% trade/trans./util.; 3.0% mfg.; 9.1% ed./health; 6.2% prof./bus. serv.; 11.0% leisure/hosp.; 3.8% finance; 17.3% constr./mining/log.; 1.3% info.; 3.9% other serv. **Unemployment** (2010): 7%. **Per cap. pers. income** (2010 prelim.): $47,851. **New private housing** (2010): 2,298 units/$435.2 mil. **Commercial banks** (2010): 44; deposits: $11.6 bil. **Savings institutions** (2010): 3; deposits: $470 mil.

Federal govt. Fed. civ. employees (Mar. 2011): 5,906; **avg. salary:** $60,374. **Notable fed. facilities:** Warren AFB.

Energy. Electricity production (2010 kWh by source): coal: 41.6 bil; gas: 93 mil; petroleum: 56 mil; hydroelectric: 1 bil; other: 1.5 bil.

State data. Motto: Equal rights. **Flower:** Indian paintbrush. **Bird:** Western meadowlark. **Tree:** Plains cottonwood. **Song:** "Wyoming." **Entered union:** July 10, 1890; rank: 44th. **State fair** at Douglas, mid-Aug.

History. Inhabited for at least 12,000 years, the region supported Shoshone, Crow, Cheyenne, Oglala Sioux, and Arapaho peoples when Europeans arrived. France's Vérendrye brothers were the first Europeans to see the region, 1742-43. John Colter, an American, traversed the Yellowstone area, 1807-08. Trappers and fur traders followed in the 1820s. Forts Laramie and Bridger became important stops on trails to the West Coast. Population grew after the Union Pacific crossed the state, 1867-68. Wyoming became a territory, 1868, and the first to extend full voting rights to women, 1869. Statehood was attained, 1890. Disputes between large landowners and small ranchers culminated in the Johnson County Cattle War, 1892; federal troops were called in to restore order. Nellie Tayloe Ross was the first woman governor to take office in the U.S., 1925. Wyoming, the least populous state, has relied on the energy, tourism, and ranching industries in recent decades. Dick Cheney, Wyoming's representative in the U.S. House, 1979-89, served as U.S. vice pres. (2001-09).

Tourist attractions. Yellowstone Natl. Park, the first U.S. national park, est. 1872; Grand Teton Natl. Park; Natl. Elk Refuge; Devils Tower Natl. Monument; Ft. Laramie Natl. Hist. Site and nearby pioneer trail ruts; Buffalo Bill Historical Center, Cody; Cheyenne Frontier Days.

Famous Wyomingites. James Bridger, William F. "Buffalo Bill" Cody, Curt Gowdy, Esther Hobart Morris, Jackson Pollock, Nellie Tayloe Ross.

Tourist information. Wyoming Travel and Tourism, 1520 Etchepare Cir., Cheyenne, WY 82007; 1-800-225-5996; www.wyomingtourism.org

Website. www.wyoming.gov

District of Columbia (DC)

People. Population (2010): 601,723; rank: 50; net change (2000-10): 5.2%. **Pop. density:** 9,856.5 per sq mi. **Racial distribution** (2010): 38.5% white; 50.7% black; 3.5% Asian; 0.3% Native Amer./AK; 0.1% Hawaiian/Pacific Islander; 2 or more races, 2.9%. **Hispanic pop.** (any race, 2010): 9.1%.

Geography. Total area: 68 sq mi; rank: 51. **Land area:** 61 sq mi; rank: 51. **Location:** at the confluence of the Potomac and Anacostia Rivers, flanked by Maryland on the N, E, and SE and by Virginia on the SW. **Climate:** hot humid summers, mild winters. **Topography:** low hills rise toward the N away from the Potomac R. and slope to the S; highest elevation, 410 ft, lowest Potomac R., 1 ft.

Economy. Chief industries: government, legal, publishing, medical, service, tourism. **Gross product** (2010): $103.3 bil. **Sales tax** (2011): 6.0%. **Broadband internet:** 61.7%. **Employment distrib.** (May 2011): 34.5% govt.; 3.7% trade/trans./util.; 0.2% mfg.; 15.2% ed./health; 21.2% prof./bus. serv.; 8.4% leisure/hosp.; 3.7% finance; 1.5% constr./mining/log.; 2.6% info.; 9% other serv. **Unemployment** (2010): 9.9%. **Per cap. pers. income** (2010 prelim.): $71,044. **New private housing** (2010): 739 units/$105.5 mil. **Commercial banks** (2010): 26; deposits: $27.1 bil. **Savings institutions** (2010): 7; deposits: $278 mil. **Lottery** (2010): total sales: $232 mil; profit: $66 mil.

Federal govt. Fed. civ. employees (Mar. 2011): 169,177; **avg. salary:** $102,611.

Energy. Electricity production: NA.

District data. Motto: Justitia omnibus (Justice for all). **Flower:** American beauty rose. **Tree:** Scarlet oak. **Bird:** Wood thrush.

History. The District of Columbia, coextensive with the city of Washington, is the seat of the U.S. federal government. It lies on the west central edge of Maryland on the Potomac River, opposite Virginia. The Piscataway, an Algonquian-speaking people, were living in the region when Europeans arrived in the 17th cent. Proposals for a "federal town" for the deliberations of the Continental Congress were made in 1783. Authorized by Congress, 1790, Pres. George Washington chose the Potomac site and persuaded landowners to sell their holdings to the government. Its area was originally 100 sq mi taken from the sovereignty of Maryland and Virginia. Virginia's portion south of the Potomac was given back to that state in 1846.

Pres. Washington chose Pierre Charles L'Enfant, a Frenchman, to plan the capital. Surveyor Andrew Ellicott finished the official map and design of the city, assisted by Benjamin Banneker, a black architect and astronomer. Washington laid the cornerstone of the north wing of the Capitol building, 1793, and Pres. John Adams moved to the new national capital, 1800. The City of Washington was incorporated, 1802. British troops invaded, 1814, setting fire to the Capitol, the President's House (as the White House was then called), and other buildings. Pres. Abraham Lincoln ended slavery in the district, 1862. Many African Americans arrived after the Civil War, but racial segregation remained legal until the mid-20th cent. After federal government expansion spurred population growth, 1930-50, an exodus to the suburbs shrank the city's population, 1950-2005.

The 23rd Amendment (1961) granted residents the right to vote for president and vice president. Congress, which has legislative authority over the District under the Constitution, approved legislation in 1970 giving the District one delegate to the House of Representatives, who could vote in committee but not on the floor. Voters approved, 1974, a congressionally drafted charter giving them the right to elect their own mayor and city council. The district won the right to levy taxes, but Congress retained power to veto council actions and approve the city budget. Security measures were dramatically increased after terrorists attacked the U.S. on Sept. 11, 2001. After a 34-year absence, major league baseball returned to the city in 2005.

Tourist attractions. See Washington, DC, Capital of the U.S.

Famous Washingtonians. Edward Albee, Frederick Douglass, John Foster Dulles, Duke Ellington, Katherine Graham, Goldie Hawn, J. Edgar Hoover, Pete Sampras, John Philip Sousa.

Tourist information. Destination DC, 901 7th St. NW, 4th Fl., Washington, DC, 20001-3719; 1-800-422-8644; www. washington.org

Website. www.dc.gov

OUTLYING U.S. AREAS

American Samoa (AS)

People. Population (2010): 55,519; net change (2000-10): –3.1%. **Pop. density:** 721 per sq mi. **Racial distrib.** (2000): 91.6% Pacific Islander; 2.8% Asian; 1.1% white; 2 or more races, 4.2%. **Languages:** Samoan, English, Tongan.

Geography. Total area: 77 sq mi. **Land area:** 77 sq mi. **Location:** most southerly of all lands under U.S. sovereign, about 2,300 mi SW of Honolulu. It is an unincorporated territory consisting of 7 small islands of the Samoan group: **Tutuila** (52.59 sq mi), **Aunu'u** (0.59 sq mi); Manu'a group: **Ta'u** (17.57 sq mi), **Olosega** (2.03 sq mi), **Ofu** (2.83 sq mi), and the atolls **Rose** (0.03 sq mi) and **Swains** (1.38 sq mi). **Climate:** marine tropical, avg. temp 82°F with little seasonal variation; avg. annual rainfall about 36 in. **Topography:** volcanic islands, rugged peaks, and limited coastal plains. About 70% of the land is bush and mountains. **Capital:** Pago Pago on Tutuila. **Airport:** Pago Pago.

Economy. Chief industries: tuna fishing and processing, trade, services, tourism. **Chief crops:** giant taro, taro, yams, coconuts, breadfruits, bananas, papayas. **Livestock** (2003): 300 cattle; 68,372 chickens; 64,208 hogs/pigs. **Commercial fishing** (2008): $9.7 mil. **Nonfuel minerals:** crushed stone, trap rock. **Unemployment** (2007): 29.8%. **Gross domestic product** (2007): $532 mil. **Commercial banks** (2010): 2; deposits: $194 mil.

Energy. Electricity production (2007): 185 mil kWh.

Fed. civ. employees (Mar. 2011): 111; **avg. salary:** $51,855.

Misc. data. Motto: Samoa Muamua le Atua (In Samoa, God is first). **Flower:** Paogo (Ula-fala). **Plant:** Ava. **Song:** "Amerika Samoa."

History. A tripartite agreement between Great Britain, Germany, and the U.S. in 1899 gave the U.S. sovereignty over the eastern islands of the Samoan group; these islands became American Samoa. Local chiefs ceded Tutuila and Aunu'u to the U.S. in 1900, and the Manu'a group and Rose Island in 1904; Swains Island was annexed in 1925. Samoa (Western), comprising the larger islands of the Samoan group, was a New Zealand mandate and UN Trusteeship until it became independent Jan. 1, 1962 (now called Samoa).

From 1900 to 1951, American Samoa was under the jurisdiction of the U.S. Navy. Since 1951, it has been under the Interior Dept. On Jan. 3, 1978, the first popularly elected Samoan governor and lieutenant governor were inaugurated. Previously, the governor was appointed by the Sec. of the Interior. American Samoa has a bicameral legislature and elects a delegate to the U.S. House of Representatives who has a voice but no vote, except in committees.

Five of the 7 islands are volcanoes. Scientists discovered a rapidly growing volcano, Vailulu'u, between Ta'u and Rose in 1975.

The tuna canning industry has been the backbone of the economy since the 1950s, but one of the two canneries closed in 2009. An 8.1 magnitude earthquake in Sept. 2009 triggered a tsunami that severely damaged Tutuila.

American Samoans are of Polynesian origin. They are nationals of the U.S. As of 2000, 91,029 lived in the U.S., including 16,166 in Hawaii, 37,498 in California, and 8,049 in Washington.

Tourist attractions. Rose Atoll; Vaitogi coast; Natl. Park of American Samoa; tropical rainforest.

Tourist information. Office of Tourism, Dept. of Commerce, American Samoa Govt., P.O. Box 1147, Pago Pago, AS 96799; (684) 699-9411; www.amsamoatourism.com

Website. www.americansamoa.gov

Guam (GU)

People. Population (2010): 159,358; net change (2000-10): 2.9%. **Pop. density:** 752 per sq mi. **Racial/ethnic distrib.** (2010 est.): 41.0% Chamorro; 30.6% Filipino; 11.7% other Pacific Islander; 3.2% white. **Languages:** English, Chamorro, Philippine/other Pacific Island languages.

Geography. Total area: 212 sq mi. **Land area:** 212 sq mi. **Location:** largest and southernmost of the Mariana Islands in the West Pacific, 3,700 mi W of Hawaii. **Climate:** tropical, with temperatures from 70° to 90° F; rainy July to Nov., avg. annual rainfall, about 80-100 in. **Topography:** coralline limestone plateau in the N; southern chain of low volcanic mountains sloping gently to the W, more steeply to coastal cliffs on the E; general elevation, 500 ft; highest point, Mt. Lamlam, 1,334 ft. **Capital:** Hagåtña. **Chief airport:** Tamuning.

Economy. Chief industries: U.S. military, tourism, construction, shipping, concrete products, printing & publishing. **Chief manuf. goods:** textiles, foods. **Chief crops:** watermelons, cucumbers, eggplant, long beans, bananas, corn. **Livestock** (2007): 112 cattle; 635 hogs/pigs; 124 goats; 533 chickens. **Commercial fishing** (2008): $499,095. **Nonfuel minerals** (est. 2006): $9.3 mil; crushed stone. **Chief port:** Apra Harbor. **Gross domestic product** (2009): $4.0 bil. **Employment distrib.** (Dec. 2008): 33.3% trade/trans; 26.7% serv.; 24.8% govt.; 10.6% constr.; 2.8% mfg.; 0.6% agric. **Unemployment** (2009): 9.3%. **Per capita income** (2005): $12,864. **Commercial banks** (2010): 6; deposits: $1.9 bil. **Savings institutions** (2010): 1; deposits: $67 mil.

Energy. Electricity production (2007): 1.7 bil kWh.

Federal govt. Fed. employees (Mar. 2011): 2,890; **avg. salary:** $55,774. **Notable fed. facilities:** *Anderson AFB.

Misc. data. Motto: Where America's day begins. **Flower:** Puti Tai Nobio (Bougainvillea). **Bird:** Ko'ko (Guam rail). **Tree:** Ifit (Intsia bijuga). **Song:** "Stand Ye Guamanians."

History. Guam was probably settled by voyagers from the Indonesian-Philippine archipelago by 3rd cent. BCE. Pottery, rice cultivation, and megalithic technology show strong East Asian cultural influence. Centralized, village clan-based communities engaged in agriculture and offshore fishing. The estimated population by the early 16th cent. was 50,000-75,000. Ferdinand Magellan arrived in the Marianas Mar. 6, 1521. They were colonized in 1668 by Spanish missionaries, who named them the Mariana Islands in honor of Maria Anna, queen of Spain. When Spain ceded Guam to the U.S., it sold the other Marianas to Germany. Japan obtained a League of Nations mandate over the German islands in 1919; in Dec. 1941 it seized Guam, which was retaken by the U.S. in July-Aug. 1944.

Guam is a self-governing organized unincorporated U.S. territory. The Organic Act of 1950 provided for a governor, elected to a 4-year term, and a 21-member unicameral legislature, elected biennially by the residents, who are American citizens. In 1970, the first governor was elected. In 1972, a U.S. law gave Guam one delegate to the U.S. House of Representatives who has a voice but no vote, except in committees. Guam's quest to change its status to a U.S. commonwealth began in the late 1970s. The Guam Commission on Self-Determination, created in 1984, developed a draft Commonwealth Act. In 1993, legislation proposing a change of status was submitted to the U.S. Congress. In 1994, the U.S. Congress passed legislation transferring 3,200 acres of land on Guam from federal to local control. The U.S. plans to move 8,000 Marines stationed in Okinawa, Japan, to Guam by 2014.

Tourist attractions. Tropical climate, oceanic marine environment; Tarzan Falls; Plaza de España; beaches; water sports; duty-free port shopping.

Tourist information. Guam Visitors Bureau, 401 Pale San Vitores Rd., Tumon, Guam 96913; (671) 646-5278; www.visitguam.org

Website. www.guam.gov

Commonwealth of the Northern Mariana Islands (MP)

People. Population (2010): 53,883; net change (2000-10): −22.2%. **Pop. density:** 293 per sq mi. **Racial/ethnic distrib.** (2000): 56.3% Asian; 36.3% Pacific Islander; 1.8% white; 0.8% other; 4.8% two or more races/ethnicities. **Languages:** Philippine languages, Chinese, Chamorro, English.

Geography. Total area: 184.2 sq mi. **Land area:** 184.2 sq mi. **Location:** between Guam and the Tropic of Cancer, the 14 islands of the Northern Marianas form a 300-mi long archipelago. The indigenous population is concentrated on the 3 largest of the 6 inhabited islands: **Saipan**, the seat of government and commerce, **Rota**, and **Tinian**. **Climate:** tropical, with avg. temperature around 82°F, moderated by northeast trade winds; avg. annual rainfall, 80-100 in. **Topography:** Limestone S islands with even terraces and coral reefs; volcanic N isles. **Capital:** Saipan. **Airport:** Saipan.

Economy. Chief industries: banking, construction, fishing, mining, tourism, apparel mfg., retail. **Chief manuf. goods:** apparel, stone, clay and glass products. **Chief crops:** bananas, cucumbers, sweet potatoes, taro, watermelons. **Livestock** (2007): 1,395 cattle; 1,483 hogs/pigs; 9,700 chickens. **Commercial fishing** (2008): $751,388. **Chief port:** Saipan. **Gross domestic product** (2007): $962 mil. **Fed. employees** (2005): 124. **Unemployment** (2005): 8.0%. **Commercial banks** (2010): 3; deposits: $430 mil. **Savings institutions** (2010): 1; deposits: $6 mil.

Energy. Electricity production (2009): 60,600 kWh.

Federal govt. Fed. employees (Mar. 2011): 187; **avg. salary:** $49,897.

Misc. data. Flower: Plumeria. **Bird:** Mariana fruit-dove. **Tree:** Flame tree. **Song:** "Gi Talo Gi Halom Tasi" (In the middle of the sea).

History. The people of the Northern Marianas are predominantly of Chamorro cultural extraction, although Carolinians and immigrants from other areas of E. Asia and Micronesia have also settled in the islands. English is among the several languages commonly spoken.

The German-controlled Northern Marianas were placed under Japanese control by a League of Nations mandate after World War I. The U.S. captured the islands during World War II. From July 18, 1947, the U.S. had administered the Northern Marianas under a trusteeship agreement with the UN Security Council. In 1975, the residents voted to become a U.S. commonwealth.

The Northern Mariana Islands has been self-governing since 1978, when a constitution drafted and adopted by the people became effective and a popularly elected bicameral legislature (2-year term), with offices of governor (4-year term) and lieut. governor, was inaugurated. Pres. Ronald Reagan proclaimed the Northern Marianas a commonwealth, 1986, and the UN formally ended its trusteeship, 1990. In 2008, U.S. law gave the islands one delegate to the U.S. House of Representatives who has a voice but no vote, except in committees.

Under the 1976 Commonwealth Covenant with the U.S., the islands are exempt from federal immigration and import laws, and minimum wage is lower than on the mainland. The garment-making industry, which has since boomed, has drawn accusations of sweatshop conditions from some critics. Legislation passed in 2007 will raise the minimum wage to the federal rate by 2015.

Tourist attractions. WWII sites; House of Taga; beaches, water sports; resorts; gambling.

Tourist information. Marianas Visitors Authority, P.O. Box 500861, Saipan, MP 96950; (670) 664-3200; www.mymarianas.com

Website. www.gov.mp

Commonwealth of Puerto Rico (PR)
(Estado Libre Asociado de Puerto Rico)

People. Population (2010): 3,725,789 (about 4.6 million additional Puerto Ricans reside in the mainland U.S.); net change (2000-10): −2.2%. **Pop. density:** 1,088.2 per sq mi. **Racial distribution** (2010): 75.8% white; 12.4% black; 0.2% Asian; 0.5% Native Amer./AK; <0.05% Hawaiian/Pacific Islander; 2 or more races, 3.3%. **Hispanic pop.** (any race, 2010): 99.0%. **Languages:** Spanish and English are joint official languages.

Geography. Total area: 5,325 sq mi. **Land area:** 3,424 sq mi. **Location:** island lying between the Atlantic to the N and the Caribbean to the S; it is easternmost of the West Indies group called the Greater Antilles, of which Cuba, Hispaniola, and Jamaica are the larger islands. **Climate:** mild, with a mean temperature of 77°F. **Topography:** mountainous throughout three-fourths of its rectangular area, surrounded by a broken coastal plain; highest peak, Cerro de Punto, 4,390 ft. **Capital:** San Juan. **Chief airport:** San Juan.

Economy. Chief industries: manufacturing, service, tourism. **Chief manuf. goods:** pharmaceuticals, medical equip., electronics, apparel, food products. **Chief crops:** pumpkins, coffee, watermelons, plantains, yams, oranges. **Livestock** (2007): 490,817 cattle; 11,137 sheep; 69,892 hogs/pigs; 5.1 mil broilers; 1.4 mil chickens. **Commercial fishing** (2008): $3.8 mil. **Broadband internet:** 74.6%. **Nonfuel minerals** (est. 2006): $228 mil; crushed stone, lime, salt, portland cement, clays (common), sand and gravel (industrial), dimension marble. **Chief ports:** San Juan, Ponce, Mayaguez. **Gross domestic product** (est. 2009): $95.7 bil. **Employment distrib.** (May 2011): 28.7% govt.; 18.7% trade/trans./util.; 9% mfg.; 12.8% ed./health; 11.7% prof./bus. serv.; 7.5% leisure/hosp.; 4.9% finance; 3.6% constr./mining/log.; 2.1% info.; 1.7% other serv. **Unemployment** (2009): 13.4%. **Per capita pers. income** (est. 2009): $14,905. **Commercial banks** (2010): 8; deposits: $50.5 bil. **Lottery** (2009): total sales: $421.18 mil; profit: $146.91 mil.

Federal govt. Fed. civ. employees (Mar. 2011): 11,356; **avg. salary:** $59,410. **Notable fed. facilities:** P.R. Natl. Guard Training Area at Camp Santiago; *U.S. Army Station at Ft. Buchanan; Intl. Inst. of Tropical Forestry; Vieques Natl. Wildlife Ref.; USGS Caribbean Water Science Ctr.

Energy. Electricity production (2009): 22.7 bil kWh.

Misc. data. Motto: Joannes Est Nomen Eius (John is his name). **Flower:** Maga. **Bird:** Reinita. **Tree:** Ceiba. **National anthem:** La Borinqueña.

History. Puerto Rico (or Borinquen, after the original Arawak Indian name, Boriquen) was visited by Christopher Columbus on his second voyage, Nov. 19, 1493. In 1508, the Spanish arrived.

Sugarcane was introduced, 1515, and slaves were imported 3 years later. Gold mining petered out, 1570. Spaniards fought off a series of British and Dutch attacks; slavery was abolished, 1873. Under the treaty of Paris, Puerto Rico was ceded to the U.S. after the Spanish-American War, 1898. In 1952 the people voted in favor of Commonwealth status.

The Commonwealth of Puerto Rico is a self-governing part of the U.S. with a primarily Hispanic culture. The island's citizens have virtually the same control over their internal affairs as do the 50 states of the U.S. However, they do not vote in national general elections, only in national primaries.

Puerto Rico is represented in the U.S. House of Representatives by a Resident Commissioner who has a voice but no vote, except in committees. No federal income tax is collected from residents on income earned from local sources in Puerto Rico. Nevertheless, as part of the U.S. legal system, Puerto Rico is subject to the provisions of the U.S. Constitution; most federal laws apply as they do in the 50 states.

Puerto Rico's famous "Operation Bootstrap," begun in the late 1940s, succeeded in changing the island from the "Poorhouse of the Caribbean" to an area with the highest per capita income in Latin America. This program encouraged manufacturing and development of the tourist trade by selective tax exemption, low-interest loans, and other incentives. Despite the marked success of Puerto Rico's development efforts over an extended period of time, per capita income in Puerto Rico is low in comparison to that of the 50 states.

In plebiscites held in 1967, 1993, and 1998, voters chose to retain Commonwealth status. Protests mounted in the late-1990s over the U.S. Navy's use of Vieques Island for live ammunition training; official military exercises there were terminated, 2003.

Tourist attractions. Ponce Museum of Art; Forts El Morro and San Cristobal; Old Walled City of San Juan; Arecibo Observatory; Cordillera Central and state parks; El Yunque Rain Forest; San Juan Cathedral; Porta Coeli Chapel and Museum of Religious Art, Interamerican Univ., San Germán; Condado Convention Center; Casa Blanca, Ponce de León family home, Puerto Rican Family Museum of 16th and 17th centuries; and Fine Arts Center, all in San Juan.

Cultural facilities and events. Festival Casals classical music concerts, mid-June; Puerto Rico Symphony Orchestra at Music Conservatory; Botanical Garden and Museum of Anthropology, Art, and History at the University of Puerto Rico; Institute of Puerto Rican Culture, at the Dominican Convent.

Famous Puerto Ricans. Julia de Burgos, Marta Casals Istomin, Pablo Casals, José Celso Barbosa, Orlando Cepeda, Roberto Clemente, José de Diego, José Feliciano, Doña Felisa Rincón de Gautier, Luis A. Ferré, José Ferrer, Commodore Diégo E. Hernández, Miguel Hernández Agosto, Rafael Hernández (El Jibarito), Rafael Hernández Colón, Raúl Julía, René Marqués, Ricky Martin, Concha Meléndez, Rita Moreno, Luis Muñoz Marín, Luis Palés Matos, Adm. Horacio Rivero.

Tourist information. The Puerto Rico Tourism Company, La Princesa Bldg. #2, Paseo La Princesa, Old San Juan, PR 00902; (800) 866-7827; www.seepuertorico.com

Website. www.gobierno.pr (in Spanish)

Virgin Islands (VI)
St. John, St. Croix, St. Thomas

People. Population (2010): 106,405; net change (2000-10): –2.0%. **Pop. density:** 788 per sq mi. **Racial distrib.** (2000): 76.2% black; 13.1% white; 1.1% Asian; 6.1% other races; 2 or more races, 3.5%. **Languages:** English (official), Spanish, Creole.

Geography. Total area: 136 sq mi. **Land area:** 135 sq mi. **Location:** 3 larger and 50 smaller islands and cays in the S and W of the V.I. group (British V.I. colony to the N and E), which is situated 70 mi E of Puerto Rico, located W of the Anegada Passage, a major channel connecting the Atlantic Ocean and the Caribbean Sea. **Climate:** subtropical; the sun tempered by gentle trade winds; humidity is low; avg. temperature, 78°F. **Topography:** St. Thomas is mainly a ridge of hills running E-W, and has little tillable land; St. Croix rises abruptly in the N but slopes to the S to flatlands and lagoons; St. John has steep, lofty hills and valleys with little level tillable land. **Capital:** Charlotte Amalie on St. Thomas. **Chief airport:** Charlotte Amalie.

Economy. Chief industries: retail, petroleum, tourism, prof. consulting. **Chief manuf. goods:** rum, stone, glass & clay products, electronics, textiles. **Chief crops:** cucumbers, coconuts, mangoes, tomatoes, bananas. **Livestock** (2007): 776 cattle; 2,981 sheep; 2,331 goats; 1,125 hogs/pigs; 699 chickens. **Commercial fishing** (2008): $8.8 mil. **Broadband internet:** 57.7%. **Nonfuel minerals:** crushed stone, limestone, traprock. **Chief port:** Charlotte Amalie. **Gross domestic product** (2007): $4.6 bil. **Employment distrib.** (May 2011): 29.5% govt.; 19.3% trade/trans./util.; 4.9% mfg.; 5.8% ed./health; 7.9% prof./bus. serv.; 16.5% leisure/hosp.; 5.3% finance; 4.4% constr./mining/log.; 1.9% info.; 4.2% other serv. **Unemployment** (June 2011): 9.4%. **Commercial banks** (2010): 4; deposits: $1.6 bil.

Energy. Electricity production (2007 est.): 776 mil kWh.

Federal govt. Fed. civ. employees (Mar. 2011): 719; **avg. salary:** $56,378.

Misc. data. Motto: United in Pride and Hope. **Flower:** Yellow cedar. **Bird:** Yellow breast. **Song:** "Virgin Islands March."

History. The islands were visited by Columbus in 1493. Spanish forces, 1555, defeated the Caribes and claimed the territory; by 1596 the native population was annihilated. First permanent settlement in the U.S. territory, 1672, by the Danes; U.S. purchased the islands, 1917, for defense purposes.

The Virgin Islands has a republican form of government, headed by a governor and lieut. governor elected, since 1970, by popular vote for 4-year terms. There is a 15-member unicameral legislature, elected by popular vote for a 2-year term. Residents of the V.I. have been U.S. citizens since 1927. Since 1973 they have elected a delegate to the U.S. House of Representatives, who has a voice but no vote, except in committees.

Tourist attractions. Magens Bay, St. Thomas; duty-free shopping; Virgin Islands Natl. Park; beaches, Indian relics, and evidence of colonial Danes.

Tourist information. USVI Division of Tourism, P.O. Box 6400, St. Thomas 00804; 1-800-372-USVI; www.usvitourism.vi

Website. ltg.gov.vi

Other Islands

Navassa lies between Haiti and Jamaica, 100 mi S of Guantanamo Bay, Cuba, in the Caribbean; it covers 1,147 acres, and is uninhabited. Claimed 1857, USCG lighthouse built 1917, now inoperative. Natl. Wildlife Refuge since 1999. Administered by the Dept. of Interior.

The three coral islands of **Wake Atoll**—**Wake, Wilkes,** and **Peale**—lie in the Pacific Ocean on a direct route from Hawaii to Hong Kong, about 2,300 mi W of Honolulu and 1,500 mi NE of Guam. The group is 4.5 mi long, 1.5 mi wide. Land area totals 2.5 sq mi. The U.S. annexed Wake Atoll Jan. 17, 1899. Japan occupied Wake 1941-45. Designated a National Historic Landmark in 1985. Wake is owned by the U.S. Air Force, administered by the Dept. of Interior, but used by the Army as a missile launch facility. The population consists of military personnel and contractors. Most infrastructure damaged by super typhoon Ioke in 2006.

The following mostly uninhabited islands are part of the **Pacific/Remote Islands National Wildlife Refuge Complex**, along with Wake Atoll, administered by the Dept. of Interior: **Midway Atoll**, acquired in 1867, has 3 main islands—Sand, Spit, and Eastern—1,250 mi WNW of Honolulu, with an area of about 1,500 acres. Naval activity ended in 1997. Has the world's largest colony of Laysan albatross. **Johnston Atoll**, 800 mi WSW of Honolulu, is 2 natural and 2 man-made islands across 107 sq mi administered by the Navy. Johnston was a nuclear test site in 1958, 1962; the Army disposed of chemical weapons 1990-2000. Cleanup ended in 2005. **Kingman Reef** is a barren, coral atoll 932 mi S of Hawaii, annexed 1922. **Palmyra Atoll** is 54 islets over 753 sq mi, 1,052 mi S of Hawaii; annexed with Hawaii in 1898. Part privately owned by the Nature Conservancy. **Jarvis Island** covers 1,086 acres, 1,300 mi S of Honolulu near the equator. West of Jarvis are **Howland and Baker Islands**, 36 mi apart and about 1,600 mi SW of Honolulu.

Attractions in Washington, DC, Capital of the U.S.

Most attractions are free. All times are subject to change. For more details call the Washington, DC, Convention and Visitors Association at 1-800-422-8644, or visit www.washington.org

Bureau of Engraving and Printing

The **Bureau of Engraving and Printing** of the U.S. Treasury Dept. is the headquarters for the making of U.S. paper money. Public tours are offered Mon.-Fri., 9-10:45 AM, 12:30-2 PM (later in summer), except on federal holidays. 14th and C Sts. SW; (866) 874-2330. **Website:** www.moneyfactory.gov

Capitol

The **United States Capitol** was originally designed by Dr. William Thornton, an amateur architect, who submitted a plan in 1793 that won him $500 and a city lot. Three other architects designed or supervised the construction of the Capitol before its completion.

The present cast iron dome at its greatest exterior height measures 135 ft, 5 in. and is topped by the bronze Statue of Freedom, which stands 19½ ft and weighs 14,985 lbs. On its base are the words *E Pluribus Unum* (Out of Many, One).

The Capitol is open to the public Mon.-Sat., 8:30 AM-4:30 PM. It is closed Jan. 1, Inauguration Day, Thanksgiving Day, and Dec. 25.

To observe debate while Congress is in session, those living in the U.S. may obtain tickets from their U.S. representative or senator. Visitors from other countries may obtain passes at the Capitol. Between Constitution & Independence Aves., at Pennsylvania Ave.; (202) 225-6827. **Website:** www.visitthecapital.gov

Federal Bureau of Investigation

The **Federal Bureau of Investigation** offers guided one-hour tours of its headquarters. Visitors learn about the history of the FBI and see weapons confiscated from famous gangsters, photos of most-wanted fugitives, the DNA laboratory, goods forfeited/seized in narcotics operations, and a sharpshooting demonstration.

Tours have been suspended for building renovation. J. Edgar Hoover Bldg., Pennsylvania Ave., between 9th and 10th Sts. NW; (202) 324-3447. **Website:** www.fbi.gov

Folger Shakespeare Library

The **Folger Shakespeare Library**, on Capitol Hill, is a research institution holding rare books and manuscripts of the Renaissance period and the largest collection of Shakespearean materials in the world. Exhibit may be visited Mon.-Sat., 10 AM-5 PM, except federal holidays. 201 E. Capitol St. SE; (202) 544-4600. **Website:** www.folger.edu

Holocaust Memorial Museum

The **U.S. Holocaust Memorial Museum** opened on Apr. 21, 1993. The museum documents the events of the Holocaust through permanent and temporary displays, interactive videos, and special lectures. The permanent exhibition is not recommended for children under age 11.

The museum is open daily, 10 AM-5:20 PM, except Yom Kippur and Dec. 25; extended hours Mon.-Thurs. (10 AM-6:20 PM) from Apr.-June. A limited number of free tickets are available at the door; advance tickets may be ordered for a small fee at 1-800-400-9373. Tickets are needed only for the permanent exhibition, only Mar. through Aug. 100 Raoul Wallenberg Pl. SW; (202) 488-0400. **Website:** www.ushmm.org

Jefferson Memorial

Dedicated Apr. 13, 1943, the **Thomas Jefferson Memorial** stands on the south shore of the Tidal Basin in West Potomac Park. It is a circular stone structure that combines architectural elements of the dome of the Pantheon in Rome and the rotunda designed by Jefferson for the Univ. of Virginia.

The memorial is open daily, 24 hrs., staffed 9:30 AM-11:30 PM. Has elevator and curb ramps for handicapped; (202) 426-6841. **Website:** www.nps.gov/thje

John F. Kennedy Center

The **John F. Kennedy Center for the Performing Arts** opened Sept. 8, 1971. Designed by Edward Durell Stone, it includes an opera house, a concert hall, several theaters, 2 restaurants, and a library. Free tours are available Mon.-Fri., 10 AM-5 PM and Sat. & Sun., 10 AM-1 PM. 2700 F St. NW; (202) 467-4600; (800) 444-1324. **Website:** www.kennedy-center.org

Korean War Veterans Memorial

Dedicated on July 27, 1995, the **Korean War Veterans Memorial** honors Americans who served in the war. Situated at the west end of the Mall, the triangular-shaped stone and steel memorial features a multiservice formation of 19 combat-ready troops clad in ponchos with the wind at their back. A granite wall, with images of men and women who served, juts into the Pool of Remembrance.

The memorial is open daily, 24 hrs., staffed 9:30 AM-11:30 PM. French Dr. SW across from Lincoln Memorial; (202) 426-6841. **Website:** www.nps.gov/kowa

Library of Congress

Established by and for Congress in 1800, the **Library of Congress** extends its services to other government agencies and libraries, scholars, and the general public. It contains more than 134 mil items in some 460 languages.

Exhibit halls are open to the public Mon.-Fri., 8:30 AM-9:30 PM; Sat., 8:30 AM-5 PM. A few areas are open on most federal holidays; all are closed Jan. 1, Thanksgiving, and Dec. 25. 101 Independence Ave. SE; (202) 707-8000. **Website:** www.loc.gov

Lincoln Memorial

Designed by Henry Bacon, the **Lincoln Memorial** in West Potomac Park is a large marble hall enclosing a statue of Abraham Lincoln seated on an armchair. The memorial was dedicated May 30, 1922. The statue was designed by Daniel Chester French and sculpted by French and the Piccirilli brothers. The text of the Gettysburg Address is in the south chamber; that of Lincoln's Second Inaugural speech is in the north chamber. Each is engraved on a stone tablet.

The memorial is open daily, 24 hrs., staffed 9:30 AM-11:30 PM, and is wheelchair-accessible. W. Potomac Park at 23rd St. NW; (202) 426-6841. **Website:** www.nps.gov/linc

National Archives and Records

Original copies of the Declaration of Independence, the Constitution, and the Bill of Rights are on display in the **National Archives** Exhibition Hall. The National Archives also holds other valuable U.S. government records and historic maps, photographs, and manuscripts. Central Research and Microfilm Research Rooms are also available to the public for genealogical research.

Exhibition Hall open daily 10 AM-5:30 PM (later in spring and summer). 7th St. & Pennsylvania Ave. NW; (202) 357-5000. **Website:** www.archives.gov

National Gallery of Art

The **National Gallery of Art** was established by Congress, Mar. 24, 1937, and opened Mar. 17, 1941. The original West building was designed by John Russell Pope. The East building, opened in 1978, was designed by I. M. Pei. Open daily, Mon.-Sat. 10 AM-5 PM, Sunday 11 AM-6 PM. Closed Jan. 1 and Dec. 25. 4th St. and Constitution Ave NW; (202) 737-4215. **Website:** www.nga.gov

Franklin Delano Roosevelt Memorial

Opened May 2, 1997, the **FDR Memorial** features 9 bronze sculptural ensembles depicting FDR, Eleanor Roosevelt, and events from the Great Depression and World War II. This 7.5-acre memorial is located near the Tidal Basin in a park-like setting and is wheelchair accessible.

Grounds, staffed daily, 8 AM-11:45 PM, except Dec. 25. 1850 W. Basin Dr. SW; (202) 426-6841. **Website:** www.nps.gov/fdrm

Smithsonian Institution

The **Smithsonian Institution**, established in 1846, is the world's largest museum complex. It holds some 137 mil artifacts and specimens in its trust. There are 15 museums and the National Zoo in the DC area. The **Smithsonian Information Center** is located in "the Castle" on the Mall. Also on the Mall are the **National Museum of American History**, the **National Museum of Natural History**, the **National Air and Space Museum**, the **National Museum of the American Indian**, the **Hirshhorn Museum and Sculpture Garden**, the **Arthur M. Sackler & Freer Galleries of Art**, the **National Museum of African Art**, and the **Arts and Industries Building** (currently closed for renovation). Located nearby are the **National Postal Museum**, the **National Museum of American Art**, the **National Portrait Gallery**, and the **Renwick Gallery**. Farther away is the **Anacostia Museum**. The **Air and Space Museum's Udvar-Hazy Center** is near Dulles Airport in Virginia.

Most museums are open daily, except Dec. 25, 10 AM-5:30 PM (later in summer); (202) 633-1000. **Website:** www.si.edu

Vietnam Veterans Memorial

Originally dedicated Nov. 13, 1982, the **Vietnam Veterans Memorial** recognizes the men and women who served in the armed forces in the Vietnam War. The names of more than 58,000 Americans who lost their lives or remain missing are inscribed on a V-shaped black-granite wall, designed by Maya Ying Lin.

Since 1982, 2 additions have been made to the Memorial. The 1st, dedicated on Nov. 11, 1984, is the Frederick Hart sculpture *Three Servicemen*. On Nov. 11, 1993, the Vietnam Women's Memorial, designed by Glenna Goodacre, was dedicated, honoring the more than 11,500 women who served in Vietnam.

The memorial is open daily, 24 hrs., staffed 9:30 AM-11:30 PM. Constitution Ave. & Bacon Dr. NW; (202) 426-6841. **Website:** www.nps.gov/vive

Washington Monument

The **Washington Monument**, dedicated in 1885, is a tapering shaft, or obelisk, of white marble, 555 ft, 5$\frac{1}{8}$ in. in height and 55 ft, 1½ in. square at base. Eight small windows, 2 on each side, are located at the 500-ft level.

(As of Sept. 30, 2011, the monument was closed to the public while damages caused during a Aug. 23, 2011, earthquake, were assessed.) Normally open daily, 9 AM-5 PM (later in summer), except July 1, Dec. 25. Free timed passes are available; advance passes are available for a small fee. 15th St. and Constitution Ave. NW; (202) 426-6841. **Website:** www.nps.gov/wamo

White House

The **White House**, the President's residence, stands on 18 acres on the south side of Pennsylvania Ave., between the Treasury and the old Executive Office Building. The walls are of sandstone, quarried at Aquia Creek, VA. The building was first made white with lime-based whitewash in 1798, but the name did not become official until 1901.

The White House is normally open for free self-guided tours of 10 or more Tues.-Thurs., 7:30-11 AM; Fri., 7:30 AM-noon; Sat., 7:30 AM-1 PM. (Tour requests must be made at least one month in advance through your member of Congress.) Only the public rooms on the ground floor and state floor may be visited. 1600 Pennsylvania Ave. The White House Visitor Center at 1450 Pennsylvania Ave. is open daily 7:30 AM-4 PM; (202) 456-7041. **Website:** www.whitehouse.gov

National World War II Memorial

The **National WWII Memorial** is dedicated to the approx. 16 mil veterans who served and the more than 400,000 who died in the war. It rests on 7.4 acres of land at the east end of the reflecting pool on the Mall. The memorial opened on Apr. 29, 2004, and was dedicated on May 29.

At the north and south entrances are 43-ft archways, representing the Atlantic and Pacific theaters. Inside the grounds is a large, oval plaza with a wall of 4,000 gold stars; each represents 100 American deaths. Fifty-six pillars ringing the center represent the states, territories, and District of Columbia. There is also a garden enclosed by a stone wall, the Circle of Remembrance.

The memorial is wheelchair-accessible and open daily, 24 hrs., staffed 9:30 AM-11:30 PM. Located on 17th St. between Constitution and Independence Aves.; (202) 426-6841. **Website:** www.nps.gov/nwwm

Attractions Near Washington, DC

Arlington National Cemetery

Arlington National Cemetery, on the former Custis-Lee estate in Arlington, VA, is the site of the **Tomb of the Unknowns** and is the final resting place of Pres. W. H. Taft and Pres. John F. Kennedy and his wife, Jacqueline Bouvier Kennedy Onassis. An eternal flame burns over the site of Kennedy's grave. Many other famous Americans are buried at Arlington, as well as more than 300,000 U.S. military personnel, from every major war.

North of the National Cemetery stands the **U.S. Marine Corps War Memorial**, also known as Iwo Jima. The memorial is a bronze statue of the raising of the U.S. flag on Mt. Suribachi, Feb. 23, 1945, during World War II, executed by Felix de Weldon from the photograph by Joe Rosenthal.

On the southern side of the Memorial Bridge, near the cemetery entrance, a memorial honoring the women in the military was dedicated Oct. 18, 1997. The **Women in Military Service for America Memorial** is a semicircular retaining wall 226 ft long with a central niche 30 ft high.

Open daily, 8 AM-5 PM (8 AM-7 PM, Apr.-Sept.), Arlington, VA; (703) 607-8000. **Website:** www.arlingtoncemetery.org

Mount Vernon

Mount Vernon, George Washington's estate, is on the south bank of the Potomac R., 16 mi from Washington, DC, in northern Virginia. The present house is believed to be an enlargement of one built by Augustine Washington in 1735. His son Lawrence renamed the estate after British Navy Adm. Edward Vernon. George Washington, Lawrence's half brother, inherited it in 1761. The estate has been restored to its 18th-century appearance and includes many original furnishings. Washington and his wife, Martha, are buried on the grounds.

Open 365 days, Apr.-Aug. 8 AM-5 PM; Mar., Sept.-Oct. 9 AM-5 PM; Nov.-Feb. 9 AM-4 PM; (703) 780-2000; (800) 429-1520. Admission: adults $15, seniors (62+) $14, children (6-11) $7, age 5 and under free. **Website:** www.mountvernon.org

The Pentagon

The **Pentagon**, headquarters of the Dept. of Defense, is the largest office building in the U.S. It houses more than 23,000 employees in offices occupying 3,705,793 sq ft. The building was severely damaged when struck by a plane Sept. 11, 2001.

Group tours available to government agencies, educational institutions, or military units by reservation only. General public must use the Pentagon website or contact their member of Congress to request a tour. Non U.S. citizens must contact their national embassy. Arlington, VA (I-395 South to Boundary Channel Drive exit); (703) 697-1776. **Website:** pentagon.afis.osd.mil

100 MOST POPULOUS U.S. CITIES

Sources: Population: Decennial Census, U.S. Census Bureau, U.S. Dept. of Commerce. Population is as of Apr. 1, 2010; population rank is indicated within parentheses. **Pop. density** specifies the number of persons per square mile (sq mi). **Employment:** Bureau of Labor Statistics, U.S. Dept. of Labor (2010). **Per capita income:** Bureau of Economic Analysis, U.S. Dept. of Commerce; figures apply to MSA (2009). **Avg. home:** National Association of Realtors®; figures represent median sales price of existing single-family homes in the metropolitan area; data not available for all cities. **Mayor** (or other city leaders) and websites: World Almanac research as of mid-2011; subject to change.

Included here are the 100 most populous U.S. cities, according to the 2010 Census. Most data are for the city proper; some, where noted, apply to the Metropolitan Statistical Area (MSA). Inc. = Incorporated; est. = Established.

Albuquerque, New Mexico

Population: 545,852 (32). **Pop. density:** 2,908. **Pop. change (2000-10):** 21.7%. **Area:** 187.7 sq mi. **Employment:** 241,557 employed; 8.0% unemployed. **Per capita income:** $35,329; change (2008-09): −0.8%. **Avg. home:** $178,700; change (2008-10): −7.2%.
Mayor: Richard J. Berry, nonpartisan
History: Founded 1706 by the Spanish; inc. 1890.
Transportation: 1 intl. airport; 1 railroad; bus system. **Communications:** 1 daily newspaper; 8 TV, 39 radio stations. **Medical facilities:** 19 major hosp. **Educational facilities:** 1 univ., 25 colleges; 139 pub. schools. **Further information:** Albuquerque Convention & Visitors Bureau, P.O. Box 26866, Albuquerque, NM 87125-6866; www.itsatrip.org; www.cabq.gov

Anaheim, California

Population: 336,265 (54). **Pop. density:** 6,748. **Pop. change (2000-10):** 2.5%. **Area:** 49.8 sq mi. **Employment:** 152,842 employed; 12.2% unemployed. **Per capita income:** $42,784; change (2008-09): −3.8%. **Avg. home:** $316,700; change (2008-10): −21.2%.
Mayor: Tom Tait, nonpartisan
History: Founded 1857; inc. 1870. Home of Disneyland, the Anaheim Ducks, and the Los Angeles Angels.
Transportation: Amtrak; Metrolink (2 stations), OCTA bus service. **Communications:** 1 daily newspaper; 2 TV, 2 radio stations (MSA). **Medical facilities:** 5 hosp.; 5 med. centers. **Educational facilities:** 11 colleges and trade schools; 65 pub. schools, 33 priv. schools. **Further information:** City Hall, 200 South Anaheim Blvd., Ste. 733, Anaheim, CA 92805; www.anaheimoc.org; www.anaheim.net

Anchorage, Alaska

Population: 291,826 (64). **Pop. density:** 171. **Pop. change (2000-10):** 12.1%. **Area:** 1,704.7 sq mi. **Employment:** 143,815 employed; 6.9% unemployed. **Per capita income:** $46,217; change (2008-09): −3.5%.
Mayor: Dan Sullivan, Republican
History: Founded 1914 as a construction camp for railroad; HQ of Alaska Defense Command, WWII. Severely damaged in earthquake, 1964. Current population center of Alaska.
Transportation: 1 intl., 1 regional airport, 2 airfields, 2 seaplane bases; 1 railroad; transit system; 1 port. **Communications:** 1 daily newspaper; 13 TV, 25 radio stations. **Medical facilities:** 5 hosp. **Educational facilities:** 2 univ., 8 colleges/trade schools; 96 pub. schools. **Further information:** Anchorage Chamber of Commerce, 1016 W. 6th Ave., Ste. 303, Anchorage, AK, 99501; www.anchoragechamber.org; www.muni.org

Arlington, Texas

Population: 365,438 (50). **Pop. density:** 3,811. **Pop. change (2000-10):** 9.8%. **Area:** 95.9 sq mi. **Employment:** 189,544 employed; 7.8% unemployed. **Per capita income:** $41,764; change (2008-09): −4.4%. **Avg. home:** $143,800; change (2008-10): −1.4%.
Mayor: Robert N. Cluck, nonpartisan
History: Settled in 1840s; inc. 1884.
Transportation: 1 muni. airport; freight railways. **Communications:** 2 TV, 1 radio station. **Medical facilities:** 7 hosp. **Educational facilities:** 1 univ., 8 colleges and trade schools; 74 pub. schools. **Further information:** Arlington Chamber of Commerce, 505 E. Border St., Arlington, TX 76010; www.arlingtontx.com; www.ci.arlington.tx.us

Atlanta, Georgia

Population: 420,003 (40). **Pop. density:** 3,154. **Pop. change (2000-10):** 0.8%. **Area:** 133.2 sq mi. **Employment:** 205,910 employed; 11.3% unemployed. **Per capita income:** $37,101; change (2008-09): −4.7%. **Avg. home:** $114,800; change (2008-10): −23.2%.
Mayor: Kasim Reed, nonpartisan
History: Founded as Terminus 1837; renamed Atlanta 1845; inc. 1847; played major role in Civil War; became permanent state capital 1877; birthplace of civil rights movement; host to 1996 Centennial Olympic Games.
Transportation: 1 intl., 2 regional airports; 1 passenger, 2 freight railroad lines; 1 rail system; 4 bus systems. **Communications:** 3 daily newspapers; 21 TV, 23 radio stations. **Medical facilities:** 18 hosp.; VA hosp.; U.S. Centers for Disease Control and Prevention; American Cancer Society. **Educational facilities:** 25 postsecondary insts.; 93 pub. schools. **Further information:** Metro Atlanta Chamber of Commerce, 235 Andrew Young Intl. Blvd. NW, Atlanta, GA 30303; www.metroatlantachamber.com; www.atlantaga.gov

Aurora, Colorado

Population: 325,078 (56). **Pop. density:** 2,101. **Pop. change (2000-10):** 17.6%. **Area:** 154.7 sq mi. **Employment:** 156,069 employed; 10.8% unemployed. **Per capita income:** $46,611; change (2008-09): −4.1%. **Avg. home:** $232,400; change (2008-10): 6.0%.
Mayor: Ed Tauer, nonpartisan
History: Founded 1891; originally called Fletcher; renamed Aurora 1907; inc. 1929. Early growth stimulated by presence of military bases; fast-growing trade, technology, and med. science center.
Transportation: adjacent to Denver Intl. Airport; bus system. **Communications:** 1 daily newspaper; 2 TV, 3 radio stations. **Medical facilities:** 3 hosp. **Educational facilities:** 2 univ., 6 colleges and tech. schools; 49 pub. schools, 4 priv. schools. **Further information:** Aurora Planning Dept., 15151 E. Alameda Pkwy., Aurora, CO 80012; www.aurorachamber.org; www.auroragov.org

Austin, Texas

Population: 790,390 (14). **Pop. density:** 2,653. **Pop. change (2000-10):** 20.4%. **Area:** 297.9 sq mi. **Employment:** 404,236 employed; 6.6% unemployed. **Per capita income:** $37,544; change (2008-09): −3.6%. **Avg. home:** $193,600; change (2008-10): 2.7%.
Mayor: Lee Leffingwell, nonpartisan
History: First permanent settlement 1835; capital of Rep. of Texas 1839; named after Stephen Austin; inc. 1840.
Transportation: 1 intl. airport; 2 railroads; bus system. **Communications:** 1 daily newspaper; 8 TV, 40 radio stations. **Medical facilities:** 26 hosp. **Educational facilities:** 5 4-year univ., 3 seminaries, 8 community college campuses, 22 trade schools; 229 pub. schools, 70 priv. schools. **Further information:** Greater Austin Chamber of Commerce, 210 Barton Springs Rd., Ste. 400, Austin, TX 78704; www.austinchamber.com; www.austintexas.org; www.ci.austin.tx.us

Bakersfield, California

Population: 347,483 (51). **Pop. density:** 2,444. **Pop. change (2000-10):** 40.6%. **Area:** 142.2 sq mi. **Employment:** 135,951 employed; 11.2% unemployed. **Per capita income:** $29,630; change (2008-09): −1.5%.
Mayor: Harvey L. Hall, nonpartisan
History: Named after Col. Thomas Baker, an early settler; inc. 1898.
Transportation: 2 airports; Amtrak; Greyhound bus service, 3 local bus systems. **Communications:** 1 daily newspaper; 7 TV, 29 radio stations. **Medical facilities:** 9 hosp. **Educational facilities:** 8 univ., 5 colleges, 4 tech. schools; 43 pub. schools. **Further information:** Greater Bakersfield Chamber of Commerce, 1725 Eye St., Bakersfield, CA 93301; www.bakersfieldchamber.org; www.bakersfieldcity.us

Baltimore, Maryland

Population: 620,961 (23). **Pop. density:** 7,671. **Pop. change (2000-10):** −4.6%. **Area:** 80.9 sq mi. **Employment:** 246,550 employed; 10.9% unemployed. **Per capita income:** $48,201; change (2008-09): −0.2%. **Avg. home:** $246,100; change (2008-10): −10.2%.
Mayor: Stephanie C. Rawlings-Blake, Democrat
History: Founded by Maryland legislature 1729; inc. 1797; War of 1812 British artillery barrage of Ft. McHenry (1814) inspired

Francis Scott Key to write "Star-Spangled Banner." Birthplace of America's railroads 1828; rebuilt after fire 1904. Site of National Aquarium.

Transportation: 1 intl. airport; 3 railroads; light rail, subway, bus systems; Inner Harbor water taxi system; 2 underwater tunnels. **Communications:** 4 daily newspapers; 8 TV, 21 radio stations. **Medical facilities:** 23 hosp. **Educational facilities:** 12 univ., 18 colleges and trade schools; 203 pub. schools. **Further information:** Greater Baltimore Committee, 111 S. Calvert St., Ste. 1700, Baltimore, MD 21202-6180; www.gbc.org; www.baltimore.org; www.baltimorecity.gov

Baton Rouge, Louisiana

Population: 229,493 (85). **Pop. density:** 2,982. **Pop. change (2000-10):** 0.7%. **Area:** 77.0 sq mi. **Employment:** 99,657 employed; 8.0% unemployed. **Per capita income:** $38,107; change (2008-09): 0.6%. **Avg. home:** $169,600; change (2008-10): 2.8%.

Mayor-President: Melvin "Kip" Holden, Democrat

History: Claimed by Spain at time of Louisiana Purchase 1803; est. independence by rebellion 1810; inc. as town 1817. Became state capital 1849; Union-held most of Civil War.

Transportation: 1 airport; 3 railroad trunk lines; 1 bus line. **Communications:** 1 daily newspaper; 13 TV, 18 radio stations. **Medical facilities:** 17 hosp. **Educational facilities:** 2 univ., 24 colleges and trade schools; 94 pub. schools, 52 priv. schools. **Further information:** Chamber of Greater Baton Rouge, 564 Laurel St., Baton Rouge, LA, 70801; www.brac.org; www.brgov.com

Birmingham, Alabama

Population: 212,237 (97). **Pop. density:** 1,453. **Pop. change (2000-10):** −12.6%. **Area:** 146.1 sq mi. **Employment:** 84,969 employed; 11.2% unemployed. **Per capita income:** $38,592; change (2008-09): −3.4%. **Avg. home:** $143,000; change (2008-10): −7.1%.

Mayor: William A. Bell, nonpartisan

History: Settled 1871 at the intersection of two major railroads, within proximity of elements needed for iron and steel production.

Transportation: 1 intl. airport, 5 air cargo cos.; 4 major rail freight lines, Amtrak; 1 bus line; 75 truck line terminals; 7 barge lines. **Communications:** 1 daily newspaper; 9 TV, 21 radio stations; 1 educational TV, 1 educational radio station. **Medical facilities:** 16 hosp.; VA hosp. **Educational facilities:** 7 univ., 16 colleges; 51 pub. schools. **Further information:** Greater Birmingham Convention and Visitors Bureau, 2200 Ninth Ave. N., Birmingham, AL 35203-1100; www.birminghamal.org; www.birminghamal.gov

Boston, Massachusetts

Population: 617,594 (24). **Pop. density:** 12,793. **Pop. change (2000-10):** 4.8%. **Area:** 48.3 sq mi. **Employment:** 301,649 employed; 7.9% unemployed. **Per capita income:** $53,553; change (2008-09): −3.3%. **Avg. home:** $357,300; change (2008-10): −1.1%.

Mayor: Thomas M. Menino, Democrat

History: Settled 1630 by John Winthrop; capital of Mass. Bay Colony; figured strongly in American Revolution, earning distinction as the "Cradle of Liberty"; inc. 1822.

Transportation: 1 intl. airport; 2 railroads; city rail, subway system; 3 underwater tunnels; port. **Communications:** 3 daily newspapers; 11 TV, 21 radio stations. **Medical facilities:** 39 hosp. **Educational facilities:** 31 univ. and colleges. **Further information:** Greater Boston Convention and Visitors Bureau, 2 Copley Pl., Ste. 105, Boston, MA 02116; www.bostonusa.com; www.cityofboston.gov

Buffalo, New York

Population: 261,310 (70). **Pop. density:** 6,471. **Pop. change (2000-10):** −10.7%. **Area:** 40.4 sq mi. **Employment:** 108,943 employed; 10.3% unemployed. **Per capita income:** $37,469; change (2008-09): 0.3%. **Avg. home:** $121,200; change (2008-10): 15.0%.

Mayor: Byron W. Brown, Democrat

History: Settled 1780 by Seneca Indians; raided twice by British in War of 1812. Served as western terminus for Erie Canal, became a center for trade and manufacturing; inc. 1832. A last stop on the Underground Railroad. Key point for Canada-U.S. political, trade, and social relations.

Transportation: 2 airports; 4 Class I railroads, regional rail system; 7 intl. ports of entry (in metro area). **Communications:** 12 TV, 43 radio stations. **Medical facilities:** 14 hosp. **Educational facilities:** 8 univ. and colleges; 70 pub. schools.

Further information: Visit Buffalo Niagara, 617 Main St., Ste. 200, Buffalo, NY 14203; www.visitbuffaloniagara.com; www.ci.buffalo.ny.us

Chandler, Arizona

Population: 236,123 (80). **Pop. density:** 3,666. **Pop. change (2000-10):** 33.7%. **Area:** 64.4 sq mi. **Employment:** 127,600 employed; 7.0% unemployed. **Per capita income:** $34,452; change (2008-09): −4.7%. **Avg. home:** $139,200; change (2008-10): −27.2%.

Mayor: Jay Tibshraeny, nonpartisan

History: Formed 1912; population doubled in 1990s as "the high-tech oasis of the Silicon Desert."

Transportation: 1 muni., 1 private airport; mass transit system. **Communications:** 1 govt. access cable channel. **Medical facilities:** 2 hosp. **Educational facilities:** 2 univ., 1 community college; 35 pub. schools, 13 charter schools. **Further information:** Chandler Chamber, 25 South Arizona Pl., Ste. 201, Chandler, AZ 85225; www.chandlerchamber.com; www.chandleraz.gov

Charlotte, North Carolina

Population: 731,424 (18). **Pop. density:** 2,457. **Pop. change (2000-10):** 35.2%. **Area:** 297.7 sq mi. **Employment:** 315,377 employed; 9.6% unemployed. **Per capita income:** $38,034; change (2008-09): −5.4%. **Avg. home:** $191,000; change (2008-10): −3.4%.

Mayor: Anthony R. Foxx, Democrat

History: Settled by Scotch-Irish immigrants 1740s; inc. 1768 and named after Queen Charlotte, George III's wife. Scene of first major U.S. gold discovery 1799.

Transportation: 1 intl. airport; 2 major railway lines; 1 bus line; 605 trucking firms. **Communications:** 2 daily newspapers; 8 TV, 13 radio stations. **Medical facilities:** 8 hosp. **Educational facilities:** 9 univ., 9 colleges; 151 pub. schools. **Further information:** Charlotte Chamber of Commerce, 330 S. Tryon St., Charlotte, NC 28202; www.charlottechamber.com; www.charmeck.org

Chesapeake, Virginia

Population: 222,209 (91). **Pop. density:** 652. **Pop. change (2000-10):** 11.6%. **Area:** 340.8 sq mi. **Employment:** 108,370 employed; 6.9% unemployed. **Per capita income:** $39,518; change (2008-09): −0.7%. **Avg. home:** $205,000; change (2008-10): −6.8%.

Mayor: Alan P. Krasnoff, Independent

History: Region settled in 1620s with first English colonies on banks of Elizabeth River; home to Great Dismal Swamp Canal, first envisioned by George Washington in 1763. Battle of Great Bridge fought here Dec. 1775; inc. 1963.

Transportation: 2 regional airports; freight rail service; bus service. **Communications:** 3 TV, 5 radio stations. **Medical facilities:** 1 hosp. **Educational facilities:** 9 univ. and colleges; 56 pub. schools and educational centers. **Further information:** City of Chesapeake, Public Communications Dept., 306 Cedar Rd., Chesapeake, VA 23322; www.cityofchesapeake.net

Chicago, Illinois

Population: 2,695,598 (3). **Pop. density:** 11,842. **Pop. change (2000-10):** −6.9%. **Area:** 227.6 sq mi. **Employment:** 1,175,029 employed; 11.0% unemployed. **Per capita income:** $44,379; change (2008-09): −3.8%. **Avg. home:** $191,400; change (2008-10): −22.1%.

Mayor: Rahm Emanuel, nonpartisan

History: Site acquired from Indians 1795; significant white settlement began with completion of Erie Canal 1825; chartered as city 1837. Boomed with arrival of railroads and canal to Mississippi R.; one-third of city destroyed by fire 1871. Major grain and livestock market.

Transportation: 2 intl. airports; major railroad system; public transit system; trucking industry. **Communications:** 16 TV, 38 radio stations. **Medical facilities:** 43 hosp. **Educational facilities:** 59 insts. of higher learning; 621 pub. schools. **Further information:** Chicago Convention & Tourism Bureau, 2301 S. Lake Shore Dr., Chicago, IL 60616; www.choosechicago.com; www.cityofchicago.org

Chula Vista, California

Population: 243,916 (77). **Pop. density:** 4,915. **Pop. change (2000-10):** 40.5%. **Area:** 49.6 sq mi. **Employment:** 80,511 employed; 12.3% unemployed. **Per capita income:** $45,706; change (2008-09): −2.8%. **Avg. home:** $385,200; change (2008-10): −0.1%.

Mayor: Cheryl Cox, nonpartisan

History: Visited by Spanish in 1542; became part of Spanish land grant in 1795; came into the U.S. during the Mexican War in 1847; inc. 1911. WWII brought aircraft industry and growth.

Transportation: bus system, DART paratransit. **Communications:** see San Diego, CA. **Medical facilities:** 2 hosp. **Educational facilities:** 5 colleges; 65 pub. schools. **Further information:** Chula Vista Chamber of Commerce, 233 Fourth Ave., Chula Vista, CA 91910; www.chulavistachamber.org; www.chulavista.gov

Cincinnati, Ohio

Population: 296,943 (62). **Pop. density:** 3,810. **Pop. change (2000-10):** −10.4%. **Area:** 77.9 sq mi. **Employment:** 144,310 employed; 10.0% unemployed. **Per capita income:** $37,967; change (2008-09): −2.5%. **Avg. home:** $128,000; change (2008-10): −2.9%.

Mayor: Mark Mallory, nonpartisan

History: Founded 1788; named after the Society of Cincinnati, an organization of Revolutionary War officers; chartered as village 1802; inc. 1819.

Transportation: 1 intl., 2 muni. airports; 3 railroads; 2 bus systems. **Communications:** 1 daily newspaper; 10 TV, 31 radio stations. **Medical facilities:** 28 hosp.; Cincinnati Children's Hosp. Medical Center; VA hosp. **Educational facilities:** 4 univ., 12 colleges, 8 tech. and 2-year colleges; 65 pub. schools. **Further information:** Chamber of Commerce, 441 Vine St., Ste. 300, Cincinnati, OH 45202; www.cincinnatichamber.com; www.cincinnatioh. gov

Cleveland, Ohio

Population: 396,815 (45). **Pop. density:** 5,107. **Pop. change (2000-10):** −17.1%. **Area:** 77.7 sq mi. **Employment:** 160,778 employed; 11.4% unemployed. **Per capita income:** $39,451; change (2008-09): −2.3%. **Avg. home:** $114,500; change (2008-10): 5.5%.

Mayor: Frank G. Jackson, nonpartisan

History: Surveyed in 1796; given recognition as village 1815; inc. 1836; annexed Ohio City 1854.

Transportation: 1 intl., 2 muni. airports; rail service; rapid transit system; major port. **Communications:** 10 TV, 23 radio stations. **Medical facilities:** 14 hosp. **Educational facilities:** 8 univ. and colleges; 127 pub. schools. **Further information:** Greater Cleveland Partnership, The Highbee Building, 100 Public Sq., Ste. 210, Cleveland, OH 44113-2291; www.gcpartnership.com; www.city. cleveland.oh.us

Colorado Springs, Colorado

Population: 416,427 (41). **Pop. density:** 2,141. **Pop. change (2000-10):** 15.4%. **Area:** 194.5 sq mi. **Employment:** 193,891 employed; 9.4% unemployed. **Per capita income:** $38,401; change (2008-09): −0.3%. **Avg. home:** $195,500; change (2008-10): −4.9%.

Mayor: Steve Bach, nonpartisan

History: Founded 1871 at the foot of Pike's Peak; inc. 1872.

Transportation: 2 airports; 1 bus line. **Communications:** 8 TV, 19 radio stations. **Medical facilities:** 9 hosp.; 8 med. centers. **Educational facilities:** 14 univ., 11 colleges; 211 pub. schools. **Further information:** Chamber of Commerce, 6 S. Tejon St., Ste. 700, Colorado Springs, CO 80903; www.coloradospringschamber. org; www.springsgov.com

Columbus, Ohio

Population: 787,033 (15). **Pop. density:** 3,624. **Pop. change (2000-10):** 10.6%. **Area:** 217.2 sq mi. **Employment:** 386,883 employed; 8.6% unemployed. **Per capita income:** $37,999; change (2008-09): −1.7%. **Avg. home:** $136,400; change (2008-10): −2.1%.

Mayor: Michael B. Coleman, Democrat

History: First settlement 1797; laid out as new capital 1812 with current name; inc. 1834.

Transportation: 1 intl., 2 muni. airports, 2 airfields; 3 railroads; 3 intercity bus lines. **Communications:** 13 TV, 20 radio stations. **Medical facilities:** 17 hosp. **Educational facilities:** 11 univ. and colleges, 8 tech. and 2-year schools; 128 pub. schools. **Further information:** Greater Columbus Chamber of Commerce, 150 S. Front St., Ste. 200, Columbus, OH 43215; www.columbus.org; www. experiencecolumbus.org; www.columbus.gov

Corpus Christi, Texas

Population: 305,215 (60). **Pop. density:** 1,900. **Pop. change (2000-10):** 10.0%. **Area:** 160.6 sq mi. **Employment:** 140,871 employed; 7.3% unemployed. **Per capita income:** $36,558; change (2008-09): −2.1%. **Avg. home:** $135,100; change (2008-10): −2.9%.

Mayor: Joe Adame, nonpartisan

History: Settled 1839; inc. 1852. One of the largest U.S. ports.

Transportation: 1 intl. airport; 3 freight railroads; 2 bus lines, metro bus system. **Communications:** 7 TV, 30 radio stations. **Medical facilities:** 8 hosp. **Educational facilities:** 1 univ., 1 college; 60 pub. schools. **Further information:** Corpus Christi Regional Economic Development Corp., 800 N. Shoreline Blvd., Ste. 1300 South, Corpus Christi, TX 78401; www.ccredc.com; www.cctexas.com

Dallas, Texas

Population: 1,197,816 (9). **Pop. density:** 3,518. **Pop. change (2000-10):** 0.8%. **Area:** 340.5 sq mi. **Employment:** 546,264 employed; 8.8% unemployed. **Per capita income:** $41,764; change (2008-09): −4.4%. **Avg. home:** $143,800; change (2008-10): −1.4%.

Mayor: Mike Rawlings, nonpartisan

History: First settled 1841; platted 1846; inc. 1871. Developed as financial and commercial center of Southwest; headquarters of regional Federal Reserve Bank; major center for distribution and high-tech manufacturing.

Transportation: 1 intl., 1 natl., 1 muni., 1 corp./charter airport, 2 airfields; Amtrak; transit system. **Communications:** 11 TV, 19 radio stations. **Medical facilities:** 33 hosp. **Educational facilities:** 12 univ. and colleges, 3 community college campuses; 225 pub. schools. **Further information:** Greater Dallas Chamber, Resource Center, 700 N. Pearl St., Ste. 1200, Dallas, TX 75201; www. dallaschamber.org; www.dallascityhall.com

Denver, Colorado

Population: 600,158 (27). **Pop. density:** 3,923. **Pop. change (2000-10):** 8.2%. **Area:** 153.0 sq mi. **Employment:** 290,731 employed; 9.7% unemployed. **Per capita income:** $46,611; change (2008-09): −4.1%. **Avg. home:** $232,400; change (2008-10): 6.0%.

Mayor: Michael Hancock, nonpartisan

History: Settled 1858 by gold prospectors and miners; inc. 1861; became territorial capital 1867; growth spurred by gold and silver boom. Became financial, industrial, cultural center of Rocky Mt. region.

Transportation: 1 intl., 1 regional, 2 muni. airports; 5 rail freight lines, Amtrak; 1 bus line. **Communications:** 22 TV, 23 radio stations. **Medical facilities:** 15 hosp. **Educational facilities:** 15 4-year univ. and colleges, 8 2-year and community colleges; 151 pub. schools. **Further information:** Denver Metro Chamber of Commerce, 1445 Market St., Denver, CO 80202-1729; www. denverchamber.org; www.denvergov.org

Detroit, Michigan

Population: 713,777 (19). **Pop. density:** 5,144. **Pop. change (2000-10):** −25.0%. **Area:** 138.8 sq mi. **Employment:** 282,100 employed; 22.7% unemployed. **Per capita income:** $37,927; change (2008-09): −4.1%.

Mayor: Dave Bing, nonpartisan

History: Founded by French 1701; controlled by British 1760; acquired by U.S. 1796; destroyed by fire 1805; fought over during War of 1812; inc. 1815; capital of state 1837-47. Auto manufacturing began 1890.

Transportation: 1 intl., 2 muni. airports; 10 railroads (4 Class I); 2 pub. transit systems; major intl. port (in Wayne County). **Communications:** 11 TV, 23 radio stations. **Medical facilities:** 38 hosp. (in MSA). **Educational facilities:** 2 univ., 2 colleges, 1 community college; 130 pub. schools. **Further information:** Detroit Regional Chamber, One Woodward Ave., Ste. 1900, P.O. Box 33840, Detroit, MI 48232-0840; www.detroitchamber.com, www. detroitmi.gov

Durham, North Carolina

Population: 228,330 (86). **Pop. density:** 2,127. **Pop. change (2000-10):** 22.1%. **Area:** 107.4 sq mi. **Employment:** 109,736 employed; 7.3% unemployed. **Per capita income:** $41,008; change (2008-09): −1.2%. **Avg. home:** $177,900; change (2008-10): −1.5%.

Mayor: William V. Bell, nonpartisan

History: Inc. 1869. Trinity College moved to Durham in 1892, renamed Duke Univ. in 1924.

Transportation: 1 intl. airport; 1 train station; 2 area bus systems. **Communications:** 5 TV, 8 radio stations. **Medical facilities:** 5 hosp. **Educational facilities:** 2 univ., 1 community college, 1 nursing school; 52 pub. schools. **Further information:** Durham Convention and Visitors Bureau, 101 E. Morgan St., Durham, NC 27701-3333; www.durhamchamber.org; www.durham-nc.com; www.durhamnc.gov

El Paso, Texas

Population: 649,121 (20). **Pop. density:** 2,543. **Pop. change (2000-10):** 15.2%. **Area:** 255.2 sq mi. **Employment:** 247,099 employed; 8.7% unemployed. **Per capita income:** $29,381; change (2008-09): 1.8%. **Avg. home:** $134,300; change (2008-10): −2.3%.

Mayor: John Cook, nonpartisan

History: First settled 1598; inc. 1873; arrival of railroad, 1881, boosted city's population and industries.
Transportation: 1 intl. airport, 1 airfield; 2 rail providers; 4 intl. ports of entry. **Communications:** 9 TV, 22 radio stations. **Medical facilities:** 16 hosp. **Educational facilities:** 2 grad. and doctoral programs, 5 univ., 2 colleges; 92 pub. schools. **Further information:** Greater El Paso Chamber of Commerce, 10 Civic Center Plz., El Paso, TX 79901; www.elpaso.com; www.elpasotexas.gov

Fort Wayne, Indiana

Population: 253,691 (74). **Pop. density:** 2,293. **Pop. change (2000-10):** 23.3%. **Area:** 110.6 sq mi. **Employment:** 111,011 employed; 11.1% unemployed. **Per capita income:** $33,669; change (2008-09): −2.7%. **Avg. home:** $97,400; change (2008-10): 5.2%.
Mayor: Tom Henry, Democrat
History: French fort 1680; U.S. fort 1794; settled by 1832; inc. 1840 prior to Wabash-Erie Canal completion 1843.
Transportation: 1 intl. airport, 1 airfield; 3 railroads; 6 bus lines. **Communications:** 11 newspapers; 6 TV, 26 radio stations. **Medical facilities:** 9 hosp. **Educational facilities:** 8 univ., 5 colleges, 3 bus. schools; 53 pub. schools. **Further information:** Chamber of Commerce, 826 Ewing St., Fort Wayne, IN 46802-2182; www.fwchamber.org; www.cityoffortwayne.org

Fort Worth, Texas

Population: 741,206 (16). **Pop. density:** 2,181. **Pop. change (2000-10):** 38.6%. **Area:** 339.8 sq mi. **Employment:** 308,828 employed; 8.5% unemployed. **Per capita income:** $41,764; change (2008-09): −4.4%. **Avg. home:** $143,800; change (2008-10): −1.4%.
Mayor: Betsy Price, nonpartisan
History: Established as military post 1849; inc. 1873; oil discovered 1917.
Transportation: 1 intl., 2 muni., 1 industrial airport, 4 airfields; 4 major railroads, Amtrak; 1 transcontinental, 1 intrastate bus line, local bus service. **Communications:** 16 TV, 71 radio stations. **Medical facilities:** 15 hosp. **Educational facilities:** 6 univ. and colleges; 144 pub. schools. **Further information:** Fort Worth Chamber of Commerce, 777 Taylor St., Ste. 900, Fort Worth, TX 76102; www.fortworthchamber.com; www.fortworthgov.org

Fremont, California

Population: 214,089 (95). **Pop. density:** 2,764 **Pop. change (2000-10):** 5.2%. **Area:** 77.5 sq mi. **Employment:** 99,287 employed; 8.2% unemployed. **Per capita income:** $59,993; change (2008-09): −3.9%. **Avg. home:** $525,300; change (2008-10): −15.5%.
Mayor: Bob Wasserman, nonpartisan
History: Area first settled by Spanish 1769; inc. 1956 with consolidation of five communities.
Transportation: Bay Area Rapid Transit System (southern terminal), intracity bus line. **Communications:** 2 radio stations. **Medical facilities:** 2 hosp.; 2 major med. facilities; 18 clinics. **Educational facilities:** 1 community college; 51 pub. schools. **Further information:** Chamber of Commerce, 39488 Stevenson Pl., Ste. 100, Fremont, CA 94539; www.fremontbusiness.com; www.fremont.gov

Fresno, California

Population: 494,665 (34). **Pop. density:** 4,418. **Pop. change (2000-10):** 15.7%. **Area:** 112.0 sq mi. **Employment:** 193,696 employed; 15.8% unemployed. **Per capita income:** $30,646; change (2008-09): −1.5%.
Mayor: Ashley Swearengin, nonpartisan
History: Founded 1872; inc. 1885.
Transportation: 1 intl., 1 muni., 1 corp./charter airport; Amtrak; 1 bus line, intracity bus system. **Communications:** 16 TV, 26 radio stations. **Medical facilities:** 9 hosp. **Educational facilities:** 9 colleges; 88 pub. schools. **Further information:** Fresno/Clovis Convention and Visitors Bureau, 1550 E. Shaw Ave., Ste. 101, Fresno, CA 93710; www.playfresno.org; www.fresno.gov

Garland, Texas

Population: 226,876 (87). **Pop. density:** 3,974. **Pop. change (2000-10):** 5.1%. **Area:** 57.1 sq mi. **Employment:** 99,400 employed; 8.6% unemployed. **Per capita income:** $41,764; change (2008-09): −4.4%. **Avg. home:** $143,800; change (2008-10): −1.4%.
Mayor: Ronald Jones, nonpartisan
History: Settled 1850s; inc. 1891.
Transportation: 30 mins. from Dallas/Ft. Worth Intl. Airport; 2 railroads. **Communications:** 2 TV, 2 radio stations. **Medical facilities:** 2 hosp. **Educational facilities:** 3 univ., 2 commu-nity colleges; 67 pub. schools. **Further information:** Chamber of Commerce, 914 S. Garland Ave., Garland, TX 75040; www.garlandchamber.com; www.ci.garland.tx.us

Glendale, Arizona

Population: 226,721 (88). **Pop. density:** 3,780. **Pop. change (2000-10):** 3.6%. **Area:** 60.0 sq mi. **Employment:** 116,636 employed; 9.4% unemployed. **Per capita income:** $34,452; change (2008-09): −4.7%. **Avg. home:** $139,200; change (2008-10): −27.2%.
Mayor: Elaine M. Scruggs, nonpartisan
History: Est. 1892; inc. 1910.
Transportation: 1 muni. airport. **Communications:** 1 TV, 4 radio stations. **Medical facilities:** 4 hosp. **Educational facilities:** 12 insts. of higher education; 82 pub. schools. **Further information:** City of Glendale Marketing/Communications Dept., 5850 W. Glendale Ave., Glendale, AZ 85301; www.glendaleazchamber.org; www.glendaleaz.com

Greensboro, North Carolina

Population: 269,666 (69). **Pop. density:** 2,131. **Pop. change (2000-10):** 20.4%. **Area:** 126.5 sq mi. **Employment:** 115,929 employed; 10.3% unemployed. **Per capita income:** $34,948; change (2008-09): −2.0%. **Avg. home:** $129,800; change (2008-10): −10.7%.
Mayor: Bill Knight, nonpartisan
History: Settled 1749; site of Revolutionary War conflict 1781 between Generals Nathanael Greene and Cornwallis; inc. 1807. Origin of civil rights sit-in movement.
Transportation: 1 intl. airport, 2 airfields; 2 railroads; Trailways/Greyhound bus service. **Communications:** 3 TV, 10 radio stations. **Medical facilities:** 2 hosp. **Educational facilities:** 1 law school, 2 univ., 4 colleges; 94 pub. schools. **Further information:** Chamber of Commerce, 342 N. Elm St., Greensboro, NC 27401; www.greensboro.org; www.greensboro-nc.gov

Henderson, Nevada

Population: 257,729 (73). **Pop. density:** 2,392. **Pop. change (2000-10):** 47.0%. **Area:** 107.7 sq mi. **Employment:** 121,851 employed; 14.0% unemployed. **Per capita income:** $36,711; change (2008-09): −6.5%. **Avg. home:** $138,000; change (2008-10): −37.4%.
Mayor: Andy A. Hafen, nonpartisan
History: Early growth spurred by WWII magnesium mining; inc. 1953.
Transportation: 1 executive airport; public bus line. **Communications:** 2 TV, 8 radio stations. **Medical facilities:** 3 hosp. **Educational facilities:** 5 colleges, 2 voc. schools; 47 pub. schools. **Further information:** City of Henderson Public Information Office, 240 Water St., Henderson, NV 89015; www.hendersonchamber.com; www.cityofhenderson.com

Hialeah, Florida

Population: 224,669 (90). **Pop. density:** 10,474. **Pop. change (2000-10):** −0.8%. **Area:** 21.5 sq mi. **Employment:** 86,765 employed; 15.9% unemployed. **Per capita income:** $42,764; change (2008-09): −3.9%. **Avg. home:** $201,900; change (2008-10): −29.2%.
Mayor: Carlos Hernandez, nonpartisan
History: Founded 1917; inc. 1925. Industrial and residential city NW of Miami; site of Hialeah Park Horse Racing Track.
Transportation: 5 mi from Miami Intl. Airport; 2 rail freight lines, Amtrak; Metrorail, Metrobus systems; access to Port of Miami. **Communications:** 2 radio stations. **Medical facilities:** 3 hosp. **Educational facilities:** 8 univ. and colleges; 25 pub. schools, 39 priv. schools. **Further information:** Hialeah-Dade Development, Inc., 501 Palm Ave., Hialeah, FL 33010; www.hialeahchamber.org; www.hialeahfl.gov

Honolulu, Hawaii

Population: 337,256 (53). **Pop. density:** 5,573. **Pop. change (2000-10):** 8.8%. **Area:** 60.5 sq mi. **Employment:** 414,515 employed; 5.6% unemployed (CDP). **Per capita income:** $45,496; change (2008-09): −0.3%. **Avg. home:** $607,600; change (2008-10): −2.6%.
Mayor: Peter Carlisle, nonpartisan
History: Europeans entered harbor 1778; declared capital of kingdom by King Kamehameha III 1850. Pearl Harbor naval base attacked by Japanese Dec. 7, 1941.
Transportation: 1 intl. airport; 2 commercial harbors. **Communications:** 15 TV, 45 radio stations. **Medical facilities:** 6 hosp. **Educational facilities:** 7 univ., 4 community colleges; 52 pub. schools. **Further information:** Oahu Visitors Bureau, 2270 Kalakaua Ave #801, Honolulu, HI 96815; www.gohawaii.com/oahu/; www.honolulu.gov

Houston, Texas

Population: 2,099,451 (4). **Pop. density:** 3,501. **Pop. change (2000-10):** 7.5%. **Area:** 599.6 sq mi. **Employment:** 984,852 employed; 8.2% unemployed. **Per capita income:** $46,570; change (2008-09): −4.8%. **Avg. home:** $155,000; change (2008-10): 2.2%.

Mayor: Annise D. Parker, Democrat

History: Founded 1836; inc. 1837; capital of Rep. of Texas 1837-39; developed rapidly after completion of channel to Gulf of Mexico 1914. World center of oil, natural gas technology.

Transportation: 1 intl., 1 natl., 1 regional, 4 muni., 2 corp./charter airports, 6 airfields; 14 mainline railroads; major bus, rail transit system; major intl. port. **Communications:** 15 TV, 70 radio stations. **Medical facilities:** 120 hosp. **Educational facilities:** 6 med. schools, 11 univ., 10 community colleges, 27 spec. schools; 298 pub. schools. **Further information:** Greater Houston Partnership, 1200 Smith St., Ste. 700, Houston, TX 77002-4400; www.houston.org; www.houstontx.gov

Indianapolis, Indiana

Population: 829,718 (11). **Pop. density:** 2,296. **Pop. change (2000-10):** 4.8%. **Area:** 361.4 sq mi. **Employment:** 368,645 employed; 10.0% unemployed. **Per capita income:** $38,532; change (2008-09): −3.3%. **Avg. home:** $123,300; change (2008-10): 10.9%.

Mayor: Gregory A. Ballard, Republican

History: Settled 1820; became capital 1825.

Transportation: 1 intl., 4 muni., 1 corp./charter airport, 2 airfields; 5 railroads; 3 interstate bus lines. **Communications:** 14 TV, 21 radio stations. **Medical facilities:** 17 hosp. **Educational facilities:** 8 univ. and colleges; 80 pub. schools. **Further information:** Indianapolis Convention & Visitors Association, 200 S. Capitol Ave., Ste. 300, Indianapolis, IN 46225-1063; www.visitindy.com; www.indygov.org

Irvine, California

Population: 212,375 (96). **Pop. density:** 3,213. **Pop. change (2000-10):** 48.4%. **Area:** 66.1 sq mi. **Employment:** 75,997 employed; 7.2% unemployed. **Per capita income:** $42,784; change (2008-09): −3.8%. **Avg. home:** $316,700; change (2008-10): −21.2%.

Mayor: Sukhee Kang, nonpartisan

History: Univ. of CA–Irvine campus announced 1959; planned city developed around campus 1960s; inc. 1971.

Transportation: 1 regional airport; Amtrak; 1 intercounty bus line. **Communications:** 2 daily newspapers; 28 TV, 74 radio stations. **Medical facilities:** 3 hosp. **Educational facilities:** 10 univ. and college campuses; 39 pub. schools. **Further information:** Irvine Chamber of Commerce, 2485 McCabe Way, Ste. 150, Irvine, CA 92614; www.irvinechamber.com; www.destinationirvine.com; www.cityofirvine.org

Irving, Texas

Population: 216,290 (94). **Pop. density:** 3,227. **Pop. change (2000-10):** 12.9%. **Area:** 67.0 sq mi. **Employment:** 101,845 employed; 8.0% unemployed. **Per capita income:** $41,764; change (2008-09): −4.4%. **Avg. home:** $143,800; change (2008-10): −1.4%.

Mayor: Beth Van Duyne, nonpartisan

History: Founded 1903; inc. 1914; remained small until 1950s.

Transportation: 2 intl. airports; 1 RR express (train service); 1 bus service. **Communications:** 9 TV, 7 radio stations. **Medical facilities:** 2 hosp. **Educational facilities:** 1 univ., 2 colleges. **Further information:** Greater Irving-Las Colinas Chamber of Commerce, 5201 N. O'Connor Blvd., Ste. 100, Irving, TX 75039; www.irvingchamber.com; www.ci.irving.tx.us

Jacksonville, Florida

Population: 821,784 (12). **Pop. density:** 1,100. **Pop. change (2000-10):** 11.7%. **Area:** 747.0 sq mi. **Employment:** 370,531 employed; 11.5% unemployed. **Per capita income:** $39,376; change (2008-09): −2.9%. **Avg. home:** $137,700; change (2008-10): −21.1%.

Mayor: Alvin Brown, Democrat

History: Settled 1816 as Cowford; renamed after Andrew Jackson 1822; inc. 1832; rechartered 1851; scene of conflicts in Seminole and Civil Wars.

Transportation: 1 intl., 3 muni. airports; 3 railroads; 2 interstate bus lines; 1 seaport. **Communications:** 15 TV, 22 radio stations. **Medical facilities:** 9 hosp. **Educational facilities:** 2 univ., 6 colleges; 172 pub. schools, 114 priv. schools. **Further information:** Chamber of Commerce, 3 Independent Dr., Jacksonville, FL 32202; www.myjaxchamber.com; www.expandinjax.com; www.coj.net

Jersey City, New Jersey

Population: 247,597 (75). **Pop. density:** 16,736. **Pop. change (2000-10):** 3.1%. **Area:** 14.8 sq mi. **Employment:** 103,700 employed; 11.1% unemployed. **Per capita income:** $52,037; change (2008-09): −4.4%. **Avg. home:** $393,700; change (2008-10): −10.1%.

Mayor: Jerramiah Healy, nonpartisan

History: Site bought from Indians 1630; chartered as town by British 1668; scene of Revolutionary War conflict 1779; chartered under present name 1838. Important station on Underground Railroad.

Transportation: intercity bus, subway system; ferry service to Manhattan. **Communications:** 2 radio stations. **Medical facilities:** 2 hosp. **Educational facilities:** 1 univ., 3 colleges; 38 pub. schools. **Further information:** Hudson County Chamber of Commerce, 857 Bergen Ave., 3rd Fl., Jersey City, NJ 07306; www.hudsonchamber.org; www.cityofjerseycity.com

Kansas City, Missouri

Population: 459,787 (37). **Pop. density:** 1,460. **Pop. change (2000-10):** 4.1%. **Area:** 315.0 sq mi. **Employment:** 207,631 employed; 10.6% unemployed. **Per capita income:** $40,438; change (2008-09): −2.2%. **Avg. home:** $141,600; change (2008-10): −1.9%.

Mayor: Sly James, nonpartisan

History: Settled by 1838 at confluence of Missouri and Kansas Rivers; inc. 1850.

Transportation: 1 intl., 1 muni. airport; major rail center; more than 300 motor freight carriers; 1 barge line. **Communications:** 9 TV, 17 radio stations. **Medical facilities:** 19 hosp. **Educational facilities:** 22 univ. and colleges. **Further information:** Greater Kansas City Chamber of Commerce, 30 W. Pershing Rd., Ste. 301, Kansas City, MO 64108; www.kcchamber.com; www.kcmo.org

Laredo, Texas

Population: 236,091 (81). **Pop. density:** 2,655. **Pop. change (2000-10):** 33.7%. **Area:** 88.9 sq mi. **Employment:** 83,352 employed; 8.0% unemployed. **Per capita income:** $23,294; change (2008-09): −1.3%.

Mayor: Raul G. Salinas, nonpartisan

History: Founded by Spanish colonists in 1755; part of U.S. from 1848. Fast growth fueled by immigration; principal port of entry into Mexico.

Transportation: 1 intl. airport; 2 railroads; 3 interstate, 2 local bus lines. **Communications:** 8 TV, 9 radio stations. **Medical facilities:** 4 hosp. **Educational facilities:** 1 univ., 1 community college, 7 voc. training centers; 62 pub. schools, 29 priv. schools. **Further information:** Laredo Chamber of Commerce, P.O. Box 790, Laredo, TX 78042; www.laredochamber.com; www.cityoflaredo.com

Las Vegas, Nevada

Population: 583,756 (30). **Pop. density:** 4,298. **Pop. change (2000-10):** 22.0%. **Area:** 135.8 sq mi. **Employment:** 237,541 employed; 15.7% unemployed. **Per capita income:** $36,711; change (2008-09): −6.5%. **Avg. home:** $138,000; change (2008-10): −37.4%.

Mayor: Oscar B. Goodman, nonpartisan

History: Occupied by Mormons 1855-57; bought by railroad 1903; city of Las Vegas inc. 1911; gambling legalized 1931.

Transportation: 1 intl., 1 muni. airport; 1 railroad; monorail, bus system. **Communications:** 19 TV, 27 radio stations. **Medical facilities:** 21 hosp. **Educational facilities:** 1 univ., 2 state colleges; 277 pub. schools in area. **Further information:** Las Vegas Chamber of Commerce, 3720 Howard Hughes Pkwy., Las Vegas, NV 89169-0916; www.lvchamber.com; www.lasvegasnevada.gov

Lexington, Kentucky

Population: 295,803 (63). **Pop. density:** 1,043. **Pop. change (2000-10):** 13.5%. **Area:** 283.7 sq mi. **Employment:** 142,844 employed; 8.1% unemployed (county). **Per capita income:** $35,715; change (2008-09): −2.5%. **Avg. home:** $143,200; change (2008-10): −0.8%.

Mayor: Jim Gray, nonpartisan

History: Site founded and named in 1775 after site of the Revolutionary War's opening battle at Lexington, MA; settled 1779; chartered 1782; inc. 1832.

Transportation: 1 regional airport; 2 railroads; city buses. **Communications:** 5 TV, 9 radio stations. **Medical facilities:** 13 hosp. **Educational facilities:** 2 univ., 4 colleges; 53 pub. schools. **Further information:** Commerce Lexington, 330 E. Main St., Lexington, KY 40507; www.commercelexington.com; lexingtonky.com

Lincoln, Nebraska

Population: 258,379 (72). **Pop. density:** 2,899. **Pop. change (2000-10):** 14.5%. **Area:** 89.1 sq mi. **Employment:** 136,612 employed; 4.1% unemployed. **Per capita income:** $37,361; change (2008-09): -1.7%. **Avg. home:** $133,600; change (2008-10): -1.2%.

Mayor: Chris Beutler, nonpartisan

History: Originally called Lancaster; chosen state capital 1867, renamed after Abraham Lincoln; inc. 1869.

Transportation: 1 regional airport; 2 railroads, Amtrak; Greyhound bus service. **Communications:** 6 TV, 14 radio stations. **Medical facilities:** 8 hosp. **Educational facilities:** 3 univ., 3 voc. tech./bus. colleges; 55 pub. schools, 30 priv. schools, 3 focus programs. **Further information:** Chamber of Commerce, P.O. Box 83006, Lincoln, NE 68501-3006; www.lcoc.com; www.lincoln.org; lincoln.ne.gov

Long Beach, California

Population: 462,257 (36). **Pop. density:** 9,191. **Pop. change (2000-10):** 0.2%. **Area:** 50.3 sq mi. **Employment:** 204,162 employed; 13.9% unemployed. **Per capita income:** $42,784; change (2008-09): -3.8%. **Avg. home:** $316,700; change (2008-10): -21.2%.

Mayor: Bob Foster, nonpartisan

History: Settled as early as 1784 by Spanish; by 1884, present site developed on harbor; inc. 1888; oil discovered 1921.

Transportation: 1 natl. airport; 3 railroads; light rail service; 4 bus cos. with 40 bus lines; major intl. port. **Communications:** 1 TV, 3 radio stations. **Medical facilities:** 7 hosp. **Educational facilities:** 1 univ., 1 community college (2 campuses); 87 pub. schools in district. **Further information:** Long Beach City Hall, 333 W. Ocean Blvd., Long Beach, CA 90802; www.lbchamber. com; www.longbeach.gov

Los Angeles, California

Population: 3,792,921 (2). **Pop. density:** 8,092. **Pop. change (2000-10):** 2.6%. **Area:** 468.7 sq mi. **Employment:** 1,647,868 employed; 13.9% unemployed. **Per capita income:** $42,784; change (2008-09): -3.8%. **Avg. home:** $316,700; change (2008-10): -21.2%.

Mayor: Antonio Villaraigosa, nonpartisan

History: Founded by Spanish 1781; captured by U.S. 1846; inc. 1850; grew rapidly after coming of railroads, 1876 and 1885. Hollywood is a district of L.A.

Transportation: 1 intl., 1 muni. airport; 3 railroads; intracity bus, rail system; major freeway system. **Communications:** 20 TV, 32 radio stations. **Medical facilities:** 30 hosp. **Educational facilities:** 87 univ. and colleges; 1,858 pub. schools, 1,120 priv. schools. **Further information:** Los Angeles Area Chamber of Commerce, 350 S. Bixel St., Los Angeles, CA 90017; www.lachamber.org; www.lacity.org

Louisville, Kentucky

Population: 741,096 (17). **Pop. density:** 2,279. **Pop. change (2000-10):** 189.2%. **Area:** 325.3 sq mi. **Employment:** 326,802 employed; 10.6% unemployed (metro-govt. area balance). **Per capita income:** $37,688; change (2008-09): -1.4%. **Avg. home:** $134,600; change (2008-10): 1.8%.

Mayor: Greg Fischer, Democrat

History: Settled 1778; named for Louis XVI of France; inc. 1828; base for Union forces in Civil War.

Transportation: 1 intl., 1 regional airport; 1 terminal, 4 railroad trunk lines; Greyhound bus station, metro bus line; 5 barge lines. **Communications:** 9 TV, 19 radio stations. **Medical facilities:** 16 hosp. **Educational facilities:** 10 univ. and colleges, 32 bus. and voc. schools. **Further information:** Greater Louisville Inc., 614 W. Main St., Ste. 6000, Louisville, KY 40202; www.greaterlouisville. com; www.louisvilleky.gov

Lubbock, Texas

Population: 229,573 (84). **Pop. density:** 1,875. **Pop. change (2000-10):** 15.0%. **Area:** 122.4 sq mi. **Employment:** 113,456 employed; 6.0% unemployed. **Per capita income:** $34,079; change (2008-09): -0.3%.

Mayor: Tom Martin, nonpartisan

History: Settled 1879; laid out 1891; inc. 1909 through merger of two towns.

Transportation: 1 intl. airport, 1 airfield; 2 railroads; bus line. **Communications:** 16 TV, 18 radio stations. **Medical facilities:** 7 hosp. **Educational facilities:** 3 univ., 1 junior college; 51 pub. schools. **Further information:** Chamber of Commerce, 1500 Broadway, 1st Fl., Lubbock, TX 79401; www.lubbockchamber. com; www.ci.lubbock.tx.us

Madison, Wisconsin

Population: 233,209 (82). **Pop. density:** 3,037. **Pop. change (2000-10):** 12.1%. **Area:** 76.8 sq mi. **Employment:** 137,375 employed; 5.5% unemployed. **Per capita income:** $43,107; change (2008-09): -2.3%. **Avg. home:** $217,700; change (2008-10): -3.9%.

Mayor: Paul R. Soglin, nonpartisan

History: Settled 1832; selected as site for state capital, named after James Madison, 1836; chartered 1856.

Transportation: 1 natl. airport, 1 airfield; 3 freight rail lines; 1 intracity, 3 intercity bus systems. **Communications:** 6 TV, 15 radio stations. **Medical facilities:** 5 hosp. **Educational facilities:** 7 univ. and colleges, incl. main campus of Univ. of Wisconsin; 46 pub. schools. **Further information:** Greater Madison Chamber of Commerce, P.O. Box 71, Madison, WI 53701-0071; www. greatermadisonchamber.com; www.cityofmadison.com

Memphis, Tennessee

Population: 646,889 (21). **Pop. density:** 2,053. **Pop. change (2000-10):** -0.5%. **Area:** 315.1 sq mi. **Employment:** 271,753 employed; 10.9% unemployed. **Per capita income:** $37,623; change (2008-09): -2.7%. **Avg. home:** $120,200; change (2008-10): 0.8%.

Mayor: A. C. Wharton, nonpartisan

History: French, Spanish, and U.S. forts by 1797; settled by 1819; inc. as town 1826, as city 1840; surrendered charter to state 1879 after yellow fever epidemics; rechartered as city 1893.

Transportation: 1 intl. airport; 5 railroads; 1 bus system. **Communications:** 9 TV, 20 radio stations. **Medical facilities:** 15 hosp. **Educational facilities:** 17 univ. and colleges; 191 pub. schools. **Further information:** Memphis Regional Chamber, 22 N. Front St., 2nd Fl., Memphis, TN 38101; www.memphischamber.com; www.cityofmemphis.org

Mesa, Arizona

Population: 439,041 (38). **Pop. density:** 3,218. **Pop. change (2000-10):** 10.8%. **Area:** 136.5 sq mi. **Employment:** 212,816 employed; 8.3% unemployed. **Per capita income:** $34,452; change (2008-09): -4.7%. **Avg. home:** $139,200; change (2008-10): -27.2%.

Mayor: Scott Smith, nonpartisan

History: Founded by Mormons 1878; inc. 1883. Population boomed fivefold 1960-80.

Transportation: 1 muni. airport, 1 airfield; metro bus service. **Communications:** 3 TV, 4 radio stations. **Medical facilities:** 7 hosp. **Educational facilities:** 5 univ., 7 colleges; 82 pub. schools. **Further information:** Convention and Visitor's Bureau and Mesa Chamber of Commerce, 120 N. Center, Mesa, AZ 85201; www. visitmesa.com; www.mesachamber.org; www.mesaaz.gov

Miami, Florida

Population: 399,457 (44). **Pop. density:** 11,136. **Pop. change (2000-10):** 10.2%. **Area:** 35.9 sq mi. **Employment:** 169,478 employed; 13.1% unemployed. **Per capita income:** $42,764; change (2008-09): -3.9%. **Avg. home:** $201,900; change (2008-10): -29.2%.

Mayor: Tomás Regalado, nonpartisan

History: Site of fort 1836; settlement began 1870; inc. 1896. Modern city developed into financial and recreation center; land speculation in 1920s added to city's growth, as did Cuban, Central and South American, and Haitian immigration since 1960.

Transportation: 1 intl., 1 regional, 1 corp. airport, 2 airfields, 1 seaplane base; Amtrak; transit rail system; 2 bus lines; 65 truck lines; seaport. **Communications:** 23 TV, 21 radio stations. **Medical facilities:** 19 hosp. **Educational facilities:** 6 univ. and colleges. **Further information:** Greater Miami Chamber of Commerce, Omni Intl. Complex, 1601 Biscayne Blvd., Miami, FL 33132; www.greatermiami.com; www.miamigov.com

Milwaukee, Wisconsin

Population: 594,833 (28). **Pop. density:** 6,188. **Pop. change (2000-10):** -0.4%. **Area:** 96.1 sq mi. **Employment:** 243,600 employed; 11.5% unemployed. **Per capita income:** $42,303; change (2008-09): -1.6%. **Avg. home:** $205,900; change (2008-10): -3.0%.

Mayor: Tom Barrett, Democrat

History: Indian trading post by 1674; settlement began 1835; inc. 1848. Famous beer industry.

Transportation: 1 intl. airport, 1 airfield; 3 railroads; 4 bus lines; major port. **Communications:** 14 TV, 19 radio stations. **Medical facilities:** 17 hosp. **Educational facilities:** 7 univ. and colleges; 182 pub. schools. **Further information:** Visit Milwaukee, 648 N. Plankinton Ave., Ste. 425, Milwaukee, WI 53203-2917; www.visitmilwaukee.org; city.milwaukee.gov

Minneapolis, Minnesota

Population: 382,578 (48). **Pop. density:** 7,088. **Pop. change (2000-10):** 0%. **Area:** 54.0 sq mi. **Employment:** 200,754 employed; 6.9% unemployed. **Per capita income:** $45,811; change (2008-09): −4.0%. **Avg. home:** $170,600; change (2008-10): −15.5%.

Mayor: R. T. Rybak, Democrat

History: Site visited by French missionary Louis Hennepin 1680; included in area of military reservations 1819; inc. 1867.

Transportation: 1 intl., 2 regional, 1 muni. airport, 1 airfield; 5 railroads. **Communications:** 10 TV, 17 radio stations. **Medical facilities:** 7 hosp. **Educational facilities:** 10 univ. and colleges; 121 pub. schools, 28 priv. schools. **Further information:** City of Minneapolis Office of Pub. Affairs, 301M City Hall, 350 S. Fifth St., Minneapolis, MN 55415; www.minneapolischamber.org; www.minneapolis.org; www.ci.minneapolis.mn.us

Nashville, Tennessee

Population: 626,681 (22). **Pop. density:** 1,319. **Pop. change (2000-10):** 10.0%. **Area:** 475.1 sq mi. **Employment:** 299,882 employed; 8.8% unemployed (metro-govt. balance). **Per capita income:** $38,656; change (2008-09): −4.0%.

Mayor: Karl Dean, nonpartisan

History: Settled 1779; first chartered 1806; became permanent state capital 1843. Home of Grand Ole Opry.

Transportation: 1 intl. airport, 2 airfields; 1 railroad; bus line; transit system of buses, trolleys. **Communications:** 15 TV, 18 radio stations. **Medical facilities:** 14 hosp. **Educational facilities:** 17 univ. and colleges; 130 pub. schools. **Further information:** Chamber of Commerce, 211 Commerce St., Ste. 100, Nashville, TN 37201; www.nashvillechamber.com; www.nashville.gov

Newark, New Jersey

Population: 277,140 (68). **Pop. density:** 11,458. **Pop. change (2000-10):** 1.3%. **Area:** 24.2 sq mi. **Employment:** 91,853 employed; 15.0% unemployed. **Per capita income:** $52,037; change (2008-09): −4.4%. **Avg. home:** $393,700; change (2008-10): −10.1%.

Mayor: Cory A. Booker, nonpartisan

History: Settled by Puritans 1666; used as supply base by Washington 1776; inc. as town 1833, as city 1836.

Transportation: 1 intl. airport; 4 railroads; subway, bus system; 1 intl. seaport. **Communications:** 1 daily newspaper; 3 TV, 5 radio stations. **Medical facilities:** 6 hosp. **Educational facilities:** 5 univ. and colleges; 2 voc. schools; 71 pub. schools, 40 priv. schools. **Further information:** Newark Public Information Office, City of Newark, 920 Broad St., Newark, NJ 07102; www.rbp.org; www.ci.newark.nj.us

New Orleans, Louisiana

Population: 343,829 (52). **Pop. density:** 2,029. **Pop. change (2000-10):** −29.1%. **Area:** 169.4 sq mi. **Employment:** 135,521 employed; 8.8% unemployed. **Per capita income:** $42,705; change (2008-09): −3.9%. **Avg. home:** $159,700; change (2008-10): −0.5%.

Mayor: Mitchell J. Landrieu, Democrat

History: Founded by French 1718; became major seaport on Mississippi R.; acquired by U.S. as part of Louisiana Purchase 1803; inc. 1805. Americans defeated British forces at Battle of New Orleans in 1815.

Transportation: 1 intl., 1 regional airport; major railroad center; streetcar, bus lines. **Communications:** 15 TV, 43 radio stations. **Medical facilities:** 13 hosp. **Educational facilities:** 6 univ., 4 colleges. **Further information:** New Orleans Metropolitan Convention & Visitors Bureau, 2020 St. Charles Ave., New Orleans, LA 70130; www.neworleanschamber.org; www.neworleanscvb.com; www.cityofno.com

New York, New York

Population: 8,175,133 (1). **Pop. density:** 27,012. **Pop. change (2000-10):** 2.1%. **Area:** 302.6 sq mi. **Employment:** 3,624,942 employed; 9.5% unemployed. **Per capita income:** $52,037; change (2008-09): −4.4%. **Avg. home:** $393,700; change (2008-10): −10.1%.

Mayor: Michael R. Bloomberg, Republican

History: Trading post est. 1624; British took control from Dutch 1664, named city New York; briefly U.S. capital; under new charter, 1898, city expanded to include five boroughs: Bronx, Brooklyn, Queens, and Staten Island, as well as Manhattan. Sept. 11, 2001, terrorist attacks destroyed World Trade Center, killed more than 2,750.

Transportation: 3 intl. airports serve area, 2 seaplane bases; 2 rail terminals; subway network that incl. 26 routes, 244 bus routes; ferry system; 4 underwater tunnels. **Communications:** 13 TV, 38 radio stations. **Medical facilities:** 70 hosp.; 6 academic med. centers. **Educational facilities:** 54 univ. and colleges; 1,198 pub. schools. **Further information:** Convention and Visitors Bureau, 810 Seventh Ave., New York, NY 10019; www.manhattancc.org; www.nycvisit.com; www.nyc.gov

Norfolk, Virginia

Population: 242,803 (78). **Pop. density:** 4,486. **Pop. change (2000-10):** 3.6%. **Area:** 54.1 sq mi. **Employment:** 90,948 employed; 9.2% unemployed. **Per capita income:** $39,518; change (2008-09): −0.7%. **Avg. home:** $205,000; change (2008-10): −6.8%.

Mayor: Paul D. Fraim, nonpartisan

History: Founded 1682; burned by colonists to prevent capture by British during Revolutionary War; rebuilt and inc. as town 1805, as city 1845. Site of world's largest naval base; major East Coast commercial port and cruise terminal.

Transportation: 1 intl., 1 corp./charter airport, 1 airfield; 2 railroads, Amtrak; 1 light rail system; bus system, free downtown shuttle. **Communications:** 5 TV, 15 radio stations. **Medical facilities:** 8 hosp. **Educational facilities:** 1 med. school, 2 univ., 2 colleges; 59 pub. schools. **Further information:** VisitNorfolk, 232 E. Main St., Norfolk, VA 23510; www.visitnorfolktoday.com; www.norfolk.gov

North Las Vegas, Nevada

Population: 216,961 (93). **Pop. density:** 2,141. **Pop. change (2000-10):** 87.9%. **Area:** 101.4 sq mi. **Employment:** 83,027 employed; 16.9% unemployed. **Per capita income:** $36,711; change (2008-09): −6.5%. **Avg. home:** $138,000; change (2008-10): −37.4%.

Mayor: Shari L. Buck, nonpartisan

History: Inc. 1946.

Transportation: nr. 1 intl. airport, 1 regional airport. **Communications:** 15 TV, 45 radio stations. **Medical facilities:** 1 hosp. **Educational facilities:** 39 pub. schools. **Further information:** North Las Vegas Chamber of Commerce, 3345 W. Craig Rd., Ste. B, North Las Vegas, NV 89032; www.northlasvegaschamber.com; www.cityofnorthlasvegas.com

Oakland, California

Population: 390,724 (47). **Pop. density:** 7,004. **Pop. change (2000-10):** −2.2%. **Area:** 55.8 sq mi. **Employment:** 168,794 employed; 16.9% unemployed. **Per capita income:** $59,993; change (2008-09): −3.9%. **Avg. home:** $525,300; change (2008-10): −15.5%.

Mayor: Jean Quan, nonpartisan

History: Area settled by Spanish 1820; inc. 1854.

Transportation: 1 intl. airport; western terminus for 2 railroads; underground, 75-mi underwater subway. **Communications:** 1 TV, 3 radio stations. **Medical facilities:** 4 hosp. **Educational facilities:** 12 East Bay univ. and colleges; 81 pub. schools. **Further information:** Oakland Metropolitan Chamber of Commerce, 475 14th St., Oakland, CA 94612-1903; www.oaklandchamber.com; www.oaklandnet.com

Oklahoma City, Oklahoma

Population: 579,999 (31). **Pop. density:** 956. **Pop. change (2000-10):** 14.6%. **Area:** 606.4 sq mi. **Employment:** 238,880 employed; 6.5% unemployed. **Per capita income:** $38,742; change (2008-09): −3.1%. **Avg. home:** $145,700; change (2008-10): 13.7%.

Mayor: Mick Cornett, nonpartisan

History: Settled during land rush in Midwest 1889; inc. 1890; became capital 1910; oil discovered 1928. Bomb in 1995 destroyed federal office bldg., killed 168 people.

Transportation: 1 military, 1 intl., 1 regional airport, 3 airfields; 3 railroads; pub. transit system; 1 major bus line. **Communications:** 15 TV, 32 radio stations. **Medical facilities:** 21 hosp. **Educational facilities:** 18 univ. and colleges; 157 pub., 32 priv. schools. **Further information:** Greater Oklahoma City Chamber of Commerce, Economic Development Division, 123 Park Ave., Oklahoma City, OK 73102; www.okccvb.org; www.greateroklahomacity.com; www.okc.gov

Omaha, Nebraska

Population: 408,958 (42). **Pop. density:** 3,218. **Pop. change (2000-10):** 4.9%. **Area:** 127.1 sq mi. **Employment:** 225,906 employed; 4.9% unemployed. **Per capita income:** $42,982; change (2008-09): −2.3%. **Avg. home:** $137,300; change (2008-10): 1.6%.

Mayor: Jim Suttle, nonpartisan

History: Founded 1854; inc. 1857. Large food-processing, telecommunications, information-processing center.

Transportation: 1 natl. airport, 1 airfield; 3 major railroads; inter-city bus line. **Communications:** 10 TV, 17 radio stations. **Medical facilities:** 12 hosp. **Educational facilities:** 5 univ., 6 colleges; 243 pub. schools, 78 priv. schools. **Further information:** Greater Omaha Chamber of Commerce, 1301 Harney St., Omaha, NE 68102; www.omahachamber.org; www.cityofomaha.org

Orlando, Florida

Population: 238,300 (79). **Pop. density:** 2,327. **Pop. change (2000-10):** 28.2%. **Area:** 102.4 sq mi. **Employment:** 121,046 employed; 11.1% unemployed. **Per capita income:** $35,279; change (2008-09): −3.7%. **Avg. home:** $134,700; change (2008-10): −35.5%.

Mayor: Buddy Dyer, nonpartisan

History: Ft. Gatlin built just south of present-day Orlando in 1838; name changed from Jernigan to Orlando 1856; inc. 1875. Walt Disney World opened in 1971.

Transportation: 2 intl., 1 regional, 1 corp./charter airport; 2 bus lines. **Communications:** 18 TV, 11 radio stations. **Medical facilities:** 3 hosp. **Educational facilities:** 5 univ. and colleges: 4 tech. schools; 153 pub. schools. **Further Information:** Orlando/Orange County Convention and Visitors Bureau, 6700 Forum Dr., Ste. 100, Orlando, FL 32821-8087; www.orlando.org; www.orlandoinfo.com; www.ci.orlando.fl.us

Philadelphia, Pennsylvania

Population: 1,526,006 (5). **Pop. density:** 11,380. **Pop. change (2000-10):** 0.6%. **Area:** 134.1 sq mi. **Employment:** 577,011 employed; 10.9% unemployed. **Per capita income:** $46,075; change (2008-09): −1.3%. **Avg. home:** $214,900; change (2008-10): −7.1%.

Mayor: Michael A. Nutter, Democrat

History: First settled by Swedes 1638; Swedes surrendered to Dutch 1654; settled by English and Scottish Quakers 1678; named Philadelphia 1682; chartered 1701; Continental Congresses convened 1774, 1775; Declaration of Independence signed here 1776; natl. capital 1790-1800; state capital 1683-1799.

Transportation: 1 intl., 2 muni. airports; 3 railroads; rail commuter, subway, El, bus, and streetcar system; major fresh water ports. **Communications:** 4 major daily newspapers; 12 TV, 42 radio stations. **Medical facilities:** 39 hosp. **Educational facilities:** 29 univ. and colleges. **Further information:** Greater Philadelphia Chamber of Commerce, Business Information Center, 200 S. Broad St., Ste. 700, Philadelphia PA 19102; www.philachamber.com; www.phila.gov

Phoenix, Arizona

Population: 1,445,632 (6). **Pop. density:** 2,798. **Pop. change (2000-10):** 9.4%. **Area:** 516.7 sq mi. **Employment:** 716,910 employed; 10.6% unemployed. **Per capita income:** $34,452; change (2008-09): −4.7%. **Avg. home:** $139,200; change (2008-10): −27.2%.

Mayor: Phil Gordon, nonpartisan

History: Founded 1867; inc. 1881; became territorial capital 1889.

Transportation: 1 intl., 2 muni. airports; 2 transcontinental, 10 intrastate railroads; pub. transit system; transcontinental bus line. **Communications:** 22 TV, 22 radio stations. **Medical facilities:** 24 hosp. **Educational facilities:** 36 insts. of higher learning; 380 pub. schools, 98 charter schools. **Further information:** Greater Phoenix Chamber of Commerce, 201 N. Central Ave., 27th Fl., Phoenix, AZ 85004; www.phoenixchamber.com; www.phoenix.gov

Pittsburgh, Pennsylvania

Population: 305,704 (59). **Pop. density:** 5,521. **Pop. change (2000-10):** −8.6%. **Area:** 55.4 sq mi. **Employment:** 140,386

employed; 8.3% unemployed. **Per capita income:** $42,298; change (2008-09): −0.6%.

Mayor: Luke Ravenstahl, Democrat

History: Settled around Ft. Pitt 1758; inc. 1816; became an inland port; by Civil War, already a center for iron production.

Transportation: 1 intl., 1 regional airport; 22 railroads; 102 light rail and intracity pub. transit bus routes, 2 inner city bus lines. **Communications:** 10 TV, 18 radio stations. **Medical facilities:** 22 hosp. **Educational facilities:** 8 univ., 3 colleges; 64 pub. schools. **Further information:** VisitPittsburgh, 120 Fifth Ave., Fifth Avenue Place, Ste. 2800, Pittsburgh, PA 15222; Pittsburgh Regional Alliance, 11 Stanwix St., 17th Fl., Pittsburgh, PA 15222; www.visitpittsburgh.com; www.pittsburghregion.org; www.pghgov.com

Plano, Texas

Population: 259,841 (71). **Pop. density:** 3,630. **Pop. change (2000-10):** 17.0%. **Area:** 71.6 sq mi. **Employment:** 136,327 employed; 7.2% unemployed. **Per capita income:** $41,764; change (2008-09): −4.4%. **Avg. home:** $143,800; change (2008-10): −1.4%.

Mayor: Phil Dyer, nonpartisan

History: Settled 1846; inc. 1873.

Transportation: 2 DART light rail stations, DART bus line. **Communications:** 1 TV, 2 radio stations. **Medical facilities:** 7 hosp. **Educational facilities:** 5 insts. of higher learning; 68 pub. schools. **Further information:** City of Plano Public Information Dept., 1520 K Ave., Ste. 320, Plano, TX 75074; Plano Chamber of Commerce, 1200 E. 15th St., Plano, TX 75074; www.planochamber.org; www.plano.gov

Portland, Oregon

Population: 583,776 (29). **Pop. density:** 4,375. **Pop. change (2000-10):** 10.3%. **Area:** 133.4 sq mi. **Employment:** 279,429 employed; 10.1% unemployed. **Per capita income:** $39,206; change (2008-09): −2.9%. **Avg. home:** $237,300; change (2008-10): −15.3%.

Mayor: Sam Adams, nonpartisan

History: Settled by pioneers 1845; developed as trading center, aided by California Gold Rush 1849; city chartered 1851.

Transportation: 1 intl. airport; 2 major rail freight lines, Amtrak; mass transit bus, light rail, and streetcar system; marine port. **Communications:** 11 TV, 25 radio stations. **Medical facilities:** 8 hosp. **Educational facilities:** 25 univ. and colleges, 1 community college. **Further information:** Portland Business Alliance, 200 SW Market St., Ste. 1770, Portland, OR 97201; www.portlandalliance.com; www.portlandonline.com

Raleigh, North Carolina

Population: 403,892 (43). **Pop. density:** 2,826. **Pop. change (2000-10):** 46.3%. **Area:** 142.9 sq mi. **Employment:** 192,471 employed; 7.6% unemployed. **Per capita income:** $38,007; change (2008-09): −4.3%. **Avg. home:** $217,600; change (2008-10): −2.6%.

Mayor: Charles Meeker, nonpartisan

History: Named after Sir Walter Raleigh; site chosen for capital 1788; laid out 1792; inc. 1795; occupied by Union Gen. William Sherman 1865.

Transportation: 1 intl. airport, 1 airfield; 3 railroads; 2 bus lines. **Communications:** 8 TV, 13 radio stations. **Medical facilities:** 7 hosp. **Educational facilities:** 6 univ. and colleges, 1 community college; 140 pub. schools (county). **Further information:** Chamber of Commerce, 800 S. Salisbury St., Raleigh, NC 27602; www.raleigh-wake.org; www.raleighchamber.org, www.raleighnc.gov

Reno, Nevada

Population: 225,221 (89). **Pop. density:** 2,186. **Pop. change (2000-10):** 24.8%. **Area:** 103.0 sq mi. **Employment:** 99,231 employed; 14.2% unemployed. **Per capita income:** $42,390; change (2008-09): −5.7%. **Avg. home:** $179,500; change (2008-10): −30.7%.

Mayor: Robert Cashell, nonpartisan

History: Founded 1857; originally named Lakes Crossing; name changed to Reno, after a Union Civil War general, 1868, with arrival of transcontinental railroad.

Transportation: 1 intl. airport, 1 airfield; Union Pacific Railroad, Amtrak; local, natl. bus lines. **Communications:** 11 TV, 14 radio stations. **Medical facilities:** 8 hosp. **Educational facilities:** 1 univ., 1 community college; 98 pub. schools. **Further information:** Reno Sparks Chamber of Commerce, 449 S. Virginia St., 2nd Fl., Reno, NV 89501; www.renosparkschamber.org; www.reno.gov

Riverside, California

Population: 303,871 (61). **Pop. density:** 3,745. **Pop. change (2000-10):** 19.1%. **Area:** 81.1 sq mi. **Employment:** 136,928 employed; 14.8% unemployed. **Per capita income:** $29,680; change (2008-09): -2.8%. **Avg. home:** $183,000; change (2008-10): -21.9%.

Mayor: Ronald O. Loveridge, nonpartisan

History: Founded 1870; inc. 1886. Known for its citrus industry; home of the parent navel orange tree, historic Mission Inn resort.

Transportation: nr. 1 intl. airport, 1 muni. airport; rail freight lines, commuter line; trolley, bus system; interstate freeways. **Communications:** 3 TV, 7 radio stations. **Medical facilities:** 3 hosp. **Educational facilities:** 1 law school, 3 univ., 1 community college. **Further information:** Chamber of Commerce, 3985 University Ave., Riverside, CA 92501; www.riverside-chamber.com; www.riversideca.gov

Rochester, New York

Population: 210,565 (98). **Pop. density:** 5,885. **Pop. change (2000-10):** -4.2%. **Area:** 35.8 sq mi. **Employment:** 84,355 employed; 10.6% unemployed. **Per capita income:** $39,036; change (2008-09): -0.9%. **Avg. home:** $118,900; change (2008-10): 1.6%.

Mayor: Thomas S. Richards, Democrat

History: First permanent settlement 1812; inc. as village 1817, as city 1834; developed as Erie Canal town.

Transportation: 1 intl. airport; Amtrak; intracity transit service; 2 bus lines; port. **Communications:** 10 TV, 17 radio stations. **Medical facilities:** 5 hosp. **Educational facilities:** 11 colleges, 3 community colleges. **Further information:** Rochester Business Alliance, 150 State St., Ste. 400, Rochester, NY 14614; www.rochesterbusinessalliance.com; www.cityofrochester.gov

Sacramento, California

Population: 466,488 (35). **Pop. density:** 4,764. **Pop. change (2000-10):** 14.6%. **Area:** 97.9 sq mi. **Employment:** 182,872 employed; 14.9% unemployed. **Per capita income:** $40,306; change (2008-09): -2.5%. **Avg. home:** $183,600; change (2008-10): -15.3%.

Mayor: Kevin Johnson, nonpartisan

History: Settled 1839; important trading center during California Gold Rush 1840s; became state capital 1854.

Transportation: 1 intl., 2 muni., 1 corp./charter airport; 2 mainline transcontinental rail carriers; bus, light rail system; port. **Communications:** 15 TV, 21 radio stations. **Medical facilities:** 10 hosp. **Educational facilities:** 7 univ. and colleges, 5 community colleges; 81 pub. schools. **Further information:** Sacramento Metropolitan Chamber of Commerce, One Capitol Mall, Ste. 300, Sacramento, CA 95814; www.metrochamber.org; www.cityofsacramento.org

St. Louis, Missouri

Population: 319,294 (58). **Pop. density:** 5,157. **Pop. change (2000-10):** -8.3%. **Area:** 61.9 sq mi. **Employment:** 138,966 employed; 12.3% unemployed. **Per capita income:** $40,728; change (2008-09): -3.6%. **Avg. home:** $131,100; change (2008-10): -1.6%.

Mayor: Francis Slay, Democrat

History: Founded 1764 as fur trading post by French; acquired by U.S. 1803; chartered as city 1822; became independent city 1876. Lies on Mississippi R., near confluence with Missouri R.

Transportation: 1 intl., 1 muni. airport, 1 airfield (outside city limits); 3rd largest rail center, 6 railroad trunk lines; bus, light rail; 550 motor freight carriers; 32 barge lines, 2nd largest inland port in nation. **Communications:** 6 TV, 24 radio stations. **Medical facilities:** 15 hosp. **Educational facilities:** 3 univ., 7 colleges and seminaries; 106 pub. schools, 40 parochial schools, 6 magnet/charter high schools. **Further information:** St. Louis Regional Chamber and Growth Assn., 1 Metropolitan Sq., Ste. 1300, St. Louis, MO 63102; www.stlrcga.org; www.explorestlouis.com; www.stlouis-mo.gov

St. Paul, Minnesota

Population: 285,068 (67). **Pop. density:** 5,484. **Pop. change (2000-10):** -0.7%. **Area:** 52.0 sq mi. **Employment:** 133,143 employed; 7.7% unemployed. **Per capita income:** $45,811; change (2008-09): -4.0%. **Avg. home:** $170,600; change (2008-10): -15.5%.

Mayor: Chris Coleman, nonpartisan

History: Founded in early 1840s as Pig's Eye Landing; became capital of Minnesota territory 1849; chartered as St. Paul 1854.

Transportation: 1 intl., 2 muni. airports; 6 major rail lines; pub. transit system; 2 interstate bus lines. **Communications:** 7 TV, 2 radio stations. **Medical facilities:** 7 hosp. **Educational facilities:** 3 law schools, 5 univ., 5 colleges, 1 art and design college, 1 tech. school; 65 pub. schools, 39 priv. schools. **Further information:** St. Paul Area Chamber of Commerce, 401 N. Robert St., Ste. 150, St. Paul, MN 55101; www.saintpaulchamber.com; www.stpaul.gov

St. Petersburg, Florida

Population: 244,769 (76). **Pop. density:** 3,964. **Pop. change (2000-10):** -1.4%. **Area:** 61.7 sq mi. **Employment:** 108,029 employed; 11.7% unemployed. **Per capita income:** $37,632; change (2008-09): -2.1%. **Avg. home:** $134,200; change (2008-10): -22.4%.

Mayor: Bill Foster, nonpartisan

History: Founded 1888; inc. 1903. Site of Salvador Dali Museum.

Transportation: 1 intl., 1 regional airport; Amtrak bus connection; county-wide pub. bus system, downtown "Looper" bus service; largest muni. marina in Florida, 1 cruise port. **Communications:** 2 daily newspapers; 1 radio station. **Medical facilities:** 8 hosp. **Educational facilities:** 1 law school; 1 univ., 1 college; 41 pub., 3 alternative/voc., 100 priv. schools. **Further information:** St. Petersburg Area Chamber of Commerce, 100 Second Ave. N., Ste. 150, St. Petersburg, FL 33701; www.stpete.com; www.stpete.org

San Antonio, Texas

Population: 1,327,407 (7). **Pop. density:** 2,880. **Pop. change (2000-10):** 16.0%. **Area:** 460.9 sq mi. **Employment:** 600,988 employed; 7.0% unemployed. **Per capita income:** $36,285; change (2008-09): -0.7%. **Avg. home:** $151,000; change (2008-10): -1.2%.

Mayor: Julián Castro, nonpartisan

History: First Spanish garrison 1718; Battle of the Alamo 1836; city subsequently captured by Texans; inc. 1837; first town meeting in Texas took place here in 1845.

Transportation: 1 intl., 1 muni. airport, 6 airfields; 2 railroads; pub. transit system; 3 bus lines. **Communications:** 16 TV, 66 radio stations. **Medical facilities:** 42 hosp. **Educational facilities:** 18 univ. and colleges; 16 pub. school districts. **Further information:** The Greater San Antonio Chamber of Commerce, 602 E. Commerce St., San Antonio, TX 78205; www.sachamber.org; www.sanantonio.gov

San Bernardino, California

Population: 209,924 (99). **Pop. density:** 3,546. **Pop. change (2000-10):** 13.2%. **Area:** 59.2 sq mi. **Employment:** 68,879 employed; 18.9% unemployed. **Per capita income:** $29,680; change (2008-09): -2.8%. **Avg. home:** $183,000; change (2008-10): -21.9%.

Mayor: Patrick J. Morris, nonpartisan

History: Named by Spanish Franciscan missionaries 1810; major Mormon settlement in the 1850s, later recalled to Utah; inc. 1854. Population grew in 1860s when gold was discovered nearby; later became a transportation hub.

Transportation: 1 intl. airport; commuter rail; local bus lines. **Communications:** 5 TV, 9 radio stations. **Medical facilities:** 3 hosp. **Educational facilities:** 3 univ.; 66 pub. schools. **Further information:** San Bernardino Convention & Visitors Bureau, 1955 Hunts Ln., Ste. 102, San Bernardino, CA 92408; www.san-bernardino.org; www.ci.san-bernardino.ca.us

San Diego, California

Population: 1,307,402 (8). **Pop. density:** 4,020. **Pop. change (2000-10):** 6.9%. **Area:** 325.2 sq mi. **Employment:** 622,247 employed; 10.5% unemployed. **Per capita income:** $45,706; change (2008-09): -2.8%. **Avg. home:** $385,200; change (2008-10): -0.1%.

Mayor: Jerry Sanders, nonpartisan

History: Claimed by Spanish 1542; first mission est. 1769; scene of conflict during Mexican-American War 1846; inc. 1850.

Transportation: 1 intl., 2 muni. airports; 1 railroad; bus, trolley system; major freeway system. **Communications:** 13 TV, 23 radio stations. **Medical facilities:** 15 hosp. **Educational facilities:** 25 univ. and colleges; 177 pub. schools. **Further information:** San Diego Regional Chamber of Commerce, 402 W. Broadway, Ste. 1000, San Diego, CA 92101; www.sdchamber.org; www.sandiego.gov

San Francisco, California

Population: 805,235 (13). **Pop. density:** 17,179. **Pop. change (2000-10):** 3.7%. **Area:** 46.9 sq mi. **Employment:** 414,410 employed; 9.5% unemployed. **Per capita income:** $59,993; change (2008-09): -3.9%. **Avg. home:** $525,300; change (2008-10): -15.5%.

Mayor: Edwin M. Lee, nonpartisan

History: Nearby Farallon Islands sighted by Spanish 1542; city settled by 1776; claimed by U.S. 1846; became major city during California Gold Rush 1849; inc. 1850. Devastated by earthquake 1906.

Transportation: 1 intl. airport; intracity railway system, 2 railway transit systems; bus service; ferry system; 1 underwater tunnel. Communications: 13 TV, 30 radio stations. Medical facilities: 5 hosp. Educational facilities: 18 univ. and colleges; 140 pub. schools, 89 priv. schools. Further information: San Francisco Visitors Information Center, 900 Market St., San Francisco, CA 94102; www.sfchamber.com; www.onlyinsanfrancisco.com; www.sfgov.org

San Jose, California

Population: 945,942 (10). Pop. density: 5,359. Pop. change (2000-10): 5.7%. Area: 176.5 sq mi. Employment: 403,257 employed; 12.4% unemployed. Per capita income: $55,169; change (2008-09): –5.5%. Avg. home: $602,400; change (2008-10): –9.8%.

Mayor: Chuck Reed, nonpartisan

History: Founded by Spanish 1777, between San Francisco and Monterey; state capital 1849-51; inc. 1850.

Transportation: 1 intl., 1 muni. airport; 2 railroads; light rail, bus system. Communications: 5 TV, 10 radio stations. Medical facilities: 5 hosp. Educational facilities: 6 univ. and colleges. Further information: San Jose Convention & Visitors Bureau, 408 Almaden Blvd., San Jose, CA 95110; www.sanjose.org; www.sanjoseca.gov

Santa Ana, California

Population: 324,528 (57). Pop. density: 11,901. Pop. change (2000-10): –4.0%. Area: 27.3 sq mi. Employment: 136,525 employed; 15.0% unemployed. Per capita income: $42,784; change (2008-09): –3.8%. Avg. home: $316,700; change (2008-10): –21.2%.

Mayor: Miguel Pulido, nonpartisan

History: Founded 1769; inc. 1869.

Transportation: 1 natl. airport; Amtrak; 5 major freeways incl. main Los Angeles-San Diego artery. Communications: 2 TV, 3 radio stations. Medical facilities: 3 hosp. Educational facilities: 1 community college. Further information: Santa Ana Chamber of Commerce, 2020 N. Broadway, #1, Santa Ana, CA 92706; www.santaanachamber.com; www.ci.santa-ana.ca.us

Scottsdale, Arizona

Population: 217,385 (92). Pop. density: 1,182. Pop. change (2000-10): 7.2%. Area: 183.9 sq mi. Employment: 119,501 employed; 6.8% unemployed. Per capita income: $34,452; change (2008-09): –4.7%. Avg. home: $139,200; change (2008-10): –27.2%.

Mayor: W. J. Lane, nonpartisan

History: Founded 1888 by Army Chaplain Winfield Scott; inc. 1951; slogan "West's Most Western Town" adopted same year.

Transportation: 1 muni. airport; regional bus, local trolley, taxi system. Communications: 5 radio stations. Medical facilities: 7 hosp. Educational facilities: 1 univ. nearby, 1 community college; 3 unified school districts. Further information: Scottsdale Convention and Visitors Bureau, Galleria Corporate Center, 4343 N. Scottsdale Rd., Ste. 170, Scottsdale, AZ 85251; www.scottsdalecvb.com; www.scottsdalechamber.com; www.scottsdaleaz.gov

Seattle, Washington

Population: 608,660 (25). Pop. density: 7,251. Pop. change (2000-10): 8.0%. Area: 83.9 sq mi. Employment: 348,146 employed; 7.8% unemployed. Per capita income: $50,378; change (2008-09): –2.4%. Avg. home: $295,700; change (2008-10): –17.2%.

Mayor: Mike McGinn, nonpartisan

History: Settled 1851; inc. 1869. Suffered severe fire 1889; played prominent role during Alaska Gold Rush 1897; growth followed opening of Panama Canal 1914. Center of aircraft industry during WWII.

Transportation: 2 intl. airports, 2 seaplane bases; 2 railroads; ferries serve Puget Sound, Alaska, Canada; cruise ships to Alaska. Communications: 23 TV, 23 AM, 43 FM radio stations. Medical facilities: 13 hosp. Educational facilities: 24 colleges. Further information: Greater Seattle Chamber of Commerce, 1301 5th Ave., Ste. 2500, Seattle, WA 98101-2611; www.seattlechamber.com; www.seattle.gov

Spokane, Washington

Population: 208,916 (100). Pop. density: 3,526. Pop. change (2000-10): 6.8%. Area: 59.3 sq mi. Employment: 92,715 employed; 9.9% unemployed. Per capita income: $34,599; change (2008-09): –0.6%. Avg. home: $172,200; change (2008-10): –9.9%.

Mayor: Mary Verner, nonpartisan

History: Settled 1872; inc. as village of Spokane Falls 1881; destroyed in fire 1889; reinc. as city of Spokane 1891.

Transportation: 1 intl. airport; 2 railroads; bus system. Communications: 5 TV, 25 radio stations. Medical facilities: 6 major hosp. Educational facilities: 9 univ. and colleges; 14 pub. school districts, 16 high schools. Further information: Spokane Regional Convention & Visitors Bureau, 801 W. Riverside, Ste. 301, Spokane, WA 99201; www.visitspokane.com; www.spokanecity.org

Stockton, California

Population: 291,707 (65). Pop. density: 4,730. Pop. change (2000-10): 19.7%. Area: 61.7 sq mi. Employment: 100,455 employed; 20.8% unemployed. Per capita income: $31,071; change (2008-09): –1.6%.

Mayor: Ann Johnston, nonpartisan

History: Site purchased 1842; settled 1849; inc. 1850. Chief distribution point for agric. products of San Joaquin Valley.

Transportation: 1 muni. airport; 4 railroads; 2 bus lines, county bus system; deepwater inland seaport. Communications: 5 TV, 8 radio stations. Medical facilities: 4 hosp.; regional burn, cancer, heart centers. Educational facilities: 9 univ. and colleges; 58 pub. schools. Further information: Stockton Convention & Visitors Bureau, P.O. Box 2336, Stockton, CA 95201; www.visitstockton.org; www.stocktongov.com

Tampa, Florida

Population: 335,709 (55). Pop. density: 2,960. Pop. change (2000-10): 10.6%. Area: 113.4 sq mi. Employment: 143,741 employed; 12.1% unemployed. Per capita income: $37,632; change (2008-09): –2.1%. Avg. home: $134,200; change (2008-10): –22.4%.

Mayor: Bob Buckhorn, nonpartisan

History: U.S. army fort on site 1824; inc. 1851. Ybor City, Tampa's Latin Quarter, a Natl. Historical Landmark District.

Transportation: 1 intl., 2 muni. airports; CSX rail, Amtrak; bus system, downtown streetcars; port. Communications: 16 TV, 11 radio stations. Medical facilities: 30 hosp. Educational facilities: 25 univ. and colleges; 254 K-12 pub. schools, 82 additional school centers (county). Further information: Greater Tampa Chamber of Commerce, P.O. Box 420, Tampa, FL 33601; www.tampachamber.com; www.tampagov.net

Toledo, Ohio

Population: 287,208 (66). Pop. density: 3,559. Pop. change (2000-10): –8.4%. Area: 80.7 sq mi. Employment: 127,674 employed; 11.8% unemployed. Per capita income: $33,178; change (2008-09): –1.0%. Avg. home: $81,500; change (2008-10): –10.6%.

Mayor: Mike Bell, nonpartisan

History: Site of Ft. Industry 1794; Battle of Ft. Meigs 1812; figured in Toledo War 1835-36 between OH and MI over borders; inc. 1837.

Transportation: 2 muni. airports; 4 railroads; 16 interstate bus lines; 53 motor freight lines. Communications: 10 TV, 11 radio stations. Medical facilities: 4 hosp. Educational facilities: 6 univ. and colleges. Further information: Toledo Area Chamber of Commerce, 300 Madison Ave., Ste. 200, Toledo, OH 43604; www.toledochamber.com; www.ci.toledo.oh.us

Tucson, Arizona

Population: 520,116 (33). Pop. density: 2,294. Pop. change (2000-10): 6.9%. Area: 226.7 sq mi. Employment: 239,306 employed; 9.9% unemployed. Per capita income: $33,833; change (2008-09): –2.2%. Avg. home: $156,600; change (2008-10): –23.3%.

Mayor: Robert E. Walkup, Republican

History: Settled 1775 by Spanish as a presidio; acquired by U.S. in Gadsden Purchase 1853; inc. 1877.

Transportation: 1 intl. airport; 2 railroads; 1 bus line; 1 trolley. Communications: 11 TV, 32 radio stations. Medical facilities: 11 hosp. Educational facilities: 1 univ., 1 community college; 222 pub. schools. Further information: Tucson Metropolitan Chamber of Commerce, 465 St. Mary's Rd., P.O. Box 991, Tucson, AZ 85701; www.tucsonchamber.org; www.visittucson.org; www.tucsonaz.gov

Tulsa, Oklahoma

Population: 391,906 (46). Pop. density: 1,992. Pop. change (2000-10): –0.3%. Area: 196.8 sq mi. Employment: 172,737 employed; 7.5% unemployed. Per capita income: $40,402;

change (2008-09): −4.1%. **Avg. home:** $132,300; change (2008-10): −3.4%.
Mayor: Dewey F. Bartlett Jr., Republican
History: Settled in 1836 by Creek Indians; modern town founded 1882; inc. 1898; oil discovered early 20th century. Emerging telecommunications hub.
Transportation: 1 intl., 1 regional airport; 5 rail lines; 2 bus lines, transit bus system. **Communications:** 5 TV, 33 radio stations. **Medical facilities:** 9 hosp. **Educational facilities:** 10 univ. and colleges; 86 pub. schools, 62 priv. schools. **Further information:** Tulsa Metro Chamber, 2 W. 2nd St., Williams Tower II, Ste. 150, Tulsa, OK 74103; www.tulsachamber.com; www.cityoftulsa.org

Virginia Beach, Virginia

Population: 437,994 (39). **Pop. density:** 1,759. **Pop. change (2000-10):** 3.0%. **Area:** 249.0 sq mi. **Employment:** 208,026 employed; 6.4% unemployed. **Per capita income:** $39,518; change (2008-09): −0.7%. **Avg. home:** $205,000; change (2008-10): −6.8%.
Mayor: William D. Sessoms Jr., nonpartisan
History: Area founded by Capt. John Smith 1607; formed by merger with Princess Anne Co. 1963.
Transportation: 1 private airfield; 1 rail line; 1 bus line. **Communications:** 6 TV, 26 radio stations. **Medical facilities:** 3 hosp. **Educational facilities:** 5 univ. and colleges; 85 pub. schools. **Further information:** Virginia Beach Dept. of Economic Development, 222 Central Park Ave., Ste. 1000, Virginia Beach, VA 23462; Virginia Beach Convention and Visitors Bureau, 2100 Parks Ave., Virginia Beach, VA 23451; www.yesvirginiabeach.com; www.vbfun.com; www.vbgov.com

Washington, District of Columbia

Population: 601,723 (26). **Pop. density:** 9,857. **Pop. change (2000-10):** 5.2%. **Area:** 61.1 sq mi. **Employment:** 300,663 employed; 9.9% unemployed. **Per capita income:** $56,984; change (2008-09): −1.4%. **Avg. home:** $325,300; change (2008-10): −5.3%.
Mayor: Vincent C. Gray, Democrat
History: U.S. capital; site on Potomac R. chosen by George Washington 1790 on land ceded from VA and MD (portion S of Potomac returned to VA 1846); Congress first met 1800; inc. 1802; sacked by British, War of 1812. 125 killed during Sept. 11, 2001 terrorist attack on the Pentagon.

Transportation: 3 intl. airports serve area; Amtrak, 6 other passenger and cargo rail lines; Metrobus/Metrorail transit system; bus line. **Communications:** 18 TV, 20 radio stations. **Medical facilities:** 17 hosp. **Educational facilities:** 10 univ. and colleges. **Further information:** DC Chamber of Commerce, 1213 K St. NW, Washington, DC 20005; www.dc chamber.org; dc.gov

Wichita, Kansas

Population: 382,368 (49). **Pop. density:** 2,400. **Pop. change (2000-10):** 11.1%. **Area:** 159.3 sq mi. **Employment:** 174,902 employed; 9.4% unemployed. **Per capita income:** $38,935; change (2008-09): −3.3%. **Avg. home:** $118,700; change (2008-10): −2.5%.
Mayor: Carl Brewer, nonpartisan
History: Founded 1864; inc. 1871. Established itself as aircraft manufacturing hub between WWI and WWII.
Transportation: 1 natl., 1 muni. airport, 4 airfields; 3 major rail freight lines; 2 bus lines. **Communications:** 8 TV, 15 radio stations. **Medical facilities:** 12 hosp. **Educational facilities:** 1 med. school, 3 univ.; 96 pub. schools. **Further information:** Chamber of Commerce, 350 W. Douglas Ave., Wichita, KS 67202; www.wichitakansas.org; www.gwedc.org; www.wichita.org

Winston-Salem, North Carolina

Population: 229,617 (83). **Pop. density:** 1,734. **Pop. change (2000-10):** 23.6%. **Area:** 132.5 sq mi. **Employment:** 96,590 employed; 9.3% unemployed. **Per capita income:** $34,996; change (2008-09): −3.8%.
Mayor: Allen Joines, Democrat
History: Salem founded 1766; Winston founded 1849; became Winston-Salem 1913. The Reynolds Building, completed 1929, used as model for Empire State Building (designed by same architects).
Transportation: 1 intl., 1 general aviation airport; local, regional mass transit system. **Communications:** 1 daily newspaper; 5 TV, 17 radio stations. **Medical facilities:** 4 hosp. **Educational facilities:** 1 med. school, 4 univ. and colleges, 1 community college; 74 pub. schools, 28 priv. schools. **Further information:** Greater Winston-Salem Chamber of Commerce, 601 W. Fourth St., Winston-Salem, NC 27101; www.winstonsalem.com; www.cityofws.org

Fastest Growing and Shrinking Big Cities, 2010

Source: Decennial Censuses, U.S. Census Bureau, U.S. Dept. of Commerce

Fastest-Growing Cities

City	2010 population	2000 population	% change
1. Gilbert, AZ	208,453	109,697	90.0
2. North Las Vegas, NV	216,961	115,488	87.9
3. Fayetteville, NC	200,564	121,015	65.7
4. Irvine, CA	212,375	143,072	48.4
5. Henderson, NV.....	257,729	175,381	47.0
6. Raleigh, NC	403,892	276,093	46.3
7. Bakersfield, CA	347,483	247,057	40.6
8. Chula Vista, CA	243,916	173,556	40.5
9. Fort Worth, TX	741,206	534,694	38.6
10. Charlotte, NC	731,424	540,828	35.2

Fastest-Shrinking Cities

City	2010 population	2000 population	% change
1. New Orleans, LA ...	343,829	484,674	−29.1
2. Detroit, MI........	713,777	951,270	−25.0
3. Cleveland, OH	396,815	478,403	−17.1
4. Birmingham, AL ...	212,237	242,820	−12.6
5. Buffalo, NY	261,310	292,648	−10.7
6. Cincinnati, OH	296,943	331,285	−10.4
7. Pittsburgh, PA.....	305,704	334,563	−8.6
8. Toledo, OH	287,208	313,619	−8.4
9. St. Louis, MO	319,294	348,189	−8.3
10. Chicago, IL	2,695,598	2,896,016	−6.9

Note: Among those with populations of 200,000 or more, based on the 2010 Census.

Race and Hispanic Origin in the Largest U.S. Cities, 2010

Source: 2010 Census, U.S. Census Bureau, U.S. Dept. of Commerce

City	White	Black	Amer. Indian, Alaska Native	Asian	Hawaiian & other Pacific Isl.	Some other race	Two or more races	Hispanic or Latino (any race)
1. New York, NY.......	44.0%	25.5%	0.7%	12.7%	0.1%	13.0%	4.0%	28.6%
2. Los Angeles, CA......	49.8	9.6	0.7	11.3	0.1	23.8	4.6	48.5
3. Chicago, IL..........	45.0	32.9	0.5	5.5	—	13.4	2.7	28.9
4. Houston, TX..........	50.5	23.7	0.7	6.0	0.1	15.7	3.3	43.8
5. Philadelphia, PA.......	41.0	43.4	0.5	6.3	—	5.9	2.8	12.3
6. Phoenix, AZ	65.9	6.5	2.2	3.2	0.2	18.5	3.6	40.8
7. San Antonio, TX.......	72.6	6.9	0.9	2.4	0.1	13.7	3.4	63.2
8. San Diego, CA	58.9	6.7	0.6	15.9	0.5	12.3	5.1	28.8
9. Dallas, TX............	50.7	25.0	0.7	2.9	—	18.1	2.6	42.4
10. San Jose, CA	42.8	3.2	0.9	32.0	0.4	15.7	5.0	33.2

— = Less than 0.05%.

UNITED STATES POPULATION

Census Origins and Methods

A census is conducted in the U.S. every 10 years. The primary purpose is to apportion seats in the House of Representatives. Census data is also used to determine the boundaries of state legislative districts.

The first U.S. census, mandated by Article 1, Section 2 of the Constitution, was conducted in 1790, a little more than a year after George Washington became president. It counted the numbers of free white males ages 16 and over (to measure how many might be available to work in industry or serve in the military), free white males under 16, free white females, all other free persons, and slaves. It took 18 months to collect the data, at a cost of about $1 million in today's dollars. The 1790 census counted a total of 3.9 million people, resulting in an increase of 41 seats (from 65 to 106) in the House of Representatives.

As the nation grew, so did the scope of the census. The first inquiries on manufacturing industries were made in 1810. Questions on agriculture, mining, and fisheries were added to the 1840 census. In 1850, the census included questions on social issues—taxation, churches, poverty, and crime.

The 1880 census had so many questions that it took the full 10 years between censuses to publish all the results. Because of this delay, Congress limited the 1900 census to questions on population, manufactures, agriculture, and mortality. Many of the dropped topics reappeared in later censuses.

Today, the secretary of commerce and the Census Bureau are directed by law to take censuses of population, housing, agriculture, irrigation, manufactures, mineral industries, other businesses (wholesale trade, retail trade, services), construction, transportation, and governments at stated intervals. They also conduct smaller-scale surveys on behalf of other federal agencies.

U.S. marshals supervised the first nine censuses and reported to the president (1790), the secretary of state (1800-40), or the secretary of the interior (1850-70). There was no continuity in personnel from one census to the next. In 1902, Congress authorized a permanent Census Office within the Interior Department. In 1903, the agency was transferred to the new Department of Commerce and Labor. When the department split in 1913, the Bureau of the Census was placed in the Commerce Department.

The Census Bureau began using statistical sampling techniques in the 1940s. Its first modern computer in the 1950s, and enumeration by mail in the 1960s, all in an effort to publish data sooner, at a lower cost, and with less burden on the public. For the 2010 Census, the Census Bureau mailed questionnaires to most housing units in the country. Follow-up interviews at nonresponding households were conducted using handheld computers rather than paper and pencil.

The 2010 Census focused on counting the population through use of a short-form questionnaire. In previous censuses, about five in six households received the short form while one in six households answered the long-form questionnaire, which asked about details such as ancestry, marital status, and occupation. The American Community Survey (ACS) replaced the need in 2010 for the long-form questionnaire. First implemented nationwide in 2005 and conducted yearly on a random sample of the population, the ACS gathers demographic, economic, and housing information on communities across the country.

U.S. Population by State and Region, 2000, 2010

Source: Decennial Censuses, U.S. Census Bureau, U.S. Dept. of Commerce
(ranked by 2010 resident population)

Rank	State	2010[1]	2000[1]	% change 2000-10	Rank	State	2010[1]	2000[1]	% change 2000-10
1.	California	37,253,956	33,871,648	10.0%	29.	Connecticut	3,574,097	3,405,565	4.9%
2.	Texas	25,145,561	20,851,820	20.6	30.	Iowa	3,046,355	2,926,324	4.1
3.	New York	19,378,102	18,976,457	2.1	31.	Mississippi	2,967,297	2,844,658	4.3
4.	Florida	18,801,310	15,982,378	17.6	32.	Arkansas	2,915,918	2,673,400	9.1
5.	Illinois	12,830,632	12,419,293	3.3	33.	Kansas	2,853,118	2,688,418	6.1
6.	Pennsylvania	12,702,379	12,281,054	3.4	34.	Utah	2,763,885	2,233,169	23.8
7.	Ohio	11,536,504	11,353,140	1.6	35.	Nevada	2,700,551	1,998,257	35.1
8.	Michigan	9,883,640	9,938,444	−0.6	36.	New Mexico	2,059,179	1,819,046	13.2
9.	Georgia	9,687,653	8,186,453	18.3	37.	West Virginia	1,852,994	1,808,344	2.5
10.	North Carolina	9,535,483	8,049,313	18.5	38.	Nebraska	1,826,341	1,711,263	6.7
11.	New Jersey	8,791,894	8,414,350	4.5	39.	Idaho	1,567,582	1,293,953	21.1
12.	Virginia	8,001,024	7,078,515	13.0	40.	Hawaii	1,360,301	1,211,537	12.3
13.	Washington	6,724,540	5,894,121	14.1	41.	Maine	1,328,361	1,274,923	4.2
14.	Massachusetts	6,547,629	6,349,097	3.1	42.	New Hampshire	1,316,470	1,235,786	6.5
15.	Indiana	6,483,802	6,080,485	6.6	43.	Rhode Island	1,052,567	1,048,319	0.4
16.	Arizona	6,392,017	5,130,632	24.6	44.	Montana	989,415	902,195	9.7
17.	Tennessee	6,346,105	5,689,283	11.5	45.	Delaware	897,934	783,600	14.6
18.	Missouri	5,988,927	5,595,211	7.0	46.	South Dakota	814,180	754,844	7.9
19.	Maryland	5,773,552	5,296,486	9.0	47.	Alaska	710,231	626,932	13.3
20.	Wisconsin	5,686,986	5,363,675	6.0	48.	North Dakota	672,591	642,200	4.7
21.	Minnesota	5,303,925	4,919,479	7.8	49.	Vermont	625,741	608,827	2.8
22.	Colorado	5,029,196	4,301,261	16.9	50.	District of Columbia	601,723	572,059	5.2
23.	Alabama	4,779,736	4,447,100	7.5	51.	Wyoming	563,626	493,782	14.1
24.	South Carolina	4,625,364	4,012,012	15.3		**United States**	**308,745,538**	**281,421,906**	**9.7**
25.	Louisiana	4,533,372	4,468,976	1.4		Northeast[2]	55,317,240	53,594,378	3.2
26.	Kentucky	4,339,367	4,041,769	7.4		Midwest[3]	66,927,001	64,392,776	3.9
27.	Oregon	3,831,074	3,421,399	12.0		South[4]	114,555,744	100,236,820	14.3
28.	Oklahoma	3,751,351	3,450,654	8.7		West[5]	71,945,553	63,197,932	13.8

Note: The U.S. resident population consists of individuals whose "usual place of residence" is in one of the 50 states or DC. It excludes overseas U.S. military personnel and civilian U.S. citizens living abroad. (1) Population figures are for Apr. 1 of decennial census year. (2) Incl. the states of the New England division (Connecticut, Maine, Massachusetts, New Hampshire, Rhode Island, Vermont) and Middle Atlantic division (New Jersey, New York, Pennsylvania). (3) Incl. the states of the East North Central division (Illinois, Indiana, Michigan, Ohio, Wisconsin) and West North Central division (Iowa, Kansas, Minnesota, Missouri, Nebraska, North Dakota, South Dakota). (4) Incl. the states of the South Atlantic division (Delaware, DC, Florida, Georgia, Maryland, North Carolina, South Carolina, Virginia, West Virginia), East South Central division (Alabama, Kentucky, Mississippi, Tennessee), and West South Central division (Arkansas, Louisiana, Oklahoma, Texas). (5) Incl. the states of the Mountain division (Arizona, Colorado, Idaho, Montana, Nevada, New Mexico, Utah, Wyoming) and Pacific division (Alaska, California, Hawaii, Oregon, Washington).

U.S. Population by Official

Source: Decennial Censuses, U.S. Census Bureau

(population figures for 1790-1860

State	1790	1800	1810	1820	1830	1840	1850	1860	1870	1880	1890	1900	1910	1920
AL[1]	...	1	9	128	310	591	772	964	996,992	1,262,505	1,513,401	1,828,697	2,138,093	2,348,174
AK	...	...	...	...	...	...	...	...	...	33,426	32,052	63,592	64,356	55,036
AZ[2]	...	...	...	...	...	...	...	...	9,658	40,440	88,243	122,931	204,354	334,162
AR	...	...	1	14	30	98	210	435	484,471	802,525	1,128,211	1,311,564	1,574,449	1,752,204
CA	...	...	...	...	...	...	93	380	560,247	864,694	1,213,398	1,485,053	2,377,549	3,426,861
CO[2]	...	...	...	...	...	...	...	34	39,864	194,327	413,249	539,700	799,024	939,629
CT	238	251	262	275	298	310	371	460	537,454	622,700	746,258	908,420	1,114,756	1,380,631
DE	59	64	73	73	77	78	92	112	125,015	146,608	168,493	184,735	202,322	223,003
DC	...	8	16	23	30	34	52	75	131,700	177,624	230,392	278,718	331,069	437,571
FL	...	...	...	...	35	54	87	140	187,748	269,493	391,422	528,542	752,619	968,470
GA	83	163	252	341	517	69	906	1,057	1,184,109	1,542,180	1,837,353	2,216,331	2,609,121	2,895,832
HI	...	...	...	...	...	...	...	...	...	...	154,001	191,909	255,912
ID[3]	...	...	...	...	...	...	...	...	14,999	32,610	88,548	161,772	325,594	431,866
IL	...	...	12	55	157	476	851	1,712	2,539,891	3,077,871	3,826,352	4,821,550	5,638,591	6,485,280
IN	...	6	25	147	343	686	988	1,350	1,680,637	1,978,301	2,192,404	2,516,462	2,700,876	2,930,390
IA	...	...	...	...	...	43	192	675	1,194,020	1,624,615	1,912,297	2,231,853	2,224,771	2,404,021
KS	...	...	...	...	...	...	...	107	364,399	996,096	1,428,108	1,470,495	1,690,949	1,769,257
KY	74	221	407	564	688	780	982	1,156	1,321,011	1,648,690	1,858,635	2,147,174	2,289,905	2,416,630
LA	...	...	77	153	216	352	518	708	726,915	939,946	1,118,588	1,381,625	1,656,388	1,798,509
ME[4]	97	152	229	298	399	502	583	628	626,915	648,936	661,086	694,466	742,371	768,014
MD	320	342	381	407	447	470	583	687	780,894	934,943	1,042,390	1,188,044	1,295,346	1,449,661
MA[4]	379	423	472	523	610	738	995	1,231	1,457,351	1,783,085	2,238,947	2,805,346	3,366,416	3,852,356
MI	...	...	5	9	32	212	398	749	1,184,059	1,636,937	2,093,890	2,420,982	2,810,173	3,668,412
MN	...	...	...	...	...	...	...	6	439,706	780,773	1,310,283	1,751,394	2,075,708	2,387,125
MS[1]	...	8	31	75	137	376	607	791	827,922	1,131,597	1,289,600	1,551,270	1,797,114	1,790,618
MO	...	...	20	67	140	384	682	1,182	1,721,295	2,168,380	2,679,185	3,106,665	3,293,335	3,404,055
MT[3]	...	...	...	...	...	...	...	...	20,595	39,159	142,924	243,329	376,053	548,889
NE	...	...	...	...	...	...	...	29	122,993	452,402	1,062,656	1,066,300	1,192,214	1,296,372
NV[2]	...	...	...	...	...	...	...	7	42,491	62,266	47,355	42,335	81,875	77,407
NH	142	184	214	244	269	285	318	326	318,300	346,991	376,530	411,588	430,572	443,083
NJ	184	211	246	278	321	373	490	672	906,096	1,131,116	1,444,933	1,883,669	2,537,167	3,155,900
NM[2]	...	...	...	...	...	...	62	94	91,874	119,565	160,282	195,310	327,301	360,350
NY	340	589	959	1,373	1,919	2,429	3,097	3,881	4,382,759	5,082,871	6,003,174	7,268,894	9,113,614	10,385,227
NC	394	478	556	639	736	753	869	993	1,071,361	1,399,750	1,617,949	1,893,810	2,206,287	2,559,123
ND[5]	...	...	...	...	...	...	...	...	2,405	36,909	190,983	319,146	577,056	646,872
OH	...	45	231	581	938	1,519	1,980	2,340	2,665,260	3,198,062	3,672,329	4,157,545	4,767,121	5,759,394
OK	...	...	...	...	...	...	...	...	...	...	258,657	790,391	1,657,155	2,028,283
OR[6]	...	...	...	...	...	...	12	52	90,923	174,768	317,704	413,536	672,765	783,389
PA	434	602	810	1,049	1,348	1,724	2,312	2,906	3,521,951	4,282,891	5,258,113	6,302,115	7,665,111	8,720,017
RI	69	69	77	83	97	109	148	175	217,353	276,531	345,506	428,556	542,610	604,397
SC	249	346	415	503	581	594	669	704	705,606	995,577	1,151,149	1,340,316	1,515,400	1,683,724
SD[5]	...	...	...	...	...	...	...	5	11,776	98,268	348,600	401,570	583,888	636,547
TN	36	106	262	423	682	829	1,003	1,110	1,258,520	1,542,359	1,767,518	2,020,616	2,184,789	2,337,885
TX	...	...	...	...	...	...	213	604	818,579	1,591,749	2,235,527	3,048,710	3,896,542	4,663,228
UT	...	...	...	...	...	...	11	40	86,786	143,963	210,779	276,749	373,351	449,396
VT	85	154	218	236	281	292	314	315	330,551	332,286	332,422	343,641	355,956	352,428
VA[7]	692	808	878	938	1,044	1,025	1,120	1,220	1,225,163	1,512,565	1,655,980	1,854,184	2,061,612	2,309,187
WA[3,6]	...	...	...	...	...	...	...	1	23,955	75,116	357,232	518,103	1,141,990	1,356,621
WV[7]	56	79	105	137	177	225	302	377	442,014	618,457	762,794	958,800	1,221,119	1,463,701
WI	...	...	...	...	...	31	305	776	1,054,670	1,315,497	1,693,330	2,069,042	2,333,860	2,632,067
WY[3]	...	...	...	...	...	...	...	...	9,118	20,789	62,555	92,531	145,965	194,402
U.S.[8]	**3,929**	**5,308**	**7,240**	**9,638**	**12,866**	**17,063**	**23,192**	**31,443**	**38,558,371**	**50,189,209**	**62,979,766**	**76,212,168**	**92,228,531**	**106,021,568**

Note: Unless otherwise noted, pop. shown is for a state's present-day area. Excl. overseas U.S. military personnel and civilian U.S. citizens living abroad. (1) 1800-10 figures for MS are for those areas of Mississippi Territory now part of present-day AL and MS. (2) 1850 figure for NM incl. parts of New Mexico Territory now part of present-day AZ, NM, CO, and NV; 1870 figure incl. parts taken in formation of Arizona Territory in 1863. (3) 1860 figure for WA incl. pop. in present-day ID and parts of MT and WY. (4) 1790-1810 figures for MA do not incl. district taken to form state of ME in 1820. (5) 1860 figure is for Dakota Territory, which comprised present-day ND and SD; 1870-80 figures are for parts of territory that became the two states in 1889. (6) Parts of Oregon Territory went to Washington Territory in 1853 and 1859. 1850 pop. in those areas listed under WA, not OR. (7) 1790-1860 figures for VA do not incl. areas taken in creation of WV in 1863. (8) 1830-40 totals incl. persons (5,318 in 1830; 6,100 in 1840) on public ships in service of U.S. not credited to any state.

Estimated Population of American Colonies, 1630-1780

Source: U.S. Census Bureau, U.S. Dept. of Commerce

(numbers in thousands)

Colony	1630	1650	1670	1690	1700	1720	1740	1750	1770	1780
Total	4.6	50.4	111.9	210.4	250.9	466.2	905.6	1,170.8	2,148.1	2,780.4
Maine (counties)[1]	0.4	1.0	...	...	...	...	...	...	31.3	49.1
New Hampshire[2]	0.5	1.3	1.8	4.2	5.0	9.4	23.3	27.5	62.4	87.8
Vermont[3]	...	...	...	...	...	...	...	...	10.0	47.6
Plymouth and Massachusetts[1,2,4]	0.9	15.6	35.3	56.9	55.9	91.0	151.6	188.0	235.3	268.6
Rhode Island[2]	...	0.8	2.2	4.2	5.9	11.7	25.3	33.2	58.2	52.9
Connecticut[2]	...	4.1	12.6	21.6	26.0	58.8	89.6	111.3	183.9	206.7
New York[2]	0.4	4.1	5.8	13.9	19.1	36.9	63.7	76.7	162.9	210.5
New Jersey[2]	...	...	1.0	8.0	14.0	29.8	51.4	71.4	117.4	139.6
Pennsylvania[2]	...	...	...	11.4	18.0	31.0	85.6	119.7	240.1	327.3
Delaware[2]	...	0.2	0.7	1.5	2.5	5.4	19.9	28.7	35.5	45.4
Maryland[2]	...	4.5	13.2	24.0	29.6	66.1	116.1	141.1	202.6	245.5
Virginia[2]	2.5	18.7	35.3	53.0	58.6	87.8	180.4	231.0	447.0	538.0
North Carolina[2]	...	...	3.9	7.6	10.7	21.3	51.8	73.0	197.2	270.1
South Carolina[2]	...	0.2	3.9	5.7	17.0	45.0	64.0	124.2	180.0
Georgia[2]	...	...	...	...	...	...	2.0	5.2	23.4	56.1
Kentucky[5]	...	...	...	...	...	...	...	...	15.7	45.0
Tennessee[6]	...	...	...	...	...	...	...	...	1.0	10.0

(1) For 1660-1750, the pop. of ME counties are included with MA. ME was annexed by MA in 1650s but became separate state in 1820. (2) One of original 13 states. (3) Admitted as state 1791. (4) Plymouth became part of Prov. of Massachusetts in 1691. (5) Admitted as state 1792. (6) Admitted as state 1796.

Census, 1790-2010
U.S. Dept. of Commerce
only are in thousands)

1930	1940	1950	1960	1970	1980	1990	2000	2010	State
2,646,248	2,832,961	3,061,743	3,266,740	3,444,165	3,893,888	4,040,587	4,447,100	4,779,736	AL
59,278	72,524	128,643	226,167	300,382	401,851	550,043	626,932	710,231	AK
435,573	499,261	749,587	1,302,161	1,770,900	2,718,215	3,665,228	5,130,632	6,392,017	AZ
1,854,482	1,949,387	1,909,511	1,786,272	1,923,295	2,286,435	2,350,725	2,673,400	2,915,918	AR
5,677,251	6,907,387	10,586,223	15,717,204	19,953,134	23,667,902	29,760,021	33,871,648	37,253,956	CA
1,035,791	1,123,296	1,325,089	1,753,947	2,207,259	2,889,964	3,294,394	4,301,261	5,029,196	CO
1,606,903	1,709,242	2,007,280	2,535,234	3,031,709	3,107,576	3,287,116	3,405,565	3,574,097	CT
238,380	266,505	318,085	446,292	548,104	594,338	666,168	783,600	897,934	DE
486,869	663,091	802,178	763,956	756,510	638,333	606,900	572,059	601,723	DC
1,468,211	1,897,414	2,771,305	4,951,560	6,789,443	9,746,324	12,937,926	15,982,378	18,801,310	FL
2,908,506	3,123,723	3,444,578	3,943,116	4,589,575	5,463,105	6,478,216	8,186,453	9,687,653	GA
368,336	422,330	499,794	632,772	768,561	964,691	1,108,229	1,211,537	1,360,301	HI
445,032	524,873	588,637	667,191	712,567	943,935	1,006,749	1,293,953	1,567,582	ID
7,630,654	7,897,241	8,712,176	10,081,158	11,113,976	11,426,518	11,430,602	12,419,293	12,830,632	IL
3,238,503	3,427,796	3,934,224	4,662,498	5,193,669	5,490,224	5,544,159	6,080,485	6,483,802	IN
2,470,939	2,538,268	2,621,073	2,757,537	2,824,376	2,913,808	2,776,755	2,926,324	3,046,355	IA
1,880,999	1,801,028	1,905,299	2,178,611	2,246,578	2,363,679	2,477,574	2,688,418	2,853,118	KS
2,614,589	2,845,627	2,944,806	3,038,156	3,218,706	3,660,777	3,685,296	4,041,769	4,339,367	KY
2,101,593	2,363,880	2,683,516	3,257,022	3,641,306	4,205,900	4,219,973	4,468,976	4,533,372	LA
797,423	847,226	913,774	969,265	992,048	1,124,660	1,227,928	1,274,923	1,328,361	ME
1,631,526	1,821,244	2,343,001	3,100,689	3,922,399	4,216,975	4,781,468	5,296,486	5,773,552	MD
4,249,614	4,316,721	4,690,514	5,148,578	5,689,170	5,737,037	6,016,425	6,349,097	6,547,629	MA
4,842,325	5,256,106	6,371,766	7,823,194	8,875,083	9,262,078	9,295,297	9,938,444	9,883,640	MI
2,563,953	2,792,300	2,982,483	3,413,864	3,804,971	4,075,970	4,375,099	4,919,479	5,303,925	MN
2,009,821	2,183,796	2,178,914	2,178,141	2,216,912	2,520,638	2,573,216	2,844,658	2,967,297	MS
3,629,367	3,784,664	3,954,653	4,319,813	4,676,501	4,916,686	5,117,073	5,595,211	5,988,927	MO
537,606	559,456	591,024	674,767	694,409	786,690	799,065	902,195	989,415	MT
1,377,963	1,315,834	1,325,510	1,411,330	1,483,493	1,569,825	1,578,385	1,711,263	1,826,341	NE
91,058	110,247	160,083	285,278	488,738	800,493	1,201,833	1,998,257	2,700,551	NV
465,293	491,524	533,242	606,921	737,681	920,610	1,109,252	1,235,786	1,316,470	NH
4,041,334	4,160,165	4,835,329	6,066,782	7,168,164	7,364,823	7,730,188	8,414,350	8,791,894	NJ
423,317	531,818	681,187	951,023	1,016,000	1,302,894	1,515,069	1,819,046	2,059,179	NM
12,588,066	13,479,142	14,830,192	16,782,304	18,236,967	17,558,072	17,990,455	18,976,457	19,378,102	NY
3,170,276	3,571,623	4,061,929	4,556,155	5,082,059	5,881,766	6,628,637	8,049,313	9,535,483	NC
680,845	641,935	619,636	632,446	617,761	652,717	638,800	642,200	672,591	ND
6,646,697	6,907,612	7,946,627	9,706,397	10,652,017	10,797,630	10,847,115	11,353,140	11,536,504	OH
2,396,040	2,336,434	2,233,351	2,328,284	2,559,229	3,025,290	3,145,585	3,450,654	3,751,351	OK
953,786	1,089,684	1,521,341	1,768,687	2,091,385	2,633,105	2,842,321	3,421,399	3,831,074	OR
9,631,350	9,900,180	10,498,012	11,319,366	11,793,909	11,863,895	11,881,643	12,281,054	12,702,379	PA
687,497	713,346	791,896	859,488	949,723	947,154	1,003,464	1,048,319	1,052,567	RI
1,738,765	1,899,804	2,117,027	2,382,594	2,590,516	3,121,820	3,486,703	4,012,012	4,625,364	SC
692,849	642,961	652,740	680,514	665,507	690,768	696,004	754,844	814,180	SD
2,616,556	2,915,841	3,291,718	3,567,089	3,923,687	4,591,120	4,877,185	5,689,283	6,346,105	TN
5,824,715	6,414,824	7,711,194	9,579,677	11,196,730	14,229,191	16,986,510	20,851,820	25,145,561	TX
507,847	550,310	688,862	890,627	1,059,273	1,461,037	1,722,850	2,233,169	2,763,885	UT
359,611	359,231	377,747	389,881	444,330	511,456	562,758	608,827	625,741	VT
2,421,851	2,677,773	3,318,680	3,966,949	4,648,494	5,346,818	6,187,358	7,078,515	8,001,024	VA
1,563,396	1,736,191	2,378,963	2,853,214	3,409,169	4,132,156	4,866,692	5,894,121	6,724,540	WA
1,729,205	1,901,974	2,005,552	1,860,421	1,744,237	1,949,644	1,793,477	1,808,344	1,852,994	WV
2,939,006	3,137,587	3,434,575	3,951,777	4,417,731	4,705,767	4,891,769	5,363,675	5,686,986	WI
225,565	250,742	290,529	330,066	332,416	469,557	453,588	493,782	563,626	WY
123,202,660	132,164,569	151,325,798	179,323,175	203,211,926	226,545,805	248,709,873	281,421,906	308,745,538	U.S.

U.S. Center of Population, 1790-2010
Source: Decennial Censuses, Geography Division, U.S. Census Bureau, U.S. Dept. of Commerce

The country's **center of population (mean)** is considered here to be the center of population gravity, or that point upon which the U.S. would balance if it were a rigid, weightless plane and the population distributed thereon, with each individual assuming an equal weight and exerting an influence on a central point proportional to his or her distance from that point.

Census year	N Lat °	'	''	W Long °	'	''	Approximate location
1790	39	16	30	76	11	12	Kent Co., MD, 23 miles east of Baltimore
1800	39	16	6	76	56	30	Howard Co., MD, 18 miles west of Baltimore
1810	39	11	30	77	37	12	Loudoun Co., VA, 40 miles northwest by west of Washington, DC
1820	39	5	42	78	33	0	Hardy Co., WV, 16 miles east of Moorefield[1]
1830	38	57	54	79	16	54	Grant Co., WV, 19 miles west-southwest of Moorefield[1]
1840	39	2	0	80	18	0	Upshur Co., WV, 16 miles south of Clarksburg[1]
1850	38	59	0	81	19	0	Wirt Co., WV, 23 miles southeast of Parkersburg[1]
1860	39	0	24	82	48	48	Pike Co., OH, 20 miles south by east of Chillicothe
1870	39	12	0	83	35	42	Highland Co., OH, 48 miles east by north of Cincinnati
1880	39	4	8	84	39	40	Boone Co., KY, 8 miles by south of Cincinnati, OH
1890	39	11	56	85	32	53	Decatur Co., IN, 20 miles east of Columbus
1900	39	9	36	85	48	54	Bartholomew Co., IN, 6 miles southeast of Columbus
1910	39	10	12	86	32	20	Monroe Co., IN, in the city of Bloomington
1920	39	10	21	86	43	15	Owen Co., IN, 8 miles south-southeast of Spencer
1930	39	3	45	87	8	6	Greene Co., IN, 3 miles northeast of Linton
1940	38	56	54	87	22	35	Sullivan Co., IN, 2 miles southeast by east of Carlisle
1950	38	50	21	88	9	33	Richland Co., IL, 8 miles north-northwest of Olney
1950[2]	38	48	15	88	22	8	Clay Co., IL, 3 miles northeast of Louisville
1960[2]	38	35	58	89	12	35	Clinton Co., IL, 6½ miles northwest of Centralia
1970[2]	38	27	47	89	42	22	St. Clair Co., IL, 5 miles east-southeast of Mascoutah
1980[2]	38	8	13	90	34	26	Jefferson Co., MO, ¼ mile west of DeSoto
1990[2]	37	52	20	91	12	55	Crawford Co., MO, 9.7 miles southeast of Steelville
2000[2]	37	41	49	91	48	34	Phelps Co., MO, 2.8 miles east of Edgar Springs
2010[2]	37	31	3	92	10	23	Texas Co., MO, 2.7 miles northeast of Plato

(1) West Virginia was set off from Virginia on Dec. 31, 1862, and admitted as a state on June 20, 1863. (2) Incl. Alaska and Hawaii.

Density of U.S. Population by State, 1930-2010

Source: Decennial Censuses, U.S. Census Bureau, U.S. Dept. of Commerce

(per square mile, land area only)

State	1930	1950	1970	1990	2010	State	1930	1950	1970	1990	2010
AL......	52.3	60.5	68.0	79.8	94.4	MT	3.7	4.1	4.8	5.5	6.8
AK......	0.1	0.2	0.5	1.0	1.2	NE......	17.9	17.3	19.3	20.5	23.8
AZ......	3.8	6.6	15.6	32.3	56.3	NV......	0.8	1.5	4.5	10.9	24.6
AR......	35.6	36.7	37.0	45.2	56.0	NH	52.0	59.6	82.4	123.9	147.0
CA......	36.4	68.0	128.1	191.0	239.1	NJ......	549.5	657.5	974.7	1,051.1	1,195.5
CO	10.0	12.8	21.3	31.8	48.5	NM	3.5	5.6	8.4	12.5	17.0
CT......	331.8	414.5	626.1	678.5	738.1	NY......	267.1	314.7	387.0	381.7	411.2
DE......	122.3	163.2	281.3	341.9	460.8	NC	65.2	83.5	104.5	136.3	196.1
DC 7,975.1		13,140.3	12,392.0	9,941.3	9,856.5	ND	9.9	9.0	9.0	9.3	9.7
FL.......	27.4	51.7	126.6	241.3	350.6	OH	162.7	194.5	260.7	265.5	282.3
GA	50.6	59.9	79.8	112.6	168.4	OK	34.9	32.6	37.3	45.9	54.7
HI	57.3	77.8	119.7	172.6	211.8	OR	9.9	15.8	21.8	29.6	39.9
ID	5.4	7.1	8.6	12.2	19.0	PA.......	215.3	234.6	263.6	265.6	283.9
IL.......	137.4	156.9	200.2	205.9	231.1	RI	665.0	766.0	915.8	970.6	1,018.1
IN	90.4	109.8	145.0	154.8	181.0	SC.......	57.8	70.4	86.2	116.0	153.9
IA	44.2	46.9	50.6	49.7	54.5	SD.......	9.1	8.6	8.8	9.2	10.7
KS.......	23.0	23.3	27.5	30.3	34.9	TN.......	63.5	79.8	95.2	118.3	153.9
KY.......	66.2	74.6	81.5	93.3	109.9	TX.......	22.3	29.5	42.9	65.0	96.3
LA.......	48.6	62.1	84.3	97.7	104.9	UT.......	6.2	8.4	12.9	21.0	33.6
ME	25.9	29.6	32.2	39.8	43.1	VT.......	39.0	41.0	48.2	61.1	67.9
MD	168.1	241.4	404.1	492.6	594.8	VA	61.3	84.0	117.7	156.7	202.6
MA	544.8	601.3	729.4	771.3	839.4	WA	23.5	35.8	51.3	73.2	101.2
MI	85.6	112.7	157.0	164.4	174.8	WV	71.9	83.4	72.6	74.6	77.1
MN	32.2	37.5	47.8	54.9	66.6	WI	54.3	63.4	81.6	90.3	105.0
MS	42.8	46.4	47.2	54.8	63.2	WY	2.3	3.0	3.4	4.7	5.8
MO	52.8	57.5	68.0	74.4	87.1	**U.S.**	**34.7**	**42.6**	**57.5**	**70.4**	**87.4**

Note: For the sake of comparison, the densities of Alaska and Hawaii in 1930 are included though they were not yet states.

U.S. Area and Population, 1790-2010

Source: Decennial Censuses, U.S. Census Bureau, U.S. Dept. of Commerce

	AREA (square miles)			POPULATION		Increase over preceding census	
Census date	Gross area[1]	Land area	Water area[1]	Number	Per sq mi of land	Number	%
1790 (Aug. 2)	891,364	864,746	24,065	3,929,214	4.5	—	—
1800 (Aug. 4)	891,364	864,746	24,065	5,308,483	6.1	1,379,269	35.1%
1810 (Aug. 6)	1,722,685	1,681,828	34,115	7,239,881	4.3	1,931,398	36.4
1820 (Aug. 7)	1,792,552	1,749,462	38,544	9,638,453	5.5	2,398,572	33.1
1830 (June 1)	1,792,552	1,749,462	38,544	12,866,020	7.4	3,227,567	33.5
1840 (June 1)	1,792,552	1,749,462	38,544	17,069,453	9.8	4,203,433	32.7
1850 (June 1)	2,991,655	2,940,042	52,705	23,191,876	7.9	6,122,423	35.9
1860 (June 1)	3,021,295	2,969,640	52,747	31,443,321	10.6	8,251,445	35.6
1870 (June 1)	3,612,299	3,540,705	68,082	39,818,449[2]	11.2[2]	8,375,128	26.6
1880 (June 1)	3,612,299	3,540,705	68,082	50,189,209	14.2	10,370,760	26.0
1890 (June 1)	3,612,299	3,540,705	68,082	62,979,766	17.8	12,790,557	25.5
1900 (June 1)	3,618,770	3,547,314	67,901	76,212,168	21.5	13,232,402	21.0
1910 (Apr. 15)	3,618,770	3,547,045	68,170	92,228,496	26.0	16,016,328	21.0
1920 (Jan. 1)	3,618,770	3,546,931	68,284	106,021,537	29.9	13,793,041	15.0
1930 (Apr. 1)	3,618,770	3,554,608	60,607	123,202,624	34.7	17,181,087	16.2
1940 (Apr. 1)	3,618,770	3,554,608	60,607	132,164,569	37.2	8,961,945	7.3
1950 (Apr. 1)	3,618,770	3,552,206	63,005	151,325,798	42.6	19,161,229	14.5
1960 (Apr. 1)	3,618,770	3,540,911	74,212	179,323,175	50.6	27,997,377	18.5
1970 (Apr. 1)	3,618,770	3,536,855	78,444	203,302,031	57.5	23,978,856	13.4
1980 (Apr. 1)	3,618,770	3,539,289	79,481	226,542,199	64.0	23,240,168	11.4
1990 (Apr. 1)	3,717,796	3,536,278	181,518	248,718,302	70.3	22,176,103	9.8
2000 (Apr. 1)	3,794,083	3,537,438	256,645	281,424,603	79.6	32,706,301	13.1
2010 (Apr. 1)	3,796,742	3,531,905	264,837	308,745,538	87.4	27,323,632	9.7

Note: Percent changes are computed on the basis of change in population since the preceding census date, so the period covered is not always exactly 10 years. Population density figures given for various years represent the area within the boundaries of the U.S. under its jurisdiction on the date in question including, in some cases, considerable areas not organized or settled and not actually covered by the census. In 1870, for example, Alaska was not covered by the census, but its area is included in density calculations. Population figures may reflect corrections made to initial tabulated census counts. (1) Figures for 1790-1980 cover inland water only. Figure for 1990 includes inland, coastal, and Great Lakes water. Figures for 2000-10 include additional territorial water as determined by presidential decree in Dec. 1998. (2) Revised to include adjustments for underenumeration in Southern states.

U.S. Congressional Apportionment by Census Year, 1850-2010
Source: Decennial Censuses, U.S. Census Bureau, U.S. Dept. of Commerce

The U.S. Constitution, in Article 1, Section 2, mandates that the population be counted every 10 years so that the number of representatives can be apportioned among the states. Every state is entitled to at least one House seat. The size of a state's resident population, both citizens and noncitizens, determines if it may send additional representatives to Congress. A congressional apportionment has been made after every decennial census except for that of 1920. Prior to 1870, slaves were counted as being only ⅗ of a person in the apportionment population. Apportionments made before the 20th century also excluded some Native Americans and armed forces personnel and federal civilian employees stationed overseas. District of Columbia residents remain excluded.

Under the provisions of a law that went into effect Nov. 15, 1941, representatives are apportioned by the method of equal proportions. In the application of this method, the apportionment is made so that the average number of people each House member represents has the least possible variation between states.

The first House of Representatives, in 1789, had 65 members as provided by the Constitution. The largest numbers were from Virginia (10), Massachusetts (8), and Pennsylvania (8). As the nation's population grew, the number of representatives was increased, but a 1911 act fixed the total membership of the House at 435. (Alaska and Hawaii each gained one House seat when they became states, temporarily raising the total to 437 representatives until after the 1960 census was conducted.)

State	2010	2000	1990	1970	1950	1900	1850	State	2010	2000	1990	1970	1950	1900	1850
AL	7	7	7	7	9	9	7	NE	3	3	3	3	4	6	NA
AK	1	1	1	1	1	NA	NA	NV	4	3	2	1	1	1	NA
AZ	9	8	6	4	2	NA	NA	NH	2	2	2	2	2	2	3
AR	4	4	4	4	6	7	2	NJ	12	13	13	15	14	10	5
CA	53	53	52	43	30	8	2	NM	3	3	3	2	2	NA	NA
CO	7	7	6	5	4	3	NA	NY	27	29	31	39	43	37	33
CT	5	5	6	6	6	5	4	NC	13	13	12	11	12	10	8
DE	1	1	1	1	1	1	1	ND	1	1	1	1	2	2	NA
FL	27	25	23	15	8	3	1	OH	16	18	19	23	23	21	21
GA	14	13	11	10	10	11	8	OK	5	5	6	6	6	5	NA
HI	2	2	2	2	1	NA	NA	OR	5	5	5	4	4	2	1
ID	2	2	2	2	2	1	NA	PA	18	19	21	25	30	32	25
IL	18	19	20	24	25	25	9	RI	2	2	2	2	2	2	2
IN	9	9	10	11	11	13	11	SC	7	6	6	6	6	7	6
IA	4	5	5	6	8	11	2	SD	1	1	1	2	2	2	NA
KS	4	4	4	5	6	8	NA	TN	9	9	9	8	9	10	10
KY	6	6	6	7	8	11	10	TX	36	32	30	24	22	16	2
LA	6	7	7	8	8	7	4	UT	4	3	3	2	2	1	NA
ME	2	2	2	2	3	4	6	VT	1	1	1	1	1	2	3
MD	8	8	8	8	7	6	6	VA	11	11	11	10	10	10	13
MA	9	10	10	12	14	14	11	WA	10	9	9	7	7	3	NA
MI	14	15	16	19	18	12	4	WV	3	3	3	4	6	6	NA
MN	8	8	8	8	9	9	2	WI	8	8	9	9	10	11	3
MS	4	4	5	5	6	8	5	WY	1	1	1	1	1	1	NA
MO	8	9	9	10	11	16	7	**Total**	**435**	**435**	**435**	**435**	**437**	**391**	**237**
MT	1	1	1	2	2	1	NA								

NA = Not applicable.

U.S. Slave and "Free Colored" Population, 1790, 1820, 1860
Source: Decennial Censuses, U.S. Census Bureau, U.S. Dept. of Commerce

	1790 census			1820 census			1860 census		
	Slaves	% slaves	Free colored[1]	Slaves	% slaves	Free colored[1]	Slaves	% slaves	Free colored[1]
Northern states[2]	**40,370**	**2.1%**	**33,016**	**18,001**	**0.3%**	**92,351**	**18**	**0%**	**225,224**
Connecticut	2,759	1.2	2,801	97	0	7,844	0	0	8,627
New Jersey	11,423	6.2	2,762	7,557	2.7	12,460	18	0	25,318
New York	21,324	6.3	4,654	10,088	0.7	29,279	0	0	49,005
Pennsylvania	3,737	0.9	6,537	211	0	30,202	0	0	56,949
Border/disputed states	**123,753**	**27.4**	**12,056**	**248,860**	**22.4**	**55,794**	**429,403**	**20.6**	**118,652**
Delaware	8,887	15.0	3,899	4,509	6.2	12,958	1,798	1.6	19,829
Kansas	—	—	—	—	—	—	2	0	625
Kentucky	11,830	16.2	114	126,732	22.5	2,759	225,483	19.5	10,684
Maryland	103,036	32.2	8,043	107,397	26.4	39,730	87,189	12.7	83,942
Missouri	—	—	—	10,222	15.4	347	114,931	9.7	3,572
Southern states	**533,774**	**35.4**	**20,301**	**1,263,780**	**37.8**	**74,381**	**3,521,110**	**34.3**	**132,760**
Alabama	—	—	—	41,879	32.7	571	435,080	45.1	2,690
Arkansas	—	—	—	1,617	11.3	59	111,115	25.5	144
Florida	—	—	—	—	—	—	61,745	44.0	932
Georgia	29,264	35.5	398	149,654	43.9	1,763	462,198	43.7	3,500
Louisiana	—	—	—	69,064	45.2	10,476	331,726	46.9	18,647
Mississippi	—	—	—	32,814	43.5	458	436,631	55.2	773
North Carolina	100,572	25.5	4,975	205,017	32.1	14,612	331,059	33.4	30,463
South Carolina	107,094	43.0	1,801	258,475	51.4	6,826	402,406	57.2	9,914
Tennessee	3,417	9.5	361	80,107	18.9	2,727	275,719	24.8	7,300
Texas	—	—	—	—	—	—	182,566	30.2	355
Virginia	293,427	39.2	12,766	425,153	39.9	36,889	490,865	30.7	58,042
Total territories[3]	—	—	—	**6,377**	**19.3**	**4,048**	**3,229**	**1.1**	**11,434**
Total states and territories	**697,897**	**17.8**	**59,466**	**1,538,125**	**16.0**	**233,504**	**3,953,760**	**12.6**	**488,070**

(1) "Free colored" was an official Census Bureau designation in these decades. All pop. figures for slaves and free colored include both blacks and those of mixed-race background. (2) Some states had negligible slave pops. that are not listed separately but are included in regional totals (relevant census years in parentheses): California (1860), Illinois (1820, 1860), Indiana (1820, 1860), Iowa (1860), Maine (1820, 1860), Massachusetts (1790, 1820, 1860), Michigan (1860), Minnesota (1860), New Hampshire (1790, 1820, 1860), Ohio (1820, 1860), Oregon (1860), Rhode Island (1790, 1820, 1860), Vermont (1820, 1860), and Wisconsin (1860). (3) Incl. Colorado (1860), Dakota (1860), District of Columbia (1820, 1860), Nebraska (1860), Nevada (1860), New Mexico (1860), Utah (1860), and Washington (1860).

Largest U.S. Metropolitan Areas by Population, 1990-2010

Source: Decennial Censuses, U.S. Census Bureau, U.S. Dept. of Commerce

(ranked by 2010 population)

Metropolitan Statistical Areas (MSAs) are defined, or delineated geographically, for federal statistical use by the Office of Management and Budget (OMB), with technical assistance from the Census Bureau. The standards used to define metropolitan areas are revised before each decennial census. Following a decennial census and between decennial census years, population estimates are used to update area boundaries.

An MSA consists of at least one urbanized area of 50,000 or more inhabitants, plus an adjacent area closely integrated socially and economically with the core as measured by commuting ties. Micropolitan Statistical Areas, which are not included in the rankings below, have at least one urban cluster with a population of at least 10,000 but no more than 50,000.

About 83.9% of the total U.S. population resided in an MSA in 2000. That represents an increase of 28.9 mil (13.9%) from 1990. The standards in current use were published in 2000. The most recent definitions, issued by the OMB in Dec. 2009, designates 374 MSAs in the U.S. and Puerto Rico.

Rank	Metropolitan Statistical Area (MSA)	Population 2010	Population 2000	Population 1990	Percent change 2000-10	Percent change 1990-2010
1.	New York-Northern New Jersey-Long Island, NY-NJ-PA	18,897,109	18,323,002	16,846,046	3.1%	12.2%
2.	Los Angeles-Long Beach-Santa Ana, CA	12,828,837	12,365,627	11,273,720	3.7	13.8
3.	Chicago-Joliet-Naperville, IL-IN-WI	9,461,105	9,098,316	8,182,076	4.0	15.6
4.	Dallas-Fort Worth-Arlington, TX	6,371,773	5,161,544	3,989,294	23.4	59.7
5.	Philadelphia-Camden-Wilmington, PA-NJ-DE-MD	5,965,343	5,687,147	5,435,468	4.9	9.7
6.	Houston-Sugar Land-Baytown, TX	5,946,800	4,715,407	3,767,335	26.1	57.9
7.	Washington-Arlington-Alexandria, DC-VA-MD-WV	5,582,170	4,796,183	4,122,914	16.4	35.4
8.	Miami-Fort Lauderdale-Pompano Beach, FL	5,564,635	5,007,564	4,056,100	11.1	37.2
9.	Atlanta-Sandy Springs-Marietta, GA	5,268,860	4,247,981	3,069,425	24.0	71.7
10.	Boston-Cambridge-Quincy, MA-NH	4,552,402	4,391,344	4,133,895	3.7	10.1
11.	San Francisco-Oakland-Fremont, CA	4,335,391	4,123,740	3,686,592	5.1	17.6
12.	Detroit-Warren-Livonia, MI	4,296,250	4,452,557	4,248,699	-3.5	1.1
13.	Riverside-San Bernardino-Ontario, CA	4,224,851	3,254,821	2,588,793	29.8	63.2
14.	Phoenix-Mesa-Glendale, AZ	4,192,887	3,251,876	2,238,480	28.9	87.3
15.	Seattle-Tacoma-Bellevue, WA	3,439,809	3,043,878	2,559,164	13.0	34.4
16.	Minneapolis-St. Paul-Bloomington, MN-WI	3,279,833	2,968,806	2,538,834	10.5	29.2
17.	San Diego-Carlsbad-San Marcos, CA	3,095,313	2,813,833	2,498,016	10.0	23.9
18.	St. Louis, MO-IL	2,812,896	2,698,687	2,580,897	4.2	9.0
19.	Tampa-St. Petersburg-Clearwater, FL	2,783,243	2,395,997	2,067,959	16.2	34.6
20.	Baltimore-Towson, MD	2,710,489	2,552,994	2,382,172	6.2	13.8
21.	Denver-Aurora-Broomfield, CO	2,543,482	2,179,240	1,666,883	16.7	52.6
22.	Pittsburgh, PA	2,356,285	2,431,087	2,468,289	-3.1	-4.5
23.	Portland-Vancouver-Hillsboro, OR-WA	2,226,009	1,927,881	1,523,741	15.5	46.1
24.	Sacramento-Arden-Arcade-Roseville, CA	2,149,127	1,796,857	1,481,102	19.6	45.1
25.	San Antonio-New Braunfels, TX	2,142,508	1,711,703	1,407,745	25.2	52.2
26.	Orlando-Kissimmee-Sanford, FL	2,134,411	1,644,561	1,224,852	29.8	74.3
27.	Cincinnati-Middletown, OH-KY-IN	2,130,151	2,009,632	1,844,917	6.0	15.5
28.	Cleveland-Elyria-Mentor, OH	2,077,240	2,148,143	2,102,248	-3.3	-1.2
29.	Kansas City, MO-KS	2,035,334	1,836,038	1,636,528	10.9	24.4
30.	Las Vegas-Paradise, NV	1,951,269	1,375,765	741,459	41.8	163.2
31.	San Jose-Sunnyvale-Santa Clara, CA	1,836,911	1,735,819	1,534,274	5.8	19.7
32.	Columbus, OH	1,836,536	1,612,694	1,405,168	13.9	30.7
33.	Charlotte-Gastonia-Rock Hill, NC-SC	1,758,038	1,330,448	1,024,643	32.1	71.6
34.	Indianapolis-Carmel, IN	1,756,241	1,525,104	1,294,217	15.2	35.7
35.	Austin-Round Rock-San Marcos, TX	1,716,289	1,249,763	846,227	37.3	102.8
36.	Virginia Beach-Norfolk-Newport News, VA-NC	1,671,683	1,576,370	1,449,389	6.0	15.3
37.	Providence-New Bedford-Fall River, RI-MA	1,600,852	1,582,997	1,509,789	1.1	6.0
38.	Nashville-Davidson-Murfreesboro-Franklin, TN	1,589,934	1,311,789	1,048,216	21.1	51.7
39.	Milwaukee-Waukesha-West Allis, WI	1,555,908	1,500,741	1,432,149	3.7	8.6
40.	Jacksonville, FL	1,345,596	1,122,750	925,213	19.8	45.4
41.	Memphis, TN-MS-AR	1,316,100	1,205,204	1,067,263	9.2	23.3
42.	Louisville-Jefferson County, KY-IN	1,283,566	1,161,975	1,055,973	10.5	21.6
43.	Richmond, VA	1,258,251	1,096,957	949,244	14.7	32.6
44.	Oklahoma City, OK	1,252,987	1,095,421	971,042	14.4	29.0
45.	Hartford-West Hartford-East Hartford, CT	1,212,381	1,148,618	1,123,678	5.6	7.9
46.	New Orleans-Metairie-Kenner, LA	1,167,764	1,316,510	1,264,391	-11.3	-7.6
47.	Buffalo-Niagara Falls, NY	1,135,509	1,170,111	1,189,288	-3.0	-4.5
48.	Raleigh-Cary, NC	1,130,490	797,071	541,100	41.8	108.9
49.	Birmingham-Hoover, AL	1,128,047	1,052,238	956,844	7.2	17.9
50.	Salt Lake City, UT	1,124,197	968,858	768,075	16.0	46.4
51.	Rochester, NY	1,054,323	1,037,831	1,002,410	1.6	5.2
52.	Tucson, AZ	980,263	843,746	666,880	-16.2	47.0
53.	Honolulu, HI	953,207	876,156	836,231	8.8	14.0
54.	Tulsa, OK	937,478	859,532	761,019	9.1	23.2
55.	Fresno, CA	930,450	799,407	667,490	16.4	39.4
56.	Bridgeport-Stamford-Norwalk, CT	916,829	882,567	827,645	3.9	10.8
57.	Albuquerque, NM	887,077	729,649	599,416	21.6	48.0
58.	Albany-Schenectady-Troy, NY	870,716	825,875	809,443	5.4	7.6
59.	Omaha-Council Bluffs, NE-IA	865,350	767,041	685,797	12.8	26.2
60.	New Haven-Milford, CT	862,477	824,008	804,219	4.7	7.2
61.	Dayton, OH	841,502	848,153	843,835	-0.8	-0.3
62.	Bakersfield-Delano, CA	839,631	661,645	543,477	26.9	54.5
63.	Oxnard-Thousand Oaks-Ventura, CA	823,318	753,197	669,016	9.3	23.1
64.	Allentown-Bethlehem-Easton, PA-NJ	821,173	740,395	686,688	10.9	19.6
65.	Baton Rouge, LA	802,484	705,973	623,853	13.7	28.6
66.	El Paso, TX	800,647	679,622	591,610	17.8	35.3
67.	Worcester, MA	798,552	750,963	709,705	6.3	12.5
68.	McAllen-Edinburg-Mission, TX	774,769	569,463	383,545	36.1	102.0
69.	Grand Rapids-Wyoming, MI	774,160	740,482	645,914	4.5	19.9
70.	Columbia, SC	767,598	647,158	548,335	18.6	40.0

Largest U.S. Cities by Population, 1850-2010

Source: Decennial Censuses, U.S. Census Bureau, U.S. Dept. of Commerce
(ranked by 2010 population)

Rank	City	2010	2000	1990	1980	1970	1950	1900	1850
1.	New York, NY	8,175,133	8,008,278	7,322,564	7,071,639	7,895,563	7,891,957	3,437,202	696,115
2.	Los Angeles, CA	3,792,621	3,694,820	3,485,398	2,968,528	2,811,801	1,970,358	102,479	1,610
3.	Chicago, IL	2,695,598	2,896,016	2,783,726	3,005,072	3,369,357	3,620,962	1,698,575	29,963
4.	Houston, TX	2,099,451	1,953,631	1,630,553	1,595,138	1,233,535	596,163	44,633	2,396
6.	Philadelphia, PA	1,526,006	1,517,550	1,585,577	1,688,210	1,949,996	2,071,605	1,293,697	121,376
5.	Phoenix, AZ	1,445,632	1,321,045	983,403	789,704	584,303	106,818	5,544	...
7.	San Antonio, TX	1,327,407	1,144,646	935,933	785,940	654,153	408,442	53,321	3,488
8.	San Diego, CA	1,307,402	1,223,400	1,110,549	875,538	697,471	334,387	17,700	...
9.	Dallas, TX	1,197,816	1,188,580	1,006,877	904,599	844,401	434,462	42,638	...
10.	San Jose, CA	945,942	894,943	782,248	629,400	459,913	95,280	21,500	...
11.	Jacksonville, FL	821,784	735,617	635,230	540,920	504,265	204,517	28,429	1,045
12.	Indianapolis, IN[1]	820,445	781,870	741,952	700,807	736,856	427,173	169,164	8,091
13.	San Francisco, CA	805,235	776,733	723,959	678,974	715,674	775,357	342,782	34,776
14.	Austin, TX	790,390	656,562	465,622	345,890	253,539	132,459	22,258	629
15.	Columbus, OH	787,033	711,470	632,910	565,021	540,025	375,901	125,560	17,882
16.	Fort Worth, TX	741,206	534,694	447,619	385,164	393,455	278,778	26,688	...
17.	Charlotte, NC	731,424	540,828	395,934	315,474	241,420	134,042	18,091	1,065
18.	Detroit, MI	713,777	951,270	1,027,974	1,203,368	1,514,063	1,849,568	285,704	21,019
19.	El Paso, TX	649,121	563,662	515,342	425,259	322,261	130,485	15,906	...
20.	Memphis, TN	646,889	650,100	610,337	646,174	623,988	396,000	102,320	8,841
21.	Baltimore, MD	620,961	651,154	736,014	786,741	905,787	949,708	508,957	169,054
22.	Boston, MA	617,594	589,141	574,283	562,994	641,071	801,444	560,892	136,881
23.	Seattle, WA	608,660	563,374	516,259	493,846	530,831	467,591	80,671	...
24.	Washington, DC	601,723	572,059	606,900	638,432	756,668	802,178	278,718	40,001
25.	Nashville-Davidson, TN[1]	601,222	545,524	510,784	455,651	426,029	174,307	80,865	10,165
26.	Denver, CO	600,158	554,636	467,610	492,686	514,678	415,786	133,859	...
27.	Louisville-Jefferson, KY[1]	597,337	256,231	269,063	298,694	361,706	369,129	204,731	43,194
28.	Milwaukee, WI	594,833	596,974	628,088	636,297	717,372	637,392	285,315	20,061
29.	Portland, OR	583,776	529,121	437,319	368,148	379,967	373,628	90,426	...
30.	Las Vegas, NV	583,756	478,434	258,295	164,674	125,787	24,624	...	...
31.	Oklahoma City, OK	579,999	506,132	444,719	404,014	368,164	243,504	10,037	...
32.	Albuquerque, NM	545,852	448,607	384,736	332,920	244,501	96,815	6,238	...
33.	Tucson, AZ	520,116	486,699	405,390	330,537	262,933	45,454	7,531	...
34.	Fresno, CA	494,665	427,652	354,202	217,491	165,655	91,669	12,470	...
35.	Sacramento, CA	466,488	407,018	369,365	275,741	257,105	137,572	29,282	6,820
36.	Long Beach, CA	462,257	461,522	429,433	361,498	358,879	250,767	2,252	...
37.	Kansas City, MO	459,787	441,545	435,146	448,028	507,330	456,622	163,752	...
38.	Mesa, AZ	439,041	396,375	288,091	152,404	63,049	16,790	722	...
39.	Virginia Beach, VA	437,994	425,257	393,069	262,199	172,106	5,390	...	...
40.	Atlanta, GA	420,003	416,474	394,017	425,022	495,039	331,314	89,872	2,572
41.	Colorado Springs, CO	416,427	360,890	281,140	215,105	135,517	45,472	21,085	...
42.	Omaha, NE	408,958	390,007	335,795	313,939	346,929	251,117	102,555	...
43.	Raleigh, NC	403,892	276,093	207,951	150,255	122,830	65,679	13,643	4,518
44.	Miami, FL	399,457	362,470	358,548	346,681	334,859	249,276	1,681	...
45.	Cleveland, OH	396,815	478,403	505,616	573,822	750,879	914,808	381,768	17,034
46.	Tulsa, OK	391,906	393,049	367,302	360,919	330,350	182,740	1,390	...
47.	Oakland, CA	390,724	399,484	372,242	339,337	361,561	384,575	66,960	...
48.	Minneapolis, MN	382,578	382,618	368,383	370,951	434,400	521,718	202,718	...
49.	Wichita, KS	382,368	344,284	304,011	279,838	276,554	168,279	24,671	...
50.	Arlington, TX	365,438	332,969	261,721	160,113	90,229	7,692	1,079	...
51.	Bakersfield, CA	347,483	247,057	174,820	105,611	69,515	34,784	4,836	...
52.	New Orleans, LA	343,829	484,674	496,938	557,927	593,471	570,445	287,104	116,375
53.	Honolulu, HI[2]	337,256	371,657	365,272	365,048	324,871	248,034	39,306	...
54.	Anaheim, CA	336,265	328,014	266,406	219,494	166,408	14,556	1,456	...
55.	Tampa, FL	335,709	303,447	280,015	271,577	277,714	124,681	15,839	...
56.	Aurora, CO	325,078	276,393	222,103	158,588	74,974	11,421	202	...
57.	Santa Ana, CA	324,528	337,977	293,742	204,023	155,710	45,533	4,933	...
58.	St. Louis, MO	319,294	348,189	396,685	452,801	622,236	856,796	575,238	77,860
59.	Pittsburgh, PA	305,704	334,563	369,879	423,959	520,089	676,806	321,616	46,601
60.	Corpus Christi, TX	305,215	277,454	257,453	232,134	204,525	108,287	4,703	...
61.	Riverside, CA	303,871	255,166	226,505	170,591	140,089	46,764	7,973	...
62.	Cincinnati, OH	296,943	331,285	364,040	385,409	453,514	503,998	325,902	115,435
63.	Lexington-Fayette, KY	295,803	260,512	225,366	204,165	108,137	55,534	26,369	8,159
64.	Anchorage, AK	291,826	260,283	226,338	174,431	48,081	11,254	...	...
65.	Stockton, CA	291,707	243,771	210,943	148,283	109,963	70,853	17,506	...
66.	Toledo, OH	287,208	313,619	332,943	354,635	383,062	303,616	131,822	3,829
67.	St. Paul, MN	285,068	287,151	272,235	270,230	309,866	311,349	163,065	1,112
68.	Newark, NJ	277,140	273,546	275,221	329,248	381,930	438,776	246,070	38,894
69.	Greensboro, NC	269,666	223,891	183,521	155,642	144,076	74,389	10,035	...
70.	Buffalo, NY	261,310	292,648	328,123	357,870	462,768	580,132	352,387	42,261
71.	Plano, TX	259,841	222,030	128,713	72,331	17,872	2,126	1,304	...
72.	Lincoln, NE	258,379	225,581	191,972	171,932	149,518	98,884	40,169	...
73.	Henderson, NV	257,729	175,381	64,942	23,376	16,400	5,717	...	...
74.	Fort Wayne, IN	253,691	205,727	173,072	172,391	178,269	133,607	45,115	4,282
75.	Jersey City, NJ	247,597	240,055	228,537	223,532	260,350	299,017	206,433	6,856
76.	St. Petersburg, FL	244,769	248,232	238,629	238,647	216,159	96,738	1,575	...
77.	Chula Vista, CA	243,916	173,556	135,163	83,927	67,901	31,339	...	...
78.	Norfolk, VA	242,803	234,403	261,229	266,979	307,951	213,513	46,624	14,326
79.	Orlando, FL	238,300	185,951	164,693	128,394	99,006	52,367	2,481	...
80.	Chandler, AZ	236,123	176,581	89,862	29,673	13,763	3,799	...	...

Rank City	2010	2000	1990	1980	1970	1950	1900	1850
81. Laredo, TX	236,091	176,576	122,899	91,449	69,024	51,910	13,429	...
82. Madison, WI	233,209	208,054	191,262	170,616	171,809	96,056	19,164	1,525
83. Winston-Salem, NC	229,617	185,776	143,485	131,885	133,683	87,811	13,650	...
84. Lubbock, TX	229,573	199,564	186,206	174,361	149,101	71,747	...	...
85. Baton Rouge, LA	229,493	227,818	219,531	220,394	165,921	125,629	11,269	3,905
86. Durham, NC	228,330	187,035	136,611	100,831	95,438	71,311	6,679	...
87. Garland, TX	226,876	215,768	180,650	138,857	81,437	10,571	819	...
88. Glendale, AZ	226,721	218,812	148,134	96,988	36,228	8,179	...	...
89. Reno, NV	225,221	180,480	134,230	100,756	72,863	32,497	4,500	...
90. Hialeah, FL	224,669	226,419	188,004	145,254	102,452	19,676	...	...
91. Paradise, NV[2]	223,167	186,070	124,682	84,818	24,477	...	...	...
92. Chesapeake, VA	222,209	199,184	151,976	114,486	89,580	...	...	...
93. Scottsdale, AZ	217,385	202,705	130,069	88,364	67,823	2,032	...	...
94. North Las Vegas, NV	216,961	115,488	47,707	42,739	46,067	...	...	...
95. Irving, TX	216,290	191,615	155,037	109,943	97,260	2,621	...	...
96. Fremont, CA	214,089	203,413	173,339	131,945	100,869	...	...	...
97. Irvine, CA	212,375	143,072	110,330	62,134	...	...	...	...
98. Birmingham, AL	212,237	242,820	265,968	284,413	300,910	326,037	38,415	...
99. Rochester, NY	210,565	219,773	231,636	241,741	295,011	332,488	162,608	36,403
100. San Bernardino, CA	209,924	185,401	164,164	117,490	104,251	63,058	6,150	...

Note: Population figures for 1950-2010 are for Apr. 1; 1850 and 1900 are for June 1. (1) Consolidated city. Population figures are for city or metro government only, i.e., exclude the populations of semi-independent incorporated places within the consolidated city. For years predating consolidation, city population figure is shown. (2) Census designated place (CDP). Although not incorporated, CDPs are recognized as statistical equivalents for census purposes.

Largest U.S. Counties by Population, 2000, 2010

Source: Decennial Censuses, U.S. Census Bureau, U.S. Dept. of Commerce

(ranked by 2010 population; figures are for Apr. 1 of decennial census year)

Rank County	2010	2000	% change	Rank County	2010	2000	% change
1. Los Angeles Co., CA	9,818,605	9,519,338	3.1%	16. Tarrant Co., TX	1,809,034	1,446,219	25.1%
2. Cook Co., IL	5,194,675	5,376,741	–3.4	17. Santa Clara Co., CA	1,781,642	1,682,585	5.9
3. Harris Co., TX	4,092,459	3,400,578	20.3	18. Broward Co., FL	1,748,066	1,623,018	7.7
4. Maricopa Co., AZ	3,817,117	3,072,149	24.2	19. Bexar Co., TX	1,714,773	1,392,931	23.1
5. San Diego Co., CA	3,095,313	2,813,833	10.0	20. New York Co., NY	1,585,873	1,537,195	3.2
6. Orange Co., CA	3,010,232	2,846,289	5.8	21. Philadelphia Co., PA	1,526,006	1,517,550	0.6
7. Kings Co., NY	2,504,700	2,465,326	1.6	22. Alameda Co., CA	1,510,271	1,443,741	4.6
8. Miami-Dade Co., FL	2,496,435	2,253,362	10.8	23. Middlesex Co., MA	1,503,085	1,465,396	2.6
9. Dallas Co., TX	2,368,139	2,218,899	6.7	24. Suffolk Co., NY	1,493,350	1,419,369	5.2
10. Queens Co., NY	2,230,722	2,229,379	0.1	25. Sacramento Co.,			
11. Riverside Co., CA	2,189,641	1,545,387	41.7	CA	1,418,788	1,223,499	16.0
12. San Bernardino Co.,				26. Bronx Co., NY	1,385,108	1,332,650	3.9
CA	2,035,210	1,709,434	19.1	27. Nassau Co., NY	1,339,532	1,334,544	0.4
13. Clark Co., NV	1,951,269	1,375,765	41.8	28. Palm Beach Co., FL	1,320,134	1,131,184	16.7
14. King Co., WA	1,931,249	1,737,034	11.2	29. Cuyahoga Co., OH	1,280,122	1,393,978	–8.2
15. Wayne Co., MI	1,820,584	2,061,162	–11.7	30. Hillsborough Co., FL	1,229,226	998,948	23.1

Note: The 10 smallest counties by 2010 population (with % change in 2000-10): (1) Loving Co., TX (pop.: 82; 22.4%); (2) Kalawao Co., HI (90; –38.8%); (3) King Co., TX (286; –19.7%); (4) Kenedy Co., TX (416; 0.5%); (5) Arthur Co., NE (460; 3.6%); (6) Blaine Co., NE (478; –18.0%); (7) Petroleum Co., MT (494; 0.2%); (8) McPherson Co., NE (539; 1.1%); (9) Grant Co., NE (614; –17.8%); (10) Loup Co., NE (632; –11.2%).

Mobility of U.S. Population by Selected Characteristics, 2009-10

Source: Annual Social and Economic Supplement, Current Population Survey, Housing and Household Economic Statistics Division, U.S. Census Bureau, U.S. Dept. of Commerce

(numbers in thousands)

	Total	Location of new residence					Total	Location of new residence			
		Same county	Diff. county, same state	Diff. state	Abroad			Same county	Diff. county, same state	Diff. state	Abroad
Age						**Marital status[1]**					
1-14 years	8,612	6,312	1,259	912	130	Married, spouse present	9,489	6,132	1,674	1,334	348
1-17 years	9,923	7,258	1,460	1,031	174	Married, spouse absent	625	396	83	96	50
18 years and older	27,616	18,758	4,794	3,297	772	Widowed	740	482	146	95	18
25 years and older	20,789	14,174	3,524	2,536	560	Divorced	3,454	2,469	567	398	21
65 years and older	1,422	873	299	224	28	Separated	1,241	885	245	99	13
85 years and older	170	107	28	31	3	Never married	13,378	9,342	2,278	1,392	366
Income[1]						**Educational attainment[2]**					
Without income	4,231	2,791	651	462	326	Not a h.s. graduate	3,012	2,245	440	218	109
Under $5,000 or loss	2,826	1,863	465	394	104	High school graduate	6,372	4,537	1,128	619	87
$5,000 to $9,999	3,018	2,082	562	319	56	Some college or					
$10,000 to $19,999	5,539	3,932	956	565	87	associate degree	5,385	3,677	1,021	611	76
$20,000 to $29,999	4,301	2,980	805	455	61	Bachelor's degree	4,169	2,641	658	704	166
$30,000 to $39,999	2,914	2,019	478	363	55	Prof. or grad. degree	1,853	1,075	274	380	122
$40,000 to $59,999	3,282	2,196	594	434	59	**Tenure**					
$60,000 to $74,999	1,162	762	200	172	28	In owner-occupied unit	10,770	7,010	2,050	1,417	293
$75,000 to $99,999	781	547	132	86	16	In renter-occupied unit[3]	26,769	19,007	4,202	2,908	653
$100,000 and over	875	534	152	163	25	**Total movers**	37,540	26,017	6,252	4,326	946

Note: Total movers consists of persons ages 1 and older who moved to a new residence in the 12 months preceding the administering of the survey. Figures may not add up to totals due to rounding. (1) Ages 15 and older. (2) Ages 25 and older. (3) Includes units occupied without payment of cash rent.

U.S. Foreign-Born Population

Source: Annual Social and Economic Supplements, Current Population Surveys, Housing and Household Economic Statistics Division, U.S. Census Bureau, U.S. Dept. of Commerce

Percentage of Population That Is Foreign-Born, 1900-2009

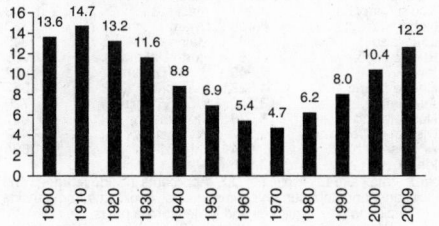

Foreign-Born Population by Region of Birth, 1995-2009
(numbers in thousands)

Region	2009[1] No.	%	2000	1995
Asia............	9,925	27.0%	7,246	6,121
Under 18.....	723	27.4	657	767
Europe	4,572	12.4	4,355	3,937
Under 18.....	251	9.5	250	232
Latin America	19,882	54.1	14,477	11,777
Under 18.....	1,467	55.6	1,684	1,481
Other[2]...........	2,371	6.5	2,301	2,658
Under 18.....	197	7.5	245	275
All regions....	**36,750**	**100.0**	**28,379**	**24,493**
Under 18	**2,638**	**100.0**	**2,837**	**2,726**

(1) Figures given as percent of total foreign-born population or of total foreign-born population under 18 years. (2) Including those born at sea.

U.S. Foreign-Born Population: Top Countries of Origin, 1880-2010

Source: American Community Survey, Decennial Censuses, U.S. Census Bureau, U.S. Dept. of Commerce
(numbers in thousands; % is of all foreign-born)

1880			1920			1960			2000			2010[4]		
Country	No.	%	Country	No.	%	Country	No.	%	Country	No.	%	Country	No.	%
Germany	1,967	29.4	Germany	1,686	12.1	Italy	1,257	12.9	Mexico	9,177	29.5	Mexico	11,711	29.3
Ireland	1,855	27.8	Italy	1,610	11.6	Germany	990	10.2	China[2]	1,519	4.9	China[2]	2,167	5.4
Gr. Britain	918	13.7	U.S.S.R.	1,400	10.1	Canada	953	9.8	Philippines	1,369	4.4	India	1,780	4.5
Canada	717	10.7	Poland	1,140	8.2	Gr. Britain	765	7.9	India	1,023	3.3	Philippines	1,778	4.4
Sweden	194	2.9	Canada	1,138	8.2	Poland	748	7.7	Vietnam	988	3.2	Vietnam	1,241	3.1
Norway	182	2.7	Gr. Britain	1,135	8.2	U.S.S.R.	691	7.1	Cuba	873	2.8	El Salvador	1,214	3.0
France	107	1.6	Ireland	1,037	7.5	Mexico	576	5.9	Korea[3]	864	2.8	Cuba	1,105	2.8
China[1]	104	1.6	Sweden	626	4.5	Ireland	339	3.5	Canada	821	2.6	Korea[3]	1,100	2.8
Switzerland	89	1.3	Austria	576	4.1	Austria	305	3.1	El Salvador	817	2.6	Dominican Republic	879	2.2
Czech.	85	1.3	Mexico	486	3.5	Hungary	245	2.5	Germany	707	2.3	Guatemala	831	2.1
Total	**6,680**	**100.0**	**Total**	**13,921**	**100.0**	**Total**	**9,738**	**100.0**	**Total**	**31,108**	**100.0**	**Total**	**39,956**	**100.0**

(1) Includes Taiwan. (2) Includes Hong Kong and Taiwan. (3) Includes North and South Korea. (4) Data based on sample and subject to sampling variability.

Language Spoken at Home by the U.S. Population, 2010

Source: American Community Survey, U.S. Census Bureau, U.S. Dept. of Commerce
(ranked by number of speakers)

Language	Number (thous.)	% of total	% English inability[1]
Total population[2]	289,215.7	100.00%	8.7%
Speak only English........	229,673.2	79.41	NA
Speak another language ...	59,542.6	20.59	42.4
Spanish or Spanish Creole...	36,995.6	12.79	44.7
Chinese	2,808.7	0.97	55.1
Tagalog..................	1,573.7	0.54	31.1
Vietnamese..............	1,381.5	0.48	60.5
French (incl. Patois, Cajun)...	1,322.7	0.46	20.5
Korean	1,137.3	0.39	55.9
German	1,067.7	0.37	16.4
Arabic..................	865.0	0.30	37.1
African languages..........	862.4	0.30	32.1
Russian.................	855.0	0.30	48.7
Other Asian languages......	839.3	0.29	30.5
French Creole.............	746.7	0.26	43.3
Other Indic languages	741.3	0.26	39.0
Italian	725.2	0.25	28.1
Portuguese or Portuguese Creole.................	688.3	0.24	40.2
Hindi	609.4	0.21	20.1
Polish	608.3	0.21	41.2
Japanese	443.5	0.15	42.4
Other Indo-European languages..............	435.6	0.15	36.9
Other Pacific Island languages..............	414.4	0.14%	38.4%
Urdu	388.9	0.13	30.7
Persian	381.4	0.13	37.0
Gujarati.................	356.4	0.12	36.3
Other Slavic languages	323.4	0.11	38.2
Greek	307.2	0.11	25.9
Other West Germanic languages..............	299.0	0.10	23.7
Serbo-Croatian...........	284.1	0.10	39.4
Armenian	240.4	0.08	45.7
Mon-Khmer, Cambodian	220.9	0.08	50.1
Hmong	211.5	0.07	42.3
Hebrew	204.6	0.07	16.4
Other Native North American languages..............	197.5	0.07	15.9
Navajo..................	172.9	0.06	23.5
Laotian.................	158.8	0.05	50.3
Yiddish	154.8	0.05	33.7
Thai....................	150.9	0.05	52.3
Other and unspecified languages..............	146.8	0.05	38.2
Scandinavian languages	131.0	0.05	10.6
Hungarian...............	90.5	0.03	30.9

NA = Not applicable or available. **Note:** Data based on sample and subject to sampling variability. (1) Speakers of other languages were asked how well they spoke English: very well, well, not well, or not at all. Figures shown here are percentage of speakers of an individual language who indicated they spoke English less than very well. (2) Ages 5 and older.

Persons Granted Legal Permanent Resident Status by State of Residence, 2010

Source: Office of Immigration Statistics, U.S. Dept. of Homeland Security
(ranked by fiscal year 2010 number)

State/territory	Number	State/territory	Number	State/territory	Number	State/territory	Number
Total	1,042,625	Arizona	18,243	Kansas	5,501	New Hampshire	2,556
California	208,446	North Carolina	16,112	Kentucky	4,930	Delaware	2,198
New York	147,999	Ohio	13,585	Oklahoma	4,627	Mississippi	1,709
Florida	107,276	Colorado	12,489	South Carolina	4,401	Alaska	1,703
Texas	87,750	Minnesota	12,408	Nebraska	4,400	Guam	1,383
New Jersey	56,920	Connecticut	12,222	Louisiana	4,397	Maine	1,349
Illinois	37,909	Nevada	10,803	Puerto Rico	4,283	North Dakota	1,058
Massachusetts	31,069	Indiana	8,539	Iowa	4,245	South Dakota	987
Virginia	28,607	Tennessee	8,156	Rhode Island	4,027	Vermont	867
Maryland	26,450	Oregon	7,997	Alabama	3,740	West Virginia	729
Georgia	24,833	Missouri	7,151	New Mexico	3,528	Montana	457
Pennsylvania	24,130	Hawaii	7,037	District of Columbia	2,897	Wyoming	452
Washington	22,283	Wisconsin	6,189	Arkansas	2,684	Other[1]	1,694
Michigan	18,579	Utah	6,085	Idaho	2,556		

Note: Applicants for legal permanent resident (LPR) status, or "green cards," may already live in the U.S. Applicants include refugees and asylees, temporary workers, foreign students, family members of U.S. citizens, and undocumented immigrants. Applicants from outside the U.S. enter on a visa and are granted LPR status upon admittance. (1) Includes U.S. territories and armed forces posts.

Persons Granted Legal Permanent Resident Status by Top Areas of Residence, 2010

Source: Office of Immigration Statistics, U.S. Dept. of Homeland Security
(ranked by fiscal year 2010 number)

Core Based Statistical Area (CBSA)[1]	Number	% of total	Core Based Statistical Area (CBSA)[1]	Number	% of total
Total	1,042,625	100.0%	Portland-Vancouver-Beaverton, OR-WA	6,732	0.6%
New York-Northern New Jersey-Long Island, NY-NJ-PA	186,086	17.8	Austin-Round Rock, TX	5,434	0.5
Los Angeles-Long Beach-Santa Ana, CA	87,443	8.4	Honolulu, HI	5,169	0.5
Miami-Fort Lauderdale-Pompano Beach, FL	69,420	6.7	Providence-New Bedford-Fall River, RI-MA	4,912	0.5
			San Antonio, TX	4,740	0.5
Washington-Arlington-Alexandria, DC-VA-MD-WV	41,322	4.0	El Paso, TX	4,646	0.4
Chicago-Naperville-Joliet, IL-IN-WI	35,109	3.4	Bridgeport-Stamford-Norwalk, CT	4,587	0.4
San Francisco-Oakland-Fremont, CA	31,761	3.0	Columbus, OH	4,460	0.4
Houston-Sugar Land-Baytown, TX	30,844	3.0	Kansas City, MO-KS	4,299	0.4
Dallas-Fort Worth-Arlington, TX	26,006	2.5	Charlotte-Gastonia-Concord, NC-SC	4,178	0.4
Boston-Cambridge-Quincy, MA-NH	24,969	2.4	Raleigh-Cary, NC	3,917	0.4
Atlanta-Sandy Springs-Marietta, GA	20,447	2.0	Nashville-Davidson–Murfreesboro–Franklin, TN	3,897	0.4
San Diego-Carlsbad-San Marcos, CA	19,769	1.9	San Juan-Caguas-Guaynabo, Puerto Rico	3,894	0.4
San Jose-Sunnyvale-Santa Clara, CA	18,619	1.8	Salt Lake City, UT	3,879	0.4
Philadelphia-Camden-Wilmington, PA-NJ-DE-MD	18,253	1.8	Hartford-West Hartford-East Hartford, CT	3,869	0.4
Seattle-Tacoma-Bellevue, WA	16,866	1.6	Indianapolis-Carmel, IN	3,606	0.3
Riverside-San Bernardino-Ontario, CA	14,926	1.4	St. Louis, MO-IL	3,553	0.3
Detroit-Warren-Livonia, MI	12,682	1.2	Jacksonville, FL	3,503	0.3
Phoenix-Mesa-Scottsdale, AZ	12,542	1.2	Worcester, MA	3,283	0.3
Orlando-Kissimmee, FL	10,676	1.0	Cleveland-Elyria-Mentor, OH	3,111	0.3
Minneapolis-St. Paul-Bloomington, MN-WI	10,434	1.0	Oxnard-Thousand Oaks-Ventura, CA	3,104	0.3
Las Vegas-Paradise, NV	9,004	0.9	Stockton, CA	3,017	0.3
Tampa-St. Petersburg-Clearwater, FL	8,818	0.8	Fresno, CA	3,010	0.3
Denver-Aurora-Broomfield, CO	8,214	0.8	Tucson, AZ	2,926	0.3
Baltimore-Towson, MD	8,207	0.8	Cincinnati-Middletown, OH-KY-IN	2,814	0.3
Sacramento–Arden-Arcade–Roseville, CA	8,047	0.8	Virginia Beach-Norfolk-Newport News, VA-NC	2,750	0.3
			Other CBSAs	195,454	18.7
			Non-CBSA or unknown	13,406	1.3

Note: Applicants for legal permanent resident (LPR) status, or "green cards," may already live in the U.S. Applicants include refugees and asylees, temporary workers, foreign students, family members of U.S. citizens, and undocumented immigrants. Applicants from outside the U.S. enter on a visa and are granted LPR status upon admittance. (1) CBSAs refer collectively to metropolitan and micropolitan statistical areas. These areas are defined for federal statistical use by the U.S. Office of Management and Budget, with technical assistance from the U.S. Census Bureau.

Unauthorized Immigrant Population in the U.S., 2000, 2010

Source: Office of Immigration Statistics, U.S. Dept. of Homeland Security
(ranked by 2010 est. population)

	Country of Birth				State of Residence		
	Est. population[1]		% change		Est. population[1]		% change
Country	2010	2000	2000-10	State	2010	2000	2000-10
All countries	10,790,000	8,460,000	27.5%	All states	10,790,000	8,460,000	27.5%
Mexico	6,640,000	4,680,000	41.9	California	2,570,000	2,510,000	2.4
El Salvador	620,000	430,000	44.2	Texas	1,770,000	1,090,000	62.4
Guatemala	520,000	290,000	79.3	Florida	760,000	800,000	-5.0
Honduras	330,000	160,000	106.3	Illinois	490,000	440,000	11.4
Philippines	280,000	200,000	40.0	Arizona	470,000	330,000	42.4
India	200,000	120,000	66.7	Georgia	460,000	220,000	109.1
Ecuador	180,000	110,000	63.6	New York	460,000	540,000	-14.8
Brazil	180,000	100,000	80.0	North Carolina	390,000	260,000	50.0
Korea[2]	170,000	180,000	-5.6	New Jersey	370,000	350,000	5.7
China	130,000	190,000	-31.6	Nevada	260,000	170,000	52.9
Other countries	1,550,000	2,000,000	-22.5	Other states	2,790,000	1,760,000	58.5

Note: Unauthorized immigrant population estimates are made using the "residual" method. The estimated size of the legally resident foreign-born population (i.e., legal permanent residents, asylees, refugees, and nonimmigrants) is subtracted from the estimated size of the total foreign-born population. Numbers may not add up to totals because of rounding. (1) In Jan. of year listed. (2) Includes North and South Korea.

U.S. Population by Age, Sex, and Household, 2010

Source: American Community Survey, U.S. Census Bureau, U.S. Dept. of Commerce

	Number	% of tot.		Number	% of tot.
Total population[1]	309,349,689	100.0%	Sex		
Age			Male	152,089,450	49.2%
Under 5 years	20,133,943	6.5	Female	157,260,239	50.8
5 to 14 years	41,159,800	13.3	**Total households[2]**	114,567,419	100.0
15 to 17 years	12,871,622	4.2	Family households	76,089,045	66.4
18 to 24 years	30,895,391	10.0	2-person household	32,547,775	28.4
25 to 34 years	40,972,083	13.2	3-person household	17,258,605	15.1
35 to 44 years	41,192,328	13.3	4-person household	14,806,321	12.9
45 to 54 years	44,929,033	14.5	5-or-more-person household	11,476,344	10.0
55 to 64 years	36,761,964	11.9	Married-couple family	55,704,781	48.6
65 years and over	40,433,525	13.1	Female HH, no husband present	14,998,476	13.1
15 to 44 years	125,931,424	40.7	Male HH, no wife present	5,385,788	4.7
18 years and over	235,184,324	76.0	Nonfamily households (total HHs)	38,478,374	33.6
Male	114,105,885	36.9	HH living alone	31,403,342	27.4
Female	121,078,439	39.1	HH 65 years and over	10,908,469	9.5
75 years and over	18,579,490	6.0	2-person household	5,766,767	5.0
85 years and over	5,560,440	1.8	3-or-more-person household	1,308,265	1.1
Median age (years)	37.2	NA	Average household size	2.63	NA

NA = Not applicable. HH = Householder. **Note:** Data based on sample and subject to sampling variability. (1) Includes population living in group quarters (both institutional and noninstitutional, e.g., correctional facilities, military barracks, university housing). (2) Number of households, not number of people living in households. Group quarters are not considered households.

Elderly U.S. Population, 1900-2050

Source: Decennial Censuses, 2008 National Population Projections, U.S. Census Bureau, U.S. Dept. of Commerce

(numbers in thousands)

	65 and over		85 and over			65 and over		85 and over	
Year[1]	Number	% tot. pop.	Number	% tot. pop.	Year[1]	Number	% tot. pop.	Number	% tot. pop.
1900[2]	3,080	4.1%	122	0.2%	2010	40,268	13.0%	5,493	1.8%
1920[2]	4,933	4.7	210	0.2	2015	46,837	14.4	6,292	1.9
1940[2]	9,019	6.8	365	0.3	2020	54,804	16.1	6,597	1.9
1960	16,560	9.2	929	0.5	2030	72,092	19.3	8,745	2.3
1980	25,549	11.3	2,240	1.0	2040	81,238	20.0	14,198	3.5
2000	34,992	12.4	4,240	1.5	2050	88,547	20.2	19,041	4.3

(1) 1900 number is for June 1 of given year. 1920 number is for Jan. 1. 1940-2010 figures are for Apr. 1. 2015-50 projections are for July 1. (2) Excludes Alaska and Hawaii.

U.S. Population Projections by Age, 2015-50

Source: 2008 National Population Projections, U.S. Census Bureau, U.S. Dept. of Commerce

(numbers in thousands)

	2015		2020		2030		2040		2050	
Age	No.	% distrib.	No.	% distrib.	No.	% distrib.	No.	% distrib.	No.	% distrib.
Total	325,540	100.0%	341,387	100.0%	373,504	100.0%	405,655	100.0%	439,010	100.0%
Under 5 years	22,076	6.8	22,846	6.7	24,161	6.5	26,117	6.4	28,148	6.4
5-14 years	43,365	13.3	45,303	13.3	48,799	13.1	51,998	12.8	56,370	12.8
15-24 years	43,551	13.4	44,353	13.0	48,914	13.1	52,909	13.0	56,593	12.9
25-34 years	44,499	13.7	46,061	13.5	47,020	12.6	51,847	12.8	56,165	12.8
35-44 years	41,301	12.7	43,664	12.8	48,223	12.9	49,545	12.2	54,696	12.5
45-54 years	43,368	13.3	41,354	12.1	44,030	11.8	48,784	12.0	50,378	11.5
55-64 years	40,543	12.5	43,003	12.6	40,266	10.8	43,216	10.7	48,111	11.0
65 years and over	46,837	14.4	54,804	16.1	72,092	19.3	81,238	20.0	88,547	20.2
85 years and over	6,292	1.9	6,597	1.9	8,745	2.3	14,198	3.5	19,041	4.3

Note: Projections are for July 1. They are based on assumptions about future births, deaths, and net international migration. Numbers exclude overseas U.S. military personnel and civilian U.S. citizens living abroad. Percent distribution may not add up to totals due to rounding.

Disability Status of U.S. Population by Age, 2010

Source: American Community Survey, U.S. Census Bureau, U.S. Dept. of Commerce

(numbers in thousands)

Disability type	Number	% of pop.	Disability type	Number	% of pop.
Total population	304,288	100.0%	**Total population (5 and over)**	284,156	100.0%
With a disability[1]	36,355	11.9	With a cognitive difficulty[2]	13,769	4.8
Under 5 years	156	0.1	5 to 17 years	2,114	0.7
Under 18 years	2,955	1.0	18 to 64 years	7,943	2.8
18 to 64 years	19,048	6.3	65 years and over	3,712	1.3
65 years and over	14,352	4.7	With an ambulatory difficulty[3]	19,519	6.9
With a hearing difficulty	10,272	3.4	5 to 17 years	347	0.1
Under 18 years	443	0.1	18 to 64 years	9,857	3.5
18 to 64 years	3,924	1.3	65 years and over	9,315	3.3
65 years and over	5,904	1.9	With a self-care difficulty[4]	7,363	2.6
With a vision difficulty	6,388	2.1	5 to 17 years	491	0.2
Under 18 years	490	0.2	18 to 64 years	3,444	1.2
18 to 64 years	3,209	1.1	65 years and over	3,428	1.2
65 years and over	2,688	0.9	**Total population (18 and over)**	230,270	100.0%
			With an independent living difficulty[5]	12,986	5.6
			18 to 64 years	6,648	2.9
			65 years and over	6,338	2.8

Note: Data based on sample and subject to sampling variability. Does not include U.S. military personnel and population in civilian institutions (i.e., facilities in which the population is under formal supervision or custody). (1) Defined by the Census Bureau as the "restriction in participation that results from a lack of fit between the individual's functional limitations and the characteristics of the physical and social environment." (2) Concentrating, remembering, or making decisions. (3) Walking or climbing stairs. (4) Dressing or bathing. (5) Doing errands alone, such as visiting a doctor's office or shopping.

Marital Status of the U.S. Population, 1960-2010

Source: Annual Social and Economic Supplements, Current Population Surveys, Housing and Household Economic Statistics Division, U.S. Census Bureau, U.S. Dept. of Commerce

(numbers in millions)

Marital status	Both sexes 2010	2000	1980	1960	Male 2010	2000	1980	1960	Female 2010	2000	1980	1960
Total.................	242.0	213.8	171.9	124.9	117.7	103.1	81.9	60.3	124.4	110.7	89.9	64.6
Married[1]...........	129.7	120.2	104.8	84.4	64.5	59.7	51.8	41.8	65.2	60.5	53.0	42.6
Never married........	74.2	60.0	44.5	27.5	40.2	32.3	24.2	15.3	34.0	27.8	20.2	12.3
Divorced	23.7	19.9	9.9	2.8	10.0	8.6	3.9	1.1	13.8	11.3	6.0	1.7
Widowed	14.3	13.7	12.7	10.2	3.0	2.6	2.0	2.1	11.4	11.1	10.8	8.1
% of total or subset pops.												
Married[1]...........	53.6%	56.2%	61.0%	67.6%	54.8%	57.9%	63.2%	69.3%	52.4%	54.7%	58.9%	65.9%
Never married........	30.7	28.1	25.9	22.0	34.2	31.3	29.6	25.3	27.4	25.1	22.5	19.0
Divorced	9.8	9.3	5.8	2.3	8.5	8.3	4.8	1.8	11.1	10.2	6.6	2.6
Widowed	5.9	6.4	7.4	8.1	2.5	2.5	2.4	3.5	9.1	10.0	12.0	12.5

Note: Total population for 1980-2010 is persons ages 15 and older; 1960 total population is persons ages 14 and older. Data is based on sample. Figures may not add up to totals due to rounding. (1) Comprises subcategories Married, spouse present; Married, spouse absent; and Separated.

Living Arrangements of Children in the U.S. by Parental Presence, 1970-2010

Source: Annual Social and Economic Supplements, Current Population Surveys, Housing and Household Economic Statistics Division, U.S. Census Bureau, U.S. Dept. of Commerce

% of children (with selected characteristic at left) living with—

Race and Hispanic origin/year	No. of children (thous.)	Both parents[3]	Total[4]	Divorced	Mother only— Married spouse absent	Never remarried	Widowed	Father only	Neither parent
White alone[1]									
1970............	58,791	90%	8%	3%	3%	Z	2%	1%	2%
1980............	52,242	83	14	7	4	1%	2	2	2
1990............	51,390	79	16	8	4	3	1	3	2
2000............	56,455	75	17	NA	NA	NA	NA	4	3
2010............	56,416	75	18	1	1	7	6	4	3
Black alone[1]									
1970............	9,422	59	30	5	16	4	4	2	10
1980............	9,375	42	44	11	16	13	4	28	12
1990............	10,018	38	51	10	12	27	2	4	8
2000............	11,412	38	49	NA	NA	NA	NA	4	9
2010............	11,272	39	50	3	1	9	32	4	8
Hispanic[2]									
1970............	4,006	78	NA	NA	NA	NA	NA	NA	NA
1980............	5,459	75	20	6	8	4	2	2	4
1990............	7,174	67	27	7	10	8	2	3	3
2000............	11,613	65	25	NA	NA	NA	NA	4	5
2010............	16,941	67	26	3	1	6	12	3	4

NA = Not available. Z = Less than 1%. **Note:** Children are defined as all persons under 18 years of age, not including those who are a family reference person or spouse. Total does not include children living in group quarters. Data based on sample. (1) One race only, not in combination with another race. (2) May be of any race. (3) Includes married and unmarried couples. (4) Includes children in the subcategory Living with mother only—separated, not shown in detail here.

Children in the U.S. by Parental Presence, 2010

Source: Annual Social and Economic Supplement, Current Population Survey, Housing and Household Economic Statistics Division, U.S. Census Bureau, U.S. Dept. of Commerce

(numbers in thousands)

	Number	% of total		Number	% of total
Total children	74,718	100.0%	Living with 1 parent.................	19,857	26.6%
			Mother only......................	17,285	23.1
Living with 2 parents................	51,823	69.4	Biological mother	16,948	22.7
Married parents	49,106	65.7	Father only	2,572	3.4
Unmarried parents	2,717	3.6	Biological father	2,443	3.3
Biological mother and father........	46,438	62.2	Living with no parents.................	3,038	4.1
Married parents	44,099	59.0	Grandparents only	1,655	2.2
Biological mother and stepfather	3,252	4.4	Other relatives only	650	0.9
Biological father and stepmother	955	1.3	Nonrelatives only	595	0.8
Biological mother and adoptive father	167	0.2	Other arrangement...............	138	0.2
Biological father and adoptive mother	33	0.0	Living with at least 1 biological parent ..	70,236	94.0
Adoptive mother and father	768	1.0	Living with at least 1 stepparent........	4,615	6.2
Other[1]........................	210	0.3	Living with at least 1 adoptive parent..	1,258	1.7

Note: Children are defined as all persons under 18 years of age, not including those who are a family reference person or spouse. Total does not include children living in group quarters. Data based on sample. (1) Includes children living with an adoptive parent and a stepparent, or two stepparents.

Unmarried-Partner Households in the U.S. by Sex of Partners, 2010

Source: American Community Survey, U.S. Census Bureau, U.S. Dept. of Commerce

Household	Number	% of total	% of cat.	Household	Number	% of total	% of cat.
Total households	114,567,419	100.0%		Female HH, female partner	305,637	0.3%	4.5%
Unmarried-partner households...	6,768,083	5.9	100.0%	Male HH, male partner	287,687	0.3	4.3
Male HH, female partner	3,070,784	2.7	45.4	All other households	107,799,336	94.1	100.0
Female HH, male partner	3,103,975	2.7	45.9				

HH = Householder. **Note:** Data based on sample and subject to sampling variability. Households do not include people living in group quarters (both institutional and noninstitutional, e.g., correctional facilities, military barracks, university housing).

U.S. Population by Sex, Race, Residence, and Median Age, 1790-2010

Source: Decennial Censuses, U.S. Census Bureau, U.S. Dept. of Commerce
(numbers in thousands, unless otherwise noted)

| | SEX | | RACE[2] | | | | RESIDENCE | | MEDIAN AGE (years) | | |
	Male	Female	White	Black Number	% tot. pop	Other	Urban[3]	Rural	All races	White[2]	Black[2]
Conterminous U.S.[1]											
1790 (Aug. 2)	NA	NA	3,172	757	19.3%	NA	202	3,728	NA	NA	NA
1810 (Aug. 6)	NA	NA	5,862	1,378	19.0	NA	525	6,714	NA	16.0	NA
1820 (Aug. 7)	4,897	4,742	7,867	1,772	18.4	NA	693	8,945	16.7	16.6	17.2
1840 (June 1)	8,689	8,381	14,196	2,874	16.8	NA	1,845	15,218	17.8	17.9	17.6
1860 (June 1)	16,085	15,358	26,923	4,442	14.1	79	6,217	25,227	19.4	19.7	17.5
1870 (June 1)	19,494	19,065	33,589	4,880	12.7	89	9,902	28,656	20.2	20.4	18.5
1880 (June 1)	25,519	24,637	43,403	6,581	13.1	172	14,130	36,059	20.9	21.4	18.0
1890 (June 1)	32,237	30,711	55,101	7,489	11.9	358	22,106	40,874	22.0	22.5	17.8
1900 (June 1)	38,816	37,178	66,809	8,834	11.6	351	30,215	45,997	22.9	23.4	19.4
1920 (Jan. 1)	53,900	51,810	94,821	10,463	9.9	427	54,253	51,768	25.3	25.5	22.3
1930 (Apr. 1)	62,137	60,638	110,287	11,891	9.7	597	69,161	54,042	26.5	26.9	23.5
1940 (Apr. 1)	66,062	65,608	118,215	12,866	9.8	589	74,705	57,459	29.0	29.5	25.3
United States											
1950 (Apr. 1)	74,833	75,864	135,150	15,045	10.0	713	96,847	54,479	30.2	30.8	26.1
1960 (Apr. 1)	88,331	90,992	158,832	18,872	10.5	1,620	125,269	54,054	29.5	30.3	23.5
1970 (Apr. 1)	98,926	104,309	178,098	22,581	11.1	2,557	149,647	53,565	28.1	28.9	22.4
1980 (Apr. 1)	110,053	116,493	194,713	26,683	11.8	5,150	167,051	59,495	30.0	30.9	24.9
1990 (Apr. 1)	121,284	127,507	208,741	30,517	12.3	9,533	187,053	61,656	32.8	33.7	27.9
2000 (Apr. 1)	138,056	143,368	195,577	35,705	12.7	13,716	222,361	59,061	35.3	38.6	30.0
2010 (Apr. 1)	151,781	156,964	196,818	37,686	12.2	18,147	NA	NA	37.2	NA	NA

NA = Not available. (1) Excludes Alaska and Hawaii. (2) New race categories were introduced in the 2000 census. Race data for 2000 and on are for one race alone, not in combination with one or more other races. "White" does not include people who reported being of Hispanic origin. "Other" comprises Asians, Native Hawaiians and other Pacific Islanders, and American Indians and Alaska Natives. Because of these changes, race data from 2000 on are not comparable to figures from previous years. (3) Residents of urban areas (densely settled areas with 50,000 or more inhabitants) as well as urban clusters (at least 2,500 but fewer than 50,000 inhabitants) were counted in the 2000 census unlike in previous decennial censuses.

U.S. Population by Race and Hispanic Origin, 2000-10

Source: Decennial Censuses, U.S. Census Bureau, U.S. Dept. of Commerce

| | 2010 census | | 2000 census | | % change, 2000-10[2] | |
	One race alone	One or more races[1]	One race alone	One or more races[1]	One race alone	One or more races
Total U.S. population	299,736,465	308,745,538	274,595,678	281,421,906	9.2%	9.7%
Race						
White	223,553,265	231,040,398	211,460,626	216,930,975	5.7	6.5
Black or African American	38,929,319	42,020,743	34,658,190	36,419,434	12.3	15.4
American Indian and Alaska Native. .	2,932,248	5,220,579	2,475,956	4,119,301	18.4	26.7
Asian	14,674,252	17,320,856	10,242,998	11,898,828	43.3	45.6
Native Hawaiian and other Pac. Isl.	540,013	1,225,195	398,835	874,414	35.4	40.1
Some other race	19,107,368	21,748,084	15,359,073	18,521,486	24.4	17.4
Hispanic origin and race						
Hispanic or Latino, any race	47,435,002	50,477,594	33,081,736	35,305,818	43.4	43.0
Not Hispanic or Latino.	252,301,463	258,267,944	241,513,942	246,116,088	4.5	4.9
White	196,817,552	201,856,108	194,552,774	198,177,900	1.2	1.9
Black or African American	37,685,848	40,123,525	33,947,837	35,383,751	11.0	13.4
American Indian and Alaska Native. .	2,247,098	4,029,675	2,068,883	3,444,700	8.6	17.0
Asian	14,465,124	16,722,710	10,123,169	11,579,494	42.9	44.4
Native Hawaiian and other Pac. Isl.	481,576	1,014,888	353,509	748,149	36.2	35.7
Some other race	604,265	1,033,866	467,770	1,770,645	29.2	−41.6

(1) Alone or in combination with one or more of the other races listed. Numbers may not add up to totals because individuals could report more than one race. (2) Columns 5 and 6 provide, respectively, a minimum-maximum range for the percent change in the population of each race.

U.S. Population by Ancestry Reported, 2010

Source: American Community Survey, U.S. Census Bureau, U.S. Dept. of Commerce

(numbers in thousands; ranked by number)

Ancestry[1]	Number	% of total	Ancestry[1]	Number	% of total	Ancestry[1]	Number	% of total
Total population	309,350	100.0%	Scottish	5,461	1.8%	West Indian (except		
German	47,902	15.5	Dutch	4,645	1.5	Hispanic groups)[4]	2,624	0.8%
Irish	34,670	11.2	Norwegian	4,470	1.4	French Canadian	2,043	0.7
English	25,926	8.4	Swedish	4,089	1.3	Welsh	1,793	0.6
American	19,976	6.5	European	3,617	1.2	Arab[5]	1,646	0.5
Italian	17,236	5.6	Scotch-Irish[2]	3,257	1.1	Other groups not listed		
Polish	9,569	3.1	Russian	2,972	1.0	here	140,733	45.5
French (except			Sub-Saharan African[3]	2,789	0.9	Unclassified or not		
Basque)	8,761	2.8				reported	36,730	11.9

Note: Data based on sample and subject to sampling variability. (1) Single ancestry or multiple ancestries with which respondents self-identified. Individual ancestries sum to more than the total population as respondents could identify more than one ancestry. Official data for race and Hispanic origin are not included here as they are tracked elsewhere by the Census Bureau. (2) People who reported Irish-Scotch ancestry are classified under "Other groups." (3) Incl. Cape Verdean, Ethiopian, Ghanian, Kenyan, Liberian, Nigerian, Senegalese, Sierra Leonean, Somalian, South African, Sudanese, Ugandan, Zimbabwean, African, and other sub-Saharan African. (4) Incl. Bahamian, Barbadian, Belizean, Bermudan, British West Indian, Dutch West Indian, Haitian, Jamaican, Trinidadian and Tobagonian, U.S. Virgin Islander, West Indian, and other West Indian. (5) Incl. Egyptian, Iraqi, Jordanian, Lebanese, Moroccan, Palestinian, Syrian, Arab, and other Arab.

U.S. Race and Minority Group Populations by Age, 2010

Source: American Community Survey, U.S. Census Bureau, U.S. Dept. of Commerce

Race and origin/age	Number	% of race	Race and origin/age	Number	% of race
White (not Hispanic or Latino)	196,929,412	100.0%	**Native Hawaiian and other**		
Under 5 years	10,219,126	5.2	**Pacific Islander**	507,916	100.0%
Under 18 years	39,638,319	20.1	Under 5 years	41,630	8.2
18 to 64 years	124,982,727	63.5	Under 18 years	148,328	29.2
65 years and over	32,308,366	16.4	18 to 64 years	332,204	65.4
85 years and over	4,700,447	2.4	65 years and over	27,384	5.4
Black or African American	38,874,625	100.0	85 years and over	1,979	0.4
Under 5 years	2,877,856	7.4	**Some other race**	14,889,440	100.0
Under 18 years	10,754,571	27.7	Under 5 years	1,420,407	9.5
18 to 64 years	24,679,032	63.5	Under 18 years	4,804,373	32.3
65 years and over	3,441,022	8.9	18 to 64 years	9,502,420	63.8
85 years and over	389,851	1.0	65 years and over	582,647	3.9
Asian	14,728,302	100.0	85 years and over	50,425	0.3
Under 5 years	881,038	6.0	**Two or more races**	8,398,368	100.0
Under 18 years	3,240,946	22.0	Under 5 years	1,314,353	15.7
18 to 64 years	10,074,292	68.4	Under 18 years	3,974,421	47.3
65 years and over	1,413,064	9.6	18 to 64 years	4,035,860	48.1
85 years and over	145,069	1.0	65 years and over	388,087	4.6
American Indian and Alaska Native	2,553,566	100.0	85 years and over	38,187	0.5
Under 5 years	200,912	7.9	**Hispanic or Latino (any race)**	50,740,089	100.0
Under 18 years	739,656	29.0	Under 5 years	5,105,856	10.1
18 to 64 years	1,628,248	63.8	Under 18 years	17,197,659	33.9
65 years and over	185,662	7.3	18 to 64 years	30,734,091	60.6
85 years and over	15,405	0.6	65 years and over	2,808,339	5.5
			85 years and over	284,007	0.6

Note: Data based on sample and subject to sampling variability. Categories are for one race alone, not in combination with any other race, unless otherwise noted.

Educational Attainment of the U.S. Population, 2010

Source: American Community Survey, U.S. Census Bureau, U.S. Dept. of Commerce

(numbers in thousands)

Race and origin/highest ed. level completed	Number[1]	% of group	Race and origin/highest ed. level completed	Number[1]	% of group
White (not Hispanic or Latino)	139,695	100.0%	**Native Hawaiian and other Pacific**		
Less than high school diploma	12,949	9.3	**Islander**	287	100.0%
High school graduate[2]	40,927	29.3	Less than high school diploma	36	12.6
Some college or associate's degree	41,928	30.0	High school graduate[2]	105	36.6
Bachelor's degree or higher	43,890	31.4	Some college or associate's degree	103	35.9
Black or African American	23,531	100.0	Bachelor's degree or higher	43	14.9
Less than high school diploma	4,254	18.1	**Some other race**	8,150	100.0
High school graduate[2]	7,459	31.7	Less than high school diploma	3,534	43.4
Some college or associate's degree	7,605	32.3	High school graduate[2]	2,189	26.9
Bachelor's degree or higher	4,213	17.9	Some college or associate's degree	1,647	20.2
Asian	9,964	100.0	Bachelor's degree or higher	780	9.6
Less than high school diploma	1,451	14.6	**Two or more races**	3,416	100.0
High school graduate[2]	1,594	16.0	Less than high school diploma	549	16.1
Some college or associate's degree	1,951	19.6	High school graduate[2]	830	24.3
Bachelor's degree or higher	4,969	49.9	Some college or associate's degree	1,153	33.7
American Indian and Alaska Native	1,504	100.0	Bachelor's degree or higher	885	25.9
Less than high school diploma	341	22.7	**Hispanic or Latino (any race)**	27,314	100.0
High school graduate[2]	462	30.7	Less than high school diploma	10,321	37.8
Some college or associate's degree	499	33.2	High school graduate[2]	7,225	26.5
Bachelor's degree or higher	201	13.4	Some college or associate's degree	6,206	22.7
			Bachelor's degree or higher	3,562	13.0

Note: Data based on sample and subject to sampling variability. Categories are for one race alone, not in combination with any other race, unless otherwise noted. (1) Population 25 years of age and over. (2) Incl. equivalency.

U.S. Population Growth by Race and Hispanic Origin, 1970-2030[1]

Source: Decennial Censuses, 2008 National Population Projections, U.S. Census Bureau, U.S. Dept. of Commerce
(numbers in millions)

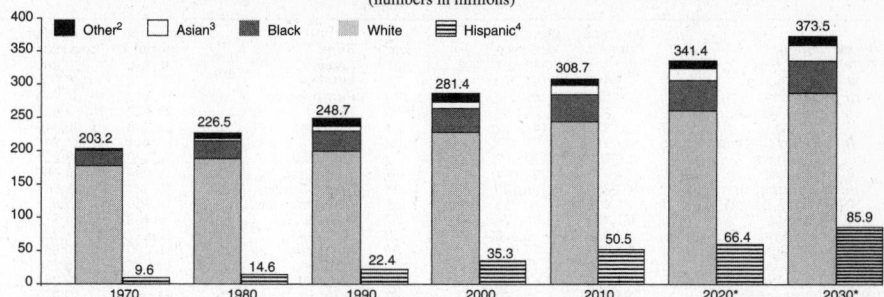

*Projected. (1) Because of changes in census questions and methods, data on race and Hispanic origin are not wholly comparable over time. (2) Includes American Indians and Alaska Natives, and other races. For 2000 and on, this category also includes Native Hawaiians and other Pacific Islanders, and persons reporting two or more races. (3) Figures for 1970-90 include Pacific Islanders. (4) May be of any race.

U.S. Race and Minority Group Percentages by State, 2010

Source: 2010 Census, U.S. Census Bureau, U.S. Dept. of Commerce

State	One race[1] (%) White	Black or African American	Asian	American Indian and Alaska Native	Native Hawaiian and other Pacific Islander	Some other race	Two or more races[1] (%)	Hispanic or Latino, any race (%)
Alabama	67.0%	26.0%	1.1%	0.5%	0.04%	0.08%	1.3%	3.9%
Alaska	64.1	3.1	5.3	14.4	1.02	0.16	6.4	5.5
Arizona	57.8	3.7	2.7	4.0	0.17	0.13	1.8	29.6
Arkansas	74.5	15.3	1.2	0.7	0.19	0.07	1.6	6.4
California	40.1	5.8	12.8	0.4	0.35	0.23	2.6	37.6
Colorado	70.0	3.8	2.7	0.6	0.11	0.15	2.0	20.7
Connecticut	71.2	9.4	3.8	0.2	0.03	0.34	1.7	13.4
Delaware	65.3	20.8	3.2	0.3	0.03	0.17	2.0	8.2
District of Columbia	34.8	50.0	3.5	0.2	0.04	0.24	2.1	9.1
Florida	57.9	15.2	2.4	0.3	0.05	0.26	1.5	22.5
Georgia	55.9	30.0	3.2	0.2	0.05	0.20	1.6	8.8
Hawaii	22.7	1.5	37.7	0.2	9.43	0.14	19.4	8.9
Idaho	84.0	0.6	1.2	1.1	0.14	0.10	1.7	11.2
Illinois	63.7	14.3	4.5	0.1	0.02	0.12	1.4	15.8
Indiana	81.5	9.0	1.6	0.2	0.03	0.13	1.5	6.0
Iowa	88.7	2.9	1.7	0.3	0.06	0.07	1.4	5.0
Kansas	78.2	5.7	2.3	0.8	0.07	0.10	2.3	10.5
Kentucky	86.3	7.7	1.1	0.2	0.05	0.11	1.5	3.1
Louisiana	60.3	31.8	1.5	0.6	0.03	0.15	1.3	4.2
Maine	94.4	1.1	1.0	0.6	0.02	0.08	1.4	1.3
Maryland	54.7	29.0	5.5	0.2	0.04	0.21	2.2	8.2
Massachusetts	76.1	6.0	5.3	0.2	0.02	0.94	1.9	9.6
Michigan	76.6	14.0	2.4	0.6	0.02	0.10	1.9	4.4
Minnesota	83.1	5.1	4.0	1.0	0.04	0.11	1.9	4.7
Mississippi	58.0	36.9	0.9	0.5	0.03	0.06	0.9	2.7
Missouri	81.0	11.5	1.6	0.4	0.10	0.09	1.8	3.5
Montana	87.8	0.4	0.6	6.1	0.06	0.05	2.2	2.9
Nebraska	82.1	4.4	1.7	0.8	0.05	0.12	1.6	9.2
Nevada	54.1	7.7	7.1	0.9	0.57	0.18	2.9	26.5
New Hampshire	92.3	1.0	2.1	0.2	0.02	0.14	1.4	2.8
New Jersey	59.3	12.8	8.2	0.1	0.02	0.31	1.5	17.7
New Mexico	40.5	1.7	1.3	8.5	0.06	0.18	1.4	46.3
New York	58.3	14.4	7.3	0.3	0.03	0.42	1.7	17.6
North Carolina	65.3	21.2	2.2	1.1	0.06	0.16	1.6	8.4
North Dakota	88.9	1.1	1.0	5.3	0.04	0.05	1.5	2.0
Ohio	81.1	12.0	1.7	0.2	0.03	0.13	1.8	3.1
Oklahoma	68.7	7.3	1.7	8.2	0.11	0.08	5.1	8.9
Oregon	78.5	1.7	3.6	1.1	0.33	0.14	2.9	11.7
Pennsylvania	79.5	10.4	2.7	0.1	0.02	0.13	1.4	5.7
Rhode Island	76.4	4.9	2.8	0.4	0.03	0.84	2.2	12.4
South Carolina	64.1	27.7	1.3	0.4	0.05	0.12	1.4	5.1
South Dakota	84.7	1.2	0.9	8.5	0.04	0.06	1.8	2.7
Tennessee	75.6	16.5	1.4	0.3	0.04	0.10	1.4	4.6
Texas	45.3	11.5	3.8	0.3	0.07	0.14	1.3	37.6
Utah	80.4	0.9	2.0	1.0	0.87	0.13	1.8	13.0
Vermont	94.3	0.9	1.3	0.3	0.02	0.09	1.6	1.5
Virginia	64.8	19.0	5.5	0.3	0.06	0.19	2.3	7.9
Washington	72.5	3.4	7.1	1.3	0.58	0.18	3.7	11.2
West Virginia	93.2	3.4	0.7	0.2	0.02	0.06	1.3	1.2
Wisconsin	83.3	6.2	2.3	0.9	0.03	0.07	1.4	5.9
Wyoming	85.9	0.8	0.8	2.1	0.06	0.08	1.5	8.9
United States	63.7	12.2	4.7	0.7	0.16	0.20	1.9	16.3

(1) Not Hispanic or Latino.

American Indian and Alaska Native Population by State, 2010

Source: 2010 Census, U.S. Census Bureau, U.S. Dept. of Commerce
(ranked by one race alone)

Rank	State	One race alone[1]	More than one race[2]	Rank	State	One race alone[1]	More than one race[2]
1.	California	362,801	360,424	27.	Kansas	28,150	30,980
2.	Oklahoma	321,687	161,073	28.	Missouri	27,376	45,000
3.	Arizona	296,529	56,857	29.	Pennsylvania	26,843	54,249
4.	New Mexico	193,222	26,290	30.	Ohio	25,292	64,832
5.	Texas	170,972	144,292	31.	Arkansas	22,248	25,340
6.	North Carolina	122,110	61,972	32.	Idaho	21,441	14,944
7.	New York	106,906	114,152	33.	Maryland	20,420	38,237
8.	Alaska	104,871	33,441	34.	Tennessee	19,994	34,880
9.	Washington	103,869	95,129	35.	South Carolina	19,524	22,647
10.	South Dakota	71,817	10,256	36.	Massachusetts	18,850	31,855
11.	Florida	71,458	91,104	37.	Indiana	18,462	31,276
12.	Montana	62,555	16,046	38.	Nebraska	18,427	11,389
13.	Michigan	62,007	77,088	39.	Mississippi	15,030	10,880
14.	Minnesota	60,916	40,984	40.	Wyoming	13,336	5,260
15.	Colorado	56,010	51,822	41.	Connecticut	11,256	19,884
16.	Wisconsin	54,526	31,702	42.	Iowa	11,084	13,427
17.	Oregon	53,203	56,020	43.	Kentucky	10,120	21,235
18.	Illinois	43,963	57,488	44.	Maine	8,568	9,914
19.	North Dakota	36,591	6,405	45.	Rhode Island	6,058	8,336
20.	Utah	32,927	17,137	46.	Delaware	4,181	5,718
21.	Georgia	32,151	51,873	47.	Hawaii	4,164	29,306
22.	Nevada	32,062	23,883	48.	West Virginia	3,787	9,527
23.	Louisiana	30,579	24,500	49.	New Hampshire	3,150	7,374
24.	Virginia	29,225	51,699	50.	Vermont	2,207	5,172
25.	New Jersey	29,026	41,690	51.	District of Columbia	2,079	4,442
26.	Alabama	28,218	28,900		United States	2,932,248	2,288,331

(1) Respondents who self-identified as American Indian and Alaska Native alone, whether or not they reported their specific tribe or tribes. (2) Respondents who self-identified as American Indian and Alaska Native in combination with one or more other races, whether or not they reported their specific tribe or tribes.

American Indian and Alaska Native Population by Selected Tribal Groupings, 2010

Source: 2010 Census, U.S. Census Bureau, U.S. Dept. of Commerce
(ranked by American Indian and Alaska Native alone, one tribal grouping only)

Tribal grouping	AIAN alone One tribal grouping only[1]	AIAN alone One or more tribal groupings[2]	AIAN alone or in combination One or more tribal groupings[3]	Tribal grouping	AIAN alone One tribal grouping only[1]	AIAN alone One or more tribal groupings[2]	AIAN alone or in combination One or more tribal groupings[3]
American Indian				Osage	8,820	9,939	18,264
Cherokee	281,218	297,118	807,927	Yakama	8,733	9,038	11,430
Navajo	155,364	161,347	191,866	Menominee	8,313	8,560	11,043
Mexican American Indian	117,282	119,435	169,698	Houma	8,157	8,228	10,747
Chippewa	111,802	114,359	168,812	Colville	8,042	8,239	10,451
Sioux	110,350	114,315	166,632	Arapaho	7,898	8,274	10,676
Choctaw	102,371	108,639	192,248	Delaware	7,760	8,124	18,038
Lumbee	62,178	62,823	73,476	Shoshone	7,628	8,200	12,624
Pueblo	48,227	50,208	60,270	Yaqui	7,464	8,593	15,233
Creek	47,936	52,459	87,310	Ute	7,240	7,968	11,153
Iroquois	39,977	41,811	79,727	Ottawa	7,205	7,968	12,869
Apache	38,206	43,933	83,661	Canadian and French American Indian	6,304	6,901	14,524
Chickasaw	27,585	29,797	51,430	Yuman	3,218	3,411	4,599
Blackfeet	26,928	31,378	103,768	Hopi	2,899	3,845	6,715
South American Indian	20,728	21,187	46,822	Tohono O'Odham	2,693	2,933	4,477
Potawatomi	20,082	20,529	33,197	Pima	2,585	2,972	4,536
Central American Indian	15,740	16,299	27,611	Cree	2,132	2,853	7,789
Puget Sound Salish	14,239	14,444	20,099	**Alaska Native**			
Seminole	13,956	16,301	31,613	Yup'ik	28,858	29,546	33,758
Spanish American Indian	13,128	13,419	19,486	Inupiat[4]	24,627	25,481	33,002
Comanche	12,066	13,215	22,861	Alaskan Athabascan	15,480	16,274	22,262
Cheyenne	11,196	12,284	18,723	Tlingit-Haida	15,066	15,899	25,755
Paiute	8,874	9,656	13,100	Aleut	11,792	12,493	19,064
				Tsimshian	2,290	2,530	3,718

AIAN = American Indian and Alaska Native. **Note:** Tribal groupings refer to the combining of individual American Indian or Alaska Native tribes. For example, the Fort Sill Apache, Mescalero Apache, and San Carlos Apache appear in the general Apache tribal grouping. The King Salmon Tribe, Native Village of Kanatak, and Sun'aq Tribe of Kodiak belong in the Aleut tribal grouping. (1) For example, Cherokee, or Navajo, or Alaskan Athabascan. (2) As in footnote 1 or in combination with one or more other tribal groupings (e.g., Apache and Navajo, or Yakama and Aleut). Individuals are included in each category. (3) As in footnote 1 or footnote 2, or in combination with any other race in addition to AIAN (e.g., Cherokee and white; or Apache, Navajo, and white; or Inupiat, white, and black or African American). (4) Classified as Eskimo in previous censuses.

Populations, ZIP, and Area Codes for U.S. Places of 10,000 or More

Source: Decennial Censuses, U.S. Census Bureau, U.S. Dept. of Commerce; NeuStar Inc.

The following is a list of places of 10,000 or more inhabitants according to the U.S. Census Bureau based on the results of the 2010 Census. Also given are 2000 census populations, if available. This list includes **places that are incorporated** under the laws of their respective states as cities, boroughs, towns, and villages. **Townships are not included.**

Census designated places (CDPs) are marked with a (c). CDP boundaries are defined by the Census Bureau and may change over time. This list also includes, in *italics*, **minor civil divisions (MCDs)** for Connecticut, Maine, Massachusetts, New Hampshire, Rhode Island, and Vermont. MCDs are not incorporated and not recognized as CDPs, but are often the primary political or administrative divisions of a county.

An **asterisk** (*) denotes that the ZIP code given is for general delivery; named streets and/or P.O. boxes within the community may use a different one; consult www.usps.com. Telephone **area codes** are given in parentheses. New phone numbers in a given area may be assigned a different area code from that of existing phone numbers in the area. These areas of **overlay** are noted. When two or more area codes are listed for one place, consult local operators for assistance. Area codes based on latest information as of Sept. 2011. For a listing in numerical order of specific area codes in the U.S., Canada, and the Caribbean, see Computers and Telecommunications chapter, page 369.

For some places listed, no area code and/or ZIP code is available. — = Not available.

Alabama

Area code (938) overlays area code (256).

ZIP	Place	Area code	2000	2010
*35007	Alabaster	(205)	22,619	30,352
*35950	Albertville	(256)	17,247	21,160
*35010	Alexander City	(256)	15,008	14,875
*36201	Anniston	(256)	24,276	23,106
*35611	Athens	(256)	18,967	21,897
*36502	Atmore	(251)	7,676	10,194
*36830	Auburn	(334)	42,987	53,380
*35020	Bessemer	(205)	29,672	27,456
*35201	Birmingham	(205)	242,820	212,237
*35040	Calera	(205)	3,158	11,620
*35215	Center Point	(205)	—	16,921
35043	Chelsea	(205)	2,949	10,183
*35055	Cullman	(256)	13,995	14,775
36526	Daphne	(251)	16,581	21,570
*36601	Decatur	(256)	53,929	55,683
*36301	Dothan	(334)	57,737	65,496
*36330	Enterprise	(334)	21,178	26,562
*36027	Eufaula	(334)	13,908	13,137
35064	Fairfield	(205)	12,381	11,117
*36532	Fairhope	(251)	12,480	15,326
*35630	Florence	(256)	36,264	39,319
*36535	Foley	(251)	7,590	14,618
35214	Forestdale (c)	(205)	10,509	10,162
*35967	Fort Payne	(256)	12,938	14,012
*35901	Gadsden	(256)	38,978	36,856
35071	Gardendale	(205)	11,626	13,893
35640	Hartselle	(256)	12,019	14,255
*35080	Helena	(205)	10,296	16,793
*35209	Homewood	(205)	25,043	25,167
*35244	Hoover	(205)	62,742	81,619
*35023	Hueytown	(205)	15,364	16,105
*35801	Huntsville	(205)	158,216	180,105
35210	Irondale	(205)	9,813	12,349
36265	Jacksonville	(256)	8,404	12,548
*35501	Jasper	(205)	14,052	14,352
35094	Leeds	(205)	10,455	11,773
*35758	Madison	(256)	29,329	42,938
36054	Millbrook	(334)	10,386	14,640
*36601	Mobile	(251)	198,915	195,111
*36104	Montgomery	(334)	201,568	205,764
35004	Moody	(205)	8,053	11,726
*35223	Mountain Brook	(205)	20,604	20,413
*35661	Muscle Shoals	(256)	11,924	13,146
*35476	Northport	(205)	19,435	23,330
*36801	Opelika	(334)	23,498	26,477
36203	Oxford	(256)	14,592	21,348
*36360	Ozark	(334)	15,119	14,907
35124	Pelham	(205)	14,369	21,352
*35125	Pell City	(205)	9,565	12,695
*36867	Phenix City	(334)	28,265	32,822
35127	Pleasant Grove	(205)	9,983	10,110
*36067	Prattville	(334)	24,303	33,960
36610	Prichard	(251)	28,633	22,659
36206	Saks (c)	(256)	10,698	10,744
36571	Saraland	(251)	12,288	13,405
*35768	Scottsboro	(256)	14,762	14,770
*36701	Selma	(334)	20,512	20,756
*35150	Sylacauga	(256)	12,616	12,749
*35160	Talladega	(256)	15,143	15,676
36619	Tillman's Corner (c)	(251)	15,685	17,398
*36081	Troy	(334)	13,935	18,033
35173	Trussville	(205)	12,924	19,933
*35401	Tuscaloosa	(205)	77,906	90,468
*35216	Vestavia Hills	(205)	24,476	34,033

Alaska (907)

ZIP	Place	2000	2010
*99501	Anchorage	260,283	291,826
99711	Badger (c)	—	19,482
*99708	College (c)	11,402	12,964
*99701	Fairbanks	30,224	31,535
*99801	Juneau	30,711	31,275
99654	Knik-Fairview (c)	7,049	14,923

Arizona

ZIP	Place	Area code	2000	2010
85086	Anthem (c)	(623)	—	21,700
*85120	Apache Junction	(480)	31,814	35,840
85123	Arizona City (c)	(520)	4,385	10,475
*85323	Avondale	(623)	35,883	76,738
*85326	Buckeye	(623)	6,537	50,876
*86442	Bullhead City	(928)	33,769	39,540
86322	Camp Verde	(928)	9,451	10,873
*85122	Casa Grande	(520)	25,224	48,571
85704	Casas Adobes (c)	(520)	54,011	66,795
85718	Catalina Foothills (c)	(520)	53,794	50,796
*85225	Chandler	(480)	176,581	236,123
86323	Chino Valley	(928)	7,835	10,817
85128	Coolidge	(520)	7,786	11,825
86326	Cottonwood	(928)	9,179	11,265
*85607	Douglas	(520)	14,312	17,378
85746	Drexel Heights (c)	(520)	23,849	27,749
85335	El Mirage	(623)	7,609	31,797
85131	Eloy	(520)	10,375	16,631
*86004	Flagstaff	(928)	52,894	65,870
85132	Florence	(520)	17,054	25,536
85705	Flowing Wells (c)	(520)	15,050	16,419
*86427	Fort Mohave (c)	(928)	—	14,364
85367	Fortuna Foothills (c)	(928)	20,478	26,265
*85268	Fountain Hills	(480)	20,235	22,489
*85299	Gilbert	(480)	109,697	208,453
*85302	Glendale	(623)	218,812	226,721
85118	Gold Canyon (c)	(480)	—	10,159
*85338	Goodyear	(623)	18,911	65,275
*85622	Green Valley (c)	(520)	17,283	21,391
*86401	Kingman	(928)	20,069	28,068
*86403	Lake Havasu City	(928)	41,938	52,527
85653	Marana	(520)	13,556	34,961
*85139	Maricopa	(520)	—	43,482
*85201	Mesa	(480)	396,375	439,041
86401	New Kingman-Butler (c)	(928)	14,810	12,134
*85087	New River (c)	(623)	10,740	14,952
*85621	Nogales	(520)	20,878	20,837
*85737	Oro Valley	(520)	29,700	41,011
85253	Paradise Valley	(480)	13,664	12,820
*85541	Payson	(928)	13,620	15,301
*85345	Peoria	(623)	108,364	154,065
85034	Phoenix	(480)/(602)/(623)	1,321,045	1,445,632
*86301	Prescott	(928)	33,938	39,843
*86314	Prescott Valley	(928)	23,535	38,822
*85142	Queen Creek	(480)	4,316	26,361
85648	Rio Rico (c)	(520)	—	18,962
*85629	Sahuarita	(520)	3,242	25,259
85349	San Luis	(928)	15,322	25,505
*85142	San Tan Valley (c)	(480)	—	81,321
*85251	Scottsdale	(480)	202,705	217,385
*86336	Sedona	(928)	10,192	10,031
*85901	Show Low	(928)	7,695	10,660
*85635	Sierra Vista	(520)	37,775	43,888
85650	Sierra Vista Southeast (c)	(520)	14,348	14,797
85350	Somerton	(928)	7,266	14,287
*85351	Sun City (c)	(623)	38,309	37,499
*85375	Sun City West (c)	(623)	26,344	24,535
*85248	Sun Lakes (c)	(480)	11,936	13,975
*85374	Surprise	(623)	30,848	117,517
85749	Tanque Verde (c)	(520)	16,195	16,901
*85282	Tempe	(480)	158,625	161,719
*85726	Tucson	(520)	486,699	520,116
85735	Tucson Estates (c)	(520)	9,755	12,192
85641	Vail (c)	(520)	2,484	10,208
86326	Verde Village[1] (c)	(928)	10,610	11,605
*85364	Yuma	(928)	77,515	93,064

(1) Formerly Cottonwood-Verde Village CDP.

Arkansas

ZIP	Place	Area code	2000	2010
*71923	Arkadelphia	(870)	10,912	10,714
*72501	Batesville	(870)	9,445	10,248
*72714	Bella Vista	(479)	—	26,461
*72015	Benton	(501)	21,906	30,681
72712	Bentonville	(479)	19,730	35,301

ZIP	Place	Area code	2000	2010
*72315	Blytheville	(870)	18,272	15,620
*72022	Bryant	(501)	9,764	16,688
72023	Cabot	(501)	15,261	23,776
*71701	Camden	(870)	13,154	12,183
*72032	Conway	(501)	43,167	58,908
*71730	El Dorado	(870)	21,530	18,884
*72701	Fayetteville	(479)	58,047	73,580
*72335	Forrest City	(870)	14,774	15,371
*72901	Fort Smith	(479)	80,268	86,209
*72601	Harrison	(870)	12,152	12,943
72342	Helena-West Helena	(870)	—	12,282
*71801	Hope	(870)	10,616	10,095
*71901	Hot Springs	(501)	35,750	35,193
*72076	Jacksonville	(501)	29,916	28,364
*72401	Jonesboro	(870)	55,515	67,263
*72201	Little Rock	(501)	183,133	193,524
*71753	Magnolia	(870)	10,858	11,577
*72104	Malvern	(501)	9,021	10,318
72364	Marion	(870)	8,901	12,345
*72113	Maumelle	(501)	10,557	17,163
*72653	Mountain Home	(870)	11,012	12,448
*72114	North Little Rock	(501)	60,433	62,304
*72450	Paragould	(870)	22,017	26,113
*71601	Pine Bluff	(870)	55,085	49,083
*72756	Rogers	(479)	38,829	55,964
*72801	Russellville	(479)	23,682	27,920
*72143	Searcy	(501)	18,928	22,858
*72120	Sherwood	(501)	21,511	29,523
*72761	Siloam Springs	(479)	10,843	15,039
*72764	Springdale	(479)	45,798	69,797
71854	Texarkana	(870)	26,448	29,919
*72956	Van Buren	(479)	18,986	22,791
*72301	West Memphis	(870)	27,666	26,245

California

Area code (442) overlays area code (760). Area code (707) overlays area code (714). Area code (747) overlays area code (818).

ZIP	Place	Area code	2000	2010
92301	Adelanto	(760)	18,130	31,765
*91376	Agoura Hills	(818)	20,537	20,330
*94501	Alameda	(510)	72,259	73,812
94507	Alamo (c)	(925)	15,626	14,570
94706	Albany	(510)	16,444	18,539
*91802	Alhambra	(626)	85,804	83,089
92656	Aliso Viejo	(949)	—	47,823
*91901	Alpine (c) (San Diego Co.)	(619)	13,143	14,236
*91003	Altadena (c)	(626)	42,610	42,777
95127	Alum Rock (c)	(408)	13,479	15,536
94589	American Canyon	(707)	9,774	19,454
*92803	Anaheim	(714)	328,014	336,265
95843	Antelope (c)	(916)	—	45,770
*94509	Antioch	(925)	90,532	102,372
*92307	Apple Valley	(760)	54,239	69,135
*91006	Arcadia	(626)	53,054	56,364
*95521	Arcata	(707)	16,651	17,231
95825	Arden-Arcade (c)	(916)	96,025	92,186
*93420	Arroyo Grande	(805)	15,851	17,252
*90701	Artesia	(562)	16,380	16,522
93203	Arvin	(661)	12,956	19,304
94577	Ashland (c)	(510)	20,793	21,925
*93422	Atascadero	(805)	26,411	28,310
95301	Atwater	(209)	23,113	28,168
*95603	Auburn	(530)	12,462	13,330
93204	Avenal	(559)	14,674	15,505
91746	Avocado Heights (c)	(626)	15,148	15,411
91702	Azusa	(626)	44,712	46,361
*93302	Bakersfield	(661)	247,057	347,483
91706	Baldwin Park	(626)	75,837	75,390
92220	Banning	(951)	23,562	29,603
*92312	Barstow	(760)	21,119	22,639
94565	Bay Point (c)	(925)	21,534	21,349
92223	Beaumont	(951)	11,384	36,877
90201	Bell	(323)	36,664	35,477
*90202	Bell Gardens	(213)/(323)/(562)	44,054	42,072
*90706	Bellflower	(562)	72,878	76,616
94002	Belmont	(650)	25,123	25,835
94510	Benicia	(707)	26,865	26,997
*94704	Berkeley	(510)	102,743	112,580
*90210	Beverly Hills	(213)/(310)/(323)	33,784	34,109
*92314	Big Bear City (c)	(909)	—	12,304
92316	Bloomington (c)	(951)	19,318	23,851
*92225	Blythe	(760)	12,155	20,817
*91902	Bonita	(619)	12,401	12,538
92021	Bostonia (c)	(619)	15,169	15,379
92227	Brawley	(760)	22,052	24,953
*92822	Brea	(562)/(714)	35,410	39,282
*94513	Brentwood	(925)	23,302	51,481
*90622	Buena Park	(714)	78,282	80,530
*91510	Burbank (Los Angeles Co.)	(818)	100,316	103,340
94010	Burlingame	(650)	28,158	28,806
*91372	Calabasas	(818)	20,033	23,058
*92231	Calexico	(760)	27,109	38,572
*93504	California City	(760)	8,385	14,120

ZIP	Place	Area code	2000	2010
*93010	Camarillo	(805)	57,077	65,201
95682	Cameron Park (c)	(530)	14,549	18,228
*95008	Campbell	(408)	38,138	39,349
92058	Camp Pendleton South (c)	(760)	8,854	10,616
92587	Canyon Lake	(951)	9,952	10,561
*92008	Carlsbad	(760)	78,247	105,328
*95608	Carmichael (c)	(916)	49,742	61,762
*93013	Carpinteria	(805)	14,194	13,040
*90745	Carson	(310)	89,730	91,714
92077	Casa de Oro-Mt. Helix (c)	(619)	18,874	18,762
*91384	Castaic (c)	(661)	—	19,015
*94546	Castro Valley (c)	(510)	57,292	61,388
*92235	Cathedral City	(760)	42,647	51,200
95307	Ceres	(209)	34,609	45,417
90703	Cerritos	(562)	51,488	49,041
94541	Cherryland (c)	(510)	13,837	14,728
*95926	Chico	(530)	59,954	86,187
*91708	Chino	(909)	67,168	77,983
91709	Chino Hills	(909)	66,787	74,799
93610	Chowchilla	(559)	11,127	18,720
*91910	Chula Vista	(619)	173,556	243,916
91702	Citrus (c)	(626)	10,581	10,866
*95621	Citrus Heights	(916)	85,071	83,301
91711	Claremont	(909)	33,998	34,926
94517	Clayton	(925)	10,762	10,897
95422	Clearlake	(707)	13,142	15,250
*93612	Clovis	(559)	68,468	95,631
92236	Coachella	(760)	22,724	40,704
93210	Coalinga	(559)	11,668	13,380
*92324	Colton	(909)	47,662	52,154
90040	Commerce	(323)	12,568	12,823
*90221	Compton	(310)	93,493	96,455
*94520	Concord	(925)	121,780	122,067
*93212	Corcoran	(559)	14,458	24,813
92877	Corona	(951)	124,966	152,374
*92118	Coronado	(619)	24,100	18,912
*92628	Costa Mesa	(714)/(949)	108,724	109,960
92679	Coto de Caza (c).	(949)	13,057	14,866
*91722	Covina	(626)	46,837	47,796
92325	Crestline (c)	(909)	10,218	10,770
90201	Cudahy	(323)	24,208	23,805
*90230	Culver City	(310)	38,816	38,883
*95014	Cupertino	(408)	50,546	58,302
90630	Cypress	(714)	46,229	47,802
*94015	Daly City	(415)/(650)	103,621	101,123
*92629	Dana Point	(949)	35,110	33,351
*94526	Danville	(925)	41,715	42,039
*95616	Davis	(530)	60,308	65,622
90250	Del Aire (c)	(310)/(323)	9,012	10,001
*93215	Delano	(661)	38,824	53,041
95315	Delhi (c)	(209)	8,022	10,755
*92240	Desert Hot Springs	(760)	16,582	25,938
91765	Diamond Bar	(909)	56,287	55,544
93618	Dinuba	(559)	16,844	21,453
*94514	Discovery Bay (c)	(925)	8,981	13,352
95620	Dixon	(707)	16,103	18,351
90239	Downey	(562)	107,323	111,772
*91009	Duarte	(626)	21,486	21,321
94568	Dublin	(925)	29,973	46,036
92343	East Hemet (c)	(951)	14,823	17,418
90022	East Los Angeles (c).	(323)	124,283	126,496
94303	East Palo Alto	(650)	29,506	28,155
90221	East Rancho Domínguez (c).	(310)/(323)	—	15,135
91775	East San Gabriel (c)	(626)	14,512	14,874
*91752	Eastvale (c).	(909)/(951)	—	53,668
*92020	El Cajon	(619)	94,869	99,478
*92244	El Centro	(760)	37,835	42,598
94530	El Cerrito	(510)	23,171	23,549
95762	El Dorado Hills (c).	(916)	18,016	42,108
*91734	El Monte	(626)	115,965	113,475
*93446	El Paso de Robles (Paso Robles)	(805)	24,297	29,793
90245	El Segundo	(310)	16,033	16,654
*94803	El Sobrante (c) (Contra Costa Co.)	(510)	12,260	12,669
92503	El Sobrante (c) (Riverside Co.)	(714)/(909)	—	12,723
*95624	Elk Grove	(916)	—	153,015
*94608	Emeryville	(510)	6,882	10,080
*92024	Encinitas	(760)	58,014	59,518
*92025	Escondido	(760)	133,559	143,911
*95501	Eureka	(707)	26,128	27,191
93221	Exeter	(559)	9,168	10,334
94533	Fairfield	(707)	96,178	105,321
95628	Fair Oaks (c)	(916)	28,008	30,912
94541	Fairview (c)	(510)	9,470	10,003
*92028	Fallbrook (c)	(760)	29,100	30,534
93223	Farmersville	(559)	8,737	10,588
*93015	Fillmore	(805)	13,643	15,002
90001	Florence-Graham (c)	(323)	60,197	63,387
95828	Florin (c)	(916)	27,653	47,513
*95630	Folsom	(916)	51,884	72,203
*92334	Fontana	(909)	128,929	196,069

ZIP	Place	Area code	2000	2010
95841	Foothill Farms (c)	(916)	17,426	33,121
95540	Fortuna	(707)	10,497	11,926
94404	Foster City	(650)	28,803	30,567
*92728	Fountain Valley	(714)	54,978	55,313
*94537	Fremont	(510)	203,413	214,089
92563	French Valley (c)	(951)	—	23,067
*93706	Fresno	(559)	427,652	494,665
*92834	Fullerton	(714)	126,003	135,161
95632	Galt	(209)	19,472	23,647
95215	Garden Acres (c)	(209)	9,747	10,648
*92842	Garden Grove	(714)	165,196	170,883
*90247	Gardena	(310)	57,746	58,829
*95020	Gilroy	(408)	41,464	48,821
92509	Glen Avon (c)	(951)	14,853	20,199
*91209	Glendale	(818)	194,973	191,719
*91741	Glendora	(626)	49,415	50,073
*93116	Goleta	(805)	—	29,888
92324	Grand Terrace	(951)	11,626	12,040
95746	Granite Bay (c)	(916)	19,388	20,402
*95945	Grass Valley	(530)	10,922	12,860
93927	Greenfield	(831)	12,583	16,330
93433	Grover Beach	(805)	13,067	13,156
91745	Hacienda Heights (c)	(626)	53,122	54,038
94019	Half Moon Bay	(650)	11,842	11,324
*93230	Hanford	(559)	41,686	53,967
90716	Hawaiian Gardens (c)	(562)	14,779	14,254
*90250	Hawthorne	(310)/(323)	84,112	84,293
*94544	Hayward	(510)	140,030	144,186
95448	Healdsburg	(707)	10,722	11,254
92546	Hemet	(951)	58,812	78,657
94547	Hercules	(510)	19,488	24,060
90254	Hermosa Beach	(310)	18,566	19,506
*92340	Hesperia	(760)	62,582	90,173
92346	Highland	(909)	44,605	53,104
94010	Hillsborough	(650)	10,825	10,825
*95023	Hollister	(831)	34,413	34,928
92879	Home Gardens (c)	(909)	9,461	11,570
*92647	Huntington Beach	(714)	189,594	189,992
90255	Huntington Park	(323)	61,348	58,114
92251	Imperial	(760)	7,560	14,758
*91932	Imperial Beach	(619)	26,992	26,324
92201	Indio	(760)	49,116	76,036
*90301	Inglewood	(310)/(323)	112,580	109,673
*92619	Irvine	(714)/(949)	143,072	212,375
93117	Isla Vista (c)	(805)	18,344	23,096
93630	Kerman	(559)	8,551	13,544
93930	King City	(831)	11,094	12,874
93631	Kingsburg	(559)	9,199	11,382
*91011	La Cañada Flintridge	(818)	20,318	20,246
*91214	La Crescenta-Montrose (c)	(818)	18,532	19,653
*90631	La Habra	(562)/(949)	58,974	60,239
*91941	La Mesa	(619)	54,749	57,065
*90638	La Mirada	(562)/(714)	46,783	48,527
90623	La Palma	(562)/(714)	15,408	15,568
91977	La Presa (c)	(619)	32,721	34,169
*91747	La Puente	(626)	41,063	39,816
*92253	La Quinta	(760)	23,694	37,467
95401	La Riviera (c)	(916)	10,273	10,802
91750	La Verne	(909)	31,638	31,063
92694	Ladera Ranch (c)	(949)	—	22,980
94549	Lafayette	(925)	23,908	23,893
*92652	Laguna Beach	(949)	23,727	22,723
*92654	Laguna Hills	(949)	31,178	30,344
*92607	Laguna Niguel	(949)	61,891	62,979
*92654	Laguna Woods	(949)	16,507	16,192
92352	Lake Arrowhead (c)	(909)	8,934	12,424
*92531	Lake Elsinore	(951)	28,928	51,821
92630	Lake Forest	(949)	58,707	77,264
*93535	Lake Los Angeles (c)	(661)	11,523	12,328
92530	Lakeland Village (c)	(909)/(951)	5,626	11,541
92040	Lakeside (c)	(619)	19,560	20,648
*90714	Lakewood	(562)	79,345	80,048
93241	Lamont (c)	(661)	13,296	15,120
*93539	Lancaster	(661)	118,718	156,633
*94939	Larkspur	(415)	12,014	11,926
95330	Lathrop	(209)	10,445	18,023
*90260	Lawndale	(310)	31,711	32,769
*91945	Lemon Grove	(619)	24,918	25,320
95824	Lemon Hill (c)	(916)	—	13,729
93245	Lemoore	(559)	19,712	24,531
90304	Lennox (c)	(310)	22,950	22,753
95648	Lincoln	(916)	11,205	42,819
95901	Linda (c)	(530)	13,474	17,773
93247	Lindsay	(559)	10,297	11,768
95062	Live Oak (c) (Santa Cruz Co.)	(831)	16,628	17,158
*94550	Livermore	(925)	73,345	80,968
95334	Livingston	(209)	10,473	13,058
*95240	Lodi	(209)	56,999	62,134
92354	Loma Linda	(951)	18,681	23,261
90717	Lomita	(310)	20,046	20,256
*93436	Lompoc	(805)	41,103	42,434
*90801	Long Beach	(310)/(562)	461,522	462,257
*90720	Los Alamitos	(562)/(949)	11,536	11,449
*94022	Los Altos	(650)	27,693	28,976
*90086	Los Angeles	(213)/(310)/(323)/(818)	3,694,820	3,792,621
93665	Los Banos	(209)	25,869	35,972
*95030	Los Gatos	(408)	28,592	29,413
*93402	Los Osos (c)	(805)	—	14,276
90262	Lynwood	(213)/(310)/(323)	69,845	69,772
*93638	Madera	(559)	43,207	61,416
95954	Magalia (c)	(530)	10,569	11,310
*90265	Malibu	(310)	12,575	12,645
*90266	Manhattan Beach	(310)	33,852	35,135
95336	Manteca	(209)	49,258	67,096
93933	Marina	(831)	25,101	19,718
94553	Martinez	(925)	35,866	35,824
95901	Marysville	(530)	12,268	12,072
90270	Maywood	(323)	28,083	27,395
93250	McFarland	(661)	9,618	12,707
95521	McKinleyville (c)	(707)	13,599	15,177
93640	Mendota	(559)	7,890	11,014
92586	Menifee	(951)	—	77,519
*94025	Menlo Park	(650)	30,785	32,026
*95340	Merced	(209)	63,893	78,958
*94941	Mill Valley	(415)	13,600	13,903
94030	Millbrae	(650)	20,718	21,532
*95035	Milpitas	(408)	62,698	66,790
91752	Mira Loma (c)	(951)	17,617	21,930
92690	Mission Viejo	(949)	93,102	93,305
*95350	Modesto	(209)	188,856	201,165
91017	Monrovia	(626)	36,929	36,590
91763	Montclair	(909)	33,049	36,664
90640	Montebello	(323)	62,150	62,500
*93940	Monterey	(831)	29,674	27,810
91754	Monterey Park	(323)/(626)/(818)	60,051	60,269
*93021	Moorpark	(805)	31,415	34,421
94556	Moraga	(925)	16,290	16,016
*92552	Moreno Valley	(951)	142,381	193,365
95037	Morgan Hill	(408)	33,556	37,882
*93442	Morro Bay	(805)	10,350	10,234
94041	Mountain View	(650)	70,708	74,066
*92564	Murrieta	(951)	44,282	103,466
92407	Muscoy (c)	(909)	8,919	10,644
*94558	Napa	(707)	72,585	76,915
*91950	National City	(619)	54,260	58,582
94560	Newark	(510)	42,471	42,573
95360	Newman	(209)	7,093	10,224
*92658	Newport Beach	(949)	70,032	85,186
93444	Nipomo (c)	(805)	12,626	16,714
91760	Norco	(951)	24,157	27,063
95603	North Auburn (c)	(530)	11,847	13,022
94025	North Fair Oaks (c)	(650)	15,440	14,687
95660	North Highlands (c)	(916)	44,187	42,694
92705	North Tustin (c)	(714)/(949)	—	24,917
*90650	Norwalk	(562)	103,298	105,549
*94947	Novato	(415)	47,630	51,904
*91377	Oak Park (c)	(805)/(818)	2,320	13,811
95361	Oakdale	(209)	15,503	20,675
*94617	Oakland	(510)	399,484	390,724
94561	Oakley	(925)	25,619	35,432
*92056	Oceanside	(760)	161,029	167,086
93308	Oildale (c)	(661)	27,885	32,684
95961	Olivehurst (c)	(530)	11,061	13,656
*91761	Ontario	(909)	158,007	163,924
*92863	Orange	(714)	128,821	136,416
95662	Orangevale (c)	(916)	26,705	33,960
*93457	Orcutt (c)	(805)	28,830	28,905
94563	Orinda	(925)	17,599	17,643
*95965	Oroville	(530)	13,004	15,546
93030	Oxnard	(805)	170,358	197,899
93950	Pacific Grove	(831)	15,522	15,041
94044	Pacifica	(650)	38,390	37,234
*92260	Palm Desert	(760)	41,155	48,445
92262	Palm Springs	(760)	42,807	44,552
93590	Palmdale	(661)	116,670	152,750
*94303	Palo Alto	(650)	58,598	64,403
*90274	Palos Verdes Estates	(310)	13,340	13,438
*95969	Paradise	(530)	26,408	26,218
90723	Paramount	(562)	55,266	54,098
95823	Parkway (c)	(916)	—	14,670
93648	Parlier	(559)	11,145	14,494
*91109	Pasadena	(323)/(626)/(818)	133,936	137,122
	Paso Robles. See El Paso de Robles			
95363	Patterson	(209)	11,606	20,413
92509	Pedley (c)	(951)	11,207	12,672
*92572	Perris	(951)	36,189	68,386
*94952	Petaluma	(707)	54,548	57,941
*92371	Phelan (c)	(760)	—	14,304
*90660	Pico Rivera	(562)	63,428	62,942
*94611	Piedmont	(510)	10,952	10,667
94564	Pinole	(510)	19,039	18,390
94565	Pittsburg	(925)	56,769	63,264
*92871	Placentia	(714)	46,488	50,533
*95667	Placerville	(530)	9,610	10,389
94523	Pleasant Hill	(925)	32,837	33,152
*94566	Pleasanton	(925)	63,654	70,285
*91769	Pomona	(909)	149,473	149,058
*93041	Port Hueneme	(805)	21,845	21,723

ZIP	Place	Area code	2000	2010
*93257	Porterville	(559)	39,615	54,165
*92064	Poway	(858)	48,044	47,811
93907	Prunedale (c)	(831)	16,432	17,560
*93536	Quartz Hill (c)	(661)	9,890	10,912
92065	Ramona	(760)	15,691	20,292
*95670	Rancho Cordova	(916)	—	64,776
*91729	Rancho Cucamonga	(909)	127,743	165,269
92270	Rancho Mirage	(760)	13,249	17,218
90275	Rancho Palos Verdes	(310)	41,145	41,643
91941	Rancho San Diego (c)	(619)	20,155	21,208
92688	Rancho Santa Margarita	(949)	47,214	47,853
96080	Red Bluff	(530)	13,147	14,076
*96049	Redding	(530)	80,865	89,861
*92373	Redlands	(909)	63,591	68,747
*90277	Redondo Beach	(310)	63,261	66,748
*94063	Redwood City	(650)	75,402	76,815
93654	Reedley	(559)	20,756	24,194
*92377	Rialto	(909)	91,873	99,171
*94802	Richmond	(510)	99,216	103,701
*93556	Ridgecrest	(760)	24,927	27,616
95673	Rio Linda (c)	(916)	10,466	15,106
95366	Ripon	(209)	10,146	14,297
95367	Riverbank	(209)	15,826	22,678
*92502	Riverside	(951)	255,166	303,871
*95677	Rocklin	(916)	36,330	56,974
*94928	Rohnert Park	(707)	42,236	40,971
93560	Rosamond (c)	(661)	14,349	18,150
93314	Rosedale (c)	(661)	8,445	14,058
*91770	Rosemead	(626)	53,505	53,764
95826	Rosemont (c)	(916)	22,904	22,681
*95678	Roseville	(916)	79,921	118,788
90720	Rossmoor (c)	(714)	10,298	10,244
91748	Rowland Heights (c)	(626)	48,553	48,993
*92519	Rubidoux (c)	(951)	29,180	34,280
*95814	Sacramento	(916)	407,018	466,488
95368	Salida (c)	(209)	12,560	13,722
*93907	Salinas	(831)	151,060	150,441
*94960	San Anselmo	(415)	12,378	12,336
*92401	San Bernardino	(909)	185,401	209,924
*94066	San Bruno	(650)	40,165	41,114
*93001	San Buenaventura (Ventura)	(805)	100,916	106,433
*94070	San Carlos	(650)	27,718	28,406
*92674	San Clemente	(949)	49,936	63,522
*92138	San Diego	(619)/(858)	1,223,400	1,307,402
92065	San Diego Country Estates (c)	(760)	9,262	10,109
91773	San Dimas	(909)	34,980	33,371
*91341	San Fernando	(818)	23,564	23,645
*94142	San Francisco	(415)	776,733	805,235
*91778	San Gabriel	(626)	39,804	39,718
*92581	San Jacinto	(951)	23,779	44,199
*95113	San Jose	(408)	894,943	945,942
*92690	San Juan Capistrano	(949)	33,826	34,593
*94577	San Leandro	(510)	79,452	84,950
*94580	San Lorenzo (c)	(510)	21,898	23,452
*93401	San Luis Obispo	(805)	44,174	45,119
*92069	San Marcos	(760)	54,977	83,781
*91108	San Marino	(626)	12,945	13,147
*94402	San Mateo	(650)	92,482	97,207
94806	San Pablo	(510)	30,215	29,139
*94915	San Rafael	(415)	56,063	57,713
94583	San Ramon	(925)	44,722	72,148
93657	Sanger	(559)	18,931	24,270
*92711	Santa Ana	(714)/(949)	337,977	324,528
*93102	Santa Barbara	(805)	92,325	88,410
*95050	Santa Clara	(408)	102,361	116,468
*91380	Santa Clarita	(661)	151,088	176,320
*95060	Santa Cruz	(831)	54,593	59,946
90670	Santa Fe Springs	(562)	17,438	16,223
*93454	Santa Maria	(805)	77,423	99,553
*90401	Santa Monica	(310)	84,084	89,736
*93060	Santa Paula	(805)	28,598	29,231
*95402	Santa Rosa	(707)	147,595	167,815
*92071	Santee	(619)	52,975	53,413
*95070	Saratoga	(408)	29,843	29,926
*95066	Scotts Valley	(831)	11,385	11,580
90740	Seal Beach	(562)	24,157	24,168
93955	Seaside	(831)	31,696	33,025
93662	Selma	(559)	19,444	23,219
*93263	Shafter	(661)	12,736	16,988
*96019	Shasta Lake	(916)	9,008	10,164
*91025	Sierra Madre	(626)	10,578	10,917
*90806	Signal Hill	(562)	9,333	11,016
*93065	Simi Valley	(805)	111,351	124,237
92075	Solana Beach	(858)	12,979	12,867
93960	Soledad	(831)	11,263	25,738
95476	Sonoma	(707)	9,128	10,648
91733	South El Monte	(626)	21,144	20,116
90280	South Gate	(323)/(562)	96,375	94,396
*96151	South Lake Tahoe	(530)	23,609	21,403
*91030	S. Pasadena	(213)/(323)/(626)/(818)	24,292	25,619
*94080	South San Francisco	(650)	60,552	63,632
91744	South San Jose Hills (c)	(626)	20,218	20,551
90605	South Whittier (c)	(562)	55,193	57,156
*91977	Spring Valley (c)	(619)	26,663	28,205

ZIP	Place	Area code	2000	2010
*94309	Stanford (c)	(650)	13,315	13,809
90680	Stanton	(714)	37,403	38,186
*95208	Stockton	(209)	243,771	291,707
*94585	Suisun City	(707)	26,118	28,111
93543	Sun Village (c)	(661)	—	11,565
*94086	Sunnyvale	(408)	131,760	140,081
96130	Susanville	(530)	13,541	17,947
94941	Tamalpais-Homestead Val. (c)	(415)	10,691	10,735
*93581	Tehachapi	(661)	10,957	14,414
*92589	Temecula	(951)	57,716	100,097
92883	Temescal Valley (c)	(951)	—	22,535
91780	Temple City	(626)	33,377	35,558
*91359	Thousand Oaks	(805)	117,005	126,683
*90503	Torrance	(310)	137,946	145,438
95376	Tracy	(209)	56,929	82,922
*96161	Truckee	(916)	13,864	16,180
*93274	Tulare	(559)	43,994	59,278
*95380	Turlock	(209)	55,810	68,549
*92781	Tustin	(714)/(949)	67,504	75,540
*92277	Twentynine Palms	(760)	14,764	25,048
*95482	Ukiah	(707)	15,497	16,075
94587	Union City	(510)	66,869	69,516
*91785	Upland	(909)	68,393	73,732
*95687	Vacaville	(707)	88,625	92,428
91744	Valinda (c)	(626)	21,776	22,822
*94590	Vallejo	(707)	116,760	115,942
92343	Valle Vista (c)	(951)	10,488	14,578
	Ventura. See San Buenaventura			
*92393	Victorville	(760)	64,029	115,903
90043	View Park-Windsor Hills (c)	(310)	10,958	11,075
91722	Vincent (c)	(925)	15,097	15,922
95829	Vineyard (c)	(916)	10,109	24,836
*93291	Visalia	(559)	91,565	124,442
*92083	Vista	(760)	89,857	93,834
*91788	Walnut	(626)	30,004	23,172
*94596	Walnut Creek	(925)	64,296	64,173
90255	Walnut Park (c)	(213)	16,180	15,966
93280	Wasco	(661)	21,263	25,545
*95076	Watsonville	(831)	44,265	51,199
90502	West Carson (c)	(310)	21,138	21,699
*91790	West Covina	(626)	105,080	106,098
90069	West Hollywood	(310)/(323)	35,716	34,399
91746	West Puente Valley (c)	(626)	22,589	22,636
*95691	West Sacramento	(916)	31,615	48,744
*90606	West Whittier-Los Nietos (c)	(562)	24,164	25,540
*92685	Westminster	(714)	88,207	89,701
90047	Westmont (c)	(323)	31,623	31,853
*90605	Whittier	(562)	83,680	85,331
92595	Wildomar	(951)	14,064	32,176
90222	Willowbrook (c)	(323)	34,138	35,983
95492	Windsor	(707)	22,744	26,801
92040	Winter Gardens (c)	(619)	19,771	20,631
95388	Winton (c)	(209)	8,832	10,613
92504	Woodcrest (c)	(909)/(951)	8,342	14,347
*95695	Woodland	(530)	49,151	55,468
*92885	Yorba Linda	(714)	58,918	64,234
*95991	Yuba City	(530)	36,758	64,925
92399	Yucaipa	(909)	41,207	51,367
*92286	Yucca Valley	(760)	16,865	20,700

Colorado

Area code (720) overlays area code (303).

ZIP	Place	Area code	2000	2010
*80004	Arvada	(303)	102,153	106,433
*80017	Aurora	(303)	276,393	325,078
80221	Berkley (c)	(970)	10,743	11,207
*80908	Black Forest (c)	(719)	8,143	13,116
*80302	Boulder	(303)	94,673	97,385
*80601	Brighton	(303)	20,905	33,352
*80020	Broomfield	(303)	38,272	55,889
*81212	Cañon City	(719)	15,431	16,400
80108	Castle Pines North	(303)	—	10,360
*80104	Castle Rock	(303)	20,224	48,231
*80015	Centennial	(303)	—	100,377
80111	Cherry Creek (c)	(303)	—	11,120
81222	Cimarron Hills (c)	(719)	15,194	16,161
81520	Clifton (c)	(970)	17,345	19,889
*80903	Colorado Springs	(719)	360,890	416,427
80120	Columbine (c)	(303)	24,095	24,280
80022	Commerce City	(303)	20,991	45,913
80304	Dakota Ridge (c)	(303)	—	32,005
*80202	Denver	(303)	554,636	600,158
*81301	Durango	(970)	13,922	16,887
81632	Edwards (c)	(970)	8,257	10,266
*80110	Englewood	(303)	31,727	30,255
80516	Erie	(303)	6,291	18,135
80620	Evans	(970)	9,514	18,537
80221	Federal Heights	(303)	12,065	11,467
*80520	Firestone	(303)	1,908	10,147
80913	Fort Carson (c)	(719)	10,566	13,813
*80525	Fort Collins	(970)	118,652	143,986
*80701	Fort Morgan	(970)	11,034	11,315
80817	Fountain	(719)	15,197	25,846
*81521	Fruita	(970)	6,478	12,646

ZIP	Place	Area code	2000	2010
*80401	Golden	(303)	17,159	18,867
*81501	Grand Junction	(970)	41,986	58,566
*80631	Greeley	(970)	76,930	92,889
*80111	Greenwood Village	(303)	11,035	13,925
80163	Highlands Ranch (c)	(303)	70,931	96,713
80127	Ken Caryl (c)	(303)	30,887	32,438
80026	Lafayette	(303)	23,197	24,453
*80226	Lakewood	(303)	144,126	142,980
*80126	Littleton	(303)	40,340	41,737
*80124	Lone Tree	(303)	4,873	10,218
*80501	Longmont	(303)	71,093	86,270
80027	Louisville	(303)	18,937	18,376
*80538	Loveland	(970)	50,608	66,859
*81401	Montrose	(970)	12,344	19,132
*80233	Northglenn	(303)	31,575	35,789
*80134	Parker	(303)	23,558	45,297
*81003	Pueblo	(719)	102,121	106,595
81007	Pueblo West (c)	(719)	16,899	29,637
80911	Security-Widefield (c)	(719)	29,845	32,882
80221	Sherrelwood (c)	(303)	17,657	18,287
*80477	Steamboat Springs	(970)	9,815	12,088
80751	Sterling	(970)	11,360	14,777
80027	Superior	(303)	9,011	12,483
80134	The Pinery (c)	(303)	7,253	10,517
*80229	Thornton	(303)	82,384	118,772
80229	Welby (c)	(303)	12,973	14,846
*80030	Westminster	(303)	100,940	106,114
*80033	Wheat Ridge	(303)	32,913	30,166
*80550	Windsor	(970)	9,896	18,644

Connecticut

Area code (475) overlays area code (203). See introductory note.

ZIP	Place	Area code	2000	2010
06401	Ansonia	(203)	18,554	19,249
06001	Avon	(860)	15,832	18,098
06037	Berlin	(860)	18,215	19,866
06801	Bethel	(203)	18,067	18,584
06002	Bloomfield	(860)	19,587	20,486
06405	Branford	(203)	28,683	28,026
*06602	Bridgeport	(203)	139,529	144,229
*06010	Bristol	(860)	60,062	60,477
06804	Brookfield	(203)	15,664	16,452
06019	Canton	(860)	8,840	10,292
*06410	Cheshire	(203)	28,543	29,261
06413	Clinton	(860)	13,094	13,260
*06415	Colchester	(860)	14,551	16,068
06238	Coventry	(860)	11,504	12,435
06416	Cromwell	(860)	12,871	14,005
*06810	Danbury	(203)	74,848	80,893
06820	Darien	(203)	19,607	20,732
06418	Derby	(203)	12,391	12,902
*06424	East Hampton	(860)	13,352	12,959
*06108	East Hartford	(860)	49,575	51,252
*06512	East Haven	(203)	28,189	29,257
06333	East Lyme	(860)	18,118	19,159
*06088	East Windsor	(860)	9,818	11,162
06029	Ellington	(860)	12,921	15,602
*06082	Enfield	(860)	45,212	44,654
*06825	Fairfield	(203)	57,340	59,404
*06032	Farmington	(860)	23,641	25,340
06033	Glastonbury	(860)	31,876	34,427
06035	Granby	(860)	10,347	11,282
*06830	Greenwich	(203)	61,101	61,171
06351	Griswold	(860)	10,807	11,951
06340	Groton	(860)	39,907	40,115
06437	Guilford	(203)	21,398	22,375
*06514	Hamden	(203)	56,913	60,960
*06101	Hartford	(860)	121,578	124,775
*06239	Killingly	(860)	16,472	17,370
06339	Ledyard	(860)	14,687	15,051
06443	Madison	(203)	17,858	18,269
*06040	Manchester	(860)	54,740	58,241
*06250	Mansfield	(860)	20,720	26,543
*06450	Meriden	(203)	58,244	60,868
06457	Middletown	(860)	43,167	47,648
*06460	Milford	(203)	50,594	51,271
06461	Milford	(203)	52,305	52,759
06468	Monroe	(203)	19,247	19,479
06353	Montville	(860)	18,546	19,571
06770	Naugatuck	(203)	30,989	31,862
*06050	New Britain	(860)	71,538	73,206
*06840	New Canaan	(203)	19,395	19,738
06812	New Fairfield	(203)	13,953	13,881
*06511	New Haven	(203)	123,626	129,779
06320	New London	(860)	25,671	27,620
06776	New Milford	(860)	27,121	28,142
*06101	Newington	(860)	29,306	30,562
06470	Newtown	(203)	25,031	27,560
06471	North Branford	(203)	13,906	14,407
06473	North Haven	(203)	23,035	24,093
*06856	Norwalk	(203)	82,951	85,603

ZIP	Place	Area code	2000	2010
06360	Norwich	(860)	36,117	40,493
06475	Old Saybrook	(860)	10,367	10,242
06477	Orange	(203)	13,233	13,956
06478	Oxford	(203)	9,821	12,683
06374	Plainfield	(860)	14,619	15,405
06062	Plainville	(860)	17,328	17,716
06782	Plymouth	(860)	11,634	12,243
06877	Ridgefield	(203)	23,643	24,638
06067	Rocky Hill	(860)	17,966	19,709
*06483	Seymour	(203)	15,454	16,540
06484	Shelton	(203)	38,101	39,559
*06070	Simsbury	(860)	23,234	23,511
06071	Somers	(860)	10,417	11,444
*06074	South Windsor	(860)	24,412	25,709
06488	Southbury	(203)	18,567	19,904
06489	Southington	(860)	39,728	43,069
*06075	Stafford	(860)	11,307	12,087
*06904	Stamford	(203)	117,083	122,643
06378	Stonington	(860)	17,906	18,545
*06268	Storrs (c)	(860)	10,996	15,344
*06602	Stratford	(203)	49,976	51,384
*06078	Suffield	(860)	13,552	15,735
06084	Tolland	(860)	13,146	15,052
*06790	Torrington	(860)	35,202	36,383
06611	Trumbull	(203)	34,243	36,018
06066	Vernon	(860)	28,063	29,179
*06492	Wallingford	(203)	43,026	45,135
06492	Wallingford Center (c)	(203)	17,509	18,209
*06702	Waterbury	(203)	107,271	110,366
*06385	Waterford	(860)	19,152	19,517
06795	Watertown	(860)	21,661	22,514
*06101	West Hartford	(860)	63,589	63,268
06516	West Haven	(203)	52,360	55,564
06883	Weston	(203)	10,037	10,179
*06880	Westport	(203)	25,749	26,391
*06101	Wethersfield	(860)	26,271	26,668
06226	Willimantic (c)	(860)	15,823	17,737
06897	Wilton	(203)	17,633	18,062
*06094	Winchester	(860)	10,664	11,242
*06280	Windham	(860)	22,857	25,268
*06095	Windsor	(860)	28,237	29,044
06096	Windsor Locks	(860)	12,043	12,498
*06716	Wolcott	(203)	15,215	16,680

Delaware (302)

ZIP	Place	2000	2010
19701	Bear (c)	17,593	19,371
19713	Brookside (c)	14,806	14,353
*19901	Dover	32,135	36,047
19702	Glasgow (c)	12,840	14,303
19707	Hockessin (c)	12,902	13,527
19709	Middletown	6,161	18,871
*19711	Newark	28,547	31,454
19808	Pike Creek Valley (c)	—	11,217
19977	Smyrna	5,679	10,023
*19899	Wilmington	72,664	70,851

District of Columbia (202)

ZIP	Place	2000	2010
*20090	Washington	572,059	601,723

Florida

Area code (321) overlays area code (407). Area code (754) overlays area code (954). Area code (786) overlays area code (305).

ZIP	Place	Area code	2000	2010
*32828	Alafaya (c)	(407)	—	78,113
*32714	Altamonte Springs	(407)	41,200	41,496
33572	Apollo Beach (c)	(813)	7,444	14,055
*32712	Apopka	(407)	26,642	41,542
*32233	Atlantic Beach	(904)	13,368	12,655
33823	Auburndale	(863)	11,032	13,507
*33160	Aventura	(305)	25,267	35,762
32807	Azalea Park (c)	(407)	11,073	12,556
*33830	Bartow	(863)	15,340	17,298
34667	Bayonet Point (c)	(727)	23,577	23,467
33507	Bayshore Gardens (c)	(941)	17,350	16,323
*33756	Bellair-Meadowbrook Terrace (c)	(904)	16,539	13,343
33430	Belle Glade	(561)	14,906	14,467
*34420	Belleview (c)	(352)	21,201	23,355
33509	Bloomingdale (c)	(813)	19,839	22,711
*33431	Boca Raton	(561)	74,764	84,392
34135	Bonita Springs	(239)	32,797	43,914
*33436	Boynton Beach	(561)	60,389	68,217
*34206	Bradenton	(941)	49,504	49,546
*33509	Brandon (c)	(813)	77,895	103,483
32503	Brent (c)	(850)	22,257	21,804
33142	Brownsville (c)	(305)	14,393	15,313
34743	Buenaventura Lakes (c)	(407)	—	26,079
32404	Callaway	(850)	14,233	14,405
*33920	Cape Coral	(239)	102,286	154,305

ZIP	Place	Area code	2000	2010
*33618	Carrollwood (c)	(813)	—	33,365
*32707	Casselberry	(407)	22,629	26,241
33558	Cheval (c)	(813)	7,602	10,702
33624	Citrus Park (c)	(813)	20,226	24,252
*33758	Clearwater	(727)	108,787	107,685
*34711	Clermont	(352)	9,333	28,742
*32922	Cocoa	(321)	16,412	17,140
*32931	Cocoa Beach	(321)	12,482	11,231
*33097	Coconut Creek	(954)	43,566	52,909
32809	Conway (c)	(407)	14,394	13,467
*33328	Cooper City	(954)	27,939	28,547
*33114	Coral Gables	(305)	42,249	46,780
*33075	Coral Springs	(954)	117,549	121,096
33157	Coral Terrace (c)	(305)	24,380	24,376
33015	Country Club (c)	(305)	36,310	47,105
33196	Country Walk (c)	(305)	10,653	15,997
*32536	Crestview	(850)	14,766	20,978
33189	Cutler Bay	(305)	—	40,286
33919	Cypress Lake (c)	(239)	12,072	11,846
*33004	Dania Beach	(954)	—	29,639
*33329	Davie	(954)	75,720	91,992
*32114	Daytona Beach	(386)	64,112	61,005
*32713	DeBary	(386)	15,559	19,320
*33441	Deerfield Beach	(954)	64,583	75,018
*32720	DeLand	(386)	20,904	27,031
*33444	Delray Beach	(561)	60,020	60,522
*32783	Deltona	(407)	69,543	85,182
*32541	Destin	(850)	11,119	12,305
32836	Doctor Phillips (c)	(407)	9,548	10,981
*33178	Doral	(305)	—	45,704
*34698	Dunedin	(727)	35,691	35,321
33610	East Lake (c)	(813)	29,394	30,962
33619	East Lake-Orient Park (c)	(813)	5,703	22,753
32583	East Milton (c)	(850)	—	11,074
*32132	Edgewater	(386)	18,668	20,750
33614	Egypt Lake-Leto (c)	(813)	32,782	35,282
34680	Elfers (c)	(727)	13,161	13,986
*34295	Englewood (c)	(941)	16,196	14,863
32534	Ensley (c)	(850)	18,752	20,602
*33928	Estero (c)	(239)	9,503	22,612
32726	Eustis	(352)	15,106	18,558
32804	Fairview Shores (c)	(305)	13,898	10,239
*32034	Fernandina Beach	(904)	10,549	11,487
32514	Ferry Pass (c)	(850)	27,176	28,921
33547	Fish Hawk (c)	(813)	1,991	14,087
32003	Fleming Island (c)	(904)	—	27,126
*33034	Florida City	(305)	7,843	11,245
32960	Florida Ridge (c)	(772)	15,217	18,164
32714	Forest City (c)	(407)	12,612	13,854
*33310	Fort Lauderdale	(954)	152,397	165,521
*33902	Fort Myers	(239)	48,208	62,298
*34981	Fort Pierce	(772)	37,516	41,590
*32548	Fort Walton Beach	(850)	19,973	19,507
33172	Fountainbleau (c)	(305)	59,549	59,764
34747	Four Corners (c)	(863)	—	26,116
*32259	Fruit Cove (c)	(904)	16,077	29,362
34232	Fruitville (c)	(941)	12,741	13,224
*32602	Gainesville	(352)	95,447	124,354
33534	Gibsonton (c)	(813)	8,752	14,234
33138	Gladeview (c)	(954)	14,468	11,535
33143	Glenvar Heights (c)	(305)	16,243	16,898
34116	Golden Gate (c)	(239)	20,951	23,961
33055	Golden Glades (c)	(305)	32,623	33,145
32733	Goldenrod (c)	(407)	12,871	12,039
32560	Gonzalez (c)	(850)	11,365	13,273
33170	Goulds (c)	(305)	7,453	10,103
*33454	Greenacres	(561)	27,569	37,573
33581	Gulf Gate Estates (c)	(941)	11,647	10,911
*33737	Gulfport	(727)	12,527	12,029
*33844	Haines City	(863)	13,174	20,535
*33009	Hallandale Beach	(305)/(954)	—	37,113
*33010	Hialeah	(305)	226,419	224,669
*33016	Hialeah Gardens	(305)	19,297	21,744
33846	Highland City (c)	(863)	2,051	10,834
*33455	Hobe Sound (c)	(772)	11,376	11,521
*34690	Holiday (c)	(727)	21,904	22,403
*32125	Holly Hill	(386)	12,119	11,659
33022	Hollywood	(954)	139,357	140,768
*33030	Homestead	(305)	31,909	60,512
34447	Homosassa Springs (c)	(352)	12,458	13,791
34787	Horizon West (c)	(352)	—	14,000
*34667	Hudson (c)	(727)	12,765	12,158
32837	Hunters Creek (c)	(407)	9,369	14,321
*34142	Immokalee (c)	(239)	19,763	24,154
33908	Iona (c)	(239)	11,756	15,369
33162	Ives Estates (c)	(305)	17,586	19,525
*32203	Jacksonville	(904)	735,617	821,784
*32250	Jacksonville Beach	(904)	20,990	21,362
33568	Jasmine Estates (c)	(727)	18,213	18,989
*34957	Jensen Beach (c)	(772)	11,100	11,707
*33458	Jupiter	(561)	39,328	55,156
33478	Jupiter Farms (c)	(561)	—	11,994
33183	Kendale Lakes (c)	(305)	56,901	56,148
*33256	Kendall (c)	(305)	75,226	75,371
33193	Kendall West (c)	(305)	38,034	36,154
33149	Key Biscayne	(305)	10,507	12,344
*33037	Key Largo (c)	(305)	11,886	10,433
*33040	Key West	(305)	25,478	24,649
33556	Keystone (c)	(813)	14,627	24,039
*34744	Kissimmee	(407)	47,814	59,682
32159	Lady Lake	(352)	11,828	13,926
34786	Lake Butler (c)	(407)	7,062	15,400
32055	Lake City	(386)	9,980	12,046
33612	Lake Magdalene (c)	(813)	28,755	28,509
*32746	Lake Mary	(407)	11,458	13,822
*33853	Lake Wales	(863)	10,194	14,225
33461	Lake Worth	(561)	35,133	34,910
*33804	Lakeland	(863)	78,452	91,422
33801	Lakeland Highlands (c)	(863)	12,557	11,056
32073	Lakeside (c)	(904)	30,927	30,943
34951	Lakewood Park (c)	(772)	10,458	11,323
*34639	Land O'Lakes (c)	(813)	20,971	31,996
*33445	Lantana	(561)	9,437	10,423
*33770	Largo	(727)	69,371	77,648
*33313	Lauderdale Lakes	(954)	31,705	32,593
*33313	Lauderhill	(727)	57,585	66,887
33714	Lealman (c)	(727)	—	19,879
*34748	Leesburg	(352)	15,956	20,117
*33936	Lehigh Acres (c)	(239)	33,430	86,784
*33033	Leisure City (c)	(305)	22,152	22,655
33074	Lighthouse Point	(954)	10,767	10,344
32810	Lockhart (c)	(407)	12,944	13,060
32750	Longwood	(407)	13,745	13,657
*33549	Lutz (c)	(813)	17,081	19,344
32444	Lynn Haven	(850)	12,451	18,493
*32751	Maitland	(407)	12,019	15,751
33550	Mango (c)	(813)	8,842	11,313
34145	Marco Island	(239)	—	16,413
*33093	Margate	(954)	53,909	53,284
32824	Meadow Woods (c)	(407)	11,286	25,558
*32901	Melbourne	(321)	71,382	76,068
32953	Merritt Island (c)	(321)	36,090	34,743
*33101	Miami	(305)	362,470	399,457
*33152	Miami Beach	(305)	87,933	87,779
33023	Miami Gardens	(305)	—	107,167
*33014	Miami Lakes	(305)	—	29,361
*33138	Miami Shores	(305)	10,380	10,493
*33266	Miami Springs	(305)	13,712	13,809
*32068	Middleburg (c)	(904)	10,338	13,008
*32563	Midway (c)	(850)	—	16,115
*33023	Miramar	(954)	72,739	122,041
*32757	Mount Dora	(352)	9,418	12,370
32526	Myrtle Grove (c)	(850)	17,211	15,870
*34102	Naples	(239)	20,976	19,537
32566	Navarre (c)	(850)	—	31,378
*34653	New Port Richey	(727)	16,117	14,911
34653	New Port Richey East (c)	(727)	9,916	10,036
*32168	New Smyrna Beach	(386)	20,048	2,464
32578	Niceville	(850)	11,684	12,749
*33918	North Fort Myers (c)	(239)	40,214	39,407
*33068	North Lauderdale	(954)	32,264	41,023
*33261	North Miami	(305)	59,880	58,786
*33160	North Miami Beach	(305)	40,786	41,523
33408	North Palm Beach	(561)	12,064	12,015
*34287	North Port	(941)	22,797	57,357
33624	Northdale (c)	(813)	—	22,079
*33860	Oak Ridge (c)	(407)	22,349	22,685
33307	Oakland Park	(954)	30,966	41,363
32065	Oakleaf Plantation (c)	(904)	—	20,315
*34478	Ocala	(352)	45,943	56,315
34761	Ocoee	(407)	24,391	35,579
*33163	Ojus (c)	(305)	16,642	18,036
34677	Oldsmar	(813)	11,910	13,591
*33265	Olympia Heights (c)	(305)	13,452	13,488
*33054	Opa-Locka	(305)	14,951	15,219
*32763	Orange City	(386)	6,604	10,599
*32802	Orlando	(407)	185,951	238,300
32174	Ormond Beach	(386)	36,301	38,137
*32765	Oviedo	(407)	26,316	33,342
32571	Pace (c)	(850)	7,393	20,039
*32177	Palatka	(386)	10,033	10,558
*32905	Palm Bay	(321)	79,413	103,190
*33408	Palm Beach Gardens	(561)	35,058	48,452
*34990	Palm City (c)	(772)	20,097	23,120
*32135	Palm Coast	(386)	32,732	75,180
*34683	Palm Harbor (c)	(727)	59,248	57,439
*33601	Palm River-Clair Mel (c)	(813)	17,589	21,024
33406	Palm Springs	(561)	11,699	18,928
32082	Palm Valley (c)	(904)	19,860	20,019
*34221	Palmetto	(941)	12,571	12,606
33157	Palmetto Bay	(305)	—	23,410
33157	Palmetto Estates (c)	(305)	13,675	13,535
*32401	Panama City	(850)	36,417	36,484
32417	Panama City Beach	(850)	7,671	12,018
*33067	Parkland	(954)	13,835	23,962
33029	Pembroke Pines	(954)	137,427	154,750
*32502	Pensacola	(850)	56,255	51,923
*32809	Pine Castle (c)	(407)	8,803	10,805
32858	Pine Hills (c)	(407)	41,764	60,076
*33156	Pinecrest	(305)	19,055	18,223
*33781	Pinellas Park	(727)	45,658	49,079

ZIP	Place	Area code	2000	2010
33168	Pinewood (c)	(305)	16,523	16,520
*33566	Plant City	(813)	29,915	34,721
*33318	Plantation	(954)	82,934	84,955
*34758	Poinciana (c)	(407)	13,647	53,193
*33060	Pompano Beach	(954)	78,191	99,845
*33952	Port Charlotte (c)	(941)	46,451	54,392
*32129	Port Orange	(904)	45,823	56,048
32927	Port St. John (c)	(321)	12,112	12,267
*34981	Port St. Lucie	(772)	88,769	164,603
34992	Port Salerno (c)	(772)	10,141	10,091
*33032	Princeton (c)	(305)	10,090	22,038
*33950	Punta Gorda	(941)	14,344	16,641
33177	Richmond West (c)	(305)	28,082	31,973
*33569	Riverview (c)	(813)	12,035	71,050
*33419	Riviera Beach	(561)	29,884	32,488
*32955	Rockledge	(321)	20,170	24,926
*33411	Royal Palm Beach	(561)	21,523	34,140
*33570	Ruskin (c)	(813)	8,321	17,208
*34695	Safety Harbor	(727)	17,203	16,884
*32084	Saint Augustine	(904)	11,592	12,975
*34769	Saint Cloud	(407)	20,074	35,183
*33733	Saint Petersburg	(727)	248,232	244,769
33912	San Carlos Park (c)	(239)	16,317	16,824
*32771	Sanford	(407)	38,291	53,570
*34230	Sarasota	(941)	52,715	51,917
33577	Sarasota Springs (c)	(941)	15,875	14,395
32937	Satellite Beach	(321)	9,577	21,929
*32958	Sebastian	(772)	16,181	21,929
*33870	Sebring	(863)	9,667	10,491
*33770	Seminole	(813)	10,890	17,233
34610	Shady Hills (c)	(727)	7,798	11,523
33505	South Bradenton (c)	(941)	21,587	22,178
32121	South Daytona	(386)	13,177	12,252
*33243	South Miami	(305)	10,741	11,657
33157	South Miami Heights (c)	(305)	33,522	35,696
33595	South Venice (c)	(941)	13,539	13,949
32824	Southchase (c)	(407)	4,633	15,921
*34604	Spring Hill (c)	(352)	69,078	98,621
*34994	Stuart	(772)	14,633	15,593
*33573	Sun City Center (c)	(813)	—	19,258
33160	Sunny Isles Beach	(305)	—	20,832
*33325	Sunrise	(954)	85,779	84,439
*33283	Sunset (c)	(305)	17,150	16,389
33144	Sweetwater	(305)	—	13,499
*32301	Tallahassee	(850)	150,624	181,376
*33320	Tamarac	(954)	55,588	60,427
33144	Tamiami (c)	(305)	54,788	55,271
*33601	Tampa	(813)	303,447	335,709
*34689	Tarpon Springs	(727)	21,003	23,484
32778	Tavares	(352)	9,700	13,951
*33687	Temple Terrace	(813)	20,918	24,541
33412	The Acreage (c)	(561)	—	38,704
33186	The Crossings (c)	(305)	23,557	22,758
33196	The Hammocks (c)	(305)	47,379	51,003
*32162	The Villages (c)	(352)	8,333	51,442
33592	Thonotosassa (c)	(813)	6,091	13,014
33186	Three Lakes (c)	(305)	6,955	15,047
*32780	Titusville	(321)	40,670	43,761
32615	Town 'n' Country (c)	(813)	72,523	78,442
34655	Trinity (c)	(813)	4,279	10,907
33613	University (c) (Hillsborough Co.)	(813)	—	41,163
32826	University (c) (Orange Co.)	(407)	—	31,084
33165	University Park (c)	(305)	26,538	26,995
32401	Upper Grand Lagoon (c)	(850)	10,889	13,963
*33594	Valrico (c)	(813)	6,582	35,545
*34285	Venice	(941)	17,764	20,748
*32960	Vero Beach	(772)	17,705	15,220
32960	Vero Beach South (c)	(772)	20,362	23,092
32955	Viera East (c)	(321)	—	10,757
33901	Villas (c)	(239)	11,346	11,569
32507	Warrington (c)	(850)	15,207	14,531
32779	Wekiwa Springs (c)	(407)	23,169	21,998
*33414	Wellington (c)	(561)	38,216	56,508
*33544	Wesley Chapel (c)	(813)	5,691	44,092
33714	West Lealman (c)	(727)	—	15,651
33138	West Little River (c)	(305)	32,498	34,699
*32912	West Melbourne	(321)	9,824	18,355
*33416	West Palm Beach	(561)	82,103	99,919
33023	West Park (c)	(954)	—	14,156
32505	West Pensacola (c)	(850)	21,939	21,339
33626	Westchase (c)	(813)	11,116	21,747
33165	Westchester (c)	(305)	30,271	29,862
33326	Weston	(954)	49,286	65,333
33165	Westwood Lakes (c)	(305)	12,005	11,838
*33305	Wilton Manors	(954)	12,697	11,632
*34787	Winter Garden	(407)	14,351	34,568
*33880	Winter Haven	(863)	26,487	33,874
*32789	Winter Park	(407)	24,090	27,852
*32707	Winter Springs	(407)	31,666	33,282
32092	World Golf Village (c)	(904)	—	12,310
32547	Wright (c)	(850)	21,697	23,127
*32097	Yulee (c)	(904)	8,392	11,491
*33540	Zephyrhills	(813)	10,833	13,288

Georgia

Area codes (470) and (678) overlay area code (770). Area code (762) overlays area code (706).

ZIP	Place	Area code	2000	2010
*30101	Acworth	(770)	13,422	20,425
*31706	Albany	(229)	76,939	77,434
*30004	Alpharetta	(770)	34,854	57,551
*31709	Americus	(229)	17,013	17,041
*30603	Athens-Clarke County	(706)	100,266	115,452
*30301	Atlanta	(404)	416,474	420,003
*30903	Augusta-Richmond County	(706)	195,182	195,844
*39818	Bainbridge	(229)	11,722	12,697
30032	Belvedere Park (c)	(404)	18,945	15,152
*31520	Brunswick	(912)	15,600	15,383
*30518	Buford	(404)	10,668	12,225
*30701	Calhoun	(706)	10,667	15,650
30032	Candler-McAfee (c)	(404)	28,294	23,025
*30114	Canton	(770)	7,709	22,958
*30117	Carrollton	(770)	19,843	24,388
*30120	Cartersville	(770)	15,925	19,731
*30337	College Park	(404)	20,382	13,942
*31908	Columbus	(706)	—	189,885
*30013	Conyers	(404)	10,689	15,195
*31015	Cordele	(229)	11,608	11,147
*30014	Covington	(770)	11,547	13,118
31805	Cusseta-Chattahoochee County	(706)	—	11,267
*30132	Dallas	(770)	5,056	11,544
*30720	Dalton	(706)	27,912	33,128
*30030	Decatur	(404)	18,147	19,335
*31533	Douglas	(912)	10,639	11,589
*30134	Douglasville	(404)	20,065	30,961
30333	Druid Hills (c)	(404)	12,741	14,568
*31021	Dublin	(478)	15,857	16,201
*30096	Duluth	(404)	22,122	26,600
*30338	Dunwoody	(770)	—	46,267
30364	East Point	(404)	39,595	33,712
30809	Evans (c)	(706)	17,727	29,011
30213	Fairburn	(770)	5,464	12,950
*30214	Fayetteville	(404)	11,148	15,945
*30297	Forest Park	(404)	21,447	18,468
*30501	Gainesville	(770)	25,578	33,804
31754	Georgetown (c)	(912)	10,599	11,823
*30223	Griffin	(770)	23,451	23,643
30813	Grovetown	(706)	6,089	11,216
*31313	Hinesville	(912)	30,392	33,437
*31546	Jesup	(912)	9,279	10,214
30097	Johns Creek	(770)	—	76,728
*30144	Kennesaw	(404)	21,675	29,783
31548	Kingsland	(912)	10,506	15,946
*30240	LaGrange	(706)	25,998	29,588
*30045	Lawrenceville	(404)	22,397	28,546
*30047	Lilburn	(404)	11,307	11,596
30122	Lithia Springs (c)	(770)	—	15,491
30052	Loganville	(770)	5,435	10,458
30126	Mableton (c)	(404)	29,733	37,115
*31201	Macon	(478)	97,255	91,351
*30060	Marietta	(404)	58,748	56,579
30907	Martinez (c)	(706)	27,749	35,795
*30253	McDonough	(770)	8,493	22,084
*31061	Milledgeville	(478)	18,757	17,715
30004	Milton	(770)	—	32,661
*30655	Monroe	(770)	11,407	13,234
*31768	Moultrie	(229)	14,387	14,268
30087	Mountain Park (c)	(404)	11,753	11,554
*30263	Newnan	(770)	16,242	33,039
*30319	North Atlanta (c)	(404)	38,579	40,456
30033	North Decatur (c)	(404)	15,270	16,698
30033	North Druid Hills (c)	(404)	18,852	18,947
*30269	Peachtree City	(404)	31,580	34,364
31069	Perry	(478)	9,602	13,839
31322	Pooler	(912)	6,239	19,140
30127	Powder Springs	(404)	12,481	13,940
30074	Redan (c)	(404)	33,841	33,015
*30274	Riverdale	(404)	12,478	15,134
*30161	Rome	(706)	34,980	36,303
*30077	Roswell	(404)	79,334	88,346
31558	Saint Marys	(912)	13,761	17,121
31522	Saint Simons (c)	(912)	13,381	12,743
30358	Sandy Springs	(404)	—	93,853
*31402	Savannah	(912)	131,510	136,286
30079	Scottdale (c)	(404)	9,803	10,631
*30080	Smyrna	(404)	40,999	51,271
*30078	Snellville	(404)	15,351	18,242
*30458	Statesboro	(912)	22,698	28,422
*30281	Stockbridge	(404)	9,853	25,636
30518	Sugar Hill	(770)	11,399	18,522
30024	Suwanee	(770)	8,725	15,355
*31792	Thomasville	(229)	18,162	18,413
*31794	Tifton	(229)	15,060	16,350
*30084	Tucker (c)	(404)	26,532	27,581
30291	Union City	(404)	11,621	19,456
*31603	Valdosta	(229)	43,724	54,518

ZIP	Place	Area code	2000	2010
*30474	Vidalia	(912)	10,491	10,473
30180	Villa Rica	(770)	4,134	13,956
*31088	Warner Robins	(478)	48,804	66,588
*31501	Waycross	(912)	15,333	14,649
31410	Wilmington Island (c)	(912)	14,213	15,138
30680	Winder	(770)	10,201	14,099
*30188	Woodstock	(770)	10,050	23,896

Hawaii (808)

ZIP	Place	2000	2010
96821	East Honolulu (c)	—	49,914
96706	Ewa Beach (c)	14,650	14,955
96706	Ewa Gentry (c)	4,939	22,690
96701	Halawa (c)	13,891	14,014
96749	Hawaiian Paradise Park (c)	7,051	11,404
*96720	Hilo (c)	40,759	43,263
*96732	Kahului (c)	20,146	26,337
96740	Kailua (c) (Hawaii Co.)	9,870	11,975
96734	Kailua (c) (Honolulu Co.)	36,513	38,635
96744	Kaneohe (c)	34,970	34,597
96746	Kapaa (c)	9,472	10,699
*96707	Kapolei (c)	—	15,186
96753	Kihei (c)	16,749	20,881
96706	Makakilo (c)	13,156	18,248
96789	Mililani Mauka (c)	—	21,039
96789	Mililani Town (c)	28,608	27,629
96792	Nanakuli (c)	10,814	12,666
96782	Pearl City (c)	30,976	47,698
96797	Royal Kunia (c)	—	14,525
96857	Schofield Barracks (c)	14,428	16,370
*96820	Urban Honolulu (c)	371,657	337,256
*96786	Wahiawa (c)	16,151	17,821
96792	Waianae (c)	10,506	13,177
96793	Wailuku (c)	12,296	15,313
96701	Waimalu (c)	29,371	13,730
96797	Waipahu (c)	33,108	38,216
96797	Waipio (c)	11,672	11,674

Idaho (208)

ZIP	Place	2000	2010
*83401	Ammon	6,187	13,816
83221	Blackfoot	10,419	11,899
*83707	Boise	185,787	205,671
83318	Burley	9,316	10,345
*83605	Caldwell	25,967	43,237
83202	Chubbuck	9,700	13,922
*83814	Coeur d'Alene	34,514	44,137
83616	Eagle	11,085	19,908
*83714	Garden City	10,624	10,972
83835	Hayden	9,159	13,294
*83402	Idaho Falls	50,730	56,813
*83634	Kuna	5,382	15,210
83501	Lewiston	30,904	31,894
*83642	Meridian	34,919	75,092
*83843	Moscow	21,291	23,800
*83647	Mountain Home	11,143	14,206
*83653	Nampa	51,867	81,557
*83201	Pocatello	51,466	54,255
*83854	Post Falls	17,247	27,574
*83440	Rexburg	17,257	25,484
*83301	Twin Falls	34,469	44,125

Illinois

Area code (224) overlays area code (847). Area code (331) overlays area code (630). Area code (779) overlays area code (815). Area code (872) overlays area code (312).

ZIP	Place	Area code	2000	2010
60101	Addison	(630)	35,914	36,942
*60102	Algonquin	(847)	23,276	30,046
60803	Alsip	(708)	19,725	19,277
62002	Alton	(618)	30,496	27,865
60002	Antioch	(847)	8,788	14,430
*60005	Arlington Heights	(847)	76,031	75,101
*60505	Aurora	(630)	142,990	197,899
*60010	Barrington	(847)	10,168	10,327
*60103	Bartlett	(630)	36,706	41,208
*60510	Batavia	(630)	23,866	26,045
*60083	Beach Park	(847)	10,072	13,638
*62220	Belleville	(618)	41,410	44,478
60104	Bellwood	(708)	20,535	19,071
61008	Belvidere	(815)	20,820	25,585
*60106	Bensenville	(630)	20,703	18,352
60402	Berwyn	(708)	54,016	56,657
*60108	Bloomingdale	(630)	21,675	22,018
*61701	Bloomington	(309)	64,808	76,610
*60406	Blue Island	(708)	23,463	23,706
*60440	Bolingbrook	(630)	56,321	73,366
60914	Bourbonnais	(815)	15,256	18,631
60915	Bradley	(815)	12,784	15,895
60455	Bridgeview	(708)	15,335	16,446
60513	Brookfield	(708)	19,085	18,978
60089	Buffalo Grove	(847)	42,909	41,496

ZIP	Place	Area code	2000	2010
60459	Burbank	(708)	27,902	28,925
60527	Burr Ridge	(630)	10,408	10,559
62206	Cahokia	(618)	16,391	15,241
60409	Calumet City	(708)	39,071	37,042
61520	Canton	(309)	15,288	14,704
*62901	Carbondale	(618)	20,681	25,902
*60188	Carol Stream	(630)	40,438	39,711
60110	Carpentersville	(847)	30,586	37,691
60013	Cary	(847)	15,531	18,271
62801	Centralia	(618)	14,136	13,032
*61821	Champaign	(217)	67,518	81,055
60410	Channahon	(815)	7,344	12,560
61920	Charleston	(217)	21,039	21,838
62629	Chatham	(217)	8,583	11,500
*60607	Chicago	(312)/(773)	2,896,016	2,695,598
*60411	Chicago Heights	(708)	32,776	30,276
60415	Chicago Ridge	(708)	14,127	14,305
60804	Cicero	(708)	85,616	83,891
62234	Collinsville	(618)	24,707	25,579
60478	Country Club Hills	(708)	16,169	16,541
60435	Crest Hill	(815)	13,329	20,837
60445	Crestwood	(708)	11,251	10,950
*60014	Crystal Lake	(815)	38,000	40,473
*61832	Danville	(217)	33,904	33,027
60561	Darien	(630)	22,860	22,086
*62525	Decatur	(217)	81,860	76,122
60015	Deerfield	(847)	18,420	18,225
60115	DeKalb	(815)	39,018	43,862
*60018	Des Plaines	(847)	58,720	58,364
61021	Dixon	(815)	15,941	15,733
60419	Dolton	(708)	25,614	23,153
*60515	Downers Grove	(630)	48,724	47,833
61244	East Moline	(309)	20,333	21,302
*61611	East Peoria	(309)	22,638	23,402
*62201	East St. Louis	(618)	31,542	27,006
*62025	Edwardsville	(618)	21,491	24,293
62401	Effingham	(217)	12,384	12,328
*60120	Elgin	(847)	94,487	108,188
*60009	Elk Grove Village	(847)	34,727	33,127
60126	Elmhurst	(630)	42,762	44,121
60707	Elmwood Park	(708)	25,405	24,883
*60201	Evanston	(847)	74,239	74,486
60805	Evergreen Park	(708)	20,821	19,852
*62208	Fairview Heights	(618)	15,034	17,078
*60130	Forest Park	(708)	15,688	14,167
60020	Fox Lake	(847)	9,178	10,579
60423	Frankfort	(815)	10,391	17,782
*60131	Franklin Park	(847)	19,434	18,333
61032	Freeport	(815)	26,443	25,638
60030	Gages Lake (c)	(847)	10,415	10,198
*61401	Galesburg	(309)	33,706	32,195
60134	Geneva	(630)	19,515	21,495
62034	Glen Carbon	(618)	10,425	12,934
*60137	Glen Ellyn	(630)	26,999	27,450
*60139	Glendale Heights	(630)	31,765	34,208
*60025	Glenview	(847)	41,847	44,692
62035	Godfrey	(618)	16,286	17,982
62040	Granite City	(618)	31,301	29,849
60030	Grayslake	(847)	18,506	20,957
60031	Gurnee	(847)	28,834	31,295
60133	Hanover Park	(630)	38,278	37,973
*60426	Harvey	(708)	30,000	25,282
60429	Hazel Crest	(708)	14,816	14,100
62948	Herrin	(618)	11,298	12,501
*60457	Hickory Hills	(708)	13,926	14,049
*60035	Highland Park	(847)	31,365	29,763
*60521	Hinsdale	(630)	17,349	16,816
*60195	Hoffman Estates	(847)	49,495	51,895
*60491	Homer Glen	(708)	—	24,220
*60430	Homewood	(708)	19,543	19,323
60142	Huntley	(847)	5,730	24,291
*62650	Jacksonville	(217)	18,940	19,446
*60436	Joliet	(815)	106,221	147,433
60458	Justice	(708)	12,193	12,926
60901	Kankakee	(815)	27,491	27,537
61443	Kewanee	(309)	12,944	12,916
60525	La Grange	(708)	15,608	15,550
60526	La Grange Park	(708)	13,295	13,579
60045	Lake Forest	(847)	20,059	19,375
*60102	Lake in the Hills	(847)	23,152	28,965
*60047	Lake Zurich	(847)	18,104	19,631
60438	Lansing	(708)	28,332	28,331
*60439	Lemont	(630)	13,098	16,000
*60048	Libertyville	(847)	20,742	20,315
62656	Lincoln	(217)	15,369	14,504
*60645	Lincolnwood	(847)	12,359	12,590
60046	Lindenhurst	(847)	12,539	14,462
60532	Lisle	(630)	21,182	22,390
*60441	Lockport	(815)	15,191	24,839
*60148	Lombard	(630)	42,322	43,165
*61130	Loves Park	(815)	20,044	23,996
60534	Lyons	(708)	10,255	10,729
*61115	Machesney Park	(815)	20,759	23,499
61455	Macomb	(309)	18,558	19,288

ZIP	Place	Area code	2000	2010
62959	Marion	(618)	16,035	17,193
*60426	Markham	(708)	12,620	12,508
*60443	Matteson	(708)	12,928	19,009
61938	Mattoon	(217)	18,291	18,555
*60153	Maywood	(708)	26,987	24,090
*60050	McHenry	(815)	21,501	26,992
*60160	Melrose Park	(708)	23,171	25,411
60445	Midlothian	(708)	14,315	14,819
60447	Minooka	(815)	3,971	10,924
60448	Mokena	(708)	14,583	18,740
*61265	Moline	(309)	43,768	43,483
60538	Montgomery	(630)	5,471	18,438
60450	Morris	(815)	11,928	13,636
61550	Morton	(309)	15,198	16,267
60053	Morton Grove	(847)	22,451	23,270
60056	Mount Prospect	(847)	56,265	54,167
62864	Mount Vernon	(618)	16,269	15,277
60060	Mundelein	(847)	30,935	31,064
*60540	Naperville	(630)	128,358	141,853
60451	New Lenox	(815)	17,771	24,394
60714	Niles	(847)	30,068	29,803
*61761	Normal	(309)	45,386	52,497
*60634	Norridge	(708)	14,582	14,572
60542	North Aurora	(630)	10,585	16,760
*60064	North Chicago	(847)	35,918	32,574
*60062	Northbrook	(847)	33,435	33,170
60164	Northlake	(708)	11,878	12,323
62269	O'Fallon	(618)	21,910	28,281
60452	Oak Forest	(708)	28,051	27,962
*60303	Oak Lawn	(708)	55,245	56,690
*60303	Oak Park	(708)	52,524	51,878
*60462	Orland Park	(708)	51,077	56,767
60543	Oswego	(630)	13,326	30,355
61350	Ottawa	(815)	18,307	18,768
*60067	Palatine	(847)	65,479	68,557
60463	Palos Heights	(708)	11,260	12,515
60465	Palos Hills	(708)	17,665	17,484
60466	Park Forest	(708)	23,462	21,975
60068	Park Ridge	(847)	37,775	37,480
*61554	Pekin	(309)	33,857	34,094
*61601	Peoria	(309)	112,936	115,007
61354	Peru	(815)	9,835	10,295
*60544	Plainfield	(815)	13,038	39,581
60545	Plano	(630)	5,633	10,856
61764	Pontiac	(815)	11,864	11,931
60070	Prospect Heights	(847)	17,081	16,256
*62301	Quincy	(217)	40,366	40,633
61866	Rantoul	(217)	12,857	12,941
60471	Richton Park	(708)	12,533	13,646
60305	River Forest	(708)	11,635	11,172
60171	River Grove	(708)	10,668	10,227
60827	Riverdale	(708)	15,055	13,549
*61201	Rock Island	(309)	39,684	39,018
*61125	Rockford	(815)	150,115	152,871
60008	Rolling Meadows	(847)	24,604	24,099
*60446	Romeoville	(815)	21,153	39,680
61073	Roscoe	(815)	6,244	10,785
60172	Roselle	(630)	23,115	22,763
60073	Round Lake	(847)	5,842	18,289
60073	Round Lake Beach	(847)	25,859	28,175
*60174	Saint Charles	(630)	27,896	32,974
60411	Sauk Village	(708)	10,411	10,506
*60194	Schaumburg	(847)	75,386	74,227
*60176	Schiller Park	(847)	11,850	11,793
*62269	Shiloh	(618)	7,643	12,651
*60436	Shorewood	(815)	7,686	15,615
60077	Skokie	(847)	63,348	64,784
60177	South Elgin	(847)	16,100	21,985
60473	South Holland	(708)	22,147	22,030
*62703	Springfield	(217)	111,454	116,250
61081	Sterling	(815)	15,451	15,370
60107	Streamwood	(630)	36,407	39,858
61364	Streator	(815)	14,190	13,710
60501	Summit	(708)	10,637	11,054
*62221	Swansea	(618)	10,579	13,430
60178	Sycamore	(815)	12,020	17,519
62568	Taylorville	(217)	11,427	11,246
60477	Tinley Park	(708)	48,401	56,703
*61801	Urbana	(217)	36,395	41,250
60061	Vernon Hills	(847)	20,120	25,113
60181	Villa Park	(630)	22,075	21,904
60555	Warrenville	(630)	13,363	13,140
61571	Washington	(309)	10,841	15,134
60084	Wauconda	(847)	9,448	13,603
*60085	Waukegan	(847)	87,901	89,078
*60185	West Chicago	(630)	23,469	27,086
60154	Westchester	(708)	16,824	16,718
60558	Western Springs	(708)	12,493	12,975
60559	Westmont	(630)	24,554	24,685
*60187	Wheaton	(630)	55,416	52,894
60090	Wheeling	(847)	34,496	37,648
60091	Wilmette	(847)	27,651	27,087
60093	Winnetka	(847)	12,419	12,187
*60191	Wood Dale	(630)	13,535	13,770
62095	Wood River	(618)	11,296	10,657
60517	Woodridge	(630)	30,934	32,971
60098	Woodstock	(815)	20,151	24,770
60482	Worth	(708)	11,047	10,789
60560	Yorkville	(630)	6,189	16,921
60099	Zion	(847)	22,866	24,413

Indiana

ZIP	Place	Area code	2000	2010
*46011	Anderson	(765)	59,734	56,129
46706	Auburn	(260)	12,074	12,731
46123	Avon	(317)	6,248	12,446
47421	Bedford	(812)	13,768	13,413
46107	Beech Grove	(317)	14,880	14,192
*47408	Bloomington	(812)	69,291	80,405
46112	Brownsburg	(317)	14,520	21,285
*46032	Carmel	(317)	37,733	79,191
46303	Cedar Lake	(219)	9,279	11,560
46304	Chesterton	(219)	10,488	13,068
*47129	Clarksville	(812)	21,400	21,724
*47201	Columbus	(812)	39,059	44,061
47331	Connersville	(765)	15,411	13,481
*47933	Crawfordsville	(765)	15,243	15,915
*46307	Crown Point	(219)	19,806	27,317
46311	Dyer	(219)	13,895	16,390
46312	East Chicago	(219)	32,414	29,698
*46515	Elkhart	(574)	51,874	50,949
*47708	Evansville	(812)	121,582	117,429
*46038	Fishers	(317)	37,835	76,794
*46802	Fort Wayne	(260)	205,727	253,691
*46041	Frankfort	(765)	16,662	16,422
46131	Franklin	(317)	19,463	23,712
*46401	Gary	(219)	102,746	80,294
*46526	Goshen	(574)	29,383	31,719
46530	Granger (c)	(574)	28,284	30,465
46135	Greencastle	(765)	9,880	10,326
46140	Greenfield	(317)	14,600	20,602
47240	Greensburg	(812)	10,260	11,492
*46142	Greenwood	(317)	36,037	49,791
46319	Griffith	(219)	17,334	16,893
*46320	Hammond	(219)	83,048	80,830
*46322	Highland	(219)	23,546	23,727
46342	Hobart	(219)	25,363	29,059
46750	Huntington	(260)	17,450	17,391
*46206	Indianapolis	(317)	781,870	829,718
*47546	Jasper	(812)	12,100	15,038
*47130	Jeffersonville	(812)	27,362	44,953
*46902	Kokomo	(765)	46,113	45,468
46350	La Porte	(219)	21,621	22,053
*47901	Lafayette	(765)	56,397	67,140
46405	Lake Station	(219)	13,948	12,572
46226	Lawrence	(317)	38,915	46,001
46052	Lebanon	(765)	14,222	15,792
*46947	Logansport	(574)	19,684	18,396
47250	Madison	(812)	12,004	11,967
*46952	Marion	(765)	31,320	29,948
46151	Martinsville	(765)	11,698	11,828
*46401	Merrillville	(219)	30,560	35,246
*46360	Michigan City	(219)	32,900	31,479
*46544	Mishawaka	(574)	46,557	48,252
*47302	Muncie	(765)	67,430	70,085
46321	Munster	(219)	21,511	23,603
*47150	New Albany	(812)	37,603	36,372
47362	New Castle	(765)	17,780	18,114
46774	New Haven	(260)	12,406	14,794
*46060	Noblesville	(317)	28,590	51,969
*46970	Peru	(765)	12,994	11,417
46168	Plainfield	(317)	18,396	24,631
46563	Plymouth	(574)	9,840	10,033
46368	Portage	(219)	33,496	36,828
47907	Purdue University (c)	(765)	—	12,183
*47374	Richmond	(765)	39,124	36,812
46373	Saint John	(219)	8,382	14,850
46375	Schererville	(219)	24,851	29,243
47274	Seymour	(812)	18,101	17,503
46176	Shelbyville	(765)	17,951	19,191
*46624	South Bend	(574)	107,789	101,168
46224	Speedway	(317)	12,881	11,812
*47808	Terre Haute	(812)	59,614	60,785
*46383	Valparaiso	(219)	27,428	31,730
47591	Vincennes	(812)	18,701	18,423
46992	Wabash	(260)	11,743	10,666
*46580	Warsaw	(574)	12,415	13,559
47501	Washington	(812)	11,380	11,509
*46580	West Lafayette	(765)	28,778	29,596
46074	Westfield	(317)	9,293	30,068
46077	Zionsville	(317)	8,775	14,160

Iowa

ZIP	Place	Area code	2000	2010
50009	Altoona	(515)	10,345	14,541
*50010	Ames	(515)	50,731	58,965
*50021	Ankeny	(515)	27,117	45,582
52722	Bettendorf	(563)	31,275	33,217

ZIP	Place	Area code	2000	2010
*50036	Boone	(515)	12,803	12,661
52601	Burlington	(319)	26,839	25,663
*50613	Cedar Falls	(319)	36,145	39,260
*52401	Cedar Rapids	(319)	120,758	126,326
*52732	Clinton	(563)	27,772	26,885
50325	Clive	(515)	12,855	15,447
52241	Coralville	(319)	15,123	18,907
*51501	Council Bluffs	(712)	58,268	62,230
*52802	Davenport	(563)	98,359	99,685
*50318	Des Moines	(515)	198,682	203,433
*52001	Dubuque	(563)	57,686	57,637
50501	Fort Dodge	(515)	25,136	25,206
52627	Fort Madison	(319)	10,715	11,051
50125	Indianola	(515)	12,998	14,782
*52240	Iowa City	(319)	62,220	67,862
50131	Johnston	(515)	8,649	17,278
52632	Keokuk	(319)	11,427	10,780
52302	Marion	(319)	26,294	34,768
50158	Marshalltown	(641)	26,009	27,552
*50401	Mason City	(641)	29,172	28,079
52761	Muscatine	(563)	22,697	22,886
50208	Newton	(641)	15,579	15,254
52317	North Liberty	(319)	5,367	13,374
52577	Oskaloosa	(641)	10,938	11,463
52501	Ottumwa	(641)	24,998	25,023
50219	Pella	(641)	9,832	10,352
*51101	Sioux City	(712)	85,013	82,684
51301	Spencer	(712)	11,317	11,233
*50322	Urbandale	(515)	29,072	39,463
*50701	Waterloo	(319)	68,747	68,406
50263	Waukee	(515)	5,126	13,790
*50265	West Des Moines	(515)	46,403	56,609

Kansas

ZIP	Place	Area code	2000	2010
67002	Andover	(316)	6,698	11,791
67005	Arkansas City	(620)	11,963	12,415
66002	Atchison	(913)	10,232	11,021
67337	Coffeyville	(620)	11,021	10,295
67037	Derby	(316)	17,807	22,158
*67801	Dodge City	(620)	25,176	27,340
67042	El Dorado	(316)	12,057	13,021
66801	Emporia	(620)	26,760	24,916
*67846	Garden City	(620)	28,451	26,658
*66030	Gardner	(913)	9,396	19,123
67530	Great Bend	(620)	15,345	15,995
*67601	Hays	(785)	20,013	20,510
67060	Haysville	(316)	8,502	10,826
*67501	Hutchinson	(620)	40,787	42,080
*66441	Junction City	(785)	18,886	23,353
*66102	Kansas City	(913)	146,866	145,786
66043	Lansing	(913)	9,199	11,265
*66044	Lawrence	(785)	80,098	87,643
*66048	Leavenworth	(913)	35,420	35,251
*66209	Leawood	(913)	27,656	31,867
*66214	Lenexa	(913)	40,238	48,190
*67901	Liberal	(620)	19,666	20,525
*66502	Manhattan	(785)	44,831	52,281
67460	McPherson	(620)	13,770	13,155
*66202	Merriam	(913)	11,008	11,003
*67114	Newton	(316)	17,190	19,132
*66061	Olathe	(913)	92,962	125,872
66067	Ottawa	(785)	11,921	12,649
*66204	Overland Park	(913)	149,080	173,372
67357	Parsons	(620)	11,514	10,500
*66762	Pittsburg	(620)	19,243	20,233
*66208	Prairie Village	(913)	22,072	21,447
*67401	Salina	(785)	45,679	47,707
*66203	Shawnee	(913)	47,996	62,209
*66601	Topeka	(785)	122,377	127,473
*67202	Wichita	(316)	344,284	382,368
67156	Winfield	(620)	12,206	12,301

Kentucky

ZIP	Place	Area code	2000	2010
*41101	Ashland	(606)	21,981	21,684
40004	Bardstown	(502)	10,374	11,700
*40403	Berea	(859)	9,851	13,561
42101	Bowling Green	(270)	49,296	58,067
41005	Burlington (c)	(859)	10,779	15,926
41011	Covington	(859)	43,370	40,640
40422	Danville	(859)	15,477	16,218
*42701	Elizabethtown	(270)	22,542	28,531
*41018	Erlanger	(859)	16,676	18,082
*41042	Florence	(859)	23,551	29,951
42223	Fort Campbell North (c)	(270)	14,338	13,685
40121	Fort Knox (c)	(270)	12,377	10,124
41075	Fort Thomas	(859)	16,495	16,325
*40601	Frankfort	(502)	27,741	25,527
40324	Georgetown	(502)	18,080	29,098
*42141	Glasgow	(270)	13,019	14,028
*42420	Henderson	(270)	27,373	28,757
*42240	Hopkinsville	(270)	30,089	31,577
41051	Independence	(859)	14,982	24,757
*40269	Jeffersontown	(502)	26,633	26,595
*40342	Lawrenceburg	(502)	9,014	10,505
*40507	Lexington-Fayette	(859)	260,512	295,803
*40232	Louisville-Jefferson Co. (balance)	(502)	(1)	597,337
*40252	Lyndon	(502)	9,369	11,002
42431	Madisonville	(270)	19,307	19,591
42066	Mayfield	(270)	10,349	10,024
40965	Middlesborough	(606)	10,384	10,334
42071	Murray	(270)	14,950	17,741
*41071	Newport	(859)	17,048	15,273
*40356	Nicholasville	(859)	19,680	28,015
*42301	Owensboro	(270)	54,067	57,265
*42003	Paducah	(270)	26,307	25,024
*40160	Radcliff	(502)	21,961	21,688
*40475	Richmond	(859)	27,152	31,364
*40207	Saint Matthews	(502)	15,852	17,472
*40066	Shelbyville	(502)	10,085	14,045
40256	Shively	(502)	15,157	15,264
*42501	Somerset	(606)	11,352	11,196
*40391	Winchester	(859)	16,724	18,368

(1) Louisville merged with Jefferson County in 2003.

Louisiana

ZIP	Place	Area code	2000	2010
*70510	Abbeville	(337)	11,887	12,257
*71301	Alexandria	(318)	46,342	47,723
70714	Baker	(225)	13,793	13,895
71220	Bastrop	(318)	12,988	11,365
*70821	Baton Rouge	(225)	227,818	229,493
70360	Bayou Blue (c)	(985)	—	12,352
*70364	Bayou Cane (c)	(985)	17,046	19,355
*70037	Belle Chase (c)	(504)	9,848	12,679
*70427	Bogalusa	(985)	13,365	12,232
*71111	Bossier City	(318)	56,461	61,315
70818	Central	(225)	—	26,864
*70043	Chalmette (c)	(504)	32,069	16,751
70433	Claiborne (c)	(985)	9,830	11,507
*70526	Crowley	(337)	14,225	13,265
*70726	Denham Springs	(225)	8,757	10,215
70634	DeRidder	(337)	9,808	10,578
70047	Destrehan (c)	(985)	11,260	11,535
70072	Estelle (c)	(504)	15,880	16,377
70535	Eunice	(337)	11,499	10,398
70810	Gardere (c)	(225)	8,992	10,580
*70053	Gretna	(504)	17,423	17,736
*70401	Hammond	(985)	17,639	20,019
*70058	Harvey (c)	(504)	22,226	20,348
*70360	Houma	(985)	32,393	33,727
70121	Jefferson (c)	(504)	11,843	11,193
70546	Jennings	(337)	10,986	10,383
*70062	Kenner	(504)	70,517	66,702
*70501	Lafayette	(337)	110,257	120,623
*70601	Lake Charles	(337)	71,757	71,993
*70068	Laplace (c)	(985)	27,684	29,872
70070	Luling (c)	(985)	11,512	12,119
*70471	Mandeville	(985)	10,489	11,560
*70072	Marrero (c)	(504)	36,165	33,141
*70009	Metairie (c)	(504)	146,136	138,481
*71055	Minden	(318)	13,027	13,082
*71207	Monroe	(318)	53,107	48,815
*70380	Morgan City	(985)	12,703	12,404
70611	Moss Bluff (c)	(337)	10,535	11,557
*71457	Natchitoches	(318)	17,865	18,323
*70560	New Iberia	(337)	32,623	30,617
*70140	New Orleans	(504)	484,674	343,829
*70570	Opelousas	(337)	22,860	16,634
*71360	Pineville	(318)	13,829	14,555
70394	Raceland (c)	(985)	10,224	10,193
70123	River Ridge (c)	(504)	14,588	13,494
*71270	Ruston	(318)	20,546	21,859
70817	Shenandoah (c)	(318)	17,070	18,399
*71102	Shreveport	(318)	200,145	199,311
*70458	Slidell	(985)	25,695	27,068
*70663	Sulphur	(337)	20,512	20,410
70056	Terrytown (c)	(504)	25,430	23,319
*70301	Thibodaux	(985)	14,431	14,566
70056	Timberlane (c)	(504)	11,405	10,243
70094	Waggaman (c)	(504)	9,435	10,015
*71291	West Monroe	(318)	13,250	13,065
70058	Woodmere	(504)	13,058	12,080
70791	Zachary	(225)	11,275	14,960

Maine (207)

See introductory note.

ZIP	Place	2000	2010
*04210	Auburn	23,203	23,055
*04330	Augusta	18,560	19,136
*04401	Bangor	31,473	33,039

ZIP	Place	2000	2010
*04005	Biddeford	20,942	21,277
04011	Brunswick	21,172	20,278
04011	Brunswick (c)	14,816	15,175
04105	Falmouth	10,310	11,185
04038	Gorham	14,141	16,381
04043	Kennebunk	10,476	10,798
*04240	Lewiston	35,690	36,592
*04473	Orono	9,112	10,362
*04101	Portland	64,249	66,194
04072	Saco	16,822	18,482
04073	Sanford	20,806	20,798
*04074	Scarborough	16,970	18,919
*04106	South Portland	23,324	25,002
*04901	Waterville	15,605	15,722
*04092	Westbrook	16,142	17,494
*04062	Windham	14,904	17,001
03909	York	12,854	12,529

Maryland

Area code (240) overlays area code (301). Area code (443) overlays area code (410).

ZIP	Place	Area code	2000	2010
21001	Aberdeen	(410)	13,842	14,959
20607	Accokeek (c)	(301)	7,349	10,573
*20783	Adelphi (c)	(301)	14,998	15,086
*21401	Annapolis	(410)	35,838	38,394
21403	Annapolis Neck (c)	(410)	—	10,950
21227	Arbutus (c)	(410)	20,116	20,483
*21012	Arnold (c)	(410)	23,422	23,106
*20916	Aspen Hill (c)	(301)	50,228	48,759
21220	Ballenger Creek (c)	(410)	13,518	18,274
*21203	Baltimore	(410)	651,154	620,961
*21014	Bel Air	(410)	10,080	10,120
21050	Bel Air North (c)	(410)	25,798	30,568
21014	Bel Air South (c)	(410)	39,711	47,709
*20705	Beltsville (c)	(301)	15,690	16,772
20603	Bennsville (c)	(301)	7,325	11,923
*20814	Bethesda (c)	(301)	55,277	60,858
*20715	Bowie	(410)	50,269	54,727
21225	Brooklyn Park (c)	(410)	10,938	14,373
20705	Calverton (c)	(301)	12,610	17,724
21613	Cambridge	(410)	10,911	12,326
*20748	Camp Springs (c)	(301)	17,968	19,096
21234	Carney (c)	(410)	28,264	29,941
*21228	Catonsville (c)	(410)	39,820	41,567
20657	Chesapeake Ranch Estates (c)	(301)	—	10,519
20782	Chillum (c)	(301)	34,252	33,513
20735	Clinton (c)	(301)	26,064	35,970
20904	Cloverly (c)	(301)	7,835	15,126
21030	Cockeysville (c)	(410)	19,388	20,776
*20914	Colesville (c)	(301)	19,810	14,647
*20740	College Park	(301)	24,657	30,413
*21045	Columbia (c)	(410)	88,254	99,615
21114	Crofton (c)	(410)	20,091	27,348
*21502	Cumberland	(301)	21,518	20,859
20872	Damascus (c)	(301)	11,430	15,257
21222	Dundalk (c)	(410)	62,306	63,597
20737	East Riverdale (c)	(301)	14,961	15,509
*21601	Easton	(410)	11,708	15,945
21040	Edgewood (c)	(410)	23,378	25,562
21784	Eldersburg (c)	(410)	27,741	30,531
21075	Elkridge (c)	(410)	22,042	15,593
*21921	Elkton	(410)	11,893	15,443
*21043	Ellicott City (c)	(410)	56,397	65,834
21221	Essex (c)	(410)	39,078	39,262
20904	Fairland (c)	(301)	21,738	23,681
21061	Ferndale (c)	(410)	16,056	16,746
20747	Forestville (c)	(301)	12,707	12,353
*20744	Fort Washington (c)	(301)	23,845	23,717
*21701	Frederick	(301)	52,767	65,239
*20877	Gaithersburg	(301)	52,613	59,933
20874	Germantown (c)	(301)	55,419	86,395
20745	Glassmanor (c)	(301)	—	17,295
*21061	Glen Burnie (c)	(410)	38,922	67,639
20906	Glenmont (c)	(301)	—	13,529
20769	Glenn Dale (c)	(301)	12,609	13,466
*20770	Greenbelt	(301)	21,456	23,068
*21740	Hagerstown	(301)	36,687	39,662
21740	Halfway (c)	(301)	10,065	10,701
21078	Havre de Grace	(410)	11,331	12,952
20748	Hillcrest Heights (c)	(301)	16,359	16,469
*20780	Hyattsville	(301)	14,733	17,557
21043	Ilchester (c)	(410)	—	23,476
21085	Joppatowne (c)	(410)	11,391	12,616
20902	Kemp Mill (c)	(301)	9,956	12,564
*20772	Kettering (c)	(301)	11,008	12,790
*21122	Lake Shore (c)	(410)	13,065	19,477
20785	Landover (c)	(301)	—	23,078
*20787	Langley Park (c)	(301)	16,214	18,755
*20706	Lanham (c)	(301)	—	10,157
*20774	Largo (c)	(301)	8,408	10,709
*20707	Laurel	(301)	19,960	25,115
20653	Lexington Park (c)	(410)	11,021	11,626

ZIP	Place	Area code	2000	2010
21090	Linthicum (c)	(410)	7,539	10,324
21207	Lochearn (c)	(410)	25,269	25,333
20724	Maryland City (c)	(301)	6,814	16,093
21093	Mays Chapel (c)	(410)	11,427	11,420
21220	Middle River (c)	(410)	23,958	25,191
21207	Milford Mill (c)	(410)	26,527	29,042
*20886	Montgomery Village (c)	(301)	38,051	32,032
20784	New Carrollton	(301)	12,589	12,135
*20815	North Bethesda (c)	(301)	38,610	43,828
20878	North Potomac (c)	(301)	23,044	24,410
21811	Ocean Pines (c)	(410)	10,496	11,710
21113	Odenton (c)	(410)	20,534	37,132
*20832	Olney (c)	(301)	31,438	33,844
21206	Overlea (c)	(410)	12,148	12,275
21117	Owings Mills (c)	(410)	20,193	30,622
*20745	Oxon Hill (c)	(301)	—	17,722
21234	Parkville (c)	(410)	31,118	30,734
21401	Parole (c)	(410)	14,031	15,922
*21122	Pasadena (c)	(410)	12,093	24,287
*21128	Perry Hall (c)	(410)	28,705	28,474
*21282	Pikesville (c)	(410)	29,123	30,764
*20850	Potomac (c)	(301)	44,822	44,965
21133	Randallstown (c)	(301)	30,870	32,430
20855	Redland (c)	(301)	16,998	17,242
*21136	Reisterstown (c)	(410)	22,438	25,968
*21122	Riviera Beach (c)	(410)	12,695	12,677
*20850	Rockville	(301)	47,388	61,209
20772	Rosaryville (c)	(301)	12,322	10,697
21237	Rosedale (c)	(410)	19,199	19,257
21221	Rossville (c)	(410)	11,515	15,147
*21801	Salisbury	(410)	23,743	30,343
*20706	Seabrook (c)	(301)	—	17,287
21144	Severn (c)	(410)	35,076	44,231
21146	Severna Park (c)	(410)	28,507	37,634
*20907	Silver Spring (c)	(301)	76,540	71,452
20707	South Laurel (c)	(301)	20,479	26,112
*20746	Suitland (c)	(301)	—	25,825
21842	Summerfield (c)	(410)	—	10,898
*20913	Takoma Park	(301)	17,299	16,715
*21204	Towson (c)	(410)	51,793	55,197
20854	Travilah (c)	(301)	7,442	12,159
*20602	Waldorf (c)	(301)	22,312	67,752
20743	Walker Mill (c)	(301)	11,104	11,302
*21157	Westminster	(410)	16,731	18,590
*20902	Wheaton (c)	(301)	—	48,284
20903	White Oak (c)	(301)	20,973	17,403
21207	Woodlawn (c) (Baltimore Co.)	(410)	36,079	37,879

Massachusetts

Area code (339) overlays area code (781). Area code (351) overlays area code (978). Area code (774) overlays area code (508). Area code (857) overlays area code (617). See introductory note.

ZIP	Place	Area code	2000	2010
02351	Abington	(781)	14,605	15,985
*01720	Acton	(978)	20,331	21,924
*02743	Acushnet	(508)	10,161	10,303
01001	Agawam	(413)	28,144	28,438
01913	Amesbury	(978)	16,450	16,283
*01002	Amherst	(413)	34,874	37,819
*01002	Amherst Center (c)	(413)	17,050	19,065
*01810	Andover	(978)	31,247	33,201
*02205	Arlington	(781)	42,389	42,844
01721	Ashland	(508)	14,674	16,593
*01331	Athol	(978)	11,299	11,584
02703	Attleboro	(508)	42,068	43,593
01501	Auburn	(508)	15,901	16,188
*02630	Barnstable Town	(508)	—	45,193
*01730	Bedford	(781)	12,595	13,320
01007	Belchertown	(413)	12,968	14,649
02019	Bellingham	(508)	15,314	16,332
*02478	Belmont	(617)	24,194	24,729
01915	Beverly	(978)	39,862	39,502
*01821	Billerica	(978)	38,981	40,243
*02205	Boston	(617)	589,141	617,594
*02532	Bourne	(508)	18,721	19,754
*02185	Braintree	(781)	33,828	35,744
*02324	Bridgewater	(508)	25,185	26,563
*02303	Brockton	(508)	94,304	93,810
02446	Brookline	(617)	57,107	58,732
*01803	Burlington	(781)	22,876	24,498
02139	Cambridge	(617)	101,355	105,162
02021	Canton	(781)	20,775	21,561
*02330	Carver	(508)	11,163	11,509
01507	Charlton	(508)	11,263	12,981
01824	Chelmsford	(978)	33,858	33,802
02150	Chelsea	(617)	35,080	35,177
*01020	Chicopee	(413)	54,653	55,298
01510	Clinton	(978)	13,435	13,606
01742	Concord	(978)	16,993	17,668
01923	Danvers	(978)	25,212	26,493
*02714	Dartmouth	(508)	30,666	34,032
*02026	Dedham	(781)	23,464	24,729
02638	Dennis	(508)	15,973	14,207
01826	Dracut	(978)	28,562	29,457

ZIP	Place	Area code	2000	2010
01571	Dudley	(508)	10,036	11,390
*02332	Duxbury	(781)	14,248	15,059
02333	East Bridgewater	(508)	12,974	13,794
*01028	East Longmeadow	(413)	14,100	15,720
01027	Easthampton	(413)	15,994	16,053
*02334	Easton	(508)	22,299	23,112
02149	Everett	(617)	38,037	41,667
02719	Fairhaven	(508)	16,159	15,873
*02722	Fall River	(508)	91,938	88,857
*02540	Falmouth	(508)	32,660	31,531
01420	Fitchburg	(978)	39,102	40,318
02035	Foxborough	(508)	16,246	16,865
*01701	Framingham	(508)	66,910	68,318
02038	Franklin	(508)	29,560	31,635
*01440	Gardner	(978)	20,770	20,228
01930	Gloucester	(978)	30,273	28,789
01519	Grafton	(508)	14,894	17,765
*01301	Greenfield	(413)	18,168	17,456
*01450	Groton	(978)	9,547	10,646
*02339	Hanover	(781)	13,164	13,879
*02341	Hanson	(781)	9,495	10,209
02645	Harwich	(508)	12,386	12,243
*01830	Haverhill	(978)	58,969	60,879
*02043	Hingham	(781)	19,882	22,157
02343	Holbrook	(781)	10,785	10,791
01520	Holden	(508)	15,621	17,346
01746	Holliston	(508)	13,801	13,547
*01040	Holyoke	(413)	39,838	39,880
01748	Hopkinton	(508)	13,346	14,925
01749	Hudson	(508)	18,113	19,063
01749	Hudson (c)	(978)	14,388	14,907
02045	Hull	(781)	11,050	10,293
01938	Ipswich	(978)	12,987	13,175
02364	Kingston	(781)	11,780	12,629
02347	Lakeville	(508)	9,821	10,602
*01842	Lawrence	(978)	72,043	76,377
01524	Leicester	(508)	10,471	10,970
01453	Leominster	(978)	41,303	40,759
*02420	Lexington	(781)	30,355	31,394
*01028	Longmeadow	(413)	15,633	15,784
01853	Lowell	(978)	105,167	106,519
01056	Ludlow	(413)	21,209	21,103
*01462	Lunenburg	(978)	9,401	10,086
*01901	Lynn	(781)	89,050	90,329
01940	Lynnfield	(781)	11,542	11,596
02148	Malden	(781)	56,340	59,450
*02048	Mansfield	(508)	22,414	23,184
01945	Marblehead	(781)	20,377	19,808
01752	Marlborough	(508)	36,255	38,499
*02050	Marshfield	(781)	24,324	25,132
02649	Mashpee	(508)	12,946	14,006
01754	Maynard	(978)	10,433	10,106
02052	Medfield	(508)	12,273	12,024
*02155	Medford	(781)	55,765	56,173
02053	Medway	(508)	12,448	12,752
02176	Melrose	(781)	27,134	26,983
01844	Methuen Town	(978)	43,789	47,255
*02346	Middleborough	(508)	19,941	23,116
01757	Milford	(508)	26,799	27,999
01757	Milford (c)	(508)	24,230	25,055
*01527	Millbury	(508)	12,784	13,261
02186	Milton	(617)	26,062	27,003
01760	Natick	(508)	32,170	33,006
*02494	Needham	(781)	28,911	28,886
*02740	New Bedford	(508)	93,768	95,072
01950	Newburyport	(978)	17,189	17,416
*02456	Newton	(617)	83,829	85,146
02056	Norfolk	(508)	10,460	11,227
01247	North Adams	(413)	14,681	13,708
01845	North Andover	(978)	27,202	28,352
*02760	North Attleborough	(508)	27,143	28,712
*01864	North Reading	(978)	13,837	14,892
*01060	Northampton	(413)	28,978	28,549
01532	Northborough	(508)	14,013	14,155
01534	Northbridge	(508)	13,182	15,707
*02766	Norton	(508)	18,036	19,031
02061	Norwell	(781)	9,765	10,506
02062	Norwood	(781)	28,587	28,602
01540	Oxford	(508)	13,352	13,709
01069	Palmer	(413)	12,497	12,140
*01960	Peabody	(978)	48,129	51,251
*02359	Pembroke	(781)	16,927	17,837
01463	Pepperell	(978)	11,142	11,497
*01201	Pittsfield	(413)	45,793	44,737
*02360	Plymouth	(508)	51,701	56,468
*02169	Quincy	(617)	88,025	92,271
02368	Randolph	(781)	30,963	32,112
*02767	Raynham	(508)	11,739	13,383
01867	Reading	(781)	23,708	24,747
02769	Rehoboth	(508)	10,172	11,608
02151	Revere	(781)	47,283	51,755
*02370	Rockland	(781)	17,670	17,489
*01970	Salem	(978)	40,407	41,340
*02563	Sandwich	(508)	20,136	20,675
*01906	Saugus	(781)	26,078	26,628
*02066	Scituate	(781)	17,863	18,133
02771	Seekonk	(508)	13,425	13,722
02067	Sharon	(781)	17,408	17,612
*01545	Shrewsbury	(508)	31,640	35,608
*02725	Somerset	(508)	18,234	18,165
*02143	Somerville	(617)	77,478	75,754
01075	South Hadley	(413)	17,196	17,514
01550	Southbridge	(508)	17,214	16,719
01562	Spencer	(508)	11,691	11,688
*01101	Springfield	(413)	152,082	153,060
02180	Stoneham	(781)	22,219	21,437
02072	Stoughton	(781)	27,149	26,962
01776	Sudbury	(978)	16,841	17,659
01907	Swampscott	(781)	14,412	13,787
02777	Swansea	(508)	15,901	15,865
*02780	Taunton	(508)	55,976	55,874
01876	Tewksbury	(978)	28,851	28,961
01879	Tyngsborough	(978)	11,081	11,292
01569	Uxbridge	(508)	11,156	13,457
01880	Wakefield	(781)	24,804	24,932
02081	Walpole	(508)	22,824	24,070
*02451	Waltham	(781)	59,226	60,632
02571	Wareham	(508)	20,335	21,822
*02471	Watertown	(781)	32,986	31,915
01778	Wayland	(508)	13,100	12,994
01570	Webster	(508)	16,415	16,767
01570	Webster (c)	(508)	11,600	11,412
*02457	Wellesley	(781)	26,613	27,982
*01089	West Springfield	(413)	27,899	28,391
01581	Westborough	(508)	17,997	18,272
*01085	Westfield	(413)	40,072	41,094
01886	Westford	(978)	20,754	21,951
02493	Weston	(781)	11,469	11,261
02790	Westport	(508)	14,183	15,532
02090	Westwood	(781)	14,117	14,618
*02188	Weymouth	(781)	53,988	53,743
02382	Whitman	(781)	13,882	14,489
01095	Wilbraham	(413)	13,473	14,219
01887	Wilmington	(978)	21,363	22,325
01475	Winchendon	(978)	9,611	10,300
01890	Winchester	(781)	20,810	21,374
02152	Winthrop	(617)	18,303	17,497
*01801	Woburn	(781)	37,258	38,120
*01613	Worcester	(508)	172,648	181,045
*02093	Wrentham	(508)	10,554	10,955
*02675	Yarmouth	(508)	24,807	23,793

Michigan

Area code (947) overlays area code (248).

ZIP	Place	Area code	2000	2010
49221	Adrian	(517)	21,574	21,133
*48101	Allen Park	(313)	29,376	28,210
49401	Allendale (c)	(616)	11,555	17,579
49707	Alpena	(989)	11,304	10,483
*48106	Ann Arbor	(734)	114,024	113,934
*48321	Auburn Hills	(248)	19,837	21,412
*49016	Battle Creek	(269)	53,364	52,347
48707	Bay City	(989)	36,817	34,932
48505	Beecher (c)	(810)	12,793	10,232
*49022	Benton Harbor	(269)	11,182	10,038
48072	Berkley	(248)	15,531	14,970
49307	Big Rapids	(231)	10,849	10,601
*48012	Birmingham	(248)	19,291	20,103
48509	Burton	(810)	30,308	29,999
49601	Cadillac	(231)	10,000	10,355
*48017	Clawson	(248)	12,732	11,825
49036	Coldwater	(517)	12,697	10,945
49321	Comstock Park (c)	(616)	10,674	10,088
49508	Cutlerville (c)	(616)	15,114	14,370
*48120	Dearborn	(313)	97,775	98,153
*48127	Dearborn Heights	(313)	58,264	57,774
*48231	Detroit	(313)	951,270	713,777
*49506	East Grand Rapids	(616)	10,764	10,694
*48826	East Lansing	(517)	46,525	48,459
48021	Eastpointe	(586)	34,077	32,442
49829	Escanaba	(906)	13,140	12,616
*48333	Farmington	(248)	10,423	10,372
*48333	Farmington Hills	(248)	82,111	79,740
48430	Fenton	(810)	10,582	11,756
48220	Ferndale	(248)	22,105	19,900
*48501	Flint	(810)	124,943	102,434
49506	Forest Hills (c)	(616)	20,942	25,867
48026	Fraser	(586)	15,297	14,480
*48135	Garden City	(734)	30,047	27,692
49417	Grand Haven	(616)	11,168	10,412
49501	Grand Rapids	(616)	197,800	188,040
*49418	Grandville	(616)	16,263	15,378
48230	Grosse Pointe Park	(313)	12,443	11,555
48230	Grosse Pointe Woods	(313)	17,080	16,135
*48212	Hamtramck	(313)	22,976	22,423
48225	Harper Woods	(313)	14,254	14,236
48840	Haslett (c)	(517)	11,283	19,220

ZIP	Place	Area code	2000	2010
48030	Hazel Park	(248)	18,963	16,422
48203	Highland Park	(313)	16,746	11,776
*49423	Holland	(616)	35,048	33,051
48842	Holt (c)	(517)	11,315	23,973
48141	Inkster	(313)/(734)	30,115	25,369
48846	Ionia	(616)	10,569	11,394
*49204	Jackson	(517)	36,316	33,534
*49428	Jenison (c)	(616)	17,211	16,538
*49001	Kalamazoo	(269)	77,145	74,262
*49518	Kentwood	(616)	45,255	48,707
*48901	Lansing	(517)	119,128	114,297
48146	Lincoln Park	(313)	40,008	38,144
*48150	Livonia	(734)	100,545	96,942
48071	Madison Heights	(248)	31,101	29,694
49855	Marquette	(906)	19,661	21,355
48122	Melvindale	(313)	10,735	10,715
*48640	Midland	(989)	41,685	41,863
*48161	Monroe	(734)	22,076	20,733
*48046	Mount Clemens	(586)	17,312	16,314
*48804	Mount Pleasant	(989)	25,946	26,016
*49440	Muskegon	(231)	40,105	38,401
49444	Muskegon Heights	(231)	12,049	10,856
*48047	New Baltimore	(586)	7,405	12,084
49120	Niles	(269)	12,204	11,600
49505	Northview (c)	(616)	14,730	28,497
*49441	Norton Shores	(231)	22,527	23,994
*48376	Novi	(248)	47,386	55,224
48237	Oak Park	(248)	29,793	23,319
*48805	Okemos (c)	(517)	20,216	21,369
*48867	Owosso	(989)	15,713	15,194
*48343	Pontiac	(248)	66,337	59,515
*48061	Port Huron	(810)	32,338	30,184
*49081	Portage	(269)	44,897	46,292
*48192	Riverview	(734)	13,272	12,486
*48308	Rochester	(248)	10,467	12,711
*48306	Rochester Hills	(248)	68,825	70,995
48174	Romulus	(313)/(734)	22,979	23,989
48066	Roseville	(586)	48,129	47,299
*48068	Royal Oak	(248)	60,062	57,236
*48605	Saginaw	(989)	61,799	51,508
*48080	Saint Clair Shores	(313)	63,096	59,715
*49783	Sault Sainte Marie	(906)	16,542	14,144
48178	South Lyon	(248)	10,036	11,327
*48037	Southfield	(248)	78,296	71,739
48195	Southgate	(734)	30,136	30,047
*48311	Sterling Heights	(586)	124,471	129,699
49091	Sturgis	(269)	11,285	10,994
*48180	Taylor	(313)/(734)	65,868	63,131
*49684	Traverse City	(231)	14,532	14,674
48183	Trenton	(734)	19,584	18,853
*48099	Troy	(248)	80,959	80,980
49534	Walker	(616)	21,842	23,537
*48090	Warren	(586)	138,247	134,056
48917	Waverly (c)	(517)	16,194	23,925
48184	Wayne	(734)	19,051	17,593
*48185	Westland	(313)/(734)	86,602	84,094
48393	Wixom	(248)	13,263	13,498
48183	Woodhaven	(734)	12,530	12,875
*48192	Wyandotte	(734)	28,006	25,883
*49509	Wyoming	(616)	69,368	72,125
*48197	Ypsilanti	(734)	22,362	19,435

Minnesota

ZIP	Place	Area code	2000	2010
56007	Albert Lea	(507)	18,356	18,016
56308	Alexandria	(320)	8,820	11,070
*55304	Andover	(763)	26,588	30,598
*55303	Anoka	(612)	18,076	17,142
55124	Apple Valley	(952)	45,527	49,084
55912	Austin	(507)	23,314	24,718
*56601	Bemidji	(218)	11,917	13,431
55309	Big Lake	(763)	6,063	10,060
*55014	Blaine	(651)	44,942	57,186
*55420	Bloomington	(952)	85,172	82,893
*55401	Brainerd	(218)	13,178	13,590
*55429	Brooklyn Center	(763)	29,172	30,104
*55443	Brooklyn Park	(763)	67,388	75,781
55313	Buffalo	(763)	10,097	15,453
*55337	Burnsville	(651)	60,220	60,306
55316	Champlin	(763)	22,193	23,089
55317	Chanhassen	(952)	20,321	22,952
55318	Chaska	(952)	17,449	23,770
55720	Cloquet	(218)	11,201	12,124
55421	Columbia Heights	(612)	18,520	19,496
*55433	Coon Rapids	(763)	61,607	61,476
55016	Cottage Grove	(651)	30,582	34,589
*55428	Crystal	(763)	22,698	22,151
*55806	Duluth	(218)	86,918	86,265
55121	Eagan	(651)	63,557	64,206
*55005	East Bethel	(763)	10,941	11,626
*55344	Eden Prairie	(612)	54,901	60,797
*55424	Edina	(952)	47,425	47,941
55330	Elk River	(763)	16,447	22,974
*56031	Fairmont	(507)	10,889	10,666
55021	Faribault	(507)	20,818	23,352
55024	Farmington	(651)	12,365	21,086
*56537	Fergus Falls	(218)	13,471	13,138
55025	Forest Lake	(651)	6,798	18,375
*55432	Fridley	(763)	27,449	27,208
*55427	Golden Valley	(763)	20,281	20,371
*55304	Ham Lake	(763)	12,710	15,296
55033	Hastings	(651)	18,204	22,172
*55746	Hibbing	(218)	17,071	16,361
55343	Hopkins	(952)	17,145	17,591
55038	Hugo	(651)	6,363	13,332
55350	Hutchinson	(320)	13,080	14,178
*55076	Inver Grove Heights	(651)	29,751	33,880
*55044	Lakeville	(952)	43,128	55,954
*55014	Lino Lakes	(651)	16,791	20,216
56001	Mankato	(507)	32,427	39,309
*55311	Maple Grove	(763)	50,365	61,567
*55109	Maplewood	(651)	34,947	38,018
56258	Marshall	(507)	12,735	13,680
*55118	Mendota Heights	(651)	11,434	11,071
*55440	Minneapolis	(612)	382,618	382,578
*55345	Minnetonka	(952)	51,301	49,734
*55362	Monticello	(763)	7,868	12,759
*56560	Moorhead	(218)	32,177	38,065
55112	Mounds View	(763)	12,738	12,155
55112	New Brighton	(651)	22,206	21,456
*54427	New Hope	(763)	20,873	20,339
56073	New Ulm	(507)	13,594	13,522
55056	North Branch	(651)	8,023	10,125
*55002	North Mankato	(507)	11,798	13,394
55109	North Saint Paul	(651)	11,929	11,460
55057	Northfield	(507)	17,147	20,007
*55128	Oakdale	(651)	26,653	27,378
*55330	Otsego	(763)	6,389	13,571
55060	Owatonna	(507)	22,434	25,599
*55446	Plymouth	(763)	65,894	70,576
*55372	Prior Lake	(952)	15,917	22,796
55303	Ramsey	(763)	18,510	23,668
55066	Red Wing	(651)	16,116	16,459
55423	Richfield	(612)	34,439	35,228
*55422	Robbinsdale	(763)	14,123	13,953
*55901	Rochester	(507)	85,806	106,769
55068	Rosemount	(651)	14,619	21,874
*55113	Roseville	(651)	33,690	33,660
*56301	Saint Cloud	(320)	59,107	65,842
*55426	Saint Louis Park	(952)	44,126	45,250
55376	Saint Michael	(763)	9,099	16,399
*55101	Saint Paul	(651)	287,151	285,068
56082	Saint Peter	(507)	9,747	11,196
56377	Sartell	(320)	9,641	15,876
56379	Sauk Rapids	(320)	10,213	12,773
*55378	Savage	(952)	21,115	26,911
*55379	Shakopee	(612)	20,568	37,076
55126	Shoreview	(651)	25,924	25,043
*55075	South Saint Paul	(651)	20,167	20,160
*55082	Stillwater	(651)	15,143	18,225
*55127	Vadnais Heights	(651)	13,069	12,302
*55387	Waconia	(952)	6,814	10,697
*55118	West Saint Paul	(651)	19,405	19,540
*55110	White Bear Lake	(651)	24,325	23,797
56201	Willmar	(320)	18,351	19,610
*55987	Winona	(507)	27,069	27,592
*55125	Woodbury	(651)	46,463	61,961
56187	Worthington	(507)	11,283	12,764

Mississippi

Area code (769) overlays area code (601).

ZIP	Place	Area code	2000	2010
*39530	Biloxi	(228)	50,644	44,054
*39042	Brandon	(601)	16,436	21,705
*39601	Brookhaven	(601)	9,861	12,513
39272	Byram	(601)		11,489
39046	Canton	(601)	12,911	13,189
*38614	Clarksdale	(662)	20,645	17,962
38732	Cleveland	(662)	13,841	12,334
*39056	Clinton	(601)	23,347	25,216
*39701	Columbus	(662)	25,944	23,640
*38834	Corinth	(662)	14,054	14,573
39553	Gautier	(228)	11,681	18,572
*38701	Greenville	(662)	41,633	34,400
*38930	Greenwood	(662)	18,425	15,205
38901	Grenada	(662)	14,879	13,092
*39501	Gulfport	(228)	71,127	67,793
*39401	Hattiesburg	(601)	44,779	45,989
38632	Hernando	(662)	6,812	14,090
38637	Horn Lake	(662)	14,099	26,066
*38751	Indianola	(662)	12,066	10,683
*39205	Jackson	(601)	184,256	173,514
*39440	Laurel	(601)	18,393	18,540
39560	Long Beach	(228)	17,320	14,792
*39110	Madison	(601)	14,692	24,149
*39648	McComb	(601)	13,337	12,790
*39302	Meridian	(601)	39,968	41,148
*39563	Moss Point	(228)	15,851	13,704

ZIP	Place	Area code	2000	2010
*39120	Natchez	(601)	18,464	15,792
*39564	Ocean Springs	(228)	17,225	17,442
38654	Olive Branch	(662)	21,054	33,484
38655	Oxford	(662)	11,756	18,916
*39567	Pascagoula	(228)	26,200	22,392
*39288	Pearl	(601)	21,961	25,092
39465	Petal	(601)	7,579	10,454
39466	Picayune	(601)	10,535	10,878
*39157	Ridgeland	(601)	20,173	24,047
*38671	Southaven	(662)	28,977	48,982
*39759	Starkville	(662)	21,869	23,888
*38801	Tupelo	(662)	34,211	34,546
*39180	Vicksburg	(601)	26,407	23,856
39773	West Point	(662)	12,145	11,307
39194	Yazoo City	(662)	14,550	11,403

Missouri

ZIP	Place	Area code	2000	2010
63123	Affton (c)	(314)	20,535	20,307
63010	Arnold	(636)	19,965	20,808
*63011	Ballwin	(636)	31,283	30,404
63137	Bellefontaine Neighbors	(314)	11,271	10,860
64012	Belton	(816)	21,730	23,116
*64015	Blue Springs	(816)	48,080	52,575
*65613	Bolivar	(417)	9,143	10,325
*65616	Branson	(417)	6,050	10,520
*63044	Bridgeton	(314)	15,550	11,550
*63701	Cape Girardeau	(573)	35,349	37,941
64836	Carthage	(417)	12,668	14,378
*63017	Chesterfield	(636)	46,802	47,484
*63105	Clayton	(314)	12,825	15,939
*65201	Columbia	(573)	84,531	108,500
*63128	Concord (c)	(314)	16,689	16,421
63126	Crestwood	(314)	11,863	11,912
63141	Creve Coeur	(314)	16,500	17,833
*63366	Dardenne Prairie	(636)	4,384	11,494
63025	Eureka	(636)	7,676	10,189
64024	Excelsior Springs	(816)	10,847	11,084
63640	Farmington	(573)	13,924	16,240
*63135	Ferguson	(314)	22,406	21,203
63028	Festus	(636)	9,660	11,602
*63033	Florissant	(314)	50,497	52,158
65473	Fort Leonard Wood (c)	(573)	13,666	15,061
65251	Fulton	(573)	12,128	12,790
*64118	Gladstone	(816)	26,365	25,410
64029	Grain Valley	(816)	5,160	12,854
64030	Grandview	(816)	24,881	24,475
63401	Hannibal	(573)	17,757	17,916
64701	Harrisonville	(816)	8,946	10,019
*63042	Hazelwood	(314)	26,206	25,703
*64050	Independence	(816)	113,288	116,830
63755	Jackson	(573)	11,947	13,758
*65101	Jefferson City	(573)	39,636	43,079
63136	Jennings	(314)	15,469	14,712
*64801	Joplin	(417)	45,504	50,150
*64108	Kansas City	(816)	441,545	459,787
63857	Kennett	(573)	11,260	10,932
63501	Kirksville	(660)	16,988	17,505
63122	Kirkwood	(314)	27,324	27,540
63367	Lake Saint Louis	(636)	10,169	14,545
65536	Lebanon	(417)	12,155	14,474
*64063	Lee's Summit	(816)	70,700	91,364
63125	Lemay (c)	(314)	17,215	16,645
*64068	Liberty	(816)	26,232	29,149
*63011	Manchester	(636)	19,161	18,094
65340	Marshall	(660)	12,433	13,065
63043	Maryland Heights	(314)	25,756	27,472
64468	Maryville	(816)	10,581	11,972
63129	Mehlville (c)	(314)	28,822	28,380
65265	Mexico	(573)	11,320	11,543
65270	Moberly	(660)	11,945	13,974
*64850	Neosho	(417)	10,505	11,835
65714	Nixa	(417)	12,124	19,022
63366	O'Fallon	(636)	46,169	79,329
63129	Oakville (c)	(314)	35,309	36,143
63034	Old Jamestown (c)	(314)	—	19,184
63114	Overland	(314)	16,838	16,062
65721	Ozark	(417)	9,665	17,820
*63901	Poplar Bluff	(573)	16,651	17,023
64083	Raymore	(816)	11,146	19,206
*64133	Raytown	(816)	30,388	29,526
65738	Republic	(417)	8,438	14,751
*65401	Rolla	(573)	16,367	19,559
63074	Saint Ann	(314)	13,607	13,020
*63301	Saint Charles	(636)	60,321	65,794
*64501	Saint Joseph	(816)	73,990	76,780
*63166	Saint Louis	(314)	348,189	319,294
*63376	Saint Peters	(636)	51,381	52,575
*65301	Sedalia	(660)	20,339	21,387
63801	Sikeston	(573)	16,992	16,318
63138	Spanish Lake (c)	(314)	21,337	19,650
*65801	Springfield	(417)	151,580	159,498
63011	Town and Country	(314)	10,894	10,815
63379	Troy	(314)	6,737	10,540
63084	Union	(636)	7,757	10,204

ZIP	Place	Area code	2000	2010
63130	University City	(314)	37,428	35,371
64093	Warrensburg	(660)	16,340	18,838
63090	Washington	(636)	13,243	13,982
64870	Webb City	(417)	9,812	10,996
63119	Webster Groves	(314)	23,230	22,995
63385	Wentzville	(636)	6,896	29,070
*65775	West Plains	(417)	10,866	11,986
*63011	Wildwood	(314)	32,884	35,517

Montana (406)

ZIP	Place	2000	2010
*59101	Billings	89,847	104,170
*59718	Bozeman	27,509	37,280
*59701	Butte-Silver Bow	33,892	33,525
59401	Great Falls	56,690	58,505
*59601	Helena	25,780	28,190
*59901	Kalispell	14,223	19,927
*59801	Missoula	57,053	66,788

Nebraska
Area code (531) overlays area code (402).

ZIP	Place	Area code	2000	2010
68310	Beatrice	(402)	12,496	12,459
*68108	Bellevue	(402)	44,382	50,137
68108	Chalco (c)	(402)	10,736	10,994
*68601	Columbus	(402)	20,971	22,111
*68025	Fremont	(402)	25,174	26,397
*68802	Grand Island	(308)	42,940	48,520
68901	Hastings	(402)	24,064	24,907
*68847	Kearney	(308)	27,431	30,787
68128	La Vista	(402)	11,699	15,758
68850	Lexington	(308)	10,011	10,230
*68501	Lincoln	(402)	225,581	238,379
68701	Norfolk	(402)	23,516	24,210
*69101	North Platte	(308)	23,878	24,733
*68005	Omaha	(402)	390,007	408,958
*68046	Papillion	(402)	16,363	18,894
*69361	Scottsbluff	(308)	14,732	15,039
68776	South Sioux City	(402)	11,925	13,353

Nevada

ZIP	Place	Area code	2000	2010
*89005	Boulder City	(702)	14,966	15,023
*89701	Carson City	(775)	52,457	55,274
*89801	Elko	(775)	16,708	18,297
89139	Enterprise (c)	(702)	14,676	108,481
89408	Fernley	(775)	—	19,368
89410	Gardnerville Ranchos (c)	(775)	11,054	11,312
*89015	Henderson	(702)	175,381	257,729
*89125	Las Vegas	(702)	478,434	583,756
89024	Mesquite	(702)	9,389	15,276
*89030	North Las Vegas	(702)	115,488	216,961
89041	Pahrump (c)	(775)	24,631	36,441
89109	Paradise (c)	(702)	186,070	223,167
*89501	Reno	(775)	180,480	225,221
89441	Spanish Springs (c)	(775)	9,018	15,064
*89431	Sparks	(775)	66,346	90,264
89815	Spring Creek (c)	(702)	10,548	12,361
89147	Spring Valley (c)	(702)	117,390	178,395
89135	Summerlin South (c)	(702)	3,735	24,085
89433	Sun Valley (c)	(775)	19,461	19,299
89110	Sunrise Manor (c)	(702)	156,120	189,372
89122	Whitney (c)	(702)	18,273	38,585
89101	Winchester (c)	(702)	26,958	27,978

New Hampshire (603)
See introductory note.

ZIP	Place	2000	2010
03031	Amherst	10,769	11,201
03110	Bedford	18,274	21,203
03570	Berlin	10,331	10,051
03743	Claremont	13,151	13,355
*03301	Concord	40,687	42,695
03038	Derry	34,021	33,109
03038	Derry (c)	22,661	22,015
*03820	Dover	26,884	29,987
03824	Durham	12,664	14,638
03824	Durham (c)	12,904	10,345
03833	Exeter	14,058	14,306
03045	Goffstown	16,929	17,651
*03842	Hampton	14,937	15,430
03755	Hanover	10,850	11,260
03106	Hooksett	11,721	13,451
03051	Hudson	22,928	24,467
*03431	Keene	22,563	23,409
03246	Laconia	16,411	15,951
*03766	Lebanon	12,568	13,151
03053	Londonderry	23,236	24,129
03053	Londonderry (c)	11,417	11,037
*03103	Manchester	107,006	109,565
03054	Merrimack	25,119	25,494
03055	Milford	13,535	15,115
*03060	Nashua	86,605	86,494

ZIP	Place	2000	2010
03076	Pelham	10,914	12,897
*03801	Portsmouth	20,784	20,779
03077	Raymond	9,674	10,138
*03867	Rochester	28,461	29,752
03079	Salem	28,112	28,776
03878	Somersworth	11,477	11,766
03087	Windham	10,709	13,592

New Jersey

Area code (551) overlays area code (201). Area code (848) overlays area code (732). Area code (862) overlays area code (973).

ZIP	Place	Area code	2000	2010
07712	Asbury Park	(732)	16,930	16,116
*08401	Atlantic City	(609)	40,517	39,558
07001	Avenel (c)	(732)	17,552	17,011
07002	Bayonne	(201)	61,842	63,024
08722	Beachwood	(732)	10,375	11,045
*08031	Bellmawr	(856)	11,262	11,583
07621	Bergenfield	(201)	26,247	26,764
07922	Berkeley Heights (c)	(908)	13,407	13,183
08805	Bound Brook	(732)	10,155	10,402
08807	Bradley Gardens (c)	(908)	—	14,206
08302	Bridgeton	(856)	22,771	25,349
08015	Browns Mills (c)	(609)	11,257	11,223
*08101	Camden	(856)	79,904	77,344
07008	Carteret	(732)	20,709	22,844
08002	Cherry Hill Mall (c)	(856)	13,238	14,171
07010	Cliffside Park	(201)	23,007	23,594
*07015	Clifton	(973)	78,672	84,136
08108	Collingswood	(856)	14,326	13,926
07067	Colonia (c)	(732)	17,811	17,795
*07801	Dover	(973)	18,188	18,157
07628	Dumont	(201)	17,503	17,479
*07019	East Orange	(973)	69,824	64,270
*07724	Eatontown	(732)	14,008	12,709
08043	Echelon (c)	(856)	10,440	10,743
*07207	Elizabeth	(908)	120,568	124,969
*07407	Elmwood Park	(201)	18,925	19,403
*07631	Englewood	(201)	26,203	27,147
07410	Fair Lawn	(201)/(973)	31,637	32,457
07022	Fairview (Bergen Co.)	(201)	13,255	13,835
07932	Florham Park	(973)	8,857	11,696
08863	Fords (c)	(732)	15,032	15,187
07024	Fort Lee	(201)	35,461	35,345
07417	Franklin Lakes	(201)	10,422	10,590
07728	Freehold	(732)	10,976	12,052
07026	Garfield	(973)	29,786	30,487
08028	Glassboro	(856)	19,068	18,579
07452	Glen Rock	(201)	11,546	11,601
*08030	Gloucester City	(856)	11,484	11,456
08053	Greentree (c)	(856)	11,536	11,367
07093	Guttenberg	(201)	10,807	11,176
*07602	Hackensack	(201)	42,677	43,010
08033	Haddonfield	(856)	11,659	11,593
08690	Hamilton Square (c)	(609)	—	12,784
08037	Hammonton	(609)	12,604	14,791
07029	Harrison	(973)	14,424	13,620
07604	Hasbrouck Heights	(201)	11,662	11,842
*07506	Hawthorne	(973)	18,218	18,791
08904	Highland Park	(732)	13,999	13,982
*07642	Hillsdale	(201)	10,087	10,219
07030	Hoboken	(201)	38,577	50,005
08753	Holiday City-Berkeley (c)	(732)	13,884	12,831
07843	Hopatcong	(973)	15,888	15,147
08830	Iselin (c)	(732)	16,698	18,695
*07303	Jersey City	(201)	240,055	247,597
07734	Keansburg	(732)	10,732	10,105
*07032	Kearny	(201)/(973)	40,513	40,684
08701	Lakewood (c)	(732)	36,065	53,805
07035	Lincoln Park	(973)	10,930	10,521
07036	Linden	(732)/(908)	39,394	40,499
08021	Lindenwold	(856)	17,414	17,613
07643	Little Ferry	(201)	10,800	10,626
07644	Lodi	(201)/(973)	23,971	24,136
07740	Long Branch	(732)	31,340	30,719
07940	Madison	(973)	16,530	15,845
08835	Manville	(908)	10,343	10,344
08053	Marlton (c)	(856)	10,260	10,133
08619	Mercerville (c)	(609)	—	13,230
08840	Metuchen	(732)	12,840	13,574
08846	Middlesex	(732)	13,717	13,635
08332	Millville	(856)	26,847	28,400
08057	Moorestown-Lenola (c)	(856)	13,860	14,217
*07960	Morristown	(973)	18,544	18,411
*08901	New Brunswick	(732)	48,573	55,181
07646	New Milford	(201)	16,400	16,341
07974	New Providence	(908)	11,907	12,171
*07102	Newark	(973)	273,546	277,140
07031	North Arlington	(201)	15,181	15,392
*07060	North Plainfield	(908)	21,103	21,936
07436	Oakland	(201)	12,466	12,754
*08050	Ocean Acres (c)	(609)	13,155	16,142
08226	Ocean City	(609)	15,378	11,701

ZIP	Place	Area code	2000	2010
08857	Old Bridge (c)	(732)	22,833	23,753
07650	Palisades Park	(201)	17,073	19,622
*07652	Paramus	(201)	25,737	26,342
07055	Passaic	(973)	67,861	69,781
*07510	Paterson	(973)	149,222	146,199
08070	Pennsville (c)	(856)	11,657	11,888
*08861	Perth Amboy	(732)	47,303	50,814
08865	Phillipsburg	(908)	15,166	14,950
08021	Pine Hill	(856)	10,880	10,233
*07061	Plainfield	(908)	47,829	49,808
*08232	Pleasantville	(609)	19,012	20,249
08742	Point Pleasant	(732)	19,306	18,392
07442	Pompton Lakes	(973)	10,640	11,097
*08540	Princeton	(609)	14,203	12,307
08536	Princeton Meadows (c)	(609)	13,436	13,834
07065	Rahway	(732)	26,500	27,346
07446	Ramsey	(201)	14,351	14,473
*07701	Red Bank	(732)	11,844	12,206
07657	Ridgefield	(201)	10,830	11,032
07660	Ridgefield Park	(201)	12,873	12,729
*07451	Ridgewood	(201)/(973)	24,936	24,958
07456	Ringwood	(973)	12,396	12,228
07661	River Edge	(201)	10,946	11,340
07751	Robertsville (c)	(732)	—	11,297
07203	Roselle	(908)	21,274	21,085
07204	Roselle Park	(908)	13,281	13,297
*08872	Sayreville	(732)	40,377	42,704
*07094	Secaucus	(201)	15,931	16,264
07078	Short Hills (c)	(973)	—	13,165
08244	Somers Point	(609)	11,614	10,795
*08873	Somerset (c)	(732)	23,040	22,083
08876	Somerville	(908)	12,423	12,098
07080	South Plainfield	(732)/(908)	21,810	23,385
*08882	South River	(732)	15,322	16,008
08003	Springdale (c)	(856)	14,409	14,518
*07901	Summit	(908)	21,131	21,457
07670	Tenafly	(201)	13,806	14,488
*07724	Tinton Falls	(732)	15,053	17,892
*08753	Toms River (c)	(732)	86,327	88,791
*07512	Totowa	(973)	9,892	10,804
*08650	Trenton	(609)	85,403	84,913
*07087	Union City	(201)	67,088	66,455
07043	Upper Montclair (c)	(973)	—	11,565
08406	Ventnor City	(609)	12,910	10,650
*08360	Vineland	(856)	56,271	60,724
07057	Wallington	(201)/(973)	11,583	11,335
07465	Wanaque	(201)/(973)	10,266	11,116
07728	West Freehold (c)	(732)/(908)	12,498	13,613
07093	West New York	(201)	45,768	49,708
*07091	Westfield	(732)/(908)	29,644	30,316
*07675	Westwood	(201)	10,999	10,908
08094	Williamstown (c)	(609)/(856)	11,812	15,567
07095	Woodbridge (c)	(732)/(908)	18,309	19,265
*08096	Woodbury	(856)	10,307	10,174
*07424	Woodland Park	(973)	—	11,819

New Mexico

ZIP	Place	Area code	2000	2010
*88310	Alamogordo	(575)	35,582	30,403
*87101	Albuquerque	(505)	448,607	545,852
*88210	Artesia	(575)	10,692	11,301
*88220	Carlsbad	(575)	25,625	26,138
*88021	Chaparral (c)	(505)	6,117	14,631
*88101	Clovis	(575)	32,667	37,775
*88030	Deming	(575)	14,116	14,855
*87532	Espanola	(505)	9,688	10,224
*87401	Farmington	(505)	37,844	45,877
*87301	Gallup	(505)	20,209	21,678
*88240	Hobbs	(575)	28,657	34,122
*88001	Las Cruces	(575)	74,267	97,618
*87701	Las Vegas	(505)	14,565	13,753
87544	Los Alamos (c)	(505)	11,909	12,019
87031	Los Lunas	(505)	10,034	14,835
*88260	Lovington	(575)	9,471	11,009
87107	North Valley (c)	(505)	11,923	11,333
*88130	Portales	(575)	11,131	12,280
*87124	Rio Rancho	(505)	51,765	87,521
*88201	Roswell	(575)	45,293	48,366
*87501	Santa Fe	(505)	62,203	67,947
*88061	Silver City	(575)	10,545	10,315
87105	South Valley (c)	(505)	39,060	40,976
*88063	Sunland Park	(575)	13,309	14,106

New York

Area codes (347) and (929) overlay area code (718). Area codes (646) and (917) overlay area code (212).

ZIP	Place	Area code	2000	2010
*12201	Albany	(518)	95,658	97,856
12010	Amsterdam	(518)	18,355	18,620
*13021	Auburn	(315)	28,574	27,687
11702	Babylon	(631)	12,615	12,166
11510	Baldwin (c)	(516)	23,455	24,033
*14020	Batavia	(585)	16,256	15,465

ZIP	Place	Area code	2000	2010
11706	Bay Shore (c)	(631)	23,852	26,337
12508	Beacon	(845)	13,808	15,541
11710	Bellmore (c)	(516)	16,441	16,218
11714	Bethpage (c)	(516)	16,543	16,429
*13902	Binghamton	(607)	47,380	47,376
11716	Bohemia (c)	(631)	9,871	10,180
11717	Brentwood (c)	(631)	53,917	60,664
14610	Brighton (c)	(585)	35,584	36,609
*14240	Buffalo	(716)	292,648	261,310
*14424	Canandaigua	(585)	11,264	10,545
11720	Centereach (c)	(631)	27,285	31,578
11722	Central Islip (c)	(516)	31,950	34,450
14225	Cheektowaga (c)	(716)	79,988	75,178
12047	Cohoes	(518)	15,521	16,168
11725	Commack (c)	(631)	36,367	36,124
11726	Copiague (c)	(631)	21,922	22,993
11727	Coram (c)	(631)	34,923	39,113
*14830	Corning	(607)	10,842	11,183
13045	Cortland	(607)	18,740	19,204
11729	Deer Park (c)	(631)	28,316	27,745
14043	Depew	(716)	16,629	15,303
11746	Dix Hills (c)	(631)	26,024	26,892
10522	Dobbs Ferry	(914)	10,622	10,875
*14048	Dunkirk	(716)	13,131	12,563
11730	East Islip (c)	(631)	14,078	14,475
11758	East Massapequa (c)	(516)	19,565	19,069
11554	East Meadow (c)	(516)	37,461	38,132
11731	East Northport (c)	(631)	20,845	20,217
11772	East Patchogue (c)	(631)	20,824	22,469
10709	Eastchester (c)	(914)	18,564	19,554
14226	Eggertsville (c)	(716)	—	15,019
*14901	Elmira	(607)	30,940	29,200
11003	Elmont (c)	(516)	32,657	33,198
11731	Elwood (c)	(631)	10,916	11,177
*13760	Endicott	(607)	13,038	13,392
13762	Endwell (c)	(607)	11,706	11,446
13219	Fairmount (c)	(315)	10,795	10,224
*11001	Floral Park	(516)	15,967	15,863
13603	Fort Drum (c)	(315)	12,123	12,955
11768	Fort Salonga (c)	(631)	9,634	10,008
11010	Franklin Square (c)	(516)	29,342	29,320
14063	Fredonia	(716)	10,706	11,230
11520	Freeport	(516)	43,783	42,860
13069	Fulton	(315)	11,855	11,896
*11530	Garden City	(516)	21,672	22,371
14456	Geneva	(315)	13,617	13,261
11542	Glen Cove	(516)	26,622	26,964
12801	Glens Falls	(518)	14,354	14,700
12078	Gloversville	(518)	15,413	15,665
14616	Greece (c)	(585)	14,614	14,519
11740	Greenlawn (c)	(631)	13,286	13,742
11946	Hampton Bays (c)	(631)	12,236	13,603
10528	Harrison	(914)	24,154	27,472
*11788	Hauppauge (c)	(631)	20,100	20,882
10927	Haverstraw	(845)	10,117	11,910
*11551	Hempstead	(516)	56,554	53,891
*11802	Hicksville (c)	(516)	41,260	41,547
11741	Holbrook (c)	(631)	27,512	27,195
11742	Holtsville (c)	(631)	17,006	19,714
11743	Huntington (c)	(631)	18,403	18,046
11746	Huntington Station (c)	(631)	29,910	33,029
14617	Irondequoit (c)	(585)	52,354	51,692
11751	Islip (c)	(631)	20,575	18,689
*14850	Ithaca	(607)	29,287	30,014
*14702	Jamestown	(716)	31,730	31,146
10535	Jefferson Valley-Yorktown	(914)	14,891	14,142
11753	Jericho (c)	(516)	13,045	13,567
13790	Johnson City	(607)	15,535	15,174
*14217	Kenmore	(716)	16,426	15,423
11754	Kings Park (c)	(631)	16,146	17,282
*12401	Kingston	(845)	23,456	23,893
10950	Kiryas Joel	(845)	13,138	20,175
14218	Lackawanna	(716)	19,064	18,141
11755	Lake Grove	(631)	10,250	11,163
11779	Lake Ronkonkoma (c)	(631)	19,701	20,155
*14086	Lancaster	(716)	11,188	10,352
11756	Levittown (c)	(516)	53,067	51,881
11757	Lindenhurst	(631)	27,819	27,253
*14094	Lockport	(716)	22,279	21,165
11561	Long Beach	(516)	35,462	33,275
11563	Lynbrook	(516)	19,911	19,427
10543	Mamaroneck (c)	(914)	18,752	18,929
11949	Manorville (c)	(631)	11,131	14,314
11758	Massapequa (c)	(516)	22,652	21,685
11762	Massapequa Park	(516)	17,499	17,008
13662	Massena	(315)	11,209	10,936
11950	Mastic (c)	(631)	15,436	15,481
11951	Mastic Beach (c)	(631)	11,543	12,930
11763	Medford (c)	(631)	21,985	24,142
11747	Melville (c)	(631)	14,533	18,985
11566	Merrick (c)	(516)	22,764	22,097
11953	Middle Island (c)	(631)	9,702	10,483
*10940	Middletown	(845)	25,388	28,086
11764	Miller Place (c)	(631)	10,580	12,339
11501	Mineola	(516)	19,234	18,799
10952	Monsey (c)	(845)	14,504	18,412
10549	Mount Kisco	(914)	9,983	10,877
11766	Mount Sinai (c)	(631)	8,734	12,118
*10551	Mount Vernon	(914)	68,381	67,292
10954	Nanuet (c)	(845)	16,707	17,882
11767	Nesconset (c)	(631)	11,992	13,387
11590	New Cassel (c)	(516)	13,298	14,059
10956	New City (c)	(845)	34,038	33,559
*10802	New Rochelle	(914)	72,182	77,062
*10001	New York	(212)/(718)	8,008,278	8,175,133
*12550	Newburgh	(845)	28,259	28,866
*14302	Niagara Falls	(716)	55,593	50,193
11701	North Amityville (c)	(631)	16,572	17,862
11703	North Babylon (c)	(631)	17,877	17,509
11706	North Bay Shore (c)	(631)	14,992	18,944
11710	North Bellmore (c)	(516)	20,079	19,941
11757	North Lindenhurst (c)	(631)	11,767	11,652
11758	North Massapequa (c)	(516)	19,152	17,886
11566	North Merrick (c)	(516)	11,844	12,272
11040	North New Hyde Park (c)	(516)	14,542	14,899
14120	North Tonawanda	(716)	33,262	31,568
11580	North Valley Stream (c)	(516)	15,789	16,628
11793	North Wantagh (c)	(516)	12,156	11,960
11572	Oceanside (c)	(516)	32,733	32,109
13669	Ogdensburg	(315)	12,364	11,128
14760	Olean	(585)/(716)	15,347	14,452
13421	Oneida	(315)	10,987	11,393
13820	Oneonta	(607)	13,292	13,901
10562	Ossining	(914)	24,010	25,060
13126	Oswego	(315)	17,954	18,142
11772	Patchogue	(631)	11,919	11,798
10965	Pearl River (c)	(845)	15,553	15,876
10566	Peekskill	(914)	22,441	23,583
11803	Plainview (c)	(516)	25,637	26,217
*12901	Plattsburgh	(518)	18,816	19,989
10573	Port Chester	(914)	27,867	28,967
11050	Port Washington (c)	(516)	15,215	15,846
*12601	Poughkeepsie	(845)	29,871	32,736
11961	Ridge (c)	(631)	13,380	13,336
11901	Riverhead (c)	(631)	10,513	13,299
*14692	Rochester	(585)	219,773	210,565
*11571	Rockville Centre	(516)	24,568	24,023
11778	Rocky Point (c)	(631)	10,185	14,014
*13440	Rome	(315)	34,950	33,725
11779	Ronkonkoma (c)	(631)	20,029	19,082
11575	Roosevelt (c)	(516)	15,854	16,258
12303	Rotterdam (c)	(518)	20,536	20,652
10580	Rye	(914)	14,955	15,720
11780	Saint James (c)	(631)	13,268	13,338
13454	Salisbury (c)	(315)	12,341	12,093
12866	Saratoga Springs	(518)	26,186	26,586
11782	Sayville (c)	(631)	16,735	16,853
10583	Scarsdale	(914)	17,823	17,166
*12301	Schenectady	(518)	61,821	66,135
11783	Seaford (c)	(516)	15,791	15,294
11784	Selden (c)	(631)	21,861	19,851
11733	Setauket-East Setauket (c)	(631)	15,931	15,477
11967	Shirley (c)	(631)	25,395	27,854
11787	Smithtown (c)	(631)	26,901	26,470
11735	South Farmingdale (c)	(516)	15,061	14,486
10977	Spring Valley	(845)	25,464	31,347
*11790	Stony Brook (c)	(631)	13,727	13,740
10980	Stony Point (c)	(845)	11,744	12,147
*10901	Suffern	(845)	11,006	10,723
11791	Syosset (c)	(516)	18,544	18,829
*13220	Syracuse	(315)	147,306	145,170
10591	Tarrytown	(914)	11,090	11,277
11776	Terryville (c)	(631)	10,589	11,849
*14150	Tonawanda	(716)	16,136	15,130
*12180	Troy	(518)	49,170	50,129
11553	Uniondale (c)	(516)	23,011	24,759
*13504	Utica	(315)	60,651	62,235
*11582	Valley Stream	(516)	36,368	37,511
11793	Wantagh (c)	(516)	18,971	18,871
*13601	Watertown	(315)	26,705	27,023
*11704	West Babylon (c)	(631)	43,452	43,213
10993	West Haverstraw	(845)	10,295	10,165
11552	West Hempstead (c)	(516)	18,713	18,862
11795	West Islip (c)	(631)	28,907	28,335
14224	West Seneca (c)	(716)	45,943	44,711
*11590	Westbury	(516)	14,263	15,146
*10602	White Plains	(914)	53,077	56,853
11797	Woodbury (c)	(516)	—	10,686
11598	Woodmere (c)	(516)	16,447	17,121
11798	Wyandanch (c)	(631)	10,546	11,647
*10702	Yonkers	(914)	196,086	195,976

North Carolina

Area code (980) overlays area code (704).

ZIP	Place	Area code	2000	2010
28315	Albemarle	(910)	15,680	15,903
*27502	Apex	(919)	20,212	37,476
27263	Archdale	(336)	9,014	11,415
*27203	Asheboro	(336)	21,672	25,012

ZIP	Place	Area code	2000	2010
*28802	Asheville	(828)	68,889	83,393
28012	Belmont	(704)	8,705	10,076
*28607	Boone	(828)	13,472	17,122
*27215	Burlington	(336)	44,917	49,963
27510	Carrboro	(919)	16,782	19,582
*27511	Cary	(919)	94,536	135,234
*27514	Chapel Hill	(919)	48,715	57,233
*28204	Charlotte	(704)	540,828	731,424
*27520	Clayton	(919)	6,973	16,116
27012	Clemmons	(336)	13,827	18,627
*28025	Concord	(704)	55,977	79,066
28031	Cornelius	(704)	11,969	24,866
*28036	Davidson	(704)	7,139	10,944
*27701	Durham	(919)	187,035	22,830
*27288	Eden	(336)	15,908	15,527
*27909	Elizabeth City	(252)	17,188	18,683
*28302	Fayetteville	(910)	121,015	200,564
27526	Fuquay-Varina	(919)	7,898	17,937
27529	Garner	(919)	17,757	25,745
*28052	Gastonia	(704)	66,277	71,741
*27530	Goldsboro	(919)	39,043	36,437
27253	Graham	(336)	12,833	14,153
*27420	Greensboro	(336)	223,891	269,666
*27834	Greenville	(252)	60,476	84,554
28075	Harrisburg	(704)	4,493	11,526
*28532	Havelock	(252)	22,442	20,735
*27536	Henderson	(252)	16,095	15,368
*28739	Hendersonville	(828)	10,420	13,137
*28603	Hickory	(828)	37,222	40,010
*27260	High Point	(336)	85,839	104,371
27540	Holly Springs	(919)	9,192	24,661
28348	Hope Mills	(910)	11,237	15,176
*28070	Huntersville	(704)	24,960	46,773
28079	Indian Trail	(704)	11,905	33,518
*28540	Jacksonville	(910)	66,715	70,145
*28081	Kannapolis	(704)	36,910	42,625
*27284	Kernersville	(336)	17,126	23,123
28086	Kings Mountain	(704)	9,693	10,296
*28502	Kinston	(252)	23,688	21,677
*27545	Knightdale	(919)	5,958	11,401
*28352	Laurinburg	(910)	15,874	15,962
28451	Leland	(910)	1,938	13,527
*28645	Lenoir	(828)	16,793	18,228
27023	Lewisville	(336)	8,826	12,639
*27292	Lexington	(336)	19,953	18,931
*28092	Lincolnton	(704)	9,965	10,486
*28358	Lumberton	(910)	20,795	21,542
*28105	Matthews	(704)	22,127	27,198
27302	Mebane	(919)	7,284	11,393
28227	Mint Hill	(704)	14,922	22,722
*28110	Monroe	(704)	26,228	32,797
28115	Mooresville	(704)	18,823	32,711
*28655	Morganton	(828)	17,310	16,918
27560	Morrisville	(919)	5,208	18,576
*27030	Mount Airy	(336)	8,484	10,388
28120	Mount Holly	(704)	9,618	13,656
28411	Murraysville (c)	(910)	7,279	14,215
*28562	New Bern	(252)	23,128	29,524
28658	Newton	(828)	12,560	12,968
*28374	Pinehurst	(910)	9,706	13,124
28399	Piney Green (c)	(910)	11,658	13,293
*27611	Raleigh	(919)	276,093	403,892
*27320	Reidsville	(336)	14,485	14,520
27870	Roanoke Rapids	(252)	16,957	15,754
*27801	Rocky Mount	(252)	55,893	57,477
*28144	Salisbury	(704)	26,462	33,662
*27330	Sanford	(919)	23,220	28,094
*28150	Shelby	(704)	19,477	20,323
27577	Smithfield	(919)	11,510	10,966
*28387	Southern Pines	(910)	10,918	12,334
*28390	Spring Lake	(910)	8,098	11,964
28104	Stallings	(704)	3,189	13,831
*28677	Statesville	(704)	23,320	24,532
27358	Summerfield	(336)	7,018	10,232
27886	Tarboro	(252)	11,138	11,415
*27360	Thomasville	(336)	19,788	26,757
*27587	Wake Forest	(919)	12,588	30,117
*28402	Wilmington	(910)	75,838	106,476
*27893	Wilson	(252)	44,405	49,167
*27102	Winston-Salem	(336)	185,776	229,617

North Dakota (701)

ZIP	Place	2000	2010
*58501	Bismarck	55,532	61,272
*58601	Dickinson	16,010	17,727
*58102	Fargo	90,599	105,549
*58201	Grand Forks	49,321	52,838
*58401	Jamestown	15,527	15,427
58554	Mandan	16,718	18,331
*58701	Minot	36,567	40,888
58078	West Fargo	14,940	25,830
*58801	Williston	12,512	14,716

Ohio

Area code (234) overlays area code (330). Area code (567) overlays area code (419).

ZIP	Place	Area code	2000	2010
*44309	Akron	(330)	217,074	199,110
44601	Alliance	(330)	23,253	22,322
44001	Amherst	(440)	11,797	12,021
44805	Ashland	(419)	21,249	20,362
*44004	Ashtabula	(440)	20,962	19,124
45701	Athens	(740)	21,342	23,832
44202	Aurora	(330)	13,556	15,548
44515	Austintown (c)	(330)	31,627	29,677
44011	Avon	(440)	11,446	21,193
44012	Avon Lake	(440)	18,145	22,581
44203	Barberton	(330)	27,899	26,550
44140	Bay Village	(440)	16,087	15,651
44122	Beachwood	(216)	12,186	11,953
45434	Beavercreek	(937)	37,984	45,193
44146	Bedford	(216)/(440)	14,214	13,074
*44146	Bedford Heights	(216)/(440)	11,375	10,751
43311	Bellefontaine	(937)	13,069	13,370
44017	Berea	(440)	18,970	19,093
43209	Bexley	(614)	13,203	13,057
*45242	Blue Ash	(513)	12,513	12,114
44513	Boardman (c)	(330)	37,215	35,376
*43402	Bowling Green	(419)	29,636	30,028
44141	Brecksville	(440)	13,382	13,656
45211	Bridgetown (c)	(513)	—	14,407
44147	Broadview Heights	(440)	15,967	19,400
44142	Brook Park	(216)/(440)	21,218	19,212
44144	Brooklyn	(216)	11,586	11,169
44212	Brunswick	(330)	33,388	34,255
44820	Bucyrus	(419)	13,224	12,362
*43725	Cambridge	(740)	11,520	10,635
*44711	Canton	(330)	80,806	73,007
*45822	Celina	(419)	10,303	10,400
*45458	Centerville (Montgomery Co.)	(937)	23,024	23,999
45601	Chillicothe	(740)	21,796	21,901
*45202	Cincinnati	(513)	331,285	296,943
43113	Circleville	(740)	13,485	13,314
45315	Clayton	(937)	13,347	13,209
*44101	Cleveland	(216)	478,403	396,815
*44118	Cleveland Heights	(216)	49,958	46,121
*43216	Columbus	(614)	711,470	787,033
44030	Conneaut	(440)	12,485	12,841
43812	Coshocton	(740)	11,682	11,216
*44222	Cuyahoga Falls	(330)	49,374	49,652
*45401	Dayton	(937)	166,179	141,527
43512	Defiance	(419)	16,465	16,494
43015	Delaware	(740)	25,243	34,753
*45247	Dent (c).	(513)	7,612	10,497
44622	Dover	(330)	12,210	12,826
*43016	Dublin	(614)/(740)	31,392	41,751
*44112	East Cleveland	(216)	27,217	17,843
43920	East Liverpool	(330)	13,089	11,195
*44095	Eastlake	(440)	20,255	18,577
*44035	Elyria	(440)	55,953	54,533
*45322	Englewood	(937)	12,235	13,465
*44117	Euclid	(216)	52,717	48,920
45324	Fairborn	(937)	32,052	32,352
*45011	Fairfield	(513)	42,097	42,510
44126	Fairview Park	(440)	17,572	16,826
*45839	Findlay	(419)	38,967	41,202
45224	Finneytown (c)	(513)	13,492	12,741
45240	Forest Park	(513)	19,463	18,720
45230	Forestville (c)	(513)	10,978	10,532
44830	Fostoria	(419)	13,931	13,441
45005	Franklin	(513)	11,396	11,771
43420	Fremont	(419)	17,375	16,734
43230	Gahanna	(614)	32,636	33,248
44833	Galion	(419)	11,341	10,512
*44125	Garfield Heights	(216)	30,734	28,849
44232	Green	(330)	22,817	25,699
45331	Greenville	(937)	13,294	13,227
43123	Grove City	(614)	27,075	35,575
*45011	Hamilton	(513)	60,690	62,477
43056	Heath	(740)	8,527	10,310
43026	Hilliard	(614)/(740)	24,230	28,435
45424	Huber Heights	(937)	38,212	38,101
*44236	Hudson	(330)	22,439	22,262
45638	Ironton	(740)	11,211	11,129
*44240	Kent	(330)	27,906	28,904
*45429	Kettering	(937)	57,502	56,163
44107	Lakewood	(216)	56,646	52,131
43130	Lancaster	(740)	35,335	38,780
45036	Lebanon	(513)	16,962	20,033
*45802	Lima	(419)	40,081	38,771
*44052	Lorain	(440)	68,652	64,097
45140	Loveland	(513)	11,677	12,081
44124	Lyndhurst	(216)/(440)	15,279	14,001
*44056	Macedonia	(330)	9,224	11,188
*45248	Mack (c)	(513)	—	11,585
*44901	Mansfield	(419)	49,346	47,821
44137	Maple Heights	(216)	26,156	23,138

ZIP	Place	Area code	2000	2010
45750	Marietta	(740)	14,515	14,085
*43302	Marion	(740)	35,318	36,837
*43040	Marysville	(937)	15,942	22,094
45040	Mason	(513)	22,016	30,712
*44646	Massillon	(330)	31,325	32,149
43537	Maumee	(419)	15,237	14,286
44124	Mayfield Heights	(440)	19,386	19,155
*44256	Medina	(330)	25,139	26,678
*44060	Mentor	(440)	50,278	47,159
*45343	Miamisburg	(937)	19,489	20,181
44130	Middleburg Heights	(216)/(440)	15,542	15,946
*45042	Middletown	(513)	51,605	48,694
45211	Monfort Heights (c)	(513)	—	11,948
*45050	Monroe	(513)	7,133	12,442
45242	Montgomery	(513)	10,163	10,251
43050	Mount Vernon	(740)	14,375	16,990
44657	New Franklin	(330)	2,191	14,227
44663	New Philadelphia	(330)	17,056	17,288
*43055	Newark	(740)	46,279	47,573
44446	Niles	(330)	20,932	19,266
*44720	North Canton	(330)	16,369	17,488
44070	North Olmsted	(440)	34,113	32,718
*44039	North Ridgeville	(440)	22,338	29,465
44133	North Royalton	(440)	28,648	30,444
45239	Northbrook (c)	(513)	11,076	10,668
*44203	Norton	(330)	11,523	12,085
44857	Norwalk	(419)	16,238	17,012
*45212	Norwood	(513)	21,675	19,207
*43616	Oregon	(419)	19,355	20,291
45056	Oxford	(513)	21,943	21,371
44077	Painesville	(440)	17,503	19,563
*44129	Parma	(216)/(440)	85,655	81,601
44130	Parma Heights	(216)/(440)	21,659	20,718
43062	Pataskala	(740)	10,249	14,962
*43551	Perrysburg	(419)	16,945	20,623
43147	Pickerington	(614)/(740)	9,792	18,291
45356	Piqua	(937)	20,738	20,522
*45662	Portsmouth	(740)	20,909	20,226
43065	Powell	(614)	6,247	11,500
44266	Ravenna	(330)	11,771	11,724
*45215	Reading	(513)	11,292	10,385
43068	Reynoldsburg	(614)/(740)	32,069	35,893
44143	Richmond Heights	(216)/(440)	10,944	10,546
45431	Riverside	(937)	23,545	25,201
44116	Rocky River	(440)	20,735	20,213
44460	Salem	(330)	12,197	12,303
*44870	Sandusky	(419)	27,844	25,793
44131	Seven Hills	(216)/(440)	12,080	11,804
*44122	Shaker Heights	(216)	29,405	28,448
*45241	Sharonville	(513)	13,804	13,560
*45365	Sidney	(937)	20,211	21,229
44139	Solon	(440)	21,802	23,348
*44121	South Euclid	(216)	23,537	22,295
45066	Springboro	(513)	12,380	17,409
45246	Springdale	(513)	10,563	11,223
*45501	Springfield	(937)	65,358	60,608
*43952	Steubenville	(740)	19,015	18,659
44224	Stow	(330)	32,139	34,837
44241	Streetsboro	(330)	12,311	16,028
*44136	Strongsville	(440)	43,858	44,750
44471	Struthers	(330)	11,756	10,713
43560	Sylvania	(419)	18,670	18,965
44278	Tallmadge	(330)	16,390	17,537
44883	Tiffin	(419)	18,135	17,963
*43601	Toledo	(419)	313,619	287,208
45067	Trenton	(513)	8,746	11,869
*45426	Trotwood	(937)	27,420	24,431
*45373	Troy	(937)	21,999	25,058
44087	Twinsburg	(330)	17,006	18,795
*44122	University Heights	(216)	14,146	13,539
*43221	Upper Arlington	(614)	33,686	33,771
43078	Urbana	(937)	11,613	11,793
45377	Vandalia	(937)	14,603	15,246
45891	Van Wert	(419)	10,690	10,846
*44089	Vermilion	(440)	10,927	10,594
*44281	Wadsworth	(330)	18,437	21,567
*44481	Warren	(330)	46,832	41,557
*44122	Warrensville Heights	(216)	15,109	13,542
43160	Washington Court House	(740)	—	14,192
*45449	West Carrollton City	(937)	13,818	13,143
*43081	Westerville	(614)	35,318	36,120
44145	Westlake	(440)	31,719	32,729
45239	White Oak (c)	(513)	13,277	19,167
43213	Whitehall	(614)	19,201	18,062
44092	Wickliffe	(440)	13,484	12,750
*44094	Willoughby	(440)	22,621	22,268
*44095	Willowick	(440)	14,361	14,171
45177	Wilmington	(937)	11,921	12,520
44691	Wooster	(330)	24,811	26,119
43085	Worthington	(614)	14,125	13,575
45385	Xenia	(937)	24,164	25,719
*44501	Youngstown	(330)	82,026	66,982
*43701	Zanesville	(740)	25,586	25,487

Oklahoma

As of Apr. 1, 2011, area code (539) overlays area code (918).

ZIP	Place	Area code	2000	2010
*74820	Ada	(580)	15,691	16,810
*73521	Altus	(580)	21,447	19,813
*73401	Ardmore	(580)	23,711	24,283
*74003	Bartlesville	(918)	34,748	35,750
73008	Bethany	(405)	20,307	19,051
74008	Bixby	(918)	13,336	20,884
*74012	Broken Arrow	(918)	74,859	98,850
*73018	Chickasha	(405)	15,850	16,036
73020	Choctaw	(405)	9,377	11,146
*74017	Claremore	(918)	15,873	18,581
*73115	Del City	(405)	22,128	21,332
*73533	Duncan	(580)	22,505	23,431
*74701	Durant	(580)	13,549	15,856
*73034	Edmond	(405)	68,315	81,405
*73644	Elk City	(580)	10,510	11,693
73036	El Reno	(405)	16,212	16,749
*73701	Enid	(580)	47,045	49,379
*74033	Glenpool	(918)	8,123	10,808
73044	Guthrie	(405)	9,925	10,191
*73942	Guymon	(580)	10,472	11,442
74037	Jenks	(918)	9,557	16,924
*73501	Lawton	(580)	92,757	96,867
*74501	McAlester	(918)	17,783	18,383
*74354	Miami	(918)	13,704	13,570
*73140	Midwest City	(405)	54,088	54,371
*73153	Moore	(405)	41,138	55,081
*74401	Muskogee	(918)	38,310	39,223
73064	Mustang	(405)	13,156	17,395
*73069	Norman	(405)	95,694	110,925
*73125	Oklahoma City	(405)	506,132	579,999
74447	Okmulgee	(918)	13,022	12,321
*74055	Owasso	(918)	18,502	28,915
*74601	Ponca City	(580)	25,919	25,387
74063	Sand Springs	(918)	17,451	18,906
*74066	Sapulpa	(918)	19,166	20,544
*74801	Shawnee	(405)	28,692	29,857
*74074	Stillwater	(405)	39,065	45,688
*74464	Tahlequah	(918)	14,458	15,753
*74103	Tulsa	(918)	393,049	391,906
*73112	Warr Acres	(405)	9,735	10,043
73096	Weatherford	(580)	9,859	10,833
*73801	Woodward	(580)	11,853	12,051
*73099	Yukon	(405)	21,043	22,709

Oregon

Area code (458) overlays area code (541). Area code (971) overlays area code (503).

ZIP	Place	Area code	2000	2010
*97321	Albany	(541)	40,852	50,158
*97006	Aloha (c)	(503)	41,741	49,425
97601	Altamont (c)	(541)	19,603	19,257
97520	Ashland	(541)	19,522	20,078
*97005	Beaverton	(503)	76,129	89,803
*97701	Bend	(541)	52,029	76,639
97229	Bethany (c)	(503)	—	20,646
97013	Canby	(503)	12,790	15,829
97291	Cedar Mill (c)	(503)	12,597	14,546
97502	Central Point	(541)	12,493	17,169
97420	Coos Bay	(541)	15,374	15,967
97113	Cornelius	(503)	9,652	11,869
*97333	Corvallis	(541)	49,322	54,462
97338	Dallas	(503)	12,459	14,583
*97009	Damascus	(503)	—	10,539
*97440	Eugene	(541)	137,893	156,185
97116	Forest Grove	(503)	17,708	21,083
97301	Four Corners (c)	(503)	13,922	15,947
97027	Gladstone	(503)	11,438	11,497
*97526	Grants Pass	(541)	23,003	34,533
*97030	Gresham	(503)	90,205	105,594
*97015	Happy Valley	(503)	4,519	13,903
97303	Hayesville (c)	(503)	18,222	19,936
*97838	Hermiston	(541)	13,154	16,745
*97123	Hillsboro	(503)	70,186	91,611
97307	Keizer	(503)	32,203	36,478
*97601	Klamath Falls	(541)	19,462	20,840
97850	La Grande	(541)	12,327	13,082
*97034	Lake Oswego	(503)	35,278	36,619
97355	Lebanon	(541)	12,950	15,518
97741	McMinnville	(503)	26,499	32,187
*97501	Medford	(541)	63,154	74,907
*97269	Milwaukie	(503)	20,490	20,291
97132	Newberg	(503)	18,064	22,068
97268	Oak Grove (c)	(503)	12,808	16,629
*97006	Oak Hills (c)	(503)	9,050	11,333
97267	Oatfield (c)	(503)	15,750	13,415
97914	Ontario	(541)	10,985	11,366
97045	Oregon City	(503)	25,754	31,859
97801	Pendleton	(541)	16,354	16,612
*97028	Portland	(503)	529,121	583,776
97756	Redmond	(541)	13,481	26,215

ZIP	Place	Area code	2000	2010
97470	Roseburg	(541)	20,017	21,181
97051	Saint Helens	(503)	10,019	12,883
*97309	Salem	(503)	136,924	154,637
97140	Sherwood	(503)	11,791	18,194
*97477	Springfield	(541)	52,864	59,403
97058	The Dalles[1]	(541)	12,156	13,620
*97281	Tigard	(503)	41,223	48,035
97060	Troutdale	(503)	13,777	15,962
97062	Tualatin	(503)	22,791	26,054
97068	West Linn	(503)	22,261	25,109
97070	Wilsonville	(503)	13,991	19,509
97071	Woodburn	(503)	20,100	24,080

(1) Listed as City of The Dalles in 2000 Census.

Pennsylvania

Area code (267) overlays area code (215). Area code (484) overlays area code (610). Area code (878) overlays area code (412).

ZIP	Place	Area code	2000	2010
*18105	Allentown	(610)	106,632	118,032
15101	Allison Park (c)	(412)/(724)	—	21,552
*16603	Altoona	(814)	49,523	46,320
19003	Ardmore (c)	(610)	12,616	12,455
15234	Baldwin	(412)	19,999	19,767
18603	Berwick	(570)	10,774	10,477
15102	Bethel Park	(412)	33,556	32,313
*18016	Bethlehem	(610)	71,329	74,982
*17815	Bloomsburg	(570)	12,375	14,855
19008	Broomall (c)	(610)	11,046	10,789
*16001	Butler	(724)	15,121	13,757
*17013	Carlisle	(717)	17,970	18,682
15108	Carnot-Moon (c)	(412)	10,637	11,372
17201	Chambersburg	(717)	17,862	20,268
*19013	Chester	(610)	36,854	33,972
19320	Coatesville	(610)	10,838	13,100
17109	Colonial Park (c)	(717)	13,259	13,229
17512	Columbia	(717)	10,311	10,400
19023	Darby	(610)	10,299	10,687
19026	Drexel Hill (c)	(610)	29,364	28,043
*18512	Dunmore	(570)	14,018	14,057
*18042	Easton	(610)	26,263	26,800
17022	Elizabethtown	(717)	11,887	11,545
*18049	Emmaus	(610)	11,313	11,211
17522	Ephrata	(717)	13,213	13,394
*16501	Erie	(814)	103,717	101,786
16063	Fernway (c)	(724)	12,188	12,414
15237	Franklin Park	(412)	11,364	13,470
18052	Fullerton (c)	(610)	14,268	14,925
*15601	Greensburg	(724)	15,889	14,892
*17331	Hanover	(717)	14,535	15,289
*17105	Harrisburg	(717)	48,950	49,528
*18201	Hazleton	(570)	23,329	25,340
16148	Hermitage	(724)	16,157	16,220
17033	Hershey (c)	(717)	12,771	14,257
19044	Horsham (c)	(215)	14,779	14,842
*15701	Indiana	(724)	14,895	13,975
15025	Jefferson Hills	(412)	9,666	10,619
15907	Johnstown	(814)	23,906	20,978
19406	King of Prussia (c)	(610)	18,511	19,936
18704	Kingston	(570)	13,855	13,182
*17604	Lancaster	(717)	56,348	59,322
19446	Lansdale	(215)	16,071	16,269
19050	Lansdowne	(610)	11,044	10,620
*17042	Lebanon	(717)	24,461	25,477
*19055	Levittown (c)	(215)	53,966	52,983
15068	Lower Burrell	(724)	12,608	11,761
*15134	McKeesport	(412)	24,040	19,731
*16335	Meadville	(814)	13,685	13,388
*15146	Monroeville	(412)/(724)	29,349	28,386
18936	Montgomeryville (c)	(215)	12,031	12,624
18707	Mountain Top (c)	(570)	15,269	10,982
15120	Munhall	(412)	12,264	11,406
*15668	Murraysville	(412)/(724)	18,872	20,079
18634	Nanticoke	(570)	10,955	10,465
16108	New Castle	(724)	26,309	23,273
15068	New Kensington	(724)	14,701	13,116
*19403	Norristown	(610)	31,282	34,324
16301	Oil City	(814)	11,504	10,557
*19104	Philadelphia	(215)	1,517,550	1,526,006
*19460	Phoenixville	(610)	14,788	16,440
15233	Pittsburgh	(412)	334,563	305,704
15239	Plum	(412)	26,940	27,126
19464	Pottstown	(610)	21,859	22,377
17901	Pottsville	(570)	15,549	14,324
*19612	Reading	(610)	81,207	88,082
15857	Saint Marys	(814)	14,502	13,070
*18505	Scranton	(570)	76,415	76,089
*16146	Sharon	(724)	16,328	14,038
17404	Shiloh (c)	(717)	10,192	11,218
15129	South Park Twp. (c)	(814)	14,340	13,416
*16804	State College	(814)	38,420	42,034
15401	Uniontown	(724)	12,422	10,372
15241	Upper Saint Clair (c)	(412)	20,053	19,229
15301	Washington (Wash. Co.)	(724)	15,268	13,663
*17268	Waynesboro	(717)	9,614	10,568
17315	Weigelstown (c)	(717)	10,117	12,875

ZIP	Place	Area code	2000	2010
*19380	West Chester	(610)	17,861	18,461
*15122	West Mifflin	(412)	22,464	20,313
18052	Whitehall (Allegheny Co.)	(412)	14,444	13,944
*18703	Wilkes-Barre	(570)	43,123	41,498
15221	Wilkinsburg	(412)	19,196	15,930
*17701	Williamsport	(570)	30,706	29,381
19090	Willow Grove (c)	(215)	16,234	15,726
19610	Wyomissing	(610)	8,587	10,461
19050	Yeadon	(610)	11,762	11,443
*17405	York	(717)	40,862	27,793

Rhode Island (401)

See introductory note.

ZIP	Place	2000	2010
02806	Barrington	16,819	16,310
02809	Bristol	22,469	22,954
02830	Burrillville	15,796	15,955
02863	Central Falls	18,928	19,376
02816	Coventry	33,668	35,014
*02905	Cranston	79,269	80,387
02864	Cumberland	31,840	33,506
02818	East Greenwich	12,948	13,146
02914	East Providence	48,688	47,037
02919	Johnston	28,195	28,769
02865	Lincoln	20,898	21,105
02842	Middletown	17,334	16,150
02882	Narragansett	16,361	15,868
02840	Newport	26,475	24,672
02843	Newport East (c)	11,463	11,769
02852	North Kingstown	26,326	26,486
02908	North Providence	32,411	32,078
02896	North Smithfield	10,618	11,967
*02860	Pawtucket	72,958	71,148
02871	Portsmouth	17,149	17,389
*02904	Providence	173,618	178,042
02857	Scituate	10,324	10,329
02917	Smithfield	20,613	21,430
02879	South Kingstown	27,921	30,639
02878	Tiverton	15,260	15,780
02864	Valley Falls (c)	11,599	11,547
02885	Warren	11,360	10,611
*02886	Warwick	85,808	82,672
02893	West Warwick	29,581	29,191
02891	Westerly	22,966	22,787
02891	Westerly (c)	17,682	17,936
02895	Woonsocket	43,224	41,186

South Carolina

ZIP	Place	Area code	2000	2010
*29801	Aiken	(803)	25,337	29,524
*29621	Anderson	(864)	25,514	26,686
*29906	Beaufort	(843)	12,950	12,361
29611	Berea (c)	(864)	14,158	14,295
*29910	Bluffton	(843)	1,275	12,530
29033	Cayce	(803)	12,150	12,528
*29402	Charleston	(843)	96,650	120,083
*29631	Clemson	(864)	11,939	13,905
*29201	Columbia	(803)	116,278	129,272
*29526	Conway	(843)	11,788	17,103
29204	Dentsville (c)	(803)	13,009	14,062
*29640	Easley	(864)	17,754	19,993
29681	Five Forks (c)	(864)	8,064	14,140
*29501	Florence	(843)	30,248	37,056
29206	Forest Acres	(803)	10,558	10,361
*29715	Fort Mill	(803)	7,587	10,811
*29341	Gaffney	(864)	12,968	12,414
29605	Gantt (c)	(864)	13,962	14,229
29445	Goose Creek	(843)	29,208	35,938
*29602	Greenville	(864)	56,002	58,409
*29646	Greenwood	(864)	22,071	23,222
*29650	Greer	(864)	16,843	25,515
*29406	Hanahan	(843)	12,937	17,997
*29928	Hilton Head Island	(843)	33,862	37,099
29063	Irmo	(803)	11,039	11,097
29456	Ladson (c)	(843)	13,264	13,790
*29072	Lexington	(803)	9,793	17,870
29662	Mauldin	(864)	15,224	22,889
*29465	Mount Pleasant	(843)	47,609	67,843
*29575	Myrtle Beach	(843)	22,759	27,109
29108	Newberry	(803)	10,580	10,277
*29841	North Augusta	(803)	17,574	21,348
*29410	North Charleston	(843)	79,641	97,471
*29582	North Myrtle Beach	(843)	10,974	13,752
29073	Oak Grove (c)	(803)	8,183	10,291
*29115	Orangeburg	(803)	12,765	13,964
29611	Parker (c)	(864)	10,760	11,431
29935	Port Royal	(843)	3,950	10,678
29020	Red Hill (c)	(843)	10,509	13,223
*29730	Rock Hill	(803)	49,765	66,154
29417	Saint Andrews (c)	(843)	21,814	20,493
29210	Seven Oaks (c)	(803)	15,755	15,144
*29681	Simpsonville	(864)	14,352	18,238
29577	Socastee (c)	(843)	14,295	19,952

ZIP	Place	Area code	2000	2010
*29306	Spartanburg	(864)	39,673	37,013
*29483	Summerville	(843)	27,752	43,392
*29150	Sumter	(803)	39,643	40,524
29687	Taylors (c)	(864)	20,125	21,617
29607	Wade Hampton (c)	(864)	20,458	20,622
*29169	West Columbia	(803)	13,064	14,988

South Dakota (605)

ZIP	Place		2000	2010
*57401	Aberdeen		24,658	26,091
*57006	Brookings		18,504	22,056
*57350	Huron		11,893	12,592
57301	Mitchell		14,558	15,254
57501	Pierre		13,876	13,646
*57701	Rapid City		59,607	67,956
*57101	Sioux Falls		123,975	153,888
*57783	Spearfish		8,606	10,494
57069	Vermillion		9,765	10,571
57201	Watertown		20,237	21,482
*57078	Yankton		13,528	14,454

Tennessee

ZIP	Place	Area code	2000	2010
38002	Arlington	(901)	2,569	11,517
*37303	Athens	(423)	13,220	13,458
*38184	Bartlett	(901)	40,543	54,613
*37027	Brentwood	(615)	23,445	37,060
*37621	Bristol	(423)	24,821	26,702
38012	Brownsville	(731)	10,748	10,292
*37401	Chattanooga	(423)	155,554	167,674
*37040	Clarksville	(931)	103,455	132,929
*37311	Cleveland	(423)	37,192	41,285
*38017	Collierville	(901)	31,872	43,965
*38401	Columbia	(931)	33,055	34,681
*38501	Cookeville	(931)	23,923	30,435
38555	Crossville	(931)	8,981	10,795
*37055	Dickson	(615)	12,244	14,538
*38024	Dyersburg	(731)	17,452	17,145
37412	East Ridge	(423)	20,640	20,979
*37643	Elizabethton	(423)	13,372	14,176
*37922	Farragut	(865)	17,720	20,676
*37064	Franklin	(615)	41,842	62,487
37066	Gallatin	(615)	23,230	30,278
*38138	Germantown	(901)	37,348	38,844
*37072	Goodlettsville	(615)	13,780	15,921
*37743	Greeneville	(423)	15,198	15,062
*37075	Hendersonville	(615)	40,620	51,372
*38301	Jackson	(731)	59,643	65,211
*37601	Johnson City	(423)	55,469	63,152
*37662	Kingsport	(423)	44,905	48,205
*37950	Knoxville	(865)	173,890	178,874
*37086	La Vergne	(615)	18,687	32,588
38002	Lakeland	(901)	6,862	12,430
38464	Lawrenceburg	(931)	10,796	10,428
*37087	Lebanon	(615)	20,235	26,190
37091	Lewisburg	(931)	10,413	11,100
37355	Manchester	(931)	8,294	10,102
38237	Martin	(731)	10,515	11,473
37801	Maryville	(865)	23,120	27,465
*37110	McMinnville	(931)	12,749	13,605
*38101	Memphis	(901)	650,100	646,889
37343	Middle Valley (c)	(423)	11,854	12,684
*38053	Millington	(901)	10,433	10,176
*37813	Morristown	(423)	24,965	29,137
*37122	Mount Juliet	(615)	12,366	23,671
*37130	Murfreesboro	(615)	68,816	108,755
*37202	Nashville-Davidson	(615)	545,524	601,222
*37830	Oak Ridge	(865)	27,387	29,330
38242	Paris	(731)	9,763	10,156
37148	Portland	(615)	8,458	11,480
37415	Red Bank	(423)	12,418	11,651
*37862	Sevierville	(865)	11,757	14,807
*37160	Shelbyville	(931)	16,105	20,335
37167	Smyrna	(615)	25,569	39,974
*37379	Soddy-Daisy	(423)	11,530	12,714
37174	Spring Hill	(931)	7,715	29,036
37172	Springfield	(615)	14,329	16,440
*37388	Tullahoma	(931)	17,994	18,655
*38261	Union City	(731)	10,876	10,895
37188	White House	(615)	7,220	10,255

Texas

Area codes (281) and (832) overlay area code (713). Area code (430) overlays area code (903). Area code (682) overlays area code (817). Area codes (972) and (469) overlay area code (214).

ZIP	Place	Area code	2000	2010
*79604	Abilene	(325)	115,930	117,063
75001	Addison	(214)	14,166	13,056
78516	Alamo	(956)	14,760	18,353
77039	Aldine (c)	(713)	13,979	15,869
*78332	Alice	(361)	19,010	19,104
*75002	Allen	(214)	43,554	84,246
78574	Alton	(956)	4,384	12,341

ZIP	Place	Area code	2000	2010
*77511	Alvin	(713)	21,413	24,236
*79105	Amarillo	(806)	173,627	190,695
79714	Andrews	(432)	9,652	11,088
*77515	Angleton	(979)	18,130	18,862
*76004	Arlington	(817)	332,969	365,438
77346	Atascocita (c)	(281)	35,757	65,844
*75751	Athens	(903)	11,297	12,710
*78712	Austin	(512)	656,562	790,390
*76020	Azle	(817)	9,600	10,947
75180	Balch Springs	(214)	19,375	23,728
*77414	Bay City	(979)	18,667	17,614
*77520	Baytown	(713)	66,430	71,802
*77707	Beaumont	(409)	113,866	118,296
*76021	Bedford	(817)	47,152	46,979
*78102	Beeville	(361)	13,129	12,863
*77401	Bellaire	(713)	15,642	16,855
76513	Belton	(254)	14,623	18,216
*76126	Benbrook	(817)	20,208	21,234
*79720	Big Spring	(432)	25,233	27,282
*78006	Boerne	(830)	6,178	10,471
75418	Bonham	(903)	9,990	10,127
*79007	Borger	(806)	14,302	13,251
*77833	Brenham	(979)	13,507	15,716
*78520	Brownsville	(956)	139,722	175,023
*76801	Brownwood	(325)	18,813	19,288
78717	Brushy Creek (c)	(903)	15,371	21,764
*77801	Bryan	(979)	65,660	76,201
76354	Burkburnett	(940)	10,927	10,811
*76028	Burleson	(817)	20,976	36,690
*79015	Canyon	(806)	12,875	13,303
78130	Canyon Lake (c)	(830)	16,870	21,262
*75006	Carrollton	(214)	109,576	119,097
*75104	Cedar Hill	(214)	32,093	45,028
*78613	Cedar Park	(512)	26,049	48,937
77530	Channelview (c)	(713)	29,685	38,289
78108	Cibolo	(210)	3,035	15,349
77450	Cinco Ranch (c)	(281)	11,196	18,274
*76031	Cleburne	(817)	26,005	29,337
77015	Cloverleaf (c)	(713)	23,508	22,942
77531	Clute	(979)	10,424	11,211
*77840	College Station	(979)	67,890	93,857
76034	Colleyville	(817)	19,636	22,807
*77301	Conroe	(936)	36,811	56,207
78109	Converse	(210)	11,508	18,198
*75019	Coppell	(214)	35,958	38,659
76522	Copperas Cove	(254)	29,592	32,032
*76205	Corinth	(940)	11,325	19,935
*78469	Corpus Christi	(361)	277,454	305,215
*75110	Corsicana	(903)	24,485	23,770
76036	Crowley	(817)	7,467	12,838
*75221	Dallas	(214)	1,188,580	1,197,816
77536	Deer Park	(713)	28,520	32,010
*78840	Del Rio	(830)	33,867	35,591
*75020	Denison	(903)	22,773	22,682
*76201	Denton	(940)	80,537	113,383
*75115	DeSoto	(214)	37,646	49,047
77539	Dickinson	(281)	17,093	18,680
78537	Donna	(956)	14,768	15,798
79029	Dumas	(806)	13,747	14,691
*75138	Duncanville	(214)	36,081	38,524
*78852	Eagle Pass	(830)	22,413	26,248
*78539	Edinburg	(956)	48,465	77,100
77437	El Campo	(979)	10,945	11,602
*79910	El Paso	(915)	563,662	649,121
*75119	Ennis	(214)	16,045	18,513
*76039	Euless	(817)	46,005	51,277
*75381	Farmers Branch	(214)	27,508	28,616
*75022	Flower Mound	(214)	50,702	64,669
76119	Forest Hill	(817)	12,949	12,355
75126	Forney	(214)	5,588	14,661
76544	Fort Hood (c)	(254)	33,711	29,589
*76161	Fort Worth	(817)	534,694	741,206
77498	Four Corners (c)	(281)	2,954	12,382
78624	Fredericksburg	(830)	8,911	10,530
*77541	Freeport	(979)	12,708	12,049
77545	Fresno (c)	(281)	6,603	19,069
*77546	Friendswood	(281)	29,037	35,805
*75034	Frisco	(214)	33,714	116,989
*76240	Gainesville	(940)	15,538	16,002
77547	Galena Park	(713)	10,592	10,887
*77550	Galveston	(409)	57,247	47,743
*75040	Garland	(214)	215,768	226,876
*76528	Gatesville	(254)	15,591	15,751
*76626	Georgetown	(512)	28,339	47,400
75154	Glenn Heights	(214)	7,224	11,278
*75051	Grand Prairie	(214)	127,427	175,396
*76051	Grapevine	(817)	42,059	46,334
77479	Greatwood (c)	(281)	6,640	11,538
*75401	Greenville	(903)	23,960	25,557
77619	Groves	(409)	15,733	16,144
*76117	Haltom City	(817)	39,018	42,409
*76548	Harker Heights	(254)	17,308	26,700
*78550	Harlingen	(956)	57,564	64,849
*75652	Henderson	(903)	11,273	13,712

ZIP	Place	Area code	2000	2010
79045	Hereford	(806)	14,597	15,370
76643	Hewitt	(254)	11,085	13,549
78557	Hidalgo	(956)	7,322	11,198
75067	Highland Village	(214)	12,173	15,056
*79927	Horizon City	(915)	5,233	16,735
*77052	Houston	(713)	1,953,631	2,099,451
*77338	Humble	(713)	14,579	15,133
*77340	Huntsville	(936)	35,078	38,548
*76053	Hurst	(817)	36,273	37,337
78634	Hutto	(512)	1,250	14,698
*75015	Irving	(214)	191,615	216,290
77029	Jacinto City	(281)	10,320	10,553
75766	Jacksonville	(903)	13,868	14,544
78729	Jollyville (c)	(512)	15,813	16,151
*77449	Katy	(713)	11,775	14,102
*76248	Keller	(817)	27,345	39,627
*78028	Kerrville	(830)	20,425	22,347
*75662	Kilgore	(903)	11,301	12,975
*76540	Killeen	(254)	86,911	127,921
*78363	Kingsville	(361)	25,575	26,213
78640	Kyle	(512)	5,314	28,016
78572	La Homa (c)	(956)	10,433	11,985
77568	La Marque	(409)	13,682	14,509
*77571	La Porte	(713)	31,880	33,800
77566	Lake Jackson	(979)	26,386	26,849
78734	Lakeway	(512)	8,002	11,391
*75146	Lancaster	(214)	25,894	36,361
*78401	Laredo	(956)	176,576	236,091
*77573	League City	(281)	45,444	83,560
*78641	Leander	(512)	7,596	26,521
*78268	Leon Valley	(210)	9,239	10,151
*79336	Levelland	(806)	12,866	13,542
*75067	Lewisville	(214)	77,737	95,290
75068	Little Elm	(214)	3,646	25,898
*78233	Live Oak	(210)	9,156	13,131
78644	Lockhart	(512)	11,615	12,698
*75606	Longview	(903)	73,344	80,455
*79408	Lubbock	(806)	199,564	229,573
*75901	Lufkin	(936)	32,709	35,067
77657	Lumberton	(409)	8,731	11,943
76063	Mansfield	(817)	28,031	56,368
*75670	Marshall	(903)	23,935	23,523
*78501	McAllen	(956)	106,414	129,877
*75070	McKinney	(214)	54,369	131,117
78570	Mercedes	(956)	13,649	15,570
*75149	Mesquite	(214)	124,523	139,824
*79701	Midland	(432)	94,996	111,147
76065	Midlothian	(214)	7,480	18,037
*76067	Mineral Wells	(940)	16,946	16,788
*78572	Mission	(956)	45,408	77,058
77083	Mission Bend (c)	(713)	30,831	36,501
*77489	Missouri City	(713)	52,913	67,358
*75455	Mount Pleasant	(903)	13,935	15,564
*75094	Murphy	(214)	3,099	17,708
*75961	Nacogdoches	(936)	29,914	32,996
77627	Nederland	(409)	17,422	17,547
*78130	New Braunfels	(830)	36,494	57,740
77479	New Territory (c)	(281)	13,861	15,186
*76161	North Richland Hills	(817)	55,635	63,343
*79761	Odessa	(432)	90,943	99,940
*77630	Orange	(409)	18,643	18,595
*75801	Palestine	(903)	17,598	18,712
*79065	Pampa	(806)	17,887	17,994
*75460	Paris	(903)	25,898	25,171
*77501	Pasadena	(713)	141,674	149,043
*77581	Pearland	(713)	37,640	91,252
78721	Pecan Grove (c)	(254)	13,551	15,963
*78660	Pflugerville	(512)	16,335	46,936
78577	Pharr	(956)	46,660	70,400
*79072	Plainview	(806)	22,336	22,194
*75074	Plano	(214)	222,030	259,841
*77640	Port Arthur	(409)	57,755	53,818
77979	Port Lavaca	(361)	12,035	12,248
77651	Port Neches	(409)	13,601	13,040
78374	Portland	(361)	14,827	15,099
*78580	Raymondville	(965)	9,733	11,284
*75154	Red Oak	(972)	4,301	10,769
76140	Rendon (c)	(817)	9,022	12,552
*75080	Richardson	(214)	91,802	99,223
*77469	Richmond	(713)	11,081	11,679
78582	Rio Grande City	(956)	11,923	13,834
76701	Robinson	(254)	7,845	10,509
78380	Robstown	(361)	12,727	11,487
*75087	Rockwall	(214)	17,976	37,490
77471	Rosenberg	(713)	24,043	30,618
*78681	Round Rock	(512)	61,136	99,887
*75088	Rowlett	(214)	44,503	56,199
75048	Sachse	(214)	9,751	20,329
*76179	Saginaw	(817)	12,374	19,806
*76902	San Angelo	(325)	88,439	93,200
*78265	San Antonio	(210)	1,144,646	1,327,407
78586	San Benito	(956)	23,444	24,250
79849	San Elizario (c)	(915)	11,046	13,603
78589	San Juan	(956)	26,229	33,856

ZIP	Place	Area code	2000	2010
*78666	San Marcos	(512)	34,733	44,894
*77510	Santa Fe	(409)	9,548	12,222
*78154	Schertz	(210)	18,694	31,465
77586	Seabrook	(281)	9,443	11,952
75159	Seagoville	(214)	10,823	14,835
*78155	Seguin	(830)	22,011	25,175
*75090	Sherman	(903)	35,082	38,251
77459	Sienna Plantation (c)	(281)	1,896	13,721
*79549	Snyder	(325)	10,783	11,202
79927	Socorro	(915)	27,152	32,013
77587	South Houston	(713)	15,833	16,983
76092	Southlake	(817)	21,519	26,575
*77373	Spring (c)	(713)	36,385	54,298
*77477	Stafford	(713)	15,681	17,693
*76401	Stephenville	(254)	14,921	17,123
*77478	Sugar Land	(713)	63,328	78,817
*75482	Sulphur Springs	(903)	14,551	15,449
79556	Sweetwater	(325)	11,415	10,906
76574	Taylor	(512)	13,575	15,191
*76501	Temple	(254)	54,514	66,102
*75160	Terrell	(214)	13,606	15,816
*75501	Texarkana	(903)	34,782	36,411
*77590	Texas City	(409)	41,521	45,099
*75056	The Colony	(214)	26,531	36,328
77387	The Woodlands (c)	(713)	55,649	93,847
78260	Timberwood Park (c)	(830)	5,889	13,447
*77375	Tomball	(713)	9,089	10,753
*75702	Tyler	(903)	83,650	96,900
*78148	Universal City	(830)	14,849	18,530
75205	University Park	(214)	23,324	23,068
*78801	Uvalde	(830)	14,929	15,751
*76384	Vernon	(940)	11,660	11,002
*77901	Victoria	(361)	60,603	62,592
*77662	Vidor	(409)	11,440	10,579
*76702	Waco	(254)	113,726	124,805
76148	Watauga	(817)	21,908	23,497
*75165	Waxahachie	(214)	21,426	29,621
*76086	Weatherford	(817)	19,000	25,250
77598	Webster	(281)	9,083	10,400
78728	Wells Branch (c)	(512)	11,271	12,120
*78596	Weslaco	(956)	26,935	35,670
79764	West Odessa (c)	(432)	17,799	22,707
77005	West University Place	(713)	14,211	14,757
76108	White Settlement	(817)	14,831	16,116
*76307	Wichita Falls	(940)	104,197	104,553
75098	Wylie	(214)	15,132	104,553

Utah

Area code (385) overlays area code (801).

ZIP	Place	Area code	2000	2010
84003	American Fork	(801)	21,941	26,263
*84010	Bountiful	(801)	41,301	42,552
84302	Brigham City	(435)	17,411	17,899
*84720	Cedar City	(435)	20,527	28,857
84014	Centerville	(801)	14,585	15,335
*84015	Clearfield	(801)	25,974	30,112
84015	Clinton	(801)	12,585	20,246
84121	Cottonwood Heights	(801)	—	33,433
84020	Draper	(801)	25,220	42,274
84043	Eagle Mountain	(801)	2,157	21,415
84025	Farmington	(801)	12,081	18,275
*84032	Heber City	(435)	7,291	11,362
84065	Herriman	(801)	1,523	21,785
84003	Highland	(801)	8,172	15,523
*84117	Holladay	(801)	14,561	26,472
84737	Hurricane	(435)	8,250	13,748
84037	Kaysville	(801)	20,351	27,300
84118	Kearns (c)	(801)	33,659	35,731
84041	Layton	(801)	58,474	67,311
84043	Lehi	(801)	19,028	47,407
84042	Lindon	(801)	8,363	10,070
*84321	Logan	(435)	42,670	48,174
84044	Magna (c)	(801)	22,770	26,505
84047	Midvale	(801)	27,029	27,964
*84109	Millcreek (c)	(801)	30,377	62,139
*84157	Murray	(801)	34,024	46,746
*84404	North Ogden	(801)	15,026	17,357
84054	North Salt Lake	(801)	8,749	16,322
*84401	Ogden	(801)	77,226	82,825
*84057	Orem	(801)	84,324	88,328
*84651	Payson	(801)	12,716	18,294
84062	Pleasant Grove	(801)	23,468	33,509
*84601	Provo	(801)	105,166	112,488
84065	Riverton	(801)	25,011	38,753
*84067	Roy	(801)	32,885	36,884
*84770	Saint George	(435)	49,663	72,897
*84101	Salt Lake City	(801)	181,743	186,440
84070	Sandy	(801)	88,418	87,461
84043	Saratoga Springs	(801)	1,003	17,781
84095	South Jordan	(801)	29,437	50,418
84403	South Ogden	(801)	14,377	16,532
84165	South Salt Lake	(801)	22,038	23,617
84660	Spanish Fork	(801)	20,246	34,691
84663	Springville	(801)	20,424	29,466

ZIP	Place	Area code	2000	2010
84075	Syracuse	(801)	9,398	24,331
84118	Taylorsville	(801)	57,439	58,652
84074	Tooele	(435)	22,502	31,605
84780	Washington	(435)	8,186	18,761
84401	West Haven	(801)	3,976	10,272
*84084	West Jordan	(801)	68,336	109,712
*84170	West Valley City	(801)	108,896	129,480

Vermont (802)
See introductory note.

ZIP	Place	2000	2010
05201	Bennington	15,737	15,764
*05301	Brattleboro	12,005	12,046
*05401	Burlington	38,889	42,417
*05446	Colchester	16,986	17,067
*05451	Essex	18,626	19,587
05468	Milton	9,479	10,352
*05701	Rutland	17,292	16,495
*05403	South Burlington	15,814	17,904

Virginia
Area code (571) overlays area code (703).

ZIP	Place	Area code	2000	2010
*22313	Alexandria	(703)	128,283	139,966
22003	Annandale (c)	(703)	54,994	41,008
*22210	Arlington (c)	(703)	189,453	207,627
22041	Bailey's Crossroads (c)	(703)	23,166	23,643
*24060	Blacksburg	(540)	39,573	42,620
23235	Bon Air (c)	(804)	16,213	16,366
23112	Brandermill (c)	(804)	—	13,173
*24203	Bristol	(276)	17,367	17,835
20148	Broadlands (c)	(703)	—	12,313
20111	Buckhall (c)	(703)	—	16,293
20109	Bull Run (c)	(703)	11,337	14,983
*22015	Burke (c)	(703)	57,737	41,055
22015	Burke Centre (c)	(703)	—	17,326
24069	Cascades (c)	(434)	—	11,912
24018	Cave Spring (c)	(540)	24,941	24,922
*20120	Centreville (c)	(703)	48,661	71,135
*20151	Chantilly (c)	(703)	41,041	23,039
*22906	Charlottesville	(434)	45,049	43,475
22026	Cherry Hill (c)	(703)	—	16,000
*23320	Chesapeake	(757)	199,184	222,209
*23831	Chester (c)	(804)	17,890	20,987
*24073	Christiansburg	(540)	16,947	21,041
23834	Colonial Heights	(804)	16,897	17,411
20165	Countryside (c)	(703)	—	10,072
*22701	Culpeper	(540)	9,664	16,379
22193	Dale City (c)	(703)	55,971	65,969
*24541	Danville	(434)	48,411	43,055
20170	Dranesville (c)	(703)	—	11,921
23222	East Highland Park (c)	(804)	12,488	14,796
*22030	Fairfax	(703)	21,498	22,565
22039	Fairfax Station (c)	(703)	—	12,030
22033	Fair Oaks (c)	(703)	—	30,223
*22046	Falls Church (c)	(703)	10,377	12,332
22308	Fort Hunt (c)	(703)	12,923	16,045
22310	Franconia (c)	(703)	31,907	18,245
20171	Franklin Farm (c)	(703)	—	19,288
*22404	Fredericksburg	(540)	19,279	24,286
22630	Front Royal	(540)	13,589	14,440
*20155	Gainesville (c)	(703)	4,382	11,481
*23060	Glen Allen (c)	(804)	12,562	14,774
22066	Great Falls (c)	(703)	8,549	15,427
22306	Groveton (c)	(703)	21,296	14,598
*23670	Hampton	(757)	146,437	137,436
*22801	Harrisonburg	(540)	40,468	48,914
*20170	Herndon	(703)	21,655	23,292
23075	Highland Springs (c)	(804)	15,137	15,711
24019	Hollins (c)	(540)	14,309	14,673
23860	Hopewell	(804)	22,354	22,591
22303	Huntington (c)	(703)	8,325	11,267
22306	Hybla Valley (c)	(703)	16,721	15,801
22043	Idylwood (c)	(703)	16,005	17,288
22038	Kings Park West (c)	(703)	—	13,390
22315	Kingstowne (c)	(703)	—	15,556
22191	Lake Ridge (c)	(540)	30,404	41,058
23228	Lakeside (c)	(804)	11,157	11,849
20176	Lansdowne (c)	(703)	—	11,253
23060	Laurel (c)	(804)	14,875	16,713
*20175	Leesburg	(703)	28,311	42,616
22312	Lincolnia (c)	(703)	15,788	22,855
20136	Linton Hall (c)	(703)	8,620	35,725
*22079	Lorton (c)	(703)	17,786	18,610
20165	Lowes Island (c)	(703)	—	10,756
*24506	Lynchburg	(434)	65,269	75,568
24572	Madison Heights (c)	(434)	11,584	11,285
*20110	Manassas	(703)	35,135	37,821
20113	Manassas Park	(703)	10,290	14,273
23235	Manchester (c)	(804)	—	10,804
*24112	Martinsville	(276)	15,416	13,821
22191	Marumsco (c)	(703)	—	35,036
*22101	McLean (c)	(703)	38,929	48,115
20171	McNair (c)	(703)	—	17,513

ZIP	Place	Area code	2000	2010
23234	Meadowbrook (c)	(804)	—	18,312
*23111	Mechanicsville (c)	(804)	30,464	36,348
*22116	Merrifield (c)	(703)	11,170	15,212
22026	Montclair (c)	(703)	15,728	19,570
22121	Mount Vernon (c)	(703)	28,582	12,416
22191	Neabsco (c)	(703)	—	12,068
22122	Newington (c)	(703)	19,784	12,943
22153	Newington Forest (c)	(703)	—	12,442
*23607	Newport News	(757)	180,150	180,719
*23501	Norfolk	(757)	234,403	242,803
22124	Oakton (c)	(703)	29,348	34,166
*23804	Petersburg	(804)	33,740	32,420
23662	Poquoson	(757)	11,566	12,150
*23707	Portsmouth	(757)	100,565	95,535
*24141	Radford	(540)	15,859	16,408
*20190	Reston (c)	(703)	56,407	58,404
*23232	Richmond	(804)	197,790	204,214
*24022	Roanoke	(540)	94,911	97,032
24281	Rose Hill (c) (Fairfax Co.)	(276)	15,058	20,226
*24153	Salem	(540)	24,747	24,802
23233	Short Pump (c)	(804)	182	24,729
20152	South Riding (c)	(703)	—	24,256
*22150	Springfield (c)	(703)	30,417	30,484
*24402	Staunton	(540)	23,853	23,746
*20164	Sterling (c)	(703)	—	27,822
20109	Sudley (c)	(703)	7,719	16,203
*23434	Suffolk	(757)	63,677	84,585
20164	Sugarland Run (c)	(703)	—	11,799
24502	Timberlake (c)	(434)	10,683	12,183
23229	Tuckahoe (c)	(804)	43,242	44,990
22101	Tysons Corner (c)	(703)	18,540	19,627
*22180	Vienna (c)	(703)	14,453	15,687
*23450	Virginia Beach	(757)	425,257	437,994
23888	Wakefield (c)	(757)	1,038	11,275
22980	Waynesboro	(540)	19,520	21,006
22042	West Falls Church (c)	(703)	—	29,207
22152	West Springfield (c)	(703)	28,378	22,460
*23185	Williamsburg	(757)	11,998	14,068
*22601	Winchester	(540)	23,585	26,203
24592	Wolf Trap (c)	(703)	14,001	16,131
24381	Woodlawn (c) (Fairfax Co.)	(276)	—	20,804

Washington

ZIP	Place	Area code	2000	2010
98520	Aberdeen	(360)	16,461	16,896
*98221	Anacortes	(360)	14,557	15,778
98223	Arlington	(360)	11,713	17,926
98335	Artondale (c)	(253)	8,630	12,653
*98002	Auburn	(253)	40,314	70,180
98110	Bainbridge Island	(206)	20,308	23,025
98604	Battle Ground	(360)	9,296	17,571
*98009	Bellevue	(425)	109,569	122,363
98225	Bellingham	(360)	67,171	80,885
*98390	Bonney Lake	(253)	9,687	17,374
98011	Bothell	(425)	30,150	33,505
98036	Bothell West (c)	(425)	—	16,607
*98337	Bremerton	(360)	37,259	37,729
98178	Bryn Mawr-Skyway (c)	(206)	13,977	15,645
98166	Burien (c)	(206)	31,881	33,313
98607	Camas	(360)	12,534	19,355
98531	Centralia	(360)	14,742	16,336
99004	Cheney	(509)	8,832	10,590
98072	Cottage Lake (c)	(206)	24,330	22,494
98042	Covington (c)	(253)	13,783	17,575
*98198	Des Moines	(206)	29,267	29,673
98031	East Hill-Meridian (c)	(253)/(425)	29,308	29,878
98056	East Renton Highlands (c)	(425)	13,264	11,140
98802	East Wenatchee	(509)	5,757	13,190
98204	Eastmont (c)	(425)	—	20,101
*98020	Edmonds	(425)	39,515	39,709
98387	Elk Plain (c)	(253)	15,697	14,205
*98926	Ellensburg	(509)	15,414	18,174
98022	Enumclaw (c)	(360)	11,116	10,669
*98201	Everett	(425)	91,488	103,019
98058	Fairwood (c) (King Co.)	(253)/(425)	—	19,102
*98002	Federal Way	(253)	83,259	89,306
98248	Ferndale	(360)	8,758	11,415
98597	Five Corners (c)	(360)	12,207	18,159
98433	Fort Lewis (c)	(253)	19,089	11,046
98375	Frederickson (c)	(253)	5,758	18,719
98338	Graham (c)	(253)	8,739	23,491
98930	Grandview	(509)	8,377	10,862
98665	Hazel Dell (c)	(360)	—	19,435
98011	Inglewood-Finn Hill (c)	(425)	22,661	22,707
*98027	Issaquah (c)	(425)	11,212	30,434
98626	Kelso	(360)	11,895	11,925
98028	Kenmore (c)	(425)	18,678	20,460
*99336	Kennewick	(509)	54,693	73,917
*98031	Kent	(253)/(425)	79,524	92,411
98033	Kingsgate (c)	(425)	12,222	13,065
*98033	Kirkland	(425)	45,054	48,787
98029	Klahanie (c)	(425)	—	10,674
*98509	Lacey	(360)	31,226	42,393
98155	Lake Forest Park	(206)	13,142	12,598
98042	Lake Morton-Berrydale (c)	(253)/(425)	9,659	10,160

ZIP	Place	Area code	2000	2010
98258	Lake Stevens	(425)	6,361	28,069
98391	Lake Tapps (c)	(253)	—	11,859
98002	Lakeland North (c)	(253)	15,085	12,942
98002	Lakeland South (c)	(253)	11,436	11,574
*98498	Lakewood	(253)	58,211	58,163
98632	Longview	(360)	34,660	36,648
98264	Lynden	(360)	9,020	11,951
*98046	Lynnwood	(425)	33,847	35,836
98290	Maltby (c)	(360)/(425)	8,267	10,830
98038	Maple Valley	(425)	14,209	22,684
98012	Martha Lake (c)	(425)	12,633	15,473
*98270	Marysville	(360)	25,315	60,020
98040	Mercer Island	(206)	22,036	22,699
*98082	Mill Creek	(425)	11,525	18,244
98012	Mill Creek East (c)	(425)	—	15,709
*98272	Monroe	(360)	13,795	20,366
98837	Moses Lake	(509)	14,953	20,366
*98273	Mount Vernon	(360)	26,232	31,743
98043	Mountlake Terrace	(425)	20,362	19,909
98275	Mukilteo	(425)	18,019	20,254
*98059	Newcastle	(425)	7,737	10,380
98037	North Lynnwood (c)	(425)	—	16,574
*98277	Oak Harbor	(360)	19,795	22,075
*98501	Olympia	(360)	42,514	46,478
98662	Orchards (c)	(360)	17,852	19,556
98444	Parkland (c)	(253)	24,053	35,803
*99301	Pasco	(509)	32,066	59,781
*98362	Port Angeles	(360)	18,397	19,038
*98366	Port Orchard	(360)	7,693	11,144
98390	Prairie Ridge (c)	(360)	11,688	11,464
*99163	Pullman	(509)	24,675	29,799
*98371	Puyallup	(253)	33,011	37,022
*98052	Redmond	(425)	45,256	54,144
98058	Renton	(425)	50,052	90,927
*99352	Richland	(509)	38,708	48,058
98686	Salmon Creek (c)	(360)	16,767	19,686
*98074	Sammamish	(425)	34,104	45,780
*98148	SeaTac	(206)	25,496	26,909
*98101	Seattle	(206)/(425)	563,374	608,660
98284	Sedro-Woolley	(360)	8,658	10,540
*98133	Shoreline	(206)	53,025	53,007
98208	Silver Firs (c).	(206)/(425)	—	20,891
*98315	Silverdale (c).	(360)	15,816	19,204
*98065	Snoqualmie	(425)	1,613	10,670
98373	South Hill (c)	(253)	31,623	52,431
98387	Spanaway (c)	(253)	21,588	27,227
*99210	Spokane	(509)	195,629	208,916
*99211	Spokane Valley	(509)	—	89,755
98944	Sunnyside	(509)	13,905	15,858
*98402	Tacoma	(253)	193,556	198,397
*98138	Tukwila	(206)	17,181	19,107
*98501	Tumwater	(360)	12,698	17,371
98053	Union Hill-Novelty Hill (c)	(425)	11,265	18,805
98467	University Place	(253)	29,933	31,144
*98661	Vancouver	(360)	143,560	161,791
*98013	Vashon (c)	(206)	10,123	10,624
99362	Walla Walla	(509)	29,686	31,731
98671	Washougal	(360)	8,595	14,095
*98801	Wenatchee	(509)	27,856	31,925
*99353	West Richland	(509)	8,385	11,811
98166	White Center (c)	(206)	20,975	13,495
*98072	Woodinville	(425)	9,194	10,938
*98903	Yakima	(509)	71,845	91,067

West Virginia (304)

Area code (681) overlays area code (304).

ZIP	Place	2000	2010
*25801	Beckley	17,254	17,614
24701	Bluefield	11,451	10,447
*25301	Charleston	53,421	51,400
*26301	Clarksburg	16,743	16,578
*26554	Fairmont	19,097	18,704
*25704	Huntington	51,475	49,138
*25401	Martinsburg	14,972	17,227
*26505	Morgantown	26,809	29,660
*26101	Parkersburg	33,099	31,492
25177	Saint Albans	11,567	11,044
*25303	South Charleston	13,390	13,450
25569	Teays Valley (c)	12,704	13,175
*26105	Vienna	10,861	10,749
26062	Weirton	20,411	19,746
26003	Wheeling	31,419	28,486

Wisconsin

Area code (534) overlays area code (715).

ZIP	Place	Area code	2000	2010
54301	Allouez	(920)	15,443	13,975
*54911	Appleton	(920)	70,087	72,623
*54304	Ashwaubenon	(920)	17,634	16,963
53913	Baraboo	(608)	10,711	12,048
53916	Beaver Dam	(920)	15,169	16,214
54311	Bellevue	(920)	—	14,570

ZIP	Place	Area code	2000	2010
*53511	Beloit	(608)	35,775	36,966
*53045	Brookfield	(262)	38,649	37,920
*53209	Brown Deer	(414)	12,170	11,999
53105	Burlington	(262)	9,936	10,464
53108	Caledonia	(262)	—	24,705
53012	Cedarburg	(262)	10,908	11,412
*54729	Chippewa Falls	(715)	12,925	13,661
53110	Cudahy	(414)	18,429	18,267
54115	De Pere	(920)	20,559	23,800
*54703	Eau Claire	(715)	61,704	65,883
53121	Elkhorn	(262)	7,305	10,084
*53711	Fitchburg	(608)	20,501	25,260
*54935	Fond du Lac	(920)	42,203	43,021
53538	Fort Atkinson	(920)	11,621	12,368
53132	Franklin	(414)	29,494	35,451
53022	Germantown	(262)	18,260	19,749
*53209	Glendale	(414)	13,367	12,872
53024	Grafton	(262)	10,312	11,459
*54303	Green Bay	(920)	102,313	104,057
53129	Greendale	(414)	14,405	14,046
*53220	Greenfield	(414)	35,476	36,720
53027	Hartford	(262)	10,905	14,223
*54303	Howard	(920)	13,546	17,399
*54016	Hudson	(715)	8,775	12,719
*53545	Janesville	(608)	59,498	63,575
54130	Kaukauna	(920)	12,983	15,462
*53140	Kenosha	(262)	90,352	99,218
*54601	La Crosse	(608)	51,818	51,320
53089	Lisbon (Waukesha Co.)	(262)	9,359	10,157
54140	Little Chute	(920)	10,476	10,449
*53714	Madison	(608)	208,054	233,209
*54220	Manitowoc	(920)	34,053	33,736
54143	Marinette	(715)	11,749	10,968
*54449	Marshfield	(715)	18,800	19,118
54952	Menasha	(920)	16,331	17,353
*53051	Menomonee Falls	(262)	32,647	35,626
54751	Menomonie	(715)	14,937	16,264
*53097	Mequon	(262)	21,823	23,132
53562	Middleton	(608)	15,770	17,442
*53201	Milwaukee	(414)	596,974	594,833
53566	Monroe	(608)	10,843	10,827
53406	Mount Pleasant	(262)	—	26,197
53150	Muskego	(414)	21,397	24,135
*54956	Neenah	(920)	24,507	25,501
*53186	New Berlin	(262)	38,220	39,584
53154	Oak Creek	(414)	28,456	34,451
53066	Oconomowoc	(262)	12,382	15,759
54650	Onalaska	(608)	14,839	17,736
*54901	Oshkosh	(920)	62,916	66,083
53072	Pewaukee (city)	(262)	11,783	13,195
53818	Platteville	(608)	9,989	11,224
*53158	Pleasant Prairie	(262)	16,136	19,719
54467	Plover	(715)	10,520	12,123
53074	Port Washington	(262)	10,467	11,250
53901	Portage	(608)	9,728	10,324
*53401	Racine	(262)	81,855	78,860
*53076	Richfield	(262)	—	11,300
54022	River Falls	(715)	12,560	15,000
*53081	Sheboygan	(920)	50,792	49,288
53211	Shorewood	(414)	13,763	13,162
53172	South Milwaukee	(414)	21,256	21,156
*54481	Stevens Point	(715)	24,551	26,717
53589	Stoughton	(608)	12,354	12,611
*54173	Suamico	(920)	—	11,346
*53590	Sun Prairie	(608)	20,369	29,364
54880	Superior	(715)	27,368	27,244
53089	Sussex	(262)	8,828	10,518
*54241	Two Rivers	(920)	12,639	11,712
53593	Verona	(608)	7,052	10,619
*53094	Watertown	(920)	21,598	23,861
*53186	Waukesha	(262)	64,825	70,718
53597	Waunakee	(608)	8,995	12,097
53963	Waupun	(920)	10,718	11,340
*54403	Wausau	(715)	38,426	39,106
*53213	Wauwatosa	(414)	47,271	46,396
*53214	West Allis	(414)	61,254	60,411
*53095	West Bend	(262)	28,152	31,078
*54476	Weston	(715)	12,079	14,868
*53217	Whitefish Bay	(414)	14,163	14,110
53190	Whitewater	(262)	13,437	14,390
*54494	Wisconsin Rapids	(715)	18,435	18,367

Wyoming (307)

ZIP	Place	2000	2010
*82609	Casper	49,644	55,316
*82009	Cheyenne	53,011	59,466
*82930	Evanston	11,507	12,359
*82716	Gillette	19,646	29,087
*82935	Green River	11,808	12,515
*82072	Laramie	27,204	30,816
82501	Riverton	9,310	10,615
*82901	Rock Springs	18,708	23,036
82801	Sheridan	15,804	17,444

WORLD HISTORY

Chronology of World History

Note: In this section, the notation BCE (before the common era) is applied to years dating to the traditional BC (before Christ) era, and CE (common era) is applied to AD (anno domini) dates. This notation is now preferred in scientific and academic publications. The traditional Gregorian Calendar system and its dates and years are unaltered except by these labels.

Other abbreviations used in this chapter include the following: KYA = thousand years ago, MYA = million years ago, BP = years before the present, c. = circa, fl. = flourished, r. = ruled, b. = born, d. = died.

Prehistory: Our Ancestors Emerge

Reviewed by G. A. Clark, Ph.D., Sept. 2008

Evidence of the origins of *Homo sapiens sapiens*, the genus, species and subspecies to which all living humans belong, comes from a small, but increasing, number of fossils, from genetic and anatomical studies, and from interpretation of the geological and archaeological records. The latest evidence suggests that humans evolved from apelike primate ancestors that lived in eastern and central Africa 7-5 million years ago (MYA). Although all humans living today are members of a single species, the fossil record confirms that our ancestors coexisted with a number of similar species throughout our evolutionary history. Current theories trace the first hominin[1] (upright, bipedal, humanlike primate) to Africa, where several distinct genera appeared 6-4 MYA. They lived in a variety of environments throughout most of the continent, including swampy forest margins, woodlands, and open savannas (usually near lakes or springs). In addition to *Australopithecus afarensis*—better known as "Lucy," a 3.2 MYA Ethiopian specimen found in 1974—these earliest hominins include such recent discoveries as *Sahelanthropus* (c. 6.5 MYA, from Chad), *Ardipithecus* (c. 5 MYA, Kenya), *Kenyanthropus* (c. 3.5 MYA, Kenya), and *Orrorin* (c. 5 MYA, Kenya). Later, between 4 and 3 MYA, these earliest hominins gave rise to at least two groups of savanna/lake-edge adapted "man-apes." Called australopithecines, they are divided into "gracile" and "robust" lineages, both containing a number of species. The robust australopithecines were characterized by enormous molar and premolar teeth; they probably went extinct around 1 MYA, or slightly thereafter. Although it is uncertain from which australopithecine species humans descended, the most likely species are usually assigned to the gracile lineage.

Our genus, *Homo*, arose 3-2 MYA, when hominins began to produce primitive stone tools. The oldest tools are dated to c. 2.5 MYA from the Kada Gona site, in Ethiopia, and were used for scraping and cutting meat, sinew, and wood. It is not known whether these early hominins had the ability to speak, but they were social animals, lived in groups of 12-20 individuals, aggregated and dispersed seasonally, had campsites, and subsisted by gathering plants and small animals and by scavenging other kills. A closer ancestor, *Homo ergaster*, appeared in E Africa around 1.9 MYA and was the first to leave the continent, spreading throughout Eurasia by c. 1.8 MYA. *H. ergaster* is sometimes grouped with *H. erectus*, a species first identified in the 1890s on the island of Java. It was capable of hunting large and medium-sized hoofed animals, such as antelopes and horses, learned to make and control fire—by c. 500 thousand years ago (KYA) in Europe, possibly earlier in Africa—and almost certainly had primitive language skills.

After about 350 KYA, Europe provides a particularly rich set of fossil evidence usually assigned to *H. erectus*. By a near-universal consensus, this species gave rise to the Neanderthals, who appeared c. 200 KYA. Neanderthals were human-like in most respects: they could speak, were proficient hunters of large game, had sophisticated tools and weapons and a developed social organization, and were well adapted to the harsh climates of Ice Age Europe. Recent advances in molecular biology support the theory that Neanderthals were a distinct population or species that in some places coexisted, but evidently did not interbreed with early modern humans (also called Crô-Magnons). *H. antecessor*, a new species (c. 870 KYA) identified at the Trinchera Dolina site in north-central Spain, might help clarify the relationship between the earliest representatives of *Homo* in western Europe, and the Neanderthals. A similar situation may have occurred in E Asia, where more primitive *Homo* species coexisted with early modern humans after c. 40 KYA, and possibly as recently as 18 KYA, on the island of Flores, in Indonesia.

Since 2004, excavations at Liang Bua cave on Flores have recovered the remains of 12-15 tiny hominins dated between c. 95-18 KYA. Popularly called "hobbits" because of their diminutive stature (3.5 ft. tall at adulthood) and large, broad feet, they had brains averaging less than one-third the size of even the smallest modern human brains, yet were accompanied by thousands of stone artifacts, evidence for the hunting of stegodons (dwarfed elephants), and clear signs of fire. Dubbed *H. floresiensis*, they probably represent a normal-sized *H. erectus* population that colonized Flores some 800 KYA and subsequently became dwarfed because of limited habitat. One probable implication is that the cognitive capacities of Middle Pleistocene hominins have been seriously underestimated.

Genetic evidence indicates that the first *Homo sapiens* originated in E Africa between 200 and 100 KYA. The oldest modern human fossils are dated to c. 160 KYA and were found at the Herto site in Ethiopia's Middle Awash valley. The species quickly spread, displacing, extinguishing, out-competing, and/or genetically "swamping" the archaic humans it encountered. Modern humans were living in Israel by c. 100 KYA, and in Romania by c. 35 KYA. Migration from Asia to Australia took place as early as 60 KYA. First confirmation for the crossing from Asia to the Americas by the Bering land bridge dates to the end of the last Ice Age, at 14 KYA. However, genetic data suggests that small, isolated groups of hunter-gatherers arrived in the Americas up to 4,000 years earlier, settling in both continents. Their arrival was rapidly followed by the extinction of the indigenous Pleistocene megafauna (e.g., mammoths, mastodonts), due either to overexploitation by humans, an extraterrestrial impact c. 12,900 years ago, or a combination of both.

As human cognitive capacities slowly expanded over the Pleistocene (1.7-0.01 MYA), a variety of behavioral modes—in toolmaking, diet, shelter, social arrangements, and spiritual expression—arose as humans adapted to different geographic and climatic zones. By about 13,000 years ago, sites from all over the world show seasonal migration patterns and efficient exploitation of a wide range of plant and animal foods, some of which were eventually domesticated.

The ability to make fire at will enormously expanded the human food niche. Fire-making possibly began as early as 1 MYA in Africa and is clearly documented throughout Eurasia after c. 500 KYA. Hearths were found in northern Israel by c. 750 KYA, and by 465 KYA in southwestern France. Fire-hardened wooden throwing spears c. 3 m long were fashioned by big-game hunters 400 KYA at the Schoeningen lignite mine in Germany. Scraping tools, dated after 750 KYA in Europe, N Africa, the Middle East, and Central Asia, suggest the preparation of hides for clothing. The oldest relatively unambiguous evidence of personal adornment, perforated shell beads, dates to c. 120 KYA at Skhul Cave on Mount Carmel in Israel. Although they were probably invented much earlier, impressions in burnt clay from the Czech Republic document the ability to weave cloth baskets and nets by 28 KYA. By the time Australia was settled, human ancestors had learned to navigate in boats over considerable distances in open water. The earliest-known bone tools were fashioned some 90 KYA at Semliki, in the Congo basin, by fishermen who crafted sophisticated bone harpoons to catch giant catfish.

Cave paintings in Lascaux, France, discovered in 1940, have been carbon-dated to 11,000 to 30,000 years BP.

About 60 KYA, the earliest immigrants to Australia carved and painted designs on rocks. Although the painted caves of Cosquer and Chauvet in southern France have (contested) radiocarbon dates of c. 32 KYA, painting, engraving and bodily decoration flourished in Europe 15 KYA, along with stone and ivory sculpture. More than 200 western European caves show remarkable examples of naturalistic wall painting. A few musical instruments—bone flutes with precisely bored holes—have been found in sites dated after 40 KYA. Over the course of the Upper Pleistocene (c. 130-12 KYA), the number of people surviving long enough to become grandparents slowly increased. With more adults available to provide child care, humans began to develop more complex, multigenerational social systems. The "reach" of social memory increased accordingly. Shortly after 12 KYA, among widely separated foraging communities in both hemispheres, a series of dramatic technological and social changes occurred, marking the Neolithic, or New Stone, Age. As the world climate became drier and warmer, population/resource imbalances ensued, creating the conditions that selected for increased human interference in the life cycles of certain plants and animals. This interference ultimately resulted in the appearance of domestication economies. Domesticated plants and animals encouraged population growth and the appearance of permanent settlements, which in turn reduced birth spacing and spurred more population growth. Reliance upon domesticated plants and animals, coupled with technological advances like pottery-making, precipitated a dramatic increase in world population and social complexity. Genetic research suggests that mutations related to traits currently found in some human populations, such as Europeans' unusually light skin pigmentation and ability to process lactose, arose after c. 12 KYA.

Sites in the Americas, southeast Europe, and the Middle East show roughly contemporaneous (12-10 KYA) evidence of Neolithic domestication economies; similar evidence of E and S Asian, W European, and sub-Saharan African Neolithic adaptations dates to 10-7 KYA. From W Asian sources, farming and the herding of sheep and goats spread rapidly throughout the Mediterranean basin, perhaps in as short a time interval as 100-200 years. The variety of crops—wheat, barley, rice, maize, squash, beans and tubers—and a mix of other characteristics suggest that this adaptation occurred independently in as many as 12 or 13 places in both hemispheres. Evidence for fermented beverages likewise coincides with the early Neolithic settled farming lifestyle. Northern Chinese farmers concocted a winelike drink from rice, honey, and fruit between 9,000 and 8,000 years ago. In highland W Asia, in what is today Iran, vintners were fermenting grapes and making wine by c. 7400 KYA. The plants and animals associated with the Neolithic Revolution provided the basis for all subsequent social and cultural evolution worldwide.

---

(1) Although "hominid" was standard usage several decades ago, "hominin" is now more commonly used in reference to human ancestors because of new developments in the interpretation of primate evolution.

Earliest Civilizations: 4000-1000 BCE

Mesopotamia. If history began with writing, the first chapter opened in Mesopotamia, the Tigris-Euphrates river valley. The Sumerians used clay tablets with pictographs to keep records after 4000 BCE. A **cuneiform** (wedge-shaped) script evolved by 3000 BCE as a full syllabic alphabet. Neighboring peoples adapted the script for their own use.

Sumerian life centered, from 4000 BCE, on large cities (Eridu, Ur, Uruk, Nippur, Kish, and Lagash) organized around temples and priestly bureaucracies, with surrounding plains watered by vast irrigation works and worked with traction plows. Sailboats, wheeled vehicles, potter's wheels, and kilns were used. Copper was smelted and tempered from c. 4000 BCE; bronze was produced not long after. Ores, as well as precious stones and metals, were obtained through long-distance ship and caravan trade. Iron was used from c. 2000 BCE. Improved ironworking, developed partly by the Hittites, became widespread by 1200 BCE.

Sumerian political primacy passed among cities and their kingly dynasties. Semitic-speaking peoples, with cultures derived from the Sumerian, founded a succession of dynasties that ruled in Mesopotamia and neighboring areas for most of 1,800 years; among them were the **Akkadians** (first under Sargon I, c. 2350 BCE), the Amorites (whose laws, codified by **Hammurabi**, c. 1792-1750 BCE, have biblical parallels), and the Assyrians, with interludes of rule by the Hittites, Kassites, and Mitanni.

Mesopotamian learning, preserved in vast libraries, was practically oriented. Scribes maintained lists of astronomical phenomena, plants, animals, and stones were maintained; medical texts listed ailments and herbal cures. The Sumerians worshiped anthropomorphic gods representing natural forces. Sacrifices were made at **ziggurats**, or huge stepped temples.

The Syria-Palestine area, site of some of the earliest urban remains (Jericho, 7000 BCE), and of the recently uncovered **Ebla** civilization (fl. 2500 BCE), experienced Egyptian cultural and political influence along with Mesopotamian. The **Phoenician** coast was an active commercial center. A phonetic alphabet was invented here before 1600 BCE. It became the ancestor of many other alphabets.

Egypt. Agricultural villages along the Nile River were united, then by around 3300 BCE into two kingdoms, Upper and Lower Egypt, unified (c. 3100 BCE) under the pharaoh Menes. A bureaucracy supervised construction of canals and monuments (**pyramids** starting 2700 BCE). Control over Nubia in the S was asserted from 2600 BCE. Brilliant **Old Kingdom** period achievements in architecture, sculpture, and painting reached their height during the 3rd and 4th dynasties. **Hieroglyphic writing** appeared by 3200 BCE, recording a sophisticated literature that included religious writings, philosophy, history, and science. An ordered hierarchy of gods, including totemistic animal elements, was served by a powerful priesthood in Memphis. The pharaoh was identified with the falcon god Horus. Other trends included belief in an afterlife and short-lived quasi-monotheistic reforms introduced by the pharaoh **Akhenaton** (c. 1379-1362 BCE), also the husband of Nefertiti.

After a period of dominance by Semitic Hyksos from Asia (c. 1700-1550 BCE), the **New Kingdom** established an empire in Syria. Egypt became increasingly embroiled in Asiatic wars and diplomacy. Conquered by Persia in 525 BCE, it eventually faded away as an independent culture.

India. An urban civilization with an as-yet undeciphered writing system stretched across the Indus Valley and along the Arabian Sea c. 3000-1500 BCE. Major sites are Harappa and **Mohenjo-Daro** in Pakistan, well-planned geometric cities with underground sewers and vast granaries. The entire region may have been ruled as a single state. Bronze was used, and arts and crafts were well developed. Religious life apparently took the form of fertility cults. Indus civilization was probably in decline when it was destroyed by **Aryans** who arrived from the NW, speaking an Indo-European language. Led by a warrior aristocracy whose legendary deeds are in the **Rig Veda**, the Aryans spread E and S, bringing their sky gods, priestly (Brahman) ritual, and the beginnings of the caste system; local customs and beliefs were assimilated by the conquerors.

Europe. On Crete, the Bronze Age **Minoan civilization** emerged c. 2500 BCE. A prosperous economy and richly decorative

The Great Sphinx of Giza is believed to have been built during Egypt's 4th dynasty (c. 2575-2465 BCE).

art was supported by seaborne commerce. Mycenae and other cities in mainland Greece and Asia Minor (e.g., Troy) preserved elements of the culture until c. 1200 BCE. Cretan Linear A script (c. 2000-1700 BCE) remains undeciphered; Linear B script (c. 1300-1200 BCE) records an early Greek dialect. The possible connection between Mycenaean monumental stonework and the megalithic monuments of W Europe, Iberia, and Malta (c. 4000-1500 BCE) is unclear.

China. Proto-Chinese neolithic cultures had long covered N and SE China when the first large political state was organized in the N by the **Shang dynasty** (c. 1523 BCE). Shang kings called themselves Sons of Heaven, and they presided over a cult of human and animal sacrifice to ancestors and nature gods. The Chou dynasty, starting c. 1027 BCE, expanded the area of the Sons of Heaven's dominion, but feudal states exercised

most temporal power. A writing system with 2,000 characters was already in use under the Shang, with **pictographs** later supplemented by phonetic characters. Many of its principles and symbols, despite changes in spoken Chinese, were preserved in later writing systems. Technical advances allowed urban specialists to create fine ceramic and jade products, and bronze casting after 1500 BCE was the most advanced in the world. Bronze artifacts discovered in N Thailand date from 3600 BCE, hundreds of years before similar Middle Eastern finds.

Americas. Olmecs settled (1500 BCE) on the Gulf coast of Mexico and developed the first known civilization in the W Hemisphere. Temple cities and huge stone sculpture date from 1200 BCE. A rudimentary calendar and writing system existed. Olmec religion—centering on a jaguar god—and art forms influenced later Meso-American cultures.

Formation of Classical Societies: 1000-400 BCE

Greece. After a period of decline during the Dorian Greek invasions (1200-1000 BCE), the Aegean area developed a unique civilization. Drawing on Mycenaean traditions, Mesopotamian learning (weights and measures, lunisolar calendar, astronomy, musical scales), the Phoenician alphabet (modified for Greek), and Egyptian art, **Greek city-states** saw a rich elaboration of intellectual life. The two great epic poems attributed to **Homer**, the *Iliad* and the *Odyssey*, were probably composed around the 8th cent. BCE. Long-range commerce was aided by metal coinage (introduced by the Lydians in Asia Minor before 700 BCE); colonies were founded around the Mediterranean (Cumae in Italy in 760 BCE; Massalia in France c. 600 BCE) and Black Sea shores.

Philosophy, starting with Ionian speculation on the nature of matter (Thales, c. 634-546 BCE), continued by other "Pre-Socratics" (e.g., Heraclitus, c. 535-415 BCE; Parmenides, b. c. 515 BCE), reached a high point in Athens in the rationalist idealism of **Plato** (c. 428-347 BCE), a disciple of **Socrates** (c. 469-399 BCE; executed for alleged impiety), and in **Aristotle** (384-322 BCE), a pioneer in many fields, from natural sciences to logic, ethics, and metaphysics. The **arts** were highly valued. Architecture culminated in the **Parthenon** (438 BCE) by Phidias (fl. 490-430 BCE). Poetry (Sappho, c. 610-580 BCE; Pindar, c. 518-438 BCE) and **drama** (Aeschylus, 525-456 BCE; Sophocles, c. 496-406 BCE; Euripides, c. 484-406 BCE) thrived. Male beauty and strength, a chief artistic theme, were celebrated at the national games at Olympia.

Ruled by local tyrants or **oligarchies,** the Greeks were not politically united, but managed to resist inclusion in the Persian Empire—Persian king Darius was defeated at Marathon (490 BCE), his son Xerxes at Salamis (480 BCE), and the Persian army at Plataea (479 BCE). Democracy sprouted in Athens as statesman Pericles (495-429 BCE) sought participation in government from all citizens. Local warfare was common; the **Peloponnesian Wars** (431-404 BCE) ended in Sparta's victory over Athens. Greek political power subsequently waned, but Greek cultural forms spread far and wide.

Hebrews. Nomadic Hebrew tribes entered Canaan before 1200 BCE, settling among other Semitic peoples speaking the same language. They brought from the desert a **monotheistic** faith said to have been revealed to Abraham in Canaan c. 1800 BCE and Moses at Mt. Sinai c. 1250 BCE, after the Hebrews' escape from bondage in Egypt. David (r. 1000-961 BCE) and Solomon (r. 961-922 BCE) united them in a kingdom that briefly dominated the area. **Phoenicians** to the N founded Mediterranean colonies (Carthage, c. 814 BCE) and sailed into the Atlantic.

A temple in Jerusalem became the national religious center, with sacrifices performed by a hereditary priesthood. Polytheistic influences, especially of the fertility cult of Baal, were opposed by **prophets** (Elijah, Amos, Isaiah).

Divided into **two kingdoms** after Solomon, the Hebrews were unable to resist the revived Assyrian empire, which conquered Israel, the N kingdom, in 722 BCE. Judah, the S kingdom, was conquered in 586 BCE by the Babylonians under Nebuchadnezzar II. With the fixing of most of the biblical canon by the mid-4th cent. BCE and the emergence of rabbis, Judaism successfully survived the loss of Hebrew autonomy. A Jewish kingdom was revived under the Hasmoneans (168-42 BCE).

China. During the **Eastern Chou** dynasty (770-256 BCE), Chinese culture spread E to the sea and S to the Yangtze R.

Large feudal states on the periphery of the empire contended for preeminence but continued to recognize the Son of Heaven (king), who retained a purely ritual role enriched with courtly music and dance. In the Age of Warring States (403-221 BCE), when the first sections of the **Great Wall** were built, the Ch'in state in the W gained supremacy and finally united all of China.

Iron tools entered China c. 500 BCE, and casting techniques were advanced, aiding agriculture. Peasants owned their land and owed civil and military service to nobles. China's cities grew in number and size; barter remained the chief trade medium.

Intellectual ferment among noble scribes and officials produced the Classical Age of Chinese literature and philosophy. **Confucius** (551-479 BCE) urged a restoration of a supposedly harmonious social order of the past through proper conduct in accordance with one's station and through filial and ceremonial piety. The *Analects* attributed to him are revered throughout E Asia.

Among other thinkers, **Mencius** (d. 289 BCE) added the view that the Mandate of Heaven can be removed from an unjust dynasty. The Legalists sought to curb the supposed natural wickedness of people through new institutions and harsh laws. The Naturalists emphasized the balance of opposites—yin, yang—in the world. **Taoists** sought mystical knowledge through meditation and disengagement.

India. The political and cultural center of India shifted from the Indus to the Ganges River Valley. Buddhism, Jainism, and mystical revisions of orthodox Vedism all developed c. 500-300 BCE. The *Upanishads*, last part of the *Veda*, urged escape from the cycle of rebirth into the physical world. Vedism remained the preserve of the Brahman caste.

In contrast, **Buddhism,** founded by Siddhartha Gautama (c. 563-c. 483 BCE)—Buddha ("Enlightened One")—appealed to merchants in the urban centers and took hold at first (and most lastingly) on the geographic fringes of Indian civilization. The classic Indian epics were composed in this era: the *Ramayana* perhaps c. 300 BCE, the *Mahabharata* over a period starting around 400 BCE.

The Parthenon, a Doric temple, is part of the Acropolis in Athens, which took shape in Greece in the 5th century BCE.

China's Great Wall, first built during the Age of Warring States (403-221 BCE), was rebuilt, extended, and modified over thousands of years to protect China from invaders.

N India was divided into a large number of monarchies and aristocratic republics, probably derived from tribal groupings, when the Magadha kingdom was formed in Bihar c. 542 BCE. It soon became the dominant power. The **Maurya** dynasty, founded by Chandragupta c. 321 BCE, expanded the kingdom, uniting most of N India in a centralized bureaucratic empire. The third Mauryan king, **Asoka** (reigned c. 274-236 BCE), con-quered most of the subcontinent. He converted to Buddhism and inscribed its tenets on pillars throughout India and downplayed the caste system.

Before its final decline in India, Buddhism developed into a popular worship of heavenly Bodhisattvas ("enlightened beings"), and it produced a refined architecture (the Great Stupa [shrine] at Sanchi, 100 CE) and sculpture (Gandhara reliefs, 1-400 CE).

Persia. Aryan peoples (Persians, Medes) dominated the area of present Iran by the beginning of the 1st millennium BCE. The prophet **Zoroaster** (born c. 628 BCE) introduced a dualistic religion in which the forces of good (Ahura Mazda, "Lord of Wisdom") and evil (Ahriman) battle for dominance; individuals are judged by their actions and earn damnation or salvation. Zoroaster's hymns (*Gathas*) are included in the *Avesta*, the Zoroastrian scriptures. A version of this faith became the established religion of the Persian Empire.

Africa. Nubia, periodically occupied by Egypt since about 2600 BCE, ruled Egypt c. 750-661 BCE and survived as an independent Egyptianized kingdom (**Kush**; capital Meroe) for 1,000 years. The Iron Age Nok culture flourished c. 500 BCE-200 CE on the Benue Plateau of **Nigeria**.

Americas. The Chavin culture controlled N Peru c. 900 BCE to 200 BCE. Its ceremonial centers, featuring the jaguar god, survived long after. Its architecture, ceramics, and textiles had influenced other Peruvian cultures. **Mayan civilization** began to develop in Central America as early as 1500 BCE.

Great Empires Unite the Classical World: 400 BCE-400 CE

Persia. Cyrus, ruler of a small kingdom in Persia from 559 BCE, united the Persians and Medes within 10 years and con-quered Asia Minor and Babylonia in another 10. His son Cam-byses, followed by **Darius** (r. 522-486 BCE), added vast lands to the E and N as far as the Indus Valley and Central Asia, as well as Egypt and Thrace. The whole empire was ruled by an international bureaucracy and army, with Persians holding the chief positions. The resources and styles of all the subject civili-zations were exploited to create a rich syncretic art.

The kingdom of Macedon, which under Philip II dominated the Greek world and Egypt, was passed on to his son **Alexander** in 336 BCE. Within 13 years, Alexander had conquered all the Persian dominions. Imbued by his tutor Aristotle with Greek ideals, Alexander encouraged colonization, and Greek-style cit-ies were founded. After his death in 323 BCE, wars of succession divided the empire into three significant dynasties—the **Antigonids** in Asia Minor and Macedon, the **Ptolemies** in Egypt, and the **Seleucids** in Mesopotamia. In the ensuing 300 years (the **Hellenistic Era**), a cosmopolitan Greek-oriented culture perme-ated the ancient world from W Europe to the borders of India, absorbing native elites everywhere.

Hellenistic philosophy stressed the private individual's search for happiness. The Cynics followed Diogenes (c. 372-287 BCE), who stressed self-sufficiency and restriction of desires and expressed contempt for luxury and social convention. Zeno (c. 335-c. 263 BCE) and the **Stoics** exalted reason, identified it with virtue, and counseled an ascetic disregard for misfortune. The **Epicureans** tried to build lives of moderate pleasure with-out political or emotional involvement. Hellenistic arts imitated life realistically, especially in sculpture and literature (comedies of Menander, 342-292 BCE).

The sciences thrived, especially at Alexandria, where the Ptolemies financed a great library and museum. Fields of study included mathematics (**Euclid**'s geometry, c. 300 BCE; astronomy (heliocentric theory of Aristarchus, 310-230 BCE; Julian calendar, 45 BCE; **Ptolemy**'s *Almagest*, c. 150 CE); geo-graphy (world map of Eratosthenes, 276-194 BCE); hydraulics (**Archimedes**, 287-212 BCE); medicine (Galen, 130-200 CE); and chemistry. Inventors refined uses for siphons, valves, gears, springs, screws, levers, cams, and pulleys.

A restored Persian empire under the **Parthians** (northern Ira-nian tribesmen) controlled the eastern Hellenistic world from 250 BCE to 229 CE. The Parthians and the succeeding **Sassa-nian dynasty** (c. 224-651 CE) fought with Rome periodically. The Sassanians revived Zoroastrianism as a state religion and patronized a nationalistic artistic and scholarly renaissance.

Rome. The city of Rome was founded, according to leg-end, by Romulus in 753 BCE. Through military expansion and colonization, and by granting citizenship to conquered tribes, the city annexed all of Italy S of the Po R. in the 100-year period before 268 BCE. The Latin and other Italic tribes were annexed first, followed by the **Etruscans** (founders of a great civilization, N of Rome) and the Greek colonies in the S. With a large standing army and reserve forces of several hundred thousand, Rome was able to defeat **Carthage** in the three **Punic Wars** (264-241 BCE, 218-201 BCE, 149-146 BCE), despite the invasion of Italy by **Hannibal** (218 BCE), thus gain-ing Sicily and territory in Spain and N Africa.

Rome exploited local disputes to conquer Greece and Asia Minor in the 2nd cent. BCE and Egypt in the 1st (after the defeat and suicide of **Antony and Cleopatra,** 30 BCE). The Mediterranean civilized world, up to the disputed Par-thian border, was now Roman and remained so for 500 years. Less civilized regions were added to the Empire: Gaul (conquered by **Julius Caesar,** 58-51 BCE), Britain (43 CE), and Dacia NE of the Danube (107 CE).

The original aristocratic republican government, with demo-cratic features added in the 5th and 4th cent. BCE, deteriorated under the pressures of empire and class conflict (**Gracchus** brothers, social reformers, murdered in 133 BCE and 121 BCE; slave revolts in 135 BCE and 71 BCE). After a series of civil wars (Marius vs. Sulla, 88-82 BCE; Caesar vs. **Pompey,** 49-45 BCE; triumvirate vs. Caesar's assassins, 44-43 BCE; Antony vs. Octa-vian, 32-30 BCE), the empire came under the rule of a deified monarch (first emperor, **Augustus,** 27 BCE-14 CE).

Provincials (nearly all granted citizenship by Caracalla, 212 CE) came to dominate the army and civil service. Traditional **Roman law,** systematized and interpreted by independent jurists, and local self-rule in provincial cities were supplanted by a vast tax-collecting bureaucracy in the 3rd and 4th cent. The legal rights of women, children, and slaves were strengthened.

Roman innovations in **civil engineering** included water mills, windmills, and rotary mills and use of cement that hardened under water. Monumental architecture (baths, theaters, temples) relied on the arch and the dome. The network of roads (some still standing) stretched 53,000 mi, passing through mountain tunnels as long as 3.5 mi. Aqueducts brought water to cities; underground sewers removed waste.

Roman art and literature were derivative of Greek models. Innovations were made in sculpture (naturalistic busts, equestrian statues), decorative wall painting (as at Pompeii), satire (**Juve-nal,** 60-127 CE), history (**Tacitus,** 56-120 CE), prose romance

(**Petronius**, d. 66 CE). Gladiatorial contests dominated public amusements, which were supported by the state.

India. The **Gupta** monarchs reunited N India c. 320 CE. Their peaceful and prosperous reign saw a revival of Hindu religious thought and Brahman power. The old Vedic traditions were combined with devotion to many indigenous deities (who were seen as manifestations of Vedic gods). Caste lines were reinforced, and Buddhist practices gradually dis-appeared or were integrated with **Hindu** traditions. The art (often erotic), architecture, and literature of the period, patronized by the Gupta court, are considered among India's finest achievements (Kalidasa, poet and dramatist, fl. c. 400 CE). Mathematical innovations included use of the zero and decimal numbers. Invasions by White Huns from the NW destroyed the empire c. 550 CE. Rich cultures also developed in S India during this period. Emotional Tamil religious poetry contributed to the Hindu revival. The Pallava kingdom controlled much of S India c. 350-880 CE and helped to spread Indian civilization to SE Asia.

China. The Ch'in ruler Shih Huang Ti (r. 221-210 BCE), known as the First Emperor, centralized political authority.

standardized the written language, laws, weights, measures, and coinage, and conducted a census, but tried to destroy most philosophical texts. The **Han** dynasty (202 BCE-220 CE) instituted the Mandarin bureaucracy, which lasted 2,000 years. Local officials were selected by examination in Confucian classics and trained at the imperial university and provincial schools.

The invention of **paper** facilitated this bureaucratic system. Agriculture was promoted, but peasants bore most of the tax burden. Irrigation was improved, water clocks and sundials were used, astronomy and mathematics thrived, and landscape painting was perfected.

With the expansion S and W (to nearly the present borders of today's China), trade was opened with India, SE Asia, and the Middle East, over sea and caravan routes. Indian missionaries brought Mahayana Buddhism to China by the 1st cent. CE and spawned a variety of sects. Taoism was revived and merged with popular superstitions. **Taoist and Buddhist monasteries** and convents multiplied in the turbulent centuries after the collapse of the Han dynasty.

Monotheism Spreads: 1-750 CE

Roman Empire. Polytheism was practiced in the Roman Empire, and religions indigenous to particular Middle Eastern nations became international. Roman citizens worshiped **Isis** of Egypt, **Mithras** of Persia, **Demeter** of Greece, and the great mother **Cybele** of Phrygia. Their cults centered on mysteries (secret ceremonies) and the promise of an afterlife, symbolized by the death and rebirth of the god. The Jews of the empire preserved their monotheistic religion, Judaism, the world's oldest (c. 1300 BCE) continuous religion. Its teachings are contained in the Bible (the Old Testament). 1st-cent. CE Judaism embraced several sects, including the **Sadducees**, mostly drawn from the Temple priesthood, who were culturally Hellenized; the **Pharisees**, who upheld the full range of traditional customs and practices as of equal weight to literal scriptural law and elaborated synagogue worship; and the **Essenes**, an ascetic, millenarian sect. Messianic fervor led to repeated, unsuccessful rebellions against Rome (66-70, 135 CE). As a result, the Temple in Jerusalem was destroyed and the population decimated; this event marked the beginning of the Diaspora (living in exile). To preserve the faith, a program of codification of law was begun at the academy of Yavneh. The work continued for some 500 years in Palestine and in Babylonia, ending in the final redaction (c. 600) of the **Talmud**, a huge collection of legal and moral debates, rulings, liturgy, biblical exegesis, and legendary materials.

Christianity. Emerging as a distinct sect by the second half of the 1st cent. CE, Christianity is based on the teachings of **Jesus**, whom believers considered the Savior (Messiah or Christ) and son of God. Missionary activities of the Apostles and such early leaders as **Paul of Tarsus** spread the faith. Intermittent persecution, as in Rome under Nero in 64 CE, on grounds of suspected disloyalty, failed to disrupt the Christian communities. Each congregation, generally urban and of plebeian character, was tightly organized under a leader (bishop), elders (presbyters or priests), and assistants (deacons). The four **Gospels** (accounts of the life and teachings of Jesus) and the Acts of the Apostles were written down in the late 1st and early 2nd cent. and circulated along with letters of Paul and other Christian leaders. An authoritative canon of these writings was not fixed until the 4th cent.

A school for priests was established at Alexandria in the 2nd cent. Its teachers (**Origen**, c. 182-251) helped define doctrine and promote the faith in Greek-style philosophicalworks. Neoplatonism underwent Christian coloration in the writings of Church Fathers such as **Augustine** (354-430). Christian hermits began to associate in monasteries, first in Egypt (St. Pachomius, c. 290-345), then in other E lands, then in the W (**St. Benedict's rule**, 529). Devotion to saints, especially Mary, mother of Jesus, spread. Under **Constantine** (r. 306-37), Christianity became in effect the established religion of the Empire. Pagan temples were expropriated, state funds were used to build churches and support the hierarchy, and laws were adjusted in accordance with Christian ideas. Pagan worship was banned by the end of the 4th cent., and severe restrictions were placed on Judaism.

The newly established church was rocked by doctrinal disputes, often exacerbated by regional rivalries. Chief heresies (as defined by church councils, backed by imperial authority) were **Arianism**, which denied the divinity of Jesus; **Monophysitism**, denying the human nature of Christ; **Donatism**, which regarded as invalid any sacraments administered by sinful clergy; and **Pelagianism**, which denied the necessity of unmerited divine aid (grace) for salvation.

Islam. The earliest Arab civilization emerged by the end of the 2nd millennium BCE in the watered highlands of Yemen. Seaborne and caravan trade in frankincense and myrrh connected the area with the Nile and Fertile Crescent. The Minaean, Sabean (Sheba), and Himyarite states successively held sway. By Muhammad's time (7th cent. CE), the region was a province of Sassanian Persia. In the N, the Nabataean kingdom at Petra and the kingdom of Palmyra were Aramaicized, Romanized, and finally absorbed, as neighboring Judea had been, into the Roman Empire. Nomads shared the central region with a few trading towns and oases. Wars between tribes and raids on communities were common and were celebrated in a poetic tradition that by the 6th cent. helped establish a classic literary Arabic.

About 610, **Muhammad**, a 40-year-old Arab man of Mecca, emerged as a prophet. He proclaimed a revelation from the one true God, calling on contemporaries to abandon idolatry and restore the faith of Abraham. He introduced his religion as **Islam**, meaning "submission" to the one God, Allah, as a continuation of the biblical faith of Abraham, Moses, and Jesus, all respected as prophets in this history. His teachings, recorded in the **Koran** (al-Qur'an in Arabic), in many ways were inclusive of Abrahamic monotheistic ideas known to the Jews and Christians in Arabia. A key aspect of the Abrahamic connection was insistence on justice in society, which led to severe opposition among the aristocrats in Mecca. As conditions worsened for Muhammad and his followers, he decided in 622 to make a *hegira* (flight) to Medina, 200 mi to the N. This event marks the beginning of the Muslim lunar calendar. Hostilities between Mecca and Medina increased, and in 629 Muhammad conquered Mecca. By the time he died in 632, nearly all the Arabian peninsula accepted his political and religious leadership.

After his death the majority of Muslims (later known as **Sunni** Muslims) recognized the leadership of the **caliph** (successor) Abu Bakr (632-34), followed by Umar (634-44), Uthman (644-56), and Ali (656-60). A minority, the **Shiites**, insisted instead on the leadership of Ali, Muhammad's cousin and son-in-law. By 644, **Muslim rule** over Arabia was confirmed. Muslim armies had threatened the Byzantine and Persian empires, which were weakened by wars and disaffection among subject peoples (including Coptic and Syriac Christians opposed to the Byzantine Orthodox establishment). Syria, Palestine, Egypt, Iraq, and Persia fell to Muslim armies. The new administration assimilated existing systems in the region; hence the conquered peoples participated in running the empire. The Koran recognized the so-called Peoples of the Book, i.e.,

Christians, Jews, and Zoroastrians, as tolerated monotheists, and Muslim policy was relatively tolerant to minorities living as "protected" peoples. An expanded tax system, based on conquests of the Persian and Byzantine empires, provided revenue to organize campaigns against neighboring non-Muslim regions.

Under the **Umayyads** (661-750) and **Abbasids** (750-1256), territorial expansion led Muslim armies across N Africa and into Spain (711). Muslim armies in the W were stopped at Tours, France, in 732 by the Frankish ruler **Charles Martel**. Asia Minor, the Indus Valley, and Transoxiana were conquered in the E. The conversion of conquered peoples to Islam was gradual. In many places the official Arabic language supplanted the local tongues. But in the eastern regions the Arab rulers and their armies adopted Persian cultures and language as part of their Muslim identity.

Disputes over succession and pious opposition to injustices in society, led to a number of oppositional movements, which also led to the factionalization of Muslim community. The **Shiites** supported leadership candidates descended from Muhammad, believing them to be carriers of some kind of divine authority. The **Kharijites** supported an egalitarian system derived from the Koran, opposing and even engaging in battle against those who did not agree with them.

New Peoples Enter World History: 400-900 CE

Barbarian invasions. Germanic tribes infiltrated S and E from their Baltic homeland during the 1st millennium BCE, reaching S Germany by 100 BCE and the Black Sea by 214 CE. Organized into large federated tribes under elected kings, most resisted Roman domination and raided the empire in time of civil war (Goths took Dacia in 214, raided Thrace in 251-69). Germanic troops and commanders dominated the Roman armies by the end of the 4th cent. **Huns**, invaders from Asia, entered Europe in 372, driving more Germans into the W empire. Emperor Valens allowed Visigoths to cross the Danube in 376. Huns under Attila (d. 453) raided Gaul, Italy, and the Balkans.

The W empire, weakened by overtaxation and social stagnation, was overrun in the 5th cent. Gaul was effectively lost in 406-07, Spain in 409, Britain in 410, Africa in 429-39. Rome was sacked in 410 by Visigoths under Alaric and in 455 by Vandals. The **last western emperor**, Romulus Augustulus, was deposed in 476 by the Germanic chief Odovacar.

Celts. Celtic cultures, which in pre-Roman times covered most of W Europe, were confined almost entirely to the British Isles after the Germanic invasions. **St. Patrick** completed (c. 457-92) the conversion of Ireland and a strong monastic tradition took hold. Irish monastic missionaries in Scotland, England, and the continent (Columba, c. 521-97; Columbanus, c. 543-615) helped restore Christianity after the Germanic invasions. **Monasteries** became centers of classic and Christian learning and presided over the recording of a Christianized Celtic mythology, elaborated by secular writers and bards. An intricate decorative art style developed, especially in book illumination (Lindisfarne Gospels, c. 700; Book of Kells, 8th cent.).

Successor states. The Visigothic kingdom in Spain (from 419) and much of France (to 507) saw continuation of Roman administration, language, and law (Breviary of Alaric, 506) until its destruction by the Muslims (711). The Vandal kingdom in Africa (from 429) was conquered by the Byzantines in 533. Italy was ruled successively by an Ostrogothic kingdom under Byzantine suzerainty (489-554), direct Byzantine government, and German Lombards (568-774). The Lombards divided the peninsula with the Byzantines and papacy under the dynamic reformer **Pope Gregory the Great** (590-604) and successors.

King Clovis (r. 481-511) united the Franks on both sides of the Rhine and, after his conversion to Christianity, defeated the Arian heretics, Burgundians (after 500), and Visigoths (507) with the support of native clergy and the papacy. Under the **Merovingian** kings, a feudal system emerged: power was fragmented among hierarchies of military landowners. Social stratification, which in late Roman times had acquired legal, hereditary sanction, was reinforced.

The **Carolingians** (747-987) expanded the kingdom and restored central power. **Charlemagne** (r. 768-814) conquered nearly all the Germanic lands, including Lombard Italy, and was crowned emperor by Pope Leo III in Rome in 800. A centuries-long decline in commerce and arts was reversed under Charlemagne's patronage. He welcomed Jews to his kingdom, which became a center of Jewish learning (Rashi, 1040-1105). He sponsored the Carolingian Renaissance of learning under the Anglo-Latin scholar Alcuin (c. 732-804), who reformed church liturgy.

Byzantine Empire. Under **Diocletian** (r. 284-305) the Roman empire had been divided into two parts to facilitate administration and defense. **Constantine** founded (330) **Constantinople** (at old Byzantium) as a fully Christian city. Commerce and taxation financed a sumptuous, orientalized court, a class of hereditary bureaucratic families, and magnificent urban construction (Hagia Sophia, 532-37). The city's fortifications and naval innovations repelled assaults by Goths, Huns, Slavs, Bulgars, Avars, Arabs, and Scandinavians. Greek replaced Latin as the official language by c. 700. **Byzantine art**, a solemn, sacral, and stylized variation of late classical styles (mosaics at the Church of San Vitale, Ravenna, Italy, 526-48), was a starting point for medieval art in E and W Europe.

Justinian (r. 527-65) reconquered parts of Spain, N Africa, and Italy, codified **Roman law** (Codex Justinianus [529] was medieval Europe's chief legal text), closed the Platonic Academy at Athens, and ordered all pagans to convert. Lombards in Italy and Arabs in Africa retook most of his conquests. The Isaurian dynasty from Anatolia (from 717) and the Macedonian dynasty (867-1054) restored military and commercial power. The Iconoclast controversy (726-843) over the permissibility of images helped alienate the Eastern Church from the papacy.

Abbasid Empire. Baghdad (established 762), became seat of the **Abbasid dynasty** (established 750), while Umayyads continued to rule in Spain. A brilliant cosmopolitan civilization emerged, inaugurating a Muslim-Arab golden age. Arabic was the lingua franca of the empire; intellectual sources from Persian, Sanskrit, Greek, and Syriac were rendered into Arabic. Christians and Jews equally participated in this translation movement, which also involved interaction between Jewish legal thought and Islamic law, as much as between Christian theology and Muslim scholasticism. Persian-style court life, with art and music, flourished at the court of **Harun al-Rashid** (786-809), celebrated in the masterpiece known to English readers as The Arabian Nights. The sciences, medicine, and mathematics were pursued at Baghdad, Cordova, and Cairo (est. 969). The culmination of this intellectual synthesis in Islamic civilization came with the scientific and philosophical works of **Avicenna** (Ibn Sina, 980-1037), **Averroes** (Ibn Rushd, 1126-98), and **Maimonides** (1135-1204), a Jew who wrote in Arabic. This intellectual tradition was translated into Latin and opened a new period in Christian thought.

The decentralization of the **Abbasid** empire, from 874, led to the establishment of various Muslim dynasties under different ethnic groups. Persians, Berbers, and Turks ruled different regions, retaining connection with the Abbasid caliph at the religious level. The Abbasid period also saw various religious movements against the orthodox position held by governing authorities. This situation in Muslim religion led to the establishment of different legal, theological, and mystical schools of thought. The most influential mass movement was **Sufism**, which aimed at the reaching out of the average individual in quest of a spiritual path. Al-Ghazali (1058-1111) is credited with reconciling personal Sufism with orthodox Sunni tradition.

Africa. Immigrants from Saba in S Arabia helped set up the **Axum** kingdom in Ethiopia in the 1st cent. (their language, Ge'ez, is preserved by the Ethiopian Church). In the 3rd cent., when the kingdom became Christianized, it defeated Kushite Meroe and expanded its influence into Yemen. Axum was the center of a vast ivory trade and controlled the Red Sea coast until c. 1100. Arab conquest in Egypt cut Axum's political and economic ties with Byzantium.

The pyramid of Kukulkan (El Castillo) at Chichen Itza is one of the preeminent existing examples of Mayan architecture in present-day Mexico.

The Iron Age entered W Africa by the end of the 1st millennium BCE. **Ghana**, the first known sub-Saharan state, ruled in the upper Senegal-Niger region c. 400-1240, controlling the trade of gold from mines in the S to trans-Sahara caravan routes to the N. The **Bantu** peoples, probably of W African origin, began to spread E and S perhaps 2,000 years ago, displacing the Pygmies and Bushmen of central and S Africa during a 1,500-year period.

Japan. The advanced Neolithic Yayoi period, when irrigation, rice farming, and iron and bronze casting techniques were introduced from China or Korea, persisted to c. 400 CE. The myriad Japanese states were then united by the **Yamato** clan, under an emperor who acted as chief priest of the animistic Shinto cult. Japanese political and military intervention by the 6th cent. in Korea, then under strong Chinese influence, quickened a Chinese cultural invasion of Japan, bringing Buddhism, the Chinese language (which long remained a literary and governmental medium), Chinese ideographs, and Buddhist styles in painting, sculpture, literature, and architecture (7th cent., Horyuji temple at Nara). The Taika Reforms (646) tried unsuccessfully to centralize Japan according to Chinese bureaucratic and Buddhist philosophical values.

A nativist reaction against the Buddhist **Nara** period (710-94) ushered in the **Heian** period (794-1185) centered at the new capital, Kyoto. Japanese elegance and simplicity modified Chinese styles in architecture, scroll painting, and literature; the writing system was also simplified. The courtly novel *Tale of Genji* (1010-20) testifies to the enhanced role of women in medieval Japanese literature and culture.

Southeast Asia. The historic peoples of SE Asia began arriving some 2,500 years ago from China and Tibet, displacing scattered aborigines. Their agriculture relied on rice and yams. Indian cultural influences were strongest; literacy and Hindu and Buddhist ideas followed the S India-China trade route. From the S tip of Indochina, the kingdom of **Funan** (1st-7th cent.) traded as far W as Persia. It was absorbed by Chenla, itself conquered by the **Khmer Empire** (600-1300). The Khmers, under Hindu god-kings (Surya-varman II, 1113-c. 1150), built the monumental Angkor Wat temple center for the royal phallic cult. The **Nam-Viet** kingdom in Annam, dominated by China and Chinese culture for 1,000 years, emerged in the 10th cent., growing at the expense of the Khmers, who also lost ground in the NW to the new, highly organized **Thai** kingdom. On Sumatra, the **Srivijaya** Empire controlled vital sea lanes (7th to 10th cent.). A Buddhist dynasty, the Sailendras, ruled central **Java** (8th-9th cent.), building at Borobudur one of the largest stupas (dome-shaped Buddhist shrine) in the world.

China. The Sui dynasty (581-618) ushered in a period of commercial, artistic, and scientific achievement in China, continuing under the **Tang** dynasty (618-906). Inventions like the magnetic compass, gunpowder, the abacus, and printing were introduced or perfected. Medical innovations included cataract surgery. The state, from its cosmopolitan capital, Chang-an, supervised foreign trade, which exchanged Chinese silks, porcelains, and art for spices and ivory over Central Asian caravan routes and sea routes reaching Africa. A golden age of poetry bequeathed valuable works to later generations (Tu Fu, 712-70; Li Po, 701-62). Landscape painting flourished.

Commercial and industrial expansion continued under the **Northern Sung** dynasty (960-1126), facilitated by paper money and credit notes. But commerce never achieved respectability; government monopolies expropriated successful merchants. The population, long stable at 50 million, doubled in 200 years with the introduction of early-ripening rice and the double harvest. In art, native Chinese styles were revived.

Americas. From 300 to 600 a Native American empire stretched from the Valley of Mexico to Guatemala, centering on the huge city **Teotihuacán** (founded 100 BCE). To the S, in Guatemala, a high **Mayan** civilization developed (150-900) around hundreds of rural ceremonial centers. The Mayans improved on Olmec writing and the calendar and pursued astronomy and mathematics. In South America, a widespread pre-Inca culture grew from **Tiahuanacu**, Bolivia, near Lake Titicaca (Gateway of the Sun doorway, c. 700).

Christian Europe Regroups and Expands: 900-1300

Scandinavia. Pagan Danish and Norse (Viking) adventurers, traders, and pirates raided the coasts of the British Isles (Dublin, c. 831), France, and even the Mediterranean for over 200 years beginning in the late 8th cent. Inland settlement in the W was limited to Great Britain (King Canute, 994-1035) and Normandy, settled (911) under Rollo, as a fief of France. Vikings also reached Iceland (874), Greenland (c. 986), and North America (**Leif Ericson** and others, c. 1000). Norse traders (**Varangians**) developed Russian river commerce from the 8th to the 11th cent. and helped set up a state at Kiev in the late 9th cent. Conversion to Christianity occurred in the 10th cent., reaching Sweden 100 years later. In the 11th cent. Norman bands conquered S Italy and Sicily, and Duke **William of Normandy** conquered (1066) England, bringing feudal government and the French language, essential elements in later English civilization.

Central and East Europe. Slavs began to expand from about 150 CE in all directions in Europe, and by the 7th cent. they reached as far S as the Adriatic and Aegean seas. In the Balkan Peninsula they dislocated Romanized local populations or assimilated newcomers (Bulgarians, a Turkic people). The first **Slavic states** were Moravia (628) in Central Europe and the Bulgarian state (680) in the Balkans. Missions of St. Methodius and Cyril (whose Greek-based cyrillic alphabet is still used by some S and E Slavs) converted (863) Moravia.

The Eastern Slavs, part-civilized under the overlordship of the Turkish-Jewish **Khazar** trading empire (7th-10th cent.), gravitated toward Constantinople by the 9th cent. The **Kievan** state adopted (989) Eastern Christianity under Prince Vladimir. King Boleslav I (992-1025) began **Poland**'s long history of conquest. The Magyars (**Hungarians**), in present-day Hungary since 896, accepted (1001) Latin Christianity.

Germany. The German kingdom that emerged after the breakup of Charlemagne's W Empire remained a confederation of largely autonomous states. Otto I, a Saxon who was king from 936, established the **Holy Roman Empire**—a union of Germany and N Italy—in alliance with Pope John XII, who crowned (962) him emperor; he defeated (955) the Magyars. Imperial power was greatest under the **Hohenstaufens** (1138-1254), despite the growing opposition of the papacy, which ruled central Italy and the Lombard League cities. Frederick II (1194-1250) improved administration and patronized the arts; after his death, German influence was removed from Italy.

Christian Spain. From its N mountain redoubts, Christian rule slowly migrated S through the 11th cent., when Muslim unity collapsed. After the capture (1085) of **Toledo**, the kingdoms of Portugal, Castile, and Aragon undertook repeated crusades of reconquest, finally completed in 1492. Elements of Islamic civilization persisted in recaptured areas, influencing all Western Europe.

Crusades. Pope **Urban II** called for a crusade (1095) to restore Asia Minor to Byzantium and the Holy Land to Christendom, respectively. This first crusade captured Jerusalem and led to the foundation of four Frankish states in the Levant. The defeat inflicted upon crusaders at the Battle of Hattin (1187) by **Saladin** (c. 1137-93), the Kurdish ruler of Egypt and Syria, effectively negated territorial gains. Many crusades followed until 1291. The 4th crusade sacked Constantinople (1204). Other crusades were launched against Christian heretics (Albigensian Crusade, 1229), pagans, and enemies of the papacy.

Economy. The agricultural base of European life benefited from improvements in **plow design** (c. 1000) and by draining of lowlands and clearing of forests, leading to a rural population increase. Towns grew in N Italy, Flanders, and N Germany (Hanseatic League). Improvements in **loom design** permitted factory textile production. **Guilds** dominated urban trades from the 12th cent. Banking (centered in Italy, 12th-15th cent.) facilitated long-distance trade.

The Church. The split between the Eastern and Western churches was formalized in 1054. Western and Central Europe was divided into 500 bishoprics under one united hierarchy, but conflicts between secular and church authorities were frequent (German **Investiture Controversy**, 1075-1122). Clerical power was first strengthened through the international monastic reform begun at Cluny in 910. Popular religious enthusiasm often expressed itself in heretical movements (Waldensians from 1173), but was channeled by the **Dominican** (1215) and **Franciscan** (1223) friars into the religious mainstream.

Arts. **Romanesque** architecture (9th to mid-12th cent.) expanded on late Roman models, using the rounded arch and massed stone to support enlarged basilicas. Painting and sculpture followed Byzantine models. The literature of **chivalry** was exemplified by the epic (*Chanson de Roland*, c. 1100) and by courtly love poems of the troubadours of Provence and minnesingers of Germany. **Gothic** architecture emerged in France (choir of St. Denis, c. 1140) and spread along with French cultural influence. Rib vaulting and pointed arches were used to combine soaring heights with delicacy, and they freed walls for display of stained glass. Exteriors were covered with painted relief sculpture and embellished with elaborate architectural detail.

Learning. Law, medicine, and philosophy were advanced at independent **universities** (Bologna, Paris, 12th cent.), originally corporations of students and masters. Twelfth-cent. translations of Greek classics, especially Aristotle, encouraged an analytic approach. Scholastic philosophy, from Anselm (1033-1109) to **Aquinas** (1225-74), attempted to understand revelation through reason.

Apogee of Central Asian Power and the Spread of Islam: 1250-1500

Turks. Turkic peoples, of Central Asian ancestry, were a military threat to the Byzantine and Persian Empires from the 6th cent. After several waves of invasions, during which most of the Turks adopted Islam, the **Seljuk Turks** took (1055) Baghdad. They ruled Persia, Iraq and, after 1071, Asia Minor, where massive numbers of Turks settled. The empire was divided in the 12th cent. into smaller states ruled by Seljuks, Kurds, and Mamluks (a military caste of former Turk, Kurd, and Circassian slaves), which governed Egypt and the Middle East until the Ottoman era (c. 1290-1922).

Osman I (r. c. 1290-1326) and succeeding sultans united Anatolian Turkish warriors in a militaristic state that waged holy war against Byzantine and Balkan Christians. Most of the Balkans had been subdued, and Anatolia united, when Constantinople fell (1453). By the mid-16th cent., Hungary, the Middle East, and N Africa had been conquered. The Turkish advance was stopped at Vienna (1529) and at the naval battle of Lepanto (1571) by Spain, Venice, and the papacy.

The **Ottoman state** was governed in accordance with orthodox Muslim law. Greek, Armenian, and Jewish communities were segregated and were ruled by religious leaders responsible for taxation; they dominated trade. State offices and most army ranks were filled by slaves through a system of child conscription among Christians.

India. Mahmud of Ghazni (971-1030) led repeated Turkish raids into N India. Turkish power was consolidated in 1206 with the start of the **Sultanate at Delhi**. Centralization of state power under the early Delhi sultans went far beyond traditional Indian practice. Muslim rule of most of the subcontinent lasted until the British conquest 600 years later.

Mongols. Genghis Khan (c. 1167-1227) first united the feuding Mongol tribes, and built their armies into an effective offensive force around a core of highly mobile cavalry. He and his immediate successors created the largest land empire in history; by 1279 it stretched from the E coast of Asia to the Danube, from the Siberian steppes to the Arabian Sea. East-West trade and contacts were facilitated (Marco Polo, c. 1254-1324). The western Mongols were Islamized by 1295; successor states soon lost their Mongol character by assimilation. They were briefly reunited under the Turk Tamerlane (1336-1405).

Kublai Khan ruled China from his new capital Beijing (established c. 1264). Naval campaigns against Japan (1274, 1281) and Java (1293) were defeated, the latter by the Hindu-Buddhist maritime kingdom of Majapahit. The **Yuan** dynasty used Mongols and other foreigners (including Europeans) in official posts and tolerated the return of Nestorian Christianity (suppressed 841-45) and the spread of Islam in the S and W. A native reaction expelled the Mongols in 1367-68.

Russia. The Kievan state in Russia, weakened by the decline of Byzantium and the rise of the Catholic Polish-Lithuanian state, was overrun (1238-40) by the Mongols. Only the northern trading republic of Novgorod remained independent. The grand dukes of Moscow emerged as leaders of a coalition of princes that eventually (by 1481) defeated the Mongols. After the fall of Constantinople in 1453, the **Tsars** (Caesars) at Moscow (from Ivan III, r. 1462-1505) set up an independent Russian Orthodox Church. Commerce failed to revive. The isolated Russian state remained agrarian, with the peasant class falling into serfdom.

Persia. A revival of Persian literature, making use of the Arab alphabet and literary forms, began in the 10th cent. (epic of Firdausi, 935-1020). An art revival, influenced by Chinese styles introduced after the Mongols came to power in Iran, began in the 13th cent. Persian cultural and political forms, and often the Persian language, were used for centuries by Turkish and Mongol elites from the Balkans to India. Persian mystics from Rumi (1207-73) to Jami (1414-92) promoted **Sufism** in their poetry.

Africa. Two militant Islamic Berber dynasties emerged from the Sahara to carve out empires from the Sahel to central Spain—the **Almoravids** (c. 1050-1140) and the fanatical **Almohads** (c. 1125-1269). The Ghanaian empire was replaced in the upper Niger by Mali (c. 1230-1340), whose Muslim rulers imported Egyptians to help make **Timbuktu** a center of commerce (in gold, leather, and slaves) and learning. The Songhay empire (to 1590) replaced Mali. To the S, forest kingdoms produced refined artworks (Ife terra cotta, **Benin** bronzes).

Other **Muslim states** in Nigeria (Hausas) and Chad originated in the 11th cent. and continued in some form until the 19th-cent. European conquest. Less-developed Bantu kingdoms existed across central Africa.

Some 40 Muslim Arab-Persian trading colonies and city-states were established all along the E African coast from the 10th cent. (Kilwa, Mogadishu). The interchange with Bantu peoples produced the **Swahili** language and culture. Gold, palm oil, and slaves were brought from the interior, stimulating the growth of the Monamatapa kingdom of the Zambezi (15th cent.). The Christian Ethiopian empire (from 13th cent.) continued the traditions of Axum.

Southeast Asia. Islam was introduced into Malaya and the Indonesian islands by Arab, Persian, and Indian traders. Coastal Muslim cities and states (starting before 1300) soon dominated the interior. Chief among these was the **Malacca** state (c. 1400-1511), on the Malay peninsula.

Arts and Statecraft Thrive in Europe: 1350-1600

Italy. Distinctive Italian achievements in literature and fine arts during the late Middle Ages (**Dante**, 1265-1321; **Giotto**, 1276-1337) led to the vigorous new styles of the Renaissance (14th-16th cent.). Patronized by the rulers of the quarreling petty states of Italy (**Medicis** in Florence and the papacy, c. 1400-1737), the plastic arts perfected realistic techniques, including **perspective** (Masaccio, 1401-28; Leonardo **da Vinci**, 1452-1519). Classical motifs were used in architecture, and increased talent and expense were put into secular buildings. The Florentine dialect was refined as a national literary language (**Petrarch**, 1304-74). Greek refugees from the E strengthened the respect of humanist scholars for the classic sources. Soon an international movement aided by the spread of **printing** (Gutenberg, c. 1397-1468), **humanism** was optimistic about the power of human reason (Erasmus of Rotterdam, 1466-1536, **More**'s *Utopia*, 1516) and valued individual effort in the arts and in politics (**Machiavelli**, 1469-1527).

France. The French monarchy, strengthened in its repeated struggles with powerful nobles (Burgundy, Flanders, Aquitaine) by alliances with the growing commercial towns, consolidated bureaucratic control under Philip IV (r. 1285-1314) and extended French influence into Germany and Italy (popes at Avignon, France, 1309-1417). The **Hundred Years War** (1337-1453) ended English dynastic claims in France (battles of Crécy, 1346, and Poitiers, 1356; Joan of Arc executed, 1431). A French Renaissance, dating from royal invasions (1494, 1499) of Italy, was encouraged at the court of Francis I (r. 1515-47), who centralized taxation and law. French vernacular literature consciously asserted its independence (La Pléiade, 1549).

England. The evolution of England's unique political institutions began with the **Magna Carta** (1215), by which King John guaranteed the privileges of nobles and church against the monarchy and assured jury trial. After the **Wars of the Roses** (1455-85), the **Tudor** dynasty reasserted royal prerogatives (Henry VIII, r. 1509-47), but the trend toward independent departments and ministerial government also continued. English trade (wool exports from c. 1340) was protected by the nation's growing maritime power (**Spanish Armada** destroyed, 1588).

English replaced French and Latin in the late 14th cent. in law and literature (**Chaucer**, c. 1340-1400) and English translation of the Bible began (Wycliffe, 1380s). **Elizabeth I** (r. 1558-1603) presided over a confident flowering of poetry (Spenser, 1552-99), drama (**Shakespeare**, 1564-1616), and music.

German Empire. From among a welter of minor feudal states, church lands, and independent cities, the **Habsburgs** assembled a far-flung territorial domain, based in Austria from 1276. Family members held the title of Holy Roman Emperor from 1438 to the Empire's dissolution in 1806, but failed to centralize its domains, leaving Germany disunited for centuries. Resistance to Turkish expansion brought Hungary under Austrian control from the 16th cent. The Netherlands, Luxembourg, and Burgundy were added in 1477, curbing French expansion.

The Flemish painting tradition of naturalism, technical proficiency, and bourgeois subject matter began in the 15th cent. (Jan **van Eyck**, c. 1390-1441), the earliest northern manifestation of the Renaissance. Albrecht **Dürer** (1471-1528) typified the merging of late Gothic and Italian trends in 16th-cent. German art. Imposing civic architecture flourished in the prosperous commercial cities.

Black Death. The bubonic plague reached Europe from the E in 1348, killing up to half the population by 1350 (and recurring periodically in most areas until the early 18th cent.). Labor scarcity forced wages to rise and brought greater freedom to the peasantry, making possible **peasant uprisings** (Jacquerie in France, 1358; Wat Tyler's rebellion in England, 1381).

Spain. Despite the unification of Castile and Aragon in 1479, the two countries retained separate governments, and the nobility, especially in Aragon and Catalonia, retained many privileges. Spanish lands in Italy (Naples, Sicily) and the Netherlands entangled the country in European wars through the mid-17th cent., while explorers, traders, and conquerors built up a Spanish empire in the Americas and the Philippines.

From the late 15th cent., a **golden age** of literature and art produced works of social satire (plays of Lope de Vega, 1562-1635; **Cervantes**, 1547-1616), as well as spiritual intensity (**El Greco**, 1541-1614; **Velazquez**, 1599-1660).

Explorations. Organized European maritime exploration began, seeking to evade the Venice-Ottoman monopoly of E trade and to promote Christianity. Beginning in 1418, expeditions from Portugal explored the W coast of Africa, until Vasco da Gama rounded the Cape of Good Hope in 1497 and reached India. A Portuguese trading empire was consolidated by the seizure of Goa (1510) and Malacca (1551). Japan was reached in 1542. The voyages of Christopher **Columbus** (1492-1504) uncovered a world new to Europeans, which Spain hastened to subdue. Navigation schools in Spain and Portugal, the development of large sailing ships (carracks) mounted with cannons, and the invention (c. 1475) of the rifle aided European penetration.

Mughals and Safavids. E of the Ottoman Empire, two Muslim dynasties ruled unchallenged in the 16th and 17th cent. The Mughal dynasty of India, founded by Persianized Turkish invaders from the NW under Babur, dates from their 1526 conquest of the Delhi Sultanate. The dynasty ruled most of India for more than 200 years, surviving nominally until 1857. **Akbar** (r. 1556-1605) consolidated administration at his glorious court, where the Urdu language (Persian-influenced Hindi) developed. Trade relations with Europe increased. Under Shah Jahan (1629-58), a secularized art fusing Hindu and Muslim elements flourished in miniature painting and in architecture (**Taj Mahal**). **Sikhism** (founded c. 1519) combined elements of both faiths. Suppression of Hindus and Shi'ite Muslims in S India in the late 17th cent. weakened the empire.

Fanatical devotion to the Shi'ite sect characterized the Safavids (1502-1736) of Persia and led to hostilities with the

Queen Elizabeth I, who ruled England for more than 40 years (1558-1603), presided over the age in which Shakespeare, Spenser, and Marlowe flourished.

Sunni Ottomans for more than a century. The prosperity and the strength of the empire are evidenced by the mosques at its capital city, **Isfahan**. The Safavids enhanced Iranian national consciousness.

China. The **Ming** emperors (1368-1644), the last native dynasty in China, wielded unprecedented personal power, while the Confucian bureaucracy began to suffer from inertia. European trade (Portuguese monopoly through **Macao** from 1557) was strictly controlled. Jesuit scholars and scientists (Matteo Ricci, 1552-1610) introduced some Western science; their writings familiarized the West with China. Chinese technological inven-

tiveness declined from this era, but the arts thrived, especially in the areas of painting and ceramics.

Japan. After the decline of the first hereditary *shogunate* (chief generalship) at **Kamakura** (1185-1333), fragmentation of power accelerated, as did the consequent social mobility. Under Kamakura and the Ashikaga shogunate (1338-1573), the *daimyos* (lords) and *samurai* (warriors) grew more powerful and promoted a martial ideology. Japanese pirates and traders plied the China coast. Popular Buddhist movements included the nationalist Nichiren sect (from c. 1250) and **Zen** (brought from China, 1191), which stressed meditation and a disciplined esthetic (tea ceremony, gardening, martial arts, *No* drama).

Reformed Europe Expands Overseas: 1500-1700

Reformation. Theological debate and protests against real and perceived clerical corruption existed in the medieval Christian world, expressed by such dissenters as John **Wycliffe** (c. 1320-84) and his followers (the Lollards) in England, and **Huss** (burned as a heretic, 1415) in Bohemia.

Martin **Luther** (1483-1546) preached that faith alone leads to salvation, without the mediation of clergy or good works. He attacked the authority of the pope, rejected priestly celibacy, and recommended individual study of the Bible (which he translated into German c. 1525). His 95 Theses (1517) led to his excommunication (1521). John **Calvin** (1509-64) said that God's elect were predestined for salvation and all others for damnation; good conduct and success were signs of election. Calvin in Geneva and John **Knox** (1505-72) in Scotland established theocratic states.

Henry VIII asserted English national authority and secular power by breaking away (1534) from the Catholic Church, creating what would become the Anglican Church. Monastic property was confiscated, and some Protestant doctrines given official sanction.

Religious wars. A century and a half of religious wars began with a S German peasant uprising (1524), repressed with Luther's support. Radical sects—democratic, pacifist, millenarian—arose (Anabaptists ruled Münster, 1534-35) and were suppressed violently. Civil war in France from 1562 between **Huguenots** (Protestant nobles and merchants) and Catholics ended with the 1598 **Edict of Nantes**, tolerating Protestants (revoked 1685). Habsburg attempts to restore Catholicism in Germany were resisted in 25 years of fighting; the 1555 Peace of Augsburg guarantee of religious independence to local princes and cities was confirmed only after the **Thirty Years' War** (1618-48), when much of Germany was devastated by local and foreign armies (Sweden, France).

A Catholic Reformation, or **Counter-Reformation**, met the Protestant challenge, defining an official theology at the Council of Trent (1545-63). The **Jesuit** order (Society of Jesus), founded in 1534 by Ignatius Loyola (1491-1556), helped reconvert large areas of Poland, Hungary, and S Germany and sent missionaries to the New World, India, and China, while the **Inquisition** suppressed heresy in Catholic countries. A revival of religious fervor appeared in devotional literature (Teresa of Avila, 1515-82) and in grandiose **Baroque** art (Bernini, 1598-1680).

Scientific Revolution. The late nominalist thinkers (Ockham, c. 1300-49) of Paris and Oxford challenged Aristotelian orthodoxy, allowing for a freer scientific approach. At the same time, metaphysical values, such as the Neoplatonic faith in an orderly, mathematical cosmos, still motivated and directed inquiry. Nicolaus **Copernicus** (1473-1543) promoted the heliocentric theory, which was confirmed when Johannes **Kepler** (1571-1630) discovered the mathematical laws describing the elliptical orbits of the planets. The traditional Christian-Aristotelian belief that the heavens and the earth were fundamentally different collapsed when **Galileo Galilei** (1564-1642) discovered moving sunspots, irregular moon topography, and moons around Jupiter, though he did face religious opposition (Galileo's retraction, 1633). He and Sir Isaac **Newton** (1642-1727) developed a mechanics that unified cosmic and earthly phenomena. Newton and Gottfried von **Leibniz** (1646-1716) invented calculus. René **Descartes**

(1596-1650), best known for his influential philosophy, also invented analytic geometry.

An explosion of **observational science** included the discovery of blood circulation (Harvey, 1578-1657) and microscopic life (Leeuwenhoek, 1632-1723), and advances in anatomy (Vesalius, 1514-64, dissected corpses) and chemistry (Boyle, 1627-91). Scientific research institutes were founded in Florence (1657), London (**Royal Society**, 1660), Paris (1666). Inventions proliferated (Savery's steam engine, 1696).

Arts. Mannerist trends of the High Renaissance (**Michelangelo**, 1475-1564) exploited virtuosity, grace, novelty, and exotic subjects and poses. The notion of artistic genius was promoted. Private connoisseurs entered the art market. These trends were elaborated in the 17th cent. **Baroque** era on a grander scale. Dynamic movement in painting and sculpture was emphasized by sharp lighting effects, rich materials (colored marble, gilt), and realistic details. Curved facades, broken lines, rich detail, and ceiling decoration characterized Baroque architecture. Monarchs, princes, and prelates, usually Catholic, used Baroque art to enhance and embellish their authority, as in royal portraits (Velazquez, 1599-1660; Van Dyck, 1599-1641).

National styles emerged. In France, a taste for rectilinear order and serenity (Poussin, 1594-1665), linked to the new rational philosophy, was expressed in classical forms. The influence of **classical values** in French literature (tragedies of **Racine**, 1639-99) gave rise to the "battle of the Ancients and Moderns." New forms included the essay (**Montaigne**, 1533-92) and novel (*Princesse de Cleves*, La Fayette, 1678).

Martin Luther, one of the primary catalysts of Protestantism, was excommunicated by Pope Leo X in 1521 over his 95 Theses (1517).

Dutch painting of the 17th cent. was unique in its wide social distribution. The Flemish tradition of undemonstrative realism reached its peak in **Rembrandt** (1606-69) and Jan Vermeer (1632-75).

Economy. European economic expansion, known as the **commercial revolution**, was stimulated by new trade with the East, by New World gold and silver, and by a doubling of population (50 million in 1450, 100 million in 1600). **New business and financial techniques** were developed and refined, such as joint-stock companies, insurance, and letters of credit and exchange. The Bank of Amsterdam (1609) and the Bank of England (1694) broke the old monopoly of private banking families. The rise of a business mentality was typified by the spread of clock towers in cities in the 14th cent. By the mid-15th cent., portable clocks were available; the first watch was invented in 1502.

By 1650, most governments had adopted the **mercantile system**, in which they sought to amass metallic wealth by protecting merchants' foreign and colonial trade monopolies. The rise in prices and the new coin-based economy undermined craft guild and feudal manorial systems. Expanding industries (clothweaving, mining) benefited from technical advances. Coal replaced wood as the chief fuel; it was used to fuel new 16th-cent. blast furnaces making cast iron.

New World. The **Aztecs** united much of the Meso-American area in a militarist empire by 1519, from their capital, Tenochtitlán (pop. 300,000), which was the center of a cult requiring ritual human sacrifice. Most of the civilized areas of South America were ruled by the centralized Inca Empire (1476-1534), stretching 2,000 mi from Ecuador to NW Argentina. Lavish and sophisticated traditions in pottery, weaving, sculpture, and architecture were maintained in both regions.

These empires, beset by revolts, fell in two short campaigns to gold-seeking Spanish forces based in the Antilles and Panama. Hernán **Cortés** took Mexico (1519-21); Francisco **Pizarro**, Peru (1532-35). From these centers, land and sea expeditions claimed most of North and South America for Spain. The indigenous high cultures did not survive the impact of **Christian missionaries** and the new upper class of whites and mestizos. Although the Spanish administration intermittently concerned itself with their welfare, the population was reduced by European diseases and remained impoverished at most levels. New World silver and such native products as potatoes, tobacco, corn, peanuts, chocolate, and rubber exercised a major economic influence on Europe.

Brazil, which the Portuguese reached in 1500 and settled after 1530, and the Caribbean colonies of several European nations developed a plantation economy where sugarcane, tobacco, cotton, coffee, rice, indigo, and lumber were grown by slaves. From the early 16th to late 19th cent., 10 million Africans were transported to **slavery** in the Americas and Caribbean islands.

Netherlands. The urban, Calvinist N provinces of the Netherlands rebelled (1568) against Habsburg Spain and founded an oligarchic mercantile republic. Their control of the Baltic grain market enabled them to exploit Mediterranean food shortages. Religious refugees—French and Belgian Protestants, Iberian Jews—added to the commercial talent pool. After Spain absorbed Portugal (1580), the Dutch seized Portuguese possessions and created a vast but short-lived commercial empire in Brazil, the Antilles, Africa, India, Ceylon, Malacca, Indonesia, and Taiwan. The Dutch also challenged or supplanted Portuguese traders in China and Japan. Revolution in 1640 restored Portuguese independence.

England. Anglicanism became firmly established under **Elizabeth I** after a brief Catholic interlude under "Bloody Mary" (1553-58). But religious and political conflicts led to a rebellion (1642) by Parliament. Forces of the Roundheads (Puritans) defeated the Cavaliers (Royalists); Charles I was beheaded (1649). The new Commonwealth was ruled as a military dictatorship by Oliver **Cromwell**, who also brutally crushed (1649-51) an Irish rebellion. Conflicts within the Puritan camp (democratic Levelers defeated, 1649) aided the Stuart restoration (1660), but Parliament was strengthened and the peaceful **"Glorious Revolution"** (1688) advanced political and religious liberties (writings of **Locke**, 1632-1704). British privateers (Drake, 1540-96) challenged Spanish control of the New World and penetrated Asian trade routes (Madras taken, 1639). North American colonies (Jamestown, 1607; Plymouth, 1620) provided an outlet for private enterprise and religious dissenters from Europe.

France. Emerging from the religious civil wars in 1628, France regained military and commercial great power status (under the ministries of **Richelieu**, Mazarin, and Colbert). Under **Louis XIV** (r. 1643-1715), royal absolutism triumphed over nobles and local *parlements* (defeat of Fronde, 1648-53). Permanent colonies were founded in Canada (1608), the Caribbean (1626), and India (1674).

Sweden. Sweden seceded from the Scandinavian Union in 1523. The thinly populated agrarian state (with copper, iron, and timber exports) was united by the Vasa kings, whose conquests by the mid-17th cent. made Sweden the dominant Baltic power. The empire collapsed in the Great Northern War (1700-21).

Poland. After the union with Lithuania in 1447, Poland ruled vast territories from the Baltic to the Black Sea, resisting German and Turkish incursions. Catholic nobles failed to gain the loyalty of their Orthodox Christian subjects in the E; commerce and trades were practiced by German and Jewish immigrants. The bloody 1648-49 Cossack uprising began the kingdom's dismemberment.

China. A new dynasty, the **Manchus**, invaded from the NE, seized power in 1644, and expanded Chinese control to its greatest extent in Central and SE Asia. Trade and diplomatic contact with Europe grew, carefully controlled by China. New crops (sweet potato, maize, peanut) allowed economic and population growth (pop. 300 million, in 1800). Traditional arts and literature were pursued with increased sophistication (*Dream of the Red Chamber*, novel, mid-18th cent.).

Japan. Tokugawa Ieyasu, shogun from 1603, finally unified and pacified feudal Japan. Hereditary nobles (daimyos and samurai) monopolized government office and the professions. An urban merchant class grew, literacy spread, and a cultural renaissance occurred (**haiku**, a verse innovation of the poet Basho, 1644-94). Fear of European domination led to persecution of Christian converts from 1597 and to stringent isolation from outside contact from 1640.

Philosophy, Industry, and Revolution: 1700-1800

Science and Reason. Greater faith in reason and empirical observation, instead of tradition and religious beliefs, espoused since the Renaissance (Francis Bacon, 1561-1626), was bolstered by scientific discoveries. René **Descartes** (1596-1650) used a rationalistic approach modeled on geometry and introspection to discover "self-evident" truths as a foundation of knowledge. Sir Isaac **Newton** emphasized induction from experimental observation. Baruch de **Spinoza** (1632-77), who called for political and intellectual freedom, developed a systematic rationalistic philosophy in his classic work *Ethics*.

French philosophers assumed leadership of the **Enlightenment** in the 18th cent. Montesquieu (1689-1755) used British history to support his notions of limited government. **Voltaire's** (1694-1778) diaries and novels of exotic travel illustrated the intellectual trends toward secular ethics and relativism. Jean-Jacques **Rousseau's** (1712-78) radical concepts of the **social contract** and of the inherent goodness of the common man gave impetus to antimonarchical republicanism. The *Encyclopedia* (1751-72, edited by Diderot and d'Alembert), designed as a monument to reason, was largely devoted to practical technology.

In England, ideals of liberty were connected with empiricist philosophy and science in the followers of John Locke. But British empiricism, especially as developed by the skeptical David **Hume** (1711-76), radically reduced the role of reason in philosophy, as did the evolutionary approach to law and politics of Edmund Burke (1729-97) and the utilitarian ethics of Jeremy Bentham (1748-1832). Adam Smith (1723-90) and other **physiocrats** called for a rationalization of economic activity by removing artificial barriers to a supposedly natural free exchange of goods known as **laissez-faire**.

German writers participated in the new philosophical trends popularized by Christian von Wolff (1679-1754). Immanuel **Kant's** (1724-1804) transcendental idealism, unifying an

The storming of the Bastille fortress (1789) marked the beginning of the French Revolution.

empirical epistemology with a priori moral and logical concepts, directed German thought away from skepticism. Italian contributions included work on electricity (Galvani, 1737-98; Volta, 1745-1827), the pioneer historiography of Vico (1668-1744), and writings on penal reform (Beccaria, 1738-94). Benjamin Franklin (1706-90) was celebrated in Europe for his varied achievements.

The growth of the *press* (*Spectator*, 1711-12) and the wide distribution of realistic but sentimental *novels* attested to the increase of a large bourgeois public.

Arts. Rococo art, characterized by extravagant decorative effects, asymmetries copied from organic models, and artificial pastoral subjects, was favored by the continental aristocracy for most of the cent. (Watteau, 1684-1721) and had musical analogies in the ornamentalized polyphony of late Baroque. The **Neoclassical** art after 1750, associated with the new scientific archaeology, was more streamlined and was infused with the supposed moral and geometric rectitude of the Roman Republic (David, 1748-1825). In England, **town planning** on a grand scale began.

Industrial Revolution in England. Agricultural improvements, such as the sowing drill (1701) and livestock breeding, were implemented on the large fields provided by enclosure of common lands by private owners. Profits from agriculture and from colonial and foreign trade (1800 volume, £54 million) were channeled through hundreds of banks and the **Stock Exchange** (established 1773) into new industrial processes.

The Newcomen steam pump (1712) aided coal mining. Coal fueled the new efficient steam engines patented by James Watt in 1769, and coke-smelting produced cheap, sturdy iron for machinery by the 1730s. The **flying shuttle** (1733) and **spinning jenny** (c. 1764) were used in the large new cotton textile factories, where women and children were much of the work force. Goods were transported cheaply over **canals** (2,000 mi; built 1760-1800).

American Revolution. The British colonies in North America attracted a mass immigration of religious dissenters and poor people throughout the 17th and 18th cent., coming from the British Isles, Germany, the Netherlands, and other countries. The population reached 3 million non-natives by the 1770s. The indigenous population was greatly reduced by European diseases and by wars with the various colonies. British attempts to control colonial trade and to tax the colonists to pay for the costs of colonial administration and defense clashed with local self-government and eventually provoked the colonies to a successful rebellion.

Central and East Europe. The monarchs of the three states that dominated E Europe—Austria, Prussia, and Russia—accepted the advice and legitimation of philosophes in creating modern, centralized institutions in their kingdoms, which were enlarged by the division (1772-95) of Poland.

Under **Frederick II** (called the Great) (r. 1740-86) Prussia, with its efficient modern army, doubled in size. State monopolies and tariff protection fostered industry, and some legal reforms were introduced. Austria's heterogeneous realms were unified under **Maria Theresa** (r. 1740-80) and **Joseph II** (r. 1780-90). Reforms in education, law, and religion were enacted, and the Austrian serfs were freed (1781). With its defeat in the Seven Years' War in 1763, Austria failed to regain Silesia, which had been seized by Prussia, but it was compensated by expansion to the E and S (Hungary, Slavonia, 1699; Galicia, 1772).

Russia, whose borders continued to expand, adopted some Western bureaucratic and economic policies under **Peter I** (r. 1682-1725) and **Catherine II** (r. 1762-96). Trade and cultural contacts with the West multiplied from the new Baltic Sea capital, **St. Petersburg** (est. 1703).

French Revolution. The growing French middle class lacked political power and resented aristocratic tax privileges, especially in light of the successful American Revolution. Peasants lacked adequate land and were burdened with feudal obligations to nobles. War with Britain led to the loss of French Canada and drained the treasury, finally forcing the king to call the **Estates-General** in 1789 for the first time since 1614, in an atmosphere of food riots (poor crop in 1788).

Aristocratic resistance to absolutism was soon overshadowed by the reformist Third Estate (middle class), which proclaimed itself the **National Constituent Assembly** June 17 and took the "Tennis Court oath" on June 20 to secure a constitution. The storming of the **Bastille** on July 14, 1789, by Parisian artisans was followed by looting and seizure of aristocratic property throughout France. Assembly reforms included abolition of class and regional privileges, a Declaration of Rights, suffrage by taxpayers (75% of male population), and the **Civil Constitution of the Clergy** providing for election and loyalty oaths for priests. A republic was declared Sept. 22, 1792, in spite of royalist pressure from Austria and Prussia, which had declared war in April (joined by Britain the next year). Louis XVI was beheaded Jan. 21, 1793, and Queen Marie Antoinette was beheaded Oct. 16, 1793.

Royalist uprisings in La Vendée and military reverses led to institution of a **reign of terror** in which tens of thousands of opponents of the Revolution and criminals were executed. Radical reforms in the **Convention** period (Sept. 1793-Oct. 1795) included the abolition of colonial slavery, economic measures to aid the poor, support of public education, and a short-lived de-Christianization.

Division among radicals (execution of Hebert, Danton, and Robespierre, 1794) aided the ascendancy of a moderate **Directory**, which consolidated military victories. **Napoleon Bonaparte** (1769-1821), a popular young general, exploited political divisions and participated in a coup Nov. 9, 1799, making himself first consul (dictator).

India. Sikh and Hindu rebels (Rajputs, Marathas) and Afghans destroyed the power of the Mughals during the 18th cent. After France's defeat (1763) in the Seven Years' War, Britain was the primary European trade power in India. Its control of inland **Bengal** and **Bihar** was recognized (1765) by the Mughal shah, who granted the **British East India Co.** (under Clive, 1725-74) the right to collect land revenue there. Despite objections from Parliament (1784 India Act), the company's involvement in local wars and politics led to repeated acquisitions of new territory. The company exported Indian textiles, sugar, and indigo.

Nationalism Gathers Momentum: 1800-40

French ideals and empire spread. Inspired by the ideals of the French Revolution, and supported by the expanding French armies, new republican regimes arose near France: the **Batavian** Republic in the Netherlands (1795-1806), the **Helvetic** Republic in Switzerland (1798-1803), the **Cisalpine** Republic in N Italy (1797-1805), the **Ligurian** Republic in Genoa (1797-1805), and the **Parthenopean** Republic in S Italy

(1799). A Roman Republic existed briefly in 1798 after Pope Pius VI was arrested by French troops. In Italy and Germany, new nationalist sentiments were stimulated both in imitation of and in reaction to developments in France (anti-French and anti-Jacobin peasant uprisings in Italy, 1796-99).

From 1804, when Napoleon declared himself emperor, to 1812, a succession of military victories (Austerlitz, 1805;

Jena, 1806) extended his control over most of Europe, through puppet states (**Confederation of the Rhine** united W German states for the first time and **Grand Duchy of Warsaw** revived Polish national hopes), expansion of the empire, and alliances.

Among the lasting reforms initiated under Napoleon's absolutist reign were: establishment of the Bank of France, centralization of tax collection, codification of law along Roman models (Code Napoléon), and reform and extension of secondary and university education. In an 1801 concordat, the papacy recognized the effective autonomy of the French Catholic Church.

Napoleon's continental successes were offset by British victory under Adm. Horatio Nelson in the **Battle of Trafalgar** (1805). In all, some 400,000 French soldiers were killed in the Napoleonic Wars, along with about 600,000 foreign troops.

Last gasp of old regime. The disastrous 1812 invasion of Russia exposed Napoleon's overextension. After Napoleon's 1814 exile at Elba, his armies were defeated (1815) at **Waterloo**, by British and Prussian troops.

At the **Congress of Vienna**, the monarchs and princes of Europe redrew their boundaries, to the advantage of Prussia (in Saxony and the Ruhr), Austria (in Illyria and Venetia), and Russia (in Poland and Finland). British conquest of Dutch and French colonies (S Africa, Ceylon, Mauritius) was recognized, and France, under the restored Bourbons, retained its expanded 1792 borders. The settlement brought 50 years of international peace to Europe.

But the Congress was unable to check the advance of liberal ideals and of nationalism among the smaller European nations. The 1825 **Decembrist** uprising by liberal officers in Russia was easily suppressed. But an independence movement in **Greece**, stirred by commercial prosperity and a cultural revival, succeeded in expelling Ottoman rule by 1831, with the aid of Britain, France, and Russia.

A constitutional monarchy was secured in France by the **1830 Revolution**; Louis Philippe became king. The revolutionary contagion spread to **Belgium**, which gained its independence (1830) from the Dutch monarchy, to **Poland**, whose rebellion was defeated (1830-31) by Russia, and to Germany.

Romanticism. A new style in intellectual and artistic life replaced Neoclassicism and Rococo after the mid-18th cent. By the early 19th cent., Romanticism prevailed in Europe.

Rousseau had begun the reaction against rationalism; in education (*Émile*, 1762) he stressed subjective spontaneity over regularized instruction. German writers (Lessing, 1729-81; Herder, 1744-1803) favorably compared the German folk song to classical forms and began a cult of Shakespeare, whose passion and "natural" wisdom was a model for the romantic *Sturm und Drang* (Storm and Stress) movement. Goethe's *Sorrows of Young Werther* (1774) set the model for the tragic, passionate genius.

A new interest in **Gothic architecture** in England after 1760 (Walpole, 1717-97) spread through Europe, associated with an aesthetic Christian and mystic revival (Blake, 1757-1827). Celtic, Norse, and German mythology and folk tales were revived or imitated (Grimm's Fairy Tales, 1812-22). The medieval revival (Scott's *Ivanhoe*, 1819) led to a new interest in history, stressing national differences and organic growth (**Carlyle**, 1795-1881; Michelet, 1798-1874), corresponding to theories of natural evolution (Lamarck's *Philosophie Zoologique*, 1809; Lyell's *Geology*, 1830-33). A reaction against classicism characterized the English **romantic poets** (beginning with **Wordsworth**, 1770-1850). Revolution and war fed an emphasis on freedom and conflict, expressed by both poets (**Byron**, 1788-1824; **Hugo**, 1802-85) and philosophers (**Hegel**, 1770-1831).

Wild gardens replaced the formal French variety, and painters favored rural, stormy, and mountainous landscapes (**Turner**, 1775-1851; **Constable**, 1776-1837). Clothing became freer, with wigs, hoops, and ruffles discarded. Originality and genius were expected in the life and work of inspired artists (Murger's *Scenes from Bohemian Life*, 1847-49). Exotic locales and themes (as in Gothic horror stories) were used in art and literature (Delacroix, 1798-1863; **Poe**, 1809-49). Music exhibited the new dramatic style and a breakdown of classical forms (**Beethoven**, 1770-1827). The use of folk melodies and modes aided the growth of distinct national traditions (Glinka in Russia, 1804-57).

Latin America. Francois **Toussaint L'Ouverture** led a successful slave revolt in Haiti, which subsequently became the first Latin American state to achieve independence (1804). The mainland Spanish colonies won their independence (1810-24), under such leaders as Simón **Bolívar** (1783-1830). Brazil became an independent empire (1822) under the Portuguese prince regent. A new class of military officers divided power with large landholders and the church.

United States. Territory under U.S. control nearly doubled in size with the **Louisiana Purchase** (1803). Heavy immigration and exploitation of ample natural resources fueled rapid economic growth. The spread of the franchise, public education, and antislavery sentiment were signs of a widespread democratic ethic.

China. Failure to keep pace with Western arms technology exposed China to greater European influence and hampered efforts to bar imports of opium, which had damaged Chinese society and drained wealth overseas. In the **Opium War** (1839-42), Britain forced China to expand trade opportunities and to cede Hong Kong.

Triumph of Progress: 1840-80

Idea of progress. As a result of the cumulative scientific, economic, and political changes of the preceding eras, the idea took hold among literate people in the West that continuing growth and improvement was the usual state of human and natural life.

Charles **Darwin's** statement of the **theory of evolution** and survival of the fittest (*On the Origin of Species*, 1859), defended by intellectuals and scientists against theological objections, was taken as confirmation that progress was the natural direction of life. The controversy helped define popular ideas of the dedicated scientist and of science's increasing control over the world (Foucault's demonstration of earth's rotation, 1851; **Pasteur's** germ theory, 1861).

Liberals following Ricardo (1772-1823) in their faith that unrestrained competition would bring continuous economic expansion sought to adjust political life to new social realities and believed that unregulated competition of ideas would yield truth (**Mill**, 1806-73). In England, successive reform bills (1832, 1867, 1884) gave representation to the new industrial towns and extended the franchise to the middle and lower classes and to Catholics, Dissenters, and Jews. On both sides of the Atlantic, reformists tried to improve conditions for the mentally ill (**Dix**, 1802-87), women (Anthony, 1820-1906), and prisoners. Slavery was barred in the British Empire (1833), the U.S. (1865), and Brazil (1888).

Socialist theories based on ideas of human perfectibility or progress were widely disseminated. Utopian socialists such as Saint-Simon (1760-1825) envisaged an orderly, just society directed by a technocratic elite. A model factory town, New Lanark, Scotland, was set up by utopian Robert Owen (1771-1858), and communal experiments were tried in the U.S. (Brook Farm, MA, 1841-47). Bakunin's (1814-76) anarchism represented the opposite extreme of total freedom. Karl Marx (1818-83) posited the inevitable triumph of socialism in industrial countries through a dialectical process of class conflict.

Spread of industry. The technical processes and managerial innovations of the English industrial revolution spread to Europe (especially Germany) and the U.S., causing an explosion of industrial production, demand for raw materials, and competition for markets. Inventors, both trained and self-taught, provided means for larger-scale production (Bessemer steel, 1856; sewing machine, 1846). Many inventions were shown at the universal prosperity-themed 1851 London Great Exhibition at the **Crystal Palace**.

Local specialization and long-distance trade were aided by a revolution in transportation and communication. Railroads were first introduced in the 1820s in England and the U.S. Over 150,000 mi of track had been laid worldwide by 1880, with another 100,000 mi laid in the next decade. Steamships were

Charles Darwin's *On the Origin of Species* **(1859) was based on his travels more than 20 years earlier on the British survey ship HMS** *Beagle.*

improved (*Savannah* crossed Atlantic, 1819). The **telegraph,** perfected by 1844 (Morse), connected the Old and New Worlds by cable in 1866 and quickened the pace of international commerce and politics. The first commercial **telephone** exchange went into operation in the U.S. in 1878.

The new class of industrial workers, uprooted from their rural homes, lacked job security and suffered from dangerous overcrowding at work and at home. Many responded by organizing **trade unions** (legalized in England, 1824; France, 1884). The U.S. Knights of Labor had 700,000 members by 1886. The First International (1864-76) tried to unite workers worldwide around a Marxist program. The quasi-Socialist Paris Commune uprising (1871) was violently suppressed. Acts to reduce child labor and regulate conditions were passed (1833-50 in England). Social security measures were introduced by the Bismarck regime (1883-89) in Germany.

Revolutions of 1848. Among the causes of the continent-wide revolutions were an international collapse of credit and resulting unemployment, bad harvests in 1845-47, and a cholera epidemic. The new urban proletariat and expanding bourgeoisie demanded greater political roles. Republics were proclaimed in France, Rome, and Venice. Nationalist feelings reached fever pitch in the Habsburg empire, as Hungary declared independence under Kossuth, a Slav Congress demanded equality, and Piedmont tried to drive Austria from Lombardy. A national liberal assembly at Frankfurt called for German unification.

But riots fueled bourgeois fear of socialism (**Marx** and **Engels,** *Communist Manifesto,* 1848), and peasants remained conservative. The old establishment—the Papacy, the Habsburgs with the help of the Czarist Russian army—was able to rout the revolutionaries by 1849. The French Republic succumbed to a renewed monarchy by 1852 (Emperor Napoleon III).

Great nations unified. Using the "blood and iron" tactics of Bismarck from 1862, Prussia controlled N Germany by 1867 (war with Denmark, 1864; Austria, 1866). After

defeating France in 1870 (annexation of Alsace-Lorraine), it won the allegiance of S German states. A new **German Empire** was proclaimed (1871). **Italy,** inspired by Giuseppe Mazzini (1805-72) and Giuseppe Garibaldi (1807-82), was unified by the reformed Piedmont kingdom through uprisings, plebiscites, and war.

The **United States** its area expanded after the 1846-48 Mexican War, defeated (1861-65) a secession attempt by Southern states in the **Civil War.** Canadian provinces were united in an autonomous **Dominion of Canada** (1867). Control in **India** was removed from the East India Co. and centralized under British administration after the 1857-58 Sepoy rebellion, laying the groundwork for the modern Indian state. Queen Victoria was named Empress of India (1876).

Europe dominates Asia. The Ottoman Empire began to collapse in the face of Balkan nationalisms and European imperial incursions in N Africa (**Suez Canal,** 1869). The Turks had lost control of most of both regions by 1882. Russia completed its expansion S by 1884 (despite the temporary setback of the **Crimean War** with Turkey, Britain, and France, 1853-56), taking Turkestan, all the Caucasus, and Chinese areas in the E and sponsoring Balkan Slavs against the Turks. A succession of reformist and reactionary regimes presided over a slow modernization (serfs freed, 1861). Persian independence suffered as Russia and British India competed for influence.

China was forced to sign a series of unequal treaties with European powers and Japan. Overpopulation and an inefficient dynasty brought misery and caused rebellions (Taiping, Muslims) leaving tens of millions dead. **Japan** was forced by the U.S. (Commodore Perry's visits, 1853-54) and Europe to end its isolation. The Meiji restoration (1868) gave power to a Westernizing oligarchy. Intensified empire-building gave Burma to Britain (1824-85) and Indochina to France (1862-95). Christian missionary activity followed imperial and trade expansion in Asia.

Respectability. Fine arts were expected to reflect and encourage good morals and manners among the Victorians. Prudery, exaggerated delicacy, and familial piety were exemplified by **Bowdler's** expurgated Shakespeare edition (1818). Government-supported mass education sought to inculcate a work ethic as a means to escape poverty (Horatio **Alger,** 1832-99).

The official **Beaux Arts** school in Paris set an international style of imposing public buildings (Paris Opera, 1861-74; Vienna Opera, 1861-69) and uplifting statues (Bartholdi's Statue of Liberty, 1884). Realist painting, influenced by photography (Daguerre, 1837), appealed to a new mass audience with social or historical narrative (Wilkie, 1785-1841; Poynter, 1836-1919) or with serious religious, moral, or social messages (pre-Raphaelites, Millet's *Angelus,* 1858), often drawn from ordinary life. The **Impressionists** (Monet, 1840-1926; Pissarro, 1830-1903; Renoir, 1841-1919) rejected the formalism, sentimentality, and precise techniques of academic art in favor of a spontaneous, undetailed rendering of the world through careful representation of the effect of natural light on objects.

Realistic **novelists** presented the full panorama of social classes and personalities, but retained sentimentality and moral judgment (**Dickens,** 1812-70; **Eliot,** 1819-80; **Tolstoy,** 1828-1910; **Balzac,** 1799-1850).

Veneer of Stability: 1880-1900

Imperialism triumphant. The vast **African** interior, visited by European explorers (Barth, 1821-65; Livingstone, 1813-73), was conquered by the European powers in rapid, competitive thrusts from their coastal bases after 1880, mostly for domestic political and international strategic reasons. W African Muslim kingdoms (Fulani), Arab slave traders (Zanzibar), and Bantu military confederations (Zulu) were alike subdued. Only Christian Ethiopia (defeat of Italy, 1896) and Liberia resisted successfully. France (W Africa) and Britain ("Cape to Cairo," **Boer War,** 1899-1902) were the major beneficiaries. The ideology of "the white man's burden" (Kipling, *Barrack Room Ballads,* 1892) or of a "civilizing mission" (France) justified the conquests.

W European foreign capital investment soared to nearly $40 billion by 1914, but most was in E Europe (France, Germany), the Americas (Britain), and Europe's colonies. The foundation of the modern interdependent world economy was laid, with cartels dominating raw material trade.

An industrious world. Industrial and technological proficiency characterized the two new great powers—Germany and the U.S. Coal and iron deposits enabled Germany to reach second- or third-place status in iron, steel, and shipbuilding by the 1900s. German electrical and chemical industries were world leaders. The U.S. post-Civil War boom (interrupted by financial panics—1884, 1893, 1896) was shaped by massive immigration from S and E Europe from 1880, government subsidy of railroads, and huge private monopolies (Standard Oil,

1870; U.S. Steel, 1901). The **Spanish-American War**, 1898 (Philippine Insurrection, 1899-1902), and the **Open Door policy** in China (1899) made the U.S. a world power.

England led in **urbanization**, with London the world capital of finance, insurance, and shipping. Sewer systems (Paris, 1850s), electric subways (London, 1890), parks, and bargain department stores helped improve living standards for most of the urban population of the industrial world.

Westernization of Asia. Asian reaction to European economic, military, and religious incursions took the form of imitation of Western techniques and adoption of Western ideas of progress and freedom. The Chinese "self-strengthening" movement of the 1860s and 1870s included rail, port, and arsenal improvements and metal and textile mills. Reformers such as **K'ang Yu-wei** (1858-1927) won liberalizing reforms in 1898, right after the European and Japanese "scramble for concessions."

A universal education system in Japan and importation of foreign industrial, scientific, and military experts aided Japan's rapid modernization after 1868, under the authoritarian Meiji regime. Japan's victory in the **Sino-Japanese War** (1894-95) put Formosa and Korea in its power.

In India, the British alliance with the remaining princely states masked reform sentiment among the Westernized urban elite; higher education had been conducted largely in English for 50 years. The **Indian National Congress**, founded in 1885, demanded a larger government role for Indians.

Fin-de-siècle **sophistication.** Naturalist writers pushed realism to its extreme limits, adopting a quasi-scientific attitude and writing about formerly taboo subjects such as sex, crime, extreme poverty, and corruption (Flaubert, 1821-80; Zola, 1840-1902; Hardy, 1840-1928). Unseen or repressed psychological motivations were explored in the clinical and theoretical works of Sigmund **Freud** (1856-1939) and in works of fiction (**Dostoyevsky**, 1821-81; James, 1843-1916; Schnitzler, 1862-1931).

A contempt for bourgeois life or a desire to shock a complacent audience was shared by the French **symbolist** poets (Verlaine, 1844-96; Rimbaud, 1854-91), by neopagan English writers (Swinburne, 1837-1909), by continental dramatists (**Ibsen**, 1828-1906), and by satirists (**Wilde**, 1854-1900). The German philosopher Friedrich **Nietzsche** (1844-1900) was influential in his elitism and pessimism.

Postimpressionist art neglected long-cherished conventions of representation (**Cézanne**, 1839-1906) and showed a willingness to learn from primitive and non-European art (**Gauguin**, 1848-1903; Japanese prints).

Racism. Gobineau (1816-82) gave a pseudobiological foundation to modern racist theories, which spread in Europe in the latter 19th cent., along with **Social Darwinism**, the belief that societies are and should be organized as a struggle for survival of the fittest. The medieval period was interpreted as an era of natural Germanic rule (Chamberlain, 1855-1927), and notions of racial superiority were associated with German national aspirations (Treitschke, 1834-96). **Anti-Semitism**, with a new racist rationale, became a significant political force in Germany (Anti-Semitic Petition, 1880), Austria (Lueger, 1844-1910), and France (**Dreyfus affair**, 1894-1906).

Last Respite: 1900-09

Alliances. While the peace of Europe (and its dependencies) continued to hold (1907 **Hague Conference** extended the rules of war and international arbitration procedures), imperial rivalries, protectionist trade practices (in Germany and France), and the escalating arms race (British *Dreadnought* battleship launched; Germany widens Kiel canal, 1906) exacerbated minor disputes (German-French Moroccan "crises," 1905, 1911).

Security was sought through balance-of-power alliances: **Triple Alliance** (Germany, Austria-Hungary, Italy; renewed in 1902 and 1907); Anglo-Japanese Alliance (1902), Franco-Russian Alliance (1899), **Entente Cordiale** (Britain, France, 1904), Anglo-Russian Treaty (1907), German-Ottoman friendship.

Ottomans decline. The inefficient, corrupt Ottoman government was unable to resist further loss of territory. Nearly all European lands were lost in 1912 to Serbia, Greece, Montenegro, and Bulgaria. Italy took Libya and the Dodecanese islands the same year, and Britain took Kuwait (1899) and the Sinai (1906). The **Young Turk** revolution in 1908 forced the sultan to restore a constitution, and it introduced some social reform, industrialization, and secularization.

British Empire. British trade and cultural influence remained dominant in the empire, but constitutional reforms presaged its eventual dissolution. The colonies of **Australia** were united in 1901 under a self-governing commonwealth. **New Zealand** acquired dominion status in 1907. The old Boer republics joined Cape Colony and Natal in the self-governing Union of **South Africa** in 1910.

The 1909 Indian Councils Act enhanced the role of elected province legislatures in **India**. The Muslim League (founded 1906) sought separate communal representation.

East Asia. Japan exploited its growing industrial power to expand its empire. Victory in the 1904-05 war against Russia (naval battle of Tsushima, 1905) assured Japan's domination of **Korea** (annexed 1910) and Manchuria (Port Arthur taken, 1905).

In China, central authority began to crumble (empress died, 1908). Reforms (Confucian exam system ended 1905, modernization of the army, building of railroads) were inadequate, and secret societies of reformers and nationalists, inspired by the Westernized **Sun Yat-sen** (1866-1925), fomented periodic uprisings in the S.

Siam, whose independence had been guaranteed by Britain and France in 1896, was split into spheres of influence by those countries in 1907.

Russia. The population of the Russian Empire approached 150 million in 1900. Reforms in education, in law, and in local institutions (*zemstvos*) and an industrial boom starting in the 1880s (oil, railroads) created the beginnings of a modern state, despite the autocratic tsarist regime. Liberals (1903 Union of Liberation), Socialists (Social Democrats founded 1898, Bolsheviks split off 1903), and populists (Social Revolutionaries founded 1901) were periodically repressed, and national minorities were persecuted (anti-Jewish pogroms, 1903, 1905-06).

An industrial crisis after 1900 and harvest failures aggravated poverty among urban workers, and the 1904-05 defeat by Japan (which checked Russia's Asian expansion) sparked the **Revolution of 1905-06**. A **Duma** (parliament) was created under Tsar Nicholas II, and agricultural reform (under Stolypin, prime minister, 1906-11) created a large class of land-owning peasants (*kulaks*).

The world shrinks. Developments in transportation and communication and mass population movements helped create an awareness of an interdependent world. Early **automobiles** (Daimler, Benz, 1885) were experimental or were designed as luxuries. Assembly-line mass production (Ford Motor Co., 1903) made the invention practical, and by 1910

Nicholas II, the last Russian tsar, was forced to abdicate in 1917 and was executed along with his family in 1918.

nearly 500,000 motor vehicles were registered in the U.S. alone. **Heavier-than-air flights** began in 1903 in the U.S. (Wright brothers' *Flyer*), preceded by glider, balloon, and model plane advances in several countries. Trade was advanced by improvements in **ship design** (gyrocompass, 1910), speed (*Lusitania* crossed Atlantic in five days, 1907), and reach (Panama Canal begun, 1904).

The first transatlantic **radio** telegraphic transmission occurred in 1901, six years after Marconi discovered radio. Radio transmission of human speech had been made in 1900. Telegraphic transmission of photos was achieved in 1904, lending immediacy to news reports. **Phonographs**, popularized by Caruso's recordings (starting 1902), made for quick international spread of musical styles (ragtime). **Motion pictures**, perfected in the 1890s (Dickson, Lumière brothers), became a popular and artistic medium after 1900; newsreels appeared in 1909.

Emigration from crowded European centers soared in the decade: 9 million migrated to the U.S., and millions more went to Siberia, Canada, Argentina, Australia, South Africa, and Algeria. Some 70 million Europeans emigrated in the century before 1914. Several million Chinese, Indians, and Japanese migrated to SE Asia, where their urban skills often enabled them to take a predominant economic role.

Social reform. The social and economic problems of the poor were kept in the public eye by realist fiction writers (Dreiser's *Sister Carrie*, 1900; Gorky's *Lower Depths*, 1902; Sinclair's *The Jungle*, 1906), journalists (U.S. **muckrakers**—Steffens, Tarbell), and artists (Ashcan school). Frequent labor strikes and occasional assassinations by anarchists or radicals (Empress Elizabeth of Austria, 1898; King Umberto I of Italy, 1900; U.S. Pres. McKinley, 1901; Russian Interior Min.

Plehve, 1904; Portugal's King Carlos, 1908) added to social tension and fear of revolution.

But democratic reformism prevailed. In Germany, Bernstein's (1850-1932) **revisionist Marxism**, downgrading revolution, was accepted by the powerful Social Democrats and trade unions. The British Fabian Society (the Webbs, Shaw) and the Labour Party (founded 1906) worked for reforms such as social security and union rights (1906), while woman suffragists grew more militant. U.S. **progressives** fought big business (Pure Food and Drug Act, 1906). In France, the 10-hour work day (1904) and separation of church and state (1905) were reform victories, as was universal suffrage in Austria (1907).

Arts. An unprecedented period of experimentation, centered in France, produced several **new painting styles:** Fauvism exploited bold color areas (Matisse, *Woman With Hat*, 1905); expressionism reflected powerful inner emotions (the Brücke group, 1905); Cubism combined several views of an object on one flat surface (Picasso, *Demoiselles*, 1906-07); futurism tried to depict speed and motion (Italian Futurist Manifesto, 1910). **Architects** explored new uses of steel structures, with facades either neoclassical (Adler and Sullivan in U.S.), curvilinear Art Nouveau (Gaudi's Casa Mila, 1905-10), or functionally streamlined (Wright's Robie House, 1909).

Music and dance shared the experimental spirit. Ruth St. Denis (1877-1968) and Isadora Duncan (1878-1927) pioneered modern dance, while Sergei Diaghilev in Paris revitalized classic ballet from 1909. Composers explored atonal music (Debussy, 1862-1918) and dissonance (Schoenberg, 1874-1951) or revolutionized classical forms (Stravinsky, 1882-1971), often showing jazz or folk music influences.

War and Revolution: 1910-19

War threatens. Germany under Wilhelm II sought a political and imperial role consonant with its industrial strength, challenging Britain's world supremacy and threatening France, which was still nursing the loss (1871) of Alsace-Lorraine. Austria wanted to curb an expanded Serbia (after 1912) and the threat it posed to its own Slav lands. Russia feared Austrian and German political and economic aims in the Balkans and Turkey.

An accelerated arms race resulted from these circumstances. The German standing army rose to more than 2 million men by 1914. Russia and France had more than a million each, and Austria and the British Empire nearly a million each. Dozens of enormous battleships were built by the powers after 1906.

The **assassination of Austrian Archduke Franz Ferdinand** by a Serbian nationalist, June 28, 1914, was the pretext for war. The system of alliances made the conflict Europe-wide; Germany's invasion of Belgium to outflank France forced Britain to enter the war. Patriotic fervor was nearly unanimous among all classes in most countries.

World War I. German forces were stopped in France in one month. The rival armies dug **trench networks**. Artillery and improved machine guns prevented either side from any lasting advance despite repeated assaults (600,000 dead at **Verdun**, Feb.-July 1916). Poison gas, used by Germany in 1915, proved ineffective. The entrance of more than 1 million U.S. troops tipped the balance after mid-1917, forcing Germany to sue for peace the next year. The formal armistice was signed on Nov. 11, 1918.

In the E, the Russian armies were thrown back (battle of **Tannenberg**, Aug. 20, 1914), and the war grew unpopular in Russia. An allied attempt to relieve Russia through Turkey failed (**Gallipoli**, 1915). The **Russian Revolution** (1917) abolished the monarchy. The new Bolshevik regime signed the capitulatory Brest-Litovsk peace in Mar. 1918. Italy entered the war on the allied side in May 1915 but was pushed back by Oct. 1917. A renewed offensive with Allied aid in Oct.-Nov. 1918 forced Austria to surrender.

The British Navy successfully blockaded Germany, which responded with submarine U-boat attacks; **unrestricted submarine warfare** against neutrals after Jan. 1917 helped bring the U.S. into the war. Other battlefields included Palestine and

Mesopotamia, both of which Britain wrested from the Turks in 1917, and the African and Pacific colonies of Germany, most of which fell to Britain, France, Australia, Japan, and South Africa.

Settlement. At the **Paris Peace Conference** (Jan.-June 1919), concluded by the **Treaty of Versailles**, and in subsequent negotiations and local wars (Russian-Polish War, 1920), the **map of Europe** was redrawn with a nod to U.S. Pres. Woodrow Wilson's principle of self-determination. Austria and Hungary were separated, and much of their land was given to Yugoslavia (formerly Serbia), Romania, Italy, and the newly independent Poland and Czechoslovakia. Germany lost territory in the W, N, and E, while Finland and the Baltic states were detached from Russia. Turkey lost nearly all its Arab lands to British-sponsored

Both sides in World War I developed elaborate networks of dug-in trenches from which to fight.

Arab states or to direct French and British rule. Belgium's sovereignty was recognized.

From 1916, the civilian populations and economies of both sides were mobilized to an unprecedented degree. Hardships intensified among fighting nations in 1917 (French mutiny crushed in May). More than 10 million soldiers died in the war. A huge **reparations** burden and partial demilitarization were imposed on Germany. Pres. Wilson obtained approval for a League of Nations, but the U.S. Senate refused to allow the U.S. to join.

Russian revolution. Military defeats and high casualties caused a contagious lack of confidence in Tsar Nicholas, who was forced to abdicate Mar. 1917. A liberal provisional government failed to end the war, and massive desertions, riots, and fighting between factions followed. A moderate socialist government under Aleksandr Kerensky was overthrown (Nov. 1917) in a violent coup by the **Bolsheviks** in Petrograd under **Lenin**, who later disbanded the elected Constituent Assembly.

The Bolsheviks brutally suppressed all opposition and ended the war with Germany in Mar. 1918. Civil war broke out in the summer between the Red Army (the Bolsheviks and their supporters), and monarchists, anarchists, minority nationalities (Ukrainians, Georgians, Poles), and others. Small U.S., British, French, and Japanese units also opposed the Bolsheviks (1918-19; Japan in Vladivostok to 1922). The civil war, anarchy, and pogroms devastated the country until the 1920 Red Army victory. The **Communist Party** leadership retained absolute power.

Other European revolutions. An unpopular monarchy in **Portugal** was overthrown in 1910. The new republic took severe anticlerical measures in 1911.

After a century of Home Rule agitation, during which **Ireland** was devastated by famine (1 million dead, 1846-47) and emigration, republican militants staged an unsuccessful uprising in Dublin during **Easter 1916**. The execution of the leaders and

mass arrests by the British won popular support for the rebels. The **Irish Free State**, comprising all but the six N counties, achieved dominion status in 1922.

In the aftermath of the world war, radical revolutions were attempted in Germany (**Spartacist** uprising, Jan. 1919), **Hungary** (Kun regime, 1919), and elsewhere. All were suppressed or failed for lack of support.

Chinese revolution. The Manchu Dynasty was overthrown and a republic proclaimed in Oct. 1911. First Pres. Sun Yat-sen resigned in favor of strongman Yuan Shih-k'ai. Sun organized the parliamentarian **Kuomintang** party.

Students launched protests on May 4, 1919, against League of Nations concessions in China to Japan. Nationalist, liberal, and socialist ideas and political groups spread. The **Communist Party** was founded in 1921. A Communist regime took power in Mongolia with Soviet support in 1921.

India restive. Indian objections to British rule erupted in nationalist riots as well as in the nonviolent tactics of Mahatma **Gandhi** (1869-1948). Nearly 400 unarmed demonstrators were shot at **Amritsar** in Apr. 1919. Britain approved limited self-rule that year.

Mexican revolution. Under the long Diaz dictatorship (1877-1911) the economy advanced, but Indian and mestizo lands were confiscated, and concessions to foreigners (mostly U.S.) damaged the middle class. A **revolution in 1910** led to civil wars and U.S. intervention (1914, 1916-17). Land reform and a more democratic constitution (1917) were achieved.

Sciences. Scientific specialization prevailed by the 20th cent. Advances in knowledge and technological aptitude increased with the geometric rise in the number of practitioners. Physicists challenged common-sense views of causality, observation, and a mechanistic universe, putting science further beyond popular grasp (**Einstein**'s general theory of relativity, 1916; Bohr's quantum mechanics, 1913; Heisenberg's uncertainty principle, 1927).

Aftermath of War: 1920-29

U.S. Easy credit, technological ingenuity, and war-related industrial decline in Europe caused a long economic boom, in which ownership of new products—**autos, phones, radios**—became more democratized. **Prosperity**, an increase in women workers, women's suffrage (19th Amendment ratified, 1920), and drastic change in fashion (**flappers**, mannish bob for women, clean-shaven men) created a wide perception of social change, despite prohibition of alcoholic beverages (1919-33). Union membership and strikes increased. Fear of radicals led to Palmer raids (1919-20) and the Sacco-Vanzetti case (1921-27).

Europe sorts itself out. Germany's liberal **Weimar constitution** (1919) could not guarantee a stable government in the face of rightist violence (Rathenau assassinated, 1922) and Communist refusal to cooperate with Socialists. Reparations and Allied occupation of the Rhineland caused staggering inflation that destroyed middle-class savings, but economic expansion resumed after mid-decade, aided by U.S. loans. A sophisticated, **innovative culture** developed in architecture and design (Bauhaus, 1919-28), film (Lang, M, 1931), painting (Grosz), music (Weill, Threepenny Opera, 1928), theater (Brecht, A Man's a Man, 1926), criticism (Benjamin), philosophy (Jung), and fashion. This culture was considered decadent and socially disruptive by rightists.

England elected its first Labour governments (Jan. 1924, June 1929). A 10-day general strike in support of coal miners failed in May 1926. In **Italy**, strikes, political chaos, and violence by small Fascist bands culminated in the Oct. 1922 Fascist March on Rome, which established **Mussolini**'s dictatorship. Strikes were outlawed (1926), and Italian influence was pressed in the Balkans (Albania made a protectorate, 1926). A conservative dictatorship was also established in **Portugal** in a 1926 military coup.

Czechoslovakia, the only stable democracy to emerge from the war in Central or E Europe, faced opposition from Germans (in the Sudetenland), Ruthenians, and some Slovaks. As the industrial heartland of the old Habsburg empire, it remained fairly prosperous. With French backing, it formed the Little Entente with Yugoslavia (1920) and **Romania** (1921) to block Austrian or Hungarian irredentism. Croats and Slovenes in

Yugoslavia demanded a federal state until King Alexander I proclaimed (1929) a royal dictatorship. Poland faced internal nationality problems as well (Germans, Ukrainians, Jews); Pilsudski ruled as dictator from 1926. The Baltic states were threatened by traditionally dominant ethnic Germans and by Soviet-supported Communists.

An economic collapse and famine in **Russia** (1921-22) claimed 5 million lives. The New Economic Policy (1921) allowed land ownership by peasants and some private commerce and industry. **Stalin** was absolute ruler within four years of Lenin's death (1924). He inaugurated a brutal collectivization program (1929-32) and used foreign Communist parties for Soviet state advantage.

Internationalism. Revulsion against World War I led to pacifist legislation, to the Kellogg-Briand Pact renouncing aggressive war (1928), and to **naval disarmament** pacts (Washington, 1922; London, 1930). But the League of Nations was able to arbitrate only minor disputes (Greece-Bulgaria, 1925).

Middle East. Mustafa Kemal (**Ataturk**) led **Turkish** nationalists in resisting Italian, French, and Greek military advances (1919-23). The sultanate was abolished (1922), and elaborate reforms were passed, including secularization of law and adoption of the Latin alphabet. Ethnic conflict led to persecution of **Armenians** (more than 1 million dead in 1915, 1 million expelled), Greeks (forced Greek-Turk population exchange, 1923), and Kurds (1925 uprising).

With evacuation of the Turks from **Arab** lands, the puritanical Wahabi dynasty of E Arabia conquered (1919-25) what is now Saudi Arabia. British, French, and Arab dynastic and nationalist maneuvering resulted in the creation of two more Arab monarchies in 1921—Iraq and Transjordan (both under British control)—and two French mandates—Syria and Lebanon. Jewish immigration into British-mandated **Palestine**, inspired by the Zionist movement, was resisted by Arabs, at times violently (1921, 1929 massacres).

Reza Khan ruled **Persia** after his 1921 coup (shah from 1925), centralized control, and created the trappings of a modern secular state.

In 1922, English archaeologist Howard Carter discovered the **tomb** of the boy pharaoh **Tutankhamen** in the Valley of the Kings in Egypt.

China. The Kuomintang under **Chiang Kai-shek** (1887-1975) subdued the warlords by 1928. The Communists were brutally suppressed after their alliance with the Kuomintang was broken in 1927. Relative peace thereafter allowed for industrial and financial improvements, with some Russian, British, and U.S. cooperation.

Arts. Nearly all bounds of subject matter, style, and attitude were broken in the arts of the period. **Abstract** art first took inspiration from natural forms or narrative themes (Kandinsky from 1911) and then worked free of any representational aims

(Malevich's suprematism, 1915-19; Mondrian's geometric style from 1917). The **Dada** movement (from 1916) mocked artistic pretension with absurd collages and constructions. Paradox, illusion, and psychological taboos were exploited by **surrealists** by the late 1920s (Dali, Magritte). Architectural schools celebrated industrial values, whether vigorous abstract constructivism (Tatlin, *Monument to 3rd International*, 1919) or the machined, streamlined **Bauhaus** style, which was extended to many design fields (Helvetica typeface).

Prose writers explored revolutionary narrative modes related to dreams (Kafka's *Trial*, 1925), internal monologue (Joyce's *Ulysses*, 1922), and word play (Stein's *Making of Americans*, 1925). Poets and novelists wrote of modern alienation (Eliot's *Waste Land*, 1922) and aimlessness ("The Lost Generation").

Rise of Totalitarians: 1930-39

Depression. A worldwide financial panic and economic depression began with the Oct. 1929 U.S. stock market crash and the May 1931 failure of the Austrian Credit-Anstalt. A credit crunch caused international bankruptcies and **unemployment**: 12 million jobless by 1932 in the U.S., 5.6 million in Germany, 2.7 million in England. Governments responded with **tariff restrictions** (Smoot-Hawley Act, 1930; Ottawa Imperial Conference, 1932), which dried up world trade. Government public works programs were vitiated by deflationary budget balancing.

Germany. Years of agitation by violent extremists were brought to a head by the Depression. Nazi leader Adolf Hitler was named chancellor in Jan. 1933 and given dictatorial power by the Reichstag in March. Opposition parties were disbanded, strikes banned, and all aspects of economic, cultural, and religious life were brought under central government and Nazi party control and manipulated by sophisticated propaganda. Severe persecution of Jews began (**Nuremberg Laws**, Sept. 1935). Many Jews, political opponents, and others were sent to concentration camps (Dachau, 1933), where thousands died or were killed. Public works, renewed conscription (1935), arms production, and a four-year plan (1936) all but ended unemployment.

Italy's Benito Mussolini and Germany's Adolf Hitler affirmed their full political and military alliance with the Pact of Steel (1939).

Hitler's expansionism started with reincorporation of the Saar (1935), occupation of the **Rhineland** (Mar. 1936), and annexation of Austria (Mar. 1938). At **Munich** (Sept. 1938) Britain and France attempted to appease Hitler and avoid war by successfully encouraging Czechoslovakia's surrender of the Sudetenland settlement.

Russia. Rapid industrialization was achieved through successive **5-year plans** starting in 1928, using severe labor discipline and mass forced labor. Industry was financed by a decline in living standards and exploitation of agriculture, which was almost totally collectivized by the early 1930s (*kolkhoz* [collective farm]; *sovkhoz* [state farm], often in newly worked lands). Successive **purges** increased the role of professionals and management at the expense of workers. Millions perished in a series of manufactured disasters: extermination (1929-34) of kulaks (peasant landowners), severe famine (1932-33), party purges and show trials (Great Purge, 1936-38), suppression of nationalities, and poor conditions in labor camps.

Spain. An industrial revolution during World War I created an urban proletariat, which was attracted to socialism and anarchism; Catalan nationalists challenged central authority. The five years after King Alfonso left Spain in Apr. 1931 were dominated by tension between intermittent leftist and anticlerical governments and clericals, monarchists, and other rightists. Anarchist and Communist rebellions were crushed, but a July 1936 extreme right rebellion led by Gen. Francisco **Franco** and aided by Nazi Germany and Fascist Italy succeeded, after a three-year **civil war** (more than 1 million dead in battles and atrocities). The war polarized international public opinion.

Italy. Despite propaganda for the ideal of the Corporate State, few domestic reforms were attempted. An entente with Hungary and Austria (Mar. 1934), a pact with Germany and Japan (Nov. 1937), and intervention by 50,000-75,000 troops in Spain (1936-39) sealed Italy's identification with the fascist bloc (anti-Semitic laws after Mar. 1938). Ethiopia was conquered (1935-36), and Albania annexed (Jan. 1939) in conscious imitation of ancient Rome.

Eastern Europe. Repressive regimes fought for power against an active opposition (liberals, socialists, Communists, peasants, Nazis). Minority groups and Jews were restricted within national boundaries that did not coincide with ethnic population patterns. In the destruction of **Czechoslovakia**, Hungary occupied S Slovakia (Nov. 1938) and Ruthenia (Mar. 1939), and a pro-Nazi regime took power in the rest of Slovakia. Other boundary disputes (e.g., Poland-Lithuania, Yugoslavia-Bulgaria, and Romania-Hungary) doomed attempts to build joint fronts against Germany or Russia. Economic depression was severe.

East Asia. After a period of liberalism in **Japan**, nativist militarists dominated the government with peasant support. Manchuria was seized (Sept. 1931-Feb. 1932), and a puppet state was set up (Manchukuo). Adjacent Jehol (Inner Mongolia) was occupied in 1933. **China** proper was invaded in July 1937; large areas were conquered by Oct. 1938. Hundreds of thousands of rapes, murders, and other atrocities were attributed to the Japanese.

Communist forces left Kuomintang-besieged strongholds in the S of China in a Long March (1934-35) to the N. The Kuomintang-Communist civil war was suspended in Jan. 1937 in the face of threatening Japan.

Democracies. The Roosevelt Administration, in office Mar. 1933, embarked on an extensive program of **New Deal** social

Mahatma Gandhi led efforts for Indian autonomy and independence for more than 25 years.

works, wage-and-hour laws, and assistance to farmers. Isolationist sentiment (1937 Neutrality Act) prevented U.S. intervention in Europe, but military expenditures were increased in 1939.

French political instability and polarization prevented resolution of economic and international security questions. The **Popular Front** government under Leon Blum (June 1936-Apr. 1938) passed social reforms (40-hr. work week) and raised arms spending. National coalition governments, which ruled Britain from Aug. 1931, brought economic recovery but failed to define a consistent international policy until Chamberlain's government (from May 1937), which practiced **appeasement** of Germany and Italy.

India. Twenty years of agitation for autonomy and then for independence (Gandhi's **salt march**, 1930) achieved some constitutional reform (extended provincial powers, 1935) despite Muslim-Hindu strife. Social issues assumed prominence with peasant uprisings (1921), strikes (1928), Gandhi's efforts for untouchables (1932 "fast unto death"), and social and agrarian reform by the provinces after 1937.

Arts. The streamlined, geometric design motifs of Art Deco (from 1925) prevailed through the 1930s. **Abstract art** flourished (Moore sculptures from 1931) alongside a new **realism** related to social and political concerns (Socialist Realism, the official Soviet style from 1934; Mexican muralist Rivera, 1886-1957; and Orozco, 1883-1949), which were also expressed in fiction and poetry (Steinbeck's *Grapes of Wrath*, 1939; Sandburg's *The People, Yes*, 1936). Modern architecture (International Style, 1932) was unchallenged in its use of artificial materials (concrete, glass), lack of decoration, and monumentality (Rockefeller Center, 1929-40). Larger-than-life U.S.-made films captured a worldwide audience *(Gone With the Wind, The Wizard of Oz,* both 1939).

reform and economic stimulation, including protection for labor unions (heavy industries organized), Social Security, public

War, Hot and Cold: 1940-49

War in Asia-Pacific. Japan occupied Indochina in Sept. 1940, dominated Thailand in Dec. 1941, and attacked Hawaii (**Pearl Harbor**), the Philippines, Hong Kong, and Malaya on Dec. 7, 1941 (precipitating U.S. entrance into the war). Indonesia was attacked in Jan. 1942, and Burma was conquered in Mar. 1942. The Battle of **Midway** (June 1942) turned back the Japanese advance. "Island-hopping" battles (**Guadalcanal**, Aug. 1942-Jan. 1943; **Leyte Gulf**, Oct. 1944; **Iwo Jima**, Feb.-Mar. 1945; **Okinawa**, Apr. 1945) and massive bombing raids on Japan from June 1944 wore out Japanese defenses. U.S. atom bombs, dropped Aug. 6 and 9 on **Hiroshima** and **Nagasaki**, forced Japan to agree, on Aug. 14, to surrender; formal surrender was on Sept. 2, 1945.

War in Europe. The Nazi-Soviet nonaggression pact (Aug. 1939) freed Germany to attack Poland (Sept. 1939). Britain and France, which had guaranteed Polish independence, declared war on Germany. Russia seized E Poland (Sept. 1939), attacked Finland (Nov. 1939), and took the Baltic states (July 1940). Mobile German forces staged *blitzkrieg* attacks during Apr.-June 1940, conquering neutral Denmark, Norway, and the Low Countries and defeating France; 350,000 British and French troops were evacuated at **Dunkirk**, France (May). The **Battle of Britain** (June-Dec. 1940) denied Germany air superiority. German-Italian campaigns won the Balkans by Apr. 1941. Three million Axis troops **invaded Russia** in June 1941, marching through Ukraine to the Caucasus, and through White Russia and the Baltic republics to Moscow and Leningrad.

Russian winter counterthrusts (1941-42 and 1942-43) stopped the German advance (**Stalingrad**, Sept. 1942-Feb. 1943). Sustaining great casualties, the Russians drove the Axis from all E Europe and the Balkans in the next two years. Invasions of N Africa (Nov. 1942), Italy (Sept. 1943), and **Normandy** (launched on D-Day, June 6, 1944) brought U.S., British, Free French, and allied troops to Germany by spring 1945. In Feb. 1945, the three Allied leaders, Winston **Churchill** (Britain), Joseph **Stalin** (USSR), and Franklin D. **Roosevelt** (U.S.), met in Yalta to discuss strategy and resolve political issues, including the postwar Allied occupation of Germany. Germany surrendered May 7, 1945.

Atrocities. The war brought 20th-cent. cruelty to its peak. The Nazi regime systematically killed an estimated 5-6 million Jews, including some 3 million who died in death camps, (e.g.,

Auschwitz). Gypsies, political opponents, people with mental or physical disabilities, and others deemed undesirable were also murdered by the Nazis, as were vast numbers of Slavs.

German bombs killed 70,000 British civilians. More than 100,000 Chinese civilians were killed by Japanese forces in the capture and occupation of Nanking. Severe retaliation by the Soviet army, E European partisans, Free French, and others took a heavy toll. U.S. and British bombing of Germany killed hundreds of thousands, as did U.S. bombing of Japan (80,000-200,000 at Hiroshima alone). Some 45 million people died in the war.

Settlement. The **United Nations** charter was signed in San Francisco on June 26, 1945, by 50 nations. The International Tribunal at **Nuremberg** convicted 22 German leaders for war crimes in Sept. 1946; 23 Japanese leaders were convicted in Nov. 1948. Postwar border changes included large gains in territory for the USSR, losses for Germany, a shift to the W in Polish borders, and minor losses for Italy. Communist regimes, supported by Soviet troops, took power in most of E Europe, including Soviet-occupied Germany (GDR, aka East Germany, proclaimed Oct. 1949). Japan lost all overseas lands.

Recovery. Basic political and social changes were imposed on Japan and W Germany by the Western allies (Japan constitution adopted, Nov. 1946; W German basic law, May 1949). U.S. **Marshall Plan** aid ($12 billion, 1947-51) spurred W European economic recovery after a period of severe inflation and strikes in Europe and the U.S. The British Labour Party introduced a national health service and nationalized basic industries in 1946.

Cold War. Western fears of further Soviet advances (Cominform formed in Oct. 1947; Czechoslovakia coup, Feb. 1948; Berlin blockade, Apr. 1948-Sept. 1949) led to the formation of **NATO**. Civil War in Greece and Soviet pressure on Turkey led to U.S. aid under the **Truman Doctrine** (Mar. 1947). Other anti-Communist security pacts were the Organization of American States (Apr. 1948) and the SE Asia Treaty Organization (Sept. 1954). A new wave of **Soviet purges** and repression intensified in the last years of Stalin's rule, extending to E Europe (Slansky trial in Czechoslovakia, 1951). Only Yugoslavia resisted Soviet control (expelled by Cominform, June 1948; U.S. aid, June 1949).

Mao Zedong became chief of state when the People's Republic of China was proclaimed in 1949.

China, Korea. Communist forces emerged from World War II strengthened by the Soviet takeover of industrial Manchuria. In four years of fighting, the Kuomintang was driven from the mainland; the People's Republic of China was proclaimed

Oct. 1, 1949. Korea was divided by USSR and U.S. occupation forces. Separate republics were proclaimed in the two zones in Aug.-Sept. 1948.

India. India and Pakistan became independent dominions on Aug. 15, 1947. Millions of Hindu and Muslim refugees were created by the partition; riots (1946-47) took hundreds of thousands of lives; Mahatma **Gandhi** was assassinated in Jan. 1948. Burma became completely independent in Jan. 1948; Ceylon took dominion status in Feb.

Middle East. The UN approved partition of Palestine into Jewish and Arab states. **Israel** was proclaimed a state, May 14, 1948. Arabs rejected partition, but failed to defeat Israel in war (May 1948-July 1949). Immigration from Europe and the Middle East swelled Israel's Jewish population. British and French forces left Lebanon and Syria in 1946. Transjordan occupied most of Arab Palestine.

Southeast Asia. Communists and others fought against restoration of French rule in **Indochina** from 1946; a non-Communist government was recognized by France in Mar. 1949, but fighting continued. Both Indonesia and the Philippines became independent; the former in 1949 after four years of war with Netherlands, the latter in 1946. Philippine economic and military ties with the U.S. remained strong; a Communist-led peasant rising was checked in 1948.

Arts. New York became the center of the world art market; **abstract expressionism** was the chief mode (Pollock from 1943, de Kooning from 1947). Literature and philosophy explored **existentialism** (Camus's *The Stranger*, 1942; Sartre's *Being and Nothingness*, 1943). Non-Western attempts to revive or create regional styles (Senghor's Négritude, Mishima's novels) only confirmed the emergence of a universal culture. Radio and phonograph records spread American popular music (swing, bebop) around the world.

The American Decade: 1950-59

Polite decolonization. The peaceful decline of European political and military power in Asia and Africa accelerated in the 1950s. Nearly all of N Africa was freed by 1956, but France fought a bitter war to retain Algeria, with its large European minority, until 1962. **Ghana**, independent in 1957, led a parade of new black African nations (more than 2 dozen by 1962), which altered the political character of the UN. Ethnic disputes often exploded in the new nations after decolonization (UN troops in Cyprus, 1964; **Nigerian civil war**, 1967-70). Leaders of the new states, mostly sharing socialist ideologies, tried to create an Afro-Asian bloc (Bandung Conference, 1955), but Western economic influence and U.S. political ties remained strong (Baghdad Pact, 1955).

Trade. World trade volume soared, in an atmosphere of monetary stability assured by international accords (**Bretton Woods**, 1944). In Europe, economic integration advanced (**European Economic Community**, 1957; European Free Trade Association, 1960). Comecon (1949) coordinated the economies of Soviet-bloc countries.

U.S. Economic growth produced an abundance of consumer goods (9.3 million motor vehicles sold, 1955). Suburban housing changed life patterns for middle and working classes (Levittown, NY, 1947-51). Pres. Dwight **Eisenhower**'s landslide election victories (1952, 1956) reflected consensus politics. A system of alliances and military bases bolstered U.S. influence on all continents. Trade and payments surpluses were balanced by overseas investments and foreign aid ($50 billion, 1950-59).

USSR. In the "thaw" after Stalin's death in 1953, relations with the West improved (evacuation of Vienna, Geneva summit conference, both 1955). Repression of scientific and cultural life eased, and many prisoners were freed culminating in **de-Stalinization** (1956). Nikita **Khrushchev**'s leadership aimed at consumer sector growth, but farm production lagged, despite the virgin lands program (from 1954). Soviet crushing of the 1956 Hungarian revolution, the 1960 U-2 spy plane episode, and other incidents renewed East-West tension and domestic curbs.

Eastern Europe. Resentment of Russian domination and Stalinist repression combined with nationalist, economic, and

religious factors to produce periodic violence. E Berlin workers rioted (1953), Polish workers rioted in Poznan (June 1956), and a broad-based **revolution** broke out in **Hungary** (Oct. 1956). All were suppressed by Soviet force or threats (at least 7,000 dead in Hungary), but Poland was allowed to restore private ownership of farms, and a degree of personal and economic freedom returned to Hungary. Yugoslavia experimented with worker self-management and a market economy.

Korea. The 1945 division of Korea along the 38th parallel left industry in the N, which was organized into a militant regime and armed by the USSR. The S was politically disunited. More than 60,000 N Korean troops invaded the S on June 25, 1950. The U.S., backed by the UN Security Council, sent troops. **UN troops** reached the Chinese border in Nov. Some 200,000 Chinese troops crossed the Yalu R. and drove back UN forces. By spring 1951 battle lines had become stabilized near the original 38th parallel border, but heavy fighting continued. Finally, an armistice was signed on July 27, 1953. U.S. troops remained in the S, and U.S. economic and military aid continued. The war stimulated rapid economic recovery in Japan.

China. Starting in 1952, industry, agriculture, and social institutions were forcibly collectivized. In a massive purge, as many as several million people were executed as Kuomintang supporters or as class and political enemies. The **Great Leap Forward** (1958-60) unsuccessfully tried to force the pace of development by substituting labor for investment.

Indochina. Ho Chi Minh's forces, aided by the USSR and the new Chinese Communist government, fought French and pro-French Vietnamese forces to a standstill and captured the strategic **Dien Bien Phu** camp in May 1954. The Geneva Agreements divided Vietnam in half pending elections (never held) and recognized Laos and Cambodia as independent. The U.S. aided the anti-Communist Republic of Vietnam in the S.

Middle East. Arab revolutions placed leftist, militantly nationalist regimes in power in Egypt (1952) and Iraq (1958). But Arab unity attempts failed (United Arab Republic joined Egypt, Syria, Yemen, 1958-61). Arab refusal to recognize Israel (Arab League economic blockade began Sept. 1951) led to a permanent **state of war**, with repeated incidents (Gaza,

1955). Israel occupied Sinai, and Britain and France took (Oct. 1956) the Suez Canal, but were replaced by the UN Emergency Force. The Mossadegh government in Iran nationalized (May 1951) the British-owned oil industry in May, but was overthrown (Aug. 1953) in a U.S.-aided coup.

Latin America. Argentinian dictator Juan **Perón**, in office 1946, crushed opposition and enforced land reform, some nationalization, welfare state measures, and curbs on the Roman Catholic Church. A Sept. 1955 coup deposed Perón. The 1952 revolution in Bolivia brought land reform, nationalization of tin mines, and improvement in the status of Native Americans, who nevertheless remained poor. The Batista regime in Cuba was overthrown (Jan. 1959) by Fidel **Castro**, who imposed a Communist dictatorship, aligned Cuba with the USSR and improved education and health care. A U.S.-backed anti-Castro invasion (**Bay of Pigs**, Apr. 1961) was crushed. Self-government advanced in the British Caribbean.

Technology. Large outlays on research and development in the U.S. and the USSR focused on military applications (H-bomb in U.S., 1952; USSR, 1953; Britain, 1957; intercontinental missiles, late 1950s). Soviet launching of the **Sputnik** satellite (Oct. 4, 1957) spurred increases in U.S. science education funds (National Defense Education Act).

Literature and film. Alienation from social and literary conventions reached an extreme in the theater of the absurd (Beckett's *Waiting for Godot*, 1952), the "new novel" (Robbe-Grillet's *Voyeur*, 1955), and avant-garde film (Antonioni's *L'Avventura*, 1960). U.S. beatniks (Kerouac's *On the Road*, 1957) and others rejected the supposed conformism of Americans (Riesman's *The Lonely Crowd*, 1950).

Rising Expectations: 1960-69

Economic boom. The longest sustained economic boom on record spanned almost the entire decade in the capitalist world; the closely watched GNP figure doubled (1960-70) in the U.S., fueled by Vietnam War-related budget deficits. The **General Agreement on Tariffs and Trade** (1967) stimulated W European prosperity, which spread to peripheral areas (Spain, Italy, E Germany). Japan became a top economic power. Foreign investment aided the industri-alization of Brazil. There were limited Soviet economic reform attempts.

Reform and radicalization. Pres. John F. **Kennedy**, inaugurated 1961, emphasized youthful idealism and vigor; his assassination Nov. 22, 1963, was a national trauma. A series of political and social reform movements took root in the U.S. and other countries. Blacks demonstrated nonviolently and with partial success against segregation and poverty (1963 March on Washington; 1964 **Civil Rights Act**), but some urban areas erupted in extensive riots (Watts, 1965; Detroit, 1967; **Martin Luther King** assassination, Apr. 4, 1968). New concern for the poor (Harrington's *Other America*, 1963) helped lead to Pres. Lyndon Johnson's **"Great Society"** programs (Medicare, Water Quality Act, Higher Education Act, all 1965). Concern for the **environment** surged (Carson's *Silent Spring*, 1962).

Feminism revived as a cultural and political movement (Friedan's *Feminine Mystique*, 1963; National Organization for Women founded 1966), and a movement for homosexual rights emerged (Stonewall riot in NYC, 1969). Pope John XXIII called the **Second Vatican Council** (1962-65), which liberalized Roman Catholic liturgy and some other aspects of Catholicism. Opposition to U.S. involvement in Vietnam, especially among university students (**Moratorium** protest, Nov. 1969), turned violent (Weatherman Chicago riots, Oct. 1969). **New Left** and Marxist theories became popular, and membership in radical groups (Students for a Democratic Society, Black Panthers) increased. Maoist groups, especially in Europe, called for total transformation of society. In France, students sparked a nationwide strike affecting 10 million workers in May-June 1968, but an electoral reaction barred revolutionary change.

China. China's revolutionary militancy under **Mao** Zedong caused disputes with the USSR under "revisionist" Khrushchev, starting in 1960. The two powers exchanged fire in 1969 border disputes. China used force to capture (1962) areas disputed with India. The **"Great Proletarian Cultural Revolution"** tried to impose a utopian egalitarian program in China and spread revolution abroad; political struggle, often violent, convulsed China in 1965-68.

Indochina. Communist-led guerrillas aided by N Vietnam fought from 1960 against the S Vietnam government of Ngo Dinh Diem (killed 1963). The U.S. military role increased after the 1964 Tonkin Gulf incident. U.S. forces there peaked at 543,400 in Apr. 1969. Massive numbers of N Vietnamese troops also fought. Laotian and Cambodian neutrality were threatened by Communist insurgencies, with N Vietnamese aid, and U.S. intrigues.

Developing world. A bloc of authoritarian leftist regimes among the newly independent nations emerged in political opposition to the U.S.-led Western alliance and came to dominate the conference of nonaligned nations (Belgrade, 1961; Cairo, 1964; Lusaka, 1970). Soviet political ties and military bases were established in Cuba, Egypt, Algeria, Guinea, and other countries whose leaders were regarded as revolutionary heroes by opposition groups in pro-Western or colonial countries. Some leaders were ousted in coups by pro-Western groups—Zaire's Patrice Lumumba (killed 1961), Ghana's Kwame Nkrumah (exiled 1966), and Indonesia's Sukarno (effectively ousted in 1965 after a Communist coup failed).

Middle East. Arab-Israeli tension erupted into a brief war June 1967. Israel emerged from the war as a major regional power. Military shipments before and after the war brought much of the Arab world into the Soviet political sphere. Most Arab states broke U.S. diplomatic ties, while Communist countries cut their ties to Israel. Intra-Arab disputes continued: Egypt and Saudi Arabia supported rival factions in a bloody Yemen civil war 1962-70; Lebanese troops fought Palestinian commandos 1969.

East Europe. To stop the large-scale exodus of citizens, E German authorities built (Aug. 1961) a **fortified wall across Berlin**. Soviet sway in the Balkans was weakened by Albania's support of China (USSR broke ties in Dec. 1961) and Romania's assertion (1964) of industrial and foreign policy autonomy. Liberalization (spring 1968) in Czechoslovakia was crushed with massive force by troops of five Warsaw Pact countries. W German treaties (1970) with the USSR and Poland facilitated the transfer of German technology and confirmed postwar boundaries.

Arts and styles. The boundary between fine and popular arts was blurred to some extent by Pop Art (Warhol) and rock musicals (*Hair*, 1968). Informality and exaggeration prevailed in fashion (beards, miniskirts). A nonpolitical "counterculture" developed, rejecting traditional bourgeois life goals and personal habits, and use of marijuana and hallucinogens spread (**Woodstock** festival, Aug. 1969). Indian influence was felt in religion (Ram Dass) and fashion, and **The Beatles**, who brought unprecedented sophistication to rock music, became for many a symbol of the decade.

Science. Achievements in space (**humans on the moon**, July 1969) and electronics (lasers, integrated circuits) encouraged a faith in scientific solutions to problems in agriculture ("green revolution"), medicine (heart transplants, 1967), and other areas. Harmful technology, it was believed, could be controlled (1963 Limited Test Ban Treaty, 1968 Nuclear Nonproliferation Treaty).

A 1961 meeting between Soviet Premier Nikita Khrushchev and Pres. John F. Kennedy did little to diffuse Cold War tensions.

Disillusionment: 1970-79

U.S.: Caution and neoconservatism. A relatively sluggish economy, energy shortages, and environmental problems contributed to a "limits of growth" philosophy. Suspicion of science and technology killed or delayed major projects (supersonic transport dropped, 1971; Seabrook nuclear power plant protests, 1977-78) and was fed by the Three Mile Island nuclear reactor accident (Mar. 1979).

There were signs of growing mistrust of big government and less support for new social policies. School busing and racial quotas were opposed (Bakke decision, June 1978); the proposed Equal Rights Amendment for women languished; civil rights legislation aimed at protecting homosexuals was opposed (Dade County referendum, June 1977).

Completion of Communist forces' takeover of **South Vietnam** (evacuation of U.S. civilians, Apr. 1975), revelations of Central Intelligence Agency misdeeds (Rockefeller Commission report, June 1975), and **Watergate** scandals (Nixon resigned in Aug. 1974) reduced faith in U.S. moral and material capacity to influence world affairs. Revelations of Soviet crimes (Solzhenitsyn's *Gulag Archipelago*, 1974) and Soviet intervention in Africa helped foster a revival of anti-Communist sentiment.

Economy sluggish. The 1960s boom faltered in the 1970s; a severe recession in the U.S. and Europe (1974-75) followed a huge oil price hike (Dec. 1973). Monetary instability (U.S. cut ties to gold in Aug. 1971), the decline of the dollar, and protectionist moves by industrial countries (1977-78) threatened trade. Business investment and spending for research declined. Severe inflation plagued many countries (25% in Britain, 1975; 18% in U.S., 1979).

China picks up pieces. After the 1976 deaths of Mao Zedong and Zhou Enlai, struggle for the leadership succession was won by pragmatists. A nationwide purge of orthodox Maoists was carried out, and the **Gang of Four**, led by Mao's widow, Chiang Ching, arrested. The new leaders freed more than 100,000 political prisoners and reduced public adulation of Mao. Political and trade ties were expanded with Japan, Europe, and the U.S. in the late 1970s, as relations worsened with the USSR, Cuba, and Vietnam (four-week invasion by China, 1979). Ideological guidelines in industry, science, education, and the armed forces, which the ruling faction said had caused chaos and decline, were reversed (bonuses to workers, Dec. 1977; exams for college entrance, Oct. 1977). Severe restrictions on cultural expression were eased.

Europe. European unity moves (EEC-EFTA trade accord, 1972) faltered as economic problems appeared (Britain floated pound, 1972; France floated franc, 1974). Germany and Switzerland curbed guest workers from S Europe. Greece and Turkey quarreled over Cyprus and Aegean oil rights.

All non-Communist Europe was under democratic rule after free elections (June 1976) in **Spain** seven months after the death of Franco. The conservative, colonialist regime in **Portugal** was overthrown in Apr. 1974. In **Greece** the seven-year-old military dictatorship yielded power in 1974. N Europe, though ruled mostly by Socialists (**Swedish** Socialists unseated in 1976 after 44 years in power), turned more conservative. The **British** Labour government imposed (1975) wage curbs and suspended nationalization schemes. Terrorism in **Germany** (1972 Munich Olympics killings) led to laws curbing some civil liberties. **French** "new philosophers" rejected leftist ideologies, and the Socialist-Communist coalition lost a 1978 election bid.

Religion and politics. The improvement in **Muslim** countries' political fortunes in the 1950s (with the exception of Central Asia under Soviet and Chinese rule) and the growth of Arab oil wealth were followed by a resurgence of traditional religious fervor. Libyan dictator Muammar al-Qaddafi mixed Islamic laws with socialism and called for Muslim return to Spain and Sicily. The illegal Muslim Brotherhood in **Egypt** was accused of violence, while extreme groups bombed (1977) theaters to protest Western and secular values.

In **Turkey**, the National Salvation Party was the first Islamic group to share (1974) power since secularization in the 1920s. In **Iran**, Ayatollah Ruhollah **Khomeini** led a revolution that deposed the secular shah (Jan. 1979) and created an Islamic republic. Religiously motivated Muslims took part in an insurrection in Saudi Arabia that briefly seized (1979) the Grand Mosque in Mecca. Muslim puritan opposition to **Pakistan** Pres. Zulfikar Ali-Bhutto helped lead to his overthrow in July 1977. Muslim solidarity, however, could not prevent Pakistan's eastern province (**Bangladesh**) from declaring (Dec. 1971) independence after a bloody civil war.

Muslim and Hindu resentment of coerced sterilization in **India** helped defeat the Indira Gandhi government, which was replaced (Mar. 1977) by a coalition including religious Hindu parties. Muslims in the S **Philippines**, aided by Libya, rebelled against central rule from 1973.

The Buddhist Soka Gakkai movement launched (1964) the Komeito party in **Japan**, which became a major opposition party in 1972 and 1976 elections.

Evangelical Protestant groups grew in the U.S. A revival of interest in Orthodox Christianity occurred among **Russian** intellectuals (Solzhenitsyn). The secularist **Israeli** Labor party, after decades of rule, was ousted in 1977 by conservatives led by Menachem Begin; religious militants founded settlements on the disputed West Bank, part of biblically promised Israel. U.S. Reform Judaism revived many previously discarded traditional practices.

Religious wars raged intermittently in **Northern Ireland** (Catholic vs. Protestant, 1969-97) and **Lebanon** (Christian vs. Muslim, 1975-90), while religious militancy complicated the Israel-Arab dispute (1973 Israel-Arab war). The Camp David Accords in 1978, negotiated by Egyptian Pres. Anwar al-Sadat, Israeli Prime Min. Menachem Begin, and U.S. Pres. Jimmy Carter, facilitated the landmark 1979 **Egypt-Israel peace treaty**, but increased militancy on the West Bank impeded further progress.

Latin America. Repressive conservative regimes strengthened their hold on most of the continent, with a violent coup against the elected (Sept. 1973) Allende government in **Chile**, a 1976 military coup in **Argentina**, and coups against reformist regimes in **Bolivia** (1971, 1979) and **Peru** (1976). In Central America increasing liberal and leftist militancy led to the ouster (1979) of the Somoza regime of **Nicaragua** and to civil conflict in **El Salvador**.

Indochina. Communist victories in Vietnam, Cambodia, and Laos by May 1975 led to new turmoil. The **Pol Pot** regime ordered millions of city-dwellers to resettle in rural areas, in a program of forced labor and terrorism that cost more than 1 million lives (1975-79) and caused hundreds of thousands of ethnic Chinese and others to flee. The Vietnamese invasion of Cambodia (1979) swelled the refugee population and contributed to widespread starvation.

Russian expansion. Soviet influence, checked in some countries (troops ousted by Egypt, 1972), was projected farther afield, often with the use of Cuban troops (Angola, 1975-89; Ethiopia, 1977-88) and aided by a growing navy, a merchant fleet, and international banking ability. Détente with the West—1972 Berlin pact, 1972 strategic arms pact (**SALT**)—gave way to a more antagonistic relationship in the late 1970s, exacerbated by the Soviet invasion (1979) of **Afghanistan**.

Africa. The last remaining European colonies were granted independence (**Spanish Sahara**, 1976; **Djibouti**, 1977) and, after 10 years of civil war and many negotiation sessions, a black government took over (1979) in Zimbabwe (Rhodesia); white domination remained in **South Africa**. Great power involvement in local wars (Russia in **Angola**, **Ethiopia**; **France in Chad**, **Zaire**, **Mauritania**) and the use of tens of thousands of Cuban troops were denounced by some African leaders. Ethnic or tribal clashes made Africa a locus of sustained warfare during the late 1970s.

Arts. Traditional modes of painting, architecture, and music received increased popular and critical attention in the 1970s. These more conservative styles coexisted with modernist works in an atmosphere of increased variety and tolerance.

The fall of Saigon (1975) marked the end of the war in Vietnam as Americans and some South Vietnamese evacuated the city.

Revitalization of Capitalism, Demand for Democracy: 1980-89

USSR, Eastern Europe. The late 1980s saw the remaking of the Soviet state and the beginning of the disintegration of the Soviet empire. After the deaths of Gen. Sec. Leonid **Brezhnev** (1982) and two successors (Andropov in 1984 and Chernenko in 1985), the harsh treatment of dissent and restriction of emigration, and the Soviet invasion (Dec. 1979) of Afghanistan, Gen. Sec. Mikhail **Gorbachev** (in office 1985-1991) promoted *glasnost* and *perestroika*—economic, political, and social reform. Supported by the Communist Party (July 1988), he signed (Dec. 1987) the INF disarmament treaty, and he pledged (1988) to cut the military budget. Military withdrawal from Afghanistan was completed in Feb. 1989, and the Soviet people chose (Mar. 1989) part of the new Congress of People's Deputies from competing candidates. By decade's end the **Cold War** appeared to be fading away.

In **Poland**, Solidarity, the labor union founded (1980) by Lech Walesa, was outlawed in 1982 and then legalized in 1988, after years of unrest. Poland's first free election brought the Communist takeover brought **Solidarity** victory (June 1989); Tadeusz Mazowiecki, a Walesa adviser, became (Aug. 1989) prime minister in a government with the Communists. In the fall of 1989 the failure of Marxist economies in **Hungary**, **East Germany**, **Czechoslovakia**, **Bulgaria**, and **Romania** brought the collapse of the Communist monopoly and a demand for democracy. In a historic step, the **Berlin Wall** was opened in Nov. 1989.

U.S. The **"Reagan Years"** (1981-88) brought the **longest economic boom** yet in U.S. history via budget and tax cuts, deregulation, "junk bond" financing, leveraged buyouts, and mergers and takeovers. However, there was a stock market crash (Oct. 1987), and federal budget deficits and the trade deficit increased. Foreign policy showed a **strong anti-Communist stance**, via increased defense spending, aid to anti-Communists in Central America, invasion of Cuba-threatened Grenada, and championing of the MX missile system and "Star Wars" missile defense program. Four Reagan-Gorbachev summits (1985-88) climaxed in the INF treaty (1987), as the Cold War began to wind down. The **Iran Contra affair** (Oliver North's testimony, July 1987) was a major political scandal. In 1988, Vice Pres. George H. W. Bush was elected to succeed Ronald Reagan as president.

Middle East. The Middle East remained militarily unstable, with sharp divisions along economic, political, racial, and religious lines. In **Iran**, the Islamic revolution of 1979 created a strong anti-U.S. stance (hostage crisis, Nov. 1979-Jan. 1981). In Sept. 1980, **Iraq** repudiated its border agreement with Iran and began major hostilities that led to an eight-year war in which hundreds of thousands were killed.

Libya's support for international terrorism induced the U.S. to close (May 1981) its diplomatic mission there and embargo (Mar. 1982) Libyan oil. The U.S. accused Libyan leader Muammar al-Qaddafi of aiding (Dec. 1985) terrorists in Rome and Vienna airport attacks. Following attack on a West Berlin disco frequented by U.S. military, U.S. bombed targets in Libya (Apr. 1986).

Israel affirmed (July 1980) all Jerusalem as its capital, destroyed (June 1981) an Iraqi atomic reactor, and invaded Lebanon, citing terrorism from the Palestine Liberation Organization; PLO withdrew after cease-fire. A **Palestinian uprising** began (Dec. 1987) in Israeli-occupied Gaza and spread to the West Bank; troops responded with force, killing 300 by the end of 1988, with 6,000 more in detention camps.

Israeli withdrawal from **Lebanon** began in Feb. 1985 and ended in June 1985, as Lebanon continued to be torn by military and political conflict. Artillery duels (Mar.-Apr. 1989) between Christian East Beirut and Muslim West Beirut left 200 dead and 700 wounded.

Latin America. In **Nicaragua**, the leftist Sandinista National Liberation Front, in power after the 1979 civil war, faced problems as a result of Nicaragua's military aid to leftist guerrillas in El Salvador and U.S. backing of antigovernment contras. The U.S. CIA admitted (1984) having directed the mining of Nicaraguan ports, and the U.S. sent humanitarian (1985) and military (1986) aid. Profits from **secret arms sales** to Iran were found (1987) diverted to contras. Cease-fire talks between the Sandinista government and contras came in 1988, and elections were held in Nicaragua in Feb. 1990.

In **El Salvador**, a military coup (Oct. 1979) failed to halt extreme right-wing violence and left-wing terrorism. Archbishop Oscar Romero was assassinated in Mar. 1980; from Jan. to June some 4,000 civilians were killed in the civil unrest. In 1984, newly elected Pres. José Napoleon Duarte worked to stem human rights abuses, but violence continued.

In **Chile**, Gen. Augusto Pinochet yielded the presidency after a democratic election (Dec. 1989), but remained as head of the army. He had ruled the country since 1973, imposing harsh measures against leftists and dissidents.

Africa. The 1980s saw continuing economc decline in virtually all African countries, a result of accelerating desertification, the world economic recession, heavy indebtedness to overseas creditors, rapid population growth, and political instability. Some 60 million Africans faced prolonged hunger in 1981. Much of Africa had one of the worst **droughts** ever in 1983, and by year's end, one-third of the population, or about 150 million, were near **famine**. Live Aid, a marathon rock concert, was presented in July 1985, and the U.S. and Western nations sent aid in Sept. 1985. Economic hardship fueled political unrest and coups. Wars in Ethiopia and Sudan and military strife in several other nations continued. **HIV/AIDS** took a heavy toll.

Anti-apartheid sentiment gathered force in **South Africa** as demonstrations and violent police response grew. White voters approved (Nov. 1983) the first constitution to give "Coloureds" (people of mixed-race background) and Asians a voice, while still excluding blacks (70% of the population). The U.S. imposed economic sanctions in Aug. 1985, and 11 Western nations followed in Sept. P. W. **Botha**, 1980s president, was succeeded by F. W. **de Klerk**, in Sept. 1989, who promised "evolutionary" change via negotiation with the black population.

Asia and the Pacific. Benazir **Bhutto** became the first woman to lead a majority-Muslim nation as prime minister of **Pakistan** (Dec. 1988). The "people power" revolt in the **Philippines** ousted Ferdinand **Marcos** (Feb. 1986) after two decades as president; replaced by Corazon **Aquino.**

During the 1980s **China's** Communist government and paramount leader **Deng Xiaoping** pursued far-reaching changes, expanding commercial and technical ties to the industrialized world and increasing the role of market forces in stimulating urban development. Apr. 1989 brought new demands for political reforms; student demonstrators camped out in **Tiananmen Square**, Beijing, in a massive peaceful protest. Some 100,000 students and workers marched, and at least 20 other cities saw protests. In response, martial law was imposed; army troops crushed the demonstration in and around Tiananmen Square on June 3-4, with death toll estimates of 500-7,000, up to 10,000 dissidents arrested, 31 people tried and executed. The conciliatory Communist Party chief was ousted; the Politburo adopted (July 1989) reforms against official corruption.

Japan's relations with other nations, especially the U.S., were dominated by **trade imbalances favoring Japan**. Western Europe and the U.S. accused Japan of restrictive trade policies. A scandal involving illegal political contributions and stock trading led to the resignation (May 1989) of Prime Min. Noboru Takeshita, of the ruling and dominant Liberal Democratic Party.

Europe. With the addition of Greece, Portugal, and Spain, the European Community became a common market of more than 300 million people, the West's largest trading entity. Margaret **Thatcher** became the first British prime minister in the 20th cent. to win a third consecutive term (1987). France

The Berlin Wall, which had divided East and West Berlin since 1961, was opened in Nov. 1989.

elected (1981) its first socialist president, François **Mitterrand**, who was reelected in 1988. Elections in 1983 brought **Italy** its first socialist premier, Bettino **Craxi**.

International terrorism. With the 1979 **overthrow of the shah** of Iran and with instablity in the Middle East, terrorism became a prominent tactic. In 1979-81, Iranian militants held 52 **U.S. hostages in Iran** for 444 days; in 1983 a TNT-laden suicide terrorist blew up U.S. Marine headquarters in Beirut,

killing 241 Americans, and a truck bomb blew up a French paratroop barracks, killing 58. The **Achille Lauro** cruise ship was hijacked in 1985, and an American passenger killed; the U.S. subsequently intercepted the Egyptian plane flying the terrorists to safety. Incidents rose to 700 in 1985, and to 1,000 in 1988. **Assassinated leaders** included Egypt's Pres. Anwar al-**Sadat** (1981), India's Prime Min. Indira **Gandhi** (1984), and Lebanese Premier Rashid **Karami** (1987).

Post-Cold War World: 1990-99

Soviet Empire breakup. The breakup of the Soviet Union into 15 independent states began in earnest with declarations of independence adopted by the Baltic republics of **Lithuania, Latvia,** and **Estonia** during an abortive coup against reformist leader Mikhail **Gorbachev** (Aug. 1991). Other republics soon took the same step. In Dec. 1991, **Russia, Ukraine,** and **Belarus** declared the Soviet Union dead; Gorbachev resigned, and the Soviet Parliament went out of existence. The Warsaw Pact and the Council for Mutual Economic Assistance (Comecon) were disbanded. Most of the former Soviet republics joined in a loose confederation called the **Commonwealth of Independent States.** Russia's people soon suffered severe economic hardship as the nation, under Pres. Boris **Yeltsin,** moved to revamp the economy and adopt a free market system. In Oct. 1993, **anti-Yeltsin forces** occupied the Parliament building and were ousted by the army; about 140 people died in the fighting.

The Muslim republic of **Chechnya** declared independence from the rest of Russia, but this was met with an invasion by Russian troops (Dec. 1994). After almost 21 months of vicious fighting, a cease-fire took hold in 1996, and the Russians withdrew. In 1999 Russia forcibly suppressed Muslim insurgents in Dagestan and entered Chechnya, again fighting separatist rebels there. Yeltsin resigned Dec. 31, 1999, to be replaced by Vladimir **Putin** (elected in his own right, Mar. 2000).

Europe. Yugoslavia broke apart, and hostilities ensued among the republics along ethnic and religious lines. **Croatia, Slovenia,** and **Macedonia** declared independence (1991), followed by **Bosnia-Herzegovina** (1992). **Serbia** and **Montenegro** remained as the republic of Yugoslavia. Bitter fighting followed, especially in Bosnia, where Serbs reportedly engaged in **"ethnic cleansing"** of the Muslim population; a peace plan (Dayton accord, 1995), brokered by the U.S., was signed by **Bosnia, Serbia,** and **Croatia,** with NATO responsible for policing its implementation. In spring 1999, NATO conducted a bombing campaign aimed at stopping Yugoslavia from its campaign to drive out ethnic Albanians from the **Kosovo** region; a peace accord was reached in June under which NATO peacekeeping troops entered Kosovo.

The **two Germanys were reunited** after 45 years (Oct. 1990). The union was greeted with jubilation, but economic stresses followed. West German chancellor Helmut **Kohl,** a Christian Democrat, lost power after 16 years, in Sept. 1998 elections; Gerhard **Schröder,** a Social Democrat, took over. Czechoslovakia broke apart peacefully (Jan. 1993), becoming the **Czech Republic** and **Slovakia.** In Poland, Lech **Walesa** was elected president (Dec. 1991) but was defeated in his bid for a second term (Nov. 1995).

NATO approved the **Partnership for Peace** Program (Jan. 1994) coordinating the defense of E and Central European countries; Russia joined the program later that year. NATO signed a pact with **Russia** (1997) providing for NATO expansion into the former Soviet-bloc countries; a similar treaty was set up with **Ukraine.** The **Czech Republic, Hungary,** and **Poland** became members in Jan. 1999; in that year NATO celebrated its 50th anniversary. Efforts toward European unity continued with adoption of a single market (Jan. 1993) and conversion of the European Community to the **European Union** as the Maastricht Treaty took effect (Nov. 1993). Agreement was reached for 11 EU members to participate in Economic and Monetary Union, adopting a common currency (**euro**) in Jan. 1999.

An intraparty revolt forced Margaret **Thatcher** out as prime minister of **Great Britain,** to be succeeded by John **Major** (Nov. 1990); seven years later, Labour was returned to power under Tony **Blair** (May 1997). The divorce of Prince **Charles and Diana,** followed by the death of Diana in a car accident (Aug. 1997), made headlines around the world. Talks on peace in **Northern Ireland** that included participation of Sinn Fein, political arm of the IRA, led to a ground-breaking peace plan, approved in an all-Ireland vote (May 1998). In Dec. 1999, Northern Ireland was

granted home rule under a power-sharing cabinet. In **Scotland** voters overwhelmingly approved establishment of a regional legislature (1997), and in **Wales** voters narrowly approved establishment of a local assembly (1997). In a historic innovation, the Church of England ordained 32 women as priests (Mar. 1994).

Middle East. In Aug. 1990, **Iraq**'s Saddam Hussein ordered his troops to invade **Kuwait.** The UN approved military action (Nov. 1990), and an international military force, led by the U.S., bombed Iraq (Jan. 1991) and launched a land attack, crushing the invasion (Feb. 1991). After Iraq accepted the allied terms of a cease-fire (Apr. 1991), U.S. troops withdrew, but "nofly" zones were set up over N Iraq to protect the Kurds and over S Iraq to protect Shiite Muslims. The **UN** imposed **sanctions** on Iraq for failure to abide by the cease-fire. Iraq's reported failure to cooperate with UN arms inspectors seeking to eliminate **"weapons of mass destruction"** led to air strikes by the U.S. and Britain (1998, 2001).

The last Western hostages were freed in **Lebanon,** June 1992. **Israel** and the **PLO** signed a peace accord (Sept. 1993) providing for Palestinian self-government in the West Bank and Gaza Strip. Prime Min. Yitzhak **Rabin** and Foreign Min. Shimon **Peres** of Israel and Yasir **Arafat** of the PLO received the Nobel Peace Prize for their efforts (1994). Six Arab nations relaxed their boycott against Israel (1994), and Israel and **Jordan** signed a peace treaty (Oct. 1994). Rabin was assassinated (Nov. 1995) by an Israeli opponent of the peace process. After new elections (May 1996), Benjamin **Netanyahu** became prime minister. Arafat was elected to the presidency of the Palestinian Authority (Jan. 1996). A Labour government under Ehud **Barak** took power after May 1999 elections.

King **Hussein** of Jordan died (Feb. 1999), to be succeeded by his son Abdullah.

Asia and the Pacific. Hong Kong was returned to **China** (July 1997) after 156 years as a British colony, and **Macao** reverted to Chinese sovereignty (Dec. 1999) after over 400 years of Portuguese rule. Both were to retain their legal and capitalist economic systems for 50 years. **Jiang** Zemin, general secretary of the Chinese Communist Party, assumed the additional post of president of China (Mar. 1993) and emerged as the key leader after the death of leader **Deng** Xiaoping (Feb. 1997). China released from prison—and exiled—some well-known dissidents but continued to earn criticism for widespread **human rights** abuses. In Nov. 1999 the U.S. and China signed a landmark pact normalizing trade relations.

After years of prosperity, **Thailand, Indonesia,** and **South Korea** in 1997 began to suffer economic reverses that had a worldwide ripple effect. These countries received billion-dollar IMF bailout packages. In **Indonesia,** protests over mismanagement led to the resignation of Pres. Suharto (May 1998) after 32 years of nearly autocratic rule. Abdurraham Wahid was elected (Oct. 1999) in the country's first fully democratic elections. In a referendum (Aug. 1999), **East Timor** voted overwhelmingly for independence from Indonesia; pro-Indonesian militias then rampaged through the territory, but a multinational **peacekeeping force** was allowed to help restore order (Sept. 1999). In **South Korea,** former dissident **Kim** Dae-jung was elected president (Dec. 1997). Two previous presidents, Roh Tae Woo and Chun Doo Hwan, were convicted of crimes committed in office but were granted amnesty.

In Japan members of a religious cult released the nerve gas sarin on five **Tokyo** subway cars, killing 12 people and injuring more than 5,500 (Mar. 1995). Tamil rebels continued their armed conflict in **Sri Lanka.** In **Afghanistan** the **Taliban,** an extreme Islamic fundamentalist group, gained control of Kabul (Sept. 1996) and, eventually, most of the country. In **North Korea,** longtime dictator **Kim Il Sung** died (July 1994), to be succeeded by his son, **Kim Jong Il.**

In the same year the country signed an agreement with the U.S. setting a timetable for North Korea to eliminate its **nuclear program**. The country also suffered a severe drought, and widespread starvation was feared.

India was beset by riots following destruction of a mosque by Hindu militants (Dec. 1992); Indian army troops repeatedly clashed with pro-independence demonstrators in the disputed Muslim region of **Kashmir**, exacerbating relations with **Pakistan**. Uneasy relations between India and Pakistan reached a new level when both nations conducted nuclear tests in 1998. Conflict in Pakistan between government and the military led to a bloodless coup (Oct. 1999).

Africa. South Africa's Pres. F. W. **de Klerk** released dissident Nelson **Mandela** from prison (Feb. 1990), after 27 years, and lifted a ban on the black nationalist African National Congress. The white minority government repealed its apartheid laws (1990, 1991). Mandela was elected president (Apr. 1994), and a new nonracial constitution became law (Dec. 1996). Thabo **Mbeki**, the ANC's candidate to succeed Mandela, was elected president in June 1999. In **Nigeria**, Gen. Olusegun Obasanjo was elected president (Feb. 1999), to become the country's first civilian leader in 15 years.

The decades-long rule of **Mobutu** Sese Seko in **Zaire** came to an end (May 1997) at the hands of rebel forces led by Laurent **Kabila**; an ailing Mobutu fled the country and soon after died. Kabila changed the country's name back to **Democratic Republic of the Congo**; conditions remained unstable.

After the presidents of **Burundi** and **Rwanda** were killed in an airplane crash (Apr. 1994), violence erupted in Rwanda between Hutu and Tutsi factions; hundreds of thousands were slain in genocidal fashion. The conflict spread to refugee camps in neighboring Zaire and Burundi. Factional fighting also erupted in **Somalia** after Pres. Muhammad Siad Barre was ousted (Jan. 1991). The UN sent a U.S.-led **peacekeeping force**, but it was unsuccessful in restoring order. Some soldiers of the peacekeeping force were killed, including 23 Pakistanis (June 1993) and 18 U.S. Rangers (Oct. 1993). The UN ended its mission (Mar. 1995) with no durable government in place. **Liberia** endured factional fighting that lasted almost five years and claimed over 150,000 lives; a cease-fire was concluded in Aug. 1995. The World Health Organization reported (1995) that Africa accounted for 70% of **AIDS** cases worldwide.

A 16-year civil war appeared to end in **Angola** (May 1991) when the government signed a peace accord with the rebel UNITA faction. But despite the inauguration of a national unity government (Apr. 1997), insurgents continued to fight and gain territory. **Namibia** officially became independent in Mar. 1990 after almost 20 years under UN trusteeship. In **Algeria**, the army cancelled a second round of parliamentary elections (Jan. 1992) after the Islamic party won a first round. Ensuing violence by **Islamic fundamentalists** claimed thousands of lives; a peace plan was worked out in 1999.

North America. The **North American Free Trade Agreement** (NAFTA), liberalizing trade between the U.S., Canada, and Mexico, went into effect Jan. 1, 1994. In **Canada**, the Progressive Conservative Party suffered a crushing defeat in general elections (Oct. 1993), and liberal Jean **Chrétien** became prime minister. The map of Canada was altered in Apr. 1999 to create a new territory, **Nunavut**, out of an area that had been part of Northwest Territories.

In the U.S.'s 1992 presidential election, Dem. Bill **Clinton** defeated Pres. George H. W. Bush, but Republicans gained control of Congress in 1994 midterm elections. Clinton won reelection in 1996; despite scandals, the new administration remained popular, aided by economic prosperity. Clinton proposed (Feb. 1998) the first balanced federal budget in nearly 30 years. In Dec. 1998 Clinton was **impeached** by the U.S. House on charges related to the Monica Lewinsky scandal; he was acquitted by the Senate in Feb. 1999.

In **Mexico**, Ernesto Zedillo of the ruling PRI party was elected president (July 1994) after the party's first candidate was assassinated. The country soon faced a crisis affecting the value of the peso, but recovered with the help of a bailout package from the U.S. A peasant revolt spearheaded by the **Zapatista National Liberation Army** erupted in the state of Chiapas (Jan. 1994) and was suppressed.

Central America and the Caribbean. In **Haiti**, Jean-Bertrand **Aristide** was elected president (Dec. 1990) but

was ousted in a military coup after nine months in office. A delegation headed by former U.S. Pres. Jimmy Carter arranged (Sept. 1994) for the junta to step aside for Aristide, who served until 1996. In **Nicaragua**, Violetta Chamorro defeated Daniel **Ortega** in the presidential election (Feb. 1990), thus ousting the Sandinistas. In **Panama**, U.S. troops invaded and overthrew the government of Manuel **Noriega** (Dec. 1989). Noriega was captured Jan. 1990; convicted and jailed on drug-related charges in U.S. in 1992, and in France in 2010. On Dec. 31, 1999, Panama assumed full control of the **Panama Canal**, in accord with a treaty with the U.S. In **El Salvador** (1992) and **Guatemala** (1996) the governments signed agreements with rebel factions.

South America. Alberto **Fujimori** was elected president of **Peru** in June 1990 and, despite his suppression of the constitution (1992), was reelected in 1995. Peru succeeded in capturing (Sept. 1992) the leader of the Shining Path guerrilla movement. Leftist guerrillas took hostages at an ambassador's residence in Lima (Dec. 1996); one hostage was killed during a government assault rescuing the rest (Apr. 1997). Peronist Pres. Carlos Saúl **Menem** served as **Argentina**'s president for much of the decade (elected 1989, reelected 1995), imposing economic austerity.

Former Chilean Pres. Gen. Augusto **Pinochet** continued to head the army until Mar. 1998; he was arrested in London (Oct. 1998) on human rights charges but was judged unfit for trial and returned to Chile (Mar. 2000). In **Brazil**, Fernando Henrique **Cardoso** was elected president (Oct. 1994) and reelected in 1998 despite an economic slump; the IMF announced a $42 billion aid package (Nov. 1998). In **Venezuela** two coup attempts were thwarted during 1992, but coup leader Hugo **Chavez**, a leftist populist, was elected president in Dec. 1998.

The first UN Conference on Environment and Development, or **Earth Summit**, was held (June 1992) in Rio de Janeiro.

Terrorism. The U.S. was a prominent target of terrorism linked to Middle Eastern sources. A bomb exploded in a garage beneath New York City's **World Trade Center**, killing six people (Feb. 1993). Bombs set off outside **U.S. embassies** in Kenya and Tanzania killed over 220 people (Aug. 1998); the U.S. retaliated with missiles fired at alleged terrorist-linked sites in Afghanistan and Sudan. In the U.S.'s deadliest instance of domestic terrorism, 168 people were killed in the bombing of a federal building in **Oklahoma City**, OK (Apr. 1995).

Science and technology. The powerful **Hubble Space Telescope** was launched in Apr. 1990. U.S. space shuttle *Atlantis* docked with the orbiting Russian space station *Mir* (June 1995) in first of several joint missions. In Nov. 1998 the first component for a new **International Space Station** was launched into space from Kazakhstan.

Scottish scientist Ian Wilmut announced (Feb. 1997) the **cloning** of a sheep, nicknamed Dolly—the first mammal successfully cloned from a cell from an adult animal.

Tim Berners-Lee launched the first **World Wide Web** server (1990). User-friendly graphical browsers (Mosaic, 1993; Netscape, 1994) and affordable Internet service providers followed, expanding the reach of the **Internet**.

F. W. De Klerk and Nelson Mandela shared the Nobel Peace Prize in 1993 for negotiating the South African transition to nonracial democracy.

Opening a New Century: 2000-10

Terrorism and crime. Soon after the century opened, in Oct. 2000, 17 American sailors were killed aboard the USS *Cole* in Aden, **Yemen**, when a small boat exploded alongside it in a terrorist attack. But terrorism reached a new level on **Sept. 11, 2001**, when hijackers crashed two jetliners into the twin towers of the **World Trade Center** in New York City and another into the **Pentagon** outside Washington, DC, with a fourth crashing in a Pennsylvania field. The attacks, which destroyed both towers and damaged the Pentagon, killed about 3,000 people. Saudi exile Osama **bin Laden** and his **al-Qaeda** terrorist network, based in **Afghanistan** and backed by the Taliban government there, emerged as responsible.

Among many other incidents generally tied to Islamic radicals, a car bomb on the Indonesian island of **Bali** (Oct. 2002) killed about 200. **Commuter trains** were bombed in **Madrid**, Spain, killing 191 (Mar. 2004); elections held a week later ousted Spain's premier. **Subway trains** and a bus were bombed in **London** (July 2005); 56 people died in all. Eight explosions killed 207 on **commuter trains** in **Mumbai**, India (July 2006); also in Mumbai (Nov. 2008), terrorists launched coordinated attacks on sites frequented by foreigners, killing some 170. Bombs in Kampala, **Uganda**, killed over 70 people gathered to watch **World Cup soccer** final (July 2010). **Chechen** separatist guerrillas were implicated in an attack on a Moscow movie theater (Oct. 2002; over 100 hostages died), bombings in Moscow's subways (Feb. 2004, Mar. 2010; about 100 killed in all); explosions on two Russian planes (Aug. 2004; 89 died), and the takeover of a school in Beslan (Aug.-Sept. 2004; over 330 died).

Other attacks were reportedly foiled, as in Aug. 2006, when British authorities announced having thwarted a plot to detonate **liquid explosives** on transatlantic flights. In Dec. 2009 a Nigerian man—reportedly aided by al-Qaeda in Yemen—attempted to ignite explosives in his underwear, on a Detroit-bound international flight; the incident raised security questions.

Piracy was an increasing threat; some 445 attacks were reported worldwide in 2010 alone. Many occurred in the seas near **Somalia**, a haven for pirates.

Global economic crisis. A global recession, beginning in late 2007, gathered steam, and a financial meltdown, beginning in Sept. 2008, sent shock waves through industrialized and developing countries alike. Soaring food and **fuel prices** in early 2008 led to unrest in some areas, including an attempted general strike in **Egypt** and riots in **Haiti** (Apr. 2008). Housing values fell, unemployment rose, and governments faced rising budget deficits. Among many ripple effects around the world, **Iceland**'s banking system collapsed (Oct. 2008), rescued by loans and austerity measures. **Dubai**'s state-controlled investment company Dubai World could not meet payments on $59 bil debt; bailed out (Dec. 2009) by a loan from Abu Dhabi. Spending cuts, pension reforms, tax hikes, and other **austerity** measures spurred wide-scale protests in several European countries. The **European Union**, with help from the IMF, provided loan packages to bail out **Greece** (May 2010) and **Ireland** (Nov. 2010).

War in Iraq and Afghanistan. The U.S., with Great Britain, launched an invasion of **Iraq** (Mar. 2003), aimed at ousting the regime of Saddam **Hussein**. Troops took control of Baghdad and other cities, and U.S. Pres. George W. **Bush** declared major combat ended by May 1, but insurgents caused continuing casualties among troops and civilians. Searches for **weapons of mass destruction**, cited as major grounds for the invasion, yielded no results. Interim government installed, June 2004. Saddam Hussein was captured by U.S. troops (Dec. 2003) and tried by Iraqi authorities for crimes against humanity; he was convicted and executed (Dec. 2006).

Photographic evidence that U.S. soldiers at **Abu Ghraib** prison in Iraq abused detainees arose in Apr. 2004. Despite threats by insurgents, Iraqis turned out in large numbers to vote in **elections** for a transitional assembly (Jan. 2005),

democratic constitution (Oct. 2005), and parliament (Dec. 2005); negotiations produced a Shiite coalition government under Nouri **al-Maliki** (May 2006). With sectarian and **insurgent violence** intensifying, Bush announced (Jan. 2007) a **"surge"** of additional U.S. troops; military and civilian casualties declined sharply from mid-2007 onward, aided by a cease-fire with Shiite militias and shift in Sunni clan support for al-Qaeda. The Iraqi cabinet approved (Nov. 2008) U.S. troop presence, after a UN mandate expired. Under U.S. Pres. Barack **Obama**, combat troops withdrew from cities in mid-2009, as planned. Last combat unit withdrew from Iraq, Aug. 2010, but 50,000 U.S. troops remained. Mar. 2010 elections led eventually to formation of a new coalition government under Maliki, with Sunni support.

In **Afghanistan**, a U.S.-led military coalition ousted the **Taliban**, and a transitional government was installed (Dec. 2001), but Taliban insurgency continued, with heavy military and civilian casualties. NATO assumed control of multinational forces in Aug. 2003. Afghans elected Hamid **Karzai** (Nov. 2004) as head of what proved to be a weak central government. The next presidential election (Aug. 2009) was marked by widespread **vote-rigging**; Karzai was reelected after his main opponent withdrew from a runoff, citing transparency issues. In 2007-10, Taliban and other Islamist militants stepped up activities, often operating from safe havens inside **Pakistan**. The U.S. increased its troop strength in Afghanistan (2009), and coalition forces launched a major offensive in Helmund province, Feb. 2010.

Asia. Gen. Pervez **Musharraf**, brought to power in a 1999 coup, assumed **Pakistan**'s presidency in June 2001 and retained office through elections denounced by protesters as illegitimate. In the wake of the terrorist attacks of Sept. 11, 2001, Pakistan pledged cooperation fighting **Taliban** and **al-Qaeda** militants; attacks by militants and counterattacks by Pakistani forces caused heavy casualties over succeeding years. **Pakistan** and **India** restored ties (May 2003) and declared a cease-fire in disputed territory (Nov. 2003), but relations remained tense. An attack on a convoy carrying former Pakistani Prime Min. Benazir **Bhutto** (Oct. 2007) killed about 140 people; she was later assassinated (Dec. 2007) at a political rally. But her party won in parliamentary elections (Feb. 2008), and her widower, Asif Ali **Zardari**, was elected president (Sept. 2008) following Musharraf's resignation. In May 2009, after a cease-fire broke down, the government launched a major offensive against Taliban insurgents in the Swat Valley. Monsoon rains and **floods** (July-Aug. 2010) inundated nearly one-fifth of the country, leaving millions homeless.

Iran was censured (Dec. 2003) by the UN Intl. Atomic Energy Agency for covering up aspects of its **nuclear weapons** program, which it claimed was for peaceful purposes. Iran continued to enrich uranium in defiance of IAEA deadlines and tested missiles said to be capable of reaching Israel. Pres. Mahmoud **Ahmadinejad** was declared the landslide winner in June 2009 elections widely perceived to have been rigged. **Protests** by hundreds of thousands were crushed by police and Basij paramilitaries; many were injured, some killed, and dissidents were tried en masse (Aug. 2009).

Protests in **Kyrgyzstan** (Mar. 2005) against election fraud brought down Pres. Askar Akayev (in a **"tulip revolution"**), leading to the election of Kumanbek Bakiyev. He was, ousted in turn (Apr. 2010), after clashes between protesters and security forces left at least 85 people dead. In June 2010, despite ethnic violence (up to 2,000 killed), a referendum was held and new constitution approved.

South Korean Pres. Kim Dae-jung and **North Korean** ruler Kim Jong Il held a summit meeting and agreed to seek peace and reunification (June 2000), but tensions rose after North Korea admitted conducting a covert **nuclear weapons** development program (Oct. 2002). North Korea withdrew (Jan. 2003) from the Nuclear Nonproliferation Treaty. Multi-nation talks were held in Beijing; North Korea agreed (Feb. 2007) to end its nuclear program in exchange for an

One of the deadliest natural disasters in recorded history, the 2004 tsunami killed more than 200,000 people in 11 countries.

aid package, but subsequently reneged, conducting tests in Apr.-May 2009. An explosion tied to North Korea sank a South Korean Navy ship in the Yellow Sea (Mar. 2010), killing 46 sailors. North Korea shelled a South Korean island (Nov. 2010), killing four persons.

With the retirement of **China**'s Pres. Jiang Zemin, **Hu Jin-tao** was named Communist party chief (Nov. 2002) and president (Mar. 2003). China's rapidly expanding economy took a hit with several product recall scandals (pet food, Mar. 2007; toys, Aug.-Sept. 2007; infant formula, Sept. 2008). A massive **earthquake** killed nearly 70,000 in Sichuan province (May 2008). In **Japan**, the Liberal Democrats, in virtually uninterrupted power since the 1950s, were routed in parliamentary elections (Aug. 2009).

A massive **tsunami** in the Indian Ocean (Dec. 2004) devastated parts of Indonesia, Thailand, India, Sri Lanka, and other Asian and African nations, leaving some 200,000 dead. An **earthquake** struck the disputed territory of **Kashmir** and parts of Pakistan and India (Oct. 2005); nearly 80,000 were killed.

Myanmar's military junta cracked down on hundreds of thousands of antigovernment protesters, raiding monasteries and arresting protest leaders and others (Sept. 2007). More than 80,000 people were killed in a **cyclone** in Myanmar (May 2008); the regime thwarted aid agencies. **Sri Lanka** government forces launched a stepped-up offensive in 2008 against **Tamil guerrillas**, leading them to declare an end (May 2009) to a rebellion that since 1983 had claimed at least 80,000 lives. The military carried out a bloodless coup in **Thailand** (Sept. 2006), ousting Prem. Thaksin Shinawatra; civilian rule was restored after Dec. 2007 elections. "Red Shirt" Thaksin supporters stormed the Parliament building and occupied a fortified compound in Bangkok (Apr. 2010); more than 50 were killed in clashes with security forces (May 2010). A UN-sponsored **Cambodia war crimes** tribunal issued its first verdict, July 2010, convicting a former prison warden for mass tortures and killings under Khmer Rouge rule in the 1970s.

Under a Labor government led by Prime Min. Kevin Rudd, **Australia** ended its combat mission in Iraq (July 2008); Rudd was displaced (June 2010) by his deputy, Julia **Gillard**, who became Australia's first female prime minister.

Middle East. The peace process languished as violence between Israelis and Palestinians escalated, with **suicide bombings** by Palestinians and retaliation by Israeli armed forces. Israel launched a major West Bank offensive (Mar. 2002), and withdrew in early May but, after another wave of suicide bombings, reoccupied much of the West Bank. The U.S., Russia, UN, and EU initiated (Apr. 2003) a **"road map"** plan for peace negotiations, but little progress was made. After Palestinian leader Yasir Arafat's death (Nov. 2004), Mahmoud Abbas was elected in his place. Israeli Prime Min. Ariel **Sharon** decided in 2005 to pull troops and settlers out of the **Gaza Strip**, angering his own party's right wing. He formed a new party and, after being disabled by a stroke (Jan. 2006), was succeeded by an ally, Ehud **Olmert**, who led a coalition government following elections (Apr. 2006). The militant Palestinian party **Hamas** won a parliamentary majority over the long-ruling **Fatah** party (Jan. 2006), casting the peace process into increasing doubt.

Israel launched air and ground attacks on **Lebanon** (July 2006) in response to a raid into N Israel by Lebanon-based **Hezbollah** guerrillas; a cease-fire was declared a month later. In reaction to Hamas rocket and mortar attacks, Israel launched an aerial and ground offensive in the **Gaza Strip** (Dec. 2008), which killed an estimated 1,300 Palestinians. Olmert resigned as prime minister (effective Sept. 2008) amid corruption inquiries, and Feb. 2009 elections led to a coalition government headed by former Prime Min. Benjamin **Netanyahu**, a conservative. Enforcing a **blockade of Gaza**, Israeli commandos, May 2010, intercepted and boarded six vessels carrying aid and activists; nine activists were killed in a confrontation on one ship.

Europe. By early 2002 the **euro** was the common currency in 12 EU nations. The EU admitted 10 E European nations (May 2004); 2 more joined in Jan. 2007. A treaty to establish a new **EU constitution** was defeated (May-June 2005) by voters in France and the Netherlands. But a modified plan, known as the **Treaty of Lisbon**, came into force in Dec. 2009, after Irish voters, who had earlier rejected it, approved it (Oct. 2009).

In Oct. 2000, Yugoslav strongman Slobodan **Milosevic** yielded power to Vojislav **Kostunica**, who had declared himself president in the face of anti-Milosevic protests after a disputed election. Milosevic surrendered to Serbian authorities; he went on trial (Feb. 2002) for **war crimes** allegedly committed during 1990s ethnic conflicts in the Balkans but died (Mar. 2006) before a verdict was reached. Former Bosnian Serb leader Radovan Karadzic was also arraigned on war crimes charges (July 2008). **Kosovo** unilaterally declared independence (Feb. 2008).

Germany elected its first East German and first female chancellor (Nov. 2005); Angela **Merkel**, a Christian Democrat, succeeded Socialist Gerhard **Schröder**. Rioting shook France's immigrant communities in 300 cities and towns (Nov. 2005); over 3,000 arrests were made. A Danish newspaper's publication of cartoon **caricatures of Muhammad** sparked violent worldwide protests by Muslims (Jan.-Feb. 2006). **Polish** Pres. Lech **Kaczynski** and 95 others were killed in a plane crash (Apr. 2010).

British Prime Min. Tony **Blair** won reelection twice (2001, 2005), becoming the first-ever Labour prime minister to earn three straight terms. He stepped down in June 2007, to be succeeded by fellow Labourite Gordon **Brown**. But Conservatives were returned to power in a coalition government under David **Cameron** (May 2010). **France** underwent a leadership change with the election (May 2007) of conservative Nicolas **Sarkozy** as president. France rejoined NATO's military command (Apr. 2009) under Sarkozy after a break of more than 40 years. French legislation banning face-hiding **veils** in public won final passage, Sept. 2010, and yielded criticism.

Vladimir **Putin**, in power in Russia since 1999, was constitutionally barred from a new term as president in 2008; his protégé, Dmitri **Medvedev** was elected (May 2008) and named prime minister. Russian troops invaded the Georgian province of **South Ossetia** (Aug. 2008); a cease-fire was negotiated by French Pres. Sarkozy. Russia and U.S. signed

After seven years, the last U.S. combat troops left Iraq in 2010, reducing American presence to around 50,000 support troops.

New START arms control accord (Apr. 2010). In **Ukraine**, a tainted presidential runoff election (Nov. 2004) led to the country's "orange revolution" and a recount that gave power to nationalist Viktor **Yushchenko**. But his pro-Russian opponent, Viktor **Yanukovich**, captured back the presidency in Feb. 2010.

Africa. Ethiopia and Eritrea signed a **peace treaty** (Dec. 2000). Laurent **Kabila**, president of the **Dem. Rep. of Congo**, was shot to death by a bodyguard (Jan. 2001). Liberian Pres. Charles **Taylor** went into exile (Aug. 2003) as part of a deal to end a 14-year-old civil war; other accords were reached aimed at ending civil wars in **Angola** (Apr. 2002) and **Côte d'Ivoire** (Jan. 2003). **Libya** agreed (Dec. 2003) to abandon programs pursuing weapons of mass destruction.

A peace agreement in **Dem. Rep. of Congo** (Apr. 2003) did not end violence there; the nation agreed to work with Rwanda to disarm Hutu rebels (Nov. 2007). In **Sudan** a power-sharing accord between the Muslim-led government and rebels from the Christian south was signed, Jan. 2005, giving the south limited autonomy, with a referendum on independence slated for 2011. But a rebellion in the **Darfur** area of western Sudan led to large-scale violence. Arab militias (**janjaweed**), reportedly backed by the government, were accused of displacing over 2 million people in acts bordering on **genocide**, and by Sept. 2009 more than 300,000 people had been killed. The International Criminal Court issued an arrest warrant for Sudanese Pres. Omar Hassan Ahmad al-**Bashir**, for war crimes (Mar. 2009), but he remained in power, winning reelection (Apr. 2010) when his main opponent dropped out citing fraud.

Zimbabwean Pres. Robert **Mugabe** pulled his country out of the Commonwealth (Dec. 2003) after the group reaffirmed suspension of **Zimbabwe** for alleged fraud in the 2002 election. Violence sparked in **Kenya** (Jan. 2008) and Zimbabwe (Apr. 2008) after disputed elections in each nation. As Mugabe continued in power in Zimbabwe, unemployment there topped 90% and hyperinflation left the currency virtually worthless. **Guinea-Bissau**'s defense chief and then its president were assassinated in turn by rival groups (Mar. 2009); **Niger**'s president was ousted in a coup (Feb. 2010).

Americas and the Caribbean. The long-supreme **Institutional Revolutionary Party** lost power in **Mexico** with the election of two successive presidents from a center-right party, Vicente **Fox** and Felipe **Calderón** (July 2000, 2006). Calderón launched a crackdown on drug trafficking (Dec. 2006); from then through the end of 2010, more than 30,000 people were killed in violence fueled by warring **drug cartels**. In **Peru**, Pres. Alberto **Fujimori** stepped down during his 3rd term (Nov. 2000) amid scandal and did not seek reelection.

In Jan. 2001, Republican George W. **Bush** was inaugurated as **U.S. president**, after one of the closest and most controversial elections in U.S. history; he was reelected in Nov. 2004. Democrats claimed the White House with the Nov. 2008 election of Barack **Obama**, the first-ever black U.S. president.

In **Brazil**, reformist candidate Luis Inacio Lula **da Silva** won a runoff (Oct. 2002) to become president and was reelected in 2006; his chosen successor, Dilma **Rousseff**, was

elected in 2010. **Chile** was ruled by Socialist governments under Ricardo Lagos Escobar (from 2000) and Michelle **Bachelet** (from 2006), followed by conservative Sebastián **Piñera** (2010). Over 500 Chileans were killed in a Feb. 2010 earthquake; all 33 **men trapped in a mine** in N Chile were kept alive and successfully rescued (Oct. 2010) after almost 10 weeks underground.

In **Venezuela**, Pres. Hugo **Chavez** regained power after a 48-hr. coup (Dec. 2002) and consolidated it, in part through a referendum (Feb. 2009) that gave him new authority and eliminated presidential term limits. In **Bolivia**, Evo **Morales**, another leftist populist, won election as president (Dec. 2005) and passage of a new constitution (Jan. 2009) that gave the federal government control over resources and gave new rights to indigenous peoples. In **Honduras**, leftist opposition leader Manuel **Zelaya** was elected president (Nov. 2005) but was ousted by the military (June 2009) after he had sought constitutional changes; Porfirio (Pepe) **Lobo**, a conservative landowner, was elected (Nov. 2009) to succeed him.

Argentina was beset by economic problems; its **default** on IMF loans led (Sept. 2003) to a massive **debt-refinancing** agreement, but the money was repaid. Peronist presidents held power during the decade. **Haiti** was wracked by anti-government protests, leading to the resignation of Jean-Bertrand **Aristide** in Feb. 2004; a UN peacekeeping mission was brought in. Haiti was struck by **tropical storms**, including Hurricane Jeanne (Sept. 2004; over 3,000 killed), and by a **devastating earthquake** (Jan. 2010) that killed more than 200,000.

For the first time in 12 years, the Liberal Party handed control of **Canada**'s government to the Conservative Party, led by Prime Min. Stephen **Harper** (Jan. 2006). After 47 years in office, Cuban Pres. Fidel **Castro** ceded administrative powers to his brother, Raul Castro, to undergo surgery (July 2006); he formally resigned in Feb. 2008.

Religion. Pope **John Paul II** died, Apr. 2005, after 26 years in the papacy; German cardinal Joseph Ratzinger was elected as his successor, taking the name **Benedict XVI**. During the decade, reports of **sexual abuse** by Catholic priests going back generations, and evidence of inaction by church officials, made news in the U.S., Ireland, Belgium, Brazil, Germany, the Netherlands, and elsewhere. The Vatican (July 2010) issued revised rules for handling sexual abuse allegations.

Science and technology. The U.S. **space shuttle** *Columbia* broke up on reentering Earth's atmosphere (Feb. 2003), killing all seven crew members. NASA space shuttle program resumed with the July 2005 launch of *Discovery*. The Phoenix *Mars Lander* verified the presence of water ice on **Mars** (June 2008).

China, Oct. 2010, unveiled the Tianhe-1A **supercomputer**, said to be the world's fastest. **Internet** penetration and access to technology expanded exponentially, as more than one-fifth of the world's population had regular web access by the decade's end. Online commerce, social networking (Facebook, 2004; Twitter, 2006), and file-sharing services became commonplace. **WikiLeaks**, a controversial organization formed in 2007 to publish materials not available publicly, began disseminating secret government documents related to the Iraq and Afghanistan wars (Apr., July 2010), as well as confidential U.S. diplomatic cables (Nov. 2010).

Environment and health. The **Kyoto Protocol** (drawn up in 1997) took effect for 141 ratifying nations, Feb. 2005, requiring industrialized nations to achieve targeted reductions by 2012 in emissions of **greenhouse gases** linked to global warming. At a conference in Copenhagen (Dec. 2009), nations agreed only on nonbinding targets beyond 2012. A NASA report (Jan. 2010) found that 2000-09 had the **warmest average global temperatures** since modern records began in the 1880s.

The 13th International **AIDS Conference**, held in Durban, South Africa (July 2000), focused on ways of controlling AIDS in developing countries. Worldwide AIDS estimates were revised downward (Nov. 2007); they now showed new infections had peaked in the late 1990s. An epidemic of **swine flu**, or influenza A (H1N1), broke out in Mexico (Apr. 2009) and spread around the globe; World Health Organization estimated over 18,000 deaths by pandemic's conclusion (Aug. 2010).

HISTORICAL FIGURES

Note: Information accurate as of Sept. 2011.

Ancient Greeks and Romans

Greeks

Aeschines, orator, 389-314 BCE
Aeschylus, dramatist, 525-456 BCE
Aesop, fableist, c. 620-c. 560 BCE
Alcibiades, politician, 450-404 BCE
Anacreon, poet, c. 582-c. 485 BCE
Anaxagoras, philosopher, c. 500-428 BCE
Anaximander, philosopher, 611-546 BCE
Anaximenes, philosopher, c. 570-500 BCE
Antiphon, speechwriter, c. 480-411 BCE
Apollonius, mathematician, c. 265-170 BCE
Archimedes, mathematician, 287-212 BCE
Aristophanes, dramatist, c. 448-380 BCE
Aristotle, philosopher, 384-322 BCE
Athenaeus, scholar, fl. c. 200
Callicrates, architect, fl. 5th cent. BCE
Callimachus, poet, c. 305-240 BCE
Cratinus, comic dramatist, 520-421 BCE
Democritus, philosopher, c. 460-370 BCE
Demosthenes, orator, 384-322 BCE
Diodorus, historian, fl. 20 BCE
Diogenes, philosopher, 372-c. 287 BCE
Dionysius, historian, d. c. 7 BCE
Empedocles, philosopher, c. 490-430 BCE
Epicharmus, dramatist, c. 530-440 BCE
Epictetus, philosopher, c. 55-c. 135
Epicurus, philosopher, 341-270 BCE
Eratosthenes, scientist, 276-194 BCE
Euclid, mathematician, fl. c. 300 BCE
Euripides, dramatist, c. 484-406 BCE
Galen, physician, 129-216
Heraclitus, philosopher, c. 540-c. 475 BCE
Herodotus, historian, c. 484-420 BCE

Hesiod, poet, 8th cent. BCE
Hippocrates, physician, c. 460-377 BCE
Homer, poet, fl. c. 8th cent. BCE
Isocrates, orator, 436-338 BCE
Menander, dramatist, 342-292 BCE
Parmenides, philosopher, b. c. 515 BCE
Pericles, statesman, c. 495-429 BCE
Phidias, sculptor, c. 500-435 BCE
Pindar, poet, c. 518-c. 438 BCE
Plato, philosopher, c. 428-347 BCE
Plutarch, biographer, c. 46-120
Polybius, historian, c. 200-c. 118 BCE
Praxiteles, sculptor, 400-330 BCE
Pythagoras, phil., math., c. 580-c. 500 BCE
Sappho, poet, c. 610-c. 580 BCE
Simonides, poet, 556-c. 468 BCE
Socrates, philosopher, 469-399 BCE
Solon, statesman, 640-560 BCE
Sophocles, dramatist, c. 496-406 BCE
Strabo, geographer, c. 63 BCE-24 CE
Thales, philosopher, c. 634-546 BCE
Themistocles, politician, c. 524-c. 460 BCE
Theocritus, poet, c. 310-250 BCE
Theophrastus, phil., c. 372-c. 287 BCE
Thucydides, historian, fl. 5th cent. BCE
Timon, philosopher, c. 320-c. 230 BCE
Xenophon, historian, c. 434-c. 355 BCE
Zeno, philosopher, c. 335-c. 263 BCE

Romans

Ammianus, historian, c. 330-395
Apuleius, satirist, c. 124-c. 170
Boethius, scholar, c. 480-524
Caesar, Julius, leader, 100-44 BCE

Catiline, politician, c. 108-62 BCE
Cato (Elder), statesman, 234-149 BCE
Catullus, poet, c. 84-54 BCE
Cicero, orator, 106-43 BCE
Claudian, poet, c. 370-c. 404
Ennius, poet, 239-170 BCE
Gellius, author, c. 130-c. 165
Horace, poet, 65-8 BCE
Juvenal, satirist, 60-127
Livy, historian, 59 BCE-17 CE
Lucan, poet, 39-65
Lucilius, poet, c. 180-c.102 BCE
Lucretius, poet, c. 99-c. 55 BCE
Martial, epigrammatist, c. 38-c. 103
Nepos, historian, c. 100-c. 25 BCE
Ovid, poet, 43 BCE-17 CE
Persius, satirist, 34-62
Plautus, dramatist, c. 254-c. 184 BCE
Pliny the Elder, scholar, 23-79
Pliny the Younger, author, 62-113
Quintilian, rhetorician, c. 35-c. 97
Sallust, historian, 86-34 BCE
Seneca, philosopher, 4 BCE-65 CE
Silius, poet, c. 25-101
Statius, poet, c. 45-c. 96
Suetonius, biographer, c. 69-c. 122
Tacitus, historian, 56-120
Terence, dramatist, 195/185-c. 159 BCE
Tibullus, poet, c. 55-c. 19 BCE
Vergil, poet, 70-19 BCE
Vitruvius, architect, fl. 1st cent. BCE

Roman Rulers

From Romulus to the end of the Empire in the West. Rulers in the East sat in Constantinople and, for a brief period, in Nicaea, until the capture of Constantinople by the Turks in 1453, when Byzantium was succeeded by the Ottoman Empire.

The Kingdom

BCE
753 Romulus (Quirinus)
715 Numa Pompilius
673 Tullus Hostilius
641 Ancus Marcius
616 L. Tarquinius Priscus
579 Servius Tullius
534 L. Tarquinius Superbus

The Republic

509 Consulate established
509 Quaestorship instituted
498 Dictatorship introduced
494 Plebeian Tribunate created
494 Plebeian Aedileship created
444 Consular Tribunate organized
435 Censorship instituted
366 Praetorship established
366 Curule Aedileship created
362 Military Tribunate elected
326 Proconsulate introduced
311 Naval Duumvirate elected
217 Dictatorship of Fabius Maximus
133 Tribunate of Tiberius Gracchus
123 Tribunate of Gaius Gracchus
82 Dictatorship of Sulla
60 First Triumvirate formed
(Caesar, Pompeius, Crassus)
47 Dictatorship of Caesar
43 Second Triumvirate formed
(Octavianus, Antonius, Lepidus)

The Empire

27 Augustus (Octavian)
CE
14 Tiberius I
37 Caligula
41 Claudius I
54 Nero
68 Galba
69 Otho, Vitellius
69 Vespasianus

79 Titus
81 Domitianus
96 Nerva
98 Trajanus
117 Hadrianus
138 Antoninus Pius
161 Marcus Aurelius and Lucius Verus
169 Marcus Aurelius (alone)
180 Commodus
193 Pertinax; Julianus I
193 Septimius Severus
211 Caracalla and Geta
212 Caracalla (alone)
217 Macrinus
218 Elagabalus (Heliogabalus)
222 Alexander Severus
235 Maximinus I (the Thracian)
238 Gordianus I and Gordianus II;
Pupienus and Balbinus
238 Gordianus III
244 Philippus (the Arabian)
249 Decius
251 Gallus and Volusianus
253 Aemilianus
253 Valerianus and Gallienus
258 Gallienus (alone)
268 Claudius Gothicus
270 Quintillus
270 Aurelianus
275 Tacitus
276 Florianus
276 Probus
282 Carus
283 Carinus and Numerianus
286 Diocletianus and Maximianus
305 Galerius and Constantius I
306 Galerius, Maximinus II, Severus I
307 Galerius, Maximinus II,
Constantinus I, Licinius, Maxentius
311 Maximinus II, Constantinus I,
Licinius, Maxentius
314 Maximinus II, Constantinus I, Licinius
314 Constantinus I and Licinius
324 Constantinus I (the Great)

337 Constantinus II, Constans I,
Constantius II
340 Constantinus II and Constans I
350 Constantius II (alone)
361 Julianus II (the Apostate)
363 Jovianus

West (Rome) and East (Constantinople)

364 Valentinianus I (West),
Valens (East)
367 Valentinianus I with Gratianus
(West), Valens (East)
375 Gratianus with Valentinianus II
(West), Valens (East)
378 Gratianus with Valentinianus II
(West), Theodosius I (East)
383 Valentinianus II (West),
Theodosius I (East)
394 Theodosius I (the Great)
395 Honorius (West), Arcadius (East)
408 Honorius (West),
Theodosius II (East)
423 Valentinianus III (West),
Theodosius II (East)
450 Valentinianus III (West),
Marcianus (East)
455 Maximus (West), Avitus (West);
Marcianus (East)
456 Avitus (West), Marcianus (East)
457 Majorianus (West), Leo I (East)
461 Severus II (West), Leo I (East)
467 Anthemius (West), Leo I (East)
472 Olybrius (West), Leo I (East)
473 Glycerius (West), Leo I (East)
474 Julius Nepos (West), Leo II (East)
475 Romulus Augustulus (West),
Zeno (East)
476 End of Empire in West with
deposing of Romulus Augustulus by
Germanic chief Odovacar, who
proclaimed self king. Odovacar
murdered by King Theodoric of
Ostrogoths, 493

Rulers of England and Great Britain

Reign began	ENGLAND Name	Age at death[1]
	Saxons and Danes	
829	Egbert, king of Wessex, won allegiance of all English	NA
839	Ethelwulf, son of Egbert, king of Wessex, Sussex, Kent, Essex	NA
858	Ethelbald, eldest son of Ethelwulf, displaced father in Wessex.	NA
860	Ethelbert, 2nd son of Ethelwulf, united Kent and Wessex.	NA
866	Ethelred I, 3rd son of Ethelwulf, king of Wessex, fought Danes	NA
871	Alfred (the Great), 4th son of Ethelwulf, defeated Danes, fortified London	52
899	Edward (the Elder), son of Alfred, united English, claimed Scotland	55
924	Athelstan (the Glorious), eldest son of Edward, king of Mercia, Wessex	45
940	Edmund, 3rd son of Edward, king of Wessex, Mercia.	25
946	Edred, 4th son of Edward	32
955	Edwy (the Fair), eldest son of Edmund, king of Wessex.	18
959	Edgar (the Peaceful), 2nd son of Edmund, ruled all English.	32
975	Edward (the Martyr), eldest son of Edgar, murdered by stepmother.	17
978; 1014[2]	Ethelred II (the Unready), 2nd son of Edgar, married Emma of Normandy.	48
1016	Edmund II (Ironside), son of Ethelred II, king of London.	27
1016	Canute (the Dane), son of Sweyn, who conquered English territory; gave Wessex to Edmund II; married Emma, Ethelred II's widow.	40
1035	Harold I (Harefoot), illegitimate son of Canute	NA
1040	Hardecanute, son of Canute by Emma, also king of Denmark	24
1042	Edward (the Confessor), son of Ethelred II, canonized 1161	62
1066	Harold II, Edward's brother-in-law, last Saxon king.	44
	House of Normandy	
1066	William I (the Conqueror), son of Duke Robert I of Normandy, defeated Harold II at Hastings	60
1087	William II (Rufus), 3rd son of William I, killed by arrow while hunting; possibly assassination	43
1100	Henry I (Beauclerc), youngest son of William I	67
	House of Blois	
1135	Stephen, son of Adela, daughter of William I, and Count of Blois.	50
	House of Plantagenet	
1154	Henry II, son of Geoffrey Plantagenet (Angevin) by Matilda, daughter of Henry I.	56
1189	Richard I (Coeur de Lion), son of Henry II, crusader.	42
1199	John (Lackland), son of Henry II, approved Magna Carta, 1215.	50
1216	Henry III, son of John, acceded at 9, under regency until 1227	65
1272	Edward I (Longshanks), son of Henry III.	68
1307	Edward II, son of Edward I, deposed by Parliament	43
1327	Edward III (of Windsor), son of Edward II	65
1377	Richard II, grandson of Edward III, minor until 1389, deposed	33
	House of Lancaster	
1399	Henry IV, son of John of Gaunt, duke of Lancaster, son of Edward III	47
1413	Henry V, son of Henry IV, victor over French at Agincourt	34
1422; 1470	Henry VI, son of Henry V, overthrown by Edward IV in 1461 but was returned to throne in 1470. Deposed, died in Tower of London, 1471	49
	House of York	
1461; 1471	Edward IV, great-great-grandson of Edward III, son of duke of York. Acclaimed king by Parliament, 1461. Driven into exile in 1470 but defeated enemies to regain throne, 1471	40
1483	Edward V, son of Edward IV, murdered in Tower of London	13
1483	Richard III, brother of Edward IV, fell in battle at Bosworth Field against Henry Tudor	32
	House of Tudor	
1485	Henry VII, son of Edmund Tudor, earl of Richmond, whose father had married the widow of Henry V. Descended from Edward III through mother, Margaret Beaufort, via John of Gaunt. By marrying daughter of Edward IV, united Lancaster and York.	53
1509	Henry VIII, 2nd son of Henry VII, by Elizabeth, daughter of Edward IV	56
1547	Edward VI, son of Henry VIII, by Jane Seymour, his 3rd queen. Ruled under regents, was forced to name Lady Jane Grey his successor. Council of State proclaimed her queen, July 10, 1553. Mary Tudor won Council, was proclaimed queen, July 19. Mary had Lady Jane Grey beheaded for treason, 1554.	16
1553	Mary I, daughter of Henry VIII, by his 1st wife, Catherine of Aragon.	43
1558	Elizabeth I, daughter of Henry VIII, by his 2nd wife, Anne Boleyn	69
	GREAT BRITAIN	
	House of Stuart	
1603	James I (James VI of Scotland), son of Mary, Queen of Scots. First to call self king of Great Britain; this became official with Act of Union, 1707	59
1625	Charles I, only surviving son of James I.	48
	Commonwealth	
1649	Declared upon execution of Charles I	
	Protectorate	
1653	Oliver Cromwell, served on Council of State, executive body of Commonwealth, following overthrow of monarchy. Named Lord Protector upon creation of Protectorate by 1653 Instrument of Government	59
1658	Richard Cromwell, 3rd son of Oliver Cromwell. Resigned as Lord Protector amid civil war, 1659. Died 1712. . . .	86
	House of Stuart (restored)	
1660	Charles II, eldest son of Charles I, Restoration put him back on throne, died without issue	55
1685	James II, 2nd son of Charles I, deposed 1688.	68
1689	William III, son of William, Prince of Orange, by Mary, daughter of Charles I. Offered joint rule of throne with wife by Parliament.	51
1689	Mary II, eldest daughter of James II, wife of William III, died 1694	33
1702	Anne, 2nd daughter of James II, sister-in-law of William III, assumed throne on William's death	49
	House of Hanover	
1714	George I, son of Elector of Hanover, by Sophia, granddaughter of James I.	67
1727	George II, only son of George I, married Caroline of Brandenburg.	77
1760	George III, grandson of George II, married Charlotte of Mecklenburg	81
1820	George IV, eldest son of George III, prince regent from Feb. 1811	67
1830	William IV, 3rd son of George III, married Adelaide of Saxe-Meiningen	71
1837	Victoria, daughter of Edward, 4th son of George III; married Prince Albert of Saxe-Coburg and Gotha, 1840, who became prince consort.	81

Reign began		Age at death[1]
	House of Saxe-Coburg and Gotha	
1901	Edward VII, eldest son of Victoria, married Alexandra, Princess of Denmark	68
	House of Windsor[3]	
1910	George V, 2nd son of Edward VII, married Princess Mary of Teck	70
1936	Edward VIII, eldest son of George V, acceded Jan. 20, abdicated Dec. 11.	77
1936	George VI, 2nd son of George V, married Lady Elizabeth Bowes-Lyon	56
1952	Elizabeth II, elder daughter of George VI, acceded Feb. 6	

NA = Age/birth date not certain. (1) Except where noted, year of death is year of accession of succeeding ruler. (2) King Sweyn I of Denmark invaded England in 1013 and declared himself king. Ethelred II reclaimed the throne upon Sweyn's death in 1014. (3) Name adopted by proclamation of George V, July 17, 1917.

Rulers of Scotland

Reign began	Name
846	Kenneth I MacAlpin, first Scot to rule both Scots and Picts
1005	Malcolm II Mackenneth
1034	Duncan I, first general ruler
1040	Macbeth, seized kingdom, slain by Malcolm III MacDuncan
1057	Malcolm III MacDuncan (Canmore), eldest son of Duncan I. Married Margaret, Saxon princess who had fled from Normans
1093	Donald Bane, younger brother of Malcolm III
1094	Duncan II, eldest son of Malcolm III by first wife
1095	Donald Bane (restored)
1097	Edgar, 4th son of Malcolm III and Queen Margaret, moved court to Edinburgh
1107	Alexander I, brother of Edgar
1124	David I, brother of Edgar
1153	Malcolm IV (the Maiden), grandson of David I
1165	William (the Lion), brother of Malcolm IV
1214	Alexander II, son of William
1249	Alexander III, son of Alexander II, defeated Norse, regained the Hebrides
1286	Margaret (Maid of Norway), granddaughter of Alexander III, child of Eric of Norway, grandniece of Edward I of England. Died 1290 at age 8. (Interregnum, 1290-92)
1292	John Balliol, proclaimed king of Scotland by Edward I of England. (Interregnum, 1296-1306[1])
1306	Robert Bruce (the Bruce), victor at Bannockburn, 1314. Treaty with England and secured throne, 1328
1329	David II, only son of Robert Bruce
1371	Robert II (the Steward), grandson of Robert Bruce, son of Walter, the steward of Scotland. First of so-called Stuart line
1390	Robert III, son of Robert II
1406	James I, son of Robert III
1437	James II, son of James I
1460	James III, eldest son of James II
1488	James IV, eldest son of James III
1513	James V, eldest son of James IV
1542	Mary (Queen of Scots), daughter of James V, became queen before she was 1 week old. Married Francis II, son of Henry II of France, 1558. Francis died in 1560. Married her cousin, Henry Stewart, Lord Darnley, 1565; married James Hepburn, Earl of Bothwell, 1567. Imprisoned by Elizabeth I; beheaded, 1587
1567	James VI, son of Mary and Lord Darnley, became James I, king of England on death of Elizabeth, 1603. Although thrones were thus united, legislative union of Scotland and England did not become official until the Act of Union, 1707

(1) Edward I decreed annexation of Scotland to England, 1296. William Wallace led resistance, 1297-1305.

Prime Ministers of Great Britain

Designations in parentheses describe each government.

W = Whig; T = Tory; Cl = Coalition; P = Peelite; Li = Liberal; C = Conservative; La = Labour

Entered office	Name	Entered office	Name	Entered office	Name
1721	Sir Robert Walpole (W)[1]	1830	Earl Grey (W)	1915	Herbert H. Asquith (Cl)
1742	Earl of Wilmington (W)	1834	Viscount Melbourne (W)	1916	David Lloyd George (Cl)
1743	Henry Pelham (W)	1834	Sir Robert Peel (C)	1922	Andrew Bonar Law (C)
1754	Duke of Newcastle (W)	1835	Viscount Melbourne (W)	1923	Stanley Baldwin (C)
1756	Duke of Devonshire (W)	1841	Sir Robert Peel (C)	1924	James Ramsay MacDonald (La)
1757	Duke of Newcastle (W)	1846	Lord (later Earl) John Russell (W)	1924	Stanley Baldwin (C)
1762	Earl of Bute (T)	1852	Earl of Derby (C)	1929	James Ramsay MacDonald (La)
1763	George Grenville (W)	1852	Earl of Aberdeen (P)	1931	James Ramsay MacDonald (Cl)
1765	Marquess of Rockingham (W)	1855	Viscount Palmerston (Li)	1935	Stanley Baldwin (Cl)
1766	William Pitt the Elder (Earl of Chatham) (W)	1858	Earl of Derby (C)	1937	Neville Chamberlain (Cl)
		1859	Viscount Palmerston (Li)	1940	Winston Churchill (Cl)
1768	Duke of Grafton (W)	1865	Earl Russell (W)	1945	Winston Churchill (C)
1770	Frederick North (Lord North) (T)	1866	Earl of Derby (C)	1945	Clement Attlee (La)
1782	Marquess of Rockingham (W)	1868	Benjamin Disraeli (C)	1951	Sir Winston Churchill (C)
1782	Earl of Shelburne (W)	1868	William E. Gladstone (Li)	1955	Sir Anthony Eden (C)
1783	Duke of Portland (Cl)	1874	Benjamin Disraeli (C)	1957	Harold Macmillan (C)
1783	William Pitt the Younger (T)	1880	William E. Gladstone (Li)	1963	Sir Alec Douglas-Home (C)
1801	Henry Addington (T)	1885	Marquess of Salisbury (C)	1964	Harold Wilson (La)
1804	William Pitt the Younger (T)	1886	William E. Gladstone (Li)	1970	Edward Heath (C)
1806	William Wyndham Grenville, Baron Grenville (W)	1886	Marquess of Salisbury (C)	1974	Harold Wilson (La)
		1892	William E. Gladstone (Li)	1976	James Callaghan (La)
1807	Duke of Portland (T)	1894	Earl of Rosebery (Li)	1979	Margaret Thatcher (C)
1809	Spencer Perceval (T)	1895	Marquess of Salisbury (C)	1990	John Major (C)
1812	Earl of Liverpool (T)	1902	Arthur J. Balfour (C)	1997	Tony Blair (La)
1827	George Canning (T)	1905	Sir Henry Campbell-Bannerman (Li)	2007	Gordon Brown (La)
1827	Viscount Goderich (T)			2010	David Cameron (Cl)
1828	Duke of Wellington (T)	1908	Herbert H. Asquith (Li)		

Note: The Conservative Party was formed in 1834, an outgrowth of the Tory party. (1) Walpole is commonly regarded as the first prime minister of Britain, though the title was not commonly used then and did not become official until 1905.

Rulers of France: Kings, Queens, Presidents

Caesar to Charlemagne

Julius Caesar subdued the Gauls, native tribes of Gaul (France), 58 to 51 BCE. The Romans ruled 500 years. The Franks, a Teutonic tribe, reached the Somme from the east c. 250 CE. By the 5th century the Merovingian Franks ousted the Romans. In 451, with the help of Visigoths, Burgundians, and others, they defeated Attila and the Huns at Chalons-sur-Marne.

Childeric I became leader of the Merovingians, 458. His son Clovis I (Chlodwig, Ludwig, Louis), crowned 481, founded the dynasty. After defeating the Alemanni (Germans), 496, he was baptized a Christian and made Paris his capital. His line ruled until Childeric III was deposed, 751.

The West Merovingians were called Neustrians, the eastern Austrasians. Pepin of Herstal (687-714), major domus, or head of the palace, of Austrasia, took over Neustria as dux (leader) of the Franks. Pepin's son, Charles, called Martel (the Hammer), defeated the Saracens at Tours-Poitiers, 732; was succeeded by his son, Pepin the Short, 741, who deposed Childeric III and ruled as king until 768.

His son, Charlemagne, or Charles the Great (742-814), became king of the Franks, 768, with his brother Carloman, who died 771. Charlemagne ruled France, Germany, parts of Italy, Spain, and Austria, and enforced Christianity. Crowned Emperor of the Romans by Pope Leo III in St. Peter's, Rome, Dec. 25, 800. Succeeded by son, Louis I the Pious, 814. At death, 840, Louis left empire to sons, Lothair (Roman emperor); Pepin I (king of Aquitaine); Louis II (of Germany); Charles the Bald (France). They quarreled and, by the Treaty of Verdun, 843, divided the empire.

The date preceding each entry is year of accession.

The Carolingians

843 Charles I (the Bald), Roman emperor, 875
877 Louis II (the Stammerer), son
879 Louis III (d. 882) and Carloman, brothers
885 Charles II (the Fat), Roman emperor, 881
888 Eudes (Odo), elected by nobles
898 Charles III (the Simple), son of Louis II, defeated by Robert
922 Robert, brother of Eudes, killed in war
923 Rudolph (Raoul), duke of Burgundy
936 Louis IV, son of Charles III
954 Lothair, son, aged 13, defeated by Capet
986 Louis V (the Sluggard), left no heirs

The Capets

987 Hugh Capet, son of Hugh the Great
996 Robert II (the Pious), his son
1031 Henry I, son
1060 Philip I (the Fair), son
1108 Louis VI (the Fat), son
1137 Louis VII (the Younger), son
1180 Philip II (Augustus), son, crowned at Reims
1223 Louis VIII (the Lion), son
1226 Louis IX, son, arbitrated disputes with English King Henry III; led crusades, 1248 (captured in Egypt, 1250) and 1270, when he died of plague in Tunis. Canonized 1297 as St. Louis
1270 Philip III (the Hardy), son
1285 Philip IV (the Fair), son, king at 17
1314 Louis X (the Headstrong), son. His posthumous son, John I, lived and reigned only 5 days.
1316 Philip V (the Tall), brother of Louis X
1322 Charles IV (the Fair), brother of Louis X

House of Valois

1328 Philip VI (of Valois), grandson of Philip III
1350 John II (the Good), his son, retired to England
1364 Charles V (the Wise), son
1380 Charles VI (the Beloved), son
1422 Charles VII (the Victorious), son. In 1429 Joan of Arc (Jeanne d'Arc) defeated English at Orleans and Patay and had Charles crowned at Reims, July 17. Joan was captured May 24, 1430, and executed May 30, 1431, at Rouen for heresy. Charles ordered her rehabilitation, effected 1455.
1461 Louis XI (the Cruel), son, civil reformer
1483 Charles VIII (the Affable), son
1498 Louis XII, great-grandson of Charles V
1515 Francis I, of Angouleme, nephew, son-in-law. Fought 4 major wars, was patron of the arts
1547 Henry II, son, killed at a joust. Husband of Catherine de Médicis (1519-89) and lover of Diane de Poitiers (1499-1566). Catherine was born in Florence, daughter of Lorenzo de Medici. By marriage to Henry II she became the mother of Francis II, Charles IX, Henry III, and Queen Margaret (Reine Margot), wife of Henry IV (of Navarre).

1559 Francis II, son. Betrothed in 1548 at age 4 to Mary, Queen of Scots, aged 6; they were married 1558. Francis died 1560, aged 16. Mary returned to rule Scotland, 1561.
1560 Charles IX, brother
1574 Henry III, brother, assassinated

House of Bourbon

1589 Henry IV, of Navarre, assassinated. Made enemies when he gave tolerance to Protestants by Edict of Nantes, 1598. He was grandson of Queen Margaret of Navarre, literary patron. Married Margaret of Valois, daughter of Henry II and Catherine de Médicis; was divorced. In 1600, he married Marie de Médicis, who became Regent of France, 1610-17, for her son, Louis XIII; she was exiled by Richelieu, 1631.
1610 Louis XIII (the Just), son (1601-43), married Anne of Austria. His chief minister (1622-42), Cardinal Richelieu, determined his policies.
1643 Louis XIV (the Sun King), son; was king 72 years. Until 1661, Anne of Austria was regent, with Cardinal Mazarin as chief minister; after that, Louis ruled absolutely. Known for his lavish court and patronage of the arts, he exhausted a prosperous country in wars for thrones and territory.
1715 Louis XV (the Beloved), great-grandson. Married a Polish princess, lost Canada to the English. His favorite mistresses, Mme. de Pompadour and Mme. Du Barry, influenced policies. Mme. Pompadour's saying "Après moi, le déluge" (After me, the deluge) often incorrectly attributed to Louis XV
1774 Louis XVI, grandson, married Marie Antoinette, daughter of Empress Maria Therese of Austria. King and queen beheaded by Revolution, 1793. Their son, called Louis XVII, died in prison, never ruled

First Republic

1792 National Convention of the French Revolution
1795 Directory, under Barras and others
1799 Consulate, Napoleon Bonaparte, first consul. Elected consul for life, 1802

First Empire

1804 Napoleon I (Napoleon Bonaparte), emperor. Josephine (de Beauharnais), empress, 1804-09; Marie Louise, empress, 1810-14. Her son, Francois (1811-32), titular king of Rome, later duke de Reichstadt and Napoleon II, never ruled. Napoleon abdicated 1814; died in exile, 1821.

House of Bourbon (restored)

1814 Louis XVIII, king, brother of Louis XVI
1824 Charles X, brother, reactionary, deposed by the July Revolution, 1830

House of Orleans

1830 Louis-Philippe (the Citizen King)

Second Republic

1848 Louis Napoleon Bonaparte, president, nephew of Napoleon I

Second Empire

1852 Napoleon III (Louis Napoleon Bonaparte), emperor, Eugenie (de Montijo), empress. Lost Franco-Prussian war, deposed 1870. Son, Prince Imperial (1856-79), died in Zulu War. Eugenie died 1920.

Third Republic: Presidents

1871 Thiers, Louis Adolphe (1797-1877)
1873 MacMahon, Marshal Patrice M. de (1808-93)
1879 Grevy, Paul J. (1807-91)
1887 Sadi-Carnot, M. (1837-94), assassinated
1894 Casimir-Perier, Jean P. P. (1847-1907)
1895 Faure, François Felix (1841-99)
1899 Loubet, Emile (1838-1929)
1906 Fallieres, C. Armand (1841-1931)
1913 Poincare, Raymond (1860-1934)
1920 Deschanel, Paul (1856-1922)
1920 Millerand, Alexandre (1859-1943)
1924 Doumergue, Gaston (1863-1937)
1931 Doumer, Paul (1857-1932), assassinated
1932 Lebrun, Albert (1871-1950), resigned 1940
1940 Vichy govt. under German armistice: Henri Philippe Petain (1856-1951), chief of state, 1940-44. Provisional govt. after liberation: Charles de Gaulle (1890-1970), Oct. 1944-Jan. 21, 1946; Felix Gouin (1884-1977), Jan. 23, 1946; Georges Bidault (1899-1983), June 24, 1946.

Fourth Republic: Presidents

1947 Auriol, Vincent (1884-1966)
1954 Coty, Rene (1882-1962)

Fifth Republic: Presidents

1959 De Gaulle, Charles Andre J. M. (1890-1970)
1969 Pompidou, Georges (1911-74)
1974 Giscard d'Estaing, Valery (1926-)
1981 Mitterrand, François (1916-96)
1995 Chirac, Jacques (1932-)
2007 Sarkozy, Nicolas (1955-)

Rulers of Middle Europe; Rise and Fall of Dynasties; Rulers of Germany

Carolingian Dynasty

Charles (the Great), or Charlemagne, ruled France, Italy, and Middle Europe; established Ostmark (later Austria); crowned Roman emperor by pope in Rome, 800 CE; died 814.

Louis I (Ludwig) (the Pious), son, crowned by Charlemagne 814; died 840.

Louis II (the German), son, succeeded to East Francia (Germany) 843-76.

Charles (the Fat), son, inherited East Francia and West Francia (France) 876; reunited empire, crowned emperor by pope, 881; deposed 887.

Arnulf, nephew, 887-99, partition of empire.

Louis (the Child), 899-911, last direct descendant of Charlemagne.

Conrad I, duke of Franconia, first elected German king, 911-18, founded House of Franconia.

Saxon Dynasty; First Reich

Henry I (the Fowler), duke of Saxony, 919-36.

Otto I (the Great), 936-73, son, crowned Holy Roman Emperor by pope, 962.

Otto II, 973-83, son, failed to oust Greeks and Arabs from Sicily.

Otto III, 983-1002, son, crowned emperor at 16.

Henry II (the Saint), duke of Bavaria, 1002-24, great-grandson of Otto the Great.

House of Franconia

Conrad II, 1024-39, elected king of Germany.

Henry III (the Black), 1039-56, son, deposed 3 popes, annexed Burgundy.

Henry IV, 1056-1106, son, regency by his mother, Agnes of Poitou. Banned by Pope Gregory VII, he did penance at Canossa.

Henry V, 1106-25, son, last of Salian Dynasty.

Lothair, Duke of Saxony, 1125-37. Crowned emperor in Rome, 1134.

House of Hohenstaufen

Conrad III, duke of Swabia, 1138-52, in 2nd Crusade.

Frederick I, Barbarossa, 1152-90, nephew.

Henry VI, 1190-96, took lower Italy from Normans. Son became king of Sicily.

Philip of Swabia, 1197-1208, brother.

Otto IV, of House of Welf, 1198-1215, deposed.

Frederick II, 1215-50, son of Henry VI; king of Sicily; crowned king of Jerusalem in 5th Crusade.

Conrad IV, 1250-54, son, lost lower Italy to Charles of Anjou.

Conradin, 1252-68, son, king of Jerusalem and Sicily, beheaded. Last Hohenstaufen.

(Interregnum, 1254-73. Rise of the Electors.)

Transition

Rudolph I, of Hapsburg, 1273-91, defeated King Ottocar II of Bohemia. Bequeathed duchy of Austria to son Albert.

Adolph of Nassau, 1292-98, killed in war with Albert of Austria.

Albert I, king of Germany, 1298-1308, eldest son of Rudolph I.

Henry VII, of Luxemburg, 1308-13, crowned emperor in Rome; seized Bohemia, 1310.

Louis IV, of Bavaria (Wittelsbach), 1314-47. Also elected was Frederick of Austria, 1314-30 (Hapsburg). Abolition of papal sanction for election of Holy Roman Emperor.

Charles IV, of Luxemburg, 1347-78, grandson of Henry VII, German emperor and king of Bohemia, Lombardy, Burgundy, took Mark of Brandenburg.

Wenceslaus, 1378-1400, deposed.

Rupert, duke of Palatine, 1400-10.

Sigismund, 1411-37.

Hungary

Stephen I, House of Arpad, 997-1038. Crowned king, 1000; converted Magyars; canonized 1083. After several centuries of feuds Charles Robert of Anjou became Charles I, 1308-42.

Louis I (the Great), son, 1342-82, joint ruler of Poland with Casimir III, 1370. Defeated Turks.

Mary, daughter, 1382-95, ruled with husband, Sigismund of Luxemburg, 1387-1437, also king of Bohemia. As brother of Wenceslaus he succeeded Rupert as Holy Roman Emperor, 1410.

Albert, 1438-39, son-in-law of Sigismund, also Roman emperor as Albert II (see under Hapsburg).

Ulaszlo I of Poland, 1440-44.

Ladislaus V, posthumous son of Albert II, 1444-57. John Hunyadi (Janos Hunyadi), governor (1446-52), fought Turks, Czechs; died 1456.

Matthias I (Corvinus), son of Hunyadi, 1458-90. Shared rule of Bohemia, captured Vienna, 1485, annexed Austria, Styria, Carinthia.

Ulaszlo II (king of Bohemia), 1490-1516.

Louis II, son, aged 10, 1516-26. Wars with Suleiman, Turk. In 1527, Hungary split between Ferdinand I, Archduke of Austria, brother-in-law of Louis II, and John Zapolya of Transylvania. After Turkish invasion, 1547, Hungary split between Ferdinand, Prince John Sigismund (Transylvania), and the Turks.

House of Hapsburg

Albert V, of Austria, Hapsburg, crowned king of Hungary, Jan. 1438; Roman emperor, Mar. 1438, as Albert II; died 1439.

Frederick III, cousin, 1440-93, fought Turks.

Maximilian I, son, 1493-1519, assumed title of Holy Roman Emperor (German), 1493.

Charles V, grandson, 1519-56. King of Spain with mother co-regent, crowned Roman emperor at Aix, 1520. Confronted Luther at Worms; attempted church reform and religious conciliation; abdicated 1556.

Ferdinand I, king of Bohemia, 1526; of Hungary, 1527; disputed. German king, 1531. Crowned Roman emperor on abdication of brother Charles V, 1556.

Maximilian II, son, 1564-76.

Rudolph II, son, 1576-1612.

Matthias, brother, 1612-19, king of Bohemia and Hungary.

Ferdinand II, of Styria, king of Bohemia, 1617; of Hungary, 1618; Roman emperor, 1619. Bohemian Protestants deposed him, elected Frederick V of Palatine, starting Thirty Years War.

Ferdinand III, son, king of Hungary, 1625, Bohemia, 1627; Roman emperor, 1637. Peace of Westphalia, 1648, ended war.

Leopold I, son, 1658-1705.

Joseph I, son, 1705-11.

Charles VI, brother, 1711-40.

Maria Theresa, daughter, 1740-80, archduchess of Austria, queen of Hungary and Bohemia; ousted pretender, Charles VII, crowned 1742; in 1745 obtained election of her husband Francis I as Roman emperor and co-regent (d. 1765). Fought Seven Years' War with Frederick II of Prussia. Mother of Marie Antoinette.

Joseph II, son, 1765-90, Roman emperor, reformer; powers restricted by Empress Maria Theresa until her death, 1780. First partition of Poland.

Leopold II, brother, 1790-92.

Francis II, son, 1792-1835. Fought Napoleon. Proclaimed first hereditary emperor of Austria, 1804. Forced to abdicate as Roman, 1806; last use of title.

Ferdinand I, son, 1835-48, abdicated during revolution.

Austro-Hungarian Monarchy

Francis Joseph I, nephew, 1848-1916, emperor of Austria, king of Hungary. Dual monarchy of Austria-Hungary formed, 1867. After assassination of heir, Archduke Francis Ferdinand, June 28, 1914, Austrian diplomacy precipitated World War I.

Charles I, grand-nephew, 1916-18, last emperor of Austria and king of Hungary. Abdicated Nov. 11-13, 1918, died 1922.

Rulers of Prussia

Nucleus of Prussia was the Mark of Brandenburg. First margrave Albert the Bear (Albrecht), 1134-70. First Hohenzollern margrave was Frederick, burgrave of Nuremberg, 1417-40.

Frederick William, 1640-88, the Great Elector. Frederick III, son, 1688-1713, crowned King Frederick of Prussia, 1701.

Frederick William I, 1713-40.

Frederick II (the Great), son, 1740-86, annexed Silesia, part of Austria.

Frederick William II, nephew, 1786-97.

Frederick William III, son, 1797-1840, Napoleonic wars.

Frederick William IV, son, 1840-61. Uprising of 1848 and first parliament and constitution.

Second and Third Reich

William I, 1861-88, brother. Annexation of Schleswig and Hanover; Franco-Prussian war, 1870-71; proclamation of German Reich, Jan. 18, 1871, at Versailles; William, German emperor (Deutscher Kaiser); Bismarck, chancellor.

Frederick III, son, 1888.

William II, son, 1888-1918, led Germany in World War I; abdicated as German emperor and king of Prussia, Nov. 9, 1918. Died in exile in Netherlands, June 4, 1941. Minor rulers of Bavaria, Saxony, Wurttemberg also abdicated.

Germany proclaimed republic at Weimar, July 1, 1919. Presidents included Frederick Ebert, 1919-25; Paul von Hindenburg-Beneckendorff, 1925, reelected 1932, died Aug. 2, 1934. Adolf Hitler, chancellor, chosen successor as Leader-Chancellor (Führer-Reichskanzler) of Third Reich. Annexed Austria, Mar. 1938. Precipitated World War II, 1939-45. Suicide Apr. 30, 1945.

Germany After 1945

Following World War II, Germany was split between democratic West and Soviet-dominated East. West German chancellors: Konrad Adenauer, 1949-63; Ludwig Erhard, 1963-66; Kurt Georg Kiesinger, 1966-69; Willy Brandt, 1969-74; Helmut Schmidt, 1974-82; Helmut Kohl, 1982-90. East German Communist party leaders: Walter Ulbricht, 1946-71; Erich Honecker, 1971-89; Egon Krenz, 1989-90.

Germany reunited Oct. 3, 1990. Post-reunification chancellors: Helmut Kohl, 1990-98; Gerhard Schröder, 1998-2005; Angela Merkel, 2005- .

Rulers of Poland

House of Piasts

Mieszko I, 963-92; Poland Christianized 966. Expansion under 3 Boleslavs: Boleslav I, 992-1025, son, crowned king 1024; Boleslav II, 1058-79, great-grandson, exiled after killing bishop Stanislav, who became chief patron saint of Poland; Boleslav III, 1106-38, nephew, divided Poland among 4 sons, eldest suzerain.

Feudal division, 1138-1306. Founding in Prussia of military order Teutonic Knights, 1226. Invasion by Tartars/Mongols, 1226.

Vladislav I, 1306-33, reunited most Polish territories, crowned king 1320. Casimir III (the Great), 1333-70, son, developed economy, cultural life, foreign policy.

House of Anjou

Louis I, 1370-82, nephew, was also Louis I of Hungary. Jadwiga, 1384-99, daughter, married Jagiello, grand duke of Lithuania, 1386.

House of Jagiellonians

Vladislav II, 1386-1434; Christianized Lithuania, founded personal union between Poland and Lithuania. Defeated Teutonic Knights at Grunwald, 1410.

Vladislav III, 1434-44, son, simultaneously king of Hungary. Fought Turks; killed 1444 in Battle of Varna.

Casimir IV, 1446-92, brother, competed with Hapsburgs, put son Vladislav on throne of Bohemia, later also of Hungary (Ulaszlo II).

Sigismund I, 1506-48, son, patronized science and arts; his and son's reign "Golden Age."

Sigismund II, 1548-72, son, established 1569 real union of Poland and Lithuania (lasted until 1795).

Elective Kings

Polish nobles in 1572 proclaimed Poland a republic headed by king to be elected by whole nobility.

Stephen Batory, 1576-86, duke of Transylvania, married Ann, sister of Sigismund II August. Fought Russians.

Sigismund III Vasa, 1587-1632, nephew of Sigismund II. 1592-98 also king of Sweden. Generals fought Russians, Turks.

Vladislav II Vasa, 1632-48, son. Fought Russians.

John II Casimir Vasa, 1648-68 (abdicated), brother. Fought Cossacks, Swedish (the "Deluge"), Russians, Turks, Tatars.

John III Sobieski, 1674-96. Won Vienna from besieging Turks, 1683.

Stanislav II, 1764-95, last king. Encouraged reforms; first modern constitution in Europe, 1791. Poland partitioned among Russia (1772), Prussia (1793), Austria (1795). Unsuccessful insurrection against foreign invasion, 1794, under Thaddeus Kosciusko, American-Polish general.

1795-1918: Poland Under Foreign Rule

Grand Duchy of Warsaw created by Napoleon I, Frederick August of Saxony grand duke, 1807-15.

Congress of Vienna proclaimed part of Poland kingdom in personal union with Russia, 1815.

Polish uprisings against Russia (1830, 1863) and Austria (1846, 1848) all repressed.

1918-39: Second Republic

Head of State Jozef Pilsudski, 1918-22. Presidents: Gabriel Narutowicz, 1922, assassinated; Stanislav Wojciechowski, 1922-26, abdicated after Pilsudski's coup d'état; Ignacy Moscicki, 1926-39, ruled (with Pilsudski until his death, 1935) as virtual dictator.

1939-45: Poland Under Foreign Occupation

Nazi and Soviet invasion, Sept. 1939. Polish government-in-exile first in France, then in England. Vladislav Raczkiewicz, president; Gen. Vladislav Sikorski, then Stanislav Mikolajczyk, prime ministers. Soviet-sponsored Polish Committee of National Liberation proclaimed at Lublin, July 1944, transformed into government Jan. 1, 1945.

Poland After 1945

Communist party ruled in Poland until Aug. 1989, when democratic Solidarity party, led by Lech Walesa, gained control of government. Walesa was elected president in 1990, but lost the office to former communist Aleksander Kwasniewski in 1995.

He was succeeded by Lech Kaczynski, 2005, who died in a plane crash (Apr. 2010). Bronislaw Komorowski was inaugurated Aug. 6, 2010, for a 5-year term. (Komorowski and Grzegorz Schetyna served as acting presidents, respectively, before Komorowski was inaugurated.) Donald Tusk was sworn in as prime minister in Nov. 2007, taking over from Jaroslaw Kaczynski, the then-president's identical twin.

Rulers of Denmark, Sweden, Norway

Denmark

Earliest rulers invaded Britain. King Canute, who ruled in London 1016-35, was most famous. The Valdemars furnished kings until the 15th century. In 1282 the Danes won the first national assembly, Danehof, from King Erik V.

Most redoubtable medieval character was Margaret, daughter of Valdemar IV, born 1353, married at 10 to King Haakon VI of Norway. In 1376 she had her first infant son, Olaf, made king of Denmark. After his death, 1387, she was regent of Denmark and Norway. In 1388, Sweden accepted her as sovereign. In 1389, she made her grand-nephew, Duke Erik of Pomerania, titular king of Denmark, Sweden, and Norway, with herself as regent. In 1397, she effected the Union of Kalmar of the three kingdoms and had Erik VII crowned. In 1439, the three kingdoms deposed him and elected, 1440, Christopher of Bavaria king (Christopher III). On his death, 1448, the union broke up.

Succeeding rulers were unable to enforce their claims as rulers of Sweden until 1520, when Christian II conquered Sweden. He was thrown out 1522, and in 1523, Gustavus Vasa united Sweden. Denmark continued to dominate Norway until the Napoleonic wars, when Frederick VI, 1808-39, joined the Napoleonic cause after Britain destroyed the Danish fleet, 1807. In 1814, he was forced to cede Norway to Sweden and Helgoland to Britain, receiving Lauenburg. Successors Christian VIII, 1839; Frederick VII, 1848; Christian IX, 1863; Frederick VIII, 1906; Christian X, 1912; Frederick IX, 1947; Margrethe II, 1972.

Sweden

Early kings ruled at Uppsala, but did not dominate the country. Sverker, c. 1130-c. 1156, united the Swedes and Goths. In 1435 Sweden obtained the Riksdag, or parliament. After the Union of Kalmar, 1397, the Danes either ruled or harried the country until Christian II of Denmark conquered it anew, 1520. This led to a rising under Gustavus Vasa, who ruled Sweden 1523-60, and established an independent kingdom. Charles IX, 1599-1611, crowned 1604, conquered Moscow. Gustavus II Adolphus, 1611-32, was called the

Lion of the North. Later rulers: Christina, 1632; Charles X Gustavus, 1654; Charles XI, 1660; Charles XII (invader of Russia and Poland, defeated at Poltava, June 28, 1709), 1697; Ulrika Eleanora, sister, elected queen, 1718; Frederick I (of Hesse), her husband, 1720; Adolphus Frederick, 1751; Gustavus III, 1771; Gustavus IV Adolphus, 1792; Charles XIII, 1809. (Union with Norway began 1814.) Charles XIV John, 1818 (he was Jean Bernadotte, Napoleon's Prince of Pontecorvo, elected 1810 to succeed Charles XIII). Charles XIV John founded the present dynasty, the House of Bernadotte: Oscar I, 1844; Charles XV, 1859; Oscar II, 1872; Gustavus V, 1907; Gustav VI Adolf, 1950; Carl XVI Gustaf, 1973.

Norway

Overcoming many rivals, Harald Haarfager, 872-930, conquered Norway, Orkneys, and Shetlands. Olaf I, great-grandson, 995-1000, brought Christianity into Norway, Ice-land, and Greenland. In 1035 Magnus the Good also became king of Denmark. Haakon V, 1299-1319, had married his daughter to Erik of Sweden. Their son, Magnus, became ruler of Norway and Sweden at 6. His son, Haakon VI, married Margaret of Denmark; their son Olaf IV became king of Norway and Denmark, followed by Margaret's regency and the Union of Kalmar, 1397.

In 1450, Norway became subservient to Denmark. Christian IV, 1588-1648, founded Christiania, now Oslo. After Napoleonic wars, when Denmark ceded Norway to Sweden, a strong nationalist movement forced recognition of Norway as an independent kingdom united with Sweden under the Swedish kings, 1814-1905. In 1905, the union was dissolved, and Prince Charles of Denmark became Haakon VII. He died Sept. 21, 1957; succeeded by son, Olav V. Olav V died Jan. 17, 1991; succeeded by son, Harald V.

Rulers of the Netherlands and Belgium

The Netherlands (Holland)

William Frederick, Prince of Orange, led a revolt against French rule, 1813; crowned king, 1815. Belgium seceded Oct. 4, 1830, after a revolt. The secession was ratified by the two kingdoms by treaty, Apr. 19, 1839.

Succession: William II, son, 1840; William III, son, 1849; Wilhelmina, daughter of William III and his 2nd wife, Princess Emma of Waldeck, 1890; Wilhelmina abdicated, Sept. 4, 1948, in favor of daughter, Juliana. Juliana abdicated, Apr. 30, 1980, in favor of daughter, Beatrix.

Belgium

A national congress elected Prince Leopold of Saxe-Coburg as king; he took the throne July 21, 1831, as Leopold I.

Succession: Leopold II, son, 1865; Albert I, nephew, 1909; Leopold III, son, 1934; Prince Charles, regent 1944; Leopold returned 1950, yielded powers to son Baudouin, prince royal, Aug. 6, 1950, abdicated July 16, 1951. Baudouin I took throne July 17, 1951, died July 31, 1993; succeeded by brother, Albert II.

Rulers of Modern Italy

After the fall of Napoleon in 1814, the Congress of Vienna, 1815, restored Italy as a political patchwork, comprising the Kingdom of Naples and Sicily, the Papal States, and smaller units. Piedmont and Genoa were awarded to Sardinia, ruled by King Victor Emmanuel I of Savoy.

United Italy emerged under the leadership of Camillo, Count di Cavour (1810-61), Sardinian prime minister. Agitation was led by Giuseppe Mazzini (1805-72) and Giuseppe Garibaldi (1807-82), soldier; Victor Emmanuel I abdicated 1821. After a brief regency for a brother, Charles Albert was king, 1831-49; abdicated upon defeat by the Austrians at Novara. Succeeded by Victor Emmanuel II, 1849-61.

In 1859 France forced Austria to cede Lombardy to Sardinia, which gave rights to Savoy and Nice to France. In 1860, Garibaldi led 1,000 volunteers in a campaign, took Sicily and expelled the king of Naples. In 1860 the House of Savoy annexed Tuscany, Parma, Modena, Romagna, the Two Sicyls, the Marches, and Umbria. Victor Emmanuel assumed the title of king of Italy at Turin Mar. 17, 1861.

In 1866, Victor Emmanuel allied with Prussia in the Austro-Prussian War, and with Prussia's victory, received Venetia. On Sept. 20, 1870, his troops under Gen. Raffaele Cadorna entered Rome and took over the Papal States, ending the temporal power of the Roman Catholic Church.

Succession: Umberto I, 1878, assassinated 1900; Victor Emmanuel III, 1900, abdicated 1946, died 1947; Humbert II, 1946, ruled a month. In 1921 Benito Mussolini (1883-1945) formed the Fascist party; he became prime minister Oct. 31, 1922. He entered World War II as an ally of Hitler. He was deposed July 25, 1943.

At a plebiscite June 2, 1946, Italy voted for a republic; Premier Alcide de Gasperi became chief of state June 13, 1946. On June 28, 1946, the Constituent Assembly elected Enrico de Nicola, Liberal, provisional president. Successive presidents: Luigi Einaudi, elected May 11, 1948; Giovanni Gronchi, Apr. 29, 1955; Antonio Segni, May 6, 1962; Giuseppe Saragat, Dec. 28, 1964; Giovanni Leone, Dec. 29, 1971; Alessandro Pertini, July 9, 1978; Francesco Cossiga, July 3, 1985; Oscar Luigi Scalfaro, May 28, 1992; Carlo Azeglio Ciampi, May 18, 1999; Giorgio Napolitano, May 15, 2006.

Rulers of Spain

From 8th to 11th centuries, Spain was dominated by the Moors (Arabs and Berbers). The Christian reconquest established small kingdoms (Asturias, Aragon, Castile, Catalonia, Leon, Navarre, and Valencia). In 1474, Isabella, b. 1451, became Queen of Castile and Leon. Her husband, Ferdinand, b. 1452, inherited Aragon, 1479, with Catalonia, Valencia, and the Balearic Islands, became Ferdinand V of Castile. By Isabella's request Pope Sixtus IV established the Inquisition, 1478. Last Moorish kingdom, Granada, fell 1492. Columbus opened New World of colonies, 1492. Isabella died 1504, succeeded by her daughter, Juana (the Mad), but Ferdinand ruled until his death in 1516.

Charles I, b. 1500, son of Juana, grandson of Ferdinand and Isabella, and of Maximilian I of Hapsburg, succeeded later as Holy Roman Emperor, Charles V, 1520; abdicated 1556. Philip II, son, 1556-98, inherited only Spanish throne; conquered Portugal, fought Turks, sent Armada against England. Married to Mary I of England, 1554-58. Succession: Philip III, 1598-1621; Philip IV, 1621-65; Charles II, 1665-1700, left Spain to Philip of Anjou, grandson of Louis XIV, who as Philip V, 1700-46, founded Bourbon dynasty; Ferdinand VI, 1746-59; Charles III, 1759-88; Charles IV, 1788-1808, abdicated.

Napoleon now dominated politics and made his brother Joseph king of Spain, 1808, but the Spanish ousted him in 1813. Ferdinand VII, 1808, 1814-33, lost American colonies (except Cuba, Puerto Rico); succeeded by daughter Isabella II, aged 3, with wife Maria Christina of Naples regent until 1843. Isabella deposed by revolution, 1868. Elected king by the Cortes (parliament), Amadeo of Savoy, 1870, abdicated 1873. First republic, 1873-74. Alfonso XII, son of Isabella, 1875-85. His posthumous son was Alfonso XIII, with his mother, Queen Maria Christina, regent. Spanish-American War, 1898, Spain lost Cuba, gave up Puerto Rico, Philippines, Sulu Isls., Marianas. Alfonso took throne, 1902, aged 16; married British Princess Victoria Eugenia of Battenberg, 1906. Dictatorship of Primo de Rivera, 1923-30, precipitated revolution of 1931. Alfonso agreed to leave without formal abdication. Monarchy abolished; the second republic established, with socialist backing. Niceto Alcala Zamora was president until 1936, when Manuel Azaña was chosen.

In July 1936, the army in Morocco revolted against the government and Gen. Francisco Franco led the troops into Spain. The revolution succeeded by Feb. 1939, when Azaña resigned. Franco became chief of state, with provisions that if he was incapacitated, the Regency Council by two-thirds vote could propose a king to the Cortes, which needed to have a two-thirds majority to elect him.

Alfonso XIII died in Rome, 1941, aged 54. His property and citizenship had been restored.

A law restoring the monarchy was approved in a 1947 referendum. Prince Juan Carlos, b. 1938, grandson of Alfonso XIII, was designated by Franco and the Cortes in 1969 as future king and chief of state. Franco died in office, Nov. 20, 1975; Juan Carlos I proclaimed king, Nov. 22.

Rulers of Russia; Leaders of the USSR and Russian Federation

First ruler to consolidate Slavic tribes was Rurik, leader of the Russians who established himself at Novgorod, 862 CE. He and his immediate successors had Scandinavian affiliations. They moved to Kiev after 972 and ruled as dukes of Kiev. In 988, Vladimir was converted and adopted the Byzantine Greek Orthodox service, later modified by Slav influences. Important as organizer and lawgiver was Yaroslav, 1019-54, whose daughters married kings of Norway, Hungary, and France. His grandson, Vladimir II (Monomakh), 1113-25, was progenitor of several rulers, but in 1169, Andrew Bogolubski overthrew Kiev and began the line known as grand dukes of Vladimir.

Of the grand dukes of Vladimir, Alexander Nevsky, 1246-63, had a son, Daniel, first to be called duke of Muscovy (Moscow), who ruled 1263-1303. His successors became grand dukes of Muscovy. After Dmitri III Donskoi defeated the Tatars in 1380, they also became grand dukes of all Russia. Tatar independence and considerable territorial expansion were achieved under Ivan III, 1462-1505.

Tsars of Muscovy: Ivan III was referred to in church ritual as tsar. He married Sofia, niece of the last Byzantine emperor. His successor, Basil III, died in 1533 when Basil's son Ivan was only 3. He became Ivan IV (the Terrible), crowned 1547 as Tsar of all the Russias, ruled until 1584. Under the weak rule of his son, Feodor I, 1584-98, Boris Godunov had control. The dynasty died, and after years of tribal strife and intervention by Polish and Swedish armies, the Russians united under 17-year-old Michael Romanov, distantly related to Ivan IV's first wife. He ruled 1613-45, established the Romanov line. Fourth ruler after Michael was Peter I.

Tsars, or Emperors, of Russia (Romanovs): Peter I (the Great), 1682-1725, took title of emperor in 1721. His successors and dates of accession were Catherine, his widow, 1725; Peter II, his grandson, 1727; Anne, Duchess of Courland, 1730, daughter of Peter the Great's brother, Tsar Ivan V; Ivan VI, 1740, great-grandson of Ivan V, while still a child, kept in prison and murdered, 1764; Elizabeth, daughter of Peter I, 1741; Peter III, grandson of Peter I, 1761, deposed 1762 for his consort, Catherine II (the Great), former princess of Anhalt Zerbst (Germany); Paul I, her son, 1796, killed 1801; Alexander I, son of Paul, 1801, defeated Napoleon; Nicholas I, his brother, 1825; Alexander II, son of Nicholas, 1855, assassinated 1881 by terrorists; Alexander III, son, 1881. Nicholas II, son, 1894-1917, last tsar of Russia, was forced to abdicate by the March 1917 Revolution that followed losses to Germany in WWI. The tsar, empress, tsarevich (crown prince), and tsar's 4 daugh-

ters were murdered by the Bolsheviks in Yekaterinburg, July 16, 1918.

Provisional Government: premiers, Prince Georgi Lvov, followed by Alexander Kerensky, 1917.

Union of Soviet Socialist Republics

Bolshevik Revolution, Nov. 7, 1917, removed Kerensky from power; council of People's Commissars formed; Lenin (Vladimir Ilyich Ulyanov) became premier. Lenin died Jan. 21, 1924. Aleksei Rykov (executed 1938) and V. M. Molotov held the office, but actual ruler was Joseph Stalin (Joseph Vissarionovich Dzhugashvili), general secretary of the Central Committee of the Communist Party. Stalin became president of the Council of Ministers (premier) May 7, 1941; died Mar. 5, 1953. Succeeded by Georgi M. Malenkov as head of the Council and premier. Malenkov also briefly served as first secretary of Central Committee before giving up position to Nikita S. Khrushchev. Malenkov resigned Feb. 8, 1955, became deputy premier, was dropped July 3, 1957. Marshal Nikolai A. Bulganin became premier Feb. 8, 1955, was demoted, and Khrushchev became premier Mar. 27, 1958.

Khrushchev was ousted Oct. 14-15, 1964, replaced by Leonid I. Brezhnev as first secretary of the party and by Aleksei N. Kosygin as premier. On June 16, 1977, Brezhnev also took office as president. He died Nov. 10, 1982; 2 days later the Central Committee elected former KGB head Yuri V. Andropov president. Andropov died Feb. 9, 1984; on Feb. 13, Konstantin U. Chernenko chosen by Central Committee as its general secretary. Chernenko died Mar. 10, 1985; Mar. 11, he was succeeded as general secretary by Mikhail Gorbachev, who replaced Andrei Gromyko as president on Oct. 1, 1988. Gorbachev resigned Dec. 25, 1991, and the Soviet Union officially disbanded the next day. Each of the 15 former Soviet constituent republics became independent.

Post-Soviet Russia

Boris Yeltsin was sworn in July 10, 1991, as Russia's first elected president. With the Dec. 1991 dissolution of the Soviet Union, Russia (officially Russian Federation) became a founding member of the Commonwealth of Independent States. On Dec. 31, 1999, Yeltsin stepped down as president; he named Vladimir Putin his interim successor. Putin won a presidential election Mar. 26, 2000, and was reelected Mar. 14, 2004. Because Russia's constitution limits presidents to two terms of rule, Putin had to relinquish his office in 2008. His successor, Dmitry Medvedev, was sworn in May 7, 2008. A day later, Medvedev's nomination of Putin as prime minister was confirmed.

Leaders in the South American Wars of Liberation

Francisco Antonio Gabriel Miranda (1750-1816), Jose Francisco de San Martin (1778-1850), and Simon Bolivar (1783-1830) led early 19th-century struggles of South American nations to free themselves from Spain. All three, and their contemporaries, operated in periods of factional strife.

Miranda, a Venezuelan who had served with the French in the American Revolution and commanded parts of the French Revolutionary armies in the Netherlands, attempted to start a revolt in Venezuela in 1806 but failed. In 1810, with British and American backing, he returned and was briefly dictator, until the British withdrew their support. In 1812 he was overcome by royalists in Venezuela and taken prisoner, dying in a Spanish prison in 1816.

San Martin was born in Argentina and during 1789-1811, served in campaigns of the Spanish armies in Europe and Africa. He first joined the independence movement in Argentina in 1812 and in 1817 invaded Chile with 4,000 men over the mountain passes. Here he and Gen. Bernardo O'Higgins (1778-1842) defeated the Spaniards at Chacabuco, 1817; O'Higgins was named Liberator and became first director of Chile, 1817-23. In 1821 San Martin occupied Lima and Callao, Peru, and became protector of Peru.

Bolivar was born in Venezuela, the son of an aristocratic family. He first served under Miranda in 1812. In 1813, he

captured Caracas, where he was named Liberator. Forced out the following year by civil strife, he led a campaign that captured Bogota in 1814. In 1817 he was again in control of Venezuela and was named dictator. He organized Nueva Granada with the help of Gen. Francisco de Paula Santander (1792-1840). By joining Nueva Granada, Venezuela, and the area that is now Panama and Ecuador, the republic of Colombia was formed, with Bolivar as president. After numerous setbacks, he decisively defeated the Spaniards in the Second Battle of Carabobo, Venezuela, June 24, 1821.

In May 1822, Gen. Antonio Jose de Sucre, Bolivar's lieutenant, took Quito. Bolivar went to Guayaquil to confer with San Martin, who resigned as protector of Peru. With a new army of Colombians and Peruvians, Bolivar defeated the Spaniards in a battle at Junin in 1824 and cleared Peru.

De Sucre organized Charcas (Upper Peru) as Republica Bolivar (now Bolivia) and acted as president in place of Bolivar, who wrote its constitution. De Sucre defeated the Spanish faction of Peru at Ayacucho, Dec. 19, 1824.

Continued civil strife finally caused the Colombian federation to break apart. Santander turned against Bolivar, but the latter defeated him and banished him. In 1828, Bolivar gave up the presidency he had held precariously for 14 years. He became ill from tuberculosis and died Dec. 17, 1830. He is buried in the national pantheon in Caracas.

Governments of China

Where dynastic dates overlap, the rulers or events referred to appeared in different areas of China.

Years in power	Government
c. 1994–c. 1766 BCE	Hsia dynasty, first hereditary Chinese dynasty
c. 1766–c. 1027 BCE	Shang dynasty
c. 1027–770 BCE	Western Chou dynasty, capital near site of present-day Xi'an
770–256 BCE	Eastern Chou dynasty, new capital established at Luoyang
403–221 BCE	Period of the Warring States
221–206 BCE	Ch'in dynasty, quasi-feudal states unified for first time; name of China derived from this dynasty
206 BCE–9 CE	Earlier, or Western Han dynasty, founded by rebel leader Liu Pang, zenith of power under Emperor Wu Ti, 140-87 BCE, Chinese state expanded
9–23	Hsin dynasty, established by courtier Wang Mang, who deposed infant emperor for whom he had been acting as regent
25–220	Later, or Eastern Han dynasty
220–265[1]	Wei dynasty, established by son of Han general Ts'ao Ts'ao
221–263[1]	Shu Han dynasty in southwest China
222–280[1]	Wu dynasty in southeast China
265–317	Western Chin dynasty, established by Ssu-ma Yen, Wei dynasty general
317–420	Eastern Chin dynasty, established by prince of Ssu-ma family
420–589	Southern dynasties, four short-lived dynasties with capital at Chien-k'ang (present-day Nanjing)
589–618	Sui dynasty, reunified China; first emperor was Yang Chien, military servant who usurped throne of non-Chinese Northern Chou, 581
618–906	T'ang dynasty, founded by Li Yuan, who led rebellion against the Sui. Early rulers included former imperial concubine Empress Wu, 683-705; Hsuan Tsung, 712-56
907–960	Five Dynasties, period of disunion with short-lived dynasties in North China, 10 independent states mostly in South China
907–1125	Liao dynasty, of Khitan Mongols, capital at Yen-ching (present-day Beijing)
960–1126	Northern Sung dynasty, established by military leader Chao K'uang-yin, capital at Kaifeng
1122–1234	Chin dynasty, of Juchen people of Manchuria; drove Sung out of northern China
1127–1279	Southern Sung dynasty, capital at Lin-an (present-day Hangzhou)
1279–1368	Yuan dynasty, of Mongols; Kublai Khan, grandson of Genghis Khan, high point of Mongol power
1368–1644	Ming dynasty, founded by rebel leader Chu Yuan-chang, former Buddhist monk. Country again under Chinese rule, capital in present-day Nanjing, then Beijing after defeat of Mongolian tribes
1644–1912	Manchu, or Ch'ing dynasty, under Manchu rule with capital at Chiang-ning (present-day Nanjing). Power of Chinese empire reached highest point in its 2,000-year history. Last imperial dynasty; Hsuan T'ung, or Pu Yi, last emperor. Sun Yat-sen led revolution, 1911. Republic of China formed, 1912
1912–1949	Rep. of China, Gen. Yüan Shih-k'ai elected first president. Power passed to provincial warlords with Yüan's death, 1916. Gen. Chiang Kai-shek sought to reunify China under Kuomintang (Nationalist party) rule, 1926; Kuomintang established new national government at Nanjing, 1928. War with Japan, then civil war, led to Nationalist authority collapse, Communist declaration of People's Rep. of China, 1949

(1) Also known as the period of the Three Kingdoms because of warfare between the Wei, Shu Han, and Wu dynasties.

Leaders of People's Republic of China Since 1949

Name	Title/position, years in power
Mao Zedong	Chairman, 1949-59; Chinese Communist Party (CPC) Chairman, 1949-76
Zhou Enlai	Premier, 1949-76; foreign minister, 1949-76
Deng Xiaoping	Deputy Premier, 1952-66, 1973-76; "paramount leader," 1977-97
Liu Shaoqi	Chairman, 1959-68
Hua Guofeng	Premier, 1976-80; CPC Chairman, 1976-81
Hu Yaobang	CPC General Secretary, 1980-87; CPC Chairman 1981-82
Zhao Ziyang	Premier, 1980-87; CPC General Secretary, 1987-89
Li Xiannian	President, 1983-88
Yang Shangkun	President, 1988-93
Li Peng	Premier, 1988-98
Jiang Zemin	CPC General Secretary, 1989-2002; President, 1993-2003
Zhu Rongji	Premier, 1998-2003
Hu Jintao	CPC General Secretary, 2002- ; President, 2003-
Wen Jiabao	Premier, 2003-

Historical Periods of Japan

Years in power	Period	Founding event
c. 300–592	Yamato	Conquest of Yamato plain, c. 300 CE
592–710	Asuka	Accession of Empress Suiko, 592
710–794	Nara	Heijo (Nara) completed, 710; capital moved to Nagaoka, 784
794–1185	Heian	Heian (Kyoto) completed, 794
858–1160	Fujiwara	Fujiwara-no-Yoshifusa became regent, 858
1160–1185	Taira	Taira-no-Kiyomoro assumed control, 1160; Minamoto-no-Yoritomo victor over Taira, 1185
1192–1333	Kamakura	Yoritomo became shogun, 1192
1334–1392	Namboku	Emperor Godaigo restored, 1334; Godaigo established Southern Court at Yoshino, 1336
1392–1573	Muromachi	Unification of Southern and Northern Courts, 1392
1467–1600	Sengoku	Onin war began, 1467
1573–1603	Momoyama	Oda Nobunaga entered Kyoto, 1568, deposed last Ashikaga shogun, 1573. Tokugawa Ieyasu victor at Sekigahara, 1600
1603–1867	Edo	Ieyasu became shogun, 1603
1868–1912	Meiji	Emperor Mutsuhito (Meiji) ascended throne, 1867; Meiji Restoration and Charter Oath, 1868
1912–1926	Taisho	Accession of Emperor Yoshihito, 1912
1926–1989	Showa	Accession of Emperor Hirohito, 1926
1989–	Heisei	Accession of Emperor Akihito, 1989

WORLD EXPLORATION AND GEOGRAPHY

Early Explorers of the Western Hemisphere

Reviewed by G. A. Clark, Ph.D., Aug. 2008

In light of recent discoveries, theories about how and when the first people arrived in the Western Hemisphere are being reconsidered. Genetic evidence suggests that beginning around 14,000 years before the present (BP), the earliest immigrants crossed a 1,000-km wide "land bridge" between Siberia and Alaska in small groups and spread rapidly south through the Americas, arriving at S America's southern tip by c. 10,700 BP. Kennewick Man, found in 1996 in Washington's Columbia River Gorge, dates to 9,600-9,200 BP, and Luzia, dating to 11,500 BP from Brazil, are examples of these early arrivals. Modern Native Americans appear to be descended from peoples indigenous to N and central Asia who arrived in subsequent waves of migration. A growing body of genetic, skeletal, and linguistic evidence documents their migration throughout the Americas.

Archaeologists have confirmed evidence of habitation by 12,900 BP at sites located on the shores of ancient lakes at an elevation of 17,400 feet in Chile's Atacama Desert. There is also growing support for the settlement of Chile's Monte Verde site, dated to c. 12,500 BP, and eight other 13th-millennium sites in Brazil, Chile, and Argentina. One theory on their migration holds that a glacier covered much of N America from c. 20,000 to 13,000 BP, so those who settled in S America might have traveled there in small boats skirting the pack ice along the west coast, or spread from N to S America through a controversial 'ice-free corridor' in what today is western Canada. Other theories hold that they arrived before continental glaciation blocked migration from the north, or migrated from Iberia in skin boats. Controversial skeletal evidence from a burial at Santana do Riacho in Brazil (9,460 BP) suggests that some of the early immigrants who came via the land bridge from Siberia may have originated in Africa.

Long before Europeans arrived, the Americas were—for the most part—populated by hunter-gatherers and small-scale horticulturalists. In a few areas (SE U.S., Mesoamerica, coastal Peru and Chile), complex chiefdoms and state-level societies had appeared. Irrigation canals dating to 4,700 provide evidence for the origins of large-scale agriculture along the western slopes of Peru's Andes Mountains. The earliest known state in the Americas occupied a 700-sq mi area spanning four river valleys in coastal Peru between 3,500 and 500 BP.

Norsemen (Vikings sailing out of Iceland and Greenland), led by Leif Ericson, are usually credited with having been the first Europeans to reach America, with at least five voyages occurring about 1000 CE to areas they called Helluland, Markland, and Vinland—possibly what are known today as Baffin Island, Labrador, and either Newfoundland or somewhere farther south in New England. L'Anse aux Meadows, on the northern tip of Newfoundland, is the only documented settlement, with evidence of a small village with a church dating to c. 1000 CE. The Norsemen tried to import farming and herding economies, but these efforts failed after a few centuries, and Greenland and Newfoundland were abandoned by Europeans.

Sustained contact between the hemispheres began with the first voyage of Christopher Columbus (born Cristoforo Colombo, c. 1451, near Genoa, Italy). Columbus made four voyages to the New World while sailing for the Spanish monarchs Ferdinand II and Isabella. He left Palos, Spain, Aug. 3, 1492, with 88 men and landed at San Salvador (Watling Islands, Bahamas), Oct. 12, 1492. His fleet included three vessels, the Niña, Pinta, and Santa María. He also visited Cuba, Hispaniola, and many smaller Caribbean islands, then populated by the now-extinct Taino Indians. A second expedition left Cadíz, Spain, Sept. 25, 1493, with 17 ships and 1,400 men, reaching the island of Dominica, in the Lesser Antilles, on Nov. 3, 1493. His third voyage took him from Sanlucar, Spain (May 30, 1498, with six ships), to the island of Trinidad and to the adjacent coast of S America, where he made landfall at the mouth of the Orinoco River. A fourth voyage departed Cadíz on May 9, 1502, and reached the E coast of Mexico, Honduras, Panama, and what he christened Santiago (the present-day island of Jamaica). Columbus died in Valladolid, Spain, on May 20, 1506, still convinced he had reached Asia by sailing west.

In N America, John and Sebastian Cabot, Italian explorers sailing for the English crown, reached Newfoundland and possibly Nova Scotia in 1497. John's second voyage (1498), seeking the fabled Northwest Passage, a new trade route to Asia, resulted in the loss of his entire fleet. For most of the 16th century, exploration of the New World was dominated by the empires of Spain and Portugal.

In 1497 and 1499, Amerigo Vespucci (for whom the Americas are named), an Italian explorer sailing for Spain, passed along the N and E coasts of South America. He was the first to argue that these lands were previously unknown and not part of Asia.

Other early explorations are listed below.

Year	Explorer	Nationality (sponsor, if different)	Area reached or explored
1497-98	Vasco da Gama	Portuguese	Cape of Good Hope (Africa), India
1499	Alonso de Ojeda	Spanish	N South American coast, Venezuela
1500, Feb.	Vicente Yañez Pinzon	Spanish	S American coast, Amazon R.
1500, Apr.	Pedro Álvarez Cabral	Portuguese	Brazil
1501	Rodrigo de Bastidas	Spanish	Central America
1513	Vasco Núñez de Balboa	Spanish	Panama, Pacific Ocean
1513	Juan Ponce de León	Spanish	Florida, Yucatán Peninsula
1515	Juan de Solis	Spanish	Río de la Plata
1519	Alonso de Pineda	Spanish	Mouth of Mississippi R.
1519	Hernán Cortés	Spanish	Mexico
1519-20	Ferdinand Magellan	Portuguese (Spanish)	Straits of Magellan, Tierra del Fuego
1524	Giovanni da Verrazano	Italian (French)	Atlantic coast, incl. New York Harbor
1528	Álvar Núñez Cabeza de Vaca	Spanish	Texas coast and interior
1532	Francisco Pizarro	Spanish	Peru
1534	Jacques Cartier	French	Canada, Gulf of St. Lawrence
1536	Pedro de Mendoza	Spanish	Buenos Aires
1539	Francisco de Ulloa	Spanish	California coast
1539-41	Hernando de Soto	Spanish	Mississippi R., near Memphis, TN
1539	Marcos de Niza	Italian (Spanish)	SW United States
1540	Francisco de Coronado	Spanish	SW United States
1540	Hernando de Alarcón	Spanish	Colorado R.
1540	Garcia Lopez de Cárdenas	Spanish	Colorado, Grand Canyon
1541	Francisco de Orellana	Spanish	Amazon R.
1542	Juan Rodriguez Cabrillo	Portuguese (Spanish)	W Mexico, San Diego Harbor
1565	Pedro Menéndez de Avilés	Spanish	St. Augustine, FL
1576	Sir Martin Frobisher	English	Frobisher Bay, Canada
1577-80	Sir Francis Drake	English	California coast
1582	Antonio de Espejo	Spanish	Southwest U.S. (New Mexico)
1584	Philip Amadas & Arthur Barlowe (for Raleigh)	English	Virginia
1585-87	Sir Walter Raleigh's men	English	Roanoke Isl., NC
1595	Sir Walter Raleigh	English	Orinoco R.
1603-09	Samuel de Champlain	French	Canadian interior, Lake Champlain
1607	Capt. John Smith	English	Atlantic coast
1609-10	Henry Hudson	English (Dutch)	Hudson R., Hudson Bay
1634	Jean Nicolet	French	Lake Michigan, Wisconsin
1673	Jacques Marquette, Louis Jolliet	French	Mississippi R., S to Arkansas
1682	René-Robert Cavelier, sieur de La Salle	French	Mississippi R., S to Gulf of Mexico
1727-29	Vitus Bering	Danish (Russian)	Bering Strait, Alaska
1789	Sir Alexander Mackenzie	Canadian	NW Canada
1804-06	Meriwether Lewis and William Clark	American	Missouri R., Rocky Mts., Columbia R.

Arctic Exploration

Early Explorers

1587: John Davis (Eng.). Davis Strait to Sanderson's Hope, 72°12′N.

1596: Willem Barents and Jacob van Heemskerck (Holland). Discovered Bear Isl., touched NW tip of Spitsbergen, 79°49′N, rounded Novaya Zemlya, wintered at Ice Haven.

1607: Henry Hudson (Eng.). North along Greenland's E coast to Cape Hold-with-Hope, 73°30′, then N of Spitsbergen to 80°23′. Explored Hudson's Touches (Jan Mayen).

1616: William Baffin and Robert Bylot (Eng.). Baffin Bay to Smith Sound.

1728: Vitus Bering (Dan./Russ.). Sailed through strait (Bering) proving Asia and America are separate.

1733-40: Great Northern Expedition (Russ.). Surveyed Siberian Arctic coast.

1741: Vitus Bering (Dan./Russ.). Sighted Alaska, named Mount St. Elias. His lieutenant, Chirikof, explored coast.

1771: Samuel Hearne (Brit., Hudson's Bay Co.). Overland from Prince of Wales Fort (Churchill) on Hudson Bay to mouth of Coppermine R.

1778: James Cook (Brit.). Through Bering Strait to Icy Cape, AK, and North Cape, Siberia.

1789: Alexander Mackenzie (North West Co., Brit.). Montreal to mouth of Mackenzie River.

1806: William Scoresby (Brit.). N of Spitsbergen to 81°30′.

1820-23: Ferdinand von Wrangel (Russ.). Surveyed Siberian Arctic coast. His exploration joined James Cook's at North Cape, confirming separation of the continents.

1878-79: (Nils) Adolf Erik Nordenskjöld (Swed.). The 1st to navigate the Northeast Passage—an ocean route connecting Europe's North Sea, along the Arctic coast of Asia and through the Bering Sea, to the Pacific Ocean.

1881: The U.S. steamer *Jeannette*, led by Lt. Cmdr. George W. DeLong, was trapped in ice and crushed, June 1881. DeLong and 11 others died; 12 survived.

1888: Fridtjof Nansen (Nor.) crossed Greenland icecap.

1893-96: Nansen in *Fram* drifted from New Siberian Isls. to Spitsbergen; tried polar dash in 1895, reached Franz Josef Land, 86°14′N.

1897: Salomon A. Andrée (Swed.) and 2 others started in balloon from Spitsbergen, July 11, to drift across pole to U.S., and disappeared. Aug. 6, 1930, their bodies were found on White Isl., 82°57′N, 29°52′E.

1903-06: Roald Amundsen (Nor.) 1st to sail whole length of the Northwest Passage—an ocean route linking the Atlantic Ocean to the Pacific via Canada's marine waterways.

North Pole Exploration

Robert E. Peary explored Greenland's coast, 1891-92; tried for North Pole, 1893. In 1900 he reached northern limit of Greenland and 83°50′N; in 1902 he reached 84°17′N; in 1906 he went from Ellesmere Isl. to 87°06′N. He sailed in the *Roosevelt*, July 1908, to winter off Cape Sheridan, Grant Land. The dash for the North Pole began Mar. 1 from Cape Columbia, Ellesmere Isl. Peary reportedly reached the pole, 90°N, Apr. 6, 1909; however, later research suggests he may have fallen short of his goal by c. 30-60 mi. The first surface expedition independently

confirmed to have reached the N Pole was that of Ralph Plaisted in 1968 (see below).

Peary had several support groups carrying supplies until the last group turned back at 87°47′N. Peary, Matthew Henson, and 4 Eskimos proceeded with dog teams and sleds. They were said to have crossed the pole several times, then built an igloo there and remained 36 hours. Started south, Apr. 7 at 4 PM, for Cape Columbia.

1914: Donald MacMillan (U.S.). Northwest, 200 mi, from Axel Heiberg Isl. to seek Peary's Crocker Land.

1915-17: Vihjalmur Stefansson (Can.). Discovered Borden, Brock, Meighen, and Lougheed Isls.

1918-20: Roald Amundsen (Nor.) sailed the Northeast Passage.

1925: Amundsen and Lincoln Ellsworth (U.S.) reached 87°44′N in attempt to fly to N Pole from Spitsbergen.

1926: Richard E. Byrd and Floyd Bennett (U.S.) reputedly flew over North Pole, May 9. (Claim to have reached the pole is in dispute, however.)

1926: Amundsen, Ellsworth, and Umberto Nobile (It.) flew from Spitsbergen over N Pole May 12, to Teller, AK, in dirigible *Norge*.

1928: Nobile crossed N Pole in airship, May 24; crashed, May 25. Amundsen died attempting a rescue.

North Pole Exploration Records

1958: On Aug. 3, submarine *Nautilus*, under Comdr. William R. Anderson, crossed the N Pole beneath the ice.

1960: In Aug., the nuclear-powered U.S. submarine *Seadragon* (Comdr. George P. Steele 2nd) made the 1st E-W underwater transit through the Northwest Passage. Traveling submerged for the most part, it took 6 days to make the 850-mi trek from Baffin Bay to the Beaufort Sea.

1968: On Apr. 19, Ralph Plaisted (U.S.) and 3 amateur explorers on snowmobiles became the 1st independently confirmed surface expedition to reach the N Pole.

1977: On Aug. 16, the Soviet nuclear icebreaker *Arktika* became the 1st surface ship to reach the N Pole.

1978: On Apr. 30, Naomi Uemura (Jpn.) became the 1st person to reach the N Pole alone, traveling by dog sled in a 54-day, 600-mi trek over the frozen Arctic.

1982: In Apr., Sir Ranulph Fiennes and Charles Burton, Brit. explorers, reached the N Pole and became the 1st to circle the Earth from pole to pole. They had reached the S Pole 16 months earlier. The 52,000-mi trek took 3 years, involved 23 people, and cost an estimated $18 mil.

1986: On May 2, 6 explorers reached the N Pole assisted only by dogs. They became the 1st to reach the pole without aerial logistics support since at least 1909. The explorers, Amer. Will Steger, Paul Schurke, Ann Bancroft, and Geoff Carroll, and Can. Brent Boddy and Richard Weber, completed the 500-mi journey in 56 days.

1995: On June 15, Weber and Russ. Mikhail Malakhov became the 1st pair to make it to the N Pole and back without any mechanical assistance. The 940-mi trip, made entirely on skis, took 121 days.

2003: On May 20, Pen Hadow (Brit.) became the 1st to reach the N Pole from Canada, solo and without resupply. The 377-mi journey across the ice took 64 days.

2006: On April 16, Prince Albert II of Monaco became the 1st royal to reach the N Pole.

Antarctic Exploration

Antarctica has been approached since 1773-75, when Capt. James Cook (Brit.) reached 71°10′S. Many sea and landmarks bear names of early explorers. Fabian von Bellingshausen (Russ.) discovered Peter I and Alexander I Isls., 1819-21. Nathaniel Palmer (U.S.) traveled throughout Palmer Peninsula, 60°W, 1820, without realizing that this was a continent. Capt. John Davis (U.S.) made the 1st known landing on the continent on Feb. 7, 1821. Later, in 1823, James Weddell (Brit.) found Weddell Sea, 74°15′S, the southernmost point that had been reached.

First to announce existence of the continent of Antarctica was Charles Wilkes (U.S.), who followed the coast for 1,500 mi, 1840. Adelie Coast, 140°E, was found by Dumont d'Urville (Fr.), 1840. Ross Ice Shelf was found by James Clark Ross (Brit.), 1841-42.

1895: Leonard Kristensen (Nor.) landed a party on the coast of Victoria Land. They were the 1st ashore on the main continental mass. C. E. Borchgrevink, a member of that party, returned in 1899 with a Brit. expedition, 1st to winter on Antarctica.

1902-04: Robert Falcon Scott (Brit.) explored Edward VII Peninsula to 82°17′S, 146°33′E from McMurdo Sound.

1908-09: Ernest Shackleton (Brit.) 1st to use Manchurian ponies in Antarctic sledging. He reached 88°23′S, discovering a route onto the plateau by way of the Beardmore Glacier and pioneering the way to the pole.

1911: Roald Amundsen (Nor.) with 4 men and dog teams reached the S Pole, Dec. 14.

1912: Scott reached the pole from Ross Isl., Jan. 18, with 4 companions. None of Scott's party survived. Their bodies and expedition notes were found, Nov. 12.

1928: 1st person to use an airplane over Antarctica was Sir George Hubert Wilkins (Austral.).

1929: Richard E. Byrd (U.S.) established Little America on Bay of Whales. On 1,600-mi airplane flight begun Nov. 28, he crossed S Pole, Nov. 29, with 3 others.

1934-35: Byrd led 2nd expedition to Little America, explored 450,000 sq mi, wintered alone at 80°08´S.

1934-37: John Rymill led British Graham Land Expedition; discovered Palmer Penin. is part of mainland.

1935: Lincoln Ellsworth (U.S.) flew S along E Coast of Palmer Penin., then crossed continent to Little America, making 4 landings.

1939-41: U.S. Navy plane flights discovered about 150,000 sq mi of new land.

1940: Byrd charted most of coast between Ross Sea and Palmer Penin.

1946-47: U.S. Navy undertook Operation Highjump, commanded by Byrd, included 13 ships and 4,000 men. Airplanes photomapped coastline and penetrated beyond peak.

1946-48: Ronne Antarctic Research Expedition Comdr., Finn Ronne, USNR, determined the Antarctic to be only one continent with no strait between Weddell Sea and Ross Sea; explored 250,000 sq mi of land by flights to 79°S.

1955-57: U.S. Navy's Operation Deep Freeze led by Adm. Byrd. Supporting U.S. scientific efforts for the International Geophysical Year (IGY), the operation established 5 coastal stations fronting the Indian, Pacific, and Atlantic oceans and 3 interior stations; explored more than 1 mil sq mi in Wilkes Land.

1957-58: During the IGY, July 1957 through Dec. 1958, scientists from 12 countries conducted Antarctic research at a network of some 60 stations on Antarctica.

Dr. Vivian E. Fuchs (Brit.) led a 12-person Trans-Antarctic Expedition on the 1st land crossing of Antarctica. Starting from the Weddell Sea, they reached Scott Station, Mar. 2, 1958, after traveling 2,158 mi in 98 days.

1958: A group of 5 U.S. scientists led by Edward C. Thiel, seismologist, moving by tractor from Ellsworth Station on Weddell Sea, identified a huge mountain range 5,000 ft above the ice sheet and 9,000 ft above sea level. The range,

originally seen by a Navy plane, was named the Dufek Massif, for Rear Adm. George Dufek.

1959: Argentina, Australia, Belgium, Chile, France, Japan, New Zealand, Norway, South Africa, USSR, UK, and U.S. signed a treaty suspending territorial claims for 30 yrs. and reserving the continent, S of 60°S, for research.

1961-62: Scientists discovered the Bentley Trench, running from Ross Ice Shelf into Marie Byrd Land, near the end of the Ellsworth Mts., toward the Weddell Sea.

1962: U.S. nuclear power plant went online at McMurdo Sound; operated until 1972.

1963: On Feb. 22, a U.S. plane made the region's longest nonstop flight from McMurdo Station south past the pole to Shackleton Mts., SE to the "Area of Inaccessibility," and back to McMurdo Station, covering 3,600 mi in 10 hrs.

1964: New Zealanders mapped the mountain area from Cape Adare W some 400 mi to Pennell Glacier.

1985: Igor A. Zotikov, a Russian researcher, discovered sediments in the Ross Ice Shelf that seem to support the continental drift theory. Ocean Drilling Project finds that the ice sheets of E Antarctica are 37 mil years old.

1989: Victoria Murden and Shirley Metz became both the 1st women and the 1st Americans to reach the S Pole overland when they arrived with 9 others on Jan. 17, 1989.

1991: 24 nations approved a protocol to the 1959 Antarctica Treaty, Oct. 4. New conservation provisions, including banning oil and other mineral exploration for 50 yrs.

1994: On Dec. 25, after 50-day trek, Liv Arnesen (Nor.) became 1st woman to ski alone and unaided to the S Pole.

1995: On Dec. 22, Borge Ousland (Nor.) reached the S Pole on skis, becoming 1st to reach both N and S Poles solo.

1996-97: Ousland became 1st person to traverse Antarctica alone; reached S Pole Dec. 19, 1996; traveled 1,675 mi in 64 days, ending Jan. 18, 1997.

2000-01: On Feb. 11, Ann Bancroft and Arnesen became 1st women to ski unaided across Antarctica. The 1,717-mi journey took 94 days.

2008: On Dec. 26, Christian Eide, Rune Midtgaard, Morten Andvig, and Mads Agerup (all Nor.) reached the S Pole unaided in a record 24 days, 8 hrs., 50 mins.

Volcanoes

Source: *Volcanoes of the World*, Geoscience Press; Global Volcanism Network, Smithsonian Institution

Roughly 540 volcanoes are known to have erupted during historical times. Nearly 75% of these historically active volcanoes lie along the so-called **Ring of Fire**, running along the W coast of the Americas from the southern tip of Chile to Alaska, down the E coast of Asia from Kamchatka to Indonesia, and continuing from New Guinea to New Zealand. The Ring of Fire marks the boundary between the mobile tectonic plates underlying the Pacific Ocean and those of the surrounding continents. Other active regions occur along rift zones, where plates pull apart, as in Iceland, or where molten material moves up from the mantle over local "hot spots," as in Hawaii. The vast majority of the earth's volcanism occurs at submarine rift zones. For more information on volcanoes, see the Smithsonian Institution's global volcanism website at www.volcano.si.edu.

Notable Volcanic Eruptions

Approximately 7,000 years ago, Mazama, a 9,900-ft volcano in southern Oregon, erupted violently, ejecting large amounts of ash and pumice and voluminous pyroclastic flows. The ash spread over the entire northwestern U.S. and as far away as Saskatchewan, Can. During the eruption, the top of the mountain collapsed, leaving a caldera 6 mi across and about a half mile deep, which filled with rainwater to form what is now called Crater Lake.

In 79 CE, Vesuvio, or Vesuvius, a 4,190-ft volcano overlooking Naples Bay, became active after several centuries of apparent inactivity. On Aug. 24 of that year, a heated mud and ash flow swept down the mountain, engulfing the cities of Pompeii, Herculaneum, and Stabiae with debris more than 60 ft deep. About 10% of the population of the three towns were killed.

In 1883, an eruption similar to the Mazama eruption occurred on the island of Krakatau. At least 2,000 people died in pyroclastic flows on Aug. 26. The next day, the 2,640-ft peak of the volcano collapsed to 1,000 ft below sea level, sinking most of the island and killing over 3,000. A tsunami (tidal wave) generated by the collapse killed more than 31,000 people in Java and Sumatra, and eventually reached England. Ash from the eruption colored sunsets around the world for 2 years. A similar, even more powerful eruption had taken place 68 years earlier at Mt. Tambora on the Indonesian island of Sumbawa.

Date	Volcano	Deaths (est.)	Date	Volcano	Deaths (est.)
Aug. 24, 79 CE	Mt. Vesuvius, Italy	16,000	May 8, 1902	Mt. Pelée, Martinique	28,000
1586	Kelut, Java, Indon.	10,000	Jan. 30, 1911	Mt. Taal, Phil.	1,400
Dec. 15, 1631	Mt. Vesuvius, Italy	4,000	May 19, 1919	Mt. Kelut, Java, Indon.	5,000
Aug. 12, 1772	Mt. Papandayan, Java, Indon.	3,000	Jan. 17-21, 1951	Mt. Lamington, New Guinea	3,000
June 8, 1783	Laki, Iceland	9,350	May 18, 1980	Mt. St. Helens, U.S.	57
May 21, 1792	Mt. Unzen, Japan	14,500	Mar. 28, 1982	El Chichon, Mex.	1,880
Apr. 10-12, 1815	Mt. Tambora, Sumbawa, Indon.	92,000[1]	Nov. 13, 1985	Nevado del Ruiz, Colombia	23,000
Aug. 26-28, 1883	Krakatau, Indon.	36,000	Aug. 21, 1986	Lake Nyos, Cameroon	1,700
Apr. 24, 1902	Santa María, Guatemala	1,000[2]	June 15, 1991	Mt. Pinatubo, Luzon, Phil.	800[3]

(1) Of these, 10,000 were directly related to the eruption; an additional 82,000 were the result of starvation and disease brought on by the event. (2) An additional 3,000 deaths due to a malaria outbreak are sometimes attributed to the eruption. (3) Of these, about 500 were associated with post-eruption lahars (volcanic mudflows), in addition to the 300 deaths caused directly by the eruption.

Notable Active Volcanoes

Active volcanoes display a wide range of activity. In this table, years are given for last display of eruptive activity, as of Sept. 2011; the list does not include submarine volcanoes. An eruption may involve explosive ejection of new or old fragmental material, escape of liquid lava, or both. Volcanoes are listed by height, which does not reflect eruptive magnitude.

Africa

Volcano (latest eruption)	Location	Height (ft)
Mt. Cameroon (2000)	Cameroon	13,435
Nyiragongo (2011)	Congo	11,384
Nyamuragira (2010)	Congo	10,033
Mt. Oku [Lake Nyos] (1986)	Cameroon	9,878
Ol Doinyo Lengai (2010)	Tanzania	9,718
Fogo (1995)	Cape Verde Isls.	9,281
Piton de la Fournaise (2010)	Réunion Isl., Indian O.	8,635
Karthala (2007)	Comoros	7,746
Erta Ale (2011)	Ethiopia	2,011

Antarctica

Volcano (latest eruption)	Location	Height (ft)
Erebus (2011)	Ross Isl.	12,447
Deception Island (1970)	S. Shetland Isl.	1,890

Asia and Oceania

Volcano (latest eruption)	Location	Height (ft)
Kliuchevskoi (2011)	Kamchatka, Russia	15,863
Kerinci (2009)	Sumatra, Indon.	12,467
Fuji (1708)	Honshu, Japan	12,388
Rinjani (2010)	Lesser Sunda Isl., Indon.	12,224
Tolbachik (1976)	Kamchatka, Russia	12,080
Semeru (2011)	Java, Indon.	12,060
Slamet (2009)	Java, Indon.	11,247
Raung (2008)	Java, Indon.	10,932
Shiveluch (2011)	Kamchatka, Russia	10,771
On-take (1980)	Honshu, Japan	10,049
Merapi (2010)	Java, Indon.	9,737
Bezymianny (2011)	Kamchatka, Russia	9,455
Peuet Sague (2000)	Sumatra, Indon.	9,190
Ruapehu (2007)	New Zealand	9,176
Heard (2008)	Indian Ocean	9,006
Changbaishan (1903)	China/Korea	9,003
Asama (2009)	Honshu, Japan	8,425
Dieng (2009)	Java, Indon.	8,415
Mayon (2010)	Luzon, Phil.	8,077
Sinabung (2010)	Sumatra, Indon.	8,071
Kanlaon (2006)	Negros Isl., Phil.	7,989
Niigata-Yake-yama (1998)	Honshu, Japan	7,874
Kizimen (2011)	Kamchatka, Russia	7,795
Alaid (1996)	Kuril Isls., Russia	7,674
Ulawun (2011)	Papua New Guinea	7,657
Tengger Caldera (2011)	Java, Indon.	7,641
Chokai (1974)	Honshu, Japan	7,326
Galunggung (1984)	Java, Indon.	7,113
Azuma (1977)	Honshu, Japan	6,676
Tongariro (Ngauruhoe) (1977)	New Zealand	6,489
Sangeang Api (1988)	Lesser Sunda Isl., Indon.	6,394
Nasu (1963)	Honshu, Japan	6,283
Karkar (1979)	Papua New Guinea	6,033
Gorely (2010)	Kamchatka, Russia	6,001
Bandai (1888)	Honshu, Japan	5,968
Tiatia (2010)	Kuril Isls., Russia	5,968
Manam (2011)	Papua New Guinea	5,928
Kuju (1996)	Kyushu, Japan	5,876
Karangetang (Api Siau) (2011)	Sangihe Isls., Indon.	5,853
Soputan (2008)	Sulawesi, Indon.	5,853
Bagana (2011)	Papua New Guinea	5,741
Kelut (2008)	Java, Indon.	5,679
Adatara (1996)	Honshu, Japan	5,636
Gamalama (2003)	Halmahera, Indon.	5,627
Kirishima (2011)	Kyushu, Japan	5,577
Gamkonora (2007)	Halmahera, Indon.	5,364
Aso (2011)	Kyushu, Japan	5,223
Lokon-Empung (2011)	Sulawesi, Indon.	5,184
Bulusan (2011)	Luzon, Phil.	5,134
Karymsky (2011)	Kamchatka, Russia	5,039
Unzen (1996)	Kyushu, Japan	4,921
Akan (2008)	Hokkaido, Japan	4,918
Sarychev Peak (2009)	Kuril Isls., Russia	4,908
Pinatubo (1993)	Luzon, Phil.	4,875
Lopevi (2008)	Vanuatu	4,636
Akita-Yake-yama (1997)	Honshu, Japan	4,482
Dukono (2011)	Halmahera, Indon.	4,380
Ambrym (2011)	Vanuatu	4,377
Langila (2010)	Papua New Guinea	4,363
Ibu (2011)	Halmahera, Indon.	4,347
Awu (2004)	Sangihe Isls., Indon.	4,331
Akademia Nauk (1996)	Kamchatka, Russia	3,871
Ekarma (2010)	Kuril Isls., Russia	3,839
Ebeko (2010)	Kuril Isls., Russia	3,793
Komaga-take (2000)	Hokkaido, Japan	3,711
Sakura-jima (2011)	Kyushu, Japan	3,665
Tinakula (2011)	Solomon Isls.	2,792
Miyake-jima (2010)	Izu Isls., Japan	2,674
Krakatau (2011)	Indonesia	2,667
Suwanose-jima (2011)	Ryukyu Isls., Japan	2,621
Gaua (2010)	Vanuatu	2,615
Oshima (1990)	Izu Isls., Japan	2,507
Yasur (2011)	Tanna Isl., Vanuatu	1,184
Barren Island (2011)	Andaman Isls., India	1,161

Central America and Caribbean

Volcano (latest eruption)	Location	Height (ft)
Tacaná (1986)	Guatemala	13,320
Acatenango (1972)	Guatemala	13,044
Santa María (2011)	Guatemala	12,375
Fuego (2011)	Guatemala	12,346
Irazú (1994)	Costa Rica	11,260
Turrialba (2011)	Costa Rica	10,958
Poás (2011)	Costa Rica	8,884
Pacaya (2010)	Guatemala	8,373
Santa Ana (2005)	El Salvador	7,812
San Miguel (2002)	El Salvador	6,988
Rincón de la Vieja (1998)	Costa Rica	6,286
San Cristóbal (2011)	Nicaragua	5,725
Concepción (2011)	Nicaragua	5,577
Arenal (2010)	Costa Rica	5,479
Soufrière Guadeloupe (1977)	Guadeloupe Isl.	4,813
Pelée (1932)	Martinique	4,583
Momotombo (1905)	Nicaragua	4,255
Soufrière St. Vincent (1979)	St. Vincent	4,003
Soufrière Hills (2011)	Montserrat	3,002
Masaya (2008)	Nicaragua	2,083

North America

Volcano (latest eruption)	Location	Height (ft)
Pico de Orizaba (1846)	Mexico	18,619
Popocatépetl (2011)	Mexico	17,802
Rainier (1894)	Washington	14,409
Shasta (1786)	California	14,163
Wrangell (2002)	Alaska	14,163
Colima (2011)	Mexico	12,631
Lassen Peak (1917)	California	10,456
Redoubt (2009)	Alaska	10,197
Iliamna (1876)	Alaska	10,016
Shishaldin (2004)	Aleutian Isl., AK	9,373
St. Helens (2008)	Washington	8,363
Pavlof (2007)	Alaska	8,264
Veniaminof (2008)	Alaska	8,225
Katmai (1912)	Alaska	6,716
Makushin (1995)	Aleutian Isl., AK	5,905
Great Sitkin (1974)	Aleutian Isl., AK	5,709
Cleveland (2010)	Aleutian Isl., AK	5,676
Gareloi (1989)	Aleutian Isl., AK	5,161
Korovin (Atka complex) (2007)	Aleutian Isl., AK	5,029
Akutan (1992)	Aleutian Isl., AK	4,275
Augustine (2006)	Alaska	4,108
Kiska (1990)	Aleutian Isl., AK	4,003
El Chichón (1982)	Mexico	3,773
Okmok (2008)	Aleutian Isl., AK	3,520

South America

Volcano (latest eruption)	Location	Height (ft)
Llullaillaco (1877)	Argentina-Chile	22,109
Guallatiri (1960)	Chile	19,918
Tupungatito (1987)	Argentina-Chile	19,685
Cotopaxi (1940)	Ecuador	19,393
El Misti (1985)	Peru	19,101
Láscar (2007)	Chile	18,346
Nevado del Huila (2011)	Colombia	17,598
Nevado del Ruiz (1991)	Colombia	17,457
Sangay (2011)	Ecuador	17,159
Irruputuncu (1995)	Chile-Bolivia	16,939
Tungurahua (2011)	Ecuador	16,479
Guagua Pichincha (2009)	Ecuador	15,695
Puracé (1977)	Colombia	15,256
Galeras (2010)	Colombia	14,029
Planchón-Peteroa (2011)	Chile	13,474
Reventador (2011)	Ecuador	11,686
Llaima (2009)	Chile	10,253
Villarrica (2011)	Chile	9,340
Cerro Hudson (1991)	Chile	6,250
Fernandina (2009)	Galápagos Isls., Ecuador	4,842

Europe

Volcano (latest eruption)	Location	Height (ft)
Etna (2011)	Italy	10,925
Vesuvius (1944)	Italy	4,203
Stromboli (2011)	Italy	3,031
Santorini (1950)	Greece	1,204

Mid-Atlantic

Volcano (latest eruption)	Location	Height (ft)
Jan Mayen (1985)	N Atlantic O., Norway	7,470
Grímsvötn (2011)	Iceland	5,659
Eyjafjallajökull (2010)	Iceland	5,466
Hekla (2000)	Iceland	4,892
Krafla (1984)	Iceland	2,694

Mid-Pacific

Volcano (latest eruption)	Location	Height (ft)
Mauna Loa (1984)	Hawaii, HI	13,681
Haleakala (1750)	Maui, HI	10,023
Kilauea (2010)	Hawaii, HI	4,009

Mountains
North America
Source: U.S. Geological Survey, U.S. Dept. of the Interior. Survey dates and elevation sources may differ.

Peak, state/prov., country	Height (ft)	Peak, state/prov., country	Height (ft)	Peak, state/prov., country	Height (ft)
McKinley (Denali), AK	20,320	Alverstone, AK-YT, U.S.-Can.	14,500	Belford, CO	14,204
Logan, Yukon, Canada	19,551	Whitney, CA	14,500	Princeton, CO	14,204
Pico de Orizaba, Mexico	18,619	University Peak, AK	14,470	Crestone Needle, CO	14,203
St. Elias, AK-YT, U.S.-Can.	18,008	Elbert, CO	14,440	Yale, CO	14,203
Popocatépetl, Mexico	17,802	Massive, CO	14,428	Bross, CO	14,179
Foraker, AK	17,400	Harvard, CO	14,427	Kit Carson, CO	14,171
Iztaccihuatl, Mexico	17,343	Rainier, WA	14,416	El Diente Peak, CO	14,165
Lucania, Yukon, Canada	17,147	Williamson, CA	14,376	Point Success, WA	14,164
King, Yukon, Canada	16,971	La Plata Peak, CO	14,368	Shasta, CA	14,163
Steele, Yukon, Canada	16,644	Blanca Peak, CO	14,351	Wrangell, AK	14,163
Bona, AK	16,500	Uncompahgre Peak, CO	14,315	Maroon Peak, CO	14,163
Blackburn, AK	16,390	Crestone Peak, CO	14,300	Tabeguache, CO	14,162
Sanford, AK	16,237	Lincoln, CO	14,293	Oxford, CO	14,160
Vancouver, AK-YT, U.S.-Can.	15,979	Antero, CO	14,276	Sill, CA	14,159
South Buttress, AK	15,885	Grays Peak, CO	14,276	Sneffels, CO	14,156
Wood, Yukon, Canada	15,885	Torreys Peak, CO	14,273	Democrat, CO	14,155
Churchill, AK	15,638	Castle Peak, CO	14,272	Capitol Peak, CO	14,137
Fairweather, AK-BC, U.S.-Can.	15,300	Quandary Peak, CO	14,272	Liberty Cap, WA	14,118
Zinantecatl (Toluca), Mexico	15,016	Evans, CO	14,270	Pikes Peak, CO	14,111
Hubbard, AK-YT, U.S.-Can.	14,950	Longs Peak, CO	14,260	Snowmass, CO	14,098
Bear, AK	14,831	McArthur, Yukon, CA	14,253	Russell, CA	14,094
Walsh, Yukon, Canada	14,780	White Mt. Peak, CA	14,252	Eolus, CO	14,089
East Buttress, AK	14,730	Wilson, CO	14,252	Windom, CO	14,088
Matlalcueyetl, Mexico	14,636	North Palisade, CA	14,248	Columbia, CO	14,080
Hunter, AK	14,573	Cameron, CO	14,245	Missouri, CO	14,074
Browne Tower, AK	14,530	Shavano, CO	14,236	Augusta, AK	14,070

The highest point in the West Indies is in the Dominican Republic, Pico Duarte (10,417 ft).

Other Notable U.S. Mountains

Peak, state	Height (ft)	Peak, state	Height (ft)	Peak, state	Height (ft)
Gannett Peak, WY	13,810	Adams, WA	12,281	Clingmans Dome, NC-TN	6,643
Grand Teton, WY	13,775	San Gorgonio, CA	11,503	Washington, NH	6,289
Kings, UT	13,534	Hood, OR	11,240	Rogers, VA	5,729
Cloud, WY	13,171	Lassen, CA	10,461	Marcy, NY	5,344
Wheeler, NM	13,166	Granite, CA	10,325	Katahdin, ME	5,269
Boundary, NV	13,146	Guadalupe, TX	8,751	Spruce Knob, WV	4,863
Granite, MT	12,804	Olympus, WA	7,973	Mansfield, VT	4,393
Borah, ID	12,661	Harney, SD	7,244	Black Mountain, KY	4,145
Humphreys, AZ	12,637	Mitchell, NC	6,683		

South America

Peak, country	Height (ft)	Peak, country	Height (ft)	Peak, country	Height (ft)
Aconcagua, Argentina	22,831	Coropuna, Peru	21,083	Solo, Argentina	20,492
Ojos del Salado, Arg.-Chile	22,595	Laudo, Argentina	20,997	Polleras, Argentina	20,456
Bonete, Argentina	22,546	Ancohuma, Bolivia	20,958	Pular, Chile	20,423
Tupungato, Argentina-Chile	22,310	Ausangate, Peru	20,945	Chani, Argentina	20,341
Pissis, Argentina	22,241	Toro, Argentina-Chile	20,932	Aucanquilcha, Chile	20,295
Mercedario, Argentina	22,211	Illampu, Bolivia	20,873	Juncal, Argentina-Chile	20,276
Huascaran, Peru	22,205	Tres Cruces, Argentina-Chile	20,853	Negro, Argentina	20,184
Llullaillaco, Argentina-Chile	22,109	Huandoy, Peru	20,852	Quela, Argentina	20,128
El Libertador, Argentina	22,047	Parinacota, Bolivia-Chile	20,768	Condoriri, Bolivia	20,095
Cachi, Argentina	22,047	Tortolas, Argentina-Chile	20,745	Palermo, Argentina	20,079
Yerupaia, Peru	21,765	Ampato, Peru	20,702	Solimana, Peru	20,068
Incahuasi, Argentina-Chile	21,720	Chimborazo, Ecuador	20,702	San Juan, Argentina-Chile	20,049
Galan, Argentina	21,654	El Condor, Argentina	20,669	Sierra Nevada, Argentina-Chile	20,023
El Muerto, Argentina-Chile	21,457	Salcantay, Peru	20,574	Antofalla, Argentina	20,013
Sajama, Bolivia	21,391	Huancarhuas, Peru	20,531	Marmolejo, Argentina-Chile	20,013
Nacimiento, Argentina	21,302	Famatina, Argentina	20,505	Chachani, Peru	19,931
Illimani, Bolivia	21,201	Pumasillo, Peru	20,492		

Africa

Peak, country	Height (ft)	Peak, country	Height (ft)	Peak, country	Height (ft)
Kilimanjaro, Tanzania	19,341	Meru, Tanzania	14,977	Guna, Ethiopia	13,881
Kenya, Kenya	17,057	Karisimbi, Congo-Rwanda	14,787	Gughe, Ethiopia	13,780
Margherita Pk., Uganda-Congo	16,763	Elgon, Kenya-Uganda	14,178	Toubkal, Morocco	13,661
Ras Dashan, Ethiopia	15,158	Batu, Ethiopia	14,131	Cameroon, Cameroon	13,435

Australia, New Zealand, SE Asian Islands

Peak, country	Height (ft)	Peak, country	Height (ft)	Peak, country	Height (ft)
Jaya, New Guinea	16,500	Wilhelm, New Guinea	14,793	Cook, New Zealand	12,349
Trikora, New Guinea	15,585	Kinabalu, Malaysia	13,455	Semeru, Java, Indonesia	12,060
Mandala, New Guinea	15,420	Kerinci, Sumatra, Indon.	12,467	Kosciusko, Australia	7,310

Height of Mount Everest

Mt. Everest, the world's highest mountain, was considered 29,002 ft when Edmund Hillary and Tenzing Norgay became the 1st climbers to scale it, in 1953. This triangulation figure had been accepted since 1850. In 1954 the Surveyor General of the Republic of India set the height at 29,028 ft, plus or minus 10 ft because of snow; this figure was also accepted by the National Geographic Society.

In 1999, a team of climbers sponsored by Boston's Museum of Science and the National Geographic Society measured the height at the summit using sophisticated satellite-based technology. This new measurement, of 29,035 ft, was accepted by the National Geographic Society and other authorities, including the U.S. National Imagery and Mapping Agency.

As of the end of 2010, more than 55 years after the 1st climbers had reached the summit, some 3,142 more had followed, and about 219 had died in the attempt.

Europe

Peak, country	Height (ft)	Peak, country	Height (ft)	Peak, country	Height (ft)
Alps		Dent D'Herens, Switzerland	13,686	Schalihorn, Switzerland	13,040
		Breithorn, It.-Switzerland	13,665	Scerscen, Switzerland	13,028
Mont Blanc, France-Italy	15,781	Bishorn, Switzerland	13,645	Eiger, Switzerland	13,025
Monte Rosa (highest peak		Jungfrau, Switzerland	13,642	Jagerhorn, Switzerland	13,024
of group), Switzerland	15,203	Ecrins, France	13,461	Rottalhorn, Switzerland	13,022
Dom, Switzerland	14,911	Monch, Switzerland	13,448		
Liskamm, It.-Switzerland	14,852	Pollux, Switzerland	13,422	**Pyrenees**	
Weisshorn, Switzerland	14,780	Schreckhorn, Switzerland	13,379	Aneto, Spain	11,168
Taschhorn, Switzerland	14,733	Ober Gabelhorn, Switzerland	13,330	Posets, Spain	11,073
Matterhorn, It.-Switzerland	14,692	Gran Paradiso, Italy	13,323	Perdido, Spain	11,007
Dent Blanche, Switzerland	14,293	Bernina, It.-Switzerland	13,284	Vignemale, France-Spain	10,820
Nadelhorn, Switzerland	14,196	Fiescherhorn, Switzerland	13,283	Long, Spain	10,479
Grand Combin, Switzerland	14,154	Grunhorn, Switzerland	13,266	Estats, Spain	10,304
Lenzpitze, Switzerland	14,088	Lauteraarhorn, Switzerland	13,261	Montcalm, Spain	10,105
Finsteraarhorn, Switzerland	14,022	Durrenhorn, Switzerland	13,238		
Castor, Switzerland	13,865	Allalinhorn, Switzerland	13,213	**Caucasus (Europe-Asia)**	
Zinalrothorn, Switzerland	13,849	Weissmies, Switzerland	13,199	Elbrus, Russia	18,510
Hohberghom, Switzerland	13,842	Lagginhorn, Switzerland	13,156	Shkhara, Georgia	17,064
Alphubel, Switzerland	13,799	Zupo, Switzerland	13,120	Dykh Tau, Russia	17,054
Rimpfischhom, Switzerland	13,776	Fletschhorn, Switzerland	13,110	Kashtan Tau, Russia	16,877
Aletschorn, Switzerland	13,763	Adlerhorn, Switzerland	13,081	Janqi, Georgia	16,565
Strahlhorn, Switzerland	13,747	Gletscherhorn, Switzerland	13,068	Kazbek, Georgia	16,558

Asia (Mainland)

Peak, country/region	Height (ft)	Peak, country/region	Height (ft)	Peak, country/region	Height (ft)
Everest, Nepal-Tibet	29,035	Kungur, Xinjiang, China	25,325	Gauri Sankar, Nepal-Tibet	23,440
K2 (Godwin Austen), Kashmir	28,250	Tirich Mir, Pakistan	25,230	Badrinath, India	23,420
Kanchenjunga, India-Nepal	28,208	Makalu II, Nepal-Tibet	25,120	Nunkun, Kashmir	23,410
Lhotse I (Everest), Nepal-Tibet	27,923	Minya Konka, China	24,900	Lenin Peak, Tajikistan	23,406
Makalu I, Nepal-Tibet	27,824	Kula Gangri, Bhutan-Tibet	24,784	Pyramid, India-Nepal	23,400
Lhotse II (Everest), Nepal-Tibet	27,560	Changtzu (Everest), Nepal-Tibet	24,780	Api, Nepal	23,399
Dhaulagiri, Nepal	26,810	Muz Tagh Ata, Xinjiang, China	24,757	Pauhunri, India-Tibet	23,385
Manaslu I, Nepal	26,760	Skyang Kangri, Kashmir	24,750	Trisul, India	23,360
Cho Oyu, Nepal-Tibet	26,750	Ismail Semani Peak,Tajikistan	24,590	Kangto, India-Tibet	23,260
Nanga Parbat, Kashmir	26,660	Jongsang Peak, India-Nepal-		Nyenchhe Thanglha, Tibet	23,255
Annapurna I, Nepal	26,504	China	24,472	Trisuli, India	23,210
Gasherbrum, Kashmir	26,470	Jengish Chokusu, Xinjiang,		Pumori, Nepal-Tibet	23,190
Broad, Kashmir	26,400	China-Kyrgyzstan	24,406	Dunagiri, India	23,184
Gosainthan Nepal-Tibet	26,287	Sia Kangri, Kashmir	24,350	Lombo Kangra, Tibet	23,165
Annapurna II, Nepal	26,041	Haramosh Peak, Pakistan	24,270	Saipal, Nepal	23,100
Gyachung Kang, Nepal-Tibet	25,910	Istoro Nal, Pakistan	24,240	Macha Pucchare, Nepal	22,958
Disteghil Sar, Kashmir	25,868	Kirat Chuli, India-Nepal	24,165	Numbar, Nepal	22,817
Himalchuli, Nepal	25,801	Chomo Lhari, Bhutan-Tibet	24,040	Kanjiroba, Nepal	22,580
Nuptse (Everest), Nepal-Tibet	25,726	Chamlang, Nepal	24,012	Ama Dablam, Nepal	22,350
Masherbrum, Kashmir	25,660	Kabru, India-Nepal	24,002	Cho Polu, Nepal	22,093
Nanda Devi, India	25,645	Alung Gangri, Tibet	24,000	Lingtren, Nepal-Tibet	21,972
Rakaposhi, Kashmir	25,550	Baltoro Kangri, Kashmir	23,990	Khumbutse, Nepal-Tibet	21,785
Kamet, India-Tibet	25,447	Mussu Shan, Xinjiang, China	23,890	Hlako Gangri, Tibet	21,266
Namcha Barwa, Tibet	25,445	Mana, India	23,860	Mt. Grosvenor, China	21,190
Gurla Mandhata, Tibet	25,355	Baruntse, Nepal	23,688	Thagchhab Gangri, Tibet	20,970
Ulugh Muz Tagh, Xinjiang,		Nepal Peak, India-Nepal	23,500	Damavand, Iran	18,406
China-Tibet	25,340	Amne Machin, China	23,490	Ararat, Turkey	16,854

Antarctica

Peak	Height (ft)	Peak	Height (ft)	Peak	Height (ft)
Vinson Massif	16,066	Miller	13,650	Falla	12,549
Tyree	15,919	Long Gables	13,620	Rucker	12,520
Shinn	15,750	Dickerson	13,517	Goldthwait	12,510
Gardner	15,375	Giovinetto	13,412	Morris	12,500
Epperly	15,100	Wade	13,400	Erebus	12,450
Kirkpatrick	14,855	Fisher	13,386	Campbell	12,434
Elizabeth	14,698	Fridtjof Nansen	13,350	Don Pedro Christophersen	12,355
Markham	14,290	Wexler	13,202	Lysaght	12,326
Bell	14,117	Lister	13,200	Huggins	12,247
Mackellar	14,098	Shear	13,100	Sabine	12,200
Anderson	13,957	Odishaw	13,008	Astor	12,175
Bentley	13,934	Donaldson	12,894	Mohl	12,172
Kaplan	13,878	Ray	12,808	Frankes	12,064
Andrew Jackson	13,750	Sellery	12,779	Jones	12,040
Sidley	13,720	Waterman	12,730	Gjelsvik	12,008
Ostenso	13,710	Anne	12,703	Coman	12,000
Minto	13,668	Press	12,566		

Important Islands and Their Areas

Figures are for total areas in square miles. Boldface figure in parentheses shows rank among the world's 10 largest individual islands. Because some islands have not been surveyed accurately, some areas shown are estimates. Some "islands" listed are island groups. Only the largest islands in a group are listed individually. Only islands over 10 sq mi in area are listed.

Antarctica

Adelaide	1,400
Alexander	16,700
Berkner	18,500
Roosevelt	2,900

Arctic Ocean

Akimski, Nunavut	1,159
Amund Ringnes, NU	2,029
Axel Heiberg, NU	16,671
Baffin, NU (5)	195,928
Banks, Northwest Territories	27,038
Bathurst, NU	6,194
Bolshevik, Russia	4,368
Bolshoy Lyakhovsky, Russia	1,776
Borden, NWT-NU	1,079
Bylot, NU	4,273
Coats, NU	2,123
Cornwallis, NU	2,701
Devon, NU	21,331
Disko, Greenland	3,312
Ellef Ringnes, NU	4,361
Ellesmere, NU (10)	75,767
Faddayevskiy, Russia	1,930
Franz Josef Land, Russia	8,000
Iturup (Etorofu), Russia	2,596
King William, NU	5,062
Komsomolets, Russia	3,477
Mackenzie King, NWT	1,949
Mansel, NU	1,228
Melville, NWT-NU	16,274
Milne Land, Greenland	1,400
New Siberian Isls., Russia	14,500
Kotelnyy, Russia	4,504
Novaya Zemlya, Russia (2 isls.)	31,730
Oktyabrskoy, Russia	5,471
Prince Charles, NWT	3,676
Prince of Wales, NU	12,872
Prince Patrick, NWT	6,119
Somerset, NU	9,570
Southampton, NU	15,913
Svalbard (tot. group)	23,957
Nordaustlandet	5,410
Spitsbergen	15,060
Traill, Greenland	1,300
Victoria, NWT-NU (9)	83,897
Wrangel, Russia	2,800

Atlantic Ocean

Anticosti, QC, Can.	3,068
Ascension, UK	34
Azores, Portugal (tot. group)	868
Faial	67
San Miguel	291
Bahama Isls. (tot. group)	5,382
Andros, Bahamas	2,300
Bermuda Isls., UK (tot. group)	21
Bioko Isl., Equatorial Guinea	785
Block Island, RI, U.S.	21
Canary Islands, Spain (tot. group)	2,807
Fuerteventura	688
Gran Canaria	592
Tenerife	795
Cape Breton, NS, Can.	3,981
Cape Verde Isls.	1,557
Caviana, Pará, Brazil	1,918
Channel Isls., UK (tot. group)	75
Guernsey	24
Jersey	45
Faroe Isls., Denmark	540
Falkland Isls., UK (tot. group)	4,700
East Falkland	2,550
West Falkland	1,750
Great Britain, UK (8)	88,407
Greenland, Denmark (1)	840,000
Gurupá, Pará, Brazil	1,878
Hebrides, Scotland	2,744
Iceland	39,699
Ireland (tot. group)	32,589
Irish Republic	27,137
Northern Ireland, UK	5,452
Isle of Man, UK	221
Isle of Wight, England	147
Long Island, NY, U.S.	1,320
Madeira Islands, Portugal	306

Atlantic Ocean (cont.)

Marajo, Brazil	15,444
Martha's Vineyard, MA, U.S.	89
Mount Desert, ME, U.S.	104
Nantucket, MA, U.S.	45
Newfoundland, Canada	42,031
Orkney Isls., Scotland	390
Prince Edward, Canada	2,185
St. Helena, UK	160
Shetland Isls., Scotland	587
Skye, Scotland	670
South Georgia, UK	1,450
Tierra del Fuego, Chile, Arg.	18,800
Tristan da Cunha, UK	40

Baltic Sea

Aland Isls., Finland	590
Bornholm, Denmark	227
Gotland, Sweden	1,159

Caribbean Sea

Antigua	108
Aruba, Netherlands	75
Barbados	166
Cuba	42,804
Isle of Youth	926
Cayman Isls., UK	100
Curaçao, Netherlands	171
Dominica	290
Guadeloupe, France	687
Hispaniola (Haiti and Dominican Rep.)	29,389
Jamaica	4,244
Martinique, France	436
Puerto Rico, U.S.	3,339
Tobago	116
Trinidad	1,864
Virgin Isls., UK	59
Virgin Isls., U.S.	134

East Indies

Bali, Indonesia	2,171
Bangka, Indonesia	4,375
Borneo, Indonesia-Malaysia-Brunei (3)	280,100
Bougainville, Papua New Guinea	3,880
Buru, Indonesia	3,670
Celebes, Indonesia	69,000
Flores, Indonesia	5,500
Halmahera, Indonesia	6,865
Java (Jawa), Indonesia	48,900
Madura, Indonesia	2,113
Moluccas, Indonesia	32,307
New Britain, Papua New Guinea	14,093
New Guinea, Indon.-PNG (2)	306,000
New Ireland, PNG	3,707
Seram, Indonesia	6,621
Sumba, Indonesia	4,306
Sumbawa, Indonesia	5,965
Sumatra, Indonesia (6)	165,000
Timor, Indon.–Timor-Leste	13,094
Yos Sudarsa, Indonesia	4,500

Indian Ocean

Andaman Isls., India	2,500
Kerguelen, France	2,247
Madagascar (4)	226,658
Mauritius	720
Pemba, Tanzania	380
Reunion, France	970
Seychelles	176
Sri Lanka	25,332
Zanzibar, Tanzania	640

Mediterranean Sea

Balearic Isls., Spain	1,927
Corfu, Greece	229
Corsica, France	3,369
Crete, Greece	3,189
Cyprus	3,572
Elba, Italy	86
Euboea, Greece	1,411
Malta	95
Rhodes, Greece	540
Sardinia, Italy	9,301
Sicily, Italy	9,926

Pacific Ocean

Admiralty, AK, U.S.	1,709
Aleutian Isls., AK, U.S. (tot. group)	6,912
Adak	275
Amchitka	116
Attu	350
Kanaga	142
Kiska	106
Tanaga	195
Umnak	686
Unalaska	1,051
Unimak	1,571
Baranof, AK, U.S.	1,636
Chichagof, AK, U.S.	2,062
Chiloe, Chile	3,241
Christmas, Kiribati	94
Diomede (Big), Russia	11
Easter Isl., Chile	69
Fiji (tot. group)	7,056
Vanua Levu	2,242
Viti Levu	4,109
Galapagos Isls., Ecuador	3,043
Graham Isl., BC, Can.	2,456
Guadalcanal, Solomon Isls.	2,180
Guam, U.S.	210
Hainan, China	13,000
Hawaiian Isls., HI, U.S. (tot. group)	6,428
Hawaii	4,028
Oahu	600
Hong Kong, China	31
Hoste, Chile	1,590
Japan (tot. group)	145,914
Hokkaido	30,144
Honshu (7)	87,805
Kyushu	14,114
Okinawa	459
Shikoku	7,049
Kangaroo, South Australia	1,680
Kodiak, AK, U.S.	3,485
Kupreanof, AK, U.S.	1,084
Marquesas Isls., France	492
Marshall Isls.	70
Melville, N Terr., Australia	2,240
Micronesia	271
New Caledonia, France	6,530
New Zealand (tot. group)	103,363
Chatham Isls.	373
North	43,911
South	58,084
Stewart	649
North Mariana Isls., U.S.	179
Nunivak, AK, U.S.	1,600
Palau	188
Philippines (tot. group)	115,831
Leyte	2,787
Luzon	40,680
Mindanao	36,775
Mindoro	3,690
Negros	4,907
Palawan	4,554
Panay	4,446
Samar	5,050
Prince of Wales, AK, U.S.	2,770
Revillagigedo, AK, U.S.	1,134
Riesco, Chile	1,973
St. Lawrence, AK, U.S.	1,780
Sakhalin, Russia	29,500
Samoa Isls. (tot. group)	1,177
American Samoa, U.S.	77
Savaii, Samoa	659
Tutuila, U.S.	55
Upolu, Samoa	432
Santa Catalina, CA, U.S.	75
Santa Ines, Chile	1,407
Tahiti, France	402
Taiwan, China (tot. group)	13,892
Jinmen Dao (Quemoy)	56
Tasmania, Australia	26,178
Tonga Isls.	290
Vancouver Isl., BC, Can.	12,079
Vanuatu	4,707
Wellington, Chile	2,549

Persian Gulf

Bahrain	217

Notable Deserts of the World

Deserts are defined as regions of the Earth receiving less than 10 in. of precipitation annually, usually in combination with an evaporation rate exceeding precipitation.

In addition to areas listed below, the continent of Antarctica, with an area of about 5.4 mil sq mi (roughly doubled by ice in winter), is generally considered a desert. Annual precipitation averages 8 in. along the coast and far less in the deep interior; however, there is little evaporation.

Arabian (Eastern), 86,000 sq mi in Egypt between the Nile R. and Red Sea, extending southward into Sudan
Atacama, 600-mi-long area rich in nitrate and copper deposits in N Chile
Chihuahuan, 140,000 sq mi in TX, NM, AZ, and Mexico
Dasht-e Kavir, approx. 500 mi long by approx. 200 mi wide in N central Iran
Dasht-e Lut, approx. 300 mi long by 200 mi wide in S central Iran
Death Valley, 3,300 sq mi in CA and NV
Gibson, 120,000 sq mi in the interior of W Australia
Gobi, 500,000 sq mi in Mongolia and China
Great Sandy, 150,000 sq mi in W Australia
Great Victoria, 150,000 sq mi in SW Australia
Kalahari, 100,000 sq mi in southern Africa
Kara Kum, 115,000 sq mi in Turkmenistan
Kyzyl Kum, 115,000 sq mi in Kazakhstan and Uzbekistan
Libyan, 425,000 sq mi in the Sahara, extending from Libya through SW Egypt into Sudan

Mojave, 15,000 sq mi in southern CA
Namib, long narrow area (varies from 30-100 mi wide) extending 800 mi along SW coast of Africa
Nubian, 157,000 sq mi in the Sahara in NE Sudan
Painted Desert, section of high plateau in northern AZ extending 200 mi SE from Grand Canyon
Patagonia, 300,000 sq mi in S Argentina
Rub al-Khali (Empty Quarter), 225,000 sq mi in the S Arabian Peninsula
Sahara, 3,500,000 sq mi in N Africa, extending westward to the Atlantic. Largest desert in the world.
Sonoran, 70,000 sq mi in southwestern AZ and southeastern CA extending into NW Mexico
Syrian, 100,000-sq-mi area extending over much of N Saudi Arabia, E Jordan, S Syria, and W Iraq
Taklamakan, 140,000 sq mi in Xinjiang Prov., China
Thar (Great Indian), 100,000-sq-mi arid area extending 400 mi along India-Pakistan border

Areas and Average Depths of Oceans, Seas, and Gulfs

Geographers and mapmakers recognize at least four major bodies of water: the Pacific, Atlantic, Indian, and Arctic Oceans. The Atlantic and Pacific Oceans are considered divided at the equator into the N and S Atlantic and the N and S Pacific. The Arctic Ocean is the name for waters N of the continental landmasses in the region of the Arctic Circle. The International Hydrographic Organization delimited a fifth world ocean in 2000. The Southern Ocean extends from the coast of Antarctica north to 60° south latitude, encompassing portions of the Atlantic, Indian, and Pacific Oceans.

Body of water	Area (sq mi)	Avg. depth (ft)	Body of water	Area (sq mi)	Avg. depth (ft)
Pacific Ocean	60,060,869	14,040	Sea of Japan	391,100	5,468
Atlantic Ocean	29,637,962	11,810	Hudson Bay	281,900	305
Indian Ocean	26,469,609	12,800	East China Sea	256,600	620
Southern Ocean	7,848,295	14,450	Andaman Sea	218,100	3,667
Arctic Ocean	5,427,050	4,300	Black Sea	196,100	3,906
South China Sea	1,148,500	4,802	Red Sea	174,900	1,764
Caribbean Sea	971,400	8,448	North Sea	164,900	308
Mediterranean Sea	969,100	4,926	Baltic Sea	147,500	180
Bering Sea	873,000	4,893	Yellow Sea	113,500	121
Gulf of Mexico	582,100	5,297	Persian Gulf	88,800	328
Sea of Okhotsk	537,500	3,192	Gulf of California	59,100	2,375

Principal Ocean Depths

Source: National Imagery and Mapping Agency, U.S. Dept. of Defense

Body of water	Location (lat.)	Location (long.)	Depth (meters)	Depth (fathoms)	(ft)
Pacific Ocean					
Marianas Trench	11°22′ N	142°36′ E	10,924	5,973	35,840
Tonga Trench	23°16′ S	174°44′ W	10,800	5,906	35,433
Philippine Trench	10°38′ N	126°36′ E	10,057	5,499	32,995
Kermadec Trench	31°53′ S	177°21′ W	10,047	5,494	32,963
Bonin Trench	24°30′ N	143°24′ E	9,994	5,464	32,788
Kuril Trench	44°15′ N	150°34′ E	9,750	5,331	31,988
Izu Trench	31°05′ N	142°10′ E	9,695	5,301	31,808
New Britain Trench	06°19′ S	153°45′ E	8,940	4,888	29,331
Yap Trench	08°33′ N	138°02′ E	8,527	4,663	27,976
Japan Trench	36°08′ N	142°43′ E	8,412	4,600	27,599
Peru-Chile Trench	23°18′ S	71°14′ W	8,064	4,409	26,457
Palau Trench	07°52′ N	134°56′ E	8,054	4,404	26,424
Aleutian Trench	50°51′ N	177°11′ E	7,679	4,199	25,194
New Hebrides Trench	20°36′ S	168°37′ E	7,570	4,139	24,836
North Ryukyu Trench	24°00′ N	126°48′ E	7,181	3,927	23,560
Mid. America Trench	14°02′ N	93°39′ W	6,662	3,643	21,857
Atlantic Ocean					
Puerto Rico Trench	19°55′ N	65°27′ W	8,605	4,705	28,232
S Sandwich Trench	55°42′ S	25°56′ W	8,325	4,552	27,313
Romanche Gap	0°13′ S	18°26′ W	7,728	4,226	25,354
Cayman Trench	19°12′ N	80°00′ W	7,535	4,120	24,721
Brazil Basin	09°10′ S	23°02′ W	6,119	3,346	20,076
Indian Ocean					
Java Trench	10°19′ S	109°58′ E	7,125	3,896	23,376
Ob' Trench	09°45′ S	67°18′ E	6,874	3,759	22,553
Diamantina Trench	35°50′ S	105°14′ E	6,602	3,610	21,660
Vema Trench	09°08′ S	67°15′ E	6,402	3,501	21,004
Agulhas Basin	45°20′ S	26°50′ E	6,195	3,387	20,325
Arctic Ocean					
Eurasia Basin	82°23′ N	19°31′ E	5,450	2,980	17,881
Mediterranean Sea					
Ionian Basin	36°32′ N	21°06′ E	5,150	2,816	16,896

Note: Greater depths have been reported in some areas but have not been officially confirmed by research vessels.

Major World Rivers

For N American rivers, see separate table.

River	Source or upper limit of length	Outflow	Length (mi)
Africa			
Chari	Bamingui-Bangoran region, Central African Republic	Lake Chad	650
Congo	Junction of Lualaba and Luava Rivers, Congo	Atlantic Ocean	2,720
Cubango (fmr. Okavango)	Central Angola	Okavango Delta	1,000
Gambia	Fouta Djallon massif, Guinea	Atlantic Ocean	700
Kasai	Central Angola	Congo River	1,100
Limpopo	Junction of Marico and Ngotwane Rivers, South Africa	Indian Ocean	1,100
Lualaba	SE Congo	Congo River	1,100
Niger	Fouta Djallon plateau, Guinea	Gulf of Guinea	2,600
Nile	Luvironza River, Burundi	Mediterranean Sea	4,160
Orange	Maluti mountains, N Lesotho	Atlantic Ocean	1,300
Sénégal	Junction of Bafing and Bakoy Rivers, Mali	Atlantic Ocean	1,000
Ubangi	Junction of Uele and Bomu Rivers, Congo	Congo River	700
Zambezi	NW Zambia	Indian Ocean	1,700
Asia			
Amu Darya	Junction of Wakhsh and Panj Rivers, Tajikistan	Aral Sea	1,660
Amur	Junction of Shilka and Argun Rivers, China-Russia	Tartar Strait	1,780
Angara	Lake Baykal, Russia	Yenisei River	1,150
Ayeyarwady (fmr. Irrawaddy)	Junction of Mali and Nmai Rivers, Myanmar	Andaman Sea	1,000
Brahmaputra	Kailas range, Himalayas, SW Tibet	Bay of Bengal	1,800
Chang-Jiang	Tibetan plateau, SW Qinghai, China	East China Sea	3,450
Euphrates	Junction of Kara (Sarasu) and Murat Rivers, Turkey	Shatt al-Arab	1,700
Ganges	Gangotri glacier, Himalayas, India	Bay of Bengal	1,560
Godavari	W Ghats, Maharashtra, India	Bay of Bengal	900
Hsi (see Xi He)			
Huang-He	Kunlun mountains, Qinghai, China	Yellow Sea	3,000
Indus	Kailas range, Himalayas, Tibet	Arabian Sea	1,900
Irtysh	Kazakhstan-Russia	Ob River	2,650
Jordan	Junction of Dan, Banias, and Hazbani streams, Israel	Dead Sea	200
Kolyma	Kolyma and Cherskogo ranges, Russia	Arctic Ocean	1,500
Krishna	W Ghats, Maharashtra, India	Bay of Bengal	800
Kura	NE Turkey	Caspian Sea	950
Lena	W Baikal range, Russia	Laptev Sea	2,648
Mekong	E Tibetan Plateau, China	South China Sea	2,700
Narmada	Madhya Pradesh, India	Arabian Sea	775
Ob	Junction of Biya and Katun Rivers, Russia	Gulf of Ob	2,300
Salween	E Tibet, China	Gulf of Martaban	1,750
Songhua Jiang	Changbai mountains, Jilin, China	Amur River	1,150
Sungari (see Songhua Jiang)			
Sutlej	Kailas range, Himalayas, Tibet	Indus River	900
Syr	Junction of Naryn and Kara Darya Rivers, Uzbekistan	Aral Sea	1,380
Tarim	Junction of Kashi and Yarkant Rivers, China	Lop Nor	1,300
Tigris	Taurus mountains, Turkey	Shatt al-Arab	1,150
Xi He	E Yunnan, China	South China Sea	1,250
Yamuna	Uttarkashi dist., Uttar Pradesh, India	Ganges River	850
Yangtze (see Chang-Jiang)			
Yellow (see Huang-He)			
Yenisei	Kyzyl, Tuva Republic, Russia	Kara Sea	2,500
Australia			
Darling	Eastern Highlands, NE New South Wales/SE Queensland	Murray River	1,702
Murray	Australian Alps, SE New South Wales	Southern Ocean	1,609
Murrumbidgee	Australian Alps, SE New South Wales	Murray River	1,050
Europe			
Buh, Southern	NW of Khmel'nyts'kyy, Ukraine	Black Sea	532
Buh, Western	ENE of Zolochiv, Ukraine	Wisla River	500
Danube	Brege and Brigach Rivers, Black Forest, SW Germany	Black Sea	1,770
Dnieper	W of Sychevka, Smolensk, Russia	Black Sea	1,420
Dniester	Carpathian mountains, Ukraine	Black Sea	850
Don	SE of Tula, Russia	Sea of Azov	1,200
Drava	Carnic Alps, N Italy	Danube River	450
Dvina, North	Near Veliki Ustyug, Vologda, Russia	White Sea	465
Dvina, West	Valdai Hills, Russia	Gulf of Riga	635
Ebro	Cantabrian mountains, N Spain	Mediterranean Sea	575
Elbe	Giant mountains, NW Czech Republic	North Sea	725
Garonne	Central Pyrenees, Spain	Bay of Biscay	402
Kama	Ural mountains, N of Kuliga, Russia	Volga River	1,260
Loire	Mt. Gerbier-de-Jonc, Vivrais mountains, France	Atlantic Ocean	630
Marne	Langres plateau, NE France	Seine River	325
Meuse	Langres plateau, NE France	North Sea	560
Oder	Sudetes mountains, NE Czech Republic	Baltic Sea	562
Oka	S of Orël, Russia	Volga River	925
Pechora	N Ural mountains, Russia	Barents Sea	1,120
Po	Cottian Alps, Piedmont, NW Italy	Adriatic Sea	405
Rhine	Swiss Alps	North Sea	820

River	Source or upper limit of length	Outflow	Length (mi)
Rhône	Rhône glacier, NE Valais, Switzerland	Mediterranean Sea	505
Seine	Langres Plateau, N Burgundy, France	English Channel	480
Shannon	Near Cuilcagh Mountain, NW Cavan County, Ireland	Atlantic Ocean	240
Tagus	E of Madrid, Spain	Atlantic Ocean	585
Thames	4 headstreams in the Cotswold Hills, Gloucestershire, England	North Sea	210
Tiber	Etruscan Apennines, Italy	Tyrrhenian Sea	251
Tisza	N of Rakhiv, W Ukraine	Danube River	700
Ural	S Ural mountains, NE Bashkortostan, Russia	Caspian Sea	1,580
Volga	Valday Hills, Smolensk, Russia	Caspian Sea	2,290
Weser	Junction of Fulda and Werra Rivers, Germany	North Sea	273
Wisla	W Beskid range, Carpathian mountains, SW Poland	Gulf of Gdansk	665
South America			
Amazon	Junction of Ucayali and Marañón Rivers, Andes mountains, Peru	Atlantic Ocean	3,900
Araguaía	Serra des Araras, Goiás-Mato Grosso, Brazil	Tocantins River	1,100
Beni	Cordillera Real, La Paz, Bolivia	Madeira River	1,000
Caquetá-Japura	Andes mountains, SW Colombia	Amazon River	1,750
Juruá	Cerros de Canchyuaya, E Peru	Amazon River	1,500
Madeira	Junction of Beni and Mamoré Rivers, Bolivia	Amazon River	2,100
Magdalena	Cordillera Central, SW Colombia	Caribbean Sea	1,000
Negro	SE Colombia	Amazon River	1,400
Orinoco	Near Mt. Delgado Chalbaud, Guiana Highlands, S Venezuela	Atlantic Ocean	1,600
Paraguay	Central Mato Grosso highlands, Brazil	Paraná River	1,584
Paraná	Junction of Paranaíba and Rio Grande, SE Brazil	Rio de la Plata	2,485
Pilcomayo	E of Lake Poopó, Bolivia	Paraguay River	1,000
Purus	Andes mountains, E Peru	Amazon River	2,100
Putumayo	Andes mountains, S Colombia	Amazon River	1,000
Rio de la Plata	Estuary of Paraná and Uruguay Rivers, Argentina-Uruguay	Atlantic Ocean	170
São Francisco	Serra de Canastra, SW Minas Gerais, Brazil	Atlantic Ocean	1,800
Tocantins	S central Goiás, Brazil	Para River	1,640
Ucayali	Junction of Apurímac and Urubamba Rivers, E Peru	Marañón River	1,000
Uruguay	S Brazil	Rio de la Plata	1,000
Xingu	Central Mato Grosso, Brazil	Amazon River	1,230

Major Rivers in North America

River	Source or upper limit of length	Outflow	Length (mi)
Alabama	Gilmer County, GA	Mobile River	729
Albany	Lake St. Joseph, ON, Can.	James Bay	610
Allegheny	Potter County, PA.	Ohio River	325
Altamaha-Ocmulgee	Junction of Yellow and South Rivers, Newton Co., GA	Atlantic Ocean	392
Apalachicola-Chattahoochee	Towns County, GA	Gulf of Mexico	524
Arkansas	Lake County, CO	Mississippi River	1,459
Assiniboine	Eastern Saskatchewan	Red River	450
Attawapiskat	Attawapiskat, ON, Can.	James Bay	465
Back (NWT)	Contwoyto Lake, NWT	Chantrey Inlet, Arctic Ocean	605
Big Black (MS)	Webster County, MS	Mississippi River	330
Brazos	Junction of Salt and Double Mountain Forks, Stonewall Co., TX	Gulf of Mexico	950
Canadian	Las Animas County, CO	Arkansas River	906
Cedar (IA)	Dodge County, MN	Iowa River	329
Cheyenne	Junction of Antelope Creek and Dry Fork, Converse Co., WY	Missouri River	290
Churchill, Lab.	Lake Ashuanipi, NL, Can.	Atlantic Ocean	532
Churchill, Man.	Methy Lake, SK, Can.	Hudson Bay	1,000
Cimarron	Colfax County, NM	Arkansas River	600
Colorado (AZ)	Rocky Mountain Natl. Park, CO (90 mi in Mexico)	Gulf of California	1,450
Colorado (TX)	West Texas	Matagorda Bay	862
Columbia	Columbia Lake, BC, Can.	Pacific Ocean, bet. OR and WA	1,243
Columbia, Upper	Columbia Lake, BC, Can.	Mouth of Snake River	890
Connecticut	Third Connecticut Lake, NH	Long Island Sound, CT	407
Coppermine (NWT)	Lac de Gras, NWT	Coronation Gulf, Arctic Ocean	525
Cumberland	Letcher County, KY	Ohio River	720
Delaware	Schoharie County, NY	Liston Point, Delaware Bay	390
Fraser	Near Mount Robson (on Continental Divide)	Strait of Georgia	850
Gila	Catron County, NM	Colorado River	649
Green (UT-WY)	Junction of Wells and Trail Creeks, Sublette County, WY	Colorado River	730
Hudson	Henderson Lake, Essex County, NY	Upper NY Bay	306
Illinois	St. Joseph County, IN	Mississippi River	420
James (ND-SD)	Wells County, ND	Missouri River	710
James (VA)	Junction of Jackson and Cowpasture Rivers, Botetourt Co., VA	Hampton Roads	340
Kanawha-New	Junction of North and South Forks of New River, NC	Ohio River	352
Kentucky	Junction of North and Middle Forks, Lee County, KY	Ohio River	259
Klamath	Lake Ewauna, Klamath Falls, OR.	Pacific Ocean	250

River	Source or upper limit of length	Outflow	Length (mi)
Kootenay	Kootenay Lake, BC, Can.	Columbia River	485
Koyukuk	Endicott Mountains, AK	Yukon River	470
Kuskokwim	Alaska Range	Kuskokwim Bay	724
Liard	Southern Yukon, AK	Mackenzie River	693
Little Missouri	Crook County, WY	Missouri River	560
Mackenzie	Great Slave Lake, NWT	Arctic Ocean	1,060
Milk	Junction of North and South Forks, AB, Can.	Missouri River	625
Minnesota	Big Stone Lake, MN	Mississippi River	332
Mississippi	Lake Itasca, MN	Gulf of Mexico	2,340
Mississippi-Missouri-Red Rock	Source of Red Rock, Beaverhead Co., MT	Gulf of Mexico	3,710
Missouri	Junction of Jefferson, Madison, and Gallatin Rivers, Gallatin Co., MT	Mississippi River	2,315
Missouri-Red Rock	Source of Red Rock, Beaverhead Co., MT	Mississippi River	2,540
Mobile-Alabama-Coosa	Gilmer County, GA	Mobile Bay	774
Nelson (MB)	Lake Winnipeg, MB, Can.	Hudson Bay	410
Neosho	Morris County, KS	Arkansas River, OK	460
Niobrara	Niobrara County, WY	Missouri River, NE	431
North Canadian	Union County, NM	Canadian River, OK	800
North Platte	Junction of Grizzly and Little Grizzly Creeks, Jackson Co., CO	Platte River, NE	618
Ohio	Junction of Allegheny and Monongahela Rivers, Pittsburgh, PA	Mississippi River	981
Ohio-Allegheny	Potter County, PA	Mississippi River	1,310
Osage	East-central Kansas	Missouri River	500
Ottawa	Lake Capimitchigama, QC, Can.	St. Lawrence River	790
Ouachita	Polk County, AR	Black River	605
Peace	Junction of Finlay and Parsnip Rivers, BC	Slave River	1,210
Pearl	Neshoba County, MS	Gulf of Mexico	411
Pecos	Mora County, NM	Rio Grande	926
Pee Dee-Yadkin	Watauga County, NC	Winyah Bay	435
Pend Oreille-Clark Fork	Near Butte, MT	Columbia River	531
Platte	Junction of North and South Platte Rivers, NE.	Missouri River	310
Porcupine	Ogilvie Mountains, AK	Yukon River, AK	569
Potomac	Garrett County, MD	Chesapeake Bay	383
Powder	Junction of South and Middle Forks, WY	Yellowstone River	375
Red (OK-TX-LA)	Curry County, NM.	Mississippi River	1,290
Red River of the North	Junction of Otter Tail and Bois de Sioux Rivers, Wilkin Co., MN	Lake Winnipeg	545
Republican	Junction of North Fork and Arikaree River, NE	Kansas River	445
Rio Grande	San Juan County, CO.	Gulf of Mexico	1,900
Roanoke	Junction of N and S Forks, Montgomery Co., VA.	Albemarle Sound	380
Rock (IL-WI)	Dodge County, WI	Mississippi River	300
Sabine	Junction of South and Caddo Forks, Hunt Co., TX	Sabine Lake	380
Sacramento	Siskiyou County, CA.	Suisun Bay	377
St. Francis	Iron County, MO.	Mississippi River	425
St. John	Northwestern Maine	Bay of Fundy	418
St. Lawrence	Lake Ontario, ON-NY	Gulf of St. Lawrence, Atlantic Ocean	800
Saguenay	Lake St. John, QC, Can.	St. Lawrence River	434
Salmon (ID)	Custer County, ID.	Snake River	420
San Joaquin	Junction of South and Middle Forks, Madera Co., CA	Suisun Bay	350
San Juan	Silver Lake, Archuleta County, CO.	Colorado River	360
Santee-Wateree-Catawba	McDowell County, NC	Atlantic Ocean	538
Saskatchewan, North.	Rocky Mountains, AB, Can.	Saskatchewan R.	800
Saskatchewan, South	Rocky Mountains, AB, Can.	Saskatchewan R.	865
Savannah	Junction of Seneca and Tugaloo Rivers, Anderson Co., SC	Atlantic Ocean, GA-SC	314
Severn (ON)	Sandy Lake, ON, Can.	Hudson Bay	610
Smoky Hill	Cheyenne County, CO	Kansas River, KS	540
Snake	Teton County, WY	Columbia River, WA	1,038
South Platte	Junction of S and Middle Forks, Park County, CO	Platte River	424
Susitna	Alaska Range	Cook Inlet	313
Susquehanna	Huyden Creek, Otsego County, NY	Chesapeake Bay	447
Tallahatchie	Tippah County, MS.	Yazoo River	301
Tanana	Wrangell Mountains, AK.	Yukon River	659
Tennessee	Junction of French Broad and Holston Rivers, TN	Ohio River	652
Tennessee-French Broad	Courthouse Creek, Transylvania County, NC	Ohio River	886
Tombigbee	Prentiss County, MS.	Mobile River	525
Trinity	North of Dallas, TX.	Galveston Bay	360
Wabash	Darke County, OH	Ohio River	512
Washita	Hemphill County, TX.	Red River, OK	500
White (AR-MO)	Madison County, AR.	Mississippi River	722
Willamette	Douglas County, OR.	Columbia River	309
Wind-Bighorn	Junction of Wind and Little Wind Rivers, Fremont Co., WY (Source of Wind R. is Togwotee Pass, Teton Co., WY)	Yellowstone River	338
Wisconsin	Lac Vieux Desert, Vilas County, WI	Mississippi River	430
Yellowstone	Park County, WY	Missouri River	682
Yukon	McNeil R., YT	Bering Sea	1,979

Major Natural Lakes of the World

Source: Geological Survey, U.S. Dept. of the Interior; GeoAccess Division, Natural Resources Canada

A lake is generally defined as a body of water surrounded by land. By this definition some bodies of water that are called seas, such as the Caspian Sea and the Aral Sea, are really lakes. In the following table, the word *lake* is omitted when it is part of the name.

Name	Continent	Area (sq mi)	Length (mi)	Maximum depth (ft)	Elevation (ft)
Caspian Sea[1]	Asia-Europe	143,244	760	3,363	−92
Superior	North America	31,700	350	1,330	600
Victoria	Africa	26,828	250	270	3,720
Huron	North America	23,000	206	750	579
Michigan	North America	22,300	307	923	579
Aral Sea[1]	Asia	13,000[2]	260	180	125
Tanganyika	Africa	12,700	420	4,823	2,534
Baykal	Asia	12,162	395	5,315	1,493
Great Bear	North America	12,096	192	1,463	512
Nyasa (Malawi)	Africa	11,150	360	2,280	1,550
Great Slave	North America	11,031	298	2,015	513
Erie	North America	9,910	241	210	570
Winnipeg	North America	9,417	266	200	713
Ontario	North America	7,340	193	802	245
Balkhash[1]	Asia	7,115	376	85	1,115
Ladoga	Europe	6,835	124	738	13
Maracaibo	South America	5,217	133	115	sea level
Onega	Europe	3,710	145	328	108
Eyre[1]	Australia	3,600[3]	90	4	−52
Titicaca	South America	3,200	122	922	12,500
Nicaragua	North America	3,100	102	230	102
Athabasca	North America	3,064	208	407	700
Reindeer	North America	2,568	143	720	1,106
Tonle Sap	Asia	2,500[3]	70	45	NA
Turkana (Rudolf)	Africa	2,473	154	240	1,230
Issyk Kul[1]	Asia	2,355	115	2,303	5,279
Torrens[1]	Australia	2,230[3]	130	(3)	92
Vanern	Europe	2,156	91	328	144
Nettilling	North America	2,140	67	(3)	95
Winnipegosis	North America	2,075	141	38	830
Albert	Africa	2,075	100	168	2,030
Nipigon	North America	1,872	72	540	1,050
Gairdner[1]	Australia	1,840[3]	90	(3)	112
Urmia[1]	Asia	1,815	90	49	4,180
Manitoba	North America	1,799	140	21	813
Chad	Africa	500+[4]	175	24	787

NA = Not available (1) Salt lake. (2) The diversion of feeder rivers since the 1960s has devastated the Aral—once the world's 4th-largest lake (26,000 sq mi). By 2000, the Aral had effectively become three lakes, with the total area shown. (3) Subject to great seasonal variation. (4) Once 4th-largest lake in Africa (about 10,000 sq mi in the 1960s), Chad had shrunk to around 5% of its original size as of 2006 as a result of irrigation and long-term drought.

The Great Lakes

Source: National Ocean Service, National Oceanic and Atmospheric Administration, U.S. Dept. of Commerce

The Great Lakes form the world's **largest body of fresh water** (in surface area), and with their connecting waterways are the largest inland water transportation unit. Draining the great North Central basin of the U.S., they enable shipping to reach the Atlantic via their outlet, the St. Lawrence R., and to reach the Gulf of Mexico via the Illinois Waterway, from Lake Michigan to the Mississippi R. A third outlet connects with the Hudson R. and then the Atlantic via the New York State Barge Canal System. Traffic on the Illinois Waterway and the NYS Barge Canal System is limited to recreational boating and small shipping vessels.

Only one of the lakes, Lake Michigan, is wholly in the U.S.; the others are shared with Canada. Ships move from the shores of Lake Superior to Whitefish Bay at the east end of the lake, then through the Soo Locks, in Sault Ste. Marie, MI, through the St. Mary's R. and into Lake Huron. To reach Gary and the Port of Indiana and South Chicago, IL, ships move W from Lake Huron to Lake Michigan through the Straits of Mackinac. Lake Superior is 601 ft above low water datum at Rimouski, Quebec, on the International Great Lakes Datum (1985). From Duluth, MN, to the east end of Lake Ontario is 1,156 mi.

	Superior	Michigan	Huron	Erie	Ontario
Length in mi	350	307	206	241	193
Breadth in mi	160	118	183	57	53
Deepest soundings in ft	1,333	923	750	210	802
Volume of water in cu mi	2,935	1,180	850	116	393
Area (sq mi) water surface—U.S.	20,600	22,300	9,100	4,980	3,460
Canada	11,100	NA	13,900	4,930	3,880
Area (sq mi) entire drainage basin—U.S.	16,900	45,600	16,200	18,000	15,200
Canada	32,400	NA	35,500	4,720	12,100
Total area (sq mi), U.S. and Canada	81,000	67,900	74,700	32,630	34,850
Low water datum above mean water level at Rimouski, Quebec, avg. level in ft (1985)	601.10	577.50	577.50	569.20	243.30
Latitude, N	46°25′	41°37′	43°00′	41°23′	43°11′
	49°00′	46°06′	46°17′	42°52′	44°15′
Longitude, W	84°22′	84°45′	79°43′	78°51′	76°03′
	92°06′	88°02′	84°45′	83°29′	79°53′
National boundary line in mi	282.8	None	260.8	251.5	174.6
United States shoreline (mainland only) in mi	863	1,400	580	431	300

NA = Not applicable.

Notable Waterfalls

Source: National Geographic Society

The earth has thousands of waterfalls, some of considerable magnitude. Their magnitude is determined not only by height but also by volume of flow, steadiness of flow, crest width, whether the water drops sheerly or over a sloping surface, and whether it descends in one leap or in a succession of leaps. A series of low falls flowing over a considerable distance is known as a cascade. Waterfalls are highly variable and few authoritative figures exist. For more information and some alternative measurements, see the World Waterfall Database at www.worldwaterfalldatabase.com.

Estimated mean annual flow, in cubic feet per second, of major waterfalls is as follows: Niagara, 212,200; Paulo Afonso, 100,000; Urubupunga, 97,000; Iguazu, 61,000; Patos-Maribondo, 53,000; Victoria, 35,400; and Kaieteur, 23,400.

Height = total drop in feet in one or more leaps. # = falls of more than one leap; * = falls that diminish greatly seasonally; ** = falls that reduce to a trickle or are dry for part of each year. If the river names are not shown, they are same as the falls. R. = river; (C) = cascade.

Name, location	Height (ft)	Name, location	Height (ft)	Name, location	Height (ft)
Africa		**Norway**		**Kentucky**	
Angola		Mardalsfossen#**	2,154	Cumberland	68
Ruacana, Cunene R.	406	Skykje**	984	**Maryland**	
Lesotho		Vetti, Morka-Koldedola R.	900	Great, Potomac R. (C)*	76
Maletsunyane*	630	**Sweden**		**Minnesota**	
South Africa		Handol#	345	Minnehaha**	53
Augrabies, Orange R.*	480	**Switzerland**		**New Jersey**	
Tugela#	2,800	Giessbach (C)	984	Great, Passaic R.	70
Tanzania-Zambia		Reichenbach#	820	**New York**	
Kalambo*	704	Staubbach	984	Taughannock*	215
Zimbabwe-Zambia		Trümmelbach#	1,312	**Oregon**	
Victoria, Zambezi R.*	343	**North America**		Multnomah#	850
Asia and Oceania		**Canada**		**Tennessee**	
Australia		Alberta		Fall Creek	256
New South Wales		Panther, Nigel Creek	600	**Washington**	
Wentworth	614	British Columbia		Sluiskin, Paradise R.	300
Wollomombi	722	Della#	1,444	Snoqualmie**	268
Queensland		Takakkaw, Daly Glacier#	833	**Wisconsin**	
Tully**	984	Quebec		Big Manitou, Black R. (C)*	165
Wallaman, Stony Creek#	1,137	Montmorency	276	**Wyoming**	
India		**Canada-United States**		Tower	132
Sivasamudram	320	Niagara (American)	194	Yellowstone (upper)*	109
Jog, Sharavati R.*	830	Niagara (Horseshoe)	187	Yellowstone (lower)*	308
Japan		**United States**			
Kegon, L. Chuzenji*	350	Alabama		**South America**	
New Zealand		Noccalula Falls	90	**Argentina-Brazil**	
Helena	722	California		Iguazú	269
Sutherland, Arthur R.#	1,904	Feather*	640	**Brazil**	
Europe		Yosemite National Park		Cachoeira da Fumaça*	1,312
Austria		Bridalveil*	620	Paulo Afonso, São Francisco R.	275
Gastein#	487	Illilouette*	370	**Colombia**	
Krimml#	1,246	Nevada, Merced R.*	594	Tequendama, Bogota R.*	482
France		Ribbon**	1,612	**Ecuador**	
Gavarnie*	1,385	Silver Strand, Meadow		Agoyan, Pastaza R.*	200
Great Britain		Brook**	574	**Guyana**	
Scotland		Vernal, Merced R.*	317	Kaieteur, Potaro R.	741
Glomach	370	Yosemite#**	2,425	King George VI, Kamarang R.	1,600
Wales		Colorado		Marina, Ipobe R.#	500
Pistyll Rhaeadr	240	Seven Falls, S. Cheyenne		**Venezuela**	
Italy		Creek#	300	Angel#*	3,212
Toce (C)	470	Hawaii		Cuquenan	2,000
		Akaka, Kolekole Str.	420		
		Idaho			
		Shoshone, Snake R.**	212		

Latitude, Longitude, and Altitude of U.S. and Canadian Cities

Source: U.S. geographic positions, U.S. altitudes provided by Geological Survey, U.S. Dept. of the Interior. Canadian geographic positions and altitudes provided by Natural Resources Canada.

City, state/province	Lat. N °	'	"	Long. W °	'	"	Elev. (ft)	City, state/province	Lat. N °	'	"	Long. W °	'	"	Elev. (ft)
Abilene, TX	32	26	55	99	43	58	1,718	Belleville, Ont.	44	14	0	77	21	0	320
Akron, OH	41	4	53	81	31	9	1,050	Bellingham, WA	48	45	35	122	29	13	100
Albany, NY	42	39	9	73	45	24	20	Berkeley, CA	37	52	18	122	16	18	150
Albuquerque, NM	35	5	4	106	39	2	4,955	Billings, MT	45	47	0	108	30	0	3,124
Alert, NU	82	30	0	62	22	0	100	Biloxi, MS	30	23	45	88	53	7	25
Allentown, PA	40	36	30	75	29	26	350	Binghamton, NY	42	5	55	75	55	6	865
Amarillo, TX	35	13	19	101	49	51	3,685	Birmingham, AL	33	31	14	86	48	9	600
Anchorage, AK	61	13	5	149	54	1	101	Bismarck, ND	46	48	30	100	47	0	1,700
Ann Arbor, MI	42	16	15	83	43	35	880	Bloomington, IL	40	29	3	88	59	37	829
Asheville, NC	35	36	3	82	33	15	2,134	Boise, ID	43	36	49	116	12	9	2,730
Ashland, KY	38	28	42	82	38	17	558	Boston, MA	42	21	30	71	3	37	20
Atlanta, GA	33	44	56	84	23	17	1,050	Bowling Green, KY	36	59	25	86	26	37	510
Atlantic City, NJ	39	21	51	74	25	24	8	Brandon, Man.	49	54	35	99	57	03	1,343
Augusta, GA	33	28	15	81	58	30	414	Brantford, Ont.	43	08	0	80	16	0	815
Augusta, ME	44	18	38	69	46	48	45	Brattleboro, VT	42	51	3	72	33	30	240
Austin, TX	30	16	1	97	44	34	501	Bridgeport, CT	41	10	1	73	12	19	10
Bakersfield, CA	35	22	24	119	1	4	408	Brockton, MA	42	5	0	71	1	8	112
Baltimore, MD	39	17	25	76	36	45	100	Buffalo, NY	42	53	11	78	52	43	585
Bangor, ME	44	48	4	68	46	42	158	Burlington, Ont.	43	23	10	79	50	15	640
Baton Rouge, LA	30	27	2	91	9	16	53	Burlington, VT	44	28	33	73	12	45	113
Battle Creek, MI	42	19	16	85	10	47	820	Butte, MT	46	0	14	112	32	2	5,549
Bay City, MI	43	35	40	83	53	20	595	Calgary, Alta.	51	03	0	114	05	0	3,557
Beaumont, TX	30	5	9	94	6	6	20	Cambridge, MA	42	22	30	71	6	22	30

City, state/province	Lat. N °	′	″	Long. W °	′	″	Elev. (ft)
Canton, OH	40	47	56	81	22	43	1,100
Carson City, NV	39	9	50	119	45	59	4,730
Cedar Rapids, IA	42	0	30	91	38	38	730
Central Islip, NY	40	47	26	73	12	8	88
Champaign, IL	40	6	59	88	14	36	740
Charleston, SC	32	46	35	79	55	52	118
Charleston, WV	38	20	59	81	37	58	606
Charlotte, NC	35	13	37	80	50	36	850
Charlottetown, P.E.I.	46	14	25	63	08	05	160
Chattanooga, TN	35	2	44	85	18	35	685
Cheyenne, WY	41	8	24	104	49	11	6,067
Chicago, IL	41	51	0	87	39	0	596
Churchill, Man.	58	43	30	94	07	0	94
Cincinnati, OH	39	9	43	84	27	25	683
Cleveland, OH	41	29	58	81	41	44	690
Colorado Springs, CO	38	50	2	104	49	15	6,008
Columbia, MO.	38	57	6	92	20	2	758
Columbia, SC.	34	0	2	81	2	6	314
Columbus, GA.	32	27	39	84	59	16	300
Columbus, OH.	39	57	40	82	59	56	800
Concord, NH.	43	12	29	71	32	17	288
Corpus Christi, TX	27	48	1	97	23	46	35
Dallas, TX.	32	47	0	96	48	0	463
Dawson, Yukon	64	03	45	139	25	50	1,214
Dayton, OH.	39	45	32	84	11	30	750
Daytona Beach, FL.	29	12	38	81	1	23	10
Decatur, IL.	39	50	25	88	57	17	670
Denver, CO.	39	44	21	104	59	3	5,260
Des Moines, IA.	41	36	2	93	36	32	803
Detroit, MI.	42	19	53	83	2	45	585
Dodge City, KS.	37	45	10	100	1	0	2,550
Dubuque, IA	42	30	2	90	39	52	620
Duluth, MN	46	47	0	92	6	23	610
Durham, NC	35	59	38	78	53	56	394
Eau Claire, WI	44	48	41	91	29	54	850
Edmonton, Alta.	53	33	0	113	28	0	2,200
Elizabeth, NJ	40	39	50	74	12	40	38
El Paso, TX.	31	45	31	106	29	11	3,695
Enid, OK.	36	23	44	97	52	41	1,246
Erie, PA	42	7	45	80	5	7	650
Eugene, OR.	44	3	8	123	5	8	419
Eureka, CA.	40	48	8	124	9	45	44
Evansville, IN	37	58	29	87	33	21	388
Fairbanks, AK.	64	50	16	147	42	59	440
Fall River, MA.	41	42	5	71	9	20	200
Fargo, ND.	46	52	38	96	47	22	900
Flagstaff, AZ.	35	11	53	111	39	2	6,900
Flint, MI.	43	0	45	83	41	15	750
Ft. Smith, AR.	35	23	9	94	23	54	446
Ft. Wayne, IN.	41	7	50	85	7	44	781
Ft. Worth, TX.	32	43	31	97	19	14	670
Fredericton, N.B.	45	56	43	66	40	0	67
Fresno, CA.	36	44	52	119	46	17	296
Gadsden, AL.	34	0	51	86	0	24	554
Gainesville, FL.	29	39	5	82	19	30	183
Gallup, NM.	35	31	41	108	44	31	6,508
Galveston, TX.	29	18	4	94	47	51	10
Gary, IN	41	35	36	87	20	47	600
Grand Junction, CO	39	3	50	108	33	0	4,597
Grand Rapids, MI	42	57	48	85	40	5	610
Great Falls, MT.	47	30	1	111	18	0	3,334
Green Bay, WI	44	31	9	88	1	11	594
Greensboro, NC	36	4	21	79	47	32	770
Greenville, SC	34	51	9	82	23	39	966
Guelph, Ont.	43	33	0	80	15	0	1,100
Gulfport, MS	30	22	2	89	5	34	25
Halifax, N.S.	44	52	0	63	43	0	477
Hamilton, OH.	39	23	58	84	33	41	600
Hamilton, Ont.	43	14	0	79	57	0	780
Harrisburg, PA.	40	16	25	76	53	5	320
Hartford, CT	41	45	49	72	41	8	40
Helena, MT.	46	35	34	112	2	7	4,090
Hilo, HI	19	43	47	155	5	24	38
Honolulu, HI	21	18	25	157	51	30	18
Houston, TX	29	45	47	95	21	47	40
Huntsville, AL	34	43	49	86	35	10	641
Indianapolis, IN	39	46	6	86	9	29	717
Iowa City, IA	41	39	40	91	31	48	685
Jackson, MI	42	14	45	84	24	5	940
Jackson, MS.	32	17	55	90	11	5	294
Jacksonville, FL	30	19	55	81	39	21	12
Jersey City, NJ	40	43	41	74	4	41	83
Johnstown, PA	40	19	36	78	55	20	1200
Joplin, MO.	37	5	3	94	30	47	990
Juneau, AK.	58	18	7	134	25	11	50
Kalamazoo, MI.	42	17	30	85	35	14	755
Kansas City, KS.	39	6	51	94	37	38	750
Kansas City, MO.	39	5	59	94	34	42	740

City, state/province	Lat. N °	′	″	Long. W °	′	″	Elev. (ft)
Kenosha, WI	42	35	5	87	49	16	610
Key West, FL	24	33	19	81	46	58	8
Kingston, Ont.	44	18	0	76	28	0	305
Kitchener, Ont.	43	27	0	80	29	0	1,040
Knoxville, TN	35	57	38	83	55	15	889
Lafayette, IN.	40	25	0	86	52	31	567
Lancaster, PA.	40	2	16	76	18	21	368
Lansing, MI.	42	43	57	84	33	20	830
Laredo, TX.	27	30	22	99	30	26	414
Las Vegas, NV.	36	10	30	115	8	11	2,000
Lawrence, MA.	42	42	25	71	9	49	50
Lethbridge, Alta.	49	42	0	112	49	0	3,047
Lexington, KY.	37	59	19	84	28	40	955
Lihue, HI.	21	58	52	159	22	16	206
Lima, OH.	40	44	33	84	6	19	875
Lincoln, NE.	40	48	0	96	40	0	1,150
Little Rock, AR	34	44	47	92	17	22	350
London, Ont.	42	59	0	81	14	0	875
Los Angeles, CA.	34	3	8	118	14	34	330
Louisville, KY.	38	15	15	85	45	34	462
Lowell, MA.	42	38	0	71	19	0	102
Lubbock, TX	33	34	40	101	51	17	3,195
Macon, GA	32	50	26	83	37	57	400
Madison, WI	43	4	23	89	24	4	863
Manchester, NH	42	59	44	71	27	19	175
Marshall, TX.	32	32	41	94	22	2	410
Medicine Hat, Alta.	50	03	0	110	40	0	2,352
Memphis, TN.	35	8	58	90	2	56	254
Meriden, CT.	41	32	17	72	48	27	190
Miami, FL.	25	46	26	80	11	38	11
Milwaukee, WI.	43	2	20	87	54	23	634
Minneapolis, MN.	44	58	48	93	15	49	815
Minot, ND.	48	13	57	101	17	45	1,555
Mobile, AL.	30	41	39	88	2	35	16
Moncton, N.B.	46	06	57	64	48	11	232
Montgomery, AL.	32	22	0	86	18	0	250
Montpelier, VT.	44	15	36	72	34	33	525
Montréal, Que.	45	31	0	73	39	0	221
Moose Jaw, Sask.	50	24	0	105	32	0	1,892
Muncie, IN	40	11	36	85	23	11	952
Nashville, TN	36	9	57	86	47	4	440
Natchez, MS.	31	33	37	91	24	11	230
Newark, NJ.	40	44	8	74	10	22	95
New Britain, CT	41	39	40	72	46	48	200
New Haven, CT	41	18	29	72	55	43	40
New Orleans, LA	29	57	16	90	4	30	11
New York, NY.	40	42	51	74	0	23	55
Niagara Falls, Ont.	43	06	0	79	04	0	589
Nome, AK.	64	30	4	165	24	23	25
Norfolk, VA.	36	50	48	76	17	8	10
North Bay, Ont.	46	19	0	79	28	0	1,200
Oakland, CA.	37	48	16	122	16	11	42
Ogden, UT.	41	13	23	111	58	23	4,299
Oklahoma City, OK.	35	28	3	97	30	58	1,195
Omaha, NE.	41	15	31	95	56	15	1,040
Orlando, FL.	28	32	17	81	22	46	106
Ottawa, Ont.	45	16	0	75	45	0	382
Paducah, KY.	37	5	0	88	36	0	345
Pasadena, CA.	34	8	52	118	8	37	865
Paterson, NJ.	40	55	0	74	10	20	70
Pensacola, FL.	30	25	16	87	13	1	32
Peoria, IL.	40	41	37	89	35	20	470
Peterborough, Ont.	44	18	0	78	19	0	628
Philadelphia, PA.	39	57	8	75	9	51	40
Phoenix, AZ	33	26	54	112	4	24	1,090
Pierre, SD.	44	22	6	100	21	2	1,484
Pittsburgh, PA.	40	26	26	79	59	46	770
Pittsfield, MA.	42	27	0	73	14	45	1,039
Pocatello, ID.	43	52	17	112	26	41	4,464
Pt. Arthur, TX.	29	53	55	93	55	43	10
Portland, ME.	43	39	41	70	15	21	25
Portland, OR.	45	31	25	122	40	30	50
Portsmouth, NH.	43	4	18	70	45	47	21
Portsmouth, VA.	36	50	7	76	17	55	10
Prince Rupert, B.C.	54	19	0	130	19	0	116
Providence, RI	41	49	26	71	24	48	80
Provo, UT.	40	14	2	111	39	28	4,549
Pueblo, CO.	38	15	16	104	36	31	4,662
Québec City, Que.	46	49	0	71	13	0	244
Racine, WI.	42	43	34	87	46	58	630
Raleigh, NC	35	46	19	78	38	20	350
Rapid City, SD	44	4	50	103	13	50	3,247
Reading, PA.	40	20	8	75	55	38	266
Regina, Sask.	50	27	0	104	37	0	1,894

City, state/province	Lat. N °	′	″	Long. W °	′	″	Elev. (ft)
Reno, NV	39	31	47	119	48	46	4,498
Richmond, VA.	37	33	13	77	27	38	190
Roanoke, VA.	37	16	15	79	56	30	940
Rochester, MN	44	1	18	92	28	11	990
Rochester, NY	43	9	17	77	36	57	515
Rockford, IL	42	16	16	89	5	38	715
Sacramento, CA	38	34	54	121	29	36	20
Saginaw, MI	43	25	10	83	57	3	595
St. Catharines, Ont.	43	10	0	79	15	0	321
St. Cloud, MN	45	33	39	94	9	44	1,040
St. John, N.B.	45	15	33	66	02	20	357
St. John's, Nfld.	47	34	0	52	44	0	461
St. Joseph, MO.	39	46	7	94	50	47	850
St. Louis, MO	38	37	38	90	11	52	455
St. Paul, MN.	44	56	40	93	5	35	780
St. Petersburg, FL	27	46	14	82	40	46	44
Salem, OR	44	56	35	123	2	2	154
Salina, KS.	38	50	25	97	36	40	1,225
Salt Lake City, UT.	40	45	39	111	53	25	4,266
San Antonio, TX	29	25	26	98	29	36	650
San Bernardino, CA	34	6	30	117	17	20	1,200
San Diego, CA	32	42	55	117	9	23	40
San Francisco, CA	37	46	30	122	25	6	63
San Jose, CA	37	20	22	121	53	38	87
San Juan, P.R.	18	28	6	66	6	22	8
Santa Barbara, CA	34	25	15	119	41	50	50
Santa Cruz, CA.	36	58	27	122	1	47	20
Santa Fe, NM	35	41	13	105	56	14	6,989
Sarasota, FL	27	20	10	82	31	51	27
Saskatoon, Sask.	52	07	0	106	38	0	1,653
Sault Ste. Marie, Ont.	46	31	0	84	20	0	630
Savannah, GA	32	5	0	81	6	0	42
Schenectady, NY	42	48	51	73	56	24	245
Seattle, WA.	47	36	23	122	19	51	350
Sheboygan, WI.	43	45	3	87	42	52	630
Sherbrooke, Que.	45	24	0	71	54	0	792
Sheridan, WY	44	47	50	106	57	20	3,742
Shreveport, LA	32	31	30	93	45	0	209
Sioux City, IA	42	30	0	96	24	0	1,117
Sioux Falls, SD	43	32	48	96	43	48	1,442
South Bend, IN	41	41	0	86	15	0	725
Spartanburg, SC.	34	56	58	81	55	56	816
Spokane, WA	47	39	32	117	25	30	2,000
Springfield, IL	39	48	6	89	38	37	610
Springfield, MA	42	6	5	72	35	25	70
Springfield, MO.	37	12	55	93	17	53	1,300
Springfield, OH.	39	55	27	83	48	32	1,000
Stamford, CT	41	3	12	73	32	21	35
Steubenville, OH.	40	22	11	80	38	3	1,060
Stockton, CA.	37	57	28	121	17	23	15
Sudbury, Ont.	46	31	0	80	54	0	1,140
Superior, WI	46	43	15	92	6	14	642
Sydney, N.S.	46	09	0	60	11	0	203
Syracuse, NY	43	2	53	76	8	52	400
Tacoma, WA.	47	15	11	122	26	35	380
Tallahassee, FL	30	26	17	84	16	51	188
Tampa, FL	27	56	50	82	27	31	48
Terre Haute, IN.	39	28	0	87	24	50	501
Texarkana, TX	33	25	30	94	2	51	324
Thunder Bay, Ont.	48	24	0	89	19	0	653
Timmins, Ont.	48	28	0	81	20	0	967
Toledo, OH.	41	39	50	83	33	19	615
Topeka, KS.	39	2	54	95	40	40	1,000
Toronto, Ont.	43	37	39	79	23	46	251
Trenton, NJ	40	13	1	74	44	36	54
Trois-Rivières, Que.	46	21	0	72	33	0	198
Troy, NY	42	43	42	73	41	32	35
Tucson, AZ	32	13	18	110	55	33	2,390
Tulsa, OK	36	9	14	95	59	33	804
Urbana, IL	40	6	38	88	12	26	725
Utica, NY	43	6	3	75	13	59	415
Vancouver, B.C.	49	15	0	123	7	0	14
Victoria, B.C.	48	26	0	123	22	0	63
Waco, TX	31	32	57	97	8	47	405
Walla Walla, WA.	46	3	53	118	20	31	1,000
Washington, DC	38	53	42	77	2	12	25
Waterloo, IA	42	29	34	92	20	34	850
West Palm Beach, FL	26	42	54	80	3	13	21
Wheeling, WV.	40	3	50	80	43	16	672
Whitehorse, Yukon	60	43	0	135	03	0	2,305
White Plains, NY.	41	2	2	73	45	48	220
Wichita, KS.	37	41	32	97	20	14	1,305
Wilkes-Barre, PA	41	14	45	75	52	54	550
Wilmington, DE.	39	44	45	75	32	49	100
Wilmington, NC.	34	13	32	77	56	42	50
Windsor, Ont.	42	18	0	83	01	0	622
Winnipeg, Man.	49	54	39	97	14	36	783
Winston-Salem, NC	36	5	59	80	14	40	912
Worcester, MA	42	15	45	71	48	10	480
Yakima, WA	46	36	8	120	30	17	1,066
Yellowknife, N.W.T.	62	27	20	114	21	0	675
Youngstown, OH	41	5	59	80	38	59	861
Yuma, AZ	32	43	31	114	37	25	160
Zanesville, OH	39	56	25	82	0	48	710

Latitude and Longitude of World Cities

Source: National Imagery Mapping Agency, U.S. Dept. of Defense

City, country	Lat. °	′	Long. °	′
Athens, Greece	37	59 N	23	44 E
Bangkok, Thailand	13	45 N	100	31 E
Beijing, China	39	56 N	116	24 E
Berlin, Germany	52	31 N	13	25 E
Bogotá, Colombia	04	36 N	74	05 W
Buenos Aires, Argentina	34	36 S	58	28 W
Cairo, Egypt	30	03 N	31	15 E
Jakarta, Indonesia	06	10 S	106	48 E
Jerusalem, Israel	31	46 N	35	14 E
Johannesburg, South Africa	26	12 S	28	05 E
Kathmandu, Nepal	27	43 N	85	19 E
Kiev, Ukraine	50	26 N	30	31 E
London, UK (Greenwich)	51	30 N	00	00
Manila, Philippines	14	35 N	121	00 E
Mexico City, Mexico	19	24 N	99	09 W
Moscow, Russia	55	45 N	37	35 E
Mumbai (Bombay), India	18	58 N	72	50 E
New Delhi, India	28	36 N	77	12 E
Panama City, Panama	08	58 N	79	32 W
Paris, France	48	52 N	02	20 E
Quito, Ecuador	00	13 S	78	30 W
Rio de Janeiro, Brazil	22	43 S	43	13 W
Rome, Italy	41	53 N	12	30 E
Santiago, Chile	33	27 S	70	40 W
Seoul, South Korea	37	34 N	127	00 E
Sydney, Australia	33	53 S	151	12 E
Tehran, Iran	35	40 N	51	26 E
Tokyo, Japan	35	42 N	139	46 E
Warsaw, Poland	52	15 N	21	00 E
Wellington, New Zealand	41	18 S	174	47 E

Highest and Lowest Continental Altitudes

Source: National Geographic Society

Continent	Highest point	Elev. (ft)	Continent	Lowest point	Ft below sea level
Asia	Mount Everest, Nepal-Tibet	29,035	Antarctica	Bentley Subglacial Trench	8,327[1]
South America	Mount Aconcagua, Argentina	22,834	Asia	Dead Sea, Israel-Jordan	1,348
North America	Mount McKinley, Alaska	20,320	Africa	Lake Assal, Djibouti	512
Africa	Kilimanjaro, Tanzania	19,341	North America	Death Valley, California	282
Europe	Mount Elbrus, Russia	18,510	South America	Valdes Peninsula, Argentina	131
Antarctica	Vinson Massif	16,066	Europe	Caspian Sea, Azerbaijan	92
Australia	Mount Kosciusko, New South Wales	7,310	Australia	Lake Eyre, South Australia	52

(1) Estimated level of the continental floor. Lower points that have yet to be discovered may exist further beneath the ice.

RELIGION

Memberships of Religious Groups in the U.S.

Source: *2011 Yearbook of American & Canadian Churches*, © National Council of Churches in the U.S.A., except where indicated. Figures are the latest available and generally are based on reports made by officials of each group. Figures from other sources may vary. Reporting practices vary from one denomination to another. Many groups keep careful records; others only estimate. Not all groups report annually. Membership figures, for the most part, are inclusive and do not refer solely to full communicants or confirmed members. Groups reporting fewer than 5,000 members or providing no data in recent years are not included.

Religious group (houses of worship)	Members
Adventist Churches	
Advent Christian Ch. (294)	23,629
Seventh-day Adventist Ch. (4,892)	1,043,606
Agnostics	38,695,319[1]
American Catholic Ch. (Syro-Antiochian) (100)	33,000[1]
American Evangelical Christian Chs. (192)	17,400
Anglo-Lutheran Catholic Church (18)	11,000
Apostolic Catholic Church (12)	5,737
Apostolic Catholic Orthodox Ch. (11)	8,500
Apostolic Christian Churches of America (90)	12,850
Apostolic Episcopal Church (200)	12,000
Apostolic Orthodox Catholic Ch. of N.A. (25)	15,900
Atheists	1,328,803[1]
Baha'i Faith	525,046[1]
Baptist Churches	
Alliance of Baptists (127)	65,000
American Baptist Assn. (1,600)	100,000
American Baptist Chs. in the U.S.A. (5,402)	1,310,505
Baptist Bible Fellowship Intl. (4,200)	115,000
Baptist Missionary Assn. of America (1,287)	126,056
Conservative Baptist Assn. of America (1,200)	200,000
Converge Worldwide (formerly Baptist Gen. Conf.) (1,100)	16,000
Free Will Baptists, National Assn. of (2,369)	185,798
General Baptists, General Assn. of (900)	45,721
Natl. Baptist Convention, U.S.A., Inc. (9,000)	5,000,000
Natl. Baptist Convention of America, Inc.	3,500,000
Natl. Missionary Baptist Conv. of America (280)	449,000[1]
Natl. Primitive Baptist Conv., Inc. (1,565)	600,000
North American Baptist Conference (272)	47,150
Progressive National Baptist Conv. Inc. (1,500)	1,010,000
Regular Baptist Chs., General Assn. of (1,321)	132,700
Separate Baptists in Christ (90)	10,700[1]
Seventh Day Baptist General Conf., USA/Canada (98)	6,300
Southern Baptist Convention (45,010)	16,160,088
Berean Fellowship of Chs. (56)	12,000
Brethren (German Baptists)	
Brethren Ch. (Ashland, OH) (112)	10,227
Church of the Brethren (1,047)	121,781
Brethren in Christ Church (232)	20,739
Buddhists	4,047,598[1]
Calvary Chapel	10,000
Christian and Missionary Alliance (2,021)	432,471
Christian Brethren (Plymouth Brethren) (1,145)	86,000
Christian Church (Disciples of Christ) (3,691)	658,869
Christian Chs. and Chs. of Christ (5,007)	1,174,000[1]
Christian Congregation, Inc. (1,496)	122,181
Christian Union (107)	4,014
Church of Christ	8,000
Church of Christ (Holiness) U.S.A. (148)	11,468
Church of Christ, Scientist (2,206)	848,000[1]
Church of Jesus Christ (Bickertonites) (71)	42,869
Church of the Living God (170)	42,000
Church of the Nazarene (5,063)	645,846
Church of the United Brethren in Christ, USA (200)	20,500
Churches of Christ (13,000)	1,639,495
Churches of Christ in Christian Union (230)	11,234
Churches of God	
Church of God (Anderson, IN) (2,192)	250,202
Church of God (Seventh Day), Denver, CO (210)	11,000
Church of God, Mountain Assembly, Inc. (3,390)	7,000
Church of God by Faith, Inc. (149)	35,000
Church of God of Prophecy (1,860)	89,674
Churches of God (Gen. Conf.) (321)	32,691
Community Churches, Intl. Council of (137)	69,276
Congregational Christian Chs., Natl. Assn. of (432)	65,392
Conservative Congregational Christian Conf. (298)	42,296
Eastern Orthodox Churches	
American Carpatho-Russian Orthodox Greek Catholic Ch.	12,451
Antiochian Orthodox Christian Archdiocese of North America (256)	430,000
Armenian Apostolic Ch., Dioceses of America (63)	65,000
Armenian Apostolic Ch. of America (38)	350,000
Coptic Orthodox Ch. (100)	300,000
Greek Orthodox Archdiocese of America (560)	1,500,000

Religious group (houses of worship)	Members
Malankara Orthodox Syrian Ch., Diocese of America (80)	30,000
Mar Thoma Syrian Ch. of India (80)	43,500
Orthodox Ch. in America (750)	131,000
Patriarchal Parishes of the Russian Orthodox Ch. in the U.S.A. (31)	17,000
Russian Orthodox Ch. Outside of Russia (190)	480,000
Serbian Orthodox Ch. in the U.S.A. and Canada (68)	67,000
Syriac-Greek Antiochian Orthodox Catholic Ch. (207)	20,020
Syrian (Syriac) Orthodox Ch. of Antioch (32)	32,500
Ukrainian Orthodox Ch. of the U.S.A. (118)	50,000
Episcopal Church (6,895)	2,006,343
Ethnic religionists	1,109,997[1]
Evangelical Church (133)	12,475
Evangelical Church Alliance	295,001
Evangelical Congregational Church (139)	17,834
Evangelical Covenant Church (783)	114,283
Evangelical Free Church of America (1,475)	356,000
Fellowship of Grace Brethren Churches (444)	60,400[1]
Friends	
Evangelical Friends Intl.—N.A. Region (284)	38,428
Friends General Conference (832)	32,000
Friends United Meeting (600)	36,302
Philadelphia Yearly Meeting of the Religious Society of Friends (103)	11,511
Religious Society of Friends (Conservative) (1,200)	104,000
Full Gospel Fellowship of Churches and Ministers Intl. (1,273)	432,632
General Church of the New Jerusalem (37)	7,052
Grace Gospel Fellowship (235)	101,000[1]
Hindus	1,478,555[1]
Jains	87,351[1]
Jehovah's Witnesses (13,021):	1,162,686
Jews	6-6.4 mil[2]
Jewish Reconstructionist Federation (100)	(2)
Union for Reform Judaism (1,000)	(2)
Union of Orthodox Jewish Congregations of America (1,500)	(2)
United Synagogue of Conservative Judaism (850)	(2)
Latter-day Saints (Mormons)	
Ch. of Jesus Christ of Latter-day Saints (13,474)	6,058,907
Community of Christ (935)	178,328
Reorg. Ch. of Jesus Christ of Latter-day Saints (1,402)	254,000[1]
Liberal Catholic Church—Province of the United States of America (21)	5,800
Lutheran Churches	
American Assn. of Lutheran Chs. (70)	16,000
Apostolic Lutheran Ch. of America (56)	7,300[1]
Ch. of the Lutheran Brethren of America (106)	13,433
Ch. of the Lutheran Confession (87)	8,390
Evangelical Lutheran Ch. In America (10,348)	4,542,868
Evangelical Lutheran Synod (131)	19,868
Free Lutheran Congregations, Assn. of (280)	44,473
Independent Evangelical Lutheran Chs., Assn. of (35)	7,576
Latvian Evangelical Lutheran Ch. in America (60)	10,950
Lutheran Ch.—Missouri Synod (LCMS) (6,178)	2,312,111
Wisconsin Evangelical Lutheran Synod (1,279)	389,545
Mennonite Churches	
Beachy Amish Mennonite Chs. (201)	11,611
Ch. of God in Christ (Mennonite) (148)	14,672
Fellowship of Evangelical Chs. (45)	7,137
Hutterian Brethren (444)	43,000
Mennonite Brethren Chs., Gen. Conf. of (464)	111,000[1]
Mennonite Ch. USA (920)	104,864
Old Order Amish Ch. (898)	80,820
Old Order (Wisler) Mennonite Ch. (47)	7,100
Methodist Churches	
African Methodist Episcopal Ch. (4,100)	2,500,000
African Methodist Episcopal Zion Ch. (3,393)	1,400,000
Christian Methodist Episcopal Ch. (3,500)	850,000
Evangelical Methodist Ch. (108)	7,348
Free Methodist Ch. of North America (1,053)	75,586
Southern Methodist Ch. (101)	6,000
United Methodist Ch. (33,855)	7,774,931
Wesleyan Ch. (1,716)	139,008

Religious group (houses of worship)	Members
Metropolitan Community Churches, Universal Fellowship of (115).	15,666
Missionary Church (431)	38,206
Moravian Ch. in America (Northern Prov.) (86)	20,508
Muslims.	2,595,000[3]
New Apostolic Church of North America, Natl. Org. of the (298)	36,404
New religionists	1,662,962[1]
Old Catholic Orthodox Church (11)	11,470
Pentecostal Churches	
Apostolic Faith Mission Ch. of God (16).	6,880
Assemblies of God (12,371).	2,914,669
Bible Fellowship Ch. (63)	7,661
Ch. of God (Cleveland, TN) (6,654)	1,076,254
Ch. of God in Christ (15,300)	5,499,875
Ch. of God of Prophecy (1,860)	89,674
Congregational Holiness Ch. (225)	25,000
Elim Assemblies Fellowship (242)	41,400[1]
Intl. Ch. of the Foursquare Gospel (1,875).	353,995
Intl. Pentecostal Holiness Ch. (2,024).	330,054
Open Bible Churches (279)	45,000
Pentecostal Assemblies of the World, Inc. (1,750).	1,500,000
Pentecostal Ch. of God (1,134)	98,579
Pentecostal Free Will Baptist Ch., Inc. (200)	20,000[1]
United House of Prayer (161)	1,632,000[1]
United Pentecostal Ch. Intl. (4,358).	646,304
United Pentecostal Chs. of Christ (62).	7,059
Polish National Catholic Ch. of America (126)	60,000

Religious group (houses of worship)	Members
Presbyterian Churches	
Associate Reformed Presbyterian Ch. (General Synod) (296)	39,681
Cumberland Presbyterian Ch. (643)	65,591
Cumberland Presbyterian Ch. in America (740)	76,500[1]
Evangelical Presbyterian Ch. (207)	89,190
Korean Presbyterian Ch. Abroad (302)	55,000
Orthodox Presbyterian Ch. (271).	29,421
Presbyterian Ch. (U.S.A.) (10,657)	2,770,730
Presbyterian Ch. in America (1,719)	341,210
Reformed Presbyterian Ch. of North America (81) . .	6,641
Reformed Catholic Church (100)	57,000
Reformed Churches	
Christian Reformed Ch. in North America (803)	183,940
Hungarian Reformed Ch. in America (27)	6,000
Netherlands Reformed Congregations (26)	10,080
Protestant Reformed Chs. in America (30)	7,651
Reformed Ch. in America (896)	250,938
United Ch. of Christ (5,287)	1,080,199
Reformed Episcopal Church (149)	15,573
Roman Catholic Church (18,372)	68,503,456
Romanian Orthodox Church in America (32)	9,700
Romanian Orthodox Episcopate of America (64)	10,635
Salvation Army (1,241).	400,055
Shintoists	64,154[1]
Sikhs	285,877[1]
Spiritists	230,479[1]
Taoists (or Daoists)	12,706[1]
Vineyard U.S.A. (556)	189,000
Unitarian Universalist Assn. of Congregations (1,048)	221,367
Zoroastrians	18,048[1]

(1) Source: World Christian Database. (2) About 35% of Jews classify themselves as Reform, 26% as Conservative, 10% as Orthodox, 2% as Reconstructionist, the rest as "just Jewish." Source: Ira M. Sheskin, Univ. of Miami, director, Jewish Demography Project; I. Sheskin and Arnold Dashefsky, "Jewish Population of the United States, 2010," in *Current Jewish Population Reports, No. 2010-11*, pub. by North American Jewish Data Bank, Assn. for Social Scientific Study of Jewry, and Jewish Federations of North America. (3) Source: Pew Research Center.

World Adherents of Religions by Continental Area, Mid-2010

Source: *2011 Encyclopædia Britannica Book of the Year.* All figures are estimates.

Religion (no. of countries)	Africa	Asia	Europe	Latin America	Northern America	Oceania	World
Baha'is (221)	2,178,000	3,433,000	142,000	902,000	572,000	110,000	7,337,000
Buddhists (150)	258,000	455,412,000	1,777,000	760,000	3,845,000	573,000	462,625,000
Chinese folk religionists (119)	133,000	455,762,000	438,000	189,000	781,000	101,000	454,404,000
Christians (232)	488,880,000	350,822,000	584,809,000	544,592,000	283,308,000	28,205,000	2,280,616,000
Roman Catholics (232)	170,484,000	139,526,000	276,688,000	470,622,000	84,400,000	8,941,000	1,150,661,000
Protestants (231) . . .	136,631,000	88,765,000	67,710,000	58,769,000	60,206,000	7,714,000	419,795,000
Independents (229). . . .	98,239,000	146,423,000	10,839,000	42,669,000	71,227,000	1,271,000	370,668,000
Orthodox (220)	44,507,000	15,832,000	200,620,000	1,038,000	7,262,000	968,000	270,227,000
Anglicans (136)	50,215,000	865,000	26,428,000	865,000	2,795,000	4,883,000	86,051,000
Marginal (217)	3,667,000	3,136,000	4,113,000	11,239,000	11,820,000	668,000	34,643,000
Unaffiliated (226)	25,560,000	4,052,000	25,416,000	6,039,000	53,512,000	4,446,000	119,025,000
Doubly affiliated (174)	*−40,423,000*	*−47,777,000*	*−27,005,000*	*−46,649,000*	*−7,914,000*	*−686,000*	*−170,454,000*
Confucianists (16).	20,200	6,433,000	15,500	490	0	47,600	6,516,790
Ethnic religionists (145)	109,592,000	153,565,000	1,150,000	3,802,000	1,246,000	368,000	269,723,000
Hindus (125).	2,945,000	935,753,000	991,000	789,000	1,867,000	526,000	942,871,000
Jains (19)	95,100	5,056,000	18,800	1,400	102,000	3,200	5,276,500
Jews (139)	134,000	5,980,000	1,914,000	963,000	5,720,000	113,000	14,824,000
Muslims (209).	421,938,820	1,083,354,900	40,174,000	1,599,000	5,598,000	524,000	1,553,188,720
New religionists (119). . .	117,000	59,611,000	364,000	1,744,000	1,747,000	101,000	63,684,000
Shintoists (8).	0	2,700,000	0	7,800	64,200	0	2,772,000
Sikhs (55)	74,000	22,496,000	500,000	6,900	613,000	48,600	23,738,500
Spiritists (55).	2,900	2,100	143,000	13,330,000	247,000	7,600	13,732,600
Taoists (6)	0	8,412,000	0	0	12,700	4,400	8,429,100
Zoroastrians (27)	980	148,000	5,700	0	21,400	2,500	178,580
Other religionists (79) . . .	85,000	245,000	275,000	120,000	690,000	12,000	1,427,000
Nonreligious/agnostic (238)	5,995,000	504,352,000	84,652,000	16,941,410	43,211,700	4,629,100	659,781,210
Atheists (220)	594,000	116,204,000	15,390,000	2,901,000	2,013,000	462,000	137,564,000

Note: Continental areas. Following current UN demographic terminology, which divides the world into the 6 major areas shown. "Asia" is defined here to include the former Soviet Central Asian states, while "Europe" includes all of Russia, extending to the Pacific coast. **Countries.** Figures in parentheses indicate the number of sovereign and nonsovereign countries where the religion or type of belief has a statistically significant following. **Adherents.** As defined in the 1948 Universal Declaration of Human Rights, a person's religion is self-declared. Totals here are enumerated following methodology of the *World Christian Encyclopedia*, 2nd ed. (2001), and *World Christian Trends* (2001), using recent censuses, polls, literature, and other data. Figures may conflict with estimates elsewhere. **Buddhists.** 56% Mahayana, 38% Theravada (Hinayana), 6% Tantrayana (Lamaism). **Chinese folk religionists.** Followers of traditional Chinese religion (may involve worship of local deities, ancestor veneration, Confucian ethics, universism, divination, and Buddhist or Taoist elements, among other beliefs and practices). **Christians.** Followers of Jesus Christ. Unaffiliated Christians profess Christian beliefs but are not named on specific church rolls; Independents consider themselves post-denominational and thus independent from historic, organized mainstream Christianity. Marginal Christians belong to churches that profess Christianity but regard themselves as on the margins of mainstream Christianity; these people include Unitarians, Mormons, Jehovah's Witnesses, and Christian Science adherents. Doubly-affiliated Christians are baptized members of two denominations. **Confucianists.** Non-Chinese followers of Confucius and Confucianism, mostly Koreans in Korea. **Ethnic religionists.** Followers of local, tribal, animistic, or shamanistic religions, generally belonging to a single ethnic group. **Hindus.** 68% Vaishnavites, 27% Shaivites, 2% neo-Hindus and reform Hindus. **Jews.** Adherents of Judaism. **Muslims.** 84% Sunni Muslims, 14% Shia Muslims (Shi'ites), 2% other schools. **New religionists.** Followers of Asian 20th-cent. New Religions, New Religious movements, radical new crisis religions, and non-Christian syncretistic mass religions. **Other religionists.** Including various small religions, quasi-religions, parareligions, religious or mystic systems, religious or semireligious brotherhoods, and the like.

Episcopal Church Liturgical Colors and Calendar, 2011-15

The most common liturgical colors in the Episcopal Church are: **White**—Christmas Day through First Sunday after Epiphany; Maundy Thursday (as an alternative to crimson at the Eucharist); from the Vigil of Easter to the Day of Pentecost (Whitsunday); Trinity Sunday; Feasts of the Lord (except Holy Cross Day); the Confession of St. Peter; the Conversion of St. Paul; St. Joseph; St. Mary Magdalene; St. Mary the Virgin; St. Michael and All Angels; All Saints' Day; St. John the Evangelist; memorials of other saints who were not martyred; Independence Day and Thanksgiving Day; weddings and funerals. **Red**—the Day of Pentecost; Holy Cross Day; feasts of apostles and evangelists (except those previously mentioned); feasts and memorials of martyrs (including Holy Innocents' Day). **Violet**—Advent and Lent. **Crimson** or oxblood (dark red)—Holy Week. **Green**—the seasons after Epiphany and after Pentecost. **Black**—optional alternative for funerals and Good Friday.

The days of fasting are Ash Wednesday and Good Friday. Other days of special devotion (penitence) include the 40 days of Lent. Ember Days are days of prayer for the church's ministry. They fall on the Wednesday, Friday, and Saturday after the first Sunday in Lent, the Day of Pentecost, Holy Cross Day, and Dec. 13. Rogation Days, the three days before Ascension Day, are days of prayer for God's blessing on the crops, on commerce and industry, and for conservation of the Earth's resources.

Days, etc.	2011	2012	2013	2014	2015
Golden Number	17	18	19	1	2
Sunday Letter	B	AG	F	E	D
Sundays after Epiphany	9	7	5	8	6
Ash Wednesday	Mar. 9	Feb. 22	Feb. 13	Mar. 5	Feb. 18
First Sunday in Lent	Mar. 13	Feb. 26	Feb. 17	Mar. 9	Feb. 22
Passion/Palm Sunday	Apr. 17	Apr. 1	Mar. 24	Apr. 13	Mar. 29
Good Friday	Apr. 22	Apr. 6	Mar. 29	Apr. 18	Apr. 3
Easter Day	Apr. 24	Apr. 8	Mar. 31	Apr. 20	Apr. 5
Ascension Day	June 2	May 17	May 9	May 29	May 14
The Day of Pentecost	June 12	May 27	May 19	June 8	May 24
Trinity Sunday	June 19	June 3	May 26	June 15	May 31
Numbered Proper of 2 Pentecost	#8	#5	#4	#7	#5
First Sunday of Advent	Nov. 27	Dec. 2	Dec. 1	Nov. 30	Nov. 29

Greek Orthodox Movable Ecclesiastical Dates, 2011-15

Feast days and fasting days are determined annually on the basis of the date of Holy Pascha (Easter). This ecclesiastical cycle begins with the first day of the Triodion and ends with the Sunday of All Saints, a total of 18 weeks.

Days, etc.	2011	2012	2013	2014	2015
Triodion begins	Feb. 13	Feb. 5	Feb. 24	Feb. 9	Feb. 1
1st Saturday of Souls	Feb. 26	Feb. 18	Mar. 9	Feb. 22	Feb. 14
Meat Fare	Feb. 27	Feb. 19	Mar. 10	Feb. 23	Feb. 15
2nd Saturday of Souls	Mar. 5	Feb. 25	Mar. 16	Mar. 1	Feb. 21
Lent begins	Mar. 7	Feb. 27	Mar. 18	Mar. 3	Feb. 23
St. Theodore—3rd Saturday of Souls	Mar. 12	Mar. 3	Mar. 23	Mar. 8	Feb. 28
Sunday of Orthodoxy	Mar. 13	Mar. 4	Mar. 24	Mar. 9	Mar. 1
Saturday of Lazarus	Apr. 16	Apr. 7	Apr. 27	Apr. 12	Apr. 4
Palm Sunday	Apr. 17	Apr. 8	Apr. 28	Apr. 13	Apr. 5
Holy (Good) Friday	Apr. 22	Apr. 13	May 3	Apr. 18	Apr. 10
Western Easter	Apr. 24	Apr. 8	Mar. 31	Apr. 20	Apr. 5
Orthodox Easter	Apr. 24	Apr. 15	May 5	Apr. 20	Apr. 12
Ascension	June 2	May 24	June 13	May 29	May 21
Saturday of Souls	June 11	June 2	June 22	June 7	May 30
Pentecost	June 12	June 3	June 23	June 8	May 31
All Saints	June 19	June 10	June 30	June 15	June 7
Fast of Holy Apostles (first day)	June 20	June 11	—	June 16	June 8

Important Islamic Dates, 1432-1436 AH (2010-15)

The Islamic calendar is a strict lunar calendar reckoned from the year of the Hijra (Anno Hegirae, or AH)—Muhammad's flight from Mecca to Medina, in 622 CE. Each year consists of 12 lunar months of 29 or 30 days beginning and ending with each new moon's visible crescent. Common years have 354 days; leap years have 355 days. Some Muslim countries employ a conventionalized calendar with the leap day added to the last month, Dhûl Hijjah, but for religious purposes the leap date is taken into account by tracking each new moon sighting. Holy days begin at sunset on the day previous to the day cited. The actual dates of holy days may also vary slightly from what is cited below, depending on the locality and the times of actual moon sightings as determined by different authorities.

Day (date)	(1432) 2010-11	(1433) 2011-12	(1434) 2012-13	(1435) 2013-14	(1436) 2014-15
New Year's Day (Muharram 1)	Dec. 7, 2010	Nov. 26, 2011	Nov. 15, 2012	Nov. 4, 2013	Oct. 25 2014
Ashura (Muharram 10)	Dec. 16, 2010	Dec. 5, 2011	Nov. 24, 2012	Nov. 13, 2013	Nov. 3, 2014
Mawlid (Rabi'l 12)	Feb. 15, 2011	Feb. 4, 2012	Jan. 24, 2013	Jan. 13, 2014	Jan. 3, 2015
Ramadan begins (Ramadan 1)	Aug. 1, 2011	July 20, 2012	July 9, 2013	June 28, 2014	June 18, 2015
Eid al-Fitr (Shawwal 1)	Aug. 30, 2011	Aug. 19, 2012	Aug. 8, 2013	July 29, 2014	July 17, 2015
Eid al-Adha (Dhûl-Hijjah 10)	Nov. 6, 2011	Oct. 26, 2012	Oct. 15, 2013	Oct. 4, 2014	Sept. 23, 2015

Jewish Holy Days, Festivals, and Fasts, 5771-5775 (2010-15)

The Jewish calendar consists of 12 lunar months, alternating between 29 and 30 days. It is lunisolar, and adjusts for the solar cycle by adding an extra month (Adar II) in the 3rd, 6th, 8th, 11th, 14th, 17th, and 19th years of a 19-year cycle. The calendar starts on the day of Creation, reckoned in the 2nd-3rd cent. BCE as Tishrei 1, 3,761 years before the common era.

The religious calendar begins with the month Nisan, from which all other months are counted, and the civil calendar with Tishrei. The months are 1) Nisan; 2) Iyar; 3) Sivan; 4) Tammuz; 5) Av (also Abh); 6) Elul; 7) Tishrei; 8) Cheshvan (also Marcheshvan); 9) Kislev; 10) Tevet (also Tebeth); 11) Shevat (also Shebhat); 12) Adar; 12a) Adar Sheni (II), added in leap years. The names are Aramaic versions of the Babylonian months, adopted during the Jews' exile in Babylon in the 4th cent. BCE. Rosh Hashanah, the New Year, begins on Tishrei 1 (Sept.-Oct.). Yom Kippur is the holiest day of the year. All holidays listed below begin at sunset on the previous day, except where noted.

Holiday	Date on Jewish cal.	(5771) 2010-11		(5772) 2011-12		(5773) 2012-13		(5774) 2013-14		(5775) 2014-15	
Rosh Hashanah (New Year)	Tishrei 1	Sept. 9	Thu.	Sept. 29	Thu.	Sept. 17	Mon.	Sept. 5	Thu.	Sept. 25	Thu.
	Tishrei 2	Sept. 10	Fri.	Sept. 30	Fri.	Sept. 18	Tue.	Sept. 6	Fri.	Sept. 26	Fri.
Fast of Gedalya[1]	Tishrei 3	Sept. 12	Sun.*	Oct. 2	Sun.*	Sept. 19	Wed.	Sept. 8	Sun.*	Sept. 28	Sun.*
Yom Kippur (Day of Atonement). .	Tishrei 10	Sept. 18	Sat.	Oct. 8	Sat.	Sept. 26	Wed.	Sept. 14	Sat.	Oct. 4	Sat.
Sukkot.	Tishrei 15	Sept. 23	Thu.	Oct. 13	Thu.	Oct. 1	Mon.	Sept. 19	Thu.	Oct. 9	Thu.
	Tishrei 21	Sept. 29	Wed.	Oct. 19	Wed.	Oct. 7	Sun.	Sept. 25	Wed.	Oct. 15	Wed.
Shemini Atzeret	Tishrei 22	Sept. 30	Thu.	Oct. 20	Thu.	Oct. 8	Mon.	Sept. 26	Thu.	Oct. 16	Thu.
Simchat Torah	Tishrei 23	Oct. 1	Fri.	Oct. 21	Fri.	Oct. 9	Tue.	Sept. 27	Fri.	Oct. 17	Fri.
Hanukkah	Kislev 25	Dec. 2	Thu.	Dec. 21	Wed.	Dec. 9	Sun.	Nov. 28	Thu.	Dec. 17	Wed.
	Tevet 2 or 3	Dec. 9	Thu.	Dec. 28	Wed.	Dec. 16	Sun.	Dec. 5	Thu.	Dec. 24	Wed.
Fast of the 10th of Tevet[1]	Tevet 10	Dec. 17	Fri.	Jan. 5	Thu.	Dec. 23	Sun.	Dec. 13	Fri.	Jan. 1	Thu.
Tu B'Shevat	Shevat 15	Jan. 20	Thu.	Feb. 8	Wed.	Jan. 26	Sat.	Jan. 16	Thu.	Feb. 4	Wed.
Ta'anis Esther (Fast of Esther)[1] . .	Adar 13	Mar. 17	Thu.*	Mar. 7	Wed.	Feb. 21	Thu.*	Mar. 13	Thu.	Mar. 4	Wed.
Purim	Adar 14	Mar. 20	Sun.	Mar. 8	Thu.	Feb. 24	Sun.	Mar. 16	Sun.*	Mar. 5	Thu.
Pesach (Passover)	Nisan 15	Apr. 19	Tue.	Apr. 7	Sat.	Mar. 26	Tue.	Apr. 15	Tue.	Apr. 4	Sat.
	Nisan 22	Apr. 26	Tue.	Apr. 14	Sat.	Apr. 2	Tue.	Apr. 22	Tue.	Apr. 11	Sat.
Lag B'Omer	Iyar 18	May 22	Sun.	May 10	Thu.	Apr. 28	Sun.	May 18	Sun.	May 7	Thu.
Shavuot (Pentecost)	Sivan 6	June 8	Wed.	May 27	Sun.	May 15	Wed.	June 4	Wed.	May 24	Sun.
	Sivan 7	June 9	Thu.	May 28	Mon.	May 16	Thu.	June 5	Thu.	May 25	Mon.
Fast of the 17th Day of Tammuz[1]	Tammuz 17	July 19	Tue.	July 8	Sun.	June 25	Tue.	July 15	Tue.	July 5	Sun.*
Fast of the 9th Day of Av	Av 9	Aug. 9	Tue.	July 29	Sun.	July 16	Tue.	Aug. 5	Tue.	July 26	Sun.*

*Date changed to avoid Sabbath. (1) "Minor fasts" begin at dawn.

Ash Wednesday and Easter Sunday (Western Churches), 1901-2100

Year	Ash Wed.	Easter Sunday	Year	Ash Wed.	Easter Sunday	Year	Ash Wed.	Easter Sunday	Year	Ash Wed.	Easter Sunday	Year	Ash Wed.	Easter Sunday
1901	Feb. 20	Apr. 7	1941	Feb. 26	Apr. 13	1981	Mar. 4	Apr. 19	2021	Feb. 17	Apr. 4	2061	Feb. 23	Apr. 10
1902	Feb. 12	Mar. 30	1942	Feb. 18	Apr. 5	1982	Feb. 24	Apr. 11	2022	Mar. 2	Apr. 17	2062	Feb. 8	Mar. 26
1903	Feb. 25	Apr. 12	1943	Mar. 10	Apr. 25	1983	Feb. 16	Apr. 3	2023	Feb. 22	Apr. 9	2063	Feb. 28	Apr. 15
1904	Feb. 17	Apr. 3	1944	Feb. 23	Apr. 9	1984	Mar. 7	Apr. 22	2024	Feb. 14	Mar. 31	2064	Feb. 20	Apr. 6
1905	Mar. 8	Apr. 23	1945	Feb. 14	Apr. 1	1985	Feb. 20	Apr. 7	2025	Mar. 5	Apr. 20	2065	Feb. 11	Mar. 29
1906	Feb. 28	Apr. 15	1946	Mar. 6	Apr. 21	1986	Feb. 12	Mar. 30	2026	Feb. 18	Apr. 5	2066	Feb. 24	Apr. 11
1907	Feb. 13	Mar. 31	1947	Feb. 19	Apr. 6	1987	Mar. 4	Apr. 19	2027	Feb. 10	Mar. 28	2067	Feb. 16	Apr. 3
1908	Mar. 4	Apr. 19	1948	Feb. 11	Mar. 28	1988	Feb. 17	Apr. 3	2028	Mar. 1	Apr. 16	2068	Mar. 7	Apr. 22
1909	Feb. 24	Apr. 11	1949	Mar. 2	Apr. 17	1989	Feb. 8	Mar. 26	2029	Feb. 14	Apr. 1	2069	Feb. 27	Apr. 14
1910	Feb. 9	Mar. 27	1950	Feb. 22	Apr. 9	1990	Feb. 28	Apr. 15	2030	Mar. 6	Apr. 21	2070	Feb. 12	Mar. 30
1911	Feb. 1	Apr. 16	1951	Feb. 7	Mar. 25	1991	Feb. 13	Mar. 31	2031	Feb. 26	Apr. 13	2071	Mar. 4	Apr. 19
1912	Feb. 21	Apr. 7	1952	Feb. 27	Apr. 13	1992	Mar. 4	Apr. 19	2032	Feb. 11	Mar. 28	2072	Feb. 24	Apr. 10
1913	Feb. 5	Mar. 23	1953	Feb. 18	Apr. 5	1993	Feb. 24	Apr. 11	2033	Mar. 2	Apr. 17	2073	Feb. 8	Mar. 26
1914	Feb. 25	Apr. 12	1954	Mar. 3	Apr. 18	1994	Feb. 16	Apr. 3	2034	Feb. 22	Apr. 9	2074	Feb. 28	Apr. 15
1915	Feb. 17	Apr. 4	1955	Feb. 23	Apr. 10	1995	Mar. 1	Apr. 16	2035	Feb. 7	Mar. 25	2075	Feb. 20	Apr. 7
1916	Mar. 8	Apr. 23	1956	Feb. 15	Apr. 1	1996	Feb. 21	Apr. 7	2036	Feb. 27	Apr. 13	2076	Mar. 4	Apr. 19
1917	Feb. 21	Apr. 8	1957	Mar. 6	Apr. 21	1997	Feb. 12	Mar. 30	2037	Feb. 18	Apr. 5	2077	Feb. 24	Apr. 11
1918	Feb. 13	Mar. 31	1958	Feb. 19	Apr. 6	1998	Feb. 25	Apr. 12	2038	Mar. 10	Apr. 25	2078	Feb. 16	Apr. 3
1919	Mar. 5	Apr. 20	1959	Feb. 11	Mar. 29	1999	Feb. 17	Apr. 4	2039	Feb. 23	Apr. 10	2079	Mar. 8	Apr. 23
1920	Feb. 18	Apr. 4	1960	Mar. 2	Apr. 17	2000	Mar. 8	Apr. 23	2040	Feb. 15	Apr. 1	2080	Feb. 21	Apr. 7
1921	Feb. 9	Mar. 27	1961	Feb. 15	Apr. 2	2001	Feb. 28	Apr. 15	2041	Mar. 6	Apr. 21	2081	Feb. 12	Mar. 30
1922	Mar. 1	Apr. 16	1962	Mar. 7	Apr. 22	2002	Feb. 13	Mar. 31	2042	Feb. 19	Apr. 6	2082	Mar. 4	Apr. 19
1923	Feb. 14	Apr. 1	1963	Feb. 27	Apr. 14	2003	Mar. 5	Apr. 20	2043	Feb. 11	Mar. 29	2083	Feb. 17	Apr. 4
1924	Mar. 5	Apr. 20	1964	Feb. 12	Mar. 29	2004	Feb. 25	Apr. 11	2044	Mar. 2	Apr. 17	2084	Mar. 8	Apr. 26
1925	Feb. 25	Apr. 12	1965	Mar. 3	Apr. 18	2005	Feb. 9	Mar. 27	2045	Feb. 22	Apr. 9	2085	Feb. 28	Apr. 15
1926	Feb. 17	Apr. 4	1966	Feb. 23	Apr. 10	2006	Mar. 1	Apr. 16	2046	Feb. 7	Mar. 25	2086	Feb. 13	Mar. 31
1927	Mar. 2	Apr. 17	1967	Feb. 8	Mar. 26	2007	Feb. 21	Apr. 8	2047	Feb. 27	Apr. 14	2087	Mar. 5	Apr. 20
1928	Feb. 22	Apr. 8	1968	Feb. 28	Apr. 14	2008	Feb. 6	Mar. 23	2048	Feb. 19	Apr. 5	2088	Feb. 25	Apr. 11
1929	Feb. 13	Mar. 31	1969	Feb. 19	Apr. 6	2009	Feb. 25	Apr. 12	2049	Mar. 3	Apr. 18	2089	Feb. 16	Apr. 3
1930	Mar. 5	Apr. 20	1970	Feb. 11	Mar. 29	2010	Feb. 17	Apr. 4	2050	Feb. 23	Apr. 10	2090	Mar. 1	Apr. 16
1931	Feb. 18	Apr. 5	1971	Feb. 24	Apr. 11	2011	Mar. 9	Apr. 24	2051	Feb. 15	Apr. 2	2091	Feb. 21	Apr. 8
1932	Feb. 10	Mar. 27	1972	Feb. 16	Apr. 2	2012	Feb. 22	Apr. 8	2052	Mar. 6	Apr. 21	2092	Feb. 13	Mar. 30
1933	Mar. 1	Apr. 16	1973	Mar. 7	Apr. 22	2013	Feb. 13	Mar. 31	2053	Feb. 19	Apr. 6	2093	Feb. 25	Apr. 12
1934	Feb. 14	Apr. 1	1974	Feb. 27	Apr. 14	2014	Mar. 5	Apr. 20	2054	Feb. 11	Mar. 29	2094	Feb. 17	Apr. 4
1935	Mar. 6	Apr. 21	1975	Feb. 12	Mar. 30	2015	Feb. 18	Apr. 5	2055	Mar. 3	Apr. 18	2095	Mar. 9	Apr. 24
1936	Feb. 26	Apr. 12	1976	Mar. 3	Apr. 18	2016	Feb. 10	Mar. 27	2056	Feb. 16	Apr. 2	2096	Feb. 29	Apr. 15
1937	Feb. 10	Mar. 28	1977	Feb. 23	Apr. 10	2017	Mar. 1	Apr. 16	2057	Mar. 7	Apr. 22	2097	Feb. 13	Mar. 31
1938	Mar. 2	Apr. 17	1978	Feb. 8	Mar. 26	2018	Feb. 14	Apr. 1	2058	Feb. 27	Apr. 14	2098	Mar. 5	Apr. 20
1939	Feb. 22	Apr. 9	1979	Feb. 28	Apr. 15	2019	Mar. 6	Apr. 21	2059	Feb. 12	Mar. 30	2099	Feb. 25	Apr. 12
1940	Feb. 7	Mar. 24	1980	Feb. 20	Apr. 6	2020	Feb. 26	Apr. 12	2060	Mar. 3	Apr. 18	2100	Feb. 10	Mar. 28

Roman Catholic Hierarchy

Source: U.S. Catholic Conference; Holy See Press

Supreme Pontiff

At the head of the Roman Catholic Church is the supreme pontiff, Pope Benedict XVI, Joseph Ratzinger, born in Marktl am Inn, in Bavaria, Germany, on Apr. 16, 1927; ordained priest on June 29, 1951, named archbishop of Munich and Feising in Mar. 1977 and elevated to cardinal three months later. In 1981, he was appointed prefect of the Congregation for the Doctrine of the Faith, and confirmed as dean of the College of Cardinals on Nov. 30, 2002. He was elected pope by the College of Cardinals on Apr. 19, 2005.

Chronological List of Popes

Source: Annuario Pontificio

The Roman Catholic Church named the Apostle Peter as founder of the church in Rome and the first pope. He arrived there c. 42, was martyred there c. 67, and was ultimately canonized as a saint. The **pope's temporal title** is Sovereign of the State of Vatican City. The **pope's spiritual titles** are Bishop of Rome, Vicar of Jesus Christ, Successor of St. Peter, Prince of the Apostles, Supreme Pontiff of the Universal Church, Patriarch of the West, Primate of Italy, Archbishop and Metropolitan of the Roman Province.

Table lists year of accession of each pope. The **names of antipopes** are in italics and followed by an *. Antipopes were illegitimate claimants to the papal throne.

Year	Pope	Year	Pope	Year	Pope	Year	Pope	Year	Pope
	St. Peter	526	St. Felix IV (III)	872	John VIII	1100	*Theodoric**	1417	Martin V
67	St. Linus	530	Boniface II	882	Marinus I	1102	*Albert**	1431	Eugene IV
76	St. Anacletus	530	*Dioscorus**	884	St. Adrian III	1105	*Sylvester IV**	1439	*Felix V**
	or Cletus	533	John II	885	Stephen V (VI)	1118	Gelasius II	1447	Nicholas V
88	St. Clement I	535	St. Agapitus I	891	Formosus	1118	*Gregory VIII**	1455	Callistus III
97	St. Evaristus	536	St. Silverius, Martyr	896	Boniface VI	1119	Callistus II	1458	Pius II
105	St. Alexander I	537	Vigilius	896	Stephen VI (VII)	1124	Honorius II	1464	Paul II
115	St. Sixtus I	556	Pelagius I	897	Romanus	1124	*Celestine II**	1471	Sixtus IV
125	St. Telesphorus	561	John III	897	Theodore II	1130	Innocent II	1484	Innocent VIII
136	St. Hyginus	575	Benedict I	898	John IX	1130	*Anacletus II**	1492	Alexander VI
140	St. Pius I	579	Pelagius II	900	Benedict IV	1138	*Victor IV**	1503	Pius III
155	St. Anicetus	590	St. Gregory I	903	Leo V	1143	Celestine II	1503	Julius II
166	St. Soter	604	Sabinian	903	*Christopher**	1144	Lucius II	1513	Leo X
175	St. Eleutherius	607	Boniface III	904	Sergius III	1145	Bl. Eugene III	1522	Adrian VI
189	St. Victor I	608	St. Boniface IV	911	Anastasius III	1153	Anastasius IV	1523	Clement VII
199	St. Zephyrinus	615	St. Deusdedit	913	Landus	1154	Adrian IV	1534	Paul III
217	St. Callistus I		or Adeodatus	914	John X	1159	Alexander III	1550	Julius III
217	*St. Hippolytus**	619	Boniface V	928	Leo VI	1159	*Victor IV**	1555	Marcellus II
222	St. Urban I	625	Honorius I	928	Stephen VII (VIII)	1164	*Paschal III**	1555	Paul IV
230	St. Pontian	640	Severinus	931	John XI	1168	*Callistus III**	1559	Pius IV
235	St. Anterus	640	John IV	936	Leo VII	1179	*Innocent III**	1566	St. Pius V
236	St. Fabian	642	Theodore I	939	Stephen VIII (IX)	1181	Lucius III	1572	Gregory XIII
251	St. Cornelius	649	St. Martin I, Martyr	942	Marinus II	1185	Urban III	1585	Sixtus V
251	*Novatian**	654	St. Eugene I	946	Agapitus II	1187	Gregory VIII	1590	Urban VII
253	St. Lucius I	657	St. Vitalian	955	John XII	1187	Clement III	1590	Gregory XIV
254	St. Stephen I	672	Adeodatus II	963	Leo VIII	1191	Celestine III	1591	Innocent IX
257	St. Sixtus II	676	Donus	964	Benedict V	1198	Innocent III	1592	Clement VIII
259	St. Dionysius	678	St. Agatho	965	John XIII	1216	Honorius III	1605	Leo XI
269	St. Felix I	682	St. Leo II	973	Benedict VI	1227	Gregory IX	1605	Paul V
275	St. Eutychian	684	St. Benedict II	974	*Boniface VII**	1241	Celestine IV	1621	Gregory XV
283	St. Caius	685	John V	974	Benedict VII	1243	Innocent IV	1623	Urban VIII
296	St. Marcellinus	686	Conon	983	John XIV	1254	Alexander IV	1644	Innocent X
308	St. Marcellus I	687	*Theodore**	985	John XV	1261	Urban IV	1655	Alexander VII
309	St. Eusebius	687	*Paschal**	996	Gregory V	1265	Clement IV	1667	Clement IX
311	St. Melchiades	687	St. Sergius I	997	*John XVI**	1271	Bl. Gregory X	1670	Clement X
314	St. Sylvester I	701	John VI	999	Sylvester II	1276	Bl. Innocent V	1676	Bl. Innocent XI
336	St. Marcus	705	John VII	1003	John XVII	1276	Adrian V	1689	Alexander VIII
337	St. Julius I	708	Sisinnius	1004	John XVIII	1276	John XXI	1691	Innocent XII
352	Liberius	708	Constantine	1009	Sergius IV	1277	Nicholas III	1700	Clement XI
355	*Felix II**	715	St. Gregory II	1012	Benedict VIII	1281	Martin IV	1721	Innocent XIII
366	St. Damasus I	731	St. Gregory III	1012	*Gregory**	1285	Honorius IV	1724	Benedict XIII
366	*Ursinus**	741	St. Zachary	1024	John XIX	1288	Nicholas IV	1730	Clement XII
384	St. Siricius	752	Stephen II (III)[1]	1032	Benedict IX	1294	St. Celestine V	1740	Benedict XIV
399	St. Anastasius I	757	St. Paul I	1045	Sylvester III	1294	Boniface VIII	1758	Clement XIII
401	St. Innocent I	767	*Constantine**	1045	Benedict IX	1303	Bl. Benedict XI	1769	Clement XIV
417	St. Zosimus	768	*Philip**	1045	Gregory VI	1305	Clement V	1775	Pius VI
418	St. Boniface I	768	Stephen III (IV)	1046	Clement II	1316	John XXII	1800	Pius VII
418	*Eulalius**	772	Adrian I	1047	Benedict IX	1328	*Nicholas V**	1823	Leo XII
422	St. Celestine I	795	St. Leo III	1048	Damasus II	1334	Benedict XII	1829	Pius VIII
432	St. Sixtus III	816	Stephen IV (V)	1049	St. Leo IX	1342	Clement VI	1831	Gregory XVI
440	St. Leo I	817	St. Paschal I	1055	Victor II	1352	Innocent VI	1846	Pius IX
461	St. Hilary	824	Eugene II	1057	Stephen IX (X)	1362	Bl. Urban V	1878	Leo XIII
468	St. Simplicius	827	Valentine	1058	*Benedict X**	1370	Gregory XI	1903	St. Pius X
483	St. Felix III (II)	827	Gregory IV	1059	Nicholas II	1378	Urban VI	1914	Benedict XV
492	St. Gelasius I	844	*John**	1061	Alexander II	1378	*Clement VII**	1922	Pius XI
496	Anastasius II	844	Sergius II	1061	*Honorius II**	1389	Boniface IX	1939	Pius XII
498	St. Symmachus	847	St. Leo IV	1073	St. Gregory VII	1394	*Benedict XIII**	1958	John XXIII
498	*Lawrence** (501-505)	855	Benedict III	1080	*Clement III**	1404	Innocent VII	1963	Paul VI
514	St. Hormisdas	855	*Anastasius**	1086	Bl. Victor III	1406	Gregory XII	1978	John Paul I
523	St. John I, Martyr	858	St. Nicholas I	1088	Bl. Urban II	1409	*Alexander V**	1978	John Paul II
		867	Adrian II	1099	Paschal II	1410	*John XXIII**	2005	Benedict XVI

Bl. = Blessed (1) After St. Zachary, a Roman priest named Stephen was elected, but died before assuming the papacy. Another Stephen was then elected to succeed Zachary as Stephen II. He is sometimes listed as Stephen III.

College of Cardinals
Source: U.S. Conference of Catholic Bishops

Members of the Sacred College of Cardinals are chosen by the pope to be his chief assistants and advisers in the administration of the church. Among their duties is the election of the pope.

In its present form, the College of Cardinals dates from the 12th century. The first cardinals, from about the 6th century, were deacons and priests of the leading churches of Rome and were bishops of neighboring dioceses. The title of cardinal was limited to members of the college in 1567. The number of cardinals was set at 70 in 1586 by Pope Sixtus V. From 1959 Pope John XXIII began to increase the number; however, the number eligible to participate in papal elections was limited to 120. Previous limitations were set aside by Pope John Paul II when he created new cardinals. In 1918 the Code of Canon Law specified that all cardinals must be priests. Pope John XXIII in 1962 established a rule that all cardinals must be bishops, but exceptions can be made. In 1971, Pope Paul VI decreed that at age 80 cardinals must retire from curial departments and offices and from participation in papal elections.

As of Aug. 2011, there were 194 cardinals, of whom 114 remained eligible to vote.

North American Cardinals

Name	Office	Born	Named cardinal
Luis Aponte Martínez[1]	Archbishop emeritus of San Juan	1922	1973
William W. Baum[1]	Archbishop emeritus of Washington, DC	1926	1976
Anthony J. Bevilacqua[1]	Archbishop emeritus of Philadelphia	1923	1991
Raymond L. Burke	Prefect, Supreme Tribunal of the Apostolic Signature	1948	2010
Daniel N. DiNardo	Archbishop of Galveston-Houston	1949	2007
Edward M. Egan	Archbishop emeritus of New York	1932	2001
John Patrick Foley	Grand Master of the Knights of the Holy Sepulcher	1935	2007
Francis E. George	Archbishop of Chicago	1937	1998
William Henry Keeler[1]	Archbishop emeritus of Baltimore	1931	1994
Bernard F. Law	Archbishop emeritus of Boston	1931	1985
William Levada	Prefect, Congregation for the Doctrine of the Faith	1936	2006
Javier Lozano Barragán[1]	Pres, emeritus, Pontifical Council for Health Care Workers	1933	2003
Roger Mahony	Archbishop emeritus of Los Angeles	1936	1991
Adam Joseph Maida[1]	Archbishop emeritus of Detroit	1930	1994
Theodore McCarrick[1]	Archbishop emeritus of Washington, DC	1930	2001
Sean O'Malley	Archbishop of Boston	1944	2006
Marc Ouellet	Prefect, Congregation of Bishops	1944	2003
Justin F. Rigali	Archbishop emeritus of Philadelphia	1935	2003
Norberto Rivera Carrera	Archbishop of Mexico City	1942	1998
José Francisco Robles Ortega	Archbishop of Monterrey, Mexico	1949	2007
Juan Sandoval Íñiguez	Archbishop of Guadalajara	1933	1994
James F. Stafford	Archbishop emeritus of Denver	1932	1998
Edmund C. Szoka[1]	Archbishop emeritus of Detroit	1927	1988
Jean-Claude Turcotte	Archbishop of Montreal	1936	1994
Donald W. Wuerl	Archbishop of Washington, DC	1940	2010

(1) Ineligible to take part in papal elections (as of Aug. 2011).

The Ten Commandments

In the Hebrew Bible (Old Testament) the Ten Commandments (also called the Decalogue, from the Greek meaning "ten words") were revealed by God to Moses on Mt. Sinai. They form the covenant between God and the Israelites and the moral code that is the basis for the Jewish and Christian religions. The Ten Commandments appear in two places in the Old Testament—Exodus 20:1-17 and Deuteronomy 5:6-21.

Most Protestant, Anglican, and Orthodox Christians follow Jewish tradition, as here, which considers the introduction ("I am the Lord . . .") the first commandment and makes the prohibition against idolatry the second. Roman Catholic and Lutheran traditions combine I and II and split the last commandment into two that separately prohibit coveting of a neighbor's wife and a neighbor's goods. This arrangement alters the numbering of the other commandments by one.

Following is the text of the Ten Commandments as it appears in Exodus 20:1-17, in the King James version of the Bible [Roman numerals added]:

And God spake all these words, saying,

I. I *am* the LORD thy God, which have brought thee out of the land of Egypt, out of the house of bondage. Thou shalt have no other gods before me.

II. Thou shalt not make unto thee any graven image, or any likeness of *any thing* that *is* in heaven above, or that *is* in the earth beneath, or that *is* in the water under the earth. Thou shalt not bow down thyself to them, nor serve them: for I the LORD thy God *am* a jealous God, visiting the iniquity of the fathers upon the children unto the third and fourth *generation* of them that hate me; and shewing mercy unto thousands of them that love me, and keep my commandments.

III. Thou shalt not take the name of the LORD thy God in vain: for the LORD will not hold him guiltless that taketh his name in vain.

IV. Remember the sabbath day, to keep it holy. Six days shalt thou labour, and do all thy work: but the seventh day *is* the sabbath of the LORD thy God: *in it* thou shalt not do any work, thou, nor thy son, nor thy daughter, thy manservant, nor thy maidservant, nor thy cattle, nor thy stranger that *is* within thy gates: for *in* six days the LORD made heaven and earth, the sea, and all that in them *is*, and rested the seventh day: wherefore the LORD blessed the sabbath day, and hallowed it.

V. Honour thy father and thy mother: that thy days may be long upon the land which the LORD thy God giveth thee.

VI. Thou shalt not kill.

VII. Thou shalt not commit adultery.

VIII. Thou shalt not steal.

IX. Thou shalt not bear false witness against thy neighbour.

X. Thou shalt not covet thy neighbour's house, thou shalt not covet thy neighbour's wife, nor his manservant, nor his maidservant, nor his ox, nor his ass, nor any thing that *is* thy neighbour's.

Major Christian Denominations:

Brackets indicate some features that tend to

Denomination	Origins	Organization	Authority	Special rites
Baptists	In radical Reformation, objections to infant baptism, demands for church and state separation; John Smyth, English Separatist, in 1609; Roger Williams, 1638, Providence, RI.	Congregational; each local church is autonomous.	Scripture; some Baptists, particularly in the South, interpret the Bible literally.	[Baptism, usually early teen years and after, by total immersion]; Lord's Supper.
Church of Christ (Disciples)	Among evangelical Presbyterians in KY (1804) and PA (1809), in distress over Protestant factionalism and decline of fervor; organized in 1832.	Congregational.	["Where the Scriptures speak, we speak; where the Scriptures are silent, we are silent."]	Adult baptism; Lord's Supper (weekly).
Episcopalians	Henry VIII separated English Catholic Church from Rome, 1534, for political reasons; Protestant Episcopal Church in U.S. founded in 1789.	[Diocesan bishops, in apostolic succession, are elected by parish representatives; the national Church is headed by General Convention and Presiding Bishop; part of the Anglican Communion.]	Scripture as interpreted by tradition, especially 39 Articles (1563); tri-annual convention of bishops, priests, and lay people.	Infant baptism, Eucharist, and other sacraments; sacrament taken to be symbolic, but as having real spiritual effect.
Jehovah's Witnesses	Founded in 1870 in PA by Charles Taze Russell; incorporated as Watch Tower Bible and Tract Society of PA, 1884; name Jehovah's Witnesses adopted in 1931.	A governing body located in NY coordinates worldwide activities; each congregation cared for by a body of elders; each Witness considered a minister.	The Bible.	Baptism by immersion; annual Lord's Meal ceremony.
Latter-day Saints (Mormons)	In a vision of the Father and the Son reported by Joseph Smith (1820s) in NY; Smith also reported receiving new scripture on golden tablets: the Book of Mormon.	Theocratic; 1st Presidency (church president, 2 counselors), 12 Apostles preside over international church; local congregations headed by lay priesthood leaders.	Revelation to living prophet (church president). The Bible, Book of Mormon, and other revelations to Smith and his successors.	Baptism, at age 8; laying on of hands (which confers the gift of the Holy Ghost); Lord's Supper; temple rites: baptism for the dead, marriage for eternity, others.
Lutherans	Begun by Martin Luther in Wittenberg, Germany, in 1517; objection to Catholic doctrine of salvation and sale of indulgences; break complete, 1519.	Varies from congregational to episcopal; in U.S., a combination of regional synods and congregational polities is most common.	Scripture alone; the Book of Concord (1580), which includes the three Ecumenical Creeds, subscribed to as a correct exposition of Scripture.	Infant baptism; Lord's Supper; Christ's true body and blood present "in, with, and under the bread and wine."
Methodists	Rev. John Wesley began movement in 1738, within Church of England; first U.S. denomination, Baltimore (1784).	Conference and superintendent system; [in United Methodist Church, general superintendents are bishops—not a priestly order, only an office—who are elected for life].	Scripture as interpreted by tradition, reason, and experience.	Baptism of infants or adults; Lord's Supper commanded; other rites: marriage, ordination, solemnization of personal commitments.
Orthodox	Developed in original Christian proselytizing; broke with Rome in 1054 after centuries of doctrinal disputes and diverging traditions.	Synods of bishops in autonomous, usually national, churches elect a patriarch, archbishop, or metropolitan; these men, as a group, are the heads of the church.	Scripture, tradition, and the first seven church councils up to Nicaea II in 787; bishops in council have authority in doctrine and policy.	Seven sacraments: infant baptism and anointing, Eucharist, ordination, penance, marriage, and anointing of the sick.
Pentecostal	In Topeka, KS, (1901) and Los Angeles (1906), in reaction to perceived loss of evangelical fervor among Methodists and others.	Originally a movement, not a formal organization. Pentecostalism now has a variety of organized forms and continues also as a movement.	Scripture; individual charismatic leaders, the teachings of the Holy Spirit.	[Spirit baptism, especially as shown in "speaking in tongues"; healing and sometimes exorcism]; adult baptism; Lord's Supper.
Presbyterians	In 16th-cent. Calvinist reformation; differed with Lutherans over sacraments, church government; John Knox founded Scotch Presbyterian church about 1560.	[Highly structured representational system of ministers and lay persons (presbyters) in local, regional, and national bodies (synods).]	Scripture.	Infant baptism; Lord's Supper; bread and wine symbolize Christ's spiritual presence.
Roman Catholics	Traditionally, founded by Jesus who named St. Peter the first vicar; developed in early Christian proselytizing, especially after the conversion of imperial Rome in the 4th cent.	[Hierarchy with supreme power vested in pope elected by cardinals]; councils of bishops advise on matters of doctrine and policy.	[The pope, when speaking for the whole church in matters of faith and morals; and tradition (which is expressed in church councils and in part contained in Scripture).]	Mass; seven sacraments: baptism, reconciliation, Eucharist, confirmation, marriage, ordination, and anointing of the sick (unction).
United Church of Christ	[By ecumenical union, in 1957, of Congregationalists and Evangelical & Reformed, representing both Calvinist and Lutheran traditions.]	Congregational; a General Synod, representative of all congregations, sets general policy.	Scripture.	Infant baptism; Lord's Supper.

How Do They Differ?

distinguish a denomination sharply from others.

Practice	Ethics	Doctrine	Other	Denomination
Worship style varies from staid to evangelistic; extensive missionary activity.	Usually opposed to alcohol and tobacco; some tendency toward a perfectionist ethical standard.	[No creed; true church is of believers only, who are all equal.]	Believing no authority can stand between the believer and God, the Baptists are strong supporters of church and state separation.	**Baptists**
Tries to avoid any rite not considered part of the 1st-cent. church; some congregations may reject instrumental music.	Some tendency toward perfectionism; increasing interest in social action programs.	Simple New Testament faith; avoids any elaboration not firmly based on Scripture.	Highly tolerant in doctrinal and religious matters; strongly supportive of scholarly education.	**Church of Christ (Disciples)**
Formal, based on *Book of Common Prayer*, updated 1979; services range from austerely simple to highly liturgical.	Tolerant, sometimes permissive; some social action programs.	Scripture; the "historic creeds," which include the Apostles, Nicene, and Athanasian, and the *Book of Common Prayer*; ranges from Anglo-Catholic to low church, with Calvinist influences.	Strongly ecumenical, holding talks with many branches of Christendom.	**Episcopalians**
Meetings are held in Kingdom Halls and members' homes for study and worship; [extensive door-to-door visitations].	High moral code; stress on marital fidelity and family values; avoidance of tobacco and blood transfusions.	[God, by his first creation, Christ, will soon destroy all wickedness; 144,000 faithful ones will rule in heaven with Christ over others on a paradise earth.]	Total allegiance proclaimed only to God's kingdom or heavenly government by Christ; main periodical, *The Watchtower*, is printed in 115 languages.	**Jehovah's Witnesses**
Simple service with prayers, hymns, sermon; private temple ceremonies may be more elaborate.	Temperance; strict moral code; [tithing]; a strong work ethic with communal self-reliance; [strong missionary activity]; family emphasis.	Jesus Christ is the Son of God, the Eternal Father. Jesus' atonement saves all humans; those who are obedient to God's laws may become joint-heirs with Christ in God's kingdom.	Mormons believe theirs is the true church of Jesus Christ, restored by God through Joseph Smith. Official name: The Church of Jesus Christ of Latter-day Saints.	**Latter-day Saints (Mormons)**
Relatively simple, formal liturgy with emphasis on the sermon.	Generally conservative in personal and social ethics; doctrine of "two kingdoms" (worldly and holy) supports conservatism in secular affairs.	Salvation by grace alone through faith; Lutheranism has made major contributions to Protestant theology.	Though still somewhat divided along ethnic lines (German, Swedish, etc.), main divisions are between fundamentalists and liberals.	**Lutherans**
Worship style varies widely by denomination, local church, geography.	Originally pietist and perfectionist; always strong social activist elements.	No distinctive theological development; 25 articles abridged from Church of England's 39, not binding.	In 1968, The United Methodist Church was formed by the union of The Methodist Church and The Evangelical United Brethren Church.	**Methodists**
Elaborate liturgy, usually in the vernacular, though extremely traditional; the liturgy is the essence of Orthodoxy; veneration of icons.	Tolerant; little stress on social action; divorce, remarriage permitted in some cases; bishops are celibate; priests need not be.	Emphasis on Christ's resurrection, rather than crucifixion; the Holy Spirit proceeds from God the Father only.	Orthodox Church in America originally under Patriarch of Moscow, was granted autonomy in 1970; Greek Orthodox do not recognize this autonomy.	**Orthodox**
Loosely structured service with rousing hymns and sermons, culminating in spirit baptism.	Usually, emphasis on perfectionism, with varying degrees of tolerance.	Simple traditional beliefs, usually Protestant, with emphasis on the immediate presence of God in the Holy Spirit.	Once confined to lower-class "holy rollers," Pentecostalism now appears in mainline churches and has established middle-class congregations.	**Pentecostal**
A simple, sober service in which the sermon is central.	Traditionally, a tendency toward strictness, with firm church- and self-discipline; otherwise tolerant.	Emphasizes the sovereignty and justice of God; no longer dogmatic.	Although traces of belief in predestination (that God has foreordained salvation for the "elect") remain, this idea is no longer a central element in Presbyterianism.	**Presbyterians**
Relatively elaborate ritual centered on the Mass; also rosary recitation, novenas, etc.	Traditionally strict but increasingly tolerant in practice; divorce and remarriage not accepted, but annulments sometimes granted; celibate clergy, except in Eastern rite.	Highly elaborated; salvation by merit gained through grace; dogmatic; special veneration of Mary, the mother of Jesus.	Relatively rapid change followed Vatican Council II; Mass now in vernacular; more stress on social action, tolerance, ecumenism.	**Roman Catholics**
Usually simple service with emphasis on the sermon.	Tolerant; some social action emphasis.	Standard Protestant; "Statement of Faith" (1959) is not binding.	Two main churches in the 1957 union represented earlier unions with small groups of almost every Protestant denomination.	**United Church of Christ**

Books of the Bible

Old Testament—Standard Protestant List

Genesis	I Kings	Ecclesiastes	Obadiah
Exodus	II Kings	Song of Solomon	Jonah
Leviticus	I Chronicles	Isaiah	Micah
Numbers	II Chronicles	Jeremiah	Nahum
Deuteronomy	Ezra	Lamentations	Habakkuk
Joshua	Nehemiah	Ezekiel	Zephaniah
Judges	Esther	Daniel	Haggai
Ruth	Job	Hosea	Zechariah
I Samuel	Psalms	Joel	Malachi
II Samuel	Proverbs	Amos	

New Testament List

Matthew	Ephesians	Hebrews
Mark	Philippians	James
Luke	Colossians	I Peter
John	I Thessalonians	II Peter
Acts	II Thessalonians	I John
Romans	I Timothy	II John
I Corinthians	II Timothy	III John
II Corinthians	Titus	Jude
Galatians	Philemon	Revelation

The standard Protestant Old Testament consists of the same 39 books as in the Bible of Judaism, but the latter is organized differently. The Old Testament used by Roman Catholics has 7 additional "deuterocanonical" books, plus some additional parts of books. The 7 are **Tobit, Judith, Wisdom, Sirach (Ecclesiastics), Baruch, I Maccabees**, and **II Maccabees**. Both Catholic and Protestant versions of the New Testament have 27 books, with the same names.

Figures in the Hebrew Bible (Old Testament)

Aaron: First of Hebrew high priests; brother of Moses and Miriam.

Abel: Second son of Adam and Eve; slain by Cain.

Abraham: Founder of monotheism; patriarch; also called Abram.

Adam: First human according to Genesis.

Amos: Herdsman; prophesized against social injustice and oppression of the poor.

Bathsheba: Seduced by King David; mother of King Solomon.

Cain: Tiller of the soil; son of Adam and Eve; killed his brother Abel.

Cyrus: Persian ruler; sent Jews home from exile.

Daniel: Cast into lion's den by Nebuchadnezzar; saved.

David: Israel's greatest king; shepherd, warrior, musician, psalmist.

Deborah: Prophet and judge; ruled over Israel.

Elijah: Great prophet; was victorious over the priests of the Phoenician god, Baal.

Elisha: Prophet; successor to Elijah.

Esther: Jewish wife of the king of Persia; saved Jews from annihilation.

Eve: First woman according to Genesis.

Ezekiel: Visionary; prophesized hope to exiled Jews in Babylon.

Ezra: Great Jewish leader; rededicated worship and Torah law after exile.

Goliath: Giant Philistine warrior; slain by David.

Hannah: Childless; promised child to God; mother to the prophet Samuel.

Hosea: Enacted prophecy; asked God's forgiveness for Israel's unfaithfulness.

Isaac: Son of Abraham and Sarah; saved from sacrificial altar.

Isaiah: Highly educated prophet; avoided war with Assyria; Israel destroyed; Jerusalem survived.

Jacob: Son of Isaac; father of the Twelve Tribes; renamed "Israel" by angel.

Jeremiah: Confronted leaders; urged surrender to Babylon.

Jezebel: Phoenician queen of King Ahab; had Israelite prophets killed.

Job: "Blameless" man; lost family and possessions but not his faith.

Jonah: Swallowed by a great fish; prophesied destruction of Nineveh, averted when the people repented.

Jonathan: Son of King Saul; friend of David.

Joseph: Favorite of Jacob; interpreted Pharaoh's dreams; brought Hebrews to Egypt.

Josiah: Reformist king; repaired Temple; restored worship; reintroduced Passover.

Joshua: Successor of Moses; led Hebrews into Canaan.

Leah: Matriarch; older sister of Rachel; Jacob's wife.

Micah: Prophet; predicted the end of war and beginning of peace.

Miriam: Prophet and great leader of the Hebrews; sister to Moses and Aaron.

Moses: Most important Hebrew prophet; leader of the Israelites; received the Torah.

Nathan: Prophet; confronted King David over his seduction of Bathsheba.

Nebuchadnezzar: Babylonian king; destroyed Jerusalem.

Nehemiah: Led Jews back to Jerusalem from Babylonian exile.

Noah: A man of great faith who, according to Genesis, saved his family and two of every living thing on Earth from a great flood.

Rachel: Matriarch; younger sister of Leah; Jacob's wife; Joseph's mother.

Rebecca: Matriarch; wife of Isaac; mother of Jacob.

Ruth: Moabite convert; ancestor of David.

Samuel: Prophet; anointed Saul king of Israel and later anointed David to succeed him.

Samson: Judge and military leader of Israel; possessed superhuman strength.

Sarah: First matriarch of Israel; wife of Abraham; mother of Isaac.

Saul: First king of Israel; father of Jonathan.

Solomon: King of Israel at its zenith; known for great wisdom.

Zechariah: Prophet; encouraged rebuilding of Temple destroyed by Babylonians.

Figures in the New Testament

Andrew: One of the Twelve Apostles; brother of Peter and former fisherman; one of the earlier disciples.

Barabbas: Imprisoned with Jesus; set free by Pilate on Passover.

Barnabas: Disciple of Jesus; closely connected with Paul.

Bartholomew: A lesser-known member of the Twelve Apostles; cheerful and prayed often.

Cornelius: A Roman convert; defended by Peter, allowing Gentiles to become Christians.

Elizabeth: Mother of John the Baptist; relation of the Virgin Mary.

Gabriel: Archangel; appeared to the Virgin Mary to announce that she was to give birth to the messiah.

Herod: Two Herods appear in the New Testament: Herod the Great ordered the death of children around the time of Jesus's birth; his son, Herod, imprisoned John the Baptist and later had him beheaded.

James: One of the Twelve; brother of John the apostle.

Jesus: Central figure of the Gospels; believed to be the Messiah and son of God; crucified by the Romans.

John (Baptist): Known as John the Baptist; important prophet and forerunner to Jesus; relation of the Virgin Mary.

John (Apostle): Beloved disciple of Jesus; one of the Twelve; possible author of fourth Gospel; brother of James.

Joseph: Husband of the Virgin Mary; descendant of King David.

Judas Iscariot: Betrayer of Jesus; prominent member of the Apostles; committed suicide.

Judas Thaddeus: One of the Twelve; also called Jude to distinguish him from Judas Iscariot.

Lazarus: Brother of the disciples Martha and Mary of Bethany; raised from the dead at their request; possibly the same Lazarus who appears in Jesus's parable of the rich man.

Luke: Traditional author of the Gospel of Luke; possibly a follower of Paul.

Mark: Traditional author of the Gospel of Mark; possibly a disciple of Peter.

Matthew: One of the Twelve; possible author of the Gospel of Matthew; a former tax collector.

Mary Magdalene: Important female disciple of Jesus; witness to his death and resurrection.

Mary, the mother of Jesus: Traditionally believed to be a virgin who conceived without sin; wife of Joseph.

Matthias: Often included on lists of the Twelve Apostles as the apostle who replaced Judas Iscariot after his betrayal.

Paul (Saul): Writer of nearly a quarter of the New Testament; a former persecutor of Christians, converted after a vision; played a significant role in spreading Christianity.

Peter: Considered the foremost of the Twelve Apostles; traditionally the first pope and "rock" of the Christian church; author of epistles; also called Simon and Simon Peter.

Philip: One of the Twelve; considered pragmatic and sensible.

Pilate, Pontius: A Roman prefect; played large role in the trial and crucifixion of Jesus.

Simon: One of the Twelve; known as "the Zealot" to distinguish from Simon Peter.

Stephen: Fervently preached that Jesus was the Messiah; stoned to death by angry mob, including Saul; important figure in Saul's conversion.

Thomas: One of the Twelve; known as "Doubting Thomas" because he did not believe Jesus had risen until he could touch him.

Timothy: A disciple closely connected with Paul; recipient of epistles.

Zacharias: Father of John the Baptist; husband of Elizabeth; struck dumb when he doubted his barren wife could become pregnant.

Major Non-Christian World Religions

Source: Islam reviewed by Natana Delong-Bas, Lecturer in Islamic Studies, Boston College; Hinduism and Judaism reviewed by Anthony Padovano, PhD, STD, Prof. of Literature & Relig. Studies, Ramapo College, NJ, Adj. Prof. of Theol., Fordham U., NYC; Baha'i reviewed by the Baha'i Community Relations Center; Sikhism reviewed by The Sikh Coalition of New York, NY.

Islam

Founded: Muhammad received his first revelation in 610 CE.

Founder: Muhammad (c. 570-632), the Prophet.

Sacred texts: Two texts constitute the Muslim sacred canon, the *Qur'an* and the *Hadith*. The Qur'an provides the foundation for Islamic religion and culture. It is regarded as the final, perfect, and complete word of God as revealed to Muhammad over the course of his life. Received by Muhammad in the Arabic language, it is memorized in Arabic by adherents regardless of their native language. It is divided into 114 chapters of unequal length, the shortest containing only 3 verses, and the longest containing 306 verses. The Qur'an is the ultimate source of everything Islamic, from metaphysics to theology to sacred history, to ethics and law, to art. The Hadith, which describes Muhammad's actions, attitudes and teachings, complements the Qur'an. Due to its long history of oral transmission, the Hadith's lessons are seen as somewhat vulnerable to human error; it does not contain God's unadulterated voice as does the Qur'an, but functions as a powerful spiritual and behavioral code nonetheless.

Organization: Muhammad was both the last prophet and a statesman. Muslim leaders have often assumed both civil and moral functions within Islamic states. Within the larger community, there are cultural and national groups, held together by a common religious law, the *Shari'a*. Muslims believe that God is the ultimate lawgiver and that human beings cannot devise laws that oppose divine laws; still, the Shari'a is approached differently in different parts of the Islamic world. Over the centuries, Sunnis have developed four major schools of law: the Hanafi, the Shafi'i, the Hanbali, and the Maliki schools. The Ja'fari school is the most important and well-known Shiite school. Before the 20th century, religious scholars known as the ulama held much legal power. Judges (qadis) and law-interpreters (muftis) are people learned in religious law who lead congregational prayers in mosques and perform other religious duties.

Practice: Five duties (of both men and women), known as the "Pillars of Islam," are regarded as cardinal in Islam and as central to the life of the Islamic community. In accordance with Islam's absolute commitment to monotheism, the first duty is the profession of faith (the *Shahadah*): "There is no God but Allah and Muhammad is His Prophet." A Muslim must profess this belief publicly at least once in his or her lifetime; it defines the membership of an individual in the Islamic community. The second duty is that of five daily prayers organized in intervals throughout the day: sunrise, early afternoon, late afternoon, immediately after sunset, and before midnight. During prayer, Muslims face the *Kaaba*, a small, cube-shaped structure in the courtyard of *al-Haram* (the "inviolate place"), at the Grand Mosque of Mecca. All five prayers in Islam are congregational and are to be offered in a mosque, but they may be offered individually if one cannot be present with a congregation. Congregational prayer is required only at the early afternoon prayer on Friday for men. The third cardinal duty of a Muslim is to pay alms, or *zakat*, which should be 2.5% of one's total wealth. This was originally the tax levied by Muhammad on the wealthy members of the community, primarily to help the poor. Only when zakat has been paid is the rest of a Muslim's property considered purified and legitimate. The fourth duty is the fast of the lunar month of Ramadan. During the fasting month, one must abstain from eating, drinking, smoking, impure thoughts, and sexual intercourse from dawn until sunset, and feed at least one poor person, if able. The fifth duty is the pilgrimage to the Kaaba, which a Muslim must undertake, with exceptions for poverty and ill health, at least once during his or her lifetime.

Divisions: There are two major groups: the majority Sunni (84% of the worldwide Muslim population) and the minority Shiites (14%). Sects first appeared in Islam at the time of Muhammad's death. The group that came to be known as Sunni accepted Abu Bakr, an early convert, as his successor (caliph), while a smaller number, which became the Shi'a, believed that Ali ibn Abi Talib, the son-in-law and first cousin of the prophet, should have become his successor (Imam). Imams are believed to interpret the Qur'an infallibly. **Shiites** fall into three major branches: Fivers, Seveners, and Twelvers, reflecting the number of Imams they recognize. Twelvers believe that the 12th Imam has lived an invisible existence since 874, and will return as the Mahdi (a messiah figure) who will usher in a 1,000-year reign of peace and justice. **Sufism** (mystical dimension of Islam) emphasizes personal relation to God and obedience informed by love of God; it is prevalent among both Sunni and Shiites.

Location: W Africa to Philippines, across a band including E Africa, Central Asia and W China, India, Malaysia, Indonesia. Islam has several million adherents in North America and about 30 mil in Europe.

Beliefs: Strictly monotheistic. God is creator of the universe, omnipotent, omniscient, just, forgiving, and merciful. God revealed the Qur'an to Muhammad to guide humanity to truth and justice. Those who sincerely "submit" (literal meaning of "islam") to God attain salvation.

World's Largest Muslim Populations, 2010

Source: Pew Research Center

Rank	Country	Muslim population	% of country pop.
1.	Indonesia	204,847,000	88.1%
2.	Pakistan	178,097,000	96.4
3.	India	177,286,000	14.6
4.	Bangladesh	148,607,000	90.4
5.	Egypt	80,024,000	94.7
6.	Nigeria	75,728,000	47.9
7.	Iran	74,819,000	99.6
8.	Turkey	74,660,000	98.6
9.	Algeria	34,780,000	98.2
10.	Morocco	32,381,000	99.9
11.	Iraq	31,108,000	98.9
12.	Sudan	30,855,000	71.4
13.	Afghanistan	29,047,000	99.8
14.	Ethiopia	28,721,000	33.8
15.	Uzbekistan	26,833,000	96.5
16.	Saudi Arabia	25,493,000	97.1
17.	Yemen	24,023,000	99.0
18.	China	23,308,000	1.8
19.	Syria	20,895,000	92.8
20.	Malaysia	17,139,000	61.4

Baha'i

Founded: Mid-19th century.

Founder: Mirza Husayn-Ali Nuri (1817-92), later known as Baha'u'llah (Arabic for "Glory of God").

Sacred texts: The writings of Baha'u'llah and of his herald the Bab (Siyyid Ali-Muhammad, 1819-50). The primary text is *Kitab-i-Aqdas* (Most Holy Book).

Organization: The Baha'i administrative system consists of elected nine-member councils at the local, national, and international levels. There are also more than 180 National Spiritual Assemblies and an elected, international governing body known as the Universal House of Justice.

Practice: Prayer, meditation, and fasting are key components of the Baha'i Faith. Work performed in a spirit of service to humanity is considered an important form of worship. The Baha'i Faith has no clergy and minimal ritual and congregational worship.

Divisions: In a religion in which unity is perhaps the central spiritual value, the Baha'i Faith has avoided separating into sects with differentiated theologies and practices.

Location: Worldwide, with practitioners in 236 countries.

Beliefs: God has progressively revealed His will and purpose through a series of Divine manifestations including Jesus, Buddha, Muhammad, Zoroaster, and Baha'u'llah. Baha'u'llah's teachings include the oneness of humanity, the equality of men and women, the harmony of science and religion, the abandonment of all forms of prejudice, and the elimination of extremes of poverty and wealth.

Buddhism

Founded: About 525 BCE, reportedly near Benares, India.

Founder: Gautama Siddhartha (c. 563-483 BCE), the Buddha, who achieved enlightenment through intense meditation.

Sacred texts: The *Tripitaka*, a collection of the Buddha's teachings, rules of monastic life, and philosophical commentaries on the teachings; also a vast body of Buddhist teachings and commentaries, many of which are called *sutras*.

Organization: The basic institution is the *sangha*, or monastic order, through which traditions are passed down. Monastic life tends to be democratic and anti-authoritarian.

Practice: Varies widely according to the sect, and ranges from austere meditation to magical chanting and elaborate temple rites. Many practices, such as exorcism of devils, reflect pre-Buddhist beliefs.

Divisions: A variety of sects grouped into three primary branches: Theravada, which emphasizes the importance of pure thought and deed; Mahayana (includes Zen and Soka-gakkai), which ranges from philosophical schools to belief in the saving grace of higher beings or ritual practices and to practical meditative disciplines; and Vajrayana, or Tantrism, a combination of belief in ritual magic and sophisticated philosophy.

Location: Mainly in Asia, from Sri Lanka to Japan.

Beliefs: Life is suffering, and there is no ultimate reality behind it. The cycle of birth and rebirth continues because of desire and attachment to the unreal "self." Meditation and deeds will end the cycle and achieve Nirvana (nothingness, enlightenment).

Hinduism

Founded: About 1500 BCE by Aryans who migrated to India, where their Vedic religion intermixed with the practices and beliefs of the natives.

Sacred texts: The *Veda*, including the *Upanishads*, a collection of rituals and commentaries; a vast number of epic stories about gods, heroes, and saints, including the *Bhagavadgita*, a part of the *Mahabharata*, and the *Ramayana*.

Organization: None, strictly speaking. Generally, rituals should be performed or assisted by Brahmins, the priestly caste, but in practice, simpler rituals can be performed by anyone. Brahmins are the final judges of ritual purity, the vital element in Hindu life. Temples and religious organizations are usually presided over by Brahmins.

Practice: Primarily passage rites (e.g., initiation, marriage, death, etc.) and daily devotions. Of the public rites, the *puja*, a ceremonial dinner for a god, is the most common.

Divisions: There is no concept of orthodoxy in Hinduism, which presents a variety of sects. The three major living traditions are those devoted to the gods Vishnu and Shiva and to the goddess Shakti. Numerous folk beliefs and practices, often in amalgamation with the above groups, exist side by side with philosophical schools.

Location: Mainly India, Nepal, Malaysia, Guyana, Suriname, and Sri Lanka.

Beliefs: There is only one divine principle; the many gods are only aspects of that unity. Life in all its forms is an aspect of the divine, but it appears as a separation from the divine, a meaningless cycle of birth and rebirth (*samsara*)

determined by the purity or impurity of past deeds (*karma*). To improve one's karma or escape samsara by pure acts, thought, and/or devotion is the aim of every Hindu.

Judaism

Founded: About 2000 BCE.

Founder: Abraham is regarded as the founding patriarch.

Sacred texts: The five books of Moses (the Torah), the basic source of teachings.

Organization: Originally theocratic, Judaism has evolved into a congregational polity. The basic institution is the local synagogue or temple, operated by the congregation and led by a rabbi of their choice. Chief rabbis in France and Great Britain have authority only over those who accept it; in Israel, the two chief rabbis have civil authority in family law.

Practice: Among traditional practitioners, almost all areas of life are governed by strict discipline. Sabbath and holidays are marked by observances, and attendance at public worship is considered especially important. Chief annual observances are Passover, celebrating liberation of the Israelites from Egypt and marked by the Seder meal in homes, and the 10 days from Rosh Hashanah (New Year) to Yom Kippur (Day of Atonement), a period of penitence.

Divisions: Judaism is an unbroken spectrum from ultraconservative to ultraliberal, largely reflecting different points of view regarding the binding character of the prohibitions and duties—particularly the dietary and Sabbath observations—traditionally prescribed for the daily life of the Jew.

Location: Mainly in Israel and the U.S.

Beliefs: Strictly monotheistic. God is the creator and ruler of the universe. God established a particular relationship with the Hebrew people: by obeying a divine law God gave them, they would be a special witness to God's mercy and justice. Judaism stresses ethical behavior (and, among the traditional, careful ritual obedience) as true worship of God.

Sikhism

Founded: Late 15th century in South Asia.

Founder: Guru Nanak Dev ji, Sikhism's first Guru.

Sacred texts: The *Guru Granth Sahib* was compiled by the Sikh Gurus and contains their experiences of the Divine. It also contains writing by other saintly figures of different faiths.

Organization: Each Sikh must make her or his own spiritual journey and not depend on clergy. Congregational prayer led by both men and women takes place in local *Gurudwaras*. Harmandir Sahib in Amritsar, Punjab (northern India), is the central place of worship.

Practice: Prayers are required in the morning, evening, and before sleeping. The most important mode of congregational prayer is the singing of hymns from the Guru Granth Sahib. The "Five Ks" are five articles of faith required of all Sikhs: *Kes* (uncut hair), *Kangha* (comb), *Kara* (steel bracelet), *Kirpan* (sword), and *Kaccha* (short pants).

Divisions: The last living Guru, Guru Gobind Singh (1666-1708) crystallized the practices and beliefs of the faith and determined that no future living Guru was needed. Today the religion is guided by joint sovereignty of Guru Granth and Guru Panth. Guru Granth is the Sikh scripture, as the spiritual manifestation of the Guru, while the Guru Panth is the collectivity of all initiated Sikhs worldwide, as the physical manifestation of the Guru.

Location: Many Sikhs are from Punjabi backgrounds. The Punjab region was divided between India and Pakistan with the end of British rule.

Beliefs: Sikhism preaches a message of devotion, remembrance of God at all times, truthful living, equality between all human beings, and social justice, while emphatically denouncing superstitions and blind rituals. Sikhism is a monotheistic religion based on revelation.

Gods and Goddesses in Egyptian, Norse, and Classical Mythology

Source: World Almanac research

Major Gods and Goddesses of Ancient Egypt

Name	Relations	Sphere or position	Emblem/attribute
Ra (Re)/Atum/Amon	Self-created	The sun, creation	Hawk
Thoth (Djeheuty)	Son of Ra	The moon, wisdom, writing	Ibis/baboon
Ptah	Creator of Atum	Creation, craftsmen	——
Osiris	Brother of Set(h) & Isis	The underworld (dead), fertility, resurrection, vegetation	Bull
Isis	Sister/consort of Osiris	The underworld (dead)	——
Set(h)	Brother of Osiris	Evil, trickery, chaos	Boar, pig
Horus (several)	Sons of Osiris & Isis and Ra & Hathor	The earth	Falcon
Hathor	Consort of Ra	Motherhood, love	Cow
Anubis	Son of Osiris	Embalmer and judge of the dead	Jackal/dog

Major Norse Gods and Goddesses

Name	Relations	Sphere or position	Emblem/attribute
Odin	Father of the Aesir (gods)	War and death, poetry, wisdom, magic	Spear, mead, ring/one-eyed
Thor	Son of Odin	Thunder, lightning, rain; champion of the gods	Hammer, belt
Njord	Father of Freyja & Freyr	Wind and sea, wealth and prosperity	——
Frigg	Wife of Odin	Marriage and motherhood, home	——
Freyja (Freya)	Daughter of Njord	Fertility, birth, crops	Necklace
Freyr	Son of Njord	Agriculture, sun, rain	Magic ship, golden boar
Tyr	Son of Odin[1]	Justice, war	Spear/one-handed
Heimdall	Son of nine giantesses	Watchman of the gods; keen sight and hearing	Horn
Balder (Baldur)	Son of Odin	Light, purity	——
Loki	Son of giants; father of Hel (goddess of death), Jormungand (serpent encompassing the world), Fenrir (the wolf)	Malicious trickster	——

(1) Referred to as the son of Hymir in some mythologies.

Major Gods and Goddesses of the Classical World

Greek name	Roman name	Relations	Sphere or position
Aphrodite	Venus	Daughter of Zeus & Dione	Love
Apollo	——	Son of Zeus & Leto	Healing, poetry, light
Ares	Mars	Son of Zeus & Hera	War
Artemis	Diana	Daughter of Zeus & Leto	Hunting, chastity
Athena	Minerva	Daughter of Zeus & Metis	Wisdom, crafts, war
Cronus	Saturn	Father of Zeus	Titans' ruler
Demeter	Ceres	Sister of Zeus	Agriculture, fertility
Dionysus	Bacchus	Son of Zeus & Semele	Wine, fertility, ecstasy
Eros	Cupid	Son of Ares & Aphrodite	Love
Hades	Pluto	Brother of Zeus	The underworld, death
Hephaestus	Vulcan	Son of Zeus & Hera	Fire
Hera	Juno	Wife & sister of Zeus	Women, marriage
Hermes	Mercury	Son of Zeus & Maia	Travel, commerce, gods' messenger
Hestia	Vesta	Sister of Zeus	The hearth
Pan	——	Son of Hermes & a wood nymph	Forests, flocks, shepherds
Persephone	Proserpina	Daughter of Zeus & Demeter	Grain
Poseidon	Neptune	Brother of Zeus	The sea
Rhea	Ops	Mother of Zeus	The earth
Uranus	Uranus	Father of the Titans (elder gods)	The heavens
Zeus	Jupiter	Son of Cronus & Rhea	Ruler of the gods

LANGUAGE

New Words in English

The following words and definitions were provided by Merriam-Webster Inc., publishers of *Merriam-Webster's Collegiate Dictionary, Eleventh Edition*, released in 2003. The words are among those that the Merriam-Webster editors decided had achieved enough currency in English to be added to the latest (2011) printing of the dictionary.

beer pong: a game in which a set of beer-containing cups is placed at two ends of a table and in which a player scores by bouncing or tossing a Ping-Pong ball into an opponent's cup, from which the opponent then has to drink the beer

biowaste: waste (as manure, sawdust, or food scraps) that is composed chiefly of organic matter

bromance: a close nonsexual friendship between men

crowdsourcing: the practice of obtaining needed services, ideas, or content by soliciting contributions from a large group of people and especially from the online community

cube farm: an office in which employees work in cubicles

cyberbullying: the electronic posting of mean-spirited messages about a person (as a student), often done anonymously

duathlon: a three-part long distance race typically having a running phase, a bicycling phase, and a final running phase

eco-friendly: not environmentally harmful

elliptical trainer: a stationary exercise device on which the user stands on two small rimmed platforms and moves them forward and back in an approximately elliptical path

factory farm: a farm in which large numbers of livestock are raised indoors in conditions intended to maximize production at minimal cost

fist bump: a gesture in which two people bump their fists together (as in greeting or celebration)

gap year: a one-year hiatus from academic studies to allow for nonacademic activities

honor killing: the traditional practice in some countries of killing a family member who is believed to have brought shame on the family

hypermiling: the use of fuel-saving techniques (as lower speeds and frequent coasting) to maximize a vehicle's fuel mileage

Kobe beef: highly marbled premium beef from Japanese cattle that is noted for exceptional tenderness and flavor

microblogging: blogging done with severe space or size constraints typically by posting frequent brief messages about personal activities

mojito: a cocktail made of rum, sugar, mint, lime juice, and soda water

netbook: a small portable computer designed primarily for wireless Internet access

oracy: proficiency in oral expression and comprehension

parkour: the sport of traversing environmental obstacles by running, climbing, or leaping rapidly and efficiently

pixelated: (of an image) displayed in such a manner that individual pixels are discernible

robocall: a telephone call from an automated source that delivers a prerecorded message to a large number of people

skeevy: morally or physically repulsive: disgusting

smartphone: a cell phone that includes additional software functions (as e-mail or an Internet browser)

social media: forms of electronic communication through which users create online communities to share information, ideas, personal messages, and other content (as videos)

swine flu: influenza A of humans that is caused by a different strain of an orthomyxovirus subtype from those found in swine and that is marked especially by fever, sore throat, cough, chills, body ache, fatigue, and sometimes diarrhea and vomiting

text message: a short message sent electronically, usually from one cell phone to another

tweet: to post a message to the Twitter online message service

viral marketing: marketing designed to disseminate information very rapidly by making it likely to be passed from person to person via electronic means

X factor: a circumstance, quality, or person that has a strong but unpredictable influence

Words About Words

allegory: extended use of symbols, in the form of characters, animals, or events, that represent ideas or themes. Ex.: John Bunyan, *Pilgrim's Progress*

alliteration: repetition of same, initial consonant sounds of two or more words in sequence or in short intervals. Ex.: "I have stood still and stopped the sound of feet." —Robert Frost, "Acquainted with the Night"

antithesis: an expression in which contrasting ideas are intentionally juxtaposed, usually in parallel structure. Ex.: "The world will little note, nor long remember, what we say here, but it can never forget what they did here." —Abraham Lincoln, Gettysburg Address

assonance: repetition of same or similar vowel sounds in words located near each other. Ex.: "Green as a dream, and deep as death." —Rupert Brooke, "The Old Vicarage, Grantchester"

back-formation: creation of a word from an existing word, whose forms seem to suggest that the previously existing word derived from the newer word. Ex.: The verb "edit" is a back-formation of the word "editor."

cliché: a saying or expression that has been used so often it has lost its effect. Ex.: work like a dog

euphemism: a mild, indirect expression used instead of a plainer one that might be harsh, unpleasant, or offensive. Ex.: restroom instead of toilet; pass away, or pass, instead of die

hyperbole: exaggeration for emphasis or effect. Ex.: "And fired the shot heard round the world." —Ralph Waldo Emerson, "Concord Hymn"

irony: deliberate use of an expression in which the literal or surface meaning is contrary to what is meant, often opposite meaning that can be inferred. Ex.: "Yet Brutus says he was ambitious; / And Brutus is an honorable man." —William Shakespeare, *Julius Caesar*

litotes: intentional understatement made by negating the opposite of what is meant. Ex.: This was no small matter.

metaphor: a stated equivalence between two dissimilar things or a reference to one thing rather than another, so as to imply a comparison. Ex.: "Life is a tale told by an idiot, full of sound and fury, signifying nothing." —Shakespeare, *Macbeth*

metonymy: substitution of one word for another that it suggests. Ex.: The pen is mightier than the sword.

onomatopoeia: words that imitate the sounds they describe. Ex.: buzz, murmur

oxymoron: juxtaposition of contradictory words. Ex.: deafening silence

paradox: a statement that is phrased to seem contradictory, odd, or opposed to common sense or expectation, while being presented as true. Ex.: "What a pity that youth must be wasted on the young." —George Bernard Shaw

personification: treatment of objects or abstractions as if they were persons. Ex.: "Because I could not stop for Death— / He kindly stopped for me." —Emily Dickinson, "Because I Could Not Stop for Death"

simile: a comparison between two dissimilar things using the words "like" or "as." Ex.: "My love is like a red, red rose" —Robert Burns, "A Red, Red Rose"

spoonerism: play on words in which the initial sounds of two or more words are transposed, creating different phrases whose meanings when compared can be humorous. Ex.: blushing crow instead of crushing blow

synecdoche: a form of metonymy; the use of a part for the whole, or the whole for the part. Ex.: All hands on deck!

tautology: useless, often unwitting repetition of the same idea in different wording. Ex.: close proximity. In logic, a proposition that would be self-contradictory to deny. Ex.: All bachelors are male.

National Spelling Bee

The annual Scripps National Spelling Bee competition, conducted by The E.W. Scripps Company and other newspapers since 1941, was instituted by *The Courier-Journal* of Louisville, KY, in 1925. Students under 16 who are not beyond the 8th grade are eligible to compete at the local level for a chance to advance to the national competition in Washington, DC. The 2011 winner was Sukanya Roy, of South Abington Township, PA. Runners-up were Laura Newcombe, of Toronto, ON, Canada (2nd place) and Arvind Mahankali, of Forest Hills, NY, and Joanna Ye, of Carlisle, PA (tied for 3rd place).

Here are the last words given and spelled correctly at the National Spelling Bee in recent years.

1981	sarcophagus	1988	elegiacal	1994	antediluvian	2000	demarche	2006	Ursprache
1982	psoriasis	1989	spoliator	1995	xanthosis	2001	succedaneum	2007	serrefine
1983	Purim	1990	fibranne	1996	vivisepulture	2002	prospicience	2008	guerdon
1984	luge	1991	antipyretic	1997	euonym	2003	pococurante	2009	Laodicean
1985	milieu	1992	lyceum	1998	chiaroscurist	2004	autochthonous	2010	stromuhr
1986	odontalgia	1993	kamikaze	1999	logorrhea	2005	appoggiatura	2011	cymotrichous
1987	staphylococci								

Names of the Days

ENGLISH	RUSSIAN	HEBREW	FRENCH	ITALIAN	SPANISH	GERMAN	JAPANESE
Sunday	voskresenye	yom rishon	dimanche	domenica	domingo	Sonntag	nichiyoubi
Monday	ponedelnik	yom sheni	lundi	lunedì	lunes	Montag	getsuyoubi
Tuesday	vtornik	yom shlishi	mardi	martedì	martes	Dienstag	kayoubi
Wednesday	sreda	yom ravii	mercredi	mercoledì	miércoles	Mittwoch	suiyoubi
Thursday	chetverg	yom hamishi	jeudi	giovedì	jueves	Donnerstag	mokuyoubi
Friday	pyatnitsa	yom shishi	vendredi	venerdì	viernes	Freitag	kinyoubi
Saturday	subbota	shabbat	samedi	sabato	sábado	Samstag	doyoubi

Foreign Words and Phrases

(A = Arabic; F = French; Ger = German; Gr = Greek; I = Italian; J = Japanese; L = Latin; R = Russian; S = Spanish; Y = Yiddish)

à bientôt (F; ah-bee-en-TOH): so long; see you soon
ad hoc (L; ad-HOK): for the end or purpose at hand; impromptu
ad hominem (L; ad-HOH-mee-nem): argument that criticizes an opponent, often unfairly, rather than addressing an issue directly
al fresco (I; ahl-FRAYS-koh): outdoors
angst (G; angkst): feeling of anxiety or dread
anime (J: A-nuh-may): Japanese-style animation
antebellum (L; AHN-teh-BEL-lum): pre-war
aperçu(s) (F; ah-per-SOO): first perception or insight; outline
au courant (F; oh-koo-RAHN): up-to-date, fashionable
belles lettres (F; bel-LET-truh): writing aspiring to artistic merit
bête noire (F; bet-NWAHR): a thing or person viewed with particular dislike or fear
bildungsroman (Ger; BIL-doongs-roh-mahn): novel embodying coming-of-age story
bodega (S; boh-DAY-gah): grocery store
bonhomie (F; boh-noh-MEE): friendliness
bon vivant (F; bon-vee-VAHN): a person with refined tastes, especially for food and drink
bourgeois (F; boo-ZHWAH): middle-class; conventional; materialistic
carte blanche (F; kahrt-BLANSH): full discretionary power
casus belli (L; KAH-soos-BEL-lee): reason for going to war
cause célèbre (F; kawz-suh-LEB): a notorious incident
cognoscenti (I; kahn-yuh-SHEN-tee): experts; connoisseurs
comme il faut (F; cum-eel-FOH): proper; as it should be
contretemps (F; kon-truh-TAHN): awkward situation
coup de grâce (F; kooh-duh-GRAHS): the decisive final blow
cum laude/magna cum laude/summa cum laude (L; kuhm-LOU-day; MAG-na ... ; SOO-ma ...): with praise or honor/with great praise or honor/with the highest praise or honor
de facto (L; day-FAK-toh): in fact, if not by law
de jure (L; dee-JOOR-ee, day-YOOR-ay): in accordance with right or law
de rigueur (F; duh-ree-GUR): necessary according to convention or etiquette
détente (F; day-TAHNT): an easing of strained relations
deus ex machina (L; DAY-uhs-eks-MAH-keh-nah): person/event that provides a solution unexpectedly or suddenly, espec. (in literature) a contrived solution to a plot
doppelgänger (G; DAH-pul-gang-ur): a double or ghostly counterpart of a person
double entendre (F; DOO-blahn-TAHN-druh): expression with a double meaning, one meaning of which is often risqué
éminence grise (F; ay-meh-nahns-GREEZ): one who wields power behind the scenes
enfant terrible (F; ahn-FAHN-te-REE-bluh): one who is noteworthy for embarrassing or unconventional behavior
ennui (F; ah-NOOEE): boredom; world-weariness; annoyance
e pluribus unum (L; eh-PLOO-ree-boos-OO-noom): out of many, one (US motto)
ersatz (Ger; EHR-zats): artificial; being a (usually inferior) substitute
ex post facto (L; eks-pohst-FAK-toh): retroactive(ly)
fait accompli (F; fayt-uh-kom-PLEE): an accomplished fact
fatwa (A; FAHT-wah): in Islam, a legal or religious decree
faux pas (F; foh-PAH): false step; breach of etiquette
habeas corpus (L; HAY-bee-ahs-KOR-pus): an order for a prisoner to be brought to court to challenge his or her detention
hoi polloi (Gr; hoy-puh-LOY): the masses
impresario (I; im-prah-SAH-ri-oh): manager, promoter, or sponsor of a musical or theatrical program or company

imprimatur (L; im-prah-MAH-toor): approval or official permission to print, espec. by the Roman Catholic church
in loco parentis (L; in-LOH-koh-puh-REN-tis): in place of parent
in medias res (L; in-MAY-dee-oos-rays): into the middle of things
intelligentsia (R; in-te-luh-JEN-see-uh): elite social class made up of intellectuals and educated people
ipso facto (L; ip-soh-FAK-toh): by that fact itself
je ne sais quoi (F; zhuh-nuh-say-KWAH): literally, "I don't know what"; the little something that eludes description
jihad (A; jih-HAHD): Islamic holy war; struggle in devotion to Islam
joie de vivre (F; zhwah-duh-VEEV-ruh): zest for life
leitmotif (Ger; lyt-moh-TEEF): the central theme or idea, particularly in art and literature
mano a mano (S; MAH-noh-ah-MAH-noh): hand to hand; in direct combat
mea culpa (L; MAY-uh-CUL-puh): through my fault
mensch (Y; MENTSCH): an upright, noble, admirable person
modus operandi (L; MOH-duhs-op-uh-RAN-dee): method of operation
mujahideen (A; moo-jah-ha-DEEN): Islamic holy warrior
noblesse oblige (F; noh-BLES-oh-BLEEZH): the obligation of nobility to help the less fortunate
nolo contendere (L; NOH-loh-kohn-TEN-duh-ree): a plea of no contest to charges, without admitting guilt
non compos mentis (L; non-KOM-puhs-MEN-tis): not of sound mind
non sequitur (L; non-SEH-kwi-tour): a conclusion that does not logically follow from what preceded it
nouveau riche (F; noo-voh-REESH): a newly rich person, espec. one who spends money conspicuously
ombudsman (Swedish; AHM-budz-muhn): person who receives, investigates, and settles complaints
par excellence (F; par-ek-seh-LANS): best of all; incomparable
parvenu (F; par-vuh-NOO): upstart
persona non grata (L; per-SOH-nah-non-GRAH-tah): unwelcome person
pièce de résistance (F; pee-es-duh-ray-ZEES-tonz): the outstanding item in a series or group
prima facie (L; pry-muh-FAY-shee-ee; pry-muh-FAY-shuh): true at first glance; presumptively valid
pro bono (L; proh-BOH-noh): (legal work) donated for the public good
quid pro quo (L; kwid-proh-KWOH): something given or received for something else
raison d'être (F; RAY-zohnn-DET-ruh): reason for being
savoir faire (F; sav-wahr-FAIR): dexterity in social affairs
schadenfreude (Ger; SHAH-duhn-froy-deh): joy at another's misfortune
schlemiel (Y; shleh-MEEL): an unlucky, bungling person
schlepp (Y; SHLEP): move slowly, tediously, drag oneself along
semper fidelis (L; SEM-puhr-fee-DAY-lis): always faithful
sobriquet (F; SOH-bri-kay): nickname or informal descriptive name for someone
sotto voce (L; sah-toh-VOH-chee); in a low voice
sui generis (L; soo-ee-JEN-er-is); unique; one of a kind
terra firma (L; TER-uh-FUR-muh): solid ground
troika (R; TROY-kuh): group of three, espec. a ruling group
verboten (Ger; ver-BOH-ten): forbidden
vis-à-vis (F; vee-zuh-VEE): compared with; with regard to
voir dire (F; vwar-DEER): examination by lawyers or judge to determine the suitability of a witness or a prospective juror
zeitgeist (Ger; ZITE-gyste): the general intellectual, moral, and cultural climate of an era

Names for Animal Young

calf: cattle, elephant, hippo, camel, others
cheeper: grouse, partridge, quail
chick: chicken, penguin, other birds
cockerel: rooster
codling, sprag: codfish
colt: horse, zebra (male)
cria: llama, alpaca
cub: lion, bear, shark, fox, others
cygnet: swan
duckling: duck
elver: eel
ephyra: jellyfish
eyas: hawk, others
fawn: deer, antelope
filly: horse, zebra (female)

fingerling, fry: fish generally
fledgling, nestling: birds generally
foal: horse, zebra, others
gosling: goose
heifer: cow
hoglet: hedgehog
joey: kangaroo, opossum, wombat, other marsupials
kid: goat
kit: beaver, rabbit, ferret, wolverine, others
kitten: cat, other small mammals
lamb: sheep
larva: frog, sea urchin, insects generally
parr, smolt, grilse: salmon

peachick: peafowl
piglet, shoat, farrow, suckling: pig
polliwog, tadpole: frog
poult: turkey
puggle: echidna
pullet: hen
pup: dog, fox, seal, rat, others
spat: oyster, other bivalves
spiderling: spider
spike, blinker, tinker: mackerel
squab: pigeon
whelp: dog, tiger, other carnivorous mammals
yearling: cattle, sheep, horse, others

Names for Animal Collectives

alligators: congregation
ants: army, colony, swarm
apes: shrewdness, troop
bats: colony
bears: sleuth, sloth
bees: colony, swarm, hive, grist
birds: flight, volery
boars/swine: singular, sounder
buffalo: gang, obstinacy
butterflies: flutter
buzzards: wake
camels: caravan, flock, train
cats: clowder, cluster, glaring, pounce
cattle: drove
cheetahs: coalition
clams, oysters: bed
cockroaches: intrusion
cranes: sedge, siege
crocodiles: bask, nest, float
crows: murder, horde
dolphins: pod
doves: dule, pitying
ducks: brace, team
eagles: convocation, aerie
ferrets: business
finches: charm

fish: school, shoal
flamingos: stand, flamboyance
foxes: skulk
geese: flock, gaggle, skein
giraffes: corps, herd, tower
goats: tribe, trip
gorillas: band, whoop
grasshoppers: cloud
hares: down, husk, trip
hawks: cast, kettle
hedgehogs: array, prickle
hippopotamuses: bloat
horses: pair, team
hounds: cry, mute, pack
hyenas: cackle
iguanas: mess
jellyfish: smack
kangaroos: mob, troop
larks: exaltation
leopards: leap
lions: pride
locusts: plague, swarm
moles: labor
monkeys: troop
mules: barren, span
nightingales: watch

otters: romp
owls: parliament
oxen: yoke
peacocks: muster
pheasants: nest, nide, bouquet
ponies: string
raccoons: gaze
ravens: unkindness
rhinoceroses: crash
seals: pod
sheep: flock, drove, hurtle
snakes: nest
squirrels: dray, scurry
starlings: flock, murmuration
swans: bevy
tigers: streak
toads: knot
trout: hover
turkeys: rafter
turtles: bale
vultures: committee
whales: gam, herd, pod
woodchucks: fall
woodpeckers: descent
zebras: herd, zeal

Some Common Abbreviations and Acronyms

Acronyms are pronounceable words formed from first letters (or syllables) of other words. Some **abbreviations** below (e.g., AIDS, NATO) are thus acronyms. Some acronyms are words coined as abbreviations and written in lowercase (e.g., sonar, yuppie). Acronyms do not have periods; usage for other abbreviations varies, but periods have become less common. Capitalization usage may vary from what is shown here. Some acronyms may have other, typically less common, meanings not given here. Italicized words preceding parenthetical definitions below are Latin unless otherwise noted. See also Computers and Telecommunications, Weights and Measures, and other chapters.

AA: Alcoholics Anonymous; Associate in Arts; administrative assistant
ABA: American Bar Association
AC: alternating current; air-conditioning
ACLU: American Civil Liberties Union
AD: *anno Domini* (in the year of the Lord)
ADD: attention deficit disorder
AFL-CIO: American Federation of Labor and Congress of Industrial Organizations
AFSCME: American Federation of State, County, and Municipal Employees
AI: artificial intelligence
AIDS: acquired immune deficiency syndrome
ALA: American Library Association
a.m. OR **AM:** *ante meridiem* (before noon)
APO: army post office
APR: annual percentage rate
ARM: adjustable rate mortgage
ASCAP: American Society of Composers, Authors, and Publishers
ASCII: American Standard Code for Information Interchange
ATM: automated teller machine
Ave.: Avenue
AWOL: absent without leave
BA: Bachelor of Arts
bbl: barrel(s)
BC: before Christ
BCE: before the Common Era; before the Christian Era
bpd: barrels per day
BS: Bachelor of Science
Btu: British thermal unit(s)
bu: bushel(s)
BYOB: bring your own bottle
C: Celsius, centigrade
c: *circa* (about); copyright
CAT: computerized axial tomography
CD: compact disc
CDC: Centers for Disease Control and Prevention; Community Development Corporation
CE: Common Era; Christian Era
CEO: chief executive officer
cf.: *confer* (compare)
CFO: chief financial officer
CIA: Central Intelligence Agency
CIF: cost, insurance, and freight

COD: cash (or collect) on delivery
COL or **Col.:** Colonel
COLA: cost of living adjustment
COO: chief operating officer
CPA: certified public accountant
CPI: consumer price index
CPL or **Cpl.:** Corporal
CPR: cardiopulmonary resuscitation
CPU: central processing unit
CST: central standard time
CV: curriculum vitae
DA: district attorney
DC: direct current
DD: Doctor of Divinity
DDS: Doctor of Dental Surgery
DEA: Drug Enforcement Agency
DHS: Department of Homeland Security
DMD: Doctor of Dental Medicine
DMZ: demilitarized zone
DNA: deoxyribonucleic acid
DNR: do not resuscitate
DOA: dead on arrival
DOB: date of birth
dpi: dots per inch
DPT: diphtheria, pertussis, tetanus
DUI: driving under the influence
DVD: digital video disc
DVM: Doctor of Veterinary Medicine
DWI: driving while intoxicated
ed.: edited; edition; editor
EEG: electroencephalogram
e.g.: *exempli gratia* (for example)
EKG: electrocardiogram
EOE: equal opportunity employer
EP: extended play
EPA: Environmental Protection Agency
ERA: Equal Rights Amendment; earned run average
ESL: English as a second language
ESP: extrasensory perception
Esq.: Esquire
EST: eastern standard time
et al.: *et alii* (and others)
etc.: *et cetera* (and so forth)
EU: European Union
F: Fahrenheit
Fannie Mae: Federal National Mortgage Association
FAQ: frequently asked questions
FBI: Federal Bureau of Investigation

FDA: Food and Drug Administration
FDIC: Federal Deposit Insurance Corporation
FEMA: Federal Emergency Management Agency
ff.: and those following
FICA: Federal Insurance Contributions Act (Social Security)
fl.: *floruit* (flourished), used for hist. figures when life dates uncertain
Freddie Mac: Federal Home Loan Mortgage Corporation
FTP: file transfer protocol
FY: fiscal year
FYI: for your information
GATT: General Agreement on Tariffs and Trade
GB: gigabyte(s)
GDP: gross domestic product
GED: general equivalency diploma; General Educational Development (Tests)
GMT: Greenwich mean time
GOP: Grand Old Party (Republican Party)
GPS: Global Positioning System
GUI: graphical user interface
hazmat: HAZardous MATerial
HDTV: high-definition television
HIV: human immunodeficiency virus
HMO: health maintenance organization
HMS: His/Her Majesty's Ship (UK)
Hon.: the Honorable
HOV: high-occupancy vehicle
HRH: Her (His) Royal Highness (UK)
HTML: hypertext markup language
HTTP: hypertext transfer protocol
HUD: Department of Housing and Urban Development
HVAC: heating, ventilating, and air-conditioning
Hz: hertz
ibid: *ibidem* (in the same place)
i.e.: *id est* (that is)
ICU: intensive care unit
IM: instant messaging
IMF: International Monetary Fund
INS: Immigration and Naturalization Service
IPO: initial public offering
IQ: intelligence quotient
IRA: individual retirement account; Irish Republican Army

IRS: Internal Revenue Service
ISBN: International Standard Book Number
ISP: Internet service provider
IVF: in vitro fertilization
JD: *Juris Doctor* (Doctor of Law)
k: karat
K: kelvin
kWh: kilowatt-hour(s)
laser: Light Amplification by Stimulated Emission of Radiation
LGBT: lesbian, gay, bisexual, and transgender
LLP: limited liability partnership
loc. cit.: *loco citato* (in the place cited)
LSAT: Law School Admission Test
LT or Lt.: Lieutenant
MA: Master of Arts
MB: megabyte(s)
MBA: Master of Business Administration
MCAT: Medical College Admission Test
MD: *Medicinae Doctor* (Doctor of Medicine)
MIA: missing in action
modem: MOdulator-DEModulator
MP: member of Parliament (UK)
mph: miles per hour
MRI: magnetic resonance imaging
ms, mss: manuscript(s)
MS: Master of Science; multiple sclerosis
MSG: monosodium glutamate
MST: mountain standard time
MVP: most valuable player
NA: not applicable; not available
NAACP: National Association for the Advancement of Colored People
NAFTA: North American Free Trade Agreement
NASA: National Aeronautics and Space Administration
NATO: North Atlantic Treaty Organization
NB or n.b.: *nota bene* (note carefully)
NCAA: National Collegiate Athletic Association
NEA: National Education Association

NIH: National Institutes of Health
NOW: National Organization for Women
NPR: National Public Radio
NRA: National Rifle Association
obs.: obsolete
OED: Oxford English Dictionary
op: *opus* (work)
OMB: Office of Management and Budget
OPEC: Organization of Petroleum Exporting Countries
OTC: over-the-counter
p, pp: page(s)
PA: public address
PAC: political action committee
PC: personal computer; politically correct
PDA: Personal Digital Assistant
PhD: *Philosophiae Doctor* (doctor of philosophy)
PIN: personal identification number
p.m. or PM: *post meridiem* (after noon)
PPO: preferred provider organization, a type of healthcare provider network
PS: *post scriptum* (postscript)
PST: Pacific standard time
pt: part(s); pint(s); point(s)
PVT or Pvt.: Private
QC: Queen's Council (UK)
QED: *quod erat demonstrandum* (which was to be demonstrated)
q.v.: *quod vide* (which see)
radar: RAdio Detecting And Ranging
RAM: random access memory
RCMP: Royal Canadian Mounted Police
REM: rapid eye movement
Rev.: Reverend
rev.: revised; reviewed
RIP: *requiescat in pace* (may he/she rest in peace)
RN: Registered Nurse
RNA: ribonucleic acid
ROM: read only memory
ROTC: Reserve Officers' Training Corps
rpm: revolutions per minute

RSVP: *répondez s'il vous plaît* (Fr.) (please reply)
SARS: severe acute respiratory syndrome
SASE: self-addressed stamped envelope
SEC: Securities and Exchange Commission
SETI: Search for Extraterrestrial Intelligence
SGT or Sgt.: Sergeant
SIDS: sudden infant death syndrome
SJ: Society of Jesus (Jesuits)
sonar: SOund NAvigation and Ranging
SPCA: Society for the Prevention of Cruelty to Animals
SSI: Supplementary Security Income
St.: Saint; Street
TB: tuberculosis; terabyte(s)
TBA: to be announced
TBD: to be determined
TEFL: teaching English as a foreign language
UFO: unidentified flying object
UPC: Universal Product Code
URL: Universal Resource Locator
USDA: United States Department of Agriculture
USS: United States ship
UTC: coordinated universal time
var.: variant
VAT: value-added tax
VCR: videocassette recorder
viz: *videlicet* (namely)
VP: vice president
W: watt(s)
WHO: World Health Organization
WMD: weapon of mass destruction
WPM: words per minute
WWW: World Wide Web
YMCA: Young Men's Christian Association
YWCA: Young Women's Christian Association
YTD: year to date
yuppie: young urban professional
ZIP: zone improvement plan (U.S. Postal Service)

Eponyms
(words named for people)

boycott: to avoid trade or dealings with, as a protest; after Charles C. Boycott, an English land agent in County Mayo, Ireland, ostracized in 1880 for refusing to reduce rents

derby: a stiff felt hat with a dome-shaped crown and narrow rolled brim; after Edward Stanley, 12th Earl of Derby, who in 1780 founded the Derby horse race, to which these hats are worn

derrick: a type of crane consisting of a boom connected to the base of an upright mast; after Derrick, early 17th-cent. English hangman who used a gallows that operated via cables and pulleys

draconian: harsh or severe; after Draco, statesman who codified the laws in Athens in 621 BCE

gerrymander: to draw an election district in such a way as to favor a political party; after Elbridge Gerry, who created (1812) just such an election district (shaped like a salamander) during his governorship of Massachusetts

guillotine: a machine for beheading; after Joseph Guillotin, French physician who proposed its use in 1789 as more humane than hanging

Luddite: one who opposes new technology; from Ned Ludd, leader of a group of textile workers in England who destroyed machinery in the early 1800s

maudlin: excessively sentimental; from scriptural figure Mary Magdalene, who is often shown weeping in depictions

milquetoast: a timid, unassertive person; after Caspar Milquetoast, comic strip character created by American Harold Tucker Webster in 1924

Pollyanna: an overly optimistic person; based on the title character of a 1913 novel by American writer Eleanor Porter

salmonella: group of bacteria that can cause infections when contaminated food or water is consumed; named after Daniel Elmer Salmon, American veterinarian and public health official

sandwich: two or more slices of bread with a filling in-between; after John Montagu, 4th Earl of Sandwich (1718-92), who supposedly ate these at the gaming table

shrapnel: originally, a projectile with lead balls designed to inflict maximum damage in explosions, later pieces of shell casings; from Henry Shrapnel (1761-1842), British artillery officer who designed the projectile

silhouette: an outline image; from Étienne de Silhouette (1709-67), a stingy French finance minister

Zamboni: an ice resurfacing machine; after American inventor Frank Zamboni, who owned an ice skating rink

Palindromes and Anagrams

A **palindrome** is a sequence of letters (or other symbols) that read the same backward and forward. Words such as *radar* and *racecar* are familiar palindromes, as are names such as Hannah, and phrases such as "Madam, I'm Adam" and "A man, a plan, a canal, Panama!" Certain dates, such as 11/02/2011, are also palindromes.

An **anagram** is a word or word sequence made by rearranging all the letters of another word or word sequence. Websites can be consulted that generate large numbers of anagrams for a given expression ("world almanac" has over 2,500 anagrams), but most, even if technically made up of words, make little sense. The best anagrams not only make some sense but fit the subject in a clever or amusing way. Ex.: stipend = spend it!; archaeologists = goal is to search; Elvis Aaron Presley = Seen alive? Sorry, pal; The Leaning Tower of Pisa = I spot one giant flaw here.

Top 10 First Names of Americans by Decade or Year of Birth

Source: U.S. Social Security Administration

BOYS

1880-1889	John, William, Charles, George, James, Frank, Joseph, Harry, Henry, Edward
1890-1899	John, William, George, James, Charles, Joseph, Frank, Robert, Harry, Henry
1900-1909	John, William, James, George, Joseph, Charles, Robert, Frank, Edward, Henry
1910-1919	John, William, James, Robert, Joseph, Charles, George, Edward, Frank, Walter
1920-1929	John, Robert, James, William, Charles, George, Joseph, Richard, Edward, Donald
1930-1939	Robert, James, John, William, Richard, Charles, Donald, George, Thomas, Joseph
1940-1949	James, Robert, John, William, Richard, David, Charles, Thomas, Michael, Ronald
1950-1959	Michael, James, Robert, John, David, William, Steven, Richard, Thomas, Mark
1960-1969	Michael, John, David, James, Robert, Mark, Steven, William, Jeffrey, Richard
1970-1979	Michael, Christopher, Jason, David, James, John, Brian, Robert, Steven, William
1980-1989	Michael, Christopher, Matthew, Joshua, David, Daniel, James, John, Robert, Brian
1990-1999	Michael, Christopher, Matthew, Joshua, Nicholas, Jacob, Andrew, Daniel, Brandon, Tyler
2000-2009	Jacob, Michael, Joshua, Matthew, Daniel, Christopher, Andrew, Ethan, Joseph, William
2010	Jacob, Ethan, Michael, Jayden, William, Alexander, Noah, Daniel, Aiden, Anthony

GIRLS

1880-1889	Mary, Anna, Elizabeth, Catherine, Margaret, Emma, Bertha, Minnie, Florence, Clara
1890-1899	Mary, Anna, Margaret, Helen, Catherine, Elizabeth, Florence, Ruth, Rose, Ethel
1900-1909	Mary, Helen, Margaret, Anna, Ruth, Catherine, Elizabeth, Dorothy, Marie, Mildred
1910-1919	Mary, Helen, Dorothy, Margaret, Ruth, Catherine, Mildred, Anna, Elizabeth, Frances
1920-1929	Mary, Dorothy, Betty, Helen, Margaret, Ruth, Virginia, Catherine, Doris, Frances
1930-1939	Mary, Betty, Barbara, Shirley, Patricia, Dorothy, Joan, Margaret, Carol, Nancy
1940-1949	Mary, Linda, Barbara, Patricia, Carol, Sandra, Nancy, Sharon, Judith, Susan
1950-1959	Deborah, Mary, Linda, Patricia, Susan, Barbara, Karen, Nancy, Donna, Catherine
1960-1969	Lisa, Deborah, Mary, Karen, Michelle, Susan, Kimberly, Lori, Teresa, Linda
1970-1979	Jennifer, Michelle, Amy, Melissa, Kimberly, Lisa, Angela, Heather, Kelly, Sarah
1980-1989	Jessica, Jennifer, Ashley, Sarah, Amanda, Stephanie, Nicole, Melissa, Katherine, Megan
1990-1999	Ashley, Jessica, Sarah, Brittany, Emily, Kaitlyn, Samantha, Megan, Brianna, Katherine
2000-2009	Emily, Madison, Emma, Olivia, Hannah, Abigail, Isabella, Samantha, Elizabeth, Ashley
2010	Isabella, Sophia, Emma, Olivia, Ava, Emily, Abigail, Madison, Chloe, Mia

Origins of Popular American Given Names

Source: Dr. Cleveland Kent Evans, Bellevue University, Bellevue, NE; World Almanac research

Boys

Alexander: Gr. *Alexandros*, "defender of man"

Andrew: Gr. *andreios*, "manly"

Anthony: Roman *Antonius*, possibly from Gr. *anthos*, "flower"

Benjamin: Heb. *Binyamin*, "son of the right hand"

Brandon: Eng. place name, "gorse-covered hill"

Brian: Irish, perhaps Celtic *Brigonos*, "high" or "noble"

Charles: Ger. *ceorl*, "free man"

Christopher: Gr. *Khristophoros*, "bearing Christ [in one's heart]"

Daniel: Heb. "God is my judge"

David: Heb. "beloved," perhaps "darling"

Edward: Old Eng. *Eadweard*, "wealth-ward"

Elijah: Heb. "the Lord is my God"

Ethan: Heb. "solid, firm"

Frank: Ger. "Frenchman"

George: Gr. *georgos*, "soil tiller, farmer"

Henry: Ger. *Haimric*, "home-power"

Jack: nickname for John

Jacob: Heb. *Yaakov*, "God protects" or "supplanter"

James: Late Lat. *Iacomus*, form of Jacob

Jason: Gr. *Iason*, "healer"

Jayden: prob. from Jay (short form for many *J* names) and Hayden (Old Eng. "little hollow")

Jeffrey: Norman Fr., from Ger. *Gaufrid*, "land-peace," or *Gisfrid*, "pledge-peace"

John: Heb. *Yohanan*, "God is gracious"

Jonathan: Heb. "God has given"

José: Heb. and Aramaic *Yose*, variant of Joseph

Joseph: Heb. *Yosef*, "[God] shall add"

Joshua: Heb. *Yoshua*, "God saves"

Logan: Gaelic "little hollow"

Mark: Lat. *Marcus*, perhaps from Mars, Roman god of war

Mason: Fr. "stone worker, " related to Old Eng. "work"

Matthew: Heb. *Mattathia*, "gift of God"

Michael: Heb. "who could ever be like God?"

Nathan: Heb. "God has given"; modern short form of Nathaniel or Jonathan

Nicholas: Gr. *Nikolaos*, "victory-people"

Noah: Heb. "rest"

Patrick: Lat. *Patricius*, "belonging to the noble class"

Richard: Ger. "power-hardy"

Robert: Ger. *Hrodberht*, "fame-bright"

Ryan: prob. from Irish surname, Gaelic "king"

Samuel: Heb. *Shemuel*, "God heard"

Sean: Gaelic form of John

Steven: Gr. *stephanos*, "crown" or "garland"

Thomas: Aramaic "twin"

Tyler: Old Eng. *tigeler*, "tile layer"

William: Ger. *Wilhelm*, "will-helmet"

Girls

Abigail: Heb. "my father is joy"

Addison: Eng. "son of Adam"

Alexandra, Sandra: fem. forms of Alexander

Alexis: Gr. "helper" or "defender"

Alyssa: variant of Alicia (Eng., Span.) or Alice (Eng., Fr.); may mean "noble"

Amanda: 17th-cent. invention from Lat. "lovable"

Amy: Old Fr. *Amee*, "beloved"

Andrea: fem. form of Andrew

Angela: Gr. *angelos*, "messenger [of God]"

Anna: Lat., Gr. form of Hannah; variants include Ann (Eng.), Ana (Span.), Anne (Eng., Fr., Ger.)

Ashley: Eng. place name, "ash grove"

Ava: prob. modern form of Eva, Lat. form of Heb. *Eve*, "to breathe"

Barbara: Gr. *barbarus*, "foreign"

Brianna: modern fem. form of Brian

Brittany: place name, Fr. province settled by Britons

Carol: form of Charles

Chloe: Gr. "young shoot," "blooming"

Claire, Clara: Lat. *clarus*, "famous"

Deborah: Heb. "bee"

Donna: Ital. "lady"

Dorothy: Gr. *Dorothea*, "gift of God"

Elizabeth: Heb. *Elisheba*, perhaps "God is my oath" or "God is good fortune"

Ella: prob. variant or nickname for Eleanor or Ellen

Emily: Roman *Aemilia*, possibly from Lat. *aemulus*, "rival"

Emma: Ger. *ermen*, "whole" or "entire"

Frances: fem. form of Francis, "a Frenchman"

Grace: Lat. *gratia*, "grace, blessing"

Hailey: Eng. place name, "hay clearing"

Hannah: Heb. "He has favored me"

Heather: Middle Eng. *hathir*, "heather"

Helen: Gr. *Helene*, possibly "sunbeam"

Isabella, Isabel: Lat., Sp. variant of Elizabeth

Jennifer: Cornish form of Welsh *Gwenhwyfar*, "fair-smooth"

Jessica: Shakesp. invention, prob. fem. form of Jesse, Heb. "God exists"

Judith: Heb. "Jewish woman"

Julia: fem. form of Julius, Roman family name, or Lat. "youthful"

Kaitlyn: American spelling of Caitlin, the Irish form of Katherine

Karen: Danish form of Katherine

Katherine: Egyptian *Aikaterine*, later modified to resemble Gr. *katharos*, "pure"

Kelly: Irish Gaelic *Ceallagh*, perhaps "churchgoer" or "bright-headed"

Kimberly: Eng. place name, "Cyneburgh's clearing"
Laura: Lat. *laurus*, "laurel"
Linda: Sp. "pretty" or Ger. "tender"
Lily: for the flower, suggesting purity, innocence
Lisa: nickname for Elizabeth
Madison: Middle Eng. surname, "son of Madeline or Maud"
Margaret: Gr. *margaron*, "pearl"
Maria, Marie, Mary: Lat., Fr., Eng. forms for Heb. *Maryam*, perhaps "seeress" or "wished-for child"
Megan: Welsh form of Margaret

Melissa: Gr. "bee"
Mia: Nordic or Ital., short for Maria and other names
Michelle: Fr. fem. form of Michael
Nancy: medieval Eng. nickname for Agnes (Gr. *hagnos*, "holy"), later also for Ann
Natalie: Fr., from Lat. *natalia*, "birthday [of Christ]"
Nicole: Fr. fem. form of Nicholas
Olivia: Lat. *oliva*, "olive tree"
Patricia: Lat. fem. form of Patrick
Rachel: Heb. "ewe"

Rose: Ger. *hros*, "horse," or Lat. *rosa*, "rose"
Ruth: Heb., perhaps "companion"
Samantha: colonial American invention, prob. combining Sam from Samuel with *-antha* from Gr. *anthos*, "flower"
Sarah: Heb. "princess"
Sharon: Biblical place name, Heb. "plain"
Sophia: Gr. "wisdom"
Stephanie: Fr. fem. form of Steven
Susan: Eng. form of Heb. *Shoshana*, "lily"
Teresa: Sp., perhaps "woman from Therasia"
Victoria: fem. form of Victor, from Lat. *vincere*, "to conquer"

30 Most Common Last Names in the U.S. Population

Source: 2000 Census, U.S. Census Bureau, U.S. Dept. of Commerce

Rank	Name	Frequency[1] (%)	Rank	Name	Frequency[1] (%)	Rank	Name	Frequency[1] (%)	Rank	Name	Frequency[1] (%)
1.	Smith	0.881	9.	Rodriguez	0.298	17.	Martin	0.249	24.	Harris	0.220
2.	Johnson	0.688	10.	Wilson	0.290	18.	Jackson	0.247	25.	Clark	0.203
3.	Williams	0.569	11.	Martinez	0.287	19.	Thompson	0.239	26.	Lewis	0.189
4.	Brown	0.512	12.	Anderson	0.283	20.	White	0.237	27.	Robinson	0.186
5.	Jones	0.505	13.	Taylor	0.267	21.	Lopez	0.230	28.	Walker	0.186
6.	Miller	0.418	14.	Thomas	0.263	22.	Lee	0.225	29.	Perez	0.181
7.	Davis	0.398	15.	Hernandez	0.262	23.	Gonzalez	0.222	30.	Hall	0.176
8.	Garcia	0.318	16.	Moore	0.259						

(1) Percent of people in the sample population with the name shown. The sample population consists of nearly 2.7 mil respondents to the 2000 census.

Pen Names

Woody Allen	Allen Stewart Konigsberg
Maya Angelou	Marguerite Johnson
Richard Bachman	Stephen King
Currer, Ellis, and Acton Bell	Charlotte, Emily, and Anne Brontë
Nellie Bly	Elizabeth Jane Cochrane Seaman
John le Carré	David John Moore Cornwell
Lewis Carroll	Charles Lutwidge Dodgson
Colette	Sidonie Gabrielle Colette
George Eliot	Mary Ann or Marian Evans
Maksim Gorky	Aleksey Maksimovich Peshkov
O. Henry	William Sydney Porter
Hergé	Georges Rémi
P. D. James	Phyllis Dorothy James White
Ann Landers	Esther Pauline Lederer
André Maurois	Émile Herzog
Molière	Jean Baptiste Poquelin
Toni Morrison	Chloe Anthony Wofford
Pablo Neruda	Neftalí Ricardo Reyes Basoalto
Frank O'Connor	Michael Donovan
George Orwell	Eric Arthur Blair
Ouida	Marie Louise de la Ramée
Ellery Queen	Frederic Dannay and Manfred B. Lee
Ayn Rand	Alice Rosenbaum
Anne Rice	Howard Allen O'Brien
Nora Roberts/J. D. Robb	Eleanor Marie Robertson
Saki	Hector Hugh Munro
George Sand	Amandine Lucie Aurore Dupin
Dr. Seuss	Theodor Seuss Geisel
Lemony Snicket	Daniel Handler
Stendhal	Marie-Henri Beyle
Mark Twain	Samuel Clemens
Voltaire	François Marie Arouet

American Manual Alphabet

In the American Manual Alphabet, each letter of the alphabet is represented by a position of the fingers. This system was originally developed in France by Charles Michel de l'Epee in the 1700s. Laurent Clerc and Thomas Gallaudet further refined it into the American Manual Alphabet.

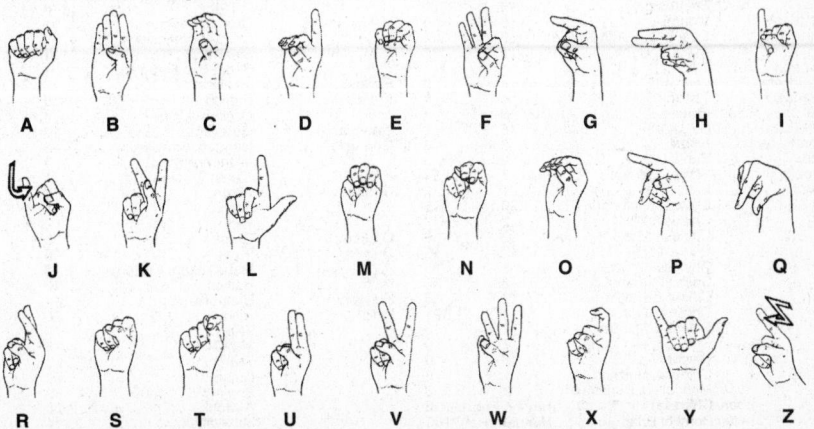

Commonly Misspelled English Words

accidentally	cemetery	eligible	innocuous	miniature	permissible	separate
accommodate	changeable	eliminate	innovative	miscellaneous	perseverance	sheriff
accumulate	collectible	embarrass	inoculate	Mississippi	personnel	sincerely
acknowledgment	commitment	environment	irresistible	misspelled	possess	stubbornness
acquainted	committee	existence	jewelry	mnemonic	potatoes	supersede
acquire	connoisseur	fascinating	judgment	mysterious	prescient	temperament
a lot	conscience	February	laboratory	necessary	privilege	temperature
already	conscientious	fluorescent	leisure	noticeable	propaganda	transferred
amateur	conscious	forty	license	occasionally	questionnaire	truly
appearance	convenience	gauge	liaison	occurrence	receipt	twelfth
appropriate	deceive	government	lieutenant	omitted	receive	vaccinate
assimilate	defendant	grammar	lightning	opportunity	recommend	vacillate
bureau	definitely	harass	liquefy	optimistic	rhythm	vacuum
business	desirable	humorous	maintenance	parallel	ridiculous	vicious
calendar	desperate	incidentally	marriage	patience	sacrilegious	Wednesday
canceled	deterrent	independent	medieval	performance	seize	weird
Caribbean	eighth	indispensable	millennium	permanent	sergeant	wholly

The Principal Languages of the World

Source: Database of *Ethnologue: Languages of the World, 16th Edition.* www.ethnologue.com. M. Paul Lewis, editor. Copyright © 2009, SIL International. Used by permission.

The following tables count only first language (or mother tongue) speakers. All figures are estimates, made for the latest edition, published in 2009.

Languages Spoken by the Most People

This table combines macrolanguages and individual languages, e.g., the Chinese and Arabic macrolanguages combine all the individual varieties listed in the next table. Ranked by millions of speakers.

Language	Speakers (millions)	Language	Speakers (millions)	Language	Speakers (millions)
Chinese	1,213	Russian	144	French	68
Spanish	329	Japanese	122	Marathi	68
English	328	German	90	Korean	66
Arabic	221	Javanese	85	Tamil	66
Hindi	182	Lahnda	78	Italian	62
Bengali	181	Telugu	70	Urdu	61
Portuguese	178	Vietnamese	69		

Individual Languages Spoken by at Least 2 Million People

A "hub" country is the country of origin, not necessarily the country where the most speakers reside (e.g., Portugal is the hub country of Portuguese, although more Portuguese speakers live in Brazil). Number of speakers listed is worldwide total for each language. Hub countries are listed alphabetically; within a hub, individual languages are ranked by millions of speakers.

Hub	Language	Countries	Speakers (millions)	Hub	Language	Countries	Speakers (millions)
Afghanistan	Farsi, Eastern	3	8	China (cont'd)	Chinese, Pu-Xian	3	3
	Hazaragi	4	2		Nuosu	1	2
Albania	Albanian, Tosk	10	3	Congo, Dem. Rep.	Luba-Kasai	1	6
Algeria	Arabic, Algerian Spoken	6	22		Koongo	3	5
	Kabyle	3	3		Kituba	1	4
Angola	Umbundu	2	4		Lingala	3	2
	Kimbundu	1	3	Côte d'Ivoire	Baoulé	1	2
Armenia	Armenian	30	6	Croatia	Croatian	14	6
Austria	Bavarian	4	13	Czech Republic	Czech	12	9
Azerbaijan	Azerbaijani, North	10	7	Denmark	Danish	8	6
Bangladesh	Bengali	10	181	Egypt	Arabic, Egyptian Spoken	10	54
	Rangpuri	2	15		Arabic, Sa'idi Spoken	1	19
	Chittagonian	1	13	Ethiopia	Amharic	6	18
	Sylheti	10	10		Oromo, West Central	2	9
Belarus	Belarusan	16	9		Tigrigna	6	6
Belgium	Vlaams	5	6		Oromo, Eastern	1	5
Bolivia	Quechua, South Bolivian	2	4		Oromo, Borana-Arsi-Guji	3	4
	Aymara, Central	4	2		Sidamo	1	3
Bosnia and					Sebat Bet Gurage	1	2
Herzegovina	Bosnian	4	2	Finland	Finnish	7	5
Botswana	Tswana	4	5	France	French	60	68
Brazil	Hunsrik	5	3		Occitan	4	2
Bulgaria	Bulgarian	16	9	Georgia	Georgian	13	4
Burkina Faso	Mòoré	7	5	Germany	German, Standard	43	90
Burundi	Rundi	4	5		Mainfränkisch	1	5
Cambodia	Khmer, Central	7	14		Saxon, Upper	1	2
Cameroon	Beti	1	2	Ghana	Abron	2	23
China	Chinese, Mandarin	20	845		Akan	1	8
	Chinese, Wu	2	77		Éwé	2	3
	Chinese, Yue	20	56	Greece	Greek	38	13
	Chinese, Min Nan	10	47	Guinea	Pular	6	3
	Chinese, Jinyu	1	45		Maninkakan, Eastern	3	2
	Chinese, Xiang	2	36	Haiti	Haitian	10	8
	Chinese, Hakka	17	30	Hungary	Hungarian	14	13
	Chinese, Gan	1	21	India	Hindi	20	182
	Chinese, Min Bei	2	10		Telugu	10	70
	Chinese, Min Dong	7	9		Marathi	5	68
	Uighur	15	9		Tamil	17	66
	Chinese, Huizhou	1	5		Gujarati	20	47
	Mongolian, Peripheral	2	3		Bhojpuri	3	39
	Chinese, Min Zhong	1	3		Awadhi	2	38
	Bouyei	4	3		Malayalam	11	36

Hub	Language	Countries	Speakers (millions)
India (cont'd)	Kannada	3	35
	Maithili	2	35
	Oriya	2	32
	Panjabi, Eastern	12	28
	Assamese	4	17
	Chhattisgarhi	1	15
	Haryanvi	1	13
	Magahi	1	13
	Deccan	1	13
	Degaru	1	13
	Malvi	1	10
	Kanauji	1	10
	Dhundari	1	9
	Bagheli	2	8
	Varhadi-Nagpuri	1	7
	Santali	4	6
	Lambadi	1	6
	Kashmiri	4	6
	Marwari	3	6
	Mewati	1	5
	Hadothi	1	5
	Konkani	2	4
	Merwari	1	4
	Mina	1	4
	Konkani, Goan	3	4
	Godwari	1	3
	Shekhawati	1	3
	Garhwali	1	3
	Indian Sign Language	3	3
	Kumaoni	1	2
	Dogri	1	2
	Bagri	2	2
	Kurux	3	2
	Mewari	1	2
Indonesia	Javanese	5	85
	Sunda	1	34
	Indonesian	6	23
	Madura	2	14
	Minangkabau	1	6
	Musi	1	4
	Aceh	1	4
	Banjar	2	4
	Bugis	2	4
	Bali	1	3
	Betawi	1	3
	Malay, Central	1	2
	Sasak	1	2
	Batak Toba	1	2
Iran	Farsi, Western	27	24
	Azerbaijani, South	8	13
	Domari	14	4
	Gilaki	1	3
	Mazanderani	1	3
	Kurdish, Southern	2	3
Iraq	Arabic, Mesopotamian Spoken	5	15
	Arabic, North Mesopotamian Spoken	4	6
	Kurdish, Central	2	4
	Arabic, Gulf Spoken	10	4
Israel	Hebrew	8	5
Italy	Italian	34	62
	Lombard	3	9
	Napoletano-Calabrese	1	7
	Venetian	4	6
	Sicilian	1	5
	Piemontese	3	3
	Emiliano-Romagnolo	2	2
Jamaica	Jamaican Creole English	7	3
Japan	Japanese	25	122
Jordan	Arabic, South Levantine Spoken	9	6
Kazakhstan	Kazakh	14	8
Kenya	Gikuyu	1	7
	Dholuo	2	4
	Kamba	1	4
	Ekegusii	2	2
Korea, South	Korean	33	66
Kyrgyzstan	Kyrgyz	9	3
Laos	Lao	7	3
Lesotho	Sotho, Southern	4	6
Libya	Arabic, Libyan Spoken	3	4
Lithuania	Lithuanian	19	3
Macedonia	Macedonian	9	2
Madagascar	Malagasy, Plateau	4	8
Malawi	Nyanja	6	9
Malaysia	Malay	7	9
	Malay, Kedah	2	3

Hub	Language	Countries	Speakers (millions)
Mali	Bamanankan	7	3
Mauritania	Hassaniyya	8	3
Mongolia	Mongolian, Halh	5	2
Morocco	Arabic, Moroccan Spoken	10	21
	Tamazight, Central Atlas	3	3
	Tachelhit	3	3
Mozambique	Makhuwa	1	3
	Ndau	2	2
Myanmar (Burma)	Burmese	5	32
	Shan	3	3
Nepal	Nepali	5	14
Netherlands	Dutch	12	22
Niger	Zarma	4	2
Nigeria	Hausa	13	25
	Yoruba	6	19
	Igbo	1	18
	Kanuri, Central	6	6
	Tiv	2	2
Norway	Norwegian	1	5
Pakistan	Panjabi, Western	7	63
	Urdu	23	61
	Sindhi	8	21
	Seraiki	3	14
	Pashto, Northern	7	10
	Pashto, Central	1	8
	Balochi, Southern	4	3
	Pashto, Southern	6	3
	Brahui	4	2
Paraguay	Guaraní, Paraguayan	2	5
Philippines	Filipino	1	25
	Tagalog	8	24
	Cebuano	2	16
	Ilocano	2	7
	Hiligaynon	2	6
	Waray-Waray	1	3
	Bicolano, Central	1	3
Poland	Polish	23	40
Portugal	Portuguese	37	178
Romania	Romanian	20	23
Russia	Russian	33	144
	Tatar	19	7
Rwanda	Rwanda	4	8
Saudi Arabia	Arabic, Najdi Spoken	7	10
	Arabic, Hijazi Spoken	2	6
Senegal	Wolof	6	4
	Pulaar	6	4
Serbia	Serbian	22	7
	Albanian, Gheg	9	4
Slovakia	Slovak	12	5
Somalia	Somali	13	14
South Africa	Zulu	6	10
	Xhosa	3	8
	Afrikaans	12	5
	Sotho, Northern	2	4
	Tsonga	4	4
Spain	Spanish	44	329
	Catalan-Valencian-Balear	18	12
	Galician	2	3
Sri Lanka	Sinhala	8	16
Sudan	Arabic, Sudanese Spoken	6	17
Swaziland	Swati	4	2
Sweden	Swedish	8	8
Switzerland	German, Swiss	5	6
Syria	Arabic, North Levantine Spoken	16	14
Tajikistan	Tajiki	8	4
Tanzania	Sukuma	1	5
Thailand	Thai	5	20
	Thai, Northeastern	1	15
	Thai, Northern	2	6
	Thai, Southern	1	5
Tunisia	Arabic, Tunisian Spoken	5	9
Turkey	Turkish	36	51
	Kurdish, Northern	32	9
Turkmenistan	Turkmen	14	7
Uganda	Ganda	1	4
	Nyankore	1	2
	Soga	1	2
Ukraine	Ukrainian	27	37
United Kingdom	English	112	328
Uzbekistan	Uzbek, Northern	12	19
Vietnam	Vietnamese	23	69
Yemen	Arabic, Sanaani Spoken	1	8
	Arabic, Ta'izzi-Adeni Spoken	8	7
Zambia	Bemba	4	4
Zimbabwe	Shona	5	11

BUILDINGS, BRIDGES, AND TUNNELS

Tallest Buildings in the World

Source: Phorio, phorio.com; Council on Tall Buildings and Urban Habitat, Illinois Inst. of Technology, www.ctbuh.org

Structures under construction and topped out architecturally are denoted by an asterisk (*). Year in parentheses is date of completion or projected completion. Only buildings that are completed or under construction and topped out as of Sept. 2011 are included here. Height is generally measured from the lowest significant open-air pedestrian entrance to the architectural top, including penthouses, spires, and other decorative features that are an integral part of the design. Stories generally counted from street level.

Building	Ht. (ft)	Stories
Burj Khalifa, Dubai, United Arab Emirates (2010)	2,720	163
*Makkah Royal Clock Tower Hotel, Makkah, Saudi Arabia (2011)	1,972	95
Taipei 101, Taipei, Taiwan (2004)	1,667	101
Shanghai World Financial Center, Shanghai, China (2008)	1,614	101
International Commerce Centre, Hong Kong, China (2010)	1,588	108
Petronas Tower I, Kuala Lumpur, Malaysia (1998)	1,483	88
Petronas Tower II, Kuala Lumpur, Malaysia (1998)	1,483	88
Zifeng Tower, Nanjing, China (2010)	1,476	66
Willis Tower, Chicago, United States (1974)	1,451	108
*Kingkey 100, Shenzhen, China (2012)	1,449	100
Guangzhou International Finance Center, Guangzhou, China (2010)	1,439	103
Trump International Hotel & Tower, Chicago, U.S. (2009)	1,389	98
Jin Mao Building, Shanghai, China (1999)	1,380	88
*Princess Tower, Dubai, UAE (2011)	1,358	101
*Al Hamra Firdous Tower, Kuwait City, Kuwait (2011)	1,354	77
Two International Finance Centre, Hong Kong, China (2003)	1,352	88
CITIC Plaza, Guangzhou, China (1997)	1,280	80
*23 Marina, Dubai, UAE (2011)	1,276	90
Shun Hing Square, Shenzhen, China (1996)	1,260	69
Empire State Building, New York, U.S. (1931)	1,250	102
*Elite Residence, Dubai, UAE (2012)	1,250	87
*Emirates Park Towers Hotel & Spa 1, Dubai, UAE (2011)	1,234	77
*Emirates Park Towers Hotel & Spa 2, Dubai, UAE (2011)	1,234	77
Central Plaza, Hong Kong, China (1992)	1,227	78
Bank of China Tower, Hong Kong, China (1990)	1,205	72
Bank of America Tower, New York, U.S. (2009)	1,200	54
Almas Tower, Dubai, UAE (2008)	1,181	68
*The Pinnacle, Guangzhou, China (2012)	1,181	60
Emirates Office Tower, Dubai, UAE (2000)	1,163	54
Tuntex Sky Tower, Kaohsiung, Taiwan (1998)	1,140	85
Aon Center, Chicago, U.S. (1973)	1,136	83
The Center, Hong Kong, China (1998)	1,135	73
The Torch, Dubai, UAE (2011)	1,132	80
John Hancock Center, Chicago, U.S. (1969)	1,128	100
Tianjin World Financial Center, Tianjin, China (2011)	1,106	76
*Hanoi Landmark Tower, Hanoi, Vietnam (2011)	1,103	70
Shanghai Shimao International Plaza, Shanghai, China (2006)	1,094	60
Rose Rayhaan by Rotana, Dubai, UAE (2007)	1,093	72
Minsheng Bank Building, Wuhan, China (2008)	1,087	68
*Ryugyong Hotel, Pyongyang, North Korea (2012)	1,083	105
China World Tower, Beijing, China (2009)	1,083	74
Hanging Village of Huaxi, Jiangyin, China (2011)	1,076	74
*Al Yaqoub Tower, Dubai, UAE (2011)	1,076	69
The Index, Dubai, UAE (2010)	1,070	80
*The Landmark, Abu Dhabi, UAE (2011)	1,063	72
Q1, Gold Coast, Australia (2005)	1,058	78
Wenzhou Trade Center, Wenzhou, China (2011)	1,056	68
Burj al Arab Hotel, Dubai, UAE (1999)	1,053	60
Nina Tower I, Hong Kong, China (2007)	1,046	80
Chrysler Building, New York, U.S. (1930)	1,046	77
New York Times Tower, New York, U.S. (2007)	1,046	52
HHHR Tower, Dubai, UAE (2010)	1,042	72
Bank of America Plaza, Atlanta, U.S. (1992)	1,039	55
U.S. Bank Tower, Los Angeles, U.S. (1990)	1,018	73
Ocean Heights, Dubai, UAE (2010)	1,017	83
Menara Telekom Headquarters, Kuala Lumpur, Malaysia (2001)	1,017	59
*Pearl River Tower, Guangzhou, China (2011)	1,016	71
Jumeirah Emirates Towers Hotel, Dubai, UAE (2000)	1,014	56
AT&T Corporate Center, Chicago, U.S. (1989)	1,007	60
*Infinity Tower, Dubai, UAE (2012)	1,005	75
JPMorganChase Tower, Houston, U.S. (1982)	1,002	75
*Etihad Tower 2, Abu Dhabi, UAE (2011)	1,002	70
NE Asia Trade Tower, New Songdo City, Incheon, South Korea (2011)	1,001	68
Baiyoke Tower II, Bangkok, Thailand (1997)	997	85
Two Prudential Plaza, Chicago, U.S. (1990)	995	64
*Leatop Plaza, Guangzhou, China (2011)	993	64
Wells Fargo Plaza, Houston, U.S. (1983)	992	71
Kingdom Centre, Riyadh, Saudi Arabia (2002)	992	41
The Address Downtown Dubai, Dubai, UAE (2008)	991	63
Capital City Moscow Tower, Moscow, Russia (2010)	990	76
*Doosan Haewundae Zenith Tower A, Busan, South Korea (2011)	988	80
Arraya Tower, Kuwait City, Kuwait (2009)	984	60
Aspire Tower, Doha, Qatar (2007)	984	36
One Island East, Hong Kong, China (2008)	979	69
First Bank Tower, Toronto, Canada (1975)	978	72
Eureka Tower, Melbourne, Australia (2006)	975	91
Comcast Center, Philadelphia, U.S. (2008)	974	57
Landmark Tower, Yokohama, Japan (1993)	972	73
Emirates Crown, Dubai, UAE (2008)	971	63
Khalid Al Attar Tower 2, Dubai, UAE (2011)	965	66
311 S. Wacker Dr., Chicago, U.S. (1990)	961	65
Sky Tower, Abu Dhabi, UAE (2011)	959	74
*Haeundae I'Park Marina Tower 2, Busan, South Korea (2011)	958	72
SEG Plaza, Shenzhen, China (2000)	957	71
70 Pine St., New York, U.S. (1932)	952	67
*Global Trade Plaza, Dongguan, China (2011)	948	68
Key Tower, Cleveland, U.S. (1991)	947	57
Plaza 66, Shanghai, China (2001)	945	66
One Liberty Place, Philadelphia, U.S. (1987)	945	61
*Chongqing Poly Tower, Chongqing, China (2012)	941	58
Sulafa Tower, Dubai, UAE (2010)	935	75
*YingLi Tower, Chongqing, China (2012)	935	60
Millennium Tower, Dubai, UAE (2006)	935	59
Tomorrow Square, Shanghai, China (2003)	934	58
Columbia Center, Seattle, U.S. (1985)	933	76
Trump Ocean Club, Panama City, Panama (2011)	932	68
Chongqing World Trade Center, Chongqing, China (2005)	929	60
Cheung Kong Centre, Hong Kong, China (1999)	928	63
The Trump Building, New York, U.S. (1930)	927	71

Tallest Free-Standing Towers in the World

Structures under construction as of Sept. 2011 are denoted by an asterisk (*). Year is date of completion or projected completion.

Tower	Ht. (ft)	Year	Tower	Ht. (ft)	Year
*Tokyo Sky Tree, Tokyo, Japan	2,080	2012	Kiev TV Tower, Kiev, Ukraine	1,263	1974
Canton Tower, Guangzhou, China	1,969	2010	Tashkent Tower, Tashkent, Uzbekistan	1,230	1985
CN Tower, Toronto, ON, Canada	1,815	1976	Liberation Tower, Kuwait City, Kuwait	1,220	1996
Ostankino Tower, Moscow, Russia	1,772	1967	Alma-Ata Tower, Almaty, Kazakhstan	1,217	1982
Oriental Pearl Television Tower, Shanghai, China	1,535	1995	TV Tower, Riga, Latvia	1,208	1987
Milad Tower, Tehran, Iran	1,427	2008	Berliner Fernsehturm, Berlin, Germany	1,207	1969
Manara Kuala Lumpur, Kuala Lumpur, Malaysia	1,379	1996	Stratosphere Tower, Las Vegas, NV, U.S.	1,149	1996
Tianjin Radio & TV Tower, Tianjin, China	1,362	1991	West Pearl Tower, Chengdu, China	1,112	2004
Henan Province Radio & Television Emission Tower, Zhengzhou, China	1,273	2010	Macau Tower, Macau, China	1,109	2001
Central Radio & TV Tower, Beijing, China	1,268	1992	Europaturm, Frankfurt, Germany	1,106	1979

Tall Buildings in Selected North American Cities

Source: Phorio, phorio.com; Council on Tall Buildings and Urban Habitat, Illinois Inst. of Technology, www.ctbuh.org

List includes freestanding towers and other structures that do not have stories and are not technically considered buildings. Structures still under construction as of Sept. 2011 are denoted by an asterisk (*). Year in parentheses is date of completion or projected completion. Height is generally measured from the lowest significant open-air pedestrian entrance to the architectural top, including penthouses, spires, and other decorative features that are an integral part of the design. Stories generally counted from street level. NA = Not available or not applicable.

Building/structure	Ht. (ft)	Stories	Building/structure	Ht. (ft)	Stories
Atlanta, GA			191 Peachtree Tower (1991)	770	50
Bank of America Plaza (incl. spire), 600 Peachtree St. NE (1992)	1,039	55	Westin Peachtree Plaza, 210 Peachtree St. NW (1976)[2]	723	73
SunTrust Plaza, 303 Peachtree St. NE (1993)[1]	867	60	Georgia Pacific Tower, 133 Peachtree St. NE (1981)	697	51
One Atlantic Center, 1201 W. Peachtree St. (1987)	820	50	Promenade II (incl. spire), 1230 Peachtree St. NE (1989)	691	40

Building/structure	Ht. (ft)	Stories
AT&T Building, 675 W. Peachtree St. (1980)	677	47
Sovereign, 3344 Peachtree (2008)	665	48
1180 Peachtree (2006)	657	41
GLG Grand/Four Seasons Hotel, 75 14th St. NE (1992)	609	53
The Mansion on Peachtree, 3376 Peachtree Rd. NE (2008)	580	42
Atlantic, 270 17th St. NW (2009)	577	46
State of Georgia Bldg., 2 Peachtree St. NW (1967)[3]	556	44
Marriott Marquis, 265 Peachtree Center Ave. NE (1985)	554	52
Viewpoint, 855 Peachtree St. NE (2008)	501	36
Twelve Centennial Park Tower I (incl. spire), 400 W. Peachtree St. NW (2007)	491	39
1075 Peachtree Office Tower (2010)	488	38
Park Avenue Condominiums, 750 Park Ave. NE (2000)	486	42
Terminus 100, 3280 Peachtree Rd. NE, Buckhead (2007)	485	26
Paramount at Buckhead, 3445 Stratford Rd. NE (2004)	478	40
3630 Peachtree Rd. (2009)	469	40
Centennial Tower, 101 Marietta St. (1976)	459	36
Equitable Building, 100 Peachtree St. NW (1967)	453	34
Spire, 860 Peachtree St. (2005)	453	28
Buckhead Grand, 3338 Peachtree Rd. NE (2004)	451	38
(1) 902 ft incl. antenna. (2) 883 ft incl. antenna. (3) 599 ft incl. antenna.		

Atlantic City, NJ

Building/structure	Ht. (ft)	Stories
*Revel Entertainment Resort Tower (2012)	709	56
Harrah's Waterfront Tower, 777 Harrah's Blvd. (2008)	525	44
Trump Taj Mahal-Chairman Tower, 1000 Boardwalk (2008)	467	41
The Water Club at Borgata (2008)	457	39
Borgata Hotel and Casino, 1 Borgata Way (2003)	431	42
Trump Taj Mahal I, 1000 Boardwalk (1990)	429	42

Austin, TX

Building/structure	Ht. (ft)	Stories
Austonian, 200 Congress Ave. (2010)	683	56
360 (incl. spire), 360 Nueces St. (2008)	563	44
Frost Bank Tower, 401 N. Congress Ave. (2004)	516	33
W Hotel and Residences, 200 Lavaca St. (2010)	477	37
Spring, 300 Bowie St. (2009)	433	43
Ashton, 101 Colorado St. (2009)	416	37

Baltimore, MD

Building/structure	Ht. (ft)	Stories
Legg Mason Building, 100 Light St. (1973)	529	40
Bank of America, 10 Light St. (1924)	509	37
William Donald Schaefer Tower, 6 St. Paul Pl. (1992)	493	29
Commerce Place, 1 South St. (1992)	454	31
Marriott Baltimore Inner Harbor East, 700 Aliceanna St. (2001)	430	32
100 E. Pratt St. (1992)	418	28
World Trade Center, 401 E. Pratt St. (1977)	405	32

Bellevue, WA

Building/structure	Ht. (ft)	Stories
Bellevue Towers Two, 106 NE 4th St. (2008)	450	43
Lincoln Tower One, 604 Bellevue Way (2005)	450	42
Bellevue Towers One, 106 NE 4th St. (2008)	430	42
Eddie Bauer at Lincoln Square, 770 Bellevue Way NE (2007)	412	27

Boston, MA

Building/structure	Ht. (ft)	Stories
Hancock Place, 200 Clarendon St. (1976)	790	62
Prudential Tower, 800 Boylston St. (1964)[1]	750	52
Federal Reserve Building, 600 Atlantic Ave. (1978)	604	32
BNY Mellon Center at One Boston Place, 201 Washington St. (1970)	602	41
One International Place, 100 Oliver St. (1987)	600	46
100 Federal St. (1971)	591	37
One Financial Center, 10 Dewey Sq. (1984)	590	46
111 Huntington Ave. (2002)	564	36
Two International Place (1993)	538	35
One Post Office Square (1981)	525	40
1 Federal St. (1975)	520	38
Exchange Place, 53 State St. (1984)	510	39
Sixty State Street (1977)	509	38
1 Beacon St. (1972)	507	36
State Street Financial Center (incl. spire), 1 Lincoln St. (2003)	503	36
28 State St. (1970)	500	40
Marriott's Custom House, 3 McKinley Sq. (1915)	496	32
John Hancock Building, 175 Berkeley St. (1949)	495	26
(1) 836 ft incl. antenna.		

Calgary, AB, Canada

Building/structure	Ht. (ft)	Stories
*The Bow (2012)	774	58
Petro Canada Centre West Tower, 150 6th Ave. SW (1984)	705	53
Eighth Avenue Place East Tower, 8th Ave. and 5th St. SW (2011)	691	51
Bankers Hall West Tower, 888 3rd St. SW (2000)	645	50
Bankers Hall East Tower, 855 2nd St. SW (1989)	645	50
Calgary Tower, 101 9th Ave. SW (1967)	626	NA
Centennial Place 1 (incl. spire), 520 3rd Ave. SW (2010)	599	40
TransCanada Tower, 450 1st St. SW (2001)	581	38
Canterra Tower, 400 3rd Ave. SW (1988)	580	46

Building/structure	Ht. (ft)	Stories
Jamieson Place (incl. spires), 302 4th Ave. SW (2009)	568	38
First Canadian Centre, 350 7th Ave. SW (1982)	547	41
Western Canadian Place-North Tower, 707 6th St. SW (1983)	538	41
Canada Trust, Calgary Eatons Centre, 421 7th Ave. SW (1991)	530	40
Scotia Square, 700 2nd St. SW (1976)	509	41
Nexen Building, 801 7th Ave. SW (1982)	500	37

Charlotte, NC

Building/structure	Ht. (ft)	Stories
Bank of America Corporate Center, 100 N. Tryon St. (1992)	871	60
Duke Energy Center, 534 S. Tryon St. (2010)	786	48
The Vue, 400 W. 5th St. (2010)	677	50
Hearst Tower, 214 N. Tryon St. (2002)	659	47
One Wachovia Center, 301 S. College St. (1988)	588	42
Bank of America Plaza, 101 S. Tryon St. (1974)	503	40
1 Bank of America Center, 130 N. College St. (2010)	484	32
121 W. Trade St. (1990)	462	32

Chicago, IL

Building/structure	Ht. (ft)	Stories
Willis Tower, 233 S. Wacker Dr. (1974)[1]	1,451	108
Trump International Hotel & Tower (incl. spire), 401 N. Wabash Ave. (2009)	1,389	98
Aon Center, 200 E. Randolph St. (1973)	1,136	83
John Hancock Center, 875 N. Michigan Ave. (1969)[2]	1,128	100
AT&T Corporate Center (incl. spires), 227 W. Monroe St. (1989)	1,007	60
Two Prudential Plaza (incl. spire), 180 N. Stetson Ave. (1990)	995	64
311 S. Wacker Dr. (1990)	961	65
900 N. Michigan Ave. (1989)	871	66
Aqua, 225 N. Columbus Dr. (2009)	859	86
Water Tower Place, 845 N. Michigan Ave. (1976)	859	74
Chase Tower, 21 S. Clark St. (1969)	850	60
Park Tower, 800 N. Michigan Ave. (2000)	844	68
The Legacy at Millennium Park, 21-39 S. Wabash (2010)	818	73
300 N. LaSalle (2009)	785	60
3 First National Plaza, 70 W. Madison St. (1981)	767	57
Chicago Title and Trust Center, 161 N. Clark St. (1992)	756	50
Blue Cross Headquarters, 300 E. Randolph St. (2010)	744	54
One Museum Park, 1215 S. Prairie Ave. (2009)	726	62
Olympia Centre, 737 N. Michigan Ave. (1986)	725	63
Elysian, 940 N. Rush St. (2009)	701	60
330 N. Wabash Ave. (1973)	695	52
111 S. Wacker Dr. (2005)	681	51
181 W. Madison St. (1990)	680	50
Hyatt Center, 71 S. Wacker (2005)	679	48
One Magnificent Mile, 980 N. Michigan Ave. (1983)	673	57
340 on the Park, 340 W. Randolph St. (2007)	672	64
United Bldg., 77 W. Wacker Dr. (1992)	668	49
UBS Tower, 1 N. Wacker Dr. (2001)	652	50
Daley Center, 55 W. Washington St. (1965)	648	32
55 E. Erie St. (2004)	647	56
Lake Point Tower, 505 N. Lake Shore Dr. (1968)	645	70
River East Center, 350 E. Illinois St. (2001)	644	58
Grand Plaza I (incl. spire), 540 N. State St. (2003)	641	57
155 N. Wacker Dr. (2009)	638	45
Leo Burnett Building, 35 W. Wacker Dr. (1989)	635	46
The Heritage at Millennium Park, 125 N. Wabash Ave. (2005)	631	57
NBC Tower (incl. spire), 455 N. Cityfront Plaza Dr. (1989)	627	37
353 N. Clark (2009)	623	44
Millennium Centre, 33 W. Ontario St. (2003)	610	58
Chicago Place, 700 N. Michigan Ave. (1991)	608	49
Board of Trade (incl. statue), 141 W. Jackson Blvd. (1930)	605	44
CNA Plaza, 325 S. Wabash St. (1972)	601	44
One Prudential Plaza, 130 E. Randolph St. (1955)[3]	601	41
Heller International Tower, 500 W. Monroe St. (1992)	600	45
One Madison Plaza, 200 W. Madison St. (1982)	599	44
One Museum Park West, 201 E. Roosevelt Rd. (2010)	595	54
1000 Lake Shore Plz. (1964)	590	55
The Clare at Water Tower, 55 East Pearson St. (2008)	589	52
Citigroup Center, 500 W. Madison St. (1987)	588	42
Mid Continental Plaza, 55 E. Monroe St. (1972)	583	49
Smurfit-Stone Building, 150 N. Michigan Ave. (1983)	582	41
North Pier Apartments, 474 N. Lake Shore Dr. (1990)	581	61
Citadel Center, 131 S. Dearborn St. (2003)	580	39
The Fordham, 25 E. Superior St. (2003)	574	52
190 S. LaSalle St. (1987)	573	40
One S. Dearborn (2005)	571	39
Onterie Center, 446 E. Ontario St. (1986)	570	58
Chicago Temple, 77 W. Washington St. (1924)	568	23
Palmolive Bldg. (incl. beacon), 919 N. Michigan Ave. (1929)	565	37
Marina City I, 300 N. State St. (1964)	562	61
Marina City II, 301 N. Dearborn St. (1964)	562	61
Huron Plaza Apartments, 30 E. Huron St. (1983)	560	56

Building/structure	Ht. (ft)	Stories
Boeing International Headquarters, 100 N. Riverside Plz. (1990)	560	36
The Parkshore, 195 N. Harbor Dr. (1991)	556	56
North Harbor Tower, 175 N. Harbor Dr. (1988)	556	55
Civic Opera Building, 20 N. Wacker Dr. (1929)	555	45
Streeter Place, 351 E. Ohio St. (2009)	554	55
Newberry Plaza, 1000 N. State St. (1974)	553	53
Michigan Plaza South, 205 N. Michigan Ave. (1985)	553	46
30 N. LaSalle St. (1975)	553	44
Pittsfield Building, 55 E. Washington St. (1927)	551	38
Harbor Point, 155 N. Harbor Dr. (1975)	550	54
One S. Wacker Dr. (1982)	550	40
Kluczynski Federal Bldg., 230 S. Dearborn St. (1975)	545	45
Park Millennium, 222 N. Columbus Dr. (2002)	544	57
USG Building, 125 S. Franklin St. (1992)	538	35
The Pinnacle, 21 E. Huron St. (2004)	535	48
LaSalle National Bank, 135 S. LaSalle St. (1934)	535	45
Park Place Tower, 655 W. Irving Park Rd. (1971)	531	56
One N. LaSalle St. (1930)	530	48
The Elysees, 111 E. Chestnut St. (1973)	529	56
River Plaza, 405 N. Wabash St. (1977)	524	56
35 E. Wacker Dr. (1927)	523	40
Unitrin Building, 1 E. Wacker Dr. (1962)	522	41
Mather Tower, 75 E. Wacker Dr. (1928)	521	41
Chicago Mercantile Exchange, 10 S. Wacker Dr. (1987)	520	40
Chicago Mercantile Exchange, 30 S. Wacker Dr. (1983)	520	40
The Columbian, 1180 S. Michigan Ave. (2008)	517	47
191 N. Wacker Dr. (2002)	516	37
401 E. Ontario St. (1990)	515	51
One Financial Place, 440 S. LaSalle St. (1985)	515	39
The Streeter, 345 E. Ohio St. (2006)	514	50
Park Tower Condominiums, 5415 N. Sheridan Rd. (1973)	513	54
600 N. Lake Shore Dr. (2009)	513	47
LaSalle-Wacker Building, 221 N. LaSalle St. (1930)	512	41
Harris Bank III, 115 S. LaSalle St. (1974)	510	38
321 N. Clark St. (1987)	510	35
215 West, 215 W. Washington St. (2010)	509	50
400 E. Ohio St. (1982)	505	50
Carbide & Carbon Bldg., 230 N. Michigan Ave. (1929)	503	37
One Superior Place, 1 W. Superior St. (1999)	502	52
120 N. LaSalle St. (1992)	501	39
10 S. LaSalle St. (1986)	501	37
The Tides, 360 E. South Water St. (2008)	500	51
200 S. Wacker St. (1981)	500	41

(1) 1,729 ft incl. antenna. (2) 1,499 ft incl. antenna. (3) 912 ft incl. antenna.

Cincinnati, OH

Building/structure	Ht. (ft)	Stories
Great American Tower at Queen City Square, 301 E. 4th St. (2011)	665	40
Carew Tower, 441 Vine St. (1931)[1]	574	49
PNC Tower, 1 W. 4th St. (1913)	495	31
Scripps Center, 312 Walnut St. (1990)	468	36
Fifth Third Tower, 511 Walnut St. (1969)	423	32
The Center at 600 Vine (1984)	418	29
Chemed Center, 255 5th St. (1990)	410	32

(1) 623 ft incl. antenna.

Cleveland, OH

Building/structure	Ht. (ft)	Stories
Key Tower (incl. spire), 127 Public Sq. (1991)	947	57
Terminal Tower, 50 Public Sq. (1930)[1]	708	52
200 Public Sq. (1985)	658	46
Tower at Erieview, 1301 E. 9th St. (1964)	529	40
One Cleveland Center, 1375 E. 9th St. (1983)	450	31
Fifth Third Center, 600 Superior Ave. (1991)	446	28
Carl B. Stokes Federal Courthouse, 801 W. Superior Ave. (2002)	430	24
Justice Center, 1250 Ontario St. (1976)	420	26
Federal Building, 1240 E. 9th St. (1967)	419	32
National City Center, 1900 E. 9th St. (1980)	410	35

(1) 771 ft incl. flagpole.

Columbus, OH

Building/structure	Ht. (ft)	Stories
James A. Rhodes State Office Tower, 30 E. Broad St. (1973)	624	41
Leveque-Lincoln Tower, 50 W. Broad St. (1927)	555	47
William Green Building, 30 W. Spring St. (1990)	530	33
Huntington Center, 41 S. High St. (1983)	512	37
Vern Riffe State Office Tower, 77 S. High St. (1988)	503	33
One Nationwide Plaza (1976)	485	40
Franklin County Courthouse, 373 S. High St. (1991)	464	27
AEP Building, One Riverside Plz. (1983)	456	31
Borden Building, 180 E. Broad St. (1974)	438	34
Three Nationwide Plaza (1989)	408	27

Dallas, TX

Building/structure	Ht. (ft)	Stories
Bank of America Plaza, 901 Main St. (1985)	921	72
Renaissance Tower (incl. spire), 1201 Elm St. (1974)	886	56
Comerica Bank Tower, 1717 Main St. (1987)	787	60
JP Morgan Chase Tower, 2200 Ross Ave. (1987)	738	55
Fountain Place, 1445 Ross Ave. (1986)	720	58
Trammel Crow Center, 2001 Ross Ave. (1984)	686	50
1700 Pacific Ave. (1983)	655	50
Thanksgiving Tower, 1600 Pacific Ave. (1982)	645	50
Energy Plaza, 1601 Bryan St. (1983)	629	49

Building/structure	Ht. (ft)	Stories
Elm Place, 1401 Elm St. (1965)	628	52
Gables Republic Tower (incl. spire), 300 N. Ervay (1954)	602	36
Republic Center Tower II, 325 N. St. Paul (1964)	598	50
One AT&T Plaza, 208 S. Akard St. (1984)	580	37
One Lincoln Plaza, 500 Akard St. (1984)	579	45
*Museum Tower, 2112 Flora St. (2013)	560	42
Cityplace Center East, 2711 N. Haskell Ave. (1989)	560	42
Reunion Tower, 300 Reunion Blvd. (1976)	560	NA
Sheraton Dallas Hotel Center Tower, 400 Olive St. (1959)	550	42
Mercantile Building (incl. spire), 1700 Main St. (1943)	523	31
Bryan Tower, 2001 Bryan St. (1973)	512	40
Harwood Center, 1999 Bryan St. (1982)	483	36
KPMG Centre, 717 N. Harwood St. (1980)	481	34
San Jacinto Tower, 2121 San Jacinto St. (1982)	456	33
Renaissance Hotel, 2222 Stemmons Fwy. (1983)	451	29

Denver, CO

Building/structure	Ht. (ft)	Stories
Republic Plaza, 330 17th St. (1984)	714	56
1801 California St. (1982)	709	52
Wells Fargo Center, 1700 Lincoln Ave. (1983)	698	50
Four Seasons Hotel and Private Residences, 1111 14th St. (2010)	639	45
1999 Broadway (1985)	544	43
707 17th St. (1981)	522	42
555 17th St. (1978)	507	40
Hyatt Regency Denver at the Colorado Convention Center, 650 15th St. (2005)	489	37
Spire, 1434 Champa St. (2009)	483	41
Broadway (1980)	448	36
17th Street Plaza, 1225 17th St. (1982)	438	32
First Interstate Tower North, 633 17th St. (1974)	434	32
Brooks Towers, 1020 15th St. (1968)	420	42
Denver Place South Tower, 999 18th St. (1981)	416	34
One Tabor Center, 1200 17th St. (1984)	408	32
Johns Manville Plaza, 717 17th St. (1978)	404	29

Detroit, MI

Building/structure	Ht. (ft)	Stories
Marriott Hotel, Renaissance Center I (1977)[1]	727	70
One Detroit Center, 500 Woodward Ave. (1991)	619	43
Penobscot Building, 633 Griswold Ave. (1928)[2]	565	47
Renaissance Center 100 Tower (1976)	508	39
Renaissance Center 200 Tower (1976)	508	39
Renaissance Center 300 Tower (1976)	508	39
Renaissance Center 400 Tower (1976)	508	39
Guardian Building, 500 Griswold Ave. (1929)	496	40
Book Tower, 1249 Washington Blvd. (1925)	475	38
150 W. Jefferson Ave. (1988)	455	29
Fisher Building, 3011 W. Grand Blvd. (1928)	444	28
Cadillac Tower, 65 Cadillac Sq. (1928)	437	40
David Stott Building, 1150 Griswold St. (1928)	436	38
One Woodward Avenue (1963)	430	30

(1) 755 ft incl. antenna. (2) 665 ft incl. antenna.

Edmonton, AB, Canada

Building/structure	Ht. (ft)	Stories
Epcor Tower (2011)	490	28
Manulife Place, 10170-101 St. (1983)	480	36
Telus Plaza South, 10020-100 St. (1971)	441	34
Bell Tower, 10104-103 Ave. (1982)	426	34
Commerce Place, 10155-102 St. (1990)	404	27

Fort Lauderdale, FL

Building/structure	Ht. (ft)	Stories
Las Olas River House 1, 333 Las Olas Way (2004)	452	42
110 Tower, 110 SE 6th St. (1988)	410	30
Bank of America Plaza, 401 E. Las Olas Blvd. (2002)	408	23

Fort Worth, TX

Building/structure	Ht. (ft)	Stories
Burnett Plaza, 801 Cherry St. (1983)	567	40
D.R. Horton Tower, 301 Commerce St. (1984)	547	38
Carter Burgess Plaza, 777 Main St. (1982)	525	40
The Tower, 400 Throckmorton St. (1974)	488	36
Wells Fargo Tower, 201 Main St. (1982)	477	33
Omni Convention Center Hotel, 1300 Houston St. (2009)	447	33

Hartford, CT

Building/structure	Ht. (ft)	Stories
City Place I, 185 Asylum St. (1980)	535	38
Travelers Tower, 26 Grove St. (1919)	527	24
Goodwin Square, 225 Asylum St. (1990)	522	30
Hartford 21, 221 Trumbull St. (2006)	440	36

Honolulu, HI

Building/structure	Ht. (ft)	Stories
First Hawaiian Center, 999 Bishop St. (1996)	429	30
Moana Pacific East Tower, 1288 Kapiolani Blvd. (2008)	422	46
Moana Pacific West Tower, 1288 Kapiolani Blvd. (2008)	422	46
Nauru Tower, 1330 Ala Moana Blvd. (1991)	418	44
Hokua Tower, 1288 Ala Moana Blvd. (2006)	418	40
Ko'olani, 1189 Waimanu St. (2006)	416	47
Hawaiki Tower, 88 Piikoi St. (1999)	400	45
One Waterfront Tower-Makai, 425 South St. (1990)	400	45
One Waterfront Tower-Mauka, 415 South St. (1990)	400	45
One Archer Lane, 801 S. King St. (1998)	400	41
Imperial Plaza, 725 Kapiolani Blvd. (1992)	400	40

Building/structure	Ht. (ft)	Stories
Houston, TX		
JPMorganChase Tower, 600 Travis St. (1982)	1,002	75
Wells Fargo Plaza, 1000 Louisiana St. (1983)	992	71
Williams Tower, 2800 Post Oak Blvd. (1982)	901	64
Bank of America Center, 700 Louisiana St. (1983)	780	56
Texaco Heritage Plaza, 1111 Bagby St. (1987)	762	53
Enterprise Plaza, 1100 Louisiana St. (1980)[1]	756	55
Centerpoint Energy Plaza, 1111 Louisiana St. (1996)	741	47
Continental Center I, 1600 Smith St. (1984)	732	55
Fulbright Tower, 1301 McKinney St. (1982)	725	52
One Shell Plaza, 900 Louisiana St. (1970)[2]	714	50
1400 Smith St. (1983)	691	50
3 Allen Center, 333 Clay St. (1980)	685	50
One Houston Center, 1221 McKinney St. (1978)	678	47
First City Tower, 1001 Fannin St. (1984)	662	47
BG Group Place, 811 Main St. (2011)	630	46
San Felipe Plaza, 5847 San Felipe Blvd. (1984)	625	45
ExxonMobil Building, 800 Bell Ave. (1962)	606	44
1500 Louisiana St. (2002)	600	40
America General Center, 2929 Allen Pkwy. (1983)	590	42
Two Houston Center, 909 Fannin St. (1974)	579	40
San Jacinto Column, La Porte (1939)	570	NA
Marathon Oil Tower, 5555 San Felipe Blvd. (1983)	562	41
Wedge International Tower, 1415 Louisiana St. (1983)	550	44
KBR Tower, 601 Jefferson St. (1973)	550	40
Pennzoil Place I, 700 Milam St. (1976)	523	36
Pennzoil Place II, 700 Louisiana St. (1976)	523	36
Devon Energy Center, 1200 Smith St. (1978)	521	36
RRI Energy Plaza, 1000 Main St. (2003)	518	36
Total Plaza, 1201 Louisiana St. (1971)	518	35
The Huntington, 2121 Kirby Dr. (1982)	503	34
El Paso Energy Building, 1010 Milam St. (1962)	502	33
One Park Place, 1500 McKinney St. (2009)	501	37
Memorial Hermann Tower, 929 Gessner Rd. (2009)	500	35
Hess Tower, 1501 McKinney St. (2010)	490	29
O'Quinn Medical Tower, 6624 Fannin St. (1991)	477	29
5 Greenway Plz. (1973)	465	31
717 Texas Ave. (2003)	453	34
One Allen Center, 500 Dallas St. (1974)	452	34

(1) 782 ft incl. antenna. (2) 999 ft incl. antenna.

Building/structure	Ht. (ft)	Stories
Indianapolis, IN		
Chase Tower, 111 Monument Cir. (1990)[1]	701	49
One America Tower, 200 N. Illinois St. (1982)	533	38
One Indiana Square, 200 N. Delaware St. (1970)	504	36
Market Tower, 10 W. Market St. (1988)	421	32
300 N. Meridian Building (1988)	408	28
First Indiana Plaza, 135 N. Pennsylvania St. (1988)	401	29

(1) 811 ft incl. antenna.

Building/structure	Ht. (ft)	Stories
Jacksonville, FL		
Bank of America Tower, 50 N. Laura St. (1990)	617	42
Modis Tower, 1 Independent Dr. (1975)	535	37
The Peninsula, 1357 Riverplace Blvd. (2006)	437	38
AT&T Tower, 424 N. Pearl St. (1983)	435	27
Riverplace Tower, 1301 Riverplace Blvd. (1967)	433	28
Jersey City, NJ		
30 Hudson St. (2004)	781	42
101 Hudson St. (1992)	548	42
Trump Plaza I, 88 Morgan St. (2008)	532	55
Newport Tower, 525 Washington Blvd. (1990)	531	37
Exchange Place Center (incl. spire), 10 Exchange Pl. (1990)	516	32
Hudson Green East Tower, 77 Hudson St. (2009)	509	48
Hudson Green West Tower, 77 Hudson St. (2010)	501	48
Harborside Financial Plaza 5, 33 Hudson St. (2002)	480	34
Monaco North Tower, 475 Washington Blvd. (2011)	455	47
Monaco South Tower, 475 Washington Blvd. (2011)	455	47
Crystal Point, 2 2nd St. (2009)	436	42
Newport Office Center VII, 480 Washington Blvd. (2002)	430	32
Marbella Apartments, 425 Washington Blvd. (2003)	427	40
Kansas City, MO		
One Kansas City Place (incl. spire), 1200 Main St. (1988)	623	42
Town Pavilion, 1111 Main St. (1986)	591	38
Power & Light Building, 1330 Baltimore Ave. (1931)	481	34
909 Walnut St. (1931)	454	35
City Hall, 414 E. 12th St. (1937)	443	29
1201 Walnut St. (1991)	427	30
Hyatt Regency Crown Center, 2345 McGee St. (1980)	425	45
Commerce Tower, 911 Main St. (1965)	407	32
City Center Square, 1100 Main St. (1977)	404	30
Las Vegas, NV		
Stratosphere Tower, 2000 Las Vegas Blvd. S. (1996)	1,149	NA
*Fontainebleau Resort Hotel, 2755 Las Vegas Blvd. S. (2012)	735	63
The Palazzo, 3339 Las Vegas Blvd. S. (2007)	642	53
Encore at Wynn Las Vegas, 3145 Las Vegas Blvd. S. (2008)	631	52
Trump International Hotel and Tower 1, 3128 Las Vegas Blvd. S. (2008)	622	64
Wynn Las Vegas, 3145 Las Vegas Blvd. S. (2005)	613	45
Cosmopolitan Casino Spa Tower, Las Vegas Blvd. and Harmon Ave. (2010)	603	52
Cosmopolitan Beach Resort Tower, Las Vegas Blvd. and Harmon Ave. (2010)	603	50
Aria Resort and Casino (2009)	600	60
Planet Hollywood Towers, 3667 Las Vegas Blvd. S. (2009)	597	50
VDARA, 2551 W. Harmon Ave. (2009)	556	55
Eiffel Tower, Paris Hotel and Casino, 3645 Las Vegas Blvd. S. (1998)	540	NA
Mandarin Oriental Hotel Las Vegas, 3750 Las Vegas Blvd. S. (2009)	539	47
New York, New York Hotel and Casino, 3790 Las Vegas Blvd. S. (1997)	529	48
Palms Place, 4321 W. Flamingo Rd. (2008)	518	50
Bellagio Hotel and Casino, 3600 Las Vegas Blvd. S. (1998)	508	36
Sky Las Vegas, 2780 Las Vegas Blvd. S. (2007)	500	45
THEhotel, Mandalay Bay, 3950 S. Las Vegas Blvd. (2003)	485	43
Panorama Tower III, S. Dean Martin Dr. (2009)	483	42
Mandalay Bay Hotel and Casino, 3950 S. Las Vegas Blvd. (1999)	480	43
Turnberry Place IV, 2777 Paradise Rd. (2006)	477	38
Turnberry Place III, 2777 Paradise Rd. (2004)	477	38
Turnberry Place II, 2777 Paradise Rd. (2002)	477	38
Turnberry Place I, 2777 Paradise Rd. (2001)	477	38
The Signature at MGM Grand Tower III, 155 E. Harmon Ave. (2007)	475	38
The Signature at MGM Grand Tower I, 155 E. Harmon Ave. (2006)	475	38
The Signature at MGM Grand Tower II, 155 E. Harmon Ave. (2006)	475	38
The Venetian, 3355 Las Vegas Blvd. W. (1999)	475	35
Allure Las Vegas I, 200 W. Sahara Ave. (2007)	466	41
Palms Resort-Fantasy Tower, 4321 W. Flamingo Rd. (2006)	457	40
Turnberry Towers West Tower, 222 Karen Ave. (2008)	453	45
Turnberry Towers East Tower, 222 Karen Ave. (2007)	453	45
Los Angeles, CA		
U.S. Bank Tower, 633 W. 5th St. (1990)	1,018	73
Aon Center, 707 Wilshire Blvd. (1974)	858	62
Two California Plaza, 350 S. Grand Ave. (1992)	750	52
Gas Company Tower, 555 W. 5th St. (1991)	749	52
Bank of America Plaza, 333 South Hope St. (1975)	735	55
777 Tower, 777 S. Figueroa St. (1991)	725	53
Wells Fargo Tower, 333 S. Grand Ave. (1983)	723	54
Figueroa at Wilshire, 601 S. Figueroa St. (1989)	717	52
City National Tower, 555 S. Flower St. (1971)	699	52
Paul Hastings Tower, 515 S. Flower St. (1971)	699	52
L.A. Live Hotel and Condominiums, 900 W. Olympic Blvd. (2010)	667	54
Citigroup Center, 444 S. Flower St. (1979)	625	48
611 Place, 611 W. 6th St. (1967)	620	42
KPMG Tower, 355 S. Grand Ave. (1984)	606	45
One California Plaza, 300 S. Grand Ave. (1985)	578	42
Century Plaza Tower 1, 2029 Century Park East (1973)	571	44
Century Plaza Tower 2, 2049 Century Park East (1973)	571	44
Ernst & Young, LLP Plaza, 725 S. Figueroa St. (1986)	534	41
AIG-SunAmerica Center, 1999 Ave. of the Stars (1989)	533	39
TCW Tower, 865 S. Figueroa St. (1990)	517	37
Union Bank Plaza, 445 S. Figueroa St. (1968)	516	40
10 Universal City Plz. (1984)	506	36
Louisville, KY		
AEGON Center, 400 W. Market St. (1992)	549	35
PNC Tower, 101 S. 5th St. (1972)	512	40
PNC Plaza, 5th and Jefferson (1971)	420	30
Humana Center, 500 W. Main St. (1985)	417	27
Memphis, TN		
100 North Main Building (1965)	430	38
Morgan Keegan Tower, 50 Front St. (1985)	403	21
Clark Tower, 5100 Poplar Ave. (1972)	400	34
Mexico City, Mexico		
*Torre Reforma (2012)	800	57
Torre Mayor, Paseo de la Reforma 505 (2003)	738	55
*Torre BBVA Bancomer (2013)	725	50
Torre Ejecutiva Pemex, Marina Nacional 329 Col. Huasteca (1984)	693	51
*Reforma 432 (2015)	676	54
Torre Altus, Paseo de los Laureles 416 (1999)	640	42
Torre Latino Americana (incl. spire), Eje Central Lazaro Cardenas 2 (1956)	597	45
World Trade Center, Montecito 38 Col. Napoles (1972)	565	50
Arcos Torre II, Paeo de los Tamarindos 400 (2008)	529	35
Arcos Torre I, Paeo de los Tamarindos 400 (1997)	529	35
Torre Altaire I (2009)	498	42
*Torre New York Life, Paseo de la Reforma 342 (2012)	492	32
Torre Libertad, Paseo de la Reforma 439 (2009)	492	31
Torre Lomas, Paseo de las Palmas 800 (1988)	481	36
Santa Fe Flats, Av. Sante Fe 443 (2005)	461	37

Building/structure	Ht. (ft)	Stories
Miami, FL		
Four Seasons Hotel & Tower, 1441 Brickell Ave (2003)	789	64
Wachovia Financial Center, 200 S. Biscayne Blvd. (1983)	764	55
900 Biscayne Bay, 900 Biscayne Blvd. (2008)	712	65
Marquis, 1100 Biscayne Blvd. (2009)	679	63
Met 2 Office Tower, 200 SE 3rd St. (2010)	655	47
Mint at Riverfront, 90 SW 3rd St. (2009)	631	55
Infinity at Brickell, 60 SW 13th St. (2008)	630	52
Miami Tower, 100 SE Second St. (1987)	625	47
Marinablue, 888 Biscayne Blvd. (2007)	615	57
Plaza on Brickell Tower I, 901 Brickell Ave. (2007)	610	56
Icon Brickell North Tower, 495 Brickell Ave. (2008)	586	58
Icon Brickell South Tower, 495 Brickell Ave. (2008)	586	58
Ten Museum Park, 1040 Biscayne Blvd. (2007)	585	50
Paramount at Edgewater Square, 2066 N. Bayshore Dr. (2009)	555	47
50 Biscayne Blvd. (2007)	554	55
Quantum on the Bay South Tower, 1900 N. Bayshore Dr. (2008)	554	51
Opera Tower, 1750 N. Bayshore Dr. (2007)	543	56
Everglades on the Bay North Tower, 244 Biscayne Blvd. (2008)	538	49
Everglades on the Bay South Tower, 244 Biscayne Blvd. (2008)	538	49
Quantum on the Bay North Tower, 1900 N. Bayshore Dr. (2008)	536	44
Jade at Brickell Bay, 1331 Brickell Bay Dr. (2004)	528	49
Plaza on Brickell Tower II, 901 Brickell Ave. (2007)	525	48
Santa Maria, 1643 Brickell Ave. (1997)	520	51
The Ivy, 90-95 SW 3rd St. (2008)	512	45
Stephen P. Clark Center, 111 NW 1 St. (1985)	510	28
Met 2 Marriott Marquis, 200 SE 3rd St. (2010)	502	41
Wind, 330 S. Miami Ave. (2008)	501	41
1450 BRICKELL (2010)	500	34
Avenue Brickell Tower, 1060 Brickell Ave. (2007)	495	47
One Brickell Square, 2 S. Biscayne Blvd. (1973)	492	39
Espirito Santo Plaza, 1301 Brickell Ave. (2004)	487	36
Brickell World Plaza at 600 Brickell (2011)	484	40
Miami Center, 201 S. Biscayne Blvd. (1983)	484	34
Asia, 900 Brickell Key Blvd. (2007)	483	36
Brickell on the River North, 27 SE 5th St. (2005)	482	42
Three Tequesta Point, 848 Brickell Key Dr. (2001)	480	46
Latitude on the River, 615 SW 2nd Ave. (2007)	476	44
Viceroy, 495 Brickell Ave. (2009)	465	46
One Miami East Tower, 205 S. Brickell Ave. (2005)	460	44
701 Brickell Ave. (1986)	450	33
Miami Beach, FL		
Blue Diamond Tower, 4779 Collins Ave. (2000)	559	44
Green Diamond Tower, 4775 Collins Ave. (2000)	559	44
Akoya, 6365 Collins Ave. (2004)	492	47
Portofino Tower, 300 South Pointe Dr. (1997)	484	44
The Continuum on South Beach, South Tower, 1 South Pointe Dr. (2002)	474	40
ICON at South Beach, 450 Alton Rd. (2004)	423	43
The Continuum on South Beach, North Tower, 200 South Pointe Dr. (2008)	415	37
Murano Grande at Portofino, 400 Alton Rd. (2003)	407	37
Murano at Portofino, 1000 South Pointe Dr. (2001)	402	38
Milwaukee, WI		
U.S. Bank Center, 777 E. Wisconsin Ave. (1973)	601	42
100 E. Wisconsin Ave. (1989)	549	37
University Club Tower, 825 N. Prospect Ave. (2007)	446	36
Milwaukee Center, 111 E. Kilbourn Ave. (1987)	426	29
411 Building, 411 E. Wisconsin Ave. (1983)	408	30
Minneapolis, MN		
IDS Tower, 80 8th St. South (1973)[1]	792	55
Capella Tower, 225 South 6th St. (1992)	776	56
Wells Fargo Center, 90 7th St. South (1988)	775	56
33 South 6th St. (1983)	668	52
Campbell Mithun Tower, 222 9th St. South (1985)	582	42
U.S. Bank Plaza I, 200 South 6th St. (1981)	561	40
RBC Plaza, 60 South 6th St. (1992)	539	40
Fifth Street Towers II, 150 5th St. South (1988)	504	36
Ameriprise Financial Center, 707 2nd Ave. South (2000)	498	31
Target Plaza South, 1020 Nicollet Mall (2001)	492	33
Plaza VII, 45 7th St. South (1987)	475	36
The Carlyle, 100 3rd Ave. South (2007)	469	41
US Bancorp Center, 800 Nicollet Mall (2000)	468	32
AT&T Tower, 901 Marquette Ave. (1991)	467	33
Accenture Tower, 333 7th St. South (1987)	455	33
Foshay Tower, 821 Marquette Ave. (1929)	448	32
Qwest Building, 224 5th St. South (1932)	416	30
Fifty South Sixth (2001)	404	30
Hennepin Co. Government Ctr., 300 South 6th St. (1977)	404	24
(1) 910 ft incl. antenna.		
Mississauga, ON, Canada		
Absolute World Tower 1, 50 Absolute Ave. (2011)	589	56
Absolute World Tower 2, 30 Absolute Ave. (2011)	529	50

Building/structure	Ht. (ft)	Stories
One Park Tower, 4200 Confederation Pkwy. (2008)	466	38
Chicago, 385 Prince of Wales Dr. (2010)	410	41
Monterrey, Mexico		
Dataflux Tower, San Pedro Garza Garcia (2000)	597	43
Centro de Gobierno Plaza Civica (2010)	591	36
*Torre Helicon, San Pedro Garza Garcia (2012)	512	33
Torre Commercial America, San Pedro Garza Garcia (1994)	427	35
Montréal, QC, Canada		
1250 Boulevard Rene Levesque (incl. spire) (1992)	743	47
1000 Rue de la Gauchetiere (1992)	673	51
Tour de la Bourse, 800 Place Victoria (1964)	624	47
1 Place Villa Marie (1962)	616	43
La Tour CIBC, 1155 Rene Levesque Blvd. (1962)[1]	604	43
Montreal Tower (1987)	574	NA
Tour McGill College, 1501 McGill College (1992)	519	38
Le Complexe Desjardins Sud (1975)	498	40
Tour KPMG, 600 Maisonneuve (1987)	479	34
Marriott Chateau Champlain, 1 Place du Canada (1967)	454	38
(1) 740 ft incl. antenna.		
Nashville, TN		
AT&T Building, 333 Commerce St. (1994)	617	33
Fifth Third Center, 424 Church St. (1986)	490	31
William R. Snodgrass Tennessee Tower, 311 7th Ave. North (1970)	452	31
The Pinnacle, 150 3rd Ave. South (2010)	435	29
Nashville Life & Casualty Tower, 401 Church St. (1957)	409	30
Nashville City Center, 511 Union St. (1987)	402	27
New Orleans, LA		
One Shell Square, 701 Poydras St. (1972)	697	51
CapitalOne Center, 201 St. Charles Ave. (1985)	645	53
Plaza Tower, 1001 Howard Ave. (1969)	531	45
Energy Centre, 1100 Poydras St. (1984)	530	39
First Bank & Trust Tower, 909 Poydras St. (1987)	481	36
Sheraton New Orleans, 500 Canal St. (1985)	478	47
New Orleans Marriott, 555 Canal St. (1972)	450	42
Texaco Center, 400 Poydras St. (1983)	442	33
Canal Place One, 365 Canal St. (1979)	439	32
1010 Common St. (1971)	438	31
World Trade Center, 2 Canal St. (1965)	407	33
1450 Poydras St. (1989)	406	26
New York, NY		
*One World Trade Center (incl. spire) (2013)	1,776	104
*Two World Trade Center, 200 Greenwich St. (NA)	1,349	88
Empire State Building, 350 5th Ave. (1931)[1]	1,250	102
*Three World Trade Center (incl. spires), 175 Greenwich St. (NA)	1,240	71
Bank of America (incl. spire), One Bryant Park (2009)	1,200	55
Chrysler Building (incl. spire), 405 Lexington Ave. (1930)	1,046	77
New York Times Tower (incl. spire), 620 8th Ave. (2007)	1,046	52
*One57, 157 W. 57th St. (2013)	1,005	75
*Four World Trade Center, 150 Greenwich St. (2012)	977	64
American International Bldg. (incl. spire), 70 Pine St. (1932)	952	67
The Trump Building, 40 Wall St. (1930)	927	71
Citigroup Center, 153 E. 53rd St. (1977)	915	59
New York by Gehry at Eight Spruce Street (2011)	870	76
Trump World Tower, 845 UN Plz. (2001)	861	72
GE Building, 30 Rockefeller Ctr. (1933)	850	70
Cityspire Center, 150 W. 56th St. (1989)	814	75
One Chase Manhattan Plaza (1960)	813	60
4 Times Sq. (1999)[2]	809	48
MetLife Building, 200 Park Ave. (1963)	808	59
Bloomberg Tower, 731 Lexington Ave. (2005)[3]	806	54
Woolworth Building, 233 Broadway (1913)	792	57
1 Worldwide Plaza, 935 8th Ave. (1989)	778	47
Carnegie Hall Tower, 152 W. 57th St. (1991)	757	60
383 Madison Ave. (2001)	755	47
AXA Center, 787 7th Ave. (1985)	752	51
One Penn Plaza, 250 W. 34th St. (1972)	750	57
1251 Ave. of the Americas (1971)	750	54
Time Warner Center North Tower, 10 Columbus Cir. (2004)	749	55
Time Warner Center South Tower, 10 Columbus Cir. (2004)	749	55
Goldman Sachs HQ, 200 Murray St. (2010)	749	44
60 Wall St. (1989)	745	55
One Astor Plaza, 1515 Broadway (1970)	745	54
1 Liberty Plaza, 165 Broadway (1973)	743	54
20 Exchange Pl. (1931)	741	57
7 World Trade Center (2006)	741	52
Three World Financial Center, 200 Vesey St. (1986)	739	51
1540 Broadway (incl. spire) (1990)	732	42
Times Square Tower, 1459 Broadway (2004)	726	47

Building/structure	Ht. (ft)	Stories
Metropolitan Tower, 142 W. 57th St. (1985)	716	68
JPMorganChase World HQ, 270 Park Ave. (1960)	707	52
General Motors Building, 767 5th Ave. (1968)	705	50
Metropolitan Life Tower, 1 Madison Ave. (1909)	700	50
500 5th Ave. (1931)	697	60
Americas Tower, 1177 Ave. of the Americas (1992)	692	48
Solow Building, 9 W. 57th St. (1974)	689	49
HSBC Bank Building, 140 Broadway (1967)	688	52
55 Water St. (1972)	687	53
277 Park Ave. (1963)	687	50
1585 Broadway (1989)	685	42
Random House/Park Imperial, 1739 Broadway (2003)	684	52
Four Seasons Hotel, 57 E. 57th St. (1993)	682	52
McGraw Hill, 1221 Ave. of the Americas (1972)	674	51
Barclay Tower, 10 Barclay St. (2007)	673	56
Lincoln Building, 60 E. 42nd St. (1930)	673	53
Citicorp, 1 Court Sq., Queens (1990)	673	50
Paramount Plaza, 1633 Broadway (1970)	670	48
Trump Tower, 725 5th Ave. (1982)	664	58
Bank of New York Building, 1 Wall St. (1932)	654	50
Silver Towers East, 600 W. 42nd St. (2009)	653	58
Silver Towers West, 600 W. 42nd St. (2009)	653	58
599 Lexington Ave. (1986)	653	51
712 5th Ave. (1990)	650	53
Chanin Building, 122 E. 42nd St. (1929)	649	56
245 Park Ave. (1967)	648	47
Sony Building, 550 Madison Ave. (1983)	647	37
Two World Financial Center, 225 Liberty St. (1986)	645	44
570 Lexington Ave. (1931)	642	50
1 New York Plaza, 1 Water St. (1969)	640	50
1 MiMA Tower, 440 W. 42nd St. (2011)	638	63
1 Dag Hammarskjold Plaza, 885 2nd Ave. (1972)	637	48
345 Park Ave. (1968)	634	44
400 5th Ave. (2010)	632	58
Mercantile Building, 10 E. 40th St. (1929)	632	48
W New York Downtown Hotel & Residences, 123 Washington St. (2010)	631	57
Grace Plaza, 1114 Ave. of the Americas (1972)	630	50
Home Insurance Plaza, 59 Maiden Ln. (1966)	630	44
1095 Ave. of the Americas (1970)	630	40
101 Park Ave. (1982)	629	49
Central Park Place, 301 W. 57th St. (1988)	628	56
888 7th Ave. (1971)	628	45
Burlington House, 1345 Ave. of the Americas (1969)	625	50
Waldorf-Astoria, 301 Park Ave. (1931)	625	47
One Madison Park, 20 E. 23rd St. (2010)	621	51
Olympic Tower, 645 5th Ave. (1976)	620	51
425 Fifth Ave. (2003)	618	55
The Epic, 125 W. 31st St. (2007)	615	58
919 3rd Ave. (1970)	615	47
Tower 49, 12 E. 49th St. (1985)	615	44
750 7th Ave. (incl. spire) (1989)	615	35
New York Life, 51 Madison Ave. (1928)	615	33
Eventi, 851 6th Ave. (2010)	614	46
Credit Lyonnais Bldg., 1301 Ave. of the Americas (1964)	609	46
The Orion, 350 W. 42nd St. (2006)	604	58
590 Madison Ave. (1983)	603	41
Eleven Times Square, 644 8th Ave. (2011)	601	40
1166 Ave. of the Americas (1974)	600	44
Hearst Magazine Tower, 959 8th Ave. (2006)	597	46
3 Lincoln Center, 160 W. 66th St. (1993)	595	60
Trump Palace, 200 E. 69th St. (1991)	594	54
Celanese Building, 1211 Ave. of the Americas (1973)	592	45
The London NYC, 151 W. 54th St. (1990)	590	54
Thurgood Marshall U.S. Court House, 505 Pearl St. (1936)	590	37
The Millenium Hilton Hotel, 55 Church St. (1992)	588	58
Sky House, 11 E. 29th St. (2008)	588	55
Museum Tower Apartments, 21 W. 53rd St. (1985)	588	52
Time-Life Building, 1271 Ave. of the Americas (1959)	587	48
Jacob K. Javits Federal Bldg., 26 Federal Plz. (1967)	587	41
W Times Square, 1567 Broadway (2000)	584	53
Trump International Hotel & Tower, 15 Columbus Cir. (1970)	583	44
Stevens Tower, 1185 Ave. of the Americas (1971)	580	42
Municipal Building, 1 Centre St. (1914)	580	34
520 Madison Ave. (1981)	577	43
One World Financial Center, 200 Liberty St. (1985)	577	37
Merchandise Mart, 41 Madison Ave. (1973)	576	42
Park Avenue Plaza, 55 E. 52nd St. (1981)	575	44
Lehman Building, 745 7th Ave. (2001)	575	38
One Financial Square, 33 Old Slip (1987)	575	37
Marriott Marquis Times Square, 1535 Broadway (1985)	574	50
299 Park Ave. (1967)	574	42
5 Times Square, 590 7th Ave. (2002)	574	40
Socony Mobil Building, 150 E. 42nd St. (1956)	572	42
1290 Ave. of the Americas (1963)	571	43
780 3rd Ave. (1983)	570	49
600 3rd Ave. (1971)	570	42
450 Lexington Ave. (1991)	568	38
Paramount Tower, 240 E. 39th St. (1998)	567	51
230 Park Ave. (1928)	565	35
New York Palace Hotel, 455 Madison Ave. (1980)	563	51
Continental Bank Building, 30 Broad St. (1932)	562	48
Park Avenue Tower, 65 E. 55th St. (1986)	561	36
Nelson Tower, 450 7th Ave. (1931)	560	46
Sherry-Netherland, 781 5th Ave. (1927)	560	40
623 5th Ave. (1990)	560	36
South Park Tower, 124 W. 60th St. (1986)	558	51
100 UN Plaza, 327 E. 48th St. (1986)	557	52
Continental Can, 633 3rd Ave. (1962)	557	39
3 Park Ave. (1975)	556	42
Continental Center, 180 Maiden Ln. (1983)	555	41
Sperry & Hutchinson Bldg., 330 Madison Ave. (1964)	555	41
Reuters Building, 3 Times Sq. (2001)[4]	555	30
Tower 111, 885 6th Ave. (2011)	554	48
The Belvedere, 10 E. 29th St. (1999)	554	48
Inmont Building, 1345 Ave. of the Americas (1970)	552	45
Downtown by Phillipe Starck, 15 Broad St. (1927)	551	42
*Hyatt Times Square, 135 W. 45th St. (2013)	550	53
Biltmore Tower, 267 W. 47th St. (2003)	550	51
Unysys Building, 605 3rd Ave. (1963)	550	44
2 Grand Central Tower, 140 E. 45th St. (1982)	550	43
*250 W. 55th St. (2015)	550	40
The Tower at 15 Central Park West (2008)	550	35
AT&T Long Lines Building, 33 Thomas St. (1974)	550	29

(1) 1,455 ft incl. antenna. (2) 1,118 ft incl. antenna. (3) 941 ft incl. antenna. (4) 659 ft incl. antenna.

Oklahoma City, OK

Building/structure	Ht. (ft)	Stories
*Devon Energy Tower, 325 W. Sheridan Ave. (2013)	844	52
Chase Tower, 100 N. Broadway Ave. (1971)	500	36
First National Center (incl. spire), 120 N. Robinson St. (1931)	493	33
City Place, 204 N. Robinson St. (1931)	440	32
Oklahoma Tower, 210 Park Ave. (1982)	434	31

Orlando, FL

Building/structure	Ht. (ft)	Stories
SunTrust Center Tower, 200 S. Orange Ave. (1988)	441	31
Peabody Orlando Expansion Tower (incl. spire), 9801 International Dr. (2010)	428	31
Vue at Lake Eola, 136 E. Robinson St. (2007)	426	35
Orange County Courthouse, 425 N. Orange Ave. (1997)	416	24
Bank of America Center, 390 N. Orange Ave. (1988)	409	28

Philadelphia, PA

Building/structure	Ht. (ft)	Stories
Comcast Center, 1701 JFK Blvd. (2008)	974	57
One Liberty Place (incl. spire), 1650 Market St. (1987)	945	61
Two Liberty Place (incl. spire), 1601 Chestnut St. (1989)	848	58
Mellon Bank Center, 1735 Market St. (1990)	792	54
Three Logan, 1717 Arch St. (1991)	725	53
G. Fred DiBona Jr. Building, 1901 Market St. (1990)	625	45
Commerce Square #2, 2001 Market St. (1992)	572	40
Commerce Square #1, 2005 Market St. (1990)	572	40
City Hall (incl. statue) (1901)	548	7
Residences at Ritz-Carlton, 1416 S. Penn Sq. (2009)	518	46
1818 Market St. (1974)	500	40
The St. James, 700 Walnut St. (2004)	498	45
Loews Philadelphia Hotel, 12 S. 12th St. (1932)[1]	492	39

(1) 748 ft incl. antenna.

Pittsburgh, PA

Building/structure	Ht. (ft)	Stories
U.S. Steel Tower, 600 Grant St. (1970)	841	64
One Mellon Bank Center, 500 Grant St. (1983)	725	54
One PPG Place (1984)	635	40
Fifth Avenue Place, 120 5th Ave. (1987)	616	32
One Oxford Centre, 301 Grant St. (1982)	615	46
Gulf Tower, 707 Grant St. (1932)	582	44
University of Pittsburgh Cathedral of Learning, 4200 5th Ave. (1936)	535	42
3 Mellon Bank Center, 525 Wm. Penn Way (1951)	520	41
Freemarkets Center, 210 6th Ave. (1968)	511	39
Grant Building, 330 Grant St. (1930)	485	40
Koppers Building, 436 7th Ave. (1929)	475	34
Two PNC Plaza, 620 Liberty Ave. (1975)	445	34
EQT Plaza, 625 Liberty Ave. (1987)	430	32
One PNC Plaza, 249 5th Ave. (1972)	424	30
Regional Enterprise Tower, 425 6th Ave. (1953)	410	30

Portland, OR

Building/structure	Ht. (ft)	Stories
Wells Fargo Center, 1300 SW 5th Ave. (1973)	546	40
U.S. Bancorp Tower, 111 SW 5th Ave. (1983)	536	42
Koin Tower, 222 SW Columbia St. (1984)	509	31
Pacwest Center, 1211 SW 5th Ave. (1984)	418	30

Raleigh, NC

Building/structure	Ht. (ft)	Stories
RBC Plaza (incl. spire), 300 Fayetteville St. (2008)	538	32
2 Hanover Square, 434 Fayetteville St. Mall (1991)	431	29
Wachovia Capitol Center, 150 Fayetteville St. Mall (1991)	400	30

St. Louis, MO

Building/structure	Ht. (ft)	Stories
Gateway Arch (1965)	630	NA
Metropolitan Square Tower, 211 N. Broadway (1988)	593	42

Building/structure	Ht. (ft)	Stories
AT&T Center, 900 Pine St. (1984)	588	44
Thomas F. Eagleton Fed. Courthouse, 111 S. 10th St. (2000)	557	29
One U.S. Bank Plaza, 505 N. 7th St. (1976)	484	35
Laclede Gas Building, 720 Olive St. (1969)	400	31

St. Paul, MN

Wells Fargo Place, 30 E. 7th St. (1987)	471	36
Galtier Plaza Jackson Tower, 168 E. 6th St. (1986)	443	46
First National Bank, 332 Minnesota St. (1930)	417	32

San Antonio, TX

Tower of the Americas, 600 Hemisphere Way (1968)	622	NA
Marriott Rivercenter (incl. spires), 101 Bowie St. (1988)	546	38
Weston Centre, 112 Pecan St. (1988)	444	32
Grand Hyatt San Antonio, 600 E. Market St. (2008)	424	34
Tower Life Building, 310 S. St. Mary's St. (1929)[1] (1) 504 ft incl. antenna.	404	30

San Diego, CA

One American Plaza, 600 W. Broadway (1991)	500	34
Symphony Tower, 759 B St. (1989)	499	34
Manchester Grand Hyatt, One Market Pl. (1992)	497	40
Electra, 701 W. Broadway (2008)	475	43
Pinnacle Museum Tower, 500 Front St. (2005)	455	35
Emerald Plaza, 400 W. Broadway (1990)	450	30
Manchester Grand Hyatt Tower 2, One Market Pl. (2003)	446	32
Harbor Club East, 200 Harbor Dr. (1992)	424	41
Harbor Club West, 100 Harbor Dr. (1992)	424	41
Vantage Point, 1200 10th Ave. (2009)	420	41
The Grande North at Santa Fe Place, 1205 Pacific Hwy. (2005)	420	39
The Grande South at Santa Fe Place, 1199 Pacific Hwy. (2004)	420	39
Advanced Equities Plaza, 655 Broadway (2005)	412	23

San Francisco, CA

Sutro Tower (1972)	977	NA
Transamerica Pyramid, 600 Montgomery St. (1972)	853	48
555 California St. (1969)	779	52
345 California Center (1986)	695	48
Millennium Tower, 301 Mission St. (2009)	645	58
One Rincon Hill South Tower, 425 First St. (2008)	605	54
101 California St. (1982)	600	48
50 Fremont Center (1985)	600	43
Chevron Tower, 575 Market St. (1975)	573	40
Four Embarcadero Center, 55 Clay St. (1984)	570	45
One Embarcadero Center, 355 Clay St. (1970)	569	45
44 Montgomery St. (1967)	565	43
Spear Tower, 1 Market St. (1976)	565	42
One Sansome Street (1984)	550	43
Shaklee Terrace Building, 444 Market St. (1982)	537	38
First Market Tower, 525 Market St. (1972)	529	38
McKesson Plaza, 1 Post St. (1969)	529	38
425 Market St. (1973)	524	38
Telsis Tower, 1 Montgomery St. (1982)	500	38
333 Bush St. (1986)	495	43
Hilton San Francisco & Towers, 201 Mason St. (1971)	493	46
Pacific Gas & Electric Building, 77 Beale St. (1971)	492	34

Seattle, WA

Columbia Center, 701 5th Ave. (1985)	933	76
1201 Third Avenue Tower, 1201 3rd Ave. (1988)	772	55
Two Union Square, 601 Union St. (1989)	740	56
Seattle Municipal Tower, 700 5th Ave. (1990)	722	57
Safeco Plaza, 1001 4th Ave. (1969)	630	50
City Centre, 1420 5th Ave. (1989)	606	44
Space Needle, 203 6th Ave. (1962)	605	NA
Russell Investments Center, 1301 2nd Ave. (2006)	598	42
Wells Fargo Center, 999 3rd Ave. (1983)	574	47
Bank of America Fifth Avenue Plaza, 800 5th Ave. (1981)	543	42
901 5th Ave. (1973)	536	41
Rainier Tower, 1301 5th Ave. (1977)	514	31
Fourth & Madison Building, 915 4th Ave. (2003)	512	40
1918 8th Ave. (2009)	500	36
1000 2nd Ave. (1986)	493	40
Henry M. Jackson Building, 915 2nd Ave. (1974)	487	37
Qwest Plaza, 1600 7th Ave. (1976)	466	33
Smith Tower, 506 2nd Ave. (1914)	462	38
One Union Square, 600 University Ave. (1981)	456	36
Olive 8 (2009)	455	39
1111 3rd Ave. (1980)	454	34

Sunny Isles Beach, FL

Jade on the Beach Condominiums, 17001 Collins Ave. (2008)	574	51
Trump Royale, 18201 Collins Ave. (2008)	551	43
Trump Palace, 18101 Collins Ave. (2005)	551	43

Building/structure	Ht. (ft)	Stories
Aqualina Ocean Residences, 17875 Collins Ave. (2004)	550	51
Jade Ocean, 17121 Collins Ave. (2009)	543	51
The Pinnacle, 17555 Collins Ave. (1999)	476	40
La Perla Ocean Residences, 16701 Collins Ave. (2006)	447	42
Ocean Four Condominiums, 17201 Collins Ave. (2008)	446	42
Ocean Two Condominiums I, 19111 Collins Ave. (2001)	426	40
Ocean Two Condominiums II, 19111 Collins Ave. (2001)	426	40
Ocean Three Condominiums, 18911 Collins Ave. (2003)	405	37

Tampa, FL

Regions Building, 100 N. Tampa St. (1992)	579	42
Bank of America Plaza, 101 E. Kennedy Blvd. (1986)	577	42
One Tampa City Center, 201 N. Franklin St. (1981)	537	39
SunTrust Financial Center, 401 E. Jackson St. (1992)	525	36
Element, 808 N. Franklin St. (2009)	460	34
Park Tower, 400 N. Tampa St. (1973)	458	36
Rivergate Tower, 400 N. Ashley Dr. (1988)	454	33

Toronto, ON, Canada

CN Tower, 310 Front St. West (1976)	1,815	NA
First Bank Tower, 100 King St. West (1975)[1]	978	72
*Trump Intl. Hotel & Tower (incl. spire), 333 Bay St. (2012)	922	59
Scotia Tower, 40 King's St. West (1989)	902	68
*Aura at College Park, 388 Yonge St. (2014)	874	75
Brookfield Place (incl. spire), 161 Bay St. (1990)	856	53
Commerce Court West, 199 Bay St. (1973)[2]	784	57
TD Centre-Toronto Dominion Bank Tower, 66 Wellington St. West (1967)	730	56
*Ice Condos at York Centre 2, 16 York St. (2015)	710	65
Bay-Adelaide Center West Tower, 335 Bay St. (2010)	704	52
*Living Shangri-La Toronto, 180 University Ave. (2012)	702	65
Ritz-Carlton Hotel and Residences, 185 Wellington St. West (2011)	687	54
BCE Place, Bay-Wellington Tower, 181 Bay St. (1991)	679	49
*L Tower, 1 Front St. (2012)	673	57
*Four Seasons Private Residences West, 48 Yorkville Ave. (2011)	623	55
*Ice Condos at York Centre 1, 16 York St. (2013)	610	55
RBC Centre, 155 Wellington St. West (2009)	607	42
TD Centre-Royal Trust Tower, 77 King St. West (1969)	600	46
Maple Leaf Square North Tower, 65 Bremner Blvd. (2010)	595	54
1 King West (2005)	578	51
Success Tower 2, 33 Bay St. (2010)	569	55
Royal Bank Plaza-South Tower, 200 Bay St. (1976)	567	41
Maple Leaf Square South Tower, 55 Bremner Blvd. (2010)	562	50
*Hullmark Centre I, 4789 Yonge St. (2014)	551	45
44 Charles St. West (1974)	545	51
Quantum 2, 2195 Yonge St. (2008)	541	51
Residences @ College Park I, 763 Bay St. (2006)	535	51
*Burano, 832 Bay St. (2012)	535	50
Success Tower 1, 18 Harbour St. (2011)	531	52
*X2, 580 Jarvis St. (2014)	529	44
The Uptown, 35 Balmuto St. (2011)	518	48
Festival Tower, 330 King St. West (2011)	514	42
*Three Hundred, 300 Front St. West (2013)	512	52
TD Centre, 79 Wellington St. West (1985)	504	39
35 Mariner (2005)	503	49
Montage, 20 Fort York Blvd. (2009)	502	48
(1) 1,116 ft incl. antenna. (2) 942 ft incl. antenna.		

Tulsa, OK

BOK Tower, 1 E. 2nd St. (1975)	667	52
Cityplex Central Tower, 2448 E. 81st St. (1979)	648	60
First Place Tower, 15 E. 5th St. (1973)	516	40
Mid-Continent Tower, 401 S. Boston St. (1984)	513	36
Bank of America Center, 15 W. 6th St. (1967)	412	32
320 S. Boston St. (1928)	400	22

Vancouver, BC, Canada

Shangri-La Vancouver, 1120 W. Georgia St. (2009)	659	59
*The Private Residences at Hotel Georgia, 699 Howe St. (2012)	517	48
One Wall Centre, 1000 Burrard St. (2001)	491	48
Shaw Tower, 298 Thurlow St. (2004)	489	40
Harbour Centre, 555 W. Hastings St. (1977)	481	30
The Melville, 1189 Melville St. (2007)	464	43
Royal Centre, 1055 W. Georgia St. (1973)	461	37
Fairmont Pacific Rim Vancouver, 1011 W. Cordova St. (2010)	460	46
Five Bentall Centre, 550 Burrard St. (2007)	460	34
Park Place, 666 Burrard St. (1984)	459	35
Four Bentall Centre, 500 Burrard St. (1981)	454	35
200 Granville Sq. (1973)	454	30
Scotia Tower, 650 W. Georgia St. (1977)	452	35

Other Tall Buildings in North America

Source: Phorio, phorio.com; Council on Tall Buildings and Urban Habitat, Illinois Inst. of Technology, www.ctbuh.org

List includes freestanding towers and other structures that do not have stories and are not technically considered buildings. Structures still under construction as of Sept. 2011 are denoted by an asterisk (*). Year in parentheses is date of completion or projected completion. Height is generally measured from the lowest significant open-air pedestrian entrance to the architectural top, including penthouses, spires, and other decorative features that are an integral part of the design. Stories generally counted from street level. NA = Not available or not applicable.

Building/structure	City	Ht. (ft)	Stories	Building/structure	City	Ht. (ft)	Stories
RSA Battle House Tower (incl. spire) (2007)	Mobile, AL	745	35	Ravinia #3 (1991)	Dunwoody, GA	444	33
*Riu Hotel (2012)	Guadalajara, Mex.	689	50	Trump Hollywood (2009)	Hollywood, FL.	443	40
The Tower at First National				Xerox Tower (1967)	Rochester, NY	443	30
Center (2002)	Omaha, NE.	634	45	One Summit Square (1981)	Fort Wayne, IN	442	27
801 Grand (1991)	Des Moines, IA.	630	44	Anadarko Tower (2002)	The Woodlands, TX	439	32
Erastus Corning II Tower (1973)	Albany, NY	589	44	Harbert Plaza (1989)	Birmingham, AL	437	32
Niagara Falls Hilton Phase 2	Niagara Falls, ON,			Trump Plaza (2007)	New Rochelle, NY	435	40
(2009)	Can.	581	58	The Palisades (2001)	Fort Lee, NJ	434	41
Concourse Corporate Center V				Bank of America Bldg. (1927)	Providence, RI	428	26
(incl. spire) (1988)	Sandy Springs, GA.	570	34	GM Building (1969)	Mobile, AL.	424	33
Washington Monument (1884)	Washington, DC	555	NA	Wells Fargo Center (1991)	Sacramento, CA	423	30
Concourse Corporate Center				Wells Fargo Center (1998)	Salt Lake City, UT.	422	26
VI (incl. spire) (1991)	Sandy Springs, GA.	553	34	CanWest Global Place (1990)	Winnipeg, MB, Can.	420	33
Torre Aura Altitude (2008)	Zapopan, Mex.	548	44	L.D.S. Church Office Bldg.			
Metropolitan Tower (1986)	Little Rock, AK	546	40	(1972)	Salt Lake City, UT.	420	28
One HSBC Center (1970)	Buffalo, NY	529	38	Landmark Place (1974)	Hamilton, ON, Can.	418	43
Vehicle Assembly Building				Oakbrook Terrace Tower (1985)	Oakbrook, IL.	418	31
(1965)	Cape Canaveral, FL.	526	40	Hidden Bay 1 (2000)	Aventura, FL.	417	40
Skylon (1965)	Niagara Falls, ON,			Galaxy Towers 1-3 (1976)	Guttenburg, NJ.	415	44
	Can.	520	NA	Edifice Marie-Guyart (1972)	Quebec, QC, Can.	415	31
The Westin Virginia Beach				RSA Towers (1996)	Montgomery, AL	415	24
Town Center and Residences				One Seagate (1982)	Toledo, OH	411	32
(2007)	Virginia Beach, VA.	508	38	One Shoreline Plaza South			
The Beach Club Tower 2 (2006)	Hallendale Beach, FL.	505	50	Tower (1988)	Corpus Christi, TX	411	28
Mohegan Sun Sky Tower (2002)	Montville, CT	487	34	Silver Legacy (1995)	Reno, NV	410	30
Chase Tower (1972)	Phoenix, AZ	486	40	Lexington Financial Ctr. (1987)	Lexington, KY	410	30
The Residences at Ritz-				One Financial Plaza (1973)	Providence, RI	410	28
Carlton Westchester North				Winston Tower (1965)	Winston-Salem, NC	410	26
Tower (2009)	White Plains, NY	484	44	The Plaza in Clayton			
The Residences at Ritz-				Residential Tower (2002)	Clayton, MO	409	30
Carlton Westchester South				Kettering Tower (1970)	Dayton, OH.	408	30
Tower (2008)	White Plains, NY	484	44	U.S. Bank Center (1976)	Phoenix, AZ	407	31
Woodmen Tower (1969)	Omaha, NE.	478	30	River House Condominiums			
Natl. Newark Bldg. (1931)	Newark, NJ.	465	36	(2008)	Grand Rapids, MI.	406	34
100 N. Main St. (1995)	Winston-Salem, NC	460	34	Richardson Building (1969)	Winnipeg, MB, Can.	406	34
State Capitol (1932)	Baton Rouge, LA	460	34	Ordway Building (1985)	Oakland, CA.	404	28
The Tower (1988)	Burbank, CA.	460	32	Three Lakeway Center (1987)	Metairie, LA	403	34
Ruan Center (1974)	Des Moines, IA.	457	36	Prudential (1975)	Southfield, MI	402	32
Wachovia Tower (1986)	Birmingham, AL	454	34	U.S. Bank Tower (2008)	Sacramento, CA	402	25
Regions Center (1975)	Little Rock, AK	454	30	Bausch & Lomb Place (1995)	Rochester, NY	401	20
James Monroe Building (1981)	Richmond, VA.	449	29	Tower on the Maumee (1970)	Toledo, OH	400	30
Eleven80 (1930)	Newark, NJ.	448	35	Monarch Place (1987)	Springfield, MA.	400	26
The Westin Diplomat (2002)	Hollywood, FL.	444	39	SunTrust Plaza (1984)	Richmond, VA.	400	24

Notable North American Bridges

Source: World Almanac research; Office of Bridge Technology, Federal Highway Administration, U.S. Dept. of Transportation

All bridges accommodate vehicles; vehicles and railroads; or vehicles, railroads, and pedestrians. Asterisk (*) designates a bridge that carries only railroads. Year is date of completion or projected completion. Span of bridge is the distance between its main supports. As of mid-2011.

Year	Bridge	Location	Main span (ft)	Year	Bridge	Location	Main span (ft)
	Suspension			2013	San Francisco-Oakland Bay		
1964	Verrazano-Narrows	New York, NY	4,260		(Self-Anchored		
1937	Golden Gate	San Francisco Bay, CA	4,200		Suspension		
1957	Mackinac	Straits of Mackinac, MI	3,800		[SAS] Span)[2]	San Francisco Bay, CA.	1,263
1931	George Washington	New York, NY-Fort Lee, NJ	3,500	1931	St. Johns	Willamette R.,	
2007	Tacoma Narrows (new)	Tacoma, WA	2,800			Portland, OR	1,207
1950	Tacoma Narrows	Tacoma, WA	2,800	1929	Mount Hope	Portsmouth-Bristol, RI.	1,200
2003	Al Zampa Memorial (new				**Cantilever**		
	Carquinez)	Carquinez Strait, CA	2,388	1917	Quebec	Quebec City, QC, Can.	1,800
1936	San Francisco-Oakland Bay	San Francisco-Yerba		1974	Commodore Barry	Chester, PA-Bridgeport, NJ	1,644
	(West Span)[1]	Buena Isl., CA	2,310	1988	Crescent City Connection	Mississippi R., New	
1939	Bronx-Whitestone	East R., New York, NY	2,300			Orleans, LA	1,575
1970	Pierre Laporte	Quebec City, QC, Can.	2,190	1958	Crescent City Connection	Mississippi R., New	
1951/Delaware Mem. (twin)	Pennsville, NJ-					Orleans, LA	1,575
68		New Castle, DE	2,150	1995	Veterans Memorial	Mississippi R., Gramercy,	
1957	Walt Whitman	Philadelphia, PA	2,000			LA	1,460
1929	Ambassador	Detroit, MI-Windsor, ON,		1936	San Francisco-Oakland Bay	Yerba Buena Isl.-	
		Canada	1,850		(East Span)[2]	Oakland, CA.	1,400
1961	Throgs Neck	New York, NY	1,801	1968	Baton Rouge	Mississippi R., LA	1,235
1926	Benjamin Franklin	Phila., PA-Camden, NJ.	1,750	1955	Tappan Zee (I-287)	Hudson R., Tarrytown, NY	1,212
1924	Bear Mountain	Hudson R., Peekskill, NY.	1,632	1930	Lewis and Clark	Longview, WA-Rainier, OR	1,200
1969	Claiborne Pell/Newport	Narragansett Bay, RI	1,600	1909	Queensboro	East R., New York, NY	1,182
1952/William Preston Lane Jr.				1958	Carquinez Strait		
73	Memorial (twin)	Sandy Point, MD.	1,600		(eastbound)	San Francisco Bay, CA.	1,100
1903	Williamsburg	East R., New York, NY.	1,600	1930	Jacques Cartier	Montreal, QC, Canada	1,097
1883	Brooklyn	East R., New York, NY	1,596	1968	Isaiah D. Hart	Jacksonville, FL	1,088
1938	Lions Gate	Vancouver, BC, Canada.	1,550	1956	Richmond-San Rafael (twin)	San Francisco Bay, CA.	1,070
1963	Vincent Thomas	L.A. Harbor, CA	1,500	1980	Newburgh-Beacon (south).	Hudson R., NY	1,000
1930	Mid-Hudson	Poughkeepsie, NY	1,495	1963	Newburgh-Beacon (north).	Hudson R., NY	1,000
1909	Manhattan	East R., New York, NY	1,470	1950	Martin Luther King Jr.	St. Louis, MO	963
1955	Angus L. Macdonald	Halifax, NS, Canada	1,447	1975	Caruthersville	Mississippi R., MO-TN	920
1970	A. Murray MacKay	Halifax, NS, Canada.	1,400	1988	Carl D. Perkins (U.S. 23)	Ohio R., Scioto Co., OH-KY	900
1936	Triborough (Harlem R.			1981	William S. Ritchie	Ohio R., Ravenswood, WV	900
	Lift/Bronx Crossing/			1977	Saint Marys	Saint Marys, WV-OH.	900
	East R. Suspension)	East R., New York, NY	1,380				

Year	Bridge	Location	Main span (ft)
1969	Silver Memorial	Pt. Pleasant, WV-OH	900
1941/ 88	Natchez-Vidalia (twin)	Mississippi R., Natchez, MS	875
1938	Blue Water	Pt. Huron, MI-ON, Can.	871

Simple Truss

Year	Bridge	Location	Main span (ft)
1977	Jennings Randolph	Chester, WV-E. Liverpool, OH	745
1929	Irvin S. Cobb (U.S. 45)	Ohio R., Brookport, IL-Paducah, KY	716
1923	*Tanana R.	Nenana, AK	700
1967	Williamstown-Marietta (I-77)	Ohio R., WV-OH	650
1917	*MacArthur	E. St. Louis, IL-St. Louis, MO	647
1992	Discovery	Missouri R., MO	625
1958	*Castleton	Hudson R., NY	598
1938	Easton-Phillipsburg	Delaware R., PA	550
1930	Swindell	Pittsburgh, PA	545
1951	Rankin	Pittsburgh, PA	525
1906	Donora-Webster	Donora-Webster, PA	515

Steel Truss

Year	Bridge	Location	Main span (ft)
1990	Glade Creek	Beckley WV	785
1973	U.S. 190, Atchafalaya R.	Krotz Springs, LA	780
1971	I-95, Piscataqua R.	Portsmouth, NH-Kittery, ME	756
1972	LA 1, Atchafalaya R.	Simmesport, LA	720
1957	Robert O. Norris	Middlesex Co., VA	648
1978	Atchafalaya R.	Morgan City, LA	607
1968	Reedy Point	Delaware City, DE	600
1960	Summit	Summit, DE	600
1910	McKinley, Mississippi R.	St. Louis, MO-Venice, IL	517
1972	Norbert F. Beckey	Mississippi R., Muscatine, IA-IL	512
1896	Newport	Ohio R., KY	511

Continuous Truss

Year	Bridge	Location	Main span (ft)
1966	Astoria	Columbia R., OR-WA	1,232
1976	Francis Scott Key	Baltimore, MD	1,200
1981	Ravenswood	Ohio R., Ravenswood, WV	902
1995	Taylor-Southgate	Ohio R., Cincinnati, OH-KY	850
1943	Julien Dubuque (U.S. 20)	Mississippi R., IA-IL	845
1966	Charles Braga	Fall River, MA	840
1956	Earle C. Clements (twin) (KY 56)	Ohio R., IL-KY	825
1953	John E. Mathews	Jacksonville, FL	810
1992	Cooper R.	Charleston, SC	800
1957	Kingston-Rhinecliff	Hudson R., NY	800
1950	Maurice J. Tobin	Boston, MA	800
1940	Gov. Nice Mem., Potomac R.	Newburg, MD-Dahlgren, VA	800
1986	Rochester-Monaca	Rochester-Monaca, PA	780
1917	*Sciotoville (twin)	Sciotoville, OH-KY	775
1981	Sewickley	Sewickley, PA	750
1974	Carroll C. Cropper (I-275)	Ohio R., IN-KY	750
1940	Glover Cary	Ohio R., Owensboro, KY-IN	750
1984	13th Street	Ohio R., Ashland, KY-OH	740
1959	Monaca-E. Rochester	Monaca-E. Rochester, PA	730
1976	Betsy Ross	Philadelphia, PA	729
1929	Milton-Madison	Ohio R., KY-IN	727
1967	Matthew E. Welsh	Ohio R., Mauckport, IN-KY	725
1962	U.S. 41 Twin, Ohio R.	Evansville, IN-Henderson, KY	720
1994	Robert C. Byrd	Huntington, WV	720
1970	Vanport	Vanport, PA	715
1962	Champlain	Montreal, QC, Canada	707
1973	Girard Point	Philadelphia, PA	700
1963	John F. Kennedy (I-65)	Ohio R., Louisville, KY-Jeffersonville, IN	700
1956	DE R.-PA Turnpike	Delaware R., NJ-PA	682
1949	George C. Platt Memorial	Philadelphia, PA	680
1938	Rainbow	Port Arthur-Orange, TX	680
1946	Chester	Mississippi R., IL-MO	670
1994	Williamstown-Marietta	Ohio R., WV-OH	650

Continuous Box and Plate Girder

Year	Bridge	Location	Main span (ft)
2010	Kanawha R. (I-64)	S. Charleston-Dunbar, WV	760
1977	LA 27, Intracoastal Canal	Gibbstown, LA	750
1976	LA 82, Intracoastal Canal	Forked Isl., LA	750
1967	San Mateo-Hayward #2	San Francisco Bay, CA	750
1969	San Diego-Coronado (twin)	San Diego Bay, CA	660
1967	B. F. Dickmann (Poplar St.)	Mississippi R., St. Louis, MO-IL	647
1992/94	Acosta (twin)	Jacksonville, FL	630
1981	Douglas	Juneau, AK	620
1976	Wax L. Outlet	Calumet, LA	618
1981	Glenn Jackson (I-205)	Columbia R., OR-WA	600

Continuous Plate

Year	Bridge	Location	Main span (ft)
1973	Sidney Sherman (I-610)	Houston, TX	630
1997	SR 114, Tennessee R.	Clifton, TN	525
1992	SR 76, Tennessee R.	Paris, TN	525
1981	IL 23, Ilinois R.	Ottawa, IL	510
1968	I-45, Trinity R.	Dallas, TX	480
1978	Antioch, San Joaquin R.	Contra Costa/Sacramento Co. CA	460

Year	Bridge	Location	Main span (ft)
1977	Thomas Johnson Memorial	Solomons, MD	451
1992	Cuba Landing	Tennessee R., TN	450
1979	Lewis (U.S. 67)	Missouri R., St. Louis, MO	450
1975	I-129, Missouri R.	Sioux City, IA-NE	450
1967	I-90, Mississippi R.	La Crosse, WI	450

Cable-Stayed

Year	Bridge	Location	Main span (ft)
2011	John James Audubon	Pointe Coupee-West Feliciana, LA	1,583
2005	Arthur Ravenel Jr.	Charleston, SC	1,546
1986	Alex Fraser	Vancouver, BC, Can.	1,526
2014	New Mississippi R. (I-70)	St. Louis, MO-IL	1,500
2010	U.S. 82, Mississippi R.	Greenville, MS-Lake Village, AR	1,378
1994	Clark	Alton, IL-MO	1,360
1988	Dame Point	Jacksonville, FL	1,300
2003	Sidney Lanier	Brunswick, GA	1,250
1995	Fred Hartman	Houston Ship Channel, Baytown, TX	1,250
2007	Veterans' Glass City Skyway	Maumee R., Toledo, OH	1,225
1983	Hale Boggs Memorial	Luling, LA	1,222
2002	William Natcher	Ohio R., Owensboro, KY-IN	1,200
1987	Sunshine Skyway	Tampa Bay, FL	1,200
2012	Margaret Hunt Hill	Trinity R., Dallas, TX	1,198
1988	Tampico	Panuco R., Mexico	1,181
2006	Penobscot Narrows	Bucksport, ME	1,161
2003	Bill Emerson Memorial	Cape Girardeau, MO-IL	1,150
1988	Skybridge[3]	Vancouver, BC, Canada	1,115
1991	Talmadge Memorial	Savannah, GA	1,100
2000	Maysville (William H. Harsha)	Savannah, GA	1,050
1993	Mezcala	Ohio R., KY-Aberdeen, OH	1,024
1978	Pasco-Kennewick	Columbia R., Pasco, WA	981
2011	Indian River Inlet (SR 1)	Rehoboth Beach, DE	950

Steel Arch

Year	Bridge	Location	Main span (ft)
1977	New River Gorge	Fayetteville, WV	1,700
1931	Bayonne (Kill Van Kull)	Bayonne, NJ-New York, NY	1,675
1973	Fremont	Portland, OR	1,255
1964	Port Mann	Vancouver, BC, Can.	1,200
1967	Laviolette	Trois-Rivières, QC, Can.	1,100
1990	Roosevelt Lake	Roosevelt Lake, AZ	1,080
1959	Glen Canyon	Page, AZ	1,028
1962	Lewiston-Queenston	Lewiston, NY-Queenston, ON, Can.	1,001
1976	Perrine	Twin Falls, ID	993
1916	*Hell Gate	East R., New York, NY	978
1941	Rainbow	Niagara Falls, NY-ON, Can.	950
1997	Blue Water	Port Huron, MI-ON, Can.	922
1977	Moundsville	Ohio R., WV	912
1973	Hernando DeSoto (I-40) (twin)	Mississippi R., AR-TN	900
2008	Blennerhassett (U.S. 50)	Parkersburg, WV-OH	878
1936	Henry Hudson	Harlem R., New York, NY	840
1966	Bob Cummings-Lincoln Trail	Ohio R., IN-KY	825
1978	I-57, Mississippi R.	Cairo, IL	821
1980	I-65, Mobile R.	Mobile, AL	800
1961	Sherman Minton (I-64)	New Albany, IN-Louisville, KY	800
1978	I-470, Ohio R.	Wheeling, WV	780
1932	West End	Pittsburgh, PA	780
1995	Navajo	Marble Canyon, AZ	726
1959	Thaddeus Kosciusko (twin)	Mohawk R., Albany, NY	600
1917	Detroit-Superior High Level	Cuyahoga R., Cleveland, OH	591
2004	Gateway Boulevard	Nashville, TN	545
1874	Eads	Mississippi R., St. Louis, MO-IL	520

Concrete Arch

Year	Bridge	Location	Main span (ft)
2010	Mike O'Callaghan-Pat Tillman Mem. (U.S. 93)	Colorado R., AZ-NV	1,060
1994	Natchez Trace Parkway	Franklin, TN	582
1993	Lake Street	Minneapolis-St. Paul, MN	556
1971	Fred Redmon (twin)	Selah, WA	549
1968	Cowlitz R.	Mossyrock, WA	520

Segmental Concrete

Year	Bridge	Location	Main span (ft)
1997	Confederation[4]	Prince Edward Isl.-NB, Can.	820
1978	Shubenacadie R.	S. Maitland, NS, Can.	790
1982	Jesse H. Jones Mem.	Houston, TX	750
1992	Jamestown-Verrazano	Narragansett Bay, RI	674
2002	Vietnam Veterans Memorial	James R., Richmond, VA	672
1986	Umatilla	Columbia R., OR-WA	660
2007	Benicia-Martinez (new)	Carquinez Strait, CA	659
1978	Stanislaus R.	Parrots Ferry, CA	640
1981	Juneau-Douglas	Gastineau Channel, AK	620
2010	Allegheny R. (I-76) (twin)	Nr. Oakmont, PA	532
1991	Veterans Mem. Centennial	Coeur d'Alene, ID	520
2008	I-35W St. Anthony Falls[5]	Minneapolis, MN	504

Year Bridge	Location	Main span (ft)
Twin Concrete Trestle[6]		
1956/Lake Pontchartrain		
69 Causeway (twin)	Metairie-Mandeville LA	126,034
1979 Manchac Swamp	Manchac, LA	120,384
1972 Atchafalaya Swamp Frwy.	Baton Rouge, LA	93,984
Concrete Slab Dam[6]		
1928 Conowingo Dam	Susquehanna R., MD	4,648
1952 John H. Kerr	Mecklenburg Co., VA	2,785
1936 Hoover Dam	Lake Mead, NV	1,324
Movable Bridges		
Vertical Lift		
1959 *Arthur Kill	New York, NY-Elizabeth, NJ	558
1965 Pennsylvania Railroad	Kirkwood-Mt. Pleas., DE	548
1935 *Cape Cod Canal	Buzzards Bay, MA	544
1896 *Delair	Pennsauken, NJ-Phila., PA	542
1937 Marine Pkwy. Gil Hodges		
Mem.	Jamaica Bay, New York, NY	540
1931 Burlington-Bristol	Delaware R., NJ-PA	540
1958 Columbia R. Interstate (I-5)	Portland, OR-Vancouver, WA	531
1908 *Willamette R.	Portland, OR	521
1968 Second Narrows	Vancouver, BC, Canada	493
1911 *Armour-Swift-Burlington	Missouri R., Kansas City, MO	428
1945 *Harry S Truman	Kansas City, MO.	427
1955 Roosevelt Island	East R., New York, NY	418
1980 U.S. 17, James R.	Isle of Wight Co., VA	415
1932 *M-K-T RR	Missouri R., MO	414
1969 Cape Fear Memorial	Wilmington, NC.	408
1930 Aerial Lift.	Duluth, MN	386

Year Bridge	Location	Main span (ft)
Bascule		
2006/		
08 Woodrow Wilson (twin)	Potomac R., VA-MD	366
1940 Charles Berry Memorial	Lorain, OH	333
1917 Market St./Chief		
John Ross	Chattanooga, TN	306
2003 *SW 2nd Avenue	Miami, FL	302
1956/1st Ave. S., Duwamish R.		
96 (twin)	Seattle, WA.	300
1955 Chehalis R.	Aberdeen, WA	288
1968 Elizabeth R.	Chesapeake, VA.	280
1913 Broadway	Portland, OR.	278
Swing		
1927 Santa Fe, Mississippi R.	Ft. Madison, IA	525
1952 George P. Coleman Mem.	Yorktown, VA	500
1991 SW Spokane St.	Seattle, WA.	480
1899 *C.M.&N. RR	Chicago, IL	474
1913 Rt. 82, Connecticut R.	E. Haddam, CT.	465
1914 *Coos Bay RR	Coos Bay, OR.	458
1936 Umpqua R.	Reedsport, OR	430
1930 Rigolets Pass	New Orleans, LA	400
Floating Pontoon		
1963 Evergreen Pt.	Seattle, WA.	7,578
1993 Lacey V. Murrow[7]	Seattle, WA.	6,620
1961 Hood Canal	Hood Canal, WA.	6,521
1989 Third Lake Washington.	Seattle, WA.	5,811

Other Notable North American Bridges

Year Bridge	Type	Location	Main span (ft)
2002 Croatan Sound[6]	Continuous post-tensioned girder	Manteo, NC	5.2 mi
1987 Powder Point[6]	Tropical hardwood	Duxbury, MA	2,200
1901 Hartland[6,8]	Covered	St. John R., Hartland, NB, Canada	1,282
1997 Second Blue Water.	Continuous tied arch.	Pt. Huron, MI-Pt. Edward, ON, Canada	922
1983 Jefferson Barracks (I-255)	Tied arch.	Mississippi R., IL-MO	910
1916 C&O RR	Steel girder	Portsmouth, OH	775
1936 Yaquina Bay	Steel braced and concrete tied arches	Newport, OR	600
1962 International	Arch truss	Sault Ste. Marie, MI-ON, Canada	430

(1) Two complete bridges end-to-end, each with a main span of 2,310 ft, which share a common anchor point in the middle of San Francisco Bay. (2) The East Span cantilever bridge will be demolished upon completion and rerouting of traffic onto replacement structures, including the SAS span, which will be the world's longest single-tower, self-anchored suspension bridge. (3) World's longest cable-stayed bridge carrying mass transit only. (4) World's longest bridge crossing ice-covered water, with total length of 8 mi (5) Replaces the bridge that collapsed on Aug. 1, 2007. (6) Length listed is total length of bridge. (7) Replaces the original Lacey V. Murrow bridge, which opened in 1940 and sank in 1990. (8) World's longest covered bridge.

Oldest U.S. Bridges in Continuous Use

Built in 1697, the stone-arch Frankford Ave. Bridge crosses Pennypack Creek in Philadelphia, PA. A 3-span bridge with a total length of 154 ft, it was constructed as part of the King's Road, which eventually connected Philadelphia to New York.

The oldest covered bridge, completed in 1829, is the double-span, 256-ft. Bath-Haverhill Bridge, which spans the Ammonoosuc River between the towns of Bath and Haverhill, NH. The bridge was bypassed in 1999. It has since reopened to pedestrian traffic only.

Notable World Bridges

Source: World Almanac research; Laboratory of Bridge Engineering, Aalto Univ. School of Science and Technology

Bridges under construction as of mid-2011 denoted by asterisk (*). Year is date of completion or projected completion. Span of bridge is the distance between its main supports.

Year Bridge	Location	Main span (ft)
Suspension		
1998 Akashi Kaikyo	Japan	6,532
2009 Xihoumen	China	5,413
1998 Storebælt (Great Belt, East Bridge)	Denmark	5,328
2012 *Gwangyang	South Korea	5,069
2005 Runyang Yangtze R. (south)	China	4,888
1981 Humber	England	4,626
1999 Jiangyin Yangtze R.	China	4,544
1997 Tsing Ma	China	4,518
2013 *Hardanger	Norway	4,298
2007 Yangluo Yangtze R.	China	4,199
1997 Höga Kusten	Sweden	3,970
2011 *Aizhai	China	3,858
2014 *Ulsan Grand	South Korea	3,773
2008 Huangpu	China	3,635
1988 Minami Bisan-Seto	Japan	3,609
1988 Fatih Sultan Mehmet (Bosphorus II)	Turkey	3,576
2010 Baling R.	China	3,570
2011 *Taizhou Yangtze R.[1]	China	3,543
1973 Bosphorus	Turkey	3,524
1999 Kurushima III	Japan	3,379
1999 Kurushima II	Japan	3,346
1966 Ponte 25 de Abril, Tagus R.[2]	Portugal	3,323
1964 Forth Road	Scotland	3,300

(1) Two spans of 3,543 ft each. (2) Road and rail bridge.

Year Bridge	Location	Main span (ft)
Steel Arch		
2009 Chongqing Chaotianmen Yangtze R.	China	1,811
2003 Lupu	China	1,804
1932 Sydney Harbour	Australia	1,650
2005 Wushan Yangtze R.	China	1,614
2013 *Chenab (rail)[1]	India	1,575

Year Bridge	Location	Main span (ft)
2007 Xinguang	China	1,404
2007 Caiyuanba	China	1,378
2008 Airport	Japan	1,247
2000 Yajisha	China	1,181
1962 Bridge of the Americas	Panama	1,128
1967 Zdakov	Czech Republic	1,083
1961 Runcorn-Widnes	England	1,082
1935 Birchenough	Zimbabwe	1,080

(1) When completed, it will be the world's highest arch bridge.

Year Bridge	Location	Main span (ft)
Concrete Arch		
1997 Wanxian	China	1,378
1980 Krk I	Croatia	1,280
1995 Jiangjiehe	China	1,083
1996 Yongjiang	China	1,024
1964 Gladesville	Australia	1,000
1965 Amizade	Brazil-Paraguay	951
2003 Infant Dom Henrique	Portugal	919
1984 Bloukrans	South Africa	892
1963 Arrábida	Portugal	886
1943 Sandö	Sweden	866

Year Bridge	Location	Main span (ft)
Cantilever		
1890 Forth Rail[1]	Scotland	1,710
1974 Minato	Japan	1,673
1943 Howrah	India	1,500

(1) Two spans of 1,710 ft each.

Year Bridge	Location	Main span (ft)
Box Girder		
2006 Shibanpo	China	1,083
1974 Pres. Costa e Silva (Rio-Niterói)	Brazil	984
1978 Neckar Valley Viaduct, Weitingen	Germany	863
1956 Sava I	Serbia	856
1966 Zoobrücke	Germany	850

Year	Bridge	Location	Main span (ft)
	Cable-Stayed[1]		
2008	Sutong Yangtze R.	China	3,570
2009	Stonecutters	China	3,340
2009	Edong	China	3,038
1999	Tatara	Japan	2,920
1995	Pont de Normandie	France	2,808
2010	Jingyue Yangtze R.	China	2,677
2009	Second Incheon	South Korea	2,625
2009	Shanghai Yangtze R.	China	2,395
2009	Minpu	China	2,323
2001	Second Nanjing Yangtze R.	China	2,060
2000	Third Wuhan Yangtze R. (Baishazhou)	China	2,028
2002	Qingzhou Minjiang R.	China	1,985
1993	Yangpu	China	1,975
1998	Meiko Chuo	Japan	1,936
1997	Xupu	China	1,936

Year	Bridge	Location	Main span (ft)
2004	Rion-Antirion	Greece	1,837
1991	Skarnsundet	Norway	1,739
1999	Shantou Queshi	China	1,699
1995	Tsurumi Tsubasa	Japan	1,673
2008	Tianxingzhou Yangtze R.[2]	China	1,654
2002	Jingsha	China	1,640
2000	Øresund	Denmark-Sweden	1,608
1991	Ikuchi	Japan	1,608
1994	Higashi Kobe	Japan	1,591
1998	Zhanjiang	China	1,575
1997	Ting Kau	China	1,558
1999	Seohae Grand	South Korea	1,542
1989	Yokohama Bay	Japan	1,509

(1) Although its main span is not among the world's longest for cable-stayed bridges, Hangzhou Bay is one of the world's longest (22.4 mi) transoceanic bridges. (2) Road and rail bridge.

World's Longest Railway Tunnels

Source: World Almanac research

Tunnel planned or under construction as of mid-2011 denoted by asterisk (*). Year is date of completion or projected completion.

Tunnel	Year	Length (mi)	Operating railway	Location
*Gotthard Base	2016-17	35.4	Swiss Federal Railways (SBB)	Switzerland-Italy
*Brenner Base	2025	34.2	Austrian Federal Railways (ÖBB)	Austria-Italy
Seikan	1988	33.5	Japan Railways Group	Japan
*Mont d'Ambin Base	2015	33.0	Réseau Ferré de France (RFF) & Rete Ferroviaria Italiana (RFI)	France-Italy
English Channel	1994	31.1	Eurotunnel	UK-France
Lötschberg Base	2007	21.0	BLS Lötschbergbahn AG	Switzerland
Guadarrama	2007	17.6	Renfe	Spain
Taihang	2009	17.3	China's Ministry of Railways	China
Hakkoda	2010	16.4	Japan Railways Group	Japan
Iwate-Ichinohe	2002	16.0	Japan Railways Group	Japan
*Pajares	2011-13	15.5	Renfe	Spain
Daishimizu	1982	13.8	Japan Railways Group	Japan
Wushaoling	2006	12.5	China's Ministry of Railways	China
Simplon No. 1 and 2	1906/22	12.3	BLS Lötschbergbahn AG	Switzerland-Italy
Vereina	1999	11.8	Rhätische Bahn (RhB)	Switzerland
London Tunnels (Channel Tunnel Link)	2007	11.8	London & Continental Railways (LCR)	UK-France
Shin-Kanmon	1975	11.6	Japan Railways Group	Japan
Apennine	1934	11.5	Ferrovie dello Stato (FS)	Italy
Qinling	2002	11.5	China's Ministry of Railways	China
Vaglia	2006	10.4	Ferrovie dello Stato (FS)	Italy
Rokko	1972	10.1	Japan Railways Group	Japan
Furka Base	1982	9.6	Matterhorn Gotthard Railway	Switzerland
Haruna	1982	9.6	Japan Railways Group	Japan
*Ceneri Base	2019	9.6	Swiss Federal Railways (SBB)	Switzerland

Underwater Vehicular Tunnels in North America

Source: World Almanac research

(more than 5,000 ft in length; year is date of completion)

Year	Name	Location	Waterway	Length (ft)
1950	Brooklyn Battery (twin)	New York, NY	East River	9,117
1927	Holland (twin)	New York, NY-Jersey City, NJ	Hudson River	8,558/8,371
1937/1945/ 1957	Lincoln (center/north/south tubes)	New York, NY-Weehawken, NJ	Hudson River	8,216/7,482/8,006
1985	Fort McHenry (twin)	Baltimore, MD	Patapsco River	7,920
1957/1976	Hampton Roads (twin)	Hampton, VA	Hampton Roads	7,479
1957	Baltimore Harbor (twin)	Baltimore, MD	Baltimore Harbor	7,392
1940	Queens Midtown (twin)	New York, NY	East River	6,414
1934	Sumner	Boston, MA	Boston Harbor	5,653
1964	Thimble Shoal	Northampton Co., VA	Chesapeake Bay	5,552
1964	Chesapeake Channel	Northampton Co., VA	Chesapeake Bay	5,237
1930	Detroit-Windsor	Detroit, MI-Windsor, ON, Canada	Detroit River	5,160
1961	Callahan	Boston, MA	Boston Harbor	5,070

Land Vehicular Tunnels in the U.S.

Source: World Almanac research; Federal Highway Administration, U.S. Dept. of Transportation

(more than 3,000 ft in length)

Name	Location	Length (ft)
Anton Anderson Memorial[1]	Whittier, AK	13,300
Edwin Johnson Memorial (eastbound)	I-70, Clear Creek Co., CO	8,960
Eisenhower Mem. (westbound)	I-70, Summit Co., CO	8,939
Ted Williams[2]	MA Turnpike, Boston, MA	8,448
Thomas P. O'Neill Jr.	I-93, Boston, MA	7,920
Allegheny (twin)	PA Turnpike	6,070
Liberty (twin)	Pittsburgh, PA	5,920
Zion-Mount Carmel	Zion Natl. Park, UT	5,808
East River Mountain (twin)	I-77, Rocky Gap, VA-Bluefield, WV	5,412
Tuscarora Mountain (twin)	PA Turnpike	5,326
Tetsuo Harano (twin)	H-3 Freeway, HI	5,165
Kittatinny Mountain (twin)	PA Turnpike	4,727
Lehigh (twin)	PA Turnpike, NE Extension	4,461

Name	Location	Length (ft)
Cumberland Gap (twin)	U.S. 25E, KY-TN	4,600
Blue Mountain (twin)	PA Turnpike	4,339
Wawona	Yosemite Natl. Pk., CA	4,233
Big Walker Mountain (twin)	Bland Co., VA	4,229
Squirrel Hill	Pittsburgh, PA	4,225
Hanging Lake (twin)	Glenwood Canyon, CO	4,000
Caldecott (3 tubes)[3]	Oakland, CA	3,771/3,610/3,610
Fort Pitt (twin)	Pittsburgh, PA	3,614
Mount Baker	Seattle, WA	3,456
Dingess	Mingo Co., WV	3,400
Mall	Washington, DC	3,400

(1) Vehicle and rail. (2) Total length of tunnel is 8,448 ft; 3,960 ft of tunnel is underwater. (3) Construction began in 2010 on a fourth tube that will be 3,389 ft in length. The projected completion date is 2013-14.

Major U.S. Dams and Reservoirs
Source: 2009 National Inventory of Dams, U.S. Army Corps of Engineers

Highest U.S. Dams

Rank	Dam	River	State	Type	Height[1] Feet	Meters	Year completed
1.	Oroville	Feather	California	E	770	235	1968
2.	Hoover	Colorado	Nevada	A	730	221	1935
3.	Dworshak	N. Fork Clearwater	Idaho	G	717	219	1973
4.	Glen Canyon	Colorado	Arizona	A	710	216	1963
5.	New Bullards Bar	North Yuba	California	A	645	197	1970
6.	New Melones	Stanislaus	California	R	625	191	1979
7.	Mossyrock	Cowlitz	Washington	A	606	185	1968
8.	Shasta	Sacramento	California	G	602	183	1945
9.	Don Pedro	Tuolumne	California	G	585	178	1971
10.	Hungry Horse	S. Fork Flathead	Montana	A	564	172	1952

E = Embankment, Earthfill; R = Embankment, Rockfill; G = Gravity; A = Arch. **Note:** Does not include tailings or other mining dams. (1) Vertical distance between lowest points on dam's crest and original streambed.

Largest U.S. Embankment Dams

Rank	Dam	River	State	Volume Cubic yards (thousands)	Cubic meters (thousands)	Year completed
1.	Fort Peck	Missouri	Montana	125,628	96,049	1957
2.	Diamond Valley Lake	Domenigoni Valley Creek	California	110,551	84,523	2000
3.	Oahe	Missouri	South Dakota	92,000	70,339	1966
4.	Oroville	Feather	California	80,000	61,164	1968
5.	B. F. Sisk	San Luis Creek	California	77,664	59,378	1967
6.	Garrison	Missouri	North Dakota	66,500	50,843	1953
7.	Scotts Flat	Deer Creek	California	66,300	50,690	1948
8.	Cochiti	Rio Grande	New Mexico	65,000	49,696	1975
9.	Herbert Hoover	North New River Canal	Florida	54,700	41,821	1965
10.	Fort Randall	Missouri	South Dakota	50,200	38,381	1954

Note: All earthfill.

Largest-Capacity U.S. Reservoirs

Rank	Dam	Reservoir	State	Max. reservoir capacity Acre feet (thousands)	Cubic meters (thousands)	Year completed
1.	Glen Canyon	Lake Powell	Arizona	29,875	36,850,270	1963
2.	Hoover	Lake Mead	Nevada	28,537	35,199,872	1935
3.	Garrison	Lake Sakakawea	North Dakota	24,500	30,220,305	1953
4.	Oahe	Lake Oahe	South Dakota	23,600	29,110,172	1966
5.	Fort Peck	Fort Peck Lake	Montana	19,100	23,559,503	1957
6.	Grand Coulee	Lake Roosevelt	Washington	9,386	11,577,461	1941
7.	Herbert Hoover	Lake Okeechobee	Florida	8,519	10,508,032	1965
8.	Sam Rayburn	Sam Rayburn Lake	Texas	6,520	8,042,302	1965
9.	Wright Patman	Wright Patman Lake	Texas	6,505	8,023,799	1954
10.	Fort Randall	Lake Francis Case	South Dakota	6,300	7,770,936	1954

Major Dams and Reservoirs of the World
Source: Intl. Commission on Large Dams, *World Register of Dams*
Asterisk (*) designates structure is planned or under construction as of mid-2010.

World's Highest Dams

Rank	Dam	Country	Height above lowest formation Meters	Feet
1.	Gaolandoh	India	618	2,028
2.	Rio Grande	Argentina	410	1,345
3.	*Rogun	Tajikistan	335	1,099
4.	Nurek	Tajikistan	300	984
5.	Xiaowan (Yunnan Gorge)	China	292	958
6.	Grand Dixence	Switzerland	285	935
7.	Inguri	Georgia	272	892
8.	Vajont	Italy	262	860
9.	Manuel M. Torres	Mexico	261	856
	*Tehri	India	261	856
11.	Alvaro Obregon	Mexico	260	853
12.	Mauvoisin	Switzerland	250	820
13.	Mica	Canada	243	797
	Alberto Lleras C	Colombia	243	797
15.	Sayano-Shushenskaya	Russia	242	794

World's Largest Embankment Dams

Rank	Dam	Country	Volume cubic meters (thousands)
1.	Tarbela	Pakistan	127,908
2.	Diamond Valley Lake	U.S.	84,522
3.	Yacyreta	Argentina/Paraguay	81,000
4.	Tucurui	Brazil	80,865
5.	Ataturk	Turkey	80,500
6.	Rogun*	Tajikistan	75,500
7.	Fort Peck	U.S.	73,436
8.	Guri	Venezuela	70,000
9.	Parambikulam	India	69,165
10.	High Island West	China	67,000
11.	Gardiner	Canada	65,440
12.	Mangla	Pakistan	64,991
13.	Afsluitdijk	Netherlands	63,400
14.	Oroville	U.S.	61,164
15.	B. F. Sisk	U.S.	59,378

World's Largest-Capacity Reservoirs

Rank	Dam	Country	Max. capacity cubic meters (millions)
1.	Kariba	Zimbabwe/Zambia	180,600
2.	Bratsk	Russia	169,000
3.	High Aswan	Egypt	162,000
4.	Akosombo (Lake Volta)	Ghana	150,000
5.	Daniel-Johnson	Canada	141,851
6.	Guri	Venezuela	135,000
7.	W. A. C. Bennett	Canada	74,300
8.	Krasnoyarsk	Russia	73,300
9.	Zeya	Russia	68,400
10.	Robert-Bourassa (La Grande 2)	Canada	61,715
11.	La Grande 3	Canada	60,020
12.	Ust-Ilim	Russia	59,300
13.	Boguchany	Russia	58,200
14.	Kuibyshev	Russia	58,000
15.	Serra da Mesa	Brazil	54,400

World's Largest-Capacity Hydro Plants

Rank	Dam	Country	Rated capacity planned (MW)
1.	San Xia (Three Gorges Dam)	China	18,200
2.	Itaipu	Brazil/Paraguay	12,600
3.	Guri (Raúl Leoni)	Venezuela	10,000
4.	Tucuruí	Brazil	8,370
5.	Sayano-Shushenskaya	Russia	6,400
6.	Itaipu	Paraguay	6,300
7.	Krasnoyarsk	Russia	6,000
8.	Bratsk	Russia	4,500
9.	Longtan (Guangxi, Tian'e)	China	4,200
	Xiaowan (Yunnan)	China	4,200
11.	Ust-Ilim	Russia	3,840
12.	Ilha Solteira	Brazil	3,444
13.	Ertan	China	3,300
14.	Yacyreta	Argentina/Paraguay	3,100
15.	Xingo	Brazil	3,000

Timeline of Selected Architectural Styles and Structures
Asterisk (*) denotes part of World Heritage Site.

Style and period	Location; characteristics; significant examples
Mesopotamian c. 3500–539 BCE	City-states of Sumer, Akkad, Babylon, Assyria (modern-day Iraq). Mud brick rectangular temples on oval platforms with simple corbel vaults, later ziggurats. Painted terra-cotta mosaics and murals; carved reliefs on columns and walls. **Ziggurat of Nanna**, Ur (Muqayyar, Iraq), ordered by Ur-Nammu, c. 2100 BCE **Anu Ziggurat and White Temple**, Uruk (Warka, Iraq), c. 3000 BCE
Egyptian c. 3000–30 BCE	Along Nile R. Mud brick and limestone tombs and massive, geometric pyramids, post-and-lintel construction. Highly decorative with colorful hieroglyphics, carvings, columns, obelisks, paintings, and sculpture. ***Stepped Pyramid of Pharaoh Zoser** (Saqqara), by Imhotep, c. 2737–2717 BCE ***Great Pyramid of Khufu** (Giza), c. 2250 BCE ***Great Temple of Amon-Ra** (Karnak), c. 1530–300 BCE ***Mortuary Temple of Queen Hatshepsut**, Deir el Bahari (Thebes), by Senenmut, c. 1479–1458 BCE
Three Dynasties c. 2100–221 BCE	China. Single-level mudbrick or mud-smeared timber structures on earthen platforms with thatched roofs. Later, bracketed wooden-framed structures with brick-tiled floors, roofs with overhanging eaves. **City of Erlitou** (Yanshi, China), c. 1900–1500 BCE
Minoan c. 1800–1450 BCE	Crete. Palaces, tombs in monumental style adapted from Mesopotamia and Egypt. Multi-level stone palaces with large central court, no fortifications. Walls made of doors (*polythyron*); stone porticoes and lintels; wooden ceilings and columns; beehive-shaped tombs (*tholi*). **Palace at Knossos** (Heraklion, Crete), c. 1700 BCE
Mycenaean c. 1600–1100 BCE	Greece. Adapted Minoan style, with large stone masonry, huge walls, and fortified citadels with complex palaces (*megaron*). ***Treasury of Atreus** (Mycenae, Greece), c. 1250 BCE
Olmec c. 1200–400 BCE	Mexico Gulf Coast. Many religious structures, including stone temple-pyramids centered in cities; also large stone sculptures and mosaic pavement with natural and animistic themes. **Great Pyramid** (La Venta, Mexico), c. 800–400 BCE
Mayan c. 900 BCE–900 CE	Central America. Religious structures with plaster-surfaced stone temple-pyramids with stairs, containing tombs. Decorative animistic and geometric relief sculptures, lintels, and stone monuments with hieroglyphics. ***Pyramid of the Magician** (Uxmal, Mexico), c. 700–910 CE **North Acropolis** (Tikal, Guatemala), c. 200 BCE
Greek c. 750–323 BCE	Greek peninsula, Asia Minor, North Africa, western Mediterranean. Religious, civic buildings in monumental style, inspired by Egypt, based on strict rules of form and human proportion; many ornamental details. Marble and limestone structures (including rectangular temples) with pediment, colonnaded porticos in diverse regional styles, defined by "orders" of architecture like Ionic, Doric, Corinthian. Most early buildings with timber supports; solid stone in later temples. ***Parthenon, Acropolis** (Athens, Greece), by Ictinus and Callicrates, 447–436 BCE ***Temple of Zeus** (Olympia, Greece), by Libon of Elis, mid-5th cent. BCE **Mausoleum of Halicarnassus** (Bodrum, Turkey), by Pythis, c. 353 BCE (destroyed) ***Temple of Apollo Epicurius** (Bassae, Greece), by Ictinus, c. 420 BCE
Achaemenid c. 550–334 BCE	Persian Empire (Eastern Mediterranean to Indus R.). Palatial complexes influenced by cultures absorbed by the empire; limestone and mud brick complexes on raised stone terraces with ornamental stairways, rectangular pillared audience halls with porticoes and corner towers; pleasure gardens (*bâgh*) as focal point of architecture. ***Pasargadae** (Iran), founded by Cyrus II, after 547 BCE ***Persepolis** (Iran), founded by Darius I, around 518 BCE
Roman c. 500 BCE–400 CE	Roman Empire. Civic and religious structures with grandiose limestone brick and concrete construction in systematic, practical layout. Adapted Greek orders in many structures, including circular temples and large covered halls (basilica), but emphasized movement with rounded arches and domes, geometric vaults. ***Pantheon** (Rome, Italy), ordered by Emperor Hadrian, 118–128 CE ***Colosseum** (Rome, Italy), ordered by Emperor Vespasian, 70–82 CE ***Roman Forum** (Rome, Italy), 500s BCE–608 CE
Qin and Han c. 221 BCE–220 CE	China. Massive public works, palaces, tombs, and planned cities; systematic layout and design determined by divination techniques (geomancy). Multi-storied timber palace complexes with gardens, courtyards laid along a long hall with a south-north axis for weather; decorative roof with overhanging eaves. ***The Great Wall** (China), ordered by Qin Shi Huang, 220 BCE–c. 1600 CE ***Mausoleum of the First Qin Emperor** (Xianyang [Xi'an], China), c. 210 BCE
Sassanian 226–651 CE	Iran. Mud brick, mortared rubble, and stone palaces on platforms. Tall, vaulted entry chambers with one open side (*iwans*). Three-aisled hall chambers covered with rudimentary barrel vaults. Parabolic domes abandoned for square courtyards in later Sassanian period. **Palace of Ardashir I** (Firuzabad, Iran), c. 224 **Taq-i Kisra** (Arch of Khosrau] (Ctesiphon, Iraq), c. 260 or c. 550
Byzantine 330–1453	Byzantine Empire, Italy, Russia. Religious structures with masonry construction based on Roman architecture, many salvaged pieces of old structures. Centralized cross-in-square layout, with large central dome supported by vaults. Highly decorative, with iconographic frescoes, glass mosaics. ***Hagia Sophia** (Istanbul, Turkey), by Anthemius and Isidorus, 532–37 ***St. Mark's Basilica** (Venice, Italy), ordered by Domenico Contarini, 1063–94
Sui and Tang 581–906	China. Includes influences from other cultures; geomancy used to enhance harmony and social status. Rectangular, multi-story modular timber structures with interlinking corridors; single-eaved roofs with exposed beams. **Daming Palace** (Xi'an, China), 634 (destroyed) ***Hall of the Great Buddha**, Foguang Temple (Wutai Mountain), ordered rebuilt by Xuan Zhong, 857
Early Islamic (Umayyad) 692–c. 1000	Syria, Middle East, North Africa, southern Spain. Mosques in adapted Sassanian style. Austere exteriors; simple columned halls with minarets and mihrab, walled courtyards and gardens, onion domes. Highly decorative interiors with patterned marble, mosaics. **Dome of the Rock** [Qubbat al-Sakhra] (Jerusalem), ordered by Abd al-Malik, 692 ***Great Mosque of Córdoba** (Spain), ordered by Abd al-Rahman I, 784–86
Khmer c. 880–1200s	Indochina. Hindu or Buddhist temple complexes, including brick, later sandstone beehive-shaped shrines with arches atop terraced temple "mountains" symbolizing Mount Meru, Hindu and Buddhist "Mountain of the Gods." Concentric layout of structures mimics the cosmos, relating religious narrative in carved reliefs. ***Angkor Wat** (Cambodia), begun by Suryavarman II, 12th cent.
Romanesque (Norman) c. 900s–1100s	Western Europe. Churches and monasteries in localized Roman style; many reused material from Roman structures. Austere, heavy, simple masonry construction with thick walls, concealed buttresses, small windows, barrel arches, and vaults. Churches like Roman basilica with arched central nave, lower side aisles, apse, transept form Latin cross. Monumental art and ornaments with Christian narrative throughout, especially on façade and portals. ***Durham Cathedral** (England, UK), ordered by Bishop William de Saint-Calais, 1093–1133 ***Cathedral, Baptistery, and "Leaning" Tower** (Pisa, Italy), by various architects, begun in 1063, tower not completed until 1372

Style and period	Location; characteristics; significant examples
Gothic c. 1100s-1500s	France, Europe. Cathedrals meant to inspire spirituality with design like Roman basilica: pointed arches and spires that reach toward heavens, skeletal masonry, revealed structure like flying buttresses, ribbed vaults to allow better lighting, large stained-glass windows. **Abbey Church of Saint-Denis** (France), ordered by Abbot Suger, 1136-47 *****Cathedral of Notre-Dame** (Paris, France), ordered by Bishop Maurice de Sully, 1163-1351 *****Chartres Cathedral** (France), 1194-1260 *****Cologne Cathedral** (Cologne, Germany), ordered by Archbishop Konrad von Hochstaden, 1248-1880 *****St. Vitus Cathedral** (Prague, Czech Republic), by Matthias of Arras, later Peter Parler, 1344-1929
Yüan and Ming 1279-1644	China. Mongol-influenced timber and some brick structures, influenced by geomancy. Emphasized monumental mass in sprawling yet low-lying structures with simple rectangular pavilions, great halls, elaborate wooden latticework, carved and painted details. *****Forbidden City** (Beijing, China), ordered by Emperor Yung Lo, 1406-20
Renaissance 1420s-1520s	Italy. The rebirth or rediscovery of ancient Roman design, grounded in a scholarly approach to architecture. Followed rules of proportion in perspective and symmetry, classical orders, and simple but perfected geometric forms; emphasis on human scale. *****Pazzi Chapel** (Florence, Italy), by Filippo Brunelleschi, 1429-61 *****Palazzo Medici-Riccardi** (Florence, Italy), by Michelozzo di Bartolomeo, 1444-60 *****Tempietto San Pietro** (Rome, Italy), by Donato Bramante, 1502-10 **Villa Almerico Capra "La Rotonda"** (near Vicenza, Italy), by Andrea Palladio, later Vincenzo Scamozzi, 1566-1610
Mughal 1526-1858	India. Monumental palaces and mosques, blending Hindu and Islamic architecture. Sandstone with marble inlay; highly decorative, with semi-precious stones, vegetal and Koranic motifs. Formulaic four-part pleasure gardens (*charbâgh*), exemplified by grounds of Taj Mahal. *****Humayun Tomb** (Delhi, India), by Sayyid Muhammad, 1562-72 *****Taj Mahal** (Agra, India), ordered by Emperor Shah Jahan, 1631-48
Baroque 1630s-1700s	Italy, later Western Europe. Elaborate and theatrical religious and civic structures, focused on dramatic overall effect. Complex geometric shapes and elaborate sculptures meant to be viewed from many angles. **St. Carlo alle Quattro Fontane** (Rome, Italy), by Francesco Borromini, 1638-41 *****Palace of Versailles** (Versailles, France), royal hunting lodge (built 1631-34) expanded under Louis XIV, 1661-1710 **Church of San Lorenzo** (Turin, Italy), by Guarino Guarini, 1666-79 **Church of St. John of Nepomuk "Asamkirche"** (Munich, Germany), by Cosmas Damian and Egid Quirin Asam, 1733-46
Rococo 1690s-1700s	Europe. Mostly interior, simplified but still fanciful Baroque designs; ornate with natural motifs, gold trim, light and creamy colors, asymmetrical designs and unusual materials. *****Sanssouci Palace** (Potsdam, Germany), by Georg Wenzeslaus von Knobelsdorff, 1745-47
Neoclassicism 1750-1830	Europe, Americas. Civic, commercial, and religious structures; chaste, non-decorative designs in reaction to Baroque excess. Grounded in Enlightenment-era principles and simple, strict adherence to classic (Greek, Roman, Renaissance) forms and details. Palladian style in England, Federal style in U.S. **Chiswick House** (Chiswick, England), by Richard Boyle, 1725-29 *****Monticello** (Charlottesville, VA), by Thomas Jefferson, 1768-1809
Neo-Gothic 1837-1900s	Britain and U.S. Civic, commercial, and religious structures utilizing Gothic forms in new commercial enterprises like railway stations and hotels. Traditional masonry façade disguised modern structural material like iron and glass. *****Westminster Palace** (London, England, UK), by Charles Barry and A.W.N. Pugin, 1840-47 **Hotel fronting St. Pancras Railway Station** (London, England, UK), by George Gilbert Scott, 1865-71
Arts and Crafts 1850s-1930s	England and U.S. Residential structures made of brick and other indigenous materials with pastoral and traditional elements like gabled roofs. Conceived as a reaction against homogenization of style following the Industrial Revolution. **Red House** (Bexley Heath, England, UK), by Philip Webb, 1859 **Tigbourne Court** (Surrey, England, UK), by Edwin Lutyens, 1898
Beaux-Arts 1870s-1930s	France, U.S. Grandiose, highly decorative style, using a mix of classical forms taught at the Ecole des Beaux-Arts (School of Fine Arts) in Paris: columns, wall projections, elaborate rooftops, high-relief decoration. **Boston Public Library** (Boston, MA), by McKim, Mead, and White, 1888-95 **Grand Central Terminal** (New York, NY), Reed & Stem and Warren & Wetmore, 1903-13
Art Noveau 1884-1905	Europe (esp. Brussels, Belgium, France). Civic and residential structures using industrial products like metal and glass to mimic natural forms; airy, fluid, and ornate. **Hôtel Tassel** (Brussels, Belgium), by Victor Horta, 1892-93 **Entrances to Métro (subway)** (Paris, France), by Hector Guimard, 1900
Prairie 1893-1917	U.S. Mostly residences, some civic buildings in adapted Arts and Crafts style. Inspired by American Midwest and small-town values. Frank Lloyd Wright most notable architect of the style. Buildings centered on chimney, with overhanging eaves and horizontal emphasis, long bands of windows. **Robie House** (Chicago, IL), by Frank Lloyd Wright, 1908-10 **National Farmer's Bank** (Owatonna, MN), by Louis Sullivan, 1906-08
Futurism 1913-14	Italy. Purely theoretical style that produced no actual structures; emphasized concrete, glass, and steel construction, pure geometric forms and straight lines, and exposed structure and utilities. **La Citta Nuova** (sketches), by Antonio Sant'Elia, 1913
Constructivism 1914-20s	Russia, Europe. Public buildings based on socialist philosophies. Purely utilitarian industrial design, modern materials. **Rusakov Club** (Moscow, Russia), by Konstantin Melnikov, 1927-28
De Stijl 1917-31	Netherlands. Building and fixtures designed as a complete, sculpture-like piece of art; emphasis on primary colors, simple but asymmetrical geometry. Name is Dutch for "The Style." **Schröder House** (Utrecht, Netherlands), by Gerrit Thomas Rietveld, 1923-24
Bauhaus 1919-33	Weimar Republic Germany. Art and design school founded by Walter Gropius with philosophy that the machine is the modern medium. Concrete, glass, and steel construction that united industrial crafts and fine arts with simple geometric forms and colors. **Bauhaus** (Dessau, Germany), by Walter Gropius, 1925-26
International Style 1920s-70s	Asia, Europe, North America. Reinforced concrete and steel structures, mostly commercial buildings with some residences and civic structures. Post-and-slab construction meant walls no longer supported weight so façades could be continuous strip (ribbon) glass "curtain-walls" with modular interiors. Emphasis on simple forms; glass, marble, and stainless steel; minimal decoration. **Philadelphia Savings Fund Society Building** (Philadelphia, PA), by George Howe and William Lescaze, 1926-32 **Villa Savoye** (Poissy, France), by Le Corbusier, 1928-31 **Seagram Building** (New York, NY), by Ludwig Mies Van Der Rohe with Philip Johnson, 1954-58
Art Deco 1925-30s	Europe, U.S. Traditional, symmetric, elegant construction (like Beaux-Arts) whimsically mixed with modern styles like geometric forms and steel or chrome features. **Chrysler Building** (New York, NY), by William van Alen, 1928-30 **Empire State Building** (New York, NY), by Shreve, Lamb, & Harmon, 1930-31
Postmodernism 1970s-present	Asia, Europe, N. America. Playful reaction against generic, mainstream "orthodox modern architecture," according to Venturi. Token references to traditional architectural elements like pediments or gables on houses; aim to present, Venturi wrote, "old clichés in new settings." **Vanna Venturi House** (Philadelphia, PA), by Robert Venturi, 1962 **Public Service Building** (Portland, OR), by Michael Graves, 1980-83

INTERNATIONAL STATISTICS

World Population Growth

Although the population of the world in ancient times can only be very roughly estimated, it is believed that there were perhaps 50 mil people in the world in 1000 BCE. The United Nations Population Division estimates a figure of 300 mil for 1 CE; this diagram shows estimated population growth since then.

While figures for other centuries may vary, all sources indicate that the world's population began growing more rapidly in the 18th and 19th centuries and increased at an even greater rate in the 20th century. According to the UN, the total population reached 1 bil in 1804; rose to 2 bil 123 years later, in 1927; to 3 bil 33 years after that, in 1960; to 4 bil in 1974; to 5 bil in 1987; and to 6 bil in 1999. The UN put the world population in mid-2011 at about 6.95 bil. It is expected to reach 7 bil in Oct. 2011.

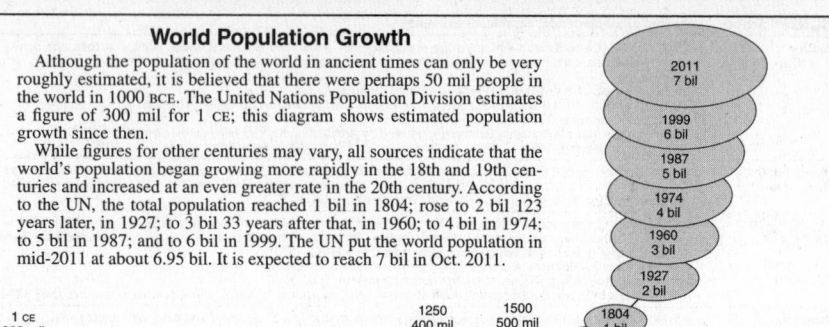

Area and Population of the World by Continent/Region

Source: International Data Base, International Programs Center, U.S. Census Bureau, U.S. Dept. of Commerce; *The World Factbook*, Central Intelligence Agency

Land area figures are those used by the U.S. Census Bureau. Geographical (continental) regions are as defined by the United Nations. Figures may not add up to totals due to rounding.

Continent/ region	Land area (sq km)	(sq mi)	% of Earth's land	Population (midyear) 1950	1975	2000	2011	% of world total, 2011	2025[1]
Asia	31,119,378	12,015,259	23.6	1,437,565,483	2,413,319,639	3,693,639,590	4,181,136,147	60.2	4,715,450,477
Africa	29,641,857	11,444,785	22.5	227,958,258	416,549,998	806,960,070	1,052,302,753	15.1	1,431,477,668
Europe	22,167,994	8,559,110	16.8	547,118,727	678,592,963	730,355,070	735,705,115	10.6	729,754,203
Northern America	20,407,482	7,879,373	15.5	165,945,185	238,783,486	313,397,878	345,213,803	5.0	389,046,607
Latin America and the Caribbean. .	20,104,280	7,762,306	15.2	165,442,794	322,225,213	519,897,589	596,296,221	8.6	682,725,711
Oceania	8,490,744	3,278,295	6.4	12,476,128	21,114,852	30,419,374	35,389,950	0.5	41,261,391
Antarctica[2]	14,000,000	5,405,430	10.6	NA	NA	NA	NA	NA	NA
World	**131,931,734**	**50,939,127**	**100.0**	**2,556,506,575**	**4,090,586,151**	**6,094,669,571**	**6,946,043,989**	**100.0**	**7,989,716,057**

NA = Not applicable. (1) Projected. (2) Antarctica has no indigenous inhabitants; researchers stay for various periods of time.

Current Population and Projections for All Countries and Territories

Source: International Data Base, International Programs Center, U.S. Census Bureau, U.S. Dept. of Commerce; *The World Factbook*, Central Intelligence Agency

(midyear figures)

Country/area	2011	2025	2050	Country/area	2011	2025	2050
Afghanistan	29,757,566	41,117,073	63,795,418	Cameroon	19,711,291	25,522,447	34,908,839
Albania	2,994,667	3,104,932	2,824,012	Canada	34,030,589	37,558,781	41,135,648
Algeria	34,994,937	40,290,081	44,163,403	Cape Verde	516,100	619,168	741,842
American Samoa	67,242	79,477	98,269	Cayman Islands	51,384	67,661	91,118
Andorra	84,825	85,112	74,765	Central African			
Angola	17,544,728	25,673,282	45,888,061	Republic	4,950,027	6,637,613	10,338,863
Anguilla	15,094	19,749	26,980	Chad	10,758,945	13,914,726	20,473,601
Antigua and				Chile	16,888,760	18,585,122	19,386,517
Barbuda	87,884	103,830	122,930	China[1]	1,336,718,015	1,394,638,699	1,303,723,332
Argentina	41,769,726	47,164,630	53,511,279	Colombia	44,725,543	51,194,904	56,227,630
Armenia	2,967,975	3,044,164	2,943,441	Comoros	721,886	905,545	1,169,893
Aruba	106,113	126,130	150,730	Congo, Dem. Rep. of	71,712,867	99,162,003	144,805,434
Australia	21,766,711	25,053,669	29,012,740	Congo Republic	4,243,929	6,161,500	9,598,623
Austria	8,217,280	8,189,560	7,520,950	Cook Islands	11,124	7,621	5,460
Azerbaijan	9,397,279	10,533,598	11,209,644	Costa Rica	4,576,562	5,353,218	6,065,989
Bahamas, The	313,312	349,116	371,219	Cote d'Ivoire	21,504,162	27,651,498	37,111,782
Bahrain	1,214,705	1,579,899	1,847,072	Croatia	4,483,804	4,374,007	3,864,201
Bangladesh	158,570,535	197,673,655	250,155,274	Cuba	11,087,330	10,784,894	9,161,479
Barbados	286,705	297,015	282,041	Curaçao	144,688	153,501	150,128
Belarus	9,577,552	9,033,301	7,738,613	Cyprus	1,120,489	1,329,908	1,392,078
Belgium	10,431,477	10,453,261	9,882,599	Czech Republic	10,190,213	9,844,275	8,540,221
Belize	321,115	411,007	543,690	Denmark	5,529,888	5,697,913	5,575,147
Benin	9,325,032	13,564,964	22,118,545	Djibouti	757,074	1,016,919	1,395,810
Bermuda	68,679	72,851	69,874	Dominica	72,969	74,374	64,772
Bhutan	708,427	820,143	951,873	Dominican Republic	9,956,648	11,702,846	13,690,264
Bolivia	10,118,683	12,463,434	16,003,638	Ecuador	15,007,343	17,867,616	21,102,550
Bosnia and				Egypt	82,079,636	103,742,157	137,872,522
Herzegovina	4,622,163	4,535,296	3,891,669	El Salvador	6,071,774	6,288,430	6,181,181
Botswana	2,065,398	2,425,114	2,871,345	Equatorial Guinea	668,225	935,553	1,428,139
Brazil	203,429,773	231,886,946	260,692,493	Eritrea	5,939,484	7,987,458	11,381,250
Brunei	401,890	498,756	638,157	Estonia	1,282,963	1,149,245	861,913
Bulgaria	7,093,635	6,257,716	4,651,477	Ethiopia	90,873,739	140,139,507	278,283,137
Burkina Faso	16,751,455	25,384,628	47,429,509	Faroe Islands	49,267	53,200	57,112
Burundi	10,216,190	15,464,910	27,148,888	Fiji	883,125	956,003	1,013,636
Cambodia	14,701,717	18,037,946	22,338,891	Finland	5,259,250	5,251,272	4,819,615
				France	65,102,719	68,481,838	69,768,223

Country/area	2011	2025	2050
French Polynesia	271,687	305,484	324,712
Gabon	1,576,665	2,063,339	3,229,741
Gambia, The	1,797,860	2,369,298	3,210,223
Gaza Strip	1,657,155	2,350,255	3,392,849
Georgia	4,585,874	4,341,061	3,784,724
Germany	81,471,834	79,226,209	71,541,906
Ghana	24,791,073	30,919,184	40,242,893
Gibraltar	28,956	29,753	28,423
Greece	10,760,136	10,670,697	10,035,935
Greenland	57,670	57,174	49,356
Grenada	108,419	114,741	114,205
Guam	183,286	214,034	243,857
Guatemala	13,824,463	17,564,073	22,995,434
Guernsey	65,068	67,710	66,521
Guinea	10,601,009	15,240,839	26,407,254
Guinea-Bissau	1,596,677	2,061,262	2,894,545
Guyana	744,768	786,286	888,494
Haiti	9,719,932	11,252,370	13,352,710
Honduras	8,143,564	10,143,648	12,948,839
Hong Kong	7,122,508	7,354,531	6,172,725
Hungary	9,976,062	9,615,020	8,489,811
Iceland	311,058	337,632	350,922
India	1,189,172,906	1,396,046,308	1,656,553,632
Indonesia	245,613,043	278,502,882	313,020,847
Iran	77,891,220	90,481,226	100,044,564
Iraq	30,399,572	40,387,147	56,316,329
Ireland	4,670,976	5,417,947	6,333,836
Isle of Man	84,655	92,606	92,840
Israel	7,473,052	8,984,285	10,828,462
Italy	61,016,804	62,591,055	61,415,852
Jamaica	2,868,380	3,151,611	3,554,571
Japan	127,469,543	123,385,521	107,209,536
Jersey	94,161	104,140	107,581
Jordan	6,508,271	7,945,150	11,243,177
Kazakhstan	17,304,513	19,809,426	22,237,156
Kenya	41,943,504	53,196,255	70,755,460
Kiribati	100,743	117,779	139,738
Korea, North	24,457,492	26,242,210	26,969,396
Korea, South	48,754,657	49,372,307	43,368,983
Kosovo	1,825,632	1,999,461	2,222,619
Kuwait	2,595,628	3,169,497	3,863,453
Kyrgyzstan	5,587,443	6,678,722	8,237,623
Laos	6,477,211	7,971,675	10,068,995
Latvia	2,204,708	1,992,516	1,544,073
Lebanon	4,143,101	4,307,087	4,155,101
Lesotho	1,924,886	1,970,540	1,920,225
Liberia	3,786,764	5,283,774	8,192,118
Libya	6,597,960	8,342,156	10,871,760
Liechtenstein	36,422	40,505	43,610
Lithuania	3,535,547	3,355,985	2,787,516
Luxembourg	503,302	586,296	720,603
Macao	573,003	630,434	620,184
Macedonia	2,077,328	2,119,511	1,990,728
Madagascar	21,926,221	32,431,146	56,513,827
Malawi	15,879,252	22,859,677	37,406,745
Malaysia	28,728,607	34,683,300	42,928,546
Maldives	394,999	388,681	444,429
Mali	14,159,904	20,240,154	32,367,436
Malta	408,333	421,239	395,639
Marshall Islands	67,182	83,203	103,092
Mauritania	3,281,634	4,425,089	6,536,272
Mauritius	1,303,717	1,412,384	1,441,100
Mayotte	209,530	235,576	266,801
Mexico	113,724,226	130,198,692	147,907,650
Micronesia	106,836	98,948	74,483
Moldova	3,694,121	3,176,863	2,261,208
Monaco	30,539	31,706	29,810
Mongolia	3,133,318	3,725,352	4,340,496
Montenegro	661,807	635,537	577,654
Montserrat	5,140	5,529	5,707
Morocco	31,968,361	36,484,418	42,026,448
Mozambique	22,948,858	32,306,018	58,998,457
Myanmar (Burma)	53,999,804	61,747,758	70,673,160
Namibia	2,147,585	2,283,845	2,149,815
Nauru	9,322	10,008	11,995
Nepal	29,391,883	36,622,606	45,984,605
Netherlands	16,653,734	17,572,113	17,906,594
New Caledonia	256,275	307,452	370,511
New Zealand	4,290,347	4,775,930	5,198,992
Nicaragua	5,666,301	6,493,913	7,233,620
Niger	16,468,886	27,062,502	55,304,449
Nigeria	165,822,569	234,362,895	402,425,535
Northern Mariana Islands	46,050	52,564	66,017
Norway	4,691,849	4,916,787	4,966,385
Oman	3,027,959	3,981,057	5,401,957

Country/area	2011	2025	2050
Pakistan	187,342,721	228,385,138	290,847,790
Palau	20,956	22,102	22,894
Panama	3,460,462	4,117,882	4,859,334
Papua New Guinea	6,187,591	7,823,210	10,110,027
Paraguay	6,459,058	7,602,853	8,840,105
Peru	29,248,943	33,283,408	36,943,693
Philippines	101,833,938	128,921,424	171,964,187
Poland	38,441,588	37,349,696	32,084,570
Portugal	10,760,305	10,806,202	9,933,334
Puerto Rico	3,989,133	4,054,536	3,679,836
Qatar	1,849,252	2,562,764	2,558,854
Romania	21,904,551	20,872,127	18,060,354
Russia	138,739,892	128,180,396	109,187,353
Rwanda	11,370,425	16,080,729	27,506,207
Saint Barthélemy	7,367	7,056	6,527
Saint Helena	7,700	7,888	7,296
Saint Kitts and Nevis	50,314	55,405	56,362
Saint Lucia	161,557	168,519	162,356
Saint Martin	30,615	33,048	34,601
Saint Pierre and Miquelon	5,888	5,030	3,516
Saint Vincent and the Grenadines	103,869	100,409	93,507
Samoa	193,161	210,369	245,010
San Marino	31,817	35,203	35,178
São Tomé and Principe	179,506	227,395	309,457
Saudi Arabia	26,131,703	31,877,311	40,250,628
Senegal	12,643,799	17,580,816	27,244,158
Serbia	7,310,555	6,845,638	5,869,146
Seychelles	89,188	98,843	100,391
Sierra Leone	5,363,669	7,500,140	13,593,862
Singapore	5,246,787	6,732,999	8,609,518
Sint Maarten	38,486	46,560	53,001
Slovakia	5,477,038	5,458,581	4,943,616
Slovenia	2,000,092	1,907,560	1,596,947
Solomon Islands	571,890	747,001	1,015,731
Somalia	9,925,640	13,274,251	22,626,120
South Africa	49,004,031	48,714,478	49,400,628
South Sudan	8,260,490[2]	NA	NA
Spain	46,754,784	51,415,437	52,490,640
Sri Lanka	21,283,913	23,563,343	25,166,733
Sudan[3]	45,047,502	63,116,874	97,164,847
Suriname	553,159	636,782	717,936
Swaziland	1,370,424	1,585,439	1,834,151
Sweden	9,088,728	9,315,507	9,084,788
Switzerland	7,639,961	7,774,334	7,296,092
Syria	22,517,750	26,536,400	33,657,629
Taiwan	23,071,779	23,213,741	20,161,286
Tajikistan	7,627,200	9,510,130	12,132,365
Tanzania	42,746,620	53,427,873	66,843,312
Thailand	66,720,153	70,643,689	69,611,256
Timor-Leste	1,177,834	1,498,319	1,954,611
Togo	6,771,993	9,741,450	16,583,950
Tonga	105,916	104,648	78,995
Trinidad and Tobago	1,227,505	1,183,838	1,023,741
Tunisia	10,629,186	11,849,537	12,180,271
Turkey	78,785,548	90,498,016	100,955,188
Turkmenistan	4,997,503	5,800,391	6,607,083
Turks and Caicos Islands	44,819	61,293	84,240
Tuvalu	10,544	11,819	13,423
Uganda	34,612,250	56,744,814	128,007,514
Ukraine	45,134,707	41,037,583	33,573,842
United Arab Emirates	5,148,664	7,063,346	8,018,904
United Kingdom	62,698,362	67,243,723	71,153,797
United States	311,050,977	351,352,771	422,554,384
Uruguay	3,308,535	3,431,610	3,495,238
Uzbekistan	28,128,600	31,823,964	35,116,374
Vanuatu	224,564	264,047	312,153
Vatican City	832	NA	NA
Venezuela	27,635,743	33,188,608	40,255,592
Vietnam	90,549,390	102,458,828	111,173,583
Virgin Islands, British	30,391	41,324	59,618
Virgin Islands, U.S.	109,666	107,114	92,343
Wallis and Futuna	15,398	16,023	15,598
West Bank	2,568,555	3,328,248	4,376,251
Western Sahara	507,160	735,697	1,173,350
Yemen	24,133,492	32,650,107	45,780,651
Zambia	13,881,336	20,671,760	38,371,544
Zimbabwe	12,084,304	17,370,260	25,198,196
World[4]	6,946,044,821	7,989,716,057	9,441,101,083

NA = Not available. (1) Not including the populations of Hong Kong and Macao, listed separately in this table. (2) 2008 est. (3) Includes the population of South Sudan. (4) Total projected populations do not include countries for which populations are not available.

Population of the World's Largest Urban Areas

Source: *World Population Prospects* and *World Urbanization Prospects*, Dept. of Economic and Social Affairs, UN Population Division

Population figures are midyear estimates for urban agglomerations, i.e., whole metropolitan areas comprising an urban center and surrounding settlements of lower density. The UN releases revised and updated numbers every two years. Numbers for 2010-20 are projected population counts. Data may differ from figures elsewhere in *The World Almanac*.

(ranked by mid-2010 population)

		Population (thous.)					Rate of change (%)			Pop. of urban aggl. as % of country's
Rank	Urban aggl., country	1975	2000	2010	2015	2020	1975-2000	2000-10	2010-20	2010 pop.
1.	Tokyo, Japan	26,614.7	34,449.9	36,668.5	37,049.2	37,087.7	29.4%	6.4%	1.1%	28.9%
2.	Delhi, India	4,426.0	15,730.4	22,156.8	24,159.8	26,272.2	255.4	40.9	18.6	1.8
3.	São Paulo, Brazil	9,614.0	17,099.2	20,262.5	21,300.0	21,627.8	77.9	18.5	6.7	10.4
4.	Mumbai (Bombay), India	7,082.0	16,085.7	20,040.9	21,796.7	23,718.5	127.1	24.6	18.4	1.7
5.	Mexico City, Mexico	10,689.7	18,021.6	19,460.2	20,077.7	20,476.0	68.6	8.0	5.2	17.6
6.	New York-Newark, NY-NJ, U.S.	15,880.3	17,845.9	19,425.1	19,968.4	20,373.6	12.4	8.8	4.9	6.1
7.	Shanghai, China	5,626.6	13,224.3	16,575.1	17,840.1	19,093.5	135.0	25.3	15.2	1.2
8.	Kolkata (Calcutta), India	7,887.8	13,058.1	15,552.1	16,923.7	18,448.9	65.5	19.1	18.6	1.3
9.	Dhaka, Bangladesh	2,221.1	10,284.9	14,648.4	16,623.0	18,721.3	363.1	42.4	27.8	8.9
10.	Karachi, Pakistan	3,989.2	10,021.2	13,124.8	14,817.7	16,693.4	151.2	31.0	27.2	7.1
11.	Buenos Aires, Argentina	8,744.6	11,847.0	13,074.4	13,401.1	13,606.2	35.5	10.4	4.1	32.2
12.	Los Angeles-Long Beach-Santa Ana, CA, U.S.	8,925.5	11,813.5	12,762.1	13,155.8	13,463.0	32.4	8.0	5.5	4.0
13.	Beijing, China	4,827.9	9,757.0	12,385.3	13,334.9	14,296.1	102.1	26.9	15.4	0.9
14.	Rio de Janeiro, Brazil	7,557.4	10,802.8	11,949.6	12,404.3	12,616.7	42.9	10.6	5.6	6.1
15.	Manila, Philippines	4,999.3	9,958.3	11,628.3	12,587.2	13,687.0	99.2	16.8	17.7	12.4

National Rankings by Population, Area, Population Density, 2011

Source: International Data Base, International Programs Center, U.S. Census Bureau, U.S. Dept. of Commerce; *The World Factbook*, Central Intelligence Agency

Pop. figures are for midyear. The world had an estimated pop. of 6.9 mil in mid-2011. China was the most populous nation, with nearly $^1/_5$ of the world total. A country's land area does not include its inland water. Rankings by total area, which includes inland water, may differ. For total area, refer to a country's entry in the Nations chapter. Pop. density is calculated using land area figures.

Largest Populations

Rank	Country	Population
1.	China[1]	1,336,718,015
2.	India	1,189,172,906
3.	United States	311,050,977
4.	Indonesia	245,613,043
5.	Brazil	203,429,773
6.	Pakistan	187,342,721
7.	Nigeria	165,822,569
8.	Bangladesh	158,570,535
9.	Russia	138,739,892
10.	Japan	127,469,543
11.	Mexico	113,724,226
12.	Philippines	101,833,938
13.	Ethiopia	90,873,739
14.	Vietnam	90,549,390
15.	Egypt	82,079,636

Smallest Populations

Rank	Country	Population
1.	Vatican City	832
2.	Nauru	9,322
3.	Tuvalu	10,544
4.	Palau	20,956
5.	Monaco	30,539
6.	San Marino	31,817
7.	Liechtenstein	36,422
8.	Saint Kitts and Nevis	50,314
9.	Marshall Islands	67,182
10.	Dominica	72,969
11.	Andorra	84,825
12.	Antigua and Barbuda	87,884
13.	Seychelles	89,188
14.	Kiribati	100,743
15.	Saint Vincent and the Grenadines	103,869

Largest Land Areas

Rank	Country	Area (sq mi)	Area (sq km)
1.	Russia	6,323,482	16,377,742
2.	China	3,694,959	9,569,901
3.	United States	3,531,905	9,147,593
4.	Canada	3,511,023	9,093,507
5.	Brazil	3,266,199	8,459,417
6.	Australia	2,966,153	7,682,300
7.	India	1,147,956	2,973,193
8.	Argentina	1,056,642	2,736,690
9.	Kazakhstan	1,042,360	2,699,700
10.	Algeria	919,595	2,381,741
11.	Congo, Dem. Rep. of	875,312	2,267,048
12.	Saudi Arabia	830,000	2,149,690
13.	Mexico	750,561	1,943,945
14.	Sudan	718,723	1,861,484
15.	Indonesia	699,451	1,811,569

Smallest Land Areas

Rank	Country	Area (sq mi)	Area (sq km)
1.	Vatican City	0.17	0.44
2.	Monaco	0.77	2
3.	Nauru	8.1	21
4.	Tuvalu	10	26
5.	San Marino	24	61
6.	Liechtenstein	62	160
7.	Marshall Islands	70	181
8.	Saint Kitts and Nevis	101	261
9.	Maldives	115	298
10.	Malta	122	316
11.	Grenada	133	344
12.	Saint Vincent and the Grenadines	150	389
13.	Barbados	166	430
14.	Antigua and Barbuda	171	443
15.	Seychelles	176	455

Most Densely Populated

Rank	Country	Persons per sq mi	Persons per sq km
1.	Monaco	39,547.8	15,269.5
2.	Singapore	19,780.4	7,637.2
3.	Vatican City	4,897.4	1,890.9
4.	Bahrain	4,139.6	1,598.3
5.	Maldives	3,433.0	1,325.5
6.	Malta	3,346.8	1,292.2
7.	Bangladesh	3,155.1	1,218.2
8.	Taiwan	1,852.3	715.2
9.	Barbados	1,726.9	666.8
10.	Mauritius	1,663.4	642.2
11.	San Marino	1,350.9	521.6
12.	Korea, South	1,302.9	503.0
13.	Netherlands	1,272.6	491.4
14.	Rwanda	1,193.8	460.9
15.	Nauru	1,149.7	443.9

Most Sparsely Populated

Rank	Country	Persons per sq mi	Persons per sq km
1.	Mongolia	5.2	2.0
2.	Namibia	6.8	2.6
3.	Australia	7.3	2.8
4.	Iceland	8.0	3.1
5.	Mauritania	8.2	3.2
6.	Suriname	9.2	3.5
7.	Botswana	9.4	3.6
8.	Canada	9.7	3.7
9.	Libya	9.7	3.7
10.	Guyana	9.8	3.8
11.	Gabon	15.8	6.1
12.	Kazakhstan	16.6	6.4
13.	Central African Republic	20.6	7.9
14.	Russia	21.9	8.5
15.	Chad	22.1	8.5

(1) Total pop. does not include mid-2011 pops. of Hong Kong (7,122,508) and Macao (573,003).

Countries Ranked by Gross Domestic Product and Per Capita GDP, 2010

Source: *The World Factbook*, Central Intelligence Agency

GDP figures are 2010 estimates unless otherwise noted. Data may differ from estimates made by the U.S. Bureau of Economic Analysis. International GDP estimates are derived from purchasing power parity calculations, which involve the use of international dollar price weights applied to quantities of goods and services produced in a given economy. Per capita GDP is calculated using the estimated population size in a given year.

GDP (in mil)

	Highest			Lowest	
1.	U.S.	$14,660,000	1.	Tuvalu	$36
2.	China[1]	10,090,000	2.	Nauru[2]	60
3.	Japan	4,310,000	3.	Marshall Islands[3]	134
4.	India	4,060,000	4.	Palau[4]	164
5.	Germany	2,940,000	5.	Micronesia[5]	238
6.	Russia	2,223,000	6.	São Tomé and Príncipe	311
7.	UK	2,173,000	7.	Kiribati	618
8.	Brazil	2,172,000	8.	St. Kitts and Nevis	684
9.	France	2,145,000	9.	Tonga	751
10.	Italy	1,774,000	10.	Dominica	758
11.	Mexico	1,567,000	11.	Comoros	800
12.	Korea, South	1,459,000	12.	Monaco[6]	976
13.	Spain	1,369,000	13.	Samoa	1,055
14.	Canada	1,330,000	14.	St. Vincent and the Grenadines	1,069
15.	Indonesia	1,030,000	15.	Grenada	1,098
16.	Turkey	960,500	16.	San Marino[7]	1,137
17.	Australia	882,400	17.	Vanuatu	1,137
18.	Taiwan	821,800	18.	Antigua and Barbuda	1,425
19.	Iran	818,700	19.	Solomon Islands	1,627
20.	Poland	721,300	20.	Liberia	1,691

Per capita GDP

	Highest			Lowest	
1.	Qatar	$179,000	1.	Burundi	$300
2.	Liechtenstein[3]	141,100		Congo, Dem. Rep. of	300
3.	Luxembourg	82,600	3.	Liberia	500
4.	Singapore	62,100		Zimbabwe	500
5.	Norway	54,600	5.	Somalia	600
6.	Brunei	51,600		Eritrea	600
7.	United Arab Emirates	49,600	7.	Niger	700
8.	Kuwait	48,900		Central African Republic	700
9.	U.S.	47,200	9.	Malawi	800
10.	Andorra[7]	46,700	10.	Sierra Leone	900
11.	Switzerland	42,600		Madagascar	900
12.	Australia	41,000		Afghanistan	900
13.	Austria	40,400		Togo	900
14.	Netherlands	40,300	14.	Guinea	1,000
	Bahrain	40,300		Ethiopia	1,000
16.	Canada	39,400		Comoros	1,000
17.	Sweden	39,100		Mozambique	1,000
18.	Iceland	38,300	18.	Guinea-Bissau	1,100
19.	Belgium	37,800		Rwanda	1,100
20.	Ireland	37,300	20.	Mali	1,200
				Haiti	1,200
				Burkina Faso	1,200
				Nepal	1,200

(1) Does not include Hong Kong, which had an estimated GDP of $325.8 bil and a per capita GDP of $45,900 in 2010, or Macao, with an estimated GDP of $18.5 bil and a per capita GDP of $33,000 in 2009. (2) 2005 est. (3) 2008 est. (4) 2008 est. in 2010 USD; incl. U.S. subsidy. (5) 2008 est.; supplemented by grant aid, averaging perhaps $100 mil annually. (6) 2006 est. (7) 2009 or 2009 est.

Gold Reserves of Selected Central Banks and Governments, 1975-2010

Source: *International Financial Statistics*, International Monetary Fund

(in mil fine troy ounces)

Year end	All countries[1]	Canada	China[2]	France	Germany[3]	India	Italy	Japan	Netherlands	Russia	Switzerland	UK	U.S.
1975	1,188.0	22.0	NA	100.9	117.6	7.0	82.5	21.1	54.3	NA	83.2	21.0	274.7
1980	1,152.2	21.0	12.8	81.9	95.2	8.6	66.7	24.2	43.9	NA	83.3	18.8	264.3
1985	1,147.4	20.1	12.7	81.9	95.2	9.4	66.7	24.2	43.9	NA	83.3	19.0	262.7
1990	1,144.2	14.8	12.7	81.9	95.2	10.7	66.7	24.2	43.9	NA	83.3	18.9	261.9
1995	1,115.3	3.4	12.7	81.9	95.2	12.8	66.7	24.2	34.8	9.4	83.3	18.4	261.7
2000	1,062.9	1.2	12.7	97.2	111.5	11.5	78.8	24.5	29.3	12.4	77.8	15.7	261.6
2001	1,053.9	1.1	16.1	97.2	111.1	11.5	78.8	24.6	28.4	13.6	70.7	11.4	262.0
2002	1,042.1	0.6	19.3	97.2	110.8	11.5	78.8	24.6	27.4	12.5	61.6	10.1	262.0
2003	1,024.3	0.1	19.3	97.2	110.6	11.5	78.8	24.6	25.0	12.5	52.5	10.1	261.5
2004	1,007.7	0.1	19.3	96.0	110.4	11.5	78.8	24.6	25.0	12.4	43.5	10.0	261.6
2005	988.4	0.1	19.3	90.9	110.2	11.5	78.8	24.6	22.3	12.4	41.5	10.0	261.6
2006	976.7	0.1	19.3	87.4	110.0	11.5	78.8	24.6	20.6	12.9	41.5	10.0	261.5
2007	960.5	0.1	19.3	83.7	109.9	11.5	78.8	24.6	20.0	14.5	36.8	10.0	261.5
2008	960.4	0.1	19.3	80.1	109.7	11.5	78.8	24.6	19.7	16.7	33.4	10.0	261.5
2009	977.1	0.1	33.9	78.3	109.5	17.9	78.8	24.6	19.7	20.9	33.4	10.0	261.5
2010	981.7	0.1	33.9	78.3	109.3	17.9	78.8	24.6	19.7	25.4	33.4	10.0	261.5

NA = Not available. (1) Covers International Monetary Fund members with reported gold holdings. (2) Figures are for mainland China only and do not include Hong Kong nor Macao. (3) West Germany prior to 1991.

Consumer Price Changes in Selected Countries, 1975-2010

Source: *International Financial Statistics*, International Monetary Fund

(annual average % change)

Country	1975-80	1980-85	1995-96	1996-97	1997-98	1998-99	1999-2000	2000-01	2002-03	2004-05	2006-07	2008-09	2009-10
Canada	8.7%	7.4%	1.6%	1.6%	1.0%	1.7%	2.7%	2.3%	2.8%	2.2%	2.1%	0.3%	1.8%
China[1]	NA	NA	8.3	2.8	−0.9	−1.4	0.3	0.5	1.2	1.8	4.8	−0.7	3.3
France	10.5	9.6	2.0	1.2	0.7	0.5	1.7	1.6	2.1	1.8	1.5	0.1	1.5
Germany[2]	4.1	3.9	1.5	1.8	1.0	0.6	1.5	2.0	1.1	2.0	2.1	0.3	1.1
Italy	16.3	13.7	4.0	2.0	2.0	1.7	2.5	2.8	2.7	2.0	1.8	0.8	1.5
Japan	6.5	2.7	0.1	1.7	0.6	−0.3	−0.7	−0.7	−0.3	−0.3	0.1	−1.4	−0.7
Spain	18.6	12.2	3.6	2.0	1.8	2.3	3.4	3.6	3.0	3.4	2.8	−0.4	1.9
Sweden	10.5	9.0	0.5	0.5	−0.1	0.5	0.9	2.4	1.9	0.5	2.2	−0.3	1.2
Switzerland	2.3	4.3	0.8	0.5	0.1	0.7	1.5	1.0	0.6	1.2	0.7	−0.5	0.7
United Kingdom	14.4	7.2	2.4	3.1	3.4	1.6	2.9	1.8	2.9	2.8	4.3	−0.6	3.3
United States	8.9	5.5	3.0	2.3	1.6	2.2	3.4	2.8	2.3	3.4	2.9	−0.4	1.6

NA = Not available. (1) Figures are for mainland China only and do not include Hong Kong nor Macao. (2) West Germany prior to 1991.

Hourly Compensation Costs in Manufacturing in Selected Countries, 1975-2009

Source: Division of Foreign Labor Statistics, U.S. Bureau of Labor Statistics, U.S. Dept. of Labor

For production workers (engaged in assembly, shipping, and maintenance, among other activities) in manufacturing only. Compensation includes all direct pay (overtime and bonuses), paid benefits, and social insurance expenditures and labor taxes.

(in U.S. dollars)

Country/area	1975	1980	1985	1990	1995	2000	2009	Country/area	1975	1980	1985	1990	1995	2000	2009
Australia	5.80	8.73	8.48	13.57	15.23	14.15	30.50	Luxembourg	6.24	11.54	7.47	15.97	23.54	17.49	31.88
Austria	4.55	8.96	7.66	17.92	25.50	20.00	39.14	Mexico	1.80	2.71	1.95	1.94	1.85	3.02	3.81
Belgium	6.34	12.89	9.02	19.62	28.34	22.32	42.80	Netherlands	6.57	12.03	8.73	17.99	24.02	18.67	38.99
Brazil	NA	NA	NA	NA	NA	3.56	6.81	New Zealand	3.30	5.49	4.60	8.57	10.33	8.33	15.69
Canada	6.40	9.02	11.40	16.62	16.80	16.78	26.40	Norway	7.01	11.88	10.51	21.68	24.74	22.17	45.50
Czech Republic	NA	NA	NA	NA	2.54	2.85	9.51	Philippines	NA	NA	NA	NA	0.89	0.69	1.17
Denmark	6.23	10.82	8.03	18.29	24.87	21.45	44.99	Poland	NA	NA	NA	NA	NA	2.75	6.14
Finland	4.99	8.50	8.22	20.68	22.73	17.73	36.88	Portugal	1.79	2.33	1.73	4.23	5.86	5.01	9.60
France	4.72	9.33	7.85	16.17	20.02	15.96	30.42	Singapore	0.84	1.55	2.57	3.81	7.71	7.39	9.23
Germany[1]	5.16	10.05	7.85	18.05	26.17	19.62	34.80	Spain	2.49	5.79	4.59	11.23	12.60	10.57	23.70
Hong Kong[2]	0.77	1.54	1.77	3.30	4.89	5.50	5.82	Sri Lanka	0.28	0.22	0.28	0.35	0.48	0.48	NA
Hungary	NA	NA	NA	NA	2.56	2.36	6.44	Sweden	7.10	12.37	9.56	20.71	21.45	20.25	31.82
Ireland	3.71	6.80	6.54	12.78	14.83	13.53	31.09	Switzerland	6.14	11.17	9.74	21.02	29.43	21.29	37.99
Israel	2.02	3.41	3.65	7.70	9.41	11.38	16.06	Taiwan	0.39	1.04	1.50	3.89	5.96	6.16	6.20
Italy	4.70	8.20	7.67	18.01	16.71	14.53	30.67	United Kingdom	3.25	7.29	6.05	12.11	13.39	16.60	23.35
Japan	2.95	5.41	6.24	12.52	23.34	21.69	25.36	United States	6.19	9.67	12.76	14.88	17.24	19.73	26.19
Korea, South	0.33	0.98	1.28	3.79	7.54	8.54	12.39	OECD countries[3]	4.26	7.10	7.11	12.66	15.78	14.59	23.45

NA = Not available. (1) 1975-90 data are for former West Germany; 1995-present data for unified Germany. (2) Part of China since 1997. (3) Australia, Canada, Japan, South Korea, Mexico, New Zealand, U.S., and all European countries covered in this table are Organisation for Economic Co-operation and Development (OECD) countries. 1975-95 data exclude the Czech Republic, Hungary, and Poland.

Unemployment Rates in Selected Countries, 1970-2010

Source: Division of International Labor Comparisons, U.S. Bureau of Labor Statistics, U.S. Dept. of Labor

Year	U.S.	Australia	Canada	France	Germany[1]	Italy	Japan	Netherlands	Sweden	UK
1970	4.9%	1.7%	5.7%	2.5%	0.5%	3.2%	1.2%	NA	1.5%	NA
1975	8.5	4.9	6.9	3.7	3.4	3.4	1.9	5.1%	1.6	4.5%
1980	7.1	6.1	7.3	5.7	2.8	4.4	2.0	6.0	2.0	6.9
1985	7.2	8.3	10.1	9.1	7.2	6.0	2.5	9.6	2.8	11.4
1990	5.6	6.7	7.7	8.0	5.0	7.0	2.0	7.6	1.8	7.1
1991	6.8	9.3	9.8	8.3	5.6	6.9	2.0	7.1	3.2	8.9
1992	7.5	10.5	10.6	9.1	6.7	7.3	2.1	6.8	5.8	10.0
1993	6.9	10.6	10.8	10.2	8.0	9.8	2.4	6.3	9.4	10.4
1994	6.1	9.4	9.6	10.8	8.5	10.7	2.6	6.9	9.6	9.5
1995	5.6	8.2	8.6	10.2	8.2	11.3	2.9	7.1	9.1	8.7
1996	5.4	8.2	8.8	10.7	9.0	11.3	3.1	6.6	9.9	8.1
1997	4.9	8.3	8.4	10.9	9.9	11.4	3.1	5.6	10.1	7.0
1998	4.5	7.7	7.7	10.5	9.3	11.5	3.8	4.4	8.4	6.3
1999	4.2	6.9	7.0	10.1	8.5	11.0	4.2	3.5	7.1	6.0
2000	4.0	6.3	6.1	8.6	7.8	10.2	4.4	3.1	5.8	5.5
2001	4.7	6.8	6.5	7.9	7.9	9.2	4.5	2.5	5.0	5.1
2002	5.8	6.4	7.0	8.0	8.6	8.7	4.9	3.1	5.1	5.2
2003	6.0	5.9	6.9	8.6	9.3	8.5	4.6	4.1	5.8	5.0
2004	5.5	5.4	6.4	9.0	10.3	8.1	4.2	5.0	6.6	4.8
2005	5.1	5.0	6.0	9.0	11.2	7.8	3.8	5.3	7.7	4.9
2006	4.6	4.8	5.5	8.9	10.3	6.9	3.6	4.3	7.0	5.5
2007	4.6	4.4	5.2	8.1	8.7	6.2	3.6	3.6	6.1	5.4
2008	5.8	4.2	5.3	7.5	7.6	6.8	3.7	3.1	6.0	5.7
2009	9.3	5.6	7.3	9.2	7.8	7.9	4.8	3.7	8.2	7.7
2010	9.6	5.2	7.1	9.4	7.2	8.6	4.8	4.5	8.3	7.9

Note: Unemployment rates are for the civilian labor force, seasonally adjusted. U.S. unemployment rate concepts are applied to unemployment data from other countries in order to make comparisons. As a result of revisions in survey methodology, some data may not be fully comparable across time. NA = Not available. (1) For former West Germany only, through 1990; data from 1991 on are for unified Germany.

Tax Payments in Selected Countries, 2010

Source: *Taxing Wages 2009-2010*, Organisation for Economic Co-operation and Development

Excluding taxes not listed here, such as sales tax. Rates apply to a single person without children at an average earnings level.

(as % of gross wage earnings, in dollars with equal purchasing power; ranked by size of total payment)

Country	Total payment[1]	Income tax	Soc. sec. contribs.	Gross wage earnings	Country	Total payment[1]	Income tax	Soc. sec. contribs.	Gross wage earnings
Belgium	42.1%	28.1%	14.0%	$47,617	United States	22.9%	15.3%	7.7%	$43,040
Germany	39.2	18.7	20.5	51,935	Portugal	22.9	11.9	11.0	27,723
Denmark	38.6	27.9	10.7	46,235	Czech Republic	22.5	11.5	11.0	21,549
Slovenia	33.1	11.0	22.1	26,438	Canada	22.2	14.9	7.3	35,871
Austria	32.7	14.7	18.1	46,911	Ireland	21.8	14.4	7.3	44,993
Netherlands	31.9	16.4	15.6	52,581	Australia	21.6	21.6	0.0	41,231
Hungary	31.2	14.2	17.0	18,967	Spain	21.6	15.2	6.4	34,545
Italy	29.8	20.3	9.5	35,847	Slovak Republic	21.5	8.1	13.4	18,142
Finland	29.1	22.0	7.1	41,915	Japan	20.8	7.7	13.1	43,626
Norway	28.7	20.9	7.8	49,991	Estonia	19.4	16.6	2.8	18,440
France	27.8	14.1	13.7	38,828	Greece	18.8	2.8	16.0	24,112
Turkey	27.1	12.1	15.0	19,783	New Zealand	16.9	16.9	0.0	31,152
Luxembourg	26.4	14.2	12.2	53,561	Israel	16.5	8.6	7.8	31,747
United Kingdom	25.5	16.3	9.2	53,623	Switzerland	16.0	10.0	6.1	50,170
Iceland	25.3	24.7	0.6	32,464	Korea, South	11.9	4.1	7.8	43,049
Sweden	24.7	17.7	7.0	40,902	Chile	7.0	0.0	7.0	11,552
Poland	24.6	6.7	17.8	20,051	Mexico	5.6	4.3	1.4	10,996

(1) Figures may not add up to totals due to rounding.

Refugees and People in a Refugee-Like Situation, 2010

Source: *UNHCR Global Trends 2010*, United Nations High Commissioner for Refugees (UNHCR)

Refugees are persons recognized under the 1951 UN Convention Relating to the Status of Refugees; its 1967 Protocol; the 1969 OAU (Org. of African Unity) Refugee Convention; in accordance with the UNHCR Statute; or persons granted or receiving similar protection. Persons outside of their country or territory of origin who face protection risks similar to those of refugees—but for whom refugee status has not been ascertained—are described as being in a refugee-like situation. Data were generally provided by governments based on their definitions and data collection methods. The UNHCR made estimates where government figures were absent.

Only countries hosting 50,000 or more refugees and people in a refugee-like situation are shown. Only countries of origin with 5,000 or more refugees and people in a refugee-like situation are shown, in decreasing order. Totals include those in countries not listed. As of year-end 2010.

Place of asylum	Origin of most refugees and asylum seekers	Number
Africa		**2,183,955**
Cameroon	Central African Republic, Chad	104,275
Chad	Sudan, Central African Republic	347,939
Congo, Dem. Rep. of	Angola, Rwanda, Burundi	166,366
Congo Republic	Dem. Rep. of the Congo, Rwanda	133,112
Ethiopia	Somalia, Eritrea, Sudan	154,295
Kenya	Somalia, Ethiopia, Sudan	402,905
Rwanda	Dem. Rep. of the Congo	55,398
South Africa	Somalia, Dem. Rep. of the Congo, Angola	57,899
Sudan	Eritrea, Chad, Dem. Rep. of the Congo, Ethiopia	178,308
Tanzania	Dem. Rep. of the Congo, Burundi	109,286
Uganda	Dem. Rep. of the Congo, Sudan, Rwanda, Somalia	135,801
Americas		**803,990**
Canada	Sri Lanka, China, Colombia, Pakistan, India, Mexico	165,549
Ecuador	Colombia	121,249
United States	China, Colombia, Haiti, Ethiopia, India, Cameroon, Russia, Armenia, Albania, Venezuela, Indonesia, Iraq, Iran	264,574
Venezuela	Colombia	201,547
Asia and Pacific		**4,014,115**
Bangladesh	Myanmar	229,253
China (incl. HK, Macao)	Vietnam	300,986
India	China, Sri Lanka, Afghanistan	184,821
Malaysia	Myanmar	81,516
Nepal	Bhutan, Tibetan	89,808
Pakistan	Afghanistan	1,900,621
Thailand	Myanmar	96,675
Europe		**1,606,639**
France	Sri Lanka, Cambodia, Dem. Rep. of the Congo, Turkey, Serbia-Kosovo, Russia, Vietnam, Laos	200,687
Germany	Serbia-Kosovo, Turkey, Iraq, Russia, Afghanistan, Vietnam, Bosnia and Herzegovina, Iran, Ukraine, Lebanon, Sri Lanka, Syria, Pakistan, Azerbaijan, Macedonia, Dem. Rep. of the Congo, stateless[1]	594,269
Italy	Eritrea, Somalia	56,397
Netherlands	Iraq, Somalia, Afghanistan	74,961
Serbia-Kosovo	Croatia, Bosnia and Herzegovina	73,608
Sweden	Iraq, Somalia, Serbia-Kosovo	82,629
United Kingdom	Somalia, Afghanistan, Iraq, Zimbabwe, Iran, Eritrea, Sri Lanka, Serbia-Kosovo, Turkey	238,150
Middle East and North Africa		**1,940,987**
Algeria	Western Sahara	94,144
Egypt	Occupied Palestinian Territory[2], Sudan, Iraq, Somalia	95,056
Iran	Afghanistan, Iraq	1,073,366
Jordan	Iraq	450,915
Syria	Iraq	1,005,472
Yemen	Somalia	190,092
TOTAL		**10,549,686**

(1) Persons not considered nationals by any state under the operation of its laws. (2) Palestinians under the UNHCR mandate only.

Internally Displaced Persons, 2010

Source: *Global Overview of Trends and Developments*, Internal Displacement Monitoring Centre, Norwegian Refugee Council

Internally displaced persons (IDPs) are people who have been forced to flee due to armed conflict or human rights violations but who have not crossed into another country. As such, they are not protected by international refugee law and legally remain under the protection of their home country. Ests. are latest available and may comprise only registered IDPs or those displaced from a certain area of a country.

Country	Number	Country	Number	Country	Number
Afghanistan	309,000+	India	650,000+	Peru	150,000
Armenia	8,000+	Indonesia	200,000	Philippines	15,000+
Azerbaijan	<593,000	Iraq	2.8 mil	Russia	6,500-78,000
Bosnia and Herzegovina	113,400	Kenya	250,000	Senegal	10,000-40,000
Burundi	<100,000	Kosovo	18,300	Serbia[3]	225,000
Central African Republic	192,000	Kyrgyzstan	75,000	Somalia	1.5 mil
Chad	131,000	Lebanon[2]	76,000+	Sri Lanka	220,000+
Colombia[1]	3.6 mil-5.2 mil	Libya	218,000	Sudan[4]	4.5 mil-5.2 mil
Congo, Dem. Rep. of	1.7 mil	Macedonia	650	Syria	433,000+
Congo	<7,800	Mexico	120,000	Turkey	954,000-1.2 mil
Croatia	2,300	Myanmar	446,000+	Uganda	73,239+
Cyprus	<208,000	Nepal	50,000	Uzbekistan	3,400
Eritrea	10,000	Occupied Palestinian		Yemen[5]	250,000+
Ethiopia	300,000	Territory	160,000+	Zimbabwe	570,000-1 mil
Georgia	<258,000	Pakistan	980,000+	**Total**	**27.5 mil**

Note: The number of IDPs in the following countries was undetermined: Algeria, Angola, Bangladesh, Côte d'Ivoire, Guatemala, Israel, Laos, Liberia, Niger, Nigeria, Rwanda, Timor-Leste, Togo, and Turkmenistan. (1) Low end of range cumulative since 2000; high end since 1985. (2) Prior to July 2006, an est. 50,000-600,000 were displaced by the 1975-90 civil war and Israeli invasions. (3) Incl. an est. 20,000 unregistered Roma in Serbia and 20,000 IDPs in Kosovo. (4) Incl. 220,000 IDPs newly displaced in 2010 in South Sudan. (5) Political unrest and counterinsurgency operations have displaced 20,000+ from late 2010 to mid-2011.

Estimated HIV Infection and Reported AIDS Cases, 2009

Source: Joint United Nations Programme on HIV/AIDS (UNAIDS), World Health Organization

The percentage of people living with HIV/AIDS worldwide has stabilized since 2000. But the numbers of those infected continue to rise, in part due to greater access to antiretroviral therapy, particularly in low- and middle-income countries. In 2009, there were an estimated 2.6 mil new cases of HIV infection and 1.8 mil AIDS-related deaths. One out of four deaths is from tuberculosis. About 2.5 mil of those living with HIV/AIDS in 2009 were children under 15 years of age. Sub-Saharan Africa remained the world's worst affected region, with approximately two-thirds of the total population living with HIV/AIDS and nearly three-quarters (72.2%) of all AIDS-related deaths in 2009. About $15.9 bil was spent globally on HIV/AIDS treatment and prevention in 2009, less than the estimated $26.8 bil needed to fund services in 2010.

Estimates of the number of HIV/AIDS cases and deaths are made based on all available data, including surveys of pregnant women visiting prenatal clinics, household surveys, monitoring of at-risk population groups, and birth and death records.

Current and New HIV/AIDS Cases and Deaths by Region, 2009

Region	Number living with HIV/AIDS[1]	Percent of total[2]	New HIV infections	AIDS-related deaths
Sub-Saharan Africa	22,500,000	67.6%	1,800,000	1,300,000
South and South-East Asia	4,100,000	12.3	270,000	260,000
North America	1,500,000	4.5	70,000	26,000
Eastern Europe and Central Asia	1,400,000	4.2	130,000	76,000
Central and South America	1,400,000	4.2	92,000	58,000
Western and Central Europe	820,000	2.5	31,000	8,500
East Asia	770,000	2.3	82,000	36,000
Middle East and North Africa	460,000	1.4	75,000	24,000
Caribbean	240,000	0.7	17,000	12,000
Oceania	57,000	0.2	4,500	1,400
World[3]	33,300,000	100.0	2,600,000	1,800,000

(1) Includes adults (ages 15 and older) and children (under 15). (2) Population within a region living with HIV/AIDS as a percentage of population worldwide living with HIV/AIDS. (3) Figures may not add up to totals because of rounding.

Infectious Disease, Sanitation, and Water Quality, 2008

Source: *Global Burden of Disease* and *World Health Statistics*, World Health Organization (WHO)

According to the World Health Organization, 13% of the world's population, or 884 mil people, lacked access to improved sources of drinking water in 2008. The majority of those without access, about 84%, lived in a rural area. WHO estimates in that same year, 17%, or 1.1 bil people, lacked access to improved sanitation facilities. The population in unserved areas are at increased risk of contracting a variety of infectious and parasitic diseases such as diarrhea, malaria, trachoma, and hepatitis A.

Listed below are nations with the highest death rates from infectious and parasitic diseases and the poorest access to improved sanitation and water. Rankings and death rates for G8 countries and China are included for comparison. With the exception of China and Russia, these nations have near-universal (99% or greater) access to improved water and sanitation. In 2008, 55% of China's population had access to improved sanitation, and 89% had access to improved water. In Russia, the figures were 87% and 96%, respectively. (Sanitation figures was not available for Italy.)

Deaths from Infectious and Parasitic Diseases, 2008
(per 100,000 population; ranked by deaths from infectious and parasitic diseases)

Rank	Country	Infectious and parasitic diseases	Tuberculosis	Diarrheal diseases	All causes
1.	Zimbabwe	931.4	50.6	36.3	1,467.5
2.	Lesotho	793.3	29.4	41.7	1,558.8
3.	Chad	787.3	66.8	210.9	1,716.9
4.	Swaziland	770.4	32.5	48.6	1,504.4
5.	Central African Republic	754.9	46.2	113.5	1,670.5
6.	Sierra Leone	733.7	128.5	156.0	1,502.3
7.	South Africa	727.6	39.3	71.6	1,344.7
8.	Malawi	719.3	23.7	101.5	1,626.7
9.	Mozambique	697.0	39.5	82.2	1,558.7
10.	Congo, Dem. Rep. of	687.4	78.8	187.5	1,606.8
91.	Russia	53.3	18.0	0.3	1,473.7
123.	China	23.4	11.8	1.4	715.7
124.	United States	22.9	0.2	2.3	817.5
130.	Japan	20.8	3.1	1.8	892.5
136.	France	18.8	1.1	2.2	841.8
144.	Germany	16.0	0.5	1.7	1,009.1
149.	Italy	14.0	0.7	0.3	975.7
151.	United Kingdom	13.4	0.7	5.0	960.2
154.	Canada	12.8	0.3	3.2	704.3

Lowest Access to Improved Sanitation Facilities, 2008
Improved sanitation facilities incl. public sewer connections, septic system connections, and ventilated improved pit latrines.

Rank	Country	% of pop. with access
1.	Niger	9%
2.	Chad	9
3.	Madagascar	11
4.	Burkina Faso	11
5.	Ethiopia	12
6.	Togo	12
7.	Benin	12
8.	Sierra Leone	13
9.	Ghana	13
10.	Eritrea	14

Lowest Access to Improved Drinking-Water Sources, 2008
Improved water sources incl. household connections, public standpipes, and dug wells protected from outside contamination.

Rank	Country	% of pop. with access
1.	Somalia	30%
2.	Ethiopia	38
3.	Madagascar	41
4.	Papua New Guinea	41
5.	Equatorial Guinea (2005)	43
6.	Mozambique	47
7.	Afghanistan	48
8.	Niger	48
9.	Mauritania	49
10.	Sierra Leone	49

Foreign Development Aid Donors, 2009-10

Source: Development Assistance Committee (DAC), Organisation for Economic Co-operation and Development (OECD)

Listed are the amounts of official development assistance (ODA) (grants or loans) each DAC member country disbursed in a given year to developing countries. The numbers represent net, not gross, disbursements. They include both bilateral ODA (aid given directly to an aid recipient) and multilateral ODA (aid given to agencies like the World Bank). Countries are ranked by the size of their ODA as a percentage of their 2010 gross national income (GNI). 2010 figures are preliminary.

	Donor	ODA as % of GNI 2010	ODA as % of GNI 2009	ODA in mil of current U.S. dollars 2010	ODA in mil of current U.S. dollars 2009		Donor	ODA as % of GNI 2010	ODA as % of GNI 2009	ODA in mil of current U.S. dollars 2010	ODA in mil of current U.S. dollars 2009
1.	Norway	1.10%	1.06%	$4,582.23	$4,085.84	15.	Austria	0.32%	0.30%	$1,198.94	$1,141.78
2.	Luxembourg	1.09	1.04	399.20	414.73	16.	Australia	0.32	0.29	3,848.91	2,761.61
3.	Sweden	0.97	1.12	4,526.62	4,548.23	17.	Portugal	0.29	0.23	648.10	512.71
4.	Denmark	0.90	0.88	2,866.63	2,809.88	18.	New Zealand	0.26	0.28	352.83	309.28
5.	Netherlands	0.81	0.82	6,350.60	6,426.08	19.	United States	0.21	0.21	30,154.29	28,831.34
6.	Belgium	0.64	0.55	3,000.23	2,609.60	20.	Japan	0.20	0.18	11,045.22	9,456.93
7.	United Kingdom	0.56	0.51	13,763.07	11,282.61	21.	Greece	0.17	0.19	500.03	607.27
8.	Finland	0.55	0.54	1,335.36	1,290.18	22.	Italy	0.15	0.16	3,110.87	3,297.49
9.	Ireland	0.53	0.54	895.15	1,005.78	23.	Korea	0.12	0.10	1,167.74	816.04
10.	France	0.50	0.47	12,915.62	12,600.02		**Total DAC**	**0.32**	**0.31**	**128,728.34**	**119,780.95**
11.	Spain	0.43	0.46	5,916.59	6,584.11		**Total G7[1]**	**0.28**	**0.26**	**88,843.96**	**81,547.76**
12.	Switzerland	0.41	0.45	2,295.22	2,310.07		**EU institutions**	**NA**	**NA**	**12,985.87**	**13,443.66**
13.	Germany	0.38	0.35	12,723.05	12,079.30						
14.	Canada	0.33	0.30	5,131.84	4,000.07						

(1) Canada, France, Germany, Italy, Japan, the UK, and the U.S.

Recipients of U.S. Official Development Assistance, 2008-09

Source: Development Assistance Committee (DAC), Organisation for Economic Co-operation and Development (OECD)

(in mil of current U.S. dollars; ranked by 2009 figures)

	Country	2009	2008		Country	2009	2008
1.	Afghanistan	$2,979.93	$2,111.58	11.	Uganda	$366.88	$352.88
2.	Iraq	2,346.31	2,741.99	12.	Nigeria	354.03	363.89
3.	Sudan	954.64	848.16	13.	Haiti	319.56	259.09
4.	Palestinian Administered Areas	844.31	490.60	14.	Tanzania	283.65	246.95
5.	Ethiopia	726.04	811.37	15.	Georgia	279.12	402.10
6.	Colombia	652.34	636.09	16.	Mozambique	255.61	226.66
7.	Pakistan	613.04	350.63	17.	Zimbabwe	249.74	222.90
8.	Kenya	590.21	439.43	18.	Congo, Dem. Rep. of	238.69	196.63
9.	South Africa	523.74	378.66	19.	Zambia	231.86	226.49
10.	Jordan	394.61	384.05	20.	Cote d'Ivoire	230.66	88.82
					All developing countries	**25,173.65**	**23,848.21**

Nuclear Powers of the World

As of Aug. 2011, eight countries were acknowledged nuclear powers: the **UK, France, China, India, Pakistan, Russia, North Korea,** and the **U.S.** In addition, **Israel** is suspected of having an arsenal. **Iran** was suspected of developing nuclear weapons despite the country's claims that it was focusing on nuclear energy. More than 40 nations have the knowledge or technology to produce nuclear weapons. All—except Israel, India, and Pakistan—have signed the Nuclear Non-Proliferation Treaty (NPT). North Korea announced its withdrawal Jan. 10, 2003, following its expulsion of Intl. Atomic Energy Agency (IAEA) inspectors in late Dec. 2002.

At six-party talks with China, Japan, Russia, South Korea, and the U.S. on Sept. 19, 2005, North Korea agreed to a draft accord whereby it would scrap its nuclear weapons program in exchange for aid. Left unresolved was Pyongyang's continuing demand for donors to provide light-water nuclear reactors for "peaceful uses."

After further negotiations broke down, North Korea conducted its first-ever nuclear test Oct. 9, 2006. It returned to a new round of talks in Dec. 2006 and agreed to a deal in Feb. 2007: in exchange for closing its main nuclear facility and taking steps toward disabling its nuclear weapons program, the country would receive economic aid and diplomatic recognition. Though North Korea seemed willing to take conciliatory steps, the next round of talks, in Dec. 2008, ended in deadlock. North Korea conducted a second nuclear test May 25, 2009, earning it additional UN sanctions. The country

may have produced enough plutonium for about 10 nuclear bombs. But the U.S. believes North Korea currently lacks the capability to weaponize them.

Despite UN sanctions dating back to Dec. 2006, Iran has refused to suspend its activities in the enrichment of uranium. Iran argued that as an NPT signatory, it had a right to pursue the peaceful application of nuclear technology. The IAEA maintained that Iran has withheld information on the extent of its nuclear activities.

In Sept. 2009, the U.S., along with France and Britain, accused Iran of building a secret uranium enrichment facility. Iran acknowledged the existence of the facility as a backup to its main enrichment site. Iran began loading fuel into its first nuclear power plant on Aug. 21, 2010. Under an agreement between the two countries, Russia would supply Iran with low-enriched uranium, which Iran would send back once it was spent. A computer virus apparently targeting Iran's nuclear program came to public attention in 2010. Researchers said the Stuxnet program, which targets specific computer hardware, may have disrupted operations at Iran's nuclear facility. Newspapers reported that the worm may have been created in a joint U.S.-Israeli operation.

Several countries abandoned their nuclear ambitions. **South Africa** announced in 1993 that it had built seven fission weapons (one was under construction) but had dismantled all of them. In the 1980s, **Argentina** and **Brazil** had active nuclear weapons programs but abandoned them by mutual treaty and signed the NPT.

Estimated Numbers of Nuclear Weapons by Country, 1945-2011

Source: *Bulletin of the Atomic Scientists*; Carnegie Endowment for International Peace; Federation of American Scientists (FAS); Natural Resources Defense Council (NRDC); Nuclear Threat Initiative (NTI); Stockholm International Peace Research Institute (SIPRI)

Year	United States	USSR/Russia	United Kingdom	France	China	Israel[1]	India	Pakistan	Total
1945	6	—	—	—	—	—	—	—	6
1950	369	5	—	—	—	—	—	—	374
1960	20,434	1,605	30	—	—	—	—	—	22,069
1970	26,662	11,643	280	36	75	8	—	—	38,696
1980	24,304	30,062	350	250	280	31	—	—	55,246
1990	21,004	37,000	300	505	430	53	—	—	59,239
1995	12,144	27,000	300	500	400	63	—	—	40,344
2000	10,577	21,000	185	470	400	72	—	—	32,632
2011	8,500[2]	11,000[3]	225	300	240	80	80-100	80-110	20,500

(1) Israel is widely presumed to have a nuclear capability although it has never confirmed nor denied its nuclear status. (2) About 2,150 are considered operational. The rest include warheads in reserve or marked for dismantlement. (3) About 4,500 are considered active or operational. Includes warheads that have been retired and are awaiting dismantlement.

Nuclear Arms Treaties and Negotiations: A Historical Overview

Aug. 5, 1963: Partial (Limited) Test Ban Treaty signed by U.S., USSR, and Britain in Moscow, went into effect Oct. 10, 1963. Prohibited parties from testing or participating in the testing of nuclear weapons in the atmosphere, in outer space, and under water.

Jan. 27, 1967: Treaty on Principles Governing the Activities of States in the Exploration and Use of Outer Space, including the Moon and Other Celestial Bodies (or the **Outer Space Treaty**) opened to signatures, went into effect Oct. 10, 1967. Banned the introduction of nuclear weapons or any other weapons of mass destruction into space.

July 1, 1968: Nuclear Nonproliferation Treaty (NPT) opened to signatures, went into effect Mar. 5, 1970. With the U.S., USSR, and Great Britain as major signers, the treaty limited the spread of nuclear material for military purposes by agreement not to help non-nuclear nations get or make nuclear weapons.

On May 11, 1995, at an NPT review conference, parties to the treaty voted to extend it indefinitely. As of Sept. 2011, 190 countries were party to the treaty, not including North Korea, which withdrew in 2003. Israel, India, and Pakistan were not signatories.

May 26, 1972: The **Strategic Arms Limitation Talks (SALT I)** led to the signing of two agreements by the U.S. and USSR in Moscow: the **Treaty on the Limitation of Anti-Ballistic Missile Systems** (or **ABM Treaty**) and the **Interim Agreement on Certain Measures with Respect to the Limitation of Strategic Offensive Arms.** These treaties set a cap on the numbers of intercontinental ballistic missile (ICBM) launchers and submarine-launched ballistic missile (SLBM) launchers.

July 3, 1974: Treaty on the Limitation of Underground Nuclear Weapon Tests (or **Threshold Test Ban Treaty**) signed by the U.S. and USSR in Moscow. Limited underground testing of nuclear weapons to yields of 150 kilotons or less. On May 28, 1976, U.S. and Russia signed the **Peaceful Nuclear Explosions Treaty,** governing explosions occurring outside weapons test sites. Both treaties entered into force Dec. 11, 1990.

June 18, 1979: Strategic Offensive Arms Limitation Treaty (or **SALT II**) signed by the U.S. and USSR in Vienna. Limited each side to 2,400 missile launchers and heavy bombers; ceiling to apply until Jan. 1, 1985. Treaty also set a sub-ceiling of 1,320 ICBMs and SLBMs with multiple warheads on each side. Following Dec. 1979 Soviet invasion of Afghanistan, Pres. Jimmy Carter withdrew SALT II from Senate consideration for ratification.

Dec. 8, 1987: Intermediate-Range Nuclear Forces (INF) Treaty signed by the U.S. and USSR in Washington, DC. Eliminated all U.S. and Soviet intermediate- and shorter-range nuclear missiles from Europe and Asia. Entered into force June 1, 1988.

July 31, 1991: Strategic Arms Reduction Treaty (START I) signed by the USSR and U.S. in Moscow, to reduce strategic offensive arms by about 30% in three phases over seven years. This was the first treaty to mandate reductions by the superpowers.

With the Soviet Union breakup in Dec. 1991, four former republics became independent nations with strategic nuclear weapons: Russia, Ukraine, Kazakhstan, and Belarus. Under the **Lisbon Protocol** of May 1992, Ukraine, Kazakhstan, and Belarus agreed to accede to the NPT as non-nuclear-weapon states, to destroy or transfer their nuclear weapons to Russia, and to ratify START I. START I expired on Dec. 5, 2009.

Jan. 3, 1993: START II signed by the U.S. and Russia in Moscow, ratified by the two countries on Jan. 26, 1996, and Apr. 14, 2000, respectively. Called for reductions in their long-range nuclear arsenals. Both sides withdrew from the treaty before it went into force.

Sept. 24, 1996: Comprehensive Test Ban Treaty (CTBT) signed by the U.S. and Russia in New York City. The CTBT banned all nuclear weapons tests and other nuclear explosions. It was intended to prevent the nuclear powers from developing more advanced weapons, while limiting the ability of other states to acquire such devices. As of Sept. 2011, the CTBT had been signed by 182 nations. It had been ratified by 155, including France, Russia, and the UK but neither the U.S. nor China. It will enter into force only after all Annex 2 states—the 44 states with nuclear technology capabilities at the time of final treaty negotiations—ratify it; only 35 have done so.

Dec. 13, 2001: The U.S. announced its intention to withdraw from the **ABM Treaty** in 180 days, arguing that it hindered the government in protecting itself from "future terrorist or rogue state missile attacks." Russia responded by withdrawing from START II, stating that U.S. withdrawal from the ABM Treaty effectively invalidated START II.

May 24, 2002: Strategic Offensive Reductions Treaty (SORT or Moscow Treaty) signed by the U.S. and Russia in Moscow, entered into force June 1, 2003. Committed both countries to cutting nuclear arsenals to 1,700-2,200 warheads each, down from about 6,000, by Dec. 31, 2012. SORT terminated upon entry into force of the New START Treaty.

Apr. 8, 2010: New START Treaty signed by the U.S. and Russia and entered into force on Feb. 5, 2011. It limited each country's arsenal of deployed strategic nuclear warheads to 1,550.

Major International Organizations

African Union (AU), inaugurated July 9, 2002, in Durban, South Africa, following disbanding of the Organization of African Unity. It consists of the same 53 members, i.e., all countries of Africa except Morocco, which left the OAU after it admitted Western Sahara (Sahrawi Arab Dem. Rep.), a territory claimed by Morocco. The organization is focused on achieving greater socioeconomic integration and unity among its member states. The founders provided for a peer review committee to oversee member states' adherence to standards of good government, respect for human rights, and financial transparency. The AU's founding document authorized the organization to intervene to stop genocide, war crimes, or human rights abuses within individual member nations. **Headquarters:** Addis Ababa, Ethiopia. **Website:** www.au.int

Asia-Pacific Economic Cooperation (APEC), founded Nov. 1989 as a forum to further cooperation on trade and investment between nations of the region and the rest of the world. Its 21 members are Australia, Brunei, Canada, Chile, China, Hong Kong, Indonesia, Japan, Malaysia, Mexico, New Zealand, Papua New Guinea, Peru, Philippines, Russia, Singapore, South Korea, Taiwan, Thailand, the U.S., and Vietnam. **Headquarters:** Singapore. **Website:** www.apec.org

Association of Southeast Asian Nations (ASEAN), formed Aug. 8, 1967, to promote economic, social, and cultural cooperation and development among states of the Southeast Asian region. Its members are Brunei, Cambodia, Indonesia, Laos, Malaysia, Myanmar, Philippines, Singapore, Thailand, and Vietnam. **Headquarters:** Jakarta, Indonesia. **Website:** www.asean.org

Caribbean Community and Common Market (CARICOM), established Aug. 1, 1973. Its aim is to increase cooperation in economics, health, education, culture, science and technology, and tax administration, as well as the coordination of foreign policy. Its 15 members are Antigua and Barbuda, The Bahamas, Barbados, Belize, Dominica, Grenada, Guyana, Haiti, Jamaica, Montserrat, St. Kitts and Nevis, St. Lucia, St. Vincent and the Grenadines, Suriname, and Trinidad and Tobago. Anguilla, Bermuda, British Virgin Islands, Cayman Islands, and Turks and Caicos Islands are associate members. **Headquarters:** Georgetown, Guyana. **Website:** www.caricom.org

The Commonwealth, originally called the British Commonwealth of Nations, then the Commonwealth of Nations, is an association of nations and dependencies that were once parts of the former British Empire. The British monarch is the symbolic head of the Commonwealth.

There are 54 independent nations in the Commonwealth. Rwanda joined most recently, in Nov. 2009. Regular members include the UK and 15 other nations recognizing the British monarch, represented by a governor-general, as their head of state, and member countries in good standing with their own heads of state. Pakistan was suspended from the councils of the Commonwealth in Oct. 1999, following a military coup, but regained its member status Mar. 2004. Zimbabwe was suspended in Mar. 2002, following election and land redistribution controversies; it withdrew from the Commonwealth in 2003. In Sept. 2009, Fiji's military regime was suspended. The Commonwealth facilitates consultation among members through meetings of ministers and through a permanent secretariat. **Headquarters:** London, UK. **Website:** www.thecommonwealth.org

Commonwealth of Independent States (CIS), an alliance established in Dec. 1991, made up of former Soviet constituent republics. Its members are Armenia, Azerbaijan, Belarus, Kazakhstan, Kyrgyzstan, Moldova, Russia, Tajikistan, Turkmenistan, Ukraine, and Uzbekistan. Georgia withdrew from the organization in Aug. 2009 following fighting with Russia over disputed territory. Policy is set through coordinating bodies such as the Council of the Heads of States and Council of the Heads of Governments. **Headquarters:** Minsk, Belarus. **Website:** www.cis.minsk.by

European Free Trade Association (EFTA), created May 3, 1960, to promote expansion of free trade. By Dec. 31, 1966, tariffs and quotas between member nations had been eliminated. Members entered into free trade agreements with the EU in 1972 and 1973. In 1992, EFTA and EU agreed to create a single market—with free flow of goods, services, capital, and labor—among nations of the two organizations. Its members are Iceland, Liechtenstein, Norway, and Switzerland. **Headquarters:** Geneva, Switzerland. **Website:** www.efta.int

European Union (EU), known as the European Community (EC) until 1994, comprises three organizations with common membership: the European Economic Community (Common Market), the European Coal and Steel Community, and the European Atomic Energy Community (Euratom). A merger of the three communities' executives went into effect July 1, 1967. As of Sept. 2011, there were 27 EU members: the 12 original members (Belgium, Denmark, France, Germany, Greece, Ireland, Italy, Luxembourg, Netherlands, Portugal, Spain, and UK), three that entered Jan. 1, 1995 (Austria, Finland, Sweden), 10 that joined on May 1, 2004 (Cyprus, Czech Republic, Estonia, Hungary, Latvia, Lithuania, Malta, Poland, Slovakia, Slovenia), and two that joined Jan. 1, 2007 (Bulgaria, Romania). Croatia, Iceland, Macedonia, Montenegro, and Turkey were candidate countries. Some 70 nations in Africa, the Caribbean, and the Pacific are affiliated under the Lomé Convention. **Headquarters:** Brussels, Belgium. **Website:** europa.eu

The EU aims to integrate the economies, coordinate social developments, and bring about political union of the member states. The Council of the Union, European Commission, European Parliament, and European Courts of Justice and of Auditors comprise the permanent structure. Effective Dec. 31, 1992, there are no restrictions on the movement of goods, services, capital, workers, and tourists within the EU. There are also common agricultural, fisheries, and nuclear research policies.

Leaders of the member nations (12 at the time), meeting Dec. 9-11, 1991, in Maastricht, the Netherlands, committed the organization to launching a common currency (the euro) by 1999; sought to establish common foreign policies; laid the groundwork for a common defense policy; gave the organization a leading role in social policy (Britain was not included in this plan); pledged increased aid for poorer member nations; and slightly increased the powers of the 567-member European Parliament. The treaties went into effect Nov. 1, 1993, following ratification by all 12 members.

In June 1998 the European Central Bank was established. In Jan. 1999, 11 of the then-15 EU countries began using the euro for some purposes. By Feb. 2002, national currencies in those 11 countries and Greece were removed from circulation and replaced with the euro as the only currency of legal tender. EU peacekeeping forces replaced NATO troops in Macedonia, Mar. 31, 2003, the first such mission for the organization.

A "Treaty Establishing a Constitution for Europe" was signed Oct. 2004 by EU members but was never ratified. The Treaty of Lisbon, which amended existing EU and EC treaties, was signed Dec. 2007. The Treaty of Lisbon went into force Dec. 1, 2009.

Group of Eight (G-8), established Sept. 22, 1985; forum of seven major industrial democracies (Canada, France, Germany, Italy, Japan, the UK, and U.S.) and (later) Russia, which meet periodically to discuss economic and other issues. At its annual summit in May 1998, the name was changed to G-8 from G-7. The seven were still free to meet without Russia on some issues, especially those relating to global finance. The presidency rotates yearly among members. The 2005 summit was held in Perthshire, Scotland. It was interrupted by the July 7 bombings in London but concluded as scheduled.

International Criminal Police Organization (INTERPOL), created 1923 as the International Criminal Police Commission before changing its name in 1956, is the world's largest international police organization. Promotes mutual assistance among all police authorities within the limits of the law existing in different countries. There were 188 member nations as of Aug. 2011. **Headquarters:** Lyon, France. **Website:** www.interpol.int

League of Arab States (Arab League), created Mar. 22, 1945. The League promotes economic, social, political, and military cooperation, mediates disputes, and represents Arab states in certain international negotiations. Its members are Algeria, Bahrain, Comoros, Djibouti, Egypt, Iraq, Jordan, Kuwait, Lebanon, Libya, Mauritania, Morocco, Oman, Palestine (considered an independent state by the League), Qatar, Saudi Arabia, Somalia, Sudan, Syria, Tunisia, United Arab Emirates, and Yemen. **Headquarters:** Cairo, Egypt. **Website:** www.arableagueonline.org

North Atlantic Treaty Organization (NATO), created by treaty (signed Apr. 4, 1949; in effect Aug. 24, 1949). Its 28 members as of Sept. 2011 are Albania, Belgium, Bulgaria, Canada, Croatia, Czech Republic, Denmark, Estonia, France, Germany, Greece, Hungary, Iceland, Italy, Latvia, Lithuania, Luxembourg, Netherlands, Norway, Poland, Portugal, Romania, Slovakia, Slovenia, Spain, Turkey, UK, and U.S. Several of these states are former Warsaw Pact Eastern European nations.

Members have agreed to settle disputes by peaceful means, to develop their capacity to resist armed attack, to regard an attack on one as an attack on all, and to take necessary action to repel an attack under Article 51 of the UN Charter. **Headquarters:** Brussels, Belgium. **Website:** www.nato.int

The NATO structure consists of the North Atlantic Council (NAC), the Defense Planning Committee, the Military Committee (realigned in June 2003 and consisting of two commands: Allied Command Operations and Allied Command Transformation), the Nuclear Planning Group, and the Canada-U.S. Regional Planning Group. France detached itself from the military command structure in 1966.

With the end of the cold war in the early 1990s, members put greater stress on political action and on creating a rapid deployment force to react to local crises. By the mid-1990s, 27 nations, including Russia and other former Soviet republics, had joined with NATO in the so-called Partnership for Peace (PfP; drafted Dec. 1993), which provided for limited joint military exercises, peacekeeping missions, and information exchange. NATO has proceeded gradually toward extending full membership to former Eastern bloc nations. On Mar. 12, 1999, three former Warsaw Pact members, Hungary, Poland, and the Czech Republic, formally became members. NATO and Russia signed a cooperation pact May 28, 2002, forming a NATO-Russia Council, and NATO invited seven former eastern-bloc nations to join the alliance, Nov. 21.

A NATO-led multinational force was deployed to help keep the peace in Bosnia and Herzegovina in 1995; in 1999, another force was deployed in Kosovo. Following the terrorist attacks on the U.S., the NATO Council agreed, Sept. 12, 2001, to invoke for the first time Article 5 of the treaty, which stipulates mutual defense of alliance members. NATO assumed control of the International Security Assistance Force in Afghanistan (ISAF), Aug. 2003, marking the first time NATO led a mission outside Europe.

Organization of American States (OAS), formed in Bogotá, Colombia, Apr. 30, 1948. It has a Permanent Council, Inter-American Council for Integral Development, Juridical Committee, and Commission on Human Rights. A general assembly meets annually.

Its 35 members are Antigua and Barbuda, Argentina, The Bahamas, Barbados, Belize, Bolivia, Brazil, Canada, Chile, Colombia, Costa Rica, Cuba, Dominica, Dominican Republic, Ecuador, El Salvador, Grenada, Guatemala, Guyana, Haiti, Honduras, Jamaica, Mexico, Nicaragua, Panama, Paraguay, Peru, St. Kitts and Nevis, St. Lucia, St. Vincent and the Grenadines, Suriname, Trinidad and Tobago, U.S., Uruguay, and Venezuela. **Headquarters:** Washington, DC. **Website:** www.oas.org

Organization for Economic Cooperation and Development (OECD), established Dec. 14, 1960, to promote the economic and social welfare of all its member countries and to stimulate efforts on behalf of developing nations. The OECD also collects and disseminates economic and environmental information. Its 34 members are Australia, Austria, Belgium, Canada, Chile, Czech Republic, Denmark, Estonia, Finland, France, Germany, Greece, Hungary, Iceland, Ireland, Israel, Italy, Japan, Luxembourg, Mexico, Netherlands, New Zealand, Norway, Poland, Portugal, Slovakia, Slovenia, South Korea, Spain, Sweden, Switzerland, Turkey, UK, and the U.S. **Headquarters:** Paris, France. **Website:** www.oecd.org

Organization of Petroleum Exporting Countries (OPEC), created Sept. 14, 1960, by Iran, Iraq, Kuwait, Saudi Arabia, and Venezuela. This group made up of most but not all the major petroleum exporting nations seeks to stabilize the oil market and set world oil prices by controlling production. In addition to the founding countries, members include Algeria, Angola, Ecuador, Indonesia (suspended membership starting in Jan. 2009), Libya, Nigeria, Qatar, and United Arab Emirates. Gabon is a former member. **Headquarters:** Vienna, Austria. **Website:** www.opec.org

Organization for Security and Cooperation in Europe (OSCE), established in 1972 as the Conference on Security and Cooperation in Europe; current name adopted 1995. The group, formed by NATO and Warsaw Pact members, seeks improved East-West relations through a commitment to nonaggression and human rights, and cooperation in economics, science and technology, cultural exchange, and environmental protection. There were 56 member states as of Aug. 2011, making it the world's largest regional security organization. **Headquarters:** Vienna, Austria. **Website:** www.osce.org

United Nations

The 66th regular session of the United Nations General Assembly opened Sept. 13, 2011, attended by world leaders and other delegates from 193 nations. The UN headquarters is in New York, NY, between First Ave. and Roosevelt Dr. and E. 42nd St. and E. 48th St.

Proposals to establish an organization for maintenance of world peace led to the convening of the United Nations Conference on International Organization in San Francisco, Apr. 25-June 26, 1945, where the UN charter was drawn. It was signed June 26 by 50 nations and by Poland, one of the original 51 members, on Oct. 15, 1945. It went into effect Oct. 24, 1945, upon ratification by the permanent members of the Security Council and a majority of the other signatories.

Purposes. To maintain international peace and security; to develop friendly relations among nations; to achieve international cooperation in solving economic, social, cultural, and humanitarian problems and in promoting respect for human rights and basic freedoms; to be a center for harmonizing the actions of nations in attaining these common ends.

Visitors to the UN. The UN headquarters is open to the public every day except New Year's Day, President's Day, Good Friday, Memorial Day, Independence Day, Eid al-Fitr, Labor Day, Eid al-Adha, Thanksgiving, and Christmas. The headquarters may also close on days when meetings between heads of state and government are held.

Guided tours are conducted weekdays from 9:45 PM to 4:45 PM. Groups of 15 or more require reservations, which should be made by e-mailing unitg@un.org or calling (212) 963-4440. For safety reasons, children under 5 are not admitted on tours.

United Nations Secretaries General

Took office	Secretary, nation		Took office	Secretary, nation
1946	Trygve Lie, Norway		1982	Javier Pérez de Cuéllar, Peru
1953	Dag Hammarskjöld, Sweden		1992	Boutros Boutros-Ghali, Egypt
1961	U Thant, Burma (Myanmar)		1997	Kofi Annan, Ghana
1972	Kurt Waldheim, Austria		2007	Ban Ki-moon, South Korea

Six Main Organs of the United Nations

The United Nations consists of six principal organs, 15 agencies, and many programs and other bodies. The six principal organs are the General Assembly, the Security Council, the Secretariat, the Economic and Social Council, the Trusteeship Council, and the Intl. Court of Justice.

General Assembly. The General Assembly is composed of representatives of all the member nations. Each nation is entitled to one vote. The General Assembly meets in regular annual sessions and in special session when convoked at the request of the Security Council or a majority of UN members. On important questions a two-thirds majority of members present and voting is required; on other questions a simple majority is sufficient.

The General Assembly must approve the UN budget and apportion expenses among members. A member in arrears can lose its vote if the amount of arrears equals or exceeds the amount of the contributions due for the preceding two full years. **Website:** www.un.org/ga/

Security Council. The Security Council consists of 15 members, five with permanent seats. The remaining 10 are elected for two-year terms by the General Assembly.

The permanent members of the Council are China, France, Russia, United Kingdom, and the United States. Nonpermanent members with terms expiring Dec. 31, 2011, are Bosnia and Herzegovina, Brazil, Gabon, Lebanon, and Nigeria; those with terms expiring Dec. 31, 2012, are Colombia, Germany, India, Portugal, and South Africa.

The Security Council has the primary responsibility within the UN for maintaining international peace and security. The Council may investigate any dispute that threatens international peace and security.

Any UN member may, if invited by the Council, participate in its discussions, and a nation not a UN member may appear if it is a party to a dispute. Decisions on procedural questions are made by an affirmative vote of nine members. On all other matters the affirmative vote of nine members must include the concurring votes of all permanent members (giving them veto power). A party to a dispute must refrain from voting.

The Security Council directs the various peacekeeping forces deployed throughout the world. **Website:** www.un.org/Docs/sc/

Secretariat. The Secretariat has an international staff (about 44,000 as of mid-2010) that carries out the day-to-day operations of the UN and is headed by the secretary general. The secretary general is the chief administrative officer of the UN, and is appointed by the General Assembly, on the recommendation of the Security Council, for a five-year, renewable term. The Secretary General reports to the General Assembly and may bring to the attention of the Security Council any matter that threatens international peace. **Website:** www.un.org/en/mainbodies/secretariat/

Economic and Social Council. The Economic and Social Council consists of 54 members elected by the General Assembly for overlapping three-year terms. The council is responsible for carrying out UN functions with regard to international economic, social, cultural, educational, health, and related matters. It meets once a year. **Website:** www.un.org/ecosoc/

Trusteeship Council. The Trusteeship Council, made up of the five permanent Security Council members, supervised the administration of UN trust territories. All 11 trust territories have since attained their right to self-determination. The Council formally suspended its work on Nov. 1, 1994, with Palau's independence. **Website:** www.un.org/en/mainbodies/trusteeship/

International Court of Justice (World Court). The International Court of Justice is the principal judicial organ of the UN. The Court has jurisdiction over cases that UN members or parties to the court's statute submit to it. In addition to rendering judgments, the Court gives advisory opinions.

The court's 15 judges are elected to nine-year terms by the General Assembly and the Security Council. No two judges come from the same nation, and they represent the world's principal legal systems. Once elected, the judges no longer act as representatives of a government. The Court remains permanently in session, except during vacations. All questions are decided by a majority. The International Court of Justice sits in The Hague, Netherlands. **Website:** www.icj-cij.org

The text of the UN **Charter** may be read online at www.un.org/en/documents/charter/index.shtml.

Selected Specialized and Related Agencies

These specialized and related agencies are autonomous, with their own memberships and organs, and at the same time have a functional relationship or working agreement with the UN (headquarters), except for UNICEF and UNHCR, which report directly to the Economic and Social Council and to the General Assembly.

Food and Agriculture Org. (FAO) helps developing countries modernize farms, forests, and fisheries; improves food distribution and marketing; and educates on nutrition. (Viale delle Terme di Caracalla, 00153 Rome, Italy) **Website:** www.fao.org

International Atomic Energy Agency (IAEA) aims to promote safe, peaceful uses of atomic energy. (P.O. Box 100, Wagramer Strasse 5, A-1400, Vienna, Austria) **Website:** www.iaea.org

International Civil Aviation Org. (ICAO) promotes international civil aviation standards and regulations. (999 University St., Montreal, Quebec H3C 5H7, Canada) **Website:** www.icao.int

International Fund for Agricultural Development (IFAD) seeks to alleviate poverty in rural areas in developing countries. (Via Paolo di Dono, 44, 00142 Rome, Italy) **Website:** www.ifad.org

International Labor Org. (ILO) aims to promote decent and productive employment practices, the improvement of labor conditions, social security, and vocational training. (4 Route des Morillons, CH-1211 Geneva 22, Switzerland) **Website:** www.ilo.org

International Maritime Org. (IMO) aims to promote cooperation on technical matters affecting international shipping. (4 Albert Embankment, London, SE1 7SR, UK) **Website:** www.imo.org

International Monetary Fund (IMF) aims to promote international monetary cooperation, currency stabilization, and the expansion of international trade. (700 19th St. NW, Washington, DC 20431) **Website:** www.imf.org

International Telecommunication Union (ITU) regulates all aspects of global communication, including setting standards for radio, telegraph, telephone, and space radio-communications, and allocating radio frequencies. (Place des Nations, 1211 Geneva 20, Switzerland) **Website:** www.itu.int

Office of the High Commissioner for Human Rights (OHCHR) seeks to uphold human rights standards by monitoring areas of concern, investigating abuses, and working with government institutions to improve conditions. (52 Rue des Pâquis, CH-1201 Geneva, Switzerland) **Website:** www.ohchr.org

United Nations Children's Fund (UNICEF) provides financial aid and development assistance to programs for children and mothers in developing countries. (3 United Nations Plaza, New York, NY 10017) **Website:** www.unicef.org

United Nations Educational, Scientific, and Cultural Org. (UNESCO) aims to promote collaboration among nations through education, science, and culture. (7, Place de Fontenoy, 75352 Paris 07 SP and 1, Rue Miollis, 75732 Paris Cedex 15, France) **Website:** www.unesco.org

United Nations High Commissioner for Refugees (UNHCR) provides essential assistance for refugees. (Case Postale 2500, CH-1211 Geneva 2 Depot, Switzerland) **Website:** www.unhcr.org

United Nations Industrial Development Org. (UNIDO) helps developing and transitional nations pursue sustainable industrial development while promoting international industrial cooperation. (Vienna Intl. Centre, Wagramerstr. 5, P.O. Box 300, A-1400 Vienna, Austria) **Website:** www.unido.org

Universal Postal Union (UPU) aims to perfect postal services and promote international collaboration. (International Bureau, P.O. Box, 3000 Berne 15, Switzerland) **Website:** www.upu.int

World Bank Group encompasses two development institutions and three affiliates focused on worldwide poverty reduction. The **International Bank for Reconstruction and Development (IBRD)** provides loans and technical assistance for projects in developing member countries and encourages co-financing for projects from other sources. The **International Development**

Association (IDA) provides funds for development projects on concessionary terms to poorer developing member countries. The **International Finance Corporation (IFC)** promotes the growth of the private sector in developing member countries; encourages the development of local capital markets; and stimulates the international flow of private capital. The **Multilateral Investment Guarantee Agency (MIGA)** promotes investment in developing countries; guarantees investments to protect investors from noncommercial risks, such as nationalization; and advises governments on attracting private investment. The **International Center for the Settlement of Investment Disputes (ICSID)** provides conciliation and arbitration services for disputes between foreign investors and host governments that arise out of an investment. (1818 H St. NW, Washington, DC 20433) **Website:** www.worldbank.org

World Health Org. (WHO) aims for the attainment of the highest possible level of health. (Avenue Appia 20, 1211 Geneva 27, Switzerland) **Website:** www.who.int

World Intellectual Property Org. (WIPO) seeks to protect, through international cooperation, literary, industrial, scientific, and artistic works. (34, Chemin des Colombettes, CH-1211 Geneva 20, Switzerland) **Website:** www.wipo.int

World Meteorological Org. (WMO) aims to coordinate and improve world meteorological work. (7bis, Avenue de la Paix, Case Postale 2300, CH-1211 Geneva 2, Switzerland) **Website:** www.wmo.int

World Tourism Org. (UNWTO) promotes responsible, sustainable, and universally accessible tourism with the aim of fostering economic development and international understanding. (Capitán Haya 42, 28020 Madrid, Spain) **Website:** www.unwto.org

World Trade Org. (WTO) administers trade agreements and treaties between nations, examines members' trade regimes, keeps track of various trade measures and statistics, and attempts to settle trade disputes. (Centre William Rappard, Rue de Lausanne 154, CH-1211 Geneva 21, Switzerland) **Website:** www.wto.org

Ongoing UN Peacekeeping Missions, 2011

Source: Dept. of Peacekeeping Operations (DPKO), United Nations Secretariat, UN

Unless otherwise noted, numbers are for peacekeeping operations only, as of July 31, 2011. The DPKO also directs what it calls political or peacebuilding missions. Year given in graphic is the year each mission started.

Uniformed personnel (troops, police, military observers)	98,022	Total personnel serving in 16 DPKO-led peace operations	121,822
Countries contributing uniformed personnel	114	Peacekeeping operations since 1948	66
International civilian personnel (as of June 30, 2011)	5,707	Total fatalities in peacekeeping operations since 1948	2,918[1]
Local civilian personnel (as of June 30, 2011)	13,870	Est. total cost of operations, 1948 to June 30, 2010	$69 bil

(1) Incl. fatalities for all UN peace operations.

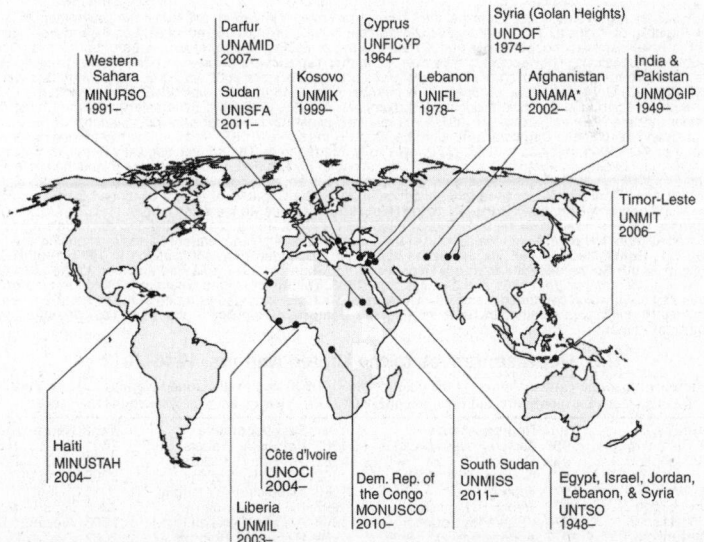

Western Sahara
MINURSO
1991–

Darfur
UNAMID
2007–

Kosovo
UNMIK
1999–

Sudan
UNISFA
2011–

Cyprus
UNFICYP
1964–

Lebanon
UNIFIL
1978–

Syria (Golan Heights)
UNDOF
1974–

Afghanistan
UNAMA*
2002–

India & Pakistan
UNMOGIP
1949–

Timor-Leste
UNMIT
2006–

Haiti
MINUSTAH
2004–

Côte d'Ivoire
UNOCI
2004–

Liberia
UNMIL
2003–

Dem. Rep. of the Congo
MONUSCO
2010–

South Sudan
UNMISS
2011–

Egypt, Israel, Jordan, Lebanon, & Syria
UNTSO
1948–

*Political mission directed and supported by the Dept. of Peacekeeping Operations.

Roster of the United Nations

Listed below are the 193 members of the United Nations, with the years in which they were admitted (as of Sept. 2011). Vatican City, Kosovo, and China (Taiwan)[1] are not members. Taiwan's repeated bids for UN membership have so far been unsuccessful. Vatican City is a permanent observer.

Member	Year	Member	Year	Member	Year	Member	Year
Afghanistan	1946	Dominica	1978	Libya	1955	Saint Vincent and the	
Albania	1955	Dominican Republic	1945	Liechtenstein	1990	Grenadines	1980
Algeria	1962	Ecuador	1945	Lithuania	1991	Samoa	1976
Andorra	1993	Egypt[4]	1945	Luxembourg	1945	San Marino	1992
Angola	1976	El Salvador	1945	Macedonia[2,7]	1993	São Tomé and Príncipe	1975
Antigua and Barbuda	1981	Equatorial Guinea	1968	Madagascar	1960	Saudi Arabia	1945
Argentina	1945	Eritrea	1993	Malawi	1964	Senegal	1960
Armenia	1992	Estonia	1991	Malaysia[8]	1957	Serbia[2,9]	2000
Australia	1945	Ethiopia	1945	Maldives	1965	Seychelles	1976
Austria	1955	Fiji	1970	Mali	1960	Sierra Leone	1961
Azerbaijan	1992	Finland	1955	Malta	1964	Singapore[8]	1965
Bahamas, The	1973	France	1945	Marshall Islands	1991	Slovakia[3]	1993
Bahrain	1971	Gabon	1960	Mauritania	1961	Slovenia[2]	1992
Bangladesh	1974	Gambia, The	1965	Mauritius	1968	Solomon Islands	1978
Barbados	1966	Georgia	1992	Mexico	1945	Somalia	1960
Belarus	1945	Germany[5]	1973	Micronesia	1991	South Africa[11]	1945
Belgium	1945	Ghana	1957	Moldova	1992	South Sudan[12]	2011
Belize	1981	Greece	1945	Monaco	1993	Spain	1955
Benin	1960	Grenada	1974	Mongolia	1961	Sri Lanka	1955
Bhutan	1971	Guatemala	1945	Montenegro[2,9]	2006	Sudan[12]	1956
Bolivia	1945	Guinea	1958	Morocco	1956	Suriname	1975
Bosnia and		Guinea-Bissau	1974	Mozambique	1975	Swaziland	1968
Herzegovina[2]	1992	Guyana	1966	Myanmar (Burma)	1948	Sweden	1946
Botswana	1966	Haiti	1945	Namibia	1990	Switzerland	2002
Brazil	1945	Honduras	1945	Nauru	1999	Syria[3]	1945
Brunei	1984	Hungary	1955	Nepal	1955	Tajikistan	1992
Bulgaria	1955	Iceland	1946	Netherlands	1945	Tanzania[13]	1961
Burkina Faso	1960	India	1945	New Zealand	1945	Thailand	1946
Burundi	1962	Indonesia[6]	1950	Nicaragua	1945	Timor-Leste	2002
Cambodia	1955	Iran	1945	Niger	1960	Togo	1960
Cameroon	1960	Iraq	1945	Nigeria	1960	Tonga	1999
Canada	1945	Ireland	1955	Norway	1945	Trinidad and Tobago	1962
Cape Verde	1975	Israel	1949	Oman	1971	Tunisia	1956
Central African Rep.	1960	Italy	1955	Pakistan	1947	Turkey	1945
Chad	1960	Jamaica	1962	Palau	1994	Turkmenistan	1992
Chile	1945	Japan	1956	Panama	1945	Tuvalu	2000
China[1]	1945	Jordan	1955	Papua New Guinea	1975	Uganda	1962
Colombia	1945	Kazakhstan	1992	Paraguay	1945	Ukraine	1945
Comoros	1975	Kenya	1963	Peru	1945	United Arab Emirates	1971
Congo, Dem. Rep.	1960	Kiribati	1999	Philippines	1945	United Kingdom	1945
Congo, Republic of the	1960	Korea, North	1991	Poland	1945	United States	1945
Costa Rica	1945	Korea, South	1991	Portugal	1955	Uruguay	1945
Côte d'Ivoire	1960	Kuwait	1963	Qatar	1971	Uzbekistan	1992
Croatia[2]	1992	Kyrgyzstan	1992	Romania	1955	Vanuatu	1981
Cuba	1945	Laos	1955	Russia[10]	1945	Venezuela	1945
Cyprus	1960	Latvia	1991	Rwanda	1962	Vietnam	1977
Czech Republic[3]	1993	Lebanon	1945	Saint Kitts and Nevis	1983	Yemen[14]	1947
Denmark	1945	Lesotho	1966	Saint Lucia	1979	Zambia	1964
Djibouti	1977	Liberia	1945			Zimbabwe	1980

(1) The General Assembly (GA) voted in 1971 to expel the Chinese government in Taiwan and admit the government in Beijing. (2) The Socialist Federal Republic of Yugoslavia was an original UN member. After four of its six republics (Bosnia and Herzegovina, Croatia, Macedonia, and Slovenia) declared independence in 1991-92, the two remaining republics, Montenegro and Serbia, reconstituted as the Federal Republic of Yugoslavia. They sought to take over the former Yugoslavia's UN seat in 1992 but were expelled a few months later by GA vote. The Federal Republic of Yugoslavia was granted membership in 2000. In 2003, the country changed its name to Serbia and Montenegro. (3) Czechoslovakia, an original UN member from 1945 to 1992, was succeeded by both the Czech Republic and Slovakia in 1993. (4) Egypt and Syria were original UN members. In 1958, Egypt and Syria established the United Arab Republic and continued under a single UN membership. In 1961, Syria resumed separate membership following independence. (5) The Federal Republic of Germany and the German Democratic Republic became UN members in 1973. In 1990, the two formed one sovereign state. (6) Withdrew from the UN in 1965; rejoined in 1966. (7) Provisionally referred to as The Former Yugoslav Republic of Macedonia within the UN pending settlement of Greece's objection to its constitutional name. (8) The Federation of Malaya joined the UN in 1957. In 1963, it changed its name to Malaysia following the accession of Singapore, Sabah, and Sarawak. Singapore became an independent UN member in 1965. (9) After Montenegro declared independence in 2006, the Republic of Serbia continued Serbia and Montenegro's UN membership. Montenegro was admitted to the UN as the Republic of Montenegro the same month. (10) The USSR was an original UN member. After the USSR's dissolution in 1991, Russia informed the UN it would continue the Soviet Union's membership in the Security Council and all other UN organs with the support of the Commonwealth of Independent States (comprising most of the former Soviet republics). (11) Readmitted in 1994. Its delegation had been suspended from participation in 1974 because of apartheid. (12) The Republic of South Sudan seceded from the Republic of the Sudan in 2011 and was admitted to the UN the same year. (13) Tanganyika was a UN member from 1961 and Zanzibar from 1963. The two countries united in 1964 to form the United Republic of Tanganyika and Zanzibar, which continued a single UN membership. It later changed its name to the United Republic of Tanzania. (14) The Yemen Arab Republic was admitted in 1947; the People's Democratic Republic of Yemen in 1967. In 1990, the two nations formed the Republic of Yemen.

U.S. Representatives to the United Nations, 1946-2011

The U.S. Representative to the United Nations is the chief of the U.S. Mission to the United Nations in New York and holds the rank and status of Ambassador Extraordinary and Plenipotentiary (A.E.P.). Year given is the year each took office.

Year	Representative	Year	Representative	Year	Representative	Year	Representative
1946	Edward R. Stettinius Jr.	1968	James Russell Wiggins	1985	Vernon A. Walters	2001	John D. Negroponte
1946	Herschel V. Johnson (act.)	1969	Charles W. Yost	1989	Thomas R. Pickering	2004	John C. Danforth
1947	Warren R. Austin	1971	George H. W. Bush	1992	Edward J. Perkins	2005	Anne W. Patterson (act.)
1953	Henry Cabot Lodge Jr.	1973	John A. Scali	1993	Madeleine K. Albright		
1960	James J. Wadsworth	1975	Daniel P. Moynihan	1997	Bill Richardson	2005	John R. Bolton
1961	Adlai E. Stevenson	1976	William W. Scranton	1998	A. Peter Burleigh (act.)	2006	Alejandro D. Wolff (act.)
1965	Arthur J. Goldberg	1977	Andrew Young	1999	Richard C. Holbrooke	2007	Zalmay M. Khalilzad
1968	George W. Ball	1979	Donald McHenry	2001	James B. Cunningham (act.)	2009	Susan E. Rice
		1981	Jeane J. Kirkpatrick				

International Criminal Court

The International Criminal Court (ICC) was created when 120 nations signed the Rome Statute on July 17, 1998. Its mission is to try individuals accused of genocide, war crimes, or other crimes against humanity, which was undertaken in the past by temporary tribunals. The statute came into force on July 1, 2002. As of Aug. 23, 2011, 115 nations were state parties to the Rome Statute of the ICC. China, Russia, and the U.S. have not yet joined.

The ICC, unlike the World Court, is not part of the UN. It is an independent international agency with its own administration and budget, which is made up of funds from member states and voluntary contributions by other institutions, international groups, individuals, and corporations. It consists of 18 judges elected by member nations. An absolute majority of these 18 judges elect three from among themselves to serve as president, first vice president, and second vice president in three-year, renewable terms. A Registry handles the nonjudicial aspects of

administration. The Office of the Prosecutor reviews, investigates, and, prosecutes cases referred to it by a state or by the UN Security Council.

The following situations are currently under investigation by the ICC prosecutor: the situation in the Dem. Rep. of the Congo; in Kenya; in Uganda; in Darfur, Sudan; and in the Central African Republic. The UN Security Council, on Feb. 26, 2011, decided to refer the situation in Libya since Feb. 15 to the prosecutor of the ICC.

Though jurisdiction is limited to member nations, the ICC is a court of last resort. It may also initiate cases involving nonmember nations if it deems the country's authorities have not taken steps to investigate or prosecute a case. The ICC is based in The Hague, Netherlands, though it may sit elsewhere. (Office of the Prosecutor, P.O. Box 19519, 2500 CM The Hague, Netherlands) **Website:** icc-cpi.int

Geneva Conventions

The Geneva Conventions are four international treaties governing the protection of civilians in times of war, the treatment of prisoners of war, and the care of the wounded and sick in the armed forces. The first convention, covering the sick and wounded in war, was concluded in Geneva, Switzerland, in 1864, at a conference convened by the Swiss government at the urging of the International Committee of the Red Cross. The convention was amended and expanded in 1906. In 1929, two more conventions covering the wounded and prisoners of war were signed. Outrage at the treatment of prisoners and civilians during WWII by some belligerents, notably Germany and Japan, prompted the conclusion, on Aug. 12, 1949, of four new conventions. Three of these restated and strengthened the previous conventions. The fourth codified general principles of international law governing the treatment of civilians in wartime.

The 1949 convention for civilians provided for special safeguards for wounded persons, children under 15 years of age,

pregnant women, and the elderly. Discrimination on racial, religious, national, or political grounds was forbidden. Torture, collective punishment, reprisals, unwarranted destruction of property, and forced use of civilians for an occupier's armed forces were also prohibited. Also included was a pledge for the humane treatment, adequate feeding, and delivery of supplies to prisoners. They were not to be forced to disclose more than minimal information. Two additional protocols were adopted in June 1977 dealing with the protection of victims, especially civilians, in international and non-international armed conflicts. (A third protocol, adopted in 2005, created the Red Crystal emblem for use along with the Red Cross and Red Crescent.)

Most countries have formally accepted all or most of the humanitarian conventions as binding. As of 2006, all of the then 194 nations had signed onto the 1949 Conventions. However, there is no permanent international machinery in place to enforce these treaties.

Genocide

Source: Convention on the Prevention and Punishment of the Crime of Genocide, United Nations Treaty Series 277; Rome Statute of the International Criminal Court

The term "genocide" (literally "murder of a race") was coined by Prof. Raphael Lemkin (1900-59) in 1944 and refers to the intentional destruction or attempted destruction of a national, ethnic, racial, or religious group, whether in wartime or peacetime. Genocide is defined as killing members of a group, causing serious bodily harm to members of a group, or otherwise attempting to bring about a group's destruction, including efforts to prevent births or transfer children away from a group. Although the legal definition of genocide does not extend to political groups, the term is often used colloquially to refer to large-scale political violence.

The prohibition against genocide is part of customary international law and is codified in the Convention on the Prevention and Punishment of the Crime of Genocide ("Genocide Convention"), entered into force on Jan. 12, 1951. Today, more than 130 nations, including the U.S., are parties to it.

Genocide is also prohibited by the domestic laws of many nations.

The first modern trials for genocide were conducted by the Allies after WWII. Although the charter of the Nuremberg Tribunal, the international court set up to try Nazi war criminals, did not use the term genocide, its definition of "crimes against humanity" included persecution on racial or religious grounds. More recently, the UN Security Council created ad hoc tribunals to try those responsible for genocide and other serious crimes in the former Yugoslavia and in Rwanda. The International Criminal Court (ICC) also has jurisdiction to try perpetrators of genocide. In Mar. 2005, the Security Council referred the situation in Darfur, Sudan, to the ICC prosecutor. The ICC has since issued two arrest warrants for Sudanese Pres. Omar Hassan al-Bashir on multiple counts of genocide, crimes against humanity, and war crimes.

Examples of Genocides Since 1900

Year	Event	Location	Est. deaths
1915	Extermination of Armenians by the Young Turks	Turkey/Ottoman Empire	1,000,000+
1930s	Intentional infliction of famine on Ukraine	Soviet Union (Ukraine)	6,000,000-7,000,000
1933-45	Attempted destruction of European Jewry (Holocaust)	Europe	6,000,000
1975-79	Khmer Rouge campaign of extermination under Pol Pot[1]	Cambodia	1,500,000-2,000,000
1981-83	Army and paramilitary killings of indigenous Mayan during civil war	Guatemala	200,000+
1988	Anfal Campaign (named by the Iraqi government) against Iraqi Kurds	Iraq	100,000-200,000
1992-95	Ethnic killings during the breakup of Yugoslavia, chiefly Serbs against Bosnian Muslims	Bosnia-Herzegovina, Serbia, Croatia	200,000
1994	Hutu massacre of Tutsis	Rwanda	800,000
2003-present	Rebel group and government-backed Arab militia attacks on non-Arab southern tribes, black population[2]	Darfur region, Sudan	200,000-400,000

Note: Estimates based on historical evidence. The legal definition of "genocide" does not include politically motivated mass killings. Therefore, instances of mass violence against political or class enemies, such as Josef Stalin's purges in the 1930s, which killed some 20 mil Soviets, and Mao Zedong's Cultural Revolution, which killed several mil Chinese, are not included. (1) The mass killings from Cambodia's Khmer Rouge regime are often spoken of as genocide, though many of the murders were politically or class motivated. (2) In 2005, a UN commission concluded that although the "international offenses ... that have been committed in Darfur may be no less serious and heinous than genocide," it did not term the situation there a genocide.

NATIONS OF THE WORLD

As of mid-2011, there were **196 nations** in the world. This number includes three nations that are not members of the United Nations—Kosovo, Taiwan, and Vatican City (the Holy See). Certain regions and territories that are not independent nations can be found under the entry for the governing nation.

Sources: FAOSTAT, Statistics Division, Economic and Social Development Dept. and Fisheries and Aquaculture Dept., Food and Agriculture Organization of the UN (FAO); *Global Report: UNAIDS Report on the Global AIDS Epidemic 2010*, Joint United Nations Programme on HIV/AIDS (UNAIDS) and World Health Organization (WHO); International Civil Aviation Organization (ICAO); International Data Base, U.S. Census Bureau; *International Energy Annual*, Energy Information Administration (EIA), U.S. Dept. of Energy; *International Financial Statistics*, International Monetary Fund (IMF); ITU World Telecommunication/ICT Indicators Database, International Telecommunication Union (ITU); *The Military Balance*, International Institute for Strategic Studies; *Oil & Gas Journal*, PennWell Corp.; *Statistical Yearbook*, UN Statistics Division; United Nations Educational, Scientific, and Cultural Organization (UNESCO); *UNWTO World Tourism Barometer* © UNWTO, 9284402711, World Tourism Organization (WTO); U.S. Dept. of State; Ward's Automotive Group, a division of Penton Media Inc.; The World Bank; *The World Factbook*, Central Intelligence Agency (CIA); *World Population Prospects* and *World Urbanization Prospects*, Dept. of Economic and Social Affairs, UN Population Division.

Note: Because of rounding or incomplete enumeration, percentages may not add up to 100%. FY = Fiscal year. NA = Not available/not applicable. **Population, age distrib.**, and **pop. density** figures are mid-2011 estimates, unless otherwise noted. Percent of total population living in **urban** areas—not percent of land area urbanized—as defined by each country were projections for mid-2010. **Principal languages** are ranked with the most widely spoken language first. Population figures for **capitals** are mid-2009 estimates; for **cities (urban aggl.)**, they were projections for mid-2010. Urban agglomerations, i.e., whole metropolitan areas comprising an urban center and surrounding settlements of lower density, are shown in descending order by population. **Defense budget** and **active troops** figures are from mid-2010 unless otherwise noted. Selected **industries** are ranked by value of annual output. **Chief crops** are listed in descending order of importance. **Crude oil reserves** are Jan. 1, 2011, estimates unless otherwise noted. **Arable land** is land that is under temporary crops, temporary meadows for mowing or pasture, market and kitchen gardens or is temporarily fallow. The latest available data is given as a percentage of a country's land area. **Livestock** figures are for 2009. **Fish catch** figures, which include capture production as well as the farming of fish, mollusks, and crustaceans for commercial, industrial, and recreational or subsistence purposes, are for 2009. **Electricity prod.** numbers indicate net generation, not gross generation; they are for 2008 unless otherwise noted. **Labor force** estimates are latest available; percentages for a country may not add up to 100% if data is incomplete. **GDP** data are actual figures or estimates for 2010 unless otherwise noted; data are based on purchasing power parity calculations, involving use of international dollar price weights applied to quantities of goods and services produced. **Imports** and **exports** estimates are from 2010 unless otherwise noted; trade partners, which are listed in order in order of importance with percentages of total dollar value, are latest available. **Tourism** figures are latest available and represent receipts from international tourism. **Budget** figures are actual or estimated expenditures for 2010 unless otherwise noted. They are calculated on an exchange rate basis, not purchasing power parity terms. Figures for **total reserves less gold** and **gold** are from 2010 unless otherwise noted. **CPI change**, or consumer price index change, measures the percent change in the CPI between 2009 and 2010 unless otherwise noted. **Railways** figure is latest available and represents total length of railway network. **Motor vehicle** statistics are latest available; cars and commercial vehicles are included in figures. **Civil aviation** statistics measure the number of passengers carried a certain distance on scheduled flights operated by airlines registered in a country; they are the latest available. Airport figures represent the total number of airports with paved, usable runways in a country as of 2010 unless otherwise noted. The amount of cargo and number of containers and ship visits handled annually are considered in determining **chief ports** listed. **TV sets** (in both businesses and households), **radios** (receivers used for broadcast to the general public), and **daily newspaper circ.** figures are latest available. **Telephone lines** and **Internet** data are for 2010 unless otherwise noted. The number of Internet users comprise all who access the Internet regardless of device used, such as mobile phones. **Life expect.** is at birth for persons born in 2011. **Natural inc.** measures the difference between the number of **births** and the number of **deaths** in 2011. **Infant mortality** measures the probability of a child dying between birth and exact age 1, in 2011. **HIV rate** is the estimated number of persons, ages 15-49, living with HIV in 2009, divided by the total 2009 population aged 15-49. **Education** figures and **literacy** rates are latest available. Literacy rates of adults aged 15 and older, generally measure the percent of population able to read and write simple statements on everyday life, not the (smaller) percent able to read and write to carry out effectively activities within the community; some countries define as literate those who have completed a certain number of years of schooling. **Embassy** addresses are for Wash., DC, area code (202), unless otherwise noted.

See pages 457-72 for full-color maps and flags of all nations.

Afghanistan
Islamic Republic of Afghanistan

People: Population: 29,757,566. **Age distrib.:** <15: 43.7%; 65+: 2.5%. **Pop. density:** 118.2 per sq mi, 45.6 per sq km. **Urban:** 22.6%. **Ethnic groups:** Pashtun 42%, Tajik 27%, Hazara 9%, Uzbek 9%, Aimak 4%, Turkmen 3%, Baloch 2%. **Principal languages:** Afghan Persian or Dari (official), Pashto (official), Turkic languages (Uzbek, Turkmen), 30 minor languages (Balochi, Pashai). **Chief religions:** Sunni 80%, Shi'a 19%.

Geography: Total area: 251,827 sq mi, 652,230 sq km; **Land area:** 251,827 sq mi, 652,230 sq km. **Location:** In SW Asia, NW of the Indian subcontinent. **Neighbors:** Pakistan on E, S; Iran on W; Turkmenistan, Tajikistan, Uzbekistan on N. The NE tip touches China. **Topography:** The country is landlocked and mountainous, much of it over 4,000 ft above sea level. The Hindu Kush Mts. tower 16,000 ft above Kabul and reach a height of 25,000 ft to the E. Trade with Pakistan flows through the 35-mi-long Khyber Pass. The climate is dry, with extreme temperatures, and there are large desert regions. **Capital:** Kabul, 3,573,000.

Government: Type: Islamic republic. **Head of state and gov.:** Pres. Hamid Karzai; b. Dec. 24, 1957; in office: June 19, 2002. **Local divisions:** 32 provinces. **Defense budget (2009):** $205 mil. **Active troops:** 136,106.

Economy: Industries: textiles, soap, furniture, shoes. **Chief crops:** opium, wheat, fruits, nuts. **Natural resources:** nat. gas, petroleum, coal, copper, chromite, talc, barites, sulfur, lead, zinc, iron ore, salt, prec. and semiprec. stones. **Arable land:** 11.9%. **Livestock:** cattle: 4.7 mil; chickens: 10.2 mil; goats: 5.8 mil; sheep: 12.3 mil. **Fish catch:** 1,000 metric tons. **Electricity prod.:** 832 mil kWh. **Labor force:** agric. 78.6%, industry 5.7%, services 15.7%.

Finance: Monetary unit: Afghani (AFN) (Sept. 2011: 43.33 = $1 U.S.). **GDP:** $27.4 bil; **per capita GDP:** $900; **GDP growth:** 8.2%. **Imports (2008 est.):** $5.3 bil; U.S. 24.9%, Pakistan 22.3%, India 7.7%, Germany 5.1%, Russia 4.3%. **Exports (2009 est.):** $547 mil (not incl. illicit exports or reexports); U.S. 24.9%, India 24.2%, Pakistan 23.9%, Tajikistan 8.9%. **Tourism:** NA. **Budget (FY09/10 est.):** $3.3 bil (not incl. $2.6 bil from Reconstruction Trust Fund and $63 mil from Law and Order Trust Fund). **Total reserves less gold:** NA. **CPI change:** NA.

Transport: Motor vehicles: 27.5 vehicles per 1,000 pop. **Civil aviation:** 19 airports. **Chief ports:** Kheyrabad, Shir Khan.

Communications: TV sets: 80 per 1,000 pop. **Radios:** 129 per 1,000 pop. **Telephone lines:** 0.5 per 100 pop. **Internet:** 4 users per 100 pop.

Health: Life expect.: 48.1 male; 50.6 female. **Births:** 39.5 (per 1,000 pop.). **Deaths:** 14.8 (per 1,000 pop.). **Natural inc.:** 2.47%. **Infant mortality:** 123.9 (per 1,000 live births). **HIV rate:** NA.

Education: Compulsory: ages 7-15. **Literacy:** 18.2%.

Major intl. organizations: UN (FAO, IBRD, ILO, IMF, WHO), WTO (observer).

Embassy: 2341 Wyoming Ave. NW 20008; 483-6410.

Website: www.president.gov.af

Afghanistan, occupying a favored invasion route since antiquity, has been variously known as Ariana or Bactria (in ancient times) and Khorasan (in the Middle Ages). Foreign empires alternated rule with local emirs and kings until the 18th cent., when a unified kingdom was established. In 1973, a military coup ushered in a republic.

Pro-Soviet leftists took power in a bloody 1978 coup and concluded an economic and military treaty with the USSR. In Dec. 1979 the USSR began a massive airlift into Kabul and backed a new coup, leading to installation of a more pro-Soviet leader. Soviet forces fanned out over Afghanistan and waged a protracted guerrilla war with Muslim rebels, in which some 15,000 Soviet troops reportedly died.

A UN-mediated agreement was signed Apr. 14, 1988, providing for withdrawal of Soviet troops, a neutral Afghan state, and repatriation of refugees. Afghan rebels rejected the pact. The Soviets completed their troop withdrawal Feb. 15, 1989; fighting between Afghan rebels and government forces ensued. Communist Pres. Najibullah resigned Apr. 16, 1992, as competing guerrilla forces advanced on Kabul. The rebels achieved power Apr. 28, ending 14 years of Soviet-backed regimes. More than 2 mil Afghans had been killed and 6 mil had left the country since 1979.

Following the rebel victory there were clashes between moderates and Islamic fundamentalists. Burhanuddin Rabbani, a guerrilla leader, became president June 28, 1992, but fierce fighting continued around Kabul and elsewhere. The Taliban, an insurgent Islamic radical faction, captured Kabul in Sept. 1996. The Taliban executed former Pres. Najibullah and empowered Islamic religious police to enforce codes of dress and behavior that were especially restrictive to women. Rabbani and other ousted leaders fled to the north.

Victories in the northern cities of Mazar-e Sharif, Aug. 8, 1998, and Taloqan, Aug. 8-11, gave the Taliban control over more than 90% of the country. On Aug. 20, U.S. cruise missiles struck southeast of Kabul, hitting facilities the U.S. said were terrorist training camps run by a wealthy Saudi, Osama bin Laden. The UN imposed sanctions Nov. 14, 1999, when Afghanistan refused to turn over bin Laden to the U.S. for prosecution; a UN ban on all military aid to the Taliban took effect Jan. 19, 2001.

After the Sept. 11, 2001, attacks on the World Trade Center and Pentagon, the U.S., blaming bin Laden, demanded that the Taliban surrender him and shut down his al-Qaeda terrorist network. When the Taliban refused, the U.S., with British assistance, began bombing Afghanistan Oct. 7, as part of Operation Enduring Freedom.

Supported by the U.S., the opposition Northern Alliance recaptured Mazar-e Sharif Nov. 9 and took Kabul 4 days later; the Taliban forces abandoned Kandahar, their last stronghold, to southern tribesmen Dec. 7. A power-sharing agreement signed by 4 anti-Taliban factions, including the Northern Alliance, provided for an interim government headed by Hamid Karzai, a Pashtun tribal leader. The UN authorized Dec. 20 a multinational security force.

Meeting June 13, 2002, in Kabul, a traditional council (loya jirga) chose Karzai to head a new transitional government. The U.S. announced the end of major combat operations in Afghanistan, May 1, 2003, but resistance continued, with relief and reconstruction workers targeted. NATO officially assumed control of peacekeeping forces (ISAF) Aug. 11. A new constitution took effect Jan. 26, 2004.

The most intense fighting in more than 4 years erupted Mar. 2006 with a new wave of suicide bombings, rocket and mortar attacks, and other strikes by Taliban insurgents against military and civilian targets. Erosion of government authority led to an increase in opium growing; the Taliban, local warlords, and some Karzai associates were accused of profiting from the drug trade. A record poppy crop of 8,200 metric tons in 2007 made Afghanistan the source of 93% of the world's illicit opium; drought, blight, and local suppression efforts cut estimated output to 3,600 metric tons by 2010. According to UN estimates, about 3% of the adult population used opiates in 2010.

Operating from sanctuaries across the border in Pakistan, Islamist suicide bombers and Taliban insurgents stepped up their activities during 2007-11. Violence escalated in the run-up to the presidential election Aug. 20, 2009; on that day, Taliban attacks, intended to suppress turnout, killed at least 30 people. Preliminary results released Sept. 8 showed Karzai above 50% of the vote, but a UN-backed commission overseeing the tally ordered a recount, citing "clear and convincing evidence of fraud" at numerous polling stations; a runoff election scheduled for Nov. 7 was canceled when Karzai's lone remaining opponent dropped out of the race. Karzai was sworn in for a second full term Nov. 19, despite growing U.S. doubts about his ability to prosecute the war and root out corruption. Weak turnout, allegations of vote-buying, and Taliban attacks marred parliamentary elections Sept. 18, 2010. After a decade-long manhunt, U.S. commandos killed bin Laden shortly after midnight May 2, 2011, in Abbottabad, Pakistan. Insurgents retaliated Aug. 6 by shooting down a Chinook transport helicopter, killing 30 Americans (including 22 Navy SEALs) and 8 Afghans. Other violence included the killing July 12 of Ahmed Wali Karzai, the powerful half-brother of Pres. Karzai; a truck bombing Sept. 11 in Wardak Province that killed 5 Afghan civilians and wounded 77 NATO soldiers; attacks Sept. 13 on the U.S. embassy, NATO headquarters, and other targets in Kabul; and the assassination Sept. 20 of former Pres. Rabbani, a leader in government-backed peace talks with the Taliban.

Between Jan. 2009 and June 2011, the number of U.S. troops in Afghanistan rose from about 36,000 to 99,000, while the number of allied foreign forces under ISAF increased from nearly 32,000 to more than 42,000. The U.S. on June 22, 2011, outlined a timetable calling for a pullout of 10,000 U.S. troops by the end of 2011 and another 23,000 by Sept. 2012; the combined total of 33,000 roughly equaled the "surge" in U.S. troops that had been announced by Pres. Obama in Dec. 2009. Canada ended its combat mission July 2011, and other coalition partners including the UK and France also began troop pullouts, with all U.S. forces scheduled to be withdrawn by the end of 2014.

Intensification of hostilities between coalition forces and insurgents led to a steep increase in casualties. Coalition military fatalities rose from 295 in 2008 to 521 in 2009, 711 in 2010, and more than 400 during Jan.-Aug. 2011; of more than 2,600 coalition military deaths since Operation Enduring Freedom began in Oct. 2001, over 1,700 were from the U.S., about 380 from the UK, and nearly 160 from Canada. According to the UN, 1,462 Afghan civilians were killed and 2,144 wounded during the first 6 months of 2011; the combined total was 10% higher than the corresponding period in 2010. By Mar. 2011, the U.S. Congress had appropriated more than $440 bil for the Afghanistan war and related military activities.

Albania
Republic of Albania

People: Population: 2,994,667. **Age distrib.:** <15: 21.4%; 65+: 10.5%. **Pop. density:** 283.1 per sq mi, 109.3 per sq km. **Urban:** 51.9%. **Ethnic groups:** Albanian 95%, Greek 3%. **Principal languages:** Albanian (official; derived from Tosk dialect), Greek. **Chief religions:** Muslim 70%, Albanian Orthodox 20%, Roman Catholic 10%.

Geography: Total area: 11,100 sq mi, 28,748 sq km; **Land area:** 10,578 sq mi, 27,398 sq km. **Location:** SE Europe, on SE coast of Adriatic Sea. **Neighbors:** Greece on S; Montenegro, Kosovo, Serbia on N; Macedonia on E. **Topography:** Apart from a narrow coastal plain, Albania consists of hills and mountains covered with scrub forest, cut by small E-W rivers. **Capital:** Tirana (Tiranë), 433,000.

Government: Type: Republic. **Head of state:** Pres. Bamir Topi; b. Apr. 24, 1957; in office: July 24, 2007. **Head of gov.:** Prime Min. Sali Berisha; b. Oct. 15, 1944; in office: Sept. 11, 2005. **Local divisions:** 12 counties divided into 36 districts. **Defense budget:** $195 mil. **Active troops:** 14,245.

Economy: Industries: food proc., textiles and clothing, lumber. **Chief crops:** wheat, corn, potatoes, vegetables, fruits, sugar beets, grapes. **Natural resources:** petroleum, nat. gas, coal, bauxite, chromite, copper, iron ore, nickel, salt, timber, hydropower. **Crude oil reserves:** 199.1 mil bbls. **Arable land:** 22.3%. **Livestock:** cattle: 494,000; chickens: 5.1 mil; goats: 772,000; pigs: 160,300; sheep: 1.8 mil. **Fish catch:** 8,128 metric tons. **Electricity prod.:** 3.8 bil kWh. **Labor force:** agric. 47.8%, industry 23%, services 29.2%.

Finance: Monetary unit: Lek (ALL) (Sept. 2011: 98.94 = $1 U.S.). **GDP:** $23.9 bil (country has an informal and unreported sector that may be as large as 50% of official GDP); **per capita GDP:** $8,000; **GDP growth:** 3.5%. **Imports:** $4.6 bil; Italy 28%, Greece 13%, China 6.3%, Turkey 5.6%, Germany 5.6%. **Exports:** $1.6 bil; Italy 50.8%, Kosovo 6.2%, Turkey 5.9%, China 5.5%, Greece 5.4%. **Tourism:** $1.6 bil. **Budget:** $3.6 bil. **Total reserves less gold:** $2.5 bil. **Gold:** 50,606 oz t. **CPI change:** 3.5%.

Transport: Railways: 211 mi. **Civil aviation:** 105.6 mil pass.-mi; 4 airports. **Chief ports:** Durres, Sarande, Shengjin, Vlore.

Communications: TV sets: 190 per 1,000 pop. **Radios:** 585 per 1,000 pop. **Telephone lines:** 10.4 per 100 pop. **Daily newspaper circ.:** 24.4 per 1,000 pop. **Internet:** 45 users per 100 pop.

Health: Life expect.: 74.8 male; 80.3 female. **Births:** 12.2 (per 1,000 pop.). **Deaths:** 6.2 (per 1,000 pop.). **Natural inc.:** 0.60%. **Infant mortality:** 14.6 (per 1,000 live births). **HIV rate:** NA.

Major intl. organizations: UN (FAO, IBRD, ILO, IMF, IMO, WHO), NATO, OSCE, WTO.

Education: Compulsory: ages 6-13. **Literacy:** 95.9%.

Embassy: 2100 S St. NW 20008; 223-4942.

Website: www.km.gov.al

Ancient Illyria was conquered by Romans, Slavs, and Turks (15th cent.); the Turks Islamized the population. Independent Albania was proclaimed in 1912; the republic was formed in 1920. King Zog I ruled 1925-39, until Italy invaded.

Communist partisans took over in 1944, allied Albania with the USSR, then broke with the USSR in 1960 over de-Stalinization. Later, China provided billions of dollars in assistance, but cut off aid in 1978 when Albania attacked its policies after the death of Chinese ruler Mao Zedong. Large-scale purges of officials occurred during the 1970s.

Enver Hoxha, the nation's ruler for 4 decades, died Apr. 11, 1985. Eventually the new regime introduced some liberalization, including measures in 1990 providing for freedom to travel abroad. Efforts were begun to improve ties with the outside world.

Albania's former Communists were routed in elections Mar. 1992, amid economic collapse and social unrest. Sali Berisha was elected as the first non-Communist president since WWII. Berisha's party claimed a landslide victory in disputed parliamentary elections, May 26 and June 2, 1996. Public protests over the collapse of fraudulent investment schemes in Jan. 1997 led to armed rebellion and anarchy. The UN Security Council, Mar. 28, authorized a 7,000-member force to restore order. Socialists and their allies won parliamentary elections, June 29 and July 6, and international peacekeepers completed their pullout by Aug. 11.

During NATO's air war against Yugoslavia, Mar.-June 1999, Albania hosted some 465,000 Kosovar refugees. Victory by a pro-Berisha coalition in elections July 3, 2005, ended 8 years of Socialist rule. Albania became a full member of NATO Apr. 1, 2009; the nation formally applied for EU membership Apr. 28. Following parliamentary elections June 28, 2009, Berisha retained his office as prime minister.

Algeria
People's Democratic Republic of Algeria

People: Population: 34,994,937. **Age distrib.:** <15: 24.2%; 65+: 5.2%. **Pop. density:** 38.1 per sq mi, 14.7 per sq km. **Urban:** 66.5%. **Ethnic groups:** Arab-Berber 99%. **Principal languages:** Arabic (official), French, Berber dialects. **Chief religions:** Sunni Muslim (official) 99%, Christian & Jewish 1%.

Geography: Total area: 919,595 sq mi, 2,381,741 sq km; **Land area:** 919,595 sq mi, 2,381,741 sq km. **Location:** In NW Africa, from Medit. Sea into Sahara Desert. **Neighbors:** Morocco, Western Sahara on W; Mauritania, Mali, Niger on S; Libya, Tunisia on E. **Topography:** The Tell, located on the coast, comprises fertile plains 50-100 mi wide, with a moderate climate and adequate rain. Two major chains of Atlas Mts., running roughly E-W and reaching 7,000 ft, enclose a dry plateau region. Below lies the Sahara, mostly desert with major mineral resources. **Capital:** Algiers, 2,740,000. **Cities (urban aggl.):** Oran, 769,562.

Government: Type: Republic. **Head of state:** Pres. Abdelaziz Bouteflika; b. Mar. 2, 1937; in office: Apr. 27, 1999. **Head of gov.:** Prime Min. Ahmed Ouyahia; b. July 2, 1952; in office: June 23, 2008. **Local divisions:** 48 provinces. **Defense budget:** $5.67 bil. **Active troops:** 147,000.

Economy: Industries: petroleum, nat. gas, light industries, mining, electrical, petrochemical, food proc. **Chief crops:** wheat, barley, oats, grapes, olives, citrus, fruits. **Natural resources:** petroleum, nat. gas, iron ore, phosphates, uranium, lead, zinc. **Crude oil reserves:** 12.2 bil bbls. **Arable land:** 3.1%. **Livestock:** cattle: 1.7 mil; chickens: 125 mil; goats: 3.8 mil; pigs: 5,700; sheep: 20 mil. **Fish catch:** 130,112 metric tons. **Electricity prod.** (2009): 40.1 bil kWh. **Labor force:** agric. 14%, industry 13.4%, constr. and public works 10%, trade 14.6%, govt. 32%, other 16%.

Finance: Monetary unit: Dinar (DZD) (Sept. 2011: 73.30 = $1 U.S.). **GDP:** $251.1 bil; **per capita GDP:** $7,300; **GDP growth:** 3.3%. **Imports:** $37.1 bil; France 15.1%, China 11.6%, Italy 9.1%, Spain 7.3%, Germany 6.8%, U.S. 4.9%, Tajikistan 4.3%, Turkey 4.3%. **Exports:** $52.7 bil; U.S. 22.9%, Italy 12.6%, Spain 11.9%, France 9.8%, Netherlands 7.2%, Canada 5.4%, Turkey 4.4%. **Tourism:** $267 mil. **Budget:** $85.6 bil. **Total reserves less gold:** $162.6 bil. **Gold:** 5.6 mil oz t. **CPI change:** 3.9%.

Transport: Railways: 2,469 mi. **Motor vehicles:** 112.6 vehicles per 1,000 pop. **Civil aviation:** 2.4 bil pass.-mi; 57 airports. **Chief ports:** Algiers, Annaba, Oran.

Communications: TV sets: 190 per 1,000 pop. **Radios:** 229 per 1,000 pop. **Telephone lines:** 8.2 per 100 pop. **Internet:** 12.5 users per 100 pop.

Health: Life expect.: 72.8 male; 76.3 female. **Births:** 16.7 (per 1,000 pop.). **Deaths:** 4.7 (per 1,000 pop.). **Natural inc.:** 1.20%. **Infant mortality:** 25.8 per 1,000 live births). **HIV rate:** 0.1%.

Education: Compulsory: ages 6-14. **Literacy:** 72.6%.

Major intl. organizations: UN (FAO, IBRD, ILO, IMF, IMO, WHO), AL, AU, OPEC, WTO (observer).

Embassy: 2118 Kalorama Rd. NW 20008; 265-2800.

Website: www.premier-ministre.gov.dz or www.algeria-us.org

Earliest known inhabitants were ancestors of Berbers, followed by Phoenicians, Romans, Vandals, and, finally, Arabs. Turkey ruled 1518 to 1830, when France took control. Large-scale European immigration followed. Arab nationalists launched a guerrilla war, 1954, that more than 400,000 French troops were unable to suppress. After French Pres. Charles de Gaulle came to power, 1958, colonial rule ended, nearly all Europeans left, and Algeria declared independence July 5, 1962. Ahmed Ben Bella ruled until 1965, when an army coup installed Col. Houari Boumedienne, a former guerrilla leader who held power until his death in 1978.

Hundreds died in antigovernment riots protesting economic hardship in Oct. 1988. In 1989, voters approved a new constitution, which cleared the way for a multiparty system. The government canceled the Jan. 1992 elections that Islamic fundamentalists were expected to win, and banned all nonreligious activities at Algeria's 10,000 mosques. Pres. Mohammed Boudiaf was assassinated June 29, 1992. Over the next 7 years, Muslim fundamentalists carried out attacks on high-ranking officials, security forces, foreigners, and others; pro-government death squads also were active.

Liamine Zeroual won the presidential election of Nov. 16, 1995. A new constitution banning Islamic political parties and increasing the president's powers passed in a referendum on Nov. 28, 1996. Abdelaziz Bouteflika, who became president after a flawed election on Apr. 15, 1999, made peace with rebels and won approval for an amnesty plan in a referendum on Sept. 16. Some 100 people died and thousands were injured in violent protests Apr.-June 2001, chiefly by Algeria's Berber minority. Bouteflika was reelected Apr. 8, 2004, in a landslide; opponents charged fraud.

An earthquake in northern Algeria, May 21, 2003, claimed over 2,200 lives and left 200,000 people homeless. Under a reconciliation plan approved by referendum Sept. 29, 2005, the government in Mar. 2006 began freeing Islamists jailed for their role in the 1990s civil war, in which up to 200,000 people were killed, and 8,000 "disappeared."

Radical Islamists bombed 2 police stations Oct. 30, 2006, and 7 more police stations Feb. 13, 2007. A group known as al-Qaeda in the Islamic Maghreb (AQIM) carried out suicide bombings Apr. 11 at the Government Palace and a police station in Algiers, killing 33 people; more than 50 died in suicide bombings at Batna, Sept. 6, and Dellys, Sept. 8. Car bombs Dec. 11, 2007, killed 17 UN staff members and at least 20 others in Algiers. A surge in AQIM violence in Aug. 2008 left more than 100 people dead.

Parliament Nov. 12, 2008, amended the constitution to abolish presidential term limits, clearing the way for Bouteflika to run for a 3rd term. He claimed more than 90% of the vote in an election Apr. 9, 2009, denounced as fraudulent by opposition parties. As "Arab Spring" uprisings swept across N Africa in early 2011, the Bouteflika government suppressed street protests in Algiers Feb. 12, and used oil revenues to raise salaries of teachers, police, and other discontented civil servants. A suicide attack Aug. 26 near a military academy in Cherchell, west of Algiers, killed at least 18 people and wounded more than 20.

Andorra
Principality of Andorra

People: Population: 84,825. **Age distrib.:** <15: 15.6%; 65+: 13%. **Pop. density:** 469.4 per sq mi, 181.3 per sq km. **Urban:** 88%. **Ethnic groups:** Spanish 43%, Andorran 33%, Portuguese 11%, French 7%. **Principal languages:** Catalan (official), French, Castilian, Portuguese. **Chief religion:** Roman Catholic (predominant).

Geography: Total area: 181 sq mi, 468 sq km; **Land area:** 181 sq mi, 468 sq km. **Location:** SW Europe, in Pyrenees Mts. **Neighbors:** Spain on S, France on N. **Topography:** High mountains and narrow valleys cover the country. **Capital:** Andorra la Vella, 25,000.

Government: Type: Parliamentary co-principality. **Heads of state:** President of France and Bishop of Urgel (Spain), as co-princes. **Head of gov.:** Antoni Martí Petit; b. 1963; in office: May 12, 2011. **Local divisions:** 7 parishes. **Defense budget/active troops:** NA. Defense is responsibility of France and Spain.

Economy: Industries: tourism, cattle raising, timber, banking, tobacco, furniture. **Chief crops:** rye, wheat, barley, oats, vegetables. **Natural resources:** hydropower, mineral water, timber, iron ore, lead. **Arable land:** 2.1%. **Labor force:** agric. 0.4%, industry 4.7%, services 94.9%.

Finance: Monetary unit: Euro (EUR) (Sept. 2011: 0.71 = $1 U.S.). **GDP** (2009 est.): $3.3 bil; **per capita GDP** (2009 est.): $46,700; **GDP growth** (2009 est.): 3.8%. **Imports** (2009): $1.5 bil; NA. **Exports** (2009): $64 mil; NA. **Tourism:** NA. **Budget** (2009): $868.4 mil. **Total reserves less gold:** NA. **CPI change:** NA.

Communications: TV sets: 440 per 1,000 pop. **Radios:** 243 per 1,000 pop. **Telephone lines:** 45 per 100 pop. **Internet:** 81 users per 100 pop.

Health: Life expect.: 80.4 male; 84.6 female. **Births:** 9.7 (per 1,000 pop.). **Deaths:** 6.4 (per 1,000 pop.). **Natural inc.:** 0.33%. **Infant mortality:** 3.8 (per 1,000 live births). **HIV rate:** NA.

Education: Compulsory: ages 6-16. **Literacy:** 100%.

Major intl. organizations: UN (FAO, WHO), OSCE, WTO (observer).

Embassy: 2 UN Plaza, 27th Fl., New York, NY 10017; (212) 750-8064.

Website: www.andorra.ad

France and the bishop of Urgel held joint sovereignty over Andorra from 1278 to 1993. Voters chose to adopt a parliamentary system Mar. 14, 1993, although co-princes remain heads of state.

Tourism, especially skiing, is the economic mainstay. A free port, Andorra attracts more than 9 mil visitors annually.

Angola
Republic of Angola

People: Population: 17,544,728. **Age distrib.:** <15: 44.3%; 65+: 2.9%. **Pop. density:** 36.4 per sq mi, 14.1 per sq km. **Urban:** 58.5%. **Ethnic groups:** Ovimbundu 37%, Kimbundu 25%, Bakongo 13%, mestico (mixed European and native African) 2%, European 1%. **Principal languages:** Portuguese (official), Bantu, other African languages. **Chief religion:** indigenous beliefs 47%, Roman Catholic 38%, Protestant 15%.

Geography: Total area: 481,354 sq mi, 1,246,700 sq km; **Land area:** 481,354 sq mi, 1,246,700 sq km. **Location:** In SW Africa on Atlantic coast. **Neighbors:** Namibia on S, Zambia on E, Congo-Kinshasa on N; Cabinda, an enclave separated from rest of country by short Atlantic coast of Congo-Kinshasa, borders Congo-Brazzaville. **Topography:** Mostly plateau elevated 3,000-5,000 ft above sea level, rising from a narrow coastal strip. There is also a temperate highland area in the west-central region, a desert in S, and a tropical rain forest covering Cabinda. **Capital:** Luanda, 4,511,000. **Cities (urban aggl.):** Huambo, 1,034,410.

Government: Type: Republic. **Head of state and gov.:** Pres. José Eduardo dos Santos; b. Aug. 28, 1942; in office: Sept. 20, 1979. **Local divisions:** 18 provinces. **Defense budget:** $2.74 bil. **Active troops:** 107,000.

Economy: Industries: petroleum, mining, cement, metal prods., fish and food proc. **Chief crops:** bananas, sugarcane, coffee, sisal, corn, cotton, manioc, tobacco. **Natural resources:** petroleum, diamonds, iron ore, phosphates, copper, feldspar, gold, bauxite, uranium. **Crude oil reserves:** 9.5 bil bbls. **Arable land:** 3.2%. **Livestock:** cattle: 5 mil; chickens: 7.1 mil; goats: 2.5 mil; pigs: 788,000; sheep: 350,000. **Fish catch:** 272,473 metric tons. **Electricity prod.:** 3.9 bil kWh. **Labor force:** agric. 85%, industry and services 15%.

Finance: Monetary unit: Kwanza (AOA) (Sept. 2011: 93.58 = $1 U.S.). **GDP:** $107.3 bil; **per capita GDP:** $8,200; **GDP growth:** 1.6%. **Imports:** $18.1 bil; Portugal 19.7%, China 15.1%, U.S. 9%, Brazil 8.7%, France 4.1%, South Africa 4.2%. **Exports:** $51.7 bil; China 37%, U.S. 24.5%, India 8.7%, France 8.3%. **Tourism:** $534 mil. **Budget:** $37.4 bil. **Total reserves less gold:** $19.7 bil. **CPI change:** 14.5%.

Transport: Railways: 1,717 mi. **Motor vehicles:** 9.2 vehicles per 1,000 pop. **Civil aviation:** 422.5 mil pass.-mi; 31 airports. **Chief ports:** Cabinda, Lobito, Luanda, Namibe.

Communications: TV sets: 140 per 1,000 pop. **Radios:** 81 per 1,000 pop. **Telephone lines:** 1.6 per 100 pop. **Daily newspaper circ.:** 2.2 per 1,000 pop. **Internet:** 10 users per 100 pop.

Health: Life expect.: 53.1 male; 55.3 female. **Births:** 39.6 (per 1,000 pop.). **Deaths:** 12.3 (per 1,000 pop.). **Natural inc.:** 2.72%. **Infant mortality:** 85.3 (per 1,000 live births). **HIV rate:** 2%.

Education: Compulsory: ages 6-11. **Literacy:** 70%.

Major intl. organizations: UN (FAO, IBRD, ILO, IMF, WHO), AU, OPEC, WTO.

Embassy: 2100-2108 16th St. NW 20009; 785-1156.

Website: www.governo.gov.ao or www.angola.org

From the early centuries CE to 1500, Bantu tribes penetrated most of the region. Portuguese came in 1583, allied with the Bakongo kingdom in the north, and developed the slave trade. Large-scale colonization did not begin until the 20th cent., when 400,000 Portuguese immigrated.

A guerrilla war begun in 1961 lasted until 1975, when Portugal granted independence. Fighting then erupted between three rival rebel groups—the National Front, based in Zaire (now Congo), the Soviet-backed Popular Movement for the Liberation of Angola (MPLA), and the National Union for the Total Independence of Angola (UNITA), aided by the U.S. and South Africa.

Cuban troops and Soviet aid helped the MPLA win control of most of the country by 1976, although fighting continued through the 1980s. A peace accord between the MPLA government and UNITA was signed May 1, 1991.

Elections were held in Sept. 1992, but fighting again broke out, as UNITA rejected the results. UNITA signed a new peace treaty with the government, Nov. 20, 1994, but the rebels were slow to demobilize. The UN Security Council voted, Aug. 28, 1997, to impose sanctions on UNITA. The UN ended its mission in Angola in Mar. 1999, as the civil war continued.

As of 2001, the UN estimated that the war with UNITA had claimed some 1 mil lives and left another 2.5 mil people homeless. Rebel leader Jonas Savimbi was killed by government troops Feb. 22, 2002. UNITA agreed to a truce Apr. 4, 2002, ending the 27-year-long civil war. Fighting continued, however, between government forces and separatist guerrillas in oil-rich Cabinda; rebels there agreed to a cease-fire July 2006.

With proven petroleum reserves estimated at more than 9 bil barrels, Angola is one of Africa's leading oil producers. Mismanagement and corruption led to the diversion of up to $4.2 bil in oil revenues during 1997-2002, according to a Human Rights Watch report. The ruling MPLA claimed victory in voting Sept. 5-6, 2008, in Angola's first parliamentary elections in 16 years. Parliament approved Jan. 21, 2010, a new constitution augmenting the power of MPLA leader José Eduardo dos Santos, who has held Angola's presidency since 1979.

Antigua and Barbuda

People: Population: 87,884. **Age distrib.:** <15: 25.8%; 65+: 6.8%. **Pop. density:** 513.8 per sq mi, 198.6 per sq km. **Urban:** 30.3%. **Ethnic groups:** black 91%, mixed 4%, white 2%. **Principal languages:** English (official), local dialects. **Chief religions:** Anglican 26%, Seventh-Day Adventist 12%, Pentecostal 11%, Moravian 11%, Roman Catholic 10%, Methodist 8%, Baptist 5%, Church of God 5%, other Christian 5%.

Geography: Total area: 171 sq mi, 443 sq km; **Land area:** 171 sq mi, 443 sq km. **Location:** E Caribbean. **Neighbors:** St. Kitts & Nevis to W, Guadeloupe (Fr.) to S. **Topography:** These are mostly low-lying and limestone coral islands. Antigua is mostly hilly with an indented coast; Barbuda is a flat island with a large lagoon on W. **Capital:** St. John's, 27,000.

Government: Type: Constitutional monarchy with British-style parliament. **Head of state:** Queen Elizabeth II; represented by Gov.-Gen. Dame Louise Agnetha Lake-Tack; b. July 26, 1944; in office: July 17, 2007. **Head of gov.:** Prime Min. Baldwin Spencer; b. Oct. 8, 1948; in office: Mar. 24, 2004. **Local divisions:** 6 parishes, 2 dependencies. **Defense budget:** $33 mil. **Active troops:** 170.

Economy: Industries: tourism, constr., light mfg. **Chief crops:** cotton, fruits, vegetables, bananas, coconuts. **Natural resources:** negligible. **Arable land:** 18.2%. **Livestock:** cattle: 14,600; chickens: 110,000; goats: 37,000; pigs: 3,000; sheep: 20,000. **Fish catch:** 2,490 metric tons. **Electricity prod.:** 115 mil kWh. **Labor force:** agric. 7%, industry 11%, services 82%.

Finance: Monetary unit: East Caribbean Dollar (XCD) (Sept. 2011: 2.70 = $1 U.S.). **GDP:** $1.4 bil; per capita GDP: $16,400; **GDP growth:** –4.1%. **Imports** (2007 est.): $522.8 mil; NA. **Exports** (2007 est.): $84.3 mil; NA. **Tourism:** $306 mil. **Budget** (2009 est.): $293.4 mil. **Total reserves less gold:** $136.6 mil. **CPI change:** 2.9%.

Transport: Civil aviation: 76.4 mil pass.-mi; 2 airports. **Chief port:** Saint John's.

Communications: TV sets: 465 per 1,000 pop. **Radios:** 497 per 1,000 pop. **Telephone lines:** 47.1 per 100 pop. **Internet:** 80 users per 100 pop.

Health: Life expect.: 73.5 male; 77.6 female. **Births:** 16.3 (per 1,000 pop.). **Deaths:** 5.7 (per 1,000 pop.). **Natural inc.:** 1.06%. **Infant mortality:** 14.6 (per 1,000 live births). **HIV rate:** NA.

Education: Compulsory: ages 5-16. **Literacy:** 99%.

Major intl. organizations: UN (FAO, IBRD, ILO, IMF, WHO), Caricom, the Commonwealth, OAS, OECS, WTO.

Embassy: 3216 New Mexico Ave. NW 20016; 362-5122.

Website: www.ab.gov.ag

Columbus landed on Antigua in 1493. The British colonized it in 1632. The British associated state of Antigua achieved independence as Antigua and Barbuda on Nov. 1, 1981. Tourism, which accounts for more than 25% of GDP, was hit hard by the worldwide recession in 2008-10. The economy suffered a further blow when Robert Allen Stanford, a Texas businessman, was charged by U.S. authorities Feb. 17, 2009, with employing his Antigua-based Stanford International Bank to carry out a fraudulent $8 bil investment scheme.

Argentina
Argentine Republic

People: Population: 41,769,726. **Age distrib.:** <15: 25.4%; 65+: 11%. **Pop. density:** 39.5 per sq mi, 15.3 per sq km. **Urban:** 92.4%. **Ethnic groups:** white (mostly Spanish & Italian) 97%; mestizo (mixed white & Amerindian), Amerindian, other non-white groups 3%. **Principal languages:** Spanish (official), Italian, English, German, French. **Chief religions:** nominally Roman Catholic 92%, Protestant 2%, Jewish 2%.

Geography: Total area: 1,073,518 sq mi, 2,780,400 sq km; **Land area:** 1,056,642 sq mi, 2,736,690 sq km. **Location:** Occupies most of southern S. America. **Neighbors:** Chile on W; Bolivia, Paraguay on N; Brazil, Uruguay on NE. **Topography:** Mountains in W are the Andean, Central, Misiones, and Southern ranges. Aconcagua is the highest peak in the Western Hemisphere, alt. 22,834 ft. E of the Andes are heavily wooded plains, called the Gran Chaco in N, and the fertile, treeless Pampas in the central region. Patagonia, in S, is bleak and arid. Rio de la Plata, an estuary in NE, 170 by 140 mi, is mostly fresh water, from 2,485-mi Parana and 1,000-mi Uruguay rivers. **Capital:** Buenos Aires, 12,988,000 (the Senate has approved moving the capital to the Patagonia Region). **Cities (urban aggl.):** Córdoba, 1,492,788; Rosario, 1,231,298.

Government: Type: Republic. **Head of state and gov.:** Pres. Cristina Fernández de Kirchner; b. Feb. 19, 1953; in office: Dec. 10, 2007. **Local divisions:** 23 provinces, 1 federal district. **Defense budget:** $2.6 bil. **Active troops:** 73,100.

Economy: Industries: food proc., motor vehicles, consumer durables, textiles, chemicals and petrochemicals. **Chief crops:** sunflower seeds, lemons, soybeans, grapes, corn. **Natural resources:** lead, zinc, tin, copper, iron ore, manganese, petroleum, uranium. **Crude oil reserves:** 2.5 bil bbls. **Arable land:** 11.3%. **Livestock:** cattle: 50.8 mil; chickens: 96 mil; goats: 4.3 mil; pigs: 2.3 mil; sheep: 15.8 mil. **Fish catch:** 862,543 metric tons. **Electricity prod.:** 115.4 bil kWh. **Labor force:** agric. 5%, industry 23%, services 72%.

Finance: Monetary unit: Peso (ARS) (Sept. 2011: 4.20 = $1 U.S.). **GDP:** $596 bil; per capita GDP: $14,700; **GDP growth:** 7.5%. **Imports:** $56.4 bil; Brazil 31.1%, U.S. 13.3%, China 12.4%, Germany 5.1%. **Exports:** $68.5 bil; Brazil 20.5%, Chile 7.9%, U.S. 6.6%, China 6.6%, Netherlands 4.3%. **Tourism:** $4.9 bil. **Budget:** $86.9 bil. **Total reserves less gold:** $49.7 bil. **Gold:** 1.8 mil oz t. **CPI change:** 10.8%.

Transport: Railways: 22,970 mi. **Motor vehicles:** 218.9 vehicles per 1,000 pop. **Civil aviation:** 7.3 bil pass.-mi; 156 airports. **Chief ports:** Bahia Blanca, Buenos Aires, La Plata, Punta Colorado.

Communications: TV sets: 325 per 1,000 pop. **Radios:** 681 per 1,000 pop. **Telephone lines:** 24.7 per 100 pop. **Daily newspaper circ.:** 35.5 per 1,000 pop. **Internet:** 36 users per 100 pop.

Health: Life expect.: 73.7 male; 80.4 female. **Births:** 17.5 (per 1,000 pop.). **Deaths:** 7.4 (per 1,000 pop.). **Natural inc.:** 1.02%. **Infant mortality:** 10.8 (per 1,000 live births). **HIV rate:** 0.5%.

Education: Compulsory: ages 5-14. **Literacy:** 97.7%.

Major intl. organizations: UN (FAO, IBRD, ILO, IMF, WHO), OAS, WTO.

Embassy: 1600 New Hampshire Ave. NW 20009; 238-6401.

Website: www.argentina.ar

Nomadic Indians roamed the Pampas when Spaniards arrived, 1515-16, led by Juan Diaz de Solis. Nearly all the Indians were killed by the late 19th cent. The colonists won independence, 1816, and a long period of disorder ended in a strong centralized government.

Large-scale Italian, German, and Spanish immigration in the decades after 1880 spurred modernization. Social reforms were enacted in the 1920s, but military coups prevailed, 1930-46, until the election of Gen. Juan Perón as president.

Perón, with his wife, Eva Duarte (d. 1952), effected labor reforms but also suppressed speech and press freedoms, closed religious schools, and ran the country into debt. A 1955 coup exiled Perón, who was followed by a series of military and civilian regimes. Perón returned in 1973 and was once more elected president. He died 10 months later, succeeded by his wife Isabel, who had been elected vice president, and who became the first woman head of state in the Western Hemisphere.

A military junta seized Mrs. Perón in 1976 amid charges of corruption. Under a continuing state of siege, the army conducted a "dirty war" against guerrillas and leftists in which an estimated 30,000 people "disappeared."

Argentine troops seized control of the British-held Falkland Islands (Islas Malvinas) on Apr. 2, 1982. The British imposed an air and sea blockade around the Falklands. Fighting began May 1. British troops landed on East Falkland May 21. Argentine troops surrendered, June 14; Argentine Pres. Leopoldo Galtieri resigned June 17.

Democratic rule returned in 1983. On Dec. 9, 1985, 5 former junta members were found guilty of murder and human rights abuses during the "dirty war" period.

Buenos Aires Mayor Fernando de la Rúa won the presidential election Oct. 24, 1999. A prolonged recession and a debt of more than $130 bil left Argentina facing an economic crisis in 2001, which austerity measures and IMF aid failed to remedy. After widespread rioting and looting Dec. 19, de la Rúa resigned.

A 2-week period of protests and political upheavals abated when Congress, Jan. 1, 2002, chose a Peronist, Eduardo Alberto Duhalde, to finish de la Rúa's term. Further economic decline and renewed protests led Duhalde July 2 to schedule an early presidential election for Mar. 2003; another Peronist, Néstor Kirchner, took office May 25, 2003. Kirchner moved to end corruption and human rights abuses among the military and police. A new IMF aid deal, approved Sept. 10, 2003, rescued Argentina from default.

Fire at a Buenos Aires nightclub, Dec. 30, 2004, killed 194 people. The supreme court, June 14, 2005, overturned amnesty laws that had barred prosecution for "dirty war" crimes committed while the military ruled Argentina. Robust economic growth, 2004-05, allowed Argentina to repay its $9.57 bil debt to the IMF, Jan. 3, 2006.

After Pres. Kirchner declined to seek a second term, his wife, Cristina Fernández de Kirchner, ran as the Peronist candidate and was elected president Oct. 28, 2007. Responding to mass protests by farmers, Argentina's senate voted July 17, 2008, to block Kirchner's proposed tax increase on agricultural exports. A candidate slate led by Néstor Kirchner suffered a humiliating defeat in legislative elections June 28, 2009, as the Peronists lost control of both houses of Congress. Argentina July 2010 became the first Latin American country to extend full marriage rights to same-sex couples.

Néstor Kirchner died Oct. 27, 2010. As Argentina approached national elections Oct. 2011, the nation enjoyed robust economic growth, but inflation was estimated at 30% in 2010.

Armenia
Republic of Armenia

People: Population: 2,967,975. **Age distrib.:** <15: 17.6%; 65+: 10.1%. **Pop. density:** 272.6 per sq mi, 105.2 per sq km. **Urban:** 64.2%. **Ethnic groups:** Armenian (official) 98%, Yezidi (Kurd) 1%. **Principal languages:** Armenian (official), Yezidi, Russian. **Chief religions:** Armenian Apostolic 95%, other Christian 4%, Yezidi 1%.

Geography: Total area: 11,484 sq mi, 29,743 sq km; **Land area:** 10,889 sq mi, 28,203 sq km. **Location:** SW Asia. **Neighbors:** Georgia on N, Azerbaijan on E, Iran on S, Turkey on W. **Topography:** Mountainous with many peaks above 10,000 ft. **Capital:** Yerevan, 1,110,000.

Government: Type: Republic. **Head of state:** Pres. Serzh Sargsyan; b. June 30, 1954; in office: Apr. 9, 2008. **Head of gov.:** Prime Min. Tigran Sargsyan; b. Jan. 29, 1960; in office; Apr. 9, 2008. **Local divisions:** 10 provinces, 1 city. **Defense budget:** $434 mil. **Active troops:** 48,570.

Economy: Industries: diamond proc., machine tools, forging-pressing machines, elec. motors, tires, knitted wear. **Chief crops:** fruits (espec. grapes), vegetables. **Natural resources:** gold, copper, molybdenum, zinc, bauxite. **Arable land:** 16.1%. **Livestock:** cattle: 584,779; chickens: 4 mil; goats: 32,580; pigs: 84,801; sheep: 526,638. **Fish catch:** 5,893 metric tons. **Electricity prod.:** 5.9 bil kWh. **Labor force:** agric. 46.2%, industry 15.6%, services 38.2%.

Finance: Monetary unit: Dram (AMD) (Sept. 2011: 369.72 = $1 U.S.). **GDP:** $16.9 bil; **per capita GDP:** $5,700; **GDP growth:** 2.6%. **Imports:** $3 bil; Russia 24%, China 8.7%, Ukraine 6.1%, Turkey 5.4%, Germany 5.4%, Iran 4.1%. **Exports:** $846 mil; Germany 16.5%, Russia 15.4%, U.S. 9.6%, Bulgaria 8.6%, Georgia 7.6%, Netherlands 7.5%, Belgium 6.7%, Canada 4.9% **Tourism:** $403 mil. **Budget:** $2.6 bil. **Total reserves less gold:** $1.9 bil. **CPI change:** 8.2%.

Transport: Railways: 540 mi. **Civil aviation:** 667.4 mil pass.-mi; 10 airports.

Communications: TV sets: 293 per 1,000 pop. **Radios:** 270 per 1,000 pop. **Telephone lines:** 19.1 per 100 pop. **Daily newspaper circ.:** 7.6 per 1,000 pop. **Internet:** 37 users per 100 pop.

Health: Life expect.: 69.6 male; 77.3 female. **Births:** 12.9 (per 1,000 pop.). **Deaths:** 8.5 (per 1,000 pop.). **Natural inc.:** 0.44%. **Infant mortality:** 18.9 (per 1,000 live births). **HIV rate:** 0.1%.

Education: Compulsory: ages 7-14. **Literacy:** 99.5%.

Major intl. organizations: UN (FAO, IBRD, ILO, IMF, WHO), CIS, OSCE, WTO.

Embassy: 2225 R St. NW 20008; 319-1976.

Website: www.gov.am

Ancient Armenia extended into parts of what are now Turkey and Iran. Present-day Armenia was set up as a Soviet republic Apr. 2, 1921. It joined Georgian and Azerbaijan SSRs Mar. 12, 1922, to form the Transcaucasian SFSR, which became part of the USSR Dec. 30, 1922. Armenia became a constituent republic of the USSR Dec. 5, 1936. An earthquake struck Armenia Dec. 7,

1988; approximately 55,000 were killed and several cities and towns were left in ruins.

Armenia declared independence Sept. 23, 1991, and became an independent state when the USSR disbanded Dec. 26, 1991. Both mostly Christian Armenia and mostly Muslim Azerbaijan claimed Nagorno-Karabakh, an enclave in Azerbaijan that has an ethnic Armenian majority; it seceded from Azerbaijan in 1988. A 1992-94 war that cost 30,000 lives ended in a cease-fire with Armenian forces in control of the enclave. Voters in the breakaway region approved a pro-independence constitution Dec. 10, 2006, but the referendum was rejected by the EU and OSCE.

Voters approved, July 5, 1995, a new constitution increasing presidential powers. Pres. Levon Ter-Petrosian won reelection on Sept. 22, 1996, amid claims of fraud; he resigned Feb. 3, 1998, in a conflict over Nagorno-Karabakh. Robert Kocharian, a nationalist born in the disputed region, won the presidency on Mar. 30, 1998. Gunmen stormed Parliament Oct. 27, 1999, killing Prime Min. Vazgen Sarkissian and 7 others. Kocharian won a second term Mar. 5, 2003, in a runoff vote viewed as flawed by opposition groups and Western observers.

Prime Min. Andranik Margaryan died of a heart attack Mar. 25, 2007, and was replaced by Def. Min. Serzh Sargsyan. He defeated Ter-Petrosian in the presidential election of Feb. 19, 2008; opposition protests in Yerevan were forcibly suppressed Mar. 1, and a 20-day state of emergency followed. Sargsyan took office Apr. 9, 2008.

Seeking to bridge long-standing bitterness over the killing of more than 1 mil Armenians by Ottoman Turks in 1915-18, Armenian and Turkish negotiators signed a treaty Oct. 10, 2009, intended to normalize relations between their two countries; renewed friction with Turkey led Armenia to halt ratification of the treaty Apr. 22, 2010.

Australia
Commonwealth of Australia

People: Population: 21,766,711. **Age distrib.:** <15: 18.3%; 65+: 14%. **Pop. density:** 7.3 per sq mi, 2.8 per sq km. **Urban:** 89.1%. **Ethnic groups:** white 92%, Asian 7%, aboriginal & other 1%. **Principal languages:** English, Chinese, Italian, Greek, Arabic, Vietnamese. **Chief religions:** Roman Catholic 26%, Anglican 19%, Uniting Church 6%, Presbyterian & Reformed 3%, Eastern Orthodox 3%, other Christian 8%, Buddhist 2%, Muslim 2%, none 19%.

Geography: Total area: 2,988,902 sq mi, 7,741,220 sq km; **Land area:** 2,966,153 sq mi, 7,682,300 sq km. **Location:** SE of Asia, Indian O. is W and S, Pacific O. (Coral, Tasman seas) is E; they meet N of Australia in Timor and Arafura seas. Tasmania lies 150 mi S of Victoria state, across Bass Strait. **Neighbors:** Nearest are Indonesia, Papua New Guinea on N; Solomons, Fiji, and New Zealand on E. **Topography:** An island continent. The Great Dividing Range along the E coast has Mt. Kosciusko, 7,310 ft. The W plateau rises to 2,000 ft, with arid areas in the Great Sandy and Great Victoria deserts. The NW part of Western Australia and Northern Terr. are arid and hot. The NE has heavy rainfall and Cape York Peninsula has jungles. **Capital:** Canberra, 384,000. **Cities (urban aggl.):** Sydney, 4,428,978; Melbourne, 3,852,684; Brisbane, 1,970,306; Perth, 1,598,862; Adelaide, 1,167,533.

Government: Type: Democratic, federal state system. **Head of state:** Queen Elizabeth II, represented by Gov.-Gen. Quentin Bryce; b. Dec. 23, 1942; in office: Sept. 5, 2008. **Head of gov.:** Prime Min. Julia Gillard; b. Sept. 29, 1961; in office: June 24, 2010. **Local divisions:** 6 states, 2 territories. **Defense budget:** $24.5 mil. **Active troops:** 56,552.

Economy: Industries: mining, industrial and transp. equip., food proc., chemicals, steel. **Chief crops:** wheat, barley, sugarcane, fruits. **Natural resources:** bauxite, coal, iron ore, copper, tin, gold, silver, uranium, nickel, tungsten, rare earth elements, mineral sands, lead, zinc, diamonds, nat. gas, petroleum. **Crude oil reserves:** 3.3 bil bbls. **Other resources:** Wool (world's leading producer), beef. **Arable land:** 6.1%. **Livestock:** cattle: 27.9 mil; chickens: 95.4 mil; goats: 3.2 mil; pigs: 2.3 mil; sheep: 72.7 mil. **Fish catch:** 239,460 metric tons. **Electricity prod.** (2009): 232 bil kWh. **Labor force:** agric. 3.6%, industry 21.1%, services 75%.

Finance: Monetary unit: Dollar (AUD) (Sept. 2011: 0.95 = $1 U.S.). **GDP:** $882.4 bil; **per capita GDP:** $41,000; **GDP growth:** 2.7%. **Imports:** $200.4 bil; China 17.9%, U.S. 11.3%, Japan 8.4%, Thailand 5.8%, Singapore 5.5%, Germany 5.3%. **Exports:** $210.7 bil; China 21.8%, Japan 19.2%, South Korea 7.9%, India 7.5%, U.S. 4.9%, UK 4.4%, New Zealand 4.1% **Tourism:** $30.1 bil. **Budget:** $426.5 bil. **Total reserves less gold:** $38.7 bil. **Gold:** 2.6 mil oz t. **CPI change:** 2.8%.

Transport: Railways: 23,889 mi. **Motor vehicles:** 705.6 vehicles per 1,000 pop. **Civil aviation:** 62.5 bil pass.-mi; 326 airports. **Chief ports:** Brisbane, Darwin, Fremantle, Geelong, Gladstone, Melbourne, Newcastle, Sydney.

Communications: TV sets: 659 per 1,000 pop. **Radios:** 1,885 per 1,000 pop. **Telephone lines:** 38.9 per 100 pop. **Daily newspaper circ.:** 155.1 per 1,000 pop. **Internet:** 76 users per 100 pop.

Health: Life expect.: 79.4 male; 84.4 female. **Births:** 12.3 (per 1,000 pop.). **Deaths:** 6.9 (per 1,000 pop.). **Natural inc.:** 0.55%. **Infant mortality:** 4.6 (per 1,000 live births). **HIV rate:** 0.1%.

Education: Compulsory: ages 5-15. **Literacy:** 99%.

Major intl. organizations: UN and all of its specialized agencies, APEC, the Commonwealth, OECD, WTO.
Embassy: 1601 Massachusetts Ave. NW 20036; 797-3000.
Website: www.australia.gov.au

Australia harbors many plant and animal species not found elsewhere, including kangaroos, koalas, platypuses, dingoes (wild dogs), Tasmanian devils (raccoon-like marsupials), wombats (bear-like marsupials), and barking and frilled lizards.

Capt. James Cook explored the eastern coast in 1770, when the continent was inhabited by a variety of indigenous peoples. The first European settlers, beginning in 1788, were mostly convicts, soldiers, and government officials. By 1830, Britain had claimed the entire continent, and the immigration of free settlers began to accelerate. The Commonwealth was proclaimed Jan. 1, 1901. Northern Terr. was granted limited self-rule July 1, 1978.

State/territory, capital	Area (sq mi)	Population (Dec. 2010 est.)
New South Wales, Sydney	309,500	7,272,200
Victoria, Melbourne	87,900	5,585,600
Queensland, Brisbane	666,990	4,548,700
Western Australia, Perth	975,100	2,317,100
South Australia, Adelaide	379,900	1,650,400
Tasmania, Hobart	26,200	509,300
Australian Capital Terr., Canberra	900	361,900
Northern Terr., Darwin	519,800	229,900

Racially discriminatory immigration policies were abandoned in 1973, after 3 mil Europeans (half British) had entered since 1945. Indigenous peoples, 90% of them aborigines, number more than 500,000; in the Northern Territory they account for about 28% of the population and hold about 46% of the land. They remain economically disadvantaged.

Australia's agricultural success makes the country among the top exporters of beef, lamb, wool, and wheat. Major mineral deposits have been developed, largely for export. Industrialization has been completed.

The Labor Party won a majority in Feb. 1983 general elections and was reelected in 1984, 1987, 1990, and 1993. After an election that focused mainly on economic issues, conservatives swept into power in elections Mar. 2, 1996. Incumbent Prime Min. John Howard retained power in the 1998, 2001, and 2004 elections.

Australia led an international peacekeeping force into Timor in Sept. 1999. In a referendum Nov. 6, voters rejected a proposal that would have made Australia a republic. Sydney hosted the Olympics Sept. 15-Oct. 1, 2000.

Australian troops fought in U.S.-led military operations in Afghanistan (2001) and Iraq (2003). Some 2,000 Australian peacekeepers began arriving in the Solomon Isl., July 24, 2003; nearly all had been withdrawn by mid-2005. In race riots in Sydney suburbs, Dec. 11-12, 2005, thousands of white youths assaulted people of Middle Eastern ancestry, who then retaliated against whites. Australian troops were dispatched, 2006, to suppress disorder in the Solomon Isl. in Apr. and Timor in May. As of mid-2011, about 3,300 Australian troops were serving overseas, including 1,550 in Afghanistan and 380 in Timor.

Pledging to pull combat troops out of Iraq and to ratify the Kyoto Protocol against global warming, Kevin Rudd led the Labor Party to victory in parliamentary elections Nov. 24, 2007. Australia's combat mission in Iraq ended July 31, 2008. Quentin Bryce, the nation's first female governor-general, was sworn in Sept. 5, 2008. "Black Saturday" bushfires Feb. 7 in Victoria State claimed 173 lives and burned at least 1.1 mil acres.

After a series of policy missteps that eroded his popularity and alienated his Labor supporters, Rudd was forced out June 24, 2010, by his deputy, Julia Gillard, who became Australia's first female prime minister. Inconclusive parliamentary elections Aug. 21 led to the formation of a minority government headed by Gillard, with Rudd as foreign minister. Downpours from Cyclone Tasha and other storms flooded Queensland in late Dec. 2010 and early Jan. 2011, with three-fourths of the state declared a disaster zone. By late Jan. the flood death toll had reached 35, and property damage was estimated at more than AUD $5 bil.

Australian External Territories

Norfolk Isl., area 14 sq mi, pop. (2011 est.) 2,169, was taken over, 1914. The soil is very fertile, suitable for citrus, bananas, and coffee. Many of the inhabitants are descendants of the *Bounty* mutineers, moved to Norfolk 1856 from Pitcairn Isl. Australia offered the island limited home rule in 1978. **Website:** www.info.gov.nf

Coral Sea Isls. territory, area less than 1.2 sq mi, is administered from Norfolk Isl.

Ashmore and Cartier Isls., area 1.9 sq mi, in the Indian O., came under Australian authority 1934 and are administered as part of Northern Territory. **Heard Isl. and McDonald Isls.,** area 159 sq mi, are administered by the Dept. of Science.

Cocos (Keeling) Isls., 27 small coral islands in the Indian O. 1,750 mi NW of Australia. Pop. (2010 est.) 596; area 5 sq mi. The residents voted to become part of Australia, Apr. 1984.

Christmas Isl., area 52 sq mi, pop (2010 est.) 1,402; 230 mi S of Java, was transferred by Britain in 1958. It has phosphate deposits.

Australian Antarctic Territory was claimed by Australia in 1933, including 2,362,000 sq mi of territory S of 60th parallel S lat. and between 160th-45th meridians E long. It does not include Adelie Coast.

Austria
Republic of Austria

People: Population: 8,217,280. **Age distrib.:** <15: 14%; 65+: 18.2%. **Pop. density:** 258.1 per sq mi, 99.7 per sq km. **Urban:** 67.6%. **Ethnic groups:** Austrian 91%, fmr. Yugoslav (incl. Croatian, Slovene, Serb, Bosniak) 4%, Turk 2%. **Principal languages:** German (official), Turkish, Serbian, Croatian (official in Burgenland). **Chief religions:** Roman Catholic 74%, Protestant 5%, Muslim 4%, none 12%.

Geography: Total area: 32,383 sq mi, 83,871 sq km; **Land area:** 31,832 sq mi, 82,445 sq km. **Location:** In S Central Europe. **Neighbors:** Switzerland, Liechtenstein on W; Germany, Czech Rep. on N; Slovakia, Hungary on E; Slovenia, Italy on S. **Topography:** Austria is primarily mountainous, with the Alps and foothills covering the western and southern provinces. The eastern provinces and Vienna are located in the Danube River Basin. **Capital:** Vienna, 1,693,000.

Government: Type: Federal republic. **Head of state:** Pres. Heinz Fischer; b. Oct. 9, 1938; in office: July 8, 2004. **Head of gov.:** Chancellor Werner Faymann; b. May 4, 1960; in office: Dec. 2, 2008. **Local divisions:** 9 bundeslaender (states). **Defense budget:** $2.81 bil. **Active troops:** 25,900.

Economy: Industries: constr., machinery, vehicles and parts, food, metals, chemicals. **Chief crops:** grains, potatoes, wine, fruits. **Natural resources:** oil, coal, lignite, timber, iron ore, copper, zinc, antimony, magnesite, tungsten, graphite, salt, hydropower. **Crude oil reserves:** 50 mil bbls. **Arable land:** 16.6%. **Livestock:** cattle: 2 mil; chickens: 14.5 mil; goats: 62,500; pigs: 3.1 mil; sheep: 333,181. **Fish catch:** 2,491 metric tons. **Electricity prod.** (2009): 63 bil kWh. **Labor force:** agric. 5.5%, industry 27.5%, services 67%.

Finance: Monetary unit: Euro (EUR) (Sept. 2011: 0.71 = $1 U.S.). **GDP:** $332 bil; **per capita GDP:** $40,400; **GDP growth:** 2%. **Imports:** $156 bil; Germany 45.1%, Switzerland 6.8%, Italy 6.7%, Netherlands 4%. **Exports:** $157.4 bil; Germany 31%, Italy 8.2%, Switzerland 4%. **Tourism:** $18.7 bil. **Budget:** $189.4 bil. **Total reserves less gold:** $9.6 bil. **Gold:** 9 mil oz t. **CPI change:** 1.8%.

Transport: Railways: 3,976 mi. **Motor vehicles:** 579.5 vehicles per 1,000 pop. **Civil aviation:** 9.2 bil pass.-mi; 25 airports. **Chief ports:** Enns, Krems, Linz, Vienna.

Communications: TV sets: 656 per 1,000 pop. **Radios:** 752 per 1,000 pop. **Telephone lines:** 38.7 per 100 pop. **Daily newspaper circ.:** 311.4 per 1,000 pop. **Internet:** 72.7 users per 100 pop.

Health: Life expect.: 76.9 male; 82.8 female. **Births:** 8.7 (per 1,000 pop.). **Deaths:** 10.1 (per 1,000 pop.). **Natural inc.:** −0.15%. **Infant mortality:** 4.3 (per 1,000 live births). **HIV rate:** 0.3%.

Education: Compulsory: ages 6-14. **Literacy:** 98%.

Major intl. organizations: UN and all of its specialized agencies, EU, OECD, OSCE, WTO.

Embassy: 3524 International Ct. NW 20008; 895-6700.

Website: www.austria.gv.at

Rome conquered Austrian lands from Celtic tribes around 15 BC. In 788 the territory was incorporated into Charlemagne's empire. By 1300, the House of Hapsburg had gained control; they added vast territories in all parts of Europe to their realm in the next few hundred years.

Austrian dominance of Germany was undermined in the 18th cent. and ended by Prussia by 1866. But the Congress of Vienna, 1815, confirmed Austrian control of a large empire in southeast Europe consisting of Germans, Hungarians, Slavs, Italians, and others. The dual Austro-Hungarian monarchy was established in 1867, giving autonomy to Hungary and almost 50 years of peace.

World War I, started after the June 28, 1914, assassination of Archduke Franz Ferdinand, the Hapsburg heir, by a Serbian nationalist, destroyed the empire. By 1918 Austria was reduced to a small republic, with the borders it has today.

Nazi Germany, ruled by the Austrian-born Adolf Hitler, annexed Austria Mar. 13, 1938. The republic was reestablished in 1945, under Allied occupation. Full independence and neutrality were restored in 1955. Austria joined the EU Jan. 1, 1995.

The rise of the right-wing, anti-immigrant Austrian Freedom Party challenged the dominance of the Austrian Social Democratic Party in the late 1990s. When Freedom Party members joined the cabinet, Feb. 4, 2000, the EU imposed political sanctions on Austria for 7 months. Social Democrats won the parliamentary elections of Oct. 1, 2006; they held onto their plurality in elections Sept. 28, 2008, although far-right parties made gains.

Azerbaijan
Republic of Azerbaijan

People: Population: 9,397,279. **Age distrib.:** <15: 22.8%; 65+: 6.3%. **Pop. density:** 294.6 per sq mi, 113.7 per sq km. **Urban:** 51.9%. **Ethnic groups:** Azeri 91%, Dagestani 2%, Russian 2%, Armenian 2%. **Principal languages:** Azerbaijani (Azeri) (official), Lezgi, Russian, Armenian. **Chief religions:** Muslim 93%, Russian Orthodox 3%, Armenian Orthodox 2%.

Geography: Total area: 33,436 sq mi, 86,600 sq km; **Land area:** 31,903 sq mi, 82,629 sq km. **Location:** SW Asia. **Neighbors:** Russia, Georgia on N; Iran on S; Armenia on W; Caspian Sea on E. **Topography:** The Great Caucasus Mts. in N, Karabakh Upland in W border the Kur-Abas lowland; climate is arid except in the subtropical SE. **Capital:** Baku, 1,950,000.

Government: Type: Republic. **Head of state:** Pres. Ilham Aliyev; b. Dec. 24, 1961; in office: Oct. 31, 2003. **Head of gov.:** Prime Min. Artur Rasizade; b. Feb. 26, 1935; in office: Nov. 4, 2003. **Local division:** 59 rayons, 11 cities, 1 autonomous republic. **Defense budget:** $1.59 bil. **Active troops:** 66,940.

Economy: Industries: petroleum and nat. gas, petroleum prods., oil field equip.; steel, iron ore; cement. **Chief crops:** cotton, grain, rice, grapes. **Natural resources:** petroleum, nat. gas, iron ore, nonferrous metals, bauxite. **Crude oil reserves:** 7 bil bdls. **Arable land:** 22.7%. **Livestock:** cattle: 2.3 mil; chickens: 21.5 mil; goats: 590,935; pigs: 10,299; sheep: 7.7 mil. **Fish catch:** 1,303 metric tons. **Electricity prod.:** 22.6 bil kWh. **Labor force:** agric. 38.3%, industry 12.1%, services 49.6%.

Finance: Monetary unit: New Manat (AZN) (Sept. 2011: 0.79 = $1 U.S.). **GDP:** $90.8 bil; **per capita GDP:** $10,900; **GDP growth:** 5%. **Imports:** $7 bil; Russia 17.5%, Turkey 14.8%, Germany 9%, Ukraine 8.4%, China 7.9%, UK 4.5%, U.S. 4.3%. **Exports:** $28.1 bil; Italy 25.8%, U.S. 11.9%, France 9%, Israel 8.4%, Russia 5.1%, Indonesia 4.5%. **Tourism:** $621 mil. **Budget:** $14.6 bil. **Total reserves less gold:** $6.4 bil. **CPI change:** 5.7%.

Transport: Railways: 1,813 mi. **Motor vehicles:** 110 vehicles per 1,000 pop. **Civil aviation:** 791.6 mil pass.-mi; 27 airports. **Chief port:** Baku.

Communications: TV sets: 216 per 1,000 pop. **Radios:** 214 per 1,000 pop. **Telephone lines:** 16.3 per 100 pop. **Daily newspaper circ.:** 16.1 per 1,000 pop. **Internet:** 36 users per 100 pop.

Health: Life expect.: 68.1 male; 74.4 female. **Births:** 17.4 (per 1,000 pop.). **Deaths:** 7.2 (per 1,000 pop.). **Natural inc.:** 1.02%. **Infant mortality:** 29.9 (per 1,000 live births). **HIV rate:** 0.1%.

Education: Compulsory: ages 6-17. **Literacy:** 99.5%.

Major intl. organizations: UN (FAO, IBRD, ILO, IMF, WHO), CIS, OSCE, WTO (observer).

Embassy: 2741 34th St. NW 20008; 337-3500.

Website: www.president.az

Azerbaijan was the home of Scythian tribes and part of the Roman Empire. Overrun by Turks in the 11th cent. and conquered by Russia in 1806 and 1813, it joined the USSR Dec. 30, 1922, and became a constituent republic in 1936. Azerbaijan declared independence Aug. 30, 1991, and became an independent state when the Soviet Union disbanded Dec. 26, 1991.

Nagorno-Karabakh, an enclave with a majority population of ethnic Armenians, seceded from Azerbaijan in 1988, triggering a war between mostly Muslim Azerbaijan and most Christian Armenia, 1992-94, in which 30,000 lives were lost (see Armenia).

Voters approved a new constitution expanding presidential powers, Nov. 12, 1995. Pres. Haydar Aliyev, a pro-Russian former Communist, was reelected Oct. 11, 1998, but international monitors called the vote seriously flawed.

The dying Pres. Aliyev named his son Ilham prime minister Aug. 4, 2003. The younger Aliyev won the presidential election of Oct. 15, in a vote considered fraudulent by international observers; he responded to violent protests Oct. 16 by arresting hundreds of opposition leaders and their supporters. Serious abuses also marred the parliamentary elections of Nov. 6, 2005, won by parties loyal to Aliyev. The opening May 25, 2005, of the Baku-Tbilisi-Ceyhan pipeline, providing an outlet for Azerbaijan's vast Caspian oil reserves, transformed the nation's economy.

Pres. Ilham Aliyev won a second term Oct. 15, 2008, in an election boycotted by the main opposition parties. A constitutional amendment abolishing presidential term limits was approved by referendum Mar. 18, 2009. Azerbaijan holds strategic importance as a transit point for U.S. troops and supplies bound for Afghanistan.

The Bahamas
Commonwealth of The Bahamas

People: Population: 313,312. **Age distrib.:** <15: 24.4%; 65+: 6.3%. **Pop. density:** 81.1 per sq mi, 31.3 per sq km. **Urban:** 84.1%. **Ethnic groups:** black 85%, white 12%, Asian & Hispanic 3%. **Principal languages:** English (official), Creole (among Haitian immigrants). **Chief religions:** Baptist 35%, Anglican 15%, Roman Catholic 14%, Pentecostal 8%, Church of God 5%, Methodist 4%, other Christian 15%.

Geography: Total area: 5,359 sq mi, 13,880 sq km; **Land area:** 3,865 sq mi, 10,010 sq km. **Location:** In Atlantic O., E of Florida. **Neighbors:** Nearest are U.S. on W, Cuba on S. **Topography:** Nearly 700 islands (29 inhabited) and over 2,000 islets in the W Atlantic O. extend 760 mi NW to SE. **Capital:** Nassau, 248,000.

Government: Type: Parliamentary democracy. **Head of state:** Queen Elizabeth II, represented by Gov.-Gen. Sir Arthur Foulkes; b. May 11, 1928; in office: Apr. 14, 2010. **Head of gov.:** Prime Min. Hubert Alexander Ingraham; b. Aug. 4, 1947; in office: May 4, 2007. **Local divisions:** 21 districts. **Defense budget:** $46 mil. **Active troops:** 860.

Economy: Industries: tourism, banking, cement, oil transshipment, salt, rum. **Chief crops:** citrus, vegetables. **Natural resources:** salt, aragonite, timber. **Arable land:** 0.8%. **Livestock:** cattle: 750; chickens: 3 mil; goats: 14,500; pigs: 5,000; sheep: 6,500. **Fish catch:** 9,106 metric tons. **Electricity prod.** (2009): 1.9 bil kWh. **Labor force:** agric. 5%, industry 5%, tourism 50%, other services 40%.

Finance: Monetary unit: Dollar (BSD) (Sept. 2011: 1.00 = $1 U.S.). **GDP:** $8.9 bil; **per capita GDP:** $28,700; **GDP growth:** 0.5%. **Imports** (2006): $2.4 bil; U.S. 23.1%, Venezuela 18.9%, Japan 12.3%, South Korea 11.5%, Singapore 5%, India 4.8%. **Exports** (2006): $674 mil; U.S. 39.3%, Singapore 20.4%, Poland 13.2%, Germany 6.8%. **Tourism:** $2.1 bil. **Budget** (FY04/05): $1.03 bil. **Total reserves less gold:** $1.04 bil. **CPI change:** 1.3%.

Transport: Motor vehicles: 397.7 vehicles per 1,000 pop. **Civil aviation:** 171.5 mil pass.-mi; 23 airports. **Chief ports:** Freeport, Nassau.

Communications: TV sets: 248 per 1,000 pop. **Radios:** 746 per 1,000 pop. **Telephone lines:** 37.7 per 100 pop. **Internet:** 43 users per 100 pop.

Health: Life expect.: 68.8 male; 73.6 female. **Births:** 16.1 (per 1,000 pop.). **Deaths:** 6.9 (per 1,000 pop.). **Natural inc.:** 0.92%. **Infant mortality:** 13.5 (per 1,000 live births). **HIV rate:** 3.1%.

Education: Compulsory: ages 5-16. **Literacy:** NA.

Major intl. organizations: UN (FAO, IBRD, ILO, IMF, WHO), Caricom, the Commonwealth, OAS, WTO (observer).

Embassy: 2220 Massachusetts Ave. NW 20008; 319-2660.

Website: www.bahamas.gov.bs

Christopher Columbus first set foot in the New World on San Salvador (Watling Isl.) in 1492, when Arawak Indians inhabited the islands. British settlement began in 1647; the islands became a British colony in 1783. Internal self-government was granted in 1964; full independence within the Commonwealth was attained July 10, 1973. International banking and investment management have become major industries alongside tourism.

Bahrain
Kingdom of Bahrain

People: Population: 1,214,705. **Age distrib.:** <15: 20.5%; 65+: 2.6%. **Pop. density:** 4,139.6 per sq mi, 1,598.3 per sq km. **Urban:** 88.6%. **Ethnic groups:** Bahraini 62%, non-Bahraini 38%. **Principal languages:** Arabic (official), English, Farsi, Urdu. **Chief religions:** Muslim (Shi'a & Sunni) 81%, Christian 9%.

Geography: Total area: 293 sq mi, 760 sq km; **Land area:** 293 sq mi, 760 sq km. **Location:** SW Asia, in Persian Gulf. **Neighbors:** Nearest are Saudi Arabia on W, Qatar on E. **Topography:** Bahrain Island, and several adjacent, smaller islands, are flat, hot, and humid, with little rain. **Capital:** Manama, 163,000.

Government: Type: Constitutional monarchy. **Head of state:** King Hamad bin Isa al-Khalifa; b. Jan. 28, 1950; in office: as emir Mar. 6, 1999; as king Feb. 14, 2002. **Head of gov.:** Prime Min. Khalifa bin Sulman al-Khalifa; b. Nov. 24, 1936; in office: Jan. 19, 1970. **Local divisions:** 12 municipalities. **Defense budget:** $742 mil. **Active troops:** 8,200.

Economy: Industries: petroleum proc. and refining, aluminum smelting, iron pelletization, fertilizers, Islamic and offshore banking. **Chief crops:** fruits, vegetables. **Natural resources:** oil, nat. gas, fish, pearls. **Crude oil reserves:** 124.6 mil bbls. **Arable land:** 1.7%. **Livestock:** cattle: 10,000; chickens: 525,000; goats: 19,000; sheep: 40,000. **Fish catch:** 16,360 metric tons. **Electricity prod.:** 11.2 bil kWh. **Labor force:** agric. 1%, industry 79%, services 20%.

Finance: Monetary unit: Dinar (BHD) (Sept. 2011: 0.38 = $1 U.S.). **GDP:** $29.7 bil; **per capita GDP:** $40,300; **GDP growth:** 4.1%. **Imports:** $12.1 bil; Saudi Arabia 23.1%, France 9.9%, U.S. 8%, China 5.7%, Japan 5.2%, Germany 5.1%, UK 4.4%. **Exports:** $15.1 bil; NA. **Tourism:** $1.1 bil. **Budget:** $5.9 bil. **Total reserves less gold:** NA. **Gold:** 150,000 oz t. **CPI change:** 2%.

Transport: Motor vehicles: 400.3 vehicles per 1,000 pop. **Civil aviation:** 8.7 bil pass.-mi; 4 airports. **Chief ports:** Mina, Salman, Sitrah.

Communications: TV sets: 414 per 1,000 pop. **Radios:** 544 per 1,000 pop. **Telephone lines:** 18.1 per 100 pop. **Internet:** 55 users per 100 pop.

Health: Life expect.: 76.0 male; 80.3 female. **Births:** 14.6 (per 1,000 pop.). **Deaths:** 2.6 (per 1,000 pop.). **Natural inc.:** 1.20%. **Infant mortality:** 10.4 (per 1,000 live births). **HIV rate:** NA.

Education: Compulsory: ages 6-14. **Literacy:** 91.4%.

Major intl. organizations: UN (FAO, IBRD, ILO, IMF, WHO), AL, WTO.

Embassy: 3502 International Dr. NW 20008; 342-1111.

Website: www.bahrain.bh

Long ruled by the Khalifa family, Bahrain was a British protectorate from 1861 to Aug. 15, 1971, when it regained independence.

Pearls, shrimp, fruits, and vegetables were the mainstays of the economy until oil was discovered in 1932. Crude oil production has declined since the 1970s, but natural gas output has grown and international banking has thrived. Shiite dissidents have clashed with the Sunni-led government since 1996.

Emir Hamad bin Isa al-Khalifa proclaimed himself king Feb. 14, 2002. Local elections in May 2002 marked the first time Bahraini women were allowed to vote and run for office. The first female judge was appointed June 6, 2006. The monarchy forcefully suppressed "Arab Spring" mass demonstrations Feb.-Mar. 2011; to bolster security, a Gulf Cooperation Council force of 1,600, led by Saudi Arabia, entered Bahrain Mar. 14, and the government recruited hundreds of additional former soldiers and police from Pakistan.

Bangladesh

People's Republic of Bangladesh

People: Population: 158,570,535. **Age distrib.:** <15: 34.3%; 65+: 4.7%. **Pop. density:** 3,155.1 per sq mi, 1,218.2 per sq km. **Urban:** 28.1%. **Ethnic groups:** Bengali 98%. **Principal languages:** Bangla, or Bengali (official), English. **Chief religions:** Muslim 89.5%, Hindu 9.6%.

Geography: Total area: 55,598 sq mi, 143,998 sq km; **Land area:** 50,258 sq mi, 130,168 sq km. **Location:** In S Asia, on N bend of Bay of Bengal. **Neighbors:** India nearly surrounds country on W, N, E; Myanmar on SE. **Topography:** The country is mostly a low plain cut by the Ganges and Brahmaputra rivers and their delta. The land is alluvial and marshy along the coast, with hills only in the extreme SE and NE. A tropical monsoon climate prevails, among the rainiest in the world. **Capital:** Dhaka, 14,251,000. **Cities (urban aggl.):** Chittagong, 4,961,826; Khulna, 1,682,330.

Government: Type: Parliamentary democracy. **Head of state:** Pres. Zillur Rahman; b. Mar. 9, 1929; in office: Feb. 12, 2009. **Head of gov.:** Prime Min. Sheikh Hasina; b. Sept. 28, 1947; in office: Jan. 6, 2009. **Local divisions:** 6 divisions. **Defense budget:** $1.32 bil. **Active troops:** 157,053.

Economy: Industries: cotton textiles, jute, garments, tea proc., paper newsprint, cement, chem. fertilizer, light engineering, sugar. **Chief crops:** rice, jute, tea, wheat, sugarcane, potatoes, tobacco, pulses, oilseeds, spices. **Natural resources:** nat. gas, timber, coal. **Crude oil reserves:** 28 mil bbls. **Arable land:** 58.1%. **Livestock:** cattle: 23 mil; chickens: 221.3 mil; goats: 60.6 mil; sheep: 1.7 mil. **Fish catch:** 2.9 mil metric tons. **Electricity prod.:** 32.9 bil kWh. **Labor force:** agric. 45%, industry 30%, services 25%.

Finance: Monetary unit: Taka (BDT) (Sept. 2011: 74.25 = $1 U.S.). **GDP:** $258.6 bil; **per capita GDP:** $1,700; **GDP growth:** 6%. **Imports:** $21.3 bil; China 16.2%, India 12.6%, Singapore 7.6%, Japan 4.6%, Malaysia 4.5%. **Exports:** $16.2 bil; U.S. 20.2%, Germany 12.7%, UK 8.6%, France 6.5%, Netherlands 5.9%. **Tourism:** $81 mil. **Budget:** $15.9 bil. **Total reserves less gold:** $10.6 bil. **Gold:** 434,400 oz t. **CPI change:** 8.1%.

Transport: Railways: 1,629 mi. **Motor vehicles:** 0.7 vehicles per 1,000 pop. **Civil aviation:** 2.7 bil pass.-mi; 15 airports. **Chief ports:** Chittagong, Mongla Port.

Communications: TV sets: 106 per 1,000 pop. **Radios:** 64 per 1,000 pop. **Telephone lines:** 0.6 per 100 pop. **Internet:** 3.7 users per 100 pop.

Health: Life expect.: 67.9 male; 71.7 female. **Births:** 23.0 (per 1,000 pop.). **Deaths:** 5.8 (per 1,000 pop.). **Natural inc.:** 1.72%. **Infant mortality:** 50.7 (per 1,000 live births). **HIV rate:** <0.1%.

Education: Compulsory: ages 6-10. **Literacy:** 55.9%.

Major intl. organizations: UN (FAO, IBRD, ILO, IMF, WHO), the Commonwealth, WTO.

Embassy: 3510 International Dr. NW 20008; 244-0183.

Website: www.bangladesh.gov.bd

Muslim invaders conquered the formerly Hindu area in the 12th cent. British rule lasted from the 18th cent. to 1947, when East Bengal became part of Pakistan.

Opposing domination by West Pakistan, the Awami League, based in the East, won control of the National Assembly in 1971. Assembly sessions were postponed; riots broke out. Pakistani troops attacked Mar. 25; Bangladesh independence was proclaimed the next day. In the ensuing civil war, 1 mil died and 10 mil fled to India.

War between India and Pakistan broke out Dec. 3, 1971. Pakistan surrendered in the East on Dec. 16. Mujibur Rahman, known as Sheikh Mujib, became prime minister; he was killed in a coup Aug. 15, 1975.

On May 30, 1981, Pres. Ziaur Rahman was killed in an unsuccessful coup attempt by army rivals. Vice Pres. Abdus Sattar assumed the presidency but was ousted in a coup led by army chief of staff Gen. H. M. Ershad, Mar. 1982. Ershad declared Bangladesh an Islamic Republic in 1988; a parliamentary system of government was adopted in 1991. A cyclone struck Apr. 1991, killing over 131,000 people and causing $2.7 bil in damages.

Political turmoil led to the resignation, Mar. 30, 1996, of Prime Min. Khaleda Zia, the widow of Ziaur Rahman. Sheikh Mujib's daughter, known as Sheikh Hasina, led the country after the June 12, 1996 election. Floods in July-Sept. 1998 inundated most of the country, killed over 1,400 people (many through disease), and stranded at least 30 mil.

Khaleda Zia returned to power following the parliamentary elections of Oct. 1, 2001. Floods July-Aug. 2004 caused at least 950

deaths and $7 bil in property damage. Militant Islamists set off more than 400 small bombs in over 50 cities and towns, Aug. 17, 2005, killing 3 people. Another wave of jihadist bombings, killed 22 Nov. 29-Dec. 8, 2005. A Bangladeshi economist, Muhammad Yunus, won the 2006 Nobel Peace Prize for using very small loans (microcredit) to help alleviate poverty, a severe problem in this densely populated country.

Escalating political violence led Pres. Iajuddin Ahmed to declare a state of emergency Jan. 11, 2007. A military-backed caretaker government filed criminal charges against Khaleda Zia and Sheikh Hasina, but failed in an attempt to force the two former prime ministers into exile. Cyclone Sidr struck Nov. 15, 2007, damaging more than 1.5 mil homes and affecting 8.9 mil people; the confirmed death toll reached nearly 3,400.

The Awami League triumphed in parliamentary elections Dec. 29, 2008, and Sheikh Hasina was sworn in as prime minister Jan. 6, 2009, ending 2 years of emergency rule. A mutiny Feb. 25-26, 2009, at the Dhaka headquarters of the Bangladesh Rifles, a border force, left 74 people dead, according to official figures. A fire that raged through a crowded residential area of Dhaka June 3, 2010, killed at least 117.

Barbados

People: Population: 286,705. **Age distrib.:** <15: 18.9%; 65+: 9.8%. **Pop. density:** 1,726.9 per sq mi, 666.8 per sq km. **Urban:** 44.5%. **Ethnic groups:** black 93%, white 3%, mixed 3%, East Indian 1%. **Principal language:** English. **Chief religions:** Protestant 63%, Roman Catholic 4%, other Christian 7%.

Geography: Total area: 166 sq mi, 430 sq km; **Land area:** 166 sq mi, 430 sq km. **Location:** In Atlantic O., farthest E of West Indies. **Neighbors:** Nearest are St. Lucia and St. Vincent & the Grenadines to the W. **Topography:** The island lies alone in the Atlantic almost completely surrounded by coral reefs. Highest point is Mt. Hillaby, 1,115 ft. **Capital:** Bridgetown, 112,000.

Government: Type: Parliamentary democracy. **Head of state:** Queen Elizabeth II, represented by Gov.-Gen. Sir Clifford Husbands; b. Aug. 5, 1926; in office: June 1, 1996. **Head of gov.:** Prime Min. Freundel Stuart; b. Apr. 27, 1951; in office: Oct. 23, 2010. **Local divisions:** 11 parishes and Bridgetown. **Defense budget:** $34 mil. **Active troops:** 610.

Economy: Industries: tourism, sugar, light mfg., component assembly. **Chief crops:** sugarcane, vegetables, cotton. **Natural resources:** petroleum, fish, nat. gas. **Crude oil reserves:** 1.8 mil bbls. **Other resources:** Fish. **Arable land:** 37.2%. **Livestock:** cattle: 11,000; chickens: 3.6 mil; goats: 5,200; pigs: 20,000; sheep: 11,500. **Fish catch:** 3,496 metric tons. **Electricity prod.:** 1.01 bil kWh. **Labor force:** agric. 10%, industry 15%, services 75%.

Finance: Monetary unit: Dollar (BBD) (Sept. 2011: 2.00 = $1 U.S.). **GDP:** $6.2 bil; **per capita GDP:** $21,800; **GDP growth:** −0.5%. **Imports** (2006): $1.6 bil; Trinidad and Tobago 28.9%, U.S. 28.3%, China 6.4%, Colombia 5.2%, UK 4.4%. **Exports** (2006): $385 mil; Trinidad and Tobago 19.1%, U.S. 9.8%, Saint Lucia 8.9%, Venezuela 6.8%, UK 5.9%, Saint Vincent and the Grenadines 5.5%, Antigua and Barbuda 4.5%, France 4.3%, Saint Kitts and Nevis 4.2%, Jamaica 4%. **Tourism:** $1.1 bil. **Budget** (2000 est.): $886 mil. **Total reserves less gold:** $833.5 mil. **CPI change:** 5.8%.

Transport: Motor vehicles: 342.6 vehicles per 1,000 pop. **Civil aviation:** 1 airport. **Chief port:** Bridgetown.

Communications: TV sets: 291 per 1,000 pop. **Radios:** 287 per 1,000 pop. **Telephone lines:** 50.3 per 100 pop. **Internet:** 70.2 users per 100 pop.

Health: Life expect.: 72.1 male; 76.6 female. **Births:** 12.4 (per 1,000 pop.). **Deaths:** 8.4 (per 1,000 pop.). **Natural inc.:** 0.40%. **Infant mortality:** 11.9 (per 1,000 live births). **HIV rate:** 1.4%.

Education: Compulsory: ages 5-15. **Literacy:** NA.

Major intl. organizations: UN (FAO, IBRD, ILO, IMF, WHO), Caricom, the Commonwealth, OAS, WTO.

Embassy: 2144 Wyoming Ave. NW 20008; 939-9200.

Website: www.barbados.gov.bb

Barbados was probably named by Portuguese sailors in reference to bearded fig trees. An English ship visited in 1605, and British settlers arrived on the uninhabited island in 1627. Slaves worked the sugar plantations until slavery was abolished in 1834. Self-rule came gradually, with full independence proclaimed Nov. 30, 1966. British traditions have remained.

When Prime Min. David Thompson died Oct. 23, 2010, he was succeeded by his deputy, Freundel Stuart.

Belarus

Republic of Belarus

People: Population: 9,577,552. **Age distrib.:** <15: 14.2%; 65+: 14.1%. **Pop. density:** 122.3 per sq mi, 47.2 per sq km. **Urban:** 74.7%. **Ethnic groups:** Belarusian 81%, Russian 11% , Polish 4, Ukrainian 2%. **Principal languages:** Belarusian (official), Russian (official). **Chief religions:** Eastern Orthodox 80%, other (incl. Roman Catholic, Protestant, Jewish, Muslim) 20%.

Geography: Total area: 80,155 sq mi, 207,600 sq km; **Land area:** 78,340 sq mi, 202,900 sq km. **Location:** E Europe. **Neighbors:** Poland on W; Latvia, Lithuania on N; Russia on E; Ukraine on S. **Topography:** Belarus is a landlocked country consisting mostly of hilly lowland with significant marsh areas in S. **Capital:** Minsk, 1,837,000.

Government: Type: Republic. **Head of state:** Pres. Aleksandr Lukashenko; b. Aug. 30, 1954; in office: July 20,1994. **Head of gov.:** Prime Min. Mikhail Myasnikovich; b. May 6, 1950; in office: Dec. 28, 2010. **Local divisions:** 6 oblasts and 1 municipality. **Defense budget:** $716 mil. **Active troops:** 72,940.

Economy: Industries: machine tools, tractors, trucks, earthmovers, motorcycles. **Chief crops:** grain, potatoes, vegetables, sugar beets, flax. **Natural resources:** timber, peat, oil, nat. gas, granite, dolomitic limestone, marl, chalk, sand, gravel, clay. **Crude oil reserves:** 198 mil bbls. **Arable land:** 27.3%. **Livestock:** cattle: 4.1 mil; chickens: 29.2 mil; goats: 73,200; pigs: 3.7 mil; sheep: 52,500. **Fish catch:** 5,050 metric tons. **Electricity prod.:** 32.9 bil kWh. **Labor force:** agric. 14%, industry 34.7%, services 51.3%.

Finance: Monetary unit: Ruble (BYR) (Sept. 2011: 5,213.00 = $1 U.S.). **GDP:** $131.2 bil; **per capita GDP:** $13,600; **GDP growth:** 7.6%. **Imports:** $29.8 bil; Russia 58.5%, Germany 7.8%, Ukraine 4.5%. **Exports:** $24.5 bil; Russia 31.6%, Netherlands 17.3%, Ukraine 8%, Latvia 7.8%, Germany 4.6%. **Tourism:** $411 mil. **Budget:** $24.3 bil. **Total reserves less gold:** $3.4 bil. **Gold:** 1.1 mil oz t. **CPI change:** 7.7%.

Transport: Railways: 3,441 mi. **Motor vehicles:** 256.3 vehicles per 1,000 pop. **Civil aviation:** 272.2 mil pass.-mi; 35 airports. **Chief port:** Mazyr.

Communications: TV sets: 386 per 1,000 pop. **Radios:** 340 per 1,000 pop. **Telephone lines:** 43.1 per 100 pop. **Daily newspaper circ.:** 81.3 per 1,000 pop. **Internet:** 31.7 users per 100 pop.

Health: Life expect.: 65.6 male; 77.2 female. **Births:** 9.8 (per 1,000 pop.). **Deaths:** 13.8 (per 1,000 pop.). **Natural inc.:** –0.40%. **Infant mortality:** 6.3 (per 1,000 live births). **HIV rate:** 0.3%.

Education: Compulsory: ages 6-14. **Literacy:** 99.7%.

Major intl. organizations: UN (FAO, IBRD, ILO, IMF, WHO), CIS, OSCE, WTO (observer).

Embassy: 1619 New Hampshire Ave. NW 20009; 986-1604.

Website: www.president.gov.by

Belarus became a constituent republic of the USSR in 1922, although the western region was controlled by Poland. Overrun by German armies in 1941, Belarus was recaptured by Soviet troops in 1944. Following WWII, Belarus increased in area through Soviet annexation of part of NE Poland. Belarus declared independence Aug. 25, 1991. It became an independent state when the Soviet Union disbanded Dec. 26, 1991.

A new constitution was adopted, Mar. 15, 1994, after which Aleksandr Lukashenko was elected president. Russia and Belarus signed a pact Apr. 2, 1996, linking their political and economic systems. An authoritarian constitution enacted in Nov. gave Pres. Lukashenko vast new powers. Since then, Lukashenko and his supporters have retained power in elections criticized as seriously flawed by Western observers.

The IMF agreed Jan. 2009 to extend $2.5 bil in credits to help Belarus weather the global economic downturn. A dispute over natural gas deliveries from Russia was resolved June 24, 2010, after Belarus settled its $200 mil energy debt. Belarus agreed July 5 to form a customs union with Russia and Kazakhstan. Lukashenko crushed protests that followed the presidential election of Dec. 19, 2010, in which he claimed nearly 80% of the vote; the U.S. and EU imposed sanctions on Lukashenko and other Belarus officials Jan. 31, 2011.

Belgium
Kingdom of Belgium

People: Population: 10,431,477. **Age distrib.:** <15: 15.9%; 65+: 18%. **Pop. density:** 892.3 per sq mi, 344.5 per sq km. **Urban:** 97.4%. **Ethnic groups:** Fleming 58%, Walloon 31%, mixed or other 11%. **Principal languages:** Dutch, French, German (all official). **Chief religions:** Roman Catholic 75%, other (incl. Protestant) 25%.

Geography: Total area: 11,787 sq mi, 30,528 sq km; **Land area:** 11,690 sq mi, 30,278 sq km. **Location:** In W Europe, on North Sea. **Neighbors:** France on W and S, Luxembourg on SE, Germany on E, Netherlands on N. **Topography:** Mostly flat, the country is trisected by the Scheldt and Meuse, major commercial rivers. The land becomes hilly and forested in the SE (Ardennes) region. **Capital:** Brussels, 1,892,000. **Cities (urban aggl.):** Antwerpen, 965,297.

Government: Type: Parliamentary democracy under a constitutional monarch. **Head of state:** King Albert II; b. June 6, 1934; in office: Aug. 9, 1993. **Head of gov.:** Prime Min. Yves Leterme; b. Oct. 6, 1960; in office: Nov. 25, 2009. **Local divisions:** 10 provinces and Brussels. **Defense budget:** $3.64 bil. **Active troops:** 37,882.

Economy: Industries: engineering and metal prods., motor vehicle assembly, transp. equip., scientific instruments, processed food and beverages, chemicals, metals, textiles, glass, petroleum. **Chief crops:** sugar beets, vegetables, fruits, grain, tobacco. **Natural resources:** constr. materials, silica sand, carbonates. **Arable land:** 27.7%. **Livestock:** cattle: 2.6 mil; chickens: 33.2 mil; goats: 31,668; pigs: 6.3 mil; sheep: 126,219. **Fish catch:** 22,298 metric tons. **Electricity prod.** (2009): 84.2 bil kWh. **Labor force:** agric. 2%, industry 25%, services 73%.

Finance: Monetary unit: Euro (EUR) (Sept. 2011: 0.71 = $1 U.S.). **GDP:** $394.3 bil; **per capita GDP:** $37,800; **GDP growth:** 2%. **Imports:** $281.7 bil; Netherlands 17.9%, Germany 17.1%, France 11.7%, Ireland 6.3%, U.S. 5.7%, UK 5.1%, China 4.1%. **Exports:** $279.2 bil; Germany 19.6%, France 17.7%, Netherlands

11.8%, UK 7.2%, U.S. 5.4%, Italy 4.8%. **Tourism:** $10.2 bil. **Budget:** $242.6 bil. **Total reserves less gold:** $16.5 bil. **Gold:** 7.3 mil oz t. **CPI change:** 2.2%.

Transport: Railways: 2,009 mi. **Motor vehicles:** 571.6 vehicles per 1,000 pop. **Civil aviation:** 4.4 bil pass.-mi; 27 airports. **Chief ports:** Antwerp (one of the world's busiest), Gent, Liege, Zeebrugge.

Communications: TV sets: 585 per 1,000 pop. **Radios:** 791 per 1,000 pop. **Telephone lines:** 43.3 per 100 pop. **Daily newspaper circ.:** 164.7 per 1,000 pop. **Internet:** 79.3 users per 100 pop.

Health: Life expect.: 76.4 male; 82.8 female. **Births:** 10.1 (per 1,000 pop.). **Deaths:** 10.6 (per 1,000 pop.). **Natural inc.:** –0.05%. **Infant mortality:** 4.3 (per 1,000 live births). **HIV rate:** 0.2%.

Education: Compulsory: ages 6-18. **Literacy:** 99%.

Major intl. organizations: UN and all of its specialized agencies, EU, NATO, OECD, OSCE, WTO.

Embassy: 3330 Garfield St. NW 20008; 333-6900.

Website: www.belgium.be

Belgium derives its name from the Belgae, the first recorded inhabitants, probably Celts. The land was ruled for 1800 years by conquerors, including Rome, the Franks, Burgundy, Spain, Austria, and France. After 1815, Belgium was made a part of the Netherlands, but it became an independent constitutional monarchy in 1830.

Belgian neutrality was violated by Germany in both world wars. King Leopold III surrendered to Germany, May 28, 1940. After the war, he was forced by political pressure to abdicate in favor of his son, King Baudouin. Baudouin was succeeded by his brother, Albert II, Aug. 9, 1993.

The Flemings of northern Belgium speak Dutch, while French is the language of the Walloons in the south. The language difference has been a perennial source of controversy between the 2 groups. Parliament has passed measures aimed at transferring power from the central government to 3 regions—Wallonia, Flanders, and Brussels. Constitutional changes in 1993 made Belgium a federal state.

After elections June 10, 2007, rivalries between Flemings and Walloons led to a 9-month political stalemate. Controversy over the sale of troubled bank Fortis NV to BNP Paribas of France led to the resignation of Prime Min. Yves Leterme, Dec. 19, 2008, and his replacement by former Budget Min. Herman Van Rompuy. Leterme returned to office after Van Rompuy was chosen Nov. 19, 2009, to become president of the EU. Elections June 13, 2010, led to another prolonged political deadlock while Leterme remained caretaker prime minister.

Belize

People: Population: 321,115. **Age distrib.:** <15: 36.8%; 65+: 3.5%. **Pop. density:** 36.5 per sq mi, 14.1 per sq km. **Urban:** 52.2%. **Ethnic groups:** mestizo 49%, Creole 25%, Maya 11%, Garifuna 6%. **Principal languages:** Spanish, Creole, Mayan dialects, English (official), Garifuna (Carib), German. **Chief religions:** Roman Catholic 50%, Protestant 27%, none 9%.

Geography: Total area: 8,867 sq mi, 22,966 sq km; **Land area:** 8,805 sq mi, 22,806 sq km. **Location:** Eastern coast of Central America. **Neighbors:** Mexico on N, Guatemala on W and S. **Topography:** Belize has swampy lowlands in N, Maya Mts. in S, coral reefs and cays near coast. Climate is tropical. **Capital:** Belmopan, 20,000.

Government: Type: Parliamentary democracy. **Head of state:** Queen Elizabeth II, represented by Gov.-Gen. Sir Colville Young; b. Nov. 20, 1932; in office: Nov. 17, 1993. **Head of gov.:** Prime Min. Dean Barrow; b. Mar. 2, 1951; in office: Feb. 8, 2008. **Local divisions:** 6 districts. **Defense budget:** $19 mil. **Active troops:** 1,050.

Economy: Industries: garment prod., food proc., tourism, constr., oil. **Chief crops:** bananas, cacao, citrus, sugar. **Natural resources:** timber, fish, hydropower. **Crude oil reserves:** 6.7 mil bbls. **Arable land:** 3.1%. **Livestock:** cattle: 91,129; chickens: 1.5 mil; goats: 180; pigs: 17,038; sheep: 13,018. **Fish catch:** 14,642 metric tons. **Electricity prod.:** 215.5 mil kWh. **Labor force:** agric. 10.2%, industry 18.1%, services 71.7%.

Finance: Monetary unit: Dollar (BZD) (Sept. 2011: 2.03 = $1 U.S.). **GDP:** $2.7 bil; **per capita GDP:** $8,400; **GDP growth:** 2%. **Imports:** $740 mil; U.S. 34%, Mexico 12.9%, Cuba 8.6%, Guatemala 6.8%, Spain 6.1%, China 4.4%. **Exports:** $404 mil; U.S. 27.8%, UK 27%, Costa Rica 11.1%, Nigeria 4.4%, Côte d'Ivoire 4%. **Tourism:** $256 mil. **Budget:** $418 mil. **Total reserves less gold:** $218 mil. **CPI change:** 0.9%.

Transport: Motor vehicles: 93.3 vehicles per 1,000 pop. **Civil aviation:** 4 airports. **Chief ports:** Belize City, Big Creek.

Communications: TV sets: 445 per 1,000 pop. **Radios:** 590 per 1,000 pop. **Telephone lines:** 9.7 per 100 pop. **Internet:** 14 users per 100 pop.

Health: Life expect.: 66.5 male; 70.0 female. **Births:** 26.4 (per 1,000 pop.). **Deaths:** 5.9 (per 1,000 pop.). **Natural inc.:** 2.06%. **Infant mortality:** 22.0 (per 1,000 live births). **HIV rate:** 2.3%.

Education: Compulsory: ages 5-14. **Literacy:** 70.3%.

Major intl. organizations: UN (FAO, IBRD, ILO, IMF, WHO), Caricom, the Commonwealth, OAS, WTO.

Embassy: 2535 Massachusetts Ave. NW 20008; 332-9636.

Website: www.belize.gov.bz

Belize (formerly British Honduras) was Britain's last colony on the American mainland; independence was achieved Sept. 21, 1981. Relations with neighboring Guatemala, initially tense, have improved in recent years. Belize has become a center for drug trafficking between Colombia and the U.S.

Benin
Republic of Benin

People: Population: 9,325,032. **Age distrib.:** <15: 44.7%; 65+: 2.7%. **Pop. density:** 218.3 per sq mi, 84.3 per sq km. **Urban:** 42%. **Ethnic groups:** Fon & related 39%, Adja & related 15%, Yoruba & related 12%, Bariba & related 9%, Peulh & related 7%, Ottamari & related 6%, Yoa-Lokpa & related 4%, Dendi & related 3%. **Principal languages:** French (official), Fon, Yoruba, tribal languages. **Chief religions:** Christian 43%, Muslim 24%, Vodoun 17%.
Geography: Total area: 43,484 sq mi, 112,622 sq km; **Land area:** 42,711 sq mi, 110,622 sq km. **Location:** In W Africa on Gulf of Guinea. **Neighbors:** Togo on W; Burkina Faso, Niger on N; Nigeria on E. **Topography:** Most of Benin is flat and covered with dense vegetation. The coast is hot, humid, and rainy. **Capital:** Porto-Novo (official), 276,000; Cotonou (seat), 815,000.
Government: Type: Republic. **Head of state:** Pres. Boni Yayi; b. July 1, 1952; in office: Apr. 6, 2006. **Head of gov.:** Prime Min. Pascal Koupaki; b. 1951; in office: May 28, 2011. **Local divisions:** 12 departments. **Defense budget:** $53 mil. **Active troops:** 4,750.
Economy: Industries: textiles, food proc., constr. materials, cement. **Chief crops:** cotton, corn, cassava, yams, beans. **Natural resources:** oil, limestone, marble, timber. **Crude oil reserves:** 8 mil bbls. **Arable land:** 22.1%. **Livestock:** cattle: 2 mil; chickens: 16 mil; goats: 1.6 mil; pigs: 355,600; sheep: 810,300. **Fish catch:** 39,328 metric tons. **Electricity prod.:** 128 mil kWh. **Labor force:** NA.
Finance: Monetary unit: CFA BCEAO Franc (XOF) (Sept. 2011: 468.55 = $1 U.S.). **GDP:** $14 bil; **per capita GDP:** $1,500; **GDP growth:** 2.5%. **Imports:** $1.8 bil; China 35.8%, U.S. 7.3%, France 7.2%, Thailand 6.5%, Malaysia 5.5%, Netherlands 4.7%. **Exports:** $1.1 bil; India 26%, China 20.7%, Niger 6.7%, Nigeria 6.3%, Namibia 4%. **Tourism:** $131 mil. **Budget:** $1.7 bil. **Total reserves less gold:** $1.2 bil. **CPI change:** 2.3%.
Transport: Railways: 272 mi. **Motor vehicles:** 3.3 vehicles per 1,000 pop. **Civil aviation:** 80.8 mil pass.-mi; 1 airport. **Chief port:** Cotonou.
Communications: TV sets: 45 per 1,000 pop. **Radios:** 323 per 1,000 pop. **Telephone lines:** 1.5 per 100 pop. **Daily newspaper circ.:** 0.4 per 1,000 pop. **Internet:** 3.1 users per 100 pop.
Health: Life expect.: 58.6 male; 61.1 female. **Births:** 38.1 (per 1,000 pop.). **Deaths:** 9.0 (per 1,000 pop.). **Natural inc.:** 2.91%. **Infant mortality:** 61.6 (per 1,000 live births). **HIV rate:** 1.2%.
Education: Compulsory: ages 6-11. **Literacy:** 41.7%.
Major intl. organizations: UN (FAO, IBRD, ILO, IMF, WHO), AU, WTO.
Embassy: 2124 Kalorama Rd. NW 20008; 232-6656.
Website: www.gouv.bz
The Kingdom of Abomey, rising to power in wars with neighboring kingdoms in the 17th cent., came under French domination in the late 19th cent., and was incorporated into French West Africa by 1904. Under the name Dahomey, the country gained independence Aug. 1, 1960; it became Benin in 1975. In the fifth coup since independence Col. Ahmed Kerekou took power in 1972; two years later he declared a socialist state with a "Marxist-Leninist" philosophy. In Dec. 1989, Kerekou announced Marxism-Leninism would no longer be the state ideology.
In Mar. 1991, Kerekou lost to Nicéphore Soglo in Benin's first free presidential election in 30 years. Kerekou defeated Soglo in Mar. 1996 to reclaim the presidency. He won reelection in a runoff Mar. 22, 2001. Boni Yayi, an economist, won a presidential runoff vote, Mar. 19, 2006. He survived an apparent assassination attempt Mar. 15, 2007.
Benin, which in 2006 signed a 5-year, $307 mil aid deal with the U.S., received a visit from Pres. Bush Feb. 16, 2008. More than 100,000 people reportedly lost their savings when a fraudulent investment scheme linked to high government officials collapsed in mid-2010. Pres. Yayi won reelection to a second 5-year term Mar. 13, 2011.

Bhutan
Kingdom of Bhutan

People: Population: 708,427. **Age distrib.:** <15: 28.9%; 65+: 5.7%. **Pop. density:** 47.8 per sq mi, 18.5 per sq km. **Urban:** 34.7%. **Ethnic groups:** Bhote 50%, ethnic Nepalese 35%, indigenous or migrant tribes 15%. **Principal languages:** Sharchhopka, Dzongkha (official), Lhotshamkha. **Chief religions:** Lamaistic Buddhist 75%, Indian- & Nepalese-influenced Hinduism 25%.
Geography: Total area: 14,824 sq mi, 38,394 sq km; **Land area:** 14,824 sq mi, 38,394 sq km. **Location:** S Asia, in eastern Himalayan Mts. **Neighbors:** India on W (Sikkim) and S, China on N. **Topography:** Bhutan is comprised of very high mountains in the N, fertile valleys in the center, and thick forests in the Duar Plain in the S. **Capital:** Thimphu, 89,000.

Government: Type: Constitutional monarchy. **Head of state:** King Jigme Khesar Namgyal Wangchuk; b. Feb. 21, 1980; in office: Dec. 14, 2006. **Head of gov.:** Prime Min. Jigmi Y. Thinley; b. Sept. 9, 1952; in office: Apr. 9, 2008. **Local divisions:** 18 districts. **Defense budget/active troops:** NA.
Economy: Industries: cement, wood prods., processed fruits, alcoholic beverages, calcium carbide, tourism. **Chief crops:** rice, corn, root crops, citrus, foodgrains. **Natural resources:** timber, hydropower, gypsum, calcium carbonate. **Arable land:** 2.0%. **Livestock:** cattle: 326,017; chickens: 240,000; goats: 31,500; pigs: 36,000; sheep: 13,109. **Fish catch:** 226 metric tons. **Electricity prod.:** 7.1 bil kWh. **Labor force:** agric 43.7%, industry 39.1%, services 17.2%.
Finance: Monetary unit: Ngultrum (BTN) (Sept. 2011: 46.07 = $1 U.S.). **GDP:** $3.9 bil; **per capita GDP:** $5,500; **GDP growth:** 6.7%. **Imports** (2008): $533 mil; NA. **Exports** (2008): $513 mil; NA. **Tourism:** $35 mil. **Budget** (FY09/10): $588 mil (nearly three-fifths financed by India's govt.). **Total reserves less gold:** $1 bil. **CPI change:** 7%.
Transport: Civil aviation: 44.7 mil pass.-mi; 1 airport.
Communications: TV sets: 12 per 1,000 pop. **Radios:** 118 per 1,000 pop. **Telephone lines:** 3.6 per 100 pop. **Internet:** 13.6 users per 100 pop.
Health: Life expect.: 66.5 male; 68.2 female. **Births:** 19.1 (per 1,000 pop.). **Deaths:** 7.1 (per 1,000 pop.). **Natural inc.:** 1.20%. **Infant mortality:** 44.5 (per 1,000 live births). **HIV rate:** 0.2%.
Education: Compulsory ages: NA. **Literacy:** 52.8%.
Major intl. organizations: UN (FAO, IBRD, IMF, WHO), WTO (observer).
Permanent UN mission: 763 United Nations Plz., New York, NY 10017; (212) 490-9660.
Website: www.bhutan.gov.bt
The region came under Tibetan rule in the 16th cent. British influence grew in the 19th cent. A Buddhist monarchy was set up in 1907. According to a 1910 treaty, Britain guided Bhutan's external affairs, while the country remained internally self-governing. Upon independence, India assumed Britain's role in a 1949 revision of the treaty.
Isolated for much of its history, Bhutan has taken steps toward modernization. King Jigme Singye Wangchuk, in power since 1972, stepped down Dec. 14, 2006, in favor of his son, Jigme Khesar Namgyal Wangchuk. Multiparty parliamentary elections took place Mar. 24, 2008, and a new constitution was ratified in July.

Bolivia
Plurinational State of Bolivia

People: Population: 10,118,683. **Age distrib.:** <15: 34.6%; 65+: 4.6%. **Pop. density:** 24.2 per sq mi, 9.3 per sq km. **Urban:** 66.5%. **Ethnic groups:** Quechua 30%, mestizo (mixed white & Amerindian) 30%, Aymara 25%, white 15%. **Principal languages:** Spanish, Quechua, Aymara (all official). **Chief religions:** Roman Catholic 95%, Protestant (Evangelical Methodist) 5%.
Geography: Total area: 424,164 sq mi, 1,098,581 sq km; **Land area:** 418,265 sq mi, 1,083,301 sq km. **Location:** In W central South America, in the Andes Mts. (one of 2 landlocked countries in South America). **Neighbors:** Peru and Chile on W, Argentina and Paraguay on S, Brazil on E and N. **Topography:** The great central plateau, at an altitude of 12,000 ft, over 500 mi long, lies between two great cordilleras having 3 of the highest peaks in South America. Lake Titicaca, on Peruvian border, is highest lake in world on which steamboats ply (12,506 ft). The E central region has semitropical forests; the llanos, or Amazon-Chaco lowlands are in E. **Capital:** La Paz (admin.), 1,642,000; Sucre (legislative), 281,000. **Cities (urban aggl.):** Santa Cruz, 1,648,651.
Government: Type: Republic. **Head of state and gov.:** Pres. Juan Evo Morales Aima; b. Oct. 26, 1959; in office: Jan. 22, 2006. **Local divisions:** 9 departments. **Defense budget:** $357 mil. **Active troops:** 46,100.
Economy: Industries: mining, smelting, petroleum, food and beverages, tobacco, handicrafts, clothing. **Chief crops:** soybeans, coffee, coca, cotton, corn, sugarcane, rice, potatoes. **Natural resources:** nat. gas, petroleum, zinc, tungsten, antimony, silver, iron, lead, gold, timber, hydropower. **Crude oil reserves:** 465 mil bbls. **Other resources:** Timber. **Arable land:** 3.4%. **Livestock:** cattle: 8.1 mil; chickens: 83.9 mil; goats: 2 mil; pigs: 2.8 mil; sheep: 9.5 mil. **Fish catch:** 8,343 metric tons. **Electricity prod.:** 6 bil kWh. **Labor force:** agric. 40%, industry 17%, services 43%.
Finance: Monetary unit: Boliviano (BOB) (Sept. 2011: 7.01 = $1 U.S.). **GDP:** $47.9 bil; **per capita GDP:** $4,800; **GDP growth:** 4.2%. **Imports:** $5.4 bil; Brazil 26.6%, Argentina 16.8%, U.S. 12.5%, Peru 9.3%, Chile 8.3%. **Exports:** $7 bil; Brazil 39.3%, U.S. 13.2%, Peru 7.6%, Colombia 6.2%, Argentina 5.4%, Japan 5.3%. **Tourism:** $310 mil. **Budget:** $10 bil. **Total reserves less gold:** $8.1 bil. **Gold:** 1.1 mil oz t. **CPI change:** 2.5%.
Transport: Railways: 2,269 mi. **Motor vehicles:** 53.7 vehicles per 1,000 pop. **Civil aviation:** 1.2 bil pass.-mi; 16 airports. **Chief port:** Puerto Aguirre.
Communications: TV sets: 155 per 1,000 pop. **Radios:** 672 per 1,000 pop. **Telephone lines:** 8.5 per 100 pop. **Internet:** 20 users per 100 pop.

Health: Life expect.: 64.8 male; 70.4 female. **Births:** 24.7 (per 1,000 pop.). **Deaths:** 6.9 (per 1,000 pop.). **Natural inc.:** 1.79%. **Infant mortality:** 42.2 (per 1,000 live births). **HIV rate:** 0.2%. **Education:** Compulsory: ages 5-17. **Literacy:** 90.7%.

Major intl. organizations: UN (FAO, IBRD, ILO, IMF, WHO), OAS, WTO.

Embassy: 3014 Massachusetts Ave. NW 20008; 483-4410.

Website: www.bolivia.gov.bo

The Incas conquered the region's earlier Indian inhabitants in the 13th cent. Spanish rule began in the 1530s and lasted until Aug. 6, 1825. The country is named after Simon Bolivar, independence fighter.

In a series of wars, Bolivia lost its Pacific coast to Chile, the oil-bearing Chaco to Paraguay, and rubber-growing areas to Brazil, 1879-1935.

Economic unrest, especially among militant mine workers, has led to continuing political instability. A reformist government under Victor Paz Estenssoro, 1951-64, nationalized tin mines and attempted to improve conditions for the Indian majority but was overthrown by a military junta. A series of coups and countercoups continued until constitutional government was restored in 1982.

U.S. pressure on the government to reduce the country's coca output, the raw material for cocaine, has led to clashes between police and coca growers and increased anti-U.S. feeling among Bolivians. Gen. Hugo Banzer Suárez, who ruled as a dictator, 1971-78, later governed as president, 1997-2001.

After an inconclusive presidential election June 30, 2002, Congress Aug. 4 chose Gonzalo Sánchez de Lozada, a U.S.-educated mining executive, as head of state. He quit Oct. 17, 2003, after a month of antigovernment protests, led by Bolivian Indians, in which over 70 people died. His successor, Vice Pres. Carlos D. Mesa Gisbert, was embroiled in controversies over energy policy.

Juan Evo Morales Aima, a leftist and coca-farmer advocate, won the presidential election, Dec. 18, 2005. He nationalized the hydrocarbon sector, launched a land-redistribution program to benefit poor farmers, and tightened ties with Venezuela and Cuba; he faced resistance and demands for autonomy from leaders of Bolivia's relatively prosperous lowland provinces. Voters Jan. 25, 2009, approved a new constitution strengthening the rights of Bolivia's indigenous majority and increasing federal control over the country's natural resources. In national elections Dec. 6, Pres. Morales easily won a second term, and his Movement Toward Socialism consolidated its hold over Bolivia's legislature.

Bosnia and Herzegovina

People: Population: 4,622,163. **Age distrib.:** <15: 14%; 65+: 15%. **Pop. density:** 233.9 per sq mi, 90.3 per sq km. **Urban:** 48.6%. **Ethnic groups:** Bosniak 48%, Serb 37%, Croat 14%. **Principal languages:** Bosnian, Croatian (both official); Serbian. **Chief religions:** Muslim 40%, Orthodox 31%, Roman Catholic 15%.

Geography: Total area: 19,767 sq mi, 51,197 sq km; **Land area:** 19,763 sq mi, 51,187 sq km. **Location:** On Balkan Peninsula in SE Europe. **Neighbors:** Serbia, Montenegro on E and SE, Croatia on N and W. **Topography:** Hilly with some mountains. About 36% of the land is forested. **Capital:** Sarajevo, 392,000.

Government: Type: Federal republic. **Heads of state:** Collective presidency with rotating leadership. **Head of gov.:** Prime Min. Nikola Spiric; b. Sept. 4, 1956; in office: Jan. 11, 2007. **Local divisions:** Muslim-Croat Federation, divided into 10 cantons; Serbian-led region (Republika Srpska); internationally supervised Brcko district. **Defense budget:** $227 mil. **Active troops:** 10,577.

Economy: Industries: steel, coal, mining, vehicle assembly, textiles, tobacco prods., wooden furniture, ammunition, domestic appliances, oil refining. **Chief crops:** wheat, corn, fruits, vegetables. **Natural resources:** coal, iron ore, bauxite, copper, lead, zinc, chromite, cobalt, manganese, nickel, clay, gypsum, salt, sand, timber, hydropower. **Arable land:** 19.5%. **Livestock:** cattle: 457,743; chickens: 17.3 mil; goats: 70,604; pigs: 529,095; sheep: 1.1 mil. **Fish catch:** 9,625 metric tons. **Electricity prod.:** 12.7 bil kWh. **Labor force:** agric. 20.5%, industry 32.6%, services 47%.

Finance: Monetary unit: Convertible Balkan (BAM) (Sept. 2011: 1.40 = $1 U.S.). **GDP:** $30.3 bil; **per capita GDP:** $6,600; **GDP growth:** 0.8%. **Imports:** $9.2 bil; Croatia 22.1%, Germany 14%, Slovenia 13.4%, Italy 11.8%, Austria 6.6%, Hungary 5.7%. **Exports:** $4.8 bil; Croatia 19%, Slovenia 18.5%, Italy 16.8%, Germany 13.4%, Austria 10.2%. **Tourism:** $593 mil. **Budget:** $7.8 bil. **Total reserves less gold:** $4.4 bil. **CPI change:** NA.

Transport: Railways: 373 mi. **Civil aviation:** 69 mil pass.-mi; 7 airports. **Chief ports:** Bosanski Samac, Brcko.

Communications: TV sets: 282 per 1,000 pop. **Radios:** 251 per 1,000 pop. **Telephone lines:** 26.6 per 100 pop. **Internet:** 52 users per 100 pop.

Health: Life expect.: 75.3 male; 82.6 female. **Births:** 8.9 (per 1,000 pop.). **Deaths:** 8.8 (per 1,000 pop.). **Natural inc.:** 0.01%. **Infant mortality:** 8.7 (per 1,000 live births). **HIV rate:** NA. **Education:** Compulsory: ages 6-15. **Literacy:** 97.8%.

Major intl. organizations: UN (FAO, IBRD, ILO, IMF, WHO), OSCE, WTO (observer).

Embassy: 2109 E St. NW 20037; 337-1500.

Website: www.fbihvlada.gov.ba

Bosnia was ruled by Croatian kings c. 958 CE, and by Hungary 1000-1200. It became organized c. 1200 and later took control of Herzegovina. The kingdom disintegrated from 1391, with the southern part becoming the independent duchy Herzegovina. It was conquered by Turks in 1463 and made a Turkish province. The area was placed under control of Austria-Hungary in 1878 and made part of the province of Bosnia and Herzegovina, which was formally annexed to Austria-Hungary, 1908. Bosnia became a province of Yugoslavia in 1918. It was reunited with Herzegovina as a federated republic in the 1946 Yugoslav constitution.

Bosnia and Herzegovina declared sovereignty Oct. 15, 1991. A referendum for independence was passed Feb. 29, 1992. Ethnic Serbs' opposition to the referendum spurred violent clashes and bombings. The U.S. and EU recognized the republic Apr. 7. Fierce three-way fighting continued between Bosnia's Serbs, Muslims, and Croats. Serb forces massacred thousands of Bosnian Muslims and engaged in ethnic cleansing, expelling Muslims and other non-Serbs from areas under Bosnian Serb control. The capital, Sarajevo, was surrounded and besieged by Bosnian Serb forces. Muslims and Croats in Bosnia reached a cease-fire Feb. 23, 1994, and signed an accord, Mar. 18, to create a Muslim-Croat confederation in Bosnia. However, by mid-1994, Bosnian Serbs controlled over 70% of the country.

As fighting continued in 1995, the balance of power began to shift toward the Muslim-Croat alliance. Massive NATO air strikes at Bosnian Serb targets beginning Aug. 30 triggered a new round of peace talks, and the siege of Sarajevo was lifted Sept. 15. The new talks produced an agreement in principle to create autonomous regions within Bosnia, with the Serb region (Republika Srpska) constituting 49% of the country. A Croat-Muslim offensive in Sept. recaptured significant territory, leaving Bosnian Serbs in control of approximately half that percentage.

A peace agreement initialed in Dayton, Ohio, Nov. 21, 1995, was signed in Paris, Dec. 14, by leaders of Bosnia, Croatia, and Serbia. Some 60,000 NATO troops (about 20,000 from the U.S.) moved in to police the accord. Meanwhile, a UN tribunal began bringing charges against suspected war criminals. Elections were held Sept. 14, 1996, for a 3-person collective presidency, for seats in a federal parliament, and for regional offices. In Dec. a revamped NATO "stabilization force" (SFOR) of over 30,000 members (more than 8,000 from the U.S.) received an 18-month mandate, which was later extended.

In a landmark verdict Aug. 2, 2001, the UN tribunal found Radislav Krstic, a Bosnian Serb general, guilty in connection with the genocide of thousands of Muslims at Srebrenica in 1995. A European Union peacekeeping force (EUFOR), with 7,000 members, assumed responsibility from SFOR, Dec. 2, 2004. Accused of complicity in the Sarajevo and Srebrenica atrocities, former Bosnian Serb leader Radovan Karadzic was arrested in Serbia, July 21, 2008, and handed over to the UN tribunal at The Hague, Netherlands. Also extradited to The Hague was Ratko Mladic, the former Bosnian Serb military commander accused of directing the Srebrenica massacre, who was arrested in Serbia May 26, 2011. As the security situation in Bosnia improved, EUFOR strength dropped to about 1,600 troops as of Aug. 2011.

Botswana

Republic of Botswana

People: Population: 2,065,398. **Age distrib.:** <15: 33.9%; 65+: 3.9%. **Pop. density:** 9.4 per sq mi, 3.6 per sq km. **Urban:** 61.1%. **Ethnic groups:** Tswana or Setswana 79%, Kalanga 11%, Basarwa 3%, other (incl. Kgalagadi & white) 7%. **Principal languages:** Setswana, Kalanga, Sekgalagadi, English (official). **Chief religions:** Christian 72%, Badimo 6%, none 21%.

Geography: Total area: 224,607 sq mi, 581,730 sq km; **Land area:** 218,816 sq mi, 566,730 sq km. **Location:** In southern Africa. **Neighbors:** Namibia on N and W, South Africa on S, Zimbabwe on NE; Botswana claims border with Zambia on N. **Topography:** The Kalahari Desert, supporting nomadic Bushmen and wildlife, spreads over SW; there are swamplands and farming areas in N, and roiling plains in E where livestock are grazed. **Capital:** Gaborone, 196,000.

Government: Type: Parliamentary republic. **Head of state and gov.:** Pres. Seretse Khama Ian Khama; b. Feb. 27, 1953; in office: Apr. 1, 2008. **Local divisions:** 10 districts, 4 town councils. **Defense budget:** $628 mil. **Active troops:** 9,000.

Economy: Industries: diamonds, copper, nickel, salt, soda ash, potash, coal, iron ore, silver. **Chief crops:** sorghum, maize, millet, beans, sunflowers, groundnuts. **Natural resources:** diamonds, copper, nickel, salt, soda ash, potash, coal, iron ore, silver. **Arable land:** 0.4%. **Livestock:** cattle: 2.5 mil; chickens: 5 mil; goats: 2 mil; pigs: 13,302; sheep: 169,603. **Fish catch:** 86 metric tons. **Electricity prod.:** 593 mil kWh. **Labor force:** NA.

Finance: Monetary unit: Pula (BWP) (Sept. 2011: 6.81 = $1 U.S.). **GDP:** $28.5 bil; **per capita GDP:** $14,000; **GDP growth:** 8.6%. **Imports:** $4.5 bil; NA. **Exports:** $4.4 bil; NA. **Tourism:** $452 mil. **Budget:** $5.9 bil. **Total reserves less gold:** $7.9 bil. **CPI change:** 6.9%.

Transport: Railways: 552 mi. **Motor vehicles:** 123.3 vehicles per 1,000 pop. **Civil aviation:** 70.2 mil pass.-mi; 9 airports.

Communications: TV sets: 44 per 1,000 pop. **Radios:** 734 per 1,000 pop. **Telephone lines:** 6.9 per 100 pop. **Daily newspaper circ.:** 41.5 per 1,000 pop. **Internet:** 6 users per 100 pop.

Health: Life expect.: 58.8 male; 57.3 female. **Births:** 22.3 (per 1,000 pop.). **Deaths:** 10.6 (per 1,000 pop.). **Natural inc.:** 1.17%. **Infant mortality:** 11.1 (per 1,000 live births). **HIV rate:** 24.8%.

Education: Compulsory: ages 6-15. **Literacy:** 84.1%.

Major intl. organizations: UN (FAO, IBRD, ILO, IMF, WHO), AU, the Commonwealth, WTO.

Embassy: 1531-1533 New Hampshire Ave. NW 20036; 244-4990.

Website: www.gov.bw

First inhabited by Bushmen, then Bantus, the region became the British protectorate of Bechuanaland in 1886. The country became fully independent Sept. 30, 1966, as Botswana.

Cattle raising and mining (diamonds, copper, nickel) have contributed to economic growth; the economy is closely tied to South Africa's. According to the UN, nearly 25% of the adult population has HIV/AIDS. Pres. Festus Mogae transferred power Apr. 1, 2008, to Seretse Khama Ian Khama, son of Botswana's independence leader and first president (1966-80), Sir Seretse Khama. In power since independence, the Botswana Democratic Party dominated national elections Oct. 16, 2009, and Ian Khama was sworn in for a full term Oct. 20.

Brazil
Federative Republic of Brazil

People: Population: 203,429,773. **Age distrib.:** <15: 26.2%; 65+: 6.7%. **Pop. density:** 62.3 per sq mi, 24 per sq km. **Urban:** 86.5%. **Ethnic groups:** white 54%, mixed white & black) 39%, black 6%. **Principal languages:** Portuguese (official), Spanish, minor Amerindian languages. **Chief religions:** Roman Catholic (nominal) 74%, Protestant 15%, Spiritualist 1%, none 7%.

Geography: Total area: 3,287,612 sq mi, 8,514,877 sq km; **Land area:** 3,266,199 sq mi, 8,459,417 sq km. **Location:** Occupies E half of South America. **Neighbors:** French Guiana, Suriname, Guyana, Venezuela on N; Colombia, Peru, Bolivia, Paraguay, on W; Argentina, Uruguay on S. **Topography:** Brazil's Atlantic coastline stretches 4,603 mi. In N is the heavily wooded Amazon basin covering half the country. Its network of rivers is navigable for 15,814 mi. The Amazon itself flows 2,093 mi in Brazil, all navigable. The NE region is semiarid scrubland, heavily settled and poor. The S central region, favored by climate and resources, has almost half of the population, produces 75% of farm goods and 80% of industrial output. The narrow coastal belt includes most of the major cities. Almost the entire country has a tropical or semitropical climate. **Capital:** Brasília, 3,789,000. **Cities (urban aggl.):** São Paulo, 20,262,493; Rio de Janeiro, 11,949,619; Belo Horizonte, 5,852,358.

Government: Type: Federal republic. **Head of state and gov.:** Pres. Dilma Rousseff; b. Dec. 14, 1947; in office: Jan. 1, 2011. **Local divisions:** 26 states, 1 federal district (Brasília). **Defense budget:** $34.7 bil. **Active troops:** 318,480.

Economy: Industries: textiles, shoes, chemicals, cement, lumber, iron ore, tin, steel, aircraft, motor vehicles and parts. **Chief crops:** coffee, soybeans, wheat, rice, corn, sugarcane, cocoa, citrus. **Natural resources:** bauxite, gold, iron ore, manganese, nickel, phosphates, platinum, tin, rare earth elements, uranium, petroleum hydropower, timber. **Crude oil reserves:** 12.9 bil bbls. **Arable land:** 7.2%. **Livestock:** cattle: 205.3 mil; chickens: 1.2 bil; goats: 9.2 mil; pigs: 38 mil; sheep: 16.8 mil. **Fish catch:** 1.2 mil metric tons. **Electricity prod.** (2009): 461.1 bil kWh. **Labor force:** agric. 20%, industry 14%, services 66%.

Finance: Monetary unit: Real (BRL) (Sept. 2011: 1.66 = $1 U.S.). **GDP:** $2.2 tril; **per capita GDP:** $10,800; **GDP growth:** 7.5%. **Imports:** $187.7 bil; U.S. 16.1%, China 12.6%, Argentina 8.8%, Germany 7.7%, Japan 4.3%. **Exports:** $199.7 bil; China 12.5%, U.S. 10.5%, Argentina 8.4%, Netherlands 5.4%, Germany 4.1%. **Tourism:** $5.9 bil. **Budget:** $552.6 bil. **Total reserves less gold:** $287.1 bil. **Gold:** 1.1 mil oz t. **CPI change:** 5%.

Transport: Railways: 17,733 mi. **Motor vehicles:** 149.2 vehicles per 1,000 pop. **Civil aviation:** 46 bil pass.-mi; 726 airports. **Chief ports:** Ilha Grande, Paranaguá, Rio Grande, Santos, São Sebastião, Tubarão.

Communications: TV sets: 279 per 1,000 pop. **Radios:** 255 per 1,000 pop. **Telephone lines:** 21.6 per 100 pop. **Daily newspaper circ.:** 35.5 per 1,000 pop. **Internet:** 40.7 users per 100 pop.

Health: Life expect.: 69.0 male; 76.3 female. **Births:** 17.8 (per 1,000 pop.). **Deaths:** 6.4 (per 1,000 pop.). **Natural inc.:** 1.14%. **Infant mortality:** 21.2 (per 1,000 live births). **HIV rate:** NA.

Education: Compulsory: ages 7-14. **Literacy:** 90%.

Major intl. organizations: UN and most of its specialized agencies, OAS, WTO.

Embassy: 3006 Massachusetts Ave. NW 20008; 238-2700.

Website: www.brasil.gov.br

Pedro Alvares Cabral, a Portuguese navigator, is generally credited as the first European to reach Brazil, in 1500. The country was thinly settled by various Indian tribes. Only a few have survived to the present, mostly in the Amazon basin.

In the next centuries, Portuguese colonists gradually pushed inland, bringing along large numbers of African slaves. (Slavery was not abolished until 1888.) The King of Portugal, fleeing

before Napoleon's army, moved the seat of government to Brazil in 1808. Brazil thereupon became a kingdom under Dom Joao VI. After Joao VI returned to Portugal, his son Pedro proclaimed the independence of Brazil, Sept. 7, 1822, and was crowned emperor. The second emperor, Dom Pedro II, was deposed in 1889, and a republic proclaimed, called the United States of Brazil. In 1967 the country was renamed the Federative Republic of Brazil.

A military junta took control in 1930; dictatorial power was assumed by Getulio Vargas, until finally forced out by the military in 1945. A democratic regime prevailed 1945-64, during which time the capital was moved from Rio de Janeiro to Brasília. Military-backed governments ruled Brazil for the next 20 years. Censorship was imposed, and much of the opposition was suppressed amid charges of torture.

Brazil became the leading industrial power of Latin America by the 1970s, while agricultural output soared. By the 1990s, Brazil had one of the world's largest economies; income was poorly distributed, however, and more than one out of four Brazilians continued to survive on less than $1 a day. Despite protective environmental legislation, development has destroyed much of the Amazon ecosystem.

Democratic presidential elections were held in 1985 as the nation returned to civilian rule. Fernando Collor de Mello was elected president in Dec. 1989. In Sept. 1992, Collor was impeached for corruption. He resigned on Dec. 29 as his trial was beginning, and Itamar Franco, who had been acting president, was sworn in as president. In elections held on Oct. 3, 1994, Fernando Henrique Cardoso was elected president. Reelected Oct. 4, 1998, he guided Brazil through a series of financial crises.

A new civil code guaranteeing legal equality for women was enacted Aug. 15, 2001. The IMF approved a $30 bil loan to Brazil Aug. 7, 2002; by then, Brazil's debt already exceeded $260 bil. Luiz Inácio Lula da Silva, a union leader and reformer, won a presidential runoff Oct. 27, 2002, with 61% of the vote. Brazil's space program suffered a setback when a rocket exploded on its launchpad Aug. 22, 2003, killing 21 people; the country successfully launched its first rocket into space Oct. 23, 2004.

A top aide to Pres. Lula resigned June 16, 2005, amid allegations the ruling party bribed legislators in exchange for votes; despite this and other scandals, the highly popular Lula won a second presidential term Oct. 29, 2006. The nation, which already meets many of its energy needs through biofuels, reported huge new offshore oil finds in 2007-08. The International Olympic Committee Oct. 2, 2009, chose Rio de Janeiro to host the 2016 Olympic Games. Lula's former chief of staff, Dilma Rousseff, won a runoff election Oct. 31, 2010, with 56% of the vote; she took office as Brazil's first woman president Jan. 1, 2011.

Brunei
Brunei Darussalam

People: Population: 401,890. **Age distrib.:** <15: 25.5%; 65+: 3.5%. **Pop. density:** 197.7 per sq mi, 76.3 per sq km. **Urban:** 75.7%. **Ethnic groups:** Malay 66%, Chinese 11%, indigenous 3%. **Principal languages:** Malay (official), English, Chinese. **Chief religions:** Muslim (official) 67%, Buddhist 13%, Christian 10%, other (incl. indigenous beliefs) 10%.

Geography: Total area: 2,226 sq mi, 5,765 sq km; **Land area:** 2,033 sq mi, 5,265 sq km. **Location:** In SE Asia, on the N coast of the island of Borneo; it is surrounded on its landward side by the Malaysian state of Sarawak. **Topography:** Brunei has a narrow coastal plain, with mountains in E, hilly lowlands in W. There are swamps in W and NE. Climate is tropical. **Capital:** Bandar Seri Begawan, 22,000.

Government: Type: Independent sultanate. **Head of state and gov.:** Sultan Sir Muda Hassanal Bolkiah Mu'izzadin Waddaulah; b. July 15, 1946; in office: Jan. 1, 1984 (sultan since Oct. 5, 1967). **Local divisions:** 4 districts. **Defense budget:** $372 mil. **Active troops:** 7,000.

Economy: Industries: petroleum, petroleum refining, liquefied nat. gas, constr. **Chief crops:** rice, vegetables, fruits. **Natural resources:** petroleum, nat. gas, timber. **Crude oil reserves:** 1.1 bil bbls. **Arable land:** 0.6%. **Livestock:** cattle: 1,000; chickens: 16 mil; goats: 3,000; pigs: 1,300; sheep: 3,800. **Fish catch:** 2,791 metric tons. **Electricity prod.:** 3.2 bil kWh. **Labor force:** agric. 4.2%, industry 62.8%, services 33%.

Finance: Monetary unit: Dollar (BND) (Sept. 2011: 1.21 = $1 U.S.). **GDP:** $20.4 bil; **per capita GDP:** $51,600; **GDP growth:** 4.1%. **Imports** (2008 est.): $2.6 bil; Singapore 37.1%, Malaysia 19%, Japan 7%, China 6%, Thailand 5%, U.S. 4.3%, UK 4.1%. **Exports** (2008): $10.7 bil; Japan 46.8%, South Korea 13.7%, Indonesia 9%, Australia 8.9%, India 6.9%, New Zealand 4.6%. **Tourism:** $254 mil. **Budget** (2008 est.): $4 bil. **Total reserves less gold:** $1.6 bil. **CPI change:** NA.

Transport: Motor vehicles: 279.6 vehicles per 1,000 pop. **Civil aviation:** 2.1 bil pass.-mi; 2 airports. **Chief ports:** Lumut, Muara, Seria.

Communications: TV sets: 629 per 1,000 pop. **Radios:** 300 per 1,000 pop. **Telephone lines:** 20 per 100 pop. **Daily newspaper circ.:** 68.4 per 1,000 pop. **Internet:** 50 users per 100 pop.

Health: Life expect.: 73.9 male; 78.5 female. **Births:** 17.9 (per 1,000 pop.). **Deaths:** 3.4 (per 1,000 pop.). **Natural inc.:** 1.45%. **Infant mortality:** 11.5 (per 1,000 live births). **HIV rate:** NA.

Education: Compulsory: ages 6-14. **Literacy:** 95.3%.

Major intl. organizations: UN and some of its specialized agencies, APEC, ASEAN, the Commonwealth, WTO.

Embassy: 3520 International Ct. NW 20008; 237-1838.

Website: www.gov.bn

The Sultanate of Brunei was a powerful state in the early 16th cent., with authority over all of the island of Borneo as well as parts of the Sulu Islands and the Philippines. In 1888, a treaty placed the state under the protection of Great Britain.

Brunei became a fully sovereign and independent state on Jan. 1, 1984. Much of the country's oil wealth has been squandered by members of the royal family.

Bulgaria
Republic of Bulgaria

People: Population: 7,093,635. **Age distrib.:** <15: 13.9%; 65+: 18.2%. **Pop. density:** 169.3 per sq mi, 65.4 per sq km. **Urban:** 71.5%. **Ethnic groups:** Bulgarian 84%, Turk 9%, Roma 5%, other (incl. Macedonian, Armenian, Tatar, Circassian) 2%. **Principal languages:** Bulgarian (official), Turkish, Roma. **Chief religions:** Bulgarian Orthodox 83%, Muslim 12%, other Christian 1%.

Geography: Total area: 42,811 sq mi, 110,879 sq km; **Land area:** 41,888 sq mi, 108,489 sq km. **Location:** SE Europe, in E Balkan Peninsula on Black Sea. **Neighbors:** Romania on N; Serbia, Macedonia on W; Greece, Turkey on S. **Topography:** The Stara Planina (Balkan) Mts. stretch E-W across the center of the country, with the Danubian plain on N, the Rhodope Mts. on SW, and Thracian Plain on SE. **Capital:** Sofia, 1,192,000.

Government: Type: Republic. **Head of state:** Pres. Georgi Parvanov; b. June 28, 1957; in office: Jan. 22, 2002. **Head of gov.:** Prime Min. Boyko Borisov; b. June 13, 1959; in office: July 27, 2009. **Local divisions:** 28 provinces. **Defense budget:** $609 mil. **Active troops:** 31,315.

Economy: Industries: utilities; food, beverages, tobacco. **Chief crops:** vegetables, fruits, tobacco, wine grapes, wheat, barley, sunflowers, sugar beets. **Natural resources:** bauxite, copper, lead, zinc, coal, timber. **Crude oil reserves:** 15 mil bbls. **Arable land:** 28.9%. **Livestock:** cattle: 564,904; chickens: 15.8 mil; goats: 429,834; pigs: 783,649; sheep: 1.5 mil. **Fish catch:** 15,701 metric tons. **Electricity prod.:** 41.7 bil kWh. **Labor force:** agric. 7.1%, industry 35.2%, services 57.7%.

Finance: Monetary unit: Lev (BGN) (Sept. 2011: 1.40 = $1 U.S.). **GDP:** $96.8 bil; **per capita GDP:** $13,500; **GDP growth:** 0.2%. **Imports:** $22.8 bil; Russia 13.4%, Germany 12.2%, Italy 7.7%, Greece 6.1%, Romania 5.6%, Turkey 5.4%, Ukraine 4.8%, Austria 4.1%. **Exports:** $19.3 bil; Germany 11.3%, Greece 9.6%, Italy 9.3%, Romania 8.6%, Turkey 7.3%, Belgium 5.7%, France 4.5%. **Tourism:** $3.6 bil. **Budget:** $17.5 bil. **Total reserves less gold:** $15.4 bil. **Gold:** 1.3 mil oz t. **CPI change:** 2.4%.

Transport: Railways: 2,579 mi. **Motor vehicles:** 454.1 vehicles per 1,000 pop. **Civil aviation:** 775.5 mil pass.-mi; 130 airports. **Chief ports:** Burgas, Varna.

Communications: TV sets: 429 per 1,000 pop. **Radios:** 553 per 1,000 pop. **Telephone lines:** 29.4 per 100 pop. **Daily newspaper circ.:** 79 per 1,000 pop. **Internet:** 46.2 users per 100 pop.

Health: Life expect.: 70.0 male; 77.4 female. **Births:** 9.3 (per 1,000 pop.). **Deaths:** 14.3 (per 1,000 pop.). **Natural inc.:** –0.50%. **Infant mortality:** 16.7 (per 1,000 live births). **HIV rate:** 0.1%.

Education: Compulsory: ages 7-14. **Literacy:** 98.3%.

Major intl. organizations: UN (FAO, IBRD, ILO, IMF, WHO), EU, NATO, OSCE, WTO.

Embassy: 1621 22nd St. NW 20008; 387-0174.

Website: www.government.bg

Bulgaria was settled by Slavs in the 6th cent. Turkic Bulgars arrived in the 7th cent., merged with the Slavs, became Christians by the 9th cent., and set up powerful empires in the 10th and 12th centuries. Ottomans prevailed in 1396 and ruled for nearly 500 years.

An 1876 revolt led to an independent kingdom in 1908. Bulgaria expanded after the first Balkan War but lost its Aegean coastline in WWI, when it sided with Germany. Bulgaria joined the Axis in WWII but withdrew in 1944. Communists took power with Soviet aid; monarchy was abolished Sept. 8, 1946.

On Nov. 10, 1989, Communist Party leader and head of state Todor Zhivkov, who had held power for 35 years, resigned. In Jan. 1990, Parliament voted to revoke the constitutionally guaranteed dominant role of the Communist Party. A new constitution took effect July 13, 1991.

Bulgaria's deteriorating economy provoked nationwide strikes and demonstrations in Jan. 1997. The Union of Democratic Forces, an anti-Communist group, won national elections on Apr. 19. The UDF lost the elections of June 17, 2001, to a party headed by the former king, Simeon II. Socialist opposition leader Georgi Parvanov won a presidential runoff vote Nov. 18, 2001; he was reelected Oct. 29, 2006.

Bulgaria became a full member of NATO, Apr. 2, 2004, and entered the European Union, Jan. 1, 2007. Boyko Borisov, mayor of Sofia, became prime minister after his center-right party won parliamentary elections July 5, 2009.

Burkina Faso

People: Population: 16,751,455. **Age distrib.:** <15: 45.8%; 65+: 2.5%. **Pop. density:** 158.5 per sq mi, 61.2 per sq km. **Urban:** 25.7%. **Ethnic groups:** Mossi 40%+, other (incl. Gurunsi, Senufo, Lobi, Bobo, Mande, Fulani) approx. 60%. **Principal languages:** French (official), native African Sudanic-family languages. **Chief religions:** Muslim 61%, Catholic 19%, animist 15%, Protestant 4%.

Geography: Total area: 105,869 sq mi, 274,200 sq km; **Land area:** 105,715 sq mi, 273,800 sq km. **Location:** In W Africa, S of the Sahara. **Neighbors:** Mali on NW; Niger on NE; Benin, Togo, Ghana, Côte d'Ivoire on S. **Topography:** Landlocked Burkina Faso is in the savanna region of W Africa. The N is arid, hot, and thinly populated. **Capital:** Ouagadougou, 1,777,000.

Government: Type: Republic. **Head of state:** Pres. Blaise Compaoré; b. Feb. 3, 1951; in office: Oct. 15, 1987. **Head of gov.:** Prime Min. Luc Adolphe Tiao; b. June 4, 1954; in office: Apr. 18, 2011. **Local divisions:** 45 provinces. **Defense budget:** $97 mil. **Active troops:** 11,200.

Economy: Industries: cotton lint, beverages, agric. proc., soap, cigarettes, textiles, gold. **Chief crops:** cotton, peanuts, shea nuts, sesame, sorghum, millet. **Natural resources:** manganese, limestone, marble, gold, phosphates, pumice, salt. **Arable land:** 21.6%. **Livestock:** cattle: 9.5 mil; chickens: 37 mil; goats: 12 mil; pigs: 2 mil; sheep: 7.9 mil. **Fish catch:** 12,075 metric tons. **Electricity prod.** (2009): 664.4 mil kWh. **Labor force:** agric. 90%, industry and services 10%.

Finance: Monetary unit: CFA BCEAO Franc (XOF) (Sept. 2011: 468.55 = $1 U.S.). **GDP:** $20 bil; **per capita GDP:** $1,200; **GDP growth:** 5.8%. **Imports:** $1.5 bil; Côte d'Ivoire 24.7%, France 19.8%, Togo 5%. **Exports:** $991 mil; China 21.2%, Singapore 15%, Belgium 11.4%, Ghana 6.1%, Denmark 5.1%, Niger 4.6%, Thailand 4%. **Tourism:** NA. **Budget:** $2.3 bil. **Total reserves less gold:** $1.1 bil. **CPI change:** –0.8%.

Transport: Railways: 386 mi. **Motor vehicles:** 10.2 vehicles per 1,000 pop. **Civil aviation:** 25.5 mil pass.-mi; 2 airports.

Communications: TV sets: 19 per 1,000 pop. **Radios:** 111 per 1,000 pop. **Telephone lines:** 0.9 per 100 pop. **Internet:** 1.4 users per 100 pop.

Health: Life expect.: 51.8 male; 55.7 female. **Births:** 43.6 (per 1,000 pop.). **Deaths:** 12.7 (per 1,000 pop.). **Natural inc.:** 3.09%. **Infant mortality:** 81.4 (per 1,000 live births). **HIV rate:** 1.2%.

Education: Compulsory: ages 6-15. **Literacy:** 28.7%.

Major intl. organizations: UN and many of its specialized agencies, AU, WTO.

Embassy: 2340 Massachusetts Ave. NW 20008; 332-5577.

Website: www.gouvernement.gov.bf or www.burkinaembassy-usa.org

The Mossi people entered the area in the 11th to 13th centuries. Their kingdoms ruled until they were defeated by the Mali and Songhai empires.

French control came by 1896, but Upper Volta (renamed Burkina Faso on Aug. 4, 1984) was not established as a separate territory until 1947. Full independence came Aug. 5, 1960, and a pro-French government was elected. The military seized power in 1980. A 1987 coup established the current regime, which instituted a multiparty system in the early 1990s. Pres. Blaise Compaoré won reelection, Nov. 13, 2005, with 80% of the vote. The country, one of the world's poorest, depends heavily on foreign aid. Compaoré revamped his cabinet after antigovernment protests Mar.-Apr. 2011 by soldiers, students, merchants, and police.

Burma
See Myanmar.

Burundi
Republic of Burundi

People: Population: 10,216,190. **Age distrib.:** <15: 46%; 65+: 2.5%. **Pop. density:** 1,030.4 per sq mi, 397.8 per sq km. **Urban:** 11%. **Ethnic groups:** Hutu (Bantu) 85%, Tutsi (Hamitic) 14%, Twa (Pygmy) 1%. **Principal languages:** Kirundi, French (both official), Swahili. **Chief religions:** Christian 67%, indigenous beliefs 23%, Muslim 10%.

Geography: Total area: 10,745 sq mi, 27,830 sq km; **Land area:** 9,915 sq mi, 25,680 sq km. **Location:** In central Africa. **Neighbors:** Rwanda on N, Dem. Rep. of the Congo (formerly Zaire) on W, Tanzania on E and S. **Topography:** Much of the country is grassy highland, with mountains reaching 8,900 ft. The southernmost source of the White Nile is located in Burundi. Lake Tanganyika is the second deepest lake in the world. **Capital:** Bujumbura, 455,000.

Government: Type: Republic. **Head of state and gov.:** Pres. Pierre Nkurunziza; b. Dec. 18, 1963; in office: Aug. 26, 2005. **Local divisions:** 16 provinces. **Defense budget:** $57 mil. **Active troops:** 20,000.

Economy: Industries: light consumer goods, assembly of imported components, public works constr., food proc. **Chief crops:** coffee, cotton, tea, corn, sorghum, sweet potatoes, bananas, manioc. **Natural resources:** nickel, uranium, rare earth oxides, peat, cobalt, copper, platinum, vanadium, hydropower. **Arable land:** 35.0%. **Livestock:** cattle: 553,538; chickens: 5 mil;

goats: 1.7 mil; pigs: 202,926; sheep: 291,522. **Fish catch:** 17,900 metric tons. **Electricity prod.:** 208 mil kWh. **Labor force:** agric. 93.6%, industry 2.3%, services 4.1%.

Finance: Monetary unit: Franc (BIF) (Sept. 2011: 1,231.00 = $1 U.S.). **GDP:** $3.4 bil; **per capita GDP:** $300; **GDP growth:** 3.9%. **Imports:** $336 mil; Saudi Arabia 15.4%, Belgium 10.2%, China 9.8%, Uganda 7.9%, Kenya 6.9%, France 4.9%, Germany 4%. **Exports:** $71 mil; Germany 26%, Belgium 11.2%, Sweden 10.8%, Pakistan 7.6%, U.S. 4.6%. **Tourism:** NA. **Budget:** $476.2 mil. **Total reserves less gold:** $330.7 mil. **Gold:** 961 oz t. **CPI change:** 6.4%.

Transport: Motor vehicles: 5.9 vehicles per 1,000 pop. **Civil aviation:** 1 airport. **Chief port:** Bujumbura.

Communications: TV sets: 36 per 1,000 pop. **Radios:** 166 per 1,000 pop. **Telephone lines:** 0.4 per 100 pop. **Internet:** 2.1 users per 100 pop.

Health: Life expect.: 57.1 male; 60.5 female. **Births:** 41.0 (per 1,000 pop.). **Deaths:** 9.6 (per 1,000 pop.). **Natural inc.:** 3.14%. **Infant mortality:** 61.8 (per 1,000 live births). **HIV rate:** 3.3%.

Education: Compulsory: ages 7-12. **Literacy:** 66.6%.

Major intl. organizations: UN (FAO, IBRD, ILO, IMF, WHO), AU, WTO.

Embassy: 2233 Wisconsin Ave. NW, Ste. 212, 20007; 342-2574. **Website:** www.burundi-gov.bi or www.burundiembassy-usa.org

The pygmy Twa were the first inhabitants, followed by Bantu Hutus, who were conquered in the 16th cent. by the Tutsi (Watusi), probably from Ethiopia. Under German control in 1899, the area fell to Belgium in 1916, which exercised successively a League of Nations mandate and UN trusteeship over Ruanda-Urundi (now the two countries of Rwanda and Burundi). Burundi became independent July 1, 1962.

An unsuccessful Hutu rebellion in 1972-73 left 10,000 Tutsi and 150,000 Hutu dead. Over 100,000 Hutu fled to Tanzania and Zaire (now Congo). In the 1980s, Burundi's Tutsi-dominated regime pledged itself to ethnic reconciliation and democratic reform. In the nation's first democratic presidential election, in June 1993, a Hutu, Melchior Ndadaye, was elected. He was killed in an attempted coup, Oct. 21, 1993. At least 150,000 Burundians died as a result of ethnic conflict during the next three years. Pres. Cyprien Ntaryamira, elected Jan. 1994, was killed with the president of Rwanda in a mysterious plane crash, Apr. 6. The incident sparked massive carnage in Rwanda; violence in Burundi, initially far more limited, intensified in 1995. Ethnic strife continued after a military coup, July 25, 1996. Former South African Pres. Nelson Mandela mediated peace talks from Dec. 1999; most warring groups signed a draft peace treaty in Arusha, Tanzania, Aug. 28, 2000. Coup attempts were suppressed Apr. 18 and July 23, 2001. A power-sharing government headed by Pierre Buyoya was sworn in Nov. 1, 2001, but clashes with rebels continued.

Domitien Ndayizeye, a Hutu, became president Apr. 30, 2003. The UN Security Council authorized, May 21, 2004, a 5,650-member peacekeeping force (ONUB) for Burundi. Approval of a power-sharing constitution by referendum, Feb. 28, 2005, paved the way for local and parliamentary elections. Pierre Nkurunziza, former leader of a Hutu rebel group, became president Aug. 26, 2005. ONUB was succeeded, Jan. 1, 2007, by the UN Integrated Office in Burundi (BINUB). Under a reconciliation accord reached Dec. 4, 2008, remaining Hutu rebels began to disarm and demobilize. Candidates opposing Nkurunziza dropped out of the June 28, 2010, presidential election, claiming the vote was rigged.

Cambodia
Kingdom of Cambodia

People: Population: 14,701,717. **Age distrib.:** <15: 32.2%; 65+: 3.8%. **Pop. density:** 215.7 per sq mi, 83.3 per sq km. **Urban:** 20.1%. **Ethnic groups:** Khmer 90%, Vietnamese 5%, Chinese 1%. **Principal languages:** Khmer (official), French, English. **Chief religions:** Buddhist (official) 96%, Muslim 2%.

Geography: Total area: 69,898 sq mi, 181,035 sq km; **Land area:** 68,153 sq mi, 176,515 sq km. **Location:** SE Asia, on Indochina Peninsula. **Neighbors:** Thailand on W and N, Laos on NE, Vietnam on E. **Topography:** The central area, formed by the Mekong R. basin and Tonle Sap lake, is level. Hills and mountains are in SE, a long escarpment separates the country from Thailand on NW. 76% of the area is forested. **Capital:** Phnom Penh, 1,519,000.

Government: Type: Constitutional monarchy. **Head of state:** King Norodom Sihamoni; b. May 14, 1953; in office: Oct. 14, 2004. **Head of gov.:** Prime Min. Samdech Hun Sen; b. Aug. 5, 1952; in office: Nov. 30, 1998. **Local divisions:** 20 provinces and 4 municipalities. **Defense budget:** $274 mil. **Active troops:** 124,300.

Economy: Industries: tourism, garments, constr., rice milling, fishing, wood and wood prods., rubber, cement, gem mining, textiles. **Chief crops:** rice, rubber, corn, vegetables, cashews, tapioca. **Natural resources:** oil and gas, timber, gems, iron ore, manganese, phosphates, hydropower potential. **Arable land:** 22.1%. **Livestock:** cattle: 3.6 mil; chickens: 17 mil; pigs: 2.2 mil. **Fish catch:** 515,000 metric tons. **Electricity prod.:** 1.4 bil kWh. **Labor force:** agric. 57.6%, industry 15.9%, services 26.5%.

Finance: Monetary unit: Riel (KHR) (Sept. 2011: 4,088.00 = $1 U.S.). **GDP:** $30.2 bil; **per capita GDP:** $2,100; **GDP growth:** 6%. **Imports:** $6 bil; China 22.6%, Vietnam 12.7%, Hong Kong 12.4%, Thailand 11.9%, South Korea 5.4%, Singapore 5.4%. **Exports:**

$4.7 bil; Hong Kong 33%, U.S. 31.2%, Singapore 9.7%. **Tourism:** $1.3 bil. **Budget:** $2.1 bil. **Total reserves less gold:** $3.3 bil. **Gold:** 399,832 oz t. **CPI change:** 4%.

Transport: Railways: 429 mi. **Civil aviation:** 157.2 mil pass.-mi; 6 airports. **Chief ports:** Phnom Penh, Kampong Saom.

Communications: TV sets: 8 per 1,000 pop. **Radios:** 112 per 1,000 pop. **Telephone lines:** 2.5 per 100 pop. **Internet:** 1.3 users per 100 pop.

Health: Life expect.: 60.3 male; 65.1 female. **Births:** 25.4 (per 1,000 pop.). **Deaths:** 8.1 (per 1,000 pop.). **Natural inc.:** 1.73%. **Infant mortality:** 55.5 (per 1,000 live births). **HIV rate:** 0.5%.

Education: Compulsory ages: NA. **Literacy:** 77.6%.

Major intl. organizations: UN (FAO, IBRD, ILO, IMF, WHO), ASEAN, WTO.

Embassy: 4530 16th St. NW 20011; 726-7742.
Website: www.cambodia.gov.kh

Early kingdoms dating from that of Funan in the 1st cent. CE culminated in the great Khmer empire that flourished from the 9th cent. to the 13th, encompassing present-day Thailand, Cambodia, Laos, and southern Vietnam. The peripheral areas were lost to invading Siamese and Vietnamese, and France established a protectorate in 1863. Independence came in 1953.

Prince Norodom Sihanouk, king 1941-55 and head of state from 1960, tried to maintain neutrality during the Vietnam War. The U.S. bombed Cambodia, 1969-73, targeting suspected border sanctuaries of Vietnamese insurgents.

In 1970, pro-U.S. Prem. Lon Nol seized power, demanding removal of 40,000 North Vietnamese troops; the monarchy was abolished. Sihanouk formed a government-in-exile in Beijing, and open war began between the government and Communist Khmer Rouge guerrillas. The U.S. provided heavy military and economic aid.

Khmer Rouge forces captured Phnom Penh Apr. 17, 1975. Cities were depopulated and their residents executed or condemned to forced labor. An estimated 1.7 mil people died in "killing fields" or from other hardships under Khmer Rouge rule, 1975-79.

Severe border fighting broke out with Vietnam in 1978 and developed into a full-fledged Vietnamese invasion. Formation of a Vietnamese-backed government was announced, Jan. 8, 1979, one day after the capture of Phnom Penh. Thousands of refugees fled to Thailand, and widespread starvation was reported. Vietnamese troops remained in Cambodia during the 1980s, meeting resistance from Khmer Rouge guerrillas, especially along the Thai border. Vietnam withdrew nearly all its troops by Sept. 1989.

Following UN-sponsored elections in Cambodia that ended May 28, 1993, the 2 leading parties agreed to share power in an interim government. On Sept. 21, a constitution reestablishing a mon-archy was adopted by the National Assembly. It took effect Sept. 24, with Sihanouk as king. The Khmer Rouge, which had boycotted the elections, opposed the new government, but the insurgents weakened and splintered by 1996.

Co-Prime Min. Hun Sen staged a coup July 5, 1997, ousting his rival, Prince Norodom Ranariddh. Pol Pot, the Khmer Rouge leader who held power during the late 1970s, was denounced by his former comrades at a show trial, July 25, 1997, and sentenced to house arrest; he died Apr. 15, 1998. Sihanouk abdicated because of poor health and was succeeded, Oct. 14, 2004, by his son Norodom Sihamoni.

Arrested in 1999, former Khmer Rouge military chief Ta Mok died July 21, 2006, before he could stand trial for genocide and crimes against humanity. Hun Sen's party retained power through a series of flawed elections; the most recent, on July 27, 2008, was described by international observers as a notable improvement over previous votes. On July 26, 2010, a UN-backed war crimes tribunal convicted a former prison warden known as Duch for overseeing the killing and torture of more than 14,000 inmates under Khmer Rouge rule. The tribunal Sept. 16, 2010, announced the indictment of former Pres. Khieu Samphan (arrested 2007) and 3 other senior Khmer Rouge leaders. A panic and stampede on a crowded Phnom Penh bridge Nov. 22, 2010, killed 353 people and injured nearly 400 others.

Cameroon
Republic of Cameroon

People: Population: 19,711,291. **Age distrib.:** <15: 40.5%; 65+: 3.3%. **Pop. density:** 108 per sq mi, 41.7 per sq km. **Urban:** 58.4%. **Ethnic groups:** Cameroon Highlanders 31%, Equatorial Bantu 19%, Kirdi 11%, Fulani 10%, NW Bantu 8%, E Nigritic 7%, other African 13%. **Principal languages:** 24 major African language groups; English, French (both official). **Chief religions:** indigenous beliefs 40%, Christian 40%, Muslim 20%.

Geography: Total area: 183,568 sq mi, 475,440 sq km; **Land area:** 182,514 sq mi, 472,710 sq km. **Location:** Between W and central Africa. **Neighbors:** Nigeria on NW; Chad, Central African Republic on E; Congo, Gabon, Equatorial Guinea on S. **Topography:** A low coastal plain with rain forests is in S; plateaus in center lead to forested mountains in W, including Mt. Cameroon, 13,435 ft; grasslands in N lead to marshes around Lake Chad. **Capital:** Yaoundé, 1,739,000. **Cities (urban aggl.):** Douala, 2,124,806.

Government: Type: Republic. **Head of state:** Pres. Paul Biya; b. Feb. 13, 1933; in office: Nov. 6, 1982. **Head of gov.:** Prime Min.

Philemon Yang; b. June 14, 1947; in office: June 30, 2009. **Local divisions:** 10 provinces. **Defense budget:** $346 mil. **Active troops:** 14,100.

Economy: Industries: petroleum prod. and refining, aluminum prod., food proc., light consumer goods, textiles, lumber. **Chief crops:** coffee, cocoa, cotton, rubber, bananas, oilseed, grains, root starches. **Natural resources:** petroleum, bauxite, iron ore, timber, hydropower. **Crude oil reserves:** 200 mil bbls. **Arable land:** 12.6%. **Livestock:** cattle: 6 mil; chickens: 33 mil; goats: 4.4 mil; pigs: 1.4 mil; sheep: 3.8 mil. **Fish catch:** 138,400 metric tons. **Electricity prod.:** 5.4 bil kWh. **Labor force:** agric. 70%, industry 13%, services 17%.

Finance: Monetary unit: CFA BEAC Franc (XAF) (Sept. 2011: 468.55 = $1 U.S.). **GDP:** $44.3 bil; **per capita GDP:** $2,300; **GDP growth:** 3%. **Imports:** $4.9 bil; France 21%, China 11.7%, Nigeria 10.8%, Belgium 6.6%, U.S. 4.3%. **Exports:** $4.4 bil; Netherlands 14.5%, Spain 12.6%, Italy 12.2%, China 9.4%, U.S. 6.3%, France 5.7%, Belgium 4.5%, UK 4.1%. **Tourism:** $222 mil. **Budget:** $4.3 bil. **Total reserves less gold:** $3.6 bil. **Gold** (2008): 29,954 oz t. **CPI change:** 1.3%

Transport: Railways: 613 mi. **Motor vehicles:** 14.8 vehicles per 1,000 pop. **Civil aviation:** 577.9 mil pass.-mi; 11 airports. **Chief ports:** Douala, Limboh Terminal.

Communications: TV sets: 51 per 1,000 pop. **Radios:** 131 per 1,000 pop. **Telephone lines:** 2.5 per 100 pop. **Internet:** 4 users per 100 pop.

Health: Life expect.: 53.5 male; 55.3 female. **Births:** 33.0 (per 1,000 pop.). **Deaths:** 11.8 (per 1,000 pop.). **Natural inc.:** 2.12%. **Infant mortality:** 60.9 (per 1,000 live births). **HIV rate:** 5.3%.

Education: Compulsory: ages 6-11. **Literacy:** 70.7%.

Major intl. organizations: UN (FAO, IBRD, ILO, IMF, WHO), AU, the Commonwealth, WTO.

Embassy: 2349 Massachusetts Ave. NW 20008; 265-8790.

Website: www.spm.gov.cm

Portuguese sailors were the first Europeans to reach Cameroon, in the 15th cent. The European and American slave trade was very active in the area. German control lasted from 1884 to 1916, when France and Britain divided the territory, later receiving League of Nations mandates and UN trusteeships. French Cameroon became independent Jan. 1, 1960; one part of British Cameroon joined Nigeria in 1961, the other part joined Cameroon. Stability has allowed for development of roads, railways, agriculture, and petroleum production.

Pres. Paul Biya has retained power since 1982 in a series of elections that were boycotted by opposition parties or disputed as fraudulent. Rising food and fuel costs and discontent with Biya's continued rule sparked antigovernment riots Feb. 23-29, 2008. The legislature, controlled by Biya loyalists, voted Apr. 10, 2008, to abolish a presidential term limit that had been introduced in 1996.

Canada

People: Population: 34,030,589. **Age distrib.:** <15: 15.7%; 65+: 15.9%. **Pop. density:** 9.7 per sq mi, 3.7 per sq km. **Urban:** 80.6%. **Ethnic groups:** British Isles origin 28%, French origin 23%, other European 15%, Amerindian 2%, other (mostly Asian, African, Arab) 6%, mixed background 26%. **Principal languages:** English, French (both official). **Chief religions:** Roman Catholic 43%, Protestant 23%, other Christian 4%, Muslim 2%, none 16%.

Geography: Total area: 3,855,103 sq mi, 9,984,670 sq km; **Land area:** 3,511,023 sq mi, 9,093,507 sq km. The largest country in land size in the Western Hemisphere. **Topography:** Canada stretches 3,426 mi from east to west and extends southward from the North Pole to the U.S. border. Its seacoast includes 36,356 mi of mainland and 115,133 mi of islands, including the Arctic islands almost from Greenland to near the Alaskan border. **Climate:** While generally temperate, varies from freezing winter cold to blistering summer heat. **Capital:** Ottawa, 1,170,000 (figure is for Ottawa-Gatineau area). **Cities (urban aggl.):** Toronto, 5,449,456; Montréal, 3,783,032; Vancouver, 2,220,306; Calgary, 1,182,465; Edmonton, 1,112,860.

Government: Type: Confederation with parliamentary democracy. **Head of state:** Queen Elizabeth II, represented by Gov.-Gen. David Johnston; b. June 28, 1941; in office: Oct. 1, 2010. **Head of gov.:** Prime Min. Stephen Harper; b. Apr. 30, 1959; in office: Feb. 6, 2006. **Local divisions:** 10 provinces, 3 territories. **Defense budget:** $19.9 bil. **Active troops:** 65,722.

Economy: Industries: transp. equip., chemicals, minerals, food prods., wood and paper products, fish products, petroleum and nat. gas. **Chief crops:** wheat, barley, oilseed, tobacco, fruits, vegetables. **Natural resources:** iron ore, nickel, zinc, copper, gold, lead, rare earth elements, molybdenum, potash, diamonds, silver, fish, timber, wildlife, coal, petroleum, nat. gas, hydropower. **Crude oil reserves:** 175.2 bil bbls. **Arable land:** 5.0%. **Livestock:** cattle: 13.2 mil; chickens: 165 mil; goats: 30,000; pigs: 12.2 mil; sheep: 808,200. **Fish catch:** 1.1 mil metric tons. **Electricity prod.** (2009): 604.4 bil kWh. **Labor force:** agric. 2%, mfg. 13%, constr. 6%, services 76%, other 3%.

Finance: Monetary unit: Dollar (CAD) (Sept. 2011: 0.99 = $1 U.S.). **GDP:** $1.3 tril; **per capita GDP:** $39,400; **GDP growth:** 3.1%. **Imports:** $406.4 bil; U.S. 51.1%, China 10.9%, Mexico 4.6%. **Exports:** $406.8 bil; U.S. 75.1%. **Tourism:** $15.7 bil. **Budget:** $677.7 bil. **Total reserves less gold:** $57 bil. **Gold:** 109,000 oz t. **CPI change:** 1.8%.

Transport: Railways: 28,926 mi. **Motor vehicles:** 620.9 vehicles per 1,000 pop. **Civil aviation:** 66.7 bil pass.-mi; 514 airports. **Chief ports:** Fraser River, Halifax, Hamilton, Montréal, Port-Cartier, Québec City, Saint John (New Brunswick), Sept-Isles, Vancouver.

Communications: TV sets: 731 per 1,000 pop. **Radios:** 1,052 per 1,000 pop. **Telephone lines:** 50 per 100 pop. **Daily newspaper circ:** 174.6 per 1,000 pop. **Internet:** 81.6 users per 100 pop.

Health: Life expect.: 78.8 male; 84.1 female. **Births:** 10.3 (per 1,000 pop.). **Deaths:** 8.0 (per 1,000 pop.). **Natural inc.:** 0.23%. **Infant mortality:** 4.9 (per 1,000 live births). **HIV rate:** 0.2%.

Education: Compulsory: ages 6-16. **Literacy:** 99%.

Major intl. organizations: UN and all of its specialized agencies, APEC, the Commonwealth, NAFTA, NATO, OAS, OECD, OSCE, WTO.

Embassy: 501 Pennsylvania Ave. NW 20001; 682-1740.

Website: www.canada.gc.ca

French explorer Jacques Cartier, who reached the Gulf of St. Lawrence in 1534, is generally regarded as Canada's founder. But English seaman John Cabot sighted Newfoundland in 1497, and Vikings are believed to have reached the Atlantic coast centuries before either explorer. Canadian settlement was pioneered by the French who established Quebec City (1608) and Montreal (1642) and declared New France a colony in 1663.

Britain acquired Acadia (later Nova Scotia) in 1717 and, through military victory over French forces in Canada, obtained control of Quebec (1759) and the rest of New France in 1763. The French, through the Quebec Act of 1774, retained rights to their own language, religion, and civil law. The British presence in Canada increased during the American Revolution when many colonials, calling themselves United Empire Loyalists, moved north to Canada. Fur traders and explorers led Canadians westward across the continent. Sir Alexander Mackenzie reached the Pacific in 1793 and scrawled on a rock, "From Canada by land."

In Upper and Lower Canada (later called Ontario and Quebec) and in the Maritimes, legislative assemblies appeared in the 18th cent. and reformers called for responsible government. But the War of 1812 intervened. The war, a conflict between Great Britain and the U.S. fought mainly in Upper Canada, ended in a stalemate in 1814.

In 1837 political agitation for more democratic government culminated in rebellions in Upper and Lower Canada. Britain sent Lord Durham to investigate; in a famous report (1839), he recommended union of the 2 parts into one colony called Canada. The union lasted until Confederation, July 1, 1867, when proclamation of the British North America Act (now known as the Constitution Act, 1867) launched the Dominion of Canada, consisting of Ontario, Quebec, and the former colonies of Nova Scotia and New Brunswick.

Canada's Provinces and Territories

Provinces/territories	Joined confed.	Area (sq mi)	Population (Apr. 2011 est.)	Capital	Premier	Party	In office
Alberta	1905	255,287	3,758,234	Edmonton	Ed Stelmach	Prog. Cons.	2006
British Columbia	1871	365,948	4,563,296	Victoria	Christy Clark	Liberal	2011
Manitoba	1870	250,947	1,246,396	Winnipeg	Greg Selinger	New Democratic	2009
New Brunswick	1867	28,355	753,025	Fredericton	David Alward	Prog. Cons.	2010
Newfoundland & Labrador	1949	156,649	508,410	St. John's	Kathy Dunderdale	Prog. Cons.	2010
Nova Scotia	1867	21,425	942,334	Halifax	Darrell Dexter	New Democratic	2009
Ontario	1867	412,581	13,310,859	Toronto	Dalton McGuinty	Liberal	2003
Prince Edward Island	1873	2,185	143,836	Charlottetown	Robert Ghiz	Liberal	2007
Quebec	1867	594,860	7,957,591	Québec	Jean Charest	Liberal	2003
Saskatchewan	1905	251,866	1,053,960	Regina	Brad Wall	Saskatchewan	2007
Northwest Territories[1]	1871	503,951	43,505	Yellowknife	Floyd Roland	nonpartisan	2007
Nunavut[1]	(2)	818,959	33,413	Iqaluit	Eva Aariak	nonpartisan	2008
Yukon[1]	1898	186,661	34,377	Whitehorse	Darrell Pasloski	Yukon	2011

(1) Territories also have federally appointed commissioners to represent federal interests. (2) Territory created in 1999 from eastern portion of Northwest Territories.

Since 1840 the Canadian colonies had held the right to internal self-government. The British North America Act, which was the basis for the country's written constitution, established a federal system of government on the model of a British parliament and cabinet structure under the crown. Canada was proclaimed a self-governing Dominion within the British Empire in 1931. With the ratification of the Constitution Act, 1982, Canada severed its last formal legislative link with Britain by obtaining the right to amend its constitution.

Failure in 1990 of the so-called Meech Lake Accord, 1987, which would have assured constitutional protection for Quebec's efforts to preserve its French language and culture, sparked a separatist revival in Quebec. Subsequently, the Charlottetown agreement called for constitutional changes, such as recognition of Quebec as a "distinct society" within the Canadian confederation. It was defeated by a national referendum Oct. 26, 1992.

Canada became the first nation to ratify the North American Free Trade Agreement between Canada, Mexico, and the U.S. June 23, 1993. It went into effect Jan. 1, 1994. In a Quebec referendum held Oct. 30, 1995, proponents of secession lost by a razor-thin margin. On Jan. 7, 1998, the government apologized to indigenous peoples for 150 years of mistreatment and pledged to set up a "healing fund." Canada's highest court ruled, Aug. 20, that Quebec cannot secede unilaterally, even if a majority of the province approves. Nunavut ("Our Land"), carved from Northwest Territories as a homeland for the Inuit, was established Apr. 1, 1999.

Victory by the Liberals in national elections Nov. 27, 2000, made Jean Chrétien the first Canadian prime minister in over 50 years to head a third successive majority government. Canada sent troops and warships to aid the U.S.-led coalition in Afghanistan beginning Oct. 2001, but refused to support the U.S.-led invasion of Iraq in Mar. 2003; 157 Canadian troops had been killed in Afghanistan by the time Canada's combat mission ended July 7, 2011.

Chrétien retired Dec. 12, 2003, and Paul Martin became prime minister. Weakened by a scandal involving improper payments to Quebec firms for advertising and sponsorship of cultural and sporting events, the Liberals won only 135 of 308 seats in parliamentary elections June 28, 2004. Martin stayed in office as head of a minority government. Parliament enacted a bill, July 19, 2005, making same-sex marriage (already permitted in 8 of 10 provinces) legal throughout the country. Michaëlle Jean, a Haitian-born TV journalist, was installed Sept. 27 as Canada's first black governor-general.

Twelve years of Liberal Party rule ended when Conservatives won 124 seats to the Liberals' 103 in parliamentary elections, Jan. 23, 2006. Conservative leader Stephen Harper took office Feb. 6 as head of a minority government. Police and intelligence officials in the Toronto area, June 2-3, arrested and charged 17 people with plotting terrorist attacks in Canada; their targets were said to include the House of Commons and the prime minister. The Supreme Court, Feb. 23, 2007, unanimously struck down a law under which foreign-born terrorism suspects had been indefinitely detained without charge.

Prime Min. Harper remained in office as head of a minority government after early elections Oct. 14, 2008, as Conservatives increased their plurality to 143 seats in the 308-seat House of Commons. Canada hosted the Winter Olympics Feb. 12-28, 2010, in Vancouver, BC, and the G-8 and G-20 summit meetings June 25-27 in Ontario. A vote of no-confidence Mar. 25, 2011, led to federal elections May 2 in which Harper's Conservatives gained a parliamentary majority of 166 seats. The New Democratic Party with 103 seats became the official opposition, as the Liberals plummeted to 34 seats.

Prime Ministers of Canada

Canada is a constitutional monarchy with a parliamentary system of government. It is also a federal state. Canada's official head of state, Queen Elizabeth II, is represented by a resident governor-general. However, in practice the nation is governed by the prime minister, leader of the party that commands the support of a majority of the House of Commons, dominant chamber of Canada's bicameral Parliament.

Name	Party	Term
Sir John A. Macdonald	Conservative	1867-1873
Alexander Mackenzie	Liberal	1873-1878
Sir John A. Macdonald	Conservative	1878-1891
Sir John J. C. Abbott	Conservative	1891-1892
Sir John S. D. Thompson	Conservative	1892-1894
Sir Mackenzie Bowell	Conservative	1894-1896
Sir Charles Tupper	Conservative	1896[1]
Sir Wilfrid Laurier	Liberal	1896-1911
Sir Robert Laird Borden	Cons./Union.[2]	1911-1920
Arthur Meighen	Unionist	1920-1921
W. L. Mackenzie King	Liberal	1921-1926
Arthur Meighen	Conservative	1926[3]
W. L. Mackenzie King	Liberal	1926-1930
Richard Bedford Bennett	Conservative	1930-1935

Name	Party	Term
W. L. Mackenzie King	Liberal	1935-1948
Louis St. Laurent	Liberal	1948-1957
John G. Diefenbaker	Prog. Cons.	1957-1963
Lester Bowles Pearson	Liberal	1963-1968
Pierre Elliott Trudeau	Liberal	1968-1979
Joe Clark	Prog. Cons.	1979-1980
Pierre Elliott Trudeau	Liberal	1980-1984
John Napier Turner	Liberal	1984[4]
Brian Mulroney	Prog. Cons.	1984-1993
Kim Campbell	Prog. Cons.	1993[5]
Jean Chrétien	Liberal	1993-2003
Paul Martin	Liberal	2003-2006
Stephen Harper	Conservative	2006-

(1) May-July. (2) Conservative 1911-17, Unionist 1917-20. (3) June-Sept. (4) June-Sept. (5) June-Oct.

Cape Verde
Republic of Cape Verde

People: Population: 516,100. **Age distrib.:** <15: 32.6%; 65+: 5.5%. **Pop. density:** 331.4 per sq mi, 128 per sq km. **Urban:** 61.1%. **Ethnic groups:** Creole (mulatto) 71%, African 28%, European 1%. **Principal languages:** Portuguese (official), Crioulo (blend of Portuguese & W African words). **Chief religions:** Roman Catholic (infused with indigenous beliefs), Protestant (mostly Church of the Nazarene).

Geography: Total area: 1,557 sq mi, 4,033 sq km; **Land area:** 1,557 sq mi, 4,033 sq km. **Location:** In Atlantic O., off W tip of Africa. **Neighbors:** Nearest are Mauritania, Senegal to E. **Topography:** Cape Verde Islands are 15 in number, volcanic in origin (active crater on Fogo). The landscape is eroded and stark, with vegetation mostly in interior valleys. **Capital:** Praia, 125,000.

Government: Type: Republic. **Head of state:** Pres. Jorge Carlos Fonseca; b. Oct. 20, 1950; in office: Sept. 9, 2011. **Head of gov.:** Prime Min. José Maria Neves; b. Mar. 28, 1960; in office: Feb. 1, 2001. **Local divisions:** 17 districts. **Defense budget:** $8 mil. **Active troops:** 1,200.

Economy: Industries: food and beverages, fish proc., shoes and garments, salt mining, ship repair. **Chief crops:** bananas, corn, beans, sweet potatoes, sugarcane, coffee, peanuts. **Natural resources:** salt, basalt rock, limestone, kaolin, fish, clay, gypsum. **Arable land:** 14.9%. **Livestock:** cattle: 45,000; chickens: 600,000; goats: 215,850; pigs: 231,640; sheep: 18,310. **Fish catch:** 16,828 metric tons. **Electricity prod.:** 256.5 mil kWh. **Labor force:** NA.

Finance: Monetary unit: Escudo (CVE) (Jan. 2011: 78.40 = $1 U.S.). **GDP:** $1.9 bil; **per capita GDP:** $3,800; **GDP growth:** 5.4%. **Imports:** $858 mil; Portugal 43.5%, Netherlands 15.1%, Spain 5.9%, China 5%, Italy 4.3%, Brazil 4.1%. **Exports:** $114 mil; Spain 52.1%, Portugal 21.5%, Morocco 6.9%. **Tourism:** $289 mil. **Budget:** $680.8 mil. **Total reserves less gold:** $382.2 mil. **CPI change:** 2.1%.

Transport: Civil aviation: 755.6 mil pass.-mi; 9 airports. **Chief port:** Porto Grande.

Communications: TV sets: 128 per 1,000 pop. **Radios:** 176 per 1,000 pop. **Telephone lines:** 14.5 per 100 pop. **Internet:** 30 users per 100 pop.

Health: Life expect.: 68.5 male; 73.0 female. **Births:** 21.5 (per 1,000 pop.). **Deaths:** 6.3 (per 1,000 pop.). **Natural inc.:** 1.51%. **Infant mortality:** 26.9 (per 1,000 live births). **HIV rate:** NA.

Education: Compulsory: ages 6-11. **Literacy:** 84.8%.

Major intl. organizations: UN (FAO, IBRD, ILO, IMF, WHO), AU, WTO.

Embassy: 3415 Massachusetts Ave. NW 20007; 965-6820. **Website:** www.governo.cv

The first Portuguese colonists landed in 1462; African slaves were brought soon after, and most Cape Verdeans descend from both groups. Cape Verde independence came July 5, 1975. Antonio Mascarenhas Monteiro won the nation's first free presidential election Feb. 17, 1991; he was reelected without opposition 5 years later. When Pres. Pedro Pires retired after serving two 5-year terms, 2001-11, Jorge Carlos Fonseca won a presidential runoff election Aug. 21, 2011. Remittances from Cape Verdean emigrants are a major source of income.

Central African Republic

People: Population: 4,950,027. **Age distrib.:** <15: 41%; 65+: 3.7%. **Pop. density:** 20.6 per sq mi, 7.9 per sq km. **Urban:** 38.9%. **Ethnic groups:** Baya 33%, Banda 27%, Mandjia 13%, Sara 10%, Mboum 7%, M'Baka 4%, Yakoma 4%. **Principal languages:** French (official), Sangho (lingua franca & national), tribal languages. **Chief religions:** indigenous beliefs 35%, Protestant 25%, Roman Catholic 25%, Muslim 15%.

Geography: Total area: 240,535 sq mi, 622,984 sq km; **Land area:** 240,535 sq mi, 622,984 sq km. **Location:** In central Africa. **Neighbors:** Chad on N, Cameroon on W, Congo-Brazzaville and Congo-Kinshasa (formerly Zaire) on S, Sudan on E. **Topography:** Mostly rolling plateau, average altitude 2,000 ft, with rivers draining

S to the Congo and N to Lake Chad. Open, well-watered savanna covers most of the area, with an arid area in NE, and tropical rain forest in SW. **Capital:** Bangui, 702,000.

Government: Type: Republic. **Head of state:** Pres. François Bozizé; b. Oct. 14, 1946; in office: Mar. 15, 2003. **Head of gov.:** Prime Min. Faustin Archange Touadéra; b. Apr. 21, 1957; in office: Jan. 22, 2008. **Local divisions:** 14 prefectures, 2 economic prefectures, 1 commune. **Defense budget:** $52 mil. **Active troops:** 2,150.

Economy: Industries: gold and diamond mining, logging, brewing, textiles, footwear, bicycle and motorcycle assembly. **Chief crops:** timber, cotton, coffee, tobacco, manioc, yams, millet, corn, bananas. **Natural resources:** diamonds, uranium, timber, gold, oil, hydropower. **Arable land:** 3.1%. **Livestock:** cattle: 4 mil; chickens: 6.2 mil; goats: 4.2 mil; pigs: 800,000; sheep: 304,000. **Fish catch:** 15,000 metric tons. **Electricity prod.:** 160 mil kWh. **Labor force:** NA.

Finance: Monetary unit: CFA BEAC Franc (XAF) (Sept. 2011: 468.55 = $1 U.S.). **GDP:** $3.4 bil; **per capita GDP:** $700; **GDP growth:** 3.3%. **Imports** (2007 est.): $237.3 mil; France 14.7%, U.S. 9.6%, Cameroon 9.1%, Netherlands 8.3%. **Exports** (2007 est.): $146.7 mil; Belgium 35.6%, China 12%, Morocco 11.2%, Dem. Rep. of the Congo 7.5%, France 6.3%. **Tourism:** NA. **Budget** (2009 est.): $362 mil. **Total reserves less gold:** $181.2 mil. **Gold** (2008): 11,126 oz t. **CPI change:** 1.5%.

Transport: Motor vehicles: 0.9 vehicles per 1,000 pop. **Civil aviation:** 2 airports. **Chief ports:** Bangui, Nola, Nzinga, Salo.

Communications: TV sets: 10 per 1,000 pop. **Radios:** 111 per 1,000 pop. **Telephone lines:** 0.3 per 100 pop. **Internet:** 2.3 users per 100 pop.

Health: Life expect.: 48.8 male; 51.4 female. **Births:** 36.5 (per 1,000 pop.). **Deaths:** 15.0 (per 1,000 pop.). **Natural inc.:** 2.15%. **Infant mortality:** 99.4 (per 1,000 live births). **HIV rate:** 4.7%.

Education: Compulsory: ages 6-15. **Literacy:** 55.2%.

Major intl. organizations: UN (FAO, IBRD, ILO, IMF, WHO), AU, WTO.

Embassy: 1618 22nd St. NW 20008; 483-7800.

Website: www.state.gov/p/af/ci/ct/car

Various Bantu peoples migrated through the region for centuries before French control was asserted in the late 19th cent., when the region was named Ubangi-Shari. Complete independence was attained Aug. 13, 1960.

Pres. Jean-Bedel Bokassa, who seized power in a 1965 military coup, proclaimed himself constitutional emperor of the renamed Central African Empire Dec. 1976. Bokassa's rule was characterized by ruthless authoritarianism and human rights violations. He was ousted in a bloodless coup aided by the French government, Sept. 20, 1979. In 1981, Gen. André Kolingba became head of state in another bloodless coup. Multiparty legislative and presidential elections were held in Oct. 1992 but were canceled by the government when Kolingba was losing. New elections, held in Aug. and Sept. 1993, led to the replacement of Kolingba with civilian rule under Pres. Ange-Félix Patassé.

France sent in troops to suppress army mutinies in 1996 and 1997. After thwarting several coup attempts, Patassé was ousted Mar. 15, 2003, by rebels under former army chief François Bozizé. Bozizé won a presidential runoff election May 8, 2005, but insurgent activity by Patassé loyalists and others continued in the north. A national peace conference, Dec. 8-20, 2008, paved the way for the installation of a unity government Jan. 19, 2009. Pres. Bozizé won reelection Jan. 23, 2011.

Chad
Republic of Chad

People: Population: 10,758,945. **Age distrib.:** <15: 46%; 65+: 2.9%. **Pop. density:** 22.1 per sq mi, 8.5 per sq km. **Urban:** 27.6%. **Ethnic groups:** Sara 28%, Arab 12%, Mayo-Kebbi 12%, Kanem-Bornou 9%, Ouaddai 9%, Hadjarai 7%, Tandjile 7%, Gorane 6%, Fitri-Batha 5%. **Principal languages:** French, Arabic (both official); Sara; 120+ languages & dialects. **Chief religions:** Muslim 53%, Catholic 20%, Protestant 14%, animist 7%, atheist 3%.

Geography: Total area: 495,755, sq mi, 1,284,000 sq km; **Land area:** 486,180 sq mi, 1,259,200 sq km. **Location:** In central N Africa. **Neighbors:** Libya on N; Niger, Nigeria, Cameroon on W; Central African Republic on S; Sudan on E. **Topography:** Wooded savanna, steppe, and desert in the S; part of the Sahara in the N. Southern rivers flow N to Lake Chad, surrounded by marshland. **Capital:** N'Djaména, 808,000.

Government: Type: Republic. **Head of state:** Pres. Idriss Déby Itno; b. 1952; in office: Dec. 4, 1990. **Head of gov.:** Prime Min. Emmanuel Nadingar; b. 1951; in office: Mar. 5, 2010. **Local divisions:** 14 prefectures. **Defense budget:** $129 mil. **Active troops:** 25,350.

Economy: Industries: oil, cotton textiles, meatpacking, brewing, sodium carbonate, soap, cigarettes, constr. materials. **Chief crops:** cotton, sorghum, millet, peanuts, rice, potatoes, manioc. **Natural resources:** petroleum, uranium, natron, kaolin, fish. **Crude oil reserves:** 1.5 bil bbls. **Arable land:** 3.4%. **Livestock:** cattle: 7.2 mil; chickens: 5.5 mil; goats: 6.4 mil; pigs: 29,240; sheep: 3 mil. **Fish catch:** 40,000 metric tons. **Electricity prod.:** 100 mil kWh. **Labor**

force: agric. 80% (subsistence farming, herding, fishing), industry and services 20%.

Finance: Monetary unit: CFA BEAC Franc (XAF) (Sept. 2011: 468.55 = $1 U.S.). **GDP:** $17.4 bil; **per capita GDP:** $1,600; **GDP growth:** 5.1%. **Imports:** $2.6 bil; China 16.8%, France 16%, Cameroon 11.5%, U.S. 6.9%, Italy 5.9%, Ukraine 4.8%. **Exports:** $3 bil; U.S. 89%, France 4.7%. **Tourism:** NA. **Budget:** $2.9 bil. **Total reserves less gold:** $632.4 mil. **Gold** (2008): 11,126 oz t. **CPI change** (2008-09): 10%.

Transport: Civil aviation: 8 airports.

Communications: TV sets: 9 per 1,000 pop. **Radios:** 103 per 1,000 pop. **Telephone lines:** 0.5 per 100 pop. **Internet:** 1.7 users per 100 pop.

Health: Life expect.: 47.3 male; 49.4 female. **Births:** 39.4 (per 1,000 pop.). **Deaths:** 15.5 (per 1,000 pop.). **Natural inc.:** 2.39%. **Infant mortality:** 95.3 (per 1,000 live births). **HIV rate:** 3.4%.

Education: Compulsory: ages 6-11. **Literacy:** 33.6%.

Major intl. organizations: UN (FAO, IBRD, ILO, IMF, WHO), AU, WTO.

Embassy: 2002 R St. NW 20009; 462-4009.

Website: www.dgmp.gouv.td or www.state.gov/p/af/ci/cd/

Chad was the site of Paleolithic and Neolithic cultures before the Sahara Desert formed. A succession of kingdoms and Arab slave traders dominated Chad until France took control around 1900. Independence came Aug. 11, 1960. Northern Muslim rebels have fought animist and Christian southern government and French troops from 1966, despite numerous cease-fires and peace pacts.

Rebel forces, led by Hissène Habré, captured the capital and forced Pres. Goukouni Oueddei to flee the country in June 1982. In Dec. 1990, Habré was overthrown by a Libyan-supported insurgent group, the Patriotic Salvation Movement. After approval of a new constitution Mar. 1996, Chad's first multiparty presidential election was held in June and July.

Oil began flowing July 15, 2003, through a 665-mi pipeline that allows landlocked Chad to export via Cameroon. Pres. Idriss Déby Itno won a third term, May 3, 2006, in an election boycotted by major opposition groups. Violence along the Sudan border escalated during the year, as Sudanese *janjaweed* militias and Chadian rebels attacked civilians, and Darfur rebels preyed on refugee camps. Between 140 and 700 civilians died in N'Djaména, Feb. 2-5, 2008, as more than 2,000 Chadian rebels stormed the capital and clashed with government troops in a failed coup attempt.

On Jan. 15, 2010, Chad and Sudan signed an accord aimed at normalizing relations and suppressing cross-border activities by rebel groups. Established in 2007, a UN peacekeeping force (MINURCAT) completed its mandate Dec. 31, 2010. In early 2011, camps in E Chad housed some 262,900 refugees, most from Darfur, and camps in S Chad held about 73,500 refugees, most from the Central African Republic; more than 157,000 Chadians were internally displaced. Pres. Deby won reelection Apr. 25, 2011, in a vote boycotted as fraudulent by the main opposition groups.

Chile
Republic of Chile

People: Population: 16,888,760. **Age distrib.:** <15: 22.3%; 65+: 9.6%. **Pop. density:** 58.8 per sq mi, 22.7 per sq km. **Urban:** 89%. **Ethnic groups:** white & white-Amerindian 95%, Mapuche 4%. **Principal languages:** Spanish (official), Mapudungun, German, English. **Chief religions:** Roman Catholic 70%, Evangelical 15%, Jehovah's Witnesses 1%, other Christian 1%, none 8%.

Geography: Total area: 291,933 sq mi, 756,102 sq km; **Land area:** 287,187 sq mi, 743,812 sq km. **Location:** Occupies western coast of S America. **Neighbors:** Peru on N, Bolivia on NE, Argentina on E. **Topography:** Andes Mts. on E border incl. some of the world's highest peaks; on W is 2,650-mile Pacific coast. Width varies 100-250 mi. In N is Atacama Desert, in center are agricultural regions, in S, forests and grazing lands. **Capital:** Santiago, 5,883,000. **Cities (urban aggl.):** Valparaíso, 872,591.

Government: Type: Republic. **Head of state and gov.:** Pres. Sebastián Piñera Echenique; b. Dec. 1, 1949; in office: Mar. 11, 2010. **Local divisions:** 13 regions. **Defense budget:** $2.07 bil. **Active troops:** 59,059.

Economy: Industries: copper, lithium, other minerals, foodstuffs, fish proc., iron, steel, wood and wood prods., transp. equip., cement, textiles. **Chief crops:** grapes, apples, pears, onions, wheat, corn, oats, peaches, garlic, asparagus, beans. **Natural resources:** copper, timber, iron ore, nitrates, prec. metals, molybdenum, hydropower. **Crude oil reserves:** 150 mil bbls. **Arable land:** 1.7%. **Livestock:** cattle: 3.9 mil; chickens: 43.2 mil; goats: 750,000; pigs: 2,724,640; sheep: 4 mil. **Fish catch:** 4.7 mil metric tons. **Electricity prod.:** 60.3 bil kWh. **Labor force:** agric. 13.2%, industry 23%, services 63.9%.

Finance: Monetary unit: Peso (CLP) (Sept. 2011: 463.75 = $1 U.S.). **GDP:** $257.9 bil; **per capita GDP:** $15,400; **GDP growth:** 5.3%. **Imports:** $54.2 bil; U.S. 16.8%, China 11.8%, Argentina 10.9%, Brazil 6.7%, South Korea 5.1%. **Exports:** $64.3 bil; China 23.2%, U.S. 11.3%, Japan 9.2%, South Korea 5.8%, Brazil 5.1%. **Tourism:** $1.6 bil. **Budget:** $45.1 bil. **Total reserves less gold:** $27.8 bil. **Gold:** 7,900 oz t. **CPI change:** 1.4%.

Transport: Railways: 4,401 mi. **Motor vehicles:** 170.7 vehicles per 1,000 pop. **Civil aviation:** 10.9 bil pass.-mi; 84 airports. **Chief**

ports: Coronel, Huasco, Lirquen, Puerto Ventanas, San Antonio, San Vicente, Valparaiso.

Communications: TV sets: 313 per 1,000 pop. **Radios:** 783 per 1,000 pop. **Telephone lines:** 20.2 per 100 pop. **Daily newspaper circ:** 50.6 per 1,000 pop. **Internet:** 45 users per 100 pop.

Health: Life expect.: 74.4 male; 81.1 female. **Births:** 14.3 (per 1,000 pop.). **Deaths:** 6.0 (per 1,000 pop.). **Natural inc.:** 0.84%. **Infant mortality:** 7.3 (per 1,000 live births). **HIV rate:** 0.4%.

Education: Compulsory: ages 6-13. **Literacy:** 98.6%.

Major intl. organizations: UN and all of its specialized agencies, APEC, OAS, OECD, WTO.

Embassy: 1732 Massachusetts Ave. NW 20036; 785-1746.

Website: www.gob.cl

Northern Chile was under Inca rule before the Spanish conquest, 1536-40. The southern Araucanian Indians resisted until the late 19th cent. Independence was gained 1810-18, under José de San Martin and Bernardo O'Higgins; the latter, as supreme director 1817-23, sought social and economic reforms until deposed. Chile defeated Peru and Bolivia in 1836-39 and 1879-84, gaining mineral-rich northern land.

In 1970, Salvador Allende Gossens, a Marxist, became president with a narrow plurality of the popular vote. His government improved conditions for the poor, but property seizures by leftwing extremists, poorly planned socialist economic programs, and a destabilization campaign backed by the U.S. led to political and financial chaos. A military junta seized power Sept. 11, 1973. With the presidential palace under attack, Allende refused to surrender; police said he killed himself. (A new autopsy, disclosed July 19, 2011, confirmed the original police account.) The junta, headed by Gen. Augusto Pinochet Ugarte, implemented plans to privatize the economy and "exterminate Marxism." Repression continued into the 1980s.

In Dec. 1989 voters elected a civilian president, although Pinochet continued to head the army until Mar. 10, 1998. In Mar. 1994 a Chilean human rights group estimated that human rights violations had claimed more than 3,100 lives during Pinochet's rule. Efforts to prosecute him failed when he was declared mentally unfit to stand trial by courts in Britain and Chile.

Ricardo Lagos Escobar, Chile's first Socialist president since the 1973 coup, took office Mar. 11, 2000. Chile and the U.S. signed a free trade accord June 6, 2003. Verónica Michelle Bachelet Jeria, also a Socialist, won a runoff election Jan. 15, 2006, and took office Mar. 11 as Chile's first woman president. Pinochet died Dec. 10, 2006.

Billionaire businessman Sebastián Piñera Echenique, a conservative, won a presidential runoff election Jan. 17, 2010, and took office Mar. 11. In the interim, a powerful earthquake Feb. 27, 2010, off the coast of central Chile, followed by hundreds of aftershocks, killed at least 521 people and caused up to $30 bil in property damage. Chile mounted a successful 10-week effort to rescue 33 miners trapped 2,300 feet underground by a cave-in at the San José gold and copper mine Aug. 5, 2010. A prison fire Dec. 8 in Santiago killed at least 81 inmates. Chile's economy was growing at a 6.6% annual rate in mid-2011, but lagging wages sparked labor protests against the Piñera government.

Tierra del Fuego is the largest (18,800 sq mi) island in the archipelago of the same name at the southern tip of S. America, an area of majestic mountains, tortuous channels, and high winds. It was visited 1520 by Magellan and named Land of Fire because of its many Indian bonfires. Part of the island is in Chile, part in Argentina. Punta Arenas, on a mainland peninsula, is a center of sheep raising and the world's southernmost city (pop. [2002 census] 116,005); Puerto Williams is the southernmost settlement.

China
People's Republic of China
(Statistical data do not include Hong Kong or Macao.)

People: Population: 1,336,718,015. **Age distrib.:** <15: 17.6%; 65+: 8.9%. **Pop. density:** 361.8 per sq mi, 139.7 per sq km. **Urban:** 47% (not incl. Hong Kong and Macao). **Ethnic groups:** Han Chinese 92%; Zhuang, Manchu, Hui, Miao, Uighur, Tujia, Yi, Mongol, Tibetan, Buyi, Dong, Yao, Korean, other nationalities 9%. **Principal languages:** Standard Chinese or Mandarin (Putonghua, based on Beijing dialect), Yue (Cantonese), Wu (Shanghainese), Minbei (Fuzhou), Minnan (Hokkien-Taiwanese), Xiang, Gan, Hakka dialects, minority languages. **Chief religions:** officially atheist; Daoist (Taoist), Buddhist, Christian, Muslim.

Geography: Total area: 3,705,407 sq mi, 9,596,961 sq km; **Land area:** 3,694,959 sq mi, 9,569,901 sq km. **Location:** Occupies most of the habitable mainland of E Asia. **Neighbors:** Mongolia on N; Russia on NE and NW; Afghanistan, Pakistan, Tajikistan, Kyrgyzstan, Kazakhstan on W; India, Nepal, Bhutan, Myanmar, Laos, Vietnam on S; North Korea on NE. **Topography:** Two-thirds of the vast territory is mountainous or desert; only one-tenth is cultivated. Rolling topography rises to high elevations in the N in the Daxinganlingshanmai separating Manchuria and Mongolia; the Tien Shan in Xinjiang; the Himalayan and Kunlunshanmai in the SW and in Tibet. Length is 1,860 mi from N to S, width E to W is more than 2,000 mi. The eastern half of China is one of

the world's best-watered lands. Three great river systems, the Chang (Yangtze), Huang (Yellow), and Xi, provide water for vast farmlands. **Capital:** Beijing, 12,214,000. **Cities (urban aggl.):** Shanghai, 16,575,110; Chongqing, 9,401,170; Shenzhen, 9,005,283; Guangzhou, Guangdong, 8,883,865; Tianjin, 7,884,473; Wuhan, 7,681,099; Dongguan, Guangdong, 5,346,652; Shenyang, 5,165,771.

Government: Type: Communist Party-led state. **Head of state:** Pres. Hu Jintao; b. Dec. 1942; in office: Mar. 15, 2003 (also gen. sec. of Communist Party since Nov. 15, 2002). **Head of gov.:** Premier Wen Jiabao; b. Sept. 1942; in office: Mar. 16, 2003. **Local divisions:** 22 provinces (not including Taiwan), 5 autonomous regions, and 4 municipalities, plus the special administrative regions of Hong Kong (as of July 1, 1997) and Macao (as of Dec. 20, 1999). **Defense budget:** $76.4 bil. **Active troops:** 2,285,000.

Economy: Industries: world leader in gross value of industrial output; mining and ore processing, iron, steel, aluminum, other metals, coal; machine building; armaments; textiles and apparel; petroleum; cement; chemicals; fertilizers; consumer prods. **Chief crops:** world leader in gross value of agric. output; rice, wheat, potatoes, corn, peanuts, tea, millet, barley, apples, cotton, oilseed. **Natural resources:** coal, iron ore, petroleum, nat. gas, mercury, tin, tungsten, antimony, manganese, molybdenum, vanadium, magnetite, aluminum, lead, zinc, rare earth elements, uranium, hydropower potential (world's largest). **Crude oil reserves:** 20.4 bil bbls. **Arable land:** 11.8%. **Livestock:** cattle: 84.1 mil; chickens: 4.7 bil; goats: 152.5 mil; pigs: 450.9 mil; sheep: 128.6 mil. **Fish catch:** 60.5 mil metric tons. **Electricity prod.** (2009): 3.4 tril kWh. **Labor force:** agric. 38.1%, industry 27.8%, services 34.1%.

Finance: Monetary unit: Yuan Renminbi (CNY) (Sept. 2011: 6.39 = $1 U.S.). **GDP:** $10.1 tril; **per capita GDP:** $7,600; **GDP growth:** 10.3%. **Imports:** $1.3 tril; Japan 13%, South Korea 10.2%, U.S. 7.7%, Germany 5.6%. **Exports:** $1.5 tril; U.S. 18.4%, Hong Kong 13.8%, Japan 8.2%, South Korea 4.5%, Germany 4.2%. **Tourism:** $45.8 bil. **Budget:** $1.27 tril. **Total reserves less gold:** $2.9 tril. **Gold:** 33.9 mil oz t. **CPI change:** 3.3%.

Transport: Railways: 53,438 mi. **Motor vehicles:** 46.2 vehicles per 1,000 pop. **Civil aviation:** 205.2 bil pass.-mi (incl. data for Hong Kong and Macao); 442 airports. **Chief ports:** Dalian, Guangzhou, Ningbo, Qingdao, Qinhuangdao, Shanghai, Shenzhen, Tianjin.

Communications: TV sets: 380 per 1,000 pop. **Radios:** 336 per 1,000 pop. **Telephone lines:** 22 per 100 pop. **Daily newspaper circ.:** 74.1 per 1,000 pop. **Internet:** 34.3 users per 100 pop.

Health: Life expect.: 72.7 male; 76.9 female. **Births:** 12.3 (per 1,000 pop.). **Deaths:** 7.0 (per 1,000 pop.). **Natural inc.:** 0.53%. **Infant mortality:** 16.1 (per 1,000 live births). **HIV rate:** 0.1%.

Education: Compulsory: ages 6-14. **Literacy:** 94%.

Major intl. organizations: UN (FAO, IBRD, ILO, IMF, WHO), APEC, WTO.

Embassy: 2300 Connecticut Ave. NW 20008; 328-2500.

Website: www.gov.cn

Remains of various humanlike creatures who lived as early as several hundred thousand years ago have been found in many parts of China. Neolithic agricultural settlements dotted the Huang (Yellow) R. basin from about 5000 BCE. Their language, religion, and art were the sources of later Chinese civilization.

Bronze metallurgy reached a peak and Chinese pictographic writing, similar to today's, was in use in the more developed culture of the Shang Dynasty (c. 1500 BCE-c. 1000 BCE), which ruled much of North China.

A succession of dynasties and interdynastic warring kingdoms ruled China for the next 3,000 years. They expanded Chinese political and cultural domination to the south and west, and developed a society that was technologically and culturally advanced. Rule by foreigners (Mongols in the Yuan Dynasty, 1271-1368, and Manchus in the Ch'ing Dynasty, 1644-1911) did not alter the underlying culture.

A period of relative stagnation left China vulnerable to internal and external pressures in the 19th cent. Rebellions left tens of millions dead, and Russia, Japan, Britain, and other powers exercised political and economic control in large parts of the country. China became a republic Jan. 1, 1912, following the Wuchang Uprising inspired by Dr. Sun Yat-sen, founder of the Kuomintang (Nationalist) party. By 1928, the Kuomintang, led by Chiang Kai-shek, succeeded in nominal reunification of China. About the same time, a bloody purge of Communists from the ranks of the Kuomintang fomented hostilities between the two groups.

For over 50 years, 1894-1945, China was involved in conflicts with Japan. In 1895, China ceded Korea, Taiwan, and other areas. On Sept. 18, 1931, Japan seized the Northeastern Provinces (Manchuria) and set up a puppet state called Manchukuo. Taking advantage of Chinese dissension, Japan invaded China proper July 7, 1937. On Nov. 20 the retreating Nationalist government moved its capital to Chongqing (Chungking) from Nanking (Nanjing), which Japanese troops then ravaged Dec. 13.

From 1939 the Sino-Japanese War (1937-45) became part of the broader world conflict. After its defeat in World War II, Japan gave up all seized land. Within China, conflicts involving the Kuomintang, Communists, and other factions resumed. China came under the domination of Communist armies, 1949-50. The Kuomintang government fled to Taiwan, Dec. 8, 1949.

The People's Republic of China was proclaimed in Beijing (Peking) Oct. 1, 1949, under Mao Zedong. China and the USSR signed a 30-year treaty of "friendship, alliance, and mutual assistance," Feb. 15, 1950. The U.S. refused recognition of the new regime. On Nov. 26, 1950, the People's Republic sent armies into Korea against U.S. troops and forced a stalemate in the Korean War.

After an initial period of consolidation, 1949-52, industry, agriculture, and social and economic institutions were forcibly molded according to Maoist ideals. However, frequent drastic changes in policy and violent factionalism interfered with economic development. In 1957, Mao admitted an estimated 800,000 people had been executed 1949-54; opponents claimed much higher figures.

The Great Leap Forward, 1958-60, tried to force the pace of economic development through intensive labor on huge new rural communes, and through emphasis on ideological purity. The program caused resistance and was largely abandoned.

By the 1960s, relations with the USSR deteriorated, with disagreements on borders, ideology, and leadership of world Communism. The USSR canceled aid accords, and China, with Albania, launched anti-Soviet propaganda drives.

The Great Proletarian Cultural Revolution, 1965, was an attempt to oppose pragmatism and bureaucratic power and instruct a new generation in revolutionary principles. Massive purges took place. A program of forcibly relocating millions of urban teenagers into the countryside was launched. By 1968 the movement had run its course; many purged officials returned to office in subsequent years, and reforms that had placed ideology above expertise were gradually weakened.

On Oct. 25, 1971, the UN General Assembly ousted the Taiwan government from the UN and seated the People's Republic in its place. The U.S. had supported the mainland's admission but opposed Taiwan's expulsion.

U.S. Pres. Richard Nixon visited China Feb. 21-28, 1972, on invitation from Premier Zhou Enlai, ending years of antipathy between the 2 nations. China and the U.S. opened liaison offices in each other's capitals, May-June 1973. The U.S., Dec. 15, 1978, formally recognized the People's Republic of China as the sole legal government of China; diplomatic relations between the 2 nations were established, Jan. 1, 1979.

Mao died Sept. 9, 1976. By 1978, Vice Premier Deng Xiaoping had consolidated power, succeeding Mao as "paramount leader" of China. The new ruling group modified Maoist policies in education, culture, and industry, and sought better ties with non-Communist countries. By the mid-1980s, China had enacted far-reaching economic reforms, deemphasizing centralized planning and incorporating market-oriented incentives.

Some 100,000 students and workers staged a march in Beijing to demand political reforms, May 4, 1989. As the unrest spread, martial law was imposed, May 20. Troops entered Beijing, June 3-4, and crushed the pro-democracy protests, as tanks and armored personnel carriers rolled through Tiananmen Square. It is estimated that 5,000 died, 10,000 were injured, and hundreds of students and workers were arrested.

Deng Xiaoping died Feb. 19, 1997, leaving Jiang Zemin in control as president. By agreement with the UK, Hong Kong reverted to Chinese sovereignty July 1 (see below). Portugal returned Macao to China Dec. 20, 1999.

Hu Jintao was named Communist Party general secretary at the 16th party congress, Nov. 15, 2002, and elected president by the 10th National People's Congress, Mar. 15, 2003. With the successful launch and recovery, Oct. 15-16, 2003, of the Shenzhou 5 spacecraft, China became the third nation (after the U.S. and USSR) to send a man into space.

China's industries, exports, and demand for oil have all increased rapidly since the 1980s. Reports in 2007 that China had exported hazardous pet products, toothpaste, tires, and toys focused attention on factories' quality-control problems. Zheng Xiaoyu, the former head of China's food and drug safety agency, was executed July 10 for bribe taking and dereliction of duty.

The National People's Congress Mar. 15-16, 2008, reelected Pres. Hu Jintao and Premier Wen Jiabao. A powerful earthquake rocked Sichuan Province May 12, leaving 69,226 people dead and 17,923 missing. China reportedly spent $43 bil preparing for the XXIX Summer Olympics, held in Beijing Aug. 8-24, 2008. In a new quality-control scandal, China's health ministry reported Sept. 22 that nearly 53,000 babies had been sickened by contaminated milk powder; on Dec. 1, the estimate was raised to 300,000.

Western computer security experts Jan.-Feb. 2010 blamed hackers at 2 Chinese schools for Internet attacks on Google and at least 30 other firms. An earthquake Apr. 14 killed at least 2,200 people in NW China. The government reacted angrily when the Nobel Peace Prize was awarded Oct. 8 to Liu Xiaobo, a human rights activist who had received an 11-year prison sentence in Dec. 2009.

China has invested heavily in environmental technologies, especially wind and solar power, but illegal mining and ore processing remain major public-health hazards. Rapid growth during 2009-10 made China the world's second-largest economy, ranking behind the U.S. but ahead of Japan. A report made public June 2011 by China's central bank alleged that corrupt officials had smuggled more than $120 bil out of the country from the mid-1990s to 2008. China is the largest holder of U.S. debt, with $1.17 tril in U.S. obligations as of mid-2011.

Autonomous Regions

Guangxi Zhuang is in SE China, bounded on the N by Guizhou and Hunan provinces, E and S by Guangdong, on the SW by Vietnam, and on the W by Yunnan. It produces rice in the river valleys and has valuable forest products. Pop. (2010): 46,026,629.

Inner Mongolia was organized by the People's Republic in 1947. Its boundaries have undergone frequent changes, reaching its greatest extent in 1956 (and restored in 1979), with an area of 454,600 sq mi, allegedly in order to dilute the minority Mongol population. Chinese settlers outnumber the Mongols more than 10 to 1. Pop. (2010): 24,706,321. Capital: Hohhot.

Ningxia Hui, in north central China, is about 60,000 sq mi. Pop. (2010): 6,301,350. Capital: Yinchuan. The climate is mostly semiarid, with desert areas in the N. The Huang He (Yellow R.) flows across the N, furnishing water for irrigation. Coal is mined in the E. The majority of the population is Han, and the Hui (Chinese Muslims) constitute about one-third of the population. The region experienced a significant population boom, 1950-80, which has now stabilized.

Xinjiang Uighur, in Central Asia, is 635,900 sq mi, pop. (2010): 21,813,334 (75% Uighurs, a Turkic Muslim group, with a heavy Han Chinese increase in recent years). Capital: Urumqi. It is China's richest region in strategic minerals. China has moved to crack down on Uighur separatists, whom Beijing regards as terrorists. A protest march July 5, 2009, by Uighurs in Urumqi led to violent clashes with Han Chinese; at least 197 people (mostly Han) were killed in the riots. Renewed unrest including protests by Han in early Sept. led to the dismissal of the city's top Communist official.

Tibet, 471,700 sq mi, is a thinly populated region of high plateaus and massive mountains, the Himalayas on the S, the Kunluns on the N. High passes connect with India and Nepal; roads lead into China proper. Capital: Lhasa. Average altitude is 15,000 ft. Jiachan, 15,870 ft, is believed to be the highest inhabited town on earth. Agriculture is primitive. Pop. (2010): 3,002,166 (of whom about 500,000 are Chinese). Another 4 mil Tibetans form the majority of the population of vast adjacent areas that have long been incorporated into China.

China ruled all of Tibet from the 18th cent. Independence came in 1911, but China reasserted control in 1951, and a Communist government was installed in 1953. Serfdom was abolished, but all land remained collectivized.

A Tibetan uprising within China in 1956 spread to Lhasa in 1959. The rebellion was crushed by Chinese troops, and Buddhism was almost totally suppressed. The Dalai Lama and 100,000 Tibetans fled to India.

Efforts by Chinese authorities to halt peaceful demonstrations by Tibetan monks led to anti-Chinese riots in Lhasa, Mar. 14, 2008; the Chinese government sent troops into Tibet to crush dissent, sparking international protests.

Hong Kong

Hong Kong (Xianggang), located at the mouth of the Zhu Jiang (Pearl R.) in SE China, 90 mi S of Canton (Guangzhou), was a British dependency from 1842 until July 1, 1997, when it became a Special Administrative Region of China. Its nucleus is Hong Kong Isl., 31 sq mi, occupied by the British in 1841 and formally ceded to them in 1842, on which is located the seat of government. Opposite is Kowloon Peninsula, 3 sq mi, and Stonecutters Isl., added to the territory in 1860. An additional 355 sq mi known as the New Territories, a mainland area and islands, were leased from China, 1898, for 99 years. Area 426 sq mi (total); 407 sq mi (land); pop. (2011 est.) 7,122,508. **Website:** www.gov.hk

Hong Kong is a major center for trade and banking. Per capita GDP, $45,900 (2010 est.), is among the highest in the world. Principal industries are textiles and apparel; also tourism, electronics, shipbuilding, iron and steel, fishing, cement, and small manufactures. Hong Kong's spinning mills are among the best in the world. Outside of the public sector, the labor force is engaged in the following sectors: wholesale and retail trade, restaurants, and hotels 42.9%; financing, insurance, and real estate 21.4%; community and social services 19.7%; manufacturing 6.1%; and construction 1.9%.

Hong Kong harbor was long an important British naval station and one of the world's great transshipment ports. The colony was often a place of refuge for exiles from mainland China. It was occupied by Japan during WWII.

From 1949 to 1962 Hong Kong absorbed more than a million refugees fleeing Communist China. Starting in the 1950s, cheap labor led to a boom in light manufacturing, while liberal tax policies attracted foreign investment; Hong Kong became one of the wealthiest, most productive areas in the Far East.

With the end of the 99-year lease on the New Territories drawing near, Britain and China signed an agreement, Dec. 19, 1984, under which all of Hong Kong was to be returned to China in 1997; under this agreement Hong Kong was to be allowed to keep its capitalist system for 50 years. Following the transfer of government, Hong Kong retained its street names and its currency, the Hong Kong dollar (HK$7.75 = $1 U.S.), but without the queen's picture. Official languages remained Chinese (Cantonese dialect) and English.

Hundreds of thousands of Hong Kong residents turned out July 1, 2003, to protest a proposed anti-subversion law; the bill was withdrawn Sept. 5. Another mass march, July 1, 2004, protested

Beijing's refusal to allow greater freedom. Pro-democracy candidates won a majority of the popular vote in elections, Sept. 12, but failed to gain control of the Legislative Council. After Hong Kong's chief executive, Tung Chee-hwa resigned Mar. 10, 2005, Donald Tsang was chosen to serve the remaining two years of Tung's term; he won a full 5-year term Mar. 25, 2007.

Macao

Macao, area of 11 sq mi, is an enclave, a peninsula and two small islands, at the mouth of the Xi (Pearl) R. in China. It was established as a Portuguese trading colony in 1557. In 1849, Portugal claimed sovereignty over the territory; this claim was accepted by China in an 1887 treaty. Portugal granted broad autonomy in 1976. Under a 1987 agreement, Macao reverted to China Dec. 20, 1999. As in the case of Hong Kong, the Chinese government guaranteed Macao it would not interfere in its way of life and capitalist system for a period of 50 years. Tourism is the fastest-growing economic sector; revenues from casinos and other gambling activities exceeded $23 bil in 2010. The labor force is occupied in the following areas: gambling 14.2%, restaurants and hotels 13.6%, wholesale and retail trade 12.6%, construction 9.3%, public sector 6.6%, transport and communications 5.2%, manufacturing 4.9%, and financial services 2.1%. Pop. (2011 est.): 573,003.

Colombia
Republic of Colombia

People: Population: 44,725,543. **Age distrib.:** <15: 26.7%; 65+: 6.1%. **Pop. density:** 111.5 per sq mi, 43.1 per sq km. **Urban:** 75.1%. **Ethnic groups:** mestizo 58%, white 20%, mulatto 14%, black 4%, mixed black-Amerindian 3%, Amerindian 1%. **Principal language:** Spanish (official). **Chief religion:** Roman Catholic 90%.

Geography: Total area: 439,736 sq mi, 1,138,910 sq km; **Land area:** 401,044 sq mi, 1,038,700 sq km. **Location:** At the NW corner of South America. **Neighbors:** Panama on NW, Ecuador and Peru on S, Brazil and Venezuela on E. **Topography:** Three ranges of Andes—Western, Central, and Eastern Cordilleras—run through the country from N to S. The eastern range consists mostly of high tablelands, densely populated. The Magdalena R. rises in the Andes, flows N to Caribbean, through a rich alluvial plain. Sparsely settled plains in E are drained by Orinoco and Amazon systems. **Capital:** Bogotá, 8,262,000. **Cities (urban aggl.):** Medellín, 3,593,821; Cali, 2,401,004; Barranquilla, 1,866,711.

Government: Type: Republic. **Head of state and gov.:** Pres. Juan Manuel Santos; b. Aug. 10, 1951; in office: Aug. 7, 2010. **Local divisions:** 32 departments, capital district of Bogotá. **Defense budget:** $6.18 bil. **Active troops:** 283,004.

Economy: Industries: textiles, food proc., oil, clothing and footwear, beverages, chemicals, cement. **Chief crops:** coffee, cut flowers, bananas, rice, tobacco, corn, sugarcane, cocoa beans, oilseed, vegetables. **Natural resources:** petroleum, nat. gas, coal, iron ore, nickel, gold, copper, emeralds, hydropower. **Crude oil reserves:** 1.9 bil bbls. **Arable land:** 1.6%. **Livestock:** cattle: 27.4 mil; chickens: 157 mil; goats: 1.2 mil; pigs: 1.9 mil; sheep: 3.4 mil. **Fish catch:** 191,933 metric tons. **Electricity prod.:** 51 bil kWh. **Labor force:** agric. 18%, industry 13%, services 68%.

Finance: Monetary unit: Peso (COP) (Sept. 2011: 1,790.00 = $1 U.S.). **GDP:** $435.4 bil; **per capita GDP:** $9,800; **GDP growth:** 4.3%. **Imports:** $36.3 bil; U.S. 25.5%, China 13.4%, Mexico 9.4%, Brazil 5.9%, Germany 4.1%. **Exports:** $40.2 bil; U.S. 42%, EU 12.6%, China 5.2%, Ecuador 4.5%. **Tourism:** $2.1 bil. **Budget (2011 est.):** $83.9 bil. **Total reserves less gold:** $27.8 bil. **Gold:** 220,500 oz t. **CPI change:** 2.3%.

Transport: Railways: 543 mi. **Motor vehicles:** 37.6 vehicles per 1,000 pop. **Civil aviation:** 9 bil pass.-mi; 116 airports. **Chief ports:** Barranquilla, Buenaventura, Cartagena, Puerto Bolivar, Santa Marta, Turbo.

Communications: TV sets: 291 per 1,000 pop. **Radios:** 543 per 1,000 pop. **Telephone lines:** 14.7 per 100 pop. **Daily newspaper circ.:** 22.7 per 1,000 pop. **Internet:** 36.5 users per 100 pop.

Health: Life expect.: 71.3 male; 78.0 female. **Births:** 17.5 (per 1,000 pop.). **Deaths:** 5.3 (per 1,000 pop.). **Natural inc.:** 1.22%. **Infant mortality:** 16.4 (per 1,000 live births). **HIV rate:** 0.5%.

Education: Compulsory: ages 5-14. **Literacy:** 93.2%.

Major intl. organizations: UN (FAO, IBRD, ILO, IMF, WHO), OAS, WTO.

Embassy: 2118 Leroy Pl. NW 20008; 387-8338.

Website: wsp.presidencia.gov.co

Spain subdued the local Indian kingdoms (Funza, Tunja) by the 1530s and ruled Colombia and neighboring areas as New Granada for 300 years. Independence was won by 1819. Venezuela and Ecuador broke away in 1829-30, and Panama withdrew in 1903.

Colombia is plagued by rural and urban violence. "La Violencia" of 1948-58 claimed 200,000 lives; since 1989, political killings, kidnappings, and "disappearances" have victimized many thousands of civilians, and the internally displaced population has been estimated at up to 3 mil or more. Attempts at land and social reform and progress in industrialization have not reduced massive social problems. Government activity against local drug traffickers has sparked retaliation killings of politicians and judges.

Right-wing paramilitaries launched a campaign Dec. 22, 2000, against suspected left-wing guerrillas. A hardliner, Alvaro Uribe

Vélez, whose father had been killed by leftist rebels in 1983, won a presidential election May 26, 2002. A wave of guerrilla violence as he took office led Uribe to declare a "state of unrest" Aug. 12. Police powers were increased Sept. 10 as part of a new government offensive. The constitution was amended, Nov. 30, 2004, to allow the president to seek a second consecutive term; Uribe easily won reelection May 28, 2006. Key political figures, including major allies of Uribe, were arrested in 2007 on charges of colluding with paramilitary death squads. Guerrilla strength has waned in recent years.

Former Def. Min. Juan Manuel Santos, a conservative ally of Uribe, won a presidential runoff election June 20, 2010, and took office Aug. 7.

Colombia processes at least 90% of the cocaine reaching the U.S. Since 2000, the U.S. has provided more than $8 bil to Colombia, much of it to combat the drug trade.

Comoros
Union of the Comoros

People: Population: 721,886. **Age distrib.:** <15: 42.5%; 65+: 3.6%. **Pop. density:** 836.5 per sq mi, 323 per sq km. **Urban:** 28.2%. **Ethnic groups:** Antalote, Cafre, Makoa, Oimatsaha, Sakalava. **Principal languages:** Arabic, French (both official); Shikomoro (blend of Swahili & Arabic). **Chief religion:** Sunni Muslim 98%, Roman Catholic 2%.

Geography: Total area: 863 sq mi, 2,235 sq km; **Land area:** 863 sq mi, 2,235 sq km. **Location:** 3 islands—Grande Comore (Njazidja), Anjouan (Nzwani), and Moheli (Mwali)—in the Mozambique Channel between NW Madagascar and SE Africa. **Neighbors:** Nearest are Mozambique on W, Madagascar on E. **Topography:** The islands are of volcanic origin, with an active volcano on Grande Comore. **Capital:** Moroni, 49,000.

Government: Type: Republic. **Head of state and gov.:** Pres. Ikililou Dhoinine; b. Aug. 14, 1962; in office: May 26, 2011. **Local divisions:** 3 main islands with 4 municipalities. **Defense budget/active troops:** NA.

Economy: Industries: fishing, tourism, perfume distillation. **Chief crops:** vanilla, cloves, ylang-ylang, copra, coconuts, bananas, cassava. **Natural resources:** negligible. **Arable land:** 43.0%. **Livestock:** cattle: 50,000; chickens: 520,000; goats: 118,000; sheep: 23,000. **Fish catch:** 20,450 metric tons. **Electricity prod.:** 52 mil kWh. **Labor force:** agric. 80%, industry and services 20%.

Finance: Monetary unit: Franc (KMF) (Sept. 2011: 351.87 = $1 U.S.). **GDP:** $800 mil; **per capita GDP:** $1,000; **GDP growth:** 2.1%. **Imports (2006):** $143 mil; France 16.8%, Pakistan 14.3%, UAE 8.5%, China 6.8%, India 5.6%, Kenya 4.9%. **Exports (2006):** $32 mil; Turkey 27.3%, France 22.2%, Singapore 18.9%, Italy 6.6%, Saudi Arabia 5.4%. **Tourism:** NA. **Budget:** NA. **Total reserves less gold** $145.3 mil. **Gold:** 579 oz t. **CPI change (2008-09):** -0.1%.

Transport: Civil aviation: 4 airports. **Chief ports:** Mayotte, Mutsamudu.

Communications: TV sets: 31 per 1,000 pop. **Radios:** 159 per 1,000 pop. **Telephone lines:** 2.9 per 100 pop. **Internet:** 5.1 users per 100 pop.

Health: Life expect.: 60.2 male; 64.6 female. **Births:** 32.8 (per 1,000 pop.). **Deaths:** 8.4 (per 1,000 pop.). **Natural inc.:** 2.43%. **Infant mortality:** 70.9 (per 1,000 live births). **HIV rate:** 0.1%.

Education: Compulsory: ages 6-13. **Literacy:** 74.2%.

Major intl. organizations: UN (FAO, IBRD, ILO, IMF, WHO), AL, AU, WTO (observer).

Permanent UN Mission: 866 United Nations Plz., Ste. 418, New York, NY 10017; (212) 750-1637.

Website: www.beit-salam.km

The islands were controlled by Muslim sultans until the French acquired them 1841-1909. They became a French overseas territory in 1947. A 1974 referendum favored independence, with only the Christian island of Mayotte preferring association with France. The French National Assembly decided to allow each of the islands to decide its own fate. The Comore Chamber of Deputies declared independence July 6, 1975, with Ahmed Abdallah as president. In a referendum in 1976, Mayotte voted to remain French.

A leftist regime that seized power from Abdallah in 1975 was deposed in a pro-French 1978 coup in which he regained the presidency. In Nov. 1989, Pres. Abdallah was assassinated; soon after, a multiparty system was instituted. A Sept. 1995 military coup, assisted by French mercenaries, ousted Pres. Said Mohamed Djohar. French troops invaded, Oct. 4, and forced coup leaders to surrender.

Attempts to work out a new constitutional relationship between Grande Comore, Anjouan, and Moheli have been ongoing since Anjouan and Moheli seceded from the Comoros in 1997. Unrest on Grande Comore culminated in a military coup, Apr. 30, 1999. Anjouans endorsed secession in a disputed vote Jan. 23, 2000.

Irregularities marred the presidential runoff election of Apr. 14, 2002, won by Azali Assoumani, who led the 1999 coup. Elections for national and island assemblies took place Mar.-Apr. 2004. Ahmed Abdallah Mohamed Sambi won a presidential runoff vote, May 14, 2006. Each of the 3 islands elected its own president in 2002 and 2007. Anjouan's leader, Col. Mohamed Bacar, who had refused to relinquish power after the central government ruled his 2007 election illegal, was forced to flee when Comorian and African Union troops took control of the island, Mar. 25-26, 2008.

A Yemeni Airbus A310 jetliner en route from Sana'a', Yemen, plunged into rough seas June 30, 2009, while trying to land at Moroni; the crash killed 152 of the 153 people on board. Sambi's Vice Pres. Ikililou Dhoinine won a presidential runoff election Dec. 26, 2010.

Congo
Democratic Republic of the Congo

(Congo, officially Democratic Republic of the Congo, is also known as Congo-Kinshasa. It should not be confused with Republic of the Congo, commonly called Congo Republic, and also known as Congo-Brazzaville.)

People: Population: 71,712,867. **Age distrib.:** <15: 44.4%; 65+: 2.6%. **Pop. density:** 81.9 per sq mi, 31.6 per sq km. **Urban:** 35.2%. **Ethnic groups:** 200+ groups, majority Bantu. Four largest tribes (Mongo, Luba, Kongo [all Bantu], Mangbetu-Azande [Hamitic] 45%. **Principal languages:** French (official), Lingala (lingua franca), Kingwana (Kiswahili or Swahili dialect), Kikongo, Tshiluba. **Chief religions:** Roman Catholic 50%, Protestant 20%, Kimbanguist 10%, Muslim 10%, other (incl. syncretic sects, indigenous beliefs) 10%.

Geography: Total area: 905,355 sq mi, 2,344,858 sq km; **Land area:** 875,312 sq mi, 2,267,048 sq km. **Location:** In central Africa. **Neighbors:** Congo-Brazzaville on W; Central African Republic, Sudan on N; Uganda, Rwanda, Burundi, Tanzania on E; Zambia, Angola on S. **Topography:** Congo includes the bulk of the Congo R. basin. The vast central region is a low-lying plateau covered by rain forest. Mountainous terraces in the W, savannas in the S and SE, grasslands toward the N, and the high Ruwenzori Mts. on the E surround the central region. A short strip of territory borders the Atlantic O. **Capital:** Kinshasa, 8,401,000. **Cities (urban aggl.):** Lubumbashi, 1,542,945; Mbuji-Mayi, 1,488,468; Kananga, 878,263.

Government: Type: Republic. **Head of state:** Pres. Joseph Kabila; b. June 24, 1971; in office: Jan. 26, 2001. **Head of gov.:** Prime Min. Adolphe Muzito; b. 1957; in office: Oct. 10, 2008. **Local divisions:** 10 provinces, 1 city. **Defense budget:** $197 mil. **Active troops:** 159,000.

Economy: Industries: mining, mineral proc., consumer prods., timber, cement. **Chief crops:** coffee, sugar, palm oil, rubber, tea, cotton, cocoa, quinine, cassava, manioc, bananas, plantains, peanuts, root crops, corn, fruits. **Natural resources:** cobalt, copper, niobium, tantalum, petroleum, diamonds, gold, silver, zinc, manganese, tin, uranium, coal, hydropower, timber. **Crude oil reserves:** 180 mil bbls. **Arable land:** 3.0%. **Livestock:** cattle: 755,000; chickens: 19.8 mil; goats: 4.1 mil; pigs: 965,000; sheep: 900,000. **Fish catch:** 238,970 metric tons. **Electricity prod.:** 7.5 bil kWh. **Labor force:** NA.

Finance: Monetary unit: Franc (CDF) (Sept. 2011: 915.00 = $1 U.S.). **GDP:** $23.1 bil; **per capita GDP:** $300; **GDP growth:** 7.2%. **Imports** (2009 est.): $5.3 bil; South Africa 17.5%, Belgium 9.8%, China 9.8%, Zambia 9.2%, France 7%, Zimbabwe 6.3%, Kenya 5.3%. **Exports** (2009 est.): $3.8 bil; China 41%, Zambia 17.8%, U.S. 12.4%, Belgium 8.6%, India 5.2%. **Tourism:** NA. **Budget** (2006 est.): $2 bil. **Total reserves less gold:** $1.8 bil. **CPI change** (2007-08): 17.3%.

Transport: Railways: 2,490 mi. **Motor vehicles:** 23.9 vehicles per 1,000 pop. **Civil aviation:** 26 airports. **Chief ports:** Boma, Bukavu, Bumba, Goma, Kinshasa, Kisangani, Matadi, Mbandaka. **Communications: TV sets:** 5 per 1,000 pop. **Radios:** 379 per 1,000 pop. **Telephone lines:** 0.1 per 100 pop. **Internet:** 0.7 users per 100 pop.

Health: Life expect.: 53.9 male; 56.8 female. **Births:** 37.7 (per 1,000 pop.). **Deaths:** 11.1 (per 1,000 pop.). **Natural inc.:** 2.67%. **Infant mortality:** 78.4 (per 1,000 live births). **HIV rate:** NA. **Education:** Compulsory: ages 6-13. **Literacy:** 66.8%. **Major intl. organizations:** UN and most of its specialized agencies, AU, WTO.

Embassy: 1726 M St. NW 20036; 234-7690.
Website: www.presidentrdc.cd

The earliest inhabitants of Congo may have been the pygmies, followed by Bantus from the east and Nilotic tribes from the north. The large Bantu Bakongo kingdom ruled much of Congo and Angola when Portuguese explorers visited in the 15th cent.

Leopold II, king of the Belgians, formed an international group to exploit the Congo region in 1876. In 1877 Henry M. Stanley explored the Congo, and in 1878 the king's group sent him back to organize the region and win over the indigenous leaders. The Conference of Berlin, 1884-85, established the Congo Free State with Leopold as king and chief owner. Exploitation of Congolese laborers on the rubber plantations caused international criticism and led to granting of a colonial charter, 1908; the colony became known as the Belgian Congo. Millions of Congolese are believed to have died under brutal European rule between 1880 and 1920.

Belgian and Congolese leaders agreed Jan. 27, 1960, that Congo would become independent in June. In the first general elections, May 31, Patrice Lumumba's party won a plurality in the National Assembly. The Republic of the Congo was proclaimed June 30. Widespread violence caused Europeans and others to flee. The UN Security Council, Aug. 9, called on Belgium to

withdraw its troops and sent a UN contingent. Lumumba was dismissed as premier Sept. 5, 1960, and was murdered Jan. 17, 1961. The last UN troops left the Congo June 30, 1964.

In late 1965 Gen. Joseph D. Mobutu was named president. He later changed his name to Mobutu Sese Seko and ruled as a dictator. The country became the Democratic Republic of the Congo (1966) and the Republic of Zaire (1971). Under Mobutu, economic decline and government corruption plagued Zaire. He sought to retain power despite mounting international pressure and internal opposition.

During 1994, Zaire was inundated with refugees from the massive ethnic bloodshed in Rwanda. Ethnic violence spread to eastern Zaire in 1996. In Oct. militant Hutus, who dominated in the refugee camps, fought against rebels (mostly Tutsis) in Zaire, precipitating intervention by government troops. As a result of the fighting, Rwandan refugees abandoned the camps; hundreds of thousands returned to Rwanda, while hundreds of thousands more were dispersed throughout eastern Zaire. The rebels, led by Gen. Laurent Kabila—a former Marxist and longtime opponent of Mobutu—gained momentum and began to move west across Zaire. On May 17, 1997, Kabila's troops entered Kinshasa and Mobutu went into exile. The country again assumed the name Democratic Republic of the Congo. Mobutu died Sept. 7 in Rabat, Morocco.

Kabila, who ruled by decree, alienated UN officials, international aid donors, and former allies. Rebels assisted by Rwanda and Uganda threatened Kinshasa in Aug. 1998, but the assault was turned back with help from Angola, Namibia, and Zimbabwe. Rebel groups agreed to a cease-fire on Aug. 31, 1999, but the truce was widely violated. Kabila was assassinated Jan. 16, 2001, apparently by one of his bodyguards, and was succeeded by his son Joseph.

The overall death toll from the civil war and related causes was estimated at 3.3 mil through Nov. 2002. By then, Rwanda and Uganda had agreed to pull out their remaining troops. A power-sharing accord signed Apr. 2, 2003, led to the installation of a new Congolese government in July. A new constitution won legislative approval May 13, 2005. A UN peacekeeping force (MONUC), established in 1999, remained in the country to oversee elections, held July 30-31, 2006, the nation's first multiparty vote since 1960. Kabila defeated former rebel leader Jean-Pierre Bemba in a presidential runoff election, Oct. 29, 2006.

Hundreds reportedly died in Kinshasa, Mar. 22-23, 2007, in clashes between security forces and a militia loyal to Bemba, who fled to Europe; he was arrested in Belgium May 24, 2008, on war crimes charges. A peace deal with militia groups in eastern Congo, including one led by Tutsi rebel Gen. Laurent Nkunda, was signed Jan. 23, 2008, but Nkunda launched a new offensive Aug. 28; he was arrested by Rwandan authorities Jan. 22, 2009.

Visiting eastern Congo Aug. 11, 2009, U.S. Sec. of State Hillary Clinton announced a $17 mil program to curb rampant sexual violence in the region. The UN reported that more than 8,000 Congolese women were raped in 2009; at least 150 others in eastern Congo were gang-raped by Rwandan rebels, July 30-Aug. 3, 2010. A study published by the *American Journal of Public Health* in June 2011 estimated that more than 1,000 women were raped in Congo every day.

The MONUC peacekeeping mission, reconstituted and renamed MONUSCO as of July 1, 2010, included about 17,000 military personnel in mid-2011.

Congo Republic
Republic of the Congo

(Congo Republic, officially Republic of the Congo, is also known as Congo-Brazzaville. It should not be confused with Democratic Republic of the Congo [formerly Zaire], now commonly called Congo, and also known as Congo-Kinshasa.)

People: Population: 4,243,929. **Age distrib.:** <15: 45.6%; 65+: 2.8%. **Pop. density:** 32.2 per sq mi, 12.4 per sq km. **Urban:** 62.1%. **Ethnic groups:** Kongo 48%, Sangha 20%, Teke 17%, M'Bochi 12%, Europeans and other 3%. **Principal languages:** French (official); Lingala, Monokutuba (lingua francas); many local languages & dialects (Kikongo most widespread). **Chief religions:** Christian 50%, animist 48%, Muslim 2%.

Geography: Total area: 132,047 sq mi, 342,000 sq km; **Land area:** 131,854 sq mi, 341,500 sq km. **Location:** In W central Africa. **Neighbors:** Gabon and Cameroon on W, Central African Republic on N, Congo-Kinshasa (formerly Zaire) on E, Angola on SW. **Topography:** Much of the Congo is covered by thick forests. A coastal plain leads to the fertile Niari Valley. The center is a plateau; the Congo R. basin consists of flood plains in the lower and savanna in the upper portion. **Capital:** Brazzaville, 1,292,000.

Government: Type: Republic. **Head of state and gov.:** Pres. Denis Sassou-Nguesso; b. 1943; in office: Oct. 25, 1997. **Local divisions:** 10 regions, 6 communes. **Defense budget:** $218 mil. **Active troops:** 10,000.

Economy: Industries: petroleum extraction, cement, lumber, brewing, sugar, palm oil. **Chief crops:** cassava, sugar, rice, corn, peanuts, vegetables, coffee, cocoa. **Natural resources:** petroleum, timber, potash, lead, zinc, uranium, copper, phosphates, gold, magnesium, nat. gas, hydropower. **Crude oil reserves:** 1.6 bil bbls. **Arable land:** 1.5%. **Livestock:** cattle: 115,000; chickens: 2.4 mil; goats: 295,000; pigs: 68,000; sheep: 100,000. **Fish catch:** 61,277 metric tons. **Electricity prod.:** 452 mil kWh. **Labor force:** NA.

Finance: Monetary unit: CFA BEAC Franc (XAF) (Sept. 2011: 468.55 = $1 U.S.). **GDP:** $17.1 bil; **per capita GDP:** $4,100; **GDP growth:** 9.1%. **Imports:** $3.6 bil; France 20.9%, China 12.1%, Italy 9.7%, U.S. 9.1%, India 6.5%, Belgium 4.6%. **Exports:** $9.2 bil; U.S. 43.1%, China 23.5%, France 8.8%, India 6.2%. **Tourism:** NA. **Budget:** $2.6 bil. **Total reserves less gold:** $4.4 bil. **Gold** (2008): 11,126 oz t. **CPI change** (2008-09): 5%.

Transport: Railways: 551 mi. **Motor vehicles:** 15.7 vehicles per 1,000 pop. **Civil aviation:** 19.3 mil pass.-mi; 6 airports. **Chief ports:** Brazzaville, Djeno, Impfondo, Ouesso, Oyo, Pointe-Noire.

Communications: TV sets: 50 per 1,000 pop. **Radios:** 107 per 1,000 pop. **Telephone lines:** 0.2 per 100 pop. **Internet:** 5 users per 100 pop.

Health: Life expect.: 53.6 male; 56.3 female. **Births:** 40.6 (per 1,000 pop.). **Deaths:** 11.5 (per 1,000 pop.). **Natural inc.:** 2.91%. **Infant mortality:** 76.1 (per 1,000 live births). **HIV rate:** 3.4%.

Education: Compulsory: ages 6-15. **Literacy:** NA.

Major intl. organizations: UN (FAO, IBRD, ILO, IMF, WHO), AU, WTO.

Embassy: 4891 Colorado Ave. NW 20011; 726-5500.

Website: www.presidence.cg

The Loango Kingdom flourished in the 15th cent., as did the Anzico Kingdom of the Batekes; by the late 17th cent. they had weakened. By 1885, France established control of the region, then called the Middle Congo. Republic of the Congo gained independence Aug. 15, 1960.

After a 1963 coup sparked by trade unions, the country adopted a Marxist-Leninist stance, with the USSR and China vying for influence. France remained a dominant trade partner and source of technical assistance, however, and French-owned private enterprise retained a major economic role. In 1970, the country was renamed People's Republic of the Congo. Since the 1980s, oil has come to dominate the economy.

In 1990, Marxism was renounced and opposition parties were legalized. In 1991 the country's name was changed back to Republic of the Congo, and a new constitution was approved. A democratically elected government came into office in 1992. Factional fighting broke out in Brazzaville, June 5, 1997, and intensified during the summer, devastating the capital. Troops loyal to former Marxist dictator Denis Sassou-Nguesso took control of the city Oct. 15, 1997; he claimed lopsided victories in the presidential elections of Mar. 10, 2002, and July 12, 2009.

Costa Rica
Republic of Costa Rica

People: Population: 4,576,562. **Age distrib.:** <15: 24.6%; 65+: 6.4%. **Pop. density:** 232.1 per sq mi, 89.6 per sq km. **Urban:** 64.4%. **Ethnic groups:** white (incl. mestizo) 94%, black 3%, Amerindian 1%, Chinese 1%. **Principal languages:** Spanish (official), English. **Chief religions:** Roman Catholic 76%, Evangelical 14%, Jehovah's Witnesses 1%, none 3%.

Geography: Total area: 19,730 sq mi, 51,100 sq km; **Land area:** 19,714 sq mi, 51,060 sq km. **Location:** In Central America. **Neighbors:** Nicaragua on N, Panama on S. **Topography:** Lowlands by the Caribbean are tropical. The interior plateau, with an altitude of about 4,000 ft, is temperate. **Capital:** San José, 1,416,000.

Government: Type: Republic. **Head of state and gov.:** Pres. Laura Chinchilla Miranda; b. Mar. 28, 1959; in office: May 8, 2010. **Local divisions:** 7 provinces. **Defense budget:** $215 mil (paramilitary budget). **Active troops:** 9,800 (paramilitary).

Economy: Industries: microprocessors, food proc., medical equip., textiles and clothing, constr. materials, fertilizer, plastic prods. **Chief crops:** bananas, pineapples, coffee, melons, ornamental plants, sugar, corn, rice, beans, potatoes. **Natural resources:** hydropower. **Arable land:** 3.9%. **Livestock:** cattle: 1.3 mil; chickens: 22.1 mil; goats: 5,000; pigs: 440,000; sheep: 2,700. **Fish catch:** 46,475 metric tons. **Electricity prod.:** 9.3 bil kWh. **Labor force:** agric. 14%, industry 22%, services 64%.

Finance: Monetary unit: Colon (CRC) (Sept. 2011: 507.70 = $1 U.S.). **GDP:** $51.2 bil; **per capita GDP:** $11,300; **GDP growth:** 4.2%. **Imports:** $13.3 bil; U.S. 42.1%, Mexico 6.5%, China 6.2%, Japan 5.3%. **Exports:** $10 bil; U.S. 35.9%, China 8.8%, Netherlands 6.8%, Panama 4.6%. **Tourism:** $2.1 bil. **Budget:** $6.9 bil. **Total reserves less gold:** $4.6 bil. **Gold:** 1,987 oz t. **CPI change:** 5.7%.

Transport: Railways: 173 mi. **Motor vehicles:** 168.5 vehicles per 1,000 pop. **Civil aviation:** 1.4 bil pass.-mi; 39 airports. **Chief ports:** Caldera, Puerto Limon.

Communications: TV sets: 250 per 1,000 pop. **Radios:** 222 per 1,000 pop. **Telephone lines:** 31.8 per 100 pop. **Daily newspaper circ.:** 64.7 per 1,000 pop. **Internet:** 36.5 users per 100 pop.

Health: Life expect.: 75.1 male; 80.5 female. **Births:** 16.5 (per 1,000 pop.). **Deaths:** 4.3 (per 1,000 pop.). **Natural inc.:** 1.22%. **Infant mortality:** 9.5 (per 1,000 live births). **HIV rate:** 0.3%.

Education: Compulsory: ages 5-14. **Literacy:** 96.1%.

Major intl. organizations: UN (FAO, IBRD, ILO, IMF, WHO), OAS, WTO.

Embassy: 2114 S St. NW 20008; 234-2945.

Website: www.gobiernofacil.go.cr

Guaymi Indians inhabited the area when Spaniards arrived, 1502. Independence came in 1821. Costa Rica seceded from the Central American Federation in 1838. Since the civil war of 1948-49, there has been little violent social conflict, and free political institutions have been preserved.

Costa Rica, though still a largely agricultural country, has achieved a relatively high standard of living, and land ownership is widespread. Tourism is growing rapidly. Nobel Peace Prizewinner Óscar Arias Sánchez, president 1986-90, won a second term in a close election, Feb. 5, 2006. A decisive election victory Feb. 7, 2010, made ruling party candidate Laura Chinchilla Miranda the nation's first female president.

Côte d'Ivoire
Republic of Côte d'Ivoire

People: Population: 21,504,162. **Age distrib.:** <15: 39.8%; 65+: 3%. **Pop. density:** 175.1 per sq mi, 67.6 per sq km. **Urban:** 50.6%. **Ethnic groups:** Akan 42%, Voltaiques or Gur 18%, N Mandes 17%, Krous 11%, S Mandes 10%. **Principal languages:** French (official), 60 native dialects (Dioula most widely spoken). **Chief religions:** Muslim 39%, Christian 33%, indigenous 12%, none 17%.

Geography: Total area: 124,504 sq mi, 322,463 sq km; **Land area:** 122,782 sq mi, 318,003 sq km. **Location:** On S coast of W Africa. **Neighbors:** Liberia, Guinea on W; Mali, Burkina Faso on N; Ghana on E. **Topography:** Forests cover the W half of the country, and range from a coastal strip to halfway to the N on the E. A sparse inland plain leads to low mountains in NW. **Capital:** Yamoussoukro, 808,000; Abidjan (seat), 4,009,000.

Government: Type: Republic. **Head of state:** Pres. Alassane Ouattara; b. Jan. 1, 1942; in office: Apr. 11, 2011 (sworn in Dec. 4, 2010). **Head of gov.:** Prime Min. Guillaume Soro; b. May 8, 1972; in office: Apr. 4, 2007. **Local divisions:** 58 departments. **Defense budget:** $340 mil. **Active troops:** 17,050.

Economy: Industries: foodstuffs, beverages, wood prods., oil refining, truck and bus assembly, textiles, fertilizer. **Chief crops:** coffee, cocoa beans, bananas, palm kernels, corn, rice, manioc, sweet potatoes, sugar, cotton, rubber. **Natural resources:** petroleum, nat. gas, diamonds, manganese, iron ore, cobalt, bauxite, copper, gold. **Crude oil reserves:** 100 mil bbls. **Arable land:** 8.8%. **Livestock:** cattle: 1.5 mil; chickens: 33 mil; goats: 1.3 mil; pigs: 330,000; sheep: 1.6 mil. **Fish catch:** 49,290 metric tons. **Electricity prod.:** 5.5 bil kWh. **Labor force:** agric. 68%, industry and services NA.

Finance: Monetary unit: CFA BCEAO Franc (XOF) (Sept. 2011: 468.55 = $1 U.S.). **GDP:** $37 bil; **per capita GDP:** $1,800; **GDP growth:** 2.6%. **Imports:** $7 bil; Nigeria 20.7%, France 14.2%, China 7.2%, Thailand 5.1%. **Exports:** $10.3 bil; Netherlands 13.9%, France 10.7%, U.S. 7.8%, Germany 7.2%, Nigeria 7%, Ghana 5.6%. **Tourism:** $113 mil. **Budget:** $5.2 bil. **Total reserves less gold:** $3.6 bil. **CPI change:** 1.7%.

Transport: Railways: 410 mi. **Motor vehicles:** 5.5 vehicles per 1,000 pop. **Civil aviation:** 7 airports. **Chief ports:** Abidjan, Espoir, San-Pédro.

Communications: TV sets: 44 per 1,000 pop. **Radios:** 138 per 1,000 pop. **Telephone lines:** 1.1 per 100 pop. **Internet:** 2.6 users per 100 pop.

Health: Life expect.: 55.8 male; 57.8 female. **Births:** 31.0 (per 1,000 pop.). **Deaths:** 10.2 (per 1,000 pop.). **Natural inc.:** 2.08%. **Infant mortality:** 64.8 (per 1,000 live births). **HIV rate:** 3.4%.

Education: Compulsory: ages 6-15. **Literacy:** 55.3%.

Major intl. organizations: UN and all of its specialized agencies, AU, WTO.

Embassy: 3421 Massachusetts Ave. NW 20007; 797-0300.

Website: www.gouv.ci

A French protectorate from 1842, Côte d'Ivoire became independent in 1960. The name was officially changed from Ivory Coast, Oct. 1985. The country is a leading producer of coffee and cocoa beans.

Students and workers protested, Feb. 1990, demanding the ouster of longtime Pres. Félix Houphouët-Boigny. Côte d'Ivoire held its first multiparty presidential election Oct. 1990, and Houphouët-Boigny retained his office. He died Dec. 7, 1993. The National Assembly named a successor, Henri Konan Bédié, who was reelected Oct. 22, 1995; he was ousted in a military coup Dec. 24, 1999. The coup leader, Robert Guéi, apparently lost a presidential vote Oct. 22, 2000, but claimed victory anyway. After mass protests, he fled, and Laurent Gbagbo became president. Guéi was killed in Abidjan Sept. 19, 2002, after a mutiny broke out there and in Bouaké and Korhogo.

Agreement on power sharing was reached in Mar. 2003, and Gbagbo and former rebel leaders held a ceremony July 5, declaring that the war was over. The country remained divided, however, with rebels holding the north and government forces controlling the south. Under a new accord reached Mar. 4, 2007, rebel leader Guillaume Soro was sworn in as prime min. Apr. 4.

Both Gbagbo and his main challenger, former Prime Min. Alassane Ouattara, claimed victory after a presidential runoff election Nov. 28, 2010. Gbagbo clung to power, although the UN, U.S.,

France, and the Economic Community of West African States recognized Ouattara as the legitimate winner. A violent power struggle followed, claiming an estimated 1,500 lives and displacing at least 1 mil people. With support from French and UN forces, Ouattara loyalists captured Gbagbo in Abidjan, Apr. 11, 2011. Human Rights Watch reported June 2 that after taking power, Ouattara's troops killed at least 149 suspected Gbagbo supporters. A UN peacekeeping mission (UNOCI), authorized since 2004, had more than 9,600 military personnel in Côte d'Ivoire in mid-2011.

Croatia
Republic of Croatia

People: Population: 4,483,804. **Age distrib.:** <15: 15.1%; 65+: 16.9%. **Pop. density:** 207.5 per sq mi, 80.1 per sq km. **Urban:** 57.7%. **Ethnic groups:** Croat 90%, Serb 5%, other (incl. Bosniak, Hungarian, Slovene, Czech, Roma) 6%. **Principal languages:** Croatian (official), Serbian. **Chief religions:** Roman Catholic 88%, Orthodox 4%, Muslim 1%, none 5%.

Geography: Total area: 21,851 sq mi, 56,594 sq km; **Land area:** 21,612 sq mi, 55,974 sq km. **Location:** SE Europe, on the Balkan Peninsula. **Neighbors:** Slovenia, Hungary on N; Bosnia and Herzegovina, Serbia, Montenegro on E. **Topography:** Flat plains in NE; highlands, low mts. along Adriatic coast. **Capital:** Zagreb, 685,000.

Government: Type: Parliamentary democracy. **Head of state:** Pres. Ivo Josipovic; b. Aug. 28, 1957; in office: Feb. 18, 2010. **Head of gov.:** Prime Min. Jadranka Kosor; b. July 1, 1953; in office: July 6, 2009. **Local divisions:** 20 counties and Zagreb. **Defense budget:** $863 mil. **Active troops:** 18,600.

Economy: Industries: chemicals and plastics, machine tools, fabricated metal, electronics. **Chief crops:** wheat, corn, sugar beets, sunflower seeds, barley, alfalfa, clover, olives. **Natural resources:** oil, coal, bauxite, iron ore, calcium, gypsum, nat. asphalt, silica, mica, clays, salt, hydropower. **Crude oil reserves:** 71 mil bbls. **Arable land:** 15.5%. **Livestock:** cattle: 447,000; chickens: 6.7 mil; goats: 76,000; pigs: 1.3 mil; sheep: 619,000. **Fish catch:** 69,160 metric tons. **Electricity prod.:** 11.7 bil kWh. **Labor force:** agric. 5%, industry 31.3%, services 63.6%.

Finance: Monetary unit: Kuna (HRK) (Sept. 2011: 5.35 = $1 U.S.). **GDP:** $78.1 bil; **per capita GDP:** $17,400; **GDP growth:** −1.4%. **Imports:** $20.9 bil; Italy 15.5%, Germany 13.6%, Russia 9.3%, China 6.8%, Slovenia 5.7%, Austria 5%. **Exports:** $11.5 bil; Italy 19.1%, Bosnia and Herzegovina 13%, Germany 11.1%, Slovenia 7.5%, Austria 5.4%. **Tourism:** $8.3 bil. **Budget:** $24.3 bil. **Total reserves less gold:** $14.1 bil. **CPI change:** 1%.

Transport: Railways: 1,691 mi. **Motor vehicles:** 379.2 vehicles per 1,000 pop. **Civil aviation:** 715.2 mil pass.-mi; 23 airports. **Chief ports:** Omisalj, Ploce, Rijeka, Sibenik, Split, Vukovar.

Communications: TV sets: 550 per 1,000 pop. **Radios:** 327 per 1,000 pop. **Telephone lines:** 42 per 100 pop. **Internet:** 60.3 users per 100 pop.

Health: Life expect.: 72.2 male; 79.6 female. **Births:** 9.6 (per 1,000 pop.). **Deaths:** 11.9 (per 1,000 pop.). **Natural inc.:** −0.23%. **Infant mortality:** 6.2 (per 1,000 live births). **HIV rate:** <0.1%.

Education: Compulsory: ages 7-14. **Literacy:** 98.8%.

Major intl. organizations: UN (FAO, IBRD, ILO, IMF, WHO), NATO, OSCE, WTO.

Embassy: 2343 Massachusetts Ave. NW 20008; 588-5899. **Website:** www.vlada.hr

From the 7th cent. the area was inhabited by Croats, a south Slavic people. It was formed into a kingdom under Tomislav in 924, and joined with Hungary in 1102. The Croats became westernized and separated from Slavs under Austro-Hungarian influence. Croatia united with other Yugoslav areas to proclaim the Kingdom of Serbs, Croats, and Slovenes in 1918. A nominally independent state between 1941 and 1945, it became a constituent republic of Yugoslavia in the 1946 constitution.

On June 25, 1991, Croatia declared independence from Yugoslavia. Fighting began between ethnic Serbs and Croats, with the former gaining control of about 30% of Croatian territory. 1995. Pres. Franjo Tudjman signed a peace accord with leaders of Bosnia and Serbia in Paris, Dec. 14. The last Serb-held enclave, E Slavonia, returned to Croatian control Jan. 15, 1998. Tudjman died Dec. 10, 1999. Indicted in 2001 and arrested in 2005, former Croatian Gen. Ante Gotovina was convicted by a UN tribunal Apr. 15, 2011, and sentenced to 24 years in prison for war crimes committed in the mid-1990s. Stipe Mesic, a moderate, won a presidential runoff election Feb. 7, 2000, and was reelected Jan. 16, 2005. Croatia became a full member of NATO Apr. 1, 2009. Law professor and composer Ivo Josipovic, the nominee of the Social Democratic Party, won a presidential runoff election Jan. 10, 2010, and took office Feb. 18.

Cuba
Republic of Cuba

People: Population: 11,087,330. **Age distrib.:** <15: 17.3%; 65+: 11.7%. **Pop. density:** 261.5 per sq mi, 101 per sq km. **Urban:** 75.2%. **Ethnic groups:** white 65%, mulatto & mestizo 25%, black

10%. **Principal language:** Spanish (official). **Chief religion:** Roman Catholic (nominally, prior to Castro assuming power) 85%.

Geography: Total area: 42,803 sq mi, 110,860 sq km; **Land area:** 42,402 sq mi, 109,820 sq km. **Location:** In Caribbean, westernmost of West Indies. **Neighbors:** Bahamas, U.S. to N; Mexico to W; Jamaica to S; Haiti to E. **Topography:** Coastline is about 2,500 mi. The N coast is steep and rocky, the S coast low and marshy. Low hills and fertile valleys cover more than half the country. Sierra Maestra, in E, is the highest of 3 mountain ranges. **Capital:** Havana, 2,140,000.

Government: Type: Communist state. **Head of state and gov.:** Pres. Raúl Castro Ruz; b. June 3, 1931; in office: Feb. 24, 2008 (acting from July 31, 2006). **Local divisions:** 14 provinces, 1 special municipality. **Defense budget:** NA. **Active troops:** 49,000.

Economy: Industries: sugar, petroleum, tobacco, constr., nickel, steel, cement, agric. machinery, pharmaceuticals. **Chief crops:** sugar, tobacco, citrus, coffee, rice, potatoes, beans. **Natural resources:** cobalt, nickel, iron ore, chromium, copper, salt, timber, silica, petroleum. **Crude oil reserves:** 124 mil bbls. **Arable land:** 34.3%. **Livestock:** cattle: 3.9 mil; chickens: 30.8 mil; goats: 1.1 mil; pigs: 1.8 mil; sheep: 2.6 mil. **Fish catch:** 65,154 metric tons. **Electricity prod.:** 17 bil kWh. **Labor force:** agric. 20%, industry 19.4%, services 60.6%.

Finance: Monetary unit: Peso (CUP) (Sept. 2011: 26.50 = $1 U.S.). **GDP:** $114.1 bil; **per capita GDP:** $9,900; **GDP growth:** 1.5%. **Imports:** $10.3 bil; Venezuela 32.3%, China 12.8%, Spain 8.5%, U.S. 7%. **Exports:** $3.3 bil; China 23%, Canada 19.5%, Venezuela 10.4%, Spain 6.5%, Netherlands 4.4%. **Tourism:** $2.2 bil. **Budget:** $48.9 bil. **Total reserves less gold:** NA. **CPI change:** NA.

Transport: Railways: 5,343 mi. **Motor vehicles:** 38.4 vehicles per 1,000 pop. **Civil aviation:** 1.5 bil pass.-mi; 65 airports. **Chief ports:** Cienfuegos, Guantanamo, Havana, Mariel, Matanzas, Santiago de Cuba.

Communications: TV sets: 213 per 1,000 pop. **Radios:** 276 per 1,000 pop. **Telephone lines:** 10.3 per 100 pop. **Daily newspaper circ.:** 64.7 per 1,000 pop. **Internet:** 15.1 users per 100 pop.

Education: Compulsory: ages 6-14. **Literacy:** 99.8%.

Health: Life expect.: 75.5 male; 80.1 female. **Births:** 10.0 (per 1,000 pop.). **Deaths:** 7.5 (per 1,000 pop.). **Natural inc.:** 0.25%. **Infant mortality:** 4.9 (per 1,000 live births). **HIV rate:** 0.1%.

Major intl. organizations: UN (FAO, ILO, WHO), WTO. Cuba is an OAS member state, but its current govt. has been excluded from formal participation since 1962.

Cuban Interests Section: 2630 16th St. NW 20009; 797-8518. **Website:** www.cubagob.cu

Some 50,000 Indians lived in Cuba when it was reached by Columbus in 1492. Its name derives from the Indian Cubanacan. Except for British occupation of Havana, 1762-63, Cuba remained Spanish until 1898. A slave-based sugar plantation economy developed from the 18th cent. Sugar remains a leading export.

A 10-year uprising ended in 1878 with guarantees of rights by Spain, which Spain failed to carry out. A full-scale liberation movement under Jose Martí began Feb. 24, 1895.

The Spanish-American War began Apr. 1898, after the sinking of the USS *Maine* in Havana harbor. Spain, which lost the war, gave up all claims to Cuba. U.S. troops withdrew in 1902, but under 1903 and 1934 agreements, the U.S. continued to lease a site at Guantánamo Bay in the southeast as a naval base (see below). U.S. and other foreign investors acquired a dominant role in the economy. In 1952, former Pres. Fulgencio Batista seized control and established a dictatorship, which grew increasingly harsh and corrupt. Fidel Castro assembled a rebel band in 1956; guerrilla fighting intensified in 1958. Batista fled Jan. 1, 1959, and in the resulting political vacuum Castro took power, becoming premier Feb. 16.

The government began a program of sweeping economic and social changes, without restoring promised liberties. Opponents were imprisoned, and some were executed. Some 700,000 Cubans emigrated in the first years after the Castro takeover, mostly to the U.S. By 1960 all banks and industrial companies had been nationalized, including over $1 bil worth of U.S.-owned properties, mostly without compensation.

In 1961, some 1,400 Cubans, trained and backed by the U.S. Central Intelligence Agency, unsuccessfully tried to invade and overthrow the regime. In the fall of 1962, the U.S. learned the USSR had brought nuclear missiles to Cuba. On Oct. 22, Pres. John F. Kennedy ordered a naval blockade and demanded that the missiles be withdrawn. The crisis ended Oct. 28 when Soviet Prem. Nikita S. Khrushchev agreed to pull out the missiles immediately; in return, the U.S. ended the blockade, pledged not to invade Cuba, and quietly removed its own missiles from Turkey.

In 1977, Cuba and the U.S. signed agreements to exchange diplomats, without restoring full ties, and to regulate offshore fishing. In 1978 and 1980, the U.S. agreed to accept political prisoners released by Cuba, some of whom were criminals and mental patients. A 1987 agreement provided for 20,000 Cubans to emigrate to the U.S. each year; Cuba agreed to take back some 2,500 jailed in the U.S. since 1980. Cuba's support for left-wing regimes and liberation movements in Central America, Africa, and the Caribbean contributed to poor relations with the U.S.

Cuba's economy, hobbled by U.S. sanctions and dependent on aid from other Communist countries, was severely shaken by the collapse of the Communist bloc in the late 1980s. Stiffer trade sanctions enacted by the U.S. in 1992 made things worse. Antigovernment demonstrations in Aug. 1994 prompted Castro to loosen emigration restrictions. A new U.S.-Cuba accord in Sept. ended the exodus of "boat people" after more than 30,000 had left Cuba. In another policy shift, the U.S. announced May 2, 1995, it would admit 20,000 Cuban refugees held at Guantánamo but would send further boat people back to Cuba.

The U.S. imposed additional sanctions after Cuba, Feb. 24, 1996, shot down 2 aircraft operated by anti-Castro exiles. Cuba blamed exile groups for bombings at Havana tourist hotels, July-Sept. 1997. Pope John Paul II visited Cuba, Jan. 21-25, 1998.

On July 31, 2006, the ailing Fidel Castro yielded power to his 75-year-old brother Raúl, who then served as acting president until formally succeeding Fidel Feb. 24, 2008. Hurricanes Gustav and Ike, Aug.-Sept. 2008, devastated the sugar crop and damaged 450,000 homes, causing an estimated $5 bil in losses.

The U.S. in 2009 eased restrictions on remittances and family travel to the island but retained its embargo on trade with Cuba. The Cuban government announced plans Sept. 13, 2010, to restructure the economy by cutting more than 500,000 workers from the public payroll during the next 6 months. A Communist Party conference, Apr. 16-19, 2011, confirmed Raúl Castro as first secretary and approved economic reforms including an expansion of private property rights.

The U.S., Jan. 11, 2002, began using its naval base at Guantánamo Bay to detain prisoners captured in Afghanistan. The indefinite detention and aggressive interrogation of Afghan prisoners and others at Guantánamo were criticized by human rights groups. Pres. Obama signed Jan. 22, 2009, an executive order calling for the closure of the Guantánamo detention center within a year; as of Aug. 2011, however, 171 detainees were still being held there.

Cyprus
Republic of Cyprus

People: Population: 1,120,489. **Age distrib.:** <15: 16.2%; 65+: 10.4%. **Pop. density:** 314 per sq mi, 121.3 per sq km. **Urban:** 70.3%. **Ethnic groups:** Greek 77%, Turkish 18%. **Principal languages:** Greek, Turkish (both official); English. **Chief religions:** Greek Orthodox 78%, Muslim 18%, other (incl. Maronite, Armenian Apostolic) 4%.

Geography: Total area: 3,572 sq mi, 9,251 sq km; **Land area:** 3,568 sq mi, 9,241 sq km. **Location:** In eastern Mediterranean Sea, off Turkish coast. **Neighbors:** Nearest are Turkey on N, Syria and Lebanon on E. **Topography:** Two mountain ranges run E-W, separated by a wide, fertile plain. **Capital:** Nicosia (Lefkosia), 240,000.

Government: Type: Republic. **Head of state and gov.:** Pres. Dimitris Christofias; b. Aug. 29, 1946; in office; Feb. 28, 2008. **Local divisions:** 6 districts. **Defense budget:** $498 mil. **Active troops:** 10,000.

Economy: Industries: tourism, food and beverage proc., cement and gypsum prod., ship repair and refurb., textiles, light chemicals, metal prods. **Chief crops:** citrus, vegetables, barley, grapes, olives, vegetables. **Natural resources:** copper, pyrites, asbestos, gypsum, timber, salt, marble, clay earth pigment. **Arable land:** 9.4%. **Livestock:** cattle: 55,589; chickens: 2.9 mil; goats: 318,401; pigs: 464,932; sheep: 267,308. **Fish catch:** 4,751 metric tons. **Electricity prod.:** 4.7 bil kWh. **Labor force:** agric. 8.5%, industry 20.5%, services 71%.

Finance: Monetary unit: Euro (EUR) (Sept. 2011: 0.71 = $1 U.S.). **GDP:** $23.2 bil; **per capita GDP:** $21,000; **GDP growth:** 1%. **Imports:** $8 bil; Greece 20.1%, Italy 10.8%, UK 8.9%, Germany 8.7%, Israel 6.9%, China 5.5%, Netherlands 4.8%. **Exports:** $2.2 bil; Greece 24.4%, Germany 9.1%, UK 8.8%. **Tourism:** $2.2 bil. **Budget:** $10.6 bil. **Total reserves less gold:** $514.9 mil. **Gold:** 446,000 oz t. **CPI change:** 2.4%.

Transport: Motor vehicles: 562.2 vehicles per 1,000 pop. **Civil aviation:** 2.6 bil pass.-mi; 13 airports. **Chief ports:** Larnaca, Limassol (under govt. control); Famagusta (admin. by Turkish Cypriots). **Communications: TV sets:** 358 per 1,000 pop. **Radios:** 505 per 1,000 pop. **Telephone lines:** 37.6 per 100 pop. **Internet:** 33 users per 100 pop.

Health: Life expect.: 75.0 male; 80.7 female. **Births:** 11.4 (per 1,000 pop.). **Deaths:** 6.5 (per 1,000 pop.). **Natural inc.:** 0.50%. **Infant mortality:** 9.4 (per 1,000 live births). **HIV rate:** NA.

Education: Compulsory: ages 6-14. **Literacy:** 97.9%.
Major intl. organizations: UN (FAO, IBRD, ILO, IMF, WHO), the Commonwealth, EU, OSCE, WTO.
Embassy: 2211 R St. NW 20008; 462-5772.
Website: www.cyprus.gov.cy

The Ottoman Empire held Cyprus, 1571-1878, until it yielded control over the island to Britain. Agitation for *enosis* (union) with Greece increased after WWII, with the Turkish minority opposed, and led to violence in 1955-56. In 1959, Britain, Greece, Turkey, and Cypriot leaders approved a plan for an independent republic, with constitutional guarantees for the Turkish minority and permanent division of offices on an ethnic basis.

Archbishop Makarios III, formerly the leader of the *enosis* movement, was elected president, and full independence became final Aug. 16, 1960. Further communal strife led the UN to send a peacekeeping force (UNFICYP) in 1964; its mandate has been repeatedly renewed.

The Cypriot National Guard, led by officers from the army of Greece, seized the government July 15, 1974. On July 20, Turkey invaded the island; Greece mobilized its forces but did not intervene. By Aug. 16, Turkish forces had occupied the northeastern 40% of the island.

Turkish Cyprus opened its border with Greek Cyprus Apr. 23, 2003, for the first time since partition. In separate referendums Apr. 24, 2004, 65% of Turkish Cypriot voters accepted a UN-sponsored reunification plan, but 76% of Greek Cypriots rejected it. Still divided, Cyprus became a full member of the EU on May 1. Dimitris Christofias won a runoff election Feb. 24, 2008, becoming the country's first Communist president. A blast July 11, 2011, at a naval base in southern Cyprus killed 13 people and knocked out the nation's largest power plant; also in mid-2011, exposure to Greece's troubled economy raised doubts about Cyprus's own credit standing.

Turkish Republic of Northern Cyprus
A declaration of independence was announced by Turkish-Cypriot leader Rauf Denktash, Nov. 15, 1983. The state is not internationally recognized, but has trade relations with some countries. Denktash was succeeded as president by Mehmet Ali Talat (2005-10) and Dervis Eroglu, who unseated Talat in the election of Apr. 18, 2010. Area of TRNC: 1,295 sq mi; pop. (2010): 287,856, nearly all Turkish. Capital: Lefkosia (Nicosia).

Czech Republic

People: Population: 10,190,213. **Age distrib.:** <15: 13.5%; 65+: 16.3%. **Pop. density:** 341.7 per sq mi, 131.9 per sq km. **Urban:** 73.5%. **Ethnic groups:** Czech 90%, Moravian 4%, Slovak 2%. **Principal languages:** Czech, Slovak. **Chief religions:** Roman Catholic 27%, Protestant 2%, unaffiliated 59%.

Geography: Total area: 30,451 sq mi, 78,867 sq km; **Land area:** 29,825 sq mi, 77,247 sq km. **Location:** In E central Europe. **Neighbors:** Poland on N, Germany on N and W, Austria on S, Slovakia on E and SE. **Topography:** Bohemia, in W, is a plateau surrounded by mountains; Moravia is hilly. **Capital:** Prague, 1,162,000.

Government: Type: Republic. **Head of state:** Pres. Vaclav Klaus; b. June 19, 1941; in office: Mar. 7, 2003. **Head of gov.:** Prime Min. Petr Necas; b. Nov. 19, 1964; in office: June 28, 2010. **Local divisions:** 13 regions and Prague. **Defense budget:** $2.55 bil. **Active troops:** 23,441.

Economy: Industries: motor vehicles, metallurgy, machinery and equip., glass, armaments. **Chief crops:** wheat, potatoes, sugar beets, hops, fruits. **Natural resources:** coal, kaolin, clay, graphite, timber. **Crude oil reserves:** 15 mil bbls. **Arable land:** 41.2%. **Livestock:** cattle: 1.3 mil; chickens: 24 mil; goats: 21,709; pigs: 1.9 mil; sheep: 196,913. **Fish catch:** 24,183 metric tons. **Electricity prod.** (2009): 77 bil kWh. **Labor force:** agric 3.1%, industry 38.6%, services 58.3%.

Finance: Monetary unit: Koruna (CZK) (Sept. 2011: 17.48 = $1 U.S.). **GDP:** $261.3 bil; **per capita GDP:** $25,600; **GDP growth:** 2.3%. **Imports:** $109.2 bil; Germany 25.6%, China 11.9%, Poland 6.5%, Russia 5.4%, Slovakia 5.2%. **Exports:** $116.5 bil; Germany 31.7%, Slovakia 8.7%, Poland 6.2%, France 5.5%, UK 4.9%, Austria 4.7%, Italy 4.5%. **Tourism:** $6.7 bil. **Budget:** $87.9 bil. **Total reserves less gold:** $41.9 bil. **Gold:** 408,300 oz t. **CPI change:** 1.4%.

Transport: Railways: 5,985 mi. **Motor vehicles:** 503.3 vehicles per 1,000 pop. **Civil aviation:** 3.9 bil pass.-mi; 44 airports. **Chief ports:** Decin, Prague, Usti nad Labem.

Communications: TV sets: 457 per 1,000 pop. **Radios:** 802 per 1,000 pop. **Telephone lines:** 21 per 100 pop. **Daily newspaper circ.:** 182.5 per 1,000 pop. **Internet:** 68.8 users per 100 pop.

Health: Life expect.: 73.9 male; 80.7 female. **Births:** 8.7 (per 1,000 pop.). **Deaths:** 10.9 (per 1,000 pop.). **Natural inc.:** −0.22%. **Infant mortality:** 3.7 (per 1,000 live births). **HIV rate:** <0.1%.

Education: Compulsory: ages 6-15. **Literacy:** 99%.
Major intl. organizations: UN (FAO, IBRD, ILO, IMF, WHO), EU, NATO, OECD, OSCE, WTO.
Embassy: 3900 Spring of Freedom St. NW 20008; 274-9100.
Website: www.czech.cz

Bohemia and Moravia were part of the Great Moravian Empire in the 9th cent. and later became part of the Holy Roman Empire. Under the kings of Bohemia, Prague in the 14th cent. was the cultural center of Central Europe. Bohemia and Hungary became part of Austria-Hungary.

In 1914-18 Thomas G. Masaryk and Eduard Benes formed a provisional government with the support of Slovak leaders including Milan Stefanik. They proclaimed the Republic of Czechoslovakia Oct. 28, 1918.

Czechoslovakia
By 1938 Nazi Germany had worked up disaffection among German-speaking citizens in Sudetenland and demanded its cession.

British Prime Min. Neville Chamberlain, with the acquiescence of France, signed with Hitler at Munich, Sept. 30, 1938, an agreement to the cession, with a guarantee of peace by Hitler and Mussolini. Germany occupied Sudetenland Oct. 1-2.

Hitler on Mar. 15, 1939, dissolved Czechoslovakia, made protectorates of Bohemia and Moravia, and supported the autonomy of Slovakia, proclaimed independent Mar. 14, 1939.

Soviet troops with some Czechoslovak contingents entered eastern Czechoslovakia in 1944 and reached Prague in May 1945; Benes returned as president. In May 1946 elections, the Communist Party won 38% of the votes. In Feb. 1948, the Communists seized power in advance of scheduled elections. The country was renamed the Czechoslovak Socialist Republic. A harsh Stalinist period followed, with complete and violent suppression of all opposition.

In Jan. 1968 a liberalization movement spread through Czechoslovakia. Antonin Novotny, long the Stalinist ruler, was deposed as party leader and succeeded by Alexander Dubcek, a Slovak, who supported democratic reforms. In July, the USSR and 4 Warsaw Pact nations demanded an end to liberalization. On Aug. 20, the Soviet, Polish, East German, Hungarian, and Bulgarian armies invaded Czechoslovakia. Despite demonstrations and riots by students and workers, press censorship was imposed and liberal leaders were ousted. On Apr. 17, 1969, Dubcek resigned as leader of the Communist Party and was succeeded by Gustav Husak. Censorship was tightened, and the Communist Party expelled a third of its members.

More than 700 leading Czechoslovak intellectuals and former party leaders signed a human rights manifesto in 1977, called Charter 77, prompting a renewed crackdown by the regime.

The police crushed the largest antigovernment protests since 1968, when tens of thousands of demonstrators took to the streets of Prague, Nov. 17, 1989. As protesters demanded free elections, the Communist Party leadership resigned Nov. 24; millions went on strike Nov. 27.

On Dec. 10, 1989, the first cabinet in 41 years without a Communist majority took power; Vaclav Havel, playwright and human rights campaigner, was chosen president, Dec. 29. In Mar. 1990 the country was officially renamed the Czech and Slovak Federal Republic. Havel failed to win reelection July 3, 1992; his bid was blocked by a Slovak-led coalition.

Slovakia declared sovereignty, July 17, 1992. Czech and Slovak leaders agreed, July 23, on a basic plan for a peaceful division of Czechoslovakia into two independent states.

Czech Republic

Czechoslovakia split into 2 separate states—the Czech Republic and Slovakia—on Jan. 1, 1993. Havel was elected president of the Czech Republic on Jan. 26. Record floods in July 1997 caused more than $1.7 bil in damage. The country became a full member of NATO on Mar. 12, 1999. Floods Aug. 2002 damaged cultural treasures in Prague.

Vaclav Klaus was chosen Feb. 28, 2003, to replace the retiring Havel. After Czech voters June 13-14, 2003, endorsed joining the EU, the nation became a full EU member May 1, 2004. Inconclusive parliamentary elections, June 2-3, 2006, led to a prolonged political deadlock, after which a minority center-right government took office Sept. 4, 2006. Center-right parties made a strong showing in parliamentary elections May 28-29, 2010.

Denmark
Kingdom of Denmark

People: Population: 5,529,888. **Age distrib.:** <15: 17.6%; 65+: 17.1%. **Pop. density:** 337.5 per sq mi, 130.3 per sq km. **Urban:** 86.9%. **Ethnic groups:** Scandinavian, Inuit, Faroese, German, Turkish, Iranian, Somali. **Principal languages:** Danish, Faroese, Greenlandic, English (predominant second language). **Chief religions:** Evangelical Lutheran (official) 95%, other Christian (incl. Protestant, Roman Catholic) 3%, Muslim 2%.

Geography: Total area: 16,639 sq mi, 43,094 sq km; **Land area:** 16,384 sq mi, 42,434 sq km. **Location:** In N Europe, separating North and Baltic seas. **Neighbors:** Germany on S, Norway on NW, Sweden on NE. **Topography:** Consists of the Jutland Peninsula and about 500 islands, 100 inhabited. Land is flat or gently rolling and is almost all in productive use. **Capital:** Copenhagen, 1,174,000.

Government: Type: Constitutional monarchy. **Head of state:** Queen Margrethe II; b. Apr. 16, 1940; in office: Jan. 14, 1972. **Head of gov.:** Prime Min. Helle Thorning-Schmidt; b. Dec. 14, 1966; in office: Oct. 3, 2011. **Local divisions:** 5 regions. **Defense budget:** $3.66 bil. **Active troops:** 18,707.

Economy: Industries: iron, steel, nonferrous metals, chemicals, food proc., machinery and transp. equip., textiles and clothing, electronics, constr., furniture and other wood prods. **Chief crops:** barley, wheat, potatoes, sugar beets. **Natural resources:** petroleum, nat. gas, fish, salt, limestone, chalk, stone, gravel and sand. **Crude oil reserves:** 812 mil bbls. **Arable land:** 57.3%. **Livestock:** cattle: 1.5 mil; chickens: 19.2 mil; pigs: 12.4 mil; sheep: 103,977. **Fish catch:** 811,882 metric tons. **Electricity prod.** (2009): 34.1 bil kWh. **Labor force:** agric. 2.5%, industry 20.2%, services 77.3%.

Finance: Monetary unit: Krone (DKK) (Sept. 2011: 5.32 = $1 U.S.). **GDP:** $201.7 bil; **per capita GDP:** $36,600; **GDP growth:** 2.1%. **Imports:** $90.8 bil; Germany 21%, Sweden 13.1%, Norway 7%, Netherlands 7%, China 6.3%, UK 5.5%. **Exports:** $99.4 bil; Germany 17.5%, Sweden 12.8%, UK 8.5%, U.S. 6%, Norway 6%, Netherlands 4.8%, France 4.5%. **Tourism:** $5.5 bil. **Budget:** $175.9 bil. **Total reserves less gold:** $73.5 bil. **Gold:** 2.1 mil oz t. **CPI change:** 2.3%.

Transport: Railways: 1,657 mi. **Motor vehicles:** 480.4 vehicles per 1,000 pop. **Civil aviation:** 5.5 bil pass.-mi; 28 airports. **Chief ports:** Aalborg, Aarhus, Copenhagen, Ensted, Esbjerg, Fredericia, Kalundborg.

Communications: TV sets: 975 per 1,000 pop. **Radios:** 1,399 per 1,000 pop. **Telephone lines:** 47.3 per 100 pop. **Daily newspaper circ.:** 352.8 per 1,000 pop. **Internet:** 88.7 users per 100 pop.

Health: Life expect.: 76.3 male; 81.1 female. **Births:** 10.3 (per 1,000 pop.). **Deaths:** 10.2 (per 1,000 pop.). **Natural inc.:** 0.01%. **Infant mortality:** 4.2 (per 1,000 live births). **HIV rate:** 0.2%.

Education: Compulsory: ages 7-16. **Literacy:** 99%.

Major intl. organizations: UN and all of its specialized agencies, EU, NATO, OECD, OSCE, WTO.

Embassy: 3200 Whitehaven St. NW 20008; 234-4300.

Website: www.denmark.dk

Danes formed a large component of the Viking raiders in the early Middle Ages. The Danish kingdom was a major power until the 17th cent., when it lost its land in southern Sweden. Norway was separated in 1815, and Schleswig-Holstein in 1864. Northern Schleswig was returned in 1920. Denmark was occupied by Nazi Germany, Apr. 1940-May 1945, but Danes helped more than 7,200 Jews escape to safety in Sweden, Sept. 1943.

Voters ratified the Maastricht Treaty, the basic document of the European Union, in May 1993, after rejecting it in 1992. On Sept. 28, 2000, Danes voted not to join the euro currency zone.

The Danish newspaper *Jyllands-Posten* published, Sept. 30, 2005, cartoon images of the prophet Muhammad, offensive to Muslims; the caricatures, republished elsewhere, triggered violent protests and a boycott of Danish products in Islamic countries in early 2006. Raids by Danish police broke up alleged Islamist bomb plots Sept. 2006 and Sept. 2007. A car bomb blast linked to al-Qaeda killed 8 people outside Denmark's embassy in Islamabad, Pakistan, June 2, 2008.

Ten years of center-right government ended Sept. 15, 2011, as a left-wing coalition won parliamentary elections. Helle Thorning-Schmidt, a Social Democrat, became Denmark's first female prime minister Oct. 3.

The **Faroe Islands** in the North Atlantic, about 300 mi NW of the Shetlands, and 850 mi from Denmark proper, 18 inhabited, have an area of 540 sq mi and pop. (2011 est.) of 49,267. They are an administrative division of Denmark, self-governing in most matters. Torshavn is the capital. Fish is a primary export (292,519 metric tons in 2006). **Website:** www.us.fo

Greenland (Kalaallit Nunaat)

Greenland, a huge island between the North Atlantic and the Polar Sea, is separated from the North American continent by Davis Strait and Baffin Bay. Its total area is 836,330 sq mi, 81% of which is ice-capped. Most of the island is a lofty plateau 9,000 to 10,000 ft in altitude. The average thickness of the cap is 1,000 ft. Scientists point to accelerated melting of Greenland's ice sheet in recent years as evidence of global warming. The population (2011 est.) is 57,670. Under the 1953 Danish constitution the colony became an integral part of the realm with representatives in the Folketing (Danish legislature). The Danish parliament, 1978, approved home rule for Greenland, effective May 1, 1979. With home rule, Greenlandic place names came into official use. The technically correct name for Greenland is now Kalaallit Nunaat; the official name for its capital is Nuuk, rather than Godthab. Fish is the principal export (120,725 metric tons in 2006). Other natural resources include coal, iron ore, lead, zinc, molybdenum, diamonds, gold, and platinum. **Website:** www.nanoq.gl

Djibouti
Republic of Djibouti

People: Population: 757,074. **Age distrib.:** <15: 35%; 65+: 3.3%. **Pop. density:** 84.6 per sq mi, 32.7 per sq km. **Urban:** 76.2%. **Ethnic groups:** Somali 60%, Afar 35%, other (incl. French, Arab, Ethiopian, Italian) 5%. **Principal languages:** French, Arabic (both official); Somali; Afar. **Chief religions:** Muslim 94%, Christian 6%.

Geography: Total area: 8,958 sq mi, 23,200 sq km; **Land area:** 8,950 sq mi, 23,180 sq km. **Location:** On E coast of Africa, separated from Arabian Peninsula by strategically vital strait of Bab el-Mandeb. **Neighbors:** Ethiopia on W and SW, Eritrea on NW, Somalia on SE. **Topography:** The territory, divided into a low coastal plain, mountains behind, and an interior plateau, is arid, sandy, and desolate. Climate is generally hot and dry. **Capital:** Djibouti, 567,000.

Government: Type: Republic. **Head of state:** Pres. Ismail Omar Guelleh; b. Nov. 27, 1947; in office: May 8, 1999. **Head of gov.:** Prime Min. Dileita Mohamed Dileita; b. Mar. 12, 1958; in office: Mar. 7, 2001. **Local divisions:** 5 districts. **Defense budget:** $10 mil. **Active troops:** 10,450.

Economy: Industries: constr., agric. proc. **Chief crops:** fruits, vegetables. **Natural resources:** potential geothermal power, gold, clay, granite, limestone, marble, salt, diatomite, gypsum, pumice, petroleum. **Arable land:** 0.1%. **Livestock:** cattle: 297,000; goats: 512,000; sheep: 466,000. **Fish catch:** 1,058 metric tons. **Electricity prod.:** 280 mil kWh. **Labor force:** NA.

Finance: Monetary unit: Franc (DJF) (Sept. 2011: 174.75 = $1 U.S.). **GDP:** $2.1 bil; **per capita GDP:** $2,800; **GDP growth:** 4.5%. **Imports** (2009 est.): $644 mil; Saudi Arabia 15.7%, China 13.9%, India 11.8%, U.S. 9.3%, Malaysia 6.9%, Japan 4.6%, Pakistan 4.3%. **Exports** (2009 est.): $100 mil; Somalia 75.3%, France 4.8%, UAE 4.1%. **Tourism:** NA. **Budget** (1999 est.): $182 mil. **Total reserves less gold:** $249 mil. **CPI change:** 4%.

Transport: Railways: 62 mi. **Civil aviation:** 3 airports. **Chief port:** Djibouti.

Communications: TV sets: 67 per 1,000 pop. **Radios:** 93 per 1,000 pop. **Telephone lines:** 2.1 per 100 pop. **Internet:** 6.5 users per 1,000 pop.

Health: Life expect.: 58.7 male; 63.7 female. **Births:** 25.3 (per 1,000 pop.). **Deaths:** 8.2 (per 1,000 pop.). **Natural inc.:** 1.70%. **Infant mortality:** 54.9 (per 1,000 live births). **HIV rate:** 2.5%.

Education: Compulsory: ages 6-14. **Literacy:** NA.

Major intl. organizations: UN (FAO, IBRD, ILO, IMF, WHO), AL, AU, WTO.

Embassy: 1156 15th St. NW, Ste. 515, 20005; 331-0270.

Website: www.presidence.dj

France gained control of the territory in stages between 1862 and 1900. As French Somaliland it became an overseas territory of France in 1945; in 1967 it was renamed the French Territory of the Afars and the Issas.

Ethiopia and Somalia have renounced their claims to the area, but each has accused the other of trying to gain control. There were clashes between Afars (ethnically related to Ethiopians) and Issas (related to Somalis) in 1976. Immigrants from both countries continued to enter the country up to independence, which came June 27, 1977.

French aid is the mainstay of the economy, as well as assistance from Arab countries. A peace accord Dec. 1994 ended a 3-year-long uprising by Afar rebels. Drought 2007-11 devastated crops and livestock. An estimated 3,000 French and 2,200 U.S. military personnel are based in Djibouti.

Dominica
Commonwealth of Dominica

People: Population: 72,969. **Age distrib.:** <15: 22.9%; 65+: 10.3%. **Pop. density:** 251.6 per sq mi, 97.2 per sq km. **Urban:** 67.2%. **Ethnic groups:** black 87%, mixed 9%, Carib Amerindian 3%. **Principal languages:** English (official), French patois. **Chief religions:** Roman Catholic 61%, Seventh-Day Adventist 6%, Pentecostal 6%, Baptist 4%, Methodist 4%, Rastafarian 1%, Church of God 1%, Jehovah's Witnesses 1%, other Christian 8%, none 6%.

Geography: Total area: 290 sq mi, 751 sq km; **Land area:** 290 sq mi, 751 sq km. **Location:** In E Caribbean, most northerly Windward Isl. **Neighbors:** Guadeloupe to N, Martinique to S. **Topography:** Mountainous, a central ridge running from N to S, terminating in cliffs; volcanic in origin, with numerous thermal springs; rich deep topsoil on leeward side, red tropical clay on windward coast. **Capital:** Roseau, 14,000.

Government: Type: Parliamentary democracy. **Head of state:** Pres. Nicholas Liverpool; b. Sept. 9, 1934; in office: Oct. 2, 2003. **Head of gov.:** Prime Min. Roosevelt Skerrit; b. June 8, 1972; in office: Jan. 8, 2004. **Local divisions:** 10 parishes. **Defense budget/active troops:** NA.

Economy: Industries: soap, coconut oil, tourism, copra, furniture, cement blocks, shoes. **Chief crops:** bananas, citrus, mangoes, root crops, coconuts, cocoa. **Natural resources:** timber, hydropower. **Arable land:** 8.0%. **Livestock:** cattle: 13,500; chickens: 190,000; goats: 9,700; pigs: 5,000; sheep: 7,600. **Fish catch:** 790 metric tons. **Electricity prod.:** 87 mil kWh. **Labor force:** agric. 40%, industry 32%, services 28%.

Finance: Monetary unit: East Caribbean Dollar (XCD) (Sept. 2011: 2.70 = 1 U.S.). **GDP:** $758 mil; **per capita GDP:** $10,400; **GDP growth:** 1%. **Imports** (2006): $296 mil; Japan 33%, U.S. 20.8%, Trinidad and Tobago 12.4%, China 6%. **Exports** (2006): $94 mil; Japan 25.5%, U.K 17.7%, Egypt 10.7%, Antigua and Barbuda 6.9%, Jamaica 6.1%, Guyana 5.8%. **Tourism:** $87 mil. **Budget** (2009): $277 mil. **Total reserves less gold:** $76.1 mil. **CPI change:** 3.3%.

Transport: Civil aviation: 2 airports. **Chief ports:** Portsmouth, Roseau.

Communications: TV sets: 230 per 1,000 pop. **Radios:** 602 per 1,000 pop. **Telephone lines:** 22.9 per 100 pop. **Daily newspaper circ.:** 39.1 per 1,000 pop. **Internet:** 47.5 users per 100 pop.

Health: Life expect.: 73.0 male; 79.1 female. **Births:** 15.6 (per 1,000 pop.). **Deaths:** 8.1 (per 1,000 pop.). **Natural inc.:** 0.76%. **Infant mortality:** 12.8 (per 1,000 live births). **HIV rate:** NA.

Education: Compulsory: ages 5-16. **Literacy:** NA.

Major intl. organizations: UN (FAO, IBRD, ILO, IMF, WHO), Caricom, the Commonwealth, OAS, OECS, WTO.

Embassy: 3216 New Mexico Ave. NW 20016; 364-6781.

Website: www.dominica.gov.dm

A British colony since 1805, Dominica was granted self-government in 1967. Independence was achieved Nov. 3, 1978.

Hurricane David struck, Aug. 30, 1979, devastating the island and destroying the banana plantations, Dominica's economic mainstay. Coups were attempted in 1980 and 1981.

Dominica participated in the 1983 U.S.-led invasion of nearby Grenada. Prime Min. Pierre Charles, 49, died of a heart attack Jan. 6, 2004, and was succeeded by Roosevelt Skerrit.

Dominican Republic

People: Population: 9,956,648. **Age distrib.:** <15: 29.5%; 65+: 6.5%. **Pop. density:** 533.7 per sq mi, 206.1 per sq km. **Urban:** 69.2%. **Ethnic groups:** mixed 73%, white 16%, black 11%. **Principal language:** Spanish (official). **Chief religion:** Roman Catholic 95%.

Geography: Total area: 18,792 sq mi, 48,670 sq km; **Land area:** 18,656 sq mi, 48,320 sq km. **Location:** In W Indies, sharing isl. of Hispaniola with Haiti. **Neighbors:** Haiti on W, Puerto Rico (U.S.) to E. **Topography:** The Cordillera Central range crosses center of the country, rising to over 10,000 ft, highest in the Caribbean. The Cibao Valley to N is major agricultural area. **Capital:** Santo Domingo, 2,138,000.

Government: Type: Republic. **Head of state and gov.:** Pres. Leonel Fernández Reyna; b. Dec. 26, 1953; in office: Aug. 16, 2004. **Local divisions:** 29 provinces and national district. **Defense budget:** $335 mil. **Active troops:** 24,500.

Economy: Industries: tourism, sugar proc., mining, textiles, cement, tobacco. **Chief crops:** sugarcane, coffee, cotton, cocoa, tobacco, rice, beans, potatoes, corn, bananas. **Natural resources:** nickel, bauxite, gold, silver. **Arable land:** 16.6%. **Livestock:** cattle: 2.7 mil; chickens: 100.5 mil; goats: 190,000; pigs: 580,000; sheep: 123,000. **Fish catch:** 15,214 metric tons. **Electricity prod.:** 14.6 bil kWh. **Labor force:** agric. 14.6%, industry 22.3%, services 63.1%.

Finance: Monetary unit: Peso (DOP) (Sept. 2011: 37.80 = $1 U.S.). **GDP:** $87.3 bil; **per capita GDP:** $8,900; **GDP growth:** 7.8%. **Imports:** $14.5 bil; U.S. 44.3%, Venezuela 6%, China 5%, Mexico 4.3%, Colombia 4.1%. **Exports:** $6.2 bil; U.S. 53.4%, Haiti 9.7%. **Tourism:** $4.2 bil. **Budget:** $8.6 bil. **Total reserves less gold:** $3.5 bil. **GDP:** 18,296 oz t. **CPI change:** 6.3%.

Transport: Railways: 88 mi. **Motor vehicles:** 131.5 vehicles per 1,000 pop. **Civil aviation:** 16 airports. **Chief ports:** Boca Chica, Puerto Plata, Santo Domingo.

Communications: TV sets: 219 per 1,000 pop. **Radios:** 185 per 1,000 pop. **Telephone lines:** 10.2 per 100 pop. **Daily newspaper circ.:** 39.1 per 1,000 pop. **Internet:** 39.5 users per 100 pop.

Health: Life expect.: 75.2 male; 79.6 female. **Births:** 19.7 (per 1,000 pop.). **Deaths:** 4.4 (per 1,000 pop.). **Natural inc.:** 1.53%. **Infant mortality:** 22.2 (per 1,000 live births). **HIV rate:** 0.9%.

Education: Compulsory: ages 5-13. **Literacy:** 88.2%.

Major intl. organizations: UN (FAO, IBRD, ILO, IMF, WHO), OAS, WTO.

Embassy: 1715 22nd St. NW 20008; 332-6280.

Website: www.presidencia.gov.do

Carib and Arawak Indians inhabited the island of Hispaniola when Columbus landed in 1492. The city of Santo Domingo, founded 1496, is the oldest settlement by Europeans in the hemisphere.

The western third of the island was ceded to France in 1697. Santo Domingo itself was ceded to France in 1795. Haitian leader Toussaint L'Ouverture seized it, 1801. Spain returned intermittently 1803-21, as several native republics came and went. Haiti ruled again, 1822-44; Spanish occupation occurred 1861-63. The country was occupied by U.S. Marines 1916-24.

In 1930, Gen. Rafael Leonidas Trujillo Molina was elected president. The brutal Trujillo era ended with his assassination in 1961. Pres. Joaquín Balaguer, appointed by Trujillo in 1960, resigned under pressure in 1962.

Juan Bosch, elected president in the first free elections in 38 years, was overthrown in 1963. On Apr. 24, 1965, Bosch's followers and others, including a few Communists, launched a revolt. Four days later U.S. Marines intervened against pro-Bosch forces. Five South American countries later sent token units as a peacekeeping force. A provisional government supervised a June 1966 election in which Balaguer defeated Bosch. Balaguer remained in office for most of the next 28 years, but his May 1994 reelection was widely denounced as fraudulent. He cut short his term and on June 30, 1996, Leonel Fernández Reyna was elected.

Hurricane Georges struck Sept. 22, 1998, causing extensive property damage and claiming more than 200 lives. The leftist candidate, Hipólito Mejía, won a presidential vote May 16, 2000. With the nation reeling from a banking scandal and soaring inflation, Fernández defeated Mejía in the election of May 16, 2004. Floods and mudslides in late May killed about 395 people. A fight between rival prison gangs led to a fire, Mar. 7, 2005, in which 136 inmates died. Torrential rains from Tropical Storm Noel, Oct. 28-31, 2007, claimed at least 87 lives. Fernández was reelected May 16, 2008.

East Timor

See Timor-Leste.

Ecuador

Republic of Ecuador

People: Population: 15,007,343. **Age distrib.:** <15: 30.1%; 65+: 6.4%. **Pop. density:** 140.4 per sq mi, 54.2 per sq km. **Urban:** 66.9%. **Ethnic groups:** mestizo (mixed Amerindian & white) 65%, Amerindian 25%, Spanish & others 7%, black 3%. **Principal languages:** Spanish (official), Amerindian languages (espec. Quechua). **Chief religion:** Roman Catholic 95%.

Geography: Total area: 109,484 sq mi, 283,561 sq km; **Land area:** 106,889 sq mi, 276,841 sq km. **Location:** In NW S. America, on Pacific coast, astride the Equator. **Neighbors:** Colombia on N, Peru on E and S. **Topography:** Two ranges of Andes run N and S, splitting country into 3 zones: hot, humid lowlands on coast; temperate highlands between ranges; and rainy, tropical lowlands to E. **Capital:** Quito, 1,801,000. **Cities (urban aggl.):** Guayaquil, 2,689,916.

Government: Type: Republic. **Head of state and gov.:** Pres. Rafael Correa; b. Apr. 6, 1963; in office: Jan. 15, 2007. **Local divisions:** 22 provinces. **Defense budget:** $1.47 bil. **Active troops:** 58,483.

Economy: Industries: petroleum, food proc., textiles, wood prods., chemicals. **Chief crops:** bananas, coffee, cocoa, rice, potatoes, manioc, plantains, sugarcane. **Natural resources:** petroleum, fish, timber, hydropower. **Crude oil reserves:** 6.5 bil bbls. **Arable land:** 4.8%. **Livestock:** cattle: 5.2 mil; chickens: 110 mil; goats: 158,081; pigs: 1.4 mil; sheep: 1.9 mil. **Fish catch:** 696,763 metric tons. **Electricity prod.:** 18.1 bil kWh. **Labor force:** agric. 8.3%, industry 21.2%, services 70.4%.

Finance: Monetary unit: U.S. Dollar (USD). **GDP:** $115 bil; **per capita GDP:** $7,800; **GDP growth:** 3.2%. **Imports:** $17.7 bil; U.S. 25.4%, Colombia 10.6%, China 7.2%, Venezuela 6.5%, Brazil 4.5%, Peru 4.5%. **Exports:** $17.4 bil; U.S. 33.6%, Panama 14.3%, Peru 6.8%, Chile 6.6%, Colombia 4.9%, Russia 4.4%, Italy 4.2%. **Tourism:** $781 mil. **Budget** (2011 est.): $18.2 bil. **Total reserves less gold:** $1.4 bil. **Gold:** 845,000 oz t. **CPI change:** 3.6%.

Transport: Railways: 600 mi. **Motor vehicles:** 52.8 vehicles per 1,000 pop. **Civil aviation:** 2.5 bil pass.-mi; 105 airports. **Chief ports:** Esmeraldas, Guayaquil, Manta, Puerto Bolívar.

Communications: TV sets: 261 per 1,000 pop. **Radios:** 517 per 1,000 pop. **Telephone lines:** 14.4 per 100 pop. **Internet:** 24 users per 100 pop.

Health: Life expect.: 72.8 male; 78.8 female. **Births:** 20.0 (per 1,000 pop.). **Deaths:** 5.0 (per 1,000 pop.). **Natural inc.:** 1.50%. **Infant mortality:** 19.7 (per 1,000 live births). **HIV rate:** 0.4%.

Education: Compulsory: ages 5-14. **Literacy:** 84.2%.

Major intl. organizations: UN (FAO, IBRD, ILO, IMF, WHO), OAS, OPEC, WTO.

Embassy: 2535 15th St. NW 20009; 234-7200.

Website: www.presidencia.gob.ec

The region, which was the northern Inca empire, was conquered by Spain in 1533. Liberation forces defeated the Spanish May 24, 1822, near Quito. Ecuador became part of the Great Colombia Republic but seceded, May 13, 1830.

Ecuadoran Indians staged protests in the 1990s to demand greater rights. A border war with Peru flared from Jan. 26, 1995, until a truce took effect Mar. 1. Vice Pres. Alberto Dahik resigned and fled Ecuador, Oct. 11, 1995, to avoid arrest on corruption charges. Elected president in a runoff, July 7, 1996, Abdalá Bucaram—a populist known as El Loco, or "The Crazy One"—imposed stiff price increases and other austerity measures. His rising unpopularity and erratic behavior led the National Congress, Feb. 6, 1997, to dismiss him for "mental incapacity."

Jamil Mahuad Witt, mayor of Quito, won a presidential runoff election July 12, 1998. In Sept. 1998 and Mar. 1999 he imposed emergency measures to cope with a continuing economic crisis. Opposed by Indian groups and military leaders, he was ousted Jan. 21, 2000, and succeeded by Vice Pres. Gustavo Noboa Bejarano. Noboa went ahead with a plan introduced by Mahuad to replace the sucre with the U.S. dollar as Ecuador's currency. Lucio Gutiérrez Borbúa, a leader in the 2000 coup, won a presidential runoff Nov. 24, 2002. Noboa, under investigation for financial mismanagement, went into exile Aug. 23, 2003.

Gutiérrez imposed economic austerity measures, purged opponents from the supreme court, Dec. 2004, and then dissolved the court, Apr. 15, 2005. With street protests rising, Congress ousted Gutiérrez Apr. 20, and Vice Pres. Alfredo Palacio González became president. The U.S. suspended free-trade talks after Ecuador, May 15, 2006, took over oil assets belonging to U.S.-based Occidental Petroleum.

Rafael Correa, a left-wing economist, won a presidential runoff vote Nov. 26, 2006. After a power struggle with the National Congress, Correa scored a major triumph when voters Apr. 15, 2007, approved his plan to convene an assembly to rewrite the constitution. The revised constitution won overwhelming approval in a national referendum Sept. 28, 2008. Early in his term, when oil revenues were high, he boosted development spending and aid to poor families; later, as oil prices dropped, he restricted imports to prevent an outflow of dollars and, in Dec. 2008, allowed Ecuador to default on part of its $10 bil foreign debt.

Correa, who won reelection Apr. 26, 2009, pressured foreign oil companies in 2010 to renegotiate contracts to increase the government's share of mineral revenues. A confrontation Sept. 30, 2010 between Correa and rebellious police officers led to a shootout between government troops and police in which 5 people were killed and at least 38 wounded. An Ecuadoran judge Feb. 14, 2011, ordered Chevron (which had absorbed Texaco in 2001) to pay $9.5 bil to clean up oil pollution from Texaco operations in Ecuador, 1965-92; the plaintiffs and defendants disputed the ruling.

The **Galápagos Islands,** pop. (2008 est.): 30,000, about 600 mi to the W, are the home of huge tortoises and other unusual animals. The oil tanker *Jessica* ran aground Jan. 16, 2001, off San Cristóbal Isl., spilling some 185,000 gallons of fuel.

Egypt

Arab Republic of Egypt

People: Population: 82,079,636. **Age distrib.:** <15: 32.7%; 65+: 4.5%. **Pop. density:** 213.6 per sq mi, 82.5 per sq km. **Urban:** 43.4%. **Ethnic groups:** Egyptian 99.6%. **Principal languages:** Arabic (official), English & French widely understood by educated classes. **Chief religions:** Muslim (mostly Sunni) 90%, Coptic 9%, other Christian 1%.

Geography: Total area: 386,662 sq mi, 1,001,450 sq km; **Land area:** 384,345 sq mi, 995,450 sq km. **Location:** NE corner of Africa. **Neighbors:** Libya on W; Sudan on S; Israel, Gaza Strip on E. **Topography:** Almost entirely desolate and barren, with hills and mountains in E and along Nile. The Nile Valley, where most of the people live, stretches 550 mi. **Capital:** Cairo, 10,902,000. **Cities (urban aggl.):** Alexandria, 4,387,282.

Government: Type: In transition. **Head of state:** Chmn., Supreme Council of the Armed Forces, Mohamed Hussein Tantawi; b. Oct. 31, 1935; in office: Feb. 11, 2011. **Head of gov.:** Prime Min. Essam Sharaf; b. 1952; in office: Mar. 3, 2011. **Local divisions:** 26 governorates. **Defense budget:** $6.24 bil. **Active troops:** 468,500.

Economy: Industries: textiles, food proc., tourism, chemicals, pharmaceuticals, hydrocarbons, constr., cement, metals. **Chief crops:** cotton, rice, corn, wheat, beans, fruits, vegetables. **Natural resources:** petroleum, nat. gas, iron ore, phosphates, manganese, limestone, gypsum, talc, asbestos, lead, rare earth elements, zinc. **Crude oil reserves:** 4.4 bil bbls. **Arable land:** 2.9%. **Livestock:** cattle: 5 mil; chickens: 96 mil; goats: 4.6 mil; pigs: 38,000; sheep: 5.5 mil. **Fish catch:** 1.1 mil metric tons. **Electricity prod.:** 123.9 bil kWh. **Labor force:** agric. 32%, industry 17%, services 51%.

Finance: Monetary unit: Pound (EGP) (Sept. 2011: 5.96 = $1 U.S.). **GDP:** $497.8 bil; **per capita GDP:** $6,200; **GDP growth:** 5.1%. **Imports:** $46.5 bil; U.S. 10.6%, China 8.7%, Germany 8%, Italy 5.9%, Turkey 5.2%, Saudi Arabia 4.5%. **Exports:** $25.3 bil; Spain 6.8%, Italy 6.7%, U.S. 6.3%, India 6.1%, Saudi Arabia 5.8%, China 4.3%, Libya 4.3%, Jordan 4%. **Tourism:** $12.5 bil. **Budget:** $64.2 bil. **Total reserves less gold:** $33.6 bil. **Gold:** 2.4 mil oz t. **CPI change:** 11.3%.

Transport: Railways: 3,158 mi. **Motor vehicles:** 43.5 vehicles per 1,000 pop. **Civil aviation:** 9.2 bil pass.-mi; 73 airports. **Chief ports:** Alexandria, Ayn Sukhnah, Damietta, El Dekheila, Port Said, Sidi Kurayr, Suez.

Communications: TV sets: 243 per 1,000 pop. **Radios:** 242 per 1,000 pop. **Telephone lines:** 11.9 per 100 pop. **Internet:** 26.7 users per 100 pop.

Health: Life expect.: 70.1 male; 75.4 female. **Births:** 24.6 (per 1,000 pop.). **Deaths:** 4.8 (per 1,000 pop.). **Natural inc.:** 1.98%. **Infant mortality:** 25.2 (per 1,000 live births). **HIV rate:** <0.1%.

Education: Compulsory: ages 6-14. **Literacy:** 66.4%.

Major intl. organizations: UN (FAO, IBRD, ILO, IMF, WHO), AL, AU, WTO.

Embassy: 3521 International Ct. NW 20008; 895-5400.

Website: www.egypt.gov.eg

Archaeological records of ancient Egyptian civilization date back to 4000 BCE. A unified kingdom arose around 3200 BCE and extended its way south into Nubia and as far north as Syria. A high culture of rulers and priests was built on an economic base of serfdom, fertile soil, and annual flooding of the Nile.

Imperial decline facilitated conquest by Asian invaders (Hyksos, Assyrians). The last native dynasty fell in 341 BCE to the Persians, who were in turn replaced by Greeks (Alexander and the Ptolemies), Romans, Byzantines, and Arabs, who introduced Islam and the Arabic language. The ancient Egyptian language is preserved only in Coptic Christian liturgy.

Egypt was ruled as part of larger Islamic empires for many centuries. Britain intervened in Egypt in 1882 and ruled the country as a protectorate, 1914-22. A 1936 treaty strengthened Egyptian autonomy, but Britain retained bases in Egypt and a condominium over the Sudan. When the state of Israel was proclaimed in 1948, Egypt joined other Arab nations invading Israel and was defeated. In 1951 Egypt abrogated the 1936 treaty; the Sudan became independent in 1956.

An uprising on July 23, 1952, overthrew King Farouk and established a republic. Lt. Col. Gamal Abdel Nasser rose to power, becoming premier in 1954 and president in 1956. Nasser emerged as the most influential leader in the Arab world at the time; within Egypt, he pushed construction of the Aswan High Dam, completed in 1970.

After guerrilla raids across its border, Israel invaded Egypt's Sinai Peninsula, Oct. 29, 1956. Egypt rejected a cease-fire demand by Britain and France; on Oct. 31 the 2 nations dropped bombs and on Nov. 5-6 landed forces. Egypt and Israel accepted a UN cease-fire; fighting ended Nov. 7. Subsequently, a UN Emergency Force guarded the border. Full-scale war with Israel broke out again, June 5, 1967; before it ended under a UN cease-fire June 10, Israel had captured Gaza and the Sinai Peninsula and taken control of the E bank of the Suez Canal.

Nasser died Sept. 28,1970, and was replaced by Vice Pres. Anwar Sadat. In a surprise attack Oct. 6, 1973, Egyptian forces crossed the Suez Canal into the Sinai. (At the same time, Syrian forces attacked Israelis on the Golan Heights.) Egypt was supplied by a USSR military airlift; the U.S. responded with an airlift to Israel. Israel counterattacked, crossed the canal, and surrounded Suez City. A UN cease-fire took effect Oct. 24. Under an agreement signed Jan. 18, 1974, Israeli forces withdrew from the canal's W bank; limited numbers of Egyptian forces occupied a strip along the E bank. A second accord was signed in 1975, with Israel yielding Sinai oil fields.

Pres. Sadat's surprise visit to Jerusalem, Nov. 1977, opened the prospect of peace with Israel. On Mar. 26, 1979, Egypt and Israel signed a formal peace treaty, ending 30 years of war, and establishing diplomatic relations. On Oct. 6, 1981, Pres. Sadat was assassinated by Muslim extremists within the army; he was succeeded by Hosni Mubarak. Israel returned control of the Sinai to Egypt in Apr. 1982.

Egyptian security forces battled a rising tide of Islamist violence in the 1990s and after. Pres. Mubarak escaped assassination in Ethiopia, June 26, 1995; Egypt blamed Sudan for the attack. On Nov. 17, 1997, near Luxor, Muslim extremists killed 58 foreign tourists and 4 Egyptians. Mubarak, who was grazed by a knife-wielding assailant Sept. 6, 1999, was confirmed by popular vote Sept. 26 for a 4th presidential term. Bombs Oct. 7, 2004, in and near Taba (a Sinai tourist site popular with Israelis) killed at least 35 people. Another 88 people were killed in bombings July 23, 2005, at Sharm el Sheikh, a Red Sea resort city.

Pressured by the U.S., Mubarak agreed to allow opposition candidates in the Sept. 7 presidential election, which he won with an 88.5% majority; turnout was only 23%. Suicide bombings at the Sinai resort town of Dahab, Apr. 24, 2006, killed at least 18 people and injured 85; security forces May 9 killed Nasser Khamis al-Mallahi, leader of the group blamed for the Taba, Sharm el Sheikh, and Dahab attacks. Constitutional amendments expanding presidential powers and barring religiously-based political parties were approved Mar. 26, 2007, in a referendum criticized as fraudulent by opposition groups and human rights observers.

Following 18 days of mass protests in which at least 846 people died in clashes between "Arab Spring" dissidents and Mubarak loyalists, Mubarak surrendered power Feb. 11, 2011, to the Supreme Council of the Armed Forces. While Islamists and pro-democracy secularists contended for influence, the transitional military regime prepared for elections in late 2011 and charged Mubarak and his associates with corruption and abuse of power. Egypt continued to adhere to the 1979 peace treaty with Israel, but improved ties with Hamas in Gaza.

The **Suez Canal**, 103 mi long, links the Mediterranean and Red seas. It was built by a French corporation 1859-69, but Britain obtained controlling interest in 1875. The last British troops were removed June 13, 1956. On July 26, Egypt nationalized the canal.

El Salvador
Republic of El Salvador

People: Population: 6,071,774. **Age distrib.: <15:** 30.6%; **65+:** 6.4%. **Pop. density:** 758.9 per sq mi, 293 per sq km. **Urban:** 64.3%. **Ethnic groups:** mestizo 90%, white 9%, Amerindian 1%. **Principal languages:** Spanish (official), Nahua. **Chief religions:** Roman Catholic 57%, Protestant 21%, Jehovah's Witnesses 2%, none 17%.

Geography: Total area: 8,124 sq mi, 21,041 sq km; **Land area:** 8,000 sq mi, 20,721 sq km. **Location:** In Central America. **Neighbors:** Guatemala on W, Honduras on N. **Topography:** A hot Pacific coastal plain in S rises to a cooler plateau and valley region, densely populated. The N is mountainous, including many volcanoes. **Capital:** San Salvador, 1,534,000.

Government: Type: Republic. **Head of state and gov.:** Pres. Mauricio Funes; b. Oct. 18, 1959; in office: June 1, 2009. **Local divisions:** 14 departments. **Defense budget:** $1.13 bil. **Active troops:** 15,500.

Economy: Industries: food proc., beverages, petroleum, chemicals, fertilizer, textiles, furniture, light metals. **Chief crops:** coffee, sugar, corn, rice, beans, oilseed, cotton, sorghum. **Natural resources:** hydropower, geothermal power, petroleum. **Arable land:** 32.7%. **Livestock:** cattle: 1.3 mil; chickens: 13.8 mil; goats: 15,000; pigs: 422,792; sheep: 5,100. **Fish catch:** 35,851 metric tons. **Electricity prod.:** 5.7 bil kWh. **Labor force:** agric. 19%, industry 23%, services 58%.

Finance: Monetary unit: Colon (SVC) (8.75 = $1 U.S.) This exchange rate has been fixed since 2001, when U.S. dollars went into circulation in El Salvador. **GDP:** $43.6 bil; **per capita GDP:** $7,200; **GDP growth:** 0.7%. **Imports:** $8 bil; U.S. 36.1%, Guatemala 10.4%, Mexico 7.4%, Honduras 4.7%, China 4.6%. **Exports:** $4.4 bil; U.S. 46.6%, Guatemala 14%, Honduras 13.4%, Nicaragua 5.5%. **Tourism:** $390 mil. **Budget:** $4.9 bil. **Total reserves less gold:** $2.6 bil. **Gold:** 233,100 oz t. **CPI change:** 1.2%.

Transport: Railways: 176 mi. **Motor vehicles:** 33.1 vehicles per 1,000 pop. **Civil aviation:** 2.2 bil pass.-mi; 4 airports. **Chief ports:** Acajutla, Puerto Cutuco.

Communications: TV sets: 227 per 1,000 pop. **Radios:** 477 per 1,000 pop. **Telephone lines:** 16.2 per 100 pop. **Daily newspaper circ.:** 38 per 1,000 pop. **Internet:** 15 users per 100 pop.

Health: Life expect: 70.2 male; 76.9 female. **Births:** 17.8 (per 1,000 pop.). **Deaths:** 5.6 (per 1,000 pop.). **Natural inc.:** 1.21%. **Infant mortality:** 20.3 (per 1,000 live births). **HIV rate:** 0.8%.

Education: Compulsory: ages 4-15. **Literacy:** 84.1%.

Major intl. organizations: UN (FAO, IBRD, ILO, IMF, WHO), OAS, WTO.

Embassy: 1400 16th St. NW, Ste. 100, 20036; 265-9671.

Website: www.presidencia.gob.sv

El Salvador became independent of Spain in 1821, and of the Central American Federation in 1839. A fight with Honduras in 1969 over the presence of 300,000 Salvadoran workers left 2,000 dead.

A military coup overthrew the government of Pres. Carlos Humberto Romero in 1979, but the ruling military-civilian junta failed to quell a rebellion by leftist insurgents, armed by Cuba and Nicaragua. Extreme right-wing death squads organized to eliminate suspected leftists were blamed for thousands of deaths in the 1980s. The Reagan administration staunchly supported the government with military aid.

After taking the lives of some 75,000 people (with thousands more "disappeared"), the 12-year civil war ended Jan. 16, 1992, as the government and leftist rebels signed a formal peace treaty. Rightist legislators in the National Assembly passed a sweeping amnesty Mar. 20, 1993, for civil war atrocities.

Members of the right-wing ARENA party held the presidency from 1989 to 2009. Mauricio Funes, a leftist and former TV journalist, won the presidential election of Mar. 15, 2009, and took office June 1. Remittances from Salvadorans working in the U.S. are a major source of income.

Equatorial Guinea
Republic of Equatorial Guinea

People: Population: 668,225. **Age distrib.: <15:** 41.5%; **65+:** 4.1%. **Pop. density:** 61.7 per sq mi, 23.8 per sq km. **Urban:** 39.7%. **Ethnic groups:** Fang 86%, Bubi 7%, Mdowe 4%, Annobon 2%, Bujeba 1%. **Principal languages:** Spanish, French (both official); Fang; Bubi. **Chief religions:** nominally Christian & predominantly Roman Catholic, pagan practices.

Geography: Total area: 10,831 sq mi, 28,051 sq km; **Land area:** 10,831 sq mi, 28,051 sq km. **Location:** Bioko Isl. off W Africa coast in Gulf of Guinea, and Rio Muni, mainland enclave. **Neighbors:** Gabon on S, Cameroon on E and N. **Topography:** Bioko Isl. consists of 2 volcanic mountains and connecting valley. Rio Muni, with over 90% of the area, has coastal plain and low hills beyond. **Capital:** Malabo, 128,000.

Government: Type: Republic. **Head of state:** Pres. Teodoro Obiang Nguema Mbasogo; b. June 5, 1942; in office: Aug. 3, 1979. **Head of gov.:** Prime Min. Ignacio Milam Tang; b. June 20, 1940; in office: July 8, 2008. **Local divisions:** 7 provinces. **Defense budget** (2008): $11 mil. **Active troops:** 1,320.

Economy: Industries: petroleum, nat. gas, sawmilling. **Chief crops:** coffee, cocoa, rice, yams, cassava, bananas, palm oil nuts. **Natural resources:** petroleum, nat. gas, timber, gold, bauxite, diamonds, tantalum, sand and gravel, clay. **Crude oil reserves:** 1.1 bil bbls. **Arable land:** 4.7%. **Livestock:** cattle: 5,100; chickens: 340,000; goats: 9,100; pigs: 6,300; sheep: 38,000. **Fish catch:** 7,722 metric tons. **Electricity prod.:** 92 mil kWh. **Labor force:** NA.

Finance: Monetary unit: CFA BEAC Franc (XAF) (Sept. 2011: 468.55 = $1 U.S.). **GDP:** $23.8 bil; **per capita GDP:** $36,600 (pop. figures uncertain; per capita GDP might be significantly lower); **GDP growth:** -0.8%. **Imports:** $5.7 bil; China 19.9%, U.S. 17%, Spain 15%, France 9.3%, Côte d'Ivoire 6.2%, Italy 4.9%. **Exports:** $10.2 bil; U.S. 29.2%, China 11.9%, Japan 8.9%, South Korea 7.9%, Spain 7.2%, Italy 5.2%. **Tourism:** NA. **Budget:** $6.98 bil. **Total reserves less gold:** $2.3 bil. **CPI change** (2007-08): 6.6%.

Transport: Civil aviation: 6 airports. **Chief ports:** Bata, Malabo.

Communications: TV sets: 116 per 1,000 pop. **Radios:** 431 per 1,000 pop. **Telephone lines:** 1.9 per 100 pop. **Internet:** 6 users per 100 pop.

Health: Life expect: 61.4 male; 63.4 female. **Births:** 35.4 (per 1,000 pop.). **Deaths:** 9.0 (per 1,000 pop.). **Natural inc.:** 2.64%. **Infant mortality:** 77.3 (per 1,000 live births). **HIV rate:** 5%.

Education: Compulsory: ages 7-11. **Literacy:** 93.3%.

Major intl. organizations: UN (FAO, IBRD, ILO, IMF, WHO), AU, WTO (observer).

Embassy: 2020 16th St. NW 20009; 518-5700.

Website: www.state.gov/p/af/ci/ek/

Fernando Po (now Bioko) Island was reached by Portugal in the late 15th cent. and ceded to Spain in 1778. Independence came Oct. 12, 1968. Riots occurred in 1969 over disputes between the island and the more backward Rio Muni province on the mainland.

Masie Nguema Biyogo, a mainlander, became president for life in 1972. His reign was one of the most brutal in Africa, resulting in a bankrupted nation; most of the nation's 7,000 Europeans emigrated. He was ousted in a military coup, Aug. 1979. Teodoro Obiang Nguema Mbasogo, leader of the coup, became president and installed his family members in key government posts. Multiparty presidential elections, held in 1996, 2002, and 2009, were seriously flawed. Oil sales, especially to the U.S., have boomed in recent years. Foreign investment in the oil sector has been extensive, but poverty remains widespread, and health conditions are poor. Human Rights Watch reported in 2011 that the Obiang regime "regularly engages in torture and arbitrary detention" of suspected dissidents.

Eritrea
State of Eritrea

People: Population: 5,939,484. **Age distrib.:** <15: 42.1%; 65+: 3.6%. **Pop. density:** 152.3 per sq mi, 58.8 per sq km. **Urban:** 21.6%. **Ethnic groups:** Tigrinya 55%, Tigre 30%, Saho 4%, Kunama 2%, Rashaida 2%, Bilen 2%, other (Afar, Beni Amir, Nera) 5%. **Principal languages:** Tigrinya, Arabic, English (all official); Tigre; Kunama; Afar; other Cushitic languages. **Chief religions:** Muslim, Coptic Christian, Roman Catholic, Protestant.

Geography: Total area: 45,406 sq mi, 117,600 sq km; **Land area:** 38,996 sq mi, 101,000 sq km. **Location:** In E Africa, on SW coast of Red Sea. **Neighbors:** Ethiopia on S, Djibouti on SE, Sudan on W. **Topography:** Includes many islands of the Dahlak Archipelago, low coastal plains in S, mountain range with peaks to 9,000 ft in N. **Capital:** Asmara, 649,000.

Government: Type: In transition. **Head of state and gov.:** Pres. Isaias Afwerki; b. Feb. 2, 1946; in office: May 24, 1993. **Local divisions:** 8 provinces. **Defense budget:** NA. **Active troops:** 201,750.

Economy: Industries: food proc., beverages, clothing and textiles. **Chief crops:** sorghum, lentils, vegetables, corn, cotton, tobacco, sisal. **Natural resources:** gold, potash, zinc, copper, salt, poss. oil and nat. gas, fish. **Arable land:** 6.8%. **Livestock:** cattle: 2 mil; chickens: 1.2 mil; goats: 1.7 mil; sheep: 2.3 mil. **Fish catch:** 3,030 metric tons. **Electricity prod.:** 269.9 mil kWh. **Labor force:** agric. 80%, industry and services 20%.

Finance: Monetary unit: Nakfa (ERN) (Sept. 2011: 15.10 = $1 U.S.). **GDP:** $3.6 bil; **per capita GDP:** $600; **GDP growth:** 2.2%. **Imports:** $738 mil; NA. **Exports:** $25 mil; NA. **Tourism:** NA. **Budget:** $920.1 mil. **Total reserves less gold (2008):** $57.9 mil. **CPI change:** NA.

Transport: Railways: 190 mi. **Civil aviation:** 4 airports. **Chief ports:** Assab, Massawa.

Communications: TV sets: 67 per 1,000 pop. **Radios:** 458 per 1,000 pop. **Telephone lines:** 1 per 100 pop. **Internet:** 5.4 users per 100 pop.

Health: Life expect: 60.4 male; 64.7 female. **Births:** 32.8 (per 1,000 pop.). **Deaths:** 8.1 (per 1,000 pop.). **Natural inc.:** 2.47%. **Infant mortality:** 41.3 (per 1,000 live births). **HIV rate:** 0.8%.

Education: Compulsory: ages 7-14. **Literacy:** 66.6%.

Major intl. organizations: UN (FAO, IBRD, ILO, IMF, WHO), AU.

Embassy: 1708 New Hampshire Ave. NW 20009; 319-1991.

Website: www.shabait.com

Eritrea was part of the Ethiopian kingdom of Aksum. It was an Italian colony from 1890 to 1941, when it was captured by the British. Following a period of British and UN supervision, Eritrea was awarded to Ethiopia as part of a federation in 1952. Ethiopia annexed Eritrea as a province in 1962. This led to a 31-year struggle for independence, which ended when Eritrea formally declared itself an independent nation May 24, 1993. A constitution was ratified in 1997 but not implemented.

A border war with Ethiopia that erupted in June 1998 intensified in May 2000, as Ethiopian troops plunged into western Eritrea; a cease-fire signed June 18 provided for a UN peacekeeping force (UNMEE) to patrol a buffer zone on Eritrean territory. A peace treaty was signed Dec. 12, 2000.

A UN report in July 2007 accused Eritrea of aiding an Islamic insurgency in Somalia. Citing Eritrean obstruction of UNMEE activities, the UN Security Council ended the peacekeeping mission as of July 31, 2008. Many thousands have fled repressive conditions in Eritrea, including all 12 players from the national soccer team, who defected to Kenya during a Dec. 2009 tournament. According to a July 2011 UN report, the Eritrean government plotted a failed attack against an African Union summit conference Jan. 30-31 in Addis Ababa, Ethiopia.

Estonia
Republic of Estonia

People: Population: 1,282,963. **Age distrib.:** <15: 15.1%; 65+: 17.7%. **Pop. density:** 78.4 per sq mi, 30.3 per sq km. **Urban:**

69.5%. **Ethnic groups:** Estonian 69%, Russian 26%, Ukrainian 2%, Belarusian 1%, Finn 1%. **Principal languages:** Estonian (official), Russian. **Chief religions:** Evangelical Lutheran 14%, Orthodox 13%, other Christian 1%, unaffiliated 34%, none 6%.

Geography: Total area: 17,463 sq mi, 45,228 sq km; **Land area:** 16,366 sq mi, 42,388 sq km. **Location:** E Europe, bordering Baltic Sea and Gulf of Finland. **Neighbors:** Russia on E, Latvia on S. **Topography:** Marshy lowland with numerous lakes and swamps; about 40% forested. Elongated hills show evidence of former glaciation. More than 800 islands on Baltic coast. **Capital:** Tallinn, 399,000.

Government: Type: Republic. **Head of state:** Pres. Toomas Hendrik Ilves; b. Dec. 26, 1953; in office: Oct. 9, 2006. **Head of gov.:** Prime Min. Andrus Ansip; b. Oct. 1, 1956; in office: Apr. 13, 2005. **Local divisions:** 15 counties. **Defense budget:** $330 mil. **Active troops:** 5,450.

Economy: Industries: engineering, electronics, wood and wood prods., textiles, information technology, telecomm. **Chief crops:** grain, potatoes, vegetables. **Natural resources:** oil shale, peat, rare earth elements, phosphorite, clay, limestone, sand, dolomite, sea mud. **Arable land:** 14.1%. **Livestock:** cattle: 237,900; chickens: 1.8 mil; goats: 3,600; pigs: 364,900; sheep: 78,200. **Fish catch:** 99,107 metric tons. **Electricity prod.:** 10 bil kWh. **Labor force:** agric. 2.8%, industry 22.7%, services 74.5%.

Finance: Monetary unit: Euro (EUR) (Sept. 2011: 0.71 = $1 U.S.). **GDP:** $24.7 bil; **per capita GDP:** $19,100; **GDP growth:** 3.1%. **Imports:** $12.2 bil; Finland 14.5%, Lithuania 10.9%, Latvia 10.6%, Germany 10.5%, Sweden 8.4%, Russia 8%, Poland 5.7%. **Exports:** $11.5 bil; Finland 18.5%, Sweden 12.5%, Latvia 9.5%, Russia 9.3%, Germany 6.1%, Lithuania 4.7%, U.S. 4.3%. **Tourism:** $1.1 bil. **Budget:** $8.2 bil. **Total reserves less gold:** $2.6 bil. **Gold:** 8,000 oz t. **CPI change:** 3%.

Transport: Railways: 743 mi. **Civil aviation:** 223.1 mil pass.-mi; 13 airports. **Chief ports:** Kuivastu, Kunda, Muuga, Sillamae, Tallinn.

Communications: TV sets: 511 per 1,000 pop. **Radios:** 1,200 per 1,000 pop. **Telephone lines:** 36 per 100 pop. **Daily newspaper circ.:** 190.6 per 1,000 pop. **Internet:** 74.1 users per 100 pop.

Health: Life expect.: 68.0 male; 79.0 female. **Births:** 10.5 (per 1,000 pop.). **Deaths:** 13.6 (per 1,000 pop.). **Natural inc.:** –0.31%. **Infant mortality:** 7.1 (per 1,000 live births). **HIV rate:** 1.2%.

Education: Compulsory: ages 7-15. **Literacy:** 99.8%.

Major intl. organizations: UN (FAO, IBRD, ILO, IMF, WHO), EU, NATO, OECD, OSCE, WTO.

Embassy: 2131 Massachusetts Ave. NW 20008; 588-0101.

Website: www.eesti.ee

Estonia was a province of imperial Russia before World War I, and was independent between World Wars I and II. It was conquered by the USSR in 1940 and incorporated as the Estonian SSR. During an abortive Soviet coup, Estonia declared immediate full independence, Aug. 20, 1991; the Soviet Union recognized its independence in Sept. 1991. The first free elections in over 50 years were held Sept. 20, 1992. The last occupying Russian troops departed by Aug. 31, 1994.

Estonia became a full member of the EU and NATO in 2004. The government accused Russia of orchestrating a cyber attack against Estonia's computer network in Apr.-May 2007. A former high-ranking defense official, Herman Simm, was convicted of treason Feb. 25, 2009, for passing Estonian and NATO security secrets to Russian agents. Estonia adopted the euro (the European common currency) on Jan. 1, 2011.

Ethiopia
Federal Democratic Republic of Ethiopia

People: Population: 90,873,739. **Age distrib.:** <15: 46.3%; 65+: 2.7%. **Pop. density:** 235.4 per sq mi, 90.9 per sq km. **Urban:** 16.7%. **Ethnic groups:** Oromo 35%, Amara 27%, Somalie 6%, Tigraway 6%, Sidama 4%, Guragie 3%, Welaita 2%, Hadiya 2%, Affar 2%, Gamo 2%, Gedeo 1%. **Principal languages:** Amarigna, (Amharic) (official); Oromigna, Tigrigna, (both official regional); Somaligna; Guaragigna; Sidamigna; Hadiyigna; English (official; major foreign language taught in schools); Arabic (official). **Chief religions:** Orthodox 44%, Muslim 34%, Protestant 19%, traditional 3%.

Geography: Total area: 426,373 sq mi, 1,104,300 sq km; **Land area:** 386,102 sq mi, 1,000,000 sq km. **Location:** In E Africa. **Neighbors:** Sudan on W; Kenya on S; Somalia, Djibouti on E; Eritrea on N. **Topography:** A high central plateau, 6,000-10,000 ft high, rises to higher mountains near the Great Rift Valley, cutting in from SW. Blue Nile and other rivers cross the plateau, which descends to plains on both W and SE. **Capital:** Addis Ababa, 2,863,000.

Government: Type: Federal republic. **Head of state:** Pres. Girma Wolde Giorgis; b. Dec. 1924; in office: Oct. 8, 2001. **Head of gov.:** Prime Min. Meles Zenawi; b. May 8, 1955; in office: Aug. 23, 1995. **Local divisions:** 9 states, 2 charted cities. **Defense budget:** $311 mil. **Active troops:** 138,000.

Economy: Industries: food proc., beverages, textiles, leather, chemicals, metals proc., cement. **Chief crops:** cereals, pulses, coffee, oilseed, cotton, sugarcane, potatoes, qat, cut flowers. **Natural resources:** gold, platinum, copper, potash, nat. gas, hydropower. **Crude oil reserves:** 430,000 bbls. **Arable land:** 13.9%. **Livestock:**

cattle: 50.9 mil; chickens: 38 mil; goats: 22 mil; pigs: 29,000; sheep: 26 mil. **Fish catch:** 17,072 metric tons. **Electricity prod.:** 3.7 bil kWh. **Labor force:** agric. 85%, industry 5%, services 10%.

Finance: Monetary unit: Birr (ETB) (Sept. 2011: 17.04 = $1 U.S.). **GDP:** $86.1 bil; **per capita GDP:** $1,000; **GDP growth:** 8%. **Imports:** $7.5 bil; China 19.8%, Saudi Arabia 8.5%, India 4.4%, U.S. 4.4%. **Exports:** $1.7 bil; China 13.3%, Germany 10%, Saudi Arabia 7.6%, U.S. 7.4%, Netherlands 6.5%, Sudan 4.5%, Belgium 4.1%. **Tourism:** $329 mil. **Budget:** $5.1 bil. **Total reserves less gold** (2009): $1.8 bil. **CPI change:** 8.1%.

Transport: Railways: 423 mi. **Motor vehicles:** 1.6 vehicles per 1,000 pop. **Civil aviation:** 6.1 bil pass.-mi; 17 airports.

Communications: TV sets: 2 per 1,000 pop. **Radios:** 171 per 1,000 pop. **Telephone lines:** 1.1 per 100 pop. **Daily newspaper circ.:** 4.6 per 1,000 pop. **Internet:** 0.8 users per 100 pop.

Health: Life expect.: 53.6 male; 58.8 female. **Births:** 43.0 (per 1,000 pop.). **Deaths:** 11.0 (per 1,000 pop.). **Natural inc.:** 3.20%. **Infant mortality:** 77.1 (per 1,000 live births). **HIV rate:** NA.

Education: Compulsory ages: NA. **Literacy:** 29.8%.

Major intl. organizations: UN (FAO, IBRD, ILO, IMF, WHO), AU, WTO (observer).

Embassy: 3506 International Dr. NW 20008; 364-1200.

Website: www.ethiopia.gov.et

Ethiopian culture was influenced by Egypt and Greece. The ancient monarchy was invaded by Italy in 1880 but maintained its independence until another Italian invasion in 1936. British forces freed the country in 1941.

A series of droughts in the 1970s killed hundreds of thousands. An army mutiny, strikes, and student demonstrations led to the dethronement, Sept. 12, 1974, of Ethiopia's last emperor, Haile Selassie I, ending his 58-year reign; he died Aug. 1975, while being held by the ruling junta, known as the Dergue. The junta dissolved parliament, abolished the monarchy, established a socialist state, redistributed land, curbed the influence of the Coptic Church, and violently suppressed opposition.

The regime, torn by bloody coups, faced uprisings by tribal and political groups aided in part by Sudan and Somalia. Ties with the U.S., once a major ally, deteriorated, while cooperation accords were signed with the USSR in 1977. In 1978, Soviet advisers and Cuban troops helped defeat Somali forces. Ethiopia and Somalia signed a peace agreement in 1988.

A worldwide relief effort began in 1984, as an extended drought threatened the country with famine; up to 1 mil people may have died as a result of starvation and disease.

The Ethiopian People's Revolutionary Democratic Front (EPRDF), an umbrella group of 6 rebel armies, launched a major push against government forces, Feb. 1991. In May, Pres. Mengistu Haile Mariam resigned, finding refuge in Zimbabwe. The EPRDF took over and set up a transitional government. Ethiopia's first multiparty general elections were held in 1995.

Eritrea, a province on the Red Sea, declared its independence May 24, 1993. Fighting along the border with Eritrea, which erupted in June 1998, intensified in May 2000, as Ethiopian forces plunged into Eritrean territory; a cease-fire was signed June 18 and a peace treaty Dec. 12. The war displaced 350,000 Ethiopians and is estimated to have cost the country nearly $3 bil.

The ruling EPRDF won parliamentary elections May 15, 2005, but opposition parties made big gains. Police opened fire on anti-government protesters in Addis Ababa, June 8, killing at least 36; the government arrested some 3,000 dissidents. Police suppression of further protests in the capital, Nov. 1-4, left at least 46 dead. As part of a crackdown on Oromo Liberation Front rebels, the government rounded up thousands of Oromo, Nov. 2005-Jan. 2006. In July 2006, Ethiopia sent troops into Somalia in response to advances by Islamist militias there. Tried in absentia, former Pres. Mengistu was convicted of genocide Dec. 12, 2006.

Drought and other food supply disruptions led Ethiopia June 2008 to appeal for $325 mil in emergency aid; the nation requested $175 mil in additional food aid Oct. 2009. Ethiopia pulled its troops out of Somalia in Jan. 2009. The EPRDF dominated parliamentary elections May 23, 2010, though the opposition contested the results and accused the EPRDF of voter fraud. As of Aug. 2011, Ethiopia housed 160,000 refugees fleeing violence and famine in Somalia.

Fiji
Republic of Fiji

People: Population: 883,125. **Age distrib.:** <15: 28.9%; 65+: 5.2%. **Pop. density:** 125.2 per sq mi, 48.3 per sq km. **Urban:** 51.9%. **Ethnic groups:** Fijian (predominantly Melanesian with Polynesian) 57%, Indian 38%, Rotuman 1%, other (European, other Pacific Islanders, Chinese) 4%. **Principal languages:** English, Fijian (both official); Hindustani. **Chief religions:** Christian 65% Hindu 28%, Muslim 6%.

Geography: Total area: 7,056 sq mi, 18,274 sq km; **Land area:** 7,056 sq mi, 18,274 sq km. **Location:** In western S Pacific O. **Neighbors:** Nearest are Vanuatu to W, Tonga to E. **Topography:** 322 isls. (106 inhabited), many mountainous, with tropical forests and large fertile areas. Viti Levu, the largest isl., has over half the total land area. **Capital:** Greater Suva, 174,000.

Government: Type: In transition. **Head of state:** Pres. Ratu Epeli Nailatikau; b. July 5, 1941; in office: Nov. 5, 2009 (acting from July 30). **Head of gov.:** Interim Prime Min. Vorege (Frank) Bainimarama; b. Apr. 27, 1954; in office: Jan. 5, 2007. **Local divisions:** 4 divisions comprising 14 provinces and 1 dependency. **Defense budget:** $55 mil. **Active troops:** 3,500.

Economy: Industries: tourism, sugar, clothing, copra, gold, silver, lumber. **Chief crops:** sugarcane, coconuts, cassava, rice, sweet potatoes, bananas. **Natural resources:** timber, fish, gold, copper, offshore oil potential, hydropower. **Arable land:** 8.8%. **Livestock:** cattle: 312,000; chickens: 3.5 mil; goats: 250,000; pigs: 145,000; sheep: 6,000. **Fish catch:** 41,455 metric tons. **Electricity prod.** (2009): 970 mil kWh. **Labor force:** agric. 70%, industry and services 30%.

Finance: Monetary unit: Dollar (FJD) (Sept. 2011: 1.77 = $1 U.S.). **GDP:** $3.9 bil; **per capita GDP:** $4,400; **GDP growth:** 0.1%. **Imports** (2006): $3.1 bil; Singapore 27.7%, Australia 19.7%, New Zealand 15.4%, China 7.7%, Thailand 4.3%. **Exports** (2006): $1.2 bil; U.S. 15.1%, Australia 12%, UK 11.1%, Samoa 5.3%, Tonga 4.7%, Japan 4.6%. **Tourism:** $422 mil. **Budget** (2006): $1.4 bil. **Total reserves less gold:** $719.3 mil. **Gold:** 800 oz t. **CPI change:** 5.5%.

Transport: Railways: 371 mi. **Motor vehicles:** 166.7 vehicles per 1,000 pop. **Civil aviation:** 2.2 bil pass.-mi; 4 airports. **Chief ports:** Lautoka, Levuka, Suva.

Communications: TV sets: 117 per 1,000 pop. **Radios:** 678 per 1,000 pop. **Telephone lines:** 15.9 per 100 pop. **Daily newspaper circ.:** 53.5 per 1,000 pop. **Internet:** 14.8 users per 100 pop.

Health: Life expect.: 68.7 male; 74.0 female. **Births:** 21.1 (per 1,000 pop.). **Deaths:** 5.9 (per 1,000 pop.). **Natural inc.:** 1.52%. **Infant mortality:** 11.0 (per 1,000 live births). **HIV rate:** 0.1%.

Education: Compulsory: ages 6-15. **Literacy:** NA.

Major intl. organizations: UN (FAO, IBRD, ILO, IMF, WHO), WTO.

Embassy: 2000 M St. NW, Ste. 710, 20036; 466-8320.

Website: www.fiji.gov.fj

A British colony since 1874, Fiji became independent Oct. 10, 1970. Cultural differences between the Indian community (descendants of contract laborers brought to the islands in the 19th cent.) and indigenous Fijians have led to political polarization. More than 100,000 Indians have left Fiji since the mid-1980s.

Military coups have been frequent in recent decades. Fiji's first Indian prime minister, Mahendra Chaudhry, took office May 19, 1999. He and other government officials were taken captive May 19, 2000, by indigenous Fijian gunmen led by George Speight. The hostage crisis culminated in a military takeover, May 29, led by Frank Bainimarama. Release of the last remaining hostages in July 2000 coincided with the installation of an interim military-backed government. Speight was later tried for treason; he was sentenced to life in prison, Feb. 18, 2002. Prime Min. Laisenia Qarase headed an elected civilian government, 2001-06. He retained his office in parliamentary voting, May 6-13, 2006, but was ousted in a military coup Dec. 5, and Bainimarama took office as interim prime minister. After a court ruled Apr. 9, 2009, that the 2006 coup was illegal, Pres. Ratu Josefa Iloilo abrogated the constitution, dissolved the judiciary, and reappointed Interim Prime Min. Bainimarama. In July, Bainimarama promised a new constitution by 2013 and legislative elections by 2014; he also named Vice Pres. Ratu Epeli Nailatikau to replace the retiring Pres. Iloilo, who died Feb. 6, 2011.

Finland
Republic of Finland

People: Population: 5,259,250. **Age distrib.:** <15: 16%; 65+: 17.8%. **Pop. density:** 44.8 per sq mi, 17.3 per sq km. **Urban:** 85.1%. **Ethnic groups:** Finn 93%, Swede 6%, Russian 1%. **Principal languages:** Finnish, Swedish (both official). **Chief religions:** Lutheran Church of Finland 83%, Orthodox Church 1%, other Christian 1%, none 15%.

Geography: Total area: 130,559 sq mi, 338,145 sq km; **Land area:** 117,304 sq mi, 303,815 sq km. **Location:** In N Europe. **Neighbors:** Norway on N, Sweden on W, Russia on E. **Topography:** South and central are generally flat areas with low hills and many lakes. The N has mountainous areas, 3,000-4,000 ft above sea level. **Capital:** Helsinki, 1,107,000.

Government: Type: Constitutional republic. **Head of state:** Pres. Tarja Halonen; b. Dec. 24, 1943; in office: Mar. 1, 2000. **Head of gov.:** Prime Min. Jyrki Katainen; b. Oct. 14, 1971; in office: June 22, 2011. **Local divisions:** 6 laanit (provinces). **Defense budget:** $3.59 bil. **Active troops:** 22,250.

Economy: Industries: metals and metal prods., electronics, machinery and scientific instruments, shipbuilding, pulp and paper, foodstuffs, chemicals, textiles. **Chief crops:** barley, wheat, sugar beets, potatoes. **Natural resources:** timber, iron ore, copper, lead, zinc, chromite, nickel, gold, silver, limestone. **Arable land:** 7.4%. **Livestock:** cattle: 918,268; chickens: 4.9 mil; goats: 5,924; pigs: 1.4 mil; sheep: 117,673. **Fish catch:** 168,219 metric tons. **Electricity prod.** (2009): 67.9 bil kWh. **Labor force:** agric. and forestry 4.9%; industry 16.7%; constr. 7.1%; commerce 19.4%; finance, insurance, and business services 12.8%; transp. and communications 6.3%; public services 32.8%.

Finance: Monetary unit: Euro (EUR) (Sept. 2011: 0.71 = $1 U.S.). **GDP:** $186 bil; **per capita GDP:** $35,400; **GDP growth:** 3.1%. **Imports:** $69.1 bil; Russia 16.2%, Germany 15.8%, Sweden 14.7%, Netherlands 7%, China 5.3%, France 4.2%. **Exports:** $73.5 bil; Germany 10.3%, Sweden 9.8%, Russia 8.9%, U.S. 7.9%, Netherlands 5.9%, UK 5.2%, China 4.1%. **Tourism:** $2.9 bil. **Budget:** $65.3 bil (central government budget). **Total reserves less gold:** $7.3 bil. **Gold:** 1.6 mil oz t. **CPI change:** 1.2%.

Transport: Railways: 3,678 mi. **Motor vehicles:** 611.6 vehicles per 1,000 pop. **Civil aviation:** 10.2 bil pass.-mi; 75 airports. **Chief ports:** Helsinki, Kotka, Naantali, Porvoo, Raahe, Rauma.

Communications: TV sets: 679 per 1,000 pop. **Radios:** 1,623 per 1,000 pop. **Telephone lines:** 23.3 per 100 pop. **Daily newspaper circ.:** 431.1 per 1,000 pop. **Internet:** 86.9 users per 100 pop.

Health: Life expect.: 75.8 male; 82.9 female. **Births:** 10.4 (per 1,000 pop.). **Deaths:** 10.2 (per 1,000 pop.). **Natural inc.:** 0.01%. **Infant mortality:** 3.4 (per 1,000 live births). **HIV rate:** 0.1%.

Education: Compulsory: ages 7-16. **Literacy:** 100%.

Major intl. organizations: UN (FAO, IBRD, ILO, IMF, WHO), EU, OECD, OSCE, WTO.

Embassy: 3301 Massachusetts Ave. NW 20008; 298-5800.

Website: www.government.fi

The early Finns probably migrated from the Ural area at about the beginning of the Christian era. Swedish settlers brought the country into Sweden, 1154 to 1809, when Finland became an autonomous grand duchy of the Russian Empire. Russian exactions created a strong national spirit; on Dec. 6, 1917, Finland declared its independence, and in 1919 it became a republic.

On Nov. 30, 1939, the Soviet Union invaded, and the Finns were forced to cede 16,173 sq mi of territory. After World War II, further cessions were exacted. In 1948, Finland signed a treaty of mutual assistance with the USSR; Finland and Russia nullified this treaty with a new pact in Jan. 1992.

Following approval by Finnish voters in an advisory referendum Oct. 16, 1994, Finland joined the EU effective Jan. 1, 1995. Pres. Tarja Halonen won a second 6-year term, Jan. 29, 2006. Former Pres. Martti Ahtisaari was awarded the Nobel Peace Prize, Oct. 10, 2008, for his efforts in mediating international conflicts. Following parliamentary elections Apr. 17, 2011, Jyrki Katainen, leader of the conservative National Coalition Party, became prime minister.

Aland, or Ahvenanmaa, constituting an autonomous province, is a group of small islands, 590 sq mi, in the Gulf of Bothnia, 25 mi from Sweden, 15 mi from Finland. Mariehamn is the chief port.

France
French Republic

People: Population: 65,102,719. **Age distrib.:** <15: 18.5%; 65+: 16.8%. **Pop. density:** 263.4 per sq mi, 101.7 per sq km. **Urban:** 85.3%. **Ethnic groups:** Celtic & Latin with Teutonic, Slavic, N African, Indochinese, Basque minorities. **Principal languages:** French (official); rapidly declining regional dialects (Provençal, Breton, Alsatian, Corsican, Catalan, Basque, Flemish). **Chief religions:** Roman Catholic 83%-88%, Muslim 5%-10%, Protestant 2%, Jewish 1%, unaffiliated 4%.

Geography: Total area: 248,573 sq mi, 643,801 sq km; **Land area:** 247,126 sq mi, 640,053 sq km. **Location:** In W Europe, between Atlantic O. and Medit. Sea. **Neighbors:** Spain, Andorra, Monaco on S; Italy, Switzerland, Germany on E; Luxembourg, Belgium on N. **Topography:** A wide plain covers more than half of the country, in N and W, drained to W by Seine, Loire, Garonne rivers. The Massif Central is a mountainous plateau in center. In E are Alps (Mt. Blanc is tallest in W Europe, 15,771 ft), the lower Jura range, and forested Vosges. The Rhone flows from Lake Geneva to Mediterranean. Pyrenees are in SW, on border with Spain. **Capital:** Paris, 10,410,000. **Cities (urban aggl.):** Marseille-Aix-en-Provence, 1,468,772; Lyon, 1,467,701; Lille, 1,032,766.

Government: Type: Republic. **Head of state:** Pres. Nicolas Sarkozy; b. Jan. 28, 1955; in office: May 16, 2007. **Head of gov.:** Prime Min. François Fillon; b. Mar. 4, 1954; in office: May 17, 2007. **Local divisions:** 22 administrative regions containing 96 departments. **Defense budget:** $42.6 bil. **Active troops:** 238,591.

Economy: Industries: machinery, chemicals, automobiles, metallurgy, aircraft, electronics, textiles, food proc., tourism. **Chief crops:** wheat, cereals, sugar beets, potatoes, wine grapes. **Natural resources:** coal, iron ore, bauxite, zinc, uranium, antimony, arsenic, potash, feldspar, fluorspar, gypsum, timber, fish. **Crude oil reserves:** 91.6 mil bbls. **Other resources:** Timber, dairy. **Arable land:** 33.5%. **Livestock:** cattle: 19.2 mil; chickens: 183 mil; goats: 1.3 mil; pigs: 14.8 mil; sheep: 7.7 mil. **Fish catch:** 664,564 metric tons. **Electricity prod.** (2009): 510 bil kWh. **Labor force:** agric. 3.8%, industry 24.3%, services 71.8%.

Finance: Monetary unit: Euro (EUR) (Sept. 2011: 0.71 = $1 U.S.). **GDP:** $2.1 tril; **per capita GDP:** $33,100; **GDP growth:** 1.5%. **Imports:** $577.7 bil; Germany 19.4%, Belgium 11.6%, Italy 8%, Netherlands 7.1%, Spain 6.7%, UK 4.9%, U.S. 4.7%, China 4.4%. **Exports:** $508.7 bil; Germany 15.9%, Italy 8.2%, Spain 7.8%, Belgium 7.4%, UK 7%, U.S. 5.7%. **Tourism:** $46.6 bil. **Budget:** $1.4 tril. **Total reserves less gold:** $55.8 bil. **Gold:** 78.3 mil oz t. **CPI change:** 1.5%.

Transport: Railways: 18,417 mi. **Motor vehicles:** 581.2 vehicles per 1,000 pop. **Civil aviation:** 94.6 bil pass.-mi (incl. airlines

based in territories and dependencies); 297 airports. **Chief ports:** Calais, Dunkerque, Le Havre, Marseille, Nantes, Paris, Rouen.

Communications: TV sets: 661 per 1,000 pop. **Radios:** 943 per 1,000 pop. **Telephone lines:** 56.1 per 100 pop. **Daily newspaper circ.:** 163.5 per 1,000 pop. **Internet:** 80.1 users per 100 pop.

Health: Life expect.: 78.0 male; 84.5 female. **Births:** 12.3 (per 1,000 pop.). **Deaths:** 8.8 (per 1,000 pop.). **Natural inc.:** 0.35%. **Infant mortality:** 3.3 (per 1,000 live births). **HIV rate:** 0.4%.

Education: Compulsory: ages 6-16. **Literacy:** 99%.

Major intl. organizations: UN and most of its specialized agencies, EU, NATO, OECD, OSCE, WTO.

Embassy: 4101 Reservoir Rd. NW 20007; 944-6195.

Website: www.gouvernement.fr

Celtic Gaul was conquered by Julius Caesar 58-51 BCE; Romans ruled for 500 years. Under Charlemagne, Frankish rule extended over much of Europe. After his death France emerged as one of the successor kingdoms.

The monarchy was overthrown by the French Revolution (1789-93) and succeeded by the First Republic, followed by the First Empire under Napoleon (1804-15), a monarchy (1814-48), the Second Republic (1848-52), the Second Empire (1852-70), the Third Republic (1871-1946), the Fourth Republic (1946-58), and the Fifth Republic (1958 to present).

France suffered severe losses in manpower and wealth in WWI, when it was invaded by Germany. By the Treaty of Versailles, France exacted return of Alsace and Lorraine, provinces seized by Germany in 1871. Germany invaded France again in May 1940, and signed an armistice with a government based in Vichy. After France was liberated by the Allies in Sept. 1944, Gen. Charles de Gaulle became head of the provisional government, serving until 1946. De Gaulle again became premier in 1958, during a crisis over Algeria, and obtained voter approval for a new constitution, ushering in the Fifth Republic. He then became president.

France had withdrawn from Indochina in 1954, and from Morocco and Tunisia in 1956. Most of its remaining African territories, including Algeria, were freed 1958-62.

In May 1968, rebellious students in Paris and other centers rioted, battled police, and were joined by workers who launched nationwide strikes. The government awarded pay increases to the strikers May 26. De Gaulle resigned from office in Apr. 1969, after losing a nationwide referendum on constitutional reform. Georges Pompidou, who was elected to succeed him, continued De Gaulle's emphasis on French independence from the U.S. and Soviet Union. After Pompidou's death, in 1974, Valery Giscard d'Estaing was elected president; he continued the basically conservative policies of his predecessors.

On May 10, 1981, France elected François Mitterrand, a Socialist, president. Under Mitterrand the government nationalized 5 major industries and most private banks. After 1986, however, when rightists won a narrow victory in the National Assembly, Mitterrand chose conservative Jacques Chirac as premier. A 2-year period of "cohabitation" ensued, and France began to pursue a privatization program in which many state-owned companies were sold. After Mitterrand was elected to a second 7-year term in 1988, he appointed a Socialist as premier. The center-right won a large majority in 1993 legislative elections, ushering in another period of "cohabitation" with a conservative premier.

Chirac won the presidency in a runoff election May 7, 1995. He cut government spending to meet budgetary goals for the introduction of a common European currency, the euro. With unemployment at nearly 13%, legislative elections completed June 1, 1997, produced a decisive victory for the leftist parties. The result was a new period of "cohabitation," this time between a conservative president and a Socialist prime minister, Lionel Jospin. France contributed 7,000 troops to the NATO-led force (KFOR) that entered Kosovo in June 1999.

French voters, disaffected by government scandals, shocked the political establishment in the first round of presidential voting Apr. 21, 2002, by giving Jean-Marie Le Pen, leader of the far-right National Front, a second place finish with 16.9% of the vote; Chirac won only 19.9%, and Jospin was third, with 16.2%. Chirac easily won the May 5 runoff, with 82%, and his center-right allies won parliamentary elections June 9 and 16. Parliament gave final approval Mar. 3, 2004, to a law barring the wearing of Islamic head scarves and other religious symbols in public schools.

Displeased with sluggish economic growth, high unemployment, and budget cuts in entitlement programs, voters showed their discontent by rejecting, May 29, 2005, a proposed EU constitution strongly supported by the Chirac government. A state of emergency was declared Nov. 8 after 12 days of riots that began in Paris and spread to some 300 French cities and towns; rioters were mainly young immigrants from N and W Africa. After a wave of mass protests and strikes, Chirac agreed, Apr. 10, 2006, to rescind a law that made it easier for employers to fire inexperienced young workers.

Campaigning as an economic reformer, the conservative, pro-American Nicolas Sarkozy won a presidential runoff election May 6, 2007. The French bank Société Générale disclosed Jan. 24, 2008, that it had lost more than $7 bil, which it blamed on a rogue trader, Jerôme Kerviel; he was sentenced to 3 years in prison and ordered to pay restitution Oct. 5, 2010.

Sarkozy responded to the global recession by unveiling Dec. 4, 2008, a $33 bil economic stimulus plan focused on infrastructure development; new measures announced Feb. 18, 2009, following labor protests, provided $3.3 bil in aid for lower-income people. Former Pres. Chirac was indicted Oct. 30 on corruption charges stemming from his tenure (1977-95) as mayor of Paris. A French court Jan. 28, 2010, acquitted former Prime Min. Dominique de Villepin of conspiring to smear Sarkozy while the two men were vying to succeed Pres. Chirac. Sarkozy's policy of shutting Roma (Gypsy) encampments and expelling thousands of Roma to Romania and Bulgaria drew public rebukes from EU allies in Sept. 2010.

France, a founding member of NATO, formally returned to the alliance's military command structure Apr. 2009 after an absence of 43 years. In mid-2011, France had about 4,000 troops fighting as part of NATO forces in Afghanistan. France participated in military operations that removed Pres. Laurent Gbagbo from power in Côte d'Ivoire, Apr. 11, and ousted Libyan leader Muammar al-Qaddafi, Aug. 23.

The island of **Corsica**, in the Mediterranean W of Italy and N of Sardinia, is a territorial collectivity and region of France comprising 2 departments. It elects a total of 2 senators and 3 deputies to the French Parliament. Area: 3,369 sq mi; pop. (2006 census): 294,118. The capital is Ajaccio, birthplace of Napoleon I. Violence by Corsican separatist groups has hurt tourism, a leading industry on the island. Corsicans rejected, 51%-49%, a limited autonomy plan in a referendum July 6, 2003.

Overseas Departments

French Guiana is on the NE coast of South America with Suriname on the W and Brazil on the E and S. Its area is 35,135 sq mi (total); 34,421 sq mi (land); pop. (2007 est.) 203,321. Guiana sends one senator and 2 deputies to the French Parliament. Guiana is administered by a prefect and has a Council General of 16 elected members; capital is Cayenne.

The famous penal colony, Devil's Island, was phased out between 1938 and 1951. The European Space Agency maintains a satellite-launching center (established by France in 1964) in the city of Kourou.

Immense forests of rich timber cover 88% of the land. Fishing (especially shrimp), forestry, and gold mining are the most important industries. Natural resources include petroleum, kaolin, niobium, tantalum, and clay.

Guadeloupe, in the West Indies' Leeward Islands, consists of 2 large islands, Basse-Terre and Grande-Terre, separated by the Salt River, plus Marie Galante and the Saintes group to the S and, to the N, Desirade. A French possession since 1635, the department is represented in the French Parliament; administration consists of a prefect (governor) as well as an elected general and regional councils. St. Barthelemy and over half of Sint Martin (the Netherlands' portion is called St. Maarten), both formerly part of Guadeloupe, voted for secession in 2003 and became separate overseas territorial collectivities in 2007.

Area of the islands is 525 sq mi; pop. (2007 est., incl. St. Barthelemy and St. Martin) 456,698, mainly descendants of slaves; capital is Basse-Terre on Basse-Terre Island. The land is fertile; sugar, rum, and bananas are exported. Tourism is an important industry.

Martinique, the northernmost of the Windward Islands, in the West Indies, has been a possession since 1635, and a department since Mar. 1946. It is represented in the French Parliament by 2 senators and 4 deputies. The island was the birthplace of Napoleon's first wife, Empress Josephine.

It has an area of 425 sq mi (total); 409 sq mi (land); pop. (2007 est.) 439,202, mostly descendants of slaves. The capital is Fort-de-France, pop. (2006): 90,347. It is a popular tourist stop. The chief exports are rum, bananas, and petroleum products. **Website:** www.region-martinique.mq

Mayotte, claimed by Comoros and administered by France, voted in 1976 to become a territorial collectivity of France. An island NW of Madagascar, area is 144 sq mi, pop. (2010 est.) 231,139. The capital is Mamoudzou. In a Mar. 29, 2009, referendum, 95% of voters endorsed a plan under which Mayotte became an overseas department of France as of Mar. 31, 2011.

Réunion is a volcanic island in the Indian O. about 420 mi E of Madagascar and has belonged to France since 1665. Area, 972 sq mi (total); 968 sq mi (land); pop. (2007 est.) 798,094, 30% of French extraction. Capital: Saint-Denis. The chief export is sugar. It elects 5 deputies, 3 senators to the French Parliament. **Website:** www.wereunion.re

Overseas Territorial Collectivities

French Polynesia, comprises 130 islands widely scattered among 5 archipelagos in the S Pacific; administered by a Council of Ministers (headed by a president). Territorial Assembly and the Council have headquarters at Papeete, on Tahiti, one of the Society Islands (which include the Windward Isls. and Leeward Isls.). Two deputies and a senator are elected to the French Parliament.

Other groups are the Marquesas Islands; the Tuamotu Archipelago; the Gambier Islands; and the Austral, or Tubuai, Islands.

Total area of the islands administered from Tahiti is 1,609 sq mi (total); 1,478 sq mi (land); pop. (2011 est.) 291,000, more than half on Tahiti. Tahiti is mountainous with a productive coastline bearing coconuts, citrus, pineapples, and vanilla. Cultured pearls are also produced.

Tahiti was visited by Capt. James Cook in 1769 and by Capt. Bligh in the *Bounty*, 1788-89. Its beauty impressed Herman Melville, Paul Gauguin, and Charles Darwin. A coalition favoring independence for French Polynesia within 20 years gained control of the territorial assembly after elections May 23, 2004.

St. Pierre and Miquelon became a territorial collectivity in 1985. It consists of 2 groups of rocky islands near the SW coast of Newfoundland, inhabited by fishermen. Fish products are the chief export. The St. Pierre group has an area of 10 sq mi; Miquelon, 83 sq mi. Total pop. (2011 est.) 5,888. Capital: Saint-Pierre. Both Mayotte and St. Pierre and Miquelon elect a deputy and a senator to the French Parliament.

St. Barthelemy and **St. Martin** became overseas territorial collectivities in 2007, with total pop. (2011 est.) of 7,367 and 30,615, respectively.

The territorial collectivity of **Wallis and Futuna** comprises 2 island groups in the SW Pacific S of Tuvalu, N of Fiji, and W of Western Samoa; became an overseas territory July 29, 1961. The islands have a total area of 55 sq mi and pop. (2011 est.) of 15,398. Alofi, attached to Futuna, is uninhabited. Capital: Mata-Utu. Chief products are copra, yams, taro roots, bananas, and coconuts. A senator and a deputy are elected to the French Parliament.

Overseas Territory and Special Collectivity

The territory of the **French Southern and Antarctic Lands** comprises Adelie Land, on Antarctica, and island groups in the Indian O. Area: 2,991 sq mi (total); 2,960 sq mi (land).

Adelie, reached 1840, has a 185-mi coastline and tapers 1,240 mi inland to the S Pole. (The U.S. does not recognize national claims in Antarctica.) It has a research station. There are 2 glaciers: Ninnis, 22 mi wide, 99 mi long, and Mentz, 11 mi by 140 mi.

The Indian O. groups are as follows: Kerguelen Archipelago, visited 1772, consists of one large and 300 small islands. The chief is 87 mi long, 74 mi wide, and has Mt. Ross, 6,429 ft tall. Principal research station is Port-aux-Français. Seals often weigh two tons; there are blue whales, coal, peat, semiprecious stones. Crozet Archipelago, reached 1772, covers 136 sq mi. Eastern Island rises to 6,560 ft. Saint Paul, in southern Indian O., has warm springs with earth at places heating to 120° to 390°F. Amsterdam is nearby; both produce cod and rock lobster. Military garrisons and meteorological stations are located on the Scattered Isls.

The special collectivity of **New Caledonia** and Dependencies is a group of islands in the Pacific O. about 1,115 mi E of Australia and approx. the same distance NW of New Zealand. Dependencies are the Loyalty Isls., Isle of Pines, Belep Archipelago, and Huon Isls.

The largest island, New Caledonia, is 6,530 sq mi. Total area of the territory is 7,172 sq mi (total); 7,056 sq mi (land); pop. (2011 est.) 256,275. The group was acquired by France in 1853.

The territory is administered by a High Commissioner. There is a popularly elected Territorial Congress. Two deputies and a senator are elected to the French Parliament. Capital: Noumea.

Mining is the chief industry. New Caledonia is one of the world's largest nickel producers. Chrome, iron, cobalt, manganese, silver, gold, lead, and copper are also found. Agric. products include yams, sweet potatoes, potatoes, manioc, corn, and coconuts.

In 1987, New Caledonian voters chose by referendum to remain within the French Republic. There were clashes between French and Melanesians (Kanaks) in 1988. An agreement Apr. 21, 1998, between France and rival New Caledonian factions specified a 15-to 20-year period of "shared sovereignty." The French constitution was amended, July 6, to allow the territory a gradual increase in autonomy; New Caledonian voters approved the plan Nov. 8, 1998, by a 72% majority.

Gabon
Gabonese Republic

People: Population: 1,576,665. **Age distrib.:** <15: 42.2%; 65+: 3.9%. **Pop. density:** 15.8 per sq mi, 6.1 per sq km. **Urban:** 86%. **Ethnic groups:** Bantu tribes (incl. Fang, Bapounou, Nzebi, Obamba). **Principal languages:** French (official), Fang, Myene, Nzebi, Bapounou/Eschira, Bandjabi. **Chief religions:** Christian 55%-75%, animist.

Geography: Total area: 103,347 sq mi, 267,667 sq km; **Land area:** 99,486 sq mi, 257,667 sq km. **Location:** On Atlantic coast of W central Africa. **Neighbors:** Equatorial Guinea, Cameroon on N; Congo on E and S. **Topography:** Heavily forested, consisting of coastal lowlands; plateaus in N, E, and S; mountains in N, SE, and center. The Ogooue R. system covers most of Gabon. **Capital:** Libreville, 619,000.

Government: Type: Republic. **Head of state:** Pres. Ali Bongo Ondimba; b. Feb. 9, 1959; in office: Oct. 16, 2009. **Head of gov.:** Prime Min. Paul Biyoghé Mba; b. Apr. 18, 1953; in office: July 17, 2009. **Local divisions:** 9 provinces. **Defense budget:** $250 mil. **Active troops:** 4,700.

Economy: Industries: petroleum extraction and refining; manganese, gold; chemicals; ship repair; food and beverages. **Chief**

crops: cocoa, coffee, sugar, palm oil, rubber. **Natural resources:** petroleum, nat. gas, diamonds, niobium, manganese, uranium, gold, timber, iron ore, hydropower. **Crude oil reserves:** 2 bil bbls. **Arable land:** 1.3%. **Livestock:** cattle: 36,500; chickens: 3.2 mil; goats: 92,000; pigs: 215,000; sheep: 196,000. **Fish catch:** 30,124 metric tons. **Electricity prod.:** 2 bil kWh. **Labor force:** agric. 60%, industry 15%, services 25%.

Finance: Monetary unit: CFA BEAC Franc (XAF) (Sept. 2011: 468.55 = $1 U.S.). **GDP:** $22.5 bil; **per capita GDP:** $14,500; **GDP growth:** 5.7%. **Imports:** $2.4 bil; France 32.2%, U.S. 7.9%, China 7.2%, Belgium 5%, Cameroon 4.6%, Netherlands 4.3%. **Exports:** $6.8 bil; U.S. 24.4%, China 13.6%, France 6.3%, Malaysia 5.9%, Spain 5.8%, Germany 5.3%, Trinidad and Tobago 4.8%, South Korea 4%. **Tourism:** NA. **Budget:** $2.9 bil. **Total reserves less gold:** $1.7 bil. **Gold** (2008): 12,837 oz t. **CPI change:** 1.5%.

Transport: Railways: 403 mi. **Civil aviation:** 578.5 mil pass.-mi; 13 airports. **Chief ports:** Gamba, Libreville, Lucinda, Owendo, Port-Gentil.

Communications: TV sets: 161 per 1,000 pop. **Radios:** 217 per 1,000 pop. **Telephone lines:** 2 per 100 pop. **Internet:** 7.2 users per 100 pop.

Health: Life expect.: 51.8 male; 53.2 female. **Births:** 35.2 (per 1,000 pop.). **Deaths:** 13.0 (per 1,000 pop.). **Natural inc.:** 2.22%. **Infant mortality:** 50.0 (per 1,000 live births). **HIV rate:** 5.2%.

Education: Compulsory: ages 6-15. **Literacy:** 87.7%.

Major intl. organizations: UN (FAO, IBRD, ILO, IMF, WHO), AU, WTO.

Embassy: 2034 20th St. NW 20009; 797-1000.

Website: www.legabon.org

France established control over the region in the second half of the 19th cent. Gabon became independent Aug. 17, 1960. Backed by France, Pres. Albert-Bernard Bongo (later Omar Bongo Ondimba) ruled the country 1967-2009, greatly enriching himself and his family. A multiparty political system was introduced in 1990, and a new constitution was enacted Mar. 14, 1991. Bongo's reelection victories in 1993, 1998, and 2003 were faulted by international observers. After he died June 8, 2009, his son Ali Bongo Ondimba, Gabon's defense minister 1999-2009, ran for the presidency. He claimed victory in a disputed election Aug. 30 and took office Oct. 16, 2009.

Gabon is one of the most prosperous African countries, thanks to abundant natural resources, foreign private investment, and government development programs.

The Gambia

Republic of The Gambia

People: Population: 1,797,860. **Age distrib.:** <15: 40%; 65+: 3.1%. **Pop. density:** 465.6 per sq mi, 179.8 per sq km. **Urban:** 58.1%. **Ethnic groups:** African 99% (incl. Mandinka 42%, Fula 18%, Wolof 16%, Jola 10%, Serahuli 9%). **Principal languages:** English (official), Mandinka, Wolof, Fula, other indigenous vernaculars. **Chief religions:** Muslim 90%, Christian 8%, indigenous beliefs 2%.

Geography: Total area: 4,361 sq mi, 11,295 sq km; **Land area:** 3,861 sq mi, 10,000 sq km. **Location:** On Atlantic coast near W tip of Africa. **Neighbors:** Surrounded on 3 sides by Senegal. **Topography:** A narrow strip of land on each side of lower Gambia R. **Capital:** Banjul, 436,000.

Government: Type: Republic. **Head of state and gov.:** Pres. Yahya Jammeh; b. May 25, 1965; in office: July 22, 1994. **Local divisions:** 5 divisions, 1 city. **Defense budget:** $7 mil. **Active troops:** 800.

Economy: Industries: peanuts, fish, and hides proc.; tourism; beverages; agric. machinery assembly. **Chief crops:** rice, millet, sorghum, peanuts, corn, sesame, cassava, palm kernels. **Natural resources:** fish, clay, silica sand, titanium, tin, zircon. **Arable land:** 40.0%. **Livestock:** cattle: 432,000; chickens: 750,000; goats: 380,000; pigs: 27,000; sheep: 209,500. **Fish catch:** 45,881 metric tons. **Electricity prod.:** 220 mil kWh. **Labor force:** agric. 75%, industry 19%, services 6%.

Finance: Monetary unit: Dalasi (GMD) (Sept. 2011: 29.40 = $1 U.S.). **GDP:** $3.5 bil; **per capita GDP:** $1,900; **GDP growth:** 5.7%. **Imports:** $306 mil; China 22.1%, Senegal 9.3%, Brazil 8.4%, Côte d'Ivoire 4.7%, Netherlands 4.6%, India 4.5%, U.S. 4.4%. **Exports:** $107 mil; India 47.5%, France 12.6%, China 10.9%, UK 7.4%. **Tourism:** $63 mil. **Budget:** $202.5 mil. **Total reserves less gold:** $201.6 mil. **CPI change:** 5%.

Transport: Civil aviation: 1 airport. **Chief port:** Banjul.

Communications: TV Sets: 14 per 1,000 pop. **Radios:** 147 per 1,000 pop. **Telephone lines:** 2.8 per 100 pop. **Internet:** 9.2 users per 100 pop.

Health: Life expect.: 61.2 male; 65.9 female. **Births:** 34.2 (per 1,000 pop.). **Deaths:** 7.7 (per 1,000 pop.). **Natural inc.:** 2.65%. **Infant mortality:** 71.7 (per 1,000 live births). **HIV rate:** 2%.

Education: Compulsory: ages 7-12. **Literacy:** 46.5%.

Major intl. organizations: UN (FAO, IBRD, ILO, IMF, WHO), AU, the Commonwealth, WTO.

Embassy: 1156 15th St. NW 20005; 785-1399.

Website: www.gambia.gm

The peoples of Gambia were at one time associated with the West African empires of Ghana, Mali, and Songhai. The area became Britain's first African possession in 1588.

Independence came Feb. 18, 1965; republic status within the Commonwealth was achieved in 1970. The country suffered from severe famine in the 1970s. Senegambia, a confederation with Senegal, lasted from 1982 to 1989.

On July 22, 1994, after 24 years in power, Pres. Dawda K. Jawara was deposed in a bloodless coup by a military officer, Yahya Jammeh. Jammeh barred political activity, detained potential opponents, and governed by decree. Despite a nominal return to constitutional government in 1996, Jammeh has retained a tight grip on power, while Gambia has remained one of the world's poorest countries. Security forces suppressed an alleged coup plot by army officers Mar. 2006. Pres. Jammeh won a third 5-year term Sept. 22, 2006; the next presidential election was scheduled for Nov. 2011.

Georgia

People: Population: 4,585,874. **Age distrib.:** <15: 15.6%; 65+: 16%. **Pop. density:** 170.4 per sq mi, 65.8 per sq km. **Urban:** 52.7%. **Ethnic groups:** Georgian 84%, Azeri 7%, Armenian 6%, Russian 2%. **Principal languages:** Georgian (official), Russian, Armenian, Azeri, Abkhaz (official in Abkhazia). **Chief religions:** Orthodox Christian (official) 84%, Muslim 10%, Armenian-Gregorian 4%.

Geography: Total area: 26,911 sq mi, 69,700 sq km; **Land area:** 26,911 sq mi, 69,700 sq km. **Location:** SW Asia, on E coast of Black Sea. **Neighbors:** Russia on N and NE, Turkey and Armenia on S, Azerbaijan on SE. **Topography:** Separated from Russia on NE by main range of Caucasus Mts. **Capital:** T'bilisi, 1,115,000.

Government: Type: Republic. **Head of state:** Pres. Mikhail Saakashvili; b. Dec. 21, 1967; in office: Jan. 25, 2004. **Head of gov.:** Prime Min. Nikoloz (Nika) Gilauri; b. Feb., 14, 1975; in office: Feb. 6, 2009. **Local divisions:** 53 rayons, 9 cities, and 2 autonomous republics. **Defense budget:** $420 mil. **Active troops:** 20,655.

Economy: Industries: steel, aircraft, machine tools, elec. appliances, mining, chemicals. **Chief crops:** citrus, grapes, tea, hazelnuts, vegetables. **Natural resources:** timber, hydropower, manganese, iron ore, copper, minor coal and oil deposits. **Crude oil reserves:** 35 mil bbls. **Arable land:** 6.4%. **Livestock:** cattle: 1.03 mil; chickens: 6.2 mil; goats: 79,400; pigs: 86,400; sheep: 690,000. **Fish catch:** 25,260 metric tons. **Electricity prod:** 8.3 bil kWh. **Labor force:** agric. 55.6%, industry 8.9%, services 35.5%.

Finance: Monetary unit: Lari (GEL) (Sept. 2011: 1.66 = $1 U.S.). **GDP:** $22.4 bil; **per capita GDP:** $4,900; **GDP growth:** 6.4%. **Imports:** $4.8 bil; Turkey 18.2%, Ukraine 9.7%, Azerbaijan 8.7%, Germany 7%, Russia 6.7%, U.S. 5.2%, China 4%. **Exports:** $2.3 bil; Turkey 20.1%, Azerbaijan 14.7%, Canada 10.4%, Armenia 7.9%, Ukraine 7.5%, Bulgaria 7.3%. **Tourism:** $659 mil. **Budget:** $3.9 bil. **Total reserves less gold:** $2.3 bil. **CPI change:** 7.1%.

Transport: Railways: 1,002 mi. **Civil aviation:** 369.1 mil pass.-mi; 18 airports. **Chief ports:** Batumi, Poti.

Communications: TV sets: 450 per 1,000 pop. **Radios:** 542 per 1,000 pop. **Telephone lines:** 13.7 per 100 pop. **Daily newspaper circ.:** 3.9 per 1,000 pop. **Internet:** 27 users per 100 pop.

Health: Life expect.: 73.8 male; 80.8 female. **Births:** 10.7 (per 1,000 pop.). **Deaths:** 9.9 (per 1,000 pop.). **Natural inc.:** 0.08%. **Infant mortality:** 15.2 (per 1,000 live births). **HIV rate:** 0.1%.

Education: Compulsory: ages 6-14. **Literacy:** 99.7%.

Major intl. organizations: UN (FAO, IBRD, ILO, IMF, WHO), CIS, OSCE, WTO.

Embassy: 2209 Massachusetts Ave. NW 20008; 387-2390.

Website: www.government.gov.ge

The region, which contained the ancient kingdoms of Colchis and Iberia, was Christianized in the 4th cent. and conquered by Arabs in the 8th cent. Annexed by Russia in 1801, Georgia was forcibly incorporated into the USSR in 1922.

Georgia declared independence Apr. 9, 1991. It emerged as an independent state when the Soviet Union disbanded Dec. 26. After a power struggle, former Soviet Foreign Min. Eduard A. Shevardnadze became president of Georgia. He survived several coup attempts and won reelection in 1995 and 2000. But parliamentary elections Nov. 2, 2003, denounced as fraudulent by opposition groups and international observers, sparked massive antigovernment protests, causing him to resign Nov. 23. Opposition leader Mikhail Saakashvili won the presidential election of Jan. 4, 2004. He survived an apparent assassination attempt along with U.S. Pres. George W. Bush in Tbilisi May 10, 2005, suppressed an alleged coup plot Sept. 6, 2006, and cracked down violently on antigovernment protests and imposed a state of emergency, Nov. 7-16, 2007; he then called early elections, Jan. 5, 2008, in which he won a renewed mandate.

Since the country gained independence, secessionist movements in the enclaves of South Ossetia and Abkhazia, supported by Russia, have challenged the Tbilisi government. Open warfare between Georgia and Russia erupted when Saakashvili sent troops Aug. 7, 2008, to suppress insurgent activity in Tskhinvali, the South Ossetian capital. Russia retaliated Aug. 8-9 by dispatching its forces to South Ossetia and Abkhazia and launching assaults on key Georgian cities. A cease-fire signed Aug. 15-16 called for withdrawal of Russian forces from Georgia proper, but allowed thousands of Russian troops to remain in the breakaway regions. On Aug. 26, Russian Pres. Dmitri Medvedev formally recognized their independence, a step protested by the U.S. and Georgia's other Western allies. International donors Oct. 22 pledged $4.55 bil in reconstruction aid, including about $1.5 bil from EU members and $1 bil from the U.S. Russia announced Aug. 11, 2010, that it had deployed antiaircraft missiles in Abkhazia. Abkhazia's pro-Russian Pres. Sergei Bagapsh died May 29, 2011; his vice president, Aleksandr Ankvab, was elected to succeed him Aug. 26.

Germany
Federal Republic of Germany

People: Population: 81,471,834. **Age distrib.:** <15: 13.3%; 65+: 20.6%. **Pop. density:** 605.2 per sq mi, 233.7 per sq km. **Urban:** 73.8%. **Ethnic groups:** German 92%, Turkish 2%, other (incl. Greek, Italian, Polish, Russian, Serbo-Croatian, Spanish) 6%. **Principal language:** German. **Chief religions:** Protestant 34%, Roman Catholic 34%, Muslim 4%, unaffiliated or other 28%.

Geography: Total area: 137,847 sq mi, 357,022 sq km; **Land area:** 134,623 sq mi, 348,672 sq km. **Location:** In central Europe. **Neighbors:** Denmark on N; Netherlands, Belgium, Luxembourg, France on W; Switzerland, Austria on S; Czech Rep., Poland on E. **Topography:** Germany is flat in N, hilly in center and W, and mountainous in Bavaria in the S. Chief rivers are Elbe, Weser, Ems, Rhine, and Main, all flowing toward North Sea, and Danube, flowing toward Black Sea. **Capital:** Berlin, 3,438,000. **Cities (urban aggl.):** Hamburg, 1,786,098; Munich, 1,349,325.

Government: Type: Federal republic. **Head of state:** Pres. Christian Wulff; b. June 19, 1959; in office: June 30, 2010. **Head of gov.:** Chancellor Angela Merkel; b. July 17, 1954; in office: Nov. 22, 2005. **Local divisions:** 16 laender (states). **Defense budget:** $41.2 bil. **Active troops:** 251,465.

Economy: Industries: among the world's largest and most technologically advanced producers of iron, steel, coal, cement, chemicals, machinery, vehicles, machine tools, electronics, food and beverages, shipbuilding, textiles. **Chief crops:** potatoes, wheat, barley, sugar beets, fruits, cabbages. **Natural resources:** coal, lignite, nat. gas, iron ore, copper, nickel, uranium, potash, salt, constr. materials, timber. **Crude oil reserves:** 276 mil bbls. **Arable land:** 34.3%. **Livestock:** cattle: 12.9 mil; chickens: 118 mil; goats: 220,000; pigs: 26.9 mil; sheep: 2.4 mil. **Fish catch:** 290,300 metric tons. **Electricity prod** (2009): 556.4 bil kWh. **Labor force:** agric. 2.4%, industry 29.7%, services 67.8%.

Finance: Monetary unit: Euro (EUR) (Sept. 2011: 0.71 = $1 U.S.). **GDP:** $2.9 tril; **per capita GDP:** $35,700; **GDP growth:** 3.5%. **Imports:** $1.1 tril; Netherlands 13%, France 8.2%, Belgium 7.2%, China 6.8%, Italy 5.6%, UK 4.7%, Austria 4.4%, U.S. 4.2%, Switzerland 4.1%. **Exports:** $1.3 tril; France 10.1%, U.S. 6.7%, UK 6.6%, Netherlands 6.6%, Italy 6.3%, Austria 5.7%, Belgium 5.2%, China 4.7%, Switzerland 4.5%. **Tourism:** $34.7 bil. **Budget:** $1.5 tril. **Total reserves less gold:** $62.3 bil. **Gold:** 109.3 mil oz t. **CPI change:** 1.1%.

Transport: Railways: 26,086 mi. **Motor vehicles:** 545.4 vehicles per 1,000 pop. **Civil aviation:** 127.6 bil pass.-mi; 330 airports. **Chief ports:** Bremen, Bremerhaven, Duisburg, Hamburg, Karlsruhe, Lubeck, Neuss-Dusseldorf, Rostock, Wilhemshaven.

Communications: TV sets: 675 per 1,000 pop. **Radios:** 558 per 1,000 pop. **Telephone lines:** 55.4 per 100 pop. **Daily newspaper circ.:** 267.5 per 1,000 pop. **Internet:** 81.9 users per 100 pop.

Health: Life expect.: 77.8 male; 82.4 female. **Births:** 8.3 (per 1,000 pop.). **Deaths:** 10.9 (per 1,000 pop.). **Natural inc.:** −0.26%. **Infant mortality:** 3.5 (per 1,000 live births). **HIV rate:** 0.1%.

Education: Compulsory: ages 6-18. **Literacy:** 99%.

Major intl. organizations: UN and all of its specialized agencies, EU, NATO, OECD, OSCE, WTO.

Embassy: 4645 Reservoir Rd. NW 20007; 298-4000.

Website: www.deutschland.de

Germany is a central European nation originally composed of numerous states, with a common language and traditions, that were united in one country in 1871. Germany was split into 2 countries from the end of WWII until 1990, when it was reunified.

History and government. Germanic tribes were defeated by Julius Caesar, 55 and 53 BCE, but Roman expansion north of the Rhine was stopped in 9 CE. Charlemagne, ruler of the Franks, consolidated Saxon, Bavarian, Rhenish, Frankish, and other lands; after him the eastern part became the German Empire. The Thirty Years' War, 1618-48, split Germany into small principalities and kingdoms.

Otto von Bismarck, Prussian chancellor, formed the North German Confederation, 1867.

In 1870 Bismarck maneuvered Napoleon III into declaring war. After the quick defeat of France, Bismarck formed the **German Empire** and on Jan. 18, 1871, in Versailles, proclaimed King Wilhelm I of Prussia German emperor (Deutscher kaiser).

The German Empire reached its peak before WWI in 1914, with 208,780 sq mi, plus overseas colonies. After losing the war in 1918, Germany ceded Alsace-Lorraine to France, West Prussia and Posen (Poznan) province to Poland, and part of Schleswig to Denmark. It lost all colonies and the ports of Memel and Danzig.

Republic of Germany, 1919-33, adopted the Weimar constitution; met reparation payments and elected Friedrich Ebert and Gen. Paul von Hindenburg presidents.

Third Reich, 1933-45, Adolf Hitler led the National Socialist German Workers' (Nazi) party after WWI. Pres. von Hindenburg named Hitler chancellor Jan. 30, 1933; on Aug. 3, 1934, the day after Hindenburg's death, the cabinet joined the offices of president and chancellor and made Hitler *fuehrer* (leader). Hitler abolished freedom of speech and assembly, and began a long series of persecutions climaxed by the murder of millions of Jews and others.

He repudiated the Versailles treaty and reparations agreements, remilitarized the Rhineland (1936), and annexed Austria (Anschluss, 1938). At Munich he made an agreement with Neville Chamberlain, British prime minister, which permitted Germany to annex part of Czechoslovakia. He signed a nonaggression treaty with the USSR, 1939, and declared war on Poland Sept. 1, 1939, precipitating WWII. With total defeat near, Hitler committed suicide in Berlin Apr. 1945. The victorious Allies voided all acts and annexations of Hitler's Reich.

Division of Germany. Germany was sectioned into 4 zones of occupation, administered by the Allied Powers (U.S., USSR, UK, and France). The USSR took control of many E German states. The territory E of the so-called Oder-Neisse line was assigned to, and later annexed by, Poland. Northern East Prussia (now Kaliningrad) was annexed by the USSR. Greater Berlin, within but not part of the Soviet zone, was administered by the 4 occupying powers under the Allied Command. In 1948 the USSR withdrew, established its single command in East Berlin, and cut off supplies. The Western Allies utilized a gigantic airlift to bring food to West Berlin, 1948-49.

In 1949, 2 separate German states were established. In May the zones administered by the Western Allies became West Germany; in Oct. the Soviet sector became East Germany. West Berlin was considered an enclave of West Germany, although its status was disputed by the Soviet bloc.

East Germany. The German Democratic Republic (East Germany) was proclaimed in the Soviet sector of Berlin Oct. 7, 1949. It was declared fully sovereign in 1954, but Soviet troops remained.

Coincident with the entrance of West Germany into the European defense community in 1952, the East German government decreed a prohibited zone 3 mi deep along its 600-mi border with West Germany and cut Berlin's telephone system in two. Berlin was further divided by erection of a fortified wall in 1961, after over 3 mil East Germans had fled to the West. The oppressive Communist regime maintained control through the state security police, known as the Stasi.

By the early 1970s, the economy of East Germany was highly industrialized, and the nation was credited with the highest standard of living among Warsaw Pact countries. But growth slowed in the late 1970s, because of shortages of natural resources and labor, and a huge debt to lenders in the West. Comparison with the lifestyle in the West caused many young people to emigrate.

In the late 1980s the government firmly resisted following the USSR's policy of openness (*glasnost*), but was faced with nationwide demonstrations demanding reform. Pres. Erich Honecker, in office since 1976, was forced to resign Oct. 18, 1989. On Nov. 9, the East German government announced its decision to open the border with the West, signaling the end of the Berlin Wall, which was the supreme emblem of the cold war. On Aug. 23, 1990, the East German parliament agreed to formal unification with West Germany; this occurred Oct. 3.

West Germany. The Federal Republic of Germany (West Germany) was proclaimed May 23, 1949, in Bonn. The occupying powers, the U.S., Britain, and France, restored civil status, Sept. 21. The Western Allies ended the state of war with Germany in 1951 (the U.S. resumed diplomatic relations July 2), while the USSR did so in 1955. The powers lifted controls, and the republic became fully independent May 5, 1955.

Dr. Konrad Adenauer, Christian Democrat, was made chancellor Sept. 15, 1949, and reelected 1953, 1957, 1961. Willy Brandt, heading a coalition of Social Democrats and Free Democrats, became chancellor Oct. 21, 1969, and pursued a policy of *Ostpolitik*, or rapprochement with East Germany and the USSR. Brandt resigned May 1974 because of a spy scandal. Terrorist acts on German soil in the 1970s included activities of the Baader-Meinhof gang and the murder of Israeli athletes by Palestinian commandos at the Olympic Games in Munich, Sept. 5, 1972.

Helmut Kohl became chancellor in 1982 and led Christian Democrats to victory in 1983 and 1987. In 1990, under Kohl's leadership, West Germany moved rapidly to reunite with East Germany.

A New Era. In May 1990, NATO ministers adopted a package of proposals on reunification, including the inclusion of the united Germany as a full member of NATO and the barring of the new Germany from having its own nuclear, chemical, or biological weapons. The merger of the 2 Germanys took place Oct. 3, and the first all-German elections since 1932 were held Dec. 2, with West German Chancellor Helmut Kohl confirmed as leader of the unified nation. Eastern Germany received over $1 tril in public and private funds from western Germany between 1990 and 1995. In 1991, Berlin again became Germany's official capital; the Bundestag (parliament) and parts of the federal executive were relocated from Bonn to Berlin in 1999.

Unemployment hit a postwar high of 12.6% in Jan. 1998. The Kohl era ended after 16 years with the defeat of the Christian Democrats in parliamentary elections Sept. 27; Gerhard Schröder, of the Social Democratic Party, became chancellor. Germany contributed 8,500 troops to the NATO-led security force (KFOR) that entered Kosovo in June 1999. Germany supplied troops for coalition military operations in Afghanistan (2001) but opposed the U.S.-led invasion of Iraq (2003).

The Christian Democrats, led by Angela Merkel, won a razor-thin plurality in the parliamentary elections of Sept. 18, 2005, and after prolonged negotiations she became chancellor Nov. 22, heading a "grand coalition" that included the Socialists.

Responding to the global recession, the government passed a 50 bil euro economic stimulus plan in early 2009. The German economy shrank 5% in 2009 but rebounded in 2010-11.

Merkel led a center-right coalition to victory in national elections Sept. 27, 2009. Christian Wulff, the Christian Democratic leader of Lower Saxony, became federal president June 30, 2010. Def. Min. Karl-Theodor zu Guttenberg, one of Germany's fastest-rising politicians, was forced to step down Mar. 1, 2011, in a plagiarism scandal. After an earthquake and tsunami in Japan caused a nuclear disaster, the Merkel government said May 30 that it would close Germany's 17 nuclear power plants by 2022.

Helgoland, an island of 130 acres in the North Sea, was taken from Denmark by a British Naval Force in 1807 and later ceded to Germany to become part of Schleswig-Holstein province in return for rights in East Africa. The heavily fortified island was surrendered to UK, May 23, 1945, demilitarized in 1947, and returned to West Germany, Mar. 1, 1952. It is a free port.

Ghana
Republic of Ghana

People: Population: 24,791,073. **Age distrib.:** <15: 36.5%; 65+: 3.6%. **Pop. density:** 282.2 per sq mi, 109 per sq km. **Urban:** 51.5%. **Ethnic groups:** Akan 45%, Mole-Dagbon 15%, Ewe 12%, Ga-Dangme 7%, Guan 4%, Gurma 4%, Grusi 3%, Mande-Busanga 1%. **Principal languages:** Asante, Ewe, Fante, English (official). **Chief religions:** Christian 69%, Muslim 16%, traditional 9%, none 6%.

Geography: Total area: 92,098 sq mi, 238,533 sq km. **Land area:** 87,851 sq mi, 227,533 sq km. **Location:** On S coast of W Africa. **Neighbors:** Côte d'Ivoire on W, Burkina Faso on N, Togo on E. **Topography:** Mostly low fertile plains and scrubland, cut by rivers and by the artificial Lake Volta. **Capital:** Accra, 2,269,000. **Cities (urban aggl.):** Kumasi, 1,834,084.

Government: Type: Republic. **Head of state and gov.:** Pres. John Atta Mills; b. July 21, 1944; in office: Jan. 7, 2009. **Local divisions:** 10 regions. **Defense budget:** $126 mil. **Active troops:** 15,500.

Economy: Industries: mining, lumbering, light mfg., aluminum smelting, food proc. **Chief crops:** cocoa, rice, cassava, peanuts, corn, shea nuts, bananas. **Natural resources:** gold, timber, industrial diamonds, bauxite, manganese, fish, rubber, hydropower, petroleum, silver, salt, limestone. **Crude oil reserves:** 660 mil bbls. **Arable land:** 19.3%. **Livestock:** cattle: 1.4 mil; chickens: 43.3 mil; goats: 4.6 mil; pigs: 521,000; sheep: 3.6 mil. **Fish catch:** 328,969 metric tons. **Electricity prod.:** 8.2 bil kWh. **Labor force:** agric. 56%, industry 15%, services 29%.

Finance: Monetary unit: Cedi (GHS) (Sept. 2011: 1.53 = $1 U.S.). **GDP:** $62 bil; **per capita GDP:** $2,500; **GDP growth:** 5.7%. **Imports:** $10.2 bil; China 16.5%, Nigeria 12.2%, U.S. 6.8%, Côte d'Ivoire 6.2%, France 5.2%, UK 4.3%. **Exports:** $7.3 bil; Netherlands 13.2%, UK 7.7%, France 5.8%, Ukraine 5.7%. **Tourism:** $968 mil. **Budget:** $7.03 bil. **Total reserves less gold (2006):** $2.1 bil. **Gold (2006):** 281,000 oz t. **CPI change:** 10.7%.

Transport: Railways: 588 mi. **Motor vehicles:** 7.3 vehicles per 1,000 pop. **Civil aviation:** 225.6 mil pass.-mi; 7 airports. **Chief ports:** Takoradi, Tema.

Communications: TV sets: 52 per 1,000 pop. **Radios:** 133 per 1,000 pop. **Telephone lines:** 1.1 per 100 pop. **Internet:** 8.6 users per 100 pop.

Health: Life expect.: 59.8 male; 62.3 female. **Births:** 27.6 (per 1,000 pop.). **Deaths:** 8.8 (per 1,000 pop.). **Natural inc.:** 1.88%. **Infant mortality:** 48.6 (per 1,000 live births). **HIV rate:** 1.8%.

Education: Compulsory: ages 6-15. **Literacy:** 66.6%.

Major intl. organizations: UN and all of its specialized agencies, AU, the Commonwealth, WTO.

Embassy: 3512 International Dr. NW 20008; 686-4520.

Website: www.ghana.gov.gh

Named for an African empire along the Niger River, 400-1240 CE, Ghana was ruled by Britain for 113 years as the Gold Coast. The UN in 1956 approved merger with the British Togoland trust territory. Independence came Mar. 6, 1957, and republic status within the Commonwealth in 1960.

Pres. Kwame Nkrumah built hospitals and schools, promoted development projects like the Volta R. hydroelectric and aluminum plants, but ran the country into debt, jailed opponents, and was accused of corruption. A 1964 referendum gave Nkrumah dictatorial powers and set up a one-party socialist state. Nkrumah was overthrown in 1966 by a police-army coup. Elections were held in

1969, but 4 further coups occurred in 1972, 1978, 1979, and 1981. The 1979 and 1981 coups, led by Flight Lieut. Jerry Rawlings, were followed by suspension of the constitution and banning of political parties. A new constitution, allowing multiparty politics, was approved in Apr. 1992.

In Feb. 1993 more than 1,000 people were killed in ethnic clashes in northern Ghana. Rawlings won the presidential election of Dec. 7, 1996. Kofi Annan, a career UN diplomat from Ghana, served as UN secretary general, 1997-2006.

Opposition leader John Agyekum Kufuor won a runoff vote Dec. 28, 2000, and was sworn in Jan. 7, 2001, marking Ghana's first peaceful transfer of power from one elected president to another. He was reelected Dec. 7, 2004. John Atta Mills, a tax law expert who had contended unsuccessfully for the presidency in 2000 and 2004, narrowly defeated the ruling party candidate, Nana Akufo-Addo, in a runoff election Dec. 28, 2008. A major offshore oil and gas find was announced June 2007; the Jubilee field, estimated to hold recoverable reserves of 1.5 bil barrels, began production Dec. 15, 2010.

Greece
Hellenic Republic

People: Population: 10,760,136. **Age distrib.:** <15: 14.2%; 65+: 19.6%. **Pop. density:** 213.3 per sq mi, 82.4 per sq km. **Urban:** 61.4%. **Ethnic groups:** Greek (citizenship) 93%, other (foreign citizenship) 7%. (Greece does not collect ethnicity data.) **Principal language:** Greek (official). **Chief religion:** Greek Orthodox (official) 98%, Muslim 1%.

Geography: Total area: 50,949 sq mi, 131,957 sq km; **Land area:** 50,443 sq mi, 130,647 sq km. **Location:** Occupies S end of Balkan Peninsula in SE Europe. **Neighbors:** Albania, Macedonia, Bulgaria on N; Turkey on E. **Topography:** About three-quarters is nonarable, with mountains in all areas. Pindus Mts. run through the country N to S. The heavily indented coastline is 9,385 mi long. Of over 2,000 islands, only 169 are inhabited, among them Crete, Rhodes, Milos, Kerkira (Corfu), Chios, Lesbos, Samos, Euboea, Delos, Mykonos. **Capital:** Athens, 3,252,000. **Cities (urban aggl.):** Thessaloníki, 837,446.

Government: Type: Parliamentary republic. **Head of state:** Pres. Karolos Papoulias; b. June 4, 1929; in office: Mar. 12, 2005. **Head of gov.:** Prime Min. George A. Papandreou; b. June 16, 1952; in office: Oct. 6, 2009. **Local divisions:** 13 regions comprising 51 prefectures. **Defense budget:** $9.66 bil. **Active troops:** 138,936.

Economy: Industries: tourism, food and tobacco proc., textiles, chemicals, metal prods., mining, petroleum. **Chief crops:** wheat, corn, barley, sugar beets, olives, tomatoes, wine grapes, tobacco, potatoes. **Natural resources:** lignite, petroleum, iron ore, bauxite, lead, zinc, nickel, magnesite, marble, salt, hydropower potential. **Crude oil reserves:** 10 mil bbls. **Arable land:** 19.8%. **Livestock:** cattle: 620,000; chickens: 31.8 mil; goats: 4.2 mil; pigs: 942,000; sheep: 9 mil. **Fish catch:** 205,305 metric tons. **Electricity prod.** (2009): 51.5 bil kWh. **Labor force:** agric. 12.4%, industry 22.4%, services 65.1%.

Finance: Monetary unit: Euro (EUR) (Sept. 2011: 0.71 = $1 U.S.). **GDP:** $318.1 bil; **per capita GDP:** $29,600; **GDP growth:** –4.5% **Imports:** $44.9 bil; Germany 13.7%, Italy 12.7%, China 7.1%, France 6.1%, Netherlands 6%, South Korea 5.7%, Belgium 4.3%, Spain 4.1%. **Exports:** $21.1 bil; Germany 11.1%, Italy 11%, Cyprus 7.3%, Bulgaria 6.7%, U.S. 4.9%, UK 4.4%, Turkey 4.2%. **Tourism:** $12.7 bil. **Budget:** $142.9 bil. **Total reserves less gold:** $1.3 bil. **Gold:** 3.6 mil oz t. **CPI change:** 4.7%.

Transport: Railways: 1,583 mi. **Motor vehicles:** 601.8 vehicles per 1,000 pop. **Civil aviation:** 4.7 bil pass.-mi; 67 airports. **Chief ports:** Agioi Theodoroi, Aspropyrgos, Pachi, Piraeus, Thessaloníki.

Communications: TV sets: 556 per 1,000 pop. **Radios:** 464 per 1,000 pop. **Telephone lines:** 45.8 per 100 pop. **Internet:** 44.4 users per 100 pop.

Health: Life expect.: 77.4 male; 82.7 female. **Births:** 9.2 (per 1,000 pop.). **Deaths:** 10.7 (per 1,000 pop.). **Natural inc.:** –0.15%. **Infant mortality:** 5.0 (per 1,000 live births). **HIV rate:** 0.1%.

Education: Compulsory: ages 6-14. **Literacy:** 97.2%.

Major intl. organizations: UN (FAO, IBRD, ILO, IMF, WHO), EU, NATO, OECD, OSCE, WTO.

Embassy: 2217 Massachusetts Ave. NW 20008; 939-1306.

Website: www.primeminister.gov.gr

The achievements of ancient Greece in art, architecture, science, mathematics, philosophy, drama, literature, and democracy became legacies for succeeding ages. Greece reached the height of its glory and power, particularly in the Athenian city-state, in the 5th cent. BCE. Greece fell under Roman rule in the 2nd and 1st centuries BCE. In the 4th cent. CE it became part of the Byzantine Empire and, after the fall of Constantinople to the Turks in 1453, part of the Ottoman Empire.

Greece won its war of independence from Turkey 1821-29, and became a kingdom. A republic was established 1924; the monarchy was restored, 1935. In Oct. 1940, Greece rejected an ultimatum from Italy, but the country was defeated and occupied by Germans, Italians, and Bulgarians. By the end of 1944 the invaders withdrew. Communist resistance forces were overcome by Royalist and British troops. A plebiscite again restored the monarchy.

Communists waged guerrilla war 1947-49 against the government but were defeated with the aid of the U.S. A period of reconstruction and rapid development followed, mainly with conservative governments under Premier Constantine Karamanlis. The Center Union, led by George Papandreou, won elections in 1963 and 1964, but King Constantine, who acceded in 1964, forced Papandreou to resign. A period of political maneuvers ended in the military takeover of Apr. 21, 1967, by Col. George Papadopoulos. King Constantine tried to reverse the consolidation of the harsh dictatorship Dec. 13, 1967, but failed and fled to Italy. Papadopoulos was ousted Nov. 25, 1973.

Greek army officers serving in the National Guard of Cyprus staged a coup on the island July 15, 1974. Turkey invaded Cyprus a week later, precipitating the collapse of the Greek junta, which was implicated in the Cyprus coup. Democratic government returned, and in 1975 the monarchy was abolished.

The 1981 electoral victory of the Panhellenic Socialist Movement (Pasok) of Andreas Papandreou brought substantial changes in Greece's internal and external policies. A scandal centered on George Kostokas, a banker and publisher, led to the arrest or investigation of leading Socialists, implicated Papandreou, and contributed to the defeat of the Socialists at the polls in 1989. However, Papandreou, who was narrowly acquitted Jan. 1992 of corruption charges, led the Socialists to a comeback victory in general elections Oct. 10, 1993.

Tensions between Greece and the Former Yugoslav Republic of Macedonia eased when the two countries agreed to normalize relations Sept. 13, 1995. The ailing Papandreou was replaced as prime minister by Costas Simitis, Jan. 18, 1996. Simitis led the Socialists to victory in the election of Sept. 22.

An earthquake that shook Athens Sept. 7, 1999, killed at least 143 people and left more than 60,000 homeless. The Socialists retained power by a narrow margin in the elections of Apr. 9, 2000. Police in 2002 cracked down on the November 17 terrorist movement, blamed for 23 killings since the mid-1970s.

The conservative New Democracy Party won parliamentary elections, Mar. 7, 2004, and Konstantinos (Costas) Karamanlis became prime minister. Athens hosted the Olympic Summer Games, Aug. 13-29, 2004. Rampant wildfires, Aug. 2007, left at least 65 people dead and caused over $1.6 bil in damage. Karamanlis kept his office after early elections Sept. 16. On Jan. 23-25, 2008, he became the first Greek government leader in 49 years to pay an official visit to Turkey.

Beset by scandals and an ailing economy, Karamanlis called early elections for Oct. 4, 2009, won by Pasok under the leadership of the U.S.-born George A. Papandreou, whose father and grandfather had headed previous Greek governments. The IMF and the 16 eurozone countries agreed May 2 on a 110 bil euro ($146 bil) loan package to prevent Greece from defaulting on its debts; in return, Greek leaders implemented an austerity plan. With default again impending, eurozone leaders agreed July 21, 2011, on another Greek bailout package, for 109 bil euros ($157 bil).

Grenada

People: Population: 108,419. **Age distrib.:** <15: 25.4%; 65+: 8.9%. **Pop. density:** 816.3 per sq mi, 315.2 per sq km. **Urban:** 39.3%. **Ethnic groups:** black 82%, mixed black & European 13%, European & East Indian 5%. **Principal languages:** English (official), French patois. **Chief religions:** Roman Catholic 53%, Anglican 14%, other Protestant 33%.

Geography: Total area: 133 sq mi, 344 sq km; **Land area:** 133 sq mi, 344 sq km. **Location:** In Caribbean, 90 mi N of Venezuela. **Neighbors:** Venezuela, Trinidad & Tobago to S; St. Vincent & the Grenadines to N. **Topography:** Main island is mountainous; country includes Carriacou and Petit Martinique isls. **Capital:** St. George's, 40,000.

Government: Type: Parliamentary democracy. **Head of state:** Queen Elizabeth II, represented by Gov.-Gen. Sir Carlyle Glean; b. Feb. 11, 1932; in office: Nov. 27, 2008. **Head of gov.:** Prime Min. Tillman Thomas; b. June 13, 1945; in office: July 9, 2008. **Local divisions:** 6 parishes, 1 dependency. **Defense budget/active troops:** NA.

Economy: Industries: food and beverages, textiles, light assembly operations, tourism, constr. **Chief crops:** bananas, cocoa, nutmeg, mace, citrus, avocados, root crops, sugarcane, corn, vegetables. **Natural resources:** timber, tropical fruit. **Arable land:** 7.4%. **Livestock:** cattle: 4,450; chickens: 270,000; goats: 7,200; pigs: 2,650; sheep: 13,200. **Fish catch:** 2,615 metric tons. **Electricity prod.** (2009): 195.4 mil kWh. **Labor force:** agric. 24%, industry 14%, services 62%.

Finance: Monetary unit: East Caribbean Dollar (XCD) (Sept. 2011: 2.70 = $1 U.S.). **GDP:** $1.1 bil; **per capita GDP:** $10,200; **GDP growth:** −1.4%. **Imports** (2006): $343 mil; Trinidad and Tobago 39.9%, U.S. 18.2%. **Exports** (2006): $38 mil; Saint Lucia 16.2%, Egypt 15.4%, Antigua and Barbuda 11%, U.S. 10%, Saint Kitts and Nevis 9.9%, Dominica 9.8%. **Tourism:** $97 mil. **Budget** (2009 est.): $215.9 mil. **Total reserves less gold:** $119.2 mil. **CPI change:** 3.4%.

Transport: Civil aviation: 3 airports. **Chief port:** Saint George's.

Communications: TV sets: 383 per 1,000 pop. **Radios:** 567 per 1,000 pop. **Telephone lines:** 27.2 per 100 pop. **Internet:** 33.5 users per 100 pop.

Health: Life expect.: 70.5 male; 75.8 female. **Births:** 17.0 (per 1,000 pop.). **Deaths:** 7.9 (per 1,000 pop.). **Natural inc.:** 0.91%. **Infant mortality:** 11.4 (per 1,000 live births). **HIV rate:** NA.

Education: Compulsory: ages 5-16. **Literacy:** NA.

Major intl. organizations: UN (FAO, IBRD, ILO, IMF, WHO), Caricom, the Commonwealth, OAS, OECS, WTO.

Embassy: 1701 New Hampshire Ave. NW 20009; 265-2561.

Website: www.gov.gd

Columbus sighted Grenada in 1498. First European settlers were French, 1650. The island was held alternately by France and England until final British occupation, 1784. Grenada became fully independent Feb. 7, 1974, during a general strike.

On Oct. 14, 1983, a military coup ousted Prime Min. Maurice Bishop, who was put under house arrest, later freed by supporters, rearrested, and, finally, on Oct. 19, executed. U.S. forces, with a token force from 6 area nations, invaded Grenada, Oct. 25. Resistance from the Grenadian army and Cuban advisors was quickly overcome as most people welcomed the invading forces. U.S. troops left Grenada in June 1985.

Hurricane Ivan slammed into Grenada, Sept. 7, 2004, killing 39 people and damaging an estimated 90% of the buildings on the island. Tillman Thomas of the National Democratic Congress became prime minister after parliamentary elections July 8, 2008.

Guatemala
Republic of Guatemala

People: Population: 13,824,463. **Age distrib.:** <15: 38.1%; 65+: 3.9%. **Pop. density:** 334.1 per sq mi, 129 per sq km. **Urban:** 49.5%. **Ethnic groups:** mestizo (mixed Amerindian-Spanish) & European 59%, K'iche 9%, Kaqchikel 8%, Mam 8%, Q'eqchi 6%, other Mayan 9%. **Principal languages:** Spanish (official), Amerindian languages (23 officially recognized). **Chief religions:** Roman Catholic, Protestant, indigenous Mayan beliefs.

Geography: Total area: 42,042 sq mi, 108,889 sq km; **Land area:** 41,374 sq mi, 107,159 sq km. **Location:** In Central America. **Neighbors:** Mexico on N and W, El Salvador on S, Honduras and Belize on E. **Topography:** The central highland and mountain areas are bordered by the narrow Pacific coast and lowlands and fertile river valleys on the Caribbean. Numerous volcanoes in S, more than half a dozen over 11,000 ft. **Capital:** Guatemala City, 1,075,000.

Government: Type: Republic. **Head of state and gov.:** Pres. Álvaro Colom Caballeros; b. June 15, 1951; in office: Jan. 14, 2008. **Local divisions:** 22 departments. **Defense budget:** $169 mil. **Active troops:** 15,212.

Economy: Industries: sugar, textiles and clothing, furniture, chemicals, petroleum, metals, rubber, tourism. **Chief crops:** sugarcane, corn, bananas, coffee, beans, cardamom. **Natural resources:** petroleum, nickel, rare woods, fish, chicle, hydropower. **Crude oil reserves:** 83.1 mil bbls. **Arable land:** 14.0%. **Livestock:** cattle: 3.1 mil; chickens: 31.4 mil; goats: 125,000; pigs: 2.7 mil; sheep: 598,300. **Fish catch:** 36,617 metric tons. **Electricity prod.:** 8.4 bil kWh. **Labor force:** agric. 50%, industry 15%, services 35%.

Finance: Monetary unit: Quetzal (GTQ) (Sept. 2011: 7.87 = $1 U.S.). **GDP:** $70.2 bil; **per capita GDP:** $5,200; **GDP growth:** 2.6%. **Imports:** $12.7 bil; U.S. 37.1%, Mexico 11.3%, China 6.3%, El Salvador 5.1%. **Exports:** $8.5 bil; U.S. 41.6%, El Salvador 9.3%, Honduras 7.9%, Mexico 6.8%. **Tourism:** $1.4 bil. **Budget:** $6.1 bil. **Total reserves less gold:** $5.6 bil. **Gold:** 221,800 oz t. **CPI change:** 3.9%.

Transport: Railways: 206 mi. **Motor vehicles:** 22.6 vehicles per 1,000 pop. **Civil aviation:** 13 airports. **Chief ports:** Puerto Quetzal, Santo Tomas de Castilla.

Communications: TV sets: 163 per 1,000 pop. **Radios:** 80 per 1,000 pop. **Telephone lines:** 10.4 per 100 pop. **Internet:** 10.5 users per 100 pop.

Health: Life expect.: 69.0 male; 72.8 female. **Births:** 27.0 (per 1,000 pop.). **Deaths:** 5.0 (per 1,000 pop.). **Natural inc.:** 2.20%. **Infant mortality:** 26.0 (per 1,000 live births). **HIV rate:** 0.8%.

Education: Compulsory: ages 7-15. **Literacy:** 74.5%.

Major intl. organizations: UN (FAO, IBRD, ILO, IMF, WHO), OAS, WTO.

Embassy: 2220 R St. NW 20008; 745-4952.

Website: www.guatemala.gob.gt

A Mayan Indian empire flourished in what is today Guatemala for over 1,000 years before Spaniards came. Guatemala was a Spanish colony 1524-1821. A republic was established in 1839.

The U.S. intervened in Guatemala in 1954 when the Central Intelligence Agency engineered the overthrow of elected Pres. Jacobo Arbenz Guzmán, a left-wing reformer. Since then, the country has experienced a variety of military and civilian governments and periods of insurgency, repression, paramilitary violence, and civil war. After military coups in 1982 and 1983, the nation returned to civilian rule in 1986.

On Sept. 19, 1996, the Guatemalan government and leftist rebels approved a peace accord; the final agreement was signed Dec. 29. During more than 35 years of armed conflict, some 200,000 people were killed or "disappeared" (and are presumed dead); most of these casualties were attributed to the government and its paramilitary allies. U.S. Pres. Bill Clinton, on a visit to Guatemala Mar. 10, 1999, apologized for aid the U.S. had given to forces which he said "engaged in violence and widespread repression."

Drought and weak export prices during 2001-02 worsened the plight of Guatemala's poor, who make up 80% of the population. Floods and mudslides from Tropical Storm Stan, Oct. 2005, killed at least 669 people; another 844 were missing and presumed dead.

After a campaign marred by violence, Álvaro Colom Caballeros, a businessman who pledged to fight poverty, won a presidential runoff election Nov. 4, 2007, and took office Jan. 14, 2008. Floods and landslides from Tropical Storm Agatha, which hit Guatemala May 29, 2010, killed more than 170 people. With Pres. Colom and his relatives constitutionally barred from running in the Sept. 2011 presidential election, his wife, Sandra Torres de Colom, declared her candidacy Mar. 8 and filed for divorce 3 days later, saying she was "getting married to the Guatemalan people"; her bid was blocked by the courts. Former Gen. Otto Pérez Molina and businessman Manuel Baldizón led after the first round of presidential balloting Sept. 11, 2011, with a runoff vote scheduled for Nov. 6. Drug trafficking, arms smuggling, police corruption, and one of the world's highest homicide rates pose ongoing threats to national stability.

Guinea
Republic of Guinea

People: Population: 10,601,009. **Age distrib.:** <15: 42.5%; 65+: 3.5%. **Pop. density:** 111.7 per sq mi, 43.1 per sq km. **Urban:** 35.4%. **Ethnic groups:** Peuhl 40%, Malinke 30%, Soussou 20%, smaller ethnic groups 10%. **Principal languages:** French (official), ethnic group-specific languages. **Chief religions:** Muslim 85%, Christian 8%, indigenous beliefs 7%.

Geography: Total area: 94,926 sq mi, 245,857 sq km; **Land area:** 94,872 sq mi, 245,717 sq km. **Location:** On Atlantic coast of W Africa. **Neighbors:** Guinea-Bissau, Senegal, Mali on N; Côte d'Ivoire on E; Liberia, Sierra Leone on S. **Topography:** A narrow coastal belt leads to mountainous middle region, source of the Gambia, Senegal, and Niger rivers. Upper Guinea, farther inland, is cooler upland. The SE is forested. **Capital:** Conakry, 1,597,000.

Government: Type: Republic. **Head of state:** Interim Pres. Alpha Condé; b. Mar. 4, 1938; in office: Dec. 21, 2010. **Head of gov.:** Prime Min. Mohamed Said Fofana; b. 1952; in office: Dec. 24 2010. **Local divisions:** 33 prefectures, 1 special zone. **Defense budget:** $58 mil. **Active troops:** 12,300.

Economy: Industries: bauxite, gold, diamonds, iron; alumina refining; light mfg. **Chief crops:** rice, coffee, pineapples, palm kernels, cassava, bananas, sweet potatoes. **Natural resources:** bauxite, iron ore, diamonds, gold, uranium, hydropower, fish, salt. **Arable land:** 11.6%. **Livestock:** cattle: 4.7 mil; chickens: 20.1 mil; goats: 1.8 mil; pigs: 90,700; sheep: 1.5 mil. **Fish catch:** 86,129 metric tons. **Electricity prod.:** 920 mil kWh. **Labor force:** agric. 76%, industry and services 24%.

Finance: Monetary unit: Franc (GNF) (Sept. 2011: 6,425.00 = $1 U.S.). **GDP:** $10.8 bil; **per capita GDP:** $1,000; **GDP growth:** 1.9%. **Imports:** $1.6 bil; China 8.6%, Netherlands 6.5%, France 4.2%, UK 4.1%. **Exports:** $1.5 bil; Spain 15.5%, Russia 8.2%, Germany 8.1%, Ireland 6.9%, U.S. 5.7%, Ukraine 6.6%, India 4.6%, Canada 4.3%. **Tourism:** NA. **Budget:** $875.4 mil. **Total reserves less gold** (2005): $95.1 mil. **Gold** (2005): 4,068 oz t. **CPI change:** 15.5%.

Transport: Railways: 736 mi. **Civil aviation:** 4 airports. **Chief ports:** Conakry, Kamsar.

Communications: TV sets: 18 per 1,000 pop. **Radios:** 81 per 1,000 pop. **Telephone lines:** 0.2 per 100 pop. **Internet:** 1 user per 100 pop.

Health: Life expect.: 56.6 male; 59.6 female. **Births:** 36.9 (per 1,000 pop.). **Deaths:** 10.5 (per 1,000 pop.). **Natural inc.:** 2.65%. **Infant mortality:** 61.0 (per 1,000 live births). **HIV rate:** 1.3%.

Education: Compulsory: ages 7-12. **Literacy:** 39.5%.

Major intl. organizations: UN and most of its specialized agencies, AU, WTO.

Embassy: 2112 Leroy Pl. NW 20008; 906-4300.

Website: www.state.gov/p/af/ci/gv/

Guinea, a French colony, attained independence Oct. 2, 1958. Sékou Touré, Guinea's first president (1958-84), turned to Communist nations for support and set up a one-party state. Thousands of opponents were jailed in the 1970s, after an unsuccessful Portuguese invasion. Many were tortured and killed.

The military took control in a bloodless coup after the Mar. 1984 death of Touré. A new constitution was approved in 1991, but movement toward democracy was slow. When presidential elections were finally held, in Dec. 1993, the incumbent, Gen. Lansana Conté, was the official winner; outside monitors called the elections flawed. Conté suppressed an army mutiny in Conakry, Feb. 2-3, 1996, and won reelection in Dec. 1998. Fighting in early 2001 along the border with Liberia and Sierra Leone created a refugee crisis in Guinea; voluntary repatriation of more than 51,000 Liberian refugees was largely completed in 2007.

Major opposition parties boycotted the presidential election Dec. 21, 2003, in which the ailing Conté won 95.6% of the vote. More than 120 died in strikes and protests Jan.-Feb. 2007, until Conté agreed to name a new prime min. from a list approved by union leaders; protests followed his ouster by Conté in May 2008.

After Conté's death Dec. 22, 2008, a military junta took power, calling itself the National Council for Democracy and Development. More than 150 people were reportedly killed Sept. 28, 2009, when Guinean troops fired into a crowd of about 50,000 antigovernment protesters in Conakry. After an assassination attempt Dec. 3, 2009, by a former aide left Pres. Moussa Dadis Camara seriously wounded, Vice Pres. Sékouba Konaté became interim head of state. Presidential elections June-Nov. 2010 led to a return to civilian government Dec. 21 with Alpha Condé as head of state.

Guinea-Bissau
Republic of Guinea-Bissau

People: Population: 1,596,677. **Age distrib.:** <15: 40.4%; 65+: 3.2%. **Pop. density:** 147.1 per sq mi, 56.8 per sq km. **Urban:** 30%. **Ethnic groups:** African 99% (incl. Balanta 30%, Fula 20%, Manjaca 14%, Mandinga 13%, Papel 7%). **Principal languages:** Portuguese (official), Crioulo, African languages. **Chief religions:** Muslim 50%, indigenous beliefs 40%, Christian 10%.

Geography: Total area: 13,948 sq mi, 36,125 sq km; **Land area:** 10,857 sq mi, 28,120 sq km. **Location:** On Atlantic coast of W Africa. **Neighbors:** Senegal on N, Guinea on E and S. **Topography:** A swampy coastal plain covers most of country; to E is a low savanna region. **Capital:** Bissau, 302,000.

Government: Type: Republic. **Head of state:** Pres. Malam Bacai Sanhá; b. May 5, 1947; in office; Sept. 8, 2009. **Head of gov.:** Prime Min. Carlos Gomes Júnior; b. Dec. 19, 1949; in office: Jan. 2, 2009. **Local divisions:** 9 regions. **Defense budget:** NA. **Active troops:** 4,458.

Economy: Industries: agric. prods. proc., beer, soft drinks. **Chief crops:** rice, corn, beans, cassava, cashew nuts, peanuts, palm kernels, cotton. **Natural resources:** fish, timber, phosphates, bauxite, clay, granite, limestone, unexploited deposits of petroleum. **Arable land:** 10.7%. **Livestock:** cattle: 620,000; chickens: 1.8 mil; goats: 415,970; pigs: 410,000; sheep: 420,000. **Fish catch:** 6,800 metric tons. **Electricity prod.:** 70 mil kWh. **Labor force:** agric. 82%, industry and services 18%.

Finance: Monetary unit: CFA BCEAO Franc (XOF) (Sept. 2011: 468.55 = $1 U.S.). **GDP:** $1.8 bil; **per capita GDP:** $1,100; **GDP growth:** 3.5%. **Imports** (2006): $200 mil; Portugal 15.6%, Senegal 15.3%, India 11.6%, Netherlands 8.4%, China 7.8%, Thailand 4.7%, Brazil 4.1%. **Exports** (2006): $133 mil; India 69.7%, Nigeria 24.1%. **Tourism:** NA. **Budget:** NA. **Total reserves less gold:** $156.4 mil. **CPI change:** 2.5%.

Transport: Civil aviation: 2 airports. **Chief ports:** Bissau, Buba, Cacheu, Farim.

Communications: TV sets: 39 per 1,000 pop. **Radios:** 41 per 1,000 pop. **Telephone lines:** 0.3 per 100 pop. **Internet:** 2.5 users per 100 pop.

Health: Life expect.: 46.8 male; 50.7 female. **Births:** 35.2 (per 1,000 pop.). **Deaths:** 15.3 (per 1,000 pop.). **Natural inc.:** 1.99%. **Infant mortality:** 96.2 (per 1,000 live births). **HIV rate:** 2.5%.

Education: Compulsory: ages 7-12. **Literacy:** 52.2%.

Major intl. organizations: UN (FAO, IBRD, ILO, IMF, WHO), AU, WTO.

Permanent UN Mission: 800 Second Ave., Ste. 400F, New York, NY 10017; (917) 770-5598.

Website: www.state.gov/p/af/ci/pu/

Portuguese mariners explored the area in the mid-15th cent.; the slave trade flourished in the 17th and 18th centuries, and colonization began in the 19th. Independence came Sept. 10, 1974, ending 13 years of guerrilla warfare against the Portuguese regime.

A Nov. 1980 coup gave army chief João Bernardo Vieira absolute power. Vieira eventually initiated political liberalization; multiparty elections were held July 3, 1994. An army uprising June 7, 1998, triggered a civil war, with Senegal and Guinea aiding the Vieira regime. After a peace accord signed on Nov. 2 broke down, rebel troops ousted Vieira on May 7, 1999.

Elections 1999-2000 brought a return to civilian rule, but top military officers staged a coup Sept. 14, 2003. Vieira won a presidential runoff election, July 24, 2005, and returned to power Oct. 1. Gen. Batista Tagme Na Waie, the nation's defense chief, was killed by a bomb Mar. 1, 2009; less than a day later, a group of soldiers murdered Vieira in his presidential palace. Political violence continued as the June 28, 2009, presidential election approached; the ruling party candidate, Malam Bacai Sanhá, won a runoff vote July 26. In recent years, Guinea-Bissau has become an important transit point for cocaine trafficking from Colombia to Europe.

Guyana
Co-operative Republic of Guyana

People: Population: 744,768. **Age distrib.:** <15: 31.9%; 65+: 4.8%. **Pop. density:** 9.8 per sq mi, 3.8 per sq km. **Urban:** 28.6%. **Ethnic groups:** East Indian 44%, black (African) 30%, mixed 17%, Amerindian 9%. **Principal languages:** English, Amerindian dialects, Creole, Caribbean Hindustani, Urdu. **Chief religions:** Hindu 28%, Pentecostal 17%, Roman Catholic 8%, Muslim 7%, Anglican 7%, Seventh-Day Adventist 5%, Methodist 2%, Jehovah's Witnesses 1%, other Christian 18%, none 4%.

Geography: Total area: 83,000 sq mi, 214,969 sq km; **Land area:** 76,004 sq mi, 196,849 sq km. **Location:** On N coast of S. America. **Neighbors:** Venezuela on W, Brazil on S, Suriname on E.

Topography: Dense tropical forests cover much of land, although flat coastal area up to 40 mi wide, where 90% of the population lives, provides rich alluvial soil for agriculture. A grassy savanna divides the 2 zones. **Capital:** Georgetown, 132,000.

Government: Type: Republic. **Head of state:** Pres. Bharrat Jagdeo; b. Jan. 23, 1964; in office: Aug. 11, 1999. **Head of gov.:** Prime Min. Samuel Hinds; b. Dec. 27, 1943; in office: Dec. 22, 1997. **Local divisions:** 10 regions. **Defense budget:** $128 mil. **Active troops:** 1,100.

Economy: Industries: bauxite, sugar, rice milling, timber, textiles, gold mining. **Chief crops:** sugarcane, rice, edible oils. **Natural resources:** bauxite, gold, diamonds, timber, shrimp, fish. **Arable land:** 2.1%. **Livestock:** cattle: 110,000; chickens: 19.9 mil; goats: 79,000; pigs: 13,500; sheep: 130,000. **Fish catch:** 44,114 metric tons. **Electricity prod.:** 820 mil kWh. **Labor force:** NA.

Finance: Monetary unit: Dollar (GYD) (Sept. 2011: 203.20 = $1 U.S.). **GDP:** $5.4 bil; **per capita GDP:** $7,200; **GDP growth:** 3.6%. **Imports:** $1.4 bil; U.S. 24.9%, Trinidad and Tobago 22.9%, Cuba 6.3%, China 5.7%. **Exports:** $814 mil; Canada 27.6%, U.S. 17%, UK 10.9%, Ukraine 5.6%, Netherlands 5.1%, Trinidad and Tobago 4.3%, Jamaica 4.3%. **Tourism:** NA. **Budget:** $655.7 mil. **Total reserves less gold:** $782.1 mil. **CPI change:** 2.1%.

Transport: Motor vehicles: 62.1 vehicles per 1,000 pop. **Civil aviation:** 10 airports. **Chief port:** Georgetown.

Communications: TV sets: 167 per 1,000 pop. **Radios:** 571 per 1,000 pop. **Telephone lines:** 19.9 per 100 pop. **Internet:** 29.9 users per 100 pop.

Health: Life expect.: 63.3 male; 71.1 female. **Births:** 17.1 (per 1,000 pop.). **Deaths:** 7.2 (per 1,000 pop.). **Natural inc.:** 0.99%. **Infant mortality:** 36.8 (per 1,000 live births). **HIV rate:** 1.2%.

Education: Compulsory: ages 6-15. **Literacy:** NA.

Major intl. organizations: UN (FAO, IBRD, ILO, IMF, WHO), Caricom, the Commonwealth, OAS, WTO.

Embassy: 2490 Tracy Pl. NW 20008; 265-6900.

Website: www.gina.gov.gy

Guyana became a Dutch possession in the 17th cent., but sovereignty passed to Britain in 1815. Indentured servants from India soon outnumbered African slaves. Guyana became independent May 26, 1966.

The Port Kaituma ambush of U.S. Rep. Leo J. Ryan and others investigating mistreatment of American followers of the Rev. Jim Jones's People's Temple cult triggered a mass suicide-execution of 911 cultists at Jonestown in the jungle, Nov. 18, 1978.

The People's National Congress, the party in power since Guyana became independent, was voted out of office with the election of Cheddi Jagan in Oct. 1992. When Pres. Jagan died Mar. 6, 1997, Prime Min. Samuel Hinds succeeded him. Jagan's widow, Janet, became prime min. Mar. 17. She won the presidency in a disputed election Dec. 15. She resigned because of ill health Aug. 11, 1999, and was succeeded by Bharrat Jagdeo, then 35, who became the youngest head of state in the Americas. He won reelection Mar. 19, 2001, and Aug. 28, 2006.

Floods from torrential rains, Jan. 2005, affected about 40% of the population. Gunmen in Georgetown killed Agric. Min. Satyadeow Sawh and two members of his family, Apr. 22, 2006. Rondell Rawlins, a gang leader suspected in the 2006 assassination plot and accused of ordering massacres in two villages that left 23 dead in early 2008, was killed in a shootout with police Aug. 28, 2008.

Haiti
Republic of Haiti

People: Population: 9,719,932. **Age distrib.:** <15: 35.9%; 65+: 3.9%. **Pop. density:** 913.4 per sq mi, 352.7 per sq km. **Urban:** 52.1%. **Ethnic groups:** black 95%, mulatto & white 5%. **Principal languages:** French, Creole (both official). **Chief religions:** Roman Catholic 80%, Protestant 16%, none 1%; roughly half of pop. practices voodoo.

Geography: Total area: 10,714 sq mi, 27,750 sq km; **Land area:** 10,641 sq mi, 27,560 sq km. **Location:** In Caribbean, occupies W third of Isl. of Hispaniola. **Neighbors:** Dominican Republic on E, Cuba to W. **Topography:** About two-thirds is mountainous. Much of rest is semiarid. Coastal areas are warm and moist. **Capital:** Port-au-Prince, 2,643,000.

Government: Type: Republic. **Head of state:** Pres. Michel Martelly; b. Feb. 12, 1961; in office: May 14, 2011. **Head of gov.:** Prime Min. Garry Conille; b. Feb. 26, 1966; in office: Oct. 4, 2011. **Local divisions:** 9 departments. **Defense budget:** NA. **Active troops:** No active armed forces.

Economy: Industries: textiles, sugar refining, flour milling, cement, light assembly of imported parts. **Chief crops:** coffee, mangoes, sugarcane, rice, corn, sorghum. **Natural resources:** bauxite, copper, calcium carbonate, gold, marble, hydropower. **Arable land:** 38.1%. **Livestock:** cattle: 1.5 mil; chickens: 5.6 mil; goats: 1.9 mil; pigs: 1 mil; sheep: 153,500. **Fish catch:** 8,392 metric tons. **Electricity prod.:** 466 mil kWh. **Labor force:** agric 38.1%, industry 11.5%, services 50.4%.

Finance: Monetary unit: Gourde (HTG) (Sept. 2011: 40.85 = $1 U.S.). **GDP:** $11.5 bil; **per capita GDP:** $1,200; **GDP growth:** –5.1%. **Imports:** $2.7 bil; U.S. 51%, Dominican Republic 19%, China 11%. **Exports:** $530.2 mil; U.S. 90.2%, Canada 4%, France

1.5%. **Tourism:** $315 mil. **Budget:** $2.6 bil. **Total reserves less gold:** $1.3 bil. **Gold:** 1,308 oz t. **CPI change:** 5.7%.

Transport: Motor vehicles: 7.2 vehicles per 1,000 pop. **Civil aviation:** 4 airports. **Chief ports:** Cap-Haitien, Gonaives, Jacmel, Port-au-Prince.

Communications: TV sets: 104 per 1,000 pop. **Radios:** 170 per 1,000 pop. **Telephone lines:** 0.5 per 100 pop. **Internet:** 8.4 users per 100 pop.

Health: Life expect.: 60.8 male; 63.5 female. **Births:** 24.4 (per 1,000 pop.). **Deaths:** 8.2 (per 1,000 pop.). **Natural inc.:** 1.62%. **Infant mortality:** 54.0 (per 1,000 live births). **HIV rate:** 1.9%.

Education: Compulsory: ages 6-11. **Literacy:** 48.7%.

Major intl. organizations: UN and most of its specialized agencies, Caricom, OAS, WTO.

Embassy: 2311 Massachusetts Ave. NW 20008; 332-4090.

Website: www.parlementhaitien.ht or www.haiti.org

Haiti, visited by Columbus in 1492 and a French colony from 1697, attained its independence, 1804, following a rebellion led by former slave Toussaint L'Ouverture. After a period of political violence, the U.S. occupied the country 1915-34.

François Duvalier, known as Papa Doc, was elected president in Sept. 1957; in 1964 he was named president for life. Upon his death in 1971, he was succeeded by his son, Jean Claude Duvalier, known as Baby Doc. Following weeks of unrest, Jean Claude fled Haiti aboard a U.S. Air Force jet Feb. 7, 1986. His departure ended the Duvalier family's brutal 28-year dictatorship, but political violence, government corruption, poverty, AIDS and other health problems, and deteriorating environmental quality have continued to plague Haiti.

Father Jean-Bertrand Aristide was elected president Dec. 1990, but in Sept. 1991, he was arrested by the military and expelled from the country. Some 35,000 Haitian refugees were intercepted by the U.S. Coast Guard as they tried to enter the U.S., 1991-92. Most were returned to Haiti. There was a new upsurge of refugees starting in late 1993.

The UN authorized, July 31, 1994, an invasion of Haiti by a multinational force. With U.S. troops already en route, a full-scale invasion was averted, Sept. 18, when military leaders agreed to step down. Aristide returned to Haiti and was restored to office Oct. 15. A UN peacekeeping force exercised responsibility in Haiti from Mar. 31, 1995, to Nov. 30, 1997. Aristide transferred power to his elected successor, René Préval, on Feb. 7, 1996.

At least 140 people died and over 160,000 were left homeless when Hurricane Georges struck Haiti Sept. 22, 1998. Aristide won the presidency Nov. 26, 2000, in an election boycotted by opposition groups. An armed uprising in early 2004 and pressure from France and the U.S. toppled Aristide, who went into exile Feb. 29. A U.S.-led contingent, sent in after the upheaval, yielded authority June 1 to a UN stabilization force (MINUSTAH).

Flooding in late May 2004 killed more than 1,000 people, and more than 2,400 were killed in Tropical Storm Jeanne in Sept. Presidential elections Feb. 7, 2006, restored Préval to power.

Skyrocketing prices for food imports sparked riots and mass protests in Apr. 2008. A succession of hurricanes and tropical storms (Fay, Gustav, Hanna, Ike), Aug.-Sept. 2008, left more than 550 Haitians dead and up to 1 mil homeless. A school collapse near Port-au-Prince Nov. 7, 2008, killed 91 students and teachers.

An earthquake Jan. 12, 2010, near Port-au-Prince caused cataclysmic damage: more than 220,000 people (including nearly 100 UN peacekeepers) were killed, at least 300,000 were injured, and many more were left homeless. With the central government paralyzed and the presidential palace and parliament building in ruins, the U.S. and other countries mounted a massive relief effort. Nearly 600,000 Haitians were still living in displacement camps 18 months later.

After the first round of presidential balloting Nov. 28, 2010, Michel Martelly, an entertainer popularly known as Sweet Micky, was initially declared ineligible for the 2nd round. Violent protests from his supporters, allegations of electoral fraud from international observers, and diplomatic pressure from the U.S. and other donor countries gained him a place in the runoff Mar. 20, 2011, which he won. Parliament twice blocked his nominees for prime minister before approving his third choice, Garry Conille, a physician and development expert. MINUSTAH uniformed personnel numbered about 12,250 in mid-2011.

Honduras
Republic of Honduras

People: Population: 8,143,564. **Age distrib.:** <15: 36.7%; 65+: 3.8%. **Pop. density:** 188.5 per sq mi, 72.8 per sq km. **Urban:** 51.6%. **Ethnic groups:** mestizo (mixed Amerindian & European) 90%, Amerindian 7%, black 2%, white 1%. **Principal languages:** Spanish (official), Amerindian dialects. **Chief religions:** Roman Catholic 97%, Protestant 3%.

Geography: Total area: 43,278 sq mi, 112,090 sq km; **Land area:** 43,201 sq mi, 111,890 sq km. **Location:** In Central America. **Neighbors:** Guatemala on W; El Salvador, Nicaragua on S. **Topography:** Caribbean coast is 500 mi long. Pacific coast, on Gulf of Fonseca, is 40 mi long. Country is mountainous, with wide fertile valleys and rich forests. **Capital:** Tegucigalpa, 1,000,000.

Government: Type: Republic. **Head of state and gov.:** Pres. Porfirio (Pepe) Lobo; b. Dec. 22, 1947; in office: Jan. 27, 2010. **Local divisions:** 18 departments. **Defense budget:** $138 mil. **Active troops:** 12,000.

Economy: Industries: sugar, coffee, woven and knit apparel, wood prods., cigars. **Chief crops:** bananas, coffee, citrus, corn, African palm. **Natural resources:** timber, gold, silver, copper, lead, zinc, iron ore, antimony, coal, fish, hydropower. **Arable land:** 9.1%. **Livestock:** cattle: 2.7 mil; chickens: 38.6 mil; goats: 24,500; pigs: 424,819; sheep: 15,000. **Fish catch:** 40,160 metric tons. **Electricity prod.:** 6.3 bil kWh. **Labor force:** agric. 39.2%, industry 20.9%, services 39.8%.

Finance: Monetary unit: Lempira (HNL) (Sept. 2011: 18.85 = $1 U.S.). **GDP:** $33.6 bil; **per capita GDP:** $4,200; **GDP growth:** 2.8%. **Imports:** $8.9 bil; U.S. 33.9%, Guatemala 10.5%, Mexico 6.8%, El Salvador 6.2%, China 4.7%, Costa Rica 4.6%. **Exports:** $5.9 bil; U.S. 40.9%, El Salvador 8.6%, Guatemala 7.2%, Germany 7%, Nicaragua 4.6%, Belgium 4.3%. **Tourism:** $650 mil. **Budget:** $3.7 bil. **Total reserves less gold:** $2.7 bil. **Gold:** 21,400 oz t. **CPI change:** 4.7%.

Transport: Railways: 47 mi. **Motor vehicles:** 15.9 vehicles per 1,000 pop. **Civil aviation:** 12 airports. **Chief ports:** La Ceiba, Puerto Cortes, San Lorenzo, Tela.

Communications: TV sets: 176 per 1,000 pop. **Radios:** 1,698 per 1,000 pop. **Telephone lines:** 8.8 per 100 pop. **Internet:** 11.1 users per 100 pop.

Health: Life expect.: 68.9 male; 72.4 female. **Births:** 25.1 (per 1,000 pop.). **Deaths:** 5.0 (per 1,000 pop.). **Natural inc.:** 2.01%. **Infant mortality:** 20.4 (per 1,000 live births). **HIV rate:** 0.8%.

Education: Compulsory: ages 6-11. **Literacy:** 83.6%.

Major intl. organizations: UN (FAO, IBRD, ILO, IMF, WHO), OAS, WTO.

Embassy: 3007 Tilden St. NW 20008; 966-7702.

Website: www.gob.hn

Mayan civilization flourished in Honduras in the 1st millennium CE. Columbus arrived in 1502. Honduras became independent after freeing itself from Spain, 1821, and from the Fed. of Central America, 1838.

Gen. Oswaldo Lopez Arellano, president for most of the period 1963-75 by virtue of one election and 2 coups, was ousted by the army in 1975 over charges of pervasive bribery by United Brands Co. of the U.S. An elected civilian government took power in 1982. Some 3,200 U.S. troops were sent to Honduras after the Honduran border was violated by Nicaraguan forces, Mar. 1988.

Already one of the poorest countries in the Western Hemisphere, Honduras was devastated in late Oct. 1998 by Hurricane Mitch, which killed at least 5,600 people and caused more than $850 mil in damage to crops and livestock.

Ricardo Maduro, a businessman who pledged to crack down on crime, won the presidency Nov. 25, 2001. He was succeeded by Manuel Zelaya Rosales of the opposition Liberal Party, who won the presidential election held Nov. 27, 2005. Seeking constitutional changes in his final year in office that may have allowed him to run for a second term, Zelaya lost a political struggle with the Honduran congress and supreme court; he was ousted by the military June 28, 2009. The U.S. and OAS refused to recognize his successor, congressional leader Roberto Micheletti Bain. Porfirio (Pepe) Lobo, a conservative landowner, defeated Liberal Party nominee Elvin Santos in the presidential election of Nov. 29, 2009, and took office Jan. 27, 2010, resolving the constitutional crisis.

Hungary
Republic of Hungary

People: Population: 9,976,062. **Age distrib.:** <15: 14.9%; 65+: 16.9%. **Pop. density:** 288.3 per sq mi, 111.3 per sq km. **Urban:** 68.1%. **Ethnic groups:** Hungarian 92%, Roma 2%. **Principal language:** Hungarian. **Chief religions:** Roman Catholic 52%, Calvinist 16%, Lutheran 3%, Greek Catholic 3%, other Christian 1%, unaffiliated 15%.

Geography: Total area: 35,918 sq mi, 93,028 sq km; **Land area:** 34,598 sq mi, 89,608 sq km. **Location:** In E central Europe. **Neighbors:** Slovakia, Ukraine on N; Austria on W; Slovenia, Serbia, Croatia on S; Romania on E. **Topography:** The Danube R. forms Slovak border in NW, then swings S to bisect the country. Eastern half of Hungary is mainly a great fertile plain, the Alfold; the W and N are hilly. **Capital:** Budapest, 1,705,000.

Government: Type: Parliamentary democracy. **Head of state:** Pres. Pál Schmitt; b. May 13, 1942; in office: Aug. 6, 2010. **Head of gov.:** Prime Min. Viktor Orbán; b. May 31, 1963; in office: May 29, 2010. **Local divisions:** 19 counties, 20 urban counties, 1 capital. **Defense budget:** $1.35 bil. **Active troops:** 29,626.

Economy: Industries: mining, metallurgy, constr. materials, processed foods, textiles, chemicals (espec. pharmaceuticals), motor vehicles. **Chief crops:** wheat, corn, sunflower seeds, potatoes, sugar beets. **Natural resources:** bauxite, coal, nat. gas, fertile soils. **Crude oil reserves:** 26.6 mil bbls. **Arable land:** 50.6%. **Livestock:** cattle: 701,000; chickens: 31.2 mil; goats: 66,000; pigs: 3.4 mil; sheep: 1.2 mil. **Fish catch:** 21,191 metric tons. **Electricity prod.** (2009): 33.9 bil kWh. **Labor force:** agric. 4.7%, industry 80.9%, services 64.4%.

Finance: Monetary unit: Forint (HUF) (Sept. 2011: 198.25 = $1 U.S.). **GDP:** $187.6 bil; **per capita GDP:** $18,800; **GDP growth:**

1.2%. **Imports:** $87.4 bil; Germany 26.1%, Russia 7.7%, China 6.8%, Austria 5.9%, Netherlands 4.4%, Poland 4.3%, Italy 4.2%. **Exports:** $93.7 bil; Germany 25.5%, Italy 5.5%, UK 5.4%, Romania 5.3%, Slovakia 5.1%, France 4.9%, Austria 4.7%. **Tourism:** $5.4 bil. **Budget:** $67.3 bil. **Total reserves less gold:** $44.8 bil. **Gold:** 98,900 oz t. **CPI change:** 4.9%.

Transport: Railways: 5,722 mi. **Motor vehicles:** 344.8 vehicles per 1,000 pop. **Civil aviation:** 2.4 bil pass.-mi; 22 airports. **Chief ports:** Baja, Budapest, Csepel, Dunaujvaros, Gyor-Gonyu, Mohacs.

Communications: TV sets: 572 per 1,000 pop. **Radios:** 473 per 1,000 pop. **Telephone lines:** 29.8 per 100 pop. **Daily newspaper circ.:** 217 per 1,000 pop. **Internet:** 65.3 users per 100 pop.

Health: Life expect.: 71.0 male; 78.8 female. **Births:** 9.6 (per 1,000 pop.). **Deaths:** 12.7 (per 1,000 pop.). **Natural inc.:** −0.31%. **Infant mortality:** 5.3 (per 1,000 live births). **HIV rate:** <0.1%.

Education: Compulsory: ages 7-16. **Literacy:** 99.4%.

Major intl. organizations: UN (FAO, IBRD, ILO, IMF, WHO), EU, NATO, OECD, OSCE, WTO.

Embassy: 3910 Shoemaker St. NW 20008; 362-6730.

Website: www.hungary.hu

Earliest settlers, chiefly Slav and Germanic, were overrun by Magyars from the east. Stephen I (997-1038) was made king by Pope Sylvester II in 1000 CE. The country suffered repeated Turkish invasions in the 15th-17th centuries. After the defeat of the Turks, 1686-97, Austria dominated, but Hungary obtained concessions until it regained internal independence in 1867, under a dual monarchy with the emperor of Austria. Defeated with the Central Powers in 1918, Hungary lost Transylvania to Romania, Croatia and Bacska to Yugoslavia, and Slovakia and Carpatho-Ruthenia to Czechoslovakia, all of which had large Hungarian minorities. A republic under Michael Karolyi and a Bolshevist revolt under Bela Kun were followed by a vote for a monarchy in 1920 with Admiral Nicholas Horthy as regent.

Hungary joined Germany in WWII, and was allowed to annex most of its lost territories. Russian troops captured the country, 1944-45. By terms of an armistice with the Allied powers Hungary agreed to give up territory acquired by the 1938 dismemberment of Czechoslovakia and to return to its borders of 1937.

A republic was declared Feb. 1, 1946. In 1947 a hard-line Communist, pro-Soviet government was installed. Demonstrations against Communist rule developed into open revolt in 1956. Soviet forces launched a massive attack Nov. 4 against Budapest with 200,000 troops, 2,500 tanks, and armored cars. About 200,000 persons fled the country. Thousands were arrested and executed.

Hungarian troops participated in the 1968 Warsaw Pact invasion of Czechoslovakia. Major economic reforms were launched early in 1968, switching from a central planning system to one based on market forces and profit.

In 1989 Parliament legalized freedom of assembly and association as Hungary shifted away from Communism. In Oct. the Communist Party was formally dissolved. The last Soviet troops left Hungary June 19, 1991. Hungary became a full member of NATO Mar. 12, 1999, and of the EU May 1, 2004.

The IMF, EU, and World Bank agreed Oct. 28, 2008, to extend $25.1 bil to rescue Hungary's economy, which was battered by the global financial crisis. With the nation still reeling from recession, the center-right Fidesz party ousted the Socialists in parliamentary elections Apr. 11-25, 2010. Parliament, dominated by Fidesz, approved Apr. 18, 2011, a fiscally and socially conservative constitution that drew criticism from the EU; the law was scheduled to take effect Jan. 1, 2012.

Iceland
Republic of Iceland

People: Population: 311,058. **Age distrib.:** <15: 20.2%; 65+: 12.7%. **Pop. density:** 8 per sq mi, 3.1 per sq km. **Urban:** 93.4%. **Ethnic groups:** Homogeneous mixture of Norse & Celt descendants 94%, pop. of foreign origin 6%. **Principal languages:** Icelandic, English, Nordic languages, German. **Chief religions:** Lutheran Church of Iceland (official) 81%, Roman Catholic 3%, Reykjavik Free Church 2%, Hafnarfjorour Free Church 2%.

Geography: Total area: 39,769 sq mi, 103,000 sq km; **Land area:** 38,707 sq mi, 100,250 sq km. **Location:** Isl. at N end of Atlantic O. **Neighbors:** Nearest is Greenland (Den.) to W. **Topography:** Recent volcanic origin. Three-quarters of surface is wasteland: glaciers, lakes, a lava desert. There are geysers and hot springs, and the climate is moderated by the Gulf Stream. **Capital:** Reykjavik, 198,000.

Government: Type: Constitutional republic. **Head of state:** Pres. Olafur Ragnar Grímsson; b. May 14, 1943; in office: Aug. 1, 1996. **Head of gov.:** Prime Min. Jóhanna Sigurdardóttir; b. Oct. 4, 1942; in office: Feb. 1, 2009. **Local divisions:** 23 counties, 14 independent towns. **Defense budget** (2009): $32 mil. **Active troops:** No armed forces; budget mainly for coast guard.

Economy: Industries: fish proc.; aluminum smelting, ferrosilicon prod.; geothermal power, hydropower; tourism. **Chief crops:** potatoes, green vegetables. **Natural resources:** fish, hydropower, geothermal power, diatomite. **Arable land:** 0.1%. **Livestock:** cattle: 73,498; chickens: 261,000; goats: 655; pigs: 43,286; sheep: 469,429. **Fish catch:** 1.2 mil metric tons. **Electricity prod.** (2009): 16.5 bil kWh. **Labor force:** agric. 4.8%, industry 22.2%, services 73%.

Finance: Monetary unit: Krona (ISK) (Sept. 2011: 114.82 = $1 U.S.). **GDP:** $11.8 bil; **per capita GDP:** $38,300; **GDP growth:** –3.5%. **Imports:** $3.7 bil; Norway 13%, Netherlands 8.6%, Germany 8.3%, Sweden 8%, Denmark 7.3%, U.S. 6.9%, China 5%, UK 4.5%, Brazil 4.1%. **Exports:** $4.6 bil; Netherlands 30.7%, UK 12.7%, Germany 11.2%, Norway 5.8%, Spain 4.8%. **Tourism:** $558 mil. **Budget:** $5.7 bil. **Total reserves less gold:** $5.7 bil. **Gold:** 63,785 oz t. **CPI change:** 5.4%.

Transport: Motor vehicles: 781.9 vehicles per 1,000 pop. **Civil aviation:** 2.3 bil pass.-mi; 6 airports. **Chief ports:** Grundartangi, Hafnarfjordur, Reykjavík.

Communications: TV sets: 505 per 1,000 pop. **Radios:** 1,077 per 1,000 pop. **Telephone lines:** 63.7 per 100 pop. **Daily newspaper circ.:** 551.6 per 1,000 pop. **Internet:** 95 users per 100 pop.

Health: Life expect.: 78.7 male; 83.2 female. **Births:** 13.3 (per 1,000 pop). **Deaths:** 7.0 (per 1,000 pop). **Natural inc.:** 0.63%. **Infant mortality:** 3.2 (per 1,000 live births). **HIV rate:** 0.3%.

Education: Compulsory: ages 6-16. **Literacy:** 99%.

Major intl. organizations: UN (FAO, IBRD, ILO, IMF, WHO), EFTA, NATO, OECD, OSCE, WTO.

Embassy: 1156 15th St. NW, Ste. 1200, 20005; 265-6653.

Website: www.iceland.is

Iceland was an independent republic from 930 to 1262, when it joined with Norway. Its language has maintained its purity for 1,000 years. The Althing, or assembly, established in 930, is the world's oldest surviving parliament. Danish rule lasted 1380-1918; the last ties with the Danish crown were severed in 1941.

A continuous 55-year U.S. military presence in Iceland ended with the closure of the Keflavík naval air station in Sept. 2006. Iceland's banking system and currency collapsed amid the global financial crisis in Oct. 2008. More than $10 bil in loans from the IMF and European governments restored financial stability; austerity measures were imposed, and the nation entered a deep recession. Political unrest sparked by soaring inflation and unemployment led to the installation Feb. 1, 2009, of a center-left government, which swept to victory in elections Apr. 25. Parliament July 16 approved a plan for Iceland to seek EU membership. A major eruption Apr. 14, 2010, of the Eyjafjallajökull volcano disrupted European air traffic, affecting about 10 mil passengers and 100,000 flights during the next 6 days.

India
Republic of India

People: Population: 1,189,172,906. **Age distrib.:** <15: 29.7%; 65+: 5.5%. **Pop. density:** 1,035.9 per sq mi, 400 per sq km. **Urban:** 30%. **Ethnic groups:** Indo-Aryan 72%, Dravidian 25%, Mongoloid and other 3%. **Principal languages:** Hindi (most widely spoken & primary tongue); 14 other official languages (Bengali, Telugu, Marathi, Tamil, Urdu, Gujarati, Malayalam, Kannada, Oriya, Punjabi, Assamese, Kashmiri, Sindhi, Sanskrit); English (crucial for national, political, commercial communication); Hindustani (popular variant of Hindi/Urdu widely spoken throughout N). **Chief religions:** Hindu 81%, Muslim 13%, Christian 2%, Sikh 2%.

Geography: Total area: 1,269,219 sq mi, 3,287,263 sq km; **Land area:** 1,147,956 sq mi, 2,973,193 sq km. **Location:** Occupies most of Indian subcontinent in S Asia. **Neighbors:** Pakistan on W; China, Nepal, Bhutan on N; Myanmar, Bangladesh on E. **Topography:** The Himalaya Mts., highest in world, stretch across India's northern borders. Below, the Ganges Plain is wide, fertile, and among the most densely populated regions of the world. Area below includes Deccan Peninsula. Close to one quarter of area is forested. The climate varies from tropical heat in S to near-Arctic cold in N. Rajasthan Desert is NW; NE Assam Hills get 400 in. of rain a year. **Capital:** New Delhi, 21,720,000 (figure is for Delhi urban aggl.). **Cities (urban aggl.):** Mumbai (Bombay), 20,040,868; Kolkata (Calcutta), 15,552,080; Chennai (Madras), 7,546,954; Bangalore, 7,217,570; Hyderabad, 6,750,650; Ahmadabad, 5,717,173.

Government: Type: Federal republic. **Head of state:** Pres. Pratibha Patil; b. Dec. 19, 1934; in office: July 25, 2007. **Head of gov.:** Prime Min. Manmohan Singh; b. Sept. 26, 1932; in office: May 22, 2004. **Local divisions:** 28 states, 6 union territories, 1 national capital territory. **Defense budget:** $38.4 bil. **Active troops:** 1,325,000.

Economy: Industries: textiles, chemicals, food proc., steel, transp. equip., cement, mining, petroleum, machinery, software, pharmaceuticals. **Chief crops:** rice, wheat, oilseed, cotton, jute, tea, sugarcane, lentils, onions, potatoes. **Natural resources:** coal (world's fourth-largest reserves), iron ore, manganese, mica, bauxite, rare earth elements, titanium ore, chromite, nat. gas, diamonds, petroleum, limestone. **Crude oil reserves:** 5.7 bil bbls. **Arable land:** 53.1%. **Livestock:** cattle: 172.5 mil; chickens: 613 mil; goats: 126 mil; pigs: 13.8 mil; sheep: 65.7 mil. **Fish catch:** 7.8 mil metric tons. **Electricity prod.** (2009): 835.3 bil kWh. **Labor force:** agric. 52%, industry 14%, services 34%.

Finance: Monetary unit: Rupee (INR) (Sept. 2011: 46.07 = $1 U.S.). **GDP:** $4.1 tril; **per capita GDP:** $3,500; **GDP growth:** 10.4%. **Imports:** $327 bil; China 11.2%, U.S. 6.5%, UAE 6%, Saudi Arabia 5.7%, Australia 4.2%, Germany 4.2%, Iran 4.1%. **Exports:** $201 bil; UAE 12.5%, U.S. 11.1%, China 6.1%, Hong Kong 4.2%, Singapore 4.1%. **Tourism:** $14.2 bil. **Budget:** $268 bil. **Total reserves less gold:** $275.3 bil. **Gold:** 17.9 mil oz t. **CPI change:** 12%.

Transport: Railways: 39,752 mi. **Motor vehicles:** 14.4 vehicles per 1,000 pop. **Civil aviation:** 53.3 bil pass.-mi; 249 airports. **Chief ports:** Chennai, Jawaharal Nehru, Kandla, Kolkata, Mumbai, Sikka, Vishakhapatnam.

Communications: TV sets: 137 per 1,000 pop. **Radios:** 120 per 1,000 pop. **Telephone lines:** 2.9 per 100 pop. **Daily newspaper circ.:** 70.9 per 1,000 pop. **Internet:** 7.5 users per 100 pop.

Health: Life expect.: 65.8 male; 68.0 female. **Births:** 21.0 (per 1,000 pop.). **Deaths:** 7.5 (per 1,000 pop.). **Natural inc.:** 1.35%. **Infant mortality:** 47.6 (per 1,000 live births). **HIV rate:** 0.3%.

Education: Compulsory: ages 6-14. **Literacy:** 62.8%.

Major intl. organizations: UN (FAO, IBRD, ILO, IMF, WHO), the Commonwealth, WTO.

Embassy: 2107 Massachusetts Ave. NW 20008; 939-7000.

Website: www.india.gov.in

India has one of the oldest civilizations in the world. Excavations trace the Indus Valley civilization back for at least 5,000 years. Paintings in the mountain caves of Ajanta, richly carved temples, the Taj Mahal in Agra, and the Kutab Minar in Delhi are among treasured relics of the past.

Aryan tribes, speaking Sanskrit, invaded from the northwest around 1500 BCE. Asoka ruled most of the Indian subcontinent in the 3rd cent. BCE, and established Buddhism. But Hinduism revived and eventually predominated. Under the Guptas, 4th-6th cent. CE, science, literature, and the arts enjoyed a golden age.

Arab invaders established a Muslim foothold in the west in the 8th cent., and Turkish Muslims gained control of North India by 1200. The Mughal emperors ruled 1526-1857.

Vasco da Gama established Portuguese trading posts 1498-1503. The Dutch followed. The British East India Co. sent Capt. William Hawkins, 1609, to get concessions from the Mughal emperor for spices and textiles. Operating as the East India Co. the British gained control of most of India. The British parliament assumed political direction; under Lord Bentinck, 1828-35, rule by rajahs was curbed. After the Sepoy troops mutinied, 1857-58, the British supported the native rulers.

Nationalism grew rapidly after WWI. The Indian National Congress and the Muslim League demanded constitutional reform. A leader emerged in Mohandas K. Gandhi (called Mahatma, or Great Soul), b. Oct. 2, 1869, assassinated Jan. 30, 1948. He advocated self-rule, nonviolence, and an end to caste discrimination against "untouchables." In 1930 he launched a program of civil disobedience, including a boycott of British goods and rejection of taxes without representation.

In 1935 Britain gave India a constitution providing a bicameral federal congress. Muhammad Ali Jinnah, head of the Muslim League, sought creation of a Muslim nation, Pakistan.

The British government partitioned British India into the dominions of India and Pakistan. India became a member of the UN in 1945, a self-governing member of the Commonwealth in 1947, and a democratic republic, Jan. 26, 1950. More than 12 mil Hindu and Muslim refugees crossed the India-Pakistan borders in 1947; about 200,000 were killed in communal fighting.

After Pakistan troops began attacks on Bengali separatists in East Pakistan, Mar. 25, 1971, some 10 mil refugees fled into India. India and Pakistan went to war Dec. 3, 1971, on both the east and west fronts. Pakistan troops in the east surrendered Dec. 16; Pakistan agreed to a cease-fire in the west Dec. 17.

Indira Gandhi, India's prime minister since Jan. 1966, invoked emergency powers in June 1975. Thousands of opponents were arrested and press censorship imposed. These and other actions, including population control through forced vasectomies, were widely resented. Opposition parties, united in the Janata coalition, won the 1977 elections.

Gandhi became prime minister for the second time, Jan. 14, 1980. She was assassinated by 2 of her Sikh bodyguards Oct. 31, 1984, in response to the government suppression of a Sikh uprising in Punjab in June 1984, which included an assault on the Golden Temple at Amritsar, the holiest Sikh shrine. Widespread rioting followed the assassination; thousands of Sikhs were killed and some 50,000 left homeless. Rajiv, Indira Gandhi's son, replaced her as prime minister. A gas leak at a Union Carbide chemical plant in Bhopal, in Dec. 1984, eventually killed some 14,000 people.

Many died in religious, ethnic, and political conflicts during the late 1980s and early '90s. To suppress the Sikh insurgency in Punjab, Indian government troops attacked the Golden Temple again in 1988. Rajiv Gandhi was swept from office in 1989 amid charges of incompetence and corruption and assassinated May 21, 1991, while campaigning to regain power. Nationwide riots followed the destruction of a 16th-cent. mosque by Hindu militants in Dec. 1992. Ethnic clashes in Assam, in northwest India, killed thousands in Feb. 1993. Bombs jolted Mumbai and Kolkata, Mar. 12-19, killing over 300.

India's first lowest-caste president, K. R. Narayanan, took office July 25, 1997. India conducted a series of nuclear tests in mid-May 1998, raising tensions with Pakistan. A cyclone that hit the state of Orissa, East India, on Oct. 29, 1999, left some 10,000 people dead. A powerful earthquake in Gujarat state on Jan. 26, 2001, claimed more than 20,000 lives.

India blamed Pakistani-sponsored terrorist groups for an Oct. 1, 2001, suicide attack on the state legislature in Jammu and Kashmir (see below), in which at least 40 people died, and a Dec. 13 assault on the Indian parliament in New Delhi that left 13 people dead. Hindu-Muslim clashes in Gujarat Feb. 27-Mar. 11, 2002, claimed more than 700 lives. A. P. J. Abdul Kalam, a Muslim scientist who spearheaded India's nuclear weapons program, became president July 25.

Led by Rajiv Gandhi's Italian-born widow, Sonia, the Congress Party won the most seats in parliamentary elections Apr.-May 2004. When Hindu nationalists objected to her candidacy, she chose not to become prime minister, and Manmohan Singh, a Sikh economist, took office instead.

The Indian Ocean tsunami of Dec. 26, 2004, left more than 10,700 people dead, some 5,600 missing, and over 647,000 displaced. Islamic extremists were suspected in 7 bombings in Mumbai, July 11, 2006, that killed more than 200 on commuter trains. Pratibha Patil took office July 25, 2007, as India's first female president. Monsoon floods, July-Sept. 2007, killed more than 2,600 people and severely damaged 575,000 homes. The next year, monsoon floods killed more than 2,200 and affected over 21.8 mil people. At least 224 died in a stampede Sept. 30, 2008, at a Hindu temple in Jodhpur. The unmanned Chandrayaan-1, India's first lunar survey mission, was launched into space Oct. 22.

Ten Pakistanis linked to the militant group Lashkar-e-Taiba stormed luxury hotels, a railway station, a Jewish center, and other sites in Mumbai, Nov. 26, 2008; by the time Indian army commandos took control 3 days later, the attackers had slaughtered 163 people. Nine of the terrorists were also killed; convicted of murder and of waging war against India, the lone surviving gunman, Ajmal Kasab, received a death sentence May 6, 2010.

In parliamentary elections Apr. 16-May 13, 2009, Prime Min. Manmohan Singh's United Progressive Alliance, headed by the Congress party, gained a resounding victory. A triple bombing in Mumbai July 13, 2011, killed 26 people and injured about 140; 11 were killed and at least 60 injured when a bomb exploded Sept. 7 outside the High Court in New Delhi. Development of high-tech industries has propelled rapid economic growth since the 1990s; nearly 200 mil people have emerged from extreme poverty, although distribution of wealth remains highly uneven.

Sikkim, bordered by Tibet, Bhutan, and Nepal, formerly British protected, became a protectorate of India in 1950. Area, 2,740 sq mi; pop. (2011 census): 607,688; capital: Gangtok. In Sept. 1974, India's parliament voted to make Sikkim an associate Indian state, absorbing it into India.

Kashmir is a predominantly Muslim region in the NW that borders India, Pakistan, Afghanistan, and China. Originally a Hindu kingdom, Muslim rule began in 1341; after almost 200 years under the Mughals, the area was incorporated into British India in 1846. Fighting broke out in the region between India and Pakistan in 1947 following independence from Britain. A cease-fire was negotiated by the UN Jan. 1, 1949; it gave Pakistan control of one-third of the area as Azad Kashmir, in the west and northwest, and India the remaining two-thirds, as the Indian state of Jammu and Kashmir. Area: 85,806 sq mi; pop. (2011 census): 12,548,926; capitals: Srinagar (summer) and Jammu (winter). Fighting in the area resumed during the 1965 and 1971 wars with Pakistan. China occupied about 14,000 sq mi in the Ladakh district after a war with India in 1962.

In the 1990s there were repeated clashes between Indian army troops and separatist fighters triggered by India's decision to impose central government rule. The clashes strained relations between India and Pakistan, whom India charged with aiding the separatists; fighting was especially heavy in May-June 1999.

A cease-fire between Indian and Pakistani troops along the line of control took effect Nov. 25, 2003, but fighting between Indian forces and Islamic militants continued. Estimates of conflict-related deaths since 1989 range from 40,000 to over 80,000. A powerful earthquake Oct. 8, 2005, killed about 80,000 and left up to 3 mil homeless in Pakistani-held Kashmir and northern Pakistan.

France, 1952-54, peacefully yielded to India its 5 colonies, former French India: Pondicherry, Karikal, Mahe, and Yanaon were merged to become Pondicherry, now **Puducherry**, area 185 sq mi; pop. (2011 census): 1,244,464; the colony of Chandernagor was incorporated into the state of **West Bengal**.

Indonesia
Republic of Indonesia

People: Population: 245,613,043. **Age distrib.:** <15: 27.3%; 65+: 6.1%. **Pop. density:** 351.2 per sq mi, 135.6 per sq km. **Urban:** 44.3%. **Ethnic groups:** Javanese 41%, Sundanese 15%, Madurese 3%, Minangkabau 3%, Betawi 2%, Bugis 2%, Banten 2%, Banjar 2%. **Principal languages:** Bahasa Indonesia (official; modified form of Malay), English, Dutch, local dialects (Javanese most widely spoken). **Chief religions:** Muslim 86%, Protestant 6%, Roman Catholic 3%, Hindu 2%.

Geography: Total area: 735,358 sq mi, 1,904,569 sq km; **Land area:** 699,451 sq mi, 1,811,569 sq km. **Location:** Archipelago SE of Asian mainland along the Equator. **Neighbors:** Malaysia on N, Papua New Guinea on E, Timor-Leste on S. **Topography:** Indonesia comprises over 13,500 islands (6,000 inhabited), including Java (one of the most densely populated areas in the world with over 2,000 persons per sq mi), Sumatra, Kalimantan (most of Borneo), Sulawesi (Celebes), and West Irian (Irian Jaya, the W half of New Guinea). Also: Bangka, Billiton, Madura, Bali, Timor. The mountains

and plateaus on the major islands have a cooler climate than the tropical lowlands. **Capital:** Jakarta, 9,121,000. **Cities (urban aggl.):** Surabaya, 2,508,768; Bandung, 2,412,271.

Government: Type: Republic. **Head of state and gov.:** Pres. Susilo Bambang Yudhoyono; b. Sept. 9, 1949; in office: Oct. 20, 2004. **Local divisions:** 30 provinces, 2 special regions, 1 capital district. **Defense budget:** $4.47 bil. **Active troops:** 302,000.

Economy: Industries: petroleum and nat. gas, textiles, apparel, footwear, mining, cement, chem. fertilizers, plywood, rubber. **Chief crops:** rice, cassava, peanuts, rubber, cocoa, coffee, palm oil, copra. **Natural resources:** petroleum, tin, nat. gas, nickel, timber, bauxite, copper, coal, gold, silver. **Crude oil reserves:** 4 bil bbls. **Arable land:** 13.0%. **Livestock:** cattle: 12.9 mil; chickens: 1.3 bil; goats: 15.8 mil; pigs: 6.9 mil; sheep: 10.2 mil. **Fish catch:** 9.8 mil metric tons. **Electricity prod.:** 141.2 bil kWh. **Labor force:** agric. 38.3%, industry 12.8%, services 48.9%.

Finance: Monetary unit: Rupiah (IDR) (Sept. 2011: 8,548.00 = $1 U.S.). **GDP:** $1 tril; **per capita GDP:** $4,200; **GDP growth:** 6.1%. **Imports:** $111.1 bil; Singapore 16.1%, China 14.5%, Japan 10.2%, U.S. 7.3%, Malaysia 5.9%, South Korea 4.9%, Thailand 4.8%. **Exports:** $146.3 bil; Japan 15.9%, China 9.9%, U.S. 9.3%, Singapore 8.8%, South Korea 7%, India 6.4%, Malaysia 5.8%. **Tourism:** $7 bil. **Budget** (2011 est.): $132.9 bil. **Total reserves less gold:** $92.9 bil. **Gold:** 2.4 mil oz t. **CPI change:** 7%.

Transport: Railways: 3,133 mi. **Motor vehicles:** 76.1 vehicles per 1,000 pop. **Civil aviation:** 19.8 bil pass.-mi; 171 airports. **Chief ports:** Banjarmasin, Belawan, Kotabaru, Krueg Geukueh, Palembang, Panjang, Sungai Pakning, Tanjung Priok.

Communications: TV sets: 161 per 1,000 pop. **Radios:** 157 per 1,000 pop. **Telephone lines:** 15.8 per 100 pop. **Internet:** 9.1 users per 100 pop.

Health: Life expect.: 68.8 male; 74.0 female. **Births:** 18.1 (per 1,000 pop.). **Deaths:** 6.3 (per 1,000 pop.). **Natural inc.:** 1.18%. **Infant mortality:** 28.0 (per 1,000 live births). **HIV rate:** 0.2%.

Education: Compulsory: ages 7-15. **Literacy:** 92.2%.

Major intl. organizations: UN and all of its specialized agencies, APEC, ASEAN, WTO.

Embassy: 2020 Massachusetts Ave. NW 20036; 775-5200.

Website: www.indonesia.go.id

Hindu and Buddhist civilization from India reached Indonesia nearly 2,000 years ago, taking root especially in Java. Islam spread along the maritime trade routes in the 15th cent., and became predominant by the 16th cent. The Dutch replaced the Portuguese as the area's most important European trade power in the 17th cent., securing territorial control over Java by 1750. The outer islands were not finally subdued until the early 20th cent.

Following Japanese occupation, 1942-45, nationalists led by Sukarno and Hatta declared independence. The Netherlands ceded sovereignty Dec. 27, 1949, after 4 years of fighting. A republic was declared, Aug. 17, 1950, with Sukarno as president. West Irian, on New Guinea, remained under Dutch control but was transferred by the UN to Indonesia in 1963.

Sukarno suspended parliament in 1960 and was named president for life in 1963. He made close alliances with Communist governments. In Sept. 1965 an attempted coup in which several military officers were murdered was successfully put down, but Sukarno was forced to cede power to the army, led by Gen. Suharto, who became acting president in 1967 and ruled Indonesia for the next 31 years. The regime blamed the coup on the Communist Party; more than 300,000 alleged Communists were killed in army-initiated massacres.

Parliament reelected Suharto to a seventh consecutive 5-year term Mar. 10, 1998, as a severe economic downturn focused public anger on nepotism, cronyism, and corruption in the Suharto regime. Price increases in May sparked mass protests and then mob violence in Jakarta and other cities, claiming some 500 lives. Suharto resigned May 21 and was succeeded by his vice president, Bacharuddin Jusuf Habibie. Abdurrahman Wahid, leader of Indonesia's largest Muslim organization, was elected president Oct. 20, 1999. In Aug. 2000, under pressure from the legislature, he agreed to share power with Vice Pres. Megawati Sukarnoputri, the daughter of the late Pres. Sukarno. Charging Wahid with incompetence and corruption, the legislature ousted him July 23, 2001, and Megawati became Indonesia's first woman president.

Clashes between Muslims and Christians in the Maluku (Molucca) Isl., 1999-2002, claimed about 5,000 lives. Ethnic violence in Kalimantan, Borneo, killed more than 400 in Feb. 2001. East Timor, a former Portuguese colony that Indonesia invaded in Dec. 1975 and controlled until Oct. 1999, became a fully independent country May 20, 2002, as Timor-Leste. Separatists in Aceh, NW Sumatra, fought repeatedly against government troops during the 1980s and '90s; peace accords were announced in Dec. 2002 and, after that deal unraveled, in July 2005. The last of 24,000 Indonesian government troops pulled out of Aceh, Dec. 29, 2005.

Investigators blamed the Islamic terrorist group Jemaah Islamiyah, an al-Qaeda affiliate, for bombings that killed 202 people, mostly foreign tourists, at nightclubs in Bali, Oct. 12, 2002, and 12 people at a Marriott hotel in Jakarta, Aug. 5, 2003. A car bomb attack outside the Australian embassy in Jakarta, Sept. 9, 2004, killed 9 people and injured more than 180. Susilo Bambang Yudhoyono, a retired general, defeated Megawati Sept. 20 in a direct presidential runoff vote.

A massive earthquake off northwest Sumatra, Dec. 26, 2004, triggered tsunamis that wreaked havoc in the Indian Ocean region. The death toll in Indonesia alone exceeded 125,000, not counting almost 40,000 missing. Another large quake off northwest Sumatra, Mar. 28, 2005, left at least 1,300 dead. On Java in 2006, an earthquake May 27 killed 5,800, left 1.5 mil homeless, and caused damage estimated at $3.1 bil; a tsunami July 17 claimed at least 650 lives.

Two leaders of the Jemaah Islamiyah terror network were arrested in June 2007. Faced with falling oil production, Indonesia left OPEC in 2008. Pres. Yudhoyono won a second 5-year term July 8, 2009, in an election generally praised by international observers. Suicide bombings at two Jakarta hotels July 17 left 9 people dead. Police confirmed Sept. 17 that Noordin Muhammad Top, sus-pected of plotting the recent Jakarta attacks and other terrorist bombings, had been killed in a shootout.

Padang, Sumatra, was hit Sept. 30, 2009, by a powerful earthquake, which also triggered mudslides in the region; at least 1,115 people were killed, and more than 135,000 homes were seriously damaged. On Oct. 25, 2010, a 7.7-magnitude earthquake in the Mentawai Islands, off the western coast of Sumatra, triggered a tsunami that killed at least 500 people and left 11,000 homeless; that same day, Mt. Merapi, a volcano near Yogyakarta in central Java, began a series of major eruptions that claimed at least 228 lives and displaced 430,500.

Iran
Islamic Republic of Iran

People: Population: 77,891,220. **Age distrib.:** <15: 24.1%; 65+: 5%. **Pop. density:** 131.7 per sq mi, 50.9 per sq km. **Urban:** 70.8%. **Ethnic groups:** Persian 51%, Azeri 24%, Gilaki & Mazandarani 8%, Kurd 7%, Arab 3%, Lur 2%, Baloch 2%, Turkmen 2%. **Principal languages:** Persian & Persian dialects (official), Turkic & Turkic dialects, Kurdish, Luri, Balochi, Arabic, Turkish. **Chief religions:** Muslim (official) Shi'a 89%, Sunni 9%) 98%, other (incl. Zoroastrian, Jewish, Christian, Baha'i) 2%.

Geography: Total area: 636,372 sq mi, 1,648,195 sq km; **Land area:** 591,352 sq mi, 1,531,595 sq km. **Location:** Between the Middle East and S Asia. **Neighbors:** Turkey, Iraq on W; Armenia, Azerbaijan, Turkmenistan on N; Afghanistan, Pakistan on E. **Topography:** Interior highlands and plains surrounded by high mountains, up to 18,000 ft. Large salt deserts cover much of area, but there are many oases and forest areas. Most of population inhabits N and NW. **Capital:** Tehran, 7,190,000. **Cities (urban aggl.):** Mashhad, 2,652,183; Esfahan, 1,741,689.

Government: Type: Islamic republic. **Religious head:** Ayatollah Sayyed Ali Khamenei; b. July 17, 1939; in office: June 4, 1989. **Head of state and gov.:** Pres. Mahmoud Ahmadinejad; b. Oct. 28, 1956; in office: Aug. 3, 2005. **Local divisions:** 28 provinces. **Defense budget:** $9.02 bil (excl. defense industry funding). **Active troops:** 523,000.

Economy: Industries: petroleum, petrochemicals, fertilizers, caustic soda, textiles, cement and other constr. materials, food proc., metal fabrication, armaments. **Chief crops:** wheat, rice, other grains, sugar beets, sugarcane, fruits, nuts, cotton. **Natural resources:** petroleum, nat. gas, coal, chromium, copper, iron ore, lead, manganese, zinc, sulfur. **Crude oil reserves:** 137 bil bbls. **Arable land:** 10.6%. **Livestock:** cattle: 8.1 mil; chickens: 513 mil; goats: 25.5 mil; sheep: 53.8 mil. **Fish catch:** 599,476 metric tons. **Electricity prod.:** 201.7 bil kWh. **Labor force:** agric. 25%, industry 31%, services 45%.

Finance: Monetary unit: Rial (IRR) (Sept. 2011: 10,603.00 = $1 U.S.). **GDP:** $818.7 bil; **per capita GDP:** $10,600; **GDP growth:** 1%. **Imports:** $59 bil; UAE 15%, China 14.5%, Germany 9.7%, South Korea 7.3%, Italy 5.2%, Russia 5.1%. **Exports:** $78.7 bil; China 16.3%, India 13.1%, Japan 11.5%, South Korea 7.1%, Turkey 4.2%. **Tourism:** $2 bil. **Budget:** $98.8 bil. **Total reserves less gold:** NA. **CPI change:** 14.8%.

Transport: Railways: 5,246 mi. **Motor vehicles:** 50.8 vehicles per 1,000 pop. **Civil aviation:** 8 bil pass.-mi; 133 airports. **Chief ports:** Assaluyeh, Bandar Abbas, Bandar-e-Eman Khomeyni.

Communications: TV sets: 170 per 1,000 pop. **Radios:** 734 per 1,000 pop. **Telephone lines:** 36.3 per 100 pop. **Internet:** 13 users per 100 pop.

Health: Life expect.: 68.6 male; 71.6 female. **Births:** 18.6 (per 1,000 pop.). **Deaths:** 5.9 (per 1,000 pop.). **Natural inc.:** 1.26%. **Infant mortality:** 42.3 (per 1,000 live births). **HIV rate:** 0.2%.

Education: Compulsory: ages 6-13. **Literacy:** 85%.

Major intl. organizations: UN (FAO, IBRD, ILO, IMF, WHO), OPEC, WTO (observer).

Iranian Interests Section: 2209 Wisconsin Ave. NW 20007; 965-4990.

Website: www.president.ir

Iran, formerly known as Persia, has been settled for thousands of years. Ancestors of the Iranians came from the east during the second millennium BCE; they were an Indo-European group related to the Aryans of India. In 549 BCE Cyrus the Great united the Medes and Persians in the Persian Empire; he conquered Babylonia in 538 BCE, and restored Jerusalem to the Jews. Alexander the Great conquered Persia in 333 BCE, but Persians regained independence

in the next century under the Parthians, themselves succeeded by Sassanian Persians in 226 CE. Arabs brought Islam to Persia in the 7th cent., replacing the indigenous Zoroastrian faith. After Persian political and cultural autonomy was reasserted in the 9th cent., arts and sciences flourished.

Turks and Mongols ruled Persia in turn from the 11th cent. to 1502, when Ismael I established the Iranian Safavid dynasty and made Shiite Islam the official religion. The dynasty lasted until 1722. The British and Russian empires vied for influence in the 19th cent.; Afghanistan was severed from Iran by Britain in 1857.

Reza Khan, a military officer, became prime min., 1923, and shah in 1925. He began modernization, curbed foreign influence, and officially changed the country's name from Persia to Iran in 1935. Fearing the shah's Axis sympathies, British and Soviet troops forced him to abdicate, 1941; he was succeeded by his son, Mohammad Reza Pahlavi. The U.S. Central Intelligence Agency had a major role in the ouster, 1953, of Prime Min. Muhammad Mossadegh, who had nationalized the oil industry.

With U.S. backing, the shah brought economic and social change to Iran (the White Revolution), but repression of opposition groups grew severe. Violent protests in 1978 eventually forced the shah to depart, Jan. 16, 1979. Shiite leader Ayatollah Ruhollah Khomeini, exiled by the shah in 1963, returned to Tehran, Feb. 1, and by Feb. 11 pro-Khomeini forces had defeated government troops. Khomeini established an Islamic theocracy.

Iranian militants seized the U.S. embassy in Tehran Nov. 4, 1979, and took hostages including 62 Americans. Despite international condemnations and U.S. efforts, including an abortive Apr. 1980 rescue attempt, the crisis continued. The U.S. broke diplomatic relations with Iran, Apr. 7. The shah died in Egypt, July 27. The hostage drama ended Jan. 20, 1981, when an accord, involving the release of frozen Iranian assets, was reached.

A dispute over the Shatt al-Arab waterway situated between Iran and Iraq led to a long and costly war between the 2 countries, 1980-88, killing hundreds of thousands of people. In Nov. 1986 it became known that the U.S., which had generally sided with Iraq during the war, had secretly shipped arms to Iran to gain that country's help in obtaining the release of U.S. hostages held in Lebanon. The revelation sparked a major scandal in the U.S. A U.S. Navy warship shot down an Iranian airliner, July 3, 1988, after mistaking it for an F-14 fighter jet; all 290 aboard the plane died.

An earthquake struck northern Iran June 21, 1990, killing more than 45,000, injuring 100,000, and leaving 400,000 homeless. Some 1 mil Kurdish refugees fled from Iraq to Iran following the Persian Gulf War of 1991. To curb Iran's alleged support for international terrorism, the U.S. in 1996 authorized sanctions on foreign companies that invest there.

Mohammad Khatami, a moderate Shiite Muslim cleric, was elected president on May 23, 1997, winning nearly 70% of the vote. During the next three years, hard-line Islamists clashed repeatedly and sometimes violently with reformers, who won a majority in parliamentary elections Feb. 18 and May 5, 2000. Inviting rapprochement with Iran, the U.S. eased some sanctions Mar. 18. Khatami was reelected June 8, 2001, with a 77% majority but continued to face resistance from religious conservatives.

The U.S.-led war in Iraq, beginning Mar. 2003, contributed to a new period of instability in Iran. An earthquake Dec. 26 in Bam, southeast Iran, killed about 26,000 people. After the Guardian Council, dominated by religious conservatives, disqualified some 2,400 reformist candidates, hard-liners won legislative elections Feb. 20, 2004.

The mayor of Tehran, Mahmoud Ahmadinejad, a religious conservative who campaigned as an economic reformer, defeated former Pres. Hashemi Rafsanjani in a runoff election June 24, 2005, and took office Aug. 3. The Bush administration, which in 2002 had called Iran part of an "axis of evil," accused the Iranian regime of seeking to build nuclear weapons, aiding Shiite militias in Iraq, and supplying rockets to Hezbollah fighters in Lebanon for use against Israel.

Seeking to halt Iran's uranium-enrichment program, which could be used for either military or civilian purposes, the UN Security Council imposed sanctions, Dec. 23, 2006, and toughened them, Mar. 24, 2007. After the Guardian Council disqualified about 1,700 reformist candidates, conservative allies of Ahmadinejad won parliamentary elections Mar.-Apr. 2008. Further talks on nuclear enrichment ended in deadlock July 20, and the U.S. imposed additional sanctions Sept. 10.

After a hard-fought campaign, Ahmadinejad claimed victory in the presidential election of June 12, 2009. His main opponent, former Prime Min. Mir Hussein Moussavi, supported by Khatami and Rafsanjani, claimed that the official count, which gave Ahmadinejad more than 62% of the total vote, was fraudulent. Huge protests by Moussavi supporters in Tehran and other major cities were crushed by police and Basij paramilitary forces. Tensions with the U.S. and European governments were heightened in late Sept. 2009 by disclosures that Iran had been secretly enriching uranium at an underground site near Qom, and by Iranian tests of medium-range missiles capable of reaching Israel or U.S. and European bases in the Persian Gulf region. In direct talks Oct. 1 with the U.S. and other world powers, Iran agreed to allow international inspection of the Qom site and other nuclear safeguards.

The UN and U.S. toughened sanctions, June-July 2010, but did not object when loading of uranium fuel began in Aug. at Iran's Bushehr nuclear power plant, built and supervised by Russia. Iran blamed Israel, the U.S., and other Western powers for carrying out cyber attacks against the country's nuclear facilities and assassination plots aimed at Iranian scientists. On Dec. 21, 2010, the U.S. announced new sanctions targeting companies linked to Iran's nuclear program. The Bushehr plant began generating electricity for the national power grid in Sept. 2011.

Iraq
Republic of Iraq

People: Population: 30,399,572. **Age distrib.:** <15: 38%; 65+: 3.1%. **Pop. density:** 180 per sq mi, 69.5 per sq km. **Urban:** 66.2%. **Ethnic groups:** Arab 75%-80%; Kurdish 15%-20%; Turkoman, Assyrian, or other 5%. **Principal languages:** Arabic (official), Kurdish (official in Kurdish regions), Turkoman, Assyrian (Neo-Aramaic), Armenian. **Chief religions:** Muslim (official): Shi'a 60%-65%, Sunni 32%-37%) 97%, Christian or other 3%.

Geography: Total area: 169,235 sq mi, 438,317 sq km; **Land area:** 168,868 sq mi, 437,367 sq km. **Location:** In Middle East, occupying most of historic Mesopotamia. **Neighbors:** Jordan, Syria on W; Turkey on N; Iran on E; Kuwait, Saudi Arabia on S. **Topography:** Mostly an alluvial plain, including the Tigris and Euphrates rivers, descending from mountains in N to desert in SW. Persian Gulf region is marshland. **Capital:** Baghdad, 5,751,000. **Cities (urban aggl.):** Mosul, 1,446,940; Erbil, 1,009,204; Basra, 923,237.

Government: Type: In transition. **Head of state:** Pres. Jalal Talabani; b. 1933; in office: Apr. 7, 2005. **Head of gov.:** Prime Min. Nouri Kamel al-Maliki; b. 1950; in office: May 20, 2006. **Local divisions:** 18 governorates (3 in Kurdish Autonomous Region). **Defense budget:** $4.9 bil. **Active troops:** 245,782.

Economy: Industries: petroleum, chemicals, textiles, leather, constr. materials, food proc, fertilizer, metal fabrication/proc. **Chief crops:** wheat, barley, rice, vegetables, dates, cotton. **Natural resources:** petroleum, nat. gas, phosphates, sulfur. **Arable land:** 10.4%. **Crude oil reserves:** 115 bil bbls. **Livestock:** cattle: 1.6 mil; chickens: 27.5 mil; goats: 1.6 mil; sheep: 7.8 mil. **Fish catch:** 53,237 metric tons. **Electricity prod.:** 34.6 bil kWh. **Labor force:** agric. 21.6%, industry 18.7%, services 59.8%.

Finance: Monetary unit: Dinar (IQD) (Sept. 2011; 1,170.50 = $1 U.S.). **GDP:** $113.4 bil; **per capita GDP:** $3,800; **GDP growth:** 0.8%. **Imports:** $42.6 bil; Turkey 23.8%, Syria 16.6%, China 8.5%, U.S. 8.3%. **Exports:** $49.1 bil; U.S. 25.2%, India 15.1%, South Korea 9.9%, Italy 9.2%, China 8.5%. **Tourism:** NA. **Budget** $72.4 bil. **Total reserves less gold:** $50.4 bil. **Gold:** 188,599 oz t. **CPI change:** 2.9%.

Transport: Railways: 1,412 mi. **Motor vehicles:** 35.7 vehicles per 1,000 pop. **Civil aviation:** 75 airports. **Chief ports:** Al Basrah, Khawr az Zubayr, Umm Qasr.

Communications: TV sets: 82 per 1,000 pop. **Radios:** 211 per 1,000 pop. **Telephone lines:** 5.1 per 100 pop. **Internet:** 5.6 users per 100 pop.

Health: Life expect.: 69.2 male; 72.0 female. **Births:** 28.8 (per 1,000 pop.). **Deaths:** 4.8 (per 1,000 pop.). **Natural inc.:** 2.40%. **Infant mortality:** 41.7 (per 1,000 live births). **HIV rate:** NA.

Education: Compulsory: ages 6-11. **Literacy:** 78.1%.

Major intl. organizations: UN (FAO, IBRD, ILO, IMF, WHO), AL, OPEC, WTO (observer).

Iraqi Interests Section: 1801 P St. NW 20036; 483-7500.

Website: www.cabinet.iq

The Tigris-Euphrates valley, formerly called Mesopotamia, was the site of one of the earliest civilizations in the world. Mesopotamia ceased to be a separate entity after the Persian, Greek, and Arab conquests. The Arabs founded Baghdad, from where the caliph ruled a vast Islamic empire in the 8th and 9th centuries. Mongol and Turkish conquests led to a decline in the region's population, economy, cultural life, and irrigation system.

Britain secured a League of Nations mandate over Iraq after WWI. Independence under a king came in 1932. Rebellious army officers killed King Faisal II, July 14, 1958, and established a leftist, pan-Arab republic, which pursued close ties with the USSR. Successive regimes were increasingly dominated by the Baath Arab Socialist Party. A Baath leader, Saddam Hussein, became president of Iraq, July 16, 1979. After purging his enemies, he ruled as a dictator for more than 2 decades, repressing Iraq's Kurds and Shiites and launching disastrous wars against 2 neighboring nations, Iran and Kuwait. Hussein sought weapons of mass destruction; Israeli planes destroyed a nuclear reactor near Baghdad June 7, 1981, claiming it could be used to produce nuclear weapons.

After skirmishing intermittently for 10 months over the sovereignty of the disputed Shatt al-Arab waterway that divides the two countries, Iraq and Iran entered into open warfare on Sept. 22, 1980. Iran repulsed early Iraqi advances, producing a long and costly stalemate; hundreds of thousands of Iraqis lost their lives during the 8-year conflict. Hussein used poison gas against Iraqi Kurds in 1988, killing more than 5,000 people in Halabja, the first mass use of poison gas against civilians since the Holocaust.

Iraq attacked and overran Kuwait Aug. 2, 1990. Backed by the UN, a U.S.-led coalition launched air and missile attacks on Iraq, Jan. 16, 1991. The coalition began a ground attack to retake Kuwait Feb. 23. Iraqi forces showed little resistance and were soundly defeated in 4 days. Some 175,000 Iraqis were taken prisoner, and Iraqi casualties were estimated at over 85,000. As part of the cease-fire agreement, Iraq agreed to scrap all poison gas and germ weapons and allow UN observers to inspect the sites. UN trade sanctions would remain in effect until Iraq complied with all terms.

Iraqi cooperation with UN weapons inspection teams was intermittent throughout the 1990s. Standoffs over inspections led to diplomatic crises 1997-98, culminating in intensive U.S. and British aerial bombardment of Iraqi military targets, Dec. 16-19, 1998. After 2 years of sporadic activity, U.S. and British warplanes struck harder at sites near Baghdad on Feb. 16, 2001.

In a speech before the UN, Sept. 12, 2002, Pres. George W. Bush demanded that Iraq eliminate weapons of mass destruction, refrain from supporting terrorism, and end repression. Despite opposition from some countries, including France, Germany, and Russia, a U.S.-led coalition launched an invasion of Iraq on the evening of Mar. 19, 2003. By Apr. 6 the British controlled Basra and other areas in the south, and the U.S. entered Baghdad Apr. 7. Hussein had disappeared, the Iraqi government had collapsed, and most of Iraq's armed forces had dissolved into the civilian population. On May 1, Pres. Bush declared that major combat there was over. Continuing searches failed to find evidence of usable chemical, biological, or nuclear weapons the U.S. and other countries claimed Iraq had stockpiled.

The U.S. initially governed Iraq through a Coalition Provisional Authority, headed by L. Paul Bremer, which was unable to maintain order in the weeks following Hussein's fall. Reconstruction efforts were hampered by guerrilla attacks from Baath remnants, Islamic extremists, and others. Bombings at UN headquarters in Baghdad, Aug. 19 and Sept. 22, 2003, led the UN to scale back its presence in Iraq. Coalition forces succeeded in neutralizing many leaders of the former regime. Two of Hussein's sons, Uday and Qusay, were killed July 22, 2003, by U.S. troops in Mosul. Saddam Hussein was captured in an underground hideout Dec. 13, 2003; tried and convicted for committing crimes against humanity in the 1980s, he was executed Dec. 30, 2006.

Photographs released in Apr. 2004 graphically showed instances of physical abuse and sexual humiliation of Iraqi inmates by U.S. military personnel at Baghdad's Abu Ghraib prison in fall 2003. The images sparked widespread condemnation and U.S. criminal proceedings against some individuals.

On June 28, 2004, U.S. authorities officially transferred sovereignty to a transitional Iraqi government. Despite threats by insurgents, an estimated 8 mil people in Iraq, mostly Shiites and Kurds, cast ballots Jan. 30, 2005, for a 275-member transitional national assembly. On Apr. 6, the assembly elected Jalal al-Talabani, a Kurd, as president; Ibrahim al-Jaafari, a Shiite, became prime minister. The insurgents launched new waves of attacks, killing hundreds of police and army recruits. Rumors of a suicide bomber set off a stampede by Shiite pilgrims in northern Baghdad Aug. 31, killing close to 1,000 people. The U.S. blamed Jordanian militant Abu Musab al-Zarqawi, leader of the terrorist group Al Qaeda in Iraq, for directing a series of kidnappings, beheadings, and suicide bombings. He was killed by a U.S. air strike, June 7, 2006.

Legislative elections were held Dec. 15, 2005, and official results announced Jan. 20, 2006, but political wrangling delayed installation of a new government, headed by Shiite leader Nouri Kamel al-Maliki, until May 20. Meanwhile, a bomb Feb. 22 that destroyed the dome of Samarra's Golden Mosque, a Shiite shrine, triggered an intensification of sectarian violence between Sunnis and Shiites, much of it in Baghdad. The Iraqi civilian death toll averaged more than 2,800 per month in 2006.

In early 2007, Lt. Gen. David H. Petraeus became the top U.S. military commander in Iraq; a "surge" elevated U.S. troop strength from 132,000 in Jan. to peak of 171,000 in Oct. Many of the reinforcements were sent to the Baghdad area. U.S. troop deaths for all of 2007 totaled 899 (the highest for any year since the war began), but military and civilian casualties dropped steadily from mid-2007 through 2008. Contributing to the reduction in violence were a cease-fire by Shiite militias and a shift by Sunni clan leaders against Al Qaeda in Iraq.

Parliament approved, Nov. 27, 2008, a status-of-forces agreement calling for the U.S. to withdraw its troops from Iraqi cities and towns by June 30, 2009, and for all U.S. forces to leave Iraq by Dec. 31, 2011. Legislative elections Mar. 7, 2010, brought gains by the Iraqiya coalition headed by former Prime Min. Iyad Allawi, a Shiite who had campaigned as a secularist to win widespread Sunni support. On Aug. 31, Pres. Barack Obama formally declared an end to the U.S. combat role, and Operation Iraqi Freedom was succeeded by Operation New Dawn. More than 9 months of political deadlock ended when Prime Min. Maliki was sworn in for a second term Dec. 21, heading a unity government that included Shiite, Sunni, and Kurdish factions. Civilian casualties, which had averaged more than 2,800 per month in 2006, declined to about 200 per month during 2010; according to Iraqi government statistics, the average monthly civilian death toll dropped to about 130 in the first half of 2011.

As of mid-2011, the U.S. troop presence in Iraq stood at 46,000. (Also present were tens of thousands of U.S. and other foreign civilian advisers and contractors.) From Mar. 2003 through Aug. 2011, operations in Iraq cost the lives of more than 4,470 U.S. service members, and another 32,000 were wounded. British troop losses totaled 179; other allies, 139. More than 115,000 Iraqi civilians and over 10,000 police and security forces were killed from June 2003 through June 2011, according to a U.S. analysis by the Brookings Institution. U.S. budgeted costs of the Iraq war exceeded $820 bil for the 2003-12 period.

Ireland

People: Population: 4,670,976. **Age distrib.:** <15: 21.1%; 65+: 11.6%. **Pop. density:** 175.6 per sq mi, 67.8 per sq km. **Urban:** 61.9%. **Ethnic groups:** Irish 87%, other white 8%, Asian 1%, black 1%, mixed 1%. **Principal languages:** English (official; generally used), Irish (Gaelic or Gaeilge) (official; spoken mainly on W coast). **Chief religions:** Roman Catholic 87%, Church of Ireland 3%, other Christian 2%, none 4%.

Geography: Total area: 27,133 sq mi, 70,273 sq km; **Land area:** 26,596 sq mi, 68,883 sq km. **Location:** In Atlantic O. just W of Great Britain. **Neighbors:** United Kingdom (Northern Ireland) on E. **Topography:** Consists of a central plateau surrounded by isolated groups of hills and mountains. Coastline is heavily indented by the Atlantic O. **Capital:** Dublin, 1,084,000.

Government: Type: Parliamentary republic. **Head of state:** Pres. Mary McAleese; b. June 27, 1951; in office: Nov. 11, 1997. **Head of gov.:** Prime Min. Enda Kenny; b. Apr. 24, 1951; in office: Mar. 9, 2011. **Local divisions:** 26 counties. **Defense budget:** $1.2 bil. **Active troops:** 10,460.

Economy: Industries: pharmaceuticals, chemicals, computer hardware and software, food prods., beverages and brewing. **Chief crops:** barley, potatoes, wheat. **Natural resources:** nat. gas, peat, copper, lead, zinc, silver, barite, gypsum, limestone, dolomite. **Arable land:** 15.8%. **Livestock:** cattle: 6.7 mil; chickens: 13.5 mil; goats: 10,100; pigs: 1.5 mil; sheep: 4.8 mil. **Fish catch:** 345,793 metric tons. **Electricity prod.** (2009): 25.5 bil kWh. **Labor force:** agric. 5%, industry 20%, services 76%.

Finance: Monetary unit: Euro (EUR) (Sept. 2011: 0.71 = $1 U.S.). **GDP:** $172.3 bil; **per capita GDP:** $37,300; **GDP growth:** –1%. **Imports:** $70.4 bil; UK 35.4%, U.S. 16.8%, Germany 6.8%, Netherlands 5.9%, France 4.8%. **Exports:** $115.7 bil; U.S. 21%, Belgium 17%, UK 16.1%, Germany 7%, France 5.4%. **Tourism:** $4.1 bil. **Budget:** $135.1 bil. **Total reserves less gold:** $1.8 bil. **Gold:** 193,000 oz t. **CPI change:** –0.9%.

Transport: Railways: 2,011 mi. **Motor vehicles:** 498.7 vehicles per 1,000 pop. **Civil aviation:** 54.4 bil pass.-mi; 16 airports. **Chief ports:** Cork, Dublin, Shannon Foynes.

Communications: TV sets: 715 per 1,000 pop. **Radios:** 695 per 1,000 pop. **Telephone lines:** 46.5 per 100 pop. **Daily newspaper circ.:** 182.4 per 1,000 pop. **Internet:** 69.9 users per 100 pop.

Health: Life expect.: 78.0 male; 82.6 female. **Births:** 16.1 (per 1,000 pop.). **Deaths:** 6.3 (per 1,000 pop.). **Natural inc.:** 0.98%. **Infant mortality:** 3.9 (per 1,000 live births). **HIV rate:** 0.2%.

Education: Compulsory: ages 6-15. **Literacy:** 99%.

Major intl. organizations: UN (FAO, IBRD, ILO, IMF, WHO), EU, OECD, OSCE, WTO.

Embassy: 2234 Massachusetts Ave. NW 20008; 462-3939.

Website: www.gov.ie

Celtic tribes invaded the islands about the 4th cent. BCE; their Gaelic culture and literature flourished and spread to Scotland and elsewhere in the 5th cent. CE, the same century in which St. Patrick converted the Irish to Christianity. Invasions by Norsemen began in the 8th cent., ended with defeat of the Danes by the Irish King Brian Boru in 1014. English invasions started in the 12th cent.; for over 700 years the Anglo-Irish struggle continued with bitter rebellions and savage repressions.

The Easter Monday Rebellion in 1916 failed but was followed by guerrilla warfare and harsh reprisals by British troops called the "Black and Tans." The Dail Eireann (Irish parliament) reaffirmed independence in Jan. 1919. The British offered dominion status to Ulster (6 counties) and southern Ireland (26 counties) Dec. 1921. The constitution of the Irish Free State, a British dominion, was adopted Dec. 11, 1922. Northern Ireland remained part of the United Kingdom (see United Kingdom—Northern Ireland).

A new constitution adopted by plebiscite came into operation Dec. 29, 1937. It declared the name of the state Eire in the Irish language (Ireland in the English) and declared it a sovereign democratic state. On Dec. 21, 1948, an Irish law declared the country a republic rather than a dominion and withdrew it from the Commonwealth. The British Parliament recognized both actions, 1949, but reasserted its claim to incorporate the 6 northeastern counties in the UK.

Irish governments have favored peaceful unification of all Ireland and cooperated with Britain against terrorist groups. After negotiators in Northern Ireland approved a peace settlement on Good Friday, Apr. 10, 1998, voters in the Irish Republic endorsed the accord, on May 22; the agreement required the removal from the Irish constitution of territorial claims on the north.

Expansion of educational opportunities and foreign investment in high-tech industries since the 1990s have boosted Ireland's prosperity. Ireland's first woman president, Mary Robinson, resigned Sept. 12, 1997, to become UN high commissioner for human rights, 1997-2002. She was succeeded as president by Mary McAleese, a law professor from Northern Ireland and the first northerner to hold the office. Implicated in a corruption inquiry, Prime Min. Bertie Ahern announced his resignation Apr. 2, 2008, after 11 years in power; the Dail Eireann May 7 chose Finance Min. Brian Cowen to succeed him.

In referendums June 12, 2008, and Oct. 2, 2009, Irish voters first rejected and then approved the Lisbon Treaty, a plan to revamp the EU. Responding to a growing scandal over abusive Catholic clergy, Pope Benedict XVI issued a public apology to victims and their families Mar. 20, 2010, and launched an official church investigation May 31 of Irish dioceses, seminaries, and religious orders.

To aid Ireland's ailing banks and prevent default after a 2008-10 financial crisis, finance ministers from EU member countries approved Nov. 28, 2010, an 85 bil euro ($115 bil) emergency loan package that obligated Ireland to impose unpopular austerity measures. Fianna Fáil, the party that had dominated Irish politics since the 1930s, suffered a crushing defeat in elections Feb. 25, 2011, and Enda Kenny, leader of the opposition Fine Gael and a critic of the bailout, became prime minister.

Israel
State of Israel

People: Population: 7,473,052. **Age distrib.:** <15: 27.6%; 65+: 10.1%. **Pop. density:** 952 per sq mi, 367.6 per sq km. **Urban:** 91.9%. **Ethnic groups:** Jewish 76% (Israel-born 67%, Europe/American-born 23%, Africa-born 6%, Asia-born 4%), non-Jewish (mostly Arab) 24%. **Principal languages:** Hebrew, Arabic (both official); English (most common foreign language). **Chief religions:** Jewish 76%, Muslim 17%, Christian 2%, Druze 2%.

Geography: Total area: 8,019 sq mi, 20,770 sq km; **Land area:** 7,849 sq mi, 20,330 sq km. **Location:** Middle East, on E end of Mediterranean Sea. **Neighbors:** Lebanon on N; Syria, West Bank, Jordan on E; Gaza Strip, Egypt on W. **Topography:** The Mediterranean coastal plain is fertile and well-watered. In the center is the Judean Plateau. A triangular-shaped semi-desert region, the Negev, extends from S of Beersheba to an apex at head of the Gulf of Aqaba. The E border drops sharply into the Jordan Rift Valley, including Lake Tiberias (Sea of Galilee) and the Dead Sea, which is c. 1,300 ft below sea level, lowest point on earth's surface. **Capital:** Jerusalem, 768,000. **Cities (urban aggl.):** Tel Aviv-Jaffa, 3,271,671; Haifa, 1,036,368.

Government: Type: Parliamentary democracy. **Head of state:** Pres. Shimon Peres; b. Aug. 1923; in office: July 15, 2007. **Head of gov.:** Prime Min. Benjamin Netanyahu; b. Oct. 21, 1949; in office: Mar. 31, 2009. **Local divisions:** 6 districts. **Defense budget:** $15.6 bil. **Active troops:** 176,500.

Economy: Industries: high-tech prods. (incl. aviation, comm., computer-aided design and manufactures) wood and paper prods., potash and phosphates, food, beverages, tobacco. **Chief crops:** citrus, vegetables, cotton. **Natural resources:** timber, potash, copper ore, nat. gas, phosphate rock, magnesium bromide, clays, sand. **Crude oil reserves:** 1.9 mil bbls. **Arable land:** 14.1%. **Livestock:** cattle: 404,000; chickens: 41.1 mil; goats: 91,000; pigs: 223,500; sheep: 430,000. **Fish catch:** 22,401 metric tons. **Electricity prod.:** 53 bil kWh. **Labor force:** agric. 2%, industry 16%, services 82%.

Finance: Monetary unit: New Shekel (ILS) (Sept. 2011: 3.67 = $1 U.S.). **GDP:** $219.4 bil; **per capita GDP:** $29,800; **GDP growth:** 4.6%. **Imports:** $55.6 bil; U.S. 12.3%, China 7.4%, Germany 7.1%, Switzerland 6.9%, Belgium 5.4%, Italy 4.5%, UK 4%. **Exports:** $54.3 bil; U.S. 35%, Hong Kong 6%, Belgium 5%. **Tourism:** $4.8 bil. **Budget:** $68.7 bil. **Total reserves less gold:** $70.9 bil. **CPI change:** 2.7%.

Transport: Railways: 606 mi. **Motor vehicles:** 324.7 vehicles per 1,000 pop. **Civil aviation:** 10.7 bil pass.-mi; 30 airports. **Chief ports:** Ashdod, Elat, Hadera, Haifa.

Communications: TV sets: 340 per 1,000 pop. **Radios:** 540 per 1,000 pop. **Telephone lines:** 44.2 per 100 pop. **Internet:** 67.2 users per 100 pop.

Health: Life expect.: 78.8 male; 83.2 female. **Births:** 19.2 (per 1,000 pop.). **Deaths:** 5.5 (per 1,000 pop.). **Natural inc.:** 1.38%. **Infant mortality:** 4.1 (per 1,000 live births). **HIV rate:** 0.2%.

Education: Compulsory: ages 5-15. **Literacy:** 91.8%.

Major intl. organizations: UN (FAO, IBRD, ILO, IMF, WHO), OECD, WTO.

Embassy: 3514 International Dr. NW 20008; 364-5500.

Website: www.gov.il

Occupying the southwest corner of the ancient Fertile Crescent, Israel contains some of the oldest known evidence of agriculture and of primitive town life. The Hebrews probably arrived early in the 2nd millennium BCE. Under King David and his successors (c. 1000 BCE-597 BCE), Judaism was developed and secured. After conquest by Babylonians, Persians, and Greeks, an independent Jewish kingdom was revived, 168 BCE, but Rome took effective control in the next century, suppressed Jewish revolts in 70 CE and 135 CE, and renamed Judea Palestine, after the earlier coastal inhabitants, the Philistines.

Arab invaders conquered Palestine in 636. The Arabic language and Islam prevailed within a few centuries, but a Jewish minority remained. The land was ruled from the 11th cent. as a part of non-Arab empires by Seljuks, Mamluks, and Ottomans (with a Crusader interval, 1098-1291).

After four centuries of Ottoman rule, the land was taken in 1917 by Britain, which pledged in the Balfour Declaration to support a Jewish homeland there. In 1920 a British Palestine Mandate was recognized; in 1922 the land east of the Jordan was detached.

Jewish immigration, begun in the late 19th cent., swelled in the 1930s with refugees from the Nazis; heavy Arab immigration from Syria and Lebanon also occurred. Arab opposition to Jewish immigration turned violent in 1920, 1921, 1929, and 1936. The UN General Assembly voted in 1947 to partition Palestine into an Arab and a Jewish state. Britain withdrew in May 1948.

Israel was declared an independent state May 14, 1948; the Arabs rejected partition. Egypt, Jordan, Syria, Lebanon, Iraq, and Saudi Arabia invaded but failed to destroy the Jewish state, which gained territory. Separate armistices with the Arab nations were signed in 1949; Jordan occupied the West Bank, Egypt occupied Gaza. Neither granted Palestinian autonomy.

After persistent terrorist raids, Israel invaded Egypt's Sinai, Oct. 29, 1956, aided briefly by British and French forces. A UN cease-fire was arranged Nov. 6.

An uneasy truce between Israel and the Arab countries lasted until 1967, when Egypt reoccupied the Gaza Strip and closed the Gulf of Aqaba to Israeli shipping. In a 6-day war that started June 5, the Israelis took the Gaza Strip, occupied the Sinai Peninsula to the Suez Canal, and captured East Jerusalem, Syria's Golan Heights, and Jordan's West Bank. Together, the West Bank and Gaza comprise the Palestinian territories, now represented by the Palestinian Authority (see below).

Egypt and Syria attacked Israel, Oct. 6, 1973 (on Yom Kippur, the most solemn day on the Jewish calendar). Israel counterattacked, driving the Syrians back, and crossed the Suez Canal. A cease-fire took effect Oct. 24 and a UN peacekeeping force went to the area. Under a disengagement agreement signed Jan. 18, 1974, Israel withdrew from the canal's west bank. Israeli forces raided Entebbe, Uganda, July 3, 1976, and rescued 103 hostages who had been seized by Arab and German terrorists.

Israel's prime ministers, including David Ben-Gurion, Golda Meir, and Yitzhak Rabin, pursued a moderate socialist program, 1948-77. In 1977, the conservative opposition, led by Menachem Begin, was voted into office for the first time. Egypt's Pres. Anwar al-Sadat visited Jerusalem Nov. 1977, and on Mar. 26, 1979, Egypt and Israel signed a formal peace treaty, ending 30 years of war. Israel returned the Sinai to Egypt in 1982.

On June 7, 1981, Israeli jets destroyed an Iraqi atomic reactor near Baghdad that, Israel claimed, would have enabled Iraq to manufacture nuclear weapons. Israeli forces invaded Lebanon, June 6, 1982, to destroy Palestine Liberation Organization (PLO) strongholds there. After massive Israeli bombing of West Beirut, the PLO agreed to evacuate the city. Israeli troops entered West Beirut after newly elected Lebanese Pres. Bashir Gemayel was assassinated on Sept. 14. Israel drew widespread condemnation when Lebanese Christian forces, Sept. 16, entered two West Beirut refugee camps and slaughtered hundreds of Palestinians.

In 1989, violence escalated over the Israeli military occupation of the West Bank and Gaza Strip. In a series of uprisings known as the first intifada, Palestinian protesters defied Israeli troops, who forcibly retaliated. During the Persian Gulf War, 1991, Iraq fired Scud missiles at Israel. The Labor Party of Yitzhak Rabin won parliamentary elections, June 23, 1992.

Ongoing peace talks led to historic agreements between Israel and the PLO, Sept. 1993. The PLO recognized Israel's right to exist; Israel recognized the PLO as the Palestinians' representative. The two sides then signed, Sept. 13, an agreement for limited Palestinian self-rule in the West Bank and Gaza. Israel and Jordan signed, July 25, 1994, in Washington, DC, a declaration ending their 46-year state of war.

Arab and Jewish extremists repeatedly challenged the peace process. On Nov. 4, 1995, an Orthodox Jewish Israeli assassinated Rabin as he left a peace rally in Tel Aviv. Support for Rabin's successor, Shimon Peres, was shaken by a series of suicide bombings and rocket attacks against Israel by Islamic militants. Emphasizing security issues, the candidate of the conservative Likud bloc, Benjamin Netanyahu, was elected prime minister on May 29, 1996.

Under an interim accord brokered by Pres. Bill Clinton and signed by Netanyahu and PLO leader Yasir Arafat at the White House, Oct. 23, 1998, Israel yielded more West Bank territory to the Palestinians, in exchange for new security guarantees. Negotiations bogged down, however, and full implementation did not begin until Sept. 1999. In the interim, Netanyahu lost by a landslide to the Labor candidate, Ehud Barak, in the election of May 17, 1999.

Israel pulled virtually all its troops out of southern Lebanon by May 24, 2000. Marathon summit talks in the U.S. between Barak and Arafat, July 11-25, failed. A second intifada began in late Sept. in Israel and the Palestinian territories. Barak called new elections for prime minister but lost Feb. 6, 2001, to Ariel Sharon, a hardliner. The bloodshed intensified during the summer, as Palestinian suicide bombers launched attacks on Israeli civilians and Israel struck at Palestinian-controlled territory and carried out an assassination campaign against suspected terrorists.

Israel launched a major West Bank offensive Mar. 29, 2002, 2 days after a suicide bomber killed 26 Israeli Jews at a Passover celebration in Netanya. Fighting was particularly fierce at the Jenin refugee camp, where 23 Israeli troops and at least 50 Palestinians were killed. A U.S.-sponsored "road map" to Middle East peace, unveiled Apr. 30, 2003, made little headway, as violence flared between Israel and Hamas militants in Gaza.

Sharon's decision to pull all Israeli settlers and troops out of Gaza (see below), approved by the cabinet Feb. 20, 2005, led to a realignment in Israeli politics. When right-wing Likud members opposed the plan, Sharon and Deputy Prime Min. Ehud Olmert broke with them and formed the centrist Kadima Party. Sharon suffered a massive stroke Jan. 4, 2006. With Sharon incapacitated, Olmert became prime minister, led Kadima to victory in Mar. 28 elections, and formed a broad coalition government.

Clashes in mid-2006 along the Gaza and Lebanon borders rapidly escalated into full-scale war. Israeli air and ground forces hit hard in Gaza, but the fiercest fighting raged on the northern front. By Aug. 14, when a UN-sponsored cease-fire took hold, the estimated death toll from the war included nearly 1,150 Lebanese, almost 200 Gaza Palestinians, and 150 Israelis. Olmert, criticized for leadership failures during the 2006 war and targeted in multiple corruption inquiries, announced July 30, 2008, that he would resign when his Kadima Party chose a replacement. Foreign Min. Tzipi Livni won a hard-fought party primary Sept. 17. Unable to form a stable government, she called early elections for Feb. 10, 2009. After a campaign overshadowed by a 3-week war between Israel and Hamas in Gaza (see below), both Kadima and Likud fell far short of a majority. On Mar. 31, Netanyahu became prime minister for a second time, heading a coalition that included Likud, Labor, the ultra-nationalist Yisrael Beitenu party, and the ultra-Orthodox Shas party.

Israel's relations with allies were strained when senior Hamas commander Mahmoud al-Mabhouh was killed Jan. 2010 in Dubai, allegedly by agents of the Israeli spy agency Mossad who entered the UAE carrying false European and Australian passports. Further criticism greeted the Israeli government's announcement, during a Mar. 9 visit by U.S. Vice-Pres. Joe Biden, that it would proceed with construction of 1,600 homes in Ramat Shlomo (a Jewish settlement in mostly Arab East Jerusalem), and the killing by Israeli commandos of 9 pro-Palestinian activists in clashes May 31 on board the *Mavi Marmara*, part of a flotilla that was seeking to break Israel's blockade of Gaza.

"Arab Spring" uprisings in 2011, which toppled the Mubarak government in neighboring Egypt and shook other Middle Eastern regimes, unsettled Israeli policy in the region. In a cross-border clash that raised tensions between Israel and Egypt, militants Aug. 18, 2011, killed 8 Israelis (6 civilians, 2 soldiers), and retaliatory fire by Israel killed at least 7 of the attackers along with at least 3 Egyptian security officers and, according to some reports, several civilians. Israel evacuated its diplomats from Egypt after thousands of protesters stormed the Israeli embassy in Cairo Sept. 9. Mass protests within Israel July-Sept. focused on social and economic inequality and the rising cost of living.

Palestinian Territories

The Palestinian territories comprise the Gaza Strip, often called Gaza, and the West Bank, both occupied by Israel in 1967. Since 1996 the Palestinian Authority has been responsible for civil government in the territories. Elected president Jan. 20, 1996, PLO leader Yasir Arafat headed the Palestinian Authority until his death Nov. 11, 2004. Mahmoud Abbas (also called Abu Mazen), who had succeeded Arafat as PLO chairman and leader of the Fatah faction, was elected president Jan. 9, 2005. A victory by Hamas militants in legislative elections Jan. 25, 2006, led to a power struggle with Abbas, who favored a negotiated settlement with Israel. In bitter fighting, Hamas ousted Fatah from Gaza, June 2007, but Abbas retained power in the West Bank. From Sept. 2000, when the second intifada began, through the end of 2008, the Israeli-Palestinian conflict claimed the lives of more than 1,060 Israelis and at least 4,900 Palestinians; nearly 600 Palestinians were killed by other Palestinians in factional fighting. Fatah and Hamas declared Apr. 27, 2011, that they had agreed to a reconciliation agreement under which the two rival factions would form a joint caretaker government and hold elections throughout Palestine within a year. In a speech Sept. 23 to the UN General Assembly, Abbas sought full UN membership of an independent Palestinian state; the U.S. and Israel opposed the request.

The **Gaza Strip** extends northeast from the Sinai Peninsula for 25 mi (40 km), with the Mediterranean Sea to the west and Israel to the east. The Palestinian Authority is responsible for civil government. Nearly all the inhabitants are Palestinian Arabs, more than 35% of whom live in refugee camps. Population (2011 est.): 1,657,155. Area: 139 sq mi.

Israel captured Gaza from Egypt in the 1967 war. It remained under Israeli occupation until May 1994, when the Israeli Defense Forces withdrew. Agreements between Israel and the PLO in 1993 and 1994 provided for interim self-rule in Gaza, but Israel retained control over security. Israel forcibly evacuated all 9,000 Jewish settlers from Gaza by Aug. 22, 2005, and the last remaining Israeli soldiers pulled out Sept. 12. Israel established a fortified barrier on its Gaza border to block Palestinian infiltrators.

After the Hamas takeover, Israel declared Gaza a "hostile entity," Sept. 19, 2007, and intensified military and economic pressures.

Hamas thwarted an Israeli blockade, Jan. 2008, by blowing up part of the border wall between Gaza and Egypt. Retaliating for Hamas rocket and mortar attacks, Israel launched an aerial assault and ground offensive in Gaza, Dec. 27, 2008-Jan. 18, 2009; investigators for B'Tselem, an Israeli human rights group, later concluded that the fighting killed 1,387 Palestinians, of whom more than half were civilians. A UN report issued Sept. 15 found evidence of war crimes committed by both sides. After the *Mavi Marmara* incident (see above), Israel June 2010 eased some restrictions on the flow of goods to Gaza. Egypt lifted the blockade along its Gaza border May 28, 2011.

The **West Bank** is located west of the Jordan R. and Dead Sea, bounded by Jordan on the east and by Israel on the north, west, and south. The Palestinian Authority administers several major cities, but Israel retains control over much land, including Jewish settlements. Population (2011 est.): 2,568,555. Area: 2,263 sq mi.

Israel captured the West Bank from Jordan in the 1967 war. An accord between Israel and the PLO expanding Palestinian self-rule in the West Bank was signed Sept. 28, 1995. Later agreements gave Palestinians full or shared control of 40% of West Bank territory.

In June 2002 the Israeli government began building a controversial security barrier in the West Bank to restrict Palestinian access to Israel and reduce infiltration by suicide bombers. In a nonbinding ruling, July 9, 2004, the World Court said the barrier violated international law. Israel has continued to allow the expansion of Jewish settlements on the West Bank, despite U.S. government calls for a settlement freeze; by mid-2011, an estimated 320,000 Jewish settlers were living in the West Bank (not including East Jerusalem, which Israel annexed in 1967).

Italy
Italian Republic

People: Population: 61,016,804. **Age distrib.:** <15: 13.8%; 65+: 20.3%. **Pop. density:** 537.3 per sq mi, 207.4 per sq km. **Urban:** 68.4%. **Ethnic groups:** Italian (incl. small clusters of German-, French-, & Slovene-Italians in N; Albanian- & Greek-Italians in S). **Principal languages:** Italian (official), German, French, Slovene. **Chief religions:** Roman Catholic 90%, other (incl. Protestant, Jewish, Muslim) 10%.

Geography: Total area: 116,348 sq mi, 301,340 sq km; **Land area:** 113,568 sq mi, 294,140 sq km. **Location:** In S Europe, jutting into Mediterranean Sea. **Neighbors:** France on W; Switzerland, Austria on N; Slovenia on E; San Marino, Vatican City. **Topography:** Occupies long boot-shaped peninsula, extending SE from the Alps into Mediterranean, with islands of Sicily and Sardinia offshore. The alluvial Po Valley drains most of N. Rest of the country is rugged and mountainous, except for intermittent coastal plains, like the Campania, S of Rome. Apennine Mts. run down through center of peninsula. **Capital:** Rome, 3,357,000. **Cities (urban aggl.):** Milan, 2,967,085; Naples, 2,275,683; Turin, 1,664,863.

Government: Type: Republic. **Head of state:** Pres. Giorgio Napolitano; b. June 29, 1925; in office: May 15, 2006. **Head of gov.:** Prime Min. Silvio Berlusconi; b. Sept. 29, 1936; in office: May 8, 2008. **Local divisions:** 20 regions divided into 103 provinces. **Defense budget:** $20.5 bil. **Active troops:** 184,609.

Economy: Industries: tourism, machinery, iron and steel, chemicals, food proc., textiles, motor vehicles. **Chief crops:** fruits, vegetables, grapes, potatoes, sugar beets, soybeans, grain, olives. **Natural resources:** coal, mercury, zinc, potash, marble, barite, asbestos, pumice, fluorspar, feldspar, pyrite (sulfur), nat. gas and crude oil reserves, fish. **Crude oil reserves:** 476.5 mil bbls. **Arable land:** 23.4%. **Livestock:** cattle: 6.4 mil; chickens: 120 mil; goats: 957,300; pigs: 9.3 mil; sheep: 8.2 mil. **Fish catch:** 416,726 metric tons. **Electricity prod.** (2009): 269.6 bil kWh. **Labor force:** agric. 4.2%, industry 30.7%, services 65.1%.

Finance: Monetary unit: Euro (EUR) (Sept. 2011: 0.71 = $1 U.S.). **GDP:** $1.8 tril; **per capita GDP:** $30,500; **GDP growth:** 1.3%. **Imports:** $459.7 bil; Germany 16.7%, France 8.9%, China 6.5%, Netherlands 5.7%, Spain 4.4%, Russia 4.1%, Belgium 4%. **Exports:** $458.4 bil; Germany 12.6%, France 11.6%, U.S. 5.9%, Spain 5.7%, UK 5.1%, Switzerland 4.7%. **Tourism:** $38.8 bil. **Budget:** $1.04 tril. **Total reserves less gold:** $47.7 bil. **Gold:** 78.8 mil oz t. **CPI change:** 1.5%.

Transport: Railways: 12,585 mi. **Motor vehicles:** 683.5 vehicles per 1,000 pop. **Civil aviation:** 24.7 bil pass.-mi; 101 airports. **Chief ports:** Augusta, Genoa, Livorno, Sarroch, Taranto, Trieste, Venice.

Communications: TV sets: 492 per 1,000 pop. **Radios:** 878 per 1,000 pop. **Telephone lines:** 35.7 per 100 pop. **Daily newspaper circ.:** 137.1 per 1,000 pop. **Internet:** 53.7 users per 100 pop.

Health: Life expect.: 79.2 male; 84.5 female. **Births:** 9.2 (per 1,000 pop.). **Deaths:** 9.8 (per 1,000 pop.). **Natural inc.:** −0.07%. **Infant mortality:** 3.4 (per 1,000 live births). **HIV rate:** 0.3%.

Education: Compulsory: ages 6-14. **Literacy:** 98.9%.

Major intl. organizations: UN and all of its specialized agencies, EU, NATO, OECD, OSCE, WTO.

Embassy: 3000 Whitehaven St. NW 20008; 612-4400.

Website: www.quirinale.it

Rome emerged as the major power in Italy after 500 BCE, dominating the Etruscans to the north and Greeks to the south. Under the Empire, which lasted until the 5th cent. CE, Rome ruled most of Western Europe, the Balkans, the Middle East, and North Africa. After Rome fell, Italy became a patchwork of kingdoms, principalities, and city-states until reunified, 1870.

The Fascist leader Benito Mussolini came to power, 1922, and aligned Italy with Nazi Germany in WWII. After Fascism was overthrown in 1943, Italy declared war on Germany and Japan and contributed to the Allied victory. It surrendered conquered lands and lost its colonies. Mussolini was killed by partisans Apr. 28, 1945. Victor Emmanuel III abdicated May 9, 1946; his son Humbert II was king until June 10, when Italy became a republic after a referendum, June 2-3. In the postwar decades, Italy had a succession of short-lived governments.

Christian Democratic leader and former prime min. Aldo Moro was abducted and murdered in 1978 by Red Brigade terrorists. The wave of left-wing political violence, including other kidnappings and assassinations, continued into the 1980s.

In the early 1990s, scandals implicated some of Italy's most prominent politicians. In Mar. 1994 voting, under reformed election rules, right-wing parties won a majority, dislodging Italy's long-powerful Christian Democratic Party. Italy led a 7,000-member peacekeeping force in Albania, Apr.-Aug. 1997, and contributed 2,000 troops to the NATO-led security force (KFOR) that entered Kosovo in June 1999.

Supporters of Silvio Berlusconi, a multibillionaire media magnate, won the parliamentary elections of May 13, 2001. Berlusconi, a close ally of the U.S., backed American-led military operations in Afghanistan (2001) and Iraq (2003). Italy pulled its last remaining troops out of Iraq in 2006; as of mid-2011, nearly 4,000 Italian troops continued to serve with the NATO mission (ISAF) in Afghanistan.

A coalition of center-left parties led by Romano Prodi scored a narrow win over Berlusconi in parliamentary voting; Berlusconi returned at the head of a center-right coalition after elections Apr. 13-14, 2008. An earthquake in the Abruzzo region of central Italy Apr. 6, 2009, battered the town of L'Aquila, killed more than 300 people, and left at least 50,000 homeless. Sluggish economic growth and rising public debt (equal to about 120% of annual GDP in mid-2011) raised investors' concerns about Italy's financial stability.

Sicily, 9,927 sq mi, pop. (2010 est.) 5,050,486, is an island 180 by 120 mi, seat of a region that embraces the island of Pantelleria, 32 sq mi, and the Lipari group, 44 sq mi, including two active volcanoes: Vulcano, 1,637 ft, and Stromboli, 3,038 ft. From prehistoric times Sicily has been settled by various peoples; a Greek state had its capital at Syracuse. Rome took Sicily from Carthage 215 BCE. Mt. Etna, an 11,053-ft active volcano, is its tallest peak.

Sardinia, 9,301 sq mi, pop. (2010 est.) 1,675,411, lies in the Mediterranean, 115 mi W of Italy and 7½ mi S of Corsica. It is 160 mi long, 68 mi wide, and mountainous, with mining of coal, zinc, lead, copper. In 1720 Sardinia was added to the possessions of the Dukes of Savoy in Piedmont and Savoy to form the Kingdom of Sardinia. Giuseppe Garibaldi is buried on the nearby isle of Caprera. **Elba**, 86 sq mi, lies 6 mi W of Tuscany. Napoleon I lived in exile on Elba 1814-15.

Jamaica

People: Population: 2,868,380. **Age distrib.:** <15: 30.1%; 65+: 7.6%. **Pop. density:** 685.9 per sq mi, 264.8 per sq km. **Urban:** 52%. **Ethnic groups:** black 91%, mixed 6%. **Principal languages:** English, English patois. **Chief religions:** Protestant 63%, Roman Catholic 3%, none 21%.

Geography: Total area: 4,244 sq mi, 10,991 sq km; **Land area:** 4,182 sq mi, 10,831 sq km. **Location:** In W Indies. **Neighbors:** Nearest are Cuba to N, Haiti to E. **Topography:** Four-fifths of country covered by mountains. **Capital:** Kingston, 580,000.

Government: Type: Constitutional monarchy with parliamentary system based on UK model. **Head of state:** Queen Elizabeth II, represented by Sir Patrick Allen; b. Feb. 7, 1951; in office: Feb. 26, 2009. **Head of gov.:** Prime Min. Bruce Golding; b. Dec. 5, 1947; in office: Sept. 11, 2007. **Local divisions:** 14 parishes. **Defense budget** (2009): $91 mil. **Active troops:** 2,830.

Economy: Industries: tourism, bauxite/alumina, agric. proc., light manufactures, rum, cement, metal, paper, chem. prods., telecom. **Chief crops:** sugarcane, bananas, coffee, citrus, yams. **Natural resources:** bauxite, gypsum, limestone. **Arable land:** 11.1%. **Livestock:** cattle: 185,000; chickens: 14.1 mil; goats: 440,000; pigs: 219,000; sheep: 520. **Fish catch:** 19,002 metric tons. **Electricity prod.:** 7.3 bil kWh. **Labor force:** agric. 17%, industry 19%, services 64%.

Finance: Monetary unit: Dollar (JMD) (Sept. 2011: 85.05 = $1 U.S.). **GDP:** $23.7 bil; **per capita GDP:** $8,300; **GDP growth:** −1.1%. **Imports:** $5.4 bil; U.S. 37.3%, Venezuela 12.6%, Trinidad and Tobago 12.5%, China 4.6%. **Exports:** $1.5 bil; U.S. 49.4%, Canada 10%, UK 9.9%. **Tourism:** $2 bil. **Budget:** $4.6 bil. **Total reserves less gold:** $2.5 bil. **CPI change:** 12.6%.

Transport: Motor vehicles: 60.2 vehicles per 1,000 pop. **Civil aviation:** 1.8 bil pass.-mi; 12 airports. **Chief ports:** Kingston, Montego Bay, Port Esquivel, Port Kaiser, Port Rhoades, Rocky Point.

Communications: TV sets: 382 per 1,000 pop. **Radios:** 23 per 1,000 pop. **Telephone lines:** 9.6 per 100 pop. **Internet:** 26.1 users per 100 pop.

Health: Life expect.: 71.8 male; 75.2 female. **Births:** 19.2 (per 1,000 pop.). **Deaths:** 6.5 (per 1,000 pop.). **Natural inc.:** 1.27%. **Infant mortality:** 14.6 (per 1,000 live births). **HIV rate:** 1.7%.

Education: Compulsory: ages 6-11. **Literacy:** 86.4%.

Major intl. organizations: UN (FAO, IBRD, ILO, IMF, WHO), Caricom, the Commonwealth, OAS, WTO.

Embassy: 1520 New Hampshire Ave. NW 20036; 452-0660.

Website: www.jis.gov.jm

Jamaica was visited by Columbus, 1494, and ruled by Spain (under whom Arawak Indians died out) until seized by Britain, 1655. Jamaica won independence Aug. 6, 1962. The island's rich musical innovations include ska and reggae. Rastafarianism is an influential religious movement.

In 1974 Jamaica sought an increase in taxes paid by U.S. and Canadian bauxite mines. The socialist government acquired 50% ownership of the companies' Jamaican interests in 1976, and was reelected that year. Rudimentary welfare state measures were passed. Relations with the U.S. improved in the 1980s when Jamaican politics entered a more conservative phase. Violence between government forces and West Kingston slum residents claimed at least 20 lives July 7-10, 2001.

At least 17 died when Hurricane Ivan hit southern Jamaica Sept. 10-11, 2004. Portia Simpson Miller, leader of the People's National Party, became Jamaica's first female prime minister, Mar. 30, 2006. The opposition Jamaica Labour Party (JLP) won the parliamentary elections of Sept. 3, 2007. Police and soldiers clashed with gang members in the Tivoli Gardens section of Kingston in May 2010, leaving 76 people dead; the alleged gang leader, Christopher (Dudus) Coke, surrendered June 22, 2010, and was extradited to the U.S., where he pleaded guilty to racketeering charges Aug. 31, 2011. The JLP revealed Sept. 25 that Prime Min. Bruce Golding would step down in Nov. as JLP leader and head of government.

Japan

People: Population: 127,469,543. **Age distrib.:** <15: 13.6%; 65+: 23.1%. **Pop. density:** 905.8 per sq mi, 349.7 per sq km. **Urban:** 66.8%. **Ethnic groups:** Japanese 98.5%, Korean 0.5%. **Principal language:** Japanese. **Chief religions:** Shintoism 84%, Buddhism 71% (observed together); Christian 2%.

Geography: Total area: 145,914 sq mi, 377,915 sq km; **Land area:** 140,728 sq mi, 364,485 sq km. **Location:** Archipelago off E coast of Asia. **Neighbors:** Russia to N, S. Korea to W. **Topography:** Consists of 4 main islands: Honshu ("mainland"), 87,805 sq mi; Hokkaido, 30,144 sq mi; Kyushu, 14,114 sq mi; and Shikoku, 7,049 sq mi. The coast, deeply indented, measures 16,654 mi. The northern islands are continuation of the Sakhalin Mts. The Kunlun range of China continues into southern islands, the ranges meeting in Japanese Alps. In a vast transverse fissure crossing Honshu E-W rises a group of volcanoes, mostly extinct or inactive, including 12,388 ft. Mt. Fuji (Fujiyama) near Tokyo. **Capital:** Tokyo, 36,507,000. **Cities (urban aggl.):** Osaka-Kobe, 11,337,016; Nagoya, 3,267,448; Fukuoka-Kitakyushu, 2,816,278; Sapporo, 2,686,681.

Government: Type: Constitutional monarchy with parliamentary democracy. **Head of state:** Emperor Akihito; b. Dec. 23, 1933; in office: Jan. 7, 1989. **Head of gov.:** Prime Min. Yoshihiko Noda; b. May 20, 1957; in office: Sept. 2, 2011. **Local divisions:** 47 prefectures. **Defense budget:** $52.8 bil. **Active troops:** 247,746.

Economy: Industries: among world's largest and technologically advanced producers of motor vehicles, electronic equip., machine tools, metals, ships, chemicals, textiles, processed foods. **Chief crops:** rice, sugar beets, vegetables, fruits. **Natural resources:** negligible mineral resources, fish. **Crude oil reserves:** 44.1 mil bbls. **Arable land:** 11.8%. **Livestock:** cattle: 4.4 mil; chickens: 285.3 mil; goats: 14,500; pigs: 9.9 mil; sheep: 14,000. **Fish catch:** 5.2 mil metric tons. **Electricity prod.:** (2009): 982.3 bil kWh. **Labor force:** agric. 3.9%, industry 26.2%, services 69.8%.

Finance: Monetary unit: Yen (JPY) (Sept. 2011: 77.57 = $1 U.S.). **GDP:** $4.3 tril; **per capita GDP:** $34,000; **GDP growth:** 3.9%. **Imports:** $636.8 bil; China 22.2%, U.S. 11%, Australia 6.3%, Saudi Arabia 5.3%, UAE 4.1%. **Exports:** $765.2 bil; China 18.9%, U.S. 16.4%, South Korea 8.1%, Hong Kong 5.5%. **Tourism:** $13.2 bil. **Budget:** $2.2 tril. **Total reserves less gold:** $1.06 tril. **Gold:** 24.6 mil oz t. **CPI change:** -0.7%.

Transport: Railways: 16,426 mi. **Motor vehicles:** 580.8 vehicles per 1,000 pop. **Civil aviation:** 79.4 bil pass.-mi; 144 airports. **Chief ports:** Chiba, Kawasaki, Kobe, Mizushima, Moji, Nagoya, Osaka, Tokyo, Tomakomai, Yokohama.

Communications: TV sets: 842 per 1,000 pop. **Radios:** 955 per 1,000 pop. **Telephone lines:** 31.9 per 100 pop. **Daily newspaper circ.:** 551.2 per 1,000 pop. **Internet:** 80 users per 100 pop.

Health: Life expect.: 80.3 male; 87.2 female. **Births:** 8.5 (per 1,000 pop.). **Deaths:** 9.1 (per 1,000 pop.). **Natural inc.:** -0.05%. **Infant mortality:** 2.3 (per 1,000 live births). **HIV rate:** <0.1%.

Education: Compulsory: ages 6-14. **Literacy:** 99%.

Major intl. organizations: UN and all its specialized agencies, APEC, OECD, WTO.

Embassy: 2520 Massachusetts Ave. NW 20008; 238-6700.

Website: www.kantei.go.jp

According to Japanese legend, the empire was founded by Emperor Jimmu, 660 BCE, but earliest records of a unified Japan date from 1,000 years later. Chinese influence was strong in the formation of Japanese civilization. Buddhism was introduced before the 6th cent. CE.

A feudal system, with locally powerful noble families and their samurai warrior retainers, dominated from 1192. Central power was held by successive families of shoguns (military dictators), 1192-1867, until recovered by Emperor Meiji, 1868. The Portuguese and Dutch had minor trade with Japan in the 16th and 17th centuries; U.S. Commodore Matthew C. Perry opened the country to U.S. trade in a treaty ratified 1854. Industrialization was begun in the late 19th cent. Japan fought China, 1894-95, gaining Taiwan. After war with Russia, 1904-05, Russia ceded the southern half of Sakhalin and gave concessions in China. Japan annexed Korea, 1910.

In WWI Japan ousted Germany from Shandong in China and took over German Pacific islands. Japan took Manchuria in 1931 and launched full-scale war in China in 1937. Japan launched war against the U.S. by attacking Pearl Harbor Dec. 7, 1941. The U.S. dropped atomic bombs on Hiroshima, Aug. 6, and Nagasaki, Aug. 9, 1945. Japan surrendered Aug. 14, 1945.

In a new constitution adopted May 3, 1947, Japan renounced the right to wage war; the emperor gave up claims to divinity; the Diet became the sole lawmaking authority. The U.S. and 48 other non-Communist nations signed a peace treaty and the U.S. a bilateral defense agreement with Japan, in San Francisco Sept. 8, 1951, restoring Japan's sovereignty as of Apr. 28, 1952.

Rebuilding after WWII, Japan emerged as one of the most powerful economies in the world, and as a leader in technology. The U.S. and Western Europe criticized Japan for its restrictive policy on imports, which eventually allowed Japan to accumulate huge trade surpluses.

On June 26, 1968, the U.S. returned to Japanese control the Bonin Isls., Volcano Isls. (including Iwo Jima), and Marcus Isls. On May 15, 1972, Okinawa, the other Ryukyu Isls., and the Daito Isls. were returned by the U.S.; it was agreed the U.S. would continue to maintain military bases on Okinawa.

The Liberal Democratic Party (LDP) governed Japan from the mid-1950s through the early 90s. On June 29, 1994, Tomiichi Murayama became Japan's first Socialist premier since 1947-48. An earthquake in the Kobe area in Jan. 1995 claimed more than 5,000 lives, injured nearly 35,000, and caused over $90 bil in property damage. With the country mired in a lengthy recession, the LDP regained power in 1996 and a series of weak LDP governments led Japan until 2009.

About 600 noncombatant troops were in Iraq Feb. 2004-July 2006, the first time since WWII that Japanese forces served in an overseas war zone. The worldwide recession of 2008-09 hit Japan hard, prompting a series of economic stimulus plans; the largest of these, unveiled Apr. 10, 2009, called for more than $150 bil in spending and tax measures. The LDP suffered a crushing defeat in parliamentary elections Aug. 30, and Yukio Hatoyama of the opposition Democratic Party of Japan (DPJ) became prime minister. His public support soon plummeted, and he was replaced June 8, 2010, by former Finance Minister Naoto Kan, who then beat back a leadership challenge, Sept. 14, from a DPJ power broker, Ichiro Ozawa.

A magnitude 9.0 earthquake and tsunami in the Pacific Ocean off Japan's east coast Mar. 11, 2011, killed more than 15,800 people with another 3,800 still listed as missing (as of Oct. 7); property damage was estimated at $325 bil. Inundated by the tsunami, the Fukushima Daiichi nuclear power plant experienced meltdowns at 3 of the plant's 6 nuclear reactors, spewing radiation over a large area and contaminating crops, beef, and seafood. Criticized for his response to the catastrophe, Prime Min. Naoto Kan submitted his resignation Aug. 26 and was succeeded by Finance Min. Yoshihiko Noda.

Jordan

Hashemite Kingdom of Jordan

People: Population: 6,508,271. **Age distrib.:** <15: 35.3%; 65+: 4.8%. **Pop. density:** 189.8 per sq mi, 73.3 per sq km. **Urban:** 78.5%. **Ethnic groups:** Arab 98%, Circassian 1%, Armenian 1%. **Principal languages:** Arabic (official), English widely understood among upper & middle classes. **Chief religions:** Sunni Muslim (official) 92%, Christian 6%.

Geography: Total area: 34,495 sq mi, 89,342 sq km; **Land area:** 34,287 sq mi, 88,802 sq km. **Location:** In Middle East. **Neighbors:** Israel, West Bank on W; Saudi Arabia on S; Iraq on E; Syria on N. **Topography:** About 88% is arid. Fertile areas are in W. Only port is on short Aqaba Gulf coast. Country shares Dead Sea (about 1,300 ft below sea level) with Israel. **Capital:** Amman, 1,088,000.

Government: Type: Constitutional monarchy. **Head of state:** King Abdullah II; b. Jan. 30, 1962; in office: Feb. 7, 1999. **Head of gov.:** Prime Min. Marouf al-Bakhit; b. 1947; in office: Feb. 9, 2011. **Local divisions:** 12 governorates. **Defense budget:** $2.53 bil. **Active troops:** 100,500.

Economy: Industries: clothing, fertilizers, potash, phosphate mining, pharmaceuticals, petroleum refining, cement, inorganic chemicals, light mfg, tourism. **Chief crops:** citrus, tomatoes, cucumbers, olives, strawberries, stone fruits. **Natural resources:** phosphates, potash, shale oil. **Crude oil reserves:** 1 mil bbls. **Arable land:** 2.3%. **Livestock:** cattle: 64,520; chickens: 25 mil; goats: 919,740; sheep: 2.1 mil. **Fish catch:** 1,009 metric tons. **Electricity prod.:** 13 bil kWh. **Labor force:** agric. 2.7%, industry 20%, services 77.4%.

Finance: Monetary unit: Dinar (JOD) (Sept. 2011: 0.71 = $1 U.S.). **GDP:** $34.5 bil; **per capita GDP:** $5,400; **GDP growth:** 3.1%. **Imports:** $13 bil; Saudi Arabia 17.5%, China 11%, U.S. 7%, Germany 6.3%, Egypt 6%. **Exports:** $7.3 bil; U.S. 17.1%, Iraq 17%,

India 13.5%, Saudi Arabia 10.5%, Syria 4.2%, UAE 4.1%. **Tourism:** $3.4 bil. **Budget:** $8.7 bil. **Total reserves less gold:** $13.1 bil. **Gold:** 410,000 oz t. **CPI change:** 5%.

Transport: Railways: 315 mi. **Motor vehicles:** 84.1 vehicles per 1,000 pop. **Civil aviation:** 4 bil pass.-mi; 16 airports. **Chief port:** Al Aqabah.

Communications: TV sets: 207 per 1,000 pop. **Radios:** 361 per 1,000 pop. **Telephone lines:** 7.8 per 100 pop. **Internet:** 38 users per 100 pop.

Health: Life expect.: 78.7 male; 81.5 female. **Births:** 26.8 (per 1,000 pop.). **Deaths:** 2.7 (per 1,000 pop.). **Natural inc.:** 2.41%. **Infant mortality:** 16.4 (per 1,000 live births). **HIV rate:** NA.

Education: Compulsory: ages 6-15. **Literacy:** 92.2%.

Major intl. organizations: UN (FAO, IBRD, ILO, IMF, WHO), AL, WTO.

Embassy: 3504 International Dr. NW 20008; 966-2664.

Website: www.kinghussein.gov.jo

From ancient times to 1922 the lands to the east of the Jordan R. were culturally and politically united with the lands to the W. Arabs conquered the area in the 7th cent.; the Ottomans took control in the 16th. Britain's 1920 Palestine Mandate covered both sides of the Jordan. In 1921, Abdullah, son of the ruler of Hejaz in Arabia, was installed by Britain as emir of an autonomous Transjordan, covering two-thirds of Palestine. An independent kingdom was proclaimed, 1946.

During the 1948 Arab-Israeli war the West Bank and East Jerusalem were added to the kingdom, which changed its name to Jordan. These territories were lost to Israel in the 1967 war, which swelled the number of Arab refugees on the East Bank.

Jordan and Israel officially agreed, July 25, 1994, to end their state of war; a formal peace treaty was signed Oct. 26. Following a prolonged bout with cancer, King Hussein died Feb. 7, 1999, ending a nearly 47-year reign; his eldest son assumed the throne as Abdullah II. From 1951 to 2010, the U.S. provided about $11.4 bil in economic and military aid to Jordan. According to government estimates, at least 450,000 refugees from the Iraq war were living in Jordan at the beginning of 2011. Abdullah II responded to 3 weeks of "Arab Spring" protests by replacing his prime minister in early Feb.

Kazakhstan
Republic of Kazakhstan

People: Population: 17,304,513. **Age distrib.:** <15: 24.2%; 65+: 6.8%. **Pop. density:** 16.6 per sq mi, 6.4 per sq km. **Urban:** 58.5%. **Ethnic groups:** Kazakh (Qazaq) 63%, Russian 24%, Uzbek 3%, Ukrainian 2%, Uighur 1%, Tatar 1%, German 1%. **Principal languages:** Kazakh (Qazaq; state language), Russian (official; used in everyday business). **Chief religions:** Muslim 47%, Russian Orthodox 44%, Protestant 2%.

Geography: Total area: 1,052,090 sq mi, 2,724,900 sq km; **Land area:** 1,042,360 sq mi, 2,699,700 sq km. **Location:** In Central Asia. **Neighbors:** Russia on N; China on E; Kyrgyzstan, Uzbekistan, Turkmenistan on S; Caspian Sea on W. **Topography:** Extends from lower reaches of Volga in Europe to Altay Mts. on Chinese border. **Capital:** Astana, 650,000. **Cities (urban aggl.):** Almaty, 1,383,158.

Government: Type: Republic. **Head of state:** Pres. Nursultan A. Nazarbayev; b. July 6, 1940; in office: Apr. 24, 1990. **Head of gov.:** Prime Min. Karim Masimov; b. June 15, 1965; in office: Jan. 10, 2007. **Local divisions:** 14 oblystar, 3 cities. **Defense budget:** $1.12 bil. **Active troops:** 49,000.

Economy: Industries: oil, coal, iron ore, manganese, chromite, lead, zinc, copper, titanium, bauxite, gold, silver, phosphates, sulfur, uranium, iron and steel; tractors and other agric. machinery, elec. motors, constr. materials. **Chief crops:** grain (mostly spring wheat), cotton. **Natural resources:** petroleum, nat. gas, coal, iron ore, manganese, chrome ore, nickel, cobalt, copper, molybdenum, lead, zinc, bauxite, gold, uranium. **Crude oil reserves:** 30 bil bbls. **Arable land:** 8.7%. **Livestock:** cattle: 6 mil; chickens: 30 mil; goats: 2.6 mil; pigs: 1.3 mil; sheep: 14.1 mil. **Fish catch:** 33,940 metric tons. **Electricity prod.** (2009): 75.6 bil kWh. **Labor force:** agric. 28.2%, industry 18.2%, services 53.6%.

Finance: Monetary unit: Tenge (KZT) (Sept. 2011: 146.96 = $1 U.S.). **GDP:** $196.4 bil; **per capita GDP:** $12,700; **GDP growth:** 7%. **Imports:** $30.1 bil; Russia 29.6%, China 26.1%, Germany 6.2%, Italy 5.6%, Ukraine 4.8%. **Exports:** $59.2 bil; China 15.6%, Russia 8.9%, France 8.5%, Germany 7.8%, Ukraine 5.1%, Romania 4.8%, Italy 4.7%, U.S. 4%. **Tourism:** $1 bil. **Budget:** $31.6 bil. **Total reserves less gold:** $25.2 bil. **Gold:** 2.2 mil oz t. **CPI change:** 7.1%.

Transport: Railways: 9,370 mi. **Civil aviation:** 1.6 bil pass.-mi; 65 airports. **Chief ports:** Aqtau, Atyrau, Oskemen.

Communications: TV sets: 497 per 1,000 pop. **Radios:** 215 per 1,000 pop. **Telephone lines:** 25 per 100 pop. **Internet:** 34 users per 100 pop.

Health: Life expect.: 64.0 male; 74.3 female. **Births:** 20.8 (per 1,000 pop.). **Deaths:** 8.6 (per 1,000 pop.). **Natural inc.:** 1.22%. **Infant mortality:** 23.8 (per 1,000 live births). **HIV rate:** 0.1%.

Education: Compulsory: ages 7-17. **Literacy:** 99.7%.

Major intl. organizations: UN (FAO, IBRD, ILO, IMF, WHO), CIS, OSCE, WTO (observer).

Embassy: 1401 16th St. NW 20036; 232-5488.

Website: www.government.kz

The region came under the Mongols' rule in the 13th cent. and gradually came under Russian rule, 1730-1853. It was admitted to the USSR as a constituent republic in 1936.

Kazakhstan declared independence Dec. 16, 1991. It became an independent state when the Soviet Union dissolved Dec. 26, 1991. The Communist Party chief, Nursultan Nazarbayev, was elected president unopposed. He boosted the economy by encouraging Western investment in the oil industry. Dissent was suppressed, and much of the nation's oil wealth was reportedly controlled by the president's family and aides.

Kazakhstan agreed, Feb. 14, 1994, to dismantle nuclear missiles. Private land ownership was legalized Dec. 26, 1995. Astana (formerly Akmola) became the nation's new capital, June 9, 1998. Reelected in 1999 and 2005, Pres. Nazarbayev was authorized to run for an unlimited number of terms under a constitutional amendment passed by parliament May 18, 2007; he claimed more than 95% of the vote in a presidential election Apr. 3, 2011, that was faulted by international election monitors.

Kenya
Republic of Kenya

People: Population: 41,943,504. **Age distrib.:** <15: 42.6%; 65+: 2.7%. **Pop. density:** 190.9 per sq mi, 73.7 per sq km. **Urban:** 22.2%. **Ethnic groups:** Kikuyu 22%, Luhya 14%, Luo 13%, Kalenjin 12%, Kamba 11%, Kisii 6%, Meru 6%, other African 15%. **Principal languages:** English, Kiswahili (both official); numerous indigenous languages. **Chief religions:** Protestant 45%, Roman Catholic 33%, Muslim 10%, indigenous beliefs 10%.

Geography: Total area: 224,081 sq mi, 580,367 sq km; **Land area:** 219,746 sq mi, 569,140 sq km. **Location:** E Africa, on coast of Indian O. **Neighbors:** Uganda on W, Tanzania on S, Somalia on E, Ethiopia on N, Sudan on NW. **Topography:** The northern three-fifths of Kenya is arid. To S, a low coastal area and a plateau varying 3,000-10,000 ft. The Great Rift Valley enters the country N-S, flanked by high mountains. **Capital:** Nairobi, 3,375,000. **Cities (urban aggl.):** Mombasa, 1,002,833.

Government: Type: Republic. **Head of state:** Pres. Mwai Kibaki; b. Nov. 15, 1931; in office: Dec. 30, 2002. **Head of gov.:** Prime Min. Raila Odinga; b. Jan. 7, 1945; in office: Apr. 17, 2008. **Local divisions:** 47 counties. **Defense budget:** $720 mil. **Active troops:** 24,120.

Economy: Industries: small-scale consumer goods (plastic, furniture, batteries, textiles, clothing, soap, cigarettes); agric. prods., horticulture; oil refining; aluminum, steel, lead; cement. **Chief crops:** tea, coffee, corn, wheat, sugarcane, fruits, vegetables. **Natural resources:** limestone, soda ash, salt, gems, fluorspar, zinc, diatomite, gypsum, wildlife, hydropower. **Arable land:** 9.5%. **Livestock:** cattle: 12.5 mil; chickens: 28.6 mil; goats: 13.9 mil; pigs: 334,689; sheep: 9.9 mil. **Fish catch:** 144,451 metric tons. **Electricity prod.:** 6.8 bil kWh. **Labor force:** agric. 75%, industry and services 25%.

Finance: Monetary unit: Shilling (KES) (Sept. 2011: 93.65 = $1 U.S.). **GDP:** $66 bil; **per capita GDP:** $1,600; **GDP growth:** 5%. **Imports:** $10.4 bil; India 12.5%, China 11.9%, UAE 9.1%, South Africa 8.1%, Saudi Arabia 6.4%, U.S. 6.1%, Japan 5%. **Exports:** $5.1 bil; UK 11.4%, Netherlands 9.9%, Uganda 9.2%, Tanzania 8.9%, U.S 6%, Egypt 4.3%. **Tourism:** $756 mil. **Budget:** $9.05 bil. **Total reserves less gold:** $4.3 bil. **Gold** 500 oz t. **CPI change:** 4%.

Transport: Railways: 1,284 mi. **Motor vehicles:** 11.5 vehicles per 1,000 pop. **Civil aviation:** 4.9 bil pass.-mi; 17 airports. **Chief ports:** Kisumu, Mombasa.

Communications: TV sets: 46 per 1,000 pop. **Radios:** 89 per 1,000 pop. **Telephone lines:** 1.1 per 100 pop. **Internet:** 21 users per 100 pop.

Health: Life expect.: 61.3 male; 64.2 female. **Births:** 33.7 (per 1,000 pop.). **Deaths:** 7.4 (per 1,000 pop.). **Natural inc.:** 2.63%. **Infant mortality:** 45.2 (per 1,000 live births). **HIV rate:** 6.3%.

Education: Compulsory: ages 6-13. **Literacy:** 87%.

Major intl. organizations: UN and all of its specialized agencies, AU, the Commonwealth, WTO.

Embassy: 2249 R St. NW 20008; 387-6101.

Website: www.primeminister.go.ke

Arab colonies exported spices and slaves from the Kenya coast as early as the 8th cent. Britain obtained control in the 19th cent. Kenya won independence Dec. 12, 1963, 4 years after the end of the violent Mau Mau uprising. Jomo Kenyatta, the country's leader since independence, died Aug. 22, 1978. He was succeeded by his vice president, Daniel arap Moi.

During the first half of the 1990s, Kenya suffered widespread unemployment and high inflation. Tribal clashes in the western provinces claimed thousands of lives and left tens of thousands homeless. Pres. Moi won a 3rd term in Dec. 1992 elections, which were marred by violence and fraud. He was reelected Dec. 29, 1997, in an election plagued by irregularities. A truck bomb explosion at the U.S. embassy in Nairobi, Aug. 7, 1998, killed more than 200 people and injured about 5,000. The U.S. blamed the attack and a near-simultaneous embassy bombing in Tanzania on al-Qaeda.

Constitutionally barred from seeking another term, Pres. Moi was succeeded Dec. 30, 2002, by Mwai Kibaki, the candidate of the opposition Democratic Party. After a disputed election Dec. 27, 2007, that drew criticism from European and Kenyan monitors, Kenya's Electoral Commission declared Kibaki the winner over challenger Raila Odinga. Weeks of factional violence followed, in which some 1,500 people died and 600,000 were displaced. Under a Feb. 28, 2008, power-sharing deal mediated by former UN Sec. Gen. Kofi Annan, Kibaki remained president and Odinga took the newly created post of prime minister.

A new constitution curtailing presidential powers, establishing a senate, and reforming regional government won approval in a referendum Aug. 4, 2010. More than 350,000 Somali refugees were living in Kenya as of Jan. 1, 2011. Drought and mismanagement led to severe food shortages during the year.

Kiribati
Republic of Kiribati

People: Population: 100,743. **Age distrib.:** <15: 33.9%; 65+: 3.7%. **Pop. density:** 321.7 per sq mi, 124.2 per sq km. **Urban:** 43.9%. **Ethnic groups:** Micronesian 99%. **Principal languages:** I-Kiribati, English (official). **Chief religions:** Roman Catholic 55%, Protestant 36%, Mormon 3%, Baha'i 2%, Seventh-Day Adventist 2%.

Geography: Total area: 313 sq mi, 811 sq km; **Land area:** 313 sq mi, 811 sq km. **Location:** 33 Micronesian islands (the Gilbert, Line, and Phoenix groups) in mid-Pacific scattered in a 2-mil sq mi chain around the point where the International Date Line formerly cut the Equator. In 1997 the Date Line was moved to follow Kiribati's E border. **Neighbors:** Nearest are Nauru to SW, Tuvalu and Tokelau Isls. to S. **Topography:** Except Banaba (Ocean) Isl., all are low-lying, with soil of coral sand and rock fragments, subject to erratic rainfall. **Capital:** Tarawa, 43,000.

Government: Type: Republic. **Head of state and gov.:** Pres. Anote Tong; b. June 11, 1952; in office: July 10, 2003. **Local divisions:** 3 units, 6 districts. **Defense budget/active troops:** NA.

Economy: Industries: fishing, handicrafts. **Chief crops:** copra, taro, breadfruit, sweet potatoes, vegetables. **Natural resources:** phosphate (production discontinued in 1979). **Arable land:** 2.5%. **Livestock:** chickens: 480,000; pigs: 12,600. **Fish catch:** 42,019 metric tons. **Electricity prod.:** 22 mil kWh. **Labor force:** agric. 2.7%, industry 32%, services 65.3%.

Finance: Monetary unit: Australia Dollar (AUD) (Sept. 2011: 0.95 = 1 U.S.). **GDP:** $618 mil; **per capita GDP:** $6,200; **GDP growth:** 1.8%. **Imports** (2004 est.): $62 mil; NA. **Exports** (2004 est.): $17 mil; NA. **Tourism:** NA. **Budget** (FY05): $59.7 mil. **Total reserves less gold:** NA. **CPI change:** NA.

Transport: Civil aviation: 4 airports. **Chief port:** Betio.

Communications: TV sets: 41 per 1,000 pop. **Radios:** 830 per 1,000 pop. **Telephone lines:** 4.1 per 100 pop. **Internet:** 9 users per 100 pop.

Health: Life expect.: 62.0 male; 66.9 female. **Births:** 22.7 per 1,000 pop.). **Deaths:** 7.4 (per 1,000 pop.). **Natural inc.:** 1.53%. **Infant mortality:** 38.9 (per 1,000 live births). **HIV rate:** NA.

Education: Compulsory: ages 6-15. **Literacy:** NA.

Major intl. organizations: UN (FAO, IBRD, ILO, IMF, WHO), the Commonwealth.

Honorary Consulate: 95 Nakolo Pl., Rm. 265, Honolulu, HI 96819; (808) 834-6775.

Website: www.parliament.gov.ki

A British protectorate since 1892, the Gilbert and Ellice Islands colony was completed with the inclusion of the Phoenix Islands, 1937. Tarawa Atoll was the scene of some of the bloodiest fighting in the Pacific during WWII.

Self-rule was granted 1971; the Ellice Islands separated from the colony in 1975 and became independent Tuvalu, 1978. Kiribati (pronounced *Kiribass*) independence was attained July 12, 1979. Under a treaty of friendship the U.S. relinquished its claims to several Line and Phoenix islands, including Christmas (Kiritimati), Canton, and Enderbury. Kiribati was admitted to the UN Sept. 14, 1999. Pres. Anote Tong won reelection Oct. 17, 2007.

Korea, North
Democratic People's Republic of Korea

People: Population: 24,457,492. **Age distrib.:** <15: 22.4%; 65+: 9.1%. **Pop. density:** 526.1 per sq mi, 203.1 per sq km. **Urban:** 60.2%. **Ethnic group:** Racially homogeneous; small Chinese community & few ethnic Japanese. **Principal language:** Korean. **Chief religions:** traditionally Buddhist & Confucianist, some Christian; autonomous religious activities almost nonexistent.

Geography: Total area: 46,540 sq mi, 120,538 sq km; **Land area:** 46,490 sq mi, 120,408 sq km. **Location:** In northern E Asia. **Neighbors:** China and Russia on N, S. Korea on S. **Topography:** Mountains and hills cover nearly all the country, with narrow valleys and small plains in between. N and E coasts are most rugged areas. **Capital:** P'yongyang, 2,828,000.

Government: Type: Communist state. **Head of state:** Kim Jong Il; b. Feb. 16, 1942; officially assumed post Oct. 8, 1997. **Head of**

gov.: Prem. Choe Yong Rim; b. Nov. 20, 1930; in office: June 7, 2010. **Local divisions:** 9 provinces, 4 special cities. **Defense budget:** NA. **Active troops:** 1,190,000.

Economy: Industries: military prods.; machine building, elec. power, chemicals; mining, metallurgy; textiles, food proc. **Chief crops:** rice, corn, potatoes, soybeans. **Natural resources:** coal, lead, tungsten, zinc, graphite, magnesite, iron ore, copper, gold, pyrites, salt, fluorspar, hydropower. **Arable land:** 22.0%. **Livestock:** cattle: 576,000; chickens: 13.9 mil; goats: 3.6 mil; pigs: 2.2 mil; sheep: 165,000. **Fish catch:** 713,350 metric tons. **Electricity prod.:** 22.5 bil kWh. **Labor force:** agric. 35%, industry and services 65%.

Finance: Monetary unit: Won (KPW) (Sept. 2011: 133.22 = $1 U.S.). **GDP** (2009 est.): $40 bil; **per capita GDP** (2009 est.): $1,800; **GDP growth** (2009 est.): –0.9%. **Imports** (2009): $3.1 bil; China 61%, South Korea 24%, Singapore 2%, India 2%. **Exports** (2009): $2 bil; South Korea 47%, China 40%, Hong Kong 2%. **Tourism:** NA. **Budget** (2007 est.): $3.3 bil. **Total reserves less gold:** NA. **CPI change:** NA.

Transport: Railways: 3,257 mi. **Civil aviation:** 25.5 mil pass.-mi; 37 airports. **Chief ports:** Chongjin, Haeju, Hungnam, Nampo, Senbong, Sonbong, Songnim, Wonsan.

Communications: TV sets: 172 per 1,000 pop. **Radios:** 157 per 1,000 pop. **Telephone lines:** 4.9 per 100 pop. **Internet:** NA.

Health: Life expect.: 65.0 male; 72.9 female. **Births:** 14.5 (per 1,000 pop.). **Deaths:** 9.1 (per 1,000 pop.). **Natural inc.:** 0.54%. **Infant mortality:** 27.1 (per 1,000 live births). **HIV rate:** NA.

Labor force: agric. 36%, industry & services 64%.

Education: Compulsory: ages 6-15. **Literacy:** 99.99%.

Major intl. organizations: UN (FAO, WHO).

Permanent UN mission: 820 Second Ave., 13th Fl., New York, NY 10017; (212) 972-3105.

Website: www.korea-dpr.com

The Democratic People's Republic of Korea was founded May 1, 1948, in the zone occupied by Russian troops after WWII. Its armies tried to conquer the south, 1950. After 3 years of fighting, with Chinese and U.S. intervention, a cease-fire was proclaimed.

For the next four decades, a hard-line Communist regime headed by Kim Il Sung kept tight control over the nation's political, economic, and cultural life. The nation used its abundant mineral and hydroelectric resources to develop its military strength and heavy industry. By the early 1990s, North Korea was widely believed to be developing nuclear weapons. The U.S. and North Korea signed an agreement, Oct. 21, 1994, providing for phased dismantling of North Korea's nuclear development program in return for U.S. energy aid and improved ties with the U.S.

Kim Il Sung died July 8, 1994. He was succeeded by his son, Kim Jong Il. Defections by high officials, a deteriorating economy, and severe food shortages plagued North Korea in the late 1990s. A first-ever summit conference in P'yongyang between North and South Korean leaders, June 13-15, 2000, marked an improvement in relations between the two nations. In a landmark summit, Sept. 2002, North Korea and Japan agreed to normalize relations.

Pres. George W. Bush, in a speech Jan. 31, 2002, included North Korea with Iraq and Iran as part of an "axis of evil." In Oct. 2002, North Korea admitted to pursuing a secret nuclear weapons program, in violation of past agreements. The U.S. insisted that North Korea end its nuclear weapons program, while P'yongyang demanded a non-aggression treaty and economic aid from the U.S. During 2003-09, as 6-nation talks sponsored by China sought to resolve the nuclear dispute, North Korea followed a zigzag course, alternately stopping and resuming its nuclear program in order to win further concessions from the U.S.

In Apr.-May 2009, North Korea suspended its participation in the 6-nation talks, expelled IAEA inspectors, tested multiple missiles, and exploded a nuclear device underground. The UN Security Council June 12 toughened sanctions on the North Korean regime. Tensions between North and South Korea increased after the sinking Mar. 26, 2010, of the South Korean warship *Cheonan* killed 46 of the 104 sailors on board; a South Korean panel including international investigators concluded May 20 that the *Cheonan* had been torpedoed by a North Korean submarine. Visits to P'yongyang by former presidents Bill Clinton, Aug. 2009, and Jimmy Carter, Aug. 2010, succeeded in gaining the release of several detained Americans. A North Korean artillery barrage killed 2 South Korean marines and 2 civilians on Yeonpyeong Isl. Nov. 23, 2010.

Korea, South
Republic of Korea

People: Population: 48,754,657. **Age distrib.:** <15: 15.7%; 65+: 11.4%. **Pop. density:** 1,302.9 per sq mi, 503 per sq km. **Urban:** 83%. **Ethnic group:** Homogeneous, except for some Chinese. **Principal languages:** Korean, English widely taught in school. **Chief religions:** Christian 26%, Buddhist 23%, none 49%.

Geography: Total area: 38,502 sq mi, 99,720 sq km; **Land area:** 37,421 sq mi, 96,920 sq km. **Location:** In northern E Asia.

Neighbors: North Korea on N. **Topography:** Mountainous, with a rugged E coast. W and S coasts are deeply indented, with many islands and harbors. **Capital:** Seoul, 9,778,000. **Cities (urban aggl.):** Busan, 3,425,291; Incheon, 2,582,967; Daegu, 2,458,372.

Government: Type: Republic. **Head of state:** Pres. Lee Myung Bak; b. Dec. 19, 1941; in office: Feb. 25, 2008. **Head of gov.:** Prime Min. Kim Hwang Sik; b. Aug. 9, 1948; in office: Oct. 1, 2010. **Local divisions:** 9 provinces, 7 special cities. **Defense budget:** $25.4 bil. **Active troops:** 655,000.

Economy: Industries: electronics, telecom., auto prod., chemicals, shipbuilding, steel. **Chief crops:** rice, root crops, barley, vegetables, fruits. **Natural resources:** coal, tungsten, graphite, molybdenum, lead, hydropower potential. **Arable land:** 16.4%. **Livestock:** cattle: 3.1 mil; chickens: 138.8 mil; goats: 260,000; pigs: 9.6 mil; sheep: 3,000. **Fish catch:** 3.2 mil metric tons. **Electricity prod.** (2009): 417.3 bil kWh. **Labor force:** agric. 7.3%, industry 24.3%, services 68.4%.

Finance: Monetary unit: Won (KRW) (Sept. 2011: 1,076.73 = $1 U.S.). **GDP:** $1.5 tril; **per capita GDP:** $30,000; **GDP growth:** 6.1%. **Imports:** $417.9 bil; China 16.8%, Japan 15.3%, U.S. 9%, Saudi Arabia 6.1%, Australia 4.6%. **Exports:** $466.3 bil; China 23.9%, U.S. 10.4%, Japan 6%, Hong Kong 5.4%. **Tourism:** $9.8 bil. **Budget:** $267.3 bil. **Total reserves less gold:** $291.5 bil. **Gold:** 464,160 oz t. **CPI change:** 2.9%.

Transport: Railways: 2,101 mi. **Motor vehicles:** 357.2 vehicles per 1,000 pop. **Civil aviation:** 51.1 bil pass.-mi; 72 airports. **Chief ports:** Busan, Incheon, Pohang, Ulsan.

Communications: TV sets: 424 per 1,000 pop. **Radios:** 1,037 per 1,000 pop. **Telephone lines:** 59.2 per 100 pop. **Internet:** 83.7 users per 100 pop.

Health: Life expect.: 75.8 male; 82.5 female. **Births:** 8.6 (per 1,000 pop.). **Deaths:** 6.3 (per 1,000 pop.). **Natural inc.:** 0.23%. **Infant mortality:** 4.2 (per 1,000 live births). **HIV rate:** <0.1%.

Education: Compulsory: ages 6-14. **Literacy:** NA.

Major intl. organizations: UN (FAO, IBRD, ILO, IMF, WHO), APEC, OECD, WTO.

Embassy: 2320 Massachusetts Ave. NW 20008; 939-5663.

Website: www.korea.net

Korea, once called the Hermit Kingdom, has a recorded history since the 1st cent. BCE. It was united in a kingdom under the Silla Dynasty, 668 CE. It was at times associated with the Chinese empire; the treaty that concluded the Sino-Japanese war of 1894-95 recognized Korea's complete independence. In 1910 Japan forcibly annexed Korea as Chosun.

At the Potsdam conference, July 1945, the 38th parallel was designated as the line dividing Soviet and U.S. occupation zones. Russian troops entered Korea Aug. 10, 1945; U.S. troops entered Sept. 8, 1945.

The South Koreans formed the Republic of Korea in May 1948 with Seoul as the capital. Dr. Syngman Rhee was chosen president. A separate, Communist regime was formed in the north; its army attacked the south in June 1950, initiating the Korean War. UN troops, under U.S. command, supported South Korea in the war, which ended in an armistice (July 1953) leaving Korea divided by a demilitarized zone (DMZ) along the 38th parallel.

Rhee's authoritarian rule became increasingly unpopular, and a movement spearheaded by college students forced his resignation Apr. 26, 1960. In an army coup May 16, 1961, Gen. Park Chung Hee became chairman of a ruling junta. He was elected president, 1963; a 1972 referendum allowed him to be reelected for an unlimited series of 6-year terms. Park was assassinated by the chief of the Korean CIA, Oct. 26, 1979.

In May 1980, Gen. Chun Doo Hwan, head of military intelligence, ordered the brutal suppression of pro-democracy demonstrations in Kwangju. On July 1, 1987, following weeks of antigovernment protests, some of them violent, Chun agreed to democratic reforms. In Dec., Roh Tae Woo, a longtime ally of Chun's, was elected president. In 1990, the nation's three largest political parties merged; some 100,000 students protested the merger as undemocratic.

Pres. Kim Young Sam took office in 1993. Convicted of mutiny, treason, and corruption, Chun was sentenced to death by a Seoul court, Aug. 26, 1996, for his role in the 1979 coup and 1980 Kwangju massacre; Roh received a 22½ year prison sentence. On Dec. 16, Chun's term was reduced to life in prison, and Roh's to 17 years.

The collapse in Jan. 1997 of the Hanbo steel firm triggered a series of corruption scandals. With currency and stock values plummeting, the nation averted default by agreeing, Dec. 4, on a $57 bil bailout from the IMF. Kim Dae Jung, a longtime dissident, won the presidential election Dec. 18. Chun and Roh were released and pardoned Dec. 22, 1997.

At an unprecedented summit meeting in P'yongyang, June 13-15, 2000, Pres. Kim Dae Jung and North Korean leader Kim Jong Il agreed to work for reconciliation and eventual reunification of their two countries. On Oct. 13, 2000, Kim Dae Jung was named the winner of the Nobel Peace Prize. Roh Moo Hyun won a presidential election Dec. 19, 2002.

A subway fire in Taegu, Feb. 18, 2003, killed 198 people; the arsonist was given a life term, and 8 subway officials charged with negligence also received prison sentences. Typhoon Maemi

battered Pusan and other areas Sept. 12-13, 2003, leaving about 130 people dead and causing at least $4.1 bil in damage.

The National Assembly, Mar. 12, 2004, impeached Pres. Roh Moo Hyun for violating political neutrality and urging voters to support the Uri Party in upcoming legislative elections; voters backed Roh Apr. 15 by electing a Uri majority, and the Constitutional Court May 14 restored Roh to office. The IAEA Sept. 2 said South Korea had acknowledged having secretly processed a small amount of uranium to near weapons-grade level in 2000, violating the Nuclear Non-Proliferation Treaty and a bilateral accord with N. Korea.

Ban Ki-Moon, South Korea's foreign minister in 2004-06, took office as UN secretary-general Jan. 1, 2007. Lee Myung Bak, a former construction executive and Seoul mayor nicknamed "The Bulldozer," won the presidential election Dec. 19. Former Pres. Roh Moo Hyun, under investigation for corruption, committed suicide May 23, 2009.

South Korea supplied a 3,600-member force to the U.S.-led coalition in Iraq; by the end of 2008, all Korean troops had been withdrawn. As of mid-2011, South Korea had 350 troops serving with coalition forces in Afghanistan, and the U.S. had about 28,500 troops stationed in South Korea.

Kosovo

Republic of Kosovo

People: Population: 1,825,632. **Age distrib.:** <15: 27.2%; 65+: 6.7%. **Pop. density:** 434.3 per sq mi, 167.7 per sq km. **Urban:** NA. **Ethnic groups:** Albanian 92%, other (incl. Serb, Bosniak, Gorani, Roma, Turk, Ashkali, Egyptian) 8%. **Principal languages:** Albanian, Serbian (both official); Bosnian; Turkish; Roma. **Chief religions:** Muslim, Serbian Orthodox, Roman Catholic.

Geography: Total area: 4,203 sq mi, 10,887 sq km. **Land area:** 4,203 sq mi, 10,887 sq km. **Location:** SE Europe between Serbia and Macedonia. **Neighbors:** Serbia on N, Montenegro on NW, Albania on SW, Macedonia on SE. **Topography:** Low flood basins surrounded by several high mountain ranges. **Capital:** Pristina.

Government: Type: Republic. **Head of state:** Pres. Atifete Jahjaga; b. Apr. 20, 1975; in office: Apr. 7, 2011. **Head of gov.:** Prime Min. Hashim Thaçi; b. Apr. 24, 1968; in office: Jan. 9, 2008. **Local divisions:** 30 municipalities. **Defense budget/active troops:** NA.

Economy: Industries: mineral mining, constr. materials, base metals, leather, machinery, appliances. **Chief crops:** wheat, corn, berries, potatoes, peppers. **Natural resources:** nickel, lead, zinc, magnesium, lignite, kaolin, chrome, bauxite. **Arable land:** NA. **Labor force:** agric. 23.6%, industry and services NA.

Finance: Monetary unit: Euro (EUR) (Sept. 2011: 0.71 = $1 U.S.). **GDP:** $12 bil; **per capita GDP:** $6,600; **GDP growth:** 4%. **Imports** (2007 est.): $2.6 bil; Germany 12.2%, Italy 9.5%, Hungary 6.8%, Slovenia 6.6%, Austria 4.9%, Romania 4%. **Exports** (2007 est.): $527 mil; Bosnia and Herzegovina 13.1%, Italy 10.9%, Germany 9.9%, Austria 5.4%, Slovenia 5.4%, Macedonia 5.1%, Russia 4.6%, Hungary 4.3%. **Tourism:** NA. **Budget:** $1.6 bil. **Total reserves less gold:** $846.4 mil. **CPI change:** NA.

Transport: Railways: 267 mi. **Civil aviation:** 4 airports.

Communications: Telephone lines: 4.9 per 100 pop. **Internet:** NA.

Health: Life expect.: 68.1 male; 72.3 female. **Births:** 18.3 (per 1,000 pop.). **Deaths:** 7.0 (per 1,000 pop.). **Natural inc.:** 1.13%. **Infant mortality:** 42.3 (per 1,000 live births). **HIV rate:** NA.

Education: Compulsory ages: NA. **Literacy:** NA.

Major intl. organizations: UN (IBRD, IMF).

Embassy: 900 19th St. NW, Ste. 400, 20006; 380-3581.

Website: www.rks-gov.net

Kosovo was part of the Roman and Byzantine empires before Serbs, a Slavic people, took control in the Middle Ages. After Ottoman Turks defeated Serb forces, 1389, Kosovo's population became predominantly Muslim and Kosovar (ethnic Albanian). Serbia regained control in the First Balkan War (1912-13). Kosovo entered the Kingdom of Serbs, Croats, and Slovenes as part of Serbia after World War I and became an autonomous province of Serbia, a constituent republic of Yugoslavia, after World War II.

Revoking provincial autonomy, Serbia began ruling Kosovo by force in 1989. Albanian secessionists proclaimed an independent Republic of Kosovo in July 1990. As Yugoslavia collapsed, the republics of Serbia (incl. Kosovo) and Montenegro proclaimed a new Federal Republic of Yugoslavia in 1992, under Pres. Slobodan Milosevic. Guerrilla attacks by the Kosovo Liberation Army in 1997 brought a ferocious counteroffensive by Serbian authorities.

Fearful that the Serbs were employing "ethnic cleansing" tactics, as they had in Bosnia, the U.S. and its NATO allies sought to pressure the Yugoslav government. When Milosevic refused to comply, NATO launched an air war against Yugoslavia, Mar.-June 1999; the Serbs retaliated by terrorizing the Kosovars and forcing hundreds of thousands to flee, mostly to Albania and Macedonia. A 50,000-member multinational force (KFOR) entered Kosovo in June, and most of the Kosovar refugees had returned by Sept. 1.

From June 1999, Kosovo was administered by a UN mission (UNMIK). When Kosovar and Serbian negotiators were unable to reach agreement on the final status of the region. Kosovo unilaterally declared independence, Feb. 17, 2008. The U.S. and most European allies immediately recognized the new country, but Serbia and Russia refused. In a nonbinding ruling, the World Court held July 22, 2010, that Kosovo's independence declaration was legal. As of Aug. 2011, KFOR had about 5,900 troops in Kosovo.

Kuwait
State of Kuwait

People: Population: 2,595,628. **Age distrib.:** <15: 25.8%; 65+: 2%. **Pop. density:** 377.3 per sq mi, 145.7 per sq km. **Urban:** 98.4%. **Ethnic groups:** Kuwaiti 45%, other Arab 35%, South Asian 9%, Iranian 4%. **Principal languages:** Arabic (official), English widely spoken. **Chief religions:** Muslim (official; Sunni 70%, Shi'a 30%) 85%, other (incl. Christian, Hindu, Parsi) 15%.

Geography: Total area: 6,880 sq mi, 17,818 sq km; **Land area:** 6,880 sq mi, 17,818 sq km. **Location:** In Middle East, at N end of Persian Gulf. **Neighbors:** Iraq on N, Saudi Arabia on S. **Topography:** Flat, very dry, and extremely hot. **Capital:** Kuwait City, 2,230,000.

Government: Type: Constitutional monarchy. **Head of state:** Emir Sheikh Sabah al-Ahmad al-Jabir as-Sabah; b. June 6, 1929; in office: Jan. 29, 2006. **Head of gov.:** Prime Min. Sheikh Nasser al-Muhammad al-Ahmad as-Sabah; b. 1940; in office: Feb. 7, 2006. **Local divisions:** 5 governorates. **Defense budget:** $3.91 bil. **Active troops:** 15,500.

Economy: Industries: petroleum, petrochemicals, cement, shipbuilding and repair, water desalination, food proc., constr. materials. **Chief crops:** NA. **Natural resources:** petroleum, fish, shrimp, nat. gas. **Crude oil reserves:** 104 bil bbls (incl. half of Neutral Zone reserves). **Arable land:** 0.6%. **Livestock:** cattle: 31,500; chickens: 33.5 mil; goats: 145,000; sheep: 900,000. **Fish catch:** 4,733 metric tons. **Electricity prod.** (2009): 49.8 bil kWh. **Labor force:** NA.

Finance: Monetary unit: Dinar (KWD) (Sept. 2011: 0.27 = $1 U.S.). **GDP:** $136.5 bil; **per capita GDP:** $48,900; **GDP growth:** 2%. **Imports:** $20.4 bil; U.S. 11.2%, China 9%, Germany 7.8%, Japan 7.2%, Saudi Arabia 6.3%, Italy 5%, France 4.8%, South Korea 4.3%, India 4.2%, UK 4%. **Exports:** $65 bil; Japan 17.2%, South Korea 15.3%, India 14.4%, U.S. 7.6%, China 6.7%, Singapore 5.3%. **Tourism:** $227 mil. **Budget:** $38.1 bil. **Total reserves less gold:** $21.2 bil. **Gold:** 2.5 mil oz t. **CPI change:** 4%.

Transport: Motor vehicles: 466.9 vehicles per 1,000 pop. **Civil aviation:** 4.8 bil pass.-mi; 4 airports. **Chief ports:** Ash Shu'aybah, Ash Shuwaykh, Az Zawr, Mina' al Ahmadi.

Communications: TV sets: 399 per 1,000 pop. **Radios:** 572 per 1,000 pop. **Telephone lines:** 20.7 per 100 pop. **Internet:** 38.3 users per 100 pop.

Health: Life expect.: 76.0 male; 78.3 female. **Births:** 21.3 (per 1,000 pop.). **Deaths:** 2.1 (per 1,000 pop.). **Natural inc.:** 1.92%. **Infant mortality:** 8.1 (per 1,000 live births). **HIV rate:** NA.

Education: Compulsory: ages 6-14. **Literacy:** 93.9%.

Major intl. organizations: UN (FAO, IBRD, ILO, IMF, WHO), AL, OPEC, WTO.

Embassy: 2940 Tilden St. NW 20008; 966-0702.

Website: www.da.gov.kw

Kuwait is ruled by the Sabah dynasty, founded 1759. Britain ran foreign relations and defense from 1899 until independence in 1961. Nearly half the population is non-Kuwaiti, including many Palestinians, and cannot vote.

Oil is the fiscal mainstay, providing most of Kuwait's income. Oil pays for free medical care, education, and social security. There are no taxes, except customs duties.

Kuwait was attacked and overrun by Iraqi forces Aug. 2, 1990. In Operation Desert Storm a U.S.-led coalition, with authorization from the UN Security Council, began bombing Iraq and Iraqi forces in Kuwait, Jan. 1991, then launched a ground assault Feb. 23. By Feb. 27, Iraqi forces were routed and Kuwait liberated. Northern Kuwait was used by U.S. and British troops as a staging area prior to the Mar. 2003 invasion of Iraq.

Political rights were extended to women, May 16, 2005; the first female cabinet member was appointed June 12. Kuwait enacted a $5.2 bil program Mar. 26, 2009, to bail out banks and investment companies battered by the global financial crisis.

Kyrgyzstan
Kyrgyz Republic

People: Population: 5,587,443. **Age distrib.:** <15: 29.3%; 65+: 5.3%. **Pop. density:** 75.5 per sq mi, 29.1 per sq km. **Urban:** 34.5%. **Ethnic groups:** Kyrgyz 65%, Uzbek 14%, Russian 13%, Dungan 1%, Ukrainian 1%, Uighur 1%. **Principal languages:** Kyrgyz (official), Uzbek, Russian (official), Dungun. **Chief religions:** Muslim 75%, Russian Orthodox 20%.

Geography: Total area: 77,202 sq mi, 199,951 sq km; **Land area:** 74,055 sq mi, 191,801 sq km. **Location:** In Central Asia. **Neighbors:** Kazakhstan on N, China on E, Uzbekistan on W, Tajikistan on S. **Topography:** Landlocked country nearly covered by Tien Shan and Pamir Mts.; avg. elevation 9,020 ft. A large lake, Issyk-Kul, in NE is 1 mi above sea level. **Capital:** Bishkek, 854,000.

Government: Type: Parliamentary republic. **Head of state:** Pres. Roza Otunbayeva; b. Aug. 23, 1950; in office: July 3, 2010 (de facto from Apr. 7). **Head of gov.:** Prime Min. Almazbek Atambayev; b. Sept. 17, 1956; in office: Dec. 17, 2010. **Local divisions:** 7 oblasts and Bishkek. **Defense budget:** $96 mil. **Active troops:** 10,900.

Economy: Industries: small machinery, textiles, food proc., cement, shoes, sawn logs, refrigerators, furniture, elec. motors. **Chief crops:** tobacco, cotton, potatoes, vegetables, grapes, fruits and berries. **Natural resources:** hydropower, gold, rare earth metals, coal, oil, nat. gas, nepheline, mercury, bismuth, lead, zinc. **Crude oil reserves:** 40 mil bbls. **Arable land:** 6.7%. **Livestock:** cattle: 1.2 mil; chickens: 4 mil; goats: 896,864; pigs: 63,328; sheep: 3.6 mil. **Fish catch:** 143 metric tons. **Electricity prod.:** 11.7 bil kWh. **Labor force:** agric. 48%, industry 12.5%, services 39.5%.

Finance: Monetary unit: Som (KGS) (Sept. 2011: 45.02 = $1 U.S.). **GDP:** $12 bil; **per capita GDP:** $2,200; **GDP growth:** −1.4%. **Imports:** $3.1 bil; China 70.8%, Russia 12.3%, Kazakhstan 4.1%. **Exports:** $1.7 bil; Russia 34.5%, Uzbekistan 21.2%, Kazakhstan 16.8%, UAE 5%, China 4.6%, Afghanistan 4.2%. **Tourism:** $284 mil. **Budget:** $1.5 bil. **Total reserves less gold:** $1.6 bil. **Gold:** 83,090 oz t. **CPI change:** 8%.

Transport: Railways: 292 mi. **Civil aviation:** 361.6 mil pass.-mi; 18 airports. **Chief port:** Balykchy.

Communications: TV sets: 224 per 1,000 pop. **Radios:** 110 per 1,000 pop. **Telephone lines:** 9.4 per 100 pop. **Daily newspaper circ.:** 0.96 per 1,000 pop. **Internet:** 20 users per 100 pop.

Health: Life expect.: 66.0 male; 74.2 female. **Births:** 23.7 (per 1,000 pop.). **Deaths:** 6.8 (per 1,000 pop.). **Natural inc.:** 1.69%. **Infant mortality:** 29.3 (per 1,000 live births). **HIV rate:** 0.3%.

Education: Compulsory: ages 7-15. **Literacy:** 99.2%.

Major intl. organizations: UN (FAO, IBRD, ILO, WHO), CIS, OSCE, WTO.

Embassy: 2360 Massachusetts Ave. NW 20008; 338-5141.

Website: www.president.kg

The region was inhabited around the 13th cent. by the Kyrgyz. It was annexed to Russia, 1864, and became a constituent republic of the USSR in 1936. Kyrgyzstan declared independence Aug. 31, 1991. It became an independent state when the USSR disbanded Dec. 26, 1991.

In power since 1990, Pres. Askar Akayev won a third 5-year term in the Oct. 29, 2000, election. Fraud by Akayev loyalists in parliamentary elections Feb.-Mar. 2005 sparked protests. Akayev fled the country, Mar. 24, and formally resigned, Apr. 4. His interim successor, former Prime Min. Kurmanbek Bakiyev, a leader of the "tulip revolution," won by a landslide in the July 10 presidential vote.

Official results of the July 23, 2009, election gave the increasingly autocratic Pres. Bakiyev 76% of the vote, but international and local monitors reported numerous irregularities. He was ousted by opposition parties Apr. 7, 2010, after clashes between protesters and government security forces left at least 85 people dead; an interim government was then led by former Foreign Min. Roza Otunbayeva. Fighting in mid-June between majority Kyrgyz and minority Uzbeks in the southern cities of Osh and Jalalabad claimed up to 2,000 lives. A June 27, 2010, referendum on a new constitution received overwhelming approval, and parliamentary elections Oct. 10, 2010, earned praise from international observers. A presidential election was scheduled for Oct. 30, 2011.

Laos
Lao People's Democratic Republic

People: Population: 6,477,211. **Age distrib.:** <15: 36.7%; 65+: 3.7%. **Pop. density:** 72.7 per sq mi, 28.1 per sq km. **Urban:** 33.2%. **Ethnic groups:** Lao 55%, Khmou 11%, Hmong 8%, other (100+ minor ethnic groups) 26%. **Principal languages:** Lao (official), French, English, various ethnic languages. **Chief religions:** Buddhist 67%, Christian 2%.

Geography: Total area: 91,429 sq mi, 236,800 sq km; **Land area:** 89,112 sq mi, 230,800 sq km. **Location:** In Indochina Peninsula in SE Asia. **Neighbors:** Myanmar, China on N; Vietnam on E; Cambodia on S; Thailand on W. **Topography:** Landlocked, dominated by jungle. High mountains along E border are source of the E-W rivers slicing across the country to the Mekong R., which defines most of W border. **Capital:** Vientiane (Viangchan), 799,000.

Government: Type: Communist. **Head of state:** Pres. Choummaly Sayasone; b. Mar. 6, 1936; in office: June 8, 2006. **Head of gov.:** Prime Min. Thongsing Thammavong; b. 1944; in office: Dec. 23, 2010. **Local divisions:** 16 provinces, 1 municipality, 1 special zone. **Defense budget** (2008): $17 mil. **Active troops:** 29,100.

Economy: Industries: mining, timber, elec. power, agric. proc., constr., garments, cement, tourism. **Chief crops:** sweet potatoes, vegetables, corn, coffee, sugarcane, tobacco, cotton, tea, peanuts, rice. **Natural resources:** timber, hydropower, gypsum, tin, gold, gems. **Arable land:** 5.9%. **Livestock:** cattle: 1.4 mil; chickens: 22.5 mil; goats: 367,450; pigs: 2.9 mil. **Fish catch:** 105,001 metric tons. **Electricity prod:** 4 bil kWh. **Labor force:** agric. 75.1%, industry and services NA.

Finance: Monetary unit: Kip (LAK) (Sept. 2011: 7,988.40 = $1 U.S.). **GDP:** $15.7 bil; **per capita GDP:** $2,500; **GDP growth:** 7.7%. **Imports:** $1.5 bil; Thailand 62.2%, China 14.3%, Vietnam 6.4%. **Exports:** $2 bil; Thailand 27.9%, China 20.1%, Vietnam 14.9%, UK

4.1%. Tourism: $268 mil. **Budget:** $1.3 bil. **Total reserves less gold:** $703.4 mil. **Gold:** 285,429 oz t. **CPI change:** 6%.
Transport: Civil aviation: 82.6 mil pass.-mi; 9 airports.
Communications: TV sets: 57 per 1,000 pop. **Radios:** 148 per 1,000 pop. **Telephone lines:** 1.7 per 100 pop. **Daily newspaper circ.:** 2.6 per 1,000 pop. **Internet:** 7 users per 100 pop.
Health: Life expect.: 60.5 male; 64.4 female. **Births:** 26.1 (per 1,000 pop.). **Deaths:** 8.1 (per 1,000 pop.). **Natural inc.:** 1.80%. **Infant mortality:** 59.5 (per 1,000 live births). **HIV rate:** 0.2%.
Education: Compulsory: ages 6-10. **Literacy:** 72.7%.
Major intl. organizations: UN (FAO, IBRD, ILO, IMF, WHO), ASEAN, WTO (observer).
Embassy: 2222 S St. NW 20008; 332-6416.
Website: www.laopdr.gov.la

Laos became a French protectorate in 1893, but regained independence as a constitutional monarchy July 19, 1949.

Conflicts among neutralist, Communist, and conservative factions created a chaotic political situation. Armed conflict increased after 1960.

The three factions formed a coalition government in June 1962, with neutralist Prince Souvanna Phouma as premier. A 14-nation conference in Geneva signed agreements, 1962, guaranteeing neutrality and independence. By 1964 the Pathet Lao had withdrawn from the coalition, and, with aid from North Vietnamese troops, renewed sporadic attacks. U.S. planes bombed the Ho Chi Minh trail, a supply line from North Vietnam to Communist forces in Laos and South Vietnam.

In 1970 the U.S. stepped up air support and military aid. After Pathet Lao military gains, Souvanna Phouma in May 1975 ordered government troops to cease fighting; the Pathet Lao took control. The Lao People's Democratic Republic was proclaimed Dec. 3, 1975.

From the mid-1970s through the 1980s, Laos relied on Vietnam for military and financial aid. After easing its finance laws in 1988, Laos attracted substantial foreign investment from Thailand, China, Vietnam, the U.S., and other nations. Laos was admitted to ASEAN on July 23, 1997. The U.S. Congress, Nov. 19, 2004, approved normalization of trade with Laos. To spur further investment, Laos opened its first stock exchange Jan. 11, 2011, in Vientiane.

Latvia
Republic of Latvia

People: Population: 2,204,708. **Age distrib.:** <15: 13.5%; 65+: 16.9%. **Pop. density:** 91.7 per sq mi, 35.4 per sq km. **Urban:** 67.7%. **Ethnic groups:** Latvian 59%, Russian 28%, Belarusian 4%, Ukrainian 3%, Polish 2%, Lithuanian 1%. **Principal languages:** Latvian (official), Russian, Lithuanian. **Chief religions:** Lutheran 20%, Orthodox 15%, other Christian 1%.
Geography: Total area: 24,938 sq mi, 64,589 sq km; **Land area:** 24,034 sq mi, 62,249 sq km. **Location:** E Europe, on Baltic Sea. **Neighbors:** Estonia on N; Lithuania, Belarus on S; Russia on E. **Topography:** Lowland with numerous lakes, marshes, and peat bogs. Principal river, W. Dvina (Daugava), rises in Russia. Glacial hills in E. **Capital:** Riga, 711,000.
Government: Type: Republic. **Head of state:** Pres. Andris Berzins; b. Dec. 10, 1944; in office: July 8, 2011. **Head of gov.:** Prime Min. Valdis Dombrovskis; b. Aug. 5, 1971; in office: Mar. 12, 2009. **Local divisions:** 26 counties, 7 municipalities. **Defense budget:** $250 mil. **Active troops:** 5,745.
Economy: Industries: processed foods, processed wood prods., textiles, processed metals, pharmaceuticals, railroad cars, synthetic fibers, electronics. **Chief crops:** grain, rapeseed, potatoes, vegetables. **Natural resources:** peat, limestone, dolomite, amber, hydropower, timber. **Arable land:** 18.8%. **Livestock:** cattle: 380,200; chickens: 4 mil; goats: 12,900; pigs: 383,700; sheep: 67,100. **Fish catch:** 163,730 metric tons. **Electricity prod.:** 5.1 bil kWh. **Labor force:** agric. 12.1%, industry 25.8%, services 61.8%.
Finance: Monetary unit: Lat (LVL) (Sept. 2011: 0.51 = $1 U.S.). **GDP:** $32.5 bil; **per capita GDP:** $14,700; **GDP growth:** –0.3%. **Imports:** $9.2 bil; Lithuania 16.4%, Germany 11.3%, Russia 10.6%, Poland 8.1%, Estonia 7.8%. **Exports:** $7.9 bil; Lithuania 15.2%, Estonia 13.7%, Russia 13.1%, Germany 8.2%, Sweden 5.7%. **Tourism:** $640 mil. **Budget:** $9.9 bil. **Total reserves less gold:** $7.3 bil. **Gold:** 248,700 oz t. **CPI change:** –1.1%.
Transport: Railways: 1,391 mi. **Motor vehicles:** 463.5 vehicles per 1,000 pop. **Civil aviation:** 904.7 mil pass.-mi; 19 airports. **Chief ports:** Riga, Ventspils.
Communications: TV sets: 855 per 1,000 pop. **Radios:** 700 per 1,000 pop. **Telephone lines:** 23.6 per 100 pop. **Daily newspaper circ.:** 154.1 per 1,000 pop. **Internet:** 68.4 users per 100 pop.
Health: Life expect.: 67.6 male; 78.1 female. **Births:** 10.0 (per 1,000 pop.). **Deaths:** 13.6 (per 1,000 pop.). **Natural inc.:** –0.36%. **Infant mortality:** 8.4 (per 1,000 live births). **HIV rate:** 0.7%.
Education: Compulsory: ages 7-15. **Literacy:** 99.8%.
Major intl. organizations: UN (FAO, IBRD, ILO, IMF, WHO), EU, NATO, OSCE, WTO.
Embassy: 2306 Massachusetts Ave. NW 20008; 328-2840.
Website: www.li.lv

Prior to 1918, Latvia was occupied by the Russians and Germans. It was an independent republic, 1918-39. The Aug. 1939

Soviet-German agreement assigned Latvia to the Soviet sphere of influence. It was officially absorbed by the USSR on Aug. 5, 1940. It was overrun by the German army in 1941, but retaken in 1945.

During an abortive Soviet coup, Latvia declared independence, Aug. 21, 1991. The last Russian troops in Latvia withdrew by Aug. 31, 1994. Responding to international pressure, Latvian voters on Oct. 3, 1998, eased citizenship laws that had discriminated against some 500,000 ethnic Russians. Latvia joined the EU and NATO in 2004.

Hit hard by recession, Latvia reached agreement Dec. 2008 on a $10.4 bil emergency loan from the EU, IMF, World Bank, and Nordic countries. Angered by the prolonged economic downturn and by the growing influence of wealthy oligarchs over Latvian politics, voters in a July 23, 2011, referendum approved a proposal to dissolve parliament, and new elections were held Sept. 17.

Lebanon
Lebanese Republic

People: Population: 4,143,101. **Age distrib.:** <15: 23%; 65+: 9%. **Pop. density:** 1,048.9 per sq mi, 405 per sq km. **Urban:** 87.2%. **Ethnic groups:** Arab 95%, Armenian 4%; many Christian Lebanese do not identify as Arab but prefer to be called Phoenician. **Principal languages:** Arabic (official), French, English, Armenian. **Chief religions:** Muslim 60%, Christian 39%.
Geography: Total area: 4,015 sq mi, 10,400 sq km; **Land area:** 3,950 sq mi, 10,230 sq km. **Location:** In Middle East, on E end of Mediterranean Sea. **Neighbors:** Syria on E, Israel on S. **Topography:** There is a narrow coastal strip, and 2 mountain ranges running N-S enclosing the fertile Beqaa Valley. The Litani R. runs S through the valley, turning W to empty into Mediterranean. **Capital:** Beirut, 1,909,000.
Government: Type: Republic. **Head of state:** Pres. Michel Suleiman; b. Nov. 21, 1948; in office: May 25, 2008. **Head of gov.:** Prime Min. Najib Mikati; b. Nov. 24, 1955; in office: June 13, 2011. **Local divisions:** 6 governorates. **Defense budget:** $1.16 bil. **Active troops:** 59,100.
Economy: Industries: banking, tourism, food proc., wine, jewelry, cement, textiles, mineral and chem. prods. **Chief crops:** citrus, grapes, tomatoes, apples, vegetables, potatoes, olives, tobacco. **Natural resources:** limestone, iron ore, salt, water (surplus in a water-deficit region). **Arable land:** 14.2%. **Livestock:** cattle: 77,000; chickens: 37.5 mil; goats: 450,000; pigs: 9,500; sheep: 330,000. **Fish catch:** 4,614 metric tons. **Electricity prod.:** 10 bil kWh. **Labor force:** NA.
Finance: Monetary unit: Pound (LBP) (Sept. 2011: 1,506.50 = $1 U.S.). **GDP:** $59.4 bil; **per capita GDP:** $14,400; **GDP growth:** 7.5%. **Imports:** $18 bil; France 10.6%, U.S. 9.2%, Syria 9.2%, Italy 6.8%, China 6.8%, Germany 5.4%, Ukraine 4.4%, Turkey 4.4%. **Exports:** $5.2 bil; Syria 25.8%, UAE 14.3%, Saudi Arabia 6.8%, Switzerland 5.6%, Qatar 4.4%. **Tourism:** $6.8 bil. **Budget:** $10.95 bil. **Total reserves less gold:** $31.5 bil. **Gold:** 9.2 mil oz t. **CPI change:** 4%.
Transport: Railways: 249 mi. **Motor vehicles:** 131.5 vehicles per 1,000 pop. **Civil aviation:** 1.7 bil pass.-mi; 5 airports. **Chief ports:** Beirut, Tripoli.
Communications: TV sets: 387 per 1,000 pop. **Radios:** 75 per 1,000 pop. **Telephone lines:** 21 per 100 pop. **Daily newspaper circ.:** 54.2 per 1,000 pop. **Internet:** 31 users per 100 pop.
Health: Life expect.: 73.5 male; 76.6 female. **Births:** 15.0 (per 1,000 pop.). **Deaths:** 6.5 (per 1,000 pop.). **Natural inc.:** 0.85%. **Infant mortality:** 15.9 (per 1,000 live births). **HIV rate:** 0.1%.
Education: Compulsory: ages 6-14. **Literacy:** 89.6%.
Major intl. organizations: UN (FAO, IBRD, ILO, IMF, WHO), AL, WTO (observer).
Embassy: 2560 28th St. NW 20008; 939-6300.
Website: www.presidency.gov.lb

Formed from five former Turkish Empire districts, Lebanon became an independent state Sept. 1, 1920, administered under French mandate 1920-41. French troops withdrew in 1946.

Under the 1943 National Covenant, all public positions were divided among the various religious communities, with Christians in the majority. By the 1970s, Muslims became the majority and demanded a larger political and economic role.

U.S. Marines intervened, May-Oct. 1958, during a Syrian-aided revolt. Continued raids against Israeli civilians, 1970-75, brought Israeli retaliation in southern Lebanon.

An estimated 60,000 were killed and billions of dollars in damage inflicted in a 1975-76 civil war. Palestinian units and leftist Muslims fought against Maronite militia (the Phalange) and other Christians. Several Arab countries provided political and arms support to the various factions, while Israel aided Christian forces. Up to 15,000 Syrian troops intervened in 1976 to fight Palestinian groups. A cease-fire was mainly policed by Syria.

Israeli forces invaded Lebanon June 6, 1982, attacking strongholds of the Palestine Liberation Organization (PLO). Israeli and Syrian forces engaged in the Bekaa Valley. On Aug. 21, the PLO evacuated west Beirut after massive Israeli bombings there. Israeli troops entered west Beirut following the Sept. 14 assassination of newly elected Lebanese Pres. Bashir Gemayel. On Sept. 16, Lebanese Christian troops entered the Sabra and Shatila refugee camps and massacred hundreds of Palestinian civilians. An agreement May 17, 1983, between Lebanon, Israel, and the U.S. (but not Syria) provided for the withdrawal of Israeli troops; at least 30,000 Syrian troops remained in Lebanon, and Israel held onto a "security zone" in the south.

In 1983, terrorist bombings became a way of life in Beirut as some 50 people were killed in an explosion at the U.S. Embassy, Apr. 18; 241 U.S. service members and 58 French soldiers died in separate Islamist suicide attacks, Oct. 23. The 1980s also witnessed kidnappings of U.S., British, French, and Soviet citizens by Islamic militants. All hostages were released by 1992.

A treaty signed May 22, 1991, between Lebanon and Syria recognized Lebanon as a separate state for the first time since the two countries gained independence in 1943.

Israeli forces conducted air raids and artillery strikes against guerrilla bases and villages in southern Lebanon, causing over 200,000 to flee their homes July 25-29, 1993. Some 500,000 civilians fled their homes in Apr. 1996 when Israel again struck suspected guerrilla bases in the south. The economy revived in the 1990s, but Syria continued to dominate Lebanon's political affairs. Israel withdrew virtually all its troops from S Lebanon by May 24, 2000, leaving Hezbollah, an Iranian-backed guerrilla group, in control of much of the region.

Rafik al-Hariri, a former prime minister (1992-98, 2000-04), was killed by a truck bomb, Feb. 14, 2005. Many Lebanese blamed Syria, which denied involvement. As anti-Syrian protests mounted, Syria pulled nearly all its troops out of Lebanon, although some intelligence agents may have remained. An anti-Syrian bloc won parliamentary elections held in May and June. A new cabinet, installed July 19, was headed by Fouad Siniora, a friend and aide to Hariri, and included a Hezbollah member.

A rocket attack and border raid by Hezbollah, July 12, 2006, in which 3 Israeli soldiers were killed and 2 captured, triggered a massive escalation of hostilities. Hezbollah, led by Sheikh Hassan Nasrallah, bombarded northern Israel with nearly 4,000 rockets, while Israeli air and ground forces assaulted suspected Hezbollah strongholds in southern Lebanon and southern Beirut. By Aug. 14, 2006, when a UN-sponsored cease-fire took hold, the war dead included nearly 1,150 Lebanese. To enforce the truce, thousands of Lebanese govt. troops began moving into southern Lebanon, and expansion of the small UN force already in Lebanon (UNIFIL) was approved.

Industry Min. Pierre Gemayel, a prominent Christian and critic of Syria, was assassinated Nov. 21, 2006. At an international conference in Paris, Jan. 25, 2007, donor countries pledged more than $7.6 bil in reconstruction aid. After more than three months of fighting in which over 400 people died, Lebanese forces Sept. 2 defeated Islamic militants at the Nahr al-Bared Palestinian refugee camp north of Tripoli. A power-sharing accord May 21, 2008, between the Siniora government and Hezbollah eased factional violence and paved the way for Army Chief Gen. Michel Suleiman to become president, ending an 18-month stalemate.

A pro-Western coalition, the March 14 Movement, led by Saad Hariri (son of the slain former prime minister), won a parliamentary majority in elections June 7, 2009. A 5-month impasse ended with the installation of Prime Min. Hariri and his cabinet (including Hezbollah) Nov. 9, 2009. After that government collapsed in Jan. 2011, a 5-month deadlock culminated in the installation June 13 of a cabinet dominated by Hezbollah and headed by Prime Min. Najib Mikati, a telecommunications billionaire. UNIFIL had about 12,350 uniformed personnel in Lebanon in mid-2011.

Lesotho
Kingdom of Lesotho

People: Population: 1,924,886. **Age distrib.:** <15: 33.5%; 65+: 5.4%. **Pop. density:** 164.2 per sq mi, 63.4 per sq km. **Urban:** 26.9%. **Ethnic groups:** Sotho 99.7%. **Principal languages:** Sesotho, English (both official); Zulu; Xhosa. **Chief religions:** Christian 80%, indigenous beliefs 20%.

Geography: Total area: 11,720 sq mi, 30,355 sq km; **Land area:** 11,720 sq mi, 30,355 sq km. **Location:** In southern Africa. **Neighbors:** Completely surrounded by Republic of South Africa. **Topography:** Landlocked and mountainous, altitudes from 5,000 to 11,000 ft. **Capital:** Maseru, 220,000.

Government: Type: Modified constitutional monarchy. **Head of state:** King Letsie III; b. July 17, 1963; in office: Feb. 7, 1996. **Head of gov.:** Prime Min. Pakalitha Mosisili; b. Mar. 14, 1945; in office: May 29, 1998. **Local divisions:** 10 districts. **Defense budget** (2008): $36 mil. **Active troops:** 2,000.

Economy: Industries: food, beverages, textiles, apparel assembly, handicrafts. **Chief crops:** corn, wheat, pulses, sorghum, barley. **Natural resources:** water, diamonds, sand, clay, building stone. **Arable land:** 11.0%. **Livestock:** cattle: 616,496; chickens: 716,000; goats: 1.01 mil; pigs: 83,705; sheep: 1.4 mil. **Fish catch:** 153 metric tons. **Electricity prod:** 200 mil kWh. **Labor force:** agric. 86% (subsistence); approx. 35% of active male wage earners work in South Africa; industry and services 14%.

Finance: Monetary unit: Loti (LSL) (Sept. 2011: 7.20 = $1 U.S.). **GDP:** $3.3 bil; **per capita GDP:** $1,700; **GDP growth:** 2.4%. **Imports:** $1.8 bil; NA. **Exports:** $985 mil; NA. **Tourism:** NA. **Budget:** $1.2 bil. **Total reserves less gold** (2006): $658.4 mil. **CPI change:** 3.6%.

Transport: Civil aviation: 3 airports.
Communications: TV sets: 44 per 1,000 pop. **Radios:** 121 per 1,000 pop. **Telephone lines:** 1.8 per 100 pop. **Internet:** 3.9 users per 100 pop.
Health: Life expect.: 51.5 male; 51.8 female. **Births:** 26.9 (per 1,000 pop.). **Deaths:** 15.2 (per 1,000 pop.). **Natural inc.:** 1.17%. **Infant mortality:** 55.0 (per 1,000 live births). **HIV rate:** 23.6%.
Education: Compulsory: ages 6-12. **Literacy:** 89.7%.
Major intl. organizations: UN (FAO, IBRD, ILO, IMF, WHO), AU, the Commonwealth, WTO.
Embassy: 2511 Massachusetts Ave. NW 20008; 797-5533.
Website: www.ads.ls

Lesotho (once called Basutoland) became a British protectorate in 1868 when Chief Moshesh sought protection against the Boers. Independence came Oct. 4, 1966. Most of Lesotho's GNP is provided by citizens working in South Africa. Livestock raising is a major industry; diamonds are the chief export.

In Mar. 1990, King Moshoeshoe was exiled by the military government. Letsie III became king Nov. 12. In Mar. 1993, Ntsu Mokhehle, a civilian, was elected prime minister, ending 23 years of military rule. After a series of violent disturbances, the king dismissed the Mokhehle government Aug. 17, 1994; constitutional rule was restored Sept. 14.

Letsie abdicated and Moshoeshoe was reinstated Jan. 25, 1995. Moshoeshoe died in an automobile accident, Jan. 15, 1996. Letsie was reinstated Feb. 7, 1996. South Africa and Botswana sent troops Sept. 22, 1998, to help suppress violent antigovernment protests.

According to UN estimates, more than 20% of the population between the ages of 15 and 49 has HIV/AIDS. Cultivation of marijuana for smuggling to South Africa is a significant source of income.

Liberia
Republic of Liberia

People: Population: 3,786,764. **Age distrib.:** <15: 44.3%; 65+: 2.9%. **Pop. density:** 101.8 per sq mi, 39.3 per sq km. **Urban:** 47.8%. **Ethnic groups:** Kpelle 20%, Bassa 13%, Gio 8%, Mano 8%, Kru 6%, Lorma 5%, Kissi 5%, Gola 4%. **Principal languages:** English (official), about 20 ethnic languages. **Chief religions:** Christian 86%, Muslim 12%, none 1%.

Geography: Total area: 43,000 sq mi, 111,369 sq km; **Land area:** 37,189 sq mi, 96,320 sq km. **Location:** On SW coast of W Africa. **Neighbors:** Sierra Leone on W, Guinea on N, Côte d'Ivoire on E. **Topography:** Marshy Atlantic coastline rises to low mountains and plateaus in forested interior; 6 major rivers flow in parallel courses to the ocean. **Capital:** Monrovia, 882,000.

Government: Type: Republic. **Head of state and gov.:** Pres. Ellen Johnson-Sirleaf; b. Oct. 29, 1938; in office: Jan. 16, 2006. **Local divisions:** 15 counties. **Defense budget:** $1.59 mil. **Active troops:** 2,050.

Economy: Industries: rubber and palm oil proc., timber, diamonds. **Chief crops:** rubber, coffee, cocoa, rice, cassava, palm oil, sugarcane, bananas. **Natural resources:** iron ore, timber, diamonds, gold, hydropower. **Arable land:** 4.2%. **Livestock:** cattle: 39,000; chickens: 6.5 mil; goats: 310,500; pigs: 230,060; sheep: 252,150. **Fish catch:** 8,016 metric tons. **Electricity prod.:** 335 mil kWh. **Labor force:** agric. 70%, industry 8%, services 22%.

Finance: Monetary unit: Dollar (LRD) (Sept. 2011: 72.00 = $1 U.S.). **GDP:** $1.7 bil; **per capita GDP:** $500; **GDP growth:** 5.1%. **Imports** (2006): $7.1 bil; South Korea 41.7%, China 16%, Singapore 14.1%, Japan 12.6%. **Exports** (2006): $1.2 bil; Germany 29.3%, Poland 18%, South Africa 16.6%, Greece 7.4%, U.S. 6.5%, Norway 5.5%. **Tourism:** $123 mil. **Budget:** NA. **Total reserves less gold** (2009): $372.5 mil. **CPI change** (2008-09): 7.4%.

Transport: Railways: 267 mi. **Motor vehicles:** 14.3 vehicles per 1,000 pop. **Civil aviation:** 2 airports. **Chief ports:** Buchanan, Monrovia.
Communications: TV sets: 26 per 1,000 pop. **Radios:** 318 per 1,000 pop. **Telephone lines:** 0.2 per 100 pop. **Internet:** 0.1 users per 100 pop.
Health: Life expect.: 55.4 male; 58.6 female. **Births:** 37.3 (per 1,000 pop.). **Deaths:** 10.6 (per 1,000 pop.). **Natural inc.:** 2.66%. **Infant mortality:** 74.5 (per 1,000 live births). **HIV rate:** 1.5%.
Education: Compulsory ages: NA. **Literacy:** 59.1%.
Major intl. organizations: UN and most of its specialized agencies, AU, WTO (observer).
Embassy: 5201 16th St. NW 20011; 723-0437.
Website: www.emansion.gov.lr

Liberia was founded in 1822 by freed black slaves from the U.S. who settled at Monrovia with the aid of colonization societies. It became a republic July 26, 1847, with a constitution modeled on that of the U.S. Descendants of freed slaves dominated politics for much of the 19th and 20th centuries.

Under Pres. William V. S. Tubman, Liberia was a founding member of the UN in 1945. Tubman died in 1971 and was succeeded by his vice president, William R. Tolbert Jr. Charging rampant corruption, an Army Redemption Council of enlisted men staged a bloody predawn coup, Apr. 12, 1980, in which Pres. Tolbert was killed and replaced as head of state by Sgt. Samuel Doe, an indigenous African. In 1985, Doe was chosen president in a disputed election.

A civil war began Dec. 1989. In Sept. 1990, Pres. Doe was captured and put to death. Despite the introduction of peacekeeping forces from several countries, the conflict intensified. Factional fighting devastated Monrovia in Apr. 1996. On Sept. 3, Ruth Perry became modern Africa's first female head of state, leading a transitional government. By then, the civil war had claimed more than 150,000 lives and uprooted over half the population.

Former rebel leader Charles Taylor was elected president July 19, 1997, in Liberia's first national election in 12 years. The UN imposed sanctions May 4, 2001, to punish Liberia for aiding the Revolutionary United Front (RUF) insurgency in Sierra Leone. Taylor declared a state of emergency Feb. 8, 2002, after Liberian rebels launched raids near Monrovia.

A UN-sponsored war crimes tribunal indicted Taylor June 4, 2003, for his role in the conflict in Sierra Leone. With rebels again threatening Monrovia, Taylor resigned Aug. 11 and went into exile. The UN authorized a 15,000-member peacekeeping force (UNMIL) Sept. 19 to help stabilize the nation. A businessman, Charles Gyude Bryant, was sworn in Oct. 14 to head a power-sharing interim government. Ellen Johnson-Sirleaf won a presidential runoff election Nov. 8, 2005. Captured Mar. 29, 2006, while trying to flee Nigeria, Taylor was transferred to the Netherlands; his trial at The Hague began June 4, 2007, but was plagued by delays. UNMIL had about 9,200 uniformed personnel in Liberia in mid-2011. Presidential and legislative elections were scheduled for Oct. 11, and a verdict in the Taylor case was expected before the end of the year.

Libya
Libyan Republic

People: Population: 6,597,960. **Age distrib.:** <15: 32.8%; 65+: 4.6%. **Pop. density:** 9.7 per sq mi, 3.7 per sq km. **Urban:** 77.9%. **Ethnic groups:** Berber & Arab 97%, other (incl. Greek, Maltese, Italian, Egyptian, Pakistani, Turk, Indian, Tunisian) 3%. **Principal languages:** Arabic (official), Italian, English all widely understood in major cities. **Chief religion:** Sunni Muslim (official) 97%.

Geography: Total area: 679,362 sq mi, 1,759,540 sq km; **Land area:** 679,362 sq mi, 1,759,540 sq km. **Location:** On Mediterranean coast of N Africa. **Neighbors:** Tunisia, Algeria on W; Niger, Chad on S; Sudan, Egypt on E. **Topography:** Desert and semidesert regions cover 92% of land, with low mountains in N, higher mountains in S, and a narrow coastal zone. **Capital:** Tripoli (Tarabulus), 1,095,000.

Government: Type: In transition. **Head of state:** Chairman, Libyan Interim National Council, Mustafa Mohammed Abdul Jalil; b. 1952; in office: Aug. 23, 2011 (de facto). **Head of gov.:** Interim Prime Min. Mahmoud Jabril; b. 1952; in office: Aug. 23, 2011 (de facto). **Local divisions:** 25 municipalities. **Defense budget:** NA. **Active troops:** 76,000.

Economy: Industries: petroleum, petrochemicals, aluminum, iron and steel, food proc., textiles, handicrafts, cement. **Chief crops:** wheat, barley, olives, dates, citrus, vegetables, peanuts, soybeans. **Natural resources:** petroleum, nat. gas, gypsum. **Crude oil reserves:** 46.4 bil bbls. **Arable land:** 1.0%. **Livestock:** cattle: 185,000; chickens: 27 mil; goats: 2.5 mil; sheep: 6.5 mil. **Fish catch:** 52,356 metric tons. **Electricity prod.:** 26.9 bil kWh. **Labor force:** agric. 17%, industry 23%, services 59%.

Finance: Monetary unit: Dinar (LYD) (Sept. 2011: 1.21 = $1 U.S.). **GDP:** $90.6 bil; **per capita GDP:** $14,000; **GDP growth:** 4.2%. **Imports:** $24.5 bil; Italy 17.6%, China 10.3%, Turkey 9.3%, Germany 8.1%, South Korea 6.4%, France 5.3%, Egypt 5.1%, Tunisia 4.9%. **Exports:** $44.9 bil; Italy 37.6%, Germany 10.4%, France 8.4%, China 8.3%, Spain 7.9%, U.S. 5.2%. **Tourism:** $50 mil. **Budget:** $38.9 bil. **Total reserves less gold:** $99.6 bil. **Gold:** 4.6 mil oz t. **CPI change** (2008-09): 2.5%.

Transport: Motor vehicles: 133 vehicles per 1,000 pop. **Civil aviation:** 945.1 mil pass.-mi; 59 airports. **Chief ports:** Az Zawiyah, Ra's Lanuf, Tripoli.

Communications: TV sets: 147 per 1,000 pop. **Radios:** 270 per 1,000 pop. **Telephone lines:** 19.3 per 100 pop. **Internet:** 14 users per 100 pop.

Health: Life expect.: 75.3 male; 80.1 female. **Births:** 24.0 (per 1,000 pop.). **Deaths:** 3.4 (per 1,000 pop.). **Natural inc.:** 2.06%. **Infant mortality:** 20.1 (per 1,000 live births). **HIV rate:** NA.

Education: Compulsory: ages 6-14. **Literacy:** 88.9%.

Major intl. organizations: UN (FAO, IBRD, ILO, IMF, WHO), AL, AU, OPEC, WTO (observer).

Embassy: 2600 Virginia Ave. NW, Ste. 705, 20037; 944-9601. **Website:** www.libyanbureaudc.org

First settled by Berbers, Libya was ruled in succession by Carthage, Rome, the Vandals, and the Ottomans. Italy ruled from 1912, and Britain and France after WWII. Libya became an independent constitutional monarchy Jan. 2, 1952. In 1969 a junta led by Col. Muammar al-Qaddafi seized power.

Qaddafi ruled as a dictator, suppressing domestic dissent and engaging in armed conflicts with neighboring Egypt and Chad. During the 1980s, Libya was accused of aiding terrorists and violent revolutionary groups. The U.S. charged Qaddafi with ordering the

Apr. 5, 1986, bombing of a West Berlin discotheque, which killed 3, including a U.S. serviceman. In response, the U.S. sent warplanes to attack what it called "terrorist-related targets" in Libya, Apr. 14, including Qaddafi's barracks.

Libyan agents were accused of planting bombs that blew up Pan Am Flight 103 over Lockerbie, Scotland, killing 270 people Dec. 21, 1988, and UTA Flight 772 over Niger, killing 170 people Sept. 19, 1989. The UN imposed sanctions, Apr. 15, 1992, for Libya's failure to cooperate in the Lockerbie and UTA cases.

Libya agreed in 2003 to renounce terrorism and settle compensation cases for the families of the Lockerbie and UTA bombing victims. The UN lifted sanctions, Sept. 12, 2003. Secret talks with the U.S. and UK led to Libya's announcement Dec. 19 that it would stop developing nuclear, chemical, and biological weapons and long-range missiles. The U.S. ended most economic sanctions Apr. 23, 2004, and restored full diplomatic relations May 15, 2006. Abdel Basset Ali al-Megrahi, a former Libyan agent sentenced to life in prison in 2001 for his role in the Lockerbie bombing, was freed by Scottish authorities on humanitarian grounds Aug. 20, 2009; British officials differed as to whether a secret UK-Libya oil deal had an impact on the decision to release the ailing Megrahi, who received a jubilant welcome in Libya.

"Arab Spring" rebels gained control Feb. 2011 of much of Libya's eastern region including Benghazi, the nation's second-largest city, while Qaddafi held power in western Libya including Tripoli, the national capital. Qaddafi launched a ferocious counteroffensive in the east, but with diplomatic backing from the Arab League and the UN Security Council, NATO forces led by the U.S., France, and UK imposed an arms embargo and no-fly zone against Qaddafi. With stepped-up aid from NATO, the rebels took control of Tripoli Aug. 23 and began governing through the Libyan Interim National Council. Qaddafi eluded capture, while some members of his family fled to Algeria.

Liechtenstein
Principality of Liechtenstein

People: Population: 36,422. **Age distrib.:** <15: 16.2%; 65+: 14.3%. **Pop. density:** 589.6 per sq mi, 227.6 per sq km. **Urban:** 14.3%. **Ethnic groups:** Liechtensteiner 66%. **Principal languages:** German (official), Alemannic dialect. **Chief religions:** Roman Catholic (official) 76%, Protestant 7%.

Geography: Total area: 62 sq mi, 160 sq km; **Land area:** 62 sq mi, 160 sq km. **Location:** Central Europe, in Alps. **Neighbors:** Switzerland on W, Austria on E. **Topography:** Rhine Valley occupies one-third of country, Alps cover the rest. **Capital:** Vaduz, 5,000.

Government: Type: Hereditary constitutional monarchy. **Head of state:** Prince Hans-Adam II; b. Feb. 14, 1945; in office: Nov. 13, 1989. **Head of gov.:** Klaus Tschütscher; b. July 8, 1967; in office: Mar. 25, 2009. **Local divisions:** 11 communes. **Defense budget/active troops:** NA.

Economy: Industries: electronics, metal mfg., dental prods., ceramics, pharmaceuticals, food prods., precision instruments, tourism, optical instruments. **Chief crops:** wheat, barley, corn, potatoes. **Natural resources:** hydroelectric potential. **Arable land:** 21.9%. **Livestock:** cattle: 6,000; goats: 450; pigs: 1,800; sheep: 3,900. **Labor force:** agric. 1.5%, industry 43.5%, services 55%.

Finance: Monetary unit: Switzerland Franc (CHF) (Sept. 2011: 0.86 = $1 U.S.). **GDP** (2008): $5 bil; **per capita GDP** (2008 est.): $141,100; **GDP growth** (2008 est.): 1.8%. **Imports** (2009): $1.8 bil; NA. **Exports** (2009): $2.8 bil; NA. **Tourism:** NA. **Budget** (2008 est.): $820 mil. **Total reserves less gold:** NA. **CPI change:** NA.

Transport: Railways: 6 mi.

Communications: TV sets: 540 per 1,000 pop. **Radios:** 662 per 1,000 pop. **Telephone lines:** 54.4 per 100 pop. **Daily newspaper circ.:** 513.6 per 1,000 pop. **Internet:** 80 users per 100 pop.

Health: Life expect.: 79.3 male; 84.1 female. **Births:** 10.9 (per 1,000 pop.). **Deaths:** 6.6 (per 1,000 pop.) **Natural inc.:** 0.43%. **Infant mortality:** 4.4 (per 1,000 live births). **HIV rate:** NA.

Education: Compulsory: ages 6-14. **Literacy:** 100%.

Major intl. organizations: EFTA, OSCE, WTO.

Embassy: 2900 K St. NW, Ste. 602B, 20007; 331-0590. **Website:** www.liechtenstein.li

Liechtenstein became sovereign in 1806. It is united with Switzerland by a customs and monetary union. Nearly half of all workers commute daily from Austria, Switzerland, and Germany.

On Aug. 15, 2004, Prince Hans-Adam II assigned day-to-day responsibilities for running the tiny country to his son, Crown Prince Alois. Long regarded as a tax haven, Liechtenstein has recently agreed to ease banking secrecy laws that had impeded international tax fraud investigations.

Lithuania
Republic of Lithuania

People: Population: 3,535,547. **Age distrib.:** <15: 13.8%; 65+: 16.5%. **Pop. density:** 146.1 per sq mi, 56.4 per sq km. **Urban:** 67%. **Ethnic groups:** Lithuanian 84%, Polish 6%, Russian 5%, Belarusian 1%. **Principal languages:** Lithuanian (official), Russian, Polish. **Chief religions:** Roman Catholic 79%, Russian Orthodox 4%, Protestant 2%, none 10%.

Geography: Total area: 25,212 sq mi, 65,300 sq km; **Land area:** 24,201 sq mi, 62,680 sq km. **Location:** In E Europe, on SE coast of Baltic. **Neighbors:** Latvia on N; Belarus on E, S; Poland, Russia on W. **Topography:** Lowland with hills in W and S; fertile soil; many small lakes and rivers, with marshes espec. in N and W. **Capital:** Vilnius, 546,000.

Government: Type: Republic. **Head of state:** Pres. Dalia Grybauskaite; b. Mar. 1, 1956; in office: July 12, 2009. **Head of gov.:** Prime Min. Andrius Kubilius; b. Dec. 8, 1956; in office: Dec. 9, 2008. **Local divisions:** 10 provinces. **Defense budget:** $323 mil. **Active troops:** 10,640.

Economy: Industries: machine tools, elec. motors, TVs, refrigerators and freezers, petroleum refining, shipbuilding, furniture making, textiles. **Chief crops:** grain, potatoes, sugar beets, flax, vegetables. **Natural resources:** peat, amber. **Crude oil reserves:** 12 mil bbls. **Arable land:** 32.8%. **Livestock:** cattle: 770,900; chickens: 8.8 mil; goats: 16,600; pigs: 897,100; sheep: 47,500. **Fish catch:** 176,114 metric tons. **Electricity prod.:** 12.3 bil kWh. **Labor force:** agric. 14%, industry 29.1%, services 56.9%.

Finance: Monetary unit: Litas (LTL) (Sept. 2011: 2.47 = $1 U.S.). **GDP:** $56.6 bil; **per capita GDP:** $16,000; **GDP growth:** 1.3%. **Imports:** $20.3 bil; Russia 29.9%, Germany 11.3%, Poland 10%, Latvia 6.4%, Netherlands 4%. **Exports:** $19.3 bil; Russia 13.3%, Latvia 10.1%, Germany 9.7%, Poland 7.2%, Estonia 7%, Netherlands 5.1%, Belarus 4.7%, UK 4.4%. **Tourism:** $1 bil. **Budget:** $13.5 bil. **Total reserves less gold:** $6.6 bil. **Gold:** 187,000 oz t. **CPI change:** 1.3%.

Transport: Railways: 1,098 mi. **Civil aviation:** 577.9 mil pass.-mi; 26 airports. **Chief port:** Klaipeda.

Communications: TV sets: 518 per 1,000 pop. **Radios:** 525 per 1,000 pop. **Telephone lines:** 22.1 per 100 pop. **Daily newspaper circ.:** 107.8 per 1,000 pop. **Internet:** 62.1 users per 100 pop.

Health: Life expect.: 70.5 male; 80.5 female. **Births:** 9.3 (per 1,000 pop.). **Deaths:** 11.3 (per 1,000 pop.). **Natural inc.:** −0.20%. **Infant mortality:** 6.3 (per 1,000 live births). **HIV rate:** 0.1%.

Education: Compulsory: ages 7-15. **Literacy:** 99.7%.

Major intl. organizations: UN (FAO, IBRD, ILO, IMF, WHO), EU, NATO, OSCE, WTO.

Embassy: 4590 MacArthur Blvd. NW, Ste. 200, 20007; 234-5860. **Website:** www.lrvk.lt

Lithuania was occupied by the German army, 1914-18. It was annexed by the Soviet Russian army, but the Soviets were overthrown, 1919. In 1939 the Soviet-German treaty assigned most of Lithuania to the Soviet sphere of influence. Lithuania was annexed by the USSR Aug. 3, 1940.

Lithuania formally declared its independence from the Soviet Union Mar. 11, 1990. During an abortive Soviet coup in Aug., the Western nations recognized Lithuania's independence, which was ratified by the Soviet Union in Sept. 1991. The country became a full member of NATO and the EU in 2004. A plummeting economy spurred popular discontent and brought a rightward shift in parliamentary and presidential elections, 2008-09. In mid-2011, Lithuania had 235 troops serving with the NATO mission (ISAF) in Afghanistan.

Luxembourg
Grand Duchy of Luxembourg

People: Population: 503,302. **Age distrib.:** <15: 18.2%; 65+: 14.9%. **Pop. density:** 504.1 per sq mi, 194.6 per sq km. **Urban:** 85.2%. **Ethnic groups:** Luxembourger 63%, Portuguese 13%, French 5%, Italian 4%, German 2%, other EU 7%. **Principal languages:** Luxembourgish (national); German, French (both administrative). **Chief religions:** Roman Catholic 87%, other (incl. Protestant, Jewish, Muslim) 13%.

Geography: Total area: 998 sq mi, 2,586 sq km; **Land area:** 998 sq mi, 2,586 sq km. **Location:** In W Europe. **Neighbors:** Belgium on W, France on S, Germany on E. **Topography:** Heavy forests (Ardennes) cover N. S is a low, open plateau. **Capital:** Luxembourg, 90,000.

Government: Type: Constitutional monarchy. **Head of state:** Grand Duke Henri; b. Apr. 16, 1955; in office: Oct. 7, 2000. **Head of gov.:** Prime Min. Jean-Claude Juncker; b. Dec. 9, 1954; in office: Jan. 20, 1995. **Local divisions:** 3 districts. **Defense budget:** $556 mil. **Active troops:** 900.

Economy: Industries: banking and financial services, iron and steel, information tech., telecom., cargo trans., food proc., chemicals, metal prods., engineering, tires, glass, aluminum, tourism. **Chief crops:** grapes, barley, oats, potatoes, wheat, fruits. **Natural resources:** iron ore (no longer exploited). **Arable land:** 23.9%. **Livestock:** cattle: 196,470; chickens: 97,000; goats: 3,130; pigs: 80,217; sheep: 8,824. **Electricity prod.** (2009): 2.7 bil kWh. **Labor force:** agric. 2.2%, industry 17.2%, services 80.6%.

Finance: Monetary unit: Euro (EUR) (Sept. 2011: 0.71 = $1 U.S.). **GDP:** $41.1 bil; **per capita GDP:** $82,600; **GDP growth:** 3.4%. **Imports:** $23.7 bil; Belgium 27.5%, Germany 23.2%, China 18.5%, France 8.8%, Netherlands 5%. **Exports:** $17.8 bil; Germany 20.2%, France 16.3%, Belgium 11.2%, UK 7.9%, Italy 7.6%, Netherlands 4.4%. **Tourism:** $4.1 bil. **Budget:** $22.1 bil. **Total reserves less gold:** $747.1 mil. **Gold:** 72,000 oz t. **CPI change:** 2.3%.

Transport: Railways: 171 mi. **Motor vehicles:** 753.4 vehicles per 1,000 pop. **Civil aviation:** 255.4 mil pass.-mi; 1 airport. **Chief port:** Mertert.

Communications: TV sets: 605 per 1,000 pop. **Radios:** 683 per 1,000 pop. **Telephone lines:** 53.7 per 100 pop. **Daily newspaper circ.** (2004): 254.5 per 1,000 pop. **Internet:** 90.6 users per 100 pop.

Health: Life expect.: 76.4 male; 83.1 female. **Births:** 11.7 (per 1,000 pop.). **Deaths:** 8.5 (per 1,000 pop.). **Natural inc.:** 0.32%. **Infant mortality:** 4.4 (per 1,000 live births). **HIV rate:** 0.3%.

Education: Compulsory: ages 6-15. **Literacy:** 100%.

Major intl. organizations: UN (FAO, IBRD, ILO, IMF, WHO), EU, NATO, OECD, OSCE, WTO.

Embassy: 2200 Massachusetts Ave. NW 20008; 265-4171.

Website: www.gouvernement.lu

Luxembourg, founded about 963, was ruled by Burgundy, Spain, Austria, and France from 1448 to 1815. It left the Germanic Confederation in 1866. Overrun by Germany in two world wars, Luxembourg ended its neutrality in 1948, when a customs union with Belgium and Netherlands was adopted.

Luxembourg was one of the six founding members (1951) of what became the European Union. Prime Min. Jean-Claude Juncker is the EU's longest-serving head of government.

Macedonia
Former Yugoslav Republic of Macedonia

People: Population: 2,077,328. **Age distrib.:** <15: 18.5%; 65+: 11.6%. **Pop. density:** 211.5 per sq mi, 81.7 per sq km. **Urban:** 59.3%. **Ethnic groups:** Macedonian 64%, Albanian 25%, Turkish 4%, Roma 3%, Serb 2%. **Principal languages:** Macedonian, Albanian (both official); Turkish; Roma; Serbian. **Chief religions:** Macedonian Orthodox 65%, Muslim 33%.

Geography: Total area: 9,928 sq mi, 25,713 sq km; **Land area:** 9,820 sq mi, 25,433 sq km. **Location:** In SE Europe. **Neighbors:** Bulgaria on E, Greece on S, Albania on W, Serbia on N. **Topography:** Macedonia is a landlocked, mostly mountainous country, with deep river valleys, 3 large lakes; country is bisected by Vardar R. **Capital:** Skopje, 480,000.

Government: Type: Republic. **Head of state:** Pres. Gjorge Ivanov; b. May 2, 1960; in office: May 12, 2009. **Head of gov.:** Prime Min. Nikola Gruevski; b. Aug. 31, 1970; in office: Aug. 27, 2006. **Local divisions:** 123 municipalities. **Defense budget:** $140 mil. **Active troops:** 8,000.

Economy: Industries: food proc., beverages, textiles, chemicals, iron, steel, cement, energy, pharmaceuticals. **Chief crops:** grapes, tobacco, vegetables, fruits. **Natural resources:** iron ore, copper, lead, zinc, chromite, manganese, nickel, tungsten, gold, silver, asbestos. **Arable land:** 16.7%. **Livestock:** cattle: 252,521; chickens: 2.2 mil; goats: 94,016; pigs: 193,840; sheep: 455,356. **Fish catch:** 1,799 metric tons. **Electricity prod.:** 6 bil kWh. **Labor force:** agric. 19.9%, industry 22.1%, services 58%.

Finance: Monetary unit: Denar (MKD) (Sept. 2011: 43.62 = $1 U.S.). **GDP:** $20 bil (country has a large informal sector); **per capita GDP:** $9,700; **GDP growth:** 0.7%. **Imports:** $5.1 bil; Germany 10.3%, Russia 9.8%, Greece 8.7%, Italy 7.2%, China 5.7%, Turkey 5%, Bulgaria 4.8%. **Exports:** $3.2 bil; Germany 16.7%, Greece 10.8%, Italy 8.1%, Bulgaria 8.1%, Croatia 5.7%. **Tourism:** $198 mil. **Budget:** $3.01 bil. **Total reserves less gold:** $2 bil. **Gold:** 218,239 oz t. **CPI change:** 2.1%.

Transport: Railways: 434 mi. **Civil aviation:** 54.1 mil pass.-mi; 10 airports.

Communications: TV sets: 296 per 1,000 pop. **Radios:** 207 per 1,000 pop. **Telephone lines:** 20.1 per 100 pop. **Daily newspaper circ.:** 88.8 per 1,000 pop. **Internet:** 51.9 users per 100 pop.

Health: Life expect.: 72.6 male; 77.9 female. **Births:** 11.9 (per 1,000 pop.). **Deaths:** 8.9 (per 1,000 pop.). **Natural inc.:** 0.30%. **Infant mortality:** 8.5 (per 1,000 live births). **HIV rate:** NA.

Education: Compulsory: ages 7-14. **Literacy:** 97.1%.

Major intl. organizations: UN (FAO, IBRD, ILO, IMF, WHO) OSCE, WTO.

Embassy: 2129 Wyoming Ave. NW 20008; 667-0501.

Website: www.vlada.mk

Macedonia was ruled by Muslim Turks from 1389 to 1912. In 1913, the area was incorporated into Serbia, which in 1918 became part of the Kingdom of Serbs, Croats, and Slovenes (later Yugoslavia). In 1946, Macedonia became a constituent republic of Yugoslavia.

Macedonia declared its independence Sept. 8, 1991, and was admitted to the UN in 1993. Greece, which objected to Macedonia's use of what it considered a Hellenic name and symbols, imposed a trade blockade on the landlocked nation; the 2 countries agreed to normalize relations Sept. 13, 1995.

By the end of NATO's air war against Yugoslavia, Mar.-June 1999, Macedonia had a Kosovar refugee population of more than 250,000; over 90% had been repatriated by Sept. 1. Boris Trajkovski, candidate of the ruling center-right coalition, won a presidential runoff vote Nov. 14.

Ethnic Albanian guerrillas launched an offensive Mar. 2001 in NW Macedonia. An accord signed Aug. 13 paved the way for the introduction of a NATO peacekeeping force. A law broadening the rights of ethnic Albanians was enacted Jan. 24, 2002. A 320-member EU force replaced the NATO peacekeepers, Mar.-Dec. 2003.

After Trajkovski died in a plane crash Feb. 26, 2004, Prime Min. Branko Crvenkovski won a presidential runoff vote Apr. 28. Prime

Min. Nikola Gruevski's governing coalition retained power after parliamentary elections June 1, 2008, and June 5, 2011. Gjorge Ivanov won a presidential runoff vote Apr. 5, 2009, and took office May 12. Greece has blocked Macedonia's bid to join NATO because of the continuing dispute over Macedonia's name.

Madagascar
Republic of Madagascar

People: Population: 21,926,221. **Age distrib.:** <15: 43.1%; 65+: 3%. **Pop. density:** 97.7 per sq mi, 37.7 per sq km. **Urban:** 30.2%. **Ethnic groups:** Malayo-Indonesian (Merina & related Betsileo), Cotiers (mixed African, Malayo-Indonesian, & Arab), French, Indian, Creole, Comoran. **Principal languages:** French, Malagasy (both official); English. **Chief religions:** indigenous beliefs 52%, Christian 41%, Muslim 7%.

Geography: Total area: 226,658 sq mi, 587,041 sq km; **Land area:** 224,534 sq mi, 581,540 sq km. **Location:** In Indian O., off SE coast of Africa. **Neighbors:** Comoro Isls. to NW, Mozambique to W. **Topography:** Humid coastal strip in E, fertile valleys in mountainous center plateau region, and a wider coastal strip on W. **Capital:** Antananarivo, 1,816,000.

Government: Type: In transition. **Head of state:** Pres. Andry Rajoelina; b. May 30, 1974; in office: Mar. 17, 2009. **Head of gov.:** Prime Min. Albert Camille Vital; b. July 18, 1952; in office: Dec. 20, 2009. **Local divisions:** 6 provinces. **Defense budget:** $56 mil. **Active troops:** 13,500.

Economy: Industries: meat proc., seafood, soap, breweries, tanneries, sugar, textiles, glassware, cement, auto assembly plant. **Chief crops:** coffee, vanilla, sugarcane, cloves, cocoa, rice, cassava, beans, bananas, peanuts. **Natural resources:** graphite, chromite, coal, bauxite, rare earth elements, salt, quartz, tar sands, semiprec. stones, mica, fish, hydropower. **Arable land:** 5.1%. **Livestock:** cattle: 9.8 mil; chickens: 26 mil; goats: 1.3 mil; pigs: 1.4 mil; sheep: 725,000. **Fish catch:** 144,599 metric tons. **Electricity prod.:** 1.1 bil kWh. **Labor force:** NA.

Finance: Monetary unit: Ariary (MGA) (Sept. 2011: 1,978.00 = $1 U.S.). **GDP:** $19.4 bil; **per capita GDP:** $900; **GDP growth:** –2%. **Imports:** $2 bil; Thailand 18.6%, China 15.3%, France 5.8%, South Africa 4.8%, U.S. 4.6%, India 4.4%. **Exports:** $1.4 bil; France 32.1%, U.S. 16.1%, Germany 6.4%, China 5%. **Tourism:** $308 mil. **Budget:** $1.5 bil. **Total reserves less gold:** $1.2 bil. **CPI change:** 9.2%.

Transport: Railways: 531 mi. **Motor vehicles:** 6.3 vehicles per 1,000 pop. **Civil aviation:** 508.9 mil pass.-mi; 27 airports. **Chief ports:** Antsiranana, Mahajanga, Toamasina, Toliara.

Communications: TV sets: 37 per 1,000 pop. **Radios:** 268 per 1,000 pop. **Telephone lines:** 0.8 per 100 pop. **Internet:** 1.7 users per 100 pop.

Health: Life expect.: 61.6 male; 65.7 female. **Births:** 37.5 (per 1,000 pop.). **Deaths:** 7.8 (per 1,000 pop.). **Natural inc.:** 2.97%. **Infant mortality:** 51.5 (per 1,000 live births). **HIV rate:** 0.2%.

Education: Compulsory: ages 6-14. **Literacy:** 64.5%.

Major intl. organizations: UN (FAO, IBRD, ILO, IMF, WHO), AU, WTO.

Embassy: 2374 Massachusetts Ave. NW 20008; 265-5525.

Website: www.madagascar-presidency.gov.mg

Madagascar was settled 2,000 years ago by Malayan-Indonesian people, whose descendants still predominate. A unified kingdom ruled in the 18th and 19th centuries. The island became a French protectorate, 1885, and a colony 1896. Independence came June 26, 1960.

Discontent with inflation and French domination led to a coup in 1972. The new regime nationalized French-owned financial interests, closed French bases and a U.S. space-tracking station, and obtained Chinese aid. The government conducted a program of arrests, expulsion of foreigners, and repression of strikes, 1979.

In 1990, Madagascar ended a ban on multiparty politics that had been in place since 1975. Albert Zafy was elected president in 1993, ending the 17-year rule of Adm. Didier Ratsiraka. After Zafy was impeached by the legislature, Madagascar's constitutional court removed him from office, Sept. 5, 1996. A cholera epidemic, then cyclones in Feb. and Apr. 2000, claimed 1,600 lives.

Marc Ravalomanana won a power struggle with Ratsiraka that followed a disputed presidential election Dec. 16, 2001; he was reelected with a 55% majority Dec. 3, 2006. Cyclone Ivan hit Feb. 17, 2008, killing at least 83 people and leaving 145,000 homeless. A power struggle between Ravalomanana and Antananarivo Mayor Andry Rajoelina, backed by the military, culminated in Rajoelina's installation as head of a transitional regime, Mar. 17, 2009. The African Union suspended Madagascar and pushed for a power-sharing arrangement, but accords signed in Aug. and Nov. 2009 were abrogated by Rajoelina. The transitional government suppressed a coup attempt launched by dissident military officers Nov. 17, 2010, the same day voters approved a new constitution that would allow Rajoelina to hold power indefinitely.

Malawi
Republic of Malawi

People: Population: 15,879,252. **Age distrib.:** <15: 45.1%; 65+: 2.7%. **Pop. density:** 437.2 per sq mi, 168.8 per sq km. **Urban:** 19.8%. **Ethnic groups:** Chewa 33%, Lomwe 18%, Yao 14%, Ngoni

12%, Tumbuka 9%, Nyanja 6%, Sena 4%, Tonga 2%, Ngonde 1%. **Principal languages:** Chichewa (official), Chinyanja, Chiyao, Chitumbuka, Chisena, Chilomwe, Chitonga. **Chief religions:** Christian 83%, Muslim 13%, none 3%.

Geography: Total area: 45,747 sq mi, 118,484 sq km; **Land area:** 36,324 sq mi, 94,080 sq km. **Location:** In SE Africa. **Neighbors:** Zambia on W, Mozambique on S and E, Tanzania on N. **Topography:** Malawi stretches 560 mi N-S along Lake Malawi (Lake Nyasa), most of which belongs to Malawi. High plateaus and mountains line the Rift Valley the length of the nation. **Capital:** Lilongwe, 821,000. **Cities (urban aggl.):** Blantyre-Limbe, 856,156.

Government: Type: Republic. **Head of state and gov.:** Pres. Bingu wa Mutharika; b. Feb. 24, 1934; in office: May 24, 2004. **Local divisions:** 3 regions, 26 districts. **Defense budget (2008):** $43 mil. **Active troops:** 5,300.

Economy: Industries: tobacco, tea, sugar, sawmill prods., cement, consumer goods. **Chief crops:** tobacco, sugarcane, cotton, tea, corn, potatoes, cassava, sorghum, pulses, groundnuts. **Natural resources:** limestone, hydropower, uranium, coal, bauxite. **Arable land:** 28.4%. **Livestock:** cattle: 1.03 mil; chickens: 15.7 mil; goats: 3.5 mil; pigs: 1.6 mil; sheep: 191,500. **Fish catch:** 70,945 metric tons. **Electricity prod.:** 1.7 bil kWh. **Labor force:** agric. 90%, industry and services 10%.

Finance: Monetary unit: Kwacha (MWK) (Sept. 2011: 152.50 = $1 U.S.). **GDP:** $13 bil; **per capita GDP:** $800; **GDP growth:** 6.6%. **Imports:** $1.7 bil; South Africa 38.2%, India 7.7%, Zambia 6.5%, China 5.8%, France 4.8%, Tanzania 4.6%. **Exports:** $1.2 bil; Germany 11.5%, India 8.5%, South Africa 7.2%, Russia 7.1%, Zimbabwe 7.1%, U.S. 7%, Netherlands 6.3%. **Tourism:** NA. **Budget:** $1.8 bil. **Total reserves less gold (2009):** $149.4 mil. **Gold (2009):** 12,800 oz t. **CPI change:** 7.4%.

Transport: Railways: 495 mi. **Motor vehicles:** 2 vehicles per 1,000 pop. **Civil aviation:** 124.3 mil pass.-mi; 6 airports. **Chief ports:** Chilumba, Chipoka, Monkey Bay, Nkhata Bay, Nkhotakota.

Communications: TV sets: 11 per 1,000 pop. **Radios:** 3 per 1,000 pop. **Telephone lines:** 1.1 per 100 pop. **Internet:** 2.3 users per 100 pop.

Health: Life expect.: 50.9 male; 52.5 female. **Births:** 40.9 (per 1,000 pop.). **Deaths:** 13.2 (per 1,000 pop.). **Natural inc.:** 2.76%. **Infant mortality:** 81.0 (per 1,000 live births). **HIV rate:** 11%.

Education: Compulsory: ages 6-13. **Literacy:** 73.7%.

Major intl. organizations: UN (FAO, IBRD, ILO, IMF, WHO), AU, the Commonwealth, WTO.

Embassy: 1029 Vermont Ave. NW, Ste. 1000, 20005; 721-0270.

Website: www.malawi.gov.mw

Bantus came to the land in the 16th cent., Arab slavers in the 19th. The area became the British protectorate Nyasaland in 1891. It became independent July 6, 1964, and a republic in 1966.

After 3 decades as a one-party state under Pres. Hastings Kamuzu Banda, Malawi adopted a new constitution and, in multiparty elections held May 17, 1994, chose a new leader, Bakili Muluzi.

Bingu wa Mutharika, candidate of the ruling United Democratic Front, won a disputed presidential election May 20, 2004. In an ongoing power struggle, an effort by his former political allies to impeach him was halted by Malawi's Constitutional Court, Oct. 26, 2005. Mutharika won reelection May 19, 2009. Clashes between police and antigovernment protesters July 2011 left at least 19 people dead.

Malaysia

People: Population: 28,728,607. **Age distrib.:** <15: 29.6%; 65+: 5%. **Pop. density:** 226.4 per sq mi, 87.4 per sq km. **Urban:** 72.2%. **Ethnic groups:** Malay 50%, Chinese 24%, indigenous 11%, Indian 7%. **Principal languages:** Bahasa Malaysia (official), English, Chinese dialects, Tamil, Telugu, Malayalam, Panjabi, Thai. **Chief religions:** Muslim (official) 60%; Buddhist 19%; Christian 9%; Hindu 6%; Confucianism, Taoism, other traditional Chinese religions 3%.

Geography: Total area: 127,355 sq mi, 329,847 sq km; **Land area:** 126,895 sq mi, 328,657 sq km. **Location:** On SE tip of Asia, plus N coast of the island of Borneo. **Neighbors:** Thailand, Brunei on N; Indonesia on S. **Topography:** Most of W Malaysia is covered by tropical jungle, including the central mountain range that runs N-S through the peninsula. W coast is marshy, the E coast, sandy. E Malaysia has a wide, swampy coastal plain, with interior jungles and mountains. **Capital:** Kuala Lumpur (financial), 1,493,000; Putrajaya (admin.), NA. **Cities (urban aggl.):** Klang, 1,128,023.

Government: Type: Constitutional monarchy. **Head of state:** Paramount Ruler Al-Wathiqu Billah Tuanku Mizan Zainal Abidin ibni al-Marhum Sultan Mahmud al-Muktafi Billah Shah; b. Jan. 22, 1962; in office: Dec. 13, 2006. **Head of gov.:** Prime Min. Najib Razak; b. July 23, 1953; in office: Apr. 3, 2009. **Local divisions:** 13 states, 3 federal territories. **Defense budget:** $2.81 bil. **Active troops:** 109,000.

Economy: Industries: rubber and palm oil proc. and mfg., light mfg., pharmaceuticals, medical technology, electronics, tin mining and smelting, logging, timber proc. **Chief crops:** rubber, palm oil, cocoa, rice, coconuts, pepper. **Natural resources:** tin, petroleum, timber, copper, iron ore, nat. gas, bauxite. **Crude oil reserves:** 4 bil bbls. **Arable land:** 5.5%. **Livestock:** cattle: 800,000; chickens: 205 mil; goats: 336,000; pigs: 2.1 mil; sheep: 116,000. **Fish catch:**

1.9 mil metric tons. **Electricity prod.** (2009): 101.1 bil kWh. **Labor force:** agric. 13%, industry 36%, services 51%.

Finance: Monetary unit: Ringgit (MYR) (Sept. 2011: 2.98 = $1 U.S.). **GDP:** $414.4 bil; **per capita GDP:** $14,700; **GDP growth:** 7.2%. **Imports:** $174.3 bil; China 12.6%, Japan 12.6%, Singapore 11.4%, U.S. 10.7%, Thailand 6.2%, Indonesia 5.6%. **Exports:** $210.3 bil; Singapore 13.4%, China 12.6%, Japan 10.4%, U.S. 9.5%, Thailand 5.3%, Hong Kong 5.1%. **Tourism:** $18.3 bil. **Budget:** $46.3 bil. **Total reserves less gold:** $104.9 bil. **Gold:** 1.2 mil oz t. **CPI change:** 1.7%.

Transport: Railways: 1,149 mi. **Motor vehicles** 345.3 vehicles per 1,000 pop. **Civil aviation:** 28.3 bil pass.-mi; 38 airports. **Chief ports:** Bintulu, George Town (Penang), Johor Bahru, Port Kelang, Tanjung Pelepas.

Communications: TV sets: 224 per 1,000 pop. **Radios:** 425 per 1,000 pop. **Telephone lines:** 16.1 per 100 pop. **Daily newspaper circ.:** 109.3 per 1,000 pop. **Internet:** 55.3 users per 100 pop.

Health: Life expect.: 71.1 male; 76.7 female. **Births:** 21.1 (per 1,000 pop.). **Deaths:** 4.9 (per 1,000 pop.). **Natural inc.:** 1.62%. **Infant mortality:** 15.0 (per 1,000 live births). **HIV rate:** 0.5%.

Education: Compulsory: ages 6-11. **Literacy:** 92.5%.

Major intl. organizations: UN (FAO, IBRD, ILO, IMF, WHO), APEC, ASEAN, the Commonwealth, WTO.

Embassy: 3516 International Ct. NW 20008; 572-9700.

Website: www.malaysia.gov.my

European traders appeared in the 16th cent.; Britain established control in 1867. Malaysia was created Sept. 16, 1963. It included Malaya (which had become independent in 1957 after the suppression of Communist rebels), plus the formerly British Singapore, Sabah (N Borneo), and Sarawak (NW Borneo). Singapore was separated in 1965, in order to end tensions between Chinese, the majority in Singapore, and Malays in control of the Malaysian government.

A monarch is elected by a council of hereditary rulers of the Malayan states every five years.

Abundant natural resources have bolstered prosperity, and foreign investment has aided industrialization and trade. Work on a federal administrative center at Putrajaya, south of Kuala Lumpur, began in 1995; it is linked by rail with Kuala Lumpur's city center and international airport and with Cyberjaya, a hub for high-tech manufacturing and research.

Mahathir bin Mohamad dominated Malaysian politics as prime minister, 1981-2003. His successor, Abdullah Ahmad Badawi, took office Oct. 31, 2003, and led his National Front coalition to a resounding win in parliamentary elections Mar. 21, 2004. The Indian Ocean tsunami of Dec. 26, 2004, left at least 68 people dead and 8,000 displaced in Malaysia. Recession and scandals plagued Malaysia as National Front leader Najib Razak took office as prime min. Apr. 3, 2009.

Maldives
Republic of Maldives

People: Population: 394,999. **Age distrib.:** <15: 21.5%; 65+: 4.1%. **Pop. density:** 3,433 per sq mi, 1,325.5 per sq km. **Urban:** 40.1%. **Ethnic groups:** South Indian, Sinhalese, Arab. **Principal languages:** Dhivehi (official), English spoken by most govt. officials. **Chief religion:** Sunni Muslim (official).

Geography: Total area: 115 sq mi, 298 sq km; **Land area:** 115 sq mi, 298 sq km. **Location:** In Indian O., SW of India. **Neighbors:** Nearest is India on N. **Topography:** 19 atolls with 1,190 islands, 198 inhabited. None of the islands are over 5 sq mi in area, and all are nearly flat. **Capital:** Male, 120,000.

Government: Type: Republic. **Head of state and gov.:** Pres. Mohamed (Anni) Nasheed; b. May 17, 1967; in office: Nov. 11, 2008. **Local divisions:** 19 atolls and Male capital atoll. **Defense budget/active troops:** NA.

Economy: Industries: tourism, fish proc., shipping, boat building, coconut proc., garments. **Chief crops:** coconuts, corn, sweet potatoes. **Natural resources:** fish. **Arable land:** 13.3%. **Fish catch:** 116,895 metric tons. **Electricity prod.:** 260 mil kWh. **Labor force:** agric. 11%, industry 23%, services 65%.

Finance: Monetary unit: Rufiyaa (MVR) (Sept. 2011: 15.16 = $1 U.S.). **GDP:** $2.9 bil; **per capita GDP:** $6,900; **GDP growth:** 8%. **Imports** (2009 est.): $967 mil; Singapore 24.6%, UAE 15.7%, India 11.4%, Malaysia 7.7%, Sri Lanka 5.4%, Thailand 5.3%, China 4.3%. **Exports** (2009 est.): $163 mil; France 16.9%, Thailand 15.1%, Italy 13.4%, UK 13.1%, Sri Lanka 12.3%. **Tourism:** $714 mil. **Budget:** $758 mil. **Total reserves less gold:** $364.3 mil. **CPI change:** 6.1%.

Transport: Civil aviation: 28 mil pass.-mi; 3 airports. **Chief port:** Male.

Communications: TV sets: 131 per 1,000 pop. **Radios:** 131 per 1,000 pop. **Telephone lines:** 15.2 per 100 pop. **Internet:** 28.3 users per 100 pop.

Health: Life expect.: 72.2 male; 76.8 female. **Births:** 14.8 (per 1,000 pop.). **Deaths:** 3.7 (per 1,000 pop.). **Natural inc.:** 1.11%. **Infant mortality:** 27.5 (per 1,000 live births). **HIV rate:** <0.1%.

Education: Compulsory: ages 6-12. **Literacy:** 98.4%.

Major intl. organizations: UN (FAO, IBRD, IMF, WHO), the Commonwealth, WTO.

Embassy: 800 2nd Ave., Ste. 400E, New York, NY 10017; (212) 599-6194.

Website: www.presidencymaldives.gov.mv

A British protectorate since 1887, the nation achieved independence July 26, 1965; long a sultanate, Maldives became a republic in 1968. Tourism and fishing are the most important sectors of the economy. Rising sea levels threaten the country, which comprises at least 1,200 small, low-lying coral islands.

The Indian Ocean tsunami of Dec. 26, 2004, killed at least 82 people and displaced more than 21,600 in Maldives. Pres. Maumoon Abdul Gayoom, in office 1978-2008, lost a runoff vote Oct. 29, 2008, to pro-democracy leader and former political prisoner Mohamed (Anni) Nasheed.

Mali
Republic of Mali

People: Population: 14,159,904. **Age distrib.:** <15: 47.3%; 65+: 3%. **Pop. density:** 30.1 per sq mi, 11.6 per sq km. **Urban:** 35.9%. **Ethnic groups:** Mande (Bambara, Malinke, Soninke) 50%, Peul 17%, Voltaic 12%, Songhai 6%, Tuareg & Moor 10%. **Principal languages:** French (official), Bambara, numerous African languages. **Chief religions:** Muslim 90%, Christian 1%, indigenous beliefs 9%.

Geography: Total area: 478,841 sq mi, 1,240,192 sq km; **Land area:** 471,118 sq mi, 1,220,190 sq km. **Location:** In interior of W Africa. **Neighbors:** Mauritania, Senegal on W; Guinea, Côte d'Ivoire, Burkina Faso on S; Niger on E; Algeria on N. **Topography:** Landlocked grassy plain in upper basins of the Senegal and Niger rivers, extending N into the Sahara. **Capital:** Bamako, 1,628,000.

Government: Type: Republic. **Head of state:** Pres. Amadou Toumani Touré; b. Nov. 4, 1948; in office: June 8, 2002. **Head of gov.:** Prime Min. Cissé Mariam Kaïdama Sidibé; b. Jan. 4, 1948; in office: Apr. 3, 2011. **Local divisions:** 8 regions, 1 capital district. **Defense budget:** $208 mil. **Active troops:** 7,350.

Economy: Industries: food proc., constr., phosphate and gold mining. **Chief crops:** cotton, millet, rice, corn, vegetables, peanuts. **Natural resources:** gold, phosphates, kaolin, salt, limestone, uranium, gypsum, granite, hydropower. **Arable land:** 5.2%. **Livestock:** cattle: 8.7 mil; chickens: 35 mil; goats: 10.7 mil; pigs: 79,100; sheep: 10.2 mil. **Fish catch:** 100,796 metric tons. **Electricity prod.:** 490 mil kWh. **Labor force:** agric. 80%, industry and services 20%.

Finance: Monetary unit: CFA BCEAO Franc (XOF) (Sept. 2011: 468.55 = $1 U.S.). **GDP:** $16.8 bil; **per capita GDP:** $1,200; **GDP growth:** 4.5%. **Imports** (2006): $2.4 bil; Senegal 12.8%, France 10.9%, Côte d'Ivoire 9.4%, China 5.9%, South Korea 4.8%. **Exports** (2006): $294 mil; China 20.9%, Thailand 7.4%, Morocco 5.8%, South Korea 5.7%, Indonesia 4.9%, Burkina Faso 4.2%, France 4.1%. **Tourism:** $192 mil. **Budget** (2006 est.): $1.8 bil. **Total reserves less gold:** $1.3 bil. **CPI change:** 1.1%.

Transport: Railways: 368 mi. **Motor vehicles:** 1.7 vehicles per 1,000 pop. **Civil aviation:** 8 airports. **Chief port:** Koulikoro.

Communications: TV sets: 49 per 1,000 pop. **Radios:** 132 per 1,000 pop. **Telephone lines:** 0.7 per 100 pop. **Internet:** 2.7 users per 100 pop.

Health: Life expect.: 51.0 male; 54.3 female. **Births:** 45.6 (per 1,000 pop.). **Deaths:** 14.3 (per 1,000 pop.). **Natural inc.:** 3.13%. **Infant mortality:** 111.4 (per 1,000 live births). **HIV rate:** 1%.

Education: Compulsory: ages 7-15. **Literacy:** 26.2%.

Major intl. organizations: UN and most of its specialized agencies, AU, WTO.

Embassy: 2130 R St. NW 20008; 332-2249.

Website: www.primature.gov.ml

Until the 15th cent. the area was part of the great Mali Empire. Timbuktu (Tombouctou) was a center of Islamic study. French rule was secured, 1898. The Sudanese Rep. and Senegal became independent as the Mali Federation June 20, 1960, but Senegal withdrew, and the Sudanese Rep. was renamed Mali.

A socialist regime led, 1960-68, by Pres. Modibo Keita, was toppled by a coup. Famine struck in 1973-74, killing as many as 100,000 people. Drought conditions returned in the 1980s.

The military, Mar. 26, 1991, overthrew the government of Pres. Moussa Traoré, who had ruled since 1968. Oumar Konare, a coup leader, was elected president, Apr. 26, 1992. The government and a Tuareg rebel group signed a peace accord June 1994. Twice condemned to death for crimes committed in office, Traoré had his sentences commuted to life imprisonment Dec. 1997 and Sept. 1999; he was pardoned May 2002.

Amadou Toumani Touré, who led the 1991 coup, was elected president May 12, 2002, and reelected Apr. 29, 2007. Mali's first female prime minister, Cissé Mariam Kaïdama Sidibé, took office Apr. 3, 2011.

Malta
Republic of Malta

People: Population: 408,333. **Age distrib.:** <15: 15.7%; 65+: 15.8%. **Pop. density:** 3,346.8 per sq mi, 1,292.2 per sq km. **Urban:** 94.7%. **Ethnic groups:** Maltese (descendants of ancient Carthaginians & Phoenicians with strong Italian, other Mediterranean elements). **Principal languages:** Maltese, English (both official). **Chief religion:** Roman Catholic (official) 98%.

Geography: Total area: 122 sq mi, 316 sq km; **Land area:** 122 sq mi, 316 sq km. **Location:** In center of Mediterranean Sea. **Neighbors:** Nearest is Italy on N. **Topography:** Isl. of Malta is 95 sq mi; other islands in the group: Gozo, 26 sq mi; Comino, 1 sq mi. Coastline is heavily indented. Low hills cover the interior. **Capital:** Valletta, 199,000.

Government: Type: Parliamentary democracy. **Head of state:** Pres. George Abela; b. Apr. 22, 1948; in office: Apr. 4, 2009. **Head of gov.:** Prime Min. Lawrence Gonzi; b. July 1, 1953; in office: Mar. 23, 2004. **Local divisions:** 3 regions comprising 67 local councils. **Defense budget:** $57 mil. **Active troops:** 1,954.

Economy: Industries: tourism, electronics, shipbuilding and repair, constr., food and beverages, pharmaceuticals. **Chief crops:** potatoes, cauliflower, grapes, wheat, barley, tomatoes, citrus, cut flowers, green peppers. **Natural resources:** limestone, salt. **Arable land:** 25.0%. **Livestock:** cattle: 17,777; chickens: 500,000; goats: 6,361; pigs: 65,511; sheep: 12,843. **Fish catch:** 4,142 metric tons. **Electricity prod.:** 2.2 bil kWh. **Labor force:** agric. 1.3%, industry 24.8%, services 73.9%.

Finance: Monetary unit: Euro (EUR) (Sept. 2011: 0.71 = $1 U.S.). **GDP:** $10.4 bil; **per capita GDP:** $25,600; **GDP growth:** 3.7%. **Imports:** $5.2 bil; Italy 25.2%, UK 12.2%, France 10.2%, Germany 9%, Netherlands 5.1%. **Exports** (2010): $3.1 bil; Germany 13.8%, Singapore 11.7%, France 11.6%, U.S. 9.4%, Hong Kong 6.5%, UK 6.1%, Italy 5.5%, Libya 5%. **Tourism:** $1.1 bil. **Budget:** $3.3 bil. **Total reserves less gold:** $535.8 mil. **Gold:** 3,100 oz t. **CPI change:** 1.5%.

Transport: Motor vehicles: 681.3 vehicles per 1,000 pop. **Civil aviation:** 2 bil pass.-mi; 1 airport. **Chief ports:** Marsaxlokk (Malta Freeport), Valletta.

Communications: TV sets: 554 per 1,000 pop. **Radios:** 664 per 1,000 pop. **Telephone lines:** 59.4 per 100 pop. **Internet:** 63 users per 100 pop.

Health: Life expect.: 77.5 male; 82.1 female. **Births:** 10.4 (per 1,000 pop.). **Deaths:** 8.6 (per 1,000 pop.). **Natural inc.:** 0.18%. **Infant mortality:** 3.7 (per 1,000 live births). **HIV rate:** 0.1%.

Education: Compulsory: ages 5-15. **Literacy:** 92.4%.

Major intl. organizations: UN (FAO, IBRD, ILO, IMF, WHO), the Commonwealth, EU, OSCE, WTO.

Embassy: 2017 Connecticut Ave. NW 20008; 462-3611.

Website: www.gov.mt

Malta was ruled by Phoenicians, Romans, Arabs, Normans, the Knights of Malta, France, and Britain (since 1814). It became independent Sept. 21, 1964. Malta became a republic in 1974. The withdrawal of the last British sailors, Apr. 1, 1979, ended 179 years of British military presence on the island.

From 1971 to 1987 and again from 1996 to 1998, Malta was governed by the socialist Labour Party; the Nationalist Party, which pressed for Malta's entry into the EU, held office 1987-96 and won parliamentary elections in 1998, 2003, and 2008. Malta became a full member of the EU May 1, 2004.

Marshall Islands
Republic of the Marshall Islands

People: Population: 67,182. **Age distrib.:** <15: 38.2%; 65+: 3%. **Pop. density:** 961.3 per sq mi, 371.2 per sq km. **Urban:** 71.8%. **Ethnic groups:** Marshallese 92%, mixed Marshallese 6%. **Principal languages:** Marshallese, English (both official). **Chief religions:** Protestant 55%, Assembly of God 26%, Roman Catholic 8%, Bukot nan Jesus 3%, Mormon 2%, other Christian 4%, none 2%.

Geography: Total area: 70 sq mi, 181 sq km; **Land area:** 70 sq mi, 181 sq km. **Location:** In N Pacific Ocean; composed of two 800-mi-long parallel chains of coral atolls. **Neighbors:** Nearest are Micronesia on W, Nauru and Kiribati to S. **Topography:** Marshall Islands are low coral limestone and sand islands. **Capital:** Majuro, 30,000.

Government: Type: Republic in free association with the U.S. **Head of state and gov.:** Pres. Iroij Jurelang Zedkaia; b. July 13, 1950; in office: Nov. 2, 2009. **Local divisions:** 33 municipalities. **Defense budget/active troops:** NA.

Economy: Industries: copra, tuna proc., tourism, craft items. **Chief crops:** coconuts, tomatoes, melons, taro, breadfruit, fruits. **Natural resources:** coconut prods., marine prods., deep-seabed minerals. **Arable land:** 11.1%. **Fish catch:** 46,933 metric tons. **Labor force:** agric. 21.4%, industry 20.9%, services 57.7%.

Finance: Monetary unit: U.S. Dollar (USD). **GDP** (2008 est.): $133.5 mil; **per capita GDP** (2008 est.): $2,500; **GDP growth** (2008 est.): −0.3%. **Imports** (2008 est.): $79.4 mil; NA. **Exports** (2008 est.): $19.4 mil; NA. **Tourism:** NA. **Budget** (2008): $1.2 bil. **Total reserves less gold:** NA. **CPI change:** NA.

Transport: Civil aviation: 0.6 mil pass.-mi; 4 airports. **Chief port:** Majuro.

Communications: Telephone lines: 8.1 per 100 pop. **Internet:** NA.

Health: Life expect.: 69.7 male; 74.0 female. **Births:** 29.1 (per 1,000 pop.). **Deaths:** 4.4 (per 1,000 pop.). **Natural inc.:** 2.47%. **Infant mortality:** 23.7 (per 1,000 live births). **HIV rate:** NA.

Education: Compulsory: ages 6-14. **Literacy:** NA.

Major Intl. organizations: UN (FAO, IBRD, IMF, WHO).

Embassy: 2433 Massachusetts Ave. NW 20008; 234-5414.

Website: www.rmigovernment.org

The Marshall Islands were a German possession until WWI and were administered by Japan between the World Wars. After WWII, they were administered by the U.S. as part of the UN Trust Territory of the Pacific Islands. During 1946-58, Bikini and Enewetak atolls were used as test sites for U.S. nuclear weapons, including the hydrogen bomb.

The Compact of Free Association, ratified by the U.S. on Oct. 21, 1986, gave the islands their independence. In the compact, the U.S. agreed to provide financial aid to the islands, maintain their defense, and compensate victims of nuclear testing; it was renewed Dec. 2003. The Marshall Islands joined the UN Sept. 17, 1991. Amata Kabua, the islands' first and only president since 1979, died Dec. 19, 1996. His cousin Imata Kabua, elected president Jan. 13, 1997, was succeeded by Kessai Note on Jan. 10, 2000; Litokwa Tomeing, Jan. 14, 2008; and Jurelang Zedkaia, Nov. 2, 2009.

Mauritania
Islamic Republic of Mauritania

People: Population: 3,281,634. **Age distrib.:** <15: 40.4%; 65+: 3.5%. **Pop. density:** 8.2 per sq mi, 3.2 per sq km. **Urban:** 41.4%. **Ethnic groups:** mixed Moor/black 40%, Moor 30%, black 30%. **Principal languages:** Arabic (official & national); Pulaar, Soninke, Wolof (all national); French; Hassaniya. **Chief religion:** Muslim 100%.

Geography: Total area: 397,955 sq mi, 1,030,700 sq km; **Land area:** 397,955 sq mi, 1,030,700 sq km. **Location:** In NW Africa. **Neighbors:** Western Sahara on N; Algeria, Mali on E; Senegal on S. **Topography:** Fertile Senegal R. valley in the S gives way to a wide central region of sandy plains and scrub trees. N is arid and extends into the Sahara. **Capital:** Nouakchott, 709,000.

Government: Type: Republic. **Head of state:** Pres. Mohamed Ould Abdel Aziz; b. Dec. 20, 1956; in office: Aug. 5. 2009. **Head of gov.:** Prime Min. Moulaye Ould Mohamed Laghdaf; b. 1957; in office: Aug. 14, 2008. **Local divisions:** 12 regions, 1 capital district. **Defense budget** (2008): $20 mil. **Active troops:** 15,870.

Economy: Industries: fish proc.; oil prod.; iron ore, gold, copper mining. **Chief crops:** dates, millet, sorghum, rice, corn. **Natural resources:** iron ore, gypsum, copper, phosphate, diamonds, gold, oil, fish. **Crude oil reserves:** 100 mil bbls. **Arable land:** 0.4%. **Livestock:** cattle: 1.7 mil; chickens: 4.3 mil; goats: 5.6 mil; sheep: 8.9 mil. **Fish catch:** 178,541 metric tons. **Electricity prod.:** 547 mil kWh. **Labor force:** agric. 50%, industry 10%, services 40%.

Finance: Monetary unit: Ouguiya (MRO) (Sept. 2011: 276.00 = $1 U.S.). **GDP:** $6.7 bil; **per capita GDP:** $2,100; **GDP growth:** 4.7%. **Imports:** $1.5 bil; France 13.7%, China 12.6%, Netherlands 9.9%, Brazil 5.3%, Belgium 4.7%. **Exports** (2006): $1.4 bil; China 43.8%, Italy 9.6%, Japan 7.5%, Côte d'Ivoire 6.1%, Spain 5.5%, Netherlands 4.3%. **Tourism:** NA. **Budget** (2007 est.): $770 mil. **Total reserves less gold:** $271.7 mil. **Gold:** 11,500 oz t. **CPI change:** 6.3%.

Transport: Motor vehicles: 7.2 vehicles per 1,000 pop. **Civil aviation:** 39.8 mil pass.-mi; 9 airports. **Chief ports:** Nouadhibou, Nouakchott.

Communications: TV sets: 46 per 1,000 pop. **Radios:** 384 per 1,000 pop. **Telephone lines:** 2.1 per 100 pop. **Internet:** 3 users per 100 pop.

Health: Life expect.: 58.9 male; 63.4 female. **Births:** 33.2 (per 1,000 pop.). **Deaths:** 8.8 (per 1,000 pop.). **Natural inc.:** 2.44%. **Infant mortality:** 60.4 (per 1,000 live births). **HIV rate:** 0.7%.

Education: Compulsory: ages 6-11. **Literacy:** 57.5%.

Major intl. organizations: UN (FAO, IBRD, ILO, IMF, WHO), AL, AU, WTO.

Embassy: 2129 Leroy Pl. NW 20008; 232-5700.

Website: www.mauritania.mr

Mauritania was a French protectorate from 1903. It became independent Nov. 28, 1960, and annexed the south of former Spanish Sahara (now Western Sahara) in 1976. Mauritania signed a peace treaty with the Saharan guerrillas of the Polisario Front, 1979, and renounced its own claim to the region.

Maaouiya Ould Sid Ahmed Taya took power in a military coup in 1984. Taya, a U.S. ally, was toppled in a bloodless coup, Aug. 3, 2005. During Jan.-June 2006, up to 10,000 people tried to emigrate in handmade boats from Mauritania to Spain's Canary Islands; more than 1,700 died. Civilian rule was restored, 2006-07, but a military coup, Aug. 6, 2008, toppled the elected government. The coup leader, Gen. Mohamed Ould Abdel Aziz, won a disputed presidential election July 18, 2009. Security concerns, including a rising threat from the group al-Qaeda in the Islamic Maghreb, led the U.S. Peace Corps to pull its volunteers out of Mauritania in Aug.

Major oil finds have recently been developed. Although slavery has been repeatedly abolished, most recently in 1981, thousands of Mauritanians continued to live under conditions of servitude; legislation mandating prison terms for slaveholders was enacted Aug. 8, 2007.

Mauritius
Republic of Mauritius

People: Population: 1,303,717. **Age distrib.:** <15: 21.8%; 65+: 7.5%. **Pop. density:** 1,663.4 per sq mi, 642.2 per sq km. **Urban:**

41.8%. **Ethnic groups:** Indo-Mauritian 68%, Creole 27%, Sino-Mauritian 3%, Franco-Mauritian 2%. **Principal languages:** Creole, Bhojpuri, French, English (official). **Chief religions:** Hindu 48%, Roman Catholic 24%, Muslim 17%, other Christian 9%.

Geography: Total area: 788 sq mi, 2,040 sq km; **Land area:** 784 sq mi, 2,030 sq km. **Location:** In Indian O., 500 mi E of Madagascar. **Neighbors:** Nearest is Madagascar to W. **Topography:** A volcanic island nearly surrounded by coral reefs. A central plateau is encircled by mountain peaks. **Capital:** Port Louis, 149,000.

Government: Type: Republic. **Head of state:** Pres. Sir Anerood Jugnauth; b. Mar. 29, 1930; in office: Oct. 7, 2003. **Head of gov.:** Prime Min. Navinchandra Ramgoolam; b. July 14, 1947; in office: July 5, 2005. **Local divisions:** 9 districts, 3 dependencies. **Defense budget** (2009): $41 mil. **Active troops:** 2,000 (paramilitary only).

Economy: Industries: food proc. (largely sugar milling), textiles, clothing, mining, chemicals. **Chief crops:** sugarcane, tea, corn, potatoes, bananas, pulses. **Natural resources:** fish. **Arable land:** 42.9%. **Livestock:** cattle: 7,237; chickens: 13.7 mil; goats: 26,014; pigs: 14,108; sheep: 12,000. **Fish catch:** 8,113 metric tons. **Electricity prod.:** 2.4 bil kWh. **Labor force:** agric. and fishing 9%; constr. and industry 30%; transp. and communication 7%; trade, restaurants, hotels 22%; finance 6%; other services 25%.

Finance: Monetary unit: Rupee (MUR) (Sept. 2011: 27.60 = $1 U.S.). **GDP:** $18.1 bil; **per capita GDP:** $14,000; **GDP growth:** 4%. **Imports** (2006): $3.9 bil; India 18.7%, China 12.6%, France 11.8%, South Africa 8.7%. **Exports:** $2 bil; UK 27%, France 21.2%, U.S. 8.3%, Madagascar 6.4%, Italy 5.5%, South Africa 4.6%, Spain 4.6%. **Tourism:** $1.3 bil. **Budget:** $2.6 bil. **Total reserves less gold:** $2.4 bil. **Gold:** 125,781 oz t. **CPI change:** 2.9%.

Transport: Motor vehicles: 160.8 vehicles per 1,000 pop. **Civil aviation:** 3.5 bil pass.-mi; 2 airports. **Chief port:** Port Louis.

Communications: TV sets: 370 per 1,000 pop. **Radios:** 78 per 1,000 pop. **Telephone lines:** 29.8 per 100 pop. **Daily newspaper circ.:** 77.2 per 1,000 pop. **Internet:** 24.9 users per 100 pop.

Health: Life expect.: 71.0 male; 78.1 female. **Births:** 14.0 (per 1,000 pop.). **Deaths:** 6.7 (per 1,000 pop.). **Natural inc.:** 0.73%. **Infant mortality:** 11.5 (per 1,000 live births). **HIV rate:** 1%.

Education: Compulsory: ages 5-16. **Literacy:** 87.9%.

Major intl. organizations: UN and all of its specialized agencies, AU, the Commonwealth, WTO.

Embassy: 4301 Connecticut Ave. NW, Ste. 441, 20008; 244-1491.

Website: www.gov.mu

Mauritius was uninhabited when settled in 1638 by the Dutch, who introduced sugarcane. France took over in 1721, bringing African slaves. Britain ruled from 1810 to Mar. 12, 1968, bringing Indian workers for the sugar plantations.

Mauritius formally severed its association with the British crown Mar. 12, 1992.

Mexico
United Mexican States

People: Population: 113,724,226. **Age distrib.:** <15: 28.2%; 65+: 6.6%. **Pop. density:** 151.5 per sq mi, 58.5 per sq km. **Urban:** 77.8%. **Ethnic groups:** mestizo (Amerindian-Spanish) 60%, Amerindian or predominantly Amerindian 30%, white 9%. **Principal languages:** Spanish, indigenous languages (incl. various Mayan, Nahuatl, & others). **Chief religions:** Roman Catholic 77%, Protestant 6%, none 3%.

Geography: Total area: 758,449 sq mi, 1,964,375 sq km; **Land area:** 750,561 sq mi, 1,943,945 sq km. **Location:** In southern N. America. **Neighbors:** U.S. on N, Guatemala and Belize on S. **Topography:** The Sierra Madre Occidental Mts. run NW-SE near the west coast; the Sierra Madre Oriental Mts. run near Gulf of Mexico. They join S of Mexico City. Between the 2 ranges lies the dry central plateau, 5,000 to 8,000 ft alt., rising toward the S, with temperate vegetation. Coastal lowlands are tropical. About 45% of land is arid. **Capital:** Mexico City, 19,319,000. **Cities** (urban aggl.): Guadalajara, 4,402,412; Monterrey, 3,895,876; Puebla, 2,315,422; Tijuana, 1,663,686; Toluca de Lerdo, 1,582,142; León de los Aldamas, 1,570,650.

Government: Type: Federal republic. **Head of state and gov.:** Pres. Felipe de Jesús Calderón Hinojosa; b. Aug. 18, 1962; in office: Dec. 1, 2006. **Local divisions:** 31 states, 1 federal district. **Defense budget:** $4.6 bil (excl. paramilitaries). **Active troops:** 280,250.

Economy: Industries: food and beverages, tobacco, chemicals, iron and steel, petroleum, mining, textiles, clothing, motor vehicles, consumer durables, tourism. **Chief crops:** corn, wheat, soybeans, rice, beans, cotton, coffee, fruits, tomatoes. **Natural resources:** petroleum, silver, copper, gold, lead, zinc, nat. gas, timber. **Crude oil reserves:** 10.4 bil bbls. **Arable land:** 12.9%. **Livestock:** cattle: 32 mil; chickens: 510 mil; goats: 8.9 mil; pigs: 15.2 mil; sheep: 7.8 mil. **Fish catch:** 1.8 mil metric tons. **Electricity prod.** (2009): 239.1 bil kWh. **Labor force:** agric. 13.7%, industry 23.4%, services 62.9%.

Finance: Monetary unit: Peso (MXN) (Sept. 2011: 12.50 = $1 U.S.). **GDP:** $1.6 tril; **per capita GDP:** $13,900; **GDP growth:** 5.5%. **Imports:** $306 bil; U.S. 48%, China 13.9%, Japan 4.9%, South Korea 4.7%, Germany 4.2%. **Exports:** $303 bil; U.S. 80.6%. **Tourism:** $11.9 bil. **Budget:** $267 bil. **Total reserves less gold:** $120.3 bil. **Gold:** 226,984 oz t. **CPI change:** 4.2%.

Transport: Railways: 10,666 mi. **Motor vehicles:** 267.1 vehicles per 1,000 pop. **Civil aviation:** 17.4 bil pass.-mi; 250 airports. **Chief ports:** Altamira, Coatzacoalcos, Manzanillo, Salina Cruz, Veracruz.

Communications: TV sets: 274 per 1,000 pop. **Radios:** 324 per 1,000 pop. **Telephone lines:** 17.5 per 100 pop. **Internet:** 31 users per 100 pop.

Health: Life expect.: 73.7 male; 79.4 female. **Births:** 19.1 (per 1,000 pop.). **Deaths:** 4.9 (per 1,000 pop.). **Natural inc.:** 1.43%. **Infant mortality:** 17.3 (per 1,000 live births). **HIV rate:** 0.3%.

Education: Compulsory: ages 6-15. **Literacy:** 93.4%.

Major intl. organizations: UN (FAO, IBRD, ILO, IMF, WHO), APEC, NAFTA, OAS, OECD, WTO.

Embassy: 1911 Pennsylvania Ave. NW 20006; 728-1600.

Website: www.presidencia.gob.mx

Mexico was the site of advanced Indian civilizations. The Mayans, an agricultural people, moved up from Yucatan, built huge stone pyramids, and invented a calendar. The Toltecs were overcome by the Aztecs, who founded Tenochtitlan 1325 CE, now Mexico City. Hernán Cortés, Spanish conquistador, destroyed the Aztec empire, 1519-21. After 3 centuries of Spanish rule the people rose, under Fr. Miguel Hidalgo y Costilla, 1810, Fr. Morelos y Pavón, 1812, and Gen. Agustín Iturbide, who made himself emperor as Agustín I, 1822. A republic was declared in 1823.

Mexican territory extended into the present American Southwest and California until Texas revolted and established a republic in 1836. The U.S.-Mexican War, 1846-48, resulted in the loss by Mexico of the lands north of the Rio Grande.

French arms supported an Austrian archduke on the throne of Mexico as Maximilian I, 1864-67, but pressure from the U.S. forced France to withdraw. Dictatorial rule by Porfirio Díaz, president 1877-80, 1884-1911, led to a period of rebellion and factional fighting. A new constitution, Feb. 5, 1917, brought reform.

The Institutional Revolutionary Party (PRI) dominated politics from 1929 until the late 1990s. Radical opposition, including some guerrilla activity, was contained by strong measures. Some gains in agriculture, industry, and social services were achieved, but much of the work force remained jobless or underemployed. Although prospects brightened with the discovery of vast oil reserves, inflation and a drop in world oil prices aggravated Mexico's economic problems in the 1980s. Mexico reached agreement with the U.S. and Canada on the North American Free Trade Agreement (NAFTA) Aug. 12, 1992; it took effect Jan. 1, 1994.

Guerrillas of the Zapatista National Liberation Army (EZLN) launched an uprising, Jan. 1, 1994, in southern Mexico. A tentative peace accord was reached Mar. 2. The presidential candidate of the governing PRI, Luis Donaldo Colosio Murrieta, was assassinated at a political rally in Tijuana, Mar. 23. The new PRI candidate, Ernesto Zedillo Ponce de León, won election Aug. 21 and was inaugurated Dec. 1, 1994.

An austerity plan and pledges of aid from the U.S. saved Mexico's currency from collapse in early 1995. Popular Revolutionary Army guerrillas launched coordinated attacks on government targets in Aug. 1996. In elections July 6, 1997, the PRI failed to win a congressional majority for the first time since 1929.

In the presidential election of July 2, 2000, the PRI lost for the first time in over 7 decades; the winner, Vicente Fox Quesada of the National Action Party (PAN), took office Dec. 1, 2000. Hurricane Wilma hit Cancún Oct. 21, 2005, causing $2 bil damage.

Results of the July 2, 2006, presidential vote gave the PAN candidate, conservative Felipe Calderón Hinojosa, a slim margin over former Mexico City mayor Andrés Manuel López Obra-dor, nominee of the leftist Democratic Revolutionary Party. Claiming vote fraud, López Obrador and his supporters held massive protests, but Calderón was declared the winner and took office Dec. 1, 2006. Despite a government crackdown on drug cartels, drug-related violence intensified, including an arson attack on a Monterrey casino Aug. 25, 2011, that killed 52 people, mostly women; the cumulative death toll in the drug war exceeded 42,000, Dec. 2006-Sept. 2011.

Micronesia
Federated States of Micronesia

People: Population: 106,836. **Age distrib.:** <15: 33.6%; 65+: 3%. **Pop. density:** 394.2 per sq mi, 152.2 per sq km. **Urban:** 22.7%. **Ethnic groups:** Chuukese 49%, Pohnpeian 24%, Kosraean 6%, Yapese 5%, Yap outer islands 5%, Asian 2%, Polynesian 2%. **Principal languages:** English (official & common), Chuukese, Kosraen, Pohnpeian, Yapese, Ulithian, Woleaian, Nukuoro, Kapingamarangi. **Chief religions:** Roman Catholic 52%, Congregational 40%.

Geography: Total area: 271 sq mi, 702 sq km; **Land area:** 271 sq mi, 702 sq km. **Location:** Consists of 607 islands in W Pacific Ocean. **Topography:** Includes both high mountainous islands and low coral atolls; volcanic outcroppings on Pohnpei, Kosrae, and Truk. Climate is tropical. **Capital:** Palikir, 7,000.

Government: Type: Republic in free association with U.S. **Head of state and gov.:** Pres. Emanuel (Manny) Mori; b. Dec. 25, 1948; in office: May 11, 2007. **Local divisions:** 4 states. **Defense budget/active troops:** NA.

Economy: Industries: tourism, constr., fish proc., specialized aquaculture, craft items. **Chief crops:** black pepper, tropical fruits and vegetables, coconuts, bananas, cassava, kava, citrus, betel nuts, sweet potatoes. **Natural resources:** timber, marine prods., deep-sea-bed minerals, phosphate. **Arable land:** 2.9%. **Livestock:** cattle: 14,000; chickens: 190,000; goats: 4,100; pigs: 33,000. **Fish catch:** 27,856 metric tons. **Labor force:** agric. 0.9%, industry 34.4%, services 64.7% (two-thirds govt. employees).

Finance: Monetary unit: U.S. dollar (USD). **GDP** (2008 est.): $238.1 mil (supplemented by grant aid, averaging perhaps $100 mil annually); **per capita GDP** (2008 est.): $2,200; **GDP growth** (2005 est.): 0.3%. **Imports** (2004): $132.7 mil; NA. **Exports** (2004 est.): $14 mil; NA. **Tourism:** NA. **Budget** (FY07 est.): $152.7 mil. **Total reserves less gold:** $55.8 mil. **CPI change:** NA.

Transport: Civil aviation: 6 airports. **Chief port:** Colonia.

Communications: TV sets: 27 per 1,000 pop. **Radios:** 47 per 1,000 pop. **Telephone lines:** 7.6 per 100 pop. **Internet:** 20 users per 100 pop.

Health: Life expect.: 69.6 male; 73.6 female. **Births:** 22.2 (per 1,000 pop.). **Deaths:** 4.4 (per 1,000 pop.). **Natural inc.:** 1.79%. **Infant mortality:** 24.3 (per 1,000 live births). **HIV rate:** NA.

Education: Compulsory: ages 6-13. **Literacy:** NA.

Major intl. organizations: UN (FAO, IBRD, IMF, WHO).

Embassy: 1725 N St. NW 20036; 223-4383.

Website: micronesia.fm

The Federated States of Micronesia, formerly known as the Caroline Islands, was ruled successively by Spain, Germany, Japan, and the U.S. The nation gained independence under a compact of free association with the U.S., Nov. 1986, and was admitted to the UN, Sept. 17, 1991. Micronesian officials have repeatedly warned of the dangers to their country of rising sea levels linked to global climate change.

Moldova

Republic of Moldova

People: Population: 3,694,121. **Age distrib.:** <15: 17.5%; 65+: 10.6%. **Pop. density:** 290.9 per sq mi, 112.3 per sq km. **Urban:** 47%. **Ethnic groups:** Moldovan/Romanian 78%, Ukrainian 8%, Russian 6%, Gagauz 4%, Bulgarian 2%. **Principal languages:** Moldovan (official; virtually same as Romanian), Russian, Gagauz. **Chief religions:** Eastern Orthodox 98%, Jewish 1.5%.

Geography: Total area: 13,070 sq mi, 33,851 sq km; **Land area:** 12,699 sq mi, 32,891 sq km. **Location:** In E Europe. **Neighbors:** Romania on W; Ukraine on N, E, and S. **Topography:** Country is landlocked; mainly hilly plains, with steppelands in S near Black Sea. **Capital:** Chisinau (Kishinev), 650,000.

Government: Type: Republic. **Head of state:** Pres. Marian Lupu; b. June 20, 1966; in office: Dec. 30, 2010 (acting). **Head of gov.:** Prime Min. Vladimir Filat; b. May 6, 1969; in office: Sept. 25, 2009. **Local divisions:** 9 counties, 1 municipality, 1 autonomous territory. **Defense budget:** $16 mil. **Active troops:** 5,354.

Economy: Industries: sugar, vegetable oil, food proc., agric. machinery, foundry equip. **Chief crops:** vegetables, fruits, grapes, grain, sugar beets, sunflower seeds, tobacco. **Natural resources:** lignite, phosphorites, gypsum, limestone. **Arable land:** 55.2%. **Livestock:** cattle: 218,000; chickens: 18,0 mil; goats: 104,000; pigs: 284,000; sheep: 762,000. **Fish catch:** 6,307 metric tons. **Electricity prod.:** 3.4 bil kWh. **Labor force:** agric. 40.6%, industry 16%, services 43.3%.

Finance: Monetary unit: Leu (MDL) (Sept. 2011: 11.36 = $1 U.S.). **GDP:** $11 bil; **per capita GDP:** $2,500; **GDP growth:** 6.9%. **Imports:** $3.7 bil; Ukraine 14%, Russia 11.4%, Romania 9.5%, Germany 7.7%, China 7.5%, Italy 7.1%, Turkey 5.3%, Kazakhstan 5.1%, Belarus 4.2%. **Exports:** $1.5 bil; Russia 22.3%, Romania 18.7%, Italy 10.8%, Ukraine 6.3%, Belarus 6.3%, Germany 5.9%, UK 4.7%. **Tourism:** $162 mil. **Budget:** $2.5 bil. **Total reserves less gold:** $1.7 bil. **CPI change:** 7.4%.

Transport: Railways: 739 mi. **Civil aviation:** 330.6 mil pass.-mi; 5 airports.

Communications: TV sets: 310 per 1,000 pop. **Radios:** 39 per 1,000 pop. **Telephone lines:** 32.5 per 100 pop. **Internet:** 40 users per 100 pop.

Health: Life expect.: 65.3 male; 73.3 female. **Births:** 12.6 (per 1,000 pop.). **Deaths:** 12.6 (per 1,000 pop.). **Natural inc.:** -0.01%. **Infant mortality:** 14.0 (per 1,000 live births). **HIV rate:** 0.4%.

Education: Compulsory: ages 7-15. **Literacy:** 98.5%.

Major intl. organizations: UN (FAO, IBRD, ILO, IMF, WHO), CIS, OSCE, WTO.

Embassy: 2101 S St. NW 20008; 667-1130.

Website: www.moldova.md

In 1918, Romania annexed all of Bessarabia that Russia had acquired from Turkey in 1812 by the Treaty of Bucharest. In 1924, the Soviet Union established the Moldavian Autonomous Soviet Socialist Republic on the eastern bank of the Dniester. It was merged with the Romanian-speaking districts of Bessarabia in 1940 to form the Moldavian SSR.

During WWII, Romania, allied with Germany, occupied the area. It was recaptured by the USSR in 1944. Moldova declared independence Aug. 27, 1991. It became an independent state when the USSR disbanded Dec. 26, 1991.

Fighting erupted Mar. 1992 in the Trans-Dniester region between Moldovan security forces and Slavic separatists—ethnic Russians and ethnic Ukrainians—who feared Moldova would merge with neighboring Romania. In a plebiscite on Mar. 6, 1994, voters in Moldova supported independence, without unification with Romania.

Defying the Moldovan government, voters in the breakaway Trans-Dniester region held legislative elections and approved a separatist constitution Dec. 24, 1995. A peace accord with Trans-Dniester separatists was signed in Moscow May 8, 1997. In a referendum Sept. 17, 2006, Trans-Dniester voters overwhelmingly supported independence from Moldova and eventual union with Russia. The Communists gained legislative majorities in 2001 and 2005 but were outpolled by a fragile coalition of pro-Western parties in 2009 and 2010 elections. When a deadlocked parliament failed to agree on a president, a constitutional referendum providing for direct presidential elections was held Sept. 5, 2010. Although 88% of voters supported it, the measure failed to pass because of insufficient turnout.

Monaco

Principality of Monaco

People: Population: 30,539. **Age distrib.:** <15: 12.3%; 65+: 26.9%. **Pop. density:** 39,547.8 per sq mi, 15,269.5 per sq km. **Urban:** 100%. **Ethnic groups:** French 47%, Monegasque 16%, Italian 16%. **Principal languages:** French (official), English, Italian, Monegasque. **Chief religion:** Roman Catholic 90%.

Geography: Total area: 0.77 sq mi, 2 sq km; **Land area:** 0.77 sq mi, 2 sq km. **Location:** On NW Mediterranean coast. **Neighbors:** France to W, N, E. **Topography:** Monaco-Ville sits atop a high promontory, the rest of the principality rises from the port up the hillside. **Capital:** Monaco, 33,000.

Government: Type: Constitutional monarchy. **Head of state:** Prince Albert II; b. Mar. 14, 1958; in office: Apr. 6, 2005. **Head of gov.:** Min. of State Michel Roger; b. Mar. 9, 1949; in office: Mar. 29, 2010. **Local divisions:** 4 quarters. **Defense budget/active troops:** NA.

Economy: Industries: tourism, constr., small-scale industrial and consumer prods. **Chief crops:** none. **Natural resources:** none. **Arable land:** None. **Fish catch:** 1 metric ton. **Labor force:** NA.

Finance: Monetary unit: Euro (EUR) (Sept. 2011: 0.71 = $1 U.S.). **GDP** (2006 est.): $976.3 mil; **per capita GDP** (2006 est.): $30,000; **GDP growth:** NA. **Imports** (2005): $916.1 mil; NA. **Exports** (2005): $716.3 mil; NA. (Full customs integration with France. Also participates in EU market system through customs union with France.) **Tourism:** NA. **Budget** (2005 est.): $920.6 mil. **Total reserves less gold:** NA. **CPI change:** NA.

Transport: Civil aviation: 1.9 mil pass.-mi; 1 heliport. **Chief port:** Monaco.

Communications: TV sets: 758 per 1,000 pop. **Telephone lines:** 96.4 per 100 pop. **Internet:** 80 users per 100 pop.

Health: Life expect.: 85.8 male; 93.8 female. **Births:** 6.9 (per 1,000 pop.). **Deaths:** 8.3 (per 1,000 pop.). **Natural inc.:** -0.13%. **Infant mortality:** 1.8 (per 1,000 live births). **HIV rate:** NA.

Education: Compulsory: ages 6-16. **Literacy:** 99%.

Major intl. organizations: UN (FAO, WHO), OSCE.

Embassy: 2314 Wyoming Ave. NW 20008; 234-1530.

Website: www.gouv.mc

An independent principality for over 300 years, Monaco has belonged to the House of Grimaldi since 1297, except during the French Revolution. It was placed under the protectorate of Sardinia in 1815, and under France, 1861. The Prince of Monaco was an absolute ruler until the 1911 constitution. Monaco was admitted to the UN on May 28, 1993.

Monaco is noted for its mild climate, magnificent scenery, and elegant casinos. Prince Rainier III, who ruled Monaco from 1949 and turned it into one of Europe's top tourist spots, died Apr. 6, 2005, and was succeeded by his son, Albert II.

Mongolia

People: Population: 3,133,318. **Age distrib.:** <15: 27.3%; 65+: 4%. **Pop. density:** 5.2 per sq mi, 2 per sq km. **Urban:** 62%. **Ethnic groups:** Mongol (mostly Khalkha) 95%, Turkic (mostly Kazakh) 5%. **Principal languages:** Khalkha Mongol, Turkic, Russian. **Chief religions:** Buddhist Lamaist 50%, Shamanist & Christian 6%, Muslim 4%, none 40%.

Geography: Total area: 603,909 sq mi, 1,564,116 sq km; **Land area:** 599,831 sq mi, 1,553,556 sq km. **Location:** In E Central Asia. **Neighbors:** Russia on N, China on E, W, and S. **Topography:** Mostly a high plateau with mountains, salt lakes, and vast grasslands. Arid lands in S are part of the Gobi Desert. **Capital:** Ulaanbaatar, 949,000.

Government: Type: Republic. **Head of state:** Pres. Tsakhiagiin Elbegdorj; b. Mar. 30, 1963; in office: June 18, 2009. **Head of gov.:** Prime. Min. Sukhbaatar Batbold; b. 1963; in office: Oct. 29, 2009. **Local divisions:** 18 provinces, 3 municipalities. **Defense budget** (2008): $51 mil. **Active troops:** 10,000.

Economy: Industries: constr. and constr. materials, mining, oil, food and beverages, animal prods. proc. **Chief crops:** wheat, barley, vegetables, forage crops. **Natural resources:** oil, coal, copper, molybdenum, tungsten, phosphates, tin, nickel, zinc, fluorspar, gold, silver, iron. **Arable land:** 0.6%. **Livestock:** cattle: 2.6 mil; chickens: 399,000; goats: 19.7 mil; pigs: 25,808; sheep: 19.3 mil. **Fish catch:** 90 metric tons. **Electricity prod.:** 3.9 bil kWh. **Labor force:** agric. 34%, industry 5%, services 61%.

Finance: Monetary unit: Tughrik (MNT) (Sept. 2011: 1,247.50 = $1 U.S.). **GDP:** $11 bil; **per capita GDP:** $3,600; **GDP growth:** 6.1%. **Imports** (2010): $3.3 bil; Russia 33.2%, China 30.5%, Japan 6%, South Korea 5.5%. **Exports** (2010): $2.9 bil; China 84.8%, Canada 3.6%, Russia 2.7%. **Tourism:** $244 mil. **Budget:** $2.3 bil. **Total reserves less gold:** $2.2 bil. **Gold:** 64,792 oz t. **CPI change:** 10.1%.

Transport: Railways: 1,186 mi. **Civil aviation:** 379 mil pass.-mi; 14 airports.

Communications: TV sets: 88 per 1,000 pop. **Radios:** 328 per 1,000 pop. **Telephone lines:** 7 per 100 pop. **Daily newspaper circ.:** 19.6 per 1,000 pop. **Internet:** 10.2 users per 100 pop.

Health: Life expect.: 65.9 male; 70.9 female. **Births:** 20.9 (per 1,000 pop.). **Deaths:** 6.0 (per 1,000 pop.). **Natural inc.:** 1.49%. **Infant mortality:** 37.3 (per 1,000 live births). **HIV rate:** <0.1%.

Education: Compulsory: ages 7-15. **Literacy:** 97.5%.

Major intl. organizations: UN (FAO, IBRD, ILO, IMF, WHO), WTO.

Embassy: 2833 M St. NW 20007; 333-7117.

Website: www.pmis.gov.mn

One of the world's oldest countries, Mongolia reached the zenith of its power in the 13th cent. when Genghis Khan and his successors conquered all of China and extended their influence as far west as Hungary and Poland. In later centuries, the empire dissolved and Mongolia became a province of China.

With the advent of the 1911 Chinese revolution, Mongolia, with Russian backing, declared its independence. A Communist regime was established July 11, 1921. In 1990, the Mongolian Communist Party yielded its monopoly on power. A new constitution took effect Feb. 12, 1992.

Mongolia contributed troops to U.S.-led operations in Afghanistan (2001) and Iraq (2003); more than 100 Mongolian troops remained in Afghanistan in mid-2011. Riots followed parliamentary elections June 29, 2008, won by the ruling Mongolian People's Revolutionary Party (MPRP). In presidential voting May 24, 2009, former Prime Min. Tsakhiagiin Elbergdorj (1998, 2004-06), the Democratic Party candidate, defeated the MPRP's incumbent Pres. Nambaryn Enkhbayar. Exploitation of vast mineral resources is expected to boost Mongolia's GDP at annual rates of more than 10% in 2011 and over 20% by 2013.

Montenegro

People: Population: 661,807. **Age distrib.:** <15: 15.5%; 65+: 13.5%. **Pop. density:** 127.4 per sq mi, 49.2 per sq km. **Urban:** 61.5%. **Ethnic groups:** Montenegrin 43%, Serbian 32%, Bosniak 8%, Albanian 5%, other (Muslim, Croat, Roma) 12%. **Principal languages:** Serbian, Montenegrin (official), Bosnian, Albanian. **Chief religions:** Orthodox 74%, Muslim 18%, Roman Catholic 4%, atheist 1%.

Geography: Total area: 5,333 sq mi, 13,812 sq km; **Land area:** 5,194 sq mi, 13,452 sq km. **Location:** On Balkan Peninsula in SE Europe. **Neighbors:** Bosnia and Herzegovina on N and W; Serbia on E; Albania on SE; Adriatic Sea on SW; Croatia on W. **Topography:** Most terrain is rugged and mountainous, with few arable regions, mostly along the Zeta R.; narrow coastline is highly indented. **Capital:** Podgorica, 144,000.

Government: Type: Republic. **Head of state:** Pres. Filip Vujanovic; b. Sept. 1, 1954; in office: May 22, 2003. **Head of gov.:** Prime Min. Igor Luksic; b. June 14, 1976; in office: Dec. 29, 2010. **Local divisions:** 21 municipalities. **Defense budget:** $35 mil. **Active troops:** 3,127.

Economy: Industries: steelmaking, aluminum, agric. proc., consumer goods, tourism. **Chief crops:** tobacco, potatoes, citrus, olives, grapes. **Natural resources:** bauxite, hydroelectricity. **Arable land:** 12.9%. **Livestock:** cattle: 100,835; chickens: 417,000; pigs: 12,377; sheep: 199,764. **Fish catch:** 2,981 metric tons. **Electricity prod.:** 2.7 bil kWh. **Labor force:** agric. 2%, industry 30%, services 68%.

Finance: Monetary unit: Euro (EUR) (Sept. 2011: 0.71 = $1 U.S.). **GDP:** $6.7 bil; **per capita GDP:** $10,100; **GDP growth:** 1.1%. **Imports** (2003): $601.7 mil; Italy 17.2%, Slovenia 14.4%, Germany 9.9%, China 7.8%, Austria 7.7%, Russia 6.1%, Greece 4%, Hungary 4%. **Exports** (2003): $171.3 mil; Italy 27.9%, Greece 21.6%, Slovenia 11.3%, Hungary 8.5%, U.S. 7.6%, Egypt 4.8%. **Tourism:** $660 mil. **Budget:** NA. **Total reserves less gold:** $556.2 mil. **CPI change:** 0.7%.

Transport: Railways: 155 mi. **Civil aviation:** 4 airports. **Chief port:** Bar.

Communications: Telephone lines: 26.8 per 100 pop. **Internet:** 52 users per 100 pop.

Health: Life expect.: 74.8 male; 80.9 female. **Births:** 11.0 (per 1,000 pop.). **Deaths:** 8.9 (per 1,000 pop.). **Natural inc.:** 0.21%. **Infant mortality:** 9.6 (per 1,000 live births). **HIV rate:** NA.

Education: Compulsory: ages 6-14. **Literacy:** NA.

Major intl. organizations: UN (FAO, ILO, WHO), OSCE, WTO (observer).

Embassy: 1610 New Hampshire Ave. NW 20009; 234-6108.

Website: www.gov.me

Part of the medieval Serbian Kingdom, Montenegro preserved its autonomy for centuries because of its mountainous terrain. After WWI, it was part of the Kingdom of Serbs, Croats, and Slovenes, later renamed Yugoslavia. Italian forces occupied parts of Montenegro during WWII. In 1945, with the establishment of a federal Yugoslavia under Communist rule, Montenegro became one of 6 constituent republics.

In Apr. 1992, after 4 other republics had declared independence, Montenegro and Serbia reconstituted themselves as the Federal Republic of Yugoslavia. Because of its ties with Serbia, Montenegro was a target of NATO air strikes during the Kosovo war, Mar.-June 1999. The republic sought closer ties with the West, however, and worked to reduce its political and economic dependence on Serbia. A referendum on independence passed May 21, 2006, with barely more than the 55% majority required. Montenegro declared independence June 3, 2006, and was admitted as a UN member June 28. It applied Dec. 15, 2008, to join the EU.

Morocco
Kingdom of Morocco

People: Population: 31,968,361. **Age distrib.:** <15: 27.8%; 65+: 6.1%. **Pop. density:** 185.5 per sq mi, 71.6 per sq km. **Urban:** 58.2%. **Ethnic groups:** Arab-Berber 99%. **Principal languages:** Arabic (official), Berber dialects, French (lang. of business, govt., diplomacy). **Chief religions:** Muslim 99%, Christian 1%.

Geography: Total area: 172,414 sq mi, 446,550 sq km; **Land area:** 172,317 sq mi, 446,300 sq km. **Location:** On NW coast of Africa. **Neighbors:** Western Sahara on S, Algeria on E, Spain on N. **Topography:** Consists of 5 natural regions: mountain ranges (Riff in the N, Middle Atlas, Upper Atlas, and Anti-Atlas); rich plains in W; alluvial plains in SW; well-cultivated plateaus in the center; a pre-Sahara arid zone extending from SE. **Capital:** Rabat, 1,770,000. **Cities (urban aggl.):** Casablanca (Dar-el-Beida), 3,283,605; Fès, 1,065,496; Marrakech, 928,019.

Government: Type: Constitutional monarchy. **Head of state:** King Mohammed VI; b. Aug. 21, 1963; in office: July 23, 1999. **Head of gov.:** Prime Min. Abbas El Fassi; b. Sept. 18, 1940; in office: Sept. 19, 2007. **Local divisions:** 16 regions. **Defense budget:** $3.19 bil. **Active troops:** 195,800.

Economy: Industries: phosphate rock mining and proc., food proc., leather goods, textiles, constr., energy, tourism. **Chief crops:** barley, wheat, citrus, grapes, vegetables, olives. **Natural resources:** phosphates, iron ore, manganese, lead, zinc, fish, salt. **Crude oil reserves:** 680,000 bbls. **Arable land:** 18.0%. **Livestock:** cattle: 2.9 mil; chickens: 165 mil; goats: 5.3 mil; pigs: 8,000; sheep: 17.5 mil. **Fish catch:** 1.2 mil metric tons. **Electricity prod.:** 19.5 bil kWh. **Labor force:** agric. 44.6%, industry 19.8%, services 35.5%.

Finance: Monetary unit: Dirham (MAD) (Sept. 2011: 8.05 = $1 U.S.). **GDP:** $151.4 bil; **per capita GDP:** $4,800; **GDP growth:** 3.2%. **Imports:** $34.2 bil; France 17%, Spain 14.9%, China 7.5%, Italy 6.8%, Germany 6.4%, U.S. 5.7%, Saudi Arabia 5.1%. **Exports:** $14.5 bil; Spain 22.1%, France 20.1%, India 4.9%. **Tourism:** $6.7 bil. **Budget:** $27.1 bil. **Total reserves less gold:** $22.6 bil. **Gold:** 708,765 oz t. **CPI change:** 1%.

Transport: Railways: 1,284 mi. **Motor vehicles:** 58.8 vehicles per 1,000 pop. **Civil aviation:** 6 bil pass.-mi; 32 airports. **Chief ports:** Casablanca, Jorf Lasfar, Mohammedia, Safi, Tangier.

Communications: TV sets: 174 per 1,000 pop. **Radios:** 246 per 1,000 pop. **Telephone lines:** 11.7 per 100 pop. **Daily newspaper circ.:** 11.7 per 1,000 pop. **Internet:** 49 users per 100 pop.

Health: Life expect.: 72.8 male; 79.1 female. **Births:** 19.2 (per 1,000 pop.). **Deaths:** 4.8 (per 1,000 pop.). **Natural inc.:** 1.44%. **Infant mortality:** 27.5 (per 1,000 live births). **HIV rate:** 0.1%.

Education: Compulsory: ages 6-14. **Literacy:** 56.1%.

Major intl. organizations: UN (FAO, IBRD, ILO, IMF, WHO), AL, WTO.

Embassy: 1601 21st St. NW 20009; 462-7979.

Website: www.maroc.ma

Berbers were the original inhabitants, followed by Carthaginians and Romans. Arabs conquered in 683. In the 11th and 12th centuries, a Berber empire ruled all northwest Africa and most of Spain from Morocco.

Part of Morocco came under Spanish rule in the 19th cent.; France controlled the rest in the early 20th. Tribal uprisings lasted from 1911 to 1933. The country became independent Mar. 2, 1956. Tangier, an internationalized seaport, was turned over to Morocco, 1956. Ifni, a Spanish enclave, was ceded in 1969. Morocco annexed the disputed territory of Western Sahara during the second half of the 1970s.

King Hassan II assumed the throne in 1961, reigning until his death on July 23, 1999; he was immediately succeeded by his eldest son. A bicameral legislature was established in 1997.

Five terrorist attacks in Casablanca May 16, 2003, left 45 people dead, including 12 suicide bombers; the government blamed Salafia Jihadia, a group connected with al-Qaeda. An earthquake Feb. 24, 2004, killed at least 629 people in the vicinity of al-Hoceima, northern coastal Morocco. Following a series of suicide bombings in 2007, the government stepped up its campaign against militant Islamists. Following "Arab Spring" street demonstrations Feb.-Mar. 2011, the monarchy implemented modest constitutional reforms.

Western Sahara

Western Sahara, formerly the protectorate of Spanish Sahara, is bounded on the N by Morocco, the NE by Algeria, the E and S by Mauritania, and the W by the Atlantic Ocean. Phosphates are the major resource. Population (2011 est.): 507,160; capital: Laayoune (El Aaiún). Area: 102,703 sq mi.

Spain withdrew from its protectorate in Feb. 1976. On Apr. 14, 1976, Morocco annexed over 70,000 sq mi, with the remainder annexed by Mauritania. The Polisario Front guerrilla movement, which had proclaimed the region independent Feb. 27, launched attacks with Algerian support. After Mauritania signed a treaty with Polisario on Aug. 5, 1979, Morocco occupied Mauritania's portion of Western Sahara.

After years of bitter fighting, Morocco controlled the main urban areas, but Polisario guerrillas moved freely in the vast, sparsely populated deserts. The two sides implemented a cease-fire in 1991, when a UN peacekeeping force (MINURSO) was established with a mandate to prepare for a referendum on self-determination as early as 1992; in mid-2011, MINURSO had about 230 uniformed personnel in Western Sahara, but a referendum had still not been held.

Mozambique
Republic of Mozambique

People: Population: 22,948,858. **Age distrib.:** <15: 45.9%; 65+: 3%. **Pop. density:** 75.6 per sq mi, 29.2 per sq km. **Urban:** 38.4%. **Ethnic groups:** African (Makhuwa, Tsonga, Lomwe, Sena, others) 99.7%. **Principal languages:** Emakhuwa, Portuguese (official), Xichangana, Cisena, Elomwe, Echuwabo, other Mozambican languages. **Chief religions:** Catholic 28%, Muslim 18%, Zionist Christian 16%, Evangelical Pentacostal 11%, Anglican 1%, none 19%.

Geography: Total area: 308,642 sq mi, 799,380 sq km; **Land area:** 303,623 sq mi, 786,380 sq km. **Location:** On SE coast of Africa. **Neighbors:** Tanzania on N; Malawi, Zambia, Zimbabwe on W; South Africa, Swaziland on S. **Topography:** Coastal lowlands comprise nearly half the country with plateaus rising in steps to the mountains along W border. **Capital:** Maputo, 1,589,000. **Cities (urban aggl.):** Matola, 793,486.

Government: Type: Republic. **Head of state:** Pres. Armando Guebuza; b. Jan. 20, 1943; in office: Feb. 2, 2005. **Head of gov.:** Prime Min. Aires Ali; b. Dec. 6, 1955; in office: Jan. 16, 2010. **Local divisions:** 10 provinces and Maputo municipality. **Defense budget** (2009): $73 mil. **Active troops:** 11,200.

Economy: Industries: food, beverages, chemicals, aluminum, petroleum prods., textiles, cement. **Chief crops:** cotton, cashew nuts, sugarcane, tea, cassava, corn, coconuts, sisal, citrus and tropical fruits, potatoes, sunflowers. **Natural resources:** coal, titanium, nat. gas, hydropower, tantalum, graphite. **Arable land:** 6.4%. **Livestock:** cattle: 1.2 mil; chickens: 18 mil; goats: 4.3 mil; pigs: 1.3 mil; sheep: 181,899. **Fish catch:** 68,361 metric tons. **Electricity prod.:** 15 bil kWh. **Labor force:** agric. 81%, industry 6%, services 13%.

Finance: Monetary unit: Metical (MZN) (Sept. 2011: 26.80 = $1 U.S.). **GDP:** $21.8 bil; **per capita GDP:** $1,000; **GDP growth:** 7%. **Imports:** $3.5 bil; South Africa 33.5%, Netherlands 8.4%, India 5.9%, China 4.2%. **Exports:** $2.5 bil; Netherlands 47.6%, South Africa 11.6%. **Tourism:** $197 mil. **Budget:** $2.9 bil. **Total reserves less gold:** $2.2 bil. **Gold:** 75,200. **CPI change:** 12.7%.

Transport: Railways: 2,975 mi. **Motor vehicles:** 3 vehicles per 1,000 pop. **Civil aviation:** 343 mil pass.-mi; 23 airports. **Chief ports:** Beira, Maputo, Nacala.

Communications: TV sets: 21 per 1,000 pop. **Radios:** 63 per 1,000 pop. **Telephone lines:** 0.4 per 100 pop. **Daily newspaper circ.:** 2.7 per 1,000 pop. **Internet:** 4.2 users per 100 pop.

Health: Life expect.: 51.0 male; 52.6 female. **Births:** 39.6 (per 1,000 pop.). **Deaths:** 13.0 (per 1,000 pop.). **Natural inc.:** 2.66%. **Infant mortality:** 79.0 (per 1,000 live births). **HIV rate:** 11.5%.

Education: Compulsory: ages 6-12. **Literacy:** 55.1%.

Major intl. organizations: UN (FAO, IBRD, ILO, IMF, WHO), AU, the Commonwealth, WTO.

Embassy: 1525 New Hampshire Ave. NW 20036; 293-7146.

Website: www.mozambique.mz

The first Portuguese post on the Mozambique coast was established in 1505, on the trade route to the East. Mozambique became independent June 25, 1975, after a 10-year war against Portuguese colonial domination. The 1974 revolution in Portugal paved the way for an orderly transfer of power to Frelimo (Front for the Liberation of Mozambique).

The Frelimo government, headed by Pres. Samora Machel, a former guerrilla commander, provided for a gradual transition to a Communist system. Most of the country's whites emigrated. In the 1980s, severe drought and civil war caused famine and heavy loss of life. Pres. Machel was killed in a plane crash just inside the South African border, Oct. 19, 1986. Frelimo formally abandoned Marxist-Leninism in 1989, and a new constitution, effective Nov. 30, 1990, provided for multiparty elections and a free-market economy.

On Oct. 4, 1992, a peace agreement was signed aimed at ending hostilities between the government and the rebel Mozambican National Resistance (MNR). Repatriation of 1.7 mil Mozambican refugees officially ended June 1995. In Mar. 1999 the heaviest floods in four decades left nearly 200,000 people stranded. Even worse flooding in Feb.-Mar. 2000 claimed more than 600 lives, displaced over 1 mil people, and devastated the economy.

Frelimo retained its hold under Pres. Joaquim Chissano (in office 1986-2005) and his successor, Pres. Armando Guebuza, elected Dec. 1-2, 2004. Flooding of the Zambezi River basin, followed by Cyclone Favio, killed at least 45 people and left more than 170,000 people homeless in Feb. 2007. Another flood crisis, Jan.-Mar. 2008, claimed some 700 lives and displaced 650,000 people. Despite robust economic growth during 2000-11, average per capita income remains low and poverty is widespread. Guebuza won reelection with a 75% majority Oct. 28, 2009.

Myanmar (*formerly* Burma)
Republic of the Union of Myanmar

People: Population: 53,999,804. **Age distrib.:** <15: 27.5%; 65+: 5%. **Pop. density:** 214 per sq mi, 82.6 per sq km. **Urban:** 33.6%. **Ethnic groups:** Burman 68%, Shan 9%, Karen 7%, Rakhine 4%, Chinese 3%, Indian 2%, Mon 2%. **Principal languages:** Burmese (official), ethnic minority languages. **Chief religions:** Buddhist 89%, Christian 4%, Muslim 4%, animist 1%.

Geography: Total area: 261,228 sq mi, 676,578 sq km; **Land area:** 252,321 sq mi, 653,508 sq km. **Location:** Between S and SE Asia, on Bay of Bengal. **Neighbors:** Bangladesh, India on W; China, Laos, Thailand on E. **Topography:** Mountains surround Myanmar on W, N, and E, and dense forests cover much of the nation. N-S rivers provide habitable valleys and communications, especially the Irrawaddy, navigable for 900 mi. Country has a tropical monsoon climate. **Capital:** Rangoon (Yangon), 4,259,000; Nay Pyi Taw (admin.), 992,000. **Cities (urban aggl.):** Mandalay, 1,034,167.

Government: Type: Presidential republic dominated by the military. **Head of state and gov.:** Pres. Thein Sein; b. Apr. 20, 1945; in office: Mar. 30, 2011. **Local divisions:** 7 states, 7 divisions. **Defense budget:** $1.9 bil. **Active troops:** 406,000.

Economy: Industries: agric. proc.; wood and wood prods.; copper, tin, tungsten, iron; cement, constr. materials; pharmaceuticals. **Chief crops:** rice, pulses, beans, sesame, groundnuts, sugarcane. **Natural resources:** petroleum, timber, tin, antimony, zinc, copper, tungsten, lead, coal, marble, limestone, prec. stones, nat. gas, hydropower. **Crude oil reserves:** 50 mil bbls. **Arable land:** 16.9%. **Livestock:** cattle: 13 mil; chickens: 125 mil; goats: 2.8 mil; pigs: 7.8 mil; sheep: 535,000. **Fish catch:** 3.5 mil metric tons. **Electricity prod.:** 6.4 bil kWh. **Labor force:** agric. 70%, industry 7%, services 23%.

Finance: Monetary unit: Kyat (MMK) (Sept. 2011: 6.41 = $1 U.S.) (official; black market rate may vary widely). **GDP:** $76.5 bil; **per capita GDP:** $1,400; **GDP growth:** 5.3%. **Imports:** $4.5 bil (figure grossly underestimated due to value of consumer goods, diesel fuel, other products smuggled in from Thailand, China, Malaysia, India); China 35.4%, Thailand 23.9%, Singapore 13.8%, South Korea 6.3%. **Exports:** $7.8 bil (official export figure grossly underestimated due to value of timber, gems, narcotics, rice, other products smuggled to Thailand, China, Bangladesh); Thailand 43.1%, India 18.4%, China 9.9%, Japan 5.2%. **Tourism:** NA. **Budget:** $2.95 bil. **Total reserves less gold** (2006): $1.2 bil. **Gold** (2006): 231,400 oz t. **CPI change:** 7.7%.

Transport: Railways: 3,126 mi. **Motor vehicles:** 0.5 vehicles per 1,000 pop. **Civil aviation:** 913.4 mil pass.-mi; 37 airports. **Chief ports:** Moulmein, Rangoon (Yangon), Sittwe.

Communications: TV sets: 7 per 1,000 pop. **Radios:** 203 per 1,000 pop. **Telephone lines:** 1.3 per 100 pop. **Internet** (2009): 0.2 users per 100 pop.

Health: Life expect.: 62.6 male; 67.3 female. **Births:** 19.3 (per 1,000 pop.). **Deaths:** 8.2 (per 1,000 pop.). **Natural inc.:** 1.12%. **Infant mortality:** 49.2 (per 1,000 live births). **HIV rate:** 0.6%.

Education: Compulsory: ages 5-9. **Literacy:** 92%.

Major intl. organizations: UN (FAO, IBRD, ILO, IMF, WHO), ASEAN, WTO.

Embassy: 2300 S St. NW 20008; 332-3344.

Website: www.mofa.gov.mm

The Burmese arrived from Tibet before the 9th cent., displacing earlier cultures, and a Buddhist monarchy was established by the 11th. Burma was conquered by the Mongol dynasty of China in 1272, then ruled by Shans as a Chinese tributary, until the 16th cent. Britain subjugated Burma in three wars, 1824-84, and ruled the country as part of India until 1937, when Burma became self-governing. Independence outside the Commonwealth was achieved Jan. 4, 1948.

Gen. Ne Win dominated politics from 1962 to 1988, first as military ruler, then as constitutional president. His regime drove Indians from the civil service and Chinese from commerce. Economic socialization was advanced, isolation from foreign countries enforced. In 1987 Burma, once the richest nation in Southeast Asia, was granted less-developed status by the UN.

Ne Win resigned July 1988, following antigovernment riots. In Sept. the military seized power, under Gen. Saw Maung. In 1989 the country's name was changed to Myanmar.

The first free multiparty elections in 30 years took place May 27, 1990, with the main opposition party winning a decisive victory, but the military refused to hand over power. A key opposition leader, Aung San Suu Kyi, awarded the Nobel Peace Prize in 1991, was held under house arrest, 1989-95, 2000-02, and 2003-10. Because of the regime's poor human rights record and continued harassment of Aung San Suu Kyi and her supporters, the U.S. imposed sanctions. The Indian Ocean tsunami of Dec. 26, 2004, killed at least 61 people in Myanmar.

Public anger over soaring fuel costs in Aug. 2007 triggered new challenges to the military regime. In late Sept., thousands of Buddhist monks led mass protests in Yangon; security forces cracked down by raiding monasteries, arresting monks, and firing on demonstrators. On Sept. 25, the U.S. announced tougher sanctions against junta leaders. Cyclone Nargis, May 2-3, 2008, left at least 84,537 people dead, with an estimated 53,836 missing.

Parliamentary elections Nov. 7, 2010, dominated by the military, led to the dissolution of the ruling State Peace and Development Council and a nominal return to return to civilian government, Mar. 30, 2011.

Namibia
Republic of Namibia

People: Population: 2,147,585. **Age distrib.:** <15: 34.2%; 65+: 4.1%. **Pop. density:** 6.8 per sq mi, 2.6 per sq km. **Urban:** 38%. **Ethnic groups:** black 88%, white 6%, mixed 7%; about 50% of pop. belong to Ovambo tribe. **Principal languages:** English (official), Afrikaans (common), German, indigenous languages (incl. Oshivambo, Herero, Nama). **Chief religions:** Christian 80%-90%, indigenous beliefs 10%-20%.

Geography: Total area: 318,261 sq mi, 824,292 sq km; **Land area:** 317,874 sq mi, 823,290 sq km. **Location:** In southern Africa on coast of Atlantic O. **Neighbors:** Angola on N; Botswana, Zambia on E; South Africa on S. **Topography:** Three distinct regions incl. Namib desert along the Atlantic coast, a mountainous central plateau with woodland savanna, and Kalahari desert in E. True forests found in NE. There are 4 rivers, but little other surface water. **Capital:** Windhoek, 342,000.

Government: Type: Republic. **Head of state:** Pres. Hifikepunye Pohamba; b. Aug. 18, 1935; in office: Mar. 21, 2005. **Head of gov.:** Prime Min. Nahas Angula; b. Aug. 22, 1943; in office: Mar. 21, 2005. **Local divisions:** 13 regions. **Defense budget:** $408 mil. **Active troops:** 9,200.

Economy: meatpacking, fish proc., dairy prods., mining. **Chief crops:** millet, sorghum, peanuts, grapes. **Natural resources:** diamonds, copper, uranium, gold, silver, lead, tin, lithium, cadmium, tungsten, zinc, salt, hydropower, fish. **Arable land:** 1.0%. **Livestock:** cattle: 2.5 mil; chickens: 4.9 mil; goats: 2 mil; pigs: 50,000; sheep: 2.7 mil. **Fish catch:** 370,106 metric tons. **Electricity prod.:** 2.2 bil kWh. **Labor force:** agric. 16.3%, industry 22.4%, services 61.3%; formal sector only. About half of population unemployed. About two-thirds of people live in rural areas and rely on subsistence agric.

Finance: Monetary unit: Dollar (NAD) (Sept. 2011: 7.19 = $1 U.S.). **GDP:** $14.6 bil; **per capita GDP:** $6,900; **GDP growth:** 4.4%. **Imports:** $5.2 bil; NA. **Exports:** $4.3 bil; NA. **Tourism:** $438 mil. **Budget:** $3.8 bil. **Total reserves less gold:** $1.7 bil. **CPI change:** 4.5%.

Transport: Railways: 1,632 mi. **Motor vehicles:** 82.4 vehicles per 1,000 pop. **Civil aviation:** 1 bil pass.-mi; 21 airports. **Chief ports:** Luderitz, Walvis Bay.

Communications: TV sets: 78 per 1,000 pop. **Radios:** 62 per 1,000 pop. **Telephone lines:** 6.7 per 100 pop. **Daily newspaper circ.:** 28.0 per 1,000 pop. **Internet:** 6.5 users per 100 pop.

Health: Life expect.: 52.5 male; 51.9 female. **Births:** 21.5 (per 1,000 pop.). **Deaths:** 13.0 (per 1,000 pop.). **Natural inc.:** 0.85%. **Infant mortality:** 45.6 per 1,000 live births). **HIV rate:** 13.1%.

Education: Compulsory: ages 7-16. **Literacy:** 88.5%.

Major intl. organizations: UN (FAO, IBRD, ILO, IMF, WHO), AU, the Commonwealth, WTO.

Embassy: 1605 New Hampshire Ave. NW 20009; 986-0540.

Website: www.grnnet.gov.na

Namibia was declared a German protectorate in 1890 and officially called South-West Africa. South Africa seized the territory from Germany in 1915 during WWI; the League of Nations gave South Africa a mandate over the territory in 1920. In 1966, the Marxist South-West Africa People's Organization (SWAPO) launched a guerrilla war for independence. The UN General Assembly named the area Namibia in 1968.

After many years of guerrilla warfare, South Africa, Angola, and Cuba signed a U.S.-mediated agreement Dec. 22, 1988, to end South African administration of Namibia and provide for a ceasefire and transition to independence, in accordance with a 1978 UN plan. A separate accord between Cuba and Angola provided for a phased withdrawal of Cuban troops from Namibia. A constitution providing for multiparty government was adopted Feb. 9, 1990, and Namibia gained independence Mar. 21.

Walvis Bay, the principal deepwater port, had been turned over to South African administration in 1922. It remained in South African hands after independence, but South Africa turned control of the port back to Namibia, as of Mar. 1, 1994. Separatist violence flared in the Caprivi Strip in the late 1990s. In 2009, severe flooding in northern Namibia claimed at least 85 lives by mid-Apr. SWAPO, the leading political group since independence, dominated the general election held Nov. 27-28, 2009.

Nauru
Republic of Nauru

People: Population: 9,322. **Age distrib.:** <15: 33%; 65+: 1.6%. **Pop. density:** 1,149.7 per sq mi, 443.9 per sq km. **Urban:** 100%. **Ethnic groups:** Nauruan 58%, other Pacific Islander 26%, Chinese 8%, European 8%. **Principal languages:** Nauruan (official; English widely understood, spoken, used for most govt. and commercial purposes). **Chief religions:** Nauru Congregational 35%, Roman Catholic 33%, Nauru Independent Church 10%, none 5%.

Geography: Total area: 8.1 sq mi, 21 sq km; **Land area:** 8.1 sq mi, 21 sq km. **Location:** In W Pacific O. just S of Equator. **Neighbors:** Nearest is Kiribati to E. **Topography:** Mostly a plateau bearing high-grade phosphate deposits, surrounded by a sandy shore and coral reef in concentric rings. **Capital:** No official capital; govt. offices in Yaren District, 10,000.

Government: Type: Republic. **Head of state and gov.:** Pres. Marcus Stephen; b. Oct. 1, 1969; in office: Dec. 19, 2007. **Local divisions:** 14 districts. **Defense budget/active troops:** NA.

Economy: Industries: phosphate mining, offshore banking, coconut prods. **Chief crops:** coconuts. **Natural resources:** phosphates, fish. **Arable land:** None. **Livestock:** chickens: 5,000; pigs: 3,000. **Fish catch:** 220 metric tons. **Electricity prod.:** 32 mil kWh. **Labor force:** Mining phosphates, public administration, education, transportation.

Finance: Monetary unit: Australia Dollar (AUD) (Sept. 2011: 0.95 = $1 U.S.). **GDP** (2005 est.): $60 mil; **per capita GDP** (2005 est.): $5,000; **GDP growth:** NA. **Imports** (2004 est.): $20 mil; NA. **Exports** (2005 est.): $64,000; NA. **Tourism:** NA. **Budget** (2005): $13.5 mil. **Total reserves less gold:** NA. **CPI change:** NA.

Transport: Civil aviation: 220 mil pass.-mi; 1 airport. **Chief port:** Nauru.

Communications: TV sets: 1 per 1,000 pop. **Radios:** 618 per 1,000 pop. **Telephone lines** (2009): 17.8 per 100 pop. **Internet:** 6 users per 100 pop.

Health: Life expect.: 61.3 male; 68.8 female. **Births:** 27.8 (per 1,000 pop.). **Deaths:** 6.1 (per 1,000 pop.). **Natural inc.:** 2.17%. **Infant mortality:** 8.7 (per 1,000 live births). **HIV rate:** NA.

Education: Compulsory: ages 6-16. **Literacy:** NA.

Major intl. organizations: UN (FAO, WHO), the Commonwealth.

Permanent UN mission: 800 2nd Ave., Ste. 400A, New York, NY 10017; (212) 937-0074.

Website: gov.nr

The island was discovered in 1798 by the British but was formally annexed to the German Empire in 1886. After WWI, Nauru became a League of Nations mandate administered by Australia. During WWII the Japanese occupied the island. In 1947 Nauru was made a UN trust territory, administered by Australia. It became an independent republic Jan. 31, 1968, and was admitted to the UN Sept. 14, 1999.

Phosphate exports provided Nauru with per capita revenues that were among the highest in the Third World. Phosphate reserves, however, are nearly depleted, and environmental damage from strip-mining has been severe. Lax banking practices have made Nauru a haven for money laundering. Nauru defaulted on a loan payment for its real estate holdings in Australia and was virtually bankrupt by 2004, when financial reforms were implemented. Rising seas linked to global climate change have eroded the coastline of this tiny island nation.

Nepal
Federal Democratic Republic of Nepal

People: Population: 29,391,883. **Age distrib.:** <15: 34.6%; 65+: 4.4%. **Pop. density:** 531 per sq mi, 205 per sq km. **Urban:** 18.6%. **Ethnic groups:** Chhettri 16%, Brahman-Hill 13%, Magar 7%, Tharu 7%, Tamang 6%, Newar 5%, Muslim 4%, Kami 4%, Yadav 4%. **Principal languages:** Nepali (official), Maithali, Bhojpuri, Tharu (Dagaura/Rana), Tamang, Newar, Magar, Awadhi, English spoken by many in govt. and business. **Chief religions:** Hindu 81%, Buddhist 11%, Muslim 4%, Kirant 4%.

Geography: Total area: 56,827 sq mi, 147,181 sq km; **Land area:** 55,348 sq mi, 143,351 sq km. **Location:** Astride the Himalaya Mts. **Neighbors:** China on N, India on S. **Topography:** The Himalayas stretch across the N, the hill country with its fertile valleys extends across the center, while S border region is part of the flat, subtropical Ganges Plain. **Capital:** Kathmandu, 990,000.

Government: Type: Republic. **Head of state:** Pres. Ram Baran Yadav; b. Feb. 4, 1948; in office: July 23, 2008. **Head of gov.:** Prime Min. Baburam Bhattarai; b. June 18, 1954; in office: Aug. 29, 2011. **Local divisions:** 5 regions subdivided into 14 zones. **Defense budget:** $245 mil. **Active troops:** 95,753.

Economy: Industries: tourism; carpets; textiles; small rice, jute, sugar, and oilseed mills. **Chief crops:** pulses, rice, corn, wheat, sugarcane, jute, root crops. **Natural resources:** quartz, water, timber, hydropower, lignite, copper, cobalt, iron ore. **Arable land:** 16.7%. **Livestock:** cattle: 7.2 mil; chickens: 24.5 mil; goats: 8.5 mil; pigs: 1.04 mil; sheep: 802,993. **Fish catch:** 48,230 metric tons. **Electricity prod.:** 3.1 bil kWh. **Labor force:** agric. 75%, industry 7%, services 18%.

Finance: Monetary unit: Rupee (NPR). **GDP:** $35.8 bil; **per capita GDP:** $1,200; **GDP growth:** 4.6%. **Imports** (2009): $5.3 bil; India 52.5%, China 15.1%. **Exports** (2009): $849 mil; India 58.2%, U.S. 8.2%, Bangladesh 6.3%, Germany 5.1%. **Tourism:** $350 mil. **Budget** (FY10): $4.6 bil. **Total reserves less gold** (2005): $1.5 bil. **Gold** (2005): 129,081 oz t. **CPI change:** 10%.

Transport: Railways: 37 mi. **Civil aviation:** 533.1 mil pass.-mi; 11 airports.

Communications: TV sets: 21 per 1,000 pop. **Radios:** 39 per 1,000 pop. **Telephone lines:** 2.8 per 100 pop. **Internet:** 6.8 users per 100 pop.

Japan Catastrophe A 9.0-magnitude earthquake—the most powerful ever recorded in Japan and fourth largest worldwide since 1900—struck Mar. 11, 2011, near Honshu, Japan. A tsunami triggered by the quake slammed into the northeast coast that same day, with waves destroying coastal structures and sweeping debris inland.

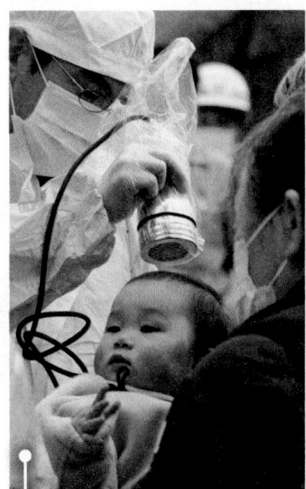

Continued Catastrophe The Mar. 11, 2011, disasters knocked out cooling systems at Japan's six-reactor Fukushima Daiichi nuclear power plant, causing a series of explosions and fires, with radiation threatening plant workers and nearby residents.

Afghanistan Departure Begins Pres. Barack Obama announced June 22, 2011, that 10,000 troops would leave Afghanistan by the end of 2011.

Power Transfer Iraqi Army officials took control in 2011 of forward operating bases that had previously been under the control of the U.S. and other coalition forces.

More Secrets Leaked WikiLeaks, the controversial activist group dedicated to publishing confidential documents online, led by Julian Assange, began releasing 779 secret U.S. military documents related to terrorism detainees held at Guantánamo Bay, Cuba, Apr. 24, 2011.

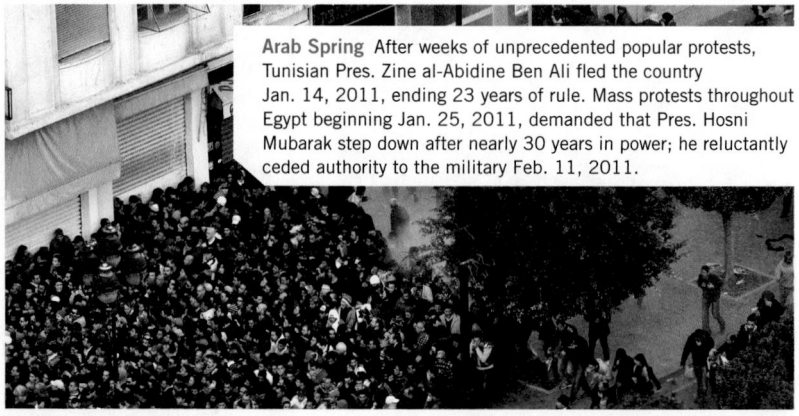

Arab Spring After weeks of unprecedented popular protests, Tunisian Pres. Zine al-Abidine Ben Ali fled the country Jan. 14, 2011, ending 23 years of rule. Mass protests throughout Egypt beginning Jan. 25, 2011, demanded that Pres. Hosni Mubarak step down after nearly 30 years in power; he reluctantly ceded authority to the military Feb. 11, 2011.

People Protest in Syria Arab Spring protesters staged mass demonstrations in many cities in 2011, but the regime of Syrian Pres. Bashar al-Assad resisted calls from the international community, including Saudi King Abdullah and Pres. Barack Obama in Aug., to step down from power, using troops and tanks to beat protesters back.

Libyan Liberation Ceremonies in the former Green Square (renamed Martyrs' Square) in Tripoli, Libya, Sept. 12, 2011, marked the ousting of the government of Muammar al-Qaddafi, which had ruled since 1969.

Terrorism in Norway A lone far-right extremist July 22, 2011, carried out terrorist attacks in and around Oslo, Norway's capital, that left 77 people dead, including 69 at an island camp sponsored by the Labor Party.

New Nation South Sudan celebrated its newly independent status July 9, 2011.

African Famine The United Nations predicted that a famine in Somalia, formally declared in July, could last through Dec. 2011, with starvation threatening millions.

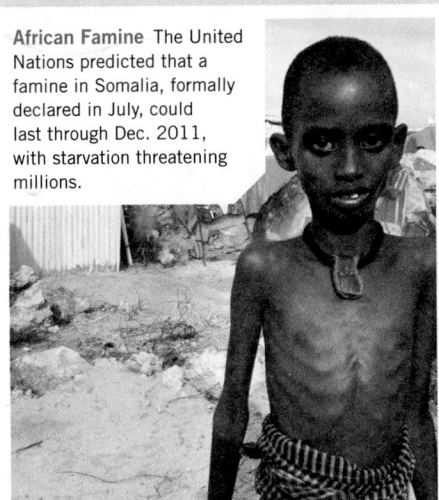

Phone Hacking Scandal Powerful News Corp. chair Rupert Murdoch appeared with son James Murdoch July 19, 2011, before the British parliament to give evidence in an ongoing phone-hacking and corruption scandal.

JAMES MURDOCH   RUPERT MURDOCH

London Calling Riots broke out in Tottenham, London, Aug. 6, 2011, after a peaceful protest against the police killing of a man during an arrest attempt erupted in violence.

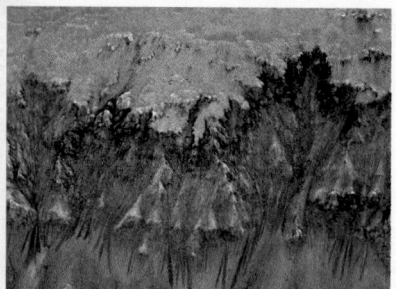

Water on Mars National Aeronautics and Space Administration (NASA) researchers announced Aug. 4, 2011, that they had found the strongest evidence yet for the present existence of salty liquid water on the surface of Mars.

Oldest Americans Texas A&M's Michael Waters published research Mar. 25, 2011, of fossil evidence discovered near Austin, TX, that may prove human civilization existed in North America 15,500 years ago, or 2,500 years earlier than previously thought.

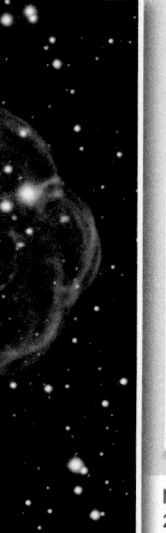

Newbie Nebula Researchers confirmed July 25, 2011, that Matthias Kronberger, a member of the amateur astronomy group Deep Sky Hunters, had discovered a new planetary nebula.

Farewell *Atlantis* The final shuttle flight docked with the International Space Station July 10, as part of the final mission July 8-21, 2011, in the U.S.'s 30-year shuttle program.

Don't Mess With Texas A&M
Danielle Adams carried the Aggies to victory over Notre Dame Apr. 5, 2011, in the NCAA women's Final Four championship game; it was the first basketball championship for any Texas A&M team.

Canucks Collapse Goalie Tim Thomas and the Boston Bruins shut out the Vancouver Canucks in Game 7 to claim the NHL Stanley Cup June 15, 2011.

Tigers Stall Ducks Heisman Trophy-winner Cam Newton led Auburn to the school's first college championship since 1957 with a BCS Championship win over the Oregon Ducks Jan. 10, 2011, in Glendale, AZ.

Mr. Rodgers' Neighborhood Super Bowl MVP Aaron Rodgers led the Green Bay Packers to the Super Bowl XLV win over the Pittsburgh Steelers Feb. 6, 2011, in Arlington, TX.

Mavericks Beat Heat Dirk Nowitzki and the Dallas Mavericks veteran roster combined to beat the young talent (including high-profile 2010 acquisitions Chris Bosh and LeBron James) of the Miami Heat June 12, 2011, in the NBA Finals.

Yankee Milestone NY Yankee shortstop Derek Jeter smacked a solo home run for his 3,000th career hit July 9, 2011.

World Champion Women Japan earned a stunning championship win at the women's World Cup July 17, 2011, defeating the U.S. on penalty kicks in Frankfurt, Germany. The win capped a determined effort by Japan, which made its first-ever appearance in the final of a major international soccer tournament. Japan's Homare Sawa scored a game-tying goal, after the U.S.'s Abby Wambach scored on a header for a 2-1 lead in the 104th minute.

Five in a Row Jimmie Johnson claimed an unprecedented fifth consecutive NASCAR title Nov. 21, 2010, by placing second in the Ford 400 in Florida.

"Blade Runner" South Africa's Oscar Pistorius competed in the World Athletics Championships in South Korea in Aug. 2011 and became the first amputee to win an able-bodied world track medal when South Africa claimed silver in the 400-m relay Sept. 2.

Labor Lockout The four-month NFL player lockout delayed the official start of NFL team training camps; until a deal was reached July 25, 2011, many players organized their own informal team practices.

Novice No More Serbia's Novak Djokovic defeated Spain's Rafael Nadal Sept. 12, 2011, in Flushing, NY, to claim the U.S. Open title and his third Grand Slam victory of the year.

Warren Christopher
OCT. 27, 1925-MAR. 18, 2011

Jackie Cooper
SEPT. 15, 1922-MAY 3, 2011

Peter Falk
SEPT. 16, 1927-JUNE 23, 2011

Geraldine Ferraro
AUG. 26, 1935-MAR. 26, 2011

Betty Ford
APR. 8, 1918-JULY 8, 2011

Farley Granger
JULY 1, 1925-MAR. 27, 2011

Harmon Killebrew
JUNE 29, 1936-MAY 17, 2011

Jack LaLanne
SEPT. 26, 1914-JAN. 23, 2011

Leslie Nielsen
FEB. 11, 1926-NOV. 28, 2010

Jane Russell
JUNE 21, 1921-FEB. 28, 2011

Randy Savage
NOV. 15, 1952-MAY 20, 2011

Gil Scott-Heron
APR. 1, 1949-MAY 27, 2011

Sargent Shriver
NOV. 9, 1915-JAN. 18, 2011

Elizabeth Taylor
FEB. 27, 1932-MAR. 23, 2011

Grete Waitz
OCT. 1, 1953-APR. 19, 2011

Amy Winehouse
SEPT. 14, 1983-JULY 23, 2011

Health: Life expect.: 64.9 male; 67.4 female. **Births:** 22.2 (per 1,000 pop.). **Deaths:** 6.8 (per 1,000 pop.). **Natural inc.:** 1.54%. **Infant mortality:** 44.5 (per 1,000 live births). **HIV rate:** 0.4%.

Education: NA. **Literacy:** 59.1%.

Major intl. organizations: UN (FAO, IBRD, ILO, IMF, WHO), WTO.

Embassy: 2131 Leroy Pl. NW 20008; 667-4550.

Website: www.nepalgov.gov.np

Nepal was originally a group of petty principalities, the inhabitants of one of which, the Gurkhas, became dominant about 1769. In 1951 King Tribhubana Bir Bikram, member of the Shah family, ended the system of rule by hereditary premiers of the Ranas family, who had kept the kings virtual prisoners, and established a cabinet system of government. Polygamy, child marriage, and the caste system were officially abolished in 1963. Political parties were legalized in 1990.

Nine members of Nepal's royal family, including King Birendra and Queen Aishwarya, died as the result of a massacre on the night of June 1, 2001. An official inquiry blamed the carnage on a 10th family member, Crown Prince Dipendra, who reportedly shot himself that night and died 3 days later, allowing Birendra's brother Gyanendra Bir Bikram Shah Dev to take the throne.

Citing the government's failure to stop a Maoist insurgency, King Gyanendra assumed absolute authority, Feb. 1, 2005. After weeks of pro-democracy demonstrations, in which police killed at least 12 protesters, the king agreed Apr. 24, 2006, to reinstate parliament, which had not met for 4 years. A new government, led by Prime Min. Girija Prasad Koirala, signed a peace accord with Maoist rebels Nov. 21, ending a decade-long civil war that had claimed 13,000 lives.

Under a draft constitution that made Koirala acting head of state, Maoists joined an interim parliament Jan. 15, 2007, and entered the cabinet Apr. 1. The king was stripped of most powers. A constituent assembly voted May 28, 2008, to abolish the monarchy and make Nepal a republic. After months of political wrangling, Maoist leader Pushpa Kamal Dahal, popularly known as Prachanda, became prime min. Aug. 18. On May 3, 2009, Prachanda moved to fire Nepal's army chief, who had refused orders to integrate some 19,000 former Maoist rebels into the armed forces; when Pres. Ram Baran Yadav countermanded the firing, Prachanda resigned May 4. After two more short-lived governments, Baburam Bhattarai, also a Maoist, was sworn as prime min. Aug. 29, 2011.

Netherlands
Kingdom of the Netherlands

People: Population: 16,653,734. **Age distrib.:** <15: 17.4%; 65+: 16%. **Pop. density:** 1,272.6 per sq mi, 491.4 per sq km. **Urban:** 82.9%. **Ethnic groups:** Dutch 80%, EU 5%, Indonesian 2%, Turkish 2%, Surinamese 2%, Moroccan 2%. **Principal languages:** Dutch, Frisian (both official). **Chief religions:** Roman Catholic 30%, Dutch Reformed 11%, Calvinist 6%, Muslim 6%, other Protestant 3%, none 42%.

Geography: Total area: 16,040 sq mi, 41,543 sq km; **Land area:** 13,086 sq mi, 33,893 sq km. **Location:** In NW Europe on North Sea. **Neighbors:** Germany on E, Belgium on S. **Topography:** Land is flat, an average alt. of 37 ft above sea level, with much land below sea level reclaimed and protected by some 1,500 mi of dikes. Since 1920 the government has been draining the IJsselmeer, formerly the Zuiderzee. **Capital:** Amsterdam, 1,048,914; The Hague ('s-Gravenhage) (seat), 629,000. **Cities (urban aggl.):** Rotterdam, 1,009,963.

Government: Type: Parliamentary democracy under a constitutional monarch. **Head of state:** Queen Beatrix; b. Jan. 31, 1938; in office: Apr. 30, 1980. **Head of gov.:** Prime Min. Mark Rutte; b. Feb. 14, 1967; in office: Oct. 14, 2010. **Seat of govt.:** The Hague. **Local divisions:** 12 provinces. **Defense budget:** $11.3 bil. **Active troops:** 37,368.

Economy: Industries: agroindustries, metal and engineering prods., elec. machinery and equip., chemicals, petroleum, constr., microelectronics, fishing. **Chief crops:** grains, potatoes, sugar beets, fruits, vegetables. **Natural resources:** nat. gas, petroleum, peat, limestone, salt, sand and gravel. **Crude oil reserves:** 310 mil bbls. **Arable land:** 31.3%. **Livestock:** cattle: 4 mil; chickens: 97 mil; goats: 416,000; pigs: 12.1 mil; sheep: 1.1 mil. **Fish catch:** 437,703 metric tons. **Electricity prod.** (2009): 105.7 bil kWh. **Labor force:** agric. 2%, industry 18%, services 80%.

Finance: Monetary unit: Euro (EUR) (Sept. 2011: 0.71 = $1 U.S.). **GDP:** $676.9 bil; **per capita GDP:** $40,300; **GDP growth:** 1.7%. **Imports:** $408.4 bil; Germany 16.8%, China 11.7%, Belgium 8.7%, U.S. 7.8%, UK 6%, Russia 4.5%, France 4.4%. **Exports:** $451.3 bil; Germany 25.8%, Belgium 12.6%, France 9.2%, UK 8.1%, Italy 5.1%. **Tourism:** $13 bil. **Budget:** $399.3 bil. **Total reserves less gold:** $18.5 bil. **Gold:** 19.7 mil oz t. **CPI change:** 1.3%.

Transport: Railways: 1,799 mi. **Motor vehicles:** 533.6 vehicles per 1,000 pop. **Civil aviation:** 56 bil pass.-mi (incl. airlines based in territories and dependencies); 20 airports. **Chief ports:** Amsterdam, Ijmuiden, Moerdijk, Rotterdam, Terneuzen, Vlissingen.

Communications: TV sets: 767 per 1,000 pop. **Radios:** 978 per 1,000 pop. **Telephone lines:** 43.2 per 100 pop. **Daily newspaper circ.:** 307.5 per 1,000 pop. **Internet:** 90.7 users per 100 pop.

Health: Life expect.: 78.8 male; 83 female. **Births:** 11 (per 1,000 pop.). **Deaths:** 8.3 (per 1,000 pop.). **Natural inc.:** 0.27%. **Infant mortality:** 3.8 (per 1,000 live births). **HIV rate:** 0.2%.

Education: Compulsory: ages 5-17. **Literacy:** 99%.

Major intl. organizations: UN and all of its specialized agencies, EU, NATO, OECD, OSCE, WTO.

Embassy: 4200 Linnean Ave. NW 20008; 877-DUTCHHELP.

Website: www.government.nl

Julius Caesar conquered the region in 55 BCE, when it was inhabited by Celtic and Germanic tribes. After the empire of Charlemagne fell apart, the Netherlands (Holland, Belgium, Flanders) split among counts, dukes, and bishops, passed to Burgundy and thence to Spain. William the Silent, prince of Orange, led a confederation of the northern provinces, called Estates, in the Union of Utrecht, 1579; in 1581 they repudiated allegiance to Spain. The rise of the Dutch republic to naval, economic, and artistic eminence came in the 17th cent.

After a period of French hegemony, 1795-1813, the Congress of Vienna in 1815 formed a kingdom of the Netherlands, including Belgium, under William I. In 1830, the Belgians seceded and formed a separate kingdom.

The Netherlands maintained its neutrality in WWI, but was invaded and brutally occupied by Germany, 1940-45. In 1949, after several years of fighting, the Netherlands granted independence to Indonesia.

The murder May 6, 2002, of right-wing populist leader Pim Fortuyn, 9 days before legislative elections, marked the first political assassination in modern Dutch history. The killing of filmmaker Theo van Gogh, Nov. 2, 2004, by an Islamic extremist also shocked many Dutch. On Apr. 30, 2009, the national Queen's Day holiday, a Dutch motorist in Apeldoorn aimed his car at an open-topped bus carrying Queen Beatrix and other royal family members; they were unhurt, but 7 bystanders died, as did the driver. The anti-Islamic, right-wing Freedom Party, headed by Geert Wilders, gained in parliamentary elections June 9, 2010.

Netherlands Dependencies

The **Netherlands Antilles** consists of 2 island groups in the West Indies. **Curaçao** and **Bonaire** are near the coast of Venezuela; **Sint Eustatius**, **Saba**, and the southern part of **Sint Maarten** are southeast of Puerto Rico. The northern two-thirds of St. Maarten belongs to French Guadeloupe; the French call the island Saint Martin. Total area of the 2 groups is 371 sq mi, incl. Bonaire (111), Curaçao (171), St. Eustatius (8), Saba (5), St. Maarten (13). St. Maarten suffered extensive damage from Hurricane Luis, Sept. 1995. Total pop. of the Netherlands Antilles (2010 est.) was 228,693. Willemstad, on Curaçao, is the capital. The principal industry is the refining of crude oil from Venezuela. Tourism is also an important industry, as is shipbuilding. Constitutional changes effective Oct. 10, 2010, dissolved the Netherlands Antilles as a political entity and elevated Curaçao and St. Maarten to the status of "autonomous countries" within the Kingdom of the Netherlands. Bonaire, St. Eustatius, and Saba were classified as special municipalities.

Aruba, about 26 mi west of Curaçao, was separated from the Netherlands Antilles on Jan. 1, 1986; it is an autonomous component of the Netherlands, with a status similar to Curaçao and St. Maarten. Area: 69 sq mi; pop. (2011 est.): 106,113; capital: Oranjestad. Chief industries are oil refining and tourism. **Website:** www.kabga.aw

New Zealand

People: Population: 4,290,347. **Age distrib.:** <15: 20.4%; 65+: 13.3%. **Pop. density:** 41.5 per sq mi, 16 per sq km. **Urban:** 86.2%. **Ethnic groups:** European 57%, Asian 8%, Maori 7%, Pacific Islander 5%, mixed 10%. **Principal languages:** English, Maori (both official); Samoan; French; Hindi; Yue; Northern Chinese; NZ sign language (official). **Chief religions:** Anglican 14%; Roman Catholic 13%; Presbyterian, Congregational, & Reformed 10%; Christian (no denomination specified) 5%; Methodist 3%; Pentecostal 2%; other Christian 4%; Maori Christian 2%; Hindu 2%; Buddhist 1%; Baptist 1%; none 32%.

Geography: Total area: 103,363 sq mi, 267,710 sq km; **Land area:** 103,363 sq mi, 267,710 sq km. **Location:** In SW Pacific O. **Neighbors:** Nearest are Australia on W, Fiji and Tonga on N. **Topography:** Each of the 2 main islands (North and South Isls.) is mainly hilly and mountainous. The E coasts consist of fertile plains, especially the broad Canterbury Plains on South Isl. A volcanic plateau is in center of North Isl. South Isl. has glaciers and 15 peaks over 10,000 ft. **Capital:** Wellington, 391,000. **Cities (urban aggl.):** Auckland, 1,404,431.

Government: Type: Parliamentary democracy. **Head of state:** Queen Elizabeth II, represented by Gov.-Gen. Sir Jeremiah (Jerry) Mateparae; b. Nov. 14, 1954; in office: Aug. 31, 2011. **Head of gov.:** Prime Min. John Key; b. Aug. 9, 1961; in office: Nov. 19, 2008. **Local divisions:** 16 regions. **Defense budget:** $1.59 bil. **Active troops:** 9,673.

Economy: Industries: food proc., wood and paper prods., textiles, machinery, transp. equip., banking and insurance, tourism, mining. **Chief crops:** wheat, barley, potatoes, pulses, fruits, vegetables. **Natural resources:** nat. gas, iron ore, sand, coal, timber, hydropower, gold, limestone. **Crude oil reserves:** 112.5 mil bbls. **Arable land:** 1.8%. **Livestock:** cattle: 10 mil; chickens: 13.1 mil; goats: 82,229; pigs: 322,788; sheep: 32.4 mil. **Fish catch:** 543,258 metric tons. **Electricity prod.** (2009): 42 bil kWh. **Labor force:** agric. 7%, industry 19%, services 74%.

Finance: Monetary unit: Dollar (NZD) (Sept. 2011: 1.21 = $1 U.S.). **GDP:** $117.8 bil; **per capita GDP:** $27,700; **GDP growth:** 1.5%. **Imports:** $30.2 bil; Australia 18.4%, China 15.1%, U.S. 10.5%, Japan 7.2%, Germany 4.2%, Singapore 4.1%. **Exports:** $33.2 bil; Australia 23.4%, U.S. 9.6%, China 9.2%, Japan 7.1%, UK 4.2%. **Tourism:** $4.9 bil. **Budget:** $62.2 bil. **Total reserves less gold:** $16.7 bil. **CPI change:** 2.9%.

Transport: Railways: 2,565 mi. **Motor vehicles:** 729.4 vehicles per 1,000 pop. **Civil aviation:** 16.1 bil pass.-mi; 40 airports. **Chief ports:** Auckland, Lyttelton, Manukau Harbor, Marsden Point, Tauranga, Wellington.

Communications: TV sets: 615 per 1,000 pop. **Radios:** 1,006 per 1,000 pop. **Telephone lines:** 42.8 per 100 pop. **Daily newspaper circ.:** 182.5 per 1,000 pop. **Internet:** 83 users per 100 pop.

Health: Life expect.: 78.6 male; 82.7 female. **Births:** 13.7 (per 1,000 pop.). **Deaths:** 7.2 (per 1,000 pop.). **Natural inc.:** 0.65%. **Infant mortality:** 4.8 (per 1,000 live births). **HIV rate:** 0.1%.

Education: Compulsory: ages 5-16. **Literacy:** 99%.

Major intl. organizations: UN (FAO, IBRD, ILO, IMF, WHO), APEC, the Commonwealth, OECD, WTO.

Embassy: 37 Observatory Cir. NW 20008; 328-4800.

Website: newzealand.govt.nz

The Maori, a Polynesian group from the eastern Pacific, reached New Zealand before and during the 14th cent. The first European to sight New Zealand was Dutch navigator Abel Janszoon Tasman, but the Maori refused to allow him to land. British Capt. James Cook explored the coasts, 1769-70.

British sovereignty was proclaimed and Maori land rights were recognized in the Treaty of Waitangi, 1840, with organized settlement beginning in the same year. Representative institutions were granted in 1853. The Maori wars, or New Zealand Wars, ended in 1870 with British victory. The colony became a dominion in 1907 and gained full independence in 1947. It is a member of the Commonwealth. The Maori make up about 15% of the population; 7 of 122 members of the House of Representatives are directly elected from Maori constituencies, but Maori may also run in other districts.

A progressive tradition in politics dates back to the 19th cent., when New Zealand was internationally known for social experimentation; much of the nation's economy has been deregulated since the 1980s. Jenny Shipley of the National Party became the nation's first female prime minister, Dec. 8, 1997. The Labour Party, led by Helen Clark, won the general elections of Nov. 27, 1999, and July 27, 2002. New Zealand supplied small troop contingents to coalition forces in Iraq and Afghanistan.

The legislature legalized prostitution June 2003. In July, New Zealand contributed troops to the Australian-led force in the Solomon Islands. A measure establishing a Supreme Court and ending appeals to the UK Privy Council passed Oct. 14. A major settlement of Maori land claims dating from the 19th cent. was signed June 25, 2008. With the country in recession, Clark called new elections Nov. 8, which were won by the National Party, led by John Key.

A South Island earthquake Sept. 3, 2010, damaged 100,000 homes and other structures in and around Christchurch; property losses were estimated at $2.7 bil. An explosion Nov. 19 at the Pike River coal mine on South Island claimed the lives of 29 men. Another Christchurch quake, Feb. 22, 2011, killed 181 people and destroyed about one-third of the central business district, causing damage estimated at $11 bil.

New Zealand comprises **North Island**, 43,911 sq mi; **South Island**, 58,084 sq mi; **Stewart Island**, 649 sq mi; **Chatham Isls.**, 373 sq mi; and several groups of smaller islands.

In 1965, the **Cook Islands** (2011 est. pop.: 11,124; area: 91 sq mi), halfway between New Zealand and Hawaii, became self-governing. New Zealand retains responsibility for defense and foreign affairs. **Niue** attained the same status in 1974; it lies 400 mi W (2011 est. pop.: 1,311; area: 100 sq mi). Cyclone Heta devastated Niue Jan. 6, 2004. **Tokelau** (2011 est. pop.: 1,384; area: 4 sq mi) comprises 3 atolls 300 mi N of Samoa. Two referendums on Tokelau self-government, held Feb. 13-15, 2006, and Oct. 20-24, 2007, failed to gain the required two-thirds majority.

Ross Dependency, administered by New Zealand since 1923, comprises 160,000 sq mi of Antarctic territory.

Nicaragua
Republic of Nicaragua

People: Population: 5,666,301. **Age distrib.:** <15: 31.7%; 65+: 4.5%. **Pop. density:** 122.3 per sq mi, 47.2 per sq km. **Urban:** 57.3%. **Ethnic groups:** mestizo (mixed Amerindian & white) 69%, white 17%, black 9%, Amerindian 5%. **Principal languages:** Spanish (official), Miskito, English & indigenous languages on Atlantic coast. **Chief religions:** Roman Catholic 59%, Evangelical 22%, Moravian 2%, none 16%.

Geography: Total area: 50,336 sq mi, 130,370 sq km; **Land area:** 46,328 sq mi, 119,990 sq km. **Location:** In Central America. **Neighbors:** Honduras on N, Costa Rica on S. **Topography:** Both Caribbean and Pacific coasts are over 200 mi long. Cordillera Mts., with many volcanic peaks, run NW-SE through middle of the country. Between this and a volcanic range to the E lie Lakes Managua and Nicaragua. **Capital:** Managua, 943,626.

Government: Type: Republic. **Head of state and gov.:** Pres. Daniel Ortega Saavedra; b. Nov. 11, 1945; in office: Jan. 10, 2007. **Local divisions:** 15 departments, 2 autonomous regions. **Defense budget:** $38 mil. **Active troops:** 12,000.

Economy: Industries: food proc., chemicals, machinery and metal prods., knit and woven apparel, petroleum refining and distribution, beverages, footwear, wood. **Chief crops:** coffee, bananas, sugarcane, cotton, rice, corn, tobacco, sesame, soya, beans. **Natural resources:** gold, silver, copper, tungsten, lead, zinc, timber, fish. **Arable land:** 15.8%. **Livestock:** cattle: 3.6 mil; chickens: 18 mil; goats: 7,100; pigs: 475,000; sheep: 6,300. **Fish catch:** 54,801 metric tons. **Electricity prod.:** 3.4 bil kWh. **Labor force:** agric. 28%, industry 19%, services 53%.

Finance: Monetary unit: Cordoba (NIO) (Sept. 2011: 22.62 = $1 U.S.). **GDP:** $17.7 bil; **per capita GDP:** $3,000; **GDP growth:** 4.5%. **Imports:** $4.7 bil; U.S. 19.9%, Venezuela 16.9%, Costa Rica 9.2%, China 7.5%, Mexico 7%, Guatemala 6.2%, El Salvador 4.8%. **Exports:** $3.2 bil; U.S. 32.4%, El Salvador 14.3%, Venezuela 8.6%, Honduras 7.2%, Costa Rica 6.2%, Guatemala 4.4%, Mexico 4.1%. **Tourism:** $309 mil. **Budget:** $1.5 bil. **Total reserves less gold:** $1.8 bil. **CPI change:** 5.5%.

Transport: Motor vehicles: 33.9 vehicles per 1,000 pop. **Civil aviation:** 11 airports. **Chief ports:** Bluefields, Corinto.

Communications: TV sets: 129 per 1,000 pop. **Radios:** 273 per 1,000 pop. **Telephone lines:** 4.5 per 100 pop. **Internet:** 10 users per 100 pop.

Health: Life expect.: 69.8 male; 74.1 female. **Births:** 19.5 (per 1,000 pop.). **Deaths:** 5 (per 1,000 pop.). **Natural inc.:** 1.44%. **Infant mortality:** 22.6 (per 1,000 live births). **HIV rate:** 0.2%.

Education: Compulsory: ages 6-11. **Literacy:** 78%.

Major intl. organizations: UN and most of its specialized agencies, OAS, WTO.

Embassy: 1627 New Hampshire Ave. NW 20009; 939-6570.

Website: www.presidencia.gob.ni

Nicaragua, inhabited by various Indian tribes, was conquered by Spain in 1552. After gaining independence from Spain, 1821, Nicaragua was united for a short period with Mexico, then with the United Provinces of Central America, finally becoming an independent republic, 1838. U.S. Marines occupied the country at times in the early 20th cent., the last time from 1926 to 1933.

Gen. Anastasio Somoza Debayle held the presidency 1967-72, 1974-79. Martial law was imposed in Dec. 1974, after officials were kidnapped by the Marxist Sandinista guerrillas. Nationwide antigovernment strikes touched off a civil war, 1978, which ended when Somoza fled Nicaragua and the Sandinistas took control of Managua in July 1979. Somoza was assassinated in Paraguay, Sept. 17, 1980.

Relations with the U.S. were strained as a result of Nicaragua's aid to leftist guerrillas in El Salvador and U.S. backing of anti-Sandinista contra guerrilla groups. In 1983 the contras launched a major offensive; the Sandinistas imposed rule by decree. In 1985 the U.S. House rejected Pres. Reagan's request for military aid to the contras. The subsequent diversion of funds to the contras from the proceeds of a secret arms sale to Iran caused a major scandal in the U.S.

In a stunning upset, Violeta Barrios de Chamorro defeated Sandinista leader Daniel Ortega Saavedra in national elections, Feb. 25, 1990. Arnoldo Alemán Lacayo, a conservative former mayor of Managua, defeated Ortega in the presidential election of Oct. 20, 1996. Up to 2,000 people died Oct. 30, 1998, in a mudslide caused by rains from Hurricane Mitch.

Drought and a drop in coffee prices plunged Nicaragua into an economic crisis in 2001. Enrique Bolaños Geyer, a conservative businessman, won the presidency that year. Convicted Dec. 7, 2003, on corruption charges, former Pres. Alemán was fined $10 mil and received a 20-year sentence, which he was allowed to serve under house arrest. Ortega won the presidential election of Nov. 5, 2006. After taking office Jan. 10, 2007, he irritated the U.S. by cultivating ties with Venezuela and Iran, which offered aid to the financially hard-pressed country. Hurricane Felix, a Category 5 storm that struck Sept. 4, 2007, killed more than 100 people. Presidential and legislative elections were scheduled for Nov. 2011.

Niger
Republic of Niger

People: Population: 16,468,886. **Age distrib.:** <15: 49.6%; 65+: 2.3%. **Pop. density:** 33.7 per sq mi, 13 per sq km. **Urban:** 17.1%. **Ethnic groups:** Haoussa 55%, Djerma Sonrai 21%, Tuareg 9%, Peuhl 9%, Kanouri Manga 5%. **Principal languages:** French (official), Hausa, Djerma. **Chief religions:** Muslim 80%, other (incl. indigenous beliefs, Christian) 20%.

Geography: Total area: 489,191 sq mi, 1,267,000 sq km; **Land area:** 489,076 sq mi, 1,266,700 sq km. **Location:** In interior of N Africa. **Neighbors:** Libya, Algeria on N; Mali, Burkina Faso on W; Benin, Nigeria on S; Chad on E. **Topography:** Mostly arid desert and mountains. A narrow savanna in S and Niger R. basin in the SW contain most of the population. **Capital:** Niamey, 1,047,686.

Government: Type: Republic. **Head of state:** Pres. Mahamadou Issoufou; b. 1952; in office: Apr. 7, 2011. **Head of gov.:** Prime Min. Brigi Rafini; b. Apr. 7, 1953; in office: Apr. 7, 2011. **Local divisions:** 7 departments, 1 capital district. **Defense budget** (2009): $64 mil. **Active troops:** 5,300.

Economy: Industries: uranium mining, cement, brick, soap, textiles, food proc., chemicals, slaughterhouses. **Chief crops:** cowpeas, cotton, peanuts, millet, sorghum, cassava, rice. **Natural resources:** uranium, coal, iron ore, tin, phosphates, gold, molybdenum, gypsum, salt, petroleum. **Arable land:** 11.8%. **Livestock:** cattle: 9.3 mil; chickens: 11 mil; goats: 13.1 mil; pigs: 40,000; sheep: 10.5 mil. **Fish catch:** 29,954 metric tons. **Electricity prod.:** 200 mil kWh. **Labor force:** agric. 90%, industry 6%, services 4%.

Finance: Monetary unit: CFA BCEAO Franc (XOF) (Sept. 2011: 468.55 = $1 U.S.). **GDP:** $11.1 bil; **per capita GDP:** $700; **GDP growth:** 7.5%. **Imports** (2006): $800 mil; China 19.7%, France 15.8%, Netherlands 7.6%, French Polynesia 6.1%, Nigeria 5.4%, Algeria 4.3%, Côte d'Ivoire 4.1%, U.S. 4%. **Exports** (2006): $428 mil; France 52.9%, Nigeria 22.5%, U.S. 18.3%. **Tourism:** $66 mil. **Budget** (2002 est.): $320 mil. **Total reserves less gold:** $760.3 mil. **CPI change:** 0.8%.

Transport: Motor vehicles: 7.8 vehicles per 1,000 pop. **Civil aviation:** 10 airports.

Communications: TV sets: 12 per 1,000 pop. **Radios** 235 per 1,000 pop. **Telephone lines:** 0.5 per 100 pop. **Daily newspaper circ.:** 0.2 per 1,000 pop. **Internet:** 0.8 users per 100 pop.

Health: Life expect.: 52.1 male; 54.7 female. **Births:** 50.5 (per 1,000 pop.). **Deaths:** 14.1 (per 1,000 pop.). **Natural inc.:** 3.64%. **Infant mortality:** 112.2 (per 1,000 live births). **HIV rate:** 0.8%.

Education: Compulsory: ages 7-12. **Literacy:** 28.7%.

Major intl. organizations: UN (FAO, IBRD, ILO, IMF, WHO), AU, WTO

Embassy: 2204 R St. NW 20008; 483-4224.

Website: www.gouv.ne

Niger was part of ancient and medieval African empires. European explorers reached the area in the late 18th cent. The French colony of Niger was established 1900-22, after the defeat of Tuareg fighters, who had invaded the area from the north a century before. The country became independent Aug. 3, 1960.

In 1993, Niger held its first free and open elections since independence; an opposition leader, Mahamane Ousmane, won the presidency. A peace accord Apr. 24, 1995, ended a Tuareg rebellion that began in 1990. A coup, Jan. 27, 1996, followed by a disputed presidential election in July, left the military in control of Niger. On Apr. 9, 1999, Gen. Ibrahim Bare Mainassara, Niger's president since 1996, was assassinated, apparently by members of his security team. Elections were held Oct. 17 and Nov. 24, 1999, under a new constitution, approved by referendum July 18, that restored civilian rule.

One of the world's poorest countries, Niger experienced severe food shortages in 2005 after locusts and drought ruined the grain harvest. A resurgence of Tuareg rebel activity in June 2007 brought a major government counteroffensive. Popularly elected in 1999 and 2004, Pres. Mamadou Tandja invoked emergency powers in 2009, seeking to remain in office for a 3rd 5-year term; he was overthrown by a military junta Feb. 18, 2010. Civilian rule returned following Jan.-Mar. 2011 elections.

Nigeria
Federal Republic of Nigeria

People: Population: 165,822,569. **Age distrib.:** <15: 44%; 65+: 3%. **Pop. density:** 471.6 per sq mi, 182.1 per sq km. **Urban:** 49.8%. **Ethnic groups:** 250+ ethnic groups: Hausa & Fulani 29%, Yoruba 21%, Igbo (Ibo) 18%, Ijaw 10%, Kanuri 4%, Ibibio 4%, Tiv 3% most populous, politically influential groups. **Principal languages:** English (official), Hausa, Yoruba, Igbo (Ibo), Fulani, 500+ indigenous languages. **Chief religions:** Muslim 50%, Christian 40%, indigenous beliefs 10%.

Geography: Total area: 356,669 sq mi, 923,768 sq km; **Land area:** 351,649 sq mi, 910,768 sq km. **Location:** On S coast of W Africa. **Neighbors:** Benin on W, Niger on N, Chad and Cameroon on E. **Topography:** 4 E-W regions divide Nigeria: a coastal mangrove swamp 10-60 mi wide, a tropical rain forest 50-100 mi wide, a plateau of savanna and open woodland, and semi-desert in N. **Capital:** Abuja, 1,995,187. **Cities (urban aggl.):** Lagos, 10,577,672; Kano, 3,394,649; Ibadan, 2,836,665.

Government: Type: Federal republic. **Head of state and gov.:** Pres. Goodluck Jonathan; b. Nov. 20, 1957; in office: May 6, 2010 (acting from Feb. 9). **Local divisions:** 36 states, 1 capital territory. **Defense budget:** $1.55 bil. **Active troops:** 80,000.

Economy: Industries: crude oil; coal, tin, columbite; rubber prods.; wood; hides and skins; textiles; cement and other constr. materials. **Chief crops:** cocoa, peanuts, cotton, palm oil, corn, rice, sorghum, millet, cassava, yams, rubber. **Natural resources:** nat. gas, petroleum, tin, iron ore, coal, limestone, niobium, lead, zinc. **Crude oil reserves:** 37.2 bil bbls. **Arable land:** 37.3%. **Livestock:** cattle: 16.4 mil; chickens: 184.5 mil; goats: 55.1 mil; pigs: 7.2 mil; sheep: 34.7 mil. **Fish catch:** 751,006 metric tons. **Electricity prod.:** 20.1 bil kWh. **Labor force:** agric. 70%, industry 10%, services 20%.

Finance: Monetary unit: Naira (NGN) (Sept. 2011: 155.65 = $1 U.S.). **GDP:** $377.9 bil; **per capita GDP:** $2,500; **GDP growth:** 8.4%. **Imports** (2006): China 13.9%, U.S. 9.3%, Netherlands 8.6%, UK 4.9%, France 4.4%. **Exports** (2006): U.S. 34%, India 9.8%, Brazil 9%, Spain 6.8%, France 4.5%. **Tourism:** $608 mil. **Budget:** $29.6 bil. **Total reserves less gold:** $34.9 bil. **Gold:** 687,000 oz t. **CPI change:** 13.7%.

Transport: Railways: 2,178 mi. **Motor vehicles** 8.3 vehicles per 1,000 pop. **Civil aviation:** 1.2 bil pass.-mi; 38 airports. **Chief ports:** Calabar, Lagos.

Communications: TV sets: 67 per 1,000 pop. **Radios:** 602 per 1,000 pop. **Telephone lines:** 0.7 per 100 pop. **Internet:** 28.4 users per 100 pop.

Health: Life expect.: 48.5 male; 54.9 female. **Births:** 39.7 (per 1,000 pop.). **Deaths:** 13.8 (per 1,000 pop.). **Natural inc.:** 2.59%. **Infant mortality:** 75.8 (per 1,000 live births). **HIV rate:** 3.6%.

Education: Compulsory: ages 6-14. **Literacy:** 60.8%.

Major intl. organizations: UN (FAO, IBRD, ILO, IMF, WHO), AU, the Commonwealth, OPEC, WTO.

Embassy: 3519 International Ct. NW 20008; 986-8400.

Website: www.nigeria.gov.ng

Early cultures in Nigeria date back to at least 700 BCE. From the 12th to the 14th centuries, more advanced cultures developed in the Yoruba area, at Ife, and in the north, where Muslim influence prevailed. Portuguese and British slavers appeared from the 15th-16th centuries. Britain seized Lagos, 1861, and gradually extended control inland until 1900. Nigeria became independent Oct. 1, 1960, and a republic Oct. 1, 1963.

On May 30, 1967, the Eastern Region seceded, proclaiming itself the Republic of Biafra, plunging the country into civil war. Casualties in the war were estimated at over 1 mil, including many "Biafrans" (mostly Ibos) who died of starvation despite international efforts to provide relief. The secessionists, after steadily losing ground, capitulated Jan. 12, 1970.

Nigeria emerged as one of the world's leading oil exporters in the 1970s, but much of the revenue has been squandered through corruption and mismanagement. Oil spills have polluted much of the Niger Delta region, and rebel activities there have been extensive.

After 13 years of military rule, the nation made a peaceful return to civilian government, Oct. 1979. Military rule resumed, Dec. 31, 1983; a second coup came in 1985. Headed by Gen. Ibrahim Babangida, the military regime held elections June 12, 1993, but annulled the vote June 23 when it appeared that Moshood Abiola would win. Riots followed and many were killed. Babangida resigned and appointed a civilian to head an interim government, Aug. 26, but that government was ousted Nov. 17 in a coup led by Gen. Sani Abacha. On June 11, 1994, Abiola declared himself president; he was jailed June 23.

Abacha's brutal rule ended June 8, 1998, when he died of an apparent heart attack. Abiola died in prison July 7, as Abacha's successor, Gen. Abdulsalam Abubakar, was reportedly preparing to free him. Abiola's death sparked riots in Lagos and other cities; on July 20, Abubakar promised elections and a return to civilian rule. Olusegun Obasanjo (a former military ruler) won the presidential vote Feb. 27, 1999, Nigeria's first civilian government in 15 years.

An oil fire that exploded from a ruptured pipeline in southern Nigeria, Oct. 17, 1998, killed at least 700 people who were scavenging for fuel. The imposition of strict Islamic law in northern states led to clashes, Jan.-Mar. 2000, in which at least 800 people died. Fighting between Muslims and Christians Sept. 7-12, 2001, and Oct. 13-14, 2001, claimed an estimated 600 lives; another 200 people died when soldiers went on a rampage in SE Nigeria Oct. 22-24, 2001.

At least 1,000 people were killed Jan. 27, 2002, when an army weapons depot in Lagos exploded; many of the victims drowned in a drainage canal while fleeing the blasts. Controversy over Nigeria's plans to host a Miss World pageant sparked sectarian riots in Kaduna, Nov. 20-24, leaving more than 200 people dead and 1,100 injured. Obasanjo won reelection Apr. 19, 2003. Christian militia members massacred about 630 Muslims at Yelwa, central Nigeria, May 2, 2004. Obasanjo's chosen successor, Umaru Musa Yar'Adua, won a landslide victory Apr. 21, 2007, in a presidential election marred by violence and described as "not credible" by international monitors. Clashes between government security forces and Boko Haram, a radical Islamist sect in NE Nigeria, killed up to 800 people in late July 2009. After prolonged illness, for which he sought medical treatment in Saudi Arabia, Pres. Yar'Adua died May 5, 2010, and was succeeded by Vice-Pres. Goodluck Jonathan, a southern Christian. After he won reelection Apr. 16, 2011, over Muhammadu Buhari, a northern-based Muslim, riots in 12 northern provinces left more than 800 people dead. Nigeria's security police blamed members of Boko Haram for an Aug. 26 car bombing at UN headquarters in Abuja that killed 23 people and injured more than 100.

Norway
Kingdom of Norway

People: Population: 4,691,849. **Age distrib.:** <15: 18%; 65+: 16%. **Pop. density:** 39.9 per sq mi, 15.4 per sq km. **Urban:** 79.4%. **Ethnic groups:** Norwegian (incl. Sami) 94%, other European 4%. **Principal languages:** Bokmal Norwegian, Nynorsk Norwegian (both official); Sami (official in 6 municipalities). **Chief religion:** Church of Norway 86%, Muslim 2%, Pentecostal 1%, Roman Catholic 1%, other Christian 2%.

Geography: Total area: 125,021 sq mi, 323,802 sq km; **Land area:** 117,484 sq mi, 304,282 sq km. **Location:** W part of Scandinavian peninsula in NW Europe (extends farther north than any European land). **Neighbors:** Sweden, Finland, Russia on E. **Topography:** Highly indented coast is lined with tens of thousands of islands. Mountains and plateaus cover most of the country, which is only 25% forested. **Capital:** Oslo, 88,435.

Government: Type: Hereditary constitutional monarchy. **Head of state:** King Harald V; b. Feb. 21, 1937; in office: Jan. 17, 1991. **Head of gov.:** Prime Min. Jens Stoltenberg; b. Mar. 16, 1959; in office: Oct. 17, 2005. **Local divisions:** 19 provinces. **Defense budget:** $5.77 bil. **Active troops:** 26,450.

Economy: Industries: petroleum and gas, food proc., shipbuilding, pulp and paper prods., metals, chemicals, timber, mining, textiles, fishing. **Chief crops:** barley, wheat, potatoes. **Natural resources:** petroleum, nat. gas, iron ore, copper, lead, zinc, titanium, pyrites, nickel, fish, timber, hydropower. **Crude oil reserves:** 5.7 bil bbls. **Arable land:** 2.7%. **Livestock:** cattle: 877,711; chickens: 3.8 mil; goats: 67,767; pigs: 839,346; sheep: 2.3 mil. **Fish catch:** 3.5 mil metric tons. **Electricity prod.:** (2009): 129.9 bil kWh. **Labor force:** agric. 2.9%, industry 21.1%, services 76%.

Finance: Monetary unit: Krone (NOK) (Sept. 2011: 5.39 = $1 U.S.). **GDP:** $255.3 bil; **per capita GDP:** $54,600; **GDP growth:** 0.4%. **Imports:** $74 bil; Sweden 13.9%, Germany 12.9%, China 7.8%, Denmark 6.8%, U.S. 6.2%, UK 6%. **Exports:** $137 bil; UK 24.3%, Germany 13.4%, Netherlands 10.9%, France 8.5%, Sweden 5.8%, U.S. 4.8%. **Tourism:** $4.8 bil. **Budget:** $187 bil. **Total reserves less gold:** $52.8 bil. **CPI change:** 2.4%.

Transport: Railways: 2,590 mi. **Motor vehicles:** 601 vehicles per 1,000 pop. **Civil aviation:** 5.5 bil pass.-mi; 67 airports. **Chief ports:** Bergen, Borg Havn, Haugesund, Maaloy, Mongstad, Narvik, Oslo, Sture.

Communications: TV sets: 1,554 per 1,000 pop. **Radios:** 913 per 1,000 pop. **Telephone lines:** 34.9 per 100 pop. **Daily newspaper circ.:** 516 per 1,000 pop. **Internet:** 93.4 users per 100 pop.

Health: Life expect.: 77.5 male; 83 female. **Births:** 10.8 (per 1,000 pop.). **Deaths:** 9.2 (per 1,000 pop.). **Natural inc.:** 0.16%. **Infant mortality:** 3.5 (per 1,000 live births). **HIV rate:** 0.1%.

Education: Compulsory: ages 6-16. **Literacy:** 100%.

Major intl. organizations: UN and all of its specialized agencies, EFTA, NATO, OECD, OSCE, WTO.

Embassy: 2720 34th St. NW 20008; 333-6000.

Website: www.norway.no

The first ruler of Norway was Harald the Fairhaired, who came to power in 872 CE. Between 800 and 1000, Norway's Vikings raided and occupied widely dispersed parts of Europe.

The country was united with Denmark 1381-1814, and with Sweden, 1814-1905. In 1905, the country became independent with Prince Charles of Denmark as king.

Norway remained neutral during WWI. Germany attacked Norway Apr. 9, 1940, and held it until liberation May 8, 1945. The country abandoned its neutrality after the war, and joined NATO. In a referendum Nov. 28, 1994, Norwegian voters rejected European Union membership.

Abundant hydroelectric resources provided the base for industrialization, giving Norway one of the highest living standards in the world. The country is a leading producer and exporter of crude oil, with extensive reserves in the North Sea.

A center-left bloc headed by Labor Party leader Jens Stoltenberg won parliamentary elections Sept. 12, 2005, and remained in power after elections Sept. 13-14, 2009. A right-wing extremist, Anders Behring Breivik, confessed to carrying out mass killings July 22, 2011, in which he killed 8 people with a car bomb near government buildings in central Oslo, and shot 69 at an island camp sponsored by the Labor Party's youth wing. As of mid-2011, more than 400 Norwegian soldiers were serving with the NATO command in Afghanistan.

Svalbard is a group of mountainous islands in the Arctic O., area 23,956 sq mi, pop. (2011 est.) 2,019. The largest, Spitsbergen (formerly called West Spitsbergen), 15,060 sq mi, seat of the governor, is about 370 mi N of Norway. By a treaty signed in Paris, 1920, major European powers recognized the sovereignty of Norway, which incorporated it in 1925.

Jan Mayen, area 146 sq mi, is a volcanic island located about 565 mi W-NW of Norway; it was annexed in 1929.

Oman
Sultanate of Oman

People: Population: 3,027,959. **Age distrib.:** <15: 31.2%; 65+: 3.1%. **Pop. density:** 25.3 per sq mi, 9.8 per sq km. **Urban:** 73%. **Ethnic groups:** Arab, Baluchi, South Asian (Indian, Pakistani, Sri Lankan, Bangladeshi), African. **Principal languages:** Arabic (official), English, Baluchi, Urdu, Indian dialects. **Chief religions:** Ibadhi Muslim 75%, other (incl. Sunni Muslim, Shi'a Muslim, Hindu) 25%.

Geography: Total area: 119,499 sq mi, 309,500 sq km; **Land area:** 119,499 sq mi, 309,500 sq km. **Location:** On SE coast of Arabian peninsula. **Neighbors:** United Arab Emirates, Saudi Arabia, Yemen on W. **Topography:** A narrow coastal plain up to 10 mi wide, a range of barren mountains reaching 9,900 ft, and a wide, stony, mostly waterless plateau, avg. alt. 1,000 ft. Also, an exclave at the tip of the Musandam peninsula controls access to the Persian Gulf. **Capital:** Muscat, 634,000.

Government: Type: Absolute monarchy. **Head of state and gov.:** Sultan Qabus bin Said; b. Nov. 18, 1940; in office: July 23, 1970 (also prime min. since Jan. 2, 1972). **Local divisions:** 6 regions and 2 governorates. **Defense budget** (2009): $4.02 bil. **Active troops:** 42,600.

Economy: Industries: crude oil production and refining, nat. gas, constr., cement, copper, steel, chemicals, optic fiber. **Chief crops:** dates, limes, bananas, alfalfa, vegetables. **Natural resources:** petroleum, copper, asbestos, marble, limestone, chromium, gypsum, nat. gas. **Crude oil reserves:** 5.5 bil bbls. **Arable land:** 0.3%. **Livestock:** cattle: 325,500; chickens: 4.2 mil; goats: 1.7 mil; sheep: 381,000. **Fish catch:** 158,669 metric tons. **Electricity prod.** (2009): 17.6 bil kWh. **Labor force:** NA.

Finance: Monetary unit: Rial (OMR) (Sept. 2011: 0.39 = $1 U.S.). **GDP:** $75.8 bil; **per capita GDP:** $25,600; **GDP growth:** 4.2%. **Imports:** $19.3 bil; UAE 23.8%, Japan 15%, U.S. 6.5%, India 5.9%, China 4.8%, Germany 4.3%. **Exports:** $36.1 bil; China 20.1%, South Korea 15.5%, Japan 12.5%, UAE 11.6%, India 9.6%, Thailand 7.9%. **Tourism:** $700 mil. **Budget:** $20.1 bil. **Total reserves less gold:** $13 bil. **Gold:** 600 oz t. **CPI change:** 3.2%.

Transport: Motor vehicles: 149.5 vehicles per 1,000 pop. **Civil aviation:** 2.7 bil pass.-mi; 11 airports. **Chief ports:** Mina' Qabus, Salalah.

Communications: TV sets: 620 per 1,000 pop. **Radios:** 72 per 1,000 pop. **Telephone lines:** 10.2 per 100 pop. **Internet:** 62.6 users per 100 pop.

Health: Life expect.: 72.4 male; 76.2 female. **Births:** 24.2 (per 1,000 pop.). **Deaths:** 3.5 (per 1,000 pop.). **Natural inc.:** 2.07%. **Infant mortality:** 15.5 (per 1,000 live births). **HIV rate:** 0.1%.

Education: NA. **Literacy:** 86.6%.

Major intl. organizations: UN (FAO, IBRD, ILO, IMF, WHO), AL, WTO.

Embassy: 2535 Belmont Rd. NW 20008; 387-1980.

Website: www.omanet.om

Oman was originally called Muscat and Oman. A long history of rule by other lands, including Portugal in the 16th cent., ended with the ouster of the Persians in 1744. By the early 19th cent., Muscat and Oman was one of the most important countries in the region, controlling much of the Persian and Pakistan coasts.

British influence was confirmed in a 1951 treaty, and Britain helped suppress an uprising by traditionally rebellious interior tribes against control by Muscat in the 1950s.

On July 23, 1970, Sultan Said bin Taimur was overthrown by his son, Sultan Qabus bin Said, who changed the nation's name to Sultanate of Oman. Petroleum and natural gas are major sources of income. Although Oman has strong military and economic ties to the U.S., it has also cultivated favorable relations with Iran. Sultan Qabus shuffled his cabinet after "Arab Spring" protests Feb. 2011.

Pakistan
Islamic Republic of Pakistan

People: Population: 187,342,721. **Age distrib.:** <15: 35.4%; 65+: 4.2%. **Pop. density:** 629.4 per sq mi, 243 per sq km. **Urban:** 35.9%. **Ethnic groups:** Punjabi 45%, Pashtun (Pathan) 15%, Sindhi 14%, Sariaki 8%, Muhajir 8%, Balochi 4%. **Principal languages:** Punjabi, Sindhi, Siraiki, Pashtu, Urdu (official), Balochi, Hindko, Brahui, English (official; lingua franca of elite, most govt. ministries), Burushaski. **Chief religion:** Muslim (Sunni 75%, Shi'a 20%) 95%, other (incl. Christian, Hindu) 5%.

Geography: Total area: 307,374 sq mi, 796,095 sq km; **Land area:** 297,637 sq mi, 770,875 sq km. **Location:** In W part of South Asia. **Neighbors:** Iran on W, Afghanistan and China on N, India on E. **Topography:** The Indus R. rises in the Hindu Kush and Himalaya Mts. in the N (highest is K2, or Godwin Austen, 28,250 ft, 2nd highest in world), then flows over 1,000 mi through fertile valley and empties into Arabian Sea. Thar Desert, Eastern Plains flank Indus Valley. **Capital:** Islamabad, 855,648. **Cities (urban agg.):** Karachi, 13,124,793; Lahore, 7,131,864; Faisalabad, 2,849,206.

Government: Type: Republic. **Head of state:** Pres. Asif Ali Zardari; b. July 26, 1955; in office: Sept. 9, 2008. **Head of gov.:** Prime Min. Syed Yousaf Raza Gilani; b. June 9, 1952; in office: Mar. 25, 2008. **Local divisions:** 4 provinces and 1 capital territory, plus federally administered tribal areas. **Defense budget:** $5.2 bil. **Active troops:** 617,000.

Economy: Industries: textiles and apparel, food proc., pharmaceuticals, constr. materials, paper prods., fertilizer, shrimp. **Chief crops:** cotton, wheat, rice, sugarcane, fruits, vegetables. **Natural resources:** nat. gas, limited petroleum, poor quality coal, iron ore, copper, salt, limestone. **Crude oil reserves:** 313 mil bbls. **Arable land:** 26.5%. **Livestock:** cattle: 33 mil; chickens: 295 mil; goats: 58.3 mil; sheep: 27.4 mil. **Fish catch:** 684,461 metric tons. **Electricity prod.** (2009): 89.2 bil kWh. **Labor force:** agric. 43%, industry 20.3%, services 36.6%.

Finance: Monetary unit: Rupee (PKR) (Sept. 2011: 87.40 = $1 U.S.). **GDP:** $464.9 bil; **per capita GDP:** $2,500; **GDP growth:** 4.8%. **Imports:** $32.7 bil; China 11.9%, Saudi Arabia 11%, UAE 10.9%, U.S. 5.7%, Kuwait 5.7%, Malaysia 5.1%, Japan 4.1%, Germany 4%. **Exports:** $20.3 bil; U.S. 18.1%, UAE 8.4%, Afghanistan 7.7%, China 5.6%, UK 5.3%, Germany 4%. **Tourism:** $362 mil. **Budget:** $36.2 bil. **Total reserves less gold:** $14.3 bil. **Gold:** 2.1 mil oz t. **CPI change:** 13.9%.

Transport: Railways: 4,841 mi. **Motor vehicles:** 12 vehicles per 1,000 pop. **Civil aviation:** 8.1 bil pass.-mi; 101 airports. **Chief ports:** Karachi, Port Muhammad Bin Qasim.

Communications: TV sets: 81 per 1,000 pop. **Radios:** 83 per 1,000 pop. **Telephone lines:** 2 per 100 pop. **Daily newspaper circ.:** 50.3 per 1,000 pop. **Internet:** 16.8 users per 100 pop.

Health: Life expect.: 64.2 male; 67.9 female. **Births:** 24.8 (per 1,000 pop.). **Deaths:** 6.9 (per 1,000 pop.). **Natural inc.:** 1.79%. **Infant mortality:** 63.3 (per 1,000 live births). **HIV rate:** 0.1%.

Education: Compulsory: ages 5-9. **Literacy:** 55.5%.

Major intl. organizations: UN (FAO, IBRD, ILO, IMF, WHO), the Commonwealth, WTO.

Embassy: 3517 International Ct. NW 20008; 243-6500.

Website: www.pakistan.gov.pk

Pakistan shares the 5,000-year history of the India-Pakistan subcontinent. At present-day Harappa and Mohenjo Daro, the Indus Valley Civilization, with large cities and elaborate irrigation systems, flourished c. 4,000-2,500 BCE. Aryan invaders from the northwest conquered the region around 1,500 BCE, forging the Vedic civilization that dominated the region for over a thousand years. Other invaders from the west followed. The first Arab invasion, 712 CE, introduced Islam. Present-day Pakistan and India were part of the Mughal empire from 1526 to 1857. Muslim power faded by the end of the 19th cent. as the British gained control.

Muhammad Ali Jinnah (1876-1948) was the principal architect of Pakistan. When the British withdrew Aug. 14, 1947, the Islamic majority areas of India acquired self-government as Pakistan, with dominion status in the Commonwealth. Pakistan was divided into 2 sections, West Pakistan and East Pakistan. The 2 areas were nearly 1,000 mi apart on opposite sides of India. Kashmir, a predominantly Muslim region divided between Pakistan and India, has remained a source of conflict between the two countries.

The Awami League, which had sought regional autonomy for East Pakistan for several years, won a majority in Dec. 1970 elections to a constituent assembly. On Mar. 1, 1971, Pakistan's military-dominated government postponed the assembly. Rioting and strikes broke out in the East. On Mar. 25, government troops launched attacks in the East. The Easterners, aided by India, proclaimed the independent nation of Bangladesh. In months of widespread fighting, thousands were killed. Some 10 mil Easterners fled into India. Full-scale war between India and Pakistan had spread to both the East and West fronts by Dec. 3. Pakistan troops in the East surrendered Dec. 16; Pakistan agreed to a cease-fire in the West Dec. 17. On July 3, 1972, Pakistan and India signed a pact agreeing to withdraw troops from their borders and resolve problems peacefully.

Zulfikar Ali Bhutto, leader of the Pakistan People's Party, which had won the most West Pakistan votes in Dec. 1970 elections, became president Dec. 20, 1971. Bhutto was overthrown in a military coup July 1977. Convicted of complicity in a 1974 political murder, he was executed Apr. 4, 1979. Millions of Afghan refugees flooded into Pakistan after the USSR invaded Afghanistan Dec. 1979; during 2002-10, some 3.6 mil refugees were repatriated, but 1.7 mil remained.

Pres. Mohammad Zia ul-Haq was killed when his plane exploded in Aug. 1988. Following Nov. elections, Benazir Bhutto, daughter of Zulfikar Ali Bhutto, was named prime minister, becoming the first woman leader of a Muslim nation. She was accused of corruption and dismissed by the president, Aug. 1990. Bhutto returned to power Oct. 1993 but was dismissed again, Nov. 1996, amid further corruption charges. Responding to nuclear weapons tests by India, Pakistan conducted its own tests in 1998; the U.S. imposed economic sanctions on both countries.

Growing conflict between Prime Min. Nawaz Sharif and the military climaxed in his firing on Oct. 12, 1999, of army chief Gen. Pervez Musharraf, whose supporters staged a bloodless coup. Musharraf assumed the presidency June 20, 2001. Following the Sept. 11, 2001, terrorist attacks on the U.S., Pres. Musharraf, Sept. 19, pledged cooperation with the U.S. in fighting Taliban and al-Qaeda militants within Pakistan's own tribal areas and in neighboring Afghanistan. In return, the U.S. waived its 1998 sanctions and offered Pakistan financial aid and debt relief. A referendum Apr. 30, 2002, extended Musharraf's rule for 5 years; many observers called the vote rigged.

Accused of selling atomic secrets to Iran, Libya, and North Korea, Pakistan's top nuclear scientist, Abdul Qadeer Khan, made a televised apology, Feb. 4, 2004, and said his actions were unauthorized. He received a pardon from Musharraf Feb. 5. An earthquake that rocked Pakistan and the Pakistani-held region of Kashmir Oct. 8, 2005, killed about 80,000 people and left up to 3 mil homeless.

Musharraf's grip weakened in 2007, as his efforts to oust Pakistan's chief justice sparked mass protests by pro-democracy demonstrators. Musharraf survived an assassination attempt (at least the 4th in 5 years) when gunmen fired on his plane July 6. He retained the presidency in an electoral-college vote Oct. 6, 2007, after his main opponents boycotted the election. More than 140 people died Oct. 18 when suicide bombers struck a convoy carrying Benazir Bhutto from the Karachi airport after more than 8 years in exile. Musharraf imposed emergency rule Nov. 3 and suspended the constitution, while Pakistan's Supreme Court debated the constitutionality of his reelection. Musharraf gave up his army post Nov. 25, was sworn in as civilian president the next day, and lifted emergency rule Dec. 16. Bhutto was assassinated Dec. 27 after a rally in Rawalpindi.

Headed by Bhutto's widower, Asif Ali Zardari, the Pakistan Peoples Party led in parliamentary elections Feb. 18, 2008. Musharraf

resigned Aug. 18 under threat of impeachment, and Zardari became president Sept. 9. Meanwhile, the security situation continued to deteriorate, as U.S. and Pakistani forces clashed with the Taliban near the Afghan border, and Islamists executed new suicide attacks. The government announced Feb. 16, 2009, a truce conceding de facto control of the strategic Swat Valley to the Taliban. The cease-fire broke down in May, when government forces launched an offensive that reclaimed most of the region; the fighting displaced nearly 2 mil civilians. Catastrophic floods and monsoon rains, July-Aug. 2010, inundated one-fifth of Pakistan, leaving more than 1,750 people dead and displacing up to 20 mil

From early 2007 to Aug. 2011, terrorist attacks, sectarian clashes, and armed conflict between Islamic insurgents and government forces killed more than 12,000 civilians and injured over 23,000. In Karachi alone, ethnic violence claimed about 1,000 lives during Jan.-Aug. 2011. Extremists targeted proponents of religious tolerance, including Punjab's provincial Gov. Salman Taseer, a Zardari ally who was assassinated Jan. 4, and Shahbaz Bhatti, the only Christian in the federal cabinet, who was ambushed and killed Mar. 2.

A decade-long international manhunt came to an end shortly after midnight May 2, 2011, when U.S. commandos killed al-Qaeda leader Osama bin Laden at his fortified compound in Abbottabad, less than a mile from the Pakistan Military Academy at Kakul. The raid, carried out by helicopter from Jalalabad, Afghanistan, was launched without prior warning to Pakistani authorities.

Palau
Republic of Palau

People: Population: 20,956. **Age distrib.:** <15: 21.5%; 65+: 6.5%. **Pop. density:** 118.2 per sq mi, 45.7 per sq km. **Urban:** 83.4%. **Ethnic groups:** Palauan (Micronesian with Malayan & Melanesian) 70%, Filipino 15%, Chinese 5%, other Asian 2%, white 2%, Carolinian 1%, other Micronesian 1%. **Principal languages:** Palauan (official on most islands); Filipino; English; Chinese; Carolinian; Japanese; Sonsorolese, Tobi, Angaur (all also official in certain states). **Chief religions:** Roman Catholic 42%, Protestant 23%, Modekngei 9%, Seventh-Day Adventist 5%, none 16%.

Geography: Total area: 177 sq mi, 459 sq km; **Land area:** 177 sq mi, 459 sq km. **Location:** Archipelago (26 islands, more than 300 islets) in W Pacific Ocean, about 530 mi SE of the Philippines. **Neighbors:** Micronesia to E, Indonesia to S. **Topography:** A mountainous main island and low coral atolls, usually fringed with large barrier reefs. **Capital:** Melekeok, 391; Koror (former), 12,000.

Government: Type: Republic in free association with the U.S. **Head of state and gov.:** Pres. Johnson Toribiong; b. July 22, 1946; in office: Jan. 15, 2009. **Local divisions:** 16 states. **Defense budget/active troops:** NA.

Economy: Industries: tourism, craft items, constr., garment making. **Chief crops:** coconuts, copra, cassava, sweet potatoes. **Natural resources:** forests, minerals (espec. gold), marine prods., deep-seabed minerals. **Arable land:** 2.2%. **Fish catch:** 1,012 metric tons. **Labor force:** agric. 20%, industry and services NA.

Finance: Monetary unit: U.S. Dollar (USD). **GDP** (2008 est.): $164 mil (in 2010 USD; incl. U.S. subsidy); **per capita GDP** (2008 est.): $8,100; **GDP growth** (2005 est.): 5.5%. **Imports** (2004 est.): $107.3 mil; NA. **Exports** (2004 est.): $5.9 mil; NA. **Tourism:** $93 mil. **Budget** (2008 est.): $99.5 mil. **Total reserves less gold:** NA.

Transport: Civil aviation: 1 airport. **Chief port:** Koror.

Communications: TV sets: 98 per 1,000 pop. **Telephone lines:** 34.1 per 100 pop. **Internet:** NA.

Health: Life expect.: 68.6 male; 75.1 female. **Births:** 10.7 (per 1,000 pop.). **Deaths:** 7.9 (per 1,000 pop.). **Natural inc.:** 0.29%. **Infant mortality:** 12.4 (per 1,000 live births). **HIV rate:** NA.

Education: Compulsory: ages 6-14. **Literacy:** 91.9%.

Major intl. organizations: UN (FAO, IBRD, ILO, IMF, WHO).

Embassy: 1700 Pennsylvania Ave. NW, Ste. 400, 20006; 452-6814.

Website: www.palaugov.net

Spain acquired the Palau Islands in 1886 and sold them to Germany in 1899. Japan seized them in 1914. American forces occupied the islands in 1944; in 1947, they became part of the U.S.-administered UN Trust Territory of the Pacific Islands. In 1981 Palau became an autonomous republic; the republic ratified a compact of free association with the U.S. in 1993 and became an independent nation on Oct. 1, 1994. On Nov. 1, 2009, the government of Pres. Johnson Toribiong accepted resettlement of 6 Uighur (Chinese Muslim) detainees who had been held by the U.S. at Guantánamo Bay, Cuba, after their capture in Pakistan and Afghanistan in 2001.

Panama
Republic of Panama

People: Population: 3,460,462. **Age distrib.:** <15: 28.6%; 65+: 7.2%. **Pop. density:** 120.6 per sq mi, 46.5 per sq km. **Urban:** 74.8%. **Ethnic groups:** mestizo (mixed Amerindian & white) 70%, Amerindian & mixed (West Indian) 14%, white 10%, Amerindian 6%. **Principal languages:** Spanish (official), English. **Chief religions:** Roman Catholic 85%, Protestant 15%.

Geography: Total area: 29,120 sq mi, 75,420 sq km; **Land area:** 28,703 sq mi, 74,340 sq km. **Location:** In Central America. **Neighbors:** Costa Rica on W, Colombia on E. **Topography:** 2 mountain ranges run the length of the isthmus. Tropical rain forests cover the Caribbean coast and E Panama. **Capital:** Panama City, 1,378,470.

Government: Type: Republic. **Head of state and gov.:** Pres. Ricardo Martinelli Berrocal; b. Mar. 11, 1952; in office: July 1, 2009. **Local divisions:** 9 provinces, 5 territories. **Defense budget:** $230 mil. **Active troops:** 12,000 (paramilitary only).

Economy: Industries: constr., brewing, cement and other constr. materials, sugar milling. **Chief crops:** bananas, rice, corn, coffee, sugarcane, vegetables. **Natural resources:** copper, mahogany forests, shrimp, hydropower. **Arable land:** 7.4%. **Livestock:** cattle: 1.6 mil; chickens: 16.5 mil; goats: 6,300; pigs: 272,700. **Fish catch:** 228,509 metric tons. **Electricity prod.:** 6.2 bil kWh. **Labor force:** agric. 17.6%, industry 8.8%, services 73.6%.

Finance: Monetary unit: Balboa (PAB) (Sept. 2011: 1.00 = $1 U.S.). **GDP:** $44.4 bil; **per capita GDP:** $13,000; **GDP growth:** 7.5%. **Imports:** $16.1 bil; Japan 27.5%, China 14%, Singapore 12.8%, South Korea 9.6%, U.S. 9.3%, Ecuador 4.2%. **Exports:** $12.5 bil; Venezuela 22.1%, South Korea 17.7%, Greece 6.2%, Ecuador 6.1%, India 5.6%, U.S. 5.2%. (Imports and exports incl. the Colon Free Zone). **Tourism:** $1.7 bil. **Budget:** $7.1 bil. **Total reserves less gold:** $2.7 bil. **CPI change:** 3.5%.

Transport: Railways: 47 mi. **Motor vehicles:** 138.7 vehicles per 1,000 pop. **Civil aviation:** 5.2 bil pass.-mi; 54 airports. **Chief ports:** Balboa, Colon, Cristobal.

Communications: TV sets: 219 per 1,000 pop. **Radios:** 293 per 1,000 pop. **Telephone lines:** 15.7 per 100 pop. **Daily newspaper circ.:** 65.1 per 1,000 pop. **Internet:** 42.8 users per 100 pop.

Health: Life expect.: 75 male; 80.7 female. **Births:** 19.4 (per 1,000 pop.). **Deaths:** 4.7 (per 1,000 pop.). **Natural inc.:** 1.48%. **Infant mortality:** 11.6 (per 1,000 live births). **HIV rate:** 0.9%.

Education: Compulsory: ages 6-14. **Literacy:** 93.6%.

Major intl. organizations: UN (FAO, IBRD, ILO, IMF, WHO), OAS, WTO.

Embassy: 2862 McGill Ter. NW 20008; 483-1407.

Website: www.presidencia.gob.pa

The coast of Panama was sighted by Rodrigo de Bastidas, sailing with Columbus for Spain in 1501, and was visited by Columbus in 1502. Vasco Núñez de Balboa crossed the isthmus and "discovered" the Pacific Ocean, Sept. 13, 1513. Spanish colonies were ravaged by Francis Drake, 1572-95, and Henry Morgan, 1668-71. Morgan destroyed the old city of Panama which had been founded in 1519. Freed from Spain, Panama joined Colombia in 1821.

Panama declared independence from Colombia Nov. 3, 1903, with U.S. support. Panama granted use, occupation, and control of the Canal Zone to the U.S. by treaty, ratified Feb. 26, 1904. In 1978, a new treaty provided for a gradual takeover by Panama of the canal, and withdrawal of U.S. troops, to be completed before the end of the century.

Pres. Eric Arturo Delvalle was ousted by the National Assembly, Feb. 26, 1988, after he tried to fire the head of the Panama Defense Forces, Gen. Manuel Antonio Noriega, who was under U.S. federal indictment on drug charges. U.S. troops invaded Panama Dec. 20, 1989, and Noriega surrendered Jan. 3, 1990.

The U.S. handed over control of the Panama Canal to Panama Dec. 31, 1999. A $5.3-bil plan to widen the canal was approved by national referendum Oct. 22, 2006; construction on the 7-year project began Sept. 3, 2007. Ricardo Martinelli Berrocal, a conservative supermarket magnate, was elected president May 3, 2009, and took office July 1. After spending 2 decades in a U.S. prison, Noriega was extradited to France Apr. 26, 2010, where he was convicted of money laundering July 7 and received a 7-year sentence.

Papua New Guinea

Independent State of Papua New Guinea

People: Population: 6,187,591. **Age distrib.:** <15: 36.4%; 65+: 3.6%. **Pop. density:** 35.4 per sq mi, 13.7 per sq km. **Urban:** 12.5%. **Ethnic groups:** Melanesian, Papuan, Negrito, Micronesian, Polynesian. **Principal languages:** Tok Pisin, English, Hiri Motu (all official); some 860 indigenous languages spoken. **Chief religions:** Roman Catholic 27%, Evangelical Lutheran 20%, United Church 12%, Seventh-Day Adventist 10%, Pentecostal 9%, Evangelical Alliance 5%, Anglican 3%, Baptist 3%, other Protestant 9%.

Geography: Total area: 178,704 sq mi, 462,840 sq km; **Land area:** 174,850 sq mi, 452,860 sq km. **Location:** SE Asia, occupying E half of island of New Guinea and about 600 nearby islands. **Neighbors:** Indonesia on W, Australia on S. **Topography:** Thickly forested mts. cover much of center of the country, with lowlands along the coasts. Included are some islands of Bismarck and Solomon groups, such as Admiralty Isls., New Ireland, New Britain, and Bougainville. **Capital:** Port Moresby, 314,000.

Government: Type: Parliamentary democracy. **Head of state:** Queen Elizabeth II, represented by Gov.-Gen. Sir Michael Ogio; b. July 7, 1942; in office: Feb. 25, 2011 (acting from Dec. 20, 2010). **Head of gov.:** Prime Min. Peter O'Neill; b. Feb. 13, 1965; in office: Aug. 2, 2011. **Local divisions:** 20 provinces. **Defense budget:** $43 mil. **Active troops:** 3,100.

Economy: Industries: copra crushing, palm oil proc., plywood prod., wood chip prod., mining, crude oil prod., petroleum refining. **Chief crops:** coffee, cocoa, copra, palm kernels, tea, sugar, rubber, sweet potatoes. **Natural resources:** gold, copper, silver, nat. gas, timber, oil, fisheries. **Crude oil reserves:** 88 mil bbls. **Arable land:** 0.6%. **Livestock:** cattle: 94,000; chickens: 4 mil; goats: 3,000; pigs: 1.8 mil; sheep: 7,000. **Fish catch:** 230,103 metric tons. **Electricity prod.:** 3 bil kWh. **Labor force:** agric. 85%, industry and services NA.

Finance: Monetary unit: Kina (PGK) (Sept. 2011: 2.21 = $1 U.S.). **GDP:** $14.95 bil; **per capita GDP:** $2,500; **GDP growth:** 7%. **Imports:** $3.5 bil; Australia 41.9%, China 14.8%, Singapore 9.3%, U.S. 6.2%, Japan 4.5%. **Exports:** $6 bil; Australia 29.4%, Japan 7.9%, China 4.1%. **Tourism:** NA. **Budget:** $2.8 bil. **Total reserves less gold:** $3 bil. **Gold:** 63,000 oz t. **CPI change:** 6%.

Transport: Motor vehicles: 22 vehicles per 1,000 pop. **Civil aviation:** 452.4 mil pass.-mi; 21 airports. **Chief ports:** Kimbe, Lae, Madang, Rabaul, Wewak.

Communications: TV sets: 24 per 1,000 pop. **Radios:** 191 per 1,000 pop. **Telephone lines:** 1.8 per 100 pop. **Daily newspaper circ.:** 8.6 per 1,000 pop. **Internet:** 1.3 users per 100 pop.

Health: Life expect.: 64 male; 68.6 female. **Births:** 26.4 (per 1,000 pop.). **Deaths:** 6.6 (per 1,000 pop.). **Natural inc.:** 1.99%. **Infant mortality:** 43.3 (per 1,000 live births). **HIV rate:** 0.9%.

Education: Compulsory: ages 6-14. **Literacy:** 60.1%.

Major intl. organizations: UN (FAO, IBRD, ILO, IMF, WHO), APEC, the Commonwealth, WTO.

Embassy: 1779 Massachusetts Ave. NW, Ste. 805, 20036; 745-3680.

Website: www.pm.gov.pg

Human remains have been found in the interior of New Guinea dating back at least 10,000 years and possibly much earlier. Europeans visited in the 15th cent., but actual land claims did not begin until the 19th cent., when the Dutch took control of the island's western half (now part of Indonesia). The southern half of eastern New Guinea was first claimed by Britain in 1884, and transferred to Australia in 1905. The northern half was claimed by Germany in 1884, but captured in WWI by Australia, which received a League of Nations mandate and then a UN trusteeship. The 2 territories were administered jointly after 1949, gained self-government Dec. 1, 1973, and became independent Sept. 16, 1975.

Secessionist rebels clashed with government forces on Bougainville beginning in 1988; a truce signed Oct. 10, 1997, brought a halt to the fighting, which had claimed some 20,000 lives. A tsunami killed at least 3,000 July 17, 1998. A Bougainville autonomy agreement was signed Aug. 30, 2001. Army mutinies were suppressed in Mar. 2001 and Mar. 2002. Sir Michael Somare, the nation's first prime minister (1975-80, 1982-85), regained the office in 2002 and was reelected by parliament Aug. 13, 2007. After serving a two-week suspension Apr. 2011 for filing improper financial reports, the elderly Somare took indefinite medical leave; parliament Aug. 2 elected a permanent replacement, Prime Min. Peter O'Neill.

The country has extensive energy resources; a proposed pipeline would transport natural gas to Queensland, Australia.

Paraguay

Republic of Paraguay

People: Population: 6,459,058. **Age distrib.:** <15: 28.5%; 65+: 6.1%. **Pop. density:** 42.1 per sq mi, 16.3 per sq km. **Urban:** 61.5%. **Ethnic groups:** mestizo (mixed Spanish & Amerindian) 95%. **Principal languages:** Spanish, Guaraní (both official). **Chief religions:** Roman Catholic 90%, Protestant 6%, other Christian 1%, none 1%.

Geography: Total area: 157,048 sq mi, 406,752 sq km; **Land area:** 153,399 sq mi, 397,302 sq km. **Location:** Landlocked country in central S. America. **Neighbors:** Bolivia on N, Argentina on S, Brazil on E. **Topography:** Paraguay R. bisects the country. To E are fertile plains, wooded slopes, grasslands. To W is the Gran Chaco plain, with marshes and scrub trees. Extreme W is arid. **Capital:** Asunción, 2,029,666.

Government: Type: Republic. **Head of state and gov.:** Pres. Fernando Armindo Lugo Méndez; b. May 30, 1951; in office: Aug. 15, 2008. **Local divisions:** 17 departments and capital city. **Defense budget:** $142 mil. **Active troops:** 10,650.

Economy: Industries: sugar, cement, textiles, beverages, wood prods., steel. **Chief crops:** cotton, sugarcane, soybeans, corn, wheat, tobacco, cassava, fruits, vegetables. **Natural resources:** hydropower, timber, iron ore, manganese, limestone. **Arable land:** 9.6%. **Livestock:** cattle: 11.6 mil; chickens: 18 mil; goats: 135,000; pigs: 1.2 mil; sheep: 400,000. **Fish catch:** 3,800 metric tons. **Electricity prod.:** 54.9 bil kWh. **Labor force:** agric. 26.5%, industry 18.5%, services 55%.

Finance: Monetary unit: Guarani (PYG) (Sept. 2011: 3,910.00 = $1 U.S.). **GDP:** $33.3 bil; **per capita GDP:** $5,200; **GDP growth:** 15.3%. **Imports:** $9.6 bil; China 30%, Brazil 23.3%, Argentina 15.9%, Venezuela 5.1%, Japan 4.9%, U.S. 4.1%. **Exports:** $8 bil; Brazil 20.7%, Uruguay 16.9%, Chile 11.5%, Argentina 10.8%, Russia 4%. **Tourism:** $217 mil. **Budget:** $3.4 bil. **Total reserves less gold:** $4.1 bil. **Gold:** 21,220 oz t. **CPI change:** 4.7%.

Transport: Railways: 22 mi. **Motor vehicles:** 29.7 vehicles per 1,000 pop. **Civil aviation:** 311.9 mil pass.-mi; 15 airports. **Chief ports:** Asunción, Encarnación, San Antonio, Villeta.

Communications: TV sets: 262 per 1,000 pop. **Radios:** 182 per 1,000 pop. **Telephone lines:** 6.3 per 100 pop. **Internet:** 23.6 users per 100 pop.

Health: Life expect.: 73.6 male; 78.9 female. **Births:** 17.5 (per 1,000 pop.). **Deaths:** 4.6 (per 1,000 pop.). **Natural inc.:** 1.29%. **Infant mortality:** 23 (per 1,000 live births). **HIV rate:** 0.3%.

Education: Compulsory: ages 6-14. **Literacy:** 94.6%.

Major intl. organizations: UN (FAO, IBRD, ILO, IMF, WHO), OAS, WTO.

Embassy: 2400 Massachusetts Ave. NW 20008; 483-6960.

Website: www.embaparusa.gov.py

Guaraní Indians inhabited Paraguay before Europeans came. Visited by Sebastian Cabot in 1527 and settled as a Spanish possession in 1535, Paraguay gained its independence from Spain in 1811. It lost half its population and much of its territory to Brazil, Uruguay, and Argentina in the War of the Triple Alliance, 1865-70. Large areas were won from Bolivia in the Chaco War, 1932-35. Gen. Alfredo Stroessner, a military strongman, held the presidency 1954-89, until his ouster in a military coup.

Although the country returned to civilian rule in 1993, the next 6 years were marked by a protracted power struggle involving a popular military leader, Gen. Lino César Oviedo. Accused of insubordination, he surrendered Dec. 12, 1997, but was freed Aug. 18, 1998, following the inauguration of Pres. Raúl Cubas Grau, Oviedo's successor as Colorado Party nominee. The assassination of Vice Pres. Luis María Argaña, Mar. 23, 1999, by an unidentified gunman, was widely attributed to Cubas and triggered protests and an impeachment vote; Cubas resigned Mar. 28 and was succeeded by Senate leader Luis Angel González Macchi. An attempted military coup was suppressed May 18, 2000.

Mass protests over the depressed economy led to the proclamation of a state of emergency July 15, 2002. Nicanor Duarte Frutos of the Colorado Party won the presidency, Apr. 27, 2003.

Paraguayan authorities blamed a leftist group, Patria Libre, for the Sept. 2004 kidnapping and subsequent murder of Cecilia Cubas, daughter of former Pres. Cubas. Former Pres. González Macchi was convicted of fraud and embezzlement, Dec. 4, 2006, and sentenced to 8 years in prison. Fernando Lugo, a former Catholic cleric known as the "bishop of the poor," won a presidential election Apr. 20, 2008, ending over 6 decades of Colorado rule. In response to a paternity suit, Lugo acknowledged Apr. 20, 2008, that he had fathered a child while still a Roman Catholic bishop; within the next 10 days, 2 other women came forward with similar allegations.

Peru
Republic of Peru

People: Population: 29,248,943. **Age distrib.:** <15: 28.5%; 65+: 6.4%. **Pop. density:** 59.2 per sq mi, 22.9 per sq km. **Urban:** 76.9%. **Ethnic groups:** Amerindian 45%; mestizo (mixed Amerindian & white) 37%; white 15%; black, Japanese, Chinese, & other 3%. **Principal languages:** Spanish, Quechua (both official); Aymara; Ashaninka; other native languages (incl. large number of minor Amazonian languages). **Chief religion:** Roman Catholic 81%, Evangelical 13%.

Geography: Total area: 496,225 sq mi, 1,285,216 sq km; **Land area:** 494,209 sq mi, 1,279,996 sq km. **Location:** On Pacific coast of S. America. **Neighbors:** Ecuador, Colombia on N; Brazil, Bolivia on E; Chile on S. **Topography:** An arid coastal strip, 10-100 mi wide, supports much of the population thanks to widespread irrigation. The Andes cover 27% of land area. The uplands are well-watered, as are the eastern slopes reaching the Amazon basin, which covers half the country. **Capital:** Lima, 8,940,555. **Cities (urban aggl.):** Arequipa, 789,490.

Government: Type: Republic. **Head of state:** Pres. Ollanta Humala Tasso; b. June 27, 1962; in office: July 28, 2011. **Head of gov.:** Prime Min. Salomón Lerner Ghitis; b. Feb. 4, 1946; in office: July 28, 2011. **Local divisions:** 12 regions, 24 departments, 1 constitutional province. **Defense budget:** $1.11 bil. **Active troops:** 115,000.

Economy: Industries: mining and refining of minerals, steel, metal fabrication, petroleum extraction and refining, nat. gas and nat. gas liquefaction, fishing and fish proc., cement, textiles, clothing, food proc. **Chief crops:** asparagus, coffee, cocoa, cotton, sugarcane, rice, potatoes, corn, plantains, grapes, oranges and other fruits, coca, tomatoes, barley, medicinal plants. **Natural resources:** copper, silver, gold, petroleum, timber, fish, iron ore, coal, phosphate, potash, hydropower, nat. gas. **Crude oil reserves:** 532.7 mil bbls. **Arable land:** 2.9%. **Livestock:** cattle: 5.5 mil; chickens: 137.8 mil; goats: 1.9 mil; pigs: 3.3 mil; sheep: 14.1 mil. **Fish catch:** 7 mil metric tons. **Electricity prod.:** 31.9 bil kWh. **Labor force:** agric. 0.7%, industry 23.8%, services 75.5%.

Finance: Monetary unit: Nuevo Sol (PEN) (Sept. 2011: 2.73 = $1 U.S.). **GDP:** $275.7 bil; **per capita GDP:** $9,200; **GDP growth:** 8.8%. **Imports:** $25.7 bil; U.S. 19.7%, China 15%, Brazil 7.6%, Ecuador 4.9%, Chile 4.7%, Colombia 4.3%, Japan 4.1%, Argentina 4.1%. **Exports:** $35.6 bil; U.S. 17.6%, China 15.3%, Switzerland 14.9%, Canada 8.7%, Japan 5.1%. **Tourism:** $2.3 bil. **Budget:** $29.7 bil. **Total reserves less gold:** $42.6 bil. **Gold:** 1.1 mil oz t. **CPI change:** 1.5%.

Transport: Railways: 1,255 mi. **Motor vehicles:** 51 vehicles per 1,000 pop. **Civil aviation:** 5.8 bil pass.-mi; 58 airports. **Chief ports:** Callao, Iquitos, Matarani, Paita, Pucallpa, Yurimaguas.

Communications: TV sets: 201 per 1,000 pop. **Radios:** 269 per 1,000 pop. **Telephone lines:** 10.9 per 100 pop. **Internet:** 34.3 users per 100 pop.

Health: Life expect.: 70.6 male; 74.5 female. **Births:** 19.4 (per 1,000 pop.). **Deaths:** 5.9 (per 1,000 pop.). **Natural inc.:** 1.35%. **Infant mortality:** 22.2 (per 1,000 live births). **HIV rate:** 0.4%.

Education: Compulsory: ages 6-16. **Literacy:** 89.6%.

Major intl. organizations: UN and all of its specialized agencies, APEC, OAS, WTO.

Embassy: 1700 Massachusetts Ave. NW 20036; 833-9860.

Website: www.peru.gob.pe

The powerful Inca empire had its seat at Cuzco in the Andes and covered much of S. America. A civil war had weakened the empire when Francisco Pizarro, Spanish conquistador, began raiding Peru for its wealth, 1532. In 1533 he executed the Inca ruler, Atahualpa, and enslaved the people.

Lima was the seat of Spanish viceroys until the Argentine liberator, José de San Martin, captured it in 1821; Spanish forces were ultimately routed by Simón Bolívar, 1824. For much of the 19th cent., the country was governed by military leaders. Chile defeated Peru in the War of the Pacific, 1879-83. The first half of the 20th cent. was dominated by rivalry between right-wing groups (allied with the military) and the leftist APRA party.

Peru returned to democratic leadership in 1980 but was plagued by economic problems and by leftist Shining Path (Sendero Luminoso) guerrillas. Conflict between guerrillas and government troops, 1980-2000, killed more than 69,000 people, mostly Andean Indians.

Elected president in June 1990, Alberto Fujimori, the son of Japanese immigrants, dissolved the National Congress, suspended parts of the constitution, and initiated press censorship, Apr. 5, 1992. The leader of Shining Path was captured Sept. 12. Fujimori won reelection Apr. 9, 1995, but his repressive antiterrorism tactics drew international criticism.

Fujimori's path to a 3rd term was cleared when his lone remaining challenger withdrew, charging electoral fraud, 6 days before a runoff vote on May 28, 2000. Scandals involving his top aide and intelligence chief, Vladimiro Montesinos, led Fujimori to resign his office Nov. 20 while on a visit to Japan; instead of accepting his resignation, Congress ousted him as "morally unfit." Montesinos was captured in Venezuela June 23, 2001; extradited to Peru, he was convicted in a series of criminal trials. Fujimori was arrested in Chile, Nov. 7, 2005, and extradited to Peru, Sept. 22, 2007. He was convicted in 3 separate proceedings, 2007-09, on charges that included complicity in the killings by a paramilitary death squad of at least 25 people during 1991-92.

Alan García, whose first term as president, 1985-90, had ended with the country facing hyperinflation and guerrilla war, won a presidential runoff election June 4, 2006. An earthquake rocked SW coastal Peru, Aug. 15, 2007, killing more than 500 people and leaving 200,000 homeless. In a presidential runoff election June 5, 2011, Ollanta Humala Tasso, a leftist former military officer, defeated Peruvian legislator Keiko Fujimori Higuchi, the daughter of jailed former Pres. Fujimori.

Philippines
Republic of the Philippines

People: Population: 101,833,938. **Age distrib.:** <15: 34.6%; 65+: 4.3%. **Pop. density:** 884.6 per sq mi, 341.5 per sq km. **Urban:** 48.9%. **Ethnic groups:** Tagalog 28%, Cebuano 13%, Ilocano 9%, Bisaya/Binisaya 8%, Hiligaynon Ilonggo 8%, Bikol 6%, Waray 3%. **Principal languages:** Filipino, English (both official); 8 major dialects. **Chief religions:** Roman Catholic 81%, Muslim 5%, Evangelical 3%, Iglesia ni Kristo 2%, Aglipayan 2%, other Christian 5%.

Geography: Total area: 115,831 sq mi, 300,000 sq km; **Land area:** 115,124 sq mi, 298,170 sq km. **Location:** An archipelago off SE coast of Asia. **Neighbors:** Nearest are Malaysia, Indonesia on S; Taiwan on N. **Topography:** The country consists of some 7,100 islands stretching 1,100 mi N-S. About 95% of area and population are on 11 largest islands, which are mountainous, except for the heavily indented coastlines and central plain on Luzon. **Capital:** Manila, 11,628,288. **Cities (urban aggl.):** Davao, 1,518,730; Cebu, 859,812.

Government: Type: Republic. **Head of state and gov.:** Pres. Benigno (NoyNoy) Aquino III; b. Feb. 8, 1960; in office: June 30, 2010. **Local divisions:** 79 provinces. **Defense budget:** $2.13 bil. **Active troops:** 125,000.

Economy: Industries: electronics assembly, garments, footwear, pharmaceuticals, chemicals, wood prods., food proc., petroleum refining, fishing. **Chief crops:** sugarcane, coconuts, rice, corn, bananas, cassava, pineapples, mangoes. **Natural resources:** timber, petroleum, nickel, cobalt, silver, gold, salt, copper. **Crude oil reserves:** 138.5 mil bbls. **Arable land:** 18.1%. **Livestock:** cattle: 2.6 mil; chickens: 158.4 mil; goats: 4.2 mil; pigs: 13.6 mil; sheep: 30,000. **Fish catch:** 5.1 mil metric tons. **Electricity prod.** (2009): 59.2 bil kWh. **Labor force:** agric. 33%, industry 15%, services 52%.

Finance: Monetary unit: Peso (PHP) (Sept. 2011: 42.30 = $1 U.S.). **GDP:** $351.4 bil; **per capita GDP:** $3,500; **GDP growth:** 7.3%. **Imports:** $59.9 bil; Japan 12.6%, U.S. 12%, China 8.9%, Singapore 8.6%, South Korea 6.9%, Thailand 5.7%, Indonesia 4.2%.

Exports: $50.7 bil; U.S. 17.7%, Japan 16.3%, Netherlands 9.5%, Hong Kong 8.4%, China 7.6%, Singapore 6.7%, Germany 6.6%, South Korea 4.7%. **Tourism:** $2.8 bil. **Budget:** $33.8 bil. **Total reserves less gold:** $55.4 bil. **Gold:** 5 mil oz t. **CPI change:** 3.8%. **Transport: Railways:** 618 mi. **Motor vehicles:** 30.5 vehicles per 1,000 pop. **Civil aviation:** 11.3 bil pass.-mi; 85 airports. **Chief ports:** Batangas, Cagayan de Oro, Cebu, Davao, Liman, Manila.

Communications: TV sets: 194 per 1,000 pop. **Radios:** 735 per 1,000 pop. **Telephone lines:** 7.3 per 100 pop. **Daily newspaper circ.:** 78.6 per 1,000 pop. **Internet:** 25 users per 100 pop.

Health: Life expect.: 68.7 male; 74.7 female. **Births:** 25.3 (per 1,000 pop.). **Deaths:** 5 (per 1,000 pop.) **Natural inc.:** 2.03% **Infant mortality:** 19.3 (per 1,000 live births). **HIV rate:** <0.1%.

Education: Compulsory: ages 6-12. **Literacy:** 95.4%.

Major intl. organizations: UN (FAO, IBRD, ILO, IMF, WHO), APEC, ASEAN, WTO.

Embassy: 1600 Massachusetts Ave. NW 20036; 467-9300.

Website: www.gov.ph

Originally inhabited by Malay peoples, the archipelago was visited by Magellan, 1521. The Spanish founded Manila, 1571. The islands, named for King Philip II of Spain, were ceded by Spain to the U.S. for $20 mil, 1898, following the Spanish-American War. U.S. troops suppressed a guerrilla uprising in a brutal 6-year war, 1899-1905. Japan attacked the Philippines Dec. 8, 1941, and occupied the islands during WWII. On July 4, 1946, independence was proclaimed. A republic was established.

The repressive and corrupt regime of Pres. Ferdinand Marcos and his wife, Imelda, ruled the Philippines 1965-86. The assassination of prominent opposition leader Benigno S. Aquino Jr., Aug. 21, 1983, sparked demonstrations calling for Marcos's resignation. Amid allegations of widespread election fraud, Marcos was declared the victor Feb. 16, 1986, over Corazon Aquino, widow of the slain opposition leader. Mass protests and international pressure forced Marcos to flee the country Feb. 25, and Corazon Aquino became president.

Her government was plagued by a weak economy, widespread poverty, Communist and Muslim insurgencies, and lukewarm military support. Rebel troops seized military bases and TV stations and bombed the presidential palace, Dec. 1, 1989. Government forces, with U.S. air support, defeated the attempted coup. Aquino endorsed Fidel Ramos in the May 1992 presidential election, which he won. The U.S. vacated the Subic Bay Naval Station in late 1992, ending its long military presence in the Philippines. The government signed a cease-fire agreement, Jan. 30, 1994, with Muslim separatist guerrillas, but some rebels refused to abide by the accord. A new treaty providing for expansion and development of an autonomous Muslim region on Mindanao was signed Sept. 2, 1996, formally ending a rebellion that had claimed more than 120,000 lives since 1972.

Running as a populist, Joseph (Erap) Estrada, a former movie actor, won the presidential election of May 11, 1998. Charged with bribery and corruption, he was impeached Nov. 13, 2000. When the Supreme Court ruled the presidency vacant Jan. 20, 2001, Vice Pres. Gloria Macapagal Arroyo became president.

As part of the war on terrorism, the U.S. assisted Filipino troops in combating Abu Sayyaf, an Islamic guerrilla group. Pres. Arroyo won reelection May 10, 2004. Flooding and mudslides from tropical storms, Nov.-Dec. 2004, left at least 1,060 people dead, more than 560 missing, and 880,000 displaced. Former Pres. Estrada was convicted, Sept. 12, 2007, of taking more than $85 mil in bribes and kickbacks while in office; he received a pardon from Pres. Arroyo, Oct. 25. Typhoon Fengshen, June 21-22, 2008, left at least 557 people dead and destroyed more than 90,000 homes; at least 700 more people died when the ferry *Princess of the Stars* capsized and ran aground in the storm. Tropical storms Sept.-Oct. 2009 claimed more than 900 lives and affected over 9 mil people. Benigno (NoyNoy) Aquino III, the son of former Pres. Corazon Aquino (who died Aug. 1, 2009), defeated Estrada in the presidential election of May 10, 2010, and was sworn in June 30.

Poland
Republic of Poland

People: Population: 38,441,588. **Age distrib.:** <15: 14.7%; 65+: 13.7%. **Pop. density:** 327.2 per sq mi, 126.3 per sq km. **Urban:** 61%. **Ethnic groups:** Polish 97%. **Principal language:** Polish (official). **Chief religion:** Roman Catholic 90%, Eastern Orthodox 1%.

Geography: Total area: 120,728 sq mi, 312,685 sq km; **Land area:** 117,474 sq mi, 304,255 sq km. **Location:** On Baltic Sea in E central Europe. **Neighbors:** Germany on W; Czech Rep., Slovakia on S; Lithuania, Belarus, Ukraine on E; Russia on N. **Topography:** Mostly lowlands forming part of the Northern European Plain. The Carpathian Mts. along S border rise to 8,200 ft. **Capital:** Warsaw, 1,712,264. **Cities (urban aggl.):** Cracow, 756,150.

Government: Type: Republic. **Head of state:** Pres. Bronislaw Komorowski; b. June 4, 1952; in office: Aug. 6, 2010. **Head of gov.:** Prime Min. Donald Tusk; b. Apr. 22, 1957; in office: Nov. 16, 2007. **Local divisions:** 16 provinces. **Defense budget:** $8.35 bil. **Active troops:** 100,000.

Economy: Industries: machine building, iron and steel, coal mining, chemicals, shipbuilding, food proc., glass, beverages, textiles. **Chief crops:** potatoes, fruits, vegetables, wheat. **Natural**

resources: coal, sulfur, copper, nat. gas, silver, lead, salt, amber. **Crude oil reserves:** 96.4 mil bbls. **Arable land:** 41.2%. **Livestock:** cattle: 5.7 mil; chickens: 124.1 mil; goats: 118,842; pigs: 14.3 mil; sheep: 286,376. **Fish catch:** 260,396 metric tons. **Electricity prod.:** (2009): 141.8 bil kWh. **Labor force:** agric. 17.4%, industry 29.2%, services 53.4%.

Finance: Monetary unit: Zloty (PLN) (Sept. 2011: 3.03 = $1 U.S.). **GDP:** $721.3 bil; **per capita GDP:** $18,800; **GDP growth:** 3.8%. **Imports:** $167.4 bil; Germany 28.1%, Russia 8.5%, Italy 6.6%, Netherlands 5.7%, China 5.2%, France 4.6%, Czech Republic 4%. **Exports:** $160.8 bil; Germany 26.1%, France 6.9%, Italy 6.8%, UK 6.4%, Czech Republic 5.9%, Netherlands 4.2%. **Tourism:** $9.4 bil. **Budget:** $128.4 bil. **Total reserves less gold:** $88.8 bil. **Gold:** 3.3 mil oz t. **CPI change:** 2.7%.

Transport: Railways: 12,072 mi. **Motor vehicles:** 503.8 vehicles per 1,000 pop. **Civil aviation:** 4.5 bil pass.-mi; 86 airports. **Chief ports:** Gdansk, Gdynia, Swinoujscie, Szczecin.

Communications: TV sets: 408 per 1,000 pop. **Radios:** 297 per 1,000 pop. **Telephone lines:** 24.7 per 100 pop. **Daily newspaper circ.:** 113.6 per 1,000 pop. **Internet:** 62.3 users per 100 pop.

Health: Life expect.: 72.1 male; 80.3 female. **Births:** 10 (per 1,000 pop.) **Deaths:** 10.2 (per 1,000 pop.) **Natural inc.:** –0.02%. **Infant mortality:** 6.5 (per 1,000 live births). **HIV rate:** 0.1%.

Education: Compulsory: ages 7-15. **Literacy:** 99.5%.

Major intl. organizations: UN (FAO, IBRD, ILO, IMF, WHO), EU, NATO, OECD, OSCE, WTO.

Embassy: 2640 16th St. NW 20009; 234-3800.

Website: www.poland.gov.pl

Slavic tribes in the area were converted to Latin Christianity in the 10th cent. Poland was a great power from the 14th to the 17th centuries. In 3 partitions (1772, 1793, 1795) it was apportioned among Prussia, Russia, and Austria. Overrun by the Austro-German armies in WWI, it declared its independence on Nov. 11, 1918, and was recognized as independent by the Treaty of Versailles, June 28, 1919. Large territories to the east were taken in a war with Russia, 1921.

Germany and the USSR invaded Poland Sept. 1939 and divided the country. During the war, some 6 mil Polish citizens, half of them Jews, were killed by the Nazis. In compensation for 69,860 sq mi ceded to the USSR when the war ended, Poland received approx. 40,000 sq mi of German territory east of the Oder-Neisse line comprising Silesia, Pomerania, West Prussia, and part of East Prussia. The election of 1947 was completely dominated by the Communists, who aligned themselves with the USSR.

In 12 years of rule by Stalinists, large estates were abolished, industries nationalized, schools secularized, and Roman Catholic prelates jailed. Farm production fell off. Harsh working conditions caused a riot in Poznan, June 28-29, 1956. A new Politburo, committed to a more independent Polish Communism, was named Oct. 1956, with Wladyslaw Gomulka as first secretary of the party. Collectivization of farms was ended. Gomulka agreed to permit religious liberty and religious publications, provided the church kept out of politics.

In Dec. 1970 workers in port cities rioted because of price rises and new incentive wage rules. On Dec. 20 Gomulka resigned as party leader; he was succeeded by Edward Gierek. The rules were dropped and price rises revoked.

After 2 months of labor turmoil had crippled the country, the Polish government, Aug. 30, 1980, met the demands of striking workers at the Lenin Shipyard, Gdansk. Government concessions included the right to form independent trade unions and the right to strike. By 1981, 9.5 mil workers had joined the independent trade union (Solidarity). As Solidarity's demands grew bolder, the government, spurred by fear of Soviet intervention, imposed martial law Dec. 13. Lech Walesa and other Solidarity leaders were arrested.

On Apr. 5, 1989, an accord was reached between the government and opposition factions on political and economic reforms, including free elections. Candidates endorsed by Solidarity swept the parliamentary elections, June 4. Lech Walesa became president Dec. 22, 1990.

A radical economic program designed to transform the economy into a free-market system led to inflation and unemployment. In Sept. 1993, former Communists and other leftists won a majority in the lower house of Parliament. A former Communist, Aleksander Kwasniewski, defeated Walesa in a presidential election in 1995 and was reelected 5 years later. A new constitution was approved by referendum May 25, 1997. Poland became a full member of NATO, Mar. 12, 1999, and entered the European Union May 1, 2004.

Lech Kaczynski, the conservative mayor of Warsaw, won a presidential runoff election Oct. 23, 2005. In July 2006 he appointed his identical twin brother Jaroslaw as prime min. Poland's governing coalition fell apart in 2007, and the center-right Civic Platform party, led by Donald Tusk, won parliamentary elections Oct. 21. Pres. Lech Kaczynski, his wife Maria, and many senior Polish government officials were among the 96 passengers and crew members killed in a plane crash Apr. 10, 2010, near Smolensk, in western Russia. Parliament Speaker Bronislaw Komorowski, an ally of Prime Min. Tusk, became acting president after the crash; he won a full term July 4 by defeating Kaczynski's brother Jaroslaw 53%-47% in a presidential runoff vote.

Poland pulled its contingent of 900 troops out of Iraq in Oct. 2008. Nearly 2,600 Polish troops were serving in Afghanistan as of mid-2011.

Portugal
Portuguese Republic

People: Population: 10,760,305. **Age distrib.:** <15: 16.2%; 65+: 18%. **Pop. density:** 304.7 per sq mi, 117.6 per sq km. **Urban:** 60.7%. **Ethnic groups:** homogeneous Mediterranean stock; East Europeans have immigrated since 1990. **Principal languages:** Portuguese, Mirandese (both official). **Chief religion:** Roman Catholic 85%, other Christian 2%, none 4%.

Geography: Total area: 35,556 sq mi, 92,090 sq km; **Land area:** 35,371 sq mi, 91,470 sq km. **Location:** At SW extreme of Europe. **Neighbors:** Spain on N, E. **Topography:** Portugal N of Tajus R., which bisects country NE-SW, is mountainous, cool and rainy. To the S there are drier, rolling plains, and a warm climate. **Capital:** Lisbon, 2,823,965. **Cities (urban aggl.):** Porto, 1,354,688.

Government: Type: Republic. **Head of state:** Pres. Aníbal Cavaco Silva; b. July 15, 1939; in office: Mar. 9, 2006. **Head of gov.:** Prime Min. Pedro Passos Coelho; b. July 24,1964; in office: June 21, 2011. **Local divisions:** 18 districts, 2 autonomous regions. **Defense budget:** $3.19 bil. **Active troops:** 43,340.

Economy: Industries: textiles, clothing, footwear, wood and cork, paper, chemicals, auto-parts mfg., base metals, dairy prods., wine and other foods, porcelain and ceramics, glassware, technology. **Chief crops:** grain, potatoes, tomatoes, olives, grapes. **Natural resources:** fish, forests (cork), iron ore, copper, zinc, tin, tungsten, silver, gold, uranium, marble, clay, gypsum, salt, hydropower. **Arable land:** 12.3%. **Livestock:** cattle: 1.4 mil; chickens: 39 mil; goats: 485,000; pigs: 2.3 mil; sheep: 3.1 mil. **Fish catch:** 207,058 metric tons. **Electricity prod.** (2009): 46.5 bil kWh. **Labor force:** agric. 11.7%, industry 28.5%, services 59.8%.

Finance: Monetary unit: Euro (EUR) (Sept. 2011: 0.71 = $1 U.S.). **GDP:** $247 bil; **per capita GDP:** $23,000; **GDP growth:** 1.4%. **Imports:** $68.2 bil; Spain 32.6%, Germany 13.2%, France 8.3%, Italy 5.8%, Netherlands 5.5%. **Exports:** $46.3 bil; Spain 27.3%, Germany 12.9%, France 12.4%, Angola 7%, UK 5.7%. **Tourism:** $10.1 bil. **Budget:** $110.2 bil. **Total reserves less gold:** $3.7 bil. **Gold:** 12.3 mil oz t. **CPI change:** 1.4%.

Transport: Railways: 2,062 mi. **Motor vehicles:** 542.5 vehicles per 1,000 pop. **Civil aviation:** 14.2 bil pass.-mi; 43 airports. **Chief ports:** Leixoes, Lisbon, Setubal, Sines.

Communications: TV sets: 425 per 1,000 pop. **Radios:** 299 per 1,000 pop. **Telephone lines:** 42 per 100 pop. **Internet:** 51.1 users per 100 pop.

Health: Life expect.: 75.3 male; 82 female **Births:** 9.9 (per 1,000 pop.) **Deaths:** 10.8 (per 1,000 pop.) **Natural inc.:** −0.09%. **Infant mortality:** 4.7 (per 1,000 live births) **HIV rate:** 0.6%.

Education: Compulsory: ages 6-14. **Literacy:** 94.9%.

Major intl. organizations: UN (FAO, IBRD, ILO, IMF, WHO), EU, NATO, OECD, OSCE, WTO.

Embassy: 2012 Massachusetts Ave. NW 20036; 350-5400.

Website: www.portugal.gov.pt

Portugal, an independent state since the 12th cent., was a kingdom until a revolution in 1910 drove out King Manoel II and a republic was proclaimed. From 1932 a strong, repressive government was headed by Prem. Antonio de Oliveira Salazar. Illness forced his retirement in Sept. 1968.

On Apr. 25, 1974, the government was seized by a military junta led by Gen. Antonio de Spinola, who became president. The new government reached agreements providing independence for Guinea-Bissau, Mozambique, Cape Verde Islands, Angola, and São Tomé and Príncipe. Portugal returned Macao to China on Dec. 20, 1999.

With the economy lagging, opposition Socialists, led by Jóse Sócrates, gained a parliamentary majority in 2005 and held onto a plurality in 2009. The conservative Aníbal Cavaco Silva, a former prime min., 1985-95, defeated two Socialist candidates to win the Jan. 2006 presidential election and was reelected 5 years later. After Portugal was forced to negotiate a $116 bil bailout package from international lenders to avert default, voters delivered a parliamentary election victory June 5, 2011, to the center-right Social Democratic Party, headed by Pedro Passos Coelho.

Azores Isls., in the Atlantic, 740 mi W of Portugal, have an area of 868 sq mi and a pop. (2009 est.) of 245,374. A 1951 agreement gave the U.S. rights to use defense facilities in the Azores. The **Madeira Isls.,** 350 mi off the NW coast of Africa, have an area of 306 sq mi and a pop. (2009 est.) of 247,399. Both groups were offered partial autonomy in 1976.

Qatar
State of Qatar

People: Population: 1,849,257. **Age distrib.:** <15: 12.7%; 65+: 0.8%. **Pop. density:** 413.4 per sq mi, 159.6 per sq km. **Urban:** 95.8%. **Ethnic groups:** Arab 40%, Indian 18%,Pakistani 18%, Iranian 10%. **Principal languages:** Arabic (official), English commonly used as second lang. **Chief religions:** Muslim 78%, Christian 9%.

Geography: Total area: 4,473 sq mi, 11,586 sq km; **Land area:** 4,473 sq mi, 11,586 sq km. **Location:** Middle East, occupying peninsula on W coast of Persian Gulf. **Neighbors:** Saudi Arabia on S. **Topography:** Mostly flat desert with some limestone ridges; vegetation of any kind is scarce. **Capital:** Doha (Ad-Dawhah), 427,000.

Government: Type: Traditional monarchy. **Head of state:** Emir Sheikh Hamad bin Khalifa al-Thani; b. 1952; in office: June 27, 1995. **Head of gov.:** Prime Min. Sheikh Hamad bin Jassim bin Jabr al-Thani; b. 1959; in office: Apr. 3, 2007. **Local divisions:** 9 municipalities. **Defense budget** (2008): $1.75 bil. **Active troops:** 11,800.

Economy: Industries: liquefied nat. gas, crude oil prod. and refining, ammonia, fertilizers, petrochemicals, steel reinforcing bars, cement, commercial ship repair. **Chief crops:** fruits, vegetables. **Natural resources:** petroleum, nat. gas, fish. **Crude oil reserves:** 25.4 bil bbls. **Arable land:** 1%. **Livestock:** cattle: 7,500; chickens: 4.7 mil; goats: 140,000; sheep: 148,000. **Fish catch:** 14,100 metric tons. **Electricity prod.** (2009): 19.2 bil kWh. **Labor force:** NA.

Finance: Monetary unit: Riyal (QAR) (Sept. 2011: 3.64 = $1 U.S.). **GDP:** $150.6 bil; **per capita GDP:** $179,000; **GDP growth:** 16.3%. **Imports:** $23.4 bil; U.S. 13.1%, Italy 8.1%, Japan 7.9%, Germany 7.2%, South Korea 6.3%, France 6.1%, UAE 5.5%, UK 5.5%, China 4.2%, Saudi Arabia 4.1%. **Exports:** $57.8 bil; Japan 31.3%, South Korea 16.5%, Singapore 9.1%, India 8.1%. **Tourism:** $584 mil. **Budget:** $29.7 bil. **Total reserves less gold:** $30.6 bil. **Gold:** 399,100 oz t. **CPI change:** −2.4%.

Transport: Motor vehicles: 341.5 vehicles per 1,000 pop. **Civil aviation:** 25.1 bil pass.-mi; 4 airports. **Chief ports:** Doha, Mesaieed, Ra's Laffan.

Communications: TV sets: 405 per 1,000 pop. **Radios:** 468 per 1,000 pop. **Telephone lines:** 17 per 100 pop. **Internet:** 69 users per 100 pop.

Health: Life expect.: 76 male; 80 female. **Births:** 10.4 (per 1,000 pop.) **Deaths:** 1.6 (per 1,000 pop.) **Natural inc.:** 0.89%. **Infant mortality:** 6.9 (per 1,000 live births) **HIV rate:** <0.1%.

Education: Compulsory: ages 6-17. **Literacy:** 94.7%.

Major intl. organizations: UN (FAO, IBRD, ILO, IMF, WHO), AL, OPEC, WTO.

Embassy: 2555 M St. NW 20037; 274-1600.

Website: portal.www.gov.qa

Qatar was under Bahrain's control until the Ottoman Turks took power, 1872 to 1915. In a treaty signed 1916, Qatar gave Great Britain responsibility for its defense and foreign relations. After Britain announced it would remove its military forces from the Persian Gulf area by the end of 1971, Qatar sought a federation with other British-protected states in the area; this failed and Qatar declared itself independent, Sept. 1, 1971. Crown Prince Hamad bin Khalifa al-Thani ousted his father, Emir Khalifa bin Hamad al-Thani, June 27, 1995. In municipal elections held Mar. 8, 1999, women participated for the first time as candidates and voters.

Qatar, one of the world's leading exporters of liquefied natural gas, has experienced rapid economic growth in recent years. Military ties with the U.S. have been expanding; Camp As-Sayliyah, a base near Doha, served as a command center for the U.S.-led invasion of Iraq, Mar. 2003. The influential Arab news network Al-Jazeera is based in Qatar. Qatar was chosen Dec. 2, 2010, to host the World Cup soccer tournament in 2022.

Romania

People: Population: 21,904,551. **Age distrib.:** <15: 14.8%; 65+: 14.8%. **Pop. density:** 246.8 per sq mi, 95.3 per sq km. **Urban:** 57.5%. **Ethnic groups:** Romanian 90%, Hungarian 7%, Roma 3%. **Principal languages:** Romanian (official), Hungarian, Romany. **Chief religions:** Eastern Orthodox 87%, Protestant 8%, Roman Catholic 5%.

Geography: Total area: 92,043 sq mi, 238,391 sq km; **Land area:** 88,761 sq mi, 229,891 sq km. **Location:** SE Europe, on the Black Sea. **Neighbors:** Moldova on E, Ukraine on N, Hungary and Serbia on W, Bulgaria on S. **Topography:** The Carpathian Mts. encase the north-central Transylvanian plateau. There are wide plains S and E of the mountains, through which flow the lower reaches of the rivers of Danube system. **Capital:** Bucharest, 1,934,433.

Government: Type: Republic. **Head of state:** Pres. Traian Basescu; b. Nov. 4, 1951; in office: Dec. 20, 2004. **Head of gov.:** Prime Min. Emil Boc; b. Sept. 6, 1966; in office: Dec. 22, 2008. **Local divisions:** 41 counties and Bucharest. **Defense budget:** $2.14 bil. **Active troops:** 71,745.

Economy: Industries: elec. machinery and equip., textiles and footwear, light machinery, auto assembly, mining, timber, constr. materials. **Chief crops:** wheat, corn, barley, sugar beets, sunflower seeds, potatoes, grapes. **Natural resources:** petroleum (reserves declining), timber, nat. gas, coal, iron ore, salt, hydropower. **Crude oil reserves:** 600 mil bbls. **Arable land:** 38.2%. **Livestock:** cattle: 2.7 mil; chickens: 84.4 mil; goats: 898,000; pigs: 6.2 mil; sheep: 8.9 mil. **Fish catch:** 17,151 metric tons. **Electricity prod.:** 62 bil kWh. **Labor force:** agric. 29.7%, industry 23.2%, services 47.1%.

Finance: Monetary unit: New Leu (RON) (Sept. 2011: 3.03 = $1 U.S.). **GDP:** $254.2 bil; **per capita GDP:** $11,600; **GDP growth:** −1.3%. **Imports:** $59.8 bil; Germany 17.3%, Italy 11.7%, Hungary 8.5%, France 6.1%, China 4.9%, Austria 4.8%. **Exports:** $51.9 bil; Germany 18.8%, Italy 15.4%, France 8.2%, Turkey 5%, Hungary 4.3%. **Tourism:** $1.1 bil. **Budget:** $62 bil. **Total reserves less gold:** $43.4 bil. **Gold:** 3.3 mil oz t. **CPI change:** 6.1%.

Transport: Railways: 6,701 mi. **Motor vehicles:** 224.8 vehicles per 1,000 pop. **Civil aviation:** 2.5 bil pass.-mi; 26 airports. **Chief ports:** Braila, Constanta, Galati, Midia, Tulcea.

Communications: TV sets: 885 per 1,000 pop. **Radios:** 143 per 1,000 pop. **Telephone lines:** 20.9 per 100 pop. **Daily newspaper circ.:** 70.3 per 1,000 pop. **Internet:** 39.9 users per 100 pop.

Health: Life expect.: 70.5 male; 77.7 female. **Births:** 9.6 (per 1,000 pop.) **Deaths:** 11.8 (per 1,000 pop.) **Natural inc.:** −0.23%. **Infant mortality:** 11 (per 1,000 live births). **HIV rate:** 0.1%.

Education: Compulsory: ages 7-14. **Literacy:** 97.7%.

Major intl. organizations: UN (FAO, IBRD, ILO, IMF, WHO), NATO, OSCE, WTO.

Embassy: 1607 23rd St. NW 20008; 332-4846.

Website: www.gov.ro

Romania's earliest known people merged with invading Proto-Thracians, preceding by centuries the Dacians. The Dacian kingdom was occupied by Rome, 106-271 CE; people and language were Romanized. The principalities of Wallachia and Moldavia, dominated by Turkey, were united in 1859, became Romania in 1861, and gained recognition as an independent kingdom, 1881.

After WWI, Romania acquired Bessarabia, Bukovina, Transylvania, and Banat. In 1940 it ceded Bessarabia and Northern Bukovina to the USSR, part of southern Dobrudja to Bulgaria, and northern Transylvania to Hungary. In 1941, Prem. Marshal Ion Antonescu led Romania in support of Germany against the USSR. In 1944 he was overthrown, and Romania joined the Allies. After occupation by Soviet troops, a People's Republic was proclaimed, Dec. 30, 1947.

On Aug. 22, 1965, a new constitution proclaimed Romania a Socialist Republic. Pres. Nicolae Ceausescu maintained an independent course in foreign affairs, but his domestic policies were repressive. All industry was state-owned, and state farms and cooperatives owned almost all arable land. Ceausescu's security forces fired on antigovernment demonstrators in Dec. 1989, killing hundreds, but when the army sided with the protesters, his regime fell. Charged with genocide and abuse of power, Ceausescu and his wife were executed Dec. 25, 1989.

A new constitution providing for a multiparty system took effect Dec. 8, 1991. Many of Romania's state-owned companies were privatized in 1996. Romania became a full NATO member in 2004 and entered the European Union Jan. 1, 2007. The IMF and other donors agreed to provide a $27 bil loan Mar. 25, 2009, to rescue the country from the global recession. Romania, a firm U.S. ally, pulled its remaining troops out of Iraq July 2009. About 1,950 Romanian soldiers were serving with NATO-led forces in Afghanistan in mid-2011.

Russia
Russian Federation

People: Population: 138,739,892. **Age distrib.:** <15: 15.2%; 65+: 13%. **Pop. density:** 21.9 per sq mi, 8.5 per sq km. **Urban:** 73.2%. **Ethnic groups:** Russian 80%, Tatar 4%, Ukrainian 2%, Bashkir 1%, Chuvash 1%. **Principal languages:** Russian (official), many minority languages. **Chief religions:** Russian Orthodox 15%-20%, Muslim 10%-15%, other Christian 2%.

Geography: Total area: 6,601,668 sq mi, 17,098,242 sq km; **Land area:** 6,323,482 sq mi, 16,377,742 sq km., more than 76% of total area of the former USSR and the largest country in the world. **Location:** Stretches from E Europe across N Asia to the Pacific O. **Neighbors:** Finland, Norway, Estonia, Latvia, Belarus, Ukraine on W; Georgia, Azerbaijan, Kazakhstan, China, Mongolia, N. Korea on S; Kaliningrad exclave bordered by Poland on the S, Lithuania on the N and E. **Topography:** Every type of climate except distinctly tropical. The European portion is a low plain, grassy in S, wooded in N, with Ural Mts. on E, and Caucasus Mts. on S. Urals stretch N-S for 2,500 mi. The Asiatic portion is a vast plain, with mountains on S and in E; tundra covers extreme N, with forest belt below; plains, marshes are in W, desert in SW. **Capital:** Moscow, 10,549,892. **Cities (urban aggl.):** Saint Petersburg, 4,575,272; Novosibirsk, 1,397,276; Yekaterinburg, 1,343,969; Nizhniy Novgorod, 1,267,216.

Government: Type: Federal republic. **Head of state:** Pres. Dmitri Medvedev; b. Sept. 14, 1965; in office: May 7, 2008. **Head of gov.:** Prime Min. Vladimir Putin; b. Oct. 7, 1952; in office: May 8, 2008. **Local divisions:** 7 federal districts incl. 49 provinces, 21 autonomous republics, 6 territories, 1 autonomous region, 10 autonomous districts, 2 federal cities. **Defense budget:** $41.4 bil. **Active troops:** 1,046,000.

Economy: Industries: mining and extractive industries producing coal, oil, gas, chemicals, metals; machine building; defense (incl. radar, missile prod.); transp. equip.; comm. equip.; agric. machinery, constr. equip.; elec. power generating and transmitting equip.; medical and scientific instruments; consumer durables, textiles. **Chief crops:** grain, sugar beets, sunflower seeds, vegetables, fruits. **Natural resources:** oil, nat. gas, coal, minerals, rare earth elements, timber (climate, terrain, and distance are obstacles to exploitation of resources). **Crude oil reserve:** 60 bil bbls. **Arable land:** 7.4%. **Livestock:** cattle: 21 mil; chickens: 366.3 mil; goats: 2.2 mil; pigs: 16.2 mil; sheep: 19.6 mil. **Fish catch:** 3.9 mil metric tons. **Electricity prod.:** (2009) 925.9 bil kWh. **Labor force:** agric. 10%, industry 31.9%, services 58.1%.

Finance: Monetary unit: Ruble (RUB) (Sept. 2011: 29.63 = $1 U.S.). **GDP:** $2.2 tril; **per capita GDP:** $15,900; **GDP growth:** 4%. **Imports:** $237.3 bil; China 14.2%, Germany 13.2%, Ukraine 5.6%, U.S. 5.4%, Italy 4.9%, Japan 4.5%. **Exports:** $376.7 bil; Netherlands 12.3%, Italy 7.1%, China 5.6%, Germany 4.2%. **Tourism:** $9

bil. Budget: $341.1 bil. **Total reserves less gold:** $443.6 bil. **Gold:** 25.4 mil oz t. **CPI change:** 6.9%.

Transport: Railways: 54,157 mi. **Motor vehicles:** 282.1 vehicles per 1,000 pop. **Civil aviation:** 52.1 bil pass.-mi; 593 airports. **Chief ports:** Kaliningrad, Kavkaz, Nakhodka, Novorossiysk, Primorsk, Saint Petersburg, Vostochny.

Communications: TV sets: 546 per 1,000 pop. **Radios:** 416 per 1,000 pop. **Telephone lines:** 31.5 per 100 pop. **Daily newspaper circ.:** 91.8 per 1,000 pop. **Internet:** 43 users per 100 pop.

Health: Life expect.: 59.8 male; 73.2 female. **Births:** 11.1 (per 1,000 pop.). **Deaths:** 16 (per 1,000 pop.). **Natural inc.:** −0.50%. **Infant mortality:** 10.1 (per 1,000 live births). **HIV rate:** 1%.

Education: Compulsory: ages 6-15. **Literacy:** 99.6%.

Major intl. organizations: UN (FAO, IBRD, ILO, IMF, WHO), APEC, CIS, OSCE, WTO (observer).

Embassy: 2650 Wisconsin Ave. NW 20007; 298-5700.

Website: www.gov.ru or kremlin.ru

History. Slavic tribes began migrating into Russia from the W in the 5th cent. The first Russian state, centered in Novgorod and Kiev, was founded by Scandinavian chieftains in the 9th cent. In the 13th cent., Mongols overran the country. It recovered under the grand dukes and princes of Muscovy, or Moscow, and by 1480 freed itself from the Mongols. Ivan the Terrible was first formally proclaimed Tsar (1547). Peter the Great (1682-1725) extended the domain and, in 1721, founded the Russian empire. Western ideas and the beginnings of modernization spread through the huge Russian empire in the 19th and early 20th centuries, but political evolution failed to keep pace.

Military reverses in the 1905 war with Japan and in WWI led to the breakdown of the Tsarist regime. The 1917 Revolution began in Mar. with a series of sporadic strikes for higher wages by factory workers. A provisional democratic government under Prince Georgi Lvov was established but was followed in May by a second provisional government, under Alexander Kerensky. The Kerensky government and the freely elected Constituent Assembly were overthrown in a Communist coup led by Vladimir Ilyich Lenin Nov. 7.

Soviet Union

Lenin's death Jan. 21, 1924, led to an internal power struggle eventually won by Joseph Stalin. His brutal tactics, including purge trials, mass executions, and exile of many to work camps, resulted in millions of deaths, according to most estimates.

Germany and the USSR signed a non-aggression pact Aug. 1939; Germany launched a massive invasion of the Soviet Union, June 1941. Russian winter counterthrusts, 1941-42 and 1942-43, and heroic resistance to the siege of Leningrad (now St. Petersburg) stopped the German advance. Russians drove the German forces from Eastern Europe and the Balkans in the next 2 years.

After WWII, Communists took over in countries throughout the region, extending the Soviet sphere of influence. The USSR and the U.S., the world's leading nuclear superpowers, faced off against each other as cold war rivals. After Stalin died, Mar. 5, 1953, Nikita Khrushchev gained power. In 1956 he denounced Stalin and "de-Stalinization" began.

Under Khrushchev the open antagonism of Poles and Hungarians toward domination by Moscow was brutally suppressed in 1956. He aided the Cuban revolution under Fidel Castro but withdrew Soviet missiles from Cuba during a confrontation with U.S. Pres. Kennedy, Sept.-Oct. 1962. Khrushchev was suddenly deposed, Oct. 1964, and replaced by Leonid I. Brezhnev. In Aug. 1968 Soviet forces led an invasion of Czechoslovakia, crushing liberalization there.

Massive Soviet military aid to North Vietnam in the late 1960s and early 1970s helped assure Communist victories throughout Indochina. In Dec. 1979, Soviet forces entered Afghanistan to support a pro-Soviet regime against Muslim resistance fighters aided by the U.S. In Apr. 1988, the Soviets agreed to withdraw their troops, ending a futile 8-year war.

Mikhail Gorbachev was chosen gen. sec. of the Communist Party, Mar. 1985. In 1987 he initiated a program of political and economic reforms, through openness (*glasnost*) and restructuring (*perestroika*). Gorbachev faced economic problems as well as ethnic and nationalist unrest in the republics. An apparent coup by Communist hardliners Aug. 1991 was foiled with help from Russian Republic Pres. Boris Yeltsin. On Aug. 24, Gorbachev resigned as leader of the Communist Party. Several republics declared their independence, including Russia, Ukraine, and Kazakhstan. On Aug. 29, the Soviet Parliament voted to suspend all activities of the Communist Party.

The Soviet Union officially broke up Dec. 26, 1991. The Soviet hammer and sickle flying over the Kremlin was lowered and replaced by the flag of Russia, ending the domination of the Communist Party over all areas of national life since 1917.

Russian Federation

Led by Pres. Yeltsin, Russia took steps toward privatization; immediate effects were inflation and a severe economic downturn. In June 1992, Yeltsin and U.S. Pres. George H. W. Bush agreed to massive arms reductions. Yeltsin prevailed in a power struggle with the Congress of People's Deputies, which was dominated by conservatives and former Communists, and in a referendum Dec. 12, 1993, a new constitution was approved. In Dec. 1994 the Russian government sent troops into the breakaway republic of Chechnya. A peace accord was signed with Chechen rebels Aug. 31, 1996, temporarily ending the conflict. On May 27, 1997, Yeltsin signed a "founding act" increasing cooperation with NATO and paving the way for NATO to admit Eastern European nations.

Russia's economic crisis deepened in the late 1990s, heightening tensions between parliament and Pres. Yeltsin, who had been reelected in 1996. Russia moved forcibly in Aug. 1999 to suppress Islamic rebels in Dagestan; the conflict reignited the war in neighboring Chechnya, where Russia launched a full-scale assault. Yeltsin unexpectedly resigned Dec. 31, 1999, naming Prime Min. Vladimir Putin as his interim successor. Putin defeated 10 opponents in a presidential election Mar. 26, 2000. Putin's allies won legislative elections, Dec. 7, 2003, and the president was reelected Mar. 14, 2004, with 71% support; international election monitors cited flaws on both occasions.

A bomb in Grozny, May 9, 2004, killed Chechnya's pro-Moscow president, Akhmad Kadyrov, and at least 6 others. In another terrorist act linked to the Chechnya conflict, 2 passenger planes exploded in midair after taking off from Moscow Aug. 24, killing 90 people. Chechen rebels Sept. 1, 2004, seized control of a school in Beslan, North Ossetia, taking more than 1,100 hostages. Russian troops stormed the school Sept. 3; in the end more than 330 people died, including 186 children. Putin cited the terrorist threat Sept. 13 in proposing a government overhaul that tightened his control over parliament and regional officeholders. Russian forces killed Chechen rebel leader Aslan Maskhadov, Mar. 8, 2005. Chechen guerrilla leader Shamil Basayev, who had organized the terrorist attack at Beslan, was killed July 10, 2006.

Constitutionally barred from seeking another term, Pres. Putin backed his protégé Dmitri Medvedev, who won the presidential election Mar. 2, 2008; after taking office May 7 Medvedev named Putin as prime minister. A long-simmering conflict with Georgia erupted into open warfare Aug. 7-16, as Russia dispatched troops to support secessionists in the enclaves of South Ossetia and Abkhazia and launched assaults on strategic Georgian cities; a cease-fire left thousands of Russian troops in the breakaway regions, which Pres. Medvedev recognized as independent on Aug. 26, 2008.

An economic boom fueled by oil and gas sales came to a halt in late 2008. The global financial crisis and a drop in oil prices led to turmoil on Russian financial markets, which were closed Sept. 17-18 as the government put together a $130-bil emergency rescue plan. As the crisis deepened, the government loaned banks $37 bil Oct. 7 and began buying shares to prop up the Russian stock exchange.

Russia declared Apr. 16, 2009, that it had ended counterterrorism operations in Chechnya; from June through Aug., however, there was a marked upsurge of insurgent violence in Chechnya and neighboring Dagestan and Ingushetia. Female suicide bombers from Dagestan struck 2 Moscow subway stations Mar. 29, 2010, killing 40 people and injuring dozens more. A bombing at a Moscow airport Jan. 24, 2011, killed 37.

During a visit to Russia July 6-7, 2009, U.S. Pres. Obama met with Pres. Medvedev and Prime Min. Putin. Repairing relations strained since the 2008 Georgia war, Russia and the U.S. agreed on measures to reduce nuclear stockpiles and increase military cooperation. Medvedev and Obama Apr. 8, 2010, signed a nuclear arms reduction treaty known as New START, which was ratified by the U.S. Senate Dec. 22, 2010. Following the exposure in late June of an alleged Russian spy ring operating in the U.S., 10 Russian agents arrested in the U.S. by the FBI June 27, 2010, were exchanged July 9 in Vienna, Austria, for 4 Russian prisoners convicted of having had contact with Western intelligence agencies. Russia was chosen Dec. 2, 2010, to host the World Cup soccer tournament in 2018. Medvedev announced Sept. 24, 2011, that Putin would run for president in elections Mar. 2012, with Medvedev then serving as his prime minister.

Rwanda
Republic of Rwanda

People: Population: 11,370,425. **Age distrib.:** <15: 42.9%; 65+: 2.4%. **Pop. density:** 1,193.8 per sq mi, 460.9 per sq km. **Urban:** 18.9%. **Ethnic groups:** Hutu (Bantu) 84%, Tutsi (Hamitic) 15%, Twa (Pygmy) 1%. **Principal languages:** Kinyarwanda (universal Bantu vernacular), French, English (all official); Swahili used in commercial centers. **Chief religions:** Roman Catholic 57%, Protestant 26%, Adventist 11%, Muslim 5%, none 2%.

Geography: Total area: 10,169 sq mi, 26,338 sq km; **Land area:** 9,524 sq mi, 24,668 sq km. **Location:** In C entral Africa. **Neighbors:** Uganda on N, Congo (formerly Zaire) on W, Burundi on S, Tanzania on E. **Topography:** Grassy uplands and hills cover most of country, with chain of volcanoes in the NW. The source of the Nile R. has been located in headwaters of the Kagera (Akagera) R., SW of Kigali. **Capital:** Kigali, 939,425.

Government: Type: Republic. **Head of state:** Pres. Paul Kagame; b. Oct. 23, 1957; in office: Apr. 22, 2000 (de facto from Mar. 24). **Head of gov.:** Prime Min. Bernard Makuza; b. Sept. 30, 1961; in office: Mar. 8, 2000. **Local divisions:** 12 prefectures subdivided into 155 communes. **Defense budget:** $75 mil. **Active troops:** 33,000.

Economy: Industries: cement, agric. prods., small-scale beverages, soap, furniture, shoes, plastic goods, textiles. **Chief crops:** coffee, tea, pyrethrum (insecticide made from chrysanthemums), bananas, beans, sorghum, potatoes. **Natural resources:** gold, tin ore, tungsten ore, methane, hydropower. **Arable land:** 52.7%. **Livestock:** cattle: 1.5 mil; chickens: 2 mil; goats: 1.7 mil; pigs: 310,833;

sheep: 470,000. **Fish catch:** 9,438 metric tons. **Electricity prod.:** 160 mil kWh. **Labor force:** agric. 90%, industry and services 10%.

Finance: Monetary unit: Franc (RWF) (Sept. 2011: 593.00 = $1 U.S.). **GDP:** $12.2 bil; **per capita GDP:** $1,100; **GDP growth:** 6.5%. **Imports:** $1.05 bil; Kenya 16.6%, Uganda 15%, UAE 6.9%, China 6.6%, Belgium 5.6%, Germany 4.9%, Tanzania 4.8%, Sweden 4%. **Exports:** $226 mil; Kenya 33.4%, Dem. Rep. of the Congo 13.4%, China 7%, Thailand 6.1%, U.S. 5.4%, Swaziland 5.4%, Belgium 5.1%, Pakistan 4.2%. **Tourism:** $202 mil. **Budget:** $1.4 bil. **Total reserves less gold:** $812.8 mil. **CPI change:** 2.3%.

Transport: Civil aviation: 4 airports. **Chief ports:** Cyangugu, Gisenyi, Kibuye.

Communications: TV sets: 8 per 1,000 pop. **Radios:** 854 per 1,000 pop. **Telephone lines:** 0.4 per 100 pop. **Internet:** 7.7 users per 100 pop.

Health: Life expect.: 56.6 male; 59.5 female. **Births:** 36.7 (per 1,000 pop.). **Deaths:** 9.9 (per 1,000 pop.). **Natural inc.:** 2.69%. **Infant mortality:** 64 (per 1,000 live births). **HIV rate:** 2.9%.

Education: Compulsory: ages 7-12. **Literacy:** 70.7%.

Major intl. organizations: UN (FAO, IBRD, ILO, IMF, WHO), AU, the Commonwealth, WTO.

Embassy: 1714 New Hampshire Ave. NW 20009; 232-2882.
Website: www.gov.rw

For centuries, the Tutsi dominated the Hutu (90% of the population). A civil war broke out in 1959 and Tutsi power was ended. Many Tutsi went into exile. Rwanda, which had been part of the Belgian UN trusteeship of Rwanda-Urundi, became independent July 1, 1962.

In 1963 Tutsi exiles unsuccessfully attempted to regain power; a large-scale massacre of Tutsi followed. Hutu rivalries led to a bloodless coup July 1973 in which Hutu army officer Juvénal Habyarimana took power. After another invasion and coup attempt by Tutsi exiles in 1990, a multiparty democracy was established.

Renewed ethnic strife led to an Aug. 1993 peace accord between the government and rebels of the Tutsi-led Rwandan Patriotic Front (RPF). But after Habyarimana and Burundi Pres. Cyprien Ntaryamira were killed Apr. 6, 1994, in a suspicious plane crash, massive violence broke out. More than 1 mil may have died in massacres, mostly of Tutsi by Hutu militias, and in civil warfare as the RPF sought power. About 2 mil Tutsi and Hutu fled to camps in Zaire (now Dem. Rep. of the Congo) and other countries, where many died of cholera and other diseases. French troops under a UN mandate moved into SW Rwanda June 23 to establish a "safe zone." The RPF claimed victory, installing a government in July led by a moderate Hutu president. French troops pulled out Aug. 22. A UN peacekeeping mission ended Mar. 8, 1996, but the Rwandan government and a UN-sponsored tribunal in Tanzania continued to gather evidence of crimes against humanity. More than 1 mil refugees, mostly Hutu, flooded back to Rwanda from Tanzania and Zaire in Nov. and Dec. 1996.

Firing squads in Rwanda on Apr. 24, 1998, executed 22 people convicted of genocide. Former Prime Min. Jean Kambanda pleaded guilty May 1 before the UN tribunal and received a life sentence Sept. 4, 1998. RPF leader Maj. Gen. Paul Kagame became Rwanda's first Tutsi president Apr. 22, 2000.

Rwandans in 2003 approved a new constitution, May 26, re-elected Pres. Kagame, Aug. 25, and chose a new parliament, Sept. 29-30. Former Pres. Bizimungu was sentenced to 15 years for embezzlement, June 2004; he was pardoned by Kagame and released, Apr. 6, 2007. Rwanda cut diplomatic ties with France Nov. 24, 2006, after a French judge linked Kagame and his close aides to the deaths in 1994 of Habyarimana and Ntaryamira. Diplomatic relations with France were restored Nov. 2009, when Rwanda also joined the Commonwealth.

Accused of being one of the architects of the 1994 genocide, Col. Theoneste Bagosora was convicted and sentenced to life in prison by the UN tribunal Dec. 18, 2008. A Rwandan court handed out a life sentence Jan. 20, 2009, to former Justice Min. Agnes Ntamabyariro for her role in inciting the massacres. Up to 4,000 Rwandan troops fought that month alongside Congolese forces against Hutu militias in E Congo. After a campaign criticized as repressive by human rights groups, Pres. Kagame won reelection Aug. 9, 2010, with 93% of the vote. In mid-2011, Rwanda had about 3,200 peacekeepers serving with the AU-UN Mission in Darfur (UNAMID) in Sudan.

Rwanda has experienced steady economic growth in recent years. The U.S. has funded efforts to train the Rwandan military and control HIV/AIDS and malaria.

Saint Kitts and Nevis
Federation of Saint Kitts and Nevis

People: Population: 50,314. **Age distrib.:** <15: 22.8%; 65+: 7.6%. **Pop. density:** 499.3 per sq mi, 192.8 per sq km. **Urban:** 32.4%. **Ethnic group:** predominantly black; some British, Portuguese, Lebanese. **Principal language:** English (official). **Chief religions:** Anglican, other Protestant, Roman Catholic.

Geography: Total area: 101 sq mi, 261 sq km; **Land area:** 101 sq mi, 261 sq km. **Location:** In N part of the Leeward group of Lesser Antilles in E Caribbean Sea. **Neighbors:** Antigua and Barbuda to E. **Topography:** St. Kitts has forested volcanic slopes; Nevis rises from beaches to central peak. Climate is tropical moderated by sea breezes. **Capital:** Basseterre, 13,000.

Government: Type: Constitutional monarchy. **Head of state:** Queen Elizabeth II, represented by Gov.-Gen. Sir Cuthbert M.

Sebastian; b. Oct. 22, 1921; in office: Jan. 1, 1996. **Head of gov.:** Prime Min. Denzil Douglas; b. Jan. 14, 1953; in office: July 7, 1995. **Local div.:** 14 parishes. **Defense budget/active troops:** NA.

Economy: Industries: tourism, cotton, salt, copra, clothing, footwear, beverages. **Chief crops:** sugarcane, rice, yams, vegetables, bananas. **Arable land:** 15.4%. **Livestock:** cattle: 7,500; chickens: 80,000; goats: 9,000; pigs: 6,000; sheep: 7,000. **Fish catch:** 450 metric tons. **Electricity prod.:** 130 mil kWh. **Labor force:** NA.

Finance: Monetary unit: East Caribbean Dollar (XCD) (Sept. 2011: 2.70 = $1 U.S.). **GDP:** $684 mil; **per capita GDP:** $13,700; **GDP growth:** −1.5%. **Imports** (2006): $383 mil; U.S. 43%, Trinidad and Tobago 15.1%, Italy 11.7%. **Exports** (2006): $84 mil; U.S. 64.1%, Canada 8.2%, Azerbaijan 4.4%. **Tourism:** $80 mil. **Budget** (2008 est.): $232.1 mil. **Total reserves less gold:** $168.9 mil. **CPI change:** 0.8%.

Transport: Railways: 31 mi. **Civil aviation:** 2 airports. **Chief ports:** Basseterre, Charlestown.

Communications: TV sets: 312 per 1,000 pop. **Radios:** 697 per 1,000 pop. **Telephone lines:** 39.3 per 100 pop. **Internet:** (2009) 32.9 users per 100 pop.

Health: Life expect.: 72.3 male; 77 female. **Births:** 14.1 (per 1,000 pop.). **Deaths:** 7.1 (per 1,000 pop.). **Natural inc.:** 0.7%. **Infant mortality:** 9.7 (per 1,000 live births). **HIV rate:** NA.

Education: Compulsory: ages 5-16. **Literacy:** NA.

Major intl. organizations: UN (FAO, IBRD, ILO, IMF, WHO), Caricom, the Commonwealth, OAS, OECS, WTO.

Embassy: 3216 New Mexico Ave. NW 20016; 686-2636.

Website: www.gov.kn

St. Kitts (formerly St. Christopher; known by indigenous peoples as Liamuiga) and Nevis were reached and named by Columbus in 1493. They were settled by Britain in 1623, but ownership was disputed with France until 1713. They were part of the Leeward Islands Federation, 1871-1956, and the Federation of the West Indies, 1958-62. The colony achieved self-government as an Associated State of the UK in 1967, and became fully independent Sept. 19, 1983. A secession referendum on Nevis, Aug. 10, 1998, fell short of the two-thirds majority required.

St. Kitts and Nevis are the smallest independent nation in the Western Hemisphere.

Saint Lucia

People: Population: 161,557. **Age distrib.:** <15: 22.8%; 65+: 9.7%. **Pop. density:** 690.5 per sq mi, 266.6 per sq km. **Urban:** 28%. **Ethnic groups:** black 83%, mixed 12%, East Indian 2%. **Principal languages:** English (official), French patois. **Chief religions:** Roman Catholic 68%, Seventh-Day Adventist 9%, Pentecostal 6%, Rastafarian 2%, Anglican 2%, Evangelical 2%, other Christian 5%, none 5%.

Geography: Total area: 238 sq mi, 616 sq km; **Land area:** 234 sq mi, 606 sq km. **Location:** In E Caribbean, 2nd largest of Windward Isls. **Neighbors:** Martinique to N, St. Vincent to S. **Topography:** Mountainous, volcanic in origin; Soufriere, a volcanic crater, in S. Wooded mountains run N-S to Mt. Gimie, 3,145 ft, with streams through fertile valleys. **Capital:** Castries, 15,000.

Government: Type: Constitutional monarchy. **Head of state:** Queen Elizabeth II, represented by Gov.-Gen. Dame Calliopa Pearlette Louisy; b. June 8, 1946; in office: Sept. 17, 1997. **Head of gov.:** Prime Min. Stephenson King; b. Nov. 13, 1958; in office: Sept. 9, 2007 (acting from May 1). **Local divisions:** 11 quarters. **Defense budget/active troops:** NA.

Economy: Industries: clothing, electronic components assembly, beverages, corrugated cardboard boxes, tourism. **Chief crops:** bananas, coconuts, vegetables, citrus, root crops, cocoa. **Natural resources:** forests, beaches, pumice, mineral springs, geothermal potential. **Arable land:** 4.9%. **Livestock:** cattle: 11,000; chickens: 450,000; goats: 9,500; pigs: 20,000; sheep: 10,000. **Fish catch:** 1,920 metric tons. **Electricity prod.:** (2009) 341.2 mil kWh. **Labor force:** agric. 21.7%; industry 24.7%; services 53.6%.

Finance: Monetary unit: East Caribbean Dollar (XCD) (Sept. 2011: 2.70 = $1 U.S.). **GDP:** $1.8 bil; **per capita GDP** $11,200; **GDP growth:** 0.8%. **Imports:** (2006) $791 mil; Brazil 83.8%, U.S. 4.7%, Trinidad and Tobago 4.6%. **Exports:** (2006) $288 mil; Spain 30.7%, UK 15.9%, India 13.8%, U.S. 10.2%, Peru 4.1%. **Tourism:** $326 mil. **Budget:** $393.3 mil. **Total reserves less gold:** $206.3 mil. **CPI change:** 1.8%.

Transport: Civil aviation: 2 airports. **Chief ports:** Castries, Cul-de-Sac, Vieux-Fort.

Communications: TV sets: 341 per 1,000 pop. **Radios:** 193 per 1,000 pop. **Telephone lines:** 23.6 per 100 pop. **Internet:** (2009) 83 users per 100 pop.

Health: Life expect.: 74.2 male; 79.7 female. **Births:** 14.6 (per 1,000 pop.). **Deaths:** 7 (per 1,000 pop.). **Natural inc.:** 0.76%. **Infant mortality:** 12.7 (per 1,000 live births). **HIV rate:** NA.

Education: Compulsory: ages 5-14. **Literacy:** NA.

Major intl. organizations: UN (FAO, IBRD, ILO, IMF, WHO), Caricom, the Commonwealth, OAS, OECS, WTO.

Embassy: 3216 New Mexico Ave. NW 20016; 364-6792.

Website: www.stlucia.gov.lc

St. Lucia was ceded to Britain by France at the Treaty of Paris, 1814. Self-government was granted with the West Indies Act, 1967. Independence was attained Feb. 22, 1979.

Saint Vincent and the Grenadines

People: Population: 103,869. **Age distrib.:** <15: 24.5%; 65+: 8.1%. **Pop. density:** 691.6 per sq mi, 267 per sq km. **Urban:** 49.3%. **Ethnic groups:** black 66%, mixed 19%, East Indian 6%, European 4%, Carib Amerindian 2%. **Principal languages:** English, French patois. **Chief religions:** Anglican 47%, Methodist 28%, Roman Catholic 13%, other (incl. Hindu, Seventh-Day Adventist, other Protestant) 12%.

Geography: Total area: 150 sq mi, 389 sq km; **Land area:** 150 sq mi, 389 sq km. **Location:** In E Caribbean, St. Vincent (133 sq mi) and the northern islets of the Grenadines form a part of Windward chain. **Neighbors:** St. Lucia to N, Barbados to E, Grenada to S. **Topography:** St. Vincent is volcanic, with a ridge of thickly wooded mountains running its length. **Capital:** Kingstown, 28,000.

Government: Type: Constitutional monarchy. **Head of state:** Queen Elizabeth II, represented by Sir Frederick Ballantyne; b. July 5, 1936; in office: Sept. 2, 2002. **Head of gov.:** Prime Min. Ralph Gonsalves; b. Aug. 8, 1946; in office: Mar. 29, 2001. **Local divisions:** 6 parishes. **Defense budget/active troops:** NA.

Economy: Industries: food proc., cement, furniture, clothing, starch. **Chief crops:** bananas, coconuts, sweet potatoes, spices. **Natural resources:** hydropower. **Arable land:** 12.8%. **Livestock:** cattle: 5,200; chickens: 250,000; goats: 7,500; pigs: 9,300; sheep: 13,500. **Fish catch:** 3,977 metric tons. **Electricity prod.:** 132 mil kWh. **Labor force:** agric. 26%, industry 17%, services 57%.

Finance: Monetary unit: East Caribbean Dollar (XCD) (Sept. 2011: 2.70 = $1 U.S.). **GDP:** $1.1 bil; **per capita GDP:** $10,300; **GDP growth:** −2.3%. **Imports:** (2006) $578 mil; Singapore 15.8%, Trinidad and Tobago 13.5%, U.S. 13.2%, China 12.6%, Italy 8.7%, Turkey 6.5%, France 5.5%, Romania 4.4%. **Exports:** (2006) $193 mil; Greece 46.1%, Poland 13.6%, France 10.4%. **Tourism:** $88 mil. **Budget:** $218.1 mil. **Total reserves less gold:** $112.7 mil. **CPI change:** 1%.

Transport: Civil aviation: 5 airports. **Chief port:** Kingstown.

Communications: TV sets: 341 per 1,000 pop. **Radios:** 1,025 per 1,000 pop. **Telephone lines:** 19.9 per 100 pop. **Internet:** (2009) 69.6 users per 100 pop.

Health: Life expect.: 72.3 male; 76.1 female. **Births:** 14.6 (per 1,000 pop.). **Deaths:** 7 (per 1,000 pop.). **Natural inc.:** 0.76%. **Infant mortality:** 14.3 (per 1,000 live births). **HIV rate:** NA.

Education: Compulsory: ages 5-15. **Literacy:** NA.

Major intl. organizations: UN (FAO, IBRD, ILO, IMF, WHO), Caricom, the Commonwealth, OAS, OECS, WTO.

Embassy: 3216 New Mexico Ave. NW 20016; 364-6730.

Website: www.gov.vc

Columbus landed on St. Vincent on Jan. 22, 1498 (St. Vincent's Day). Britain and France both laid claim to the island in the 17th and 18th centuries; the Treaty of Versailles, 1783, finally ceded it to Britain. Associated State status was granted 1969; independence was attained Oct. 27, 1979.

Samoa (*formerly* Western Samoa)
Independent State of Samoa

People: Population: 193,161. **Age distrib.:** <15: 35.4%; 65+: 5.2%. **Pop. density:** 177.3 per sq mi, 68.5 per sq km. **Urban:** 20.2%. **Ethnic groups:** Samoan 93%, Euronesians (mixed European, Polynesian) 7%. **Principal languages:** Samoan (Polynesian) (official), English. **Chief religions:** Congregationalist 35%, Roman Catholic 20%, Methodist 15%, Latter-Day Saints 13%, Assembly of God 7%, Seventh-Day Adventist 4%, Worship Centre 1%, other Christian 5%.

Geography: Total area: 1,093 sq mi, 2,831 sq km; **Land area:** 1,089 sq mi, 2,821 sq km. **Location:** In S Pacific O. **Neighbors:** Nearest are Fiji to SW, Tonga to S. **Topography:** Main islands, Savaii (659 sq mi) and Upolu (432 sq mi), both ruggedly mountainous, and small islands Manono and Apolima. **Capital:** Apia, 36,000.

Government: Type: Constitutional monarchy. **Head of state:** Tuiatua Tupua Tamasese Efi; b. Mar. 1, 1938; in office: June 20, 2007. **Head of gov.:** Prime Min. Tuilaepa Sailele Malielegaoi; b. Apr. 14, 1945; in office: Nov. 23, 1998. **Local divisions:** 11 districts. **Defense budget/active troops:** NA.

Economy: Industries: food proc., building materials, auto parts. **Chief crops:** coconuts, bananas, taro, yams, coffee, cocoa. **Natural resources:** forests, fish, hydropower. **Arable land:** 8.8%. **Livestock:** cattle: 30,000; chickens: 620,000; pigs: 202,000. **Fish catch:** 13,270 metric tons. **Electricity prod.:** (2009) 108 mil kWh. **Labor force:** NA.

Finance: Monetary unit: Tala (WST) (Sept. 2011: 2.22 = $1 U.S.). **GDP:** $1.1 bil; **per capita GDP:** $5,500; **GDP growth:** 0%. **Imports** (2006): $324 mil; New Zealand 24.2%, Fiji 17.4%, Singapore 12.6%, China 12%, Australia 9.9%, U.S. 6%. **Exports** (2006): $131 mil; American Samoa 40.8%, Australia 24.5%, China 5.8%, U.S. 4%. **Tourism:** $116 mil. **Budget** (FY04/05 est.): $78.1 mil. **Total reserves less gold:** $209.4 mil. **CPI change:** 0.8%.

Transport: Civil aviation: 224.9 mil pass.-mi; 1 airport. **Chief port:** Apia.

Communications: TV sets: 122 per 1,000 pop. **Radios:** 312 per 1,000 pop. **Telephone lines:** 19.3 per 100 pop. **Internet:** 7 users per 100 pop.

Health: Life expect.: 69.6 male; 75.4 female. **Births:** 22.5 (per 1,000 pop.). **Deaths:** 5.3 (per 1,000 pop.). **Natural inc.:** 1.72%. **Infant mortality:** 22.7 (per 1,000 live births). **HIV rate:** NA.
Education: Compulsory: ages 5-14. **Literacy:** 98.8%.
Major intl. organizations: UN (FAO, IBRD, ILO, IMF, WHO), the Commonwealth, WTO (observer).
Embassy: 800 Second Ave., Ste. 400J, New York, NY 10017; (212) 599-6196.
Website: www.govt.ws

Samoa (formerly known as Western Samoa to distinguish it from American Samoa, a small U.S. territory) was a German colony, 1899 to 1914, when New Zealand landed troops and took over. It became a New Zealand mandate under the League of Nations and, in 1945, a New Zealand UN Trusteeship.

An elected local government took office in Oct. 1959, and the country became fully independent Jan. 1, 1962. Malietoa Tanumafili II, Samoa's head of state since independence, died May 11, 2007, and was succeeded by Tuiatua Tupua Tamasese Efi. An earthquake and tsunami Sept. 29, 2009, left at least 143 people dead in Samoa.

San Marino
Republic of San Marino

People: Population: 31,817. **Age distrib.:** <15: 16.6%; 65+: 18%. **Pop. density:** 1,350.9 per sq mi, 521.6 per sq km. **Urban:** 94.1%. **Ethnic groups:** Sammarinese, Italian. **Principal language:** Italian. **Chief religion:** Roman Catholic.
Geography: Total area: 24 sq mi, 61 sq km; **Land area:** 24 sq mi, 61 sq km. **Location:** In N central Italy near Adriatic coast. **Neighbors:** Completely surrounded by Italy. **Topography:** The country lies on slopes of Mt. Titano. **Capital:** San Marino, 4,000.
Government: Type: Republic. **Heads of state and gov.:** Two co-regents appt. every 6 months. **Local divisions:** 9 castelli. **Defense budget/active troops:** NA.
Economy: Industries: tourism, banking, textiles, electronics, ceramics, cement, wine. **Chief crops:** wheat, grapes, corn, olives. **Natural resources:** building stone. **Arable land:** 16.7%. **Labor force:** agric. 0.2%, industry 36.3%, services 63.5%.
Finance: Monetary unit: Euro (EUR) (Sept. 2011: 0.71 = $1 U.S.). **GDP** (2009): $1.1 bil; **per capita GDP** (2009): $36,200; **GDP growth** (2009 est.): –13%. **Imports** (2009): $2.2 bil; NA. **Exports** (2009): $2.4 bil; NA. **Total reserves less gold:** $449.2 mil. **Tourism:** NA. **Budget** (2009): $940.4 mil. **Total reserves less gold** (2008): $449.2 mil. **CPI change:** NA.
Transport: NA.
Communications: TV sets: 792 per 1,000 pop. **Radios:** 1,322 per 1,000 pop. **Telephone lines:** 68.8 per 100 pop. **Internet:** (2009) 54.2 users per 100 pop.
Health: Life expect.: 80.5 male; 85.7 female. **Births:** 9 (per 1,000 pop.). **Deaths:** 7.9 (per 1,000 pop.). **Natural inc.:** 0.11%. **Infant mortality:** 4.7 (per 1,000 live births). **HIV rate:** NA.
Education: Compulsory: ages 6-16. **Literacy:** NA.
Major intl. organizations: UN (FAO, IBRD, ILO, IMF, WHO), OSCE.
Honorary Consulate: 1899 L St. NW, Ste. 500, 20036; 223-3517.
Website: www.visitsanmarino.com or www.consigliograndegenerale.sm

San Marino claims to be the oldest state in Europe and to have been founded in the 4th cent. It has had a treaty of friendship with Italy since 1862. A Communist-led coalition ruled 1947-57; a similar coalition ruled 1978-86. The Pact for San Marino, a center-right coalition, won parliamentary elections Nov. 9, 2008.

São Tomé and Príncipe
Democratic Republic of São Tomé and Príncipe

People: Population: 179,506. **Age distrib.:** <15: 44.7%; 65+: 3.2%. **Pop. density:** 482.3 per sq mi, 186.2 per sq km. **Urban:** 62.2%. **Ethnic groups:** mestico, angolares (descendants of Angolan slaves), forros (descendants of freed slaves), servicais (contract laborers fr. Angola, Mozambique, Cape Verde), tongas (children of servicais born in country), Europeans (primarily Portuguese). **Principal language:** Portuguese (official). **Chief religions:** Catholic 70%, Evangelical 3%, New Apostolic 2%, Adventist 2%, none 19%.
Geography: Total area: 372 sq mi, 964 sq km; **Land area:** 372 sq mi, 964 sq km. **Location:** In Gulf of Guinea about 125 mi off W central Africa. **Neighbors:** Gabon, Equatorial Guinea to E. **Topography:** São Tomé and Príncipe islands, part of an extinct volcano chain, are both covered by lush forests and croplands. **Capital:** São Tomé, 60,000.
Government: Type: Republic. **Head of state:** Pres. Manuel Pinto da Costa; b. Aug. 5, 1937; in office: Sept. 3, 2011. **Head of gov.:** Prime Min. Patrice Trovoada; b. Mar. 18, 1962; in office: Aug. 14, 2010. **Local divisions:** 2 provinces. **Defense budget/active troops:** NA.
Economy: Industries: light constr., textiles, soap, beer, fish proc., timber. **Chief crops:** cocoa, coconuts, palm kernels, copra, cinnamon, pepper, coffee, bananas, papayas, beans. **Natural resources:** fish, hydropower. **Arable land:** 10.4%. **Livestock:** cattle: 4,800; chickens: 420,000; goats: 5,200; pigs: 2,620; sheep: 3,000. **Fish catch:** 4,250 metric tons. **Electricity prod.:** 41 mil kWh. **Labor force:** Population mainly engaged in subsistence agric. and fishing; shortage of skilled workers.

Finance: Monetary unit: Dobra (STD) (Sept. 2011: 17,075.00 = $1 U.S.). **GDP:** $311 mil; **per capita GDP:** $1,800; **GDP growth:** 4.5%. **Imports:** $99 mil; Portugal 56.2%, Brazil 6.5%, Malaysia 6%, U.S. 4.5%, Japan 4.3%. **Exports:** $13 mil; UK 32.9%, Netherlands 26.8%, Belgium 21%, Portugal 4.3%. **Tourism:** NA. **Budget:** $38.6 mil. **Total reserves less gold** (2007): $39.3 mil. **CPI change:** 12.9%.
Transport: Civil aviation: 12.4 mil pass.-mi; 2 airports. **Chief port:** São Tomé.
Communications: TV sets: 127 per 1,000 pop. **Radios:** 106 per 1,000 pop. **Telephone lines:** 4.6 per 100 pop. **Internet:** 18.8 users per 100 pop.
Health: Life expect.: 61.9 male; 64.3 female. **Births:** 38 (per 1,000 pop.). **Deaths:** 8.2 (per 1,000 pop.). **Natural inc.:** 2.99%. **Infant mortality:** 53.2 (per 1,000 live births). **HIV rate:** NA.
Education: Compulsory: ages 7-12. **Literacy:** 88.8%.
Major intl. organizations: UN (FAO, IBRD, ILO, WHO), AU, WTO (observer).
Permanent UN mission: 460 Park Ave., 11th Fl., New York, NY 10022; (212) 317-0533.
Website: www.gov.st

The islands were discovered in 1471 by the Portuguese, who brought the first settlers—convicts and exiled Jews. Sugar planting was replaced by the slave trade as the chief economic activity until coffee and cocoa were introduced in the 19th century.

Portugal agreed, 1974, to turn the colony over to the Gabon-based Movement for the Liberation of São Tomé and Príncipe, which proclaimed as first president its East German-trained leader, Manuel Pinto da Costa. Independence came July 12, 1975. Democratic reforms were instituted in 1987. In 1991 Miguel Trovoada won the first free presidential election following Pinto da Costa's withdrawal. A military coup that ousted Trovoada Aug. 15, 1995, was reversed a week later after Angolan mediation. Trovoada defeated Pinto da Costa in a presidential runoff election, July 21, 1996.

Fradique de Menezes, a wealthy cocoa exporter, easily beat Pinto da Costa in the presidential election of July 29, 2001. The government was ousted in a military coup July 16, 2003, but was restored to power a week later and reelected July 30, 2006. After the opposition Independent Democratic Action party won parliamentary elections Aug. 1, 2010, Patrice Trovoada (son of the former president) was chosen to head the new government. Pinto da Costa returned to power after a presidential runoff vote Aug. 7, 2011. The country, long one of the world's poorest, has sought to develop large oil deposits in the Gulf of Guinea.

Saudi Arabia
Kingdom of Saudi Arabia

People: Population: 26,131,703. **Age distrib.:** <15: 29.4%; 65+: 3%. **Pop. density:** 31.5 per sq mi, 12.2 per sq km. **Urban:** 82.1%. **Ethnic groups:** Arab 90%, Afro-Asian 10%. **Principal language:** Arabic (official). **Chief religion:** Muslim 100%.
Geography: Total area: 830,000 sq mi, 2,149,690 sq km; **Land area:** 830,000 sq mi, 2,149,690 sq km. **Location:** Occupies most of Arabian Peninsula in Mid-East. **Neighbors:** Kuwait, Iraq, Jordan on N; Yemen, Oman on S; United Arab Emirates, Qatar on E. **Topography:** Bordered by Red Sea on W. The highlands on W, up to 9,000 ft, slope as arid, barren desert to the Persian Gulf on E. **Capital:** Riyadh, 4,847,840. **Cities (urban aggl.):** Jiddah, 3,233,930; Mecca (Makkah), 1,483,770; Medina, 1,103,531.
Government: Type: Monarchy with council of ministers. **Head of state and gov.:** King Abdullah bin Abdul Aziz; b. Aug. 1, 1924; in office: Aug. 1, 2005. **Local divisions:** 13 provinces. **Defense budget:** $45.24 bil. **Active troops:** 233,500.
Economy: Industries: crude oil prod., petroleum refining, basic petrochemicals, ammonia, industrial gases, caustic soda, cement, fertilizer, plastics, metals. **Chief crops:** wheat, barley, tomatoes, melons, dates, citrus. **Natural resources:** petroleum, nat. gas, iron ore, gold, copper. **Crude oil reserves:** 262.6 bil bbls (incl. half of Neutral Zone reserves). **Arable land:** 1.5%. **Livestock:** cattle: 421,000; chickens: 146 mil; goats: 4.3 mil; sheep: 8 mil. **Fish catch:** 95,061 metric tons. **Electricity prod.** (2009): 194.4 bil kWh. **Labor force:** agric. 6.7%, industry 21.4%, services 71.9%.
Finance: Monetary unit: Riyal (SAR) (Sept. 2011: 3.75 = $1 U.S.). **GDP:** $622 bil; **per capita GDP:** $24,200; **GDP growth:** 3.7%. **Imports:** $99.2 bil; U.S. 12.8%, China 10.6%, Germany 8.1%, Japan 6.4%, UK 4.9%, South Korea 4.6%, India 4.4%, France 4.2%, Italy 4%. **Exports:** $235.3 bil; Japan 15.4%, China 12.5%, U.S. 12.3%, South Korea 10.4%, India 7.7%, Singapore 4.3%. **Tourism:** $6.7 bil. **Budget:** $173.1 bil. **Total reserves less gold:** $444.7 bil. **Gold:** 10.4 mil oz t. **CPI change:** 5.3%.
Transport: Railways: 856 mi. **Motor vehicles:** 210 vehicles per 1,000 pop. **Civil aviation:** 18 bil pass.-mi; 81 airports. **Chief ports:** Ad Dammam, Al Jubayl, Jeddah, Yanbu al Bahr.
Communications: TV sets: 275 per 1,000 pop. **Radios:** 317 per 1,000 pop. **Telephone lines:** 15.2 per 100 pop. **Internet:** 41 users per 100 pop.
Health: Life expect.: 72.2 male; 76.2 female. **Births:** 19.3 (per 1,000 pop.). **Deaths:** 3.3 (per 1,000 pop.). **Natural inc.:** 1.6%. **Infant mortality:** 16.2 (per 1,000 live births). **HIV rate:** NA.
Education: Compulsory: ages 6-11. **Literacy:** 86.1%.

Major intl. organizations: UN (FAO, IBRD, ILO, IMF, WHO), AL, OPEC, WTO.

Embassy: 601 New Hampshire Ave. NW 20037; 342-3800.

Website: www.saudi.gov.sa

Before Muhammad, Arabia was divided among numerous warring tribes and small kingdoms. It was united for the first time by Muhammad, in the early 7th cent. His successors conquered the entire Near East and North Africa, bringing Islam and the Arabic language. But Arabia itself soon returned to its former status.

Nejd, in central Arabia, long an independent state and center of the Wahhabi sect, fell under Turkish rule in the 18th cent. In 1913 Ibn Saud, founder of the Saudi dynasty, overthrew the Turks and captured the Turkish province of Hasa in eastern Arabia; he took the Hejaz region in western Arabia in 1925 and most of Asir, in SW Arabia, by 1926. The discovery of oil in the 1930s transformed the nation.

The Hejaz contains the holy cities of Islam—Medina, where the Mosque of the Prophet enshrines the tomb of Muhammad, and Mecca, his birthplace. An estimated 3 mil Muslims make pilgrimage to Mecca annually. Stampedes and other disasters have killed thousands of pilgrims in recent decades.

Ibn Saud reigned until his death, Nov. 1953. Subsequent kings have been sons of Ibn Saud. The king exercises authority together with a Council of Ministers. The Islamic religious code is the law of the land. Alcohol and public entertainments are restricted, and women have an inferior legal status.

Saudi Arabia has often allied itself with the U.S. and other Western nations, and billions of dollars of advanced arms have been purchased from Britain, France, and the U.S.; however, Western support for Israel has often strained relations. Saudi units fought against Israel in the 1948 and 1973 Arab-Israeli wars. Beginning with the 1967 Arab-Israeli war, Saudi Arabia provided large annual financial gifts to Egypt; aid was later extended to Syria, Jordan, and Palestinian groups.

King Faisal played a leading role in the 1973-74 Arab oil embargo against the U.S. and other nations. Crown Prince Khalid was proclaimed king on Mar. 25, 1975, after the assassination of Faisal. Fahd became king on June 13, 1982, following Khalid's death.

After Iraq invaded Kuwait, Aug. 2, 1990, Saudi Arabia accepted the Kuwaiti royal family and more than 400,000 Kuwaiti refugees. King Fahd invited Western and Arab troops to deploy on Saudi soil before and during the 1991 Persian Gulf War.

The presence of 15 Saudis among the 19 al-Qaeda hijackers who took part in the Sept. 11, 2001, attacks on the U.S. raised tensions between the U.S. and Saudi governments, and some blamed the Saudi government for allowing Muslim extremism to flourish in Saudi Arabia. Policy differences over the Israeli-Palestinian dispute and Iraq (where Saudi jihadists supported the Sunni cause) were further irritants. The U.S. completed a pullout of its combat forces from Saudi Arabia in Sept. 2003.

Alarmed at guerrilla attacks that killed more than 100 people, mostly foreigners, in Saudi Arabia during 2003-04, the Saudi government stepped up antiterrorist activities in cooperation with the U.S. Islamist candidates on a "golden list" circulated by conservative clerics fared well in municipal council elections, Feb.-Apr. 2005; women were barred from voting in the elections, the country's first since 1963.

King Fahd died Aug. 1, 2005. He was succeeded by his half-brother, Abdullah, who had in effect ruled the Kingdom since Fahd suffered a stroke in Nov. 1995. Soaring oil revenues in 2004-08 provided funds for more than $500 bil in investments, including plans to diversify the economy and redevelop Mecca.

Hoping to contain the wave of "Arab Spring" uprisings that had challenged or toppled other entrenched regimes in North Africa and the Middle East in 2011, Saudi Arabia led a Gulf Cooperation Council force that entered Bahrain Mar. 14 to suppress protests there. The Saudis also took steps to aid monarchies in Jordan and Morocco, and sent $4 bil to assist the military council that assumed power in Egypt after the ouster of Pres. Hosni Mubarak. King Abdullah announced Sept. 25, 2011, that women would have the right to vote and run for office by 2015.

Senegal
Republic of Senegal

People: Population: 12,643,799. **Age distrib.:** <15: 43.3%; 65+: 2.9%. **Pop. density:** 170.1 per sq mi, 65.7 per sq km. **Urban:** 42.4%. **Ethnic groups:** Wolof 43%, Pular 24%, Serer 15%, Jola 4%, Mandinka 3%, Soninke 1%, European & Lebanese 1%. **Principal languages:** French (official), Wolof, Pulaar, Jola, Mandinka. **Chief religions:** Muslim 94%, Christian 5%, indigenous beliefs 1%.

Geography: Total area: 75,955 sq mi, 196,722 sq km; **Land area:** 74,336 sq mi, 192,530 sq km. **Location:** At W extreme of Africa. **Neighbors:** Mauritania on N, Mali on E, Guinea and Guinea-Bissau on S; surrounds Gambia on three sides. **Topography:** Low rolling plains cover most of Senegal, rising somewhat in SE. Swamp and jungles are in SW. **Capital:** Dakar, 2,862,879.

Government: Type: Republic. **Head of state:** Pres. Abdoulaye Wade; b. May 29, 1926; in office: Apr. 1, 2000. **Head of gov.:** Prime Min. Souleymane Ndéné Ndiaye; b. Aug. 6, 1958; in office: Apr. 30, 2009. **Local divisions:** 11 regions. **Defense budget:** $199 mil. **Active troops:** 13,620.

Economy: Industries: agric. and fish proc., phosphate mining, fertilizer prod., petroleum refining. **Chief crops:** peanuts, millet, corn, sorghum, rice, cotton, tomatoes, green vegetables. **Natural resources:** fish, phosphates, iron ore. **Arable land:** 20%. **Livestock:** cattle: 3.3 mil; chickens: 44 mil; goats: 4.6 mil; pigs: 332,260; sheep: 5.4 mil. **Fish catch:** 459,303 metric tons. **Electricity prod.:** 2.2 bil kWh. **Labor force:** agric. 77.5%, industry and services 22.5%.

Finance: Monetary unit: CFA BCEAO Franc (XOF) (Sept. 2011: 468.55 = $1 U.S.). **GDP:** $23.9 bil; **per capita GDP:** $1,900; **GDP growth:** 4.2%. **Imports:** $4.5 bil; France 20%, Nigeria 9.2%, China 9%, Thailand 5.5%, Spain 4.3%. **Exports:** $2.1 bil; Mali 19.3%, Switzerland 8.3%, India 8.2%, France 5.8%, UK 4.2%. **Tourism:** $463 mil. **Budget:** $3.3 bil. **Total reserves less gold:** $2 bil. **CPI change:** 1.3%.

Transport: Railways: 563 mi. **Civil aviation:** 612.1 mil pass.-mi; 10 airports. **Chief port:** Dakar.

Communications: TV sets: 44 per 1,000 pop. **Radios:** 536 per 1,000 pop. **Telephone lines:** 2.8 per 100 pop. **Daily newspaper circ.:** 8.7 per 1,000 pop. **Internet:** 16 users per 100 pop.

Health: Life expect.: 57.9 male; 61.8 female. **Births:** 36.7 (per 1,000 pop.). **Deaths:** 9.3 (per 1,000 pop.). **Natural inc.:** 2.75%. **Infant mortality:** 56.4 (per 1,000 live births). **HIV rate:** 0.9%.

Education: Compulsory: ages 7-12. **Literacy:** 49.7%.

Major intl. organizations: UN and all of its specialized agencies, AU, WTO.

Embassy: 2112 Wyoming Ave. NW 20008; 234-0540.

Website: www.gouv.sn

Portuguese settlers arrived in the 15th cent., but French control grew from the 17th cent. The last independent Muslim state was subdued in 1893. Senegal became an independent republic Aug. 20, 1960, but French political and economic influence remained strong. Senegambia, a loose confederation of Senegal and The Gambia, was established in 1982 but dissolved 7 years later.

Forty years of Socialist Party rule ended when Abdoulaye Wade, leader of the Senegalese Democratic Party, won a presidential runoff election Mar. 19, 2000. A Senegalese ferry capsized off the coast of The Gambia Sept. 26, 2002, killing at least 1,863 people. A peace accord signed Dec. 30, 2004, with separatists in Cassamance Province, S Senegal, sought to end a 22-year insurgency. Pres. Wade was reelected Feb. 25, 2007.

Serbia
Republic of Serbia

People: Population: 7,310,555. **Age distrib.:** <15: 15.1%; 65+: 16.5%. **Pop. density:** 244.4 per sq mi, 94.4 per sq km. **Urban:** 56.1%. **Ethnic groups:** Serb 83%, Hungarian 4%, Bosniak 2%, Romany 1%, Yugoslav 1%. **Principal languages:** Serbian (official), Hungarian, Bosniak, Romany. **Chief religions:** Serbian Orthodox 85%, Catholic 6%, Muslim 3%, Protestant 1%.

Geography: Total area: 29,913 sq mi, 77,474 sq km; **Land area:** 29,913 sq mi, 77,474 sq km. **Location:** On Balkan Peninsula in SE Europe. **Neighbors:** Croatia, Bosnia and Herzegovina on W; Hungary on N; Romania, Bulgaria on E; Montenegro, Albania, Macedonia on S. **Topography:** Terrain varies widely, with fertile plains drained by Danube and other rivers in N, limestone basins in E, ancient mountains and hills in SE, and very high coastline in Montenegro along SW. **Capital:** Belgrade (Beograd), 1,117,200.

Government: Type: Republic. **Head of state:** Pres. Boris Tadic; b. Jan. 15, 1958; in office: July 11, 2004. **Head of gov.:** Prime Min. Mirko Cvetkovic; b. Aug. 16, 1950; in office: July 7, 2008. **Local divisions:** 1 republic with 1 autonomous province. **Defense budget:** $918 mil. **Active troops:** 29,125.

Economy: Industries: base metals, furniture, food proc., machinery, chemicals, sugar, tires, clothes, pharmaceuticals. **Chief crops:** wheat, maize, sugar beets, sunflowers, raspberries. **Natural resources:** oil, gas, coal, iron ore, copper, zinc, antimony, chromite, gold, silver, magnesium, pyrite, limestone, marble, salt. **Crude oil reserves:** 77.5 mil bbls. **Arable land:** 37.7%. **Livestock:** cattle: 1 mil; chickens: 22.4 mil; goats: 143,000; pigs: 3.6 mil; sheep: 1.5 mil. **Fish catch:** 11,286 metric tons. **Electricity prod.:** 34.7 bil kWh. **Labor force:** agric. 23.9%, industry 20.5%, services 55.6%.

Finance: Monetary unit: Dinar (RSD) (Sept. 2011: 72.17 = $1 U.S.). **GDP:** $80.1 bil; **per capita GDP:** $10,900; **GDP growth:** 1.8%. **Imports:** $15.8 bil; Russia 12.8%, Germany 10.6%, Italy 8.5%, China 7.2%, Hungary 4.9%. **Exports:** $9.7 bil; Italy 11.5%, Bosnia and Herzegovina 11.2%, Germany 10.5%, Montenegro 8.4%, Romania 6.3%, Russia 5.4%, Macedonia 4.9%, Slovenia 4.4%. **Tourism:** $798 mil. **Budget:** $18.5 bil. **Total reserves less gold:** $12.7 bil. **Gold:** 421,817 oz t. **CPI change:** 6.1%.

Transport: Railways: 2,100 mi. **Civil aviation:** 588.4 mil pass.-mi; 11 airports.

Communications: TV sets: 248 per 1,000 pop. **Telephone lines:** 40.5 per 100 pop. **Internet:** 40.9 users per 100 pop.

Health: Life expect.: 71.5 male; 77.3 female. **Births:** 9.2 (per 1,000 pop.). **Deaths:** 13.9 (per 1,000 pop.). **Natural inc.:** −0.47%. **Infant mortality:** 6.5 (per 1,000 live births). **HIV rate:** 0.1%.

Education: Compulsory: ages 7-14. **Literacy:** 97.8%.

Major intl. organizations: UN (FAO, IBRD, ILO, IMF, WHO), OSCE, WTO (observer).

Embassy: 2134 Kalorama Rd. NW 20008; 332-0333.
Website: www.srbija.gov.rs

Serbia, which had since 1389 been a vassal principality of Turkey, was established as an independent kingdom by the Treaty of Berlin, 1878. After the Balkan wars, Serbia's boundaries were enlarged by the annexation of Old Serbia and Macedonia, 1913.

When the Austro-Hungarian empire collapsed after WWI, the Kingdom of Serbs, Croats, and Slovenes was formed from the former provinces of Croatia, Dalmatia, Bosnia, Herzegovina, Slovenia, Vojvodina, and the independent state of Montenegro. The name became Yugoslavia in 1929.

Nazi Germany invaded in 1941. After the Nazis were driven out in 1945, Yugoslavia became a federal republic, headed by Josip Broz, a Communist, known as Marshal Tito. He rejected Stalin's policy of dictating to all Communist nations, and he accepted economic and military aid from the West. Pres. Tito died May 4, 1980. Yugoslavia held together for a decade, then broke apart. During 1991-95, Serbia, under Pres. Slobodan Milosevic, supported ethnic Serb fighters as war raged in Croatia and in Bosnia and Herzegovina, which had declared independence. The republics of Serbia and Montenegro proclaimed a new Federal Republic of Yugoslavia Apr. 17, 1992. The UN imposed sanctions on the newly reconstituted Yugoslavia as a means of ending the bloodshed in Bosnia.

A peace agreement initialed in Dayton, OH, Nov. 21, 1995, was signed in Paris, Dec. 14, by Milosevic and leaders of Bosnia and Croatia. In May 1996, a UN tribunal in the Netherlands began trying suspected war criminals from the former Yugoslavia. Mass protests erupted when Milosevic refused to accept opposition victories in local elections Nov. 17; non-Communist governments took office in Belgrade and other cities in Feb. 1997. Barred from running for a 3rd term as Serbian president, Milosevic had himself inaugurated as president of Yugoslavia on July 23, 1997.

Efforts by Serbia to suppress a secessionist movement in Kosovo province led in Mar.-June 1999 to a war with the U.S. and its NATO allies; they accused Milosevic of pursuing a policy of ethnic cleansing against the Kosovars (ethnic Albanians), who were predominantly Muslim. NATO stationed a multinational force in Kosovo, which was placed under UN administration.

Defeated in a presidential election Sept. 24, 2000, by opposition leader Vojislav Kostunica, Milosevic initially refused to accept the result. A rising tide of mass demonstrations forced him to resign Oct. 6, and Kostunica was sworn in the next day. Charged with corruption and abuse of power, Milosevic surrendered to Serbian authorities Apr. 1, 2001. He was extradited June 28 to The Hague, Netherlands, where a UN tribunal had indicted him for war crimes. His trial began Feb. 12, 2002, but proceeded slowly. He was found dead in his prison cell Mar. 11, 2006, before a verdict was reached.

A pact to reconstitute Yugoslavia as a new union of Serbia and Montenegro took effect Feb. 4, 2003. Zoran Djindjic, premier of the Republic of Serbia, was assassinated Mar. 12 in Belgrade; the murder triggered a roundup of more than 4,500 people associated with organized crime and the Milosevic regime. Serbia's union with Montenegro disintegrated in 2006, as Montenegrins voted support for separation in a referendum May 21, and Montenegro became an independent republic June 3.

After years of fruitless negotiations, Kosovo unilaterally declared independence from Serbia Feb. 17, 2008; the new country was immediately recognized by the U.S. and most European allies, but not by Serbia and Russia. Following parliamentary elections in Serbia May 11, a pro-Western government under Mirko Cvetkovic took office July 7. Serbia, seeking EU membership, met a key requirement of European leaders July 21, 2008, by arresting former Bosnian Serb leader Radovan Karadzic, who was then extradited to the International Criminal Court in The Hague, Netherlands, on charges of genocide and crimes against humanity. Serbia's parliament passed a resolution Mar. 31, 2010, apologizing for the 1995 massacre of thousands of Muslims by Bosnian Serbs at Srebrenica; in a further effort to deal with wartime atrocities, Serbian prosecutors on Sept. 11, 2010, announced the indictment of 9 former members of the "Jackals" paramilitary unit for allegedly killing 43 ethnic Albanian civilians during the 1999 Kosovo conflict. Ratko Mladic, the former Bosnian Serb military commander accused of directing the 1995 massacre of 8,000 Bosnian Muslims in Srebrenica, was arrested in Serbia May 26, 2011, and sent to The Hague for trial.

Vojvodina is a nominally autonomous province in northern Serbia (8,304 sq mi), with a population (2008 est.) of 1,979,389, mostly Serbian. The capital is Novi Sad.

Seychelles
Republic of Seychelles

People: Population: 89,188. **Age distrib.:** <15: 21.9%; 65+: 7.2%. **Pop. density:** 507.7 per sq mi, 196 per sq km. **Urban:** 55.3%. **Ethnic groups:** mixed French, African, Indian, Chinese, Arab. **Principal languages:** Creole, English (official). **Chief religions:** Roman Catholic 82%, Anglican 6%, Hindu 2%, Seventh-Day Adventist 1%, Muslim 1%, other Christian 3%.

Geography: Total area: 176 sq mi, 455 sq km; **Land area:** 176 sq mi, 455 sq km. **Location:** In Indian O. 700 mi NE of Madagascar. **Neighbors:** Nearest are Madagascar on SW, Somalia on

NW. **Topography:** A group of 86 islands, about half of them composed of coral, the other half granite, the latter predominantly mountainous. **Capital:** Victoria, 26,000.

Government: Type: Republic. **Head of state and gov.:** Pres. James Michel, b. Aug. 18, 1944; in office: Apr. 14, 2004. **Local divisions:** 23 districts. **Defense budget:** $7 mil. **Active troops:** 200.

Economy: Industries: fishing, tourism, coconuts and vanilla proc., coir (coconut fiber) rope, boat building, printing, furniture. **Chief crops:** coconuts, cinnamon, vanilla, sweet potatoes, cassava, copra, bananas. **Natural resources:** fish, cinnamon trees. **Arable land:** 2.2%. **Livestock:** cattle: 350; chickens: 370,000; goats: 5,200; pigs: 5,175. **Fish catch:** 81,489 metric tons. **Electricity prod.:** 260 mil kWh. **Labor force:** agric. 3%, industry 23%, services 74%.

Finance: Monetary unit: Rupee (SCR) (Sept. 2011: 12.15 = $1 U.S.). **GDP:** $2.1 bil; **per capita GDP:** $23,200; **GDP growth:** 6.2%. **Imports:** $831 mil; Saudi Arabia 17.4%, Spain 7.9%, South Africa 7.1%, France 6.7%, Brazil 6.4%, Singapore 5.4%, Germany 4.1%, U.S. 4%. **Exports:** $464 mil; U.K. 28.1%, France 21%, Italy 10.7%, Japan 7.9%, Spain 5.4%. **Tourism:** $209 mil. **Budget:** $310.3 mil. **Total reserves less gold:** $235.6 mil. **CPI change:** −2.4%.

Transport: Civil aviation: 887.3 mil pass.-mi; 8 airports. **Chief port:** Victoria.

Communications: TV sets: 278 per 1,000 pop. **Radios:** 278 per 1,000 pop. **Telephone lines:** 25.5 per 100 pop. **Internet:** 41 users per 100 pop.

Health: Life expect.: 68.9 male; 78.3 female. **Births:** 15.3 (per 1,000 pop.). **Deaths:** 6.9 (per 1,000 pop.). **Natural inc.:** 0.84%. **Infant mortality:** 11.7 (per 1,000 live births). **HIV rate:** NA.

Education: Compulsory: ages 6-15. **Literacy:** 91.8%.

Major intl. organizations: UN (FAO, IBRD, ILO, IMF, WHO), AU, the Commonwealth, WTO (observer).

Embassy: 800 Second Ave., Ste. 400C, New York, NY 10017; (212) 972-1785.
Website: www.egov.sc

The islands were occupied by France in 1768 and seized by Britain in 1794. Ruled as part of Mauritius from 1814, Seychelles became a separate colony in 1903. Independence was declared June 29, 1976. The first president was ousted in a coup a year later by a socialist leader, France Albert René. A new constitution, approved June 1993, provided for a multiparty state. After nearly 27 years in power, René resigned Apr. 14, 2004, and was succeeded by Vice Pres. James Michel. He won a full 5-year term in elections July 28-30, 2006 and was reelected May 19-21, 2011.

Sierra Leone
Republic of Sierra Leone

People: Population: 5,363,669. **Age distrib.:** <15: 41.8%; 65+: 3.7%. **Pop. density:** 194 per sq mi, 74.9 per sq km. **Urban:** 38.4%. **Ethnic groups:** Temne 35%, Mende 31%, Limba 8%, Kono 5%, Kriole (descendants of freed Jamaican slaves) 2%, Mandingo 2%, Loko 2%, other (incl. Liberian refugees & small numbers of Europeans, Lebanese, Pakistanis, Indians) 15%. **Principal languages:** English (official), Mende (principal vernacular in S), Temne (principal vernacular in N), Krio (English-based Creole, a lingua franca). **Chief religions:** Muslim 60%, indigenous beliefs 30%, Christian 10%.

Geography: Total area: 27,699 sq mi, 71,740 sq km; **Land area:** 27,653 sq mi, 71,620 sq km. **Location:** On W coast of W Africa. **Neighbors:** Guinea on N and E, Liberia on S. **Topography:** The heavily-indented, 210-mi coastline has mangrove swamps. Behind are wooded hills, rising to a plateau and mountains in E. **Capital:** Freetown, 900,847.

Government: Type: Republic. **Head of state and gov.:** Pres. Ernest Bai Koroma; b. Oct. 2, 1953; in office: Sept. 17, 2007. **Local divisions:** 3 provinces, 1 area. **Defense budget:** $13 mil. **Active troops:** 10,500.

Economy: Industries: diamond mining, small-scale mfg. (beverages, textiles), petroleum refining. **Chief crops:** rice, coffee, cocoa, palm kernels, palm oil, peanuts. **Natural resources:** diamonds, titanium ore, bauxite, iron ore, gold, chromite. **Arable land:** 15.1%. **Livestock:** cattle: 350,000; chickens: 7.8 mil; goats: 540,000; pigs: 52,000; sheep: 470,000. **Fish catch:** 200,040 metric tons. **Electricity prod.:** 58 mil kWh. **Labor force:** NA.

Finance: Monetary unit: Leone (SLL) (Sept. 2011: 4,402.00 = $1 U.S.). **GDP:** $4.7 bil. **per capita GDP:** $900. **GDP growth:** 5%. **Imports:** (2006) $560 mil; South Africa 14.6%, China 7.6%, Malaysia 6.7%, U.S. 5.9%, Côte d'Ivoire 5.6%, France 5.1%, India 4.7%, UK 4.5%, Netherlands 4.1%. **Exports:** (2006) $216 mil; Belgium 27%, U.S. 12%; Netherlands 8%, UK 7.5%, Côte d'Ivoire 6.2%, China 4.4%, Greece 4.1%. **Tourism:** $22 mil. **Budget** (2000 est.): $351 mil. **Total reserves less gold:** $409 mil. **CPI change** 16.6%.

Transport: Motor vehicles: 5.9 vehicles per 1,000 pop. **Civil aviation:** 66.5 mil pass.-mi; 1 airport. **Chief ports:** Freetown, Pepel.

Communications: TV sets: 13 per 1,000 pop. **Radios:** 132 per 1,000 pop. **Telephone lines:** 0.2 per 100 pop. **Internet:** (2009) 0.3 users per 100 pop.

Health: Life expect.: 53.7 male; 58.7 female. **Births:** 38.5 (per 1,000 pop.). **Deaths:** 11.7 (per 1,000 pop.). **Natural inc.:** 2.67%. **Infant mortality:** 78.4 (per 1,000 live births). **HIV rate:** 1.6%.

Education: Compulsory: ages 6-11. **Literacy:** 40.9%.

Major intl. organizations: UN (FAO, IBRD, ILO, IMF, WHO), AU, the Commonwealth, WTO.

Embassy: 1701 19th St. NW 20009; 939-9261.

Website: www.statehouse.gov.sl

Freetown was founded in 1787 by the British government as a haven for freed slaves. Full independence arrived Apr. 27, 1961. A one-party state was established by referendum in 1978.

Mutinous soldiers ousted Pres. Joseph Momoh Apr. 30, 1992. Another coup, Jan. 16, 1996, paved the way for multiparty elections and a return to civilian rule. A peace accord, signed Nov. 30 with the Revolutionary United Front (RUF), brought a temporary halt to a civil war that had claimed over 10,000 lives in 5 years.

A coup on May 25, 1997, was met with widespread international opposition. Armed intervention by Nigeria restored Pres. Ahmad Tejan Kabbah to power on Mar. 10, 1998, but RUF rebels (who funded their operations through illicit diamond sales) mounted a guerrilla counteroffensive, killing thousands of civilians and mutilating thousands more. The Kabbah government signed a power-sharing agreement with the RUF on July 7, 1999. A UN mission (UNAMSIL) was established in Oct. to help maintain the agreement. The accord collapsed in early May 2000, as RUF guerrillas took more than 500 UN peacekeepers hostage. Rebel leader Foday Sankoh was captured in Freetown May 17. The hostages were freed by the end of May, and 233 more UN personnel behind rebel lines were rescued July 15.

A UN-sponsored disarmament program in 2001 reduced the level of violence. On Jan. 16, 2002, the government and the UN signed an agreement creating the Sierra Leone Special Court to try war crimes that had occurred from Nov. 1996 onwards. Government and rebel leaders declared an official end to the war Jan. 18; by then, the death toll had risen to more than 50,000. Kabbah won the May 14 presidential election.

Sankoh, an indicted war criminal, died in UN custody July 29, 2003. UNAMSIL, which ended Dec. 31, 2005, was succeeded by UNIOSIL, a UN mission intended to strengthen political institutions. Opposition leader Ernest Bai Koroma won a presidential runoff vote, Sept. 8, 2007. Under an anti-corruption law signed Sept. 2, 2008, Koroma became Sierra Leone's first head of state to declare all his assets. Three former RUF leaders were convicted of war crimes Feb. 25, 2009.

Singapore
Republic of Singapore

People: Population: 5,246,787. **Age distrib.:** <15: 14.4%; 65+: 7.4%. **Pop. density:** 19,780.4 per sq mi, 7,637.2 per sq km. **Urban:** 100%. **Ethnic groups:** Chinese 77%, Malay 14%, Indian 8%. **Principal languages:** Mandarin, English, Malay (all official); Hokkien; Cantonese; Teochew; Tamil (official). **Chief religions:** Buddhist 43%, Muslim 15%, Taoist 9%, Catholic 5%, Hindu 4%, other Christian 10%, none 15%.

Geography: Total area: 269 sq mi, 697 sq km; **Land area:** 265 sq mi, 687 sq km. **Location:** Off tip of Malayan Peninsula in SE Asia. **Neighbors:** Nearest are Malaysia on N, Indonesia on S. **Topography:** Singapore is a flat, formerly swampy island. The nation includes 40 nearby islets. **Capital:** Singapore, 4,836,691.

Government: Type: Republic. **Head of state:** Pres. Tony Tan Keng Yam; b. Feb. 7, 1940; in office Sept. 1, 2011. **Head of gov.:** Prime Min. Lee Hsien Loong; b. Feb. 10, 1952; in office Aug. 12, 2004. **Defense budget:** $8.34 bil. **Active troops:** 72,500.

Economy: Industries: electronics, chemicals, financial services, oil drilling equip., petroleum refining, rubber proc. and rubber prods., processed food and beverages, ship repair, offshore platform constr., life sciences. **Chief crops:** orchids, vegetables. **Natural resources:** fish. **Arable land:** 0.7%. **Livestock:** cattle: 200; chickens: 3.2 mil; goats: 650; pigs: 260,000. **Fish catch:** 5,688 metric tons. **Electricity prod.:** 39.2 bil kWh. **Labor force:** agric. 0.1%, industry 30.2%, services 69.7%.

Finance: Monetary unit: Dollar (SGD) (Sept. 2011: 1.21 = $1 U.S.). **GDP:** $291.9 bil; **per capita GDP:** $62,100; **GDP growth:** 14.5%. **Imports:** $310.4 bil; U.S. 11.9%, Malaysia 11.6%, China 10.6%, Japan 7.6%, Indonesia 5.8%, South Korea 5.7%. **Exports:** $351.2 bil; Hong Kong 11.6%, Malaysia 11.5%, China 9.8%, Indonesia 9.7%, U.S. 5.6%, South Korea 4.7%, Japan 4.6%. **Tourism:** $14.1 bil. **Budget:** $34.01 bil (incl. both operational and development expenditures) **Total reserves less gold:** $225.7 bil. **CPI change:** 2.8%.

Transport: Motor vehicles: 164.3 vehicles per 1,000 pop. **Civil aviation:** 52.5 bil pass.-mi; 8 airports. **Chief port:** Singapore.

Communications: TV sets: 213 per 1,000 pop. **Radios:** 689 per 1,000 pop. **Telephone lines:** 39 per 100 pop. **Daily newspaper circ.:** 360.8 per 1,000 pop. **Internet:** 70 users per 100 pop.

Health: Life expect.: 81.3 male; 85.8 female. **Births:** 7.6 (per 1,000 pop.). **Deaths:** 3.4 (per 1,000 pop.). **Natural inc.:** 0.42%. **Infant mortality:** 2.7 (per 1,000 live births). **HIV rate:** 0.1%.

Education: Compulsory: ages 6-11. **Literacy:** 94.7%.

Major intl. organizations: UN (IBRD, ILO, IMF, WHO), APEC, ASEAN, the Commonwealth, WTO.

Embassy: 3501 International Pl. NW 20008; 537-3100.

Website: www.gov.sg

Founded in 1819 by Sir Thomas Stamford Raffles, Singapore was a British colony until 1959, when it became autonomous within the Commonwealth. On Sept. 16, 1963, it joined with Malaya, Sarawak, and Sabah to form the Federation of Malaysia. Tensions between Malayans, dominant in the federation, and ethnic Chinese, dominant in Singapore, led to an accord under which Singapore became a separate nation, Aug. 9, 1965.

Singapore is one of the world's largest ports and a major center of manufacturing, banking, and commerce. Standards in health, education, and housing are generally high. A free trade pact with the U.S. took effect Jan. 1, 2004.

Singapore has had only 3 prime mins.: Lee Kuan Yew, who dominated national politics, 1959-90; Goh Chok Tong, 1990-2004; and Lee Kuan Yew's son, Lee Hsien Loong, who took office Aug. 12, 2004. The government, dominated by the People's Action Party (PAP), has taken strong actions to keep order and suppress dissent. Singapore's export-dependent economy was hit hard by the global downturn in 2008 but rebounded during 2009-11. Opposition parties mounted a vigorous challenge to the PAP in 2011 elections.

Slovakia
Slovak Republic

People: Population: 5,477,038. **Age distrib.:** <15: 15.6%; 65+: 12.8%. **Pop. density:** 294.9 per sq mi, 113.9 per sq km. **Urban:** 55%. **Ethnic groups:** Slovak 86%, Hungarian 10%, Roma 2%, Ruthenian/Ukrainian 1%. **Principal languages:** Slovak (official); Hungarian, Roma, Ukrainian. **Chief religions:** Roman Catholic 69%, Protestant 11%, Greek Catholic 4%, none 13%.

Geography: Total area: 18,933 sq mi, 49,035 sq km; **Land area:** 18,573 sq mi, 48,105 sq km. **Location:** In E central Europe. **Neighbors:** Poland on N, Hungary on S, Austria and Czech Rep. on W, Ukraine on E. **Topography:** Carpathian Mts. in N, fertile Danube plain in S. **Capital:** Bratislava, 428,000.

Government: Type: Republic. **Head of state:** Pres. Ivan Gasparovic; b. Mar. 27, 1941; in office: June 15, 2004. **Head of gov.:** Prime Min. Iveta Radicová; b. Dec. 7, 1956; in office: July 8, 2010. **Local divisions:** 8 departments. **Defense budget:** $1.09 bil. **Active troops:** 16,531.

Economy: Industries: metal and metal prods.; food and beverages; electricity, gas, coke, oil, nuclear fuel; chemicals and man-made fibers; machinery; paper and printing. **Chief crops:** grains, potatoes, sugar beets, hops, fruits. **Natural resources:** brown coal and lignite, iron ore, copper, manganese ore, salt. **Crude oil reserves:** 9 mil bbls. **Arable land:** 28.7%. **Livestock:** cattle: 483,810; chickens: 13.2 mil; goats: 35,686; pigs: 740,862; sheep: 361,600. **Fish catch:** 2,584 metric tons. **Electricity prod.:** (2009): 24.7 bil kWh. **Labor force:** agric. 3.5%, industry 27%, services 69.4%.

Finance: Monetary unit: Euro (EUR) (Sept. 2011: 0.71 = $1 U.S.). **GDP:** $120.2 bil; **per capita GDP:** $22,000; **GDP growth:** 4%. **Imports:** $62.4 bil; Czech Republic 19.3%, Germany 17.4%, Russia 8.7%, Hungary 7.4%, South Korea 5.9%, Austria 5.1%, Poland 5.1%, France 4.5%, Italy 4.3%. **Exports:** $64.2 bil; Germany 19.5%, Czech Republic 13.4%, France 7.6%, Hungary 7.2%, Poland 7.1%, Austria 6%, Italy 6%, UK 4.5%. **Tourism:** $2.2 bil. **Budget:** $35.01 bil. **Total reserves less gold:** $719.3 mil. **Gold:** 1.02 mil oz t. **CPI change:** 1%.

Transport: Railways: 2,251 mi. **Motor vehicles:** 350.3 vehicles per 1,000 pop. **Civil aviation:** 2.1 bil pass.-mi; 20 airports. **Chief ports:** Bratislava, Komarno.

Communications: TV sets: 437 per 1,000 pop. **Radios:** 964 per 1,000 pop. **Telephone lines:** 20.1 per 100 pop. **Daily newspaper circ.:** 125.7 per 1,000 pop. **Internet:** 79.4 users per 100 pop.

Health: Life expect.: 71.9 male; 79.9 female. **Births:** 10.5 (per 1,000 pop.). **Deaths:** 9.6 (per 1,000 pop.). **Natural inc.:** 0.09%. **Infant mortality:** 6.6 (per 1,000 live births). **HIV rate:** <0.1%.

Education: Compulsory: ages 6-14. **Literacy:** NA.

Major intl. organizations: UN (FAO, IBRD, ILO, IMF, WHO), EU, NATO, OECD, OSCE, WTO.

Embassy: 3523 International Ct. NW 20008; 237-1054.

Website: www.government.gov.sk

Slovakia was originally settled by Illyrian, Celtic, and Germanic tribes and was incorporated into Great Moravia in the 9th cent. It became part of Hungary in the 11th cent. Overrun by Czech Hussites in the 15th cent., it was restored to Hungarian rule in 1526. The Slovaks disassociated themselves from Hungary after WWI and joined the Czechs of Bohemia to form the Republic of Czechoslovakia, Oct. 28, 1918.

Germany invaded Czechoslovakia, 1939, and declared Slovakia independent. Slovakia rejoined Czechoslovakia in 1945. Czechoslovakia split into 2 separate states—the Czech Republic and Slovakia—on Jan. 1, 1993.

Slovakia attained full membership in the EU and NATO in 2004. The country adopted the euro currency as scheduled on Jan. 1, 2009, but its economy, which had been one of Europe's fastest growing, was battered by the global recession. Pres. Ivan Gasparovic won a 2nd 5-year term in a runoff election Apr. 4, 2009. A coalition of right-leaning parties took power after the parliamentary elections of June 12, 2010; they were led by Iveta Radicová, who became Slovakia's first female prime minister.

Slovenia
Republic of Slovenia

People: Population: 2,000,092. **Age distrib.:** <15: 13.4%; 65+: 16.8%. **Pop. density:** 257.1 per sq mi, 99.3 per sq km. **Urban:** 49.5%. **Ethnic groups:** Slovene 83%, Serb 2%, Croat 2%, Bosniak 1%. **Principal languages:** Slovenian; Serbo-Croatian; Italian, Hungarian (both official in some municipalities). **Chief religions:** Catholic 58%, Muslim 2%, Orthodox 2%, none 10%.

Geography: Total area: 7,827 sq mi, 20,273 sq km; **Land area:** 7,780 sq mi, 20,151 sq km. **Location:** In SE Europe. **Neighbors:** Italy on W, Austria on N, Hungary on NE, Croatia on SE, S. **Topography:** Mostly hilly; 42% forested. **Capital:** Ljubljana, 260,000.

Government: Type: Republic. **Head of state:** Pres. Danilo Türk; b. Feb. 19, 1952; in office: Dec. 22, 2007. **Head of gov.:** Prime Min. Borut Pahor; b. Nov. 2, 1963; in office: Nov. 21, 2008. **Local divisions:** 183 municipalities, 11 urban municipalities. **Defense budget:** $672 mil. **Active troops:** 7,600.

Economy: Industries: ferrous metallurgy and aluminum prods., lead and zinc smelting, electronics (incl. military), trucks, automobiles, elec. power equip., wood prods., textiles, chemicals, machine tools. **Chief crops:** potatoes, hops, wheat, sugar beets, corn, grapes. **Natural resources:** lignite coal, lead, zinc, building stone, hydropower, forests. **Arable land:** 8.7%. **Livestock:** cattle: 469,983; chickens: 4.4 mil; goats: 24,228; pigs: 432,011; sheep: 138,958. **Fish catch:** 2,344 metric tons. **Electricity prod.:** 15.6 bil kWh. **Labor force:** agric. 2.2%, industry 35%, services 62.8%.

Finance: Monetary unit: Euro (EUR) (Sept. 2011: 0.71 = $1 U.S.). **GDP:** $56.6 bil; **per capita GDP:** $28,200; **GDP growth:** –7.8%. **Imports:** $25.68 bil; Germany 16.5%, Italy 15.9%, Austria 11.8%, France 5%, Croatia 4.3%. **Exports:** $25 bil; Germany 19.4%, Italy 11.4%, Croatia 7.8%, France 7.4%, Austria 7.3%. **Tourism:** $2.3 bil. **Budget:** $25.5 bil. **Total reserves less gold:** $962.8 mil. **Gold:** 103,000 oz t. **CPI change:** 1.8%.

Transport: Railways: 763 mi. **Motor vehicles:** 569.8 vehicles per 1,000 pop. **Civil aviation:** 541.8 mil pass.-mi; 7 airports. **Chief port:** Koper.

Communications: TV sets: 371 per 1,000 pop. **Radios:** 409 per 1,000 pop. **Telephone lines:** 45 per 100 pop. **Daily newspaper circ.:** 172.8 per 1,000 pop. **Internet:** 70 users per 100 pop.

Health: Life expect.: 73.6 male; 81.2 female. **Births:** 8.9 (per 1,000 pop.). **Deaths:** 10.9 (per 1,000 pop.). **Natural inc.:** –0.2%. **Infant mortality:** 4.2 per 1,000 live births). **HIV rate:** <0.1%.

Education: Compulsory: ages 6-14. **Literacy:** 99.7%.

Major intl. organizations: UN (FAO, IBRD, ILO, IMF, WHO), EU, NATO, OECD, OSCE, WTO.

Embassy: 2410 California St. NW 20008; 386-6601.

Website: e-uprava.gov.si

The Slovenes settled in their current territory during the 6th to the 8th cent. They fell under German domination as early as the 9th cent. Modern Slovenian political history began after 1848 when the Slovenes, divided among several Austrian provinces, began their struggle for unification. In 1918 a majority of Slovenes became part of the Kingdom of Serbs, Croats, and Slovenes, later renamed Yugoslavia.

Slovenia declared independence June 25, 1991, and joined the UN May 22, 1992. It attained full membership in the EU and NATO in 2004. Slovenia adopted the euro currency Jan. 1, 2007. On Mar. 5, 2008, it became the first former Yugoslav republic to formally recognize Kosovo's independence from Serbia. A center-left coalition took office following legislative elections Sept. 21, 2008. New elections were called for Dec. 14, 2011, after the government lost a vote of no-confidence Sept. 20.

Solomon Islands

People: Population: 571,890. **Age distrib.:** <15: 37.8%; 65+: 3.9%. **Pop. density:** 52.9 per sq mi, 20.4 per sq km. **Urban:** 18.6%. **Ethnic groups:** Melanesian 95%, Polynesian 3%, Micronesian 1%. **Principal languages:** Melanesian pidgin (lingua franca in much of country), English (official, but only spoken by 1%-2% of pop.), 120 indigenous languages. **Chief religions:** Church of Melanesia 33%, Roman Catholic 19%, South Seas Evangelical 17%, Seventh-Day Adventist 11%, United Church 10%, Christian Fellowship Church 2%, other Christian 4%.

Geography: Total area: 11,157 sq mi, 28,896 sq km; **Land area:** 10,805 sq mi, 27,986 sq km. **Location:** Melanesian Archipelago in W Pacific O. **Neighbors:** Nearest is Papua New Guinea to W. **Topography:** 10 large volcanic, rugged islands; 4 groups of smaller ones. **Capital:** Honiara, 72,000.

Government: Type: Parliamentary democracy. **Head of state:** Queen Elizabeth II, represented by Gov.-Gen. Sir Frank Ofagioro Kabui; in office: July 7, 2009. **Head of gov.:** Prime Min. Danny Philip; b. 1951; in office: Aug. 25, 2010. **Local divisions:** 9 provinces and Honiara. **Defense budget/active troops:** NA.

Economy: Industries: fish (tuna), mining, timber. **Chief crops:** cocoa beans, coconuts, palm kernels, rice, potatoes, vegetables, fruits. **Natural resources:** fish, forests, gold, bauxite, phosphates, lead, zinc, nickel. **Arable land:** 0.6%. **Livestock:** cattle: 14,500; chickens: 235,000; pigs: 54,000. **Fish catch:** 26,106 metric tons. **Electricity prod.:** 78 mil kWh. **Labor force:** agric. 75%, industry 5%, services 20%.

Finance: Monetary unit: Dollar (SBD) (Sept. 2011: 7.59 = $1 U.S.). **GDP:** $1.6 bil; **per capita GDP:** $2,900; **GDP growth:** 5.6%. **Imports:** (2006) $256 mil; Singapore 24.5%, Australia 22.9%, China 6.1%, New Zealand 5.2%, Fiji 4.4%, Papua New Guinea 4.3%, Malaysia 4.3%. **Exports:** (2006) $237 mil; China 57.1%, Spain 5.1%, South Korea 4.1%. **Tourism:** $3 mil. **Budget** (2003): $75.1 mil. **Total reserves less gold:** $265.8 mil. **CPI change:** 11%.

Transport: Civil aviation: 49.7 mil pass.-mi; 2 airports. **Chief ports:** Honiara, Viru Harbor.

Communications: TV sets: 12 per 1,000 pop. **Radios:** 65 per 1,000 pop. **Telephone lines:** 1.6 per 100 pop. **Daily newspaper circ.:** 10.8 per 1,000 pop. **Internet:** 5 users per 100 pop.

Health: Life expect.: 71.6 male; 76.9 female. **Births:** 28 (per 1,000 pop.). **Deaths:** 3.9 (per 1,000 pop.). **Natural inc.:** 2.41%. **Infant mortality:** 17.8 (per 1,000 live births). **HIV rate:** NA.

Education: NA. **Literary:** 76.6%.

Major intl. organizations: UN (FAO, IBRD, ILO, IMF, WHO), the Commonwealth, WTO.

Embassy: 800 Second Ave., Ste. 400L, New York, NY 10017; (212) 599-6192.

Website: www.pmc.gov.sb

The Solomon Isls. were sighted 1568 by an expedition from Peru. Britain established a protectorate in the 1890s over most of the group, inhabited by Melanesians. The islands saw major WWII battles. They achieved self-government Jan. 2, 1976, and formal independence July 7, 1978.

A coup attempt June 5, 2000, sparked factional fighting in Honiara. Violence and lawlessness became widespread over the next 3 years. To restore order, a 2,225-member intervention force, led by Australia and authorized by the Pacific Isls. Forum, began arriving in Honiara July 24, 2003; nearly all foreign troops were removed by mid-2005.

Following elections Apr. 5, 2006, parliament's choice of Snyder Rini as prime min. led to 2 days of rioting in Honiara over alleged influence-buying by the ethnic Chinese business community. Rini resigned Apr. 26 rather than face a no-confidence vote. An earthquake and tsunami Apr. 2, 2007, claimed at least 52 lives.

Somalia

People: Population: 9,925,640. **Age distrib.:** <15: 44.7%; 65+: 2.4%. **Pop. density:** 41 per sq mi, 15.8 per sq km. **Urban:** 37.4%. **Ethnic groups:** Somali 85%, Bantu & other non-Somali 15%. **Principal languages:** Somali (official), Arabic, Italian, English. **Chief religion:** Sunni Muslim.

Geography: Total area: 246,201 sq mi, 637,657 sq km; **Land area:** 242,216 sq mi, 627,337 sq km. **Location:** Occupies eastern horn of Africa. **Neighbors:** Djibouti, Ethiopia, Kenya on W. **Topography:** The coastline extends for 1,700 mi. Hills cover the N; center and S are flat. **Capital:** Mogadishu, 1,500,000.

Government: Type: In transition. **Head of state:** Pres. Sheikh Sharif Sheikh Ahmed; b. July 25, 1964; in office: Jan. 31, 2009. **Head of gov.:** Abdiweli Mohamed Ali; in office: June 28, 2011 (acting from June 19). **Local divisions:** 18 regions. **Defense budget:** NA. **Active troops:** NA (Ethiopian trained, part of transitional fed. govt.).

Economy: Industries: few light industries incl. sugar refining, textiles, wireless comm. **Chief crops:** bananas, sorghum, corn, coconuts, rice, sugarcane, mangoes, sesame seeds, beans. **Natural resources:** uranium, iron ore, reserves, tin, gypsum, bauxite, copper, salt, nat. gas, likely oil. **Arable land:** 1.6%. **Livestock:** cattle: 5.4 mil; chickens: 3.4 mil; goats: 12.7 mil; pigs: 4,200; sheep: 13.1 mil. **Fish catch:** 30,000 metric tons. **Electricity prod.:** 315 mil kWh. **Labor force:** agric. 71%, industry and services 29%.

Finance: Monetary unit: Shilling (SOS) (Sept. 2011: 1,630.00 = $1 U.S.). **GDP:** $5.9 bil; **per capita GDP:** $600; **GDP growth:** 2.6%. **Imports:** (2006) $798 mil; Djibouti 29.9%, Kenya 7.8%, China 7.3%, Pakistan 7%, Brazil 6.4%, Yemen 4.8%, Oman 4.6%, UAE 4.5%. **Exports:** (2006) $300 mil; UAE 53%, Yemen 18.5%, Oman 13.4%. **Tourism:** NA. **Budget:** NA. **Total reserves less gold:** NA. **CPI change:** NA.

Transport: Civil aviation: 7 airports. **Chief ports:** Berbera, Kismaayo.

Communications: TV sets: 26 per 1,000 pop. **Radios:** 242 per 1,000 pop. **Telephone lines:** 1.1 per 100 pop. **Internet** (2009): 1.2 users per 100 pop.

Health: Life expect.: 48.5 male; 52.4 female. **Births:** 42.7 (per 1,000 pop.). **Deaths:** 14.9 (per 1,000 pop.). **Natural inc.:** 2.78%. **Infant mortality:** 105.6 (per 1,000 live births). **HIV rate:** 0.7%.

Education: Compulsory: ages 6-13. **Literacy:** NA.

Major intl. organizations: UN (FAO, IBRD, ILO, IMF, WHO), AL, AU.

Permanent UN mission: 425 E. 61st St., Ste. 702, New York, NY, 10021; (212) 688-9410. (Embassy ceased operation in U.S. in 1991.)

Website: www.state.gov/p/af/ci/so/

British Somaliland (present-day North Somalia) was formed in the 19th cent., as was Italian Somaliland (now central and South Somalia). Italy lost its African colonies in WWII. British Somaliland gained independence, June 26, 1960, and by prearrangement, merged July 1 with the UN Trust Territory of Somalia to create the independent Somali Republic.

On Oct. 15, 1969, Somalia's first civilian president, Abdirashid Ali Sharmarke, was assassinated. Six days later, a military group led by

Maj. Gen. Muhammad Siad Barre seized power. In 1970, he declared the country a socialist state—the Somali Democratic Republic.

Somalia has laid claim to Ogaden, the huge eastern region of Ethiopia, peopled mostly by Somalis. Some 11,000 Cuban troops with Soviet arms defeated Somali army troops and ethnic Somali rebels in Ethiopia, 1978. As many as 1.5 mil refugees entered Somalia. Guerrilla fighting in Ogaden continued until 1988, when a peace agreement was reached with Ethiopia.

After a month of fierce combat in Mogadishu between pro-government soldiers and the rebel United Somali Congress, Siad Barre was forced to flee the capital, Jan. 1991. Fighting between rival factions caused 40,000 casualties in 1991 and 1992, and by mid-1992 the civil war, drought, and banditry combined to produce a famine that threatened some 1.5 mil people with starvation.

In Dec. 1992 the UN accepted a U.S. offer of troops to safe-guard food delivery to the starving. The UN took control of the multinational relief effort from the U.S. May 4, 1993. While the operation helped alleviate the famine, there were significant U.S. and other casualties; a failed mission Oct. 3-4 left 18 U.S. troops and more than 500 Somalis dead. The U.S. withdrew its peace-keeping forces Mar. 25, 1994.

When the last UN troops pulled out Mar. 3, 1995, Mogadishu had no functioning central government, and armed factions con-trolled different regions. By 1999 a joint police force was operating in the capital, but much of the country, especially southern Soma-lia, faced continued violence and food shortages. After political and factional leaders signed a peace deal Jan. 29, 2004, a transitional parliament, Somalia's first legislature in 13 years, was inaugurated Aug. 22. Meeting in Nairobi, Kenya, the parliament chose Abdullahi Yusuf Ahmed as president; he was sworn in Oct. 14. The Indian Ocean tsunami of Dec. 26, 2004, killed at least 150 people and displaced about 5,000 in Somalia.

Because Mogadishu was held by his rivals, Pres. Yusuf moved, July 26, 2005, to make his transitional capital at Jowhar; an interim parliament convened Feb. 26, 2006, at Baidoa. On June 5, an Islamist militia took over Mogadishu, defeating secular warlords backed by the U.S. The Islamists, calling themselves the Supreme Islamic Courts Council, also held much of the central and southern regions. Pres. Yusuf escaped assassination, Sept. 18, but 8 others died in a car bomb explosion at Baidoa 5 days later.

With aid from Ethiopian troops, transitional govt. forces recap-tured Mogadishu in late Dec. 2006. The UN Security Council autho-rized, Feb. 20, 2007, an African Union peacekeeping mission to Somalia (AMISOM), but the troops were targeted by insurgents. An upsurge of fighting in Mogadishu, Feb.-Apr., killed hundreds of people and caused 350,000 to flee the capital. Bombings and kid-nappings escalated in 2007-08, as a series of cease-fires failed; the increasing violence forced international aid workers to pull out, worsening a humanitarian crisis. Many of the attacks on transitional authorities and their allies were blamed on al-Shabaab, an al-Qaeda ally that had recruited supporters in the U.S. and elsewhere.

After Pres. Yusuf resigned Dec. 29, 2008, the transitional par-liament, meeting in Djibouti Jan. 31, 2009, elected a moder-ate Islamist, Sheikh Sharif Sheikh Ahmed; by then, Ethiopia had completely withdrawn its troops from Somalia. Meanwhile, pirates intensified their operations in coastal waters in 2009, carrying out more than 200 attacks off the Horn of Africa. Activities by pirates and Islamist insurgents continued in 2010-11, disrupting efforts to relieve a famine that by mid-2011 threatened an estimated 3.7 mil Somalis. Pressured by the 9,000-member AMISOM force, al-Shabaab pulled out of Mogadishu Aug. 6, but the radical Islamists continued to control much of southern Somalia. An al-Shabaab suicide bomb attack Oct. 4, 2011, on government buildings in Mog-adishu claimed more than 100 lives.

South Africa
Republic of South Africa

People: Population: 49,004,031. **Age distrib.:** <15: 28.5%; 65+: 5.7%. **Pop. density:** 104.5 per sq mi, 40.4 per sq km. **Urban:** 61.7%. **Ethnic groups:** black African 79%, white 10%, colored 9%, Indian/Asian 3%. **Principal languages:** IsiZulu, IsiXhosa, Afri-kaans, Sepedi, English, Setswana, Sesotho, Xitsonga, isiNdebele, Tshivenda, siSwati (all official). **Chief religions:** Zion Christian 11%, Pentecostal/Charismatic 8%, Catholic 7%, Methodist 7%, Dutch Reformed 7%, Anglican 4%, Muslim 2%, other Christian 36%, none 15%.

Geography: Total area: 470,693 sq mi, 1,219,090 sq km; **Land area:** 468,909 sq mi, 1,214,470 sq km. **Location:** At south-ern extreme of Africa. **Neighbors:** Namibia, Botswana, Zimbabwe on N; Mozambique, Swaziland on E; surrounds Lesotho. **Topogra-phy:** Large interior plateau reaches close to the country's 1,739-mi coastline. There are few major rivers or lakes; rainfall sparse in W, more plentiful in E. **Capital:** Cape Town (legislative), 3,404,807; Pretoria (admin.), 1,428,987; Bloemfontein (judicial), 436,000. **Cit-ies (urban aggl.):** Johannesburg, 3,669,725; East Rand (Ekurhu-leni), 3,201,805; Durban, 2,879,233.

Government: Type: Republic. **Head of state and gov.:** Pres. Jacob Zuma; b. Apr. 12, 1942; in office: May 9, 2009. **Local divi-sions:** 9 provinces. **Defense budget:** $4.15 bil. **Active troops:** 62,082.

Economy: Industries: mining (platinum, gold, chromium), auto assembly, metalworking, machinery, textiles, iron and steel, chemi-cals, fertilizer, foodstuffs. **Chief crops:** corn, wheat, sugarcane,

fruits, vegetables. **Natural resources:** gold, chromium, antimony, coal, iron ore, manganese, nickel, phosphates, tin, rare earth ele-ments, uranium, gem diamonds, platinum, copper, vanadium, salt, nat. gas. **Crude oil reserves:** 15 mil bbls. **Arable land:** 11.8%. **Livestock:** cattle: 13.8 mil; chickens: 125 mil; goats: 6.4 mil; pigs: 1.6 mil; sheep: 25 mil. **Fish catch:** 528,277 metric tons. **Electric-ity prod.:** 238.3 bil kWh. **Labor force:** agric. 9%, industry 26%, services 65%.

Finance: Monetary unit: Rand (ZAR) (Sept. 2011: 7.19 = $1 U.S.). **GDP:** $524 bil; **per capita GDP:** $10,700; **GDP growth:** 2.8%. **Imports:** $77 bil; China 17.2%, Germany 11.2%, U.S. 7.4%, Saudi Arabia 4.9%, Japan 4.7%. **Exports:** $76.9 bil; China 10.3%, U.S. 9.2%, Japan 7.6%, Germany 7%, UK 5.5%, Switzerland 4.7%. **Tourism:** $9.1 bil. **Budget:** $126.2 bil. **Total reserves less gold:** $38.2 bil. **Gold:** 4 mil oz t. **CPI change:** 4.3%.

Transport: Railways: 12,547 mi. **Motor vehicles:** 159.5 vehi-cles per 1,000 pop. **Civil aviation:** 16.7 bil pass.-mi; 147 airports. **Chief ports:** Cape Town, Durban, Port Elizabeth, Richards Bay, Saldanha Bay.

Communications: TV sets: 195 per 1,000 pop. **Radios:** 443 per 1,000 pop. **Telephone lines:** 8.4 per 100 pop. **Daily newspaper circ.:** 29.6 per 1,000 pop. **Internet:** 12.3 users per 100 pop.

Health: Life expect.: 50.2 male; 48.4 female. **Births:** 19.5 (per 1,000 pop.). **Deaths:** 17.1 (per 1,000 pop.). **Natural inc.:** 0.24%. **Infant mortality:** 43.2 (per 1,000 live births). **HIV rate:** 17.8%.

Education: Compulsory: ages 7-15. **Literacy:** 88.7%.

Major intl. organizations: UN (FAO, IBRD, ILO, IMF, WHO), AU, the Commonwealth, WTO.

Embassy: 3051 Massachusetts Ave. NW 20008; 232-4400.

Website: www.gov.za

Bushmen and KhoiKhoi were the original inhabitants. Bantus, including Zulu, Xhosa, Swazi, and Sotho, had occupied the area from northeastern to southern South Africa before the 17th cent.

The Cape of Good Hope area was settled by the Dutch, beginning in the 17th cent. Britain seized the Cape in 1806. Many Dutch trekked north and founded 2 republics, Transvaal and Orange Free State. Diamonds were discovered, 1867, and gold, 1886. The Dutch (Boers) resented encroachments by the British and others; the Anglo-Boer War followed, 1899-1902. Britain won and, effective May 31, 1910, created the Union of South Africa, incorporating 2 British colonies (Cape and Natal) with Transvaal and Orange Free State. After a ref-erendum, the Union became the Republic of South Africa, May 31, 1961, and withdrew from the Commonwealth.

With the election victory of Daniel Malan's National Party in 1948, the policy of separate development of the races, or apart-heid, already existing unofficially, became official. Under apartheid, blacks were severely restricted to certain occupations, and paid far lower wages than whites for similar work. Only whites could vote or run for public office. Persons of Asian Indian ancestry and those of mixed race ("coloureds") had limited political rights. In 1959 the government passed acts providing for the eventual creation of several Bantu nations, or Bantustans.

Protests against apartheid were brutally suppressed. At Sharp-eville on Mar. 21, 1960, 69 black protesters were killed by govern-ment troops. At least 600 persons, mostly Bantus, were killed in 1976 riots protesting apartheid. In 1981, South Africa launched military operations in Angola and Mozambique to combat guerrilla groups. Meanwhile, the apartheid system slowly began to crumble.

In 1986, Nobel Peace Prize winner Bishop Desmond Tutu called for Western nations to apply sanctions against South Africa to force an end to apartheid. Pres. P. W. Botha announced in Apr. the end to the nation's system of racial pass laws and offered blacks an advisory role in government. On May 19, South Africa attacked 3 neighboring countries—Zimbabwe, Botswana, Zambia—to strike at guerrilla strongholds of the black nationalist African National Congress (ANC). A nationwide state of emergency was declared June 12, giving almost unlimited power to the security forces.

Some 2 mil South African black workers staged a massive strike, June 6-8, 1988. Pres. Botha, head of the government since 1978, resigned Aug. 14, 1989, and was replaced by F. W. de Klerk. In 1990 the government lifted its ban on the ANC. Anti-apartheid leader Nelson Mandela was freed Feb. 11 after more than 27 years in prison. In Feb. 1991, Pres. de Klerk pledged to end all apartheid laws.

In 1993 negotiators agreed on basic principles for a new demo-cratic constitution. South Africa's partially self-governing black territories, or "homelands," were dissolved and incorporated into a national system of 9 provinces. In elections Apr. 26-29, 1994, the ANC won 62.7% of the vote, making Mandela president. The National Party won 20.4%. The Inkatha Freedom Party won 10.5% and control of the legislature in a mainly Zulu province. By then, fighting between the ANC and Inkatha (aided, during the apartheid era, by South African defense forces) had killed more than 14,000 people in the Zulu region since the mid-1980s.

In 1995, Mandela appointed a truth commission, led by Des-mond Tutu, to document human rights abuses under apartheid. A post-apartheid constitution became law Dec. 10, 1996. The ANC won a landslide victory in elections held June 2, 1999. ANC leader Thabo Mbeki thus became South Africa's second popularly elected president. South Africa, Nov. 30, 2006, became the first country in Africa to legalize same-sex marriage.

After Mbeki's former deputy president, Jacob Zuma, defeated him in a power struggle for the ANC leadership, Mbeki resigned his presidential office, Sept. 21, 2008. Corruption charges against

Zuma were dropped Apr. 6, 2009, and he became president after the ANC swept national elections Apr. 22, 2009. South Africa became the first African nation to host the final round of the World Cup soccer competition, June-July 2010.

South Sudan
Republic of South Sudan

People: Population (2008): 8,260,490. **Age distrib.:** (2008): <15: 44.4%; 65+: 2.6%. **Pop. density (2008):** 33.2 per sq mi, 12.8 per sq km. **Urban:** NA. **Ethnic groups:** Dinka, Kakwa, Bari, Azande, Shilluk, Kuku, Murle, Mandari, Didinga, Ndogo, Bviri, Lndi, Anuak, Bongo, Lango, Dungotona, Acholi. **Principal languages:** English, Arabic (incl. Juba, Sudanese variants) (both official); Dinka; Nuer; Bari; Zande; Shilluk. **Chief religions:** animist, Christian.

Geography: Total area: 248,777 sq mi, 644,329 sq km. **Land area:** 248,777 sq mi, 644,329 sq km. **Location:** In NE Africa. **Neighbors:** Sudan on N, Uganda and Kenya on S, Ethiopia on E. **Topography:** The White Nile R. flows north through the center of the country. The river feeds the Sudd, a swampy area occupying more than 15% of the country's center; it is one of the world's largest wetlands. **Capital:** Juba.

Government: Type: Republic. **Head of state and gov.:** Salva Kiir Mayardit; b. 1951; in office: July 9, 2011. **Local divisions:** 10 states.

Economy: Industries: petroleum (nearly 75% of former Sudan's total oil output); industry and infrastructure underdeveloped. **Chief crops:** sorghum, maize, rice, millet, wheat, gum arabic, sugarcane, fruits, sweet potatoes, sunflower, cotton, sesame, cassava, beans, peanuts. **Natural resources:** petroleum; fertile soils; ecotourism, hydroelectricity potential. **Labor force:** vast majority of pop. relies on subsistence agriculture.

Finance: Monetary unit: South Sudanese Pound (SSP) (Aug. 2011: 3.31 = $1 U.S.).

Transport: Railways: 147 mi (reported to be in disrepair). **Civil aviation:** 2 airports.

Health: Infant mortality (2006): 102 (per 1,000 live births).

Major intl. organizations: UN.

Embassy: 1233 20th St. NW, Ste. 602, 20036; 293-7940.

Website: www.goss.org

South Sudan was a region of the Republic of the Sudan when that country became independent in 1956. Northerners (mostly Arab Muslims) had the dominant role, while southerners (mostly black Africans who practiced Christianity or traditional religions) were marginalized. Southern Anya Nya rebels waged war against the north, 1955-72, until an agreement reached in Addis Ababa, Ethiopia, offered regional self-government for the south. Oil was discovered in the southern region in 1978.

Civil war broke out again in 1983, with southern rebels led by the Sudan People's Liberation Movement (SPLM). Fighting and related famine cost an estimated 2 mil lives and displaced millions of southerners until a peace accord was signed in 2005. A power-sharing agreement offered autonomy for southern Sudan and allowed the south to hold an independence referendum.

Nearly 4 mil southern Sudanese cast ballots in the referendum Jan. 9-15, 2011, with almost 99% supporting secession. On July 8 the UN Security Council authorized a peacekeeping mission (UNMISS) with up to 7,900 uniformed personnel. South Sudan attained full independence July 9, 2011, and was admitted to the UN July 14. At independence, issues regarding the border with Sudan and division of oil revenues remained unresolved. South Sudan also faced challenges of poverty, underdevelopment, and factional conflict. More than 3,000 South Sudanese were killed by political and ethnic violence Jan.-Aug. 2011.

Spain
Kingdom of Spain

People: Population: 46,754,784. **Age distrib.:** <15: 15.1%; 65+: 17.1%. **Pop. density:** 242.7 per sq mi, 93.7 per sq km. **Urban:** 77.4%. **Ethnic groups:** mixed Mediterranean & Nordic. **Principal languages:** Castilian Spanish (official); Catalan, Galician, Basque (all official regionally). **Chief religion:** Roman Catholic 94%.

Geography: Total area: 195,124 sq mi, 505,370 sq km. **Land area:** 192,657 sq mi, 498,980 sq km. **Location:** In SW Europe. **Neighbors:** Portugal on W; France, Andorra on N; Morocco to S. **Topography:** The interior is a high, arid plateau broken by mountain ranges and river valleys. The NW is heavily watered, the S has lowlands and a Medit. climate. **Capital:** Madrid, 5,851,288. **Cities (urban aggl.):** Barcelona, 5,083,341; Valencia, 814,147.

Government: Type: Constitutional monarchy. **Head of state:** King Juan Carlos I de Borbon y Borbon; b. Jan. 5, 1938; in office: Nov. 22, 1975. **Head of gov.:** Prime Min. José Luis Rodríguez Zapatero; b. Aug. 4, 1960; in office: Apr. 17, 2004. **Local divisions:** 17 autonomous communities and two autonomous cities. **Defense budget:** $10.2 bil. **Active troops:** 142,212.

Economy: Industries: textiles and apparel, food and beverages, metals and metal manufactures, chemicals, shipbuilding, automobiles, machine tools, tourism, clay and refractory prods., footwear, pharmaceuticals. **Chief crops:** grain, vegetables, olives, wine grapes, sugar beets, citrus. **Natural resources:** coal, lignite, iron ore, copper, lead, zinc, uranium, tungsten, mercury, pyrites,

magnesite, fluorspar, gypsum, sepiolite, kaolin, potash, hydropower. **Crude oil reserves:** 150 mil bbls. **Arable land:** 25.1%. **Livestock:** cattle: 6 mil; chickens: 138 mil; goats: 2.3 mil; pigs: 26.3 mil; sheep: 19.7 mil. **Fish catch:** 1.2 mil metric tons. **Electricity prod.** (2009): 275.1 bil kWh. **Labor force:** agric. 4.2%, industry 24%, services 71.7%.

Finance: Monetary unit: Euro (EUR) (Sept. 2011: 0.71 = $1 U.S.). **GDP:** $1.4 tril; **per capita GDP:** $29,400; **GDP growth:** –0.1%. **Imports:** $324.6 bil; Germany 14%, France 12.8%, Italy 7.4%, China 5.7%, Netherlands 5.4%, UK 4.9%, Portugal 4.1%. **Exports:** $268.3 bil; France 19.5%, Germany 11.4%, Portugal 9.2%, Italy 8.5%, UK 6.4%. **Tourism:** $52.5 bil. **Budget:** $648.6 bil. **Total reserves less gold:** $19.1 bil. **Gold:** 9.1 mil oz t. **CPI change:** 1.9%.

Transport: Railways: 9,503 mi. **Motor vehicles:** 596.9 vehicles per 1,000 pop. **Civil aviation:** 49.8 bil pass.-mi; 97 airports. **Chief ports:** Algeciras, Barcelona, Bilbao, Cartagena, Huelva, Tarragona, Valencia.

Communications: TV sets: 556 per 1,000 pop. **Radios:** 327 per 1,000 pop. **Daily newspaper circ.:** 144.5 per 1,000 pop. **Internet:** 66.5 users per 100 pop.

Health: Life expect.: 78.2 male; 84.4 female. **Births:** 10.7 (per 1,000 pop.). **Deaths:** 8.8 (per 1,000 pop.). **Natural inc.:** 0.19%. **Infant mortality:** 3.4 (per 1,000 live births). **HIV rate:** 0.4%.

Education: Compulsory: ages 6-16. **Literacy:** 97.7%.

Major intl. organizations: UN and all of its specialized agencies, EU, NATO, OECD, OSCE, WTO.

Embassy: 2375 Pennsylvania Ave. NW 20037; 452-0100.

Website: www.lamoncloa.gob.es

Initially settled by Iberians, Basques, and Celts, Spain was successively ruled (wholly or in part) by Carthage, Rome, and the Visigoths. Muslims invaded Iberia from N Africa in 711. Reconquest of the peninsula by Christians from the N laid the foundations of modern Spain. In 1469 the kingdoms of Aragon and Castile were united by the marriage of Ferdinand II and Isabella I. Moorish rule ended with the fall of Granada, 1492. Spain's large Jewish community was expelled the same year.

Spain obtained a colonial empire with the 1492 "discovery" of America by Columbus and the conquest of Mexico by Cortés and of Peru by Pizarro. It also controlled the Netherlands and parts of Italy and Germany. Spain lost its American colonies in the early 19th cent. It lost Cuba, the Philippines, and Puerto Rico during the Spanish-American War, 1898.

Primo de Rivera became dictator, 1923. King Alfonso XIII revoked the dictatorship, 1930, but was forced into exile in 1931. A republic was proclaimed, which disestablished the church, curtailed its privileges, and secularized education. In 1936-39, a Popular Front of socialists, Communists, republicans, and anarchists governed Spain.

Army officers under Francisco Franco revolted, 1936. Franco received help and troops from Italy and Germany, while the USSR, France, and Mexico supported the republic. Some 500,000 to 1 mil died before the war's end Mar. 28, 1939. Franco was named *caudillo*, leader of the nation. Spain was officially neutral in WWII, but its cordial relations with fascist countries prompted its exclusion from the UN until 1955.

In July 1969, Franco and the Cortes (Parliament) designated Prince Juan Carlos future king and chief of state. After Franco's death, Nov. 20, 1975, Juan Carlos was sworn in as king. In free elections June 1977, moderates and democratic socialists emerged as the largest parties.

In 1981, a coup attempt by right-wing military officers was thwarted by the king. The Socialist Workers' Party, under Felipe González Márquez, won 4 consecutive general elections between 1982 and 1993 but lost in 1996 to a coalition of conservative and regional parties. Conservative Prime Min. José María Aznar, who won a parliamentary majority in the 2000 election, went against Spanish public opinion by openly supporting the U.S.-led invasion of Iraq, Mar. 2003.

Four commuter trains in central Madrid were bombed by Islamic extremists, Mar. 11, 2004, killing 191 people. The opposition Socialist Workers Party won elections 3 days later, and Socialist leader José Luis Rodríguez Zapatero, who became prime min. Apr. 17, fulfilled a campaign pledge to remove all 1,300 Spanish troops from Iraq. Spain legalized same-sex marriage, July 3, 2005.

Prime Min. Zapatero won a 2nd term in elections Mar. 9, 2008. As the financial crisis spread worldwide, Spain's banking, building, and tourism industries suffered; in May 2010, as the budget deficit mounted and unemployment surged above 20%, the government introduced austerity measures to reassure international lenders. Spain won its first World Cup international soccer championship July 11, 2010. On July 29, 2011, Zapatero called early elections for Nov. 20, 2011.

Catalonia and the Basque country were granted autonomy, Jan. 1980, following overwhelming approval in home-rule referendums. But Basque extremists pushed for independence. The Basque separatist group ETA carried out bombings that have killed about 830 since 1968. ETA declared a permanent cease-fire effective Mar. 24, 2006, after which the Spanish govt. agreed to formal peace talks. Negotiations broke down after ETA exploded a car bomb at the Madrid airport, Dec. 30, 2006, killing 2; Basque militants formally rescinded the truce, June 5, 2007, but reinstated it Sept. 5, 2010. In Catalonia, voters approved a plan for expanded home-rule, June 18, 2006.

The **Balearic Isls.** in the W Mediterranean, 1,927 sq mi, are a province of Spain; they include **Majorca** (Mallorca; capital Palma de Mallorca), **Minorca**, **Cabrera**, **Ibiza**, and **Formentera**. The **Canary Isls.**, 2,807 sq mi, in the Atlantic W of Morocco, form 2 provinces, and include the islands of Tenerife, Palma, Gomera, Hierro, Grand Canary, Fuerteventura, and Lanzarote; Las Palmas and Santa Cruz are thriving ports. More than 1,700 people died trying to get from Mauritania to the Canary Islands in rickety boats, Jan.-June 2006.

Ceuta and Melilla, small Spanish enclaves on Morocco's Mediterranean coast, gained limited autonomy in Sept. 1994. Spain has sought the return of Gibraltar, in British hands since 1704.

Sri Lanka
Democratic Socialist Republic of Sri Lanka

People: Population: 21,283,913. **Age distrib.:** <15: 24.9%; 65+: 7.9%. **Pop. density:** 852.9 per sq mi, 329.3 per sq km. **Urban:** 14.3%. **Ethnic groups:** Sinhalese 74%, Sri Lankan Moors 7%, Indian Tamil 5%, Sri Lankan Tamil 4%. **Principal languages:** Sinhala (official & national), Tamil (national), English commonly used in govt. **Chief religions:** Buddhist 69%, Muslim 8%, Hindu 7%, Christian 6%.

Geography: Total area: 25,332 sq mi, 65,610 sq km; **Land area:** 24,954 sq mi, 64,630 sq km. **Location:** In Indian O. off SE coast of India. **Neighbors:** India on NW. **Topography:** Coastal area and N half are flat; S-central area is hilly and mountainous. **Capital:** Colombo, 681,000; Sri Jayewardenepura Kotte (admin.), 123,000.

Government: Type: Republic. **Head of state:** Pres. Mahinda Rajapaksa; b. Nov. 18, 1945; in office: Nov. 19, 2005. **Head of gov.:** Dissanayake Mudiyanselage (Di Mu) Jayaratne; b. June 7, 1931; in office: Apr. 21, 2010. **Local divisions:** 9 provinces with 25 districts. **Defense budget:** $1.44 bil. **Active troops:** 160,900.

Economy: Industries: rubber proc., tea, coconuts, tobacco and other agric. commodities, telecommunications, insurance, banking, tourism, shipping, clothing, textiles, cement, petroleum refining. **Chief crops:** rice, sugarcane, grains, pulses, oilseed, spices, vegetables, fruits, tea, rubber, coconuts. **Natural resources:** limestone, graphite, mineral sands, gems, phosphates, clay, hydropower. **Arable land:** 19.1%. **Livestock:** cattle: 1.1 mil; chickens: 13.6 mil; goats: 377,460; pigs: 81,311; sheep: 8,000. **Fish catch:** 363,935 metric tons. **Electricity prod.:** 8.9 bil kWh. **Labor force:** agric. 32.7%, industry 26.3%, services 41%.

Finance: Monetary unit: Rupee (LKR) (Sept. 2011: 109.98 = $1 U.S.). **GDP:** $106.5 bil; **per capita GDP:** $5,000; **GDP growth:** 9.1%. **Imports:** $11.6 bil; India 17.5%, China 15.9%, Singapore 7.7%, Iran 7.1%. **Exports:** $7.9 bil; U.S. 20.5%, UK 12.8%, Italy 5.5%, Germany 5.3%, Belgium 4.4%, India 4%. **Tourism:** $576 mil. **Budget:** $11.2 bil. **Total reserves less gold:** $6.7 bil. **Gold:** 345,524 oz t. **CPI change:** 5.9%.

Transport: Railways: 900 mi. **Motor vehicles:** 36.5 vehicles per 1,000 pop. **Civil aviation:** 4.8 bil pass.-mi; 14 airports. **Chief port:** Colombo.

Communications: TV sets: 118 per 1,000 pop. **Radios:** 200 per 1,000 pop. **Telephone lines:** 17.2 per 100 pop. **Daily newspaper circ.:** 26.1 per 1,000 pop. **Internet:** 12 users per 100 pop.

Health: Life expect.: 72.2 male; 79.4 female. **Births:** 17.4 (per 1,000 pop.). **Deaths:** 5.9 (per 1,000 pop.). **Natural inc.:** 1.15%. **Infant mortality:** 9.7 (per 1,000 live births). **HIV rate:** <0.1%.

Education: Compulsory: ages 5-13. **Literacy:** 90.6%.

Major intl. organizations: UN (FAO, IBRD, ILO, IMF, WHO), the Commonwealth, WTO.

Embassy: 2148 Wyoming Ave. NW 20008; 483-4025.

Website: www.priu.gov.lk

The island was known to the ancient world as Taprobane (Greek for copper-colored) and later as Serendip (from Arabic). Colonists from N India subdued the indigenous Veddahs about 543 BCE; their descendants, the Buddhist Sinhalese, still form most of the population. Hindu descendants of Tamil immigrants from S India account for about one-fifth of the population.

Parts were occupied by the Portuguese in 1505 and the Dutch in 1658. The British seized the island in 1796. It became an independent member of the Commonwealth as Ceylon in 1948 and changed to Sri Lanka May 22, 1972.

Prime Min. Solomon W. R. D. Bandaranaike was assassinated Sept. 25, 1959. His widow, Mrs. Sirimavo Bandaranaike, served as prime min. 1960-65, 1970-77, 1994-2000. In 1971 the nation endured economic problems and terrorist activities by ultra-leftists, thousands of whom were executed. Massive land reform and nationalization of foreign-owned plantations took place in the mid-1970s.

Tensions between Sinhalese and Tamil separatists erupted into violence in the early 1980s. More than 60,000 died in the civil war, which continued for the next 2 decades; another 20,000, mostly young Tamils, "disappeared" after they were taken into custody by government security forces.

Pres. Ranasinghe Premadasa was assassinated May 1, 1993, by a Tamil rebel. Mrs. Bandaranaike's daughter, Chandrika Bandaranaike Kumaratunga, became prime min. after the Aug. 16, 1994, general elections. Elected president Nov. 9, Kumaratunga appointed her mother prime min. Kumaratunga, who was injured

in a suicide bomb attack at a campaign rally Dec. 18, 1999, won a second 6-year term 3 days later. In failing health, Mrs. Bandaranaike resigned Aug. 10 and died Oct. 10, 2000.

A truce accord intended to bring an end to the civil war was signed Feb. 22, 2002. The Indian Ocean tsunami of Dec. 26, 2004, left more than 31,100 dead, 4,100 missing, and 519,000 displaced in Sri Lanka.

Prime Min. Mahinda Rajapaksa of the United People's Freedom Alliance won the presidential election of Nov. 17, 2005. A resurgence of fighting by govt. forces, paramilitary groups, and Tamil rebels beginning in Dec. 2005 claimed thousands more lives during the next 3 years. The army launched a fierce offensive, eventually trapping the rebels in a small patch of territory in the northeast and displacing some 265,000 civilians; an estimated 7,000 noncombatants were killed between Jan. 20 and May 7, 2009. On May 18-19, Tamil leader Vellupillai Prabhakaran was killed, and Pres. Rajapaksa formally declared victory. He won reelection Jan. 26, 2010, with more than 57% of the total vote.

Sudan
Republic of the Sudan

(Unless otherwise noted, Sudan's data still includes South Sudan, which became independent July 9, 2011.)

People: Population: 45,047,502. **Age distrib.:** <15: 42.1%; 65+: 2.7%. **Pop. density:** 47.9 per sq mi, 18.5 per sq km. **Urban:** 40.1%. **Ethnic groups:** Sudanese Arab 70%, Fur, Beja, Nuba, Fallata. **Principal languages:** Arabic, English (both official); Nubian; Ta Bedawie; Fur. **Chief religions:** Sunni Muslim, small Christian minority.

Geography: Total area: 718,723 sq mi, 1,861,484 sq km; **Land area:** 718,723 sq mi, 1,861,484 sq km. **Location:** At E end of Sahara desert zone. **Neighbors:** Egypt on N; Libya, Chad, Central African Republic on W; Congo, Uganda, Kenya on S; Ethiopia, Eritrea on E. **Topography:** The N consists of Libyan Desert in W, and the mountainous Nubia Desert in E, with narrow Nile valley between. Center contains large, fertile, rainy areas with fields, pasture, and forest. The S has rich soil, heavy rain. **Capital:** Khartoum, 5,172,283.

Government: Type: Republic with strong military influence. **Head of state and gov.:** Pres. Gen. Omar Hassan Ahmad Al-Bashir; b. Jan. 1, 1944; in office: June 30, 1989. **Local divisions:** 26 states. **Defense budget:** NA. **Active troops:** 109,300.

Economy: Industries: oil, cotton ginning, textiles, cement, edible oils, sugar, soap distilling, shoes, petroleum refining, pharmaceuticals, armaments. **Chief crops:** cotton, groundnuts sorghum, millet, wheat, sugarcane, cassava, mangoes, papayas, bananas, sweet potatoes, sesame. **Natural resources:** petroleum; small reserves of iron ore, copper, chromium ore, zinc, tungsten, mica, silver, gold; hydropower. **Crude oil reserves:** 5 bil bbls. **Arable land:** 8.5%. **Livestock:** cattle: 41.6 mil; chickens: 42.4 mil; goats: 43.3 mil; sheep: 51.6 mil. **Fish catch:** 73,898 metric tons. **Electricity prod.:** 4.3 bil kWh. **Labor force:** agric. 80%, industry 7%, services 13%.

Finance: Monetary unit: Pound (SDG) (Sept. 2011: 2.67 = $1 U.S.). **GDP:** $100 bil; **per capita GDP:** $2,300; **GDP growth:** 5.1%. **Imports:** $8.5 bil; China 22.1%, Egypt 7.3%, Saudi Arabia 6.9%, India 5.8%, UAE 5%. **Exports:** $9.8 bil; China 60.3%, Japan 14%, Indonesia 8.6%, India 4.9%. **Tourism:** $299 mil. **Budget:** $13.2 bil. **Total reserves less gold:** (2009) $1.1 bil. **CPI change:** 13%.

Transport: Railways: 3,715 mi. **Motor vehicles:** 2.2 vehicles per 1,000 pop. **Civil aviation:** 690.3 mil; pass.-mi; 17 airports. **Chief port:** Port Sudan.

Communications: TV sets: 370 per 1,000 pop. **Radios:** 172 per 1,000 pop. **Telephone lines:** 0.9 per 100 pop. **Internet:** (2009) 9.9 users per 100 pop.

Health: Life expect.: 54.2 male; 56.7 female. **Births:** 36.1 (per 1,000 pop.). **Deaths:** 11 (per 1,000 pop.). **Infant mortality:** 68.1 (per 1,000 live births). **HIV rate:** 1.1%.

Education: Compulsory: ages 6-13. **Literacy:** 70.2%.

Major intl. organizations: UN (FAO, IBRD, ILO, IMF, WHO), AL, AU, WTO (observer).

Embassy: 2210 Massachusetts Ave. NW 20008; 338-8565.

Website: www.presidency.gov.sd or www.state.gov/p/af/ci/su/

Northern Sudan, ancient Nubia, was settled by Egyptians in antiquity. The population was converted to Coptic Christianity in the 6th cent. Arab conquests brought Islam to the area in the 15th cent. In the 1820s, Egypt took over Sudan, defeating the last of earlier empires, including the Fung. In the 1880s a revolution was led by Muhammad Ahmad, who called himself the Mahdi (leader of the faithful), and his followers, the dervishes. In 1898 an Anglo-Egyptian force crushed the Mahdi's successors.

Sudan voted for complete independence effective Jan. 1, 1956. In 1969, a Revolutionary Council took power, led by authoritarian Pres. Gaafar al-Nimeiry. He was overthrown in a bloodless coup, Apr. 6, 1985. Sudan held its first democratic parliamentary elections in 18 years in 1986, but the elected government was toppled in a bloodless military coup, June 30, 1989, led by Brig. Omar Hassan Ahmad al-Bashir. He dissolved the ruling junta and took the title of president in 1993.

During 1955-72 and 1983-2005, rebels in the south (populated largely by black Christians and followers of traditional religions) took up arms against government domination by northern Sudan, mostly Arab-Muslim. War and related famine cost an estimated 2 mil lives and displaced millions of southerners. An accord to end the rebellion in the south was signed Jan. 9, 2005.

A rebellion in the Darfur region of western Sudan led to a new crisis, 2003-11. Marauding Arab militias known as the *janjaweed*, reportedly acting in collusion with Sudanese government troops, looted and burned homes in Darfur and killed many African villagers. The African Union sent more than 7,000 peacekeepers, but fighting continued. Rebel and militia activities in both Sudan and Chad led to border clashes and further attacks on civilians. By Sept. 2009 the Darfur war had killed about 300,000 people and displaced another 2.7 mil. The UN Security Council voted July 31, 2007, to begin deploying a joint UN-African Union force of up to 26,000 peacekeepers (UNMIS), but fewer than 11,000 uniformed personnel were sent by mid-2011. The mission was succeeded by UNMISS upon South Sudan's independence in July 2011.

On Mar. 4, 2009, the International Criminal Court in The Hague, Netherlands, issued a warrant for Pres. Bashir's arrest on charges of war crimes and other crimes against humanity in Darfur. On July 12, 2010, the Court issued another warrant for Bashir's arrest for genocide, the first time it had ever accused a head of state of genocide. Bashir defied the calls for his arrest, and in Apr. 2010 won a new 5-year term in an election where his main challengers dropped out, alleging fraud.

After southern Sudanese voted overwhelmingly for secession, Jan. 9-15, 2011, South Sudan attained full independence July 9. At that time, differences over the border and the division of oil revenues between Sudan and South Sudan had not yet been resolved.

Suriname
Republic of Suriname

People: Population: 553,159. **Age distrib.:** <15: 28%; 65+: 5.6%. **Pop. density:** 9.2 per sq mi, 3.5 per sq km. **Urban:** 69.4%. **Ethnic groups:** Hindustani (known locally as East Indian) 37%, Creole 31%, Javanese 15%, Maroon (descendants of escaped slaves) 10%, Amerindian 2%, Chinese 2%, white 1%. **Principal languages:** Dutch (official), English widely spoken, Sranang Tongo (Surinamese), Caribbean Hindustani, Javanese. **Chief religions:** Hindu 27%, Protestant 25%, Roman Catholic 23%, Muslim 20%, indigenous beliefs 5%.

Geography: Total area: 63,251 sq mi, 163,820 sq km; **Land area:** 60,232 sq mi, 156,000 sq km. **Location:** On N shore of S. America. **Neighbors:** Guyana on W, Brazil on S, French Guiana on E. **Topography:** A flat Atlantic coast, where dikes permit agriculture. Inland is forest belt; to S, largely unexplored hills cover 75% of country. **Capital:** Paramaribo, 259,000.

Government: Type: Republic. **Head of state and gov.:** Pres. Désiré (Dési) Delano Bouterse; b. Oct. 13, 1945; in office: Aug. 12, 2010. **Local divisions:** 10 districts. **Defense budget:** $49 mil. **Active troops:** 1,840.

Economy: Industries: mining, alumina prod., oil, lumber, food proc., fishing. **Chief crops:** paddy rice, bananas, palm kernels, coconuts, plantains, peanuts. **Natural resources:** timber, hydropower, fish, kaolin, shrimp, bauxite, gold, small amounts of nickel, copper, platinum, iron ore. **Crude oil reserves:** 78.9 mil bbls. **Arable land:** 0.4%. **Livestock:** cattle: 50,000; chickens: 5.3 mil; goats: 4,335; pigs: 27,127; sheep: 6,000. **Fish catch:** 25,872 metric tons. **Electricity prod.:** 1.6 bil kWh. **Labor force:** agric. 8%, industry 14%, services 78%.

Finance: Monetary unit: Dollar (SRD) (Sept. 2011: 3.25 = $1 U.S.). **GDP:** $4.7 bil; **per capita GDP:** $9,700; **GDP growth:** 4.4%. **Imports** (2006 est.): $1.3 bil; U.S. 30%, Netherlands 18.7%, Trinidad and Tobago 12.7%, China 7.6%, Japan 5.7%. **Exports** (2006 est.): $1.4 bil; Canada 35.1%, Belgium 14.7%, U.S. 10%, UAE 9.8%, Norway 4.9%, Netherlands 4.7%, France 4.4%. **Tourism:** $64 mil. **Budget** (2004): $425.9 mil. **Total reserves less gold:** $638.9 mil. **Gold:** 65,491 oz t. **CPI change:** 6.9%.

Transport: Motor vehicles: 228.7 vehicles per 1,000 pop. **Civil aviation:** 1.1 bil pass.-mi; 5 airports. **Chief ports:** Paramaribo, Wageningen.

Communications: TV sets: 266 per 1,000 pop. **Radios:** 711 per 1,000 pop. **Telephone lines:** 16.2 per 100 pop. **Daily newspaper circ.:** 80.1 per 1,000 pop. **Internet:** 31.6 users per 100 pop.

Health: Life expect.: 68.5 male; 73.3 female. **Births:** 17.8 (per 1,000 pop.). **Deaths:** 6.2 (per 1,000 pop.). **Natural inc.:** 1.16%. **Infant mortality:** 29.9 (per 1,000 live births). **HIV rate:** 1%.

Education: Compulsory: ages 6-11. **Literacy:** 94.6%.

Major intl. organizations: UN (FAO, IBRD, ILO, IMF, WHO), Caricom, OAS, WTO.

Embassy: 4301 Connecticut Ave. NW, Ste. 460, 20008; 244-7488.

Website: www.gov.sr or www.surinameembassy.org

The Netherlands acquired Suriname in 1667 from Britain, in exchange for New Netherlands (New York). The 1954 Dutch constitution raised the colony to a level of equality with the Netherlands and the Netherlands Antilles. Independence was granted Nov. 25, 1975, despite objections from East Indians. Some 40% of the population (mostly East Indians) immigrated to the Netherlands in the months before independence.

Suriname's history since 1980 has been overshadowed by military coups and political intrigues. Désiré (Dési) Bouterse, who masterminded coups in 1982 and 1990, was elected president by parliament July 19, 2010; as he took office Aug. 12, he was facing trial in Suriname on charges of having executed 15 political opponents in 1982, and he had been convicted in absentia in the Netherlands, 1999, for drug trafficking. In Dec. 2010, he named his son Dino, convicted in 2005 of cocaine and arms smuggling, to lead a new counterterrorism unit. The U.S. State Dept. has labeled Suriname a transshipment point for cocaine trafficking.

Swaziland
Kingdom of Swaziland

People: Population: 1,370,424. **Age distrib.:** <15: 37.8%; 65+: 3.6%. **Pop. density:** 206.3 per sq mi, 79.7 per sq km. **Urban:** 21.4%. **Ethnic groups:** African 97%, European 3%. **Principal languages:** English used in govt., siSwati (both official). **Chief religions:** Zionist 40%, Roman Catholic 20%, Muslim 10%, other (incl. Anglican, Baha'i, Methodist, Mormon, Jewish) 30%.

Geography: Total area: 6,704 sq mi, 17,364 sq km; **Land area:** 6,643 sq mi, 17,204 sq km. **Location:** In southern Africa, near Indian O. coast. **Neighbors:** South Africa on N, W, S; Mozambique on E. **Topography:** Descends W-E in broad belts, becoming more arid in low veld region, then rising to plateau in E. **Capital:** Mbabane (admin.), 74,000; Lobamba (legislative), NA.

Government: Type: Constitutional monarchy. **Head of state:** King Mswati III; b. Apr. 19, 1968; in office: Apr. 25, 1986. **Head of gov.:** Prime Min. Barnabas Sibusiso Dlamini; b. May 15, 1942; in office: Oct. 23, 2008. **Local divisions:** 4 districts. **Defense budget/ active troops:** NA.

Economy: Industries: coal, wood pulp, sugar, soft drink concentrates, textiles and apparel. **Chief crops:** sugarcane, cotton, corn, tobacco, rice, citrus, pineapples, sorghum, peanuts. **Natural resources:** asbestos, coal, clay, cassiterite, hydropower, forests, small gold and diamond deposits, quarry stone, talc. **Arable land:** 10.2%. **Livestock:** cattle: 585,000; chickens: 3.2 mil; goats: 276,000; pigs: 30,000; sheep: 28,000. **Fish catch:** 143 metric tons. **Electricity prod.:** 470 mil kWh. **Labor force:** agric. 70%, industry and services NA.

Finance: Monetary unit: Lilangeni (SZL) (Sept. 2011: 7.18 = $1 U.S.). **GDP:** $6.1 bil; **per capita GDP:** $4,500; **GDP growth:** 2%. **Imports:** $1.6 bil; NA. **Exports:** $1.4 bil; NA. **Tourism:** NA. **Budget:** $1.4 bil. **Total reserves less gold:** $756.3 mil. **CPI change:** 4.5%.

Transport: Railways: 187 mi. **Civil aviation:** 2 airports.

Communications: TV sets: 37 per 1,000 pop. **Radios:** 362 per 1,000 pop. **Telephone lines:** 3.7 per 100 pop. **Daily newspaper circ.:** 24.2 per 1,000 pop. **Internet:** 8 users per 100 pop.

Health: Life expect.: 48.9 male; 48.4 female. **Births:** 26.6 (per 1,000 pop.). **Deaths:** 14.6 (per 1,000 pop.). **Natural inc.:** 1.2%. **Infant mortality:** 63.1 (per 1,000 live births). **HIV rate:** 25.9%.

Education: Compulsory: ages 6-12. **Literacy:** 86.9%.

Major intl. organizations: UN (FAO, IBRD, ILO, IMF, WHO), the Commonwealth, WTO.

Embassy: 1712 New Hampshire Ave. NW 20009; 234-5002.

Website: www.gov.sz

The royal house of Swaziland traces back 400 years, and is one of Africa's last ruling dynasties. The Swazis, a Bantu people, were driven to Swaziland from lands to the N by the Zulus in 1820. Their autonomy was later guaranteed by Britain and Transvaal (later part of South Africa), with Britain assuming control after 1903. Independence came Sept. 6, 1968. In 1973, the king repealed the constitution and assumed full powers.

A new constitution banning political parties took effect Oct. 13, 1978. Under a revised constitution effective Feb. 8, 2006, nonpartisan parliamentary elections were held Sept. 19, 2008. The AIDS crisis and the huge gap between rich and poor have fueled student and labor unrest in recent years.

Sweden
Kingdom of Sweden

People: Population: 9,088,728. **Age distrib.:** <15: 15.4%; 65+: 19.7%. **Pop. density:** 57.4 per sq mi, 22.1 per sq km. **Urban:** 84.7%. **Ethnic groups:** Swedes; foreign-born or immigrant Finns, Yugoslavs, Danes, Norwegians, Greeks, Turks. **Principal language:** Swedish (official). **Chief religions:** Lutheran 87%, other (incl. Roman Catholic, Orthodox, Baptist, Muslim, Jewish, Buddhist) 13%.

Geography: Total area: 173,860 sq mi, 450,295 sq km; **Land area:** 158,431 sq mi, 410,335 sq km. **Location:** On Scandinavian Peninsula in N Europe. **Neighbors:** Norway on W, Denmark on S (across Kattegat), Finland on E. **Topography:** Mountains along NW border cover 25% of Sweden, flat or rolling terrain covers central and southern areas, which include several large lakes. **Capital:** Stockholm, 1,285,387.

Government: Type: Constitutional monarchy. **Head of state:** King Carl XVI Gustaf; b. Apr. 30, 1946; in office: Sept. 19, 1973. **Head of gov.:** Prime Min. Fredrik Reinfeldt; b. Aug. 4, 1965; in office: Oct. 5, 2006. **Local divisions:** 21 counties. **Defense budget:** $5.54 bil. **Active troops:** 13,050.

Economy: Industries: iron and steel, precision equip. (bearings, radio and phone parts, armaments), wood pulp and paper prods., processed foods, motor vehicles. **Chief crops:** barley, wheat, sugar beets. **Natural resources:** iron ore, copper, lead, zinc, gold, silver, tungsten, uranium, arsenic, feldspar, timber, hydropower. **Arable land:** 6.4%. **Livestock:** cattle: 1.5 mil; chickens: 7.2 mil; pigs: 1.5 mil; sheep: 540,487. **Fish catch:** 211,953 metric tons. **Electricity prod.** (2009): 129.4 bil kWh. **Labor force:** agric. 1.1%, industry 28.2%, services 70.7%.

Finance: Monetary unit: Krona (SEK) (Sept. 2011: 6.46 = $1 U.S.). **GDP:** $354.7 bil; **per capita GDP:** $39,100; **GDP growth:** 5.5%. **Imports:** $158.6 bil; Germany 18%, Denmark 8.9%, Norway 8.7%, Netherlands 6.1%, UK 5.5%, Finland 5.2%, France 5%, China 4.8%. **Exports:** $162.6 bil; Norway 10.6%, Germany 10.2%, UK 7.4%, Denmark 7.3%, Finland 6.4%, U.S. 6.4%, France 5%, Netherlands 4.7%. **Tourism:** $11.1 bil. **Budget:** $236.6 bil. **Total reserves less gold:** $42.6 bil. **Gold:** 4 mil oz t. **CPI change:** 1.2%.

Transport: Railways: 7,228 mi. **Motor vehicles:** 533 vehicles per 1,000 pop. **Civil aviation:** 5.6 bil pass.-mi; 152 airports. **Chief ports:** Brofjorden, Göteborg, Helsingborg, Lulea, Malmö, Stockholm, Trelleborg, Visby.

Communications: TV sets: 551 per 1,000 pop. **Radios:** 931 per 1,000 pop. **Telephone lines:** 53.5 per 100 pop. **Daily newspaper circ.:** 480.6 per 1,000 pop. **Internet:** 90 users per 100 pop.

Health: Life expect.: 78.8 male; 83.5 female. **Births:** 10.2 (per 1,000 pop.). **Deaths:** 10.2 (per 1,000 pop.). **Natural inc.:** 0%. **Infant mortality:** 2.7 (per 1,000 live births). **HIV rate:** 0.1%.

Education: Compulsory: ages 7-16. **Literacy:** 99%.

Major intl. organizations: UN and all of its specialized agencies, EU, OECD, OSCE, WTO.

Embassy: 2900 K St. NW 20007; 467-2600.

Website: www.sweden.se

The Swedes have lived in present-day Sweden for at least 5,000 years, longer than nearly any other European people. Gothic tribes from Sweden played a major role in the disintegration of the Roman Empire. Other Swedes helped create the first Russian state in the 9th cent.

The Swedes were Christianized from the 11th cent., and a strong centralized monarchy developed. A parliament, the Riksdag, was first called in 1435, the earliest parliament on the European continent, with all classes of society represented.

Swedish independence from rule by Danish kings (dating from 1397) was secured by Gustavus I in a revolt, 1521-23; he built up the government and military and established the Lutheran Church. In the 17th cent. Sweden was a major European power, gaining most of the Baltic seacoast, but its international position subsequently declined. The Napoleonic wars, 1799-1815, in which Sweden acquired Norway (it became independent 1905), were the last in which Sweden participated. Armed neutrality was maintained in both world wars.

Social Democrats have governed Sweden for most of the period since World War II. Prime Min. Olof Palme was shot to death in Stockholm, Feb. 28, 1986. Accused of murdering Palme, Christer Pettersson was found guilty in 1988 and sentenced to life in prison, but his conviction was overturned on appeal the following year.

Swedish voters approved membership in the European Union Nov. 13, 1994, and Sweden entered the EU as of Jan. 1, 1995. Foreign Min. Anna Lindh died Sept. 11, 2003, after being stabbed in a Stockholm department store.

A center-right alliance led by Fredrik Reinfeldt defeated the Social Democrats in the elections of Sept. 17, 2006. Parliament voted Apr. 1, 2009, to legalize same-sex marriage. The global recession of 2008-09 led to a steep drop in orders for Swedish exports, especially cars and trucks, but the economy began to recover in mid-2009. Reinfeldt's center-right bloc won a renewed mandate in parliamentary elections Sept. 19, 2010.

Switzerland
Swiss Confederation

People: Population: 7,639,961. **Age distrib.:** <15: 15.2%; 65+: 17%. **Pop. density:** 494.7 per sq mi, 191 per sq km. **Urban:** 73.6%. **Ethnic groups:** German 65%, French 18%, Italian 10%, Romansch 1%. **Principal languages:** German, French, Italian, Romansch (all official); Serbo-Croatian; Albanian; Portuguese; Spanish; English. **Chief religions:** Roman Catholic 42%, Protestant 35%, Muslim 4%, Orthodox 2%, none 11%.

Geography: Total area: 15,937 sq mi, 41,277 sq km; **Land area:** 15,443 sq mi, 39,997 sq km. **Location:** In Alps Mts. in central Europe. **Neighbors:** France on W; Italy on S; Liechtenstein, Austria on E; Germany on N. **Topography:** The Alps cover 60% of land area; the Jura, near France, 10%. Running between, NE-SW, are midlands, 30%. **Capital:** Bern, 346,000. **Cities (urban aggl.):** Zurich, 1,150,163.

Government: Type: Federal republic. **Head of state and gov.:** 7-member Federal Council with a president chosen on a rotating basis to a nonrenewable 1-year term. Micheline Calmy-Rey, b. July 8, 1945, was named Jan. 1, 2011. **Local divisions:** 20 full cantons, 6 half cantons. **Defense budget:** $4.57 bil. **Active troops:** 25,620.

Economy: Industries: machinery, chemicals, watches, textiles, precision instruments, tourism, banking, insurance. **Chief crops:** grains, fruits, vegetables. **Natural resources:** hydropower potential, timber, salt. **Arable land:** 10.2%. **Livestock:** cattle: 1.6 mil; chickens: 8.7 mil; goats: 85,131; pigs: 1.6 mil; sheep: 431,889. **Fish catch:** 2,931 metric tons. **Electricity prod.** (2009): 64.1 bil kWh. **Labor force:** agric. 3.4%, industry 23.4%, services 73.2%.

Finance: Monetary unit: Franc (CHF) (Sept. 2011: 0.86 = $1 U.S.). **GDP:** $324.5 bil; **per capita GDP:** $42,600; **GDP growth:** 2.6%. **Imports:** $226.3 bil; Germany 32.6%, Italy 10.7%, France 9.3%, U.S. 5.8%, Netherlands 4.5%, Austria 4.3%. **Exports:** $232.6 bil; Germany 19.3%, U.S. 10.1%, Italy 8.4%, France 8.4%, UK 5%. **Tourism:** $14.8 bil. **Budget** (2011 est.): $192.7 bil (incl. federal, cantonal, and municipal accounts). **Total reserves less gold:** $223.5 bil. **Gold:** 33.4 mil oz t. **CPI change:** 0.7%.

Transport: Railways: 3,030 mi. **Motor vehicles:** 577.1 vehicles per 1,000 pop. **Civil aviation:** 18.4 bil pass.-mi; 42 airports. **Chief port:** Basel.

Communications: TV sets: 594 per 1,000 pop. **Radios:** 1,004 per 1,000 pop. **Telephone lines:** 58.6 per 100 pop. **Daily newspaper circ.:** 420 per 1,000 pop. **Internet:** 83.9 users per 100 pop.

Health: Life expect.: 78.2 male; 84.1 female. **Births:** 9.5 (per 1,000 pop.). **Deaths:** 8.7 (per 1,000 pop.). **Natural inc.:** 0.08%. **Infant mortality:** 4.1 (per 1,000 live births) **HIV rate:** 0.4%.

Education: Compulsory: ages 7-15. **Literacy:** 99%.

Major intl. organizations: UN and most of its specialized agencies, EFTA, OECD, OSCE, WTO.

Embassy: 2900 Cathedral Ave. NW 20008; 745-7900.

Website: www.ch.ch

Switzerland, the former Roman province of Helvetia, traces its modern history to 1291, when 3 cantons created a defensive league. Other cantons were subsequently admitted to the Swiss Confederation, which obtained its independence from the Holy Roman Empire through the Peace of Westphalia (1648). The cantons were joined under a federal constitution in 1848.

Switzerland has maintained an armed neutrality since 1815 and has not been involved in a foreign war since 1515. It is the seat of many UN and other international agencies but did not become a full member of the UN until Sept. 10, 2002.

Switzerland is a world banking center. Stung by charges that assets seized by the Nazis and deposited in Swiss banks in WWII had not been properly returned, the government announced, Mar. 5, 1997, a $4.7 bil fund to compensate victims of the Holocaust and other catastrophes. Swiss banks agreed Aug. 12, 1998, to pay $1.25 bil in reparations. Abortion was decriminalized by a June 2, 2002 referendum. In referendums June 5 and Sept. 25, 2005, voters backed plans harmonizing travel, asylum, law enforcement, and labor policies with the EU; more rights for same-sex couples were also endorsed June 5.

The Swiss government responded to an international financial crisis in Oct. 2008 by bailing out the troubled banking giant UBS. Bowing to pressure from U.S. tax authorities, UBS agreed in Jan. 2009 to close some 19,000 hidden offshore accounts, and pledged Aug. 19 to disclose data on accounts held by over 4,400 U.S. clients. In a referendum Nov. 29, 2009, that reflected rising anti-Muslim sentiment, 57.5% of voters approved a constitutional ban on construction of new minarets or mosques. After Japan's nuclear disaster, Mar. 2011, Switzerland approved a plan to phase out its five nuclear reactors by 2034.

Syria
Syrian Arab Republic

People: Population: 22,517,750. **Age distrib.:** <15: 35.2%; 65+: 3.8%. **Pop. density:** 317.6 per sq mi, 122.6 per sq km. **Urban:** 55.7%. **Ethnic groups:** Arab 90%; Kurds, Armenians, & other 10%. **Principal languages:** Arabic (official), Kurdish, Armenian, Aramaic, Circassian widely understood. **Chief religions:** Sunni Muslim 74%, other Muslim (incl. Alawite, Druze) 16%, Christian 10%.

Geography: Total area: 71,498 sq mi, 185,180 sq km; **Land area:** 70,900 sq mi, 183,630 sq km. **Location:** Middle East, at E end of Medit. Sea. **Neighbors:** Lebanon, Israel on W; Jordan on S; Iraq on E; Turkey on N. **Topography:** Syria has a short Medit. coastline, then stretches E and S with fertile lowlands and plains, alternating with mountains and large desert areas. **Capital:** Damascus, 2,597,093. **Cities (urban aggl.):** Aleppo (Halab), 3,086,729; Hims (Homs), 1,327,865.

Government: Type: Republic (under military regime). **Head of state:** Pres. Bashar al-Assad; b. Sept. 11, 1965; in office: July 17, 2000. **Head of gov.:** Prime Min. Adel Safar; b. 1953; in office: Apr. 14, 2011. **Local divisions:** 14 provinces. **Defense budget:** $1.89 bil. **Active troops:** 295,000.

Economy: Industries: petroleum, textiles, food proc., beverages, tobacco, phosphate rock mining, cement. **Chief crops:** wheat, barley, cotton, lentils, chickpeas, olives, sugar beets. **Natural resources:** petroleum, phosphates, chrome and manganese ores, asphalt, iron ore, rock salt, marble, gypsum, hydropower. **Crude oil reserves:** 2.5 bil bbls. **Arable land:** 25.4%. **Livestock:** cattle: 1.1 mil; chickens: 24.5 mil; goats: 1.5 mil; sheep: 21.7 mil. **Fish catch:** 15,304 metric tons. **Electricity prod.:** 38.7 bil kWh. **Labor force:** agric. 17%, industry 16%, services 67%.

Finance: Monetary unit: Pound (SYP) (Sept. 2011: 47.35 = $1 U.S.). **GDP:** $107.4 bil; **per capita GDP:** $4,800; **GDP growth:** 3.2%. **Imports:** $13.6 bil; China 10.8%, Saudi Arabia 10.1%, Turkey 7%, UAE 5%, Italy 4.9%, South Korea 4.7%, Germany 4.5%, Russia 4.2%, Lebanon 4.1%, Egypt 4.1%. **Exports:** $12.8 bil; Iraq 31.4%, Lebanon 12.7%, Germany 9.2%, Saudi Arabia 5.2%, Italy 4.7%. **Tourism:** $3.8 bil. **Budget:** $15.3 bil. **Total reserves less gold:** $19.5 bil. **Gold:** 830,000 oz t. **CPI change:** 4.4%.

Transport: Railways: 1,275 mi. **Motor vehicles:** 27.3 vehicles per 1,000 pop. **Civil aviation:** 1.6 bil pass.-mi; 29 airports. **Chief ports:** Latakia, Tartus.

Communications: TV sets: 192 per 1,000 pop. **Radios:** 267 per 1,000 pop. **Telephone lines:** 19.9 per 100 pop. **Internet:** 20.7 users per 100 pop.

Health: Life expect.: 72.3 male; 77.2 female. **Births:** 24 (per 1,000 pop.). **Deaths:** 3.7 (per 1,000 pop.). **Natural inc.:** 2.03%. **Infant mortality:** 15.6 (per 1,000 live births). **HIV rate:** NA.

Education: Compulsory: ages 6-14. **Literacy:** 84.2%.

Major intl. organizations: UN (FAO, IBRD, ILO, IMF, WHO), AL, WTO (observer).

Embassy: 2215 Wyoming Ave. NW 20008; 232-6313.

Website: parliament.sy

Syria was the center of the Seleucid empire, but later became absorbed in the Roman and Arab empires. Ottoman rule prevailed for 4 cents., until the end of WWI.

The state of Syria was formed from former Turkish districts, separated by the Treaty of Sevres, 1920, and divided into the states of Syria and Greater Lebanon. Both were administered under a French League of Nations mandate, 1920-41. Syria was proclaimed a republic by the occupying French Sept. 16, 1941, and exercised full independence Apr. 17, 1946. Syria joined the Arab invasion of Israel in 1948.

Syria joined Egypt Feb. 1958 in the United Arab Republic but seceded Sept. 1961. The Socialist Baath party and military leaders seized power Mar. 1963. The Baath, a pan-Arab organization, became the only legal party. The government has been dominated by the Alawite minority.

In the Arab-Israeli war of June 1967, Israel seized and occupied the Golan Heights, from which Syria had shelled Israeli settlements. On Oct. 6, 1973, Syria participated with Egypt in an attack on Israel, but failed to recapture the Golan Heights. Syrian troops entered Lebanon in 1976, during the Lebanese civil war, and remained a strong presence in the country. They fought Palestinian guerrillas and, later, Christian militiamen. Syria sided with Iran during the Iran-Iraq war, 1980-88.

Thousands died in the city of Hama Feb. 1982 when government forces crushed an uprising by the Muslim Brotherhood. Following Israel's invasion of Lebanon, June 6, 1982, Israeli planes destroyed 17 Syrian antiaircraft missile batteries in the Bekaa Valley, June 9. Some 25 Syrian planes were downed during the engagement. Israel and Syria agreed to a cease-fire June 11. Syria's alleged role in promoting international terrorism led to strained relations with the U.S. and Great Britain.

Syria condemned the Aug. 1990 Iraqi invasion of Kuwait and sent troops to help Allied forces in the Gulf War. In 1991, Syria accepted U.S. proposals for the terms of an Arab-Israeli peace conference. Syria subsequently participated in negotiations with Israel, but little progress was made.

Hafez al-Assad, president of Syria since 1971, died June 10, 2000, and was succeeded by his son Bashar al-Assad. Following the U.S.-led invasion of Iraq, Mar. 2003, hundreds of thousands of Iraqi refugees flooded into Syria. The U.S. pressured Syria to rein in extremists and deny safe haven to fugitive Iraqi leaders. Israeli planes hit an alleged terrorist camp near Damascus Oct. 4, 2003. The U.S. imposed limited sanctions on Syria, May 11, 2004.

The killing of former Lebanese Prime Min. Rafik al-Hariri by a truck bomb in Beirut, Feb. 14, 2005, was a catalyst for massive anti-Syrian protests in Lebanon. Syria denied responsibility for the blast but pulled nearly all its troops out of Lebanon by Apr. 26; some Syrian intelligence agents may have remained. Syria aided Hezbollah fighters in their conflict with Israel. When Israeli armed forces struck Lebanon, July-Aug. 2006, in an effort to cripple Hezbollah, about 180,000 Lebanese found temporary refuge in Syria. Four suspected Islamic militants stormed the U.S. embassy in Damascus Sept. 12 but were gunned down by Syrian security guards.

In an uncontested referendum, May 27, 2007, Syrian voters confirmed Pres. Bashar al-Assad for another 7-year term. On Sept. 6, Israel bombed a secret site in N Syria where the Israelis reportedly believed Syria and North Korea were developing a nuclear facility; both countries denied the claim. Beginning Mar. 2011, the Baathist government faced its most serious challenge in decades, as "Arab Spring" protesters staged mass demonstrations in many cities. The Assad regime used troops and tanks to enforce control in Deraa, Homs, Hama, and elsewhere. The U.S. and European Union toughened sanctions against Syria, Arab states also applied pressure, with Saudi King Abdullah on Aug. 8 telling the Syrian government to stop "the killing machine"; 10 days later, U.S. Pres. Obama called on Assad to step down.

Taiwan

People: Population: 23,071,779. **Age distrib.:** <15: 15.6%; 65+: 10.9%. **Pop. density:** 1,852.3 per sq mi, 715.2 per sq km. **Urban:** NA. **Ethnic groups:** Taiwanese (incl. Hakka) 84%, mainland Chinese 14%, indigenous 2%. **Principal languages:** Mandarin Chinese (official), Taiwanese (Min), Hakka dialects. **Chief religions:** mixture of Buddhist & Taoist 93%, Christian 5%.

Geography: Total area: 13,892 sq mi, 35,980 sq km; **Land area:** 12,456 sq mi, 32,260 sq km. **Location:** Off SE coast of China, between E and S China seas. **Neighbors:** Nearest is

China to NW. **Topography:** A mountain range forms backbone of island; the eastern half is very steep and craggy, western slope is flat, fertile, and well cultivated. **Capital:** Taipei, 2,630,000. **Cities (urban aggl.):** Kaohsiung, 1,598,000; Taichung, 1,221,000.

Government: Type: Democracy. **Head of state:** Pres. Ma Ying-jeou; b. July 13, 1950; in office: May 20, 2008. **Head of gov.:** Prime Min. Wu Den-yih; b. Jan. 30, 1948; in office: Sept. 10, 2009. **Local divisions:** 16 counties, 5 municipalities, 2 special municipalities (Taipei, Kaohsiung). **Defense budget:** $9.3 bil. **Active troops:** 290,000.

Economy: Industries: electronics, comm. and info. tech. prods., petroleum refining, armaments, chemicals, textiles, iron and steel, machinery, cement, food proc., vehicles, consumer prods., pharmaceuticals. **Chief crops:** rice, vegetables, fruits, tea, flowers. **Natural resources:** small deposits of coal, nat. gas, limestone, marble, asbestos. **Crude oil reserves:** 2.4 mil bbls. **Arable land:** 24%. **Fish catch:** 1.1 mil metric tons. **Electricity prod.:** 221.4 bil kWh. **Labor force:** agric. 5.2%, industry 35.9%, services 58.8%.

Finance: Monetary unit: New Dollar (TWD) (Sept. 2011: 29.11 = $1 U.S.). **GDP:** $821.8 bil; **per capita GDP:** $35,700; **GDP growth:** 10.8%. **Imports:** $251.4 bil; Japan 20.7%, China 14.2%, U.S. 10%, South Korea 6.4%, Saudi Arabia 4.7%. **Exports:** $274.6 bil; China 28.1%, Hong Kong 13.8%, U.S. 11.5%, Japan 6.6%, Singapore 4.4%. **Tourism:** $8.6 bil. **Budget:** $79.7 bil. **Total reserves less gold:** NA. **CPI change:** NA.

Transport: Railways: 982 mi. **Motor vehicles:** 294.4 vehicles per 1,000 pop. **Civil aviation:** 38 airports. **Chief ports:** Chilung, Hualian, Kaohsiung, Taichung.

Communications: TV sets: 444 per 1,000 pop. **Radios:** 178 per 1,000 pop. **Telephone lines:** 70.8 per 100 pop. **Internet:** 71.5 users per 100 pop.

Health: Life expect.: 75.5 male; 81.4 female. **Births:** 8.9 (per 1,000 pop.). **Deaths:** 7 (per 1,000 pop.). **Natural inc.:** 0.19%. **Infant mortality:** 5.2 (per 1,000 live births). **HIV rate:** NA.

Education: Compulsory: ages 6-14. **Literacy:** 96.1%.

Major intl. organizations: APEC, WTO.

Taipei Economic and Cultural Representative Office: 4201 Wisconsin Ave. NW 20016; 895-1800.

Website: www.taiwan.gov.tw

Large-scale Chinese immigration began in the 17th cent. The island came under mainland control after an interval of Dutch rule, 1620-62. Taiwan (also called Formosa) was ruled by Japan 1895-1945. The Kuomintang (Chinese nationalist govt.) fled to Taiwan in 1949 and established the Republic of China under Chiang Kai-shek, who ruled until his death in 1975. The U.S. provided military aid to deter a Communist invasion.

In 1971, the UN expelled Taiwan from its seat and recognized the mainland government. The U.S. officially recognized the People's Republic, Dec. 15, 1978, and severed ties with Taiwan. However, the U.S. and Taiwan have continued a strong trading relationship and maintain contact via quasi-official agencies.

Land reform, government planning, U.S. aid and investment, and free universal education brought huge advances in industry, agriculture, and living standards. In 1987 martial law was lifted after 38 years, and in 1991 the 43-year period of emergency rule ended. Taiwan held its first direct presidential election Mar. 23, 1996. An earthquake on Sept. 21, 1999, killed more than 2,300 people and injured thousands more.

Five decades of Nationalist Party rule ended with the presidential election of Mar. 18, 2000, won by Chen Shui-bian, leader of the pro-independence Democratic Progressive Party. Chen was wounded in an apparent assassination attempt Mar. 19, 2004, one day before he narrowly won a 2nd term as president. Promising increased cooperation with China, Taipei Mayor Ma Ying-jeou, candidate of the opposition Kuomintang, won the presidential election Mar. 22, 2008.

Jailed on corruption charges Nov. 12, 2008, former Pres. Chen Shui-bian was convicted and sentenced to life in prison, Sept. 11, 2009. Flooding and mudslides from Typhoon Morakot, Aug. 7-9, left at least 700 people dead or missing; criticism of the government's disaster response led to a cabinet shake-up a month later. Former Pres. Lee Teng-hui, who introduced democratic reforms 1988-2000, was indicted June 30, 2011, for allegedly embezzling $7.8 mil while in office.

Since 1949, the People's Republic has considered Taiwan a rebel province of the mainland; until 1991, Taiwan claimed to be the sole government of both. In 2003, China replaced the U.S. as Taiwan's leading trade partner. China has warned that any Taiwan move toward independence could provoke military action.

The **Penghu Isls.** (Pescadores), 49 sq mi, pop. (2011 est.) 96,597, lie between Taiwan and the mainland. **Kinmen,** fmr. **Quemoy,** pop. (2011 est.) 99,691, and **Matsu,** pop. (2006 est.) 9,786, lie just off the mainland.

Tajikistan
Republic of Tajikistan

People: Population: 7,627,200. **Age distrib.:** <15: 33.9%; 65+: 3.4%. **Pop. density:** 139.6 per sq mi, 53.9 per sq km. **Urban:** 26.3%. **Ethnic groups:** Tajik 80%, Uzbek 15%, Russian 1%, Kyrgyz 1%. **Principal languages:** Tajik (official), Russian widely used in govt. & business. **Chief religions:** Sunni Muslim 85%, Shi'a Muslim 5%.

Geography: Total area: 55,251 sq mi, 143,100 sq km; **Land area:** 54,637 sq mi, 141,510 sq km. **Location:** Central Asia. **Neighbors:** Uzbekistan on N and W, Kyrgyzstan on N, China on E, Afghanistan on S. **Topography:** Mountainous region that contains the Pamirs, Trans-Alai mountain system. **Capital:** Dushanbe, 704,000.

Government: Type: Republic. **Head of state:** Pres. Imomali Rakhmon; b. Oct. 5, 1952; in office: Nov. 6, 1994. **Head of gov.:** Prime Min. Akil Akilov; b. Feb. 2, 1944; in office: Dec. 20, 1999. **Local divisions:** 2 viloyats, 1 autonomous viloyat. **Defense budget:** $84 mil. **Active troops:** 8,800.

Economy: Industries: aluminum, cement, vegetable oil. **Chief crops:** cotton, grain, fruits, grapes, vegetables. **Natural resources:** hydropower, petroleum, uranium, mercury, brown coal, lead, zinc, antimony, tungsten, silver, gold. **Crude oil reserves:** 12 mil bbls. **Arable land:** 5.3%. **Livestock:** cattle: 1.8 mil; chickens: 3.7 mil; goats: 1.6 mil; pigs: 483; sheep: 2.6 mil. **Fish catch:** 401 metric tons. **Electricity prod.:** 16 bil kWh. **Labor force:** agric. 49.8%, industry 12.8%, services 37.4%.

Finance: Monetary unit: Somoni (TJS) (Sept. 2011: 4.76 = $1 U.S.). **GDP:** $14.7 bil; **per capita GDP:** $2,000; **GDP growth:** 6.5%. **Imports:** $3.3 bil; Russia 31.7%, Kazakhstan 11.1%, China 10.6%, Uzbekistan 5%, Ukraine 4.6%. **Exports:** $1.3 bil; China 40.2%, Turkey 15.1%, Russia 10.2%, Uzbekistan 7.1%, Iran 4.8%. **Tourism:** NA. **Budget:** $1.5 bil. **Total reserves less gold (2006)** $175.1 mil. **Gold:** 56,150 oz t. **CPI change:** 6.4%.

Transport: Railways: 423 mi. **Civil aviation:** 1.1 bil pass.-mi; 17 airports.

Communications: TV sets: 386 per 1,000 pop. **Radios:** 398 per 1,000 pop. **Telephone lines:** 5.4 per 100 pop. **Internet:** 11.6 users per 100 pop.

Health: Life expect.: 63 male; 69.3 female. **Births:** 26.3 (per 1,000 pop.). **Deaths:** 6.6 (per 1,000 pop.). **Natural inc.:** 1.97%. **Infant mortality:** 38.5 (per 1,000 live births). **HIV rate:** 0.2%.

Education: Compulsory: ages 7-15. **Literacy:** 99.7%.

Major International Organizations: UN (FAO, IBRD, ILO, IMF, WHO), CIS, OSCE, WTO (observer).

Embassy: 1005 New Hampshire Ave. NW 20037; 223-6090.

Website: www.parlament.tj

There were settled societies in the region from about 3000 BCE. Invaders have included Iranians, Arabs (who converted the population to Islam), Mongols, Uzbeks, Afghans, and Russians. The USSR gained control 1918-25. The region then was part of the Uzbek SSR until the Tajik SSR was proclaimed in 1929.

Tajikistan declared independence Sept. 9, 1991. Factional fighting led to the installation of a pro-Communist regime, Jan. 1993. A new constitution establishing a presidential system was approved by referendum Nov. 6, 1994.

Clashes between Muslim rebels, reportedly armed by Afghanistan, and troops loyal to the government (and supported by Russia) claimed an estimated 55,000 lives by mid-1997, despite a series of peace accords. Constitutional changes including legalization of Islamic political parties were approved by referendum Sept. 26, 1999. Pres. Imomali Rakhmonov won a Nov. 6 election called "a farce" by human-rights observers. Voters approved, June 22, 2003, constitutional changes giving Rakhmonov the right to serve as president until 2020. Leading opposition groups boycotted the election of Nov. 6, 2006, again won by Rakhmonov. He changed his name to Rakhmon in 2007 under a decree that banned Slavic name endings and other Soviet-era practices.

Poverty and corruption are widespread. Much of the nation's income is supplied by international donors and by remittances from young Tajiks working in Russia and Kazakhstan.

Tanzania
United Republic of Tanzania

People: Population: 42,746,620. **Age distrib.:** <15: 42%; 65+: 2.9%. **Pop. density:** 125 per sq mi, 48.3 per sq km. **Urban:** 26.4%. **Ethnic groups:** African 99% (Bantu 95%, 130+ tribes); other 1%. **Principal languages:** Kiswahili/Swahili, English primary language of commerce, admin., higher ed. (both official); Arabic widely spoken in Zanzibar; local languages. **Chief religions:** Christian 30%, Muslim 35%, indigenous beliefs 35%; 99%+ Muslim on Zanzibar.

Geography: Total area: 365,755 sq mi, 947,300 sq km; **Land area:** 342,009 sq mi, 885,800 sq km. **Location:** On coast of E Africa. **Neighbors:** Kenya, Uganda on N; Rwanda, Burundi, Congo on W; Zambia, Malawi, Mozambique on S. **Topography:** Hot, arid central plateau, surrounded by lake region in W, temperate highlands in N and S, the coastal plains. Mt. Kilimanjaro, 19,340 ft, is highest in Africa. **Capital:** Dodoma, 200,000 (planned new capital; legis. and National Assembly currently meet here); Dar es Salaam, 3,349,134.

Government: Type: Republic. **Head of state and gov.:** Pres. Jakaya Mrisho Kikwete; b. Oct. 7, 1950; in office: Dec. 21, 2005. **Local divisions:** 25 regions. **Defense budget (2008):** $183 mil. **Active troops:** 27,000.

Economy: Industries: agric. proc.; diamond, gold, iron mining; salt; soda ash; cement; oil refining; shoes; apparel. **Chief crops:** coffee, sisal, tea, cotton, pyrethrum (insecticide made from chrysanthemums), cashews, tobacco, cloves, corn, wheat. **Natural resources:**

hydropower, tin, phosphates, iron ore, coal, diamonds, gems, gold, nat. gas, nickel. **Arable land:** 11.3%. **Livestock:** cattle: 19.1 mil; chickens: 30 mil; goats: 12.6 mil; pigs: 455,000; sheep: 3.6 mil. **Fish catch:** 321,151 metric tons. **Electricity prod.:** 4.3 bil kWh. **Labor force:** agric. 80%, industry and services 20%.

Finance: Monetary unit: Shilling (TZS) (Sept. 2011: 1,625.50 = $1 U.S.). **GDP:** $58.4 bil; **per capita GDP:** $1,400; **GDP growth:** 6.5%. **Imports:** $6.3 bil; China 15.5%, India 15%, South Africa 7.6%, Kenya 6.7%, UAE 4.5%, Japan 4.2%. **Exports:** $3.8 bil; India 12.1%, China 9.4%, Japan 6.7%, Netherlands 5.9%, UAE 5.4%, Germany 4.9%. **Tourism:** $1.3 bil. **Budget:** $5.6 bil. **Total reserves less gold:** $3.9 bil. **CPI change:** 6.2%.

Transport: Railways: 2,292 mi. **Motor vehicles:** 1.9 vehicles per 1,000 pop. **Civil aviation:** 245.4 mil pass.-mi; 9 airports. **Chief ports:** Dar es Salaam, Zanzibar.

Communications: TV sets: 41 per 1,000 pop. **Radios:** 352 per 1,000 pop. **Telephone lines:** 0.4 per 100 pop. **Daily newspaper circ.:** 1.6 per 1,000 pop. **Internet:** 11 users per 100 pop.

Health: Life expect.: 51.3 male; 54.4 female. **Births:** 32.6 (per 1,000 pop.). **Deaths:** 12.1 (per 1,000 pop.). **Natural inc.:** 2.06%. **Infant mortality:** 66.9 (per 1,000 live births). **HIV rate:** 5.6%.

Education: Compulsory: ages 7-13. **Literacy:** 72.9%.

Major intl. organizations: UN and all of its specialized agencies, AU, the Commonwealth, WTO.

Embassy: 2139 R St. NW 20008; 939-6125.

Website: www.tanzania.go.tz

The Republic of Tanganyika in E Africa and the island Republic of Zanzibar, off Tanganyika's coast, both of which had recently gained independence, joined to form the United Republic of Tanzania, Apr. 26, 1964. Zanzibar retains internal self-government.

Until resigning as president in 1985, Julius K. Nyerere, a former Tanganyikan independence leader, dominated Tanzania's politics, which emphasized government planning and control of the economy, with single-party rule. In 1992 the constitution was amended to establish a multiparty system. Privatization of the economy was undertaken in the 1990s.

At least 500 people died when an overcrowded Tanzanian ferry sank in Lake Victoria, May 21, 1996. A bomb at the U.S. embassy in Dar-es-Salaam, Aug. 7, 1998, killed 11 people and injured at least 70 others. The U.S. blamed the attack and a near-simultaneous embassy bombing in Kenya on Islamic terrorists associated with Osama bin Laden.

President since 1995, Benjamin Mkapa was reelected Oct. 29, 2000. Over 280 people died in a train wreck June 24, 2002, SE of Dodoma. Jakaya Mrisho Kikwete of the ruling Chama Cha Mapinduzi (Party of the Revolution) won the Dec. 14, 2005, presidential election; he was reelected to a 2nd 5-year term Oct. 31, 2010.

Tanganyika. Arab colonization and slaving began in the 8th cent. CE; Portuguese sailors explored the coast by about 1500. Other Europeans followed.

In 1885 Germany established German East Africa, of which Tanganyika formed the bulk. It became a League of Nations mandate and, after 1946, a UN trust territory, both under Britain. It became independent Dec. 9, 1961, and a republic within the Commonwealth a year later.

Zanzibar. The Isle of Cloves, lies 23 mi off mainland Tanzania; area 640 sq mi and pop. (2002) 622,459. The island of **Pemba**, 25 mi to the NE, area 380 sq mi and pop. (2002) 362,166 is included in the administration.

Chief industry is cloves and clove oil production, of which Zanzibar and Pemba produce most of the world's supply.

Zanzibar was for centuries the center for Arab slave traders. Portugal ruled the region for 2 centuries until ousted by Arabs around 1700. Zanzibar became a British Protectorate in 1890; independence came Dec. 10, 1963. Revolutionary forces overthrew the Sultan Jan. 12, 1964. The new government ousted Western diplomats and newsmen, slaughtered thousands of Arabs, and nationalized farms. Union with Tanganyika followed.

Thailand
Kingdom of Thailand

People: Population: 66,720,153. **Age distrib.:** <15: 19.9%; 65+: 9.2%. **Pop. density:** 338.2 per sq mi, 130.6 per sq km. **Urban:** 34%. **Ethnic groups:** Thai 75%, Chinese 14%. **Principal languages:** Thai, English secondary language of elite, ethnic & regional dialects. **Chief religions:** Buddhist 95%, Muslim 5%.

Geography: Total area: 198,117 sq mi, 513,120 sq km; **Land area:** 197,256 sq mi, 510,890 sq km. **Location:** On Indochinese and Malayan peninsulas in SE Asia. **Neighbors:** Myanmar on W and N, Laos on N, Cambodia on E, Malaysia on S. **Topography:** A plateau dominates NE third of Thailand, dropping to the fertile alluvial valley of Chao Phraya R. in center. Forested mountains are in N, with narrow fertile valleys. The S peninsula region is covered by rain forests. **Capital:** Bangkok (Krung Thep), 6,976,471.

Government: Type: Constitutional monarchy. **Head of state:** King Bhumibol Adulyadej; b. Dec. 5, 1927; in office: June 9, 1946. **Head of gov.:** Prime Min. Yingluck Shinawatra; b. June 21, 1967; in office: Aug. 8, 2011. **Local divisions:** 76 provinces. **Defense budget:** $4.81 bil. **Active troops:** 305,860.

Economy: Industries: tourism, textiles and garments, agric. proc., beverages, tobacco, cement, light mfg. (jewelry, elec. appliances, computers and parts, automobiles and auto. parts); world's second-largest tungsten producer and third-largest tin producer. **Chief crops:** rice, cassava, rubber, corn, sugarcane, coconuts, soybeans. **Natural resources:** tin, rubber, nat. gas, tungsten, tantalum, timber, lead, fish, gypsum, lignite, fluorite. **Crude oil reserves:** 435 mil bbls. **Arable land:** 29.9%. **Livestock:** cattle: 6.7 mil; chickens: 228.2 mil; goats: 383,796; pigs: 7.5 mil; sheep: 40,269. **Fish catch:** 3.1 mil metric tons. **Electricity prod.:** 139 bil kWh. **Labor force:** agric. 42.4%, industry 19.7%, services 37.9%.

Finance: Monetary unit: Baht (THB) (Sept. 2011: 29.95 = $1 U.S.). **GDP:** $586.9 bil; **per capita GDP:** $8,700; **GDP growth:** 7.8%. **Imports:** $156.9 bil; Japan 18.7%, China 12.7%, Malaysia 6.4%. **Exports:** $191.3 bil; U.S. 10.9%, China 10.6%, Japan 10.3%. **Tourism:** $19.8 bil. **Budget:** $56.9 bil. **Total reserves less gold:** $167.5 bil. **Gold:** 3.2 mil oz t. **CPI change:** 3.3%.

Transport: Railways: 2,530 mi. **Motor vehicles:** 154.4 vehicles per 1,000 pop. **Civil aviation:** 33.2 bil pass.-mi; 64 airports. **Chief ports:** Bangkok, Laem Chabang, Prachuap Port, Si Racha.

Communication: TV sets: 285 per 1,000 pop. **Radios:** 229 per 1,000 pop. **Telephone lines:** 10.1 per 100 pop. **Internet:** 21.2 users per 100 pop.

Health: Life expect.: 71.2 male; 76.1 female. **Births:** 13 (per 1,000 pop.). **Deaths:** 7.3 (per 1,000 pop.). **Natural inc.:** 0.57%. **Infant mortality:** 16.4 (per 1,000 live births). **HIV rate:** 1.3%.

Education: Compulsory: ages 6-14. **Literacy:** 93.5%.

Major intl. organizations: UN (FAO, IBRD, ILO, IMF, WHO), APEC, ASEAN, WTO.

Embassy: 1024 Wisconsin Ave. NW, Ste. 401, 20007; 944-3600.

Website: www.thaigov.go.th

Thais began migrating from southern China during the 11th cent. A unified Thai kingdom was established in 1350. Known as Siam until 1939, Thailand is the only country in SE Asia never taken over by a European power, thanks to King Mongkut and his son King Chulalongkorn. Ruling successively from 1851 to 1910, they modernized the country and signed trade treaties with Britain and France. A bloodless revolution in 1932 limited the monarchy. Thailand was an ally of Japan during WWII and of the U.S. during the postwar period. For decades, the military had a dominant role in governing the country.

A steep downturn in the economy forced Thailand to seek more than $15 bil in emergency international loans in Aug. 1997. A new constitution won legislative approval Sept. 27. By the end of the 1990s, according to UN estimates, more than 750,000 people in Thailand had HIV/AIDS; a nationwide prevention campaign has reduced the number of new infections.

Following elections in Jan. 2001, Thaksin Shinawatra, a wealthy former telecommunications executive, became prime min. On Feb. 1, 2003, Thaksin launched a nationwide crackdown on methamphetamines; human rights observers criticized police tactics in the drug war, which killed more than 2,200 people by Apr. 30. The Indian Ocean tsunami of Dec. 26, 2004, left about 5,400 people dead and over 2,800 missing in Thailand.

Elections Feb. 6, 2005, gave Thaksin's party a huge majority in parliament. Facing rising opposition and accused of benefiting improperly from the sale of his family's telecom business, Thaksin called snap elections for Apr. 2, 2006, 3 years ahead of schedule; the vote, which major parties boycotted, was later ruled unconstitutional. A military junta took power in a bloodless coup Sept. 19.

Thaksin supporters won elections Dec. 23, 2007, and Samak Sundaravej became prime min. after civilian rule was restored Jan. 22, 2008. After a series of antigovernment protests paralyzed Bangkok, Prime Min. Samak imposed emergency rule Sept. 2. He was ousted a week later by Thailand's Constitutional Court, ostensibly for getting paid to host TV cooking shows while he held public office. Thaksin's brother-in-law Somchai Wongsawat became prime min. Sept. 18, but a Constitutional Court ruling Dec. 2 barred him from politics and dissolved his People Power Party because of electoral fraud.

The political turmoil continued in 2009, as mass protests by Thaksin supporters led the government to postpone a summit meeting of East Asian leaders planned for Pattaya, Apr. 11, and to declare a state of emergency in Bangkok, Apr. 12-24. Meanwhile, about 60,000 security forces in southern Thailand sought to suppress a Muslim insurgency; from Jan. 2004 to Sept. 2009, more than 3,500 people, mostly civilians, died in the fighting.

On Feb. 26, 2010, Thailand's Supreme Court ordered the seizure of about $1.4 bil of Thaksin's family assets. Thaksin supporters, known as Red Shirts, staged mass rallies in Bangkok, and on Apr. 7 a group of Red Shirts stormed the parliament building, leading the government to impose emergency rule in the capital. After the Red Shirts began to build a fortified compound in the heart of Bangkok's business district, a crackdown by Thai security forces May 14-19, 2010, left at least 54 people dead and some 470 injured. After parliamentary elections July 3, 2011, Thaksin's sister, Yingluck Shinawatra, took office as Thailand's first female prime minister.

Timor-Leste
(East Timor)
Democratic Republic of Timor-Leste

People: Population: 1,177,834. **Age distrib.:** <15: 33.8%; 65+: 3.6%. **Pop. density:** 205.1 per sq mi, 79.2 per sq km. **Urban:** 28.1%. **Ethnic groups:** Austronesian (Malayo-Polynesian), Papuan, small

Chinese minority. **Principal languages:** Tetum, Portuguese (both official); Indonesian; English; about 16 indigenous languages (incl. Tetum, Galole, Mambae, Kemak). **Chief religions:** Roman Catholic 98%, Muslim 1%, Protestant 1%.

Geography: Total area: 5,743 sq mi, 14,874 sq km. **Land area:** 5,743 sq mi, 14,874 sq km. **Location:** E half of Timor Isl. in SW Pacific O. **Neighbors:** Indonesia (West Timor) on W. **Topography:** Terrain is rugged, rising to 9,721 ft at Mt. Ramelau. **Capital:** Dili, 166,000.

Government: Type: Republic. **Head of state:** Pres. José Ramos-Horta; b. Dec. 26, 1949; in office: May 20, 2007. **Head of gov.:** Prime Min. Kay Rala Xanana Gusmão; b. June 20, 1946; in office: Aug. 8, 2007. **Local divisions:** 13 districts. **Defense budget:** NA. **Active troops:** 1,332.

Economy: Industries: printing, soap mfg., handicrafts, woven cloth. **Chief crops:** coffee, rice, corn, cassava, sweet potatoes, soybeans. **Natural resources:** gold, petroleum, nat. gas, manganese, marble. **Arable land:** 11.1%. **Livestock:** cattle: 148,000; chickens: 1 mil; goats: 137,500; pigs: 388,000; sheep: 41,500. **Fish catch:** 4,677 metric tons. **Labor force:** agric. 90%, industry and services NA.

Finance: Monetary unit: U.S. Dollar (USD). **GDP:** $3.1 bil; **per capita GDP:** $2,600; **GDP growth:** 6.1%. **Imports** (2004 est.): $202 mil; NA. **Exports** (2005 est.): $10 mil (excl. oil); NA. **Tourism:** NA. **Budget:** $838 mil.**Total reserves less gold:** $406.2 mil. **CPI change:** 6.8%.

Transport: Civil aviation: 2 airports. **Chief port:** Dili.

Communication: Telephone lines: 0.2 per 100 pop. **Internet:** 0.2 users per 100 pop.

Health: Life expect.: 65.5 male; 70.5 female. **Births:** 25.7 (per 1,000 pop.). **Deaths:** 5.9 (per 1,000 pop.). **Natural inc.:** 1.98%. **Infant mortality:** 38 (per 1,000 live births). **HIV rate:** NA.

Education: Compulsory: ages 6-14. **Literacy:** 50.6%.

Major intl. organizations: UN (FAO, IBRD, ILO, IMF, WHO).

Embassy: 4201 Connecticut Ave. NW 20008; 966-3202.

Website: www.timor-leste.gov.tl

The collapse of Portuguese rule in East Timor led to an outbreak of factional fighting in Aug. 1975 and an invasion by Indonesia in Dec. Indonesia annexed East Timor as a 27th province in 1976, despite international condemnation. In over 2 decades some 200,000 Timorese died as a result of civil war, famine, and persecution by Indonesian authorities. In a referendum held Aug. 30, 1999, under UN auspices, Timorese voted overwhelmingly for independence. Pro-Indonesian militias then went on a rampage, terrorizing the population. Under pressure, the government allowed entrance of an international peacekeeping force, which began arriving in Sept.; a UN interim administration formally took command Oct. 26, 1999.

Pro-independence forces won elections for a constituent assembly Aug. 30, 2001. Xanana Gusmão, a former guerrilla leader, won the presidential election Apr. 14, 2002. As Timor-Leste, the territory became independent May 20 and entered the UN Sept. 27. Australia and other nations sent peacekeepers to suppress a wave of gang violence that engulfed Dili in May 2006.

José Ramos-Horta, a Nobel laureate, won a presidential runoff vote May 9, 2007. After inconclusive parliamentary elections June 30, Ramos-Horta ended a political deadlock by choosing Gusmão as prime min. Renegade soldiers shot and seriously wounded Ramos-Horta in a failed coup attempt Feb. 11, 2008.

Togo
Togolese Republic

People: Population: 6,771,993. **Age distrib.:** <15: 40.9%; 65+: 3.1%. **Pop. density:** 322.5 per sq mi, 124.5 per sq km. **Urban:** 43.4%. **Ethnic groups:** African (37 tribes; Ewe, Mina, Kabre largest). **Principal languages:** French (official & lang. of commerce), Ewe & Mina (in S), Kabye & Dagomba (in N). **Chief religions:** Christian 29%, Muslim 20%, indigenous beliefs 51%.

Geography: Total area: 21,925 sq mi, 56,785 sq km; **Land area:** 20,998 sq mi, 54,385 sq km. **Location:** On S coast of W Africa. **Neighbors:** Ghana on W, Burkina Faso on N, Benin on E. **Topography:** A range of hills running SW-NE splits Togo into 2 savanna plains regions. **Capital:** Lomé, 1,667,016.

Government: Type: Republic. **Head of state:** Pres. Faure Gnassingbé; b. June 6, 1966; in office: May 4, 2005. **Head of gov.:** Prime Min. Gilbert Fossoun Houngbo; b. Feb. 4, 1961; in office: Sept. 8, 2008. **Local divisions:** 5 regions. **Defense budget:** (2009) $67 mil. **Active troops:** 8,550.

Economy: Industries: phosphate mining, agric. proc., cement, handicrafts. **Chief crops:** coffee, cocoa, cotton, yams, cassava, corn, beans, rice. **Natural resources:** phosphates, limestone, marble. **Arable land:** 40.4%. **Livestock:** cattle: 378,050; chickens: 18.3 mil; goats: 1.5 mil; pigs: 612,250; sheep: 2.1 mil. **Fish catch:** 27,132 metric tons. **Electricity prod.:** 156.9 mil kWh. **Labor force:** agric. 65%, industry 5%, services 30%.

Finance: Monetary unit: CFA BCEAO Franc (XOF) (Sept. 2011: 468.55 = $1 U.S.). **GDP:** $5.97 bil; **per capita GDP:** $900; **GDP growth:** 3.4%. **Imports:** $1.3 bil; China 17.1%, France 12.9%, Finland 9.9%, Netherlands 5.4%, Belgium 4.5%, Ghana 4.5%, Côte d'Ivoire 4%. **Exports:** $859 mil; India 13.6%, Benin 12.6%, Ghana 12.5%, Burkina Faso 11.7%, China 8.9%, Nigeria 6.1%, Niger 6%, Malaysia 4.4%. **Tourism:** $68 mil. **Budget:** $692.1 mil. **Total reserves less gold:** $714.9 mil. **CPI change:** 1.8%.

Transport: Railways: 353 mi. **Motor vehicles:** 24.2 vehicles per 1,000 pop. **Civil aviation:** 2 airports. **Chief ports:** Kpeme, Lomé.

Communications: TV sets: 26 per 1,000 pop. **Radios:** 669 per 1,000 pop. **Telephone lines:** 3.6 per 100 pop. **Internet:** 5.4 users per 100 pop.

Health: Life expect.: 60.2 male; 65.3 female. **Births:** 35.6 (per 1,000 pop.). **Deaths:** 8 (per 1,000 pop.) **Natural inc.:** 2.76%. **Infant mortality:** 51.5 (per 1,000 live births). **HIV rate:** 3.2%.

Education: Compulsory: ages 6-15. **Literacy:** 56.9%.

Major intl. organizations: UN (FAO, IBRD, ILO, IMF, WHO), AU, WTO.

Embassy: 2208 Massachusetts Ave. NW 20008; 234-4212.

Website: www.assemblee-nationale.tg or www.state.gov/p/af/ci/to/

Togoland was administered by Germany and then by France and Britain. The French sector became the republic of Togo Apr. 27, 1960. In office since 1967, Pres. Gnassingbé Eyadéma was Africa's longest-serving head of state until his death Feb. 5, 2005. His son, Faure Gnassingbé, was immediately installed as president, but other African leaders pressured Togo to hold an election, which Gnassingbé won Apr. 24. Opposition parties disputed the result, and protests led to violent clashes in Lomé.

After a shootout at his home Apr. 12, 2009, former Defense Min. Kpatcha Gnassingbé, the president's brother, sought refuge Apr. 15 at the U.S. embassy in Lomé; denied asylum, he was arrested by Togolese authorities and accused of plotting a coup. Pres. Gnassingbé won reelection Mar. 4, 2010, to a 2nd 5-year term.

Tonga
Kingdom of Tonga

People: Population: 105,916. **Age distrib.:** <15: 37.2%; 65+: 6.1%. **Pop. density:** 382.6 per sq mi, 147.7 per sq km. **Urban:** 23.4%. **Ethnic groups:** Polynesian, European. **Principal languages:** Tongan, English (both official). **Chief religion:** Christian (mostly Free Wesleyan Church).

Geography: Total area: 288 sq mi, 747 sq km; **Land area:** 277 sq mi, 717 sq km. **Location:** In western S Pacific O. **Neighbors:** Nearest are Fiji to W, Samoa to NE. **Topography:** Tonga comprises 170 volcanic and coral islands, 36 inhabited. **Capital:** Nuku'alofa, 24,000.

Government: Type: Constitutional monarchy. **Head of state:** King George Tupou V; b. May 4, 1948; in office: Sept. 11, 2006. **Head of gov.:** Prime Min. Tu'ivakano; b. Jan. 15, 1952; in office: Dec, 22, 2010. **Local divisions:** 3 island groups. **Defense budget/ active troops:** NA.

Economy: Industries: tourism, constr., fishing. **Chief crops:** squash, coconuts, copra, bananas, vanilla beans, cocoa, coffee, ginger, black pepper. **Natural resources:** fish. **Arable land:** 22.2%. **Livestock:** cattle: 11,300; chickens: 330,000; goats: 12,600; pigs: 81,200. **Fish catch:** 2,054 metric tons. **Electricity prod.:** 40 mil kWh. **Labor force:** agric. 31.8%, industry 30.6%, services 37.6%.

Finance: Monetary unit: Pa'anga (TOP) (Sept. 2011: 1.68 = $1 U.S.). **GDP:** $751 mil; **per capita GDP:** $6,100; **GDP growth:** 0.3%. **Imports** (2006): $139 mil; Fiji 34.9%, New Zealand 25.4%, U.S. 9.6%, Australia 7.7%, China 5.9%. **Exports** (2006): $22 mil; Hong Kong 27%, U.S. 24.1%, Japan 12.9%, New Zealand 7.8%, Fiji 7.7%, Samoa 6.4%, American Samoa 4.1%. **Tourism:** $16 mil. **Budget** (FY07/08 est.): $109.8 mil. **Total reserves less gold:** $104.5 mil. **CPI change:** 3.6%.

Transport: Civil aviation: 11.8 mil pass.-mi; 1 airport. **Chief port:** Nuku'alofa.

Communications: TV sets: 49 per 1,000 pop. **Radios:** 662 per 1,000 pop. **Telephone lines:** 29.8 per 100 pop. **Internet:** 12 users per 100 pop.

Health: Life expect.: 73.8 male; 76.6 female. **Births:** 25.3 (per 1,000 pop.). **Deaths:** 4.9 (per 1,000 pop.). **Natural inc.:** 2.04%. **Infant mortality:** 13.7 (per 1,000 live births). **HIV rate:** NA.

Education: Compulsory: ages 6-14. **Literacy:** 99%.

Major intl. organizations: UN (FAO, IBRD, ILO, IMF, WHO), the Commonwealth, WTO.

Embassy: 250 E. 51st St., New York, NY 10022; (917) 369-1025.

Website: pmo.gov.to

The islands were first visited by the Dutch in the early 17th cent. A series of civil wars ended in 1845 with establishment of the Tupou dynasty. In 1900 Tonga became a British protectorate. On June 4, 1970, Tonga became independent and a member of the Commonwealth. It joined the UN on Sept. 14, 1999. George Tupou V became king Sept. 11, 2006, following the death of his father, Taufa'ahau Tupou IV, who had reigned since 1965.

Trinidad and Tobago
Republic of Trinidad and Tobago

People: Population: 1,227,505. **Age distrib.:** <15: 19.5%; 65+: 8.4%. **Pop. density:** 620 per sq mi, 239.4 per sq km. **Urban:** 13.9%. **Ethnic groups:** Indian (South Asian) 40%, African 38%, mixed 21%. **Principal languages:** English (official), Caribbean Hindustani, French, Spanish, Chinese. **Chief religions:** Roman Catholic 26%, Hindu 23%, Anglican 8%, Baptist 7%, Pentecostal 7%, Muslim 6%, Seventh-Day Adventist 4%, other Christian 6%, none 2%.

Geography: Total area: 1,980 sq mi, 5,128 sq km; **Land area:** 1,980 sq mi, 5,128 sq km. **Location:** In Caribbean, off E coast of Venezuela. **Neighbors:** Nearest is Venezuela to SW. **Topography:** Three low mountain ranges cross Trinidad E-W, with a well-watered plain between N and central ranges. Parts of E and W coasts are swamps. Tobago, 116 sq mi, lies 20 mi NE. **Capital:** Port of Spain, 57,000.

Government: Type: Parliamentary democracy. **Head of state:** Pres. George Maxwell Richards; b. Dec. 1, 1931; in office: Mar. 17, 2003. **Head of gov.:** Prime Min. Kamla Persad-Bissessar; b. Apr. 22, 1952; in office: May 26, 2010. **Local div.:** 8 counties, 3 municipalities, 1 ward. **Defense budget:** $172 mil. **Active troops:** 4,063.

Economy: Industries: petroleum and petroleum prods., liquefied nat. gas, methanol, ammonia, urea, steel prods., beverages, food proc. **Chief crops:** cocoa, rice, citrus, coffee, vegetables. **Natural resources:** petroleum, nat. gas, asphalt. **Crude oil reserves:** 728.3 mil bbls. **Arable land:** 4.9%. **Livestock:** cattle: 30,700; chickens: 28.5 mil; goats: 61,430; pigs: 47,000; sheep: 3,700. **Fish catch:** 13,868 metric tons. **Electricity prod.:** 7.4 bil kWh. **Labor force:** agric. 3.8%; mfg., mining, and quarrying 12.8%; constr. and utilities 20.4%; services 62.9%.

Finance: Monetary unit: Dollar (TTD) (Sept. 2011: 6.35 = $1 U.S.). **GDP:** $26.1 bil; **per capita GDP:** $21,300; **GDP growth:** 0%. **Imports:** $8.2 bil; U.S. 32.6%, Russia 10%, Colombia 6.2%, Brazil 5.8%. **Exports:** $12.1 bil; U.S. 42.2%, Spain 7.6%, Jamaica 4.8%. **Tourism:** NA. **Budget:** $7.2 bil. **Total reserves less gold:** $9.6 bil. **Gold:** 61,702 oz t. **CPI change:** 10.5%.

Transport: Motor vehicles: 291.1 vehicles per 1,000 pop. **Civil aviation:** 1.9 bil pass.-mi; 3 airports. **Chief ports:** Port-of-Spain, Scarborough.

Communications: TV sets: 355 per 1,000 pop. **Radios:** 535 per 1,000 pop. **Telephone lines:** 21.9 per 100 pop. **Daily newspaper circ.:** 149.1 per 1,000 pop. **Internet:** 48.5 users per 100 pop.

Health: Life expect.: 68.5 male; 74.3 female. **Births:** 14.4 (per 1,000 pop.). **Deaths:** 8.3 (per 1,000 pop.). **Natural inc.:** 0.61%. **Infant mortality:** 27.7 (per 1,000 live births). **HIV rate:** 1.5%.

Education: Compulsory: ages 6-12. **Literacy:** 98.7%.

Major intl. organizations: UN (FAO, IBRD, ILO, IMF, WHO), Caricom, the Commonwealth, OAS, WTO.

Embassy: 1708 Massachusetts Ave. NW 20036; 467-6490.

Website: www.ttconnect.gov.tt

Columbus sighted Trinidad in 1498. A British possession since 1802, Trinidad and Tobago won independence Aug. 31, 1962. It became a republic in 1976.

The nation is one of the most prosperous in the Caribbean. Oil production has increased with offshore finds. Middle Eastern oil is refined and exported, mostly to the U.S.

In July 1990, some 120 Muslim extremists captured the Parliament building and TV station and took about 50 hostages, including Prime Min. Arthur N. R. Robinson, who was beaten, shot in the legs, and tied to explosives. After a 6-day siege, the rebels surrendered.

Basdeo Panday, in office 1995-2001, was the nation's first prime min. of East Indian ancestry. The country's first female prime min., Kamla Persad-Bissessar, leader of the People's Partnership coalition, took office May 26, 2010.

Tunisia
Tunisian Republic

People: Population: 10,629,186. **Age distrib.:** <15: 23.2%; 65+: 7.5%. **Pop. density:** 177.2 per sq mi, 68.4 per sq km. **Urban:** 67.3%. **Ethnic groups:** Arab 98%, European 1%, Jewish & other 1%. **Principal languages:** Arabic (official), French used in commerce. **Chief religions:** Muslim 98%, Christian 1%, Jewish & other 1%.

Geography: Total area: 63,170 sq mi, 163,610 sq km; **Land area:** 59,985 sq mi, 155,360 sq km. **Location:** On N coast of Africa. **Neighbors:** Algeria on W, Libya on E. **Topography:** The N is wooded and fertile. The central coastal plains are given to grazing and orchards. The S is arid, approaching Sahara Desert. **Capital:** Tunis, 766,750.

Government: Type: In transition. **Head of state:** Pres. Fouad Mebazaa; b. June 15, 1933; in office: Jan. 15, 2011 (interim). **Head of gov.:** Prime Min. Béji Caïd Essebsi; b. Nov. 29, 1926; in office: Feb. 27, 2011. **Local divisions:** 24 governorates. **Defense budget** (2008): $534 mil. **Active troops:** 35,800.

Economy: Industries: petroleum, mining, tourism, textiles, footwear, agribusiness. **Chief crops:** olives, olive oil, grain, tomatoes, citrus fruits, sugar beets, dates, almonds. **Natural resources:** petroleum, phosphates, iron ore, lead, zinc, salt. **Crude oil reserves:** 425 mil bbls. **Arable land:** 17.4%. **Livestock:** cattle: 679,080; chickens: 70 mil; goats: 1.5 mil; pigs: 6,000; sheep: 7.4 mil. **Fish catch:** 102,085 metric tons. **Electricity prod.:** 14.4 bil kWh. **Labor force:** agric. 18.3%, industry 31.9%, services 49.8%.

Finance: Monetary unit: Dinar (TND) (Sept. 2011: 1.39 = $1 U.S.). **GDP:** $100 bil; **per capita GDP:** $9,400; **GDP growth:** 3.7%. **Imports:** $25 bil; France 23.3%, Italy 19.1%, Germany 9.2%, Spain 4.9%. **Exports:** $16.1 bil; France 27.6%, Italy 18.7%, Germany 10.4%, Libya 6.9%, Belgium 4.5%. **Tourism:** $2.7 bil. **Budget:** $11.8 bil. **Total reserves less gold:** $9.5 bil. **Gold:** 217,000 oz t. **CPI change:** 4.4%.

Transport: Railways: 1,345 mi. **Motor vehicles:** 94.3 vehicles per 1,000 pop. **Civil aviation:** 2 bil pass.-mi; 16 airports. **Chief ports:** Bizerte, Gabes, Rades, Sfax, Skhira.

Communications: TV sets: 225 per 1,000 pop. **Radios:** 158 per 1,000 pop. **Telephone lines:** 12.3 per 1,000 pop. **Daily newspaper circ.:** 22.7 per 1,000 pop. **Internet:** 36.8 users per 100 pop.

Health: Life expect.: 73 male; 77.2 female. **Births:** 17.4 (per 1,000 pop.). **Deaths:** 5.8 (per 1,000 pop.). **Natural inc.:** 1.16%. **Infant mortality:** 25.9 (per 1,000 live births). **HIV rate:** <0.1%.

Education: Compulsory: ages 6-16. **Literacy:** 77.6%.

Major intl. organizations: UN (FAO, IBRD, ILO, IMF, WHO), AL, AU, WTO.

Embassy: 1515 Massachusetts Ave. NW 20005; 862-1850.

Website: www.tunisie.gov.tn

Site of ancient Carthage and a former Barbary state under the suzerainty of Turkey, Tunisia became a protectorate of France under a treaty signed May 12, 1881. The nation became independent Mar. 20, 1956, and ended the monarchy the following year. Habib Bourguiba, an independence leader, served as president until 1987, when he was deposed by his prime min., Zine al-Abidine Ben Ali, who then won 5 presidential elections, 1989-2009, all tightly controlled by the ruling party.

"Arab Spring" protests, which began Dec, 2010 in the town of Sidi Bouzid, succeeded in ousting Ben Ali, Jan. 14, 2011, and Parliament Speaker Fouad Mebazaa became interim president. Subsequent protests also forced the removal of holdover Prime Min. Mohamed Ghannouchi. Elections for a constituent assembly were scheduled for Oct. 23, 2011.

Turkey
Republic of Turkey

People: Population: 78,785,548. **Age distrib.:** <15: 26.6%; 65+: 6.3%. **Pop. density:** 265.1 per sq mi, 102.4 per sq km. **Urban:** 69.6%. **Ethnic groups:** Turkish 70%-75%, Kurdish 18%. **Principal languages:** Turkish (official), Kurdish, other minority languages. **Chief religion:** Muslim (mostly Sunni) 99.8%.

Geography: Total area: 302,535 sq mi, 783,562 sq km; **Land area:** 297,157 sq mi, 769,632 sq km. **Location:** Occupies Asia Minor, stretches into continental Europe; borders on Medit. and Black seas. **Neighbors:** Bulgaria, Greece on W; Georgia, Armenia on N; Iran on E; Iraq, Syria on S. **Topography:** Central Turkey has wide plateaus, with hot, dry summers and cold winters. High mountains ring the interior on all but W, with more than 20 peaks over 10,000 ft. Rolling plains are in W; mild, fertile coastal plains are in S, W. **Capital:** Ankara, 3,906,044. **Cities (urban aggl.):** Istanbul, 10,524,625; Izmir, 2,722,724; Bursa, 1,587,877.

Government: Type: Republic. **Head of state:** Pres. Abdullah Gül; b. Oct. 29, 1950; in office: Aug. 28, 2007. **Head of gov.:** Prime Min. Recep Tayyip Erdogan; b. Feb. 26, 1954; in office: Mar. 14, 2003. **Local divisions:** 81 provinces. **Defense budget:** $10.5 bil. **Active troops:** 510,600.

Economy: Industries: textiles, food proc., autos, electronics, mining, steel, petroleum, constr. **Chief crops:** tobacco, cotton, grain, olives, sugar beets, hazelnuts, pulse, citrus. **Natural resources:** coal, iron ore, copper, chromium, antimony, mercury, gold, barite, borate, strontium, emery, feldspar, limestone, magnesite. **Crude oil reserves:** 270.4 mil bbls. **Arable land:** 27.7%. **Livestock:** cattle: 10.9 mil; chickens: 244.3 mil; goats: 5.6 mil; pigs: 1,717; sheep: 24 mil. **Fish catch:** 622,679 metric tons. **Electricity prod.** (2009): 185.2 bil kWh. **Labor force:** agric. 29.5%, industry 24.7%, services 45.8%.

Finance: Monetary unit: Lira (TRY) (Sept. 2011: 1.76 = $1 U.S.). **GDP:** $960.5 bil; **per capita GDP:** $12,300; **GDP growth:** 8.2%. **Imports:** $166.3 bil; Russia 13.8%, Germany 10%, China 9%, U.S. 6.1%, Italy 5.4%, France 5%. **Exports:** $117.4 bil; Germany 9.6%, France 6.1%, UK 5.8%, Italy 5.8%, Iraq 5%. **Tourism:** $20.8 bil. **Budget:** $189.6 bil. **Total reserves less gold:** $80.7 bil. **Gold:** 3.7 mil oz t. **CPI change:** 8.6%.

Transport: Railways: 5,405 mi. **Motor vehicles:** 138.2 vehicles per 1,000 pop. **Civil aviation:** 30.8 bil pass.-mi; 88 airports. **Chief ports:** Aliaga, Diliskelesi, Eregli, Izmir, Izmit.

Communications: TV sets: 428 per 1,000 pop. **Radios:** 283 per 1,000 pop. **Telephone lines:** 22.3 per 100 pop. **Internet:** 39.8 users per 100 pop.

Health: Life expect.: 70.6 male; 74.5 female. **Births:** 17.9 (per 1,000 pop.). **Deaths:** 6.1 (per 1,000 pop.). **Natural inc.:** 1.18%. **Infant mortality:** 23.9 (per 1,000 live births). **HIV rate:** <0.1%.

Education: Compulsory: ages 6-14. **Literacy:** 90.8%.

Major intl. organizations: UN (FAO, IBRD, ILO, IMF, WHO), NATO, OECD, OSCE, WTO.

Embassy: 2525 Massachusetts Ave. NW 20008; 612-6700.

Website: www.tccb.gov.tr

Ancient inhabitants of Turkey were among the world's first agriculturalists. Such civilizations as the Hittite, Phrygian, and Lydian flourished in Asiatic Turkey (Asia Minor), as did much of Greek civilization. After the fall of Rome in the 5th cent., Constantinople (now Istanbul) was the capital of the Byzantine Empire for 1,000 years. It fell in 1453 to Ottoman Turks, who ruled a vast empire for over 400 years.

Just before WWI, Turkey, or the Ottoman Empire, ruled what is now Syria, Lebanon, Iraq, Jordan, Israel, Saudi Arabia, Yemen, and islands in the Aegean Sea. Turkey joined Germany and Austria in WWI, and its defeat resulted in the loss of much territory and the fall of the sultanate. A secular republic was established Oct. 29, 1923, with Mustafa Kemal (later Kemal Ataturk) as its first president. Ataturk led Turkey until his death in 1938.

Turkey kept neutral during most of WWII. The country became a full member of NATO in 1952 and remained a Western ally despite domestic political instability. Military coups overthrew civilian governments in 1960 and 1980. Turkey invaded nearby Cyprus July 20, 1974, to prevent that country from being united with Greece; since then, Cyprus has been divided into Greek and Turkish zones.

In recent decades, Turkish governments have contended with Kurdish separatism and the rise of militant Islam. Turkey was a member of the U.S.-led force that ousted Iraq from Kuwait, 1991. In the aftermath of the war, millions of Kurdish refugees fled to Turkey's border to escape Iraqi forces. Turkish offensives against the Kurds caused heavy casualties among guerrillas and civilians. Kurdish militants raided Turkish diplomatic missions in some 25 Western European cities June 24, 1993.

Tansu Ciller officially became Turkey's first woman prime min. July 5, 1993. The Welfare Party, an Islamic group, gained strength in the 1990s but was unable to form a government until June 1996, when it came to power in coalition with Ciller's True Path Party. The pro-Islamic government resigned June 18, 1997, under pressure from the military, which stepped up its campaign against Islamic fundamentalism in 1998.

Kurdish rebel leader Abdullah Öcalan was captured Feb. 15, 1999; convicted of terrorism June 29, he was sentenced to death by a Turkish security court. His organization, the Kurdistan Workers' Party, announced Aug. 5, 1999, that it would abandon its 14-year-old insurgency, in which more than 30,000 people died.

Earthquakes in Aug. and Nov. 1999 killed over 17,000 people. The IMF announced $7.5 bil in emergency loans Dec. 6, 2000, to help Turkey cope with a severe financial crisis. The death penalty was abolished Aug. 3, 2002, and Öcalan's sentence was commuted to life in prison Oct. 3. The Justice and Development Party (AKP), an Islamic group led by Recep Tayyip Erdogan, won elections Nov. 3.

During the U.S.-led invasion of Iraq, Mar.-Apr. 2003, Turkey, a NATO ally, refused to allow coalition forces to launch attacks on N Iraq from Turkish soil. Suicide bombings by Islamic extremists Nov. 15-20, 2003, killed 58 people and wounded about 750 at 2 synagogues, the British consulate, and the offices of a London-based bank, all in Istanbul.

Erdogan's party scored a landslide win in national elections, July 22, 2007. Overcoming objections by the military and other secularists, parliament, Aug. 28, chose an Islamic politician, Abdullah Gül, as president. An effort by secularists to ban the ruling AKP failed by one vote in Turkey's Constitutional Court July 30, 2008, but the justices cut the party's public funding in half and warned it to restrain Islamic influence on state institutions. Turkish voters Sept. 12, 2010, gave resounding approval to constitutional changes favored by the Islamic government, including a provision that would expand membership of the Constitutional Court.

The AKP gained a third consecutive general election victory June 12, 2011, amid an ongoing struggle between the military and the Erdogan government. Dozens of military officers, including some retired generals, were detained for allegedly plotting to seize power; after the nation's 4 top military commanders resigned en masse July 29, 2011, Pres Gül appointed their replacements Aug. 4, breaking with a tradition that had allowed the military to promote its own leaders.

Turkey has long sought to become a full member of the European Union, but the EU has deferred talks on accession until economic, human rights, and immigration issues are resolved. As Turkey has strengthened its ties with Islamic countries, relations with Israel, a former ally, have soured.

Turkmenistan

People: Population: 4,997,503. **Age distrib.:** <15: 27.5%; 65+: 4.1%. **Pop. density:** 27.5 per sq mi, 10.6 per sq km. **Urban:** 49.5%. **Ethnic groups:** Turkmen 85%, Uzbek 5%, Russian 4%. **Principal languages:** Turkmen (official), Russian, Uzbek. **Chief religions:** Muslim 89%, Eastern Orthodox 9%.

Geography: Total area: 188,456 sq mi, 488,100 sq km; **Land area:** 181,441 sq mi, 469,930 sq km. **Location:** Central Asia bordering Caspian Sea. **Neighbors:** Kazakhstan on N; Uzbekistan on N and E; Afghanistan, Iran on S. **Topography:** The Kara Kum Desert occupies 80% of the area. Bordered on W by Caspian Sea. **Capital:** Ashgabat (Ashkhabad), 637,000.

Government: Type: Republic with authoritarian rule. **Head of state and gov.:** Pres. Gurbanguly Berdymukhammedov; b. June 29, 1957; in office: Feb. 14, 2007 (acting from Dec. 21, 2006). **Local divisions:** 5 regions. **Defense budget:** $261 mil. **Active troops:** 22,000.

Economy: Industries: nat. gas, oil, petroleum prods., textiles, food proc. **Chief crops:** cotton, grain. **Natural resources:** petroleum, nat. gas, sulfur, salt. **Crude oil reserves:** 600 mil bbls. **Arable land:** 3.9%. **Livestock:** cattle: 2.2 mil; chickens: 14.6 mil; goats: 2.8 mil; pigs: 29,800; sheep: 13.5 mil. **Fish catch:** 15,016 metric tons. **Electricity prod.:** 14.1 bil kWh. **Labor force:** agric. 48.2%, industry 14%, services 37.8%.

Finance: Monetary unit: Manat (TMT) (Sept. 2011: 2.85 = $1 U.S.). **GDP:** $36.9 bil; **per capita GDP:** $7,500; **GDP growth:** 9.2%.
Imports: $4.9 bil; Turkey 16.1%, Russia 15.9%, China 15.6%, Germany 6.1%, UAE 5.7%, Ukraine 5.5%, U.S. 5.3%, France 4.2%.
Exports: $9.7 bil; Ukraine 22.2%, Turkey 10.1%, Hungary 6.7%, UAE 6.2%, Poland 6.1%, Afghanistan 5.8%, Iran 5.2%. **Tourism:** NA. **Budget:** $1.9 bil. **Total reserves less gold:** NA.
Transport: Railways: 1,852 mi. **Civil aviation:** 1.2 bil pass.-mi; 22 airports. **Chief port:** Turkmenbasy.
Communications: TV sets: 190 per 1,000 pop. **Radios:** 155 per 1,000 pop. **Telephone lines:** 10.3 per 100 pop. **Daily newspaper circ.:** 9.4 per 1,000 pop. **Internet:** 2.2 users per 100 pop.
Health: Life expect.: 65.6 male; 71.6 female. **Births:** 19.5 (per 1,000 pop.). **Deaths:** 6.2 (per 1,000 pop.). **Natural inc.:** 1.33%. **Infant mortality:** 42.3 (per 1,000 live births). **HIV rate:** NA.
Education: Compulsory: ages 7-15. **Literacy:** 99.6%.
Major intl. organizations: UN (FAO, IBRD, ILO, IMF, WHO), CIS, OSCE.
Embassy: 2207 Massachusetts Ave. NW 20008; 588-1500.
Website: www.turkmenistan.gov.tm

The region has been inhabited by Turkic tribes since the 10th cent. It became part of Russian Turkestan in 1881, and a constituent republic of the USSR in 1925. Turkmenistan declared independence Oct. 27, 1991, and became an independent state when the USSR disbanded Dec. 26, 1991.

Extensive oil and gas reserves place Turkmenistan in a favorable economic position. Political power centered around the former Communist Party apparatus, and authoritarian Pres. Saparmurad Niyazov (also known as Turkmenbashi) became the object of a personality cult. Niyazov died Dec. 21, 2006, and was succeeded by Gurbanguly Berdymukhammedov; he won the presidential election of Feb. 11, 2007, considered neither free nor fair by international observers.

Tuvalu

People: Population: 10,544. **Age distrib.:** <15: 30.6%; 65+: 5.4%. **Pop. density:** 1,050.3 per sq mi, 405.5 per sq km. **Urban:** 50.4%. **Ethnic group:** Polynesian 96%, Micronesian 4%. **Principal languages:** Tuvaluan, English (both official); Samoan; Kiribati. **Chief religions:** Church of Tuvalu (Congregationalist) 97%, Seventh-Day Adventist 1%, Baha'i 1%.
Geography: Total area: 10 sq mi, 26 sq km; **Land area:** 10 sq mi, 26 sq km. **Location:** 9 islands forming NW-SE chain 360 mi long in SW Pacific O. **Neighbors:** Nearest are Kiribati to N, Fiji to S. **Topography:** The islands are all low-lying atolls, nowhere rising more than 15 ft above sea level, composed of coral reefs. **Capital:** Funafuti, 5,000.
Government: Type: Constitutional monarchy, with a parliamentary democracy. **Head of state:** Queen Elizabeth II, represented by Gov.-Gen. Sir Iakoba Italeli; b. 1936; in office: Apr. 16, 2010. **Head of gov.:** Prime Min. Willy Telavi; b. July 7, 1958; in office: Dec. 24, 2010. **Defense budget/active troops:** NA.
Economy: Industries: fishing, tourism, copra. **Chief crops:** coconuts. **Natural resources:** fish. **Arable land:** none. **Livestock:** chickens: 45,000; pigs: 13,600. **Fish catch:** 4,198 metric tons. **Labor force:** Mainly exploitation of the sea, reefs, and atolls; wages sent home by those abroad (mostly workers in phosphate industry and sailors).
Finance: Monetary unit: Dollar (TVD) (Sept. 2011: 0.95 = $1 U.S.). **GDP:** $36 mil; **per capita GDP:** $3,400; **GDP growth:** 0.2%. **Imports** (2005): $12.9 mil; NA. **Exports** (2004 est.): $1 mil; NA. **Tourism:** NA. **Budget** (2006): $23.1 mil. **Total reserves less gold:** NA.
Transport: Civil aviation: 1 airport (unpaved runway). **Chief port:** Funafuti.
Communications: TV sets: 9 per 1,000 pop. **Telephone lines:** 16.5 per 100 pop. **Internet:** 25 users per 100 pop.
Health: Life expect.: 62.7 male; 66.9 female. **Births:** 23.2 (per 1,000 pop.). **Deaths:** 9.2 (per 1,000 pop.). **Natural inc.:** 1.4%. **Infant mortality:** 34.5 (per 1,000 live births). **HIV rate:** NA.
Education: Compulsory: ages 7-14. **Literacy:** NA.
Major intl. organizations: UN (FAO, ILO, WHO), the Commonwealth.
Permanent UN Mission: 800 Second Ave., Ste. 400D, New York, NY 10017; (212) 490-0534.
Website: www.timelesstuvalu.com

The Ellice Islands separated from the British Gilbert and Ellice Islands Colony in 1975 and became Tuvalu; independence came Oct. 1, 1978. In 2000, Tuvalu joined the United Nations.

Uganda

Republic of Uganda

People: Population: 34,612,250. **Age distrib.:** <15: 49.9%; 65+: 2.1%. **Pop. density:** 454.8 per sq mi, 175.6 per sq km. **Urban:** 13.3%. **Ethnic groups:** Baganda 17%, Banyakole 10%, Basoga 8%, Bakiga 7%, Iteso 6%, Langi 6%, Acholi 5%, Bagisu 5%, Lugbara 4%, Bunyoro 3%. **Principal languages:** English (official), Ganda or Luganda and other Niger-Congo languages,

Nilo-Saharan languages, Swahili, Arabic. **Chief religions:** Roman Catholic 42%, Protestant 42%, Muslim 12%.
Geography: Total area: 93,065 sq mi, 241,038 sq km; **Land area:** 76,101 sq mi, 197,100 sq km. **Location:** In E Central Africa. **Neighbors:** Sudan on N, Congo (formerly Zaire) on W, Rwanda and Tanzania on S, Kenya on E. **Topography:** Most of Uganda is a high plateau 3,000-6,000 ft high, with high Ruwenzori range in W (Mt. Margherita 16,763 ft), volcanoes in SW; NE is arid, W and SW rainy. Lakes Victoria, Edward, Albert form much of borders. **Capital:** Kampala, 1,597,916.
Government: Type: Republic. **Head of state and gov.:** Pres. Yoweri Kaguta Museveni; b. Aug. 15, 1944; in office: Jan. 29, 1986. **Local divisions:** 56 districts. **Defense budget:** $230 mil. **Active troops:** 45,000.
Economy: Industries: sugar, brewing, tobacco, cotton textiles, cement, steel prod. **Chief crops:** coffee, tea, cotton, tobacco, cassava, potatoes, corn, millet, pulses, cut flowers. **Natural resources:** copper, cobalt, hydropower, limestone, salt, gold. **Crude oil reserves:** 1 bil bbls. **Arable land:** 33%. **Livestock:** cattle: 7.6 mil; chickens: 28.3 mil; goats: 8.8 mil; pigs: 2.3 mil; sheep: 1.8 mil. **Fish catch:** 476,654 metric tons. **Electricity prod.:** 2.2 bil kWh. **Labor force:** agric. 82%; industry 5%; services 13%.
Finance: Monetary unit: Shilling (UGX) (Sept. 2011: 2,815.00 = $1 U.S.). **GDP:** $42.2 bil; **per capita GDP:** $1,300; **GDP growth:** 5.2%. **Imports:** $4.247 bil; Kenya 15.8%, UAE 12.7%, China 9%, India 8.1%, South Africa 5.8%, France 5.2%, Japan 5%, U.S. 4.6%.
Exports: $2.9 bil; Sudan 14.3%, Kenya 9.5%, UAE 8%, Rwanda 7.9%, Dem. Rep. of the Congo 7.3%, Netherlands 6%, Belgium 6%, Germany 5.5%, Italy 4.6%. **Tourism:** $798 mil. **Budget:** $2.9 bil. **Total reserves less gold:** $2.8 bil. **CPI change:** 4%.
Transport: Railways: 773 mi. **Motor vehicles:** 3.2 vehicles per 1,000 pop. **Civil aviation:** 213.8 mil pass.-mi; 5 airports. **Chief ports:** Entebbe, Jinja, Port Bell.
Communications: TV sets: 22 per 1,000 pop. **Radios:** 888 per 1,000 pop. **Telephone lines:** 1 per 100 pop. **Internet:** 12.5 users per 100 pop.
Health: Life expect.: 52.2 male; 54.3 female. **Births:** 47.5 (per 1,000 pop.). **Deaths:** 11.7 (per 1,000 pop.). **Natural inc.:** 3.58%. **Infant mortality:** 62.5 (per 1,000 live births). **HIV rate:** 6.5%.
Education: Compulsory: ages 6-12. **Literacy:** 71.4%.
Major intl. organizations: UN (FAO, IBRD, ILO, IMF, WHO), AU, the Commonwealth, WTO.
Embassy: 5911 16th St. NW 20011; 726-7100.
Websites: www.statehouse.go.ug

Britain obtained a protectorate over Uganda in 1894. The country became independent Oct. 9, 1962, and a republic within the Commonwealth a year later. In 1967, the traditional kingdoms, including the powerful Buganda state, were abolished.

Gen. Idi Amin seized power from Prime Min. Milton Obote in 1971. During his 8 years of dictatorial rule, he was responsible for the deaths of up to 300,000 of his opponents. In 1972 he expelled nearly all of Uganda's 45,000 Asians. Tanzanian troops and Ugandan exiles and rebels ousted Amin, Apr. 11, 1979.

Obote held the presidency from Dec. 1980 until his ouster in a military coup July 27, 1985. Guerrilla war and rampant human rights abuses plagued Uganda under Obote's regime.

Conditions improved after Yoweri Museveni took power in Jan. 1986. In 1993 the Buganda and other traditional monarchies were restored, but only for ceremonial purposes. Uganda helped Laurent Kabila seize power in the Congo (formerly Zaire) in 1997 but sent troops in 1998 to aid insurgents seeking his ouster. A withdrawal accord was signed Sept. 6, 2002.

Pres. Museveni won reelection Mar. 12, 2001, and Feb. 23, 2006; opponents disputed the latter result, citing what they claimed were trumped-up charges of treason, terrorism, and rape lodged against Museveni's main rival, Kizza Besigye. Museveni again defeated Besigye in a presidential election Feb. 18, 2011, described as flawed by European observers.

An ongoing insurgency in N Uganda has killed more than 100,000 people and forced up to 2 mil to flee. The Lord's Resistance Army (LRA), a rebel group, has fought the Museveni govt. since 1986 and has abducted some 30,000 children to serve as soldiers and sex slaves. Peace talks brokered by Sudan began July 2006; as talks continued through 2007, the violence diminished, and many refugees returned to their homes. A cease-fire accord was signed Feb. 23, 2008, but Ugandan and Congolese troops (with aid from the U.S.) launched a new offensive against the LRA in late 2008. Al-Shabaab, an Islamist group based in Somalia and linked to al-Qaeda, claimed responsibility for suicide bombings July 11, 2010, that killed 76 people as they watched a World Cup soccer match on outdoor video screens in Kampala. Rising food and fuel prices spurred protests in 2011 against Museveni's entrenched regime.

Ukraine

People: Population: 45,134,707. **Age distrib.:** <15: 13.7%; 65+: 15.5%. **Pop. density:** 201.8 per sq mi, 77.9 per sq km. **Urban:** 68.8%. **Ethnic groups:** Ukrainian 78%, Russian 17%. **Principal languages:** Ukrainian (official), Russian. **Chief religions:** Ukrainian

Orthodox (Kiev patriarchate) 50%, Ukrainian Orthodox (Moscow patriarchate) 26%, Ukrainian Greek Catholic 8%, Ukrainian Autocephalous Orthodox 7%, Roman Catholic 2%, Protestant 2%.

Geography: Total area: 233,032 sq mi, 603,550 sq km; **Land area:** 223,681 sq mi, 579,330 sq km. **Location:** In E Europe. **Neighbors:** Belarus on N; Russia on NE and E; Moldova and Romania on SW; Hungary, Slovakia, and Poland on W. **Topography:** Part of the E European plain. Mountainous areas include the Carpathians in the SW and Crimean chain in the S. Arable black soil constitutes a large part of the country. **Capital:** Kyiv (Kiev), 2,804,781. **Cities (urban aggl.):** Kharkiv, 1,452,786; Dnipropetrovsk, 1,003,697; Odesa, 1,009,172.

Government: Type: Republic. **Head of state:** Pres. Viktor Yanukovych; b. July 9, 1950; in office: Feb. 25, 2010. **Head of gov.:** Prime Min. Mykola Azarov; b. Dec. 17, 1947; in office: Mar. 11, 2010. **Local divisions:** 24 oblasts, 2 municipalities, 1 autonomous republic. **Defense budget:** $1.43 bil. **Active troops:** 129,925.

Economy: Industries: coal, elec. power, metals, machinery and transp. equip., chemicals, food proc. **Chief crops:** grain, sugar beets, sunflower seeds, vegetables. **Natural resources:** iron ore, coal, manganese, nat. gas, petroleum, salt, sulfur, graphite, titanium, magnesium, kaolin, nickel, mercury, timber. **Crude oil reserves:** 395 mil bbls. **Arable land:** 56.1%. **Livestock:** cattle: 5.1 mil; chickens: 158.8 mil; goats: 631,200; pigs: 6.5 mil; sheep: 1.1 mil. **Fish catch:** 239,435 metric tons. **Electricity prod.:** 181.3 bil kWh. **Labor force:** agric. 15.8%, industry 18.5%, services 65.7%.

Finance: Monetary unit: Hryvnia (UAH) (Sept. 2011: 8.00 = $1 U.S.). **GDP:** $305.2 bil. **per capita GDP:** $6,700; **GDP growth:** 4.2%. **Imports:** $53.5 bil; Russia 29.1%; Germany 8.5%; China 6%, Poland 4.8%, Kazakhstan 4.5%. **Exports:** $49.7 bil; Russia 21.4%, Turkey 5.4%. **Tourism:** $3.8 bil. **Budget:** $49.8 bil (planned and consolidated). **Total reserves less gold:** $33.3 bil. **Gold:** 885,000 oz t. **CPI change:** 9.4%.

Transport: Railways: 13,474 mi. **Motor vehicles:** 201.8 vehicles per 1,000 pop. **Civil aviation:** 3.7 bil pass.-mi; 189 airports. **Chief ports:** Feodosiya, Kerch, Mariupol, Mykolayiv, Odesa, Yuzhnyy.

Communications: TV sets: 433 per 1,000 pop. **Radios:** 283 per 1,000 pop. **Telephone lines:** 28.5 per 100 pop. **Daily newspaper circ.:** 131 per 1,000 pop. **Internet:** 23 users per 100 pop.

Health: Life expect.: 62.8 male; 74.8 female. **Births:** 9.6 (per 1,000 pop.). **Deaths:** 15.7 (per 1,000 pop.). **Natural inc.:** −0.61%. **Infant mortality:** 8.5 (per 1,000 live births). **HIV rate:** 1.1%.

Education: Compulsory: ages 6-17. **Literacy:** 99.7%.

Major intl. organizations: UN (FAO, IBRD, ILO, IMF, WHO), CIS, OSCE, WTO.

Embassy: 3350 M St. NW 20007; 333-0606.

Website: www.kmu.gov.ua

Ukrainians' Slavic ancestors inhabited the region well before the first cent. CE. In the 9th cent., the princes of Kiev established a strong state called Kievan Rus, which included much of present-day Ukraine. Internal conflicts led to the disintegration of the Ukrainian state by the 13th cent. Mongol rule was supplanted by Poland and Lithuania in the 14th and 15th centuries. The N Black Sea coast and Crimea came under Turkish control in 1478. Ukrainian Cossacks, starting in the late 16th cent., rebelled against the occupiers of Ukraine: Russia, Poland, and Turkey.

An independent Ukrainian National Republic was proclaimed on Jan. 22, 1918. But in 1921, Ukraine's neighbors occupied and divided Ukrainian territory. In 1922, Ukraine became a constituent republic of the USSR. In 1932-33, the Soviet government engineered a famine in eastern Ukraine, resulting in the deaths of 6-7 mil Ukrainians. During WWII the Ukrainian nationalist underground fought both Nazi and Soviet forces. Over 5 mil Ukrainians died in the war. With the reoccupation of Ukraine by Soviet troops in 1944 came a renewed wave of repression.

The world's worst nuclear power plant disaster occurred in Chernobyl, Ukraine, in Apr. 1986; many thousands were killed or disabled as a result of the radiation leak. The plant was finally shut down Dec. 15, 2000.

Ukrainian independence was restored in Dec. 1991 with the dissolution of the Soviet Union. In the post-Soviet period Ukraine was burdened with a deteriorating economy. Following a 1994 accord with Russia and the U.S., Ukraine's large nuclear arsenal was transferred to Russia for destruction.

President since 1994, Leonid Kuchma attempted to engineer the election in 2004 of his handpicked successor, Prime Min. Viktor Yanukovych, also favored by Russia. The main challenger, Viktor Yushchenko, a former prime min., was poisoned in Sept. with dioxin, but continued to campaign. Official results of a runoff vote Nov. 21 showed a win for Yanukovych. Yushchenko supporters, calling the election fraudulent, staged massive protests (the "orange revolution"), and the vote was annulled. An election rerun Dec. 26 gave the victory to Yushchenko.

Yushchenko's Our Ukraine party fared poorly in parliamentary elections Mar. 26, 2006, and the resurgent Yanukovych, whose party won the vote, returned as prime min. Aug. 4. The two rivals

then engaged in a year-long political struggle. A report released Feb. 19, 2007, by the International Organization for Migration estimated that 117,000 Ukrainians had been trafficked abroad as forced laborers or prostitutes since 1991.

Following elections Sept. 30, 2007, Yulia Tymoshenko, a former Orange Revolution ally of Yushchenko, became prime min. Dec. 18. She lost to Yanukovych defeated Tymoshenko in a presidential runoff election Feb. 7, 2010. The installation of a pro-Russian government in Ukraine led to a rapid improvement in relations with Moscow. In what her supporters and some international observers viewed as a politically motivated prosecution, former Prime Min. Tymoshenko went on trial June 24, 2011, for abusing her powers while she held office 2007-10.

United Arab Emirates

People: Population: 5,148,664. **Age distrib.:** <15: 20.4%; 65+: 0.9%. **Pop. density:** 159.5 per sq mi, 61.6 per sq km. **Urban:** 84.1%. **Ethnic groups:** Emirati 19%, other Arab & Iranian 23%, South Asian 50%, other expatriates (incl. Westerners & E Asians) 8%. (Less than 20% are UAE citizens.) **Principal languages:** Arabic (official), Persian, English, Hindi, Urdu. **Chief religions:** Muslim 96% (Shi'a 16%), other (incl. Christian, Hindu) 4%.

Geography: Total area: 32,278 sq mi, 83,600 sq km; **Land area:** 32,278 sq mi, 83,600 sq km. **Location:** Middle East, on S shore of the Persian Gulf. **Neighbors:** Saudi Arabia on W and S, Oman on E. **Topography:** A barren, flat coastal plain gives way to uninhabited sand dunes on S. Hajar Mts. on E. **Capital:** Abu Dhabi, 666,000. **Cities (urban aggl.):** Dubai, 1,566,878.

Government: Type: Federation of emirates. **Head of state:** Pres. Sheikh Khalifa ibn Zaid an-Nahayan; b. 1948; in office: Nov. 3, 2004. **Head of gov.:** Prime Min. Sheikh Muhammad ibn Rashid al-Maktum; b. 1949; in office: Jan. 5, 2006. **Local divisions:** 7 autonomous emirates: Abu Dhabi, Ajman, Dubai, Fujaira, Ras al-Khaimah, Sharjah, Umm al-Qaiwain. **Defense budget:** $7.96 bil. **Active troops:** 51,000.

Economy: Industries: petroleum and petrochemicals, fishing, aluminum, cement, fertilizers, commercial ship repair, constr. materials. **Chief crops:** dates, vegetables, watermelons. **Natural resources:** petroleum, nat. gas. **Crude oil reserves:** 97.8 bil bbls. **Arable land:** 0.8%. **Livestock:** cattle: 62,000; chickens: 15.5 mil; goats: 1.7 mil; sheep: 620,000. **Fish catch:** 77,705 metric tons. **Electricity prod.** (2009): 80.9 bil kWh. **Labor force:** agric. 7%, industry 15%, services 78%.

Finance: Monetary unit: Dirham (AED) (Sept. 2011: 3.67 = $1 U.S.). **GDP:** $246.8 bil; **per capita GDP:** $49,600; **GDP growth:** 3.2%. **Imports:** $159 bil; India 15%, China 13.5%, U.S. 8.8%, Germany 6.1%, Japan 4.7%. **Exports:** $195.8 bil; Japan 17.5%, India 11.9%, South Korea 7.2%, Iran 6.9%, Thailand 5.2%. **Tourism:** $8.6 bil. **Budget:** $60.02 bil. **Total reserves less gold:** $42.8 bil. **CPI change:** NA.

Transport: Motor vehicles: 86.6 vehicles per 1,000 pop. **Civil aviation:** 89.4 bil pass.-mi; 25 airports. **Chief ports:** Al Fujayrah, Khawr Fakkan, Mina' Jabal Ali, Mina' Rashid, Mina', Saqr, Mina' Zayid.

Communications: TV sets: 197 per 1,000 pop. **Radios:** 1,455 per 1,000 pop. **Telephone lines:** 19.7 per 100 pop. **Internet:** 78 users per 100 pop.

Health: Life expect.: 73.9 male; 79.2 female. **Births:** 15.9 (per 1,000 pop.). **Deaths:** 2.1 (per 1,000 pop.). **Natural inc.:** 1.38%. **Infant mortality:** 11.9 (per 1,000 live births). **HIV rate:** NA.

Education: Compulsory: ages 6-14. **Literacy:** 90%.

Major intl. organizations: UN (FAO, IBRD, ILO, IMF, WHO), AL, OPEC, WTO.

Embassy: 3522 International Ct. NW, Ste. 400, 20008; 243-2400.

Website: www.government.ae

The 7 "Trucial Sheikdoms" gave Britain control of defense and foreign relations in the 19th cent. They merged to become an independent state Dec. 2, 1971. Oil revenues have made the UAE one of the world's wealthiest countries. Foreigners make up more than 80% of the population and nearly all the private work force.

International banking, investment, and construction boomed during the late 1990s and early 2000s; holdings of Abu Dhabi's largest government-sponsored investment fund were estimated at $550 bil in Oct. 2008. But the global recession grounded Dubai's high-flying economy. On Mar. 25, 2010, Dubai's government was forced to extend up to $9.5 bil in loans to help its state-controlled investment company, Dubai World, avoid default.

United Kingdom
United Kingdom of Great Britain and Northern Ireland

People: Population: 62,698,362. **Age distrib.:** <15: 17.3%; 65+: 16.5%. **Pop. density:** 671.2 per sq mi, 259.2 per sq km. **Urban:** 79.6%. **Ethnic groups:** white 92% (English 84%, Scottish 9%, Welsh 5%, N Irish 3%), black 2%, Indian 2%, Pakistani 1%, mixed 1%. **Principal languages:** English; Scots, Scottish Gaelic,

Welsh, Irish, Cornish (all recognized regional languages). **Chief religions:** Christian 72%, Muslim 3%.

Geography: Total area: 94,058 sq mi, 243,610 sq km; **Land area:** 93,410 sq mi, 241,930 sq km. **Location:** Off NW coast of Europe, across English Channel, Strait of Dover, North Sea. **Neighbors:** Ireland to W, France to SE. **Topography:** England is mostly rolling land, rising to Uplands of southern Scotland. Lowlands are in center of Scotland, granite Highlands are in N. Coast is heavily indented, especially on W. British Isles have milder climate than N Europe due to Gulf Stream and ample rainfall. Severn, 220 mi, and Thames, 215 mi, are longest rivers. **Capital:** London, 8,631,325. **Cities (urban aggl.):** Birmingham, 2,302,186; Manchester, 2,252,873; West Yorkshire, 1,546,599; Glasgow, 1,170,003.

Government: Type: Constitutional monarchy. **Head of state:** Queen Elizabeth II; b. Apr. 21, 1926; in office: Feb. 6, 1952. **Head of gov.:** Prime Min. David Cameron; b. Oct. 9, 1966; in office: May 11, 2010. **Local divisions:** 467 local authorities, including England: 387; Wales: 22; Scotland: 32; Northern Ireland: 26. **Defense budget:** $56.5 bil. **Active troops:** 178,470.

Economy: Industries: machine tools, elec. power equip., automation equip., railroad equip., shipbuilding, aircraft, motor vehicles and parts, electronics and comm. equip., metals, chemicals, coal, petroleum, paper and paper prods. **Chief crops:** cereals, oilseed, potatoes, vegetables. **Natural resources:** coal, petroleum, nat. gas, iron ore, lead, zinc, gold, tin, limestone, salt, clay, chalk, gypsum, potash, silica sand, slate. **Crude oil reserves:** 2.9 bil bbls. **Arable land:** 25%. **Livestock:** cattle: 9.9 mil; chickens: 159.3 mil; goats: 95,000; pigs: 4.6 mil; sheep: 32 mil. **Fish catch:** 770,086 metric tons. **Electricity prod.** (2009): 346 bil kWh. **Labor force:** agric. 1.4%, industry 18.2%, services 80.4%.

Finance: Monetary unit: Pound (GBP) (Sept. 2011: 0.63 = $1 U.S.). **GDP:** $2.2 tril; **per capita GDP:** $34,800; **GDP growth:** 1.3%. **Imports:** $546.5 bil; Germany 12.9%, U.S. 9.7%, China 8.9%, Netherlands 7%, France 6.7%, Belgium 4.9%, Norway 4.8%. **Exports:** $405.6 bil; U.S. 14.7%, Germany 11.1%, France 8%, Netherlands 7.8%, Ireland 6.9%, Belgium 4.7%. **Tourism:** $30.6 bil. **Budget:** $1.2 tril. **Total reserves less gold:** $68.3 bil. **Gold:** 10 mil oz t. **CPI change:** 3.3%.

Transport: Railways: 10,224 mi. **Motor vehicles:** 568 vehicles per 1,000 pop. **Civil aviation:** 143.3 bil pass.-mi; 306 airports. **Chief ports:** Dover, Felixstowe, Immingham, Liverpool, London, Southampton, Teesport.

Communications: TV sets: 1,105 per 1,000 pop. **Radios:** 2,059 per 1,000 pop. **Telephone lines:** 53.7 per 100 pop. **Daily newspaper circ.:** 289.8 per 1,000 pop. **Internet:** 85 users per 100 pop.

Health: Life expect.: 78 male; 82.3 female. **Births:** 12.3 (per 1,000 pop.). **Deaths:** 9.3 (per 1,000 pop.). **Natural inc.:** 0.3%. **Infant mortality:** 4.6 (per 1,000 live births). **HIV rate:** 0.2%.

Education: Compulsory: ages 5-16. **Literacy:** 99%.

Major intl. organizations: UN and all of its specialized agencies, the Commonwealth, EU, NATO, OECD, OSCE, WTO.

Embassy: 3100 Massachusetts Ave. NW 20008; 588-6500.

Website: www.direct.gov.uk

The United Kingdom of Great Britain and Northern Ireland comprises England, Wales, Scotland, and Northern Ireland.

Queen and Royal Family. The ruling sovereign is Elizabeth II of the House of Windsor, b. Apr. 21, 1926, elder daughter of King George VI. She succeeded to the throne Feb. 6, 1952, and was crowned June 2, 1953. She was married Nov. 20, 1947, to Lt. Philip Mountbatten, b. June 10, 1921, former Prince of Greece. He was created Duke of Edinburgh, and given the title H.R.H., Nov. 19, 1947; he was named Prince of the United Kingdom and Northern Ireland Feb. 22, 1957. Prince Charles Philip Arthur George, b. Nov. 14, 1948, is the Prince of Wales and heir apparent. His first son, William Philip Arthur Louis, b. June 21, 1982, is second in line to the throne.

Parliament is the legislative body for the UK, with certain powers over dependent units. It consists of 2 houses: The **House of Commons** has 650 members, elected by direct ballot and divided as follows: England, 533; Wales, 40; Scotland, 59; Northern Ireland, 18. Following a drastic reduction in 1999 in the number of hereditary peerages, the **House of Lords** (Oct. 2011) comprised 826 members: 92 hereditary peers, 710 life peers, and 24 archbishops and bishops of the Church of England.

Resources and Industries. Great Britain's major occupations are manufacturing and trade. Metals and metal-using industries contribute more than 50% of exports. Of about 60 mil acres of land in England, Wales, and Scotland, 46 mil are farmed, of which 17 mil are arable, the rest pastures. Large oil and gas fields have been found in the North Sea. Commercial oil production began in 1975. There are large deposits of coal.

Britain imports all of its cotton, rubber, sulphur, about 80% of its wool, half of its food and iron ore, also certain amounts of paper, tobacco, chemicals. Manufactured goods made from these basic materials have been exported since the industrial age began. Main exports are machinery, chemicals, textiles, clothing, autos and trucks, iron and steel, locomotives, ships, jet aircraft, farm machinery, drugs, radio, TV, radar and navigation equipment, scientific instruments, arms, whisky.

Religion and Education. The Church of England is Protestant Episcopal. The queen is its temporal head, with rights of appointments to archbishoprics, bishoprics, and other offices. There are 2 provinces, Canterbury and York, each headed by an archbishop. The most famous church is Westminster Abbey (1050-1760), site of coronations, tombs of Elizabeth I, Mary, Queen of Scots, kings, poets, and of the Unknown Warrior.

The most celebrated British universities are Oxford and Cambridge, each dating to the 13th cent. There are about 70 other universities.

History. Recent research indicates that Britain was separated from the European continent at least 200,000 years ago by a catastrophic flood that created the English Channel. Migrants across the Channel included the Celts, who arrived 2,500 to 3,000 years ago. Their language survives in Welsh and Gaelic enclaves.

England was added to the Roman Empire in 43 CE. After the withdrawal of Roman legions in 410, waves of Jutes, Angles, and Saxons arrived from German lands. They contended with Danish raiders for control from the 8th through 11th centuries. The last successful invasion was by French speaking Normans in 1066, who united the country with their dominions in France.

Opposition by nobles to royal authority forced King John to agree to the Magna Carta in 1215, a guarantee of rights and the rule of law. In the ensuing decades, the foundations of the parliamentary system were laid.

English dynastic claims to large parts of France led to the Hundred Years War, 1338-1453, and the defeat of England. A long civil war, the War of the Roses, lasted 1455-85, and ended with the establishment of the powerful Tudor monarchy. A distinct English civilization flourished. The economy prospered over long periods of domestic peace unmatched in continental Europe. Religious independence was secured when the Church of England was separated from the authority of the pope in 1534.

During the reign of Queen Elizabeth I, 1558-1603, England became a major naval power, leading to the founding of colonies in the new world and the expansion of trade with Europe and the Orient. Scotland was united with England when James VI of Scotland was crowned James I of England in 1603.

A struggle between Parliament and the Stuart kings led to a bloody civil war, 1642-49, and the establishment of a republic under the Puritan Oliver Cromwell. The monarchy was restored in 1660, but the "Glorious Revolution" of 1688 confirmed the sovereignty of Parliament: a Bill of Rights was granted 1689.

In the 18th cent., parliamentary rule was strengthened. Technological and entrepreneurial innovations led to the Industrial Revolution. The 13 N American colonies were lost but replaced by growing empires in Canada and India. Britain's role in the defeat of Napoleon, 1815, strengthened its position as the leading world power.

The extension of the franchise in 1832 and 1867, the formation of trade unions, and the development of universal public education were among the drastic social changes that accompanied the spread of industrialization and urbanization in the 19th cent. Large parts of Africa and Asia were added to the empire during the reign of Queen Victoria, 1837-1901.

Though victorious in WWI, Britain suffered huge casualties and economic dislocation. Ireland became independent in 1921, and independence movements became active in India and other colonies. The country suffered major bombing damage in WWII but rallied by Prime Min. Winston Churchill, held out against Germany until Allied victory was achieved, 1945.

Industrial growth continued in the postwar period, but Britain lost its leadership position to other powers. Labour governments passed socialist programs nationalizing some basic industries and expanding social security. Prime Min. Margaret Thatcher's Conservative governments, 1979-90, revived the role of private enterprise. Her Conservative successor, John Major, held power 1990-97. The UK sent military forces to the Persian Gulf War, 1991. The Channel Tunnel linking Britain to the Continent was inaugurated May 6, 1994.

On May 1, 1997, the Labour Party swept into power, making Tony Blair, 43, Britain's youngest prime min. since 1812. Diana, Princess of Wales, died in a car crash in Paris, Aug. 31. Britain played a leading role in the NATO air war against Yugoslavia, Mar.-June 1999, and contributed 12,000 troops to the multinational security force in Kosovo (KFOR).

Blair led Labour to another landslide election victory June 7, 2001. After the Sept. 11 attacks on the U.S., Britain took an important role in the U.S.-led war against terrorism. The UK participated in the bombing of Afghanistan that began Oct. 7, 2001; 9,500 UK troops were serving in Afghanistan as of Sept. 2011, with more than 380 fatalities recorded since the war started.

Overcoming dissent within his own cabinet, Blair committed British troops to the U.S.-led invasion of Iraq, Mar.-Apr. 2003. UK forces, which numbered 46,000 at the height of combat operations, had been almost entirely pulled out by mid-2009, with nearly 180 deaths reported.

In elections May 5, 2005, Blair became the first Labour prime min. to win 3 consecutive terms. Suicide bombings on 3 London underground trains and a bus, July 7, 2005, left 56 people dead and hundreds injured; police identified the bombers as 4 British Muslim men (3 of Pakistani origin). British authorities announced Aug. 10, 2006, that they had thwarted a plot to use liquid explosives to blow up passenger aircraft flying the UK-U.S. route.

Blair stepped down June 27, 2007, and was succeeded by Gordon Brown. Failed car bombings in London, June 29, 2007, and at Glasgow Airport in Scotland, June 30, led to the arrest in Britain of 7 suspects, mostly foreign-born medical workers. Severe floods June-Aug. in central England caused at least $2 bil in damage. Responding Oct. 13, 2008, to the worldwide financial crisis, Prime Min. Brown initiated a plan to partially nationalize 3 of Britain's largest banks and support them with a capital infusion of up to $63 bil. Michael Martin, Labour speaker of the House of Commons, resigned May 19, 2009, amid revelations that parliamentarians of all parties had padded their salaries with questionable expense claims.

In the wake of Britain's deepest recession since WWII, voters rejected Brown and the Labour Party in parliamentary elections May 6, 2010. Conservatives and Liberal Democrats formed the first coalition government in 70 years, with Conservative leader David Cameron becoming prime min. and Liberal Democratic leader Nick Clegg deputy prime min. A phone hacking scandal involving illegal interception by newspapers of telephone voicemail and emails led to the closure July 10, 2011, of the popular tabloid News of the World (owned by a subsidiary of Rupert Murdoch's News Corp.) and the arrest 2 days earlier of the paper's former editor, Andy Coulson, who until Jan. 2011 had served as communications director for Prime Min. Cameron.

Wales

The Principality of Wales in western Britain has an area of 8,019 sq mi and a population (2010 est.) of 3,006,400. Cardiff is the capital, pop. (2010 est., city proper) 341,054.

Less than 20% of Wales residents speak English and Welsh; about 32,000 speak Welsh solely. A 1979 referendum rejected, 4-1, the creation of an elected Welsh assembly; a similar proposal passed by a thin margin on Sept. 18, 1997. Elections for the 60-seat assembly were held in 1997, 2003, 2007, and 2011.

Early Anglo-Saxon invaders drove Celtic peoples into the mountains of Wales, terming them Waelise (Welsh, or foreign). There they developed a distinct nationality. Members of the ruling house of Gwynedd in the 13th cent. fought England but were crushed, 1283. Edward of Caernarvon, son of Edward I of England, was created Prince of Wales, 1301.

Scotland

Scotland, a kingdom now united with England and Wales in Great Britain, occupies the northern 37% of the main British island, and the Hebrides, Orkney, Shetland, and smaller islands. Length 275 mi, breadth approx. 150 mi, area 30,414 sq mi, pop. (2010 est.) 5,222,100.

The Lowlands, a belt of land approx. 60 mi wide from the Firth of Clyde to the Firth of Forth, divide the farming region of the Southern Uplands from the granite Highlands of the N; they contain 75% of the population and most of the industry. The Highlands, famous for hunting and fishing, have been opened to industry by many hydroelectric power stations.

Edinburgh, pop. (2010 est., city proper) 486,120, is the capital. Glasgow, pop. (2010 est., city proper) 592,820, is Britain's greatest industrial center. It is a shipbuilding complex on the Clyde and an ocean port. Aberdeen, pop. (2010 est.) 217,120, NE of Edinburgh, is a major port, center of granite industry, fish-processing, and North Sea oil exploration. Dundee, pop. (2010 est.) 144,290, NE of Edinburgh, is an industrial and fish-processing center. About 90,000 persons speak Gaelic as well as English.

History. Scotland was called Caledonia by the Romans who battled early Celtic tribes and occupied southern areas from the 1st to the 4th centuries. Missionaries from Britain introduced Christianity in the 4th cent.; St. Columba, an Irish monk, converted most of Scotland in the 6th cent.

The Kingdom of Scotland was founded in 1018. William Wallace and Robert Bruce both defeated English armies 1297 and 1314, respectively.

In 1603 James VI of Scotland, son of Mary, Queen of Scots, succeeded to the throne of England as James I, and effected the Union of the Crowns. In 1707 Scotland received representation in the British Parliament, resulting from the union of former separate Parliaments. Its executive in the British cabinet is the Secretary of State for Scotland. The growing Scottish National Party urges independence. A 1979 referendum on the creation of an elected Scottish assembly was defeated, but a proposal to create a regional legislature with limited taxing authority passed by a landslide

Sept. 11, 1997. Elections for the 129-seat parliament were held 1999, 2003, 2007, and 2011; in the 2011 vote, Scottish Nationalist candidates won a majority.

Memorials of Robert Burns, Sir Walter Scott, John Knox, and Mary, Queen of Scots, draw many tourists, as do the beauties of the Trossachs, Loch Katrine, Loch Lomond, and abbey ruins.

Industries. Engineering products are the most important industry, with growing emphasis on office machinery, autos, electronics, and other consumer goods. Oil has been discovered offshore in the North Sea, stimulating on-shore support industries.

Scotland produces fine woolens, worsteds, tweeds, silks, fine linens, and jute. It is known for its special breeds of cattle and sheep. Fisheries have large hauls of herring, cod, whiting. Whisky is a major export.

The Hebrides are a group of about 500 islands, 100 inhabited, off the W coast. The **Inner Hebrides** include Skye, Mull, and Iona, the last famous for the arrival of St. Columba, 563 CE. The **Outer Hebrides** include Lewis and Harris. Industries include sheep raising and weaving. The **Orkney Isls.**, c. 90, are to the NE. The capital is Kirkwall, on Pomona Isl. Fish curing, sheep raising, and weaving are occupations. NE of the Orkneys are the 200 **Shetland Isls.**, 24 inhabited, home of Shetland ponies. The Orkneys and Shetlands are centers for the North Sea oil industry.

Northern Ireland

Northern Ireland was constituted in 1920 from 6 of the 9 counties of Ulster, the NE corner of Ireland. Area 5,452 sq mi, pop. (2010 est.) 1,799,392. Capital and chief industrial center, Belfast, pop. (2010 est., city proper) 268,745.

Industries. Shipbuilding, including large tankers, has long been an important industry, centered in Belfast, the largest port. Linen manufacture is also important, along with apparel, rope, and twine. Growing diversification has added engineering products, synthetic fibers, and electronics. There are large numbers of cattle, hogs, and sheep. Potatoes, poultry, and dairy foods are also produced.

Government and History. An act of the British Parliament, 1920, divided Northern from Southern Ireland, each with a parliament and government. When Ireland became a dominion, 1921, and later a republic, Northern Ireland chose to remain a part of the United Kingdom. It elects 18 members to the House of Commons.

During 1968-69, large demonstrations were conducted by Roman Catholics who charged they were discriminated against in voting rights, housing, and employment. The Catholics, a minority comprising about a third of the population, demanded abolition of property qualifications for voting in local elections. Violence and terrorism intensified, involving branches of the Irish Republican Army (outlawed in the Irish Republic), Protestant groups, police, and British troops. Between 1969 and 2001 more than 3,500 were killed in sectarian violence in Northern Ireland, Ireland, England, and elsewhere. For most of this period, the Northern Ireland parliament was suspended, and Britain imposed direct rule.

A settlement reached on Good Friday, Apr. 10, 1998, provided for restoration of home rule and election of a 108-member assembly with safeguards for minority rights. Both Ireland and Great Britain agreed to give up their constitutional claims on Northern Ireland. The accord was approved May 22 by voters in Northern Ireland and the Irish Republic, and elections to the assembly were held June 25. IRA dissidents seeking to derail the agreement were responsible for a bomb at Omagh Aug. 15 that killed 29 people and injured over 330.

London transferred authority to a Northern Ireland power-sharing government Dec. 2, 1999. Delays in IRA disarmament led to several suspensions of self-government. The IRA stated July 28, 2005, that it had renounced violence and ordered all units to disarm. In response, the British began reducing their military presence in the region. On Sept. 26, an international monitoring group reported that the IRA had apparently scrapped its entire arsenal. The Northern Ireland legislature, suspended for 3½ years, reconvened May 15, 2006. Elections were held in 2007 and 2011.

Religion and Education. Northern Ireland is about 58% Protestant, 42% Roman Catholic. Education is compulsory between the ages of 5 and 16 years.

Channel Islands

The Channel Islands, area 75 sq mi, off the NW coast of France, the only parts of the one-time Dukedom of Normandy belonging to England, are Jersey, Guernsey and the dependencies of Guernsey—Alderney, Brechou, Greed Sark, Little Sark, Herm, Jethou, and Lihou. **Jersey**, area 45 sq mi, pop. (2011 est.) 94,161, and **Guernsey**, area 30 sq mi, pop. (2011 est.) 65,068, have separate legal existences and lieutenant governors named by the Crown. The islands were the only British soil occupied by German troops in WWII. **Websites:** www.gov.je; www.gov.gg

Isle of Man

The Isle of Man, area 221 sq mi, pop. (2011 est.) 84,655, is in the Irish Sea, 20 mi from Scotland, 30 mi from Cumberland. It is rich in lead and iron. The island has its own laws and a lieutenant governor appointed by the Crown. The Tynwald (legislature) consists of the Legislative Council, partly elected, and House of Keys, elected. Capital: Douglas. Farming, tourism, and fishing (kippers, scallops) are chief occupations. Man is famous for the Manx tailless cat. **Website:** www.gov.im

Gibraltar

Gibraltar, a dependency on the S coast of Spain, guards the entrance to the Mediterranean. The Rock of Gibraltar has been in British possession since 1704; it is 2.5 mi long, ¾ of a mi wide and 1,396 ft in height; a narrow isthmus connects it with the mainland. Pop. (2011 est.) 28,956. **Website:** www.gibraltar.gov.gi

Gibraltar has historically been an object of contention between Britain and Spain. In 1967, residents voted with near unanimity to remain under British rule. A new constitution, May 30, 1969, increased Gibraltarian control of domestic affairs (the UK continues to handle defense and internal security matters). Following a 1984 agreement between Britain and Spain, the border, closed by Spain in 1969, was fully reopened in Feb. 1985. A UN General Assembly resolution requested Britain to end Gibraltar's colonial status by Oct. 1, 1996. A plan for the UK and Spain to share sovereignty was rejected by Gibraltar voters, Nov. 7, 2002. Residents approved a new constitution Nov. 30, 2006.

British West Indies

Swinging in a vast arc from the coast of Venezuela NE, then N and NW toward Puerto Rico are the Leeward Islands, forming a coral and volcanic barrier sheltering the Caribbean from the open Atlantic. Many of the islands are self-governing British possessions. Universal suffrage was instituted 1951-54; ministerial systems were set up 1956-60.

The **Leeward Isls.** still associated with the UK are **Montserrat,** area 39 sq mi, pop. (2011 est.) 5,140, capital Plymouth; the **British Virgin Isls.,** 58 sq mi, pop. (2011 est.) 30,391, capital Road Town; and **Anguilla,** the most northerly of Leeward Islands, 35 sq mi, pop. (2011 est.) 15,094, capital The Valley. Montserrat has been devastated by the Soufrière Hills volcano, which began erupting July 18, 1995.

The three **Cayman Isls.,** a dependency, lie S of Cuba, NW of Jamaica. Pop. (2011 est.) 51,384, most of it on Grand Cayman. It is a free port; in the 1970s Grand Cayman became a tax-free refuge for foreign funds and branches of many Western banks were opened there. Total area 102 sq mi, capital George Town.

The **Turks and Caicos Isls.** are a dependency at the SE end of the Bahama Islands. Of about 30 islands, only 6 are inhabited; area 366 sq mi, pop. (2011 est.) 44,819; capital Grand Turk. Salt, shellfish, and conch shells are the main exports.

Bermuda

Bermuda is a British dependency governed by a royal governor and an assembly, dating from 1620, the oldest legislative body among British dependencies. Capital is Hamilton. **Website:** www.gov.bm

It is a group of about 150 small islands of coral formation, 20 inhabited, comprising 21 sq mi in the western Atlantic, 580 mi E of N. Carolina. Pop. (2011 est.) 68,679 (about 55% of African descent). Pop. density is high.

Tourism is the major industry. Bermuda is also a haven for the offshore insurance industry. Exports include petroleum products, medicine. In a referendum Aug. 15, 1995, voters rejected independence by nearly a 3-to-1 majority.

Hurricane Fabian, the most potent storm to reach Bermuda in 50 years, struck Sept. 5, 2003; 4 people were missing and presumed dead, and damage was estimated at over $300 mil.

South Atlantic

The **Falkland Isls.,** a dependency, lie 300 mi E of the Strait of Magellan at the southern end of S. America.

The Falklands, or Islas Malvinas, include 2 large islands and about 200 smaller ones, area 4,700 sq mi, pop. (2008 est.) 3,140, capital Stanley. The licensing of foreign fishing vessels has become the major source of revenue. Sheep-grazing is a main industry; wool is the principal export. There are indications of large oil and gas deposits. The islands are also claimed by Argentina, though 97% of inhabitants are of British origin. Argentina invaded the islands Apr. 2, 1982. The British responded by sending a task force to the area, landing their main force on the Falklands, May 21, and forcing an Argentine surrender at Port Stanley, June 14. A pact resuming commercial air service with Argentina was signed July 14, 1999. **Website:** www.falklands.gov.fk

British Antarctic Territory, south of 60° S lat., formerly a dependency of the Falkland Isls., was made a separate colony in 1962 and includes the South Shetland Isls., the South Orkneys, and the Antarctic Peninsula. A chain of meteorological stations is maintained.

South Georgia and the **South Sandwich Isls.,** formerly administered by the Falkland Isls., became a separate dependency in 1985. Total area of 1,507 sq mi. South Georgia, with no permanent population, is about 800 mi SE of the Falklands; the South Sandwich Isls. are uninhabited, about 470 mi SE of South Georgia.

St. Helena, an island 1,200 mi off the W coast of Africa and 1,800 mi E of S. America, 160 sq mi and pop. (2011 est.) 7,700.

Flax, lace, and rope-making are the chief industries. After Napoleon Bonaparte was defeated at Waterloo the Allies exiled him to St. Helena, where he lived from Oct. 16, 1815, to his death, May 5, 1821. Capital is Jamestown. **Website:** www.sainthelena.gov.sh

Tristan da Cunha is the principal island in a group of islands of volcanic origin, total area 40 sq mi, halfway between the Cape of Good Hope and S. America. A volcanic peak 6,760 ft high erupted in 1961. The 262 inhabitants were removed to England, but most returned in 1963. The islands are dependencies of St. Helena. Pop. (2010 est.): 265.

Ascension is an island of volcanic origin, 34 sq mi in area, 700 mi NW of St. Helena, through which it is administered. It is a communications relay center for Britain, and has a U.S. satellite tracking center. Pop. (2010) was 884, half of them communications workers. The island is noted for sea turtles. **Website:** www.ascension-island.gov.ac.

British Indian Ocean Territory

Formed Nov. 1965, embracing islands formerly dependencies of Mauritius or Seychelles: the Chagos Archipelago (including Diego Garcia), Aldabra, Farquhar, and Des Roches. The latter 3 were transferred to Seychelles, which became independent in 1976. Total area 21,004 sq mi, land area 23 sq mi. No permanent civilian population remains; the UK and the U.S. maintain a military presence.

Pacific Ocean

Pitcairn Isl. is in the Pacific, halfway between S. America and Australia. The island was discovered in 1767 by Philip Carteret but was not inhabited until 23 years later when the mutineers of the *Bounty* landed there. The 2011 pop. was 48. It is a British dependency and is administered by a British High Commissioner in New Zealand and a local Council. The uninhabited islands of Henderson, Ducie, and Oeno are in the Pitcairn group, area 18 sq mi. **Website:** www.government.pn

United States
United States of America

People: Population: 311,050,977 (incl. 50 states & Dist. of Columbia). (Note: U.S. pop. figures may differ elsewhere in *The World Almanac*.) **Age distrib.:** <15: 20%; 65+: 13.2%. **Pop. density:** 88.1 per sq mi, 34 per sq km. **Urban:** 82.3%. **Ethnic groups:** white 80%, black 13%, Asian 4%, Amerindian & Alaska native 1%. (Hispanic, any race 15%.) **Principal languages:** English, Spanish, other Indo-European, Asian & Pacific Island, Hawaiian (official in Hawaii). **Chief religions:** Protestant 51%, Roman Catholic 24%, Mormon 2%, Jewish 2%, other Christian 2%, none 4%.

Geography: Total area: 3,794,100 sq mi, 9,826,675 sq km; **Land area:** 3,531,905 sq mi, 9,147,593 sq km. **Topography:** Vast central plain, mountains in W, hills and low mountains in E. **Capital:** Washington, DC, 4,459,904.

Government: Federal republic, strong democratic tradition. **Head of state and gov.:** Pres. Barack Obama; b. Aug. 4, 1961; in office: Jan. 20, 2009. **Local divisions:** 50 states and Dist. of Columbia. **Defense budget:** $722.14 bil. **Active troops:** 1,563,996.

Economy: Industries: petroleum, steel, motor vehicles, aerospace, telecommunications, chemicals, electronics, food proc., consumer goods, lumber, mining. **Chief crops:** wheat, corn, other grains, fruits, vegetables, cotton. **Natural resources:** coal, copper, lead, molybdenum, phosphates, rare earth elements, uranium, bauxite, gold, iron, mercury, nickel, potash, silver, tungsten, zinc, petroleum, nat. gas, timber. **Crude oil reserves** (2009): 20.7 bil bbls. **Arable land:** 17.8%. **Livestock:** cattle: 94.5 mil; chickens: 2.1 bil; goats: 3.1 mil; pigs: 67.1 mil; sheep: 5.7 mil. **Fish catch:** 4.7 mil metric tons. **Electricity prod.** (2009): 3.95 tril kWh. **Labor force** (excl. unemployed): farming, forestry, and fishing 0.7%; mfg., extraction, transp., and crafts 20.3%; managerial, professional, and technical 37.3%; sales and office 24.2%; other services 17.6%.

Finance: Monetary unit: Dollar (USD). **GDP:** $14.7 tril; **per capita GDP:** $47,200; **GDP growth:** 2.8%. **Imports:** $1.9 tril; China 19.3%, Canada 14.2%, Mexico 11.1%, Japan 6.1%, Germany 4.5%. **Exports:** $1.3 tril; Canada 19.4%, Mexico 12.2%, China 6.6%, Japan 4.8%, UK 4.3%, Germany 4.1%. **Tourism:** $103.5 bil. **Budget:** $3.4 tril. **Total reserves less gold:** $121.4 bil. **Gold:** 261.5 mil oz t. **CPI change:** 1.6%.

Transport: Railways: 139,679 mi. **Motor vehicles:** 809.3 vehicles per 1,000 pop. **Civil aviation:** 762.8 bil pass.-mi (incl. airlines based in territories and dependencies); 5,194 airports.

Communications: TV sets: 844 per 1,000 pop. **Radios:** 145 per 1,000 pop. **Telephone lines:** 48.7 per 100 pop. **Daily newspaper circ.:** 193.2 per 1,000 pop. **Internet:** 79 users per 100 pop.

Health: Life expect.: 75.9 male; 80.9 female. **Births:** 13.7 (per 1,000 pop.). **Deaths:** 8.4 (per 1,000 pop.). **Natural inc.:** 0.53%. **Infant mortality:** 6.1 (per 1,000 live births). **HIV rate:** 0.6%.

Education: Compulsory: ages 6-17. **Literacy:** 99%.

Major intl. organizations: UN (FAO, IBRD, ILO, IMF, WHO), APEC, NAFTA, NATO, OAS, OECD, OSCE, WTO.

Website: www.usa.gov

See also U.S. History chapter; Chronology of the Year's Events.

Uruguay
Oriental Republic of Uruguay

People: Population: 3,308,535. **Age distrib.:** <15: 22.2%; 65+: 13.7%. **Pop. density:** 49 per sq mi, 18.9 per sq km. **Urban:** 92.5%. **Ethnic groups:** white 88%, mestizo 8%, black 4%. **Principal languages:** Spanish (official), Portunol, Brazilero. **Chief religions:** Roman Catholic 47%, non-Catholic Christian 11%, nondenominational 23%, atheist or agnostic 17%.

Geography: Total area: 68,037 sq mi, 176,215 sq km; **Land area:** 67,574 sq mi, 175,015 sq km. **Location:** In southern S. America, on Atlantic O. **Neighbors:** Argentina on W, Brazil on N. **Topography:** Uruguay is composed of rolling, grassy plains and hills, well watered by rivers flowing W to Uruguay R. **Capital:** Montevideo, 1,634,809.

Government: Type: Republic. **Head of state and gov.:** Pres. José (Pepe) Mujica; b. May 20, 1935; in office: Mar. 1, 2010. **Local divisions:** 19 departments. **Defense budget:** $431 mil. **Active troops:** 24,621.

Economy: Industries: food proc., elec. machinery, transp. equip., petroleum prods., textiles, chemicals, beverages. **Chief crops:** soybeans, cellulose, rice, wheat. **Natural resources:** hydropower, minor minerals, fish. **Arable land:** 10.7%. **Livestock:** cattle: 12.5 mil; chickens: 16 mil; goats: 16,700; pigs: 200,000; sheep: 8.7 mil. **Fish catch:** 81,502 metric tons. **Electricity prod.:** 8.5 bil kWh. **Labor force:** agric. 13%, industry 14%, services 73%.

Finance: Monetary unit: Peso (UYU) (Sept. 2011: 18.70 = $1 U.S.). **GDP:** $48 bil; **per capita GDP:** $13,700; **GDP growth:** 8.5%. **Imports:** $8.3 bil; Brazil 18.6%, Argentina 16.7%, China 13.5%, Venezuela 9.1%, U.S. 8.3%, Russia 4.2%. **Exports:** $6.7 bil; Brazil 21%, Nueva Palmira Free Zone 10.2%, Argentina 7.5%, Chile 5.5%, Russia 5.3%. **Tourism:** $1.5 bil. **Budget:** $17.9 bil. **Total reserves less gold:** $7.6 bil. **Gold:** 8,459 oz t. **CPI change:** 6.7%.

Transport: Railways: 1,020 mi. **Motor vehicles:** 222.7 vehicles per 1,000 pop. **Civil aviation:** 610.2 mil pass.-mi; 9 airports. **Chief port:** Montevideo.

Communications: TV sets: 381 per 1,000 pop. **Radios:** 603 per 1,000 pop. **Telephone lines:** 28.6 per 100 pop. **Internet:** 43.4 users per 100 pop.

Health: Life expect.: 73.1 male; 79.5 female. **Births:** 13.5 (per 1,000 pop.). **Deaths:** 9.6 (per 1,000 pop.). **Natural inc.:** 0.39%. **Infant mortality:** 9.7 (per 1,000 live births). **HIV rate:** 0.5%.

Education: Compulsory: ages 6-15. **Literacy:** 98.3%.

Major intl. organizations: UN (FAO, IBRD, ILO, IMF, WHO), OAS, WTO.

Embassy: 1913 I St. NW 20006; 331-1313.

Website: portal.gub.uy

Spanish settlers began to supplant the indigenous Charrua Indians in 1624. Portuguese from Brazil arrived later, but Uruguay was attached to the Spanish Viceroyalty of Rio de la Plata in the 18th cent. Rebels fought against Spain beginning in 1810. An independent republic was declared Aug. 25, 1825. To suppress Tupamaro guerrilla activities, a repressive military regime took power in 1973. Constitutional government was restored in 1985.

Uruguay's standard of living remains one of the highest in S. America, and political and labor conditions now rank among the freest. José (Pepe) Mujica, a former guerrilla who transformed his Marxist Tupamaro movement into a mainstream political party, won a presidential runoff election Nov. 29, 2009, and took office Mar. 1, 2010.

Uzbekistan
Republic of Uzbekistan

People: Population: 28,128,600. **Age distrib.:** <15: 26.5%; 65+: 4.7%. **Pop. density:** 171.3 per sq mi, 66.1 per sq km. **Urban:** 36.2%. **Ethnic groups:** Uzbek 80%, Russian 6%, Tajik 5%, Kazakh 3%, Karakalpak 3%, Tatar 2%. **Principal languages:** Uzbek (official), Russian, Tajik. **Chief religions:** Muslim (mostly Sunni) 88%, Eastern Orthodox 9%.

Geography: Total area: 172,742 sq mi, 447,400 sq km; **Land area:** 164,248 sq mi, 425,400 sq km. **Location:** Central Asia. **Neighbors:** Kazakhstan on N and W; Kyrgyzstan, Tajikistan on E; Afghanistan, Turkmenistan on S. **Topography:** Mostly plains and desert. **Capital:** Tashkent, 2,209,647.

Government: Type: Republic with authoritarian rule. **Head of state:** Pres. Islam A. Karimov; b. Jan. 30, 1938; in office: Mar. 24, 1990. **Head of gov.:** Prime Min. Shavkat Mirziyaev; b. 1957; in office: Dec. 11, 2003. **Local divisions:** 12 regions, 1 autonomous republic, 1 city. **Defense budget:** $1.42 bil. **Active troops:** 67,000.

Economy: Industries: textiles, food proc., machine building, metallurgy, gold, petroleum, nat. gas, chemicals. **Chief crops:** cotton, vegetables, fruits, grain. **Natural resources:** nat. gas, petroleum, coal, gold, uranium, silver, copper, lead, zinc, tungsten, molybdenum. **Crude oil reserves:** 594 mil bbls. **Arable land:** 10.1%. **Livestock:** cattle: 8 mil; chickens: 29.1 mil; goats: 2.2 mil; pigs: 92,000; sheep: 11.4 mil. **Fish catch:** 9,469 metric tons. **Electricity prod.** (2009): 47.4 bil kWh. **Labor force:** agric. 44%, industry 20%, services 36%.

Finance: Monetary unit: Som (UZS) (Sept. 2011: 1,750.00 = $1 U.S.). **GDP:** $85.9 bil; **per capita GDP:** $3,100; **GDP growth:** 8.5%. **Imports:** $9.4 bil; Russia 22.1%, China 20.3%, South Korea 15%, Germany 6%, Ukraine 5.3%, Kazakhstan 4.6%. **Exports:** $13.1 bil; Ukraine 30.5%, Russia 15.8%, Turkey 7.7%, Kazakhstan 7.4%, Bangladesh 7%, China 6.5%. **Tourism:** $99 mil. **Budget:** $12.3 bil. **Total reserves less gold:** NA.

Transport: Railways: 2,265 mi. **Civil aviation:** 3 bil pass.-mi; 33 airports. **Chief port:** Termiz.

Communications: TV sets: 226 per 1,000 pop. **Radios:** 456 per 1,000 pop. **Telephone lines:** 6.8 per 100 pop. **Internet:** 20 users per 100 pop.

Health: Life expect.: 69.5 male; 75.7 female. **Births:** 17.4 (per 1,000 pop.). **Deaths:** 5.3 (per 1,000 pop.). **Natural inc.:** 1.21%. **Infant mortality:** 21.9 (per 1,000 live births). **HIV rate:** 0.1%.

Education: Compulsory: ages 7-18. **Literacy:** 99.3%.

Major intl. organizations: UN (FAO, IBRD, ILO, IMF, WHO), CIS, OSCE, WTO (observer).

Embassy: 1746 Massachusetts Ave. NW 20036; 887-5300.

Website: www.gov.uz

The region was overrun by the Mongols under Genghis Khan in 1220. In the 14th cent., Uzbekistan became the center of a native Timurid empire. In later centuries Muslim feudal states emerged. Russian military conquest began in the 19th cent. Uzbek SSR became a Soviet republic in 1925.

Uzbekistan declared independence Aug. 29, 1991. It became an independent republic when the Soviet Union disbanded Dec. 26, 1991. Since then, the authoritarian government of Uzbekistan has been led by a former Communist, Islam A. Karimov.

Attacks by Islamic militants, Mar.-July 2004, killed more than 50 people. In June 2004, Russia's OAO Lukoil signed a $1 bil deal to develop Uzbekistan's natural gas fields. Militants bombed the U.S. and Israeli embassies in Tashkent, July 30.

After armed dissidents at Andizhan, east Uzbekistan, attacked government buildings and freed hundreds of prisoners, May 12-13, 2005, Uzbek security forces opened fire on rebels and unarmed demonstrators, killing many. Karimov then launched a general crackdown on human rights activists. Irritated by U.S. human rights pressures, Karimov ordered the U.S. to vacate an airbase used to support operations in Afghanistan; the U.S. pullout was completed Nov. 21. Meeting in Moscow a week earlier, Karimov and Russian Pres. Vladimir Putin signed a military cooperation agreement.

Karimov remained in office following the formal expiration of his presidential term Jan. 22, 2007; despite a 2-term limit under the constitution, he ran for a 3rd term Dec. 23 and won with an 88.1% majority. Sanctions imposed by the EU on Uzbek officials after the 2005 Andizhan shootings were lifted Oct. 13, 2008.

Vanuatu
Republic of Vanuatu

People: Population: 224,564. **Age distrib.:** <15: 29.6%; 65+: 4.3%. **Pop. density:** 47.7 per sq mi, 18.4 per sq km. **Urban:** 25.6%. **Ethnic groups:** Ni-Vanuatu 99%. **Principal languages:** Local languages (100+); pidgin; English, French (both official). **Chief religions:** Presbyterian 31%, Anglican 13%, Roman Catholic 13%, Seventh-Day Adventist 11%, indigenous beliefs 6%, other Christian 14%, none 1%.

Geography: Total area: 4,706 sq mi, 12,189 sq km; **Land area:** 4,706 sq mi, 12,189 sq km. **Location:** SW Pacific, 1,200 mi. NE of Brisbane, Australia. **Neighbors:** Fiji to E, Solomon Isls. to NW. **Topography:** Dense forest with narrow coastal strips of cultivated land. **Capital:** Port Vila, 44,000.

Government: Type: Republic. **Head of state:** Pres. Iolu Johnson Abil; b. 1942; in office: Sept. 2, 2009. **Head of gov.:** Prime Min. Sato Kilman; in office: June 26, 2011. **Local divisions:** 6 provinces. **Defense budget/active troops:** NA.

Economy: Industries: food and fish freezing, wood proc., meat canning. **Chief crops:** copra, coconuts, cocoa, coffee, taro, yams, fruits, vegetables. **Natural resources:** manganese, forests, fish. **Arable land:** 1.6%. **Livestock:** cattle: 170,000; chickens: 800,000; goats: 19,000; pigs: 89,000. **Fish catch:** 144,652 metric tons. **Electricity prod.:** 43 mil kWh. **Labor force:** agric. 65%, industry 5%, services 30%.

Finance: Monetary unit: Vatu (VUV) (Sept. 2011: 91.96 = $1 U.S.). **GDP:** $1.1 bil; **per capita GDP:** $5,100; **GDP growth:** 2.2%. **Imports:** (2006) $156 mil; Japan 17.5%, Australia 13.7%, Singapore 12.2%, China 11.3%, New Zealand 7%, Poland 6.7%, France 5.9%, Fiji 5.6%. **Exports:** (2006) $40 mil; Thailand 57.7%, Japan 13.3%, Poland 12.8%. **Tourism:** NA. **Budget** (2005 est.): $72.2 mil. **Total reserves less gold:** $161.4 mil. **CPI change:** 2.8%.

Transport: Motor vehicles: 64.6 vehicles per 1,000 pop. **Civil aviation:** 141.1 mil pass.-mi; 3 airports. **Chief port:** Port-Vila.

Communications: TV sets: 13 per 1,000 pop. **Radios:** 344 per 1,000 pop. **Telephone lines:** 2.1 per 100 pop. **Daily newspaper circ.:** 14.3 per 1,000 pop. **Internet:** 8 users per 100 pop.

Health: Life expect.: 63 male; 66.4 female. **Births:** 20.9 (per 1,000 pop.). **Deaths:** 7.4 (per 1,000 pop.). **Natural inc.:** 1.34%. **Infant mortality:** 46.9 (per 1,000 live births). **HIV rate:** NA.

Education: Compulsory: ages 6-12. **Literacy:** 82%.

Major intl. organizations: UN (FAO, IBRD, ILO, IMF, WHO), the Commonwealth, WTO (observer).

Permanent UN mission: 800 Second Ave., Ste. 400B, New York, NY 10017; (212) 661-4323.

Website: www.governmentofvanuatu.gov.vu

The Anglo-French condominium of the New Hebrides, administered jointly by France and Great Britain since 1906, became the independent Republic of Vanuatu on July 30, 1980. Vanuatu is located in the Ring of Fire, a zone where earthquakes and volcanic eruptions are frequent.

Vatican City (The Holy See)

People: Population: 832. **Pop. density:** 4,897.4 per sq mi, 1,890.9 per sq km. **Urban:** 100%. **Ethnic groups:** Italian, Swiss, other. **Principal languages:** Italian, Latin, French, various others. **Chief religion:** Roman Catholic.

Geography: Total area: 0.17 sq mi, 0.44 sq km; **Land area:** 0.17 sq mi, 0.44 sq km. **Location:** In Rome, Italy. **Neighbors:** Completely surrounded by Italy.

Economy: Industries: printing; coins, medals, postage stamps prod.; mosaics and staff uniforms; worldwide banking and financial activities. **Labor force:** Essentially services with small amount of industry; nearly all dignitaries, priests, nuns, guards, and approx. 3,000 lay workers live outside the Vatican.

Finance: Monetary unit: Euro (EUR) (Sept. 2011: 0.71 = $1 U.S.). **Budget** (2008): $356.8 mil.

Apostolic Nunciature: 3339 Massachusetts Ave. NW 20008; 333-7121.

Website: www.vatican.va

The popes for many centuries, with brief interruptions, held temporal sovereignty over mid-Italy (the so-called Papal States), comprising an area of some 16,000 sq mi, with a population in the 19th cent. of more than 3 mil. This territory was incorporated in the new Kingdom of Italy (1861), the sovereignty of the pope being confined to the palaces of the Vatican and the Lateran in Rome and the villa of Castel Gandolfo, by an Italian law, May 13, 1871.

A Treaty of Conciliation, a concordat, and a financial convention were signed Feb. 11, 1929, by Cardinal Gasparri and Premier Mussolini. The documents established the independent state of Vatican City and gave the Roman Catholic church special status in Italy. The treaty (Lateran Agreement) was made part of the Constitution of Italy (Article 7) in 1947. Italy and the Vatican signed an agreement in 1984 on revisions of the concordat; the accord eliminated Roman Catholicism as the state religion and ended required religious education in Italian schools.

Vatican City includes the Basilica of Saint Peter, the Vatican Palace and Museum covering over 13 acres, the Vatican gardens, and neighboring buildings between Viale Vaticano and the church. Thirteen buildings in Rome, outside the boundaries, enjoy extraterritorial rights; these buildings house congregations or officers necessary for the administration of the Holy See.

The legal system is based on the code of canon law, the apostolic constitutions, and laws especially promulgated for the Vatican City by the pope. The Secretariat of State represents the Holy See in its diplomatic relations.

The present sovereign of the State of Vatican City is Pope Benedict XVI, born Joseph Ratzinger in Marktl am Inn, Germany, Apr. 16, 1927, elected Apr. 19, 2005.

Venezuela
Bolivarian Republic of Venezuela

People: Population: 27,635,743. **Age distrib.:** <15: 29.5%; 65+: 5.4%. **Pop. density:** 81.1 per sq mi, 31.3 per sq km. **Urban:** 93.4%. **Ethnic groups:** Spanish, Italian, Portuguese, Arab, German, African, indigenous. **Principal languages:** Spanish (official), indigenous dialects. **Chief religion:** Roman Catholic (nominally) 96%, Protestant 2%.

Geography: Total area: 352,144 sq mi, 912,050 sq km; **Land area:** 340,561 sq mi, 882,050 sq km. **Location:** On Carib. coast of S. America. **Neighbors:** Colombia on W, Brazil on S, Guyana on E. **Topography:** Flat coastal plain and Orinoco Delta are bordered by Andes Mts. and hills. Plains, called llanos, extend between mountains and Orinoco. Guiana Highlands and plains are S of Orinoco, which stretches 1,600 mi and drains 80% of country. **Capital:** Caracas, 3,089,964. **Cities (urban aggl.):** Maracaibo, 2,192,078; Valencia, 1,769,558; Barquisimeto, 1,179,887; Maracay, 1,057,156.

Government: Type: Federal republic. **Head of state and gov.:** Pres. Hugo Rafael Chávez Frías; b. July 28, 1954; in office: Feb. 2,

1999. **Local divisions:** 23 states, 1 federal district (Caracas), 1 federal dependency (72 islands). **Defense budget:** $3.33 bil. **Active troops:** 115,000.

Economy: Industries: petroleum, constr. materials, food proc., textiles, iron ore mining, steel, aluminum, motor vehicle assembly. **Chief crops:** corn, sorghum, sugarcane, rice, bananas, vegetables, coffee. **Natural resources:** petroleum, nat. gas, iron ore, gold, bauxite, other minerals, hydropower, diamonds. **Crude oil reserves:** 211.2 bil bbls. **Arable land:** 3.1%. **Livestock:** cattle: 16.9 mil; chickens: 115 mil; goats: 1.4 mil; pigs: 3.3 mil; sheep: 550,000. **Fish catch:** 310,423 metric tons. **Electricity prod.** (2009): 123.4 bil kWh. **Labor force:** agric. 13%, industry 23%, services 64%.

Finance: Monetary unit: Bolívar Fuerte (VEF) (Sept. 2011: 4.30 = $1 U.S.). **GDP:** $345.2 bil. **GDP per capita GDP:** $12,700; **GDP growth:** −1.9%. **Imports:** $31.4 bil; U.S. 27.1%, Colombia 11.8%, China 8.6%, Brazil 8.4%. **Exports:** $64.9 bil; U.S. 37.8%, China 5.8%, Singapore 4.9%, Cuba 4.3%. **Tourism:** $618 mil. **Budget:** $56.5 bil. **Total reserves less gold:** $13.1 bil. **Gold:** 11.8 mil oz t. **CPI change:** 29.1%.

Transport: Railways: 501 mi. **Motor vehicles:** 115.6 vehicles per 1,000 pop. **Civil aviation:** 1.6 bil pass.-mi; 129 airports. **Chief ports:** La Guaira, Maracaibo, Puerto Cabello, Punta Cardon.

Communications: TV sets: 208 per 1,000 pop. **Radios:** 291 per 1,000 pop. **Telephone lines:** 24.4 per 100 pop. **Daily newspaper circ.:** 93.3 per 1,000 pop. **Internet:** 35.6 users per 100 pop.

Health: Life expect.: 70.8 male; 77.2 female. **Births:** 20.1 (per 1,000 pop.). **Deaths:** 5.2 (per 1,000 pop.). **Natural inc.:** 1.49%. **Infant mortality:** 20.6 (per 1,000 live births). **HIV rate:** NA.

Education: Compulsory: ages 3-16. **Literacy:** 95.2%.

Major intl. organizations: UN (FAO, IBRD, ILO, IMF, WHO), OAS, OPEC, WTO.

Embassy: 1099 30th St. NW 20007; 342-2214.

Website: www.presidencia.gob.ve or venezuela-us.org

Columbus first set foot on the South American continent on the peninsula of Paria, Aug. 1498. Alonso de Ojeda, 1499, was the first European to see Lake Maracaibo. He called the land Venezuela, or Little Venice, because the Indians had houses on stilts. Spanish colonialists dominated Venezuela until Simón Bolívar's victory near Carabobo in June 1821. The republic was formed after secession from the Colombian Federation in 1830. Military strongmen ruled Venezuela for much of its history. Since 1959, the country has had democratically elected governments.

Oil accounts for more than 75% of export earnings and about half of government revenues. The government, Jan. 1, 1976, nationalized the oil industry with compensation. Attempts to reduce dependence on the hydrocarbon sector have met with limited success. The country has large reserves of natural gas; a large new gas find in the Gulf of Venezuela was announced Sept. 2009.

An attempted coup by midlevel military officers was thwarted by loyalist troops Feb. 4, 1992. A second coup attempt was thwarted in Nov. Pres. Carlos Andrés Pérez was removed from office on corruption charges, May 1993; he was convicted, May 1996, of mismanaging a $17 mil secret government fund.

A 1992 coup leader, Hugo Chávez, who ran as a populist, was elected president Dec. 6, 1998. Voters on Dec. 15, 1999, approved a new constitution greatly increasing his powers.

Popular among the poor, Chávez alienated some middle- and upper-class Venezuelans with his program of economic and political reform, and his foreign policy antagonized the U.S. Gunfire erupted at a mass protest Apr. 11, 2002, in Caracas, killing at least 17 people. Chávez was forced to relinquish power, but when an interim government issued decrees suspending democratic institutions, Chávez loyalists rebelled; the coup fell apart, and the president reclaimed his office Apr. 14. Opponents of Chávez organized strikes and recall efforts, 2003-04, but failed to oust him.

Chávez countered U.S. attempts to isolate him diplomatically and militarily by solidifying ties with other Latin American leftist leaders and with Iran and Russia. With the economy surging, he captured a 63% majority in the Dec. 3, 2006, presidential election. On Jan. 31, 2007, the legislature granted him the power to rule by decree. Constitutional changes abolishing presidential term limits were rejected by Venezuelan voters Dec. 2, 2007, but approved Feb. 15, 2009. Emboldened by the victory, Chávez pressured domestic critics and consolidated his control over the armed forces. He traveled repeatedly to Cuba for cancer treatments in 2011.

Vietnam
Socialist Republic of Vietnam

People: Population: 90,549,390. **Age distrib.:** <15: 25.2%; 65+: 5.5%. **Pop. density:** 756.4 per sq mi, 292 per sq km. **Urban:** 30.4%. **Ethnic groups:** Kinh (Viet) 86%, Tay 2%, Thai 2%, Muong 2%, Khmer 2%, Mong 1%, Nung 1%. **Principal languages:** Vietnamese (official), English increasingly favored as second language, French, Chinese, Khmer, mountain area languages (Mon-Khmer, Malayo-Polynesian). **Chief religions:** Buddhist 9%, Catholic 7%, Hoa Hao 2%, Cao Dai 1%, none 81%.

Geography: Total area: 127,881 sq mi, 331,210 sq km; **Land area:** 119,719 sq mi, 310,070 sq km. **Location:** SE Asia, on E coast of Indochinese Peninsula. **Neighbors:** China on N; Laos, Cambodia on W. **Topography:** Vietnam is long and narrow, with 1,400-mi coast. About 22% of country is readily arable, including densely settled Red R. valley in N, narrow coastal plains in center, and the wide, often marshy Mekong R. Delta in S. The rest consists of semi-arid plateaus and barren mountains, with some stretches of tropical rain forest. **Capital:** Hanoi (Hà Nội), 2,814,417. **Cities (urban aggl.):** Ho Chi Minh City, 6,167,090; Hai Phòng, 1,969,884.

Government: Type: Communist. **Head of state:** Pres. Truong Tan Sang; b. Jan. 21, 1949; in office: July 25, 2011. **Head of gov.:** Prime Min. Nguyen Tan Dung; b. Nov. 17, 1949; in office: June 27, 2006. **Local divisions:** 58 provinces, 3 cities, 1 capital region. **Defense budget:** $2.41 bil. **Active troops:** 482,000.

Economy: Industries: food proc., garments, shoes, machine-building, mining, coal, steel, cement, chemical fertilizer. **Chief crops:** paddy rice, coffee, rubber, cotton, tea, pepper, soybeans, cashews, sugarcane, peanuts, bananas. **Natural resources:** phosphates, coal, manganese, rare earth elements, bauxite, chromate, offshore oil and gas deposits, timber, hydropower. **Crude oil reserves:** 600 mil bbls. **Arable land:** 20.3%. **Livestock:** cattle: 6.1 mil; chickens: 196.1 mil; goats: 1.4 mil; pigs: 27.6 mil. **Fish catch:** 4.8 mil metric tons. **Electricity prod.:** 70 bil kWh. **Labor force:** agric. 53.9%, industry 20.3%, services 25.8%.

Finance: Monetary unit: Dong (VND) (Sept. 2011: 20,800.00 = $1 U.S.). **GDP:** $276.6 bil; **per capita GDP:** $3,100; **GDP growth:** 6.8%. **Imports:** $84.3 bil; China 23.8%, South Korea 11.6%, Japan 10.8%, Taiwan 8.4%, Thailand 6.7%, Singapore 4.9%. **Exports:** $72 bil; U.S. 20%, Japan 10.7%, China 9.8%, South Korea 4.3%. **Tourism:** $4.5 bil. **Budget:** $29.7 bil. **Total reserves less gold:** $12.5 bil. **CPI change:** 8.9%.

Transport: Railways: 1,458 mi. **Motor vehicles:** 3.8 vehicles per 1,000 pop. **Civil aviation:** 10.2 bil pass.-mi; 37 airports. **Chief ports:** Da Nang, Hai Phong, Ho Chi Minh City, Quy Nhon.

Communications: TV sets: 208 per 1,000 pop. **Radios:** 109 per 1,000 pop. **Telephone lines:** 18.7 per 100 pop. **Internet:** 27.6 users per 100 pop.

Health: Life expect.: 69.7 male; 74.9 female. **Births:** 17.1 (per 1,000 pop.). **Deaths:** 6 (per 1,000 pop.). **Natural inc.:** 1.11%. **Infant mortality:** 20.9 (per 1,000 live births). **HIV rate:** 0.4%.

Education: Compulsory: ages 6-14. **Literacy:** 92.8%.

Major intl. organizations: UN (FAO, IBRD, ILO, IMF, WHO), APEC, ASEAN, WTO.

Embassy: 1233 20th St. NW, Ste. 400, 20036; 861-0737.

Website: www.na.gov.vn

Settled by Viets from central China, Vietnam was held by China, 111 BCE-939 CE, and was a vassal state during subsequent periods. Conquest by France began in 1858 and ended in 1884 with the protectorates of Tonkin and Annam in the N and the colony of Cochin-China in the S.

Japan occupied Vietnam in 1940. A number of groups formed the Vietminh (Independence) League, headed by Ho Chi Minh, Communist guerrilla leader. In Aug. 1945 the Vietminh forced out Bao Dai, former emperor of Annam, head of a Japan-sponsored regime. France, seeking to reestablish colonial control, battled Communist and nationalist forces, 1946-54, and was defeated at Dienbienphu, May 8, 1954.

Separate states formed in N. and S. Vietnam, with Communists under Ho Chi Minh (backed by Russia and China) controlling N. Vietnam and a non-Communist government (backed by the U.S.) established in S. Vietnam, with its capital at Saigon. N. Vietnam aided Vietcong guerrillas who sought to take over S. Vietnam. The U.S. committed hundreds of thousands of troops to defend S. Vietnam and launched massive bombing raids against N. Vietnam and border areas of Laos and Cambodia. Casualties of the war were as follows—combat deaths: U.S. 47,369; S. Vietnam more than 200,000; other allied forces 5,225. Total U.S. fatalities numbered more than 58,000. Vietnamese civilian casualties were more than 1 mil. The war displaced more than 6.5 mil in S. Vietnam.

A cease-fire agreement was signed in Paris Jan. 27, 1973, by the U.S., N. and S. Vietnam, and the Vietcong. It was never implemented. The Saigon regime surrendered Apr. 30, 1975. N. Vietnam assumed control, and began transforming society along Communist lines. The country was officially reunited July 2, 1976.

Conditions in the region remained unstable after the Vietnam War ended. Heavy fighting with Cambodia took place, 1977-80. Relations with China soured as 140,000 ethnic Chinese left Vietnam charging discrimination; China cut off economic aid. Reacting to Vietnam's invasion of Cambodia, China attacked 4 Vietnamese border provinces, Feb. 1979.

Vietnam announced economic reforms aimed at reducing central control of the economy in 1987. Citing Hanoi's cooperation in returning remains of U.S. soldiers killed in the Vietnam War, the U.S. announced an end, Feb. 3, 1994, to a 19-year-old U.S. embargo on trade with Vietnam. The U.S. extended full diplomatic recognition to Vietnam July 11, 1995. The U.S. has become Vietnam's top export market, with total annual trade over $15 bil between the two countries.

Yemen
Republic of Yemen

People: Population: 24,133,492. **Age distrib.:** <15: 43%; 65+: 2.6%. **Pop. density:** 118.4 per sq mi, 45.7 per sq km. **Urban:** 31.8%. **Ethnic groups:** predominantly Arab; Afro-Arab, South Asian, European. **Principal language:** Arabic (official). **Chief religion:** Muslim (incl. Sunni, Shi'a).

Geography: Total area: 203,850 sq mi, 527,968 sq km; **Land area:** 203,850 sq mi, 527,968 sq km. **Location:** Middle East, on S coast of the Arabian Peninsula. **Neighbors:** Saudi Arabia on N, Oman on E. **Topography:** A sandy coastal strip leads to well-watered fertile mountains in interior. **Capital:** Sana'a', 2,342,043.

Government: Type: In transition. **Head of state:** Pres. Ali Abdullah Saleh; b. Mar. 21, 1942; in office: May 22, 1990. **Head of gov.:** Prime Min. Ali Muhammad Mujawar; b. 1953; in office: Apr. 7, 2007. **Local divisions:** 19 governorates and capital region. **Defense budget:** $2.02 bil. **Active troops:** 66,700.

Economy: Industries: crude oil prod. and petroleum refining, small-scale prod. of cotton textiles and leather goods, food proc., handicrafts. **Chief crops:** grains, fruits, vegetables, pulses, qat, coffee, cotton. **Natural resources:** petroleum; fish; rock salt; marble; small deposits of coal, gold, lead, nickel, copper. **Crude oil reserves:** 3 bil bbls. **Arable land:** 2.2%. **Livestock:** cattle: 1.6 mil; chickens: 58 mil; goats: 8.9 mil; sheep: 9.1 mil. **Fish catch:** 127,132 metric tons. **Electricity prod.:** 6.2 bil kWh. **Labor force:** Most people employed in agric. and herding; services, constr., industry, and commerce account for less than one-fourth of labor force.

Finance: Monetary unit: Rial (YER) (Sept. 2011: 214.00 = $1 U.S.). **GDP:** $63.4 bil; **per capita GDP:** $2,700; **GDP growth:** 8%. **Imports:** $8.4 bil; China 13.4%, UAE 11.8%, India 8.5%, Saudi Arabia 5.6%, U.S. 4.4%, Brazil 4.3%, Turkey 4.3%, Kuwait 4.2%, France 4.1%. **Exports:** $7.5 bil; China 23%, India 21.4%, Thailand 19.4%, South Africa 6.8%, Japan 6.1%, UAE 5.5%. **Tourism:** $496 mil. **Budget:** $9.3 bil. **Total reserves less gold:** $5.9 bil. **Gold:** 50,000 oz t. **CPI change:** 11.2%.

Transport: Motor vehicles: 28.1 vehicles per 1,000 pop. **Civil aviation:** 1.9 bil pass.-mi; 17 airports. **Chief ports:** Aden, Al Hudaydah, Al Mukalla.

Communications: TV sets: 344 per 1,000 pop. **Radios:** 64 per 1,000 pop. **Telephone lines:** 4.4 per 100 pop. **Daily newspaper circ.:** 4.1 per 1,000 pop. **Internet:** 10.9 users per 100 pop.

Health: Life expect.: 61.7 male; 65.9 female. **Births:** 33.5 (per 1,000 pop.). **Deaths:** 7 (per 1,000 pop.). **Natural inc.:** 2.65%. **Infant mortality:** 55.1 (per 1,000 live births). **HIV rate:** NA.

Education: Compulsory: ages 6-14. **Literacy:** 62.4%.

Major intl. organizations: UN (FAO, IBRD, ILO, IMF, WHO), AL, WTO (observer).

Embassy: 2319 Wyoming Ave. NW 20008; 965-4760.

Website: www.yemen.gov.ye or www.yemenembassy.org

Yemen's territory once was part of the ancient biblical Kingdom of Sheba, or Saba. Yemen became independent in 1918, after centuries of Ottoman Turkish rule.

Imam Yahya ibn Muhammad ruled, 1904-48, and after his assassination was succeeded by his son, Imam Ahmed, 1948-62. Army officers headed by Brig. Gen. Abdullah al-Salal declared the country to be the Yemen Arab Republic, Sept. 1962. Ahmed's heir, the Imam Mohamad al-Badr, fled to the mountains where tribesmen joined royalist forces, aided by the Saudi monarchy. Fighting between royalists and republicans killed about 150,000 people until hostilities ended in 1970.

Meanwhile, South Yemen, formed from the British colony of Aden and the British protectorate of South Arabia, became independent Nov. 1967. A Marxist state and a Soviet ally, it took the name People's Democratic Republic of Yemen in 1970. More than 300,000 Yemenis fled from the S to the N after independence, contributing to 2 decades of hostility between the 2 states.

The 2 countries were formally united May 21, 1990, but regional clan-based rivalries led to full-scale civil war in 1994. Secessionists declared a breakaway state in South Yemen, May 21, 1994, but northern troops captured the former southern capital of Aden in July. A new constitution was approved Sept. 28.

Yemen, the ancestral home of Osama bin Laden, has been caught in a crossfire between the U.S. and Islamic extremists. While on a refueling stop in Aden, Oct. 12, 2000, the destroyer U.S.S. Cole was bombed, leaving 17 Americans dead and more than 3 dozen injured. The U.S. government blamed the attack on terrorists associated with bin Laden.

Clashes beginning in June 2004 between Yemeni government forces and Shiite rebels led by an anti-U.S. cleric, Hussein al-Houthi, left more than 200 people dead. The government announced Sept. 10 that Yemeni troops had killed al-Houthi. Incumbent Pres. Ali Abdullah Saleh was reelected Sept. 20, 2006.

During 2007-10, Shiite rebels in the northwest, secessionists in the south, al-Qaeda militants in the east, and pirates in coastal waters challenged Yemeni government authority. Emboldened by the success of "Arab Spring" protests in Tunisia and Egypt in early 2011, mass demonstrations in Yemeni cities demanded Pres. Saleh's resignation, and the U.S. and Gulf Arab nations also pressed him to depart. Saleh was severely wounded June 3 in a rocket attack on the presidential compound in Sana'a'. Vice Pres. Abd al-Rab Mansur al-Hadi served as acting president June 4-Sept. 23, 2011, while Saleh received extended medical treatment in Saudi Arabia. After a 2-year manhunt, Anwar al-Awlaki, an American citizen and radical Muslim cleric linked to several plots against the U.S., was killed Sept. 30, 2011, by a U.S. missile in northern Yemen.

Zambia
Republic of Zambia

People: Population: 13,881,336. **Age distrib.:** <15: 46.7%; 65+: 2.5%. **Pop. density:** 48.4 per sq mi, 18.7 per sq km. **Urban:** 35.7%. **Ethnic groups:** African 99.5%. **Principal languages:** Bemba, Nyanja, Tonga, Lozi, Lunda, Kaonde, Luvale, English (all official); Chewa; Nsenga; Tumbuka; Lala. **Chief religions:** Christian 50%-75%, Muslim & Hindu 24%-49%, indigenous beliefs 1%.

Geography: Total area: 290,587 sq mi, 752,618 sq km; **Land area:** 287,028 sq mi, 743,398 sq km. **Location:** In S central Africa. **Neighbors:** Congo on N; Tanzania, Malawi, Mozambique on E; Zimbabwe, Namibia on S; Angola on W. **Topography:** Mostly high plateau covered with thick forests and drained by several important rivers, including the Zambezi. **Capital:** Lusaka, 1,450,759.

Government: Type: Republic. **Head of state and gov.:** Pres. Michael Sata; b. 1937; in office: Sept. 23, 2011. **Local divisions:** 9 provinces. **Defense budget:** $276 mil. **Active troops:** 15,100.

Economy: Industries: copper mining and proc., constr., foodstuffs, beverages, chemicals, textiles, fertilizer, horticulture. **Chief crops:** corn, sorghum, rice, peanuts, sunflower seeds, vegetables, flowers, tobacco, cotton, sugarcane, cassava, coffee. **Natural resources:** copper, cobalt, zinc, lead, coal, emeralds, gold, silver, uranium, hydropower. **Arable land:** 4.5%. **Livestock:** cattle: 2.9 mil; chickens: 30 mil; goats: 2 mil; pigs: 340,000; sheep: 200,000. **Fish catch:** 93,221 metric tons. **Electricity prod.:** 9.6 bil kWh. **Labor force:** agric. 85%, industry 6%, services 9%.

Finance: Monetary unit: Kwacha (ZMK) (Sept. 2011: 4,972.00 = $1 U.S.). **GDP:** $20.04 bil; **per capita GDP:** $1,500; **GDP growth:** 7.6%. **Imports:** $4.9 bil; South Africa 40.2%, Dem. Rep. of the Congo 12.9%, Kuwait 10.6%, China 4.7%. **Exports:** $6.5 bil; Switzerland 47.1%, China 11.2%, South Africa 9.2%, Dem. Rep. of the Congo 7%. **Tourism:** $98 mil. **Budget:** $3.7 bil. **Total reserves less gold:** $2.1 bil. **CPI change:** 8.5%.

Transport: Railways: 1,340 mi (incl. part of Tanzania-Zambia Railway Authority). **Motor vehicles:** 20.7 vehicles per 1,000 pop. **Civil aviation:** 12.4 mil pass.-mi; 8 airports. **Chief port:** Mpulungu.

Communications: TV sets: 64 per 1,000 pop. **Radios:** 145 per 1,000 pop. **Telephone lines:** 0.7 per 100 pop. **Daily newspaper circ.:** 4.9 per 1,000 pop. **Internet:** 6.7 users per 100 pop.

Health: Life expect.: 51.1 male; 53.6 female. **Births:** 44.1 (per 1,000 pop.). **Deaths:** 12.6 (per 1,000 pop.). **Natural inc.:** 3.15%. **Infant mortality:** 66.6 (per 1,000 live births). **HIV rate:** 13.5%.

Education: Compulsory: ages 7-13. **Literacy:** 70.9%.

Major intl. organizations: UN (FAO, IBRD, ILO, IMF, WHO), AU, the Commonwealth, WTO.

Embassy: 2419 Massachusetts Ave. NW 20008; 265-9717.

Website: www.statehouse.gov.zm

Ruled by the British as Northern Rhodesia, the country became the independent republic of Zambia within the Commonwealth Oct. 24, 1964. Independence leader Kenneth Kaunda governed the country as president, 1964-91. A Zambian government corporation in 1970 took over 51% of 2 foreign-owned copper-mining companies. Privately-held land and other enterprises were nationalized in 1975. In the 1980s and 1990s lowered copper prices hurt the economy and severe drought caused famine.

Food riots erupted in June 1990, as the nation suffered its worst violence since independence. Elections held Oct. 1991 brought an end to Kaunda's one-party rule. The new government sought to sell state enterprises, including the copper industry. Pres. Frederick Chiluba won reelection Nov. 18, 1996, but international observers cited harassment of opposition parties. A coup attempt was suppressed Oct. 28, 1997.

Thwarted in his effort to change the constitution to allow himself to run for a 3rd term, Chiluba endorsed Levy Patrick Mwanawasa, who won a disputed election Dec. 27, 2001. Food shortages threatened more than 2 mil Zambians in 2002; the government refused to distribute shipments of U.S. grain because it was genetically modified. In a hard-fought election, Sept. 28, 2006, Mwanawasa won a 2nd term. Accused of embezzling state funds while he was president, Chiluba was ordered to pay $58 mil by a British court, June 7, 2007; he was acquitted by a Zambian court, Aug. 17, 2009, of misusing $500,000 in public money.

Pres. Mwanawasa suffered a stroke June 29, 2008, and died Aug. 19. Vice-Pres. Rupiah Banda became acting pres. He won the presidency by a narrow margin in an election Oct. 30, 2008, but lost to opposition leader Michael Sata Sept. 20, 2011.

The country has made progress in treating HIV/AIDS, which afflicts nearly 1 mil adults in Zambia.

Zimbabwe
Republic of Zimbabwe

People: Population: 12,084,304. **Age distrib.:** <15: 41.9%; 65+: 3.8%. **Pop. density:** 80.9 per sq mi, 31.2 per sq km. **Urban:** 38.3%. **Ethnic groups:** African 98% (Shona 82%, Ndebele 14%), mixed & Asian 1%. **Principal languages:** English (official), Shona, Sindebele, minor tribal dialects. **Chief religions:** Syncretic (Christian & indigenous beliefs) 50%, Christian 25%, indigenous beliefs 24%, Muslim & other 1%.

Geography: Total area: 150,872 sq mi, 390,757 sq km; **Land area:** 149,362 sq mi, 386,847 sq km. **Location:** In southern Africa. **Neighbors:** Zambia on N, Botswana on W, South Africa on S, Mozambique on E. **Topography:** High plateau country, rising to mountains on E border, sloping down on other borders. **Capital:** Harare, 1,631,594.

Government: Type: In transition. **Head of state.:** Pres. Robert Gabriel Mugabe; b. Feb. 21, 1924; in office: Dec. 31, 1987. **Head of gov.:** Prime Min. Morgan Tsvangirai; b. Mar. 10, 1952; in office: Feb. 11, 2009. **Local divisions:** 8 provinces, 2 cities. **Defense budget:** $98.3 mil. **Active troops:** 29,000.

Economy: Industries: mining, steel, wood prods., cement, chemicals, fertilizer, clothing and footwear. **Chief crops:** corn, cotton, tobacco, wheat, coffee, sugarcane, peanuts. **Natural resources:** coal, chromium ore, asbestos, gold, nickel, copper, iron ore, vanadium, lithium, tin, platinum group metals. **Arable land:** 10.8%. **Livestock:** cattle: 5 mil; chickens: 32.5 mil; goats: 2.9 mil; pigs: 630,000; sheep: 380,000. **Fish catch:** 13,152 metric tons. **Electricity prod.:** 7.7 bil kWh. **Labor force:** agric. 66%, industry 10%, services 24%.

Finance: Monetary unit: Use of the Zimbabwe dollar (ZWD) was suspended in 2009; the South African rand and U.S. dollar are currently in use. **GDP:** $5.5 bil; **per capita GDP:** $500; **GDP growth:** 9%. **Imports:** $4 bil; South Africa 61%, China 5.7%. **Exports:** $2.5 bil; Dem. Rep. of the Congo 15.3%, South Africa 13.9%, Botswana 13.7%, China 9.5%, Netherlands 5.6%, UK 5.1%. **Tourism:** $634 mil. **Budget:** $2.3 bil. **CPI change** (2006-07): 24,411%.

Transport: Railways: 2,129 mi. **Motor vehicles:** 40.6 vehicles per 1,000 pop. **Civil aviation:** 436.8 mil pass.-mi; 19 airports. **Chief ports:** Binga, Kariba.

Communications: TV sets: 71 per 1,000 pop. **Radios:** 135 per 1,000 pop. **Telephone lines:** 3 per 100 pop. **Internet:** 11.5 users per 100 pop.

Health: Life expect.: 49.9 male; 49.3 female. **Births:** 31.9 (per 1,000 pop.). **Deaths:** 13.6 (per 1,000 pop.). **Natural inc.:** 1.83%. **Infant mortality:** 29.5 (per 1,000 live births). **HIV rate:** 14.3%.

Education: Compulsory: ages 6-12. **Literacy:** 91.9%.

Major intl. organizations: UN (FAO, IBRD, ILO, IMF, WHO), AU, WTO.

Embassy: 1608 New Hampshire Ave. NW 20009; 332-7100.

Website: www.zim.gov.zw

Britain took over the area as Southern Rhodesia in 1923 from the British South Africa Co. (which, under Cecil Rhodes, had conquered it by 1897) and granted internal self-government. Under a 1961 constitution, voting was restricted to keep whites in power.

On Nov. 11, 1965, Prime Min. Ian D. Smith announced his country's unilateral declaration of independence. Britain termed the act illegal and demanded that the country (known as Rhodesia until 1980) enfranchise the black African majority. The UN imposed sanctions and, in May 1968, a trade embargo, as black nationalist groups launched guerrilla attacks.

After the country held its first universal-franchise election, Apr. 21, 1979, all parties accepted a cease-fire, Dec. 5. The country changed its name to Zimbabwe upon independence, Apr. 18, 1980. Robert Mugabe, the nation's first prime min., became executive president in 1987.

From the late 1990s, Mugabe's rule became increasingly repressive. A land redistribution campaign triggered violent attacks in Apr. 2000 against some white farmers. (Whites made up less than 1% of the population but held 70% of the land.) International observers criticized Mugabe for relying on fraud and intimidation to win the presidential election of Mar. 9-11, 2002. The EU, the U.S., and the Commonwealth imposed sanctions on the Mugabe regime. In May 2005, Mugabe launched Operation Murambatsvina ("Drive out rubbish"), razing shanty dwellings and illegal street markets in urban areas and leaving some 700,000 people homeless. During 2006-08, inflation soared to a yearly rate of more than 100,000%.

Using force to intimidate his opponents, Mugabe clung to power after a widely discredited presidential election, Mar. 29, 2008, and June 27 runoff vote. A power-sharing deal was reached Sept. 15, 2008, and after prolonged and difficult negotiations, opposition leader Morgan Tsvangirai was sworn in as prime min. Feb. 11, 2009.

SPORTS

Sports Highlights, 2011

Led by Heisman Trophy-winning junior quarterback Cam Newton, Auburn completed an undefeated season to win the **2011 BCS National Championship Game**, 22-19 over Oregon, at Univ. of Phoenix Stadium in Glendale, Ariz. Jan. 10. It was the second straight year that a team from Alabama captured the national title, and the fifth consecutive championship for the Southeastern Conference.

The Vince Lombardi Trophy returned to Titletown as the Green Bay Packers held off the Pittsburgh Steelers, 31-25, in **Super Bowl XLV** at Cowboys Stadium in Arlington, TX, Feb. 6. Green Bay jumped out to a 14-0 lead and never trailed. Quarterback Aaron Rodgers threw for 304 yards and three touchdowns to win MVP honors.

The Univ. of Connecticut won the **NCAA men's basketball championship** Apr. 4 with a 53-41 drubbing of upstart Butler Univ. at Reliant Stadium in Houston. It was the third title for the Huskies, and the second straight loss for Butler, which had shocked sports fans by reaching the finals the previous year before losing to Duke. UConn point guard Kemba Walker scored 141 points over the six games and was named most outstanding player. The tournament expanded from 65 to 68 teams for the first time, and upsets were abundant: for the first time ever, none of the top eight seeds reached the Final Four.

Danielle Adams scored 30 points (22 of them in the second half) to lead Texas A&M to its first **NCAA basketball championship** with a 76-70 victory over Notre Dame Apr. 5 at Conseco Fieldhouse in Indianapolis. The senior center was named most outstanding player. Notre Dame reached the title game by defeating top-ranked Connecticut, 73-62 in the semifinals. The Lady Huskies saw their 90-game winning streak (the longest ever in college basketball) end earlier in the season with a loss to Stanford Dec. 31, 2010.

Charl Schwartzel, a 26-year-old South African, birdied the last four holes to win the **Masters Championship** in Augusta, GA, Apr. 10. The final round featured a scramble in which eight different players held a share of the lead over the last nine holes. Northern Ireland's Rory McIlroy started that day with a four-stroke lead only to shoot an 8-over-par 80. It marked the first time ever an American did not hold one of golf's four major trophies or the Ryder Cup.

McIlroy redeemed himself by winning the **U.S. Open** at Congressional Country Club in Bethesda, MD, June 19. The 22-year-old led the entire way, finishing with a record-breaking 16-under-par 268 and defeating his nearest competitor by eight strokes. The previous 72-hole record at the U.S. Open was 272, set by Tiger Woods in 2000 at Pebble Beach.

McIlroy's 42-year-old countryman Darren Clarke won his first major at the 140th **British Open Championship**, at Royal St. George's in Sandwich, Kent, England, July 17. Clarke outlasted the rain and runs by Americans Dustin Johnson and Phil Mickelson to finish 5-under.

Keegan Bradley, a 25-year-old American rookie playing in his first-ever **PGA Championship**, shocked the Atlanta Athletic Club field Aug. 14 by rallying from five shots down with three holes remaining to win the tournament.

Thoroughbred racing's three jewels once again went to three different horses in 2011. Animal Kingdom, a 20-1 longshot, captured the **Kentucky Derby** May 7 before a record crowd of 164,858 at Churchill Downs. But jockey John Velazquez couldn't repeat the feat May 21 at Pimlico in Baltimore, as Shackleford took the **Preakness Stakes** by

half a length. Neither horse did well in New York's **Belmont Stakes** June 11, won by yet another longshot, Ruler on Ice.

The Boston Bruins won their first **Stanley Cup** championship in 39 years June 15, shutting out the Vancouver Canucks 4-0 in Game 7 at Rogers Arena in Vancouver, BC, Canada. Boston goalie Tim Thomas made 37 saves in the deciding game and a record 798 in the 2011 postseason to capture the Conn Smythe Trophy for the most valuable player in the playoffs.

The Dallas Mavericks upset the heavily favored Miami Heat in six games to win their first ever **NBA Championship**, June 12 at American Airlines Arena in Miami, FL. It was also the first title in the 13-year career of Mavericks veteran forward Dirk Nowitzki, who averaged 26 points and 9.7 rebounds in the finals and was named MVP of the championship.

Japan won the **Women's World Cup** soccer tournament with a thrilling shootout victory over the U.S. in the final, held in Frankfurt, Germany, July 17. Japan's Homare Sawa took the Golden Boot award for top scorer with five goals and the Golden Ball award as the tournament's top player.

The Philadelphia Phillies ran away with **Major League Baseball**'s National League East, the Milwaukee Brewers won their first-ever NL Central championship, and the surprising Arizona Diamondbacks took out the defending champion San Francisco Giants for the NL West crown. The New York Yankees won the American League East for the 12th time in 16 years; the Texas Rangers won the AL West for the second straight year; and the Detroit Tigers took the AL Central behind the stellar pitching of Justin Verlander. Both wild cards were decided on the final day of the season in thrilling fashion. The Boston Red Sox blew a nine-game AL lead in Sept., allowing the Tampa Bay Rays to claim the fourth playoff spot in the bottom of the 12th inning against the Yankees in game 162. The Atlanta Braves suffered a similar collapse, surrendering the last NL playoff spot to the St. Louis Cardinals, who were 8.5 games back on Sept. 1.

With a solo home run, Derek Jeter became the first Yankee ever to reach 3,000 hits July 9; his teammate of 17 years, Mariano Rivera, broke the record for most career saves (602) Sept. 19; Minnesota's Jim Thome hit two home runs Aug. 15 to join the 600 career home run club.

Serbia's Novak Djokovic took over tennis's No. 1 ranking with victories in three of the four Grand Slam tournaments in 2011. He defeated Andy Murray to win the **Australian Open** (Jan. 30), and Spain's Rafael Nadal in both **Wimbledon** (July 3) and the **U.S. Open** (Sept. 12). Nadal won his sixth **French Open** (June 5) tying Björn Borg for most ever. On the women's side, Belgium's Kim Clijsters took the Australian Open (Jan. 29), and three unheralded players won their first Grand Slam titles: China's Li Na at the French Open (June 4); Petra Kvitova of the Czech Republic at Wimbledon (July 2), and Australia's Samantha Stosur at the U.S. Open (Sept. 11).

Owners in both the NFL and NBA locked out their players in 2011. The 136-day NFL lockout ended just in time for the start of the 2011 season; the new 10-year collective bargaining agreement included a salary scale for rookies and a $120 mil salary cap, but did not extend the season from 16 to 18 games, as owners had hoped. The NBA closed its doors July 1 and as of Sept. 30, had still not resolved issues related to luxury taxes, revenue sharing, and franchises that perpetually lose money.

World Almanac Editors' Picks: Greatest Sports Upsets

Sports fans noted no shortage of unlikely champions in 2011, as exemplified by the graying Dallas Mavericks' improbable win over the Miami Heat juggernaut in the NBA Finals. From the gridiron, ring, and links to the ice, court, and diamond, here are 10 other moments that left the sports world stunned.

Horse Tale

Saratoga, NY: Aug. 13, 1919

Antigambling laws and the first World War had all but destroyed thoroughbred racing in the U.S. when along came a horse named Man o' War. In 1919 and 1920, he won 20 of 21 races, many by fantastic margins—including the Triple Crown of the Kentucky Derby, Preakness, and Belmont Stakes. Over the course of 16 months, Man o' War made the United States the epicenter of the sport. He was as big a star in his day as Babe Ruth. The only blemish on Man o' War's record was a stakes race in Saratoga during the summer of 1919. The horse that went off with 100-to-1 odds and beat him by a half-length was named—what else?—Upset!

Sweep Victory

Cleveland, OH: Oct. 2, 1954

The 7-4 final score of decisive Game Four barely hinted at the remarkable story of the 1954 World Series. The Cleveland Indians had looked invincible as they took the field in the Series opener against the NY Giants in New York. Cleveland was coming off a record-setting 111-win season with a pitching staff that boasted future Hall of Famers and a lineup bristling with power hitters. The Giants had National League MVP Willie Mays, a lot of heart, and not much else. In Game One, Mays saved the day with an eye-popping over-the-shoulder catch that's still considered the greatest ever. Pinch-hitter Dusty Rhodes came off the bench in the 10th inning to win the game with a three-run home run. Rhodes also drove in the deciding runs in pinch-hit appearances in Games Two and Three. But the Giants didn't need Rhodes in the finale, as they completed their World Series sweep with an easy 7-4 victory.

You Don't Know Jack

San Francisco, CA: June 19, 1955

Golfer Jack Fleck was a man who understood perseverance. He survived the bankruptcy of his family's farm as a boy and the horrors of D-Day as a young man. At the age of 33, he had yet to win a single tournament as a pro. That changed in the 1955 U.S. Open when, after 72 holes, he found himself dead even with his idol, Ben Hogan, who was aiming for his fifth U.S. Open win. This development was so utterly unexpected that NBC actually ended its TV coverage of the tournament while Fleck still had two holes to go! Fleck defeated Hogan by three strokes in a playoff the next day to complete the greatest upset in golf history.

Do You Believe in Miracles?

Lake Placid, NY: Feb. 22, 1980

Hands down, the best hockey team in the world in 1980 was the Soviet Union's national squad. They regularly beat the world's top pro teams—including a 6-0 wipeout of NHL All-Stars in 1979. They also defeated the U.S. Olympians 10-3 in an exhibition less than two weeks before their rematch in Lake Placid. This time the winner would go on to play for the gold medal. For two periods, the Soviets outshot and outplayed the Americans, but led only 3-2. In the final period, with Team USA on a power play, Mark Johnson scored to tie the game. Less than two minutes later, captain Mike Eruzione threaded a wrist shot into the net for a 4-3 lead. For the final 10 minutes, the Soviets were turned away time and again by the Americans' desperate defense. Team USA followed this amazing win by beating Finland for the gold medal.

Hoya Destroyas

Lexington, KY: Apr. 1, 1985

Experts were calling Georgetown one of the greatest college hoops teams in history before the Hoyas took the floor for the 1985 NCAA Final against the Villanova Wildcats—a team they had already beaten twice that season. The Hoyas had just demolished powerful St. John's in the semifinals, in what many believed to be that year's "real" championship game. But Villanova hung tough and held a one-point lead at halftime. The Wildcats missed only one shot in the second half—and only six in the entire game—as they held off a furious charge by Georgetown in the closing minutes. Guards Harold Jensen and Dwayne McClain hit clutch shots in the final minutes as Villanova pulled off an epic upset 66-64.

Teenage Dream

Paris, France: June 5, 1989

No one at the 1989 French Open expected Ivan Lendl to lose—especially not to the 17-year-old American Michael Chang. Lendl, the top-ranked player in the world, had already banked three singles championships on the red clay of Roland Garros. After dropping the first two sets in the Round of 16 match with Lendl, Chang battled back to tie the score. Fighting cramps and exhaustion in a grueling fifth set, Chang used every trick in his bag including, at one point, serving underhand. He maneuvered Lendl out of position and either banged home winners or forced the Czech star into uncharacteristic errors. Lendl lost the match on a double-fault, and Chang reeled off three more victories to become the youngest, and unlikeliest, French Open champion.

Busted by Douglas

Tokyo, Japan: Feb. 11, 1990

No fighter was more intimidating than Mike Tyson in 1990. Every time the undefeated 23-year-old heavyweight stepped into the ring, there was a chance his opponent would hit the canvas before the end of the first round. A winter fight with Buster Douglas was slated to be a warm-up for Tyson's anticipated showdown with the No. 1 contender, Evander Holyfield. Not surprisingly, Douglas fought like he had nothing to lose. He was actually ahead on points when Tyson floored him in the 8th round. Tyson looked to finish the job in the next two rounds, but Douglas hung tough and stopped Tyson with a thunderous uppercut in the 10th. Douglas pinned Tyson against the ropes and knocked him out to become undisputed heavyweight champion.

Solid Gold

Salt Lake City, UT: Feb. 21, 2002

Sarah Hughes was no ice princess. She was not known for her artistic skating, nor did her technical precision turn many heads. Heading into her long program at the 2002 Olympics, Hughes was in fourth place. In skating terms, that meant she had almost no chance of winning the gold. Hughes *did* have something favorites Michelle Kwan and Sasha Cohen (her teammates) and Russian Irina Slutskaya did not—the ability to elevate her game when a gold medal was within her grasp. Hughes nailed seven flawless triple jumps, took a seat, and watched in astonishment as Kwan and Cohen fell and Slutskaya turned in a lackluster performance. When the scores were tallied, Hughes was the Olympic champion.

David Stuns Goliath

Ann Arbor, MI: Sept. 1, 2007

In college football, early September is a time for powerhouse teams to schedule "tune-up" games against weaker opponents. That's the only reason Appalachian State, a Division I-AA school, was even on the same field as the No. 5-ranked Division I-A Michigan Wolverines. As the game unfolded, however, it became increasingly clear that it was the Mountaineers who were doing the tuning-up. Appalachian State scored 21 second-quarter points to grab a 28-17 halftime lead. The Wolverines came roaring back in the second half and lined up to kick the winning field goal with time running out. But the Mountaineers' Corey Lynch broke through to block the kick and preserve a 34-32 victory. It was the first time a Division I-AA school had ever beaten a nationally ranked Division I team.

Giant Shock

Phoenix, AZ: Feb. 3, 2008

Nineteen-and-oh. That's the historic mark the New England Patriots were gunning for as they took the field against the underdog New York Giants in Super Bowl XLII. An undefeated, 16-game regular season plus two playoff victories had put the Pats in line to become the first team since the 1972 Dolphins to complete a perfect season. But New York's relentless pass rush and a desperate fourth-quarter pass completion from Eli Manning to David Tyree gave the Giants a chance to win the game with under a minute left. Manning flipped a perfect pass to Plaxico Burress in the end zone to seal a 17-14 win. The same New York fans who had booed Manning in December now cheered him as the Super Bowl MVP.

2012 Summer Olympic Games
London, England, UK, July 27-Aug. 12, 2012

An estimated 10,500 athletes from 204 nations were expected to compete for medals in 302 events in the XXX Summer Olympiad July 27-Aug. 12, 2012. London, England, was hosting the Games for the third time, an Olympic record; the city had previously hosted the Olympic Games in 1908 and 1948. The Olympic Park complex, located in London's East End, is the main site of the games and includes the 80,000-seat Olympic Stadium, where the track-and-field events and opening and closing ceremonies will take place.

The number of events is the same as that of the Summer Games in Beijing in 2008, but the International Olympic Committee (IOC) elected to drop baseball and softball, bringing the number of sports included in the games to 26 from 28. Women were to compete for medals in boxing for the first time, and a mixed-doubles event was added to the tennis competitions.

General Olympic Information

The modern Olympic Games, first held in Athens, Greece, in 1896, were the result of efforts by Baron Pierre de Coubertin, a French educator, to promote interest in education and culture and to foster better international understanding through love of athletics. His inspiration was the ancient Greek Olympic Games, most notable of the four Panhellenic celebrations. The games were combined patriotic, religious, and athletic festivals held every four years. The first such recorded festival was held in 776 BCE, when the Greeks began to keep their calendar by "Olympiads," or four-year spans between the games.

Baron de Coubertin enlisted 13 nations to send athletes to the first modern Olympics in 1896; now athletes from more than 200 nations and territories compete in the Summer Olympics. The Winter Olympic Games were started in 1924.

Symbol: Five rings or circles, linked to represent the sporting friendship of all peoples. They also symbolize 5 geographic areas—Europe, Asia, Africa, Australia, and America. Each ring is a different color—blue, yellow, black, green, and red—which, with the color white, represent the colors of the world's flags.

Flag: The symbol of the 5 rings on a plain white background.

Creed: "The most important thing in the Olympic Games is not to win but to take part, just as the most important thing in life is not the triumph but the struggle. The essential thing is not to have conquered but to have fought well."

Motto: "Citius, Altius, Fortius." Latin meaning "swifter, higher, stronger."

Oath: "In the name of all the competitors I promise that we shall take part in these Olympic Games, respecting and abiding by the rules which govern them, committing ourselves to a sport without doping and without drugs, in the true spirit of sportsmanship, for the glory of sport and the honor of our teams."

Flame: The modern version of the flame was adopted in 1936. The torch used to kindle it is first lit by the sun's rays at Olympia, Greece, then carried to the site of the Games by relays of runners. Ships and planes are used when necessary.

Winter Olympic Games Sites, 1924-2018

1924	Chamonix, France	1956	Cortina d'Ampezzo, Italy	1980	Lake Placid, NY, U.S.	2006	Turin, Italy
1928	St. Moritz, Switzerland	1960	Squaw Valley, CA, U.S.	1984	Sarajevo, Yugoslavia	2010	Vancouver, BC, Canada
1932	Lake Placid, NY, U.S.	1964	Innsbruck, Austria	1988	Calgary, AB, Canada	2014	Sochi, Russia
1936	Garmisch-Partenkirchen, Germany	1968	Grenoble, France	1992	Albertville, France	2018	PyeongChang, South Korea
1948	St. Moritz, Switzerland	1972	Sapporo, Japan	1994	Lillehammer, Norway		
1952	Oslo, Norway	1976	Innsbruck, Austria	1998	Nagano, Japan		
				2002	Salt Lake City, UT, U.S.		

Summer Olympic Games Sites, 1896-2016

1896	Athens, Greece	1928	Amsterdam, Netherlands	1964	Tokyo, Japan	1992	Barcelona, Spain
1900	Paris, France	1932	Los Angeles, CA, U.S.	1968	Mexico City, Mexico	1996	Atlanta, GA, U.S.
1904	St. Louis, MO, U.S.	1936	Berlin, Germany	1972	Munich, W. Germany	2000	Sydney, Australia
1906	Athens, Greece*	1948	London, England	1976	Montreal, QC, Canada	2004	Athens, Greece
1908	London, England	1952	Helsinki, Finland	1980	Moscow, USSR	2008	Beijing, China
1912	Stockholm, Sweden	1956	Melbourne, Australia	1984	Los Angeles, CA, U.S.	2012	London, England
1920	Antwerp, Belgium	1960	Rome, Italy	1988	Seoul, South Korea	2016	Rio de Janeiro, Brazil
1924	Paris, France						

*Games not recognized by International Olympic Committee. Games VI (1916), XII (1940), and XIII (1944) were not celebrated.

2008 Summer Olympic Games Final Medal Standings

Country	G	S	B	T	Country	G	S	B	T	Country	G	S	B	T
United States	36	38	36	110	Czech Republic	3	3	0	6	Estonia	1	1	0	2
China	51	21	28	100	Slovakia	3	2	1	6	Portugal	1	1	0	2
Russia	23	21	28	72	Georgia	3	0	3	6	Iran	1	0	1	2
Great Britain	19	13	15	47	North Korea	2	1	3	6	Trinidad and Tobago	0	2	0	2
Australia	14	15	17	46	Argentina	2	0	4	6	Algeria	0	1	1	2
Germany	16	10	15	41	Switzerland	2	0	4	6	Bahamas	0	1	1	2
France	7	16	17	40	Uzbekistan	1	2	3	6	Colombia	0	1	1	2
South Korea	13	10	8	31	Armenia	0	0	6	6	Kyrgyzstan	0	1	1	2
Italy	8	10	10	28	Slovenia	1	2	2	5	Morocco	0	1	1	2
Japan	7	5	15	27	Bulgaria	1	1	3	5	Tajikistan	0	1	1	2
Ukraine	7	5	15	27	Indonesia	1	1	3	5	Bahrain	1	0	0	1
Cuba	2	11	11	24	Sweden	0	4	1	5	Cameroon	1	0	0	1
Belarus	4	5	10	19	Croatia	0	2	3	5	Panama	1	0	0	1
Spain	5	10	3	18	Lithuania	0	2	3	5	Tunisia	1	0	0	1
Canada	3	9	6	18	Mongolia	2	2	0	4	Chile	0	1	0	1
Netherlands	7	5	4	16	Thailand	2	2	0	4	Ecuador	0	1	0	1
Brazil	3	4	8	15	Zimbabwe	1	3	0	4	Iceland	0	1	0	1
Kenya	5	5	4	14	Finland	1	1	2	4	Malaysia	0	1	0	1
Kazakhstan	2	4	7	13	Greece	0	2	2	4	Singapore	0	1	0	1
Jamaica	6	3	2	11	Nigeria	0	1	3	4	South Africa	0	1	0	1
Poland	3	6	1	10	Taiwan	0	0	4	4	Sudan	0	1	0	1
Hungary	3	5	2	10	Mexico	2	0	1	3	Vietnam	0	1	0	1
Norway	3	5	2	10	Latvia	1	1	1	3	Afghanistan	0	0	1	1
New Zealand	3	1	5	9	India	1	0	2	3	Egypt	0	0	1	1
Romania	4	1	3	8	Austria	0	1	2	3	Israel	0	0	1	1
Turkey	1	4	3	8	Ireland	0	1	2	3	Mauritius	0	0	1	1
Ethiopia	4	1	2	7	Serbia	0	1	2	3	Moldova	0	0	1	1
Denmark	2	2	3	7	Belgium	1	1	0	2	Togo	0	0	1	1
Azerbaijan	1	2	4	7	Dominican Rep.	1	1	0	2	Venezuela	0	0	1	1

Summer Olympic Games Champions, 1896-2008

*Olympic record; (w) wind-aided

The 1980 games were boycotted by 62 nations, including the U.S. The 1984 games were boycotted by the USSR and most Eastern bloc nations. East and West Germany competed separately, 1968-88. The 1992 Unified Team consisted of 12 former Soviet republics. The 1992 Independent Olympic Participants (I.O.P.) were from Serbia, Montenegro, and Macedonia.

Not all sports are listed here, and many events are omitted, even within listed sports, particularly if the event has not been held in more recent Games.

Baseball (Men)

1992	Cuba, Taiwan, Japan	2000	United States, Cuba, S. Korea	2008	S. Korea, Cuba, United States
1996	Cuba, Japan, United States	2004	Cuba, Australia, Japan		

Boxing

Weight class limits have changed many times since the first Olympic boxing events were held in 1904. The following were used in the 2008 Olympic Games.

Lt. Flyweight (48 kg/106 lbs)

1968	Francisco Rodriguez, Venezuela
1972	Gyorgy Gedo, Hungary
1976	Jorge Hernandez, Cuba
1980	Shamil Sabyrov, USSR
1984	Paul Gonzalez, United States
1988	Ivailo Hristov, Bulgaria
1992	Rogelio Marcelo, Cuba
1996	Daniel Petrov, Bulgaria
2000	Brahim Asloum, France
2004	Yan Bhartelemy Varela, Cuba
2008	Zou Shiming, China

Flyweight (51 kg/112 lbs)

1904	George Finnegan, United States
1920	William Di Gennara, United States
1924	Fidel LaBarba, United States
1928	Antal Kocsis, Hungary
1932	Istvan Enekes, Hungary
1936	Willi Kaiser, Germany
1948	Pascual Perez, Argentina
1952	Nathan Brooks, United States
1956	Terence Spinks, Great Britain
1960	Gyula Torok, Hungary
1964	Fernando Atzori, Italy
1968	Ricardo Delgado, Mexico
1972	Georgi Kostadinov, Bulgaria
1976	Leo Randolph, United States
1980	Peter Lessov, Bulgaria
1984	Steve McCrory, United States
1988	Kim Kwang Sun, S. Korea
1992	Su Choi Choi, N. Korea
1996	Maikro Romero, Cuba
2000	Wijan Ponlid, Thailand
2004	Yuriorkis Gamboa Toledano, Cuba
2008	Somjit Jongjohor, Thailand

Bantamweight (54 kg/119 lbs)

1904	Oliver Kirk, United States
1908	A. Henry Thomas, Great Britain
1920	Clarence Walker, South Africa
1924	William Smith, South Africa
1928	Vittorio Tamagnini, Italy
1932	Horace Gwynne, Canada
1936	Ulderico Sergo, Italy
1948	Tibor Csik, Hungary
1952	Pentti Hamalainen, Finland
1956	Wolfgang Behrendt, E. Germany
1960	Oleg Grigoryev, USSR
1964	Takao Sakurai, Japan
1968	Valery Sokolov, USSR
1972	Orlando Martinez, Cuba
1976	Yong-Jo Gu, N. Korea
1980	Juan Hernandez, Cuba
1984	Maurizio Stecca, Italy
1988	Kennedy McKinney, United States
1992	Joel Casamayor, Cuba
1996	Istvan Kovacs, Hungary
2000	Guillermo Rigondeaux, Cuba
2004	Guillermo Rigondeaux, Cuba
2008	Badar-Uugan Enkhbat, Mongolia

Featherweight (57 kg/125 lbs)

1904	Oliver Kirk, United States
1908	Richard Gunn, Great Britain
1920	Paul Fritsch, France
1924	John Fields, United States
1928	Lambertus van Klaveren, Netherlands
1932	Carmelo Robledo, Argentina
1936	Oscar Casanovas, Argentina
1948	Ernesto Formenti, Italy
1952	Jan Zachara, Czechoslovakia
1956	Vladimir Safronov, USSR
1960	Francesco Musso, Italy
1964	Stanislav Stephashkin, USSR
1968	Antonin Roldan, Mexico
1972	Boris Kousnetsov, USSR
1976	Angel Herrera, Cuba
1980	Rudi Fink, E. Germany
1984	Meldrick Taylor, United States
1988	Giovanni Parisi, Italy
1992	Andreas Tews, Germany
1996	Somluck Kamsing, Thailand
2000	Bekzat Sattarkhanov, Kazakhstan
2004	Alexei Tichtchenko, Russia
2008	Vasyl Lomachenko, Ukraine

Lightweight (60 kg/132 lbs)

1904	Harry Spanger, United States
1908	Frederick Grace, Great Britain
1920	Samuel Mosberg, United States
1924	Hans Nielsen, Denmark
1928	Carlo Orlandi, Italy
1932	Lawrence Stevens, South Africa
1936	Imre Harangi, Hungary
1948	Gerald Dreyer, South Africa
1952	Aureliano Bolognesi, Italy
1956	Richard McTaggart, Great Britain
1960	Kazimierz Pazdzior, Poland
1964	Jozef Grudzien, Poland
1968	Ronald Harris, United States
1972	Jan Szczepanski, Poland
1976	Howard Davis, United States
1980	Angel Herrera, Cuba
1984	Pernell Whitaker, United States
1988	Andreas Zuelow, E. Germany
1992	Oscar De La Hoya, United States
1996	Hocine Soltani, Algeria
2000	Mario Kindelan, Cuba
2004	Mario Kindelan, Cuba
2008	Alexey Tishchenko, Russia

Lt. Welterweight (64 kg/141 lbs)

1952	Charles Adkins, United States
1956	Vladimir Yengibaryan, USSR
1960	Bohumil Nemecek, Czechoslovakia
1964	Jerzy Kulej, Poland
1968	Jerzy Kulej, Poland
1972	Ray Seales, United States
1976	Ray Leonard, United States
1980	Patrizio Oliva, Italy
1984	Jerry Page, United States
1988	Viatcheslav Janovski, USSR
1992	Hector Vinent, Cuba
1996	Hector Vinent, Cuba

2000	Mahamadkadyz Abdullaev, Uzbekistan
2004	Manus Boonjumnong, Thailand
2008	Felix Diaz, Dominican Republic

Welterweight (69 kg/152 lbs)

1904	Albert Young, United States
1920	Albert Schneider, Canada
1924	Jean Delarge, Belgium
1928	Edward Morgan, New Zealand
1932	Edward Flynn, United States
1936	Sten Suvio, Finland
1948	Julius Torma, Czechoslovakia
1952	Zygmunt Chychia, Poland
1956	Nicolae Linca, Romania
1960	Giovanni Benvenuti, Italy
1964	Marian Kasprzyk, Poland
1968	Manfred Wolke, E. Germany
1972	Emilio Correa, Cuba
1976	Jochen Bachfeld, E. Germany
1980	Andres Aldama, Cuba
1984	Mark Breland, United States
1988	Robert Wangila, Kenya
1992	Michael Carruth, Ireland
1996	Oleg Saitov, Russia
2000	Oleg Saitov, Russia
2004	Artayev Bakhtiyar, Kazakhstan
2008	Bakhyt Sarsekbayev, Kazakhstan

Lt. Middleweight (71 kg/156 lbs)

1952	Laszlo Papp, Hungary
1956	Laszlo Papp, Hungary
1960	Wilbert McClure, United States
1964	Boris Lagutin, USSR
1968	Boris Lagutin, USSR
1972	Dieter Kottysch, W. Germany
1976	Jerzy Rybicki, Poland
1980	Armando Martinez, Cuba
1984	Frank Tate, United States
1988	Park Si Hun, S. Korea
1992	Juan Lemus, Cuba
1996	David Reid, United States
2000	Yermakhan Ibraimov, Kazakhstan

Middleweight (75 kg/165 lbs)

1904	Charles Mayer, United States
1908	John Douglas, Great Britain
1920	Harry Mallin, Great Britain
1924	Harry Mallin, Great Britain
1928	Piero Toscani, Italy
1932	Carmen Barth, United States
1936	Jean Despeaux, France
1948	Laszlo Papp, Hungary
1952	Floyd Patterson, United States
1956	Gennady Schatkov, USSR
1960	Edward Crook, United States
1964	Valery Popenchenko, USSR
1968	Christopher Finnegan, Great Britain
1972	Vyacheslav Lemechev, USSR
1976	Michael Spinks, United States
1980	Jose Gomez, Cuba
1984	Joon-Sup Shin, S. Korea
1988	Henry Maske, E. Germany
1992	Ariel Hernandez, Cuba

Middleweight (75 kg/165 lbs)
- 1996 Ariel Hernandez, Cuba
- 2000 Jorge Gutierrez, Cuba
- 2004 Gaydarbek Gaydarbekov, Russia
- 2008 James Degale, Great Britain

Lt. Heavyweight (81 kg/178 lbs)
- 1920 Edward Eagan, United States
- 1924 Harry Mitchell, Great Britain
- 1928 Victor Avendano, Argentina
- 1932 David Carstens, South Africa
- 1936 Roger Michelot, France
- 1948 George Hunter, South Africa
- 1952 Norvel Lee, United States
- 1956 James Boyd, United States
- 1960 Cassius Clay, United States
- 1964 Cosimo Pinto, Italy
- 1968 Dan Poznyak, USSR
- 1972 Mate Parlov, Yugoslavia
- 1976 Leon Spinks, United States
- 1980 Slobodan Kacar, Yugoslavia
- 1984 Anton Josipovic, Yugoslavia
- 1988 Andrew Maynard, United States

- 1992 Torsten May, Germany
- 1996 Vassili Jirov, Kazakhstan
- 2000 Alexander Lebziak, Russia
- 2004 Andre Ward, United States
- 2008 Zhang Xiaoping, China

Heavyweight (91 kg/201 lbs)
- 1984 Henry Tillman, United States
- 1988 Ray Mercer, United States
- 1992 Felix Savon, Cuba
- 1996 Felix Savon, Cuba
- 2000 Felix Savon, Cuba
- 2004 Odlanier Solis Fonte, Cuba
- 2008 Rakhim Chakhkiev, Russia

Super Heavyweight
(91+ kg/201+ lbs)
(known as heavyweight, 1904-80)
- 1904 Samuel Berger, United States
- 1908 Albert Oldham, Great Britain
- 1920 Ronald Rawson, Great Britain

- 1924 Otto von Porat, Norway
- 1928 Arturo Rodriguez Jurado, Argentina
- 1932 Santiago Lovell, Argentina
- 1936 Herbert Runge, Germany
- 1948 Rafael Iglesias, Argentina
- 1952 H. Edward Sanders, United States
- 1956 T. Peter Rademacher, United States
- 1960 Franco De Piccoli, Italy
- 1964 Joe Frazier, United States
- 1968 George Foreman, United States
- 1972 Teofilo Stevenson, Cuba
- 1976 Teofilo Stevenson, Cuba
- 1980 Teofilo Stevenson, Cuba
- 1984 Tyrell Biggs, United States
- 1988 Lennox Lewis, Canada
- 1992 Roberto Balado, Cuba
- 1996 Vladimir Klitchko, Ukraine
- 2000 Audley Harrison, Great Britain
- 2004 Alexander Povetkin, Russia
- 2008 Roberto Cammarelle, Italy

Gymnastics—Men

Floor Exercises
- 1932 István Pelle, Hungary
- 1936 Georges Miez, Switzerland
- 1948 Ferenc Pataki, Hungary
- 1952 William Thoresson, Sweden
- 1956 Valentin Muratov, USSR
- 1960 Nobuyuki Aihara, Japan
- 1964 Franco Menichelli, Italy
- 1968 Sawao Kato, Japan
- 1972 Nikolay Andrianov, USSR
- 1976 Nikolay Andrianov, USSR
- 1980 Roland Brückner, E. Germany
- 1984 Li Ning, China
- 1988 Serguei Kharikov, USSR
- 1992 Xiaosahuang Li, China
- 1996 Ioannis Melissanidis, Greece
- 2000 Igors Vihrovs, Latvia
- 2004 Kyle Shewfelt, Canada
- 2008 Zou Kai, China

Horizontal Bars
- 1896 Hermann Weingärtner, Germany
- 1904 Anton Heida, United States; Edward Hennig, United States (tie)
- 1924 Leon Stukelj, Yugoslavia
- 1928 Georges Miez, Switzerland
- 1932 Dallas Denver Bixler, United States
- 1936 Aleksanteri Saarvala, Finland
- 1948 Josef Stadler, Switzerland
- 1952 Jakob (Jack) Günthard, Switzerland
- 1956 Takashi Ono, Japan
- 1960 Takashi Ono, Japan
- 1964 Boris Shakhlin, USSR
- 1968 Mikhail Voronin, USSR; Akinori Nakayama, Japan (tie)
- 1972 Mitsuo Tsukahara, Japan
- 1976 Mitsuo Tsukahara, Japan
- 1980 Stoyan Deltchev, Bulgaria
- 1984 Shinji Morisue, Japan
- 1988 Valeri Lioukine, USSR; Vladimir Artemov, USSR (tie)
- 1992 Trent Dimas, United States
- 1996 Andreas Wecker, Germany
- 2000 Alexei Nemov, Russia
- 2004 Igor Cassina, Italy
- 2008 Zou Kai, China

Individual All-Round
- 1900 Gustave Sandras, France
- 1904 Julius Lenhart, United States
- 1908 G. Alberto Braglia, Italy
- 1912 G. Alberto Braglia, Italy
- 1920 Giorgio Zampori, Italy
- 1924 Leon Stukelj, Yugoslavia
- 1928 Georges Miez, Switzerland
- 1932 Romeo Neri, Italy
- 1936 Karl-Alfred Schwarzmann, Germany
- 1948 Veikko Huhtanen, Finland
- 1952 Viktor Ivanovich Chukarin, USSR
- 1956 Viktor Ivanovich Chukarin, USSR
- 1960 Boris Shakhlin, USSR
- 1964 Yukio Endo, Japan
- 1968 Sawao Kato, Japan
- 1972 Sawao Kato, Japan

Individual All-Round
- 1976 Nikolay Andrianov, USSR
- 1980 Aleksandr Dityatin, USSR
- 1984 Koji Gushiken, Japan
- 1988 Vladimir Artemov, USSR
- 1992 Vitaly Scherbo, Unified Team (Belarus)
- 1996 Li Xiaosahuang, China
- 2000 Alexei Nemov, Russia
- 2004 Paul Hamm, United States
- 2008 Yang Wei, China

Parallel Bars
- 1896 Alfred Flatow, Germany
- 1904 George Eyser, United States
- 1924 August Güttinger, Switzerland
- 1928 Ladislav Vacha, Czechoslovakia
- 1932 Romeo Neri, Italy
- 1936 Konrad Frey, Germany
- 1948 Michael Reusch, Switzerland
- 1952 Hans Eugster, Switzerland
- 1956 Viktor Ivanovich Chukarin, USSR
- 1960 Boris Shakhlin, USSR
- 1964 Yukio Endo, Japan
- 1968 Akinori Nakayama, Japan
- 1972 Sawao Kato, Japan
- 1976 Sawao Kato, Japan
- 1980 Aleksandr Tkachev, USSR
- 1984 Barthold Wayne Conner, United States
- 1988 Vladimir Artemov, USSR
- 1992 Vitaly Scherbo, Unified Team (Belarus)
- 1996 Roustam Sharipov, Ukraine
- 2000 Li Xiaopeng, China
- 2004 Valeri Goncharov, Ukraine
- 2008 Li Xiaopeng, China

Pommel Horse
- 1896 Louis Zutter, Switzerland
- 1904 Anton Heida, United States
- 1924 Josef Wilhelm, Switzerland
- 1928 Hermann Hänggi, Switzerland
- 1932 István Pelle, Hungary
- 1936 Konrad Frey, Germany
- 1948 Heikki Savolainen, Finland; Paavo Johannes Aaltonen, Finland; Veikko Huhtanen, Finland (tie)
- 1952 Viktor Ivanovich Chukarin, USSR
- 1956 Boris Shakhlin, USSR
- 1960 Eugen Georg Oskar Ekman, Finland; Boris Shakhlin, USSR (tie)
- 1964 Miroslav Cerar, Yugoslavia
- 1968 Miroslav Cerar, Yugoslavia
- 1972 Viktor Klimenko, USSR
- 1976 Zoltan Magyar, Hungary
- 1980 Zoltan Magyar, Hungary
- 1984 Li Ning, China; Peter Glen Vidmar, United States (tie)
- 1988 Zsolt Borkai, Hungary; Dmitri Bilozerchev, USSR; Lubomir Geraskov, Bulgaria (tie)
- 1992 Pae Gil-Su, North Korea; Vitaly Scherbo, Unified Team (Belarus) (tie)
- 1996 Li Donghua, Switzerland

Pommel Horse
- 2000 Marius Daniel Urzica, Romania
- 2004 Teng Haibin, China
- 2008 Xiao Qin, China

Rings
- 1896 Ioannis Mitropoulos, Greece
- 1904 Hermann Glass, United States
- 1924 Francesco Martino, Italy
- 1928 Leon Stukelj, Yugoslavia
- 1932 George Julius Gulack, United States
- 1936 Alois Hudec, Czechoslovakia
- 1948 Karl Frei, Switzerland
- 1952 Grant Shaginyan, USSR
- 1956 Albert Azaryan, USSR
- 1960 Albert Azaryan, USSR
- 1964 Takuji Hayata, Japan
- 1968 Akinori Nakayama, Japan
- 1972 Akinori Nakayama, Japan
- 1976 Nikolay Andrianov, USSR
- 1980 Aleksandr Dityatin, USSR
- 1984 Li Ning, China; Koji Gushiken, Japan (tie)
- 1988 Holger Behrendt, E. Germany; Dmitri Bilozerchev, USSR (tie)
- 1992 Vitaly Scherbo, Unified Team (Belarus)
- 1996 Juri Chechi, Italy
- 2000 Szilveszter Csollany, Hungary
- 2004 Dimosthenis Tampakos, Greece
- 2008 Chen Yibing, China

Team Competition
- 1904 United States, United States, United States
- 1908 Sweden, Norway, Finland
- 1912 Italy, Hungary, Great Britain
- 1920 Italy, Belgium, France
- 1924 Italy, France, Switzerland
- 1928 Switzerland, Czechoslovakia, Yugoslavia
- 1932 Italy, United States, Finland
- 1936 Germany, Switzerland, Finland
- 1948 Finland, Switzerland, Hungary
- 1952 USSR, Switzerland, Finland
- 1956 USSR, Japan, Finland
- 1960 Japan, USSR, Italy
- 1964 Japan, USSR, Unified Team of Germany
- 1968 Japan, USSR, E. Germany
- 1972 Japan, USSR, E. Germany
- 1976 Japan, USSR, E. Germany
- 1980 USSR, E. Germany, Hungary
- 1984 United States, China, Japan
- 1988 USSR, E. Germany, Japan
- 1992 Unified Team, China, Japan
- 1996 Russia, China, Ukraine
- 2000 China, Ukraine, Russia
- 2004 Japan, United States, Romania
- 2008 China, Japan, United States

Trampoline
- 2000 Alexander Moskalenko, Russia
- 2004 Yuri Nikitin, Ukraine
- 2008 Lu Chunlong, China

Vault		
1896 Carl Schumann, Germany	1956 Helmut Bantz, Unified Team of	1980 Nikolay Andrianov, USSR
1904 George Eyser, United States;	Germany;	1984 Lou Yun, China
Anton Heida, United States (tie)	Valentin Muratov, USSR (tie)	1988 Lou Yun, China
1924 Frank Kriz, United States	1960 Takashi Ono, Japan;	1992 Vitaly Scherbo, Unified Team
1928 Eugen Mack, Switzerland	Boris Shakhlin, USSR (tie)	(Belarus)
1932 Savino Guglielmetti, Italy	1964 Haruhiro Yamashita, Japan	1996 Alexei Nemov, Russia
1936 Karl-Alfred Schwarzmann, Germany	1968 Mikhail Voronin, USSR	2000 Gervasio Deferr, Spain
1948 Paavo Johannes Aaltonen, Finland	1972 Klaus Köste, E. Germany	2004 Gervasio Deferr, Spain
1952 Viktor Ivanovich Chukarin, USSR	1976 Nikolay Andrianov, USSR	2008 Leszek Blanik, Poland

Gymnastics—Women

Balance Beam	Individual All-Round	Trampoline
1952 Nina Bocharova, USSR	1952 Mariya Gorokhovskaya, USSR	2000 Irina Karavaeva, Russia
1956 Agnes Keleti, Hungary	1956 Larisa Latynina, USSR	2004 Anna Dogonadze, Germany
1960 Eva Vechtova-Bosakova,	1960 Larisa Latynina, USSR	2008 He Wenna, China
Czechoslovakia	1964 Vera Caslavska, Czechoslovakia	
1964 Vera Caslavska, Czechoslovakia	1968 Vera Caslavska, Czechoslovakia	Uneven Bars
1968 Natalya Kuchinskaya, USSR	1972 Lyudmila Turischeva, USSR	1952 Margit Korondi, Hungary
1972 Olga Korbut, USSR	1976 Nadia Comaneci, Romania	1956 Agnes Keleti, Hungary
1976 Nadia Comaneci, Romania	1980 Elena Davydova, USSR	1960 Polina Astakhova, USSR
1980 Nadia Comaneci, Romania	1984 Mary-Lou Retton, United States	1964 Polina Astakhova, USSR
1984 Ecaterina Szabo, Romania;	1988 Elena Shushunova, USSR	1968 Vera Caslavska, Czechoslovakia
Simona Pauca, Romania (tie)	1992 Tatiana Goutsou, Unified Team	1972 Karin Janz, E. Germany
1988 Daniela Silivas, Romania	1996 Lilia Podkopayeva, Ukraine	1976 Nadia Comaneci, Romania
1992 Tatiana Lyssenko, Unified Team	2000 Simona Amanar, Romania	1980 Maxi Gnauck, E. Germany
(Ukraine)	2004 Carly Patterson, United States	1984 Julianne Lyn McNamara, United
1996 Shannon Miller, United States	2008 Nastia Liukin, United States	States; Yan-Hong Ma, China (tie)
2000 Liu Xuan, China		1988 Daniela Silivas, Romania
2004 Catalina Ponor, Romania	Team Competition	1992 Lu Li, China
2008 Shawn Johnson, United States	1928 Netherlands, Italy, Great Britain	1996 Svetlana Khorkina, Russia
	1936 Germany, Czechoslovakia, Hungary	2000 Svetlana Khorkina, Russia
Floor Exercises	1948 Czechoslovakia, Hungary,	2004 Emilie LePennec, France
1952 Agnes Keleti, Hungary	United States	2008 He Kexin, China
1956 Agnes Keleti, Hungary;	1952 USSR, Hungary, Czechoslovakia	
Larisa Latynina, USSR (tie)	1956 USSR, Hungary, Romania	Vault
1960 Larisa Latynina, USSR	1960 USSR, Czechoslovakia, Romania	1952 Ekaterina Kalinchuk, USSR
1964 Larisa Latynina, USSR	1964 USSR, Czechoslovakia, Japan	1956 Larisa Latynina, USSR
1968 Vera Caslavska, Czechoslovakia;	1968 USSR, Czechoslovakia,	1960 Margarita Nikolaeva, USSR
Larisa Petrik, USSR (tie)	E. Germany	1964 Vera Caslavska, Czechoslovakia
1972 Olga Korbut, USSR	1972 USSR, E. Germany, Hungary	1968 Vera Caslavska, Czechoslovakia
1976 Nelli Kim, USSR	1976 USSR, Romania, E. Germany	1972 Karin Janz, E. Germany
1980 Nelli Kim, USSR;	1980 USSR, Romania, E. Germany	1976 Nelli Kim, USSR
Nadia Comaneci, Romania (tie)	1984 Romania, United States, China	1980 Natalia Shaposhnikova, USSR
1984 Ecaterina Szabo, Romania	1988 USSR, Romania, E. Germany	1984 Ecaterina Szabo, Romania
1988 Daniela Silivas, Romania	1992 Unified Team, Romania,	1988 Svetlana Boginskaya, USSR
1992 Lavinia Corina Milosovici, Romania	United States	1992 Henrietta Onodi, Hungary; Lavinia
1996 Lilia Podkopayeva, Ukraine	1996 United States, Russia, Romania	Corina Milosovici, Romania (tie)
2000 Elena Zamolodchikova, Russia	2000 Romania, Russia, China	1996 Simona Amanar, Romania
2004 Catalina Ponor, Romania	2004 Romania, United States, Russia	2000 Elena Zamolodchikova, Russia
2008 Sandra Izbasa, Romania	2008 China, United States, Romania	2004 Monica Rosu, Romania
		2008 Hong Un Jong, N. Korea

Soccer

Men	Men	Men
1900 Great Britain, France, Belgium	1956 USSR, Yugoslavia, Bulgaria	1992 Spain, Poland, Ghana
1904 Canada, United States, United	1960 Yugoslavia, Denmark, Hungary	1996 Nigeria, Argentina, Brazil
States	1964 Hungary, Czechoslovakia,	2000 Cameroon, Spain, Chile
1908 Great Britain, Denmark, Netherlands	Unified Team of Germany	2004 Argentina, Paraguay, Italy
1912 Great Britain, Denmark, Netherlands	1968 Hungary, Bulgaria, Japan	2008 Argentina, Nigeria, Brazil
1920 Belgium, Spain, Netherlands	1972 Poland; Hungary; USSR;	
1924 Uruguay, Switzerland, Sweden	E. Germany (tie for bronze)	Women
1928 Uruguay, Argentina, Italy	1976 E. Germany, Poland, USSR	1996 United States, China, Norway
1936 Italy, Austria, Norway	1980 Czechoslovakia, E. Germany, USSR	2000 Norway, United States, Germany
1948 Sweden, Yugoslavia, Denmark	1984 France, Brazil, Yugoslavia	2004 United States, Brazil, Germany
1952 Hungary, Yugoslavia, Sweden	1988 USSR, Brazil, W. Germany	2008 United States, Brazil, Germany

Swimming and Diving—Men

50-Meter Freestyle	Time	100-Meter Freestyle	Time
1988 Matt Biondi, United States	0:22.14	1936 Ferenc Csik, Hungary	0:57.6
1992 Aleksandr Popov, Unified Team	0:21.91	1948 Wally Ris, United States	0:57.3
1996 Aleksandr Popov, Russia	0:22.13	1952 Clark Scholes, United States	0:57.4
2000 Anthony Ervin, United States	0:21.98	1956 Jon Henricks, Australia	0:55.4
2000 Gary Hall Jr., United States	0:21.98	1960 John Devitt, Australia	0:55.2
2004 Gary Hall Jr., United States	0:21.93	1964 Don Schollander, United States	0:53.4
2008 Cesar Cielo Filho, Brazil	0:21.30*	1968 Mike Wenden, Australia	0:52.2
		1972 Mark Spitz, United States	0:51.22
100-Meter Freestyle	Time	1976 Jim Montgomery, United States	0:49.99
1896 Alfred Hajos, Hungary	1:22.2	1980 Jorg Woithe, E. Germany	0:50.40
1904 Zoltan de Halmay, Hungary (100 yds)	1:02.8	1984 Rowdy Gaines, United States	0:49.80
1908 Charles Daniels, United States	1:05.6	1988 Matt Biondi, United States	0:48.63
1912 Duke P. Kahanamoku, United States	1:03.4	1992 Aleksandr Popov, Unified Team	0:49.02
1920 Duke P. Kahanamoku, United States	1:01.4	1996 Aleksandr Popov, Russia	0:48.74
1924 John Weissmuller, United States	0:59.0	2000 Pieter van den Hoogenband, Netherlands	0:48.30
1928 John Weissmuller, United States	0:58.6	2004 Pieter van den Hoogenband, Netherlands	0:48.17
1932 Yasuji Miyazaki, Japan	0:58.2	2008 Alain Bernard, France	0:47:21

200-Meter Freestyle	Time
1968 Mike Wenden, Australia	1:55.2
1972 Mark Spitz, United States	1:52.78
1976 Bruce Furniss, United States	1:50.29
1980 Sergei Kopliakov, USSR	1:49.81
1984 Michael Gross, W. Germany	1:47.44
1988 Duncan Armstrong, Australia	1:47.25
1992 Yevgeny Sadovyi, Unified Team	1:46.70
1996 Danyon Loader, New Zealand	1:47.63
2000 Pieter van den Hoogenband, Netherlands	1:45.35
2004 Ian Thorpe, Australia	1:44.71
2008 Michael Phelps, United States	1:42.96*

400-Meter Freestyle	Time
1904 C. M. Daniels, United States (440 yds)	6:16.2
1908 Henry Taylor, Great Britain	5:36.8
1912 George Hodgson, Canada	5:24.4
1920 Norman Ross, United States	5:26.8
1924 John Weissmuller, United States	5:04.2
1928 Albert Zorilla, Argentina	5:01.6
1932 Clarence Crabbe, United States	4:48.4
1936 Jack Medica, United States	4:44.5
1948 William Smith, United States	4:41.0
1952 Jean Boiteux, France	4:30.7
1956 Murray Rose, Australia	4:27.3
1960 Murray Rose, Australia	4:18.3
1964 Don Schollander, United States	4:12.2
1968 Mike Burton, United States	4:09.0
1972 Brad Cooper, Australia	4:00.27
1976 Brian Goodell, United States	3:51.93
1980 Vladimir Salnikov, USSR	3:51.31
1984 George DiCarlo, United States	3:51.23
1988 Ewe Dassler, E. Germany	3:46.95
1992 Yevgeny Sadovyi, Unified Team	3:45.00
1996 Danyon Loader, New Zealand	3:47.97
2000 Ian Thorpe, Australia	3:40.59*
2004 Ian Thorpe, Australia	3:43.10
2008 Park Taehwan, S. Korea	3:41.86

1,500-Meter Freestyle	Time
1908 Henry Taylor, Great Britain	22:48.4
1912 George Hodgson, Canada	22:00.0
1920 Norman Ross, United States	22:23.2
1924 Andrew Charlton, Australia	20:06.6
1928 Arne Borg, Sweden	19:51.8
1932 Kusuo Kitamura, Japan	19:12.4
1936 Noboru Terada, Japan	19:13.7
1948 James McLane, United States	19:18.5
1952 Ford Konno, United States	18:30.3
1956 Murray Rose, Australia	17:58.9
1960 Jon Konrads, Australia	17:19.6
1964 Robert Windle, Australia	17:01.7
1968 Mike Burton, United States	16:38.9
1972 Mike Burton, United States	15:52.58
1976 Brian Goodell, United States	15:02.40
1980 Vladimir Salnikov, USSR	14:58.27
1984 Michael O'Brien, United States	15:05.20
1988 Vladimir Salnikov, USSR	15:00.40
1992 Kieren Perkins, Australia	14:43.48
1996 Kieren Perkins, Australia	14:56.40
2000 Grant Hackett, Australia	14:48.33
2004 Grant Hackett, Australia	14:43.40
2008 Oussama Mellouli, Tunisia	14:40.84

100-Meter Backstroke	Time
1904 Walter Brack, Germany (100 yds)	1:16.8
1908 Arno Bieberstein, Germany	1:24.6
1912 Harry Hebner, United States	1:21.2
1920 Warren Kealoha, United States	1:15.2
1924 Warren Kealoha, United States	1:13.2
1928 George Kojac, United States	1:08.2
1932 Masaji Kiyokawa, Japan	1:08.6
1936 Adolph Kiefer, United States	1:05.9
1948 Allen Stack, United States	1:06.4
1952 Yoshi Oyakawa, United States	1:05.4
1956 David Thiele, Australia	1:02.2
1960 David Thiele, Australia	1:01.9
1968 Roland Matthes, E. Germany	0:58.7
1972 Roland Matthes, E. Germany	0:56.58
1976 John Naber, United States	0:55.49
1980 Bengt Baron, Sweden	0:56.33
1984 Rick Carey, United States	0:55.79
1988 Daichi Suzuki, Japan	0:55.05
1992 Mark Tewksbury, Canada	0:53.98
1996 Jeff Rouse, United States	0:54.10
2000 Lenny Krayzelburg, United States	0:53.72
2004 Aaron Peirsol, United States	0:54.06
2008 Aaron Peirsol, United States	0:52.54*

200-Meter Backstroke	Time
1964 Jed Graef, United States	2:10.3
1968 Roland Matthes, E. Germany	2:09.6
1972 Roland Matthes, E. Germany	2:02.82

200-Meter Backstroke	Time
1976 John Naber, United States	1:59.19
1980 Sandor Wladar, Hungary	2:01.93
1984 Rick Carey, United States	2:00.23
1988 Igor Polianski, USSR	1:59.37
1992 Martin Lopez-Zubero, Spain	1:58.47
1996 Brad Bridgewater, United States	1:58.54
2000 Lenny Krayzelburg, United States	1:56.76
2004 Aaron Peirsol, United States	1:54.95
2008 Ryan Lochte, United States	1:53.94*

100-Meter Breaststroke	Time
1968 Don McKenzie, United States	1:07.79
1972 Nobutaka Taguchi, Japan	1:04.94
1976 John Hencken, United States	1:03.11
1980 Duncan Goodhew, Great Britain	1:03.44
1984 Steve Lundquist, United States	1:01.65
1988 Adrian Moorhouse, Great Britain	1:02.04
1992 Nelson Diebel, United States	1:01.50
1996 Fred Deburghgraeve, Belgium	1:00.60
2000 Domenico Fioravanti, Italy	1:00.46
2004 Kosuke Kitajima, Japan	1:00.08
2008 Kosuke Kitajima, Japan	0:58.91*

200-Meter Breaststroke	Time
1908 Frederick Holman, Great Britain	3:09.2
1912 Walter Bathe, Germany	3:01.8
1920 Haken Malmroth, Sweden	3:04.4
1924 Robert Skelton, United States	2:56.6
1928 Yoshiyuki Tsuruta, Japan	2:48.8
1932 Yoshiyuki Tsuruta, Japan	2:45.4
1936 Tetsuo Hamuro, Japan	2:41.5
1948 Joseph Verdeur, United States	2:39.3
1952 John Davies, Australia	2:34.4
1956 Masura Furukawa, Japan	2:34.7
1960 William Mulliken, United States	2:37.4
1964 Ian O'Brien, Australia	2:27.8
1968 Felipe Munoz, Mexico	2:28.7
1972 John Hencken, United States	2:21.55
1976 David Wilkie, Great Britain	2:15.11
1980 Robertas Zhulpa, USSR	2:15.85
1984 Victor Davis, Canada	2:13.34
1988 Jozsef Szabo, Hungary	2:13.52
1992 Mike Barrowman, United States	2:10.16
1996 Norbert Rozsa, Hungary	2:12.57
2000 Domenico Fioravanti, Italy	2:10.87
2004 Kosuke Kitajima, Japan	2:09.44
2008 Kosuke Kitajima, Japan	2:07.64*

100-Meter Butterfly	Time
1968 Doug Russell, United States	0:55.9
1972 Mark Spitz, United States	0:54.27
1976 Matt Vogel, United States	0:54.35
1980 Par Arvidsson, Sweden	0:54.92
1984 Michael Gross, W. Germany	0:53.08
1988 Anthony Nesty, Suriname	0:53.00
1992 Pablo Morales, United States	0:53.32
1996 Denis Pankratov, Russia	0:52.27
2000 Lars Froelander, Sweden	0:52.00
2004 Michael Phelps, United States	0:51.25
2008 Michael Phelps, United States	0:50.58*

200-Meter Butterfly	Time
1956 William Yorzyk, United States	2:19.3
1960 Michael Troy, United States	2:12.8
1964 Kevin J. Berry, Australia	2:06.6
1968 Carl Robie, United States	2:08.7
1972 Mark Spitz, United States	2:00.70
1976 Mike Bruner, United States	1:59.23
1980 Sergei Fesenko, USSR	1:59.76
1984 Jon Sieben, Australia	1:57.04
1988 Michael Gross, W. Germany	1:56.94
1992 Mel Stewart, United States	1:56.26
1996 Denis Pankratov, Russia	1:56.51
2000 Tom Malchow, United States	1:55.35
2004 Michael Phelps, United States	1:54.04
2008 Michael Phelps, United States	1:52.03*

200-Meter Individual Medley	Time
1968 Charles Hickcox, United States	2:12.0
1972 Gunnar Larsson, Sweden	2:07.17
1984 Alex Baumann, Canada	2:01.42
1988 Tamas Darnyi, Hungary	2:00.17
1992 Tamas Darnyi, Hungary	2:00.76
1996 Attila Czene, Hungary	1:59.91
2000 Massimiliano Rosolino, Italy	1:58.98
2004 Michael Phelps, United States	1:57.14
2008 Michael Phelps, United States	1:54.23*

400-Meter Individual Medley	Time
1964 Dick Roth, United States	4:45.4
1968 Charles Hickcox, United States	4:48.4
1972 Gunnar Larsson, Sweden	4:31.98

400-Meter Individual Medley	Time
1976 Rod Strachan, United States	4:23.68
1980 Aleksandr Sidorenko, USSR	4:22.89
1984 Alex Baumann, Canada	4:17.41
1988 Tamas Darnyi, Hungary	4:14.75
1992 Tamas Darnyi, Hungary	4:14.23
1996 Tom Dolan, United States	4:14.90
2000 Tom Dolan, United States	4:11.76
2004 Michael Phelps, United States	4:08.26
2008 Michael Phelps, United States	4:03.84*

4x100-Meter Freestyle Relay	Time
1964 United States	3:31.2
1968 United States	3:31.7
1972 United States	3:26.42
1984 United States	3:19.03
1988 United States	3:16.53
1992 United States	3:16.74
1996 United States	3:15.41
2000 Australia	3:13.67
2004 South Africa	3:13.17
2008 United States	3:08.24*

4x200-Meter Freestyle Relay	Time
1908 Great Britain	10:55.6
1912 Australia	10:11.6
1920 United States	10:04.4
1924 United States	9:53.4
1928 United States	9:36.2
1932 Japan	8:58.4
1936 Japan	8:51.5
1948 United States	8:46.0
1952 United States	8:31.1
1956 Australia	8:23.6
1960 United States	8:10.2
1964 United States	7:52.1
1968 United States	7:52.33
1972 United States	7:35.78
1976 United States	7:23.22
1980 USSR	7:23.50
1984 United States	7:15.69
1988 United States	7:12.51
1992 Unified Team	7:11.95
1996 United States	7:14.84
2000 Australia	7:07.05
2004 United States	7:07.33
2008 United States	6:58.56*

4x100-Meter Medley Relay	Time
1960 United States	4:05.4
1964 United States	3:58.4
1968 United States	3:54.9
1972 United States	3:48.16
1976 United States	3:42.22
1980 Australia	3:45.70
1984 United States	3:39.30
1988 United States	3:36.93
1992 United States	3:36.93
1996 United States	3:34.84
2000 United States	3:33.73
2004 United States	3:30.68
2008 United States	3:29.34*

10-Kilometer Marathon	Time
2008 Maarten van der Weijden, Netherlands	1:51:51.6

Platform Diving	Points
1904 Dr. G. E. Sheldon, United States	112.75
1908 Hjalmar Johansson, Sweden	183.75
1912 Erik Adlerz, Sweden	73.94
1920 Clarence Pinkston, United States	100.67
1924 Albert White, United States	97.46
1928 Pete Desjardins, United States	98.74
1932 Harold Smith, United States	124.80
1936 Marshall Wayne, United States	113.58
1948 Sammy Lee, United States	130.05
1952 Sammy Lee, United States	156.28
1956 Joaquin Capilla, Mexico	152.44
1960 Robert Webster, United States	165.56
1964 Robert Webster, United States	148.58
1968 Klaus Dibiasi, Italy	164.18
1972 Klaus Dibiasi, Italy	504.12
1976 Klaus Dibiasi, Italy	600.51
1980 Falk Hoffmann, E. Germany	835.65
1984 Greg Louganis, United States	710.91
1988 Greg Louganis, United States	638.61
1992 Sun Shuwei, China	677.31
1996 Dmitri Sautin, Russia	692.34
2000 Tian Liang, China	724.53
2004 Hu Jia, China	748.08
2008 Matthew Mitcham, Australia	537.95

Springboard Diving	Points
1908 Albert Zurner, Germany	85.50
1912 Paul Guenther, Germany	79.23
1920 Louis Kuehn, United States	675.40
1924 Albert White, United States	97.46
1928 Pete Desjardins, United States	185.04
1932 Michael Galitzen, United States	161.38
1936 Richard Degener, United States	163.57
1948 Bruce Harlan, United States	163.64
1952 David Browning, United States	205.29
1956 Robert Clotworthy, United States	159.56
1960 Gary Tobian, United States	170.00
1964 Kenneth Sitzberger, United States	159.90
1968 Bernie Wrightson, United States	170.15
1972 Vladimir Vasin, USSR	594.09
1976 Phil Boggs, United States	619.52
1980 Aleksandr Portnov, USSR	905.02
1984 Greg Louganis, United States	754.41
1988 Greg Louganis, United States	730.80
1992 Mark Lenzi, United States	676.53
1996 Xiong Ni, China	701.46
2000 Xiong Ni, China	708.72
2004 Peng Bo, China	787.30
2008 He Chong, China	572.90

Synchronized Platform	Points
2004 Tian Liang and Yang Jinghui, China	383.88
2008 Lin Yue and Huo Liang, China	468.18

Synchronized Springboard	Points
2004 Nikolaos Siranidis and Thomas Bimis, Greece	353.34
2008 Wang Feng and Qin Kai, China	469.08

Swimming and Diving—Women

50-Meter Freestyle	Time
1988 Kristin Otto, E. Germany	0:25.49
1992 Yang Wenyi, China	0:24.76
1996 Amy Van Dyken, United States	0:24.87
2000 Inge de Bruijn, Netherlands	0:24.32
2004 Inge de Bruijn, Netherlands	0:24.58
2008 Britta Steffen, Germany	0:24.06*

100-Meter Freestyle	Time
1912 Fanny Durack, Australia	1:22.2
1920 Ethelda Bleibtrey, United States	1:13.6
1924 Ethel Lackie, United States	1:12.4
1928 Albina Osipowich, United States	1:11.0
1932 Helene Madison, United States	1:06.8
1936 Hendrika Mastenbroek, Holland	1:05.9
1948 Greta Andersen, Denmark	1:06.3
1952 Katalin Szoke, Hungary	1:06.8
1956 Dawn Fraser, Australia	1:02.0
1960 Dawn Fraser, Australia	1:01.2
1964 Dawn Fraser, Australia	0:59.5
1968 Jan Henne, United States	1:00.0
1972 Sandra Neilson, United States	0:58.59
1976 Kornelia Ender, E. Germany	0:55.65
1980 Barbara Krause, E. Germany	0:54.79
1984 Carrie Steinseifer, United States	0:55.92
Nancy Hogshead, United States (tie)	0:55.92

100-Meter Freestyle	Time
1988 Kristin Otto, E. Germany	0:54.93
1992 Zhuang Yong, China	0:54.64
1996 Li Jingyi, China	0:54.50
2000 Inge de Bruijn, Netherlands	0:53.83
2004 Jodie Henry, Australia	0:53.84
2008 Britta Steffen, Germany	0:53.12*

200-Meter Freestyle	Time
1968 Debbie Meyer, United States	2:10.5
1972 Shane Gould, Australia	2:03.56
1976 Kornelia Ender, E. Germany	1:59.26
1980 Barbara Krause, E. Germany	1:58.33
1984 Mary Wayte, United States	1:59.23
1988 Heike Friedrich, E. Germany	1:57.65
1992 Nicole Haislett, United States	1:57.90
1996 Claudia Poll, Costa Rica	1:58.16
2000 Susan O'Neill, Australia	1:58.24
2004 Camelia Potec, Romania	1:58.03
2008 Federica Pellegrini, Italy	1:54.82*

400-Meter Freestyle	Time
1924 Martha Norelius, United States	6:02.2
1928 Martha Norelius, United States	5:42.8
1932 Helene Madison, United States	5:28.5
1936 Hendrika Mastenbroek, Netherlands	5:26.4

400-Meter Freestyle

Year	Champion	Time
1948	Ann Curtis, United States	5:17.8
1952	Valerie Gyenge, Hungary	5:12.1
1956	Lorraine Crapp, Australia	4:54.6
1960	Susan Chris von Saltza, United States	4:50.6
1964	Virginia Duenkel, United States	4:43.3
1968	Debbie Meyer, United States	4:31.8
1972	Shane Gould, Australia	4:19.44
1976	Petra Thuemer, E. Germany	4:09.89
1980	Ines Diers, E. Germany	4:08.76
1984	Tiffany Cohen, United States	4:07.10
1988	Janet Evans, United States	4:03.85
1992	Dagmar Hase, Germany	4:07.18
1996	Michelle Smith, Ireland	4:07.25
2000	Brooke Bennett, United States	4:05.80
2004	Laure Manaudou, France	4:05.34
2008	Rebecca Adlington, Great Britain	4:03.22

800-Meter Freestyle

Year	Champion	Time
1968	Debbie Meyer, United States	9:24.0
1972	Keena Rothhammer, United States	8:53.68
1976	Petra Thuemer, E. Germany	8:37.14
1980	Michelle Ford, Australia	8:28.90
1984	Tiffany Cohen, United States	8:24.95
1988	Janet Evans, United States	8:20.20
1992	Janet Evans, United States	8:25.52
1996	Brooke Bennett, United States	8:27.89
2000	Brooke Bennett, United States	8:19.67
2004	Ai Shibata, Japan	8:24.54
2008	Rebecca Adlington, Great Britain	8:14.10*

100-Meter Backstroke

Year	Champion	Time
1924	Sybil Bauer, United States	1:23.2
1928	Marie Braun, Netherlands	1:22.0
1932	Eleanor Holm, United States	1:19.4
1936	Dina Senff, Netherlands	1:18.9
1948	Karen Harup, Denmark	1:14.4
1952	Joan Harrison, South Africa	1:14.3
1956	Judy Grinham, Great Britain	1:12.9
1960	Lynn Burke, United States	1:09.3
1964	Cathy Ferguson, United States	1:07.7
1968	Kaye Hall, United States	1:06.2
1972	Melissa Belote, United States	1:05.78
1976	Ulrike Richter, E. Germany	1:01.83
1980	Rica Reinisch, E. Germany	1:00.86
1984	Theresa Andrews, United States	1:02.55
1988	Kristin Otto, E. Germany	1:00.89
1992	Krisztina Egerszegi, Hungary	1:00.68
1996	Beth Botsford, United States	1:01.19
2000	Diana Mocanu, Romania	1:00.21
2004	Natalie Coughlin, United States	1:00.37
2008	Natalie Coughlin, United States	0:58.96

200-Meter Backstroke

Year	Champion	Time
1968	Pokey Watson, United States	2:24.8
1972	Melissa Belote, United States	2:19.19
1976	Ulrike Richter, E. Germany	2:13.43
1980	Rica Reinisch, E. Germany	2:11.77
1984	Jolanda De Rover, Netherlands	2:12.38
1988	Krisztina Egerszegi, Hungary	2:09.29
1992	Krisztina Egerszegi, Hungary	2:07.06
1996	Krisztina Egerszegi, Hungary	2:07.83
2000	Diana Mocanu, Romania	2:08.16
2004	Kirsty Coventry, Zimbabwe	2:09.19
2008	Kirsty Coventry, Zimbabwe	2:05.24*

100-Meter Breaststroke

Year	Champion	Time
1968	Djurdjica Bjedov, Yugoslavia	1:15.8
1972	Cathy Carr, United States	1:13.58
1976	Hannelore Anke, E. Germany	1:11.16
1980	Ute Geweniger, E. Germany	1:10.22
1984	Petra Van Staveren, Netherlands	1:09.88
1988	Tania Dangalakova, Bulgaria	1:07.95
1992	Elena Roudkovskaia, Unified Team	1:08.00
1996	Penny Heyns, South Africa	1:07.73
2000	Megan Quann, United States	1:07.05
2004	Luo Xuejuan, China	1:06.64
2008	Leisel Jones, Australia	1:05.17*

200-Meter Breaststroke

Year	Champion	Time
1924	Lucy Morton, Great Britain	3:33.2
1928	Hilde Schrader, Germany	3:12.6
1932	Clare Dennis, Australia	3:06.3
1936	Hideko Maehata, Japan	3:03.6
1948	Nelly Van Vliet, Netherlands	2:57.2
1952	Eva Szekely, Hungary	2:51.7
1956	Ursula Happe, Germany	2:53.1
1960	Anita Lonsbrough, Great Britain	2:49.5
1964	Galina Prozumenschikova, USSR	2:46.4
1968	Sharon Wichman, United States	2:44.4
1972	Beverly Whitfield, Australia	2:41.71

200-Meter Breaststroke

Year	Champion	Time
1976	Marina Koshevaia, USSR	2:33.35
1980	Lina Kachushite, USSR	2:29.54
1984	Anne Ottenbrite, Canada	2:30.38
1988	Silke Hoerner, E. Germany	2:26.71
1992	Kyoko Iwasaki, Japan	2:26.65
1996	Penny Heyns, South Africa	2:25.41
2000	Agnes Kovacs, Hungary	2:24.35
2004	Amanda Beard, United States	2:23.37
2008	Rebecca Soni, United States	2:20.22*

100-Meter Butterfly

Year	Champion	Time
1956	Shelley Mann, United States	1:11.0
1960	Carolyn Schuler, United States	1:09.5
1964	Sharon Stouder, United States	1:04.7
1968	Lynn McClements, Australia	1:05.5
1972	Mayumi Aoki, Japan	1:03.34
1976	Kornelia Ender, E. Germany	1:00.13
1980	Caren Metschuck, E. Germany	1:00.42
1984	Mary T. Meagher, United States	0:59.26
1988	Kristin Otto, E. Germany	0:59.00
1992	Qian Hong, China	0:58.62
1996	Amy Van Dyken, United States	0:59.13
2000	Inge de Bruijn, Netherlands	0:56.61*
2004	Petria Thomas, Australia	0:57.72
2008	Lisbeth Trickett, Australia	0:56.73

200-Meter Butterfly

Year	Champion	Time
1968	Ada Kok, Netherlands	2:24.7
1972	Karen Moe, United States	2:15.57
1976	Andrea Pollack, E. Germany	2:11.41
1980	Ines Geissler, E. Germany	2:10.44
1984	Mary T. Meagher, United States	2:06.90
1988	Kathleen Nord, E. Germany	2:09.51
1992	Summer Sanders, United States	2:08.67
1996	Susan O'Neill, Australia	2:07.76
2000	Misty Hyman, United States	2:05.88
2004	Otylia Jedrzejczak, Poland	2:06.05
2008	Liu Zige, China	2:04.18*

200-Meter Individual Medley

Year	Champion	Time
1968	Claudia Kolb, United States	2:24.7
1972	Shane Gould, Australia	2:23.07
1984	Tracy Caulkins, United States	2:12.64
1988	Daniela Hunger, E. Germany	2:12.59
1992	Lin Li, China	2:11.65
1996	Michelle Smith, Ireland	2:13.93
2000	Yana Klochkova, Ukraine	2:10.68
2004	Yana Klochkova, Ukraine	2:11.14
2008	Stephanie Rice, Australia	2:08.45*

400-Meter Individual Medley

Year	Champion	Time
1964	Donna de Varona, United States	5:18.7
1968	Claudia Kolb, United States	5:08.5
1972	Gail Neall, Australia	5:02.97
1976	Ulrike Tauber, E. Germany	4:42.77
1980	Petra Schneider, E. Germany	4:36.29
1984	Tracy Caulkins, United States	4:39.24
1988	Janet Evans, United States	4:37.76
1992	Krisztina Egerszegi, Hungary	4:36.54
1996	Michelle Smith, Ireland	4:39.18
2000	Yana Klochkova, Ukraine	4:33.59
2004	Yana Klochkova, Ukraine	4:34.83
2008	Stephanie Rice, Australia	4:29.45*

4x100-Meter Freestyle Relay

Year	Champion	Time
1912	Great Britain	5:52.8
1920	United States	5:11.6
1924	United States	4:58.8
1928	United States	4:47.6
1932	United States	4:38.0
1936	Netherlands	4:36.0
1948	United States	4:29.2
1952	Hungary	4:24.4
1956	Australia	4:17.1
1960	United States	4:08.9
1964	United States	4:03.8
1968	United States	4:02.5
1972	United States	3:55.19
1976	United States	3:44.82
1980	East Germany	3:42.71
1984	United States	3:43.43
1988	East Germany	3:40.63
1992	United States	3:39.46
1996	United States	3:39.29
2000	United States	3:36.61
2004	Australia	3:35.94
2008	Netherlands	3:33.76*

4x200-Meter Freestyle Relay

Year	Champion	Time
1996	United States	7:59.87
2000	United States	7:57.80

4x200-Meter Freestyle Relay	Time
2004 United States	7:53.42
2008 Australia	7:44.31*

4x100-Meter Medley Relay	Time
1960 United States	4:41.1
1964 United States	4:33.9
1968 United States	4:28.3
1972 United States	4:20.75
1976 East Germany	4:07.95
1980 East Germany	4:06.67
1984 United States	4:08.34
1988 East Germany	4:03.74
1992 United States	4:02.54
1996 United States	4:02.88
2000 United States	3:58.30
2004 Australia	3:57.32
2008 Australia	3:52.69*

10-Kilometer Marathon	Time
2008 Larisa Ilchenko, Russia	1:59:27.7

Platform Diving	Points
1912 Greta Johansson, Sweden	39.90
1920 Stefani Fryland-Clausen, Denmark	34.60
1924 Caroline Smith, United States	33.20
1928 Elizabeth B. Pinkston, United States	31.60
1932 Dorothy Poynton, United States	40.26
1936 Dorothy Poynton Hill, United States	33.93
1948 Victoria M. Draves, United States	68.87
1952 Patricia McCormick, United States	79.37
1956 Patricia McCormick, United States	84.85
1960 Ingrid Kramer, Germany	91.28
1964 Lesley Bush, United States	99.80
1968 Milena Duchkova, Czechoslovakia	109.59
1972 Ulrika Knape, Sweden	390.00
1976 Elena Vaytsekhouskaya, USSR	406.59
1980 Martina Jaschke, E. Germany	596.25
1984 Zhou Jihong, China	435.51

Platform Diving	Points
1988 Xu Yanmei, China	445.20
1992 Fu Mingxia, China	461.43
1996 Fu Mingxia, China	521.58
2000 Laura Wilkinson, United States	543.75
2004 Chantelle Newbery, Australia	590.31
2008 Chen Ruolin, China	447.70

Springboard Diving	Points
1920 Aileen Riggin, United States	539.90
1924 Elizabeth Becker, United States	474.50
1928 Helen Meany, United States	78.62
1932 Georgia Coleman United States	87.52
1936 Marjorie Gestring, United States	89.27
1948 Victoria M. Draves, United States	108.74
1952 Patricia McCormick, United States	147.30
1956 Patricia McCormick, United States	142.36
1960 Ingrid Kramer, Germany	155.81
1964 Ingrid Engel-Kramer, Germany	145.00
1968 Sue Gossick, United States	150.77
1972 Micki King, United States	450.03
1976 Jenni Chandler, United States	506.19
1980 Irina Kalinina, USSR	725.91
1984 Sylvie Bernier, Canada	530.70
1988 Gao Min, China	580.23
1992 Gao Min, China	572.40
1996 Fu Mingxia, China	547.68
2000 Fu Mingxia, China	609.42
2004 Guo Jingjing, China	633.15
2008 Guo Jingjing, China	415.35

Synchronized Platform	Points
2004 Lao Lishi and Li Ting, China	352.14
2008 Wang Xin and Chen Ruolin, China	363.54

Synchronized Springboard	Points
2004 Wu Minxia and Guo Jingjing, China	336.90
2008 Guo Jingjing and Wu Minxia, China	343.50

Tennis

Men's Singles

1896	John Boland, Great Britain
1900	Hugh Lawrence Doherty, Great Britain
1904	Beals Coleman Wright, United States
1908	Josiah George Ritchie, Great Britain
1912	Charles Lyndhurst Winslow, South Africa
1920	Louis Raymond, South Africa
1924	Vincent Richards, United States
1988	Miloslav Mecir, Czechoslovakia
1992	Marc Rosset, Switzerland
1996	Andre Agassi, United States
2000	Eugueni Kafelnikov, Russia
2004	Nicolas Massu, Chile
2008	Rafael Nadal, Spain

Men's Doubles

1896	John Boland, Great Britain & Friedrick Traun, Germany
1900	Hugh Lawrence Doherty & Reginald Frank Doherty, Great Britain
1904	Edgar Welch Leonard & Beals Coleman Wright, United States
1908	George Whiteside Hillyard & Reginald Frank Doherty, Great Britain
1912	Harry Austin Kitson & Charles Lyndhurst Winslow, South Africa
1920	Oswald Graham Noel Turnbull & Maxwell Woosnam, Great Britain
1924	Vincent Richards & Francis Townsend Hunter, United States
1988	Kenneth Flach & Robert A. Seguso, United States

Men's Doubles

1992	Boris Franz Becker & Michael Stich, Germany
1996	Mark Woodforde & Todd Woodbridge, Australia
2000	Sebastien Lareau & Daniel Nestor, Canada
2004	Fernando Gonzales & Nicolas Massu, Chile
2008	Roger Federer & Stanislas Wawrinka, Switzerland

Women's Singles

1900	Charlotte Cooper, Great Britain
1908	Dorothy Katherine Chambers, Great Britain
1912	Marguerite Broquedis, France
1920	Suzanne Lenglen, France
1924	Helen Wills, United States
1988	Steffi Graf, W. Germany
1992	Jennifer Capriati, United States
1996	Lindsay Davenport, United States
2000	Venus Williams, United States
2004	Justine Henin-Hardenne, Belgium
2008	Elena Dementieva, Russia

Women's Doubles

1920	Winifred Margaret McNair & Kathleen McKane, Great Britain
1924	Hazel Virginia Wightman & Helen Wills, United States
1988	Pamela Howard Shriver & Zina Garrison, United States
1992	Gigi Fernandez & Mary Joe Fernandez, United States
1996	Gigi Fernandez & Mary Joe Fernandez, United States
2000	Venus Williams & Serena Williams, United States
2004	Ting Li & Tian Tian Sun, China
2008	Serena Williams & Venus Williams, United States

Track and Field—Men

100-Meter Run	Time
1896 Thomas Burke, United States	12.0s
1900 Francis W. Jarvis, United States	11.0s
1904 Archie Hahn, United States	11.0s
1908 Reginald Walker, South Africa	10.8s
1912 Ralph Craig, United States	10.8s
1920 Charles Paddock, United States	10.8s
1924 Harold Abrahams, Great Britain	10.6s
1928 Percy Williams, Canada	10.8s
1932 Eddie Tolan, United States	10.3s
1936 Jesse Owens, United States	10.3s
1948 Harrison Dillard, United States	10.3s
1952 Lindy Remigino, United States	10.4s
1956 Bobby Morrow, United States	10.5s

100-Meter Run	Time
1960 Armin Hary, Germany	10.2s
1964 Bob Hayes, United States	10.0s
1968 Jim Hines, United States	9.95s
1972 Valery Borzov, USSR	10.14s
1976 Hasely Crawford, Trinidad	10.06s
1980 Allan Wells, Great Britain	10.25s
1984 Carl Lewis, United States	9.99s
1988 Carl Lewis, United States	9.92s
1992 Linford Christie, Great Britain	9.96s
1996 Donovan Bailey, Canada	9.84s
2000 Maurice Greene, United States	9.87s
2004 Justin Gatlin, United States	9.85s
2008 Usain Bolt, Jamaica	9.69s*

200-Meter Run

		Time
1900	Walter Tewksbury, United States	22.2s
1904	Archie Hahn, United States	21.6s
1908	Robert Kerr, Canada	22.6s
1912	Ralph Craig, United States	21.7s
1920	Allan Woodring, United States	22.0s
1924	Jackson Scholz, United States	21.6s
1928	Percy Williams, Canada	21.8s
1932	Eddie Tolan, United States	21.2s
1936	Jesse Owens, United States	20.7s
1948	Mel Patton, United States	21.1s
1952	Andrew Stanfield, United States	20.7s
1956	Bobby Morrow, United States	20.6s
1960	Livio Berruti, Italy	20.5s
1964	Henry Carr, United States	20.3s
1968	Tommie Smith, United States	19.83s
1972	Valeri Borzov, USSR	20.00s
1976	Donald Quarrie, Jamaica	20.23s
1980	Pietro Mennea, Italy	20.19s
1984	Carl Lewis, United States	19.80s
1988	Joe DeLoach, United States	19.75s
1992	Mike Marsh, United States	20.01s
1996	Michael Johnson, United States	19.32s
2000	Konstantinos Kenteris, Greece	20.09s
2004	Shawn Crawford, United States	19.79s
2008	Usain Bolt, Jamaica	19.30s*

400-Meter Run

		Time
1896	Thomas Burke, United States	54.2s
1900	Maxey Long, United States	49.4s
1904	Harry Hillman, United States	49.2s
1908	Wyndham Halswelle, Gr. Brit., walkover	50.0s
1912	Charles Reidpath, United States	48.2s
1920	Bevil Rudd, South Africa	49.6s
1924	Eric Liddell, Great Britain	47.6s
1928	Ray Barbuti, United States	47.8s
1932	William Carr, United States	46.2s
1936	Archie Williams, United States	46.5s
1948	Arthur Wint, Jamaica	46.2s
1952	George Rhoden, Jamaica	45.9s
1956	Charles Jenkins, United States	46.7s
1960	Otis Davis, United States	44.9s
1964	Michael Larrabee, United States	45.1s
1968	Lee Evans, United States	43.86s
1972	Vincent Matthews, United States	44.66s
1976	Alberto Juantorena, Cuba	44.26s
1980	Viktor Markin, USSR	44.60s
1984	Alonzo Babers, United States	44.27s
1988	Steven Lewis, United States	43.87s
1992	Quincy Watts, United States	43.50s
1996	Michael Johnson, United States	43.49s*
2000	Michael Johnson, United States	43.84s
2004	Jeremy Wariner, United States	44.00s
2008	LaShawn Merritt, United States	43.75s

800-Meter Run

		Time
1896	Edwin Flack, Australia	2m. 11s
1900	Alfred Tysoe, Great Britain	2m. 01.2s
1904	James Lightbody, United States	1m. 56s
1908	Mel Sheppard, United States	1m. 52.8s
1912	James Meredith, United States	1m. 51.9s
1920	Albert Hill, Great Britain	1m. 53.4s
1924	Douglas Lowe, Great Britain	1m. 52.4s
1928	Douglas Lowe, Great Britain	1m. 51.8s
1932	Thomas Hampson, Great Britain	1m. 49.8s
1936	John Woodruff, United States	1m. 52.9s
1948	Mal Whitfield, United States	1m. 49.2s
1952	Mal Whitfield, United States	1m. 49.2s
1956	Thomas Courtney, United States	1m. 47.7s
1960	Peter Snell, New Zealand	1m. 46.3s
1964	Peter Snell, New Zealand	1m. 45.1s
1968	Ralph Doubell, Australia	1m. 44.3s
1972	Dave Wottle, United States	1m. 45.9s
1976	Alberto Juantorena, Cuba	1m. 43.50s
1980	Steve Ovett, Great Britain	1m. 45.40s
1984	Joaquim Cruz, Brazil	1m. 43.00s
1988	Paul Ereng, Kenya	1m. 43.45s
1992	William Tanui, Kenya	1m. 43.66s
1996	Vebjørn Rodal, Norway	1m. 42.58s*
2000	Nils Schumann, Germany	1m. 45.08s
2004	Yuriy Borzakovskiy, Russia	1m. 44.45s
2008	Wilfred Bungei, Kenya	1m. 44.65s

1,500-Meter Run

		Time
1896	Edwin Flack, Australia	4m. 33.2s
1900	Charles Bennett, Great Britain	4m. 06.2s
1904	James Lightbody, United States	4m. 05.4s
1908	Mel Sheppard, United States	4m. 03.4s
1912	Arnold Jackson, Great Britain	3m. 56.8s
1920	Albert Hill, Great Britain	4m. 01.8s

1,500-Meter Run

		Time
1924	Paavo Nurmi, Finland	3m. 53.6s
1928	Harry Larva, Finland	3m. 53.2s
1932	Luigi Beccali, Italy	3m. 51.2s
1936	Jack Lovelock, New Zealand	3m. 47.8s
1948	Henri Eriksson, Sweden	3m. 49.8s
1952	Joseph Barthel, Luxembourg	3m. 45.2s
1956	Ron Delany, Ireland	3m. 41.2s
1960	Herb Elliott, Australia	3m. 35.6s
1964	Peter Snell, New Zealand	3m. 38.1s
1968	Kipchoge Keino, Kenya	3m. 34.9s
1972	Pekka Vasala, Finland	3m. 36.3s
1976	John Walker, New Zealand	3m. 39.17s
1980	Sebastian Coe, Great Britain	3m. 38.4s
1984	Sebastian Coe, Great Britain	3m. 32.53s
1988	Peter Rono, Kenya	3m. 35.96s
1992	Fermin Cacho Ruiz, Spain	3m. 40.12s
1996	Noureddine Morceli, Algeria	3m. 35.78s
2000	Noah Ngeny, Kenya	3m. 32.07s*
2004	Hicham el-Guerrouj, Morocco	3m. 34.18s
2008	Rashid Ramzi, Bahrain	3m. 32.94s

3,000-Meter Steeplechase

		Time
1920	Percy Hodge, Great Britain	10m. 0.4s
1924	Willie Ritola, Finland	9m. 33.6s
1928	Toivo Loukola, Finland	9m. 21.8s
1932	Volmari Iso-Hollo, Finland (about 3,450 m; extra lap by error)	10m. 33.4s
1936	Volmari Iso-Hollo, Finland	9m. 3.8s
1948	Thore Sjoestrand, Sweden	9m. 4.6s
1952	Horace Ashenfelter, United States	8m. 45.4s
1956	Chris Brasher, Great Britain	8m. 41.2s
1960	Zdzislaw Krzyszkowiak, Poland	8m. 34.2s
1964	Gaston Roelants, Belgium	8m. 30.8s
1968	Amos Biwott, Kenya	8m. 51s
1972	Kipchoge Keino, Kenya	8m. 23.6s
1976	Anders Garderud, Sweden	8m. 08.2s
1980	Bronislaw Malinowski, Poland	8m. 09.7s
1984	Julius Korir, Kenya	8m. 11.8s
1988	Julius Kariuki, Kenya	8m. 05.51s*
1992	Matthew Birir, Kenya	8m. 08.84s
1996	Joseph Keter, Kenya	8m. 07.12s
2000	Reuben Kosgei, Kenya	8m. 21.43s
2004	Ezekiel Kemboi, Kenya	8m. 05.81s
2008	Brimin Kiprop Kirpruto, Kenya	8m. 10.34s

5,000-Meter Run

		Time
1912	Hannes Kolehmainen, Finland	14m. 36.6s
1920	Joseph Guillemot, France	14m. 55.6s
1924	Paavo Nurmi, Finland	14m. 31.2s
1928	Willie Ritola, Finland	14m. 38s
1932	Lauri Lehtinen, Finland	14m. 30s
1936	Gunnar Hockert, Finland	14m. 22.2s
1948	Gaston Reiff, Belgium	14m. 17.6s
1952	Emil Zatopek, Czechoslovakia	14m. 06.6s
1956	Vladimir Kuts, USSR	13m. 39.6s
1960	Murray Halberg, New Zealand	13m. 43.4s
1964	Bob Schul, United States	13m. 48.8s
1968	Mohamed Gammoudi, Tunisia	14m. 05.0s
1972	Lasse Viren, Finland	13m. 26.4s
1976	Lasse Viren, Finland	13m. 24.76s
1980	Miruts Yifter, Ethiopia	13m. 21.0s
1984	Said Aouita, Morocco	13m. 05.59s
1988	John Ngugi, Kenya	13m. 11.70s
1992	Dieter Baumann, Germany	13m. 12.52s
1996	Venuste Niyongabo, Burundi	13m. 07.96s
2000	Millon Wolde, Ethiopia	13m. 35.49s
2004	Hicham el-Guerrouj, Morocco	13m. 14.39s
2008	Kenenisa Bekele, Ethiopia	12m. 57.82s*

10,000-Meter Run

		Time
1912	Hannes Kolehmainen, Finland	31m. 20.8s
1920	Paavo Nurmi, Finland	31m. 45.8s
1924	Willie Ritola, Finland	30m. 23.2s
1928	Paavo Nurmi, Finland	30m. 18.8s
1932	Janusz Kusocinski, Poland	30m. 11.4s
1936	Ilmari Salminen, Finland	30m. 15.4s
1948	Emil Zatopek, Czechoslovakia	29m. 59.6s
1952	Emil Zatopek, Czechoslovakia	29m. 17.0s
1956	Vladimir Kuts, USSR	28m. 45.6s
1960	Pyotr Bolotnikov, USSR	28m. 32.2s
1964	Billy Mills, United States	28m. 24.4s
1968	Naftali Temu, Kenya	29m. 27.4s
1972	Lasse Viren, Finland	27m. 38.4s
1976	Lasse Viren, Finland	27m. 40.4s
1980	Miruts Yifter, Ethiopia	27m. 42.7s
1984	Alberto Cova, Italy	27m. 47.54s

10,000-Meter Run	Time
1988 Brahim Boutaib, Morocco	27m. 21.46s
1992 Khalid Skah, Morocco	27m. 46.70s
1996 Haile Gebrselassie, Ethiopia	27m. 07.34s
2000 Haile Gebrselassie, Ethiopia	27m. 18.20s
2004 Kenenisa Bekele, Ethiopia	27m. 05.10s
2008 Kenenisa Bekele, Ethiopia	27m. 01.17s*

Marathon	Time
1896 Spiridon Loues, Greece	2h. 58m. 50s
1900 Michel Theato, France	2h. 59m. 45s
1904 Thomas Hicks, United States	3h. 28m. 63s
1908 John J. Hayes, United States	2h. 55m. 18.4s
1912 Kenneth McArthur, South Africa	2h. 36m. 54.8s
1920 Hannes Kolehmainen, Finland	2h. 32m. 35.8s
1924 Albin Stenroos, Finland	2h. 41m. 22.6s
1928 A. B. El Ouafi, France	2h. 32m. 57s
1932 Juan Zabala, Argentina	2h. 31m. 36s
1936 Kijung Son, Japan (Korean)	2h. 29m. 19.2s
1948 Delfo Cabrera, Argentina	2h. 34m. 51.6s
1952 Emil Zatopek, Czechoslovakia	2h. 23m. 03.2s
1956 Alain Mimoun, France	2h. 25m.
1960 Abebe Bikila, Ethiopia	2h. 15m. 16.2s
1964 Abebe Bikila, Ethiopia	2h. 12m. 11.2s
1968 Mamo Wolde, Ethiopia	2h. 20m. 26.4s
1972 Frank Shorter, United States	2h. 12m. 19.8s
1976 Waldemar Cierpinski, E. Germany	2h. 09m. 55s
1980 Waldemar Cierpinski, E. Germany	2h. 11m. 03s
1984 Carlos Lopes, Portugal	2h. 09m. 21s
1988 Gelindo Bordin, Italy	2h. 10m. 32s
1992 Hwang Young-Cho, S. Korea	2h. 13m. 23s
1996 Josia Thugwane, South Africa	2h. 12m. 36s
2000 Gezahgne Abera, Ethiopia	2h. 10m. 11s
2004 Stefano Baldino, Italy	2h. 10m. 55s
2008 Samuel Kamau Wansiru, Kenya	2h. 06m. 32s*

4x100-Meter Relay	Time
1912 Great Britain	42.4s
1920 United States	42.2s
1924 United States	41.0s
1928 United States	41.0s
1932 United States	40.0s
1936 United States	39.8s
1948 United States	40.6s
1952 United States	40.1s
1956 United States	39.5s
1960 Germany (U.S. disqualified)	39.5s
1964 United States	39.0s
1968 United States	38.24s
1972 United States	38.19s
1976 United States	38.33s
1980 USSR	38.26s
1984 United States	37.83s
1988 USSR (U.S. disqualified)	38.19s
1992 United States	37.40s
1996 Canada	37.69s
2000 United States	37.61s
2004 Great Britain	38.07s
2008 Jamaica	37.10s*

4x400-Meter Relay	Time
1908 United States	3m. 29.4s
1912 United States	3m. 16.6s
1920 Great Britain	3m. 22.2s
1924 United States	3m. 16s
1928 United States	3m. 14.2s
1932 United States	3m. 08.2s
1936 Great Britain	3m. 09s
1948 United States	3m. 10.4s
1952 Jamaica	3m. 03.9s
1956 United States	3m. 04.8s
1960 United States	3m. 02.2s
1964 United States	3m. 00.7s
1968 United States	2m. 56.16s
1972 Kenya	2m. 59.8s
1976 United States	2m. 58.65s
1980 USSR	3m. 01.1s
1984 United States	2m. 57.91s
1988 United States	2m. 56.16s
1992 United States	2m. 55.74s
1996 United States	2m. 55.99s
2000 United States (a)	2m. 56.35s
2004 United States	2m. 55.91s
2008 United States	2m. 55.39s*

(a) The International Olympic Committee stripped the 2000 U.S. relay team of their medals in Aug. 2008 after one of the team's members, Antonio Pettigrew, admitted to doping.

20-Kilometer Walk	Time
1956 Leonid Spirin, USSR	1h. 31m. 27.4s
1960 Vladimir Golubnichy, USSR	1h. 33m. 7.2s
1964 Kenneth Mathews, Great Britain	1h. 29m. 34.0s
1968 Vladimir Golubnichy, USSR	1h. 33m. 58.4s
1972 Peter Frenkel, E. Germany	1h. 26m. 42.4s
1976 Daniel Bautista, Mexico	1h. 24m. 40.6s
1980 Maurizio Damilano, Italy	1h. 23m. 35.5s
1984 Ernesto Canto, Mexico	1h. 23m. 13.0s
1988 Josef Pribilinec, Czechoslovakia	1h. 19m. 57.0s
1992 Daniel Plaza Montero, Spain	1h. 21m. 45.0s
1996 Jefferson Perez, Ecuador	1h. 20m. 07s
2000 Robert Korzeniowski, Poland	1h. 18m. 59.0s*
2004 Ivano Brugnetti, Italy	1h. 19m. 40s
2008 Valeriy Borchin, Russia	1h. 19m. 01s

50-Kilometer Walk	Time
1932 Thomas W. Green, Great Britain	4h. 50m. 10s
1936 Harold Whitlock, Great Britain	4h. 30m. 41.4s
1948 John Ljunggren, Sweden	4h. 41m. 52s
1952 Giuseppe Dordoni, Italy	4h. 28m. 07.8s
1956 Norman Read, New Zealand	4h. 30m. 42.8s
1960 Donald Thompson, Great Britain	4h. 25m. 30s
1964 Abdon Pamich, Italy	4h. 11m. 12.4s
1968 Christoph Hohne, E. Germany	4h. 20m. 13.6s
1972 Bern Kannenberg, W. Germany	3h. 56m. 11.6s
1980 Hartwig Gauter, E. Germany	3h. 49m. 24.0s
1984 Raul Gonzalez, Mexico	3h. 47m. 26.0s
1988 Vyacheslav Ivanenko, USSR	3h. 38m. 29.0s
1992 Andrei Perlov, Unified Team	3h. 50m. 13.0s
1996 Robert Korzeniowski, Poland	3h. 43m. 30s
2000 Robert Korzeniowski, Poland	3h. 42m. 22s
2004 Robert Korzeniowski, Poland	3h. 38m. 46s
2008 Alex Schwazer, Italy	3h. 37m. 09s*

110-Meter Hurdles	Time
1896 Thomas Curtis, United States	17.6s
1900 Alvin Kraenzlein, United States	15.4s
1904 Frederick Schule, United States	16.0s
1908 Forrest Smithson, United States	15.0s
1912 Frederick Kelly, United States	15.1s
1920 Earl Thomson, Canada	14.8s
1924 Daniel Kinsey, United States	15.0s
1928 Sydney Atkinson, South Africa	14.8s
1932 George Saling, United States	14.6s
1936 Forrest Towns, United States	14.2s
1948 William Porter, United States	13.9s
1952 Harrison Dillard, United States	13.7s
1956 Lee Calhoun, United States	13.5s
1960 Lee Calhoun, United States	13.8s
1964 Hayes Jones, United States	13.6s
1968 Willie Davenport, United States	13.33s
1972 Rod Milburn, United States	13.24s
1976 Guy Drut, France	13.30s
1980 Thomas Munkelt, E. Germany	13.39s
1984 Roger Kingdom, United States	13.20s
1988 Roger Kingdom, United States	12.98s
1992 Mark McCoy, Canada	13.12s
1996 Allen Johnson, United States	12.95s
2000 Anier Garcia, Cuba	13.00s
2004 Liu Xiang, China	12.91s*
2008 Dayron Robles, Cuba	12.93s

400-Meter Hurdles	Time
1900 J. W. B. Tewksbury, United States	57.6s
1904 Harry Hillman, United States	53.0s
1908 Charles Bacon, United States	55.0s
1920 Frank Loomis, United States	54.0s
1924 F. Morgan Taylor, United States	52.6s
1928 Lord Burghley, Great Britain	53.4s
1932 Robert Tisdall, Ireland	51.7s
1936 Glenn Hardin, United States	52.4s
1948 Roy Cochran, United States	51.1s
1952 Charles Moore, United States	50.8s
1956 Glenn Davis, United States	50.1s
1960 Glenn Davis, United States	49.3s
1964 Rex Cawley, United States	49.6s
1968 Dave Hemery, Great Britain	48.12s
1972 John Akii-Bua, Uganda	47.82s
1976 Edwin Moses, United States	47.64s
1980 Volker Beck, E. Germany	48.70s
1984 Edwin Moses, United States	47.75s
1988 Andre Phillips, United States	47.19s
1992 Kevin Young, United States	46.78s
1996 Derrick Adkins, United States	47.54s

	400-Meter Hurdles	Time	
2000	Angelo Taylor, United States	47.50s	
2004	Felix Sanchez, Dominican Republic	47.63s	
2008	Angelo Taylor, United States	47.25s	

	Discus Throw	Dist.	
1896	Robert Garrett, United States	29.15m	(95' 7")
1900	Rudolf Bauer, Hungary	36.04m	(118' 3")
1904	Martin Sheridan, United States	39.28m	(128' 10")
1908	Martin Sheridan, United States	40.89m	(134' 1")
1912	Armas Taipale, Finland	45.21m	(148' 3")
1920	Elmer Niklander, Finland	44.68m	(146' 7")
1924	Clarence Houser, United States	46.15m	(151' 4")
1928	Clarence Houser, United States	47.32m	(155' 3")
1932	John Anderson, United States	49.49m	(162' 4")
1936	Ken Carpenter, United States	50.48m	(165' 7")
1948	Adolfo Consolini, Italy	52.78m	(173' 2")
1952	Sim Iness, United States	55.03m	(180' 6")
1956	Al Oerter, United States	56.36m	(184' 11")
1960	Al Oerter, United States	59.18m	(194' 2")
1964	Al Oerter, United States	61.00m	(200' 1")
1968	Al Oerter, United States	64.78m	(212' 6")
1972	Ludvik Danek, Czechoslovakia	64.40m	(211' 3")
1976	Mac Wilkins, United States	67.50m	(221' 5")
1980	Viktor Rashchupkin, USSR	66.64m	(218' 8")
1984	Rolf Dannenberg, W. Germany	66.60m	(218' 6")
1988	Jurgen Schult, E. Germany	68.82m	(225' 9")
1992	Romas Ubartas, Lithuania	65.12m	(213' 8")
1996	Lars Riedel, Germany	69.40m	(227' 8")
2000	Virgilijus Alekna, Lithuania	69.30m	(227' 4")
2004	Virgilijus Alekna, Lithuania	69.89m	(228' 9¾")*
2008	Gerd Kanter, Estonia	68.82m	(225' 9½")

	Hammer Throw	Dist.	
1900	John Flanagan, United States	49.73m	(163' 1")
1904	John Flanagan, United States	51.22m	(168' 0")
1908	John Flanagan, United States	51.92m	(170' 4")
1912	Matt McGrath, United States	54.74m	(179' 7")
1920	Pat Ryan, United States	52.86m	(173' 5")
1924	Fred Tootell, United States	53.28m	(174' 10")
1928	Patrick O'Callaghan, Ireland	51.38m	(168' 7")
1932	Patrick O'Callaghan, Ireland	53.92m	(176' 11")
1936	Karl Hein, Germany	56.48m	(185' 4")
1948	Imre Németh, Hungary	56.06m	(183' 11")
1952	József Csérmák, Hungary	60.34m	(197' 11")
1956	Harold Connolly, United States	63.18m	(207' 3")
1960	Vasily Rudenkov, USSR	67.10m	(202' 0")
1964	Romuald Klim, USSR	69.74m	(228' 10")
1968	Gyula Zsivótsky, Hungary	73.36m	(240' 8")
1972	Anatoly Bondarchuk, USSR	75.50m	(247' 8")
1976	Yuri Syedykh, USSR	77.52m	(254' 4")
1980	Yuri Syedykh, USSR	81.80m	(268' 4")
1984	Juha Tiainen, Finland	78.08m	(256' 2")
1988	Sergei Litvinov, USSR	84.80m	(278' 2")*
1992	Andrey Abduvaliyev, Unified Team	82.54m	(270' 9")
1996	Balázs Kiss, Hungary	81.24m	(266' 6")
2000	Szymon Ziolkowski, Poland	80.02m	(262' 6")
2004	Koji Murofushi, Japan	82.91m	(272')
2008	Primoz Kozmus, Slovenia	82.02m	(269' 1")

	High Jump	Height	
1896	Ellery Clark, United States	1.81m	(5' 11¼")
1900	Irving Baxter, United States	1.90m	(6' 2¾")
1904	Samuel Jones, United States	1.80m	(5' 11")
1908	Harry Porter, United States	1.90m	(6' 2¾")
1912	Alma Richards, United States	1.93m	(6' 4")
1920	Richmond Landon, United States	1.93m	(6' 4")
1924	Harold Osborn, United States	1.98m	(6' 6")
1928	Robert W. King, United States	1.94m	(6' 4¼")
1932	Duncan McNaughton, Canada	1.97m	(6' 5½")
1936	Cornelius Johnson, United States	2.03m	(6' 8")
1948	John L. Winter, Australia	1.98m	(6' 6")
1952	Walter Davis, United States	2.04m	(6' 8¼")
1956	Charles Dumas, United States	2.12m	(6' 11½")
1960	Robert Shavlakadze, USSR	2.16m	(7' 1")
1964	Valery Brumel, USSR	2.18m	(7' 1¾")
1968	Dick Fosbury, United States	2.24m	(7' 4¼")
1972	Jüri Tarmak, USSR	2.23m	(7' 3¾")
1976	Jacek Wszola, Poland	2.25m	(7' 4½")
1980	Gerd Wessig, E. Germany	2.36m	(7' 8¾")
1984	Dietmar Mögenburg, W. Germany	2.35m	(7' 8½")
1988	Hennady Avdeyenko, USSR	2.38m	(7' 9¾")
1992	Javier Sotomayor Sanabria, Cuba	2.34m	(7' 8")
1996	Charles Austin, United States	2.39m	(7' 10")*
2000	Sergey Kliugin, Russia	2.35m	(7' 8½")
2004	Stefen Holm, Sweden	2.36m	(7' 9¾")
2008	Andrey Silnov, Russia	2.36m	(7' 9¾")

	Javelin Throw	Dist.	
1908	Erik Lemming, Sweden	54.82m	(179' 10")
1912	Erik Lemming, Sweden	60.64m	(198' 11")
1920	Jonni Myyrä, Finland	64.78m	(215' 10")
1924	Jonni Myyrä, Finland	62.96m	(206' 7")
1928	Eric Lundkvist, Sweden	66.60m	(218' 6")
1932	Matti Järvinen, Finland	72.70m	(238' 6")
1936	Gerhard Stöck, Germany	71.84m	(235' 8")
1948	Kai Tapio Rautavaara, Finland	69.76m	(228' 11")
1952	Cy Young, United States	73.78m	(242' 1")
1956	Egil Danielsen, Norway	85.70m	(281' 2")
1960	Viktor Tsibulenko, USSR	84.64m	(277' 8")
1964	Pauli Nevala, Finland	82.66m	(271' 2")
1968	Janis Lusis, USSR	90.10m	(295' 7")
1972	Klaus Wolfermann, W. Germany	90.48m	(296' 10")
1976	Miklós Németh, Hungary	94.58m	(310' 4")
1980	Dainis Kula, USSR	91.20m	(299' 2")
1984	Arto Härkönen, Finland	86.76m	(284' 8")
1988	Tapio Korjus, Finland	84.28m	(276' 6")
1992	Jan Zelezny, Czechoslovakia	89.66m	(294' 2")
1996	Jan Zelezny, Czech Republic	88.16m	(289' 3")
2000	Jan Zelezny, Czech Republic	90.17m	(295' 9½")
2004	Andreas Thorkildsen, Norway	86.50m	(283' 10")
2008	Andreas Thorkildsen, Norway	90.57m	(297' 1¾")

Note: New records were kept after javelin was modified in 1986.

	Long Jump	Dist.	
1896	Ellery Clark, United States	6.35m	(20' 10")
1900	Alvin Kraenzlein, United States	7.18m	(23' 6¾")
1904	Meyer Prinstein, United States	7.34m	(24' 1")
1908	Frank Irons, United States	7.48m	(24' 6½")
1912	Albert Gutterson, United States	7.60m	(24' 11¼")
1920	William Petterssen, Sweden	7.15m	(23' 5½")
1924	William DeHart Hubbard, U.S.	7.44m	(24' 5")
1928	Edward B. Hamm, United States	7.73m	(25' 4½")
1932	Edward Gordon, United States	7.64m	(25' ¾")
1936	Jesse Owens, United States	8.06m	(26' 5½")
1948	Willie Steele, United States	7.82m	(25' 8")
1952	Jerome Biffle, United States	7.57m	(24' 10")
1956	Gregory Bell, United States	7.83m	(25' 8¼")
1960	Ralph Boston, United States	8.12m	(26' 7¾")
1964	Lynn Davies, Great Britain	8.07m	(26' 5¾")
1968	Bob Beamon, United States	8.90m	(29' 2½")*
1972	Randy Williams, United States	8.24m	(27' ½")
1976	Arnie Robinson, United States	8.35m	(27' 4¾")
1980	Lutz Dombrowski, E. Germany	8.54m	(28' ¼")
1984	Carl Lewis, United States	8.54m	(28' ¼")
1988	Carl Lewis, United States	8.72m	(28' 7½")
1992	Carl Lewis, United States	8.67m	(28' 5½")
1996	Carl Lewis, United States	8.50m	(27' 10¾")
2000	Ivan Pedroso, Cuba	8.55m	(28' ¾")
2004	Dwight Phillips, United States	8.59m	(28' 2¼")
2008	Irving Jahir Saladino Aranda, Panama	8.34m	(27' 4¼")

	Pole Vault	Height	
1896	William Welles Hoyt, United States	3.30m	(10' 10")
1900	Irving Baxter, United States	3.30m	(10' 10")
1904	Charles Dvorak, United States	3.50m	(11' 6")
1908	A. C. Gilbert, United States; Edward Cooke Jr., United States	3.71m	(12' 2")
1920	Frank Foss, United States	4.09m	(13' 5")
1924	Lee Barnes, United States	3.95m	(12' 11½")
1928	Sabin W. Carr, United States	4.20m	(13' 9¼")
1932	William Miller, United States	4.31m	(14' 1¾")
1936	Earle Meadows, United States	4.35m	(14' 3¼")
1948	Guinn Smith, United States	4.30m	(14' 1¼")
1952	Robert Richards, United States	4.55m	(14' 11¼")
1956	Robert Richards, United States	4.56m	(14' 11½")
1960	Don Bragg, United States	4.70m	(15' 5")
1964	Fred Hansen, United States	5.10m	(16' 8¾")
1968	Bob Seagren, United States	5.40m	(17' 8½")
1972	Wolfgang Nordwig, E. Germany	5.50m	(18' ½")
1976	Tadeusz Slusarski, Poland	5.50m	(18' ½")
1980	Wladyslaw Kozakiewicz, Poland	5.78m	(18' 11½")
1984	Pierre Quinon, France	5.75m	(18' 10¼")
1988	Sergei Bubka, USSR	5.90m	(19' 4¼")
1992	Maksim Tarassov, Unified Team	5.80m	(19' ¼")
1996	Jean Galfione, France	5.92m	(19' 5")
2000	Nick Hysong, United States	5.90m	(19' 4¼")
2004	Timothy Mack, United States	5.95m	(19' 6¼")
2008	Steve Hooker, Australia	5.96m	(19' 6¾")*

Shot Put

		Dist.
1896	Robert Garrett, United States	11.22m (36' 9¾")
1900	Richard Sheldon, United States	14.10m (46' 3¼")
1904	Ralph Rose, United States	14.81m (48' 7")
1908	Ralph Rose, United States	14.21m (46' 7½")
1912	Pat McDonald, United States	15.34m (50' 4")
1920	Ville Pörhölä, Finland	14.81m (48' 7¼")
1924	L. Clarence Houser, United States	14.99m (49' 2¼")
1928	John Kuck, United States	15.87m (52' ¾")
1932	Leo Sexton, United States	16.00m (52' 6")
1936	Hans Woellke, Germany	16.20m (53' 1¾")
1948	Wilbur Thompson, United States	17.12m (56' 2")
1952	W. Parry O'Brien, United States	17.41m (57' 1½")
1956	W. Parry O'Brien, United States	18.57m (60' 11¼")
1960	William Nieder, United States	19.68m (64' 6¾")
1964	Dallas Long, United States	20.33m (66' 8½")
1968	Randy Matson, United States	20.54m (67' 4¾")
1972	Wladyslaw Komar, Poland	21.18m (69' 6")
1976	Udo Beyer, E. Germany	21.05m (69' ¾")
1980	Vladimir Kyselyov, USSR	21.35m (70' ½")
1984	Alessandro Andrei, Italy	21.26m (69' 9")
1988	Ulf Timmermann, E. Germany	22.47m (73' 8¾")*
1992	Michael Stulce, United States	21.70m (71' 2½")
1996	Randy Barnes, United States	21.62m (70' 11¼")
2000	Arsi Harju, Finland	21.29m (69' 10¼")
2004	Yuriy Bilonog, Ukraine	21.16m (69' 5¼")
2008	Tomasz Majewski, Poland	21.51m (70' 6¾")

Triple Jump

		Dist.
1896	James Connolly, United States	13.71m (44' 11¾")
1900	Meyer Prinstein, United States	14.47m (47' 5¾")
1904	Meyer Prinstein, United States	14.35m (47' 1")
1908	Timothy Ahearne, G.B.-Ireland	14.92m (48' 11½")
1912	Gustaf Lindblom, Sweden	14.76m (48' 5")
1920	Vilho Tuulos, Finland	14.50m (47' 7")
1924	Anthony Winter, Australia	15.52m (50' 11")
1928	Mikio Oda, Japan	15.21m (49' 11")
1932	Chuhei Nambu, Japan	15.72m (51' 7")
1936	Naoto Tajima, Japan	16.00m (52' 6")
1948	Arne Ahman, Sweden	15.40m (50' 6¼")
1952	Adhemar Ferreira da Silva, Brazil	16.22m (53' 2¾")
1956	Adhemar Ferreira da Silva, Brazil	16.35m (53' 7¾")
1960	Jozef Schmidt, Poland	16.81m (55' 1½")
1964	Jozef Schmidt, Poland	16.85m (55' 3½")

Triple Jump

		Dist.
1968	Viktor Saneyev, USSR	17.39m (57' ¾")
1972	Viktor Saneyev, USSR	17.35m (56' 11¼")
1976	Viktor Saneyev, USSR	17.29m (56' 8¾")
1980	Jaak Uudmae, USSR	17.35m (56' 11")
1984	Al Joyner, United States	17.26m (56' 7½")
1988	Khristo Markov, Bulgaria	17.61m (57' 9½")
1992	Mike Conley, United States	18.17m (59' 7½")*(w)
1996	Kenny Harrison, United States	18.09m (59' 4¼")*
2000	Jonathan Edwards, Britain	17.71m (58' 1¼")
2004	Christian Olsson, Sweden	17.79m (58' 4½")
2008	Nelson Evora, Portugal	17.67m (57' 11¾")

Decathlon (not held 1908)

		Points
1904	Thomas Kiely, Ireland	6,036
1912	Hugo Wieslander, Sweden (a)	7,724.49
1920	Helge Lovland, Norway	6,804.35
1924	Harold Osborn, United States	7,710.77
1928	Paavo Yrjola, Finland	8,053.29
1932	James Bausch, United States	8,462.23
1936	Glenn Morris, United States	7,900
1948	Robert Mathias, United States	7,139
1952	Robert Mathias, United States	7,887
1956	Milton Campbell, United States	7,937
1960	Rafer Johnson, United States	8,392
1964	Willi Holdorf, Germany (b)	7,887
1968	Bill Toomey, United States	8,193
1972	Nikolai Avilov, USSR	8,454
1976	Bruce Jenner, United States	8,617
1980	Daley Thompson, Great Britain	8,495
1984	Daley Thompson, Great Britain (c)	8,798
1988	Christian Schenk, E. Germany	8,488
1992	Robert Zmelik, Czechoslovakia	8,611
1996	Dan O'Brien, United States	8,824
2000	Erki Nool, Estonia	8,641
2004	Roman Sebrle, Czech Republic	8,893*
2008	Bryan Clay, United States	8,791

(a) Jim Thorpe of the U.S. won the 1912 Decathlon with 8,413 pts. but was disqualified and had to return his medals because he had played pro baseball prior to the Olympics. The IOC in 1982 posthumously restored his decathlon and pentathlon golds. (b) Former point systems used prior to 1964. (c) Scoring change effective Apr. 1985; Thompson's readjusted score is 8,847 pts.

Track and Field—Women

100-Meter Run

		Time
1928	Elizabeth Robinson, United States	12.2s
1932	Stella Walsh, Poland (a)	11.9s
1936	Helen Stephens, United States	11.5s
1948	Francina Blankers-Koen, Netherlands	11.9s
1952	Marjorie Jackson, Australia	11.5s
1956	Betty Cuthbert, Australia	11.5s
1960	Wilma Rudolph, United States	11.0s
1964	Wyomia Tyus, United States	11.4s
1968	Wyomia Tyus, United States	11.08s
1972	Renate Stecher, E. Germany	11.07s
1976	Annegret Richter, W. Germany	11.08s
1980	Lyudmila Kondratyeva, USSR	11.06s
1984	Evelyn Ashford, United States	10.97s
1988	Florence Griffith-Joyner, United States	10.54s*
1992	Gail Devers, United States	10.82s
1996	Gail Devers, United States	10.94s
2000	No winner (b)	NA
2004	Yuliya Nesterenko, Belarus	10.93s
2008	Shelly-Ann Fraser, Jamaica	10.78s

(a) A 1980 autopsy determined that Walsh was a man. (b) Marion Jones was stripped of her gold medal in 2007 due to doping; the IOC declined to award the medal to the runner-up, who was also suspected of using performance-enhancing drugs.

200-Meter Run

		Time
1948	Francina Blankers-Koen, Netherlands	24.4s
1952	Marjorie Jackson, Australia	23.7s
1956	Betty Cuthbert, Australia	23.4s
1960	Wilma Rudolph, United States	24.0s
1964	Edith McGuire, United States	23.0s
1968	Irena Szewinska, Poland	22.5s
1972	Renate Stecher, E. Germany	22.40s
1976	Barbel Eckert, E. Germany	22.37s
1980	Barbel Wockel, E. Germany	22.03s
1984	Valerie Brisco-Hooks, United States	21.81s
1988	Florence Griffith-Joyner, United States	21.34s*
1992	Gwen Torrence, United States	21.81s
1996	Marie-Jose Perec, France	22.12s
2000	Pauline Davis-Thompson, Bahamas (a)	21.84s
2004	Veronica Campbell, Jamaica	22.05s
2008	Veronica Campbell-Brown, Jamaica	21.74s

(a) Originally won by Marion Jones, U.S., who was stripped of the gold in 2007 due to doping.

400-Meter Run

		Time
1964	Betty Cuthbert, Australia	52.0s
1968	Colette Besson, France	52.0s
1972	Monika Zehrt, E. Germany	51.08s
1976	Irena Szewinska, Poland	49.29s
1980	Marita Koch, E. Germany	48.88s
1984	Valerie Brisco-Hooks, United States	48.83s
1988	Olga Bryzgina, USSR	48.65s
1992	Marie-Jose Perec, France	48.83s
1996	Marie-Jose Perec, France	48.25s*
2000	Cathy Freeman, Australia	49.11s
2004	Tonique Williams-Darling, The Bahamas	49.41s
2008	Christine Ohuruogu, Great Britain	49.62s

800-Meter Run

		Time
1928	Lina Radke, Germany	2m. 16.8s
1960	Ludmila Shevtsova, USSR	2m. 04.3s
1964	Ann Packer, Great Britain	2m. 01.1s
1968	Madeline Manning, United States	2m. 00.9s
1972	Hildegard Falck, W. Germany	1m. 58.6s
1976	Tatyana Kazankina, USSR	1m. 54.94s
1980	Nadezhda Olizarenko, USSR	1m. 53.43s*
1984	Doina Melinte, Romania	1m. 57.60s
1988	Sigrun Wodars, E. Germany	1m. 56.10s
1992	Ellen Van Langen, Netherlands	1m. 55.54s
1996	Svetlana Masterkova, Russia	1m. 57.73s
2000	Maria Mutola, Mozambique	1m. 56.15s
2004	Kelly Holmes, Great Britain	1m. 56.38s
2008	Pamela Jelimo, Kenya	1m. 54.87s

1,500-Meter Run

		Time
1972	Lyudmila Bragina, USSR	4m. 01.4s
1976	Tatyana Kazankina, USSR	4m. 05.48s
1980	Tatyana Kazankina, USSR	3m. 56.6s
1984	Gabriella Dorio, Italy	4m. 03.25s
1988	Paula Ivan, Romania	3m. 53.96s*
1992	Hassiba Boulmerka, Algeria	3m. 55.30s
1996	Svetlana Masterkova, Russia	4m. 00.83s
2000	Nouria Benida Merah, Algeria	4m. 05.10s
2004	Kelly Holmes, Great Britain	3m. 57.90s
2008	Nancy Jebet Langat, Kenya	4m. 00.23s

3,000-Meter Run	Time
1984 Maricica Puica, Romania	8m. 35.96s
1988 Tatyana Samolenko, USSR	8m. 26.53s*
1992 Elena Romanova, Unified Team	8m. 46.04s

3,000-Meter Steeplechase	Time
2008 Gulnara Galkina-Samitova, Russia	8m. 58.81s

5,000-Meter Run	Time
1996 Wang Junxia, China	14m. 59.88s
2000 Gabriela Szabo, Romania	14m. 40.79s*
2004 Meseret Defar, Ethiopia	14m. 45.65s
2008 Tirunesh Dibaba, Ethiopia	15m. 41.40s

10,000-Meter Run	Time
1988 Olga Boldarenko, USSR	31m. 44.69s
1992 Derartu Tulu, Ethiopia	31m. 06.02s
1996 Fernanda Ribeiro, Portugal	31m. 01.63s
2000 Derartu Tulu, Ethiopia	30m. 17.49s
2004 Xing Huina, China	30m. 24.36s
2008 Tirunesh Dibaba, Ethiopia	29m. 54.66s*

Marathon	Time
1984 Joan Benoit, United States	2h. 24m. 52s
1988 Rosa Mota, Portugal	2h. 25m. 40s
1992 Valentina Yegorova, Unified Team	2h. 32m. 41s
1996 Fatuma Roba, Ethiopia	2h. 26m. 05s
2000 Naoko Takahashi, Japan	2h. 23m. 14s*
2004 Mizuki Noguchi, Japan	2h. 26m. 20s
2008 Constantina Tomescu, Romania	2h. 26m. 44s

4x100-Meter Relay	Time
1928 Canada	48.4s
1932 United States	46.9s
1936 United States	46.9s
1948 Netherlands	47.5s
1952 United States	45.9s
1956 Australia	44.5s
1960 United States	44.5s
1964 Poland	43.6s
1968 United States	42.88s
1972 West Germany	42.81s
1976 East Germany	42.55s
1980 East Germany	41.60s*
1984 United States	41.65s
1988 United States	41.98s
1992 United States	42.11s
1996 United States	41.95s
2000 Bahamas	41.95s
2004 Jamaica	41.73s
2008 Russia	42.31s

4x400-Meter Relay	Time
1972 East Germany	3m. 23s
1976 East Germany	3m. 19.23s
1980 USSR	3m. 20.02s
1984 United States	3m. 18.29s
1988 USSR	3m. 15.17s*
1992 Unified Team	3m. 20.20s
1996 United States	3m. 20.91s
2000 United States	3m. 22.62s
2004 United States	3m. 19.01s
2008 United States	3m. 18.54s

10-Kilometer Walk	Time
1992 Chen Yueling, China	44m. 32s
1996 Elena Nikolayeva, Russia	41m. 49s*

20-Kilometer Walk	Time
2000 Wang Liping, China	1h. 29m. 05s
2004 Athanasia Tsoumeleka, Greece	1h. 29m. 12s
2008 Olga Kaniskina, Russia	1h. 26m. 31s*

100-Meter Hurdles	Time
1972 Annelie Ehrhardt, E. Germany	12.59s
1976 Johanna Schaller, E. Germany	12.77s
1980 Vera Komisova, USSR	12.56s
1984 Benita Brown-Fitzgerald, United States	12.84s
1988 Jordanka Donkova, Bulgaria	12.38s
1992 Paraskevi Patoulidou, Greece	12.64s
1996 Ludmila Enquist, Sweden	12.58s
2000 Olga Shishigina, Kazakhstan	12.65s
2004 Joanna Hayes, United States	12.37s*
2008 Dawn Harper, United States	12.54s

400-Meter Hurdles	Time
1984 Nawal el Moutawakii, Morocco	54.61s
1988 Debra Flintoff-King, Australia	53.17s
1992 Sally Gunnell, Great Britain	53.23s
1996 Deon Hemmings, Jamaica	52.82s
2000 Irina Privalova, Russia	53.02s
2004 Fani Halkia, Greece	52.82s
2008 Melaine Walker, Jamaica	52.64s*

Discus Throw	Dist.
1928 Halina Konopacka, Poland	39.62m (130' 0")
1932 Lillian Copeland, United States	40.58m (133' 2")
1936 Gisela Mauermayer, Germany	47.62m (156' 3")
1948 Micheline Ostermeyer, France	41.92m (137' 6")
1952 Nina Ponomareva, USSR	51.42m (168' 8")
1956 Olga Fikotová, Czechoslovakia	53.68m (176' 1")
1960 Nina Ponomareva, USSR	55.10m (180' 9")
1964 Tamara Press, USSR	57.26m (187' 10")
1968 Lia Manoliu, Romania	58.28m (191' 2")
1972 Faina Melnik, USSR	66.62m (218' 7")
1976 Evelin Jahl, E. Germany	69.00m (226' 4")
1980 Evelin Jahl, E. Germany	69.96m (229' 6")
1984 Ria Stalman, Netherlands	65.36m (214' 5")
1988 Martina Hellmann, E. Germany	72.30m (237' 2")*
1992 Maritza Martén Garcia, Cuba	70.06m (229' 10")
1996 Ilke Wyludda, Germany	69.66m (228' 6")
2000 Ellina Zvereva, Belarus	68.40m (224' 5")
2004 Natalya Sadova, Russia	67.02m (219' 9")
2008 Stephanie Brown Trafton, United States	64.74m (212' 4¾")

Hammer Throw	Dist.
2000 Kamila Skolimowska, Poland	71.16m (233' 5¾")
2004 Olga Kuzenkova, Russia	75.02m (246' 1")
2008 Aksana Miankova, Belarus	76.34m (250' 5½")*

High Jump	Height
1928 Ethel Catherwood, Canada	1.59m (5' 2½")
1932 Jean Shiley, United States	1.65m (5' 5")
1936 Ibolya Csák, Hungary	1.60m (5' 3")
1948 Alice Coachman, U. S.	1.68m (5' 6")
1952 Esther Brand, South Africa	1.67m (5' 5¾")
1956 Mildred L. McDaniel, U. S.	1.76m (5' 9¼")
1960 Iolanda Balas, Romania	1.85m (6' ¾")
1964 Iolanda Balas, Romania	1.90m (6' 2¾")
1968 Miloslava Resková, Czech.	1.82m (5' 11½")
1972 Ulrike Meyfarth, W. Germany	1.92m (6' 3½")
1976 Rosemarie Ackermann, E. Ger.	1.93m (6' 4")
1980 Sara Simeoni, Italy	1.97m (6' 5½")
1984 Ulrike Meyfarth, W. Germany	2.02m (6' 7½")
1988 Louise Ritter, United States	2.03m (6' 8")
1992 Heike Henkel, Germany	2.02m (6' 7½")
1996 Stefka Kostadinova, Bulgaria	2.05m (6' 8¾")
2000 Yelena Yelesina, Russia	2.01m (6' 7")
2004 Yelena Slesarenko, Russia	2.06m (6' 9")*
2008 Tia Hellebaut, Belgium	2.05m (6' 8¾")

Javelin Throw	Dist.
1932 "Babe" Didrikson, United States	43.68m (143' 4")
1936 Tilly Fleischer, Germany	45.18m (148' 3")
1948 Herma Bauma, Austria	45.56m (149' 6")
1952 Dana Zátopková, Czechoslovakia	50.46m (165' 7")
1956 Inese Jaunzeme, USSR	53.86m (176' 8")
1960 Elvira Ozolina, USSR	55.98m (183' 8")
1964 Mihaela Penes, Romania	60.54m (198' 7")
1968 Angéla Németh, Hungary	60.36m (198' 0")
1972 Ruth Fuchs, E. Germany	63.88m (209' 7")
1976 Ruth Fuchs, E. Germany	65.94m (216' 4")
1980 Maria Colón Ruenes, Cuba	68.40m (224' 5")
1984 Tessa Sanderson, Great Britain	69.56m (228' 2")
1988 Petra Felke, E. Germany	74.68m (245' 0")
1992 Silke Renke, Germany	68.34m (224' 2")
1996 Heli Rantanen, Finland	67.94m (222' 11")
2000 Trine Hattestad, Norway	68.91m (226' 1")
2004 Osleidys Menendez, Cuba	71.53m (234' 8")*
2008 Barbora Spotakova, Czech Republic	71.42m (234' 3¾")

Note: New records were kept after javelin was modified in 1999.

Long Jump	Dist.
1948 Olga Gyarmati, Hungary	5.69m (18' 8")
1952 Yvette Williams, New Zealand	6.24m (20' 5¼")
1956 Elzbieta Krzesinska, Poland	6.35m (20' 10")
1960 Vira Krepkina, USSR	6.37m (20' 10¾")
1964 Mary Rand, Great Britain	6.76m (22' 2¼")
1968 Viorica Viscopoleanu, Romania	6.82m (22' 4½")
1972 Heidemarie Rosendahl, W. Ger.	6.78m (22' 3")
1976 Angela Voigt, E. Germany	6.72m (22' ¾")
1980 Tatyana Kolpakova, USSR	7.06m (23' 2")
1984 Anisoara Cusmir-Stanciu, Rom.	6.96m (22' 10")
1988 Jackie Joyner-Kersee, United States	7.40m (24' 3½")*
1992 Heike Drechsler, Germany	7.14m (23' 5¼")
1996 Chioma Ajunwa, Nigeria	7.12m (23' 4½")
2000 Heike Drechsler, Germany	6.99m (22' 11¼")
2004 Tatyana Lebedeva, Russia	7.07m (23' 2½")
2008 Maurren Higa Maggi, Brazil	7.04m (23' 1¼")

Pole Vault	Height
2000 Stacy Dragila, United States	4.60m (15' 1")
2004 Elena Isinbaeva, Russia	4.91m (16' 1⅓")
2008 Elena Isinbaeva, Russia	5.05m (16' 6¾")*

Shot Put	Dist.
1948 Micheline Ostermeyer, France	13.75m (45' 1½")
1952 Galina Zybina, USSR	15.28m (50' 1½")
1956 Tamara Tyshkyevich, USSR	16.59m (54' 5¼")
1960 Tamara Press, USSR	17.32m (56' 10")
1964 Tamara Press, USSR	18.14m (59' 6¼")
1968 Margitta Gummel, E. Germany	19.61m (64' 4")
1972 Nadezhda Chizova, USSR	21.03m (69' 0")
1976 Ivanka Khristova, Bulgaria	21.16m (69' 5¼")
1980 Ilona Slupianek, E. Germany	22.41m (73' 6¼")*
1984 Claudia Losch, W. Germany	20.49m (67' 2¼")
1988 Natalya Lisovskaya, USSR	22.24m (72' 11¾")
1992 Svetlana Krivelyova, Unified Team	21.06m (69' 1¼")
1996 Astrid Kumbernuss, Germany	20.56m (67' 5½")
2000 Yanina Karolchik, Belarus	20.56m (67' 5½")
2004 Yumileidi Cumba Jay, Cuba	19.59m (64' 3¼")
2008 Valerie Vili, New Zealand	20.56m (67' 5½")

Triple Jump	Dist.
1996 Inessa Kravets, Ukraine	15.33m (50' 3½")
2000 Tereza Marinova, Bulgaria	15.20m (49' 10½")
2004 Francoise Mbango Etone, Cameroon	15.30m (50' 2⅓")
2008 Francoise Mbango Etone, Cameroon	15.39m (50' 6")*

Heptathlon	Points
1984 Glynis Nunn, Australia	6,390
1988 Jackie Joyner-Kersee, United States	7,291*
1992 Jackie Joyner-Kersee, United States	7,044
1996 Ghada Shouaa, Syria	6,780
2000 Denise Lewis, Great Britain	6,584
2004 Carolina Kluft, Sweden	6,952
2008 Nataliia Dobrynska, Ukraine	6,733

2010 Winter Olympic Games
Vancouver, BC, Canada, Feb. 12-28, 2010

More than 2,600 athletes from 82 nations met in Vancouver, BC, Canada, to compete in 86 events in the XXI Olympic Winter Games Feb. 12-28, 2010. Host nation Canada set the record for most gold medals won by a nation at a single Winter Olympics, with 14. Two of Canada's gold medals came in women's and men's hockey, the latter determined by a climactic 3-2 overtime win over the U.S. The U.S. led the overall medal count with 37. Opening ceremonies held Feb. 12 were subdued by the death of luger Nodar Kumaritashvili of Georgia, who was killed during a training run earlier that day.

Despite a well-publicized injury, U.S. alpine skier Lindsey Vonn became the first American woman to win an Olympic gold medal in the downhill event Feb. 17; Vonn also won the bronze medal in the super-G event Feb. 20. U.S. snowboarder Shaun White won his second men's halfpipe gold Feb. 17.

Figure skater Evan Lysacek Feb. 18 won the first U.S. gold medal in the men's event since 1988, defeating defending Olympic champion Yevgeny Plushenko of Russia. The women's figure skating medal was awarded to South Korean Kim Yu-Na.

Speedskater Apolo Ohno won one silver and two bronze medals, for a U.S. Winter Olympic-record career total of eight. One new medal event, ski cross, debuted at the Vancouver games, with the event's first gold medals awarded to Switzerland's Michael Schmid and Canada's Ashleigh McIvor.

2010 Final Medal Standings

Country	Gold	Silver	Bronze	Total	Country	Gold	Silver	Bronze	Total
United States	9	15	13	37	Italy	1	1	3	5
Germany	10	13	7	30	Japan	0	3	2	5
Canada	14	7	5	26	Finland	0	1	4	5
Norway	9	8	6	23	Australia	2	1	0	3
Austria	4	6	6	16	Belarus	1	1	1	3
Russia	3	5	7	15	Slovakia	1	1	1	3
South Korea	6	6	2	14	Croatia	0	2	1	3
China	5	2	4	11	Slovenia	0	2	1	3
Sweden	5	2	4	11	Latvia	0	2	0	2
France	2	3	6	11	Britain	1	0	0	1
Switzerland	6	0	3	9	Estonia	0	1	0	1
Netherlands	4	1	3	8	Kazakhstan	0	1	0	1
Czech Republic	2	0	4	6					
Poland	1	3	2	6	Total	86	87	85	258

Winter Olympic Games Champions, 1924-2010

In 1992, the Unified Team represented the former Soviet republics of Russia, Ukraine, Belarus, Kazakhstan, and Uzbekistan.

Alpine Skiing

Men's Downhill	Time
1948 Henri Oreiller, France	2:55.0
1952 Zeno Colo, Italy	2:30.8
1956 Toni Sailer, Austria	2:52.2
1960 Jean Vuarnet, France	2:06.0
1964 Egon Zimmermann, Austria	2:18.16
1968 Jean-Claude Killy, France	1:59.85
1972 Bernhard Russi, Switzerland	1:51.43
1976 Franz Klammer, Austria	1:45.73
1980 Leonhard Stock, Austria	1:45.50
1984 Bill Johnson, United States	1:45.49
1988 Pirmin Zurbriggen, Switzerland	1:59.63
1992 Patrick Ortlieb, Austria	1:50.37
1994 Tommy Moe, United States	1:45.75
1998 Jean-Luc Cretier, France	1:50.11
2002 Fritz Strobl, Austria	1:39.13
2006 Antoine Deneriaz, France	1:48.80
2010 Didier Defago, Switzerland	1:54.31

Men's Giant Slalom	Time
1952 Stein Eriksen, Norway	2:25.0
1956 Toni Sailer, Austria	3:00.1
1960 Roger Staub, Switzerland	1:48.3
1964 Francois Bonlieu, France	1:46.71
1968 Jean-Claude Killy, France	3:29.28
1972 Gustavo Thoeni, Italy	3:09.62
1976 Heini Hemmi, Switzerland	3:26.97
1980 Ingemar Stenmark, Sweden	2:40.74
1984 Max Julen, Switzerland	2:41.18
1988 Alberto Tomba, Italy	2:06.37

Men's Giant Slalom	Time
1992 Alberto Tomba, Italy	2:06.98
1994 Markus Wasmeier, Germany	2:52.46
1998 Hermann Maier, Austria	2:38.51
2002 Stephan Eberharter, Austria	2:23.28
2006 Benjamin Raich, Austria	2:35.00
2010 Carlo Janka, Switzerland	2:37.83

Men's Slalom	Time
1948 Edi Reinalter, Switzerland	2:10.3
1952 Othmar Schneider, Austria	2:00.0
1956 Toni Sailer, Austria	3:14.7
1960 Ernst Hinterseer, Austria	2:08.9
1964 Josef Stiegler, Austria	2:11.13
1968 Jean-Claude Killy, France	1:39.73
1972 Francisco Fernandez-Ochoa, Spain	1:49.27
1976 Piero Gros, Italy	2:03.29
1980 Ingemar Stenmark, Sweden	1:44.26
1984 Phil Mahre, United States	1:39.41
1988 Alberto Tomba, Italy	1:39.47
1992 Finn Christian Jagge, Norway	1:44.39
1994 Thomas Stangassinger, Austria	2:02.02
1998 Hans-Petter Buraas, Norway	1:49.31
2002 Jean-Pierre Vidal, France	1:41.06
2006 Benjamin Raich, Austria	1:43.14
2010 Giuliano Razzoli, Italy	1:39.32

Men's Super Combined	Time
1936 Franz-Pfnuer, Germany	99.25 (pts.)
1948 Henri Oreiller, France	3.27 (pts.)
1988 Hubert Strolz, Austria	36.55 (pts.)
1992 Josef Polig, Italy	14.58 (pts.)
1994 Lasse Kjus, Norway	3:17.53

Men's Super Combined

		Time
1998	Mario Reiter, Austria	3:08.06
2002	Kjetil Andre Aamodt, Norway	3:17.56
2006	Ted Ligety, United States	3:09.35
2010	Bode Miller, United States	2:44.92

Note: In 2010, a one-day super combined event replaced the traditional two-day combined event.

Men's Super Giant Slalom

		Time
1988	Franck Piccard, France	1:39.66
1992	Kjetil-Andre Aamodt, Norway	1:13.04
1994	Markus Wasmeier, Germany	1:32.53
1998	Hermann Maier, Austria	1:34.82
2002	Kjetil Andre Aamodt, Norway	1:21.58
2006	Kjetil Andre Aamodt, Norway	1:30.65
2010	Aksel Lund Svindal, Norway	1:30.34

Women's Downhill

		Time
1948	Hedi Schlunegger, Switzerland	2:28.3
1952	Trude Beiser-Jochum, Austria	1:47.1
1956	Madeleine Berthod, Switzerland	1:40.7
1960	Heidi Biebl, Germany	1:37.6
1964	Christl Haas, Austria	1:55.39
1968	Olga Pall, Austria	1:40.87
1972	Marie-Theres Nadig, Switzerland	1:36.68
1976	Rosi Mittermaier, W. Germany	1:46.16
1980	Annemarie Moser-Proell, Austria	1:37.52
1984	Michela Figini, Switzerland	1:13.36
1988	Marina Kiehl, W. Germany	1:25.86
1992	Kerrin Lee-Gartner, Canada	1:52.55
1994	Katja Seizinger, Germany	1:35.93
1998	Katja Seizinger, Germany	1:28.89
2002	Carole Montillet, France	1:39.56
2006	Michaela Dorfmeister, Austria	1:56.49
2010	Lindsey Vonn, United States	1:44.19

Women's Giant Slalom

		Time
1952	Andrea Mead Lawrence, United States	2:06.8
1956	Ossi Reichert, Germany	1:56.5
1960	Yvonne Ruegg, Switzerland	1:39.9
1964	Marielle Goitschel, France	1:52.24
1968	Nancy Greene, Canada	1:51.97
1972	Marie-Theres Nadig, Switzerland	1:29.90
1976	Kathy Kreiner, Canada	1:29.13
1980	Hanni Wenzel, Liechtenstein (2 runs)	2:41.66
1984	Debbie Armstrong, United States	2:20.98
1988	Vreni Schneider, Switzerland	2:06.49
1992	Pernilla Wiberg, Sweden	2:12.74
1994	Deborah Compagnoni, Italy	2:30.97
1998	Deborah Compagnoni, Italy	2:50.59
2002	Janica Kostelic, Croatia	2:30.01
2006	Julia Mancuso, United States	2:09.19
2010	Viktoria Rebensburg, Germany	2:27.11

Women's Slalom

		Time
1948	Gretchen Fraser, United States	1:57.2
1952	Andrea Mead Lawrence, United States	2:10.6
1956	Renee Colliard, Switzerland	1:52.3
1960	Anne Heggtveit, Canada	1:49.6
1964	Christine Goitschel, France	1:29.86
1968	Marielle Goitschel, France	1:25.86
1972	Barbara Ann Cochran, United States	1:31.24
1976	Rosi Mittermaier, W. Germany	1:30.54
1980	Hanni Wenzel, Liechtenstein	1:25.09
1984	Paoletta Magoni, Italy	1:36.47
1988	Vreni Schneider, Switzerland	1:36.69
1992	Petra Kronberger, Austria	1:32.68
1994	Vreni Schneider, Switzerland	1:56.01
1998	Hilde Gerg, Germany	1:32.40
2002	Janica Kostelic, Croatia	1:46.10
2006	Anja Paerson, Sweden	1:29.04
2010	Maria Riesch, Germany	1:42.89

Women's Super Combined

		Time
1936	Christl Cranz, Germany	97.06 (pts.)
1948	Trude Beiser-Jochum, Austria	6.58 (pts.)
1988	Anita Wachter, Austria	29.25 (pts.)
1992	Petra Kronberger, Austria	2.55 (pts.)
1994	Pernilla Wiberg, Sweden	3:05.16
1998	Katja Seizinger, Germany	2:40.74
2002	Janica Kostelic, Croatia	2:43.28
2006	Janica Kostelic, Croatia	2:51.08
2010	Maria Riesch, Germany	2:09.14

Note: In 2010, a one-day super combined event replaced the traditional two-day combined event.

Women's Super Giant Slalom

		Time
1988	Sigrid Wolf, Austria	1:19.03
1992	Deborah Compagnoni, Italy	1:21.22
1994	Diann Roffe (Steinrotter), United States	1:22.15
1998	Picabo Street, United States	1:18.02
2002	Daniela Ceccarelli, Italy	1:13.59
2006	Michaela Dorfmeister, Austria	1:32.47
2010	Andrea Fischbacher, Austria	1:20.14

Biathlon

Men's 10-Kilometer Sprint

		Time
1980	Frank Ullrich, E. Germany	32:10.69
1984	Eirik Kvalfoss, Norway	30:53.80
1988	Frank-Peter Roetsch, E. Germany	25:08.10
1992	Mark Kirchner, Germany	26:02.30
1994	Serguei Tchepikov, Russia	28:07.00
1998	Ole Einar Bjoerndalen, Norway	27:16.20
2002	Ole Einar Bjoerndalen, Norway	24:51.30
2006	Sven Fischer, Germany	26:11.6
2010	Vincent Jay, France	24:07.8

Men's 12.5-Kilometer Pursuit

		Time
2002	Ole Einar Bjoerndalen, Norway	32:34.6
2006	Vincent Defrasne, France	35:20.2
2010	Bjorn Ferry, Sweden	33:38.4

Men's 15-Kilometer Mass Start

		Time
2006	Michael Greis, Germany	47:20.0
2010	Evgeny Ustyugov, Russia	35.35.7

Men's 20-Kilometer Individual

		Time
1960	Klas Lestander, Sweden	1:33:21.6
1964	Vladimir Melanin, USSR	1:20:26.8
1968	Magnar Solberg, Norway	1:13:45.9
1972	Magnar Solberg, Norway	1:15:55.50
1976	Nikolai Kruglov, USSR	1:14:12.26
1980	Anatoly Aljabiev, USSR	1:08:16.31
1984	Peter Angerer, W. Germany	1:11:52.7
1988	Frank-Peter Roetsch, E. Germany	0:56:33.33
1992	Yevgeny Redkine, Unified Team	0:57:34.4
1994	Serguei Tarasov, Russia	0:57:25.3
1998	Halvard Hanevold, Norway	0:56:16.4
2002	Ole Einar Bjoerndalen, Norway	0:51:03.03
2006	Michael Greis, Germany	0:54:23.0
2010	Emil Hegle Svendsen, Norway	0:48:22.5

Men's 4x7.5-Kilometer Relay

		Time
1968	USSR, Norway, Sweden (40 km)	2:13:02.4
1972	USSR, Finland, E. Germany (40 km)	1:51:44.92
1976	USSR, Finland, E. Germany (40 km)	1:57:55.64
1980	USSR, E. Germany, W. Germany	1:34:03.27
1984	USSR, Norway, W. Germany	1:38:51.70
1988	USSR, W. Germany, Italy	1:22:30.00
1992	Germany, Unified Team, Sweden	1:24:43.50
1994	Germany, Russia, France	1:30:22.1
1998	Germany, Norway, Russia	1:19:43.3
2002	Norway, Germany, France	1:23:42.3
2006	Germany, Russia, France	1:21:51.5
2010	Norway, Austria, Russia	1:21:38.1

Women's 7.5-Kilometer Sprint

		Time
1992	Anfissa Restsova, Unified Team	24:29.2
1994	Myriam Bedard, Canada	26:08.8
1998	Galina Koukleva, Russia	23:08.0
2002	Kati Wilhelm, Germany	20:41.4
2006	Florence Baverel-Robert, France	22:31.4
2010	Anastazia Kuzmina, Slovakia	19:55.6

Women's 10-Kilometer Pursuit

		Time
2002	Olga Pyleva, Russia	31:07.7
2006	Kati Wilhelm, Germany	36:43.6
2010	Magdalena Neuner, Germany	30:16.0

Women's 12.5-Kilometer Mass Start

		Time
2006	Anna Carin Olofsson, Sweden	40:36.5
2010	Magdalena Neuner, Germany	35:19.6

Women's 15-Kilometer Individual

		Time
1992	Antje Misersky, Germany	51:47.2
1994	Myriam Bedard, Canada	52:06.6
1998	Ekaterina Dafovska, Bulgaria	54:52.0
2002	Andrea Henkel, Germany	47:30.0
2006	Svetlana Ishmouratova, Russia	49:24.1
2010	Tora Berger, Norway	40:52.8

Women's 4x6-Kilometer Relay

		Time
1992	France, Germany, Unified Team (22.5 km)	1:15:55.6
1994	Russia, Germany, France (30 km)	1:47:19.5
1998	Germany, Russia, Norway (30 km)	1:40:13.6
2002	Germany, Norway, Russia (30 km)	1:27:55.0
2006	Russia, Germany, France	1:16:12.5
2010	Russia, France, Germany	1:09:36.3

Bobsledding

(Driver in parentheses.)

2-Man Bobsled

		Time
1932	United States (Hubert Stevens)	8:14.74
1936	United States (Ivan Brown)	5:29.29

2-Man Bobsled	Time
1948 Switzerland (F. Endrich)	5:29.20
1952 Germany (Andreas Ostler)	5:24.54
1956 Italy (Dalla Costa)	5:30.14
1964 Great Britain (Anthony Nash)	4:21.90
1968 Italy (Eugenio Monti)	4:41.54
1972 W. Germany (Wolfgang Zimmerer)	4:57.07
1976 E. Germany (Meinhard Nehmer)	3:44.42
1980 Switzerland (Erich Schaerer)	4:09.36
1984 E. Germany (Wolfgang Hoppe)	3:25.56
1988 USSR (Janis Kipours)	3:54.19
1992 Switzerland (Gustav Weber)	4:03.26
1994 Switzerland (Gustav Weber)	3:30.81
1998 Canada (Pierre Lueders); Italy (Guenther Huber) (tie)	3:37.24
2002 Germany II (Christoph Langen)	3:10.11
2006 Germany (Andre Lange)	3:43.38
2010 Germany (Andre Lange)	3:26.65

4-Man Bobsled	Time
1924 Switzerland (Eduard Scherrer)	5:45.54
1928 United States (William Fiske) (5-man)	3:20.50
1932 United States (William Fiske)	7:53.68
1936 Switzerland (Pierre Musy)	5:19.85
1948 United States (Francis Tyler)	5:20.10
1952 Germany (Andreas Ostler)	5:07.84
1956 Switzerland (Franz Kapus)	5:10.44
1964 Canada (Victor Emery)	4:14.46
1968 Italy (Eugenio Monti) (2 races)	2:17.39
1972 Switzerland (Jean Wicki)	4:43.07
1976 E. Germany (Meinhard Nehmer)	3:40.43
1980 E. Germany (Meinhard Nehmer)	3:59.92
1984 E. Germany (Wolfgang Hoppe)	3:20.22
1988 Switzerland (Ekkehard Fasser)	3:47.51
1992 Austria (Ingo Appelt)	3:53.90
1994 Germany (Wolfgang Hoppe)	3:27.28
1998 Germany II (Christoph Langen)	2:39.41
2002 Germany II (Andre Lange)	3:07.51
2006 Germany (Andre Lange)	3:40.42
2010 United States (Steven Holcomb)	3:24.46

2-Woman Bobsled	Time
2002 United States II (Jill Bakken)	1:37.76
2006 Germany (Sandra Kiriasis)	3:49.98
2010 Canada (Kaillie Humphries)	3:32.28

Cross-Country Skiing

Men's Individual Sprint Classic	Time
2002 Tor Arne Hetland, Norway (1.5 km)	2:56.9
2006 Bjoern Lind, Sweden (1.3 km)	2:26.5
2010 Nikita Kriukov, Russia	3:36.3

Men's 10 Kilometers	Time
1992 Vegard Ulvang, Norway	27:36.0
1994 Bjoern Daehlie, Norway	24:20.1
1998 Bjoern Daehlie, Norway	27:24.5
2002 Thomas Alsgaard, Norway; Frode Estil, Norway (tie) (a)	49:48.9

(a) Awarded gold after Johann Muehlegg of Spain was stripped of gold for a drug offense.

Men's 15-Kilometer Free	Time
1924 Thorleif Haug, Norway	1:14:31
1928 Johan Grottumsbraaten, Norway	1:37:01
1932 Sven Utterstrom, Sweden	1:23:07
1936 Erik-August Larsson, Sweden	1:14:38
1948 Martin Lundstrom, Sweden	1:13:50
1952 Hallgeir Brenden, Norway	1:01:34
1956 Hallgeir Brenden, Norway	0:49:39.0
1960 Haakon Brusveen, Norway	0:51:55.5
1964 Eero Maentyranta, Finland	0:50:54.1
1968 Harald Groenningen, Norway	0:47:54.2
1972 Sven-Ake Lundback, Sweden	0:45:28.24
1976 Nikolai Balukov, USSR	0:43:58.47
1980 Thomas Wassberg, Sweden	0:41:57.63
1984 Gunde Svan, Sweden	0:41:25.6
1988 Mikhail Deviatiarov, USSR	0:41:18.9
1992 Bjoern Daehlie, Norway	0:38:01.9
1994 Bjoern Daehlie, Norway	0:35:48.8
1998 Thomas Alsgaard, Norway	1:07:01.7
2002 Andrus Veerpalu, Estonia	0:37:07.4
2006 Andrus Veerpalu, Estonia	0:38:01.3
2010 Dario Cologna, Switzerland	0:33:36.3
Note: Approx. 18-km course 1924-52.	

Men's 30-Kilometer Pursuit	Time
1956 Veikko Hakulinen, Finland	1:44:06.0
1964 Eero Maentyranta, Finland	1:30:50.7
1968 Franco Nones, Italy	1:35:39.2
1972 Vyacheslav Vedenine, USSR	1:36:31.15
1976 Sergei Saveliev, USSR	1:30:29.38
1980 Nikolai Zimyatov, USSR	1:27:02.80

Men's 30-Kilometer Pursuit	Time
1984 Nikolai Zimyatov, USSR	1:28:56.3
1988 Aleksei Prokourorov, USSR	1:24:26.3
1992 Vegard Ulvang, Norway	1:22:27.8
1994 Thomas Alsgaard, Norway	1:12:26.4
1998 Mika Myllylae, Finland	1:33:55.8
2002 Christian Hoffmann, Austria (a)	1:11:31.0
2006 Eugeni Dementiev, Russia	1:17:00.8
2010 Marcus Hellner, Sweden	1:15:11.4

(a) Awarded gold after Johann Muehlegg of Spain was stripped of gold for a drug offense.

Men's 50-Kilometer Mass Start Classic	Time
1924 Thorleif Haug, Norway	3:44:32.0
1928 Per Erik Hedlund, Sweden	4:52:03.0
1932 Veli Saarinen, Finland	4:28:00.0
1936 Elis Wiklund, Sweden	3:30:11.0
1948 Nils Karlsson, Sweden	3:47:48.0
1952 Veikko Hakulinen, Finland	3:33:33.0
1956 Sixten Jernberg, Sweden	2:50:27.0
1960 Kalevi Hamalainen, Finland	2:59:06.3
1964 Sixten Jernberg, Sweden	2:43:52.6
1968 Ole Ellefsaeter, Norway	2:28:45.8
1972 Paal Tyldum, Norway	2:43:14.75
1976 Ivar Formo, Norway	2:37:30.05
1980 Nikolai Zimyatov, USSR	2:27:24.60
1984 Thomas Wassberg, Sweden	2:15:55.8
1988 Gunde Svan, Sweden	2:04:30.9
1992 Bjorn Daehlie, Norway	2:03:41.5
1994 Vladimir Smirnov, Kazakhstan	2:07:20.3
1998 Bjorn Daehlie, Norway	2:05:08.2
2002 Mikhail Ivanov, Russia	2:06:20.8
2006 Giorgio di Centa, Italy	2:06:11.8
2010 Petter Northug, Norway	2:05:35.5

Men's 4x10-Kilometer Relay	Time
1936 Finland, Norway, Sweden	2:41:33.0
1948 Sweden, Finland, Norway	2:32:08.0
1952 Finland, Norway, Sweden	2:20:16.0
1956 USSR, Finland, Sweden	2:15:30.0
1960 Finland, Norway, USSR	2:18:45.6
1964 Sweden, Finland, USSR	2:18:34.6
1968 Norway, Sweden, Finland	2:08:33.5
1972 USSR, Norway, Switzerland	2:04:47.94
1976 Finland, Norway, USSR	2:07:59.72
1980 USSR, Norway, Finland	1:57:03.46
1984 Sweden, USSR, Finland	1:55:06.30
1988 Sweden, USSR, Czechoslovakia	1:43:58.60
1992 Norway, Italy, Finland	1:39:26.00
1994 Italy, Norway, Finland	1:41:15.00
1998 Norway, Italy, Finland	1:40:55.70
2002 Norway, Italy, Germany	1:32:45.5
2006 Italy, Germany, Sweden	1:43:45.7
2010 Sweden, Norway, Czech Republic	1:45:05.4

Men's Team Sprint	Time
2006 Bjoern Lind & Thobias Fredriksson, Sweden	17:02.9
2010 Oeystein Pettersen & Petter Northug, Norway	19:01.0

Women's Individual Sprint Classic	Time
2002 Julia Tchepalova, Russia (1.5 km)	3:10.6
2006 Chandra Crawford, Canada (1.1 km)	2:12.3
2010 Marit Bjoergen, Norway	3:39.2

Women's Team Sprint	Time
2006 Lina Andersson & Anna Dahlberg, Sweden	16:36.9
2010 Evi Sachenbacher-Stehle & Claudia Nystad, Germany	18:03.7

Women's 5 Kilometers	Time
1964 Claudia Boyarskikh, USSR	17:50.5
1968 Toini Gustafsson, Sweden	16:45.2
1972 Galina Koulacova, USSR	17:00.50
1976 Helena Takalo, Finland	15:48.69
1980 Raisa Smetanina, USSR	15:06.92
1984 Marja-Liisa Haemaelainen, Finland	17:04.0
1988 Marjo Matikainen, Finland	15:04.0
1992 Marjut Lukkarinen, Finland	14:13.8
1994 Ljubov Egorova, Russia	14:08.8
1998 Larissa Lazutina, Russia	17:37.9
2002 Beckie Scott, Canada (a)	25:09.9

(a) Awarded gold after Olga Danilova of Russia was stripped of gold and Larissa Lazutina of Russia was stripped of silver for drug offenses.

Women's 10-Kilometer Free	Time
1952 Lydia Wideman, Finland	41:40.0
1956 Lyubov Kosyreva, USSR	38:11.0
1960 Maria Gusakova, USSR	39:46.6
1964 Claudia Boyarskikh, USSR	40:24.3
1968 Toini Gustafsson, Sweden	36:46.5
1972 Galina Koulacova, USSR	34:17.82
1976 Raisa Smetanina, USSR	30:13.41

Women's 10-Kilometer Free	Time
1980 Barbara Petzold, E. Germany	30:31.54
1984 Marja-Liisa Haemaelainen, Finland	31:44.2
1988 Vida Ventsene, USSR	30:08.3
1992 Lyubov Egorova, Unified Team	25:53.7
1994 Lyubov Egorova, Russia	27:30.1
1998 Larissa Lazutina, Russia	46.06.9
2002 Bente Skari, Norway	28:05.6
2006 Kristina Smigun, Estonia	27:51.4
2010 Charlotte Kalla, Sweden	24:58.4

Women's 15-Kilometer Pursuit	Time
1992 Lyubov Egorova, Unified Team	42:20.8
1994 Manuela Di Centa, Italy	39:44.5
1998 Olga Danilova, Russia	46:55.4
2002 Stefania Belmondo, Italy	39:54.4
2006 Kristina Smigun, Estonia	42:48.7
2010 Marit Bjoergen, Norway	39:58.1

Women's 30-Kilometer Mass Start Classic	Time
1992 Stefania Belmondo, Italy	1:22:30.1
1994 Manuela Di Centa, Italy	1:25:41.6
1998 Julija Tchepalova, Russia	1:22:01.5
2002 Gabriella Paruzzi, Italy	1:30:57.1
2006 Katerina Neumannova, Czech Republic	1:22:25.4
2010 Justyna Kowalczyk, Poland	1:30:33.7

Women's 4x5-Kilometer Relay	Time
1956 Finland, USSR, Sweden (15 km)	1:09:01.0
1960 Sweden, USSR, Finland (15 km)	1:04:21.4
1964 USSR, Sweden, Finland (15 km)	0:59:20.2
1968 Norway, Sweden, USSR (15 km)	0:57:30.0
1972 USSR, Finland, Norway (15 km)	0:48:46.15
1976 USSR, Finland, E. Germany	1:07:49.75
1980 E. Germany, USSR, Norway	1:02:11.1
1984 Norway, Czechoslovakia, Finland	1:06:49.7
1988 USSR, Norway, Finland	0:59:51.1
1992 United Team, Norway, Italy	0:59:34.8
1994 Russia, Norway, Italy	0:57:12.5
1998 Russia, Norway, Italy	0:55:13.5
2002 Germany, Norway, Switzerland	0:49:30.6
2006 Russia, Germany, Italy	0:54:47.7
2010 Norway, Germany, Finland	0:55:19.5

Curling

Men

1998 Switzerland, Canada, Norway
2002 Norway, Canada, Switzerland
2006 Canada, Finland, United States
2010 Canada, Norway, Switzerland

Women

1998 Canada, Denmark, Sweden
2002 Britain, Switzerland, Canada
2006 Sweden, Switzerland, Canada
2010 Sweden, Canada, China

Figure Skating

Men's Singles

1908[1] Ulrich Salchow, Sweden
1920[1] Gillis Grafstrom, Sweden
1924 Gillis Grafstrom, Sweden
1928 Gillis Grafstrom, Sweden
1932 Karl Schaefer, Austria
1936 Karl Schaefer, Austria
1948 Richard Button, United States
1952 Richard Button, United States
1956 Hayes Alan Jenkins, United States
1960 David W. Jenkins, United States
1964 Manfred Schnelldorfer, Germany
1968 Wolfgang Schwartz, Austria
1972 Ondrej Nepela, Czechoslovakia
1976 John Curry, Great Britain
1980 Robin Cousins, Great Britain
1984 Scott Hamilton, United States
1988 Brian Boitano, United States
1992 Viktor Petrenko, Unified Team
1994 Aleksei Urmanov, Russia
1998 Ilya Kulik, Russia
2002 Alexei Yagudin, Russia
2006 Yevgeny Plushenko, Russia
2010 Evan Lysacek, United States
(1) Event held during Summer Olympic Games.

Women's Singles

1908[1] Madge Syers, Great Britain
1920[1] Magda Julin-Mauroy, Sweden
1924 Herma von Szabo-Planck, Austria

Women's Singles

1928 Sonja Henie, Norway
1932 Sonja Henie, Norway
1936 Sonja Henie, Norway
1948 Barbara Ann Scott, Canada
1952 Jeanette Altwegg, Great Britan
1956 Tenley Albright, United States
1960 Carol Heiss, United States
1964 Sjoukje Dijkstra, Netherlands
1968 Peggy Fleming, United States
1972 Beatrix Schuba, Austria
1976 Dorothy Hamill, United States
1980 Anett Poetzsch, E. Germany
1984 Katarina Witt, E. Germany
1988 Katarina Witt, E. Germany
1992 Kristi Yamaguchi, United States
1994 Oksana Baiul, Ukraine
1998 Tara Lipinski, United States
2002 Sarah Hughes, United States
2006 Shizuka Arakawa, Japan
2010 Kim Yu-Na, S. Korea
(1) Event held during Summer Olympic Games.

Pairs

1908[1] Anna Hubler & Heinrich Burger, Germany
1920[1] Ludovika & Walter Jakobsson, Finland
1924 Helene Engelman & Alfred Berger, Austria
1928 Andree Joly & Pierre Brunet, France
1932 Andree Joly & Pierre Brunet, France
1936 Maxi Herber & Ernst Baier, Germany
1948 Micheline Lannoy & Pierre Baugniet, Belgium
1952 Ria and Paul Falk, Germany
1956 Elisabeth Schwartz & Kurt Oppelt, Austria
1964 Ludmila Beloussova & Oleg Protopopov, USSR
1968 Ludmila Beloussova & Oleg Protopopov, USSR
1972 Irina Rodnina & Alexei Ulanov, USSR
1976 Irina Rodnina & Aleksandr Zaitzev, USSR
1980 Irina Rodnina & Aleksandr Zaitzev, USSR
1984 Elena Valova & Oleg Vassiliev, USSR
1988 Ekaterina Gordeeva & Sergei Grinkov, USSR
1992 Natalia Mishkutienok & Artur Dimitriev, Unified Team
1994 Ekaterina Gordeeva & Sergei Grinkov, Russia
1998 Oksana Kazakova & Artur Dmitriev, Russia
2002 Elena Berezhnaya & Anton Sikharulidze, Russia; Jamie Sale & David Pelletier, Canada (tie)
2006 Tatyana Totmianina & Maxim Marinin, Russia
2010 Shen Xue & Zhao Hongbo, China
(1) Event held during Summer Olympic Games.

Ice Dancing

1976 Ludmila Pakhomova & Aleksandr Gorschkov, USSR
1980 Natalya Linichuk & Gennadi Karponosov, USSR
1984 Jayne Torvill & Christopher Dean, Great Britain
1988 Natalia Bestemianova & Andrei Bukin, USSR
1992 Marina Klimova & Sergei Ponomarenko, Unified Team
1994 Pasha Grishuk & Evgeny Platov, Russia
1998 Pasha Grishuk & Evgeny Platov, Russia
2002 Marina Anissina & Gwendal Peizerat, France
2006 Tatyana Navka & Roman Kostomarov, Russia
2010 Tessa Virtue & Scott Moir, Canada

Freestyle Skiing

Men's Aerials	Points
1994 Andreas Schoenbaechler, Switzerland	234.67
1998 Eric Bergoust, United States	255.64
2002 Ales Valenta, Czech Republic	257.02
2006 Xiaopeng Han, China	250.77
2010 Alexei Grishin, Belarus	248.41

Men's Moguls	Points
1992 Edgar Grospiron, France	25.81
1994 Jean-Luc Brassard, Canada	27.24
1998 Jonny Moseley, United States	26.93
2002 Janne Lahtela, Finland	27.97
2006 Dale Begg-Smith, Australia	26.77
2010 Alexandre Bilodeau, Canada	26.75

Men's Ski Cross

2010 Michael Schmid, Switzerland

Women's Aerials	Points
1994 Lina Tcherjazova, Uzbekistan	166.84
1998 Nikki Stone, United States	193.00
2002 Alisa Camplin, Australia	193.47
2006 Evelyne Leu, Switzerland	202.55
2010 Lydia Lassila, Australia	214.74

Women's Moguls	Points
1992 Donna Weinbrecht, United States	23.69
1994 Stine Lise Hattestad, Norway	25.97

Women's Moguls

		Points
1998	Tae Satoya, Japan	25.06
2002	Kari Traa, Norway	25.94
2006	Jennifer Heil, Canada	26.50
2010	Hannah Kearney, United States	26.63

Women's Ski Cross

2010	Ashleigh McIvor, Canada

Ice Hockey

Men

1920[1]	Canada, United States, Czechoslovakia
1924	Canada, United States, Great Britain
1928	Canada, Sweden, Switzerland
1932	Canada, United States, Germany
1936	Great Britain, Canada, United States
1948	Canada, Czechoslovakia, Switzerland
1952	Canada, United States, Sweden
1956	USSR, United States, Canada
1960	United States, Canada, USSR
1964	USSR, Sweden, Czechoslovakia
1968	USSR, Czechoslovakia, Canada
1972	USSR, United States, Czechoslovakia
1976	USSR, Czechoslovakia, W. Germany
1980	United States, USSR, Sweden
1984	USSR, Czechoslovakia, Sweden
1988	USSR, Finland, Sweden

Men

1992	Unified Team, Canada, Czechoslovakia
1994	Sweden, Canada, Finland
1998	Czech Republic, Russia, Finland
2002	Canada, United States, Russia
2006	Sweden, Finland, Czech Republic
2010	Canada, United States, Finland

Women

1998	United States, Canada, Finland
2002	Canada, United States, Sweden
2006	Canada, Sweden, United States
2010	Canada, United States, Finland

(1) Event held during Summer Olympic Games.

Luge

Men's Singles

		Time
1964	Thomas Keohler, E. Germany	3:27.77
1968	Manfred Schmid, Austria	2:52.48
1972	Wolfgang Scheidel, E. Germany	3:27.58
1976	Detlef Guenther, E. Germany	3:27.688
1980	Bernhard Glass, E. Germany	2:54.796
1984	Paul Hildgartner, Italy	3:04.258
1988	Jens Mueller, E. Germany	3:05.548
1992	Georg Hackl, Germany	3:02.363
1994	Georg Hackl, Germany	3:21.571
1998	Georg Hackl, Germany	3:18.436
2002	Armin Zoeggeler, Italy	2:57.941
2006	Armin Zoeggeler, Italy	3:26.088
2010	Felix Loch, Germany	3:13.085

Men's Doubles

		Time
1964	Austria	1:41.62
1968	E. Germany	1:35.85
1972	Italy, E. Germany (tie)	1:28.35
1976	E. Germany	1:25.604
1980	E. Germany	1:19.331
1984	W. Germany	1:23.620
1988	E. Germany	1:31.940
1992	Germany	1:32.053
1994	Italy	1:36.720
1998	Germany	1:41.105
2002	Germany	1:26.082
2006	Austria	1:34.497
2010	Austria	1:22.705

Women's Singles

		Time
1964	Ortun Enderlein, Germany	3:24.67
1968	Erica Lechner, Italy	2:28.66
1972	Anna M. Muller, E. Germany	2:59.18
1976	Margit Schumann, E. Germany	2:50.621
1980	Vera Zozulya, USSR	2:36.537
1984	Steffi Martin, E. Germany	2:46.570
1988	Steffi Walter, E. Germany	3:03.973
1992	Doris Neuner, Austria	3:06.696
1994	Gerda Weissensteiner, Italy	3:15.517
1998	Silke Kraushaar, Germany	3:23.779

Women's Singles

		Time
2002	Sylke Otto, Germany	2:52.464
2006	Sylke Otto, Germany	3:07.979
2010	Tatjana Huefner, Germany	2:46.524

Nordic Combined

Men's 7.5-Kilometer Nordic Combined

2002	Samppa Lajunen, Finland
2006	Felix Gottwald, Austria

Men's 15-Kilometer Nordic Combined

1924	Thorleif Haug, Norway
1928	Johan Grottumsbraaten, Norway
1932	Johan Grottumsbraaten, Norway
1936	Oddbjorn Hagen, Norway
1948	Heikki Hasu, Finland
1952	Simon Slattvik, Norway
1956	Sverre Stenersen, Norway
1960	Georg Thoma, W. Germany
1964	Tormod Knutsen, Norway
1968	Franz Keller, W. Germany
1972	Ulrich Wehling, E. Germany
1976	Ulrich Wehling, E. Germany
1980	Ulrich Wehling, E. Germany
1984	Tom Sandberg, Norway
1988	Hippolyt Kempf, Switzerland
1992	Fabrice Guy, France
1994	Fred Barre Lundberg, Norway
1998	Bjarte Engen Vik, Norway
2002	Samppa Lajunen, Finland
2006	Georg Hettich, Germany

Men's 10-Kilometer Large Hill

2010	Bill Demong, United States

Men's 10-Kilometer Normal Hill

2010	Jason Lamy Chappuis, France

4x5-Kilometer Relay

1988	W. Germany, Switzerland, Austria
1992	Japan, Norway, Austria
1994	Japan, Norway, Switzerland
1998	Norway, Finland, France
2002	Finland, Germany, Austria
2006	Austria, Germany, Finland
2010	Austria, United States, Germany

Skeleton

Men

		Time
1928	Jennison Heaton, United States	3:01.8
1948	Nino Bibbia, Italy	5:23.2
2002	Jim Shea, United States	1:41.96
2006	Duff Gibson, Canada	1:55.88
2010	Jon Montgomery, Canada	3:29.73

Women

		Time
2002	Tristan Gale, United States	1:45.11
2006	Maya Pedersen, Switzerland	1:59.83
2010	Amy Williams, Great Britain	3:35.64

Ski Jumping

Normal Hill

		Points
1964	Veikko Kankkonen, Finland	229.9
1968	Jiri Raska, Czechoslovakia	216.5
1972	Yukio Kasaya, Japan	244.2
1976	Hans-Georg Aschenbach, E. Germany	252.0
1980	Toni Innauer, Austria	266.3
1984	Jens Weissflog, E. Germany	215.2
1988	Matti Nykaenen, Finland	230.5
1992	Ernst Vettori, Austria	222.8
1994	Espen Bredesen, Norway	282.0
1998	Jani Soininen, Finland	234.5
2002	Simon Ammann, Switzerland	269.0
2006	Lars Bystoel, Norway	266.5
2010	Simon Ammann, Switzerland	276.5

Large Hill

		Points
1924	Jacob Tullin Thams, Norway	18.960
1928	Alfred Andersen, Norway	19.208
1932	Birger Ruud, Norway	228.1
1936	Birger Ruud, Norway	232.0
1948	Petter Hugsted, Norway	228.1
1952	Arnfinn Bergmann, Norway	226.0

Large Hill	Points
1956 Antti Hyvarinen, Finland	227.0
1960 Helmut Recknagel, E. Germany	227.2
1964 Toralf Engan, Norway	230.7
1968 Vladimir Beloussov, USSR	231.3
1972 Wojciech Fortuna, Poland	219.9
1976 Karl Schnabl, Austria	234.8
1980 Jouko Tormanen, Finland	271.0
1984 Matti Nykaenen, Finland	231.2
1988 Matti Nykaenen, Finland	224.0
1992 Toni Nieminen, Finland	239.5
1994 Jens Weissflog, Germany	274.5
1998 Kazuyoshi Funaki, Japan	272.3
2002 Simon Ammann, Switzerland	281.4
2006 Thomas Morgenstern, Austria	276.9
2010 Simon Ammann, Switzerland	283.6

Team Large Hill	Points
1988 Finland, Yugoslavia, Norway	634.4
1992 Finland, Austria, Czechoslovakia	644.4
1994 Germany, Japan, Austria	970.1
1998 Japan, Germany, Austria	933.0
2002 Germany, Finland, Slovenia	974.1
2006 Austria, Finland, Norway	984.0
2010 Austria, Germany, Norway	1,107.9

Snowboarding

Men's Halfpipe	Points
1998 Gian Simmen, Switzerland	85.2
2002 Ross Powers, United States	46.1
2006 Shaun White, United States	46.8
2010 Shaun White, United States	48.4

Men's Parallel Giant Slalom

1998 Ross Rebagliati, Canada
2002 Philipp Schoch, Switzerland
2006 Philipp Schoch, Switzerland
2010 Jasey Jay Anderson, Canada
Note: In 2002, the Giant Slalom became the Parallel Giant Slalom.

Men's Snowboard Cross

2006 Seth Wescott, United States
2010 Seth Westcott, United States

Women's Halfpipe	Points
1998 Nicola Thost, Germany	74.6
2002 Kelly Clark, United States	47.9

Women's Halfpipe	Points
2006 Hannah Teter, United States	46.4
2010 Torah Bright, Australia	45.0

Women's Parallel Giant Slalom

1998 Karine Ruby, France
2002 Isabelle Blanc, France
2006 Daniela Meuli, Switzerland
2010 Nicolien Sauerbreij, Netherlands
Note: In 2002, the Giant Slalom became the Parallel Giant Slalom.

Women's Snowboard Cross

2006 Tanja Frieden, Switzerland
2010 Maelle Ricker, Canada

Speed Skating
*Olympic record

Men's 500 Meters	Time
1924 Charles Jewtraw, United States	0:44.0
1928 Thunberg, Finland; Evensen, Norway (tie)	0:43.4
1932 John A. Shea, United States	0:43.4
1936 Ivar Ballangrud, Norway	0:43.4
1948 Finn Helgesen, Norway	0:43.1
1952 Kenneth Henry, United States	0:43.2
1956 Evgeniy Grishin, USSR	0:40.2
1960 Evgeniy Grishin, USSR	0:40.2
1964 Terry McDermott, United States	0:40.1
1968 Erhard Keller, W. Germany	0:40.3
1972 Erhard Keller, W. Germany	0:39.44
1976 Evgeny Kulikov, USSR	0:39.17
1980 Eric Heiden, United States	0:38.03
1984 Sergei Fokichev, USSR	0:38.19
1988 Uwe-Jens Mey, E. Germany	0:36.45
1992 Uwe-Jens Mey, Germany	0:37.14
1994 Aleksandr Golubev, Russia	0:36.33

Men's 500 Meters	Time
1998 Hiroyasu Shimizu, Japan	0:35.59
2002 Casey FitzRandolph, United States	0:34.42*
2006 Joey Cheek, United States	0:34.82
2010 Mo Tae-Bum, S. Korea	0:34.906

Men's 1,000 Meters	Time
1976 Peter Mueller, United States	1:19.32
1980 Eric Heiden, United States	1:15.18
1984 Gaetan Boucher, Canada	1:15.80
1988 Nikolai Guiliaev, USSR	1:13.03
1992 Olaf Zinke, Germany	1:14.85
1994 Dan Jansen, United States	1:12.43
1998 Ids Postma, Netherlands	1:10.64
2002 Gerard van Velde, Netherlands	1:07.18*
2006 Shani Davis, United States	1:08.89
2010 Shani Davis, United States	1:08.94

Men's 1,500 Meters	Time
1924 Clas Thunberg, Finland	2:20.8
1928 Clas Thunberg, Finland	2:21.1
1932 John A. Shea, United States	2:57.5
1936 Charles Mathiesen, Norway	2:19.2
1948 Sverre Farstad, Norway	2:17.6
1952 Hjalmar Andersen, Norway	2:20.4
1956 Grishin; Mikhailov, both USSR (tie)	2:08.6
1960 Aas, Norway; Grishin, USSR (tie)	2:10.4
1964 Ants Anston, USSR	2:10.3
1968 Cornetis Verkerk, Netherlands	2:03.4
1972 Ard Schenk, Netherlands	2:02.96
1976 Jan Egil Storholt, Norway	1:59.38
1980 Eric Heiden, United States	1:55.44
1984 Gaetan Boucher, Canada	1:58.36
1988 Andre Hoffmann, E. Germany	1:52.06
1992 Johann Koss, Norway	1:54.81
1994 Johann Koss, Norway	1:51.29
1998 Aadne Sondral, Norway	1:47.87
2002 Derek Parra, United States	1:43.95*
2006 Enrico Fabris, Italy	1:45.97
2010 Mark Tuitert, Netherlands	1:45.57

Men's 5,000 Meters	Time
1924 Clas Thunberg, Finland	8:39.0
1928 Ivar Ballangrud, Norway	8:50.5
1932 Irving Jaffee, United States	9:40.8
1936 Ivar Ballangrud, Norway	8:19.6
1948 Reidar Liaklev, Norway	8:29.4
1952 Hjalmar Andersen, Norway	8:10.6
1956 Boris Shilkov, USSR	7:48.7
1960 Viktor Kosichkin, USSR	7:51.3
1964 Knut Johannesen, Norway	7:38.4
1968 F. Anton Maier, Norway	7:22.4
1972 Ard Schenk, Netherlands	7:23.61
1976 Sten Stensen, Norway	7:24.48
1980 Eric Heiden, United States	7:02.29
1984 Sven Tomas Gustafson, Sweden	7:12.28
1988 Tomas Gustafson, Sweden	6:44.63
1992 Geir Karlstad, Norway	6:59.97
1994 Johann Koss, Norway	6:34.96
1998 Gianni Romme, Netherlands	6:22.20
2002 Jochem Uytdehaage, Netherlands	6:14.66
2006 Chad Hedrick, United States	6:14.68
2010 Sven Kramer, Netherlands	6:14.60*

Men's 10,000 Meters	Time
1924 Julius Skutnabb, Finland	18:04.8
1928 Event not held because of thawing of ice	
1932 Irving Jaffee, United States	19:13.6
1936 Ivar Ballangrud, Norway	17:24.3
1948 Ake Seyffarth, Sweden	17:26.3
1952 Hjalmar Andersen, Norway	16:45.8
1956 Sigvard Ericsson, Sweden	16:35.9
1960 Knut Johannesen, Norway	15:46.6
1964 Jonny Nilsson, Sweden	15:50.1
1968 Jonny Hoeglin, Sweden	15:23.6
1972 Ard Schenk, Netherlands	15:01.35
1976 Piet Kleine, Netherlands	14:50.59
1980 Eric Heiden, United States	14:28.13
1984 Igor Malkov, USSR	14:39.90
1988 Tomas Gustafson, Sweden	13:48.20
1992 Bart Veldkamp, Netherlands	14:12.12
1994 Johann Koss, Norway	13:30.55
1998 Gianni Romme, Netherlands	13:15.33
2002 Jochem Uytdehaage, Netherlands	12:58.92
2006 Bob de Jong, Netherlands	13:01.57
2010 Lee Seung-Hoon, S. Korea	12:58.55*

Men's Team Pursuit

		Time
2006	Italy, Canada, Netherlands	3:44.46
2010	Canada, United States, Netherlands	3:41.37

Women's 500 Meters

		Time
1960	Helga Haase, Germany	0:45.9
1964	Lydia Skoblikova, USSR	0:45.0
1968	Ludmila Titova, USSR	0:46.1
1972	Anne Henning, United States	0:43.33
1976	Sheila Young, United States	0:42.76
1980	Karin Enke, E. Germany	0:41.78
1984	Christa Rothenburger, E. Germany	0:41.02
1988	Bonnie Blair, United States	0:39.10
1992	Bonnie Blair, United States	0:40.33
1994	Bonnie Blair, United States	0:39.25
1998	Catriona Le May-Doan, Canada	0:38.21
2002	Catriona Le May Doan, Canada	0:37.30*
2006	Svetlana Zhurova, Russia	0:38.23
2010	Lee Sang-Hwa, S. Korea	0:37.850

Women's 1,000 Meters

		Time
1960	Klara Guseva, USSR	1:34.1
1964	Lydia Skoblikova, USSR	1:33.2
1968	Carolina Geijssen, Netherlands	1:32.6
1972	Monika Pflug, W. Germany	1:31.40
1976	Tatiana Averina, USSR	1:28.43
1980	Natalya Petruseva, USSR	1:24.10
1984	Karin Enke, E. Germany	1:21.61
1988	Christa Rothenburger, E. Germany	1:17.65
1992	Bonnie Blair, United States	1:21.90
1994	Bonnie Blair, United States	1:18.74
1998	Marianne Timmer, Netherlands	1:16.51
2002	Chris Witty, United States	1:13.83*
2006	Marianne Timmer, Netherlands	1:16.05
2010	Christine Nesbitt, Canada	1:16.56

Women's 1,500 Meters

		Time
1960	Lydia Skoblikova, USSR	2:52.2
1964	Lydia Skoblikova, USSR	2:22.6
1968	Kaija Mustonen, Finland	2:22.4
1972	Dianne Holum, United States	2:20.85
1976	Galina Stepanskaya, USSR	2:16.58
1980	Anne Borckink, Netherlands	2:10.95
1984	Karin Enke, E. Germany	2:03.42
1988	Yvonne van Gennip, Netherlands	2:00.68
1992	Jacqueline Boerner, Germany	2:05.87
1994	Emese Hunyady, Austria	2:02.19
1998	Marianne Timmer, Netherlands	1:57.58
2002	Anni Friesinger, Germany	1:54.02*
2006	Cindy Klassen, Canada	1:55.27
2010	Ireen Wust, Netherlands	1:56.89

Women's 3,000 Meters

		Time
1960	Lydia Skoblikova, USSR	5:14.3
1964	Lydia Skoblikova, USSR	5:14.9
1968	Johanna Schut, Netherlands	4:56.2
1972	Christina Baas-Kaiser, Netherlands	4:52.14
1976	Tatiana Averina, USSR	4:45.19
1980	Bjoerg Eva Jensen, Norway	4:32.13
1984	Andrea Schoene, E. Germany	4:24.79
1988	Yvonne van Gennip, Netherlands	4:11.94
1992	Gunda Niemann, Germany	4:19.90

Women's 3,000 Meters

		Time
1994	Svetlana Bazhanova, Russia	4:17.43
1998	Gunda Niemann-Stirnemann, Germany	4:07.29
2002	Claudia Pechstein, Germany	3:57.70*
2006	Ireen Wust, Netherlands	4:02.43
2010	Martina Sablikova, Czech Republic	4:02.53

Women's 5,000 Meters

		Time
1988	Yvonne van Gennip, Netherlands	7:14.13
1992	Gunda Niemann, Germany	7:31.57
1994	Claudia Pechstein, Germany	7:14.37
1998	Claudia Pechstein, Germany	6:59.61
2002	Claudia Pechstein, Germany	6:46.91*
2006	Clara Hughes, Canada	6:59.07
2010	Martina Sablikova, Czech Republic	6:50.91

Women's Team Pursuit

		Time
2006	Germany, Canada, Russia	3:01.25
2010	Germany, Japan, Poland	3:02.82

Speed Skating (Short Track)
*Olympic record

Men's 500 Meters

		Time
1998	Takafumi Nishitani, Japan	0:42.862
2002	Marc Gagnon, Canada	0:41.802
2006	Apolo Anton Ohno, United States	0:41.935
2010	Charles Hamelin, Canada	0:40.981

Men's 1,000 Meters

		Time
1992	Kim Ki-Hoon, S. Korea	1:30.76
1994	Kim Ki-Hoon, S. Korea	1:34.57
1998	Dong-Sung Kim, S. Korea	1:32.375
2002	Steven Bradbury, Australia	1:29.109
2006	Hyun-Soo Ahn, S. Korea	1:26.739
2010	Lee Jung-Su, S. Korea	1:23.747*

Men's 1,500 Meters

		Time
2002	Apolo Anton Ohno, United States	2:18.541
2006	Hyun-Soo Ahn, S. Korea	2:25.341
2010	Lee Jung-Su, S. Korea	2:17.611

Men's 5,000-Meter Relay

		Time
1992	S. Korea, Canada, Japan	7:14.02
1994	Italy, United States, Australia	7:11.74
1998	Canada, S. Korea, China	7:06.075
2002	Canada, Italy, China	6:51.579
2006	S. Korea, Canada, United States	6:43.376*
2010	Canada, S. Korea, United States	6:44.224

Women's 500 Meters

		Time
1992	Cathy Turner, United States	0:47.04
1994	Cathy Turner, United States	0:45.98
1998	Annie Perreault, Canada	0:46.568
2002	Yang Yang (A), China	0:44.187
2006	Meng Wang, China	0:44.345
2010	Wang Meng, China	0:43.048

Women's 1,000 Meters

		Time
1998	Chun Lee-Kyung, S. Korea	1:42.776
2002	Yang Yang (A), China	1:36.391
2006	Sun-Yu Jin, S. Korea	1:32.859
2010	Wang Meng, China	1:29.213

Women's 1,500 Meters

		Time
2002	Gi-Hyun Ko, S. Korea	2:31.581
2006	Sun-Yu Jin, S. Korea	2:23.494
2010	Zhou Yang, China	2:16.993*

Women's 3,000 Meter Relay

		Time
1992	Canada, United States, Unified Team	4:36.62
1994	S. Korea, Canada, United States	4:26.64
1998	S. Korea, China, Canada	4:16.26
2002	S. Korea, China, Canada	4:12.793
2006	S. Korea, Canada, Italy	4:17.040
2010	China, Canada, United States	4:06.610*

Paralympic Games

The first Olympic games for disabled athletes were held in Rome after the 1960 Summer Olympics; use of the name "paralympic" began with the 1964 games in Tokyo. The Paralympics are held by the Olympic host country in the same year and usually the same city and venue(s). A goal of the Paralympics is to provide elite competition to athletes with functional disabilities that prevent their involvement in the Olympics. In 1976 the first Winter Paralympics were held, in Ornskoldsvik, Sweden.

The XIII Paralympic Summer Games were held Sept. 6-17, 2008, in Beijing, China. Nearly 4,000 athletes from a record 146 nations competed in 472 events in 20 sports including, for the first time, rowing. The XIV Paralympic Summer Games, scheduled to be held in London, England, UK, Aug. 29-Sept. 9, 2012, expected an even greater turnout, with 4,200 athletes from 150 nations.

The X Paralympic Winter Games were held Mar. 12-21, 2010, in Vancouver, Canada. More than 500 athletes from 44 nations to competed in 5 sports. Russia dominated the total medal count with 38, while Germany won the most gold medals, with 13.

Special Olympics

Special Olympics is an international program of year-round sports training and athletic competition for people with intellectual disabilities. All 50 U.S. states, Washington, DC, and the U.S. Virgin Islands have chapter offices. In addition, there are accredited Special Olympics programs in more than 185 countries. Persons wishing to volunteer or find out more can contact Special Olympics, 1133 19th St. NW, Washington, DC 20036; www.specialolympics.org.

The 13th Special Olympics World Summer Games were held June 25-July 4, 2011, in Athens, Greece. Around 7,000 athletes from 170 nations competed in 21 sports: aquatics (swimming, diving), athletics (track and field, marathon), badminton, basketball, bocce, bowling, cycling, equestrian sports, football, golf, gymnastics, handball, judo, kayaking, powerlifting, roller skating, sailing, softball, table tennis, tennis, and volleyball.

The 10th Special Olympics World Winter Games are scheduled to be held in PyeongChang, South Korea, Jan. 26-Feb. 6, 2013. More than 2,500 athletes from 105 countries are expected to compete in alpine skiing, cross-country skiing, figure skating, floor hockey, snowboarding, snowshoeing, and speed skating events.

TRACK AND FIELD
World Track and Field Outdoor Records
As of Oct. 1, 2011.

The International Association of Athletics Federations, the world body of track and field, recognizes only records in metric distances, except for the mile. * = Pending ratification.

Men's Records
Running

Event	Record	Holder	Nationality	Date	Location
100 meters	9.58 s.	Usain Bolt	Jamaica	Aug. 16, 2009	Berlin, Germany
200 meters	19.19 s.	Usain Bolt	Jamaica	Aug. 20, 2009	Berlin, Germany
400 meters	43.18 s.	Michael Johnson	U.S.	Aug. 26, 1999	Seville, Spain
800 meters	1 min., 41.01 s.	David Lekuta Rudisha	Kenya	Aug. 29, 2010	Rieti, Italy
1,000 meters	2 min., 11.96 s.	Noah Ngeny	Kenya	Sept. 5, 1999	Rieti, Italy
1,500 meters	3 min., 26.00 s.	Hicham El Guerrouj	Morocco	July 14, 1998	Rome, Italy
1 mile	3 min., 43.13 s.	Hicham El Guerrouj	Morocco	July 7, 1999	Rome, Italy
2,000 meters	4 min., 44.79 s.	Hicham El Guerrouj	Morocco	Sept. 7, 1999	Berlin, Germany
3,000 meters	7 min., 20.67 s.	Daniel Komen	Kenya	Sept. 1, 1996	Rieti, Italy
3,000 meter stpl	7 min., 53.63 s.	Saif Saaeed Shaheen	Qatar	Sept. 3, 2004	Brussels, Belgium
5,000 meters	12 min., 37.35 s.	Kenenisa Bekele	Ethiopia	May 31, 2004	Hengelo, Netherlands
10,000 meters	26 min., 17.53 s.	Kenenisa Bekele	Ethiopia	Aug. 26, 2005	Brussels, Belgium
20,000 meters	56 min., 26.00 s.	Haile Gebrselassie	Ethiopia	June 27, 2007	Ostrava, Czech Rep.
25,000 meters	1 hr., 12 min., 25.4 s.	Moses Cheruiyot Mosop	Kenya	June 3, 2011	Eugene, OR
Marathon	2 hr., 3 min., 38 s.*	Patrick Makau Musyoki	Kenya	Sept. 25, 2011	Berlin, Germany

Hurdles

Event	Record	Holder	Nationality	Date	Location
110 meters	12.87 s.	Dayron Robles	Cuba	June 12, 2008	Ostrava, Czech Rep.
400 meters	46.78 s.	Kevin Young	U.S.	Aug. 6, 1992	Barcelona, Spain

Relay Races

Event	Record	Holder	Nationality	Date	Location
400 m (4×100)	37.04 s.*	(Carter, Frater, Blake, Bolt)	Jamaica	Sept. 4, 2011	Daegu, S. Korea
800 m (4×200)	1 min., 18.68 s.	(Marsh, Burrell, Heard, Lewis)	U.S.	Apr. 17, 1994	Walnut, CA
1,600 m (4×400)	2 min., 54.29 s.[1]	(Valmon, Watts, Reynolds, Johnson)	U.S.	Aug. 22, 1993	Stuttgart, Germany
3,200 m (4×800)	7 min., 2.43 s.	(Mutua, Yiampoy, Kombich, Bungei)	Kenya	Aug. 25, 2006	Brussels, Belgium

(1) IAAF voted in Aug. 2008 to revoke a world record set by the U.S. team in 1998; one of the team's members, Antonio Pettigrew, admitted to doping in May 2008.

Field Events

Event	Record	Holder	Nationality	Date	Location
High jump	2.45 m (8' ½")	Javier Sotomayor	Cuba	July 27, 1993	Salamanca, Spain
Long jump	8.95 m (29' 4½")	Mike Powell	U.S.	Aug. 30, 1991	Tokyo, Japan
Triple jump	18.29 m (60' ¼")	Jonathan Edwards	UK	Aug. 7, 1995	Göteborg, Sweden
Pole vault	6.14 m (20' 1¾")	Sergey Bubka	Ukraine	July 31, 1994	Sestriere, Italy
Shot put	23.12 m (75' 10¼")	Randy Barnes	U.S.	May 20, 1990	Westwood, CA
Discus	74.08 m (243' 0")	Jürgen Schult	E. Germany	June 6, 1986	Neubrandenburg, E. Germany
Hammer	86.74 m (284' 7")	Yuriy Sedykh	USSR	Aug. 30, 1986	Stuttgart, W. Germany
Javelin	98.48 m (323' 1")	Jan Zelezný	Czech Rep.	May 25, 1996	Stuttgart, W. Germany
Decathlon	9,026 pts.	Roman Šebrle	Czech Rep.	May 27, 2001	Götzis, Austria

Women's Records
Running

Event	Record	Holder	Nationality	Date	Location
100 meters	10.49 s.	Florence Griffith-Joyner	U.S.	July 16, 1988	Indianapolis, IN
200 meters	21.34 s.	Florence Griffith-Joyner	U.S.	Sept. 29, 1988	Seoul, S. Korea
400 meters	47.60 s.	Marita Koch	E. Germany	Oct. 6, 1985	Canberra, Australia
800 meters	1 min., 53.28 s.	Jarmila Kratochvílová	Czechoslovakia	July 26, 1983	Munich, W. Germany
1,000 meters	2 min., 28.98 s.	Svetlana Masterkova	Russia	Aug. 23, 1996	Brussels, Belgium
1,500 meters	3 min., 50.46 s.	Qu Yunxia	China	Sept. 11, 1993	Beijing, China
1 mile	4 min., 12.56 s.	Svetlana Masterkova	Russia	Aug. 14, 1996	Zurich, Switzerland
2,000 meters	5 min., 25.36 s.	Sonia O'Sullivan	Ireland	July 8, 1994	Edinburgh, Scotland, UK
3,000 meters	8 min., 6.11 s.	Wang Junxia	China	Sept. 13, 1993	Beijing, China
3,000 meter stpl.	8 min., 58.81 s.	Gulnara Galkina-Samitova	Russia	Aug. 17, 2008	Beijing, China

Event	Record	Holder	Nationality	Date	Location
5,000 meters	14 min., 11.15 s.	Tirunesh Dibaba	Ethiopia	June 6, 2008	Oslo, Norway
10,000 meters	29 min., 31.78 s.	Wang Junxia	China	Sept. 8, 1993	Beijing, China
20,000 meters	1 h., 5 min., 26.6 s.	Tegla Loroupe	Kenya	Sept. 3, 2000	Borgholzhausen, Germany
30,000 meters	1 h., 45 min., 50.0 s.	Tegla Loroupe	Kenya	June 6, 2003	Warstein, Germany
Marathon	2 h., 15 min., 25.0 s.	Paula Radcliffe	UK	Apr. 13, 2003	London, England, UK

Hurdles

Event	Record	Holder	Nationality	Date	Location
100 meters	12.21 s.	Yordanka Donkova	Bulgaria	Aug. 20, 1988	Stara Zagora, Bulgaria
400 meters	52.34 s.	Yuliya Pechenkina	Russia	Aug. 8, 2003	Tula, Russia

Relay Races

Event	Record	Holder	Nationality	Date	Location
400 m (4×100)	41.37 s.	(Gladisch, Rieger, Auerswald, Goehr)	E. Germany	Oct. 6, 1985	Canberra, Australia
800 m (4×200)	1 min., 27.46 s.	U.S. "Blue" (Jenkins, Colander, Perry, Jones)	U.S.	Apr. 29, 2000	Philadelphia, PA
1,600 m (4×400)	3 min., 15.17 s.	(Ledovskaya, Nazarova, Pinigina, Bryzgina)	USSR	Oct. 1, 1988	Seoul, S. Korea
3,200 m (4×800)	7 min., 50.17 s.	(Olizarenko, Gurina, Borisova, Podyalovskaya)	USSR	Aug. 5, 1984	Moscow, USSR

Field Events

Event	Record	Holder	Nationality	Date	Location
High jump	2.09 m (6' 10¼")	Stefka Kostadinova	Bulgaria	Aug. 30, 1987	Rome, Italy
Long jump	7.52 m (24' 8¼")	Galina Chistyakova	USSR	June 11, 1988	Leningrad, Russia
Triple jump	15.50 m (50' 10¼")	Inessa Kravets	Ukraine	Aug. 10, 1995	Göteborg, Sweden
Pole vault	5.06 m (16' 7¾")	Yelena Isinbaeva	Russia	Aug. 28, 2009	Zürich, Switzerland
Shot put	22.63 m (74' 3")	Natalya Lisovskaya	USSR	June 7, 1987	Moscow, Russia
Discus	76.80 m (252' 0")	Gabriele Reinsch	E. Germany	July 9, 1988	Neubrandenburg, E. Germany
Hammer	79.42 m (260' 4½")	Betty Heidler	Germany	May 21, 2011	Halle, Germany
Javelin	72.28 m (237' 1¾")	Barbora Špotáková	Czech Rep.	Sept. 13, 2008	Stuttgart, Germany
Heptathlon	7,291 pts.	Jackie Joyner-Kersee	U.S.	Sept. 24, 1988	Seoul, S. Korea

World Track and Field Indoor Records

As of Oct. 1, 2011.

The International Association of Athletics Federations first recognized world indoor track and field records on Jan. 1, 1987. World indoor bests set prior to Jan. 1, 1987, were subject to approval as world records providing they met the IAAF world records criteria, including drug testing. Criteria for indoor and outdoor records are the same, except that a track performance cannot be set on an indoor track longer than 200 meters. (a) = altitude. * = Pending ratification.

Men's Records

Event	Record	Holder	Nationality	Date	Location
50 meters	5.56 s. (a)	Donovan Bailey	Canada	Feb. 9, 1996	Reno, NV
60 meters	6.39 s.	Maurice Greene	U.S.	Mar. 3, 2001	Atlanta, GA
200 meters	19.92 s.	Frank Fredericks	Namibia	Feb. 18, 1996	Liévin, France
400 meters	44.57 s.	Kerron Clement	U.S.	Mar. 12, 2005	Fayetteville, AR
800 meters	1 min., 42.67 s.	Wilson Kipketer	Denmark	Mar. 9, 1997	Paris, France
1,000 meters	2 min., 14.96 s.	Wilson Kipketer	Denmark	Feb. 20, 2000	Birmingham, England, UK
1,500 meters	3 min., 31.18 s.	Hicham El Guerrouj	Morocco	Feb. 2, 1997	Stuttgart, Germany
1 mile	3 min., 48.45 s.	Hicham El Guerrouj	Morocco	Feb. 12, 1997	Ghent, Belgium
3,000 meters	7 min., 24.90 s.	Daniel Komen	Kenya	Feb. 6, 1998	Budapest, Hungary
5,000 meters	12 min., 49.60 s.	Kenenisa Bekele	Ethiopia	Feb. 20, 2004	Birmingham, England, UK
50-meter hurdles	6.25 s.	Mark McKoy	Canada	Mar. 5, 1986	Kobe, Japan
60-meter hurdles	7.30 s.	Colin Jackson	UK	Mar. 6, 1994	Sindelfingen, Germany
High jump	2.43 m (7' 11½")	Javier Sotomayor	Cuba	Mar. 4, 1989	Budapest, Hungary
Long jump	8.79 m (28' 10¼")	Carl Lewis	U.S.	Jan. 27, 1984	New York, NY
Triple jump	17.92 m (58' 9½")*	Teddy Tamgho	France	Mar. 6, 2011	Paris, France
Pole vault	6.15 m (20' 2")	Sergey Bubka	Ukraine	Feb. 21, 1993	Donetsk, Ukraine
Shot put	22.66 m (74' 4¼")	Randy Barnes	U.S.	Jan. 20, 1989	Los Angeles, CA

Women's Records

Event	Record	Holder	Nationality	Date	Location
50 meters	5.96 s.	Irina Privalova	Russia	Feb. 9, 1995	Madrid, Spain
60 meters	6.92 s.	Irina Privalova	Russia	Feb. 9, 1995	Madrid, Spain
200 meters	21.87 s.	Merlene Ottey	Jamaica	Feb. 13, 1993	Liévin, France
400 meters	49.59 s.	Jarmila Kratochvílová	Czechoslovakia	Mar. 7, 1982	Milan, Italy
800 meters	1 min., 55.82 s.	Jolanda Batageli	Slovenia	Mar. 3, 2002	Vienna, Austria
1,000 meters	2 min., 30.94 s.	Maria de Lurdes Mutola	Mozambique	Feb. 25, 1999	Stockholm, Sweden
1,500 meters	3 min., 58.28 s.	Yelena Soboleva	Russia	Feb. 18, 2006	Moscow, Russia
1 mile	4 min., 17.14 s.	Doina Melinte	Romania	Feb. 9, 1990	E. Rutherford, NJ
3,000 meters	8 min., 23.72 s.	Meseret Defar	Ethiopia	Feb. 3, 2007	Stuttgart, Germany
5,000 meters	14 min., 24.37 s.	Meseret Defar	Ethiopia	Feb. 18, 2009	Stockholm, Sweden
50-meter hurdles	6.58 s.	Cornelia Oschkenat	E. Germany	Feb. 20, 1988	Berlin, Germany
60-meter hurdles	7.68 s.	Susanna Kallur	Sweden	Feb. 10, 2008	Karlsruhe, Germany
High jump	2.08 m (6' 10")	Kajsa Bergqvist	Sweden	Feb. 4, 2006	Arnstadt, Germany
Long jump	7.37 m (24' 2¼")	Heike Drechsler	E. Germany	Feb. 13, 1988	Vienna, Austria
Triple jump	15.36 m (50' 4¾")	Tatyana Lebedeva	Russia	Mar. 3, 2004	Budapest, Hungary
Pole vault	5.00 m (16' 4¾")	Yelena Isinbaeva	Russia	Feb. 15, 2009	Donetsk, Ukraine
Shot put	22.50 m (73' 10")	Helena Fibingerová	Czechoslovakia	Feb. 19, 1977	Jablonec, Czechoslovakia

COLLEGE BASKETBALL
2011 Men's NCAA Tournament: UConn Triumphs Over Butler

The Univ. of Connecticut Huskies defeated the Butler Univ. Bulldogs (Indianapolis, IN), 53-41, in Houston to claim the NCAA Men's Division I national basketball title Apr. 4, 2011. This was the third national championship for head coach Jim Calhoun, who at age 68 was the oldest coach to win the NCAA championship. Butler went into the second half with a 22-19 lead but had a 18.8% shooting percentage in the game—the worst in championship history—and were outscored 26-2 in the paint. Star Huskies guard Kemba Walker scored 16 points and was named the tournament's most outstanding player.

NCAA Division I Basketball Champions, 1943-2011

Year	Champion	Coach	Final opponent	Score	Most outstanding player	Site
1943	Wyoming	Everett Shelton	Georgetown	46-34	Ken Sailors, Wyoming	New York, NY
1944	Utah	Vadal Peterson	Dartmouth	42-40[1]	Arnold Ferrin, Utah	New York, NY
1945	Oklahoma St.[2]	Henry Iba	NYU	49-45	Bob Kurland, Oklahoma St.	New York, NY
1946	Oklahoma St.[2]	Henry Iba	North Carolina	43-40	Bob Kurland, Oklahoma St.	New York, NY
1947	Holy Cross	Alvin Julian	Oklahoma	58-47	George Kaftan, Holy Cross	New York, NY
1948	Kentucky	Adolph Rupp	Baylor	58-42	Alex Groza, Kentucky	New York, NY
1949	Kentucky	Adolph Rupp	Oklahoma St.	46-36	Alex Groza, Kentucky	Seattle, WA
1950	CCNY	Nat Holman	Bradley	71-68	Irwin Dambrot, CCNY	New York, NY
1951	Kentucky	Adolph Rupp	Kansas St.	68-58	Bill Spivey, Kentucky	Minneapolis, MN
1952	Kansas	Forrest Allen	St. John's	80-63	Clyde Lovellette, Kansas	Seattle, WA
1953	Indiana	Branch McCracken	Kansas	69-68	B. H. Born, Kansas	Kansas City, MO
1954	La Salle	Kenneth Loeffler	Bradley	92-76	Tom Gola, La Salle	Kansas City, MO
1955	San Francisco	Phil Woolpert	La Salle	77-63	Bill Russell, San Francisco	Kansas City, MO
1956	San Francisco	Phil Woolpert	Iowa	83-71	Hal Lear, Temple	Evanston, IL
1957	North Carolina	Frank McGuire	Kansas	54-53[1]	Wilt Chamberlain, Kansas	Kansas City, MO
1958	Kentucky	Adolph Rupp	Seattle	84-72	Elgin Baylor, Seattle	Louisville, KY
1959	California	Pete Newell	West Virginia	71-70	Jerry West, West Virginia	Louisville, KY
1960	Ohio St.	Fred Taylor	California	75-55	Jerry Lucas, Ohio St.	San Francisco, CA
1961	Cincinnati	Edwin Jucker	Ohio St.	70-65[1]	Jerry Lucas, Ohio St.	Kansas City, MO
1962	Cincinnati	Edwin Jucker	Ohio St.	71-59	Paul Hogue, Cincinnati	Louisville, KY
1963	Loyola (IL)	George Ireland	Cincinnati	60-58[1]	Art Heyman, Duke	Louisville, KY
1964	UCLA	John Wooden	Duke	98-83	Walt Hazzard, UCLA	Kansas City, MO
1965	UCLA	John Wooden	Michigan	91-80	Bill Bradley, Princeton	Portland, OR
1966	Texas-El Paso[3]	Don Haskins	Kentucky	72-65	Jerry Chambers, Utah	College Park, MD
1967	UCLA	John Wooden	Dayton	79-64	Lew Alcindor, UCLA	Louisville, KY
1968	UCLA	John Wooden	North Carolina	78-55	Lew Alcindor, UCLA	Los Angeles, CA
1969	UCLA	John Wooden	Purdue	92-72	Lew Alcindor, UCLA	Louisville, KY
1970	UCLA	John Wooden	Jacksonville	80-69	Sidney Wicks, UCLA	College Park, MD
1971	UCLA	John Wooden	Villanova*	68-62	Howard Porter, Villanova*	Houston, TX
1972	UCLA	John Wooden	Florida St.	81-76	Bill Walton, UCLA	Los Angeles, CA
1973	UCLA	John Wooden	Memphis[4]	87-66	Bill Walton, UCLA	St. Louis, MO
1974	North Carolina St.	Norm Sloan	Marquette	76-64	David Thompson, NC St.	Greensboro, NC
1975	UCLA	John Wooden	Kentucky	92-85	Richard Washington, UCLA	San Diego, CA
1976	Indiana	Bob Knight	Michigan	86-68	Kent Benson, Indiana	Philadelphia, PA
1977	Marquette	Al McGuire	North Carolina	67-59	Butch Lee, Marquette	Atlanta, GA
1978	Kentucky	Joe Hall	Duke	94-88	Jack Givens, Kentucky	St. Louis, MO
1979	Michigan St.	Jud Heathcote	Indiana St.	75-64	Magic Johnson, Michigan St.	Salt Lake City, UT
1980	Louisville	Denny Crum	UCLA*	59-54	Darrell Griffith, Louisville	Indianapolis, IN
1981	Indiana	Bob Knight	North Carolina	63-50	Isiah Thomas, Indiana	Philadelphia, PA
1982	North Carolina	Dean Smith	Georgetown	63-62	James Worthy, N. Carolina	New Orleans, LA
1983	North Carolina St.	Jim Valvano	Houston	54-52	Hakeem Olajuwon, Houston	Albuquerque, NM
1984	Georgetown	John Thompson	Houston	84-75	Patrick Ewing, Georgetown	Seattle, WA
1985	Villanova	Rollie Massimino	Georgetown	66-64	Ed Pinckney, Villanova	Lexington, KY
1986	Louisville	Denny Crum	Duke	72-69	Pervis Ellison, Louisville	Dallas, TX
1987	Indiana	Bob Knight	Syracuse	74-73	Keith Smart, Indiana	New Orleans, LA
1988	Kansas	Larry Brown	Oklahoma	83-79	Danny Manning, Kansas	Kansas City, MO
1989	Michigan	Steve Fisher	Seton Hall	80-79[1]	Glen Rice, Michigan	Seattle, WA
1990	UNLV	Jerry Tarkanian	Duke	103-73	Anderson Hunt, UNLV	Denver, CO
1991	Duke	Mike Krzyzewski	Kansas	72-65	Christian Laettner, Duke	Indianapolis, IN
1992	Duke	Mike Krzyzewski	Michigan	71-51	Bobby Hurley, Duke	Minneapolis, MN
1993	North Carolina	Dean Smith	Michigan	77-71	Donald Williams, N. Carolina	New Orleans, LA
1994	Arkansas	Nolan Richardson	Duke	76-72	Corliss Williamson, Arkansas	Charlotte, NC
1995	UCLA	Jim Harrick	Arkansas	89-78	Ed O'Bannon, UCLA	Seattle, WA
1996	Kentucky	Rick Pitino	Syracuse	76-67	Tony Delk, Kentucky	E. Rutherford, NJ
1997	Arizona	Lute Olson	Kentucky	84-79[1]	Miles Simon, Arizona	Indianapolis, IN
1998	Kentucky	Tubby Smith	Utah	78-69	Jeff Sheppard, Kentucky	San Antonio, TX
1999	Connecticut	Jim Calhoun	Duke	77-74	Richard Hamilton, Connecticut	St. Petersburg, FL
2000	Michigan St.	Tom Izzo	Florida	89-76	Mateen Cleaves, Michigan St.	Indianapolis, IN
2001	Duke	Mike Krzyzewski	Arizona	82-72	Shane Battier, Duke	Minneapolis, MN
2002	Maryland	Gary Williams	Indiana	64-52	Juan Dixon, Maryland	Atlanta, GA
2003	Syracuse	Jim Boeheim	Kansas	81-78	Carmelo Anthony, Syracuse	New Orleans, LA
2004	Connecticut	Jim Calhoun	Georgia Tech	82-73	Emeka Okafor, Connecticut	San Antonio, TX
2005	North Carolina	Roy Williams	Illinois	75-70	Sean May, North Carolina	St. Louis, MO
2006	Florida	Billy Donovan	UCLA	73-57	Joakim Noah, Florida	Indianapolis, IN
2007	Florida	Billy Donovan	Ohio State	84-75	Corey Brewer, Florida	Atlanta, GA
2008	Kansas	Bill Self	Memphis	75-68[1]	Mario Chalmers, Kansas	San Antonio, TX
2009	North Carolina	Roy Williams	Michigan State	89-72	Wayne Ellington, North Carolina	Detroit, MI
2010	Duke	Mike Krzyzewski	Butler	61-59	Kyle Singler, Duke	Indianapolis, IN
2011	Connecticut	Jim Calhoun	Butler	53-41	Kemba Walker, Connecticut	Houston, TX

*Declared ineligible after the tournament. (1) Overtime. (2) Then known as Oklahoma A&M. (3) Then known as Texas Western. (4) Then known as Memphis State.

2011 Men's NCAA Basketball Tournament

EAST REGIONALS

(1) Ohio St. 75
(16) Texas-San Antonio 46 — Ohio St. 98
(8) George Mason 61 — George Mason 66 — Ohio St. 60
(9) Villanova 57

(5) West Virginia 84 — West Virginia 63 — Kentucky 76
(12) Clemson 76
(4) Kentucky 59 — Kentucky 71 — Kentucky 62
(13) Princeton 57

(6) Xavier 55 — Marquette 66 — Kentucky 55
(11) Marquette 66
(3) Syracuse 77 — Syracuse 62 — Marquette 63
(14) Indiana St. 60

(7) Washington 68 — Washington 83 — N. Carolina 69
(10) Georgia 65
(2) North Carolina 102 — N. Carolina 86 — N. Carolina 81
(15) Long Island 87

WEST REGIONALS

(1) Duke 87 — Duke 73
(16) Hampton 45
(8) Michigan 75 — Michigan 71 — Duke 77
(9) Tennessee 45

(5) Arizona 77 — Arizona 70 — Arizona 63
(12) Memphis 75
(4) Texas 85 — Texas 69 — Arizona 93
(13) Oakland 81

(6) Cincinnati 78 — Cincinnati 58 — Connecticut 56
(11) Missouri 63
(3) Connecticut 81 — Connecticut 69 — Connecticut 74
(14) Bucknell 52

(7) Temple 66 — Temple 64 — Connecticut 65
(10) Penn St. 64
(2) San Diego St. 68 — San Diego St. 71 — San Diego St. 67
(15) Northern Colorado 50

SOUTHWEST REGIONALS

(1) Kansas 72 — Kansas 73
(16) Boston Univ. 53
(8) UNLV 62 — Illinois 59 — Kansas 77
(9) Illinois 73

(5) Vanderbilt 66 — Richmond 65 — Kansas 61
(12) Richmond 69
(4) Louisville 61 — Morehead St. 48 — Richmond 57
(13) Morehead St. 62

(6) Georgetown 56 — VCU 94 — VCU 62
(11) VCU 74
(3) Purdue 65 — Purdue 76 — VCU 72
(14) St. Peter's 43

(7) Texas A&M 50 — Florida St. 71 — VCU 71
(10) Florida St. 57
(2) Notre Dame 69 — Notre Dame 57 — Florida St. 71
(15) Akron 56

SOUTHEAST REGIONALS

(1) Pittsburgh 74 — Pittsburgh 70
(16) UNC Asheville 51
(8) Butler 60 — Butler 71 — Butler 61
(9) Old Dominion 58

(5) Kansas St. 73 — Kansas St. 65 — Butler 74
(12) Utah St. 68
(4) Wisconsin 72 — Wisconsin 70 — Wisconsin 54
(13) Belmont 58

(6) St. John's (NY) 71 — Gonzaga 67 — Butler 70
(11) Gonzaga 86
(3) BYU 74 — BYU 89 — BYU 74
(14) Wofford 66

(7) UCLA 78 — UCLA 65 — Florida 71
(10) Michigan St. 76
(2) Florida 79 — Florida 73 — Florida 83
(15) UC Santa Barbara 51

Kentucky 55

Connecticut 56

Connecticut 53
Butler 41

VCU 62

Butler 70

Men's Basketball Final Division I Conference Standings, 2010-11

Team	Conf. W	L	Total W	L
America East				
Vermont	13	3	23	9
Boston Univ.*	12	4	21	14
Albany	9	7	16	16
Maine	9	7	15	15
Stony Brook	8	8	15	17
Hartford	7	9	11	20
New Hampshire	6	10	11	18
Binghamton	4	12	8	23
UMBC	4	12	5	25
Atlantic Coast				
North Carolina	14	2	29	8
Duke*	13	3	32	5
Florida State	11.	5	23	11
Clemson	9	7	22	12
Virginia Tech	9	7	22	12
Boston College	9	7	21	13
Maryland	7	9	19	14
Virginia	7	9	16	15
Miami (FL)	6	10	21	15
NC State	5	11	15	16
Georgia Tech	5	11	13	18
Wake Forest	1	15	8	24
Atlantic Sun				
Belmont*	19	1	30	5
E. Tennessee State	16	4	24	12
Jacksonville	13	7	20	12
Lipscomb	12	8	17	13
Mercer	11	9	15	18
North Florida	10	10	15	19
Florida Gulf Coast	7	13	10	20
Campbell	6	14	12	19
Kennesaw State	6	14	8	23
Stetson	6	14	8	23
SC Upstate	4	16	5	25
Atlantic 10				
Xavier*	15	1	24	8
Temple	14	2	26	8
Richmond	13	3	29	8
Duquesne	10	6	19	13
George Washington	10	6	17	14
Rhode Island	9	7	20	14
State Bonaventure	8	8	16	15
Dayton	7	9	22	14
Massachusetts	7	9	15	15
La Salle	6	10	15	18
St. Louis	6	10	12	19
Saint Joseph's	4	12	11	22
Charlotte	2	14	10	20
Fordham	1	15	7	21
Big East				
Pittsburgh	15	3	28	6
Notre Dame	14	4	27	7
Syracuse	12	6	27	8
Louisville	12	6	25	10
St. John's (NY)	12	6	21	12
Cincinnati	11	7	26	9
West Virginia	11	7	21	12
Georgetown	10	8	21	11
Connecticut*	9	9	32	9
Villanova	9	9	21	12
Marquette	9	9	22	15
Seton Hall	7	11	13	18
Rutgers	5	13	15	17
Providence	4	14	15	17
South Florida	3	15	10	23
DePaul	1	17	7	24
Big Sky				
N. Colorado*	13	3	21	11
Montana	12	4	21	11
Weber State	11	5	18	14
N. Arizona	9	7	19	13
Montana State	7	9	13	18
E. Washington	7	9	9	20
Portland State	5	11	14	16
Idaho State	4	12	9	20
Sacramento State	4	12	7	21

Team	Conf. W	L	Total W	L
Big South				
Coastal Carolina	16	2	28	6
Liberty	13	5	19	13
NC-Asheville*	11	7	20	14
VMI	10	8	18	13
Charleston Southern	9	9	16	16
Winthrop	9	9	13	17
Presbyterian	7	11	13	18
High Point	7	11	12	19
Gardner-Webb	6	12	11	21
Radford	2	16	5	24
Big 10				
Ohio State*	16	2	34	3
Purdue	14	4	26	8
Wisconsin	13	5	25	9
Michigan	9	9	21	14
Illinois	9	9	20	14
Michigan State	9	9	19	15
Penn State	9	9	19	15
Northwestern	7	11	20	14
Minnesota	6	12	17	14
Iowa	4	14	11	20
Indiana	3	15	12	20
Big 12				
Kansas*	14	2	35	3
Texas	13	3	28	8
Texas A&M	10	6	24	9
Kansas State	10	6	23	11
Missouri	8	8	23	11
Colorado	8	8	24	14
Nebraska	7	9	19	13
Baylor	7	9	18	13
Oklahoma State	6	10	20	14
Oklahoma	5	11	14	18
Texas Tech	5	11	13	19
Iowa State	3	13	16	16
Big West				
Long Beach State	14	2	22	12
Cal. Poly	10	6	15	15
CSU Northridge	9	7	14	18
UC Santa Barbara*	8	8	18	14
Pacific (CA)	8	8	16	15
CSU Fullerton	7	9	11	20
UC Irvine	6	10	13	19
UC Riverside	6	10	12	19
UC Davis	4	12	10	20
Colonial Athletic				
George Mason	16	2	27	7
Old Dominion*	14	4	27	7
Hofstra	14	4	21	12
VCU	12	6	28	12
Drexel	11	7	21	10
James Madison	10	8	21	12
Delaware	8	10	14	17
NC-Wilmington	7	11	13	18
Georgia State	6	12	12	19
Northeastern	6	12	11	20
William & Mary	4	14	10	22
Towson	0	18	4	26
Conference USA				
UAB*	12	4	22	9
UTEP	11	5	25	10
Tulsa	11	5	19	13
Memphis	10	6	25	10
Southern Miss.	9	7	22	10
Marshall	9	7	22	12
East Carolina	8	8	18	16
SMU	8	8	20	15
Central Florida	6	10	21	12
Rice	5	11	14	18
Houston	4	12	12	18
Tulane	3	13	13	17
Great West				
Utah Valley	11	2	19	11
North Dakota*	11	4	19	13
NJ Tech	9	4	15	15
South Dakota	9	6	18	15
Chicago State	3	10	6	26
Houston Baptist	3	11	5	26
UT-Pan American	2	11	6	25

Team	Conf. W	L	Total W	L
Horizon League				
Cleveland State	13	5	27	9
Butler*	13	5	28	10
Wis.-Milwaukee	13	5	19	14
Valparaiso	12	6	23	12
Wright State	10	8	19	14
Detroit	10	8	17	16
Green Bay	8	10	14	18
Loyola (IL.)	7	11	16	15
Youngstown State	2	16	9	21
Illinois-Chicago	2	16	7	24
Ivy League[1]				
Princeton[2]	13	2	25	7
Harvard	12	3	23	7
Yale	8	6	15	13
Penn	7	7	13	15
Columbia	6	8	15	13
Cornell	6	8	10	18
Brown	4	10	11	17
Dartmouth	1	13	5	23
Metro Atlantic Athletic				
Fairfield	15	3	25	8
Rider	13	5	23	11
Iona	13	5	25	12
St. Peter's*	11	7	20	14
Loyola (MD)	10	8	15	15
Canisius	9	9	15	15
Siena	8	10	13	18
Niagara	5	13	9	23
Manhattan	3	15	6	25
Marist	3	15	6	27
Mid-American				
East Division				
Kent State	12	4	24	12
Miami (OH)	11	5	16	17
Akron*	9	7	23	13
Ohio	9	7	19	16
Buffalo	8	8	20	14
Bowling Green	8	8	14	19
West Division				
Western Michigan	11	5	21	13
Ball State	10	6	19	13
Central Michigan	7	9	10	21
Northern Illinois	5	11	9	21
Eastern Michigan	5	11	9	22
Toledo	1	15	4	28
Mid-Eastern Athletic				
Bethune-Cookman	13	3	21	13
Hampton*	11	5	24	9
Coppin State	11	5	16	14
Morgan State	10	6	17	14
North Carolina A&T	9	7	15	17
Norfolk State	8	8	12	20
Florida A&M	7	9	12	20
SC State	5	11	10	22
Delaware State	5	11	9	21
MD-E. Shore	5	11	9	22
Howard	4	12	6	24
Missouri Valley				
Missouri State	15	3	26	9
Wichita State	14	4	29	8
Indiana State*	12	6	20	14
Creighton	10	8	23	16
N. Iowa	10	8	20	14
Evansville	9	9	16	16
Drake	7	11	13	18
Southern Illinois	5	13	13	19
Illinois State	4	14	12	19
Bradley	4	14	12	20
Mountain West				
San Diego State*	14	2	34	3
BYU	14	2	32	5
UNLV	11	5	24	9
Colorado State	9	7	19	13
New Mexico	8	8	22	13
Air Force	6	10	16	16
Utah	6	10	13	18
Wyoming	3	13	10	21
TCU	1	15	11	22

Team	Conf. W	L	Total W	L
Northeast				
Long Island*	16	2	27	6
Quinnipiac	13	5	22	10
Robert Morris	12	6	18	14
Central Conn. State	11	7	19	12
St. Francis (NY)	10	8	15	15
Wagner	9	9	13	17
Mount St. Mary's	9	9	11	21
Bryant	7	11	9	21
St. Francis (PA)	7	11	9	21
Sacred Heart	6	12	11	18
Monmouth	5	13	9	21
Fairleigh Dickinson	3	15	5	24
Ohio Valley				
Murray State	14	4	23	9
Morehead State*	13	5	25	10
Austin Peay	13	5	20	14
Tennessee Tech	12	6	20	13
Tennessee State	10	8	14	16
Eastern Kentucky	9	9	15	16
Tennessee-Martin	6	12	12	21
SE Missouri State	6	12	10	22
Eastern Illinois	4	14	9	20
Jacksonville State	3	15	5	25
Pacific 10				
Arizona	14	4	30	8
UCLA	13	5	23	11
Washington*	11	7	24	11
USC	10	8	19	15
California	10	8	18	15
Washington State	9	9	22	13
Oregon	7	11	21	18
Stanford	7	11	15	16
Oregon State	5	13	11	20
Arizona State	4	14	12	19
Patriot League				
Bucknell*	13	1	25	9
American	11	3	22	9
Holy Cross	7	7	8	21
Lehigh	6	8	16	15
Lafayette	6	8	13	19
Navy	6	8	11	20
Colgate	4	10	7	23
Army	3	11	11	19
Southeastern				
East Division				
Florida	13	3	29	8
Kentucky*	10	6	29	9
Vanderbilt	9	7	23	11
Georgia	9	7	21	12
Tennessee	8	8	19	15
South Carolina	5	11	14	16

Team	Conf. W	L	Total W	L
West Division				
Alabama	12	4	25	12
Mississippi State	9	7	17	14
Mississippi	7	9	20	14
Arkansas	7	9	18	13
Auburn	4	12	11	20
LSU	3	13	11	21
Southern				
North Division				
Western Carolina	12	6	18	15
Chattanooga	12	6	16	16
Appalachian State	10	8	16	15
Elon	7	11	14	17
NC-Greensboro	6	12	7	24
Samford	4	14	12	19
South Division				
Charleston	14	4	26	11
Wofford*	14	4	21	13
Furman	12	6	22	11
Davidson	10	8	18	15
Citadel	6	12	10	22
Georgia Southern	1	17	5	27
Southland				
East Division				
McNeese State	11	5	21	12
Northwestern State	10	6	18	14
SE Louisiana	9	7	15	14
Nicholls State	8	8	14	14
Lamar	7	9	13	17
Central Arkansas	1	15	5	24
West Division				
Sam Houston	9	6	18	13
Texas State	10	6	16	16
Stephen F. Austin	9	7	18	11
Texas-San Antonio*	9	7	20	14
Texas-Arlington	7	9	13	16
Texas A&M-Corpus Christi	5	11	10	21
Southwestern Athletic				
Texas Southern	16	2	19	13
Jackson State	12	6	17	15
Mississippi Valley	12	6	13	19
Alabama State*	11	7	17	18
Alabama A&M	10	8	13	15
Grambling	8	10	12	21
Prairie View	7	11	10	22
Arkansas-Pine Bluff	7	11	7	24
Alcorn State	4	14	4	24
Southern	3	15	4	26
Summit League				
Oakland*	17	1	25	10
Oral Roberts	13	5	19	16

Team	Conf. W	L	Total W	L
Indiana Univ.-Purdue	12	6	19	14
Indiana Univ.-Purdue				
Fort Wayne	11	7	18	12
South Dakota State	10	8	19	12
Missouri-Kansas City	9	9	16	14
North Dakota State	8	10	14	15
Southern Utah	7	11	11	19
Western Illinois	2	16	7	23
Centenary	1	17	1	29
Sun Belt				
East Division				
Florida Atlantic	13	3	21	11
Middle Tenn. State.	10	6	16	16
Western Kentucky	8	8	16	16
South Alabama	6	10	12	16
Troy	6	10	8	21
Florida International	5	11	11	19
West Division				
Arkansas State	11	5	17	15
LA-Lafayette	11	5	14	15
Denver	9	7	13	17
North Texas	8	8	22	11
Arkansas-Little Rock*	7	9	19	17
LA-Monroe	2	14	7	24
West Coast				
St. Mary's (CA)	11	3	25	9
Gonzaga*	11	3	25	10
San Francisco	10	4	19	15
Santa Clara	8	6	24	14
Portland	7	7	20	12
Pepperdine	5	9	12	21
Loyola-Marymount	2	12	11	21
San Diego	2	12	6	24
Western Athletic				
Utah State*	15	1	30	4
Boise State	10	6	22	13
Idaho	9	7	18	14
New Mexico State	9	7	16	17
Hawaii	8	8	19	13
Nevada	8	8	13	19
Fresno State	6	10	14	17
San Jose State	5	11	17	16
Louisiana Tech	2	14	12	20
Independents[1]				
Seattle	—	—	11	20
SIU-Edwardsville	—	—	8	21
Savannah State	—	—	12	18
Longwood	—	—	12	19
NC Central	—	—	15	15
CSU Bakersfield	—	—	9	19

* = Conference tournament champion. (1) Schools do not participate in a tournament. (2) Defeated Harvard in a single-game playoff to get NCAA tournament seed.

All-Time Winningest Division I College Basketball Teams

Team	Yrs.	Won	Lost	Pct.	Team	Yrs.	Won	Lost	Pct.	Team	Yrs.	Won	Lost	Pct.
Kentucky	108	2,052	638	0.763	W. Kentucky	92	1,639	793	0.671	Arizona	106	1,595	880	0.644
North Carolina	101	2,033	720	0.733	St. John's (NY)	104	1,724	884	0.656	Missouri State	99	1,548	845	0.643
Kansas	113	2,038	796	0.718	Louisville	97	1,632	844	0.655	Villanova	91	1,551	858	0.642
UNLV	53	1,107	438	0.713	Illinois	106	1,650	868	0.652	Murray State	86	1,451	811	0.641
Duke	106	1,944	822	0.702	Utah	103	1,664	875	0.651	Arkansas	88	1,519	840	0.638
UCLA	92	1,709	744	0.690	Notre Dame	106	1,701	920	0.645	Connecticut	108	1,549	855	0.638
Syracuse	110	1,810	811	0.690	Temple	115	1,766	966	0.645					

Note: Through 2010-11 season; winningest teams by percentage.

National Invitation Tournament Champions

The National Invitation Tournament (NIT), first played in 1938, is the oldest U.S. basketball tournament. The first National Collegiate Athletic Association (NCAA) national championship tournament was played one year later. In Aug. 2005, the NCAA agreed to purchase the NIT from the five New York City-area colleges that had run the NIT.

Year	Champion	Year	Champion	Year	Champion	Year	Champion	Year	Champion
1938	Temple	1953	Seton Hall	1968	Dayton	1983	Fresno State	1998	Minnesota
1939	Long Island Univ.	1954	Holy Cross	1969	Temple	1984	Michigan	1999	California
1940	Colorado	1955	Duquesne	1970	Marquette	1985	UCLA	2000	Wake Forest
1941	Long Island Univ.	1956	Louisville	1971	North Carolina	1986	Ohio State	2001	Tulsa
1942	West Virginia	1957	Bradley	1972	Maryland	1987	So. Mississippi	2002	Memphis
1943	St. John's (NY)	1958	Xavier (OH)	1973	Virginia Tech	1988	Connecticut	2003	St. John's (NY)
1944	St. John's (NY)	1959	St. John's (NY)	1974	Purdue	1989	St. John's (NY)	2004	Michigan
1945	DePaul	1960	Bradley	1975	Princeton	1990	Vanderbilt	2005	South Carolina
1946	Kentucky	1961	Providence	1976	Kentucky	1991	Stanford	2006	South Carolina
1947	Utah	1962	Dayton	1977	St. Bonaventure	1992	Virginia	2007	West Virginia
1948	St. Louis	1963	Providence	1978	Texas	1993	Minnesota	2008	Ohio State
1949	San Francisco	1964	Bradley	1979	Indiana	1994	Villanova	2009	Penn State
1950	CCNY	1965	St. John's (NY)	1980	Virginia	1995	Virginia Tech	2010	Dayton
1951	Brigham Young	1966	Brigham Young	1981	Tulsa	1996	Nebraska	2011	Wichita State
1952	La Salle	1967	Southern Illinois	1982	Bradley	1997	Michigan		

John R. Wooden Award
Awarded to the nation's outstanding men's college basketball player by the Los Angeles Athletic Club since 1977; awarded under the same name to women since 2004.

1977 Marques Johnson, UCLA	1992 Christian Laettner, Duke
1978 Phil Ford, North Carolina	1993 Calbert Cheaney, Indiana
1979 Larry Bird, Indiana State	1994 Glenn Robinson, Purdue
1980 Darrell Griffith, Louisville	1995 Ed O'Bannon, UCLA
1981 Danny Ainge, Brigham Young	1996 Marcus Camby, Massachusetts
1982 Ralph Sampson, Virginia	1997 Tim Duncan, Wake Forest
1983 Ralph Sampson, Virginia	1998 Antawn Jamison, North Carolina
1984 Michael Jordan, North Carolina	1999 Elton Brand, Duke
1985 Chris Mullin, St. John's (NY)	2000 Kenyon Martin, Cincinnati
1986 Walter Berry, St. John's (NY)	2001 Shane Battier, Duke
1987 David Robinson, Navy	2002 Jay Williams, Duke
1988 Danny Manning, Kansas	2003 T. J. Ford, Texas
1989 Sean Elliott, Arizona	2004 (M) Jameer Nelson, St. Joseph's
1990 Lionel Simmons, La Salle	(W) Alana Beard, Duke
1991 Larry Johnson, UNLV	

2005 (M) Andrew Bogut, Utah
(W) Seimone Augustus, LSU
2006 (M) J. J. Redick, Duke
(W) Seimone Augustus, LSU
2007 (M) Kevin Durant, Texas
(W) Candace Parker, Tennessee
2008 (M) Tyler Hansbrough, N. Carolina
(W) Candace Parker, Tennessee
2009 (M) Blake Griffin, Oklahoma
(W) Maya Moore, Connecticut
2010 (M) Evan Turner, Ohio State
(W) Tina Charles, Connecticut
2011 (M) Jimmer Fredette, BYU
(W) Maya Moore, Connecticut

Most Coaching Victories in the NCAA Basketball Tournament
(Through 2011 tournament. Coaches active in 2010-11 season in **bold**.)

Coach, school(s), first/last appearance	Wins	Tournaments	Championships
Mike Krzyzewski; Duke, 1984/2011	79	27	4
Dean Smith, North Carolina, 1967/1997	65	27	2
Roy Williams; Kansas, N. Carolina; 1990/2011	58	21	2
Jim Calhoun; Northeastern, Connecticut; 1981/2011	49	22	3
John Wooden, UCLA, 1950/1975	47	16	10
Lute Olson; Iowa, Arizona; 1979/2007	46	27	1
Bob Knight; Indiana, Texas Tech; 1973/2007	45	28	3
Jim Boeheim; Syracuse, 1977/2011	45	28	1
Denny Crum, Louisville, 1972/2000	42	23	2
Rick Pitino; Boston, Providence, Kentucky, Louisville; 1983/2011	38	17	1

2011 Women's NCAA Tournament: Texas A&M Claims First Title
The Texas A&M Aggies Apr. 5, 2011, defeated the Notre Dame Fighting Irish, 76-70, in Indianapolis, IN, to claim the Women's Division I basketball title for the school for the first time. Aggies star center Danielle Adams started slow, then dominated the rest of the game, scoring 22 of her 30 points (the second-most ever in a championship game) in the second half.

NCAA Division I Women's Basketball Champions, 1982-2011

Year	Champion	Coach	Final opponent	Score	Most outstanding player	Site
1982	Louisiana Tech	Sonja Hogg	Cheyney	76-62	Janice Lawrence, La. Tech	Norfolk, VA
1983	USC	Linda Sharp	Louisiana Tech	69-67	Cheryl Miller, USC	Norfolk, VA
1984	USC	Linda Sharp	Tennessee	72-61	Cheryl Miller, USC	Los Angeles, CA
1985	Old Dominion	Marianne Stanley	Georgia	70-65	Tracy Claxton, Old Dominion	Austin, TX
1986	Texas	Jody Conradt	USC	97-81	Clarissa Davis, Texas	Lexington, KY
1987	Tennessee	Pat Summitt	Louisiana Tech	67-44	Tonya Edwards, Tennessee	Austin, TX
1988	Louisiana Tech	Leon Barmore	Auburn	56-54	Erica Westbrooks, La. Tech	Tacoma, WA
1989	Tennessee	Pat Summitt	Auburn	76-60	Bridgette Gordon, Tennessee	Tacoma, WA
1990	Stanford	Tara VanDerveer	Auburn	88-81	Jennifer Azzi, Stanford	Knoxville, TN
1991	Tennessee	Pat Summitt	Virginia	70-67 (OT)	Dawn Staley, Virginia	New Orleans, LA
1992	Stanford	Tara VanDerveer	W. Kentucky	78-62	Molly Goodenbour, Stanford	Los Angeles, CA
1993	Texas Tech	Marsha Sharp	Ohio St.	84-82	Sheryl Swoopes, Texas Tech	Atlanta, GA
1994	North Carolina	Sylvia Hatchell	Louisiana Tech	60-59	Charlotte Smith, North Carolina	Richmond, VA
1995	Connecticut	Geno Auriemma	Tennessee	70-64	Rebecca Lobo, Connecticut	Minneapolis, MN
1996	Tennessee	Pat Summitt	Georgia	83-65	Michelle Marciniak, Tennessee	Charlotte, NC
1997	Tennessee	Pat Summitt	Old Dominion	68-59	Chamique Holdsclaw, Tennessee	Cincinnati, OH
1998	Tennessee	Pat Summitt	Louisiana Tech	93-75	Chamique Holdsclaw, Tennessee	Kansas City, MO
1999	Purdue	Carolyn Peck	Duke	62-45	Ukari Figgs, Purdue	San Jose, CA
2000	Connecticut	Geno Auriemma	Tennessee	71-52	Shea Ralph, Connecticut	Philadelphia, PA
2001	Notre Dame	Muffet McGraw	Purdue	68-66	Ruth Riley, Notre Dame	St. Louis, MO
2002	Connecticut	Geno Auriemma	Oklahoma	82-70	Swin Cash, Connecticut	San Antonio, TX
2003	Connecticut	Geno Auriemma	Tennessee	73-68	Diana Taurasi, Connecticut	Atlanta, GA
2004	Connecticut	Geno Auriemma	Tennessee	70-61	Diana Taurasi, Connecticut	New Orleans, LA
2005	Baylor	Kim Mulkey-Robertson	Michigan State	84-62	Sophia Young, Baylor	Indianapolis, IN
2006	Maryland	Brenda Frese	Duke	78-75 (OT)	Laura Harper, Maryland	Boston, MA
2007	Tennessee	Pat Summitt	Rutgers	59-46	Candace Parker, Tennessee	Cleveland, OH
2008	Tennessee	Pat Summitt	Stanford	64-48	Candace Parker, Tennessee	Tampa Bay, FL
2009	Connecticut	Geno Auriemma	Louisville	76-54	Tina Charles, Connecticut	St. Louis, MO
2010	Connecticut	Geno Auriemma	Stanford	53-47	Maya Moore, Connecticut	San Antonio, TX
2011	Texas A&M	Gary Blair	Notre Dame	76-70	Danielle Adams, Texas A&M	Indianapolis, IN

Wade Trophy
Awarded by the National Assn. for Girls and Women in Sport for character, leadership, and player performance.

Year	Player, school	Year	Player, school	Year	Player, school
1978	Carol Blazejowski, Montclair St.	1990	Jennifer Azzi, Stanford	2002	Sue Bird, Connecticut
1979	Nancy Lieberman, Old Dominion	1991	Daedra Charles, Tennessee	2003	Diana Taurasi, Connecticut
1980	Nancy Lieberman, Old Dominion	1992	Susan Robinson, Penn St.	2004	Alana Beard, Duke
1981	Lynette Woodard, Kansas	1993	Karen Jennings, Nebraska	2005	Seimone Augustus, LSU
1982	Pam Kelly, Louisiana Tech	1994	Carol Ann Shudlick, Minnesota	2006	Seimone Augustus, LSU
1983	LaTaunya Pollard, Long Beach St.	1995	Rebecca Lobo, Connecticut	2007	Candace Parker, Tennessee
1984	Janice Lawrence, Louisiana Tech	1996	Jennifer Rizzotti, Connecticut	2008	Candice Wiggins, Stanford
1985	Cheryl Miller, USC	1997	DeLisha Milton, Florida	2009	Maya Moore, Connecticut
1986	Kamie Ethridge, Texas	1998	Ticha Penicheiro, Old Dominion	2010	Maya Moore, Connecticut
1987	Shelly Pennefeather, Villanova	1999	Stephanie White-McCarty, Purdue	2011	Maya Moore, Connecticut
1988	Teresa Weatherspoon, Louisiana Tech	2000	Edwina Brown, Texas		
1989	Clarissa Davis, Texas	2001	Jackie Stiles, SW Missouri St.		

2011 Women's NCAA Basketball Tournament

DALLAS REGIONAL

(1) Baylor 66
(16) Prairie View 30

Baylor 82

(8) Houston 73
(9) West Virginia 79

West Virginia 68

Baylor 86

(5) Green Bay 59
(12) Arkansas-Little Rock 55

Green Bay 65

(4) Michigan St. 69
(13) Northern Iowa 66

Michigan St. 56

Green Bay 76

Baylor 46

(6) Georgia 56
(11) Middle Tenn. 41

Georgia 61

(3) Florida St. 76
(14) Samford 46

Florida St. 59

Georgia 38

Texas A&M 63

(7) Rutgers 76
(10) Louisiana Tech 51

Rutgers 48

Texas A&M 58

(2) Texas A&M 87
(15) McNeese St. 47

Texas A&M 70

Texas A&M 79

SPOKANE REGIONAL

(1) Stanford 86
(16) UC Davis 59

Stanford 75

(8) Texas Tech 50
(9) St. John's (NY) 55

St. John's (NY) 49

Stanford 72

(5) North Carolina 82
(12) Fresno St. 68

North Carolina 86

(4) Kentucky 66
(13) Hampton 62

Kentucky 74

North Carolina 65

Stanford 83

(6) Iowa 86
(11) Gonzaga 92

Gonzaga 87

(3) UCLA 55
(14) Montana 47

UCLA 75

Gonzaga 76

Stanford 62

(7) Louisville 81
(10) Vanderbilt 62

Louisville 85

Gonzaga 60

(2) Xavier 72
(15) South Dakota St. 56

Xavier 75

Louisville 69

PHILADELPHIA REGIONAL

(1) Connecticut 75
(16) Hartford 39

Connecticut 64

(8) Kansas St. 45
(9) Purdue 53

Purdue 40

Connecticut 68

(5) Georgetown 65
(12) Princeton 49

Georgetown 79

(4) Maryland 70
(13) St. Francis (PA) 48

Maryland 57

Georgetown 63

Connecticut 75

(6) Penn St. 75
(11) Dayton 66

Penn St. 73

(3) DePaul 56
(14) Navy 43

DePaul 75

DePaul 63

Connecticut 63

(7) Iowa St. 64
(10) Marist 74

Marist 66

Duke 40

(2) Duke 90
(15) UT Martin 45

Duke 71

Duke 70

DAYTON REGIONAL

(1) Tennessee 99
(16) Stetson 34

Tennessee 79

(8) Marquette 68
(9) Texas 65

Marquette 70

Tennessee 85

(5) Georgia Tech 69
(12) Bowling Green 58

Georgia Tech 60

(4) Ohio St. 80
(13) Central Florida 69

Ohio St. 67

Ohio St. 75

Tennessee 59

(6) Oklahoma 86
(11) James Madison 72

Oklahoma 88

(3) Miami 80
(14) Gardner-Webb 62

Miami 83

Oklahoma 53

Notre Dame 72

(7) Arizona St. 45
(10) Temple 63

Temple 64

Notre Dame 73

(2) Notre Dame 67
(15) Utah 54

Notre Dame 77

Notre Dame 78

Texas A&M 76
Notre Dame 70

COLLEGE FOOTBALL

BCS Championship: Auburn Defeats Oregon for 2010 BCS Title

The Auburn Univ. Tigers defeated the Univ. of Oregon Ducks, 22-19, in Glendale, AZ, to win the Bowl Championship Series (BCS) national title game Jan. 10, 2011. With the win, the Tigers, coached by Gene Chizik, claimed their first football title since 1957. Auburn junior quarterback Cam Newton, the 2010 Heisman Trophy winner, played most of the game with a back injury; Newton announced Jan. 13, 2011, that he would forgo his senior season at Auburn to enter the NFL draft. Auburn finished the season with a 14-0 record and topped the final AP poll, followed by Texas Christian Univ. (TCU) (13-0), the nation's only other undefeated FBS team.

National College Football Champions, 1936-2010

The official champion, as determined by the BCS National Championship game (BCS No. 1 vs. BCS No. 2), is listed starting 2006. For years preceding 2006, the unofficial champion, as selected by the AP poll of writers and USA Today/ESPN (until 1991, UPI; 1991-1996 USA Today/CNN) poll of coaches, is listed. Where the polls disagreed, both teams are listed (AP winner first). The AP poll started in 1936; the UPI poll in 1950.

1936 Minnesota	1951 Tennessee	1966 Notre Dame	1981 Clemson	1996 Florida
1937 Pittsburgh	1952 Michigan St.	1967 USC	1982 Penn St.	1997 Michigan/Nebraska
1938 Texas Christian	1953 Maryland	1968 Ohio St.	1983 Miami (FL)	1998 Tennessee
1939 Texas A&M	1954 Ohio St./UCLA	1969 Texas	1984 Brigham Young	1999 Florida St.
1940 Minnesota	1955 Oklahoma	1970 Nebraska/Texas	1985 Oklahoma	2000 Oklahoma
1941 Minnesota	1956 Oklahoma	1971 Nebraska	1986 Penn St.	2001 Miami (FL)
1942 Ohio St.	1957 Auburn/Ohio St.	1972 USC	1987 Miami (FL)	2002 Ohio State
1943 Notre Dame	1958 Louisiana St.	1973 Notre Dame/Alabama	1988 Notre Dame	2003 LSU/USC
1944 Army	1959 Syracuse	1974 Oklahoma/USC	1989 Miami (FL)	2004 USC
1945 Army	1960 Minnesota	1975 Oklahoma	1990 Colorado/GA Tech	2005 Texas
1946 Notre Dame	1961 Alabama	1976 Pittsburgh	1991 Miami (FL)/Washington	2006 Florida
1947 Notre Dame	1962 USC	1977 Notre Dame	1992 Alabama	2007 LSU
1948 Michigan	1963 Texas	1978 Alabama/USC	1993 Florida St.	2008 Florida
1949 Notre Dame	1964 Alabama	1979 Alabama	1994 Nebraska	2009 Alabama
1950 Oklahoma	1965 Alabama/Mich. St.	1980 Georgia	1995 Nebraska	2010 Auburn

2010 Final Standings

Bowl Championship Series		Associated Press Poll		USA Today Coaches' Poll	
Rank, team	**Rank, team**	**Rank, team**	**Rank, team**	**Rank, team**	**Rank, team**
1. Auburn	14. Oklahoma State	1. Auburn	14. Michigan State	1. Auburn	14. Michigan State
2. Oregon	15. Nevada	2. TCU	15. Mississippi State	2. TCU	15. Virginia Tech
3. TCU	16. Alabama	3. Oregon	16. Virginia Tech	3. Oregon	16. Florida State
4. Stanford	17. Texas A&M	4. Stanford	17. Florida State	4. Stanford	17. Mississippi State
5. Wisconsin	18. Nebraska	5. Ohio State	18. Missouri	5. Ohio State	18. Missouri
6. Ohio State	19. Utah	6. Oklahoma	19. Texas A&M	6. Oklahoma	19. Nebraska
7. Oklahoma	20. South Carolina	7. Wisconsin	20. Nebraska	7. Boise St.	20. Central Florida
8. Arkansas	21. Mississippi	8. LSU	21. Central Florida	8. Wisconsin	21. Texas A&M
9. Michigan State	State	9. Boise State	22. South Carolina	9. LSU	22. South Carolina
10. Boise State	22. West Virginia	10. Alabama	23. Maryland	10. Oklahoma State	23. Utah
11. LSU	23. Florida State	11. Nevada	24. Tulsa	11. Alabama	24. Maryland
12. Missouri	24. Hawaii	12. Arkansas	25. North Carolina	12. Arkansas	25. North Carolina
13. Virginia Tech	25. Central Florida	13. Oklahoma State	State	13. Nevada	State

Note: As of Jan. 11, 2011 (after all bowl games).

Annual Results of Major Bowl Games

(Dates indicate year the game was played; bowl games are generally played in late Dec. or early Jan.)

Rose Bowl, Pasadena, CA

1902	(Jan.) Michigan 49, Stanford 0	1948	Michigan 49, USC 0	1980	USC 17, Ohio St. 16
1916	Washington St. 14, Brown 0	1949	Northwestern 20, California 14	1981	Michigan 23, Washington 6
1917	Oregon 14, Pennsylvania 0	1950	Ohio St. 17, California 14	1982	Washington 28, Iowa 0
1918-19	Service teams	1951	Michigan 14, California 6	1983	UCLA 24, Michigan 14
1920	Harvard 7, Oregon 6	1952	Illinois 40, Stanford 7	1984	UCLA 45, Illinois 9
1921	California 28, Ohio St. 0	1953	USC 7, Wisconsin 0	1985	USC 20, Ohio St. 17
1922	Wash. & Jeff. 0, California 0	1954	Mich. St. 28, UCLA 20	1986	UCLA 45, Iowa 28
1923	USC 14, Penn St. 3	1955	Ohio St. 20, USC 7	1987	Arizona St. 22, Michigan 15
1924	Navy 14, Washington 14	1956	Mich. St. 17, UCLA 14	1988	Mich. St. 20, USC 17
1925	Notre Dame 27, Stanford 10	1957	Iowa 35, Oregon St. 19	1989	Michigan 22, USC 14
1926	Alabama 20, Washington 19	1958	Ohio St. 10, Oregon 7	1990	USC 17, Michigan 10
1927	Alabama 7, Stanford 7	1959	Iowa 38, California 12	1991	Washington 46, Iowa 34
1928	Stanford 7, Pittsburgh 6	1960	Washington 44, Wisconsin 8	1992	Washington 34, Michigan 14
1929	Georgia Tech 8, California 7	1961	Washington 17, Minnesota 7	1993	Michigan 38, Washington 31
1930	USC 47, Pittsburgh 14	1962	Minnesota 21, UCLA 3	1994	Wisconsin 21, UCLA 16
1931	Alabama 24, Wash. St. 0	1963	USC 42, Wisconsin 37	1995	Penn St. 38, Oregon 20
1932	USC 21, Tulane 12	1964	Illinois 17, Washington 7	1996	USC 41, Northwestern 32
1933	USC 35, Pittsburgh 0	1965	Michigan 34, Oregon St. 7	1997	Ohio St. 20, Arizona St. 17
1934	Columbia 7, Stanford 0	1966	UCLA 14, Mich. St. 12	1998	Michigan 21, Wash. St. 16
1935	Alabama 29, Stanford 13	1967	Purdue 14, USC 13	1999	Wisconsin 38, UCLA 31
1936	Stanford 7, SMU 0	1968	USC 14, Indiana 3	2000	Wisconsin 17, Stanford 9
1937	Pittsburgh 21, Washington 0	1969	Ohio St. 27, USC 16	2001	Washington 34, Purdue 24
1938	California 13, Alabama 0	1970	USC 10, Michigan 3	2002	Miami (FL) 37, Nebraska 14
1939	USC 7, Duke 3	1971	Stanford 27, Ohio St. 17	2003	Oklahoma 34, Washington St. 14
1940	USC 14, Tennessee 0	1972	Stanford 13, Michigan 12	2004	USC 28, Michigan 14
1941	Stanford 21, Nebraska 13	1973	USC 42, Ohio St. 17	2005	Texas 38, Michigan 37
1942*	Oregon St. 20, Duke 16	1974	Ohio St. 42, USC 21	2006	Texas 41, USC 38
1943	Georgia 9, UCLA 0	1975	USC 18, Ohio St. 17	2007	USC 32, Michigan 18
1944	USC 29, Washington 0	1976	UCLA 23, Ohio St. 10	2008	USC 49, Illinois 17
1945	USC 25, Tennessee 0	1977	USC 14, Michigan 6	2009	USC 38, Penn State 24
1946	Alabama 34, USC 14	1978	Washington 27, Michigan 20	2010	Ohio St. 26, Oregon 17
1947	Illinois 45, UCLA 14	1979	USC 17, Michigan 10	2011	TCU 21, Wisconsin 19

*Played in Durham, NC.

Orange Bowl, Miami, FL

1935 (Jan.) Bucknell 26, Miami (FL) 0
1936 Catholic U. 20, Mississippi 19
1937 Duquesne 13, Mississippi St. 12
1938 Auburn 6, Michigan St. 0
1939 Tennessee 17, Oklahoma 0
1940 Georgia Tech 21, Missouri 7
1941 Mississippi St. 14, Georgetown 7
1942 Georgia 40, TCU 26
1943 Alabama 37, Boston Coll. 21
1944 LSU 19, Texas A&M 14
1945 Tulsa 26, Georgia Tech 12
1946 Miami (FL) 13, Holy Cross 6
1947 Rice 8, Tennessee 0
1948 Georgia Tech 20, Kansas 14
1949 Texas 41, Georgia 28
1950 Santa Clara 21, Kentucky 13
1951 Clemson 15, Miami (FL) 14
1952 Georgia Tech 17, Baylor 14
1953 Alabama 61, Syracuse 6
1954 Oklahoma 7, Maryland 0
1955 Duke 34, Nebraska 7
1956 Oklahoma 20, Maryland 6
1957 Colorado 27, Clemson 21
1958 Oklahoma 48, Duke 21
1959 Oklahoma 21, Syracuse 6
1960 Georgia 14, Missouri 0

1961 Missouri 21, Navy 14
1962 LSU 25, Colorado 7
1963 Alabama 17, Oklahoma 0
1964 Nebraska 13, Auburn 7
1965 Texas 21, Alabama 17
1966 Alabama 39, Nebraska 28
1967 Florida 27, Georgia Tech 12
1968 Oklahoma 26, Tennessee 24
1969 Penn St. 15, Kansas 14
1970 Penn St. 10, Missouri 3
1971 Nebraska 17, LSU 12
1972 Nebraska 38, Alabama 6
1973 Nebraska 40, Notre Dame 6
1974 Penn St. 16, LSU 9
1975 Notre Dame 13, Alabama 11
1976 Oklahoma 14, Michigan 6
1977 Ohio St. 27, Colorado 10
1978 Arkansas 31, Oklahoma 6
1979 Oklahoma 31, Nebraska 24
1980 Oklahoma 24, Florida St. 7
1981 Oklahoma 18, Florida St. 17
1982 Clemson 22, Nebraska 15
1983 Nebraska 21, LSU 20
1984 Miami (FL) 31, Nebraska 30
1985 Washington 28, Oklahoma 17
1986 Oklahoma 25, Penn St. 10

1987 Oklahoma 42, Arkansas 8
1988 Miami (FL) 20, Oklahoma 14
1989 Miami (FL) 23, Nebraska 3
1990 Notre Dame 21, Colorado 6
1991 Colorado 10, Notre Dame 9
1992 Miami (FL) 22, Nebraska 0
1993 Florida St. 27, Nebraska 14
1994 Florida St. 18, Nebraska 16
1995 Nebraska 24, Miami (FL) 17
1996 Florida St. 31, Notre Dame 26
1996 (Dec.) Nebraska 41, Virginia Tech 21
1998 (Jan.) Nebraska 42, Tennessee 17
1999 Florida 31, Syracuse 10
2000 Michigan 35, Alabama 34 (OT)
2001 Oklahoma 13, Florida St. 2
2002 Florida 56, Maryland 23
2003 USC 38, Iowa 17
2004 Miami (FL) 16, Florida State 14
2005 USC 55, Oklahoma 19
2006 Penn St. 26, Florida St. 23 (3 OT)
2007 Louisville 24, Wake Forest 13
2008 Kansas 24, Virginia Tech 21
2009 Virginia Tech 20, Cincinnati 7
2010 Iowa 24, Georgia Tech 14
2011 Stanford 40, Virginia Tech 12

Sugar Bowl, New Orleans, LA

1935 (Jan.) Tulane 20, Temple 14
1936 TCU 3, LSU 2
1937 Santa Clara 21, LSU 14
1938 Santa Clara 6, LSU 0
1939 TCU 15, Carnegie Tech 7
1940 Texas A&M 14, Tulane 13
1941 Boston Coll. 19, Tennessee 13
1942 Fordham 2, Missouri 0
1943 Tennessee 14, Tulsa 7
1944 Georgia Tech 20, Tulsa 18
1945 Duke 29, Alabama 26
1946 Oklahoma A&M 33, St. Mary's 13
1947 Georgia 20, N. Carolina 10
1948 Texas 27, Alabama 7
1949 Oklahoma 14, N. Carolina 6
1950 Oklahoma 35, LSU 0
1951 Kentucky 13, Oklahoma 7
1952 Maryland 28, Tennessee 13
1953 Georgia Tech 24, Mississippi 7
1954 Georgia Tech 42, West Virginia 19
1955 Navy 21, Mississippi
1956 Georgia Tech 7, Pittsburgh 0
1957 Baylor 13, Tennessee 7
1958 Mississippi 39, Texas 7
1959 LSU 7, Clemson 0
1960 Mississippi 21, LSU 0
*Played in Atlanta, GA.

1961 Mississippi 14, Rice 6
1962 Alabama 10, Arkansas 3
1963 Mississippi 17, Arkansas 13
1964 Alabama 12, Mississippi 7
1965 LSU 13, Syracuse 10
1966 Missouri 20, Florida 18
1967 Alabama 34, Nebraska 7
1968 LSU 20, Wyoming 13
1969 Arkansas 16, Georgia 2
1970 Mississippi 27, Arkansas 22
1971 Tennessee 34, Air Force 13
1972 Oklahoma 40, Auburn 22
1972 (Dec.) Oklahoma 14, Penn St. 0
1973 Notre Dame 24, Alabama 23
1974 Nebraska 13, Florida 10
1975 Alabama 13, Penn St. 6
1977 (Jan.) Pittsburgh 27, Georgia 3
1978 Alabama 35, Ohio St. 6
1979 Alabama 14, Penn St. 7
1980 Alabama 24, Arkansas 9
1981 Georgia 17, Notre Dame 10
1982 Pittsburgh 24, Georgia 20
1983 Penn St. 27, Georgia 23
1984 Auburn 9, Michigan 7
1985 Nebraska 28, LSU 10
1986 Tennessee 35, Miami (FL) 7

1987 Nebraska 30, LSU 15
1988 Syracuse 16, Auburn 16
1989 Florida St. 13, Auburn 7
1990 Miami (FL) 33, Alabama 25
1991 Tennessee 23, Virginia 22
1992 Notre Dame 39, Florida 28
1993 Alabama 34, Miami (FL) 13
1994 Florida 41, West Virginia 7
1995 Florida St. 23, Florida 17
1995 (Dec.) Virginia Tech 28, Texas 10
1997 (Jan.) Florida 52, Florida St. 20
1998 Florida St. 31, Ohio St. 14
1999 Ohio St. 24, Texas A&M 14
2000 Florida St. 46, Virginia Tech 29
2001 Miami (FL) 37, Florida 20
2002 LSU 47, Illinois 34
2003 Georgia 26, Florida St. 13
2004 LSU 21, Oklahoma 14
2005 Auburn 16, Virginia Tech 13
2006 West Virginia 38, Georgia 35*
2007 LSU 41, Notre Dame 14
2008 Georgia 41, Hawaii 10
2009 Utah 31, Alabama 17
2010 Florida 51, Cincinnati 24
2011 Ohio St. 31, Arkansas 26

Chick-fil-A Bowl, Atlanta, GA

(Known as the Peach Bowl, 1968-97; Chick-fil-A Peach Bowl, 1998-2005.)

1968 (Dec.) LSU 31, Florida St. 27
1969 W. Virginia 14, S. Carolina 3
1970 Arizona St. 48, N. Carolina 26
1971 Mississippi 41, Georgia Tech 18
1972 N. Carolina St. 49, W. Virginia 13
1973 Georgia 17, Maryland 16
1974 Vanderbilt 6, Texas Tech 6
1975 W. Virginia 13, N. Carolina St. 10
1976 Kentucky 21, N. Carolina 0
1977 N. Carolina St. 24, Iowa St. 14
1978 Purdue 41, Georgia Tech 21
1979 Baylor 24, Clemson 18
1981 (Jan.) Miami (FL) 20, Virginia Tech 10
1981 (Dec.) W. Virginia 26, Florida 6
1982 Iowa 28, Tennessee 22

1983 Florida St. 28, N. Carolina 3
1984 Virginia 27, Purdue 22
1985 Army 31, Illinois 29
1986 Va. Tech 25, N. Carolina St. 24
1988 (Jan.) Tennessee 28, Indiana 22
1988 (Dec.) N. Carolina St. 28, Iowa 23
1989 Syracuse 19, Georgia 18
1990 Auburn 27, Indiana 23
1992 (Jan.) E. Carolina 37, NC St. 34
1993 N. Carolina 21, Mississippi St. 17
1993 (Dec.) Clemson 14, Kentucky 13
1995 (Jan.) N. Carolina St. 28, Miss. St. 24
1995 (Dec.) Virginia 34, Georgia 27
1996 LSU 10, Clemson 7

1998 (Jan.) Auburn 21, Clemson 17
1998 (Dec.) Georgia 35, Virginia 33
1999 Mississippi St. 27, Clemson 9
2000 LSU 28, Georgia Tech 14
2001 North Carolina 16, Auburn 10
2002 Maryland 30, Tennessee 3
2003 Clemson 27, Tennessee 14
2004 Miami (FL) 27, Florida 10
2005 LSU 40, Miami (FL) 3
2006 Georgia 31, Virginia Tech 24
2007 Auburn 23, Clemson 20 (OT)
2008 LSU 38, Georgia Tech 3
2009 Virginia Tech 37, Tennessee 14
2010 Florida St. 26, South Carolina 17

Cotton Bowl, Dallas, TX

1937 (Jan.) TCU 16, Marquette 6
1938 Rice 28, Colorado 14
1939 St. Mary's 20, Texas Tech 13
1940 Clemson 6, Boston Coll. 3
1941 Texas A&M 13, Fordham 12
1942 Alabama 29, Texas A&M 21
1943 Texas 14, Georgia Tech 7
1944 Randolph Field 7, Texas 7
1945 Oklahoma A&M 34, TCU 0
1946 Texas 40, Missouri 27
1947 Arkansas 0, LSU 0
1948 SMU 13, Penn St. 13
1949 SMU 21, Oregon 13
1950 Rice 27, North Carolina 13
1951 Tennessee 20, Texas 14
1952 Kentucky 20, TCU 7
1953 Texas 16, Tennessee 0
1954 Rice 28, Alabama 6
1955 Georgia Tech 14, Arkansas 6

1956 Mississippi 14, TCU 13
1957 TCU 28, Syracuse 27
1958 Navy 20, Rice 7
1959 TCU 0, Air Force 0
1960 Syracuse 23, Texas 14
1961 Duke 7, Arkansas 6
1962 Texas 12, Mississippi 7
1963 LSU 13, Texas 0
1964 Texas 28, Navy 6
1965 Arkansas 10, Nebraska 7
1966 LSU 14, Arkansas 7
1966 (Dec.) Georgia 24, SMU 9
1968 (Jan.) Texas A&M 20, Alabama 16
1969 Texas 36, Tennessee 13
1970 Texas 21, Notre Dame 17
1971 Notre Dame 24, Texas 11
1972 Penn St. 30, Texas 6
1973 Texas 17, Alabama 13
1974 Nebraska 19, Texas 3

1975 Penn St. 41, Baylor 20
1976 Arkansas 31, Georgia 10
1977 Houston 30, Maryland 21
1978 Notre Dame 38, Texas 10
1979 Notre Dame 35, Houston 34
1980 Houston 17, Nebraska 14
1981 Alabama 30, Baylor 2
1982 Texas 14, Alabama 12
1983 SMU 7, Pittsburgh 3
1984 Georgia 10, Texas 9
1985 Boston Coll. 45, Houston 28
1986 Texas A&M 36, Auburn 16
1987 Ohio St. 28, Texas A&M 12
1988 Texas A&M 35, Notre Dame 10
1989 UCLA 17, Arkansas 3
1990 Tennessee 31, Arkansas 27
1991 Miami (FL) 46, Texas 3
1992 Florida St. 10, Texas A&M 2
1993 Notre Dame 28, Texas A&M 3

1994 Notre Dame 24, Texas A&M 21
1995 USC 55, Texas Tech 14
1996 Colorado 38, Oregon 6
1997 Brigham Young 19, Kansas St. 15
1998 UCLA 29, Texas A&M 23
1999 Texas 38, Mississippi St. 11

2000 Arkansas 27, Texas 6
2001 Kansas St. 35, Tennessee 21
2002 Oklahoma 10, Arkansas 3
2003 Texas 35, LSU 20
2004 Mississippi 31, Oklahoma St. 28
2005 Tennessee 38, Texas A&M 7

2006 Alabama 13, Texas Tech 10
2007 Auburn 17, Nebraska 14
2008 Missouri 38, Arkansas 7
2009 Mississippi 47, Texas Tech 34
2010 Mississippi 21, Oklahoma St. 7
2011 LSU 41, Texas A&M 24

Fiesta Bowl, Glendale, AZ
(Played in Tempe, AZ, 1971-2006.)

1971 (Dec.) Arizona St. 45, Florida St. 38
1972 Arizona St. 49, Missouri 35
1973 Arizona St. 28, Pittsburgh 7
1974 Okla. St. 16, Brigham Young 6
1975 Arizona St. 17, Nebraska 14
1976 Oklahoma 41, Wyoming 7
1977 Penn St. 42, Arizona St. 30
1978 UCLA 10, Arkansas 10
1979 Pittsburgh 16, Arizona 10
1980 Penn St. 31, Ohio St. 19
1982 (Jan.) Penn St. 26, USC 10
1983 Arizona St. 32, Oklahoma 21
1984 Ohio St. 28, Pittsburgh 23
1985 UCLA 39, Miami (FL) 37

1986 Michigan 27, Nebraska 23
1987 Penn St. 14, Miami (FL) 10
1988 Florida St. 31, Nebraska 28
1989 Notre Dame 34, W. Virginia 21
1990 Florida St. 41, Nebraska 17
1991 Louisville 34, Alabama 7
1992 Penn St. 42, Tennessee 17
1993 Syracuse 26, Colorado 22
1994 Arizona 29, Miami (FL) 0
1995 Colorado 41, Notre Dame 24
1996 Nebraska 62, Florida 24
1997 Penn St. 38, Texas 15
1997 (Dec.) Kansas St. 35, Syracuse 18

1999 (Jan.) Tennessee 23, Florida St. 16
2000 Nebraska 31, Tennessee 21
2001 Oregon St. 41, Notre Dame 9
2002 Oregon 38, Colorado 16
2003 Ohio St. 31, Miami (FL) 24 (2 OT)
2004 Ohio St. 35, Kansas St. 28
2005 Utah 35, Pittsburgh 7
2006 Ohio St. 34, Notre Dame 20
2007 Boise St. 43, Oklahoma 42 (OT)
2008 West Virginia 48, Oklahoma 28
2009 Texas 24, Ohio State 21
2010 Boise St. 17, TCU 10
2011 Oklahoma 48, Connecticut 20

Gator Bowl, Jacksonville, FL

1946 (Jan.) Wake Forest 26, S. Carolina 14
1947 Oklahoma 34, N. Carolina St. 13
1948 Maryland 20, Georgia 20
1949 Clemson 24, Missouri 23
1950 Maryland 20, Missouri 7
1951 Wyoming 20, Washington & Lee 7
1952 Miami (FL) 14, Clemson 0
1953 Florida 14, Tulsa 13
1954 Texas Tech 35, Auburn 13
1954 (Dec.) Auburn 33, Baylor 13
1955 Vanderbilt 25, Auburn 13
1956 Georgia Tech 21, Pittsburgh 14
1957 Tennessee 3, Texas A&M 0
1958 Mississippi 7, Florida 3
1960 (Jan.) Arkansas 14, Georgia Tech 7
1960 (Dec.) Florida 13, Baylor 12
1961 Penn St. 30, Georgia Tech 15
1962 Florida 17, Penn St. 7
1963 N. Carolina 35, Air Force 0
1965 (Jan.) Florida St. 36, Okla. 19
1965 (Dec.) GA Tech 31, Texas Tech 21
1966 Tennessee 18, Syracuse 12

1967 Penn St. 17, Florida St. 17
1968 Missouri 35, Alabama 10
1969 Florida 14, Tennessee 13
1971 (Jan.) Auburn 35, Mississippi 28
1971 (Dec.) Georgia 7, N. Carolina 3
1972 Auburn 24, Colorado 3
1973 Texas Tech 28, Tennessee 19
1974 Auburn 27, Texas 3
1975 Maryland 13, Florida 0
1976 Notre Dame 20, Penn St. 9
1977 Pittsburgh 34, Clemson 3
1978 Clemson 17, Ohio St. 15
1979 N. Carolina 17, Michigan 15
1980 Pittsburgh 37, S. Carolina 9
1981 N. Carolina 31, Arkansas 27
1982 Florida St. 31, West Virginia 12
1983 Florida 14, Iowa 6
1984 Oklahoma St. 21, S. Carolina 14
1985 Florida St. 34, Oklahoma St. 23
1986 Clemson 27, Stanford 21
1987 LSU 30, S. Carolina 13
1989 (Jan.) Georgia 34, Michigan St. 27

1989 (Dec.) Clemson 27, W. Virginia 7
1991 (Jan.) Michigan 35, Mississippi 3
1991 (Dec.) Oklahoma 48, Virginia 14
1992 Florida 27, N. Carolina St. 10
1993 Alabama 24, N. Carolina 10
1994 Tennessee 45, Virginia Tech 23
1996 (Jan.) Syracuse 41, Clemson 0
1997 N. Carolina 20, W. Virginia 13
1998 N. Carolina 42, Virginia Tech 3
1999 Georgia Tech 35, Notre Dame 28
2000 Miami (FL) 28, Georgia Tech 13
2001 Virginia Tech 41, Clemson 20
2002 Florida St. 30, Virginia Tech 17
2003 N. Carolina St. 28, Notre Dame 6
2004 Maryland 41, West Virginia 7
2005 Florida St. 30, West Virginia 18
2006 Virginia Tech 35, Louisville 24
2007 West Virginia 38, Georgia Tech 35
2008 Texas Tech 31, Virginia 28
2009 Nebraska 26, Clemson 21
2010 Florida St. 33, West Virginia 21
2011 Mississippi St. 52, Michigan 14

Liberty Bowl, Memphis, TN

1959 (Dec.) Penn St. 7, Alabama 0
1960 Penn St. 41, Oregon 12
1961 Syracuse 15, Miami (FL) 14
1962 Oregon St. 6, Villanova 0
1963 Mississippi St. 16, N. Carolina St. 12
1964 Utah 32, West Virginia 6
1965 Mississippi 13, Auburn 7
1966 Miami (FL) 14, Virginia Tech 7
1967 N. Carolina St. 14, Georgia 7
1968 Mississippi 34, Virginia Tech 17
1969 Colorado 47, Alabama 33
1970 Tulane 17, Colorado 3
1971 Tennessee 14, Arkansas 13
1972 Georgia Tech 31, Iowa St. 30
1973 N. Carolina St. 31, Kansas 18
1974 Tennessee 7, Maryland 3
1975 USC 20, Texas A&M 0
1976 Alabama 36, UCLA 6

1977 Nebraska 21, N. Carolina 17
1978 Missouri 20, LSU 15
1979 Penn St. 9, Tulane 6
1980 Purdue 28, Missouri 25
1981 Ohio St. 31, Navy 28
1982 Alabama 21, Illinois 15
1983 Notre Dame 19, Boston Coll. 18
1984 Auburn 21, Arkansas 15
1985 Baylor 21, LSU 7
1986 Tennessee 21, Minnesota 14
1987 Georgia 20, Arkansas 17
1988 Indiana 34, S. Carolina 10
1989 Mississippi 42, Air Force 29
1990 Air Force 23, Ohio St. 11
1991 Air Force 38, Mississippi St. 15
1992 Mississippi 13, Air Force 0
1993 Louisville 18, Michigan St. 7
1994 Illinois 30, East Carolina 0

1995 East Carolina 19, Stanford 13
1996 Syracuse 30, Houston 17
1997 So. Mississippi 41, Pittsburgh 7
1998 Tulane 41, Brigham Young 27
1999 So. Mississippi 23, Colorado St. 17
2000 Colorado St. 22, Louisville 17
2001 Louisville 28, BYU 10
2002 TCU 17, Colorado St. 3
2003 Utah 17, So. Mississippi 0
2004 Louisville 44, Boise St. 40
2005 Tulsa 31, Fresno St. 24
2006 South Carolina 44, Houston 36
2007 Mississippi State 10, UCF 3
2009 (Jan.) Kentucky 25, East Carolina 19
2010 Arkansas 20, East Carolina 17 (OT)
2010 (Dec.) Central Florida 10, Georgia 6

Sun Bowl, El Paso, TX

1936 (Jan.) Hardin-Simmons 14, New Mexico St. 14
1937 Hardin-Simmons 34, Texas Mines 6
1938 West Virginia 7, Texas Tech 6
1939 Utah 26, New Mexico 0
1940 Catholic U. 0, Arizona St. 0
1941 Western Reserve 26, Arizona St. 13
1942 Tulsa 6, Texas Tech 0
1943 2d Air Force 13, Hardin-Simmons 7
1944 Southwestern (TX) 7, New Mexico 0
1945 Southwestern (TX) 35, Univ. of Mexico 0
1946 New Mexico 34, Denver 24
1947 Cincinnati 18, Virginia Tech 6
1948 Miami (OH) 13, Texas Tech 12
1949 West Virginia 21, Texas Mines 12
1950 Texas Western 33, Georgetown 20
1951 West Texas St. 14, Cincinnati 13
1952 Texas Tech 25, Pacific (CA) 14
1953 Pacific (CA) 26, S. Mississippi 7
1954 Texas Western 37, S. Miss. 14
1955 Texas Western 47, Florida St. 20
1956 Wyoming 21, Texas Tech 14
1957 Geo. Washington 13, TX Western 0
1958 Louisville 34, Drake 20
1958 (Dec.) Wyoming 14, Hardin-Simmons 6

1959 New Mexico St. 28, N. Texas St. 8
1960 New Mexico St. 20, Utah St. 13
1961 Villanova 17, Wichita 9
1962 West Texas St. 15, Ohio U. 14
1963 Oregon 21, SMU 14
1964 Georgia 7, Texas Tech 0
1965 Texas Western 13, TCU 12
1966 Wyoming 28, Florida St. 20
1967 UTEP 14, Mississippi 7
1968 Auburn 34, Arizona 10
1969 Nebraska 45, Georgia 6
1970 Georgia Tech. 17, Texas Tech 9
1971 LSU 33, Iowa St. 15
1972 North Carolina 32, Texas Tech 28
1973 Missouri 34, Auburn 17
1974 Mississippi St. 26, North Carolina 24
1975 Pittsburgh 33, Kansas 19
1977 (Jan.) Texas A&M 37, Florida 14
1977 (Dec.) Stanford 24, LSU 14
1978 Texas 42, Maryland 0
1979 Washington 14, Texas 7
1980 Nebraska 31, Mississippi St. 17
1981 Oklahoma 40, Houston 14
1982 North Carolina 26, Texas 10
1983 Alabama 28, SMU 7
1984 Maryland 28, Tennessee 27

1985 Georgia 13, Arizona 13
1986 Alabama 28, Washington 6
1987 Oklahoma St. 35, West Virginia 33
1988 Alabama 29, Army 28
1989 Pittsburgh 31, Texas A&M 28
1990 Michigan St. 17, USC 16
1991 UCLA 6, Illinois 3
1992 Baylor 20, Arizona 15
1993 Oklahoma 41, Texas Tech 10
1994 Texas 35, North Carolina 31
1995 Iowa 38, Washington 18
1996 Stanford 38, Michigan St. 0
1997 Arizona St. 17, Iowa 7
1998 TCU 28, USC 19
1999 Oregon 24, Minnesota 20
2000 Wisconsin 21, UCLA 20
2001 Washington St. 33, Purdue 27
2002 Purdue 34, Washington 24
2003 Minnesota 31, Oregon 30
2004 Arizona St. 27, Purdue 23
2005 UCLA 50, Northwestern 38
2006 Oregon St. 39, Missouri 38
2007 Oregon 56, South Florida 21
2008 Oregon State 3, Pittsburgh 0
2009 Oklahoma 31, Stanford 27
2010 Notre Dame 33, Miami (FL) 17

Other Bowl Results, Dec. 2010-Jan. 2011

Alamo Bowl, San Antonio, TX: Oklahoma St. 36, Arizona 10

Armed Forces Bowl, Ft. Worth, TX: Army 16, SMU 14

Capital One Bowl, Orlando, FL: Alabama 49, Michigan St. 7

Champs Sports Bowl, Orlando, FL: NC State 23, West Virginia 7

Compass Bowl, Birmingham, AL: Pittsburgh 27, Kentucky 10

GoDaddy.Com Bowl, Mobile, AL: Miami (OH) 35, Middle Tennessee St. 21

Hawaii Bowl, Honolulu, HI: Tulsa 62, Hawaii 35

Holiday Bowl, San Diego, CA: Washington 19, Nebraska 7

Humanitarian Bowl, Boise, ID: Northern Illinois 40, Fresno St. 17

Independence Bowl, Shreveport, LA: Air Force 14, Georgia Tech 7

Insight Bowl, Tempe, AZ: Iowa 27, Missouri 24

Kraft Fight Hunger Bowl, San Francisco, CA: Nevada 20, Boston Coll. 13

Las Vegas Bowl, Las Vegas, NV: Boise St. 26, Utah 3

Little Caesars Bowl, Detroit, MI: Florida International 34, Toledo 32

Meineke Car Care Bowl, Charlotte, NC: South Florida 31, Clemson 26

Military Bowl, Washington, DC: Maryland 51, East Carolina 20

Music City Bowl, Nashville, TN: North Carolina 30, Tennessee 27 (2 OT)

New Mexico Bowl, Albuquerque, NM: BYU 52, UTEP 24

New Orleans Bowl, New Orleans, LA: Troy 48, Ohio 21

Outback Bowl, Tampa, FL: Florida 37, Penn St. 24

Pinstripe Bowl, Bronx, NY: Syracuse 36, Kansas St. 34

Poinsettia Bowl, San Diego, CA: San Diego St. 35, Navy 14

St. Petersburg Bowl, St. Petersburg, FL: Louisville 31, Southern Mississippi 28

Texas Bowl, Houston, TX: Illinois 38, Baylor 14

TicketCity Bowl, Dallas, TX: Texas Tech 45, Northwestern 38

All-Time NCAA Division I-A (FBS) Statistical Leaders

(At end of 2010 season. Prior to 2002, postseason games were not included in NCAA final football statistics or records. Beginning with the 2002 season, all postseason games were included. Career rushing yards per game rankings do not include active players.)

Career Rushing Yards

Player, team	Yrs.	Carries	Yds.	Avg.
Ron Dayne, Wisconsin	1996-99	1,115	6,397	5.74
Ricky Williams, Texas	1995-98	1,011	6,279	6.21
Tony Dorsett, Pittsburgh	1973-76	1,074	6,082	5.66
DeAngelo Williams, Memphis	2002-05	969	6,026	6.22
Charles White, USC	1976-79	1,023	5,598	5.47

Career Passing Yards

Player, team	Yrs.	Comp./att.	Yds.
Timmy Chang, Hawaii	2000-04	1,388/2,436	17,072
Graham Harrell, Texas Tech	2005-08	1,403/2,010	15,793
Ty Detmer, BYU	1988-91	958/1,530	15,031
Colt Brennan, Hawaii	2005-07	1,115/1,584	14,193
Case Keenum, Houston	2007-10	1,118/1,626	13,586

Career Rushing Yards/Game (min. 2,500 yds.)

Player, team	Yrs.	Carries	Yds.	Avg./game
Ed Marinaro, Cornell	1969-71	918	4,715	174.6
O. J. Simpson, USC	1967-68	621	3,214	164.4
Herschel Walker, Georgia	1980-82	994	5,259	159.4
Garrett Wolfe, N. Illinois	2004-06	807	5,164	156.5
LeShon Johnson, N. Illinois	1992-93	592	3,314	150.6

Career Receiving Yards

Player, team	Yrs.	Rec.	Yds.	Avg.
Trevor Insley, Nevada	1996-99	298	5,005	16.8
Marcus Harris, Wyoming	1993-96	259	4,518	17.4
Rashaun Woods, Oklahoma St.	2000-03	293	4,414	15.1
Ryan Yarborough, Wyoming	1990-93	229	4,357	19.0
Troy Edwards, Louisiana Tech	1996-98	280	4,352	15.5

All-Time Division I-A (FBS) Team Won-Lost Records

Team	Years	Won	Lost	Tied	Pct.	Total
Michigan	131	884	308	36	0.735	1,228
Notre Dame	122	845	295	42	0.733	1,182
Ohio St.	121	830	309	53	0.719	1,192
Texas	118	850	325	33	0.717	1,208
Oklahoma	116	811	304	53	0.717	1,168
Boise St. (1996)	43	365	145	2	0.715	512
Alabama[1]	116	823	319	43	0.713	1,185
USC[1]	118	774	308	54	0.705	1,136
Nebraska	121	837	345	40	0.701	1,222
Tennessee	114	788	340	53	0.690	1,181
Penn St.	124	818	357	41	0.690	1,216
Florida St.[1]	64	476	231	17	0.669	724
Georgia	117	737	396	54	0.644	1,187
LSU	117	720	389	47	0.643	1,156
Miami (FL)	84	560	320	19	0.633	899
Auburn	118	703	400	47	0.632	1,150
Florida	104	662	379	40	0.631	1,081
South Fla. (2000)	14	103	62	0	0.624	165
Miami (OH)	122	660	394	44	0.621	1,098
Arizona St.	98	555	348	24	0.612	927
Washington	121	662	413	50	0.611	1,125
Virginia Tech	117	678	431	46	0.607	1,155
Central Mich.	110	573	366	36	0.606	975
Colorado	121	671	442	36	0.600	1,149
West Virginia	118	691	454	45	0.600	1,190

Note: As of end of 2010 season. Includes senior college only. Bowl and playoff games are included, and each tie game is computed as half won and half lost. Teams listed with years in parentheses indicates reclassification to Division I-A (FBS). The year in parentheses is the first year of Division I-A (FBS) membership. Tiebreaker rule began with 1996 season. (1) Record adjusted by action of the NCAA Committee on Infractions.

Heisman Trophy Winners, 1935-2010

Awarded annually to the nation's outstanding college football player by the Downtown Athletic Club.

1935 Jay Berwanger, Chicago, HB	1961 Ernest Davis, Syracuse, HB	1986 Vinny Testaverde, Miami (FL), QB
1936 Larry Kelley, Yale, E	1962 Terry Baker, Oregon St., QB	1987 Tim Brown, Notre Dame, WR
1937 Clinton Frank, Yale, HB	1963 Roger Staubach, Navy, QB	1988 Barry Sanders, Oklahoma St., RB
1938 David O'Brien, Texas Christian, QB	1964 John Huarte, Notre Dame, QB	1989 Andre Ware, Houston, QB
1939 Nile Kinnick, Iowa, HB	1965 Mike Garrett, USC, HB	1990 Ty Detmer, BYU, QB
1940 Tom Harmon, Michigan, HB	1966 Steve Spurrier, Florida, QB	1991 Desmond Howard, Michigan, WR
1941 Bruce Smith, Minnesota, HB	1967 Gary Beban, UCLA, QB	1992 Gino Torretta, Miami (FL), QB
1942 Frank Sinkwich, Georgia, HB	1968 O. J. Simpson, USC, RB	1993 Charlie Ward, Florida St., QB
1943 Angelo Bertelli, Notre Dame, QB	1969 Steve Owens, Oklahoma, RB	1994 Rashaan Salaam, Colorado, RB
1944 Leslie Horvath, Ohio St., QB	1970 Jim Plunkett, Stanford, QB	1995 Eddie George, Ohio St., RB
1945 Felix Blanchard, Army, FB	1971 Pat Sullivan, Auburn, QB	1996 Danny Wuerffel, Florida, QB
1946 Glenn Davis, Army, HB	1972 Johnny Rodgers, Nebraska, RB-WR	1997 Charles Woodson, Michigan, CB
1947 John Lujack, Notre Dame, QB	1973 John Cappelletti, Penn St., RB	1998 Ricky Williams, Texas, RB
1948 Doak Walker, SMU, HB	1974 Archie Griffin, Ohio St., RB	1999 Ron Dayne, Wisconsin, QB
1949 Leon Hart, Notre Dame, E	1975 Archie Griffin, Ohio St., RB	2000 Chris Weinke, Florida St., QB
1950 Vic Janowicz, Ohio St., HB	1976 Tony Dorsett, Pittsburgh, RB	2001 Eric Crouch, Nebraska, QB
1951 Richard Kazmaier, Princeton, HB	1977 Earl Campbell, Texas, RB	2002 Carson Palmer, USC, QB
1952 Billy Vessels, Oklahoma, HB	1978 Billy Sims, Oklahoma, RB	2003 Jason White, Oklahoma, QB
1953 John Lattner, Notre Dame, HB	1979 Charles White, USC, RB	2004 Matt Leinart, USC, QB
1954 Alan Ameche, Wisconsin, FB	1980 George Rogers, S. Carolina, RB	2005 Reggie Bush, USC, RB[1]
1955 Howard Cassady, Ohio St., HB	1981 Marcus Allen, USC, RB	2006 Troy Smith, Ohio State, QB
1956 Paul Hornung, Notre Dame, QB	1982 Herschel Walker, Georgia, RB	2007 Tim Tebow, Florida, QB
1957 John Crow, Texas A&M, HB	1983 Mike Rozier, Nebraska, RB	2008 Sam Bradford, Oklahoma, QB
1958 Pete Dawkins, Army, HB	1984 Doug Flutie, Boston College, QB	2009 Mark Ingram, Alabama, RB
1959 Billy Cannon, LSU, HB	1985 Bo Jackson, Auburn, RB	2010 Cam Newton, Auburn, QB
1960 Joe Bellino, Navy, HB		

(1) Bush forfeited the trophy voluntarily Sept. 14, 2010, following revelations of NCAA rules violations while Bush was at USC.

All-Time Division I-A (FBS) Coaching Victories

Joe Paterno	401	Hayden Fry	232	Dan McGugin	197	Johnny Majors	185
Bobby Bowden	377	**Frank Beamer**	240	Fielding Yost	196	Darrell Royal	184
Paul "Bear" Bryant	323	**Mack Brown**	219	Howard Jones	194	Dick Tomey	183
Glenn "Pop" Warner	319	Jess Neely	207	John Cooper	192	Gil Dobie	180
Amos Alonzo Stagg	314	Warren Woodson	203	John Vaught	190	Jackie Sherrill	180
LaVell Edwards	257	Don Nehlen	202	George Welsh	188	Carl Snavely	180
Tom Osborne	255	Eddie Anderson	201	Dennis Franchione	187	Jerry Claiborne	179
Lou Holtz	249	Vince Dooley	201	John Heisman	186	Carmen Cozza	179
Woody Hayes	238	Jim Sweeney	200	**Steve Spurrier**	186	Ben Schwartzwalder	178
Bo Schembechler	234	Dana X. Bible	198				

Note: Coaches active in 2010 shown in bold. Total victories through Jan. 10, 2011, including bowl games; coaches must have at least 10 seasons coaching BCS schools to be eligible.

College Football Coach of the Year, 1935-2010

The Division I-A (FBS) Coach of the Year has been selected by the American Football Coaches Assn. (AFCA) since 1935 and selected by the Football Writers Assn. of America (FWAA) since 1957. When polls disagree, both winners are indicated.

1935 Lynn Waldorf, Northwestern
1936 Dick Harlow, Harvard
1937 Edward Mylin, Lafayette
1938 Bill Kern, Carnegie Tech
1939 Eddie Anderson, Iowa
1940 Clark Shaughnessy, Stanford
1941 Frank Leahy, Notre Dame
1942 Bill Alexander, Georgia Tech
1943 Amos Alonzo Stagg, Pacific (CA)
1944 Carroll Widdoes, Ohio St.
1945 Bo McMillin, Indiana
1946 Earl "Red" Blaik, Army
1947 Fritz Crisler, Michigan
1948 Bennie Oosterbaan, Michigan
1949 Bud Wilkinson, Oklahoma
1950 Charlie Caldwell, Princeton
1951 Chuck Taylor, Stanford
1952 Biggie Munn, Michigan St.
1953 Jim Tatum, Maryland
1954 Henry "Red" Sanders, UCLA
1955 Duffy Daugherty, Michigan St.
1956 Bowden Wyatt, Tennessee
1957 Woody Hayes, Ohio St.
1958 Paul Dietzel, LSU
1959 Ben Schwartzwalder, Syracuse
1960 Murray Warmath, Minnesota
1961 Paul "Bear" Bryant, Ala. (AFCA); Darrell Royal, Texas (FWAA)
1962 John McKay, USC
1963 Darrell Royal, Texas
1964 Ara Parseghian, Notre Dame, & Frank Broyles, Arkansas (AFCA); Ara Parseghian (FWAA)

1965 Tommy Prothro, UCLA (AFCA); Duffy Daugherty, Mich. St. (FWAA)
1966 Tom Cahill, Army
1967 John Pont, Indiana
1968 Joe Paterno, Penn St. (AFCA); Woody Hayes, Ohio St. (FWAA)
1969 Bo Schembechler, Michigan
1970 Charles McClendon, LSU, and Darrell Royal, Texas (AFCA); Alex Agase, Northwestern (FWAA)
1971 Paul "Bear" Bryant, Alabama (AFCA); Bob Devaney, Nebraska (FWAA)
1972 John McKay, USC
1973 Paul "Bear" Bryant, Alabama (AFCA); Johnny Majors, Pittsburgh (FWAA)
1974 Grant Teaff, Baylor
1975 Frank Kush, Arizona St. (AFCA); Woody Hayes, Ohio St. (FWAA)
1976 Johnny Majors, Pittsburgh
1977 Don James, Washington (AFCA); Lou Holtz, Arkansas (FWAA)
1978 Joe Paterno, Penn St.
1979 Earle Bruce, Ohio St.
1980 Vince Dooley, Georgia
1981 Danny Ford, Clemson
1982 Joe Paterno, Penn St.
1983 Ken Hatfield, Air Force (AFCA); Howard Schnellenberger, Miami (FL) (FWAA)
1984 LaVell Edwards, Brigham Young
1985 Fisher De Berry, Air Force
1986 Joe Paterno, Penn St.
1987 Dick MacPherson, Syracuse

1988 Don Nehlen, W. Virginia (AFCA); Lou Holtz, Notre Dame (FWAA)
1989 Bill McCartney, Colorado
1990 Bobby Ross, Georgia Tech
1991 Don James, Washington
1992 Gene Stallings, Alabama
1993 Barry Alvarez, Wisconsin (AFCA); Terry Bowden, Auburn (FWAA)
1994 Tom Osborne, Nebraska (AFCA); Rich Brooks, Oregon (FWAA)
1995 Gary Barnett, Northwestern
1996 Bruce Snyder, Arizona St.
1997 Mike Price, Washington St.
1998 Phillip Fulmer, Tennessee
1999 Frank Beamer, Virginia Tech
2000 Bob Stoops, Oklahoma
2001 Larry Coker, Miami (FL), & Ralph Friedgen, Maryland (AFCA); Ralph Friedgen, Maryland (FWAA)
2002 Jim Tressel, Ohio St.
2003 Pete Carroll, USC (AFCA); Nick Saban, LSU (FWAA)
2004 Tommy Tuberville, Auburn (AFCA); Urban Meyer, Utah (FWAA)
2005 Joe Paterno, Penn St. (AFCA); Charlie Weis, Notre Dame (FWAA)
2006 Jim Grobe, Wake Forest (AFCA); Greg Schiano, Rutgers (FWAA)
2007 Mark Mangino, Kansas
2008 Kyle Whittingham, Utah (AFCA); Nick Saban, Alabama (FWAA)
2009 Gary Patterson, TCU
2010 Chip Kelly, Oregon

NCAA Div. I-A (FBS) Football Conference Champions, 1980-2010

Atlantic Coast
1980 North Carolina
1981 Clemson
1982 Clemson
1983 Maryland
1984 Maryland
1985 Maryland
1986 Clemson
1987 Clemson
1988 Clemson
1989 Virginia, Duke
1990 Georgia Tech
1991 Clemson
1992 Florida St.
1993 Florida St.
1994 Florida St.
1995 Virginia, Florida St.
1996 Florida St.
1997 Florida St.
1998 Florida St., Georgia Tech
1999 Florida St.
2000 Florida St.
2001 Maryland
2002 Florida St.
2003 Florida St.
2004 Virginia Tech
2005 Florida St.
2006 Wake Forest
2007 Virginia Tech
2008 Virginia Tech
2009 Georgia Tech
2010 Virginia Tech

Big East
1991 Miami (FL), Syracuse
1992 Miami (FL)
1993 West Virginia
1994 Miami (FL)
1995 Virginia Tech, Miami (FL)
1996 Virginia Tech, Miami (FL), Syracuse
1997 Syracuse
1998 Syracuse
1999 Virginia Tech
2000 Miami (FL)
2001 Miami (FL)
2002 Miami (FL)
2003 Miami (FL), West Virginia
2004 Boston College, Pittsburgh, Syracuse, W. Virginia
2005 West Virginia
2006 Louisville
2007 Connecticut, West Virginia
2008 Cincinnati
2009 Cincinnati
2010 Connecticut, Pittsburgh, West Virginia

Big Ten
1980 Michigan
1981 Iowa, Ohio St.
1982 Michigan
1983 Illinois
1984 Ohio St.
1985 Iowa
1986 Michigan, Ohio St.
1987 Michigan St.
1988 Michigan
1989 Michigan
1990 Iowa, Illinois, Mich., Mich. St.
1991 Michigan
1992 Michigan
1993 Ohio St., Wisconsin
1994 Penn St.
1995 Northwestern
1996 Northwestern, Ohio St.
1997 Michigan
1998 Michigan, Ohio St., Wisconsin
1999 Wisconsin
2000 Michigan, Northwestern, Purdue
2001 Illinois
2002 Iowa, Ohio St.
2003 Michigan
2004 Iowa, Michigan
2005 Penn St., Ohio St.
2006 Ohio St.
2007 Ohio St.
2008 Penn St., Ohio St.
2009 Ohio St.
2010 Wisconsin

Big 12
1996 Texas
1997 Nebraska
1998 Texas A&M
1999 Nebraska
2000 Oklahoma
2001 Colorado
2002 Oklahoma
2003 Kansas St.
2004 Oklahoma
2005 Texas
2006 Oklahoma
2007 Oklahoma
2008 Oklahoma
2009 Texas
2010 Oklahoma

Conference USA
1996 Houston, So. Mississippi
1997 So. Mississippi
1998 Tulane
1999 So. Mississippi
2000 Louisville
2001 Louisville
2002 Cincinnati, TCU
2003 So. Mississippi
2004 Louisville
2005 Tulsa
2006 Houston
2007 Central Florida
2008 East Carolina
2009 East Carolina
2010 Central Florida

Mid-American Athletic
1980 Central Michigan
1981 Toledo
1982 Bowling Green
1983 Northern Illinois
1984 Toledo
1985 Bowling Green
1986 Miami (OH)
1987 E. Michigan
1988 W. Michigan
1989 Ball St.
1990 Central Michigan
1991 Bowling Green
1992 Bowling Green
1993 Ball St.
1994 Central Michigan
1995 Toledo
1996 Ball St.
1997 Marshall
1998 Marshall
1999 Marshall
2000 Marshall
2001 Toledo
2002 Marshall
2003 Miami (OH)
2004 Toledo
2005 Akron
2006 Central Michigan
2007 Central Michigan
2008 Buffalo
2009 Central Michigan
2010 Miami (OH)

Mountain West
1999 BYU, Colorado St., Utah
2000 Colorado St.
2001 BYU
2002 Colorado St.
2003 Utah
2004 Utah
2005 TCU
2006 BYU, TCU
2007 BYU
2008 Utah
2009 TCU
2010 TCU

Pacific Ten
1980 Washington
1981 Washington
1982 UCLA
1983 UCLA
1984 USC
1985 UCLA
1986 Arizona St.
1987 UCLA, USC
1988 USC

1989 USC
1990 Washington
1991 Washington
1992 Stanford, Washington
1993 Arizona, UCLA, USC
1994 Oregon
1995 USC, Washington
1996 Arizona St.
1997 UCLA, Washington St.
1998 UCLA
1999 Stanford
2000 Oregon, Oregon St., Washington
2001 Oregon
2002 USC, Washington St.
2003 USC
2004 USC
2005 USC
2006 California, USC
2007 Arizona St., USC

2008 USC
2009 Oregon
2010 Oregon

Southeastern
1980 Georgia
1981 Alabama, Georgia
1982 Georgia
1983 Auburn
1984 Florida (title vacated)
1985 Tennessee
1986 LSU
1987 Auburn
1988 Auburn, LSU
1989 Ala., Auburn, Tenn.
1990 Tennessee
1991 Florida
1992 Alabama
1993 Florida
1994 Florida
1995 Florida
1996 Florida
1997 Tennessee
1998 Tennessee

1999 Alabama
2000 Florida
2001 LSU
2002 Georgia
2003 LSU
2004 Auburn
2005 Georgia
2006 Florida
2007 LSU
2008 Florida
2009 Alabama
2010 Auburn

Sun Belt
2001 Middle Tenn. St., North Texas
2002 North Texas
2003 North Texas
2004 North Texas
2005 Arkansas St., LA-Lafayette, LA-Monroe
2006 Middle Tenn. St., Troy

2007 Florida Atlantic, Troy
2008 Troy
2009 Troy
2010 Florida Intl., Troy

Western Athletic
1980 Brigham Young (BYU)
1981 BYU
1982 BYU
1983 BYU
1984 BYU
1985 Air Force, BYU
1986 San Diego St.
1987 Wyoming
1988 Wyoming
1989 BYU
1990 BYU
1991 BYU
1992 BYU, Fresno St., Hawaii
1993 BYU, Fresno St., Wyoming

1994 Colorado St.
1995 Air Force, BYU, Colorado St., Utah
1996 BYU
1997 Colorado St.
1998 Air Force
1999 Fresno St., Hawaii, TCU
2000 TCU, UTEP
2001 Louisiana Tech
2002 Boise State
2003 Boise State
2004 Boise State
2005 Boise State, Nevada
2006 Boise State
2007 Hawaii
2008 Boise State
2009 Boise State
2010 Boise State, Hawaii, Nevada

NCAA Div. I-AA (FCS) Football Conference Champions, 1990-2010

Big Sky
1990 Nevada
1991 Nevada
1992 Eastern Wash., Idaho
1993 Montana
1994 Boise St.
1995 Montana
1996 Montana
1997 Eastern Wash.
1998 Montana
1999 Montana
2000 Montana
2001 Montana
2002 Idaho St., Montana, Montana St., No. Arizona
2003 Montana, Montana St., No. Arizona
2004 Eastern Wash., Montana
2005 Eastern Wash., Montana, Montana St.
2006 Montana
2007 Montana
2008 Montana, Weber St.
2009 Montana
2010 Eastern Wash., Montana St.

Big South
2002 Gardner-Webb
2003 Gardner-Webb
2004 Coastal Carolina
2005 Charleston Southern, Coastal Carolina
2006 Coastal Carolina
2007 Liberty
2008 Liberty
2009 Liberty, Stony Brook
2010 Coastal Carolina, Liberty, Stony Brook

Colonial Athletic Association
2007 Massachusetts, Richmond
2008 James Madison
2009 Richmond, Villanova
2010 Delaware, William & Mary

Great West
2004 Cal. Poly
2005 Cal. Poly, UC Davis
2006 North Dakota St.
2007 South Dakota St.
2008 Cal. Poly
2009 UC Davis
2010 Southern Utah

Ivy League
1990 Cornell, Dartmouth
1991 Dartmouth

1992 Dartmouth, Princeton
1993 Pennsylvania
1994 Pennsylvania
1995 Princeton
1996 Dartmouth
1997 Harvard
1998 Pennsylvania
1999 Brown, Yale
2000 Pennsylvania
2001 Harvard
2002 Pennsylvania
2003 Pennsylvania
2004 Harvard
2005 Brown
2006 Princeton, Yale
2007 Harvard
2008 Harvard, Brown
2009 Pennsylvania
2010 Pennsylvania

Mid-Eastern Athletic
1990 Florida A&M
1991 North Carolina A&T
1992 North Carolina A&T
1993 Howard
1994 South Carolina St.
1995 Florida A&M
1996 Florida A&M
1997 Hampton
1998 Florida A&M, Hampton
1999 North Carolina A&T
2000 Florida A&M
2001 Florida A&M
2002 Bethune-Cookman
2003 North Carolina A&T
2004 Hampton, South Carolina St.
2005 Hampton
2006 Hampton
2007 Delaware St.
2008 South Carolina St.
2009 South Carolina St.
2010 Bethune-Cookman, Florida A&M, South Carolina St.

Missouri Valley
1990 Northern Iowa
1991 Northern Iowa
1992 Northern Iowa
1993 Northern Iowa
1994 Northern Iowa
1995 Eastern Illinois, N. Iowa
1996 Northern Iowa
1997 Western Illinois
1998 Western Illinois
1999 Illinois St.
2000 Western Illinois
2001 Northern Iowa

2002 W. Illinois, W. Kentucky
2003 N. Iowa, S. Illinois
2004 Southern Illinois
2005 N. Iowa, S. Illinois, Youngstown St.
2006 Youngstown St.
2007 Northern Iowa
2008 N. Iowa, S. Illinois
2009 Southern Illinois
2010 Northern Iowa

Northeast
1996 Monmouth, Robert Morris
1997 Robert Morris
1998 Monmouth, Robert Morris
1999 Robert Morris
2000 Robert Morris
2001 Sacred Heart
2002 Albany
2003 Albany, Monmouth
2004 Central Conn. St., Monmouth
2005 Central Conn. St., Stony Brook
2006 Monmouth
2007 Albany
2008 Albany
2009 Central Conn. St.
2010 Central Conn. St., Robert Morris

Ohio Valley
1990 E. Kentucky, Middle Tenn. St.
1991 Middle Tenn. St.
1992 Middle Tenn. St.
1993 Eastern Kentucky
1994 Eastern Kentucky
1995 Murray St.
1996 Murray St.
1997 Eastern Kentucky
1998 Tennessee St.
1999 Tennessee St.
2000 Western Kentucky
2001 Eastern Illinois
2002 E. Illinois, Murray St.
2003 Jacksonville St.
2004 Jacksonville St.
2005 Eastern Illinois
2006 E. Illinois, Tenn.-Martin
2007 Eastern Kentucky
2008 Eastern Kentucky
2009 Eastern Illinois
2010 SE Missouri St.

Patriot
1990 Holy Cross
1991 Holy Cross

1992 Lafayette
1993 Lehigh
1994 Lafayette
1995 Lehigh
1996 Bucknell
1997 Colgate
1998 Lehigh
1999 Colgate, Lehigh
2000 Lehigh
2001 Lehigh
2002 Colgate, Fordham
2003 Colgate
2004 Lafayette, Lehigh
2005 Colgate, Lafayette
2006 Colgate, Lafayette, Lehigh
2007 Fordham
2008 Colgate
2009 Holy Cross
2010 Lehigh

Pioneer
1993 Dayton
1994 Butler, Dayton
1995 Drake
1996 Dayton
1997 Dayton
1998 Drake
1999 Dayton
2000 Dayton, Drake, Valparaiso
2001 Dayton
2002 Dayton
2003 Valparaiso
2004 Drake
2005 San Diego
2006 San Diego
2007 Dayton, San Diego
2008 Jacksonville
2009 Butler, Dayton
2010 Dayton, Jacksonville

Southern
1990 Furman
1991 Appalachian St.
1992 Citadel
1993 Georgia Southern
1994 Marshall
1995 Appalachian St.
1996 Marshall
1997 Georgia Southern
1998 Georgia Southern
1999 Appalachian St., Furman, Georgia Southern
2000 Georgia Southern
2001 Furman, Southern
2002 Georgia Southern
2003 Wofford
2004 Furman, Georgia Southern

2005 Appalachian St.
2006 Appalachian St.
2007 Appalachian St., Wofford
2008 Appalachian St.
2009 Appalachian St.
2010 Appalachian St., Wofford

Southland
1990 La.-Monroe
1991 McNeese St.
1992 La.-Monroe
1993 McNeese St.
1994 North Texas
1995 McNeese St.
1996 Troy St.
1997 McNeese St., Northwestern St.
1998 Northwestern St.
1999 Stephen F. Austin, Troy
2000 Troy
2001 McNeese St., Sam Houston St.
2002 McNeese St.
2003 McNeese St.
2004 Northwestern St., Sam Houston St.
2005 Nicholls St., Texas St.
2006 McNeese St.
2007 McNeese St.
2008 Texas State
2009 McNeese St., Stephen F. Austin
2010 Stephen F. Austin

Southwestern Athletic
1990 Jackson St.
1991 Alabama St.
1992 Alcorn St.
1993 Southern
1994 Alcorn St., Grambling St.
1995 Jackson St.
1996 Jackson St.
1997 Southern
1998 Southern
1999 Southern
2000 Grambling St.
2001 Grambling St.
2002 Grambling St.
2003 Southern
2004 Alabama St.
2005 Grambling St.
2006 Alabama A&M
2007 Jackson St.
2008 Grambling St.
2009 Prairie View A&M
2010 Texas Southern

Note: Missouri Valley Conference was known as Gateway Football Conference, 1992-2007, and as Gateway Collegiate Athletic Conference, 1985-91.

Selected NCAA Division I Teams

(Conferences and coaches listed are as of Sept. 2011.)

Team	Nickname	Team colors	Conference	Basketball coach	Football coach
Air Force	Falcons	Blue & silver	Mountain West	Jeff Reynolds	Troy Calhoun
Akron	Zips	Blue & gold	Mid-American	Keith Dambrot	Rob Ianello
Alabama	Crimson Tide	Crimson & white	Southeastern	Anthony Grant	Nick Saban
Appalachian State*	Mountaineers	Black & gold	Southern	Jason Capel	Jerry Moore
Arizona	Wildcats	Cardinal & navy	Pac-12	Sean Miller	Mike Stoops
Arizona State	Sun Devils	Maroon & gold	Pac-12	Herb Sendek	Dennis Erickson
Arkansas	Razorbacks	Cardinal & white	Southeastern	Mike Anderson	Bobby Petrino
Arkansas State	Red Wolves	Scarlet & black	Sun Belt	John Brady	Hugh Freeze
Army	Black Knights	Black, gold, & gray	Independent	Zach Spiker	Rich Ellerson
Auburn	Tigers	Burnt orange & navy	Southeastern	Tony Barbee	Gene Chizik
Ball State	Cardinals	Cardinal & white	Mid-American	Billy Taylor	Pete Lembo
Baylor	Bears	Green & gold	Big 12	Scott Drew	Art Briles
Boise State	Broncos	Blue & orange	Mountain West	Leon Rice	Chris Petersen
Boston College	Eagles	Maroon & gold	Atlantic Coast	Steve Donahue	Frank Spaziani
Bowling Green	Falcons	Orange & brown	Mid-American	Louis Orr	Dave Clawson
Brigham Young (BYU)	Cougars	Dark blue & white	Independent#	Dave Rose	Bronco Mendenhall
Brown*	Bears	Brown, cardinal, & white	Ivy League	Jesse Agel	Phil Estes
California	Golden Bears	Blue & gold	Pac-12	Mike Montgomery	Jeff Tedford
Central Michigan	Chippewas	Maroon & gold	Mid-American	Ernie Zeigler	Dan Enos
Cincinnati	Bearcats	Red & black	Big East	Mick Cronin	Butch Jones
Citadel*	Bulldogs	Blue & white	Southern	Chuck Driesell	Kevin Higgins
Clemson	Tigers	Burnt orange & purple	Atlantic Coast	Brad Brownell	Dabo Swinney
Colgate*	Raiders	Maroon, gray, & white	Patriot League	Matt Langel	Dick Biddle
Colorado	Buffaloes	Silver, gold, & black	Big 12	Tad Boyle	Jon Embree
Colorado State	Rams	Green & gold	Mountain West	Tim Miles	Steve Fairchild
Columbia*	Lions	Columbia blue & white	Ivy League	Kyle Smith	Norries Wilson
Connecticut	Huskies	Blue & white	Big East	Jim Calhoun	Paul Pasqualoni
Cornell*	Big Red	Carnelian & white	Ivy League	Bill Courtney	Kent Austin
Dartmouth*	Big Green	Dartmouth green & white	Ivy League	Paul Cormier	Buddy Teevens
Delaware*	Fightin' Blue Hens	Blue & gold	Colonial Athletic	Monté Ross	K. C. Keeler
Duke	Blue Devils	Royal blue & white	Atlantic Coast	Mike Krzyzewski	David Cutcliffe
East Carolina	Pirates	Purple & gold	Conference USA	Jeff Lebo	Ruffin McNeill
Eastern Illinois*	Panthers	Blue & gray	Ohio Valley	Mike Miller	Bob Spoo
Eastern Kentucky*	Colonels	Maroon & white	Ohio Valley	Jeff Neubauer	Dean Hood
Eastern Michigan	Eagles	Dark green & white	Mid-American	Rob Murphy	Ron English
Eastern Washington*	Eagles	Red & white	Big Sky	Jim Hayford	Beau Baldwin
Florida	Gators	Orange & blue	Southeastern	Billy Donovan	Will Muschamp
Florida A&M*	Rattlers	Orange & green	Mid-Eastern Athletic	Clemon Johnson	Joe Taylor
Florida State	Seminoles	Garnet & gold	Atlantic Coast	Leonard Hamilton	Jimbo Fisher
Fresno State	Bulldogs	Red & blue	Western Athletic[1]	Rodney Terry	Pat Hill
Furman*	Paladins	Purple & white	Southern	Jeff Jackson	Bruce Fowler
Georgia	Bulldogs	Red & black	Southeastern	Mark Fox	Mark Richt
Georgia Southern*	Eagles	Blue & white	Southern	Charlton Young	Jeff Monken
Georgia Tech	Yellow Jackets	Old gold & white	Atlantic Coast	Brian Gregory	Paul Johnson
Harvard*	Crimson	Crimson & white	Ivy League	Tommy Amaker	Tim Murphy
Hawaii	Warriors	Green, black, white, silver	Western Athletic[1]	Gib Arnold	Greg McMackin
Holy Cross*	Crusaders	Royal purple	Patriot League	Milan Brown	Tom Gilmore
Houston	Cougars	Scarlet & white	Conference USA	James Dickey	Kevin Sumlin
Howard*	Bison	Blue, red, & white	Mid-Eastern Athletic	Kevin Nickelberry	Gary Harrell
Idaho	Vandals	Silver & gold	Western Athletic	Don Verlin	Robb Akey
Illinois	Fighting Illini	Orange & blue	Big Ten	Bruce Weber	Ron Zook
Illinois State*	Redbirds	Red & white	Missouri Valley	Tim Jankovich	Brock Spack
Indiana	Hoosiers	Cream & crimson	Big Ten	Tom Crean	Kevin Wilson
Indiana State*	Sycamores	Blue & white	Missouri Valley	Greg Lansing	Trent Miles
Iowa	Hawkeyes	Old gold & black	Big Ten	Fran McCaffery	Kirk Ferentz
Iowa State	Cyclones	Cardinal & gold	Big 12	Fred Hoiberg	Paul Rhoads
Jackson State*	Tigers	Blue & white	Southwestern Athletic	Tevester Anderson	Rick Comegy
James Madison*	Dukes	Purple & gold	Colonial Athletic	Matt Brady	Mickey Matthews
Kansas	Jayhawks	Crimson & blue	Big 12	Bill Self	Turner Gill
Kansas State	Wildcats	Royal purple	Big 12	Frank Martin	Bill Snyder
Kent State	Golden Flashes	Navy blue & gold	Mid-American	Rob Senderoff	Darrell Hazell
Kentucky	Wildcats	Blue & white	Southeastern	John Calipari	Joker Phillips
Lafayette*	Leopards	Maroon & white	Patriot League	Fran O'Hanlon	Frank Tavani
Lehigh*	Mountain Hawks	Brown & white	Patriot League	Brett Reed	Andy Coen
Liberty*	Flames	Red, white, & blue	Big South	Dale Layer	Danny Rocco
Louisiana State (LSU)	Fighting Tigers	Purple & gold	Southeastern	Trent Johnson	Les Miles
Louisiana Tech	Bulldogs	Red & blue	Western Athletic	Michael White	Sonny Dykes
Louisiana-Lafayette	Ragin' Cajuns	Vermilion & white	Sun Belt	Bob Marlin	Mark Hudspeth
Louisiana-Monroe	Warhawks	Maroon & gold	Sun Belt	Keith Richard	Todd Berry
Louisville	Cardinals	Red, black, & white	Big East	Rick Pitino	Charlie Strong
Maine*	Black Bears	Blue & white	Colonial Athletic#	Ted Woodward	Jack Cosgrove
Marshall	Thundering Herd	Kelly green & white	Conference USA	Tom Herrion	Doc Holliday
Maryland	Terrapins	Red, white, black, gold	Atlantic Coast	Mark Turgeon	Randy Edsall
Massachusetts*	Minutemen	Maroon & white	Colonial Athletic[1]	Derek Kellogg	Kevin Morris
Memphis	Tigers	Blue & gray	Conference USA	Josh Pastner	Larry Porter
Miami (Florida)	Hurricanes	Orange, green, & white	Atlantic Coast	Jim Larranaga	Al Golden
Miami (Ohio)	RedHawks	Red & white	Mid-American	Charlie Coles	Don Treadwell
Michigan	Wolverines	Maize & blue	Big Ten	John Beilein	Brady Hoke
Michigan State	Spartans	Green & white	Big Ten	Tom Izzo	Mark Dantonio
Mid. Tennessee State	Blue Raiders	Royal blue & white	Sun Belt	Kermit Davis	Rick Stockstill
Minnesota	Golden Gophers	Maroon & gold	Big Ten	Tubby Smith	Jerry Kill
Mississippi	Rebels	Cardinal red & navy blue	Southeastern	Andy Kennedy	Houston Nutt
Mississippi State	Bulldogs	Maroon & white	Southeastern	Rick Stansbury	Dan Mullen
Missouri	Tigers	Old gold & black	Big 12	Frank Haith	Gary Pinkel

Team	Nickname	Team colors	Conference	Basketball coach	Football coach
Montana*	Grizzlies	Copper, silver, & gold	Big Sky	Wayne Tinkle	Robin Pflugrad
Montana State*	Bobcats	Blue & gold	Big Sky	Brad Huse	Rob Ash
Morgan State*	Bears	Blue & orange	Mid-Eastern Athletic	Todd Bozeman	Donald Hill-Eley
Murray State*	Racers	Navy blue & gold	Ohio Valley	Steve Prohm	Chris Hatcher
Navy	Midshipmen	Navy blue & gold	Independent	Ed DeChellis	Ken Niumatalolo
Nebraska	Cornhuskers	Scarlet & cream	Big Ten	Doc Sadler	Bo Pelini
Nevada	Wolf Pack	Cobalt blue & silver	Western Athletic[1]	David Carter	Chris Ault
Nevada-Las Vegas (UNLV)	Rebels	Scarlet & gray	Mountain West	Dave Rice	Bobby Hauck
New Hampshire*	Wildcats	Blue & white	Colonial Athletic#	Bill Herrion	Sean McDonnell
New Mexico	Lobos	Cherry & silver	Mountain West	Steve Alford	Mike Locksley
New Mexico State	Aggies	Crimson & white	Western Athletic	Marvin Menzies	DeWayne Walker
Nicholls State*	Colonels	Red & gray	Southland	J. P. Piper	Charlie Stubbs
North Carolina	Tar Heels	Carolina blue & white	Atlantic Coast	Roy Williams	Everett Withers
North Carolina State	Wolfpack	Red & white	Atlantic Coast	Mark Gottfried	Tom O'Brien
North Texas	Mean Green	Green & white	Sun Belt	Johnny Jones	Dan McCarney
Northern Illinois	Huskies	Cardinal & black	Mid-American	Mark Montgomery	Dave Doeren
Northern Iowa*	Panthers	Purple & gold	Missouri Valley	Ben Jacobson	Mark Farley
Northwestern	Wildcats	Purple & white	Big Ten	Bill Carmody	Pat Fitzgerald
Northwestern State*	Demons	Purple, white, & orange	Southland	Mike McConathy	Bradley Dale Peveto
Notre Dame	Fighting Irish	Gold & blue	Independent#	Mike Brey	Brian Kelly
Ohio	Bobcats	Hunter green & white	Mid-American	John Groce	Frank Solich
Ohio State	Buckeyes	Scarlet & gray	Big Ten	Thad Matta	Luke Fickell
Oklahoma	Sooners	Crimson & cream	Big 12	Lon Kruger	Bob Stoops
Oklahoma State	Cowboys	Orange & black	Big 12	Travis Ford	Mike Gundy
Oregon	Ducks	Green & yellow	Pac-12	Dana Altman	Chip Kelly
Oregon State	Beavers	Orange & black	Pac-12	Craig Robinson	Mike Riley
Penn State	Nittany Lions	Blue & white	Big Ten	Patrick Chambers	Joe Paterno
Pennsylvania*	Quakers	Red & blue	Ivy League	Jerome Allen	Al Bagnoli
Pittsburgh	Panthers	Blue & gold	Big East	Jamie Dixon	Todd Graham
Princeton*	Tigers	Orange & black	Ivy League	Mitch Henderson	Bob Surace
Purdue	Boilermakers	Old gold & black	Big Ten	Matt Painter	Danny Hope
Rhode Island*	Rams	Keaney blue, dark blue, white	Colonial Athletic#	Jim Baron	Joe Trainer
Rice	Owls	Blue & gray	Conference USA	Ben Braun	David Bailiff
Richmond*	Spiders	Red & blue	Colonial Athletic#	Chris Mooney	Latrell Scott
Rutgers	Scarlet Knights	Scarlet	Big East	Mike Rice	Greg Schiano
Sam Houston State*	Bearkats	Orange & white	Southland	Jason Hooten	Willie Fritz
San Diego State	Aztecs	Scarlet & black	Mountain West	Steve Fisher	Rocky Long
San Jose State	Spartans	Gold & blue	Western Athletic	George Nessman	Mike MacIntyre
SE Missouri State*	Redhawks	Red & black	Ohio Valley	Dickey Nutt	Tony Samuel
South Carolina	Gamecocks	Garnet & black	Southeastern	Darrin Horn	Steve Spurrier
South Carolina State*	Bulldogs	Garnet & blue	Mid-Eastern Athletic	Tim Carter	Oliver Pough
South Florida	Bulls	Green & gold	Big East	Stan Heath	Skip Holtz
Southern California (USC)	Trojans	Cardinal & gold	Pac-12	Kevin O'Neill	Lane Kiffin
Southern Illinois*	Salukis	Maroon & white	Missouri Valley	Chris Lowery	Dale Lennon
Southern Methodist (SMU)	Mustangs	Crimson & blue	Conference USA	Matt Doherty	June Jones
Southern Mississippi	Golden Eagles	Black & gold	Conference USA	Larry Eustachy	Larry Fedora
Stanford	Cardinal	Red & white	Pac-12	Johnny Dawkins	David Shaw
Stephen F. Austin*	Lumberjacks	Purple & white	Southland	Danny Kaspar	J. C. Harper
Syracuse	Orange	Orange	Big East	Jim Boeheim	Doug Marrone
Temple	Owls	Cherry & white	Mid-American#	Fran Dunphy	Steve Addazio
Tennessee	Volunteers	Orange & white	Southeastern	Cuonzo Martin	Derek Dooley
Tennessee State*	Tigers	Royal blue & white	Ohio Valley	John Cooper	Rod Reed
Tennessee Tech*	Golden Eagles	Purple & gold	Ohio Valley	Mike Sutton	Watson Brown
Texas	Longhorns	Burnt orange & white	Big 12	Rick Barnes	Mack Brown
Texas A&M	Aggies	Maroon & white	Big 12	Billy Kennedy	Mike Sherman
Texas Christian (TCU)	Horned Frogs	Purple & white	Mountain West[1]	Jim Christian	Gary Patterson
Texas Southern*	Tigers	Maroon & gray	Southwestern Athletic	Tony Harvey	Kevin Ramsey
Texas State*	Bobcats	Maroon & gold	Southland[1]	Doug Davalos	Dennis Franchione
Texas Tech	Red Raiders	Scarlet & black	Big 12	Billy Gillispie	Tommy Tuberville
Toledo	Rockets	Midnight blue & gold	Mid-American	Tod Kowalczyk	Tim Beckman
Troy	Trojans	Cardinal, black, & silver	Sun Belt	Don Maestri	Larry Blakeney
Tulane	Green Wave	Olive green & sky blue	Conference USA	Ed Conroy	Bob Toledo
Tulsa	Golden Hurricane	Blue, gold, & crimson	Conference USA	Doug Wojcik	Bill Blankenship
UCLA	Bruins	Blue & gold	Pacific Ten	Ben Howland	Rick Neuheisel
Utah	Utes	Crimson & white	Pac-12	Larry Krystkowiak	Kyle Whittingham
Utah State	Aggies	Navy blue & white	Western Athletic	Stew Morrill	Gary Andersen
UTEP (Texas-El Paso)	Miners	Orange, blue, white, silver	Conference USA	Tim Floyd	Mike Price
Vanderbilt	Commodores	Black & gold	Southeastern	Kevin Stallings	James Franklin
Villanova*	Wildcats	Blue & white	Colonial Athletic#	Jay Wright	Andy Talley
Virginia	Cavaliers	Orange & navy blue	Atlantic Coast	Tony Bennett	Mike London
Virginia Tech	Hokies	Burnt orange & maroon	Atlantic Coast	Seth Greenberg	Frank Beamer
Wake Forest	Demon Deacons	Old gold & black	Atlantic Coast	Jeff Bzdelik	Jim Grobe
Washington	Huskies	Purple & gold	Pac-12	Lorenzo Romar	Steve Sarkisian
Washington State	Cougars	Crimson & gray	Pac-12	Ken Bone	Paul Wulff
Weber State*	Wildcats	Royal purple & white	Big Sky	Randy Rahe	Ron McBride
West Virginia	Mountaineers	Old gold & blue	Big East	Bob Huggins	Dana Holgorsen
Western Illinois*	Leathernecks	Purple & gold	Missouri Valley#	Jim Molinari	Mark Hendrickson
Western Kentucky	Hilltoppers	Red & white	Sun Belt	Ken McDonald	Willie Taggart
Western Michigan	Broncos	Brown & gold	Mid-American	Steve Hawkins	Bill Cubit
William & Mary*	Tribe	Green, gold, & silver	Colonial Athletic	Tony Shaver	Jimmye Laycock
Wisconsin	Badgers	Cardinal & white	Big Ten	Bo Ryan	Bret Bielema
Wyoming	Cowboys	Brown & gold	Mountain West	Larry Shyatt	Dave Christensen
Yale*	Bulldogs, Elis	Yale blue & white	Ivy League	James Jones	Tom Williams
Youngstown State*	Penguins	Red & white	Missouri Valley#	Jerry Slocum	Eric Wolford

* = Football Championship Subdivision (FCS) team (formerly known as I-AA). # = Team competes in conference listed in football, but not basketball. (1) Team is expected to change conferences on July 1, 2012. Fresno State, Hawaii, Nevada: Mountain West. Massachusetts: Mid-American. TCU: Big East. Texas State: Western Athletic.

COLLEGE BASEBALL/SOFTBALL

NCAA Men's Baseball Division I Champions, 1947-2011

1947 California	1959 Oklahoma St.	1972 USC	1985 Miami (FL)	1999 Miami (FL)
1948 Southern California	1960 Minnesota	1973 USC	1986 Arizona	2000 LSU
	1961 USC	1974 USC	1987 Stanford	2001 Miami (FL)
1949 Texas	1962 Michigan	1975 Texas	1988 Stanford	2002 Texas
1950 Texas	1963 USC	1976 Arizona	1989 Wichita St.	2003 Rice
1951 Oklahoma	1964 Minnesota	1977 Arizona St.	1990 Georgia	2004 Cal. St.-Fullerton
1952 Holy Cross	1965 Arizona St.	1978 USC	1991 LSU	2005 Texas
1953 Michigan	1966 Ohio St.	1979 Cal. St.-Fullerton	1992 Pepperdine	2006 Oregon St.
1954 Missouri	1967 Arizona St.	1980 Arizona	1993 LSU	2007 Oregon St.
1955 Wake Forest	1968 USC	1981 Arizona St.	1994 Oklahoma	2008 Fresno St.
1956 Minnesota	1969 Arizona St.	1982 Miami (FL)	1995 Cal. St.-Fullerton	2009 LSU
1957 California	1970 USC	1983 Texas	1996 LSU	2010 South Carolina
1958 USC	1971 USC	1984 Cal. St.-Fullerton	1997 LSU	2011 South Carolina
			1998 USC	

NCAA Women's Softball Division I Champions, 1982-2011

1982 UCLA	1988 UCLA	1994 Arizona	2000 Oklahoma	2006 Arizona
1983 Texas A&M	1989 UCLA	1995 UCLA	2001 Arizona	2007 Arizona
1984 UCLA	1990 UCLA	1996 Arizona	2002 California	2008 Arizona St.
1985 UCLA	1991 Arizona	1997 Arizona	2003 UCLA	2009 Washington
1986 Cal St. Fullerton	1992 UCLA	1998 Fresno St.	2004 UCLA	2010 UCLA
1987 Texas A&M	1993 Arizona	1999 UCLA	2005 Michigan	2011 Arizona St.

COLLEGE HOCKEY

NCAA Men's Hockey Champions, 1948-2011

1948 Michigan	1961 Denver	1974 Minnesota	1987 North Dakota	2000 North Dakota
1949 Boston College	1962 Michigan Tech	1975 Michigan Tech	1988 Lake Superior St.	2001 Boston College
1950 Colorado College	1963 North Dakota	1976 Minnesota	1989 Harvard	2002 Minnesota
1951 Michigan	1964 Michigan	1977 Wisconsin	1990 Wisconsin	2003 Minnesota
1952 Michigan	1965 Michigan Tech	1978 Boston Univ.	1991 N. Michigan	2004 Denver
1953 Michigan	1966 Michigan State	1979 Minnesota	1992 Lake Superior St.	2005 Denver
1954 Rensselaer	1967 Cornell	1980 North Dakota	1993 Maine	2006 Wisconsin
1955 Michigan	1968 Denver	1981 Wisconsin	1994 Lake Superior St.	2007 Michigan State
1956 Michigan	1969 Denver	1982 North Dakota	1995 Boston Univ.	2008 Boston College
1957 Colorado College	1970 Cornell	1983 Wisconsin	1996 Michigan	2009 Boston Univ.
1958 Denver	1971 Boston Univ.	1984 Bowling Green	1997 North Dakota	2010 Boston College
1959 North Dakota	1972 Boston Univ.	1985 Rensselaer	1998 Michigan	2011 Minnesota-Duluth
1960 Denver	1973 Wisconsin	1986 Michigan State	1999 Maine	

NCAA Women's Hockey Champions, 2001-11

2001 Minnesota-Duluth	2004 Minnesota	2006 Wisconsin	2008 Minnesota-Duluth	2010 Minnesota-Duluth
2002 Minnesota-Duluth	2005 Minnesota	2007 Wisconsin	2009 Wisconsin	2011 Wisconsin
2003 Minnesota-Duluth				

COLLEGE LACROSSE

NCAA Division I Lacrosse Champions, 1982-2011

Year	Men	Women	Year	Men	Women	Year	Men	Women
1982	North Carolina	Massachusetts	1992	Princeton	Maryland	2002	Syracuse	Princeton
1983	Syracuse	Delaware	1993	Syracuse	Virginia	2003	Virginia	Princeton
1984	Johns Hopkins	Temple	1994	Princeton	Princeton	2004	Syracuse	Virginia
1985	Johns Hopkins	New Hampshire	1995	Syracuse	Maryland	2005	Johns Hopkins	Northwestern
1986	North Carolina	Maryland	1996	Princeton	Maryland	2006	Virginia	Northwestern
1987	Johns Hopkins	Penn St.	1997	Princeton	Maryland	2007	Johns Hopkins	Northwestern
1988	Syracuse	Temple	1998	Princeton	Maryland	2008	Syracuse	Northwestern
1989	Syracuse	Penn St.	1999	Virginia	Maryland	2009	Syracuse	Northwestern
1990	Vacated	Harvard	2000	Syracuse	Maryland	2010	Duke	Maryland
1991	North Carolina	Virginia	2001	Princeton	Maryland	2011	Virginia	Northwestern

COLLEGE SOCCER

NCAA Soccer Champions, 1982-2010

Year[1]	Men	Women	Year[1]	Men	Women	Year[1]	Men	Women
1982	Indiana	North Carolina	1991	Virginia	North Carolina	2001	North Carolina	Santa Clara
1983	Indiana	North Carolina	1992	Virginia	North Carolina	2002	UCLA	Portland
1984	Clemson	North Carolina	1993	Virginia	North Carolina	2003	Indiana	North Carolina
1985	UCLA	George Mason	1994	Virginia	North Carolina	2004	Indiana	Notre Dame
1986	Duke	North Carolina	1995	Wisconsin	Notre Dame	2005	Maryland	Portland
1987	Clemson	North Carolina	1996	St. John's (NY)	North Carolina	2006	UC Santa Barbara	North Carolina
1988	Indiana	North Carolina	1997	UCLA	North Carolina	2007	Wake Forest	USC
1989	Santa Clara/ Virginia (tie)	North Carolina	1998	Indiana	Florida	2008	Maryland	North Carolina
			1999	Indiana	North Carolina	2009	Virginia	North Carolina
1990	UCLA	North Carolina	2000	Connecticut	North Carolina	2010	Akron	Notre Dame

(1) NCAA Championships began in 1959 for men, in 1982 for women.

COLLEGE WRESTLING

NCAA Division I Wrestling Champions, 1964-2011

Year	Champion	Year	Champion	Year	Champion	Year	Champion	Year	Champion
1964	Oklahoma State	1974	Oklahoma	1984	Iowa	1994	Oklahoma State	2003	Oklahoma State
1965	Iowa State	1975	Iowa	1985	Iowa	1995	Iowa	2004	Oklahoma State
1966	Oklahoma State	1976	Iowa	1986	Iowa	1996	Iowa	2005	Oklahoma State
1967	Michigan State	1977	Iowa State	1987	Iowa State	1997	Iowa	2006	Oklahoma State
1968	Oklahoma State	1978	Iowa	1988	Arizona State	1998	Iowa	2007	Minnesota
1969	Iowa State	1979	Iowa	1989	Oklahoma State	1999	Iowa	2008	Iowa
1970	Iowa State	1980	Iowa	1990	Oklahoma State	2000	Iowa	2009	Iowa
1971	Oklahoma State	1981	Iowa	1991	Iowa	2001	Minnesota	2010	Iowa
1972	Iowa State	1982	Iowa	1992	Iowa	2002	Minnesota	2011	Penn State
1973	Iowa State	1983	Iowa	1993	Iowa				

FOOTBALL

NFL 2010: QBs, Offense, and Labor Talks Take Center Stage

The National Football League's 2010 season featured thrilling offensive feats, but contract talks between players and owners overshadowed most record-breaking performances. League owners and players continued attempts to agree on a new collective bargaining agreement, originally scheduled to expire Mar. 3, 2011.

On the field, quarterback Aaron Rodgers led the Green Bay Packers to Super Bowl victory over the Pittsburgh Steelers Feb. 6, 2011, at Cowboys Stadium in Arlington, TX, in a season that featured a record 11,283 total points. Teams averaged over 44 points per game, the highest in 45 years, and a record 22 quarterbacks threw for 3,000 or more yards. New England's Tom Brady led all QBs with a league-high 36 TD passes and a 111.0 passer rating, the fifth highest single-season total in history. Stellar quarterbacks were accompanied by other offensive standouts: Houston running back Arian Foster led the league and set franchise records in rushing yards (1,616) and rushing TDs (16), while wide receiver Roddy White of the Atlanta Falcons topped the NFL with a team-record 115 receptions.

In the AFC, QB Peyton Manning set a single-season NFL record with 450 pass completions and rallied his Indianapolis Colts to four straight wins to end the season and earn their ninth consecutive playoff berth. The Colts lost the wild card playoff game to the NY Jets, who went on to topple New England in the AFC divisional round. The Jets dropped the AFC championship game for the second year in a row, this time to Pittsburgh, sending the Steelers on their NFL record-tying eighth trip to the Super Bowl.

The Bears won the NFC North and reached the conference final with a 35-24 win over Seattle, which had taken the NFC West title despite a losing record. Green Bay clinched the last NFC wild card playoff slot on the final day of the season, then defeated Philadelphia and Atlanta before stopping the Chicago Bears in the NFC title game. The Packers became the 10th NFC franchise to reach the Super Bowl in the last 10 seasons.

The Minnesota Vikings saw some late-season drama when the inflatable roof at the Metrodome collapsed Dec. 12, 2010, under the weight of a heavy snow storm. The Vikings played their remaining two home games at Detroit's Ford Field and the Univ. of Minnesota's TCF Bank Stadium. Their game Dec. 13 against the NY Giants became a noteworthy event when Vikings veteran QB Brett Favre did not play due to an injured shoulder, snapping his NFL-record streak of 297 consecutive regular-season games started. Favre, the league's all-time passing leader, played one more game but announced his retirement for the third time shortly after the season, ending a 20-year career.

NFL Final Standings, 2010

AMERICAN FOOTBALL CONFERENCE

East Division	W	L	T	Pct	Pts	Opp	Div
#New England	14	2	0	.875	518	313	5-1
*New York Jets	11	5	0	.688	367	304	4-2
Miami	7	9	0	.438	273	333	2-4
Buffalo	4	12	0	.250	283	425	1-5

North Division	W	L	T	Pct	Pts	Opp	Div
Pittsburgh	12	4	0	.750	375	232	5-1
*Baltimore	12	4	0	.750	357	270	4-2
Cleveland	5	11	0	.313	271	332	1-5
Cincinnati	4	12	0	.250	322	395	2-4

South Division	W	L	T	Pct	Pts	Opp	Div
Indianapolis	10	6	0	.625	435	388	4-2
Jacksonville	8	8	0	.500	353	419	3-3
Houston	6	10	0	.375	390	427	3-3
Tennessee	6	10	0	.375	356	339	2-4

West Division	W	L	T	Pct	Pts	Opp	Div
Kansas City	10	6	0	.625	366	326	2-4
San Diego	9	7	0	.563	441	322	3-3
Oakland	8	8	0	.500	410	371	6-0
Denver	4	12	0	.250	344	471	1-5

NATIONAL FOOTBALL CONFERENCE

East Division	W	L	T	Pct	Pts	Opp	Div
Philadelphia	10	6	0	.625	439	377	4-2
New York Giants	10	6	0	.625	394	347	3-3
Dallas	6	10	0	.375	394	436	3-3
Washington	6	10	0	.375	302	377	2-4

North Division	W	L	T	Pct	Pts	Opp	Div
Chicago	11	5	0	.688	334	286	5-1
*Green Bay	10	6	0	.625	388	240	4-2
Detroit	6	10	0	.375	362	369	2-4
Minnesota	6	10	0	.375	281	348	1-5

South Division	W	L	T	Pct	Pts	Opp	Div
#Atlanta	13	3	0	.813	414	288	5-1
*New Orleans	11	5	0	.688	384	307	4-2
Tampa Bay	10	6	0	.625	341	318	3-3
Carolina	2	14	0	.125	196	408	0-6

West Division	W	L	T	Pct	Pts	Opp	Div
Seattle	7	9	0	.438	310	407	4-2
St. Louis	7	9	0	.438	289	328	3-3
San Francisco	6	10	0	.375	305	346	4-2
Arizona	5	11	0	.313	289	434	1-5

* = Wild card qualifier for playoffs. # = Top playoff seed in conference.

Note: Indianapolis finished ahead of Kansas City based on a week 5 win over the Chiefs. Pittsburgh finished ahead of Baltimore based on better record within the division. Philadelphia finished ahead of the NY Giants based on head-to-head sweep (2-0). Green Bay earned the second NFC wild card berth based on a strength-of-victory tiebreaker over the NY Giants and Tampa Bay. Seattle finished ahead of St. Louis based on better record within the division.

2010 Playoff Seedings
AFC: 1. New England (14-2), 2. Pittsburgh (12-4), 3. Indianapolis (10-6), 4. Kansas City (10-6), 5. Baltimore (12-4), 6. NY Jets (11-5)
NFC: 1. Atlanta (13-3), 2. Chicago (11-5), 3. Philadelphia (10-6), 4. Seattle (7-9), 5. New Orleans (11-5), 6. Green Bay (10-6)

2010 Playoffs
AFC Wild Card Playoff Games: NY Jets 17, Indianapolis 16; Baltimore 30, Kansas City 7
AFC Divisional Playoff Games: Pittsburgh 31, Baltimore 24; NY Jets 28, New England 21
AFC Championship Game: Pittsburgh 24, NY Jets 19
NFC Wild Card Playoff Games: Seattle 41, New Orleans 36; Green Bay 21, Philadelphia 16
NFC Divisional Playoff Games: Green Bay 48, Atlanta 21; Chicago 35, Seattle 24
NFC Championship Game: Green Bay 21, Chicago 14
Super Bowl XLV at Cowboys Stadium, Arlington, TX: Green Bay 31, Pittsburgh 25
AFC-NFC Pro Bowl at Aloha Stadium, Honolulu, HI: NFC 55, AFC 41

NFL Individual Leaders: American Football Conference, 2010

(* = rookie)

PASSING	Att	Comp	Pct comp	Yds	Yds/Att	Long	TD	Pct TD	Int	Rating
Tom Brady, New England	492	324	65.9	3,900	7.9	79T	36	7.3	4	111.0
Philip Rivers, San Diego	541	357	66.0	4,710	8.7	59T	30	5.5	13	101.8
Ben Roethlisberger, Pittsburgh	389	240	61.7	3,200	8.2	56T	17	4.4	5	97.0
Joe Flacco, Baltimore	489	306	62.6	3,622	7.4	67	25	5.1	10	93.6
Matt Cassel, Kansas City	450	262	58.2	3,116	6.9	75T	27	6.0	7	93.0
Matt Schaub, Houston	574	365	63.6	4,370	7.6	60	24	4.2	12	92.0
Peyton Manning, Indianapolis	679	450	66.3	4,700	6.9	73T	33	4.9	17	91.9
David Garrard, Jacksonville	366	236	64.5	2,734	7.5	75	23	6.3	15	90.8
Kyle Orton, Denver	498	293	58.8	3,653	7.3	71	20	4.0	9	87.5
Jason Campbell, Oakland	329	194	59.0	2,387	7.3	73T	13	4.0	8	84.5
Carson Palmer, Cincinnati	586	362	61.8	3,970	6.8	78T	26	4.4	20	82.4

PASSING	Att	Comp	Pct comp	Yds	Yds/Att	Long	TD	Pct TD	Int	Rating
Kerry Collins, Tennessee	278	160	57.6	1,823	6.6	80T	14	5.0	8	82.2
Ryan Fitzpatrick, Buffalo	441	255	57.8	3,000	6.8	65T	23	5.2	15	81.8
Chad Henne, Miami	490	301	61.4	3,301	6.7	57T	15	3.1	19	75.4
Mark Sanchez, NY Jets	507	278	54.8	3,291	6.5	74T	17	3.4	13	75.3

RUSHING YARDS	Yds	Att	Avg	Long	TD
Arian Foster, Houston	1,616	327	4.9	74T	16
Jamaal Charles, Kansas City	1,467	230	6.4	80	5
Chris Johnson, Tennessee	1,364	316	4.3	76T	11
Maurice Jones-Drew, Jacksonville	1,324	299	4.4	37	5
Rashard Mendenhall, Pittsburgh	1,273	324	3.9	50T	13
Ray Rice, Baltimore	1,220	307	4.0	50	5
Peyton Hillis, Cleveland	1,177	270	4.4	48	11
Darren McFadden, Oakland	1,157	223	5.2	57T	7
Cedric Benson, Cincinnati	1,111	321	3.5	26	7
BenJarvus Green-Ellis, New England	1,008	229	4.4	33T	13

RECEPTIONS	Rec	Yds	Avg	Long	TD
Reggie Wayne, Indianapolis	111	1,355	12.2	50	6
Andre Johnson, Houston	86	1,216	14.1	60	8
Brandon Marshall, Miami	86	1,014	11.8	46	3
Wes Welker, New England	86	848	9.9	35	7
Steve Johnson, Buffalo	82	1,073	13.1	45	10
Davone Bess, Miami	79	820	10.4	29	5
Brandon Lloyd, Denver	77	1,448	18.8	71	11
Dwayne Bowe, Kansas City	72	1,162	16.1	75T	15
Terrell Owens, Cincinnati	72	983	13.7	78T	9
Benjamin Watson, Cleveland	68	763	11.2	44	3

SCORING—KICKERS	PAT	FG	Long	Pts
Sebastian Janikowski, Oakland	43/43	33/41	59	142
Adam Vinatieri, Indianapolis	51/51	26/28	48	129
Nick Folk, NY Jets	37/37	30/39	56	127
Neil Rackers, Houston	43/43	27/30	57	124
Billy Cundiff, Baltimore	39/39	26/29	49	117
Dan Carpenter, Miami	25/25	30/41	60	115

SCORING—NON-KICKERS	TD	Rush	Rec	2-Pt	Pts
Arian Foster, Houston (RB)	18	16	2	0	108
Dwayne Bowe, Kansas City (WR)	15	0	15	0	90
BenJarvus Green-Ellis, New England (RB)	13	13	0	0	78
Peyton Hillis, Cleveland (RB)	13	11	2	0	78
Rashard Mendenhall, Pittsburgh (RB)	13	13	0	0	78
Chris Johnson, Tennessee (RB)	12	11	1	0	72

INTERCEPTIONS	No.	Yds	Avg	Long	TD
Ed Reed, Baltimore	8	183	22.9	44	0
*Devin McCourty, New England	7	110	15.7	50	0
Troy Polamalu, Pittsburgh	7	101	14.4	45T	1
*Joe Haden, Cleveland	6	101	16.8	62	0
*Eric Berry, Kansas City	4	102	25.5	54T	1
Antoine Cason, San Diego	4	51	12.8	28	0
Derek Cox, Jacksonville	4	14	3.5	14	0
Michael Griffin, Tennessee	4	50	12.5	28	0
Leon Hall, Cincinnati	4	19	4.8	22	0

KICKOFF RETURNS	No.	Yds	Avg	Long	TD
*David Reed, Baltimore	21	616	29.3	103T	1
Brad Smith, NY Jets	50	1,432	28.6	97T	2
Brandon Tate, New England	41	1,057	25.8	103T	2
*Marc Mariani, Tennessee	60	1,530	25.5	98T	1
*Eric Decker, Denver	22	556	25.3	51	0
*Emmanuel Sanders, Pittsburgh	25	628	25.1	48	0

PUNTING	No.	Yds	Long	Avg
Shane Lechler, Oakland	77	3,618	68	47.0
Mike Scifres, San Diego	52	2,430	67	46.7
Brandon Fields, Miami	73	3,369	69	46.2
Daniel Sepulveda, Pittsburgh	56	2,550	62	45.5
Britton Colquitt, Denver	86	3,835	63	44.6
Dustin Colquitt, Kansas City	88	3,908	72	44.4

PUNT RETURNS	No.	Yds	Avg	Long	TD
Julian Edelman, New England	21	321	15.3	94T	1
*Marc Mariani, Tennessee	27	329	12.2	87T	1
Eddie Royal, Denver	25	298	11.9	33	0
Davone Bess, Miami	25	284	11.4	47	0
Jim Leonhard, NY Jets	21	238	11.3	32	0
Mike Thomas, Jacksonville	34	358	10.5	78T	1

SACKS: Tamba Hali, Kansas City, 14.5; Cameron Wake, Miami, 14.0; Jason Babin, Tennessee, 12.5; Robert Mathis, Indianapolis, 11.0; Shaun Phillips, San Diego, 11.0; Terrell Suggs, Baltimore, 11.0; James Harrison, Pittsburgh, 10.5; Dwight Freeney, Indianapolis, 10.0; LaMarr Woodley, Pittsburgh, 10.0; *Carlos Dunlap, Cincinnati, 9.5; Kamerion Wimbley, Oakland, 9.0; Mario Williams, Houston, 8.5.

NFL Individual Leaders: National Football Conference, 2010

(* = rookie)

PASSING	Att	Comp	Pct comp	Yds	Yds/Att	Long	TD	Pct TD	Int	Rating
Aaron Rodgers, Green Bay	475	312	65.7	3,922	8.3	86T	28	5.9	11	101.2
Michael Vick, Philadelphia	372	233	62.6	3,018	8.1	91T	21	5.6	6	100.2
Josh Freeman, Tampa Bay	474	291	61.4	3,451	7.3	64	25	5.3	6	95.9
Matt Ryan, Atlanta	571	357	62.5	3,705	6.5	46	28	4.9	9	91.0
Drew Brees, New Orleans	658	448	68.1	4,620	7.0	80T	33	5.0	22	90.9
Jon Kitna, Dallas	318	209	65.7	2,365	7.4	71T	16	5.0	12	88.9
Jay Cutler, Chicago	432	261	60.4	3,274	7.6	89T	23	5.3	16	86.3
Eli Manning, NY Giants	539	339	62.9	4,002	7.4	92T	31	5.8	25	85.3
Alex Smith, San Francisco	342	204	59.6	2,370	6.9	62T	14	4.1	10	82.1
Shaun Hill, Detroit	416	257	61.8	2,686	6.5	75T	16	3.8	12	81.3
Donovan McNabb, Washington	472	275	58.3	3,377	7.2	76	14	3.0	15	77.1
*Sam Bradford, St. Louis	590	354	60.0	3,512	6.0	49	18	3.1	15	76.5
Matt Hasselbeck, Seattle	444	266	59.9	3,001	6.8	87T	12	2.7	17	73.2
Brett Favre, Minnesota	358	217	60.6	2,509	7.0	53T	11	3.1	19	69.9
Derek Anderson, Arizona	327	169	51.7	2,065	6.3	43	7	2.1	10	65.9
*Jimmy Clausen, Carolina	299	157	52.5	1,558	5.2	55T	3	1.0	9	58.4

RUSHING YARDS	Yds	Att	Avg	Long	TD
Michael Turner, Atlanta	1,371	334	4.1	55	12
Adrian Peterson, Minnesota	1,298	283	4.6	80T	12
Steven Jackson, St. Louis	1,241	330	3.8	42T	6
Ahmad Bradshaw, NY Giants	1,235	276	4.5	48T	8
LeSean McCoy, Philadelphia	1,080	207	5.2	62	7
Matt Forte, Chicago	1,069	237	4.5	68T	6
*LeGarrette Blount, Tampa Bay	1,007	201	5.0	53	6
Frank Gore, San Francisco	853	203	4.2	64	3
Brandon Jacobs, NY Giants	823	147	5.6	73	9
Felix Jones, Dallas	800	185	4.3	34	1

RECEPTIONS	Rec	Yds	Avg	Long	TD
Roddy White, Atlanta	115	1,389	12.1	46	10
Jason Witten, Dallas	94	1,002	10.7	33	9
Santana Moss, Washington	93	1,115	12.0	56	6
Larry Fitzgerald, Arizona	90	1,137	12.6	41	6
Danny Amendola, St. Louis	85	689	8.1	36	3
Marques Colston, New Orleans	84	1,023	12.2	43	7
Hakeem Nicks, NY Giants	79	1,052	13.3	46T	11
LeSean McCoy, Philadelphia	78	592	7.6	40	2
Chris Cooley, Washington	77	849	11.0	35	3
Calvin Johnson, Detroit	77	1,120	14.5	87T	12

SCORING—KICKERS	PAT	FG	Long	Pts
David Akers, Philadelphia	47/47	32/38	50	143
Matt Bryant, Atlanta	44/44	28/31	51	128
Josh Brown, St. Louis	26/27	33/39	53	125
David Buehler, Dallas	42/44	24/32	53	114
Mason Crosby, Green Bay	46/46	22/28	56	112
Robbie Gould, Chicago	35/35	25/30	54	110

SCORING—NON-KICKERS	TD	Rush	Rec	2-Pt	Pts
Adrian Peterson, Minnesota (RB)	13	12	1	0	78
Calvin Johnson, Detroit (WR)	12	0	12	1	74
Greg Jennings, Green Bay (WR)	12	0	12	0	72
Michael Turner, Atlanta (RB)	12	12	0	0	72
Hakeem Nicks, NY Giants (WR)	11	0	11	0	66
*Mike Williams, Tampa Bay (WR)	11	0	11	0	66

INTERCEPTIONS	No.	Yds	Avg	Long	TD
Asante Samuel, Philadelphia	7	70	10.0	33	0
DeAngelo Hall, Washington	6	92	15.3	92T	1
Aqib Talib, Tampa Bay	6	91	15.2	45T	0
Tramon Williams, Green Bay	6	87	14.5	64	0
Charles Godfrey, Carolina	5	112	22.4	38	0
Brent Grimes, Atlanta	5	84	16.8	36	0
Chris Harris, Chicago	5	69	13.8	39	0
William Moore, Atlanta	5	117	23.4	34	0
Terence Newman, Dallas	5	16	3.2	30	0
Gerald Sensabaugh, Dallas	5	26	5.2	10	0
Alphonso Smith, Detroit	5	48	9.6	42T	0
Terrell Thomas, NY Giants	5	56	11.2	28	0
*Earl Thomas, Seattle	5	68	13.6	34	0
Charles Tillman, Chicago	5	127	25.4	56	0

KICKOFF RETURNS	No.	Yds	Avg	Long	TD
Eric Weems, Atlanta	40	1,100	27.5	102T	1
LaRod Stephens-Howling, Arizona	57	1,548	27.2	102T	2
Stefan Logan, Detroit	55	1,448	26.3	105T	1
Micheal Spurlock, Tampa Bay	44	1,129	25.7	89T	1
Leon Washington, Seattle	57	1,461	25.6	101T	3
*Brandon Banks, Washington	46	1,155	25.1	96T	1

PUNTING	No.	Yds	Long	Avg
Mat McBriar, Dallas	65	3,115	65	47.9
Andy Lee, San Francisco	91	4,203	64	46.2
Thomas Morstead, New Orleans	57	2,618	64	45.9
Donnie Jones, St. Louis	94	4,276	63	45.5
*Matt Dodge, NY Giants	72	3,222	69	44.8
Nick Harris, Detroit	90	4,018	66	44.6

PUNT RETURNS	No.	Yds	Avg	Long	TD
Devin Hester, Chicago	33	564	17.1	89T	1
Ted Ginn, San Francisco	24	321	13.4	78T	1
Stefan Logan, Detroit	30	362	12.1	71	0
DeSean Jackson, Philadelphia	20	231	11.6	65T	1
Danny Amendola, St. Louis	40	452	11.3	42	0
*Brandon Banks, Washington	38	431	11.3	53	0

SACKS: DeMarcus Ware, Dallas, 15.5; Clay Matthews, Green Bay, 13.5; John Abraham, Atlanta, 13.0; Charles Johnson, Carolina, 11.5; Justin Tuck, NY Giants, 11.5; Osi Umenyiora, NY Giants, 11.5; Jared Allen, Minnesota, 11.0; Chris Clemons, Seattle, 11.0; James Hall, St. Louis, 10.5; Trent Cole, Philadelphia, 10.0; *Ndamukong Suh, Detroit, 10.0; Raheem Brock, Seattle, 9.0; Cliff Avril, Detroit, 8.5; Chris Long, St. Louis, 8.5; Brian Orakpo, Washington, 8.5; Justin Smith, San Francisco, 8.5.

Super Bowl XLV: Green Bay 31, Pittsburgh 25

The Green Bay Packers beat the Pittsburgh Steelers in Super Bowl XLV for their record 13th NFL title and 4th during the Super Bowl era. Aaron Rodgers threw three touchdown passes for 304 yards and no interceptions and was voted Super Bowl MVP. Rodgers threw for a combined 1,094 yards with nine TD passes and just two interceptions in leading the Packers to three playoff road victories and a Super Bowl victory. The 27-year-old quarterback completed 24 of 39 passes against a Steelers' defense that topped the NFL in lowest average points allowed (14.5 PPG) and a league-low 62.8 rushing yards per game. Green Bay took a quick 14-0 lead in the first quarter on Rodgers' 29-yard TD pass to Jordy Nelson and a 37-yard interception return by cornerback Nick Collins just 24 seconds later. The Packers extended their lead to 21-3 in the second on a 21-yard touchdown pass to wideout Greg Jennings. The Steelers began to close the gap when Ben Roethlisberger hit veteran Hines Ward with an eight-yard scoring toss late in the first half, and Rashard Mendenhall added an eight-yard scoring run in the third to trail 21-17. Mendenhall rushed for a modest 63 yards, but it surpassed the Packers' entire team total of 50 yards rushing. The Steelers again threatened to overtake the Pack when Mike Wallace caught a 25-yard TD pass from Roethlisberger in the fourth quarter, and a successful two-point conversion pulled Pittsburgh to within three at 28-25. A late field goal by Mason Crosby gave Green Bay a six-point lead and the Steelers, making their third Super Bowl trip in six seasons, failed in a late effort to tie. Green Bay, under the guidance of fifth-year head coach Mike McCarthy, is just the second number-6 seed in postseason history to reach the Super Bowl, joining the 2005 Steelers, who were victorious in Super Bowl XL. Pittsburgh is tied with the Dallas Cowboys for most Super Bowl appearances with eight, and still tops the NFL with six all-time Super Bowl victories.

Quarters

Team	1	2	3	4	Total
Pittsburgh	0	10	7	8	25
Green Bay	14	7	0	10	31

Scoring

Green Bay: Jordy Nelson, 29-yard pass from Aaron Rodgers (Mason Crosby PAT)

Green Bay: Nick Collins, 37-yard interception return (Mason Crosby PAT)

Pittsburgh: Shaun Suisham, 33-yard field goal

Green Bay: Greg Jennings, 21-yard pass from Aaron Rodgers (Mason Crosby PAT)

Pittsburgh: Hines Ward, 8-yard pass from Ben Roethlisberger (Shaun Suisham PAT)

Pittsburgh: Rashard Mendenhall, 8-yard run (Shaun Suisham PAT)

Green Bay: Greg Jennings, 8-yard pass from Aaron Rodgers (Mason Crosby PAT)

Pittsburgh: Mike Wallace, 25-yard pass from Ben Roethlisberger (Antwaan Randle El rush)

Green Bay: Mason Crosby, 23-yard field goal

Individual Statistics

Rushing: Pittsburgh—Mendenhall, 14-63; Roethlisberger, 4-31; Redman, 2-19; Moore, 3-13. Green Bay—Starks, 11-52; Rodgers, 2-minus-2.

Passing: Pittsburgh—Roethlisberger, 25-40, 263 yards, 2 TD, 2 Int. Green Bay—Rodgers, 24-39, 304 yards, 3 TD, 0 Int.

Receiving: Pittsburgh—Wallace, 9-89; Ward, 7-78; Randle El, 2-50; Sanders, 2-17; Miller, 2-12; Spaeth, 1-9; Mendenhall, 1-7; Brown, 1-1. Green Bay—Nelson, 9-140; Jones, 5-50; Jennings, 4-64; Driver, 2-28; Jackson, 1-14; Quarless, 1-5; Hall, 1-2; Crabtree, 1-1.

Missed Field Goals: Pittsburgh—1 (Suisham, 52).

Team Statistics

	Steelers	Packers
1st downs	19	15
Total net yards	387	338
Rushes-yards	23-126	13-50
Passing yards, net	261	288
Punt returns-yards	4-5	1-0
Kickoff returns-yards	6-111	3-63
Interception return-yards	0-0	2-38
Field goals made-attempts	1-2	1-1
Att.-comp.-int.	25-40-2	24-39-0
Sacked-yards lost	1-2	3-16
Punts-average	3-51.0	6-40.5
Fumbles-lost	1-1	1-0
Penalties-yards	6-55	7-67
Time of possession	33:25	26:35

Total attendance: 103,219   **Game length:** 3:32

Future Super Bowl Sites

No.	Site	Date	No.	Site	Date
XLVI	Lucas Oil Stadium, Indianapolis, IN.	Feb. 5, 2012	XLVIII	New Meadowlands Stadium,	
XLVII	Louisiana Superdome, New Orleans, LA	Feb. 2013		East Rutherford, NJ.	Feb. 2014

Super Bowl Results, 1967-2011

No.	Year	Winner	Opponent	Winning coach	Site
I	1967	*Green Bay Packers, 35	Kansas City Chiefs, 10	Vince Lombardi	Memorial Coliseum, Los Angeles, CA
II	1968	Green Bay Packers, 33	*Oakland Raiders, 14	Vince Lombardi	Orange Bowl, Miami, FL
III	1969	*NY Jets, 16	Baltimore Colts, 7	Weeb Ewbank	Orange Bowl, Miami, FL
IV	1970	Kansas City Chiefs, 23	*Minnesota Vikings, 7	Hank Stram	Tulane Stadium, New Orleans, LA
V	1971	Baltimore Colts, 16	*Dallas Cowboys, 13	Don McCafferty	Orange Bowl, Miami, FL
VI	1972	Dallas Cowboys, 24	*Miami Dolphins, 3	Tom Landry	Tulane Stadium, New Orleans, LA
VII	1973	*Miami Dolphins, 14	Washington Redskins, 7	Don Shula	Memorial Coliseum, Los Angeles, CA
VIII	1974	*Miami Dolphins, 24	Minnesota Vikings, 7	Don Shula	Rice Stadium, Houston, TX
IX	1975	*Pittsburgh Steelers, 16	Minnesota Vikings, 6	Chuck Noll	Tulane Stadium, New Orleans, LA
X	1976	Pittsburgh Steelers, 21	*Dallas Cowboys, 17	Chuck Noll	Orange Bowl, Miami, FL
XI	1977	*Oakland Raiders, 32	Minnesota Vikings, 14	John Madden	Rose Bowl, Pasadena, CA
XII	1978	*Dallas Cowboys, 27	Denver Broncos, 10	Tom Landry	Superdome, New Orleans, LA
XIII	1979	Pittsburgh Steelers, 35	*Dallas Cowboys, 31	Chuck Noll	Orange Bowl, Miami, FL
XIV	1980	Pittsburgh Steelers, 31	*L.A. Rams, 19	Chuck Noll	Rose Bowl, Pasadena, CA
XV	1981	Oakland Raiders, 27	*Philadelphia Eagles, 10	Tom Flores	Superdome, New Orleans, LA
XVI	1982	*San Francisco 49ers, 26	Cincinnati Bengals, 21	Bill Walsh	Silverdome, Pontiac, MI
XVII	1983	Washington Redskins, 27	*Miami Dolphins, 17	Joe Gibbs	Rose Bowl, Pasadena, CA
XVIII	1984	*L.A. Raiders, 38	Washington Redskins, 9	Tom Flores	Tampa Stadium, Tampa, FL
XIX	1985	*San Francisco 49ers, 38	Miami Dolphins, 16	Bill Walsh	Stanford Stadium, Stanford, CA
XX	1986	*Chicago Bears, 46	New England Patriots, 10	Mike Ditka	Superdome, New Orleans, LA
XXI	1987	NY Giants, 39	*Denver Broncos, 20	Bill Parcells	Rose Bowl, Pasadena, CA
XXII	1988	*Washington Redskins, 42	Denver Broncos, 10	Joe Gibbs	Jack Murphy Stadium, San Diego, CA
XXIII	1989	*San Francisco 49ers, 20	Cincinnati Bengals, 16	Bill Walsh	Joe Robbie Stadium, Miami, FL
XXIV	1990	San Francisco 49ers, 55	*Denver Broncos, 10	George Seifert	Superdome, New Orleans, LA
XXV	1991	NY Giants, 20	*Buffalo Bills, 19	Bill Parcells	Tampa Stadium, Tampa, FL
XXVI	1992	*Washington Redskins, 37	Buffalo Bills, 24	Joe Gibbs	Metrodome, Minneapolis, MN
XXVII	1993	Dallas Cowboys, 52	*Buffalo Bills, 17	Jimmy Johnson	Rose Bowl, Pasadena, CA
XXVIII	1994	*Dallas Cowboys, 30	Buffalo Bills, 13	Jimmy Johnson	Georgia Dome, Atlanta, GA
XXIX	1995	*San Francisco 49ers, 49	San Diego Chargers, 26	George Seifert	Joe Robbie Stadium, Miami, FL
XXX	1996	*Dallas Cowboys, 27	Pittsburgh Steelers, 17	Barry Switzer	Sun Devil Stadium, Tempe, AZ
XXXI	1997	Green Bay Packers, 35	*New England Patriots, 21	Mike Holmgren	Superdome, New Orleans, LA
XXXII	1998	Denver Broncos, 31	*Green Bay Packers, 24	Mike Shanahan	Qualcomm Stadium, San Diego, CA
XXXIII	1999	Denver Broncos, 34	*Atlanta Falcons, 19	Mike Shanahan	Pro Player Stadium, Miami, FL
XXXIV	2000	*St. Louis Rams, 23	Tennessee Titans, 16	Dick Vermeil	Georgia Dome, Atlanta, GA
XXXV	2001	Baltimore Ravens, 34	*NY Giants, 7	Brian Billick	Raymond James Stadium, Tampa, FL
XXXVI	2002	New England Patriots, 20	*St. Louis Rams, 17	Bill Belichick	Superdome, New Orleans, LA
XXXVII	2003	*Tampa Bay Buccaneers, 48	Oakland Raiders, 21	Jon Gruden	Qualcomm Stadium, San Diego, CA
XXXVIII	2004	New England Patriots, 32	*Carolina Panthers, 29	Bill Belichick	Reliant Stadium, Houston, TX
XXXIX	2005	New England Patriots, 24	*Philadelphia Eagles, 21	Bill Belichick	Alltel Stadium, Jacksonville, FL
XL	2006	Pittsburgh Steelers, 21	*Seattle Seahawks, 10	Bill Cowher	Ford Field, Detroit, MI
XLI	2007	Indianapolis Colts, 29	*Chicago Bears, 17	Tony Dungy	Dolphin Stadium, Miami, FL
XLII	2008	*NY Giants, 17	New England Patriots, 14	Tom Coughlin	Univ. of Phoenix Stadium, Glendale, AZ
XLIII	2009	Pittsburgh Steelers, 27	*Arizona Cardinals, 23	Mike Tomlin	Raymond James Stadium, Tampa, FL
XLIV	2010	*New Orleans Saints, 31	Indianapolis Colts, 17	Sean Payton	Sun Life Stadium, Miami Gardens, FL
XLV	2011	*Green Bay Packers, 31	Pittsburgh Steelers, 25	Mike McCarthy	Cowboys Stadium, Arlington, TX

*Team that won the coin toss. All teams that won the toss elected to receive, except the 2009 Cardinals and 2011 Packers, who deferred their choice to receive in the 2nd half.

Super Bowl Single-Game Statistical Leaders

Passing Yards

	Year	Att/comp	Yds	TD
Kurt Warner, Rams	2000	45/24	414	2
Kurt Warner, Cardinals	2009	43/31	377	3
Kurt Warner, Rams	2002	44/28	365	1
Donovon McNabb, Eagles	2005	51/30	357	3
Joe Montana, 49ers	1989	36/23	357	2

Passing Touchdowns

	Year	Att/comp	Yds	TD
Steve Young, 49ers	1995	36/24	325	6
Joe Montana, 49ers	1990	29/22	297	5
Troy Aikman, Cowboys	1993	30/22	273	4
Doug Williams, Redskins	1988	29/18	340	4
Terry Bradshaw, Steelers	1979	30/17	318	4

Receiving Yards

	Year	Rec	Yds	TD
Jerry Rice, 49ers	1989	11	215	1
Ricky Sanders, Redskins	1988	9	193	2
Isaac Bruce, Rams	2000	6	162	1

Scoring

	Year	Points	
Terrell Davis, Broncos	1998	18	3 TDs
Jerry Rice, 49ers	1995	18	3 TDs
Ricky Watters, 49ers	1995	18	3 TDs
Jerry Rice, 49ers	1990	18	3 TDs
Roger Craig, 49ers	1985	18	3 TDs
Don Chandler, Packers	1968	15	4 FG, 3 PATs

Rushing Yards

	Year	Att	Yds	TD
Timmy Smith, Redskins	1988	22	204	2
Marcus Allen, Raiders	1984	20	191	2
John Riggins, Redskins	1983	38	166	1

Super Bowl MVPs, 1967-2011

1967 Bart Starr, Green Bay	1982 Joe Montana, San Francisco	1997 Desmond Howard, Green Bay
1968 Bart Starr, Green Bay	1983 John Riggins, Washington	1998 Terrell Davis, Denver
1969 Joe Namath, NY Jets	1984 Marcus Allen, L.A. Raiders	1999 John Elway, Denver
1970 Len Dawson, Kansas City	1985 Joe Montana, San Francisco	2000 Kurt Warner, St. Louis
1971 Chuck Howley, Dallas	1986 Richard Dent, Chicago	2001 Ray Lewis, Baltimore
1972 Roger Staubach, Dallas	1987 Phil Simms, NY Giants	2002 Tom Brady, New England
1973 Jake Scott, Miami	1988 Doug Williams, Washington	2003 Dexter Jackson, Tampa Bay
1974 Larry Csonka, Miami	1989 Jerry Rice, San Francisco	2004 Tom Brady, New England
1975 Franco Harris, Pittsburgh	1990 Joe Montana, San Francisco	2005 Deion Branch, New England
1976 Lynn Swann, Pittsburgh	1991 Ottis Anderson, NY Giants	2006 Hines Ward, Pittsburgh
1977 Fred Biletnikoff, Oakland	1992 Mark Rypien, Washington	2007 Peyton Manning, Indianapolis
1978 Randy White, Harvey Martin, Dallas	1993 Troy Aikman, Dallas	2008 Eli Manning, NY Giants
1979 Terry Bradshaw, Pittsburgh	1994 Emmitt Smith, Dallas	2009 Santonio Holmes, Pittsburgh
1980 Terry Bradshaw, Pittsburgh	1995 Steve Young, San Francisco	2010 Drew Brees, New Orleans
1981 Jim Plunkett, Oakland	1996 Larry Brown, Dallas	2011 Aaron Rodgers, Green Bay

First-Round Selections in the 2011 NFL Draft

Team	Player	Pos.	College	Team	Player	Pos.	College
1. Carolina Panthers . .	Cam Newton	QB	Auburn	19. NY Giants	Prince		
2. Denver Broncos . . .	Von Miller	LB	Texas A&M		Amukamara . . .	CB	Nebraska
3. Buffalo Bills	Marcell Dareus . .	DT	Alabama	20. Tampa Bay			
4. Cincinnati Bengals	A.J. Green	WR	Georgia	Buccaneers	Adrian Clayborn . .	DL	Iowa
5. Arizona Cardinals .	Patrick Peterson	CB	Louisiana	21. Cleveland			
			State	Browns[5]	Phil Taylor	DL	Baylor
6. Atlanta Falcons[1] . . .	Julio Jones	WR	Alabama	22. Indianapolis Colts . .	Anthony		
7. San Francisco					Castonzo	OL	Boston Coll.
49ers[2]	Aldon Smith	DE	Missouri	23. Philadelphia			
8. Tennessee Titans . .	Jake Locker	QB	Washington	Eagles	Danny Watkins . . .	OL	Baylor
9. Dallas Cowboys . . .	Tyron Smith	OT	USC	24. New Orleans			
10. Jacksonville				Saints	Cameron Jordan . .	DE	California
Jaguars[2]	Blaine Gabbert . .	QB	Missouri	25. Seattle Seahawks .	James Carpenter	OL	Alabama
11. Houston Texans . . .	J.J. Watt	DE	Wisconsin	26. Kansas City			
12. Minnesota Vikings	Christian			Chiefs[6]	Jonathan Baldwin	WR	Pittsburgh
	Ponder	QB	Florida State	27. Baltimore Ravens . .	Jimmy Smith	CB	Colorado
13. Detroit Lions	Nick Fairley	DT	Auburn	28. New Orleans			
14. St. Louis Rams . . .	Robert Quinn . . .	DE	North Carolina	Saints[7]	Mark Ingram	RB	Alabama
15. Miami Dolphins . . .	Mike Pouncey . . .	OL	Florida	29. Chicago Bears . . .	Gabe Carimi	OL	Wisconsin
16. Washington				30. NY Jets	Muhammad		
Redskins[3]	Ryan Kerrigan . . .	DE	Purdue		Wilkerson	DT	Temple
17. New England				31. Pittsburgh			
Patriots[4]	Nate Solder	OL	Colorado	Steelers	Cam Heyward . .	DT	Ohio State
18. San Diego				32. Green Bay			
Chargers	Corey Liuget . . .	DT	Illinois	Packers	Derek Sherrod . . .	OL	Mississippi State

(1) From Cleveland. (2) From Washington. (3) From Jacksonville. (4) From Oakland. (5) From Kansas City. (6) From Atlanta through Cleveland. (7) From New England.

Number One NFL Draft Choices, 1936-2011

Year	Team	Player, pos., college	Year	Team	Player, pos., college
1936	Philadelphia	Jay Berwanger, HB, Chicago	1974	Dallas	Ed "Too Tall" Jones, DE, Tenn. St.
1937	Philadelphia	Sam Francis, FB, Nebraska	1975	Atlanta	Steve Bartkowski, QB, California
1938	Cleveland Rams . .	Corbett Davis, FB, Indiana	1976	Tampa Bay	Lee Roy Selmon, DE, Oklahoma
1939	Chicago Cards . . .	Ki Aldrich, C, TCU	1977	Tampa Bay	Ricky Bell, RB, USC
1940	Chicago Cards . . .	George Cafego, HB, Tennessee	1978	Houston	Earl Campbell, RB, Texas
1941	Chicago Bears . . .	Tom Harmon, HB, Michigan	1979	Buffalo	Tom Cousineau, LB, Ohio St.
1942	Pittsburgh	Bill Dudley, HB, Virginia	1980	Detroit	Billy Sims, RB, Oklahoma
1943	Detroit	Frank Sinkwich, HB, Georgia	1981	New Orleans	George Rogers, RB, S. Carolina
1944	Boston Yanks	Angelo Bertelli, QB, Notre Dame	1982	New England	Kenneth Sims, DT, Texas
1945	Chicago Cards . . .	Charley Trippi, HB, Georgia	1983	Baltimore Colts . . .	John Elway, QB, Stanford
1946	Boston Yanks	Frank Dancewicz, QB, Notre Dame	1984	New England	Irving Fryar, WR, Nebraska
1947	Chicago Bears . . .	Bob Fenimore, HB, Oklahoma St.	1985	Buffalo	Bruce Smith, DE, Virginia Tech
1948	Washington	Harry Gilmer, QB, Alabama	1986	Tampa Bay	Bo Jackson, RB, Auburn
1949	Philadelphia	Chuck Bednarik, C, Pennsylvania	1987	Tampa Bay	Vinny Testaverde, QB, Miami (FL)
1950	Detroit	Leon Hart, E, Notre Dame	1988	Atlanta	Aundray Bruce, LB, Auburn
1951	NY Giants	Kyle Rote, HB, SMU	1989	Dallas	Troy Aikman, QB, UCLA
1952	L.A. Rams	Bill Wade, QB, Vanderbilt	1990	Indianapolis	Jeff George, QB, Illinois
1953	San Francisco . . .	Harry Babcock, E, Georgia	1991	Dallas	Russell Maryland, DL, Miami (FL)
1954	Cleveland	Bobby Garrett, QB, Stanford	1992	Indianapolis	Steve Emtman, DL, Washington
1955	Baltimore Colts . . .	George Shaw, QB, Oregon	1993	New England	Drew Bledsoe, QB, Washington St.
1956	Pittsburgh	Gary Glick, DB, Colorado State	1994	Cincinnati	Dan Wilkinson, DT, Ohio St.
1957	Green Bay	Paul Hornung, QB, Notre Dame	1995	Cincinnati	Ki-Jana Carter, RB, Penn State
1958	Chicago Cards . . .	King Hill, QB, Rice	1996	NY Jets	Keyshawn Johnson, WR, USC
1959	Green Bay	Randy Duncan, QB, Iowa	1997	St. Louis	Orlando Pace, T, Ohio St.
1960	L.A. Rams	Billy Cannon, HB, LSU	1998	Indianapolis	Peyton Manning, QB, Tennessee
1961	Minnesota	Tommy Mason, HB, Tulane	1999	Cleveland	Tim Couch, QB, Kentucky
1962	Washington	Ernie Davis, HB, Syracuse	2000	Cleveland	Courtney Brown, DE, Penn State
1963	L.A. Rams	Terry Baker, QB, Oregon St.	2001	Atlanta	Michael Vick, QB, Virginia Tech
1964	San Francisco . . .	Dave Parks, E, Texas Tech	2002	Houston	David Carr, QB, Fresno St.
1965	NY Giants	Tucker Frederickson, HB, Auburn	2003	Cincinnati	Carson Palmer, QB, USC
1966	Atlanta	Tommy Nobis, LB, Texas	2004	San Diego	Eli Manning, QB, Mississippi
1967	Baltimore Colts . . .	Bubba Smith, DT, Michigan St.	2005	San Francisco . . .	Alex D. Smith, QB, Utah
1968	Minnesota	Ron Yary, T, USC	2006	Houston	Mario Williams, DE, NC State
1969	Buffalo	O. J. Simpson, RB, USC	2007	Oakland	JaMarcus Russell, QB, LSU
1970	Pittsburgh	Terry Bradshaw, QB, LA Tech	2008	Miami	Jake Long, OT, Michigan
1971	New England	Jim Plunkett, QB, Stanford	2009	Detroit	Matthew Stafford, QB, Georgia
1972	Buffalo	Walt Patulski, DE, Notre Dame	2010	St. Louis	Sam Bradford, QB, Oklahoma
1973	Houston	John Matuszak, DE, Tampa	2011	Carolina	Cam Newton, QB, Auburn

American Football League Champions, 1960-69

Year	Eastern (W-L-T)	Western (W-L-T)	Championship
1960	Houston Oilers (10-4-0)	L.A. Chargers (10-4-0)	Houston 24, L.A. 16
1961	Houston Oilers (10-3-1)	San Diego Chargers (12-2-0)	Houston 10, San Diego 3
1962	Houston Oilers (11-3-0)	Dallas Texans (11-3-0)	Dallas 20, Houston 17 (2 OT)
1963	Boston Patriots (7-6-1)[1]	San Diego Chargers (11-3-0)	San Diego 51, Boston 10
1964	Buffalo Bills (12-2-0)	San Diego Chargers (8-5-1)	Buffalo 20, San Diego 7
1965	Buffalo Bills (10-3-1)	San Diego Chargers (9-2-3)	Buffalo 23, San Diego 0
1966	Buffalo Bills (9-4-1)	Kansas City Chiefs (11-2-1)	Kansas City 31, Buffalo 7
1967	Houston Oilers (9-4-1)	Oakland Raiders (13-1-0)	Oakland 40, Houston 7
1968	NY Jets (11-3-0)	Oakland Raiders (12-2-0)[2]	NY 27, Oakland 23
1969	NY Jets (10-4-0)	Oakland Raiders (12-1-1)	Kansas City 17, Oakland 7[3]

(1) Defeated Buffalo Bills in divisional playoff. (2) Defeated Kansas City Chiefs in divisional playoff. (3) Kansas City defeated NY Jets, and Oakland Raiders defeated Houston Oilers in divisional playoffs.

National Football League Champions, 1933-69

Year	East (W-L-T)	West (W-L-T)	Championship
1933	NY Giants (11-3-0)	Chicago Bears (10-2-1)	Chicago Bears 23, NY 21
1934	NY Giants (8-5-0)	Chicago Bears (13-0-0)	NY 30, Chicago Bears 13
1935	NY Giants (9-3-0)	Detroit Lions (7-3-2)	Detroit 26, NY 7
1936	Boston Redskins (7-5-0)	Green Bay Packers (10-1-1)	Green Bay 21, Boston 6
1937	Washington Redskins (8-3-0)	Chicago Bears (9-1-1)	Washington 28, Chicago Bears 21
1938	NY Giants (8-2-1)	Green Bay Packers (8-3-0)	NY 23, Green Bay 17
1939	NY Giants (9-1-1)	Green Bay Packers (9-2-0)	Green Bay 27, NY 0
1940	Washington Redskins (9-2-0)	Chicago Bears (8-3-0)	Chicago Bears 73, Washington 0
1941	NY Giants (8-3-0)	Chicago Bears (10-1-1)[1]	Chicago Bears 37, NY 9
1942	Washington Redskins (10-1-1)	Chicago Bears (11-0-0)	Washington 14, Chicago Bears 6
1943	Washington Redskins (6-3-1)	Chicago Bears (8-1-1)	Chicago Bears, 41, Washington 21
1944	NY Giants (8-1-1)	Green Bay Packers (8-2-0)	Green Bay 14, NY 7
1945	Washington Redskins (8-2-0)	Cleveland Rams (9-1-0)	Cleveland 15, Washington 14
1946	NY Giants (7-3-1)	Chicago Bears (8-2-1)	Chicago Bears 24, NY 14
1947	Philadelphia Eagles (8-4-0)[1]	Chicago Cardinals (9-3-0)	Chicago Cardinals 28, Philadelphia 21
1948	Philadelphia Eagles (9-2-1)	Chicago Cardinals (11-1-0)	Philadelphia 7, Chicago Cardinals 0
1949	Philadelphia Eagles (11-1-0)	L.A. Rams (8-2-2)	Philadelphia 14, L.A. 0
1950	Cleveland Browns (10-2-0)[1]	L.A. Rams (9-3-0)[1]	Cleveland 30, L.A. 28
1951	Cleveland Browns (11-1-0)	L.A. Rams (8-4-0)	L.A. 24, Cleveland 17
1952	Cleveland Browns (8-4-0)	Detroit Lions (9-3-0)[1]	Detroit 17, Cleveland 7
1953	Cleveland Browns (11-1-0)	Detroit Lions (10-2-0)	Detroit 17, Cleveland 16
1954	Cleveland Browns (9-3-0)	Detroit Lions (9-2-1)	Cleveland 56, Detroit 10
1955	Cleveland Browns (9-2-1)	L.A. Rams (8-3-1)	Cleveland 38, L.A. 14
1956	NY Giants (8-3-1)	Chicago Bears (9-2-1)	NY 47, Chicago Bears 7
1957	Cleveland Browns (9-2-1)	Detroit Lions (8-4-0)[1]	Detroit 59, Cleveland 14
1958	NY Giants (9-3-0)[1]	Baltimore Colts (9-3-0)	Baltimore 23, NY 17[2]
1959	NY Giants (10-2-0)	Baltimore Colts (9-3-0)	Baltimore 31, NY 16
1960	Philadelphia Eagles (10-2-0)	Green Bay Packers (8-4-0)	Philadelphia 17, Green Bay 13
1961	NY Giants (10-3-1)	Green Bay Packers (11-3-0)	Green Bay 37, NY 0
1962	NY Giants (12-2-0)	Green Bay Packers (13-1-0)	Green Bay 16, NY 7
1963	NY Giants (11-3-0)	Chicago Bears (11-1-2)	Chicago 14, NY 10
1964	Cleveland Browns (10-3-1)	Baltimore Colts (12-2-0)	Cleveland 27, Baltimore 0
1965	Cleveland Browns (11-3-0)	Green Bay Packers (10-3-1)[1]	Green Bay 23, Cleveland 12
1966	Dallas Cowboys (10-3-1)	Green Bay Packers (12-2-0)	Green Bay 34, Dallas 27
1967	Dallas Cowboys (9-5-0)	Green Bay Packers (9-4-1)	Green Bay 21, Dallas 17
1968	Cleveland Browns (10-4-0)	Baltimore Colts (13-1-0)	Baltimore 34, Cleveland 0
1969	Cleveland Browns (10-3-1)	Minnesota Vikings (12-2-0)	Minnesota 27, Cleveland 7

(1) Won divisional playoff. (2) Won at 8:15 of sudden death overtime period.

NFL Divisional Champions and Wild Cards, 1970-95

The American Football League and National Football League officially merged in 1966. At the beginning of the 1970 season, the two leagues became the AFC and NFC conferences in the new NFL. Regular-season records are in parentheses.

AMERICAN FOOTBALL CONFERENCE

Year	Eastern	Central	Western	Wild card
1970	Baltimore Colts (11-2-1)	Cincinnati Bengals (8-6-0)	Oakland Raiders (8-4-2)	Miami Dolphins (10-4-0)
1971	Miami Dolphins (10-3-1)	Cleveland Browns (9-5-0)	Kansas City Chiefs (10-3-1)	Baltimore Colts (10-4-0)
1972	Miami Dolphins (14-0-0)	Pittsburgh Steelers (11-3-0)	Oakland Raiders (10-3-1)	Cleveland Browns (10-4-0)
1973	Miami Dolphins (12-2-0)	Cincinnati Bengals (10-4-0)	Oakland Raiders (9-4-1)	Pittsburgh Steelers (10-4-0)
1974	Miami Dolphins (11-3-0)	Pittsburgh Steelers (10-3-1)	Oakland Raiders (12-2-0)	Buffalo Bills (9-5-0)
1975	Baltimore Colts (10-4-0)	Pittsburgh Steelers (12-2-0)	Oakland Raiders (11-3-0)	Cincinnati Bengals (11-3-0)
1976	Baltimore Colts (11-3-0)	Pittsburgh Steelers (10-4-0)	Oakland Raiders (13-1-0)	New England Patriots (11-3-0)
1977	Baltimore Colts (10-4-0)	Pittsburgh Steelers (9-5-0)	Denver Broncos (12-2-0)	Oakland Raiders (11-3-0)
1978	New England Patriots (11-5-0)	Pittsburgh Steelers (14-2-0)	Denver Broncos (10-6-0)	Houston Oilers (10-6-0) Miami Dolphins (11-5-0)
1979	Miami Dolphins (10-6-0)	Pittsburgh Steelers (12-4-0)	San Diego Chargers (12-4-0)	Houston Oilers (11-5-0) Denver Broncos (10-6-0)
1980	Buffalo Bills (11-5-0)	Cleveland Browns (11-5-0)	San Diego Chargers (11-5-0)	Houston Oilers (11-5-0) Oakland Raiders (11-5-0)
1981	Miami Dolphins (11-4-1)	Cincinnati Bengals (12-4-0)	San Diego Chargers (10-6-0)	Buffalo Bills (10-6-0) NY Jets (10-5-1)
1982	Strike abbreviated season. See note.			
1983	Miami Dolphins (12-4-0)	Pittsburgh Steelers (10-6-0)	L.A. Raiders (12-4-0)	Denver Broncos (9-7-0) Seattle Seahawks (9-7-0)
1984	Miami Dolphins (14-2-0)	Pittsburgh Steelers (9-7-0)	Denver Broncos (13-3-0)	L.A. Raiders (11-5-0) Seattle Seahawks (12-4-0)
1985	Miami Dolphins (12-4-0)	Cleveland Browns (8-8-0)	L.A. Raiders (12-4-0)	New England Patriots (11-5-0) NY Jets (11-5-0)

AMERICAN FOOTBALL CONFERENCE

Year	Eastern	Central	Western	Wild card
1986	New England Patriots (11-5-0)	Cleveland Browns (12-4-0)	Denver Broncos (11-5-0)	Kansas City Chiefs (10-6-0) NY Jets (10-6-0)
1987	Indianapolis Colts (9-6-0)	Cleveland Browns (10-5-0)	Buffalo Bills (12-4-0)	Houston Oilers (9-6-0) Seattle Seahawks (9-6-0)
1988	Buffalo Bills (12-4-0)	Cincinnati Bengals (12-4-0)	Seattle Seahawks (9-7-0)	Cleveland Browns (10-6-0) Houston Oilers (10-6-0)
1989	Buffalo Bills (9-7-0)	Cleveland Browns (9-6-1)	Denver Broncos (11-5-0)	Houston Oilers (9-7-0) Pittsburgh Steelers (9-7-0)
1990	Buffalo Bills (13-3-0)	Cincinnati Bengals (9-7-0)	L.A. Raiders (12-4-0)	Houston Oilers (9-7-0) Kansas City Chiefs (11-5-0) Miami Dolphins (12-4-0)
1991	Buffalo Bills (13-3-0)	Houston Oilers (11-5-0)	Denver Broncos (12-4-0)	Kansas City Chiefs (11-5-0) Miami Dolphins (12-4-0) NY Jets (8-8-0)
1992	Miami Dolphins (11-5-0)	Pittsburgh Steelers (11-5-0)	San Diego Chargers (11-5-0)	Buffalo Bills (11-5-0) Houston Oilers (10-6-0) Kansas City Chiefs (10-6-0)
1993	Buffalo Bills (12-4-0)	Houston Oilers (12-4-0)	Kansas City Chiefs (11-5-0)	Denver Broncos (9-7-0) L.A. Raiders (10-6-0) Pittsburgh Steelers (9-7-0)
1994	Miami Dolphins (10-6-0)	Pittsburgh Steelers (12-4-0)	San Diego Chargers (11-5-0)	Cleveland Browns (11-5-0) Kansas City Chiefs (9-7-0) New England Patriots (10-6-0)
1995	Buffalo Bills (10-6-0)	Pittsburgh Steelers (11-5-0)	Kansas City Chiefs (13-3-0)	Miami Dolphins (9-7-0) Indianapolis Colts (9-7-0) San Diego Chargers (9-7-0)

NATIONAL FOOTBALL CONFERENCE

Year	Eastern	Central	Western	Wild card
1970	Dallas Cowboys (10-4-0)	Minnesota Vikings (12-2-0)	San Francisco 49ers (10-3-1)	Detroit Lions (10-4-0)
1971	Dallas Cowboys (11-3-0)	Minnesota Vikings (11-3-0)	San Francisco 49ers (9-5-0)	Washington Redskins (9-4-1)
1972	Washington Redskins (11-3-0)	Green Bay Packers (10-4-0)	San Francisco 49ers (8-5-1)	Dallas Cowboys (10-4-0)
1973	Dallas Cowboys (10-4-0)	Minnesota Vikings (12-2-0)	L.A. Rams (12-2-0)	Washington Redskins (10-4-0)
1974	St. Louis Cardinals (10-4-0)	Minnesota Vikings (10-4-0)	L.A. Rams (10-4-0)	Washington Redskins (10-4-0)
1975	St. Louis Cardinals (11-3-0)	Minnesota Vikings (12-2-0)	L.A. Rams (12-2-0)	Dallas Cowboys (10-4-0)
1976	Dallas Cowboys (11-3-0)	Minnesota Vikings (11-2-1)	L.A. Rams (10-3-1)	Washington Redskins (10-4-0)
1977	Dallas Cowboys (12-2-0)	Minnesota Vikings (9-5-0)	L.A. Rams (10-4-0)	Chicago Bears (9-5-0)
1978	Dallas Cowboys (12-4-0)	Minnesota Vikings (8-7-1)	L.A. Rams (12-4-0)	Atlanta Falcons (9-7-0) Philadelphia Eagles (9-7-0)
1979	Dallas Cowboys (11-5-0)	Tampa Bay Buccaneers (10-6-0)	L.A. Rams (9-7-0)	Chicago Bears (10-6-0) Philadelphia Eagles (11-5-0)
1980	Philadelphia Eagles (12-4-0)	Minnesota Vikings (9-7-0)	Atlanta Falcons (12-4-0)	Dallas Cowboys (12-4-0) L.A. Rams (11-5-0)
1981	Dallas Cowboys (12-4-0)	Tampa Bay Buccaneers (9-7-0)	San Francisco 49ers (13-3-0)	NY Giants (9-7-0) Philadelphia Eagles (10-6-0)
1982	Strike abbreviated season. See note.			
1983	Washington Redskins (14-2-0)	Detroit Lions (9-7-0)	San Francisco 49ers (10-6-0)	Dallas Cowboys (12-4-0) L.A. Rams (9-7-0)
1984	Washington Redskins (11-5-0)	Chicago Bears (10-6-0)	San Francisco 49ers (15-1-0)	L.A. Rams (10-6-0) NY Giants (9-7-0)
1985	Dallas Cowboys (10-6-0)	Chicago Bears (15-1-0)	L.A. Rams (11-5-0)	NY Giants (10-6-0) San Francisco 49ers (10-6-0)
1986	NY Giants (14-2-0)	Chicago Bears (14-2-0)	San Francisco 49ers (10-5-1)	L.A. Rams (10-6-0) Washington Redskins (12-4-0)
1987	Washington Redskins (11-4-0)	Chicago Bears (11-4-0)	San Francisco 49ers (13-2-0)	Minnesota Vikings (8-7-0) New Orleans Saints (12-3-0)
1988	Philadelphia Eagles (10-6-0)	Chicago Bears (12-4-0)	San Francisco 49ers (10-6-0)	L.A. Rams (10-6-0) Minnesota Vikings (11-5-0)
1989	NY Giants (12-4-0)	Minnesota Vikings (10-6-0)	San Francisco 49ers (14-2-0)	L.A. Rams (11-5-0) Philadelphia Eagles (11-5-0)
1990	NY Giants (13-3-0)	Chicago Bears (11-5-0)	San Francisco 49ers (14-2-0)	New Orleans Saints (8-8-0) Philadelphia Eagles (10-6-0) Washington Redskins (10-6-0)
1991	Washington Redskins (14-2-0)	Detroit Lions (12-4-0)	New Orleans Saints (11-5-0)	Atlanta Falcons (10-6-0) Chicago Bears (11-5-0) Dallas Cowboys (11-5-0)
1992	Dallas Cowboys (13-3-0)	Minnesota Vikings (11-5-0)	San Francisco 49ers (14-2-0)	New Orleans Saints (12-4-0) Philadelphia Eagles (11-5-0) Washington Redskins (9-7-0)
1993	Dallas Cowboys (12-4-0)	Detroit Lions (10-6-0)	San Francisco 49ers (10-6-0)	Green Bay Packers (9-7-0) Minnesota Vikings (9-7-0) NY Giants (11-5-0)
1994	Dallas Cowboys (12-4-0)	Minnesota Vikings (10-6-0)	San Francisco 49ers (13-3-0)	Chicago Bears (9-7-0) Detroit Lions (9-7-0) Green Bay Packers (9-7-0)
1995	Dallas Cowboys (12-4-0)	Green Bay Packers (11-5-0)	San Francisco 49ers (11-5-0)	Philadelphia Eagles (10-6-0) Detroit Lions (10-6-0) Atlanta Falcons (9-7-0)

Note: A strike shortened the 1982 season from 16 to 9 games. The top 8 teams in each conference played in a tournament to determine the conference champion. AFC—Miami Dolphins, New England Patriots, L.A. Raiders, Cleveland Browns, NY Jets, Cincinnati Bengals, San Diego Chargers, Pittsburgh Steelers. NFC—Washington Redskins, Detroit Lions, Green Bay Packers, St. Louis Cardinals, Dallas Cowboys, Tampa Bay Buccaneers, Minnesota Vikings, Atlanta Falcons.

NFL Playoff Results, 1996-2010

Year	Conference	Division	Winner (W-L-T)	Playoffs[1]	Year
1996	American	Eastern	New England Patriots (11-5-0)	Jacksonville* 30, Denver 27	1996
		Central	Pittsburgh Steelers (10-6-0)	New England 28, Pittsburgh 3	
		Western	Denver Broncos (13-3-0)	New England 20, Jacksonville* 6	
	National	Eastern	Dallas Cowboys (10-6-0)	Green Bay 35, San Francisco* 14	
		Central	Green Bay Packers (13-3-0)	Carolina 26, Dallas 17	
		Western	Carolina Panthers (12-4-0)	Green Bay 30, Carolina 13	
1997	American	Eastern	New England Patriots (10-6-0)	Pittsburgh 7, New England 6	1997
		Central	Pittsburgh Steelers (11-5-0)	Denver* 14, Kansas City 10	
		Western	Kansas City Chiefs (13-3-0)	Denver* 24, Pittsburgh 21	
	National	Eastern	NY Giants (10-5-1)	San Francisco 38, Minnesota* 22	
		Central	Green Bay Packers (13-3-0)	Green Bay 21, Tampa Bay* 7	
		Western	San Francisco 49ers (13-3-0)	Green Bay 23, San Francisco 10	
1998	American	Eastern	NY Jets (12-4-0)	Denver 38, Miami* 3	1998
		Central	Jacksonville Jaguars (11-5-0)	NY Jets 34, Jacksonville 24	
		Western	Denver Broncos (14-2-0)	Denver 23, NY Jets 10	
	National	Eastern	Dallas Cowboys (10-6-0)	Atlanta 20, San Francisco* 18	
		Central	Minnesota Vikings (15-1-0)	Minnesota 41, Arizona* 21	
		Western	Atlanta Falcons (14-2-0)	Atlanta 30, Minnesota 27 (OT)	
1999	American	Eastern	Indianapolis Colts (13-3-0)	Jacksonville 62, Miami* 7	1999
		Central	Jacksonville Jaguars (14-2-0)	Tennessee* 19, Indianapolis 16	
		Western	Seattle Seahawks (9-7-0)	Tennessee* 33, Jacksonville 14	
	National	Eastern	Washington Redskins (10-6-0)	Tampa Bay 14, Washington 13	
		Central	Tampa Bay Buccaneers (11-5-0)	St. Louis 49, Minnesota* 37	
		Western	St. Louis Rams (13-3-0)	St. Louis 11, Tampa Bay 6	
2000	American	Eastern	Miami Dolphins (11-5-0)	Oakland 27, Miami 0	2000
		Central	Tennessee Titans (13-3-0)	Baltimore* 24, Tennessee 10	
		Western	Oakland Raiders (12-4-0)	Baltimore* 16, Oakland 3	
	National	Eastern	NY Giants (12-4-0)	Minnesota 34, New Orleans 16	
		Central	Minnesota Vikings (11-5-0)	NY Giants 20, Philadelphia* 10	
		Western	New Orleans Saints (10-6-0)	NY Giants 41, Minnesota 0	
2001	American	Eastern	New England Patriots (11-5-0)	New England 16, Oakland 13	2001
		Central	Pittsburgh Steelers (13-3-0)	Pittsburgh 27, Baltimore 10	
		Western	Oakland Raiders (10-6-0)	New England 24, Pittsburgh 17	
	National	Eastern	Philadelphia Eagles (11-5-0)	Philadelphia 33, Chicago 19	
		Central	Chicago Bears (13-3-0)	St. Louis 45, Green Bay* 17	
		Western	St. Louis Rams (14-2-0)	St. Louis 29, Philadelphia 24	
2002	American	East	NY Jets (9-7-0)		2002
		North	Pittsburgh Steelers (10-5-1)	Oakland 30, NY Jets 10	
		South	Tennessee Titans (11-5-0)	Tennessee 34, Pittsburgh 31	
		West	Oakland Raiders (11-5-0)	Oakland 41, Tennessee 24	
	National	East	Philadelphia Eagles (12-4-0)		
		North	Green Bay Packers (12-4-0)	Philadelphia 20, Atlanta* 6	
		South	Tampa Bay Buccaneers (12-4-0)	Tampa Bay 31, San Francisco 6	
		West	San Francisco 49ers (10-6-0)	Tampa Bay 27, Philadelphia 10	
2003	American	East	New England Patriots (14-2-0)		2003
		North	Baltimore Ravens (10-6-0)	Indianapolis 38, Kansas City 31	
		South	Indianapolis Colts (12-4-0)	New England 17, Tennessee* 14	
		West	Kansas City Chiefs (13-3-0)	New England 24, Indianapolis 14	
	National	East	Philadelphia Eagles (12-4-0)		
		North	Green Bay Packers (10-6-0)	Carolina 29, St. Louis 23	
		South	Carolina Panthers (11-5-0)	Philadelphia 20, Green Bay 17	
		West	St. Louis Rams (12-4-0)	Carolina 14, Philadelphia 3	
2004	American	East	New England Patriots (14-2-0)		2004
		North	Pittsburgh Steelers (15-1-0)	Pittsburgh 20, NY Jets* 17 (OT)	
		South	Indianapolis Colts (12-4-0)	New England 20, Indianapolis 3	
		West	San Diego Chargers (12-4-0)	New England 41, Pittsburgh 27	
	National	East	Philadelphia Eagles (13-3-0)		
		North	Green Bay Packers (10-6-0)	Atlanta 47, St. Louis* 17	
		South	Atlanta Falcons (11-5-0)	Philadelphia 27, Minnesota* 14	
		West	Seattle Seahawks (9-7-0)	Philadelphia 27, Atlanta 10	
2005	American	East	New England Patriots (10-6-0)		2005
		North	Cincinnati Bengals (11-5-0)	Denver 27, New England 13	
		South	Indianapolis Colts (14-2-0)	Pittsburgh* 21, Indianapolis 18	
		West	Denver Broncos (13-3-0)	Pittsburgh* 34, Denver 17	
	National	East	NY Giants (11-5-0)		
		North	Chicago Bears (11-5-0)	Seattle 20, Washington* 10	
		South	Tampa Bay Buccaneers (11-5-0)	Carolina* 29, Chicago 21	
		West	Seattle Seahawks (13-3-0)	Seattle 34, Carolina* 14	
2006	American	East	New England Patriots (12-4-0)		2006
		North	Baltimore Ravens (13-3-0)	Indianapolis 15, Baltimore 6	
		South	Indianapolis Colts (12-4-0)	New England 24, San Diego 21	
		West	San Diego Chargers (14-2-0)	Indianapolis 38, New England 34	
	National	East	Philadelphia Eagles (10-6-0)		
		North	Chicago Bears (13-3-0)	New Orleans 27, Philadelphia 24	
		South	New Orleans Saints (10-6-0)	Chicago 27, Seattle 24 (OT)	
		West	Seattle Seahawks (9-7-0)	Chicago 39, New Orleans 14	

Year	Conference	Division	Winner (W-L-T)	Playoffs[1]	Year
2007	American	East	New England Patriots (16-0-0)		2007
		North	Pittsburgh Steelers (10-6-0)	New England 31, Jacksonville* 20	
		South	Indianapolis Colts (13-3-0)	San Diego 28, Indianapolis 24	
		West	San Diego Chargers (11-5-0)	New England 21, San Diego 12	
	National	East	Dallas Cowboys (13-3-0)		
		North	Green Bay Packers (13-3-0)	Green Bay 42, Seattle 20	
		South	Tampa Bay Buccaneers (9-7-0)	NY Giants* 21, Dallas 17	
		West	Seattle Seahawks (10-6-0)	NY Giants* 22, Green Bay 20	
2008	American	East	Miami Dolphins (11-5-0)		2008
		North	Pittsburgh Steelers (12-4-0)	Baltimore* 13, Tennessee 10	
		South	Tennessee Titans (13-3-0)	Pittsburgh 35, San Diego 24	
		West	San Diego Chargers (8-8-0)	Pittsburgh 23, Baltimore* 14	
	National	East	NY Giants (12-4-0)		
		North	Minnesota Vikings (10-6-0)	Arizona 33, Carolina 13	
		South	Carolina Panthers (12-4-0)	Philadelphia* 23, NY Giants 11	
		West	Arizona Cardinals (9-7-0)	Arizona 32, Philadelphia* 25	
2009	American	East	New England Patriots (10-6-0)		2009
		North	Cincinnati Bengals (10-6-0)	Indianapolis 20, Baltimore 3	
		South	Indianapolis Colts (14-2-0)	NY Jets* 17, San Diego 14	
		West	San Diego Chargers (13-3-0)	Indianapolis 30, NY Jets* 17	
	National	East	Dallas Cowboys (11-5-0)		
		North	Minnesota Vikings (12-4-0)	New Orleans 45, Arizona 14	
		South	New Orleans Saints (13-3-0)	Minnesota 34, Dallas 3	
		West	Arizona Cardinals (10-6-0)	New Orleans 31, Minnesota 28 (OT)	
2010	American	East	New England Patriots (14-2-0)		2010
		North	Pittsburgh Steelers (12-4-0)	Pittsburgh 31, Baltimore* 24	
		South	Indianapolis Colts (10-6-0)	NY Jets* 28, New England 21	
		West	Kansas City Chiefs (10-6-0)	Pittsburgh 24, NY Jets* 19	
	National	East	Philadelphia Eagles (10-6-0)		
		North	Chicago Bears (11-5-0)	Green Bay* 48, Atlanta 21	
		South	Atlanta Falcons (13-3-0)	Chicago 35, Seattle 24	
		West	Seattle Seahawks (7-9-0)	Green Bay* 21, Chicago 14	

*Wild card team. (1) Only the final two conference playoff rounds are shown.

American Football Conference Leaders, 1960-2010
(American Football League, 1960-69)

Passing (based on QB rating points)						Receptions			
Player, team	Att	Comp	YG	TD	Year	Player, team	Rec	YG	TD
Jack Kemp, L.A. Chargers	406	211	3,018	20	1960	Lionel Taylor, Denver	92	1,235	12
George Blanda, Houston	362	187	3,330	36	1961	Lionel Taylor, Denver	100	1,176	4
Len Dawson, Dallas Texans	310	189	2,759	29	1962	Lionel Taylor, Denver	77	908	4
Tobin Rote, San Diego	286	170	2,510	20	1963	Lionel Taylor, Denver	78	1,101	10
Len Dawson, Kansas City	354	199	2,879	30	1964	Charley Hennigan, Houston	101	1,546	8
John Hadl, San Diego	348	174	2,798	20	1965	Lionel Taylor, Denver	85	1,131	6
Len Dawson, Kansas City	284	159	2,527	26	1966	Lance Alworth, San Diego	73	1,383	13
Daryle Lamonica, Oakland	425	220	3,228	30	1967	George Sauer, NY Jets	75	1,189	6
Len Dawson, Kansas City	224	131	2,109	17	1968	Lance Alworth, San Diego	68	1,312	10
Greg Cook, Cincinnati	197	106	1,854	15	1969	Lance Alworth, San Diego	64	1,003	4
Daryle Lamonica, Oakland	356	179	2,516	22	1970	Marlin Briscoe, Buffalo	57	1,036	8
Bob Griese, Miami	263	145	2,089	19	1971	Fred Biletnikoff, Oakland	61	929	9
Earl Morrall, Miami	150	83	1,360	11	1972	Fred Biletnikoff, Oakland	58	802	7
Ken Stabler, Oakland	260	163	1,997	14	1973	Fred Willis, Houston	57	371	1
Ken Anderson, Cincinnati	328	213	2,667	18	1974	Lydell Mitchell, Baltimore Colts	72	544	2
Ken Anderson, Cincinnati	377	228	3,169	21	1975	Reggie Rucker, Cleveland	60	770	3
						Lydell Mitchell, Baltimore Colts	60	554	4
Ken Stabler, Oakland	291	194	2,737	27	1976	MacArthur Lane, Kansas City	66	686	1
Bob Griese, Miami	307	180	2,252	22	1977	Lydell Mitchell, Baltimore Colts	71	620	4
Terry Bradshaw, Pittsburgh	368	207	2,915	28	1978	Steve Largent, Seattle	71	1,168	8
Dan Fouts, San Diego	530	332	4,082	24	1979	Joe Washington, Baltimore Colts	82	750	3
Brian Sipe, Cleveland	554	337	4,132	30	1980	Kellen Winslow, San Diego	89	1,290	9
Ken Anderson, Cincinnati	479	300	3,754	29	1981	Kellen Winslow, San Diego	88	1,075	10
Ken Anderson, Cincinnati	309	218	2,495	12	1982	Kellen Winslow, San Diego	54	721	6
Dan Marino, Miami	296	173	2,210	20	1983	Todd Christensen, L.A. Raiders	92	1,247	12
Dan Marino, Miami	564	362	5,084	48	1984	Ozzie Newsome, Cleveland	89	1,001	5
Ken O'Brien, NY Jets	488	297	3,888	25	1985	Lionel James, San Diego	86	1,027	6
Dan Marino, Miami	623	378	4,746	44	1986	Todd Christensen, L.A. Raiders	95	1,153	8
Bernie Kosar, Cleveland	389	241	3,033	22	1987	Al Toon, NY Jets	68	976	5
Boomer Esiason, Cincinnati	388	223	3,572	28	1988	Al Toon, NY Jets	93	1,067	5
Boomer Esiason, Cincinnati	455	258	3,525	28	1989	Andre Reed, Buffalo	88	1,312	9
Jim Kelly, Buffalo	346	219	2,829	24	1990	Haywood Jeffires, Houston	74	1,048	8
						Drew Hill, Houston	74	1,019	5

Passing (based on QB rating points) / Receptions

Player, team	Att	Comp	YG	TD	Year	Player, team	Rec	YG	TD
Jim Kelly, Buffalo	474	304	3,844	33	1991	Haywood Jeffires, Houston	100	1,181	7
Warren Moon, Houston	346	224	2,521	18	1992	Haywood Jeffires, Houston	90	913	9
John Elway, Denver	551	348	4,030	25	1993	Reggie Langhorne, Indianapolis	85	1,038	3
Dan Marino, Miami	615	385	4,453	30	1994	Ben Coates, New England	96	1,174	7
Jim Harbaugh, Indianapolis	314	200	2,575	17	1995	Carl Pickens, Cincinnati	99	1,234	17
John Elway, Denver	466	287	3,328	26	1996	Carl Pickens, Cincinnati	100	1,180	12
Mark Brunell, Jacksonville	435	264	3,281	18	1997	Tim Brown, Oakland	104	1,408	5
Vinny Testaverde, NY Jets	421	259	3,256	29	1998	O. J. McDuffie, Miami	90	1,050	7
Peyton Manning, Indianapolis	533	331	4,135	26	1999	Jimmy Smith, Jacksonville	116	1,636	6
Brian Griese, Denver	336	216	2,688	19	2000	Marvin Harrison, Indianapolis	102	1,413	14
Rich Gannon, Oakland	549	361	3,828	27	2001	Rod Smith, Denver	113	1,343	11
Chad Pennington, NY Jets	399	275	3,120	22	2002	Marvin Harrison, Indianapolis	143	1,722	11
Steve McNair, Tennessee	400	250	3,215	24	2003	LaDainian Tomlinson, San Diego	100	725	4
Peyton Manning, Indianapolis	497	336	4,557	49	2004	Tony Gonzalez, Kansas City	102	1,258	7
Peyton Manning, Indianapolis	453	305	3,747	28	2005	Chad Johnson, Cincinnati	97	1,432	9
Peyton Manning, Indianapolis	557	362	4,397	31	2006	Andre Johnson, Houston	103	1,147	5
Tom Brady, New England	578	398	4,806	50	2007	Wes Welker, New England	112	1,175	8
Philip Rivers, San Diego	478	312	4,009	34	2008	Andre Johnson, Houston	115	1,575	8
Philip Rivers, San Diego	486	317	4,254	28	2009	Wes Walker, New England	123	1,348	4
Tom Brady, New England	492	324	3,900	36	2010	Reggie Wayne, Indianapolis	111	1,355	6

Scoring / Rushing

Player, team	TD	PAT	FG	Pts	Year	Player, team	Yds	Att	TD
Gene Mingo, Denver	6	33	18	123	1960	Abner Haynes, Dallas Texans	875	156	9
Gino Cappelletti, Boston	8	48	17	147	1961	Billy Cannon, Houston	948	200	6
Gene Mingo, Denver	4	32	27	137	1962	Cookie Gilchrist, Buffalo	1,096	214	13
Gino Cappelletti, Boston	2	35	22	113	1963	Clem Daniels, Oakland	1,099	215	3
Gino Cappelletti, Boston	7	36	25	155	1964	Cookie Gilchrist, Buffalo	981	230	6
Gino Cappelletti, Boston	9	27	17	132	1965	Paul Lowe, San Diego	1,121	222	7
Gino Cappelletti, Boston	6	35	16	119	1966	Jim Nance, Boston	1,458	299	11
George Blanda, Oakland	0	56	20	116	1967	Jim Nance, Boston	1,216	269	7
Jim Turner, NY Jets	0	43	34	145	1968	Paul Robinson, Cincinnati	1,023	238	8
Jim Turner, NY Jets	0	33	32	129	1969	Dickie Post, San Diego	873	182	6
Jan Stenerud, Kansas City	0	26	30	116	1970	Floyd Little, Denver	901	209	3
Garo Yepremian, Miami	0	33	28	117	1971	Floyd Little, Denver	1,133	284	6
Bobby Howfield, NY Jets	0	40	27	121	1972	O. J. Simpson, Buffalo	1,251	292	6
Roy Gerela, Pittsburgh	0	36	29	123	1973	O. J. Simpson, Buffalo	2,003	332	12
Roy Gerela, Pittsburgh	0	33	20	93	1974	Otis Armstrong, Denver	1,407	263	9
O. J. Simpson, Buffalo	23	0	0	138	1975	O. J. Simpson, Buffalo	1,817	329	16
Toni Linhart, Baltimore Colts	0	49	20	109	1976	O. J. Simpson, Buffalo	1,503	290	8
Errol Mann, Oakland	0	39	20	99	1977	Mark van Eeghen, Oakland	1,273	324	7
Pat Leahy, NY Jets	0	41	22	107	1978	Earl Campbell, Houston	1,450	302	13
John Smith, New England	0	46	23	115	1979	Earl Campbell, Houston	1,697	368	19
John Smith, New England	0	51	26	129	1980	Earl Campbell, Houston	1,934	373	13
Jim Breech, Cincinnati	0	49	22	115	1981	Earl Campbell, Houston	1,376	361	10
Nick Lowery, Kansas City	0	37	26	115					
Marcus Allen, L.A. Raiders	14	0	0	84	1982	Freeman McNeil, NY Jets	786	151	6
Gary Anderson, Pittsburgh	0	38	27	119	1983	Curt Warner, Seattle	1,449	335	13
Gary Anderson, Pittsburgh	0	45	24	117	1984	Earnest Jackson, San Diego	1,179	296	8
Gary Anderson, Pittsburgh	0	40	33	139	1985	Marcus Allen, L.A. Raiders	1,759	380	11
Tony Franklin, New England	0	44	32	140	1986	Curt Warner, Seattle	1,481	319	13
Jim Breech, Cincinnati	0	25	24	97	1987	Eric Dickerson, L.A. Rams-Ind.	1,288*	283	6
Scott Norwood, Buffalo	0	33	32	129	1988	Eric Dickerson, Indianapolis	1,659	388	14
David Treadwell, Denver	0	39	27	120	1989	Christian Okoye, Kansas City	1,480	370	12
Nick Lowery, Kansas City	0	37	34	139	1990	Thurman Thomas, Buffalo	1,297	271	11
Pete Stoyanovich, Miami	0	28	31	121	1991	Thurman Thomas, Buffalo	1,407	288	7
Pete Stoyanovich, Miami	0	34	30	124	1992	Barry Foster, Pittsburgh	1,690	390	11
Jeff Jaeger, L.A. Raiders	0	27	35	132	1993	Thurman Thomas, Buffalo	1,315	355	6
John Carney, San Diego	0	33	34	135	1994	Chris Warren, Seattle	1,545	333	9
Norm Johnson, Pittsburgh	0	39	34	141	1995	Curtis Martin, New England	1,487	368	14
Cary Blanchard, Indianapolis	0	27	36	135	1996	Terrell Davis, Denver	1,538	345	13
Mike Hollis, Jacksonville	0	41	31	134	1997	Terrell Davis, Denver	1,750	369	15
Steve Christie, Buffalo	0	41	33	140	1998	Terrell Davis, Denver	2,008	392	21
Mike Vanderjagt, Indianapolis	0	43	34	145	1999	Edgerrin James, Indianapolis	1,553	369	13
Matt Stover, Baltimore	0	30	35	135	2000	Edgerrin James, Indianapolis	1,709	387	13
Mike Vanderjagt, Indianapolis	0	41	28	125	2001	Priest Holmes, Kansas City	1,555	327	8
Priest Holmes, Kansas City	24	0	0	144	2002	Ricky Williams, Miami	1,853	383	16
Priest Holmes, Kansas City	27	0	0	162	2003	Jamal Lewis, Baltimore	2,066	387	14
Adam Vinatieri, New England	0	48	31	141	2004	Curtis Martin, NY Jets	1,697	371	12
Shayne Graham, Cincinnati	0	47	28	131	2005	Larry Johnson, Kansas City	1,750	336	20
LaDainian Tomlinson, San Diego	31	0	0	186	2006	LaDainian Tomlinson, San Diego	1,815	348	28
Randy Moss, New England	23	0	0	138	2007	LaDainian Tomlinson, San Diego	1,474	315	15
Stephen Gostkowski, New England	0	40	36	148	2008	Thomas Jones, NY Jets	1,312	290	13
Nate Kaeding, San Diego	0	50	32	146	2009	Chris Johnson, Tennessee	2,006	358	14
Sebastian Janikowski, Oakland	0	43	33	142	2010	Arian Foster, Houston	1,616	327	16

*Includes 277 yards after being traded to NFC; 1,011 yards led AFC.

National Football Conference Leaders, 1960-2010

(National Football League, 1960-69)

Passing (based on QB rating points) Player, team	Att	Comp	YG	TD	Year	Receptions Player, team	Rec	YG	TD
Milt Plum, Cleveland	250	151	2,297	21	1960	Raymond Berry, Baltimore Colts	74	1,298	10
Milt Plum, Cleveland	302	177	2,416	18	1961	Jim Phillips, L.A. Rams	78	1,092	5
Bart Starr, Green Bay	285	178	2,438	12	1962	Bobby Mitchell, Washington	72	1,384	11
Y. A. Tittle, NY Giants	367	221	3,145	36	1963	Bobby Joe Conrad, St. Louis Cardinals	73	967	10
Bart Starr, Green Bay	272	163	2,144	15	1964	Johnny Morris, Chicago	93	1,200	10
Rudy Bukich, Chicago	312	176	2,641	20	1965	Dave Parks, San Francisco	80	1,344	12
Bart Starr, Green Bay	251	156	2,257	14	1966	Charley Taylor, Washington	72	1,119	12
Sonny Jurgensen, Washington	508	288	3,747	31	1967	Charley Taylor, Washington	70	990	9
Earl Morrall, Baltimore Colts	317	182	2,909	26	1968	Clifton McNeil, San Francisco	71	994	7
Sonny Jurgensen, Washington	442	274	3,102	22	1969	Dan Abramowicz, New Orleans	73	1,015	7
John Brodie, San Francisco	378	223	2,941	24	1970	Dick Gordon, Chicago	71	1,026	13
Roger Staubach, Dallas	211	126	1,882	15	1971	Bob Tucker, NY Giants	59	791	4
Norm Snead, NY Giants	325	196	2,307	17	1972	Harold Jackson, Philadelphia	62	1,048	4
Roger Staubach, Dallas	286	179	2,428	23	1973	Harold Carmichael, Philadelphia	67	1,116	9
Sonny Jurgensen, Washington	167	107	1,185	11	1974	Charles Young, Philadelphia	63	696	3
Fran Tarkenton, Minnesota	425	273	2,994	25	1975	Chuck Foreman, Minnesota	73	691	9
James Harris, L.A. Rams	158	91	1,460	8	1976	Drew Pearson, Dallas	58	806	6
Roger Staubach, Dallas	361	210	2,620	18	1977	Ahmad Rashad, Minnesota	51	681	2
Roger Staubach, Dallas	413	231	3,190	25	1978	Rickey Young, Minnesota	88	704	5
Roger Staubach, Dallas	461	267	3,586	27	1979	Ahmad Rashad, Minnesota	80	1,156	9
Ron Jaworski, Philadelphia	451	257	3,529	27	1980	Earl Cooper, San Francisco	83	567	4
Joe Montana, San Francisco	488	311	3,565	19	1981	Dwight Clark, San Francisco	85	1,105	4
Joe Thiesmann, Washington	252	161	2,033	13	1982	Dwight Clark, San Francisco	60	913	5
Steve Bartkowski, Atlanta	432	274	3,167	22	1983	Roy Green, St. Louis Cardinals	78	1,227	14
						Charlie Brown, Washington	78	1,225	8
						Earnest Gray, NY Giants	78	1,139	5
Joe Montana, San Francisco	432	279	3,630	28	1984	Art Monk, Washington	106	1,372	7
Joe Montana, San Francisco	494	303	3,653	27	1985	Roger Craig, San Francisco	92	1,016	6
Tommy Kramer, Minnesota	372	208	3,000	24	1986	Jerry Rice, San Francisco	86	1,570	15
Joe Montana, San Francisco	398	266	3,054	31	1987	J. T. Smith, St. Louis Cardinals	91	1,117	8
Wade Wilson, Minnesota	332	204	2,746	15	1988	Henry Ellard, L.A. Rams	86	1,414	10
Joe Montana, San Francisco	386	271	3,521	26	1989	Sterling Sharpe, Green Bay	90	1,423	12
Phil Simms, NY Giants	311	184	2,284	15	1990	Jerry Rice, San Francisco	100	1,502	13
Steve Young, San Francisco	279	180	2,517	17	1991	Michael Irvin, Dallas	93	1,523	8
Steve Young, San Francisco	402	268	3,465	25	1992	Sterling Sharpe, Green Bay	108	1,461	13
Steve Young, San Francisco	462	314	4,023	29	1993	Sterling Sharpe, Green Bay	112	1,274	11
Steve Young, San Francisco	461	324	3,969	35	1994	Cris Carter, Minnesota	122	1,256	7
Brett Favre, Green Bay	570	359	4,413	38	1995	Herman Moore, Detroit	123	1,686	14
Steve Young, San Francisco	316	214	2,410	14	1996	Jerry Rice, San Francisco	108	1,254	8
Steve Young, San Francisco	356	241	3,029	19	1997	Herman Moore, Detroit	104	1,293	8
Randall Cunningham, Minnesota	425	259	3,704	34	1998	Frank Sanders, Arizona	89	1,145	3
Kurt Warner, St. Louis	499	325	4,353	41	1999	Muhsin Muhammad, Carolina	96	1,253	8
Trent Green, St. Louis	240	145	2,063	16	2000	Muhsin Muhammad, Carolina	102	1,183	6
Kurt Warner, St. Louis	546	375	4,830	36	2001	Keyshawn Johnson, Tampa Bay	106	1,266	1
Brad Johnson, Tampa Bay	451	281	3,049	22	2002	Randy Moss, Minnesota	106	1,347	7
Daunte Culpepper, Minnesota	454	295	3,479	25	2003	Torry Holt, St. Louis	117	1,696	12
Daunte Culpepper, Minnesota	548	379	4,717	39	2004	Joe Horn, New Orleans	94	1,399	11
						Torry Holt, St. Louis	94	1,372	10
Matt Hasselbeck, Seattle	449	294	3,459	24	2005	Steve Smith, Carolina	103	1,563	12
						Larry Fitzgerald, Arizona	103	1,409	10
Drew Brees, New Orleans	554	356	4,418	26	2006	Mike Furrey, Detroit	98	1,086	6
Tony Romo, Dallas	520	335	4,211	36	2007	Larry Fitzgerald, Arizona	100	1,409	10
Kurt Warner, Arizona	598	401	4,583	30	2008	Larry Fitzgerald, Arizona	96	1,431	12
Drew Brees, New Orleans	514	363	4,388	34	2009	Steve Smith, NY Giants	107	1,220	7
Aaron Rodgers, Green Bay	475	312	3,922	28	2010	Roddy White, Atlanta	115	1,389	10

Scoring Player, team	TD	PAT	FG	Pts	Year	Rushing Player, team	Yds	Att	TD
Paul Hornung, Green Bay	15	41	15	176	1960	Jim Brown, Cleveland	1,257	215	9
Paul Hornung, Green Bay	10	41	15	146	1961	Jim Brown, Cleveland	1,408	305	8
Jim Taylor, Green Bay	19	0	0	114	1962	Jim Taylor, Green Bay	1,474	272	19
Don Chandler, NY Giants	0	52	18	106	1963	Jim Brown, Cleveland	1,863	291	12
Lenny Moore, Baltimore Colts	20	0	0	120	1964	Jim Brown, Cleveland	1,446	280	7
Gale Sayers, Chicago	22	0	0	132	1965	Jim Brown, Cleveland	1,544	289	17
Bruce Gossett, L.A. Rams	0	29	28	113	1966	Gale Sayers, Chicago	1,231	229	8
Jim Bakken, St. Louis Cardinals	0	36	27	117	1967	Leroy Kelly, Cleveland	1,205	235	11
Leroy Kelly, Cleveland	20	0	0	120	1968	Leroy Kelly, Cleveland	1,239	248	16
Fred Cox, Minnesota	0	43	26	121	1969	Gale Sayers, Chicago	1,032	236	8
Fred Cox, Minnesota	0	35	30	125	1970	Larry Brown, Washington	1,125	237	5
Curt Knight, Washington	0	27	29	114	1971	John Brockington, Green Bay	1,105	216	4
Chester Marcol, Green Bay	0	29	33	128	1972	Larry Brown, Washington	1,216	285	8
David Ray, L.A. Rams	0	40	30	130	1973	John Brockington, Green Bay	1,144	265	3
Chester Marcol, Green Bay	0	19	25	94	1974	Lawrence McCutcheon, L.A. Rams	1,109	236	3
Chuck Foreman, Minnesota	22	0	0	132	1975	Jim Otis, St. Louis Cardinals	1,076	269	5
Mark Moseley, Washington	0	31	22	97	1976	Walter Payton, Chicago	1,390	311	13

Scoring Player, team	TD	PAT	FG	Pts	Year	Rushing Player, team	Yds	Att	TD
Walter Payton, Chicago	16	0	0	96	1977	Walter Payton, Chicago	1,852	339	14
Frank Corral, L.A. Rams	0	31	29	118	1978	Walter Payton, Chicago	1,395	333	11
Mark Moseley, Washington	0	39	25	114	1979	Walter Payton, Chicago	1,610	369	14
Ed Murray, Detroit	0	35	27	116	1980	Walter Payton, Chicago	1,460	317	6
Ed Murray, Detroit	0	46	25	121	1981	George Rogers, New Orleans	1,674	378	13
Rafael Septien, Dallas	0	40	27	121					
Wendell Tyler, L.A. Rams	13	0	0	78	1982	Tony Dorsett, Dallas	745	177	5
Mark Moseley, Washington	0	62	33	161	1983	Eric Dickerson, L.A. Rams	1,808	390	18
Ray Wersching, San Francisco	0	56	25	131	1984	Eric Dickerson, L.A. Rams	2,105	379	14
Kevin Butler, Chicago	0	51	31	144	1985	Gerald Riggs, Atlanta	1,719	397	10
Kevin Butler, Chicago	0	36	28	120	1986	Eric Dickerson, L.A. Rams	1,821	404	11
Jerry Rice, San Francisco	23	0	0	138	1987	Charles White, L.A. Rams	1,374	324	11
Mike Cofer, San Francisco	0	40	27	121	1988	Herschel Walker, Dallas	1,514	361	5
Mike Cofer, San Francisco	0	49	29	136	1989	Barry Sanders, Detroit	1,470	280	14
Chip Lohmiller, Washington	0	41	30	131	1990	Barry Sanders, Detroit	1,304	255	13
Chip Lohmiller, Washington	0	56	31	149	1991	Emmitt Smith, Dallas	1,563	365	12
Morten Andersen, New Orleans	0	33	29	120	1992	Emmitt Smith, Dallas	1,713	373	18
Chip Lohmiller, Washington	0	30	30	120					
Jason Hanson, Detroit	0	28	34	130	1993	Emmitt Smith, Dallas	1,486	283	9
Fuad Reveiz, Minnesota	0	30	34	132	1994	Barry Sanders, Detroit	1,883	331	7
Emmitt Smith, Dallas	22	0	0	132					
Emmitt Smith, Dallas	25	0	0	150	1995	Emmitt Smith, Dallas	1,773	377	25
John Kasay, Carolina	0	34	37	145	1996	Barry Sanders, Detroit	1,553	307	11
Richie Cunningham, Dallas	0	24	34	126	1997	Barry Sanders, Detroit	2,053	335	11
Gary Anderson, Minnesota	0	59	35	164	1998	Jamal Anderson, Atlanta	1,846	410	14
Jeff Wilkins, St. Louis	0	64	20	124	1999	Stephen Davis, Washington	1,405	290	17
Marshall Faulk, St. Louis	26	0	0	156	2000	Robert Smith, Minnesota	1,521	295	7
Marshall Faulk, St. Louis	21	0	0	128	2001	Stephen Davis, Washington	1,432	356	5
Jay Feely, Atlanta	0	42	32	138	2002	Deuce McAllister, New Orleans	1,388	325	13
Jeff Wilkins, St. Louis	0	46	39	163	2003	Ahman Green, Green Bay	1,883	355	15
David Akers, Philadelphia	0	41	27	122	2004	Shaun Alexander, Seattle	1,696	353	16
Shaun Alexander, Seattle	28	0	0	168	2005	Shaun Alexander, Seattle	1,880	370	27
Robbie Gould, Chicago	0	47	32	143	2006	Frank Gore, San Francisco	1,695	312	8
Mason Crosby, Green Bay	0	48	31	141	2007	Adrian Peterson, Minnesota	1,341	238	12
David Akers, Philadelphia	0	45	33	144	2008	Adrian Peterson, Minnesota	1,760	363	10
David Akers, Philadelphia	0	43	32	139	2009	Steven Jackson, St. Louis	1,416	324	4
David Akers, Philadelphia	0	47	32	143	2010	Michael Turner, Atlanta	1,371	334	12

NFL MVP and Rookies of the Year, 1957-2010

The Most Valuable Player, Offensive Rookie of the Year, and Defensive Rookie of the Year are a few of the many awards given out annually by the Associated Press according to the results of balloting by a nationwide panel of media. Many other organizations give out annual awards honoring the NFL's best players.

Year	NFL Most Valuable Player Award	Offensive Rookie of the Year	Defensive Rookie of the Year
1957	Jim Brown, Cleveland	NA	NA
1958	Jim Brown, Cleveland	NA	NA
1959	Charley Conerly, NY Giants	NA	NA
1960	Norm Van Brocklin, Philadelphia	NA	NA
1961	Paul Hornung, Green Bay	NA	NA
1962	Jim Taylor, Green Bay	NA	NA
1963	Y. A. Tittle, NY Giants	NA	NA
1964	Johnny Unitas, Baltimore	NA	NA
1965	Jim Brown, Cleveland	NA	NA
1966	Bart Starr, Green Bay	NA	NA
1967	Johnny Unitas, Baltimore	Mel Farr, Detroit	Lem Barney, Detroit
1968	Earl Morrall, Baltimore	Earl McCullouch, Detroit	Claude Humphrey, Atlanta
1969	Roman Gabriel, Los Angeles	Calvin Hill, Dallas	Joe Greene, Pittsburgh
1970	John Brodie, San Francisco	Dennis Shaw, Buffalo	Bruce Taylor, San Francisco
1971	Alan Page, Minnesota	John Brockington, Green Bay	Isiah Robertson, Los Angeles
1972	Larry Brown, Washington	Franco Harris, Pittsburgh	Willie Buchanon, Green Bay
1973	O. J. Simpson, Buffalo	Chuck Foreman, Minnesota	Wally Chambers, Chicago
1974	Ken Stabler, Oakland	Don Woods, San Diego	Jack Lambert, Pittsburgh
1975	Fran Tarkenton, Minnesota	Mike Thomas, Washington	Robert Brazile, Houston
1976	Bert Jones, Baltimore	Sammy White, Minnesota	Mike Haynes, New England
1977	Walter Payton, Chicago	Tony Dorsett, Dallas	A. J. Duhe, Miami
1978	Terry Bradshaw, Pittsburgh	Earl Campbell, Houston	Al Baker, Detroit
1979	Earl Campbell, Houston	Ottis Anderson, St. Louis	Jim Haslett, Buffalo
1980	Brian Sipe, Cleveland	Billy Sims, Detroit	Buddy Curry, Atlanta; Al Richardson, Atlanta
1981	Ken Anderson, Cincinnati	George Rogers, New Orleans	Lawrence Taylor, NY Giants
1982	Mark Moseley, Washington	Marcus Allen, Los Angeles	Chip Banks, Cleveland
1983	Joe Theismann, Washington	Eric Dickerson, Los Angeles	Vernon Maxwell, Baltimore
1984	Dan Marino, Miami	Louis Lipps, Pittsburgh	Bill Maas, Kansas City
1985	Marcus Allen, Los Angeles	Eddie Brown, Cincinnati	Duane Bickett, Indianapolis
1986	Lawrence Taylor, NY Giants	Rueben Mayes, New Orleans	Leslie O'Neal, San Diego
1987	John Elway, Denver	Troy Stradford, Miami	Shane Conlan, Buffalo
1988	Boomer Esiason, Cincinnati	John Stephens, New England	Erik McMillan, NY Jets
1989	Joe Montana, San Francisco	Barry Sanders, Detroit	Derrick Thomas, Kansas City
1990	Joe Montana, San Francisco	Emmitt Smith, Dallas	Mark Carrier, Chicago
1991	Thurman Thomas, Buffalo	Leonard Russell, New England	Mike Croel, Denver

Year	NFL Most Valuable Player Award	Offensive Rookie of the Year	Defensive Rookie of the Year
1992	Steve Young, San Francisco	Carl Pickens, Cincinnati	Dale Carter, Kansas City
1993	Emmitt Smith, Dallas	Jerome Bettis, Los Angeles	Dana Stubblefield, San Francisco
1994	Steve Young, San Francisco	Marshall Faulk, Indianapolis	Tim Bowens, Miami
1995	Brett Favre, Green Bay	Curtis Martin, New England	Hugh Douglas, NY Jets
1996	Brett Favre, Green Bay	Eddie George, Houston	Simeon Rice, Arizona
1997	Brett Favre, Green Bay; Barry Sanders, Detroit	Warrick Dunn, Tampa Bay	Peter Boulware, Baltimore
1998	Terrell Davis, Denver	Randy Moss, Minnesota	Charles Woodson, Oakland
1999	Kurt Warner, St. Louis	Edgerrin James, Indianapolis	Jevon Kearse, Tennessee
2000	Marshall Faulk, St. Louis	Mike Anderson, Denver	Brian Urlacher, Chicago
2001	Kurt Warner, St. Louis	Anthony Thomas, Chicago	Kendrell Bell, Pittsburgh
2002	Rich Gannon, Oakland	Clinton Portis, Denver	Julius Peppers, Carolina
2003	Peyton Manning, Indianapolis; Steve McNair, Tennessee	Anquan Boldin, Arizona	Terrell Suggs, Baltimore
2004	Peyton Manning, Indianapolis	Ben Roethlisberger, Pittsburgh	Jonathan Vilma, NY Jets
2005	Shaun Alexander, Seattle	Cadillac Williams, Tampa Bay	Shawne Merriman, San Diego
2006	LaDainian Tomlinson, San Diego	Vince Young, Tennessee	DeMeco Ryans, Houston
2007	Tom Brady, New England	Adrian Peterson, Minnesota	Patrick Willis, San Francisco
2008	Peyton Manning, Indianapolis	Matt Ryan, Atlanta	Jerod Mayo, New England
2009	Peyton Manning, Indianapolis	Percy Harvin, Minnesota	Brian Cushing, Houston
2010	Tom Brady, New England	Sam Bradford, St. Louis	Ndamukong Suh, Detroit

The Sporting News NFL All-Pro Team, 2010

Offense: Quarterback: Tom Brady, New England. Running back: Arian Foster, Houston; Maurice Jones-Drew, Jacksonville. Wide receiver: Roddy White, Atlanta; Andre Johnson, Houston. Tight end: Jason Witten, Dallas. Tackle: Joe Thomas, Cleveland; Jake Long, Miami. Guard: Chris Snee, NY Giants; Jahri Evans, New Orleans. Center: Nick Mangold, NY Jets.

Defense: Linebacker: Clay Matthews, Green Bay; James Harrison, Pittsburgh; Cameron Wake, Miami. Defensive end: Julius Peppers, Chicago; John Abraham, Atlanta. Defensive tackle: Haloti Ngata, Baltimore; Ndamukong Suh, Detroit. Cornerback: Asante Samuel, Philadelphia; Devin McCourty, New England. Safety: Troy Polamalu, Pittsburgh; Ed Reed, Baltimore.

Special Teams: Kicker: David Akers, Philadelphia. Kick returner: Leon Washington, Seattle. Punter: Shane Lechler, Oakland. Punt returner: Devin Hester, Chicago.

All-Time Professional (NFL and AFL) Football Records

(at end of 2010 season; * = active in 2010; (a) includes AFL statistics; ** = 2-point conversions scored)

Leading Lifetime Scorers

Player	Yrs.	TD	PAT	FG	Total
Morten Andersen.....	25	0	849	565	2,544
Gary Anderson	23	0	820	538	2,434
John Carney*........	23	0	628	478	2,062
Matt Stover	19	0	591	471	2,004
George Blanda (a)....	26	9	942	335	2,002
Jason Elam	17	0	675	436	1,983
Jason Hanson*	19	0	573	439	1,890
John Kasay*	19	0	524	433	1,823
Norm Johnson	18	0	638	366	1,736
Nick Lowery	18	0	562	383	1,711
Jan Stenerud (a)	19	0	580	373	1,699
Adam Vinatieri*	15	0	565**	364	1,657
Eddie Murray	19	0	538	352	1,594
Al Del Greco	17	0	543	347	1,584
Ryan Longwell*	14	0	566	339	1,583
Steve Christie	15	0	468	336	1,476
Pat Leahy	18	0	558	304	1,470
Jim Turner (a)	16	1	521	304	1,439
Matt Bahr	17	0	522	300	1,422
Olindo Mare*	14	0	436	328	1,420

Leading Lifetime Touchdown Scorers

Player	Yrs.	Rush	Rec	Ret	TD
Jerry Rice	20	10	197	1	208
Emmitt Smith	15	164	11	0	175
LaDainian Tomlinson*..	10	144	15	0	159
Terrell Owens*	15	3	153	0	156
Randy Moss*	13	0	153	1	154
Marcus Allen	16	123	21	1	145
Marshall Faulk	12	100	36	0	136
Cris Carter	16	0	130	1	131
Marvin Harrison	13	0	128	0	128
Jim Brown	9	106	20	0	126
Walter Payton	13	110	15	0	125
John Riggins	14	104	12	0	116
Lenny Moore	12	63	48	2	113
Shaun Alexander......	9	100	12	0	112
Barry Sanders	10	99	10	0	109
Tim Brown	17	1	100	4	105
Don Hutson	11	3	99	3	105
Steve Largent	14	1	100	0	101
Franco Harris	13	91	9	0	100
Curtis Martin	11	90	10	0	100

Points, season: 186, LaDainian Tomlinson, San Diego Chargers, 2006 (31 TDs).
Points, game: 40, Ernie Nevers, Chicago Cardinals vs. Chicago Bears, Nov. 28, 1929 (6 TDs, 4 PATs).
Touchdowns, season: 31, LaDainian Tomlinson, San Diego Chargers, 2006.
Touchdowns, game: 6, Ernie Nevers, Chicago Cardinals vs. Chicago Bears, Nov. 28, 1929 (6 rushing); Dub Jones, Cleveland Browns vs. Chicago Bears, Nov. 25, 1951 (4 rushing, 2 pass receptions); Gale Sayers, Chicago Bears vs. San Francisco 49ers, Dec. 12, 1965 (4 rushing, 1 pass reception, 1 punt return).
Points after TD, season: 74, Stephen Gostkowski, New England Patriots, 2007.
Consecutive points after TD: 422, Matt Stover, Baltimore Ravens-Indianapolis Colts, 1996-2009.
Field goals, season: 40, Neil Rackers, Arizona Cardinals, 2005.
Field goals, game: 8, Rob Bironas, Tennessee Titans vs. Houston Texans, Oct. 21, 2007.
Field goals, career: 565, Morten Andersen, New Orleans Saints-Atlanta Falcons-NY Giants-Kansas City Chiefs-Minnesota Vikings-Atlanta Falcons, 1982-2007.
Longest field goal: 63 yards, Tom Dempsey, New Orleans Saints vs. Detroit Lions, Nov. 8, 1970; Jason Elam, Denver Broncos vs. Jacksonville Jaguars, Oct. 25, 1998.

Defensive Records

Interceptions, career: 81, Paul Krause, Washington Redskins-Minnesota Vikings, 1964-79.
Interceptions, season: 14, Dick "Night Train" Lane, L.A. Rams, 1952.
Touchdowns, career: 12, Rod Woodson, Pittsburgh Steelers-San Francisco 49ers-Baltimore Ravens-Oakland Raiders, 1987-2003.
Touchdowns, season: 4, Ken Houston, Houston Oilers, 1971; Jim Kearney, Kansas City Chiefs, 1972; Eric Allen, Philadelphia Eagles, 1993.
Sacks, career (since 1982): 200, Bruce Smith, Buffalo Bills-Washington Redskins, 1985-2003.
Sacks, season (since 1982): 22.5, Michael Strahan, NY Giants, 2001.

Leading Lifetime Rushers
(ranked by rushing yards; * = active in 2010)

Player	Yrs.	Att	Yds	Avg	Long	TD	Player	Yrs.	Att	Yds	Avg	Long	TD
Emmitt Smith	15	4,409	18,355	4.2	75	164	Edgerrin James	11	3,028	12,246	4.0	72	80
Walter Payton	13	3,838	16,726	4.4	76	110	Marcus Allen	16	3,022	12,243	4.1	61	123
Barry Sanders	10	3,062	15,269	5.0	85	99	Franco Harris	13	2,949	12,120	4.1	75	91
Curtis Martin	11	3,518	14,101	4.0	70	90	Thurman Thomas	13	2,877	12,074	4.2	80	65
Jerome Bettis	13	3,479	13,662	3.9	71	91	Fred Taylor*	13	2,534	11,695	4.6	80	66
LaDainian Tomlinson*	10	3,099	13,404	4.3	85	144	John Riggins	14	2,916	11,352	3.9	66	104
Eric Dickerson	11	2,996	13,259	4.4	85	90	Corey Dillon	10	2,618	11,241	4.3	96	82
Tony Dorsett	12	2,936	12,739	4.3	99	77	O. J. Simpson	11	2,404	11,236	4.7	94	61
Jim Brown	9	2,359	12,312	5.2	80	106	Warrick Dunn	12	2,669	10,967	4.1	90	49
Marshall Faulk	12	2,836	12,279	4.3	71	100	Ricky Watters	10	2,622	10,643	4.1	57	78

Yards gained, season: 2,105, Eric Dickerson, L.A. Rams, 1984.
Yards gained, game: 296, Adrian Peterson, Minnesota Vikings vs. San Diego Chargers, Nov. 4, 2007.
Rushing TDs, career: 164, Emmitt Smith, Dallas Cowboys-Arizona Cardinals, 1990-2004.
Rushing TDs, season: 28, LaDainian Tomlinson, San Diego Chargers, 2006.
Rushing TDs, game: 6, Ernie Nevers, Chicago Cardinals vs. Chicago Bears, Nov. 28, 1929.
Rushing attempts, game: 45, Jamie Morris, Washington Redskins vs. Cincinnati Bengals, Dec. 17, 1988 (OT).
Longest run from scrimmage: 99 yards, Tony Dorsett, Dallas Cowboys vs. Minnesota Vikings, Jan. 3, 1983 (TD).

Leading Lifetime Receivers
(ranked by number of receptions; * = active in 2010)

Player	Yrs.	No.	Yds	Avg	Long	TD	Player	Yrs.	No.	Yds	Avg	Long	TD
Jerry Rice	20	1,549	22,895	14.8	96	197	Art Monk	16	940	12,721	13.5	79	68
Marvin Harrison	13	1,102	14,580	13.2	80	128	Derrick Mason*	14	924	11,891	12.9	79	66
Cris Carter	16	1,101	13,899	12.6	80	130	Torry Holt	11	920	13,382	14.5	85	74
Tim Brown	17	1,094	14,934	13.7	80	100	Keenan McCardell	16	883	11,373	12.9	76	63
Terrell Owens*	15	1,078	15,934	14.8	98	153	Jimmy Smith	12	862	12,287	14.3	75	67
Tony Gonzalez*	14	1,069	12,463	11.7	73	88	Muhsin Muhammad	14	860	11,438	13.3	72	62
Isaac Bruce	16	1,024	15,208	14.9	80	91	Irving Fryar	17	851	12,785	15.0	80	84
Randy Moss*	13	954	14,858	15.6	82	153	Rod Smith	12	849	11,389	13.4	85	68
Hines Ward*	13	954	11,702	12.3	85	83	Larry Centers	14	827	6,797	8.2	54	28
Andre Reed	16	951	13,198	13.9	83	87	Steve Largent	14	819	13,089	16.0	74	100

Yards gained, career: 22,895, Jerry Rice, San Francisco 49ers-Oakland Raiders-Seattle Seahawks, 1985-2004.
Yards gained, season: 1,848, Jerry Rice, San Francisco 49ers, 1995.
Yards gained, game: 336, Willie "Flipper" Anderson, L.A. Rams vs. New Orleans Saints, Nov. 26, 1989 (OT).
Pass receptions, season: 143, Marvin Harrison, Indianapolis Colts, 2002.
Pass receptions, game: 21, Brandon Marshall, Denver Broncos vs. Indianapolis Colts, Dec. 13, 2009 (200 yards).
Touchdown receptions, career: 197, Jerry Rice, San Francisco 49ers-Oakland Raiders-Seattle Seahawks, 1985-2004.
Touchdown receptions, season: 23, Randy Moss, New England Patriots, 2007.
Touchdown receptions, game: 5, Bob Shaw, Chicago Cardinals vs. Baltimore Colts, Oct. 2, 1950; Kellen Winslow, San Diego Chargers vs. Oakland Raiders, Nov. 22, 1981; Jerry Rice, San Francisco 49ers vs. Atlanta Falcons, Oct. 14, 1990.

Leading Lifetime Passers
(minimum 1,500 attempts; ranked by quarterback rating points; * = active in 2010)

Player	Yrs.	Att	Comp	Yds	TD	Int	Pts[1]	Player	Yrs.	Att	Comp	Yds	TD	Int	Pts[1]
Aaron Rodgers*	6	1,611	1,038	12,723	87	32	98.4	Matt Schaub*	7	1,987	1,288	15,457	83	52	91.5
Philip Rivers*	7	2,455	1,564	19,661	136	58	97.2	Chad Pennington	11	2,471	1,632	17,823	102	64	90.1
Steve Young	15	4,149	2,667	33,124	232	107	96.8	Daunte Culpepper	11	3,199	2,016	24,153	149	106	87.8
Tony Romo*	7	2,070	1,326	16,650	118	62	95.5	Jeff Garcia	11	3,676	2,264	25,537	161	83	87.5
Tom Brady*	11	4,710	2,996	34,744	261	103	95.2	Carson Palmer*	7	3,217	2,024	22,694	154	100	86.9
Peyton Manning*	13	7,210	4,682	54,828	399	198	94.9	Dan Marino	17	8,358	4,967	61,361	420	252	86.4
Kurt Warner	12	4,070	2,666	32,344	208	128	93.7	Trent Green	11	3,740	2,266	28,475	162	114	86.0
Ben Roethlisberger*	7	2,800	1,766	22,502	144	86	92.5	Brett Favre*	20	10,169	6,300	71,838	508	336	86.0
Joe Montana	15	5,391	3,409	40,551	273	139	92.3	David Garrard*	9	2,281	1,406	16,003	89	54	85.8
Drew Brees*	10	4,822	3,145	35,266	235	132	91.7	Donovan McNabb*	12	5,218	3,076	36,250	230	115	85.7

(1) Rating points based on performances in the following categories: percentage of completions, percentage of touchdown passes, percentage of interceptions, and average gain per pass attempt.

Most yards gained, career: 71,838, Brett Favre, Atlanta Falcons-Green Bay Packers-NY Jets-Minnesota Vikings, 1991-2010.
Most yards gained, season: 5,084, Dan Marino, Miami Dolphins, 1984.
Most yards gained, game: 554, Norm Van Brocklin, L.A. Rams vs. NY Yanks, Sept. 28, 1951 (27 completions in 41 attempts).
Most touchdowns passing, career: 508, Brett Favre, Atlanta Falcons-Green Bay Packers-NY Jets-Minnesota Vikings, 1991-2010.
Most touchdowns passing, season: 50, Tom Brady, New England Patriots, 2007.
Most touchdowns passing, game: 7, Sid Luckman, Chicago Bears vs. NY Giants, Nov. 14, 1943; Adrian Burk, Philadelphia Eagles vs. Washington Redskins, Oct. 17, 1954; George Blanda, Houston Oilers vs. NY Titans, Nov. 19, 1961; Y. A. Tittle, NY Giants vs. Washington Redskins, Oct. 28, 1962; Joe Kapp, Minnesota Vikings vs. Baltimore Colts, Sept. 28, 1969.
Most passes completed, career: 6,300, Brett Favre, Atlanta Falcons-Green Bay Packers-NY Jets-Minnesota Vikings, 1991-2010.
Most passes completed, season: 450, Peyton Manning, Indianapolis Colts, 2010.
Most passes completed, game: 45, Drew Bledsoe, New England Patriots vs. Minnesota Vikings, Nov. 13, 1994 (OT).

All-Time NFL Coaching Victories

(at end of 2010 season; ranked by overall career wins; * = active in 2010)

Coach	Team	Yrs.	Regular Season W	L	T	Pct.	Overall W	L	T	Pct.
Don Shula	Colts, Dolphins	33	328	156	6	.677	347	173	6	.666
George Halas	Bears	40	318	148	31	.682	324	151	31	.682
Tom Landry	Cowboys	29	250	162	6	.607	270	178	6	.603
Earl "Curly" Lambeau	Packers, Chi. Cardinals, Redskins	33	226	132	22	.631	229	134	22	.631
Chuck Noll	Steelers	23	193	148	1	.566	209	156	1	.572
Marty Schottenheimer	Browns, Chiefs, Redskins, Chargers	21	200	126	1	.613	205	139	1	.596
Dan Reeves	Broncos, Giants, Falcons	23	190	165	2	.535	201	174	2	.536
Chuck Knox	Rams, Bills, Seahawks	22	186	147	1	.558	193	158	1	.550
Bill Parcells	Giants, Patriots, Jets, Cowboys	19	172	130	1	.569	183	138	1	.570
Bill Belichick*	Browns, Patriots	16	162	94	0	.633	177	100	0	.639
Mike Holmgren	Packers, Seahawks	17	161	111	0	.592	174	122	0	.588
Joe Gibbs	Redskins	21	154	94	0	.621	171	101	0	.629
Paul Brown	Browns, Bengals	21	166	100	6	.624	170	108	6	.612
Bud Grant	Vikings	18	158	96	5	.621	168	108	5	.608
Bill Cowher	Steelers	15	149	90	1	.623	161	99	1	.619
Mike Shanahan*	Raiders, Broncos, Redskins	17	152	108	0	.585	160	113	0	.586
Marv Levy	Chiefs, Bills	17	143	112	0	.561	154	120	0	.562
Steve Owen	Giants	23	151	100	17	.602	153	108	17	.586
Tony Dungy	Buccaneers, Colts	13	139	69	0	.668	148	79	0	.652
Jeff Fisher*	Oilers, Titans	17	142	120	0	.542	147	126	0	.538

NFL Stadiums, 2010

(G = Grass, S = Synthetic, A = AstroPlay, D = DD Grassmaster (grass), F = FieldTurf, N = Natural grass,
SS = Sportfield Softtop, SM = Sportexe Momentum)

Team: stadium, location, surface (year built)	Capacity[1]
Bears: Soldier Field[2], Chicago, IL, M (1924)	61,500
Bengals: Paul Brown Stadium, Cincinnati, OH, S (2000)	65,515
Bills: Ralph Wilson Stadium, Orchard Park, NY, A (1973)	73,967
Broncos: INVESCO Field at Mile High, Denver, CO, D (2001)	76,125
Browns: Cleveland Browns Stadium, Cleveland, OH, G (1999)	73,300
Buccaneers: Raymond James Stadium, Tampa, FL, G (1998)	65,908
Cardinals: University of Phoenix Stadium, Glendale, AZ, G (2006)	65,000
Chargers: Qualcomm Stadium[3], San Diego, CA, G (1967)	70,000 (approx.)
Chiefs: Arrowhead Stadium, Kansas City, MO, G (1972)	79,416
Colts: Lucas Oil Stadium, Indianapolis, IN, F (2008)	63,000
Cowboys: Cowboys Stadium, Arlington, TX, SS (2009)	80,000 (expandable to 100,000 for special events)
Dolphins: Sun Life Stadium[4], Miami Gardens, FL, G (1987)	75,192
Eagles: Lincoln Financial Field, Philadelphia, PA, N (2003)	69,144
Falcons: Georgia Dome, Atlanta, GA, F (1992)	71,228
49ers: Candlestick Park[5], San Francisco, CA, N (1960)	69,732
Giants: New Meadowlands Stadium, E. Rutherford, NJ, F (2010)	82,500
Jaguars: EverBank Field[6], Jacksonville, FL, G (1995)	67,246
Jets: New Meadowlands Stadium, E. Rutherford, NJ, F (2010)	82,500
Lions: Ford Field, Detroit, MI, F (2002)	64,500
Packers: Lambeau Field[7], Green Bay, WI, DD (1957)	72,928
Panthers: Bank of America Stadium[8], Charlotte, NC, G (1996)	73,778
Patriots: Gillette Stadium, Foxboro, MA, F (2002)	68,756
Raiders: O.co Coliseum[9], Oakland, CA, G (1966)	63,132
Rams: Edward Jones Dome[10], St. Louis, MO, F (1995)	66,000
Ravens: M & T Bank Stadium[11], Baltimore, MD, SM (1998)	71,008
Redskins: FedEx Field[12], Landover, MD, N (1997)	91,704
Saints: Louisiana Superdome, New Orleans, LA, SM (1975)	68,000
Seahawks: Qwest Field[13], Seattle, WA, F (2002)	67,000
Steelers: Heinz Field, Pittsburgh, PA, DD (2001)	65,050
Texans: Reliant Stadium, Houston, TX, G (2002)	71,054
Titans: LP Field[14], Nashville, TN, N (1999)	69,143
Vikings: Mall of America Field at Hubert H. Humphrey Metrodome[15], Minneapolis, MN, F (1982)	64,121

(1) As of the start of the 2010 season. (2) Renovation in 2002 replaced interior of stadium. (3) Formerly San Diego Stadium (1967-80); San Diego Jack Murphy Stadium (1981-97). (4) Formerly Joe Robbie Stadium (1987-96); Pro Player Stadium (1996-2005); Land Shark Stadium (2009). (5) Formerly Candlestick Park (1960-94); 3Com Park at Candlestick Point (1995-2004). (6) Formerly ALLTEL Stadium (1997-2007); Jacksonville Municipal Stadium (1946-97, 2007-09). (7) Formerly City Stadium (1957-65). Renovation completed in 2003 added 11,625 seats. (8) Formerly Ericsson Stadium (1996-2003). (9) Formerly Oakland-Alameda County Coliseum (1966-98); Network Associates Coliseum (1998-2004); McAfee Stadium (2004-08); Oakland Coliseum (2008-11). (10) Formerly Trans World Dome (1995-2001); full name: Edward Jones Dome at America's Center. (11) Formerly PSINet Stadium (1998-2002); Ravens Stadium (2002-03). (12) Formerly Jack Kent Cooke Stadium (1997-99). (13) Formerly Seahawks Stadium (2002-04). (14) Formerly Adelphia Coliseum (1999-2002). (15) Formerly Hubert H. Humphrey Metrodome (1982-2009).

National Football League Franchise Origins

(Founding year, league. Home stadium location; subsequent history.)

Arizona Cardinals: 1920, American Professional Football Association (APFA)[1]. Chicago, 1920-59; St. Louis, 1960-87; Tempe, AZ, 1988-2005; Glendale, AZ, 2006-present.

Atlanta Falcons: 1966, NFL. Atlanta, 1966-present.

Baltimore Ravens: 1996, NFL. Baltimore, 1996-present.

Buffalo Bills: 1960, American Football League (AFL)[2]. Buffalo, 1960-72; Orchard Park, NY, 1973-present.

Carolina Panthers: 1995, NFL. Clemson, SC, 1995; Charlotte, NC, 1996-present.

Chicago Bears: 1920, APFA. Decatur, IL, 1920; Chicago, 1921-present.

Cincinnati Bengals: 1968, AFL. Cincinnati, 1968-present.

Cleveland Browns: 1946, All-America Football Conference (AAFC)[3]. Cleveland, 1946-95; 1999-present.

Dallas Cowboys: 1960, NFL. Dallas, 1960-70; Irving, TX, 1971-2008; Arlington, TX, 2009-present.

Denver Broncos: 1960, AFL. Denver, 1960-present.

Detroit Lions: 1930, NFL. Portsmouth, OH, 1930-33; Detroit, 1934-74; Pontiac, MI, 1975-2001; Detroit, 2002-present.

Green Bay Packers: 1921, APFA. Green Bay, WI, 1921-present.

Houston Texans: 2002, NFL. Houston, 2002-present.

Indianapolis Colts: 1953, NFL. Baltimore, 1953-83; Indianapolis, 1984-present.

Jacksonville Jaguars: 1995, NFL. Jacksonville, FL, 1995-present.

Kansas City Chiefs: 1960, AFL. Dallas, 1960-62; Kansas City, MO, 1963-present.

Miami Dolphins: 1966, AFL. Miami, 1966-2002; Miami Gardens, FL, 2003-present.

Minnesota Vikings: 1961, NFL. Bloomington, MN, 1961-81; Minneapolis, 1982-present.

New England Patriots: 1960, AFL. Boston, 1960-70; Foxboro, MA, 1971-present.

New Orleans Saints: 1967, NFL. New Orleans, 1967-2004; Baton Rouge and San Antonio, 2005; New Orleans, 2006-present.

NY Giants: 1925, NFL. NY, 1925-73, 1975; New Haven, CT, 1973-74; E. Rutherford, NJ, 1976-present.

NY Jets: 1960, AFL. NY, 1960-83; E. Rutherford, NJ, 1984-present.

Oakland Raiders: 1960, AFL. San Francisco, 1960-61; Oakland, CA, 1962-81; Los Angeles, 1982-94; Oakland, CA, 1995-present.

Philadelphia Eagles: 1933, NFL. Philadelphia, 1933-present.

Pittsburgh Steelers: 1933, NFL. Pittsburgh, 1933-present.

St. Louis Rams: 1937, NFL. Cleveland, 1936-45; Los Angeles, 1946-79; Anaheim, CA, 1980-94; St. Louis, 1995-present.

San Diego Chargers: 1960, AFL. Los Angeles, 1960; San Diego, 1961-present.

Seattle Seahawks: 1976, NFL. Seattle, 1976-present.

San Francisco 49ers: 1946, AAFC. San Francisco, 1946-present.

Tampa Bay Buccaneers: 1976, NFL. Tampa, 1976-present.

Tennessee Titans: 1960, AFL. Houston, 1969-96; Memphis, 1997; Nashville, 1998-present.

Washington Redskins: 1932, NFL. Boston, 1932-36; Washington, DC, 1937-96; Landover, MD, 1997-present.

(1) The American Professional Football Association (APFA) was formed in 1920 to standardize the rules of professional football. In 1922, the name was changed to the National Football League (NFL). (2) The most successful of 4 separate leagues called the American Football League or AFL (1926; 1936-37; 1940-41; 1960-69). Congress approved an NFL/AFL merger in 1966. Baltimore, Cleveland, and Pittsburgh agreed to join the 10 incoming AFL teams to form the American Football Conference. The NFL began play in 1970 with 26 teams. (3) The All-America Football Conference, 1946-49. In 1950, 3 of its teams joined the NFL (Baltimore, Cleveland, and San Francisco). The Baltimore franchise failed, but the NFL awarded the city a second one, also called the Colts, in 1953.

Pro Football Hall of Fame, Canton, OH
(Asterisk indicates member elected in Feb. 2011 and inducted Aug. 6, 2011.)

Herb Adderley	Carl Eller	David "Deacon" Jones	Art Monk	Bruce Smith
Troy Aikman	John Elway	Stan Jones	Joe Montana	Emmitt Smith
George Allen	Weeb Ewbank	Henry Jordan	Warren Moon	Jackie Smith
Marcus Allen	*Marshall Faulk	Sonny Jurgensen	Lenny Moore	John Stallworth
Lance Alworth	Tom Fears	Jim Kelly	Marion Motley	Bart Starr
Doug Atkins	Jim Finks	Leroy Kelly	Mike Munchak	Roger Staubach
Morris "Red" Badgro	Ray Flaherty	Walt Kiesling	Anthony Munoz	Ernie Stautner
Lem Barney	Len Ford	Frank "Bruiser" Kinard	George Musso	Jan Stenerud
Cliff Battles	Dr. Daniel Fortmann	Paul Krause	Bronko Nagurski	Dwight Stephenson
Sammy Baugh	Dan Fouts	Earl "Curly" Lambeau	Joe Namath	Hank Stram
Chuck Bednarik	Benny Friedman	Jack Lambert	Earle "Greasy" Neale	Ken Strong
Bert Bell	Frank Gatski	Tom Landry	Ernie Nevers	Joe Stydahar
Bobby Bell	Bill George	Dick "Night Train" Lane	Ozzie Newsome	Lynn Swann
Raymond Berry	Joe Gibbs	Jim Langer	Ray Nitschke	Fran Tarkenton
Elvin Bethea	Frank Gifford	Willie Lanier	Chuck Noll	Charley Taylor
Charles Bidwill	Sid Gillman	Steve Largent	Leo Nomellini	Jim Taylor
Fred Biletnikoff	Otto Graham	Yale Lary	Merlin Olsen	Lawrence "LT" Taylor
George Blanda	Red Grange	Dante Lavelli	Jim Otto	Derrick Thomas
Mel Blount	Bud Grant	Bobby Layne	Steve Owen	Emmitt Thomas
Terry Bradshaw	Darrell Green	Dick LeBeau	Alan Page	Thurman Thomas
Bob Brown	Joe Greene	Alphonse "Tuffy"	Clarence "Ace" Parker	Jim Thorpe
Jim Brown	Forrest Gregg	Leemans	Jim Parker	Andre Tippett
Paul Brown	Bob Griese	Marv Levy	Walter Payton	Y. A. Tittle
Roosevelt Brown	Russ Grimm	Bob Lilly	Joe Perry	George Trafton
Willie Brown	Lou Groza	Floyd Little	Pete Pihos	Charley Trippi
Buck Buchanan	Joe Guyon	Larry Little	Fritz Pollard	Emlen Tunnell
Nick Buoniconti	George Halas	James Lofton	John Randle	Clyde "Bulldog" Turner
Dick Butkus	Jack Ham	Vince Lombardi	Hugh "Shorty" Ray	Johnny Unitas
Earl Campbell	Dan Hampton	Howie Long	Dan Reeves	Gene Upshaw
Tony Canadeo	*Chris Hanburger	Ronnie Lott	Mel Renfro	Norm Van Brocklin
Joe Carr	John Hannah	Sid Luckman	Jerry Rice	Steve Van Buren
Harry Carson	Franco Harris	Roy "Link" Lyman	*Les Richter	Doak Walker
Dave Casper	Bob Hayes	Tom Mack	John Riggins	Bill Walsh
Guy Chamberlin	Mike Haynes	John Mackey	Jim Ringo	Paul Warfield
Jack Christiansen	Ed Healey	John Madden	Andy Robustelli	Bob Waterfield
Earl "Dutch" Clark	Mel Hein	Tim Mara	Art Rooney	Mike Webster
George Connor	Ted Hendricks	Wellington Mara	Dan Rooney	Roger Wehrli
Jim Conzelman	Wilbur "Pete" Henry	Gino Marchetti	Pete Rozelle	Arnie Weinmeister
Lou Creekmur	Arnold Herber	Dan Marino	*Ed Sabol	Randy White
Larry Csonka	Bill Hewitt	George Preston	Bob St. Clair	Reggie White
Al Davis	Gene Hickerson	Marshall	Barry Sanders	Dave Wilcox
Willie Davis	Clarke Hinkle	Bruce Mathews	Charlie Sanders	Bill Willis
Len Dawson	Elroy "Crazylegs" Hirsch	Ollie Matson	*Deion Sanders	Larry Wilson
Fred Dean	Paul Hornung	Don Maynard	Gale Sayers	Ralph Wilson Jr.
Joe DeLamielleure	Ken Houston	George McAfee	Joe Schmidt	Kellen Winslow
*Richard Dent	Cal Hubbard	Mike McCormack	Tex Schramm	Alex Wojciechowicz
Eric Dickerson	Sam Huff	Randall McDaniel	Lee Roy Selmon	Willie Wood
Dan Dierdorf	Lamar Hunt	Tommy McDonald	*Shannon Sharpe	Rod Woodson
Mike Ditka	Don Hutson	Hugh McElhenny	Billy Shaw	Rayfield Wright
Art Donovan	Michael Irvin	Johnny "Blood" McNally	Art Shell	Ron Yary
Tony Dorsett	Rickey Jackson	Mike Michalske	Don Shula	Steve Young
John "Paddy" Driscoll	Jimmy Johnson	Wayne Millner	O. J. Simpson	Jack Youngblood
Bill Dudley	John Henry Johnson	Bobby Mitchell	Mike Singletary	Gary Zimmerman
Glen "Turk" Edwards	Charlie Joiner	Ron Mix	Jackie Slater	

BASEBALL

Playoff Results, 2011

National League Division Series (NLDS): St. Louis (wild card) defeated Philadelphia, 3 games to 2. Milwaukee defeated Arizona, 3 games to 2.
National League Championship Series (NLCS): St. Louis defeated Milwaukee, 4 games to 2.

American League Division Series (ALDS): Texas defeated Tampa Bay (wild card), 3 games to 1. Detroit defeated NY Yankees, 3 games to 2.
American League Championship Series (ALCS): Texas defeated Detroit, 4 games to 2.

World Series, 2011

The St. Louis Cardinals won their second World Series title in five years with a heart-pounding victory over the Texas Rangers. Twice, the Rangers were a strike away from winning the title in Game 6, but the Cards survived each time with a 10-9 win in 11 innings. Cardinals third baseman David Freese, who delivered the game-tying triple in the ninth and game-winning home run in Game 6, batted .348 in the series with seven RBI and won World Series MVP. Second baseman Ian Kinsler led Texas with a .360 batting average (9-for-25), while Rangers catcher Mike Napoli hit .350 with a pair of home runs and 10 RBI. Texas became the first team to lose in back-to-back World Series since the Atlanta Braves in 1991-92 and the first AL team since the 1963-64 Yankees.

Game 1

Wednesday, Oct. 19 at Busch Stadium, St. Louis, MO

	1	2	3	4	5	6	7	8	9	R	H	E
Texas Rangers	0	0	0	0	2	0	0	0	0	2	6	0
St. Louis Cardinals	0	0	2	0	1	0	0	X		3	6	0

Winning pitcher: Chris Carpenter
Losing pitcher: C. J. Wilson
Save: Jason Motte
Attendance: 46,406

Right-hander Chris Carpenter pitched six strong innings and an army of relievers shut down a powerful Texas offense as the St. Louis Cardinals defeated the Rangers, 3-2, in Game 1 of the 2011 World Series Oct. 19, 2011, at Busch Stadium in St. Louis. The Cardinals scored first in the fourth inning on Lance Berkman's two-out single to right that drove home Albert Pujols, who had been hit by a pitch, and Matt Holliday, who had doubled. But Texas quickly tied the game in the top of the fifth on Mike Napoli's two-run home run to right field off Carpenter, who scattered five hits and struck out four. C. J. Wilson allowed just four hits in 5 2/3 innings, but walked six batters in the loss, his third decision of the 2011 postseason. The Cardinals scored the go-ahead run in the bottom of the sixth inning on a pinch-hit single by Allen Craig off Rangers reliever Alexi Ogando. Five Cardinals relievers—Fernando Salas, Marc Rzepczynski, Octavio Dotel, Arthur Rhodes, and Jason Motte—limited the Rangers to just one hit in the final three innings and Motte retired the side in order in the ninth to earn a save.

Game 2

Thursday, Oct. 20 at Busch Stadium, St. Louis, MO

	1	2	3	4	5	6	7	8	9	R	H	E
Texas Rangers	0	0	0	0	0	0	0	0	2	2	5	1
St. Louis Cardinals	0	0	0	0	0	1	0	0		1	6	0

Winning pitcher: Mike Adams
Losing pitcher: Jason Motte
Save: Neftali Feliz
Attendance: 47,288

Game 2 began as a classic pitching duel and ended with a dramatic comeback. The Texas Rangers hit two consecutive sacrifice flies in the ninth to rally to a 2-1 win over St. Louis Oct. 20, 2011, at Busch Stadium in St. Louis, MO, tying the best-of-seven series at one game apiece. Right-hander Jason Motte started the ninth inning for the Cardinals with a 1-0 lead. He allowed a leadoff single to Ian Kinsler, who stole second and advanced to third on a single by Elvis Andrus. Andrus went to second on the play after the relay throw from right-center field evaded Albert Pujols and bounced towards the third base dugout. Arthur Rhodes relieved Motte and allowed a game-tying sacrifice fly to Josh Hamilton that scored Kinsler and allowed Andrus to advance to third. Lance Lynn then relieved Rhodes to face Michael Young, who put the Rangers ahead for good with another sacrifice fly to score Andrus. Until the ninth inning, it looked like Cardinals pinch-hitter Allen Craig would be the hero for the second straight night. As he did in Game 1, Craig delivered a pinch-hit RBI single for the Cardinals, again off Rangers reliever Alexi Ogando, for the game's first run. Ogando entered the game in relief of Texas starter Colby Lewis, who allowed just two hits through the first six innings, but gave up singles to David Freese and Nick Punto in the seventh before Ogando took over and allowed Craig's go-ahead single. The Cardinals' 25-year-old starter Jaime Garcia allowed just three hits and struck out seven Texas batters in seven innings. Neftali Feliz earned a save for Texas. He gave up a leadoff walk to Yadier Molina in the bottom of the ninth, but promptly struck out Punto and Skip Schumaker and got Rafael Furcal to fly out to right to end the game.

Game 3

Saturday, Oct. 22 at Rangers Ballpark in Arlington, Arlington, TX

	1	2	3	4	5	6	7	8	9	R	H	E
St. Louis Cardinals	1	0	0	4	3	4	2	1	1	16	15	0
Texas Rangers	0	0	0	3	3	0	1	0	0	7	13	3

Winning pitcher: Lance Lynn
Losing pitcher: Matt Harrison
Attendance: 51,462

Albert Pujols stamped his name in the record books, becoming the third player in history to hit three home runs in a single World Series game. The St. Louis first baseman also tied World Series records with five hits and six RBI in the game. Pujols's first home run, a three-run shot in the sixth off Texas reliever Alexi Ogando, gave the Cardinals an 11-6 lead. He then belted a two-run home run off Mike Gonzalez in the seventh and added a solo shot of Darren Oliver in the ninth. Pujols joined Babe Ruth (Game 4 of 1926 and 1928 series) and Reggie Jackson (Game 6, 1977) as the only players to hit three home runs in a World Series game. While runs had been scarce in the first two games of the Series, both offenses erupted in Game 3; neither St. Louis starter Kyle Lohse nor Texas's Matt Harrison made it out of the fourth inning. St. Louis took a 5-0 lead in the top of the fourth, but home runs by Michael Young and Nelson Cruz in the bottom half cut the margin to 5-3. Cardinal catcher Yadier Molina, who had four RBI, capped a three-run fifth for St. Louis with a two-run double. Texas then rang up three more runs in its half of the fifth to make it an 8-6 ballgame before St. Louis pulled away for good. Pujols's six RBI matched the World Series record held by two NY Yankees: second baseman Bobby Richardson (Game 3, 1960) and designated hitter Hideki Matsui (Game 6, 2009).

Game 4
Sunday, Oct. 23 at Rangers Ballpark in Arlington, Arlington, TX

	1	2	3	4	5	6	7	8	9	R	H	E
St. Louis Cardinals	0	0	0	0	0	0	0	0	0	0	2	0
Texas Rangers	1	0	0	0	3	0	0	X		4	6	0

Winning pitcher: Derek Holland
Losing pitcher: Edwin Jackson
Attendance: 51,539

The best answer for the St. Louis Cardinals' Game 3 power surge turned out to be Texas Rangers left-hander Derek Holland, who allowed only two hits and struck out seven in 8 1/3 innings as the Rangers tied the series at two games apiece. Lance Berkman had both of St. Louis's hits off Holland, who retired the side in order five times. No Cardinal reached third base all night; St. Louis's best chance to score came in the ninth inning, when Holland allowed a one-out walk to Rafael Furcal. Rangers closer Neftali Feliz came into the game and walked Allen Craig, but retired Albert Pujols on a flyout to center field and struck out Matt Holliday to end the game. The Rangers took a 1-0 lead in the first against St. Louis starter Edwin Jackson on an RBI double by Texas slugger Josh Hamilton, who had hit just .083 in the first three games. Jackson left the game with one out in the sixth after walking Nelson Cruz and David Murphy, then Ranger catcher Mike Napoli hit the first pitch from reliever Mitchell Boggs into the left field stands for his second home run of the Series.

Game 5
Monday, Oct. 24 at Rangers Ballpark in Arlington, Arlington, TX

	1	2	3	4	5	6	7	8	9	R	H	E
St. Louis Cardinals	0	2	0	0	0	0	0	0	0	2	7	1
Texas Rangers	0	0	1	0	0	1	0	2	X	4	9	2

Winning pitcher: Darren Oliver
Losing pitcher: Octavio Dotel
Save: Neftali Feliz
Attendance: 51,459

Mike Napoli's two-run, bases-loaded double in the bottom of the eighth snapped a 2-2 tie and lifted the Texas Rangers to within one victory of its first championship Oct. 24. Michael Young led off the eighth inning for Texas with a double off Octavio Dotel, who then intentionally walked Nelson Cruz. Cardinals' manager Tony La Russa brought in left-hander Mark Rzepczynski to face lefty David Murphy, who loaded the bases with an infield hit that caromed off Rzepczynski's knee. La Russa later blamed poor communication with his bullpen for inserting Rzepczynski to face the right hand-hitting Napoli. In the ninth, Rangers closer Neftali Feliz hit the leadoff batter, Allen Craig, but Napoli caught Craig trying to steal second as Albert Pujols struck out. Feliz then walked Matt Holliday, but struck out Lance Berkman to end the game for his sixth save in the postseason. The Cardinals had taken an early 2-0 lead in the second inning when Texas starter C. J. Wilson walked Holliday and Berkman. Yadier Molina's single scored Holliday and Skip Schumacher's groundout brought Berkman home. Rangers pitchers issued nine walks in the game, including intentionally walking Cardinals first baseman Pujols three times. Cardinals ace Chris Carpenter scattered six hits through seven innings but allowed the Rangers to draw even on solo home runs by Mitch Moreland and Adrian Beltre. St. Louis stranded 12 runners and was just 1-for-12 with men in scoring position.

Game 6
Thursday, Oct. 27 at Busch Stadium, St. Louis, MO

	1	2	3	4	5	6	7	8	9	10	11	R	H	E
Texas Rangers	1	1	0	1	1	0	3	0	0	2	0	9	15	2
St. Louis Cardinals	2	0	0	1	0	1	0	1	2	2	1	10	13	3

Winning pitcher: Jake Westbrook
Losing pitcher: Mark Lowe
Attendance: 47,325

In both the 9th and 10th innings, the Texas Rangers were a strike away from their first World Series championship in the 51-year franchise history, but the St. Louis Cardinals refused to lose. Cardinal third baseman David Freese's two-run triple off of Rangers closer Neftali Feliz resuscitated the Cardinals in the ninth, and Lance Berkman tied the game again with two out in the 10th after Josh Hamilton's home run gave Texas another two-run lead it could not protect. In the 11th, Missouri-native Freese ended one of the most thrilling games in World Series history with a leadoff home run off reliever Mark Lowe. The four-and-a-half-hour epic featured six lead changes, but the game's early innings were characterized by sloppy defense. Each team scored an unearned run in the fourth inning, the Rangers took the lead again in the fifth after Freese dropped a popup, and the Cardinals tied it in the sixth after a throwing error by Michael Young. The Rangers broke a 4-4 tie in the seventh with a three-run outburst that included back-to-back solo home runs by Adrian Beltre and Nelson Cruz and took a 7-5 lead into the bottom of the ninth. But Feliz, who had not blown a save since Aug. 6, gave up a one-out double to Albert Pujols and walked Berkman to set up Freese's heroics. Freese hit a two-out triple on a 1-2 count that sailed over the head of Cruz in right field to tie the game at 7-7. Undaunted, the Rangers went ahead, 9-7, in the top of the 10th when Hamilton hit a two-run home run to right, his first home run of the 2011 postseason. The Cardinals quickly responded in the bottom of the inning when Daniel Descalso and Jon Jay hit back-to-back singles off Darren Oliver. After Cardinals pitcher Kyle Lohse came in and delivered a successful sacrifice bunt, the Cards cut the lead to 9-8 on a Ryan Theriot groundout. St. Louis again was down to its last strike when Berkman hit a two-out, game-tying single to center off Scott Feldman to force an 11th inning.

Game 7
Friday, Oct. 28 at Busch Stadium, St. Louis, MO

	1	2	3	4	5	6	7	8	9	R	H	E
Texas Rangers	2	0	0	0	0	0	0	0	0	2	6	0
St. Louis Cardinals	2	0	1	0	2	0	1	0	X	6	7	1

Winning pitcher: Chris Carpenter
Losing pitcher: Matt Harrison
Attendance: 47,399

Cardinals ace Chris Carpenter rebounded from a shaky start and third baseman David Freese delivered another clutch hit to lead St. Louis to a 6-2 victory over the Texas Rangers in Game 7, clinching the 11th World Series championship in franchise history. A rainout of Game 6 allowed Carpenter, the Game 1 and Game 5 starter, to come back on three days' rest for Game 7. He earned his second win of the Series by scattering six hits in six-plus innings and ended the 2011 postseason with a perfect 4-0 record. The right-hander got into trouble in the first inning, surrendering back-to-back RBI doubles to Texas's Josh Hamilton and Michael Young, but allowed only three more hits before leav-ing the game in the seventh inning. The Cardinals tied the score in the bottom half of the first inning off Texas starter Matt Harrison, who issued consecutive walks to Albert Pujols and Lance Berk-man to set up David Freese, who hit a two-run double to left-center. St. Louis took the lead for good in the bottom of the third, when outfielder Allen Craig smacked his third home run of the series. The Cardinals extended their lead to 5-2 in the fifth inning when Rangers reliever Scott Feldman walked Yadier Molina with the bases loaded, and C. J. Wilson hit Rafael Furcal with a pitch to force in another run. Molina added an insurance run with an RBI single in the seventh that scored Berkman.

Major League Baseball, 2011: Memorable Milestones; Exciting Final Day

Major League Baseball had its share of memorable moments in 2011, including new career milestones reached by several veterans. With a home run July 9, 2011, NY Yankee shortstop Derek Jeter became the 28th player in MLB history to reach 3,000 career hits. Fellow Yankee veteran Mariano Rivera broke Trevor Hoffman's MLB record with his 602nd save Sept. 19, 2011, at Yankee Stadium. The Minnesota Twins' Jim Thome became the eighth player ever to reach 600 career home runs when he hit two Aug. 15, 2011; Thome, who was a rookie with Cleveland in 1991, was traded there less than two weeks later.

Both leagues' wild-card races came down to the final day of the season, Sept. 28, 2011. The Tampa Bay Rays and Boston Red Sox were tied for the AL wild-card playoff position after the Rays came back from nine games out Sept. 3. In the regular-season finales, the Red Sox blew a ninth-inning lead and lost to the Baltimore Orioles, as the Rays defeated the AL East champion NY Yankees in the 12th inning and claimed the wild-card slot. In the National League, the St. Louis Cardinals and Atlanta Braves were tied with 89-72 records on the last day of the regular season. The Braves, who led St. Louis in the Wild Card by 8½ games Sept. 5, dropped a ninth-inning lead against Philadelphia and lost in 13 innings Sept. 28, 2011, as the Cardinals shut out the Houston Astros, 8-0, to claim the NL wild-card slot.

The AL East champion NY Yankees earned their 16th postseason berth in the last 17 years and finished with the best record in the AL (97-65). Yankee outfielder Curtis Granderson led the league in RBI (119) and runs scored (136) and hit a career-high 41 home runs. The Detroit Tigers won the AL Central Division due in large part to right-hander Justin Verlander, who led the majors with 24 wins and 250 strikeouts. Tigers first baseman Miguel Cabrera won the AL batting title with a .344 average and led the league in on-base percentage (.448). The Texas Rangers won the team's second straight AL West crown on the strength of a powerful offense that boasted five players with at least 25 home runs.

In the National League, Roy Halladay and Cliff Lee anchored a Philadelphia pitching staff that led the majors with a 3.02 team ERA and carried the Phillies to a club-record 102 victories and their fifth consecutive NL East title. In the Central Division, the Milwaukee Brewers claimed their first division crown since 1982. After a slow start, the Arizona Diamondbacks emerged triumphant from their battle with the defending champion San Francisco Giants for supremacy in the NL West.

Despite tumultuous off-the-field headlines related to team ownership, the L.A. Dodgers boasted some top performances in 2011. Dodger outfielder Matt Kemp led the National League with 39 homers and 126 RBI but fell short of the Triple Crown when his .324 batting average was good for third in the league behind the Brewers' Ryan Braun (.332) and the NY Mets' Jose Reyes (.337). Dodger left-hander Clayton Kershaw tied the Diamondbacks' Ian Kennedy with a league-high 21 wins, and led the NL with a 2.28 ERA and 248 strikeouts.

National League Final Standings, 2011

(* = wild card team)

Eastern Division

	W	L	Pct.	GB	Home	Road	vs. East	vs. Central	vs. West	vs. AL
Philadelphia	102	60	.630	—	52-29	50-31	43-29	27-16	23-9	9-6
Atlanta	89	73	.549	13	47-34	42-39	36-36	22-17	21-15	10-5
Washington	80	81	.497	21½	44-36	36-45	36-36	20-19	16-19	8-7
NY Mets	77	85	.475	25	34-47	43-38	33-39	19-20	16-17	9-9
Florida	72	90	.444	30	31-47	41-43	32-40	20-20	12-20	8-10

Central Division

	W	L	Pct.	GB	Home	Road	vs. East	vs. Central	vs. West	vs. AL
Milwaukee	96	66	.593	—	57-24	39-42	20-14	51-29	19-14	6-9
St. Louis*	90	72	.556	6	45-36	45-36	22-13	44-35	16-17	8-7
Cincinnati	79	83	.488	17	42-39	37-44	13-20	42-37	18-14	6-12
Pittsburgh	72	90	.444	24	36-45	36-45	12-22	39-41	13-20	8-7
Chicago Cubs	71	91	.438	25	39-42	32-49	15-18	34-46	17-17	5-10
Houston	56	106	.346	40	31-50	25-56	10-21	28-50	14-24	4-11

Western Division

	W	L	Pct.	GB	Home	Road	vs. East	vs. Central	vs. West	vs. AL
Arizona	94	68	.580	—	51-30	43-38	18-14	23-17	43-29	10-8
San Francisco	86	76	.531	8	46-35	40-41	13-20	20-22	43-29	10-5
L.A. Dodgers	82	79	.509	11½	42-39	40-40	15-17	22-20	39-33	6-9
Colorado	73	89	.451	21	38-43	35-46	15-18	22-20	28-44	8-7
San Diego	71	91	.438	23	35-46	36-45	19-19	19-18	27-45	6-9

American League Final Standings, 2011

(* = wild card team)

Eastern Division

	W	L	Pct.	GB	Home	Road	vs. East	vs. Central	vs. West	vs. NL
NY Yankees	97	65	.599	—	52-29	45-36	39-33	22-14	23-13	13-5
Tampa Bay*	91	71	.562	6	47-34	44-37	42-30	21-17	16-18	12-6
Boston	90	72	.556	7	45-36	45-36	38-34	21-16	21-14	10-8
Toronto	81	81	.500	16	42-39	39-42	33-39	18-15	22-17	8-10
Baltimore	69	93	.426	28	39-42	30-51	28-44	22-20	12-18	7-11

Central Division

	W	L	Pct.	GB	Home	Road	vs. East	vs. Central	vs. West	vs. NL
Detroit	95	67	.586	—	50-31	45-36	20-16	50-22	18-18	7-11
Cleveland	80	82	.494	15	44-37	36-45	19-18	36-36	14-21	11-7
Chicago White Sox	79	83	.488	16	36-45	43-38	17-20	32-40	19-16	11-7
Kansas City	71	91	.438	24	40-41	31-50	16-21	32-40	18-17	5-13
Minnesota	63	99	.389	32	33-48	30-51	10-29	30-42	15-18	8-10

Western Division

	W	L	Pct.	GB	Home	Road	vs. East	vs. Central	vs. West	vs. NL
Texas	96	66	.593	—	52-29	44-37	22-22	25-18	40-17	9-9
L.A. Angels	86	76	.531	10	45-36	41-40	21-23	25-18	27-30	13-5
Oakland	74	88	.457	22	43-38	31-50	20-23	20-24	26-31	8-10
Seattle	67	95	.414	29	39-45	28-50	17-26	20-24	21-36	9-9

National League Statistics, 2011

Individual statistics. Players recording fewer than 150 at-bats (batters) or fewer than 70 innings or 10 saves (pitchers) are not listed here. * = changed teams within NL during season; entry includes statistics for more than one team. # = changed teams to or from AL during season; entry includes only NL statistics. Team Batting and Team Pitching includes players not shown separately.

Team Batting

Team	AVG	AB	R	H	HR	RBI
St. Louis Cardinals	.273	5,532	762	1,513	162	726
New York Mets	.264	5,600	718	1,477	108	676
Milwaukee Brewers	.261	5,447	721	1,422	185	693
Colorado Rockies	.258	5,544	735	1,429	163	697
Houston Astros	.258	5,598	615	1,442	95	579
Los Angeles Dodgers . . .	.257	5,436	644	1,395	117	613
Chicago Cubs	.256	5,549	654	1,423	148	610
Cincinnati Reds	.256	5,612	735	1,438	183	697
Philadelphia Phillies	.253	5,579	713	1,409	153	693
Arizona Diamondbacks . .	.250	5,421	731	1,357	172	702
Florida Marlins	.247	5,508	625	1,358	149	596
Pittsburgh Pirates	.244	5,421	610	1,325	107	580
Atlanta Braves	.243	5,528	641	1,345	173	606
San Francisco Giants . . .	.242	5,486	570	1,327	121	534
Washington Nationals . . .	.242	5,441	624	1,319	154	594
San Diego Padres	.237	5,417	593	1,284	91	563

Team Pitching

Team	ERA	IP	H	BB	SO	SV
Philadelphia Phillies	3.02	1,477	1,320	404	1,299	47
San Francisco Giants . . .	3.20	1,468	1,260	559	1,316	52
San Diego Padres	3.42	1,449.1	1,324	521	1,139	44
Atlanta Braves	3.48	1,479.2	1,332	521	1,332	52
Los Angeles Dodgers . . .	3.54	1,432	1,287	507	1,265	40
Washington Nationals . . .	3.58	1,449.1	1,403	477	1,049	49
Milwaukee Brewers	3.63	1,441.2	1,348	440	1,257	47
St. Louis Cardinals	3.74	1,462	1,461	448	1,098	47
Arizona Diamondbacks . .	3.80	1,443.1	1,414	442	1,058	58
Florida Marlins	3.95	1,459.2	1,403	500	1,218	40
Pittsburgh Pirates	4.04	1,449.1	1,513	535	1,031	43
Cincinnati Reds	4.16	1,467.2	1,414	539	1,112	39
New York Mets	4.19	1,448	1,482	514	1,126	43
Chicago Cubs	4.33	1,434.1	1,439	580	1,224	40
Colorado Rockies	4.43	1,447.2	1,471	522	1,118	41
Houston Astros	4.51	1,435	1,477	560	1,191	25

Arizona Diamondbacks

Batters	AVG	AB	R	H	HR	RBI	SO	SB
Gerardo Parra	.292	445	55	130	8	46	82	15
Justin Upton	.289	592	105	171	31	88	126	21
Miguel Montero	.282	493	65	139	18	86	97	1
Willie Bloomquist . .	.266	350	44	93	4	26	51	20
Stephen Drew	.252	321	44	81	5	45	74	4
Paul Goldschmidt . .	.250	156	28	39	8	26	53	4
Ryan Roberts	.249	482	86	120	19	65	98	18
Xavier Nady	.248	206	26	51	4	35	46	2
Chris Young#	.236	567	89	134	20	71	139	22
Lyle Overbay*	.234	394	43	92	9	47	88	2
Juan Miranda	.213	174	18	37	7	23	48	0
Kelly Johnson#	.209	430	59	90	18	49	132	13

Pitchers	ERA	W	L	IP	H	BB	SO	SV
J. J. Putz	2.17	2	2	58	41	12	61	45
Ian Kennedy	2.88	21	4	222	186	55	198	0
Josh Collmenter . . .	3.38	10	10	154.1	137	28	100	0
David Hernandez . . .	3.38	5	3	69.1	49	30	77	11
Daniel Hudson	3.49	16	12	222	217	50	169	0
Joe Saunders	3.69	12	13	212	210	67	108	0
Zach Duke	4.93	3	4	76.2	101	19	32	1
Jason Marquis*	4.43	8	6	132	154	43	76	0

Manager: Kirk Gibson

Chicago Cubs

Batters	AVG	AB	R	H	HR	RBI	SO	SB
Reed Johnson	.309	246	33	76	5	28	63	2
Starlin Castro	.307	674	91	207	10	66	96	22
Aramis Ramirez . . .	.306	565	80	173	26	93	69	1
Darwin Barney	.276	529	66	146	2	43	67	9
Marlon Byrd	.276	446	51	123	9	35	78	3
Kosuke Fukudome# .	.273	293	33	80	3	13	57	2
Jeff Baker	.269	201	20	54	3	23	46	0
Blake DeWitt	.265	230	21	61	5	26	31	1
Alfonso Soriano . . .	.244	475	50	116	26	88	113	2
Geovany Soto	.228	421	46	96	17	54	124	0
Carlos Pena	.225	493	72	111	28	80	161	2
Tyler Colvin	.150	206	17	31	6	20	58	0

Pitchers	ERA	W	L	IP	H	BB	SO	SV
Sean Marshall	2.26	6	6	75.2	66	17	79	5
Jeff Samardzija	2.97	8	4	88	64	50	87	0
Matt Garza	3.32	10	10	198	186	63	197	0
Carlos Marmol	4.01	2	6	74	54	48	99	34
Rodrigo Lopez	4.42	6	6	97.2	116	29	54	0
Ryan Dempster	4.80	10	14	202.1	211	82	191	0
Carlos Zambrano . .	4.82	9	7	145.2	154	56	101	0
Randy Wells	4.99	7	6	135.1	141	47	82	0
Casey Coleman . . .	6.40	3	9	84.1	102	46	75	0

Manager: Mike Quade

Atlanta Braves

Batters	AVG	AB	R	H	HR	RBI	SO	SB
Michael Bourn*	.294	656	94	193	2	50	140	61
Freddie Freeman . . .	.282	571	67	161	21	76	142	4
Chipper Jones	.275	455	56	125	18	70	80	2
Brian McCann	.270	466	51	126	24	71	89	3
Matt Diaz*	.263	251	16	66	0	20	52	5
David Ross	.263	152	14	40	6	23	51	0
Martin Prado	.260	551	66	143	13	57	52	4
Jordan Schafer* . . .	.242	302	46	73	2	13	70	22
Alex Gonzalez	.241	564	59	136	15	56	126	2
Eric Hinske	.233	236	24	55	10	28	71	0
Dan Uggla	.233	600	88	140	36	82	156	1
Nate McLouth	.228	267	35	61	4	16	54	4
Jason Heyward	.227	396	50	90	14	42	93	9

Pitchers	ERA	W	L	IP	H	BB	SO	SV
Eric O'Flaherty	0.98	2	4	73.2	59	21	67	0
Jonny Venters	1.84	6	2	88	53	43	96	5
Craig Kimbrel	2.10	4	3	77	48	32	127	46
Jair Jurrjens	2.96	13	6	152	142	44	90	0
Tim Hudson	3.22	16	10	215	189	56	158	0
Cristhian Martinez .	3.36	1	3	77.2	56	19	58	0
Tommy Hanson	3.60	11	7	130	106	46	142	0
Brandon Beachy . . .	3.68	7	3	141.2	125	46	169	0
Mike Minor	4.14	5	3	82.2	93	30	77	0
Derek Lowe	5.05	9	17	187	212	70	137	0

Manager: Fredi Gonzalez

Cincinnati Reds

Batters	AVG	AB	R	H	HR	RBI	SO	SB
Joey Votto	.309	599	101	185	29	103	129	8
Brandon Phillips . . .	.300	610	94	183	18	82	85	14
Ramon Hernandez .	.282	298	28	84	12	36	41	0
Ryan Hanigan	.267	266	27	71	6	31	32	0
Miguel Cairo	.265	245	33	65	8	33	36	3
Jay Bruce	.256	585	84	150	32	97	158	8
Chris Heisey	.254	279	44	71	18	50	78	6
Edgar Renteria	.251	299	34	75	5	36	65	4
Drew Stubbs	.243	604	92	147	15	44	205	40
Scott Rolen	.242	252	31	61	5	36	36	1
Fred Lewis	.230	183	20	42	3	19	38	2
Paul Janish	.214	336	27	72	0	23	46	3
Jonny Gomes*	.209	311	41	65	14	43	105	7

Pitchers	ERA	W	L	IP	H	BB	SO	SV
Johnny Cueto	2.31	9	5	156	123	47	104	0
Francisco Cordero .	2.45	5	3	69.2	49	22	42	37
Sam LeCure	3.71	2	1	77.2	57	21	73	0
Nick Masset	3.71	3	6	70.1	76	31	62	1
Mike Leake	3.86	12	9	167.2	159	38	118	0
Homer Bailey	4.43	9	7	132	136	33	106	0
Travis Wood	4.84	6	6	106	118	40	76	0
Dontrelle Willis	5.00	1	6	75.2	78	37	57	0
Bronson Arroyo . . .	5.07	9	12	199	227	45	108	0
Edinson Volquez . .	5.71	5	7	108.2	106	65	104	0

Manager: Dusty Baker

Colorado Rockies

Batters	AVG	AB	R	H	HR	RBI	SO	SB
Todd Helton	.302	421	59	127	14	69	71	0
Troy Tulowitzki	.302	537	81	162	30	105	79	9
Carlos Gonzalez	.295	481	92	142	26	92	105	20
Seth Smith	.284	476	67	135	15	59	93	10
Mark Ellis#	.274	263	34	72	6	25	43	7
Dexter Fowler	.266	481	84	128	5	45	130	12
Chris Nelson	.250	180	20	45	4	16	35	3
Eric Young	.247	198	34	49	0	10	38	27
Jonathan Herrera	.242	281	28	68	3	14	40	4
Ty Wigginton	.242	401	52	97	15	47	84	8
Chris Iannetta	.238	345	51	82	14	55	89	6
Jose Lopez*	.216	231	23	50	8	21	28	2
Ryan Spilborghs	.210	200	22	42	3	22	49	2

Pitchers	ERA	W	L	IP	H	BB	SO	SV
Matt Belisle	3.25	10	4	72	77	14	58	0
Jhoulys Chacin	3.62	11	14	194	168	87	150	0
Huston Street	3.86	1	4	58.1	62	9	55	29
Juan Nicasio	4.14	4	4	71.2	73	18	58	0
Ubaldo Jimenez#	4.46	6	9	123	118	51	118	0
Jason Hammel	4.76	7	13	170.1	175	68	94	1
Aaron Cook	6.03	3	10	97	127	37	48	0
Esmil Rogers	7.05	6	6	83	110	47	63	0

Manager: Jim Tracy

Florida Marlins

Batters	AVG	AB	R	H	HR	RBI	SO	SB
Emilio Bonifacio	.296	565	78	167	5	36	129	40
Omar Infante	.276	579	55	160	7	49	67	4
Greg Dobbs	.275	411	38	113	8	49	83	0
Gaby Sanchez	.266	572	72	152	19	78	97	3
Bryan Petersen	.265	204	18	54	2	10	49	7
Mike Stanton	.262	516	79	135	34	87	166	5
Logan Morrison	.247	462	54	114	23	72	99	2
Hanley Ramirez	.243	338	55	82	10	45	66	20
Chris Coghlan	.230	269	33	62	5	22	49	7
John Buck	.227	466	41	106	16	57	115	0
Jose Lopez*	.216	231	23	50	8	21	28	2

Pitchers	ERA	W	L	IP	H	BB	SO	SV
Edward Mujica	2.96	9	6	76	64	14	63	0
Anibal Sanchez	3.67	8	9	196.1	187	64	202	0
Javier Vazquez	3.69	13	11	192.2	178	50	162	0
Leo Nunez	4.06	1	4	64.1	57	21	55	36
Ricky Nolasco	4.67	10	12	206	244	44	148	0
Chris Volstad	4.89	5	13	165.2	187	49	117	0

Managers: Edwin Rodriguez, Jack McKeon

Houston Astros

Batters	AVG	AB	R	H	HR	RBI	SO	SB
Hunter Pence*	.314	606	84	190	22	97	124	8
Jason Bourgeois	.294	238	30	70	1	16	24	31
Michael Bourn*	.294	656	94	193	2	50	140	61
Brian Bogusevic	.287	164	22	47	4	15	40	4
Jimmy Paredes	.286	168	16	48	2	18	47	5
Jeff Keppinger*	.277	379	39	105	6	35	24	0
Jose Altuve	.276	221	26	61	2	12	29	7
Matt Downs	.276	199	29	55	10	41	47	0
Carlos Lee	.275	585	66	161	18	94	60	4
J. D. Martinez	.274	208	29	57	6	35	48	0
Brett Wallace	.259	336	37	87	5	29	91	1
Chris Johnson	.251	378	32	95	7	42	97	2
Clint Barmes	.244	446	47	109	12	39	88	3
Jordan Schafer*	.242	302	46	73	2	13	70	22
Angel Sanchez	.240	288	35	69	1	28	44	3
Humberto Quintero	.240	262	22	63	2	25	53	1
Bill Hall*	.211	185	24	39	2	14	63	3
Jason Michaels	.199	156	10	31	2	10	31	1
Carlos Corporan	.188	154	9	29	0	11	49	0

Pitchers	ERA	W	L	IP	H	BB	SO	SV
Mark Melancon	2.78	8	4	74.1	65	26	66	20
Wilton Lopez	2.79	2	6	71	72	18	56	0
Wandy Rodriguez	3.49	11	11	191	182	69	166	0
Bud Norris	3.77	6	11	186	177	70	176	0
Brett Myers	4.46	7	14	216	226	57	160	0
Aneury Rodriguez	5.27	1	6	85.1	83	32	64	0
J.A. Happ	5.35	6	15	156.1	157	83	134	0
Jordan Lyles	5.36	2	8	94	107	26	67	0

Manager: Brad Mills

Los Angeles Dodgers

Batters	AVG	AB	R	H	HR	RBI	SO	SB
Matt Kemp	.324	602	115	195	39	126	159	40
Dee Gordon	.304	224	34	68	0	11	27	24
Andre Ethier	.292	487	67	142	11	62	103	0
Jamey Carroll	.290	452	52	131	0	17	58	10
James Loney	.288	531	56	153	12	65	67	4
Aaron Miles	.275	454	49	125	3	45	49	4
Juan Rivera#	.274	219	24	60	5	46	35	2
Xavier Paul*	.255	243	30	62	2	20	62	16
Tony Gwynn	.256	312	37	80	2	22	61	22
Jerry Sands	.253	198	20	50	4	26	51	3
Casey Blake	.252	202	32	51	4	26	50	1
Rod Barajas	.230	305	29	70	16	47	71	0
Juan Uribe	.204	270	21	55	4	28	60	2
Rafael Furcal*	.231	333	44	77	8	28	39	9
Dioner Navarro	.193	176	13	34	5	17	35	0

Pitchers	ERA	W	L	IP	H	BB	SO	SV
Clayton Kershaw	2.28	21	5	233.1	174	54	248	0
Javy Guerra	2.31	2	2	46.2	37	18	38	21
Hiroki Kuroda	3.07	13	16	202	196	49	161	0
Ted Lilly	3.97	12	14	192.2	172	51	158	0
Chad Billingsley	4.21	11	11	188	189	84	152	0

Manager: Don Mattingly

Milwaukee Brewers

Batters	AVG	AB	R	H	HR	RBI	SO	SB
Ryan Braun	.332	563	109	187	33	111	93	33
Nyjer Morgan	.304	378	61	115	4	37	70	13
Prince Fielder	.299	569	95	170	38	120	106	1
Corey Hart	.285	492	80	140	26	63	114	7
Jerry Hairston*	.270	337	43	91	5	31	46	3
Mark Kotsay	.270	233	18	63	3	31	27	3
Rickie Weeks	.269	453	77	122	20	49	107	9
Jonathan Lucroy	.265	430	45	114	12	59	99	2
Yuniesky Betancourt	.252	556	51	140	13	68	63	4
Carlos Gomez	.225	231	37	52	8	24	64	16
Casey McGehee	.223	546	46	122	13	67	104	0
Craig Counsell	.178	157	19	28	1	9	21	2

Pitchers	ERA	W	L	IP	H	BB	SO	SV
John Axford	1.95	2	2	73.2	59	25	86	46
Francisco Rodriguez*	2.64	6	2	71.2	67	26	79	23
Kameron Loe	3.50	4	7	72	65	16	61	1
Yovani Gallardo	3.52	17	10	207.1	193	59	207	0
Shaun Marcum	3.54	13	7	200.2	175	57	158	0
Randy Wolf	3.69	13	10	212.1	214	66	134	0
Zack Greinke	3.83	16	6	171.2	161	45	201	0
Marco Estrada	4.08	4	8	92.2	83	29	88	0
Chris Narveson	4.45	11	8	161.2	160	65	126	0

Manager: Ron Roenicke

New York Mets

Batters	AVG	AB	R	H	HR	RBI	SO	SB
Jose Reyes	.337	537	101	181	7	44	41	39
Daniel Murphy	.320	391	49	125	6	49	42	5
Carlos Beltran*	.300	520	78	156	22	84	98	4
Lucas Duda	.292	301	38	88	10	50	57	1
Ruben Tejada	.284	328	31	93	0	36	50	5
Ronny Paulino	.268	228	19	61	2	19	38	0
Josh Thole	.268	340	22	91	3	40	47	0
Angel Pagan	.262	478	68	125	7	56	62	32
Justin Turner	.260	435	49	113	4	51	59	7
Nick Evans	.256	176	26	45	4	25	48	0
David Wright	.254	389	60	99	14	61	97	13
Willie Harris	.246	240	36	59	2	23	62	5
Jason Bay	.245	444	59	109	12	57	109	11
Jason Pridie	.231	208	28	48	4	20	64	7

Pitchers	ERA	W	L	IP	H	BB	SO	SV
Francisco Rodriguez*	2.64	6	2	71.2	67	26	79	23
R. A. Dickey	3.28	8	13	208.2	202	54	134	0
Jonathon Niese	4.40	11	11	157.1	178	44	138	0
Dillon Gee	4.43	13	6	160.2	150	71	114	0
Chris Capuano	4.55	11	12	186	198	53	168	0
Mike Pelfrey	4.74	7	13	193.2	220	65	105	0

Manager: Terry Collins

Philadelphia Phillies

Batters	AVG	AB	R	H	HR	RBI	SO	SB
Hunter Pence*	.314	606	84	190	22	97	124	8
Carlos Ruiz	.283	410	49	116	6	40	48	1
Shane Victorino	.279	519	95	145	17	61	63	19
Placido Polanco	.277	469	46	130	5	50	44	3
John Mayberry	.273	267	37	73	15	49	55	8
Jimmy Rollins	.268	567	87	152	16	63	59	30
Chase Utley	.259	398	54	103	11	44	47	14
Ryan Howard	.253	557	81	141	33	116	172	1
Wilson Valdez	.249	273	39	68	1	30	41	3
Domonic Brown	.245	184	28	45	5	19	35	3
Raul Ibanez	.245	535	65	131	20	84	106	2
Ben Francisco	.244	250	24	61	6	34	42	4
Michael Martinez	.196	209	25	41	3	24	35	3

Pitchers	ERA	W	L	IP	H	BB	SO	SV
Roy Halladay	2.35	19	6	233.2	208	35	220	0
Ryan Madson	2.37	4	2	60.2	54	16	62	32
Cliff Lee	2.40	17	8	232.2	197	42	238	0
Cole Hamels	2.79	14	9	216	169	44	194	0
Vance Worley	3.01	11	3	131.2	116	46	119	0
Kyle Kendrick	3.22	8	6	114.2	110	30	59	0
Roy Oswalt	3.69	9	10	139	153	33	93	0

Manager: Charlie Manuel

Pittsburgh Pirates

Batters	AVG	AB	R	H	HR	RBI	SO	SB
Ryan Doumit	.303	218	17	66	8	30	35	0
Alex Presley	.298	215	27	64	4	20	40	9
Neil Walker	.273	596	76	163	12	83	112	9
Josh Harrison	.272	195	21	53	1	16	24	4
Jose Tabata	.266	334	53	89	4	21	61	16
Matt Diaz*	.263	251	16	66	0	20	52	5
Andrew McCutchen	.259	572	87	148	23	89	126	23
Xavier Paul*	.255	243	30	62	2	20	62	16
Ronny Cedeno	.249	413	43	103	2	32	93	2
Garrett Jones	.243	423	51	103	16	58	104	6
Ryan Ludwick*	.237	490	56	116	13	75	124	1
Lyle Overbay*	.234	394	43	92	9	47	88	2
Michael McKenry	.222	180	17	40	2	11	49	0
Brandon Wood#	.220	236	25	52	7	31	65	0
Pedro Alvarez	.191	235	18	45	4	19	80	1

Pitchers	ERA	W	L	IP	H	BB	SO	SV
Joel Hanrahan	1.83	1	4	68.2	56	16	61	40
Jeff Karstens	3.38	9	9	162.1	163	33	96	0
Paul Maholm	3.66	6	14	162.1	160	50	97	0
Daniel McCutchen	3.72	5	3	84.2	87	33	47	0
Jose Veras	3.80	2	4	71	54	34	79	1
Charlie Morton	3.83	10	10	171.2	186	77	110	0
James McDonald	4.21	9	9	171	176	78	142	0
Kevin Correia	4.79	12	11	154	175	39	77	0

Manager: Clint Hurdle

San Diego Padres

Batters	AVG	AB	R	H	HR	RBI	SO	SB
Jesus Guzman	.312	247	33	77	5	44	43	9
Chase Headley	.289	381	43	110	4	44	92	13
Nick Hundley	.288	281	34	81	9	29	74	1
Chris Denorfia	.277	307	38	85	5	19	49	11
Cameron Maybin	.264	516	82	136	9	40	125	40
Orlando Hudson	.246	398	54	98	7	43	84	19
Will Venable	.246	370	49	91	9	44	92	26
Jason Bartlett	.245	554	61	136	2	40	98	23
Ryan Ludwick*	.237	490	56	116	13	75	124	1
Brad Hawpe	.231	195	19	45	4	19	68	0
Kyle Blanks	.229	170	21	39	7	26	51	2
Alberto Gonzalez	.215	247	18	53	1	32	37	1
Logan Forsythe	.213	150	12	32	0	12	33	3
Rob Johnson	.190	179	9	34	3	16	58	3

Pitchers	ERA	W	L	IP	H	BB	SO	SV
Heath Bell	2.44	3	4	62.2	51	21	51	43
Cory Luebke	3.29	6	10	139.2	105	44	154	0
Dustin Moseley	3.30	3	10	120	117	36	64	0
Mat Latos	3.47	9	14	194.1	168	62	185	0
Chad Qualls	3.51	6	8	74.1	73	20	43	0
Aaron Harang	3.64	14	7	170.2	175	58	124	0
Tim Stauffer	3.73	9	12	185.2	180	53	128	0
Clayton Richard	3.88	5	9	99.2	104	38	53	0
Wade LeBlanc	4.63	5	6	79.2	84	28	51	0

Manager: Bud Black

San Francisco Giants

Batters	AVG	AB	R	H	HR	RBI	SO	SB
Pablo Sandoval	.315	426	55	134	23	70	63	2
Carlos Beltran*	.300	520	78	156	22	84	88	4
Freddy Sanchez	.289	239	21	69	3	24	35	0
Buster Posey	.284	162	17	46	4	21	30	3
Nate Schierholtz	.278	335	42	93	9	41	61	7
Jeff Keppinger*	.277	379	39	105	6	35	24	0
Aubrey Huff	.246	521	45	128	12	59	90	5
Cody Ross	.240	405	54	97	14	52	96	5
Miguel Tejada	.239	322	28	77	4	26	35	4
Aaron Rowand	.233	331	34	77	4	21	84	2
Pat Burrell	.230	183	17	42	7	21	67	0
Mike Fontenot	.227	220	22	50	4	21	48	5
Brandon Belt	.225	187	21	42	9	18	57	3
Andres Torres	.221	348	50	77	4	19	95	19
Bill Hall*	.211	185	24	39	2	14	63	3
Brandon Crawford	.204	196	22	40	3	21	31	1
Chris Stewart	.204	162	20	33	3	10	18	0
Eli Whiteside	.197	213	14	42	4	17	59	2

Pitchers	ERA	W	L	IP	H	BB	SO	SV
Ryan Vogelsong	2.71	13	7	179.2	164	61	139	0
Tim Lincecum	2.74	13	14	217	176	86	220	0
Matt Cain	2.88	12	11	221.2	177	63	179	0
Brian Wilson	3.11	6	4	55	50	31	54	36
Madison Bumgarner	3.21	13	13	204.2	202	46	191	0
Guillermo Mota	3.81	2	2	80.1	71	30	77	1
Jonathan Sanchez	4.26	4	7	101.1	80	66	102	0

Manager: Bruce Bochy

St. Louis Cardinals

Batters	AVG	AB	R	H	HR	RBI	SO	SB
Allen Craig	.315	200	33	63	11	40	40	5
Yadier Molina	.305	475	55	145	14	65	44	4
Lance Berkman	.301	488	90	147	31	94	93	2
Albert Pujols	.299	579	105	173	37	99	58	9
David Freese	.297	333	41	99	10	55	75	1
Jon Jay	.297	455	56	135	10	37	81	6
Matt Holliday	.296	446	83	132	22	75	93	2
Skip Schumaker	.283	367	34	104	2	38	50	0
Ryan Theriot	.271	442	46	120	1	47	41	4
Daniel Descalso	.264	326	35	86	1	28	65	2
Rafael Furcal*	.231	333	44	77	8	28	39	9
Colby Rasmus#	.246	338	61	83	11	40	77	5

Pitchers	ERA	W	L	IP	H	BB	SO	SV
Fernando Salas	2.28	5	6	75	50	21	75	24
Kyle Lohse	3.39	14	8	188.1	178	42	111	0
Chris Carpenter	3.45	11	9	237.1	243	55	191	0
Jaime Garcia	3.56	13	7	194.2	207	50	156	0
Edwin Jackson#	3.58	5	2	78	91	23	51	0
Kyle McClellan	4.19	12	7	141.2	143	43	76	0
Jake Westbrook	4.66	12	9	183.1	208	73	104	0

Manager: Tony La Russa

Washington Nationals

Batters	AVG	AB	R	H	HR	RBI	SO	SB
Michael Morse	.303	522	73	158	31	95	126	2
Ryan Zimmerman	.289	395	52	114	12	49	73	3
Jerry Hairston*	.270	337	43	91	5	31	46	3
Wilson Ramos	.267	389	48	104	15	52	76	0
Ian Desmond	.253	584	65	148	8	49	139	25
Laynce Nix	.250	324	38	81	16	44	82	2
Roger Bernadina	.243	309	40	75	7	27	63	17
Rick Ankiel	.239	380	46	91	9	37	96	10
Danny Espinosa	.236	573	72	135	21	66	166	17
Jayson Werth	.232	561	69	130	20	58	160	19
Alex Cora	.224	156	12	35	0	6	23	2
Jonny Gomes*	.209	311	41	65	14	43	105	7
Adam LaRoche	.172	151	15	26	3	15	37	1

Pitchers	ERA	W	L	IP	H	BB	SO	SV
Tyler Clippard	1.83	3	0	88.1	48	26	104	0
Drew Storen	2.75	6	3	75.1	57	20	74	43
Jordan Zimmermann	3.18	8	11	161.1	154	31	124	0
John Lannan	3.70	10	13	184.2	194	76	106	0
Tom Gorzelanny	4.03	4	6	105	102	33	95	0
Jason Marquis*	4.43	8	6	132	154	43	76	0
Livan Hernandez	4.47	8	13	175.1	199	46	99	0

Managers: Jim Riggleman, Davey Johnson

American League Team Statistics, 2011

Individual statistics. Players recording fewer than 150 at-bats (batters) or fewer than 70 innings or 10 saves (pitchers) are not listed here. * = changed teams within AL during season; entry includes statistics for more than one team. # = changed teams to or from NL during season; entry includes only AL statistics. Team Batting and Team Pitching includes players not shown separately.

Team Batting

Team	BA	AB	R	H	HR	RBI
Texas Rangers	.283	5,659	855	1,599	210	807
Boston Red Sox	.280	5,710	875	1,600	203	842
Detroit Tigers	.277	5,563	787	1,540	169	750
Kansas City Royals. . .	.275	5,672	730	1,560	129	705
New York Yankees. . .	.263	5,518	867	1,452	222	836
Baltimore Orioles	.257	5,585	708	1,434	191	684
Los Angeles Angels . .	.253	5,513	667	1,394	155	629
Chicago White Sox . . .	.252	5,502	654	1,387	154	625
Cleveland Indians. . . .	.250	5,509	704	1,380	154	671
Toronto Blue Jays . . .	.249	5,559	743	1,384	186	704
Minnesota Twins	.247	5,487	619	1,357	103	572
Oakland Athletics	.244	5,452	645	1,330	114	612
Tampa Bay Rays.	.244	5,436	707	1,324	172	674
Seattle Mariners	.233	5,421	556	1,263	109	534

Team Pitching

Team	ERA	IP	H	BB	SO	SV
Los Angeles Angels . .	3.57	1,465	1,388	476	1,058	39
Tampa Bay Rays.	3.58	1,449	1,263	504	1,143	32
Oakland Athletics	3.71	1,447.2	1,380	519	1,160	39
New York Yankees. . . .	3.73	1,458.1	1,423	507	1,222	47
Texas Rangers	3.79	1,441.1	1,327	461	1,179	38
Seattle Mariners	3.90	1,483	1,369	436	1,088	39
Detroit Tigers	4.04	1,440	1,406	492	1,115	52
Chicago White Sox . .	4.10	1,460	1,463	439	1,220	42
Boston Red Sox	4.20	1,457.1	1,366	540	1,213	36
Cleveland Indians . . .	4.23	1,453.1	1,482	463	1,024	38
Toronto Blue Jays . . .	4.32	1,458.2	1,433	540	1,169	33
Kansas City Royals . .	4.44	1,451.1	1,487	557	1,080	37
Minnesota Twins	4.58	1,421.2	1,564	480	940	32
Baltimore Orioles . . .	4.89	1,446.2	1,568	535	1,044	32

Baltimore Orioles

Batters	AVG	AB	R	H	HR	RBI	SO	SB
Vladimir Guerrero . . .	.290	562	60	163	13	63	56	2
Nick Markakis.	.284	641	72	182	15	73	75	12
Adam Jones	.280	567	68	159	25	83	113	12
J. J. Hardy.	.269	527	76	142	30	80	92	0
Chris Davis*	.266	199	25	53	5	19	63	1
Robert Andino	.263	457	63	120	5	36	83	13
Matt Wieters	.262	500	72	131	22	68	84	1
Nolan Reimold.	.247	267	40	66	13	45	57	7
Derrek Lee#	.246	334	39	82	12	41	83	2
Brian Roberts	.221	163	18	36	3	19	21	6
Mark Reynolds	.221	534	84	118	37	86	196	6
Felix Pie	.220	164	15	36	0	7	32	3
Luke Scott	.220	209	24	46	9	22	54	1

Pitchers	ERA	W	L	IP	H	BB	SO	SV
Jim Johnson	2.67	6	5	91	80	21	58	9
Jeremy Guthrie	4.33	9	17	208	213	66	130	0
Kevin Gregg	4.37	0	3	59.2	58	40	53	22
Zach Britton	4.61	11	11	154.1	162	62	97	0
Tommy Hunter*	4.68	4	4	84.2	100	15	45	0
Alfredo Simon	4.90	4	9	115.2	128	40	83	0
Jake Arrieta	5.05	10	8	119.1	115	59	93	0
Jo-Jo Reyes*	5.57	7	11	140.2	176	48	87	0
Brad Bergesen	5.70	2	7	101	119	32	61	0
Chris Jakubauskas . .	5.72	2	2	72.1	93	29	52	0
Manager: Buck Showalter								

Chicago White Sox

Batters	AVG	AB	R	H	HR	RBI	SO	SB
Alejandro De Aza . . .	.329	152	29	50	4	23	34	12
Paul Konerko	.300	543	69	163	31	105	89	1
A. J. Pierzynski	.287	464	38	133	8	48	33	0
Juan Pierre	.279	639	80	178	2	50	41	27
Alexei Ramirez	.269	614	81	165	15	70	84	7
Brent Lillibridge. . . .	.258	186	38	48	13	29	62	10
Carlos Quentin	.254	421	53	107	24	77	84	1
Omar Vizquel	.251	167	18	42	0	8	18	1
Brent Morel	.245	413	44	101	10	41	57	5
Gordon Beckham	.230	499	60	115	10	44	111	5
Alex Rios	.227	537	64	122	13	44	68	11
Mark Teahen*	.200	160	14	32	4	14	45	0
Adam Dunn	.159	415	36	66	11	42	177	0

Pitchers	ERA	W	L	IP	H	BB	SO	SV
Chris Sale	2.79	2	2	71	52	27	79	8
Sergio Santos	3.55	4	5	63.1	41	29	92	30
Mark Buehrle	3.59	13	9	205.1	221	45	109	0
Philip Humber	3.75	9	9	163	151	41	116	0
Edwin Jackson#	3.92	7	7	121.2	134	39	97	0
John Danks	4.33	8	12	170.1	182	46	135	0
Gavin Floyd	4.37	12	13	193.2	180	45	151	0
Jake Peavy	4.92	7	7	111.2	117	24	95	0
Manager: Ozzie Guillen								

Boston Red Sox

Batters	AVG	AB	R	H	HR	RBI	SO	SB
Adrian Gonzalez. . . .	.338	630	108	213	27	117	119	1
Jacoby Ellsbury	.321	660	119	212	32	105	98	39
David Ortiz	.309	525	84	162	29	96	83	1
Dustin Pedroia	.307	635	102	195	21	91	85	26
Marco Scutaro	.299	395	59	118	7	54	36	4
Josh Reddick	.280	254	41	71	7	28	50	1
Kevin Youkilis	.258	431	68	111	17	80	100	3
Mike Aviles*	.255	286	31	73	7	39	44	14
Carl Crawford	.255	506	65	129	11	56	104	18
Jed Lowrie	.252	309	40	78	6	36	60	1
Conor Jackson*	.244	352	32	86	5	43	53	3
Darnell McDonald. . .	.236	157	26	37	6	24	33	2
Jarrod Saltalamacchia	.235	358	52	84	16	56	119	1
J. D. Drew	.222	248	23	55	4	22	58	0
Jason Varitek	.221	222	32	49	11	36	67	0

Pitchers	ERA	W	L	IP	H	BB	SO	SV
Alfredo Aceves	2.61	10	2	114	84	42	80	2
Josh Beckett	2.89	13	7	193	146	52	175	0
Jonathan Papelbon. .	2.94	4	1	64.1	50	10	87	31
Daniel Bard	3.33	2	9	73	46	24	74	1
Jon Lester.	3.47	15	9	191.2	166	75	182	0
Clay Buchholz.	3.48	6	3	82.2	76	31	60	0
Erik Bedard*	3.62	5	9	129.1	118	48	125	0
Tim Wakefield	5.12	7	8	154.2	163	47	93	0
John Lackey	6.41	12	12	160	203	56	108	0
Manager: Terry Francona								

Cleveland Indians

Batters	AVG	AB	R	H	HR	RBI	SO	SB
Travis Hafner	.280	325	41	91	13	57	78	0
Asdrubal Cabrera . . .	.273	604	87	165	25	92	119	17
Michael Brantley. . . .	.266	451	63	120	7	46	76	13
Shelley Duncan	.260	223	29	58	11	47	56	0
Shin-Soo Choo	.259	313	37	81	8	36	78	12
Jim Thome*	.256	277	32	71	15	50	92	0
Lonnie Chisenhall. . .	.255	212	27	54	7	22	49	1
Jack Hannahan	.250	320	38	80	8	40	80	2
Kosuke Fukudome# . .	.249	237	26	59	5	22	53	2
Matt LaPorta	.247	352	34	87	11	53	87	1
Orlando Cabrera#. . .	.244	324	35	79	4	38	40	6
Ezequiel Carrera . . .	.243	202	27	49	0	14	35	10
Carlos Santana	.239	552	84	132	27	79	133	5
Lou Marson	.230	243	26	56	1	19	68	4
Grady Sizemore	.224	268	34	60	10	32	85	0
Austin Kearns	.200	150	18	30	2	7	48	0

Pitchers	ERA	W	L	IP	H	BB	SO	SV
Justin Masterson. . .	3.21	12	10	216	211	65	158	0
Chris Perez.	3.32	4	7	59.2	46	26	39	36
Josh Tomlin.	4.25	12	7	165.1	157	21	89	0
Carlos Carrasco . . .	4.62	8	9	124.2	130	40	85	0
Fausto Carmona	5.25	7	15	188.2	205	60	109	0
Manager: Manny Acta								

Detroit Tigers

Batters	AVG	AB	R	H	HR	RBI	SO	SB
Miguel Cabrera	.344	572	111	197	30	105	89	2
Victor Martinez	.330	540	76	178	12	103	51	1
Jhonny Peralta	.299	525	68	157	21	86	95	0
Alex Avila	.295	464	63	137	19	82	131	3
Wilson Betemit*	.285	323	40	92	8	46	105	4
Brennan Boesch	.283	428	75	121	16	54	83	5
Delmon Young*	.268	473	54	127	12	64	85	1
Ramon Santiago	.260	258	29	67	5	30	38	0
Casper Wells*	.237	215	30	51	11	27	71	3
Ryan Raburn	.256	387	53	99	14	49	114	1
Magglio Ordonez	.255	329	33	84	5	32	41	2
Andy Dirks	.251	219	34	55	7	28	36	5
Austin Jackson	.249	591	90	147	10	45	181	22
Don Kelly	.245	257	35	63	7	28	32	2
Scott Sizemore*	.245	368	50	90	11	56	112	5
Brandon Inge	.197	269	29	53	3	23	74	1

Pitchers	ERA	W	L	IP	H	BB	SO	SV
Jose Valverde	2.24	2	4	72.1	52	34	69	49
Justin Verlander	2.40	24	5	251	174	57	250	0
Doug Fister*	2.83	11	13	216.1	193	37	146	0
David Pauley*	3.16	5	6	74	64	22	44	0
Max Scherzer	4.43	15	9	195	207	56	174	0
Phil Coke	4.47	3	9	108.2	118	40	69	1
Rick Porcello	4.75	14	9	182	210	46	104	0
Brad Penny	5.30	11	11	181.2	222	62	74	0
Charlie Furbush*	5.48	4	10	85.1	97	30	67	0

Manager: Jim Leyland

Kansas City Royals

Batters	AVG	AB	R	H	HR	RBI	SO	SB
Melky Cabrera	.305	658	102	201	18	87	94	20
Alex Gordon	.303	611	101	185	23	87	139	17
Eric Hosmer	.293	523	66	153	19	78	82	11
Billy Butler	.291	597	74	174	19	95	95	2
Wilson Betemit*	.285	323	40	92	8	46	105	4
Jeff Francoeur	.285	601	77	171	20	87	123	22
Mike Moustakas	.263	338	26	89	5	30	51	2
Mike Aviles*	.255	286	31	73	7	39	44	14
Chris Getz	.255	380	50	97	0	26	45	21
Alcides Escobar	.254	548	69	139	4	46	73	26
Brayan Pena	.248	222	17	55	3	24	24	0
Johnny Giavotella	.247	178	20	44	2	21	32	5
Matt Treanor*	.214	196	24	42	3	22	53	2

Pitchers	ERA	W	L	IP	H	BB	SO	SV
Bruce Chen	3.77	12	8	155	152	50	97	0
Joakim Soria	4.03	5	5	60.1	60	17	60	28
Felipe Paulino#	4.11	4	6	124.2	123	48	119	0
Luke Hochevar	4.68	11	11	198	192	62	128	0
Jeff Francis	4.82	6	16	183	224	39	91	0
Danny Duffy	5.64	4	8	105.1	119	51	87	0

Manager: Ned Yost

Los Angeles Angels

Batters	AVG	AB	R	H	HR	RBI	SO	SB
Alberto Callaspo	.288	475	54	137	6	46	48	8
Howard Kendrick	.285	537	86	153	18	63	119	14
Erick Aybar	.279	556	71	155	10	59	68	30
Maicer Izturis	.276	449	51	124	5	38	65	9
Peter Bourjos	.271	502	72	136	12	43	124	22
Torii Hunter	.262	580	80	152	23	82	125	5
Mark Trumbo	.254	539	65	137	29	87	120	9
Bobby Abreu	.253	502	54	127	8	60	113	21
Vernon Wells	.218	505	60	110	25	66	86	9

Batters	AVG	AB	R	H	HR	RBI	SO	SB
Hank Conger	.209	177	14	37	6	19	37	0
Jeff Mathis	.174	247	18	43	3	22	75	1

Pitchers	ERA	W	L	IP	H	BB	SO	SV
Jered Weaver	2.41	18	8	235.2	182	56	198	0
Jordan Walden	2.98	5	5	60.1	49	26	67	32
Dan Haren	3.17	16	10	238.1	211	33	192	0
Ervin Santana	3.38	11	12	228.2	207	72	178	0
Tyler Chatwood	4.75	6	11	142	166	71	74	0
Joel Pineiro	5.13	7	7	145.2	182	38	62	0

Manager: Mike Scioscia

Minnesota Twins

Batters	AVG	AB	R	H	HR	RBI	SO	SB
Joe Mauer	.287	296	38	85	3	30	38	0
Michael Cuddyer	.284	529	70	150	20	70	95	11
Jason Kubel	.273	366	37	100	12	58	86	1
Delmon Young*	.268	473	54	127	12	64	85	1
Ben Revere	.267	450	56	120	0	30	41	34
Denard Span	.264	284	37	75	2	16	36	6
Alexi Casilla	.260	323	52	84	2	21	45	15
Jim Thome*	.256	277	32	71	15	50	92	0
Danny Valencia	.246	564	63	139	15	72	102	2
Trevor Plouffe	.238	286	47	68	8	31	71	3
Justin Morneau	.227	264	19	60	4	30	44	0
Tsuyoshi Nishioka	.226	221	14	50	0	19	43	2
Luke Hughes	.223	287	31	64	7	30	79	3
Rene Tosoni	.203	172	20	35	5	22	42	0
Matt Tolbert	.198	207	22	41	0	11	31	3
Drew Butera	.167	234	19	39	2	23	42	0

Pitchers	ERA	W	L	IP	H	BB	SO	SV
Scott Baker	3.14	8	6	134.2	126	32	123	0
Matt Capps	4.25	4	7	65.2	66	13	34	15
Carl Pavano	4.30	9	13	222	262	40	102	0
Anthony Swarzak	4.32	4	7	102	111	26	55	0
Nick Blackburn	4.49	7	10	148.1	183	54	76	0
Joe Nathan	4.84	2	1	44.2	38	14	43	14
Francisco Liriano	5.09	9	10	134.1	125	75	112	0
Brian Duensing	5.23	9	14	161.2	193	52	115	0

Manager: Ron Gardenhire

New York Yankees

Batters	AVG	AB	R	H	HR	RBI	SO	SB
Robinson Cano	.302	623	104	188	28	118	96	8
Derek Jeter	.297	546	84	162	6	61	81	16
Alex Rodriguez	.276	373	67	103	16	62	80	4
Eduardo Nunez	.265	309	38	82	5	30	37	22
Eric Chavez	.263	160	16	42	2	26	34	0
Curtis Granderson	.262	583	136	153	41	119	169	25
Nick Swisher	.260	526	81	137	23	85	125	2
Brett Gardner	.259	510	87	132	7	36	93	49
Mark Teixeira	.248	589	90	146	39	111	110	4
Andruw Jones	.247	190	27	47	13	33	62	0
Russell Martin	.237	417	57	99	18	65	81	8
Jorge Posada	.235	344	34	81	14	44	76	0

Pitchers	ERA	W	L	IP	H	BB	SO	SV
Mariano Rivera	1.91	1	2	61.1	47	8	60	44
CC Sabathia	3.00	19	8	237.1	230	61	230	0
Freddy Garcia	3.62	12	8	146.2	152	45	96	0
Ivan Nova	3.70	16	4	165.1	163	57	98	0
Bartolo Colon	4.00	8	10	164.1	172	40	135	0
A. J. Burnett	5.15	11	11	190.1	190	83	173	0
Phil Hughes	5.79	5	5	74.2	84	27	47	0

Manager: Joe Girardi

Oakland Athletics

Batters	AVG	AB	R	H	HR	RBI	SO	SB
Jemile Weeks	.303	406	50	123	2	36	62	22
Ryan Sweeney	.265	264	34	70	1	25	48	1
Coco Crisp	.264	531	69	140	8	54	65	49
Cliff Pennington	.264	515	57	136	8	58	104	14
Hideki Matsui	.251	517	58	130	12	72	84	1
Josh Willingham	.246	488	69	120	29	98	150	4
Scott Sizemore*	.245	368	50	90	11	56	112	5
Conor Jackson*	.244	352	32	86	5	43	53	3
David DeJesus	.240	442	60	106	10	46	86	4
Kurt Suzuki	.237	460	54	109	14	44	64	2
Mark Ellis#	.217	217	21	47	1	16	32	7
Daric Barton	.212	236	27	50	0	21	47	2

Pitchers	ERA	W	L	IP	H	BB	SO	SV
Gio Gonzalez	3.12	16	12	202	175	91	197	0
Andrew Bailey	3.24	0	4	41.2	34	12	41	24
Brandon McCarthy	3.32	9	9	170.2	168	25	123	0
Guillermo Moscoso	3.38	8	10	128	102	38	74	0
Brian Fuentes	3.70	2	8	58.1	52	20	42	12
Brett Anderson	4.00	3	6	83.1	86	25	61	0
Trevor Cahill	4.16	12	14	207.2	214	82	147	0
Rich Harden	5.12	4	4	82.2	87	31	91	0

Managers: Bob Geren, Bob Melvin

Seattle Mariners

Batters	AVG	AB	R	H	HR	RBI	SO	SB
Mike Carp	.276	290	27	80	12	46	81	0
Dustin Ackley	.273	333	39	91	6	36	79	6
Ichiro Suzuki	.272	677	80	184	5	47	69	40
Kyle Seager	.258	182	22	47	3	13	36	3
Jack Wilson#	.249	173	22	43	0	11	27	5
Brendan Ryan	.248	436	51	108	3	39	87	13
Casper Wells*	.237	215	30	51	11	27	71	3
Adam Kennedy	.234	380	36	89	7	38	67	8
Justin Smoak	.234	427	38	100	15	55	105	0
Franklin Gutierrez	.224	322	26	72	1	19	56	13
Miguel Olivo	.224	477	54	107	19	62	140	6
Jack Cust	.213	225	19	48	3	23	87	0
Chone Figgins	.188	288	24	54	1	15	42	11
Michael Saunders	.149	161	16	24	2	8	56	6

Pitchers	ERA	W	L	IP	H	BB	SO	SV
Brandon League	2.79	1	5	61.1	56	10	45	37
Doug Fister*	2.83	11	13	216.1	193	37	146	0
David Pauley*	3.16	5	6	74	64	22	44	0
Felix Hernandez	3.47	14	14	233.2	218	67	222	0
Erik Bedard*	3.62	5	9	129.1	118	48	125	0
Michael Pineda	3.74	9	10	171	133	55	173	0
Jason Vargas	4.25	10	13	201	205	59	131	0
Blake Beavan	4.27	5	6	97	106	15	42	0
Charlie Furbush*	5.48	4	10	85.1	97	30	67	0

Manager: Eric Wedge

Tampa Bay Rays

Batters	AVG	AB	R	H	HR	RBI	SO	SB
Casey Kotchman	.306	500	44	153	10	48	66	2
Matt Joyce	.277	462	69	128	19	75	106	13
Ben Zobrist	.269	588	99	158	20	91	128	19
Johnny Damon	.261	582	79	152	16	73	92	19
Desmond Jennings	.259	247	44	64	10	25	59	20
Evan Longoria	.244	483	78	118	31	99	93	3
B. J. Upton	.243	560	82	136	23	81	161	36
Sam Fuld	.240	308	41	74	3	27	49	20
John Jaso	.224	246	26	55	5	27	36	1
Sean Rodriguez	.223	373	45	83	8	36	87	11
Elliot Johnson	.194	160	20	31	4	17	53	6
Reid Brignac	.193	249	18	48	1	15	63	3
Kelly Shoppach	.176	221	23	39	11	22	79	0

Tampa Bay Rays (continued)

Pitchers	ERA	W	L	IP	H	BB	SO	SV
Kyle Farnsworth	2.18	5	1	57.2	45	12	51	25
James Shields	2.82	16	12	249.1	195	65	225	0
Jeremy Hellickson	2.95	13	10	189	146	72	117	0
David Price	3.49	12	13	224.1	192	63	218	0
Jeff Niemann	4.06	11	7	135.1	131	37	105	0
Wade Davis	4.45	11	10	184	190	63	105	0

Manager: Joe Maddon

Texas Rangers

Batters	AVG	AB	R	H	HR	RBI	SO	SB
Michael Young	.338	631	88	213	11	106	78	6
Mike Napoli	.320	369	72	118	30	75	85	4
Endy Chavez	.301	256	37	77	5	27	30	10
Josh Hamilton	.298	487	80	145	25	94	93	8
Adrian Beltre	.296	487	82	144	32	105	53	1
Elvis Andrus	.279	587	96	164	5	60	74	37
David Murphy	.275	404	46	111	11	46	61	11
Yorvit Torrealba	.273	396	40	108	7	37	65	0
Chris Davis*	.266	199	25	53	5	19	63	1
Nelson Cruz	.263	475	64	125	29	87	116	9
Mitch Moreland	.259	464	60	120	16	51	92	2
Ian Kinsler	.255	620	121	158	32	77	71	30
Matt Treanor*	.214	196	24	42	3	22	53	2

Pitchers	ERA	W	L	IP	H	BB	SO	SV
Neftali Feliz	2.74	2	3	62.1	42	30	54	32
C. J. Wilson	2.94	16	7	223.1	191	74	206	0
Matt Harrison	3.39	14	9	185.2	180	57	126	0
Alexi Ogando	3.51	13	8	169	149	43	126	0
Derek Holland	3.95	16	5	198	201	67	162	0
Colby Lewis	4.40	14	10	200.1	187	56	169	0
Tommy Hunter*	4.68	4	4	84.2	100	15	45	0

Manager: Ron Washington

Toronto Blue Jays

Batters	AVG	AB	R	H	HR	RBI	SO	SB
Jose Bautista	.302	513	105	155	43	103	111	9
Brett Lawrie	.293	150	26	44	9	25	31	7
Yunel Escobar	.290	513	77	149	11	48	70	3
Jose Molina	.281	171	19	48	3	15	44	2
Edwin Encarnacion	.272	481	70	131	17	55	77	8
Eric Thames	.262	362	58	95	12	37	88	2
Corey Patterson#	.252	317	44	80	6	33	65	13
Adam Lind	.251	499	56	125	26	87	107	1
John McDonald#	.250	168	19	42	2	20	18	2
Juan Rivera#	.243	247	22	60	6	28	41	3
Rajai Davis	.238	320	44	76	1	29	63	34
Aaron Hill#	.225	396	38	89	6	45	53	16
Travis Snider	.225	187	23	42	3	30	56	9
J. P. Arencibia	.219	443	47	97	23	78	133	1
Mark Teahen*	.200	160	14	32	4	14	45	0
Mike McCoy	.198	197	26	39	2	10	41	12

Pitchers	ERA	W	L	IP	H	BB	SO	SV
Ricky Romero	2.92	15	11	225	176	80	178	0
Frank Francisco	3.55	1	4	50.2	49	18	53	17
Carlos Villanueva	4.04	6	4	107	103	32	68	0
Jesse Litsch	4.44	6	3	75	69	28	66	1
Brandon Morrow	4.72	11	11	179.1	162	69	203	0
Brett Cecil	4.73	4	11	123.2	122	42	87	0
Jon Rauch	4.85	5	4	52	56	14	36	11
Jo-Jo Reyes*	5.57	7	11	140.2	176	48	87	0
Kyle Drabek	6.06	4	5	78.2	87	55	51	0

Manager: John Farrell

Major League Leaders, 2011

National League

Batting Average: Jose Reyes, NY Mets, .337; Ryan Braun, Milwaukee, .332; Matt Kemp, L.A. Dodgers, .324; Hunter Pence, Houston-Philadelphia, .314; Joey Votto, Cincinnati, .309.

Runs Scored: Matt Kemp, L.A. Dodgers, 115; Ryan Braun, Milwaukee, 109; Albert Pujols, St. Louis, 105; Justin Upton, Arizona, 105; Jose Reyes, NY Mets, 101; Joey Votto, Cincinnati, 101.

Runs Batted In: Matt Kemp, L.A. Dodgers, 126; Prince Fielder, Milwaukee, 120; Ryan Howard, Philadelphia, 116; Ryan Braun, Milwaukee, 111; Troy Tulowitzki, Colorado, 105.

Hits: Starlin Castro, Chicago Cubs, 207; Matt Kemp, L.A. Dodgers, 195; Michael Bourn, Houston/Atlanta, 193; Hunter Pence, Houston-Philadelphia, 190; Ryan Braun, Milwaukee, 187.

Doubles: Joey Votto, Cincinnati, 40; Carlos Beltran, NY Mets-San Francisco, 39; Justin Upton, Arizona, 39; Ryan Braun, Milwaukee, 38; Carlos Lee, Houston, 38; Hunter Pence, Houston-Philadelphia, 38; Brandon Phillips, Cincinnati, 38; Chris Young, Arizona, 38.

Triples: Jose Reyes, NY Mets, 16; Shane Victorino, Philadelphia, 16; Dexter Fowler, Colorado, 15; Michael Bourn, Houston-Atlanta, 10; Starlin Castro, Chicago Cubs, 9; Seth Smith, Colorado, 9.

Home Runs: Matt Kemp, L.A. Dodgers, 39; Prince Fielder, Milwaukee, 38; Albert Pujols, St. Louis, 37; Dan Uggla, Atlanta, 36; Mike Stanton, Florida, 34.

Stolen Bases: Michael Bourn, Houston-Atlanta, 61; Emilio Bonifacio, Florida, 40; Matt Kemp, L.A. Dodgers, 40; Cameron Maybin, San Diego, 40; Drew Stubbs, Cincinnati, 40.

Pitching Wins: Ian Kennedy, Arizona, 21-4; Clayton Kershaw, L.A. Dodgers, 21-5; Roy Halladay, Philadelphia, 19-6; Cliff Lee, Philadelphia, 17-8; Yovani Gallardo, Milwaukee, 17-10.

Earned Run Average: Clayton Kershaw, L.A. Dodgers, 2.28; Roy Halladay, Philadelphia, 2.35; Cliff Lee, Philadelphia, 2.40; Ryan Vogelsong, San Francisco, 2.71; Tim Lincecum, San Francisco, 2.74.

Strikeouts: Clayton Kershaw, L.A. Dodgers, 248; Cliff Lee, Philadelphia, 238; Roy Halladay, Philadelphia, 220; Tim Lincecum, San Francisco, 220; Yovani Gallardo, Milwaukee, 207.

Saves: John Axford, Milwaukee, 46; Craig Kimbrel, Atlanta, 46; J. J. Putz, Arizona, 45; Heath Bell, San Diego, 43; Drew Storen, Washington.

American League

Batting Average: Miguel Cabrera, Detroit, .344; Adrian Gonzalez, Boston, .338; Michael Young, Texas, .338; Victor Martinez, Detroit, .330; Jacoby Ellsbury, Boston, .321.

Runs Scored: Curtis Granderson, NY Yankees, 136; Ian Kinsler, Texas, 121; Jacoby Ellsbury, Boston, 119; Miguel Cabrera, Detroit, 111; Adrian Gonzalez, Boston, 108.

Runs Batted In: Curtis Granderson, NY Yankees, 119; Robinson Cano, NY Yankees, 118; Adrian Gonzalez, Boston, 117; Mark Teixeira, NY Yankees, 111; Michael Young, Texas, 106.

Hits: Adrian Gonzalez, Boston, 213; Michael Young, Texas, 213; Jacoby Ellsbury, Boston, 212; Melky Cabrera, Kansas City, 201; Miguel Cabrera, Detroit, 197.

Doubles: Miguel Cabrera, Detroit, 48; Jeff Francoeur, Kansas City, 47; Robinson Cano, NY Yankees, 46; Jacoby Ellsbury, Boston, 46; Ben Zobrist, Tampa Bay, 46.

Triples: Peter Bourjos, L.A. Angels, 11; Austin Jackson, Detroit, 11; Curtis Granderson, NY Yankees, 10; Erick Aybar, LA Angels, 8; Alcides Escobar, Kansas City, 8; Brett Gardner, NY Yankees, 8; Jemile Weeks, Oakland, 8.

Home Runs: Jose Bautista, Toronto, 43; Curtis Granderson, NY Yankees, 41; Mark Teixeira, NY Yankees, 39; Mark Reynolds, Baltimore, 37; Adrian Beltre, Texas, 32; Jacoby Ellsbury, Boston, 32; Ian Kinsler, Texas, 32.

Stolen Bases: Coco Crisp, Oakland, 49; Brett Gardner, NY Yankees, 49; Ichiro Suzuki, Seattle, 40; Jacoby Ellsbury, Boston, 39; Elvis Andrus, Texas, 37.

Pitching Wins: Justin Verlander, Detroit, 24-5; CC Sabathia, NY Yankees, 19-8; Jered Weaver, L.A. Angels, 18-8; Gio Gonzalez, Oakland, 16-12; Dan Haren, L.A. Angels, 16-10; Derek Holland, Texas, 16-5; Ivan Nova, NY Yankees, 16-4; James Shields, Tampa Bay, 16-12; C. J. Wilson, Texas, 16-7.

Earned Run Average: Justin Verlander, Detroit, 2.40; Jered Weaver, L.A. Angels, 2.41; James Shields, Tampa Bay, 2.82; Doug Fister, Seattle/Detroit, 2.83; Josh Beckett, Boston, 2.89.

Strikeouts: Justin Verlander, Detroit, 250; CC Sabathia, NY Yankees, 230; James Shields, Tampa Bay, 225; Felix Hernandez, Seattle, 222; David Price, Tampa Bay, 218.

Saves: Jose Valverde, Detroit, 49; Mariano Rivera, NY Yankees, 44; Brandon League, Seattle, 37; Chris Perez, Cleveland, 36; Neftali Feliz, Texas, 32; Jordan Walden, L.A. Angels, 32.

All-Time Major League Single-Season Leaders

Source: www.mlb.com; * = player active in 2011 season; records for "modern" era beginning 1901

Home Runs	HR
Barry Bonds (2001)	73
Mark McGwire (1998)	70
Sammy Sosa (1998)	66
Mark McGwire (1999)	65
Sammy Sosa (2001)	64

Runs Scored	R
Babe Ruth (1921)	177
Lou Gehrig (1936)	167
Lou Gehrig (1931)	163
Babe Ruth (1928)	163
Chuck Klein (1930)	158
Babe Ruth (1920, 1927)	158

Hits	H
Ichiro Suzuki* (2004)	262
George Sisler (1920)	257
Lefty O'Doul (1929)	254
Bill Terry (1930)	254
Al Simmons (1925)	253
Rogers Hornsby (1922)	250
Chuck Klein (1930)	250

Runs Batted In	RBI
Hack Wilson (1930)	191
Lou Gehrig (1931)	184
Hank Greenberg (1937)	183
Jimmie Foxx (1938)	175
Lou Gehrig (1927)	175

Batting Average	AVG
Nap Lajoie (1901)	.426
Rogers Hornsby (1924)	.424
George Sisler (1922)	.420
Ty Cobb (1911)	.420
Ty Cobb (1912)	.410

Stolen Bases	SB
Rickey Henderson (1982)	130
Lou Brock (1974)	118
Vince Coleman (1985)	110
Vince Coleman (1987)	109
Rickey Henderson (1983)	108

Walks (Batter)	BB
Barry Bonds (2004)	232
Barry Bonds (2002)	198
Barry Bonds (2001)	177
Babe Ruth (1923)	170
Mark McGwire (1998)	162
Ted Williams (1947, 1949)	162

Strikeouts (Batter)	SO
Mark Reynolds* (2009)	223
Mark Reynolds* (2010)	211
Drew Stubbs* (2011)	205
Mark Reynolds* (2008)	204
Adam Dunn* (2010)	199
Ryan Howard* (2007, 2008)	199

Earned Run Average	ERA
Dutch Leonard (1914)	0.96
Mordecai "Three Finger" Brown (1906)	1.04
Bob Gibson (1968)	1.12
Christy Mathewson (1909)	1.14
Walter Johnson (1913)	1.14

Wins	W
Jack Chesbro (1904)	41
Ed Walsh (1908)	40
Christy Mathewson (1908)	37
Walter Johnson (1913)	36
Joe McGinnity (1904)	35

Strikeouts	K
Nolan Ryan (1973)	383
Sandy Koufax (1965)	382
Randy Johnson (2001)	372
Nolan Ryan (1974)	367
Randy Johnson (1999)	364

Saves	SV
Francisco Rodriguez* (2008)	62
Bobby Thigpen (1990)	57
Eric Gagne (2003)	55
John Smoltz (2002)	55
Trevor Hoffman (1998)	53
Randy Myers (1993)	53
Mariano Rivera* (2004)	53

All-Time Major League Leaders

Source: www.mlb.com; * = player active in 2011 season; career records for players in "modern" era beginning 1901 may include some statistics from preceding years.

Games

Player	Games
Pete Rose	3,562
Carl Yastrzemski	3,308
Hank Aaron	3,298
Rickey Henderson	3,081
Ty Cobb	3,035
Eddie Murray	3,026
Stan Musial	3,026
Cal Ripken Jr.	3,001
Willie Mays	2,992
Barry Bonds	2,986

At Bats

Player	At Bats
Pete Rose	14,053
Hank Aaron	12,364
Carl Yastrzemski	11,988
Cal Ripken Jr.	11,551
Ty Cobb	11,429
Eddie Murray	11,336
Robin Yount	11,008
Dave Winfield	11,003
Stan Musial	10,972
Rickey Henderson	10,961

Runs Batted In

Hank Aaron	2,297
Babe Ruth	2,213
Barry Bonds	1,996
Lou Gehrig	1,995
Stan Musial	1,951
Ty Cobb	1,938
Jimmie Foxx	1,922
Eddie Murray	1,917
Willie Mays	1,903
Alex Rodriguez*	1,893

Runs

Player	Runs
Rickey Henderson	2,295
Ty Cobb	2,246
Barry Bonds	2,227
Hank Aaron	2,174
Babe Ruth	2,174
Pete Rose	2,165
Willie Mays	2,062
Stan Musial	1,949
Lou Gehrig	1,888
Tris Speaker	1,881

Stolen Bases

Rickey Henderson	1,406
Lou Brock	938
Billy Hamilton	912
Ty Cobb	892
Tim Raines	808
Vince Coleman	752
Eddie Collins	745
Max Carey	738
Honus Wagner	722
Arlie Latham	707

Triples

Sam Crawford	309
Ty Cobb	297
Honus Wagner	252
Tris Speaker	222
Jake Beckley	221
Fred Clarke	220
Roger Connor	218
Dan Brouthers	196
Joe Kelley	194
Paul Waner	191

Batting Average

Ty Cobb	.367
Rogers Hornsby	.358
Joe Jackson	.356
Ed Delahanty	.350
Tris Speaker	.345
Billy Hamilton	.344
Ted Williams	.344
Dan Brouthers	.343
Harry Heilmann	.342
Babe Ruth	.342

Walks (Batter)

Barry Bonds	2,258
Rickey Henderson	2,190
Babe Ruth	2,062
Ted Williams	2,019
Joe Morgan	1,865
Carl Yastrzemski	1,845
Mickey Mantle	1,733
Jim Thome*	1,725
Mel Ott	1,708
Frank Thomas	1,667

Strikeouts

Nolan Ryan	5,714
Randy Johnson	4,875
Roger Clemens	4,672
Steve Carlton	4,136
Bert Blyleven	3,701
Tom Seaver	3,640
Don Sutton	3,574
Gaylord Perry	3,534
Walter Johnson	3,508
Greg Maddux	3,371

Saves

Mariano Rivera*	603
Trevor Hoffman	601
Lee Smith	478
John Franco	424
Billy Wagner	422
Dennis Eckersley	390
Jeff Reardon	367
Troy Percival	358
Randy Myers	347
Rollie Fingers	341

Shutouts

Walter Johnson	110
Grover Alexander	90
Christy Mathewson	79
Cy Young	76
Eddie Plank	69
Warren Spahn	63
Nolan Ryan	61
Tom Seaver	61
Bert Blyleven	60
Don Sutton	58

Losses

Player	L
Cy Young	316
Nolan Ryan	292
Walter Johnson	279
Phil Niekro	274
Gaylord Perry	265
Don Sutton	256
Jack Powell	254
Eppa Rixey	251
Bert Blyleven	250

All-Time Home Run Leaders

Source: www.mlb.com; * = player active in 2011 season

Player	HR	Player	HR	Player	HR	Player	HR
Barry Bonds	762	Mike Schmidt	548	Willie Stargell	475	Mike Piazza	427
Hank Aaron	755	Mickey Mantle	536	Carlos Delgado	473	Billy Williams	426
Babe Ruth	714	Jimmie Foxx	534	Dave Winfield	465	Andruw Jones*	420
Willie Mays	660	Willie McCovey	521	Jose Canseco	462	Darrell Evans	414
Ken Griffey Jr.	630	Frank Thomas	521	Chipper Jones*	454	Duke Snider	407
Alex Rodriguez*	629	Ted Williams	521	Carl Yastrzemski	452	Andres Galarraga	399
Sammy Sosa	609	Ernie Banks	512	Jeff Bagwell	449	Al Kaline	399
Jim Thome*	604	Eddie Mathews	512	Vladimir Guerrero*	449	Dale Murphy	398
Frank Robinson	586	Mel Ott	511	Albert Pujols*	445	Joe Carter	396
Mark McGwire	583	Gary Sheffield	509	Dave Kingman	442	Paul Konerko*	396
Harmon Killebrew	573	Eddie Murray	504	Andre Dawson	438	Jim Edmonds	393
Rafael Palmeiro	569	Lou Gehrig	493	Juan Gonzalez	434	Graig Nettles	390
Reggie Jackson	563	Fred McGriff	493	Cal Ripken Jr.	431	Johnny Bench	389
Manny Ramirez*	555	Stan Musial	475	Jason Giambi*	428	Dwight Evans	385

Players With 3,000 Major League Hits

Source: www.mlb.com; * = player active in 2011 season

Player	Hits	Player	Hits	Player	Hits	Player	Hits
Pete Rose	4,256	Paul Molitor	3,319	Paul Waner	3,152	Rod Carew	3,053
Ty Cobb	4,191	Eddie Collins	3,315	Robin Yount	3,142	Lou Brock	3,023
Hank Aaron	3,771	Willie Mays	3,283	Tony Gwynn	3,141	Rafael Palmeiro	3,020
Stan Musial	3,630	Eddie Murray	3,255	Dave Winfield	3,110	Cap Anson	3,011
Tris Speaker	3,514	Nap Lajoie	3,242	Derek Jeter*	3,088	Wade Boggs	3,010
Carl Yastrzemski	3,419	Cal Ripken Jr.	3,184	Craig Biggio	3,060	Al Kaline	3,007
Honus Wagner	3,415	George Brett	3,154	Rickey Henderson	3,055	Roberto Clemente	3,000

50 Home Run Club

Only Mark McGwire and Barry Bonds hit 70 or more home runs in a season. Five players—including Babe Ruth and Roger Maris—hit 60 or more, a feat Sammy Sosa accomplished for the third time in 2001. Those five are at the pinnacle of a select group of players to have hit 50 or more homers in a season. The following list shows each time a player achieved this mark.

HR	Player, team	Year	HR	Player, team	Year
73	Barry Bonds, San Francisco Giants	2001	54	David Ortiz, Boston Red Sox	2006
70	Mark McGwire, St. Louis Cardinals	1998	54	Alex Rodriguez, NY Yankees	2007
66	Sammy Sosa, Chicago Cubs	1998	54	Babe Ruth, NY Yankees	1920
65	Mark McGwire, St. Louis Cardinals	1999	54	Babe Ruth, NY Yankees	1928
64	Sammy Sosa, Chicago Cubs	2001	52	George Foster, Cincinnati Reds	1977
63	Sammy Sosa, Chicago Cubs	1999	52	Mickey Mantle, NY Yankees	1956
61	Roger Maris, NY Yankees	1961	52	Willie Mays, San Francisco Giants	1965
60	Babe Ruth, NY Yankees	1927	52	Mark McGwire, Oakland A's	1996
59	Babe Ruth, NY Yankees	1921	52	Alex Rodriguez, Texas Rangers	2001
58	Jimmie Foxx, Philadelphia Athletics	1932	52	Jim Thome, Cleveland Indians	2002
58	Hank Greenberg, Detroit Tigers	1938	51	Cecil Fielder, Detroit Tigers	1990
58	Ryan Howard, Philadelphia Phillies	2006	51	Andruw Jones, Atlanta Braves	2005
58	Mark McGwire, Oakland A's/St. Louis Cardinals	1997	51	Ralph Kiner, Pittsburgh Pirates	1947
57	Luis Gonzalez, Arizona Diamondbacks	2001	51	Willie Mays, NY Giants	1955
57	Alex Rodriguez, Texas Rangers	2002	51	Johnny Mize, NY Giants	1947
56	Ken Griffey Jr., Seattle Mariners	1997	50	Brady Anderson, Baltimore Orioles	1996
56	Ken Griffey Jr., Seattle Mariners	1998	50	Albert Belle, Cleveland Indians	1995
56	Hack Wilson, Chicago Cubs	1930	50	Prince Fielder, Milwaukee Brewers	2007
54	Jose Bautista, Toronto Blue Jays	2010	50	Jimmie Foxx, Boston Red Sox	1938
54	Ralph Kiner, Pittsburgh Pirates	1949	50	Sammy Sosa, Chicago Cubs	2000
54	Mickey Mantle, NY Yankees	1961	50	Greg Vaughn, San Diego Padres	1998

Pitchers With 300 Major League Wins

Source: www.mlb.com

Pitcher	Wins	Pitcher	Wins	Pitcher	Wins	Pitcher	Wins
Cy Young	511	Kid Nichols	361	Eddie Plank	326	Charley Radbourn	310
Walter Johnson	417	Greg Maddux	355	Nolan Ryan	324	Mickey Welch	309
Grover Alexander	373	Roger Clemens	354	Don Sutton	324	Tom Glavine	305
Christy Mathewson	373	Tim Keefe	342	Phil Niekro	318	Randy Johnson	303
Warren Spahn	363	Steve Carlton	329	Gaylord Perry	314	Lefty Grove	300
Pud Galvin	361	John Clarkson	327	Tom Seaver	311	Early Wynn	300

Official Major League Perfect Games Since 1901

Date	Pitcher	Teams	Date	Pitcher	Teams
5/5/1904	Cy Young	Boston 3 vs. Phil. 0 (AL)	9/16/1988	Tom Browning	Cincinnati 1 vs. L.A. 0 (NL)
10/2/1908	Addie Joss	Clev. 1 vs. Chicago 0 (AL)	7/28/1991	Dennis Martinez	Montréal 2 vs. L.A. 0 (NL)
4/30/1922	Charlie Robertson	Chicago 2 vs. Detroit 0 (AL)	7/28/1994	Kenny Rogers	Texas 4 vs. California 0 (AL)
10/8/1956	Don Larsen	NY 2 (AL) vs. Brooklyn 0* (NL)	5/17/1998	David Wells	NY 4 vs. Minn. 0 (AL)
6/21/1964	Jim Bunning	Phil. 6 vs. NY 0 (NL)	7/18/1999	David Cone	NY 6 vs. Montréal 0 (AL)
9/9/1965	Sandy Koufax	L.A. 1 vs. Chicago 0 (NL)	5/18/2004	Randy Johnson	Arizona 2 vs. Atlanta 0 (NL)
5/8/1968	Catfish Hunter	Oakland 4 vs. Minn. 0 (AL)	7/23/2009	Mark Buehrle	Chicago 5 vs. Tampa Bay 0 (AL)
5/15/1981	Len Barker	Clev. 3 vs. Toronto 0 (AL)	5/9/2010	Dallas Braden	Oakland 4 vs. Tampa Bay 0 (AL)
9/30/1984	Mike Witt	California 1 vs. Texas 0 (AL)	5/29/2010	Roy Halladay	Phil. 1 vs. Florida 0 (NL)

*World Series game

Most Career Major League No-Hitters

No.	Pitcher
7	Nolan Ryan
4	Sandy Koufax
3	Larry Corcoran, Bob Feller, Cy Young
2	Jim Bunning, Steve Busby, Carl Erskine, Bob Forsch, Pud Galvin, Roy Halladay, Ken Holtzman, Randy Johnson, Addie Joss, Dutch Leonard, Jim Maloney, Christy Mathewson, Hideo Nomo, Allie Reynolds, Frank Smith, Warren Spahn, Bill Stoneman, Virgil Trucks, Johnny Vander Meer, Justin Verlander, Ed Walsh, Don Wilson

Home Run Leaders, by Season, 1901-2011

* = All-time single-season record for league since beginning of "modern" era in 1901

	National League			American League	
Year	Player, team	HR	Year	Player, team	HR
1901	Sam Crawford, Cincinnati	16	1901	Napoleon Lajoie, Philadelphia	14
1902	Thomas Leach, Pittsburgh	6	1902	Socks Seybold, Philadelphia	16
1903	James Sheckard, Brooklyn	9	1903	Buck Freeman, Boston	13
1904	Harry Lumley, Brooklyn	9	1904	Harry Davis, Philadelphia	10
1905	Fred Odwell, Cincinnati	9	1905	Harry Davis, Philadelphia	8
1906	Timothy Jordan, Brooklyn	12	1906	Harry Davis, Philadelphia	12
1907	David Brain, Boston	10	1907	Harry Davis, Philadelphia	8
1908	Timothy Jordan, Brooklyn	12	1908	Sam Crawford, Detroit	7
1909	Red Murray, New York	7	1909	Ty Cobb, Detroit	9
1910	Fred Beck, Boston; Frank Schulte, Chicago	10	1910	Jake Stahl, Boston	10
1911	Frank Schulte, Chicago	21	1911	J. Franklin Baker, Philadelphia	11
1912	Henry Zimmerman, Chicago	14	1912	J. Franklin Baker, Phil.; Tris Speaker, Boston	10
1913	Gavvy Cravath, Philadelphia	19	1913	J. Franklin Baker, Philadelphia	12
1914	Gavvy Cravath, Philadelphia	19	1914	J. Franklin Baker, Philadelphia	9
1915	Gavvy Cravath, Philadelphia	24	1915	Robert Roth, Chicago-Cleveland	7
1916	Dave Robertson, NY; Fred (Cy) Williams, Chi.	12	1916	Wally Pipp, New York	12
1917	Dave Robertson, NY; Gavvy Cravath, Phil.	12	1917	Wally Pipp, New York	9
1918	Gavvy Cravath, Philadelphia	8	1918	Babe Ruth, Boston; Tilly Walker, Philadelphia	11
1919	Gavvy Cravath, Philadelphia	12	1919	Babe Ruth, Boston	29
1920	Cy Williams, Philadelphia	15	1920	Babe Ruth, New York	54
1921	George Kelly, New York	23	1921	Babe Ruth, New York	59
1922	Rogers Hornsby, St. Louis	42	1922	Ken Williams, St. Louis	39
1923	Cy Williams, Philadelphia	41	1923	Babe Ruth, New York	41

	National League			American League	
Year	**Player, team**	**HR**	**Year**	**Player, team**	**HR**
1924	Jacques Fournier, Brooklyn	27	1924	Babe Ruth, New York	46
1925	Rogers Hornsby, St. Louis	39	1925	Bob Meusel, New York	33
1926	Hack Wilson, Chicago	21	1926	Babe Ruth, New York	47
1927	Hack Wilson, Chicago; Cy Williams, Philadelphia	30	1927	Babe Ruth, New York	60
1928	Hack Wilson, Chicago; Jim Bottomley, St. Louis	31	1928	Babe Ruth, New York	54
1929	Chuck Klein, Philadelphia	43	1929	Babe Ruth, New York	46
1930	Hack Wilson, Chicago	56	1930	Babe Ruth, New York	49
1931	Chuck Klein, Philadelphia	31	1931	Babe Ruth, New York; Lou Gehrig, New York	46
1932	Chuck Klein, Philadelphia; Mel Ott, New York	38	1932	Jimmie Foxx, Philadelphia	58
1933	Chuck Klein, Philadelphia	28	1933	Jimmie Foxx, Philadelphia	48
1934	Rip Collins, St. Louis; Mel Ott, New York	35	1934	Lou Gehrig, New York	49
1935	Walter Berger, Boston	34	1935	Jimmie Foxx, Phil.; Hank Greenberg, Detroit	36
1936	Mel Ott, New York	33	1936	Lou Gehrig, New York	49
1937	Mel Ott, New York; Joe Medwick, St. Louis	31	1937	Joe DiMaggio, New York	46
1938	Mel Ott, New York	36	1938	Hank Greenberg, Detroit	58
1939	John Mize, St. Louis	28	1939	Jimmie Foxx, Boston	35
1940	John Mize, St. Louis	43	1940	Hank Greenberg, Detroit	41
1941	Dolph Camilli, Brooklyn	34	1941	Ted Williams, Boston	37
1942	Mel Ott, New York	30	1942	Ted Williams, Boston	36
1943	Bill Nicholson, Chicago	29	1943	Rudy York, Detroit	34
1944	Bill Nicholson, Chicago	33	1944	Nick Etten, New York	22
1945	Tommy Holmes, Boston	28	1945	Vern Stephens, St. Louis	24
1946	Ralph Kiner, Pittsburgh	23	1946	Hank Greenberg, Detroit	44
1947	Ralph Kiner, Pittsburgh; John Mize, New York	51	1947	Ted Williams, Boston	32
1948	Ralph Kiner, Pittsburgh; John Mize, New York	40	1948	Joe DiMaggio, New York	39
1949	Ralph Kiner, Pittsburgh	54	1949	Ted Williams, Boston	43
1950	Ralph Kiner, Pittsburgh	47	1950	Al Rosen, Cleveland	37
1951	Ralph Kiner, Pittsburgh	42	1951	Gus Zernial, Chicago-Philadelphia	33
1952	Ralph Kiner, Pittsburgh; Hank Sauer, Chicago	37	1952	Larry Doby, Cleveland	32
1953	Ed Mathews, Milwaukee	47	1953	Al Rosen, Cleveland	43
1954	Ted Kluszewski, Cincinnati	49	1954	Larry Doby, Cleveland	32
1955	Willie Mays, New York	51	1955	Mickey Mantle, New York	37
1956	Duke Snider, Brooklyn	43	1956	Mickey Mantle, New York	52
1957	Hank Aaron, Milwaukee	44	1957	Roy Sievers, Washington	42
1958	Ernie Banks, Chicago	47	1958	Mickey Mantle, New York	42
1959	Ed Mathews, Milwaukee	46	1959	Rocky Colavito, Cleve.; Harmon Killebrew, Wash.	42
1960	Ernie Banks, Chicago	41	1960	Mickey Mantle, New York	40
1961	Orlando Cepeda, San Francisco	46	1961	Roger Maris, New York	61*
1962	Willie Mays, San Francisco	49	1962	Harmon Killebrew, Minnesota	48
1963	Hank Aaron, Milwaukee; Willie McCovey, S.F.	44	1963	Harmon Killebrew, Minnesota	45
1964	Willie Mays, San Francisco	47	1964	Harmon Killebrew, Minnesota	49
1965	Willie Mays, San Francisco	52	1965	Tony Conigliaro, Boston	32
1966	Hank Aaron, Atlanta	44	1966	Frank Robinson, Baltimore	49
1967	Hank Aaron, Atlanta	39	1967	Carl Yastrzemski, Boston; Harmon Killebrew, Minn.	44
1968	Willie McCovey, San Francisco	36	1968	Frank Howard, Washington	44
1969	Willie McCovey, San Francisco	45	1969	Harmon Killebrew, Minnesota	49
1970	Johnny Bench, Cincinnati	45	1970	Frank Howard, Washington	44
1971	Willie Stargell, Pittsburgh	48	1971	Bill Melton, Chicago	33
1972	Johnny Bench, Cincinnati	40	1972	Dick Allen, Chicago	37
1973	Willie Stargell, Pittsburgh	44	1973	Reggie Jackson, Oakland	32
1974	Mike Schmidt, Philadelphia	36	1974	Dick Allen, Chicago	32
1975	Mike Schmidt, Philadelphia	38	1975	George Scott, Milwaukee; Reggie Jackson, Oak.	36
1976	Mike Schmidt, Philadelphia	38	1976	Graig Nettles, New York	32
1977	George Foster, Cincinnati	52	1977	Jim Rice, Boston	39
1978	George Foster, Cincinnati	40	1978	Jim Rice, Boston	46
1979	Dave Kingman, Chicago	48	1979	Gorman Thomas, Milwaukee	45
1980	Mike Schmidt, Philadelphia	48	1980	Reggie Jackson, New York; Ben Oglivie, Milw.	41
1981	Mike Schmidt, Philadelphia	31	1981	Bobby Grich, California; Tony Armas, Oakland; Dwight Evans, Boston; Eddie Murray, Baltimore	22
1982	Dave Kingman, New York	37	1982	Gorman Thomas, Milw.; Reggie Jackson, Cal.	39
1983	Mike Schmidt, Philadelphia	40	1983	Jim Rice, Boston	39
1984	Mike Schmidt, Philadelphia; Dale Murphy, Atlanta	36	1984	Tony Armas, Boston	43
1985	Dale Murphy, Atlanta	37	1985	Darrell Evans, Detroit	40
1986	Mike Schmidt, Philadelphia	37	1986	Jesse Barfield, Toronto	40
1987	Andre Dawson, Chicago	49	1987	Mark McGwire, Oakland	49
1988	Darryl Strawberry, New York	39	1988	Jose Canseco, Oakland	42
1989	Kevin Mitchell, San Francisco	47	1989	Fred McGriff, Toronto	36
1990	Ryne Sandberg, Chicago	40	1990	Cecil Fielder, Detroit	51
1991	Howard Johnson, New York	38	1991	Cecil Fielder, Detroit; Jose Canseco, Oakland	44
1992	Fred McGriff, San Diego	35	1992	Juan Gonzalez, Texas	43
1993	Barry Bonds, San Francisco	46	1993	Juan Gonzalez, Texas	46
1994	Matt Williams, San Francisco	43	1994	Ken Griffey Jr., Seattle	40
1995	Dante Bichette, Colorado	40	1995	Albert Belle, Cleveland	50
1996	Andres Galarraga, Colorado	47	1996	Mark McGwire, Oakland	52
1997[1]	Larry Walker, Colorado	49	1997[1]	Ken Griffey Jr., Seattle	56
1998	Mark McGwire, St. Louis	70	1998	Ken Griffey Jr., Seattle	56
1999	Mark McGwire, St. Louis	65	1999	Ken Griffey Jr., Seattle	48
2000	Sammy Sosa, Chicago	50	2000	Troy Glaus, Anaheim	47
2001	Barry Bonds, San Francisco	73*	2001	Alex Rodriguez, Texas	52
2002	Sammy Sosa, Chicago	49	2002	Alex Rodriguez, Texas	57
2003	Jim Thome, Philadelphia	47	2003	Alex Rodriguez, Texas	47
2004	Adrian Beltre, Los Angeles	48	2004	Manny Ramirez, Boston	43
2005	Andruw Jones, Atlanta	51	2005	Alex Rodriguez, New York	48
2006	Ryan Howard, Philadelphia	58	2006	David Ortiz, Boston	54
2007	Prince Fielder, Milwaukee	50	2007	Alex Rodriguez, New York	54
2008	Ryan Howard, Philadelphia	48	2008	Miguel Cabrera, Detroit	37
2009	Albert Pujols, St. Louis	47	2009	Carlos Pena, Tampa Bay; Mark Teixeira, New York	39
2010	Albert Pujols, St. Louis	42	2010	Jose Bautista, Toronto	54
2011	Matt Kemp, Los Angeles	39	2011	Jose Bautista, Toronto	43

(1) In 1997, Mark McGwire hit 58 home runs, 34 with the Oakland Athletics (AL) and 24 with the St. Louis Cardinals (NL).

Runs Batted In Leaders, by Season, 1907-2011

* = All-time single-season record for league since beginning of "modern" era in 1901

Year	National League Player, team	RBI	Year	American League Player, team	RBI
1907	Sherwood Magee, Philadelphia	85	1907	Ty Cobb, Detroit	116
1908	Honus Wagner, Pittsburgh	109	1908	Ty Cobb, Detroit	108
1909	Honus Wagner, Pittsburgh	100	1909	Ty Cobb, Detroit	107
1910	Sherwood Magee, Philadelphia	123	1910	Sam Crawford, Detroit	120
1911	Frank Schulte, Chicago	121	1911	Ty Cobb, Detroit	144
1912	Henry Zimmerman, Chicago	103	1912	J. Franklin Baker, Philadelphia	133
1913	Gavvy Cravath, Philadelphia	128	1913	J. Franklin Baker, Philadelphia	126
1914	Sherwood Magee, Philadelphia	103	1914	Sam Crawford, Detroit	104
1915	Gavvy Cravath, Philadelphia	115	1915	Sam Crawford, Detroit; Robert Veach, Detroit	112
1916	Henry Zimmerman, Chicago-NewYork	83	1916	Del Pratt, St. Louis	103
1917	Henry Zimmerman, New York	102	1917	Robert Veach, Detroit	103
1918	Sherwood Magee, Philadelphia	76	1918	Robert Veach, Detroit	78
1919	Hi Myers, Boston	73	1919	Babe Ruth, Boston	114
1920	George Kelly, NY; Rogers Hornsby, St. Louis	94	1920	Babe Ruth, New York	137
1921	Rogers Hornsby, St. Louis	126	1921	Babe Ruth, New York	171
1922	Rogers Hornsby, St. Louis	152	1922	Ken Williams, St. Louis	155
1923	Emil Meusel, New York	125	1923	Babe Ruth, New York	131
1924	George Kelly, New York	136	1924	Goose Goslin, Washington	129
1925	Rogers Hornsby, St. Louis	143	1925	Bob Meusel, New York	138
1926	Jim Bottomley, St. Louis	120	1926	Babe Ruth, New York	146
1927	Paul Waner, Pittsburgh	131	1927	Lou Gehrig, New York	175
1928	Jim Bottomley, St. Louis	136	1928	Babe Ruth, New York; Lou Gehrig, New York	142
1929	Hack Wilson, Chicago	159	1929	Al Simmons, Philadelphia	157
1930	Hack Wilson, Chicago	191*	1930	Lou Gehrig, New York	174
1931	Chuck Klein, Philadelphia	121	1931	Lou Gehrig, New York	184*
1932	Don Hurst, Philadelphia	143	1932	Jimmie Foxx, Philadelphia	169
1933	Chuck Klein, Philadelphia	120	1933	Jimmie Foxx, Philadelphia	163
1934	Mel Ott, New York	135	1934	Lou Gehrig, New York	165
1935	Walter Berger, Boston	130	1935	Hank Greenberg, Detroit	170
1936	Joe Medwick, St. Louis	138	1936	Hal Trosky, Cleveland	162
1937	Joe Medwick, St. Louis	154	1937	Hank Greenberg, Detroit	183
1938	Joe Medwick, St. Louis	122	1938	Jimmie Foxx, Boston	175
1939	Frank McCormick, Cincinnati	128	1939	Ted Williams, Boston	145
1940	John Mize, St. Louis	137	1940	Hank Greenberg, Detroit	150
1941	Dolph Camilli, Brooklyn	120	1941	Joe DiMaggio, New York	125
1942	John Mize, New York	110	1942	Ted Williams, Boston	137
1943	Bill Nicholson, Chicago	128	1943	Rudy York, Detroit	118
1944	Bill Nicholson, Chicago	122	1944	Vern Stephens, St. Louis	109
1945	Dixie Walker, Brooklyn	124	1945	Nick Etten, New York	111
1946	Enos Slaughter, St. Louis	130	1946	Hank Greenberg, Detroit	127
1947	John Mize, New York	138	1947	Ted Williams, Boston	114
1948	Stan Musial, St. Louis	131	1948	Joe DiMaggio, New York	155
1949	Ralph Kiner, Pittsburgh	127	1949	Ted Williams, Boston; Vern Stephens, Boston	159
1950	Del Ennis, Philadelphia	126	1950	Walt Dropo, Boston; Vern Stephens, Boston	144
1951	Monte Irvin, New York	121	1951	Gus Zernial, Chicago-Philadelphia	129
1952	Hank Sauer, Chicago	121	1952	Al Rosen, Cleveland	105
1953	Roy Campanella, Brooklyn	142	1953	Al Rosen, Cleveland	145
1954	Ted Kluszewski, Cincinnati	141	1954	Larry Doby, Cleveland	126
1955	Duke Snider, Brooklyn	136	1955	Ray Boone, Detroit; Jackie Jensen, Boston	116
1956	Stan Musial, St. Louis	109	1956	Mickey Mantle, New York	130
1957	Hank Aaron, Milwaukee	132	1957	Roy Sievers, Washington	114
1958	Ernie Banks, Chicago	129	1958	Jackie Jensen, Boston	122
1959	Ernie Banks, Chicago	143	1959	Jackie Jensen, Boston	112
1960	Hank Aaron, Milwaukee	126	1960	Roger Maris, New York	112
1961	Orlando Cepeda, San Francisco	142	1961	Roger Maris, New York	142
1962	Tommy Davis, Los Angeles	153	1962	Harmon Killebrew, Minnesota	126
1963	Hank Aaron, Milwaukee	130	1963	Dick Stuart, Boston	118
1964	Ken Boyer, St. Louis	119	1964	Brooks Robinson, Baltimore	118
1965	Deron Johnson, Cincinnati	130	1965	Rocky Colavito, Cleveland	108
1966	Hank Aaron, Atlanta	127	1966	Frank Robinson, Baltimore	122
1967	Orlando Cepeda, St. Louis	111	1967	Carl Yastrzemski, Boston	121
1968	Willie McCovey, San Francisco	105	1968	Ken Harrelson, Boston	109
1969	Willie McCovey, San Francisco	126	1969	Harmon Killebrew, Minnesota	140
1970	Johnny Bench, Cincinnati	148	1970	Frank Howard, Washington	126
1971	Joe Torre, St. Louis	137	1971	Harmon Killebrew, Minnesota	119
1972	Johnny Bench, Cincinnati	125	1972	Dick Allen, Chicago	113
1973	Willie Stargell, Pittsburgh	119	1973	Reggie Jackson, Oakland	117
1974	Johnny Bench, Cincinnati	129	1974	Jeff Burroughs, Texas	118
1975	Greg Luzinski, Philadelphia	120	1975	George Scott, Milwaukee	109
1976	George Foster, Cincinnati	121	1976	Lee May, Baltimore	109
1977	George Foster, Cincinnati	149	1977	Larry Hisle, Minnesota	119
1978	George Foster, Cincinnati	120	1978	Jim Rice, Boston	139
1979	Dave Winfield, San Diego	118	1979	Don Baylor, California	139
1980	Mike Schmidt, Philadelphia	121	1980	Cecil Cooper, Milwaukee	122
1981	Mike Schmidt, Philadelphia	91	1981	Eddie Murray, Baltimore	78
1982	Dale Murphy, Atlanta; Al Oliver, Montréal	109	1982	Hal McRae, Kansas City	133
1983	Dale Murphy, Atlanta	121	1983	Cecil Cooper, Milwaukee; Jim Rice, Boston	126
1984	Gary Carter, Montréal; Mike Schmidt, Phil.	106	1984	Tony Armas, Boston	123
1985	Dave Parker, Cincinnati	125	1985	Don Mattingly, New York	145
1986	Mike Schmidt, Philadelphia	119	1986	Joe Carter, Cleveland	121
1987	Andre Dawson, Chicago	137	1987	George Bell, Toronto	134
1988	Will Clark, San Francisco	109	1988	Jose Canseco, Oakland	124
1989	Kevin Mitchell, San Francisco	125	1989	Ruben Sierra, Texas	119
1990	Matt Williams, San Francisco	122	1990	Cecil Fielder, Detroit	132

National League			American League		
Year	Player, team	RBI	Year	Player, team	RBI
1991	Howard Johnson, New York	117	1991	Cecil Fielder, Detroit	133
1992	Darren Daulton, Philadelphia	109	1992	Cecil Fielder, Detroit	124
1993	Barry Bonds, San Francisco	123	1993	Albert Belle, Cleveland	129
1994	Jeff Bagwell, Houston	116	1994	Kirby Puckett, Minnesota	112
1995	Dante Bichette, Colorado	128	1995	Albert Belle, Cleveland; Mo Vaughn, Boston	126
1996	Andres Galarraga, Colorado	150	1996	Albert Belle, Cleveland	148
1997	Andres Galarraga, Colorado	140	1997	Ken Griffey Jr., Seattle	147
1998	Sammy Sosa, Chicago	158	1998	Juan Gonzalez, Texas	157
1999	Mark McGwire, St. Louis	147	1999	Manny Ramirez, Cleveland	165
2000	Todd Helton, Colorado	147	2000	Edgar Martinez, Seattle	145
2001	Sammy Sosa, Chicago	160	2001	Bret Boone, Seattle	141
2002	Lance Berkman, Houston	128	2002	Alex Rodriguez, Texas	142
2003	Preston Wilson, Colorado	141	2003	Carlos Delgado, Toronto	145
2004	Vinny Castilla, Colorado	131	2004	Miguel Tejada, Baltimore	150
2005	Andruw Jones, Atlanta	128	2005	David Ortiz, Boston	148
2006	Ryan Howard, Philadelphia	149	2006	David Ortiz, Boston	137
2007	Matt Holliday, Colorado	137	2007	Alex Rodriguez, New York	156
2008	Ryan Howard, Philadelphia	146	2008	Josh Hamilton, Texas	130
2009	Prince Fielder, Milwaukee; Ryan Howard, Phil.	141	2009	Mark Teixeira, New York	122
2010	Albert Pujols, St. Louis	118	2010	Miguel Cabrera, Detroit	126
2011	Matt Kemp, Los Angeles	126	2011	Curtis Granderson, New York	119

Batting Champions, by Season, 1901-2011

* = All-time single-season record for league since beginning of "modern" era in 1901

National League			American League		
Year	Player, team	AVG	Year	Player, team	AVG
1901	Jesse C. Burkett, St. Louis	.382	1901	Napoleon Lajoie, Philadelphia	.426*
1902	Clarence Beaumont, Pittsburgh	.357	1902	Ed Delahanty, Washington	.376
1903	Honus Wagner, Pittsburgh	.355	1903	Napoleon Lajoie, Cleveland	.355
1904	Honus Wagner, Pittsburgh	.349	1904	Napoleon Lajoie, Cleveland	.381
1905	James Seymour, Cincinnati	.377	1905	Elmer Flick, Cleveland	.306
1906	Honus Wagner, Pittsburgh	.339	1906	George Stone, St. Louis	.358
1907	Honus Wagner, Pittsburgh	.350	1907	Ty Cobb, Detroit	.350
1908	Honus Wagner, Pittsburgh	.354	1908	Ty Cobb, Detroit	.324
1909	Honus Wagner, Pittsburgh	.339	1909	Ty Cobb, Detroit	.377
1910	Sherwood Magee, Philadelphia	.331	1910¹	Ty Cobb, Detroit	.385
1911	Honus Wagner, Pittsburgh	.334	1911	Ty Cobb, Detroit	.420
1912	Henry Zimmerman, Chicago	.372	1912	Ty Cobb, Detroit	.410
1913	Jacob Daubert, Brooklyn	.350	1913	Ty Cobb, Detroit	.390
1914	Jacob Daubert, Brooklyn	.329	1914	Ty Cobb, Detroit	.368
1915	Larry Doyle, New York	.320	1915	Ty Cobb, Detroit	.369
1916	Hal Chase, Cincinnati	.339	1916	Tris Speaker, Cleveland	.386
1917	Edd Roush, Cincinnati	.341	1917	Ty Cobb, Detroit	.383
1918	Zach Wheat, Brooklyn	.335	1918	Ty Cobb, Detroit	.382
1919	Edd Roush, Cincinnati	.321	1919	Ty Cobb, Detroit	.384
1920	Rogers Hornsby, St. Louis	.370	1920	George Sisler, St. Louis	.407
1921	Rogers Hornsby, St. Louis	.397	1921	Harry Heilmann, Detroit	.394
1922	Rogers Hornsby, St. Louis	.401	1922	George Sisler, St. Louis	.420
1923	Rogers Hornsby, St. Louis	.384	1923	Harry Heilmann, Detroit	.403
1924	Rogers Hornsby, St. Louis	.424*	1924	Babe Ruth, New York	.378
1925	Rogers Hornsby, St. Louis	.403	1925	Harry Heilmann, Detroit	.393
1926	Eugene Hargrave, Cincinnati	.353	1926	Henry Manush, Detroit	.378
1927	Paul Waner, Pittsburgh	.380	1927	Harry Heilmann, Detroit	.398
1928	Rogers Hornsby, Boston	.387	1928	Goose Goslin, Washington	.379
1929	Lefty O'Doul, Philadelphia	.398	1929	Lew Fonseca, Cleveland	.369
1930	Bill Terry, New York	.401	1930	Al Simmons, Philadelphia	.381
1931	Chick Hafey, St. Louis	.349	1931	Al Simmons, Philadelphia	.390
1932	Lefty O'Doul, Brooklyn	.368	1932	Dale Alexander, Detroit-Boston	.367
1933	Chuck Klein, Philadelphia	.368	1933	Jimmie Foxx, Philadelphia	.356
1934	Paul Waner, Pittsburgh	.362	1934	Lou Gehrig, New York	.363
1935	Arky Vaughan, Pittsburgh	.385	1935	Buddy Myer, Washington	.349
1936	Paul Waner, Pittsburgh	.373	1936	Luke Appling, Chicago	.388
1937	Joe Medwick, St. Louis	.374	1937	Charlie Gehringer, Detroit	.371
1938	Ernie Lombardi, Cincinnati	.342	1938	Jimmie Foxx, Boston	.349
1939	John Mize, St. Louis	.349	1939	Joe DiMaggio, New York	.381
1940	Debs Garms, Pittsburgh	.355	1940	Joe DiMaggio, New York	.352
1941	Pete Reiser, Brooklyn	.343	1941	Ted Williams, Boston	.406
1942	Ernie Lombardi, Boston	.330	1942	Ted Williams, Boston	.356
1943	Stan Musial, St. Louis	.357	1943	Luke Appling, Chicago	.328
1944	Dixie Walker, Brooklyn	.357	1944	Lou Boudreau, Cleveland	.327
1945	Phil Cavarretta, Chicago	.355	1945	George Stirnweiss, New York	.309
1946	Stan Musial, St. Louis	.365	1946	Mickey Vernon, Washington	.353
1947	Harry Walker, St. Louis-Phil.	.363	1947	Ted Williams, Boston	.343
1948	Stan Musial, St. Louis	.376	1948	Ted Williams, Boston	.369
1949	Jackie Robinson, Brooklyn	.342	1949	George Kell, Detroit	.343
1950	Stan Musial, St. Louis	.346	1950	Billy Goodman, Boston	.354
1951	Stan Musial, St. Louis	.355	1951	Ferris Fain, Philadelphia	.344
1952	Stan Musial, St. Louis	.336	1952	Ferris Fain, Philadelphia	.327
1953	Carl Furillo, Brooklyn	.344	1953	Mickey Vernon, Washington	.337
1954	Willie Mays, New York	.345	1954	Roberto Avila, Cleveland	.341
1955	Richie Ashburn, Philadelphia	.338	1955	Al Kaline, Detroit	.340
1956	Hank Aaron, Milwaukee	.328	1956	Mickey Mantle, New York	.353
1957	Stan Musial, St. Louis	.351	1957	Ted Williams, Boston	.388
1958	Richie Ashburn, Philadelphia	.350	1958	Ted Williams, Boston	.328
1959	Hank Aaron, Milwaukee	.355	1959	Harvey Kuenn, Detroit	.353
1960	Dick Groat, Pittsburgh	.325	1960	Pete Runnels, Boston	.320
1961	Roberto Clemente, Pittsburgh	.351	1961	Norm Cash, Detroit	.361
1962	Tommy Davis, Los Angeles	.346	1962	Pete Runnels, Boston	.326

	National League			American League	
Year	Player, team	AVG	Year	Player, team	AVG
1963	Tommy Davis, Los Angeles	.326	1963	Carl Yastrzemski, Boston	.321
1964	Roberto Clemente, Pittsburgh	.339	1964	Tony Oliva, Minnesota	.323
1965	Roberto Clemente, Pittsburgh	.329	1965	Tony Oliva, Minnesota	.321
1966	Matty Alou, Pittsburgh	.342	1966	Frank Robinson, Baltimore	.316
1967	Roberto Clemente, Pittsburgh	.357	1967	Carl Yastrzemski, Boston	.326
1968	Pete Rose, Cincinnati	.335	1968	Carl Yastrzemski, Boston	.301
1969	Pete Rose, Cincinnati	.348	1969	Rod Carew, Minnesota	.332
1970	Rico Carty, Atlanta	.366	1970	Alex Johnson, California	.329
1971	Joe Torre, St. Louis	.363	1971	Tony Oliva, Minnesota	.337
1972	Billy Williams, Chicago	.333	1972	Rod Carew, Minnesota	.318
1973	Pete Rose, Cincinnati	.338	1973	Rod Carew, Minnesota	.350
1974	Ralph Garr, Atlanta	.353	1974	Rod Carew, Minnesota	.364
1975	Bill Madlock, Chicago	.354	1975	Rod Carew, Minnesota	.359
1976	Bill Madlock, Chicago	.339	1976	George Brett, Kansas City	.333
1977	Dave Parker, Pittsburgh	.338	1977	Rod Carew, Minnesota	.388
1978	Dave Parker, Pittsburgh	.334	1978	Rod Carew, Minnesota	.333
1979	Keith Hernandez, St. Louis	.344	1979	Fred Lynn, Boston	.333
1980	Bill Buckner, Chicago	.324	1980	George Brett, Kansas City	.390
1981	Bill Madlock, Pittsburgh	.341	1981	Carney Lansford, Boston	.336
1982	Al Oliver, Montréal	.331	1982	Willie Wilson, Kansas City	.332
1983	Bill Madlock, Pittsburgh	.323	1983	Wade Boggs, Boston	.361
1984	Tony Gwynn, San Diego	.351	1984	Don Mattingly, New York	.343
1985	Willie McGee, St. Louis	.353	1985	Wade Boggs, Boston	.368
1986	Tim Raines, Montréal	.334	1986	Wade Boggs, Boston	.357
1987	Tony Gwynn, San Diego	.370	1987	Wade Boggs, Boston	.363
1988	Tony Gwynn, San Diego	.313	1988	Wade Boggs, Boston	.366
1989	Tony Gwynn, San Diego	.336	1989	Kirby Puckett, Minnesota	.339
1990	Willie McGee, St. Louis	.335	1990	George Brett, Kansas City	.329
1991	Terry Pendleton, Atlanta	.319	1991	Julio Franco, Texas	.341
1992	Gary Sheffield, San Diego	.330	1992	Edgar Martinez, Seattle	.343
1993	Andres Galarraga, Colorado	.370	1993	John Olerud, Toronto	.363
1994	Tony Gwynn, San Diego	.394	1994	Paul O'Neill, New York	.359
1995	Tony Gwynn, San Diego	.368	1995	Edgar Martinez, Seattle	.356
1996	Tony Gwynn, San Diego	.353	1996	Alex Rodriguez, Seattle	.358
1997	Tony Gwynn, San Diego	.372	1997	Frank Thomas, Chicago	.347
1998	Larry Walker, Colorado	.363	1998	Bernie Williams, New York	.339
1999	Larry Walker, Colorado	.379	1999	Nomar Garciaparra, Boston	.357
2000	Todd Helton, Colorado	.372	2000	Nomar Garciaparra, Boston	.372
2001	Larry Walker, Colorado	.350	2001	Ichiro Suzuki, Seattle	.350
2002	Barry Bonds, San Francisco	.370	2002	Manny Ramirez, Boston	.349
2003	Albert Pujols, St. Louis	.359	2003	Bill Mueller, Boston	.326
2004	Barry Bonds, San Francisco	.362	2004	Ichiro Suzuki, Seattle	.372
2005	Derrek Lee, Chicago	.335	2005	Michael Young, Texas	.331
2006	Freddy Sanchez, Pittsburgh	.344	2006	Joe Mauer, Minnesota	.347
2007	Matt Holliday, Colorado	.340	2007	Magglio Ordonez, Detroit	.363
2008	Chipper Jones, Atlanta	.364	2008	Joe Mauer, Minnesota	.328
2009	Hanley Ramirez, Florida	.342	2009	Joe Mauer, Minnesota	.365
2010	Carlos Gonzalez, Colorado	.336	2010	Josh Hamilton, Texas	.359
2011	Jose Reyes, New York	.377	2011	Miguel Cabrera, Detroit	.344

(1) Some baseball researchers have concluded that Ty Cobb actually hit .382 in 1910 while Napoleon Lajoie, Cleveland, hit .383.

Earned Run Average Leaders, by Season, 1977-2011

	National League					American League			
Year	Pitcher, team	G	IP	ERA	Year	Pitcher, team	G	IP	ERA
1977	John Candelaria, Pittsburgh	33	230.2	2.34	1977	Frank Tanana, California	31	241.1	2.54
1978	Craig Swan, New York	29	207.1	2.43	1978	Ron Guidry, New York	35	273.2	1.74
1979	J. R. Richard, Houston	38	292.1	2.71	1979	Ron Guidry, New York	33	236.1	2.78
1980	Don Sutton, Los Angeles	32	212.1	2.21	1980	Rudy May, New York	41	175.1	2.47
1981	Nolan Ryan, Houston	21	149	1.69	1981	Dave Righetti, New York	15	105.1	2.05
1982	Steve Rogers, Montréal	35	277	2.40	1982	Rick Sutcliffe, Cleveland	34	216	2.96
1983	Atlee Hammaker, San Francisco	23	172.1	2.25	1983	Rick Honeycutt, Texas	25	174.2	2.42
1984	Alejandro Pena, Los Angeles	28	199.1	2.48	1984	Mike Boddicker, Baltimore	34	261.1	2.79
1985	Dwight Gooden, New York	35	276.2	1.53	1985	Dave Stieb, Toronto	36	265	2.48
1986	Mike Scott, Houston	37	275.1	2.22	1986	Roger Clemens, Boston	33	254	2.48
1987	Nolan Ryan, Houston	34	211.2	2.76	1987	Jimmy Key, Toronto	36	261	2.76
1988	Joe Magrane, St. Louis	24	165.1	2.18	1988	Allan Anderson, Minnesota	30	202.1	2.45
1989	Scott Garrelts, San Francisco	30	193.1	2.28	1989	Bret Saberhagen, Kansas City	36	262.1	2.16
1990	Danny Darwin, Houston	48	162.2	2.21	1990	Roger Clemens, Boston	31	228.1	1.93
1991	Dennis Martinez, Montréal	31	222	2.39	1991	Roger Clemens, Boston	35	271.1	2.62
1992	Bill Swift, San Francisco	30	164.2	2.08	1992	Roger Clemens, Boston	32	246.2	2.41
1993	Greg Maddux, Atlanta	36	267	2.36	1993	Kevin Appier, Kansas City	34	238.2	2.56
1994	Greg Maddux, Atlanta	25	202	1.56	1994	Steve Ontiveros, Oakland	27	115.1	2.65
1995	Greg Maddux, Atlanta	28	209.2	1.63	1995	Randy Johnson, Seattle	30	214.1	2.48
1996	Kevin Brown, Florida	32	233	1.89	1996	Juan Guzman, Toronto	27	187.2	2.93
1997	Pedro Martinez, Montréal	31	241.1	1.90	1997	Roger Clemens, Toronto	34	264	2.05
1998	Greg Maddux, Atlanta	34	251	2.22	1998	Roger Clemens, Toronto	33	234.2	2.65
1999	Randy Johnson, Arizona	35	271.2	2.48	1999	Pedro Martinez, Boston	31	213.1	2.07
2000	Kevin R. Brown, Los Angeles	33	230	2.58	2000	Pedro Martinez, Boston	29	217	1.74
2001	Randy Johnson, Arizona	35	249.2	2.49	2001	Freddy Garcia, Seattle	34	238.2	3.05
2002	Randy Johnson, Arizona	35	260	2.32	2002	Pedro Martinez, Boston	30	199.1	2.26
2003	Jason Schmidt, San Francisco	29	207.2	2.34	2003	Pedro Martinez, Boston	29	186.2	2.22
2004	Jake Peavy, San Diego	27	166.1	2.27	2004	Johan Santana, Minnesota	34	228	2.61
2005	Roger Clemens, Houston	32	211.1	1.87	2005	Kevin Millwood, Cleveland	30	192	2.86
2006	Roy Oswalt, Houston	33	220.2	2.98	2006	Johan Santana, Minnesota	34	233.2	2.77
2007	Jake Peavy, San Diego	34	223.1	2.54	2007	John Lackey, Los Angeles	33	224	3.01
2008	Johan Santana, New York	34	234.1	2.53	2008	Cliff Lee, Cleveland	31	223.1	2.54
2009	Chris Carpenter, St. Louis	28	192.2	2.24	2009	Zack Greinke, Kansas City	33	229.1	2.16
2010	Josh Johnson, Florida	28	183.2	2.30	2010	Felix Hernandez, Seattle	34	249.2	2.27
2011	Clayton Kershaw, Los Angeles	33	233.1	2.28	2011	Justin Verlander, Detroit	34	251	2.40

Note: ERA is computed by multiplying earned runs allowed by 9, then dividing by innings pitched.

Strikeout Leaders, by Season, 1901-2011

* = All-time single-season record for league since beginning of "modern" era in 1901

	National League			American League	
Year	Pitcher, team	SO	Year	Pitcher, team	SO
1901	Noodles Hahn, Cincinnati	239	1901	Cy Young, Boston	158
1902	Vic Willis, Boston	225	1902	Rube Waddell, Philadelphia	210
1903	Christy Mathewson, New York	267	1903	Rube Waddell, Philadelphia	302
1904	Christy Mathewson, New York	212	1904	Rube Waddell, Philadelphia	349
1905	Christy Mathewson, New York	206	1905	Rube Waddell, Philadelphia	287
1906	Fred Beebe, Chicago-St. Louis	171	1906	Rube Waddell, Philadelphia	196
1907	Christy Mathewson, New York	178	1907	Rube Waddell, Philadelphia	232
1908	Christy Mathewson, New York	259	1908	Ed Walsh, Chicago	269
1909	Orval Overall, Chicago	205	1909	Frank Smith, Chicago	177
1910	Earl Moore, Philadelphia	185	1910	Walter Johnson, Washington	313
1911	Rube Marquard, New York	237	1911	Ed Walsh, Chicago	255
1912	Grover Alexander, Philadelphia	195	1912	Walter Johnson, Washington	303
1913	Tom Seaton, Philadelphia	168	1913	Walter Johnson, Washington	243
1914	Grover Alexander, Philadelphia	214	1914	Walter Johnson, Washington	225
1915	Grover Alexander, Philadelphia	241	1915	Walter Johnson, Washington	203
1916	Grover Alexander, Philadelphia	167	1916	Walter Johnson, Washington	228
1917	Grover Alexander, Philadelphia	200	1917	Walter Johnson, Washington	188
1918	Hippo Vaughn, Chicago	148	1918	Walter Johnson, Washington	162
1919	Hippo Vaughn, Chicago	141	1919	Walter Johnson, Washington	147
1920	Grover Alexander, Chicago	173	1920	Stan Coveleski, Cleveland	133
1921	Burleigh Grimes, Brooklyn	136	1921	Walter Johnson, Washington	143
1922	Dazzy Vance, Brooklyn	134	1922	Urban Shocker, St. Louis	149
1923	Dazzy Vance, Brooklyn	197	1923	Walter Johnson, Washington	130
1924	Dazzy Vance, Brooklyn	262	1924	Walter Johnson, Washington	158
1925	Dazzy Vance, Brooklyn	221	1925	Lefty Grove, Philadelphia	116
1926	Dazzy Vance, Brooklyn	140	1926	Lefty Grove, Philadelphia	194
1927	Dazzy Vance, Brooklyn	184	1927	Lefty Grove, Philadelphia	174
1928	Dazzy Vance, Brooklyn	200	1928	Lefty Grove, Philadelphia	183
1929	Pat Malone, Chicago	166	1929	Lefty Grove, Philadelphia	170
1930	Bill Hallahan, St. Louis	177	1930	Lefty Grove, Philadelphia	209
1931	Bill Hallahan, St. Louis	159	1931	Lefty Grove, Philadelphia	175
1932	Dizzy Dean, St. Louis	191	1932	Red Ruffing, New York	190
1933	Dizzy Dean, St. Louis	199	1933	Lefty Gomez, New York	163
1934	Dizzy Dean, St. Louis	195	1934	Lefty Gomez, New York	158
1935	Dizzy Dean, St. Louis	190	1935	Tommy Bridges, Detroit	163
1936	Van Lingle Mungo, Brooklyn	238	1936	Tommy Bridges, Detroit	175
1937	Carl Hubbell, New York	159	1937	Lefty Gomez, New York	194
1938	Clay Bryant, Chicago	135	1938	Bob Feller, Cleveland	240
1939	Claude Passeau, Philadelphia-Chicago	137	1939	Bob Feller, Cleveland	246
	Bucky Walters, Cincinnati	137			
1940	Kirby Higbe, Philadelphia	137	1940	Bob Feller, Cleveland	261
1941	John Vander Meer, Cincinnati	202	1941	Bob Feller, Cleveland	260
1942	John Vander Meer, Cincinnati	186	1942	Tex Hughson, Boston	113
				Bobo Newsom, Washington	113
1943	John Vander Meer, Cincinnati	174	1943	Allie Reynolds, Cleveland	151
1944	Bill Voiselle, New York	161	1944	Hal Newhouser, Detroit	187
1945	Preacher Roe, Pittsburgh	148	1945	Hal Newhouser, Detroit	212
1946	Johnny Schmitz, Cincinnati	135	1946	Bob Feller, Cleveland	348
1947	Ewell Blackwell, Cincinnati	193	1947	Bob Feller, Cleveland	196
1948	Harry Brecheen, St. Louis	149	1948	Bob Feller, Cleveland	164
1949	Warren Spahn, Boston	151	1949	Virgil Trucks, Detroit	153
1950	Warren Spahn, Boston	191	1950	Bob Lemon, Cleveland	170
1951	Warren Spahn, Boston	164	1951	Vic Raschi, New York	164
	Don Newcombe, Brooklyn	164			
1952	Warren Spahn, Boston	183	1952	Allie Reynolds, New York	160
1953	Robin Roberts, Philadelphia	198	1953	Billy Pierce, Chicago	186
1954	Robin Roberts, Philadelphia	185	1954	Bob Turley, Baltimore	185
1955	Sam Jones, Chicago	198	1955	Herb Score, Cleveland	245
1956	Sam Jones, Chicago	176	1956	Herb Score, Cleveland	263
1957	Jack Sanford, Philadelphia	188	1957	Early Wynn, Cleveland	184
1958	Sam Jones, St. Louis	225	1958	Early Wynn, Chicago	179
1959	Don Drysdale, Los Angeles	242	1959	Jim Bunning, Detroit	201
1960	Don Drysdale, Los Angeles	246	1960	Jim Bunning, Detroit	201
1961	Sandy Koufax, Los Angeles	269	1961	Camilo Pascual, Minnesota	221
1962	Don Drysdale, Los Angeles	232	1962	Camilo Pascual, Minnesota	206
1963	Sandy Koufax, Los Angeles	306	1963	Camilo Pascual, Minnesota	202
1964	Bob Veale, Pittsburgh	250	1964	Al Downing, New York	217
1965	Sandy Koufax, Los Angeles	382*	1965	Sam McDowell, Cleveland	325
1966	Sandy Koufax, Los Angeles	317	1966	Sam McDowell, Cleveland	225
1967	Jim Bunning, Philadelphia	253	1967	Jim Lonborg, Boston	246
1968	Bob Gibson, St. Louis	268	1968	Sam McDowell, Cleveland	283
1969	Ferguson Jenkins, Chicago	273	1969	Sam McDowell, Cleveland	279
1970	Tom Seaver, New York	283	1970	Sam McDowell, Cleveland	304
1971	Tom Seaver, New York	289	1971	Mickey Lolich, Detroit	308
1972	Steve Carlton, Philadelphia	310	1972	Nolan Ryan, California	329
1973	Tom Seaver, New York	251	1973	Nolan Ryan, California	383*
1974	Steve Carlton, Philadelphia	240	1974	Nolan Ryan, California	367
1975	Tom Seaver, New York	243	1975	Frank Tanana, California	269
1976	Tom Seaver, New York	235	1976	Nolan Ryan, California	327
1977	Phil Niekro, Atlanta	262	1977	Nolan Ryan, California	341
1978	J. R. Richard, Houston	303	1978	Nolan Ryan, California	260
1979	J. R. Richard, Houston	313	1979	Nolan Ryan, California	223
1980	Steve Carlton, Philadelphia	286	1980	Len Barker, Cleveland	187
1981	Fernando Valenzuela, Los Angeles	180	1981	Len Barker, Cleveland	127
1982	Steve Carlton, Philadelphia	286	1982	Floyd Bannister, Seattle	209
1983	Steve Carlton, Philadelphia	275	1983	Jack Morris, Detroit	232
1984	Dwight Gooden, New York	276	1984	Mark Langston, Seattle	204
1985	Dwight Gooden, New York	268	1985	Bert Blyleven, Cleveland-Minnesota	206
1986	Mike Scott, Houston	306	1986	Mark Langston, Seattle	245
1987	Nolan Ryan, Houston	270	1987	Mark Langston, Seattle	262
1988	Nolan Ryan, Houston	228	1988	Roger Clemens, Boston	291
1989	Jose DeLeon, St. Louis	201	1989	Nolan Ryan, Texas	301

	National League			American League	
Year	Pitcher, team	SO	Year	Pitcher, team	SO
1990	David Cone, New York	233	1990	Nolan Ryan, Texas	232
1991	David Cone, New York	241	1991	Roger Clemens, Boston	241
1992	John Smoltz, Atlanta	215	1992	Randy Johnson, Seattle	241
1993	Jose Rijo, Cincinnati	227	1993	Randy Johnson, Seattle	308
1994	Andy Benes, San Diego	189	1994	Randy Johnson, Seattle	204
1995	Hideo Nomo, Los Angeles	236	1995	Randy Johnson, Seattle	294
1996	John Smoltz, Atlanta	276	1996	Roger Clemens, Boston	257
1997	Curt Schilling, Philadelphia	319	1997	Roger Clemens, Toronto	292
1998	Curt Schilling, Philadelphia	300	1998	Roger Clemens, Toronto	271
1999	Randy Johnson, Arizona	364	1999	Pedro Martinez, Boston	313
2000	Randy Johnson, Arizona	347	2000	Pedro Martinez, Boston	284
2001	Randy Johnson, Arizona	372	2001	Hideo Nomo, Boston	220
2002	Randy Johnson, Arizona	334	2002	Pedro Martinez, Boston	239
2003	Kerry Wood, Chicago	266	2003	Esteban Loaiza, Chicago	207
2004	Randy Johnson, Arizona	290	2004	Johan Santana, Minnesota	265
2005	Jake Peavy, San Diego	216	2005	Johan Santana, Minnesota	238
2006	Aaron Harang, Cincinnati	216	2006	Johan Santana, Minnesota	245
2007	Jake Peavy, San Diego	240	2007	Scott Kazmir, Tampa Bay	239
2008	Tim Lincecum, San Francisco	265	2008	A. J. Burnett, Toronto	231
2009	Tim Lincecum, San Francisco	261	2009	Justin Verlander, Detroit	269
2010	Tim Lincecum, San Francisco	231	2010	Jered Weaver, Los Angeles	250
2011	Clayton Kershaw, Los Angeles	248	2011	Justin Verlander, Detroit	250

Victory Leaders, by Season, 1901-2011

* = All-time single-season record for league since beginning of "modern" era in 1901

	National League			American League	
Year	Pitcher, team	Wins	Year	Pitcher, team	Wins
1901	Bill Donavan, Brooklyn	25	1901	Cy Young, Boston	33
1902	Jack Chesbro, Pittsburgh	28	1902	Cy Young, Boston	32
1903	Joe McGinnity, New York	31	1903	Cy Young, Boston	28
1904	Joe McGinnity, New York	35	1904	Jack Chesbro, New York	41*
1905	Christy Mathewson, New York	31	1905	Rube Waddell, Philadelphia	27
1906	Joe McGinnity, New York	27	1906	Al Orth, New York	27
1907	Christy Mathewson, New York	24	1907	Doc White, Chicago; Addie Joss, Cleveland	27
1908	Christy Mathewson, New York	37*	1908	Ed Walsh, Chicago	40
1909	Mordecai Brown, Chicago	27	1909	George Mullin, Detroit	29
1910	Christy Mathewson, New York	27	1910	Jack Coombs, Philadelphia	31
1911	Grover Alexander, Chicago	28	1911	Jack Coombs, Philadelphia	28
1912	Rube Marquard, New York; Larry Cheney, Chicago	26	1912	Joe Wood, Boston	34
1913	Tom Seaton, Philadelphia	27	1913	Walter Johnson, Washington	36
1914	Grover Alexander, Philadelphia	27	1914	Walter Johnson, Washington	28
1915	Grover Alexander, Philadelphia	31	1915	Walter Johnson, Washington	27
1916	Grover Alexander, Philadelphia	33	1916	Walter Johnson, Washington	25
1917	Grover Alexander, Philadelphia	30	1917	Eddie Cicotte, Chicago	28
1918	Hippo Vaughn, Chicago	22	1918	Walter Johnson, Washington	23
1919	Jesse Barnes, New York	25	1919	Eddie Cicotte, Chicago	29
1920	Grover Alexander, Philadelphia	27	1920	Jim Bagby, Cleveland	31
1921	Burleigh Grimes, Brooklyn; Wilbur Cooper, Pitt.	22	1921	Urban Shocker, St. Louis; Carl Mays, New York	27
1922	Eppa Rixey, Cincinnati	25	1922	Eddie Rommel, Philadelphia	27
1923	Dolf Luque, Cincinnati	27	1923	George Uhle, Cleveland	26
1924	Dazzy Vance, Brooklyn	28	1924	Walter Johnson, Washington	23
1925	Dazzy Vance, Brooklyn	22	1925	Eddie Rommel, Philadelphia; Ted Lyons, Chicago	21
1926	Flint Rhem, St. Louis; Remy Kremer, Pitt.; Lee Meadows, Pitt.; Pete Donohue, Cincinnati	20	1926	George Uhle, Cleveland	27
1927	Charlie Root, Chicago	26	1927	Ted Lyons, Chicago; Waite Hoyt, New York	22
1928	Burleigh Grimes, Pittsburgh; Larry Benton, NY Giants	25	1928	George Pipgras, New York; Lefty Grove, Philadelphia	24
1929	Pat Malone, Chicago	22	1929	George Earnshaw, Philadelphia; Ted Lyons, Chicago	24
1930	Pat Malone, Chicago; Remy Kremer, Pitt.	20	1930	Lefty Grove, Philadelphia	28
1931	Heine Meine, Pittsburgh	19	1931	Lefty Grove, Philadelphia	31
1932	Lon Warneke, Chicago	22	1932	Alvin Crowder, Washington	26
1933	Carl Hubbell, New York	23	1933	Lefty Grove, Philadelphia; Alvin Crowder, Washington	24
1934	Dizzy Dean, St. Louis	30	1934	Lefty Gomez, New York	26
1935	Dizzy Dean, St. Louis	28	1935	Wes Ferrell, Boston	25
1936	Carl Hubbell, New York	26	1936	Tommy Bridges, Detroit	23
1937	Carl Hubbell, New York	22	1937	Lefty Gomez, New York	21
1938	Bill Lee, Chicago	22	1938	Red Ruffing, New York	21
1939	Bucky Walters, Cincinnati	27	1939	Bob Feller, Cleveland	24
1940	Bucky Walters, Cincinnati	22	1940	Bob Feller, Cleveland	27
1941	Whit Wyatt, Brooklyn; Kirby Higbe, Brooklyn	22	1941	Bob Feller, Cleveland	25
1942	Mort Cooper, St. Louis	22	1942	Tex Hughson, Boston	22
1943	Rip Sewell, Pittsburgh; Mort Cooper, St. Louis; Elmer Riddle, Cincinnati	21	1943	Dizzy Trout, Detroit; Spurgeon Chandler, New York	20
1944	Bucky Walters, Cincinnati	23	1944	Hal Newhouser, Detroit	29
1945	Red Barrett, Boston-St. Louis	23	1945	Hal Newhouser, Detroit	25
1946	Howie Pollet, St. Louis	21	1946	Hal Newhouser, Detroit; Bob Feller, Cleveland	26
1947	Ewell Blackwell, Cincinnati	22	1947	Bob Feller, Cleveland	20
1948	Johnny Sain, Boston	24	1948	Hal Newhouser, Detroit	21
1949	Warren Spahn, Boston	21	1949	Mel Parnell, Boston	25
1950	Warren Spahn, Boston	21	1950	Bob Lemon, Cleveland	23
1951	Sal Maglie, New York; Larry Jansen, New York	23	1951	Bob Feller, Cleveland	22
1952	Robin Roberts, Philadelphia	28	1952	Bobby Shantz, Philadelphia	24
1953	Warren Spahn, Milwaukee; Robin Roberts, Phil.	23	1953	Bob Porterfield, Washington	22
1954	Robin Roberts, Philadelphia	23	1954	Early Wynn, Bob Lemon, Cleveland	23
1955	Robin Roberts, Philadelphia	23	1955	Frank Sullivan, Boston; Whitey Ford, New York; Bob Lemon, Cleveland	18
1956	Don Newcombe, Brooklyn	27	1956	Frank Lary, Detroit	21
1957	Warren Spahn, Milwaukee	21	1957	Billy Pierce, Chicago; Jim Bunning, Detroit	20
1958	Warren Spahn, Milwaukee; Bob Friend, Pitt.	22	1958	Bob Turley, New York	21
1959	Lew Burdette, Warren Spahn, Milwaukee; Sam Jones, NY Giants	21	1959	Early Wynn, Chicago	22
1960	Warren Spahn, Milwaukee; Ernie Broglio, St. Louis	21	1960	Jim Perry, Cleveland; Chuck Estrada, Baltimore	18
1961	Warren Spahn, Milwaukee; Joey Jay, Cincinnati	21	1961	Whitey Ford, New York	25
1962	Don Drysdale, Los Angeles	25	1962	Ralph Terry, New York	23

	National League			American League	
Year	Pitcher, team	Wins	Year	Pitcher, team	Wins
1963	Juan Marichal, San Francisco; Sandy Koufax, L.A.	25	1963	Whitey Ford, New York	24
1964	Larry Jackson, Chicago	24	1964	Gary Peters, Chicago; Dean Chance, Los Angeles	20
1965	Sandy Koufax, Los Angeles	26	1965	Mudcat (Jim) Grant, Minnesota	21
1966	Sandy Koufax, Los Angeles	27	1966	Jim Kaat, Minnesota	25
1967	Mike McCormick, San Francisco; Sandy Koufax, L.A.	22	1967	Earl Wilson, Detroit; Jim Lonborg, Boston	22
1968	Juan Marichal, San Francisco	26	1968	Denny McLain, Detroit	31
1969	Tom Seaver, New York	25	1969	Denny McLain, Detroit	24
1970	Gaylord Perry, San Francisco; Bob Gibson, St. Louis	23	1970	Jim Perry, Minnesota; Mike Cuellar, Dave McNally, Baltimore	24
1971	Ferguson Jenkins, Chicago	24	1971	Mickey Lolich, Detroit	25
1972	Steve Carlton, Philadelphia	27	1972	Wilbur Wood, Chicago; Gaylord Perry, Cleveland	24
1973	Ron Bryant, San Francisco	24	1973	Wilbur Wood, Chicago	24
1974	Phil Niekro, Atlanta; Andy Messersmith, L.A.	20	1974	Ferguson Jenkins, Texas; Jim "Catfish" Hunter, Oakland	25
1975	Tom Seaver, New York	22	1975	Jim Palmer, Baltimore; Jim "Catfish" Hunter, NY	23
1976	Randy Jones, San Diego	22	1976	Jim Palmer, Baltimore	22
1977	Steve Carlton, Philadelphia	23	1977	Jim Palmer, Baltimore; Dave Goltz, Minnesota; Dennis Leonard, Kansas City	20
1978	Gaylord Perry, San Diego	21	1978	Ron Guidry, New York	25
1979	Phil Niekro, Atlanta; Joe Niekro, Houston	21	1979	Mike Flanagan, Baltimore	23
1980	Steve Carlton, Philadelphia	24	1980	Steve Stone, Baltimore	25
1981	Tom Seaver, Cincinnati	14	1981	Pete Vuckovich, Milwaukee; Dennis Martinez, Balt.; Steve McCatty, Oakland; Jack Morris, Detroit	14
1982	Steve Carlton, Philadelphia	23	1982	La Marr Hoyt, Chicago	19
1983	John Denny, Philadelphia	19	1983	La Marr Hoyt, Chicago	24
1984	Joaquin Andujar, St. Louis	20	1984	Mike Boddicker, Baltimore	20
1985	Dwight Gooden, New York	24	1985	Ron Guidry, New York	22
1986	Fernando Valenzuela, Los Angeles	21	1986	Roger Clemens, Boston	24
1987	Rick Sutcliffe, Chicago	18	1987	Dave Stewart, Oakland; Roger Clemens, Boston	20
1988	Danny Jackson, Cincinnati; Orel Hershiser, L.A.	23	1988	Frank Viola, Minnesota	24
1989	Mike Scott, Houston	20	1989	Bret Saberhagen, Kansas City	23
1990	Doug Drabek, Pittsburgh	22	1990	Bob Welch, Oakland	27
1991	John Smiley, Pittsburgh; Tom Glavine, Atlanta	20	1991	Bill Gullickson, Detroit; Scott Erickson, Minnesota	20
1992	Greg Maddux, Chicago; Tom Glavine, Atlanta	20	1992	Jack Morris, Toronto; Kevin Brown, Texas	21
1993	Tom Glavine, Atlanta; John Burkett, San Francisco	22	1993	Jack McDowell, Chicago	22
1994	Greg Maddux, Atlanta	16	1994	Jimmy Key, New York	17
1995	Greg Maddux, Atlanta	19	1995	Mike Mussina, Baltimore	19
1996	John Smoltz, Atlanta	24	1996	Andy Pettitte, New York	21
1997	Denny Neagle, Atlanta	20	1997	Roger Clemens, Toronto	21
1998	Tom Glavine, Atlanta	20	1998	Rick Helling, Texas; Roger Clemens, Toronto; David Cone, New York	20
1999	Mike Hampton, Houston	22	1999	Pedro Martinez, Boston	23
2000	Tom Glavine, Atlanta	21	2000	David Wells, Toronto; Tim Hudson, Oakland	20
2001	Matt Morris, St. Louis; Curt Schilling, Arizona	22	2001	Mark Mulder, Oakland	21
2002	Randy Johnson, Arizona	24	2002	Barry Zito, Oakland	23
2003	Russ Ortiz, Atlanta	21	2003	Roy Halladay, Toronto	22
2004	Roy Oswalt, Houston	20	2004	Curt Schilling, Boston	21
2005	Dontrelle Willis, Florida	22	2005	Bartolo Colon, Los Angeles	21
2006	Aaron Harang, Cincinnati; Derek Lowe, L.A.; Brad Penny, L.A.; John Smoltz, Atlanta; Brandon Webb, Arizona; Carlos Zambrano, Chicago	16	2006	Johan Santana, Minnesota; Chien-Ming Wang, New York	19
2007	Jake Peavy, San Diego	19	2007	Josh Beckett, Boston	20
2008	Brandon Webb, Arizona	22	2008	Cliff Lee, Cleveland	22
2009	Adam Wainwright, St. Louis	19	2009	Felix Hernandez, Seattle; CC Sabathia, New York; Justin Verlander, Detroit	19
2010	Roy Halladay, Philadelphia	21	2010	CC Sabathia, New York	21
2011	Ian Kennedy, Arizona; Clayton Kershaw, L.A.	21	2011	Justin Verlander, Detroit	24

Cy Young Award Winners, 1956-2010

Year	Pitcher, team	Year	Pitcher, team	Year	Pitcher, team
1956	Don Newcombe, Brooklyn	1978	(NL) Gaylord Perry, San Diego	1995	(NL) Greg Maddux, Atlanta
1957	Warren Spahn, Milwaukee		(AL) Ron Guidry, NY		(AL) Randy Johnson, Seattle
1958	Bob Turley, NY	1979	(NL) Bruce Sutter, Chicago	1996	(NL) John Smoltz, Atlanta
1959	Early Wynn, Chicago		(AL) Mike Flanagan, Baltimore		(AL) Pat Hentgen, Toronto
1960	Vernon Law, Pittsburgh	1980	(NL) Steve Carlton, Philadelphia	1997	(NL) Pedro Martinez, Montréal
1961	Whitey Ford, NY		(AL) Steve Stone, Baltimore		(AL) Roger Clemens, Toronto
1962	Don Drysdale, L.A.	1981	(NL) Fernando Valenzuela, L.A.	1998	(NL) Tom Glavine, Atlanta
1963	Sandy Koufax, L.A.		(AL) Rollie Fingers, Milwaukee		(AL) Roger Clemens, Toronto
1964	Dean Chance, L.A.	1982	(NL) Steve Carlton, Philadelphia	1999	(NL) Randy Johnson, Arizona
1965	Sandy Koufax, L.A.		(AL) Pete Vuckovich, Milwaukee		(AL) Pedro Martinez, Boston
1966	Sandy Koufax, L.A.	1983	(NL) John Denny, Philadelphia	2000	(NL) Randy Johnson, Arizona
1967	(NL) Mike McCormick, San Francisco		(AL) LaMarr Hoyt, Chicago		(AL) Pedro Martinez, Boston
	(AL) Jim Lonborg, Boston	1984	(NL) Rick Sutcliffe, Chicago	2001	(NL) Randy Johnson, Arizona
1968	(NL) Bob Gibson, St. Louis		(AL) Willie Hernandez, Detroit		(AL) Roger Clemens, NY
	(AL) Denny McLain, Detroit	1985	(NL) Dwight Gooden, NY	2002	(NL) Randy Johnson, Arizona
1969	(NL) Tom Seaver, NY		(AL) Bret Saberhagen, Kansas City		(AL) Barry Zito, Oakland
	(AL) (tie) Denny McLain, Detroit; Mike Cuellar, Baltimore	1986	(NL) Mike Scott, Houston	2003	(NL) Eric Gagne, L.A.
			(AL) Roger Clemens, Boston		(AL) Roy Halladay, Toronto
1970	(NL) Bob Gibson, St. Louis	1987	(NL) Steve Bedrosian, Philadelphia	2004	(NL) Roger Clemens, Houston
	(AL) Jim Perry, Minnesota		(AL) Roger Clemens, Boston		(AL) Johan Santana, Minnesota
1971	(NL) Ferguson Jenkins, Chicago	1988	(NL) Orel Hershiser, L.A.	2005	(NL) Chris Carpenter, St. Louis
	(AL) Vida Blue, Oakland		(AL) Frank Viola, Minnesota		(AL) Bartolo Colon, L.A.
1972	(NL) Steve Carlton, Philadelphia	1989	(NL) Mark Davis, San Diego	2006	(NL) Brandon Webb, Arizona
	(AL) Gaylord Perry, Cleveland		(AL) Bret Saberhagen, Kansas City		(AL) Johan Santana, Minnesota
1973	(NL) Tom Seaver, NY	1990	(NL) Doug Drabek, Pittsburgh	2007	(NL) Jake Peavy, San Diego
	(AL) Jim Palmer, Baltimore		(AL) Bob Welch, Oakland		(AL) CC Sabathia, Cleveland
1974	(NL) Mike Marshall, L.A.	1991	(NL) Tom Glavine, Atlanta	2008	(NL) Tim Lincecum, San Francisco
	(AL) Jim "Catfish" Hunter, Oakland		(AL) Roger Clemens, Boston		(AL) Cliff Lee, Cleveland
1975	(NL) Tom Seaver, NY	1992	(NL) Greg Maddux, Chicago	2009	(NL) Tim Lincecum, San Francisco
	(AL) Jim Palmer, Baltimore		(AL) Dennis Eckersley, Oakland		(AL) Zack Greinke, Kansas City
1976	(NL) Randy Jones, San Diego	1993	(NL) Greg Maddux, Atlanta	2010	(NL) Roy Halladay, Philadelphia
	(AL) Jim Palmer, Baltimore		(AL) Jack McDowell, Chicago		(AL) Felix Hernandez, Seattle
1977	(NL) Steve Carlton, Philadelphia	1994	(NL) Greg Maddux, Atlanta		
	(AL) Sparky Lyle, NY		(AL) David Cone, Kansas City		

Most Valuable Players, 1931-2010

As selected by the Baseball Writers' Assn. of America. Prior to 1931, MVP honors were named by various sources.

National League

Year	Player, team	Year	Player, team	Year	Player, team
1931	Frank Frisch, St. Louis	1958	Ernie Banks, Chicago	1984	Ryne Sandberg, Chicago
1932	Chuck Klein, Philadelphia	1959	Ernie Banks, Chicago	1985	Willie McGee, St. Louis
1933	Carl Hubbell, New York	1960	Dick Groat, Pittsburgh	1986	Mike Schmidt, Philadelphia
1934	Dizzy Dean, St. Louis	1961	Frank Robinson, Cincinnati	1987	Andre Dawson, Chicago
1935	Gabby Hartnett, Chicago	1962	Maury Wills, Los Angeles	1988	Kirk Gibson, Los Angeles
1936	Carl Hubbell, New York	1963	Sandy Koufax, Los Angeles	1989	Kevin Mitchell, San Francisco
1937	Joe Medwick, St. Louis	1964	Ken Boyer, St. Louis	1990	Barry Bonds, Pittsburgh
1938	Ernie Lombardi, Cincinnati	1965	Willie Mays, San Francisco	1991	Terry Pendleton, Atlanta
1939	Bucky Walters, Cincinnati	1966	Roberto Clemente, Pittsburgh	1992	Barry Bonds, Pittsburgh
1940	Frank McCormick, Cincinnati	1967	Orlando Cepeda, St. Louis	1993	Barry Bonds, San Francisco
1941	Dolph Camilli, Brooklyn	1968	Bob Gibson, St. Louis	1994	Jeff Bagwell, Houston
1942	Mort Cooper, St. Louis	1969	Willie McCovey, San Francisco	1995	Barry Larkin, Cincinnati
1943	Stan Musial, St. Louis	1970	Johnny Bench, Cincinnati	1996	Ken Caminiti, San Diego
1944	Martin Marion, St. Louis	1971	Joe Torre, St. Louis	1997	Larry Walker, Colorado
1945	Phil Cavarretta, Chicago	1972	Johnny Bench, Cincinnati	1998	Sammy Sosa, Chicago
1946	Stan Musial, St. Louis	1973	Pete Rose, Cincinnati	1999	Chipper Jones, Atlanta
1947	Bob Elliott, Boston	1974	Steve Garvey, Los Angeles	2000	Jeff Kent, San Francisco
1948	Stan Musial, St. Louis	1975	Joe Morgan, Cincinnati	2001	Barry Bonds, San Francisco
1949	Jackie Robinson, Brooklyn	1976	Joe Morgan, Cincinnati	2002	Barry Bonds, San Francisco
1950	Jim Konstanty, Philadelphia	1977	George Foster, Cincinnati	2003	Barry Bonds, San Francisco
1951	Roy Campanella, Brooklyn	1978	Dave Parker, Pittsburgh	2004	Barry Bonds, San Francisco
1952	Hank Sauer, Chicago	1979	(tie) Keith Hernandez, St. Louis;	2005	Albert Pujols, St. Louis
1953	Roy Campanella, Brooklyn		Willie Stargell, Pittsburgh	2006	Ryan Howard, Philadelphia
1954	Willie Mays, New York	1980	Mike Schmidt, Philadelphia	2007	Jimmy Rollins, Philadelphia
1955	Roy Campanella, Brooklyn	1981	Mike Schmidt, Philadelphia	2008	Albert Pujols, St. Louis
1956	Don Newcombe, Brooklyn	1982	Dale Murphy, Atlanta	2009	Albert Pujols, St. Louis
1957	Hank Aaron, Milwaukee	1983	Dale Murphy, Atlanta	2010	Joey Votto, Cincinnati

American League

Year	Player, team	Year	Player, team	Year	Player, team
1931	Lefty Grove, Philadelphia	1958	Jackie Jensen, Boston	1985	Don Mattingly, New York
1932	Jimmie Foxx, Philadelphia	1959	Nellie Fox, Chicago	1986	Roger Clemens, Boston
1933	Jimmie Foxx, Philadelphia	1960	Roger Maris, New York	1987	George Bell, Toronto
1934	Mickey Cochrane, Detroit	1961	Roger Maris, New York	1988	Jose Canseco, Oakland
1935	Hank Greenberg, Detroit	1962	Mickey Mantle, New York	1989	Robin Yount, Milwaukee
1936	Lou Gehrig, New York	1963	Elston Howard, New York	1990	Rickey Henderson, Oakland
1937	Charlie Gehringer, Detroit	1964	Brooks Robinson, Baltimore	1991	Cal Ripken Jr., Baltimore
1938	Jimmie Foxx, Boston	1965	Zoilo Versalles, Minnesota	1992	Dennis Eckersley, Oakland
1939	Joe DiMaggio, New York	1966	Frank Robinson, Baltimore	1993	Frank Thomas, Chicago
1940	Hank Greenberg, Detroit	1967	Carl Yastrzemski, Boston	1994	Frank Thomas, Chicago
1941	Joe DiMaggio, New York	1968	Denny McLain, Detroit	1995	Mo Vaughn, Boston
1942	Joe Gordon, New York	1969	Harmon Killebrew, Minnesota	1996	Juan Gonzalez, Texas
1943	Spurgeon Chandler, New York	1970	John "Boog" Powell, Baltimore	1997	Ken Griffey Jr., Seattle
1944	Hal Newhouser, Detroit	1971	Vida Blue, Oakland	1998	Juan Gonzalez, Texas
1945	Hal Newhouser, Detroit	1972	Dick Allen, Chicago	1999	Ivan Rodriguez, Texas
1946	Ted Williams, Boston	1973	Reggie Jackson, Oakland	2000	Jason Giambi, Oakland
1947	Joe DiMaggio, New York	1974	Jeff Burroughs, Texas	2001	Ichiro Suzuki, Seattle
1948	Lou Boudreau, Cleveland	1975	Fred Lynn, Boston	2002	Miguel Tejada, Oakland
1949	Ted Williams, Boston	1976	Thurman Munson, New York	2003	Alex Rodriguez, Texas
1950	Phil Rizzuto, New York	1977	Rod Carew, Minnesota	2004	Vladimir Guerrero, Los Angeles
1951	Yogi Berra, New York	1978	Jim Rice, Boston	2005	Alex Rodriguez, New York
1952	Bobby Shantz, Philadelphia	1979	Don Baylor, California	2006	Justin Morneau, Minnesota
1953	Al Rosen, Cleveland	1980	George Brett, Kansas City	2007	Alex Rodriguez, New York
1954	Yogi Berra, New York	1981	Rollie Fingers, Milwaukee	2008	Dustin Pedroia, Boston
1955	Yogi Berra, New York	1982	Robin Yount, Milwaukee	2009	Joe Mauer, Minnesota
1956	Mickey Mantle, New York	1983	Cal Ripken Jr., Baltimore	2010	Josh Hamilton, Texas
1957	Mickey Mantle, New York	1984	Willie Hernandez, Detroit		

Rookie of the Year, 1949-2010

(as selected by the Baseball Writers' Assn. of America)

1947—Combined selection—Jackie Robinson, Brooklyn, 1B; 1948—Combined selection—Alvin Dark, Boston (NL), SS.

National League

Year	Player, team, position	Year	Player, team, position	Year	Player, team, position
1949	Don Newcombe, Brooklyn, P	1971	Earl Williams, Atlanta, C	1991	Jeff Bagwell, Houston, 1B
1950	Sam Jethroe, Boston, OF	1972	Jon Matlack, NY, P	1992	Eric Karros, L.A., 1B
1951	Willie Mays, NY, OF	1973	Gary Matthews, San Francisco, OF	1993	Mike Piazza, L.A., C
1952	Joe Black, Brooklyn, P	1974	Bake McBride, St. Louis, OF	1994	Raul Mondesi, L.A., OF
1953	Jim Gilliam, Brooklyn, 2B	1975	John Montefusco, San Francisco, P	1995	Hideo Nomo, L.A., P
1954	Wally Moon, St. Louis, OF	1976	(tie) Butch Metzger, San Diego, P;	1996	Todd Hollandsworth, L.A., OF
1955	Bill Virdon, St. Louis, OF		Pat Zachry, Cincinnati, P	1997	Scott Rolen, Philadelphia, 3B
1956	Frank Robinson, Cincinnati, OF	1977	Andre Dawson, Montréal, OF	1998	Kerry Wood, Chicago, P
1957	Jack Sanford, Philadelphia, P	1978	Bob Horner, Atlanta, 3B	1999	Scott Williamson, Cincinnati, P
1958	Orlando Cepeda, San Francisco, 1B	1979	Rick Sutcliffe, L.A., P	2000	Rafael Furcal, Atlanta, SS
1959	Willie McCovey, San Francisco, 1B	1980	Steve Howe, L.A., P	2001	Albert Pujols, St. Louis, OF
1960	Frank Howard, L.A., OF	1981	Fernando Valenzuela, L.A., P	2002	Jason Jennings, Colorado, P
1961	Billy Williams, Chicago, OF	1982	Steve Sax, L.A., 2B	2003	Dontrelle Willis, Florida, P
1962	Ken Hubbs, Chicago, 2B	1983	Darryl Strawberry, NY, OF	2004	Jason Bay, Pittsburgh, OF
1963	Pete Rose, Cincinnati, 2B	1984	Dwight Gooden, NY, P	2005	Ryan Howard, Philadelphia, 1B
1964	Richie Allen, Philadelphia, 3B	1985	Vince Coleman, St. Louis, OF	2006	Hanley Ramirez, Florida, SS
1965	Jim Lefebvre, L.A., 2B	1986	Todd Worrell, St. Louis, P	2007	Ryan Braun, Milwaukee, OF
1966	Tommy Helms, Cincinnati, 2B	1987	Benito Santiago, San Diego, C	2008	Geovany Soto, Chicago, C
1967	Tom Seaver, NY, P	1988	Chris Sabo, Cincinnati, 3B	2009	Chris Coghlan, Florida, OF
1968	Johnny Bench, Cincinnati, C	1989	Jerome Walton, Chicago, OF	2010	Buster Posey, San Francisco, C
1969	Ted Sizemore, L.A., 2B	1990	Dave Justice, Atlanta, 1B		
1970	Carl Morton, Montréal, P				

American League

Year	Player, team, position	Year	Player, team, position	Year	Player, team, position
1949	Roy Sievers, St. Louis, OF	1970	Thurman Munson, NY, C	1990	Sandy Alomar Jr., Cleveland, C
1950	Walt Dropo, Boston, 1B	1971	Chris Chambliss, Cleveland, 1B	1991	Chuck Knoblauch, Minnesota, 2B
1951	Gil McDougald, NY, 3B	1972	Carlton Fisk, Boston, C	1992	Pat Listach, Milwaukee, SS
1952	Harry Byrd, Philadelphia, P	1973	Al Bumbry, Baltimore, OF	1993	Tim Salmon, California, OF
1953	Harvey Kuenn, Detroit, SS	1974	Mike Hargrove, Texas, 1B	1994	Bob Hamelin, Kansas City, DH
1954	Bob Grim, NY, P	1975	Fred Lynn, Boston, OF	1995	Marty Cordova, Minnesota, OF
1955	Herb Score, Cleveland, P	1976	Mark Fidrych, Detroit, P	1996	Derek Jeter, NY, SS
1956	Luis Aparicio, Chicago, SS	1977	Eddie Murray, Baltimore, DH	1997	Nomar Garciaparra, Boston, SS
1957	Tony Kubek, NY, IF-OF	1978	Lou Whitaker, Detroit, 2B	1998	Ben Grieve, Oakland, OF
1958	Albie Pearson, Washington, OF	1979	(tie) John Castino, Minnesota, 3B;	1999	Carlos Beltran, Kansas City, OF
1959	Bob Allison, Washington, OF		Alfredo Griffin, Toronto, SS	2000	Kazuhiro Sasaki, Seattle, P
1960	Ron Hansen, Baltimore, SS	1980	Joe Charboneau, Cleveland, OF	2001	Ichiro Suzuki, Seattle, OF
1961	Don Schwall, Boston, P	1981	Dave Righetti, NY, P	2002	Eric Hinske, Toronto, 3B
1962	Tom Tresh, NY, IF-OF	1982	Cal Ripken Jr., Baltimore, SS	2003	Angel Berroa, Kansas City, SS
1963	Gary Peters, Chicago, P	1983	Ron Kittle, Chicago, OF	2004	Bobby Crosby, Oakland, SS
1964	Tony Oliva, Minnesota, OF	1984	Alvin Davis, Seattle, 1B	2005	Huston Street, Oakland, P
1965	Curt Blefary, Baltimore, OF	1985	Ozzie Guillen, Chicago, SS	2006	Justin Verlander, Detroit, P
1966	Tommie Agee, Chicago, OF	1986	Jose Canseco, Oakland, OF	2007	Dustin Pedroia, Boston, 2B
1967	Rod Carew, Minnesota, 2B	1987	Mark McGwire, Oakland, 1B	2008	Evan Longoria, Tampa Bay, 3B
1968	Stan Bahnsen, NY, P	1988	Walt Weiss, Oakland, SS	2009	Andrew Bailey, Oakland, P
1969	Lou Piniella, Kansas City, OF	1989	Gregg Olson, Baltimore, P	2010	Neftali Feliz, Texas, P

Major League Pennant Winners, 1901-75

	National League						American League			
Year	Winner	Won	Lost	Pct	Manager	Year	Winner	Won	Lost	Pct	Manager
1901	Pittsburgh	90	49	.647	Clarke	1901	Chicago	83	53	.610	Griffith
1902	Pittsburgh	103	36	.741	Clarke	1902	Philadelphia	83	53	.610	Mack
1903	Pittsburgh	91	49	.650	Clarke	1903	Boston	91	47	.659	Collins
1904	New York	106	47	.693	McGraw	1904	Boston	95	59	.617	Collins
1905	New York	105	48	.686	McGraw	1905	Philadelphia	92	56	.622	Mack
1906	Chicago	116	36	.763	Chance	1906	Chicago	93	58	.616	Jones
1907	Chicago	107	45	.704	Chance	1907	Detroit	92	58	.613	Jennings
1908	Chicago	99	55	.643	Chance	1908	Detroit	90	63	.588	Jennings
1909	Pittsburgh	110	42	.724	Clarke	1909	Detroit	98	54	.645	Jennings
1910	Chicago	104	50	.675	Chance	1910	Philadelphia	102	48	.680	Mack
1911	New York	99	54	.647	McGraw	1911	Philadelphia	101	50	.669	Mack
1912	New York	103	48	.682	McGraw	1912	Boston	105	47	.691	Stahl
1913	New York	101	51	.664	McGraw	1913	Philadelphia	96	57	.627	Mack
1914	Boston	94	59	.614	Stallings	1914	Philadelphia	99	53	.651	Mack
1915	Philadelphia	90	62	.592	Moran	1915	Boston	101	50	.669	Carrigan
1916	Brooklyn	94	60	.610	Robinson	1916	Boston	91	63	.591	Carrigan
1917	New York	98	56	.636	McGraw	1917	Chicago	100	54	.649	Rowland
1918	Chicago	84	45	.651	Mitchell	1918	Boston	75	51	.595	Barrow
1919	Cincinnati	96	44	.686	Moran	1919	Chicago	88	52	.629	Gleason
1920	Brooklyn	93	61	.604	Robinson	1920	Cleveland	98	56	.636	Speaker
1921	New York	94	59	.614	McGraw	1921	New York	98	55	.641	Huggins
1922	New York	93	61	.604	McGraw	1922	New York	94	60	.610	Huggins
1923	New York	95	58	.621	McGraw	1923	New York	98	54	.645	Huggins
1924	New York	93	60	.608	McGraw	1924	Washington	92	62	.597	Harris
1925	Pittsburgh	95	58	.621	McKechnie	1925	Washington	96	55	.636	Harris
1926	St. Louis	89	65	.578	Hornsby	1926	New York	91	63	.591	Huggins
1927	Pittsburgh	94	60	.610	Bush	1927	New York	110	44	.714	Huggins
1928	St. Louis	95	59	.617	McKechnie	1928	New York	101	53	.656	Huggins
1929	Chicago	98	54	.645	McCarthy	1929	Philadelphia	104	46	.693	Mack
1930	St. Louis	92	62	.597	Street	1930	Philadelphia	102	52	.662	Mack
1931	St. Louis	101	53	.656	Street	1931	Philadelphia	107	45	.704	Mack
1932	Chicago	90	64	.584	Hornsby, Grimm	1932	New York	107	47	.695	McCarthy
1933	New York	91	61	.599	Terry	1933	Washington	99	53	.651	Cronin
1934	St. Louis	95	58	.621	Frisch	1934	Detroit	101	53	.656	Cochrane
1935	Chicago	100	54	.649	Grimm	1935	Detroit	93	58	.616	Cochrane
1936	New York	92	62	.597	Terry	1936	New York	102	51	.667	McCarthy
1937	New York	95	57	.625	Terry	1937	New York	102	52	.662	McCarthy
1938	Chicago	89	63	.586	Grimm, Hartnett	1938	New York	99	53	.651	McCarthy
1939	Cincinnati	97	57	.630	McKechnie	1939	New York	106	45	.702	McCarthy
1940	Cincinnati	100	53	.654	McKechnie	1940	Detroit	90	64	.584	Baker
1941	Brooklyn	100	54	.649	Durocher	1941	New York	101	53	.656	McCarthy
1942	St. Louis	106	48	.688	Southworth	1942	New York	103	51	.669	McCarthy
1943	St. Louis	105	49	.682	Southworth	1943	New York	98	56	.636	McCarthy
1944	St. Louis	105	49	.682	Southworth	1944	St. Louis	89	65	.578	Sewell
1945	Chicago	98	56	.636	Grimm	1945	Detroit	88	65	.575	O'Neill
1946	St. Louis	98	58	.628	Dyer	1946	Boston	104	50	.675	Cronin
1947	Brooklyn	94	60	.610	Shotton	1947	New York	97	57	.630	Harris
1948	Boston	91	62	.595	Southworth	1948	Cleveland	97	58	.626	Boudreau
1949	Brooklyn	97	57	.630	Shotton	1949	New York	97	57	.630	Stengel
1950	Philadelphia	91	63	.591	Sawyer	1950	New York	98	56	.636	Stengel
1951	New York	98	59	.624	Durocher	1951	New York	98	56	.636	Stengel
1952	Brooklyn	96	57	.627	Dressen	1952	New York	95	59	.617	Stengel
1953	Brooklyn	105	49	.682	Dressen	1953	New York	99	52	.656	Stengel
1954	New York	97	57	.630	Durocher	1954	Cleveland	111	43	.721	Lopez
1955	Brooklyn	98	55	.641	Alston	1955	New York	96	58	.623	Stengel
1956	Brooklyn	93	61	.604	Alston	1956	New York	97	57	.630	Stengel
1957	Milwaukee	95	59	.617	Haney	1957	New York	98	56	.636	Stengel
1958	Milwaukee	92	62	.597	Haney	1958	New York	92	62	.597	Stengel
1959	Los Angeles	88	68	.564	Alston	1959	Chicago	94	60	.610	Lopez
1960	Pittsburgh	95	59	.617	Murtaugh	1960	New York	97	57	.630	Stengel
1961	Cincinnati	93	61	.604	Hutchinson	1961	New York	109	53	.673	Houk
1962	San Francisco	103	62	.624	Dark	1962	New York	96	66	.593	Houk
1963	Los Angeles	99	63	.611	Alston	1963	New York	104	57	.646	Houk
1964	St. Louis	93	69	.574	Keane	1964	New York	99	63	.611	Berra

		National League							American League			
Year	Winner	Won	Lost	Pct	Manager		Year	Winner	Won	Lost	Pct	Manager
1965	Los Angeles	97	65	.599	Alston		1965	Minnesota	102	60	.630	Mele
1966	Los Angeles	95	67	.586	Alston		1966	Baltimore	97	63	.606	Bauer
1967	St. Louis	101	60	.627	Schoendienst		1967	Boston	92	70	.568	Williams
1968	St. Louis	97	65	.599	Schoendienst		1968	Detroit	103	59	.636	Smith
1969	NY Mets	100	62	.617	Hodges		1969	Baltimore	109	53	.673	Weaver
1970	Cincinnati	102	60	.630	Anderson		1970	Baltimore	108	54	.667	Weaver
1971	Pittsburgh	97	65	.599	Murtaugh		1971	Baltimore	101	57	.639	Weaver
1972	Cincinnati	95	59	.617	Anderson		1972	Oakland	93	62	.600	Williams
1973	NY Mets	82	79	.509	Berra		1973	Oakland	94	68	.580	Williams
1974	Los Angeles	102	60	.630	Alston		1974	Oakland	90	72	.556	Dark
1975	Cincinnati	108	54	.667	Anderson		1975	Boston	95	65	.594	Johnson

Major League Pennant Winners, 1976-2011

National League

		East					West				Pennant
Year	Winner	W	L	Pct	Manager	Winner	W	L	Pct	Manager	winner
1976	Philadelphia	101	61	.623	Ozark	Cincinnati	102	60	.630	Anderson	Cincinnati
1977	Philadelphia	101	61	.623	Ozark	Los Angeles	98	64	.605	Lasorda	Los Angeles
1978	Philadelphia	90	72	.556	Ozark	Los Angeles	95	67	.586	Lasorda	Los Angeles
1979	Pittsburgh	98	64	.605	Tanner	Cincinnati	90	71	.559	McNamara	Pittsburgh
1980	Philadelphia	91	71	.562	Green	Houston	93	70	.571	Virdon	Philadelphia
1981(a)	Philadelphia	34	21	.618	Green	Los Angeles	36	21	.632	Lasorda	(c)
1981(b)	Montréal	30	23	.566	Williams, Fanning	Houston	33	20	.623	Virdon	Los Angeles
1982	St. Louis	92	70	.568	Herzog	Atlanta	89	73	.549	Torre	St. Louis
1983	Philadelphia	90	72	.556	Corrales, Owens	Los Angeles	91	71	.562	Lasorda	Philadelphia
1984	Chicago	96	65	.596	Frey	San Diego	92	70	.568	Williams	San Diego
1985	St. Louis	101	61	.623	Herzog	Los Angeles	95	67	.586	Lasorda	St. Louis
1986	NY Mets	108	54	.667	Johnson	Houston	96	66	.593	Lanier	New York
1987	St. Louis	95	67	.586	Herzog	San Francisco	90	72	.556	Craig	St. Louis
1988	NY Mets	100	60	.625	Johnson	Los Angeles	94	67	.584	Lasorda	Los Angeles
1989	Chicago	93	69	.571	Zimmer	San Francisco	92	70	.568	Craig	San Francisco
1990	Pittsburgh	95	67	.586	Leyland	Cincinnati	91	71	.562	Piniella	Cincinnati
1991	Pittsburgh	98	64	.605	Leyland	Atlanta	94	68	.580	Cox	Atlanta
1992	Pittsburgh	96	66	.593	Leyland	Atlanta	98	64	.605	Cox	Atlanta
1993	Philadelphia	97	65	.599	Leyland	Atlanta	104	58	.642	Cox	Philadelphia

Year	Division	Winner	W	L	Pct	Manager	Playoffs	Pennant winner
1994(d)	East	Montréal	74	40	.649	Alou	—	—
	Central	Cincinnati	66	48	.579	Johnson		
	West	Los Angeles	58	56	.509	Lasorda		
1995	East	Atlanta	90	54	.625	Cox	Atlanta 3, Colorado* 1	Atlanta
	Central	Cincinnati	85	59	.590	Johnson	Cincinnati 3, Los Angeles 0	
	West	Los Angeles	78	66	.542	Lasorda	Atlanta 4, Cincinnati 0	
1996	East	Atlanta	96	66	.593	Cox	Atlanta 3, Los Angeles* 0	Atlanta
	Central	St. Louis	88	74	.543	La Russa	St. Louis 3, San Diego 0	
	West	San Diego	91	71	.562	Bochy	Atlanta 4, St. Louis 3	
1997	East	Atlanta	101	61	.623	Cox	Atlanta 3, Houston 0	Florida*(e)
	Central	Houston	84	78	.519	Dierker	Florida* 3, San Francisco 0	
	West	San Francisco	90	72	.556	Baker	Florida* 4, Atlanta 2	
1998	East	Atlanta	106	56	.654	Cox	Atlanta 3, Chicago* 0	San Diego
	Central	Houston	102	60	.630	Dierker	San Diego 3, Houston 1	
	West	San Diego	98	64	.605	Bochy	San Diego 4, Atlanta 2	
1999	East	Atlanta	103	59	.636	Cox	Atlanta 3, Houston 1	Atlanta
	Central	Houston	97	65	.599	Dierker	New York* 3, Arizona 1	
	West	Arizona	100	62	.617	Showalter	Atlanta 4, New York* 2	
2000	East	Atlanta	95	67	.586	Cox	St. Louis 3, Atlanta 0	New York*(f)
	Central	St. Louis	95	67	.586	La Russa	New York* 3, San Francisco 1	
	West	San Francisco	97	65	.599	Baker	New York* 4, St. Louis 1	
2001	East	Atlanta	88	74	.543	Cox	Atlanta 3, Houston 0	Arizona
	Central	Houston	93	69	.574	Dierker	Arizona 3, St. Louis* 2	
	West	Arizona	92	70	.568	Brenly	Arizona 4, Atlanta 1	
2002	East	Atlanta	101	59	.631	Cox	St. Louis 3, Arizona 0	San Francisco*(g)
	Central	St. Louis	97	65	.599	La Russa	San Francisco* 3, Atlanta 2	
	West	Arizona	98	64	.605	Brenly	San Francisco* 4, St. Louis 1	
2003	East	Atlanta	101	61	.623	Cox	Chicago 3, Atlanta 2	Florida*(i)
	Central	Chicago	88	74	.543	Baker	Florida* 3, San Francisco 1	
	West	San Francisco	100	61	.621	Alou	Florida* 4, Chicago 3	
2004	East	Atlanta	96	66	.593	Cox	Houston* 3, Atlanta 2	St. Louis
	Central	St. Louis	105	57	.648	La Russa	St. Louis 3, Dodgers 1	
	West	Los Angeles	93	69	.594	Tracy	St. Louis 4, Houston* 3	
2005	East	Atlanta	90	72	.556	Cox	St. Louis 3, San Diego 0	Houston*(j)
	Central	St. Louis	100	62	.617	La Russa	Houston* 3, St. Louis 2	
	West	San Diego	82	80	.506	Bochy	Houston* 4, St. Louis 2	
2006	East	New York	97	65	.599	Randolph	New York 3, Los Angeles* 0	St. Louis
	Central	St. Louis	83	78	.516	La Russa	St. Louis 3, San Diego 1	
	West	San Diego	88	74	.543	Bochy	St. Louis 4, New York 3	
2007	East	Philadelphia	89	73	.549	Manuel	Colorado* 3, Philadelphia 0	Colorado*(m)
	Central	Chicago	85	77	.525	Piniella	Arizona 3, Chicago 0	
	West	Arizona	90	72	.556	Melvin	Colorado* 4, Arizona 0	
2008	East	Philadelphia	92	70	.568	Manuel	Philadelphia 3, Milwaukee* 1	Philadelphia
	Central	Chicago	97	64	.602	Piniella	Los Angeles 3, Chicago 0	
	West	Los Angeles	84	78	.519	Torre	Philadelphia 4, Los Angeles 1	
2009	East	Philadelphia	93	69	.574	Manuel	Philadelphia 3, Colorado* 1	Philadelphia
	Central	St. Louis	91	71	.562	La Russa	Los Angeles 3, St. Louis 0	
	West	Los Angeles	95	67	.586	Torre	Philadelphia 4, Los Angeles 1	
2010	East	Philadelphia	97	65	.599	Manuel	San Francisco 3, Atlanta* 1	San Francisco
	Central	Cincinnati	91	71	.562	Baker	Philadelphia 3, Cincinnati 0	
	West	San Francisco	92	70	.568	Bochy	San Francisco 4, Philadelphia 2	
2011	East	Philadelphia	102	60	.630	Manuel	Milwaukee 3, Arizona 2	St. Louis*(n)
	Central	Milwaukee	96	66	.593	Roenicke	St. Louis* 3, Philadelphia 2	
	West	Arizona	94	68	.580	Gibson	St. Louis* 4, Milwaukee 2	

American League

Year	East Winner	W	L	Pct	Manager	West Winner	W	L	Pct	Manager	Pennant winner
1976	New York	97	62	.610	Martin	Kansas City	90	72	.556	Herzog	New York
1977	New York	100	62	.617	Martin	Kansas City	102	60	.630	Herzog	New York
1978	New York	100	63	.613	Martin, Lemon	Kansas City	92	70	.568	Herzog	New York
1979	Baltimore	102	57	.642	Weaver	California	88	74	.543	Fregosi	Baltimore
1980	New York	103	59	.636	Howser	Kansas City	97	65	.599	Frey	Kansas City
1981(a)	New York	34	22	.607	Michael	Oakland	37	23	.617	Martin	(c)
1981(b)	Milwaukee	31	22	.585	Rodgers	Kansas City	30	23	.566	Frey, Howser	New York
1982	Milwaukee	95	67	.586	Rodgers, Kuenn	California	93	69	.574	Mauch	Milwaukee
1983	Baltimore	98	64	.605	Altobelli	Chicago	99	63	.611	La Russa	Baltimore
1984	Detroit	104	58	.642	Anderson	Kansas City	84	78	.519	Howser	Detroit
1985	Toronto	99	62	.615	Cox	Kansas City	91	71	.562	Howser	Kansas City
1986	Boston	95	66	.590	McNamara	California	92	70	.568	Mauch	Boston
1987	Detroit	98	64	.605	Anderson	Minnesota	85	77	.525	Kelly	Minnesota
1988	Boston	89	73	.549	McNamara, Morgan	Oakland	104	58	.642	La Russa	Oakland
1989	Toronto	89	73	.549	Williams, Gaston	Oakland	99	63	.611	La Russa	Oakland
1990	Boston	88	74	.543	Morgan	Oakland	103	59	.636	La Russa	Oakland
1991	Toronto	91	71	.562	Gaston	Minnesota	95	67	.586	Kelly	Minnesota
1992	Toronto	96	66	.593	Gaston	Oakland	96	66	.593	La Russa	Toronto
1993	Toronto	95	67	.586	Gaston	Chicago	94	68	.580	Lamont	Toronto

Year	Division	Winner	W	L	Pct	Manager	Playoffs	Pennant winner
1994(d)	East	New York	70	43	.619	Showalter	—	—
	Central	Chicago	67	46	.593	Lamont		
	West	Texas	52	62	.456	Kennedy		
1995	East	Boston	86	58	.597	Kennedy	Cleveland 3, Boston 0	Cleveland
	Central	Cleveland	100	44	.694	Hargrove	Seattle 3, New York* 2	
	West	Seattle	79	66	.545	Piniella	Cleveland 4, Seattle 2	
1996	East	New York	92	70	.568	Torre	Baltimore* 3, Cleveland 1	New York
	Central	Cleveland	99	62	.615	Hargrove	New York 3, Texas 1	
	West	Texas	90	72	.556	Oates	New York 4, Baltimore* 1	
1997	East	Baltimore	98	64	.605	Johnson	Baltimore 3, Seattle 1	Cleveland
	Central	Cleveland	86	75	.534	Hargrove	Cleveland 3, New York* 2	
	West	Seattle	90	72	.556	Piniella	Cleveland 4, Baltimore 2	
1998	East	New York	114	48	.704	Torre	New York 3, Texas 0	New York
	Central	Cleveland	89	73	.549	Hargrove	Cleveland 3, Boston* 1	
	West	Texas	88	74	.543	Oates	New York 4, Cleveland 2	
1999	East	New York	98	64	.605	Torre	New York 3, Texas 0	New York
		Cleveland	97	65	.599	Hargrove	Boston* 3, Cleveland 2	
	West	Texas	95	67	.586	Oates	New York 4, Boston* 1	
2000	East	New York	87	74	.540	Torre	New York 3, Oakland 2	New York
	Central	Chicago	95	67	.586	Manuel	Seattle* 3, Chicago 0	
	West	Oakland	91	70	.565	Howe	New York 4, Seattle* 2	
2001	East	New York	95	65	.594	Torre	Seattle 3, Cleveland 2	New York
	Central	Cleveland	91	71	.562	Manuel	New York 3, Oakland* 2	
	West	Seattle	116	46	.716	Piniella	New York 4, Seattle 1	
2002	East	New York	103	58	.640	Torre	Anaheim* 3, New York 1	Anaheim*(h)
	Central	Minnesota	94	67	.584	Gardenhire	Minnesota 3, Oakland 2	
	West	Oakland	103	59	.636	Howe	Anaheim* 4, Minnesota 1	
2003	East	New York	101	61	.623	Torre	New York 3, Minnesota 1	New York
	Central	Minnesota	90	72	.556	Gardenhire	Boston* 3, Oakland 2	
	West	Oakland	96	66	.593	Macha	New York 4, Boston* 3	
2004	East	New York	101	61	.623	Torre	New York 3, Minnesota 1	Boston*(k)
	Central	Minnesota	92	70	.568	Gardenhire	Boston* 3, Anaheim 0	
	West	Anaheim	92	70	.568	Scioscia	Boston* 4, New York 3	
2005	East	New York	95	67	.586	Torre	Chicago 3, Boston* 0	Chicago
	Central	Chicago	99	63	.611	Guillen	Los Angeles 3, New York 2	
	West	Los Angeles	95	67	.586	Scioscia	Chicago 4, Los Angeles 1	
2006	East	New York	97	65	.599	Torre	Oakland 3, Minnesota 0	Detroit*(l)
	Central	Minnesota	96	66	.593	Gardenhire	Detroit* 3, New York 1	
	West	Oakland	93	69	.574	Macha	Detroit* 4, Oakland 0	
2007	East	Boston	96	66	.593	Francona	Boston 3, Los Angeles 0	Boston
	Central	Cleveland	96	66	.593	Wedge	Cleveland 3, New York* 1	
	West	Los Angeles	94	68	.580	Scioscia	Boston 4, Cleveland 3	
2008	East	Tampa Bay	97	65	.599	Maddon	Tampa Bay 3, Chicago 1	Tampa Bay
	Central	Chicago	89	74	.546	Guillen	Boston* 3, Los Angeles 1	
	West	Los Angeles	100	62	.617	Scioscia	Tampa Bay 4, Boston* 3	
2009	East	New York	103	59	.636	Girardi	New York 3, Minnesota 0	New York
	Central	Minnesota	87	76	.534	Gardenhire	Los Angeles 3, Boston* 0	
	West	Los Angeles	97	65	.599	Scioscia	New York 4, Los Angeles 2	
2010	East	Tampa Bay	96	66	.593	Maddon	New York* 3, Minnesota 0	Texas
	Central	Minnesota	94	68	.580	Gardenhire	Texas 3, Tampa Bay 2	
	West	Texas	90	72	.556	Washington	Texas 4, New York* 2	
2011	East	New York	97	65	.599	Girardi	Detroit 3, New York 2	Texas
	Central	Detroit	95	67	.586	Leyland	Texas 3, Tampa Bay* 1	
	West	Texas	96	66	.593	Washington	Texas 4, Detroit 2	

*Wild card team. (a) First half. (b) Second half. (c) Montréal, L.A., NY Yankees, and Oakland won the divisional playoffs. (d) In Aug. 1994, a players' strike began that caused the cancellation of the remainder of the season, the playoffs, and the World Series. Teams listed as division "winners" for 1994 were leading their divisions at the time of the strike. (e) Florida manager: Jim Leyland. (f) New York manager: Bobby Valentine. (g) San Francisco manager: Dusty Baker. (h) Anaheim manager: Mike Scioscia. (i) Florida manager: Jack McKeon. (j) Houston manager: Phil Garner. (k) Boston manager: Terry Francona. (l) Detroit manager: Jim Leyland. (m) Colorado manager: Clint Hurdle. (n) St. Louis manager: Tony La Russa.

Rawlings Gold Glove Awards, 2010 and All-Time Leaders

National League

Bronson Arroyo, Cincinnati, P
Yadier Molina, St. Louis, C
Albert Pujols, St. Louis, 1B
Brandon Phillips, Cincinnati, 2B
Scott Rolen, Cincinnati, 3B

Troy Tulowitzki, Colorado, SS
Michael Bourn, Houston, OF
Carlos Gonzalez, Colorado, OF
Shane Victorino, Philadelphia, OF

American League

Mark Buehrle, Chicago, P
Joe Mauer, Minnesota, C
Mark Teixeira, NY, 1B
Robinson Cano, NY, 2B

Evan Longoria, Tampa Bay, 3B
Derek Jeter, NY, SS
Carl Crawford, Tampa Bay, OF
Franklin Gutierrez, Seattle, OF
Ichiro Suzuki, Seattle, OF

The following are the players at each position who have won the most Gold Gloves since the award was instituted in 1957.

Pitcher:
Greg Maddux 18
Jim Kaat 16

Catcher:
Ivan Rodriguez 13
Johnny Bench 10

First base:
Keith Hernandez 11
Don Mattingly 9

Second base:
Roberto Alomar 10
Ryne Sandberg 9
Bill Mazeroski 8
Frank White 8

Third base:
Brooks Robinson 16
Mike Schmidt 10

Shortstop:
Ozzie Smith 13
Omar Vizquel 11

Outfield:
Roberto Clemente . . . 12
Willie Mays 12
Al Kaline 10
Ken Griffey Jr. 10
Andruw Jones 10
Ichiro Suzuki 10

World Series Results, 1903-2011

1903 Boston AL 5, Pittsburgh NL 3	1940 Cincinnati NL 4, Detroit AL 3	1976 Cincinnati NL 4, New York AL 0
1904 No series	1941 New York AL 4, Brooklyn NL 1	1977 New York AL 4, Los Angeles NL 2
1905 New York NL 4, Philadelphia AL 1	1942 St. Louis NL 4, New York AL 1	1978 New York AL 4, Los Angeles NL 2
1906 Chicago AL 4, Chicago NL 2	1943 New York AL 4, St. Louis NL 1	1979 Pittsburgh NL 4, Baltimore AL 3
1907 Chicago NL 4, Detroit AL 0, 1 tie	1944 St. Louis NL 4, St. Louis AL 2	1980 Philadelphia NL 4, Kansas City AL 2
1908 Chicago NL 4, Detroit AL 1	1945 Detroit AL 4, Chicago NL 3	1981 Los Angeles NL 4, New York AL 2
1909 Pittsburgh NL 4, Detroit AL 3	1946 St. Louis NL 4, Boston AL 3	1982 St. Louis NL 4, Milwaukee AL 3
1910 Philadelphia AL 4, Chicago NL 1	1947 New York AL 4, Brooklyn NL 3	1983 Baltimore AL 4, Philadelphia NL 1
1911 Philadelphia AL 4, New York NL 2	1948 Cleveland AL 4, Boston NL 2	1984 Detroit AL 4, San Diego NL 1
1912 Boston AL 4, New York NL 3, 1 tie	1949 New York AL 4, Brooklyn NL 1	1985 Kansas City AL 4, St. Louis NL 3
1913 Philadelphia AL 4, New York NL 1	1950 New York AL 4, Philadelphia NL 0	1986 New York NL 4, Boston AL 3
1914 Boston NL 4, Philadelphia AL 0	1951 New York AL 4, New York NL 2	1987 Minnesota AL 4, St. Louis NL 3
1915 Boston AL 4, Philadelphia NL 1	1952 New York AL 4, Brooklyn NL 3	1988 Los Angeles NL 4, Oakland AL 1
1916 Boston AL 4, Brooklyn NL 1	1953 New York AL 4, Brooklyn NL 2	1989 Oakland AL 4, San Francisco NL 0
1917 Chicago AL 4, New York NL 2	1954 New York NL 4, Cleveland AL 0	1990 Cincinnati NL 4, Oakland AL 0
1918 Boston AL 4, Chicago NL 2	1955 Brooklyn NL 4, New York AL 3	1991 Minnesota AL 4, Atlanta NL 3
1919 Cincinnati NL 5, Chicago AL 3	1956 New York AL 4, Brooklyn NL 3	1992 Toronto AL 4, Atlanta NL 2
1920 Cleveland AL 5, Brooklyn NL 2	1957 Milwaukee NL 4, New York AL 3	1993 Toronto AL 4, Philadelphia NL 2
1921 New York NL 5, New York AL 3	1958 New York AL 4, Milwaukee NL 3	1994 No series
1922 New York NL 4, New York AL 0, 1 tie	1959 Los Angeles NL 4, Chicago AL 2	1995 Atlanta NL 4, Cleveland AL 2
1923 New York AL 4, New York NL 2	1960 Pittsburgh NL 4, New York AL 3	1996 New York AL 4, Atlanta NL 2
1924 Washington AL 4, New York NL 3	1961 New York AL 4, Cincinnati NL 1	1997 Florida NL 4, Cleveland AL 3
1925 Pittsburgh NL 4, Washington AL 3	1962 New York AL 4, San Francisco NL 3	1998 New York AL 4, San Diego NL 0
1926 St. Louis NL 4, New York AL 3	1963 Los Angeles NL 4, New York AL 0	1999 New York AL 4, Atlanta NL 0
1927 New York AL 4, Pittsburgh NL 0	1964 St. Louis NL 4, New York AL 3	2000 New York AL 4, New York NL 1
1928 New York AL 4, St. Louis NL 0	1965 Los Angeles NL 4, Minnesota AL 3	2001 Arizona NL 4, New York AL 3
1929 Philadelphia AL 4, Chicago NL 1	1966 Baltimore AL 4, Los Angeles NL 0	2002 Anaheim AL 4, San Francisco NL 3
1930 Philadelphia AL 4, St. Louis NL 2	1967 St. Louis NL 4, Boston AL 3	2003 Florida NL 4, New York AL 2
1931 St. Louis NL 4, Philadelphia AL 3	1968 Detroit AL 4, St. Louis NL 3	2004 Boston AL 4, St. Louis NL 0
1932 New York AL 4, Chicago NL 0	1969 New York NL 4, Baltimore AL 1	2005 Chicago AL 4, Houston NL 0
1933 New York NL 4, Washington AL 1	1970 Baltimore AL 4, Cincinnati NL 1	2006 St. Louis NL 4, Detroit AL 1
1934 St. Louis NL 4, Detroit AL 3	1971 Pittsburgh NL 4, Baltimore AL 3	2007 Boston AL 4, Colorado NL 0
1935 Detroit AL 4, Chicago NL 2	1972 Oakland AL 4, Cincinnati NL 3	2008 Philadelphia NL 4, Tampa Bay AL 1
1936 New York AL 4, New York NL 2	1973 Oakland AL 4, New York NL 3	2009 New York AL 4, Philadelphia NL 2
1937 New York AL 4, New York NL 1	1974 Oakland AL 4, Los Angeles NL 1	2010 San Francisco NL 4, Texas AL 1
1938 New York AL 4, Chicago NL 0	1975 Cincinnati NL 4, Boston AL 3	2011 St. Louis NL 4, Texas AL 3
1939 New York AL 4, Cincinnati NL 0		

World Series Most Valuable Player, 1955-2011

Year	Player, position, team	Year	Player, position, team	Year	Player, position, team
1955	Johnny Podres, P, Brooklyn	1975	Pete Rose, 3B, Cincinnati	1993	Paul Molitor, DH, Toronto
1956	Don Larsen, P, NY (AL)	1976	Johnny Bench, C, Cincinnati	1994	No series
1957	Lew Burdette, P, Milwaukee (NL)	1977	Reggie Jackson, OF, NY (AL)	1995	Tom Glavine, P, Atlanta
1958	Bob Turley, P, NY (AL)	1978	Bucky Dent, SS, NY (AL)	1996	John Wetteland, P, NY (AL)
1959	Larry Sherry, P, Los Angeles (NL)	1979	Willie Stargell, 1B, Pittsburgh	1997	Livan Hernandez, P, Florida
1960[1]	Bobby Richardson, 2B, NY (AL)	1980	Mike Schmidt, 3B, Philadelphia	1998	Scott Brosius, 3B, NY (AL)
1961	Whitey Ford, P, NY (AL)	1981	Ron Cey, 3B, Los Angeles;	1999	Mariano Rivera, P, NY (AL)
1962	Ralph Terry, P, NY (AL)		Pedro Guerrero, OF, Los Angeles;	2000	Derek Jeter, SS, NY (AL)
1963	Sandy Koufax, P, Los Angeles (NL)		Steve Yeager, C, Los Angeles	2001	Curt Schilling, P, Arizona;
1964	Bob Gibson, P, St. Louis	1982	Darrell Porter, C, St. Louis		Randy Johnson, P, Arizona
1965	Sandy Koufax, P, Los Angeles (NL)	1983	Rick Dempsey, C, Baltimore	2002	Troy Glaus, 3B, Anaheim
1966	Frank Robinson, OF, Baltimore	1984	Alan Trammell, SS, Detroit	2003	Josh Beckett, P, Florida
1967	Bob Gibson, P, St. Louis	1985	Bret Saberhagen, P, Kansas City	2004	Manny Ramirez, OF, Boston
1968	Mickey Lolich, P, Detroit	1986	Ray Knight, 3B, NY (NL)	2005	Jermaine Dye, OF, Chicago (AL)
1969	Donn Clendenon, 1B, NY (NL)	1987	Frank Viola, P, Minnesota	2006	David Eckstein, SS, St. Louis
1970	Brooks Robinson, 3B, Baltimore	1988	Orel Hershiser, P, Los Angeles	2007	Mike Lowell, 3B, Boston
1971	Roberto Clemente, OF, Pittsburgh	1989	Dave Stewart, P, Oakland	2008	Cole Hamels, P, Philadelphia
1972	Gene Tenace, C, Oakland	1990	Jose Rijo, P, Cincinnati	2009	Hideki Matsui, DH, NY (AL)
1973	Reggie Jackson, OF, Oakland	1991	Jack Morris, P, Minnesota	2010	Edgar Renteria, SS, San Francisco
1974	Rollie Fingers, P, Oakland	1992	Pat Borders, C, Toronto	2011	David Freese, 3B, St. Louis

(1) Richardson won the MVP although Pittsburgh beat New York.

World Series Won-Lost Records, by Franchise

Since beginning of "modern" era in 1901. Figures represent overall Series wins, not individual games.

Team	Wins	Losses	Team	Wins	Losses
New York Yankees	27	13	Toronto Blue Jays	2	0
St. Louis Cardinals	11	7	New York Mets	2	2
Philadelphia/Kansas City/Oakland A's	9	5	Cleveland Indians	2	3
Boston Red Sox	7	4	Philadelphia Phillies	2	5
Brooklyn/Los Angeles Dodgers	6	12	Chicago Cubs	2	8
New York/San Francisco Giants	6	12	L.A./California/Anaheim/L.A. Angels	1	0
Pittsburgh Pirates	5	2	Arizona Diamondbacks	1	0
Cincinnati Reds	5	4	Kansas City Royals	1	1
Detroit Tigers	4	6	Houston Astros	0	1
Chicago White Sox	3	2	Seattle Pilots/Milwaukee Brewers	0	1
Washington Senators/Minnesota Twins	3	3	Tampa Bay Rays	0	1
St. Louis Browns/Baltimore Orioles	3	4	Colorado Rockies	0	1
Boston/Milwaukee/Atlanta Braves	3	6	San Diego Padres	0	2
Florida Marlins	2	0	Texas Rangers	0	2

All-Time World Series Career Leaders

(through 2011)

Batting Leaders

Batter (min. 50 PA)	Hits	AB	AVG	Batter (min. 50 PA)	Hits	AB	AVG
1. Johnny "Pepper" Martin	23	55	.418	6. Marquis Grissom	30	77	.390
2. Paul Molitor	23	55	.418	7. Thurman Munson	25	67	.373
3. Lance Berkman	16	39	.410	8. George Brett	19	51	.373
4. Hal McRae	18	45	.400	9. Hank Aaron	20	55	.364
5. Lou Brock	34	87	.391	10. Frank "Home Run" Baker	33	91	.363

Games Played

Yogi Berra	75
Mickey Mantle	65
Elston Howard	54
Hank Bauer	53
Gil McDougald	53
Phil Rizzuto	52
Joe DiMaggio	51
Frankie Frisch	50
Pee Wee Reese	44
Roger Maris	41
Babe Ruth	41

Runs Batted In

Mickey Mantle	40
Yogi Berra	39
Lou Gehrig	35
Babe Ruth	33
Joe DiMaggio	30
Bill Skowron	29
Duke Snider	26
Hank Bauer	24
Bill Dickey	24
Reggie Jackson	24
Gil McDougald	24

Hits

Yogi Berra	71
Mickey Mantle	59
Frankie Frisch	58
Joe DiMaggio	54
Derek Jeter	50
Hank Bauer	46
Pee Wee Reese	46
Gil McDougald	45
Phil Rizzuto	45
Lou Gehrig	43

Home Runs

Mickey Mantle	18
Babe Ruth	15
Yogi Berra	12
Duke Snider	11
Lou Gehrig	10
Reggie Jackson	10
Joe DiMaggio	8
Frank Robinson	8
Bill Skowron	8
Hank Bauer	7
Goose Goslin	7
Gil McDougald	7
Chase Utley	7

Runs

Mickey Mantle	42
Yogi Berra	41
Babe Ruth	37
Derek Jeter	32
Lou Gehrig	30
Joe DiMaggio	27
Roger Maris	26
Elston Howard	25
Gil McDougald	23
Jackie Robinson	22

Stolen Bases

Lou Brock	14
Eddie Collins	14
Frank Chance	10
Dave Lopes	10
Phil Rizzuto	10
Frankie Frisch	9
Kenny Lofton	9
Honus Wagner	9
Johnny Evers	8
Roberto Alomar	7
Rickey Henderson	7
Pepper Martin	7
Joe Morgan	7
Joe Tinker	7

Pitching Leaders

Games Pitched

Mariano Rivera	24
Whitey Ford	22
Mike Stanton	20
Rollie Fingers	16
Jeff Nelson	16
Allie Reynolds	15
Bob Turley	15
Clay Carroll	14
Clem Labine	13
Andy Pettitte	13
Mark Wohlers	13
Waite Hoyt	12
Catfish Hunter	12
Art Nehf	12

Wins

Whitey Ford	10
Bob Gibson	7
Allie Reynolds	7
Red Ruffing	7
Chief Bender	6
Lefty Gomez	6
Waite Hoyt	6
Three Finger Brown	5
Jack Coombs	5
Catfish Hunter	5
Christy Mathewson	5
Herb Pennock	5
Andy Pettitte	5
Vic Raschi	5

Strikeouts

Whitey Ford	94
Bob Gibson	92
Allie Reynolds	62
Sandy Koufax	61
Red Ruffing	61
Chief Bender	59
George Earnshaw	56
Andy Pettitte	56
John Smoltz	52
Roger Clemens	49
Waite Hoyt	49
Christy Mathewson	48
Bob Turley	46

Saves

Mariano Rivera	11
Rollie Fingers	6
Johnny Murphy	4
Robb Nen	4
Allie Reynolds	4
John Wetteland	4
Roy Face	3
Neftali Feliz	3
Firpo Marberry	3
Will McEnaney	3
Tug McGraw	3
Jonathan Papelbon	3
Herb Pennock	3
Troy Percival	3
Kent Tekulve	3
Todd Worrell	3

All-Star Baseball Games, 1933-2011

Year	Winner, score	Host team	Year	Winner, score	Host team	Year	Winner, score	Host team
1933*	American, 4-2	Chicago (AL)	1960*	National, 5-3	Kansas City	1985	National, 6-1	Minnesota
1934*	American, 9-7	New York (NL)	1960*	National, 6-0	New York (AL)	1986	American, 3-2	Houston
1935*	American, 4-1	Cleveland	1961*	National, 5-4[3]	San Francisco	1987	National, 2-0[5]	Oakland
1936*	National, 4-3	Boston (NL)	1961*	Called–rain, 1-1	Boston	1988	American, 2-1	Cincinnati
1937*	American, 8-3	Washington	1962*	National, 3-1[3]	Washington	1989	American, 5-3	California
1938*	National, 4-1	Cincinnati	1962*	American, 9-4	Chicago (NL)	1990	American, 2-0	Chicago (NL)
1939*	American, 3-1	New York (AL)	1963*	National, 5-3	Cleveland	1991	American, 4-2	Toronto
1940*	National, 4-0	St. Louis (NL)	1964*	National, 7-4	New York (NL)	1992	American, 13-6	San Diego
1941*	American, 7-5	Detroit	1965*	National, 6-5	Minnesota	1993	American, 9-3	Baltimore
1942	American, 3-1	New York (NL)	1966*	National, 2-1[3]	St. Louis	1994	National, 8-7[3]	Pittsburgh
1943	American, 5-3	Philadelphia (AL)	1967*	National, 2-1[4]	California	1995	National, 3-2	Texas
1944	National, 7-1	Pittsburgh	1968	National, 1-0	Houston	1996	National, 6-0	Philadelphia
1945	Not played		1969*	National, 9-3	Washington	1997	American, 3-1	Cleveland
1946*	American, 12-0	Boston (AL)	1970	National, 5-4[2]	Cincinnati	1998	American, 13-8	Colorado
1947*	American, 2-1	Chicago (NL)	1971	American, 6-4	Detroit	1999	American, 4-1	Boston
1948*	American, 5-2	St. Louis (AL)	1972	National, 4-3[3]	Atlanta	2000	American, 6-3	Atlanta
1949*	American, 11-7	Brooklyn	1973	National, 7-1	Kansas City	2001	American, 4-1	Seattle
1950*	National, 4-3[1]	Chicago (AL)	1974	National, 7-2	Pittsburgh	2002	Tie, 7-7[6]	Milwaukee
1951*	National, 8-3	Detroit	1975	National, 6-3	Milwaukee	2003	American, 7-6[7]	Chicago (AL)
1952*	National, 3-2	Philadelphia (NL)	1976	National, 7-1	Philadelphia	2004	American, 9-4	Houston
1953*	National, 5-1	Cincinnati	1977	National, 7-5	New York (AL)	2005	American, 7-5	Detroit
1954*	American, 11-9	Cleveland	1978	National, 7-3	San Diego	2006	American, 3-2	Pittsburgh
1955*	National, 6-5[2]	Milwaukee	1979	National, 7-6	Seattle	2007	American, 5-4	San Francisco
1956*	National, 7-3	Washington	1980	National, 4-2	Los Angeles (NL)	2008	American, 4-3[4]	New York (AL)
1957*	American, 6-5	St. Louis	1981	National, 5-4	Cleveland	2009	American, 4-3	St. Louis
1958*	American, 4-3	Baltimore	1982	National, 4-1	Montréal	2010	National, 3-1	Los Angeles (AL)
1959*	National, 5-4	Pittsburgh	1983	American, 13-3	Chicago (AL)	2011	National, 5-1	Arizona
1959*	American, 5-3	Los Angeles (AL)	1984	National, 3-1	San Francisco			

*Day game. (1) 14 innings. (2) 12 innings. (3) 10 innings. (4) 15 innings. (5) 13 innings. (6) Commissioner's decision—game called in the 11th inning when both teams ran out of pitchers. (7) Under rule change beginning in 2003, league winning All-Star game earned World Series home-field advantage.

Baseball Stadiums

National League

Team	Stadium (year opened)	Surface	LF	Center	RF	Seating capacity[1]
Arizona Diamondbacks	Chase Field (1998)	Grass	330	407	335	48,633
Atlanta Braves	Turner Field (1997)	Grass	335	400	330	49,586
Chicago Cubs	Wrigley Field (1914)	Grass	355	400	353	41,160
Cincinnati Reds	Great American Ball Park (2003)	Grass	328	404	325	42,319
Colorado Rockies	Coors Field (1995)	Grass	347	415	350	50,490
Florida Marlins	Sun Life Stadium (1987)	Grass	330	434	345	38,560
Houston Astros	Minute Maid Park (2000)	Grass	315	435	326	40,963
Los Angeles Dodgers	Dodger Stadium (1962)	Grass	330	395	330	56,000
Milwaukee Brewers	Miller Park (2001)	Grass	344	400	345	41,900
New York Mets	Citi Field (2009)	Grass	335	408	330	41,800
Philadelphia Phillies	Citizens Bank Park (2004)	Grass	330	401	329	43,651
Pittsburgh Pirates	PNC Park at North Shore (2001)	Grass	325	399	320	38,362
St. Louis Cardinals	Busch Stadium (2006)	Grass	336	400	335	43,975
San Diego Padres	PETCO Park (2004)	Grass	336	396	322	42,691
San Francisco Giants	AT&T Park (2000)	Grass	339	399	309	41,915
Washington Nationals	Nationals Park (2008)	Grass	336	404	335	41,525

American League

Team	Stadium (year opened)	Surface	LF	Center	RF	Seating capacity[1]
Baltimore Orioles	Oriole Park at Camden Yards (1992)	Grass	333	400	318	45,971
Boston Red Sox	Fenway Park (1912)	Grass	310	420	302	37,065[2]
Chicago White Sox	U.S. Cellular Field (1991)	Grass	330	400	335	40,615
Cleveland Indians	Progressive Field (1994)	Grass	325	405	325	43,441
Detroit Tigers	Comerica Park (2000)	Grass	345	420	330	41,255
Kansas City Royals	Kauffman Stadium (1973)	Grass	330	410	330	37,903
Los Angeles Angels	Angel Stadium of Anaheim (1966)	Grass	333	404	333	45,389
Minnesota Twins	Target Field (2010)	Grass	339	404	328	39,500
New York Yankees	Yankee Stadium (2009)	Grass	318	408	314	50,329
Oakland Athletics	O.co Coliseum (1968)	Grass	330	400	330	35,067
Seattle Mariners	Safeco Field (1999)	Grass	331	405	326	47,447
Tampa Bay Rays	Tropicana Field (1990)	Astroturf	315	404	322	34,078
Texas Rangers	Rangers Ballpark in Arlington (1994)	Grass	332	400	325	49,170
Toronto Blue Jays	Rogers Centre (1989)	Turf	328	400	328	49,260

(1) As of 2011 season. (2) For daytime games; night game capacity is 37,493.

Major League Franchise Shifts and Additions

1953: Boston Braves (NL) became Milwaukee Braves.
1954: St. Louis Browns (AL) became Baltimore Orioles.
1955: Philadelphia Athletics (AL) became Kansas City Athletics.
1958: New York Giants (NL) became San Francisco Giants.
1958: Brooklyn Dodgers (NL) became L.A. Dodgers.
1961: Washington Senators (AL) became Minnesota Twins.
1961: L.A. Angels (renamed California Angels in 1965 and Anaheim Angels in 1997) enfranchised by the American League.
1961: Washington Senators enfranchised by the American League (a new team, replacing the former Washington club, whose franchise was moved to Minneapolis-St. Paul).
1962: Houston Colt .45's (renamed the Houston Astros in 1965) enfranchised by the National League.
1962: New York Mets enfranchised by the National League.
1966: Milwaukee Braves (NL) became Atlanta Braves.
1968: Kansas City Athletics (AL) became Oakland Athletics.

1969: Kansas City Royals and Seattle Pilots enfranchised by the American League; Montréal Expos and San Diego Padres enfranchised by the National League.
1970: Seattle Pilots (AL) became Milwaukee Brewers.
1971: Washington Senators (AL) became Texas Rangers (Dallas-Fort Worth area).
1977: Toronto Blue Jays and Seattle Mariners enfranchised by the American League.
1993: Colorado Rockies (Denver) and Florida Marlins (Miami) enfranchised by the National League.
1998: Tampa Bay Devil Rays (renamed Tampa Bay Rays in 2007) began play in the American League; Arizona Diamondbacks (Phoenix) began play in the National League (both teams enfranchised in 1995). Milwaukee Brewers moved from the AL to the NL.
2005: Montréal Expos (NL) became Washington Nationals; Anaheim Angels became Los Angeles Angels of Anaheim.

Little League World Series, 1947-2011

The Little League World Series is played annually in Williamsport, PA.

Year	Winning team; opponent	Score	Year	Winning team; opponent	Score
1947	Williamsport, PA; Lock Haven, PA	16-7	1980	Taiwan; Tampa, FL	4-3
1948	Lock Haven, PA; St. Petersburg, FL	6-5	1981	Taiwan; Tampa, FL	4-2
1949	Hammonton, NJ; Pensacola, FL	5-0	1982	Kirkland, WA; Taiwan	6-0
1950	Houston, TX; Bridgeport, CT	2-1	1983	Marietta, GA; Dominican Republic	3-1
1951	Stamford, CT; Austin, TX	3-0	1984	South Korea; Altamonte Springs, FL	6-2
1952	Norwalk, CT; Monongahela, PA	4-3	1985	South Korea; Mexico	7-1
1953	Birmingham, AL; Schenectady, NY	1-0	1986	Taiwan; Tucson, AZ	12-0
1954	Schenectady, NY; Colton, CA	7-5	1987	Taiwan; Irvine, CA	21-1
1955	Morrisville, PA; Merchantville, NJ	4-3	1988	Taiwan; Pearl City, HI	10-0
1956	Roswell, NM; Delaware, NJ	3-1	1989	Trumbull, CT; Chinese Taipei	5-2
1957	Mexico; La Mesa, CA	4-0	1990	Taiwan; Shippensburg, PA	9-0
1958	Mexico; Kankakee, IL	10-1	1991	Taiwan; Danville, CA	11-0
1959	Hamtramck, MI; Auburn, CA	12-0	1992	Long Beach, CA; Philippines	6-0[1]
1960	Levittown, PA; Ft. Worth, TX	5-0	1993	Long Beach, CA; Panama	3-2
1961	El Cajon, CA; El Campo, TX	4-2	1994	Venezuela; Northridge, CA	4-3
1962	San Jose, CA; Kankakee, IL	3-0	1995	Taiwan; Spring, TX	17-3
1963	Granada Hills, CA; Stratford, CT	2-1	1996	Taiwan; Cranston, RI	13-3
1964	Staten Island, NY; Mexico	4-0	1997	Mexico; Mission Viejo, CA	5-4
1965	Windsor Locks, CT; Ontario, Canada	3-1	1998	Toms River, NJ; Japan	12-9
1966	Houston, TX; W. New York, NJ	8-2	1999	Japan; Phenix City, AL	5-0
1967	Tokyo, Japan; Chicago, IL	4-1	2000	Venezuela; Bellaire, TX	3-2
1968	Osaka, Japan; Richmond, VA	1-0	2001	Japan; Apopka, FL	2-1
1969	Taiwan; Santa Clara, CA	5-0	2002	Louisville, KY; Japan	1-0
1970	Wayne, NJ; Campbell, CA	2-0	2003	Japan; East Boynton Beach, FL	10-1
1971	Taiwan; Gary, IN	12-3	2004	Curaçao; Conejo Valley of Thousand Oaks, CA	5-2
1972	Taiwan; Hammond, IN	6-0	2005	Ewa Beach, HI; Curaçao, Neth. Antilles	7-6
1973	Taiwan; Tucson, AZ	12-0	2006	Columbus, GA; Japan	2-1
1974	Taiwan; Red Bluff, CA	12-1	2007	Macon, GA; Japan	3-2
1975	Lakewood, NJ; Tampa, FL	4-3	2008	Waipahu, HI; Mexico	12-3
1976	Tokyo, Japan; Campbell, CA	10-3	2009	Chula Vista, CA; Taiwan	6-3
1977	Taiwan; El Cajon, CA	7-2	2010	Japan; Waipahu, HI	4-1
1978	Taiwan; Danville, CA	11-1	2011	Huntington Beach, CA; Hamamatsu, Japan	2-1
1979	Taiwan; Campbell, CA	2-1			

(1) Philippines won 15-4, but was disqualified for using ineligible players. Long Beach was awarded title by forfeit 6-0 (1 run per inning).

Manager of the Year, 1983-2010

1983	(NL) Tommy Lasorda, L.A.	1993	(NL) Dusty Baker, San Francisco	2002	(NL) Tony La Russa, St. Louis
	(AL) Tony La Russa, Chicago		(AL) Gene Lamont, Chicago		(AL) Mike Scioscia, Anaheim
1984	(NL) Jim Frey, Chicago	1994	(NL) Felipe Alou, Montréal	2003	(NL) Jack McKeon, Florida
	(AL) Sparky Anderson, Detroit		(AL) Buck Showalter, NY		(AL) Tony Pena, Kansas City
1985	(NL) Whitey Herzog, St. Louis	1995	(NL) Don Baylor, Colorado	2004	(NL) Bobby Cox, Atlanta
	(AL) Bobby Cox, Toronto		(AL) Lou Piniella, Seattle		(AL) Buck Showalter, Texas
1986	(NL) Hal Lanier, Houston	1996	(NL) Bruce Bochy, San Diego	2005	(NL) Bobby Cox, Atlanta
	(AL) John McNamara, Boston		(AL) (tie) Joe Torre, NY;		(AL) Ozzie Guillen, Chicago
1987	(NL) Buck Rodgers, Montréal		Johnny Oates, Texas	2006	(NL) Joe Girardi, Florida
	(AL) Sparky Anderson, Detroit	1997	(NL) Dusty Baker, San Francisco		(AL) Jim Leyland, Detroit
1988	(NL) Tommy Lasorda, L.A.		(AL) Davey Johnson, Baltimore	2007	(NL) Bob Melvin, Arizona
	(AL) Tony La Russa, Oakland	1998	(NL) Larry Dierker, Houston		(AL) Eric Wedge, Cleveland
1989	(NL) Don Zimmer, Chicago		(AL) Joe Torre, NY	2008	(NL) Lou Piniella, Chicago
	(AL) Frank Robinson, Baltimore	1999	(NL) Jack McKeon, Cincinnati		(AL) Joe Maddon, Tampa Bay
1990	(NL) Jim Leyland, Pittsburgh		(AL) Jimy Williams, Boston	2009	(NL) Jim Tracy, Colorado
	(AL) Jeff Torborg, Chicago	2000	(NL) Dusty Baker, San Francisco		(AL) Mike Scioscia, L.A.
1991	(NL) Bobby Cox, Atlanta		(AL) Jerry Manuel, Chicago	2010	(NL) Bud Black, San Diego
	(AL) Tom Kelly, Minnesota	2001	(NL) Larry Bowa, Philadelphia		(AL) Ron Gardenhire, Minnesota
1992	(NL) Jim Leyland, Pittsburgh		(AL) Lou Piniella, Seattle		
	(AL) Tony La Russa, Oakland				

National Baseball Hall of Fame and Museum, Cooperstown, NY

Player must generally be retired for five complete seasons before being eligible for induction. Four players—Babe Ruth (1936), Lou Gehrig (1939), Joe DiMaggio (1955), and Roberto Clemente (1973)—were inducted less than 5 years after retirement or, in Clemente's case, death. # = Players chosen in first year of Hall of Fame eligibility or under special circumstances earlier. * = 2011 inductee.

#Aaron, Hank "The Hammer"	Connor, Roger	Hartnett, Gabby	Mathews, Eddie	Selee, Frank
Alexander, Grover Cleveland "Old Pete"	Cooper, Andy	Harvey, Doug	Mathewson, Christy[1]	Sewell, Joe
	Coveleski, Stan	Heilmann, Harry	#Mays, Willie	Simmons, Al
*Alomar, Roberto	Crawford, Sam	#Henderson, Rickey	Mazeroski, Bill	Sisler, George
Alston, Walt	Cronin, Joe	Herman, Billy	McCarthy, Joe	Slaughter, Enos
Anderson, George "Sparky"	Cummings, W. A. "Candy"	Herzog, Whitey	McCarthy, Thomas	Smith, Hilton
Anson, Cap	Cuyler, Hazen "Kiki"	Hill, Pete	#McCovey, Willie	#Smith, Ozzie
Aparicio, Luis	Dandridge, Ray	Hooper, Harry	McGinnity, Joe	Snider, Duke
Appling, Luke	Davis, George "Gorgeous"	Hornsby, Rogers	McGowan, Bill	Southworth, Billy
Ashburn, Richie	Dawson, Andre	Hoyt, Waite	McGraw, John	#Spahn, Warren
Averill, Earl	Day, Leon	Hubbard, Cal	McKechnie, Bill	Spalding, Albert
Baker, Frank "Home Run"	Dean, Jay Hanna "Dizzy"	Hubbell, Carl	McPhee, John "Bid"	Speaker, Tris
Bancroft, Dave	Delahanty, Ed	Huggins, Miller	Medwick, Joe	#Stargell, Willie
#Banks, Ernie	Dickey, Bill	Hulbert, William	Mendez, Jose	Stearnes, Norman
Barlick, Al	Dihigo, Martín	Hunter, James "Catfish"	Miller, Jon	"Turkey"
Barrow, Edward G.	DiMaggio, Joe	Irvin, Monte	Mize, Johnny	Stengel, Casey
Beckley, Jake	#Doby, Larry	#Jackson, Reggie	#Molitor, Paul	Sutter, Bruce
Bell, James "Cool Papa"	Doerr, Bobby	Jackson, Travis	#Morgan, Joe	Suttles, George "Mule"
#Bench, Johnny	Dreyfuss, Barney	Jenkins, Ferguson	#Murray, Eddie	Sutton, Don
Bender, Charles "Chief"	Drysdale, Don	Jennings, Hugh	#Musial, Stan	Taylor, Ben
Berra, Lawrence "Yogi"	Duffy, Hugh	Johnson, Byron "Ban"	Newhouser, Hal	Terry, Bill
*Blyleven, Bert	Durocher, Leo	Johnson, Walter[1]	Nichols, Bill	Thompson, Sam
#Boggs, Wade	#Eckersley, Dennis	Johnson, William "Judy"	Niekro, Phil	Tinker, Joe
Bottomley, Jim	Evans, Billy	Joss, Addie	O'Malley, Walter	Torriente, Cristobal
Boudreau, Lou	Evers, John	#Kaline, Al	O'Rourke, James	Traynor, Harold J. "Pie"
Bresnahan, Roger	Ewing, Buck	Keefe, Timothy	Ott, Mel	Vance, Arthur "Dazzy"
#Brett, George	Faber, Urban "Red"	Keeler, William	Paige, Satchel	Vaughan, Joseph "Arky"
#Brock, Lou	#Feller, Bob	Kell, George	#Palmer, Jim	Veeck, Bill
Brouthers, Dan	Ferrell, Rick	Kelley, Joe	Pennock, Herb	Waddell, Rube
Brown, Mordecai "Three Finger"	Fingers, Rollie	Kelly, George	Perez, Tony	Wagner, Honus[1]
	Fisk, Carlton	Kelly, King	Perry, Gaylord	Wallace, Roderick
Brown, Ray	Flick, Elmer H.	Killebrew, Harmon	Peters, Nick	"Bobby"
Brown, Willard	Ford, Whitey	Kiner, Ralph	Plank, Ed	Walsh, Ed
Bulkeley, Morgan C.	Foster, Andrew "Rube"	Klein, Chuck	Pompez, Alex	Waner, Lloyd
Bunning, Jim	Foster, Bill	Klem, Bill	Posey, Cum(berland)	Waner, Paul
Burkett, Jesse C.	Fox, Nellie	#Koufax, Sandy	#Puckett, Kirby	Ward, John
Campanella, Roy	Foxx, Jimmie	Kubek, Tony	Radbourn, Charlie	Weaver, Earl
#Carew, Rod	Frick, Ford	Kuhn, Bowie	Reese, Pee Wee	Weiss, George
Carey, Max	Frisch, Frank	Lajoie, Napoleon	Rice, Jim	Welch, Mickey
#Carlton, Steve	Galvin, James "Pud"	Landis, Kenesaw M.	Rice, Sam	Wells, Willie
Carter, Gary	#Gehrig, Lou	Lasorda, Tom	Rickey, Branch	Wheat, Zach
Cartwright, Alexander	Gehringer, Charles	Lazzeri, Tony	#Ripken, Cal, Jr.	White, Sol
Cepeda, Orlando	#Gibson, Bob	Lemon, Bob	Rixey, Eppa	Wilhelm, Hoyt
Chadwick, Henry	Gibson, Josh	Leonard, Buck	Rizzuto, Phil "Scooter"	Wilkinson, J. L.
Chance, Frank	Giles, Warren	Lindstrom, Fred	Roberts, Robin	Williams, Billy
Chandler, Albert "Happy"	*Gillick, Pat	Lloyd, Pop	#Robinson, Brooks	Williams, Dick
Charleston, Oscar	Gomez, Lefty	Lombardi, Ernie	#Robinson, Frank	Williams, Joe "Smokey Joe"
Chesbro, John	Gordon, Joe	Lopez, Al	#Robinson, Jackie	
Chylak, Nestor	Goslin, Leon "Goose"	Lyons, Ted	Robinson, Wilbert	#Williams, Ted
Clarke, Fred	Gossage, Rich	Mack, Connie	Rogan, Joe "Bullet"	Willis, Vic
Clarkson, John	Grant, Frank	Mackey, James "Biz"	Roush, Edd	Wilson, Hack
#Clemente, Roberto	Greenberg, Hank	MacPhail, Larry	Ruffing, Red	Wilson, Jud
Cobb, Ty[1]	Griffith, Clark	MacPhail, Lee	Rusie, Amos	#Winfield, Dave
Cochrane, Mickey	Grimes, Burleigh	Madden, Bill	#Ruth, Babe[1]	Wright, George
Collins, Eddie	Grove, Lefty	Manley, Effa	#Ryan, Nolan	Wright, Harry
Collins, James	#Gwynn, Tony	#Mantle, Mickey	Sandberg, Ryne	Wynn, Early
Combs, Earle	Hafey, Charles "Chick"	Manush, Henry	Santop, Louis	#Yastrzemski, Carl
Comiskey, Charles A.	Haines, Jesee	Maranville, Walter "Rabbit"	Schalk, Ray	Yawkey, Tom
Conlan, John "Jocko"	Hamilton, Bill		#Schmidt, Mike	Young, Cy
Connolly, Thomas H.	Hanlon, Ned	Marichal, Juan	Schoendienst, Red	Youngs, Ross
	Harridge, Will	Marquard, Rube	#Seaver, Tom	#Yount, Robin
	Harris, Bucky			

(1) Player inducted in 1936 (the year the Hall of Fame began).

BASKETBALL

Dallas Mavericks Win First-Ever NBA Title, Defeating Hyped Heat

The Miami Heat's superstar roster grabbed its share of headlines during the 2010-11 season, but the Dallas Mavericks prevailed in the NBA Finals, defeating the Heat, four games to two, to capture the franchise's first championship June 12, 2011, at American Airlines Arena in Miami, FL. Veteran Maverick forward Dirk Nowitzki was voted Finals MVP, averaging 26 points and 9 rebounds in the series, as the Mavericks avenged a loss to Miami in the 2006 NBA Finals.

The 2010-11 NBA season seemingly began in the summer of 2010, with Cleveland Cavaliers superstar LeBron James's much-hyped announcement that he was leaving Cleveland, where he played for seven seasons, and signing with Miami. With an all-star lineup that included forward Chris Bosh, who also signed with the Heat in 2010 after seven seasons in Toronto, and guard Dwyane Wade, Miami's 58-24 regular-season record topped the Southeast Division.

Led by 22-year-old Derrick Rose (the league's youngest-ever MVP), the Chicago Bulls earned the top seed in the East with an NBA-best 62-20 record, but Miami defeated Chicago in the Eastern Conference finals. Chicago's 21-game improvement over the previous season earned Tom Thibodeau the Coach of the Year award in his first season as an NBA head coach.

Head coach Phil Jackson announced his retirement after Dallas swept his defending champion L.A. Lakers in the Western Conference semifinals; Jackson left with an NBA coaching-record 11 NBA titles. Shortly after the Boston Celtics were eliminated from the playoffs, center Shaquille O'Neal retired after 19 seasons. O'Neal, who won three titles with Jackson in L.A. and a fourth as a member of the 2006 Miami championship squad, was fifth on the NBA all-time scoring list with 28,596 career points.

Oklahoma City Thunder forward Kevin Durant led the league in scoring for the second straight year (27.7 PPG), but the team lost to the Mavericks in the Western Conference finals. L.A. Clippers forward Blake Griffin, with a rookie-best 22.5 points and 12.1 rebounds per game, became the league's first unanimous Rookie of the Year since David Robinson (1990). The New Jersey Nets and Toronto Raptors played the NBA's first regular-season games in Europe in Mar. 2011 at the O2 Arena in London, England. The Nets also joined Yao Ming and the Houston Rockets in a pair of exhibition games in China in Oct. 2010.

Final Standings, 2010-11

(playoff seeding in parentheses)

Eastern Conference

Atlantic Division	W	L	PCT	GB
Boston (3)	56	26	.683	—
New York (5)	42	40	.512	14
Philadelphia (7)	41	41	.500	15
New Jersey	24	58	.293	32
Toronto	22	60	.268	34

Central Division	W	L	PCT	GB
Chicago (1)	62	20	.756	—
Indiana (8)	37	45	.451	25
Milwaukee	35	47	.427	27
Detroit	30	52	.366	32
Cleveland	19	63	.232	43

Southeast Division	W	L	PCT	GB
Miami (2)	58	24	.707	—
Orlando (4)	52	30	.634	6
Atlanta (5)	44	38	.537	14
Charlotte	34	48	.415	24
Washington	23	59	.280	35

Western Conference

Northwest Division	W	L	PCT	GB
Oklahoma City (4)	55	27	.671	—
Denver (5)	50	32	.610	5
Portland (6)	48	34	.585	7
Utah	39	43	.476	16
Minnesota	17	65	.207	38

Pacific Division	W	L	PCT	GB
L.A. Lakers (2)	57	25	.695	—
Phoenix	40	42	.488	17
Golden State	36	46	.439	21
L.A. Clippers	32	50	.390	25
Sacramento	24	58	.293	33

Southwest Division	W	L	PCT	GB
San Antonio (1)	61	21	.744	—
Dallas (3)	57	25	.695	4
New Orleans (7)	46	36	.561	13
Memphis (8)	46	36	.561	15
Houston	43	39	.524	18

Note: New Orleans earned the No. 7 seed in the West over Memphis due to a better division record.

NBA Playoff Results, 2011

Eastern Conference
Chicago defeated Indiana, 4 games to 1
Miami defeated Philadelphia, 4 games to 1
Boston defeated New York, 4 games to 0
Atlanta defeated Orlando, 4 games to 2
Miami defeated Boston, 4 games to 1
Chicago defeated Atlanta, 4 games to 2
Miami defeated Chicago, 4 games to 1

Western Conference
Memphis defeated San Antonio, 4 games to 2
L.A. Lakers defeated New Orleans, 4 games to 2
Dallas defeated Portland, 4 games to 2
Oklahoma City defeated Denver, 4 games to 1
Dallas defeated L.A. Lakers, 4 games to 0
Oklahoma City defeated Memphis, 4 games to 3
Dallas defeated Oklahoma City, 4 games to 1

Championship
Dallas defeated Miami, 4 games to 2 (84-92, 95-93, 86-88, 86-83, 112-103, 105-95)

NBA Regular Season Individual Highs, 2010-11

Minutes, game: 57, Channing Frye, Phoenix v. L.A. Lakers, Mar. 22 (3 OT)
Points, game: 51, LeBron James, Miami v. Orlando, Feb. 3
Field goals, game: 19, Blake Griffin, L.A. Clippers v. Indiana, Jan. 17; Paul Millsap, Utah v. Miami, Nov. 9 (OT)
Field goal attempts, game: 33, Kobe Bryant, L.A. Lakers v. Indiana, Nov. 28; Derrick Rose, Chicago v. Phoenix, Nov. 24 (2 OT); Nick Young, Washington v. Oklahoma City, Jan. 28 (2 OT)
3-pointers, game: 10, Ty Lawson, Denver v. Minnesota, Apr. 9
3-pt. attempts, game: 16, J.R. Smith, Denver v. Detroit, Mar. 12
Free throws, game: 18, Chauncey Billups, New York v. Orlando, Mar. 1; DeMarcus Cousins, Sacramento v. Oklahoma City, Apr. 11; Kevin Love, Minnesota v. Golden State, Feb. 27; Kevin Martin, Houston v. Utah, Mar. 20; Derrick Rose, Chicago v. Indiana, Mar. 18 (OT)

Free throw attempts, game: 24, Dwight Howard, Orlando v. Cleveland, Nov. 26; Dwight Howard, Orlando v. Milwaukee, Mar. 16 (OT)
Rebounds, game: 31, Kevin Love, Minnesota v. New York, Nov. 12
Assists, game: 24, Rajon Rondo, Boston v. New York, Oct. 29
Steals, game: 9, John Wall, Washington v. Philadelphia, Nov. 2 (OT)
Blocks, game: 12, JaVale McGee, Washington v. Chicago, Mar. 15
Minutes played, season: 3,226, Monta Ellis, Golden State
Off. rebounds, season: 330, Kevin Love, Minnesota
Def. rebounds, season: 789, Dwight Howard, Orlando
Personal fouls, season: 332, DeMarcus Cousins, Sacramento

NBA Finals Composite Box Scores, 2011

Dallas Mavericks	FGM	FGA	FTM	FTA	Off. reb	Tot. reb	AST	AVG	Miami Heat	FGM	FGA	FTM	FTA	Off. reb	Tot. reb	AST	AVG
Dirk Nowitzki	52	125	45	46	2	58	12	26.0	Dwyane Wade	59	108	34	49	15	42	31	26.5
Jason Terry	38	77	21	28	3	12	19	18.0	Chris Bosh	38	92	35	45	15	44	6	18.5
Shawn Marion	34	71	14	17	14	38	14	13.7	LeBron James	43	90	12	20	6	43	41	17.8
Tyson Chandler	19	32	20	32	24	53	4	9.7	Mario Chalmers	20	47	17	23	2	16	21	11.8
Jose Barea	21	55	5	7	4	13	19	8.8	Udonis Haslem	18	40	4	5	7	31	4	6.7
Jason Kidd	14	36	6	8	2	27	38	7.7	Eddie House	3	9	0	0	0	4	1	4.5
DeShawn Stevenson	13	24	3	4	1	9	2	7.0	Mike Bibby	7	20	0	0	1	7	5	3.8
Ian Mahinmi	3	5	3	5	3	5	0	3.0	Mike Miller	7	23	0	0	3	17	5	3.5
Brendan Haywood	1	3	3	6	2	7	0	1.7	Juwan Howard	3	5	3	6	3	6	1	1.8
Brian Cardinal	2	3	1	2	0	1	1	1.4	Joel Anthony	4	14	0	0	12	21	2	1.3
Peja Stojakovic	1	5	0	0	0	3	0	0.5									

NBA Finals MVP, 1969-2011

1969 Jerry West, L.A. Lakers	1983 Moses Malone, Philadelphia	1998 Michael Jordan, Chicago
1970 Willis Reed, New York	1984 Larry Bird, Boston	1999 Tim Duncan, San Antonio
1971 Lew Alcindor (Kareem Abdul-	1985 Kareem Abdul-Jabbar, L.A. Lakers	2000 Shaquille O'Neal, L.A. Lakers
Jabbar), Milwaukee	1986 Larry Bird, Boston	2001 Shaquille O'Neal, L.A. Lakers
1972 Wilt Chamberlain, L.A. Lakers	1987 Magic Johnson, L.A. Lakers	2002 Shaquille O'Neal, L.A. Lakers
1973 Willis Reed, New York	1988 James Worthy, L.A. Lakers	2003 Tim Duncan, San Antonio
1974 John Havlicek, Boston	1989 Joe Dumars, Detroit	2004 Chauncey Billups, Detroit
1975 Rick Barry, Golden State	1990 Isiah Thomas, Detroit	2005 Tim Duncan, San Antonio
1976 JoJo White, Boston	1991 Michael Jordan, Chicago	2006 Dwyane Wade, Miami
1977 Bill Walton, Portland	1992 Michael Jordan, Chicago	2007 Tony Parker, San Antonio
1978 Wes Unseld, Washington	1993 Michael Jordan, Chicago	2008 Paul Pierce, Boston
1979 Dennis Johnson, Seattle	1994 Hakeem Olajuwon, Houston	2009 Kobe Bryant, L.A. Lakers
1980 Magic Johnson, L.A. Lakers	1995 Hakeem Olajuwon, Houston	2010 Kobe Bryant, L.A. Lakers
1981 Cedric Maxwell, Boston	1996 Michael Jordan, Chicago	2011 Dirk Nowitzki, Dallas
1982 Magic Johnson, L.A. Lakers	1997 Michael Jordan, Chicago	

NBA Finals All-Time Statistical Leaders

(At the end of the 2011 NBA Finals. * = Active in 2010-11 season. Minimum 10 games played.)

Scoring average leader	GP	FG	FT	PTS	AVG	Scoring average leader	GP	FG	FT	PTS	AVG
Rick Barry	10	138	87	363	36.3	Bob Pettit	25	241	227	709	28.4
Michael Jordan	35	438	258	1,176	33.6	Hakeem Olajuwon	17	187	91	467	27.5
*Dwyane Wade	12	124	109	367	30.6	Elgin Baylor	44	442	277	1,161	26.4
Jerry West	55	612	455	1,679	30.5	Julius Erving	22	216	128	561	25.5
*Shaquille O'Neal	30	340	185	865	28.8	*Kobe Bryant	37	333	223	937	25.3

Games played		Rebounds		Assists	
Bill Russell	70	Bill Russell	1,718	Magic Johnson	584
Sam Jones	64	Wilt Chamberlain	862	Bob Cousy	400
Kareem Abdul-Jabbar	56	Elgin Baylor	593	Bill Russell	315
Jerry West	55	Kareem Abdul-Jabbar	507	Jerry West	306
Tom Heinsohn	52	Tom Heinsohn	473	Dennis Johnson	228

NBA Scoring Leaders, 1947-2011

Year	Scoring champion	PTS	AVG	Year	Scoring champion	PTS	AVG
1947	Joe Fulks, Philadelphia	1,389	23.2	1980	George Gervin, San Antonio	2,585	33.1
1948	Max Zaslofsky, Chicago	1,007	21.0	1981	Adrian Dantley, Utah	2,452	30.7
1949	George Mikan, Minneapolis	1,698	28.3	1982	George Gervin, San Antonio	2,551	32.3
1950	George Mikan, Minneapolis	1,865	27.4	1983	Alex English, Denver	2,326	28.4
1951	George Mikan, Minneapolis	1,932	28.4	1984	Adrian Dantley, Utah	2,418	30.6
1952	Paul Arizin, Philadelphia	1,674	25.4	1985	Bernard King, New York	1,809	32.9
1953	Neil Johnston, Philadelphia	1,564	22.3	1986	Dominique Wilkins, Atlanta	2,366	30.3
1954	Neil Johnston, Philadelphia	1,759	24.4	1987	Michael Jordan, Chicago	3,041	37.1
1955	Neil Johnston, Philadelphia	1,631	22.7	1988	Michael Jordan, Chicago	2,868	35.0
1956	Bob Pettit, St. Louis	1,849	25.7	1989	Michael Jordan, Chicago	2,633	32.5
1957	Paul Arizin, Philadelphia	1,817	25.6	1990	Michael Jordan, Chicago	2,753	33.6
1958	George Yardley, Detroit	2,001	27.8	1991	Michael Jordan, Chicago	2,580	31.5
1959	Bob Pettit, St. Louis	2,105	29.2	1992	Michael Jordan, Chicago	2,404	30.1
1960	Wilt Chamberlain, Philadelphia	2,707	37.9	1993	Michael Jordan, Chicago	2,541	32.6
1961	Wilt Chamberlain, Philadelphia	3,033	38.4	1994	David Robinson, San Antonio	2,383	29.8
1962	Wilt Chamberlain, Philadelphia	4,029	50.4	1995	Shaquille O'Neal, Orlando	2,315	29.3
1963	Wilt Chamberlain, San Francisco	3,586	44.8	1996	Michael Jordan, Chicago	2,465	30.4
1964	Wilt Chamberlain, San Francisco	2,948	36.5	1997	Michael Jordan, Chicago	2,431	29.6
1965	Wilt Chamberlain, San Francisco, Phil.	2,534	34.7	1998	Michael Jordan, Chicago	2,357	28.7
1966	Wilt Chamberlain, Philadelphia	2,649	33.5	1999	Allen Iverson, Philadelphia	1,284	26.8
1967	Rick Barry, San Francisco	2,775	35.6	2000	Shaquille O'Neal, L.A. Lakers	2,344	29.7
1968	Dave Bing, Detroit	2,142	27.1	2001	Allen Iverson, Philadelphia	2,207	31.1
1969	Elvin Hayes, San Diego	2,327	28.4	2002	Allen Iverson, Philadelphia	1,883	31.4
1970	Jerry West, L.A. Lakers	2,309	31.2	2003	Tracy McGrady, Orlando	2,407	32.1
1971	Lew Alcindor (Abdul-Jabbar), Milwaukee	2,596	31.7	2004	Tracy McGrady, Orlando	1,878	28.0
1972	Kareem Abdul-Jabbar, Milwaukee	2,822	34.8	2005	Allen Iverson, Philadelphia	2,302	30.7
1973	Nate Archibald, Kansas City-Omaha	2,719	34.0	2006	Kobe Bryant, L.A. Lakers	2,832	35.4
1974	Bob McAdoo, Buffalo	2,261	30.6	2007	Kobe Bryant, L.A. Lakers	2,430	31.6
1975	Bob McAdoo, Buffalo	2,831	34.5	2008	LeBron James, Cleveland	2,250	30.0
1976	Bob McAdoo, Buffalo	2,427	31.1	2009	Dwyane Wade, Miami	2,386	30.2
1977	Pete Maravich, New Orleans	2,273	31.1	2010	Kevin Durant, Oklahoma City	2,472	30.1
1978	George Gervin, San Antonio	2,232	27.2	2011	Kevin Durant, Oklahoma City	2,161	27.7
1979	George Gervin, San Antonio	2,365	29.6				

NBA Most Valuable Player, 1956-2011

1956 Bob Pettit, St. Louis	1961 Bill Russell, Boston	1966 Wilt Chamberlain, Philadelphia
1957 Bob Cousy, Boston	1962 Bill Russell, Boston	1967 Wilt Chamberlain, Philadelphia
1958 Bill Russell, Boston	1963 Bill Russell, Boston	1968 Wilt Chamberlain, Philadelphia
1959 Bob Pettit, St. Louis	1964 Oscar Robertson, Cincinnati	1969 Wes Unseld, Baltimore
1960 Wilt Chamberlain, Philadelphia	1965 Bill Russell, Boston	1970 Willis Reed, New York

1971 Lew Alcindor (Abdul-Jabbar), Milw.	1985 Larry Bird, Boston	1999 Karl Malone, Utah
1972 Kareem Abdul-Jabbar, Milwaukee	1986 Larry Bird, Boston	2000 Shaquille O'Neal, L.A. Lakers
1973 Dave Cowens, Boston	1987 Magic Johnson, L.A. Lakers	2001 Allen Iverson, Philadelphia
1974 Kareem Abdul-Jabbar, Milwaukee	1988 Michael Jordan, Chicago	2002 Tim Duncan, San Antonio
1975 Bob McAdoo, Buffalo	1989 Magic Johnson, L.A. Lakers	2003 Tim Duncan, San Antonio
1976 Kareem Abdul-Jabbar, L.A. Lakers	1990 Magic Johnson, L.A. Lakers	2004 Kevin Garnett, Minnesota
1977 Kareem Abdul-Jabbar, L.A. Lakers	1991 Michael Jordan, Chicago	2005 Steve Nash, Phoenix
1978 Bill Walton, Portland	1992 Michael Jordan, Chicago	2006 Steve Nash, Phoenix
1979 Moses Malone, Houston	1993 Charles Barkley, Phoenix	2007 Dirk Nowitzki, Dallas
1980 Kareem Abdul-Jabbar, L.A. Lakers	1994 Hakeem Olajuwon, Houston	2008 Kobe Bryant, L.A. Lakers
1981 Julius Erving, Philadelphia	1995 David Robinson, San Antonio	2009 LeBron James, Cleveland
1982 Moses Malone, Houston	1996 Michael Jordan, Chicago	2010 LeBron James, Cleveland
1983 Moses Malone, Philadelphia	1997 Karl Malone, Utah	2011 Derrick Rose, Chicago
1984 Larry Bird, Boston	1998 Michael Jordan, Chicago	

NBA Champions, 1947-2011

	Regular season		Playoffs		
Year	Eastern Conference	Western Conference	Champion	Coach	Opponent
1947	Washington Capitols	Chicago Stags	Philadelphia	Ed Gottlieb	Chicago
1948	Philadelphia Warriors	St. Louis Bombers	Baltimore	Buddy Jeannette	Philadelphia
1949	Washington Capitols	Rochester	Minneapolis	John Kundla	Washington
1950	Syracuse	Minneapolis	Minneapolis	John Kundla	Syracuse
1951	Philadelphia Warriors	Minneapolis	Rochester	Lester Harrison	New York
1952	Syracuse	Rochester	Minneapolis	John Kundla	New York
1953	New York	Minneapolis	Minneapolis	John Kundla	New York
1954	New York	Minneapolis	Minneapolis	John Kundla	Syracuse
1955	Syracuse	Ft. Wayne	Syracuse	Al Cervi	Ft. Wayne
1956	Philadelphia Warriors	Ft. Wayne	Philadelphia	George Senesky	Ft. Wayne
1957	Boston	St. Louis	Boston	Red Auerbach	St. Louis
1958	Boston	St. Louis	St. Louis	Alex Hannum	Boston
1959	Boston	St. Louis	Boston	Red Auerbach	Minneapolis
1960	Boston	St. Louis	Boston	Red Auerbach	St. Louis
1961	Boston	St. Louis	Boston	Red Auerbach	St. Louis
1962	Boston	L.A. Lakers	Boston	Red Auerbach	L.A. Lakers
1963	Boston	L.A. Lakers	Boston	Red Auerbach	L.A. Lakers
1964	Boston	San Francisco	Boston	Red Auerbach	San Francisco
1965	Boston	L.A. Lakers	Boston	Red Auerbach	L.A. Lakers
1966	Philadelphia	L.A. Lakers	Boston	Red Auerbach	L.A. Lakers
1967	Philadelphia	San Francisco	Philadelphia	Alex Hannum	San Francisco
1968	Philadelphia	St. Louis	Boston	Bill Russell	L.A. Lakers
1969	Baltimore	L.A. Lakers	Boston	Bill Russell	L.A. Lakers
1970	New York	Atlanta	New York	Red Holzman	L.A. Lakers

Year	Atlantic	Central	Midwest	Pacific	Champion	Coach	Opponent
1971	New York	Baltimore	Milwaukee	L.A. Lakers	Milwaukee	Larry Costello	Baltimore
1972	Boston	Baltimore	Milwaukee	L.A. Lakers	L.A. Lakers	Bill Sharman	New York
1973	Boston	Baltimore	Milwaukee	L.A. Lakers	New York	Red Holzman	L.A. Lakers
1974	Boston	Capital	Milwaukee	L.A. Lakers	Boston	Tom Heinsohn	Milwaukee
1975	Boston	Washington	Chicago	Golden State	Golden State	Al Attles	Washington
1976	Boston	Cleveland	Milwaukee	Golden State	Boston	Tom Heinsohn	Phoenix
1977	Philadelphia	Houston	Denver	L.A. Lakers	Portland	Jack Ramsay	Philadelphia
1978	Philadelphia	San Antonio	Denver	Portland	Washington	Dick Motta	Seattle
1979	Washington	San Antonio	Kansas City	Seattle	Seattle	Len Wilkens	Washington
1980	Boston	Atlanta	Milwaukee	L.A. Lakers	L.A. Lakers	Paul Westhead	Philadelphia
1981	Boston	Milwaukee	San Antonio	Phoenix	Boston	Bill Fitch	Houston
1982	Boston	Milwaukee	San Antonio	L.A. Lakers	L.A. Lakers	Pat Riley	Philadelphia
1983	Philadelphia	Milwaukee	San Antonio	L.A. Lakers	Philadelphia	Billy Cunningham	L.A. Lakers
1984	Boston	Milwaukee	Utah	L.A. Lakers	Boston	K. C. Jones	L.A. Lakers
1985	Boston	Milwaukee	Denver	L.A. Lakers	L.A. Lakers	Pat Riley	Boston
1986	Boston	Milwaukee	Houston	L.A. Lakers	Boston	K. C. Jones	Houston
1987	Boston	Atlanta	Dallas	L.A. Lakers	L.A. Lakers	Pat Riley	Boston
1988	Boston	Detroit	Denver	L.A. Lakers	L.A. Lakers	Pat Riley	Detroit
1989	New York	Detroit	Utah	L.A. Lakers	Detroit	Chuck Daly	L.A. Lakers
1990	Philadelphia	Detroit	San Antonio	L.A. Lakers	Detroit	Chuck Daly	Portland
1991	Boston	Chicago	San Antonio	Portland	Chicago	Phil Jackson	L.A. Lakers
1992	Boston	Chicago	Utah	Portland	Chicago	Phil Jackson	Portland
1993	New York	Chicago	Houston	Phoenix	Chicago	Phil Jackson	Phoenix
1994	New York	Atlanta	Houston	Seattle	Houston	Rudy Tomjanovich	New York
1995	Orlando	Indiana	San Antonio	Phoenix	Houston	Rudy Tomjanovich	Orlando
1996	Orlando	Chicago	San Antonio	Seattle	Chicago	Phil Jackson	Seattle
1997	Miami	Chicago	Utah	Seattle	Chicago	Phil Jackson	Utah
1998	Miami	Chicago	Utah	L.A. Lakers	Chicago	Phil Jackson	Utah
1999	Miami	Indiana	San Antonio	Portland	San Antonio	Gregg Popovich	New York
2000	Miami	Indiana	Utah	L.A. Lakers	L.A. Lakers	Phil Jackson	Indiana
2001	Philadelphia	Milwaukee	San Antonio	L.A. Lakers	L.A. Lakers	Phil Jackson	Philadelphia
2002	New Jersey	Detroit	San Antonio	Sacramento	L.A. Lakers	Phil Jackson	New Jersey
2003	New Jersey	Detroit	San Antonio	Sacramento	San Antonio	Gregg Popovich	New Jersey
2004	New Jersey	Indiana	Minnesota	L.A. Lakers	Detroit	Larry Brown	L.A. Lakers

Year	Atlantic	Central	Southeast	Northwest	Pacific	Southwest	Champion	Coach	Opponent
2005	Boston	Detroit	Miami	Seattle	Phoenix	San Antonio	San Antonio	Gregg Popovich	Detroit
2006	New Jersey	Detroit	Miami	Denver	Phoenix	San Antonio	Miami	Pat Riley	Dallas
2007	Toronto	Detroit	Miami	Utah	Phoenix	Dallas	San Antonio	Gregg Popovich	Cleveland
2008	Boston	Detroit	Orlando	Utah	L.A. Lakers	New Orleans	Boston	Glenn "Doc" Rivers	L.A. Lakers
2009	Boston	Cleveland	Orlando	Denver	L.A. Lakers	San Antonio	L.A. Lakers	Phil Jackson	Orlando
2010	Boston	Cleveland	Orlando	Denver	L.A. Lakers	Dallas	L.A. Lakers	Phil Jackson	Boston
2011	Boston	Chicago	Miami	Okla. City	L.A. Lakers	San Antonio	Dallas	Rick Carlisle	Miami

All-NBA and All-Defensive Teams, 2010-11

All-NBA Team		Position	All-Defensive Team	
First Team	Second Team		First Team	Second Team
LeBron James, Miami	Pau Gasol, L.A. Lakers	Forward	LeBron James, Miami	Andre Iguodala, Philadelphia
Kevin Durant, Oklahoma City	Dirk Nowitzki, Dallas	Forward	Kevin Garnett, Boston	Joakim Noah, Chicago
Dwight Howard, Orlando	Amar'e Stoudemire, New York	Center	Dwight Howard, Orlando	Tyson Chandler, Dallas
Kobe Bryant, L.A. Lakers	Dwyane Wade, Miami	Guard	Rajon Rondo, Boston	Tony Allen, Memphis
Derrick Rose, Chicago	Russell Westbrook, Oklahoma City	Guard	Kobe Bryant, L.A. Lakers	Chris Paul, New Orleans

NBA Coach of the Year, 1963-2011

Year	Coach, team	Year	Coach, team	Year	Coach, team
1963	Harry Gallatin, St. Louis	1980	Bill Fitch, Boston	1996	Phil Jackson, Chicago
1964	Alex Hannum, San Francisco	1981	Jack McKinney, Indiana	1997	Pat Riley, Miami
1965	Red Auerbach, Boston	1982	Gene Shue, Washington	1998	Larry Bird, Indiana
1966	Dolph Schayes, Philadelphia	1983	Don Nelson, Milwaukee	1999	Mike Dunleavy, Portland
1967	Johnny Kerr, Chicago	1984	Frank Layden, Utah	2000	Glenn "Doc" Rivers, Orlando
1968	Richie Guerin, St. Louis	1985	Don Nelson, Milwaukee	2001	Larry Brown, Philadelphia
1969	Gene Shue, Baltimore	1986	Mike Fratello, Atlanta	2002	Rick Carlisle, Detroit
1970	Red Holzman, New York	1987	Mike Schuler, Portland	2003	Gregg Popovich, San Antonio
1971	Dick Motta, Chicago	1988	Doug Moe, Denver	2004	Hubie Brown, Memphis
1972	Bill Sharman, L.A. Lakers	1989	Cotton Fitzsimmons, Phoenix	2005	Mike D'Antoni, Phoenix
1973	Tom Heinsohn, Boston	1990	Pat Riley, L.A. Lakers	2006	Avery Johnson, Dallas
1974	Ray Scott, Detroit	1991	Don Chaney, Houston	2007	Sam Mitchell, Toronto
1975	Phil Johnson, Kansas City-Omaha	1992	Don Nelson, Golden State	2008	Byron Scott, New Orleans
1976	Bill Fitch, Cleveland	1993	Pat Riley, New York	2009	Mike Brown, Cleveland
1977	Tom Nissalke, Houston	1994	Lenny Wilkens, Atlanta	2010	Scott Brooks, Oklahoma City
1978	Hubie Brown, Atlanta	1995	Del Harris, L.A. Lakers	2011	Tom Thibodeau, Chicago
1979	Cotton Fitzsimmons, Kansas City				

NBA Statistical Leaders, 2010-11

Scoring Average
(Minimum 70 games or 1,400 points)

Player, team	G	FG	FT	PTS	AVG
Kevin Durant, Oklahoma City	78	711	594	2,161	27.7
LeBron James, Miami	79	758	503	2,111	26.7
Carmelo Anthony, Denver-New York	77	684	507	1,970	25.6
Dwyane Wade, Miami	76	692	494	1,941	25.5
Kobe Bryant, L.A. Lakers	82	740	483	2,078	25.3
Amar'e Stoudemire, New York	78	744	473	1,971	25.3
Derrick Rose, Chicago	81	711	476	2,026	25.0
Monta Ellis, Golden State	80	726	340	1,929	24.1
Kevin Martin, Houston	80	553	594	1,876	23.4
Dirk Nowitzki, Dallas	73	610	395	1,681	23.0

Rebounds per Game
(Minimum 70 games or 800 rebounds)

Player, team	G	OFF	DEF	TOT	AVG
Kevin Love, Minnesota	73	330	782	1,112	15.2
Dwight Howard, Orlando	78	309	789	1,098	14.1
Zach Randolph, Memphis	75	326	588	914	12.2
Blake Griffin, L.A. Clippers	82	270	719	989	12.1
Kris Humphries, New Jersey	74	225	546	771	10.4
Pau Gasol, L.A. Lakers	82	268	568	836	10.2
David Lee, Golden State	73	217	497	714	9.8
Al Jefferson, Utah	82	235	559	794	9.7
Emeka Okafor, New Orleans	72	230	454	684	9.5
Tyson Chandler, Dallas	74	206	486	692	9.4

3-Point Field Goal Percentage
(Minimum 55 3-point field goals made)

Player, team	3-FGM	3-FGA	PCT
Matt Bonner, San Antonio	105	230	.457
Ray Allen, Boston	168	378	.444
Stephen Curry, Golden State	151	342	.442
Mike Bibby, Atlanta-Washington-Miami	153	348	.440
Richard Jefferson, San Antonio	135	307	.440
Luke Ridnour, Minnesota	81	184	.440
James Jones, Miami	123	287	.429
Arron Afflalo, Denver	105	248	.423
Anthony Morrow, New Jersey	110	260	.423
Reggie Williams, Golden State	102	241	.423

Assists per Game
(Minimum 70 games or 400 assists)

Player, team	G	AST	APG
Steve Nash, Phoenix	75	855	11.4
Rajon Rondo, Boston	68	760	11.2
Deron Williams, Utah-New Jersey	65	667	10.3
Chris Paul, New Orleans	80	782	9.8
Jose Calderon, Toronto	68	605	8.9
Raymond Felton, New York-Denver	75	625	8.3
John Wall, Washington	69	574	8.3
Jason Kidd, Dallas	80	655	8.2
Russell Westbrook, Oklahoma City	82	670	8.2
Derrick Rose, Chicago	81	623	7.7

Field Goal Percentage
(Minimum 300 field goals made)

Player, team	FGM	FGA	PCT
Nene Hilario, Denver	402	654	.615
Dwight Howard, Orlando	619	1,044	.593
Emeka Okafor, New Orleans	300	524	.573
Marcin Gortat, Orlando-Phoenix	338	603	.561
Al Horford, Atlanta	513	921	.557
Greg Monroe, Detroit	303	550	.551
JaVale McGee, Washington	332	604	.550
Serge Ibaka, Oklahoma City	335	617	.543
Thaddeus Young, Philadelphia	458	847	.541
Paul Millsap, Utah	525	988	.531

Steals per Game
(Minimum 70 games or 125 steals)

Player, team	G	STL	AVG
Chris Paul, New Orleans	80	188	2.35
Rajon Rondo, Boston	68	153	2.25
Monta Ellis, Golden State	80	168	2.10
Russell Westbrook, Oklahoma City	82	155	1.89
Tony Allen, Memphis	72	129	1.79
Mike Conley, Memphis	81	144	1.78
Jason Kidd, Dallas	80	134	1.68
Raymond Felton, New York-Denver	75	125	1.67
Trevor Ariza, New Orleans	75	120	1.60
LeBron James, Miami	79	124	1.57

Free Throw Percentage
(Minimum 125 free throws made)

Player, team	FTM	FTA	PCT
Stephen Curry, Golden State	212	227	.934
Chauncey Billups, Denver-New York	384	419	.916
Steve Nash, Phoenix	227	249	.912
D.J. Augustin, Charlotte	269	297	.906
Jodie Meeks, Philadelphia	152	170	.894
Randy Foye, L.A. Clippers	133	149	.893
Dirk Nowitzki, Dallas	395	443	.892
Kevin Martin, Houston	594	669	.888
Ray Allen, Boston	193	219	.881
Kevin Durant, Oklahoma City	594	675	.880

Blocked Shots per Game
(Minimum 70 games or 100 blocked shots)

Player, team	G	BLK	AVG
Andrew Bogut, Milwaukee	65	168	2.58
JaVale McGee, Washington	79	193	2.44
Serge Ibaka, Oklahoma City	82	198	2.42
Dwight Howard, Orlando	78	186	2.38
Darko Milicic, Minnesota	69	140	2.03
Andrew Bynum, L.A. Lakers	54	106	1.96
Amar'e Stoudemire, New York	78	150	1.92
Tim Duncan, San Antonio	76	146	1.92
Al Jefferson, Utah	82	153	1.87
DeAndre Jordan, L.A. Clippers	80	142	1.78

NBA Defensive Player of the Year, 1983-2011

1983	Sidney Moncrief, Milwaukee	1993	Hakeem Olajuwon, Houston	2002	Ben Wallace, Detroit
1984	Sidney Moncrief, Milwaukee	1994	Hakeem Olajuwon, Houston	2003	Ben Wallace, Detroit
1985	Mark Eaton, Utah	1995	Dikembe Mutombo, Denver	2004	Ron Artest, Indiana
1986	Alvin Robertson, San Antonio	1996	Gary Payton, Seattle	2005	Ben Wallace, Detroit
1987	Michael Cooper, L.A. Lakers	1997	Dikembe Mutombo, Atlanta	2006	Ben Wallace, Detroit
1988	Michael Jordan, Chicago	1998	Dikembe Mutombo, Atlanta	2007	Marcus Camby, Denver
1989	Mark Eaton, Utah	1999	Alonzo Mourning, Miami	2008	Kevin Garnett, Boston
1990	Dennis Rodman, Detroit	2000	Alonzo Mourning, Miami	2009	Dwight Howard, Orlando
1991	Dennis Rodman, Detroit	2001	Dikembe Mutombo, Philadelphia-	2010	Dwight Howard, Orlando
1992	David Robinson, San Antonio		Atlanta	2011	Dwight Howard, Orlando

NBA Rookie of the Year, 1953-2011

1953	Don Meineke, Ft. Wayne	1973	Bob McAdoo, Buffalo	1994	Chris Webber, Golden State
1954	Ray Felix, Baltimore	1974	Ernie DiGregorio, Buffalo	1995	Grant Hill, Detroit;
1955	Bob Pettit, Milwaukee	1975	Keith Wilkes, Golden State		Jason Kidd, Dallas (tie)
1956	Maurice Stokes, Rochester	1976	Alvan Adams, Phoenix	1996	Damon Stoudamire, Toronto
1957	Tom Heinsohn, Boston	1977	Adrian Dantley, Buffalo	1997	Allen Iverson, Philadelphia
1958	Woody Sauldsberry, Philadelphia	1978	Walter Davis, Phoenix	1998	Tim Duncan, San Antonio
1959	Elgin Baylor, Minneapolis	1979	Phil Ford, Kansas City	1999	Vince Carter, Toronto
1960	Wilt Chamberlain, Philadelphia	1980	Larry Bird, Boston	2000	Elton Brand, Chicago;
1961	Oscar Robertson, Cincinnati	1981	Darrell Griffith, Utah		Steve Francis, Houston (tie)
1962	Walt Bellamy, Chicago	1982	Buck Williams, New Jersey	2001	Mike Miller, Orlando
1963	Terry Dischinger, Chicago	1983	Terry Cummings, San Diego	2002	Pau Gasol, Memphis
1964	Jerry Lucas, Cincinnati	1984	Ralph Sampson, Houston	2003	Amar'e Stoudemire, Phoenix
1965	Willis Reed, New York	1985	Michael Jordan, Chicago	2004	LeBron James, Cleveland
1966	Rick Barry, San Francisco	1986	Patrick Ewing, New York	2005	Emeka Okafor, Charlotte
1967	Dave Bing, Detroit	1987	Chuck Person, Indiana	2006	Chris Paul, New Or./Okla. City
1968	Earl Monroe, Baltimore	1988	Mark Jackson, New York	2007	Brandon Roy, Portland
1969	Wes Unseld, Baltimore	1989	Mitch Richmond, Golden State	2008	Kevin Durant, Seattle
1970	Lew Alcindor (Abdul-Jabbar), Milw.	1990	David Robinson, San Antonio	2009	Derrick Rose, Chicago
1971	Dave Cowens, Boston;	1991	Derrick Coleman, New Jersey	2010	Tyreke Evans, Sacramento
	Geoff Petrie, Portland	1992	Larry Johnson, Charlotte	2011	Blake Griffin, L.A. Clippers
1972	Sidney Wicks, Portland	1993	Shaquille O'Neal, Orlando		

NBA Sixth Man Award, 1983-2011

1983	Bobby Jones, Philadelphia	1993	Clifford Robinson, Portland	2003	Bobby Jackson, Sacramento
1984	Kevin McHale, Boston	1994	Dell Curry, Charlotte	2004	Antawn Jamison, Dallas
1985	Kevin McHale, Boston	1995	Anthony Mason, New York	2005	Ben Gordon, Chicago
1986	Bill Walton, Boston	1996	Toni Kukoc, Chicago	2006	Mike Miller, Memphis
1987	Ricky Pierce, Milwaukee	1997	John Starks, New York	2007	Leandro Barbosa, Phoenix
1988	Roy Tarpley, Dallas	1998	Danny Manning, Phoenix	2008	Manu Ginobili, San Antonio
1989	Eddie Johnson, Phoenix	1999	Darrell Armstrong, Orlando	2009	Jason Terry, Dallas
1990	Ricky Pierce, Milwaukee	2000	Rodney Rogers, Phoenix	2010	Jamal Crawford, Atlanta
1991	Detlef Schrempf, Indiana	2001	Aaron McKie, Philadelphia	2011	Lamar Odom, L.A. Lakers
1992	Detlef Schrempf, Indiana	2002	Corliss Williamson, Detroit		

NBA Player Draft First-Round Picks, 2011
(June 23, 2011)

Team	Player, position, college/team	Team	Player, position, college/team
1. Cleveland[1]	Kyrie Irving, Guard, Duke	15. Indiana	Kawhi Leonard, Forward, San Diego State[5]
2. Minnesota	Derrick Williams, Forward, Arizona	16. Philadelphia	Nikola Vucevic, Forward, Southern California
3. Utah[2]	Enes Kanter, Forward, Kentucky	17. New York	Iman Shumpert, Guard, Georgia Tech
4. Cleveland	Tristan Thompson, Forward, Texas	18. Washington[6]	Chris Singleton, Forward, Florida State
5. Toronto	Jonas Valanciunas, Center, Lietuvos Rytas (Lithuania)	19. Charlotte[7]	Tobias Harris, Forward, Tennessee
6. Washington	Jan Vesely, Forward, Partizan (Adriatic League)	20. Minnesota[8]	Donatas Motiejunas, Forward, Benetton Treviso (Italy)
7. Sacramento	Bismack Biyombo, Forward, Fuenlabrada (Spain)[3]	21. Portland	Nolan Smith, Guard, Duke
8. Detroit	Brandon Knight, Guard, Kentucky	22. Denver	Kenneth Faried, Forward, Morehead State
9. Charlotte	Kemba Walker, Guard, Connecticut	23. Houston[9]	Nikola Mirotic, Forward, Real Madrid (Spain)
10. Milwaukee	Jimmer Fredette, Guard, Brigham Young[4]	24. Oklahoma City	Reggie Jackson, Guard, Boston College
11. Golden State	Klay Thompson, Guard, Washington State	25. Boston	MarShon Brooks, Guard, Providence[10]
12. Utah	Alec Burks, Guard, Colorado	26. Dallas	Jordan Hamilton, Forward, Texas[11]
13. Phoenix	Markieff Morris, Forward, Kansas	27. New Jersey[12]	JaJuan Johnson, Forward, Purdue
14. Houston	Marcus Morris, Forward, Kansas	28. Chicago[13]	Norris Cole, Guard, Cleveland State
		29. San Antonio	Cory Joseph, Guard, Texas
		30. Chicago	Jimmy Butler, Forward, Marquette

(1) From L.A. Clippers. (2) From New Jersey. (3) Rights traded to Charlotte. (4) Rights traded to Sacramento. (5) Rights traded to San Antonio. (6) From Atlanta. (7) From New Orleans via Portland; rights traded to Milwaukee. (8) From Memphis via Utah; rights traded to Houston. (9) From Orlando via Phoenix; rights traded to Chicago via Minnesota. (10) Rights traded to New Jersey. (11) Rights traded to Denver. (12) From L.A. Lakers; rights traded to Boston. (13) From Miami via Toronto; rights traded to Miami via Minnesota.

Number-One First-Round NBA Draft Picks, 1966-2011

Year	Team	Player, college/team	Year	Team	Player, college/team
1966	New York	Cazzie Russell, Michigan	1990	New Jersey	Derrick Coleman, Syracuse
1967	Detroit	Jimmy Walker, Providence	1991	Charlotte	Larry Johnson, UNLV
1968	San Diego	Elvin Hayes, Houston	1992	Orlando	Shaquille O'Neal, LSU
1969	Milwaukee	Lew Alcindor (Kareem Abdul-Jabbar), UCLA	1993	Orlando	Chris Webber[2], Michigan
1970	Detroit	Bob Lanier, St. Bonaventure	1994	Milwaukee	Glenn Robinson, Purdue
1971	Cleveland	Austin Carr, Notre Dame	1995	Golden State	Joe Smith, Maryland
1972	Portland	LaRue Martin, Loyola-Chicago	1996	Philadelphia	Allen Iverson, Georgetown
1973	Philadelphia	Doug Collins, Illinois State	1997	San Antonio	Tim Duncan, Wake Forest
1974	Portland	Bill Walton, UCLA	1998	L.A. Clippers	Michael Olowokandi, Pacific
1975	Atlanta	David Thompson[1], NC State	1999	Chicago	Elton Brand, Duke
1976	Houston	John Lucas, Maryland	2000	New Jersey	Kenyon Martin, Cincinnati
1977	Milwaukee	Kent Benson, Indiana	2001	Washington	Kwame Brown, Glynn Academy (HS)
1978	Portland	Mychal Thompson, Minnesota	2002	Houston	Yao Ming, Shanghai Sharks (China)
1979	L.A. Lakers	Earvin "Magic" Johnson, Michigan State	2003	Cleveland	LeBron James, St. Vincent-St. Mary (HS)
1980	Golden State	Joe Barry Carroll, Purdue	2004	Orlando	Dwight Howard, Southwest Atlanta Christian Academy (HS)
1981	Dallas	Mark Aguirre, DePaul			
1982	L.A. Lakers	James Worthy, North Carolina	2005	Milwaukee	Andrew Bogut, Utah
1983	Houston	Ralph Sampson, Virginia	2006	Toronto	Andrea Bargnani, Benetton Treviso (Italy)
1984	Houston	Hakeem Olajuwon, Houston	2007	Portland	Greg Oden, Ohio State
1985	New York	Patrick Ewing, Georgetown	2008	Chicago	Derrick Rose, Memphis
1986	Cleveland	Brad Daugherty, North Carolina	2009	L.A. Clippers	Blake Griffin, Oklahoma
1987	San Antonio	David Robinson, Navy	2010	Washington	John Wall, Kentucky
1988	L.A. Clippers	Danny Manning, Kansas	2011	Cleveland	Kyrie Irving, Duke
1989	Sacramento	Pervis Ellison, Louisville			

HS = High school. (1) Signed with Denver of the ABA. (2) Traded to Golden State for rights to Anfernee Hardaway and three future first-round draft choices.

All-Time NBA Statistical Leaders

(At the end of the 2010-11 season. * = Active in 2010-11 season.)

Scoring Average
(Minimum 400 games or 10,000 points)

	G	PTS	AVG
Michael Jordan	1,072	32,292	30.1
Wilt Chamberlain	1,045	31,419	30.1
*LeBron James	627	17,362	27.7
Elgin Baylor	846	23,149	27.4
Jerry West	932	25,192	27.0
Allen Iverson	914	24,368	26.7
Bob Pettit	792	20,880	26.4
George Gervin	791	20,708	26.2
Oscar Robertson	1,040	26,710	25.7
*Dwyane Wade	547	13,908	25.4

Field Goal Percentage
(Minimum 2,000 field goals made)

	FGA	FGM	PCT
Artis Gilmore	9,570	5,732	.599
*Shaquille O'Neal	19,457	11,330	.582
Mark West	4,356	2,528	.580
*Dwight Howard	6,262	3,618	.578
Steve Johnson	4,965	2,841	.572
Darryl Dawkins	6,079	3,477	.572
James Donaldson	5,442	3,105	.571
*Tyson Chandler	3,601	2,046	.568
Bo Outlaw	3,534	2,005	.567
Jeff Ruland	3,734	2,105	.564

Free Throw Percentage
(Minimum 1,200 free throws made)

	FTA	FTM	PCT
*Steve Nash	3,102	2,804	.904
Mark Price	2,362	2,135	.904
Rick Barry	4,243	3,818	.900
*Peja Stojakovic	2,500	2,237	.895
*Chauncey Billups	4,874	4,356	.894
*Ray Allen	4,540	4,056	.893
Calvin Murphy	3,864	3,445	.892
Scott Skiles	1,741	1,548	.889
Reggie Miller	7,026	6,237	.888
Larry Bird	4,471	3,960	.886

3-Point Field Goal Percentage
(Minimum 250 3-point field goals made)

	3-FGA	3-FGM	PCT
Steve Kerr	1,599	726	.454
*Anthony Morrow	751	336	.447
Hubert Davis	1,651	728	.441
*Stephen Curry	722	317	.439
*Jason Kapono	1,027	449	.437
Drazen Petrovic	583	255	.437
Tim Legler	603	260	.431
*Steve Nash	3,644	1,565	.429
B.J. Armstrong	1,026	436	.425
*Daniel Gibson	1,117	467	.418

Minutes Played

Kareem Abdul-Jabbar	57,446
Karl Malone	54,852
Elvin Hayes	50,000
Wilt Chamberlain	47,859
John Stockton	47,764
Reggie Miller	47,619
Gary Payton	47,117
*Jason Kidd	46,689
John Havlicek	46,471
Robert Parish	45,704

Field Goals Attempted

Kareem Abdul-Jabbar	28,307
Karl Malone	26,210
Michael Jordan	24,537
Elvin Hayes	24,272
John Havlicek	23,930
Wilt Chamberlain	23,497
Dominique Wilkins	21,589
*Kobe Bryant	21,370
Alex English	21,036
Hakeem Olajuwon	20,991

Points

Kareem Abdul-Jabbar	38,387
Karl Malone	36,928
Michael Jordan	32,292
Wilt Chamberlain	31,419
*Shaquille O'Neal	28,596
*Kobe Bryant	27,868
Moses Malone	27,409
Elvin Hayes	27,313
Hakeem Olajuwon	26,946
Oscar Robertson	26,710

Games Played

Robert Parish	1,611
Kareem Abdul-Jabbar	1,560
John Stockton	1,504
Karl Malone	1,476
Kevin Willis	1,424
Reggie Miller	1,389
Clifford Robinson	1,380
Gary Payton	1,335
Moses Malone	1,329
Buck Williams	1,307

Field Goals Made

Kareem Abdul-Jabbar	15,837
Karl Malone	13,528
Wilt Chamberlain	12,681
Michael Jordan	12,192
*Shaquille O'Neal	11,330
Elvin Hayes	10,976
Hakeem Olajuwon	10,749
Alex English	10,659
John Havlicek	10,513
Dominique Wilkins	9,963

Rebounds

Wilt Chamberlain	23,924
Bill Russell	21,620
Kareem Abdul-Jabbar	17,440
Elvin Hayes	16,279
Moses Malone	16,212
Karl Malone	14,968
Robert Parish	14,715
Nate Thurmond	14,464
Walt Bellamy	14,241
Wes Unseld	13,769

Personal Fouls

Kareem Abdul-Jabbar	4,657
Karl Malone	4,578
Robert Parish	4,443
Charles Oakley	4,421
Hakeem Olajuwon	4,383
Buck Williams	4,267
Elvin Hayes	4,193
Clifford Robinson	4,176
Kevin Willis	4,172
*Shaquille O'Neal	4,146
Otis Thorpe	4,146

3-Point Field Goals Attempted

*Ray Allen	6,554
Reggie Miller	6,486
*Jason Kidd	5,153
*Chauncey Billups	4,462
*Peja Stojakovic	4,392
Tim Hardaway	4,345
*Jason Terry	4,341
*Rashard Lewis	4,293
Nick Van Exel	4,278
*Paul Pierce	4,273

Assists

John Stockton	15,806
*Jason Kidd	11,578
Mark Jackson	10,334
Magic Johnson	10,141
Oscar Robertson	9,887
*Steve Nash	9,252
Isiah Thomas	9,061
Gary Payton	8,966
Rod Strickland	7,987
Maurice Cheeks	7,392

Blocks

Hakeem Olajuwon	3,830
Dikembe Mutombo	3,289
Kareem Abdul-Jabbar	3,189
Mark Eaton	3,064
David Robinson	2,954
Patrick Ewing	2,894
*Shaquille O'Neal	2,732
Tree Rollins	2,542
*Tim Duncan	2,381
Robert Parish	2,361

3-Point Field Goals Made

*Ray Allen	2,612
Reggie Miller	2,560
*Jason Kidd	1,795
*Peja Stojakovic	1,760
*Chauncey Billups	1,735
Dale Ellis	1,719
*Rashard Lewis	1,674
*Jason Terry	1,650
*Paul Pierce	1,578
*Steve Nash	1,565

Steals

John Stockton	3,265
Michael Jordan	2,514
*Jason Kidd	2,477
Gary Payton	2,445
Maurice Cheeks	2,310
Scottie Pippen	2,307
Clyde Drexler	2,207
Hakeem Olajuwon	2,162
Alvin Robertson	2,112
Karl Malone	2,085

All-Time NBA Regular Season Coaching Victories

(At the end of the 2010-11 season, ranked by wins. * = Active in 2010-11 season.)

Coach	W	L	PCT	Coach	W	L	PCT	Coach	W	L	PCT
Don Nelson	1,335	1,063	.557	Bill Fitch	944	1,106	.460	John MacLeod	707	657	.518
Lenny Wilkens	1,332	1,155	.536	Red Auerbach	938	479	.662	Red Holzman	696	604	.535
*Jerry Sloan	1,221	803	.603	Dick Motta	935	1,017	.479	Mike Fratello	667	548	.549
Pat Riley	1,210	694	.636	Jack Ramsay	864	783	.525	Chuck Daly	638	437	.593
*Phil Jackson	1,155	485	.704	Cotton Fitzsimmons	832	775	.518	*Flip Saunders	636	511	.554
*Larry Brown	1,098	904	.548	*Gregg Popovich	797	383	.675	Doug Moe	628	529	.543
*George Karl	1,036	703	.596	Gene Shue	784	861	.477	Mike Dunleavy	613	716	.461
*Rick Adelman	945	616	.605								

Naismith Memorial Basketball Hall of Fame, Springfield, MA
(* = 2011 inductee. ** = Enshrined as both a player and coach.)

Players
Abdul-Jabbar, Kareem
Archibald, Nate
Arizin, Paul
Barkley, Charles
Barlow, Thomas
Barry, Rick
Baylor, Elgin
Beckman, John
Bellamy, Walt
Belov, Sergei
Bing, Dave
Bird, Larry
Blazejowski, Carol
Borgmann, Bennie
Bradley, Bill
Brennan, Joseph
Cervi, Al
Chamberlain, Wilt
Cooper, Charles
Cooper, Cynthia
Cosic, Kresimir
Cousy, Bob
Cowens, Dave
Crawford, Joan
Cunningham, Billy
Curry, Denise
Dalipagic, Drazen
Dantley, Adrian
Davies, Bob
DeBernardi, Forrest
DeBusschere, Dave
Dehnert, Henry "Dutch"
Donovan, Anne
Drexler, Clyde
Dumars, Joe
*Edwards, Teresa
Endacott, Paul
English, Alex
Erving, Julius
Ewing, Patrick
Foster, Bud
Frazier, Walt
Friedman, Max
Fulks, Joe
Gale, Lauren
Gallatin, Harry
Gates, William "Pop"
Gervin, George
*Gilmore, Artis
Gola, Tom
Goodrich, Gail
Greer, Hal
Gruenig, Robert "Ace"
Hagan, Cliff
Hanson, Victor
Harris-Stewart, Lusia

Havlicek, John
Hawkins, Cornelius "Connie"
Hayes, Elvin
Haynes, Marques
Heinsohn, Tom
Holman, Nat
Houbregs, Bob
Howell, Bailey
Hyatt, Chuck
Issel, Dan
Jeannette, Harry "Buddy"
Johnson, Dennis
Johnson, Earvin "Magic"
Johnson, Gus
Johnson, William
Johnston, Neil
Jones, K. C.
Jones, Sam
Jordan, Michael
Krause, Ed "Moose"
Kurland, Bob
Lanier, Bob
Lapchick, Joe
Lieberman, Nancy
Lovellette, Clyde
Lucas, Jerry
Luisetti, Angelo "Hank"
Macauley, Ed
Malone, Karl
Malone, Moses
Maravich, Pete
Marcari, Hortencia
Martin, Slater
McAdoo, Bob
McCracken, Emmett "Branch"
McCracken, Jack
McDermott, Bobby
McGuire, Dick
McHale, Kevin
Meneghin, Dino
Meyers, Ann
Mikan, George
Mikkelsen, Vern
Miller, Cheryl
Monroe, Earl
*Mullin, Chris
Murphy, Calvin
Murphy, Charles "Stretch"
Olajuwon, Hakeem
Page, Harlan "Pat"
Parish, Robert
Pereira, Maciel "Ubiratan"

Petrovic, Drazen
Pettit, Bob
Phillip, Andy
Pippen, Scottie
Pollard, Jim
Ramsey, Frank
Reed, Willis
Risen, Arnie
Robertson, Oscar
Robinson, David
*Rodman, Dennis
Roosma, John
Russell, Bill
Russell, John "Honey"
*Sabonis, Arvydas
*Sanders, Tom "Satch"
Schayes, Adolph
Schmidt, Ernest
Schommer, John
Sedran, Barney
Semjonova, Uljana
**Sharman, Bill
Stockton, John
Steinmetz, Christian
Stokes, Maurice
*Tatum, Reece "Goose"
Thomas, Isiah
Thompson, David
Thompson, John
Thurmond, Nate
Twyman, Jack
Unseld, Wes
Vandivier, Robert "Fuzzy"
Wachter, Edward
Walton, Bill
Wanzer, Bobby
West, Jerry
White, Nera
**Wilkens, Lenny
Wilkins, Dominique
Woodard, Lynette
**Wooden, John
Worthy, James
Yardley, George

Coaches
Allen, Forrest C. "Phog"
Anderson, Harold
Auerbach, Arnold "Red"
Auriemma, Geno
Barmore, Leon
Barry, Justin "Sam"
Blood, Ernest
Boeheim, Jim

Brown, Larry
Calhoun, Jim
Cann, Howard
Carlson, Clifford
Carnesecca, Lou
Carnevale, Ben
Carril, Pete
Case, Everett
Chancellor, Van
Chaney, John
Conradt, Jody
Crum, Denzil
Daly, Chuck
Dean, Everett
Diaz-Miguel, Antonio
Diddle, Edgar
Drake, Bruce
Ferrandiz, Pedro
Gaines, Clarence
Gamba, Sandro
Gardner, James "Jack"
Gill, Amory "Slats"
Gomelsky, Aleksandr
Gunter, Sue
Hannum, Alex
Harshman, Marv
Haskins, Don
Hickey, Edgar
Hobson, Howard
Holzman, William "Red"
Hurley, Bob, Sr.
Iba, Hank
Jackson, Phil
Julian, Alvin
Keaney, Frank
Keogan, George
Knight, Bob
Krzyzewski, Mike
Kundla, John
Lambert, Ward
Litwack, Harry
Loeffler, Kenneth
Lonborg, Arthur "Dutch"
*Magee, Herb
McCutchan, Arad
McGuire, Al
McGuire, Frank
McLendon, John
Meanwell, Dr. Walter
Meyer, Ray
Miller, Ralph
Moore, Billie
Newell, Pete
Nikolic, Aleksandar
Novosel, Mirko

Olson, Robert "Lute"
Ramsay, John "Jack"
Riley, Pat
Rubini, Cesare
Rupp, Adolph
Rush, Cathy
Sachs, Leonard
**Sharman, Bill
Shelton, Everett
Sloan, Jerry
Smith, Dean
Stringer, C. Vivian
Summitt, Pat
Taylor, Fred
Thompson, John
*VanDerveer, Tara
Wade, Margaret
Watts, Stan
**Wilkens, Lenny
Williams, Roy
*Winter, Tex
**Wooden, John
Woolpert, Phil
Wootten, Morgan
Yow, Kay

Teams
1960 USA Men's Olympic team
1992 USA Basketball "Dream Team"
Buffalo Germans
First Team
Harlem Globetrotters
New York Renaissance
Original Celtics
Texas Western

Referees
Enright, James
Hepbron, George
Hoyt, George
Kennedy, Matthew
Leith, Lloyd
Mihalik, Zigmund "Red"
Nucatola, John
Quigley, Ernest
Rudolph, Marvin "Mendy"
Shirley, J. Dallas
Strom, Earl
Tobey, David
Walsh, David

Contributors
Abbott, Senda Berenson
Bee, Clair
Biasone, Danny
Brown, Hubert "Hubie"
Brown, Walter
Bunn, John
Buss, Jerry
Colangelo, Jerry
Davidson, Bill
Douglas, Bob
Duer, Al
Embry, Wayne
Fagan, Cliff
Fisher, Harry
Fleisher, Larry
Gavitt, David
Gottlieb, Edward
Gulick, Dr. Luther
Harrison, Lester
Hearn, Francis "Chick"
Hepp, Dr. Ferenc
Hickox, Edward
Hinkle, Tony
Irish, Edward "Ned"
Jones, R. William
Kennedy, Walter
Lemon, Meadowlark
Liston, Emil
Lloyd, Earl
Mokray, Bill
Morgan, Ralph
Morgenweck, Frank
Naismith, Dr. James
Newton, C. M.
O'Brien, John
O'Brien, Larry
Olsen, Harold
Podoloff, Maurice
Porter, Henry V.
Reid, William
Ripley, Elmer
St. John, Lynn
Saperstein, Abe
Schabinger, Arthur
Stagg, Alonzo
Stankovic, Boris
Steitz, Edward
Taylor, Chuck
Teague, Bertha
Tower, Oswald
Trester, Arthur
Wells, Clifford
Wilke, Lou
Zollner, Fred

NBA Home Courts

Team	Name (year built)	Capacity[1]	Team	Name (year built)	Capacity[1]
Atlanta	Philips Arena (1999)	18,729	Milwaukee	Bradley Center (1988)	18,717
Boston	TD Garden[2] (1995)	18,624	Minnesota	Target Center (1990)	19,356
Charlotte	Time Warner Cable Arena (2005)	19,077	New Jersey	Prudential Center (2007)	18,711
Chicago	United Center (1994)	20,917	New Orleans[4]	New Orleans Arena (1999)	17,188
Cleveland	Quicken Loans Arena (1994)	20,562	New York	Madison Square Garden (IV) (1968)	19,763
Dallas	American Airlines Center (2001)	19,200	Oklahoma City	Ford Center[5] (2002)	18,203
Denver	Pepsi Center (1999)	19,155	Orlando	Amway Center[6] (1989)	18,500
Detroit	The Palace of Auburn Hills (1988)	22,076	Philadelphia	Wells Fargo Center[7] (1996)	20,328
Golden State	ORACLE Arena[3] (1966)	19,596	Phoenix	US Airways Center[8] (1992)	18,422
Houston	Toyota Center (2003)	18,043	Portland	The Rose Garden (1995)	19,980
Indiana	Conseco Fieldhouse (1999)	18,165	Sacramento	Power Balance Pavilion[9] (1988)	17,317
L.A. Clippers	STAPLES Center (1999)	19,060	San Antonio	AT&T Center[10] (2002)	18,581
L.A. Lakers	STAPLES Center (1999)	18,997	Toronto	Air Canada Centre (1999)	19,800
Memphis	FedExForum (2004)	18,119	Utah	EnergySolutions Arena[11] (1991)	19,911
Miami	AmericanAirlines Arena (1999)	19,600	Washington	Verizon Center[12] (1997)	20,173

(1) At the end of the 2010-11 season. (2) Fleet Center, 1995-2005. (3) Oakland Coliseum Arena, 1966; Arena in Oakland, 1997-2006. (4) Because of damage to New Orleans Arena due to Hurricane Katrina, the Hornets played 35 games in the Ford Center in Oklahoma City, OK, 3 games in New Orleans Arena, and 3 games at other locations during the 2005-06 season. In 2006-07, the Hornets played 35 games at the Ford Center and 6 games in New Orleans Arena. The Hornets played 2007-08 home games in New Orleans Arena. (5) The Seattle SuperSonics relocated to Oklahoma City prior to the 2008-09 season. (6) Orlando Arena, 1989-2000; TD Waterhouse Centre, 2000-06; Amway Arena, 2006-07. (7) CoreStates Center, 1996-98; First Union Center, 1998-2003; Wachovia Center, 2003-10. (8) America West Arena, 1992-2006. (9) ARCO Arena, 1988-2011. (10) SBC Center, 2002-06. (11) Delta Center, 1991-2006. (12) MCI Center, 1997-2006.

WOMEN'S NATIONAL BASKETBALL ASSOCIATION
Minnesota Wins First WNBA Title

The Minnesota Lynx capped a near-perfect postseason with a 73-67 win over the Atlanta Dream Oct. 7, 2011, that clinched the franchise's first WNBA championship. Minnesota's Seimone Augustus scored 36 points in Game 2 and 16 points in the decisive Game 3 and earned the Finals MVP award. Lynx head coach Cheryl Reeve was voted Coach of the Year, while Minnesota forward Maya Moore earned WNBA Rookie of the Year honors.

WNBA Final Standings, 2011
(playoff seeding in parentheses; conference winner automatically gets top seed)

Eastern Conference	W	L	Pct	GB	Western Conference	W	L	Pct	GB
Indiana Fever (1)	21	13	.618	—	Minnesota Lynx (1)	27	7	.794	—
Connecticut Sun (2)	21	13	.618	—	Seattle Storm (2)	21	13	.618	6
Atlanta Dream (3)	20	14	.588	1	Phoenix Mercury (3)	19	15	.559	8
New York Liberty (4)	19	15	.559	2	San Antonio Silver Stars (4)	18	16	.529	9
Chicago Sky	14	20	.412	7	Los Angeles Sparks	15	19	.441	12
Washington Mystics	6	28	.176	15	Tulsa Shock	3	31	.088	24

WNBA Playoffs, 2011

Eastern Conference
(1) Indiana defeated (4) New York, 2 games to 1
(3) Atlanta defeated (2) Connecticut, 2 games to 0
(3) Atlanta defeated (1) Indiana, 2 games to 1

Western Conference
(1) Minnesota defeated (4) San Antonio, 2 games to 1
(3) Phoenix defeated (2) Seattle, 2 games to 1
(1) Minnesota defeated (3) Phoenix, 2 games to 0

WNBA Championship, 2011
Minnesota defeated Atlanta, 3 games to 0 (88-74, 101-95, 73-67) in the best-of-five series.

All-WNBA Teams, 2011

First team	Position	Second team	Position
Tamika Catchings, Indiana	Forward	Penny Taylor, Phoenix	Forward
Angel McCoughtry, Atlanta	Forward	Seimone Augustus, Minnesota	Forward
Tina Charles, Connecticut	Center	Sylvia Fowles, Chicago	Center
Diana Taurasi, Phoenix	Guard	Sue Bird, Seattle	Guard
Lindsay Whalen, Minnesota	Guard	Cappie Pondexter, New York	Guard

WNBA Statistical Leaders, 2011

Minutes played: 1,175, Sylvia Fowles, Chicago
Total points: 712, Angel McCoughtry, Atlanta
Points per game: 21.6, Diana Taurasi, Phoenix
Field goal pct.: .591, Sylvia Fowles, Chicago
3-point field goal pct.: .468, Jeanette Pohlen, Indiana

Free throw pct.: .909, DeWanna Bonner, Phoenix
Rebounds: 374, Tina Charles, Connecticut
Assists: 199, Lindsay Whalen, Minnesota
Steals: 78, Epiphanny Prince, Chicago
Blocked shots: 68, Sylvia Fowles, Chicago

WNBA Champions, 1997-2011

Year	Regular Season Eastern Conference	Western Conference	Champion	Playoffs Coach	Opponent
1997	Houston Comets	Phoenix Mercury	Houston	Van Chancellor	New York
1998	Cleveland Rockers	Houston Comets	Houston	Van Chancellor	Phoenix
1999	New York Liberty	Houston Comets	Houston	Van Chancellor	New York
2000	New York Liberty	Los Angeles Sparks	Houston	Van Chancellor	New York
2001	Cleveland Rockers	Los Angeles Sparks	Los Angeles	Michael Cooper	Charlotte
2002	New York Liberty	Los Angeles Sparks	Los Angeles	Michael Cooper	New York
2003	Detroit Shock	Los Angeles Sparks	Detroit	Bill Laimbeer	Los Angeles
2004	Connecticut Sun	Los Angeles Sparks	Seattle	Ann Donovan	Connecticut
2005	Connecticut Sun	Sacramento Monarchs	Sacramento	John Whisenant	Connecticut
2006	Connecticut Sun	Sacramento Monarchs	Detroit	Bill Laimbeer	Sacramento
2007	Detroit Shock	Phoenix Mercury	Phoenix	Paul Westhead	Detroit
2008	Detroit Shock	San Antonio Silver Stars	Detroit	Bill Laimbeer	San Antonio
2009	Indiana Fever	Phoenix Mercury	Phoenix	Corey Gaines	Indiana
2010	Washington Mystics	Seattle Storm	Seattle	Brian Agler	Atlanta
2011	Indiana Fever	Minnesota Lynx	Minnesota	Cheryl Reeve	Atlanta

WNBA Scoring Leaders, 1997-2011
(average points per game; 10 games minimum)

Year	Leader, team	Pts.	Avg.	Year	Leader, team	Pts.	Avg.	Year	Leader, team	Pts.	Avg.
1997	Cynthia Cooper, Houston	621	22.2	2002	Chamique Holdsclaw,			2007	Lauren Jackson, Seattle	739	23.8
1998	Cynthia Cooper, Houston	680	22.7		Washington	397	19.9	2008	Diana Taurasi, Phoenix	820	24.1
1999	Cynthia Cooper, Houston	686	22.1	2003	Lauren Jackson, Seattle	698	21.2	2009	Diana Taurasi, Phoenix	631	20.4
2000	Sheryl Swoopes, Houston	643	20.7	2004	Lauren Jackson, Seattle	634	20.5	2010	Diana Taurasi, Phoenix	702	22.6
2001	Katie Smith, Minnesota	739	23.1	2005	Sheryl Swoopes, Houston	614	18.6	2011	Diana Taurasi, Phoenix	692	21.6
				2006	Diana Taurasi, Phoenix	860	25.3				

WNBA Finals MVP

Year	Player
1997	Cynthia Cooper, Houston
1998	Cynthia Cooper, Houston
1999	Yolanda Griffith, Sacramento
2000	Sheryl Swoopes, Houston
2001	Lisa Leslie, Los Angeles
2002	Sheryl Swoopes, Houston
2003	Lauren Jackson, Seattle
2004	Lisa Leslie, Los Angeles
2005	Sheryl Swoopes, Houston
2006	Deanna Nolan, Detroit
2007	Cappie Pondexter, Phoenix
2008	Katie Smith, Detroit
2009	Diana Taurasi, Phoenix
2010	Lauren Jackson, Seattle
2011	Seimone Augustus, Minnesota

WNBA Most Valuable Player

Year	Player
1997	Cynthia Cooper, Houston
1998	Cynthia Cooper, Houston
1999	Cynthia Cooper, Houston
2000	Cynthia Cooper, Houston
2001	Lisa Leslie, Los Angeles
2002	Lisa Leslie, Los Angeles
2003	Ruth Riley, Detroit
2004	Betty Lennox, Seattle
2005	Yolanda Griffith, Sacramento
2006	Lisa Leslie, Los Angeles
2007	Lauren Jackson, Seattle
2008	Candace Parker, Los Angeles
2009	Diana Taurasi, Phoenix
2010	Lauren Jackson, Seattle
2011	Tamika Catchings, Indiana

WNBA Rookie of the Year

Year	Player
1997	No award
1998	Tracy Reid, Charlotte
1999	Chamique Holdsclaw, Washington
2000	Betty Lennox, Minnesota
2001	Jackie Stiles, Portland
2002	Tamika Catchings, Indiana
2003	Cheryl Ford, Detroit
2004	Diana Taurasi, Phoenix
2005	Temeka Johnson, Washington
2006	Seimone Augustus, Minnesota
2007	Armintie Price, Chicago
2008	Candace Parker, Los Angeles
2009	Angel McCoughtry, Atlanta
2010	Tina Charles, Connecticut
2011	Maya Moore, Minnesota

HOCKEY

Boston Bruins Capture 2011 Stanley Cup

The Boston Bruins defeated the Vancouver Canucks to win the Stanley Cup in seven games for their first championship since 1972. Bruins goalie Tim Thomas recorded a Game 7 gem June 15, 2011, with 37 saves in the 4-0 shutout win that sealed the championship. Thomas earned the Conn Smythe Trophy as playoff MVP, setting NHL records for most saves in the postseason (798) and in a Stanley Cup final (238).

The Canucks won their first Presidents' Trophy with a league-high 54 wins and 117 points in the regular season. Vancouver took seven games to eliminate its first-round opponent, the defending Stanley Cup champion Chicago Blackhawks. The Canucks then beat Nashville and San Jose to earn their first trip to the finals since 1994. The Bruins defeated the Montréal Canadiens, Philadelphia Flyers, and Tampa Bay Lightning en route to the final.

The league expanded its Premiere games schedule with six teams opening the regular season in three European cities: Carolina Hurricanes vs. Minnesota Wild in Helsinki, Finland, Oct. 7-8, 2010; Columbus Blue Jackets vs. San Jose Sharks, Oct. 8-9 in Stockholm, Sweden; and Boston Bruins vs. Phoenix Coyotes in Prague, Czech Republic, Oct. 9-10. Despite rain, the Pittsburgh Penguins and Washington Capitals played the outdoor Winter Classic on Jan. 1, 2011, at Heinz Field in Pittsburgh. Less than a week later, a concussion benched Penguins all-star center Sidney Crosby for the remainder of the season.

The Atlanta Thrashers announced May 31, 2011, that the franchise would relocate to Winnipeg, Manitoba, for the 2011-12 season. The NHL Board of Governors approved the deal in June, and the relocated team will be known as the Jets, reviving the name of a franchise that called Winnipeg home before moving to Phoenix, AZ, in 1996.

Final NHL Standings, 2010-11

Playoff seeding in parentheses; division winners automatically seeded 1, 2, or 3. As of the 2010-11 season, standings were determined by total points, then by the greater number of wins, excluding games won in shootout. Teams tied at the end of regulation time are each awarded one point. An additional point is awarded to the overtime or shootout winner.

Eastern Conference

Atlantic Division	W	L	OT	GF	GA	PTS
Philadelphia Flyers (2)	47	23	12	259	223	106
Pittsburgh Penguins (4)	49	25	8	238	199	106
New York Rangers (8)	44	33	5	233	198	93
New Jersey Devils	38	39	5	174	209	81
New York Islanders	30	39	13	229	264	73

Northeast Division	W	L	OT	GF	GA	PTS
Boston Bruins (3)	46	25	11	246	195	103
Montréal Canadiens (6)	44	30	8	216	209	96
Buffalo Sabres (7)	43	29	10	245	229	96
Toronto Maple Leafs	37	34	11	218	251	85
Ottawa Senators	32	40	10	192	250	74

Southeast Division	W	L	OT	GF	GA	PTS
Washington Capitals (1)	48	23	11	224	197	107
Tampa Bay Lightning (5)	46	25	11	247	240	103
Carolina Hurricanes	40	31	11	236	239	91
Atlanta Thrashers	34	36	12	223	269	80
Florida Panthers	30	40	12	195	229	72

Western Conference

Central Division	W	L	OT	GF	GA	PTS
Detroit Red Wings (3)	47	25	10	261	241	104
Nashville Predators (5)	44	27	11	219	194	99
Chicago Blackhawks (8)	44	29	9	258	225	97
St. Louis Blues	38	33	11	240	234	87
Columbus Blue Jackets	34	35	13	215	258	81

Northwest Division	W	L	OT	GF	GA	PTS
Vancouver Canucks (1)	54	19	9	262	185	117
Calgary Flames	41	29	12	250	237	94
Minnesota Wild	39	35	8	206	233	86
Colorado Avalanche	30	44	8	227	288	68
Edmonton Oilers	25	45	12	193	269	62

Pacific Division	W	L	OT	GF	GA	PTS
San Jose Sharks (2)	48	25	9	248	213	105
Anaheim Ducks (4)	47	30	5	239	235	99
Phoenix Coyotes (6)	43	26	13	231	226	99
Los Angeles Kings (7)	46	30	6	219	198	98
Dallas Stars	42	29	11	227	233	95

Stanley Cup Playoff Results, 2011

Eastern Conference

Washington defeated NY Rangers, 4-1
Boston defeated Montréal, 4-3
Philadelphia defeated Buffalo, 4-3
Tampa Bay defeated Pittsburgh, 4-3
Boston defeated Philadelphia, 4-0
Tampa Bay defeated Washington, 4-0
Boston defeated Tampa Bay, 4-3

Western Conference

Vancouver defeated Chicago, 4-3
San Jose defeated Los Angeles, 4-2
Nashville defeated Anaheim, 4-2
Detroit defeated Phoenix, 4-0
San Jose defeated Detroit, 4-3
Vancouver defeated Nashville, 4-2
Vancouver defeated San Jose, 4-1

Stanley Cup Final

Boston defeated Vancouver, 4-3 (0-1, 2-3 (OT), 8-1, 4-0, 0-1, 5-2, 4-0)

Stanley Cup Champions, 1927-2011

Year	Champion	Coach	Final opponent
1927	Ottawa	Dave Gill	Boston
1928	NY Rangers	Lester Patrick	Montréal Maroons
1929	Boston	Cy Denneny	NY Rangers
1930	Montréal Canadiens	Cecil Hart	Boston
1931	Montréal Canadiens	Cecil Hart	Chicago
1932	Toronto	Dick Irvin	NY Rangers
1933	NY Rangers	Lester Patrick	Toronto
1934	Chicago	Tommy Gorman	Detroit
1935	Montréal Maroons	Tommy Gorman	Toronto
1936	Detroit	Jack Adams	Toronto
1937	Detroit	Jack Adams	NY Rangers
1938	Chicago	Bill Stewart	Toronto
1939	Boston	Art Ross	Toronto
1940	NY Rangers	Frank Boucher	Toronto
1941	Boston	Cooney Weiland	Detroit
1942	Toronto	Hap Day	Detroit
1943	Detroit	Jack Adams	Boston
1944	Montréal	Dick Irvin	Chicago
1945	Toronto	Hap Day	Detroit
1946	Montréal	Dick Irvin	Boston
1947	Toronto	Hap Day	Montréal
1948	Toronto	Hap Day	Detroit
1949	Toronto	Hap Day	Detroit
1950	Detroit	Tommy Ivan	NY Rangers
1951	Toronto	Joe Primeau	Montréal
1952	Detroit	Tommy Ivan	Montréal
1953	Montréal	Dick Irvin	Boston
1954	Detroit	Tommy Ivan	Montréal
1955	Detroit	Jimmy Skinner	Montréal
1956	Montréal	Toe Blake	Detroit
1957	Montréal	Toe Blake	Boston
1958	Montréal	Toe Blake	Boston
1959	Montréal	Toe Blake	Toronto
1960	Montréal	Toe Blake	Toronto
1961	Chicago	Rudy Pilous	Detroit
1962	Toronto	Punch Imlach	Chicago
1963	Toronto	Punch Imlach	Detroit
1964	Toronto	Punch Imlach	Detroit
1965	Montréal	Toe Blake	Chicago
1966	Montréal	Toe Blake	Detroit
1967	Toronto	Punch Imlach	Montréal
1968	Montréal	Toe Blake	St. Louis
1969	Montréal	Claude Ruel	St. Louis
1970	Boston	Harry Sinden	St. Louis
1971	Montréal	Al MacNeil	Chicago
1972	Boston	Tom Johnson	NY Rangers
1973	Montréal	Scotty Bowman	Chicago
1974	Philadelphia	Fred Shero	Boston
1975	Philadelphia	Fred Shero	Buffalo
1976	Montréal	Scotty Bowman	Philadelphia
1977	Montréal	Scotty Bowman	Boston

Year	Champion	Coach	Final opponent	Year	Champion	Coach	Final opponent
1978	Montréal	Scotty Bowman	Boston	1995	New Jersey	Jacques Lemaire	Detroit
1979	Montréal	Scotty Bowman	NY Rangers	1996	Colorado	Marc Crawford	Florida
1980	NY Islanders	Al Arbour	Philadelphia	1997	Detroit	Scotty Bowman	Philadelphia
1981	NY Islanders	Al Arbour	Minnesota	1998	Detroit	Scotty Bowman	Washington
1982	NY Islanders	Al Arbour	Vancouver	1999	Dallas	Ken Hitchcock	Buffalo
1983	NY Islanders	Al Arbour	Edmonton	2000	New Jersey	Larry Robinson	Dallas
1984	Edmonton	Glen Sather	NY Islanders	2001	Colorado	Bob Hartley	New Jersey
1985	Edmonton	Glen Sather	Philadelphia	2002	Detroit	Scotty Bowman	Carolina
1986	Montréal	Jean Perron	Calgary	2003	New Jersey	Pat Burns	Anaheim
1987	Edmonton	Glen Sather	Philadelphia	2004	Tampa Bay	John Tortorella	Calgary
1988	Edmonton	Glen Sather	Boston	2005	No competition (labor dispute; season cancelled)		
1989	Calgary	Terry Crisp	Montréal	2006	Carolina	Peter Laviolette	Edmonton
1990	Edmonton	John Muckler	Boston	2007	Anaheim	Randy Carlyle	Ottawa
1991	Pittsburgh	Bob Johnson	Minnesota	2008	Detroit	Mike Babcock	Pittsburgh
1992	Pittsburgh	Scotty Bowman	Chicago	2009	Pittsburgh	Dan Bylsma	Detroit
1993	Montréal	Jacques Demers	Los Angeles	2010	Chicago	Joel Quenneville	Philadelphia
1994	NY Rangers	Mike Keenan	Vancouver	2011	Boston	Claude Julien	Vancouver

Most NHL Goals in a Season

Player	Team	Season	Goals	Player	Team	Season	Goals
Wayne Gretzky	Edmonton	1981-82	92	Jari Kurri	Edmonton	1984-85	71
Wayne Gretzky	Edmonton	1983-84	87	Mario Lemieux	Pittsburgh	1987-88	70
Brett Hull	St. Louis	1990-91	86	Bernie Nicholls	Los Angeles	1988-89	70
Mario Lemieux	Pittsburgh	1988-89	85	Brett Hull	St. Louis	1991-92	70
Phil Esposito	Boston	1970-71	76	Mike Bossy	NY Islanders	1978-79	69
Teemu Selanne	Winnipeg	1992-93	76	Mario Lemieux	Pittsburgh	1992-93	69
Alexander Mogilny	Buffalo	1992-93	76	Mario Lemieux	Pittsburgh	1995-96	69
Wayne Gretzky	Edmonton	1984-85	73	Phil Esposito	Boston	1973-74	68
Brett Hull	St. Louis	1989-90	72	Mike Bossy	NY Islanders	1980-81	68
Wayne Gretzky	Edmonton	1982-83	71	Jari Kurri	Edmonton	1985-86	68

All-Time Regular Season Leading Scorers

(Through end of 2010-11 season.)

Player	Goals	Assists	Points	Player	Goals	Assists	Points	Player	Goals	Assists	Points
Wayne Gretzky	894	1,963	2,857	Joe Sakic	625	1,016	1,641	Bryan Trottier	524	901	1,425
Mark Messier	694	1,193	1,887	Jaromir Jagr	646	953	1,599	Adam Oates	341	1,079	1,420
Gordie Howe	801	1,049	1,850	Phil Esposito	717	873	1,590	Doug Gilmour	450	964	1,414
Ron Francis	549	1,249	1,798	Ray Bourque	410	1,169	1,579	Dale Hawerchuk	518	891	1,409
Marcel Dionne	731	1,040	1,771	Mark Recchi	577	956	1,533	Jari Kurri	601	797	1,398
Steve Yzerman	692	1,063	1,755	Paul Coffey	396	1,135	1,531	Luc Robitaille	668	726	1,394
Mario Lemieux	690	1,033	1,723	Stan Mikita	541	926	1,467	Brett Hull	741	650	1,391

Hart Memorial Trophy (MVP), 1927-2011

Year	Player, team	Year	Player, team	Year	Player, team
1927	Herb Gardiner, Montréal Canadiens	1955	Ted Kennedy, Toronto	1983	Wayne Gretzky, Edmonton
1928	Howie Morenz, Montréal Canadiens	1956	Jean Beliveau, Montréal	1984	Wayne Gretzky, Edmonton
1929	Roy Worters, NY Americans	1957	Gordie Howe, Detroit	1985	Wayne Gretzky, Edmonton
1930	Nels Stewart, Montréal Maroons	1958	Gordie Howe, Detroit	1986	Wayne Gretzky, Edmonton
1931	Howie Morenz, Montréal Canadiens	1959	Andy Bathgate, NY Rangers	1987	Wayne Gretzky, Edmonton
1932	Howie Morenz, Montréal Canadiens	1960	Gordie Howe, Detroit	1988	Mario Lemieux, Pittsburgh
1933	Eddie Shore, Boston	1961	Bernie Geoffrion, Montréal	1989	Wayne Gretzky, Los Angeles
1934	Aurel Joliat, Montréal Canadiens	1962	Jacques Plante, Montréal	1990	Mark Messier, Edmonton
1935	Eddie Shore, Boston	1963	Gordie Howe, Detroit	1991	Brett Hull, St. Louis
1936	Eddie Shore, Boston	1964	Jean Beliveau, Montréal	1992	Mark Messier, NY Rangers
1937	Babe Siebert, Montréal Canadiens	1965	Bobby Hull, Chicago	1993	Mario Lemieux, Pittsburgh
1938	Eddie Shore, Boston	1966	Bobby Hull, Chicago	1994	Sergei Fedorov, Detroit
1939	Toe Blake, Montréal	1967	Stan Mikita, Chicago	1995	Eric Lindros, Philadelphia
1940	Ebbie Goodfellow, Detroit	1968	Stan Mikita, Chicago	1996	Mario Lemieux, Pittsburgh
1941	Bill Cowley, Boston	1969	Phil Esposito, Boston	1997	Dominik Hasek, Buffalo
1942	Tom Anderson, Brooklyn Americans	1970	Bobby Orr, Boston	1998	Dominik Hasek, Buffalo
1943	Bill Cowley, Boston	1971	Bobby Orr, Boston	1999	Jaromir Jagr, Pittsburgh
1944	Babe Pratt, Toronto	1972	Bobby Orr, Boston	2000	Chris Pronger, St. Louis
1945	Elmer Lach, Montréal	1973	Bobby Clarke, Philadelphia	2001	Joe Sakic, Colorado
1946	Max Bentley, Chicago	1974	Phil Esposito, Boston	2002	Jose Theodore, Montréal
1947	Maurice Richard, Montréal	1975	Bobby Clarke, Philadelphia	2003	Peter Forsberg, Colorado
1948	Buddy O'Connor, NY Rangers	1976	Bobby Clarke, Philadelphia	2004	Martin St. Louis, Tampa Bay
1949	Sid Abel, Detroit	1977	Guy Lafleur, Montréal	2006	Joe Thornton, San Jose
1950	Chuck Rayner, NY Rangers	1978	Guy Lafleur, Montréal	2007	Sidney Crosby, Pittsburgh
1951	Milt Schmidt, Boston	1979	Bryan Trottier, NY Islanders	2008	Alexander Ovechkin, Washington
1952	Gordie Howe, Detroit	1980	Wayne Gretzky, Edmonton	2009	Alexander Ovechkin, Washington
1953	Gordie Howe, Detroit	1981	Wayne Gretzky, Edmonton	2010	Henrik Sedin, Vancouver
1954	Al Rollins, Chicago	1982	Wayne Gretzky, Edmonton	2011	Corey Perry, Anaheim

Conn Smythe Trophy (MVP in Playoffs), 1965-2011

Year	Player, team	Year	Player, team	Year	Player, team
1965	Jean Beliveau, Montréal	1976	Reg Leach, Philadelphia	1987	Ron Hextall, Philadelphia
1966	Roger Crozier, Detroit	1977	Guy Lafleur, Montréal	1988	Wayne Gretzky, Edmonton
1967	Dave Keon, Toronto	1978	Larry Robinson, Montréal	1989	Al MacInnis, Calgary
1968	Glenn Hall, St. Louis	1979	Bob Gainey, Montréal	1990	Bill Ranford, Edmonton
1969	Serge Savard, Montréal	1980	Bryan Trottier, NY Islanders	1991	Mario Lemieux, Pittsburgh
1970	Bobby Orr, Boston	1981	Butch Goring, NY Islanders	1992	Mario Lemieux, Pittsburgh
1971	Ken Dryden, Montréal	1982	Mike Bossy, NY Islanders	1993	Patrick Roy, Montréal
1972	Bobby Orr, Boston	1983	Billy Smith, NY Islanders	1994	Brian Leetch, NY Rangers
1973	Yvan Cournoyer, Montréal	1984	Mark Messier, Edmonton	1995	Claude Lemieux, New Jersey
1974	Bernie Parent, Philadelphia	1985	Wayne Gretzky, Edmonton	1996	Joe Sakic, Colorado
1975	Bernie Parent, Philadelphia	1986	Patrick Roy, Montréal	1997	Mike Vernon, Detroit

Year	Player, team	Year	Player, team	Year	Player, team
1998	Steve Yzerman, Detroit	2003	Jean-Sebastien Giguere, Anaheim	2008	Henrik Zetterberg, Detroit
1999	Joe Nieuwendyk, Dallas	2004	Brad Richards, Tampa Bay	2009	Evgeni Malkin, Pittsburgh
2000	Scott Stevens, New Jersey	2006	Cam Ward, Carolina	2010	Jonathan Toews, Chicago
2001	Patrick Roy, Colorado	2007	Scott Niedermayer, Anaheim	2011	Tim Thomas, Boston
2002	Nicklas Lidstrom, Detroit				

Calder Memorial Trophy (Rookie of the Year), 1933-2011

Year	Player, team	Year	Player, team	Year	Player, team
1933	Carl Voss, Detroit	1959	Ralph Backstrom, Montréal	1985	Mario Lemieux, Pittsburgh
1934	Russ Blinco, Montréal Maroons	1960	Bill Hay, Chicago	1986	Gary Suter, Calgary
1935	Dave Schriner, NY Americans	1961	Dave Keon, Toronto	1987	Luc Robitaille, Los Angeles
1936	Mike Karakas, Chicago	1962	Bobby Rousseau, Montréal	1988	Joe Nieuwendyk, Calgary
1937	Syl Apps, Toronto	1963	Kent Douglas, Toronto	1989	Brian Leetch, NY Rangers
1938	Cully Dahlstrom, Chicago	1964	Jacques Laperriere, Montréal	1990	Sergei Makarov, Calgary
1939	Frank Brimsek, Boston	1965	Roger Crozier, Detroit	1991	Ed Belfour, Chicago
1940	Kilby MacDonald, NY Rangers	1966	Brit Selby, Toronto	1992	Pavel Bure, Vancouver
1941	John Quilty, Montréal	1967	Bobby Orr, Boston	1993	Teemu Selanne, Winnipeg
1942	Grant Warwick, NY Rangers	1968	Derek Sanderson, Boston	1994	Martin Brodeur, New Jersey
1943	Gaye Stewart, Toronto	1969	Danny Grant, Minnesota	1995	Peter Forsberg, Quebec
1944	Gus Bodnar, Toronto	1970	Tony Esposito, Chicago	1996	Daniel Alfredsson, Ottawa
1945	Frank McCool, Toronto	1971	Gilbert Perreault, Buffalo	1997	Bryan Berard, NY Islanders
1946	Edgar Laprade, NY Rangers	1972	Ken Dryden, Montréal	1998	Sergei Samsonov, Boston
1947	Howie Meeker, Toronto	1973	Steve Vickers, NY Rangers	1999	Chris Drury, Colorado
1948	Jim McFadden, Detroit	1974	Denis Potvin, NY Islanders	2000	Scott Gomez, New Jersey
1949	Pentti Lund, NY Rangers	1975	Eric Vail, Atlanta	2001	Evgeni Nabokov, San Jose
1950	Jack Gelineau, Boston	1976	Bryan Trottier, NY Islanders	2002	Dany Heatley, Atlanta
1951	Terry Sawchuk, Detroit	1977	Willi Plett, Atlanta	2003	Barret Jackman, St. Louis
1952	Bernie Geoffrion, Montréal	1978	Mike Bossy, NY Islanders	2004	Andrew Raycroft, Boston
1953	Gump Worsley, NY Rangers	1979	Bobby Smith, Minnesota	2006	Alexander Ovechkin, Washington
1954	Camille Henry, NY Rangers	1980	Ray Bourque, Boston	2007	Evgeni Malkin, Pittsburgh
1955	Ed Litzenberger, Chicago	1981	Peter Stastny, Quebec	2008	Patrick Kane, Chicago
1956	Glenn Hall, Detroit	1982	Dale Hawerchuk, Winnipeg	2009	Steve Mason, Columbus
1957	Larry Regan, Boston	1983	Steve Larmer, Chicago	2010	Tyler Myers, Buffalo
1958	Frank Mahovlich, Toronto	1984	Tom Barrasso, Buffalo	2011	Jeff Skinner, Carolina

Lady Byng Memorial Trophy (Most Gentlemanly Player), 1925-2011

Year	Player, team	Year	Player, team	Year	Player, team
1925	Frank Nighbor, Ottawa	1954	Red Kelly, Detroit	1983	Mike Bossy, NY Islanders
1926	Frank Nighbor, Ottawa	1955	Sid Smith, Toronto	1984	Mike Bossy, NY Islanders
1927	Billy Burch, NY Americans	1956	Earl Reibel, Detroit	1985	Jari Kurri, Edmonton
1928	Frank Boucher, NY Rangers	1957	Andy Hebenton, NY Rangers	1986	Mike Bossy, NY Islanders
1929	Frank Boucher, NY Rangers	1958	Camille Henry, NY Rangers	1987	Joe Mullen, Calgary
1930	Frank Boucher, NY Rangers	1959	Alex Delvecchio, Detroit	1988	Mats Naslund, Montréal
1931	Frank Boucher, NY Rangers	1960	Don McKenney, Boston	1989	Joe Mullen, Calgary
1932	Joe Primeau, Toronto	1961	Red Kelly, Toronto	1990	Brett Hull, St. Louis
1933	Frank Boucher, NY Rangers	1962	Dave Keon, Toronto	1991	Wayne Gretzky, Los Angeles
1934	Frank Boucher, NY Rangers	1963	Dave Keon, Toronto	1992	Wayne Gretzky, Los Angeles
1935	Frank Boucher, NY Rangers	1964	Ken Wharram, Chicago	1993	Pierre Turgeon, NY Islanders
1936	Doc Romnes, Chicago	1965	Bobby Hull, Chicago	1994	Wayne Gretzky, Los Angeles
1937	Marty Barry, Detroit	1966	Alex Delvecchio, Detroit	1995	Ron Francis, Pittsburgh
1938	Gordie Drillon, Toronto	1967	Stan Mikita, Chicago	1996	Paul Kariya, Anaheim
1939	Clint Smith, NY Rangers	1968	Stan Mikita, Chicago	1997	Paul Kariya, Anaheim
1940	Bobby Bauer, Boston	1969	Alex Delvecchio, Detroit	1998	Ron Francis, Pittsburgh
1941	Bobby Bauer, Boston	1970	Phil Goyette, St. Louis	1999	Wayne Gretzky, NY Rangers
1942	Syl Apps, Toronto	1971	John Bucyk, Boston	2000	Pavol Demitra, St. Louis
1943	Max Bentley, Chicago	1972	Jean Ratelle, NY Rangers	2001	Joe Sakic, Colorado
1944	Clint Smith, Chicago	1973	Gil Perreault, Buffalo	2002	Ron Francis, Carolina
1945	Bill Mosienko, Chicago	1974	John Bucyk, Boston	2003	Alexander Mogilny, Toronto
1946	Toe Blake, Montréal	1975	Marcel Dionne, Detroit	2004	Brad Richards, Tampa Bay
1947	Bobby Bauer, Boston	1976	Jean Ratelle, NYR-Boston	2006	Pavel Datsyuk, Detroit
1948	Buddy O'Connor, NY Rangers	1977	Marcel Dionne, Los Angeles	2007	Pavel Datsyuk, Detroit
1949	Bill Quackenbush, Detroit	1978	Butch Goring, Los Angeles	2008	Pavel Datsyuk, Detroit
1950	Edgar Laprade, NY Rangers	1979	Bob MacMillan, Atlanta	2009	Pavel Datsyuk, Detroit
1951	Red Kelly, Detroit	1980	Wayne Gretzky, Edmonton	2010	Martin St. Louis, Tampa Bay
1952	Sid Smith, Toronto	1981	Rick Kehoe, Pittsburgh	2011	Martin St. Louis, Tampa Bay
1953	Red Kelly, Detroit	1982	Rick Middleton, Boston		

James Norris Memorial Trophy (Outstanding Defenseman), 1954-2011

Year	Player, team	Year	Player, team	Year	Player, team
1954	Red Kelly, Detroit	1973	Bobby Orr, Boston	1992	Brian Leetch, NY Rangers
1955	Doug Harvey, Montréal	1974	Bobby Orr, Boston	1993	Chris Chelios, Chicago
1956	Doug Harvey, Montréal	1975	Bobby Orr, Boston	1994	Ray Bourque, Boston
1957	Doug Harvey, Montréal	1976	Denis Potvin, NY Islanders	1995	Paul Coffey, Detroit
1958	Doug Harvey, Montréal	1977	Larry Robinson, Montréal	1996	Chris Chelios, Chicago
1959	Tom Johnson, Montréal	1978	Denis Potvin, NY Islanders	1997	Brian Leetch, NY Rangers
1960	Doug Harvey, Montréal	1979	Denis Potvin, NY Islanders	1998	Rob Blake, Los Angeles
1961	Doug Harvey, Montréal	1980	Larry Robinson, Montréal	1999	Al MacInnis, St. Louis
1962	Doug Harvey, NY Rangers	1981	Randy Carlyle, Pittsburgh	2000	Chris Pronger, St. Louis
1963	Pierre Pilote, Chicago	1982	Doug Wilson, Chicago	2001	Nicklas Lidstrom, Detroit
1964	Pierre Pilote, Chicago	1983	Rod Langway, Washington	2002	Nicklas Lidstrom, Detroit
1965	Pierre Pilote, Chicago	1984	Rod Langway, Washington	2003	Nicklas Lidstrom, Detroit
1966	Jacques Laperriere, Montréal	1985	Paul Coffey, Edmonton	2004	Scott Niedermayer, New Jersey
1967	Harry Howell, NY Rangers	1986	Paul Coffey, Edmonton	2006	Nicklas Lidstrom, Detroit
1968	Bobby Orr, Boston	1987	Ray Bourque, Boston	2007	Nicklas Lidstrom, Detroit
1969	Bobby Orr, Boston	1988	Ray Bourque, Boston	2008	Nicklas Lidstrom, Detroit
1970	Bobby Orr, Boston	1989	Chris Chelios, Montréal	2009	Zdeno Chara, Boston
1971	Bobby Orr, Boston	1990	Ray Bourque, Boston	2010	Duncan Keith, Chicago
1972	Bobby Orr, Boston	1991	Ray Bourque, Boston	2011	Nicklas Lidstrom, Detroit

Art Ross Trophy (Leading Points Scorer), 1927-2011

Trophy first awarded in 1948. Prior years list NHL scoring leader.

Year	Player, team	Year	Player, team	Year	Player, team
1927	Bill Cook, NY Rangers	1955	Bernie Geoffrion, Montréal	1983	Wayne Gretzky, Edmonton
1928	Howie Morenz, Montréal Canadiens	1956	Jean Beliveau, Montréal	1984	Wayne Gretzky, Edmonton
1929	Ace Bailey, Toronto	1957	Gordie Howe, Detroit	1985	Wayne Gretzky, Edmonton
1930	Cooney Weiland, Boston	1958	Dickie Moore, Montréal	1986	Wayne Gretzky, Edmonton
1931	Howie Morenz, Montréal Canadiens	1959	Dickie Moore, Montréal	1987	Wayne Gretzky, Edmonton
1932	Harvey Jackson, Toronto	1960	Bobby Hull, Chicago	1988	Mario Lemieux, Pittsburgh
1933	Bill Cook, NY Rangers	1961	Bernie Geoffrion, Montréal	1989	Mario Lemieux, Pittsburgh
1934	Charlie Conacher, Toronto	1962	Bobby Hull, Chicago	1990	Wayne Gretzky, Los Angeles
1935	Charlie Conacher, Toronto	1963	Gordie Howe, Detroit	1991	Wayne Gretzky, Los Angeles
1936	Dave Schriner, NY Americans	1964	Stan Mikita, Chicago	1992	Mario Lemieux, Pittsburgh
1937	Dave Schriner, NY Americans	1965	Stan Mikita, Chicago	1993	Mario Lemieux, Pittsburgh
1938	Gordie Drillon, Toronto	1966	Bobby Hull, Chicago	1994	Wayne Gretzky, Los Angeles
1939	Toe Blake, Montréal	1967	Stan Mikita, Chicago	1995	Jaromir Jagr, Pittsburgh
1940	Milt Schmidt, Boston	1968	Stan Mikita, Chicago	1996	Mario Lemieux, Pittsburgh
1941	Bill Cowley, Boston	1969	Phil Esposito, Boston	1997	Mario Lemieux, Pittsburgh
1942	Bryan Hextall, NY Rangers	1970	Bobby Orr, Boston	1998	Jaromir Jagr, Pittsburgh
1943	Doug Bentley, Chicago	1971	Phil Esposito, Boston	1999	Jaromir Jagr, Pittsburgh
1944	Herbie Cain, Boston	1972	Phil Esposito, Boston	2000	Jaromir Jagr, Pittsburgh
1945	Elmer Lach, Montréal	1973	Phil Esposito, Boston	2001	Jaromir Jagr, Pittsburgh
1946	Max Bentley, Chicago	1974	Phil Esposito, Boston	2002	Jarome Iginla, Calgary
1947	Max Bentley, Chicago	1975	Bobby Orr, Boston	2003	Peter Forsberg, Colorado
1948	Elmer Lach, Montréal	1976	Guy Lafleur, Montréal	2004	Martin St. Louis, Tampa Bay
1949	Roy Conacher, Chicago	1977	Guy Lafleur, Montréal	2006	Joe Thornton, San Jose
1950	Ted Lindsay, Detroit	1978	Guy Lafleur, Montréal	2007	Sidney Crosby, Pittsburgh
1951	Gordie Howe, Detroit	1979	Bryan Trottier, NY Islanders	2008	Alexander Ovechkin, Washington
1952	Gordie Howe, Detroit	1980	Marcel Dionne, Los Angeles	2009	Evgeni Malkin, Pittsburgh
1953	Gordie Howe, Detroit	1981	Wayne Gretzky, Edmonton	2010	Henrik Sedin, Vancouver
1954	Gordie Howe, Detroit	1982	Wayne Gretzky, Edmonton	2011	Daniel Sedin, Vancouver

Vezina Trophy (Outstanding Goalie), 1927-2011

Before 1982, awarded to the goalie or goalies who played a minimum of 25 games for the team that allowed the fewest goals; since 1982, awarded to the most outstanding goalie, as determined by a vote of NHL general managers.

Year	Player, team	Year	Player, team	Year	Player, team
1927	George Hainsworth, Montréal Canadiens	1954	Harry Lumley, Toronto	1982	Bill Smith, NY Islanders
		1955	Terry Sawchuk, Detroit	1983	Pete Peeters, Boston
1928	George Hainsworth, Montréal Canadiens	1956	Jacques Plante, Montréal	1984	Tom Barrasso, Buffalo
		1957	Jacques Plante, Montréal	1985	Pelle Lindbergh, Philadelphia
1929	George Hainsworth, Montréal Canadiens	1958	Jacques Plante, Montréal	1986	John Vanbiesbrouck, NY Rangers
		1959	Jacques Plante, Montréal	1987	Ron Hextall, Philadelphia
1930	Tiny Thompson, Boston	1960	Jacques Plante, Montréal	1988	Grant Fuhr, Edmonton
1931	Roy Worters, NY Americans	1961	Johnny Bower, Toronto	1989	Patrick Roy, Montréal
1932	Charlie Gardiner, Chicago	1962	Jacques Plante, Montréal	1990	Patrick Roy, Montréal
1933	Tiny Thompson, Boston	1963	Glenn Hall, Chicago	1991	Ed Belfour, Chicago
1934	Charlie Gardiner, Chicago	1964	Charlie Hodge, Montréal	1992	Patrick Roy, Montréal
1935	Lorne Chabot, Chicago	1965	Sawchuk, Bower, Toronto	1993	Ed Belfour, Chicago
1936	Tiny Thompson, Boston	1966	Worsley, Hodge, Montréal	1994	Dominik Hasek, Buffalo
1937	Normie Smith, Detroit	1967	Hall, DeJordy, Chicago	1995	Dominik Hasek, Buffalo
1938	Tiny Thompson, Boston	1968	Worsley, Vachon, Montréal	1996	Jim Carey, Washington
1939	Frank Brimsek, Boston	1969	Hall, Plante, St. Louis	1997	Dominik Hasek, Buffalo
1940	Dave Kerr, NY Rangers	1970	Tony Esposito, Chicago	1998	Dominik Hasek, Buffalo
1941	Turk Broda, Toronto	1971	Giacomin, Villemure, NY Rangers	1999	Dominik Hasek, Buffalo
1942	Frank Brimsek, Boston	1972	Esposito, Smith, Chicago	2000	Olaf Kolzig, Washington
1943	Johnny Mowers, Detroit	1973	Ken Dryden, Montréal	2001	Dominik Hasek, Buffalo
1944	Bill Durnan, Montréal	1974	Bernie Parent, Philadelphia; Tony Esposito, Chicago	2002	Jose Theodore, Montréal
1945	Bill Durnan, Montréal			2003	Martin Brodeur, New Jersey
1946	Bill Durnan, Montréal	1975	Bernie Parent, Philadelphia	2004	Martin Brodeur, New Jersey
1947	Bill Durnan, Montréal	1976	Ken Dryden, Montréal	2006	Miikka Kiprusoff, Calgary
1948	Turk Broda, Toronto	1977	Dryden, Larocque, Montréal	2007	Martin Brodeur, New Jersey
1949	Bill Durnan, Montréal	1978	Dryden, Larocque, Montréal	2008	Martin Brodeur, New Jersey
1950	Bill Durnan, Montréal	1979	Dryden, Larocque, Montréal	2009	Tim Thomas, Boston
1951	Al Rollins, Toronto	1980	Sauve, Edwards, Buffalo	2010	Ryan Miller, Buffalo
1952	Terry Sawchuk, Detroit	1981	Sevigny, Larocque, Herron, Montréal	2011	Tim Thomas, Boston
1953	Terry Sawchuk, Detroit				

NHL Home Ice

Team	Name (built)	Capacity[1]	Team	Name (built)	Capacity[1]
Anaheim	Honda Center[2] (1993)	17,174	Montréal	Le Centre Bell[9] (1996)	21,273
Atlanta	Philips Arena (1999)	18,545	Nashville	Bridgestone Arena[10] (1997)	17,113
Boston	TD Garden[3] (1995)	17,565	New Jersey	Prudential Center (2007)	17,625
Buffalo	HSBC Arena[4] (1996)	18,690	NY Islanders	Nassau Veterans Mem. Col. (1972)	16,234
Calgary	Pengrowth Saddledome[5] (1983)	19,289	NY Rangers	Madison Square Garden (1968)	18,200
Carolina	RBC Center[6] (1999)	18,680	Ottawa	Scotiabank Place[11] (1996)	19,153
Chicago	United Center (1994)	19,717	Philadelphia	Wells Fargo Center[12] (1996)	19,537
Colorado	Pepsi Center (1999)	18,007	Phoenix	Jobing.com Arena[13] (2003)	17,125
Columbus	Nationwide Arena (2000)	18,144	Pittsburgh	CONSOL Energy Center (2010)	18,087
Dallas	American Airlines Center (2001)	18,532	St. Louis	Scottrade Center[14] (1994)	19,150
Detroit	Joe Louis Arena (1979)	20,066	San Jose	HP Pavilion[15] (1993)	17,562
Edmonton	Rexall Place[7] (1974)	16,839	Tampa Bay	St. Pete Times Forum[16] (1996)	19,758
Florida	BankAtlantic Center[8] (1998)	17,040	Toronto	Air Canada Centre (1995)	18,819
Los Angeles	Staples Center (1999)	18,118	Vancouver	Rogers Arena[17] (1995)	18,810
Minnesota	Xcel Energy Center	18,064	Washington	Verizon Center[18] (1997)	18,277

(1) At the end of the 2010-11 season. Atlanta announced in May 2011 that the team would move to Winnipeg, MB, Canada, beginning in the 2011-12 NHL season. (2) The Arrowhead Pond of Anaheim, 1993-2006. (3) FleetCenter, 1995-2005; TD Banknorth Garden, 2005-09. (4) Marine Midland Arena, 1996-99. (5) Olympic Saddledome, 1983-96; Canadian Airlines Saddledome, 1996-2000. (6) Raleigh Entertainment and Sports Arena, 1999-2002. (7) Northlands Col., 1974-79; Edmonton Col., 1979-98; Skyreach Centre, 1998-2003. (8) National Car Rental Center, 1998-2002; Office Depot Center, 2002-05. (9) Le Centre Molson, 1996-2002. (10) Nashville Arena, 1997-99; Gaylord Entertainment Center, 1999-2007; Sommet Center, 2007-10. (11) Corel Centre, 1996-2006. (12) CoreStates Center, 1996-98; First Union Center, 1998-2003; Wachovia Center, 2003-10. (13) Glendale Arena, 2003-06. (14) Kiel Center, 1994-2000; Savvis Center, 2000-06. (15) San Jose Arena, 1993-2001; Compaq Center, 2001-02. (16) Ice Palace, 1996-2002. (17) General Motors Place, 1995-2010. (18) MCI Center, 1997-2006.

Hockey Hall of Fame, Toronto, ON, Canada

(* = 2011 inductee.)

Players

Abel, Sid
Adams, Jack
Anderson, Glenn
Apps, Syl
Armstrong, George
Bailey, Irvine "Ace"
Bain, Dan
Baker, Hobey
Barber, Bill
Barry, Marty
Bathgate, Andy
Bauer, Bobby
*Belfour, Ed
Beliveau, Jean
Benedict, Clint
Bentley, Doug
Bentley, Max
Blake, Hector "Toe"
Boivin, Leo
Boon, Dickie
Bossy, Mike
Bouchard, Butch
Boucher, Frank
Boucher, George
Bourque, Ray
Bower, Johnny
Bowie, Russell "Dubbie"
Brimsek, Frank
Broadbent, Harry L. "Punch"
Broda, Turk
Bucyk, John
Burch, Billy
Cameron, Harry
Cheevers, Gerry
Ciccarelli, Dino
Clancy, King
Clapper, Aubrey "Dit"
Clarke, Bobby
Cleghorn, Sprague
Coffey, Paul
Colville, Neil
Conacher, Charlie
Conacher, Lionel
Conacher, Roy
Connell, Alex
Cook, Bill
Cook, Frederick "Bun"
Coulter, Art
Cournoyer, Yvan
Cowley, Bill
Crawford, Rusty
Darragh, Jack
Davidson, Scotty
Day, Clarence "Hap"
Delvecchio, Alex
Denneny, Cy
Dionne, Marcel
Drillon, Gordie
Drinkwater, Graham
Dryden, Ken
Duff, Terrance "Dick"
Dumart, Woody
Dunderdale, Tommy
Durnan, Bill
Dutton, Mervyn "Red"
Dye, Babe
Esposito, Phil
Esposito, Tony
Farrel, Arthur
Federko, Bernie
Fetisov, Viacheslav
Flaman, Fernie
Foyston, Frank
Francis, Ron

Fredrickson, Frank
Fuhr, Grant
Gadsby, Bill
Gainey, Bob
Gardiner, Chuck
Gardiner, Herb
Gardiner, Jimmy
Gartner, Mike
Geoffrion, Bernie
Gerard, Eddie
Giacomin, Eddie
Gilbert, Rod
Gillies, Clark
Gilmour, Billy
*Gilmour, Doug
Goheen, Frank "Moose"
Goodfellow, Ebbie
Goulet, Michel
Granato, Cammi
Grant, Mike
Green, Wilfred "Shorty"
Gretzky, Wayne
Griffis, Si
Hainsworth, George
Hall, Glenn
Hall, Joe
Harvey, Doug
Hawerchuk, Dale
Hay, George
Hern, Riley
Hextall, Bryan
Holmes, Hap
Hooper, Tom
Horner, Red
Horton, Tim
Howe, Gordie
*Howe, Mark
Howe, Syd
Howell, Harry
Hull, Bobby
Hull, Brett
Hutton, John "Bouse"
Hyland, Harry
Irvin, Dick
Jackson, Harvey "Busher"
James, Angela
Johnson, Ching
Johnson, Ernie
Johnson, Tom
Joliat, Aurel
Keats, Duke
Kelly, Red
Kennedy, Ted
Keon, Dave
Kharlamov, Valeri
Kurri, Jari
Lach, Elmer
Lafleur, Guy
LaFontaine, Pat
Lalonde, Newsy
Langway, Rod
Laperriere, Jacques
Lapointe, Guy
Laprade, Edgar
Larionov, Igor
Laviolette, Jack
LeSueur, Percy
Leetch, Brian
Lehman, Hughie
Lemaire, Jacques
Lemieux, Mario
Lewis, Herbie
Lindsay, Ted
Lumley, Harry
MacInnis, Al
MacKay, Mickey
Mahovlich, Frank

Malone, Joe
Mantha, Sylvio
Marshall, Jack
Maxwell, Fred
McDonald, Lanny
McGee, Frank
McGimsie, Billy
McNamara, George
Messier, Mark
Mikita, Stan
Moore, Dickie
Moran, Paddy
Morenz, Howie
Mosienko, Bill
Mullen, Joe
Murphy, Larry
Neely, Cam
*Nieuwendyk, Joe
Nighbor, Frank
Noble, Reg
O'Connor, Buddy
Oliver, Harry
Olmstead, Bert
Orr, Bobby
Parent, Bernie
Park, Brad
Patrick, Lester
Patrick, Lynn
Perreault, Gilbert
Phillips, Tom
Pilote, Pierre
Pitre, Didier
Plante, Jacques
Potvin, Denis
Pratt, Babe
Primeau, Joe
Pronovost, Marcel
Pulford, Bob
Pulford, Harvey
Quackenbush, Bill
Rankin, Frank
Ratelle, Jean
Rayner, Chuck
Reardon, Kenny
Richard, Henri
Richard, Maurice
Richardson, George
Roberts, Gordie
Robinson, Larry
Robitaille, Luc
Ross, Art
Roy, Patrick
Russel, Blair
Russell, Ernie
Ruttan, Jack
Salming, Börje
Savard, Denis
Savard, Serge
Sawchuk, Terry
Scanlan, Fred
Schmidt, Milt
Schriner, Sweeney
Seibert, Earl
Seibert, Oliver
Shore, Eddie
Shutt, Steve
Siebert, Babe
Simpson, Joe "Bullet"
Sittler, Darryl
Smith, Alf
Smith, Billy
Smith, Clint
Smith, Hooley
Smith, Tommy
Stanley, Allan
Stanley, Barney

Stastny, Peter
Stevens, Ronald Scott
Stewart, Jack
Stewart, Nels
Stuart, Bruce
Stuart, Hod
Taylor, Frederick "Cyclone"
Thompson, Cecil "Tiny"
Tretiak, Vladislav
Trihey, Harry
Trottier, Bryan
Ullman, Norm
Vezina, Georges
Walker, Jack
Walsh, Marty
Watson, Harry "Moose"
Watson, Harry Percival
Weiland, Cooney
Westwick, Harry
Whitcroft, Fred
Wilson, Gordon Allan "Phat"
Worsley, Gump
Worters, Roy
Yzerman, Steve

Builders

Adams, Charles
Adams, Weston
Ahearn, Frank
Ahearn, John "Bunny"
Allan, Sir Montagu
Allen, Keith
Arbour, Al
Ballard, Harold
Bauer, Father David
Bickell, J. P.
Bowman, Scotty
Brooks, Herbert
Brown, George
Brown, Walter
Buckland, Frank
Bush, Walter, Jr.
Butterfield, Jack
Calder, Frank
Campbell, Angus
Campbell, Clarence
Cattarinich, Joseph
Chynoweth, Ed
Costello, Murray
Dandurand, Leo
Devellano, Jim
Dilio, Frank
Dudley, George
Dunn, James
Fletcher, Cliff
Francis, Emile
Gibson, Jack
Gorman, Tommy
Gregory, Jim
Griffiths, Frank
Hanley, Bill
Hay, Charles
Hendy, Jim
Hewitt, Foster
Hewitt, William
Hotchkiss, Harley
Hume, Fred
Ilitch, Mike
Imlach, Harry "Punch"
Ivan, Tommy
Jennings, Bill
Johnson, Bob
Juckes, Gordon
Kilpatrick, John
Kilrea, Brian

Knox, Seymour
Lamoriello, Lou
Leader, Al
LeBel, Robert
Lockhart, Thomas
Loicq, Paul
Mariucci, John
Mathers, Frank
McLaughlin, Frederic
Milford, Jake
Molson, Sen. Hartland
Morrison, Ian "Scotty"
Murray, Athol "Père"
Neilson, Roger
Nelson, Francis
Norris, Bruce
Norris, James
Norris, James, Sr.
Northey, William
O'Brien, J. Ambrose
O'Neill, Brian Francis
Page, Frederick
Patrick, Craig
Patrick, Frank
Pickard, Allan
Pilous, Rudy
Poile, Bud
Pollock, Sam
Raymond, Sen. Donat
Robertson, John Ross
Robinson, Claude
Ross, Phillip
Sabetzki, Gunther
Sather, Glen
Seaman, Daryl "Doc"
Selke, Frank
Sinden, Harry
Smith, Frank
Smythe, Conn
Snider, Ed
Stanley, Lord (of Preston)
Sutherland, Capt. James T.
Tarasov, Anatoli
Torrey, Bill
Turner, Lloyd
Tutt, William
Voss, Carl
Waghorne, Fred
Wirtz, Arthur
Wirtz, Bill
Ziegler, John A., Jr.

Referees and Linesmen

Armstrong, Neil
Ashley, John
Chadwick, Bill
D'Amico, John
Elliott, Edwin "Chaucer"
Hayes, George
Hewiston, Bobby
Ion, Mickey
Pavelich, Matt
Rodden, Mike
Scapinello, Ray
Smeaton, Cooper
Storey, Red
Udvari, Frank
Van Hellemond, Andy

SOCCER

Major League Soccer, 2010

The Colorado Rapids defeated FC Dallas, 2-1, at BMO Field in Toronto, ON, Canada, to capture the MLS Cup Nov. 21, 2010. Rapids forward Conor Casey scored to tie the game early in the second half, earning the MLS Cup Most Valuable Player award, but the Rapids' winning goal was scored when Dallas defender George John accidentally redirected a shot by Rapids forward Macoumba Kandji into his own net. Colorado, one of the original MLS franchises, had finished the season fifth in the Western Conference with just 12 wins and 46 points. Dallas midfielder David Ferreira, who scored the team's only goal, won the regular season MVP award with 8 goals and 13 assists.

The two-year-old Seattle Sounders' popularity continued in 2010 as they broke their own league record with an average per-game attendance of 36,173, topping their previous mark of 30,942. The 2010 MLS All-Star Game proved to be a success at the ticket gate but not on the pitch, as a crowd of 70,728 saw the MLS All-Stars drop to Manchester United, 5-2, July 28, 2010, at Reliant Stadium in Houston, TX. Major League Soccer grew by one team in 2010 as the Philadelphia Union became the league's 16th franchise. Two more expansion teams, the Portland Timbers and Vancouver Whitecaps FC, increased MLS to 18 clubs at the start of the 2011 season.

Major League Soccer (MLS) Cup, 1996-2010

Year	Winner	Final opponent	Score	Site	MVP
1996	D.C. United	Los Angeles Galaxy	3-2 (OT)	Foxboro, MA	Marco Etcheverry
1997	D.C. United	Colorado Rapids	2-1	Washington, DC	Jaime Moreno
1998	Chicago Fire	D.C. United	2-0	Pasadena, CA	Peter Nowak
1999	D.C. United	Los Angeles Galaxy	2-0	Foxboro, MA	Ben Olsen
2000	Kansas City Wizards	Chicago Fire	1-0	Washington, DC	Tony Meola
2001	San Jose Earthquakes	Los Angeles Galaxy	2-1 (OT)	Columbus, OH	Dwayne De Rosario
2002	Los Angeles Galaxy	New England Revolution	1-0 (OT)	Foxboro, MA	Carlos Ruiz
2003	San Jose Earthquakes	Chicago Fire	4-2	Carson, CA	Landon Donovan
2004	D.C. United	Kansas City Wizards	3-2	Carson, CA	Alecko Eskandarian
2005	Los Angeles Galaxy	New England Revolution	1-0 (OT)	Frisco, TX	Guillermo Ramírez
2006	Houston Dynamo	New England Revolution	1-1 (4-3)*	Frisco, TX	Brian Ching
2007	Houston Dynamo	New England Revolution	2-1	Washington, DC	Dwayne De Rosario
2008	Columbus Crew	New York Red Bulls	3-1	Carson, CA	Guillermo Barros Schelotto
2009	Real Salt Lake	Los Angeles Galaxy	1-1 (5-4)*	Seattle, WA	Nick Rimando
2010	Colorado Rapids	FC Dallas	2-1	Toronto, ON, Canada	Conor Casey

* = Match decided in penalty kicks (shootout score in parentheses). OT = Overtime.

Major League Soccer Final Standings, 2010

(Does not include playoff games.)

Eastern Division	W	L	T	PTS	GF	GA	GD	Western Division	W	L	T	PTS	GF	GA	GD
New York Red Bulls	15	9	6	51	38	29	9	Los Angeles Galaxy	18	7	5	59	44	26	18
Columbus Crew	14	8	8	50	40	34	6	Real Salt Lake	15	4	11	56	45	20	25
Kansas City Wizards	11	13	6	39	36	35	1	FC Dallas.	12	4	14	50	42	28	14
Chicago Fire	9	12	9	36	37	38	−1	Seattle Sounders FC	14	10	6	48	39	35	4
Toronto FC	9	13	8	35	33	41	−8	Colorado Rapids . . .	12	8	10	46	44	32	12
New England								San Jose							
Revolution.	9	16	5	32	32	50	−18	Earthquakes	13	10	7	46	34	33	1
Philadelphia Union . .	8	15	7	31	35	49	−14	Houston Dynamo. . . .	9	15	6	33	40	49	−9
DC United.	6	20	4	22	21	47	−26	Chivas USA	8	18	4	28	31	45	−14

Major League Soccer Scoring Leaders, 2010

Player	Club	GP	Goals	Player	Club	GP	Goals
Chris Wondolowski	San Jose.	28	18	Sebastien Le Toux	Philadelphia	28	14
Edson Buddle.	Los Angeles	25	17	Conor Casey.	Colorado.	27	13
Dwayne De Rosario	Toronto.	27	15	Juan Pablo Angel	New York	30	13
Omar Cummings	Colorado.	29	14	Alvaro Saborio	Real Salt Lake	27	12

Women's Professional Soccer, 2011

In the team's inaugural season in the league, the Western New York Flash held the best record and won the 2011 Women's Professional Soccer (WPS) Championship. The Flash defeated the Philadelphia Independence on penalty kicks in the WPS Championship game Aug. 27, 2011, at Sahlen's Stadium in Rochester, NY. Christine Sinclair scored the Flash's lone goal in the title game. Sinclair also scored one of the five penalty kick goals during the shootout and was voted championship game MVP. Sinclair teamed with Marta—reigning two-time WPS Player of the Year, and WPS 2010 Championship MVP with FC Gold Pride—to top the league with 10 goals apiece during the regular season. Philadelphia head coach Paul Riley, who led the Independence to their second straight appearance in the championship game and dealt the Flash their only two defeats during the season, repeated as WPS Coach of the Year. Philadelphia forward Veronica Boquete scored five goals and added four assists to win the WPS Player of the Year award.

Women's Professional Soccer Final Standings, 2011

(Does not include playoff games. z = clinched WPS regular season title. y = clinched playoff berth.)

Team	W	L	T	PTS	GF	GA	GD	Team	W	L	T	PTS	GF	GA	GD
z-Western New York. . .	13	2	3	42	40	18	22	y-Boston.	5	9	4	19	19	24	−5
y-Philadelphia.	11	4	3	36	31	18	13	Sky Blue	5	9	4	19	24	29	−5
y-magicJack	9	7	2	28	29	29	0	Atlanta	1	13	4	7	7	32	−25

Women's Professional Soccer Champions

Year	Winner	Final opponent	Score	Site	MVP
2009	Sky Blue FC	Los Angeles Sol	1-0	Carson, CA	Heather O'Reilly
2010	FC Gold Pride	Philadelphia Independence	4-0	Hayward, CA	Marta
2011	Western New York Flash	Philadelphia Independence	1-1 (5-4)*	Rochester, NY	Christine Sinclair

*Match decided on penalty kicks (shootout score in parentheses).

Spain Defeats the Netherlands for 2010 Men's World Cup Title

Amid the drone of vuvuzelas, Spain earned its first-ever FIFA World Cup soccer championship with a 1-0 victory over the Netherlands July 11, 2010, in Johannesburg, South Africa. Andrés Iniesta scored in the 116th minute as Spain became the first country to be crowned World Cup champion after losing its first tournament match. Spain goalkeeper Iker Casillas allowed just two goals and was named winner of the Golden Glove award as the tournament's top goaltender.

The Netherlands fell for the third time in a World Cup championship match. The Orange lost the 1974 and 1978 World Cup finals, and now have more wins in World Cup matches (19) than any other nation without a title. Germany took third place with a 3-2 win over Uruguay in the consolation match, and Uruguay's Diego Forlán was named Best Player and Thomas Müller of Germany won the Golden Boot for most goals.

Final Round Results, 2010

```
June 26: Nelson Mandela Bay/
  Port Elizabeth
Uruguay 2, South Korea 1
                                  July 2: Johannesburg (Soccer City)
                                  Uruguay 1, Ghana 1
                                  (Uruguay won, 4-2, on penalties)
June 26: Rustenburg
Ghana 2, USA 1 (extra time)
                                                                      July 6: Cape Town
                                                                      Netherlands 3, Uruguay 2

June 28: Durban
Netherlands 2, Slovakia 1         July 2: Nelson Mandela Bay/
                                    Port Elizabeth
                                  Netherlands 2, Brazil 1
June 28: Johannesburg
  (Ellis Park Stadium)
Brazil 3, Chile 0
                                                                                                July 11: Johannesburg
                                                                                                  (Soccer City)
                                                                                                Spain 1, Netherlands 0
                                                                                                  (extra time)
June 27: Manguang/Bloemfontein
Germany 4, England 1
                                  July 3: Cape Town
                                  Germany 4, Argentina 0
June 27: Johannesburg
  (Soccer City)
Argentina 3, Mexico 1
                                                                      July 7: Durban
                                                                      Spain 1, Germany 0

June 29: Tshwane/Pretoria                                                                       Third Place Final
Paraguay 0, Japan 0                                                                             July 10: Nelson Mandela
(Paraguay won, 5-3, on penalties)  July 3: Johannesburg                                           Bay/Port Elizabeth
                                     (Ellis Park Stadium)                                       Germany 3, Uruguay 2
June 29: Cape Town                 Spain 1, Paraguay 0
Spain 1, Portugal 0
```

Men's World Cup, 1930-2010

Year	Winner	Final opponent	Score	Site	Year	Winner	Final opponent	Score	Site
1930	Uruguay	Argentina	4-2	Uruguay	1978	Argentina	Netherlands	3-1#	Argentina
1934	Italy	Czechoslovakia	2-1#	Italy	1982	Italy	W. Germany	3-1	Spain
1938	Italy	Hungary	4-2	France	1986	Argentina	W. Germany	3-2	Mexico
1950	Uruguay	Brazil	2-1	Brazil	1990	W. Germany	Argentina	1-0	Italy
1954	W. Germany	Hungary	3-2	Switzerland	1994	Brazil	Italy	0-0 (3-2)*	U.S.
1958	Brazil	Sweden	5-2	Sweden	1998	France	Brazil	3-0	France
1962	Brazil	Czechoslovakia	3-1	Chile	2002	Brazil	Germany	2-0	Japan/S. Korea
1966	England	W. Germany	4-2#	England	2006	Italy	France	1-1 (5-3)*	Germany
1970	Brazil	Italy	4-1	Mexico	2010	Spain	Netherlands	1-0#	South Africa
1974	W. Germany	Netherlands	2-1	W. Germany					

* = Match decided on penalty kicks (shootout score in parentheses). # = Match decided in extra time.

FIFA Confederations Cup South Africa, 2009

The U.S. men's soccer team created much excitement at the Confederations Cup tournament in South Africa in June 2009. In one of the greatest upset victories in U.S. men's soccer history, Jozy Altidore and Clint Dempsey each scored to support a solid effort in goal by Tim Howard as the United States beat Spain, 2-0, in the semifinals of the tournament at Bloemfontein, South Africa. Spain entered the match as the world's top-ranked team, boasting 15 consecutive victories and a 35-match unbeaten streak. The United States eventually lost to Brazil, 3-2, in the tournament final, the first-ever U.S. appearance in a FIFA tournament championship match. Dempsey and Landon Donovan scored to give the U.S. a 2-0 halftime lead, but Brazil responded with three unanswered second-half goals for its second straight Confederations Cup victory and third overall.

FIFA Confederations Cup Winners, 1997-2009

Year	Winner	Final opponent	Score	Third place	Fourth place	Site
1997	Brazil	Australia	6-0	Czech Republic	Uruguay	Saudi Arabia
1999	Mexico	Brazil	4-3	U.S.	Saudi Arabia	Mexico
2001	France	Japan	1-0	Australia	Brazil	Korea/Japan
2003	France	Cameroon	1-0	Turkey	Colombia	France
2005	Brazil	Argentina	4-1	Germany	Mexico	Germany
2009	Brazil	U.S.	3-2	Spain	South Africa	South Africa

Japan Beats U.S. to Claim 2011 Women's World Cup Championship

Japan earned a stunning championship win at the 2011 Women's World Cup, defeating the United States, 3-1, on penalty kicks July 17, 2011, in Frankfurt, Germany. The win capped a determined effort from Japan, which made its first-ever appearance in the final of a major international tournament. Japan's Homare Sawa scored the game-tying goal in extra time, after the U.S.'s Abby Wambach scored on a header for a 2-1 lead in the 104th minute. Japan's goalkeeper, Ayumi Kaihori, was stellar in the shootout, allowing just one goal and two saves in four attempts by the U.S. The 32-year-old Sawa, playing in her fifth World Cup tournament, won both the Golden Ball as the best player of the tournament and the Golden Boot with a tournament-leading five goals. The underdog Japanese squad, known as the Nadeshiko, defeated Germany, the tournament host and two-time defending champion, 1-0, in extra time in a quarterfinal match on July 9, 2011, in Wolfsburg, Germany.

The U.S. enjoyed a dramatic quarterfinal triumph July 10, 2011, beating Brazil, 5-3, on penalty kicks in Dresden. Wambach converted a header into the net off a pass from Megan Rapinoe deep into injury time of the second overtime period for a 2-2 tie. Wambach and Rapinoe then scored two of the U.S.'s five successful penalty kicks and goalkeeper Hope Solo saved one of four attempts in the shootout with Brazil. The U.S. team then advanced to its first World Cup Final since 1999 with a 3-1 win over France in Mönchengladbach on July 13, 2011. France dropped a 2-1 decision to Sweden in the match for third place July 16, 2011, in Sinsheim.

Women's World Cup Results, 2011

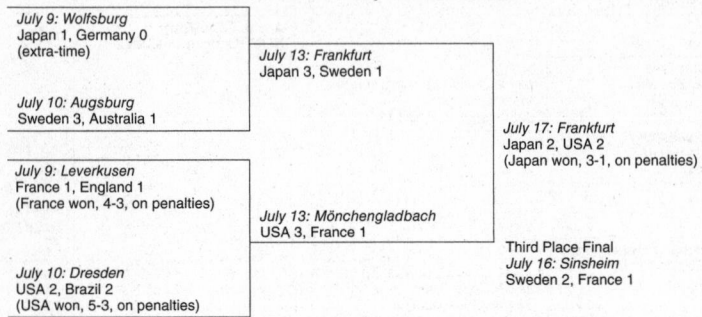

```
July 9: Wolfsburg
Japan 1, Germany 0
(extra-time)
                                July 13: Frankfurt
                                Japan 3, Sweden 1

July 10: Augsburg
Sweden 3, Australia 1
                                                        July 17: Frankfurt
                                                        Japan 2, USA 2
                                                        (Japan won, 3-1, on penalties)
July 9: Leverkusen
France 1, England 1
(France won, 4-3, on penalties)
                                July 13: Mönchengladbach
                                USA 3, France 1
                                                        Third Place Final
                                                        July 16: Sinsheim
July 10: Dresden                                        Sweden 2, France 1
USA 2, Brazil 2
(USA won, 5-3, on penalties)
```

Women's Cup, 1991-2011

Year	Winner	Final opponent	Score	Site	Third place
1991	U.S.	Norway	2-1	China	Germany
1995	Norway	Germany	2-0	Sweden	U.S.
1999	U.S.	China	0-0 (5-4)*	Pasadena, CA	Brazil
2003	Germany	Sweden	2-1#	Carson, CA	U.S.
2007	Germany	Brazil	2-0	China	U.S.
2011	Japan	U.S.	2-2 (3-1)*	Germany	Sweden

* = Match decided in penalty kicks (shootout score in parentheses). # = Match decided in extra time.

Selected European Soccer League Champions, 1950-2011

Season	English Premier League[1]	Spain: La Liga	Italy: Serie A	Germany: Bundesliga[2]
1949-50	Portsmouth FC	Atlético Madrid	Juventus	VfB Stuttgart
1950-51	Tottenham Hotspur	Atlético Madrid	AC Milan	Kaiserslautern
1951-52	Manchester United	FC Barcelona	Juventus	VfB Stuttgart
1952-53	Arsenal	FC Barcelona	Inter Milan	Kaiserslautern
1953-54	Wolverhampton Wanderers	Real Madrid	Inter Milan	Hannoverscher SV 96
1954-55	Chelsea	Real Madrid	AC Milan	Rot-Weiss Essen
1955-56	Manchester United	Athletic Bilbao	Fiorentina	Borrusia Dortmund
1956-57	Manchester United	Real Madrid	AC Milan	Borrusia Dortmund
1957-58	Wolverhampton Wanderers	Real Madrid	Juventus	Schalke 04
1958-59	Wolverhampton Wanderers	FC Barcelona	AC Milan	Eintracht Frankfurt
1959-60	Burnley FC	FC Barcelona	Juventus	Hamburg SV
1960-61	Tottenham Hotspur	Real Madrid	Juventus	FC Nuremberg
1961-62	Ipswich Town	Real Madrid	AC Milan	Cologne
1962-63	Everton	Real Madrid	Inter Milan	Borussia Dortmund
1963-64	Liverpool	Real Madrid	Bologna	FC Cologne
1964-65	Manchester United	Real Madrid	Inter Milan	Werder Bremen
1965-66	Liverpool	Atlético Madrid	Inter Milan	TSV 1860 Munich
1966-67	Manchester United	Real Madrid	Juventus	Eintracht Braunschweig
1967-68	Manchester City	Real Madrid	AC Milan	FC Nuremberg
1968-69	Leeds United	Real Madrid	Fiorentina	Bayern Munich
1969-70	Everton	Atlético Madrid	Cagliari	Borussia Mönchengladbach
1970-71	Arsenal	Valencia	Inter Milan	Borussia Mönchengladbach
1971-72	Derby County	Real Madrid	Juventus	Bayern Munich
1972-73	Liverpool	Atlético Madrid	Juventus	Bayern Munich
1973-74	Leeds United	FC Barcelona	Lazio	Bayern Munich
1974-75	Derby County	Real Madrid	Juventus	Borussia Mönchengladbach
1975-76	Liverpool	Real Madrid	Torino	Borussia Mönchengladbach
1976-77	Liverpool	Atlético Madrid	Juventus	Borussia Mönchengladbach
1977-78	Nottingham Forest	Real Madrid	Juventus	FC Cologne
1978-79	Liverpool	Real Madrid	AC Milan	Hamburg SV
1979-80	Liverpool	Real Madrid	Inter Milan	Bayern Munich

Season	English Premier League[1]	Spain: La Liga	Italy: Serie A	Germany: Bundesliga[2]
1980-81	Aston Villa	Real Sociedad	Juventus	Bayern Munich
1981-82	Liverpool	Real Sociedad	Juventus	Hamburg SV
1982-83	Liverpool	Athletic Bilbao	AS Roma	Hamburg SV
1983-84	Liverpool	Athletic Bilbao	Juventus	VfB Stuttgart
1984-85	Everton	FC Barcelona	Verona	Bayern Munich
1985-86	Liverpool	Real Madrid	Juventus	Bayern Munich
1986-87	Everton	Real Madrid	Napoli	Bayern Munich
1987-88	Liverpool	Real Madrid	AC Milan	Werder Bremen
1988-89	Arsenal	Real Madrid	Inter Milan	Bayern Munich
1989-90	Liverpool	Real Madrid	Napoli	Bayern Munich
1990-91	Arsenal	FC Barcelona	Sampdoria	FC Kaisersalutern
1991-92	Leeds United	FC Barcelona	AC Milan	VfB Stuttgart
1992-93	Manchester United	FC Barcelona	AC Milan	Werder Bremen
1993-94	Manchester United	FC Barcelona	AC Milan	Bayern Munich
1994-95	Blackburn Rovers	Real Madrid	Juventus	Borussia Dortmund
1995-96	Manchester United	Atlético Madrid	AC Milan	Borussia Dortmund
1996-97	Manchester United	Real Madrid	Juventus	Bayern Munich
1997-98	Arsenal	FC Barcelona	Juventus	FC Kaiserslautern
1998-99	Manchester United	FC Barcelona	AC Milan	Bayern Munich
1999-2000	Manchester United	Deportivo Coruña	Lazio	Bayern Munich
2000-01	Manchester United	Real Madrid	AS Roma	Bayern Munich
2001-02	Arsenal	Valencia	Juventus	Borussia Dortmund
2002-03	Manchester United	Real Madrid	Juventus	Bayern Munich
2003-04	Arsenal	Valencia	AC Milan	Werder Bremen
2004-05	Chelsea	FC Barcelona	None[3]	Bayern Munich
2005-06	Chelsea	FC Barcelona	Inter Milan	Bayern Munich
2006-07	Manchester United	Real Madrid	Inter Milan	VfB Stuttgart
2007-08	Manchester United	Real Madrid	Inter Milan	Bayern Munich
2008-09	Manchester United	FC Barcelona	Inter Milan	VfL Wolfsburg
2009-10	Chelsea	FC Barcelona	Inter Milan	Bayern Munich
2010-11	Manchester United	FC Barcelona	AC Milan	Borussia Dortmund

(1) Football league champions are listed prior to 1992, when the English Premier League formed. (2) Regional champions are listed prior to 1963, when National Bundesliga formed. (3) Juventus was stripped of the title because of match-fixing.

UEFA Champions League, 1956-2011

Year	Winner	Final opponent	Score	Year	Winner	Final opponent	Score
1956	Real Madrid	Reims	4-3	1984	Liverpool	Roma	1-1 (4-2)*
1957	Real Madrid	Fiorentina	2-0	1985	Juventus	Liverpool	1-0
1958	Real Madrid	AC Milan	3-2#	1986	Steaua	Barcelona	0-0 (2-0)*
1959	Real Madrid	Reims	2-0	1987	Porto	Bayern Munich	2-1
1960	Real Madrid	Eintracht	7-3	1988	PSV	Benfica	0-0 (6-5)*
1961	Benfica	Barcelona	3-2	1989	AC Milan	Steaua	4-0
1962	Benfica	Real Madrid	5-3	1990	AC Milan	Benfica	1-0
1963	AC Milan	Benfica	2-1	1991	Crvena Zvezda	Marseille	0-0 (5-3)*
1964	Inter Milan	Real Madrid	3-1	1992	Barcelona	Sampdoria	1-0#
1965	Inter Milan	Benfica	1-0	1993	Marseille	AC Milan	1-0
1966	Real Madrid	Partizan	2-1	1994	AC Milan	Barcelona	4-0
1967	Celtic	Inter Milan	2-1	1995	Ajax	AC Milan	1-0
1968	Manchester United	Benfica	4-1#	1996	Juventus	Ajax	1-1 (4-2)*
1969	AC Milan	Ajax	4-1	1997	Dortmund	Juventus	3-1
1970	Feyenoord	Celtic	2-1#	1998	Real Madrid	Juventus	1-0
1971	Ajax	Panathinaikos	2-0	1999	Manchester United	Bayern Munich	2-1
1972	Ajax	Inter Milan	2-0	2000	Real Madrid	Valencia	3-0
1973	Ajax	Juventus	1-0	2001	Bayern Munich	Valencia	1-1 (5-4)*
1974	Bayern Munich	Atlético	5-1[1]	2002	Real Madrid	Leverkusen	2-1
1975	Bayern Munich	Leeds	2-0	2003	AC Milan	Juventus	0-0 (3-2)*
1976	Bayern Munich	St-Etienne	1-0	2004	Porto	Monaco	3-0
1977	Liverpool	Mönchengladbach	3-1	2005	Liverpool	AC Milan	3-3 (3-2)*
1978	Liverpool	Club Brugge	1-0	2006	Barcelona	Arsenal	2-1
1979	Nottingham Forest	Malmö	1-0	2007	AC Milan	Liverpool	2-1
1980	Nottingham Forest	Hamburg	1-0	2008	Manchester United	Chelsea	1-1 (6-5)*
1981	Liverpool	Real Madrid	1-0	2009	Barcelona	Manchester United	2-0
1982	Aston Villa	Bayern Munich	1-0	2010	Inter Milan	Bayern Munich	2-0
1983	Hamburg	Juventus	1-0	2011	Barcelona	Manchester United	3-1

* = Match decided in penalty kicks (shootout score in parentheses). # = Match decided in extra time. (1) Aggregate score. First game 1-1; second, 4-0.

UEFA European Football Championships, 1960-2008

The final rounds of the 2008 UEFA European Championships were jointly hosted by Austria and Switzerland and opened June 7, 2008, in Basel, Switzerland, with the final match at Ernst Happle Stadium in Vienna, Austria, on June 29, 2008.

Year	Winner	Final opponent	Score	Site
1960	USSR	Yugoslavia	2-1#	France
1964	Spain	USSR	2-1	Spain
1968	Italy	Yugoslavia	2-0	Italy
1972	W. Germany	USSR	3-0	Belgium
1976	Czechoslovakia	W. Germany	2-2 (5-3)*	Yugoslavia
1980	W. Germany	Belgium	2-1	Italy
1984	France	Spain	2-0	France
1988	Netherlands	USSR	2-0	W. Germany
1992	Denmark	Germany	2-0	Sweden
1996	Germany	Czech Rep.	2-1#	England
2000	France	Italy	2-1#	Belgium/Neth.
2004	Greece	Portugal	1-0	Portugal
2008	Spain	Germany	1-0	Austria

* = Match decided in penalty kicks (shootout score in parentheses). # = Match decided in extra time.

GOLF

Men's All-Time Major Professional Championship Leaders

Through Oct. 2011. * = Active PGA player in 2011. (a) = Amateur.

Player	Masters	U.S. Open	British Open	PGA	Total
Jack Nicklaus	1963, '65-'66, '72, '75, '86	1962, '67, '72, '80	1966, '70, '78	1963, '71, '73, '75, '80	18
Tiger Woods*	1997, 2001-02, '05	2000, '02, '08	2000, '05-'06	1999-2000, 2006-07	14
Walter Hagen	—	1914, '19	1922, '24, '28-'29	1921, '24-'27	11
Ben Hogan	1951, '53	1948, '50-'51, '53	1953	1946, '48	9
Gary Player	1961, '74, '78	1965	1959, '68, '74	1962, '72	9
Tom Watson	1977, '81	1982	1975, '77, '80, '82-'83	—	8
Bobby Jones (a)	—	1923, '26, '29-'30	1926-27, '30	—	7
Arnold Palmer	1958, '60, '62, '64	1960	1961-62	—	7
Gene Sarazen	1935	1922, '32	1932	1922-23, '33	7
Sam Snead	1949, '52, '54	—	1946	1942, '49, '51	7
Harry Vardon	—	1900	1896, '98-'99, 1903, '11, '14	—	7
Nick Faldo	1989-90, '96	—	1987, '90, '92	—	6
Lee Trevino	—	1968, '71	1971-72	1974, '84	6

Professional Golfers' Association Leading Money Winners, 1946-2010

Year	Player	Earnings	Year	Player	Earnings	Year	Player	Earnings
1946	Ben Hogan	$42,556	1968	Billy Casper	$205,168	1990	Greg Norman	$1,165,477
1947	Jimmy Demaret	27,936	1969	Frank Beard	175,223	1991	Corey Pavin	979,430
1948	Ben Hogan	36,812	1970	Lee Trevino	157,037	1992	Fred Couples	1,344,188
1949	Sam Snead	31,593	1971	Jack Nicklaus	244,490	1993	Nick Price	1,478,557
1950	Sam Snead	35,758	1972	Jack Nicklaus	320,542	1994	Nick Price	1,499,927
1951	Lloyd Mangrum	26,088	1973	Jack Nicklaus	308,362	1995	Greg Norman	1,654,959
1952	Julius Boros	37,032	1974	Johnny Miller	353,201	1996	Tom Lehman	1,780,159
1953	Lew Worsham	34,002	1975	Jack Nicklaus	323,149	1997	Tiger Woods	2,066,833
1954	Bob Toski	65,819	1976	Jack Nicklaus	266,438	1998	David Duval	2,591,031
1955	Julius Boros	65,121	1977	Tom Watson	310,653	1999	Tiger Woods	6,616,585
1956	Ted Kroll	72,835	1978	Tom Watson	362,429	2000	Tiger Woods	9,188,321
1957	Dick Mayer	65,835	1979	Tom Watson	462,636	2001	Tiger Woods	5,687,777
1958	Arnold Palmer	42,407	1980	Tom Watson	530,808	2002	Tiger Woods	6,912,625
1959	Art Wall Jr.	53,167	1981	Tom Kite	375,699	2003	Vijay Singh	7,573,907
1960	Arnold Palmer	75,262	1982	Craig Stadler	446,462	2004	Vijay Singh	10,905,166
1961	Gary Player	64,540	1983	Hal Sutton	426,668	2005	Tiger Woods	10,628,024
1962	Arnold Palmer	81,448	1984	Tom Watson	476,260	2006	Tiger Woods	9,941,563
1963	Arnold Palmer	128,230	1985	Curtis Strange	542,321	2007	Tiger Woods	10,867,052
1964	Jack Nicklaus	113,284	1986	Greg Norman	653,296	2008	Vijay Singh	6,601,094
1965	Jack Nicklaus	140,752	1987	Curtis Strange	925,941	2009	Tiger Woods	10,508,163
1966	Billy Casper	121,944	1988	Curtis Strange	1,147,644	2010	Matt Kuchar	4,910,477
1967	Jack Nicklaus	188,988	1989	Tom Kite	1,395,278			

Masters Golf Tournament Winners, 1940-2011

First contested in 1934 as Augusta National Invitation Tournament; not played, 1943-45.

Year	Winner	Year	Winner	Year	Winner	Year	Winner	Year	Winner
1940	Jimmy Demaret	1958	Arnold Palmer	1972	Jack Nicklaus	1986	Jack Nicklaus	1999	José María
1941	Craig Wood	1959	Art Wall Jr.	1973	Tommy Aaron	1987	Larry Mize		Olazábal
1942	Byron Nelson	1960	Arnold Palmer	1974	Gary Player	1988	Sandy Lyle	2000	Vijay Singh
1946	Herman Keiser	1961	Gary Player	1975	Jack Nicklaus	1989	Nick Faldo	2001	Tiger Woods
1947	Jimmy Demaret	1962	Arnold Palmer	1976	Ray Floyd	1990	Nick Faldo	2002	Tiger Woods
1948	Claude Harmon	1963	Jack Nicklaus	1977	Tom Watson	1991	Ian Woosnam	2003	Mike Weir
1949	Sam Snead	1964	Arnold Palmer	1978	Gary Player	1992	Fred Couples	2004	Phil Mickelson
1950	Jimmy Demaret	1965	Jack Nicklaus	1979	Fuzzy Zoeller	1993	Bernhard Langer	2005	Tiger Woods
1951	Ben Hogan	1966	Jack Nicklaus	1980	Seve Ballesteros	1994	José María	2006	Phil Mickelson
1952	Sam Snead	1967	Gay Brewer Jr.	1981	Tom Watson		Olazábal	2007	Zach Johnson
1953	Ben Hogan	1968	Bob Goalby	1982	Craig Stadler	1995	Ben Crenshaw	2008	Trevor Immelman
1954	Sam Snead	1969	George Archer	1983	Seve Ballesteros	1996	Nick Faldo	2009	Angel Cabrera
1955	Cary Middlecoff	1970	Billy Casper	1984	Ben Crenshaw	1997	Tiger Woods	2010	Phil Mickelson
1956	Jack Burke	1971	Charles Coody	1985	Bernhard Langer	1998	Mark O'Meara	2011	Charl Schwartzel
1957	Doug Ford								

U.S. Open Winners, 1940-2011

First contested in 1895; not played, 1942-45.

Year	Winner	Year	Winner	Year	Winner	Year	Winner	Year	Winner
1940	Lawson Little	1958	Tommy Bolt	1972	Jack Nicklaus	1986	Ray Floyd	1999	Payne Stewart
1941	Craig Wood	1959	Billy Casper	1973	Johnny Miller	1987	Scott Simpson	2000	Tiger Woods
1946	Lloyd Mangrum	1960	Arnold Palmer	1974	Hale Irwin	1988	Curtis Strange	2001	Retief Goosen
1947	Lew Worsham	1961	Gene Littler	1975	Lou Graham	1989	Curtis Strange	2002	Tiger Woods
1948	Ben Hogan	1962	Jack Nicklaus	1976	Jerry Pate	1990	Hale Irwin	2003	Jim Furyk
1949	Cary Middlecoff	1963	Julius Boros	1977	Hubert Green	1991	Payne Stewart	2004	Retief Goosen
1950	Ben Hogan	1964	Ken Venturi	1978	Andy North	1992	Tom Kite	2005	Michael Campbell
1951	Ben Hogan	1965	Gary Player	1979	Hale Irwin	1993	Lee Janzen	2006	Geoff Ogilvy
1952	Julius Boros	1966	Billy Casper	1980	Jack Nicklaus	1994	Ernie Els	2007	Angel Cabrera
1953	Ben Hogan	1967	Jack Nicklaus	1981	David Graham	1995	Corey Pavin	2008	Tiger Woods
1954	Ed Furgol	1968	Lee Trevino	1982	Tom Watson	1996	Steve Jones	2009	Lucas Glover
1955	Jack Fleck	1969	Orville Moody	1983	Larry Nelson	1997	Ernie Els	2010	Graeme McDowell
1956	Cary Middlecoff	1970	Tony Jacklin	1984	Fuzzy Zoeller	1998	Lee Janzen	2011	Rory McIlroy
1957	Dick Mayer	1971	Lee Trevino	1985	Andy North				

British Open Winners, 1946-2011
First contested in 1860; not played, 1940-45.

Year	Winner	Year	Winner	Year	Winner	Year	Winner	Year	Winner
1946	Sam Snead	1960	Kel Nagle	1973	Tom Weiskopf	1986	Greg Norman	1999	Paul Lawrie
1947	Fred Daly	1961	Arnold Palmer	1974	Gary Player	1987	Nick Faldo	2000	Tiger Woods
1948	Henry Cotton	1962	Arnold Palmer	1975	Tom Watson	1988	Seve Ballesteros	2001	David Duval
1949	Bobby Locke	1963	Bob Charles	1976	Johnny Miller	1989	Mark Calcavecchia	2002	Ernie Els
1950	Bobby Locke	1964	Tony Lema	1977	Tom Watson	1990	Nick Faldo	2003	Ben Curtis
1951	Max Faulkner	1965	Peter Thomson	1978	Jack Nicklaus	1991	Ian Baker-Finch	2004	Todd Hamilton
1952	Bobby Locke	1966	Jack Nicklaus	1979	Seve Ballesteros	1992	Nick Faldo	2005	Tiger Woods
1953	Ben Hogan	1967	Roberto de Vicenzo	1980	Tom Watson	1993	Greg Norman	2006	Tiger Woods
1954	Peter Thomson	1968	Gary Player	1981	Bill Rogers	1994	Nick Price	2007	Padraig Harrington
1955	Peter Thomson	1969	Tony Jacklin	1982	Tom Watson	1995	John Daly	2008	Padraig Harrington
1956	Peter Thomson	1970	Jack Nicklaus	1983	Tom Watson	1996	Tom Lehman	2009	Stewart Cink
1957	Bobby Locke	1971	Lee Trevino	1984	Seve Ballesteros	1997	Justin Leonard	2010	Louis Oosthuizen
1958	Peter Thomson	1972	Lee Trevino	1985	Sandy Lyle	1998	Mark O'Meara	2011	Darren Clarke
1959	Gary Player								

PGA Championship Winners, 1940-2011
First contested in 1916; not played, 1943.

Year	Winner	Year	Winner	Year	Winner	Year	Winner	Year	Winner
1940	Byron Nelson	1956	Jack Burke	1970	Dave Stockton	1984	Lee Trevino	1998	Vijay Singh
1941	Victor Ghezzi	1957	Lionel Hebert	1971	Jack Nicklaus	1985	Hubert Green	1999	Tiger Woods
1942	Sam Snead	1958	Dow Finsterwald	1972	Gary Player	1986	Bob Tway	2000	Tiger Woods
1944	Bob Hamilton	1959	Bob Rosburg	1973	Jack Nicklaus	1987	Larry Nelson	2001	David Toms
1945	Byron Nelson	1960	Jay Hebert	1974	Lee Trevino	1988	Jeff Sluman	2002	Rich Beem
1946	Ben Hogan	1961	Jerry Barber	1975	Jack Nicklaus	1989	Payne Stewart	2003	Shaun Micheel
1947	Jim Ferrier	1962	Gary Player	1976	Dave Stockton	1990	Wayne Grady	2004	Vijay Singh
1948	Ben Hogan	1963	Jack Nicklaus	1977	Lanny Wadkins	1991	John Daly	2005	Phil Mickelson
1949	Sam Snead	1964	Bob Nichols	1978	John Mahaffey	1992	Nick Price	2006	Tiger Woods
1950	Chandler Harper	1965	Dave Marr	1979	David Graham	1993	Paul Azinger	2007	Tiger Woods
1951	Sam Snead	1966	Al Geiberger	1980	Jack Nicklaus	1994	Nick Price	2008	Padraig Harrington
1952	James Turnesa	1967	Don January	1981	Larry Nelson	1995	Steve Elkington	2009	Y.E.Yang
1953	Walter Burkemo	1968	Julius Boros	1982	Ray Floyd	1996	Mark Brooks	2010	Martin Kaymer
1954	Melvin Harbert	1969	Ray Floyd	1983	Hal Sutton	1997	Davis Love III	2011	Keegan Bradley
1955	Doug Ford								

FedEx Cup, 2007-11

The FedEx Cup, a season-long, $10-mil competition with points awarded by finishing rank in each tournament, divides the PGA Tour into a regular season lasting 33 weeks, combined with a 4-week-long playoff that ends with the Tour Championship at East Lake Golf Club in Atlanta, GA. After both finished at 8-under-par 272, Bill Haas defeated Hunter Mahan in a sudden-death playoff to win the 2011 Tour Championship and FedEx Cup title Sept. 25, 2011.

Year	Winner	Year	Winner	Year	Winner	Year	Winner	Year	Winner
2007	Tiger Woods	2008	Vijay Singh	2009	Tiger Woods	2010	Jim Furyk	2011	Bill Haas

Women's All-Time Major Professional Championship Leaders
Through Oct. 2011. * = Active in 2011 LPGA season.

Player	Kraft Nabisco[1]	LPGA	U.S. Women's Open	Women's British Open[2]	Titleholders[3]	Western Open[4]	Total
Patty Berg	—	—	1946	—	1937-39, '48, '53, '55, '57	1941, '43, '48, '51, '55, '57-'58	15
Mickey Wright	—	1958, '60-'61, '63	1958-59, '61, '64	—	1961-62	1962-63, '66	13
Louise Suggs	—	1957	1949, '52	—	1946, '54, '56, '59	1946-47, '49, '53	11
Annika Sorenstam	2001-02, '05	2003-05	1995-96, 2006	2003	—	—	10
Babe Zaharias	—	—	1948, '50, '54	—	1947, '50, '52	1940, '44-'45, '50	10
Betsy Rawls	—	1959, '69	1951, '53, '57, '60	—	—	1952, '59	8
Juli Inkster*	1984, '89	1999-2000	1999, 2002	1984	—	—	7
Karrie Webb*	2000, '06	2001	2000-01	1999, 2002	—	—	7
Pat Bradley	1986	1986	1981	1980, '85-'86	—	—	6
Betsy King	1987, '90, '97	1992	1989-90	—	—	—	6
Patty Sheehan	1996	1983-84, '93	1992, '94	—	—	—	6
Kathy Whitworth	1967, '71, '75	—	—	—	1965-66	1967	6

(1) Formerly the Nabisco Dinah Shore (1982-99) and the Nabisco Championship (2000-01); designated major in 1983. (2) In 2001, the British Open replaced the du Maurier Classic as the LPGA's 4th major; wins in column prior to 2001 are du Maurier wins. (3) Titleholders Championship was a major from 1937 to 1972. (4) Western Open was a major from 1930 to 1967.

Ladies Professional Golf Association Leading Money Winners, 1954-2010

Year	Player	Earnings	Year	Player	Earnings	Year	Player	Earnings
1954	Patty Berg	$16,011	1973	Kathy Whitworth	$82,864	1992	Dottie Mochrie	$693,335
1955	Patty Berg	16,492	1974	JoAnne Carner	87,094	1993	Betsy King	595,992
1956	Marlene Hagge	20,235	1975	Sandra Palmer	76,374	1994	Laura Davies	687,201
1957	Patty Berg	16,272	1976	Judy Rankin	150,734	1995	Annika Sorenstam	666,533
1958	Beverly Hanson	12,639	1977	Judy Rankin	122,890	1996	Karrie Webb	1,002,000
1959	Betsy Rawls	26,774	1978	Nancy Lopez	189,813	1997	Annika Sorenstam	1,236,789
1960	Louise Suggs	16,892	1979	Nancy Lopez	197,489	1998	Annika Sorenstam	1,092,748
1961	Mickey Wright	22,236	1980	Beth Daniel	231,000	1999	Karrie Webb	1,591,959
1962	Mickey Wright	21,641	1981	Beth Daniel	206,977	2000	Karrie Webb	1,876,853
1963	Mickey Wright	31,269	1982	JoAnne Carner	310,399	2001	Annika Sorenstam	2,105,868
1964	Mickey Wright	29,800	1983	JoAnne Carner	291,404	2002	Annika Sorenstam	2,863,904
1965	Kathy Whitworth	28,658	1984	Betsy King	266,771	2003	Annika Sorenstam	2,029,506
1966	Kathy Whitworth	33,517	1985	Nancy Lopez	416,472	2004	Annika Sorenstam	2,544,707
1967	Kathy Whitworth	32,937	1986	Pat Bradley	492,021	2005	Annika Sorenstam	2,588,240
1968	Kathy Whitworth	48,379	1987	Ayako Okamoto	466,034	2006	Lorena Ochoa	2,592,872
1969	Carol Mann	49,152	1988	Sherri Turner	350,851	2007	Lorena Ochoa	4,364,994
1970	Kathy Whitworth	30,235	1989	Betsy King	654,132	2008	Lorena Ochoa	2,763,193
1971	Kathy Whitworth	41,181	1990	Beth Daniel	863,578	2009	Jiyai Shin	1,807,334
1972	Kathy Whitworth	65,063	1991	Pat Bradley	763,118	2010	Na Yeon Choi	1,871,166

Kraft Nabisco Championship Winners, 1983-2011

Formerly the Colgate Dinah Shore (1972-81), the Nabisco Dinah Shore (1982-99), and the Nabisco Championship (2000-01). Designated as a major championship in 1983.

Year	Winner	Year	Winner	Year	Winner	Year	Winner	Year	Winner
1983	Amy Alcott	1989	Juli Inkster	1995	Nanci Bowen	2001	Annika Sorenstam	2006	Karrie Webb
1984	Juli Inkster	1990	Betsy King	1996	Patty Sheehan	2002	Annika Sorenstam	2007	Morgan Pressel
1985	Alice Miller	1991	Amy Alcott	1997	Betsy King	2003	Patricia Meunier-	2008	Lorena Ochoa
1986	Pat Bradley	1992	Dottie Pepper	1998	Pat Hurst		Lebouc	2009	Brittany Lincicome
1987	Betsy King	1993	Helen Alfredsson	1999	Dottie Pepper	2004	Grace Park	2010	Yani Tseng
1988	Amy Alcott	1994	Donna Andrews	2000	Karrie Webb	2005	Annika Sorenstam	2011	Stacy Lewis

LPGA Championship Winners, 1955-2011

Year	Winner	Year	Winner	Year	Winner	Year	Winner	Year	Winner
1955	Beverly Hanson	1967	Kathy Whitworth	1979	Donna Caponi	1990	Beth Daniel	2001	Karrie Webb
1956	Marlene Hagge	1968	Sandra Post	1980	Sally Little	1991	Meg Mallon	2002	Se Ri Pak
1957	Louise Suggs	1969	Betsy Rawls	1981	Donna Caponi	1992	Betsy King	2003	Annika Sorenstam
1958	Mickey Wright	1970	Shirley Englehorn	1982	Jan Stephenson	1993	Patty Sheehan	2004	Annika Sorenstam
1959	Betsy Rawls	1971	Kathy Whitworth	1983	Patty Sheehan	1994	Laura Davies	2005	Annika Sorenstam
1960	Mickey Wright	1972	Kathy Ahern	1984	Patty Sheehan	1995	Kelly Robbins	2006	Se Ri Pak
1961	Mickey Wright	1973	Mary Mills	1985	Nancy Lopez	1996	Laura Davies	2007	Suzann Pettersen
1962	Judy Kimball	1974	Sandra Haynie	1986	Pat Bradley	1997	Chris Johnson	2008	Yani Tseng
1963	Mickey Wright	1975	Kathy Whitworth	1987	Jane Geddes	1998	Se Ri Pak	2009	Anna Nordqvist
1964	Mary Mills	1976	Betty Burfeindt	1988	Sherri Turner	1999	Juli Inkster	2010	Cristie Kerr
1965	Sandra Haynie	1977	Chako Higuchi	1989	Nancy Lopez	2000	Juli Inkster	2011	Yani Tseng
1966	Gloria Ehret	1978	Nancy Lopez						

U.S. Women's Open Winners, 1946-2011

Year	Winner	Year	Winner	Year	Winner	Year	Winner	Year	Winner
1946	Patty Berg	1960	Betsy Rawls	1972	Susie Maxwell	1984	Hollis Stacy	1998	Se Ri Pak
1947	Betty Jameson	1961	Mickey Wright		Berning	1985	Kathy Baker	1999	Juli Inkster
1948	Babe Zaharias	1962	Murle Lindstrom	1973	Susie Maxwell	1986	Jane Geddes	2000	Karrie Webb
1949	Louise Suggs	1963	Mary Mills		Berning	1987	Laura Davies	2001	Karrie Webb
1950	Babe Zaharias	1964	Mickey Wright	1974	Sandra Haynie	1988	Liselotte Neumann	2002	Juli Inkster
1951	Betsy Rawls	1965	Carol Mann	1975	Sandra Palmer	1989	Betsy King	2003	Hilary Lunke
1952	Louise Suggs	1966	Sandra Spuzich	1976	JoAnne Carner	1990	Betsy King	2004	Meg Mallon
1953	Betsy Rawls	1967	Catherine Lacoste	1977	Hollis Stacy	1991	Meg Mallon	2005	Birdie Kim
1954	Babe Zaharias		(amateur)	1978	Hollis Stacy	1992	Patty Sheehan	2006	Annika Sorenstam
1955	Fay Crocker	1968	Susie Maxwell	1979	Jerilyn Britz	1993	Lauri Merten	2007	Cristie Kerr
1956	Kathy Cornelius		Berning	1980	Amy Alcott	1994	Patty Sheehan	2008	Inbee Park
1957	Betsy Rawls	1969	Donna Caponi	1981	Pat Bradley	1995	Annika Sorenstam	2009	Eun-Hee Ji
1958	Mickey Wright	1970	Donna Caponi	1982	Janet Alex	1996	Annika Sorenstam	2010	Paula Creamer
1959	Mickey Wright	1971	JoAnne Carner	1983	Jan Stephenson	1997	Alison Nicholas	2011	So Yeon Ryu

Women's British Open Winners, 1979-2011

First held as the Ladies' British Open in 1976; became the LPGA's 4th major championship in 2001, replacing the du Maurier Classic. Winners listed are for the du Maurier Classic, 1983-2000, and the Peter Jackson Classic, 1979-82.

Year	Winner	Year	Winner	Year	Winner	Year	Winner	Year	Winner
1979	Amy Alcott	1986	Pat Bradley	1993	Brandie Burton	2000	Meg Mallon	2006	Sherri Steinhauer
1980	Pat Bradley	1987	Jody Rosenthal	1994	Martha Nause	2001	Se Ri Pak	2007	Lorena Ochoa
1981	Jan Stephenson	1988	Sally Little	1995	Jenny Lidback	2002	Karrie Webb	2008	Jiyai Shin
1982	Sandra Haynie	1989	Tammie Green	1996	Laura Davies	2003	Annika Sorenstam	2009	Catriona Matthew
1983	Hollis Stacy	1990	Cathy Johnston	1997	Colleen Walker	2004	Karen Stupples	2010	Yani Tseng
1984	Juli Inkster	1991	Nancy Scranton	1998	Brandie Burton	2005	Jeong Jang	2011	Yani Tseng
1985	Pat Bradley	1992	Sherri Steinhauer	1999	Karrie Webb				

Ryder Cup, 1927-2010

Began as a biennial team competition between pro male golfers from the U.S. and Great Britain. The British team was expanded in 1973 to include players from Ireland and in 1979 from the rest of Europe. The Ryder Cup moved to even years after being postponed following the terrorist attacks of Sept. 11, 2001. Europe regained the Ryder Cup Oct. 4, 2010, at the Celtic Manor Resort in Newport, South Wales, UK. Medinah Country Club, located about 20 miles east of Chicago, IL, will host the 39th Ryder Cup Sept. 25-30, 2012.

Year	Winner, score	Year	Winner, score	Year	Winner, score	Year	Winner, score
1927	U.S., 9½-2½	1953	U.S., 6½-5½	1973	U.S., 19-13	1993	U.S., 15-13
1929	Britain-Ireland, 7-5	1955	U.S., 8-4	1975	U.S., 21-11	1995	Europe, 14½-13½
1931	U.S., 9-3	1957	Britain-Ireland, 7½-4½	1977	U.S., 12½-7½	1997	Europe, 14½-13½
1933	Britain, 6½-5½	1959	U.S., 8½-3½	1979	U.S., 17-11	1999	U.S., 14½-13½
1935	U.S., 9-3	1961	U.S., 14½-9½	1981	U.S., 18½-9½	2002	Europe, 15½-12½
1937	U.S., 8-4	1963	U.S., 23-9	1983	U.S., 14½-13½	2004	Europe, 18½-9½
1939-45	Not played	1965	U.S., 19½-12½	1985	Europe, 16½-11½	2006	Europe, 18½-9½
1947	U.S., 11-1	1967	U.S., 23½-8½	1987	Europe, 15-13	2008	U.S., 16½-11½
1949	U.S., 7-5	1969	Draw, 16-16	1989	Draw, 14-14	2010	Europe, 14½-13½
1951	U.S., 9½-2½	1971	U.S., 18½-13½	1991	U.S., 14½-13½		

Solheim Cup, 1990-2011

Europe defeated the U.S. 15-13, Sept. 23-25, 2011, at Killeen Castle in Ireland to capture the Solheim Cup. The UK's Alison Nicholas was captain of Europe's squad and LPGA veteran Rosie Jones captained the U.S. team, which had won three straight tournaments. Begun in 1990 as a biennial team competition between pro women golfers from the U.S. and Europe, competition moved to odd years in 2003 to alternate with the Ryder Cup.

Year	Winner, score	Year	Winner, score	Year	Winner, score	Year	Winner, score
1990	U.S., 11½-4½	1996	U.S., 17-11	2002	U.S., 15½-12½	2007	U.S., 16-12
1992	Europe, 11½-6½	1998	U.S., 16-12	2003	Europe, 17½-10½	2009	U.S., 16-12
1994	U.S., 13-7	2000	Europe, 14½-11½	2005	U.S., 15½-12½	2011	Europe, 15-13

TENNIS

Australian Open Singles Champions, 1969-2011

(First contested 1905 for men, 1922 for women. Became an Open Championship in 1969. Two tournaments held in 1977 in Jan. and Dec. No tournament held in 1986.)

Men's Singles

Year	Champion	Final opponent
1969	Rod Laver	Andres Gimeno
1970	Arthur Ashe	Dick Crealy
1971	Ken Rosewall	Arthur Ashe
1972	Ken Rosewall	Mal Anderson
1973	John Newcombe	Onny Parun
1974	Jimmy Connors	Phil Dent
1975	John Newcombe	Jimmy Connors
1976	Mark Edmondson	John Newcombe
1977	Roscoe Tanner	Guillermo Vilas
	Vitas Gerulaitis	John Lloyd
1978	Guillermo Vilas	John Marks
1979	Guillermo Vilas	John Sadri
1980	Brian Teacher	Kim Warwick
1981	Johan Kriek	Steve Denton
1982	Johan Kriek	Steve Denton
1983	Mats Wilander	Ivan Lendl
1984	Mats Wilander	Kevin Curren
1985	Stefan Edberg	Mats Wilander
1987	Stefan Edberg	Pat Cash
1988	Mats Wilander	Pat Cash
1989	Ivan Lendl	Miloslav Mecir
1990	Ivan Lendl	Stefan Edberg
1991	Boris Becker	Ivan Lendl
1992	Jim Courier	Stefan Edberg
1993	Jim Courier	Stefan Edberg
1994	Pete Sampras	Todd Martin
1995	Andre Agassi	Pete Sampras
1996	Boris Becker	Michael Chang
1997	Pete Sampras	Carlos Moya
1998	Petr Korda	Marcelo Rios
1999	Yevgeny Kafelnikov	Thomas Enqvist
2000	Andre Agassi	Yevgeny Kafelnikov
2001	Andre Agassi	Arnaud Clement
2002	Thomas Johansson	Marat Safin
2003	Andre Agassi	Rainer Schuettler
2004	Roger Federer	Marat Safin
2005	Marat Safin	Lleyton Hewitt
2006	Roger Federer	Marcos Baghdatis
2007	Roger Federer	Fernando Gonzalez
2008	Novak Djokovic	Jo-Wilfried Tsonga
2009	Rafael Nadal	Roger Federer
2010	Roger Federer	Andy Murray
2011	Novak Djokovic	Andy Murray

Women's Singles

Year	Champion	Final opponent
1969	Margaret Smith Court	Billie Jean King
1970	Margaret Smith Court	Kerry Melville Reid
1971	Margaret Smith Court	Evonne Goolagong
1972	Virginia Wade	Evonne Goolagong
1973	Margaret Smith Court	Evonne Goolagong
1974	Evonne Goolagong	Chris Evert
1975	Evonne Goolagong	Martina Navratilova
1976	Evonne Goolagong Cawley	Renata Tomanova
1977	Kerry Reid	Dianne Balestrat
	Evonne Goolagong Cawley	Helen Gourlay
1978	Chris O'Neill	Betsy Nagelsen
1979	Barbara Jordan	Sharon Walsh
1980	Hana Mandlikova	Wendy Turnbull
1981	Martina Navratilova	Chris Evert Lloyd
1982	Chris Evert Lloyd	Martina Navratilova
1983	Martina Navratilova	Kathy Jordan
1984	Chris Evert Lloyd	Helena Sukova
1985	Martina Navratilova	Chris Evert Lloyd
1987	Hana Mandlikova	Martina Navratilova
1988	Steffi Graf	Chris Evert
1989	Steffi Graf	Helena Sukova
1990	Steffi Graf	Mary Joe Fernandez
1991	Monica Seles	Jana Novotna
1992	Monica Seles	Mary Joe Fernandez
1993	Monica Seles	Steffi Graf
1994	Steffi Graf	Arantxa Sánchez Vicario
1995	Mary Pierce	Arantxa Sánchez Vicario
1996	Monica Seles	Anke Huber
1997	Martina Hingis	Mary Pierce
1998	Martina Hingis	Conchita Martínez
1999	Martina Hingis	Amelie Mauresmo
2000	Lindsay Davenport	Martina Hingis
2001	Jennifer Capriati	Martina Hingis
2002	Jennifer Capriati	Martina Hingis
2003	Serena Williams	Venus Williams
2004	Justine Henin	Kim Clijsters
2005	Serena Williams	Lindsay Davenport
2006	Amelie Mauresmo	Justine Henin
2007	Serena Williams	Maria Sharapova
2008	Maria Sharapova	Ana Ivanovic
2009	Serena Williams	Dinara Safina
2010	Serena Williams	Justine Henin
2011	Kim Clijsters	Li Na

French Open (Roland Garros) Singles Champions, 1968-2011

(First contested 1891 for men, 1897 for women. Became an Open Championship in 1968.)

Men's Singles

Year	Champion	Final opponent
1968	Ken Rosewall	Rod Laver
1969	Rod Laver	Ken Rosewall
1970	Jan Kodes	Zeljko Franulovic
1971	Jan Kodes	Ilie Nastase
1972	Andres Gimeno	Patrick Proisy
1973	Ilie Nastase	Nikki Pilic
1974	Björn Borg	Manuel Orantes
1975	Björn Borg	Guillermo Vilas
1976	Adriano Panatta	Harold Solomon
1977	Guillermo Vilas	Brian Gottfried
1978	Björn Borg	Guillermo Vilas
1979	Björn Borg	Victor Pecci
1980	Björn Borg	Vitas Gerulaitis
1981	Björn Borg	Ivan Lendl
1982	Mats Wilander	Guillermo Vilas
1983	Yannick Noah	Mats Wilander
1984	Ivan Lendl	John McEnroe
1985	Mats Wilander	Ivan Lendl
1986	Ivan Lendl	Mikael Pernfors
1987	Ivan Lendl	Mats Wilander
1988	Mats Wilander	Henri Leconte
1989	Michael Chang	Stefan Edberg
1990	Andres Gomez	Andre Agassi
1991	Jim Courier	Andre Agassi
1992	Jim Courier	Petr Korda
1993	Sergi Bruguera	Jim Courier
1994	Sergi Bruguera	Alberto Berasategui
1995	Thomas Muster	Michael Chang
1996	Yevgeny Kafelnikov	Michael Stich
1997	Gustavo Kuerten	Sergei Bruguera
1998	Carlos Moya	Alex Corretja
1999	Andre Agassi	Andrei Medvedev
2000	Gustavo Kuerten	Magnus Norman
2001	Gustavo Kuerten	Alex Corretja
2002	Albert Costa	Juan Carlos Ferrero
2003	Juan Carlos Ferrero	Martin Verkerk
2004	Gaston Gaudio	Guillermo Coria
2005	Rafael Nadal	Mariano Puerta
2006	Rafael Nadal	Roger Federer
2007	Rafael Nadal	Roger Federer
2008	Rafael Nadal	Roger Federer
2009	Roger Federer	Robin Soderling
2010	Rafael Nadal	Robin Soderling
2011	Rafael Nadal	Roger Federer

Women's Singles

Year	Champion	Final opponent
1968	Nancy Richey	Ann Jones
1969	Margaret Smith Court	Ann Jones
1970	Margaret Smith Court	Helga Niessen
1971	Evonne Goolagong	Helen Gourlay
1972	Billie Jean King	Evonne Goolagong
1973	Margaret Smith Court	Chris Evert
1974	Chris Evert	Olga Morozova
1975	Chris Evert	Martina Navratilova
1976	Sue Barker	Renata Tomanova
1977	Mima Jausovec	Florenza Mihai
1978	Virginia Ruzici	Mima Jausovec
1979	Chris Evert Lloyd	Wendy Turnbull
1980	Chris Evert Lloyd	Virginia Ruzici
1981	Hana Mandlikova	Sylvia Hanika
1982	Martina Navratilova	Andrea Jaeger
1983	Chris Evert Lloyd	Mima Jausovec
1984	Martina Navratilova	Chris Evert Lloyd
1985	Chris Evert Lloyd	Martina Navratilova
1986	Chris Evert Lloyd	Martina Navratilova
1987	Steffi Graf	Martina Navratilova
1988	Steffi Graf	Natalia Zvereva
1989	Arantxa Sánchez Vicario	Steffi Graf
1990	Monica Seles	Steffi Graf
1991	Monica Seles	Arantxa Sánchez Vicario
1992	Monica Seles	Steffi Graf
1993	Steffi Graf	Mary Joe Fernandez
1994	Arantxa Sánchez Vicario	Mary Pierce
1995	Steffi Graf	Arantxa Sánchez Vicario
1996	Steffi Graf	Arantxa Sánchez Vicario
1997	Iva Majoli	Martina Hingis
1998	Arantxa Sánchez Vicario	Monica Seles
1999	Steffi Graf	Martina Hingis
2000	Mary Pierce	Conchita Martínez
2001	Jennifer Capriati	Kim Clijsters
2002	Serena Williams	Venus Williams
2003	Justine Henin	Kim Clijsters
2004	Anastasia Myskina	Elena Dementieva
2005	Justine Henin	Mary Pierce
2006	Justine Henin	Svetlana Kuznetsova
2007	Justine Henin	Ana Ivanovic
2008	Ana Ivanovic	Dinara Safina
2009	Svetlana Kuznetsova	Dinara Safina
2010	Francesca Schiavone	Samantha Stosur
2011	Li Na	Francesca Schiavone

Wimbledon Champions, 1925-2011

(First contested 1877 for men, 1884 for women. Became an Open Championship in 1968. Not held 1940-45.)

Men's Singles

Year	Champion	Final opponent
1925	René Lacoste	Jean Borotra
1926	Jean Borotra	Howard Kinsey
1927	Henri Cochet	Jean Borotra
1928	René Lacoste	Henri Cochet
1929	Henri Cochet	Jean Borotra
1930	Bill Tilden	Wilmer Allison
1931	Sidney B. Wood	Francis X. Shields
1932	Ellsworth Vines	Henry Austin
1933	Jack Crawford	Ellsworth Vines
1934	Fred Perry	Jack Crawford
1935	Fred Perry	Gottfried von Cramm
1936	Fred Perry	Gottfried von Cramm
1937	Donald Budge	Gottfried von Cramm
1938	Donald Budge	Henry Austin
1939	Bobby Riggs	Elwood Cooke
1946	Yvon Petra	Geoff E. Brown
1947	Jack Kramer	Tom P. Brown
1948	Bob Falkenburg	John Bromwich
1949	Ted Schroeder	Jaroslav Drobny
1950	Budge Patty	Frank Sedgman
1951	Dick Savitt	Ken McGregor
1952	Frank Sedgman	Jaroslav Drobny
1953	Vic Seixas	Kurt Nielsen
1954	Jaroslav Drobny	Ken Rosewall
1955	Tony Trabert	Kurt Nielsen
1956	Lew Hoad	Ken Rosewall
1957	Lew Hoad	Ashley Cooper
1958	Ashley Cooper	Neale Fraser
1959	Alex Olmedo	Rod Laver
1960	Neale Fraser	Rod Laver
1961	Rod Laver	Chuck McKinley
1962	Rod Laver	Martin Mulligan
1963	Chuck McKinley	Fred Stolle
1964	Roy Emerson	Fred Stolle
1965	Roy Emerson	Fred Stolle
1966	Manuel Santana	Dennis Ralston
1967	John Newcombe	Wilhelm Bungert
1968	Rod Laver	Tony Roche
1969	Rod Laver	John Newcombe
1970	John Newcombe	Ken Rosewall
1971	John Newcombe	Stan Smith
1972	Stan Smith	Ilie Nastase
1973	Jan Kodes	Alex Metreveli
1974	Jimmy Connors	Ken Rosewall
1975	Arthur Ashe	Jimmy Connors
1976	Björn Borg	Ilie Nastase
1977	Björn Borg	Jimmy Connors
1978	Björn Borg	Jimmy Connors
1979	Björn Borg	Roscoe Tanner
1980	Björn Borg	John McEnroe
1981	John McEnroe	Björn Borg
1982	Jimmy Connors	John McEnroe
1983	John McEnroe	Chris Lewis
1984	John McEnroe	Jimmy Connors
1985	Boris Becker	Kevin Curren
1986	Boris Becker	Ivan Lendl
1987	Pat Cash	Ivan Lendl
1988	Stefan Edberg	Boris Becker
1989	Boris Becker	Stefan Edberg
1990	Stefan Edberg	Boris Becker
1991	Michael Stich	Boris Becker
1992	Andre Agassi	Goran Ivanisevic
1993	Pete Sampras	Jim Courier
1994	Pete Sampras	Goran Ivanisevic
1995	Pete Sampras	Boris Becker
1996	Richard Krajicek	MaliVai Washington
1997	Pete Sampras	Cedric Pioline
1998	Pete Sampras	Goran Ivanisevic
1999	Pete Sampras	Andre Agassi
2000	Pete Sampras	Patrick Rafter
2001	Goran Ivanisevic	Patrick Rafter
2002	Lleyton Hewitt	David Nalbandian
2003	Roger Federer	Mark Philippoussis
2004	Roger Federer	Andy Roddick
2005	Roger Federer	Andy Roddick
2006	Roger Federer	Rafael Nadal
2007	Roger Federer	Rafael Nadal
2008	Rafael Nadal	Roger Federer
2009	Roger Federer	Andy Roddick
2010	Rafael Nadal	Tomas Berdych
2011	Novak Djokovic	Rafael Nadal

Women's Singles

Year	Champion	Final opponent
1925	Suzanne Lenglen	Joan Fry
1926	Kathleen McKane Godfree	Lili de Alvarez
1927	Helen Wills	Lili de Alvarez
1928	Helen Wills	Lili de Alvarez
1929	Helen Wills	Helen Jacobs
1930	Helen Wills Moody	Elizabeth Ryan
1931	Cilly Aussem	Hilde Kranwinkel
1932	Helen Wills Moody	Helen Jacobs
1933	Helen Wills Moody	Dorothy Round
1934	Dorothy Round	Helen Jacobs
1935	Helen Wills Moody	Helen Jacobs
1936	Helen Jacobs	Hilde Kranwinkel Sperling
1937	Dorothy Round	Jadwiga Jedrzejowska
1938	Helen Wills Moody	Helen Jacobs
1939	Alice Marble	Kay Stammers
1946	Pauline Betz	Louise Brough
1947	Margaret Osborne	Doris Hart
1948	Louise Brough	Doris Hart
1949	Louise Brough	Margaret Osborne duPont
1950	Louise Brough	Margaret Osborne duPont
1951	Doris Hart	Shirley Fry
1952	Maureen Connolly	Louise Brough
1953	Maureen Connolly	Doris Hart
1954	Maureen Connolly	Louise Brough
1955	Louise Brough	Beverly Fleitz
1956	Shirley Fry	Angela Buxton
1957	Althea Gibson	Darlene Hard
1958	Althea Gibson	Angela Mortimer
1959	Maria Bueno	Darlene Hard
1960	Maria Bueno	Sandra Reynolds
1961	Angela Mortimer	Christine Truman
1962	Karen Hantze-Susman	Vera Sukova
1963	Margaret Smith	Billie Jean Moffitt
1964	Maria Bueno	Margaret Smith
1965	Margaret Smith	Maria Bueno
1966	Billie Jean King	Maria Bueno
1967	Billie Jean King	Ann Haydon Jones
1968	Billie Jean King	Judy Tegart
1969	Ann Haydon-Jones	Billie Jean King
1970	Margaret Smith Court	Billie Jean King
1971	Evonne Goolagong	Margaret Smith Court
1972	Billie Jean King	Evonne Goolagong
1973	Billie Jean King	Chris Evert
1974	Chris Evert	Olga Morozova
1975	Billie Jean King	Evonne Goolagong Cawley
1976	Chris Evert	Evonne Goolagong Cawley
1977	Virginia Wade	Betty Stove
1978	Martina Navratilova	Chris Evert
1979	Martina Navratilova	Chris Evert Lloyd
1980	Evonne Goolagong Cawley	Chris Evert Lloyd
1981	Chris Evert Lloyd	Hana Mandlikova
1982	Martina Navratilova	Chris Evert Lloyd
1983	Martina Navratilova	Andrea Jaeger
1984	Martina Navratilova	Chris Evert Lloyd
1985	Martina Navratilova	Chris Evert Lloyd
1986	Martina Navratilova	Hana Mandlikova
1987	Martina Navratilova	Steffi Graf
1988	Steffi Graf	Martina Navratilova
1989	Steffi Graf	Martina Navratilova
1990	Martina Navratilova	Zina Garrison
1991	Steffi Graf	Gabriela Sabatini
1992	Steffi Graf	Monica Seles
1993	Steffi Graf	Jana Novotna
1994	Conchita Martínez	Martina Navratilova
1995	Steffi Graf	Arantxa Sánchez Vicario
1996	Steffi Graf	Arantxa Sánchez Vicario
1997	Martina Hingis	Jana Novotna
1998	Jana Novotna	Nathalie Tauziat
1999	Lindsay Davenport	Steffi Graf
2000	Venus Williams	Lindsay Davenport
2001	Venus Williams	Justine Henin
2002	Serena Williams	Venus Williams
2003	Serena Williams	Venus Williams
2004	Maria Sharapova	Serena Williams
2005	Venus Williams	Lindsay Davenport
2006	Amelie Mauresmo	Justine Henin
2007	Venus Williams	Marion Bartoli
2008	Venus Williams	Serena Williams
2009	Serena Williams	Venus Williams
2010	Serena Williams	Vera Zvonareva
2011	Petra Kvitova	Maria Sharapova

U.S. Open Champions, 1925-2011

(First contested 1881 for men, 1887 for women. Became an Open Championship in 1970.)

Year	Men's Singles Champion	Final opponent	Year	Women's Singles Champion	Final opponent
1925	Bill Tilden	William Johnston	1925	Helen Willis	Kathleen McKane
1926	René Lacoste	Jean Borotra	1926	Molla B. Mallory	Elizabeth Ryan
1927	René Lacoste	Bill Tilden	1927	Helen Wills	Betty Nuthall
1928	Henri Cochet	Francis Hunter	1928	Helen Wills	Helen Jacobs
1929	Bill Tilden	Francis Hunter	1929	Helen Wills	M. Watson
1930	John Doeg	Francis Shields	1930	Betty Nuthall	L. A. Harper
1931	H. Ellsworth Vines	George Lott	1931	Helen Wills Moody	E. B. Whittingstall
1932	H. Ellsworth Vines	Henri Cochet	1932	Helen Jacobs	Carolin A. Babcock
1933	Fred Perry	John Crawford	1933	Helen Jacobs	Helen Wills Moody
1934	Fred Perry	Wilmer Allison	1934	Helen Jacobs	Sarah H. Palfrey
1935	Wilmer Allison	Sidney Wood	1935	Helen Jacobs	Sarah Palfrey Fabyan
1936	Fred Perry	Don Budge	1936	Alice Marble	Helen Jacobs
1937	Don Budge	Baron G. von Cramm	1937	Anita Lizana	Jadwiga Jedrzejowska
1938	Don Budge	C. Gene Mako	1938	Alice Marble	Nancye Wynne
1939	Robert Riggs	S. Welby Van Horn	1939	Alice Marble	Helen Jacobs
1940	Don McNeill	Robert Riggs	1940	Alice Marble	Helen Jacobs
1941	Robert Riggs	F. L. Kovacs	1941	Sarah Palfrey Cooke	Pauline Betz
1942	F. R. Schroeder Jr.	Frank Parker	1942	Pauline Betz	Louise Brough
1943	Joseph Hunt	Jack Kramer	1943	Pauline Betz	Louise Brough
1944	Frank Parker	William Talbert	1944	Pauline Betz	Margaret Osborne
1945	Frank Parker	William Talbert	1945	Sarah Palfrey Cooke	Pauline Betz
1946	Jack Kramer	Thomas Brown Jr.	1946	Pauline Betz	Patricia Canning
1947	Jack Kramer	Frank Parker	1947	Louise Brough	Margaret Osborne
1948	Pancho Gonzales	Eric Sturgess	1948	Margaret Osborne duPont	Louise Brough
1949	Pancho Gonzales	F. R. Schroeder Jr.	1949	Margaret Osborne duPont	Doris Hart
1950	Arthur Larsen	Herbert Flam	1950	Margaret Osborne duPont	Doris Hart
1951	Frank Sedgman	E. Victor Seixas Jr.	1951	Maureen Connolly	Shirley Fry
1952	Frank Sedgman	Gardnar Mulloy	1952	Maureen Connolly	Doris Hart
1953	Tony Trabert	E. Victor Seixas Jr.	1953	Maureen Connolly	Doris Hart
1954	E. Victor Seixas Jr.	Rex Hartwig	1954	Doris Hart	Louise Brough
1955	Tony Trabert	Ken Rosewall	1955	Doris Hart	Patricia Ward
1956	Ken Rosewall	Lewis Hoad	1956	Shirley Fry	Althea Gibson
1957	Malcolm Anderson	Ashley Cooper	1957	Althea Gibson	Louise Brough
1958	Ashley Cooper	Malcolm Anderson	1958	Althea Gibson	Darlene Hard
1959	Neale A. Fraser	Alejandro Olmedo	1959	Maria Bueno	Christine Truman
1960	Neale A. Fraser	Rod Laver	1960	Darlene Hard	Maria Bueno
1961	Roy Emerson	Rod Laver	1961	Darlene Hard	Ann Haydon
1962	Rod Laver	Roy Emerson	1962	Margaret Smith	Darlene Hard
1963	Rafael Osuna	F. A. Froehling III	1963	Maria Bueno	Margaret Smith
1964	Roy Emerson	Fred Stolle	1964	Maria Bueno	Carole Graebner
1965	Manuel Santana	Cliff Drysdale	1965	Margaret Smith	Billie Jean Moffitt
1966	Fred Stolle	John Newcombe	1966	Maria Bueno	Nancy Richey
1967	John Newcombe	Clark Graebner	1967	Billie Jean King	Ann Haydon Jones
1968	Arthur Ashe	Tom Okker	1968	Virginia Wade	Billie Jean King
1969	Rod Laver	Tony Roche	1969	Margaret Smith Court	Nancy Richey
1970	Ken Rosewall	Tony Roche	1970	Margaret Smith Court	Rosemary Casals
1971	Stan Smith	Jan Kodes	1971	Billie Jean King	Rosemary Casals
1972	Ilie Nastase	Arthur Ashe	1972	Billie Jean King	Kerry Melville
1973	John Newcombe	Jan Kodes	1973	Margaret Smith Court	Evonne Goolagong
1974	Jimmy Connors	Ken Rosewall	1974	Billie Jean King	Evonne Goolagong
1975	Manuel Orantes	Jimmy Connors	1975	Chris Evert	Evonne Goolagong Cawley
1976	Jimmy Connors	Björn Borg	1976	Chris Evert	Evonne Goolagong Cawley
1977	Guillermo Vilas	Jimmy Connors	1977	Chris Evert	Wendy Turnbull
1978	Jimmy Connors	Björn Borg	1978	Chris Evert	Pam Shriver
1979	John McEnroe	Vitas Gerulaitis	1979	Tracy Austin	Chris Evert Lloyd
1980	John McEnroe	Björn Borg	1980	Chris Evert Lloyd	Hana Mandlikova
1981	John McEnroe	Björn Borg	1981	Tracy Austin	Martina Navratilova
1982	Jimmy Connors	Ivan Lendl	1982	Chris Evert Lloyd	Hana Mandlikova
1983	Jimmy Connors	Ivan Lendl	1983	Martina Navratilova	Chris Evert Lloyd
1984	John McEnroe	Ivan Lendl	1984	Martina Navratilova	Chris Evert Lloyd
1985	Ivan Lendl	John McEnroe	1985	Hana Mandlikova	Martina Navratilova
1986	Ivan Lendl	Miloslav Mecir	1986	Martina Navratilova	Helena Sukova
1987	Ivan Lendl	Mats Wilander	1987	Martina Navratilova	Steffi Graf
1988	Mats Wilander	Ivan Lendl	1988	Steffi Graf	Gabriela Sabatini
1989	Boris Becker	Ivan Lendl	1989	Steffi Graf	Martina Navratilova
1990	Pete Sampras	Andre Agassi	1990	Gabriela Sabatini	Steffi Graf
1991	Stefan Edberg	Jim Courier	1991	Monica Seles	Martina Navratilova
1992	Stefan Edberg	Pete Sampras	1992	Monica Seles	Arantxa Sánchez Vicario
1993	Pete Sampras	Cedric Pioline	1993	Steffi Graf	Helena Sukova
1994	Andre Agassi	Michael Stich	1994	Arantxa Sánchez Vicario	Steffi Graf
1995	Pete Sampras	Andre Agassi	1995	Steffi Graf	Monica Seles
1996	Pete Sampras	Michael Chang	1996	Steffi Graf	Monica Seles
1997	Patrick Rafter	Greg Rusedski	1997	Martina Hingis	Venus Williams
1998	Patrick Rafter	Mark Philippoussis	1998	Lindsay Davenport	Martina Hingis
1999	Andre Agassi	Todd Martin	1999	Serena Williams	Martina Hingis
2000	Marat Safin	Pete Sampras	2000	Venus Williams	Lindsay Davenport
2001	Lleyton Hewitt	Pete Sampras	2001	Venus Williams	Serena Williams
2002	Pete Sampras	Andre Agassi	2002	Serena Williams	Venus Williams
2003	Andy Roddick	Juan Carlos Ferrero	2003	Justine Henin	Kim Clijsters
2004	Roger Federer	Lleyton Hewitt	2004	Svetlana Kuznetsova	Elena Dementieva
2005	Roger Federer	Andre Agassi	2005	Kim Clijsters	Mary Pierce
2006	Roger Federer	Andy Roddick	2006	Maria Sharapova	Justine Henin
2007	Roger Federer	Novak Djokovic	2007	Justine Henin	Svetlana Kuznetsova
2008	Roger Federer	Andy Murray	2008	Serena Williams	Jelena Jankovic
2009	Juan Martin del Potro	Roger Federer	2009	Kim Clijsters	Caroline Wozniacki
2010	Rafael Nadal	Novak Djokovic	2010	Kim Clijsters	Vera Zvonareva
2011	Novak Djokovic	Rafael Nadal	2011	Samantha Stosur	Serena Williams

Davis Cup, 1950-2010

Year	Result	Year	Result	Year	Result
1950	Australia 4, U.S. 1	1971	U.S. 3, Romania 2	1991	France 3, U.S. 1
1951	Australia 3, U.S. 2	1972	U.S. 3, Romania 2	1992	U.S. 3, Switzerland 1
1952	Australia 4, U.S. 1	1973	Australia 5, U.S. 0	1993	Germany 4, Australia 1
1953	Australia 3, U.S. 2	1974	South Africa (default by India)	1994	Sweden 4, Russia 1
1954	U.S. 3, Australia 2	1975	Sweden 3, Czechoslovakia 2	1995	U.S. 3, Russia 2
1955	Australia 5, U.S. 0	1976	Italy 4, Chile 1	1996	France 3, Sweden 2
1956	Australia 5, U.S. 0	1977	Australia 3, Italy 1	1997	Sweden 5, U.S. 0
1957	Australia 3, U.S. 2	1978	U.S. 4, Great Britain 1	1998	Sweden 4, Italy 1
1958	U.S. 3, Australia 2	1979	U.S. 5, Italy 0	1999	Australia 3, France 2
1959	Australia 3, U.S. 2	1980	Czechoslovakia 4, Italy 1	2000	Spain 3, Australia 1
1960	Australia 4, Italy 1	1981	U.S. 3, Argentina 1	2001	France 3, Australia 2
1961	Australia 5, Italy 0	1982	U.S. 4, France, 1	2002	Russia 3, France 2
1962	Australia 5, Mexico 0	1983	Australia 3, Sweden 2	2003	Australia 3, Spain 1
1963	U.S. 3, Australia 2	1984	Sweden 4, U.S. 1	2004	Spain 3, U.S. 2
1964	Australia 3, U.S. 2	1985	Sweden 3, W. Germany 2	2005	Croatia 3, Slovakia 2
1965	Australia 4, Spain 1	1986	Australia 3, Sweden 2	2006	Russia 3, Argentina 2
1966	Australia 4, India 1	1987	Sweden 5, India 0	2007	U.S. 4, Russia 1
1967	Australia 4, Spain 1	1988	W. Germany 4, Sweden 1	2008	Spain 3, Argentina 1
1968	U.S. 4, Australia 1	1989	W. Germany 3, Sweden 2	2009	Spain 5, Czech Republic 0
1969	U.S. 5, Romania 0	1990	U.S. 3, Australia 2	2010	Serbia 3, France 2
1970	U.S. 5, W. Germany 0				

Note: The challenge round format, which guaranteed the previous year's winner a spot in the finals at home, was eliminated in 1972.

All-Time Grand Slam Singles Titles Leaders

Men	Australian Open	French Open[1]	Wimbledon	U.S. Open	Total
Roger Federer	2004, '06-'07, '10	2009	2003-07, '09	2004-08	16
Pete Sampras	1994, '97	—	1993-95, 1997-2000	1990, '93, '95-'96, 2002	14
Roy Emerson	1961, '63-'67	1963, '67	1964-65	1961, '64	12
Björn Borg	—	1974-75, '78-'81	1976-80	—	11
Rod Laver	1960, '62, '69	1962, '69	1961-62, '68-'69	1962, '69	11
Bill Tilden	—	—	1920-21, '30	1920-25, '29	10
Rafael Nadal	2009	2005-08, '10, '11	2008, '10	2010	10
Andre Agassi	1995, 2000, '01, '03	1999	1992	1994, '99	8
Jimmy Connors	1974	—	1974, '82	1974, '76, '78, '82-'83	8
Ivan Lendl	1989-90	1984, '86-'87	—	1985-87	8
Fred Perry	1934	1935	1934-36	1933-34, '36	8
Ken Rosewall	1953, '55, '71-'72	1953, '68	—	1956, '70	8

Women					
Margaret Smith Court	1960-66, '69-'71, '73	1962, '64, '69-'70, '73	1963, '65, '70	1962, '65, '69-'70, '73	24
Steffi Graf	1988-90, '94	1987-88, '93, '95-'96, '99	1988-89, '91-'93, '95-'96	1988-89, '93, '95-'96	22
Helen Wills Moody	—	1928-30, '32	1927-30, '32-'33, '35, '38	1923-25, '27-'29, '31	19
Chris Evert	1982, '84	1974-75, '79-'80, '83, '85-'86	1974, '76, '81	1975-78, '80, '82	18
Martina Navratilova	1981, '83, '85	1982, '84	1978-79, '82-'87, '90	1983-84, '86-'87	18
Serena Williams	2003, '05, '07, '09-'10	2002	2002-03, '09-'10	1999, 2002, '08	13
Billie Jean King	1968	1972	1966-68, '72-'73, '75	1967, '71-'72, '74	12
Suzanne Lenglen	—	1920-23, '25-'26	1919-23, '25	—	12
Maureen Connolly	1953	1953-54	1952-54	1951-53	9
Monica Seles	1991-93, '96	1990-92	—	1991-92	9

Note: Players active in 2011 are in bold. (1) Prior to 1925, French Open entry was limited to members of French clubs.

RIFLE AND PISTOL CHAMPIONSHIPS

Source: National Rifle Association (NRA)

NRA Bianchi Cup National Action Pistol Championships, 2011

Action Pistol: Doug Koenig, Alburtis, PA, 1920-187X
Woman Action Pistol: Jessica Abbate, McDonough, GA, 1912-153X

Junior Action Pistol: Tiffany Piper, Auckland, New Zealand, 1893-143X

NRA National Outdoor Rifle and Pistol Championships, 2011

Pistol: Cpt. Philip W. Hemphill, Clinton, MS, 2632-113X
Civilian Pistol: John Zurek, Phoenix, AZ, 2626-115X
Woman Pistol: Judy Tant, East Lansing, MI, 2549-68X
Smallbore Rifle Prone: Staff Sgt. Michael McPhail, U.S. Army, Phenix City, AL, 4796-401X
Civilian Smallbore Rifle Prone: Mark A. Delcotto, Lexington, KY, 4796-380X
Woman Smallbore Rifle Prone: Nancy Tompkins, Prescott, AZ, 4794-375X
Smallbore Rifle NRA 3-Position: Sgt. Joseph A. Hein, U.S. Army, Phenix City, AL; 2379-153X
Civilian Smallbore Rifle NRA 3-Position: Garrett S. Spurgeon, Canton, OH, 2376-132X

Woman Smallbore Rifle NRA 3-Position: Lisette Grunwell-Lacey, Old Lyme, CT, 2369-161X
High Power Rifle: Carl R. Bernosky, Ashland, PA, 2393-160X
Civilian High Power Rifle: Carl R. Bernosky, Ashland, PA, 2939-160X
Woman High Power Rifle: Sgt. Sherri J. Gallagher, U.S. Army, Ft. Benning, GA, 2383-146X
High Power Rifle Long Range: David Tubb, Canadian, TX, 1249-68X
Woman High Power Rifle Long Range: Michelle M. Gallagher, Phoenix, AZ, 1240-64X

NRA National Indoor Rifle and Pistol Championships, 2011

Smallbore Rifle Conventional Position: Steven Hahn, Middle Grove, NY, 798-64X
Woman Smallbore Rifle Conventional Position: Lisette Grunwell-Lacey, Old Lyme, CT, 793-58X
Smallbore Rifle NRA Metric Position: Abigail Fong, New York, NY, 1174
Woman Smallbore Rifle NRA Metric Position: Abigail Fong, New York, NY, 1174
International Smallbore Rifle: Michael Liuzza, New Orleans, LA, 1170
Woman International Smallbore Rifle: Amanda Luoma, Cortland, OH, 1155
Air Rifle: Ryan Dunham-Bender, Delta Junction, AK, 590

Woman Air Rifle: Anna Hjelmevoll, Fairbanks, AK, 585
Conventional Pistol: James Henderson, Midland, GA, 892-42X
Woman Conventional Pistol: Judy Tant, East Lansing, MI, 864-20X
International Free Pistol: John Zurek, Phoenix, AZ, 548
Woman International Free Pistol: Ashley Davis, Kaysville, UT, 467
International Standard Pistol: David Lange, Glen Rock, NJ, 571
Woman International Standard Pistol: Kathy Chatterton, Glen Rock, NJ, 534
Air Pistol: John Zurek, Phoenix, AZ, 581
Woman Air Pistol: Elizabeth Callahan, Pawley's Island, SC, 556

AUTO RACING

Indianapolis 500 Winners, 1911-2011

(At Indianapolis Motor Speedway in Indianapolis, IN. * = Race record.)

Year	Winner, car[1]	Avg. mph	Year	Winner, car[1]	Avg. mph
1911	Ray Harroun, Marmon	74.602	1964	A. J. Foyt, Watson-Offy	147.350
1912	Joe Dawson, National	78.719	1965	Jim Clark, Lotus-Ford	150.686
1913	Jules Goux, Peugeot	75.933	1966	Graham Hill, Lola-Ford	144.317
1914	Rene Thomas, Delage	82.474	1967	A. J. Foyt, Coyote-Ford	151.207
1915	Ralph DePalma, Mercedes	89.840	1968	Bobby Unser, Eagle-Offy	152.882
1916	Dario Resta, Peugeot	84.001	1969	Mario Andretti, Hawk-Ford	156.867
1917-18	Not held		1970	Al Unser, P.J. Colt-Ford	155.749
1919	Howdy Wilcox, Peugeot	88.050	1971	Al Unser, P.J. Colt-Ford	157.735
1920	Gaston Chevrolet, Frontenac	88.618	1972	Mark Donohue, McLaren-Offy	162.962
1921	Tommy Milton, Frontenac	89.621	1973	Gordon Johncock, Eagle-Offy	159.036
1922	Jimmy Murphy, Duesenberg-Miller	94.484	1974	Johnny Rutherford, McLaren-Offy	158.589
1923	Tommy Milton, Miller	90.954	1975	Bobby Unser, Eagle-Offy	149.213
1924	L. L. Corum-Joe Boyer, Duesenberg	98.234	1976	Johnny Rutherford, McLaren-Offy	148.725
1925	Peter DePaolo, Duesenberg	101.127	1977	A. J. Foyt, Coyote-Foyt	161.331
1926	Frank Lockhart, Miller	95.904	1978	Al Unser, Lola-Cosworth	161.363
1927	George Souders, Duesenberg	97.545	1979	Rick Mears, Penske-Cosworth	158.899
1928	Louie Meyer, Miller	99.482	1980	Johnny Rutherford, Chaparral-Cosworth	142.862
1929	Ray Keech, Miller	97.585	1981	Bobby Unser, Penske-Cosworth	139.084
1930	Billy Arnold, Summers-Miller	100.448	1982	Gordon Johncock, Wildcat-Cosworth	162.029
1931	Louis Schneider, Stevens-Miller	96.629	1983	Tom Sneva, March-Cosworth	162.117
1932	Fred Frame, Wetteroth-Miller	104.144	1984	Rick Mears, March-Cosworth	163.612
1933	Louie Meyer, Miller	104.162	1985	Danny Sullivan, March-Cosworth	152.982
1934	Bill Cummings, Miller	104.863	1986	Bobby Rahal, March-Cosworth	170.722
1935	Kelly Petillo, Wetteroth-Offy	106.240	1987	Al Unser, March-Cosworth	162.175
1936	Louie Meyer, Stevens-Miller	109.069	1988	Rick Mears, Penske-Chevy V8	144.809
1937	Wilbur Shaw, Shaw-Offy	113.580	1989	Emerson Fittipaldi, Penske-Chevy Indy V8	167.581
1938	Floyd Roberts, Wetteroth-Miller	117.200	1990	Arie Luyendyk, Lola-Chevy Indy V8	185.981*
1939	Wilbur Shaw, Maserati	115.035	1991	Rick Mears, Penske-Chevy Indy V8	176.457
1940	Wilbur Shaw, Maserati	114.277	1992	Al Unser Jr., Galmer-Chevy Indy V8A	134.477
1941	Floyd Davis-Mauri Rose, Wetteroth-Offy	115.117	1993	Emerson Fittipaldi, Penske-Chevy Indy V8C	157.207
1942-45	Not held		1994	Al Unser Jr., Penske-Mercedes Benz	160.872
1946	George Robson, Adams-Sparks	114.820	1995	Jacques Villeneuve, Reynard-Ford Cosworth XB	153.616
1947	Mauri Rose, Deidt-Offy	116.338	1996	Buddy Lazier, Reynard-Ford Cosworth	147.956
1948	Mauri Rose, Deidt-Offy	119.814	1997	Arie Luyendyk, G Force-Aurora	145.827
1949	Bill Holland, Deidt-Offy	121.327	1998	Eddie Cheever, Dallara-Aurora	145.155
1950	Johnnie Parsons, Kurtis-Offy	124.002	1999	Kenny Brack, Dallara-Aurora	153.176
1951	Lee Wallard, Kurtis-Offy	126.244	2000	Juan Montoya, G Force-Aurora	167.607
1952	Troy Ruttman, Kuzma-Offy	128.922	2001	Helio Castroneves, Reynard-Honda	141.574
1953	Bill Vukovich, KK500A-Offy	127.740	2002	Helio Castroneves, Reynard-Honda	166.499
1954	Bill Vukovich, KK500A-Offy	130.840	2003	Gil de Ferran, G Force-Toyota	156.291
1955	Bob Sweikert, KK500C-Offy	128.213	2004	Buddy Rice, G Force-Honda	138.518
1956	Pat Flaherty, Watson-Offy	128.490	2005	Dan Wheldon, Dallara-Honda	157.603
1957	Sam Hanks, Salih-Offy	135.601	2006	Sam Hornish Jr., Dallara-Honda	157.085
1958	Jimmy Bryan, Salih-Offy	133.791	2007	Dario Franchitti, Dallara-Honda	151.774
1959	Rodger Ward, Watson-Offy	135.857	2008	Scott Dixon, Dallara-Honda	143.567
1960	Jim Rathmann, Watson-Offy	138.767	2009	Helio Castroneves, Dallara-Honda	150.318
1961	A. J. Foyt, Trevis-Offy	139.130	2010	Dario Franchitti, Dallara-Honda	161.623
1962	Rodger Ward, Watson-Offy	140.293	2011	Dan Wheldon, Dallara-Honda	170.265
1963	Parnelli Jones, Watson-Offy	143.137			

Note: The race was less than 500 mi in the following years: 1916 (300 mi), 1926 (400 mi), 1950 (345 mi), 1973 (332.5 mi), 1975 (435 mi), 1976 (255 mi), 2004 (450 mi) and 2007 (415 mi). (1) Chassis-engine.

IndyCar Series Champions, 1996-2010

A breakaway group of CART drivers began the Indy Racing League (IRL) in 1994; it awarded its first championship in 1996. Known as IndyCar Series since 2003, IRL announced it would officially change its name to IndyCar as of Jan. 1, 2011. Merged with Champ Car Series, 2008.

Year	Driver	Year	Driver	Year	Driver	Year	Driver	Year	Driver
1996	Scott Sharp, Buzz Calkins (tie)	1999	Greg Ray	2002	Sam Hornish Jr.	2005	Dan Wheldon	2008	Scott Dixon
		2000	Buddy Lazier	2003	Scott Dixon	2006	Sam Hornish Jr.	2009	Dario Franchitti
1997	Tony Stewart	2001	Sam Hornish Jr.	2004	Tony Kanaan	2007	Dario Franchitti	2010	Dario Franchitti
1998	Kenny Brack								

Champ Car World Series Vanderbilt Cup Winners, 1959-2007

U.S. Auto Club Champions, 1959-78; Championship Auto Racing Teams (CART) Champions, 1979-2003; Champ Car World Series Champions, 2004-07. Vanderbilt Cup became the series championship trophy in 2000. Merged with Indy Racing League, 2008.

Year	Driver	Year	Driver	Year	Driver	Year	Driver	Year	Driver
1959	Rodger Ward	1969	Mario Andretti	1979	Rick Mears	1989	Emerson Fittipaldi	1999	Juan Montoya
1960	A. J. Foyt	1970	Al Unser	1980	Johnny Rutherford	1990	Al Unser Jr.	2000	Gil de Ferran
1961	A. J. Foyt	1971	Joe Leonard	1981	Rick Mears	1991	Michael Andretti	2001	Gil de Ferran
1962	Rodger Ward	1972	Joe Leonard	1982	Rick Mears	1992	Bobby Rahal	2002	Cristiano da Matta
1963	A. J. Foyt	1973	Roger McCluskey	1983	Al Unser	1993	Nigel Mansell	2003	Paul Tracy
1964	A. J. Foyt	1974	Bobby Unser	1984	Mario Andretti	1994	Al Unser Jr.	2004	Sébastien Bourdais
1965	Mario Andretti	1975	A. J. Foyt	1985	Al Unser	1995	Jacques Villeneuve	2005	Sébastien Bourdais
1966	Mario Andretti	1976	Gordon Johncock	1986	Bobby Rahal	1996	Jimmy Vasser	2006	Sébastien Bourdais
1967	A. J. Foyt	1977	Tom Sneva	1987	Bobby Rahal	1997	Alex Zanardi	2007	Sébastien Bourdais
1968	Bobby Unser	1978	Tom Sneva	1988	Danny Sullivan	1998	Alex Zanardi		

NASCAR Sprint Cup Champions, 1949-2010

Strictly Stock, 1949; Grand National, 1950-70; Winston Cup, 1971-2003; Sprint Cup, 2004-present.

Year	Driver	Year	Driver	Year	Driver	Year	Driver	Year	Driver
1949	Red Byron	1962	Joe Weatherly	1975	Richard Petty	1987	Dale Earnhardt	1999	Dale Jarrett
1950	Bill Rexford	1963	Joe Weatherly	1976	Cale Yarborough	1988	Bill Elliott	2000	Bobby Labonte
1951	Herb Thomas	1964	Richard Petty	1977	Cale Yarborough	1989	Rusty Wallace	2001	Jeff Gordon
1952	Tim Flock	1965	Ned Jarrett	1978	Cale Yarborough	1990	Dale Earnhardt	2002	Tony Stewart
1953	Herb Thomas	1966	David Pearson	1979	Richard Petty	1991	Dale Earnhardt	2003	Matt Kenseth
1954	Lee Petty	1967	Richard Petty	1980	Dale Earnhardt	1992	Alan Kulwicki	2004	Kurt Busch
1955	Tim Flock	1968	David Pearson	1981	Darrell Waltrip	1993	Dale Earnhardt	2005	Tony Stewart
1956	Buck Baker	1969	David Pearson	1982	Darrell Waltrip	1994	Dale Earnhardt	2006	Jimmie Johnson
1957	Buck Baker	1970	Bobby Isaac	1983	Bobby Allison	1995	Jeff Gordon	2007	Jimmie Johnson
1958	Lee Petty	1971	Richard Petty	1984	Terry Labonte	1996	Terry Labonte	2008	Jimmie Johnson
1959	Lee Petty	1972	Richard Petty	1985	Darrell Waltrip	1997	Jeff Gordon	2009	Jimmie Johnson
1960	Rex White	1973	Benny Parsons	1986	Dale Earnhardt	1998	Jeff Gordon	2010	Jimmie Johnson
1961	Ned Jarrett	1974	Richard Petty						

NASCAR Sprint Cup Rookie of the Year, 1958-2010

Year	Driver	Year	Driver	Year	Driver	Year	Driver	Year	Driver
1958	Shorty Rollins	1969	Dick Brooks	1980	Jody Riley	1991	Bobby Hamilton	2001	Kevin Harvick
1959	Richard Petty	1970	Bill Dennis	1981	Ron Bouchard	1992	Jimmy Hensley	2002	Ryan Newman
1960	David Pearson	1971	Walter Ballard	1982	Geoff Bodine	1993	Jeff Gordon	2003	Jamie McMurray
1961	Woodie Wilson	1972	Larry Smith	1983	Sterling Marlin	1994	Jeff Burton	2004	Kasey Kahne
1962	Tom Cox	1973	Lennie Pond	1984	Rusty Wallace	1995	Ricky Craven	2005	Kyle Busch
1963	Billy Wade	1974	Earl Ross	1985	Ken Schrader	1996	Johnny Benson	2006	Denny Hamlin
1964	Doug Cooper	1975	Bruce Hill	1986	Alan Kulwicki	1997	Mike Skinner	2007	Juan Montoya
1965	Sam McQuagg	1976	Skip Manning	1987	Davey Allison	1998	Kenny Irwin	2008	Regan Smith
1966	James Hylton	1977	Ricky Rudd	1988	Ken Bouchard	1999	Tony Stewart	2009	Joey Logano
1967	Donnie Allison	1978	Ronnie Thomas	1989	Dick Trickle	2000	Matt Kenseth	2010	Kevin Conway
1968	Pete Hamilton	1979	Dale Earnhardt	1990	Rob Moroso				

Daytona 500 Winners, 1959-2011

At Daytona International Speedway in Daytona Beach, FL.

Year	Driver, car	Avg. mph	Year	Driver, car	Avg. mph	Year	Driver, car	Avg. mph
1959	Lee Petty, Oldsmobile	135.521	1977	Cale Yarborough, Chevrolet	153.218	1995	Sterling Marlin, Chevrolet	141.710
1960	Junior Johnson, Chevrolet	124.740	1978	Bobby Allison, Ford	159.730	1996	Dale Jarrett, Ford	154.308
1961	Marvin Panch, Pontiac	149.601	1979	Richard Petty, Oldsmobile	143.977	1997	Jeff Gordon, Chevrolet	148.295
1962	Fireball Roberts, Pontiac	152.529	1980	Buddy Baker, Oldsmobile	177.602	1998	Dale Earnhardt, Chevrolet	172.712
1963	Tiny Lund, Ford	151.566	1981	Richard Petty, Buick	169.651	1999	Jeff Gordon, Chevrolet	161.551
1964	Richard Petty, Plymouth	154.334	1982	Bobby Allison, Buick	153.991	2000	Dale Jarrett, Ford	155.669
1965	Fred Lorenzen, Ford	141.539	1983	Cale Yarborough, Pontiac	155.979	2001	Michael Waltrip, Chevrolet	161.783
1966	Richard Petty, Plymouth	160.627	1984	Cale Yarborough, Chevrolet	150.994	2002	Ward Burton, Dodge	142.971
1967	Mario Andretti, Ford	146.926	1985	Bill Elliott, Ford	172.265	2003	Michael Waltrip, Chevrolet	133.870
1968	Cale Yarborough, Mercury	143.251	1986	Geoff Bodine, Chevrolet	148.124	2004	Dale Earnhardt Jr., Chevrolet	156.345
1969	LeeRoy Yarbrough, Ford	160.875	1987	Bill Elliott, Ford	176.263	2005	Jeff Gordon, Chevrolet	135.173
1970	Pete Hamilton, Plymouth	149.601	1988	Bobby Allison, Buick	137.531	2006	Jimmie Johnson, Chevrolet	142.667
1971	Richard Petty, Plymouth	144.456	1989	Darrell Waltrip, Chevrolet	148.466	2007	Kevin Harvick, Chevrolet	149.335
1972	A. J. Foyt, Mercury	161.550	1990	Derrike Cope, Chevrolet	165.761	2008	Ryan Newman, Dodge	152.672
1973	Richard Petty, Dodge	157.205	1991	Ernie Irvan, Chevrolet	148.148	2009	Matt Kenseth, Ford	132.816
1974	Richard Petty, Dodge	140.894	1992	Davey Allison, Ford	160.256	2010	Jamie McMurray, Chevrolet	137.284
1975	Benny Parsons, Chevrolet	153.649	1993	Dale Jarrett, Chevrolet	154.972	2011	Trevor Bayne, Ford	130.326
1976	David Pearson, Mercury	152.181	1994	Sterling Marlin, Chevrolet	156.931			

Note: The race was less than 500 mi in the following years: 1965 (322.5 mi), 1966 (495 mi), 1974 (450 mi), 2003 (272.5 mi).

Coca-Cola 600 Winners, 1960-2011

At Charlotte Motor Speedway in Concord, NC. Known as World 600, 1960-85. * = Rain-shortened.

Year	Driver, car	Avg. mph	Year	Driver, car	Avg. mph	Year	Driver, car	Avg. mph
1960	Joe Lee Johnson, Chevrolet	107.735	1978	Darrell Waltrip, Chevrolet	138.355	1995	Bobby Labonte, Chevrolet	151.952
1961	David Pearson, Pontiac	111.633	1979	Darrell Waltrip, Chevrolet	136.674	1996	Dale Jarrett, Ford	147.581
1962	Nelson Stacy, Ford	125.552	1980	Benny Parsons, Chevrolet	119.265	1997	Jeff Gordon, Chevrolet	136.745*
1963	Fred Lorenzen, Ford	132.418	1981	Bobby Allison, Buick	129.326	1998	Jeff Gordon, Chevrolet	136.424
1964	Jim Paschal, Plymouth	125.772	1982	Neil Bonnett, Ford	130.058	1999	Jeff Burton, Ford	151.367
1965	Fred Lorenzen, Ford	121.772	1983	Neil Bonnett, Chevrolet	140.707	2000	Matt Kenseth, Ford	142.640
1966	Marvin Panch, Plymouth	135.042	1984	Bobby Allison, Buick	129.233	2001	Jeff Burton, Ford	138.107
1967	Jim Paschal, Plymouth	135.832	1985	Darrell Waltrip, Chevrolet	141.807	2002	Mark Martin, Ford	137.729
1968	Buddy Baker, Dodge	104.207*	1986	Dale Earnhardt, Chevrolet	140.406	2003	Jimmie Johnson, Chevrolet	126.198*
1969	LeeRoy Yarbrough, Mercury	134.361	1987	Kyle Petty, Ford	131.483	2004	Jimmie Johnson, Chevrolet	142.763
1970	Donnie Allison, Ford	129.680	1988	Darrell Waltrip, Chevrolet	124.460	2005	Jimmie Johnson, Chevrolet	114.698
1971	Bobby Allison, Mercury	140.422	1989	Darrell Waltrip, Chevrolet	144.077	2006	Kasey Kahne, Dodge	128.840
1972	Buddy Baker, Dodge	142.255	1990	Rusty Wallace, Pontiac	137.650	2007	Casey Mears, Chevrolet	130.222
1973	Buddy Baker, Dodge	134.890	1991	Davey Allison, Ford	138.951	2008	Kasey Kahne, Dodge	135.722
1974	David Pearson, Mercury	135.720	1992	Dale Earnhardt, Chevrolet	132.980	2009	David Reutimann, Toyota	120.809
1975	Richard Petty, Dodge	145.327	1993	Dale Earnhardt, Chevrolet	145.504	2010	Kurt Busch, Dodge	144.966
1976	David Pearson, Mercury	137.352	1994	Jeff Gordon, Chevrolet	139.445	2011	Kevin Harvick, Chevrolet	132.414
1977	Richard Petty, Dodge	137.676						

Brickyard 400 Winners, 1994-2011

At Indianapolis Motor Speedway in Indianapolis, IN.

Year	Driver, car	Avg. mph	Year	Driver, car	Avg. mph	Year	Driver, car	Avg. mph
1994	Jeff Gordon, Chevrolet	131.977	2000	Bobby Labonte, Pontiac	155.912	2006	Jimmie Johnson, Chevrolet	137.180
1995	Dale Earnhardt, Chevrolet	155.206	2001	Jeff Gordon, Chevrolet	130.790	2007	Tony Stewart, Chevrolet	117.379
1996	Dale Jarrett, Ford	139.508	2002	Bill Elliott, Dodge	125.033	2008	Jimmie Johnson, Chevrolet	115.117
1997	Ricky Rudd, Ford	130.814	2003	Kevin Harvick, Chevrolet	134.554	2009	Jimmie Johnson, Chevrolet	145.882
1998	Jeff Gordon, Chevrolet	126.772	2004	Jeff Gordon, Chevrolet	115.037	2010	Jamie McMurray, Chevrolet	136.054
1999	Dale Jarrett, Ford	148.194	2005	Tony Stewart, Chevrolet	118.782	2011	Paul Menard, Chevrolet	140.762

Irwin Tools Night Race Winners, 1961-2011

At Bristol Motor Speedway in Bristol, TN. Known as the Volunteer 500, 1961-75, '78-'79; Volunteer 400, 1976-77; Busch 500, 1980-90; Bud 500, 1991-93; Goody's 500, 1994-99; goracing.com 500, 2000; Sharpie 500, 2001-09. * = Rain-shortened.

Year	Driver, car	Avg. mph	Year	Driver, car	Avg. mph	Year	Driver, car	Avg. mph
1961	Jack Smith, Pontiac	68.373	1978	Cale Yarborough, Oldsmobile	88.628	1995	Terry Labonte, Chevrolet	81.979
1962	Bobby Johns, Pontiac	73.397	1979	Darrell Waltrip, Chevrolet	91.493	1996	Rusty Wallace, Ford	91.267
1963	Fred Lorenzen, Ford	74.844	1980	Cale Yarborough, Chevrolet	86.973	1997	Dale Jarrett, Ford	80.013
1964	Fred Lorenzen, Ford	78.044	1981	Darrell Waltrip, Buick	84.723	1998	Mark Martin, Ford	86.949
1965	Ned Jarrett, Ford	61.826	1982	Darrell Waltrip, Buick	94.318	1999	Dale Earnhardt, Chevrolet	91.276
1966	Paul Goldsmith, Plymouth	77.963	1983	Darrell Waltrip, Chevrolet	89.430*	2001	Tony Stewart, Pontiac	85.106
1967	Richard Petty, Plymouth	78.705	1984	Terry Labonte, Chevrolet	85.365	2001	Tony Stewart, Pontiac	85.106
1968	David Pearson, Ford	76.310	1985	Dale Earnhardt, Chevrolet	81.388	2002	Jeff Gordon, Chevrolet	77.097
1969	David Pearson, Ford	79.737	1986	Darrell Waltrip, Chevrolet	86.934	2003	Kurt Busch, Ford	77.421
1970	Bobby Allison, Dodge	84.880	1987	Dale Earnhardt, Chevrolet	90.373	2004	Dale Earnhardt Jr., Chevrolet	88.538
1971	Charlie Glotzbach, Chevrolet	101.074	1988	Dale Earnhardt, Chevrolet	78.775	2005	Matt Kenseth, Ford	84.678
1972	Bobby Allison, Chevrolet	92.735	1989	Darrell Waltrip, Chevrolet	85.554	2006	Matt Kenseth, Ford	90.025
1973	Benny Parsons, Chevrolet	91.342	1990	Ernie Irvan, Chevrolet	91.782	2007	Carl Edwards, Ford	89.006
1974	Cale Yarborough, Chevrolet	75.430	1991	Alan Kulwicki, Ford	82.028	2008	Carl Edwards, Ford	91.581
1975	Richard Petty, Dodge	97.016	1992	Darrell Waltrip, Ford	91.198	2009	Kyle Busch, Toyota	84.820
1976	Cale Yarborough, Chevrolet	99.175	1993	Mark Martin, Ford	88.172	2010	Kyle Busch, Toyota	99.071
1977	Cale Yarborough, Chevrolet	79.726	1994	Rusty Wallace, Ford	91.363	2011	Brad Keselowski, Dodge	96.753

NASCAR Sprint All-Star Race Winners, 1985-2011

At Charlotte Motor Speedway in Concord, NC. Known as The Winston, 1985-93, 1997-2003; The Winston Select, 1994-96; Nextel All-Star Challenge, 2004-07.

Year	Driver, car	Year	Driver, car	Year	Driver, car
1985	Darrell Waltrip, Chevrolet	1994	Geoffrey Bodine, Ford	2003	Jimmie Johnson, Chevrolet
1986	Bill Elliott, Ford	1995	Jeff Gordon, Chevrolet	2004	Matt Kenseth, Ford
1987	Dale Earnhardt, Chevrolet	1996	Michael Waltrip, Chevrolet	2005	Mark Martin, Ford
1988	Terry Labonte, Chevrolet	1997	Jeff Gordon, Chevrolet	2006	Jimmie Johnson, Chevrolet
1989	Rusty Wallace, Ford	1998	Mark Martin, Ford	2007	Kevin Harvick, Chevrolet
1990	Dale Earnhardt, Chevrolet	1999	Terry Labonte, Chevrolet	2008	Kasey Kahne, Dodge
1991	Davey Allison, Ford	2000	Dale Earnhardt Jr., Chevrolet	2009	Tony Stewart, Chevrolet
1992	Davey Allison, Ford	2001	Jeff Gordon, Chevrolet	2010	Kurt Busch, Dodge
1993	Dale Earnhardt, Chevrolet	2002	Ryan Newman, Ford	2011	Carl Edwards, Ford

Formula One Racing
World Grand Prix Champions, 1950-2010

Year	Driver, country	Year	Driver, country	Year	Driver, country
1950	Giuseppe "Nino" Farini, Italy	1971	Jackie Stewart, Scotland, UK	1990	Ayrton Senna, Brazil
1951	Juan Manuel Fangio, Argentina	1972	Emerson Fittipaldi, Brazil	1991	Ayrton Senna, Brazil
1952	Alberto Ascari, Italy	1973	Jackie Stewart, Scotland, UK	1992	Nigel Mansell, England, UK
1953	Alberto Ascari, Italy	1974	Emerson Fittipaldi, Brazil	1993	Alain Prost, France
1954	Juan Manuel Fangio, Argentina	1975	Niki Lauda, Austria	1994	Michael Schumacher, Germany
1955	Juan Manuel Fangio, Argentina	1976	James Hunt, England, UK	1995	Michael Schumacher, Germany
1956	Juan Manuel Fangio, Argentina	1977	Niki Lauda, Austria	1996	Damon Hill, England, UK
1957	Juan Manuel Fangio, Argentina	1978	Mario Andretti, United States	1997	Jacques Villeneuve, Canada
1958	Mike Hawthorne, England, UK	1979	Jody Scheckter, South Africa	1998	Mika Hakkinen, Finland
1959	Jack Brabham, Australia	1980	Alan Jones, Australia	1999	Mika Hakkinen, Finland
1960	Jack Brabham, Australia	1981	Nelson Piquet, Brazil	2000	Michael Schumacher, Germany
1961	Phil Hill, United States	1982	Keke Rosberg, Finland	2001	Michael Schumacher, Germany
1962	Graham Hill, England, UK	1983	Nelson Piquet, Brazil	2002	Michael Schumacher, Germany
1963	Jim Clark, Scotland, UK	1984	Niki Lauda, Austria	2003	Michael Schumacher, Germany
1964	John Surtees, England, UK	1985	Alain Prost, France	2004	Michael Schumacher, Germany
1965	Jim Clark, Scotland, UK	1986	Alain Prost, France	2005	Fernando Alonso, Spain
1966	Jack Brabham, Australia	1987	Nelson Piquet, Brazil	2006	Fernando Alonso, Spain
1967	Denis Hulme, New Zealand	1988	Ayrton Senna, Brazil	2007	Kimi Raikkonen, Finland
1968	Graham Hill, England, UK	1989	Alain Prost, France	2008	Lewis Hamilton, England, UK
1969	Jackie Stewart, Scotland, UK	1990	Ayrton Senna, Brazil	2009	Jenson Button, England, UK
1970	Jochen Rindt, Austria			2010	Sebastian Vettel, Germany

24 Hours of Le Mans Race, 2010

German manufacturer Audi won the 24 Hours of Le Mans on June 12, 2011, for the 7th time in the past 8 years. The team of Germany's Andre Lotterer, Switzerland's Marcel Fassler, and France's Benoit Treluyer drove the Audi No. 2 car to the win, completing 355 laps in 24 hours at Circuit de la Sarthe in Le Mans, France. Simon Pagenaud and Sebastien Bourdais of France and Portugal's Pedro Lamy guided Peugeot No. 9 to a 2nd-place finish. The Peugeot No. 8 car, driven by France's Franck Montagny, Stephane Sarrazin, and Nic Minassian took 3rd place. Audi No. 2, which battled through rainfall late in the race, became the first pole-sitting car to win the race since 2003. Fifty-six cars started the 79th edition of the race, which was first held in 1923, but only half of the cars finished.

Notable One-Mile Land Speed Records

Andy Green, a Royal Air Force pilot, broke the sound barrier and set the world's first supersonic speed record on land, Oct. 15, 1997, in Black Rock Desert, NV. Green, driving a car built by Richard Noble, had two runs at an average speed of 763.035 mph, as calculated under the rules of the Fédération Internationale de l'Automobile (FIA). That speed exceeded the speed of sound, calculated at 751.251 mph for that place and time.

Date	Driver	Car	MPH	Date	Driver	Car	MPH
1/26/1906	Marriott	Stanley (Steam)	127.659	11/19/1937	Eyston	Thunderbolt 1	311.42
3/16/1910	Oldfield	Benz	131.724	9/16/1938	Eyston	Thunderbolt 1	357.5
4/23/1911	Burman	Benz	141.732	8/23/1939	Cobb	Railton	368.9
2/12/1919	DePalma	Packard	149.875	9/16/1947	Cobb	Railton-Mobil	394.2
4/27/1920	Milton	Dusenberg	155.046	8/05/1963	Breedlove	Spirit of America	407.45
4/28/1926	Parry-Thomas	Thomas Special	170.624	10/27/1964	Arfons	Green Monster	536.71
3/29/1927	Segrave	Sunbeam	203.790	11/15/1965	Breedlove	Spirit of America	600.601
4/22/1928	Keech	White Triplex	207.552	10/23/1970	Gabelich	Blue Flame	622.407
3/11/1929	Segrave	Irving-Napier	231.446	10/09/1979	Barrett	Budweiser Rocket	638.637*
2/05/1931	Campbell	Napier-Campbell	246.086	10/04/1983	Noble	Thrust 2	633.468
2/24/1932	Campbell	Napier-Campbell	253.96	9/25/1997	Green	Thrust SSC	714.144
2/22/1933	Campbell	Napier-Campbell	272.109	10/15/1997	Green	Thrust SSC	763.035
9/03/1935	Campbell	Bluebird Special	301.13				

*Not recognized as official by sanctioning bodies.

BOXING

There are many boxing governing bodies, including the World Boxing Assn. (WBA; known as the National Boxing Assn. [NBA] until 1962), World Boxing Council (WBC), International Boxing Fed. (IBF), World Boxing Org., U.S. Boxing Assn., N. American Boxing Fed., and European Boxing Union. All have their own champions and divisions.

Boxing Champions by Class

Class (weight limit)	WBA Champion	WBC Champion	IBF Champion
Heavyweight (none)	Wladimir Klitschko, Ukraine[1] Alexander Povetkin, Russia	Vitali Klitschko, Ukraine	Wladimir Klitschko, Ukraine
Cruiserweight (200 lbs)	Guillermo Jones, Panama Yoan Pablo Hernandez, Cuba[2]	Krzysztof Wlodarczyk, Poland	Yoan Pablo Hernandez, Cuba
Light Heavyweight (175 lbs)	Beibut Shumenov, Kazakhstan	Bernard Hopkins, U.S.	Tavoris Cloud, U.S.
Super Middleweight (168 lbs)	Andre Ward, U.S.[1] Karoly Balzsay, Hungary Brian Magee, UK[2]	Carl Froch, England	Lucian Bute, Romania
Middleweight (160 lbs)	Felix Sturm, Germany[1] Gennady Golovkin, Kazakhstan Hassan N'Dam N'Jikam, Cameroon[2]	Julio Cesar Chavez Jr., Mexico	Daniel Geale, Australia
Super Welterweight/ Jr. Middleweight (154 lbs)	Miguel Cotto, Puerto Rico[1] Austin Trout, U.S. Anthony Mundine, Australia[2]	Saul Alvarez, Mexico	Cornelius Bundrage, U.S.
Welterweight (147 lbs)	Vyacheslav Senchenko, Ukraine Ismael El Massoudi, France[2]	Floyd Mayweather Jr., U.S.	Andre Berto, U.S.
Super Lightweight/ Jr. Welterweight (140 lbs)	Amir Khan, UK[1] Marcos Maidana, Argentina	Erik Morales, Mexico	Amir Khan, UK
Lightweight (135 lbs)	Juan Manuel Marquez, Mexico[1] Brandon Rios, U.S. Richard Abril, Cuba[2]	Antonio DeMarco, Mexico	Miguel Vazquez, Mexico
Super Featherweight/ Jr. Lightweight (130 lbs)	Takashi Uchiyama, Japan Jorge Solis, Mexico[2]	Takahiro Ao, Japan	John Carlos Salgado, Mexico
Featherweight (126 lbs)	Chris John, Indonesia[1] Celestino Caballero, Panama	Jhonny Gonzalez, Mexico	Billy Dib, Australia
Super Bantamweight/ Jr. Featherweight (122 lbs)	Rico Ramos, U.S.[1] Guillermo Rigondeaux, Cuba[2]	Toshiaki Nishioka, Japan	Takalani Ndlovu, South Africa
Bantamweight (118 lbs)	Anselmo Moreno, Panama[1] Koki Kameda, Japan Hugo Ruiz, Mexico[2]	Nonito Donaire, Philippines	Abner Mares, Mexico
Super Flyweight/ Jr. Bantamweight (115 lbs)	Tomonobu Shimizu, Japan Tepparith Singwancha, Thailand[2]	Suriyan Sor Rungvisai, Thailand	Rodrigo Guerrero, Mexico
Flyweight (112 lbs)	Hernan Marquez, Mexico Juan Carlos Reveco, Argentina[2]	Pongsaklek Wonjongkam, Thailand	Moruti Mthalane, South Africa
Jr. Flyweight (108 lbs)	Roman Gonzalez, Nicaragua	Adrian Hernandez, Mexico	Ulises Solis, Mexico
Strawweight/ Mini Flyweight (105 lbs)	Akira Yaegashi, Japan	Kazuto Ioka, Japan	Nkosinathi Joyi, South Africa

Note: As of Oct. 31 2011. (1) Super champion. (2) Interim champion.

Ring Champions by Years

* = Abandoned the title or was stripped of it; IBF champions listed only for heavyweight division; International Boxing Hall of Fame inductees in *italics*.

Heavyweights

1882-92	*John L. Sullivan*[1]	1978	Leon Spinks (WBC*/WBA)[5];	1994-95	Oliver McCall (WBC);
1892-97	*James J. Corbett*[2]		Ken Norton (WBC)		George Foreman (WBA*/IBF*)
1897-99	*Bob Fitzsimmons*	1978-79	*Muhammad Ali* (WBA*)	1995	Frans Botha (IBF*)
1899-1905	*James J. Jeffries*[*3]	1978-83	Larry Holmes (WBC*)[6]	1995-96	Bruce Seldon (WBA);
1905-06	Marvin Hart	1979-80	John Tate (WBA)		Frank Bruno (WBC)
1906-08	*Tommy Burns*	1980-82	Mike Weaver (WBA)	1996	*Mike Tyson* (WBC*/WBA)
1908-15	*Jack Johnson*	1982-83	Michael Dokes (WBA)	1996-97	Michael Moorer (IBF)
1915-19	*Jess Willard*	1983-84	Gerrie Coetzee (WBA)	1996-99	Evander Holyfield (WBA/IBF)
1919-26	*Jack Dempsey*	1983-85	Larry Holmes (IBF)[6]	1997-2001	*Lennox Lewis* (WBC)
1926-28	*Gene Tunney*[*]	1984	Tim Witherspoon (WBC)	1999-2001	*Lennox Lewis* (WBA*/WBC/IBF)
1928-30	Vacant	1984-85	Greg Page (WBA)	2000-01	Evander Holyfield (WBA)
1930-32	*Max Schmeling*	1984-86	Pinklon Thomas (WBC)	2001-03	John Ruiz (WBA)
1932-33	*Jack Sharkey*	1985-86	Tony Tubbs (WBA)	2001	Hasim Rahman (WBC/IBF)
1933-34	Primo Carnera	1985-87	*Michael Spinks* (IBF*)	2001-02	*Lennox Lewis* (IBF*)[7]
1934-35	*Max Baer*	1986	Tim Witherspoon (WBA)	2001-04	*Lennox Lewis* (WBC)
1935-37	*James J. Braddock*		Trevor Berbick (WBC)	2002-06	Chris Byrd (IBF)
1937-49	*Joe Louis*[*]	1986-87	*Mike Tyson* (WBC); James	2003	Roy Jones Jr. (WBA*)
1949-51	*Ezzard Charles*		"Bonecrusher" Smith (WBA)	2004-05	John Ruiz (WBA)[7];
1951-52	*Joe Walcott*	1987	Tony Tucker (IBF)		Vitali Klitschko (WBC*)
1952-56	*Rocky Marciano*[*]	1987-90	*Mike Tyson* (WBC/WBA/IBF)	2005-06	Hasim Rahman (WBC)
1956-59	*Floyd Patterson*	1990	"Buster" Douglas	2005-07	Nicolay Valuev (WBA)
1959-60	*Ingemar Johansson*		(WBA/WBC/IBF)	2006-08	Oleg Maskaev (WBC)
1960-62	*Floyd Patterson*	1990-92	Evander Holyfield	2006-	Wladimir Klitschko (IBF)
1962-64	*Sonny Liston*		(WBA/WBC/IBF)	2007-08	Ruslan Chagaev (WBA)
1964-67	*Cassius Clay*	1992-93	Riddick Bowe (WBA/IBF/WBC*)	2008	Samuel Peter (WBC)
	(*Muhammad Ali*)[4]	1992-94	*Lennox Lewis* (WBC)	2008-09	Nikolai Valuev (WBA)
1970-73	*Joe Frazier*	1993-94	Evander Holyfield (WBA/IBF)	2009-	Vitali Klitschko (WBC)
1973-74	*George Foreman*	1994	Michael Moorer (WBA/IBF)	2009-11	David Haye (WBA)
1974-78	*Muhammad Ali*			2011-	Wladimir Klitschko (WBA)

(1) London Prize Ring (bare-knuckle champion). (2) First Marquis of Queensberry champion. (3) Jeffries vacated title (1905), designated Marvin Hart and Jack Root as logical contenders. Hart def. Root in 12 rounds (1905); in turn was def. by Tommy Burns (1906), who claimed the title. Jack Johnson def. Burns (1908) and was recognized as champ. Johnson won the title by defeating Jeffries in the latter's attempted comeback (1910). (4) Title declared vacant by the WBA and others in 1967 after Ali refused military induction for religious reasons during the Vietnam War. Joe Frazier recognized as champ by six states, Mexico, and S. America. Jimmy Ellis declared champ by the WBA. Frazier KOd Ellis, Feb. 16, 1970. (5) After Spinks def. Ali, the WBC recognized Ken Norton as champ. Ali def. Spinks in 1978 rematch for WBA title, retired in 1979. (6) Holmes relinquished WBC title in Dec. 1983 to fight as champ of the new IBF. (7) James Toney def. Ruiz Apr. 30, 2005, to claim the title, but it was rescinded when Toney tested positive for steroids.

Light Heavyweights

1903	Jack Root, George Gardner	1974-77	John Conteh (WBC)	1991-92	Thomas Hearns (WBA)
1903-05	Bob Fitzsimmons	1974-78	Victor Galindez (WBA)	1992	Iran Barkley (WBA*)
1905-12	Philadelphia Jack O'Brien*	1977-78	Miguel Cuello (WBC)	1992-97	Virgil Hill (WBA)
1912-16	Jack Dillon	1978	Mate Parlov (WBC)	1994-95	Mike McCallum (WBC)
1916-20	Battling Levinsky	1978-79	Mike Rossman (WBA);	1995-96	Fabrice Tiozzo (WBC*)
1920-22	George Carpentier		Marvin Johnson (WBC)	1996-97	Roy Jones Jr. (WBC)
1922-23	Battling Siki	1979-81	Matthew Saad Muhammad	1997	Montell Griffin (WBC);
1923-25	Mike McTigue		(WBC)		Roy Jones Jr. (WBC)
1925-26	Paul Berlenbach	1979-80	Marvin Johnson (WBA)		Darius Michalczewski (WBA*)
1926-27	Jack Delaney*	1980-81	Eddie Mustafa Muhammad	1997-98	Lou Del Valle (WBA)
1927-29	Tommy Loughran*		(WBA)	1998-2003	Roy Jones Jr. (WBA*/WBC*)
1930-34	Maxie Rosenbloom	1981-83	Michael Spinks (WBA);	2003	Mehdi Sahnoune (WBA);
1934-35	Bob Olin		Dwight Muhammed-Qawi		Antonio Tarver (WBC)
1935-39	John Henry Lewis*		Braxton (WBC)	2003-04	Roy Jones Jr. (WBA/WBC*)
1939	Melio Bettina	1983-85	Michael Spinks*	2004	Antonio Tarver (WBC)
1939-41	Billy Conn*	1985-86	J. B. Williamson (WBC)	2004-06	Fabrice Tiozzo (WBA)
1941	Anton Christoforidis	1986-87	Marvin Johnson (WBA);	2005-07	Tomasz Adamek (WBC)
	(won NBA title)		Dennis Andries (WBC)	2006-07	Silvio Branco (WBA)
1941-48	Gus Lesnevich, Freddie Mills	1987	Leslie Stewart (WBA)	2007-08	Chad Dawson (WBC);
1948-50	Freddie Mills	1987-91	Virgil Hill (WBA)		Stipe Drews (WBA)
1950-52	Joey Maxim	1987	Thomas Hearns (WBC*)	2008	Hugo Hernan Garay (WBA);
1952-62	Archie Moore	1987-88	Don Lalonde (WBC)		Adrian Diaconu (WBC)
1962-63	Harold Johnson	1988	Sugar Ray Leonard (WBC*)	2009-10	Gabriel Campillo (WBA)
1963-65	Willie Pastrano	1989	Dennis Andries (WBC)	2009-11	Jean Pascal (WBC)
1965-66	Jose Torres	1989-90	Jeff Harding (WBC)	2010-	Beibut Shumenov (WBA)
1966-68	Dick Tiger	1990-91	Dennis Andries (WBC)	2011	Bernard Hopkins (WBC)
1968-74	Bob Foster*	1991-94	Jeff Harding (WBC)		

Middleweights

1884-91	Jack "Nonpareil" Dempsey	1957-58	Carmen Basilio	1988-89	Iran Barkley (WBC)
1891-97	Bob Fitzsimmons*	1958	Ray Robinson	1989-90	Roberto Duran (WBC*)
1897-1907	Tommy Ryan*	1959	Gene Fullmer (NBA);	1989-91	Mike McCallum (WBA)
1907-08	Stanley Ketchel; Billy Papke		Ray Robinson (NY)	1990-93	Julian Jackson (WBC)
1908-10	Stanley Ketchel	1960	Gene Fullmer (NBA);	1992-93	Reggie Johnson (WBA)
1911-13	Vacant		Paul Pender (NY/MA)	1993-95	Gerald McClellan (WBC*)
1913	Frank Klaus; George Chip	1961	Gene Fullmer (NBA);	1993-94	John David Jackson (WBA)
1914-17	Al McCoy		Terry Downes (NY/MA/Europe)	1994-97	Jorge Castro (WBA)
1917-20	Mike O'Dowd	1962	Gene Fullmer;	1995	Julian Jackson (WBC)
1920-23	Johnny Wilson		Dick Tiger (NBA);	1995-96	Quincy Taylor (WBC);
1923-26	Harry Greb		Paul Pender (NY/MA*)		Shinji Takehara (WBA)
1926-31	Theodore "Tiger" Flowers;	1963	Dick Tiger (universal)	1996-98	Keith Holmes (WBC)
	Mickey Walker	1963-65	Joey Giardello	1996-97	William Joppy (WBA)
1931-32	William "Gorilla" Jones (NBA)	1965-66	Dick Tiger	1997	Julio Cesar Green (WBA)
1932-37	Marcel Thil	1966-67	Emile Griffith	1998-2001	William Joppy (WBA)
1938	Al Hostak (NBA);	1967	Nino Benvenuti	1998-99	Hassine Cherifi (WBC)
	Solly Krieger (NBA)	1967-68	Emile Griffith	1999-2001	Keith Holmes (WBC)
1939-40	Al Hostak (NBA)	1968-70	Nino Benvenuti	2001	Felix Trinidad (WBA)
1941-47	Tony Zale	1970-77	Carlos Monzon*	2001-05	Bernard Hopkins (WBC, WBA)
1947-48	Rocky Graziano	1977-78	Rodrigo Valdez	2005-06	Jermain Taylor (WBA)
1948	Tony Zale; Marcel Cerdan	1978-79	Hugo Corro	2005-07	Jermain Taylor (WBA)
1949-51	Jake LaMotta	1979-80	Vito Antuofermo	2006-07	Javier Castillejo (WBA)[1]
1951	Ray Robinson;	1980	Alan Minter	2007-	Felix Sturm (WBA)
	Randy Turpin;	1980-87	Marvin Hagler	2007-10	Kelly Pavlik (WBC)
	Ray Robinson*	1987	Sugar Ray Leonard (WBC*)	2009-11	Sebastian Zbik (WBC)
1953-55	Carl "Bobo" Olson	1987-89	Sumbu Kalambay (WBA)	2010-	Sergio Gabriel Martínez (WBC)
1955-57	Ray Robinson	1987-88	Thomas Hearns (WBC)	2011	Julio Cesar Chavez Jr. (WBC)
1957	Gene Fullmer; Ray Robinson				

(1) Castillejo lost title to Mariano Carrera Dec. 2, 2006, but regained it Feb. 23, 2007, after Carrera tested positive for steroids.

Welterweights

1892-94	"Mysterious" Billy Smith	1935-38	Barney Ross	1975-76	John Stracey (WBC);
1894-96	Tommy Ryan	1938-40	Henry Armstrong		Angel Espada (WBA)
1896	Kid McCoy*	1940-41	Fritzie Zivic	1976-79	Carlos Palomino (WBC)
1900	Rube Ferns; Matty Matthews	1941-46	Fred Cochrane	1976-80	Jose "Pepino" Cuevas (WBA)
1901	Rube Ferns	1946	Marty Servo*	1979	Wilfred Benitez (WBC)
1901-04	Joe Walcott	1946-51	Ray Robinson*[1]	1979-80	Sugar Ray Leonard (WBC)
1904-06	Dixie Kid; Joe Walcott;	1951	Johnny Bratton (NBA)	1980	Roberto Duran (WBC)
	William "Honey" Mellody	1951-54	Kid Gavilan	1980-81	Thomas Hearns (WBA)
1907-11	Mike Sullivan	1954-55	Johnny Saxton	1980-82	Sugar Ray Leonard*
1911-15	Vacant	1955	Tony De Marco	1983-85	Donald Curry (WBA);
1915-19	Ted Lewis	1955-56	Carmen Basilio		Milton McCrory (WBC)
1919-22	Jack Britton	1956	Johnny Saxton	1985-86	Donald Curry
1922-26	Mickey Walker	1956-57	Carmen Basilio*	1986-87	Lloyd Honeyghan (WBC)
1926	Pete Latzo	1958	Virgil Akins	1987	Mark Breland (WBA)
1927-29	Joe Dundee	1958-60	Don Jordan	1987-88	Marlon Starling (WBA);
1929	Jackie Fields	1960-61	Benny Paret		Jorge Vaca (WBC)
1930	Jack Thompson;	1961	Emile Griffith	1988-89	Tomas Molinares (WBA);
	Tommy Freeman	1961-62	Benny Paret		Lloyd Honeyghan (WBC)
1931	Tommy Freeman;	1962-63	Emile Griffith	1989-90	Marlon Starling (WBC);
	Jack Thompson;	1963	Luis Rodriguez		Mark Breland (WBA)
	Lou Brouillard	1963-66	Emile Griffith*	1990-91	Maurice Blocker (WBC);
1932	Jackie Fields	1966-69	Curtis Cokes		Aaron Davis (WBA)
1933	Young Corbett III;	1969-70	Jose Napoles	1991	Simon Brown (WBC)
	Jimmy McLarnin	1970-71	Billy Backus	1991-92	Meldrick Taylor (WBA)
1934	Barney Ross;	1971-75	Jose Napoles	1991-93	Buddy McGirt (WBC)
	Jimmy McLarnin			1992-94	Crisanto Espana (WBA)

1993-97	Pernell Whitaker (WBC)	2002	Ricardo Mayorga (WBA)	2006-08	Floyd Mayweather Jr. (WBC);
1994-98	Ike Quartey (WBA*)	2002-03	Vernon Forrest (WBC)		Miguel Cotto (WBA)
1997-99	Oscar De La Hoya (WBC*)	2003	Ricardo Mayorga	2008	Antonio Margarito (WBA)
1998	James Page (WBA*)		(WBA/WBC)	2008-11	Andre Berto (WBC)
1999-00	Felix Trinidad (WBC*)	2003-05	Cory Spinks (WBA/WBC)	2009	Shane Mosley (WBA)
2000	Oscar De La Hoya (WBC*)	2005-06	Zab Judah (WBA/WBC)	2009-	Vyacheslav Senchenko (WBA)
2000-02	Shane Mosley (WBC)	2006	Ricky Hatton (WBA);	2011	Victor Ortiz (WBC)
2001-02	Andrew Lewis (WBA)		Carlos Baldomir (WBC)	2011	Floyd Mayweather Jr. (WBC)

(1) Robinson gained the title by defeating Tommy Bell in an elimination agreed to by the New York Commission and the National Boxing Association. Both claimed Robinson waived his title when he won the middleweight crown from LaMotta in 1951.

Lightweights

1896-99	Kid Lavigne	1965-68	Carlos Ortiz	1990-92	Pernell Whitaker*
1899-02	Frank Erne	1968-69	Teo Cruz	1992	Joey Gamache (WBA)
1902-08	Joe Gans	1969-70	Mando Ramos	1992-96	Miguel Angel Gonzalez (WBC*)
1908-10	Oscar "Battling" Nelson	1970	Ismael Laguna	1992-93	Tony Lopez (WBA)
1910-12	Ad Wolgast	1970-72	Ken Buchanan (WBA)	1993	Dingaan Thobela (WBA)
1912-14	Willie Ritchie	1971-72	Pedro Carrasco (WBC)	1993-98	Orzubek Nazarov (WBA)
1914-17	Freddie Welsh	1972-79	Roberto Duran (WBA*)	1996-97	Jean-Baptiste Mendy (WBC)
1917-25	Benny Leonard*	1972	Mando Ramos (WBC);	1997-98	Steve Johnston (WBC)
1925	Jimmy Goodrich;		Chango Carmona (WBC)	1998-99	Jean-Baptiste Mendy (WBA);
	Rocky Kansas	1972-74	Rodolfo Gonzalez (WBC)		Cesar Bazan (WBC)
1926-30	Sammy Mandell	1974-76	Ishimatsu Suzuki (WBC)	1999	Julian Lorcy (WBA);
1930	Al Singer; Tony Canzoneri	1976-78	Esteban De Jesus (WBC)		Stefano Zoff (WBA)
1930-33	Tony Canzoneri	1979-81	Jim Watt (WBC)	1999-2000	Gilberto Serrano (WBA);
1933-35	Barney Ross*	1979-80	Ernesto Espana (WBA)		Steve Johnston (WBC)
1935-36	Tony Canzoneri	1980-81	Hilmer Kenty (WBA)	2000-01	Takanori Hatakeyama (WBA)
1936-38	Lou Ambers	1981	Sean O'Grady (WBA);	2000-02	Jose Luis Castillo (WBC)
1938	Henry Armstrong		Claude Noel (WBA)	2001	Julien Lorcy (WBA)
1939	Lou Ambers	1981-83	Alexis Arguello (WBC*)	2001-02	Raul Balbi (WBA)
1940	Lew Jenkins	1981-82	Arturo Frias (WBA)	2002-03	Leonard Dorin (WBA)
1941-43	Sammy Angott	1982-84	Ray Mancini (WBA)	2002-04	Floyd Mayweather (WBC)
1944	Sammy Angott (NBA);	1983-84	Edwin Rosario (WBC)	2004	Lakva Sim (WBA)
	J. Zurita (NBA)	1984-86	Livingstone Bramble (WBA)	2004-05	Jose Luis Castillo (WBC)
1945-51	Ike Williams (NBA: later	1984-85	Jose Luis Ramirez (WBC)	2004-08	Juan Diaz (WBA)
	universal)	1985-86	Hector "Macho" Camacho	2005-06	Diego Corrales (WBC)
1951-52	James Carter		(WBC)	2006	Joel Casamayor (WBC)
1952	Lauro Salas; James Carter	1986-87	Edwin Rosario (WBA)	2006-08	David Diaz (WBC)
1953-54	James Carter	1987-88	Julio Cesar Chavez (WBA);	2008	Nate Campbell (WBA);
1954	Paddy De Marco; James Carter		Jose Luis Ramirez (WBC)		Manny Pacquiao (WBC)
1955	James Carter; Bud Smith	1988-89	Julio Cesar Chavez (WBA,	2009-	John Manuel Marquez
1956	Bud Smith; Joe Brown		WBC)		(WBA)
1956-62	Joe Brown	1989-90	Edwin Rosario (WBA);	2009-10	Edwin Valero (WBC);
1962-65	Carlos Ortiz		Pernell Whitaker (WBC)	2010-11	Humberto Soto (WBC*)
1965	Ismael Laguna	1990	Juan Nazario (WBA)	2011	Antonio DeMarco (WBC)

Featherweights

1892-1900	George Dixon (disputed)	1968-71	Shozo Saijyo (WBA)	1991-93	Park Yung Kyun (WBA);
1900-01	Terry McGovern;	1969-70	Johnny Famechon (WBC)		Paul Hodkinson (WBC)
	Young Corbett II*	1970	Vicente Salvidar (WBC)	1993	Goyo Vargas (WBC)
1901-12	Abe Attell	1970-72	Kuniaki Shibata (WBC)	1993-95	Kevin Kelley (WBC)
1912-23	Johnny Kilbane	1971-72	Antonio Gomez (WBA)	1993-96	Eloy Rojas (WBA)
1923	Eugene Criqui;	1972	Clemente Sanchez (WBC*)	1995	Alejandro Gonzalez (WBC)
	Johnny Dundee	1972-74	Ernesto Marcel (WBA*)	1995-96	Manuel Medina (WBC)
1923-25	Johnny Dundee*	1972-73	Jose Legra (WBC)	1995-99	Luisito Espinosa (WBC)
1925-27	Kid Kaplan*	1973-74	Eder Jofre (WBC*)	1996-97	Wilfredo Vasquez (WBA*)
1927-28	Benny Bass; Tony Canzoneri	1974	Ruben Olivares (WBA)	1998	Freddie Norwood (WBA)
1928-29	Andre Routis	1974-75	Bobby Chacon (WBC)	1998-99	Antonio Ceremeno (WBA)
1929-32	Battling Battalino*	1974-76	Alexis Arguello (WBA*)	1999	Cesar Soto (WBC);
1932-34	Tommy Paul (NBA)	1975	Ruben Olivares (WBC)		Naseem Hamed (WBC*);
1933-36	Freddie Miller	1975-76	David Kotey (WBC)		Freddie Norwood (WBA)
1936-37	Petey Sarron	1976-80	Danny "Little Red"	2000-01	Guty Espadas (WBC)
1937-38	Henry Armstrong*		Lopez (WBC)	2000-03	Derrick Gainer (WBA)
1938-40	Joey Archibald	1977	Rafael Ortega (WBA)	2001-04	Erik Morales (WBC)[1]
1940-41	Harry Jeffra	1977-78	Cecilio Lastra (WBA)	2003-06	Juan Manuel Marquez (WBA)
1942-48	Willie Pep	1978-85	Eusebio Pedroza (WBA)	2004-06	In-Jin Chi (WBC)
1948-49	Sandy Saddler	1980-82	Salvador Sanchez (WBC)	2006-	Chris John (WBA)
1949-50	Willie Pep	1982-84	Juan LaPorte (WBC)	2006	Takashi Koshimoto (WBC)
1950-57	Sandy Saddler*	1984	Wilfredo Gomez (WBC)	2006	Rodolfo Lopez (WBC)
1957-59	Hogan "Kid" Bassey	1984-88	Azumah Nelson (WBC)	2006-07	In-Jin Chi (WBC)
1959-63	Davey Moore	1985-86	Barry McGuigan (WBA)	2007-08	Jorge Linares (WBC)
1963-64	Ultiminio "Sugar" Ramos	1986-87	Steve Cruz (WBA)	2008	Oscar Larios (WBC)
1964-67	Vicente Saldivar*	1987-91	Antonio Esparragoza (WBA)	2009-10	Elio Rojas (WBC)
1968	Paul Rojas (WBA)	1988-90	Jeff Fenech (WBC*)	2010-11	Hozumi Hasegawa (WBC)
1968-69	Jose Legra (WBC)	1990-91	Marcos Villasana (WBC)	2011-	Jhonny Gonzalez (WBC)

(1) Marco Antonio Barrera won unan. decision over Morales, June 22, 2002, but refused WBC title. Morales regained WBC title with unan. decision over Paulie Ayala, Nov. 16, 2002. Morales moved up to Jr. Lightweight div. in 2004.

International Boxing Hall of Fame Inductees, 2011

Source: International Boxing Hall of Fame, 1 Hall of Fame Dr., Canastota, NY 13032. www.ibhof.com

Modern	Julio Cesar Chavez, 107-6-2 (88 KOs)	Kostya Tszyu, 31-2 (1 NC, 25 KOs)	Mike Tyson, 50-6 (2 NC, 44 KOs)
Old-Timer	Memphis Pal Moore, 107-25-24 (11 KOs)	Jack Root, 40-3-3 (2 NC, 28 KOs)	Dave Shade, 124-23-46 (26 ND, 1 NC, 14 KOs)
Pioneer	John Gully		
Non-participant	Ignacio "Nacho" Beristain, trainer	A. F. Bettinson, promoter	Joe Cortez, referee
Observer	Sylvester Stallone, screenwriter	Harry Carpenter, broadcaster	

Title-Changing Heavyweight Championship Bouts, 1889-2011

1889: July 8, John L. Sullivan def. Jake Kilrain, 75, Richburg, MS.

1892: Sept. 7, James J. Corbett def. John L. Sullivan, 21, New Orleans.

1897: Mar. 17, Bob Fitzsimmons def. James J. Corbett, 14, Carson City, NV.

1899: June 9, James J. Jeffries def. Bob Fitzsimmons, 11, Coney Island, NY. (Jeffries retired as champion in 1905.)

1905: July 3, Marvin Hart KOd Jack Root, 12, Reno, NV. (Jeffries refereed, gave title to Hart. Jack O'Brien also claimed the title.)

1906: Feb. 23, Tommy Burns def. Marvin Hart, 20, Los Angeles.

1908: Dec. 26, Jack Johnson KOd Tommy Burns, 14, Sydney, Australia. (Police halted contest.)

1915: Apr. 5, Jess Willard KOd Jack Johnson, 26, Havana, Cuba.

1919: July 4, Jack Dempsey KOd Jess Willard, Toledo, OH. (Willard failed to answer bell for 4th round.)

1926: Sept. 23, Gene Tunney def. Jack Dempsey, 10, Philadelphia. (Tunney retired as champion in 1928.)

1930: June 12, Max Schmeling def. Jack Sharkey, 4, New York City. (Resulted in the election of a successor to Gene Tunney.)

1932: June 21, Jack Sharkey def. Max Schmeling, 15, NYC.

1933: June 29, Primo Carnera KOd Jack Sharkey, 6, NYC.

1934: June 14, Max Baer KOd Primo Carnera, 11, NYC.

1935: June 13, James J. Braddock def. Max Baer, 15, NYC.

1937: June 22, Joe Louis KOd James J. Braddock, 8, Chicago. (Louis retired as champion in 1949.)

1949: June 22, Ezzard Charles def. Joe Walcott, 15, Chicago; NBA recognition only.

1951: July 18, Joe Walcott KOd Ezzard Charles, 7, Pittsburgh.

1952: Sept. 23, Rocky Marciano KOd Joe Walcott, 13, Philadelphia. (Marciano retired as champion in 1956.)

1956: Nov. 30, Floyd Patterson KOd Archie Moore, 5, Chicago.

1959: June 26, Ingemar Johansson KOd Floyd Patterson, 3, NYC.

1960: June 20, Floyd Patterson KOd Ingemar Johansson, 5, NYC.

1962: Sept. 25, Sonny Liston KOd Floyd Patterson, 1, Chicago.

1964: Feb. 25, Cassius Clay (Muhammad Ali) KOd Sonny Liston, 7, Miami Beach, FL. (In 1967, Ali was stripped of his title by the WBA and others for refusing military service.)

1970: Feb. 16, Joe Frazier KOd Jimmy Ellis, 5, NYC. (Frazier def. Ali in 15 rounds, Mar. 8, 1971, in NYC.)

1973: Jan. 22, George Foreman KOd Joe Frazier, 2, Jamaica.

1974: Oct. 30, Muhammad Ali KOd George Foreman, 8, Kinshasa, Zaire.

1978: Feb. 15, Leon Spinks def. Muhammad Ali, 15, Las Vegas. (WBC recognized Ken Norton as champion after Spinks refused to fight him before his rematch with Ali.); June 9, (WBC) Larry Holmes def. Ken Norton, 15, Las Vegas; Sept. 15, (WBA) Muhammad Ali def. Leon Spinks, 15, New Orleans. (Ali retired as champion in 1979.)

1979: Oct. 20, (WBA) John Tate def. Gerrie Coetzee, 15, Pretoria, South Africa.

1980: Mar. 31, (WBA) Mike Weaver KOd John Tate, 15, Knoxville, TN.

1982: Dec. 10, (WBA) Michael Dokes KOd Mike Weaver, 1, Las Vegas.

1983: Sept. 23, (WBA) Gerrie Coetzee KOd Michael Dokes, 10, Richfield, OH; in Dec., Larry Holmes relinquished the WBC title and was named champion of the newly formed IBF.

1984: Mar. 9, (WBC) Tim Witherspoon def. Greg Page, 12, Las Vegas; Aug. 31, (WBC) Pinklon Thomas def. Tim Witherspoon, 12, Las Vegas; Dec. 2, (WBA) Greg Page KOd Gerrie Coetzee, 8, Sun City, Bophuthatswana, South Africa.

1985: Apr. 29, (WBA) Tony Tubbs def. Greg Page, 15, Buffalo, NY; Sept. 21, (IBF) Michael Spinks def. Larry Holmes, 15, Las Vegas. (Spinks relinquished title in Feb. 1987.)

1986: Jan. 17, (WBA) Tim Witherspoon def. Tony Tubbs, 15, Atlanta, GA; Mar. 23, (WBC) Trevor Berbick def. Pinklon Thomas, 12, Miami; Nov. 22, (WBC) Mike Tyson KOd Trevor Berbick, 2, Las Vegas; Dec. 12, (WBA) James "Bonecrusher" Smith KOd Tim Witherspoon, 1, NYC.

1987: Mar. 7, (WBA/WBC) Mike Tyson def. James "Bonecrusher" Smith, 12, Las Vegas; May 30, (IBF) Tony Tucker KOd James "Buster" Douglas, 10, Las Vegas; Aug. 1, (WBA/WBC/IBF) Mike Tyson def. Tony Tucker, 12, Las Vegas. (Tyson became undisputed champion.)

1990: Feb. 11, (WBA/WBC/IBF) James "Buster" Douglas KOd Mike Tyson, 10, Tokyo, Japan; Oct. 25, (WBA/WBC/IBF) Evander Holyfield KOd James "Buster" Douglas, 3, Las Vegas.

1992: Nov. 13, (WBA/WBC/IBF) Riddick Bowe def. Evander Holyfield, 12, Las Vegas. (Lennox Lewis was later named WBC champion when Bowe refused to fight him.)

1993: Nov. 6, (WBA/IBF) Evander Holyfield def. Riddick Bowe, 12, Las Vegas.

1994: Apr. 22, (WBA/IBF) Michael Moorer def. Evander Holyfield, 12, Las Vegas; Sept. 24, (WBC) Oliver McCall KOd Lennox Lewis, 2, London, Eng.; Nov. 5, (WBA/IBF) George Foreman KOd Michael Moorer, 10, Las Vegas. (In Mar. 1995, Foreman was stripped of the WBA title; he relinquished the IBF title in June.)

1995: Sept. 2, (WBC) Frank Bruno def. Oliver McCall, 12, London, Eng.; Dec. 9, (IBF) Frans Botha def. Axel Schulz, 12, Las Vegas. (Botha was subsequently stripped of title.)

1996: Mar. 16, (WBC) Mike Tyson KOd Frank Bruno, 3, Las Vegas; June 22, (IBF) Michael Moorer def. Axel Schulz, 12, Dortmund, Germany; Sept. 7, (WBA/IBF) Mike Tyson KOd Bruce Seldon, 1, Las Vegas (Tyson was subsequently stripped of WBC title); Nov. 9, (WBA) Evander Holyfield KOd Mike Tyson, 11, Las Vegas.

1997: Feb. 7, (WBC) Lennox Lewis KOd Oliver McCall, 5, Las Vegas; Nov. 8, (IBF) Evander Holyfield def. Michael Moorer, 8, Las Vegas.

1999: Nov. 13, (WBA/WBC/IBF) Lennox Lewis def. Evander Holyfield, 12, Las Vegas. (Lewis became undisputed champion. In Apr. 2000, Lewis was stripped of his WBA title.)

2000: Aug. 12, (WBA) Evander Holyfield def. John Ruiz, 12, Las Vegas.

2001: Mar. 3, (WBA) John Ruiz def. Evander Holyfield, 12, Las Vegas; Apr. 1, (WBC/IBF) Hasim Rahman KOd Lennox Lewis, 5, Brakpan, South Africa; Nov. 17, (WBC, IBF) Lennox Lewis KOd Hasim Rahman, 4, Las Vegas.

2002: Dec. 14, (IBF) Chris Byrd def. Evander Holyfield, 12, Atlantic City, NJ.

2003: Mar. 1, (WBA) Roy Jones Jr. def. John Ruiz, 12, Las Vegas.

2004: Feb. 20, (WBA) Ruiz gained title when Roy Jones Jr. relinquished it; Apr. 24, (WBC) Vitali Klitschko TKOd Corrie Sanders, 8, Los Angeles, to win title vacated when champ Lennox Lewis retired in Feb.

2005: Apr. 30, (WBA) James Toney def. John Ruiz, 12, NYC (Toney tested positive for steroids; title returned to Ruiz); Nov. 9, (WBC) Hasim Rahman gained title when Vitali Klitschko retired; Dec. 17, (WBA) Nikolai Valuev def. John Ruiz, 12, Berlin, Germany.

2006: Aug. 12, (WBC) Oleg Maskaev TKOd Hasim Rahman, 12, Las Vegas.; Apr. 22, (IBF) Wladimir Klitschko TKOd Chris Byrd, 7, Mannheim, Germany.

2007: Apr. 14, (WBA) Ruslan Chagaev def. Nicolay Valuev, 12, Stuttgart, Germany.

2008: Mar. 8, (WBC) Samuel Peter TKOd Oleg Maskaev, 6, Cancun, Mexico; Aug. 30, (WBA) Nikolai Valuev def. John Ruiz, 12, Berlin, Germany; Oct. 11, (WBC) Vitali Klitschko TKOd Samuel Peter, 8, Berlin, Germany; Dec. 13, (IBF) Wladimir Klitschko TKOd Hasim Rahman, 7, Mannheim, Germany; Dec. 20, (WBA) Nikolai Valuev def. Evander Holyfield, Zurich, Switzerland.

2009: Mar. 21, (WBC) Vitali Klitschko TKOd Juan Carlos Gomez, 9, Stuttgart, Germany; June 20, (IBF) Wladimir Klitschko TKOd Ruslan Chagaev, 10, Gelsenkirchen, Germany; Nov. 7, (WBA) David Haye def. Nikolai Valuev, 12, Nuremberg, Germany.

2011: July 2, (WBA) Wladimir Klitschko def. David Haye, 12, Hamburg, Germany.

THOROUGHBRED RACING
Triple Crown Winners
Since 1920, colts have carried 126 lb in Triple Crown events; fillies, 121 lb.
(Kentucky Derby, Preakness Stakes, and Belmont Stakes)

Year	Horse	Jockey	Trainer	Year	Horse	Jockey	Trainer
1919	Sir Barton	J. Loftus	H. G. Bedwell	1946	Assault	W. Mehrtens	M. Hirsch
1930	Gallant Fox	E. Sande	J. Fitzsimmons	1948	Citation	E. Arcaro	H. A. Jones
1935	Omaha	W. Sanders	J. Fitzsimmons	1973	Secretariat	R. Turcotte	L. Laurin
1937	War Admiral	C. Kurtsinger	G. Conway	1977	Seattle Slew	J. Cruguet	W. H. Turner Jr.
1941	Whirlaway	E. Arcaro	B. A. Jones	1978	Affirmed	S. Cauthen	L. S. Barrera
1943	Count Fleet	J. Longden	G. D. Cameron				

Kentucky Derby, 1875–2011
Churchill Downs, Louisville, KY; inaug. 1875. Distance: 1-1/4 mi; 1-1/2 mi until 1896. 3-year-olds. Best time: 1:59 2/5, Secretariat (1973); 2011 time: 2:02.

Year	Winner	Jockey	Year	Winner	Jockey	Year	Winner	Jockey
1875	Aristides	O. Lewis	1920	Paul Jones	T. Rice	1966	Kauai King	D. Brumfield
1876	Vagrant	R. Swim	1921	Behave Yourself	C. Thompson	1967	Proud Clarion	R. Ussery
1877	Baden Baden	W. Walker	1922	Morvich	A. Johnson	1968	Dancer's Image[2]	R. Ussery
1878	Day Star	J. Carter	1923	Zev	E. Sande	1969	Majestic Prince	W. Hartack
1879	Lord Murphy	C. Schauer	1924	Black Gold	J. D. Mooney	1970	Dust Commander	M. Manganello
1880	Fonso	G. Lewis	1925	Flying Ebony	E. Sande	1971	Canonero II	G. Avila
1881	Hindoo	J. McLaughlin	1926	Bubbling Over	A. Johnson	1972	Riva Ridge	R. Turcotte
1882	Apollo	B. Hurd	1927	Whiskery	L. McAtee	1973	Secretariat	R. Turcotte
1883	Leonatus	W. Donohue	1928	Reigh Count	C. Lang	1974	Cannonade	A. Cordero
1884	Buchanan	I. Murphy	1929	Clyde Van Dusen	L. McAtee	1975	Foolish Pleasure	J. Vasquez
1885	Joe Cotton	E. Henderson	1930	Gallant Fox	E. Sande	1976	Bold Forbes	A. Cordero
1886	Ben Ali	P. Duffy	1931	Twenty Grand	C. Kurtsinger	1977	Seattle Slew	J. Cruguet
1887	Montrose	I. Lewis	1932	Burgoo King	E. James	1978	Affirmed	S. Cauthen
1888	Macbeth II	G. Covington	1933	Brokers Tip	D. Meade	1979	Spectacular Bid	R. Franklin
1889	Spokane	T. Kiley	1934	Cavalcade	M. Garner	1980	Genuine Risk[1]	J. Vasquez
1890	Riley	I. Murphy	1935	Omaha	W. Saunders	1981	Pleasant Colony	J. Velasquez
1891	Kingman	I. Murphy	1936	Bold Venture	I. Hanford	1982	Gato del Sol	E. Delahoussaye
1892	Azra	A. Clayton	1937	War Admiral	C. Kurtsinger	1983	Sunny's Halo	E. Delahoussaye
1893	Lookout	E. Kunze	1938	Lawrin	E. Arcaro	1984	Swale	L. Pincay
1894	Chant	F. Goodale	1939	Johnstown	J. Stout	1985	Spend a Buck	A. Cordero
1895	Halma	J. Perkins	1940	Gallahadion	C. Bierman	1986	Ferdinand	W. Shoemaker
1896	Ben Brush	W. Simms	1941	Whirlaway	E. Arcaro	1987	Alysheba	C. McCarron
1897	Typhoon II	F. Garner	1942	Shut Out	W. D. Wright	1988	Winning Colors[1]	G. Stevens
1898	Plaudit	W. Simms	1943	Count Fleet	J. Longden	1989	Sunday Silence	P. Valenzuela
1899	Manuel	F. Taral	1944	Pensive	C. McCreary	1990	Unbridled	C. Perret
1900	Lieut. Gibson	J. Boland	1945	Hoop, Jr.	E. Arcaro	1991	Strike the Gold	C. Antley
1901	His Eminence	J. Winkfield	1946	Assault	W. Mehrtens	1992	Lil E. Tee	P. Day
1902	Alan-a-Dale	J. Winkfield	1947	Jet Pilot	E. Guerin	1993	Sea Hero	J. Bailey
1903	Judge Himes	H. Booker	1948	Citation	E. Arcaro	1994	Go for Gin	C. McCarron
1904	Elwood	F. Prior	1949	Ponder	S. Brooks	1995	Thunder Gulch	G. Stevens
1905	Agile	J. Martin	1950	Middleground	W. Boland	1996	Grindstone	J. Bailey
1906	Sir Huon	R. Troxler	1951	Count Turf	C. McCreary	1997	Silver Charm	G. Stevens
1907	Pink Star	A. Minder	1952	Hill Gail	E. Arcaro	1998	Real Quiet	K. Desormeaux
1908	Stone Street	A. Pickens	1953	Dark Star	H. Moreno	1999	Charismatic	C. Antley
1909	Wintergreen	V. Powers	1954	Determine	R. York	2000	Fusaichi Pegasus	K. Desormeaux
1910	Donau	F. Herbert	1955	Swaps	W. Shoemaker	2001	Monarchos	J. Chavez
1911	Meridian	G. Archibald	1956	Needles	D. Erb	2002	War Emblem	V. Espinoza
1912	Worth	C. H. Shilling	1957	Iron Liege	W. Hartack	2003	Funny Cide	J. Santos
1913	Donerail	R. Goose	1958	Tim Tam	I. Valenzuela	2004	Smarty Jones	S. Elliot
1914	Old Rosebud	J. McCabe	1959	Tomy Lee	W. Shoemaker	2005	Giacomo	M. Smith
1915	Regret[1]	J. Notter	1960	Venetian Way	W. Hartack	2006	Barbaro	E. Prado
1916	George Smith	J. Loftus	1961	Carry Back	J. Sellers	2007	Street Sense	C. Borel
1917	Omar Khayyam	C. Borel	1962	Decidedly	W. Hartack	2008	Big Brown	K. Desormeaux
1918	Exterminator	W. Knapp	1963	Chateaugay	B. Baeza	2009	Mine That Bird	C. Borel
1919	Sir Barton	J. Loftus	1964	Northern Dancer	W. Hartack	2010	Super Saver	C. Borel
			1965	Lucky Debonair	W. Shoemaker	2011	Animal Kingdom	J. Velazquez

Only two jockeys have won the Kentucky Derby five times: Eddie Arcaro, 1938, 1941, 1945, 1948, and 1952; and Bill Hartack, 1957, 1960, 1962, 1964, and 1969. Willie Shoemaker won four times, in 1955, 1959, 1965, and 1986; and six jockeys won three times: Isaac Murphy, 1884, 1890, and 1891; Earle Sande, 1923, 1925, and 1930; Angel Cordero, 1974, 1976, and 1985; Gary Stevens, 1988, 1995, and 1997; Kent Desormeaux, 1998, 2000, and 2008; and Calvin Borel, 2007, 2009, and 2010. (1) Regret, Genuine Risk, and Winning Colors are the only fillies to have won the Derby. (2) Dancer's Image was disqualified from purse money after tests disclosed that he had run with a painkilling drug, phenylbutazone, in his system. All wagers were paid on Dancer's Image. Forward Pass was awarded first place money.

Fastest Winning Times for the Kentucky Derby
(Kentucky Derby times measured in fifths of a second according to tradition.)

Time	Horse	Jockey	Year	Time	Horse	Jockey	Year
1 min., 59 2/5 s.	Secretariat	Ron Turcotte	1973	2 min., 1 1/5 s.	Thunder Gulch	Gary Stevens	1995
1 min., 59 4/5 s.	Monarchos	Jorge Chavez	2001		Affirmed	Steve Cauthen	1978
2 min.,	Northern Dancer	Bill Hartack	1964		Lucky Debonair	Bill Shoemaker	1965
2 min., 1/5 s.	Spend a Buck	Angel Cordero Jr.	1985	2 min., 1 2/5 s.	Whirlaway	Eddie Arcaro	1941
2 min., 2/5 s.	Decidedly	Bill Hartack	1962		Barbaro	Edgar Prado	2006
2 min., 3/5 s.	Proud Clarion	Robert Ussery	1967	2 min., 1 3/5 s.	Bold Forbes	Angel Cordero Jr.	1976
2 min., 1 s.	Funny Cide	Jose Santos	2003		Hill Gail	Eddie Arcaro	1952
	War Emblem	Victor Espinoza	2002		Middleground	William Boland	1950
	Fusaichi Pegasus	Kent Desormeaux	2000				
	Grindstone	Jerry Bailey	1996				

Preakness Stakes, 1873-2011

Pimlico Race Course, Baltimore, MD; inaug. 1873. Distance: 1-3/16 mi. 3-year-olds. * = Horses ran in two divisions. Best time: 1:53 2/5, Tank's Prospect (1985), Louis Quatorze (1996), and Curlin (2007); 2011 time: 1:56.47.

Year	Winner	Jockey	Year	Winner	Jockey	Year	Winner	Jockey
1873	Survivor	G. Barbee	1921	Broomspun	F. Coltiletti	1966	Kauai King	D. Brumfield
1874	Culpepper	M. Donohue	1922	Pillory	L. Morris	1967	Damascus	W. Shoemaker
1875	Tom Ochiltree	L. Hughes	1923	Vigil	B. Marinelli	1968	Forward Pass	I. Valenzuela
1876	Shirley	G. Barbee	1924	Nellie Morse	J. Merimee	1969	Majestic Prince	W. Hartack
1877	Cloverbrook	C. Holloway	1925	Coventry	C. Kummer	1970	Personality	E. Belmonte
1878	Duke of Magenta	C. Holloway	1926	Display	J. Malben	1971	Canonero II	G. Avila
1879	Harold	L. Hughes	1927	Bostonian	A. Abel	1972	Bee Bee Bee	E. Nelson
1880	Grenada	L. Hughes	1928	Victorian	R. Workman	1973	Secretariat	R. Turcotte
1881	Saunterer	W. Costello	1929	Dr. Freeland	L. Schaefer	1974	Little Current	M. Rivera
1882	Vanguard	W. Costello	1930	Gallant Fox	E. Sande	1975	Master Derby	D. McHargue
1883	Jacobus	G. Barbee	1931	Mate	G. Ellis	1976	Elocutionist	J. Lively
1884	Knight of Ellerslie	S. H. Fisher	1932	Burgoo King	E. James	1977	Seattle Slew	J. Cruguet
1885	Tecumseh	J. McLaughlin	1933	Head Play	C. Kurtsinger	1978	Affirmed	S. Cauthen
1886	The Bard	S. H. Fisher	1934	High Quest	R. Jones	1979	Spectacular Bid	R. Franklin
1887	Dunboyne	W. Donohue	1935	Omaha	W. Saunders	1980	Codex	A. Cordero
1888	Refund	F. Littlefield	1936	Bold Venture	G. Woolf	1981	Pleasant Colony	J. Velasquez
1889	Buddhist	G. Anderson	1937	War Admiral	C. Kurtsinger	1982	Aloma's Ruler	J. Kaenel
1890	Montague	W. Martin	1938	Dauber	M. Peters	1983	Deputed Testamony	D. Miller
1894	Assignee	F. Taral	1939	Challedon	G. Seabo	1984	Gate Dancer	A. Cordero
1895	Belmar	F. Taral	1940	Bimelech	F. A. Smith	1985	Tank's Prospect	P. Day
1896	Margrave	H. Griffin	1941	Whirlaway	E. Arcaro	1986	Snow Chief	A. Solis
1897	Paul Kauvar	C. Thorpe	1942	Alsab	B. James	1987	Alysheba	C. McCarron
1898	Sly Fox	W. Simms	1943	Count Fleet	J. Longden	1988	Risen Star	E. Delahoussaye
1899	Half Time	R. Clawson	1944	Pensive	C. McCreary	1989	Sunday Silence	P. Valenzuela
1900	Hindus	H. Spencer	1945	Polynesian	W. D. Wright	1990	Summer Squall	P. Day
1901	The Parader	F. Landry	1946	Assault	W. Mehrtens	1991	Hansel	J. Bailey
1902	Old England	L. Jackson	1947	Faultless	D. Dodson	1992	Pine Bluff	C. McCarron
1903	Flocarline	W. Gannon	1948	Citation	E. Arcaro	1993	Prairie Bayou	M. Smith
1904	Bryn Mawr	E. Hildebrand	1949	Capot	T. Atkinson	1994	Tabasco Cat	P. Day
1905	Cairngorm	W. Davis	1950	Hill Prince	E. Arcaro	1995	Timber Country	P. Day
1906	Whimsical	W. Miller	1951	Bold	E. Arcaro	1996	Louis Quatorze	P. Day
1907	Don Enrique	G. Mountain	1952	Blue Man	C. McCreary	1997	Silver Charm	G. Stevens
1908	Royal Tourist	E. Dugan	1953	Native Dancer	E. Guerin	1998	Real Quiet	K. Desormeaux
1909	Effendi	W. Doyle	1954	Hasty Road	J. Adams	1999	Charismatic	C. Antley
1910	Layminster	R. Estep	1955	Nashua	E. Arcaro	2000	Red Bullet	J. Bailey
1911	Watervale	E. Dugan	1956	Fabius	W. Hartack	2001	Point Given	G. Stevens
1912	Colonel Holloway	C. Turner	1957	Bold Ruler	E. Arcaro	2002	War Emblem	V. Espinoza
1913	Buskin	J. Butwell	1958	Tim Tam	I. Valenzuela	2003	Funny Cide	J. Santos
1914	Holiday	A. Schuttinger	1959	Royal Orbit	W. Harmatz	2004	Smarty Jones	S. Elliot
1915	Rhine Maiden	D. Hoffman	1960	Bally Ache	R. Ussery	2005	Afleet Alex	J. Rose
1916	Damrosch	L. McAtee	1961	Carry Back	J. Sellers	2006	Bernardini	J. Castellano
1917	Kalitan	E. Haynes	1962	Greek Money	J. L. Rotz	2007	Curlin	R. Albarado
1918*	War Cloud	J. Loftus	1963	Candy Spots	W. Shoemaker	2008	Big Brown	K. Desormeaux
	Jack Hare Jr.	C. Peak	1964	Northern Dancer	W. Hartack	2009	Rachel Alexandra	C. Borel
1919	Sir Barton	J. Loftus	1965	Tom Rolfe	R. Turcotte	2010	Lookin At Lucky	M. Garcia
1920	Man o' War	C. Kummer				2011	Shackleford	J. Castanon

Belmont Stakes, 1867-2011

Belmont Park, Elmont, NY; inaug. 1867. Distance: 1-1/2 mi. 3-year-olds. Best time: 2:24, Secretariat (1973); 2011 time: 2:30.88.

Year	Winner	Jockey	Year	Winner	Jockey	Year	Winner	Jockey
1867	Ruthless	J. Gilpatrick	1902	Masterman	J. Bullman	1939	Johnstown	J. Stout
1868	General Duke	R. Swim	1903	Africander	J. Bullman	1940	Bimelech	F. A. Smith
1869	Fenian	C. Miller	1904	Delhi	G. Odom	1941	Whirlaway	E. Arcaro
1870	Kingfisher	W. Dick	1905	Tanya	E. Hildebrand	1942	Shut Out	E. Arcaro
1871	Harry Bassett	W. Miller	1906	Burgomaster	L. Lyne	1943	Count Fleet	J. Longden
1872	Joe Daniels	J. Rowe	1907	Peter Pan	G. Mountain	1944	Bounding Home	G. L. Smith
1873	Springbok	J. Rowe	1908	Colin	J. Notter	1945	Pavot	E. Arcaro
1874	Saxon	G. Barbee	1909	Joe Madden	E. Dugan	1946	Assault	W. Mehrtens
1875	Calvin	R. Swim	1910	Sweep	J. Butwell	1947	Phalanx	R. Donoso
1876	Algerine	W. Donohue	1913	Prince Eugene	R. Troxler	1948	Citation	E. Arcaro
1877	Cloverbrook	C. Holloway	1914	Luke McLuke	M. Buxton	1949	Capot	T. Atkinson
1878	Duke of Magenta	L. Hughes	1915	The Finn	G. Byrne	1950	Middleground	W. Boland
1879	Spendthrift	S. Evans	1916	Friar Rock	E. Haynes	1951	Counterpoint	D. Gorman
1880	Grenada	L. Hughes	1917	Hourless	J. Butwell	1952	One Count	E. Arcaro
1881	Saunterer	T. Costello	1918	Johren	F. Robinson	1953	Native Dancer	E. Guerin
1882	Forester	J. McLaughlin	1919	Sir Barton	J. Loftus	1954	High Gun	E. Guerin
1883	George Kinney	J. McLaughlin	1920	Man o' War	C. Kummer	1955	Nashua	E. Arcaro
1884	Panique	J. McLaughlin	1921	Grey Lag	E. Sande	1956	Needles	D. Erb
1885	Tyrant	P. Duffy	1922	Pillory	C. H. Miller	1957	Gallant Man	W. Shoemaker
1886	Inspector B.	J. McLaughlin	1923	Zev	E. Sande	1958	Cavan	P. Anderson
1887	Hanover	J. McLaughlin	1924	Mad Play	E. Sande	1959	Sword Dancer	W. Shoemaker
1888	Sir Dixon	J. McLaughlin	1925	American Flag	A. Johnson	1960	Celtic Ash	W. Hartack
1889	Eric	W. Hayward	1926	Crusader	A. Johnson	1961	Sherluck	B. Baeza
1890	Burlington	S. Barnes	1927	Chance Shot	E. Sande	1962	Jaipur	W. Shoemaker
1891	Foxford	E. Garrison	1928	Vito	C. Kummer	1963	Chateaugay	B. Baeza
1892	Patron	W. Hayward	1929	Blue Larkspur	M. Garner	1964	Quadrangle	M. Ycaza
1893	Comanche	W. Simms	1930	Gallant Fox	E. Sande	1965	Hail to All	J. Sellers
1894	Henry of Navarre	W. Simms	1931	Twenty Grand	C. Kurtsinger	1966	Amberoid	W. Boland
1895	Belmar	F. Taral	1932	Faireno	T. Malley	1967	Damascus	W. Shoemaker
1896	Hastings	H. Griffin	1933	Hurryoff	M. Garner	1968	Stage Door Johnny	H. Gustines
1897	Scottish Chieftain	J. Scherrer	1934	Peace Chance	W. D. Wright	1969	Arts and Letters	B. Baeza
1898	Bowling Brook	F. Littlefield	1935	Omaha	W. Saunders	1970	High Echelon	J. L. Rotz
1899	Jean Bereaud	R. R. Clawson	1936	Granville	J. Stout	1971	Pass Catcher	W. Blum
1900	Ildrim	N. Turner	1937	War Admiral	C. Kurtsinger	1972	Riva Ridge	R. Turcotte
1901	Commando	H. Spencer	1938	Pasteurized	J. Stout	1973	Secretariat	R. Turcotte

Year	Winner	Jockey	Year	Winner	Jockey	Year	Winner	Jockey
1974	Little Current	M. Rivera	1987	Bet Twice	C. Perret	2000	Commendable	P. Day
1975	Avatar	W. Shoemaker	1988	Risen Star	E. Delahoussaye	2001	Point Given	G. Stevens
1976	Bold Forbes	A. Cordero	1989	Easy Goer	P. Day	2002	Sarava	E. Prado
1977	Seattle Slew	J. Cruguet	1990	Go and Go	M. Kinane	2003	Empire Maker	J. Bailey
1978	Affirmed	S. Cauthen	1991	Hansel	J. Bailey	2004	Birdstone	E. Prado
1979	Coastal	R. Hernandez	1992	A.P. Indy	E. Delahoussaye	2005	Afleet Alex	J. Rose
1980	Temperence Hill	E. Maple	1993	Colonial Affair	J. Krone	2006	Jazil	F. Jara
1981	Summing	G. Martens	1994	Tabasco Cat	P. Day	2007	Rags to Riches	J. Velazquez
1982	Conquistador Cielo	L. Pincay	1995	Thunder Gulch	G. Stevens	2008	Da' Tara	A. Garcia
1983	Caveat	L. Pincay	1996	Editor's Note	R. Douglas	2009	Summer Bird	K. Desormeaux
1984	Swale	L. Pincay	1997	Touch Gold	C. McCarron	2010	Drosselmeyer	M. Smith
1985	Creme Fraiche	E. Maple	1998	Victory Gallop	G. Stevens	2011	Ruler On Ice	J. Valdivia Jr.
1986	Danzig Connection	C. McCarron	1999	Lemon Drop Kid	J. Santos			

Annual Leading Jockey by Earnings, 1957-2010

(Total earnings for all horses that jockey raced in year listed; does not reflect jockey's earnings.)

Year	Jockey	Earnings	Year	Jockey	Earnings	Year	Jockey	Earnings
1957	Bill Hartack	$3,060,501	1975	Braulio Baeza	$3,695,198	1993	Mike Smith	$14,024,815
1958	Willie Shoemaker	2,961,693	1976	Angel Cordero Jr.	4,709,500	1994	Mike Smith	15,979,820
1959	Willie Shoemaker	2,843,133	1977	Steve Cauthen	6,151,750	1995	Jerry Bailey	16,311,876
1960	Willie Shoemaker	2,123,961	1978	Darrel McHargue	6,029,885	1996	Jerry Bailey	19,465,376
1961	Willie Shoemaker	2,690,819	1979	Laffit Pincay Jr.	8,193,535	1997	Jerry Bailey	18,320,743
1962	Willie Shoemaker	2,916,844	1980	Chris McCarron	7,663,300	1998	Gary Stevens	19,622,855
1963	Willie Shoemaker	2,526,925	1981	Chris McCarron	8,397,604	1999	Pat Day	18,092,845
1964	Willie Shoemaker	2,649,553	1982	Angel Cordero Jr.	9,483,590	2000	Pat Day	17,479,838
1965	Braulio Baeza	2,582,702	1983	Angel Cordero Jr.	10,116,697	2001	Jerry D. Bailey	22,597,720
1966	Braulio Baeza	2,951,022	1984	Chris McCarron	12,045,813	2002	Jerry D. Bailey	19,271,814
1967	Braulio Baeza	3,088,888	1985	Laffit Pincay Jr.	13,353,299	2003	Jerry D. Bailey	23,354,960
1968	Braulio Baeza	2,835,108	1986	Jose Santos	11,329,297	2004	John R. Velazquez	22,220,261
1969	Jorge Velasquez	2,542,315	1987	Jose Santos	12,375,443	2005	John R. Velazquez	20,799,923
1970	Laffit Pincay Jr.	2,626,526	1988	Jose Santos	14,877,298	2006	Garrett K. Gomez	20,122,592
1971	Laffit Pincay Jr.	3,784,377	1989	Jose Santos	13,838,389	2007	Garrett K. Gomez	22,800,074
1972	Laffit Pincay Jr.	3,225,827	1990	Gary Stevens	13,881,198	2008	Garrett K. Gomez	23,344,351
1973	Laffit Pincay Jr.	4,093,492	1991	Chris McCarron	14,441,083	2009	Garrett K. Gomez	18,536,105
1974	Laffit Pincay Jr.	4,251,060	1992	Kent Desormeaux	14,193,006	2010	Ramon A. Dominguez	16,911,880

Breeders' Cup World Thoroughbred Championships, 1984-2010

The Breeders' Cup was inaugurated in 1984 and through 2006, consisted of seven races at one track on one day to determine thoroughbred racing's champion contenders. In 2007, it expanded to two days, and three new races debuted: the Filly and Mare Sprint, won in 2007 by Maryfield (jockey: E. Trujillo), in 2008 by Ventura (G. Gomez), in 2009 by Informed Decision (J. Leparoux), and in 2010 by Dubai Majesty (J. Theriot); the Juvenile Turf, won in 2007 by Nownownow (J. Leparoux), 2008 by Donativum (F. Dettori), 2009 by Pounced (F. Dettori), and 2010 by Pluck (G. Gomez); and the Dirt Mile, won in 2007 by Corinthian (K. Desormeaux), 2008 by Albertus Maximus (G. Gomez), 2009 by Furthest Land (J. Leparoux), and in 2010 by Dakota Phone (J. Rosario). In 2008, a "Ladies' Day" for fillies and several more races debuted: Turf Sprint, won in 2008 by Desert Code (R. Migliore), in 2009 by California Flag (J. Talamo), and in 2010 by Chamberlain Bridge (J. Theriot); Marathon, won in 2008 by Muhannak (P. Smullen), in 2009 by Man of Iron (J. Murtagh), and in 2010 by Eldaafer (J. Velazquez); and Juvenile Fillies Turf, won in 2008 by Maram (J. Lezcano), in 2009 by Tapitsfly (R. Albarado), and in 2010 by More Than Real (G. Gomez). The Ladies' Classic replaced the race formerly known as Distaff.

Classic

Distance: 1-1/4 mi.

Year	Horse	Jockey	Year	Horse	Jockey	Year	Horse	Jockey
1984	Wild Again	P. Day	1993	Arcangues	J. Bailey	2002	Volponi	P. Johnson
1985	Proud Truth	J. Velasquez	1994	Concern	J. Bailey	2003	Pleasantly Perfect	A. Solis
1986	Skywalker	L. Pincay Jr.	1995	Cigar	J. Bailey	2004	Ghostzapper	J. Castellano
1987	Ferdinand	W. Shoemaker	1996	Alphabet Soup	C. McCarron	2005	Saint Liam	J. Bailey
1988	Alysheba	C. McCarron	1997	Skip Away	M. Smith	2006	Invasor	F. Jara
1989	Sunday Silence	C. McCarron	1998	Awesome Again	P. Day	2007	Curlin	R. Albarado
1990	Unbridled	P. Day	1999	Cat Thief	P. Day	2008	Raven's Pass	F. Dettori
1991	Black Tie Affair	J. Bailey	2000	Tiznow	C. McCarron	2009	Zenyatta	M. Smith
1992	A.P. Indy	E. Delahoussaye	2001	Tiznow	C. McCarron	2010	Blame	G. Gomez

Juvenile

Distance: 1 mi, 1984-85, 1987; 1-1/16 mi, 1986 and since 1988.

Year	Horse	Jockey	Year	Horse	Jockey	Year	Horse	Jockey
1984	Chief's Crown	D. MacBeth	1993	Brocco	G. Stevens	2002	Vindication	M. Smith
1985	Tasso	L. Pincay Jr.	1994	Timber Country	P. Day	2003	Action This Day	D. Flores
1986	Capote	L. Pincay Jr.	1995	Unbridled's Song	M. Smith	2004	Wilko	F. Dettori
1987	Success Express	J. Santos	1996	Boston Harbor	J. Bailey	2005	Stevie Wonderboy	G. Gomez
1988	Is It True	L. Pincay Jr.	1997	Favorite Trick	P. Day	2006	Street Sense	C. Borel
1989	Rhythm	C. Perret	1998	Answer Lively	J. Bailey	2007	War Pass	C. Velasquez
1990	Fly So Free	J. Santos	1999	Anees	G. Stevens	2008	Midshipman	G. Gomez
1991	Arazi	P. Valenzuela	2000	Macho Uno	J. Bailey	2009	Vale of York	A. Ajtebi
1992	Gilded Time	C. McCarron	2001	Johannesburg	M. Kinane	2010	Uncle Mo	J. Velazquez

Juvenile Fillies

Distance: 1 mi, 1984-85, 1987; 1-1/16 mi, 1986 and since 1988. Outstandingly won the 1984 race by disqualification.

Year	Horse	Jockey	Year	Horse	Jockey	Year	Horse	Jockey
1984	Outstandingly	W. Guerra	1993	Phone Chatter	L. Pincay Jr.	2002	Storm Flag Flying	J. Velazquez
1985	Twilight Ridge	J. Velasquez	1994	Flanders	P. Day	2003	Halfbridled	J. Krone
1986	Brave Raj	P. Valenzuela	1995	My Flag	J. Bailey	2004	Sweet Catomine	C. Nakatani
1987	Epitome	P. Day	1996	Storm Song	C. Perret	2005	Folklore	E. Prado
1988	Open Mind	A. Cordero Jr.	1997	Countess Diana	S. Sellers	2006	Dreaming of Anna	R. Douglas
1989	Go for Wand	R. Romero	1998	Silverbulletday	G. Stevens	2007	Indian Blessing	G. Gomez
1990	Meadow Star	J. Santos	1999	Cash Run	J. Bailey	2008	Stardom Bound	M. Smith
1991	Pleasant Stage	E. Delahoussaye	2000	Caressing	J. Velazquez	2009	She Be Wild	J. Leparoux
1992	Eliza	P. Valenzuela	2001	Tempera	D. Flores	2010	Awesome Feather	J. Sanchez

Sprint

Distance: 6 furlongs.

Year	Horse	Jockey	Year	Horse	Jockey	Year	Horse	Jockey
1984	Eillo	C. Perret	1993	Cardmania	E. Delahoussaye	2002	Orientate	J. Bailey
1985	Precisionist	C. McCarron	1994	Cherokee Run	M. Smith	2003	Cajun Beat	C. Velasquez
1986	Smile	J. Vasquez	1995	Desert Stormer	K. Desormeaux	2004	Speightstown	J. Velazquez
1987	Very Subtle	P. Valenzuela	1996	Lit De Justice	C. Nakatani	2005	Silver Train	E. Prado
1988	Gulch	A. Cordero Jr.	1997	Elmhurst	C. Nakatani	2006	Thor's Echo	C. Nakatani
1989	Dancing Spree	A. Cordero Jr.	1998	Reraise	C. Nakatani	2007	Midnight Lute	G. Gomez
1990	Safely Kept	C. Perret	1999	Artax	J. Chaves	2008	Midnight Lute	G. Gomez
1991	Sheikh Albadou	P. Eddery	2000	Kona Gold	A. Solis	2009	Dancing in Silks	J. Rosario
1992	Thirty Slews	E. Delahoussaye	2001	Squirtle Squirt	J. Bailey	2010	Big Drama	Eibar Coa

Mile

Year	Horse	Jockey	Year	Horse	Jockey	Year	Horse	Jockey
1984	Royal Heroine	F. Toro	1993	Lure	M. Smith	2002	Domedriver	T. Thulliez
1985	Cozzene	W. Guerra	1994	Barathea	L. Dettori	2003	Six Perfections	J. Bailey
1986	Last Tycoon	Y. St.-Martin	1995	Ridgewood Pearl	J. Murtagh	2004	Singletary	D. Flores
1987	Miesque	F. Head	1996	Da Hoss	G. Stevens	2005	Artie Schiller	G. Gomez
1988	Miesque	F. Head	1997	Spinning World	C. Asmussan	2006	Miesque's Approval	E. Castro
1989	Steinlen	J. Santos	1998	Da Hoss	J. Velazquez	2007	Kip Deville	C. Velasquez
1990	Royal Academy	L. Piggott	1999	Silic	C. Nakatani	2008	Goldikova	O. Peslier
1991	Opening Verse	P. Valenzuela	2000	War Chant	G. Stevens	2009	Goldikova	O. Peslier
1992	Lure	M. Smith	2001	Val Royal	J. Valdivia Jr.	2010	Goldikova	O. Peslier

Filly and Mare Turf

Distance: 1-3/8 mi, 1999-2000, 2004, 2006-07; 1-1/4 mi, 2001-03, 2005, 2008-10.

Year	Horse	Jockey	Year	Horse	Jockey	Year	Horse	Jockey
1999	Soaring Softly	J. Bailey	2003	Islington	K. Fallon	2007	Lahudood	A. Garcia
2000	Perfect Sting	J. Bailey	2004	Ouija Board	K. Fallon	2008	Forever Together	J. Leparoux
2001	Banks Hill	O. Peslier	2005	Intercontinental	R. Bejarano	2009	Midday	T. Queally
2002	Starine	J. Velazquez	2006	Ouija Board (GB)	F. Dettori	2010	Shared Account	E. Prado

Ladies' Classic

Distance: 1-1/4 mi, 1984-87; 1-1/8 mi, since 1988. Race known as Distaff, 1984-2007.

Year	Horse	Jockey	Year	Horse	Jockey	Year	Horse	Jockey
1984	Princess Rooney	E. Delahoussaye	1993	Hollywood Wildcat	E. Delahoussaye	2002	Azeri	M. Smith
1985	Life's Magic	A. Cordero Jr.	1994	One Dreamer	G. Stevens	2003	Adoration	P. Valenzuela
1986	Lady's Secret	P. Day	1995	Inside Information	M. Smith	2004	Ashado	C. Velasquez
1987	Sacahuista	R. Romero	1996	Jewel Princess	C. Nakatani	2005	Pleasant Home	C. Velasquez
1988	Personal Ensign	R. Romero	1997	Ajina	M. Smith	2006	Round Pond	E. Prado
1989	Bayakoa	L. Pincay Jr.	1998	Escena	G. Stevens	2007	Ginger Punch	R. Bejarano
1990	Bayakoa	L. Pincay Jr.	1999	Beautiful Pleasure	J. Chaves	2008	Zenyatta	M. Smith
1991	Dance Smartly	P. Day	2000	Spain	V. Espinoza	2009	Life Is Sweet	G. Gomez
1992	Paseana	C. McCarron	2001	Unbridled Elaine	P. Day	2010	Unrivaled Belle	K. Desormeaux

Turf

Distance: 1-1/2 mi.

Year	Horse	Jockey	Year	Horse	Jockey	Year	Horse	Jockey
1984	Lashkari	Y. St.-Martin	1993	Kotashaan	K. Desormeaux	2003	(tie) High Chaparral	M. Kinane
1985	Pebbles	P. Eddery	1994	Tikkanen	M. Smith			Johar	A. Solis
1986	Manila	J. Santos	1995	Northern Spur	C. McCarron	2004	Better Talk Now	R. Dominguez
1987	Theatrical	P. Day	1996	Pilsudski	W. Swinburn	2005	Shirocco	C. Soumillon
1988	Great Communicator	R. Sibille	1997	Chief Bearhart	J. Santos	2006	Red Rocks	F. Dettori
			1998	Buck's Boy	S. Sellers	2007	English Channel	J. Velasquez
1989	Prized	E. Delahoussaye	1999	Daylami	L. Dettori	2008	Conduit	R. Moore
1990	In The Wings	G. Stevens	2000	Kalanisi	J. Murtagh	2009	Conduit	R. Moore
1991	Miss Alleged	E. Legrix	2001	Fantastic Light	L. Dettori	2010	Dangerous Midge	F. Dettori
1992	Fraise	P. Valenzuela	2002	High Chaparral	M. Kinane			

Eclipse Awards

The Eclipse Awards, honoring the Horse of the Year and other champions of the sport, began in 1971 and are sponsored by the *Daily Racing Form*, the National Thoroughbred Racing Association, and the National Turf Writers Assn. Prior to 1971, the *DRF* (1936-70) and the NTRA (1950-70) issued separate selections for Horse of the Year.

Eclipse Awards, 2010

Horse of the Year: Zenyatta	**Older female (4-year-old+):** Zenyatta	**Trainer:** Todd Pletcher
2-year-old male: Uncle Mo	**Male sprinter:** Big Drama	**Jockey:** Ramon Dominguez
2-year-old female: Awesome Feather	**Female sprinter:** Dubai Majesty	**Apprentice jockey:** Omar Moreno
3-year-old male: Lookin At Lucky	**Male turf horse:** Gio Ponti	**Breeder:** Adena Springs
3-year-old female: Blind Luck	**Female turf horse:** Goldikova	**Owner:** WinStar Farm
Older male (4-year-old+): Blame	**Steeplechase horse:** Slip Away	

Horse of the Year, 1936-2010

Year	Horse	Year	Horse	Year	Horse	Year	Horse
1936	Granville	1949	Capot	1960	Kelso	1971	Ack Ack
1937	War Admiral	1950	Hill Prince	1961	Kelso	1972	Secretariat
1938	Seabiscuit	1951	Counterpoint	1962	Kelso	1973	Secretariat
1939	Challedon	1952	One Count (DRF)	1963	Kelso	1974	Forego
1940	Challedon		Native Dancer (TRA)	1964	Kelso	1975	Forego
1941	Whirlaway	1953	Tom Fool	1965	Roman Brother (DRF)	1976	Forego
1942	Whirlaway	1954	Native Dancer		Moccasin (TRA)	1977	Seattle Slew
1943	Count Fleet	1955	Nashua	1966	Buckpasser	1978	Affirmed
1944	Twilight Tear	1956	Swaps	1967	Damascus	1979	Affirmed
1945	Busher	1957	Bold Ruler (DRF);	1968	Dr. Fager	1980	Spectacular Bid
1946	Assault		Dedicate (TRA)	1969	Arts and Letters	1981	John Henry
1947	Armed	1958	Round Table	1970	Fort Marcy (DRF);	1982	Conquistador Cielo
1948	Citation	1959	Sword Dancer		Personality (TRA)	1983	All Along

Year	Horse	Year	Horse	Year	Horse	Year	Horse
1984	John Henry	1991	Black Tie Affair	1998	Skip Away	2005	Saint Liam
1985	Spend A Buck	1992	A.P. Indy	1999	Charismatic	2006	Invasor
1986	Lady's Secret	1993	Kotashaan	2000	Tiznow	2007	Curlin
1987	Ferdinand	1994	Holy Bull	2001	Point Given	2008	Curlin
1988	Alysheba	1995	Cigar	2002	Azeri	2009	Rachel Alexandra
1989	Sunday Silence	1996	Cigar	2003	Mineshaft	2010	Zenyatta
1990	Criminal Type	1997	Favorite Trick	2004	Ghostzapper		

HARNESS RACING
Harness Horse of the Year, 1947-2010
(Chosen by the U.S. Trotting Assn. and the U.S. Harness Writers Assn.)

Year	Horse	Year	Horse	Year	Horse	Year	Horse
1947	Victory Song	1963	Speedy Scot	1979	Niatross	1995	CR Kay Suzie
1948	Rodney	1964	Bret Hanover	1980	Niatross	1996	Continental Victory
1949	Good Time	1965	Bret Hanover	1981	Fan Hanover	1997	Malabar Man
1950	Proximity	1966	Bret Hanover	1982	Cam Fella	1998	Moni Maker
1951	Pronto Don	1967	Nevele Pride	1983	Cam Fella	1999	Moni Maker
1952	Good Time	1968	Nevele Pride	1984	Fancy Crown	2000	Gallo Blue Chip
1953	Hi Lo's Forbes	1969	Nevele Pride	1985	Nihilator	2001	Bunny Lake
1954	Stenographer	1970	Fresh Yankee	1986	Forrest Skipper	2002	Real Desire
1955	Scott Frost	1971	Albatross	1987	Mack Lobell	2003	No Pan Intended
1956	Scott Frost	1972	Albatross	1988	Mack Lobell	2004	Rainbow Blue
1957	Torpid	1973	Sir Dalrae	1989	Matt's Scooter	2005	Rocknroll Hanover
1958	Emily's Pride	1974	Delmonica Hanover	1990	Beach Towel	2006	Glidemaster
1959	Bye Bye Byrd	1975	Savoir	1991	Precious Bunny	2007	Donato Hanover
1960	Adios Butler	1976	Keystone Ore	1992	Artsplace	2008	Somebeachsomewhere
1961	Adios Butler	1977	Green Speed	1993	Staying Together	2009	Muscle Hill
1962	Su Mac Lad	1978	Abercrombie	1994	Cam's Card Shark	2010	Rock and Roll Heaven

The Hambletonian (3-year-old trotters), 1965-2011

Year	Horse	Driver	Year	Horse	Driver
1965	Egyptian Candor	Del Cameron	1989	Park Avenue Joe	Ron Waples
1966	Kerry Way	Frank Ervin	1990	Harmonious	John Campbell
1967	Speedy Streak	Del Cameron	1991	Giant Victory	Jack Moiseyev
1968	Nevele Pride	Stanley Dancer	1992	Alf Palema	Mickey McNicholl
1969	Lindy's Pride	Howard Beissinger	1993	American Winner	Ron Pierce
1970	Timothy T	John Simpson Sr.	1994	Victory Dream	Michel Lachance
1971	Speedy Crown	Howard Beissinger	1995	Tagliabue	John Campbell
1972	Super Bowl	Stanley Dancer	1996	Continental Victory	Michel Lachance
1973	Flirth	Ralph Baldwin	1997	Malabar Man	Malvern Burroughs
1974	Christopher T	Bill Haughton	1998	Muscles Yankee	John Campbell
1975	Bonefish	Stanley Dancer	1999	Self Possessed	Mike Lachance
1976	Steve Lobell	Bill Haughton	2000	Yankee Paco	Trevor Ritchie
1977	Green Speed	Bill Haughton	2001	Scarlet Knight	Stefan Melander
1978	Speedy Somolli	Howard Beissinger	2002	Chip Chip Hooray	Eric Ledford
1979	Legend Hanover	George Sholty	2003	Amigo Hall	Mike Lachance
1980	Burgomeister	Bill Haughton	2004	Windsong's Legacy	Trond Smedshammer
1981	Shiaway St. Pat	Ray Remmen	2005	Vivid Photo	Roger Hammer
1982	Speed Bowl	Tommy Haughton	2006	Glidemaster	John Campbell
1983	Duenna	Stanley Dancer	2007	Donato Hanover	Ron Pierce
1984	Historic Freight	Ben Webster	2008	Deweycheatumnhowe	Ray Schnittker
1985	Prakas	Bill O'Donnell	2009	Muscle Hill	Brian Sears
1986	Nuclear Kosmos	Ulf Thoresen	2010	Muscle Massive	Ron Pierce
1987	Mack Lobell	John Campbell	2011	Broad Bahn	George Brennan
1988	Armbro Goal	John Campbell			

BOWLING
Professional Bowlers Association
PBA Tournament of Champions, 1965-2011

Year	Winner	Year	Winner	Year	Winner	Year	Winner
1965	Billy Hardwick	1976	Marshall Holman	1987	Pete Weber	1999	Jason Couch
1966	Wayne Zahn	1977	Mike Berlin	1988	Mark Williams	2000	Jason Couch
1967	Jim Stefanich	1978	Earl Anthony	1989	Del Ballard Jr.	2002	Jason Couch
1968	Dave Davis	1979	George Pappas	1990	Dave Ferraro	2003	Patrick Healey Jr.
1969	Jim Godman	1980	Wayne Webb	1991	David Ozio	2005	Steve Jaros
1970	Don Johnson	1981	Steve Cook	1992	Marc McDowell	2006	Chris Barnes
1971	Johnny Petraglia	1982	Mike Durbin	1993	George Branham III	2007	Tommy Jones
1972	Mike Durbin	1983	Joe Berardi	1994	Norm Duke	2008	Michael Haugen Jr.
1973	Jim Godman	1984	Mike Durbin	1996	Dave D'Entremont	2009	Patrick Allen
1974	Earl Anthony	1985	Mark Williams	1997	John Gant	2010	Kelly Kulick
1975	Dave Davis	1986	Marshall Holman	1998	Bryan Goebel	2011	Mika Koivuniemi

Note: No tournament held in 2001 or 2004.

PBA Hall of Fame Performance Inductees

Bill Allen	Don Carter	Jim Godman	George Pappas	Brian Voss
Earl Anthony	Paul Colwell	Billy Hardwick	Randy Pedersen	Wayne Webb
Mike Aulby	Steve Cook	Marshall Holman	Johnny Petraglia	Dick Weber
Del Ballard Jr.	Dave Davis	Tommy Hudson	Dick Ritger	Pete Weber
Joe Berardi	Gary Dickinson	Dave Husted	Mark Roth	Billy Welu
Ray Bluth	Norm Duke	Don Johnson	Carmen Salvino	Mark Williams
Parker Bohn III	Mike Durbin	Larry Laub	Harry Smith	Walter Ray Williams Jr.
Roy Buckley	Buzz Fazio	Amleto Monacelli	Dave Soutar	Wayne Zahn
Nelson Burton Jr.	Dave Ferraro	David Ozio	Jim Stefanich	

PBA Leading Money Winners, 1962-2011
Total winnings from tournaments only. After 2000, year shown is year the PBA season ended.

Year	Bowler	Amount	Year	Bowler	Amount	Year	Bowler	Amount
1962	Don Carter	$49,972	1979	Mark Roth	$124,517	1995	Mike Aulby	$219,792
1963	Dick Weber	46,333	1980	Wayne Webb	116,700	1996	Walter Ray Williams Jr.	241,330
1964	Bob Strampe	33,592	1981	Earl Anthony	164,735	1997	Walter Ray Williams Jr.	240,544
1965	Dick Weber	47,674	1982	Earl Anthony	134,760	1998	Walter Ray Williams Jr.	238,225
1966	Wayne Zahn	54,720	1983	Earl Anthony	135,605	1999	Parker Bohn III	240,912
1967	Dave Davis	54,165	1984	Mark Roth	158,712	2000	Norm Duke	143,325
1968	Jim Stefanich	67,377	1985	Mike Aulby	201,200	2002	Parker Bohn III	245,200
1969	Billy Hardwick	64,160	1986	Walter Ray Williams Jr.	145,550	2003	Walter Ray Williams Jr.	419,700
1970	Mike McGrath	52,049	1987	Pete Weber	175,491	2004	Mika Koivuniemi	238,590
1971	Johnny Petraglia	85,065	1988	Brian Voss	225,485	2005	Patrick Allen	350,740
1972	Don Johnson	56,648	1989	Mike Aulby	298,237	2006	Tommy Jones	301,700
1973	Don McCune	69,000	1990	Amleto Monacelli	204,775	2007	Doug Kent	200,530
1974	Earl Anthony	99,585	1991	David Ozio	225,585	2008	Norm Duke	176,855
1975	Earl Anthony	107,585	1992	Marc McDowell	174,215	2009	Norm Duke	199,130
1976	Earl Anthony	110,833	1993	Walter Ray Williams Jr.	296,370	2010	Walter Ray Williams Jr.	152,670
1977	Mark Roth	105,583	1994	Norm Duke	273,753	2011	Mika Koivuniemi	333,040
1978	Mark Roth	134,500						

Leading PBA Averages by Year, 1962-2011

Year	Bowler	Average	Year	Bowler	Average	Year	Bowler	Average
1962	Don Carter	212.84	1979	Mark Roth	221.66	1995	Mike Aulby	225.49
1963	Billy Hardwick	210.34	1980	Earl Anthony	218.53	1996	Walter Ray Williams Jr.	225.37
1964	Ray Bluth	210.51	1981	Mark Roth	216.69	1997	Walter Ray Williams Jr.	222.00
1965	Dick Weber	211.89	1982	Marshall Holman	212.84	1998	Walter Ray Williams Jr.	226.13
1966	Wayne Zahn	208.66	1983	Earl Anthony	216.64	1999	Parker Bohn III	228.04
1967	Wayne Zahn	212.34	1984	Marshall Holman	213.91	2000	Chris Barnes	220.93
1968	Jim Stefanich	211.89	1985	Mark Baker	213.71	2002	Parker Bohn III	221.54
1969	Bill Hardwick	212.95	1986	John Gant	214.37	2003	Walter Ray Williams Jr.	224.94
1970	Nelson Burton Jr.	214.90	1987	Marshall Holman	216.80	2004	Mika Koivuniemi	222.73
1971	Don Johnson	213.97	1988	Mark Roth	218.03	2005	Walter Ray Williams Jr.	227.07
1972	Don Johnson	215.29	1989	Pete Weber	215.43	2006	Norm Duke	224.29
1973	Earl Anthony	215.79	1990	Amleto Monacelli	218.15	2007	Norm Duke	228.47
1974	Earl Anthony	219.39	1991	Norm Duke	218.20	2008	Walter Ray Williams Jr.	228.34
1975	Earl Anthony	219.06	1992	Dave Ferraro	219.70	2009	Wes Malott	228.98
1976	Mark Roth	215.97	1993	Walter Ray Williams Jr.	222.98	2010	Walter Ray Williams Jr.	222.92
1977	Mark Roth	218.17	1994	Norm Duke	222.83	2011	Mika Koivuniemi	222.50
1978	Mark Roth	219.83						

United States Bowling Congress

Formed Jan. 1, 2005, from a merger of the American Bowling Congress (ABC), Women's International Bowling Congress, the Young American Bowling Alliance, and USA Bowling. Before 2006, certified games and champions are for ABC only.

Men's Career 300 Games
(As of July 31, 2011.)

Rank	Bowler, hometown	Games
1.	Fero Williams, Cincinnati, OH	123
2.	Gordon Childers, Benton, AR	122
3.	Jim Hosier, Wayne, NJ	116
4.	Andrew Neuer, Lewisburg, PA	114
5.	James Tomek, Camp Hill, PA	112
6.	Stephen Aiello, North Haledon, NJ	111
7.	Frank Massengale Jr., Hixson, TN	105
8.	Chris Hayward, Toledo, OH	104
9.	John Delp, Sinking Spring, PA	100
9.	Jack Kurent, Luzerne, PA	100

Women's Career 300 Games
(As of July 31, 2011.)

Rank	Bowler, hometown	Games
1.	Tammy Jones, Decatur, IL	39
2.	Teri Haefke, Austintown, OH	38
3.	Altramese Webb, Detroit, MI	36
4.	Jodi Musto, Schenectady, NY	33
5.	Marianne DiRupo, Succasunna, NJ	30
	Barb Staub, Cedar Rapids, IA	30
7.	Jodi Woessner, Oregon, OH	29
8.	Alisia Kellow, Louisville, KY	28
	Tish Johnson, Colorado Springs, CO	28
10.	Shannon Pluhowsky, Kettering, OH	24
	Jeanette Adams, Rancho Cordova, CA	24

USBC Masters Tournament Champions, 1980-2011

Year	Winner, hometown	Year	Winner, hometown	Year	Winner, hometown
1980	Neil Burton, St. Louis, MO	1991	Doug Kent, Canandaigua, NY	2002	Brett Wolfe, Reno, NV
1981	Randy Lightfoot, St. Charles, MO	1992	Ken Johnson, N. Richmond Hills, TX	2003	Bryon Smith, Roseburg, OR
1982	Joe Berardi, Brooklyn, NY	1993	Norm Duke, Oklahoma City, OK	2004	Walter Ray Williams Jr., FL (Jan.);
1983	Mike Lastowski, Havre de Grace, MD	1994	Steve Fehr, Cincinnati, OH		Danny Wiseman, MD (Oct.)
1984	Earl Anthony, Dublin, CA	1995	Mike Aulby, Indianapolis, IN	2005	Mike Scroggins, Amarillo, TX
1985	Steve Wunderlich, St. Louis, MO	1996	Ernie Schlegel, Vancouver, WA	2006	Doug Kent, Newark, NY
1986	Mark Fahy, Chicago, IL	1997	Jason Queen, Decatur, IL	2007	Sean Rash, Wichita, KS
1987	Rick Steelsmith, Wichita, KS	1998	Mike Aulby, Indianapolis, IN	2008	No tournament
1988	Del Ballard Jr., Richardson, TX	1999	Brian Boghosian, Middletown, CT	2009	John Nolen, Waterford, MI
1989	Mike Aulby, Indianapolis, IN	2000	Mika Koivuniemi, Finland	2010	Walter Ray Williams Jr., Ocala, FL
1990	Chris Warren, Dallas, TX	2001	Parker Bohn III, Jackson, NJ	2011	Tom Hess, Urbandale, IA

Open Champions, 2011

Regular Singles/Regular All-Events: Matt Weggen, Muscatine, IA
Regular Doubles: Chad Reiffer, Kentwood, MI, and Brandon Tarabek, Grand Rapids, MI
Regular Team: Turbo 2-N-1 Grips 1, Madison, WI
Team All-Events: K&K Bowling Services 5, Las Vegas, NV

Classified Singles: Glen Brown, Renton, WA
Classified Doubles: Velvet Sanderson, Norco, CA, and Gary Weldon, Temple City, CA
Classified All-Events: Miguel Sanchez, Chicago, IL
Classified Team: Paradise Lanes, Walden, CO

USBC Queens and Women's Champions, 2011

According to the new format introduced in 2010, USBC women's champions are selected from an all-handicap format with three divisions: Diamond (180 and higher with handicap based on 100% of 220), Ruby (150-179 with handicap based on 100% of 180), and Sapphire (149 and below with handicap based on 100% of 150). Overall champions (scratch) also are crowned.

Queens Tournament: Missy Parkin, Lake Forest, CA
Scratch Singles: Shannon Pluhowsky, Kettering, OH
Scratch Doubles: Aleta Sill, Livonia, MI, & Michelle Feldman, Auburn, NY
Scratch All-Events: Dede Davidson, Buellton, CA

Scratch Team: Shootin Nines, Indianapolis, IN
Diamond Singles: Brittany Signor, Watertown, NY
Diamond Doubles: Trish Manna & Suzy Minino, Omaha, NE
Diamond All-Events: Elizabeth HublerRike, Grand Rapids, MI
Diamond Team: Eagles Edge Pro Shop, Des Plaines, IL

CHESS
World Chess Champions, 1886-2011
Source: U.S. Chess Federation; International Chess Federation (FIDE)
Official world champions since the title was first used, as of Oct. 15, 2011.

1886-94	Wilhelm Steinitz, Austria	1972-75	Bobby Fischer, U.S.[2]
1894-1921	Emanuel Lasker, Germany	1975-85	Anatoly Karpov, USSR
1921-27	Jose R. Capablanca, Cuba	1985-2000	Garry Kasparov, USSR/Russia[3]
1927-35	Alexander Alekhine, France	1993-99	Anatoly Karpov, Russia (FIDE)[3]
1935-37	Max Euwe, Netherlands	1999-2000	Alexander Khalifman, Russia (FIDE)
1937-46	Alexander Alekhine, France[1]	2000-02	Viswanathan Anand, India (FIDE)
1948-57	Mikhail Botvinnik, USSR	2000-06	Vladimir Kramnik, Russia (classical)[4,5]
1957-58	Vassily Smyslov, USSR	2002-04	Ruslan Ponomariov, Ukraine (FIDE)
1958-59	Mikhail Botvinnik, USSR	2004-05	Rustam Kasimdzhanov, Uzbekistan (FIDE)
1960-61	Mikhail Tal, USSR	2005-06	Veselin Topalov, Bulgaria (FIDE)
1961-63	Mikhail Botvinnik, USSR	2006-07	Vladimir Kramnik, Russia[5]
1963-69	Tigran Petrosian, USSR	2007-	Viswanathan Anand, India
1969-72	Boris Spassky, USSR		

(1) After Alekhine died in 1946, the title was vacant until 1948, when Botvinnik won the 1st world championship event sanctioned by FIDE. (2) Defaulted championship after refusing to accept FIDE rules for a championship match, Apr. 1975. (3) Kasparov broke with FIDE, Feb. 26, 1993. FIDE stripped Kasparov of his FIDE title Mar. 23. Kasparov then defeated Nigel Short (Great Britain) in a world championship match played Sept.-Oct. 1993 under the auspices of a new organization the two had founded, the Professional Chess Association (PCA). FIDE held a replacement championship match between Anatoly Karpov (Russia) and Jan Timman (Netherlands), which Karpov won in Nov. 1993. The PCA folded in 1995, but Kasparov was still considered the "classical" world champion. (4) In Nov. 2000, Kramnik defeated Garry Kasparov (Russia) for the classical world championship title in London. (5) Kramnik, the classical world champion since 2000, and Veselin Topalov, FIDE champion since 2005, met at the world chess championship match in Elista, Russia, to compete for a unified championship, which Kramnik won Oct. 13, 2006.

FIGURE SKATING
U.S. and World Individual Champions, 1952-2011

U.S. Champions			World Champions	
Men	**Women**	**Year**	**Men**	**Women**
Dick Button	Tenley Albright	1952	Dick Button, U.S.	Jacqueline du Bief, France
Hayes Jenkins	Tenley Albright	1953	Hayes Jenkins, U.S.	Tenley Albright, U.S.
Hayes Jenkins	Tenley Albright	1954	Hayes Jenkins, U.S.	Gundi Busch, W. Germany
Hayes Jenkins	Tenley Albright	1955	Hayes Jenkins, U.S.	Tenley Albright, U.S.
Hayes Jenkins	Tenley Albright	1956	Hayes Jenkins, U.S.	Carol Heiss, U.S.
Dave Jenkins	Carol Heiss	1957	Dave Jenkins, U.S.	Carol Heiss, U.S.
Dave Jenkins	Carol Heiss	1958	Dave Jenkins, U.S.	Carol Heiss, U.S.
Dave Jenkins	Carol Heiss	1959	Dave Jenkins, U.S.	Carol Heiss, U.S.
Dave Jenkins	Carol Heiss	1960	Alain Giletti, France	Carol Heiss, U.S.
Bradley Lord	Laurence Owen	1961	None	None
Monty Hoyt	Barbara Roles Pursley	1962	Don Jackson, Canada	Sjoukje Dijkstra, Netherlands
Tommy Litz	Lorraine Hanlon	1963	Don McPherson, Canada	Sjoukje Dijkstra, Netherlands
Scott Allen	Peggy Fleming	1964	Manfred Schnelldorfer, W. Germany	Sjoukje Dijkstra, Netherlands
Gary Visconti	Peggy Fleming	1965	Alain Calmat, France	Petra Burka, Canada
Scott Allen	Peggy Fleming	1966	Emmerich Danzer, Austria	Peggy Fleming, U.S.
Gary Visconti	Peggy Fleming	1967	Emmerich Danzer, Austria	Peggy Fleming, U.S.
Tim Wood	Peggy Fleming	1968	Emmerich Danzer, Austria	Peggy Fleming, U.S.
Tim Wood	Janet Lynn	1969	Tim Wood, U.S.	Gabriele Seyfert, E. Germany
Tim Wood	Janet Lynn	1970	Tim Wood, U.S.	Gabriele Seyfert, E. Germany
John Misha Petkevich	Janet Lynn	1971	Ondrej Nepela, Czechoslovakia	Beatrix Schuba, Austria
Ken Shelley	Janet Lynn	1972	Ondrej Nepela, Czechoslovakia	Beatrix Schuba, Austria
Gordon McKellen Jr.	Janet Lynn	1973	Ondrej Nepela, Czechoslovakia	Karen Magnussen, Canada
Gordon McKellen Jr.	Dorothy Hamill	1974	Jan Hoffmann, E. Germany	Christine Errath, E. Germany
Gordon McKellen Jr.	Dorothy Hamill	1975	Sergei Volkov, USSR	Dianne de Leeuw, Neth.-U.S.
Terry Kubicka	Dorothy Hamill	1976	John Curry, Gr. Britain	Dorothy Hamill, U.S.
Charles Tickner	Linda Fratianne	1977	Vladimir Kovalev, USSR	Linda Fratianne, U.S.
Charles Tickner	Linda Fratianne	1978	Charles Tickner, U.S.	Anett Poetzsch, E. Germany
Charles Tickner	Linda Fratianne	1979	Vladimir Kovalev, USSR	Linda Fratianne, U.S.
Charles Tickner	Linda Fratianne	1980	Jan Hoffmann, E. Germany	Anett Poetzsch, E. Germany
Scott Hamilton	Elaine Zayak	1981	Scott Hamilton, U.S.	Denise Biellmann, Switzerland
Scott Hamilton	Rosalynn Sumners	1982	Scott Hamilton, U.S.	Elaine Zayak, U.S.
Scott Hamilton	Rosalynn Sumners	1983	Scott Hamilton, U.S.	Rosalynn Sumners, U.S.
Scott Hamilton	Rosalynn Sumners	1984	Scott Hamilton, U.S.	Katarina Witt, E. Germany
Brian Boitano	Tiffany Chin	1985	Aleksandr Fadeev, USSR	Katarina Witt, E. Germany
Brian Boitano	Debi Thomas	1986	Brian Boitano, U.S.	Debi Thomas, U.S.
Brian Boitano	Jill Trenary	1987	Brian Orser, Canada	Katarina Witt, E. Germany
Brian Boitano	Debi Thomas	1988	Brian Boitano, U.S.	Katarina Witt, E. Germany
Christopher Bowman	Jill Trenary	1989	Kurt Browning, Canada	Midori Ito, Japan
Todd Eldredge	Jill Trenary	1990	Kurt Browning, Canada	Jill Trenary, U.S.
Todd Eldredge	Tonya Harding	1991	Kurt Browning, Canada	Kristi Yamaguchi, U.S.

U.S. Champions			World Champions	
Men	Women	Year	Men	Women
Christopher Bowman	Kristi Yamaguchi	1992	Viktor Petrenko, Ukraine	Kristi Yamaguchi, U.S.
Scott Davis	Nancy Kerrigan	1993	Kurt Browning, Canada	Oksana Baiul, Ukraine
Scott Davis	Vacant[1]	1994	Elvis Stojko, Canada	Yuka Sato, Japan
Todd Eldredge	Nicole Bobek	1995	Elvis Stojko, Canada	Chen Lu, China
Rudy Galindo	Michelle Kwan	1996	Todd Eldredge, U.S.	Michelle Kwan, U.S.
Todd Eldredge	Tara Lipinski	1997	Elvis Stojko, Canada	Tara Lipinski, U.S.
Todd Eldredge	Michelle Kwan	1998	Alexei Yagudin, Russia	Michelle Kwan, U.S.
Michael Weiss	Michelle Kwan	1999	Alexei Yagudin, Russia	Maria Butyrskaya, Russia
Michael Weiss	Michelle Kwan	2000	Alexei Yagudin, Russia	Michelle Kwan, U.S.
Timothy Goebel	Michelle Kwan	2001	Yevgeny Plushenko, Russia	Michelle Kwan, U.S.
Todd Eldredge	Michelle Kwan	2002	Alexei Yagudin, Russia	Irina Slutskaya, Russia
Michael Weiss	Michelle Kwan	2003	Yevgeny Plushenko, Russia	Michelle Kwan, U.S.
Johnny Weir	Michelle Kwan	2004	Yevgeny Plushenko, Russia	Shizuka Arakawa, Japan
Johnny Weir	Michelle Kwan	2005	Stephane Lambiel, Switzerland	Irina Slutskaya, Russia
Johnny Weir	Sasha Cohen	2006	Stephane Lambiel, Switzerland	Kimmie Meissner, U.S.
Evan Lysacek	Kimmie Meissner	2007	Brian Joubert, France	Miki Ando, Japan
Evan Lysacek	Mirai Nagasu	2008	Jeffrey Buttle, Canada	Mao Asada, Japan
Jeremy Abbott	Alissa Czisny	2009	Evan Lysacek, U.S.	Yu-Na Kim, South Korea
Jeremy Abbott	Rachael Flatt	2010	Daisuke Takahashi, Japan	Mao Asada, Japan
Ryan Bradley	Alissa Czisny	2011	Patrick Chan, Canada	Miki Ando, Japan

(1) Tonya Harding was stripped of the title for her involvement in an attack on rival Nancy Kerrigan.

SKIING
Alpine World Cup Champions, 1967-2011

Year	Men's champion, country	Year	Men's champion, country	Year	Women's champion, country
1967	Jean Claude Killy, France	1998	Hermann Maier, Austria	1981	Marie-Theres Nadig, Switzerland
1968	Jean Claude Killy, France	1999	Lasse Kjus, Norway	1982	Erika Hess, Switzerland
1969	Karl Schranz, Austria	2000	Hermann Maier, Austria	1983	Tamara McKinney, U.S.
1970	Karl Schranz, Austria	2001	Hermann Maier, Austria	1984	Erika Hess, Switzerland
1971	Gustavo Thoeni, Italy	2002	Stephan Eberharter, Austria	1985	Michela Figini, Switzerland
1972	Gustavo Thoeni, Italy	2003	Stephan Eberharter, Austria	1986	Maria Walliser, Switzerland
1973	Gustavo Thoeni, Italy	2004	Hermann Maier, Austria	1987	Maria Walliser, Switzerland
1974	Piero Gros, Italy	2005	Bode Miller, U.S.	1988	Michela Figini, Switzerland
1975	Gustavo Thoeni, Italy	2006	Benjamin Raich, Austria	1989	Vreni Schneider, Switzerland
1976	Ingemar Stenmark, Sweden	2007	Aksel Lund Svindal, Norway	1990	Petra Kronberger, Austria
1977	Ingemar Stenmark, Sweden	2008	Bode Miller, U.S.	1991	Petra Kronberger, Austria
1978	Ingemar Stenmark, Sweden	2009	Aksel Lund Svindal, Norway	1992	Petra Kronberger, Austria
1979	Peter Luescher, Switzerland	2010	Carlo Janka, Switzerland	1993	Anita Wachter, Austria
1980	Andreas Wenzel, Liechtenstein	2011	Ivica Kostelic, Croatia	1994	Vreni Schneider, Switzerland
1981	Phil Mahre, U.S.			1995	Vreni Schneider, Switzerland
1982	Phil Mahre, U.S.			1996	Katja Seizinger, Germany
1983	Phil Mahre, U.S.	**Year**	**Women's champion, country**	1997	Pernilla Wiberg, Sweden
1984	Pirmin Zurbriggen, Switzerland	1967	Nancy Greene, Canada	1998	Katja Seizinger, Germany
1985	Marc Girardelli, Luxembourg	1968	Nancy Greene, Canada	1999	Alexandra Meissnitzer, Austria
1986	Marc Girardelli, Luxembourg	1969	Gertrud Gabl, Austria	2000	Renate Goetschl, Austria
1987	Pirmin Zurbriggen, Switzerland	1970	Michele Jacot, France	2001	Janica Kostelic, Croatia
1988	Pirmin Zurbriggen, Switzerland	1971	Annemarie Proell, Austria	2002	Michaela Dorfmeister, Austria
1989	Marc Girardelli, Luxembourg	1972	Annemarie Proell, Austria	2003	Janica Kostelic, Croatia
1990	Pirmin Zurbriggen, Switzerland	1973	Annemarie Proell, Austria	2004	Anja Paerson, Sweden
1991	Marc Girardelli, Luxembourg	1974	Annemarie Proell, Austria	2005	Anja Paerson, Sweden
1992	Paul Accola, Switzerland	1975	Annemarie Proell, Austria	2006	Janica Kostelic, Croatia
1993	Marc Girardelli, Luxembourg	1976	Rose Mittermaier, W. Germany	2007	Nicole Hosp, Austria
1994	Kjetil Andre Aamodt, Norway	1977	Lise-Marie Morerod, Switzerland	2008	Lindsey Vonn, U.S.
1995	Alberto Tomba, Italy	1978	Hanni Wenzel, Liechtenstein	2009	Lindsey Vonn, U.S.
1996	Lasse Kjus, Norway	1979	Annemarie Proell Moser, Austria	2010	Lindsey Vonn, U.S.
1997	Luc Alphand, France	1980	Hanni Wenzel, Liechtenstein	2011	Maria Höfl-Riesch, Germany

CYCLING
Tour de France, 2011

Cadel Evans of Australia won the 98th Tour de France, cycling's premier race, July 24, 2011. The 2,131-mile (3,430.5-km) Tour de France began July 2 with three-time champion Alberto Contador defending his title despite outstanding allegations of doping that could strip him of the previous year's Tour win. Evans, the first Australian to win the Tour, finished the race in 86 hours, 12 minutes, 22 seconds. For the first time in the history of the Tour, the other two places on the podium were ascended by brothers: Luxembourg's Andy Schleck, who came in second place for the third straight year, 1 minute, 34 seconds behind Evans, and Frank Shleck, who was 56 seconds behind his younger brother.

Tour de France Winners, 1980-2011

Year	Winner, nationality	Year	Winner, nationality	Year	Winner, nationality
1980	Zoop Zoetemelk, Netherlands	1991	Miguel Indurain, Spain	2002	Lance Armstrong, U.S.
1981	Bernard Hinault, France	1992	Miguel Indurain, Spain	2003	Lance Armstrong, U.S.
1982	Bernard Hinault, France	1993	Miguel Indurain, Spain	2004	Lance Armstrong, U.S.
1983	Laurent Fignon, France	1994	Miguel Indurain, Spain	2005	Lance Armstrong, U.S.
1984	Laurent Fignon, France	1995	Miguel Indurain, Spain	2006	Óscar Pereiro, Spain[1]
1985	Bernard Hinault, France	1996	Bjarne Riis, Denmark	2007	Alberto Contador, Spain
1986	Greg LeMond, U.S.	1997	Jan Ullrich, Germany	2008	Carlos Sastre, Spain
1987	Stephen Roche, Ireland	1998	Marco Pantani, Italy	2009	Alberto Contador, Spain
1988	Pedro Delgado, Spain	1999	Lance Armstrong, U.S.	2010	Alberto Contador, Spain
1989	Greg LeMond, U.S.	2000	Lance Armstrong, U.S.	2011	Cadel Evans, Australia
1990	Greg LeMond, U.S.	2001	Lance Armstrong, U.S.		

(1) Floyd Landis, U.S., was stripped of the title, Sept. 20, 2007, for doping. Landis lost a final appeal of the ruling June 30, 2008.

SWIMMING
World Swimming Records
Long course (50 m), as of Oct. 2011.

Men's Records
Freestyle

Distance	Time	Holder	Nationality	Location	Date
50 meters	0:20.91	César Cielo Filho	Brazil	São Paulo, Brazil	Dec. 18, 2009
100 meters	0:46.91	César Cielo Filho	Brazil	Rome, Italy	July 30, 2009
200 meters	1:42.00	Paul Biedermann	Germany	Rome, Italy	July 28, 2009
400 meters	3:40.07	Paul Biedermann	Germany	Rome, Italy	July 26, 2009
800 meters	7:32.12	Zhang Lin	China	Rome, Italy	July 29, 2009
1,500 meters	14:34.14	Yang Sun	China	Shanghai, China	July 31, 2011

Backstroke

Distance	Time	Holder	Nationality	Location	Date
50 meters	0:24.04	Liam Tancock	UK	Rome, Italy	Aug. 2, 2009
100 meters	0:51.94	Aaron Peirsol	U.S.	Indianapolis, IN	July 7, 2009
200 meters	1:51.92	Aaron Peirsol	U.S.	Rome, Italy	July 31, 2009

Breaststroke

Distance	Time	Holder	Nationality	Location	Date
50 meters	0:26.67	Cameron van der Burgh	South Africa	Rome, Italy	July 29, 2009
100 meters	0:58.58	Brenton Rickard	Australia	Rome, Italy	July 27, 2009
200 meters	2:07.31	Christian Sprenger	Australia	Rome, Italy	July 30, 2009

Butterfly

Distance	Time	Holder	Nationality	Location	Date
50 meters	0:22.43	Rafael Muñoz	Spain	Malaga, Spain	Apr. 5, 2009
100 meters	0:49.82	Michael Phelps	U.S.	Rome, Italy	Aug. 1, 2009
200 meters	1:51.51	Michael Phelps	U.S.	Rome, Italy	July 29, 2009

Individual medley

Distance	Time	Holder	Nationality	Location	Date
200 meters	1:54.00	Ryan Lochte	U.S.	Shanghai, China	July 28, 2011
400 meters	4:03.84	Michael Phelps	U.S.	Beijing, China	Aug. 10, 2008

Freestyle relay

Distance	Time	Holder	Nationality	Location	Date
400 m (4×100)	3:08.24	Phelps, Weber-Gale, Jones, Lezak	U.S.	Beijing, China	Aug. 11, 2008
800 m (4×200)	6:58.55	Phelps, Berens, Walters, Lochte	U.S.	Rome, Italy	July 31, 2009

Medley relay

Distance	Time	Holder	Nationality	Location	Date
400 m (4×100)	3:27.28	Peirsol, Shanteau, Phelps, Walters	U.S.	Rome, Italy	Aug. 2, 2009

Women's Records
Freestyle

Distance	Time	Holder	Nationality	Location	Date
50 meters	0:23.73	Britta Steffen	Germany	Rome, Italy	Aug. 2, 2009
100 meters	0:52.07	Britta Steffen	Germany	Rome, Italy	July 31, 2009
200 meters	1:52.98	Federica Pellegrini	Italy	Rome, Italy	July 29, 2009
400 meters	3:59.15	Federica Pellegrini	Italy	Rome, Italy	July 26, 2009
800 meters	8:14.10	Rebecca Adlington	UK	Beijing, China	Aug. 16, 2008
1,500 meters	15:42.54	Kate Zeigler	U.S.	Mission Viejo, CA	June 17, 2007

Backstroke

Distance	Time	Holder	Nationality	Location	Date
50 meters	0:27.06	Zhao Jing	China	Rome, Italy	July 30, 2009
100 meters	0:58.12	Gemma Spofforth	UK	Rome, Italy	July 28, 2009
200 meters	2:04.81	Kirsty Coventry	Zimbabwe	Rome, Italy	Aug. 1, 2009

Breaststroke

Distance	Time	Holder	Nationality	Location	Date
50 meters	0:29.80	Jessica Hardy	U.S.	Federal Way, WA	Aug. 7, 2009
100 meters	1:04.45	Jessica Hardy	U.S.	Federal Way, WA	Aug. 7, 2009
200 meters	2:20.12	Annamay Pierse	U.S.	Rome, Italy	July 30, 2009

Butterfly

Distance	Time	Holder	Nationality	Location	Date
50 meters	0:25.07	Therese Alshammar	Sweden	Rome, Italy	July 31, 2009
100 meters	0:56.06	Sarah Sjostrom	Sweden	Rome, Italy	July 27, 2009
200 meters	2:01.81	Liu Zige	China	Jinan, China	Oct. 21, 2009

Individual medley

Distance	Time	Holder	Nationality	Location	Date
200 meters	2:06.15	Ariana Kukors	U.S.	Rome, Italy	July 27, 2009
400 meters	4:29.45	Stephanie Rice	Australia	Beijing, China	Aug. 10, 2008

Freestyle relay

Distance	Time	Holder	Nationality	Location	Date
400 m (4×100)	3:31.72	Dekker, Kromowidjojo, Heemskerk, Veldhuis	Netherlands	Rome, Italy	July 26, 2009
800 m (4×200)	7:42.08	Yang, Zhu, Liu, Pang	China	Rome, Italy	July 30, 2009

Medley relay

Distance	Time	Holder	Nationality	Location	Date
400 m (4×100)	3:52.19	Zhao, Chen, Jiao, Li	China	Rome, Italy	Aug. 1, 2009

DOGS
2011 Iditarod Trail Sled Dog Race

John Baker won the 39th annual Iditarod Trail Sled Dog Race from Anchorage to Nome, AK, Mar. 15, 2011, capturing the $50,400 prize and a new pick-up truck. Baker finished the 1,131-mile southern route to Nome in 8 days, 18 hours, 46 minutes, and 39 seconds—the fastest time in the race's history—and became the first Alaska Native to win the race since 1976. The 2012 race was scheduled to begin Mar. 3 in Anchorage and follow the 1,112-mile course along the northern route to Nome.

Westminster Kennel Club Best-In-Show, 1989-2011

Year	Best-In-Show	Breed	Owner(s)
1989	Ch. Royal Tudor's Wild As The Wind	Doberman	Sue and Art Kemp; Richard and Carolyn Vida; Beth Wilhite
1990	Ch. Wendessa Crown Prince	Pekingese	Ed Jenner
1991	Ch. Whisperwind on a Carousel	Poodle	Joan and Frederick Hartsock
1992	Ch. Registry's Lonesome Dove	Fox Terrier	Marion and Sam Lawrence
1993	Ch. Salilyn's Condor	English Springer Spaniel	Donna and Roger Herzig
1994	Ch. Chidley Willum	Norwich Terrier	Ruth Cooper and Patricia Lussier
1995	Ch. Gaelforce Post Script	Scottish Terrier	Dr. Vandra Huber and Dr. Joe Kinnarney
1996	Ch. Clussexx Country Sunrise	Clumber Spaniel	Judith and Richard Zaleski
1997	Ch. Parsifal Di Casa Netzer	Standard Schnauzer	Rita Holloway and Gabrio Del Torre
1998	Ch. Fairewood Frolic	Norwich Terrier	Sandina Kennels
1999	Ch. Loteki Supernatural Being	Papillon	John Oulton
2000	Ch. Salilyn 'N Erin's Shameless	English Springer Spaniel	Carl Blain, Fran Sunseri, and Julia Gasow
2001	Ch. Special Times Just Right	Bichon Frise	Cecilia Ruggles, E. McDonald, and F. Werneck
2002	Ch. Surrey Spice Girl	Poodle (Miniature)	Ron L. and Barbara Scott
2003	Ch. Torum's Scarf Michael	Kerry Blue Terrier	Marilu Hanson
2004	Ch. Darbydale's All Rise Pouchcove	Newfoundland	Peggy Helming and Carol A. Bernard Bergmann
2005	Ch. Kan-Point's VJK Autumn Roses	German Shorthaired Pointer	Linda & Richard Stark; Carol Cronk; Valerie Nunes-Atkinson
2006	Ch. Rocky Top's Sundance Kid	Bull Terrier (colored)	Barbara Bishop, W. F. Poole, N. Shepherd, and R. P. Poole
2007	Ch. Felicity's Diamond Jim	English Springer Spaniel	Teresa and Allen Patton; Ruth Dehmel; D. Hadsall
2008	Ch. K-Run's Park Me In First	Beagle (15 in.)	Caroline Dowell, Eddie Dziuk, Jon Woodring, Kathy Weichert
2009	Ch. Clussexx Three D Grinchy Glee	Sussex Spaniel	Cecilia Ruggles, Beth Dowd, and Scott Sommer
2010	Ch. Roundtown Mercedes Of Maryscot	Scottish Terrier	Amelia Musser
2011	GCH Foxcliffe Hickory Wind	Scottish Deerhound	Sally Sweatt, Cecilia L. Dove, and R. Scott Dove

MARATHONS
World Marathon Majors

Five of the world's leading marathons (Berlin, Boston, Chicago, London, and New York) agreed Jan. 23, 2006, to form a series called the World Marathon Majors. Marathon runners are awarded points relative to their finish in each race in the series and in Olympic and other world championship marathons. The male and female runners with the most points at the end of each two-year cycle win $500,000. The 2009-10 World Marathon Majors series winners were Samuel Wanjiru, Kenya, and Liliya Shobukhova, Russia.

Boston Marathon Winners, 1972-2011
All times in hour:minute:second format. * = Course record.

Men's winner, country	Time	Year	Women's winner, country	Time
Olavi Suomalainen, Finland	2:15:39	1972	Nina Kuscsik, U.S.	3:10:26
Jon Anderson, U.S.	2:16:03	1973	Jacqueline Hansen, U.S.	3:05:59
Neil Cusack, Ireland	2:13:39	1974	Michiko Gorman, U.S.	2:47:11
Bill Rodgers, U.S.	2:09:55	1975	Liane Winter, West Germany	2:42:24
Jack Fultz, U.S.	2:20:19	1976	Kim Merritt, U.S.	2:47:10
Jerome Drayton, Canada	2:14:46	1977	Michiko Gorman, U.S.	2:48:33
Bill Rodgers, U.S.	2:10:13	1978	Gayle S. Barron, U.S.	2:44:52
Bill Rodgers, U.S.	2:09:27	1979	Joan Benoit, U.S.	2:35:15
Bill Rodgers, U.S.	2:12:11	1980	Jacqueline Gareau, Canada	2:34:28
Toshihiko Seko, Japan	2:09:26	1981	Allison Roe, New Zealand	2:26:46
Alberto Salazar, U.S.	2:08:52	1982	Charlotte Teske, West Germany	2:29:33
Greg Meyer, U.S.	2:09:00	1983	Joan Benoit, U.S.	2:22:43
Geoff Smith, Great Britain	2:10:34	1984	Lorraine Moller, New Zealand	2:29:28
Geoff Smith, Great Britain	2:14:05	1985	Lisa Larsen Weidenbach, U.S.	2:34:06
Robert de Castella, Australia	2:07:51	1986	Ingrid Kristiansen, Norway	2:24:55
Toshihiko Seko, Japan	2:11:50	1987	Rosa Mota, Portugal	2:25:21
Ibrahim Hussein, Kenya	2:08:43	1988	Rosa Mota, Portugal	2:24:30
Abebe Mekonnen, Ethiopia	2:09:06	1989	Ingrid Kristiansen, Norway	2:24:33
Gelindo Bordin, Italy	2:08:19	1990	Rosa Mota, Portugal	2:25:24
Ibrahim Hussein, Kenya	2:11:06	1991	Wanda Panfil, Poland	2:24:18
Ibrahim Hussein, Kenya	2:08:14	1992	Olga Markova, Russia	2:23:43
Cosmas Ndeti, Kenya	2:09:33	1993	Olga Markova, Russia	2:25:27
Cosmas Ndeti, Kenya	2:07:15	1994	Uta Pippig, Germany	2:21:45
Cosmas Ndeti, Kenya	2:09:22	1995	Uta Pippig, Germany	2:25:11
Moses Tanui, Kenya	2:09:15	1996	Uta Pippig, Germany	2:27:12
Lameck Aguta, Kenya	2:10:34	1997	Fatuma Roba, Ethiopia	2:26:23
Moses Tanui, Kenya	2:07:34	1998	Fatuma Roba, Ethiopia	2:23:21
Joseh Chebet, Kenya	2:09:52	1999	Fatuma Roba, Ethiopia	2:23:25
Elijah Lagat, Kenya	2:09:47	2000	Catherine Ndereba, Kenya	2:26:11
Lee Bong-ju, S. Korea	2:09:43	2001	Catherine Ndereba, Kenya	2:23:53
Rodgers Rop, Kenya	2:09:02	2002	Margaret Okayo, Kenya	2:20:43*
Robert Kipkoech Cheruiyot, Kenya	2:10:11	2003	Svetlana Zakharova, Russia	2:25:20
Timothy Cherigat, Kenya	2:10:37	2004	Catherine Ndereba, Kenya	2:24:27
Hailu Negussie, Ethiopia	2:11:45	2005	Catherine Ndereba, Kenya	2:25:13
Robert Kipkoech Cheruiyot, Kenya	2:07:14	2006	Rita Jeptoo, Kenya	2:23:38
Robert Kipkoech Cheruiyot, Kenya	2:14:13	2007	Lidiya Grigoryeva, Russia	2:29:18
Robert Kipkoech Cheruiyot, Kenya	2:07:46	2008	Dire Tune, Ethiopia	2:25:25
Deriba Merga, Ethiopia	2:08:42	2009	Salina Kosgei, Kenya	2:32:16
Robert Kiprono Cheruiyot, Kenya	2:05:52	2010	Teyba Erkesso, Ethiopia	2:26:11
Geoffrey Mutai, Kenya	2:03:02*	2011	Caroline Kilel, Kenya	2:22:36

Boston Marathon Winners, 1897-1971

The first Boston Marathon was held in 1897. Women were officially accepted into the race in 1972.

Year	Winner, state/country	Time	Year	Winner, state/country	Time
1897	John J. McDermott, New York	2:55:10	1935	John A. Kelley, Massachusetts	2:32:07
1898	Ronald J. MacDonald, Canada	2:42:00	1936	Ellison M. Brown, Rhode Island	2:33:40
1899	Lawrence Brignolia, Massachusetts	2:54:38	1937	Walter Young, Canada	2:33:20
1900	John Caffery, Canada	2:39:44	1938	Leslie S. Pawson, Rhode Island	2:35:34
1901	John Caffery, Canada	2:29:23	1939	Ellison M. Brown, Rhode Island	2:28:51
1902	Sammy Mellor, New York	2:43:12	1940	Gerard Cote, Canada	2:28:28
1903	John Lorden , Massachusetts	2:41:29	1941	Leslie S. Pawson, Rhode Island	2:30:38
1904	Michael Spring, New York	2:38:04	1942	Joe Smith, Massachusetts	2:26:51
1905	Frederick Lorz, New York	2:38:25	1943	Gerard Cote, Canada	2:28:25
1906	Tim Ford, Massachusetts	2:45:45	1944	Gerard Cote, Canada	2:31:50
1907	Thomas Longboat, Canada	2:24:24	1945	John A. Kelley, Massachusetts	2:30:40
1908	Thomas Morrissey, New York	2:25:43	1946	Stylianos Kyriakides, Greece	2:29:27
1909	Henri Renaud, New Hampshire	2:53:36	1947	Yun Bok Suh, Korea	2:25:39
1910	Fred Cameron, Canada	2:28:52	1948	Gerard Cote, Canada	2:31:02
1911	Clarence DeMar, Massachusetts	2:21:39	1949	Karl Leandersson, Sweden	2:31:50
1912	Michael Ryan, New York	2:21:18	1950	Kee Yong Ham, Korea	2:32:39
1913	Fritz Carlson, Minnesota	2:25:14	1951	Shigeki Tanaka, Japan	2:27:45
1914	James Duffy, Canada	2:25:14	1952	Doroteo Flores, Guatemala	2:31:53
1915	Edouard Fabre, Canada	2:31:41	1953	Keizo Yamada, Japan	2:18:51
1916	Arthur Roth, Massachusetts	2:27:16	1954	Veikko Karvonen, Finland	2:20:39
1917	Bill Kennedy, New York	2:28:37	1955	Hideo Hamamura, Japan	2:18:22
1918	Military Relay, Camp Devens	2:29:53	1956	Antti Viskari, Finland	2:14:14
1919	Carl Linder, Massachusetts	2:29:13	1957	John J. Kelley, Connecticut	2:20:05
1920	Peter Trivoulides, New York	2:29:31	1958	Franjo Mihalic, Yugoslavia	2:25:54
1921	Frank Zuna, New York	2:18:57	1959	Eino Oksanen, Finland	2:22:42
1922	Clarence DeMar, Massachusetts	2:18:10	1960	Paavo Kotila, Finland	2:20:54
1923	Clarence DeMar, Massachusetts	2:23:47	1961	Eino Oksanen, Finland	2:23:39
1924	Clarence DeMar, Massachusetts	2:29:40	1962	Eino Oksanen, Finland	2:23:48
1925	Charles Mellor, Illinois	2:33:00	1963	Aurele Vandendriessche, Belgium	2:18:58
1926	John C. Miles, Canada	2:25:40	1964	Aurele Vandendriessche, Belgium	2:19:59
1927	Clarence DeMar, Massachusetts	2:40:22	1965	Morio Shigematsu, Japan	2:16:33
1928	Clarence DeMar, Massachusetts	2:37:07	1966	Kenji Kemihara, Japan	2:17:11
1929	John C. Miles, Canada	2:33:08	1967	David McKenzie, New Zealand	2:15:45
1930	Clarence DeMar, Massachusetts	2:34:48	1968	Amby Burfoot, Connecticut	2:22:17
1931	James P. Henigan, Massachusetts	2:46:45	1969	Yoshiaki Unetani, Japan	2:13:49
1932	Paul DeBruyn, Germany	2:33:36	1970	Ron Hill, Great Britain	2:10:30
1933	Leslie S. Pawson, Rhode Island	2:31:01	1971	Alvaro Mejia, Colombia	2:18:45
1934	Dave Komonen, Canada	2:32:53			

New York City Marathon Winners, 1970-2011

All times in hour:minute:second format. * = Course record.

Men's winner, country	Time	Year	Women's winner, country	Time
Gary Muhrcke, U.S.	2:31:38	1970	No finisher	—
Norman Higgins, U.S.	2:22:54	1971	Beth Bonner, U.S.	2:55:22
Sheldon Karlin, U.S.	2:27:52	1972	Nina Kuscsik, U.S.	3:08:41
Tom Fleming, U.S.	2:19:25	1973	Nina Kuscsik, U.S.	2:57:07
Norbert Sander, U.S.	2:26:30	1974	Katherine Switzer, U.S.	3:07:29
Tom Fleming, U.S.	2:19:27	1975	Kim Merritt, U.S.	2:46:14
Bill Rodgers, U.S.	2:10:10	1976	Miki Gorman, U.S.	2:39:11
Bill Rodgers, U.S.	2:11:28	1977	Miki Gorman, U.S.	2:43:10
Bill Rodgers, U.S.	2:12:12	1978	Grete Waitz, Norway	2:32:30
Bill Rodgers, U.S.	2:11:42	1979	Grete Waitz, Norway	2:27:33
Alberto Salazar, U.S.	2:09:41	1980	Grete Waitz, Norway	2:25:42
Alberto Salazar, U.S.	2:08:13	1981	Allison Roe, New Zealand	2:25:29
Alberto Salazar, U.S.	2:09:29	1982	Grete Waitz, Norway	2:27:14
Rod Dixon, New Zealand	2:08:59	1983	Grete Waitz, Norway	2:27:00
Orlando Pizzolato, Italy	2:14:53	1984	Grete Waitz, Norway	2:29:30
Orlando Pizzolato, Italy	2:11:34	1985	Grete Waitz, Norway	2:28:34
Gianni Poli, Italy	2:11:06	1986	Grete Waitz, Norway	2:28:06
Ibrahim Hussein, Kenya	2:11:01	1987	Priscilla Welch, England	2:30:17
Steve Jones, Wales, UK	2:08:20	1988	Grete Waitz, Norway	2:28:07
Juma Ikangaa, Tanzania	2:08:01	1989	Ingrid Kristiansen, Norway	2:25:30
Douglas Wakiihuri, Kenya	2:12:39	1990	Wanda Panfil, Poland	2:30:45
Salvador Garcia, Mexico	2:09:28	1991	Liz McColgan, Scotland, UK	2:27:32
Willie Mtolo, South Africa	2:09:29	1992	Lisa Ondieki, Australia	2:24:40
Andres Espinosa, Mexico	2:10:04	1993	Uta Pippig, Germany	2:26:24
German Silva, Mexico	2:11:21	1994	Tegla Loroupe, Kenya	2:27:37
German Silva, Mexico	2:11:00	1995	Tegla Loroupe, Kenya	2:28:06
Giacomo Leone, Italy	2:09:54	1996	Anuta Catuna, Romania	2:28:43
John Kagwe, Kenya	2:08:12	1997	F. Rochat-Moser, Switzerland	2:28:43
John Kagwe, Kenya	2:08:45	1998	Franca Fiacconi, Italy	2:25:17
Joseph Chebet, Kenya	2:09:14	1999	Adriana Fernandez, Mexico	2:25:06
Abdelkhader El Mouaziz, Morocco	2:10:09	2000	Ludmila Petrova, Russia	2:25:45
Tesfaye Jifar, Ethiopia	2:07:43	2001	Margaret Okayo, Kenya	2:24:21
Rodgers Rop, Kenya	2:08:07	2002	Joyce Chepchumba, Kenya	2:25:56
Martin Lel, Kenya	2:10:30	2003	Margaret Okayo, Kenya	2:22:31*
Hendrik Ramaala, South Africa	2:09:28	2004	Paula Radcliffe, England	2:23:10
Paul Tergat, Kenya	2:09:30	2005	Jelena Prokopcuka, Latvia	2:24:41
Marilson Gomes dos Santos, Brazil	2:09:58	2006	Jelena Prokopcuka, Latvia	2:25:05
Martin Lel, Kenya	2:09:04	2007	Paula Radcliffe, England	2:23:09
Marilson Gomes dos Santos, Brazil	2:08:43	2008	Paula Radcliffe, England	2:23:56
Meb Keflezighi, U.S.	2:09:15	2009	Derartu Tulu, Ethiopia	2:28:52
Gebre Gebrmariam, Ethiopia	2:08:14	2010	Edna Kiplagat, Kenya	2:28:20
Geoffrey Mutai, Kenya	2:05:06*	2011	Firehiwot Dado, Ethiopia	2:23:15

Other Marathon Results, 2011

Los Angeles Marathon: Mar. 20. Men: Markos Geneti, Ethiopia, 2:06:35. Women: Buzunesh Deba, Ethiopia, 2:26:34.
Paris Marathon: Apr. 10. Men: Benjamin Kiptoo, Kenya, 2:06:31. Women: Priscah Jeptoo, Kenya, 2:22:55.
Rotterdam Marathon: Apr. 10. Men: Wilson Chebet, Kenya, 2.05.27. Women: Philes Ongori, Kenya, 2:24:20.

London Marathon: Apr. 17. Men: Emmanuel Mutai, Kenya, 2:04:40. Women: Mary Keitany, Kenya, 2:19:19.
Berlin Marathon: Sept. 25. Men: Patrick Makau, Kenya, 2:03:38. Women: Florence Kiplagat, Kenya, 2:19:44.
Chicago Marathon: Oct. 9. Men: Moses Mosop, Kenya, 2:05:37. Women: Liliya Shobukhova, Russia, 2:18:20.

Ironman Triathlon World Championships, 1978-2011

All times in hour:minute:second format. * = Course records. The Ironman Triathlon World Championships—a 2.4-mile ocean swim, 112-mile bike ride, and 26.2-mile run—are held annually at Kailua-Kona, Hawaii.

Men's winner, country	Time	Year	Women's winner, country	Time
Gordon Haller, U.S.	11:46:58	1978	No finisher	—
Tom Warren, U.S.	11:15:56	1979	Lyn Lemaire, U.S.	12:55:00
Dave Scott, U.S.	9:24:33	1980	Robin Beck, U.S.	11:21:24
John Howard, U.S.	9:38:29	1981	Linda Sweeney, U.S.	12:00:32
Dave Scott, U.S.	9:08:23	1982	Julie Leach, U.S.	10:54:08
Dave Scott, U.S.	9:05:57	1983	Sylviane Puntous, Canada	10:43:36
Dave Scott, U.S	8:54:20	1984	Sylvanie Puntous, Canada	10:25:13
Scott Tinley, U.S.	8:50:54	1985	Joanne Ernst, U.S.	10:25:22
Dave Scott, U.S.	8:28:37	1986	Paula Newby-Fraser, Zimbabwe	9:49:14
Dave Scott, U.S.	8:34:13	1987	Erin Baker, New Zealand	9:35:25
Scott Molina, U.S.	8:31:00	1988	Paula Newby-Fraser, Zimbabwe	9:01:01
Mark Allen, U.S.	8:09:15	1989	Paula Newby-Fraser, Zimbabwe	9:00:56
Mark Allen, U.S.	8:28:17	1990	Erin Baker, New Zealand	9:13:42
Mark Allen, U.S.	8:18:32	1991	Paula Newby-Fraser, Zimbabwe	9:07:52
Mark Allen, U.S.	8:09:08	1992	Paula Newby-Fraser, Zimbabwe	8:55:28
Mark Allen, U.S.	8:07:45	1993	Paula Newby-Fraser, Zimbabwe	8:58:23
Greg Welch, Australia	8:20:27	1994	Paula Newby-Fraser, Zimbabwe	9:20:14
Mark Allen, U.S.	8:20:34	1995	Karen Smyers, U.S.	9:16:46
Luc Van Lierde, Belgium	8:04:08	1996	Paula Newby-Fraser, Zimbabwe	9:06:49
Thomas Hellriegel, Germany	8:33:01	1997	Heather Fuhr, Canada	9:31:43
Peter Reid, Canada	8:24:20	1998	Natascha Badmann, Switzerland	9:24:16
Luc Van Lierde, Belgium	8:17:17	1999	Lori Bowden, U.S.	9:13:02
Peter Reid, Canada	8:21:01	2000	Natascha Badmann, Switzerland	9:26:16
Timothy Deboom, U.S.	8:31:18	2001	Natascha Badmann, Switzerland	9:28:37
Timothy Deboom, U.S.	8:29:56	2002	Natascha Badmann, Switzerland	9:07:54
Peter Reid, Canada	8:22:35	2003	Lori Bowden, Canada	9:11:55
Normann Stadler, Germany	8:33:29	2004	Natascha Badmann, Switzerland[1]	9:50:04
Faris al-Sultan, Germany	8:14:17	2005	Natascha Badmann, Switzerland	9:09:30
Normann Stadler, Germany	8:11:56	2006	Michellie Jones, U.S.	9:18:31
Chris McCormack, Australia	8:15:34	2007	Chrissie Wellington, UK	9:08:45
Craig Alexander, Australia	8:17:45	2008	Chrissie Wellington, UK	9:06:23
Craig Alexander, Australia	8:20:21	2009	Chrissie Wellington, UK	8:54:02*
Chris McCormack, Australia	8:10:37	2010	Mirinda Carfrae, Australia	8:58:36
Craig Alexander, Australia	8:03:56*	2011	Chrissie Wellington, UK	8:55:08

(1) First-place finisher Nina Kraft (Germany) admitted to using performance-enhancing drugs and was disqualified, Nov. 15, 2004.

SULLIVAN AWARD
James E. Sullivan Memorial Trophy Winners, 1930-2010

The James E. Sullivan Memorial Trophy, named after the former president of the Amateur Athletic Union (AAU) and inaugurated in 1930, is awarded annually by the AAU to the athlete who "by his or her performance, example and influence as an amateur, has done the most during the year to advance the cause of sportsmanship."

Year Winner	Sport	Year Winner	Sport	Year Winner	Sport
1930 Bobby Jones	Golf	1960 Rafer Johnson	Track	1989 Janet Evans	Swimming
1931 Barney Berlinger	Track	1961 Wilma Rudolph Ward	Track	1990 John Smith	Wrestling
1932 Jim Bausch	Track	1962 James Beatty	Track	1991 Mike Powell	Track
1933 Glenn Cunningham	Track	1963 John Pennel	Track	1992 Bonnie Blair	Speed
1934 Bill Bonthron	Track	1964 Don Schollander	Swimming		skating
1935 Lawson Little	Golf	1965 Bill Bradley	Basketball	1993 Charlie Ward	Football,
1936 Glenn Morris	Track	1966 Jim Ryun	Track		basketball
1937 Don Budge	Tennis	1967 Randy Matson	Track	1994 Dan Jansen	Speed
1938 Don Lash	Track	1968 Debbie Meyer	Swimming		skating
1939 Joe Burk	Rowing	1969 Bill Toomey	Track	1995 Bruce Baumgartner	Wrestling
1940 Greg Rice	Track	1970 John Kinsella	Swimming	1996 Michael Johnson	Track
1941 Leslie MacMitchell	Track	1971 Mark Spitz	Swimming	1997 Peyton Manning	Football
1942 Cornelius Warmerdam	Track	1972 Frank Shorter	Track	1998 Chamique Holdsclaw	Basketball
1943 Gilbert Dodds	Track	1973 Bill Walton	Basketball	1999 Coco Miller and	
1944 Ann Curtis	Swimming	1974 Rick Wohlhutter	Track		Kelly Miller	Basketball
1945 Doc Blanchard	Football	1975 Tim Shaw	Swimming	2000 Rulon Gardner	Wrestling
1946 Arnold Tucker	Football	1976 Bruce Jenner	Track	2001 Michelle Kwan	Figure
1947 John Kelly Jr.	Rowing	1977 John Naber	Swimming		skating
1948 Robert Mathias	Track	1978 Tracy Caulkins	Swimming	2002 Sarah Hughes	Figure
1949 Dick Button	Skating	1979 Kurt Thomas	Gymnastics		skating
1950 Fred Wilt	Track	1980 Eric Heiden	Speed	2003 Michael Phelps	Swimming
1951 Rev. Robert Richards	Track		skating	2004 Paul Hamm	Gymnastics
1952 Horace Ashenfelter	Track	1981 Carl Lewis	Track	2005 J. J. Redick	Basketball
1953 Dr. Sammy Lee	Diving	1982 Mary Decker	Track	2006 Jessica Long	Swimming
1954 Mal Whitfield	Track	1983 Edwin Moses	Track		(paralympics)
1955 Harrison Dillard	Track	1984 Greg Louganis	Diving	2007 Tim Tebow	Football
1956 Patricia McCormick	Diving	1985 Joan Benoit		2008 Shawn Johnson	Gymnastics
1957 Bobby Joe Morrow	Track		Samuelson	Marathon	2009 Amy Palmiero-	Ultra
1958 Glenn Davis	Track	1986 Jackie Joyner-Kersee	Track	Winters	marathon
1959 Parry O'Brien	Track	1987 Jim Abbott	Baseball	2010 Evan Lysacek	Figure
		1988 Florence Griffith Joyner	Track		skating

YACHTING
America's Cup

The U.S.'s BMW Oracle Racing Feb. 14, 2010, won the 33rd America's Cup when its *USA-17* yacht, skippered by Australian James Spithill, defeated two-time defending champion *Alinghi 5* of Switzerland, two races to none, in the best-of-three series off Valencia, Spain. BMW Oracle, owned by U.S. billionaire Larry Ellison, brought the America's Cup back to the U.S. for the first time since 1995. BMW Oracle in 2009 had prevailed in a lengthy court battle, winning the right to face Alinghi, owned by Swiss biotechnology billionaire Ernesto Bertarelli, in a rare best-of-three, head-to-head showdown under a provision of the Deed of Gift. (Typically, several challengers race against each other to determine who would compete against the defender for the Cup, and the America's Cup itself consists of a best-of-seven or -nine race series.)

Competition for the America's Cup grew out of the first contest to establish a world yachting championship, one of the carnival features of the London Exposition of 1851. The race covered a 60-mile course around the Isle of Wight. The prize was a cup worth about $500, donated by the Royal Yacht Squadron of England, known as America's Cup because it was first won by the U.S. yacht *America*. The title was held by American yachts until 1983.

America's Cup, 1851-2010

Year	Result	Year	Result
1851	America	1958	Columbia defeated Sceptre, England (4-0)
1870	Magic defeated Cambria, England (1-0)	1962	Weatherly defeated Gretel, Australia (4-1)
1871	Columbia (first three races) and Sappho (last two races) defeated Livonia, England (4-1)	1964	Constellation defeated Sovereign, England (4-0)
1876	Madeline defeated Countess of Dufferin, Canada (2-0)	1967	Intrepid defeated Dame Pattie, Australia (4-0)
1881	Mischief defeated Atalanta, Canada (2-0)	1970	Intrepid defeated Gretel II, Australia (4-1)
1885	Puritan defeated Genesta, England (2-0)	1974	Courageous defeated Southern Cross, Australia (4-0)
1886	Mayflower defeated Galatea, England (2-0)	1977	Courageous defeated Australia, Australia (4-0)
1887	Volunteer defeated Thistle, Scotland (2-0)	1980	Freedom defeated Australia, Australia (4-1)
1893	Vigilant defeated Valkyrie II, England (3-0)	1983	Australia II, Australia, defeated Liberty, U.S. (4-3)
1895	Defender defeated Valkyrie III, England (3-0)	1987	Stars & Stripes defeated Kookaburra III, Australia (4-0)
1899	Columbia defeated Shamrock, England (3-0)	1988	Stars & Stripes defeated New Zealand, NZ (2-0)
1901	Columbia defeated Shamrock II, England (3-0)	1992	America³ defeated Il Moro di Venezia, Italy (4-1)
1903	Reliance defeated Shamrock III, England (3-0)	1995	Black Magic 1, NZ, defeated Young America, U.S. (5-0)
1920	Resolute defeated Shamrock IV, England (3-2)	2000	New Zealand, NZ, defeated Luna Rossa, Italy (5-0)
1930	Enterprise defeated Shamrock V, England (4-0)	2003	Alinghi, Switzerland, defeated Team New Zealand, NZ (5-0)
1934	Rainbow defeated Endeavour, England (4-2)	2007	Alinghi, Switzerland, defeated Emirates Team New Zealand, NZ (5-2)
1937	Ranger defeated Endeavour II, England (4-0)	2010	USA-17 defeated Alinghi 5, Switzerland (2-0)

POWER BOATING
American Power Boat Association Gold Cup Champions, 1970-2011

Year	Boat	Driver	Year	Boat	Driver
1970	Miss Budweiser	Dean Chenoweth	1991	Winston Eagle	Mark Tate
1971	Miss Madison	Jim McCormick	1992	Miss Budweiser	Chip Hanauer
1972	Atlas Van Lines	Bill Muncey	1993	Miss Budweiser	Chip Hanauer
1973	Miss Budweiser	Dean Chenoweth	1994	Smokin' Joe's	Mark Tate
1974	Pay'N Pak	George Henley	1995	Miss Budweiser	Chip Hanauer
1975	Pay'N Pak	George Henley	1996	Pico American Dream	Dave Villwock
1976	Miss U.S.	Tom D'Eath	1997	Miss Budweiser	Dave Villwock
1977	Atlas Van Lines	Bill Muncey	1998	Miss Budweiser	Dave Villwock
1978	Atlas Van Lines	Bill Muncey	1999	Miss PICO	Chip Hanauer
1979	Atlas Van Lines	Bill Muncey	2000	Miss Budweiser	Dave Villwock
1980	Miss Budweiser	Dean Chenoweth	2001	Miss Tubby's Subs	Mike Hanson
1981	Miss Budweiser	Dean Chenoweth	2002	Miss Budweiser	Dave Villwock
1982	Atlas Van Lines	Chip Hanauer	2003	Miss Fox Hills	Mitch Evans
1983	Atlas Van Lines	Chip Hanauer	2004	Miss Detroit Yacht Club	Nate Brown
1984	Atlas Van Lines	Chip Hanauer	2005	Miss Al Deeby Dodge	Terry Troxell
1985	Miller American	Chip Hanauer	2006	Miss Beacon Plumbing	Jean Theoret
1986	Miller American	Chip Hanauer	2007	Miss Elam Plus	Dave Villwock
1987	Miller American	Chip Hanauer	2008	Race not held (wind)	
1988	Circus Circus	Chip Hanauer	2009	Miss Elam Plus	Dave Villwock
1989	Miss Budweiser	Tom D'Eath	2010	Spirit of Qatar	Dave Villwock
1990	Miss Budweiser	Tom D'Eath	2011	Spirit of Qatar	Dave Villwock

RODEO
Pro Rodeo Cowboys Association All-Around Champions, 1977-2010

Year	Winner, hometown	Earnings	Year	Winner, hometown	Earnings
1977	Tom Ferguson, Miami, OK	$76,730	1994	Ty Murray, Stephenville, TX	$246,170
1978	Tom Ferguson, Miami, OK	103,734	1995	Joe Beaver, Huntsville, TX	141,753
1979	Tom Ferguson, Miami, OK	96,272	1996	Joe Beaver, Huntsville, TX	166,103
1980	Paul Tierney, Rapid City, SD	105,568	1997	Dan Mortensen, Manhattan, MT	184,559
1981	Jimmie Cooper, Monument, NM	105,862	1998	Ty Murray, Stephenville, TX	264,673
1982	Chris Lybbert, Coyote, CA	123,709	1999	Fred Whitfield, Hockley, TX	217,819
1983	Roy Cooper, Durant, OK	153,391	2000	Joe Beaver, Huntsville, TX	225,396
1984	Dee Pickett, Caldwell, ID	122,618	2001	Cody Ohl, Stephensville, TX	296,419
1985	Lewis Feild, Elk Ridge, UT	130,347	2002	Trevor Brazile, Anson, TX	273,997
1986	Lewis Feild, Elk Ridge, UT	166,042	2003	Trevor Brazile, Anson, TX	294,839
1987	Lewis Feild, Elk Ridge, UT	144,335	2004	Trevor Brazile, Decatur, TX	253,170
1988	Dave Appleton, Arlington, TX	121,546	2005	Ryan Jarrett, Summerville, GA	263,665
1989	Ty Murray, Odessa, TX	134,806	2006	Trevor Brazile, Decatur, TX	329,924
1990	Ty Murray, Stephenville, TX	213,772	2007	Trevor Brazile, Decatur, TX	425,115
1991	Ty Murray, Stephenville, TX	244,230	2008	Trevor Brazile, Decatur, TX	419,868
1992	Ty Murray, Stephenville, TX	225,992	2009	Trevor Brazile, Decatur, TX	346,779
1993	Ty Murray, Stephenville, TX	297,896	2010	Trevor Brazile, Decatur, TX	507,921

GENERAL INDEX

Note: Page numbers in **boldface** indicate key reference. Page numbers in *italics* indicate photo or illustration captions.

QUICK REFERENCE INDEX

For complete index, see pages 979-1007.